Tolley's Yellow Tax Han
2017–18

58th Edition Part 3

Tolley's Yellow Tax Handbook 2017–18

58th Edition

Part 3

The legislation relating to—
Inheritance Tax
National Insurance Contributions
Tax Credits
Petroleum Revenue Tax
Statutes, Statutory Instruments, European legislation, Revenue Concessions, Statements of Practice, Interpretations, Decisions, and Press Releases

Consultant Editor

Anne Redston MA (Oxon) LLB FCA CTA(Fellow), Barrister

LexisNexis®

Members of the LexisNexis Group worldwide

United Kingdom	RELX (UK) Limited, trading as LexisNexis, 1-3 Strand, London WC2N 5JR
Australia	LexisNexis Butterworths, Chatswood, New South Wales
Austria	LexisNexis Verlag ARD Orac GmbH & Co KG, Vienna
Canada	LexisNexis Butterworths, Markham, Ontario
Czech Republic	Nakladatelství Orac sro, Prague
France	LexisNexis SA, Paris
Germany	LexisNexis Deutschland GmbH, Frankfurt and Munster
Hong Kong	LexisNexis Butterworths, Hong Kong
Hungary	HVG-Orac, Budapest
India	LexisNexis Butterworths, New Delhi
Italy	Giuffrè Editore, Milan
Malaysia	Malayan Law Journal Sdn Bhd, Kuala Lumpur
New Zealand	LexisNexis Butterworths, Wellington
Singapore	LexisNexis Butterworths, Singapore
South Africa	LexisNexis Butterworths, Durban
Switzerland	Stämpfli Verlag AG, Berne
USA	LexisNexis, Dayton, Ohio

First published in 1962

Published by LexisNexis UK

ISBN: 9781474304092 (for set); 9781474304146 (for Part 3)
A CIP Catalogue record for this book is available from the British Library.

Visit Tolley at www.tolley.co.uk or email the editorial department on: yellowandorange@lexisnexis.co.uk

Publishers' Note

Finance Act 2017—key dates

Budget Day	8 March 2017
Finance Bill published	20 March 2017*
Royal Assent	27 April 2017

Note that the 20 March 2017 Finance Bill was subsequently truncated in the House of Commons on 25 April 2017, allowing a shortened FA 2017 to receive Royal Assent before Parliament was dissolved on 3 May 2017 before the General Election.

Finance (No 2) Act 2017—key dates

Budget Day	8 March 2017
Finance Bill published	8 September 2017
Royal Assent	16 November 2017

Tax legislation

Tolley's Yellow and Orange Tax Handbooks are indispensable to the practitioner who needs to refer to the tax legislation as currently in force.

Each year the legislation is augmented and amended by one or more Finance Acts and lesser amendments are made from time to time by a variety of other statutes. An increasing amount of the detailed regulation of taxes is contained in statutory instruments—orders or regulations—which are also amended frequently. The Handbooks are normally published annually. They contain the text of the relevant statutes and statutory instruments as amended together with current texts of extra-statutory concessions, statements of practice, published official interpretations and decisions, selected press releases and internal guidance where available.

The Yellow Tax Handbook covers income tax, corporation tax, capital gains tax, along with annual tax on enveloped dwellings, diverted profits tax, apprenticeship levy and other direct taxes (in Parts 1a, 1b, 1c and 2a and 2b), and inheritance tax, National Insurance contributions, tax credits and petroleum revenue tax (in Part 3). The companion volume, Tolley's Orange Tax Handbook, covers value added tax (Part 1), and stamp taxes (including land and buildings transaction tax in Scotland), insurance premium tax, landfill tax (including Scottish landfill tax), aggregates levy and climate change levy (Part 2).

This edition of the Yellow Tax Handbook contains texts as they applied at 1 November 2017, although later amendments have been taken into account where possible.

Organisation

The text of the Handbook is arranged in the following order—Parts 1a, 1b, 1c: UK statutes relating to income tax, corporation tax, and capital gains tax and other direct taxes up to and including Finance (No 2) Act 2017; Part 2a: statutory instruments relating to direct taxes; Part 2b: European legislation, concessions, statements of practice, official interpretations and decisions, selected press releases, miscellaneous non-statutory material; Part 3: inheritance tax, National Insurance contributions, tax credits, and petroleum revenue tax, and destination tables for consolidation statutes.

Within each category, items are printed in chronological order. To enable individual items to be located quickly, an item reference is printed in bold type in the outside top corner of each page.

Amendments and modifications

Amendments to existing legislation which take effect for the current year are made in the text of the amended legislation. An **Amendment** note under the amended text indicates the authority for the amendment and, where appropriate, the timing of its commencement. All relevant provisions of the current Finance Act are reproduced in full but otherwise the text of provisions which merely amend other Acts is generally omitted and replaced by a note indicating the legislation amended.

Sometimes the effect of a provision is modified by a later Act or statutory instrument but the scope of the modification is limited in some way so that the original provision remains generally unaffected. In this case, the original provision is printed without modification but a **Cross reference** to the later Act or statutory instrument is provided, see below.

Prospective amendments

The Handbook sets out the text of the legislation as it applies for the current tax year. Amendments which are stated to come into effect on a specified future date, or with effect from a date to be appointed, are therefore strictly outside the scope of the current edition and are not made in the text of the Act affected. However, a **Prospective amendment** note is provided to indicate the existence of the amendment and the provision making the prospective amendment is retained in full in successive editions of the Handbook until the amendment becomes effective.

Repealed legislation

Generally, repealed legislation is omitted. However, where it may be necessary to refer to the repealed text in dealing with tax liabilities for the current year, the text is retained and is printed in italics.

Tax law rewrite statutes

The digital versions of the Yellow Tax Handbook include tables of origin/derivation. In addition, derivation/destination notes are provided under individual sections where appropriate.

Defined terms

Where a word or phrase used in the main Acts has been defined elsewhere, a cross-reference to the definition is provided in a **Definitions** note below the text.

Cross references

The notes under each section or Schedule paragraph include references to commentary in *Simon's Taxes* and to other relevant statutory provisions, statutory instruments, tax cases, published Revenue practice and other published or unpublished official and professional bodies' views. These are presented under the following headings—

Commentary—refers to paragraph number for commentary relating to the provision in *Simon's Taxes*.

Concession; Statement of Practice; HMRC interpretation; HMRC decision—refer to published official practice separately reproduced in this Handbook.

Press releases etc—refers to published or unpublished official and professional bodies' views reproduced in this Handbook or *MHA MacIntyre Hudson's Yellow Tax Guide* or elsewhere.

HMRC Manuals—refers to the views and practice of HMRC which are detailed in the Manuals published online at www.gov.uk/government/collections/hmrc-manuals.

Cross reference—refers to provisions in the same or another Act or statutory instrument.

Simon's Tax Cases—provides references to the most significant cases reported in *Simon's Tax Cases* and *Simon's First-tier Tax Decisions*. Cases decided on the previous corresponding statutory provision are marked by an asterisk.

Note—introduces other references not within any of the above categories.

Derivation/Rewrite destination—these notes provide details of the origins of legislation in consolidation/tax law rewrite statutes and, in some cases, destinations for material which has been repealed and rewritten.

November 2017

Preface

In November 2016 the Chancellor announced that there would be "a single fiscal event" in the form of an autumn budget, which would "improve external and Parliamentary scrutiny of proposed tax measures". Draft legislation was published in December 2016 and January 2017, followed by the Finance Bill in March.

However, on 18 April 2017, the Prime Minister announced a general election. The Finance Bill was truncated, and published as Finance Act 2017 only nine days later. Significant changes were pushed through Parliament with no debate at all. These include new rules for employment intermediaries, a sugar tax and reforms to disguised remuneration. The balance of the Finance Bill was held over to be reintroduced after the election, becoming Finance (No 2) Act 2017. Publication of this year's Yellow Book was delayed so as to include both Acts.

The new Acts do contain some welcome reforms. The unfair and counter-intuitive part-disposal rules which applied to life insurance bonds have been replaced, and the complex mix of case law and legislation which governed termination payments has been simplified. However, the Act also reduces the dividend allowance only a year after its introduction, and the new lower allowance is backdated six months to the beginning of the tax year. Similar backdating applies to the money purchase annual allowance. Both changes are likely to affect pensioners, already facing extraordinary complexity in their tax affairs.

Shortly before Royal Assent to the Finance (No 2) Act, the House of Lords Select Committee on the Constitution published a Report on "the Legislative Process". The Committee singles out tax legislation as particularly inaccessible, to the extent that it raises "rule of law concerns about the ability of the general public to understand the law to which they are subject". As consultant editor of the Yellow Book I entirely concur. If the Committee's sensible and practical recommendations for reform were implemented, future Finance Acts would be much improved.

In the meantime, the legislation, regulations and Statements of Practice in the Yellow Book have been organised, cross-referenced and updated for the many changes and additions since the last version, so that it is as easy as possible for practitioners to use. Perhaps, one day, the general public will also be able to locate relevant provisions within its pages.

Anne Redston

Barrister, Temple Tax Chambers

Visiting Professor, King's College London

Meaning of “the Taxes Acts”

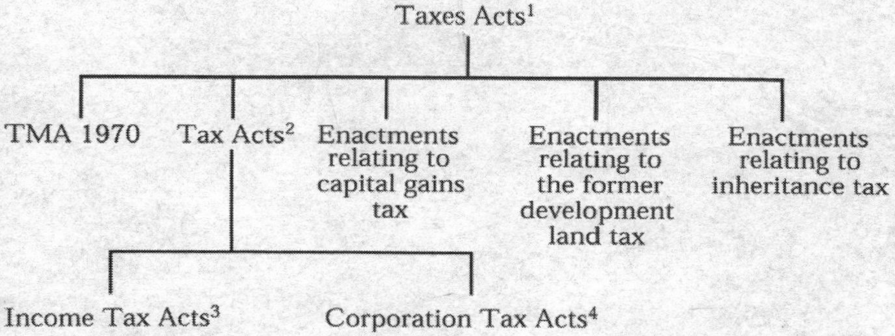

(1) Defined in TMA 1970 s 118(1).
(2) Defined in TA 1988 s 831(2).
(3) Defined in TA 1988 s 831(1)(*b*).
(4) Defined in TA 1988 s 831(1)(*a*).

See also Interpretation Act 1978 Sch 1:

“The Tax Acts” means the Income Tax Acts and the Corporation Tax Acts.

“The Income Tax Acts” means all enactments relating to income tax, including any provisions of the Corporation Tax Acts which relate to income tax.

“The Corporation Tax Acts” means the enactments relating to the taxation of the income and chargeable gains of companies and of company distributions (including provisions relating to income tax).

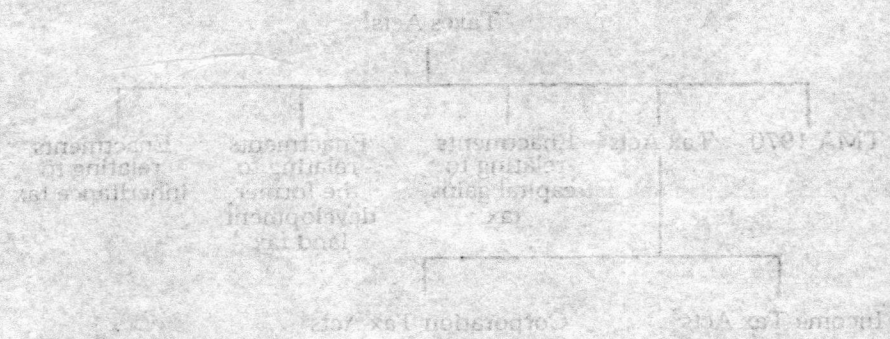

Contents

PARTS 1A, 1B, 1C

NATIONAL INSURANCE CONTRIBUTIONS

TAX CREDITS

PETROLEUM REVENUE TAX

List of abbreviations

AEA 1925	Administration of Estates Act 1925
ACT	Advance Corporation Tax
APRT	Advanced petroleum revenue tax
art	article(s)
ATED	annual tax on enveloped dwellings
BES	Business Expansion Scheme
CAA	Capital Allowances Act
CCAB	Consultative Committee of Accountancy Bodies
C&E	Customs & Excise
CGT	Capital gains tax
CGTA 1979	Capital Gains Tax Act 1979
Ch	Chapter of statute
CIOT	Chartered Institute of Taxation
col	column(s)
Comrs	Commissioners
CPA 1947	Crown Proceedings Act 1947
CRCA 2005	Commissioners for Revenue and Customs Act 2005
CRT	Composite rate tax
CSPSSA 2000	Child Support, Pensions and Social Security Act 2000
CT	Corporation tax
CTA 2009/2010	Corporation Tax Act 2009/2010
CTD	Certificates of tax deposit
CTT	Capital transfer tax
CTTA 1984	Capital Transfer Tax Act 1984
Dir	EC Directive
DLT	Development land tax
DLTA 1976	Development Land Tax Act 1976
DPT	Diverted Profits Tax
DSS	Department of Social Security
DTI	Department of Trade and Industry
DTR	Double taxation relief
EC	European Community/Communities
edn	edition

EEC	European Economic Community
EEIG	European Economic Interest Grouping
EIS	Enterprise Investment Scheme
ESC	Extra-statutory concession
ESOT	Employee share ownership trust
et seq	(et sequens) and the following
EU	European Union
FA	Finance Act
FII	Franked investment income
FIMBRA	Financial Intermediaries, Managers and Brokers Regulatory Association
F(No 2)A	Finance (No 2) Act
FSA	Friendly Societies Act
FYA	first-year allowance
GAAR	General Anti-abuse Rule
HA 1988	Housing Act 1988
HL	House of Lords
HM	Her Majesty
HMRC	Her Majesty's Revenue & Customs
HMSO	Her Majesty's Stationery Office
IA	Interpretation Act
IA 1986	Insolvency Act 1986
ICAEW	Institute of Chartered Accountants in England & Wales
IHT	Inheritance tax
IHTA 1984	Inheritance Tax Act 1984
IR	Inland Revenue
IR Comrs	Commissioners of Inland Revenue
IRRA 1890	Inland Revenue Regulation Act 1890
IT	Income tax
ITA 2007	Income Tax Act 2007
ITEPA 2003	Income Tax (Earnings and Pensions) Act 2003
ITTOIA 2005	Income Tax (trading and Other Income) Act 2005
LAUTRO	Life Assurance and Unit Trust Regulatory Organisation
LIFFE	London International Financial Futures and Options Exchange
MIRAS	Mortgage interest relief at source
NB	(nota bene) note well
NHA 1980	National Heritage Act 1980

NI	National insurance
NIC	National insurance contributions
NRCGT	Non-resident capital gains tax
OJ	Official Journal of the European Communities
OTA	Oil Taxation Act
para	paragraph(s)
PAYE	Pay as you earn
PCTA 1968	Provisional Collection of Taxes Act 1968
PR	Press release
PRP	Profit-related pay
PRT	Petroleum revenue tax
PSO	Pension Schemes Office
Pt	Part(s)
QCB	Qualifying corporate bond
r	rule(s)
RD	Revenue decision
reg	regulations
R&D	research & development
RI	Revenue Interpretation
s(s)	section(s)
SAYE	Save as you earn
Sch	Schedule
SSA	Social Security Act
SSAA 1992	Social Security Administration Act 1992
SS(C)A	Social Security (Contributions) Act
SSCBA 1992	Social Security Contributions and Benefits Act 1992
SSCPA 1992	Social Security (Consequential Provisions) Act 1992
SS(No 2)A	Social Security (No 2) Act
SSHBA	Social Security and Housing Benefits Act
SS(MP)A	Social Security (Miscellaneous Provisions) Act
SSPA 1975	Social Security Pensions Act 1975
SSPA 1991	Statutory Sick Pay Act 1991
SI	Statutory Instrument
SP	Statement of Practice
SSAP	Statement of Standard Accounting Practice
STC	Simon's Tax Cases
sub-para	sub-paragraph(s)

sub-s	sub-section(s)
SWTI	Simon's Weekly Tax Intelligence
TA	Income and Corporation Taxes Act
TaA 2000	Transport Act 2000
TCGA 1992	Taxation of Chargeable Gains Act 1992
TCA 1999	Tax Credits Act 1999
TIOPA 2010	Taxation (International and other Provisions) Act 2010
TMA 1970	Taxes Management Act 1970
TPA 2014	Taxation of Pensions Act 2014
TSBA	Trustee Savings Banks Act
UCITS	Undertakings for Collective Investment in Transferable Securities
UK	United Kingdom
VAT	Value added tax
VATA 1994	Value Added Tax Act 1994
VCT	Venture capital trust
vol	volume(s)
WDA	writing down allowance
WRA	Welfare Reform Act

TAX TABLES

INCOME TAX ALLOWANCES

	2017–18	*2016–17*
Personal allowance	£	£
basic allowance	11,500	11,000
income limit*	100,000	100,000
Personal savings allowance**		
basic rate taxpayers	1,000	1,000
higher rate taxpayers	500	500
Dividend allowance***	5,000	5,000
Trading allowance	1,000	—
Property income allowance	1,000	—

* Where income is above £100,000, the personal allowance is reduced by £1 for every £2 of income above the £100,000 limit.

** The personal savings allowance is not available to additional rate taxpayers. Savings income exceeding the allowance is taxable at the basic or higher rate as appropriate. The allowance is not a deduction in arriving at taxable income.

*** The dividend allowance is available to all taxpayers. It is not a deduction in arriving at taxable income. For the rates of tax on dividend income above the allowance, see below.

TRANSFERABLE MARRIAGE ALLOWANCE*

Maximum amount of allowance	£1,150	£1,100

* Available to married couples and civil partners who are not in receipt of married couple's allowance. A spouse or civil partner who is not liable to income tax, or not liable at the higher or additional rates, can transfer this amount of their unused personal allowance to their spouse or civil partner. The recipient must not be liable to income tax at the higher or additional rates. Relief is given at 20% (maximum of £230 for 2017–18).

MARRIED COUPLE'S ALLOWANCE* (RELIEF AT 10%)

either partner born before 6 April 1935*	8,445	8,355
income limit	28,000	27,700
minimum where income exceeds limit	3,260	3,220

* Available for civil partners.

BLIND PERSON'S ALLOWANCE

Blind person's allowance	2,320	2,290

INCOME TAX RATES

Non-savings income

Taxable income £	Band £	Rate %	Tax on band £	Total tax £
2017–18				
0–33,500	33,500	20	6,700	6,700
33,501–150,000	116,500	40	46,600	53,300
Over 150,000	—	45%	—	—
2016–17				
0–32,000	32,000	20%	6,400	6,400
32,001–150,000	118,000	40%	47,200	53,600
Over 150,000	—	45%	—	—

Trust rate of income tax for 2016–17 and 2017–18 is 45%.

Scottish Income Tax

From April 2017, the Scottish Parliament has the power to set all income tax rates and bands (except the personal allowance, which remains reserved) that will apply to Scottish taxpayers' non-savings, non-dividend income. The Scottish rates and bands are set annually by the Scottish Parliament.

Scotland: non-savings income

Taxable income £	Band £	Rate %	Tax on band £	Total tax £
2017–18				
0–31,500	31,500	20	6,300	6,300
31,501–150,000	118,500	40	47,400	53,700
Over 150,000	—	45%	—	—

Where income is above £100,000, the personal allowance is reduced by £1 for every £2 of income above the £100,000 limit.

Starting rate for savings income

Taxable income £	Band £	Rate %	Tax on band £	Total tax £
2017–18				
0–5,000	5,000	0	0	0
2016–17				
0–5,000	5,000	0	0	0

Where taxable non-savings income exceeds £5,000 the special 0% starting rate for savings income does not apply.

Income taxable at the starting rate for savings does not fall within the personal savings allowance (see above).

Dividend tax rates

Taxable income £	*Rate %*
2017–18	
0–33,500	7.5
33,501–150,000	32.5
Over 150,000	38.1
2016–17	
0–32,000	7.5
32,001–150,000	32.5
Over 150,000	38.1

A 0% rate applies to dividend income within the dividend allowance (see above).

The dividend trust rate is 38.1% for 2017–18 and 2016–17.

NATIONAL INSURANCE CONTRIBUTIONS 2017–18

Class 1 (Earnings related)

Employees	
Weekly earnings	
First £157	Nil
£157.01–£866	12%
Over £866	2%
Employers	
Weekly earnings	
First £157	Nil
Over £157	13.8%

Employers' rates for employees under 21 and apprentices under 25 are nil on earnings up to £866 per week.

Employment allowance (per employer): £3,000 a year.

Class 1A and 1B: 13.8%.

Class 2 (self-employed): flat rate £2.85 a week (small profits threshold £6,025 a year).

Class 3 (voluntary contributions): £14.25 a week.

Class 4 (self-employed): 9% of profits between £8,164 and £45,000 a year (2% of profits above £45,000 a year).

Budget 2016 announced the Government's intention to abolish Class 2 contributions from April 2018.

APPRENTICESHIP LEVY

	2017–18	*2016–17*
	£	£
Allowance (per employer)	15,000	—
Rate	0.5%	—

Effectively applies to UK employers' pay bills in excess of £3 million.

INDIVIDUAL SAVINGS ACCOUNTS

	Annual limit	*Junior ISA annual limit*	*Lifetime ISA annual limit*	*Help to Buy ISA monthly limit*
	£	£	£	£
2017–18	20,000	4,128	4,000	200
2016–17	15,240	4,080	—	200

Savings are exempt from income tax and capital gains tax.

CAPITAL GAINS TAX

	2017–18	*2016–17*
Annual exempt amount	£	£
Individuals, disabled trusts, personal representatives for year of death and two years thereafter	11,300	11,100
Trusts generally	5,650	5,550
Rates		
Individuals		
Standard rate	10%	10%
Higher rate	20%	20%
Trustees and personal representatives	20%	20%
Gains on residential property and carried interest		
Standard rate	18%	18%
Higher rate	28%	28%

Entrepreneurs' relief and investors' relief: qualifying gains charged at 10% (subject to £10 million lifetime limit).

CORPORATION TAX

Financial year to—	*31 March 2018*	*31 March 2017*
Rate	19%	20%

The main rate for ring-fence profits is 30% and the small profits rate for ring-fence profits is 19%. Ring fence profits above £300,000 but not exceeding £1.5m attract marginal relief. The marginal relief ring-fence fraction is 11/400.

BANK LEVY

	1.1.2011–28.2.2011	1.3.2011–30.4.2011	1.5.2011–31.12.2011	1.1.2012–31.12.2012	1.1.2013–31.12.2013
short-term chargeable liabilities	.05%	.1%	.075%	.088%	.130%
long-term chargeable equity and liabilities	.025%	.05%	.0375%	.044%	.065%

	1.1.2014–31.3.2015	1.4.2015–31.12.2015	1.1.2016–31.12.2016	1.1.2017–31.12.2017	1.1.2018–31.12.2018
short-term chargeable liabilities	.156%	.21%	.18%	.17%	.16%
long-term chargeable equity and liabilities	.078%	.105%	.09%	.085%	.08%

CAR BENEFIT

CO_2 emissions (2017–18) grams per kilometre	*% of list price* Petrol	*Diesel*
50	9	12
51–75	13	16
76–94	17	20
95	18	21
100	19	22
105	20	23
110	21	24
115	22	25
120	23	26
125	24	27
130	25	28
135	26	29
140	27	30
145	28	31
150	29	32
155	30	33
160	31	34
165	32	35
170	33	36
175	34	37
180	35	37
185	36	37
190 and above	37	37

A 9% charge applies for cars incapable of producing CO_2 emissions.

CAR FUEL BENEFIT

For 2017–18, car fuel benefit is calculated by applying the above car benefit percentage to a figure of £22,600.

TAX-FREE MILEAGE ALLOWANCES

Employee's own vehicle

Motorcars and vans	*2017–18*
Up to 10,000 business miles	45p
Over 10,000 business miles	25p
Passenger making same trip	5p
Motorcycles	24p
Cycles	20p

Advisory fuel rates for company car (from 1 September 2017)

Cylinder capacity	*Petrol*	*LPG*
Up to 1,400 cc	11p	7p
1,401 cc to 2,000 cc	13p	8p
Over 2,000 cc	21p	13p
	Diesel	
Up to 1,600 cc	9p	
1,601 cc to 2,000 cc	11p	
Over 2,000 cc	12p	

Hybrid cars are treated as petrol or diesel cars accordingly.

INHERITANCE TAX

Transfers made after 5 April 2017 and before 6 April 2018.

Death rates	
Nil-rate band	£325,000
Residence nil-rate band	£100,000
Rate of IHT on excess	40%

Unused nil-rate/residence nil-rate band is transferable to spouse or civil partner.

Chargeable lifetime transfers are initially charged at 20%.

Annual gifts of up to £3,000 per donor are exempt.

A reduced rate of 36% applies where 10% or more of the net estate is left to charity.

The residence nil-rate band is phased in from 6 April 2017, set at £125,000 for 2018–19, £150,000 for 2019–20 and £175,000 for 2020–21. The basic nil-rate band will remain at £325,000 until 5 April 2021. After that, both nil-rate bands will increase in line with CPI.

STAMP TAXES

Shares and marketable securities	.5%*

* Rounded up to the nearest multiple of £5 and subject to exemption where consideration is less than £1,000 or nil.

STAMP DUTY LAND TAX

Residential	*Rate*
Up to £125,000	Nil
£125,001–£250,000	2%
£250,001–£925,000	5%
£925,001–£1,500,000	10%
Over £1,500,000	12%

Rates are charged on the **portion** of the consideration that falls within each rate band.

For residential property, where consideration exceeds £500,000 a 15% rate applies if purchase by, or by a partnership including, a company or collective investment scheme enveloping the property.

Rates are increased by 3 percentage points for certain purchases including purchases of additional residential properties by individuals. Transactions under £40,000 are excluded.

Non-residential	*Rate*
Up to £150,000	Nil
£150,001–£250,000	2%
Over £250,000	5%

Rates are charged on the **portion** of the consideration that falls within each rate band.

Leases

Residential	*Non-residential*	*Rate*
Up to £125,000	Up to £150,000	Nil
Over £125,000	£150,001 to £5,000,000	1%
—	Over £5,000,000	2%

Rates are charged on the **portion** of the net present value that falls within each rate band.

LAND AND BUILDINGS TRANSACTION TAX (SCOTLAND)

Residential	*Rate*
Up to £145,000	Nil
£145,001–£250,000	2%
£250,001–£325,000	5%
£325,001–£750,000	10%
Over £750,000	12%

Rates are charged on the **portion** of the consideration that falls within each rate band.

Non-residential	*Rate*
Up to £150,000	Nil
£150,001–£350,000	3%
Over £350,000	4.5%

Rates are charged on the **portion** of the consideration that falls within each rate band.

Leases

*Residential**	*Non-residential*	*Rate*
—	Up to £150,000	Nil
—	Over £150,000	1%

*Generally, leases of residential property are exempt from LBTT.

Rates are charged on the **portion** of the net present value that falls within each rate band.

ANNUAL TAX ON ENVELOPED DWELLINGS

Property value	*Charge for the tax year 2017–18*	*Charge for the tax year 2016–17*
Over £500,000 to £1m	£3,500	£3,500
£1m – £2m	£7,050	£7,000
£2m – £5m	£23,550	£23,350
£5m – £10m	£54,950	£54,450
£10m – £20m	£110,100	£109,050
£20m +	£220,350	£218,200

VAT

Standard rate	20%
Lower rate	5%
Registration level from 1 April 2017	£85,000 pa
Deregistration limit from 1 April 2017	£83,000 pa

VAT CAR FUEL SCALE CHARGES FROM 1 MAY 2017

Description of vehicle: vehicle's CO_2 emissions figure	*VAT inclusive consideration for a 12 month prescribed accounting period (£)*	*VAT inclusive consideration for a 3 month prescribed accounting period (£)*	*VAT inclusive consideration for a 1 month prescribed accounting period (£)*
120 or less	563	140	46
125	842	211	70
130	901	224	74
135	955	238	79
140	1,013	252	84
145	1,068	267	88
150	1,126	281	93
155	1,180	295	98
160	1,239	309	102
165	1,293	323	107
170	1,351	337	111
175	1,405	351	116
180	1,464	365	121
185	1,518	379	125
190	1,577	393	131
195	1,631	408	136
200	1,689	422	140
205	1,743	436	145
210	1,802	449	149
215	1,856	463	154
220	1,914	478	159
225 or more	1,969	492	163

CAPITAL ALLOWANCES

	Rate %
Dredging (straight-line basis)	
Writing-down allowance	4
Know-how (reducing-balance basis)	
Writing-down allowance	25
Mineral extraction (reducing-balance basis)	
Writing-down allowances	
General	25
Acquisition of mineral asset	10
Patent rights (reducing-balance basis)	
Writing-down allowance	25
Plant and machinery (reducing-balance basis)	
Annual investment allowance (max £200,000)	100
First-year allowances	
Energy-saving or environmentally beneficial assets	100
New low-emission cars	100
New zero-emission goods vehicles	100
New assets for use in designated areas of enterprise zones	100
New electric charge-point equipment	100
Writing-down allowances	
General	18
Cars (other than low-emission cars)	8
Special rate expenditure (including integral features and thermal insulation)	8
Long-life assets	8
Research and development	
Allowance	100

REGISTERED PENSION SCHEMES

2017–18	£
Annual allowance	40,000
Income limit	150,000
Minimum where income exceeds limit	10,000
Lifetime allowance	£1,000,000
2016–17	£
Annual allowance	40,000
Income limit	150,000
Minimum where income exceeds limit	10,000
Lifetime allowance	£1,000,000

Any unused annual allowance can be carried forward for up to three years.

The annual allowance is tapered by £1 for every £2 of income over £150,000 (income including pension contributions), subject to a maximum reduction of £30,000.

TAX CREDITS

Annual amounts	*2017–18*	*2016–17*
	£	£
Child tax credit		
Family element	545	545
Child element (for each child)	2,780	2,780
Addition for disabled child	3,175	3,140
Severely disabled child enhancement	1,290	1,275
Working tax credit		
Basic element	1,960	1,960
Lone parent and couple element	2,010	2,010
30-hour element	810	810
Disability element	3,000	2,970
Severe disability element	1,290	1,275
Childcare element (up to 70% of costs)	Weekly	Weekly
maximum eligible cost (1 child)	175	175
maximum eligible cost (2 or more children)	300	300
Income thresholds		
Income threshold	6,420	6,420
eligible for child tax credit only	16,105	16,105
Withdrawal rate	41%	41%
Income rise disregard	2,500	2,500
Income fall disregard	2,500	2,500

Inheritance Tax

Contents

Statutes

Contents

PROBATE AND LEGACY DUTIES ACT 1808

(48 Geo. 3, c 149)

42 Confirmations of testaments not to be granted for effects not included in such inventory. Executors not to recover effects unless so included

[(1)] [2] [Subject to subsection (2) below,][2] it shall not be lawful for any commissary court in Scotland, to grant confirmation of any testament, testamentary or dative, or eik thereto, of or for any state or effects whatever of any person dying after the tenth day of October one thousand eight hundred and eight, unless the same shall be mentioned and included in some such inventory exhibited and recorded as aforesaid [nor unless that inventory shows by means of such receipt or certification as may be prescribed by the Commissioners of Inland Revenue either that the capital transfer tax payable on the delivery of the inventory has been paid or that no capital transfer tax is so payable][1]; and it shall not be competent to any executor or executors, or other person or persons, to recover any debt or other effects, in Scotland, of or belonging to any person dying after the said tenth day of October, unless the same shall have been previously included in some such inventory, exhibited and recorded as aforesaid; except the same respectively were vested in the deceased as a trustee for any other person or persons, and not beneficially; but these provisions are not, in other respects, to prejudice the law of Scotland, regarding total or partial confirmations, or the rules of succession there established.

[Provided that arrangements may be made between the Court of Session and the said Commissioners providing for the purposes of this section in such cases as may be specified that the said inventory shall be effective without such receipt or certification as aforesaid, or that some other document may be substituted for the inventory.][1]

[(2) In a case to which regulations under section 256(1)(aa) of the Inheritance Tax Act 1984 apply (excepted estates), it shall not be lawful to grant confirmation such as is mentioned in subsection (1) above except on the production of information or documents in accordance with those regulations.][2]

Notes—FA 1986 s 100(1)(*b*): any reference to the capital transfer tax (except where it relates to a liability to tax arising before 25 July 1986) has effect as a reference to inheritance tax.

Amendments—[1] The words "nor unless . . . is so payable" and the proviso were added by FA 1975 s 19(2) and Sch 4, para 38(2), (4).

[2] Sub-s (1) numbered as such, words therein substituted, and sub-s (2) inserted, by FA 2004 s 294(2) with effect from 1 November 2004 (by virtue of SI 2004/2571).

ADMINISTRATION OF ESTATES ACT 1925

(15 & 16 Geo. 5, c 23)

PART IV

DISTRIBUTION OF RESIDUARY ESTATE

46 Succession to real and personal estate on intestacy

(1) The residuary estate of an intestate shall be distributed in the manner or be held on the trusts mentioned in this section, namely—

[(i) If the intestate leaves a [spouse or civil partner][11], then in accordance with the following table:

[TABLE

(1) If the intestate leaves no issue:	the residuary estate shall be held in trust for the surviving spouse or civil partner absolutely.
(2) If the intestate leaves issue:	(A) the surviving spouse or civil partner shall take the personal chattels absolutely;
	(B) the residuary estate of the intestate (other than the personal chattels) shall stand charged with the payment of a fixed net sum, free of death duties and costs, to the surviving spouse or civil partner, together with simple interest on it from the date of the death at the rate provided for by subsection (1A) until paid or appropriated; and

(C) subject to providing for the sum and interest referred to in paragraph (B), the residuary estate (other than the personal chattels) shall be held—

(*a*) as to one half, in trust for the surviving spouse or civil partner absolutely, and

(*b*) as to the other half, on the statutory trusts for the issue of the intestate.

[The amount of the fixed net sum referred to in paragraph (B) of case (2) of this Table is to be determined in accordance with Schedule 1A.][3]][1]][7]

(ii) If the intestate leaves issue but no [spouse or civil partner][11], the residuary estate of the intestate shall be held on the statutory trusts for the issue of the intestate;

(iii) If the intestate leaves [no [spouse or civil partner][11] and no][4] issue but both parents, then the residuary estate of the intestate shall be held in trust for the father and mother in equal shares absolutely;

(iv) If the intestate leaves [no [spouse or civil partner][11] and][4] no issue but one parent, then the residuary estate of the intestate shall be held in trust for the surviving father or mother absolutely;

(v) If the intestate leaves no [[spouse or civil partner][11] and no issue and no][5] parent, then the residuary estate of the intestate shall be held in trust for the following persons living at the death of the intestate, and in the following order and manner, namely

First, on the statutory trusts for the brothers and sisters of the whole blood of the intestate; but if no person takes an absolutely vested interest under such trusts; then

Secondly, on the statutory trusts for the brothers and sisters of the half blood of the intestate; but if no person takes an absolutely vested interest under such trusts; then

Thirdly, for the grandparents of the intestate and, if more than one survive the intestate, in equal shares; but if there is no member of this class; then

Fourthly, on the statutory trusts for the uncles and aunts of the intestate (being brothers or sisters of the whole blood of a parent of the intestate); but if no person takes an absolutely vested interest under such trusts; then

Fifthly, on the statutory trusts for the uncles and aunts of the intestate (being brothers or sisters of the half blood of a parent of the intestate);

. . .[6]

(vi) In default of any person taking an absolute interest under the foregoing provisions, the residuary estate of the intestate shall belong to the Crown or to the Duchy of Lancaster or to the Duke of Cornwall for the time being, as the case may be, as bona vacantia, and in lieu of any right to escheat.

The Crown or the said Duchy or the said Duke may (without prejudice to the powers reserved by section nine of the Civil List Act 1910, or any other powers), out of the whole or any part of the property devolving on them respectively, provide, in accordance with the existing practice, for dependants, whether kindred or not, of the intestate, and other persons for whom the intestate might reasonably have been expected to make provision.

[(1A) The interest rate referred to in paragraph (B) of case (2) of the Table in subsection (1)(i) is the Bank of England rate that had effect at the end of the day on which the intestate died.][7]

(2) A husband and wife shall for all purposes of distribution or division under the foregoing provisions of this section be treated as two persons.

[(2A) Where the intestate's [spouse or civil partner][11] survived the intestate but died before the end of the period of 28 days beginning with the day on which the intestate died, this section shall have effect as respects the intestate as if the [spouse or civil partner][11] had not survived the intestate.][10]

(3) . . .[2]

(4) The interest payable on the [fixed net sum][9] payable to a surviving [spouse or civil partner][11] shall be primarily payable out of income.][8]

[(5) In subsection (1A) "Bank of England rate" means—

(*a*) the rate announced by the Monetary Policy Committee of the Bank of England as the official bank rate, or

(*b*) where an order under section 19 of the Bank of England Act 1998 (reserve powers) is in force, any equivalent rate determined by the Treasury under that section.

(6) The Lord Chancellor may by order made by statutory instrument amend the definition of "Bank of England rate" in subsection (5) (but this subsection does not affect the generality of subsection (7)(*b*)).

(7) The Lord Chancellor may by order made by statutory instrument—

(*a*) amend subsection (1A) so as to substitute a different interest rate (however specified or identified) for the interest rate for the time being provided for by that subsection;

(*b*) make any amendments of, or repeals in, this section that may be consequential on or incidental to any amendment made by virtue of paragraph (*a*).

(8) A statutory instrument containing an order under subsection (6) is subject to annulment pursuant to a resolution of either House of Parliament.

(9) A statutory instrument containing an order under subsection (7) may not be made unless a draft of the instrument has been laid before and approved by a resolution of each House of Parliament.][7]

Note—For Scotland see Succession (Scotland) Act 1964 ss 8, 9, 9A.

Cross references—SI 2009/135: sub-s (1) shall apply, in the case of persons dying on or after 1 February 2009, as if the net sums charged by paragraph (i) on the residuary estate were—

– under para (2) of the Table, £250,000; and

– under para (3) of the Table, £450,000.

Amendments—[1] In s 46(1), para (i) was substituted by the Intestates' Estates Act 1952 s 1.

[2] Sub-s (3) repealed by the Inheritance and Trustees' Powers Act 2014 s 11, Sch 4 para 1(1), (2) with effect from 1 October 2014 (by virtue of SI 2014/2039) and in relation to deaths occurring after that date. This amendment extends to England and Wales only (Inheritance and Trustees' Powers Act 2014 s 12(5)). Sub-s (3) previously read as follows—

"(3) Where the intestate and the intestate's spouse or civil partner have died in circumstances rendering it uncertain which of them survived the other and the intestate's spouse or civil partner is by virtue of section one hundred and eight-four of the Law of Property Act 1925, deemed to have survived the intestate, this section shall, nevertheless, have effect as respects the intestate as if the spouse or civil partner had not survived the intestate.".

[3] In para 2 and 3 of the Table, the words "fixed net sum" were substituted by the Family Provision Act 1966, s 1(2)(*a*) as were the words from "The fixed net sums" to the end of s 46(1)(i).

[4] In s 46(1)(iii) and 46(1)(iv), the words "no husband or wife and" were inserted by, and the words "subject to the interests of a surviving husband or wife" were repealed by, the Intestates' Estates Act 1952 s 1(3)(*a*).

[5] In s 46(1)(v), the words "husband or wife and no issue and no" were substituted for the words "issue or" by the Intestates' Estates Act 1952 s 1(3)(*b*)(i).

[6] In s 46(1)(v), the words "subject to the interests of a surviving husband of wife", and the words "but if no person takes an absolutely vested interest under such trusts: then Sixthly for the surviving husband or wife of the intestate absolutely" (which occurred at the end of s 46(1)(v)) repealed by the Intestates' Estates Act 1952 s 1(3)(*b*)(ii).

[7] In sub-s (1), Table in para (i) and following sentence substituted, sub-s (1A) substituted, and sub-ss (5)–(9) inserted by the Inheritance and Trustees' Powers Act 2014 s 1 with effect from 1 October 2014 (by virtue of SI 2014/2039) and in relation to deaths occurring after that date. This amendment extends to England and Wales only (Inheritance and Trustees' Powers Act 2014 s 12(5)). Table and following sentence previously read as follows—

"TABLE

If the intestate—

(1) leaves— (*a*) no issue, and (*b*) no parent, or brother or sister of the whole blood, or issue of a brother or sister of the whole blood	the residuary estate shall be held in trust for the surviving [spouse or civil partner][11] absolutely.
(2) leaves issue (whether or not persons mentioned in sub-paragraph (b) above also survive)	the surviving [spouse or civil partner][11] shall take the personal chattels absolutely and, in addition, the residuary estate of the intestate (other than the personal chattels) shall stand charged with the payment of a [fixed net sum][3] free of death duties and costs, to the surviving [spouse or civil partner][11] with interest thereon from the date of the death [at such rate as the Lord Chancellor may specify by order][2] until paid or appropriated, and, subject to providing for that sum and the interest thereon, the residuary estate (other than the personal chattels) shall be held— (*a*) as to one half upon trust for the surviving [spouse or civil partner][11] during his or her life, and, subject to such life interest, on the statutory trusts for the issue of the intestate, and (*b*) as to the other half, on the statutory trusts for the issue of the intestate.

(3) leaves one or more of the following, that is to say, a parent, a brother or sister of the whole blood, or issue of a brother or sister of the whole blood, but leaves no issue	the surviving [spouse or civil partner][11] shall take the personal chattels absolutely and, in addition, the residuary estate of the intestate (other than the personal chattels) shall stand charged with the payment of a [fixed net sum][3], free of death duties and costs, to the surviving [spouse or civil partner][11] with interest thereon from the date of the death at the rate of four pounds per cent per annum until paid or appropriated, and, subject to providing for that sum and the interest thereon, the residuary estate (other than the personal chattels) shall be held— (*a*) as to one half in trust for the surviving [spouse or civil partner][11] absolutely, and (*b*) as to the other half— (i) where the intestate leaves one parent or both parents (whether or not brothers or sisters of the intestate or their issue also survive) in trust for the parent absolutely or, as the case may be, for the two parents in equal shares absolutely, (ii) where the intestate leaves no parent, on the statutory trusts for the brothers and sisters of the whole blood of the intestate].

[The fixed net sums referred to in paragraphs (2) and (3) of this Table shall be of the amounts provided by or under section 1 of the Family Provision Act 1966.".

Sub-s (1A) previously read as follows—

"(1A) The power to make orders under subsection (1) above shall be exercisable by statutory instrument subject to annulment in pursuance of a resolution of either House of Parliament; and any such order may be varied or revoked by a subsequent order made under the power.".

8 S 46(3), (4) were inserted by the Intestates' Estates Act 1952 s 1(4).

9 S 46(4) the words "fixed net sum" were substituted by the Family Provision Act 1966 s 1(2)(*b*).

10 Sub-s (2A) inserted by the Law Reform (Succession) Act 1995, s 1(1), (3) with effect from 8 November 1995.

11 Words "spouse or civil partner" substituted for the words "husband or wife" by the Civil Partnership Act 2004 s 71, Sch 4 para 7 with effect from 5 December 2005, by virtue of SI 2005/3175 art 2(1).

[46A Disclaimer or forfeiture on intestacy

(1) This section applies where a person—

(*a*) is entitled in accordance with section 46 to an interest in the residuary estate of an intestate but disclaims it, or

(*b*) would have been so entitled had the person not been precluded by the forfeiture rule from acquiring it.

(2) The person is to be treated for the purposes of this Part as having died immediately before the intestate.

(3) But in a case within subsection (1)(*b*), subsection (2) does not affect the power conferred by section 2 of the Forfeiture Act 1982 (power of court to modify the forfeiture rule).

(4) In this section "forfeiture rule" has the same meaning as in the Forfeiture Act 1982.][1]

Amendments—[1] Section 46A inserted by the Estates of Deceased Persons (Forfeiture Rule and Law of Succession) Act 2011 s 1 with effect from 1 February 2012 (SI 2011/2913 art 2).

[SCHEDULE 1A

DETERMINATION OF THE FIXED NET SUM][1]

Amendments—[1] Schedule 1A inserted by the Inheritance and Trustees' Powers Act 2014 s 2, Sch 1 with effect in relation to deaths occurring after 1 October 2014 (by virtue of SI 2014/2039). This amendment extends to England and Wales only (Inheritance and Trustees' Powers Act 2014 s 12(5)).

[1 This Schedule has effect for determining the fixed net sum referred to in paragraph (B) of case (2) of the Table in section 46(1)(i).][1]

Amendments—[1] Schedule 1A inserted by the Inheritance and Trustees' Powers Act 2014 s 2, Sch 1 with effect in relation to deaths occurring after 1 October 2014 (by virtue of SI 2014/2039). This amendment extends to England and Wales only (Inheritance and Trustees' Powers Act 2014 s 12(5)).

[2 On the coming into force of this Schedule, the amount of the fixed net sum is the amount fixed by order under section 1(1)(a) of the Family Provision Act 1966 immediately before the coming into force of this Schedule.][1]

Amendments—[1] Schedule 1A inserted by the Inheritance and Trustees' Powers Act 2014 s 2, Sch 1 with effect in relation to deaths occurring after 1 October 2014 (by virtue of SI 2014/2039). This amendment extends to England and Wales only (Inheritance and Trustees' Powers Act 2014 s 12(5)).

[3—(1) The Lord Chancellor may from time to time by order made by statutory instrument specify the amount of the fixed net sum.

(2) An order under sub-paragraph (1) relates only to deaths occurring after the coming into force of the order.
(3) The first order under sub-paragraph (1) supersedes paragraph 2 of this Schedule.
(4) A statutory instrument containing an order under sub-paragraph (1) is subject to annulment pursuant to a resolution of either House of Parliament.
(5) Sub-paragraph (4) does not apply in the case mentioned in paragraph 6(3), or in the case of an instrument which also contains provision made by virtue of paragraph 8.][1]

Amendments—[1] Schedule 1A inserted by the Inheritance and Trustees' Powers Act 2014 s 2, Sch 1 with effect in relation to deaths occurring after 1 October 2014 (by virtue of SI 2014/2039). This amendment extends to England and Wales only (Inheritance and Trustees' Powers Act 2014 s 12(5)).

[**4**—(1) This paragraph applies where—
(*a*) a figure for the consumer prices index for a month has become available, and
(*b*) the consumer prices index for that month is more than 15% higher than the consumer prices index for the base month.
(2) The Lord Chancellor must, before the end of the period of 21 days beginning with the day on which the figure mentioned in subparagraph (1)(a) becomes available ("the publication date"), make an order under paragraph 3(1).
(3) But if the Lord Chancellor determines under paragraph 6 that the order should specify an amount other than that mentioned in paragraph 6(1), the Lord Chancellor is to be taken to have complied with sub-paragraph (2) if, within the period of 21 days beginning with the publication date—
(*a*) a draft of a statutory instrument containing the order is laid before each House of Parliament, and
(*b*) paragraph 6(4) is complied with.
(4) In this paragraph—
"the base month" means—
(*a*) the month in which this Schedule came into force, or
(*b*) if one or more orders under paragraph 3(1) have been made before the publication date, the most recent month for which a figure for the consumer prices index was available when the Lord Chancellor made the most recent of those orders;
"consumer prices index" means—
(*a*) the all items consumer prices index published by the Statistics Board, or
(*b*) if that index is not published for a relevant month, any substituted index or index figures published by the Statistics Board.][1]

Amendments—[1] Schedule 1A inserted by the Inheritance and Trustees' Powers Act 2014 s 2, Sch 1 with effect in relation to deaths occurring after 1 October 2014 (by virtue of SI 2014/2039). This amendment extends to England and Wales only (Inheritance and Trustees' Powers Act 2014 s 12(5)).

[**5** The Lord Chancellor must ensure that the power under paragraph 3(1) is exercised in such a way that an order is made—
(*a*) before the end of the period of 5 years beginning with the date this Schedule comes into force, and then
(*b*) before the end of the period of 5 years since the date on which the last order under paragraph 3(1) was made, and so on.][1]

Amendments—[1] Schedule 1A inserted by the Inheritance and Trustees' Powers Act 2014 s 2, Sch 1 with effect in relation to deaths occurring after 1 October 2014 (by virtue of SI 2014/2039). This amendment extends to England and Wales only (Inheritance and Trustees' Powers Act 2014 s 12(5)).

[**6**—(1) Unless the Lord Chancellor otherwise determines, an order under paragraph 3(1) must specify the amount given by paragraph 7(2) or (as the case requires) 7(3).
(2) If the Lord Chancellor does otherwise determine—
(*a*) an order under paragraph 3(1) may provide for the fixed net sum to be of any amount (including an amount equal to or lower than the previous amount), and
(*b*) the Lord Chancellor must prepare a report stating the reason for the determination.
(3) A statutory instrument containing an order under paragraph 3(1) that specifies an amount other than that mentioned in subparagraph (1) of this paragraph may not be made unless a draft of the instrument has been laid before and approved by a resolution of each House of Parliament.
(4) The Lord Chancellor must lay the report before Parliament no later than the date on which the draft of the instrument containing the order is laid before Parliament.][1]

Amendments—[1] Schedule 1A inserted by the Inheritance and Trustees' Powers Act 2014 s 2, Sch 1 with effect in relation to deaths occurring after 1 October 2014 (by virtue of SI 2014/2039). This amendment extends to England and Wales only (Inheritance and Trustees' Powers Act 2014 s 12(5)).

[**7**—(1) The amount mentioned in paragraph 6(1) is found as follows.
(2) If the consumer prices index for the current month is higher than that for the base month, the amount to be specified in the order is found by—

(*a*) increasing the amount of the previous fixed net sum by the same percentage as the percentage increase in the consumer prices index between the base month and the current month, and

(*b*) if the resulting figure is not a multiple of £1,000, rounding it up to the nearest multiple of £1,000.

(3) If the consumer prices index for the current month is the same as, or lower than, that for the base month, the amount specified in the order is to be the same as the amount of the previous fixed net sum.

(4) In this paragraph—

"the base month" means—

(*a*) in the case of the first order under paragraph 3(1), the month in which this Schedule came into force, and

(*b*) in the case of each subsequent order, the month which was the current month in relation to the previous order;

"the current month" means the most recent month for which a figure for the consumer prices index is available when the Lord Chancellor makes the order;

"consumer prices index" has the same meaning as in paragraph 4.][1]

Amendments—[1] Schedule 1A inserted by the Inheritance and Trustees' Powers Act 2014 s 2, Sch 1 with effect in relation to deaths occurring after 1 October 2014 (by virtue of SI 2014/2039). This amendment extends to England and Wales only (Inheritance and Trustees' Powers Act 2014 s 12(5)).

[8—(1) The Lord Chancellor may by order made by statutory instrument amend paragraphs 4 and 7 so as to—

(*a*) substitute for references to the consumer prices index (as defined) references to another index, and

(*b*) make amendments in those paragraphs consequential on that substitution.

(2) A statutory instrument containing an order under sub-paragraph (1) may not be made unless a draft of the instrument has been laid before and approved by a resolution of each House of Parliament.][1]

Amendments—[1] Schedule 1A inserted by the Inheritance and Trustees' Powers Act 2014 s 2, Sch 1 with effect in relation to deaths occurring after 1 October 2014 (by virtue of SI 2014/2039). This amendment extends to England and Wales only (Inheritance and Trustees' Powers Act 2014 s 12(5)).

FINANCE ACT 1930

(20 & 21 Geo. 5, c 28)

An Act to grant certain duties of Customs and Inland Revenue (including Excise), to alter other duties, and to amend the law relating to Customs and Inland Revenue (including Excise) and the National Debt, and to make further provision in connection with finance.

[1 August 1930]

PART III.
ESTATE DUTY

Rates of Estate Duty

33 Amended rates of estate duty

The scale set out in the Second Schedule to this Act shall in the case of persons dying after the commencement of this Act be substituted for the scale set out in the Fourth Schedule to the Finance Act, 1925, as the scale of rates of estate duty :

Provided that, where an interest in expectancy within the meaning of Part I of the Finance Act, 1894 (in this Part of this Act referred to as " the principal Act "), in any property (other than property deemed to pass on a death by virtue of the provisions of the next succeeding section but one of this Act) has, before the fourteenth day of April, nineteen hundred and thirty, been bona fide sold or mortgaged for full consideration in money or money's worth, then no other duty on that property shall be payable by the purchaser or mortgagee when the interest falls into possession than would have been payable if this Part of this Act had not passed, and in the case of a mortgage any higher duty payable by the mortgagor shall rank as a charge subsequent to that of the mortgagee.

Amendments—So far as not previously repealed, Part III repealed by FA 1975 s 59, Sch 13 Pt I with effect in relation to deaths occurring after 13 March 1975. The repeals made by Sch 13 Pt I have effect so far as they relate to any duty mentioned in FA 1975 s 50 (final abolition of obsolete death duties), in relation to any death, but subject to section 52(3) of that Act. Section 52(3) provides as follows—

"The repeal by this section of any enactment relating to a duty mentioned in section 50 of this Act shall not affect its operation for the purposes of any such right to repayment or allowance as is referred to in subsection (2) of that section.".

Companies

34–38

Amendments—Sections 34–39 repealed by FA 1940 s 65(8), Sch 8.

So far as not previously repealed, Part III repealed by FA 1975 s 59, Sch 13 Pt I with effect in relation to deaths occurring after 13 March 1975. The repeals made by Sch 13 Pt I have effect so far as they relate to any duty mentioned in FA 1975 s 50 (final abolition of obsolete death duties), in relation to any death, but subject to section 52(3) of that Act. Section 52(3) provides as follows—

"The repeal by this section of any enactment relating to a duty mentioned in section 50 of this Act shall not affect its operation for the purposes of any such right to repayment or allowance as is referred to in subsection (2) of that section.".

Miscellaneous

39

Amendments—Sections 34–39 repealed by FA 1940 s 65(8), Sch 8.

So far as not previously repealed, Part III repealed by FA 1975 s 59, Sch 13 Pt I with effect in relation to deaths occurring after 13 March 1975. The repeals made by Sch 13 Pt I have effect so far as they relate to any duty mentioned in FA 1975 s 50 (final abolition of obsolete death duties), in relation to any death, but subject to section 52(3) of that Act. Section 52(3) provides as follows—

"The repeal by this section of any enactment relating to a duty mentioned in section 50 of this Act shall not affect its operation for the purposes of any such right to repayment or allowance as is referred to in subsection (2) of that section.".

40 Exemption from death duties of objects of national, scientific, historic or artistic interest

(1) Where there pass on the death of a person dying after the commencement of this Act any objects to which this section applies, the value of those objects shall not be taken into account for the purpose of estimating the principal value of the estate passing on the death or the rate at which estate duty is chargeable thereon, and those objects shall, while enjoyed in kind, be exempt from death duties.

(2) In the event of the sale of any objects to which this section applies, death duties shall, subject as hereinafter provided, become chargeable on the proceeds of sale in respect of the last death on which the objects passed and, as respects estate duty, at the rate appropriate to the principal value of the estate passing on that death upon which estate duty is leviable, and with which the objects would have been aggregated if they had not been objects to which this section applies, and the person by whom or for whose benefit the objects were sold shall be accountable for the duties and shall deliver an account for the purposes thereof within one month after the sale:

Provided that death duties shall not become chargeable as aforesaid if the sale is to the National Gallery, British Museum, or any other similar national institution, any university, county council or municipal corporation in Great Britain, or the National Art Collections Fund.

[(2A) In the event of the loss of any objects to which this section applies, estate duty shall become chargeable on the value of those objects in respect of the last death on which the objects passed at the rate appropriate to the principal value of the estate passing on that death upon which estate duty is leviable, and with which the objects would have been aggregated if they had not been objects to which this section applies.

(2B) Where subsection (2A) applies, any owner of the objects—

(*a*) *shall be accountable for the estate duty, and*

(*b*) *shall deliver an account for the purposes thereof.*

(2C) The account under subsection (2B)(b) must be delivered within the period of one month beginning with—

(*a*) *in the case of a loss occurring before the coming into force of subsection (2A)—*

(i) *the coming into force of subsection (2A), or*

(ii) *if later, the date when the owner became aware of the loss;*

(*b*) *in the case of a loss occurring after the coming into force of subsection (2A)—*

(i) *the date of the loss, or*

(ii) *if later, the date when the owner became aware of the loss.*

This is subject to subsection (2E).

(2D) Subsection (2E) applies if—

(*a*) *no account has been delivered under subsection (2B),*

(*b*) *the Commissioners for Her Majesty's Revenue and Customs have by notice required an owner of the objects to confirm that the objects have not been lost,*

(*c*) *the owner has not so confirmed by the end of—*

(i) *the period of three months beginning with the day on which the notice was sent, or*

(ii) *such longer period as the Commissioners may allow, and*

(*d*) *the Commissioners are satisfied that the objects are lost.*

(2E) Where this subsection applies—

(*a*) *the objects are to be treated as lost for the purposes of subsection (2A) on the day on which the Commissioners are satisfied as specified in subsection (2D)(d),* and (*b*) *the account under subsection (2B)(b)* must be delivered within the period of one month beginning with that date.

(2F) The reference in subsection (2A) to the value of objects is to their value at the time they are lost (or treated as lost).

(2G) Subsection (2A) does not apply in relation to a loss notified to the Commissioners before the coming into force of that subsection.

(2H) In this section "owner", in relation to any objects, means a person who, if the objects were sold, would be entitled to receive (whether for their own benefit or not) the proceeds of sale or any income arising therefrom.

(2I) In this section references to the loss of objects include their theft or destruction; but do not include a loss which the Commissioners are satisfied was outside the owner's control.][3]

(3) The objects to which this section applies are such pictures, prints, books, manuscripts, works of art, scientific collections or other things not yielding income as on a claim being made to the Treasury under this section appear to them to be of national, scientific, historic or artistic interest.

(4) Nothing ,in this section shall affect the power of the Treasury under subsection (2) of section fifteen of the principal Act to remit death duties chargeable in respect of any objects to which that section applies.[1], [2]

Modifications—In its application to a sale which does not comply with IHTA 1984 Sch 5 para 6, sub-s (2) shall have effect as if the reference to the proceeds of sale were a reference to the value of the objects on that date (IHTA 1984 Sch 6 para 4).

Cross-references—See FA 2012 Sch 14 (gifts to the nation).

FA 2012 Sch 14 para 32A (qualifying gift of an object in circumstances where, had the donor instead sold the object to an individual at market value, a charge to estate duty would have arisen under this section on the proceeds of sale).

FA 2012 Sch 14 para 33 (limit on amount of duty that becomes chargeable as result of a qualifying gift).

VATA 1994 Sch 9 Group 11 (works of art—exempt supplies for VAT purposes).

Amendments—[1] Section 40 repealed by FA 1949 s 52(10), Sch 11 Pt IV except in relation to estate duty. The savings to Sch 11 Pt IV state the following—

"The repeal of any enactment by this Part of this Schedule shall not affect its operation in relation to estate duty leviable on or by reference to a death occurring before the commencement of this Act, or in relation to any legacy duty, succession duty or temporary estate duty under section six of the Customs and Inland Revenue Act, 1889, to which section twenty-seven of this Act does not apply.".

[2] So far as not previously repealed, Part III repealed by FA 1975 s 59, Sch 13 Pt I with effect in relation to deaths occurring after 13 March 1975. The repeals made by Sch 13 Pt I have effect so far as they relate to any duty mentioned in FA 1975 s 50 (final abolition of obsolete death duties), in relation to any death, but subject to section 52(3) of that Act. Section 52(3) provides as follows—

"The repeal by this section of any enactment relating to a duty mentioned in section 50 of this Act shall not affect its operation for the purposes of any such right to repayment or allowance as is referred to in subsection (2) of that section.".

[3] Sub-ss (2A)–(2I) inserted by FA 2016 s 97(1) with effect from 15 September 2016, in so far as s 40 continues to have effect.

FINANCE (NO 2) ACT 1931

(21 & 22 Geo. 5 c 49)

22 Provisions in cases where Treasury has power to borrow money

(1) Any securities issued by the Treasury under any Act may be issued with the condition that—

(*a*) so long as the securities are in the beneficial ownership of persons who are not . . . [2] resident in the United Kingdom, the interest thereon shall be exempt from income tax; and

(*b*) so long as the securities are in the beneficial ownership of persons who are neither domiciled nor . . . [2] resident in the United Kingdom, neither the capital thereof nor the interest thereon shall be liable to any taxation present or future.

(2) . . . [1]

Commentary—*Simon's Taxes* **E1.539, I9.321**.

Simon's Tax Cases—s 22(1), *Von Ernst & Cie SA v IRC* [1980] STC 111.

Cross references—See FA 1940 s 60(1) (extension of the Treasury's powers under this section).

Amendments—[1] Sub-s (2) repealed by Income Tax Act 1952 s 527 and Sch 25 Pt I.

[2] Word in sub-s (1)(*a*), (*b*) repealed by FA 2013 s 219, Sch 46 para 114(1) with effect from 17 July 2013, subject to FA 2013 Sch 46 para 114 (2)–(6).

FINANCE ACT 1940

(3 & 4 Geo. 6 c 29)

44 Purchase of annuities etc from relatives

[(1) Any disposition made by the deceased in favour of a relative of his shall be treated for the purposes of paragraph (c) of subsection (1) of section two of the Finance Act, 1894, as a gift unless—

IHT

(a) *the disposition was made, on the part of the deceased for full consideration in money or money's worth paid to him for his own use or benefit; or*

(b) *the deceased was concerned in a fiduciary capacity imposed on him otherwise than by a disposition made by him and in such a capacity only;*

and references to a gift in the other enactments relating to estate duty (including this Part of this Act) shall be construed accordingly:

Provided that where the disposition was made on the part of the deceased for partial consideration in money or money's worth paid to him for his own use or benefit, the value of the consideration shall be allowed as a deduction from the value of the property for the purpose of estate duty.

(1A) Where the deceased made a disposition of property in favour of a relative of his, the creation or disposition in favour of the deceased of an annuity or other interest limited to cease on the death of the deceased or of any other person shall not be treated for the purposes of this section or of subsection (1) of section seven of the Finance Act, 1894, as consideration for the disposition made by the deceased.

(1B) If a company to which this section applies was concerned in a transaction in relation to which it is claimed that the provisions of paragraph (z) of or the proviso to subsection (1) of this section have effect, those provisions shall have effect in relation thereto if and only if, and to the extent only to which, the Commissioners are satisfied that those provisions would have had effect in the following circumstances, namely, if the assets of the company had been held by it on trust for the members thereof and any other person to whom it is under any liability incurred otherwise than for the purposes of the business of the company wholly and exclusively, in accordance with the rights attaching to the shares and debentures of the company and the terms on which any such liability was incurred, and if the company had acted in the capacity of a trustee only with power to carry on the business of the company and to employ the assets of the company therein.

(1C) Any gift made in favour of a relative of the deceased by a company of which the deceased at the time of the gift had control within the meaning of subsection (3) of section fifty-five of this Act shall be treated for the purposes of paragraph (c) of subsection (1) of section two of the Finance Act, 1894, as a gift made by the deceased, and the property taken under the gift shall be treated as included by virtue of that paragraph in the property passing on the death of the deceased, if and to the extent to which the Commissioners are satisfied that they would fall to be so treated in the circumstances mentioned in the last foregoing subsection.][2]

(2) In this section the expression " relative " means, in relation to the deceased,—

(a) *the wife or husband of the deceased;*

(b) *the father, mother, children, uncles and aunts, of the deceased; and*

(c) *any issue of any person falling within either of the preceding paragraphs and the other party to a marriage with any such person or issue;*

and references to " children " and " issue " include references to illegitimate children and to adopted children.

(3) In this section the expression " annuity " includes any series of payments, whether interconnected or not, whether of the same or of varying amounts, and whether payable at regular intervals or otherwise, and payments of dividends or interest on shares in or debentures of a company shall be treated for the purposes of this section as a series of payments constituting an annuity limited to cease on a death if the payments are liable to cease on the death, or the amounts thereof are liable to be reduced on the death, by reason directly or indirectly of the extinguishment or any alteration of rights attaching to, or of the issue of, any shares in or debentures of a company.

(4) If the deceased has made in favour of a company to which this section applies a disposition which, if it had been made in favour of a relative of his, would have fallen within subsection (1) of this section, this section shall have effect in like manner as if the disposition had been made in favour of a relative of his, unless it is shown to the satisfaction of the Commissioners that no relative of the deceased was, at the time of the disposition or subsequently during the life of the deceased, a member of the company.

For the purposes of this subsection a person who is, or is deemed by virtue of this provision to be, a member of a company to which this section applies and which is a member of another such company shall be deemed to be a member of that other company.

(5) Where there have been associated operations effected with reference to the receiving by the deceased of any payment in respect of such an annuity or other interest as is mentioned in subsection (1) of this section, or effected with a view to enabling him to receive or to facilitating the receipt by him of any such payment, this section shall have effect in relation to each of those associated operations as it has effect in relation to the creation or disposition in favour of the deceased of such an annuity or other interest.

Amendments—[1] Section 44 repealed by FA 1975 ss 52(5), 59(5), Sch 13 Pt I in relation to deaths occurring after 13 March 1975. In so far as this repeal relates to any duty mentioned in FA 1975 s 50 (including estate duty), it has effect in relation to any death, but subject to FA 1975 s 52(3), which provides as follows—

"The repeal by this section of any enactment relating to a duty mentioned in section 50 of this Act shall not affect its operation for the purposes of any such right to repayment or allowance as is referred to in subsection (2) of that section.".

[2] Sub-ss (1)–(1C) substituted for previous sub-s (1) by FA 1950 s 46 with effect in relation to a person dying after 18 April 1950.

51 Limitation on, and prevention of duplication of, charge

(1) If it is shown to the satisfaction of the Commissioners that—

(a) the value of all such property as is mentioned in subsection (1) of section forty-six of this Act, of which the deceased made a transfer to the company, together with an amount equal to any excess of interest at the average rate on the value thereof from the date or respective dates of transfer to the death of the deceased over the aggregate amount of the benefits received by the deceased by virtue of the transfer, is less than—

(b) the value on which estate duty would be chargeable on the death under the said section if all benefits accruing to him from the company other than the benefits received by him by virtue of the transfer were disregarded,

an amount equal to the deficiency shall be deducted from the proportion of the value of the company's assets that corresponds to the benefits received by him by virtue of the transfer.

References in this subsection to benefits received by the deceased by virtue of a transfer shall be construed as references to benefits accruing to him from the company which he received or had as consideration for the transfer, or in consequence of his having received as consideration therefor shares or debentures or other property which produced any of those benefits.

[(1A) Where the following conditions are satisfied, that is to say, that the deceased has, within five years before his death, disposed of any shares in or debentures of the company for consideration in money or money's worth paid to him for his own use or benefit, and that any benefits accrued to the deceased from the company by virtue of those shares or debentures or by virtue of a power's having been exercisable by him or with his consent in relation to . those shares or debentures, then—

- (a) *if the value of the said consideration is equal to or greater than the proportion of the value of the company's assets that corresponds to the benefits that so accrued to him, or if the Commissioners are satisfied that the said proportion would not, if fully ascertained, be found to be substantially in excess of the value of the said consideration, duty on the said proportion shall not be payable;*
- (b) *in any other case, the amount on which duty is to be charged in respect of the said proportion shall be reduced by the amount of the value of the said consideration:*

Provided that, in the case of any shares or debentures—

- (i) *this subsection shall not apply where estate duty is payable on the death on their value or any part thereof or would be so payable but for an exemption from estate duty; and*
- (ii) *for the purpose of determining to what extent, if any, the disposition of them satisfies the conditions of this subsection, section fifty-six of this Act (which relates to transactions through the medium of a company), shall apply as it applies for the purposes of section three of the Finance Act, 1894.]*[2]

(2) Where any benefits accrued to the deceased from the company by virtue of any interest that he at any time had in shares in or debentures of the company, or by virtue of a power's having at any time been exercisable,by him or with his consent in relation to shares in or debentures of the company, and apart from this subsection estate duty would be payable on the death both on the value of those shares or debentures by virtue of any of the enactments relating to that duty other than section forty-six of this Act and on the proportion of the value of the company's assets that corresponds to the benefits that so accrued to him by virtue of that section,—

- (a) *if the value of the shares or debentures is equal to or greater than the said proportion, or if the Commissioners are satisfied that the said value and the said proportion would not if fully ascertained be found to be substantially different, the duty on the value of the shares or debentures shall be payable, and the duty on the said proportion shall not be payable;*
- (b) *in any other case the duty on the said proportion shall be payable, and the duty on the value of the shares or debentures shall not be payable, so however that it shall, for the purposes of the said other enactments, be deemed to have been paid by virtue of the payment of the duty on the said proportion.*

(3) References in this section to the proportion of the value of the company's assets that corresponds to any particular benefits shall be construed as references to so much of the value on which estate duty is chargeable on the death by virtue of section forty-six of this Act as is chargeable by reason of the bringing of those benefits into the computation made under subsection (2) of that section. (4) So much of any income or periodical payment or enjoyment of a kind mentioned in section forty-seven of this Act as is shown to the satisfaction of the Commissioners to have represented, or to have been such that it would if received have represented, reasonable remuneration to the deceased for any services rendered by him as the holder of an office under the company shall, notwithstanding anything in that section, not be treated for the purposes of this Part of this Act as a benefit accruing to the deceased from the company; and any liability of the company in respect of the remuneration of any person as the holder of an office under the company shall be treated for the purposes of this Part of this Act as incurred for the purposes of the business of the company wholly and exclusively to the extent to which it is shown to the satisfaction of the Commissioners that the amount thereof was reasonable, and to that extent only.[1]

Amendments—[1] Section 51 repealed by FA 1975 ss 52(5), 59(5), Sch 13 Pt I in relation to deaths occurring after 13 March 1975. In so far as this repeal relates to any duty mentioned in FA 1975 s 50 (including estate duty), it has effect in relation to any death, but subject to FA 1975 s 52(3), which provides as follows—

"The repeal by this section of any enactment relating to a duty mentioned in section 50 of this Act shall not affect its operation for the purposes of any such right to repayment or allowance as is referred to in subsection (2) of that section.".

[2] Sub-s (1A) inserted by FA 1950 s 47 with effect from 28 July 1950.

60 Extension of power of Treasury to attach exemptions from taxation to securities

(1) The power of the Treasury under section twenty-two of the Finance (No 2) Act, 1931, to issue securities with the condition as to exemption from taxation specified in that section shall extend to the issuing of securities with that condition so modified, whether as to the extent of the exemption or the cases in which the exemption is to operate, as the Treasury may specify in the terms of the issue.

(2) . . . [1]

Amendments—[1] Sub-s (2) repealed by Income Tax Act 1952 s 527 and Sch 25 Pt I.

CROWN PROCEEDINGS ACT 1947

(10 & 11 Geo. 6 c 44)

14 Summary applications to High Court in certain revenue matters

(1) Subject to and in accordance with rules of court, the Crown may apply in a summary manner to the High Court—

(*a*) for the furnishing of information required to be furnished by any person under the enactments relating to [capital transfer tax][1];

(*b*) for the delivery of accounts and [payment of capital transfer tax under the Capital Transfer Tax Act 1984.][2]

(*c*), (*d*) . . .

(2) . . .

Notes—Sub-s (1)(*c*), (*d*) and sub-s (2) are not relevant to capital transfer tax (renamed "inheritance tax" by FA 1986 s 100(1) with effect from 25 July 1986). By virtue of s 42 of this Act, this section does not apply to Scotland. By virtue of the Northern Ireland (Crown Proceedings) Order, SI 1949/1836 and FA 1975 Sch 12 para 9, this section applies to Northern Ireland. In respect of Northern Ireland only, this section reads as follows, with effect from 19 March 1981; see the Crown Proceedings (Northern Ireland) Order, SI 1981/233, arts 1(1), (5), 31.

"**14 Summary applications to High Court in certain matters concerning Northern Ireland revenue**

Subject to and in accordance with rules of court, the Crown in right of His Majesty's Government in Northern Ireland may apply in a summary manner to the High Court—

(a) for payment of any tax (being a tax to which paragraph 8 of Schedule 2 to the Northern Ireland Constitution Act 1973 does not apply) levied under any enactment such as is mentioned in section 38(7) of this Act;

(b) for the delivery of any account required to be delivered, or the furnishing of any information required to be furnished, in connection with such a tax by any such enactment or by any instrument made thereunder."

Amendments—[1] Words in sub-s (1)(*a*) substituted by FA 1975 Sch 12 para 8(*a*). By virtue of FA 1986 s 100(1), (2) CTT is known as inheritance tax with effect from 25 July 1986.

[2] Words in sub-s (1)(*b*) substituted by CTTA 1984 Sch 8 para 2 with effect from 1 January 1985. By virtue of FA 1986 s 100(1), (2) CTT is known as inheritance tax and CTTA 1984 may be cited as Inheritance Tax Act 1984 with effect from 25 July 1986.

FINANCE ACT 1950

14 Geo 6 c 15

An Act to grant certain duties and alter other duties, to make certain amendments of the law relating to purchase tax, to amend the law relating to other branches of the public revenue or to the National Debt, and to make further provision in connection with Finance.

[28 July 1950]

PART IV

ESTATE DUTY

43 Disposition or determination of life interests etc

. . . [1]

Amendments—[1] Sections 43, 45 repealed by FA 1969 s 61(6), Sch 21 Pt V with effect in relation to deaths occurring after 15 April 1969 and subject to savings in FA 1969 s 40(2).

44 Collection of duty from trustees after disposition or determination of life interest, etc

(1) Where an interest limited to cease on a death (within the meaning of section forty-three of the Finance Act, 1940) after becoming an interest in possession is disposed of or determines wholly or partly, then, whatever the nature of the property in which the interest subsisted, the following persons shall be accountable for any estate duty payable on the death by virtue of that section (in addition to any persons accountable therefor apart from this section), that is to say—

(a) *if the settlement under which the interest subsisted is in existence at the death, the trustees for the time being of that settlement; and*

(b) *if it is not, the persons who were the last trustees of that settlement.*

(2) Notwithstanding anything in the foregoing subsection or in section eight of the Finance Act, 1894, no person shall be accountable as trustee of a settlement for any estate duty payable by virtue of the said section forty-three in respect of property paid or applied to or for the benefit of a person not of full age in the exercise of any express or implied power of advancement under the settlement, where that person is not and does not become absolutely and indefeasibly entitled to any share or interest in the property comprised in the settlement, and the property so paid or applied to him or for his benefit does not exceed altogether in amount one half of his presumptive share or interest in the property so comprised.

(3) Where—

(a) *the trustees of a settlement may become accountable for estate duty payable by virtue of the said section forty-three in respect of any property; and*

(b) *it is intended that the property or any part thereof shall cease to be comprised in the settlement;*

then if the trustees obtain from the Commissioners a certificate of the amount which in the opinion of the Commissioners may properly be treated as the prospective amount of the duty, and give the Commissioners all the information and evidence required by the Commissioners in connection with the application for the certificate, no person shall be accountable as trustee of the settlement for the duty to which the certificate relates to an amount in excess of the amount certified.

(4) It is hereby declared that a person who may become accountable as trustee of a settlement for estate duty payable by virtue of the said section forty-three on property which is or has been comprised in the settlement has a lien for the prospective amount of the duty and the costs in respect thereof on any it property in his hands which is so comprised.

(5) Where the trustees of a settlement may become accountable for estate duty payable by virtue of the said section forty-three, on property which is or has been comprised in the settlement, they may refuse to execute a deed of discharge under section seventeen of the Settled Land Act, 1925, with respect to any land so comprised, or to make or concur in a conveyance of any such land to a person entitled to, it as mentioned in subsection (5) of section seven of that Act, unless they are satisfied that they are effectually indemnified against their liability by virtue of this section up to the prospective amount of the duty and the costs in respect thereof.

(6) Where land comprised in a settlement is not vested in the trustees of the settlement, but they are entitled under the last foregoing subsection to refuse to make or concur in a conveyance such as is there mentioned, they may require the person having the possession of the last or only principal vesting instrument to endorse on or annex to that instrument a memorandum that any such conveyance of land so comprised requires the concurrence of the trustees for the time being of the settlement, or, in the case of registered land, they may require the proprietor to apply for the entry on the register of a restriction to the like effect; and thereafter no such conveyance shall be made except by the, trustees for the time being or with their concurrence.

(7) References in this section to the 'prospective amount of any duty are to be taken as referring to the prospective amount of the duty on the assumption that it will become, chargeable.

(8) Subsections (1) and (2) of this section shall have effect in relation to any death occurring after the eighteenth day of April, nineteen hundred and fifty, whether or not the relevant interest is disposed of or determines after that date, so however that no person shall by virtue of the said subsection (1) be accountable as trustee of any settlement for any duty except to the extent of the property comprised in the settlement after the said eighteenth day of April; and subsection (3) of this section shall be deemed always to have had effect and to have applied with any necessary modifications to duty payable by virtue of section eleven of the Finance Act, 1900, or section thirty-nine of the Finance Act, 1930, as it applies to duty payable by virtue of section forty-three of, the Finance Act, 1940.[1]

Amendments—[1] Section 44 repealed by FA 1975 ss 52(5), 59(5), Sch 13 Pt I in relation to deaths occurring after 13 March 1975. In so far as this repeal relates to any duty mentioned in FA 1975 s 50 (including estate duty), it has effect in relation to any death, but subject to FA 1975 s 52(3), which provides as follows—

> "The repeal by this section of any enactment relating to a duty mentioned in section 50 of this Act shall not affect its operation for the purposes of any such right to repayment or allowance as is referred to in subsection (2) of that section.".

45 Parliamentary settled estates

...[1]

Amendments—[1] Sections 43, 45 repealed by FA 1969 s 61(6), Sch 21 Pt V with effect in relation to deaths occurring after 15 April 1969 and subject to savings in FA 1969 s 40(2).

46 Dispositions in favour of relatives

(1) (substitutes FA 1940 s 44(1)–(1C))

(2) Where the foregoing subsection applies—

(a) *references to subsection (1A) of the said section forty-four shall be substituted—*

(i) *for the reference to subsection (1) of that section in subsection (5) thereof; and*

(ii) *for the reference to that section in subsection (1) of section forty of the Finance Act, 1944 (which allows from the value of the property chargeable by virtue of the said section forty-four a deduction for the deceased's annuity payments, but limits the deduction to the amount specified in the Third Schedule to that Act); and*

(b) *section forty of the Finance Act, 1944, shall have effect also as if for paragraph 2 of the Third Schedule to that Act there were substituted the following paragraph:—*

"2. Where under section forty-four of the Finance Act, 1940, a deduction for partial consideration would have been allowable in respect of the annuity or other interest if subsection (1A) of that section had not applied to the disposition and if any other consideration for the disposition had not been given, the amount allowed shall not exceed the amount of that deduction."[1]

Amendments—[1] Section 46 repealed by FA 1975 ss 52(5), 59(5), Sch 13 Pt I in relation to deaths occurring after 13 March 1975. In so far as this repeal relates to any duty mentioned in FA 1975 s 50 (including estate duty), it has effect in relation to any death, but subject to FA 1975 s 52(3), which provides as follows—

"The repeal by this section of any enactment relating to a duty mentioned in section 50 of this Act shall not affect its operation for the purposes of any such right to repayment or allowance as is referred to in subsection (2) of that section.".

47 Amendment of s 51 of Finance Act 1940

(inserts FA 1940 s 51(1A))

Amendments—Section 47 repealed by FA 1975 ss 52(5), 59(5), Sch 13 Pt I in relation to deaths occurring after 13 March 1975. In so far as this repeal relates to any duty mentioned in FA 1975 s 50 (including estate duty), it has effect in relation to any death, but subject to FA 1975 s 52(3), which provides as follows—

"The repeal by this section of any enactment relating to a duty mentioned in section 50 of this Act shall not affect its operation for the purposes of any such right to repayment or allowance as is referred to in subsection (2) of that section.".

48 Objects of national, scientific, historic or artistic interest

(1) Subject to the next following subsection, section forty of the Finance Act, 1930 (which exempts from estate duty objects of national, scientific, historic or artistic interest), shall apply to objects which pass on a death occurring after the date of the passing of this Act only if an undertaking is given, by such person as the Treasury think appropriate in the circumstances of the case, that, until the objects again pass on a death or are sold—

(a) *the objects will be kept permanently in the United Kingdom, and will not leave it temporarily except- for a purpose and a period approved by the Treasury; and*

(b) *reasonable steps will be taken for the preservation of the objects; and*

(c) *reasonable facilities for examining the objects for the purpose of seeing the steps taken for their preservation, or for purposes of research, will be allowed to any person authorized by the Treasury so to examine them.*

(2) If on a claim for exemption under the said section forty it is made to appear to the Treasury that any documents for which the exemption is claimed contain information which for personal or other reasons ought to be treated as confidential, the Treasury may exclude those documents either altogether or to such extent as they think fit from any undertaking under the foregoing subsection so far as the undertaking relates to the examination of the documents for purposes of research.

(3) Where any. objects are exempted from estate duty in pursuance of an undertaking under subsection (1) of this section, and the Treasury are satisfied that at any time during the period for which the undertaking was given it has not been observed in a material respect, then estate duty shall become chargeable, on the value at that time of those objects, in respect of the death on which the exemption was given and at the rate appropriate to the principal value of the estate passing on that death upon which estate duty is leviable, and with which the objects would have been aggregated if they had not been objects to which the said section forty applies; and any person who, if the objects were sold when the duty becomes chargeable, would be entitled to receive (whether for his own benefit or not) the proceeds of sale or any income arising therefrom shall be accountable for the duty.

[(3A) But where the value of any objects is chargeable with estate duty under subsection (2A) of the said section forty (loss of objects), no estate duty shall be chargeable under this section on that value.][2]

(4) Where any objects are sold after becoming chargeable with estate duty under this section in respect of any death, the proceeds of sale shall not be chargeable with estate duty in respect of the same death under subsection (2) of the said section forty.

[(5) Where any objects are lost (within the meaning of the said section forty) after becoming chargeable with estate duty under this section in respect of any death, the value of those objects shall not be chargeable with estate duty under subsection (2A) of the said section forty.][2], [1]

Amendments—[1] Section 48 repealed by FA 1975 ss 52(5), 59(5), Sch 13 Pt I in relation to deaths occurring after 13 March 1975. In so far as this repeal relates to any duty mentioned in FA 1975 s 50 (including estate duty), it has effect in relation to any death, but subject to FA 1975 s 52(3), which provides as follows—

"The repeal by this section of any enactment relating to a duty mentioned in section 50 of this Act shall not affect its operation for the purposes of any such right to repayment or allowance as is referred to in subsection (2) of that section.".

[2] Sub-ss (3A), (5) inserted by FA 2016 s 97(2) with effect from 15 September 2016 in so far as s 48 continues to have effect.

FINANCE ACT 1969

(1969 Chapter 32)

[25 July 1969]

PART III
ESTATE DUTY

39 Objects of national, scientific, historic or artistic interest

(1) Where on any death an object to which section 40 of the Finance Act 1930 (which relates to the exemption from estate duty of objects of national, scientific, historic or artistic interest) applies has been exempted under subsection (1) of that section in pursuance of an undertaking under section 48(1) of the Finance Act 1950 as amended by section 31(7) of the Finance Act 1965 from estate duty in respect of that death, the provisions of this section shall have effect if duty subsequently becomes chargeable in relation to that object under subsection (2) [or (2A)][2] *of the said section 40 by reason of a sale or other disposal [or loss]*[2] *of the object or under subsection (3) of the said section 48 by reason of a non-observance of the undertaking.*

(2) If the event giving rise to the charge under the said subsection (2)[, (2A)][2] *or (3) occurred within the period of three years beginning with the date of the death, then, notwithstanding anything in the said section 40 or 48, the charge shall be on the principal value of the object at the date of the death, no allowance shall be made under section 31(8) of the Finance Act 1965 in determining that value, and that value shall, for all the purposes of estate duty, be aggregated with the principal value of the estate of which the object would but for the exemption have formed part as if the object had never been exempted.*

(3) If the event giving rise to the charge under the said sub-section (2)[, (2A)][2] *or (3) occurred after the expiration of the period aforesaid, then, notwithstanding anything in the said section 40 or 48, the rate at which estate duty becomes chargeable in relation to the object shall be the rate which would have been the estate rate of duty on the property comprised in the estate of which the object would have formed part on the death but for its exemption from duty if the aggregate principal value of that estate for the purposes of duty in respect of the death had been increased by [the amount in respect of which estate duty is chargeable under the said subsection]*[2]*.*

(4) Where two or more objects exempted as mentioned in subsection (1) of this section from estate duty in respect of the same death are objects which at the date of the death together formed a set, then if—

- (*a*) *there being a sale or other disposal of one of those objects, there is a sale or other disposal of another or others of them (whether by the same or by a different person) either—*
  - (i) *to the same person; or*
  - (ii) *to persons who are acting in concert or who are, in the terms of paragraph 21 of Schedule 7 to the Finance Act 1965, connected persons,*

  whether on the same or a different occasion; or
- (*b*) *there being a non-observance of the undertaking referred to in the said subsection (1) in regard to one or more of those objects, there is a further non-observance of that undertaking in regard to another or others of them whether by the same or by a different person and whether on the same or a different occasion; or*
- (*c*) *there being a non-observance of that undertaking in regard to one or more of those objects, the object or objects in question and another or others of the objects comprised in the set are sold or otherwise disposed of in such manner that paragraph (a)* of this subsection applies,

then, notwithstanding anything in subsection (4) of the said section 48, for the purpose of charging duty in accordance with this section under the said subsection (2) or (3) all the sales or other disposals referred to in paragraph (a) of this subsection, or all the non-observances referred to in paragraph (*b*) of this subsection, or, in a case falling within paragraph (*c*) of this subsection, all the non-observances and sales or other disposals there referred to, as the case may be, shall be treated as having taken place at the date of the earliest of them and to have been a sale of all the objects affected by the sales or other disposals or non-observances in question as a single item at a price equal to the aggregate amount of the proceeds of sale of any of those objects which has been sold since the death and the principal value at that earliest date of any of those objects which has not been sold since the death ; and on each occasion on which this subsection operates in relation to any sale or other disposal or non-observance, any estate duty previously charged in relation to any of the objects affected by that or any previous relevant sale or other disposal or non-observance or, by virtue of sub-section (2) of this section, on any estate of which any of those objects would have formed part but for their exemption from duty shall be adjusted accordingly.[1]

Amendments—[1] Section 39 repealed by FA 1975 ss 52(2), 59(5), Sch 13 Pt I in relation to deaths occurring after 13 March 1975. In so far as this repeal relates to any duty mentioned in FA 1975 s 50 (including estate duty), it has effect in relation to any death, but subject to FA 1975 s 52(3), which provides as follows—

"The repeal by this section of any enactment relating to a duty mentioned in section 50 of this Act shall not affect its operation for the purposes of any such right to repayment or allowance as is referred to in subsection (2) of that section.".

[2] In sub-ss (1), (2), words inserted, and in sub-s (3) words inserted and words substituted for words "the amount of the proceeds of sale or the value of the object at the time of the disposal otherwise than on sale or at the time of the non-observance of the undertaking, as the case may be", by FA 2016 s 97(3) with effect from 15 September 2016 in so far as s 39 continues to have effect.

FINANCE ACT 1975

(1975 Chapter 7)

PART III

CAPITAL TRANSFER TAX

Main charging provisions

19 Capital transfer tax

(1) . . . [1]

(2) Schedule 4 to this Act shall have effect with respect to the administration and collection of the tax.

Commentary—*Simon's Taxes* **I2.101**; *Foster* **B1.01**.

Simon's Tax Cases—*Re Clore (decd)* (No 3) [1985] STC 394.

Amendments—[1] Sub-s (1) repealed by CTTA 1984 Sch 9 with effect from 1 January 1985. By virtue of FA 1986 s 100(1), (2) CTTA 1984 may be cited as Inheritance Tax Act 1984 with effect from 25 July 1986.

Estate duty and obsolete death duties

49 Abolition of estate duty and transitional provisions

(1), (2) . . . [2]

(3) . . . [2]

(4) Where estate duty is under section 61(5) of the Finance (1909–10) Act 1910 payable on the net moneys received from the sale of timber, trees or wood when felled or cut during the period referred to therein and that period has not ended before the passing of this Act, that period shall end immediately after the first transfer of value made after the passing of this Act in which the value transferred is, or is determined by reference to, the value of the land concerned, other than a transfer exempt by virtue of paragraph 1 of Schedule 6 to this Act [or section 18 of the Capital Transfer Tax Act 1984.][1]

(5) . . . [2]

Commentary—*Simon's Taxes* **I7.401**; *Foster* **G4.01**.

Note—Sub-ss (1), (2) are not relevant to this work.

Cross references—See FA 1986 Sch 19 para 46 (transfer of value made after 30 June 1986 and which by virtue of sub-s (4) above brings to an end the period during which estate duty is payable is not a potentially exempt transfer).

Amendments—[1] Words in sub-s (4) inserted by CTTA 1984 Sch 8 para 4 with effect from 1 January 1985. By virtue of FA 1986 s 100(1), (2) CTTA 1984 may be cited as Inheritance Tax Act 1984 with effect from 25 July 1986.

[2] Sub-ss (3) and (5) repealed by CTTA 1984 Sch 9 with effect from 1 January 1985. By virtue of FA 1986 s 100(1), (2) CTTA 1984 may be cited as Inheritance Tax Act 1984 with effect from 25 July 1986.

SCHEDULES

SCHEDULE 4

ADMINISTRATION AND COLLECTION OF CAPITAL TRANSFER TAX

Section 19

Refusal of probate or administration where tax unpaid

38—(1) . . . [2]

(2) (*amends* the Probate and Legacy Duties Act 1808 s 42)

(3) . . . [1]

(4) . . . [2] . . . [1] and the amendment made by sub-paragraph (2) above have effect in relation to grants and confirmations in respect of the estates of persons dying after the passing of this Act.

Commentary—*Simon's Taxes* **I11.403**; *Foster* **L4.03**.

Cross references—See FA 1986 s 100(1), (2) (CTT to be known as inheritance tax with effect from 25 July 1986. Accordingly the references to CTT in sub-s (2) above must be read as references to inheritance tax with effect from that date).

Amendments—[1] Sub-para (3) and the words in sub-para (4) repealed by the Administration of Estates (Northern Ireland) Order, SI 1979/1575 (NI 14), Art 1 (2) and Sch 3 and the Administration of Estates (Northern Ireland) (Commencement No 2) Order 1980, SR 1980/166, with effect from 1 June 1980.

[2] Sub-para (1) and words in sub-para (4) repealed by the Senior Courts Act 1981 ss 152(4), 153(2) and Sch 7 with effect from 1 January 1982.

SCHEDULE 8

RELIEF FOR AGRICULTURAL PROPERTY

Sections 35 and 49(2)

PART I

CAPITAL TRANSFER TAX

Note—This Part of this Schedule repealed by FA 1981 s 96(3) and Sch 19 Pt IX in relation to transfers of value made after 9 March 1981. Reference to these repealed provisions may be necessary in conjunction with some of the legislation now in force.

Nature of relief

1—*(1) Where the value transferred by a chargeable transfer is determined by reference to the value of agricultural property in the United Kingdom and the conditions stated in paragraph 3 below are satisfied, then, if—*

(a) . . . [1]

(b) a person liable to pay the whole or part of the tax on the value transferred makes a claim in that behalf to the Board within two years of the transfer or such longer time as the Board may allow;

the value transferred shall be [computed in accordance with paragraph 2 below][2] *and tax shall be chargeable accordingly, but subject to the limit imposed by paragraph 5 below.*

(2) The conditions stated in paragraph 3 below shall be deemed to be satisfied with respect to a transfer of value (in this sub-paragraph referred to as the current transfer) if—

(a) not more than two years before the current transfer there was (or would have been had this Act then been in force) a transfer of value [and either that transfer or the current transfer was or would have been a transfer made on death][3]*; and*

(b) the value transferred by the earlier transfer was or would have been determined by reference to the value of the same agricultural property as in the case of the current transfer; and

(c) the conditions stated in paragraph 3 below were or would have been satisfied with respect to the earlier transfer; and

(d) the agricultural property was, at the time of the current transfer, occupied for the purposes of agriculture by the transferor or by the personal representatives of the person who was or would have been the transferor in relation to the earlier transfer [; and

[(e) the agricultural property became, through the earlier transfer, the property of the person or of the spouse of the person who is the transferor in relation to the current transfer][4].

[(2A) Where, by virtue of sub-paragraph (2) above, the conditions stated in paragraph 3 below are deemed to be satisfied but, under the earlier transfer mentioned in that sub-paragraph, the amount of the value transferred which was attributable to the agricultural property was part only of the value of that property, a like part of its agricultural value shall be substituted for the agricultural value of the property in ascertaining the part eligible for relief under paragraph 2 below.][4]

(3) In the following provisions of this Part of this Schedule, "the unreduced value", in relation to a chargeable transfer, means the value transferred, calculated before the reduction and as if no tax were chargeable on it.

Commentary—*Simon's Taxes* **I7.201, I7.202**. *Foster* **G2.01, 02**.

Cross reference—See IHTA 1984 s 116(3)(*a*) (relief for agricultural property).

Amendments—[1] Sub-para (1)(*a*) omitted by FA 1976 s 74(2) and Sch 15 Pt V in relation to chargeable transfers made after 6 April 1976;

[2] Words in sub-para (1)(*b*) substituted by FA 1976 s 74(2) in relation to chargeable transfers made after 6 April 1976.

[3] Words in sub-para (2)(*a*) inserted by FA 1976 s 74(3), (7)(*b*), in relation to chargeable transfers made on or after 29 July 1976.

[4] Sub-paras (2)(*e*), (2A) added by FA 1976 s 74(3), (7)(*b*), in relation to chargeable transfers made on or after 29 July 1976.

2 *Where the value transferred is to be computed in accordance with this paragraph there shall first be ascertained such part of the unreduced value as is attributable to the agricultural value of the agricultural property (in this Part of this Schedule referred to as the part eligible for relief) and the value transferred shall then be computed as if the part eligible for relief were [reduced by one half]*[1].

Commentary—*Simon's Taxes* **I7.202**; *Foster* **G2.02**.

Cross references—See IHTA 1984 s 116(3)(*a*) (relief for agricultural property).

Amendments—[1] Words substituted by FA 1976 s 74(4) in relation to chargeable transfers made after 6 April 1976.

Conditions for relief

3—*(1) The conditions referred to in paragraph 1(1) above are—*

(a) that the transferor was, in not less than five of the seven years ending with 5th April immediately preceding the transfer, wholly or mainly engaged in the United Kingdom in any of the capacities mentioned in sub-paragraph (2) below (or partly in one of them and partly in another or others); and

(b) subject to paragraph 4 below, that the agricultural property was at the time of the transfer occupied by him for the purposes of agriculture and either was so occupied by him throughout the two years immediately preceding the transfer or replaced other agricultural property and was so occupied by him for a period which, when added to any period during which he so occupied the replaced property, comprised at least two years in the five years immediately preceding the transfer.

(2) The capacities referred to in sub-paragraph (1) above are those of—

(a) a person who carries on farming as a trade either alone or in partnership;

(b) a person employed in farming carried on as a trade by another person;

(c) a director of a company carrying on farming in the United Kingdom as its main activity; or

(d) a person undergoing full-time education.

(3) Where not less than 75 per cent of the transferor's relevant income was immediately derived by him from his engagement in agriculture in the United Kingdom, the condition in sub-paragraph (1)(a) above shall be taken to be satisfied; and for this purpose—

(a) "relevant income" is the aggregate of income in any five of the last seven years of assessment immediately preceding the transfer which is earned income for the purposes of income tax other than income from a pension, superannuation or other allowance, deferred pay or compensation for loss of office; and

(b) the question what was the transferor's income shall be determined without regard to section 37 of the Taxes Act (aggregation of wife's income).

(4) Where the agricultural property had, at some time before the transfer, been occupied by the transferor for the purposes of agriculture and was, throughout the period between that time and the transfer, so occupied by a member of his family, the conditions in sub-paragraph (1) above shall be treated as satisfied if they would have been satisfied had the transfer occurred at that time.

(5) Where the condition in sub-paragraph (1)(b) above is satisfied but the agricultural property which was occupied by the transferor at the time of the transfer was not occupied by him for the purposes of agriculture throughout the two years immediately preceding the transfer, then if the agricultural property which it replaced had, at the time when it ceased to be so occupied, a lower agricultural value than the first-mentioned property had at the time when it was first so occupied, the part eligible for relief shall be ascertained as if the agricultural value of the first-mentioned property were reduced by applying to it the fraction of which—

(a) the numerator is that lower agricultural value; and

(b) the denominator is the agricultural value which the first-mentioned property then had.

(6) For the purposes of sub-paragraph (1) above, where the transferor became entitled to the agricultural property on the death of another person—

(a) his occupation of the agricultural property shall be deemed to have begun on the death of that person; and

(b) if that other person was the transferor's spouse and the condition stated in sub-paragraph (1)(a) above was at the time of the death satisfied with respect to the spouse, it shall be treated as having been satisfied with respect to the transferor.

(7) For the purposes of sub-paragraph (1) above occupation by a company which is controlled by the transferor shall be treated as occupation by the transferor; and for this purpose the question whether any company is controlled by the transferor shall be determined as for the purposes of paragraph 13 of Schedule 4 to this Act.

(8) For the purposes of this paragraph, occupation of any property by a Scottish partnership shall, notwithstanding section 4(2) of the Partnership Act 1890, be treated as occupation of it by the partners.

(9) For the purposes of sub-paragraph (4) above, a person is a member of the transferor's family if he is the transferor's spouse or a relative of the transferor or of the transferor's spouse or is the spouse of such a relative, and "relative" means, ancestor, lineal descendant, brother, sister, uncle, aunt, nephew or niece, "spouse" includes former spouse, and an adopted person shall be treated as the child of the person or persons by whom he was adopted and an illegitimate person as the child of his mother and reputed father.

Commentary—*Simon's Taxes* **I7.204**; *Foster* **G2.04**.

Companies

4 *So far as the value transferred is determined by reference to the value of shares in or debentures of a company it shall be taken for the purposes of this Schedule to be determined by reference to the value of any agricultural property if and only if—*

(a) the agricultural property forms part of the company's assets and part of the value of the shares or debentures can be attributed to the agricultural value of the agricultural property; and

(b) the shares or debentures gave the transferor control of the company immediately before the transfer (the question whether they did so being determined as for the purposes of paragraph 13 of Schedule 4 to this Act); and

[(bb) where the value of the shares or debentures is taken, by virtue of paragraph 9A of Schedule 10 to this Act, to be less than their value as previously determined, they would have been sufficient, without any other property to give the transferor control as mentioned in sub-paragraph (b) above; and]

(c) the main activity of the company is, and has been throughout the two years immediately preceding the transfer, farming in the United Kingdom; and

(d) the agricultural property was at the time of the transfer occupied by the company for the purposes of farming and either was so occupied by it throughout the two years immediately preceding the transfer or replaced other agricultural property and was so occupied by it for a period which, when added to any period during which it is so occupied the replaced property, comprised at least two years in the five years immediately preceding the transfer;

and the condition stated in paragraph (d) above shall replace that stated in paragraph 3(1)(b) above, and the references to that paragraph and to the transferor in paragraph 3(5) above shall be construed accordingly.

Commentary—*Simon's Taxes* **I7.206**; *Foster* **G2.06**.
Amendments—Paragraph (*bb*) inserted by FA 1976 s 74(5) in relation to chargeable transfers made after 6 April 1976.

Limitation of relief

5—*(1) Relief under this Part of this Schedule shall be given only to the extent that either—*

(a) the part eligible for relief, when added to the part eligible for relief under any previous chargeable transfer made by the same transferor, does not exceed £250,000; or

(b) the area of the agricultural property by reference to which the relief is given, together with that of any agricultural property by reference to which relief was given under previous chargeable transfers made by the same transferor, does not exceed one thousand acres.

(2) For the purposes of sub-paragraph (1)(b) above—

(a) where the transferor and some other person were together beneficially entitled to the agricultural property by reference to which the relief is given, the area of the property shall be taken to be such part thereof as corresponds to the transferor's share; and

(b) where the agricultural property by reference to which the relief is given forms part of the assets of a company, the area of the property shall be taken to be such part thereof as corresponds to the proportion which the value of the shares and debentures first mentioned in paragraph 4 above bears to the value of all the shares in and debentures of the company [and

[(c) the area of any rough grazing land shall be counted as one-sixth of its actual area.][1]

[(2A) The Board may consult the Minister of Agriculture, Fisheries and Food or, as the case may require, the Secretary of State or the Department of Agriculture for Northern Ireland on any question arising under this paragraph whether any land is rough grazing land; and paragraph 7(4) of Schedule 4 to this Act shall apply in relation to any such question as if it were a question as to the value of the land.][1]

(3) For the purposes of this paragraph chargeable transfers made by the same person on the same day shall be treated as one; and where the relief that could otherwise be given in respect of a chargeable transfer exceeds the limit imposed by this paragraph the excess shall be attributed to the agricultural properties concerned in proportion to their respective agricultural values or areas.

Commentary—*Simon's Taxes* **I7.208**; *Foster* **G2.08**.
Cross references—See IHTA 1984 s 116(3)(*a*), (4), (5) (relief for agricultural property).
Amendments—[1] Sub-paras (2)(*c*), (2A) inserted by FA 1976 s 74(6) in relation to chargeable transfers made after 6 April 1976.

Farming

6 *In this Schedule "farming" has the meaning which it would have in the Tax Acts if in those Acts "farm land" included market garden land; and for the purposes of this Schedule the question whether a person carries on farming as a trade shall be determined as for the purposes of income tax or, as the case may be, corporation tax.*

Agricultural property

7 *In this Schedule "agricultural property" means agricultural land or pasture and includes woodland if occupied with agricultural land or pasture and the occupation is ancillary to that of the agricultural land or pasture; and also includes such cottages, farm buildings and farm-houses, together with the land occupied with them, as are of a character appropriate to the property.*

Agricultural value

8 *For the purposes of this Schedule the agricultural value of any agricultural property shall be taken to be the value which would be the value of the property if the property were subject to a perpetual covenant prohibiting its use otherwise than as agricultural property.*

Commentary—*Simon's Taxes* **I7.203**; *Foster* **G2.03**.

9 . . . [1]

Amendments—[1] Repealed by FA 1976 Sch 15 Pt V in relation to chargeable transfers made after 6 April 1976.

Channel Islands and Isle of Man

10 *This part of this Schedule applies in relation to land or activities carried on in the Channel Islands or the Isle of Man as if the land were situated or the activities were carried on in the United Kingdom . . . [1].*

Commentary—*Simon's Taxes* **I7.207**; *Foster* **G2.07**.

Amendments—[1] Words repealed by FA 1976 Sch 15 Pt V in relation to chargeable transfers made after 6 April 1976.

Saving

11 *Nothing in this Part of this Schedule shall be taken to apply to the value included under section 22(5) of this Act in the value of a person's estate immediately before his death.*

Commentary—*Simon's Taxes* **I7.210**; *Foster* **G2.10**.

PART II

(The provisions of this Part relate to estate duty and are outside the scope of this work.)

INHERITANCE (PROVISION FOR FAMILY AND DEPENDANTS) ACT 1975

(1975 Chapter 63)

Miscellaneous and supplementary provisions

19 Effect, duration and form of orders

(1) Where an order is made under section 2 of this Act then for all purposes, including the purposes of the enactments relating to capital transfer tax, the will or the law relating to intestacy, or both the will and the law relating to intestacy, as the case may be, shall have effect and be deemed to have had effect as from the deceased's death subject to the provisions of the order.

(2) Any order made under section 2 or 5 of this Act in favour of—

(*a*) an applicant who was the [former spouse or former civil partner][3] of the deceased, or

(*b*) an applicant who was the husband or wife of the deceased in a case[, at the date of death, a separation order under the Family Law Act 1996 was in force in relation to the marriage with the deceased][2] and the separation was continuing, [or

(*c*) an applicant who was the civil partner of the deceased in a case where, at the date of death, a separation order under Chapter 2 of Part 2 of the Civil Partnership Act 2004 was in force in relation to their civil partnership and the separation was continuing,][3]

shall, in so far as it provides for the making of periodical payments, cease to have effect on the formation by the applicant of a subsequent marriage or civil partnership, except in relation to any arrears due under the order on the date of the formation of the subsequent marriage or civil partnership.][3]

(3) A copy of every order made under this Act [other than an order made under section 15(1) [or 15ZA(1)][3] of this Act][1] shall be sent to the principal registry of the Family Division for entry and filing, and a memorandum of the order shall be endorsed on, or permanently annexed to, the probate or letters of administration under which the estate is being administered.

Commentary—*Simon's Taxes* **I4.442** *Foster* **D4.42**.

Cross references—See IHTA 1984 s 146 (treatment of orders under certain provisions of this Act); s 236(2) (tax overpaid or underpaid in consequence of sub-s (1) above not to carry interest for any period before the order there mentioned is made).

FA 1986 s 100(1), (2) (CTT to be known as inheritance tax and CTTA 1984 may be cited as Inheritance Tax Act 1984 with effect from 25 July 1986. Accordingly the reference to CTT in sub-s (1) above must be read as a reference to inheritance tax with effect from that date).

FA 2009 Sch 53 Part 2 (late payment interest start date), Inheritance (Provision for Family and Dependants) Act 1975.

Amendments—[1] Words in sub-s (3) inserted by the Administration of Justice Act 1982 s 52.

[2] Words in sub-s (2)(*b*) substituted for words "the marriage with the deceased was the subject of a decree of judicial separation and at the date of death the decree was in force" by the Family Law Act 1996 s 66 (1), Sch 8 Pt I para 27 (1), (7), with effect from a day to be appointed, subject to savings in s 66 (2) of, and Sch 9, para 5 to, that Act.

[3] Words in sub-s (2)(*a*) and words following sub-s (2)(*c*) substituted, sub-s (2)(*c*) and preceding word, and words in sub-s (3) inserted by the Civil Partnership Act 2004 s 71, Sch 4 para 26, with effect from 5 December 2005, by virtue of SI 2005/3175 art 2(1).

FINANCE ACT 1976

(1976 Chapter 40)

PART V

MISCELLANEOUS AND SUPPLEMENTARY

131 Inter-American Development Bank

(1) The following provisions of this section shall have effect on the United Kingdom's becoming a member of the Inter-American Development Bank ("the Bank").

(2) [A security issued by the Inter-American Development Bank][1] shall be taken for the purposes of capital transfer tax . . . [2] to be situated outside the United Kingdom.

(3) . . .

Commentary—*Simon's Taxes* **I9.329**; *Foster* **J3.29**.

Note—Sub-s (3) is outside the scope of this work.

Cross references—See FA 1986 s 100(1), (2) (CTT to be known as inheritance tax with effect from 25 July 1986. Accordingly the reference to CTT in sub-s (2) above must be read as a reference to inheritance tax with effect from that date).

Amendments—[1] Words in sub-s (2) substituted by TA 1988 Sch 29 para 32 Table.

[2] Words omitted from sub-s (2) repealed by TCGA 1992 s 290(3), Sch 12.

INTERPRETATION ACT 1978

(Chapter 30)

Note—This text of this Act is reproduced in Part 1 of the *Yellow Tax Handbook*.

NATIONAL HERITAGE ACT 1980

(1980 Chapter 17)

An Act to establish a National Heritage Memorial Fund for providing financial assistance for the acquisition, maintenance and preservation of land, buildings and objects of outstanding historic and other interest; to make new provision in relation to the arrangements for accepting property in satisfaction of capital transfer tax and estate duty; to provide for payments out of public funds in respect of the loss of or damage to objects loaned to or displayed in local museums and other institutions; and for purposes connected with those matters.

[31st March 1980]

Note—By virtue of the Transfer of Functions (National Heritage) Order, SI 1992/1311 the functions under this Act which are exercisable by the Lord President alone or by the Lord President jointly with the Secretary of State are transferred, with effect from 3 July 1992, to the Secretary of State and the functions exercisable by the Lord President concurrently with the Secretary of State cease, with effect from 3 July 1992, to be exercisable by the Lord President.

PART II

PROPERTY ACCEPTED IN SATISFACTION OF TAX

9 Disposal of property accepted by Commissioners

(1) Any property accepted in satisfaction of tax shall be disposed of in such manner as [the Secretary of State][1] may direct.

(2) . . .

(3) Where [the Secretary of State][1] has determined that any property accepted in satisfaction of tax is to be disposed of under this section to any such institution or body as is mentioned in subsection (2) above or to any other person who is willing to accept it, he may direct that the disposal shall be effected by means of a transfer direct to that institution or body or direct to that other person instead of being transferred to the Commissioners.

(4) [The Secretary of State][1] may in any case direct that any property accepted in satisfaction of tax shall, instead of being transferred to the Commissioners, be transferred to a person nominated by [the Secretary of State][1]; and where property is so transferred the person to whom it is transferred shall, subject to any directions subsequently given under subsection (1) or (2) above, hold the property and manage it in accordance with such directions as may be given by [the Secretary of State][1].

(5), (6) . . .

(7) References in this section to the disposal or transfer of any property include references to leasing, sub-leasing or lending it for any period and on any terms.

Note—Omitted sub-sections are not relevant for the purposes of this part of this Handbook.

Amendment—[1] Words in sub-ss (1), (3), (4) substituted by the Transfer of Functions (National Heritage) Order, SI 1992/1311 art 12(2), Sch 2 para 5 (1), (2)(*a*)–(*d*), (4).

PART III
MISCELLANEOUS AND SUPPLEMENTARY

18 Short title, interpretation, repeals and extent

(1) This Act may be cited as the National Heritage Act 1980.

(2) In this Act—

"financial year" means the twelve months ending with 31st March;

. . . [1]

. . . [2]

(3) . . . [1]

(4) References in this Act to the making of a grant or loan or the transfer or conveyance of any property to any institution or body include references to the making of a grant or loan or the transfer or conveyance of property to trustees for that institution or body.

(5) . . .

(6) This Act extends to Northern Ireland.

Note—Sub-s (5) is not relevant for the purposes of this part of this Handbook.

Amendments—[1] Sub-s (3) and words in sub-s (2) repealed by the Transfer of Functions (Arts, Libraries and National Heritage) Order, SI 1981/207, Sch 2.

[2] Definition of "the Ministers" in sub-s (2) repealed by the Transfer of Functions (National Heritage) Order, SI 1992/1311 Sch 2 para 5(1), (2) with effect from 3 July 1992.

[SENIOR COURTS] ACT 1981

(1981 Chapter 54)

Note—This Act renamed by the Constitutional Reform Act 2005 s 59, Sch 11 Pt 1 with effect from 1 October 2009 (SI 2009/1604 art 2(*d*)). This Act was previously cited as "Supreme Court Act 1981".

109 Refusal of grant where capital transfer tax unpaid

[(1) No grant shall be made, and no grant made outside the United Kingdom shall be resealed, except—

(*a*) on the production of information or documents under regulations under section 256(1)(*aa*) of the Inheritance Tax Act 1984 (excepted estates); or

(*b*) on the production of an account prepared in pursuance of that Act showing by means of such receipt or certification as may be prescribed by the Commissioners either—

(i) that the inheritance tax payable on the delivery of the account has been paid; or

(ii) that no such tax is so payable.][2]

(2) Arrangements may be made between the President of the Family Division and the Commissioners providing for the purposes of [subsection (1)(*b*)][2] in such cases as may be specified in the arrangements that the receipt or certification of an account may be dispensed with or that some other document may be substituted for the account required by [the Inheritance Tax Act 1984][1].

[(2A) In this section and the following section, "the Commissioners" means the Commissioners of Inland Revenue.][2]

(3) . . . [2]

Cross references—See IHTA 1984 s 256(1)(*c*), (2) (regulations about accounts where documents other than an account have been produced under sub-s (2) above);

FA 1986 s 100(1), (2) (CTT to be known as inheritance tax and CTTA 1984 may be cited as Inheritance Tax Act 1984 with effect from 25 July 1986. Accordingly the references to CTT in this section must be read as references to inheritance tax and references to CTTA 1984 may be read as references to Inheritance Tax Act 1984 with effect from that date).

Amendments—[1] Words in sub-s (2) substituted by IHTA 1984 Sch 8 para 20 with effect from 1 January 1985. See the cross reference above to FA 1986 s 100(1), (2).

[2] Sub-s (1) and words in sub-s (2) substituted, sub-s (2A) inserted, and sub-s (3) repealed, by FA 2004 s 294(1) with effect from 1 November 2004 (by virtue of SI 2004/2571).

FINANCE ACT 1984

(1984 Chapter 43)

PART VI

MISCELLANEOUS AND SUPPLEMENTARY

Miscellaneous

126 Tax exemptions in relation to designated international organisations

(1) Where—

(*a*) the United Kingdom or any of the Communities is a member of an international organisation; and

(*b*) the agreement under which it became a member provides for exemption from tax in relation to the organisation, of the kind for which provision is made by this section;

the Treasury may, by order made by statutory instrument, designate that organisation for the purposes of this section.

(2) Where an organisation has been so designated, the provisions mentioned in subsection (3) below shall, with the exception of any which may be excluded by the designation order, apply in relation to that organisation.

(3) The provisions are—

(*a*) . . . [2]

(*b*) any security issued by the organisation shall be taken, for the purposes of capital transfer tax . . . [3], to be situated outside the United Kingdom; and

(*c*), (*d*) . . .

[(4) The Treasury may, by order made by statutory instrument, designate any of the Communities or the European Investment Bank for the purposes of this section, and references in subsections (2) and (3) above to an organisation designated for the purposes of this section include references to a body so designated by virtue of this subsection.][1]

[(5)] . . .

Commentary—*Simon's Taxes* **I9.329**; *Foster* **J3.29**.

Note—Words omitted from sub-s (3) are not relevant to this work.

Sub-s (5) inserted by FA 1985 s 96(1) is not relevant to this work.

Cross references—See FA 1986 s 100(1), (2) (CTT to be known as inheritance tax with effect from 25 July 1986. The reference to CTT in sub-s (3)(*b*) must be construed accordingly).

Amendments—[1] Sub-s (4) inserted by FA 1985 s 96(1).

[2] Sub-s (3)(*a*) repealed by TA 1988 s 844(4), Sch 31.

[3] Words omitted from sub-s (3)(*b*) repealed by TCGA 1992 s 290(3), Sch 12.

INHERITANCE TAX ACT 1984

(1984 Chapter 51)

Note—This Act was cited as Capital Transfer Tax Act 1984 before 25 July 1986; see FA 1986 s 100(1)(*a*).

ARRANGEMENT OF SECTIONS

PART I

GENERAL

Main charges and definitions

Rates

CHAPTER II
ESTATE ON DEATH

CHAPTER III
SALE OF SHARES ETC FROM DECEASED'S ESTATE

CHAPTER IV
SALE OF LAND FROM DECEASED'S ESTATE

PART VII
LIABILITY

General rules

Special cases

An Act to consolidate provisions of Part III of the Finance Act 1975 and other enactments relating to capital transfer tax.

[31st July 1984]

Construction—FA 1986 Pt V, other than s 100, to be construed as one with this Act; see FA 1986 s 114(5).

Note—By virtue of the Transfer of Functions (National Heritage) Order, SI 1992/1311 the functions under this Act which are exercisable by the Lord President alone or by the Lord President jointly with the Secretary of State are transferred, with effect from 3 July 1992, to the Secretary of State and the functions exercisable by the Lord President concurrently with the Secretary of State cease, with effect from 3 July 1992, to be exercisable by the Lord President.

Cross references—See the Senior Courts Act 1981 s 109 (refusal of grant where CTT (renamed inheritance tax with effect from 25 July 1986) unpaid).

FA 1986 s 100(1)–(3) (any reference in this Act (formerly cited as CTTA 1984) to CTT must be read as a reference to inheritance tax for liability to tax arising on or after 25 July 1986).

FA 2006 s 64(5), (6) (holocaust victims: if at any time before claims could have been made under any qualifying compensation scheme, a person beneficially entitled to a qualifying deposit has died, and no information in respect of that deposit was contained in any account relating to that deceased person under any provision of this Act, that deposit is to be ignored for all purposes of this Act. For this purpose "qualifying compensation scheme" and "qualifying deposit" have the same meaning as in ITTOIA 2005 s 756A).

PART I
GENERAL

Main charges and definitions

1 Charge on transfers

Capital transfer tax shall be charged on the value transferred by a chargeable transfer.

Commentary—*Simon's Taxes* **I3.111, I4.101.**

HMRC Manuals—Inheritance Tax Manual IHTM04021 (structure of the charge – main charging provisions).
IHTM14821 (associated operations).

Statement of Practice E14—Pools etc syndicates.

Simon's Tax Cases—*Re Clore (decd)* (No 3) [1985] STC 394*; *Gray (surviving executor of Lady Fox, decd) v IRC* [1994] STC 360*.

Cross references—See FA 1986 s 100(1), (2) (the reference in this section to CTT must be read as a reference to inheritance tax in respect of a liability to tax arising on or after 25 July 1986).

2 Chargeable transfers and exempt transfers

(1) A chargeable transfer is a transfer of value which is made by an individual but is not (by virtue of Part II of this Act or any other enactment) an exempt transfer.

(2) A transfer of value made by an individual and exempt only to a limited extent—

(*a*) is, if all the value transferred by it is within the limit, an exempt transfer, and

(*b*) is, if that value is partly within and partly outside the limit, a chargeable transfer of so much of that value as is outside the limit as well as an exempt transfer of so much of that value as is within the limit.

(3) Except where the context otherwise requires, references in this Act to chargeable transfers, to their making or to the values transferred by them shall be construed as including references to occasions on which tax is chargeable under Chapter III of Part III of this Act (apart from section 79), to their occurrence or to the amounts on which tax is then chargeable.

Commentary—*Simon's Taxes* **I3.102, I4.101, I5.456.**

HMRC Manuals—Inheritance Tax Manual IHTM04021 (structure of the charge – main charging provisions).
IHTM04026 (what is an exempt transfer?).
IHTM04027 (what is a chargeable transfer?).

Statement of Practice E14—Pools etc syndicates.

3 Transfers of value

(1) Subject to the following provisions of this Part of this Act, a transfer of value is a disposition made by a person (the transferor) as a result of which the value of his estate immediately after the disposition is less than it would be but for the disposition; and the amount by which it is less is the value transferred by the transfer.

(2) For the purposes of subsection (1) above no account shall be taken of the value of excluded property which ceases to form part of a person's estate as a result of a disposition.

(3) [Where the value of a person's estate is diminished, and the value—

(*a*) of another person's estate, or

(*b*) of any settled property, other than settled property treated by section 49(1) below as property to which a person is beneficially entitled, is increased][1] by the first-mentioned person's omission to exercise a right, he shall be treated for the purposes of this section as having made a disposition at the time (or latest time) when he could have exercised the right, unless it is shown that the omission was not deliberate.

(4) Except as otherwise provided, references in this Act to a transfer of value made, or made by any person, include references to events on the happening of which tax is chargeable as if a transfer of value had been made, or, as the case may be, had been made by that person; and "transferor" shall be construed accordingly.

Commentary—*Simon's Taxes* **I3.111–I3.114, I3.117, I3.254, I4.101, I5.221, I4.463.**

HMRC Manuals—Inheritance Tax Manual IHTM04021 (structure of the charge – main charging provisions).

IHTM04054–04056 (loss to estate with examples).

IHTM14531–14545 (immediately chargeable transfers).

IHTM14810 (omission to exercise a right).

IHTM17072 (transfer between pension schemes).

IHTM27211–27275 (property excluded from inheritance tax).

Statements of Practice E14—Pools etc syndicates.

E15—Close companies—group transfers.

Press releases etc—CTO letter 5-6-91 (death benefit of retirement annuity policy written in trust: policyholder failing to exercise right to annuity: CTO will not invoke s 3(3) in cases of genuine pension arrangements, but only where policyholder's intention was to increase the value of another person's estate).

Law Society 18-12-91 (loan waiver must be effected by deed).

ICAEW TAX 20/92 14-12-92 (non-resident trust: CGT on trust gains collected from settlor: settlor failing to exercise right of reimbursement under TCGA 1992 Sch 5 para 6: disposition under sub-s 3(3) occurs six years after payment of the tax, by application of Limitation Act).

Simon's Tax Cases—s 3(1), *IRC v Spencer-Nairn* [1991] STC 60*; *Reynaud v IRC* [1999] STC (SCD) 185; *Melville v IRC* [2001] STC 1247; *Marquess of Linlithgow and anor v R&C Comrs* [2010] STC 1563.

s 3(3), *R&C Comrs v Parry and ors (as personal representatives of Staveley, deceased)* [2017] UKUT 4 (TCC), [2017] STC 574.

Definitions—"Disposition" s 272; "estate", s 272; "property" s 272.

Cross references—Disapplication of sub-s 4 for the purposes of annual exemption s 19(5), small gifts s 20(3), normal expenditure out of income s 21(5) and gifts in consideration of marriage s 22(6).

Amendments—[1] Words in sub-s (3) substituted by FA 2006 s 156, Sch 20 paras 7, 8. This amendment is deemed to have come into force on 22 March 2006.

[3A Potentially exempt transfers

(1) Any reference in this Act to a potentially exempt transfer is a reference to a transfer of value—

(*a*) which is made by an individual on or after 18th March 1986 [but before 22nd March 2006][5]; and

(*b*) which, apart from this section, would be a chargeable transfer (or to the extent to which, apart from this section, it would be such a transfer); and

(*c*) to the extent that it constitutes either a gift to another individual or a gift into an accumulation and maintenance trust or a disabled trust;

. . . [6]

[(1A) Any reference in this Act to a potentially exempt transfer is also a reference to a transfer of value—

(*a*) which is made by an individual on or after 22nd March 2006,

(*b*) which, apart from this section, would be a chargeable transfer (or to the extent to which, apart from this section, it would be such a transfer), and

(*c*) to the extent that it constitutes—

(i) a gift to another individual,

(ii) a gift into a disabled trust, or

(iii) a gift into a bereaved minor's trust on the coming to an end of an immediate post-death interest.][5]

[(1B) Subsections (1) and (1A) above have effect subject to any provision of this Act which provides that a disposition (or transfer of value) of a particular description is not a potentially exempt transfer.][5]

(2) Subject to subsection (6) below, a transfer of value falls within subsection (1)(*c*) [or (1A)(*c*)(i)][5] above, as a gift to another individual,—

(*a*) to the extent that the value transferred is attributable to property which, by virtue of the transfer, becomes comprised in the estate of that other individual, . . . [2] or

(*b*) so far as that value is not attributable to property which becomes comprised in the estate of another person, to the extent that, by virtue of the transfer, the estate of that other individual is increased, . . . [2].

(3) Subject to subsection (6) below, a transfer of value falls within subsection (1)(*c*) above, as a gift into an accumulation and maintenance trust or a disabled trust, to the extent that the value transferred is attributable to property which, by virtue of the transfer, becomes settled property to which section 71 or 89 of this Act applies.

[(3A) Subject to subsection (6) below, a transfer of value falls within subsection (1A)(*c*)(ii) above to the extent that the value transferred is attributable to property which, by virtue of the transfer, becomes settled property to which section 89 below applies.][5]

[(3B) A transfer of value falls within subsection (1A)(*c*)(iii) above to the extent that the value transferred is attributable to settled property (whenever settled) that becomes property to which section 71A below applies in the following circumstances—

(*a*) under the settlement, a person ("L") is beneficially entitled to an interest in possession in the settled property,

(*b*) the interest in possession is an immediate post-death interest,

(*c*) on or after 22nd March 2006, but during L's life, the interest in possession comes to an end,

(*d*) L is beneficially entitled to the interest in possession immediately before it comes to an end, and

(*e*) on the interest in possession coming to an end, the property—

(i) continues to be held on the trusts of the settlement, and

(ii) becomes property to which section 71A below applies.][5]

(4) A potentially exempt transfer which is made seven years or more before the death of the transferor is an exempt transfer and any other potentially exempt transfer is a chargeable transfer.

(5) During the period beginning on the date of a potentially exempt transfer and ending immediately before—

(*a*) the seventh anniversary of that date, or

(*b*) if it is earlier, the death of the transferor,

it shall be assumed for the purposes of this Act that the transfer will prove to be an exempt transfer.

(6) Where, under any provision of this Act . . . [3], tax is in any circumstances to be charged as if a transfer of value had been made, that transfer shall be taken to be a transfer which is not a potentially exempt transfer.][1]

[(6A) The reference in subsection (6) above to any provision of this Act does not include section 52 below except where the transfer of value treated as made by that section is one treated as made on the coming to an end of an interest which falls within section 5(1B) below.][3]

[(7) In the application of this section to an event on the happening of which tax is chargeable under section 52 below, the reference in subsection (1)(*a*) [or (1A)(*a*)][5] above to the individual by whom the transfer of value is made is a reference to the person who, by virtue of section 3(4) above, is treated as the transferor.][4]

Commentary—*Simon's Taxes* **I3.311–I3.319, C1.425.**

HMRC Manuals—Inheritance Tax Manual IHTM04024 (example of a partly exempt transfer and partly a potentially exempt transfer).

IHTM20331 and 20332 (potentially exempt transfer treatment for the payment of renewal premiums in certain circumstances).

IHTM14319 (gifts with reservation).

IHTM04057 (what is a potentially exempt transfer?).

IHTM04066 (transferred by a potentially exempt transfer?).

IHTM04058 (when gift made to another individual or specified trust).

IHTM14515 (the charge to tax: potentially exempt transfers (pets): IHT nil rate band).

IHTM14516 (the charge to tax: potentially exempt transfers (pets): rate of tax).

IHTM14517 (the charge to tax: potentially exempt transfers (pets): taper relief).

IHTM14519 (the charge to tax: potentially exempt transfers (pets): fall in value relief).

Definitions—"Disposition" s 272; "estate", s 272; "property" s 272.

Cross references—See FA 1986 Sch 19 para 40 (where a death or other event occurs after 17 March 1986, this section does not affect the tax chargeable on a transfer of value occurring before 18 March 1986),

FA 1986 Sch 19 para 46 (notwithstanding anything in this section, a transfer of value of timber made after 30 June 1986 is not a potentially exempt transfer if estate duty deferment provision does not apply).

Amendments—[1] This section inserted by FA 1986 Sch 19 para 1.

[2] Words in sub-s (2)(*a*), (*b*) repealed by F(No 2)A 1987 s 96(1), (2)(*a*), (*b*) and Sch 9 Pt III with respect to transfers of value made after 16 March 1987.

[3] In sub-s (6) words repealed, and sub-s (6A) inserted, by FA 2010 s 53(1), (2) with effect in relation to an interest in possession to which a person is beneficially entitled if the person becomes beneficially entitled to it on or after 9 December 2009.

[4] Sub-s (7) added by F(No 2)A 1987 s 96(1), (3) with respect to transfers of value made after 16 March 1987.

[5] Words in sub-ss (1)(*a*), (2), (7) inserted, sub-ss (1A), (1B), (3A), (3B) inserted, by FA 2006 s 156, Sch 20 paras 7, 9. These amendments are deemed to have come into force on 22 March 2006.

[6] Words in sub-s (1) repealed by FA 2006 s 178, Sch 26 Pt 6. This repeal is deemed to have come into force on 22 March 2006.

4 Transfers on death

(1) On the death of any person tax shall be charged as if, immediately before his death, he had made a transfer of value and the value transferred by it had been equal to the value of his estate immediately before his death.

(2) For the purposes of this section, where it cannot be known which of two or more persons who have died survived the other or others they shall be assumed to have died at the same instant.

Commentary—*Simon's Taxes* **I4.101, I1.515, I4.453.**

HMRC Manuals—Inheritance Tax Manual IHTM12195–12197 (inheritance position in the case of simultaneous deaths).

IHTM04041 (the charging provisions).

Statement of practice E16—Missives of sale (sale of heritable property situated in Scotland, entitlement of purchaser and seller to IHT reliefs where death occurs after completion of missives and delivery of disposition of the property).
Cross reference—See IHTA 1984 s 154 (death on active service, etc).
See the Enactment of Extra-Statutory Concessions Order, SI 2009/730 (foreign-owned works of art, and decorations and awards).
Simon's Tax Cases—*Alexander v IRC* [1991] STC 112*; *RSPCA v Sharpe* [2010] STC 975.

5 Meaning of estate

(1) For the purposes of this Act a person's estate is the aggregate of all the property to which he is beneficially entitled, [except that—

(*a*) the estate of a person—

(i) does not include an interest in possession in settled property to which section 71A or 71D below applies, and

(ii) does not include an interest in possession that falls within subsection (1A) below [unless it falls within subsection (1B) below][3], and

(*b*) the][1] estate of a person immediately before his death does not include excluded property [or a foreign-owned work of art which is situated in the United Kingdom for one or more of the purposes of public display, cleaning and restoration (and for no other purpose).][2].

[(1A) An interest in possession falls within this subsection if—

(*a*) it is an interest in possession in settled property,

(*b*) the settled property is not property to which section 71A or 71D below applies,

(*c*) the person is beneficially entitled to the interest in possession,

(*d*) the person became beneficially entitled to the interest in possession on or after 22nd March 2006, and

(*e*) the interest in possession is—

(i) not an immediate post-death interest,

(ii) not a disabled person's interest, and

(iii) not a transitional serial interest.][1]

[(1B) An interest in possession falls within this subsection if the person—

(*a*) was domiciled in the United Kingdom on becoming beneficially entitled to it, and

(*b*) became beneficially entitled to it by virtue of a disposition which was prevented from being a transfer of value by section 10 below.][3]

(2) A person who has a general power which enables him, or would if he were sui juris enable him, to dispose of any property other than settled property, or to charge money on any property other than settled property, shall be treated as beneficially entitled to the property or money; and for this purpose "general power" means a power or authority enabling the person by whom it is exercisable to appoint or dispose of property as he thinks fit.

(3) In determining the value of a person's estate at any time his liabilities at that time shall be taken into account, except as otherwise provided by this Act.

(4) The liabilities to be taken into account in determining the value of a transferor's estate immediately after a transfer of value include his liability for capital transfer tax on the value transferred but not his liability (if any) for any other tax or duty resulting from the transfer.

(5) Except in the case of a liability imposed by law, a liability incurred by a transferor shall be taken into account only to the extent that it was incurred for a consideration in money or money's worth.

Commentary—*Simon's Taxes* **I3.211, I3.212, I3.231, I3.523**.
HMRC Manuals—Inheritance Tax Manual IHTM14012 (burden of tax).
IHTM23183 (valuation of a fractional share of joint property).
IHTM27211–27275 (property excluded from inheritance tax).
IHTM28381 (the law relating to debts).
IHTM04032 (how the meaning of estate is extended).
HMRC Interpretation RI 210—A bookmaker's pitch is "property to which [the deceased] is beneficially entitled".
Simon's Tax Cases—*O'Neill v IRC*, [1998] STC (SCD) 110; *Daffodil (administrator of Daffodil, decd) V IRC* [2002] STC (SCD) 224; *Curnock (personal representative of Curnock, decd) v IRC* [2003] STC (SCD) 283; *Marquess of Linlithgow and anor v R&C Comrs* [2010] STC 1563.
Definitions—"Estate", s 272; "property" s 272.
Cross references—See FA 1986 s 100(1), (2) (the reference in sub-s (4) above to CTT to be construed as a reference to inheritance tax where the liability arises on or after 25 July 1986),
FA 1986 s 103(7) (liabilities to be taken into account under this section not incumbrances).
Amendments—[1] Words in sub-s (1) substituted, and sub-s (1A) inserted, by FA 2006 s 156, Sch 20 paras 7, 10. These amendments are deemed to have come into force on 22 March 2006.
[2] Words in sub-s (1)(*b*) inserted by the Enactment of Extra-Statutory Concessions Order, SI 2009/730 art 13(1), (2) with effect in relation to deaths and ten-year anniversaries occurring on or after 6 April 2009.
[3] In sub-s (1)(*a*)(ii) words inserted, and sub-s (1B) inserted, by FA 2010 s 53(1), (3) with effect in relation to an interest in possession to which a person is beneficially entitled if the person becomes beneficially entitled to it on or after 9 December 2009.

6 Excluded property

(1) Property situated outside the United Kingdom is excluded property if the person beneficially entitled to it is an individual domiciled outside the United Kingdom.

[(1A) A holding in an authorised unit trust and a share in an open-ended investment company is excluded property if the person beneficially entitled to it is an individual domiciled outside the United Kingdom.][2]

[(1B) A relevant decoration or award is excluded property if it has never been the subject of a disposition for a consideration in money or money's worth.]

(1BA) In subsection (1B) "relevant decoration or award" means a decoration or other similar award—

(*a*) that is designed to be worn to denote membership of—

(i) an Order that is, or has been, specified in the Order of Wear published in the London Gazette ("the Order of Wear"), or

(ii) an Order of a country or territory outside the United Kingdom,

(*b*) that is, or has been, specified in the Order of Wear,

(*c*) that was awarded for valour or gallant conduct,

(*d*) that was awarded for, or in connection with, a person being, or having been, a member of, or employed or engaged in connection with, the armed forces of any country or territory,

(*e*) that was awarded for, or in connection with, a person being, or having been, an emergency responder within the meaning of section 153A (death of emergency service personnel etc), or

(*f*) that was awarded by the Crown or a country or territory outside the United Kingdom for, or in connection with, public service or achievement in public life.][6]

(1C) In subsection (1B) the reference to a disposition of the decoration or other award includes—

(*a*) a reference to a disposition of part of it, and

(*b*) a reference to a disposition of an interest in it (or in part of it).][4]

(2) Where securities have been issued by the Treasury subject to a condition authorised by section 22 of the Finance (No 2) Act 1931 (or section 47 of the Finance (No 2) Act 1915) for exemption from taxation so long as the securities are in the beneficial ownership of persons [of a description specified in the condition][1], the securities are excluded property if they are in the beneficial ownership of such a person.

(3) Where the person beneficially entitled to the rights conferred by any of the following, namely—

(*a*) war savings certificates;

(*b*) national savings certificates (including Ulster savings certificates);

(*c*) premium savings bonds;

(*d*) deposits with the National Savings Bank or with a trustee savings bank;

(*e*) a [certified SAYE savings arrangement][3] within the meaning of [section 703(1) of the Income Tax (Trading and Other Income) Act 2005][3];

is domiciled in the Channel Islands or the Isle of Man, the rights are excluded property.

(4) Property to which this subsection applies by virtue of section 155(1) [or (5A)][5] below is excluded property.

[(5) This section is subject to Schedule A1 (non-excluded overseas property).][7]

Commentary—*Simon's Taxes* **I9.321, I9.321A, I9.322, I9.328, I9.331, I9.101, I9.311**.

HMRC Manuals—Inheritance Tax Manual IHTM27211–27275 (property excluded from inheritance tax).

IHTM27272 (specific savings held by taxpayers in Channel Islands or Isle of Man).

Cross reference—See s 48(3), (4) "excluded property".

Definitions—"authorised unit trust" s 272.

Amendments—[1] Words in sub-s (2) substituted by the FA 1996 s 154(7), (9) Sch 28 para 7, for the purposes of income tax, with effect for the year 1996–97 and subsequent years of assessment, and for the purposes of corporation tax, for accounting periods ending after 31 March 1996.

[2] Sub-s (1A) inserted by FA 2003 s 186(1), (2) with effect for transfers of value or other events occurring after 15 October 2002: FA 2003 s 186(8).

[3] Words in sub-s (3)(*e*) substituted by ITTOIA 2005 s 882(1), Sch 1 paras 393, 394 with effect from 6 April 2005. ITTOIA 2005 has effect—

(a) for income tax purposes, for 2005–06 and subsequent tax years, and

(b) for corporation tax purposes, for accounting periods ending after 5 April 2005: ITTOIA 2005 s 883(1).

[4] Sub-ss (1B), (1C) inserted by the Enactment of Extra-Statutory Concessions Order, SI 2009/730 art 14 with effect in relation to transfers of value or other events occurring on or after 6 April 2009.

[5] Words in sub-s (4) inserted by FA 2012 s 220, Sch 37 para 2 with effect from 17 July 2012.

[6] Sub-ss (1B), (1BA) substituted for previous sub-s (1B) by FA 2015 s 74(1) with effect in relation to transfers of value made, or treated as made, on or after 3 December 2014.

[7] Sub-s (5) inserted by F(No 2)A 2017 s 33, Sch 10 paras 2, 3 with effect in relation to times on or after 6 April 2017, subject to transitional provisions in Sch 10 paras 10, 11.

Rates

7 Rates

(1) [Subject to subsections (2), (4) and (5) below [and to [section 8D and][6] Schedule 1A][5]][1] the tax charged on the value transferred by a chargeable transfer made by any transferor shall be charged at the following rate or rates, that is to say—

(*a*) if the transfer is the first chargeable transfer made by that transferor in the period of [seven years][1] ending with the date of the transfer, at the rate or rates applicable to that value under the . . . [2] Table in Schedule 1 to this Act;

(*b*) in any other case, at the rate or rates applicable under that Table to such part of the aggregate of—

(i) that value, and

(ii) the values transferred by previous chargeable transfers made by him in that period,

as is the highest part of that aggregate and is equal to that value.

[(2) Except as provided by subsection (4) below, the tax charged on the value transferred by a chargeable transfer made before the death of the transferor shall be charged at one-half of the rate or rates referred to in subsection (1) above.][3]

(3) In [the Table][1] in Schedule 1 to this Act any rate shown in the third column is that applicable to such portion of the value concerned as exceeds the lower limit shown in the first column but does not exceed the upper limit (if any) shown in the second column.

[(4) Subject to subsection (5) below, subsection (2) above does not apply in the case of a chargeable transfer made at any time within the period of seven years ending with the death of the transferor but, in the case of a chargeable transfer made within that period but more than three years before the death, the tax charged on the value transferred shall be charged at the following percentage of the rate or rates referred to in subsection (1) above—

(*a*) where the transfer is made more than three but not more than four years before the death, 80 per cent;

(*b*) where the transfer is made more than four but not more than five years before the death, 60 per cent;

(*c*) where the transfer is made more than five but not more than six years before the death, 40 per cent; and

(*d*) where the transfer is made more than six but not more than seven years before the death, 20 per cent][4]

[(5) If, in the case of a chargeable transfer made before the death of the transferor, the tax which would fall to be charged in accordance with subsection (4) above is less than the tax which would have been chargeable (in accordance with subsection (2) above) if the transferor had not died within the period of seven years beginning with the date of the transfer, subsection (4) above shall not apply in the case of that transfer.][4]

Commentary—*Simon's Taxes* **I1.401, I3.511, I3.521, I3.531**.

HMRC Manuals—Inheritance Tax Manual IHTM14611–14613 (taper relief).

Cross references—See FA 1986 Sch 19 para 40 (where a death or other event occurs after 17 March 1986, the amendments made to this section by FA 1986 Sch 19 (see below) do not affect the tax chargeable on a transfer of value occurring before 18 March 1986),

Sch 19 para 42 (application of this section as amended by FA 1986 Sch 19 for certain events occurring before 18 March 1986).

Amendments—[1] Words in sub-ss (1), (3) substituted by FA 1986 s 101(3) and Sch 19 para 2 with respect to transfers of value made after 17 March 1986.

[2] Word in sub-s (1)(*a*) repealed by FA 1986 s 101(3), Sch 19 para 2 and Sch 23 Pt X with respect to transfers of value made after 17 March 1986.

[3] Sub-s (2) substituted by FA 1986 s 101(3) and Sch 19 para 2 with respect to transfers of value made after 17 March 1986.

[4] Sub-ss (4), (5) inserted by FA 1986 s 101(3) and Sch 19 para 2 with respect to transfers of value made after 17 March 1986.

[5] Words inserted in sub-s (1) by FA 2012 s 209, Sch 33 paras 2, 3 with effect in cases where D's death occurs on or after 6 April 2012.

[6] In sub-s (1), words inserted by F(No 2)A 2015 s 9(1), (2) with effect from 18 November 2015.

8 Indexation of rate bands

(1) If the [consumer prices index for the month of September in any year][4] is higher than it was for the [previous September][3], then, unless Parliament otherwise determines, section 7 above and Schedule 1 to this Act shall apply to chargeable transfers made on or after 6th April in the following year with the substitution of [a new Table for the Table][1] applying (whether by virtue of this section or otherwise) to earlier chargeable transfers.

(1A) . . . [2]

(2) The new [Table][1] shall differ from the [Table][1] [it replaces][1] in that for each of the amounts specified in the first and second columns there shall be substituted amounts arrived at by increasing the previous amounts by the same percentage as the percentage increase in the [consumer prices index][4] and, if the result is not a multiple of £1,000, rounding it up to the nearest amount which is such a multiple.

(3) [In this section, "consumer prices index" means the all items consumer prices index published by the Statistics Board.][4]

(4) The Treasury shall before 6th April [1994][3] and each subsequent 6th April make an order specifying the amounts which by virtue of this section will be treated, in relation to chargeable transfers on or after that date, as specified in the [Table][1] in Schedule 1 to this Act; and any such order shall be made by statutory instrument.

Commentary—*Simon's Taxes* **I3.511, I3.532, I1.510**.

Cross references—See FA 1986 Sch 19 para 40 (where a death or other event occurs after 17 March 1986, the amendments made to this section by FA 1986 Sch 19 (see below) do not affect the tax chargeable on a transfer of value occurring before 18 March 1986);

FA 2007 s 4(3), (4) (the amendment made by FA 2007 s 4(1), (2) does not affect the application of this section by virtue of the difference between the retail prices index for September 2009, or September in any later year, and that for September in the following year. But this section does not have effect in relation to any difference between the retail prices index for the month of September 2008 and that for the month of September 2009).

FA 2010 s 8(3) (sub-s (1) above shall not have effect by virtue of any difference between the retail prices index for the month of September in 2010, 2011, 2012 or 2013 and the previous September).

FA 2014 s 117, Sch 25 para 2 (sub-s (1) above shall not have effect by virtue of any difference between the consumer prices index for the month of September in 2014, 2015 or 2016 and the previous September).

F(No 2)A 2015 s 10 (this section does not have effect by virtue of any difference between the consumer prices index for the month of September in 2017, 2018 or 2019, and the previous September).

Amendments—[1] Words in sub-ss (1), (2), (4) substituted by FA 1986 Sch 19 para 3.

[2] Sub-s (1A) repealed by FA 1988 s 136(3) and Sch 14 Pt X in relation to transfers of value made after 14 March 1988.

[3] Words in sub-ss (1), (4) substituted by FA 1993 s 197 in relation to chargeable transfers made after 5 April 1994.

[4] In sub-s (1) words substituted for words "retail prices index for the month of September in 1993 or any later year", in sub-s (2), words substituted for words "retail prices index", and sub-s (3) substituted, by FA 2012 s 208 with effect for the purposes of chargeable transfers made on or after 6 April 2015.

[8A Transfer of unused nil-rate band between spouses and civil partners

(1) This section applies where—

(*a*) immediately before the death of a person (a "deceased person"), the deceased person had a spouse or civil partner ("the survivor"), and

(*b*) the deceased person had unused nil-rate band on death.

(2) A person has unused nil-rate band on death if—

$M > VT$

where—

M is the maximum amount that could be transferred by a chargeable transfer made (under section 4 above) on the person's death if it were to be wholly chargeable to tax at the rate of nil per cent. (assuming, if necessary, that the value of the person's estate were sufficient but [that the maximum amount chargeable at nil per cent. under section 8D(2) is equal to the person's residence nil-rate amount and][2] otherwise having regard to the circumstances of the person); and

VT is the value actually transferred by the chargeable transfer so made (or nil if no chargeable transfer is so made).

(3) Where a claim is made under this section, the nil-rate band maximum at the time of the survivor's death is to be treated for the purposes of the charge to tax on the death of the survivor as increased by the percentage specified in subsection (4) below (but subject to subsection (5) and section 8C below).

(4) That percentage is—

$$\frac{E}{NRBMD} \times 100$$

where—

E is the amount by which M is greater than VT in the case of the deceased person; and

NRBMD is the nil-rate band maximum at the time of the deceased person's death.

(5) If (apart from this subsection) the amount of the increase in the nil-rate band maximum at the time of the survivor's death effected by this section would exceed the amount of that nil-rate band maximum, the amount of the increase is limited to the amount of that nil-rate band maximum.

(6) Subsection (5) above may apply either—

(*a*) because the percentage mentioned in subsection (4) above (as reduced under section 8C below where that section applies) is more than 100 because of the amount by which M is greater than VT in the case of one deceased person, or

(*b*) because this section applies in relation to the survivor by reference to the death of more than one person who had unused nil-rate band on death.

(7) In this Act "nil-rate band maximum" means the amount shown in the second column in the first row of the Table in Schedule 1 to this Act (upper limit of portion of value charged at rate of nil per cent.) and in the first column in the second row of that Table (lower limit of portion charged at next rate).][1]

Commentary—*Simon's Taxes* **I4.161A**.

HMRC Manuals—Inheritance Tax Manual IHTM43001 (basic principles: introduction).

IHTM43020 (calculating the amount to be transferred).

IHTM43030 (calculating the survivor has been married to more than one spouse: example).

IHTM43031 (calculating the survivor has been married to more than one spouse: limitation at 100%: example).

Simon's Tax Cases—*Loring and another v Woodland Trust and others* [2014] EWCA Civ 1314, [2015] STC 598.

Modification—FA 2008 s 10, Sch 4 para 10 (this section modified in relation to cases where the deceased person died before 25 July 1986 (and the survivor dies on or after 9 October 2007)).

Amendments—[1] Sections 8A–8C inserted by FA 2008 s 10, Sch 4 paras 1, 2 with effect in relation to cases where the survivor's death occurs on or after 9 October 2007.

[2] In sub-s (2), in definition of "M", words inserted by F(No 2)A 2015 s 9(1), (3) with effect from 18 November 2015.

[8B Claims under section 8A

(1) A claim under section 8A above may be made—

(*a*) by the personal representatives of the survivor within the permitted period, or

(*b*) (if no claim is so made) by any other person liable to the tax chargeable on the survivor's death within such later period as an officer of Revenue and Customs may in the particular case allow.

(2) If no claim under section 8A above has been made in relation to a person (P) by reference to whose death that section applies in relation to the survivor, the claim under that section in relation to the survivor may include a claim under that section in relation to P if that does not affect the tax chargeable on the value transferred by the chargeable transfer of value made on P's death.

(3) In subsection (1)(*a*) above "the permitted period" means—

(*a*) the period of two years from the end of the month in which the survivor dies or (if it ends later) the period of three months beginning with the date on which the personal representatives first act as such, or

(*b*) such longer period as an officer of Revenue and Customs may in the particular case allow.

(4) A claim made within either of the periods mentioned in subsection (3)(*a*) above may be withdrawn no later than one month after the end of the period concerned.][1]

Commentary—*Simon's Taxes* **I4.161A, I4.161B**.

HMRC Manuals—Inheritance Tax Manual IHTM43007 (claims and time limits).
IHTM43008 (claims by people other than the personal representatives).

Amendments—[1] Sections 8A–8C inserted by FA 2008 s 10, Sch 4 paras 1, 2 with effect in relation to cases where the survivor's death occurs on or after 9 October 2007.

[8C Section 8A and subsequent charges

(1) This section applies where—

(*a*) the conditions in subsection (1)(*a*) and (*b*) of section 8A above are met, and

(*b*) after the death of the deceased person, tax is charged on an amount under any of sections 32, 32A and 126 below by reference to the rate or rates that would have been applicable to the amount if it were included in the value transferred by the chargeable transfer made (under section 4 above) on the deceased person's death.

(2) If the tax is charged before the death of the survivor, the percentage referred to in subsection (3) of section 8A above is (instead of that specified in subsection (4) of that section)—

$$\left(\frac{E}{NRBMD} - \frac{TA}{NRBME}\right) \times 100$$

where—

E and NRBMD have the same meaning as in subsection (4) of that section;

TA is the amount on which tax is charged; and

NRBME is the nil-rate band maximum at the time of the event occasioning the charge.

(3) If this section has applied by reason of a previous event or events, the reference in subsection (2) to the fraction—

$$\frac{TA}{NRBME}$$

is to the aggregate of that fraction in respect of the current event and the previous event (or each of the previous events).

(4) If the tax is charged after the death of the survivor, it is charged as if the personal nil-rate band maximum of the deceased person were appropriately reduced.

(5) In subsection (4) above—

"the personal nil-rate band maximum of the deceased person" is the nil rate band maximum which is treated by Schedule 2 to this Act as applying in relation to the deceased person's death, increased in accordance with section 8A above where that section effected an increase in that nil-rate band maximum in the case of the deceased person (as survivor of another deceased person), and

"appropriately reduced" means reduced by the amount (if any) by which the amount on which tax was charged at the rate of nil per cent. on the death of the survivor was increased by reason of the operation of section 8A above by virtue of the position of the deceased person.][1]

Commentary—*Simon's Taxes* **I4.161A, I4.161B**.

HMRC Manuals—Inheritance Tax Manual IHTM43045 (recapture charge arising before the death of the survivor).
IHTM43046 (recapture charge arising after the death of the survivor).

Modification—FA 2008 s 10, Sch 4 para 11 (this section modified in relation to cases where the deceased person died before 25 July 1986 but on or after 13 March 1975 (and the survivor dies on or after 9 October 2007)).

Amendments—[1] Sections 8A–8C inserted by FA 2008 s 10, Sch 4 paras 1, 2 with effect in relation to cases where the survivor's death occurs on or after 9 October 2007.

[8D Extra nil-rate band on death if interest in home goes to descendants etc

(1) Subsections (2) and (3) apply for the purpose of calculating the amount of the charge to tax under section 4 on a person's death if the person dies on or after 6 April 2017.

(2) If the person's residence nil-rate amount is greater than nil, the portion of VT that does not exceed the person's residence nil-rate amount is charged at the rate of 0%.

(3) References in section 7(1) to the value transferred by the chargeable transfer under section 4 on the person's death are to be read as references to the remainder (if any) of VT.

(4) The person's residence nil-rate amount is calculated in accordance with sections 8E to 8G [(and see also section 8M)][2].

(5) For the purposes of those sections and this section—

(*a*) the "residential enhancement" is—

(i) £100,000 for the tax year 2017–18,

(ii) £125,000 for the tax year 2018–19,

(iii) £150,000 for the tax year 2019–20, and

(iv) £175,000 for the tax year 2020–21 and subsequent tax years,

but this is subject to subsections (6) and (7),

(*b*) the "taper threshold" is £2,000,000 for the tax year 2017–18 and subsequent tax years, but this is subject to subsections (6) and (7),

(*c*) TT is the taper threshold at the person's death,

(*d*) E is the value of the person's estate immediately before the person's death,

(*e*) VT is the value transferred by the chargeable transfer under section 4 on the person's death,

(*f*) the person's "default allowance" is the total of—

(i) the residential enhancement at the person's death, and

(ii) the person's brought-forward allowance (see section 8G), and

(*g*) the person's "adjusted allowance" is—

(i) the person's default allowance, less

(ii) the amount given by—

$$\frac{E - TT}{2}$$

but is nil if that amount is greater than the person's default allowance.

(6) Subsection (7) applies if—

(*a*) the consumer prices index for the month of September in any tax year ("the prior tax year") is higher than it was for the previous September, and

(*b*) the prior tax year is the tax year 2020–21 or a later tax year.

(7) Unless Parliament otherwise determines, the amount of each of—

(*a*) the residential enhancement for the tax year following the prior tax year, and

(*b*) the taper threshold for that following tax year,

is its amount for the prior tax year increased by the same percentage as the percentage increase in the index and, if the result is not a multiple of £1,000, rounded up to the nearest amount which is such a multiple.

(8) The Treasury must before 6 April 2021 and each subsequent 6 April make an order specifying the amounts that in accordance with subsections (6) and (7) are the residential enhancement and taper threshold for the tax year beginning on that date; and any such order is to be made by statutory instrument.

(9) In this section—

["consumer prices index" means the all items consumer prices index published by the Statistics Board,][2]

"tax year" means a year beginning on 6 April and ending on the following 5 April, and

"the tax year 2017–18" means the tax year beginning on 6 April 2017 (and any corresponding expression in which two years are similarly mentioned is to be read in the same way).][1]

Commentary—*Simon's Taxes* **I4.162, I4.163.**

HMRC Manuals—Inheritance Tax Manual IHTM46012 (basic definitions).

IHTM46023 (the taper threshold).

Amendments—[1] Sections 8D–8M inserted by F(No 2)A 2015 s 9(1), (4) with effect from 18 November 2015.

[2] In sub-s (4), words inserted, and in sub-s (9), definition of "consumer prices index" inserted, by FA 2016 s 93, Sch 15 paras 1, 2 with effect from 15 September 2016.

[8E Residence nil-rate amount: interest in home goes to descendants etc

(1) Subsections (2) to (7) apply if—

(*a*) the person's estate immediately before the person's death includes a qualifying residential interest, and
(*b*) N% of the interest is closely inherited, where N is a number—
(i) greater than 0, and
(ii) less than or equal to 100,

and in those subsections "NV/100" means N% of so much (if any) of the value transferred by the transfer of value under section 4 as is attributable to the interest.

(2) Where—
(*a*) E is less than or equal to TT, and
(*b*) NV/100 is less than the person's default allowance,

the person's residence nil-rate amount is equal to NV/100 and an amount, equal to the difference between NV/100 and the person's default allowance, is available for carry-forward.

(3) Where—
(*a*) E is less than or equal to TT, and
(*b*) NV/100 is greater than or equal to the person's default allowance,

the person's residence nil-rate amount is equal to the person's default allowance (and no amount is available for carry-forward).

(4) Where—
(*a*) E is greater than TT, and
(*b*) NV/100 is less than the person's adjusted allowance,

the person's residence nil-rate amount is equal to NV/100 and an amount, equal to the difference between NV/100 and the person's adjusted allowance, is available for carry-forward.

(5) Where—
(*a*) E is greater than TT, and
(*b*) NV/100 is greater than or equal to the person's adjusted allowance,

the person's residence nil-rate amount is equal to the person's adjusted allowance (and no amount is available for carry-forward).

(6) Subsections (2) to (5) have effect subject to subsection (7) [and sections 8FC and 8M(2B) to (2E)][2].

(7) Where the person's residence nil-rate amount as calculated under subsections (2) to (5) without applying this subsection is greater than VT—
[(*a*) the person's residence nil-rate amount is equal to VT,
(*b*) where E is less than or equal to TT, an amount, equal to the difference between VT and the person's default allowance, is available for carry-forward, and
(*c*) where E is greater than TT, an amount, equal to the difference between VT and the person's adjusted allowance, is available for carry-forward.][2]

(8) See also—
[section 8FC (modifications of this section where there is entitlement to a downsizing addition),][2]
section 8H (meaning of "qualifying residential interest"[, "qualifying former residential interest" and "residential property interest"][2]),
section 8J (meaning of "inherit"),
section 8K (meaning of "closely inherited"), and
section 8M (cases involving conditional exemption).][1]

Commentary—*Simon's Taxes* **I4.163, I4.164**.

Amendments—[1] Sections 8D–8M inserted by F(No 2)A 2015 s 9(1), (4) with effect from 18 November 2015.

[2] In sub-ss (6), (8), words inserted, and sub-s (7)(*a*)–(*c*) substituted for previous sub-s (7)(*a*), (*b*), by FA 2016 s 93, Sch 15 paras 1, 3 with effect from 15 September 2016. Sub-s (7)(*a*), (*b*) previously read as follows—

"(*a*) subsections (2) to (5) have effect as if each reference in them to NV/100 were a reference to VT,
(*b*) each of subsections (3) and (5) has effect as if it provided that the person's residence nil-rate amount were equal to VT (rather than the person's default allowance or, as the case may be, the person's adjusted allowance).".

[8F Residence nil-rate amount: no interest in home goes to descendants etc

(1) Subsections (2) and (3) apply if the person's estate immediately before the person's death—
(*a*) does not include a qualifying residential interest, or
(*b*) includes a qualifying residential interest but none of the interest is closely inherited.

(2) The person's residence nil-rate amount is nil.

(3) An amount—
(*a*) equal to the person's default allowance, or
(*b*) if E is greater than TT, equal to the person's adjusted allowance,

is available for carry-forward.

(4) See also—

[section 8FD (which applies instead of this section where there is entitlement to a downsizing addition),][2]
section 8H (meaning of "qualifying residential interest"[, "qualifying former residential interest" and "residential property interest"][2]),
section 8J (meaning of "inherit"),
section 8K (meaning of "closely inherited"), and
section 8M (cases involving conditional exemption).][1]

Commentary—*Simon's Taxes* **I4.163, I4.164.**

Amendments—[1] Sections 8D–8M inserted by F(No 2)A 2015 s 9(1), (4) with effect from 18 November 2015.

[2] In sub-s (4), words inserted by FA 2016 s 93, Sch 15 paras 1, 4 with effect from 15 September 2016.

[8FA Downsizing addition: entitlement: low-value death interest in home

(1) There is entitlement to a downsizing addition in calculating the person's residence nil-rate amount if each of conditions A to F is met (see subsection (8) for the amount of the addition).

(2) Condition A is that—

(*a*) the person's residence nil-rate amount is given by section 8E(2) or (4), or

(*b*) the person's estate immediately before the person's death includes a qualifying residential interest but none of the interest is closely inherited, and—

(i) where E is less than or equal to TT, so much of VT as is attributable to the person's qualifying residential interest is less than the person's default allowance, or

(ii) where E is greater than TT, so much of VT as is attributable to the person's qualifying residential interest is less than the person's adjusted allowance.

Section 8E(6) and (7) do not apply, and any entitlement to a downsizing addition is to be ignored, when deciding whether paragraph (*a*) of condition A is met.

(3) Condition B is that not all of VT is attributable to the person's qualifying residential interest.

(4) Condition C is that there is a qualifying former residential interest in relation to the person (see sections 8H(4A) to (4F) and 8HA).

(5) Condition D is that the value of the qualifying former residential interest exceeds so much of VT as is attributable to the person's qualifying residential interest.

Section 8FE(2) explains what is meant by the value of the qualifying former residential interest.

(6) Condition E is that at least some of the remainder is closely inherited, where "the remainder" means everything included in the person's estate immediately before the person's death other than the person's qualifying residential interest.

(7) Condition F is that a claim is made for the addition in accordance with section 8L(1) to (3).

(8) Where there is entitlement as a result of this section, the addition—

(*a*) is equal to the lost relievable amount (see section 8FE) if that amount is less than so much of VT as is attributable to so much of the remainder as is closely inherited, and

(*b*) otherwise is equal to so much of VT as is attributable to so much of the remainder as is closely inherited.

(9) Subsection (8) has effect subject to section 8M(2G) (reduction of downsizing addition in certain cases involving conditional exemption).

(10) See also—
section 8FC (effect of an addition: section 8E case),
section 8FD (effect of an addition: section 8F case),
section 8H (meaning of "qualifying residential interest", "qualifying former residential interest" and "residential property interest"),
section 8J (meaning of "inherit"),
section 8K (meaning of "closely inherited"), and
section 8M (cases involving conditional exemption).][1]

Commentary—*Simon's Taxes* **I4.164.**

HMRC Manuals—Inheritance Tax Manual IHTM46059 ('downsizing' addition calculations: conditions).

Amendments—[1] Sections 8FA–8FE inserted by FA 2016 s 93, Sch 15 paras 1, 5 with effect from 15 September 2016.

[8FB Downsizing addition: entitlement: no residential interest at death

(1) There is also entitlement to a downsizing addition in calculating the person's residence nil-rate amount if each of conditions G to K is met (see subsection (7) for the amount of the addition).

(2) Condition G is that the person's estate immediately before the person's death ("the estate") does not include a residential property interest.

(3) Condition H is that VT is greater than nil.

(4) Condition I is that there is a qualifying former residential interest in relation to the person (see sections 8H(4A) to (4F) and 8HA).

(5) Condition J is that at least some of the estate is closely inherited.

(6) Condition K is that a claim is made for the addition in accordance with section 8L(1) to (3).

(7) Where there is entitlement as a result of this section, the addition—

(*a*) is equal to the lost relievable amount (see section 8FE) if that amount is less than so much of VT as is attributable to so much of the estate as is closely inherited, and (*b*) otherwise is equal to so much of VT as is attributable to so much of the estate as is closely inherited.

(8) Subsection (7) has effect subject to section 8M(2G) (reduction of downsizing addition in certain cases involving conditional exemption).

(9) See also—

section 8FD (effect of an addition: section 8F case),

section 8H (meaning of "qualifying residential interest", "qualifying former residential interest" and "residential property interest"),

section 8J (meaning of "inherit"),

section 8K (meaning of "closely inherited"), and

section 8M (cases involving conditional exemption).][1]

Commentary—*Simon's Taxes* **I4.164**.

HMRC Manuals—Inheritance Tax Manual IHTM46061 (downsizing calculations: where there is no residential property interest in the estate: conditions).

Amendments—[1] Sections 8FA–8FE inserted by FA 2016 s 93, Sch 15 paras 1, 5 with effect from 15 September 2016.

[8FC Downsizing addition: effect: section 8E case

(1) Subsection (2) applies if—

(*a*) as a result of section 8FA, there is entitlement to a downsizing addition in calculating the person's residence nil-rate amount, and

(*b*) the person's residence nil-rate amount is given by section 8E.

(2) Section 8E has effect as if, in subsections (2) to (5) of that section, each reference to NV/100 were a reference to the total of—

(*a*) NV/100, and

(*b*) the downsizing addition.][1]

Commentary—*Simon's Taxes* **I4.164**.

Amendments—[1] Sections 8FA–8FE inserted by FA 2016 s 93, Sch 15 paras 1, 5 with effect from 15 September 2016.

[8FD Downsizing addition: effect: section 8F case

(1) This section applies if—

(*a*) as a result of section 8FA or 8FB, there is entitlement to a downsizing addition in calculating the person's residence nil-rate amount, and

(*b*) apart from this section, the person's residence nil-rate amount is given by section 8F.

(2) Subsections (3) to (6) apply instead of section 8F.

(3) The person's residence nil-rate amount is equal to the downsizing addition.

(4) Where—

(*a*) E is less than or equal to TT, and the downsizing addition is equal to the person's default allowance, or

(*b*) E is greater than TT, and the downsizing addition is equal to the person's adjusted allowance,

no amount is available for carry-forward.

(5) Where—

(*a*) E is less than or equal to TT, and

(*b*) the downsizing addition is less than the person's default allowance,

an amount, equal to the difference between the downsizing addition and the person's default allowance, is available for carry-forward.

(6) Where—

(*a*) E is greater than TT, and

(*b*) the downsizing addition is less than the person's adjusted allowance,

an amount, equal to the difference between the downsizing addition and the person's adjusted allowance, is available for carry-forward.][1]

Commentary—*Simon's Taxes* **I4.164**.

Amendments—[1] Sections 8FA–8FE inserted by FA 2016 s 93, Sch 15 paras 1, 5 with effect from 15 September 2016.

[8FE Calculation of lost relievable amount

(1) This section is about how to calculate the person's lost relievable amount for the purposes of sections 8FA(8) and 8FB(7).

(2) For the purposes of this section and section 8FA(5), the value of the person's qualifying former residential interest is the value of the interest at the time of completion of the disposal of the interest.

(3) In this section, the person's "former allowance" is the total of—

(*a*) the residential enhancement at the time of completion of the disposal of the qualifying former residential interest,

(*b*) any brought-forward allowance that the person would have had if the person had died at that time, having regard to the circumstances of the person at that time (see section 8G as applied by subsection (4)), and

(*c*) if the person's allowance on death includes an amount of brought-forward allowance which is greater than the amount of brought-forward allowance given by paragraph (b), the difference between those two amounts.

(4) For the purposes of calculating any brought-forward allowance that the person ("P") would have had as mentioned in subsection (3)(*b*)—

(*a*) section 8G (brought-forward allowance) applies, but as if references to the residential enhancement at P's death were references to the residential enhancement at the time of completion of the disposal of the qualifying former residential interest, and

(*b*) assume that a claim for brought-forward allowance was made in relation to an amount available for carry-forward from a related person's death if, on P's death, a claim was in fact made in relation to the amount.

(5) For the purposes of subsection (3)(*c*), where the person's allowance on death is equal to the person's adjusted allowance, the amount of brought-forward allowance included in the person's allowance on death is calculated as follows.

Step 1

Express the person's brought-forward allowance as a percentage of the person's default allowance.

Step 2

Multiply—

$$\frac{E - TT}{2}$$

by the percentage given by step 1.

Step 3

Reduce the person's brought-forward allowance by the amount given by step 2.

The result is the amount of brought-forward allowance included in the person's allowance on death.

(6) If completion of the disposal of the qualifying former residential interest occurs before 6 April 2017—

(*a*) for the purposes of subsection (3)(*a*), the residential enhancement at the time of completion of the disposal is treated as being £100,000, and

(*b*) for the purposes of subsection (3)(*b*), the amount of brought-forward allowance that the person would have had at that time is treated as being nil.

(7) In this section, the person's "allowance on death" means—

(*a*) where E is less than or equal to TT, the person's default allowance, or

(*b*) where E is greater than TT, the person's adjusted allowance.

(8) For the purposes of this section, "completion" of the disposal of a residential property interest occurs at the time of the disposal or, if the disposal is under a contract which is completed by a conveyance, at the time when the interest is conveyed.

(9) Where, as a result of section 8FA, there is entitlement to a downsizing addition in calculating the person's residence nil-rate amount, take the following steps to calculate the person's lost relievable amount.

Step 1

Express the value of the person's qualifying former residential interest as a percentage of the person's former allowance, but take that percentage to be 100% if it would otherwise be higher.

Step 2

Express QRI as a percentage of the person's allowance on death, where QRI is so much of VT as is attributable to the person's qualifying residential interest, but take that percentage to be 100% if it would otherwise be higher.

Step 3

Subtract the percentage given by step 2 from the percentage given by step 1, but take the result to be 0% if it would otherwise be negative. The result is P%.

Step 4

The person's lost relievable amount is equal to P% of the person's allowance on death.

(10) Where, as a result of section 8FB, there is entitlement to a downsizing addition in calculating the person's residence nil-rate amount, take the following steps to calculate the person's lost relievable amount.

Step 1

Express the value of the person's qualifying former residential interest as a percentage of the person's former allowance, but take that percentage to be 100% if it would otherwise be higher.

Step 2

Calculate that percentage of the person's allowance on death.

The result is the person's lost relievable amount.][1]

Commentary—*Simon's Taxes* **I4.164**.

HMRC Manuals—Inheritance Tax Manual IHTM46062 (where there is no residential property interest in the estate: calculation of the lost relievable amount).

IHTM46060 (where there is a qualifying residential interest in the estate: calculation of the lost relievable amount).

Amendments—[1] Sections 8FA–8FE inserted by FA 2016 s 93, Sch 15 paras 1, 5 with effect from 15 September 2016.

[8G Meaning of "brought-forward allowance"

(1) This section is about the amount of the brought-forward allowance (see section 8D(5)(*f*)) for a person ("P") who dies on or after 6 April 2017.

(2) In this section "related person" means a person other than P where—

(*a*) the other person dies before P, and

(*b*) immediately before the other person dies, P is the other person's spouse or civil partner.

(3) P's brought-forward allowance is calculated as follows—

(*a*) identify each amount available for carry-forward from the death of a related person (see sections 8E[, 8F and 8FD][2], and subsections (4) and (5)),

(*b*) express each such amount as a percentage of the residential enhancement at the death of the related person concerned,

(*c*) calculate the percentage that is the total of those percentages, and

(*d*) the amount that is that total percentage of the residential enhancement at P's death is P's brought-forward allowance or, if that total percentage is greater than 100%, P's brought-forward allowance is the amount of the residential enhancement at P's death,

but P's brought-forward allowance is nil if no claim for it is made under section 8L.

(4) Where the death of a related person occurs before 6 April 2017—

(*a*) an amount equal to £100,000 is treated for the purposes of subsection (3) as being the amount available for carry-forward from the related person's death, but this is subject to subsection (5), and

(*b*) the residential enhancement at the related person's death is treated for those purposes as being £100,000.

(5) If the value ("RPE") of the related person's estate immediately before the related person's death is greater than £2,000,000, the amount treated under subsection (4)(*a*) as available for carry-forward is reduced (but not below nil) by—

$$\frac{RPE - £2,000,000}{2}$$

][1]

Commentary—*Simon's Taxes* **I4.163**.

HMRC Manuals—Inheritance Tax Manual IHTM46040 (the 'brought-forward' allowance).

IHTM46041 (the brought-forward allowance: method of calculation).

Amendments—[1] Sections 8D–8M inserted by F(No 2)A 2015 s 9(1), (4) with effect from 18 November 2015.

[2] In sub-s (3)(*a*), words substituted for words "and 8F" by FA 2016 s 93, Sch 15 paras 1, 6 with effect from 15 September 2016.

[8H Meaning of "qualifying residential interest",["qualifying former residential interest" and "residential property interest"]

(1) This section applies for the purposes of sections 8E [to 8FE and section 8M][2].

(2) [A][2] "residential property interest", in relation to a person, means an interest in a dwelling-house which has been the person's residence at a time when the person's estate included that, or any other, interest in the dwelling-house.

(3) Where a person's estate immediately before the person's death includes residential property interests in just one dwelling-house, the person's interests in that dwelling-house are a qualifying residential interest in relation to the person.

(4) Where—

(*a*) a person's estate immediately before the person's death includes residential property interests in each of two or more dwelling-houses, and

(*b*) the person's personal representatives nominate one (and only one) of those dwelling-houses,

the person's interests in the nominated dwelling-house are a qualifying residential interest in relation to the person.

[(4A) Subsection (4B) or (4C) applies where—

(*a*) a person disposes of a residential property interest in a dwelling-house on or after 8 July 2015 (and before the person dies), and

(*b*) the person's personal representatives nominate—

(i) where there is only one such dwelling-house, that dwelling-house, or

(ii) where there are two or more such dwelling-houses, one (and only one) of those dwelling-houses.

(4B) Where—

(*a*) the person—

(i) disposes of a residential property interest in the nominated dwelling-house at a post-occupation time, or

(ii) disposes of two or more residential property interests in the nominated dwelling-house at the same post-occupation time or at post-occupation times on the same day, and (*b*) the person does not otherwise dispose of residential property interests in the nominated dwelling-house at post-occupation times,

the interest disposed of is, or the interests disposed of are, a qualifying former residential interest in relation to the person.

(4C) Where—

(*a*) the person disposes of residential property interests in the nominated dwelling-house at post-occupation times on two or more days, and

(*b*) the person's personal representatives nominate one (and only one) of those days,

the interest or interests disposed of at post-occupation times on the nominated day is or are a qualifying former residential interest in relation to the person.

(4D) For the purposes of subsections (4A) to (4C)—

(*a*) a person is to be treated as not disposing of a residential property interest in a dwelling-house where the person disposes of an interest in the dwelling-house by way of gift and the interest is, in relation to the gift and the donor, property subject to a reservation within the meaning of section 102 of the Finance Act 1986 (gifts with reservation), and

(*b*) a person is to be treated as disposing of a residential property interest in a dwelling-house if the person is treated as making a potentially exempt transfer of the interest as a result of the operation of section 102(4) of that Act (property ceasing to be subject to a reservation).

(4E) Where—

(*a*) a transfer of value by a person is a conditionally exempt transfer of a residential property interest, and

(*b*) at the time of the person's death, no chargeable event has occurred with respect to that interest,

that interest may not be, or be included in, a qualifying former residential interest in relation to the person.

(4F) In subsections (4B) and (4C) "post-occupation time" means a time—

(*a*) on or after 8 July 2015,

(*b*) after the nominated dwelling-house first became the person's residence, and

(*c*) before the person dies.

(4G) For the purposes of subsections (4A) to (4C), if the disposal is under a contract which is completed by a conveyance, the disposal occurs at the time when the interest is conveyed.][2]

(5) A reference in this section to a dwelling-house—

(*a*) includes any land occupied and enjoyed with it as its garden or grounds, but

(*b*) does not include, in the case of any particular person, any trees or underwood in relation to which an election is made under section 125 as it applies in relation to that person's death.

(6) If at any time when a person's estate includes an interest in a dwelling-house, the person—

(*a*) resides in living accommodation which for the person is job-related, and

(*b*) intends in due course to occupy the dwelling-house as the person's residence,

this section applies as if the dwelling-house were at that time occupied by the person as a residence.

(7) Section 222(8A) to (8D) of the 1992 Act (meaning of "job-related"), but not section 222(9) of that Act, apply for the purposes of subsection (6).][1]

Commentary—*Simon's Taxes* **I4.162, I4.164.**

HMRC Manuals—Inheritance Tax Manual IHTM46011 (basic definitions: 'qualifying residential interest' and 'residential property interests').

IHTM46030 (dwelling house).

IHTM46055 (interest in possession trust).

IHTM46056 (property subject to a reservation of benefit).

Amendments—[1] Sections 8D–8M inserted by F(No 2)A 2015 s 9(1), (4) with effect from 18 November 2015.

[2] In heading words inserted, in sub-s (1) words substituted for words "and 8F", in sub-s (2) word substituted for words "In this section", and sub-ss (4A)–(4G) inserted, by FA 2016 s 93, Sch 15 paras 1, 7 with effect from 15 September 2016.

[8HA "Qualifying former residential interest": interests in possession

(1) This section applies for the purposes of determining whether certain interests may be, or be included in, a qualifying former residential interest in relation to a person (see section 8H(4A) to (4C)).

(2) This section applies where—

(*a*) a person ("P") is beneficially entitled to an interest in possession in settled property, and

(*b*) the settled property consists of, or includes, an interest in a dwelling-house.

(3) Subsection (4) applies where—

(*a*) the trustees of the settlement dispose of the interest in the dwelling-house to a person other than P,

(*b*) P's interest in possession in the settled property subsists immediately before the disposal, and

(*c*) P's interest in possession—

(i) falls within subsection (7) throughout the period beginning with P becoming beneficially entitled to it and ending with the disposal, or

(ii) falls within subsection (8).

(4) The disposal is to be treated as a disposal by P of the interest in the dwelling-house to which P is beneficially entitled as a result of the operation of section 49(1).
(5) Subsection (6) applies where—
 (*a*) P disposes of the interest in possession in the settled property, or P's interest in possession in the settled property comes to an end in P's lifetime,
 (*b*) the interest in the dwelling-house is, or is part of, the settled property immediately before the time when that happens, and
 (*c*) P's interest in possession—
  (i) falls within subsection (7) throughout the period beginning with P becoming beneficially entitled to it and ending with the time mentioned in paragraph (*b*), or
  (ii) falls within subsection (8).
(6) The disposal, or (as the case may be) the coming to an end of P's interest in possession, is to be treated as a disposal by P of the interest in the dwelling-house to which P is beneficially entitled as a result of the operation of section 49(1).
(7) An interest in possession falls within this subsection if—
 (*a*) P became beneficially entitled to it before 22 March 2006 and section 71A does not apply to the settled property; or
 (*b*) P becomes beneficially entitled to it on or after 22 March 2006 and the interest is—
  (i) an immediate post-death interest,
  (ii) a disabled person's interest, or
  (iii) a transitional serial interest.
(8) An interest in possession falls within this subsection if P becomes beneficially entitled to it on or after 22 March 2006 and it falls within section 5(1B).][1]

Commentary—*Simon's Taxes* **I4.164**.
HMRC Manuals—Inheritance Tax Manual IHTM46055 (qualifying former residential interest: interest in possession trust).
Amendments—[1] Section 8HA inserted by FA 2016 s 93, Sch 15 paras 1, 8 with effect from 15 September 2016.

[8J Meaning of "inherited"

(1) This section explains for the purposes of sections 8E[, 8F, 8FA, 8FB and 8M][2] whether a person ("B") inherits, from a person who has died ("D"), property which forms part of D's estate immediately before D's death.
(2) B inherits the property if there is a disposition of it (whether effected by will, under the law relating to intestacy or otherwise) to B.
(3) Subsection (2) does not apply if—
 (*a*) the property becomes comprised in a settlement on D's death, or
 (*b*) immediately before D's death, the property was settled property in which D was beneficially entitled to an interest in possession.
(4) Where the property becomes comprised in a settlement on D's death, B inherits the property if—
 (*a*) B becomes beneficially entitled on D's death to an interest in possession in the property, and that interest in possession is an immediate post-death interest or a disabled person's interest, or
 (*b*) the property becomes, on D's death, settled property—
  (i) to which section 71A or 71D applies, and
  (ii) held on trusts for the benefit of B.
(5) Where, immediately before D's death, the property was settled property in which D was beneficially entitled to an interest in possession, B inherits the property if B becomes beneficially entitled to it on D's death.
(6) Where the property forms part of D's estate immediately before D's death as a result of the operation of section 102(3) of the Finance Act 1986 (gifts with reservation) in relation to a disposal of the property made by D by way of gift, B inherits the property if B is the person to whom the disposal was made.][1]

Commentary—*Simon's Taxes* **I4.162**.
HMRC Manuals—Inheritance Tax Manual IHTM46014 (basic definitions: 'inherited').
Amendments—[1] Sections 8D–8M inserted by F(No 2)A 2015 s 9(1), (4) with effect from 18 November 2015.
[2] In sub-s (1), words substituted for words "and 8F" by FA 2016 s 93, Sch 15 paras 1, 9 with effect from 15 September 2016.

[8K Meaning of "closely inherited"

(1) In relation to the death of a person ("D"), something is "closely inherited" for the purposes of sections 8E[, 8F, 8FA, 8FB and 8M][2] if it is inherited for those purposes (see section 8J) by—
 (*a*) a lineal descendant of D,
 (*b*) a person who, at the time of D's death, is the spouse or civil partner of a lineal descendant of D, or
 (*c*) a person who—
  (i) at the time of the death of a lineal descendant of D who died no later than D, was the spouse or civil partner of the lineal descendant, and

(ii) has not, in the period beginning with the lineal descendant's death and ending with D's death, become anyone's spouse or civil partner.

(2) The rules in subsections (3) to (8) apply for the interpretation of subsection (1).

(3) A person who is at any time a step-child of another person is to be treated, at that and all subsequent times, as if the person was that other person's child.

(4) Any rule of law, so far as it requires an adopted person to be treated as not being the child of a natural parent of the person, is to be disregarded (but this is without prejudice to any rule of law requiring an adopted person to be treated as the child of an adopter of the person).

(5) A person who is at any time fostered by a foster parent is to be treated, at that and all subsequent times, as if the person was the foster parent's child.

(6) Where—

(*a*) an individual ("G") is appointed (or is treated by law as having been appointed) under section 5 of the Children Act 1989, or under corresponding law having effect in Scotland or Northern Ireland or any country or territory outside the United Kingdom, as guardian (however styled) of another person, and

(*b*) the appointment takes effect at a time when the other person ("C") is under the age of 18 years,

C is to be treated, at all times after the appointment takes effect, as if C was G's child.

(7) Where—

(*a*) an individual ("SG") is appointed as a special guardian (however styled) of another person ("C") by an order of a court—

(i) that is a special guardianship order as defined by section 14A of the Children Act 1989, or

(ii) that is a corresponding order under legislation having effect in Scotland or Northern Ireland or any country or territory outside the United Kingdom, and

(*b*) the appointment takes effect at a time when C is under the age of 18 years,

C is to be treated, at all times after the appointment takes effect, as if C was SG's child.

(8) In particular, where under any of subsections (3) to (7) one person is to be treated at any time as the child of another person, that first person's lineal descendants (even if born before that time) are accordingly to be treated at that time (and all subsequent times) as lineal descendants of that other person.

(9) In subsection (4) "adopted person" means—

(*a*) an adopted person within the meaning of Chapter 4 of Part 1 of the Adoption and Children Act 2002, or

(*b*) a person who would be an adopted person within the meaning of that Chapter if, in section 66(1)(*e*) of that Act and section 38(1)(*e*) of the Adoption Act 1976, the reference to the law of England and Wales were a reference to the law of any part of the United Kingdom.

(10) In subsection (5) "foster parent" means—

(*a*) someone who is approved as a local authority foster parent in accordance with regulations made by virtue of paragraph 12F of Schedule 2 to the Children Act 1989,

(*b*) a foster parent with whom the person is placed by a voluntary organisation under section 59(1)(*a*) that Act,

(*c*) someone who looks after the person in circumstances in which the person is a privately fostered child as defined by section 66 of that Act, or

(*d*) someone who, under legislation having effect in Scotland or Northern Ireland or any country or territory outside the United Kingdom, is a foster parent (however styled) corresponding to a foster parent within paragraph (*a*) or (*b*).][1]

Commentary—*Simon's Taxes* **I4.162**.

HMRC Manuals—Inheritance Tax Manual IHTM46013 (closely inherited).
IHTM46034 (direct descendants).

Amendments—[1] Sections 8D–8M inserted by F(No 2)A 2015 s 9(1), (4) with effect from 18 November 2015.
[2] In sub-s (1), words substituted for words "and 8F" by FA 2016 s 93, Sch 15 paras 1, 10 with effect from 15 September 2016.

[8L Claims for brought-forward allowance [and downsizing addition]

(1) A claim for brought-forward allowance for a person (see section 8G) [or for a downsizing addition for a person (see sections 8FA to 8FD)][2] may be made—

(*a*) by the person's personal representatives within the permitted period, or

(*b*) (if no claim is so made) by any other person liable to the tax chargeable on the person's death within such later period as an officer of Revenue and Customs may in the particular case allow.

(2) In subsection (1)(*a*) "the permitted period" means—

(*a*) the period of 2 years from the end of the month in which the person dies or (if it ends later) the period of 3 months beginning with the date on which the personal representatives first act as such, or

(*b*) such longer period as an officer of Revenue and Customs may in the particular case allow.

(3) A claim under subsection (1) made within either of the periods mentioned in subsection (2)(*a*) may be withdrawn no later than one month after the end of the period concerned.
(4) Subsection (5) applies if—
(*a*) no claim under this section has been made for brought-forward allowance for a person ("P"),
(*b*) the amount of the charge to tax under section 4 on the death of another person ("A") would be different if a claim under subsection (1) had been made for brought-forward allowance for P, and
(*c*) the amount of the charge to tax under section 4 on the death of P, and the amount of the charge to tax under section 4 on the death of any person who is neither P nor A, would not have been different if a claim under subsection (1) had been made for brought-forward allowance for P.
(5) A claim for brought-forward allowance for P may be made—
(*a*) by A's personal representatives within the allowed period, or
(*b*) (if no claim is so made) by any other person liable to the tax chargeable on A's death within such later period as an officer of Revenue and Customs may in the particular case allow.
(6) In subsection (5)(*a*) "the allowed period" means—
(*a*) the period of 2 years from the end of the month in which A dies or (if it ends later) the period of 3 months beginning with the date on which the personal representatives first act as such, or
(*b*) such longer period as an officer of Revenue and Customs may in the particular case allow.
(7) A claim under subsection (5) made within either of the periods mentioned in subsection (6)(*a*) may be withdrawn no later than one month after the end of the period concerned.][1]

Commentary—*Simon's Taxes* **I4.163, I4.164.**
HMRC Manuals—Inheritance Tax Manual IHTM46059 (where there is a qualifying residential interest in the estate: condition F).
IHTM46061 (where there is no residential property interest in the estate: condition K).
IHTM46042 (making a claim).
Amendments—[1] Sections 8D–8M inserted by F(No 2)A 2015 s 9(1), (4) with effect from 18 November 2015.
[2] Words inserted in heading and in sub-s (1) by FA 2016 s 93, Sch 15 paras 1, 11 with effect from 15 September 2016.

[8M Residence nil-rate amount: cases involving conditional exemption

[(1) This section applies where—
(*a*) a person ("D") dies on or after 6 April 2017,
(*b*) ignoring the application of this section, D's residence nil-rate amount is greater than nil, and
(*c*) some or all of the transfer of value under section 4 on D's death is a conditionally exempt transfer of property consisting of, or including, any of the following—
(i) some or all of a qualifying residential interest;
(ii) some or all of a residential property interest, at least some portion of which is closely inherited, and which is not, and is not included in, a qualifying residential interest;
(iii) one or more closely inherited assets that are not residential property interests.
(2) Subsections (2B) to (2E) apply for the purposes of sections 8E to 8FD if—
(*a*) ignoring the application of this section, D's residence nil-rate amount is given by section 8E, and
(*b*) some or all of the transfer of value under section 4 is a conditionally exempt transfer of property mentioned in subsection (1)(*c*)(i).
(2A) In subsections (2B) to (2E), but subject to subsection (3)(*a*), "the exempt percentage of the QRI" is given by—
(X / QRI) x 100
where—
X is the attributable portion of the value transferred by the conditionally exempt transfer,
QRI is the attributable portion of the value transferred by the transfer of value under section 4, and
"the attributable portion" means the portion (which may be the whole) attributable to the qualifying residential interest.
(2B) If—
(*a*) the exempt percentage of the QRI is 100%, and
(*b*) D has no entitlement to a downsizing addition,
D's residence nil-rate amount and amount available for carry-forward are given by section 8F(2) and (3) (instead of section 8E).
(2C) If—
(*a*) the exempt percentage of the QRI is 100%, and
(*b*) D has an entitlement to a downsizing addition,
D's residence nil-rate amount and amount available for carry-forward are given by section 8FD(3) to (6) (instead of section 8E as modified by section 8FC(2)).

See also subsection (2G).

(2D) If—

(*a*) the exempt percentage of the QRI is less than 100%, and

(*b*) D has no entitlement to a downsizing addition,

D's residence nil-rate amount and amount available for carry-forward are given by section 8E but as if, in subsections (2) to (5) of that section, each reference to NV/100 were a reference to NV/100 multiplied by the percentage that is the difference between 100% and the exempt percentage of the QRI.

(2E) If—

(*a*) the exempt percentage of the QRI is less than 100%, and

(*b*) D has an entitlement to a downsizing addition,

D's residence nil-rate amount and amount available for carry-forward are given by section 8E as modified by section 8FC(2), but as if the reference to NV/100 in section 8FC(2)(*a*) were a reference to NV/100 multiplied by the percentage that is the difference between 100% and the exempt percentage of the QRI.

See also subsection (2G).

(2F) Subsection (2G) applies for the purposes of sections 8FA to 8FD if—

(*a*) some or all of the transfer of value under section 4 is a conditionally exempt transfer of property mentioned in subsection (1)(*c*)(ii) or (iii) (or both),

(*b*) D has an entitlement to a downsizing addition, and

(*c*) DA exceeds Y (see subsection (2H)).

(2G) Subject to subsection (3)(*aa*) and (*ab*), the amount of the downsizing addition is treated as reduced by whichever is the smaller of—

(*a*) the difference between DA and Y, and

(*b*) Z.

(2H) In subsections (2F) and (2G)—

DA is the amount of the downsizing addition to which D has an entitlement (ignoring the application of subsection (2G));

Y is so much (if any) of the value transferred by the transfer of value under section 4 as—

(*a*) is not transferred by a conditionally exempt transfer, and

(*b*) is attributable to—

(i) the closely inherited portion (which may be the whole) of any residential property interests that are not, and are not included in, a qualifying residential interest, or

(ii) closely inherited assets that are not residential property interests;

Z is the total of—

(*a*) the closely inherited conditionally exempt values of all residential property interests mentioned in subsection (1)(*c*)(ii), and

(*b*) so much of the value transferred by the conditionally exempt transfer as is attributable to property mentioned in subsection (1)(*c*)(iii).

(2I) For the purposes of the definition of "Z", "the closely inherited conditionally exempt value" of a residential property interest means—

(*a*) so much of the value transferred by the conditionally exempt transfer as is attributable to the interest, multiplied by

(*b*) the percentage of the interest which is closely inherited.][2]

[(3) For the purposes of calculating tax chargeable under section 32 or 32A by reference to a chargeable event related to property forming the subject-matter of the conditionally exempt transfer where D is the relevant person for the purposes of section 33—

(*a*) where subsections (2B) to (2E) apply and the chargeable event relates to property mentioned in subsection (1)(*c*)(i), in calculating the exempt percentage of the QRI, X is calculated as if the attributable portion of the value transferred by the conditionally exempt transfer had not included the portion (which may be the whole) of the qualifying residential interest on which the tax is chargeable,

(*aa*) where subsection (2G) applies and the chargeable event relates to property mentioned in subsection (1)(*c*)(ii), Z is calculated as if it had not included the portion (which may be the whole) of the closely inherited conditionally exempt value of the residential property interest on which the tax is chargeable,

(*ab*) where subsection (2G) applies and the chargeable event relates to an asset mentioned in subsection (1)(*c*)(iii) ("the taxable asset"), Z is calculated as if it had not included so much of the value transferred by the conditionally exempt transfer as is attributable to the taxable asset,][2]

(*b*) [in the cases mentioned in paragraphs (*a*), (*aa*) and (*ab*),] section 33 has effect as if for subsection (1)(*b*)(ii) there were substituted—

"(ii) if the relevant person is dead, the rate or rates that would have applied to that amount in accordance with section 8D(2) and (3) above and the appropriate provision of section 7 above if—

(*a*) that amount had been added to the value transferred on the relevant person's death, and

(*b*) the unrelieved portion of that amount had formed the highest part of that value.",

. . . [2]

(*c*) for the purposes of that substituted section 33(1)(*b*)(ii) "the unrelieved portion" of the amount on which tax is chargeable is that amount itself [reduced (but not below nil) by][2] the amount (if any) by which—

(i) D's residence nil-rate amount for the purposes of the particular calculation under section 33, exceeds

(ii) D's residence nil-rate amount for the purposes of the charge to tax under section 4 on D's death[, and

(*d*) where the chargeable event relates to property mentioned in subsection (1)(*c*)(i) and subsections (2B) to (2E) do not apply, section 33 has effect as if in subsection (1)(*b*)(ii) after "in accordance with" there were inserted "section 8D(2) and (3) above and".][2]

(4) The following provisions of this section apply if immediately before D's death there is a person ("P") who is D's spouse or civil partner.

(5) For the purposes of calculating tax chargeable under section 32 or 32A by reference to a chargeable event related to [property which forms the subject-matter of the conditionally exempt transfer where the chargeable event][2] occurs after P's death, the amount that would otherwise be D's residence nil-rate amount for those purposes is reduced by the amount (if any) by which P's residence nil-rate amount, or the residence nil-rate amount of any person who dies after P but before the chargeable event occurs, was increased by reason of an amount being available for carry-forward from D's death.

(6) Where tax is chargeable under section 32 or 32A by reference to a chargeable event related to [property which forms the subject-matter of the conditionally exempt transfer and the chargeable event][2] occurs before P's death, section 8G(3) has effect for the purpose of calculating P's brought-forward allowance as if—

(*a*) before the "and" at the end of paragraph (*c*) there were inserted—

"(*ca*) reduce that total (but not below nil) by deducting from it the recapture percentage,",

(*b*) in paragraph (*d*), before "total", in both places, there were inserted "reduced", and

(*c*) the reference to the recapture percentage were to the percentage given by—

$$\frac{TA}{REE} \times 100$$

where—

REE is the residential enhancement at the time of the chargeable event, and

TA is the amount on which tax is chargeable under section 32 or 32A.

(7) If subsection (6) has applied by reason of a previous event or events related to [property which forms the subject-matter of the conditionally exempt transfer][2], the reference in subsection (6)(*c*) to the fraction—

$$\frac{TA}{REE}$$

is to the aggregate of that fraction in respect of the current event and the previous event (or each of the previous events).][1]

Commentary—*Simon's Taxes* **I4.163, I4.164.**

HMRC Manuals—Inheritance Tax Manual IHTM46080 (estates with conditionally exempt property).

Amendments—[1] Sections 8D–8M inserted by F(No 2)A 2015 s 9(1), (4) with effect from 18 November 2015.

[2] Sub-ss (1)–(2I) substituted for previous sub-ss (1), (2), in sub-s (3) words substituted, in sub-ss (5), (6) words substituted for words "the qualifying residential interest which", and in sub-s (7) words substituted for words "the qualifying residential interest", by FA 2016 s 93, Sch 15 paras 1, 12 with effect from 15 September 2016. Sub-ss (1)–(3) previously read as follows—

"(1) This section applies where—

(*a*) the estate of a person ("D") immediately before D's death includes a qualifying residential interest,

(*b*) D dies on or after 6 April 2017, and

(*c*) some or all of the transfer of value under section 4 on D's death is a conditionally exempt transfer of property consisting of, or including, some or all of the qualifying residential interest.

(2) For the purposes of sections 8E and 8F, but subject to subsection (3), the exempt percentage of the qualifying residential interest is treated as being not closely inherited; and for this purpose "the exempt percentage" is given by—

$$\frac{X}{QRI} \times 100$$

where—

X is the attributable portion of the value transferred by the conditionally exempt transfer,

QRI is the attributable portion of the value transferred by the transfer under section 4, and

"the attributable portion" means the portion (which may be the whole) attributable to the qualifying residential interest.

(3) For the purposes of calculating tax chargeable under section 32 or 32A by reference to a chargeable event related to the qualifying residential interest where D is the relevant person for the purposes of section 33—

(*a*) in subsection (2), X is calculated as if the property forming the subject-matter of the conditionally exempt transfer had not included the property on which the tax is chargeable,

(*b*) section 33 has effect as if for subsection (1)(*b*)(ii) there were substituted—

"(ii) if the relevant person is dead, the rate or rates that would have applied to that amount in accordance with section 8D(2) and (3) above and the appropriate provision of section 7 above if—

(*a*) that amount had been added to the value transferred on the relevant person's death, and

(*b*) the unrelieved portion of that amount had formed the highest part of that value.", and

(*c*) for the purposes of that substituted section 33(1)(*b*)(ii) "the unrelieved portion" of the amount on which tax is chargeable is that amount itself less the amount (if any) by which—

(i) D's residence nil-rate amount for the purposes of the particular calculation under section 33, exceeds

(ii) D's residence nil-rate amount for the purposes of the charge to tax under section 4 on D's death.".

9 Transitional provisions on reduction of tax

The transitional provisions in Schedule 2 to this Act shall have effect in relation to any enactment by virtue of which tax is reduced by the substitution of [a new Table][1] in Schedule 1.

Commentary—*Simon's Taxes* **I11.404**.

Cross references—See FA 1986 Sch 19 para 40 (where a death or other event occurs after 17 March 1986, the amendments made to this section by FA 1986 Sch 19 (see below) do not affect the tax chargeable on a transfer of value occurring before 18 March 1986).

Amendments—[1] Words substituted by FA 1986 Sch 19 para 4.

Dispositions that are not transfers of value [(and omissions that do not give rise to deemed dispositions)]

10 Dispositions not intended to confer gratuitous benefit

(1) A disposition is not a transfer of value if it is shown that it was not intended, and was not made in a transaction intended, to confer any gratuitous benefit on any person and either—

(*a*) that it was made in a transaction at arm's length between persons not connected with each other, or

(*b*) that it was such as might be expected to be made in a transaction at arm's length between persons not connected with each other.

(2) Subsection (1) above shall not apply to a sale of [unquoted shares or unquoted debentures][1] unless it is shown that the sale was at a price freely negotiated at the time of the sale or at a price such as might be expected to have been freely negotiated at the time of the sale.

(3) In this section—

"disposition" includes anything treated as a disposition by virtue of section 3(3) above;

"transaction" includes a series of transactions and any associated operations.

Commentary—*Simon's Taxes* **I3.141–I3.148**.

HMRC Manuals—Inheritance Tax Manual IHTM04161–04167 (dispositions not intended to confer bounty).

IHTM14829 (*Re Macpherson*).

IHTM04151 (dispositions that are not transfers of value: introduction).

Concession F10—Partnership assurance policies.

Statements of Practice E14—Pools etc syndicates.

E15—Close companies—group transfers.

Press releases etc—IR 6-1-76 (accident insurance: payment to employee by employer following claim under employer's policy is covered by this section if employer and employee not connected and amount of payment is reasonable: this will normally be the case where the payment is deductible in computing the employer's profits or management expenses).

Simon's Tax Cases—*R&C Comrs v Parry and ors (as personal representatives of Staveley, deceased)* [2017] UKUT 4 (TCC), [2017] STC 574.
s 10(1), *IRC v Spencer-Nairn* [1991] STC 60*.
Definitions—"Associated operations", s 268; "unquoted", s 272.
Amendments—[1] Words in sub-s (2) substituted by FA 1987 s 58(2) and Sch 8 para 1 in relation to transfers of value made after 16 March 1987.
Words inserted in heading above s 10 by FA 2016 s 94(1), (2) with effect from 15 September 2016.

11 Dispositions for maintenance of family

(1) A disposition is not a transfer of value if it is made by one party to a marriage [or civil partnership][1] in favour of the other party or of a child of either party and is—

(*a*) for the maintenance of the other party, or
(*b*) for the maintenance, education or training of the child for a period ending not later than the year in which he attains the age of eighteen or, after attaining that age, ceases to undergo full-time education or training.

(2) A disposition is not a transfer of value if it is made in favour of a child who is not in the care of a parent of his and is for his maintenance, education or training for a period ending not later than the year in which—

(*a*) he attains the age of eighteen, or
(*b*) after attaining that age he ceases to undergo full-time education or training;

but paragraph (b) above applies only if before attaining that age the child has for substantial periods been in the care of the person making the disposition.

(3) A disposition is not a transfer of value if it is made in favour of a dependent relative of the person making the disposition and is a reasonable provision for his care or maintenance.

(4) A disposition is not a transfer of value if it is made in favour of an illegitimate child of the person making the disposition and is for the maintenance, education or training of the child for a period ending not later than the year in which he attains the age of eighteen or, after attaining that age, ceases to undergo full-time education or training.

(5) Where a disposition satisfies the conditions of the preceding provisions of this section to a limited extent only, so much of it as satisfies them and so much of it as does not satisfy them shall be treated as separate dispositions.

(6) In this section—

["civil partnership", in relation to a disposition made on the occasion of the dissolution or annulment of a civil partnership, and in relation to a disposition varying a disposition so made, includes a former civil partnership;][1]

"child" includes a step-child and an adopted child and "parent" shall be construed accordingly;

"dependent relative" means, in relation to any person—

(*a*) a relative of his, or of his spouse [or civil partner][1], who is incapacitated by old age or infirmity from maintaining himself, or
[(*b*) his mother or father or his spouse's or civil partner's mother or father;][2]

"marriage", in relation to a disposition made on the occasion of the dissolution or annulment of a marriage, and in relation to a disposition varying a disposition so made, includes a former marriage;

"year" means period of twelve months ending with 5th April.

Commentary—*Simon's Taxes* **I3.151–I3.153**.
HMRC Manuals—Inheritance Tax Manual IHTM04171–04181 (dispositions for the maintenance of the transferor's family).
Concession F12—Disposition for maintenance of dependent relative.
Definitions—"Disposition" s 272.
Cross references—FA 2004 Sch 15 para 10 (dispositions falling within this section are excluded transactions for the purposes of the charge to income tax under FA 2004 Sch 15.)
Amendments—[1] Words in sub-s (1), definition in sub-s (6) of "civil partnership" and words in definition of "dependent relative" para (*a*) inserted, by Tax and Civil Partnership Regulations, SI 2005/3229, regs 3, 4, with effect from 5 December 2005 (reg 1(1)).
[2] In sub-s (6), para (*b*) of the definition of "dependent relative" substituted by Tax and Civil Partnership Regulations, SI 2005/3229, regs 3, 4(3)(*a*)(ii), with effect in relation to dispositions made on or after 5 December 2005 (reg 1(2)).

12 Dispositions allowable for income tax or conferring [benefits under pension scheme][2]

(1) A disposition made by any person is not a transfer of value if it is allowable in computing that person's profits or gains for the purposes of income tax or corporation tax or would be so allowable if those profits or gains were sufficient and fell to be so computed.

(2) Without prejudice to subsection (1) above, a disposition made by any person is not a transfer of value if [it is a contribution under a registered pension scheme[, a qualifying non-UK pension scheme or a][3] section 615(3) scheme in respect of an employee of the person making the disposition.][1]

[(2ZA) Where a person who is a member of a registered pension scheme, a qualifying non-UK pension scheme or a section 615(3) scheme omits to exercise pension rights under the pension scheme, section 3(3) above does not apply in relation to the omission.][4]

[(2A) . . . [4]
(2B) . . . [4]

(2C) . . . [4]
(2D) . . . [4]
(2E) . . . [4]
(2F) For the purposes of this section—

(*a*) a person omits to exercise pension rights under a pension scheme if he does not become entitled to the whole or any part of a pension or lump sum (or both) under the pension scheme at a time when he was eligible to become so entitled (whether or not he does become entitled to any other benefits under the pension scheme); . . . [5]

(*b*) . . . [5]

(2G) In this section—

"entitled", in relation to a pension or lump sum, shall be construed in accordance with section 165(3) or [167(1A), or section 166(2),][6] of the Finance Act 2004;

. . . [5]

"pension" has the same meaning as in [Part 4][5] of that Act (see section 165(2) of that Act);

. . . [5]

. . . [5]

(3), (4) . . . [1]

(5) Where a disposition satisfies the conditions of the preceding provisions of this section to a limited extent only, so much of it as satisfies them and so much of it as does not satisfy them shall be treated as separate dispositions.

Commentary—*Simon's Taxes* **I3.154, I3.155**.
HMRC Manuals—IHTM04191–04193 (dispositions allowable for income tax or conferring retirement benefits).
IHTM17043 (contribution to a pension scheme for the benefit of another).
IHTM17301 (omission to exercise a right).
IHTM17302 (no IHT charge).
IHTM17303 (the legislation in detail).
Definitions—"Disposition" s 272.
Cross references—See FA 2006 Sch 22 para 12 (the reference in sub-s (2A) above to a member of a registered pension scheme having omitted to exercise pension rights under the pension scheme includes an omission before 6 April 2006 in relation to a pension scheme which on that date becomes a registered pension scheme).
Amendments—[1] Words in sub-s (2) substituted, and sub-ss (3), (4) repealed, by FA 2004 ss 203(2), 326, Sch 42 Pt 3 with effect from 6 April 2006. For transitional provisions and savings see FA 2004 Sch 36.

Words in sub-s (2) previously read as follows—

"

(*a*) it is a contribution to a retirement benefits scheme which is approved by the Board for the purposes of Chapter [I of Part XIV of the Taxes Act 1988] (occupational pension schemes) and provides benefits in respect of service which is or includes service as an employee (as defined in that Chapter) of that person; or

(*b*) it is made so as to provide—

(i) benefits on or after retirement for a person not connected with him who is or has been in his employ, or

(ii) benefits on or after the death of such a person for his widow [or surviving civil partner] or dependants,

and does not result in the recipient receiving benefits which, having regard to their form and amount, are greater than what could be provided under a scheme approved as aforesaid; [or]

[(*c*) it is a contribution under approved personal pension arrangements within the meaning of Chapter [IV of Part XIV of the Taxes Act 1988] entered into by an employee of the person making the disposition.]".

Sub-ss (3), (4) previously read as follows—

"(3) Where a person makes dispositions of the kinds described in [more than one paragraph] of subsection (2) above in respect of service by the same person, they shall be regarded as satisfying the conditions of that subsection only to the extent to which the benefits they provide do not exceed what could be provided by a disposition of the kind described in [any one] of those paragraphs.

(4) For the purposes of subsection (2)(*b*) above, the right to occupy a dwelling rent-free or at a rent less than might be expected to be obtained in a transaction at arm's length between persons not connected with each other shall be regarded as equivalent to a pension at a rate equal to the rent or additional rent that might be expected to be obtained in such a transaction.".

[2] Sub-ss (2A)–(2G) inserted, and words in Heading substituted, by FA 2006 s 160, Sch 22 paras 1, 2. These amendments are deemed to have come into force on 6 April 2006.

[3] In sub-s (2) words substituted by FA 2008 s 92, Sch 29 para 18(1), (2). This amendment is treated as having come into force on 6 April 2006.

[4] Sub-s (2ZA) inserted, and sub-ss (2A)–(2E) repealed, by FA 2011 s 65, Sch 16 paras 46, 47 with effect in relation to dispositions made (or treated as made) on or after 6 April 2011, subject to transitional provisions in FA 2011 Sch 16 Pt 3.

Sub-ss (2A)–(2E) previously read as follows—

"(2A) Subsection (2B) below applies where a person who is a member of a registered pension scheme, and who has not reached the age of 75, has omitted to exercise pension rights under the pension scheme and, if the words "(or latest time)" were omitted from subsection (3) of section 3 above,—

(a) that subsection would have treated the person as having made a disposition by reason of omitting to exercise the pension rights, but

(b) section 10 above would have prevented the disposition being a transfer of value.

(2B) Section 3(3) above does not actually treat the person as making a disposition by reason of omitting to exercise the pension rights (at the latest time when the person could have exercised them) unless the condition in subsection (2C) below is satisfied.

(2C) That condition is that—

(a) the person makes an actual pensions disposition under the pension scheme which is not prevented from being a transfer of value by section 10 above within the period of two years ending with the date of his death, and

(b) it is not shown that, when he made the actual pensions disposition, he had no reason to believe that he would die within that period.

(2D) A disposition treated by virtue of section 3(3) above as made by any person who is a member of a registered pension scheme, and who has not reached the age of 75, by reason of omitting to exercise pension rights under the pension scheme is not a transfer of value to the extent that it results in—

(a) the provision of a lump sum death benefit or pension death benefit (or both) to a relevant dependant, or

(b) the making of a payment to a charity.

(2E) A disposition made by a person who is a member of a registered pension scheme, and who has reached the age of 75, is not a transfer of value if the disposition consists in the person—

(a) making an actual pensions disposition under the pension scheme, or

(b) omitting to exercise pension rights under the pension scheme.".

[5] Sub-s (2F)(*b*) and preceding word "and" repealed, definitions in sub-s (2G) repealed, and in definition of "pension", words substituted for words "that part", by FA 2011 s 65, Sch 16 paras 49, 50 with effect in relation to dispositions made (or treated as made) on or after 6 April 2011, subject to transitional provisions in FA 2011 Sch 16 Pt 3. Sub-s (2F)(*b*) previously read as follows—

"(b) a person makes an actual pensions disposition under a registered pension scheme if he makes a disposition within section 3(1) above by doing anything in relation to, or to rights under, the pension scheme.".

Repealed definitions previously read as follows—

""lump sum death benefit" has the same meaning as in Part 4 of that Act (see section 168(2) of that Act);".

""pension death benefit" has the meaning given by section 167(2) of that Act; and"

""relevant dependant", in relation to a person, means a dependant (within the meaning given by paragraph 15 of Schedule 28 to that Act) who is the person's spouse or civil partner immediately before his death or someone who is financially dependent on the person at that time.".

[6] In sub-s (2G), in definition of "entitled", words substituted for reference "166(2)" by FA 2016 s 94(1), (3) with effect from 15 September 2016.

[12A Pension drawdown fund not used up: no deemed disposition

(1) Where a person has a drawdown fund, section 3(3) above does not apply in relation to any omission that results in the fund not being used up in the person's lifetime.

(2) For the purposes of subsection (1) above, a person has a drawdown fund if the person has—

(*a*) a member's drawdown pension fund,

(*b*) a member's flexi-access drawdown fund,

(*c*) a dependant's drawdown pension fund,

(*d*) a dependant's flexi-access drawdown fund,

(*e*) a nominee's flexi-access drawdown fund, or

(*f*) a successor's flexi-access drawdown fund, and

in respect of a money purchase arrangement under a registered pension scheme.

(3) For the purposes of subsection (1) above, a person also has a drawdown fund if sums or assets held for the purposes of a money purchase arrangement under a corresponding scheme would, if that scheme were a registered pension scheme, be the person's—

(*a*) member's drawdown pension fund,

(*b*) member's flexi-access drawdown fund,

(*c*) dependant's drawdown pension fund,

(*d*) dependant's flexi-access drawdown fund,

(*e*) nominee's flexi-access drawdown fund, or

(*f*) successor's flexi-access drawdown fund,

in respect of the arrangement.

(4) In this section—

"corresponding scheme" means—

(*a*) a qualifying non-UK pension scheme (see section 271A below), or

(*b*) a section 615(3) scheme that is not a registered pension scheme;

"money purchase arrangement" has the same meaning as in Part 4 of the Finance Act 2004 (see section 152 of that Act);

"member's drawdown pension fund", "member's flexi-access drawdown fund", "dependant's drawdown pension fund", "dependant's flexi-access drawdown fund", "nominee's flexi-access drawdown fund" and "successor's flexi-access drawdown fund" have the meaning given, respectively, by paragraphs 8, 8A, 22, 22A, 27E and 27K of Schedule 28 to that Act.][1]

Amendments—[1] Section 12A inserted by FA 2016 s 94(1), (4). This amendment has effect—

– so far as relating to a fund within sub-s (2)(*a*) or (*c*), or to a fund within sub-s (3) that corresponds to a fund within sub-s (2)(*a*) or (*c*):
  (i) where the person who has the fund dies on or after 6 April 2011, and
  (ii) is to be treated as having come into force on 6 April 2011, and

– so far as relating to a fund mentioned in sub-s (2)(*b*), (*d*), (*e*) or (*f*), or to a fund within the sub-s (3) that corresponds to a fund within sub-s (2)(*b*), (*d*), (*e*) or (*f*):
  (i) where the person who has the fund dies on or after 6 April 2015, and
  (ii) is to be treated as having come into force on 6 April 2015.

Note that, where an amount paid by way of IHT or interest on IHT is repayable as a result of the amendment made by sub-s (4), s 241(1) applies as if the last date for making a claim for repayment of the amount were 5 April 2020 if that is later than what would otherwise be the last date for that purpose (FA 2016 s 94(6)).

13 Dispositions by close companies for benefit of employees

(1) A disposition of property made to trustees by a close company whereby the property is to be held on trusts of the description specified in section 86(1) below is not a transfer of value if the persons for whose benefit the trusts permit the property to be applied include all or most of either—

(*a*) the persons employed by or holding office with the company, or

(*b*) the persons employed by or holding office with the company or any one or more subsidiaries of the company.

(2) Subsection (1) above shall not apply if the trusts permit any of the property to be applied at any time (whether during any such period as is referred to in section 86(1) below or later) for the benefit of—

(*a*) a person who is a participator in the company making the disposition, or

(*b*) any other person who is a participator in any close company that has made a disposition whereby property became comprised in the same settlement, being a disposition which but for this section would have been a transfer of value, or

(*c*) any other person who has been a participator in any such company as is mentioned in paragraph (*a*) or (*b*) above at any time after, or during the ten years before, the disposition made by that company, or

(*d*) any person who is connected with any person within paragraph (*a*), (*b*) or (*c*) above.

(3) The participators in a company who are referred to in subsection (2) above do not include any participator who—

(*a*) is not beneficially entitled to, or to rights entitling him to acquire, 5 per cent or more of, or of any class of the shares comprised in, its issued share capital, and

(*b*) on a winding-up of the company would not be entitled to 5 per cent or more of its assets.

(4) In determining whether the trusts permit property to be applied as mentioned in subsection (2) above, no account shall be taken—

(*a*) of any power to make a payment which is the income of any person for any of the purposes of income tax, or would be the income for any of those purposes of a person not resident in the United Kingdom if he were so resident, or

(*b*) if the trusts are those of a profit sharing scheme approved under [Schedule 9 to the Taxes Act 1988][2], of any power to appropriate shares in pursuance of the scheme[, or

(*c*) if the trusts are those of [a share incentive plan approved under Schedule 2 to the Income Tax (Earnings and Pensions) Act 2003][5], of any power to appropriate shares to, or acquire shares on behalf of, individuals under the plan.][4]

(5) In this section—

"close company" and "participator" have the same meanings as in Part IV of this Act;

"ordinary shares" means shares which carry either—

(*a*) a right to dividends not restricted to dividends at a fixed rate, or

(*b*) a right to conversion into shares carrying such a right as is mentioned in paragraph (*a*) above;

"subsidiary" has [the meaning given by section [1159 of and Schedule 6 to][6]][3] the [Companies Act [2006][6]][1];

and references in subsections (2) and (3) above to a participator in a company shall, in the case of a company which is not a close company, be construed as references to a person who would be a participator in the company if it were a close company.

Commentary—*Simon's Taxes* **I3.156**.

HMRC Manuals—Inheritance Tax Manual IHTM42950 (dispositions by individual: conditions).

IHTM42960 and 42961 (dispositions to a trust for employees by an individual).

IHTM04200 (conditions to be satisfied for dispositions by close companies that are not a transfer of values).

IHTM42962 (restriction of exemption).

Statement of Practice E11—Employee trusts.

Definitions—"close company", "participator", s 102(1); "disposition", "property", s 272.

Amendments—[1] Words in the definition of "subsidiary" in sub-s (5) substituted by the Companies Consolidation (Consequential Provisions) Act 1985 Sch 2 with effect from 1 July 1985.

[2] Words in sub-s (4)(*b*) substituted by TA 1988 Sch 29 para 32 Table.

[3] Words in sub-s (5) substituted by the Companies Act 1989 s 144(4), Sch 18 para 30(1), (2).

[4] Sub-s (4)(*c*) and word "or" immediately preceding it inserted by FA 2000 s 138(1), (2), with effect from 28 July 2000.

[5] In sub-s (4)(*c*), words substituted for the words "an employee share ownership plan approved under Schedule 8 to the Finance Act 2000" by ITEPA 2003 s 722, Sch 6 paras 150, 151(1)(*a*), (2) with effect, for income tax purposes, from 2003–04; and for corporation tax purposes, for accounting periods ending after 5 April 2003. For transitional provisions and savings see ITEPA 2003 s 723, Sch 7.

[6] In para (5), words substituted for words "736 of" and "1985", by the Companies Act 2006 (Consequential Amendments) (Taxes and National Insurance) Order, SI 2009/1890 art 4(1)(*f*) with effect from 1 October 2009.

[13A Dispositions by close companies to employee-ownership trusts

(1) A disposition of property made to trustees by a close company ("C") whereby the property is to be held on trusts of the description specified in section 86(1) is not a transfer of value if—

(*a*) C meets the trading requirement,

(*b*) the trusts are of a settlement which meets the all-employee benefit requirement, and

(*c*) the settlement does not meet the controlling interest requirement immediately before the beginning of the tax year in which the disposition of property occurs but does meet it at the end of that year.

(2) Sections 236I, 236J, 236K, 236M and 236T (but not 236L) of the 1992 Act apply to determine whether—

(*a*) C meets the trading requirement;

(*b*) the settlement meets the all-employee benefit requirement;

(*c*) the settlement meets the controlling interest requirement;

with references in those sections to "C" being read accordingly.

(3) In this section—

"close company" has the same meaning as in Part 4 of this Act;

"tax year" means a year beginning on 6 April and ending on the following 5 April.][1]

Commentary—*Simon's Taxes* **I3.156A, I4.223A, I5.338A**.

HMRC Manuals—Inheritance Tax Manual IHTM42997 (employee ownership trusts: conditions to be met for dispositions that are not to be treated as transfer of value).

Amendments—[1] Section 13A inserted by FA 2014 s 290, Sch 37 paras 9, 10 with effect in relation to dispositions of property made on or after 6 April 2014.

14 Waiver of remuneration

(1) Subject to subsection (2) below, the waiver or repayment of an amount of remuneration is not a transfer of value if, apart from the waiver or repayment, that amount [would be earnings, or would be treated as earnings, and would constitute employment income (see section 7(2)(*a*) or (*b*) of the Income Tax (Earnings and Pensions) Act 2003)][1].

(2) Where, apart from the waiver or repayment, the amount of the remuneration would be allowable as a deduction in computing for the purposes of income tax or corporation tax the profits or gains or losses of the person by whom it is payable or paid, this section shall apply only if, by reason of the waiver or repayment, it is not so allowed or is otherwise brought into charge in computing those profits or gains or losses.

Commentary—*Simon's Taxes* **I3.157**.

HMRC Manuals—Inheritance Tax Manual IHTM04210 (waiver or repayment of an amount of remuneration).

Amendments—[1] In sub-s (1), words substituted for the words "would be assessable to income tax under Schedule E" by ITEPA 2003 s 722, Sch 6 paras 150, 152 with effect, for income tax purposes, from 2003–04; and for corporation tax purposes, for accounting periods ending after 5 April 2003. For transitional provisions and savings see ITEPA 2003 s 723, Sch 7.

15 Waiver of dividends

A person who waives any dividend on shares of a company within twelve months before any right to the dividend has accrued does not by reason of the waiver make a transfer of value.

Commentary—*Simon's Taxes* **I3.158**.

HMRC Manuals—Inheritance Tax Manual IHTM04220 (dispositions that are not transfers of value: waiver of dividends).

16 Grant of tenancies of agricultural property

(1) The grant of a tenancy of agricultural property in the United Kingdom, the Channel Islands or the Isle of Man for use for agricultural purposes is not a transfer of value by the grantor if he makes it for full consideration in money or money's worth.

(2) Expressions used in subsection (1) above and in Chapter II of Part V of this Act have the same meaning in that subsection as in that Chapter.

Commentary—*Simon's Taxes* **I3.159**.

HMRC Manuals—Inheritance Tax Manual IHTM04230 (dispositions that are not transfers of value: grant of an agricultural tenancy).

17 Changes in distribution of deceased's estate, etc

None of the following is a transfer of value—

(*a*) a variation or disclaimer to which section 142(1) below applies;
(*b*) a transfer to which section 143 below applies;
(*c*) . . . [2]
(*d*) the renunciation of a claim to legitim [or rights under section 131 of the Civil Partnership Act 2004][1] within the period mentioned in section 147(6) below.

Commentary—*Simon's Taxes* **I3.160, I4.411, I4.451.**
HMRC Manuals—Inheritance Tax Manual IHTM04240 (dispositions that are not transfers of value: changes in the distribution of the deceased's estate).
Definitions—"Estate", s 272.
Cross references—FA 2004 Sch 15 para 16 (dispositions falling within this section to be disregarded for the purposes of FA 2004 Sch 15.)
Amendments—[1] Words inserted by Tax and Civil Partnership Regulations, SI 2005/3229, regs 3, 6, with effect from 5 December 2005 (reg 1(1)).
[2] Para (*c*) repealed by the Inheritance and Trustees' Powers Act 2014 s 11, Sch 4 para 4(*a*) with effect from 1 October 2014 (by virtue of SI 2014/2039) and in relation to deaths occurring after that date.

PART II
EXEMPT TRANSFERS

Concession A100—The capital element of any compensation paid by banks on unclaimed accounts held by Holocaust victims are exempt from tax.
Cross references—See FA 1985 s 95 (transfer of Treasury functions under this Part to the Commissioners of Inland Revenue).

CHAPTER I
GENERAL

18 Transfers between spouses [or civil partners][1]

(1) A transfer of value is an exempt transfer to the extent that the value transferred is attributable to property which becomes comprised in the estate of the transferor's spouse [or civil partner][1] or, so far as the value transferred is not so attributable, to the extent that that estate is increased.
(2) If, immediately before the transfer, the transferor but not the transferor's spouse [or civil partner][1] is domiciled in the United Kingdom the value in respect of which the transfer is exempt (calculated as a value on which no tax is chargeable) shall not exceed [the exemption limit at the time of the transfer,][2] less any amount previously taken into account for the purposes of the exemption conferred by this section.
[(2A) For the purposes of subsection (2), the exemption limit is the amount shown in the second column of the first row of the Table in Schedule 1 (upper limit of portion of value charged at rate of nil per cent).][2]
(3) Subsection (1) above shall not apply in relation to property if the testamentary or other disposition by which it is given—
(*a*) takes effect on the termination after the transfer of value of any interest or period, or
(*b*) depends on a condition which is not satisfied within twelve months after the transfer;
but paragraph (a) above shall not have effect by reason only that the property is given to a spouse [or civil partner][1] only if he survives the other spouse [or civil partner][1] for a specified period.
(4) For the purposes of this section, property is given to a person if it becomes his property or is held on trust for him.

Commentary—*Simon's Taxes* **I3.332, I4.212–I4.214.**
HMRC Manuals—Inheritance Tax Manual IHTM11031 (spouse or civil partner exemption).
IHTM11033 (spouse/civil partners domiciled outside UK).
IHTM11077 (annuities of variable amounts).
IHTM11091–11093 (exceptions where the exemption does not apply).
Simon's Tax Cases—*Holland (executor of Holland, decd) v IRC* [2003] STC (SCD) 43; *IRC v Eversden and another (executors of Greenstock, decd)* [2003] STC 822.
Definitions—"Disposition" s 272; "estate", s 272; "property" s 272.
Amendments—[1] Words in heading and sub-ss (1)–(3) inserted by the Tax and Civil Partnership Regulations, SI 2005/3229, regs 3, 7, with effect from 5 December 2005 (reg 1(1)).
[2] Words in sub-s (2) substituted and sub-s (2A) inserted by FA 2013 s 178 with effect in relation to transfers of value made on or after 6 April 2013.

19 Annual exemption

(1) Transfers of value made by a transferor in any one year are exempt to the extent that the values transferred by them (calculated as values on which no tax is chargeable) do not exceed £3,000.
(2) Where those values fall short of £3,000, the amount by which they fall short shall, in relation to the next following year, be added to the £3,000 mentioned in subsection (1) above.
(3) Where those values exceed £3,000, the excess—
(*a*) shall, as between transfers made on different days, be attributed so far as possible to a later rather than an earlier transfer, and
(*b*) shall, as between transfers made on the same day, be attributed to them in proportion to the values transferred by them.

[(3A) A transfer of value which is a potentially exempt transfer—

(*a*) shall in the first instance be left out of account for the purposes of subsections (1) to (3) above; and

(*b*) if it proves to be a chargeable transfer, shall for the purposes of those subsections be taken into account as if, in the year in which it was made, it was made later than any transfer of value which was not a potentially exempt transfer.][1]

(4) In this section "year" means period of twelve months ending with 5th April.

(5) Section 3(4) above shall not apply for the purposes of this section (but without prejudice to sections 57 and 94(5) below).

Commentary—*Simon's Taxes* **I3.322–I3.323**.

HMRC Manuals—Inheritance Tax Manual IHTM14132 (order in which exemptions apply).

IHTM14141 (annual exemption).

IHTM14142 (applying annual exemption where there is relievable property).

IHTM14143 (applying annual exemption where there are multiple transfers).

IHTM14144 (the roll-over provisions for annual exemption).

IHTM14151–14165 (schemes to exploit the annual exemption).

IHTM14343 (disapplication of annual exemption where a reservation to a gift ceases).

HMRC Interpretation RI 55—Clarification of the use of the annual exemption where a reservation of benefit ceases and the donor is treated as having made a PET (FA 1986 s 104(4)). The PET cannot be reduced by any available annual exemption.

Cross references—See FA 1986 Sch 19 para 40 (where a death or other event occurs after 17 March 1986, sub-s (3A) above does not affect the tax chargeable on a transfer of value occurring before 18 March 1986).

Amendments—[1] Sub-s (3A) inserted by FA 1986 s 101(3) and Sch 19 para 5 with respect to transfers of value made after 17 March 1986.

20 Small gifts

(1) Transfers of value made by a transferor in any one year by outright gifts to any one person are exempt if the values transferred by them (calculated as values on which no tax is chargeable) do not exceed £250.

(2) In this section "year" means period of twelve months ending with 5th April.

(3) Section 3(4) above shall not apply for the purposes of this section.

Commentary—*Simon's Taxes* **I3.324**.

HMRC Manuals—Inheritance Tax Manual IHTM14180 (small gifts exemption).

21 Normal expenditure out of income

(1) A transfer of value is an exempt transfer if, or to the extent that, it is shown—

(*a*) that it was made as part of the normal expenditure of the transferor, and

(*b*) that (taking one year with another) it was made out of his income, and

(*c*) that, after allowing for all transfers of value forming part of his normal expenditure, the transferor was left with sufficient income to maintain his usual standard of living.

(2) A payment of a premium on a policy of insurance on the transferor's life, or a gift of money or money's worth applied, directly or indirectly, in payment of such a premium, shall not for the purposes of this section be regarded as part of his normal expenditure if, when the insurance was made or at any earlier or later time, an annuity was purchased on his life, unless it is shown that—

(*a*) the purchase of the annuity, and

(*b*) the making or any variation of the insurance or of any prior insurance for which the first-mentioned insurance was directly or indirectly substituted,

were not associated operations.

(3) So much of a purchased life annuity (within the meaning of [section 423 of the Income Tax (Trading and Other Income) Act 2005][1]) as is [exempt from income tax under section 717 of that Act][1], shall not be regarded as part of the transferor's income for the purposes of this section.

(4) Subsection (3) above shall not apply to annuities purchased before 13th November 1974.

(5) Section 3(4) above shall not apply for the purposes of this section.

Commentary—*Simon's Taxes* **I3.325**.

HMRC Manuals—Inheritance Tax Manual IHTM14132 (order in which exemptions apply).

IHTM14231–14236 (normal expenditure out of income).

IHTM14241–14243 (normal expenditure).

IHTM14250 and 14251 (out of income).

IHTM20371–20377 (life policy linked with an annuity).

Press releases etc—IR letter 9-6-76 (income to be interpreted in accordance with "normal accountancy rules". This implies taking income net-of-tax).

Simon's Tax Cases—*Bennett v IRC* [1995] STC 54; *Nadin v IRC* [1997] STC (SCD) 107.

Definitions—"Associated operations", s 268.

Amendments—[1] Words in sub-s (3) substituted by ITTOIA 2005 s 882(1), Sch 1 paras 393, 395 with effect from 6 April 2005. ITTOIA 2005 has effect—

(a) for income tax purposes, for 2005–06 and subsequent tax years, and

(b) for corporation tax purposes, for accounting periods ending after 5 April 2005: ITTOIA 2005 s 883(1).

22 Gifts in consideration of marriage [or civil partnership][1]

(1) Transfers of value made by gifts in consideration of marriage [or civil partnership][1] are exempt to the extent that the values transferred by such transfers made by any one transferor in respect of any one marriage [or civil partnership][1] (calculated as values on which no tax is chargeable) do not exceed—

(*a*) in the case of gifts within subsection (2) below by a parent of a party to the marriage [or civil partnership][1], £5,000,

(*b*) in the case of other gifts within subsection (2) below, £2,500, and

(*c*) in any other case £1,000;

any excess being attributed to the transfers in proportion to the values transferred.

(2) A gift is within this subsection if—

(*a*) it is an outright gift to a child or remoter descendant of the transferor, or

(*b*) the transferor is a parent or remoter ancestor of either party to the marriage [or civil partnership][1], and either the gift is an outright gift to the other party to the marriage [or civil partnership][1] or the property comprised in the gift is settled by the gift; or

(*c*) the transferor is a party to the marriage [or civil partnership][1], and either the gift is an outright gift to the other party to the marriage [or civil partnership][1] or the property comprised in the gift is settled by the gift;

and in this section "child" includes an illegitimate child, an adopted child and a step-child and "parent", "descendant" and "ancestor" shall be construed accordingly.

(3) A disposition which is an outright gift shall not be treated for the purposes of this section as a gift made in consideration of marriage [or civil partnership][1] if, or in so far as, it is a gift to a person other than a party to the marriage [or civil partnership][1].

(4) A disposition which is not an outright gift shall not be treated for the purposes of this section as a gift made in consideration of marriage [or civil partnership][2] if the persons who are or may become entitled to any benefit under the disposition include any person other than—

[(*a*) the parties to the marriage or civil partnership, any child of the family of the parties to the marriage or civil partnership, or a spouse or civil partner of any such child;][2]

(*b*) persons becoming entitled on the failure of trusts for any such [child][2] under which trust property would (subject only to any power of appointment to a person falling within paragraph (*a*) or (*c*) of this subsection) vest indefeasibly on the attainment of a specified age or either on the attainment of such an age or on some earlier event, or persons becoming entitled (subject as aforesaid) on the failure of any limitation in tail;

[(*c*) a subsequent spouse or civil partner of a party to the marriage or civil partnership, any child of the family of the parties to any such subsequent marriage or civil partnership, or a spouse or civil partner of any such child;][2]

(*d*) persons becoming entitled under such trusts, subsisting under the law of England and Wales or of Northern Ireland, as are specified in section 33(1) of the Trustee Act 1925 or section 34(1) of the Trustee Act (Northern Ireland) 1958 (protective trusts), the principal beneficiary being a person falling within paragraph (*a*) or (*c*) of this subsection, or under such trusts, modified by the enlargement, as respects any period during which there is no such [child][2] as aforesaid in existence, of the class of potential beneficiaries specified in paragraph (ii) of the said section 33(1) or paragraph (*b*) of the said section 34(1);

(*e*) persons becoming entitled under trusts subsisting under the law of Scotland and corresponding with such trusts as are mentioned in paragraph (*d*) above;

(*f*) as respects a reasonable amount of remuneration, the trustees of the settlement.

[(4A) In subsection (4) "child of the family", in relation to parties to a marriage or civil partnership, means a child of one or both of them.][2]

(5) . . . [2]

(6) Section 3(4) above shall not apply for the purposes of this section (but without prejudice to section 57 below).

Commentary—*Simon's Taxes* **I3.326, I3.327**.

HMRC Manuals—Inheritance Tax Manual IHTM14191–14193 (gifts made in consideration of marriage or registration of civil partnership).

IHTM14201 and 14202 (*Rennell v IRC*).

IHTM14211–14221 (Inheritance Tax Act 1984 restriction of *Rennell v IRC*).

Definitions—"Disposition", s 272; "settlement", s 43.

Amendments—[1] Words in sub-ss (1)–(3) and words in heading inserted by Tax and Civil Partnership Regulations, SI 2005/3229, regs 3, 8, with effect from 5 December 2005 (reg 1(1)).

[2] Words in sub-s (4) and sub-s (4A) inserted, sub-s (4)(*a*), (*c*) substituted and sub-s (5) repealed, by Tax and Civil partnership Regulations, SI 2005/3229, regs 3, 8(5)–(7) with effect in relation to dispositions made on or after 5 December 2005 (reg 1(3)).

23 Gifts to charities [or registered clubs][4]

(1) Transfers of value are exempt to the extent that the values transferred by them are attributable to property which is given to charities [or registered clubs][4].

(2) Subsection (1) above shall not apply in relation to property if the testamentary or other disposition by which it is given—

(*a*) takes effect on the termination after the transfer of value of any interest or period, or
(*b*) depends on a condition which is not satisfied within twelve months after the transfer, or
(*c*) is defeasible;

and for this purpose any disposition which has not been defeated at a time twelve months after the transfer of value and is not defeasible after that time shall be treated as not being defeasible (whether or not it was capable of being defeated before that time).

(3) Subsection (1) above shall not apply in relation to property which is an interest in other property if—

(*a*) that interest is less than the donor's, or
(*b*) the property is given for a limited period;

and for this purpose any question whether an interest is less than the donor's shall be decided as at a time twelve months after the transfer of value.

(4) Subsection (1) above shall not apply in relation to any property if—

(*a*) the property is land or a building and is given subject to an interest reserved or created by the donor which entitles him, his spouse [or civil partner][3] or a person connected with him to possession of, or to occupy, the whole or any part of the land or building rent-free or at a rent less than might be expected to be obtained in a transaction at arm's length between persons not connected with each other, or
(*b*) the property is not land or a building and is given subject to an interest reserved or created by the donor other than—
  (i) an interest created by him for full consideration in money or money's worth, or
  (ii) an interest which does not substantially affect the enjoyment of the property by the person or body to whom it is given;

and for this purpose any question whether property is given subject to an interest shall be decided as at a time twelve months after the transfer of value.

(5) [In the case of any property which is given to charities,] [4]subsection (1) above shall not apply in relation to [the][4] property if it or any part of it may become applicable for purposes other than charitable purposes or those of a body mentioned in section 24 [or 25][2] below [or, where it is land, of a body mentioned in section 24A below][1].

[(5A) In the case of any property which is given to a registered club, subsection (1) above shall not apply in relation to the property if it or any part of it may become applicable for purposes other than—

(*a*) the purposes of the club in question;
(*b*) the purposes of another registered club;
(*c*) the purposes of the governing body of an eligible sport for the purposes of which the club in question exists; or
(*d*) charitable purposes.][4]

[(6) For the purposes of this section—

(*a*) property is given to charities if it becomes the property of charities or is held on trust for charitable purposes only; and
(*b*) property is given to registered clubs if it becomes the property of registered clubs or is held on trust for purposes of registered clubs only;

and "donor" shall be construed accordingly.

(7) For the purposes of this section "registered club" and "eligible sport" have the same meaning as in Chapter 9 of Part 13 of the Corporation Tax Act 2010.][4]

Commentary—*Simon's Taxes* **I3.333, I4.215, I3.344.**
HMRC Manuals—Inheritance Tax Manual IHTM11101–11112 (charity exemption).
IHTM11130 (newly created charities).
IHTM11171–11178 (exclusions from exemption).
Statement of practice E13—Charities.
Definitions—"Charity": see FA 2010 Sch 6.
"Disposition", "estate", "land", "property": see s 272.
Simon's Tax Cases—*Guild v IRC* [1992] STC 162*; *Routier v R&C Comrs* [2014] EWHC 3010 (Ch), [2015] STC 451.
s 23(1), *Powell-Cotton v IRC* [1992] STC 625*.
Cross reference—FA 2002 Sch 18 para 9(2) (application of this section in relation to community amateur sports clubs).
Amendments—[1] Words in sub-s (5) inserted by FA 1989 s 171(2), (6) with respect to transfers of value made after 13 March 1989.
[2] Amended by FA 1998 s 143(2) in relation to any transfer of value made on or after 17 March 1998.
[3] Words in sub-s (4)(*a*) inserted by Tax and Civil Partnership Regulations, SI 2005/3229, regs 3, 9, with effect from 5 December 2005 (reg 1(1)).
[4] Words in the title, sub-ss (1), (5) inserted, sub-(5A) inserted, sub-ss (6), (7) substituted for former sub-s (6) by CTA 2010 s 1177, Sch 1 para 189. CTA 2010 has effect for corporation tax purposes for accounting periods ending on or after 1 April 2010, and for income and capital gains tax purposes for the tax year 2010–11 and subsequent tax years.

24 Gifts to political parties

(1) Transfers of value are exempt to the extent that the values transferred by them—

(*a*) are attributable to property which becomes the property of a political party qualifying for exemption under this section, . . . [1]

(*b*) . . . [1]

(2) A political party qualifies for exemption under this section if, at the last general election preceding the transfer of value,—

(*a*) two members of that party were elected to the House of Commons, or

(*b*) one member of that party was elected to the House of Commons and not less than 150,000 votes were given to candidates who were members of that party.

(3) Subsections (2) to (5) of section 23 above shall apply in relation to subsection (1) above as they apply in relation to section 23(1).

(4) For the purposes of section 23(2) to (5) as they apply by virtue of subsection (3) above property is given to any person or body if it becomes the property of or is held on trust for that person or body, and "donor" shall be construed accordingly.

Commentary—*Simon's Taxes* **I4.216, I3.334**.

HMRC Manuals—Inheritance Tax Manual IHTM11191–11197 (gifts to political parties).

Statement of practice E13—Charities.

Press releases etc—Hansard 29-4-88 (the qualifying parties are: Conservative, Labour and Co-operative, Liberal Democrat, Scottish Nationalist, Plaid Cymru, Ulster Unionist, Democratic Unionist, Social Democratic and Labour).

Amendments—[1] Sub-s (1)(*b*) and the preceding word "and" repealed by FA 1988 s 137 and Sch 14, Part X in relation to transfers of value made after 14 March 1988.

[24A Gifts to housing associations

(1) A transfer of value is exempt to the extent that the value transferred by it is attributable to land in the United Kingdom given to a [body falling within subsection (2) below][2].

[(2) A body falls within this subsection if it is—

[(*za*) a non-profit registered provider of social housing;][3]

(*a*) a registered social landlord within the meaning of Part I of the Housing Act 1996;

(*b*) a registered housing association within the meaning of the Housing Associations Act 1985; or

(*c*) a registered housing association within the meaning of Part II of the Housing (Northern Ireland) Order 1992.][2]

(3) Subsections (2) to (5) of section 23 and subsection (4) of section 24 above shall apply in relation to subsection (1) above as they apply in relation to section 24(1).][1]

Commentary—*Simon's Taxes* **I4.217**.

HMRC Manuals—Inheritance Tax Manual IHTM11211 and 11212 (gifts to registered housing associations).

Amendments—[1] This section inserted by FA 1989 s 171(1), (6) with effect for transfers of value made after 13 March 1989.

[2] Words in sub-s (1) and whole of sub-s (2) substituted by the Housing Act 1996 (Consequential Provisions) Order, SI 1996/2325 art 5(1), Sch 2 para 12(2), (3) with effect from 1 October 1996.

[3] Sub-s (2)(*za*) inserted by the Housing and Regeneration Act 2008 s 277, Sch 9 para 7 with effect from 1 April 2010 (by virtue of SI 2010/862, art 2, subject to transitional provisions see art 2, Schedule, paras 1–4 thereto).

25 Gifts for national purposes, etc

(1) A transfer of value is an exempt transfer to the extent that the value transferred by it is attributable to property which becomes the property of a body within Schedule 3 to this Act.

(2) Subsections (2) to (5) of section 23 and subsection (4) of section 24 above shall apply in relation to subsection (1) above as they apply in relation to section 24(1), except that section 23(3) shall not prevent subsection (1) above from applying in relation to property consisting of the benefit of an agreement restricting the use of land.

[(3) A transfer of value is an exempt transfer to the extent that the value transferred by it is attributable to property that is being transferred in the circumstances described in paragraph 1 of Schedule 14 to the Finance Act 2012 (gifts to the nation).][1]

Commentary—*Simon's Taxes* **I3.336, I4.218**.

HMRC Manuals—Inheritance Tax Manual IHTM11221–11223 (gifts for national purposes).

Statement of Practice E13—Charities.

Definitions—"Property" s 272.

Amendments—[1] Sub-s (3) inserted by FA 2012 s 49, Sch 14 paras 26, 27 with effect from 17 July 2012.

26 Gifts for public benefit

Amendments—This section repealed by FA 1998 s 143(1) in relation to any transfer of value made on or after 17 March 1998.

[26A Potentially exempt transfer of property subsequently held for national purposes etc

A potentially exempt transfer which would (apart from this section) have proved to be a chargeable transfer shall be an exempt transfer to the extent that the value transferred by it is attributable to property which has been or could be designated under section 31(1) below and which, during the period beginning with the date of the transfer and ending with the death of the transferor,—

(*a*) has been disposed of by sale by private treaty to a body mentioned in Schedule 3 to this Act or has been disposed of to such a body otherwise than by sale, or

(*b*) has been disposed of in pursuance of section 230 below [or in the circumstances described in paragraph 1 of Schedule 14 to the Finance Act 2012 (gifts to the nation)][2].][1]

Commentary—*Simon's Taxes* **I3.315**.

HMRC Manuals—Inheritance Tax Manual IHTM11221 (gifts for national purposes).
Cross references—See FA 1986 Sch 19 para 40 (where a death or other event occurs after 17 March 1986, this section not to affect the tax chargeable on a transfer of value occurring before 18 March 1986).
Amendments—[1] This section inserted by FA 1986 s 101(3) and Sch 19 para 6 with respect to transfers of value made after 17 March 1986.
[2] Words in para (*b*) inserted by FA 2012 s 49, Sch 14 paras 26, 28 with effect from 17 July 2012.

27 Maintenance funds for historic buildings, etc

(1) [Subject to subsection (1A) below,][1] a transfer of value is an exempt transfer to the extent that the value transferred by it is attributable to property which by virtue of the transfer becomes comprised in a settlement and in respect of which—

(*a*) a direction under paragraph 1 of Schedule 4 to this Act has effect at the time of the transfer, or

(*b*) such a direction is given after the time of the transfer.

[(1A) Subsection (1) above does not apply in the case of a direction given after the time of the transfer unless the claim for the direction (if it is not made before that time) is made no more than two years after the date of that transfer, or within such longer period as the Board may allow.][1]

(2) Subsections (2) and (3) of section 23 and subsection (4) of section 24 above shall apply in relation to subsection (1) above as they apply in relation to section 24(1).

Commentary—*Simon's Taxes* **C1.419, I7.544, I4.220, I5.651.**
HMRC Manuals—Inheritance Tax Manual IHTM11250 (maintenance funds).
Definitions—"Board", "property" s 272; "settlement" s 43.
Amendments—[1] Words in sub-s (1), and sub-s (1A) inserted by FA 1998 s 144 in relation to transfers of value made on or after 17 March 1998.

28 Employee trusts

(1) A transfer of value made by an individual who is beneficially entitled to shares in a company is an exempt transfer to the extent that the value transferred is attributable to shares in or securities of the company which become comprised in a settlement if—

(*a*) the trusts of the settlement are of the description specified in section 86(1) below, and

(*b*) the persons for whose benefit the trusts permit the settled property to be applied include all or most of the persons employed by or holding office with the company.

(2) Subsection (1) above shall not apply unless at the date of the transfer, or at a subsequent date not more than one year thereafter, both the following conditions are satisfied, that is to say—

(*a*) the trustees—

(i) hold more than one half of the ordinary shares in the company, and

(ii) have powers of voting on all questions affecting the company as a whole which if exercised would yield a majority of the votes capable of being exercised on them; and

(*b*) there are no provisions in any agreement or instrument affecting the company's constitution or management or its shares or securities whereby the condition in paragraph (*a*) above can cease to be satisfied without the consent of the trustees.

(3) Where the company has shares or securities of any class giving powers of voting limited to either or both of the following—

(*a*) the question of winding up the company, and

(*b*) any question primarily affecting shares or securities of that class,

the reference in subsection (2)(a)(ii) above to all questions affecting the company as a whole shall be read as a reference to all such questions except any in relation to which those powers are capable of being exercised.

(4) Subsection (1) above shall not apply if the trusts permit any of the settled property to be applied at any time (whether during any such period as is referred to in section 86(1) below or later) for the benefit of—

(*a*) a person who is a participator in the company mentioned in subsection (1) above; or

(*b*) any other person who is a participator in any close company that has made a disposition whereby property became comprised in the same settlement, being a disposition which but for section 13 above would have been a transfer of value; or

(*c*) any other person who has been a participator in the company mentioned in subsection (1) above or in any such company as is mentioned in paragraph (*b*) above at any time after, or during the ten years before, the transfer of value mentioned in subsection (1) above; or

(*d*) any person who is connected with any person within paragraph (*a*), (*b*) or (*c*) above.

(5) The participators in a company who are referred to in subsection (4) above do not include any participator who—

(*a*) is not beneficially entitled to, or to rights entitling him to acquire, 5 per cent or more of, or of any class of the shares comprised in, its issued share capital, and

(*b*) on a winding-up of the company would not be entitled to 5 per cent or more of its assets.

(6) In determining whether the trusts permit property to be applied as mentioned in subsection (4) above, no account shall be taken of any power to make a payment which is the income of any person for any of the purposes of income tax, or would be the income for any of those purposes of a person not resident in the United Kingdom if he were so resident.
(7) Subsection (5) of section 13 above shall have effect in relation to this section as it has effect in relation to that section.

Commentary—*Simon's Taxes* **I4.223**.
HMRC Manuals—Inheritance Tax Manual IHTM42950 (employee benefit trusts).
Definitions—"close company", "participator", s 102(1); "settled property", s 43; "trustee", s 45.

[28A Employee-ownership trusts

(1) A transfer of value made by an individual who is beneficially entitled to shares in a company ("C") is an exempt transfer to the extent that the value transferred is attributable to shares in or securities of C which become comprised in a settlement if—
(*a*) C meets the trading requirement,
(*b*) the settlement meets the all-employee benefit requirement, and
(*c*) the settlement does not meet the controlling interest requirement immediately before the beginning of the tax year in which the transfer of value is made but does meet it at the end of that year.
(2) Sections 236I, 236J, 236K, 236M and 236T (but not 236L) of the 1992 Act apply to determine whether—
(*a*) C meets the trading requirement;
(*b*) the settlement meets the all-employee benefit requirement;
(*c*) the settlement meets the controlling interest requirement;
with references in those sections to "C" being read accordingly.
(3) In this section "tax year" means a year beginning on 6 April and ending on the following 5 April.][1]

Commentary—*Simon's Taxes* **I4.223A**.
HMRC Manuals—Inheritance Tax Manual IHTM42996 (employee ownership trusts: qualifying conditions).
IHTM42997 (employee ownership trusts: exemptions from inheritance tax).
Amendments—[1] Section 28A inserted by FA 2014 s 290, Sch 37 paras 9, 11 with effect in relation to transfers of value made on or after 6 April 2014.

29 Loans—modifications of exemptions

(1) If or to the extent that a transfer of value is a disposition whereby the use of money or other property is allowed by one person to another ("the borrower"), the preceding provisions of this Chapter shall apply to it with the following modifications.
(2) For the purposes of section 18 the borrower's estate shall be treated as increased by an amount equal to the value transferred; and section 18(3) shall not apply.
(3) For the purposes of sections 20 and 22 the transfer of value shall be treated as made by outright gift.
(4) Section 21(1) shall apply as if for the conditions stated in paragraphs (*a*) and (*b*) there were substituted the condition that the transfer was a normal one on the part of the transferor.
(5) For the purposes of sections 23 [to 25[4]]—
(*a*) the value transferred shall be treated as attributable to the property of which the borrower is allowed the use, and
(*b*) that property shall be treated as given to, or as becoming the property of, the borrower unless the use allowed includes use for purposes other than charitable purposes or those of a body mentioned in section 24 [or 25][4] [or, where it land, of a body mentioned in section 24A][2];
and sections 23(2) to (6), 24 . . . [1], (3) and (4), [24A(3),][3] [and 25(2)][4] shall not apply.

Commentary—*Simon's Taxes* **I3.342, I4.221**.
HMRC Manuals—Inheritance Tax Manual IHTM11133 (gifts to charities and registered clubs: procedure: special situations).
IHTM14236 (normal expenditure out of income: loans).
Press releases etc—Law Society's Gazette 18-12-91 (a waiver of a loan must be effected by means of a deed).
Definitions—"Charitable", "Disposition", "estate", "land", "property", s 272.
Amendments—[1] Words "(1)(*b*)" in sub-s (5) repealed by FA 1988 Sch 14 Pt X.
[2] Words in sub-s (5)(*b*) inserted by FA 1989 s 171(3), (6) with respect to transfers of value made after 13 March 1989.
[3] Words in sub-s (5) inserted by FA 1989 s 171(3), (6) with respect to transfers of value made after 13 March 1989.
[4] Words in sub-s (5) substituted by FA 1998 s 143(2) in relation to any transfer of value made on or after 17 March 1998.

[29A Abatement of exemption where claim settled out of beneficiary's own resources

(1) This section applies where—
(*a*) apart from this section the transfer of value made on the death of any person is an exempt transfer to the extent that the value transferred by it is attributable to an exempt gift, and
(*b*) the exempt beneficiary, in settlement of the whole or part of any claim against the deceased's estate, effects a disposition of property not derived from the transfer.
(2) The provisions of this Act shall have effect in relation to the transfer as if—

(*a*) so much of the relevant value as is equal to the following amount, namely the amount by which the value of the exempt beneficiary's estate immediately after the disposition is less than it would be but for the disposition, or

(*b*) where that amount exceeds the relevant value, the whole of the relevant value,

were attributable to such a gift to the exempt beneficiary as is mentioned in subsection (3) below (instead of being attributable to a gift with respect to which the transfer is exempt).

(3) The gift referred to in subsection (2) above is a specific gift with respect to which the transfer is chargeable, being a gift which satisfies the conditions set out in paragraphs (*a*) and (*b*) of section 38(1) below.

(4) In determining the value of the exempt beneficiary's estate for the purposes of subsection (2) above—

(*a*) no deduction shall be made in respect of the claim referred to in subsection (1)(*b*) above, and

(*b*) where the disposition referred to in that provision constitutes a transfer of value—

(i) no account shall be taken of any liability of the beneficiary for any tax on the value transferred, and

(ii) sections 104 and 116 below shall be disregarded.

(5) Subsection (1)(*b*) above does not apply in relation to any claim against the deceased's estate in respect of so much of any liability as is, in accordance with this Act, to be taken into account in determining the value of the estate.

(6) In this section—

"exempt gift", in relation to a transfer of value falling within subsection (1)(*a*) above, means—

(*a*) a gift with respect to which the transfer is (apart from this section) exempt by virtue of the provisions of any of sections 18 and 23 [to 28A][4] above, or

(*b*) where (apart from this section) the transfer is so exempt with respect to a gift up to a limit, so much of the gift as is within that limit;

"the exempt beneficiary", in relation to an exempt gift, means any of the following, namely—

(*a*) where the gift is exempt by virtue of section 18 above, the deceased's spouse [or civil partner][3],

(*b*) where the gift is exempt by virtue of section 23 above, any person or body—

(i) whose property the property falling within subsection (1) of that section becomes, or

(ii) by whom that property is held on trust for charitable purposes,

(*c*) where the gift is exempt by virtue of section 24 [or 25][2] above, any body whose property the property falling within subsection (1) of that section becomes,

(*d*) where the gift is exempt by virtue of section 24A above, any body to whom the land falling within subsection (1) of that section is given, and

(*e*) where the gift is exempt by virtue of section 27[, 28 or 28A][4] above, the trustees of any settlement in which the property falling within subsection (1) of that section becomes comprised;

"gift" and "specific gift" have the same meaning as in Chapter III of this Part; and

"the relevant value", in relation to a transfer of value falling within subsection (1)(*a*) above, means so much of the value transferred by the transfer as is attributable to the gift referred to in that provision.][1]

Commentary—*Simon's Taxes* **I4.445, 446.**

HMRC Manuals—Inheritance Tax Manual IHTM11133 (gifts to charities and registered clubs: procedure: special situations).
IHTM11026 (restriction of exemption where the beneficiary settles a claim against the deceased's estate from their own resources).

Definitions—"Disposition" "estate", "property" s 272; "settlement", s 43.

Amendments—[1] This section inserted by FA 1989 s 172 in relation to deaths occurring after 26 July 1989.

[2] Amended by FA 1998 s 143(2) in relation to any transfer of value made on or after 17 March 1998.

[3] Words in sub-s (6) in definition of "the exempt beneficiary" inserted by Tax and Civil Partnership Regulations, SI 2005/3229, regs 3, 10, with effect from 5 December 2005 (reg 1(1)).

[4] Words in sub-s (6) substituted by FA 2014 s 290, Sch 37 paras 9, 12 with effect in relation to transfers of value made on or after 6 April 2014.

CHAPTER II

CONDITIONAL EXEMPTION

30 Conditionally exempt transfers

(1) A transfer of value is an exempt transfer to the extent that the value transferred by it is attributable to property—

(*a*) which, on a claim made for the purpose, is designated by the Treasury under section 31 below, and

(*b*) with respect to which the requisite undertaking described in that section is given by such person as the Treasury think appropriate in the circumstances of the case [or (where the property is an area of land within subsection (1)(*d*) of that section) with respect to which the requisite undertakings described in that section are given by such person or persons as the Treasury think appropriate in the circumstances of the case][1].

(2) A transfer of value exempt with respect to any property under this section or under section 76 of the Finance Act 1976 is referred to in this Act as a conditionally exempt transfer of that property.

(3) Subsection (1) above shall not apply to a transfer of value other than one which under section 4 above a person makes on his death unless—

(*a*) the transferor or his spouse [or civil partner][4], or the transferor and his spouse [or civil partner][4] between them, have been beneficially entitled to the property throughout the six years ending with the transfer, or

(*b*) the transferor acquired the property on a death on the occasion of which there was a transfer of value under section 4 above which was itself a conditionally exempt transfer of the property.

[(3A) The provisions of this section shall be disregarded in determining under section 3A above whether a transfer of value is a potentially exempt transfer.][2]

[(3B) No claim may be made under subsection (1) above with respect to a potentially exempt transfer until the transferor has died.][2]

[(3BA) A claim under subsection (1) above must be made no more than two years after the date of the transfer of value to which it relates or, in the case of a claim with respect to a potentially exempt transfer, the date of the death, or (in either case) within such longer period as the Board may allow.][3]

[(3C) Subsection (1) above shall not apply to a potentially exempt transfer to the extent that the value transferred by it is attributable to property which has been disposed of by sale during the period beginning with the date of the transfer and ending with the death of the transferor.][2]

(4) Subsection (1) above does not apply to a transfer of value to the extent to which it is an exempt transfer under section 18 or 23 above.

Commentary—*Simon's Taxes* **I4.224, I7.501, I7.502.**

HMRC Manuals—Inheritance Tax Manual IHTM11260 (conditional exemption).

IHTM21048 (conditional exemption).

Press releases etc—IR December 1995 (Capital Taxes Office no longer need to see Inland Revenue Accounts, at the pre-grant stage, in which a claim for conditional exemption is made; interest in possession in a Heritage property which was the subject of an earlier capital tax exemption should be detailed.

Cross references—See FA 1986 Sch 19 para 40 (where a death or other event occurs after 17 March 1986, sub-ss (3A)–(3C) above not to affect the tax chargeable on a transfer of value occurring before 18 March 1986).

FA 2013 s 155 (annual tax on enveloped dwellings: dwelling conditionally exempt from IHT).

Amendments—[1] Words in sub-s (1)(*b*) added by FA 1985 Sch 26 para 1 in relation to events after 18 March 1985.

[2] Sub-ss (3A)–(3C) inserted by FA 1986 s 101(3) and Sch 19 para 7 with respect to transfers of value made after 17 March 1986.

[3] Inserted by FA 1998 Sch 25 para 2 in relation to any transfer of value or death on or after 17 March 1998.

[4] Words in sub-s (3)(*a*) inserted by Tax and Civil Partnership Regulations, SI 2005/3229, regs 3, 11, with effect from 5 December 2005 (reg 1(1)).

31 Designation and undertakings

(1) The Treasury may designate under this section—

[(*a*) any relevant object which appears to the Board to be pre-eminent for its national, scientific, historic or artistic interest;

(*aa*) any collection or group of relevant objects which, taken as a whole, appears to the Board to be pre-eminent for its national, scientific, historic or artistic interest;][6]

(*b*) any land which in the opinion of the Treasury is of outstanding scenic or historic or scientific interest;

(*c*) any building for the preservation of which special steps should in the opinion of the Treasury be taken by reason of its outstanding historic or architectural interest;

[(*d*) any area of land which in the opinion of the Treasury is essential for the protection of the character and amenities of such a building as is mentioned in paragraph (*c*) above;][1]

(*e*) any object which in the opinion of the Treasury is historically associated with such a building as is mentioned in paragraph (*c*) above.

[(1A) Where the transfer of value in relation to which the claim for designation is made is a potentially exempt transfer which (apart from section 30 above) has proved to be a chargeable transfer, the question whether any property is appropriate for designation under this section shall be determined by reference to circumstances existing after the death of the transferor.][4]

(2) In the case of property within subsection [(1)(*a*) or (*aa*)][6] above, the requisite undertaking is that, until the person beneficially entitled to the property dies or the property is disposed of, whether by sale or gift or otherwise—

(*a*) the property will be kept permanently in the United Kingdom and will not leave it temporarily except for a purpose and a period approved by the Treasury, and

(*b*) [such steps as are agreed between the Treasury and the person giving the undertaking, and are set out in it,][2] will be taken for the preservation of the property and for securing reasonable access to the public.

(3) If it appears to the Treasury, on a claim made for the purpose, that any documents which are designated or to be designated under subsection [(1)(*a*) or (*aa*)][6] above contain information which for personal or other reasons ought to be treated as confidential, they may exclude those documents, either altogether or to such extent as they think fit, from so much of an undertaking given or to be given under subsection (2)(*b*) above as relates to public access.

(4) In the case of other property within subsection (1) above, the requisite undertaking is that, until the person beneficially entitled to the property dies or the property is disposed of, whether by sale or gift or otherwise, [such steps as are agreed between the Treasury and the person giving the undertaking, and are set out in it,][2] will be taken—

(*a*) in the case of land falling within subsection (1)(*b*) above, for the maintenance of the land and the preservation of its character, and

(*b*) in the case of any other property, for the maintenance, repair and preservation of the property and, if it is an object falling within subsection (1)(*e*) above, for keeping it associated with the building concerned;

and for securing reasonable access to the public.

[(4A) In the case of an area of land within subsection (1)(*d*) above (relevant land) there is an additional requisite undertaking, which is that, until the person beneficially entitled to property falling within subsection (4C) below dies, or it is disposed of, whether by sale or gift or otherwise, specified steps will be taken for its maintenance, repair and preservation and for securing reasonable access to the public; and "specified steps" means such steps as are agreed between the Treasury and the person giving the undertaking, and are set out in it.][3]

[(4B) Where different persons are entitled (either beneficially or otherwise) to different properties falling within subsection (4C) below, subsection (4A) above shall have effect to require separate undertakings as to the maintenance, repair, preservation and access of each of the properties to be given by such persons as the Treasury think appropriate in the circumstances of the case.][3]

[(4C) The following property falls within this subsection—

(*a*) the building for the protection of whose character and amenities the relevant land is in the opinion of the Treasury essential;

(*b*) any other area (or areas) of land which, in relation to the building, falls (or fall) within subsection (1)(*d*) above and which either lies (or lie) between the relevant land and the building or is (or are) in the opinion of the Treasury physically closely connected with the relevant land or the building.][3]

[(4D) Where subsection (4A) above requires an undertaking for the maintenance, repair, preservation and access of property, such an undertaking is required notwithstanding that some other undertaking for its maintenance, repair, preservation and access is effective.][3]

[(4E) Any undertaking given in pursuance of subsection (4A) above is for the purposes of this Act given with respect to the relevant land.][3]

[(4F) It is for the person seeking the designation of relevant land to secure that any undertaking required under subsection (4A) above is given.][3]

[(4FA) For the purposes of this section, the steps agreed for securing reasonable access to the public must ensure that the access that is secured is not confined to access only where a prior appointment has been made.][7]

[(4FB) Subject to subsection (3) above, where the steps that may be set out in any undertaking include steps for securing reasonable access to the public to any property, the steps that may be agreed and set out in that undertaking may also include steps involving the publication of—

(*a*) the terms of any undertaking given or to be given for any of the purposes of this Act with respect to the property; or

(*b*) any other information relating to the property which (apart from this subsection) would fall to be treated as confidential;

and references in this Act to an undertaking for access to any property shall be construed as including references to so much of any undertaking as provides for the taking of steps involving any such publication.][7]

[(4G) In a case where—

(*a*) the transfer of value in question is a potentially exempt transfer which (apart from section 30 above) has proved to be a chargeable transfer, and

(*b*) at the time of the transferor's death an undertaking by such a person as is mentioned in section 30(1)(*b*) above given under paragraph 3(3) of Schedule 4 to this Act or under section [258 of the 1992 Act][5] is in force with respect to any property to which the value transferred by the transfer is attributable,

that undertaking shall be treated for the purposes of this Chapter as an undertaking given under section 30 above.][4]

[(5) In this section—

"national interest" includes interest within any part of the United Kingdom; and

"relevant object" means—

(*a*) a picture, print, book, manuscript, work of art or scientific object, or

(*b*) anything not falling within paragraph (*a*) above that does not yield income;
and in determining under subsection (1)(a) or (aa) above whether an object or a collection or group of objects is pre-eminent, regard shall be had to any significant association of the object, collection or group with a particular place.][6]

Commentary—*Simon's Taxes* **I7.504, C1.418, I4.224, I7.506.**
HMRC Manuals—Inheritance Tax Manual IHTM11260 (conditional exemption).
Press releases etc—Hansard 9-2-87 (details of undertakings regarding public access requirement under sub-s (4)).
IR 20-2-95 (the "V&A list" which is updated quarterly can be consulted at the Victoria & Albert Museum, National Library of Scotland, National Museum of Wales and Ulster Museum; copies can be obtained from the CTO).
Cross references—See FA 1986 Sch 19 para 40 (where a death or other event occurs after 17 March 1986, sub-ss (1A), (4G) above not to affect the tax chargeable on a transfer of value occurring before 18 March 1986).
FA 2013 s 155 (annual tax on enveloped dwellings: dwelling conditionally exempt from IHT).
Amendments—[1] Sub-s (1)(*d*) substituted by FA 1985 Sch 26 para 2(2) in relation to events after 18 March 1985.
[2] Words in sub-ss (2)(*b*), (4) substituted by FA 1985 Sch 26 para 2(3) in relation to events after 18 March 1985.
[3] Sub-ss (4A)–(4F) inserted by FA 1985 Sch 26 para 2(4) in relation to events after 18 March 1985.
[4] Sub-ss (1A), (4G) inserted by FA 1986 s 101(3) and Sch 19 para 8 with respect to transfers of value made after 17 March 1986.
[5] Words in sub-s (4G)(*b*) substituted by TCGA 1992 Sch 10 para 8(1), (2).
[6] Substituted by FA 1998 Sch 25 para 4 in relation to the making of any designation on a claim made on or after 31 July 1998.
[7] Inserted by FA 1998 Sch 25 paras 5, 6 in relation to the giving of any undertaking after 30 July 1998.

32 Chargeable events

(1) Where there has been a conditionally exempt transfer of any property, tax shall be charged under this section on the first occurrence after the transfer [(or, if the transfer was a potentially exempt transfer, after the death of the transferor)][3] of an event which under this section is a chargeable event with respect to the property.
(2) If the Treasury are satisfied that at any time an undertaking given with respect to the property under section 30 above or [subsection (5AA)][4] below has not been observed in a material respect, the failure to observe the undertaking is a chargeable event with respect to the property.
(3) If—
(*a*) the person beneficially entitled to the property dies, or
(*b*) the property is disposed of, whether by sale or gift or otherwise,
the death or disposal is, subject to [subsections (4), (4A) and (5)][6] below, a chargeable event with respect to the property.
(4) A death or disposal is not a chargeable event with respect to any property if the personal representatives of the deceased (or, in the case of settled property, the trustees or the person next entitled) within three years of the death make or, as the case may be, the disposal is—
(*a*) a disposal of the property by sale by private treaty to a body mentioned in Schedule 3 to this Act, or a disposal of it to such a body otherwise than by sale, or
(*b*) a disposal in pursuance of section 230 below,
and a death or disposal of the property after such a disposal as is mentioned in paragraph (a) or (b) above is not a chargeable event with respect to the property unless there has again been a conditionally exempt transfer of it after that disposal.
[(4A) A death or disposal is not a chargeable event with respect to any property if—
(*a*) in the case of a death, a person who became beneficially entitled to the property on the death disposes of it in the circumstances described in paragraph 1 of Schedule 14 to the Finance Act 2012 (gifts to the nation) within 3 years of the death, or
(*b*) in the case of a disposal, the disposal is made in the circumstances described in paragraph 1 of that Schedule,
and a death or disposal of the property after such a disposal as is mentioned in paragraph (a) or (b) is not a chargeable event with respect to the property unless there has again been a conditionally exempt transfer of it after that disposal.][6]
(5) A death or disposal otherwise than by sale is not a chargeable event with respect to any property if—
(*a*) the transfer of value made on the death or the disposal is itself a conditionally exempt transfer of the property, or
[(*b*) the condition specified in subsection (5AA) below is satisfied with respect to the property.][4]
[(5AA) The condition referred to in subsection (5)(*b*) above is satisfied if—
(*a*) the requisite undertaking described in section 31 above is given with respect to the property by such person as the Board think appropriate in the circumstances of the case, or
(*b*) (where the property is an area of land within section 31(1)(*d*) above) the requisite undertakings described in that section are given with respect to the property by such person or persons as the Board think appropriate in the circumstances of the case.][5]
[(5A) This section does not apply where section 32A below applies.][1]
(6)–(7) . . .[2]
Commentary—*Simon's Taxes* **I4.224, I7.513–I7.513C.**

HMRC Manuals—Inheritance Tax Manual IHTM04113 (chargeable events under s.32).
IHTM04114 (exceptions to the charge underr S.32).
Press releases etc—IR 7-5-93 (part disposal resulting from leasehold enfranchisement should not occasion a review of the retained property).
Definitions—"Conditionally exempt transfer", s 30(2); "the Board", s 272.
Cross references—See FA 1986 Sch 19 para 40 (where a death or other event occurs after 17 March 1986, sub-s (1) above as amended by FA 1986 Sch 19 para 9 not to affect the tax chargeable on a transfer of value occurring before 18 March 1986).
IHTA 1984 s 8M (modifications in relation to residence nil-rate amount).
Amendments—[1] Sub-s (5A) inserted by FA 1985 Sch 26 para 3(2) in relation to events after 18 March 1985.
[2] Sub-ss (6), (7) repealed by FA 1985 Sch 26 para 3(3) and Sch 27 Pt XI in relation to events after 18 March 1985.
[3] Words in sub-s (1) inserted by FA 1986 s 101(3) and Sch 19 para 9 with respect to transfers of value made after 17 March 1986.
[4] Words in sub-ss (2), (5)(*b*) substituted by FA 1998 Sch 25 para 7 in relation to any undertaking on or after 31 July 1998.
[5] Sub-s (5AA) inserted by FA 1998 Sch 25 para 7 in relation to any undertaking on or after 31 July 1998.
[6] In sub-s (3) words substituted for words "subsections (4) and (5)", and sub-s (4A) inserted, by FA 2012 s 49, Sch 14 paras 26, 29 with effect from 17 July 2012.

[32A Associated properties

(1) For the purposes of this section the following properties are associated with each other, namely, a building falling within section 31(1)(*c*) above and (to the extent that any of the following exists) an area or areas of land falling within section 31(1)(*d*) above in relation to the building and an object or objects falling within section 31(1)(*e*) above in relation to the building; and this section applies where there are such properties, which are referred to as associated properties.

(2) Where there has been a conditionally exempt transfer of any property (or part), tax shall be charged under this section in respect of that property (or part) on the first occurrence after the transfer [(or, if the transfer was a potentially exempt transfer, after the death of the transferor)][2] of an event which under this section is a chargeable event with respect to that property (or part).

(3) If the Treasury are satisfied that at any time an undertaking given under section 30 above or this section for the maintenance, repair, preservation, access or keeping of any of the associated properties has not been observed in a material respect, then (subject to subsection (10) below) the failure to observe the undertaking is a chargeable event with respect to the whole of each of the associated properties of which there has been a conditionally exempt transfer.

(4) If—

(*a*) the person beneficially entitled to property dies, or

(*b*) property (or part of it) is disposed of, whether by sale or gift or otherwise,

then, if the property is one of the associated properties and an undertaking for its maintenance, repair, preservation, access or keeping has been given under section 30 above or this section, the death or disposal is (subject to subsections (5) to (10) below) a chargeable event with respect to the whole of each of the associated properties of which there has been a conditionally exempt transfer.

(5) Subject to subsection (6) below, the death of a person beneficially entitled to property, or the disposal of property (or part), is not a chargeable event if the personal representatives of the deceased (or, in the case of settled property, the trustees or the person next entitled) within three years of the death make or, as the case may be, the disposal is—

(*a*) a disposal of the property (or part) concerned by sale by private treaty to a body mentioned in Schedule 3 to this Act, or to such a body otherwise than by sale, or

(*b*) a disposal of the property (or part) concerned in pursuance of section 230 below.

[(5A) The death of a person beneficially entitled to property, or the disposal of property, is not a chargeable event if—

(*a*) in the case of a death, a person who became beneficially entitled to the property on the death disposes of it in the circumstances described in paragraph 1 of Schedule 14 to the Finance Act 2012 (gifts to the nation) within 3 years of the death, or

(*b*) in the case of a disposal, the disposal is made in the circumstances described in paragraph 1 of that Schedule.][5]

(6) Where a disposal mentioned in subsection (5)(*a*) or (*b*) above is a part disposal, that subsection does not make the event non-chargeable with respect to property other than that disposed of [unless—

(*a*) the requisite undertaking described in section 31 above is given with respect to the property (or part) not disposed of by such person as the Board think appropriate in the circumstances of the case, or

(*b*) (where any of the property or part not disposed of is an area of land within section 31(1)(*d*) above) the requisite undertakings described in that section are given with respect to that property (or that part) by such person or persons as the Board think appropriate in the circumstances of the case;

and][3] in this subsection "part disposal" means a disposal of property which does not consist of or include the whole of each property which is one of the associated properties and of which there has been a conditionally exempt transfer.

(7) Where, after a relevant disposal (that is, a disposal mentioned in subsection (5)(*a*) or (*b*) [or (5A)(*a*) or (*b*)][5] above made in circumstances where that subsection applies), a person beneficially entitled to the property (or part) concerned dies or the property (or part) concerned is disposed of, the death or disposal is not a chargeable event with respect to the property (or part) concerned unless there has again been a conditionally exempt transfer of the property (or part) concerned after the relevant disposal.

(8) The death of a person beneficially entitled to property, or the disposal of property (or part) otherwise than by sale, is not a chargeable event if—

- (*a*) the transfer of value made on the death or the disposal is itself a conditionally exempt transfer of the property (or part) concerned, or
- [(*b*) the condition specified in subsection (8A) below is satisfied with respect to the property (or part) concerned.] [3]

[(8A) The condition referred to in subsection (8)(*b*) above is satisfied if—

- (*a*) the requisite undertaking described in section 31 above is given with respect to the property (or part) by such person as the Board think appropriate in the circumstances of the case, or
- (*b*) (where any of the property or part is an area of land within section 31(1)(*d*) above) the requisite undertakings described in that section are given with respect to the property (or part) by such person or persons as the Board think appropriate in the circumstances of the case.][4]

[(9) If the whole or part of any property is disposed of by sale and—

- (*a*) the requisite undertaking described in section 31 above is given with respect to the property (or part) by such person as the Board think appropriate in the circumstances of the case, or
- (*b*) (where any of the property or part is an area of land within section 31(1)(*d*) above) the requisite undertakings described in that section are given with respect to the property (or part) by such person or persons as the Board think appropriate in the circumstances of the case,

the disposal is a chargeable event only with respect to the whole or part actually disposed of (if it is a chargeable event with respect to such whole or part apart from this subsection).][3]

(10) If—

- (*a*) the Treasury are satisfied that there has been a failure to observe, as to one of the associated properties or part of it, an undertaking for the property's maintenance, repair, preservation, access or keeping, or
- (*b*) there is a disposal of one of the associated properties or part of it,

and it appears to the Treasury that the entity consisting of the associated properties has not been materially affected by the failure or disposal, they may direct that it shall be a chargeable event only with respect to the property or part as to which there has been a failure or disposal (if it is a chargeable event with respect to that property or part apart from this subsection).][1]

Commentary—*Simon's Taxes* **I7.513D**.

HMRC Manuals—Inheritance Tax Manual IHTM04115 (chargeable events under S.32A).
IHTM04116 (exceptions to the charge under S.32A).

Definitions—"Conditionally exempt transfer", s 30(2); "the Board", s 272.

Cross references—See FA 1986 Sch 19 para 40 (where a death or other event occurs after 17 March 1986, sub-s (2) above as amended by FA 1986 Sch 19 para 10 not to affect the tax chargeable on a transfer of value occurring before 18 March 1986).
IHTA 1984 s 8M (modifications in relation to residence nil-rate amount).

Amendments—[1] This section inserted by FA 1985 Sch 26 para 4 in relation to events after 18 March 1985.
[2] Words in sub-s (2) inserted by FA 1986 s 101(3) and Sch 19 para 10 with respect to transfers of value made after 17 March 1986.
[3] Substituted by FA 1998 Sch 25 para 7 in relation to the giving of any undertaking on or after 31 July 1998.
[4] Inserted by FA 1998 Sch 25 para 7 in relation to the giving of any undertaking on or after 31 July 1998.
[5] Sub-s (5A) inserted and words in sub-s (7) inserted by FA 2012 s 49, Sch 14 paras 26, 30 with effect from 17 July 2012.

33 Amount of charge under section 32

(1) Tax chargeable in respect of any property under section 32 [or 32A][1] above by reference to a chargeable event shall be charged—

- (*a*) on an amount equal to the value of the property at the time of the chargeable event; and
- (*b*) at the following rate or rates—
  - (i) if the relevant person is alive, the rate or rates that would be applicable to that amount [in accordance with section 7(2) above][2] if it were the value transferred by a chargeable transfer made by the relevant person at that time;
  - (ii) if the relevant person is dead, the rate or rates that would have applied to that amount [in accordance with the appropriate provision of section 7 above][2] if it had been added to the value transferred on his death and had formed the highest part of that value.

[(2) For the purposes of subsection (1)(*b*)(ii) above the appropriate provision of section 7 above is—

- (*a*) if the conditionally exempt transfer by the relevant person was made on death (but the property was not treated as forming part of his estate immediately before his death only by virtue of section 102(3) of the Finance Act 1986), subsection (1) of section 7; and
- (*b*) in any other case, subsection (2) of section 7.][3]

[(2ZA) In determining for the purposes of subsection (1)(*b*)(ii) the rate or rates that would have applied in accordance with subsection (1) of section 7, the effect of Schedule 1A (if it would have applied) is to be disregarded.][5]

[(2A) The rate or rates of tax determined under subsection (1)(*b*)(i) above in respect of any chargeable event shall not be affected by the death of the relevant person after that event.][3]

(3) Where the chargeable event is a disposal on sale and the sale—

(*a*) was not intended to confer any gratuitous benefit on any person, and

(*b*) was either a transaction at arm's length between persons not connected with each other or a transaction such as might be expected to be made at arm's length between persons not connected with each other,

the value of the property at the time of the chargeable event shall be taken for the purposes of subsection (1)(a) above to be equal to the proceeds of the sale.

(4) Where by virtue of section 30(4) above the conditionally exempt transfer extended only to part of the property, the amount mentioned in subsection (1)(*a*) above shall be proportionately reduced.

(5) The relevant person in relation to a chargeable event in respect of any property is—

(*a*) if there has been only one conditionally exempt transfer of the property before the event, the person who made that transfer;

(*b*) if there have been two or more such transfers and the last was before, or only one of them was within, the period of thirty years ending with the event, the person who made the last of those transfers;

(*c*) if there have been two or more such transfers within that period, the person who made whichever of those transfers the Board may select.

(6) The conditionally exempt transfers to be taken into account for the purpose of subsection (5) above in relation to a chargeable event do not include transfers made before any previous chargeable event in respect of the same property or before any event which apart from [section 32(4) or (4A)][4] above would have been such a chargeable event [or, where the property has been disposed of as mentioned in [section 32A(5) or (5A)][4] above, before any event which apart from [section 32A(5) or (5A)][4] would have been such a chargeable event][1].

(7) [Subject to subsection (8) below][2] where after a conditionally exempt transfer of any property there is a chargeable transfer the value transferred by which is wholly or partly attributable to that property, any tax charged on that value so far as attributable to that property shall be allowed as a credit—

(*a*) if the chargeable transfer is a chargeable event with respect to the property, against the tax chargeable in accordance with this section by reference to that event;

(*b*) if the chargeable transfer is not such a chargeable event, against the tax chargeable in accordance with this section by reference to the next chargeable event with respect to the property.

[(8) Where after a conditionally exempt transfer of any property there is a potentially exempt transfer the value transferred by which is wholly or partly attributable to that property and either—

(*a*) the potentially exempt transfer is a chargeable event with respect to the property, or

(*b*) after the potentially exempt transfer, but before the death of the person who is the transferor in relation to the potentially exempt transfer, a chargeable event occurs with respect to the property,

the tax charged in accordance with this section by reference to that chargeable event shall be allowed as a credit against any tax which may become chargeable, by reason of the potentially exempt transfer proving to be a chargeable transfer, on so much of the value transferred by that transfer as is attributable to the property; and subsection (7) above shall not apply with respect to any tax so becoming chargeable.][3]

Commentary—*Simon's Taxes* **I7.514–I7.514D**.

Definitions—"Conditionally exempt transfer", s 30(2); "the Board", s 272.

Cross references—See FA 1986 Sch 19 para 40 (where a death or other event occurs after 17 March 1986, the amendments to this section made by FA 1986 Sch 19 para 11 (see below) not to affect the tax chargeable on a transfer of value occurring before 18 March 1986).

IHTA 1984 s 8M (modifications in relation to residence nil-rate amount).

Amendments—[1] Words in sub-ss (1), (6) inserted by FA 1985 Sch 26 paras 5, 6.

[2] Words in sub-ss (1)(*b*)(i), (ii) substituted, and in sub-s (7) inserted, by FA 1986 s 101(3) and Sch 19 para 11 with respect to transfers of value made after 17 March 1986.

[3] Sub-ss (2), (2A) substituted for sub-s (2), and sub-s (8) added, by FA 1986 s 101(3), Sch 19 para 11 with respect to transfers of value made after 17 March 1986.

[4] In sub-s (6), words substituted for words "section 32(4)" and words "section 32A(5)" (in both places) by FA 2012 s 49, Sch 14 paras 26, 31 with effect from 17 July 2012.

[5] Sub-s (2ZA) inserted by FA 2012 s 209, Sch 33 paras 2, 4 with effect in cases where D's death occurs on or after 6 April 2012.

34 Reinstatement of transferor's cumulative total

(1) Where tax has become chargeable under section 32 [or 32A][1] above by reference to a chargeable event in respect of any property ("the relevant event") the rate or rates of tax applicable to any subsequent chargeable transfer made by the person who made the last conditionally exempt transfer

of the property before the relevant event shall be determined as if the amount on which tax has become chargeable as aforesaid were value transferred by a chargeable transfer made by him at the time of the relevant event.

(2) Where the person who made the last conditionally exempt transfer of the property before the relevant event—

(*a*) is dead, and

(*b*) is for the purposes of section 33 above the relevant person in relation to a subsequent chargeable event,

section 33(1)(b)(ii) shall have effect as if the value transferred on his death were increased by the amount on which tax has become chargeable on the occasion of the relevant event.

(3) If—

(*a*) the person who made the last conditionally exempt transfer of the property before the relevant event is not the relevant person for the purposes of section 33 above in relation to that event, and

(*b*) at the time of that event or within the previous five years the property is or has been comprised in a settlement made not more than thirty years before that event, and

(*c*) a person who is the settlor in relation to the settlement has made a conditionally exempt transfer of the property within those thirty years,

subsections (1) and (2) above shall have effect with the substitution for references to the person who made the last conditionally exempt transfer before the relevant event of a reference to any such person as is mentioned in paragraph (c) above.

(4) The conditionally exempt transfers to be taken into account for the purposes of subsection (3)(*c*) above in relation to the relevant event do not include transfers made before any previous chargeable event in respect of the same property or before any event which apart from [section 32(4) or (4A)][2] above would have been such a chargeable event [or, where the property has been disposed of as mentioned in [section 32A(5) or (5A)][2] above, before any event which apart from [section 32A(5) or (5A)][2] would have been such a chargeable event][1].

Commentary—*Simon's Taxes* **I7.514B, I7.515.**

HMRC Manuals—Inheritance Tax Manual IHTM12093 (payment of uncharged debts out of the estate).

Definitions—"Conditionally exempt transfer", s 30(2); "settlement", s 43.

Cross reference—See IHTA 1984 s 78(6) (this section not to apply to a chargeable event if the last conditionally exempt transfer of the property has been followed by a conditionally exempt occasion (within s 78) in respect of it).

Amendments—[1] Words in sub-ss (1), (4) inserted by FA 1985 Sch 26 paras 5, 6.

[2] In sub-s (4), words substituted for words "section 32(4)" and words "section 32A(5)" (in both places) by FA 2012 s 49, Sch 14 paras 26, 32 with effect from 17 July 2012.

35 Conditional exemption on death before 7th April 1976

(1) Schedule 5 to this Act shall have effect with respect to certain cases where, by virtue of sections 31 to 34 of the Finance Act 1975 the value of any property was left out of account in determining the value transferred on a death before 7th April 1976.

(2) Where there has been a transfer of value in relation to which the value of any property has been left out of account under the provisions of sections 31 to 34 of the Finance Act 1975 and, before any tax has become chargeable in respect of that property under those provisions, there is a conditionally exempt transfer of that property, then, on the occurrence of a chargeable event in respect of that property—

[(*a*) tax shall be chargeable under section 32 or 32A (as the case may be), or

(*b*) tax shall be chargeable under Schedule 5,

as the Board may elect,][2]

(3) In [section 33(7) and (8) above, references][2] to a conditionally exempt transfer of any property [include references][2] to a transfer of value in relation to which the value of any property has been left out of account under the provisions of sections 31 to 34 of the Finance Act 1975 and, in relation to such property, references to a chargeable event or to the tax chargeable in accordance with section 33 above by reference to a chargeable event include references to an event on the occurrence of which tax becomes chargeable under Schedule 5 to this Act, or to the tax so chargeable.

Commentary—*Simon's Taxes* **I7.513, I7.522.**

HMRC Manuals—Inheritance Tax Manual IHTM12091 (debts charged on property).

Definitions—"Conditionally exempt transfer", s 30(2).

Amendments—[1] Words in sub-s (3) substituted by FA 1986 Sch 19 para 12.

[2] Sub-s (2)(*a*), (*b*) substituted by FA 2016 s 97(6) with effect in relation to a chargeable event where the conditionally exempt transfer referred to in sub-s (2) or Sch 6 para 4(2) occurred after 16 March 2016. Those paras previously read as follows—

"(*a*) if there has been no conditionally exempt transfer of the property on death, tax shall be chargeable either—

(i) under section 32 or 32A above (as the case may be), or

(ii) under Schedule 5 to this Act,

as the Board may elect;

(*b*) if there has been such a conditionally exempt transfer, tax shall be chargeable under section 32 or 32A above (as the case may be) and not under that Schedule.".

[35A Variation of undertakings

(1) An undertaking given under section 30, 32 or 32A above or paragraph 5 of Schedule 5 to this Act may be varied from time to time by agreement between the Board and the person bound by the undertaking.

(2) Where [the tribunal][2] is satisfied that—

(*a*) the Board have made a proposal for the variation of such an undertaking to the person bound by the undertaking,

(*b*) that person has failed to agree to the proposed variation within six months after the date on which the proposal was made, and

(*c*) it is just and reasonable, in all the circumstances, to require the proposed variation to be made,

[the tribunal may direct that the undertaking is to have effect from a specified date][2] as if the proposed variation had been agreed to by the person bound by the undertaking.

(3) The date specified by the [tribunal][2] must not be less than sixty days after the date of [the tribunal's direction][2].

(4) A direction under this section shall not take effect if, before the date specified by the [tribunal][2], a variation different from that to which the direction relates is agreed between the Board and the person bound by the undertaking.][1]

Commentary—*Simon's Taxes* **I7.508**.

Definitions—"the Board", "the Tribunal", s 272.

Modifications—Words in sub-s (2)(*a*) deemed to be substituted, and sub-ss (5), (6) deemed to be inserted by FA 1998 Sch 25 para 10 in relation to a relevant undertaking given with respect to any property before the 31 July 1998.

Amendments—[1] Inserted by FA 1998 Sch 25 para 8 in relation to undertakings given on or after 31 July 1998.

[2] In sub-s (2), words substituted for words "a Special Commissioner", and "the Commissioner may direct that the undertaking is to have effect from a date specified by him" respectively, in sub-s (3), words substituted for "Special Commissioner" and "his direction" respectively, and in sub-s (4), word substituted for words "Special Commissioner", by the Transfer of Tribunal Functions and Revenue and Customs Appeals Order, SI 2009/56 art 3, Sch 1 paras 108, 109 with effect from 1 April 2009.

CHAPTER III

ALLOCATION OF EXEMPTIONS

36 Preliminary

Where any one or more of sections 18, 23 to 27 and 30 above apply in relation to a transfer of value but the transfer is not wholly exempt—

(*a*) any question as to the extent to which it is exempt or, where it is exempt up to a limit, how an excess over the limit is to be attributed to the gifts concerned shall be determined in accordance with sections 37 to 40 below; and

(*b*) section 41 below shall have effect as respects the burden of tax.

Commentary—*Simon's Taxes* **I4.231**.

37 Abatement of gifts

(1) Where a gift would be abated owing to an insufficiency of assets and without regard to any tax chargeable, the gift shall be treated for the purposes of the following provisions of this Chapter as so abated.

(2) Where the value attributable, in accordance with section 38 below, to specific gifts exceeds the value transferred the gifts shall be treated as reduced to the extent necessary to reduce their value to that of the value transferred; and the reduction shall be made in the order in which, under the terms of the relevant disposition or any rule of law, it would fall to be made on a distribution of assets.

Commentary—*Simon's Taxes* **I4.234, I4.241**.

HMRC Manuals—Inheritance Tax Manual IHTM12087 (abatement where there are not enough assets to pay gifts in full).

IHTM12088 (abatement caused by grossing up under s 38).

IHTM26090 (abatement where there are not enough assets to pay specific gifts in full).

IHTM26151 (exception where four stage grossing is not necessary).

IHTM26180 (abatement caused by grossing up).

Definitions—"Gift", "specific gift", s 42.

38 Attribution of value to specific gifts

(1) Such part of the value transferred shall be attributable to specific gifts as corresponds to the value of the gifts; but if or to the extent that the gifts—

(*a*) are not gifts with respect to which the transfer is exempt or are outside the limit up to which the transfer is exempt, and

(*b*) do not bear their own tax,

the amount corresponding to the value of the gifts shall be taken to be the amount arrived at in accordance with subsections (3) to (5) below.

(2) Where any question arises as to which of two or more specific gifts are outside the limit up to which a transfer is exempt or as to the extent to which a specific gift is outside that limit—

(*a*) the excess shall be attributed to gifts not bearing their own tax before being attributed to gifts bearing their own tax, and

(*b*) subject to paragraph (*a*) above, the excess shall be attributed to gifts in proportion to their values.

(3) Where the only gifts with respect to which the transfer is or might be chargeable are specific gifts which do not bear their own tax, the amount referred to in subsection (1) above is the aggregate of—

(*a*) the sum of the value of those gifts; and

(*b*) the amount of tax which would be chargeable if the value transferred equalled that aggregate.

(4) Where the specific gifts not bearing their own tax are not the only gifts with respect to which the transfer is or might be chargeable, the amount referred to in subsection (1) above is such amount as, after deduction of tax at the assumed rate specified in subsection (5) below, would be equal to the sum of the value of those gifts.

(5) For the purposes of subsection (4) above—

(*a*) the assumed rate is the rate found by dividing the assumed amount of tax by that part of the value transferred with respect to which the transfer would be chargeable on the hypothesis that—

(i) the amount corresponding to the value of specific gifts not bearing their own tax is equal to the aggregate referred to in subsection (3) above, and

(ii) the parts of the value transferred attributable to specific gifts and to gifts of residue or shares in residue are determined accordingly; and

(*b*) the assumed amount of tax is the amount that would be charged on the value transferred on the hypothesis mentioned in paragraph (*a*) above.

(6) For the purposes of this section, any liability of the transferor which is not to be taken into account under section 5(5) above [or by virtue of section 103 of the Finance Act 1986][1] shall be treated as a specific gift [and, to the extent that any liability of the transferor is abated under the said section 103, that liability shall be treated as a specific gift][1].

Commentary—*Simon's Taxes* **I4.233–I4.239**.

HMRC Manuals—Inheritance Tax Manual IHTM26020–26060 (calculating the chargeable estate).

IHTM26081–26086 (the starting value of specific gifts).

IHTM26121–26133 (grossing up).

IHTM26141–26144 (simple grossing calculations).

IHTM26151–26158 (four stage grossing calculations).

IHTM26171 and 26172 (Re Benham type grossing calculations).

Definitions—"Gift", "specific gift", s 42.

Cross references—See FA 1986 Sch 19 para 40 (where a death or other event occurs after 17 March 1986, the amendment in sub-s (6) by FA 1986 Sch 19 (see below) not to affect the tax chargeable on a transfer of value occurring before 18 March 1986).

Amendments—[1] Words in sub-s (6) inserted by FA 1986 s 101(3) and Sch 19 para 13 with respect to transfers of value made after 17 March 1986.

39 Attribution of value to residuary gifts

Such part only of the value transferred shall be attributed to gifts of residue or shares in residue as is not attributed under section 38 above to specific gifts.

Commentary—*Simon's Taxes* **I4.239, I4.239A**.

Definitions—"Gift", s 42.

[39A Operation of sections 38 and 39 in cases of business or agricultural relief

(1) Where any part of the value transferred by a transfer of value is attributable to—

(*a*) the value of relevant business property, or

(*b*) the agricultural value of agricultural property,

then, for the purpose of attributing the value transferred (as reduced in accordance with section 104 or 116 below), to specific gifts and gifts of residue or shares of residue, sections 38 and 39 above shall have effect subject to the following provisions of this section.

(2) The value of any specific gifts of relevant business property or agricultural property shall be taken to be their value as reduced in accordance with section 104 or 116 below.

(3) The value of any specific gifts not falling within subsection (2) above shall be taken to be the appropriate fraction of their value.

(4) In subsection (3) above "the appropriate fraction" means a fraction of which—

(*a*) the numerator is the difference between the value transferred and the value, reduced as mentioned in subsection (2) above, of any gifts falling within that subsection, and

(*b*) the denominator is the difference between the unreduced value transferred and the value, before the reduction mentioned in subsection (2) above, of any gifts falling within that subsection;

and in paragraph (b) above "the unreduced value transferred" means the amount which would be the value transferred by the transfer but for the reduction required by sections 104 and 116 below.

(5) If or to the extent that specific gifts fall within paragraphs (*a*) and (*b*) of subsection (1) of section 38 above, the amount corresponding to the value of the gifts shall be arrived at in accordance with subsections (3) to (5) of that section by reference to their value reduced as mentioned in subsection (2) or, as the case may be, subsection (3) of this section.

(6) For the purposes of this section the value of a specific gift of relevant business property or agricultural property does not include the value of any other gift payable out of that property; and that other gift shall not itself be treated as a specific gift of relevant business property or agricultural property.

(7) In this section—

"agricultural property" and "the agricultural value of agricultural property" have the same meaning as in Chapter II of Part V of this Act; and

"relevant business property" has the same meaning as in Chapter I of that Part.][1]

Commentary—*Simon's Taxes* **I4.240**.

HMRC Manuals—Inheritance Tax Manual IHTM26101–26104 (interaction of reliefs).

IHTM26107 (anti-avoidance provisions).

IHTM26108–26110 (the appropriate fraction).

IHTM26158 (example of four stage grossing calculation where interaction and settled property are also involved).

Definitions—"Gift", "specific gift", s 42.

Amendments—[1] This section inserted by FA 1986 s 105 with respect to transfers of value made after 17 March 1986.

40 Gifts made separately out of different funds

Where gifts taking effect on a transfer of value take effect separately out of different funds the preceding provisions of this Chapter shall be applied separately to the gifts taking effect out of each of those funds, with the necessary adjustments of the values and amounts referred to in those provisions.

Commentary—*Simon's Taxes* **I4.242**.

HMRC Manuals—Inheritance Tax Manual IHTM26211–26214 (property at more than one title).

Press releases etc—Law Society 9-5-90 (the rate of IHT used for "grossing up" should be ascertained separately for each fund).

Definitions—"Gift", s 42.

41 Burden of tax

Notwithstanding the terms of any disposition—

(*a*) none of the tax on the value transferred shall fall on any specific gift if or to the extent that the transfer is exempt with respect to the gift, and

(*b*) none of the tax attributable to the value of the property comprised in residue shall fall on any gift of a share of residue if or to the extent that the transfer is exempt with respect to the gift.

Commentary—*Simon's Taxes* **I4.243**.

HMRC Manuals—Inheritance Tax Manual IHTM26171 and 26172 (Re Benham type grossing calculations).

IHTM26201–26203 (allocating the burden of tax).

Simon's Tax Cases—*Re Benham's Will Trusts* [1995] STC 210.

s 41(*b*), *Re Ratcliffe (decd)* [1999] STC 262.

Definitions—"Disposition", s 272; "gift", s 42.

42 Supplementary

(1) In this Chapter—

"gift", in relation to any transfer of value, means the benefit of any disposition or rule of law by which, on the making of the transfer, any property becomes (or would but for any abatement become) the property of any person or applicable for any purpose;

"given" shall be construed accordingly;

"specific gift" means any gift other than a gift of residue or of a share in residue.

(2) For the purposes of this Chapter a gift bears its own tax if the tax attributable to it falls on the person who becomes entitled to the property given or (as the case may be) is payable out of property applicable for the purposes for which the property given becomes applicable.

(3) Where—

(*a*) the whole or part of the value transferred by a transfer of value is attributable to property which is the subject of two or more gifts, and

(*b*) the aggregate of the values of the property given by each of those gifts is less than the value transferred or, as the case may be, that part of it,

then for the purposes of this Chapter (and notwithstanding the definition of a gift in subsection (1) above) the value of each gift shall be taken to be the relevant proportion of the value transferred or, as the case may be, that part of it; and the relevant proportion in relation to any gift is the proportion which the value of the property given by it bears to the said aggregate.

(4) Where on the death of a person legal rights under the law of Scotland are claimed by a person entitled to claim them, they shall be treated for the purposes of this Chapter as a specific gift which bears its own tax; and in determining the value of such legal rights, any tax payable on the estate of the deceased shall be left out of account.

Commentary—*Simon's Taxes* **I4.233, I4.234**.

HMRC Manuals—Inheritance Tax Manual IHTM26003 (meaning of "gift").
IHTM26081–26086 (the starting value of specific gifts).
Press releases etc—Law Society's Gazette 22-5-85 (Deeds of variation—conditions to be satisfied by an instrument to bring it within this section).

PART III
SETTLED PROPERTY

CHAPTER I
PRELIMINARY

43 Settlement and related expressions

(1) The following provisions of this section apply for determining what is to be taken for the purposes of this Act to be a settlement, and what property is, accordingly, referred to as property comprised in a settlement or as settled property.

(2) "Settlement" means any disposition or dispositions of property, whether effected by instrument, by parol or by operation of law, or partly in one way and partly in another, whereby the property is for the time being—

(*a*) held in trust for persons in succession or for any person subject to a contingency, or

(*b*) held by trustees on trust to accumulate the whole or part of any income of the property or with power to make payments out of that income at the discretion of the trustees or some other person, with or without power to accumulate surplus income, or

(*c*) charged or burdened (otherwise than for full consideration in money or money's worth paid for his own use or benefit to the person making the disposition) with the payment of any annuity or other periodical payment payable for a life or any other limited or terminable period,

or would be so held or charged or burdened if the disposition or dispositions were regulated by the law of any part of the United Kingdom; or whereby, under the law of any other country, the administration of the property is for the time being governed by provisions equivalent in effect to those which would apply if the property were so held, charged or burdened.

(3) A lease of property which is for life or lives, or for a period ascertainable only by reference to a death, or which is terminable on, or at a date ascertainable only by reference to, a death, shall be treated as a settlement and the property as settled property, unless the lease was granted for full consideration in money or money's worth; and where a lease not granted as a lease at a rack rent is at any time to become a lease at an increased rent it shall be treated as terminable at that time.

(4) In relation to Scotland "settlement" also includes—

(*a*) an entail,

(*b*) any deed by virtue of which an annuity is charged on, or on the rents of, any property (the property being treated as the property comprised in the settlement), and

(*c*) any deed creating or reserving a proper liferent of any property whether heritable or moveable (the property from time to time subject to the proper liferent being treated as the property comprised in the settlement);

and for the purposes of this subsection "deed" includes any disposition, arrangement, contract, resolution, instrument or writing.

(5) In the application of this Act to Northern Ireland this section shall have effect as if references to property held in trust for persons included references to property standing limited to persons and as if the lease referred to in subsection (3) did not include a lease in perpetuity within the meaning of section 1 of the Renewable Leasehold Conversion Act 1849 or a lease to which section 37 of that Act applies.

Commentary—*Simon's Taxes* **I5.111–I5.122, I1.525.**
HMRC Manuals—Inheritance Tax Manual IHTM16041 and 16042 (definition of a settlement for IHT).
IHTM16191 and 16192 (leases for life).
IHTM23191 (lease for life granted gratuitously).
Concession F10—Partnership assurance policies.
Statement of Practice SP 10/79—Power for trustees to allow a beneficiary to occupy dwelling-house.
Simon's Tax Cases—s 43(2), *IRC v Lloyds Private Banking Ltd (as trustee of Irene Maude Evans, decd)* [1998] STC 559; *Rysaffe Trustee Co (CI) Ltd v IRC* [2002] STC 872; *Rysaffe Trustee Co (CI) Ltd v IRC* [2003] STC 536.
Definitions—"Trustee", s 45.

44 Settlor

(1) In this Act "settlor", in relation to a settlement, includes any person by whom the settlement was made directly or indirectly, and in particular (but without prejudice to the generality of the preceding words) includes any person who has provided funds directly or indirectly for the purpose of or in connection with the settlement or has made with any other person a reciprocal arrangement for that other person to make the settlement.

(2) Where more than one person is a settlor in relation to a settlement and the circumstances so require, this Part of this Act (except section 48(4) to (6)) shall have effect in relation to it as if the settled property were comprised in separate settlements.

Commentary—*Simon's Taxes* **I5.131, I5.132, I9.332.**
HMRC Manuals—Inheritance Tax Manual IHTM30111 (the settlor : definitions).
IHTM42251 (the settlor : who is the settlor).
IHTM42253 (more than one settlor).
"Settlement", s 43.
Simon's Tax Cases—s 44(1), *Countess Fitzwilliam v IRC* [1993] STC 502*.
Definitions—"Settlement", "settled property", s 43.

45 Trustee

In this Act "trustee", in relation to a settlement in relation to which there would be no trustees apart from this section, means any person in whom the settled property or its management is for the time being vested.

Commentary—*Simon's Taxes* **I5.133**.
HMRC Manuals—Inheritance Tax Manual IHTM16050 (the trustees).
IHTM30101 (definition and extent of liability (settled property) : trustees).

46 Interest in possession: Scotland

In the application of this Act to Scotland, any reference to an interest in possession in settled property is a reference to an interest of any kind under a settlement by virtue of which the person in right of that interest is entitled to the enjoyment of the property or would be so entitled if the property were capable of enjoyment, including an interest of an assignee under an assignation of an interest of any kind (other than a reversionary interest) in property subject to a proper liferent; and the person in right of such an interest at any time shall be deemed to be entitled to a corresponding interest in the whole or any part of the property comprised in the settlement.

Commentary—*Simon's Taxes* **I5.152, I5.812**.
HMRC Manuals—Inheritance Tax Manual IHTM16072 (introduction to proper liferents).
Definitions—"Settlement","settled property", s 43.

[46A Contract of life insurance entered into before 22nd March 2006 which on that day is settled property in which interest in possession subsists

(1) Subsections (2) and (4) below apply where—

(*a*) a settlement commenced before 22nd March 2006,
(*b*) a contract of life insurance was entered into before that day,
(*c*) a premium payable under the contract is paid, or an allowed variation is made to the contract, at a particular time on or after that day,
(*d*) immediately before that day, and at all subsequent times up to the particular time, there were rights under the contract that—
   (i) were comprised in the settlement, and
   (ii) were settled property in which a transitionally-protected interest (whether or not the same such interest throughout that period) subsisted,
(*e*) rights under the contract become, by reference to payment of the premium or as a result of the variation,—
   (i) comprised in the settlement, and
   (ii) part of the settled property in which the then-current transitionally-protected interest subsists, and
(*f*) any variation of the contract on or after 22nd March 2006 but before the particular time, so far as it is a variation that—
   (i) increased the benefits secured by the contract, or
   (ii) extended the term of the insurance provided by the contract,

was an allowed variation.

(2) For the purposes of the provisions mentioned in subsection (3) below—

(*a*) the rights mentioned in subsection (1)(*e*) above shall be taken to have become comprised in the settlement, and
(*b*) the person beneficially entitled to the then-current transitionally-protected interest shall be taken to have become beneficially entitled to his interest in possession so far as it subsists in those rights,

before 22nd March 2006.

(3) Those provisions are—

section 3A(2) above;
section 5(1A) above;
section 49(1A) and (1B) below;
section 51(1A) and (1B) below;
section 52(2A) and (3A) below;
section 53(1A) and (2A) below;

section 54(2A) and (2B) below;
section 54A(1A) below;
section 57A(1A) below;
section 58(1B) and (1C) below;
section 59(1) and (2) below;
section 80(4) below;
section 100(1A) below;
section 101(1A) below;
section 102ZA(1) of the Finance Act 1986 (gifts with reservation); and
sections 72(1A) and (2A) and 73(2A) of the 1992 Act.

(4) If payment of the premium is a transfer of value made by an individual, that transfer of value is a potentially exempt transfer.

(5) In this section—

"allowed variation", in relation to a contract, means a variation that takes place by operation of, or as a result of exercise of rights conferred by, provisions forming part of the contract immediately before 22nd March 2006;

"transitionally-protected interest" means—

(*a*) an interest in possession to which a person was beneficially entitled immediately before, and on, 22nd March 2006, or

(*b*) a transitional serial interest.][1]

Commentary—*Simon's Taxes* **I3.312, I5.208.**
HMRC Manuals—Inheritance Tax Manual IHTM20202 (contract of life insurance in existence prior to 22 march 2006).
Amendments—[1] Sections 46A, 46B inserted by FA 2006 s 156, Sch 20 paras 7, 11. These amendments are deemed to have come into force on 22 March 2006.

[46B Contract of life insurance entered into before 22nd March 2006 which immediately before that day is property to which section 71 applies

(1) Subsections (2) and (5) below apply where—

(*a*) a settlement commenced before 22nd March 2006,

(*b*) a contract of life insurance was entered into before that day,

(*c*) a premium payable under the contract is paid, or an allowed variation is made to the contract, at a particular time on or after that day,

(*d*) immediately before that day, and at all subsequent times up to the particular time, there were rights under the contract that—

(i) were comprised in the settlement, and

(ii) were settled property to which section 71 below applied,

(*e*) rights under the contract become, by reference to payment of the premium or as a result of the variation, comprised in the settlement, and

(*f*) any variation of the contract on or after 22nd March 2006 but before the particular time, so far as it was a variation that—

(i) increased the benefits secured by the contract, or

(ii) extended the term of the insurance provided by the contract,

was an allowed variation.

(2) If the rights mentioned in subsection (1)(*e*) above would, but for subsection (1A) of section 71 below, become property to which that section applies, those rights shall become settled property to which that section applies when they become comprised in the settlement.

(3) Subsection (5) below also applies where—

(*a*) a settlement commenced before 22nd March 2006,

(*b*) a contract of life insurance was entered into before that day,

(*c*) a premium payable under the contract is paid, or an allowed variation is made to the contract, at a particular time on or after that day when there are rights under the contract—

(i) that are comprised in the settlement and are settled property to which section 71A or 71D below applies,

(ii) that immediately before that day were settled property to which section 71 below applied, and

(iii) that on or after that day, but before the particular time, became property to which section 71A or 71D below applies in circumstances falling within subsection (4) below,

(*d*) rights under the contract become, by reference to payment of the premium or as a result of the variation, comprised in the settlement, and

(*e*) any variation of the contract on or after 22nd March 2006 but before the particular time, so far as it was a variation that—

(i) increased the benefits secured by the contract, or

(ii) extended the term of the insurance provided by the contract,

was an allowed variation.

(4) The circumstances referred to in subsection (3)(*c*)(iii) above are—

(*a*) in the case of property to which section 71D below applies, that the property on becoming property to which section 71D below applies ceased to be property to which section 71 below applied without ceasing to be settled property;

(*b*) in the case of property to which section 71A below applies—

(i) that the property on becoming property to which section 71A below applies ceased, by the operation of section 71(1B) below, to be property to which section 71 below applied, or

(ii) that the property, having become property to which section 71D below applied in circumstances falling within paragraph (*a*) above, on becoming property to which 71A below applies ceased, by the operation of section 71D(5)(*a*) below, to be property to which section 71D below applied.

(5) If payment of the premium is a transfer of value made by an individual, that transfer of value is a potentially exempt transfer.

(6) In this section "allowed variation", in relation to a contract, means a variation that takes place by operation of, or as a result of exercise of rights conferred by, provisions forming part of the contract immediately before 22nd March 2006.][1]

Commentary—*Simon's Taxes* **I5.526**.

HMRC Manuals—Inheritance Tax Manual IHTM20202 (contract of life insurance in existence prior to 22 march 2006). IHTM20331 (potentially exempt transfer treatment).

Amendments—[1] Sections 46A, 46B inserted by FA 2006 s 156, Sch 20 paras 7, 11. These amendments are deemed to have come into force on 22 March 2006.

47 Reversionary interest

In this Act "reversionary interest" means a future interest under a settlement, whether it is vested or contingent (including an interest expectant on the termination of an interest in possession which, by virtue of section 50 below, is treated as subsisting in part of any property) and in relation to Scotland includes an interest in the fee of property subject to a proper liferent.

Commentary—*Simon's Taxes* **I5.701**.

HMRC Manuals—Inheritance Tax Manual IHTM16231 (what is a reversion for IHT). IHTM27230 (reversionary interests).

Definitions—"Settlement", s 43.

[47A Settlement power

In this Act "settlement power" means any power over, or exercisable (whether directly or indirectly) in relation to, settled property or a settlement.][1]

Commentary—*Simon's Taxes* **I3.120, I5.741**.

Amendments—[1] This section inserted by FA 2002 s 119(1), (2), (6), (7) with effect for transfers of value after 16 April 2002. The insertion of this section by FA 2002 is also deemed always to have had effect (subject to and in accordance with the other provisions of IHTA 1984) for the purpose of determining the value, immediately before his death, of the estate of any person who died before 17 April 2002, for the purposes of the transfer of value which that person is treated by IHTA 1984 s 4(1) as having made immediately before his death.

48 Excluded property

(1) A reversionary interest is excluded property unless—

(*a*) it has at any time been acquired (whether by the person entitled to it or by a person previously entitled to it) for a consideration in money or money's worth, or

(*b*) it is one to which either the settlor or his spouse [or civil partner][3] is or has been beneficially entitled, or

(*c*) it is the interest expectant on the determination of a lease treated as a settlement by virtue of section 43(3) above[or,

(*d*) in a case where paragraphs (*a*), (*b*) and (*d*) of section 74A(1) are satisfied—

(i) it is a reversionary interest, in the relevant settled property, to which the individual is beneficially entitled, and

(ii) the individual has or is able to acquire (directly or indirectly) another interest in that relevant settled property.

Terms used in paragraph (*d*) have the same meaning as in section 74A.][5]

(2) In relation to a reversionary interest under a settlement made before 16th April 1976, subsection (1) above shall have effect with the omission of paragraph (*b*); and, if the person entitled to a reversionary interest under a settlement made on or after 16th April 1976 acquired the interest before 10th March 1981, that subsection shall have effect with the omission of the words "or has been" in paragraph (*b*).

(3) Where property comprised in a settlement is situated outside the United Kingdom—

(*a*) the property (but not a reversionary interest in the property) is excluded property unless the settlor was domiciled in the United Kingdom at the time the settlement was made, and

(*b*) section 6(1) above applies to a reversionary interest in the property but does not otherwise apply in relation to the property[;

but this subsection is subject to [subsections (3B) [to (3E)][7]][5] below [and to Schedule A1][6]][4].

[(3A) Where property comprised in a settlement is a holding in an authorised unit trust or a share in an open-ended investment company—

(*a*) the property (but not a reversionary interest in the property) is excluded property unless the settlor was domiciled in the United Kingdom at the time the settlement was made, and

(*b*) section 6(1A) above applies to a reversionary interest in the property but does not otherwise apply in relation to the property[;

but this subsection is subject to [subsections (3B) and (3E)][7] below [and to Schedule A1][6].][4]][2]

[(3B) Property is not excluded property by virtue of subsection (3) or (3A) above if—

(*a*) a person is, or has been, beneficially entitled to an interest in possession in the property at any time,

(*b*) the person is, or was, at that time an individual domiciled in the United Kingdom, and

(*c*) the entitlement arose directly or indirectly as a result of a disposition made on or after 5th December 2005 for a consideration in money or money's worth.][4]

[(3C) For the purposes of subsection (3B) above—

(*a*) it is immaterial whether the consideration was given by the person or by anyone else, and

(*b*) the cases in which an entitlement arose indirectly as a result of a disposition include any case where the entitlement arose under a will or the law relating to intestacy.][4]

[(3D) Where paragraphs (*a*) to (*d*) of section 74A(1) are satisfied, subsection (3)(*a*) above does not apply at the time they are first satisfied or any later time to make the relevant settled property (within the meaning of section 74A) excluded property.][5]

[(3E) In a case where the settlor of property comprised in a settlement is not domiciled in the United Kingdom at the time the settlement is made, the property is not excluded property by virtue of subsection (3) or (3A) above at any time in a tax year if the settlor was a formerly domiciled resident for that tax year.][7]

(4) Where securities issued by the Treasury subject to a condition of the kind mentioned in subsection (2) of section 6 above are comprised in a settlement, that subsection shall not apply to them; but the securities are excluded property if—

(*a*) a person [of a description specified in the condition in question][1] is entitled to a qualifying interest in possession in them, or

(*b*) no qualifying interest in possession subsists in them but it is shown that all known persons for whose benefit the settled property or income from it has been or might be applied, or who are or might become beneficially entitled to an interest in possession in it, are persons [of a description specified in the condition in question][1].

[This subsection is subject to Schedule A1.][6]

(5) Where—

(*a*) property ceased to be comprised in one settlement before 10th December 1981 and after 19th April 1978 and, by the same disposition, became comprised in another settlement, or

(*b*) property ceased to be comprised in one settlement after 9th December 1981 and became comprised in another without any person having in the meantime become beneficially entitled to the property (and not merely to an interest in possession in the property),

subsection (4)(b) above shall, in its application to the second settlement, be construed as requiring the matters there stated to be shown both in relation to the property comprised in that settlement and in relation to the property that was comprised in the first settlement.

(6) Subsection (5) above shall not apply where a reversionary interest in the property expectant on the termination of a qualifying interest in possession subsisting under the first settlement was settled on the trusts of the second settlement before 10th December 1981.

(7) In this section "qualifying interest in possession" has the same meaning as in Chapter III of this Part of this Act.

Commentary—*Simon's Taxes* **I5.702, I5.714, I3.452.**

HMRC Manuals—Inheritance Tax Manual IHTM16161–16163 (foreign property in a trust).

IHTM16232 (treatment of reversionary interests for IHT).

IHTM27220 (foreign settled property with non-UK domiciled settlor).

IHTM27247–27252 (specific British Government Securities: discretionary securities).

IHTM27262 (reversionary interest in exempt securities).

HMRC Interpretation RI 166—Where a settlor has added further assets to his settlement after it was made or two or more persons have contributed funds to a settlement, some of the settled property may be excluded property and some not and it is necessary to be able to attribute the settled property accordingly.

Statement of Practice E9—Excluded property.

Press releases etc—IR letter 4-2-76 (exclusion of certain reversionary interests not acquired for consideration and certain reversionary interests situated outside the UK).

IR letter 3-3-76 (reversionary interests purchased before 27-3-74: limitation of IHT charge to liability under estate duty rules).

Simon's Tax Cases—*Montagu Trust Co (Jersey) Ltd v IRC* [1989] STC 477*.

Definitions—"authorised unit trust", s 272; "qualifying interest in possession", s 59(1); "settlement", s 44.

Cross references—See IHTA 1984 s 82 (further conditions to be satisfied for sub-s 3(*a*) to apply when settlor or spouse has an initial interest in the property or in relation to property moving between settlements).

FA 2004 Sch 15 para 12 (property which is excluded property by virtue of sub-s (3)(*a*) of this section to be disregarded for the purposes of the charge to income tax under FA 2004 Sch 15.)

Amendments—[1] Words in sub-s (4)(*a*), (*b*) substituted by FA 1996 s 154(7), (9), Sch 28 para 8 for the purposes of income tax, from the year 1996–97, and for the purposes of corporation tax, for accounting periods ending after 31 March 1996.

[2] Sub-s (3A) inserted by FA 2003 s 186(1), (3) with effect for transfers of value or other events occurring after 15 October 2002: FA 2003 s 186(8).

[3] Words in sub-s (1)(*b*) inserted by Tax and Civil Partnership Regulations, SI 2005/3229, regs 3, 12, with effect from 5 December 2005 (reg 1(1)).

[4] Words in sub-ss (3), (3A) inserted, and sub-ss (3B), (3C) inserted, by FA 2006 s 157. These amendments are deemed to have come into force on 5 December 2005.

If, in consequence of these amendments, an amount of inheritance tax would (but for FA 2006 s 157(5)) fall due before the day on which FA 2006 is passed, that amount is to be treated instead as falling due at the end of the period of 14 days beginning with that day.

[5] Sub-s (1)(*d*) and preceding word inserted, in sub-s (3), words substituted for words "subsection (3B)", and sub-s (3D) inserted, by FA 2012 s 210(1), (2). These amendments are treated as having come into force on 20 June 2012 and have effect in relation to arrangements entered into on or after that day.

[6] In sub-ss (3), (3A), (4), words inserted by F(No 2)A 2017 s 33, Sch 10 paras 2, 4 with effect in relation to times on or after 6 April 2017, subject to transitional provisions in Sch 10 paras 10, 11.

[7] In sub-s (3)(*b*), words substituted for words "and (3D)", in sub-s (3A)(*b*), words substituted for words "sub-s (3B)", and sub-s (3E) inserted, by F(No 2)A 2017 s 30(4), with effect in relation to times after 5 April 2017, subject to transitional provisions in F(No 2)A 2017 s 30(10)–(12).

CHAPTER II

[INTERESTS IN POSSESSION, REVERSIONARY INTERESTS AND SETTLEMENT POWERS][1] 1

Amendments—[1] Title heading substituted by FA 2002 s 119(1), (5), (6) with effect for transfers of value after 16 April 2002. Previously the title head read "interests in possession and reversionary interests".

49 Treatment of interests in possession

(1) A person beneficially entitled to an interest in possession in settled property shall be treated for the purposes of this Act as beneficially entitled to the property in which the interest subsists.

[(1A) Where the interest in possession mentioned in subsection (1) above is one to which the person becomes beneficially entitled on or after 22nd March 2006, subsection (1) above applies in relation to that interest only if, and for so long as, it is—

(*a*) an immediate post-death interest,

(*b*) a disabled person's interest, or

(*c*) a transitional serial interest][2]

[or falls within section 5(1B) above][3].

[(1B) Where the interest in possession mentioned in subsection (1) above is one to which the person became beneficially entitled before 22nd March, subsection (1) above does not apply in relation to that interest at any time when section 71A below applies to the property in which the interest subsists.][2]

(2) Where a person becomes entitled to an interest in possession in settled property as a result of a disposition for a consideration in money or money's worth, any question whether and to what extent the giving of the consideration is a transfer of value or chargeable transfer shall be determined without regard to subsection (1) above.

[(3) . . .][1]

Commentary—*Simon's Taxes* **I5.149, I5.203, I5.141**.

HMRC Manuals—Inheritance Tax Manual IHTM16061 (introduction to interest in possession: finance act 2006 and the new trust regime).

IHTM16063–16064 (the effects of this section).

Concessions—F13: Estates of common seamen, marines or soldiers who died before 12 March 1952 which were exempt from estate duty (under FA 1894 s 8(1))—subsequent devolutions of property under wills.

Statement of Practice E6—Power to augment income.

Press releases etc—IR 12-2-76 (meaning of "interest in possession").

Definitions—"Disposition", s 272; "settled property", s 43.

Cross references—See FA 1986 Sch 19 para 40 (where a death or other event occurs on or after 18 March 1986, sub-s (3) above not to affect the tax chargeable on a transfer of value occurring before 18 March 1986).

Amendments—[1] Sub-s (3) (which was inserted by FA 1986 s 101(1), (3), Sch 19 Pt I para 14) repealed by F(No 2)A 1987 s 96(1), (4) and Sch 9 Pt III with respect to transfers of value made after 16 March 1987.

[2] Sub-ss (1A), (1B) inserted by FA 2006 s 156, Sch 20 para 4. This amendment is deemed to have come into force on 22 March 2006.

[3] In sub-s (1A) words at the end inserted by FA 2010 s 53(1), (4) with effect in relation to an interest in possession to which a person is beneficially entitled if the person becomes beneficially entitled to it on or after 9 December 2009.

[49A Immediate post-death interest

(1) Where a person ("L") is beneficially entitled to an interest in possession in settled property, for the purposes of this Chapter that interest is an "immediate post-death interest" only if the following conditions are satisfied.

(2) Condition 1 is that the settlement was effected by will or under the law relating to intestacy.

(3) Condition 2 is that L became beneficially entitled to the interest in possession on the death of the testator or intestate.

(4) Condition 3 is that—

(*a*) section 71A below does not apply to the property in which the interest subsists, and

(*b*) the interest is not a disabled person's interest.

(5) Condition 4 is that Condition 3 has been satisfied at all times since L became beneficially entitled to the interest in possession.][1]

Commentary—*Simon's Taxes* **I5.205**.

HMRC Manuals—Inheritance Tax Manual IHTM16061 (introduction to interest in possession: immediate post death interest).

Amendments—[1] Sections 49A–49E inserted by FA 2006 s 156, Sch 20 para 5. This amendment is deemed to have come into force on 22 March 2006.

[49B Transitional serial interests

Where a person is beneficially entitled to an interest in possession in settled property, for the purposes of this Chapter that interest is a "transitional serial interest" only—

(*a*) if section 49C or 49D below so provides, or

(*b*) if, and to the extent that, section 49E below so provides.][1]

Commentary—*Simon's Taxes* **I5.206**.

HMRC Manuals—Inheritance Tax Manual IHTM16061 (introduction to interest in possession: transitional serial interest).

Amendments—[1] Sections 49A–49E inserted by FA 2006 s 156, Sch 20 para 5. This amendment is deemed to have come into force on 22 March 2006.

[49C Transitional serial interest: interest to which person becomes entitled during period 22nd March 2006 to 5th [October][2] 2008

(1) Where a person ("B") is beneficially entitled to an interest in possession in settled property ("the current interest"), that interest is a transitional serial interest for the purposes of this Chapter if the following conditions are met.

(2) Condition 1 is that—

(*a*) the settlement commenced before 22nd March 2006, and

(*b*) immediately before 22nd March 2006, the property then comprised in the settlement was property in which B, or some other person, was beneficially entitled to an interest in possession ("the prior interest").

(3) Condition 2 is that the prior interest came to an end at a time on or after 22nd March 2006 but before 6th [October][2] 2008.

(4) Condition 3 is that B became beneficially entitled to the current interest at that time.

(5) Condition 4 is that—

(*a*) section 71A below does not apply to the property in which the interest subsists, and

(*b*) the interest is not a disabled person's interest.][1]

Commentary—*Simon's Taxes* **I5.206**.

HMRC Manuals—Inheritance Tax Manual IHTM16061 (introduction to interest in possession: the transitional period to 5th October 2008).

Capital Gains Manual CG36542 (IHT treatment qualifying interests in possession: transitional period to 6 April 2008).

Amendments—[1] Sections 49A–49E inserted by FA 2006 s 156, Sch 20 para 5. This amendment is deemed to have come into force on 22 March 2006.

[2] In section heading and sub-s (3), word substituted for word "April", by FA 2008 s 141(1). These amendments are treated as having come into force on 6 April 2008.

[49D Transitional serial interest: interest to which person becomes entitled on death of spouse or civil partner on or after 6th [October][2] 2008

(1) Where a person ("E") is beneficially entitled to an interest in possession in settled property ("the successor interest"), that interest is a transitional serial interest for the purposes of this Chapter if the following conditions are met.

(2) Condition 1 is that—

(*a*) the settlement commenced before 22nd March 2006, and

(*b*) immediately before 22nd March 2006, the property then comprised in the settlement was property in which a person other than E was beneficially entitled to an interest in possession ("the previous interest").

(3) Condition 2 is that the previous interest came to an end on or after 6th [October][2] 2008 on the death of that other person ("F").

(4) Condition 3 is that, immediately before F died, F was the spouse or civil partner of E.

(5) Condition 4 is that E became beneficially entitled to the successor interest on F's death.

(6) Condition 5 is that—

(*a*) section 71A below does not apply to the property in which the successor interest subsists, and

(*b*) the successor interest is not a disabled person's interest.][1]

Commentary—*Simon's Taxes* **I5.206**.

HMRC Manuals—Capital Gains Manual CG36542 (IHT treatment: qualifying interests in possession: surviving spouse or civil partner settlements).

Inheritance Tax Manual IHTM16061 (introduction to interest in possession: surviving spouse or civil partner settlements).

Amendments—[1] Sections 49A–49E inserted by FA 2006 s 156, Sch 20 para 5. This amendment is deemed to have come into force on 22 March 2006.

[2] In section heading and sub-s (3), word substituted for word "April", by FA 2008 s 141(1). These amendments are treated as having come into force on 6 April 2008.

[49E Transitional serial interest: contracts of life insurance

(1) Where—

(*a*) a person ("C") is beneficially entitled to an interest in possession in settled property ("the present interest"), and

(*b*) on C's becoming beneficially entitled to the present interest, the settled property consisted of, or included, rights under a contract of life insurance entered into before 22nd March 2006,

the present interest so far as subsisting in rights under the contract, or in property comprised in the settlement that directly or indirectly represents rights under the contract, is a "transitional serial interest" for the purposes of this Chapter if the following conditions are met.

(2) Condition 1 is that—

(*a*) the settlement commenced before 22nd March 2006, and

(*b*) immediately before 22nd March 2006—

(i) the property then comprised in the settlement consisted of, or included, rights under the contract, and

(ii) those rights were property in which C, or some other person, was beneficially entitled to an interest in possession ("the earlier interest").

(3) Condition 2 is that—

(*a*) the earlier interest came to an end at a time on or after 6th [October][2] 2008 ("the earlier-interest end-time") on the death of the person beneficially entitled to it and C became beneficially entitled to the present interest—

(i) at the earlier-interest end-time, or

(ii) on the coming to an end, on the death of the person beneficially entitled to it, of an interest in possession to which that person became beneficially entitled at the earlier-interest end-time, or

(iii) on the coming to an end of the second or last in an unbroken sequence of two or more consecutive interests in possession to the first of which a person became beneficially entitled at the earlier-interest end-time and each of which ended on the death of the person beneficially entitled to it, or

(*b*) C became beneficially entitled to the present interest—

(i) on the coming to an end, on the death of the person entitled to it, of an interest in possession that is a transitional serial interest under section 49C above, or

(ii) on the coming to an end of the second or last in an unbroken sequence of two or more consecutive interests in possession the first of which was a transitional serial interest under section 49C above and each of which ended on the death of the person beneficially entitled to it.

(4) Condition 3 is that rights under the contract were comprised in the settlement throughout the period beginning with 22nd March 2006 and ending with C's becoming beneficially entitled to the present interest.

(5) Condition 4 is that—

(*a*) section 71A below does not apply to the property in which the present interest subsists, and

(*b*) the present interest is not a disabled person's interest.][1]

Commentary—*Simon's Taxes* **I5.206**.

HMRC Manuals—Inheritance Tax Manual IHTM16061 (interest in possession: finance act 2006 and the new trust regime). Capital Gains Manual CG36542 (IHT treatment: qualifying interests in possession: life insurance trusts under IHTA/s49E).

Amendments—[1] Sections 49A–49E inserted by FA 2006 s 156, Sch 20 para 5. This amendment is deemed to have come into force on 22 March 2006.

[2] In sub-s (3), word substituted for word "April" by FA 2008 s 141(1). This amendment is treated as having come into force on 6 April 2008.

50 Interests in part, etc

(1) Where the person referred to in section 49(1) above is entitled to part only of the income (if any) of the property, the interest shall be taken to subsist in such part only of the property as bears to the whole the same proportion as the part of the income to which he is entitled bears to the whole of the income.

(2) Where the part of the income of any property to which a person is entitled is a specified amount (or the whole less a specified amount) in any period, his interest in the property shall be taken, subject to subsection (3) below, to subsist in such part (or in the whole less such part) of the property as produces that amount in that period.

(3) The Treasury may from time to time by order prescribe a higher and a lower rate for the purposes of this section; and where tax is chargeable in accordance with subsection (2) above by reference to the value of the part of a property which produces a specified amount or by reference to the value of

the remainder (but not where chargeable transfers are made simultaneously and tax is chargeable by reference to the value of that part as well as by reference to the value of the remainder) the value of the part producing that specified amount—

(*a*) shall, if tax is chargeable by reference to the value of that part, be taken to be not less than it would be if the property produced income at the higher rate so prescribed, and

(*b*) shall, if tax is chargeable by reference to the value of the remainder, be taken to be not more than it would be if the property produced income at the lower rate so prescribed;

but the value to be taken by virtue of paragraph (a) above as the value of part of a property shall not exceed the value of the whole of the property.

(4) The power to make orders under subsection (3) above shall be exercisable by statutory instrument, which shall be subject to annulment in pursuance of a resolution of the House of Commons.

(5) Where the person referred to in section 49(1) above is not entitled to any income of the property but is entitled, jointly or in common with one or more other persons, to the use and enjoyment of the property, his interest shall be taken to subsist in such part of the property as corresponds to the proportion which the annual value of his interest bears to the aggregate of the annual values of his interest and that or those of the other or others.

(6) Where, under section 43(3) above, a lease of property is to be treated as a settlement, the lessee's interest in the property shall be taken to subsist in the whole of the property less such part of it as corresponds to the proportion which the value of the lessor's interest (as determined under Part VI of this Act) bears to the value of the property.

Commentary—*Simon's Taxes* **I5.211–I5.213, I5.215.**

HMRC Manuals—Inheritance Tax Manual IHTM16101–16103 (interest in part of a fund). IHTM16211–16213 (annuities).

Statement of Practice SP 10/79—Power for trustees to allow a beneficiary to occupy dwelling-house.

Definitions—"Settlement", s 43.

Note—The CTT (Settled Property Income Yield) Order, SI 1975/610 prescribes from 8 May 1975 the 2½ per cent Consols yield and the gross dividend yield of the All-Share Index from the FT-Actuaries Share Indices (published daily in the *Financial Times*).

For the higher and lower rates of transfers of value after 15 August 1980 and before 18 February 2000, see the CTT (Settled Property Income Yield) Order, SI 1980/1000. For the higher and lower rates of transfers of value after 17 February 2000, see the Inheritance Tax (Settled Property Income Yield) Order, SI 2000/174.

51 Disposal of interest in possession

(1) Where a person beneficially entitled to an interest in possession in settled property disposes of his interest the disposal—

(*a*) is not a transfer of value, but

(*b*) shall be treated for the purposes of this Chapter as the coming to an end of his interest;

and tax shall be charged accordingly under section 52 below.

[(1A) Where the interest disposed of is one to which the person became beneficially entitled on or after 22nd March 2006, subsection (1) above applies in relation to the disposal only if the interest is—

(*a*) an immediate post-death interest,

(*b*) a disabled person's interest within section 89B(1)(*c*) or (*d*) below, or

(*c*) a transitional serial interest][1]

[or falls within section 5(1B) above][2].

(1B) Where the interest disposed of is one to which the person became beneficially entitled before 22nd March 2006, subsection (1) above does not apply in relation to the disposal if, immediately before the disposal, section 71A or 71D below applies to the property in which the interest subsists.][1]

(2) Where a disposition satisfying the conditions of section 11 above is a disposal of an interest in possession in settled property, the interest shall not by virtue of subsection (1) above be treated as coming to an end.

(3) References in this section to any property or to an interest in any property include references to part of any property or interest.

Commentary—*Simon's Taxes* **I5.225.**

HMRC Manuals—Inheritance Tax Manual IHTM04085 (settled property: the charge where an interest in possession is disposed of).

Simon's Tax Cases—s 51(1), *Powell-Cotton v IRC* [1992] STC 625*.

Definitions—"Disposition", s 272; "settled property", s 43.

Amendments—[1] Sub-ss (1A), (1B) inserted by FA 2006 s 156, Sch 20 paras 7, 12. This amendment is deemed to have come into force on 22 March 2006.

[2] In sub-s (1A) words at the end inserted by FA 2010 s 53(1), (4) with effect in relation to an interest in possession to which a person is beneficially entitled if the person becomes beneficially entitled to it on or after 9 December 2009.

52 Charge on termination of interest in possession

(1) Where at any time during the life of a person beneficially entitled to an interest in possession in settled property his interest comes to an end, tax shall be charged, subject to section 53 below, as if at that time he had made a transfer of value and the value transferred had been equal to the value of the property in which his interest subsisted.

(2) If the interest comes to an end by being disposed of by the person beneficially entitled to it and the disposal is for a consideration in money or money's worth, tax shall be chargeable under this section as if the value of the property in which the interest subsisted were reduced by the amount of the consideration; but in determining that amount the value of a reversionary interest in the property or of any interest in other property comprised in the same settlement shall be left out of account.

[(2A) Where the interest mentioned in subsection (1) or (2) above is one to which the person became beneficially entitled on or after 22nd March 2006, that subsection applies in relation to the coming to an end of the interest only if the interest is—

(*a*) an immediate post-death interest,

(*b*) a disabled person's interest, or

(*c*) a transitional serial interest][1]

[or falls within section 5(1B) above][2].

(3) Where a transaction is made between the trustees of the settlement and a person who is, or is connected with,—

(*a*) the person beneficially entitled to an interest in the property, or

(*b*) a person beneficially entitled to any other interest in that property or to any interest in any other property comprised in the settlement, or

(*c*) a person for whose benefit any of the settled property may be applied,

and, as a result of the transaction, the value of the first-mentioned property is less than it would be but for the transaction, a corresponding part of the interest shall be deemed for the purposes of this section to come to an end, unless the transaction is such that, were the trustees beneficially entitled to the settled property, it would not be a transfer of value.

[(3A) Where the interest mentioned in paragraph (*a*) of subsection (3) above is one to which the person mentioned in that paragraph became beneficially entitled on or after 22nd March 2006, that subsection applies in relation to the transaction only if the interest is—

(*a*) an immediate post-death interest,

(*b*) a disabled person's interest, or

(*c*) a transitional serial interest][1]

[or falls within section 5(1B) above][2].

(4) References in this section or section 53 below to any property or to an interest in any property include references to part of any property or interest; and—

(*a*) the tax chargeable under this section on the coming to an end of part of an interest shall be charged as if the value of the property (or part) in which the interest subsisted were a corresponding part of the whole; and

(*b*) if the value of the property (or part) to which or to an interest in which a person becomes entitled as mentioned in subsection (2) of section 53 below is less than the value on which tax would be chargeable apart from that subsection, tax shall be chargeable on a value equal to the difference.

Commentary—*Simon's Taxes* **I5.221, I5.223, I5.226, I5.227**.

HMRC Manuals—Inheritance Tax Manual IHTM14546 (settled property: when not to gross up).

IHTM16091–16093 (the effects of termination of an interest in possession).

IHTM16260 (interest for another person's life).

Statements of Practice E5—Close companies.

E6—Power to augment income.

Press releases etc—Law Society 9-5-90 (in sub-s (1) the value of the settled property is ascertained in isolation without regard to any similar property in the beneficiary's estate).

ICAEW TAX 20/92 14-12-92 (trustees' exercise of power to pay capital expenses out of income does not cause the trust to lose interest in possession status).

Simon's Tax Cases—s 52(1), *Hatton v IRC* [1992] STC 140*; *Powell-Cotton v IRC* [1992] STC 625*, *Countess Fitzwilliam v IRC* [1993] STC 502*.

Definitions—"Settlement", "settled property", s 43; "trustee", s 45.

Amendments—[1] Sub-ss (2A), (3A) inserted by FA 2006 s 156, Sch 20 paras 7, 13. These amendments are deemed to have come into force on 22 March 2006.

[2] In sub-ss (2A), (3A) words at the end inserted by FA 2010 s 53(1), (4) with effect in relation to an interest in possession to which a person is beneficially entitled if the person becomes beneficially entitled to it on or after 9 December 2009.

53 Exceptions from charge under section 52

(1) Tax shall not be chargeable under section 52 above if the settled property is excluded property.

[(1A) Tax shall not be chargeable under section 52 above if—

(*a*) the person whose interest comes to an end became beneficially entitled to the interest before 22nd March 2006,

(*b*) the interest comes to an end on or after that day, and (*c*) immediately before the interest comes to an end, section 71A or 71D below applies to the property in which the interest subsists.][2]

(2) Tax shall not be chargeable under section 52 above (except in the case mentioned in subsection (4)(*b*) of that section) if the person whose interest in the property comes to an end becomes on the same occasion beneficially entitled to the property or to another interest in possession in the property.

[(2A) Subsection (2) above applies by virtue of the person becoming beneficially entitled on or after 12 March 2008 to another interest in possession in the property only if that other interest is—

(*a*) a disabled person's interest, or

(*b*) a transitional serial interest;

and that is the case irrespective of whether the person's beneficial entitlement to the interest in possession in the property which comes to an end is one which began before, or on or after, 22 March 2006.][3]

(3) Tax shall not be chargeable under section 52 above if the interest comes to an end during the settlor's life and on the same occasion the property in which the interest subsisted reverts to the settlor.

(4) Tax shall not be chargeable under section 52 above if on the occasion when the interest comes to an end—

(*a*) the settlor's spouse [or civil partner][1], or

(*b*) where the settlor has died less than two years earlier, the settlor's widow or widower [or surviving civil partner][1],

becomes beneficially entitled to the settled property and is domiciled in the United Kingdom.

(5) Subsections (3) and (4) above shall not apply in any case where—

(*a*) the settlor or the spouse [or civil partner][1] (or in a case within subsection (4)(*b*), the widow or widower [or surviving civil partner][1]) of the settlor had acquired a reversionary interest in the property for a consideration in money or money's worth, or

(*b*) their application depends upon a reversionary interest having been transferred into a settlement on or after 10th March 1981.

(6) For the purposes of subsection (5) above a person shall be treated as acquiring an interest for a consideration in money or money's worth if he becomes entitled to it as a result of transactions which include a disposition for such consideration (whether to him or another) of that interest or of other property.

(7) Where the acquisition of the interest was before 12th April 1978, subsection (5)(*a*) above shall have effect, so far as it relates to subsection (3) above, with the omission of the reference to the spouse [or civil partner][1] of the settlor.

(8) Subsection (6) above shall not apply where the person concerned became entitled to the interest before 12th April 1978.

Commentary—*Simon's Taxes* **I5.251–I5.253A, I5.258, I5.734.**

HMRC Manuals—Inheritance Tax Manual IHTM04351–04360 (limitations and restrictions on reverter to settler provisions).
IHTM16092 (when the life tenant becomes entitled to the property on termination).
IHTM16122 (reverter to settler in lifetime).
IHTM27220 (foreign settled property with non-UK domiciled settlor).

Statements of Practice E5—Close companies.
E6—Power to augment income.

Simon's Tax Cases—s 53(3), *Hatton v IRC* [1992] STC 140*.
s 53(3), (5), *Countess Fitzwilliam v IRC* [1993] STC 502*.

Definitions—"Excluded property", s 272; "settled property", s 43; "settlor", s 44.

Amendments—[1] Words in sub-ss (4), (5), (7) inserted by Tax and Civil Partnership Regulations, SI 2005/3229, regs 3, 13, with effect from 5 December 2005 (reg 1(1)).

[2] Sub-s (1A) inserted by FA 2006 s 156, Sch 20 para 7. These amendments are deemed to have come into force on 22 March 2006.

[3] Sub-s (2A) substituted by FA 2008 s 140. This amendment is treated as having come into force on 22 March 2006 (so that FA 2006 Sch 20 para 14(3) is treated as never having had effect).

54 Exceptions from charge on death

(1) Where a person is entitled to an interest in possession in settled property which on his death, but during the settlor's life, reverts to the settlor, the value of the settled property shall be left out of account in determining for the purposes of this Act the value of the deceased's estate immediately before his death.

(2) Where on the death of a person entitled to an interest in possession in settled property—

(*a*) the settlor's spouse [or civil partner][1], or

(*b*) if the settlor has died less than two years earlier, the settlor's widow or widower [or surviving civil partner][1],

becomes beneficially entitled to the settled property and is domiciled in the United Kingdom, the value of the settled property shall be left out of account in determining for the purposes of this Act the value of the deceased's estate immediately before his death.

[(2A) Where a person becomes beneficially entitled on or after 22nd March 2006 to an interest in possession in settled property, subsections (1) and (2) above apply in relation to the interest only if it is—

(*a*) a disabled person's interest, or

(*b*) a transitional serial interest.][2]

[(2B) Where—

(*a*) a person ("B") becomes beneficially entitled on or after 22nd March 2006 to an interest in possession in settled property,

(*b*) B dies,

(*c*) the interest in possession, throughout the period beginning with when B becomes beneficially entitled to it and ending with B's death, is an immediate post-death interest,

(*d*) the settlor died before B's death but less than two years earlier, and

(*e*) on B's death, the settlor's widow or widower, or surviving civil partner, becomes beneficially entitled to the settled property and is domiciled in the United Kingdom,

the value of the settled property shall be left out of account in determining for the purposes of this Act the value of B's estate immediately before his death.][2]

(3) Subsections (5) and (6) of section 53 above shall apply in relation to subsections [(1), (2) and (2B)][2] above as they apply in relation to section 53(3) and (4)[, but as if the reference in section 53(5)(*a*) above to section 53(4)(*b*) above were to subsection (2)(*b*) or (2B) above][2].

(4) For the purposes of this section, where it cannot be known which of two or more persons who have died survived the other or others they shall be assumed to have died at the same instant.

Commentary—*Simon's Taxes* **I5.252, I5.734**.

HMRC Manuals—Inheritance Tax Manual IHTM04351–04353 (limitations and restrictions on reverter to settler provisions). IHTM04360 (settled property to settlor's spouse or civil partner).
IHTM16121 (reverter to settler on death of life tenant).

Definitions—"Settled property", s 43; "settlor", s 44.

Amendments—[1] Words in sub-s (2) inserted by Tax and Civil Partnership Regulations, SI 2005/3229, regs 3, 14, with effect from 5 December 2005 (reg 1(1)).

[2] Sub-ss (2A), (2B) inserted, and words in sub-s (3) substituted and inserted, by FA 2006 s 156, Sch 20 paras 7, 15. These amendments are deemed to have come into force on 22 March 2006.

[54A Special rate of charge where settled property affected by potentially exempt transfer

(1) If the circumstances fall within subsection (2) below, this section applies to any chargeable transfer made—

(*a*) under section 52 above, on the coming to an end of an interest in possession in settled property during the life of the person beneficially entitled to it, or

(*b*) on the death of a person beneficially entitled to an interest in possession in settled property;

and in the following provisions of this section the interest in possession mentioned in paragraph (a) or paragraph (b) above is referred to as "the relevant interest".

[(1A) Where a person becomes beneficially entitled on or after 22nd March 2006 to an interest in possession in settled property, subsection (1)(*b*) above applies in relation to the person's death only if the interest is—

(*a*) a disabled person's interest, or

(*b*) a transitional serial interest.][2]

(2) The circumstances referred to in subsection (1) above are—

(*a*) that the whole or part of the value transferred by the transfer is attributable to property in which the relevant interest subsisted and which became settled property in which there subsisted an interest in possession (whether the relevant interest or any previous interest) on the making by the settlor of a potentially exempt transfer at any time on or after 17th March 1987 and within the period of seven years ending with the date of the chargeable transfer; and

(*b*) that the settlor is alive at the time when the relevant interest comes to an end; and

(*c*) that, on the coming to an end of the relevant interest, any of the property in which that interest subsisted becomes settled property in which no qualifying interest in possession (as defined in section 59 below) subsists . . . [2]; and

(*d*) that, within six months of the coming to an end of the relevant interest, any of the property in which that interest subsisted has neither—

(i) become settled property in which a qualifying interest in possession subsists . . . [2], nor

(ii) become property to which an individual is beneficially entitled.

(3) In the following provisions of this section "the special rate property", in relation to a chargeable transfer to which this section applies, means the property in which the relevant interest subsisted or, in a case where—

(*a*) any part of that property does not fall within subsection (2)(*a*) above, or

(*b*) any part of that property does not become settled property of the kind mentioned in subsection (2)(*c*) above,

so much of that property as appears to the Board or, on appeal, to the [tribunal][3] to be just and reasonable.

(4) Where this section applies to a chargeable transfer (in this section referred to as "the relevant transfer"), the tax chargeable on the value transferred by the transfer shall be whichever is the greater of the tax that would have been chargeable apart from this section and the tax determined in accordance with subsection (5) below.

(5) The tax determined in accordance with this subsection is the aggregate of—

(*a*) the tax that would be chargeable on a chargeable transfer of the description specified in subsection (6) below, and

(*b*) so much (if any) of the tax that would, apart from this section, have been chargeable on the value transferred by the relevant transfer as is attributable to the value of property other than the special rate property.

(6) The chargeable transfer postulated in subsection (5)(*a*) above is one—

(*a*) the value transferred by which is equal to the value transferred by the relevant transfer or, where only part of that value is attributable to the special rate property, that part of that value;

(*b*) which is made at the time of the relevant transfer by a transferor who has in the preceding seven years made chargeable transfers having an aggregate value equal to the aggregate of the values transferred by any chargeable transfers made by the settlor in the period of seven years ending with the date of the potentially exempt transfer; and

(*c*) for which the applicable rate or rates are one-half of the rate or rates referred to in section 7(1) above.

(7) This section has effect subject to section 54B below.][1]

Commentary—*Simon's Taxes* **I3.526, I5.527.**

HMRC Manuals—Inheritance Tax Manual IHTM14519 (special rate for PETs where termination of interest in possession).

Definitions—"qualifying interest in possession", s 59(1); "Settled property", s 43; "settlor", s 44.

Cross references—See FA 2006 Sch 20 para 2(4) (where a chargeable transfer to which this section applies was made before 22 March 2006, this section has effect in relation to that transfer as if references in this section to IHTA 1984 s 71 were to IHTA 1984 s 71 without the amendments made by FA 2006 Sch 20 para 2(2), (3)).

FA 2006 Sch 20 para 16(4) (where a chargeable transfer to which this section applies was made before 22 March 2006, this section has effect in relation to that transfer without the amendments made by FA 2006 Sch 20 para16(3) (ie the repeal of words in sub-s (2)(*c*), (*d*)(i)).

FA 2006 Sch 20 para 20(4) (where a chargeable transfer to which this section applies was made before 22 March 2006, this section has effect in relation to that transfer as if in this section "qualifying interest in possession" has the meaning it would have apart from FA 2006 Sch 20 para 20(1)–(3)).

Amendments—[1] This section inserted by F(No 2)A 1987 s 96(1), (6) and Sch 7 para 1 with respect to transfers of value made and other events occurring after 16 March 1987.

[2] Sub-s (1A) inserted, and words in sub-s (2)(*c*), (*d*)(i) repealed, by FA 2006 ss 156, 178, Sch 20 paras 7, 16, Sch 26 Pt 6. These amendments are deemed to have come into force on 22 March 2006.

[3] In sub-s (3), word substituted for words "Special Commissioners" by the Transfer of Tribunal Functions and Revenue and Customs Appeals Order, SI 2009/56 art 3, Sch 1 paras 108, 110 with effect from 1 April 2009.

[54B Provisions supplementary to section 54A

(1) The death of the settlor, at any time after a chargeable transfer to which section 54A above applies, shall not increase the tax chargeable on the value transferred by the transfer unless, at the time of the transfer, the tax determined in accordance with subsection (5) of that section is greater than the tax that would be chargeable apart from that section.

(2) The death of the person who was beneficially entitled to the relevant interest, at any time after a chargeable transfer to which section 54A above applies, shall not increase the tax chargeable on the value transferred by the transfer unless, at the time of the transfer, the tax that would be chargeable apart from that section is greater than the tax determined in accordance with subsection (5) of that section.

(3) Where the tax chargeable on the value transferred by a chargeable transfer to which section 54A above applies falls to be determined in accordance with subsection (5) of that section, the amount referred to in paragraph (*a*) of that subsection shall be treated for the purposes of this Act as tax attributable to the value of the property in which the relevant interest subsisted.

(4) Subsection (5) below shall apply if—

(*a*) during the period of seven years preceding the date on which a chargeable transfer to which section 54A above applies ("the current transfer") is made, there has been another chargeable transfer to which that section applied, and

(*b*) the person who is for the purposes of the current transfer the settlor mentioned in subsection (2)(*a*) of that section is the settlor for the purposes of the other transfer (whether or not the settlements are the same);

and in subsections (5) and (6) below the other transfer is referred to as the "previous transfer".

(5) Where this subsection applies, the appropriate amount in relation to the previous transfer (or, if there has been more than one previous transfer, the aggregate of the appropriate amounts in relation to each) shall, for the purposes of calculating the tax chargeable on the current transfer, be taken to be the value transferred by a chargeable transfer made by the settlor immediately before the potentially exempt transfer was made.

(6) In subsection (5) above "the appropriate amount", in relation to a previous transfer, means so much of the value transferred by the previous transfer as was attributable to the value of property which was the special rate property in relation to that transfer.

(7) In this section—

"the relevant interest" has the meaning given by subsection (1) of section 54A above; and "the special rate property" has the meaning given by subsection (3) of that section.][1]

Commentary—*Simon's Taxes* **I3.527**.

HMRC Manuals—Inheritance Tax Manual IHTM14519 (special rate for PETs where termination of interest in possession).

Definitions—"Settlor", s 44.

Amendments—[1] This section inserted by F(No 2)A 1987 s 96(1), (6) and Sch 7 para 1 with respect to transfers of value made and other events occurring after 16 March 1987.

55 Reversionary interest acquired by beneficiary

(1) Notwithstanding section 5(1) above, where a person entitled to an interest (whether in possession or not) in any settled property acquires a reversionary interest expectant (whether immediately or not) on that interest, the reversionary interest is not part of his estate for the purposes of this Act.

(2) Section 10(1) above shall not apply to a disposition by which a reversionary interest is acquired in the circumstances mentioned in subsection (1) above [. . .][1].

Commentary—*Simon's Taxes* **I5.713**.

HMRC Manuals—Inheritance Tax Manual IHTM11095 (acquisition of a reversion).

IHTM16084 (restrictions when a reversionary interest is acquired).

Definitions—"Estate", s 272.

Cross references—See FA 1986 Sch 19 para 40 (where a disposition occurs after 17 March 1986, sub-s (2) above as amended by FA 1986 Sch 19 para 15 not to affect the tax chargeable on a transfer of value occurring before 18 March 1986).

Amendments—[1] Words in sub-s (2) (being words added by FA 1986 s 101(1), (3), Sch 19 para 15) repealed by F(No 2)A 1987 s 96(1), (5) and Sch 9 Pt III with respect to dispositions occurring after 16 March 1987.

[55A Purchased settlement powers

(1) Where a person makes a disposition by which he acquires a settlement power for consideration in money or money's worth—

(*a*) section 10(1) above shall not apply to the disposition;

(*b*) the person shall be taken for the purposes of this Act to make a transfer of value;

(*c*) the value transferred shall be determined without bringing into account the value of anything which the person acquires by the disposition; and

(*d*) sections 18 and 23 to 27 above shall not apply in relation to that transfer of value.

(2) For the purposes of this section, a person acquires a settlement power if he becomes entitled—

(*a*) to a settlement power;

(*b*) to exercise, or to secure or prevent the exercise of, a settlement power (whether directly or indirectly); or

(*c*) to restrict, or secure a restriction on, the exercise of a settlement power (whether directly or indirectly),

as a result of transactions which include a disposition (whether to him or another) of a settlement power or of any power of a kind described in paragraph (b) or (c) above which is exercisable in relation to a settlement power.][1]

Commentary—*Simon's Taxes* **I5.743**.

Amendments—[1] This section inserted by FA 2002 s 119(1), (3), (6) with effect for transfers of value after 16 April 2002.

56 Exclusion of certain exemptions

(1) Sections 18 and 23 to 27 above shall not apply in relation to property which is given in consideration of the transfer of a reversionary interest if, by virtue of section 55(1) above, that interest does not form part of the estate of the person acquiring it.

(2) Where a person acquires a reversionary interest in any settled property for a consideration in money or money's worth, section 18 above shall not apply in relation to the property when it becomes the property of that person on the termination of the interest on which the reversionary interest is expectant.

(3) Sections 23 to 27 above shall not apply in relation to any property if—

(*a*) the property is an interest in possession in settled property and the settlement does not come to an end in relation to that settled property on the making of the transfer of value, or

(*b*) immediately before the time when it becomes the property of the exempt body it is comprised in a settlement and, at or before that time, an interest under the settlement is or has been acquired for a consideration in money or money's worth by that or another exempt body.

(4) In subsection (3)(*b*) above "exempt body" means a charity, political party or other body within sections 23 [to 25][2] above or the trustees of a settlement in relation to which a direction under paragraph 1 of Schedule 4 to this Act has effect; and for the purposes of subsection (3)(*b*) there shall be disregarded any acquisition from a charity, political party or body within sections 23 to 25.

(5) For the purposes of subsections (2) and (3) above, a person shall be treated as acquiring an interest for a consideration in money or money's worth if he becomes entitled to it as a result of transactions which include a disposition [for such consideration][1] (whether to him or another) of that interest or of other property.
(6) Nothing in this section shall apply to a transfer of value if or to the extent that it is a disposition whereby the use of money or other property is allowed by one person to another.
(7) Subsection (2) above shall not apply where the acquisition of the reversionary interest was before 16th April 1976; and where the acquisition was on or after that date but before 12th April 1978 that subsection shall have effect—

(*a*) with the substitution for the words "section 18 above" of the words "sections 18 and 23 [to 25][2] above", and

(*b*) with the insertion after the word "person" in both places where it occurs of the words "or body".

(8) Subsection (3)(*b*) above shall not apply where the acquisition of the interest was before 12th April 1978; and subsection (5) above shall not apply where the person concerned became entitled to the interest before that date.

Commentary—*Simon's Taxes* **I5.266, I5.731–I5.733**.
HMRC Manuals—Inheritance Tax Manual IHTM11063 (settled property: exclusion from exemption in connection with a reversionary interest).
IHTM11162 (acquisition of a reversionary interest from a charity).
IHTM11164 (purchase of a reversionary interest by a charity after 12 April 1978).
IHTM16084 (restrictions when a reversionary interest is acquired).
Simon's Tax Cases—s 56(3), *Powell-Cotton v IRC* [1992] STC 625*.
Definitions—"Charity", "disposition" s 272; "settlement", "settled property", s 43; "trustees", s 272.
Amendments—[1] Words in sub-s (5) inserted by F(No 2)A 1987 Sch 7 para 2.
[2] Amended by FA 1998 s 143 in relation to any property becoming the property of any person on or after 17 March 1998.

57 Application of certain exemptions

(1) Subject to subsection (3) below, references to transfers of value in sections 19 and 22 above shall be construed as including references to events on the happening of which tax is chargeable under section 52 above, and references to the transferor and (in section 22(3) and (4)) to a disposition shall be construed accordingly.
(2) For the purposes of its application, by virtue of subsection (1) above, to the termination of interests in possession in settled property, section 22 above shall have effect as if—

(*a*) references to transfers of value made by gifts in consideration of marriage [or civil partnership][1] were references to the termination of such interests in consideration of marriage [or civil partnership][1];

(*b*) references to outright gifts were references to cases where the property ceases on the termination to be settled property; and

(*c*) references to cases where the property is settled by the gift were references to cases where it remains settled property after the termination.

(3) Subsection (1) above shall not apply to a transfer of value—

(*a*) unless the transferor has in accordance with subsection (4) below given to the trustees of the settlement a notice informing them of the availability of an exemption, and

(*b*) except to the extent specified in that notice.

(4) A notice under subsection (3) above shall be in such form as may be prescribed by the Board and shall be given before the end of the period of six months beginning with the date of the transfer of value.
(5) Section 27 above shall apply where the value transferred by a transfer of value is attributable to property which immediately after the transfer remains comprised in a settlement as it applies where property becomes comprised in a settlement by virtue of the transfer.

Commentary—*Simon's Taxes* **I3.323, I3.327, I5.266**.
HMRC Manuals—Inheritance Tax Manual IHTM10834 (settled property: excepted terminations).
IHTM16083 (settled property exemptions: annual exemptions).
Definitions—"the Board", "disposition", s 272; "settlement", "settled property", s 43.
Amendments—[1] Words in sub-s (2)(*a*) inserted by Tax and Civil Partnership Regulations, SI 2005/3229, regs 3, 15, with effect from 5 December 2005 (reg 1(1)).

[57A Relief where property enters maintenance fund

(1) Subject to the following provisions, subsection (2) below applies where—

(*a*) a person dies who immediately before his death was beneficially entitled to an interest in possession in property comprised in a settlement, and

(*b*) within two years after his death the property becomes held on trusts (whether of that or another settlement) by virtue of which a direction under paragraph 1 of Schedule 4 to this Act is given in respect of the property.

[(1A) Where the interest mentioned in subsection (1)(*a*) above is one to which the person became beneficially entitled on or after 22nd March 2006, subsection (2) below does not apply unless, immediately before the person's death, the interest was—

(*a*) an immediate post-death interest,
(*b*) a disabled person's interest, or
(*c*) a transitional serial interest][2]
[or fell within section 5(1B) above.][3]

(2) Where this subsection applies, this Act shall have effect as if the property had on the death of the deceased become subject to the trusts referred to in subsection (1)(*b*) above; and accordingly no disposition or other event occurring between the date of the death and the date on which the property becomes subject to those trusts shall, so far as it relates to the property, be a transfer of value or otherwise constitute an occasion for a charge to tax.

(3) Where property becomes held on trusts of the kind specified in paragraph (*b*) of subsection (1) above as the result of proceedings before a court and could not have become so held without such proceedings, that paragraph shall have effect as if it referred to three years instead of two.

(4) Subsection (2) above shall not apply if—
(*a*) the disposition by which the property becomes held on the trusts referred to in subsection (1)(*b*) above depends on a condition or is defeasible; or
(*b*) the property which becomes held on those trusts is itself an interest in settled property; or
(*c*) the trustees who hold the property on those trusts have, for a consideration in money or money's worth, acquired an interest under a settlement in which the property was comprised immediately before the death of the person referred to in subsection (1)(*a*) above or at any time thereafter; or
(*d*) the property which becomes held on those trusts does so for a consideration in money or money's worth, or is acquired by the trustees for such a consideration, or has at any time since the death of the person referred to in subsection (1)(*a*) above been acquired by any other person for such a consideration.

(5) If the value of the property when it becomes held on the trusts referred to in subsection (1)(*b*) above is lower than so much of the value transferred on the death of the person referred to in subsection (1)(*a*) as is attributable to the property, subsection (2) above shall apply to the property only to the extent of the lower value.

(6) For the purposes of this section, a person shall be treated as acquiring property for a consideration in money or money's worth if he becomes entitled to it as a result of transactions which include a disposition for such consideration (whether to him or another) of that or other property.][1]

Commentary—*Simon's Taxes* **I7.544**.
Definitions—"Disposition", s 272; "settled property", s 43; "trustee", s 272.
Amendments—[1] This section inserted by FA 1987 Sch 9 paras 1, 4 in relation to deaths after 16 March 1987.
[2] Sub-s (1A) inserted by FA 2006 s 156, Sch 20 paras 7, 17. This amendment is deemed to have come into force on 22 March 2006.
[3] In sub-s (1A) words at the end inserted by FA 2010 s 53(1), (5) with effect in relation to an interest in possession to which a person is beneficially entitled if the person becomes beneficially entitled to it on or after 9 December 2009.

CHAPTER III

SETTLEMENTS WITHOUT INTERESTS IN POSSESSION[, AND CERTAIN SETTLEMENTS IN WHICH INTERESTS IN POSSESSION SUBSIST][1]1

Cross references—See FA 1990 s 126(5) (certain payments and assets made or given to trustees in respect of improving safety and comfort at football grounds are not relevant property for the purposes of this Chapter).
FA 1994 s 248 (corporate Lloyd's underwriters: a corporate member's property forming part of a premiums trust fund or ancillary trust fund is not relevant property for the purpose of this Chapter).
Amendments—[1] Words in Heading inserted by FA 2006 s 156, Sch 20 paras 7, 20(5). This amendment is deemed to have come into force on 22 March 2006.

Interpretation

58 Relevant property

(1) In this Chapter "relevant property" means settled property in which no qualifying interest in possession subsists, other than—
(*a*) property held for charitable purposes only, whether for a limited time or otherwise;
(*b*) property to which section 71, [71A, 71D,][3] 73, 74 or 86 below applies [(but see subsection (1A) below)][4];
(*c*) property held on trusts which comply with the requirements mentioned in paragraph 3(1) of Schedule 4 to this Act, and in respect of which a direction given under paragraph 1 of that Schedule has effect;
[(*d*) property which is held for the purposes of a registered pension scheme[, a qualifying non-UK pension scheme or a][6] section 615(3) scheme;][1]
(*e*) property comprised in a trade or professional compensation fund; [
(*ea*) property comprised in an asbestos compensation settlement, . . . [8]][7]
[(*eb*) property comprised in a decommissioning security settlement; and][8]
(*f*) excluded property.

[(1A) Settled property to which section 86 below applies is "relevant property" for the purposes of this Chapter if—

(*a*) an interest in possession subsists in that property, and

(*b*) that interest falls within subsection (1B) or (1C) below.][4]

[(1B) An interest in possession falls within this subsection if—

(*a*) an individual is beneficially entitled to the interest in possession,

(*b*) the individual became beneficially entitled to the interest in possession on or after 22nd March 2006, and

(*c*) the interest in possession is—

(i) not an immediate post-death interest,

(ii) not a disabled person's interest, and

(iii) not a transitional serial interest.][4]

[(1C) An interest in possession falls within this subsection if—

(*a*) a company is beneficially entitled to the interest in possession,

(*b*) the business of the company consists wholly or mainly in the acquisition of interests in settled property,

(*c*) the company has acquired the interest in possession for full consideration in money or money's worth from an individual who was beneficially entitled to it,

(*d*) the individual became beneficially entitled to the interest in possession on or after 22nd March 2006, and

(*e*) immediately before the company acquired the interest in possession, the interest in possession was neither an immediate post-death interest nor a transitional serial interest.][4]

(2) The reference in subsection (1)(*d*) above to property which is . . . [2] held for the purposes of a . . . [2] scheme does not include a reference to a benefit which, having become payable under the . . . [2] scheme, becomes comprised in a settlement.

[(2A) For the purposes of subsection (1)(*d*) above—

(*a*) property applied to pay lump sum death benefits within section 168(1) of the Finance Act 2004 in respect of a member of a registered pension scheme is to be taken to be held for the purposes of the scheme from the time of the member's death until the payment is made, and

(*b*) property applied to pay lump sum death benefits in respect of a member of [a qualifying non-UK pension scheme or][6] a section 615(3) scheme is to be taken to be so held if the benefits are paid within the period of two years beginning with the earlier of the day on which the member's death was first known to the trustees or other persons having the control of the fund and the day on which they could first reasonably be expected to have known of it.][5]

(3) In subsection (1)(*e*) above "trade or professional compensation fund" means a fund which is maintained or administered by a representative association of persons carrying on a trade or profession and the only or main objects of which are compensation for or relief of losses or hardship that, through the default or alleged default of persons carrying on the trade or profession or of their agents or servants, are incurred or likely to be incurred by others.

[(4) In subsection (1)(*ea*) above "asbestos compensation settlement" means a settlement—

(*a*) the sole or main purpose of which is making compensation payments to or in respect of individuals who have, or had before their death, an asbestos-related condition, and

(*b*) which is made before 24 March 2010 in pursuance of an arrangement within subsection (5) below.

(5) An arrangement is within this subsection if it is—

(*a*) a voluntary arrangement that has taken effect under Part 1 of the Insolvency Act 1986 or Part 2 of the Insolvency (Northern Ireland) Order 1989,

(*b*) a compromise or arrangement that has taken effect under section 425 of the Companies Act 1985, Article 418 of the Companies (Northern Ireland) Order 1986 or Part 26 of the Companies Act 2006, or

(*c*) an arrangement or compromise of a kind corresponding to any of those mentioned in paragraph (*a*) or (*b*) above that has taken effect under, or as a result of, the law of a country or territory outside the United Kingdom.][7]

[(6) For the purposes of subsection (1)(eb) above a settlement is a "decommissioning security settlement" if the sole or main purpose of the settlement is to provide security for the performance of obligations under an abandonment programme.

(7) In subsection (6)—

"abandonment programme" means an abandonment programme approved under Part 4 of the Petroleum Act 1998 (including such a programme as revised);

"security" has the same meaning as in section 38A of that Act.][8]

Commentary—*Simon's Taxes* **I5.312**.

HMRC Manuals—Inheritance Tax Manual IHTM42161 (relevant property: introduction).

Statement of Practice SP 8/86—Treatment of income of discretionary trusts.

Definitions—"Charitable", "excluded property", s 272; "qualifying interest in possession", s 59(1); "settled property", "settlement", s 43.

Cross references—See FA 1994 s 248 (corporate Lloyd's underwriters: a corporate member's property forming part of a premiums trust fund or ancillary trust fund is not relevant property for the purposes of this Chapter).

Pension Protection Fund (Tax) Regulations, SI 2006/575 reg 33 (this section applies in relation to property which is held for the purposes of the Pension Protection Fund as it applies in relation to property which is held for the purposes of a registered pension scheme).

FA 2013 s 86(5) (for the purposes of this section, any reference in this section to Petroleum Act 1998 Part 4 has effect, in relation to any period before the coming into force of that Part, as a reference to Petroleum Act 1987 Part 1, and Petroleum Act 1998 s 38A is to be treated as having come into force on 20 March 1993).

Amendments—[1] Sub-s (1)(*d*) substituted by FA 2004 s 203(3) with effect from 6 April 2006. For transitional provisions and savings see FA 2004 Sch 36.

Sub-s (1)(*d*) previously read as follows—

"(*d*) property which is part of or held for the purposes of a fund or scheme to which section 151 below applies;".

[2] In sub-s (2), words "part of or" and "fund or" repealed by FA 2004 s 326, Sch 42 Pt 3 with effect from 6 April 2006. For transitional provisions and savings see FA 2004 Sch 36.

[3] References in sub-s (1)(*b*) inserted by FA 2006 s 156, Sch 20 paras 7, 18. This amendment is deemed to have come into force on 22 March 2006.

[4] Words in sub-s (1)(*b*) inserted, and sub-ss (1A)–(1C) inserted, by FA 2006 s 156, Sch 20 paras 7, 19. These amendments are deemed to have come into force on 22 March 2006.

[5] Sub-s (2A) inserted by FA 2007 s 70, Sch 20 paras 20, 24(9) with effect in relation to lump sum death benefits paid on or after 6 April 2006.

[6] Words in sub-ss (1)(*d*), (2A)(*b*) substituted by FA 2008 s 92. Sch 29 para 18(1), (3). This amendment is treated as having come into force on 6 April 2006.

[7] Sub-s (1)(*ea*) substituted for word "and" at the end of sub-s (1)(*e*), and sub-ss (4), (5) inserted, by F(No 3)A 2010 s 31, Sch 14 para 1. These amendments are treated as having come into force on 6 April 2006.

[8] In sub-s (1), word "and" at end of para (*ea*) repealed, and para (*eb*) inserted, and sub-ss (6), (7) inserted, by FA 2013 s 86(1)–(3). These amendments are treated as having come into force on 20 March 1993.

59 Qualifying interest in possession

[(1) In this Chapter "qualifying interest in possession" means—

(*a*) an interest in possession—

(i) to which an individual is beneficially entitled, and

(ii) which, if the individual became beneficially entitled to the interest in possession on or after 22nd March 2006, is an immediate post-death interest, a disabled person's interest or a transitional serial interest, or

(*b*) an interest in possession to which, where subsection (2) below applies, a company is beneficially entitled.][3]

(2) This subsection applies where—

(*a*) the business of the company consists wholly or mainly in the acquisition of interests in settled property, and

(*b*) the company has acquired the interest for full consideration in money or money's worth from an individual who was beneficially entitled to it[, and

(*c*) if the individual became beneficially entitled to the interest in possession on or after 22nd March 2006, the interest is an immediate post-death interest, or a disabled person's interest within section 89B(1)(*c*) or (*d*) below or a transitional serial interest, immediately before the company acquires it.][3]

(3) Where the acquisition mentioned in paragraph (*b*) of subsection (2) above was before 14th March 1975—

(*a*) the condition set out in paragraph (*a*) of that subsection shall be treated as satisfied if the business of the company was at the time of the acquisition such as is described in that paragraph, and

(*b*) that condition need not be satisfied [if the company is an insurance company (within the meaning of [Part 2 of the Finance Act 2012][4]) and][1] [has permission—

(i) under [Part 4A][5] of the Financial Services and Markets Act 2000, or

(ii) under paragraph 15 of Schedule 3 to that Act (as a result of qualifying for authorisation under paragraph 12(1) of that Schedule),

to effect or carry out contracts of long-term insurance.][2]

[(4) In subsection (3)(b) above "contracts of long-term insurance" means contracts which fall within Part II of Schedule 1 to the Financial Services and Markets Act 2000 (Regulated Activities) Order 2001.]

Commentary—*Simon's Taxes* **I5.203**.

HMRC Manuals—Inheritance Tax Manual IHTM16062 (definition of an interest in possession).

Press releases etc—IR 12-2-76 (meaning of "interest in possession").

Definitions—"Settled property", s 43.

Amendments—[1] Words substituted by FA 1995 s 52(4), (5), in relation to the making, on an anniversary or other occasion after 30 June 1994, of any charge to tax under s 64 or 65 of this Act.

[2] Words in sub-s (3) substituted, and sub-s (4) added, by the Financial Services and Markets Act 2000 (Consequential Amendments) (Taxes) Order, SI 2001/3629 art 5 with effect from 1 December 2001, immediately after the coming into force

of the Financial Services and Markets Act 2000 ss 411, 432(1), Sch 20. The amendments have effect in relation to the making, on an anniversary or other occasion after 30 November 2001, of any charge to tax under IHTA 1984 s 64 or 65.

3 Sub-s (1) substituted, and sub-s (2)(*c*) inserted, by FA 2006 s 156, Sch 20 paras 7, 20(1)–(3). These amendments are deemed to have come into force on 22 March 2006.

4 In sub-s (3)(*b*), words substituted for words "Chapter I of Part XII of the Taxes Act 1988" by FA 2012 s 146, Sch 16 paras 68, 69 with effect in relation to accounting periods of companies beginning on or after 1 January 2013 (subject to transitional provisions in FA 2012 Sch 17). For accounting periods straddling 1 January 2013, see FA 2012 s 149.

5 In sub-s (3)(*b*)(i), words substituted by FSA 2012 s 114(1), Sch 18 Pt 2 para 44 with effect from 1 April 2013 (by virtue of SI 2012/423, art 3, Schedule).

60 Commencement of settlement

In this Chapter references to the commencement of a settlement are references to the time when property first becomes comprised in it.

Commentary—*Simon's Taxes* **I5.321, I5.422**.
HMRC Manuals—Inheritance Tax Manual IHTM42221 (the settlement: starting date).

61 Ten-year anniversary

(1) In this Chapter "ten-year anniversary" in relation to a settlement means the tenth anniversary of the date on which the settlement commenced and subsequent anniversaries at ten-yearly intervals, but subject to subsections (2) to (4) below.

(2) The ten-year anniversaries of a settlement treated as made under section 80 below shall be the dates that are (or would but for that section be) the ten-year anniversaries of the settlement first mentioned in that section.

(3) No date falling before 1st April 1983 shall be a ten-year anniversary.

(4) Where—

(*a*) the first ten-year anniversary of a settlement would apart from this subsection fall during the year ending with 31st March 1984, and

(*b*) during that year an event occurs in respect of the settlement which could not have occurred except as the result of some proceedings before a court, and

(*c*) the event is one on which tax was chargeable under Chapter II of Part IV of the Finance Act 1982 (or, apart from Part II of Schedule 15 to that Act, would have been so chargeable),

the first ten-year anniversary shall be taken to be 1st April 1984 (but without affecting the dates of later anniversaries).

Commentary—*Simon's Taxes* **I5.321**.
HMRC Manuals—Inheritance Tax Manual IHTM42091 (no date before April 1983 is a ten year anniversary).
IHTM42231 (the settlement: initial IIP of settlor or spouse).
Definitions—"Settlement", s 43.

62 Related settlements

(1) For the purposes of this Chapter two settlements are related if and only if—

(*a*) the settlor is the same in each case, and

(*b*) they commenced on the same day,

but subject to subsection (2) below.

(2) Two settlements are not related for the purposes of this Chapter if all the property comprised in one or both of them was immediately after the settlement commenced held for charitable purposes only without limit of time (defined by a date or otherwise).

Commentary—*Simon's Taxes* **I5.326**.
HMRC Manuals—Inheritance Tax Manual IHTM42230 (related trusts).
Definitions—"charitable", s 272; "settlement", s 43; "settlor", s 44.

[62A Same-day additions

(1) For the purposes of this Chapter, there is a "same-day addition", in relation to a settlement ("settlement A"), if—

(*a*) there is a transfer of value by a person as a result of which the value immediately afterwards of the property comprised in settlement A is greater than the value immediately before,

(*b*) as a result of the same transfer of value, or as a result of another transfer of value made by that person on the same day, the value immediately afterwards of the property comprised in another settlement ("settlement B") is greater than the value immediately before,

(*c*) that person is the settlor of settlement A and settlement B,

(*d*) at any point in the relevant period, all or any part of the property comprised in settlement A was relevant property, and

(*e*) at that point, or at any other point in the relevant period, all or any part of the property comprised in settlement B was relevant property.

For exceptions, see section 62B.

(2) Where there is a same-day addition, references in this Chapter to its value are to the difference between the two values mentioned in subsection (1)(*b*).

(3) "The relevant period" means—

(*a*) in the case of settlement A, the period beginning with the commencement of settlement A and ending immediately after the transfer of value mentioned in subsection (1)(*a*), and (*b*) in the case of settlement B, the period beginning with the commencement of settlement B and ending immediately after the transfer of value mentioned in subsection (1)(*b*)).

(4) The transfer or transfers of value mentioned in subsection (1) include a transfer or transfers of value as a result of which property first becomes comprised in settlement A or settlement B; but not if settlements A and B are related settlements.

(5) For the purposes of subsection (1) above, it is immaterial whether the amount of the property comprised in settlement A or settlement B (or neither) was increased as a result of the transfer or transfers of value mentioned in that subsection.][1]

Commentary—*Simon's Taxes* **I5.442.**

Amendments—[1] Sections 62A–62C inserted by F(No 2)A 2015 s 11, Sch 1 paras 1, 2 with effect in relation to occasions on which tax falls to be charged under IHTA 1984 Pt 3 Ch 3 on or after 18 November 2015.

[62B Same day additions: exceptions

(1) There is not a same-day addition for the purposes of this Chapter if any of the following conditions is met—

(*a*) immediately after the transfer of value mentioned in section 62A(1)(*a*) all the property comprised in settlement A was held for charitable purposes only without limit of time (defined by a date or otherwise),

(*b*) immediately after the transfer of value mentioned in section 62A(1)(*b*) all the property comprised in settlement B was so held,

(*c*) either or each of settlement A and settlement B is a protected settlement (see section 62C), and

(*d*) the transfer of value, or either or each of the transfers of value, mentioned in section 62A(1)(*a*) and (*b*)—

(i) results from the payment of a premium under a contract of life insurance the terms of which provide for premiums to be due at regular intervals of one year or less throughout the contract term, or

(ii) is made to fund such a payment.

(2) If the transfer of value, or each of the transfers of value, mentioned in section 62A(1) is not the transfer of value under section 4 on the settlor's death, there is a same-day addition for the purposes of this Chapter only if conditions A and B are met.

(3) Condition A is that—

(*a*) the difference between the two values mentioned in section 62A(1)(*a*) exceeds £5,000, or

(*b*) in a case where there has been more than one transfer of value within section 62A(1)(*a*) on the same day, the difference between—

(i) the value of the property comprised in settlement A immediately before the first of those transfers, and

(ii) the value of the property comprised in settlement A immediately after the last of those transfers,

exceeds £5,000.

(4) Condition B is that—

(*a*) the difference between the two values mentioned in section 62A(1)(*b*) exceeds £5,000, or

(*b*) in a case where there has been more than one transfer of value within section 62A(1)(*b*), the difference between—

(i) the value of the property comprised in settlement B immediately before the first of those transfers, and

(ii) the value of the property comprised in settlement B immediately after the last of those transfers,

exceeds £5,000.][1]

Commentary—*Simon's Taxes* **I5.442.**

Amendments—[1] Sections 62A–62C inserted by F(No 2)A 2015 s 11, Sch 1 paras 1, 2 with effect in relation to occasions on which tax falls to be charged under IHTA 1984 Pt 3 Ch 3 on or after 18 November 2015.

[62C Protected settlements

(1) For the purposes of this Chapter, a settlement is a "protected settlement" if it commenced before 10 December 2014 and either condition A or condition B is met.

(2) Condition A is met if there have been no transfers of value by the settlor on or after 10 December 2014 as a result of which the value of the property comprised in the settlement was increased.

(3) Condition B is met if—

(*a*) there has been a transfer of value by the settlor on or after 10 December 2014 as a result of which the value of the property comprised in the settlement was increased, and

(*b*) that transfer of value was the transfer of value under section 4 on the settlor's death before 6 April 2017 and it had the result mentioned by reason of a protected testamentary disposition.

(4) In subsection (3)(*b*) "protected testamentary disposition" means a disposition effected by provisions of the settlor's will that at the settlor's death are, in substance, the same as they were immediately before 10 December 2014.][1]

Commentary—*Simon's Taxes* **I5.442.**

Amendments—[1] Sections 62A–62C inserted by F(No 2)A 2015 s 11, Sch 1 paras 1, 2 with effect in relation to occasions on which tax falls to be charged under IHTA 1984 Pt 3 Ch 3 on or after 18 November 2015.

63 Minor interpretative provisions

In this Chapter, unless the context otherwise requires—

"payment" includes a transfer of assets other than money;

"quarter" means period of three months.

Commentary—*Simon's Taxes* **I5.331, I5.332, I5.554, I5.631.**

HMRC Manuals—Inheritance Tax Manual IHTM42982 (definition of payment).

Principal charge to tax

64 Charge at ten-year anniversary

[(1)] [1] Where immediately before a ten-year anniversary all or any part of the property comprised in a settlement is relevant property, tax shall be charged at the rate applicable under sections 66 and 67 below on the value of the property or part at that time.

[(1A) For the purposes of subsection (1) above, property held by the trustees of a settlement immediately before a ten-year anniversary is to be regarded as relevant property comprised in the settlement at that time if—

(*a*) it is income of the settlement,

(*b*) the income arose before the start of the five years ending immediately before the ten-year anniversary,

(*c*) the income arose (directly or indirectly) from property comprised in the settlement that, when the income arose, was relevant property, and

(*d*) when the income arose, no person was beneficially entitled to an interest in possession in the property from which the income arose.

(1B) Where the settlor of a settlement was not domiciled in the United Kingdom at the time the settlement was made [and is not a formerly domiciled resident for the tax year in which the ten-year anniversary falls][3], income of the settlement is not to be regarded as relevant property comprised in the settlement as a result of subsection (1A) above so far as the income—

(*a*) is situated outside the United Kingdom, or

(*b*) is represented by a holding in an authorised unit trust or a share in an open-ended investment company.

(1C) Income of the settlement is not to be regarded as relevant property comprised in the settlement as a result of subsection (1A) above so far as the income—

(*a*) is represented by securities issued by the Treasury subject to a condition of the kind mentioned in subsection (2) of section 6 above, and

(*b*) it is shown that all known persons for whose benefit the settled property or income from it has been or might be applied, or who are or might become beneficially entitled to an interest in possession in it, are persons of a description specified in the condition in question.][2]

[(2) For the purposes of subsection (1) above, a foreign-owned work of art which is situated in the United Kingdom for one or more of the purposes of public display, cleaning and restoration (and for no other purpose) is not to be regarded as relevant property.][1]

Commentary—*Simon's Taxes* **I5.321.**

HMRC Manuals—Inheritance Tax Manual IHTM42081 (introduction to ten year anniversary charge).

IHTM42166 (relevant property: treatment of income after 6 April 2014).

Concession F7—Foreign owned works of art.

Simon's Tax Cases—*Rysaffe Trustee Co (CI) Ltd v IRC* [2002] STC 872, [2003] STC 536; *Gilchrist (as trustee of the JP Gilchrist 1993 Settlement) v R&C Comrs* [2014] UKUT 169 (TCC), [2014] STC 1713.

Definitions—"Relevant property", s 58(1).

Cross references—See FA 1986 Sch 19 para 43 (recalculation of tax where an occasion under s 65 below falls after 17 March 1986 in relation to a settlement in respect of which tax was last charged under this section before 18 March 1986).

Amendments—[1] Sub-s (1) numbered as such, and sub-s (2) inserted, by the Enactment of Extra-Statutory Concessions Order, SI 2009/730 art 13(1), (3) with effect in relation to deaths and ten-year anniversaries occurring on or after 6 April 2009.

[2] Sub-ss (1A)–(1C) inserted by FA 2014 s 117, Sch 25 paras 1, 4(1) with effect in relation to occasions on which tax falls to be charged under this section on or after 6 April 2014.

[3] In sub-s (1B), words inserted by F(No 2)A 2017 s 30(5), with effect in relation to times after 5 April 2017, subject to transitional provisions in F(No 2)A 2017 s 30(10)–(12).

65 Charge at other times

(1) There shall be a charge to tax under this section—

(*a*) where the property comprised in a settlement or any part of that property ceases to be relevant property (whether because it ceases to be comprised in the settlement or otherwise); and

(*b*) in a case in which paragraph (*a*) above does not apply, where the trustees of the settlement make a disposition as a result of which the value of relevant property comprised in the settlement is less than it would be but for the disposition.

(2) The amount on which tax is charged under this section shall be—

(*a*) the amount by which the value of relevant property comprised in the settlement is less immediately after the event in question than it would be but for the event, or

(*b*) where the tax payable is paid out of relevant property comprised in the settlement immediately after the event, the amount which, after deducting the tax, is equal to the amount on which tax would be charged by virtue of paragraph (*a*) above.

(3) The rate at which tax is charged under this section shall be the rate applicable under section 68 or 69 below.

(4) Subsection (1) above does not apply if the event in question occurs in a quarter beginning with the day on which the settlement commenced or with a ten-year anniversary.

(5) Tax shall not be charged under this section in respect of—

(*a*) a payment of costs or expenses (so far as they are fairly attributable to relevant property), or

(*b*) a payment which is (or will be) income of any person for any of the purposes of income tax or would for any of those purposes be income of a person not resident in the United Kingdom if he were so resident,

or in respect of a liability to make such a payment.

(6) Tax shall not be charged under this section by virtue of subsection (1)(*b*) above if the disposition is such that, were the trustees beneficially entitled to the settled property, section 10 or section 16 above would prevent the disposition from being a transfer of value.

(7) Tax shall not be charged under this section by reason only that property comprised in a settlement ceases to be situated in the United Kingdom and thereby becomes excluded property by virtue of section 48(3)(*a*) above.

[(7A) Tax shall not be charged under this section by reason only that property comprised in a settlement becomes excluded property by virtue of section 48(3A)(*a*) (holding in an authorised unit trust or a share in an open-ended investment company is excluded property unless settlor domiciled in UK when settlement made).][1]

[(7B) Tax shall not be charged under this section by reason only that property comprised in a settlement becomes excluded property by virtue of section 48(3E) ceasing to apply in relation to it.][2]

[(7C) Tax shall not be charged under this section by reason only that property comprised in a settlement ceases to any extent to be property to which paragraph 2 or 3 of Schedule A1 applies and thereby becomes excluded property by virtue of section 48(3)(*a*) above.

(7D) Tax shall not be charged under this section where property comprised in a settlement or any part of that property—

(*a*) is, by virtue of paragraph 5(2)(*a*) of Schedule A1, not excluded property for the two year period referred to in that paragraph, but

(*b*) becomes excluded property at the end of that period.][3]

(8) If the settlor of a settlement was not domiciled in the United Kingdom when the settlement was made, tax shall not be charged under this section by reason only that property comprised in the settlement is invested in securities issued by the Treasury subject to a condition of the kind mentioned in section 6(2) above and thereby becomes excluded property by virtue of section 48(4)(*b*) above.

(9) For the purposes of this section trustees shall be treated as making a disposition if they omit to exercise a right (unless it is shown that the omission was not deliberate) and the disposition shall be treated as made at the time or latest time when they could have exercised the right.

Commentary—*Simon's Taxes* **I5.322, I5.324, I5.325, I5.333, I5.335**.

HMRC Manuals—Inheritance Tax Manual IHTM42110–42114 (calculation of tax and rates before first ten year anniversary, with example).

IHTM42117 (excluded periods).

IHTM42119 (loss to the settlement basis of valuation).

IHTM42226 (property ceasing to be relevant property on class of beneficiaries closing).

IHTM42602 (foreign excluded property).

Statements of Practice E6—Power to augment income.

SP 10/79—Power for trustees to allow a beneficiary to occupy dwelling-house.

Definitions—"Disposition", s 272; "excluded property", s 272; "payment", "quarter", s 63; "relevant property", s 58(1); "settlement", "settled property", s 43; "trustee", s 45.

Cross references—See FA 1986 Sch 19 para 43 (recalculation of tax where an occasion under this section falls after 17 March 1986 in relation to a settlement in respect of which tax was last charged under s 64 above before 18 March 1986).

FA 2013 s 86(6) (there is to be no charge to tax under this section, if the only reason for such a charge would be that property ceases to be relevant property by virtue of the coming into force of FA 2013 s 86 (removal of IHT charges in respect of decommissioning security settlements)).

Amendments—[1] Sub-s (7A) inserted by FA 2013 s 175. This amendment is treated as having come into force on 16 October 2002.

[2] Sub-s (7B) inserted by F(No 2)A 2017 s 30(6) with effect in relation to times after 5 April 2017, subject to transitional provisions in F(No 2)A 2017 s 30(10)–(12).

[3] Sub-ss (7C), (7D) inserted by F(No 2)A 2017 s 33, Sch 10 paras 2, 5 with effect in relation to times on or after 6 April 2017, subject to transitional provisions in Sch 10 paras 10, 11.

Rates of principal charge

66 Rate of ten-yearly charge

(1) Subject to subsection (2) below, the rate at which tax is charged under section 64 above at any time shall be three tenths of the effective rate (that is to say the rate found by expressing the tax chargeable as a percentage of the amount on which it is charged) at which tax would be charged on the value transferred by a chargeable transfer of the description specified in subsection (3) below.

(2) Where the whole or part of the value mentioned in section 64 above is attributable to property which was not relevant property, or was not comprised in the settlement, throughout the period of ten years ending immediately before the ten-year anniversary concerned, the rate at which tax is charged on that value or part shall be reduced by one-fortieth for each of the successive quarters in that period which expired before the property became, or last became, relevant property comprised in the settlement.

[(2A) Subsection (2) above does not apply to property which is regarded as relevant property as a result of section 64(1A) (and accordingly that property is charged to tax at the rate given by subsection (1) above).][2]

(3) The chargeable transfer postulated in subsection (1) above is one—

(*a*) the value transferred by which is equal to an amount determined in accordance with subsection (4) below;

(*b*) which is made immediately before the ten-year anniversary concerned by a transferor who has in the [preceding seven years][1] made chargeable transfers having an aggregate value determined in accordance with subsection (5) below; and

(*c*) [on which tax is charged in accordance with section 7(2) of this Act][1].

(4) The amount referred to in subsection (3)(*a*) above is equal to the aggregate of—

(*a*) the value on which tax is charged under section 64 above;

(*b*) *the value immediately after it became comprised in the settlement of any property which was not then relevant property and has not subsequently become relevant property while remaining comprised in the settlement; and*[3]

(*c*) the value, immediately after a related settlement commenced, of the [relevant][3] property then comprised in it;

[(*d*) the value of any same-day addition; and

(*e*) where—

(i) an increase in the value of the property comprised in another settlement is represented by the value of a same-day addition aggregated under paragraph (*d*) above, and

(ii) that other settlement is not a related settlement,

the value immediately after that other settlement commenced of the relevant property then comprised in that other settlement;][3]

but subject to subsection (6) below.

(5) The aggregate value referred to in subsection (3)(*b*) above is equal to the aggregate of—

(*a*) the values transferred by any chargeable transfers made by the settlor in the period of [seven][1] years ending with the day on which the settlement commenced, disregarding transfers made on that day or before 27th March 1974, and

(*b*) the amounts on which any charges to tax were imposed under section 65 above in respect of the settlement in the ten years before the anniversary concerned;

but subject to subsection (6) and section 67 below.

(6) In relation to a settlement which commenced before 27th March 1974—

(*a*) subsection (4) above shall have effect with the omission of [paragraphs (*c*) to (*e*)][3]; and

(*b*) subsection (5) above shall have effect with the omission of paragraph (*a*);

and where tax is chargeable under section 64 above by reference to the first ten-year anniversary of a settlement which commenced before 9th March 1982, the aggregate mentioned in subsection (5) above shall be increased by the amounts of any distribution payments (determined in accordance with the rules applicable under paragraph 11 of Schedule 5 to the Finance Act 1975) made out of the settled property before 9th March 1982 (or, where paragraph 6, 7 or 8 of Schedule 15 to the Finance Act 1982 applied, 1st April 1983, or, as the case may be, 1st April 1984) and within the period of ten years before the anniversary concerned.

Commentary—*Simon's Taxes* **I5.401, I5.432, I5.433, I5.435, I5.436.**

HMRC Manuals—Inheritance Tax Manual IHTM42084–42087 (calculating the rate of tax).

IHTM42088 (assets that have been relevant property for less than the full ten years).

IHTM42089 (relief for double charges).

IHTM42162 (capital and income).

IHTM42164 (inheritance tax deductions).

Definitions—"Quarter", s 63; "relevant property", s 58(1); "settlement", "settled property", s 43; "settlor", s 44.

Cross references—See FA 1986 Sch 19 para 40 (where a death or other event occurs on or after 18 March 1986, the amendments to this section by FA 1986 Sch 19 (see below) not to affect the tax chargeable on a transfer of value occurring before 18 March 1986),

Sch 19 para 43 (rate of charge under this section in the case of a settlement in respect of which an occasion under s 65 above falls after 17 March 1986 and the last charge under s 64 above fell before 18 March 1986).

Amendments—[1] Words in sub-ss (3)(*b*), (5)(*a*) and whole of sub-s (3)(*c*) substituted by FA 1986 s 101(3) and Sch 19 para 16 with respect to transfers of value made or events occurring after 17 March 1986.

[2] Sub-s (2A) inserted by FA 2014 s 117, Sch 25 paras 1, 4(2) with effect in relation to occasions on which tax falls to be charged under IHTA 1984 s 64 on or after 6 April 2014.

[3] The following amendments made by F(No 2)A 2015 s 11, Sch 1 paras 1, 3 with effect in relation to occasions on which tax falls to be charged under IHTA 1984 Pt 3 Ch 3 on or after 18 November 2015—

- sub-s (4)(*b*) repealed;
- in sub-s (4)(*c*), word inserted, and sub-s (4)(*d*), (*e*) inserted; and
- in sub-s (6)(*a*), words substituted for words "paragraphs (*b*) and (*c*)".

67 Added property, etc

(1) This subsection applies where, after the settlement commenced and after 8th March 1982, but before the anniversary concerned, the settlor made a chargeable transfer as a result of which the value of the property comprised in the settlement was increased.

(2) For the purposes of subsection (1) above, it is immaterial whether the amount of the property so comprised was increased as a result of the transfer, but a transfer as a result of which the value increased but the amount did not shall be disregarded if it is shown that the transfer—

(*a*) was not primarily intended to increase the value, and

(*b*) did not result in the value being greater immediately after the transfer by an amount exceeding five per cent of the value immediately before the transfer.

(3) Where subsection (1) above applies in relation to a settlement which commenced after 26th March 1974, section 66(5)(*a*) above shall have effect as if it referred to the greater of—

(*a*) the aggregate of the values there specified, and

(*b*) the aggregate of the values transferred by any chargeable transfers made by the settlor in the period of [seven] years ending with the day on which the chargeable transfer falling within subsection (1) above was made—

(i) disregarding transfers made on that day or before 27th March 1974, and

(ii) excluding the values mentioned in subsection (5) below;

and where the settlor made two or more chargeable transfers falling within subsection (1) above, paragraph (b) above shall be taken to refer to the transfer in relation to which the aggregate there mentioned is the greatest.

(4) Where subsection (1) above applies in relation to a settlement which commenced before 27th March 1974, the aggregate mentioned in section 66(5) above shall be increased (or further increased) by the aggregate of the values transferred by any chargeable transfers made by the settlor in the period of [seven] years ending with the day on which the chargeable transfer falling within subsection (1) above was made—

(*a*) disregarding transfers made on that day or before 27th March 1974, and

(*b*) excluding the values mentioned in subsection (5) below;

and where the settlor made two or more chargeable transfers falling within subsection (1) above, this subsection shall be taken to refer to the transfer in relation to which the aggregate to be added is the greatest.

(5) The values excluded by subsections (3)(*b*)(ii) and (4)(*b*) above are—

(*a*) any value attributable to property whose value is taken into account in determining the amount mentioned in section 66(4) above; and

(*b*) any value attributable to property in respect of which a charge to tax has been made under section 65 above and by reference to which an amount mentioned in section 66(5)(*b*) above is determined.

(6) Where the property comprised in a settlement immediately before the ten-year anniversary concerned, or any part of that property, had on any occasion within the preceding ten years ceased to be relevant property then, if on that occasion tax was charged in respect of the settlement under section 65 above, the aggregate mentioned in section 66(5) above shall be reduced by an amount equal to the lesser of—

(*a*) the amount on which tax was charged under section 65 (or so much of that amount as is attributable to the part in question), and

(*b*) the value on which tax is charged under section 64 above (or so much of that value as is attributable to the part in question);

and if there were two or more such occasions relating to the property or the same part of it, this subsection shall have effect in relation to each of them.

(7) References in subsection (6) above to the property comprised in a settlement immediately before an anniversary shall, if part only of the settled property was then relevant property, be construed as references to that part.

Commentary—*Simon's Taxes* **I5.401, I5.433.**

HMRC Manuals—Inheritance Tax Manual IHTM42089 (relief for double charges).

IHTM42090 (adjusting the calculation where there are additions before the ten year anniversary).

Definitions—"relevant property", s 58(1); "settled property", "settlement" s 43.

Cross references—See FA 1986 Sch 19 para 40 (where a death or other event occurs on or after 18 March 1986, the amendments to this section by FA 1986 Sch 19 (see below) not to affect the tax chargeable on a transfer of value occurring before 18 March 1986),

Sch 19 para 43 (recalculation of tax in the case of a settlement to which property is added after 17 March 1986 and in relation to which the last periodic charge arose before 18 March 1986).

Amendments—Words in sub-ss (3)(*b*), (4) substituted by FA 1986 s 101(3) and Sch 19 para 17 with respect to a settlement to which property is added after 17 March 1986.

68 Rate before first ten-year anniversary

(1) The rate at which tax is charged under section 65 above on an occasion preceding the first ten-year anniversary after the settlement's commencement shall be the appropriate fraction of the effective rate at which tax would be charged on the value transferred by a chargeable transfer of the description specified in subsection (4) below (but subject to subsection (6) below).

(2) For the purposes of this section the appropriate fraction is three tenths multiplied by so many fortieths as there are complete successive quarters in the period beginning with the day on which the settlement commenced and ending with the day before the occasion of the charge, but subject to subsection (3) below.

(3) Where the whole or part of the amount on which tax is charged is attributable to property which was not relevant property, or was not comprised in the settlement, throughout the period referred to in subsection (2) above, then in determining the appropriate fraction in relation to that amount or part—

(*a*) no quarter which expired before the day on which the property became, or last became, relevant property comprised in the settlement shall be counted, but

(*b*) if that day fell in the same quarter as that in which the period ends, that quarter shall be counted whether complete or not.

(4) The chargeable transfer postulated in subsection (1) above is one—

(*a*) the value transferred by which is equal to an amount determined in accordance with subsection (5) below;

(*b*) which is made at the time of the charge to tax under section 65 by a transferor who has in the period of [seven][1] years ending with the day of the occasion of the charge made chargeable transfers having an aggregate value equal to that of any chargeable transfers made by the settlor in the period of [seven][1] years ending with the day on which the settlement commenced, disregarding transfers made on that day or before 27th March 1974; and

[(*c*) on which tax is charged in accordance with section 7(2) of this Act.][1]

(5) The amount referred to in subsection (4)(*a*) above is equal to the aggregate of—

(*a*) the value, immediately after the settlement commenced, of the [relevant][2] property then comprised in it;

(*b*) the value, immediately after a related settlement commenced, of the [relevant][2] property then comprised in it; . . . [2]

[(*c*) the value, immediately after it became comprised in the settlement, of property which—

(i) became comprised in the settlement after the settlement commenced and before the occasion of the charge under section 65 above, and

(ii) was relevant property immediately after it became so comprised,

whether or not the property has remained relevant property comprised in the settlement;

(*d*) the value, at the time it became (or last became) relevant property, of property which—

(i) was comprised in the settlement immediately after the settlement commenced and was not then relevant property but became relevant property before the occasion of the charge under section 65 above, or

(ii) became comprised in the settlement after the settlement commenced and before the occasion of the charge under section 65 above, and was not relevant property immediately after it became comprised in the settlement, but became relevant property before the occasion of the charge under that section,

whether or not the property has remained relevant property comprised in the settlement;

(*e*) the value of any same-day addition; and

(*f*) where—

(i) an increase in the value of the property comprised in another settlement is represented by the value of a same-day addition aggregated under paragraph (*e*) above, and

(ii) that other settlement is not a related settlement,

the value immediately after that other settlement commenced of the relevant property then comprised in that other settlement.][2]

(6) Where the settlement commenced before 27th March 1974, subsection (1) above shall have effect with the substitution of a reference to three tenths for the reference to the appropriate fraction; and in relation to such a settlement the chargeable transfer postulated in that subsection is one—

(*a*) the value transferred by which is equal to the amount on which tax is charged under section 65 above;

(*b*) which is made at the time of that charge to tax by a transferor who has in the period of [seven][1] years ending with the day of the occasion of the charge made chargeable transfers having an aggregate value equal to the aggregate of—

(i) any amounts on which any charges to tax have been imposed under section 65 above in respect of the settlement in [the period of ten years ending with that day][1]; and

(ii) the amounts of any distribution payments (determined in accordance with the rules applicable under paragraph 11 of Schedule 5 to the Finance Act 1975) made out of the settled property before 9th March 1982 (or, where paragraph 6, 7 or 8 of Schedule 15 to the Finance Act 1982 applied, 1st April 1983, or, as the case may be, 1st April 1984) and within the said period of ten years; and

[(*c*) on which tax is charged in accordance with section 7(2) of this Act.][1]

Commentary—*Simon's Taxes* **I5.421-I5.423, I5.554**.

HMRC Manuals—Inheritance Tax Manual IHTM43065 (other issues: the rate of tax on exit charges from relevant property trusts which include TNRB before the first ten year anniversary).

Simon's Tax Cases—*Russell v IRC* [1988] STC 195*.

Definitions—"Quarter", s 63; "relevant property", s 58(1).

Cross references—See FA 1986 Sch 19 para 40 (where a death or other event occurs on or after 18 March 1986, the amendments to this section by FA 1986 Sch 19 (see below) not to affect the tax chargeable on a transfer of value occurring before 18 March 1986).

Amendments—[1] Words in sub-ss (4)(*b*), (6)(*b*), and whole of sub-ss (4)(*c*), (6)(*c*) substituted by FA 1986 s 101(3) and Sch 19 para 18 with respect to transfer of value made after 17 March 1986.

[2] In sub-s 5 (*a*), (*b*), word inserted, in sub-s (5)(*b*), word "and" repealed, and sub-s (5)(*c*)–(*f*) substituted for previous sub-s (5)(*c*) by F(No 2)A 2015 s 11, Sch 1 paras 1, 4 with effect in relation to occasions on which tax falls to be charged under IHTA 1984 Pt 3 Ch 3 on or after 18 November 2015.

69 Rate between ten-year anniversaries

(1) Subject to [subsection (2A)][1] below, the rate at which tax is charged under section 65 above on an occasion following one or more ten-year anniversaries after the settlement's commencement shall be the appropriate fraction of the rate at which it was last charged under section 64 (or would have been charged apart from section 66(2)).

[(2) Subsection (2A) below applies—

(*a*) if, at any time in the period beginning with the most recent ten-year anniversary and ending immediately before the occasion of the charge under section 65 above (the "relevant period"), property has become comprised in the settlement which was relevant property immediately after it became so comprised, or

(*b*) if—

(i) at any time in the relevant period, property has become comprised in the settlement which was not relevant property immediately after it became so comprised, and

(ii) at a later time in the relevant period, that property has become relevant property, or

(*c*) if property which was comprised in the settlement immediately before the relevant period, but was not then relevant property, has at any time during the relevant period become relevant property.

(2A) Whether or not all of the property within any of paragraphs (*a*) to (*c*) of subsection (2) above has remained relevant property comprised in the settlement, the rate at which tax is charged under section 65 is to be the appropriate fraction of the rate at which it would last have been charged under section 64 above (apart from section 66(2) above) if—

(*a*) immediately before the most recent ten-year anniversary, all of that property had been relevant property comprised in the settlement with a value determined in accordance with subsection (3) below, and

(*b*) any same-day addition made on or after the most recent ten-year anniversary had been made immediately before that anniversary.][1]

(3) In the case of property within subsection (2)(*a*) above . . . [1] the value to be attributed to it for the [purposes of subsection (2A)][1] above is its value immediately after it became comprised in the settlement; and in any other case the value to be so attributed is the value of the property when it became (or last became) relevant property.

(4) For the purposes of this section the appropriate fraction is so many fortieths as there are complete successive quarters in the period beginning with the most recent ten-year anniversary and ending with the day before the occasion of the charge; but subsection (3) of section 68 above shall have effect for the purposes of this subsection as it has effect for the purposes of subsection (2) of that section.

Commentary—*Simon's Taxes* **I5.441**.

HMRC Manuals—Inheritance Tax Manual IHTM42115 (rate between ten year anniversary, with example).

Definitions—"Quarter", s 63; "relevant property", s 58(1); "settlement", s 43.

Cross references—See FA 1986 Sch 19 para 43 (rate of tax for the purposes of this section where an occasion under s 65 above falls after 17 March 1986 in the case of a settlement in respect of which the most recent ten-year anniversary fell before 18 March 1986).

Amendments—[1] In sub-s (1), words substituted for words "subsection (2); sub-ss (2), (2A) substituted for previous sub-s (2); and in sub-s (3) words repealed, and words substituted for words "purposes of subsection (2)"; by F(No 2)A 2015 s 11, Sch 1 paras 1, 5 with effect in relation to occasions on which tax falls to be charged under IHTA 1984 Pt 3 Ch 3 on or after 18 November 2015.

Special cases—charges to tax

70 Property leaving temporary charitable trusts

(1) This section applies to settled property held for charitable purposes only until the end of a period (whether defined by date or in some other way).

(2) Subject to subsections (3) and (4) below, there shall be a charge to tax under this section—

(*a*) where settled property ceases to be property to which this section applies, otherwise than by virtue of an application for charitable purposes, and

(*b*) in a case in which paragraph (*a*) above does not apply, where the trustees make a disposition (otherwise than by an application of property for charitable purposes) as a result of which the value of settled property to which this section applies is less than it would be but for the disposition.

(3) Tax shall not be charged under this section in respect of—

(*a*) a payment of costs or expenses (so far as they are fairly attributable to property to which this section applies), or

(*b*) a payment which is (or will be) income of any person for any of the purposes of income tax or would for any of those purposes be income of a person not resident in the United Kingdom if he were so resident,

or in respect of a liability to make such a payment.

(4) Tax shall not be charged under this section by virtue of subsection (2)(*b*) above if the disposition is such that, were the trustees beneficially entitled to the settled property, section 10 or section 16 above would prevent the disposition from being a transfer of value.

(5) The amount on which tax is charged under this section shall be—

(*a*) the amount by which the value of property which is comprised in the settlement and to which this section applies is less immediately after the event giving rise to the charge than it would be but for the event, or

(*b*) where the tax payable is paid out of settled property to which this section applies immediately after the event, the amount which, after deducting the tax, is equal to the amount on which tax would be charged by virtue of paragraph (*a*) above.

(6) The rate at which tax is charged under this section shall be the aggregate of the following percentages—

(*a*) 0·25 per cent for each of the first forty complete successive quarters in the relevant period,

(*b*) 0·20 per cent for each of the next forty,

(*c*) 0·15 per cent for each of the next forty,

(*d*) 0·10 per cent for each of the next forty, and

(*e*) 0·05 per cent for each of the next forty.

(7) Where the whole or part of the amount on which tax is charged under this section is attributable to property which was excluded property at any time during the relevant period then, in determining the rate at which tax is charged under this section in respect of that amount or part, no quarter throughout which that property was excluded property shall be counted.

(8) In subsections (6) and (7) above "the relevant period" means the period beginning with the later of—

(*a*) the day on which the property in respect of which tax is chargeable became (or last became) property to which this section applies, and

(*b*) 13th March 1975,

and ending with the day before the event giving rise to the charge.

(9) Where the property in respect of which tax is chargeable—

(*a*) was relevant property immediately before 10th December 1981, and

(*b*) became (or last became) property to which this section applies on or after that day and before 9th March 1982 (or, where paragraph 6, 7 or 8 of Schedule 15 to the Finance Act 1982 applied, 1st April 1983 or, as the case may be, 1st April 1984),

subsection (8) above shall have effect as if the day referred to in paragraph (a) of that subsection were the day on which the property became (or last became) relevant property before 10th December 1981.

(10) For the purposes of this section trustees shall be treated as making a disposition if they omit to exercise a right (unless it is shown that the omission was not deliberate) and the disposition shall be treated as made at the time or latest time when they could have exercised the right.

Commentary—*Simon's Taxes* **I5.643, I5.533, I5.549A, I5.554**.

HMRC Manuals—Inheritance Tax Manual IHTM04103 (settled property: charges on temporary charitable trusts). IHTM42803 (temporary charitable trusts).

Definitions—"Charitable", s 272; "excluded property" s 272; "payment", "quarter", s 63; "relevant property", s 58(1); "settled property" s 43; "trustee" s 45.

71 Accumulation and maintenance trusts

(1) Subject to [subsections (1A) to][2] (2) below, this section applies to settled property if—

(*a*) one or more persons (in this section referred to as beneficiaries) will, on or before attaining a specified age not exceeding [eighteen][3], become beneficially entitled to it . . . [3], and

(*b*) no interest in possession subsists in it and the income from it is to be accumulated so far as not applied for the maintenance, education or benefit of a beneficiary.

[(1A) This section does not apply to settled property at any particular time on or after 22nd March 2006 unless this section—

(*a*) applied to the settled property immediately before 22nd March 2006, and

(*b*) has applied to the settled property at all subsequent times up to the particular time.][2]

[(1B) This section does not apply to settled property at any particular time on or after 22nd March 2006 if, at that time, section 71A below applies to the settled property.][2]

(2) This section does not apply to settled property unless either—

(*a*) not more than twenty-five years have elapsed since the commencement of the settlement or, if it was later, since the time (or latest time) when the conditions stated in paragraphs (*a*) and (*b*) of subsection (1) above became satisfied with respect to the property, or

(*b*) all the persons who are or have been beneficiaries are or were either—

(i) grandchildren of a common grandparent, or

(ii) children, widows or widowers [or surviving civil partners][1] of such grandchildren who were themselves beneficiaries but died before the time when, had they survived, they would have become entitled as mentioned in subsection (1)(*a*) above.

(3) Subject to subsections (4) and (5) below, there shall be a charge to tax under this section—

(*a*) where settled property ceases to be property to which this section applies, and

(*b*) in a case in which paragraph (*a*) above does not apply, where the trustees make a disposition as a result of which the value of settled property to which this section applies is less than it would be but for the disposition.

(4) Tax shall not be charged under this section—

(*a*) on a beneficiary's becoming beneficially entitled to, or to an interest in possession in, settled property on or before attaining the specified age.

(*b*) on the death of a beneficiary before attaining the specified age.

(5) Subsections (3) to (8) and (10) of section 70 above shall apply for the purposes of this section as they apply for the purposes of that section (with the substitution of a reference to subsection (3)(*b*) above for the reference in section 70(4) to section 70(2)(*b*)).

(6) Where the conditions stated in paragraphs (*a*) and (*b*) of subsection (1) above were satisfied on 15th April 1976 with respect to property comprised in a settlement which commenced before that day, subsection (2)(*a*) above shall have effect with the substitution of a reference to that day for the reference to the commencement of the settlement, and the condition stated in subsection (2)(*b*) above shall be treated as satisfied if—

(*a*) it is satisfied in respect of the period beginning with 15th April 1976, or

(*b*) it is satisfied in respect of the period beginning with 1st April 1977 and either there was no beneficiary living on 15th April 1976 or the beneficiaries on 1st April 1977 included a living beneficiary, or

(*c*) there is no power under the terms of the settlement whereby it could have become satisfied in respect of the period beginning with 1st April 1977, and the trusts of the settlement have not been varied at any time after 15th April 1976.

(7) In subsection (1) above "persons" includes unborn persons; but the conditions stated in that subsection shall be treated as not satisfied unless there is or has been a living beneficiary.

(8) For the purposes of this section a person's children shall be taken to include his illegitimate children, his adopted children and his stepchildren.

Commentary—*Simon's Taxes* **13.313, 15.522, I5.511, I5.512, I5.521, I5.522, I5.524, I5.525, I5.532, I5.541, I5.542, I5.545**.

HMRC Manuals—Inheritance Tax Manual IHTM42807 (accumulation and maintenance trusts).

IHTM42808 (25 year test for accumulation and maintenance trusts).

IHTM42809 (special trusts: 25 year test for A&M trusts).

IHTM42810 (life policies in accumulation and maintenance trusts).

IHTM04099 (charges on accumulation and maintenance trusts).

Concession F8—Accumulation and maintenance settlements.

Statements of Practice E1—Powers of appointment.

SP 8/86—Treatment of income of discretionary trusts.

Press releases etc—IR 24-9-75 (entitlement of beneficiary to income in accordance with Trustee Act 1925, s 31(1)(ii) on his attaining majority satisfies sub-s (1)(*a*)).

IR letter 8-10-75 (the application of s 71 is not a once-for-all decision, but has to be kept in mind at all times. Inequality between beneficiaries is permitted. The beneficiaries need not be identified or their interests quantified in the trust deed).

Definitions—"Disposition", s 272; "settled property", "settlement", s 43; "trustee", s 45.

Cross references—See FA 2006 Sch 20 para 2(4) (where a chargeable transfer to which IHTA 1984 s 54A applies was made before 22 March 2006, that section has effect in relation to that transfer as if references in that section to this section were to this section without the amendments made by FA 2006 Sch 20 para 2(2), (3)).

FA 2006 Sch 20 para 2(5) (there is no charge to tax under this section in a case where settled property ceases, by the operation of sub-s (1B) above (as inserted by FA 2006 Sch 20 para 2(3)), to be property to which this section applies).

FA 2006 Sch 20 para 3(3) (there is no charge to tax under this section in a case where—

(a) settled property ceases, on the coming into force of FA 2006 Sch 20 para 3(1) (ie 6 April 2008), to be property to which this section applies, but

(b) this section would immediately after the coming into force of FA 2006 Sch 20 para 3(1) apply to the settled property but for the amendments made by that sub-paragraph).

Amendments—[1] Words in sub-s (2)(*b*)(ii) inserted by Tax and Civil Partnership Regulations, SI 2005/3229, regs 3, 16, with effect from 5 December 2005 (reg 1(1)).

[2] Words in sub-s (1) substituted, and sub-ss (1A), (1B) inserted, by FA 2006 s 156, Sch 20 para 2. These amendments are deemed to have come into force on 22 March 2006.

[3] In sub-s (1)(*a*), words substituted for words "twenty-five", and words "or to an interest in possession in it" repealed, with effect from 6 April 2008 but only for the purpose of determining whether, at a time on or after that day, IHTA 1984 s 71 applies to settled property.

[71A Trusts for bereaved minors

(1) This section applies to settled property (including property settled before 22nd March 2006) if—

(*a*) it is held on statutory trusts for the benefit of a bereaved minor under sections 46 and 47(1) of the Administration of Estates Act 1925 (succession on intestacy and statutory trusts in favour of issue of intestate), or

(*b*) it is held on trusts for the benefit of a bereaved minor and subsection (2) below applies to the trusts,

but this section does not apply to property in which a disabled person's interest subsists.

(2) This subsection applies to trusts—

(*a*) established under the will of a deceased parent of the bereaved minor, or

(*b*) established under the Criminal Injuries Compensation Scheme, [or

(*c*) established under the Victims of Overseas Terrorism Compensation Scheme,][2]

which secure that the conditions in subsection (3) below are met.

(3) Those conditions are—

(*a*) that the bereaved minor, if he has not done so before attaining the age of 18, will on attaining that age become absolutely entitled to—

(i) the settled property,

(ii) any income arising from it, and

(iii) any income that has arisen from the property held on the trusts for his benefit and been accumulated before that time,

(*b*) that, for so long as the bereaved minor is living and under the age of 18, if any of the settled property is applied for the benefit of a beneficiary, it is applied for the benefit of the bereaved minor, and

(*c*) that, for so long as the bereaved minor is living and under the age of 18, either—

(i) the bereaved minor is entitled to all of the income (if there is any) arising from any of the settled property, or

[(ii) if any of the income arising from any of the settled property is applied for the benefit of a beneficiary, it is applied for the benefit of the bereaved minor.][3]

(4) Trusts such as are mentioned in paragraph (*a*)[, (*b*) or (*c*)][2] of subsection (2) above are not to be treated as failing to secure that the conditions in subsection (3) above are met by reason only of—

[(*za*) the trustees' having powers that enable them to apply otherwise than for the benefit of the bereaved minor amounts (whether consisting of income or capital, or both) not exceeding the annual limit,][3]

(*a*) the trustees' having the powers conferred by section 32 of the Trustee Act 1925 (powers of advancement),

(*b*) the trustees' having those powers but free from, or subject to a less restrictive limitation than, the limitation imposed by proviso (*a*) of subsection (1) of that section,

(*c*) the trustees' having the powers conferred by section 33 of the Trustee Act (Northern Ireland) 1958 (corresponding provision for Northern Ireland),

(*d*) the trustees' having those powers but free from, or subject to a less restrictive limitation than, the limitation imposed by subsection (1)(*a*) of that section, or

(*e*) the trustees' having powers to the like effect as the powers mentioned in any of paragraphs (*a*) to (*d*) above.

[(4A) For the purposes of this section and section 71B, the "annual limit" is whichever is the lower of the following amounts—

(*a*) £3,000, and

(*b*) 3% of the amount that is the maximum value of the settled property during the period in question.

(4B) For those purposes the annual limit applies in relation to each period of 12 months that begins on 6 April.

(4C) The Treasury may by order made by statutory instrument—

(*a*) specify circumstances in which subsection (4)(za) is, or is not, to apply in relation to a trust, and

(*b*) amend the definition of "the annual limit" in subsection (4A).

(4D) An order under subsection (4C) may—

(*a*) make different provision for different cases, and

(*b*) contain transitional and saving provision.

(4E) A statutory instrument containing an order under subsection (4C) may not be made unless a draft of the instrument has been laid before, and approved by a resolution of, the House of Commons.][3]

(5) In this section "the Criminal Injuries Compensation Scheme" means—

(*a*) the schemes established by arrangements made under the Criminal Injuries Compensation Act 1995,

(*b*) arrangements made by the Secretary of State for compensation for criminal injuries in operation before the commencement of those schemes, and

(*c*) the scheme established under the Criminal Injuries Compensation (Northern Ireland) Order 2002.

(6) The preceding provisions of this section apply in relation to Scotland as if, in subsection (2) above, before "which" there were inserted "the purposes of".][1]

Commentary—*Simon's Taxes* **I5.546, I5.547, I5.253A, I5.550**.

HMRC Manuals—Inheritance Tax Manual IHTM42815 (trusts for bereaved minors).

Amendments—[1] Sections 71A–71H inserted by FA 2006 s 156, Sch 20 para 1. This amendment is deemed to have come into force on 22 March 2006.

[2] Sub-s (2)(*c*) and preceding word "or" inserted, in sub-s (4) words substituted for words "or (*b*)" by the Crime and Security Act 2010 s 48(4), Sch 2 para 2(1), (2) with effect from 8 April 2010."

[3] Sub-s (3)(*c*)(ii) substituted, and sub-ss (4)(*za*), (4A)–(4E) inserted, by FA 2013 s 216, Sch 44 paras 1, 2 with effect in relation to property transferred into settlement on or after 8 April 2013.

[71B Charge to tax on property to which section 71A applies

(1) Subject to subsections (2)[, (2B)][2] and (3) below, there shall be a charge to tax under this section—

(*a*) where settled property ceases to be property to which section 71A above applies, and

(*b*) in a case where paragraph (*a*) above does not apply, where the trustees make a disposition as a result of which the value of settled property to which section 71A above applies is less than it would be but for the disposition.

(2) Tax is not charged under this section where settled property ceases to be property to which section 71A applies as a result of—

(*a*) the bereaved minor attaining the age of 18 or becoming, under that age, absolutely entitled as mentioned in section 71A(3)(*a*) above, or

(*b*) the death under that age of the bereaved minor, or

(*c*) being paid or applied for the advancement or benefit of the bereaved minor.

[(2A) Subsection (2B) applies in a case in which—

(*a*) an amount is paid or applied otherwise than for the benefit of the bereaved minor, and

(*b*) the exemptions provided by subsection (2) of this section and subsections (3) and (4) of section 70 do not apply.

(2B) In such a case, tax is not charged under this section in respect of whichever is the lower of the following amounts—

(*a*) the amount paid or applied, and

(*b*) the annual limit.][2]

(3) Subsections (3) to (8) and (10) of section 70 above apply for the purposes of this section as they apply for the purposes of that section, but—

(*a*) with the substitution of a reference to subsection (1)(*b*) above for the reference in subsection (4) of section 70 above to subsection (2)(*b*) of that section,

(*b*) with the substitution of a reference to property to which section 71A above applies for each of the references in subsections (3), (5) and (8) of section 70 above to property to which that section applies,

(*c*) as if, for the purposes of section 70(8) above as applied by this subsection, property—

(i) which is property to which section 71A above applies,

(ii) which, immediately before it became property to which section 71A above applies, was property to which section 71 above applied, and

(iii) which, by the operation of section 71(1B) above, ceased on that occasion to be property to which section 71 above applied,

had become property to which section 71A above applies not on that occasion but on the occasion (or last occasion) before then when it became property to which section 71 above applied, and

(*d*) as if, for the purposes of section 70(8) above as applied by this subsection, property—

(i) which is property to which section 71A above applies,

(ii) which, immediately before it became property to which section 71A above applies, was property to which section 71D below applied, and

(iii) which, by the operation of section 71D(5)(*a*) below, ceased on that occasion ("the 71D-to-71A occasion") to be property to which section 71D below applied,

had become property to which section 71A above applies not on the 71D-to-71A occasion but on the relevant earlier occasion.

(4) In subsection (3)(*d*) above—

(*a*) "the relevant earlier occasion" means the occasion (or last occasion) before the 71D-to-71A occasion when the property became property to which section 71D below applied, but

(*b*) if the property, when it became property to which section 71D below applied, ceased at the same time to be property to which section 71 above applied without ceasing to be settled property, "the relevant earlier occasion" means the occasion (or last occasion) when the property became property to which section 71 above applied.][1]

Commentary—*Simon's Taxes* **I5.549, I5.549A**.

Amendments—[1] Sections 71A–71H inserted by FA 2006 s 156, Sch 20 para 1. This amendment is deemed to have come into force on 22 March 2006.

[2] In sub-s (1) words inserted, and sub-ss (2A), (2B) inserted, by FA 2013 s 216, Sch 44 paras 1, 3 with effect in relation to property transferred into settlement on or after 8 April 2013.

[71C Sections 71A and 71B: meaning of "bereaved minor"

In sections 71A and 71B above "bereaved minor" means a person—

(*a*) who has not yet attained the age of 18, and

(*b*) at least one of whose parents has died.][1]

Commentary—*Simon's Taxes* **I5.550, I5.546, I5.253A**.

HMRC Manuals—Inheritance Tax Manual IHTM42815 (trusts for bereaved minors).

Amendments—[1] Sections 71A–71H inserted by FA 2006 s 156, Sch 20 para 1. This amendment is deemed to have come into force on 22 March 2006.

[71D Age 18-to-25 trusts

(1) This section applies to settled property (including property settled before 22nd March 2006), but subject to subsection (5) below, if—

(*a*) the property is held on trusts for the benefit of a person who has not yet attained the age of 25,

(*b*) at least one of the person's parents has died, and

(*c*) subsection (2) below applies to the trusts.

(2) This subsection applies to trusts—

(*a*) established under the will of a deceased parent of the person mentioned in subsection (1)(*a*) above, or

(*b*) established under the Criminal Injuries Compensation Scheme,[or

(*c*) established under the Victims of Overseas Terrorism Compensation Scheme,][2]

which secure that the conditions in subsection (6) below are met.

(3) Subsection (4) has effect where—

(*a*) at any time on or after 22nd March 2006 but before 6th April 2008, or on the coming into force of paragraph 3(1) of Schedule 20 to the Finance Act 2006, any property ceases to be property to which section 71 above applies without ceasing to be settled property, and

(*b*) immediately after the property ceases to be property to which section 71 above applies—

(i) it is held on trusts for the benefit of a person who has not yet attained the age of 25, and

(ii) the trusts secure that the conditions in subsection (6) below are met.

(4) From the time when the property ceases to be property to which section 71 above applies, but subject to subsection (5) below, this section applies to the property (if it would not apply to the property by virtue of subsection (1) above) for so long as—

(*a*) the property continues to be settled property held on trusts such as are mentioned in subsection (3)(*b*)(i) above, and

(*b*) the trusts continue to secure that the conditions in subsection (6) below are met.

(5) This section does not apply—

(*a*) to property to which section 71A above applies,

(*b*) to property to which section 71 above, or section 89 below, applies, or

(*c*) to settled property if a person is beneficially entitled to an interest in possession in the settled property and—

(i) the person became beneficially entitled to the interest in possession before 22nd March 2006, or

(ii) the interest in possession is an immediate post-death interest, or a transitional serial interest, and the person became beneficially entitled to it on or after 22nd March 2006.

(6) Those conditions are—

(*a*) that the person mentioned in subsection (1)(*a*) or (3)(*b*)(i) above ("B"), if he has not done so before attaining the age of 25, will on attaining that age become absolutely entitled to—

(i) the settled property,

(ii) any income arising from it, and

(iii) any income that has arisen from the property held on the trusts for his benefit and been accumulated before that time,

(*b*) that, for so long as B is living and under the age of 25, if any of the settled property is applied for the benefit of a beneficiary, it is applied for the benefit of B, and

(*c*) that, for so long as B is living and under the age of 25, either—

(i) B is entitled to all of the income (if there is any) arising from any of the settled property, or

[(ii) if any of the income arising from any of the settled property is applied for the benefit of a beneficiary, it is applied for the benefit of B.][3]

[(6A) Where the income arising from the settled property is held on trusts of the kind described in section 33 of the Trustee Act 1925 (protective trusts), paragraphs (*b*) and (*c*) of subsection (6) have effect as if for "living and under the age of 25," there were substituted "under the age of 25 and the income arising from the settled property is held on trust for B,][3]

(7) For the purposes of this section, trusts are not to be treated as failing to secure that the conditions in subsection (6) above are met by reason only of—

[(*za*) the trustees' having powers that enable them to apply otherwise than for the benefit of B amounts (whether consisting of income or capital, or both) not exceeding the annual limit,][3]

(*a*) the trustees' having the powers conferred by section 32 of the Trustee Act 1925 (powers of advancement),

(*b*) the trustees' having those powers but free from, or subject to a less restrictive limitation than, the limitation imposed by proviso (*a*) of subsection (1) of that section,

(*c*) the trustees' having the powers conferred by section 33 of the Trustee Act (Northern Ireland) 1958 (corresponding provision for Northern Ireland),

(*d*) the trustees' having those powers but free from, or subject to a less restrictive limitation than, the limitation imposed by subsection (1)(*a*) of that section, or

(*e*) the trustees' having powers to the like effect as the powers mentioned in any of paragraphs (*a*) to (*d*) above.

[(7A) For the purposes of this section and section 71E, the "annual limit" is whichever is the lower of the following amounts—

(*a*) £3,000, and

(*b*) 3% of the amount that is the maximum value of the settled property during the period in question.

(7B) For those purposes the annual limit applies in relation to each period of 12 months that begins on 6 April.

(7C) The Treasury may by order made by statutory instrument—

(*a*) specify circumstances in which subsection (7)(za) is, or is not, to apply in relation to a trust, and

(*b*) amend the definition of "the annual limit" in subsection (7A).

(7D) An order under subsection (7C) may—

(*a*) make different provision for different cases, and

(*b*) contain transitional and saving provision.

(7E) A statutory instrument containing an order under subsection (7C) may not be made unless a draft of the instrument has been laid before, and approved by a resolution of, the House of Commons.][3]

(8) In this section "the Criminal Injuries Compensation Scheme" means—

(*a*) the schemes established by arrangements made under the Criminal Injuries Compensation Act 1995,

(*b*) arrangements made by the Secretary of State for compensation for criminal injuries in operation before the commencement of those schemes, and

(*c*) the scheme established under the Criminal Injuries Compensation (Northern Ireland) Order 2002.

(9) The preceding provisions of this section apply in relation to Scotland—

(*a*) as if, in subsection (2) above, before "which" there were inserted "the purposes of", and

(*b*) as if, in subsections (3)(*b*)(ii) and (4)(*b*) above, before "trusts" there were inserted "purposes of the".][1]

Commentary—*Simon's Taxes* **I5.525, I5.551, I5.552, I5.253A, 15.556.**

HMRC Manuals—Inheritance Tax Manual IHTM42816 (special trusts: age 18 to 25 trusts).

Amendments—[1] Sections 71A–71H inserted by FA 2006 s 156, Sch 20 para 1. This amendment is deemed to have come into force on 22 March 2006.

[2] Sub-s (2)(*c*) and preceding word "or" inserted by the Crime and Security Act 2010 s 48(4), Sch 2 para 2(1), (3) with effect from 8 April 2010.

[3] Sub-s (6)(*c*)(ii) substituted, and sub-ss (6A), (7)(*za*), (7A)–(7E) inserted, by FA 2013 s 216, Sch 44 paras 1, 4 with effect in relation to property transferred into settlement on or after 8 April 2013.

[71E Charge to tax on property to which section 71D applies

(1) Subject to subsections (2) to [(4A)][2] below, there shall be a charge to tax under this section—

(*a*) where settled property ceases to be property to which section 71D above applies, or

(*b*) in a case where paragraph (*a*) above does not apply, where the trustees make a disposition as a result of which the value

of the settled property to which section 71D above applies is less than it would be but for the disposition.

(2) Tax is not charged under this section where settled property ceases to be property to which section 71D above applies as a result of—

(*a*) B becoming, at or under the age of 18, absolutely entitled as mentioned in section 71D(6)(*a*) above,

(*b*) the death, under the age of 18, of B,

(*c*) becoming, at a time when B is living and under the age of 18, property to which section 71A above applies, or

(*d*) being paid or applied for the advancement or benefit of B—

(i) at a time when B is living and under the age of 18, or

(ii) on B's attaining the age of 18.

(3) Tax is not charged under this section in respect of—

(*a*) a payment of costs or expenses (so far as they are fairly attributable to property to which section 71D above applies), or

(*b*) a payment which is (or will be) income of any person for any of the purposes of income tax or would for any of those purposes be income of a person not resident in the United Kingdom if he were so resident,

or in respect of a liability to make such a payment.

(4) Tax is not charged under this section by virtue of subsection (1)(*b*) above if the disposition is such that, were the trustees beneficially entitled to the settled property, section 10 or section 16 above would prevent the disposition from being a transfer of value.

[(4A) If an amount is paid or applied otherwise than for the benefit of B and the exemptions provided by subsections (2) to (4) do not apply, tax is not charged under this section in respect of whichever is the lower of the following amounts—

(*a*) the amount paid or applied, and

(*b*) the annual limit.][2]

(5) For the purposes of this section the trustees shall be treated as making a disposition if they omit to exercise a right (unless it is shown that the omission was not deliberate) and the disposition shall be treated as made at the time or latest time when they could have exercised the right.][1]

Commentary—*Simon's Taxes* **I5.554, I5.555.**

Amendments—[1] Sections 71A–71H inserted by FA 2006 s 156, Sch 20 para 1. This amendment is deemed to have come into force on 22 March 2006.

[2] In sub-s (1) figure substituted for previous figure "(4)", and sub-s (4A) inserted, by FA 2013 s 216, Sch 44 paras 1, 5 with effect in relation to property transferred into settlement on or after 8 April 2013.

[71F Calculation of tax charged under section 71E in certain cases

(1) Where—

(*a*) tax is charged under section 71E above by reason of the happening of an event within subsection (2) below, and

(*b*) that event happens after B has attained the age of 18,

the tax is calculated in accordance with this section.

(2) Those events are—

(*a*) B becoming absolutely entitled as mentioned in section 71D(6)(*a*) above,

(*b*) the death of B, and

(*c*) property being paid or applied for the advancement or benefit of B.

(3) The amount of the tax is given by—

$$\text{Chargeable amount} \times \text{Relevant fraction} \times \text{Settlement rate}$$

(4) For the purposes of subsection (3) above, the "Chargeable amount" is—

(*a*) the amount by which the value of property which is comprised in the settlement and to which section 71D above applies is less immediately after the event giving rise to the charge than it would be but for the event, or

(*b*) where the tax is payable out of settled property to which section 71D above applies immediately after the event, the amount which, after deducting the tax, is equal to the amount on which tax would be charged by virtue of paragraph (*a*) above.

(5) For the purposes of subsection (3) above, the "Relevant fraction" is three tenths multiplied by so many fortieths as there are complete successive quarters in the period—

(*a*) beginning with the day on which B attained the age of 18 or, if later, the day on which the property became property to which section 71D above applies, and (*b*) ending with the day before the occasion of the charge.

(6) Where the whole or part of the Chargeable amount is attributable to property that was excluded property at any time during the period mentioned in subsection (5) above then, in determining the "Relevant fraction" in relation to that amount or part, no quarter throughout which that property was excluded property shall be counted.

(7) For the purposes of subsection (3) above, the "Settlement rate" is the effective rate (that is to say, the rate found by expressing the tax chargeable as a percentage of the amount on which it is charged) at which tax would be charged on the value transferred by a chargeable transfer of the description specified in subsection (8) below.

(8) The chargeable transfer postulated in subsection (7) above is one—

(*a*) the value transferred by which is equal to an amount determined in accordance with subsection (9) below,

(*b*) which is made at the time of the charge to tax under section 71E above by a transferor who has in the period of seven years ending with the day of the occasion of the charge made chargeable transfers having an aggregate value equal to that of any chargeable transfers made by the settlor in the period of seven years ending with the day on which the settlement commenced, disregarding transfers made on that day, and

(*c*) on which tax is charged in accordance with section 7(2) above.

(9) The amount referred to in subsection (8)(*a*) above is equal to the aggregate of—

(*a*) the value, immediately after the settlement commenced, of the property then comprised in it,

(*b*) the value, immediately after a related settlement commenced, of the property then comprised in it [which was property to which section 71D above applied][2], and

(*c*) the value, immediately after it became comprised in the settlement, of any property which became so comprised after the settlement commenced and before the occasion of the charge under section 71E above (whether or not it has remained so comprised).][1]

Commentary—*Simon's Taxes* **I5.554**.

Amendments—[1] Sections 71A–71H inserted by FA 2006 s 156, Sch 20 para 1. This amendment is deemed to have come into force on 22 March 2006.

[2] In sub-s (9)(*b*), words inserted by F(No 2)A 2015 s 11, Sch 1 paras 1, 6 with effect in relation to occasions on which tax falls to be charged under IHTA 1984 Pt 3 Ch 3 on or after 18 November 2015.

[71G Calculation of tax charged under section 71E in all other cases

(1) Where—

(*a*) tax is charged under section 71E above, and

(*b*) the tax does not fall to be calculated in accordance with section 71F above,

the tax is calculated in accordance with this section.

(2) The amount on which the tax is charged is—

(*a*) the amount by which the value of property which is comprised in the settlement and to which section 71D above applies is less immediately after the event giving rise to the charge than it would be but for the event, or

(*b*) where the tax is payable out of settled property to which section 71D above applies immediately after the event, the amount which, after deducting the tax, is equal to the amount on which tax would be charged by virtue of paragraph (*a*) above.

(3) The rate at which the tax is charged is the rate that would be given by subsections (6) to (8) of section 70 above—

(*a*) if the reference to section 70 above in subsection (8)(*a*) of that section were a reference to section 71D above,

(*b*) if the other references in those subsections to section 70 above were references to section 71E above, and

(*c*) if, for the purposes of section 70(8) above, property—

(i) which is property to which section 71D above applies,

(ii) which, immediately before it became property to which section 71D above applies, was property to which section 71 applied, and

(iii) which ceased on that occasion to be property to which section 71 above applied without ceasing to be settled property,

had become property to which section 71D above applies not on that occasion but on the occasion (or last occasion) before then when it became property to which section 71 above applied.][1]

Commentary—*Simon's Taxes* **I5.554**.

Amendments—[1] Sections 71A–71H inserted by FA 2006 s 156, Sch 20 para 1. This amendment is deemed to have come into force on 22 March 2006.

[71H Sections 71A to 71G: meaning of "parent"

(1) In sections 71A to 71G above "parent" includes step-parent.

(2) For the purposes of sections 71A to 71G above, a deceased individual ("D") shall be taken to have been a parent of another individual ("Y") if, immediately before D died, D had—

(*a*) parental responsibility for Y under the law of England and Wales,
(*b*) parental responsibilities in relation to Y under the law of Scotland, or
(*c*) parental responsibility for Y under the law of Northern Ireland.

(3) In subsection (2)(*a*) above "parental responsibility" has the same meaning as in the Children Act 1989.

(4) In subsection (2)(*b*) above "parental responsibilities" has the meaning given by section 1(3) of the Children (Scotland) Act 1995.

(5) In subsection (2)(*c*) above "parental responsibility" has the same meaning as in the Children (Northern Ireland) Order 1995.][1]

Commentary—*Simon's Taxes* **I5.546, I5.253A, I5.551.**

Amendments—[1] Sections 71A–71H inserted by FA 2006 s 156, Sch 20 para 1. This amendment is deemed to have come into force on 22 March 2006.

72 Property leaving employee trusts and newspaper trusts

(1) This section applies to settled property to which section 86 below applies [if—
(*a*) no interest in possession subsists in it to which an individual is beneficially entitled, and
(*b*) no company-purchased interest in possession subsists in it.][4]

[(1A) For the purposes of subsection (1)(*b*) above, an interest in possession is "company-purchased" if—
(*a*) a company is beneficially entitled to the interest in possession,
(*b*) the business of the company consists wholly or mainly in the acquisition of interests in settled property, and
(*c*) the company has acquired the interest in possession for full consideration in money or money's worth from an individual who was beneficially entitled to it.][4]

[(1B) Section 59(3) and (4) above apply for the purposes of subsection (1A)(*c*) above as for those of section 59(2)(*b*) above, but as if the references to the condition set out in section 59(2)(*a*) above were to the condition set out in subsection (1A)(*b*) above.][4]

(2) Subject to subsections [(3A),][5] (4)[, (4A)][2] and (5) below, there shall be a charge to tax under this section—
(*a*) where settled property ceases to be property to which this section applies, otherwise than by virtue of a payment out of the settled property, and
(*b*) where a payment is made out of settled property to which this section applies for the benefit of a person within subsection (3) below, or a person connected with such a person, and
(*c*) in a case in which paragraphs (*a*) and (*b*) above do not apply, where the trustees make a disposition (otherwise than by way of a payment out of the settled property) as a result of which the value of settled property to which this section applies is less than it would be but for the disposition.

(3) A person is within this subsection if—
(*a*) he has directly or indirectly provided any of the settled property otherwise than by additions not exceeding in value £1,000 in any one year; or
(*b*) in a case where the employment in question is employment by a close company, he is a participator in relation to that company and either—
(i) is beneficially entitled to, or to rights entitling him to acquire, not less than 5 per cent of, or of any class of the shares comprised in, its issued share capital, or
(ii) would, on a winding-up of the company, be entitled to not less than 5 per cent of its assets; or
(*c*) he has acquired an interest in the settled property for a consideration in money or money's worth.

[(3A) Where settled property ceases to be property to which this section applies because paragraph (*d*) of section 86(3) no longer applies, tax is not chargeable under this section by virtue of subsection (2)(*a*) if the only reason that paragraph no longer applies is that one or both of the trading requirement and the controlling interest requirement mentioned in that paragraph are no longer met with respect to the company so mentioned.][5]

(4) If the trusts are those of a profit sharing scheme approved in accordance with Schedule 9 to the [Taxes Act 1988][1], tax shall not be chargeable under this section by virtue of subsection (3)(*b*) above on an appropriation of shares in pursuance of the scheme.

[(4A) If the trusts are those of [a share incentive plan approved under Schedule 2 to the Income Tax (Earnings and Pensions) Act 2003][3], tax shall not be chargeable under this section by virtue of subsection (3)(*b*) above on an appropriation of shares to, or acquisition of shares on behalf of, an individual under the plan.][2]

(5) Subsections (3) to (10) of section 70 above shall apply for the purposes of this section as they apply for the purposes of that section (with the substitution of a reference to subsection (2)(*c*) above for the reference in section 70(4) to section 70(2)(*b*)).

(6) In this section—
(*a*) "close company" and "participator" have the same meanings as in Part IV of this Act; and

(*b*) "year" means the period beginning with 26th March 1974 and ending with 5th April 1974, and any subsequent period of twelve months ending with 5th April;

and a person shall be treated for the purposes of this section as acquiring an interest for a consideration in money or money's worth if he becomes entitled to it as a result of transactions which include a disposition for such consideration (whether to him or another) of that interest or of other property.

Commentary—*Simon's Taxes* **I5.631**.

HMRC Manuals—Inheritance Tax Manual IHTM42981–42988 (property leaving employee benefit trusts).

IHTM42990 (transfers from discretionary trusts to newspaper trusts).

Definitions—"qualifying interest in possession", s 59(1); "close company", "participator", s 102(1); "payment" s 63; "settled property", s 43.

Amendments—[1] Words in sub-s (4) substituted by TA 1988 Sch 29 para 32 Table.

[2] Words in sub-s (2) and sub-s (4A) inserted by FA 2000 s 138(1), (3), with effect from 28 July 2000.

[3] In sub-s (4A), words substituted for the words "an employee share ownership plan approved under Schedule 8 to the Finance Act 2000" by ITEPA 2003 s 722, Sch 6 paras 150, 151(1)(*b*), (2) with effect, for income tax purposes, from 2003–04; and for corporation tax purposes, for accounting periods ending after 5 April 2003. For transitional provisions and savings see ITEPA 2003 s 723, Sch 7.

[4] Words in sub-s (1) substituted, and sub-ss (1A), (1B) inserted, by FA 2006 s 156, Sch 20 paras 7, 21. These amendments are deemed to have come into force on 22 March 2006.

[5] In sub-s (2), reference inserted, and sub-s (3A) inserted, by FA 2014 s 290, Sch 37 paras 9, 13. These amendments are treated as having come into force on 6 April 2014.

73 Pre-1978 protective trusts

(1) This section applies to settled property which is held on trusts to the like effect as those specified in section 33(1)(ii) of the Trustee Act 1925 and which became held on those trusts on the failure or determination before 12th April 1978 of trusts to the like effect as those specified in section 33(1)(i).

(2) Subject to subsection (3) below, there shall be a charge to tax under this section—

(*a*) where settled property ceases to be property to which this section applies, otherwise than by virtue of a payment out of the settled property for the benefit of the principal beneficiary within the meaning of section 33 of the Trustee Act 1925, and

(*b*) in a case in which paragraph (*a*) above does not apply, where the trustees make a disposition (otherwise than by way of such a payment) as a result of which the value of settled property to which this section applies is less than it would be but for the disposition.

(3) Subsections (3) to (10) of section 70 above shall apply for the purposes of this section as they apply for the purposes of that section.

Commentary—*Simon's Taxes* **I5.623**.

HMRC Manuals—Inheritance Tax Manual IHTM42804 (special trusts: protective trusts).

Statement of practice E7—Protective trusts.

Definitions—"Disposition", s 272; "settled property", s 43; "trustee" s 45.

74 Pre-1981 trusts for disabled persons

(1) This section applies to settled property transferred into settlement before 10th March 1981 and held on trusts under which, during the life of a disabled person, no interest in possession in the settled property subsists, and which secure that any of the settled property which is applied during his life is applied only or mainly for his benefit.

(2) Subject to subsection (3) below, there shall be a charge to tax under this section—

(*a*) where settled property ceases to be property to which this section applies, otherwise than by virtue of a payment out of the settled property for the benefit of the person mentioned in subsection (1) above, and

(*b*) in a case in which paragraph (*a*) above does not apply, where the trustees make a disposition (otherwise than by way of such a payment) as a result of which the value of settled property to which this section applies is less than it would be but for the disposition.

(3) Subsections (3) to (10) of section 70 above shall apply for the purposes of this section as they apply for the purposes of that section.

(4) In this section "disabled person" means a person who—

(*a*) is by reason of mental disorder (within the meaning of the Mental Health Act 1983) incapable of administering his property or managing his affairs, or

(*b*) is in receipt of an attendance allowance under section [64 of the Social Security Contributions and Benefits Act 1992 or section 64 of the Social Security Contributions and Benefits (Northern Ireland) Act 1992][2], [or][1]

[(*c*) is in receipt of a disability living allowance under section [71 of the Social Security Contributions and Benefits Act 1992 or section 71 of the Social Security Contributions and Benefits (Northern Ireland) Act 1992][2] by virtue of entitlement to the care component at the highest or middle rate.][1]

Commentary—*Simon's Taxes* **I5.207**.

HMRC Manuals—Inheritance Tax Manual IHTM42805 (trusts for disabled persons).

Definitions—"Disposition", s 272; "payment" s 63; "settled property", s 43; "trustee" s 45.

Amendments—[1] Sub-s (4)(*c*) and the preceding word "or" inserted by the Disability Living Allowance and Disability Working Allowance Act 1991 Sch 2 para 14(1) with effect from 6 April 1992 by virtue of SI 1991/2617.

[2] Words in sub-s (4)(*b*), (*c*) substituted by the SS (Consequential Provisions) Act 1992 s 4, Sch 2 para 66 and the SS (Consequential Provisions) (Northern Ireland) Act 1992 s 4, Sch 2 para 29 with effect from 1 July 1992. Words in sub-s (4)(*c*) originally inserted by the Disability Living Allowance and Disability Working Allowance (Northern Ireland Consequential Amendments) Order, SI 1991/2874, art 4(1), (2).

[74A Arrangements involving acquisition of interest in settled property etc

(1) This section applies where—

(*a*) one or more persons enter into arrangements,

(*b*) in the course of the arrangements—

(i) an individual ("the individual") domiciled in the United Kingdom acquires or becomes able to acquire (directly or indirectly) an interest in property comprised in a settlement ("the relevant settled property"), and

(ii) consideration in money or money's worth is given by one or more of the persons mentioned in paragraph (*a*) (whether or not in connection with the acquisition of that interest or the individual becoming able to acquire it),

(*c*) there is a relevant reduction in the value of the individual's estate, and

(*d*) condition A or condition B is met.

(2) Condition A is that—

(*a*) the settlor was not domiciled in the United Kingdom at the time the settlement was made, and

(*b*) the relevant settled property is situated outside the United Kingdom at any time during the course of the arrangements.

(3) Condition B is that—

(*a*) the settlor was not an individual or a close company at the time the settlement was made, and

(*b*) condition A is not met.

(4) Subsection (6) applies if all or a part of a relevant reduction ("amount A") is attributable to the value of the individual's section 49(1) property being less than it would have been in the absence of the arrangements.

(5) "The individual's section 49(1) property" means settled property to which the individual is treated as beneficially entitled under section 49(1) by reason of the individual being beneficially entitled to an interest in possession in the property.

(6) Where this subsection applies—

(*a*) a part of that interest in possession is deemed, for the purposes of section 52, to come to an end at the relevant time, and

(*b*) that section applies in relation to the coming to an end of that part as if the reference in subsection (4)(a) of that section to a corresponding part of the whole value of the property in which the interest in possession subsists were a reference to amount A.

(7) Subsection (8) applies to so much (if any) of a relevant reduction as is not amount A ("amount B").

(8) Tax is to be charged as if the individual had made a transfer of value at the relevant time and the value transferred by it had been equal to amount B.][1]

Amendments—[1] Sections 74A–74C inserted by FA 2012 s 210(1), (3). These amendments are treated as having come into force on 20 June 2012 and have effect in relation to arrangements entered into on or after that day.

[74B Section 74A: supplementary provision

(1) A transfer of value arising by virtue of section 74A is to be taken to be a transfer which is not a potentially exempt transfer.

(2) For the purposes of section 74A—

(*a*) when determining the value transferred by a transfer of value arising by virtue of that section, no account is to be taken of section 3(2),

(*b*) nothing in section 10(1) applies to prevent such a transfer, and

(*c*) nothing in sections 102 to 102C of the Finance Act 1986 applies in relation to such a transfer.

(3) Where, ignoring this subsection, a transfer of value would arise by virtue of section 74A ("the current transfer"), the value transferred by a relevant related transfer is to be treated as reducing the value transferred by the current transfer.

But this subsection does not apply if and to the extent that the relevant related transfer has already been applied to reduce another transfer of value arising by virtue of that section.

(4) "Relevant related transfer" means—

(*a*) where the arrangements consist of a series of operations, any transfer of value constituted by one or more of those operations which occur before or at the same time as the current transfer, other than a transfer of value arising by virtue of section 74A, and

(*b*) where the arrangements consist of a single operation, any transfer of value which arises from that operation, other than a transfer of value arising by virtue of section 74A.

(5) Section 268(3) does not apply to a transfer of value arising by virtue of section 74A.

(6) Where—

(*a*) a transfer of value has arisen by virtue of section 74A, (*b*) in the course of the arrangements the individual acquires an interest in possession in settled property, and

(*c*) section 5(1B) applies to the interest in possession so that it forms part of the individual's estate,

this Act has effect as if that transfer of value had never arisen.][1]

Amendments—[1] Sections 74A–74C inserted by FA 2012 s 210(1), (3). These amendments are treated as having come into force on 20 June 2012 and have effect in relation to arrangements entered into on or after that day.

[74C Interpretation of sections 74A and 74B

(1) Subsections (2) to (4) have effect for the purposes of sections 74A and 74B.

(2) An individual has an interest in property comprised in a settlement if—

(*a*) the property, or any derived property, is or will or may become payable to, or applicable for the benefit of—

(i) the individual,

(ii) the individual's spouse or civil partner, or

(iii) a close company in relation to which the individual or the individual's spouse or civil partner is a participator or a company which is a 51% subsidiary of such a close company,

in any circumstances whatsoever, or

(*b*) a person within sub-paragraph (i), (ii) or (iii) of paragraph (*a*) enjoys a benefit deriving (directly or indirectly) from the property or any derived property.

(3) A "relevant reduction" in the value of the individual's estate occurs—

(*a*) if and when the value of the individual's estate first becomes less than it would have been in the absence of the arrangements, and

(*b*) on each subsequent occasion when the value of that estate becomes less than it would have been in the absence of the arrangements and that difference in value is greater than the sum of any previous relevant reductions.

(4) The amount of a relevant reduction is—

(*a*) in the case of a reduction within subsection (3)(*a*), the difference between the value of the estate and its value in the absence of the arrangements, and

(*b*) in the case of a reduction within subsection (3)(*b*), the amount by which the difference in value mentioned in that provision exceeds the sum of any previous relevant reductions.

(5) In sections 74A and 74B and this section—

"arrangements" includes any scheme, transaction or series of transactions, agreement or understanding, whether or not legally enforceable, and any associated operations;

"close company" has the meaning given in section 102;

"derived property", in relation to any property, means—

(*a*) income from that property,

(*b*) property directly or indirectly representing—

(i) proceeds of that property, or

(ii) proceeds of income from that property, or

(*c*) income from property which is derived property by virtue of paragraph (*b*);

"operation" includes an omission;

"participator" has the meaning given in section 102;

"the relevant time" means—

(*a*) the time the relevant reduction occurs, or

(*b*) if later, the time section 74A first applied;

"51% subsidiary" has the same meaning as in the Corporation Tax Acts (see Chapter 3 of Part 24 of the Corporation Tax Act 2010).][1]

Amendments—[1] Sections 74A–74C inserted by FA 2012 s 210(1), (3). These amendments are treated as having come into force on 20 June 2012 and have effect in relation to arrangements entered into on or after that day.

Special cases—reliefs

75 Property becoming subject to employee trusts

(1) Tax shall not be charged under section 65 above in respect of shares in or securities of a company which cease to be relevant property on becoming held on trusts of the description specified in section 86(1) below if the conditions in subsection (2) below are satisfied.

(2) The conditions referred to in subsection (1) above are—

(*a*) that the persons for whose benefit the trusts permit the settled property to be applied include all or most of the persons employed by or holding office with the company;

(*b*) that, at the date when the shares or securities cease to be relevant property or at a subsequent date not more than one year thereafter, both the conditions mentioned in subsection (2) of section 28 above (read with subsections (3) and (7)) are satisfied, without taking account of shares or securities held on other trusts; and (*c*) that the trusts do not permit any of the property to be applied at any time (whether during any such period as is referred to in section 86(1) below or later) for the benefit of any of the persons mentioned in subsection (4) of section 28 above (read with subsections (5) to (7)) or for the benefit of the settlor or of any person connected with him.

(3) In its application for the purposes of subsection (2)(*c*) above, section 28(4) shall be construed as if—

(*a*) references to section 28(1) were references to subsection (2) above, and

(*b*) references to the time of the transfer of value were references to the time when the property ceases to be relevant property.

Commentary—*Simon's Taxes* **I5.338**.

HMRC Manuals—Inheritance Tax Manual IHTM42948 (employee benefit trusts: inheritance tax operation: settled shares or securities becoming subject to employee benefit trusts).

Definitions—"relevant property", s 58(1); "settled property", s 43.

[75A Property becoming subject to employee-ownership trust

(1) Tax is not charged under section 65 in respect of shares in or securities of a company ("C") which cease to be relevant property on becoming held on trusts of the description specified in section 86(1) if the conditions in subsection (2) are satisfied.

(2) The conditions referred to in subsection (1) are—

(*a*) that C meets the trading requirement,

(*b*) that the trusts are of a settlement which meets the all-employee benefit requirement, and

(*c*) that the settlement does not meet the controlling interest requirement immediately before the beginning of the tax year in which the shares or securities cease to be relevant property but does meet it at the end of that year.

(3) Sections 236I, 236J, 236K, 236M and 236T (but not 236L) of the 1992 Act apply to determine whether—

(*a*) C meets the trading requirement;

(*b*) the settlement meets the all-employee benefit requirement;

(*c*) the settlement meets the controlling interest requirement;

with references in those sections to "C" being read accordingly.

(4) In this section "tax year" means a year beginning on 6 April and ending on the following 5 April.][1]

Commentary—*Simon's Taxes* **I5.338A, I4.223A, I3.156A**.

HMRC Manuals—Inheritance Tax Manual IHTM42997 (employee benefit trusts: employee ownership trusts: exemption from inheritance tax).

Amendments—[1] Section 75A inserted by FA 2014 s 290, Sch 37 paras 9, 14. This amendment is treated as having come into force on 6 April 2014.

76 Property becoming held for charitable purposes, etc

(1) Tax shall not be charged under this Chapter (apart from section 79 below) in respect of property which ceases to be relevant property, or ceases to be property to which section 70, 71, [71A, 71D,][3] 72, 73 or 74 above or paragraph 8 of Schedule 4 to this Act applies, on becoming—

(*a*) property held for charitable purposes only without limit of time (defined by a date or otherwise);

(*b*) the property of a political party qualifying for exemption under section 24 above; [or][1]

(*c*) the property of a body within Schedule 3 to this Act;

(*d*) . . .

(2) . . . [1]

(3) If the amount on which tax would be charged apart from this section in respect of any property exceeds the value of the property immediately after it becomes property of a description specified in paragraphs (*a*) [to (c)][2] of subsection (1) above (less the amount of any consideration for its transfer received by the trustees), that subsection shall not apply but the amount on which tax is charged shall be equal to the excess.

(4) The reference in subsection (3) above to the amount on which tax would be charged is a reference to the amount on which it would be charged—

(*a*) assuming (if it is not in fact so) that the tax is not paid out of settled property, and

(*b*) apart from Chapters I and II of Part V of this Act;

and the reference in that subsection to the amount on which tax is charged is a reference to the amount on which it would be charged on that assumption and apart from those Chapters.

(5) Subsection (1) above shall not apply in relation to any property if the disposition by which it becomes property of the relevant description is defeasible; but for this purpose a disposition which has not been defeated at a time twelve months after the property concerned becomes property of the relevant description and is not defeasible after that time shall be treated as not being defeasible, whether or not it was capable of being defeated before that time.

(6) Subsection (1) above shall not apply in relation to any property if it or any part of it may become applicable for purposes other than charitable purposes or purposes of a body mentioned in subsection (1)(*b*), [or (*c*)][2] above.

(7) Subsection (1) shall not apply in relation to any property if, at or before the time when it becomes property of the relevant description, an interest under the settlement is or has been acquired for a consideration in money or money's worth by an exempt body otherwise than from a charity or a body mentioned in subsection (1)(*b*) or (*c*) above.

(8) In subsection (7) above "exempt body" means a charity or a body mentioned in subsection (1)(*b*), [or (*c*)][2] above; and for the purposes of subsection (7) above a body shall be treated as acquiring an interest for a consideration in money or money's worth if it becomes entitled to the interest as a result of transactions which include a disposition for such consideration (whether to that body or to another person) of that interest or of other property.

Commentary—*Simon's Taxes* **I5.336**.

HMRC Manuals—Inheritance Tax Manual IHTM42811 (charitable, political and heritage trusts).

Definitions—"Charitable", s 272; "relevant property", s 58(1); "settled property", s 43.

Cross references—See FA 1985 s 95 (transfer of Treasury functions under this section to the Commissioners of Inland Revenue).

Amendments—[1] Words in sub-s (1)(*d*) and (2) repealed by FA 1998 s 143(4) in relation to property which ceases to be relevant property, or to be property to which any of IHTA 1984 ss 70–74 or Sch 4 para 8 applies, on or after 17 March 1998.

[2] Amended by FA 1998 s 143(4) in relation to property which ceases to be relevant property, or to be property to which any of IHTA 1984 ss 70–74 or Sch 4 para 8 applies, on or after 17 March 1998.

[3] References in sub-s (1) inserted by FA 2006 s 156, Sch 20 paras 7, 22. This amendment is deemed to have come into force on 22 March 2006.

Works of art, historic buildings, etc

77 Maintenance funds for historic buildings, etc

Schedule 4 to this Act shall have effect.

78 Conditionally exempt occasions

(1) A transfer of property or other event shall not constitute an occasion on which tax is chargeable under any provision of this Chapter other than section 64 if the property in respect of which the charge would have been made has been comprised in the settlement throughout the six years ending with the transfer or event, and—

(*a*) the property is, on a claim made for the purpose, designated by the Treasury under section 31 above, and

(*b*) the requisite undertaking described in that section is given with respect to the property by such person as the Treasury think appropriate in the circumstances of the case [or (where the property is an area of land within subsection (1)(*d*) of that section) the requisite undertakings described in that section are given with respect to the property by such person or persons as the Treasury think appropriate in the circumstances of the case][1].

[(1A) A claim under subsection (1) above must be made no more than two years after the date of the transfer or other event in question or within such longer period as the Board may allow.][3]

(2) References in this Chapter to a conditionally exempt occasion are to—

(*a*) a transfer or event which by virtue of subsection (1) above does not constitute an occasion on which tax is chargeable under this Chapter;

(*b*) a transfer or event which, by virtue of section 81(1) of the Finance Act 1976, did not constitute an occasion on which tax was chargeable under Chapter II of Part IV of the Finance Act 1982;

(*c*) a conditionally exempt distribution within the meaning given by section 81(2) of the Finance Act 1976 as it had effect in relation to events before 9th March 1982.

(3) Where there has been a conditionally exempt occasion in respect of any property, sections 32, [32A,][1] 33(1), [33(2ZA)][4] to (7) and 35(2) above shall have effect (and tax shall accordingly be chargeable under section 32 [or 32A][1]) as if—

(*a*) references to a conditionally exempt transfer and to such a transfer of property included references respectively to a conditionally exempt occasion and to such an occasion in respect of property;

(*b*) references to a disposal otherwise than by sale included references to any occasion on which tax is chargeable under any provision of this Chapter other than section 64;

(*c*) references to an undertaking given under section 30 above included references to an undertaking given under this section;

and the references in section 33(5) above to the person who made a conditionally exempt transfer shall have effect in relation to a conditionally exempt occasion as references to the person who is the settlor of the settlement in respect of which the occasion occurred (or if there is more than one such person, whichever of them the Board may select).

(4) Where by virtue of subsection (3) above the relevant person for the purposes of section 33 above is the settlor of a settlement, the rate (or each of the rates) mentioned in section 33(1)(*b*)(i) or (ii)—

(*a*) shall, if the occasion occurred before the first ten-year anniversary to fall after the property became comprised in the settlement concerned, be 30 per cent of what it would be apart from this subsection, and (*b*) shall, if the occasion occurred after the first and before the second ten-year anniversary to fall after the property became so comprised, be 60 per cent of what it would be apart from this subsection;

[and the appropriate provision of section 7 for the purposes of section 1(1)(b)(ii) is, if the settlement was created on his death, subsection (1) and, if not, subsection (2).][2]

(5) Where by virtue of subsection (3) above the relevant person for the purposes of section 33 above is the settlor of a settlement and that settlor died before 13th March 1975, section 33(1)(*b*) above shall have effect (subject to subsection (4) above) with the substitution for sub-paragraph (ii) of the following sub-paragraph—

"(ii) the rate or rates that would have applied to that amount ("the chargeable amount") [in accordance with the appropriate provision of section 7 above][2] if the relevant person had died when the chargeable event occurred, the value transferred on his death had been equal to the amount on which estate duty was chargeable when he in fact died, and the chargeable amount had been added to that value and had formed the highest part of it."

(6) Section 34 above shall not apply to a chargeable event in respect of property if the last conditionally exempt transfer of the property has been followed by a conditionally exempt occasion in respect of it.

Commentary—*Simon's Taxes* **I5.655, I7.531**.

HMRC Manuals—Inheritance Tax Manual IHTM42650 (other taxes and investigation: heritage).

Definitions—"the Board", s 272; "conditionally exempt transfer", s 30(2).

Cross references—See FA 1985 s 95 (transfer of Treasury functions under section 31 to the Commissioners of Inland Revenue from 25 July 1985).

FA 1986 Sch 19 para 40 (where a death or other event occurs on or after 18 March 1986, the amendments to this section by FA 1986 Sch 19 para 19 not to affect the tax chargeable on a transfer of value occurring before 18 March 1986).

FA 2013 s 155 (annual tax on enveloped dwellings: dwelling conditionally exempt from IHT).

Amendments—[1] Words in sub-s (1)(*b*) added and words in sub-s (3) inserted by FA 1985 Sch 26 para 8 in relation to events after 18 March 1985.

[2] Words in sub-ss (4), (5) substituted by FA 1986 s 101(3) and Sch 19 para 19 with respect to transfers of value made after 17 March 1986.

[3] Inserted by FA 1998 Sch 25 para 3 in relation to transfers of property made, and other events occurring, on or after 17 March 1998.

[4] Words in sub-s (3) substituted by FA 2012 s 209, Sch 33 paras 2, 5 with effect in cases where D's death occurs on or after 6 April 2012.

79 Exemption from ten-yearly charge

(1) Where property is comprised in a settlement and there has been a conditionally exempt transfer of the property on or before the occasion on which it became comprised in the settlement, section 64 above shall not have effect in relation to the property on any ten-year anniversary falling before the first occurrence after the transfer of a chargeable event with respect to the property.

(2) Where property is comprised in a settlement and there has been, on or before the occasion on which it became comprised in the settlement, a disposal of the property in relation to which subsection (4) of section [258 of the 1992 Act][2] (capital gains tax relief for works of art etc) had effect, section 64 above shall not have effect in relation to the property on any ten-year anniversary falling before the first occurrence after the disposal of an event on the happening of which the property is treated as sold under subsection (5) of the said section [258][2].

(3) Where property is comprised in a settlement and there has been no such transfer or disposal of the property as is mentioned in subsection (1) or (2) above on or before the occasion on which it became comprised in the settlement, [subsection (3A) below applies if[4]]—

(*a*) the property [is, on a claim made for the purpose,][4] designated by the Treasury under section 31 above,

[(*aa*) that claim is made during the period beginning with the date of a ten-year anniversary of the settlement ("the relevant ten-year anniversary") and ending—

(i) two years after that date, or

(ii) on such later date as the Board may allow,][4]

(*b*) the requisite undertaking described in [section 31 is given][4] [with respect to the property][1] by such person as the Treasury think appropriate in the circumstances of the case [or (where the property is an area of land within subsection (1)(*d*) of that section) the requisite undertakings described in that section [are given][4] with respect to the property by such person or persons as the Treasury think appropriate in the circumstances of the case][1], and

(*c*) the property is relevant property.

. . . [4]

[(3A) Tax is not chargeable under section 64 above in relation to the property by reference to the relevant ten-year anniversary concerned or any subsequent ten-year anniversaries; but on the first occurrence of an event which, if there had been a conditionally exempt transfer of the property immediately before that relevant ten-year anniversary, would be a chargeable event with respect to the property—

(*a*) there is a charge to tax under this subsection, and

(*b*) on any ten-year anniversary falling after that event, tax is chargeable under section 64 above in relation to the property.][4]

(4) Tax shall not be charged under [subsection (3A) above in respect of property if, after the occasion mentioned in subsection (3) above and before the occurrence mentioned in subsection (3A)][4], there has been a conditionally exempt occasion in respect of the property.

(5) The amount on which tax is charged under [subsection (3A)][4] above shall be an amount equal to the value of the property at the time of the event.

[(5A) Where the event giving rise to a charge to tax under [subsection (3A)][4] above is a disposal on sale, and the sale—

(*a*) was not intended to confer any gratuitous benefit on any person, and

(*b*) was either a transaction at arm's length between persons not connected with each other or a transaction such as might be expected to be made at arm's length between persons not connected with each other,

the value of the property at the time of that event shall be taken for the purposes of subsection (5) above to be equal to the proceeds of the sale.][3]

(6) The rate at which tax is charged under [subsection (3A)][4] above shall be the aggregate of the following percentages—

(*a*) 0·25 per cent for each of the first forty complete successive quarters in the relevant period,

(*b*) 0·20 per cent for each of the next forty,

(*c*) 0·15 per cent for each of the next forty,

(*d*) 0·10 per cent for each of the next forty, and

(*e*) 0·05 per cent for each of the next forty.

[(7) In subsection (6) above "the relevant period" means the period given by subsection (7A) below or, if shorter, the period given by subsection (7B) below.][3]

[(7A) The period given by this subsection is the period beginning with the latest of—

(*a*) the day on which the settlement commenced,

(*b*) the date of the last ten-year anniversary of the settlement to fall before the day on which the property became comprised in the settlement,

(*c*) the date of the last ten-year anniversary of the settlement to fall before the [relevant ten-year anniversary][4], and

(*d*) 13th March 1975,

and ending with the day before the event giving rise to the charge.][3]

[(7B) The period given by this subsection is the period equal in length to the number of relevant-property days in the period—

(*a*) beginning with the day that is the latest of those referred to in paragraphs (*a*) to (*d*) of subsection (7A) above, and

(*b*) ending with the day before the event giving rise to the charge.][3]

[(7C) For the purposes of subsection (7B) above, a day is a "relevant-property day" if at any time on that day the property was relevant property.][3]

(8) Subsection (9) below shall have effect where—

(*a*) by virtue of [subsection (3A)][4] above, section 64 does not have effect in relation to property [by reference to the relevant ten-year anniversary of the settlement][4],

(*b*) on that anniversary a charge to tax falls to be made in respect of the settlement under section 64, and

(*c*) the property became comprised in the settlement . . . [4] within the period of ten years ending with that anniversary.

(9) In calculating the rate at which tax is charged under section 64 above, the value of the consideration given for the property on its becoming comprised in the settlement shall be treated for the purposes of section 66(5)(*b*) above as if it were an amount on which a charge to tax was imposed in respect of the settlement under section 65 above at the time of the property becoming so comprised.

[(9A) Subsection (9B) below applies where the same event gives rise—

(*a*) to a charge under [subsection (3A)][4] above in relation to any property, and

(*b*) to a charge under section 32 or 32A above in relation to that property.][3]

[(9B) If the amount of each of the charges is the same, each charge shall have effect as a charge for one half of the amount that would be charged apart from this subsection; otherwise, whichever of the charges is lower in amount shall have effect as if it were a charge the amount of which is nil.][3]

(10) In subsection (1) above, the reference to a conditionally exempt transfer of any property includes a reference to a transfer of value in relation to which the value of any property has been left out of account under the provisions of sections 31 to 34 of the Finance Act 1975 and, in relation to such property, the reference to a chargeable event includes a reference to an event on the occurrence of which tax becomes chargeable under Schedule 5 to this Act.

Commentary—*Simon's Taxes* **I7.531**.

HMRC Manuals—Inheritance Tax Manual IHTM42650 (other taxes and investigation: heritage).

Definitions—"Conditionally exempt transfer", s 30(2); "quarter", s 63; "relevant property", s 58(1); "settlement", s 43.

Cross references—See FA 1985 s 95 (transfer of Treasury functions under section 31 to the Commissioners of Inland Revenue from 25 July 1985).

Amendments—[1] Words in sub-s (3)(*b*) inserted by FA 1985 Sch 26 para 9 in relation to events after 18 March 1985.

[2] Words in sub-s (2) substituted by TCGA 1992 Sch 10 para 8(1), (3).

[3] Sub-s (5A), (9A), (9B) inserted, and sub-ss (7)–(7C) substituted for sub-s (7), by FA 2006 s 156, Sch 20 para 34 with effect from 19 July 2006.

[4] The following amendments made by F(No 2)A 2015 s 12(1)–(7) with effect in relation to occasions on which tax would (ignoring the effect of the amendments) fall to be charged under IHTA 1984 s 64 on or after 18 November 2015—

- in sub-s (3)—
  - words substituted;
  - in paras (*a*), (*b*), words substituted; and
  - words at end repealed;
- sub-ss(3)(*aa*), (3A) inserted; and
- in sub-ss (4), (5), (5A), (6), (7A)(*c*), (8)(*a*), (*c*), (9A)(*a*), words substituted;

[79A Variation of undertakings

(1) An undertaking given under section 78 or 79 above may be varied from time to time by agreement between the Board and the person bound by the undertaking.

(2) Where [the tribunal][2] is satisfied that—

(*a*) the Board have made a proposal for the variation of such an undertaking to the person bound by the undertaking,

(*b*) that person has failed to agree to the proposed variation within six months after the date on which the proposal was made, and

(*c*) it is just and reasonable, in all the circumstances, to require the proposed variation to be made,

[the tribunal may direct that the undertaking is to have effect from a specified date][2] as if the proposed variation had been agreed to by the person bound by the undertaking.

(3) The date specified by the [tribunal][2] must not be less than sixty days after the date of [the tribunal's direction][2].

(4) A direction under this section shall not take effect if, before the date specified by the [tribunal][2], a variation different from that to which the direction relates is agreed between the Board and the person bound by the undertaking.][1]

Commentary—*Simon's Taxes* **I7.508**.

Definitions—"the Board", "the Tribunal", s 272.

Amendments—[1] Inserted by FA 1998 Sch 25 para 8 with effect in relation to undertakings given on or after 31 July 1998.

[2] In sub-s (2), words substituted for words "a Special Commissioner" and "the Commissioner may direct that the undertaking is to have effect from a date specified by him" respectively, in sub-s (3), words substituted for words "Special Commissioner" and "his direction" respectively, and in sub-s (4) words substituted for word "Special Commissioner", by the Transfer of Tribunal Functions and Revenue and Customs Appeals Order, SI 2009/56 art 3, Sch 1 paras 108, 111 with effect from 1 April 2009.

Miscellaneous

80 Initial interest of settlor or spouse [or civil partner][1]

(1) Where a settlor or his spouse [or civil partner][1] is beneficially entitled to [a qualifying interest in possession][3] in property immediately after it becomes comprised in the settlement, the property shall for the purposes of this Chapter be treated as not having become comprised in the settlement on that occasion; but when the property or any part of it becomes held on trusts under which neither of those persons is beneficially entitled to [a qualifying interest in possession][3], the property or part shall for those purposes be treated as becoming comprised in a separate settlement made by that one of them who ceased (or last ceased) to be beneficially entitled to [a qualifying interest in possession][3] in it.

(2) References in subsection (1) above to the spouse [or civil partner][1] of a settlor include references to the widow or widower [or surviving civil partner][1] of a settlor.

(3) This section shall not apply if the occasion first referred to in subsection (1) above occurred before 27th March 1974.

[(4) Where the occasion first referred to in subsection (1) above occurs on or after 22nd March 2006, this section applies—

(*a*) as though for "[a qualifying interest in possession[3]]" in each place where that appears in subsection (1) above there were substituted "a postponing interest", and

(*b*) as though, for the purposes of that subsection, each of the following were a "postponing interest"—

(i) an immediate post-death interest;

(ii) a disabled person's interest.][2]

Commentary—*Simon's Taxes* **I5.452**.

HMRC Manuals—Inheritance Tax Manual IHTM27220 (foreign settled property with non-UK domiciled settlor). IHTM42231 (initial interest in possession of settlor or spouse).

Definitions—"Settlement", s 43; "settlor", s 44.

Amendments—[1] Words in heading and sub-ss (1), (2) inserted by Tax and Civil Partnership Regulations, SI 2005/3229, regs 3, 17 with effect from 5 December 2005 (reg 1(1)).

[2] Sub-s (4) inserted by FA 2006 s 156, Sch 20 paras 7, 23. This amendment is deemed to have come into force on 22 March 2006.

[3] Words in each place substituted for words "an interest in possession" by F(No 2)A 2015 s 13(1) with effect from 19 November 2015, subject to savings in F(No 2)A 2015 s 13(3)–(7).

81 Property moving between settlements

(1) Where property which ceases to be comprised in one settlement becomes comprised in another then, unless in the meantime any person becomes beneficially entitled to the property (and not merely to an interest in possession in the property), it shall for the purposes of this Chapter be treated as remaining comprised in the first settlement.

(2) Subsection (1) above shall not apply where the property ceased to be comprised in the first settlement before 10th December 1981; but where property ceased to be comprised in one settlement before 10th December 1981 and after 26th March 1974 and, by the same disposition, became comprised in another settlement, it shall for the purposes of this Chapter be treated as remaining comprised in the first settlement.

(3) Subsection (1) above shall not apply where a reversionary interest in the property expectant on the termination of a qualifying interest in possession subsisting under the first settlement was settled on the trusts of the other settlement before 10th December 1981.

Commentary—*Simon's Taxes* **I5.453, I5.454**.

HMRC Manuals—Inheritance Tax Manual IHTM27220 (foreign settled property with non-UK domiciled settlor). IHTM42229 (property moving from one trust to another).

Definitions—"qualifying interest in possession", s 59(1); "settlement", s 43.

[81A Reversionary interests in relevant property

(1) Where a reversionary interest in relevant property to which—

(*a*) a person who acquired it for a consideration in money or money's worth, or

(*b*) the settlor or the spouse or civil partner of the settlor,

(a "relevant reversioner") is beneficially entitled comes to an end by reason of the relevant reversioner becoming entitled to an interest in possession in the relevant property, the relevant reversioner is to be treated as having made a disposition of the reversionary interest at that time.

(2) A transfer of value of a reversionary interest in relevant property to which a relevant reversioner is beneficially entitled is to be taken to be a transfer which is not a potentially exempt transfer.][1]

Commentary—*Simon's Taxes* **I1.530, I3.120, I5.711, I3.114, I5.712, I3.319**.

Amendments—[1] This section inserted by FA 2010 s 52 with effect in relation to reversionary interests to which a relevant reversioner becomes beneficially entitled on or after 9 December 2009.

82 Excluded property

[(1) In a case where, apart from this section, property to which section 80 or 81 applies would be excluded property by virtue of section 48(3)(*a*) above, that property shall not be taken to be excluded property at any time ("the relevant time") for the purposes of this Chapter (except sections 78 and 79) unless Conditions A and B are satisfied.][1]

(2) Section 65(8) above shall not have effect in relation to property to which section 80 or 81 above applies unless [Condition A][1] is satisfied (in addition to the condition in section 65(8) that the settlor was not domiciled in the United Kingdom when the settlement was made).

(3) [Condition A][1] referred to in subsections (1) and (2) above is—

(*a*) in the case of property to which section 80 above applies, that the person who is the settlor in relation to the settlement first mentioned in that section, and

(*b*) in the case of property to which subsection (1) or (2) of section 81 above applies, that the person who is the settlor in relation to the second of the settlements mentioned in the subsection concerned,

was not domiciled in the United Kingdom when that settlement was made.

[(4) Condition B referred to in subsection (1) above is—

(*a*) in the case of property to which section 80 above applies, that the person who is the settlor in relation to the settlement first mentioned in that section, and

(*b*) in the case of property to which subsection (1) or (2) of section 81 above applies, that the person who is the settlor in relation to the first or second of the settlements mentioned in that subsection,

was not a formerly domiciled resident for the tax year in which the relevant time falls.][1]

Commentary—*Simon's Taxes* **I5.452, I5.453**.

Definitions—"Excluded property", s 272.

Amendments–[1] Sub-s (1) substituted, in sub-s (2), words substituted for words "the condition in subsection (3) below", in sub-s (3), words substituted for words "The condition", and sub-s (4) inserted, by F(No 2)A 2017 s 30(7) with effect in relation to times after 5 April 2017, subject to transitional provisions in F(No 2)A 2017 s 30(10)–(12). Sub-s (1) previously read as follows—

"(1) For the purposes of this Chapter (except sections 78 and 79) property to which section 80 or 81 above applies shall not be taken to be excluded property by virtue of section 48(3)(*a*) above unless the condition in subsection (3) below is satisfied (in addition to the conditions in section 48(3) that the property is situated outside the United Kingdom and that the settlor was not domiciled there when the settlement was made).".

83 Property becoming settled on a death

Property which becomes comprised in a settlement in pursuance of a will or intestacy shall for the purposes of this Chapter be taken to have become comprised in it on the death of the testator or intestate (whether it occurred before or after the passing of this Act).

Commentary—*Simon's Taxes* **I5.161, I5.321**.
HMRC Manuals—Inheritance Tax Manual IHTM42221 (the settlement: starting date).

84 Income applied for charitable purposes

For the purposes of this Chapter (except sections 78 and 79) where the trusts on which settled property is held require part of the income of the property to be applied for charitable purposes, a corresponding part of the settled property shall be regarded as held for charitable purposes.

Commentary—*Simon's Taxes* **I5.641, I5.642**.
Definitions—"Charitable", s 272.

85 Credit for annual charges under Finance Act 1975

Any tax charged under paragraph 12(2) of Schedule 5 to the Finance Act 1975 and not already allowed as a credit under paragraph 12(3) of that Schedule or under section 125 of the Finance Act 1982 or under this section shall be allowed as a credit against tax chargeable under this Chapter (apart from section 79) in respect of the settled property or part concerned.

Commentary—*Simon's Taxes* **I5.451**.

CHAPTER IV

MISCELLANEOUS

86 Trusts for benefit of employees

(1) Where settled property is held on trusts which, either indefinitely or until the end of a period (whether defined by a date or in some other way) do not permit any of the settled property to be applied otherwise than for the benefit of—

(*a*) persons of a class defined by reference to employment in a particular trade or profession, or employment by, or office with, a body carrying on a trade, profession or undertaking, or

(*b*) persons of a class defined by reference to marriage [to or civil partnership with,][4] or relationship to, or dependence on, persons of a class defined as mentioned in paragraph (*a*) above,

then, subject to subsection (3) below, this section applies to that settled property or, as the case may be, applies to it during that period.

(2) Where settled property is held on trusts permitting the property to be applied for the benefit of persons within paragraph (*a*) or (*b*) of subsection (1) above, those trusts shall not be regarded as outside the description specified in that subsection by reason only that they also permit the settled property to be applied for charitable purposes.

(3) Where any class mentioned in subsection (1) above is defined by reference to employment by or office with a particular body, this section applies to the settled property only if—

(*a*) the class comprises all or most of the persons employed by or holding office with the body concerned, or

(*b*) the trusts on which the settled property is held are those of a profit sharing scheme approved in accordance with Schedule 9 to the [Taxes Act 1988][1][, or

(*c*) the trusts on which the settled property is held are those of [a share incentive plan approved under Schedule 2 to the Income Tax (Earnings and Pensions) Act 2003][3]][2][, or

(*d*) the settled property consists of or includes ordinary share capital of a company which meets the trading requirement and the trusts on which the settled property is held are those of a settlement which—

(i) meets the controlling interest requirement with respect to the company, and

(ii) meets the all-employee benefit requirement with respect to the company.][5]

[(3A) For the purpose of determining whether subsection (3)(*d*) is satisfied in relation to settled property which consists of or includes ordinary share capital of a company—

(*a*) section 236I of the 1992 Act applies to determine whether the company meets the trading requirement (with references to "C" being read as references to that company),

(*b*) sections 236J, 236K, 236M and 236T (but not 236L) of the 1992 Act apply to determine whether the settlement meets the all-employee benefit requirement and the controlling interest requirement (with references in those sections to "C" being read as references to that company), and (*c*) "ordinary share capital" has the meaning given by section 1119 of the Corporation Tax Act 2010.][5]

(4) Where this section applies to any settled property—

(*a*) the property shall be treated as comprised in one settlement, whether or not it would fall to be so treated apart from this section, and

(*b*) an interest in possession in any part of the settled property shall be disregarded for the purposes of this Act (except section 55) if that part is less than 5 per cent of the whole.

(5) Where any property to which this section applies ceases to be comprised in a settlement and, either immediately or not more than one month later, the whole of it becomes comprised in another settlement, then, if this section again applies to it when it becomes comprised in the second settlement, it shall be treated for all the purposes of this Act as if it had remained comprised in the first settlement.

Commentary—*Simon's Taxes* **I5.630, I5.631**.
HMRC Manuals—IHTM42901 (introduction to employee benefit trusts).
IHTM42911–42915 (conditions for relief).
IHTM42915 ("all or most" test).
IHTM42921–42937 (powers of the trust).
IHTM42940 (approved profit sharing schemes).
IHTM42945–42951 (inheritance tax operation).
IHTM42960 and 42961 (dispositions by an individual).
IHTM42971–42976 (dispositions to a trust for employees by a close company).
IHTM42981–42988 (property leaving employee benefit trusts).
IHTM42990–42991 (associated issues).
Statement of Practice E11—Employee trusts.
Definitions—"Charitable", s 272; "settled property", s 43.
Note—TA 1988 Sch 9 (referred to in sub-s (3)(*b*) above) was rewritten to ITEPA 2003 Schs 3, 4).
Amendments—[1] Words in sub-s (3)(*b*) substituted by TA 1988 Sch 29 para 32 Table.
[2] Sub-s (3)(*c*) and word "or" immediately preceding it inserted by FA 2000 s 138(1), (4), with effect from 28 July 2000.
[3] In sub-s (3)(*c*), words substituted for the words "an employee share ownership plan approved under Schedule 8 to the Finance Act 2000" by ITEPA 2003 s 722, Sch 6 paras 150, 151(1)(*c*), (2) with effect, for income tax purposes, from 2003–04; and for corporation tax purposes, for accounting periods ending after 5 April 2003. For transitional provisions and savings see ITEPA 2003 s 723, Sch 7.
[4] Words in sub-s (1)(*b*) inserted by Tax and Civil Partnership Regulations, SI 2005/3229, regs 3, 18, with effect from 5 December 2005 (reg 1(1)).
[5] Sub-ss (3)(*d*) and preceding word, (3A) inserted by FA 2014 s 290, Sch 37 paras 9, 15. This amendment is treated as having come into force on 6 April 2014.

87 Newspaper trusts

(1) In relation to property comprised in a settlement to which this section applies, section 86 above shall have effect as if newspaper publishing companies were included among the persons within paragraphs (*a*) and (*b*) of subsection (1) of that section.

(2) This section applies to a settlement if shares in a newspaper publishing company or a newspaper holding company are the only or principal property comprised in the settlement.

(3) In this section—

"newspaper publishing company" means a company whose business consists wholly or mainly in the publication of newspapers in the United Kingdom;

"newspaper holding company" means a company which—

(*a*) has as its only or principal asset shares in a newspaper publishing company, and

(*b*) has powers of voting on all or most questions affecting the publishing company as a whole which if exercised would yield a majority of the votes capable of being exercised on them;

and for the purposes of this section shares shall be treated as the principal property comprised in a settlement or the principal asset of a company if the remaining property comprised in the settlement or the remaining assets of the company are such as may be reasonably required to enable the trustees or the company to secure the operation of the newspaper publishing company concerned.

Commentary—*Simon's Taxes* **I5.648**.
HMRC Manuals—Inheritance Tax Manual IHTM42801 and 42802 (special trusts and flat rate charge).
IHTM42806 (newspaper trusts).
IHTM42990 (relationship with employee benefit trusts).

88 Protective trusts

(1) This section applies to settled property (other than property to which section 73 above applies) which is held on trusts to the like effect as those specified in section 33(1) of the Trustee Act 1925; and in this section "the principal beneficiary" and "the trust period" have the same meanings as in that section.

(2) For the purposes of this Act—

(*a*) there shall be disregarded the failure or determination, before the end of the trust period, of trusts to the like effect as those specified in paragraph (i) of the said section 33(1), and (*b*) the principal beneficiary shall be treated as beneficially entitled to an interest in possession in any property which is for the time being held on trusts to the like effect as those specified in paragraph (ii) of the said section 33(1).

[(3) Where—

(*a*) settled property became held before 22nd March 2006 on trusts to the like effect as those specified in section 33(1)(i) of the Trustee Act 1925, and

(*b*) as a result of the failure or determination of those trusts on or after 22nd March 2006, the principal beneficiary is treated by subsection (2)(*b*) above as beneficially entitled to an interest in possession,

this Act shall apply in relation to that interest in possession as if the principal beneficiary became beneficially entitled to that interest in possession before 22nd March 2006.][1]

[(4) Subsection (5) below applies where—

(*a*) settled property becomes held on or after 22nd March 2006 on trusts to the like effect as those specified in section 33(1)(i) of the Trustee Act 1925,

(*b*) the interest of the principal beneficiary under those trusts is—

(i) an immediate post-death interest,

(ii) a disabled person's interest within section 89B(1)(*c*) or (*d*) below, or

(iii) a transitional serial interest, and

(*c*) as a result of the failure or determination of those trusts, the principal beneficiary is treated by subsection (2)(*b*) above as beneficially entitled to an interest in possession.][1]

[(5) This Act shall apply—

(*a*) as if that interest in possession were a continuation of the immediate post-death interest, disabled person's interest or transitional serial interest, and

(*b*) as if the immediate post-death interest, or disabled person's interest or transitional serial interest, had not come to an end on the failure or determination of the trusts.][1]

[(6) Subsection (2) above does not apply in a case where—

(*a*) settled property becomes held on or after 22nd March 2006 on trusts to the like effect as those specified in section 33(1)(i) of the Trustee Act 1925, and

(*b*) the interest of the principal beneficiary under those trusts is—

(i) not an immediate post-death interest,

(ii) not a disabled person's interest within section 89B(1)(*c*) or (*d*) below, and

(iii) not a transitional serial interest.][1]

Commentary—*Simon's Taxes* **I5.621-I5.622.**
HMRC Manuals—Inheritance Tax Manual IHTM42801 and 42802 (special trusts and flat rate charge).
IHTM42804 (protective trusts).
Statement of Practice E7—Protective trusts.
Definitions—"Settled property", s 43.
Simon's Tax Cases—*Cholmondeley v IRC* [1986] STC 384*.
Amendments—[1] Sub-ss (3)–(6) inserted by FA 2006 s 156, Sch 20 paras 7, 24. This amendment is deemed to have come into force on 22 March 2006.

89 Trusts for disabled persons

(1) This section applies to settled property transferred into settlement after 9th March 1981 and held on trusts—

(*a*) under which, during the life of a disabled person, no interest in possession in the settled property subsists, and

[(*b*) which secure that, if any of the settled property or income arising from it is applied during the disabled person's life for the benefit of a beneficiary, it is applied for the benefit of the disabled person.][1]

(2) For the purposes of this Act the person mentioned in subsection (1) above shall be treated as beneficially entitled to an interest in possession in the settled property.

[(3) The trusts on which the settled property is held are not to be treated as falling outside subsection (1) by reason only of—

(*a*) the trustees' having powers that enable them to apply otherwise than for the benefit of the disabled person amounts (whether consisting of income or capital, or both) not exceeding the annual limit,

(*b*) the trustees' having the powers conferred by section 32 of the Trustee Act 1925 (powers of advancement),

(*c*) the trustees' having those powers but free from, or subject to a less restrictive limitation than, the limitation imposed by proviso (*a*) of subsection (1) of that section,

(*d*) the trustees' having the powers conferred by section 33 of the Trustee Act (Northern Ireland) 1958 (corresponding provision for Northern Ireland),

(*e*) the trustees' having those powers but free from, or subject to a less restrictive limitation than, the limitation imposed by subsection (1)(*a*) of that section, or

(*f*) the trustees' having powers to the like effect as the powers mentioned in any of paragraphs (*b*) to (*e*).

(3A) For the purposes of this section, the "annual limit" is whichever is the lower of the following amounts—

(*a*) £3,000, and

(*b*) 3% of the amount that is the maximum value of the settled property during the period in question.

(3B) For those purposes the annual limit applies in relation to each period of 12 months that begins on 6 April.

(3C) The Treasury may by order made by statutory instrument—

(*a*) specify circumstances in which subsection (3)(*a*) is, or is not, to apply in relation to a trust, and

(*b*) amend the definition of "the annual limit" in subsection (3A).

(3D) An order under subsection (3C) may—

(*a*) make different provision for different cases, and

(*b*) contain transitional and saving provision.

(3E) A statutory instrument containing an order under subsection (3C) may not be made unless a draft of the instrument has been laid before, and approved by a resolution of, the House of Commons.][1]

(4) The reference in subsection (1) above to a disabled person is, in relation to any settled property, a reference to a person who, when the property was transferred into settlement, [was a disabled person.][1]

[(4A) In this section "disabled person" has the meaning given by Schedule 1A to the Finance Act 2005.][1]

Commentary—*Simon's Taxes* **I5.207**.

HMRC Manuals—Inheritance Tax Manual IHTM42801 and 42802 (special trusts and flat rate charge).
IHTM42805 (trusts for disabled persons).
IHTM04102 (settled property: charges on trusts for disabled persons).
Capital Gains Manual CG36543 (2006 IHT changes: IHT treatment trusts for the disabled).

Definitions—"Settled property", s 43; "trustee", s 45.

Amendments—[1] Sub-s (1)(*b*) substituted, sub-ss (3)–(3E) substituted for previous sub-s (3), words in sub-s (4) substituted, and sub-s (4A) substituted for previous sub-ss (5), (6), by FA 2013 s 216, Sch 44 paras 1, 6 with effect in relation to property transferred into settlement on or after 8 April 2013. These amendments do not prevent property transferred into a relevant settlement on or after 8 April 2013 from being property to which IHTA 1984 s 89 or 89A applies (FA 2013 Sch 44 para 9(2)).

[89A Self-settlement by person [expected to fall within the definition of "disabled person"]

(1) This section applies to property transferred by a person ("A") into settlement on or after 22nd March 2006 if—

(*a*) A was beneficially entitled to the property immediately before transferring it into settlement,

(*b*) A satisfies the Commissioners for Her Majesty's Revenue and Customs that, when the property was transferred into settlement, A had a condition that it was at that time reasonable to expect would have such effects on A as to lead to A becoming [a person falling within any paragraph of the definition of "disabled person" in paragraph 1 of Schedule 1A to the Finance Act 2005,][2] and

(*c*) the property is held on trusts—

(i) under which, during the life of A, no interest in possession in the settled property subsists, and

(ii) which secure that Conditions 1 and 2 are met.

(2) Condition 1 is that if any of the settled property [or income arising from it][2] is applied during A's life for the benefit of a beneficiary, it is applied for the benefit of A.

(3) Condition 2 is that any power to bring the trusts mentioned in subsection (1)(*c*) above to an end during A's life is such that, in the event of the power being exercised during A's life, either—

(*a*) A or another person will, on the trusts being brought to an end, be absolutely entitled to the settled property, or

(*b*) on the trusts being brought to an end, a disabled person's interest within section 89B(1)(*a*) or (*c*) below will subsist in the settled property.

(4) If this section applies to settled property transferred into settlement by a person, the person shall be treated as beneficially entitled to an interest in possession in the settled property.

[(5) For the purposes of subsection (1)(*b*), assume—

(*a*) that A will meet any conditions as to residence or presence that are required to establish entitlement to the allowance, payment or increased pension in question,

(*b*) that there will be no provision made by regulations under any of the following—

(i) sections 67(1) and (2), 72(8), 104(3) and 113(2) of SSCBA 1992,

(ii) sections 67(1) and (2), 72(8), 104(3) and 113(2) of SSCB(NI)A 1992, and

(iii) sections 85 and 86 of WRA 2012 and the corresponding provision having effect in Northern Ireland, and

(*c*) that A will not be prevented from receiving the allowance, payment or increased pension in question by any of the following—

(i) section 113(1) of SSCBA 1992,
(ii) section 113(1) of SSCB(NI)A 1992,
(iii) section 87 of WRA 2012 and the corresponding provision having effect in Northern Ireland,
(iv) articles 61 and 64 of the Personal Injuries (Civilians) Scheme 1983 (S.I. 1983/686),
(v) article 53 of the Naval, Military and Air Forces etc.(Disablement and Death) Service Pensions Order 2006 (S.I. 2006/606), and
(vi) article 42 of the Armed Forces and Reserve Forces (Compensation Scheme) Order 2011 (S.I. 2011/517).][2]

[(6A) The trusts on which the settled property is held are not to be treated as falling outside subsection (2) by reason only of—

(*a*) the trustees' having powers that enable them to apply otherwise than for the benefit of the disabled person amounts (whether consisting of income or capital, or both) not exceeding the annual limit,
(*b*) the trustees' having the powers conferred by section 32 of the Trustee Act 1925 (powers of advancement),
(*c*) the trustees' having those powers but free from, or subject to a less restrictive limitation than, the limitation imposed by proviso (*a*) of subsection (1) of that section,
(*d*) the trustees' having the powers conferred by section 33 of the Trustee Act (Northern Ireland) 1958 (corresponding provision for Northern Ireland),
(*e*) the trustees' having those powers but free from, or subject to a less restrictive limitation than, the limitation imposed by subsection (1)(*a*) of that section, or
(*f*) the trustees' having powers to the like effect as the powers mentioned in any of paragraphs (*b*) to (*e*).

(6B) For the purposes of this section, the "annual limit" is whichever is the lower of the following amounts—

(*a*) £3,000, and
(*b*) 3% of the amount that is the maximum value of the settled property during the period in question.

(6C) For those purposes the annual limit applies in relation to each period of 12 months that begins on 6 April.

(6D) The Treasury may by order made by statutory instrument—

(*a*) specify circumstances in which subsection (6A)(*a*) is, or is not, to apply in relation to a trust, and
(*b*) amend the definition of "the annual limit" in subsection (6B).

(6E) An order under subsection (6D) may—

(*a*) make different provision for different cases, and
(*b*) contain transitional and saving provision.

(6F) A statutory instrument containing an order under subsection (6D) may not be made unless a draft of the instrument has been laid before, and approved by a resolution of, the House of Commons.][2]

(7) For the purposes of subsection (3) above, ignore—

(*a*) power to give directions as to the settled property that is exercisable jointly by the persons who between them are entitled to the entire beneficial interest in the property, and
(*b*) anything that could occur as a result of exercise of any such power.

[(8) In this section—

"SSCBA 1992" means the Social Security Contributions and Benefits Act 1992,
"SSCB(NI)A 1992" means the Social Security Contributions and Benefits (Northern Ireland) Act 1992, and
"WRA 2012" means the Welfare Reform Act 2012.][2][1]

Commentary—*Simon's Taxes* **I5.207**.
HMRC Manuals—Capital Gains Manual CG36543 (2006 IHT changes: IHT treatment trusts for the disabled).
Inheritance Tax Manual IHTM42805 (special trusts: trusts for disabled persons).
Amendments—[1] Sections 89A, 89B inserted by FA 2006 s 156, Sch 20 para 6(1), (3). This amendment is deemed to have come into force on 22 March 2006.
[2] Words in heading substituted for words "with condition expected to lead to disability", words in sub-s (1)(*b*) substituted, words in sub-s (2) inserted, sub-s (5) substituted for previous sub-ss (5), (6), sub-ss (6A)–(6F) inserted, and sub-s (8) substituted, by FA 2013 s 216, Sch 44 paras 1, 7 with effect in relation to property transferred into settlement on or after 8 April 2013. These amendments do not prevent property transferred into a relevant settlement on or after 8 April 2013 from being property to which IHTA 1984 s 89 or 89A applies (FA 2013 Sch 44 para 9(2)).

[89B Meaning of "disabled person's interest"

(1) In this Act "disabled person's interest" means—

(*a*) an interest in possession to which a person is under section 89(2) above treated as beneficially entitled,
(*b*) an interest in possession to which a person is under section 89A(4) above treated as beneficially entitled,

(*c*) an interest in possession in settled property (other than an interest within paragraph (*a*) or (*b*) above) to which a disabled person becomes beneficially entitled on or after 22nd March 2006 [if the trusts on which the settled property is held secure that, if any of the settled property is applied during the disabled person's life for the benefit of a beneficiary, it is applied for the benefit of the disabled person][3], or

(*d*) an interest in possession in settled property (other than an interest within paragraph (*a*) or (*b*) above) to which a person ("A") is beneficially entitled if—

(i) A is the settlor,

(ii) A was beneficially entitled to the property immediately before transferring it into settlement,

(iii) A satisfies Her Majesty's Commissioners for Revenue and Customs as mentioned in section 89A(1)(*b*) above,

(iv) the settled property was transferred into settlement on or after 22nd March 2006, and

(v) the trusts on which the settled property is held secure that, if any of the settled property is applied during A's life for the benefit of a beneficiary, it is applied for the benefit of A.

[(2) In subsection (1)(*c*) "disabled person" has the meaning given by Schedule 1A to the Finance Act 2005.][2]

[(2A) Where the income arising from the settled property is held on trusts of the kind described in section 33 of the Trustee Act 1925 (protective trusts), subsection (1)(*d*)(v) has effect as if for "A's life" there were substituted "the period during which the income from the property is held on trust for A".][2]

(3) Section 71D above does not apply to property in which there subsists a disabled person's interest within subsection (1)(*c*) above (but see also section 71D(5) above).][1]

Commentary—*Simon's Taxes* **I5.207**.

HMRC Manuals—Inheritance Tax Manual IHTM16061 (introduction to interests in possession: finance act 2006 and the new trust regime - disabled person's interest).

IHTM42805 (special trusts: trusts for the disabled persons).

Capital Gains Manual C36543 (2006 IHT changes: IHT treatment trusts for the disabled).

Amendments—[1] Sections 89A, 89B inserted by FA 2006 s 156, Sch 20 para 6(1), (3). This amendment is deemed to have come into force on 22 March 2006.

[2] Sub-s (2) substituted, and sub-s (2A) inserted, by FA 2013 s 216, Sch 44 paras 1, 8 with effect in relation to property transferred into settlement on or after 8 April 2013. These amendments do not prevent property transferred into a relevant settlement on or after 8 April 2013 from being property to which IHTA 1984 s 89 or 89A applies (FA 2013 Sch 44 para 9(2)).

[3] Words in sub-s (1)(*c*) inserted by FA 2013 s 216, Sch 44 paras 1, 10(1) with effect in relation to property transferred into settlement on or after 17 July 2013, subject to FA 2013 Sch 44 para 10(4), (5).

[89C Disabled person's interest: powers of advancement etc

(1) The trusts on which settled property is held are not to be treated for the purposes of section 89B(1)(*c*) or (*d*) (meaning of "disabled person's interest": cases involving an interest in possession) as failing to secure that the settled property is applied for the benefit of a beneficiary by reason only of—

(*a*) the trustees' having powers that enable them to apply otherwise than for the benefit of the beneficiary amounts (whether consisting of income or capital, or both) not exceeding the annual limit,

(*b*) the trustees' having the powers conferred by section 32 of the Trustee Act 1925 (powers of advancement),

(*c*) the trustees' having those powers but free from, or subject to a less restrictive limitation than, the limitation imposed by proviso (*a*) of subsection (1) of that section,

(*d*) the trustees' having the powers conferred by section 33 of the Trustee Act (Northern Ireland) 1958 (corresponding 45 provision for Northern Ireland),

(*e*) the trustees' having those powers but free from, or subject to a less restrictive limitation than, the limitation imposed by subsection (1)(*a*) of that section, or

(*f*) the trustees' having powers to the like effect as the powers mentioned in any of paragraphs (*b*) to (*e*).

(2) For the purposes of this section, the "annual limit" is whichever is the lower of the following amounts—

(*a*) £3,000, and

(*b*) 3% of the amount that is the maximum value of the settled property during the period in question.

(3) For those purposes the annual limit applies in relation to each period of 12 months that begins on 6 April.

(4) The Treasury may by order made by statutory instrument—

(*a*) specify circumstances in which subsection (1)(*a*) is, or is not, to apply in relation to a trust, and

(*b*) amend the definition of "the annual limit" in subsection (2).

(5) An order under subsection (4) may—

(*a*) make different provision for different cases, and

(*b*) contain transitional and saving provision.

(6) A statutory instrument containing an order under subsection (4) may not be made unless a draft of the instrument has been laid before, and approved by a resolution of, the House of Commons.][1]

Commentary—*Simon's Taxes* **I5.207**.

Amendments—[1] This section inserted by FA 2013 s 216, Sch 44 paras 1, 10(2) with effect in relation to property transferred into settlement on or after 17 July 2013, subject to FA 2013 Sch 44 para 10(4), (5).

90 Trustees' annuities, etc

Where under the terms of a settlement a person is entitled by way of remuneration for his services as trustee to an interest in possession in property comprised in the settlement, then, except to the extent that the interest represents more than a reasonable amount of remuneration—

(*a*) the interest shall be left out of account in determining for the purposes of this Act the value of his estate immediately before his death, and

(*b*) tax shall not be charged under section 52 above when the interest comes to an end.

Commentary—*Simon's Taxes* **I4.132, I5.214, I5.256**.

HMRC Manuals—Inheritance Tax Manual IHTM04410 (property excluded from charge: value left out of account: interest in possession as remuneration for services as trustee).

IHTM16221 (interest in possession for services as trustee).

Definitions—"Settlement", s 43; "trustee", s 45.

91 Administration period

(1) Where a person would have been entitled to an interest in possession in the whole or part of the residue of the estate of a deceased person had the administration of that estate been completed, the same consequences shall follow under this Act as if he had become entitled to an interest in possession in the unadministered estate and in the property (if any) representing ascertained residue, or in a corresponding part of it, on the date as from which the whole or part of the income of the residue would have been attributable to his interest had the residue been ascertained immediately after the death of the deceased person.

(2) In this section—

(*a*) "unadministered estate" means all the property for the time being held by personal representatives as such, excluding property devolving on them otherwise than as assets for the payment of debts and excluding property that is the subject of a specific disposition, and making due allowance for outstanding charges on residue and for any adjustments between capital and income remaining to be made in due course of administration;

(*b*) "ascertained residue" means property which, having ceased to be held by the personal representatives as such, is held as part of the residue;

[(*c*) subject to subsection (3) below, "charges on residue" means, in relation to the estate of a deceased person, the following liabilities properly payable out of the estate and interest payable in respect of those liabilities—

(i) funeral, testamentary and administration expenses and debts,

(ii) general legacies, demonstrative legacies, annuities and any sum payable out of the residue of the estate to which a person is entitled under the law of intestacy of any part of the United Kingdom or any other country, and

(iii) any other liabilities of the deceased person's personal representatives as such,

(*d*) "specific disposition" has the meaning given in section 947(6) of the Corporation Tax Act 2009, and

(*e*) the reference to the completion of the administration of the estate shall be construed as if it were in Chapter 3 of Part 10 of that Act.][1]

[(3) If, as between—

(*a*) persons interested under a specific disposition or in a general or demonstrative legacy or in an annuity, and

(*b*) persons interested in the residue of an estate,

any such liabilities as are mentioned in paragraph (c) of subsection (2) above fall exclusively or primarily on the property that is the subject of the specific disposition or on the legacy or annuity, only such part (if any) of those liabilities as falls ultimately on the residue shall be treated as charges on residue.

(4) In the application of this section to Scotland, "charges on residue" shall include, in addition to the liabilities specified in subsection (2)(*c*), any sums required to meet—

(*a*) claims in respect of prior rights or legal rights by a surviving spouse or civil partner, or

(*b*) claims in respect of legal rights by children.][1]

Commentary—*Simon's Taxes* **I5.161, I5.162, I5.164, I9.434**.

HMRC Manuals—Inheritance Tax Manual IHTM16220 (rights in residue of an unadministered estate).

IHTM22031 (interest in unadministered estate).

IHTM27263 (exempt securities in unadministered estates).

Note—See TA 1988 s 701(5) meaning of specific disposition; s 701(6) meaning of charges on residue (s 702 as regards application in Scotland).

Amendments—[1] Sub-s (2)(*c*)–(*e*) substituted for previous sub-s (2)(*c*), and sub-ss (3), (4) inserted, by CTA 2009 s 1322, Sch 1 paras 315, 316. CTA 2009 applies for accounting periods ending on or after 1 April 2009 (for corporation tax purposes) and for tax years 2009–10 onwards (for income and capital gains tax purposes).

92 Survivorship clauses

(1) Where under the terms of a will or otherwise property is held for any person on condition that he survives another for a specified period of not more than six months, this Act shall apply as if the dispositions taking effect at the end of the period or, if he does not survive until then, on his death (including any such disposition which has effect by operation of law or is a separate disposition of the income from the property) had had effect from the beginning of the period.

(2) Subsection (1) above does not affect the application of this Act in relation to any distribution or application of property occurring before the dispositions there mentioned take effect.

Commentary—*Simon's Taxes* **I4.453, I5.264, I5.340, I12.1131**.
HMRC Manuals—Inheritance Tax Manual IHTM16110 (survivorship clauses in a will).

93 Disclaimers

Where a person becomes entitled to an interest in settled property but disclaims the interest, then, if the disclaimer is not made for a consideration in money or money's worth, this Act shall apply as if he had not become entitled to the interest.

Commentary—*Simon's Taxes* **I5.254, I4.416**.
HMRC Manuals—Inheritance Tax Manual IHTM16137 (has someone taken up the right of occupation?).
IHTM16180 (disclaimers of interests in settled property).
IHTM35165 (disclaimer relating to an interest in settled property).
IHTM16180 (disclaimers).
Definitions—"Settled property", s 43.

PART IV
CLOSE COMPANIES

Statement of Practice E15—Close companies—group transfers.

Transfers by close companies

94 Charge on participators

(1) Subject to the following provisions of this Part of this Act, where a close company makes a transfer of value, tax shall be charged as if each individual to whom an amount is apportioned under this section had made a transfer of value of such amount as after deduction of tax (if any) would be equal to the amount so apportioned, less the amount (if any) by which the value of his estate is more than it would be but for the company's transfer; but for this purpose his estate shall be treated as not including any rights or interests in the company.

(2) For the purposes of subsection (1) above the value transferred by the company's transfer of value shall be apportioned among the participators according to their respective rights and interests in the company immediately before the transfer, and any amount so apportioned to a close company shall be further apportioned among its participators, and so on; but—

(*a*) so much of that value as is attributable to any payment or transfer of assets to any person which falls to be taken into account in computing that person's profits or gains or losses for the purposes of income tax or corporation tax (or would fall to be so taken into account but for [section 1285 of the Corporation Tax Act 2009 (exemption for UK company distributions)][2] shall not be apportioned, and

(*b*) if any amount which would otherwise be apportioned to an individual who is domiciled outside the United Kingdom is attributable to the value of any property outside the United Kingdom, that amount shall not be apportioned.

(3) In determining for the purposes of this section whether a disposition made by a close company is a transfer of value or what value is transferred by such a transfer no account shall be taken of the surrender by the company, in pursuance of section [240 or 402 of the Taxes Act 1988][1], of any relief or of the benefit of any amount of advance corporation tax paid by it.

(4) Where the amount apportioned to a person under this section is 5 per cent or less of the value transferred by the company's transfer of value then, notwithstanding section 3(4) above, tax chargeable under subsection (1) above shall be left out of account in determining, with respect to any time after the company's transfer, what previous transfers of value he has made.

(5) References in section 19 above to transfers of value made by a transferor and to the values transferred by them (calculated as there mentioned) shall be treated as including references to apportionments made to a person under this section and to the amounts for the tax on which (if charged) he would be liable.

Commentary—*Simon's Taxes* **I6.121–I6.125, I6.128**.
HMRC Manuals—Inheritance Tax Manual IHTM14851–14853 (transfers by close companies and exemptions).
IHTM14854 (foreign aspects).
IHTM04068 (transfer of value by a close company).
Statement of Practice E15—Close companies: group transfers.
Definitions—"close company", s 102(1); "estate" s 272; "participator", s 102(1).
Amendments—[1] Words in sub-s (3) substituted by TA 1988 Sch 29 para 32 Table.

2 In sub-s (2)(*a*), words substituted for words "section 208 of the Taxes Act 1988", by CTA 2009 s 1322, Sch 1 paras 315, 317. CTA 2009 applies for accounting periods ending on or after 1 April 2009 (for corporation tax purposes) and for tax years 2009–10 onwards (for income and capital gains tax purposes).

95 Participator in two companies

(1) Where—

(*a*) the value of the estate of a company ("the transferee company") is increased as the result of a transfer of value made by a close company ("the transferor company"), and

(*b*) an individual to whom part of the value transferred is apportioned under section 94 above has an interest in the transferee company (or in a company which is a participator of the transferee company or any of its participators, and so on),

subsection (2) below shall apply to the computation, for the purposes of section 94 above, of the amount to be offset, that is to say, the amount by which the value of his estate is more than it would be but for the transfer.

(2) Where this subsection applies—

(*a*) the increase in the value of the transferee company's estate shall be taken to be such part of the value transferred as accounts for the increase, and

(*b*) the increase so computed shall be apportioned among the transferee company's participators according to their respective rights and interests in the company immediately before the transfer (and, where necessary, further apportioned among their participators, and so on),

and the amount so apportioned to the individual shall be taken to be the amount to be offset.

Commentary—*Simon's Taxes* **I6.126, I6.127**.

Definitions—"Estate", s 272; "close company", "participator", s 102(1).

96 Preference shares disregarded

Where part of a close company's share capital consists of preference shares (within the meaning of [section 1023(5) of the Corporation Tax Act 2010][1] and a transfer of value made by that or any other close company has only a small effect on the value of those shares, compared with its effect on the value of other parts of the company's share capital, the preference shares shall be left out of account in determining the respective rights and interests of the participators for the purposes of sections 94 and 95 above.

Commentary—*Simon's Taxes* **I6.124**.

Definitions—"Close company", "participator", s 102(1).

Amendments—[1] Words substituted for words "section 210(4) of the Taxes Act 1988" by CTA 2010 s 1177, Sch 1 para 190. CTA 2010 has effect for corporation tax purposes for accounting periods ending on or after 1 April 2010, and for income and capital gains tax purposes for the tax year 2010–11 and subsequent tax years.

97 Transfers within group, etc

(1) Where a close company ("the transferor company") is a member, but not the [principal company][1], of a group and—

[(*a*) there is—

(i) a disposal of an asset by the transferor company, which is a disposal to which section 171(1) of the 1992 Act applies, or

(ii) by virtue of an election under section 171A(2) of that Act, a deemed transfer by the transferor company to another member of the group,][3] . . . [5]

(iii) . . . [5]

[(*aa*) the disposal is also, or [the election][4] gives rise to, a transfer of value, and][3]

(*b*) the transfer of value has only a small effect on the value of the minority participators' rights and interests in that company compared with its effect on the value of the other participators' rights and interests in the company,

the rights and interests of the minority participators shall be left out of account in determining the respective rights and interests of the transferor company's participators for the purpose of apportioning the value transferred under section 94 above.

(2) For the purposes of subsection (1) above—

[(*a*) section [170 of the 1992 Act][2] (groups of companies: definitions) applies as for the purposes of sections [171 to 181][2] of that Act][1], and

(*b*) a minority participator is a participator of the transferor company who is not, and is not a person connected with, a participator of the [principal company][1] of the group or of any of the [principal company's][1] participators;

. . . [1]

Commentary—*Simon's Taxes* **I6.124**.

HMRC Manuals—Inheritance Tax Manual IHTM04068 (transfer of value by a close company).

Statement of Practice E15—Close companies—group transfers.

Definitions—"Close company", "participator", s 102(1).

Cross references—FA 2000 Sch 29 para 14 (the main amendments made to TCGA 1992 s 170 by FA 2000 Sch 29 para 1 have effect for the purposes of this section for disposals after 31 March 2000).

Amendments—[1] Words in sub-ss (1), (2)(*b*) and whole of sub-s (2)(*a*) substituted, and words in sub-s (2) repealed, by FA 1989 s 138(6), (7), Sch 17 Pt VII with effect from 14 March 1989.

[2] Words in sub-s (2)(*a*) substituted by TCGA 1992 Sch 10 para 8(1), (4)(*b*).

[3] Sub-s (1)(*a*), (*aa*) substituted for original sub-s (1)(*a*) by FA 2001 s 106 with effect for disposals made, or transfers deemed to have been made, after 31 March 2000.

[4] Sub-s (1)(*a*)(iii) inserted, and words in sub-s (1)(*aa*) substituted, by FA 2002 s 42(3), (4) with effect—

(a) in relation to a case where a company is treated by virtue of TCGA 1992 s 179(3) as having sold and then reacquired an asset, where the company's ceasing to be a member of the group in question happens after 31 March 2002;

(b) in relation to a case where a company is so treated by virtue of TCGA 1992 s 179(6), where the relevant time (within the meaning of that subsection) is after that date.

[5] Sub-s (1)(*a*)(iii) and the immediately preceding word "or" repealed by FA 2011 s 45, Sch 10, para 8(*a*) with effect in relation to any disposal of an asset by one company ("company B") to another company ("company A") made at a time when company B is a member of a group, if—

(a) company A ceases to be a member of the group on or after 19 July 2011; or

(b) where company A ceased to be such a member before 19 July 2011 in circumstances where TCGA 1992 s 179(6)–(8) applied, company A ceases to satisfy the conditions in TCGA 1992 s 179(7) on or after 19 July 2011.

Where an early commencement election is made in relation to a group, the effective date is 1 April 2011: see FA 2011 Sch 10 para 9(4)–(8).

Alterations of capital, etc

98 Effect of alterations of capital, etc

(1) Where there is at any time—

(*a*) an alteration in so much of a close company's share or loan capital as does not consist of [quoted shares or quoted securities][2]

(*b*) an alteration in any rights attaching to [unquoted shares in or unquoted debentures of a close company][2],

the alteration shall be treated as having been made by a disposition made at that time by the participators, whether or not it would fall to be so treated apart from this section, and shall not be taken to have affected the value immediately before that time of the [unquoted shares or unquoted debentures][2].

(2) In this section "alteration" includes extinguishment.

[(3) The disposition referred to in subsection (1) above shall be taken to be one which is not a potentially exempt transfer.][1]

Commentary—*Simon's Taxes* **I6.111, I3.119, I1.537, I5.230**.

HMRC Manuals—Inheritance Tax Manual IHTM14855 (alterations in share capital, loan capital or rights).
IHTM04069 (alteration in share capital of a close company).

Press releases etc—Law Society's Gazette 11-9-91 (as regards sub-s (1)(*b*), an alteration of rights occurs when deferred shares come to rank equally, or become merged, with another class of shares. Assessments will be raised where this occurs in respect of deferred shares issued after 5 August 1991).

Definitions—"Close company", "participator", s 102(1); "quoted", "unquoted", s 272.

Amendments—[1] Sub-s (3) added by FA 1986 Sch 19 para 20.

[2] Words in sub-s (1) substituted by FA 1987 s 58 and Sch 8 para 2 in relation to events occurring after 16 March 1987.

Settled property

99 Transfers where participators are trustees

(1) Subsection (1) of section 94 above shall not apply in relation to a person who is a participator in his capacity as trustee of a settlement, but—

(*a*) the reference in subsection (2) of that section to subsection (1) shall have effect as including a reference to subsection (2) of this section, and

(*b*) in relation to tax chargeable by virtue of subsection (2) of this section, sections 94(4) and 95 above shall apply with the necessary modifications.

(2) Where any part of the value transferred by a close company's transfer of value is apportioned to a trustee of a settlement under section 94 above, then—

(*a*) if a qualifying interest in possession subsists in the settled property, a part of that interest corresponding to such part of the property as is of a value equal to the part so apportioned less the amount specified in subsection (3) below shall be treated for the purposes of Chapter II of Part III of this Act as having come to an end on the making of the transfer, and

(*b*) if no qualifying interest in possession subsists in the settled property, Chapter III of Part III of this Act shall have effect as if on the making of the transfer the trustee had made a disposition as a result of which the value of the settled property had been reduced by an amount equal to the part so apportioned less the amount specified in subsection (3) below;

and where a qualifying interest in possession subsists in part only of the settled property paragraphs (a) and (b) above shall apply with the necessary adjustments of the values and amounts referred to there.

(3) The amount referred to in paragraphs (*a*) and (*b*) of subsection (2) above is the amount (if any) by which the value of the settled property is more than it would be apart from the company's transfer, leaving out of account the value of any rights or interests in the company.

Commentary—*Simon's Taxes* **I6.127, I5.229**.

HMRC Manuals—Inheritance Tax Manual IHTM16241–16243 and 16247 (close companies and settled property). IHTM04090 (transfer of value by a close company apportioned to trustees).
Definitions—"Qualifying interest in possession", s 59(1); "close company", "participator", s 102(1); "settled property", s 43; "trustee", s 45.

100 Alterations of capital, etc where participators are trustees

(1) This section applies where, by virtue of section 98 above, an alteration in a close company's share or loan capital or of any rights attaching to shares in or debentures of a close company is treated as a disposition made by the participators, and—

(*a*) a person is a participator in his capacity as trustee of a settlement, and

(*b*) the disposition would, if the trustee were beneficially entitled to the settled property, be a transfer of value made by him, and

(*c*) at the time of the alteration an individual is beneficially entitled to an interest in possession in the whole or part of so much of the settled property as consists of [unquoted shares in or unquoted securities of the close company][1].

[(1A) Where the interest in possession is one to which the individual became beneficially entitled on or after 22nd March 2006, this section applies only if the interest in possession is—

(*a*) an immediate post-death interest,

(*b*) a disabled person's interest, or

(*c*) a transitional serial interest][2]

[or falls within section 5(1B) above][3].

(2) Where this section applies, such part of the individual's interest shall be treated for the purposes of Chapter II of Part III of this Act as having come to an end at the time of the alteration as corresponds to the relevant decrease of the value of the property in which the interest subsists, that is to say the decrease caused by the alteration.

Commentary—*Simon's Taxes* **I6.112, I5.230**.
HMRC Manuals—Inheritance Tax Manual IHTM16245 (alterations in capital or rights). IHTM16248 (example of altering rights).
Definitions—"close company", "participator", s 102(1); "unquoted", s 272.
Amendments—[1] Words in sub-s (1)(*c*) substituted by FA 1987 s 58 and Sch 8 para 3 in relation to events occurring after 16 March 1987.
[2] Sub-s (1A) inserted by FA 2006 s 156, Sch 20 paras 7, 25. This amendment is deemed to have come into force on 22 March 2006.
[3] In sub-s (1A) words at the end inserted by FA 2010 s 53(1), (6) with effect in relation to an interest in possession to which a person is beneficially entitled if the person becomes beneficially entitled to it on or after 9 December 2009.

101 Companies' interests in settled property

(1) Where a close company is entitled to an interest in possession in settled property the persons who are participators in relation to the company shall be treated for the purposes of this Act (except section 55) as being the persons entitled to that interest according to their respective rights and interests in the company.

[(1A) Where the interest in possession mentioned in subsection (1) above is one to which the company became entitled on or after 22nd March 2006 (whether or not the company was a close company when it became entitled to the interest), subsection (1) above applies in relation to the interest only if it is—

(*a*) an immediate post-death interest, or

(*b*) a transitional serial interest][1]

[or falls within section 5(1B) above][2].

[(1B) Subsection (1C) below applies where any of the participators mentioned in subsection (1) above ("the prior participator") disposes of rights and interests of his in the company to another person ("the later participator").][1]

[(1C) If and so far as the later participator is a participator in the company by virtue of having any of the rights and interests disposed of, subsection (1) above is to be applied to him only as a participator in his own right (in particular, he is not to be treated by virtue of that subsection as having entitlement to the interest in possession as a result of disposal to him of entitlement that the prior participator was treated as having by virtue of that subsection, but this is without prejudice to the application of this Act in relation to the prior participator as the person making the disposal).][1]

(2) Where—

(*a*) the participators mentioned in subsection (1) above include the trustees of a settlement, and

(*b*) a person is beneficially entitled to an interest in possession in the whole or part of the settled property by virtue of which the trustees are participators,

that person shall be treated for the said purposes as beneficially entitled to the whole or a corresponding part of the interest to which the trustees would otherwise be treated as entitled under that subsection.

Commentary—*Simon's Taxes* **I6.131, I5.229**.
HMRC Manuals—Inheritance Tax Manual IHTM16246 (close company entitled to interest in possession). IHTM04092 (the charge where a close company is entitled to an interest in possession).
Statement of Practice E5—Close companies.

Simon's Tax Cases—s 101(1), *Powell-Cotton v IRC* [1992] STC 625*.
Definitions—"close company", "participator", s 102(1).
Amendments—[1] Sub-ss (1A)–(1C) inserted by FA 2006 s 156, Sch 20 paras 7, 26. This amendment is deemed to have come into force on 22 March 2006.
[2] In sub-s (1A) words at the end inserted by FA 2010 s 53(1), (7) with effect in relation to an interest in possession to which a person is beneficially entitled if the person becomes beneficially entitled to it on or after 9 December 2009.

General

102 Interpretation

(1) In this Part of this Act—

"close company" means a company within the meaning of the Corporation Tax Acts which is (or would be if resident in the United Kingdom) a close company for the purposes of those Acts;

"participator", in relation to any company, means any person who is (or would be if the company were resident in the United Kingdom) a participator in relation to that company [within the meaning given by section 454 of the Corporation Tax Act 2010][1], other than a person who would be such a participator by reason only of being a loan creditor;

"qualifying interest in possession" has the meaning given by section 59 above.

(2) References in this Part of this Act to a person's rights and interests in a company include references to rights and interests in the assets of the company available for distribution among the participators in the event of a winding-up or in any other circumstances.

Commentary—*Simon's Taxes* **I6.102.**
HMRC Manuals—Inheritance Tax Manual IHTM42955 (definition of close company).
Amendments—[1] In sub-s (1) in the definition of "participator" words substituted for words "for the purposes of [Chapter I of Part XI of the Taxes Act 1988" by CTA 2010 s 1177, Sch 1 para 191. CTA 2010 has effect for corporation tax purposes for accounting periods ending on or after 1 April 2010, and for income and capital gains tax purposes for the tax year 2010–11 and subsequent tax years.

PART V
MISCELLANEOUS RELIEFS
CHAPTER I
BUSINESS PROPERTY

HMRC Interpretation RI 210—Where a bookmaker's pitch forms part of a deceased's business, its value may qualify for inheritance tax property relief at 100% if the statutory conditions are met.
Construction—F(No 2)A 1992 Sch 14 para 9 to be construed as if it were contained in this Chapter; see F(No 2)A 1992 Sch 14 para 9(4).
Cross references—See FA 1986 Sch 20 para 8 (disposal by way of gift of relevant business property subject to a reservation; determination of appropriate percentage of relief).

103 Preliminary

(1) In this Chapter references to a transfer of value include references to an occasion on which tax is chargeable under Chapter III of Part III of this Act (apart from section 79), and

(*a*) references to the value transferred by a transfer of value include references to the amount on which tax is then chargeable, and

(*b*) references to the transferor include references to the trustees of the settlement concerned.

(2) For the purposes of this Chapter a company and all its subsidiaries are members of a group, and "holding company" and "subsidiary" have [the meanings given by section [1159 of and Schedule 6 to][3]][2] the [Companies Act [2006][3]][1].

(3) In this Chapter "business" includes a business carried on in the exercise of a profession or vocation, but does not include a business carried on otherwise than for gain.

Commentary—*Simon's Taxes* **I7.131.**
HMRC Manuals—Inheritance Tax Manual IHTM25051–25083 (what is a business? and valuing the business).
IHTM25091–25120 (what is a partnership? and valuing a partnership interest).
IHTM25153 (meaning of "business").
Cross reference—See IHTA 1984 Part III Chapter III charge on settlements without interests in possession, subject to exemption from ten-yearly charge.
Amendments—[1] Words in sub-s (2) substituted by the Companies Consolidation (Consequential Provisions) Act 1985 Sch 2 with effect from 1 July 1985.
[2] Words in sub-s (2) substituted by the Companies Act 1989 s 144(4), Sch 18 para 30(1), (3) with effect from 1 November 1990.
[3] In para (2), words substituted for words "736 of" and "1985", by the Companies Act 2006 (Consequential Amendments) (Taxes and National Insurance) Order, SI 2009/1890 art 4(1)(*f*) with effect from 1 October 2009.

104 The relief

(1) Where the whole or part of the value transferred by a transfer of value is attributable to the value of any relevant business property, the whole or that part of the value transferred shall be treated as reduced—

(*a*) in the case of property falling within section 105(1)(*a*) [(*b*) or (*bb*)][1] below, by [100 per cent][2];

(*b*) in the case of other relevant business property, by [50 per cent][2];

but subject to the following provisions of this Chapter.

(2) For the purposes of this section, the value transferred by a transfer of value shall be calculated as a value on which no tax is chargeable.

Commentary—*Simon's Taxes* **I7.102**.

HMRC Manuals—Inheritance Tax Manual IHTM25141 (investigating relevant business property).
IHTM25151 (rate of relief).

Regulations—See IHT (Double Charges Relief) Regulations, SI 1987/1130.

Definitions—"Relevant business property", s 105.

Simon's Tax Cases—s 104, *Beckman v IRC* [2000] STC (SCD) 59.
s 104(1), *Re the Nelson Dance Family Settlement, R&C Comrs v Trustees of the Nelson Dance Family Settlement* [2009] STC 802.

Amendments—[1] Words in sub-s (1)(*a*) substituted by FA 1987 s 58 and Sch 8 para 4 in relation to transfers of value made after 16 March 1987.
[2] Percentages in sub-s (1)(*a*), (*b*) substituted by F(No 2)A 1992 Sch 14 paras 1, 8 in relation to transfers of value made after 9 March 1992.

105 Relevant business property

(1) Subject to the following provisions of this section and to sections 106, 108, [. . .][3], 112(3) and 113 below, in this Chapter "relevant business property" means, in relation to any transfer of value,—

(*a*) property consisting of a business or interest in a business;

(*b*) . . . [8] securities of a company which [are unquoted and which][5] (either by themselves or together with other such [securities owned by the transferor and any unquoted shares so owned][8] gave the transferor control of the company immediately before the transfer;

[(*bb*) any unquoted shares in a company;][6]

[(*c*) . . . ;][6]

[(*cc*) shares in or securities of a company which are quoted and which (either by themselves or together with other such shares or securities owned by the transferor) gave the transferor control of the company immediately before the transfer;][4]

(*d*) any land or building, machinery or plant which, immediately before the transfer, was used wholly or mainly for the purposes of a business carried on by a company of which the transferor then had control or by a partnership of which he then was a partner; and

(*e*) any land or building, machinery or plant which, immediately before the transfer, was used wholly or mainly for the purposes of a business carried on by the transferor and was settled property in which he was then beneficially entitled to an interest in possession.

[(1ZA) In subsection (1) above "quoted", in relation to any shares or securities, means [listed][9] on a recognised stock exchange and "unquoted", in relation to any shares or securities, means not so [listed][9].][4]

[(1A), (1B) . . .][7]

(2) Shares in or securities of a company do not fall within subsection (1) . . . [. . . [10] (*cc*)][4] above if—

(*a*) they would not have been sufficient, without other property, to give the transferor control of the company immediately before the transfer, and

(*b*) their value is taken by virtue of section 176 below to be less than the value previously determined.

[(2A) . . .][7]

(3) A business or interest in a business, or shares in or securities of a company, are not relevant business property if the business or, as the case may be, the business carried on by the company consists wholly or mainly of one or more of the following, that is to say, dealing in securities, stocks or shares, land or buildings or making or holding investments.

(4) Subsection (3) above—

[(*a*) does not apply to any property if the business concerned is wholly that of a market maker or is that of a discount house and (in either case) is carried on in the United Kingdom, and][1]

(*b*) does not apply to shares in or securities of a company if the business of the company consists wholly or mainly in being a holding company of one or more companies whose business does not fall within that subsection.

[(4A) Subsection (3) above also does not apply to any property if the business concerned is of a description set out in regulations under section 106(5) of the Finance Act 1986.][11]

(5) Shares in or securities of a company are not relevant business property in relation to a transfer of value if at the time of the transfer a winding-up order has been made in respect of the company or the company has passed a resolution for voluntary winding-up or is otherwise in process of liquidation, unless the business of the company is to continue to be carried on after a reconstruction or amalgamation and the reconstruction or amalgamation either is the purpose of the winding-up or liquidation or takes place not later than one year after the transfer of value.

(6) Land, a building, machinery or plant owned by the transferor and used wholly or mainly for the purposes of a business carried on as mentioned in subsection (1)(*d*) or (*e*) above is not relevant business property in relation to a transfer of value, unless the business or the transferor's interest in it is, or shares or securities of the company carrying on the business immediately before the transfer are, relevant business property in relation to the transfer.

[(7) In this section "market maker" means a person who—

(*a*) holds himself out at all normal times in compliance with the rules of The Stock Exchange as willing to buy and sell securities, stocks or shares at a price specified by him, and

(*b*) is recognised as doing so by the Council of The Stock Exchange.][2]

Commentary—*Simon's Taxes* **I7.102, I7.111, I7.112, I7.121–I7.123, I7.130, I7.135, I7.151, I7.161**.

HMRC Manuals—Inheritance Tax Manual IHTM25141 (investigating relevant business property).

IHTM25152 (property consisting of a business or a business interest).

IHTM25171 and 25172 (shareholdings: unquoted securities – control holding).

IHTM25191 and 25192 (shareholdings: other holdings of unquoted shares).

IHTM25221–5227 (relevant business property: land and buildings, machinery and plant).

IHTM25241–25243 (relevant business property: settled property used in the life tenant's business).

IHTM25250–25251 (relevant business property: partnership interests and woodlands syndicates).

IHTM25261–25264 (investment businesses).

IHTM25271–25280 (investment businesses: caravan sites and furnished lettings).

Regulations—FA 1986 s 106(4), (6), (8) empower the Board to make Regulations to modify the definition of "market maker" in sub-s (7) above. The Inheritance Tax (Market Makers) Regulations, SI 1992/3181 regs 2, 3, 4 make such modification in relation to transfers of value and other events occurring after 22 March 1992.

Press releases etc—IR Technical Bulletin February 1993 (milk quota: where value of agricultural land reflects value of milk quota, agricultural relief is given on that value; where milk quota valued separately, business relief is given).

IR 20-2-95 (securities on the alternative investment market are not treated as quoted for tax purposes).

Simon's Tax Cases—s 105(1)(*a*), *Beckman v IRC* [2000] STC (SCD) 59; *Re the Nelson Dance Family Settlement, R&C Comrs v Trustees of the Nelson Dance Family Settlement* [2009] STC 802.

s 105(1)(*d*), *Walker's Executors v IRC* [2001] STC (SCD) 86.

s 105(3), *Farmer and anor (executors of Farmer, decd) v IRC* [1999] STC (SCD) 321; *Grimwood Taylor v IRC* [2000] STC (SCD) 40; *Weston (executor of Weston, decd) v IRC* [2000] STC 1064; *Stedman's executors v IRC* [2002] STC (SCD) 358; *IRC v George and another (executors of Stedman, decd)* [2004] STC 147; *McCall and another (personal representatives of McClean (dec'd)) v R&C Comrs* [2009] STC 990; *Brander (representative of James (dec'd), Fourth Earl of Balfour) v R&C Comrs* [2010] STC 2666.

Definitions—"Business", s 103; "holding company", s 103; "land", s 272; "unquoted", s 272.

Cross references—See FA 1986 Sch 20 para 8(1A) (modification of sub-s (1)(*b*), (*bb*) of this section for the purposes of FA 1986 Sch 20 para 8 (gifts with reservation of agricultural and business properties));

F(No 2)A 1992 Sch 14 para 9 (commencement date of the amendments made to this section by F(No 2)A 1992 Sch 14.

Inheritance Tax (Market Makers and Discount Houses) Regulations, SI 2012/2903 (Description of "business" and "company" for the purposes of ss 105(4A) and 234(3)(c)(ii)).

Amendments—[1] Sub-s (4)(*a*) substituted by FA 1986 s 106(1), (3) in relation to transfers of value made, and other events occurring, on or after 27 October 1986 (the day on which The Stock Exchange rule prohibiting a person from carrying on business as both a broker and a jobber is abolished).

[2] Sub-s (7) inserted by FA 1986 s 106(2), (3) in relation to transfers of value made, and other events occurring. on or after 27 October 1986 (the day on which The Stock Exchange rule prohibiting a person from carrying on business as both a broker and a jobber is abolished).

[3] Number in sub-s (1) inserted by FA 1987 Sch 8 para 5 and repealed by FA 1996 Sch 41 Pt VI in relation to transfers of value occurring after 5 April 1996, and for the purpose of charging to tax any event after that date, in relation to which the transfer of value occurred before 6 April 1996.

[4] Sub-ss (1)(*cc*), (1ZA) and words in sub-s (2) inserted by F(No 2)A 1992 Sch 14 paras 2, 8 in relation to transfers of value made, and other events occurring after 9 March 1992 but subject to F(No 2)A 1992 Sch 14 para 9.

[5] Words in sub-ss (1)(*b*), (2) inserted by F(No 2)A 1992 Sch 14 paras 2, 8 in relation to transfers of value made, and other events occurring after 9 March 1992 but subject to F(No 2)A 1992 Sch 14 para 9.

[6] Sub-ss (1)(*bb*) substituted, and sub-s (1)(*c*) repealed, by FA 1996 s 184(2)(*b*), (*c*), (6)(*b*) and Sch 41 Pt VI, in relation to transfers of value occurring after 5 April 1996 and for the purpose of charging to tax any event after that date, in relation to which the transfer of value occurred before 6 April 1996.

[7] Sub-ss (1A), (1B), (2A) repealed by FA 1996 Sch 41 Pt VI with effect as for transfers of value occurring after 5 April 1996, and for the purpose of charging to tax any event after that date, in relation to which the transfer of value occurred before 6 April 1996.

[8] Words omitted from sub-s (1)(*b*) repealed, and words substituted, by FA 1996 s 184(2)(*a*), (6)(*b*) and Sch 41 Pt VI, with effect for transfers of value occurring after 5 April 1996, and for the purpose of charging to tax any event after that date, in relation to which the transfer of value occurred before 6 April 1996.

[9] Words in sub-s (1ZA) substituted by FA 1996 s 199 Sch 38 para 2 in relation to transfers made after 31 March 1996 and for the purpose of charging to tax any event after that date, in relation to which the transfer of value occurred before 1 April 1996.

[10] Sub-s (2) words repealed by FA 1996 Sch 41 Pt VI with effect for transfers of value occurring after 5 April 1996, and for the purpose of charging to tax any event after that date, in relation to which the transfer of value occurred before 6 April 1996.

[11] Sub-s (4A) inserted by the Inheritance Tax (Market Makers and Discount Houses) Regulations, SI 2012/2903 regs 3, 4 with effect from 31 December 2012. Also see cross-reference note above.

106 Minimum period of ownership

Property is not relevant business property in relation to a transfer of value unless it was owned by the transferor throughout the two years immediately preceding the transfer.

Commentary—*Simon's Taxes* **I7.113, I7.124, I7.137, I7.152**.

HMRC Manuals—Inheritance Tax Manual IHTM25301–25303 (the ownership test).
Definitions—"Relevant business property", s 105.
Cross references—See FA 1986 Sch 20 para 8(2) (gift of business property subject to a reservation; for the purposes of this section, donor's ownership treated as donee's ownership for determining whether business relief is available).

107 Replacements

(1) Property shall be treated as satisfying the condition in section 106 above if—

(*a*) it replaced other property and it, that other property and any property directly or indirectly replaced by that other property were owned by the transferor for periods which together comprised at least two years falling within the five years immediately preceding the transfer of value, and

(*b*) any other property concerned was such that, had the transfer of value been made immediately before it was replaced, it would (apart from section 106) have been relevant business property in relation to the transfer.

(2) In a case falling within subsection (1) above relief under this Chapter shall not exceed what it would have been had the replacement or any one or more of the replacements not been made.

(3) For the purposes of subsection (2) above changes resulting from the formation, alteration or dissolution of a partnership, or from the acquisition of a business by a company controlled by the former owner of the business, shall be disregarded.

[(4) Without prejudice to subsection (1) above, where any shares falling within section 105(1)(*bb*) above which are][3] owned by the transferor immediately before the transfer would under any of the provisions of sections [126 to 136 of the 1992 Act][1] be identified with other shares previously owned by him his period of ownership of the first-mentioned shares shall be treated for the purposes of section 106 above [. . .][2] as including his period of ownership of the other shares.

Commentary—*Simon's Taxes* **I7.114, I7.125, I7.137, I7.152.**
HMRC Manuals—Inheritance Tax Manual IHTM25311–25314 (replacement property).
HMRC Interpretation RI 95—Period of ownership of a farming business replaced by non-agricultural business property counts towards the minimum period of ownership condition applied to the replacement property.
Amendments—[1] Words in sub-s (4) substituted by TCGA 1992 Sch 10 para 8(1), (5).
[2] Words in sub-s (4) repealed by FA 1996 Sch 41 Pt VI, for transfers of value occurring after 5 April 1996, and for the purpose of charging to tax any event after that date, in relation to which the transfer of value occurred before 6 April 1996
[3] Words in sub-s (4) substituted by FA 1996 s 184(3), (6)(*b*) for transfers of value occurring after 5 April 1996, and for the purpose of charging to tax any event after that date, in relation to which the transfer of value occurred before 6 April 1996.

108 Successions

For the purposes of sections 106 and 107 above, where the transferor became entitled to any property on the death of another person—

(*a*) he shall be deemed to have owned it from the date of the death, and

(*b*) if that other person was his spouse [or civil partner][1] he shall also be deemed to have owned it for any period during which the spouse [or civil partner][1] owned it.

Commentary—*Simon's Taxes* **I7.115, I7.125, I7.126.**
HMRC Manuals—Inheritance Tax Manual IHTM25321 (successions).
Amendments—[1] Words in para (*b*) inserted by Tax and Civil Partnership Regulations, SI 2005/3229, regs 3, 19, with effect from 5 December 2005 (reg 1(1)).

109 Successive transfers

(1) Where—

(*a*) the whole or part of the value transferred by a transfer of value (in this section referred to as the earlier transfer) was eligible for relief under this Chapter (or would have been so eligible if such relief had been capable of being given in respect of transfers of value made at that time), and

(*b*) the whole or part of the property which, in relation to the earlier transfer, was relevant business property became, through the earlier transfer, the property of the person or of the spouse [or civil partner][1] of the person who is the transferor in relation to a subsequent transfer of value, and

(*c*) that property or part, or any property directly or indirectly replacing it, would (apart from section 106 above) have been relevant business property in relation to the subsequent transfer of value, and

(*d*) either the earlier transfer was, or the subsequent transfer of value is, a transfer made on the death of the transferor,

the property which would have been relevant business property but for section 106 above shall be relevant business property notwithstanding that section.

(2) Where the property which, by virtue of subsection (1) above, is relevant business property replaced the property or part referred to in paragraph (*c*) of that subsection, relief under this Chapter shall not exceed what it would have been had the replacement or any one or more of the replacements not been made, but section 107(3) above shall apply with the necessary modifications for the purposes of this subsection.

(3) Where, under the earlier transfer, the amount of the value transferred which was attributable to the property or part referred to in subsection (1)(*c*) above was part only of its value, a like part only of the value which (apart from this subsection) would fall to be reduced under this Chapter by virtue of this section shall be so reduced.

Commentary—*Simon's Taxes* **I7.116, I7.127, I7.152, I7.154**.
HMRC Manuals—Inheritance Tax Manual IHTM25331–25333 (successive transfers).
Definitions—"Relevant business property", s 105.
Amendments—[1] Words in sub-s (1)(*b*) inserted by Tax and Civil Partnership Regulations, SI 2005/3229, regs 3, 20, with effect from 5 December 2005 (reg 1(1)).

109A Additional requirement in case of minority shareholdings

Amendments—This section repealed by FA 1996 Sch 41 Pt VI, for transfers of value occurring after 5 April 1996, and for the purpose of charging to tax any event after that date, in relation to which the transfer of value occurred before 6 April 1996.

110 Value of business

For the purposes of this Chapter—

(*a*) the value of a business or of an interest in a business shall be taken to be its net value;

(*b*) the net value of a business is the value of the assets used in the business (including goodwill) reduced by the aggregate amount of any liabilities incurred for the purposes of the business;

(*c*) in ascertaining the net value of an interest in a business, no regard shall be had to assets or liabilities other than those by reference to which the net value of the entire business would fall to be ascertained.

Commentary—*Simon's Taxes* **I7.111, I5.275**.
HMRC Manuals—Inheritance Tax Manual IHTM25153 (meaning of "business").
IHTM25341 and 25342 (assets excluded from relief).
IHTM25250 (partnership interests).
IHTM25121 (business relief: other relevant business property).
Press releases etc—IR Technical Bulletin February 1993 (milk quota: where value of agricultural land reflects value of milk quota, agricultural relief is given on that value; where milk quota valued separately, business relief is given).
Simon's Tax Cases—*IRC v Mallender and others (executors of Drury-Lowe, deceased)* [2001] STC 514.
Definitions—"Business", s 103.

111 Value of certain shares and securities

Where a company is a member of a group and the business of any other company which is a member of the group falls within section 105(3) above, then, unless either—

(*a*) that business also falls within section 105(4), or

(*b*) that business consists wholly or mainly in the holding of land or buildings wholly or mainly occupied by members of the group whose business either does not fall within section 105(3) or falls within both section 105(3) and section 105(4),

the value of shares in or securities of the company shall be taken for the purposes of this Chapter to be what it would be if that other company were not a member of the group.

Commentary—*Simon's Taxes* **I7.131**.
HMRC Manuals—Inheritance Tax Manual IHTM25263 (business relief: holding companies).
Definitions—"Business", s 103.

112 Exclusion of value of excepted assets

(1) In determining for the purposes of this Chapter what part of the value transferred by a transfer of value is attributable to the value of any relevant business property so much of the last-mentioned value as is attributable to any excepted assets within the meaning of subsection (2) below shall be left out of account.

(2) An asset is an excepted asset in relation to any relevant business property if it was neither—

(*a*) used wholly or mainly for the purposes of the business concerned throughout the whole or the last two years of the relevant period defined in subsection (5) below, nor

(*b*) required at the time of the transfer for future use for those purposes;

but where the business concerned is carried on by a company which is a member of a group, the use of an asset for the purposes of a business carried on by another company which at the time of the use and immediately before the transfer was also a member of that group shall be treated as use for the purposes of the business concerned, unless that other company's membership of the group falls to be disregarded under section 111 above.

(3) Subsection (2) above does not apply in relation to an asset which is relevant business property by virtue only of section 105(1)(*d*) above, and an asset is not relevant business property by virtue only of that provision unless either—

(*a*) it was used as mentioned in that provision throughout the two years immediately preceding the transfer of value, or

(*b*) it replaced another asset so used and it and the other asset and any asset directly or indirectly replaced by that other asset were so used for periods which together comprised at least two years falling within the five years immediately preceding the transfer of value;

but in a case where section 109 above applies this condition shall be treated as satisfied if the asset (or it and the asset or assets replaced by it) was or were so used throughout the period between the earlier and the subsequent transfer mentioned in that section (or throughout the part of that period during which it or they were owned by the transferor or the transferor's spouse [or civil partner][1]).

(4) Where part but not the whole of any land or building is used exclusively for the purposes of any business and the land or building would, but for this subsection, be an excepted asset, or, as the case may be, prevented by subsection (3) above from being relevant business property, the part so used and the remainder shall for the purposes of this section be treated as separate assets, and the value of the part so used shall (if it would otherwise be less) be taken to be such proportion of the value of the whole as may be just.

(5) For the purposes of this section the relevant period, in relation to any asset, is the period immediately preceding the transfer of value during which the asset (or, if the relevant business property is an interest in a business, a corresponding interest in the asset) was owned by the transferor or, if the business concerned is that of a company, was owned by that company or any other company which immediately before the transfer of value was a member of the same group.

(6) For the purposes of this section an asset shall be deemed not to have been used wholly or mainly for the purposes of the business concerned at any time when it was used wholly or mainly for the personal benefit of the transferor or of a person connected with him.

Commentary—*Simon's Taxes* **I7.111, I7.119, I7.131, I7.154.**

HMRC Manuals—Inheritance Tax Manual IHTM25351–25354 (assets excluded from relief: excepted assets).

IHTM27264 (exempt securities as partnership assets).

IHTM25341 (assets excluded from relief: introduction).

IHTM25223 (relevant business property : additional user requirement).

Definitions—"business", s 103; "land", s 272; "relevant business property", s 105.

Simon's Tax Cases—*Barclays Bank Trust Co Ltd v IRC* [1998] STC (SCD) 125.

Amendments—[1] Words in sub-s (3) inserted by Tax and Civil Partnership Regulations, SI 2005/3229, regs 3, 21, with effect from 5 December 2005 (reg 1(1)).

113 Contracts for sale

Where any property would be relevant business property in relation to a transfer of value but a binding contract for its sale has been entered into at the time of the transfer, it is not relevant business property in relation to the transfer unless—

(*a*) the property is a business or interest in a business and the sale is to a company which is to carry on the business and is made in consideration wholly or mainly of shares in or securities of that company, or

(*b*) the property is shares in or securities of a company and the sale is made for the purpose of reconstruction or amalgamation.

Commentary—*Simon's Taxes* **I7.117, I7.118, I7.128, I7.129, I7.135, I7.153, I7.342.**

HMRC Manuals—Inheritance Tax Manual IHTM25291 and 25292 (contracts for sale).

Statement of Practice SP 12/80—Business relief: "buy and sell" agreements.

Definitions—"Business", s 103; "relevant business property", s 105.

[113A Transfers within seven years before death of transferor

(1) Where any part of the value transferred by a potentially exempt transfer which proves to be a chargeable transfer would (apart from this section) be reduced in accordance with the preceding provisions of this Chapter, it shall not be so reduced unless the conditions in subsection (3) are satisfied.

(2) Where—

(*a*) any part of the value transferred by any chargeable transfer, other than a potentially exempt transfer, is reduced in accordance with the preceding provisions of this Chapter, and

(*b*) the transfer is made within seven years of the death of the transferor,

then, unless the conditions in subsection (3) below are satisfied, the additional tax chargeable by reason of the death shall be calculated as if the value transferred had not been so reduced.

(3) The conditions referred to in subsections (1) and (2) above are—

(*a*) that the original property was owned by the transferee throughout the period beginning with the date of the chargeable transfer and ending with the death of the transferor; and

(*b*) [except to the extent that the original property consists of shares or securities to which subsection (3A) below applies][2] that, in relation to a notional transfer of value made by the transferee immediately before the death, the original property would (apart from section 106 above) be relevant business property.

[(3A) This subsection applies to shares or securities—

(*a*) which were quoted at the time of the chargeable transfer referred to in subsection (1) or subsection (2) above; or

(*b*) which fell within paragraph (*b*) [or (*bb*)][6] of section 105(1) above in relation to that transfer and were unquoted throughout the period referred to in subsection (3)(*a*) above.][3]

[(3B) In subsection (3A) above "quoted", in relation to any shares or securities, means [listed][8] on a recognised stock exchange and "unquoted", in relation to any shares or securities, means not so [listed][8].][5]

(4) If the transferee has died before the transferor, the reference in subsection (3) above to the death of the transferor shall have effect as a reference to the death of the transferee.
(5) If the conditions in subsection (3) above are satisfied only with respect to part of the original property, then,—
(*a*) in a case falling within subsection (1) above, only a proportionate part of so much of the value transferred as is attributable to the original property shall be reduced in accordance with the preceding provisions of this Chapter, and
(*b*) in a case falling within subsection (2) above, the additional tax shall be calculated as if only a proportionate part of so much of the value transferred as was attributable to the original property had been so reduced.
(6) Where any shares owned by the transferee immediately before the death in question—
(*a*) would under any of the provisions of sections [126 to 136 of the 1992 Act][4] be identified with the original property (or part of it), or
(*b*) were issued to him in consideration of the transfer of a business or interest in a business consisting of the original property (or part of it),
they shall be treated for the purposes of this section as if they were the original property (or that part of it).
(7) This section has effect subject to section 113B below.
[(7A) The provisions of this Chapter for the reduction of value transferred shall be disregarded in any determination for the purposes of this section of whether there is a potentially exempt or chargeable transfer in any case.][7]
(8) In this section—
"the original property" means the property which was relevant business property in relation to the chargeable transfer referred to in subsection (1) or subsection (2) above; and
"the transferee" means the person whose property the original property became on that chargeable transfer or, where on the transfer the original property became or remained settled property in which no qualifying interest in possession (within the meaning of Chapter III of Part III of this Act) subsists, the trustees of the settlement.][1]

Commentary—*Simon's Taxes* **I3.533, I7.191**.
HMRC Manuals—Inheritance Tax Manual IHTM25250 (partnership interests).
IHTM25361–25370 (lifetime transfers: additional conditions).
Definitions—"qualifying interest in possession", s 59(1); "quoted", "unquoted", s 272.
Cross references—See FA 1986 Sch 19 para 40 (where a death or other event occurs on or after 18 March 1986, this section does not affect the tax chargeable on a transfer of value occurring before 18 March 1986);
FA 1987 s 58(3) (amendments made to this Act by FA 1987 Sch 8 to be disregarded in determining under sub-s (3) above whether any property acquired by the transferee before 17 March 1987 would be relevant business property in relation to a notional transfer of value made on or after that date);
F(No 2)A 1992 Sch 14 para 9 (commencement date of the amendments made to this section by F(No 2)A 1992 Sch 14).
Amendments—[1] This section inserted by FA 1986 s 101(3) and Sch 19 para 21 in relation to transfers of value made after 17 March 1986.
[2] Words in sub-s (3)(*b*) inserted by FA 1987 s 58 and Sch 8 para 8(1) in relation to transfers of value made after 17 March 1986.
[3] Sub-s (3A) inserted by FA 1987 s 58 and Sch 8 para 8(2) in relation to transfers of value made after 16 March 1987.
[4] Words in sub-s (6)(*a*) substituted by TCGA 1992 Sch 10 para 8(1), (5).
[5] Sub-s (3B) inserted by F(No 2)A 1992 Sch 14 paras 3, 8 in relation to transfers of value made after 9 March 1992 but subject to F(No 2)A 1992 Sch 14 para 9.
[6] Words in sub-s (3A)(*b*) inserted by FA 1996 s 184(3), (6)(*b*) for transfers of value occurring after 5 April 1996, and for the purpose of charging to tax any event after that date, in relation to which the transfer of value occurred before 5 April 1996.
[7] Sub-s (7A) inserted by FA 1996 s 184(5), (6)(*a*) in relation to transfers of value after 27 November 1995.
[8] Words in sub-s (3B) substituted by FA 1996 Sch 38 para 2(*a*) for transfers of value occurring after 31 March 1996, and for the purpose of charging to tax any event after that date, in relation to which the transfer of value occurred before 1 April 1996.

[113B Application of section 113A to replacement property

(1) Subject to subsection (2) below, this section applies where—
(*a*) the transferee has disposed of all or part of the original property before the death of the transferor; and
(*b*) the whole of the consideration received by him for the disposal has been applied by him in acquiring other property (in this section referred to as "the replacement property").
(2) This section does not apply unless—
(*a*) the replacement property is acquired, or a binding contract for its acquisition is entered into, within [the allowed period][2] after the disposal of the original property (or, as the case may be, the part concerned); and
(*b*) the disposal and acquisition are both made in transactions at arm's length or on terms such as might be expected to be included in a transaction at arm's length.
(3) Where this section applies, the conditions in section 113A(3) above shall be taken to be satisfied in relation to the original property (or, as the case may be, the part concerned) if—
(*a*) the replacement property is owned by the transferee immediately before the death of the transferor; and

(*b*) throughout the period beginning with the date of the chargeable transfer and ending with the death (disregarding any period between the disposal and acquisition) either the original property or the replacement property was owned by the transferee; and

(*c*) in relation to a notional transfer of value made by the transferee immediately before the death, the replacement property would (apart from section 106 above) be relevant business property.

(4) If the transferee has died before the transferor, any reference in subsections (1) to (3) above to the death of the transferor shall have effect as a reference to the death of the transferee.

(5) In any case where—

(*a*) all or part of the original property has been disposed of before the death of the transferor or is excluded by section 113 above from being relevant business property in relation to the notional transfer of value referred to in section 113A(3)(*b*) above, and

(*b*) the replacement property is acquired, or a binding contract for its acquisition is entered into, after the death of the transferor but within [the allowed period][2] after the disposal of the original property or part, and

(*c*) the transferor dies before the transferee,

subsection (3) above shall have effect with the omission of paragraph (a), and as if any reference to a time immediately before the death of the transferor or to the death were a reference to the time when the replacement property is acquired.

(6) Section 113A(6) above shall have effect in relation to the replacement property as it has effect in relation to the original property.

(7) Where a binding contract for the disposal of any property is entered into at any time before the disposal of the property, the disposal shall be regarded for the purposes of subsections (2)(*a*) and (5)(*b*) above as taking place at that time.

(8) In this section "the original property" and "the transferee" have the same meaning as in section 113A above [and "allowed period" means the period of three years or such longer period as the Board may allow][3].][1]

Commentary—*Simon's Taxes* **I7.194**.

HMRC Manuals—Inheritance Tax Manual IHTM25250 (partnership interests).

IHTM25361–25370 (lifetime transfers: additional conditions).

HMRC Interpretation RI 95—Farming business acquired in replacement of non-agricultural business by transferee can be "relevant business property" for the purposes of sub-s (3)(*c*) above.

Definitions—"The Board", s 272; "business", s 103; "relevant business property", s 105.

Cross references—See FA 1986 Sch 19 para 40 (where a death or other event occurs on or after 18 March 1986, this section not to affect the tax chargeable on a transfer of value occurring before 18 March 1986);

FA 1987 s 58(3) (amendments made to this Act by FA 1987 Sch 8 to be disregarded in determining under sub-s (3) above whether any property acquired by the transferee before 17 March 1987 would be relevant business property in relation to a notional transfer of value made on or after that date);

F(No 2)A 1992 Sch 14 para 9 (commencement date of the amendments made to s 113A above by F(No 2)A 1992 Sch 14).

Amendments—[1] This section inserted by FA 1986 s 101(3) and Sch 19 para 21 in relation to transfers of value made after 17 March 1986.

[2] Words in sub-ss (2)(*a*), (5)(*b*) substituted by FA 1994 s 247(1), (3) in relation to transfers of value made and other events occurring after 29 November 1993.

[3] Words in sub-s (8) added by FA 1994 s 247(1), (3) in relation to transfers of value made and other events occurring after 29 November 1993.

114 Avoidance of double relief

(1) Where any part of the value transferred by a transfer of value is reduced under Chapter II of this Part of this Act by reference to the agricultural value of any property, or would be so reduced but for section 121(3), such part of the value transferred as is or would be so reduced under that Chapter shall not be reduced under this Chapter.

(2) Where the value transferred by a transfer of value is reduced under section 129 below by reference to the tax chargeable on the disposal of any trees or underwood, the value to be reduced under section 104 above shall be the value as reduced under section 129 (but subject to section 104(2) above).

Commentary—*Simon's Taxes* **I7.102, I7.174, I7.181, I7.103**.

HMRC Manuals—Inheritance Tax Manual IHTM24151 (excess of value over agricultureal value and interaction with business relief).

IHTM25121 (relationship between business and agricultural relief).

IHTM28022 (assets that qualify for both agricultural and business relief).

HMRC Interpretation RI 95—Operation of this section where agricultural property replaced with other business property (or vice versa).

CHAPTER II

AGRICULTURAL PROPERTY

Cross references—See FA 1986 Sch 20 para 8 (disposal by way of gift of agricultural property subject to a reservation; determination of appropriate percentage of relief).

FA 1995 s 154(2), (3), (5) (the cultivation of short rotation coppice, land used for such cultivation and buildings used in connection with such cultivation are regarded as agriculture, agricultural land and farm buildings for the purposes of IHTA 1984 in relation to transfers of value or other events after 5 April 1995).

115 Preliminary

(1) In this Chapter references to a transfer of value include references to an occasion on which tax is chargeable under Chapter III of Part III of this Act (apart from section 79) and—

(*a*) references to the value transferred by a transfer of value include references to the amount on which tax is then chargeable, and

(*b*) references to the transferor include references to the trustees of the settlement concerned.

(2) In this Chapter "agricultural property" means agricultural land or pasture and includes woodland and any building used in connection with the intensive rearing of livestock or fish if the woodland or building is occupied with agricultural land or pasture and the occupation is ancillary to that of the agricultural land or pasture; and also includes such cottages, farm buildings and farmhouses, together with the land occupied with them, as are of a character appropriate to the property.

(3) For the purposes of this Chapter the agricultural value of any agricultural property shall be taken to be the value which would be the value of the property if the property were subject to a perpetual covenant prohibiting its use otherwise than as agricultural property [(or, in the case of property outside the United Kingdom, the Channel Islands and the Isle of Man, if it were subject to provisions equivalent in effect to such a covenant)][1].

(4) For the purposes of this Chapter the breeding and rearing of horses on a stud farm and the grazing of horses in connection with those activities shall be taken to be agriculture and any buildings used in connection with those activities to be farm buildings.

[(5) This Chapter applies to agricultural property only if it is in—

(*a*) the United Kingdom, the Channel Islands or the Isle of Man, or

(*b*) a state, other than the United Kingdom, which is an EEA state (within the meaning given by Schedule 1 to the Interpretation Act 1978) at the time of the transfer of value in question.][1]

Commentary—*Simon's Taxes* **I5.455, I7.353, I7.302, I7.305, I7.306**.

HMRC Manuals—Inheritance Tax Manual IHTM24001 (outline of agricultural relief).

IHTM24033 (investigation of "character appropriate").

IHTM24035 (development value and other non agricultural uses).

IHTM24036 (role of Valuation Agency regarding "character appropriate").

IHTM24050 (growing crops, cultivations and unexhausted manures).

IHTM24051 (fishing and sporting rights).

IHTM24101–IHTM24102 (what are agricultural purposes?).

IHTM24163 (lifetime transfers: property is agricultural only by reference to estate as a whole).

IHTM24150 (agricultural value of agricultural property).

IHTM24030 (definition of agricultural property).

IHTM24061 (qualifying uses of land).

Press releases etc—Hansard 2-11-83 (the ownership or breeding of horses may not qualify under sub-s (2)).

Simon's Tax Cases—s 115(2), *Harrold and others (executors of Harrold, decd) v IRC* [1996] STC (SCD) 195; *Starke (executors of Brown, decd) v IRC* [1995] STC 689; *Dixon v IRC* [2002] STC (SCD) 53.

Cross references—See IHTA 1984 Part III, Chapter III charge on settlements without interest in possession, subject to exemption from ten-yearly charge.

FA 1995 s 154(2), (3), (5) (the cultivation of short rotation coppice, land used for such cultivation and buildings used in connection with such cultivation are regarded as agriculture, agricultural land and farm buildings for the purposes of IHTA 1984 in relation to transfers of value or other events after 5 April 1995).

Amendments—[1] In sub-s (3) words at the end inserted, sub-s (5) substituted by FA 2009 s 122(2), (3) with effect in relation to transfers of value where the tax payable but for s 122 (or, in the case of tax payable by instalments, the last instalment of that tax)—

(a) would have been due on or after 22 April 2009, or

(b) was paid or due on or after 23 April 2003.

116 The relief

(1) Where the whole or part of the value transferred by a transfer of value is attributable to the agricultural value of agricultural property, the whole or that part of the value transferred shall be treated as reduced by the appropriate percentage, but subject to the following provisions of this Chapter.

(2) The appropriate percentage is [100 per cent][1] if[5] . . . —

(*a*) the interest of the transferor in the property immediately before the transfer carries the right to vacant possession or the right to obtain it within the next twelve months, or

(*b*) the transferor has been beneficially entitled to that interest since before 10th March 1981 and the conditions set out in subsection (3) below are satisfied; [or][5]

[(*c*) the interest of the transferor in the property immediately before the transfer does not carry either of the rights mentioned in paragraph (*a*) above because the property is let on a tenancy beginning on or after 1st September 1995;][5]

and, subject to subsection (4) below, it is [50 per cent][2] in any other case.

[(2A) . . .][6]

(3) The conditions referred to in subsection (2)(*b*) above are—

(*a*) that if the transferor had disposed of his interest by a transfer of value immediately before 10th March 1981 and duly made a claim under paragraph 1 of Schedule 8 to the Finance Act 1975, the value transferred would have been computed in accordance with paragraph 2 of that Schedule and relief would not have been limited by paragraph 5 of that Schedule (restriction to £250,000 or one thousand acres); and

(*b*) that the transferor's interest did not at any time during the period beginning with 10th March 1981 and ending with the date of the transfer carry a right mentioned in subsection (2)(*a*) above, and did not fail to do so by reason of any act or deliberate omission of the transferor during that period.

(4) Where the appropriate percentage would be [100 per cent][3] but for a limitation on relief that would have been imposed (as mentioned in subsection (3)(*a*) above) by paragraph 5 of Schedule 8 to the Finance Act 1975 the appropriate percentage shall be [100 per cent][3] in relation to a part of the value transferred equal to the amount which would have attracted relief under that Schedule and [50 per cent][4] in relation to the remainder.

(5) In determining for the purposes of subsections (3)(*a*) and (4) above whether or to what extent relief under Schedule 8 to the Finance Act 1975 would have been limited by paragraph 5 of that Schedule, that paragraph shall be construed as if references to relief given under that Schedule in respect of previous chargeable transfers included references to—

(*a*) relief given under this Chapter by virtue of subsection (2)(*b*) or (4) above, and

(*b*) relief given under Schedule 14 to the Finance Act 1981 by virtue of paragraph 2(2)(*b*) or (4) of that Schedule,

in respect of previous chargeable transfers made on or after 10th March 1981.

[(5A) Where, in consequence of the death on or after 1st September 1995 of the tenant or, as the case may be, the last surviving tenant of any property, the tenancy—

(*a*) becomes vested in a person, as a result of his being a person beneficially entitled under the deceased tenant's will or other testamentary writing or on his intestacy, and

(*b*) is or becomes binding on the landlord and that person as landlord and tenant respectively,

subsection (2)(c) above shall have effect as if the tenancy so vested had been a tenancy beginning on the date of the death.][7]

[(5B) Where in consequence of the death on or after 1st September 1995 of the tenant or, as the case may be, the last surviving tenant of any property, a tenancy of the property or of any property comprising the whole or part of it—

(*a*) is obtained by a person under or by virtue of an enactment, or

(*b*) is granted to a person in circumstances such that he is already entitled under or by virtue of an enactment to obtain such a tenancy, but one which takes effect on a later date, or

(*c*) is granted to a person who is or has become the only or only remaining applicant, or the only or only remaining person eligible to apply, under a particular enactment for such a tenancy in the particular case,

subsection (2)(c) above shall have effect as if the tenancy so obtained or granted had been a tenancy beginning on the date of the death.][7]

[(5C) Subsection (5B) above does not apply in relation to property situate in Scotland.][7]

[(5D) If, in a case where the transferor dies on or after 1st September 1995,—

(*a*) the tenant of any property has, before the death, given notice of intention to retire in favour of a new tenant, and

(*b*) the tenant's retirement in favour of the new tenant takes place after the death but not more than thirty months after the giving of the notice,

subsection (2)(c) above shall have effect as if the tenancy granted or assigned to the new tenant had been a tenancy beginning immediately before the transfer of value which the transferor is treated by section 4(1) above as making immediately before his death.][8]

[(5E) In subsection (5D) above and this subsection—

"the new tenant" means—

(*a*) the person or persons identified in a notice of intention to retire in favour of a new tenant as the person or persons who it is desired should become the tenant of the property to which that notice relates; or

(*b*) the survivor or survivors of the persons so identified, whether alone or with any other person or persons;

"notice of intention to retire in favour of a new tenant" means, in the case of any property, a notice or other written intimation given to the landlord by the tenant, or (in the case of a joint tenancy or tenancy in common) all of the tenants, of the property indicating, in whatever terms, his or their wish that one or more persons identified in the notice or intimation should become the tenant of the property;

"the retiring tenant's tenancy" means the tenancy of the person or persons giving the notice of intention to retire in favour of a new tenant;

"the tenant's retirement in favour of the new tenant" means—

(*a*) the assignment, or (in Scotland) assignation, of the retiring tenant's tenancy to the new tenant in circumstances such that the tenancy is or becomes binding on the landlord and the new tenant as landlord and tenant respectively; or

(*b*) the grant of a tenancy of the property which is the subject of the retiring tenant's tenancy, or of any property comprising the whole or part of that property, to the new tenant and the acceptance of that tenancy by him;

and, except in Scotland, "grant" and "acceptance" in paragraph (b) above respectively include the deemed grant, and the deemed acceptance, of a tenancy under or by virtue of any enactment.][8]

(6) For the purposes of this Chapter the interest of one of two or more joint tenants or tenants in common (or, in Scotland, joint owners or owners in common) shall be taken to carry a right referred to in subsection (2)(*a*) above if the interests of all of them together carry that right.

(7) For the purposes of this section, the value transferred by a transfer of value shall be calculated as a value on which no tax is chargeable.

[(8) In its application to property outside the United Kingdom, the Channel Islands and the Isle of Man, this section has effect as if any reference to a right or obligation under the law of any part of the United Kingdom were a reference to an equivalent right or obligation under the law governing dispositions of that property.][9]

Commentary—*Simon's Taxes* **I7.301, I7.302, I7.304**; *Foster* **G3.01, 02, 04**.

HMRC Manuals—Inheritance Tax Manual IHTM24001 (outline of agricultural relief).

IHTM24071 (agricultural value of agricultural property).

IHTM24073 (treatment of mortgages and debts).

IHTM24081–24090 (the rate of agricultural relief).

IHTM24162 (lifetime transfers: value transferred greater than the value of the property transferred).

IHTM24220–24240 (IHT implications of the Agricultural Holdings Act 1986 and the Agricultural Holdings (Scotland) Act 1991).

IHTM24037 (agricultural 'property').

IHTM24141 (vacant possession and the higher rate of relief example of occupation by a company).

IHTM24143 (tenancies created on or after 1 September 1995 and the higher rate of relief).

IHTM24145 (transitional provision for relief (working farmers relief) at higher rate for let land).

Concession F17—Relief for agricultural property.

HMRC Interpretation RI 121—Relief for tenanted agricultural land.

Definitions—"Agricultural property", s 115.

Cross references—See FA 1986 Sch 20 para 8(1)(*b*), (3)(*a*) (gift of agricultural property subject to a reservation; conditions for agricultural relief and determination of the appropriate percentage for the relief).

Amendments—[1] Percentage in sub-s (2) substituted by F(No 2)A 1992 Sch 14 paras 4, 8 in relation to transfers of value and other events occurring after 9 March 1992, subject to transitional provisions in Sch 14 para 9.

[2] Percentage in sub-s (2) substituted by F(No 2)A 1992 Sch 14 paras 4, 8 in relation to transfers of value and other events occurring after 9 March 1992, subject to transitional provisions in Sch 14 para 9.

[3] Percentage in sub-s (4) substituted by F(No 2)A 1992 Sch 14 paras 4, 8 in relation to transfers of value and other events occurring after 9 March 1992, subject to transitional provisions in Sch 14 para 9.

[4] Percentage in sub-s (4) substituted by F(No 2)A 1992 Sch 14 paras 4, 8 in relation to transfers of value and other events occurring after 9 March 1992, subject to transitional provisions in Sch 14 para 9.

[5] Word "either" omitted from sub-s (2) repealed; words in sub-s (2) inserted by FA 1995 s 155(1), (2), Sch 29 Pt XI, with effect for transfers of value made, and other events occurring, after 31 August 1995.

[6] Sub-s (2A) repealed by FA 1996 s 185(3), (6) and Sch 41 Pt VI, where the death of the tenant or, the sole surviving tenant, occurs after 31 August 1995.

[7] Sub-ss (5A)–(5C) inserted by FA 1996 s 185(2), (5)(*a*) in relation to cases where the death of the tenant, or the sole surviving tenant occurs after 31 August 1995.

[8] Sub-ss (5D), (5E) inserted by FA 1996 s 185(2), (5)(*b*) in relation to cases where the death of transferor occurs after 31 August 1995.

[9] Sub-s (8) inserted by FA 2009 s 122(1), (4) with effect in relation to transfers of value where the tax payable but for s 122 (or, in the case of tax payable by instalments, the last instalment of that tax)—

(a) would have been due on or after 22 April 2009, or

(b) was paid or due on or after 23 April 2003.

117 Minimum period of occupation or ownership

Subject to the following provisions of this Chapter, section 116 above does not apply to any agricultural property unless—

(*a*) it was occupied by the transferor for the purposes of agriculture throughout the period of two years ending with the date of the transfer, or

(*b*) it was owned by him throughout the period of seven years ending with that date and was throughout that period occupied (by him or another) for the purposes of agriculture.

Commentary—*Simon's Taxes* **I7.311, I7.321, I5.272.**

HMRC Manuals—IHTM24100 (ownership: introduction).

IHTM24017 (the occupation condition).

IHTM24121–24125 (the ownership condition).

Concession F16—Agricultural property and farm cottages.

Simon's Tax Cases—*Wheatley and anor (exors of Wheatley, decd) v IRC* [1998] STC (SCD) 60.

s 117(*a*), *Harrold and ors (executors of Harrold, decd) v IRC* [1996] STC (SCD) 195; *Dixon v IRC* [2002] STC (SCD) 53; *R&C Comrs v Atkinson and anor* [2011] UKUT 506 (TCC), [2012] STC 289.

Definitions—"Agricultural property", s 115.

Cross references—See FA 1986 Sch 20 para 8(2) (gift of agricultural property subject to a reservation; for the purposes of this section, donor's ownership treated as donee's ownership for determining whether agricultural relief is available).

118 Replacements

(1) Where the agricultural property occupied by the transferor on the date of the transfer replaced other agricultural property, the condition stated in section 117(*a*) above shall be treated as satisfied if it, the other property and any agricultural property directly or indirectly replaced by the other property were occupied by the transferor for the purposes of agriculture for periods which together comprised at least two years falling within the five years ending with that date.

(2) Where the agricultural property owned by the transferor on the date of the transfer replaced other agricultural property, the condition stated in section 117(*b*) above shall be treated as satisfied if it, the other property and any agricultural property directly or indirectly replaced by the other property were, for periods which together comprised at least seven years falling within the ten years ending with that date, both owned by the transferor and occupied (by him or another) for the purposes of agriculture.

(3) In a case falling within subsection (1) or (2) above relief under this Chapter shall not exceed what it would have been had the replacement or any one or more of the replacements not been made.

(4) For the purposes of subsection (3) above changes resulting from the formation, alteration or dissolution of a partnership shall be disregarded.

Commentary—*Simon's Taxes* **I7.313, I7.322, I7.302.**

HMRC Manuals—Inheritance Tax Manual IHTM24111 (application of IHTA84/S118).

IHTM24110 (replacement property: introduction).

IHTM24112 (replacement property: limitation of relief).

IHTM24113 (replacement of property: example of limiting the relief).

IHTM24114 (replacement of property: interaction with business relief).

Definitions—"Agricultural property", s 115.

119 Occupation by company or partnership

(1) For the purposes of sections 117 and 118 above, occupation by a company which is controlled by the transferor shall be treated as occupation by the transferor.

(2) For the purposes of sections 117 and 118 above, occupation of any property by a Scottish partnership shall, notwithstanding section 4(2) of the Partnership Act 1890, be treated as occupation of it by the partners.

Commentary—*Simon's Taxes* **I7.311, I7.312.**

HMRC Manuals—Inheritance Tax Manual IHTM24072 (when is property occupied).

IHTM24124 (example of occupation by a company).

120 Successions

(1) For the purposes of section 117 above, where the transferor became entitled to any property on the death of another person—

(*a*) he shall be deemed to have owned it (and, if he subsequently occupies it, to have occupied it) from the date of the death, and

(*b*) if that other person was his spouse [or civil partner][1] he shall also be deemed to have occupied it for the purposes of agriculture for any period for which it was so occupied by his spouse [or civil partner][1], and to have owned it for any period for which his spouse [or civil partner][1] owned it.

(2) Where the transferor became entitled to his interest on the death of his spouse [or civil partner][1] on or after 10th March 1981—

(*a*) he shall for the purposes of section 116(2)(*b*) above be deemed to have been beneficially entitled to it for any period for which his spouse [or civil partner][1] was beneficially entitled to it;

(*b*) the condition set out in section 116(3)(*a*) shall be taken to be satisfied if and only if it is satisfied in relation to his spouse [or civil partner][1]; and

(*c*) the condition set out in section 116(3)(*b*) shall be taken to be satisfied only if it is satisfied both in relation to him and in relation to his spouse [or civil partner][1].

Commentary—*Simon's Taxes* **I7.3141, I7.323, I12.602.**

HMRC Manuals—Inheritance Tax Manual IHTM24121 (successions: application of IHTA84/S120).

IHTM24120 (successions: introduction).

IHTM24122 (successions: the occupation requirement).

IHTM24123 (successions: example of the occupation requirement).

IHTM24124 (successions: example of occupation by a company).

IHTM24125 (successions: application with the transitional provisions (working farmer relief).

IHTM24145 (supplementary transitional provisions).

Amendments—[1] Words inserted by Tax and Civil Partnership Regulations, SI 2005/3229, regs 3, 22, with effect from 5 December 2005 (reg 1(1)).

121 Successive transfers

(1) Where—

(*a*) the whole or part of the value transferred by a transfer of value (in this section referred to as the earlier transfer) was eligible for relief under this Chapter (or would have been so eligible if such relief had been capable of being given in respect of transfers of value made at that time), and

(*b*) the whole or part of the property which, in relation to the earlier transfer, was or would have been eligible for relief became, through the earlier transfer, the property of the person (or of the spouse [or civil partner][1] of the person) who is the transferor in relation to a subsequent transfer of value and is at the time of the subsequent transfer occupied for the purposes of agriculture either by that person or by the personal representative of the transferor in relation to the earlier transfer, and

(*c*) that property or part or any property directly or indirectly replacing it would (apart from section 117 above) have been eligible for relief in relation to the subsequent transfer of value, and

(*d*) either the earlier transfer was, or the subsequent transfer of value is, a transfer made on the death of the transferor,

the property which would have been eligible for relief but for section 117 above shall be eligible for relief notwithstanding that section.

(2) Where the property which, by virtue of subsection (1) above, is eligible for relief replaced the property or part referred to in paragraph (*c*) of that subsection, relief under this Chapter shall not exceed what it would have been had the replacement or any one or more of the replacements not been made, but section 118(4) above shall apply for the purposes of this subsection as it applies for the purposes of section 118(3).

(3) Where, under the earlier transfer, the amount of the value transferred which was attributable to the property or part referred to in subsection (1)(*c*) above was part only of its value, a like part only of the value which (apart from this subsection) would fall to be reduced under this Chapter by virtue of this section shall be so reduced.

Commentary—*Simon's Taxes* **I7.315, I7.324**.
HMRC Manuals—Inheritance Tax Manual IHTM24131 (application of IHTA84/S121).
IHTM24132 (the occupation condition).
IHTM24134 (examples of relief).
IHTM24130 (successive transfers: introduction).
IHTM24133 (successive transfers: limitatons on relief).
Amendments—[1] Words in sub-s (1)(*b*) inserted by Tax and Civil Partnership Regulations, SI 2005/3229, regs 3, 23, with effect from 5 December 2005 (reg 1(1)).

122 Agricultural property of companies

(1) Where the whole or part of the value transferred is attributable to the value of shares in or securities of a company it shall be taken for the purposes of this Chapter to be attributable (so far as appropriate) to the agricultural value of agricultural property if and only if—

(*a*) the agricultural property forms part of the company's assets and part of the value of the shares or securities can be attributed to the agricultural value of the agricultural property, and

(*b*) the shares or securities gave the transferor control of the company immediately before the transfer.

(2) Shares or securities shall not be regarded for the purposes of subsection (1)(*b*) above as giving the transferor control of a company if—

(*a*) they would not have been sufficient, without other property, to give him control of the company immediately before the transfer, and

(*b*) their value is taken by virtue of section 176 below to be less than the value previously determined.

(3) Where subsection (1) above applies—

(*a*) the references in section 116(2)(*a*) and (3)(*b*) above to the transferor's interest shall be construed as references to the company's interest, and

(*b*) section 123(1) below shall apply instead of section 117 above.

Commentary—*Simon's Taxes* **I7.331, I7.335**.
HMRC Manuals—Inheritance Tax Manual IHTM24020 (unquoted shares: introduction).
IHTM24175 (where shares or securities are original property).
IHTM24021 (unqouted shares: sales within three years of death).
IHTM24022 (unquoted shares: rate of relief).
Definitions—"Agricultural property", s 115.
Cross references—See FA 1986 Sch 20 para 8(1)(*c*), (3) (gift of securities to which sub-s (1) above applies and which are subject to a reservation; conditions for agricultural relief and determination of the appropriate percentage for the relief).
IHTA 1984 s 176 sales of related property etc

123 Provisions supplementary to section 122

(1) Section 116 above shall not apply by virtue of section 122(1) above unless—

(*a*) the agricultural property—

(i) was occupied by the company for the purposes of agriculture throughout the period of two years ending with the date of the transfer, or

(ii) was owned by the company throughout the period of seven years ending with that date and was throughout that period occupied (by the company or another) for the purposes of agriculture, and

(*b*) the shares or securities were owned by the transferor—

(i) in a case within paragraph (*a*)(i) above, throughout the period there mentioned, or

(ii) in a case within paragraph (*a*)(ii) above, throughout the period there mentioned.

(2) Subsections (1) and (2) of section 118 above shall apply in relation to the conditions stated in subsection (1)(*a*) above as they apply in relation to the conditions stated in section 117 taking references to the transferor as references to the company.

(3) Where the shares or securities owned by the transferor on the date of the transfer replaced other eligible property (that is to say, agricultural property or shares or securities the value of which is wholly or partly attributable to the value of such property) the condition stated in subsection (1)(*b*) above shall be treated as satisfied if the shares or securities, the other eligible property which they replaced and any eligible property directly or indirectly replaced by the other eligible property were owned by the transferor for periods which together comprised—

(*a*) in a case within subsection (1)(*a*)(i) above, at least two years falling within the five years ending with that date, or

(*b*) in a case within subsection (1)(*a*)(ii) above, at least seven years falling within the ten years ending with that date.

(4) Subsections (3) and (4) of section 118 above shall have effect in relation to a case falling within subsections (2) and (3) above as they have effect in relation to a case falling within subsections (1) and (2) of that section.

(5) For the purposes of subsection (1) above, a company shall be treated as having occupied the agricultural property at any time when it was occupied by a person who subsequently controls the company.

Commentary—*Simon's Taxes* **I7.333, I7.334, I7.331**.
HMRC Manuals—Inheritance Tax Manual IHTM24024 (unquoted shares: replacements).
IHTM24023 (occupation and ownership tests).
Definitions—"Agricultural property", s 115.
Cross references—See FA 1986 Sch 20 para 8(3) (gift of agricultural property (securities) subject to a reservation; certain conditions deemed as fulfilled in determining question of agricultural relief and percentage).

124 Contracts for sale

(1) Section 116 above shall not apply to agricultural property if at the time of the transfer the transferor has entered into a binding contract for its sale, except where the sale is to a company and is made wholly or mainly in consideration of shares in or securities of the company which will give the transferor control of the company.

(2) Section 116 above shall not apply by virtue of section 122(1) above if at the time of the transfer the transferor has entered into a binding contract for the sale of the shares or securities concerned, except where the sale is made for the purpose of reconstruction or amalgamation.

Commentary—*Simon's Taxes* **I7.341–I7.344**.
HMRC Manuals—Inheritance Tax Manual IHTM24040 (agricultural property: contracts and trusts for sale).
Definitions—"Agricultural property", s 115.

[124A Transfers within seven years before death of transferor

(1) Where any part of the value transferred by a potentially exempt transfer which proves to be a chargeable transfer would (apart from this section) be reduced in accordance with the preceding provisions of this Chapter, it shall not be so reduced unless the conditions in subsection (3) below are satisfied.

(2) Where—

(*a*) any part of the value transferred by any chargeable transfer, other than a potentially exempt transfer, is reduced in accordance with the preceding provisions of this Chapter, and

(*b*) the transfer is made within seven years of the death of the transferor,

then, unless the conditions in subsection (3) below are satisfied, the additional tax chargeable by reason of the death shall be calculated as if the value transferred had not been so reduced.

(3) The conditions referred to in subsections (1) and (2) above are—

(*a*) that the original property was owned by the transferee throughout the period beginning with the date of the chargeable transfer and ending with the death of the transferor (in this subsection referred to as "the relevant period") and it is not at the time of the death subject to a binding contract for sale; and

(*b*) except in a case falling within paragraph (*c*) below, that the original property is agricultural property immediately before the death and has been occupied (by the transferee or another) for the purposes of agriculture throughout the relevant period; and

(*c*) where the original property consists of shares in or securities of a company, that throughout the relevant period the agricultural property to which section 116 above applied by virtue of section 122(1) above on the chargeable transfer was owned by the company and occupied (by the company or another) for the purposes of agriculture.

(4) If the transferee has died before the transferor, the reference in subsection (3) above to the death of the transferor shall have effect as a reference to the death of the transferee.
(5) If the conditions in subsection (3) above are satisfied only with respect to part of the original property, then,—
(*a*) in a case falling within subsection (1) above, only a proportionate part of so much of the value transferred as is attributable to the original property shall be reduced in accordance with the preceding provisions of this Chapter, and
(*b*) in a case falling within subsection (2) above, the additional tax shall be calculated as if only a proportionate part of so much of the value transferred as was attributable to the original property had been so reduced.
(6) Where any shares owned by the transferee immediately before the death in question—
(*a*) would under any of the provisions of sections [126 to 136 of the 1992 Act][3] be identified with the original property (or part of it), or
(*b*) were issued to him in consideration of the transfer of agricultural property consisting of the original property (or part of it),
[his period of ownership of the original property shall be treated as including his period of ownership of the shares][2].
(7) This section has effect subject to section 124B below.
[(7A) The provisions of this Chapter for the reduction of value transferred shall be disregarded in any determination for the purposes of this section of whether there is a potentially exempt or chargeable transfer in any case.][4]
(8) In this section—
"the original property" means the property which, in relation to the chargeable transfer referred to in subsection (1) or subsection (2) above, was either agricultural property to which section 116 above applied or shares or securities of a company owning agricultural property to which that section applied by virtue of section 122(1) above; and
"the transferee" means the person whose property the original property became on that chargeable transfer or, where on the transfer the original property became or remained settled property in which no qualifying interest in possession (within the meaning of Chapter III of Part III of this Act) subsists, the trustees of the settlement.][1]

Commentary—*Simon's Taxes* **I7.381–I7.381B, I7.381C**.
HMRC Manuals—Inheritance Tax Manual IHTM24171–24180 (additional conditions for lifetime transfers).
HMRC Interpretation RI 95—Interaction of this section and s 114(1) on the replacement of agricultural property with other business property.
Definitions—"Agricultural property", s 115; "qualifying interest in possession", s 59(1).
Cross references—See FA 1986 Sch 19 para 40 (where a death or other event occurs on or after 18 March 1986, this section does not affect the tax chargeable on a transfer of value occurring before 18 March 1986).
TCGA 1992 ss 126–136 (Reorganisation of share capital, conversion of securities and reconstructions and amalgamations).
Amendments—[1] This section inserted by FA 1986 s 101(3) and Sch 19 para 22 in relation to transfers of value made after 17 March 1986.
[2] Words in sub-s (6) substituted by FA 1987 s 58 and Sch 8 para 9 in relation to transfers of value made after 16 March 1987.
[3] Words in sub-s (6)(*a*) substituted by TCGA 1992 Sch 10 para 8(1), (5).
[4] Sub-s (7A) inserted by FA 1996 s 185(4), (7) in relation to transfers of value made after 27 November 1995.

[124B Application of section 124A to replacement property
(1) Subject to subsection (2) below, this section applies where—
(*a*) the transferee has disposed of all or part of the original property before the death of the transferor; and
(*b*) the whole of the consideration received by him for the disposal has been applied by him in acquiring other property (in this section referred to as "the replacement property").
(2) This section does not apply unless—
(*a*) the replacement property is acquired, or a binding contract for its acquisition is entered into, within [the allowed period][2] after the disposal of the original property (or, as the case may be, the part concerned); and
(*b*) the disposal and acquisition are both made in transactions at arm's length or on terms such as might be expected to be included in a transaction at arm's length.
(3) Where this section applies, the conditions in section 124A(3) above shall be taken to be satisfied in relation to the original property (or, as the case may be, the part concerned) if—
(*a*) the replacement property is owned by the transferee immediately before the death of the transferor and is not at that time subject to a binding contract for sale; and
(*b*) throughout the period beginning with the date of the chargeable transfer and ending with the disposal, the original property was owned by the transferee and occupied (by the transferee or another) for the purposes of agriculture; and
(*c*) throughout the period beginning with the date when the transferee acquired the replacement property and ending with the death, the replacement property was owned by the transferee and occupied (by the transferee or another) for the purposes of agriculture; and
(*d*) the replacement property is agricultural property immediately before the death.

(4) If the transferee has died before the transferor, any reference in subsections (1) to (3) above to the death of the transferor shall have effect as a reference to the death of the transferee.

(5) In any case where—

(*a*) all or part of the original property has been disposed of before the death of the transferor or is subject to a binding contract for sale at the time of the death, and

(*b*) the replacement property is acquired, or a binding contract for its acquisition is entered into, after the death of the transferor but within [the allowed period][2] after the disposal of the original property or part, and

(*c*) the transferor dies before the transferee,

subsection (3) above shall have effect with the omission of paragraphs (a) and (c), and as if any reference to a time immediately before the death of the transferor were a reference to the time when the replacement property is acquired.

(6) Section 124A(6) above shall have effect in relation to the replacement property as it has effect in relation to the original property.

(7) Where a binding contract for the disposal of any property is entered into at any time before the disposal of the property, the disposal shall be regarded for the purposes of subsections (2)(*a*) and (5)(*b*) above as taking place at that time.

(8) In this section "the original property" and "the transferee" have the same meaning as in section 124A above [and "allowed period" means the period of three years or such longer period as the Board may allow][3].][1]

Commentary—*Simon's Taxes* **I7.381C**.

HMRC Manuals—Inheritance Tax Manual IHTM24181 (replacement property, other than shares or securities). IHTM24182 (replacement property (shares or securities).

Cross references—See FA 1986 Sch 19 para 40 (where a death or other event occurs on or after 18 March 1986, this section does not affect the tax chargeable on a transfer of value occurring before 18 March 1986).

Amendments—[1] This section inserted by FA 1986 s 101(3) and Sch 19 para 22 in relation to transfers of value made after 17 March 1986.

[2] Words in sub-ss (2)(*a*), (5)(*b*) substituted by FA 1994 s 247(2), (3) in relation to transfers of value made and other events occurring after 29 November 1993.

[3] Words in sub-s (8) added by FA 1994 s 247(2), (3) in relation to transfers of value made and other events occurring after 29 November 1993.

[124C Land in habitat schemes

(1) For the purpose of this Chapter, where any land is in a habitat scheme—

(*a*) the land shall be regarded as agricultural land;

(*b*) the management of the land in accordance with the requirements of the scheme shall be regarded as agriculture; and

(*c*) buildings used in connection with such management shall be regarded as farm buildings.

(2) For the purposes of this section land is in a habitat scheme at any time if—

(*a*) an application for aid under one of the enactments listed in subsection (3) below has been accepted in respect of the land; and

(*b*) the undertakings to which the acceptance relates have neither been terminated by the expiry of the period to which they relate nor been treated as terminated.

(3) Those enactments are—

(*a*) regulation 3(1) of the Habitat (Water Fringe) Regulations 1994;

(*b*) the Habitat (Former Set-Aside Land) Regulations 1994;

(*c*) the Habitat (Salt-Marsh) Regulation 1994;

(*d*) the Habitats (Scotland) Regulations 1994, if undertakings in respect of the land have been given under regulation 3(2)(*a*) of those Regulations;

(*e*) the Habitat Improvement Regulations (Northern Ireland) 1995, if an undertaking in respect of the land has been given under regulation 3(1)(*a*) of those Regulations.

(4) The Treasury may by order made by statutory instrument amend the list of enactments in subsection (3) above.

(5) The power to make an order under subsection (4) above shall be exercisable by statutory instrument subject to annulment in pursuance or a resolution of the House of Commons.

(6) This section has effect—

(*a*) in relation to any transfer of value made on or after 26th November 1996; and

(*b*) in relation to transfers of value made before that date, for the purposes of any charge to tax, or to extra tax, which arises by reason of an event occurring on or after 26th November 1996.][1]

Commentary—*Simon's Taxes* **I7.305, I7.311**.

HMRC Manuals—Inheritance Tax Manual IHTM24065 (the habitat scheme).

Amendments—[1] This section inserted by FA 1997 s 94.

CHAPTER III

WOODLANDS

125 The relief

(1) This section applies where—

(*a*) part of the value of a person's estate immediately before his death is attributable to the value of land . . . [1] on which trees or underwood are growing but which is not agricultural property within the meaning of Chapter II of this Part of this Act, and

(*b*) either he was beneficially entitled to the land throughout the five years immediately preceding his death, or he became beneficially entitled to it otherwise than for a consideration in money or money's worth.

[(1A) But this section applies only if the land is in the United Kingdom or another state which is an EEA state (within the meaning given by Schedule 1 to the Interpretation Act 1978) at the time of the person's death.][1]

(2) Where this section applies and the person liable for the whole or part of the tax so elects—

(*a*) the value of the trees or underwood shall be left out of account in determining the value transferred on the death, but

(*b*) tax shall be charged in the circumstances mentioned in section 126 below.

(3) An election under this section must be made by notice in writing to the Board within two years of the death or such longer time as the Board may allow.

Commentary—*Simon's Taxes* **I7.401–I7.403, I4.262, I4.127, I11.521**.

HMRC Manuals—Inheritance Tax Manual IHTM04371–04376 (details relating to woodlands).

IHTM04121 (woodlands: summary).

Definitions—"The Board", "estate", "land", s 272.

Cross references—See FA 2009 s 122 (9) (time limit for elections consequent on amendments to this section made by FA 2009 s 122 (5), (6), (see below)).

Amendments—[1] In sub-s (1), words "in the United Kingdom" repealed, and sub-s (1A) inserted, by FA 2009 s 122 (1), (5), (6), with effect in relation to transfers of value where the tax payable but for this section (or, in the case of tax payable by instalments, the last instalment of that tax)—

(a) would have been due on or after 22 April 2009, or

(b) was paid or due on or after 23 April 2003.

126 Charge to tax on disposal of trees or underwood

(1) Where under section 125 above the value of any trees or underwood has been left out of account in determining the value transferred on the death of any person, and the whole or any part of the trees or underwood is disposed of (whether together with or apart from the land on which they were growing) then, if the disposal occurs before any part of the value transferred on the death of any other person is attributable to the value of that land, tax shall be charged in accordance with sections 127 and 128 below.

(2) Subsection (1) above shall not apply to a disposal made by any person to his spouse [or civil partner][1].

(3) Where tax has been charged under this section on the disposal of any trees or underwood tax shall not again be charged in relation to the same death on a further disposal of the same trees or underwood.

Commentary—*Simon's Taxes* **I7.404, I7.405**.

HMRC Manuals—Inheritance Tax Manual IHTM04122 (the deferred charge).

Cross references—IHTA 1984 s 208 (person liable for tax under this section),

IHTA 1984 s 216(7) (delivery of accounts),

IHTA 1984 s 221(6)(*c*) (notices of determination),

IHTA 1984 s 226(4) (due date for payment of tax under this section),

IHTA 1984 s 233(1)(*c*) (interest on unpaid tax).

Amendments—[1] Words in sub-s (2) inserted by Tax and Civil Partnerships Regulations, SI 2005/3229 regs 3, 24, with effect from 5 December 2005 (reg 1(1)).

127 Amount subject to charge

(1) The amount on which tax is charged under section 126 above on a disposal of trees or underwood shall be—

(*a*) if the disposal is a sale for full consideration in money or money's worth, an amount equal to the net proceeds of the sale, and

(*b*) in any other case, an amount equal to the net value of the trees or underwood at the time of the disposal.

(2) Where, if the value of the trees or underwood had not been left out of account in determining the value transferred on the death of the person in question—

(*a*) it would have been taken into account in determining the value of any relevant business property for the purposes of relief under Chapter I of this Part of this Act in relation to the transfer of value made on his death, or

(*b*) it would have been so taken into account if this Act had then been in force,

the amount on which tax is charged under section 126 above shall be reduced by 50 per cent.

Commentary—*Simon's Taxes* **I7.404, I7.405, I7.407, I7.174.**

128 Rate of charge

[(1)] Tax charged under section 126 above on an amount determined under section 127 above shall be charged at the rate or rates at which it would have been charged on the death first mentioned in section 126 if—

(*a*) that amount, and any amount on which tax was previously charged under section 126 in relation to that death, had been included in the value transferred on death, and

(*b*) the amount on which the tax is charged had formed the highest part of that value.

[(2) In determining for the purposes of subsection (1) the rate or rates at which tax would have been charged on the amount determined under section 127, the effect of Schedule 1A (if it would have applied) is to be disregarded.][1]

Commentary—*Simon's Taxes* **I7.405**.

HMRC Manuals—Inheritance Tax Manual IHTM45051 (charges arising following the deferral of tax for woodlands or conditional exemption).

Cross reference—IHTA 1984 Sch 2 para 4 (determination of the rate of tax where there has been a reduction under Sch 1 following exemption on death).

Amendments—[1] Sub-s (1) numbered as such and sub-s (2) inserted by FA 2012 s 209, Sch 33 paras 2, 6 with effect in cases where D's death occurs on or after 6 April 2012.

129 Credit for tax charged

Where a disposal on which tax is chargeable under section 126 above is a chargeable transfer, the value transferred by it shall be calculated as if the value of the trees or underwood had been reduced by the tax chargeable under that section.

Commentary—*Simon's Taxes* **I7.406, I11.521.**

Cross reference—IHTA 1984 s 114(2) (avoidance of double relief).

130 Interpretation

(1) In this Chapter—

(*a*) references to the value transferred on a death are references to the value transferred by the chargeable transfer made on that death;

(*b*) references to the net proceeds of sale or the net value of any trees or underwood are references to the proceeds of sale or value after deduction of any expenses allowable under this Chapter so far as those expenses are not allowable for the purposes of income tax; and

(*c*) references to the disposal of any trees or underwood include references to the disposal of any interest in the trees or underwood (and references to a disposal of the same trees or underwood shall, where the case so requires, be construed as referring to a disposal of the same interest).

(2) The expenses allowable under this Chapter are, in relation to any trees or underwood the value of which has been left out of account on any death,—

(*a*) the expenses incurred in disposing of the trees or underwood; and

(*b*) the expenses incurred in replanting within three years of a disposal (or such longer time as the Board may allow) to replace the trees or underwood disposed of; and

(*c*) the expenses incurred in replanting to replace trees or underwood previously disposed of, so far as not allowable on the previous disposal.

Commentary—*Simon's Taxes* **I7.401, I7.404, I7.405.**

HMRC Manuals—Inheritance Tax Manual IHTM31492 (deductions allowable in caluculating the tax on disposal of woodlands).

CHAPTER IV

TRANSFERS WITHIN SEVEN YEARS BEFORE DEATH

Note—As a consequence of the amendment of s 131 below by FA 1986 s 101(1)(*a*), (3) and Sch 19 para 23, the cross heading above has been amended for this publication. It originally read "Transfers within three years before death".

131 The relief

(1) Subject to section 132 below, this section applies where [because of the transferor's death within seven years of the transfer, tax becomes chargeable in respect of the value transferred by a potentially exempt transfer or (by virtue of section 7(4) above) additional tax becomes chargeable in respect of the value transferred by any other chargeable transfer and (in either case)][1] all or part of the value transferred is attributable to the value of property ("the transferred property") which—

(*a*) is, at the date of the death, the property of the person ("the transferee") whose property it became on the transfer or of his spouse [or civil partner][3], or

(*b*) has, before that date, been sold by the transferee or his spouse [or civil partner][3] by a qualifying sale;

and in the following provisions of this section "the relevant date" means, in a case within paragraph (a) above, the date of the death, and in a case within paragraph (b), the date of the qualifying sale.

(2) If—

(*a*) the market value of the transferred property at the time of the chargeable transfer exceeds its market value on the relevant date, and

(*b*) a claim is made by a person liable to pay the whole or part of [the tax or, as the case may be, additional tax][1]

[the tax or, as the case may be, additional tax][1] shall be calculated as if the value transferred were reduced by the amount of the excess.

[(2ZA A claim under subsection (2)(*b*) must be made not more than 4 years after the transferor's death.][4]

[(2A) Where so much of the value transferred as is attributable to the value, or agricultural value, of the transferred property is reduced by any percentage (in this subsection referred to as "the appropriate percentage"), in accordance with Chapter I or Chapter II of this Part of this Act, references in subsection (2) above to the market value of the transferred property at any time shall have effect—

(*a*) in a case within Chapter I, as references to that market value reduced by the appropriate percentage; and

(*b*) in a case within Chapter II, as references to that market value less the appropriate percentage of the agricultural value of the transferred property at that time.][2]

(3) A sale is a qualifying sale for the purposes of this section if—

(*a*) it is at arm's length for a price freely negotiated at the time of the sale, and

(*b*) no person concerned as vendor (or as having an interest in the proceeds of the sale) is the same as or connected with any person concerned as purchaser (or as having an interest in the purchase), and

(*c*) no provision is made, in or in connection with the agreement for the sale, that the vendor (or any person having an interest in the proceeds of sale) is to have any right to acquire some or all of the property sold or some interest in or created out of it.

Commentary—*Simon's Taxes* **I3.361–I3.363, I1.510, I3.533**.

HMRC Manuals—Inheritance Tax Manual IHTM14621–14625 (fall in value relief).
IHTM14626 (what is market value?).
IHTM14627 (the claim for fall in value relief).
IHTM14629 (portfolio of assets).
IHTM27125 and 27043 (fall in value relief for foreign shares and land and buildings).

Definitions—"Purchaser", s 272.

Cross references—See FA 1986 Sch 19 para 40 (where a death or other event occurs on or after 18 March 1986, the amendments to this section by FA 1986 Sch 19 (see below) not to affect the tax chargeable on a transfer of value occurring before 18 March 1986).

Amendments—[1] Words in sub-ss (1), (2) substituted by FA 1986 s 101(1)(*a*), (3) and Sch 19 para 23 with respect to transfers of value made, and other events occurring, after 17 March 1986.

[2] Sub-s (2A) inserted by FA 1986 s 101(1)(*a*), (3) and Sch 19 para 23 with respect to transfers of value made, and other events occurring, after 17 March 1986.

[3] Words in sub-s (1) inserted by Tax and Civil Partnership Regulations, SI 2005/3229 regs 3, 25, with effect from 5 December 2005 (reg 1(1)).

[4] Sub-s (2ZA) inserted by FA 2009 s 99, Sch 51 para 6 with effect from 1 April 2011 (SI 2010/867 art 2(2)).

132 Wasting assets

(1) Section 131 above shall not apply if the transferred property is tangible movable property that is a wasting asset.

(2) The transferred property is a wasting asset for the purposes of this section if, immediately before the chargeable transfer, it had a predictable useful life not exceeding fifty years, having regard to the purpose for which it was held by the transferor; and plant and machinery shall in every case be regarded as having a predictable useful life of less than fifty years.

Commentary—*Simon's Taxes* **I3.364**.

HMRC Manuals—Inheritance Tax Manual IHTM14628 (wasting assets).

133 Shares—capital receipts

(1) If the transferred property consists of shares and at any time before the relevant date the transferee or his spouse [or civil partner][1] becomes entitled to a capital payment in respect of them, then for the purposes of section 131 above the market value of the transferred property on the relevant date shall (except where apart from this section it reflects a right to the payment) be taken to be increased by an amount equal to the payment.

(2) If at any time before the relevant date the transferee or his spouse [or civil partner][1] receives or becomes entitled to receive in respect of the transferred property a provisional allotment of shares and disposes of the rights, the amount of the consideration for the disposal shall be treated for the purposes of this section as a capital payment in respect of the transferred property.

(3) In this section "capital payment" means any money or money's worth which does not constitute income for the purposes of income tax.

Commentary—*Simon's Taxes* **I3.365**.

HMRC Manuals—Inheritance Tax Manual IHTM14641 and 14642 (shares and securities: adjustments and capital receipts).

Definitions—"Shares", s 140.

Amendments—[1] Words in sub-ss (1), (2) inserted by Tax and Civil Partnership Regulations, SI 2005/3229, regs 3, 26, with effect from 5 December 2005 (reg 1(1)).

134 Payments of calls

If the transferred property consists of shares and at any time before the relevant date the transferee or his spouse [or civil partner][1] becomes liable to make a payment in pursuance of a call in respect of them, then for the purposes of section 131 above the market value of the transferred property on the relevant date shall (except where apart from this section it reflects the liability) be taken to be reduced by an amount equal to the payment.

Commentary—*Simon's Taxes* **I3.365**.
HMRC Manuals—Inheritance Tax Manual IHTM14643 (payment of calls).
Definitions—"Shares", s 140.
Amendments—[1] Words inserted by Tax and Civil Partnership Regulations, SI 2005/3229, regs 3, 27, with effect from 5 December 2005 (reg 1(1)).

135 Reorganisation of share capital, etc

(1) This section has effect where the transferred property consists of shares in relation to which there occurs before the relevant date a transaction to which section [127 of the 1992 Act][1] applies or would apply but for section [134][1] of that Act, that is to say—

- (*a*) a reorganisation within the meaning of section [126(1)][1] of that Act,
- (*b*) the conversion of securities within the meaning of section [132][1] of that Act,
- (*c*) the issue by a company of shares in exchange for shares in another company in such circumstances that section [135][1] of that Act applies, or
- (*d*) the issue by a company of shares under such an arrangement as is referred to in section [136][1] of that Act,

or any transaction relating to a unit trust scheme which corresponds to any of the transactions referred to in paragraphs (a) to (d) above and to which section [127][1] of that Act applies by virtue of section [99][1] of that Act.

(2) In the following provisions of this section "the original shares" and "the new holding" shall be construed in accordance with section [126(1)][1].

(3) Where this section has effect the original shares and the new holding shall be treated as the same property for the purposes of this Chapter.

(4) Where this section has effect and, as part of or in connection with the transaction concerned, the transferee or his spouse [or civil partner][2] becomes liable to give any consideration for the new holding or any part of it, then for the purposes of section 131 above the market value of the transferred property on the relevant date shall (except where apart from this section it reflects the liability) be taken to be reduced by an amount equal to that consideration.

(5) For the purposes of subsection (4) above, there shall not be treated as consideration given for the new holding or any part of it—

- (*a*) any surrender, cancellation or other alteration of any of the original shares or of the rights attached thereto, or
- (*b*) any consideration consisting of any application, in paying up the new holding or any part of it, of assets of the company concerned or of any dividend or other distribution declared out of those assets but not made.

Commentary—*Simon's Taxes* **I3.365**.
HMRC Manuals—Inheritance Tax Manual IHTM14644 (changes in shareholdings).
Amendments—[1] Words in sub-ss (1), (2) substituted by TCGA 1992 Sch 10 para 8 (1), (6).
[2] Words in sub-s (4) inserted by Tax and Civil Partnership Regulations, SI 2005/3229, regs 3, 28, with effect from 5 December 2005 (reg 1(1)).

136 Transactions of close companies

(1) This section applies where the transferred property consists of shares in a close company and at any time after the chargeable transfer and before the relevant date there is a relevant transaction in relation to the shares; and for this purpose "relevant transaction" means a transaction which is—

- (*a*) the making of a transfer of value by the company, or
- (*b*) an alteration in so much of the company's share or loan capital as does not consist of [quoted shares][1] or an alteration in any rights attaching to [unquoted shares in or unquoted debentures of the company][1],

but which does not give rise to an adjustment, under any of the preceding sections of this Chapter, in the market value of the transferred property on the relevant date.

(2) Subject to subsections (3) and (4) below, where this section applies the market value of the transferred property on the relevant date shall for the purposes of section 131 above be taken to be increased by an amount equal to the difference between—

- (*a*) the market value of the transferred property at the time of the chargeable transfer, and
- (*b*) what that value would have been if the relevant transaction had occurred before rather than after that time.

(3) Where the relevant transaction is the making by the company of a transfer of value by which the value of the estate of the person who made the chargeable transfer or, if his spouse [or civil partner][2] is domiciled in the United Kingdom, his spouse [or civil partner] is increased by any amount, the increase provided for by subsection (2) above shall be reduced by that amount.
(4) Where the market value of the transferred property at the time of the chargeable transfer is less than it would have been as mentioned in subsection (2) above, that subsection shall apply as if, instead of providing for an increase, it provided for the market value on the relevant date to be reduced to what it would have been if the relevant transaction had not occurred.

Commentary—*Simon's Taxes* **I3.366**.
HMRC Manuals—Inheritance Tax Manual IHTM14645 (transactions of close companies).
Definitions—"close company", s 102(1); "quoted", "unquoted", s 272.
Amendments—[1] Words in sub-s (1)(*b*) substituted by FA 1987 s 58 and Sch 8 para 10 in relation to transfers of value made or other events occurring after 16 March 1987.
[2] Words in sub-s (3) inserted by Tax and Civil Partnership Regulations, SI 2005/3229, regs 3, 29, with effect from 5 December 2005 (reg 1(1)).

137 Interests in land

(1) Where the transferred property is an interest in land in relation to which the conditions mentioned in subsection (2) below are not satisfied, then, subject to subsections (3) and (4) below, the market value of the transferred property on the relevant date shall for the purposes of section 131 above be taken to be increased by an amount equal to the difference between—

(*a*) the market value of the interest at the time of the chargeable transfer, and
(*b*) what that market value would have been if the circumstances prevailing on the relevant date and by reason of which the conditions are not satisfied had prevailed at the time of the chargeable transfer.

(2) The conditions referred to in subsection (1) above are—

(*a*) that the interest was the same in all respects and with the same incidents at the time of the chargeable transfer and on the relevant date, and
(*b*) that the land in which the interest subsists was in the same state and with the same incidents at the time of the chargeable transfer and on the relevant date.

(3) If after the date of the chargeable transfer but before the relevant date compensation becomes payable under any enactment to the transferee or his spouse [or civil partner[1]]—

(*a*) because of the imposition of a restriction on the use or development of the land in which the interest subsists, or
(*b*) because the value of the interest is reduced for any other reason,

the imposition of the restriction or the other cause of the reduction in value shall be ignored for the purposes of subsections (1) and (2) above, but the market value of the interest on the relevant date shall be taken to be increased by an amount equal to the amount of the compensation.
(4) Where the market value of the interest at the time of the chargeable transfer is less than it would have been as mentioned in subsection (1) above, that subsection shall apply as if, instead of providing for an increase, it provided for the market value on the relevant date to be reduced to what it would have been if the change in circumstances by reason of which the conditions mentioned in subsection (2) above are not satisfied had not occurred.

Commentary—*Simon's Taxes* **I3.367**.
HMRC Manuals—Inheritance Tax Manual IHTM14661–14664 (interests in land).
Amendments—[1] Words in sub-s (3) inserted by Tax and Civil Partnership Regulations, SI 2005/3229, regs 3, 30, with effect from 5 December 2005 (reg 1(1)).

138 Leases

(1) Where the transferred property is the interest of a lessee under a lease the duration of which at the time of the chargeable transfer does not exceed fifty years, then for the purposes of section 131 above the market value of the interest on the relevant date shall be taken to be increased by an amount equal to the appropriate fraction of the market value of the interest at the time of the chargeable transfer.
(2) In subsection (1) above, "the appropriate fraction" means the fraction—

$$\frac{P(1) - P(2)}{P(1)}$$

where

P(1) is the percentage that would be derived from the Table in paragraph 1 of Schedule [8 to the 1992 Act][1] for the duration of the lease at the time of the chargeable transfer, and
P(2) is the percentage that would be so derived for the duration of the lease on the relevant date.

Commentary—*Simon's Taxes* **I3.368**.
HMRC Manuals—Inheritance Tax Manual IHTM14670 (leases).
Amendments—[1] Words in sub-s (2) substituted by TCGA 1992 Sch 10 para 8 (1), (7).

139 Other property

(1) Where the transferred property is neither shares nor an interest in land and the condition mentioned in subsection (2) below is not satisfied in relation to it, then, subject to subsections (3) and (4) below, the market value of the property on the relevant date shall for the purposes of section 131 above be taken to be increased by an amount equal to the difference between—

(*a*) the market value of the property at the time of the chargeable transfer, and

(*b*) what that value would have been if the circumstances prevailing at the relevant date and by reason of which the condition is not satisfied had prevailed at the time of the chargeable transfer.

(2) The condition referred to in subsection (1) above is that the transferred property was the same in all respects at the time of the chargeable transfer and on the relevant date.

(3) Where the market value of the transferred property at the time of the chargeable transfer is less than it would have been as mentioned in subsection (1) above, that subsection shall apply as if, instead of providing for an increase, it provided for the market value on the relevant date to be reduced to what it would have been if the property had remained the same in all respects as it was at the time of the chargeable transfer.

(4) Where the transferred property is neither shares nor an interest in land and during the period between the time of the chargeable transfer and the relevant date benefits in money or money's worth are derived from it which exceed a reasonable return on its market value at the time of the chargeable transfer, then—

(*a*) any effect of the benefits on the transferred property shall be ignored for the purposes of the preceding provisions of this section, but

(*b*) the market value of the transferred property on the relevant date shall be taken for the purposes of section 131 above to be increased by an amount equal to the said excess.

Commentary—*Simon's Taxes* **I3.369**.

HMRC Manuals—Inheritance Tax Manual IHTM14671 (other property).

Definitions—"Interest in land", "shares", s 140.

140 Interpretation

(1) In this Chapter—

"close company" has the same meaning as in Part IV of this Act;

"interest in land" does not include any estate, interest or right by way of mortgage or other security;

"shares" include securities;

and "the relevant date", "the transferee" and "the transferred property" shall be construed in accordance with section 131(1) above.

(2) For the purposes of this Chapter the market value at any time of any property is the price which the property might reasonably be expected to fetch if sold in the open market at that time; but—

(*a*) that price shall not be assumed to be reduced on the ground that the whole property is on the market at one and the same time, and

(*b*) in the case of [unquoted shares][1], it shall be assumed that in that market there is available to any prospective purchaser of the shares all the information which a prudent prospective purchaser might reasonably require if he were proposing to purchase them from a willing vendor by private treaty and at arm's length.

Commentary—*Simon's Taxes* **I8.201, I8.311, I3.365, I3.367, I3.368, I3.369**.

Definitions—"close company", s 102(1), "mortgage", "purchaser", "unquoted", s 272.

Amendments—[1] Words in sub-s (2)(*b*) substituted by FA 1987 Sch 8 para 11 in relation to transfers of value made or other events occurring after 16 March 1987.

CHAPTER V

MISCELLANEOUS

Successive charges

141 Two or more transfers within five years

(1) Where the value of a person's estate was increased by a chargeable transfer ("the first transfer") made not more than five years before—

(*a*) his death, or

(*b*) a chargeable transfer which is made by him otherwise than on his death and as to which the conditions specified in subsection (2) below are satisfied,

the tax chargeable on the value transferred by the transfer made on his death or, as the case may be, referred to in paragraph (b) above ("the later transfer") shall be reduced by an amount calculated in accordance with subsection (3) below.

(2) The conditions referred to in subsection (1)(*b*) above are—

(*a*) that the value transferred by the later transfer falls to be determined by reference to the value of settled property in which there subsists an interest in possession to which the transferor is entitled;

(*b*) that the value transferred by the first transfer also fell to be determined by reference to the value of that property; and

(*c*) that the first transfer either was or included the making of the settlement or was made after the making of the settlement.

(3) The amount referred to in subsection (1) above is a percentage of the tax charged on so much of the value transferred by the first transfer as is attributable to the increase mentioned in that subsection; and the percentage is—

(*a*) 100 per cent if the period beginning with the date of the first transfer and ending with the date of the later does not exceed one year;

(*b*) 80 per cent if it exceeds one year but does not exceed two years;

(*c*) 60 per cent if it exceeds two years but does not exceed three years;

(*d*) 40 per cent if it exceeds three years but does not exceed four years; and

(*e*) 20 per cent if it exceeds four years.

(4) Where in relation to the first transfer there is more than one later transfer, the reduction provided for by this section shall be given only in respect of the earliest of them, unless the reduction represents less than the whole of the tax charged as mentioned in subsection (3) above; and in that case a reduction may be made in respect of subsequent transfers (in chronological order) until reductions representing the whole of that tax have been made.

(5) For the purposes of subsection (4) above, a reduction made in accordance with paragraph (*a*) of subsection (3) above represents an equivalent amount of tax, a reduction made in accordance with paragraph (*b*) represents the amount of tax of which it is 80 per cent, and so on.

(6) In determining for the purposes of this section whether or to what extent the value of the transferor's estate was increased by a chargeable transfer, there shall be disregarded any excluded property consisting of a reversionary interest to which he became entitled on the occasion of or before the chargeable transfer.

(7) Where—

(*a*) the value of the transferor's estate was increased in consequence of—

(i) a gift inter vivos, or

(ii) a disposition or determination of a beneficial interest in possession in property comprised in a settlement, and

(*b*) tax under section 22(5) of the Finance Act 1975 was by reason of the gift or interest payable on a subsequent death,

this section shall apply as if the increase had been by the chargeable transfer made on the occasion of the death.

Commentary—*Simon's Taxes* **I4.172, I5.283, I5.456.**

HMRC Manuals—Inheritance Tax Manual IHTM22041–22045 (quick succession relief).

IHTM22051–22081 (calculation quick succession relief).

IHTM22091–22093 (quick succession relief: settled property).

IHTM45050 (where the estate is entitled to quick succession relief).

Definitions—"Estate", "excluded property", s 272; "reversionary interest", s 47; "settlement", s 43.

[141A Apportionment of relief under section 141

(1) This section applies if any part of the value transferred by the later transfer qualifies for the lower rate of tax in accordance with Schedule 1A.

(2) The amount of the reduction made under section 141(1) is to be apportioned in accordance with this section.

(3) For each qualifying component, the tax chargeable on so much of the value transferred by the later transfer as is attributable to property in that component ("the relevant part of the tax") is to be reduced by the appropriate proportion of the amount calculated in accordance with section 141(3).

(4) "The appropriate proportion" is a proportion equal to the proportion that—

(a) the relevant part of the tax, bears to

(b) the tax chargeable on the value transferred by the later transfer as a whole.

(5) If parts of an estate are treated under Schedule 1A as a single component, subsection (3) applies to the single component (and not to individual components forming part of the deemed single component).

(6) If, after making the reductions required by subsection (3), there remains any part of the tax chargeable on the value transferred by the later transfer that has not been reduced, the remaining part of the tax is to be reduced by so much of the amount calculated in accordance with section 141(3) as has not been used up for the purposes of making the reductions required by subsection (3).

(7) In this section—

"component" means a component of the estate, as defined in paragraph 3 of Schedule 1A;

"the later transfer" has the meaning given in section 141(1);

"qualifying component" means a component (or deemed single component) for which the donated amount is at least 10% of the baseline amount, as determined in accordance with Schedule 1A.][1]

Commentary—*Simon's Taxes* **I4.172.**

HMRC Manuals—Inheritance Tax Manual IHTM45050 (where the estate is entitled to quick succession relief).
Amendments—[1] This section inserted by FA 2012 s 209, Sch 33 paras 2, 7 with effect in cases where D's death occurs on or after 6 April 2012.

Changes in distribution of deceased's estate, etc

142 Alteration of dispositions taking effect on death

(1) Where within the period of two years after a person's death—

(*a*) any of the dispositions (whether effected by will, under the law relating to intestacy or otherwise) of the property comprised in his estate immediately before his death are varied, or

(*b*) the benefit conferred by any of those dispositions is disclaimed,

by an instrument in writing made by the persons or any of the persons who benefit or would benefit under the dispositions, this Act shall apply as if the variation had been effected by the deceased or, as the case may be, the disclaimed benefit had never been conferred.

[(2) Subsection (1) above shall not apply to a variation unless the instrument contains a statement, made by all the relevant persons, to the effect that they intend the subsection to apply to the variation.][2]

[(2A) For the purposes of subsection (2) above the relevant persons are—

(*a*) the person or persons making the instrument, and

(*b*) where the variation results in additional tax being payable, the personal representatives.

Personal representatives may decline to make a statement under subsection (2) above only if no, or no sufficient, assets are held by them in that capacity for discharging the additional tax.][2]

(3) Subsection (1) above shall not apply to a variation or disclaimer made for any consideration in money or money's worth other than consideration consisting of the making, in respect of another of the dispositions, of a variation or disclaimer to which that subsection applies.

[(3A) Subsection (1) does not apply to a variation by virtue of which any property comprised in the estate immediately before the person's death becomes property in relation to which section 23(1) applies unless it is shown that the appropriate person has been notified of the existence of the instrument of variation.

(3B) For the purposes of subsection (3A) "the appropriate person" is—

(*a*) the charity or registered club to which the property is given, or

(*b*) if the property is to be held on trust for charitable purposes or for the purposes of registered clubs, the trustees in question.][3]

(4) Where a variation to which subsection (1) above applies results in property being held in trust for a person for a period which ends not more than two years after the death, this Act shall apply as if the disposition of the property that takes effect at the end of the period had had effect from the beginning of the period; but this subsection shall not affect the application of this Act in relation to any distribution or application of property occurring before that disposition takes effect.

(5) For the purposes of subsection (1) above the property comprised in a person's estate includes any excluded property but not any property to which he is treated as entitled by virtue of section 49(1) above [or section 102 of the Finance Act 1986][1].

(6) Subsection (1) above applies whether or not the administration of the estate is complete or the property concerned has been distributed in accordance with the original dispositions.

(7) In the application of subsection (4) above to Scotland, property which is subject to a proper liferent shall be deemed to be held in trust for the liferenter.

Commentary—*Simon's Taxes* **I4.411–I4.419, I4.434, I5.254.**
HMRC Manuals—Inheritance Tax Manual IHTM35011 (introduction to instruments of variation).
IHTM35021–35029 (details of HMRC published guidelines relating to variations).
IHTM35032 (when a variation can be made).
IHTM35041–35046 (who should make the instrument).
IHTM35047 (examples where the interests of persons not party to the instrument are affected).
IHTM35051–35058 (provisions relating to elections).
IHTM35060 (Has stamp duty exemption been claimed?).
IHTM35071–35073 (meaning of estate for this section).
IHTM35081–35083 (how many variations can be attempted?).
IHTM35085 (link between this section and section 144).
IHTM35091–35110 (property redirected to the spouse).
IHTM35131–35140 (trust created by a variation).
IHTM35151–35156 (inheritance tax implications of an Instrument of Variation).
IHTM35161–35166 (details regarding disclaimers).
Statement of Practice E18—Partial disclaimers of residue.
HMRC Interpretation RI 127—Post-death variation of inheritance by survivorship.
Press releases etc—Law Society's Gazette 18-12-91 (s 142 does not require execution of a deed, but simply "an instrument in writing". In practice a deed is normally used as a "prudent precaution").
Simon's Tax Cases—s 142(1), *Soutter's Executry v IRC* [2002] STC (SCD) 385; *Wills v Gibbs* [2008] STC 808.
Definitions—"The Board", "disposition", "estate", "excluded property", "personal representatives", s 272.
Cross references—See FA 1986 Sch 19 para 40 (where a death or other event occurs on or after 18 March 1986, the amendment to this section by FA 1986 Sch 19 (see below) not to affect the tax chargeable on a transfer of value occurring before 18 March 1986).

Amendments—[1] Words in sub-s (5) added by FA 1986 Sch 19 para 24.
[2] Sub-ss (2), (2A) substituted for sub-s (2) by FA 2002 s 120(1), (4) with effect for instruments made after 31 July 2002.
[3] Sub-ss (3A), (3B) inserted by FA 2012 s 209, Sch 33 paras 2, 9 with effect in cases where the person's death occurs on or after 6 April 2012.

143 Compliance with testator's request

Where a testator expresses a wish that property bequeathed by his will should be transferred by the legatee to other persons, and the legatee transfers any of the property in accordance with that wish within the period of two years after the death of the testator, this Act shall have effect as if the property transferred had been bequeathed by the will to the transferee.

Commentary—*Simon's Taxes* **I4.451, I1.519**.
HMRC Manuals—Inheritance Tax Manual IHTM35171–35173 (compliance with a testator's request).
Simon's Tax Cases—*Harding and anor (executors of Loveday, decd) v IRC* [1997] STC (SCD) 321

144 Distribution etc from property settled by will

(1) [Subsection (2) below applies][1] where property comprised in a person's estate immediately before his death is settled by his will and, within the period of two years after his death and before any interest in possession has subsisted in the property, there occurs—

(*a*) an event on which tax would ([apart from subsection (2) below][1]) be chargeable under any provision, other than section 64 or 79, of Chapter III of Part III of this Act, or

(*b*) an event on which tax would be so chargeable but for section [65(4),][3] 75[, 75A][2] or 76 above or paragraph 16(1) of Schedule 4 to this Act.

[(1A) Where the testator dies on or after 22nd March 2006, subsection (1) above shall have effect as if the reference to any interest in possession were a reference to any interest in possession that is—

(*a*) an immediate post-death interest, or

(*b*) a disabled person's interest.][1]

(2) Where [this subsection][1] applies by virtue of an event within paragraph (*a*) of subsection (1) above, tax shall not be charged under the provision in question on that event; and in every case in which [this subsection][1] applies in relation to an event, this Act shall have effect as if the will had provided that on the testator's death the property should be held as it is held after the event.

[(3) Subsection (4) below applies where—

(*a*) a person dies on or after 22nd March 2006,

(*b*) property comprised in the person's estate immediately before his death is settled by his will, and

(*c*) within the period of two years after his death, but before an immediate post-death interest or a disabled person's interest has subsisted in the property, there occurs an event that involves causing the property to be held on trusts that would, if they had in fact been established by the testator's will, have resulted in—

(i) an immediate post-death interest subsisting in the property, or

(ii) section 71A or 71D above applying to the property.][1]

[(4) Where this subsection applies by virtue of an event—

(*a*) this Act shall have effect as if the will had provided that on the testator's death the property should be held as it is held after the event, but

(*b*) tax shall not be charged on that event under any provision of Chapter 3 of Part 3 of this Act.][1]

[(5) Subsection (4) above also applies where—

(*a*) a person dies before 22nd March 2006,

(*b*) property comprised in the person's estate immediately before his death is settled by his will,

(*c*) an event occurs—

(i) on or after 22nd March 2006, and

(ii) within the period of two years after the testator's death,

that involves causing the property to be held on trusts within subsection (6) below,

(*d*) no immediate post-death interest, and no disabled person's interest, subsisted in the property at any time in the period beginning with the testator's death and ending immediately before the event, and

(*e*) no other interest in possession subsisted in the property at any time in the period beginning with the testator's death and ending immediately before 22nd March 2006.][1]

[(6) Trusts are within this subsection if they would, had they in fact been established by the testator's will and had the testator died at the time of the event mentioned in subsection (5)(*c*) above, have resulted in—

(*a*) an immediate post-death interest subsisting in the property, or

(*b*) section 71A or 71D above applying to the property.][1]

Commentary—*Simon's Taxes* **I4.431–I4.434**.
HMRC Manuals—Inheritance Tax Manual IHTM35181–35184 (distribution from discretionary trust set up by Will).
IHTM42227 (variation of discretionary will trusts).
Capital Gains Manual CG36533 (treatment before miscellaneous situations).
IHTM46033 (more detailed guidance: inherited).
Definitions—"Estate", s 272.

Simon's Tax Cases—*Frankland v IRC* [1997] STC 1450.

Amendments—[1] Words in sub-ss (1), (2) substituted, sub-ss (1A), (3)–(6) inserted, by FA 2006 s 156, Sch 20 paras 7, 27. These amendments are deemed to have come into force on 22 March 2006.

[2] Words in sub-s (1)(*b*) inserted by FA 2014 s 290, Sch 37 paras 9, 16. This amendment is treated as having come into force on 6 April 2014.

[3] In sub-s (1)(*b*), reference inserted by F(No 2)A 2015 s 14 with effect in cases where the testator's death occurs on or after 10 December 2014.

145 Redemption of surviving spouse's or civil partner's life interest

. . .

Amendments—This section repealed by the Inheritance and Trustees' Powers Act 2014 s 11, Sch 4 para 4(*b*) with effect from 1 October 2014 (by virtue of SI 2014/2039) and in relation to deaths occurring after that date.

146 Inheritance (Provision for Family and Dependants) Act 1975

(1) Where an order is made under section 2 of the Inheritance (Provision for Family and Dependants) Act 1975 ("the 1975 Act") in relation to any property forming part of the net estate of a deceased person, then, without prejudice to section 19(1) of that Act, the property shall for the purposes of this Act be treated as if it had on his death devolved subject to the provisions of the order.

(2) Where an order is made under section 10 of the 1975 Act requiring a person to provide any money or other property by reason of a disposition made by the deceased, then—

(*a*) if that disposition was a chargeable transfer and the personal representatives of the deceased make a claim for the purpose [not more than 4 years after the date on which the order is made][1]

(i) tax paid or payable on the value transferred by that chargeable transfer (whether or not by the claimants) shall be repaid to them by the Board or, as the case may be, shall not be payable, and

(ii) the rate or rates of tax applicable to the transfer of value made by the deceased on his death shall be determined as if the values previously transferred by chargeable transfers made by him were reduced by that value;

(*b*) the money or property shall be included in the deceased's estate for the purpose of the transfer of value made by him on his death.

(3) Where the money or other property ordered to be provided under section 10 of the 1975 Act is less than the maximum permitted by that section, subsection (2)(*a*) above shall have effect in relation to such part of the value there mentioned as is appropriate.

(4) The adjustment in consequence of the provisions of this section or of section 19(1) of the 1975 Act of the tax payable in respect of the transfer of value made by the deceased on his death shall not affect—

(*a*) the amount of any deduction to be made under section 8 of that Act in respect of tax borne by the person mentioned in subsection (3) of that section, or

(*b*) the amount of tax to which regard is to be had under section 9(2) of that Act;

and where a person is ordered under that Act to make a payment or transfer property by reason of his holding property treated as part of the deceased's net estate under section 8 or 9 and tax borne by him is taken into account for the purposes of the order, any repayment of that tax shall be made to the personal representatives of the deceased and not to that person.

(5) Tax repaid under paragraph (*a*)(i) of subsection (2) above shall be included in the deceased's estate for the purposes of the transfer of value made by him on his death; and tax repaid under that paragraph or under subsection (4) above shall form part of the deceased's net estate for the purposes of the 1975 Act.

(6) Anything which is done in compliance with an order under the 1975 Act or occurs on the coming into force of such an order, and which would (apart from this subsection) constitute an occasion on which tax is chargeable under any provision, other than section 79, of Chapter III of Part III of this Act, shall not constitute such an occasion; and where an order under the 1975 Act provides for property to be settled or for the variation of a settlement, and (apart from this subsection) tax would be charged under section 52(1) above on the coming into force of the order, section 52(1) shall not apply.

(7) In subsections (2)(*a*) and (5) above references to tax include references to interest on tax.

(8) Where an order is made staying or dismissing proceedings under the 1975 Act on terms set out in or scheduled to the order, this section shall have effect as if any of those terms which could have been included in an order under section 2 or 10 of that Act were provisions of such an order.

(9) In this section any reference to, or to any provision of, the 1975 Act includes a reference to, or to the corresponding provision of, the Inheritance (Provision for Family and Dependants) (Northern Ireland) Order 1979.

Commentary—*Simon's Taxes* **I4.441–I4.444, I5.341, I5,257**.

HMRC Manuals—Inheritance Tax Manual IHTM35201–35208 (orders under the Inheritance (Provision for Family and Dependants) Act 1975).

Definitions—"Disposition", "estate", "personal representatives", s 272.

Cross references—FA 2009 Sch 53 Part 2 (late payment interest start date), Sch 54 Part 2 (repayment interest start date).

Amendments—[1] In sub-s (2)(*a*) words inserted by FA 2009 s 99, Sch 51 para 7 with effect from 1 April 2011 (by virtue of SI 2010/867 art 2(2)).

147 Scotland: legitim [etc][1]

(1) Where a testator dies leaving a surviving spouse [or civil partner][1] and a person under the age of 18 entitled to claim legitim [or rights under section 131 of the Civil Partnership Act 2004 ("section 131 rights")][1], and provision is made in his will or other testamentary document for a disposition to his spouse [or civil partner][1] which, if it could take effect, would leave insufficient property in the estate to satisfy the entitlement of that person in respect of legitim [or to section 131 rights][1], the following provisions of this section shall apply.

(2) Subject to subsections (3) and (4) below, tax shall be charged at the testator's death as if the disposition to the spouse [or civil partner][1] did not include any amount in respect of legitim [or section 131 rights][1], but if within the period mentioned in subsection (6) below the person or persons concerned renounce their claim to legitim [or section 131 rights][1], tax shall be repaid to the estate calculated on the basis that the disposition to the spouse [or civil partner][1] did include the amount renounced.

(3) The executors or judicial factor of the testator may, in accordance with the provisions of this section, elect that subsection (2) above shall not apply but that subsection (4) below shall apply.

(4) Tax shall be charged at the testator's death as if the disposition to the spouse [or civil partner][1] had taken effect, but where the person or persons concerned claim legitim [or section 131 rights][1] within the period mentioned in subsection (6) below, tax shall be charged on the amount so claimed calculated on the basis that the legitim fund had been paid out in full at the testator's death (excluding any part of the fund renounced before any claim has been made) [or on the basis that all section 131 rights had been claimed in full at the testator's death (excluding any rights renounced before any claim has been made)][1] and the tax chargeable thereon had been apportioned rateably among the persons entitled to claim legitim [or section 131 rights][1] (excluding any who have renounced as aforesaid).

(5) Where the executors or judicial factor of the testator decide to make an election under subsection (3) above they shall give notice in writing of that election to the Board within two years from the date of death of the testator or such longer period as the Board may permit.

(6) For the purposes of subsections (2) and (4) above, a person shall be treated as having claimed legitim [or section 131 rights][1] unless he has renounced his claim before attaining the age of 18 or he renounces his claim within two years of his attaining that age or such longer period as the Board may permit.

(7) Where a person dies before attaining the age of 18 or before making a renunciation under subsection (6) above the provisions of this section shall apply in relation to that person's executors or judicial factor as they would have applied in relation to that person if that person had attained the age of 18 with the substitution of the date of death of that person for the date on which a person attained that age; but where the executors or factor renounce a claim to legitim [or section 131 rights][1] in respect of a person the amount renounced shall not be treated as part of that person's estate.

(8) Where subsection (2) above applies in relation to any estate, then notwithstanding anything in section 241 below the Board may repay tax under that subsection without limit of time.

(9) Where subsection (4) above applies in relation to any estate, then notwithstanding anything in section 239 below a certificate of discharge may be given under that section in respect of the whole estate, and notwithstanding anything in section 240 below the giving of the certificate shall not preclude the Board from claiming tax under subsection (4) above without limit of time.

[(10) Where the application of subsection (4) in relation to the estate of a person means that too great an increase has been made under subsection (3) of section 8A above in the case of another person, the claim under that section in that case may be amended accordingly by the Commissioners for Her Majesty's Revenue and Customs.][2]

Commentary—*Simon's Taxes* **I4.463, I4.464**.

HMRC Manuals—Inheritance Tax Manual IHTM35211–35234 (provisions relating to legitim).

Inheritance Tax Manual IHTM30374 (special rules: Scotland - legitim).

IHTM43041 (calculating the legitim).

Definitions—"The Board"; "disposition"; "estate", s 272.

Cross references—FA 2009 Sch 53 Part 2 (late payment interest start date), Sch 54 Part 2 (repayment interest start date).

Amendments—[1] Words in sub-ss (1), (2), (4)–(7) and words in heading inserted by Tax and Civil Partnership Regulations, SI 2005/3229, regs 3, 32 (1)–(7), with effect from 5 January 2005 (reg 1(1)).

[2] Sub-s (10) inserted by FA 2008 s 10, Sch 4 para 1, 3 with effect in relation to cases where the survivor's death occurs on or after 9 October 2007.

Mutual and voidable transfers

148 Mutual transfers: exemption for donee's gift

Amendments—This section repealed by FA 1986 Sch 19 para 25 and Sch 23 Pt X where the donee's transfer is made on or after 17 March 1986.

149 Mutual transfers: relief for donor's gift

Amendments—This section repealed by FA 1986 Sch 19 para 25 and Sch 23 Pt X where the donee's transfer is made on or after 17 March 1986.

150 Voidable transfers

(1) Where on a claim made for the purpose it is shown that the whole or any part of a chargeable transfer ("the relevant transfer") has by virtue of any enactment or rule of law been set aside as voidable or otherwise defeasible—

(*a*) tax paid or payable by the claimant (in respect of the relevant transfer or any other chargeable transfer made before the claim) that would not have been payable if the relevant transfer had been void ab initio shall be repaid to him by the Board, or as the case may be shall not be payable, and

(*b*) the rate or rates of tax applicable to any chargeable transfer made after the claim by the person who made the relevant transfer shall be determined as if that transfer or that part of it had been void as aforesaid.

(2) In subsection (1)(*a*) above the reference to tax includes a reference to interest on tax.

[(3) A claim under this section must be made not more than 4 years after the claimant knew, or ought reasonably to have known, that the relevant transfer has been set aside.][1]

Commentary—*Simon's Taxes* **I3.562, I11.304**.

HMRC Manuals—Inheritance Tax Manual IHTM14890 (voidable transfers).

IHTM30372 (special rules: voidable transfers).

Definitions—"The Board", s 272.

Cross references—FA 2009 Sch 54 Part 2 (repayment interest start date).

Amendments—[1] Sub-s (3) inserted by FA 2009 s 99, Sch 51 para 8 with effect from 1 April 2011 (by virtue of SI 2010/867 art 2(2)).

Pension schemes, etc

151 Treatment of pension rights, etc

(1), (1A) . . . [1]

(2) [An interest][4] in or under a [registered pension scheme[, a qualifying non-UK pension scheme or a section][2], [3] 615(3) scheme][1] which comes to an end on the death of the person entitled to it shall be left out of account in determining for the purposes of this Act the value of his estate immediately before his death, if the interest—

(*a*) is, or is a right to, a pension or annuity, and

(*b*) is not an interest resulting (whether by virtue of the instrument establishing the [scheme][1] or otherwise) from the application of any benefit provided under the [scheme][1] otherwise than by way of a pension or annuity.

(3) Sections 49 to 53 above shall not apply in relation to an interest satisfying the conditions of paragraphs (*a*) and (*b*) of subsection (2) above.

(4) In relation to an interest in or under a [registered pension scheme[, a qualifying non-UK pension scheme or a section][3] 615(3) scheme][1], section 5(2) above shall apply as if the words "other than settled property" were omitted (in both places).

(5) Where a benefit has become payable under a [registered pension scheme[, a qualifying non-UK pension scheme or a section][3] 615(3) scheme][1], and the benefit becomes comprised in a settlement made by a person other than the person entitled to the benefit, the settlement shall for the purposes of this Act be treated as made by the person so entitled.

Commentary—*Simon's Taxes* **I4.125, I5.634**.

HMRC Manuals—Inheritance Tax Manual IHTM17103 (pensions: other provisions: ABI guidance note).

Concession F11—Property chargeable on the ceasing of an annuity.

Statement of Practice E3—Superannuation schemes.

SP 10/86—Death benefits under superannuation arrangements.

Press releases etc—IR 7-5-76 (death benefits are chargeable to IHT if they form part of the deceased's freely disposable estate or if the deceased had power to nominate or appoint beneficiaries).

CTO letter 5-6-91 (death benefit of retirement annuity policy written in trust: policyholder failing to exercise right to annuity: CTO will not invoke s 3(3) in cases of genuine pension arrangements, but only where policyholder's intention was to increase the value of another person's estate).

Cross references—FA 2004 Sch 36 Pt 4 (application of this section for the purposes of FA 2004 Sch 36 (pension schemes after 6 April 2006)).

Pension Protection Fund (Tax) Regulations, SI 2006/575 reg 34 (this section applies in relation to an interest in or under the Pension Protection Fund as it applies in relation to an interest in or under a registered pension scheme).

Amendments—[1] Sub-ss (1), (1A) repealed; in sub-ss (2), (4), (5), words substituted for the words "fund or scheme to which this section applies"; and in sub-s (2)(*b*), word substituted for the words "fund or scheme"; by FA 2004 ss 203(4), 326, Sch 42 Pt 3 with effect from 6 April 2006. For transitional provisions and savings see FA 2004 Sch 36.

Sub-ss (1), (1A) previously read as follows—

"(1) This section applies to any fund to which section [615(3) of the Taxes Act 1988] applies, to any scheme approved under section [620 or 621] of that Act, to any exempt approved scheme or statutory scheme as defined in Chapter [I of Part XIV of that Act] and to any other sponsored superannuation scheme as defined in section [624 of that Act].

[(1A) This section also applies to approved personal pension arrangements within the meaning of Chapter [IV of

Part XIV of the Taxes Act 1988]; and references in the following provisions of this section to a scheme shall be construed accordingly.]".

2 Words in sub-s (2) inserted by FA 2006 s 160, Sch 22 paras 1, 3. This amendment is deemed to have come into force on 6 April 2006.

3 Words in sub-ss (2), (4), (5) substituted, by FA 2008 s 92, Sch 29 para 18(1), (4). This amendment is treated as having come into force on 6 April 2006.

4 In sub-s (2) words substituted for words "Subject to sections 151A and 151C below, an interest" by FA 2011 s 65, Sch 16 paras 49, 51 with effect in relation to deaths occurring on or after 6 April 2011, subject to transitional provisions in FA 2011, Sch 16 Pt 3.

151A Person dying with alternatively secured pension fund

(1) This section applies where a member of a registered pension scheme has an alternatively secured pension fund in respect of an arrangement under the pension scheme immediately before his death.

[(2) Tax shall be charged on the relevant amount as if it were part of the value transferred by the transfer of value made on the member's death at the rate or rates at which it would be charged if it [and any amount on which tax was previously charged under this section in relation to the member][3] *formed the highest part of that value.]*[2]

(3) The relevant amount is—

(a) the aggregate of the amount of the sums and the value of the assets forming part of the member's alternatively secured pension fund immediately before his death [but reduced by the amount of any previously charged income tax][2]*, less*

(b) the aggregate of the amount of the sums and the value of the assets expended on dependants' benefits within the period of six months beginning with the end of the month in which his death occurs.

(4) For this purpose sums or assets are expended on dependants' benefits at any time if they (or sums or assets directly or indirectly deriving from them) are at that time—

(a) applied towards the provision of a dependants' scheme pension for a relevant dependant,

(b) applied towards the provision of a dependants' annuity for a relevant dependant,

(c) designated as available for the payment of dependants' unsecured pension to a relevant dependant, or

(d) designated as available for the payment of dependants' alternatively secured pension to a relevant dependant,

or if the sums (or sums directly or indirectly deriving from the sums or assets) are at that time paid as a charity lump sum death benefit.

[(4A) In subsection (3)(a) above "the amount of any previously charged income tax" means the amount of any liability to income tax which (after the member's death but before the time when tax is charged on the transfer of value treated as made by the member on death) has arisen by virtue of the making of an unauthorised member payment under Part 4 of the Finance Act 2004 relating to the member's alternatively secured pension fund.][2]

[(4B) Subsection (4C) below applies where the maximum [amount that could be transferred by a chargeable transfer made (under section 4 above) on the member's death if it were to be wholly chargeable at the rate of nil per cent. (assuming, if necessary, that the value of the member's estate were sufficient but otherwise having regard to the circumstances of the member)][3]*. exceeds—*

(a) the value actually transferred by [the chargeable transfer so made][3] *(or nil if there is no such chargeable transfer), less*

(b) any previously untaxed alternatively secured pension fund amount.][2]

[(4C) Where this subsection applies, tax is to be charged on the previously untaxed alternatively secured pension fund amount as if the nil rate band maximum were—

$$\frac{UNRB \times 100}{100 - MUPR}$$

where—

UNRB is the unused nil-rate band, that is the excess mentioned in subsection (4B) above, and

MUPR is the maximum unauthorised payment rate, that is the maximum aggregate rate at which tax is chargeable under Part 4 of the Finance Act 2004 in respect of an unauthorised member payment.][2]

(5) In this section—

"alternatively secured pension fund" has the same meaning as in Part 4 of the Finance Act 2004 (see paragraph 11 of Schedule 28 to that Act);

"charity lump sum death benefit" has the meaning given by paragraph 18 of Schedule 29 to that Act;

"dependants' alternatively secured pension" has the meaning given by paragraph 19 of Schedule 28 to that Act;

"dependants' annuity" has the same meaning as in Part 4 of that Act (see paragraph 17 of that Schedule);

"dependants' scheme pension" has the same meaning as in that Part of that Act (see paragraph 16 of that Schedule);

"dependants' unsecured pension" has the meaning given by paragraph 18 of that Schedule;

[*"previously untaxed alternatively secured pension fund amount"* means so much of the aggregate mentioned in subsection (3)(*a*) above as has not given rise to any liability to tax by virtue of Part 4 of the Finance Act 2004 before tax is charged on the transfer treated as made by the member on death.][2] and

"relevant dependant", in relation to a member of a registered pension scheme who dies, means a dependant (within the meaning of paragraph 15 of that Schedule) who—

(*a*) is the person's spouse or civil partner immediately before his death; or

(*b*) is financially dependent on the person at that time.][1]

[*(6) This section applies in relation to a member who would have an alternatively secured pension fund immediately before death but for sub-paragraphs (6) and (7) of paragraph 11 of Schedule 28 to the Finance Act 2004 as if those sub-paragraphs were omitted (but subject as follows).*][2]

[*(7) In the case of such a member the references in subsection (3)(a)* and (*b*) to the member's death are to the date on which the scheme administrator becomes aware of the member's death.][2, 4]

Amendments—[1] Sections 151A–151C inserted by FA 2006 s 160, Sch 22 paras 1, 4. This amendment is deemed to have come into force on 6 April 2006.

[2] Sub-s (2) substituted, words in sub-s (3) inserted, definition in sub-s (5) inserted, and sub-ss (4A)–(4C), (6), (7) inserted, by FA 2007 s 69, Sch 19 paras 19, 20, 29(8) with effect in relation to deaths, cases where scheme administrators become aware of deaths and cessations of dependency occurring on or after 6 April 2007.

[3] Words in sub-s (2) inserted by FA 2008 s 91 Sch 28 paras 6, 7(1), (2) with effect in relation to deaths occurring on or after 6 April 2008, and words in sub-s (4B) substituted by FA 2008 s 91 Sch 28 paras 6, 7(1), (3) with effect from 21 July 2008.

[4] Sections 151A–151E repealed by FA 2011 s 65, Sch 16 para 48 with effect in relation to deaths occurring on or after 6 April 2011, subject to transitional provisions in FA 2011, Sch 16 Pt 3.

[*151B Relevant dependant with pension fund inherited from member over 75*]

(1) This section applies where—

(*a*) *a relevant dependant of a person who, immediately before his death, was a member of a registered pension scheme has a dependant's unsecured pension fund, or a dependant's alternatively secured pension fund, in respect of an arrangement under the pension scheme immediately before his death or immediately before ceasing to be a relevant dependant of the member,*

(*b*) *the member had reached the age of 75 at the time of his death and had an alternatively secured pension fund in respect of an arrangement under the pension scheme immediately before his death [(or would have but for paragraph 11(6) and (7) of Schedule 28 to the Finance Act 2004)]*[2]*, and*

(*c*) *sums or assets forming part of that fund were designated as available for the payment of dependants' unsecured pension, or dependants' alternatively secured pension, to the relevant dependant within the period of six months beginning with the end of the month in which the member's death occurs.*

(2) Where this section applies tax shall be charged under this section.

(3) The amount on which tax is charged under this section shall be the aggregate of the amount of the sums and the value of the assets forming part of the dependant's unsecured pension fund, or the dependant's alternatively secured pension fund, in respect of the arrangement immediately before the relevant dependant died or ceased to be a relevant dependant of the member.

(4) But where tax is chargeable under this section by reason of the death of the relevant dependant, that amount is reduced by so much of sums forming part of the dependant's unsecured pension fund, or the dependant's alternatively secured pension fund, (or sums directly or indirectly deriving from sums or assets forming part of that fund) as are paid to a charity within the period of six months beginning with the end of the month in which his death occurs.

(5) . . . [2]

(6) In this section—

"alternatively secured pension fund" has the same meaning as in Part 4 of the Finance Act 2004 (see paragraph 11 of Schedule 28 to that Act);

"dependants' alternatively secured pension" has the meaning given by paragraph 19 of that Schedule;

"dependant's alternatively secured pension fund" has the same meaning as in that Part of that Act (see paragraph 25 of that Schedule);

"dependants' unsecured pension" has the meaning given by paragraph 18 of that Schedule;

"dependant's unsecured pension fund" has the same meaning as in that Part of that Act (see paragraph 22 of that Schedule); and

"relevant dependant", in relation to a member of a registered pension scheme who dies, means a dependant (within the meaning of paragraph 15 of that Schedule) who—

(*a*) is the person's spouse or civil partner immediately before his death; or

(*b*) is financially dependent on the person at that time.][1, 3]

Amendments—[1] Sections 151A–151C inserted by FA 2006 s 160, Sch 22 paras 1, 4. This amendment is deemed to have come into force on 6 April 2006.

[2] Words in sub-s (1)(*b*) inserted, and sub-s (5) repealed, by FA 2007 s 69, Sch 19 paras 19, 21, 29(8) with effect in relation to deaths, cases where scheme administrators become aware of deaths and cessations of dependency occurring on or after 6 April 2007.

[3] Sections 151A–151E repealed by FA 2011 s 65, Sch 16 para 48 with effect in relation to deaths occurring on or after 6 April 2011, subject to transitional provisions in FA 2011, Sch 16 Pt 3.

[151BA Rate or rates of charge under section 151B

(1) Tax charged under section 151B above shall be charged at the rate or rates at which it would be charged on the death of the member if the amount mentioned in subsection (3) of that section (as reduced under subsection (4) of that section) [less the amount of any previously charged income tax (within the meaning of subsection (4A) of section 151A) constituted the relevant amount for the purposes of subsection (2) of that section, but subject as follows.][4]

(2) . . . [4]

(3) The rate or rates at which tax is charged [is to be determined on the assumption that the references in section 151A(4A) and (5)][4] *to the time when tax is charged on the transfer treated as made by the member on death were to the time when tax is charged under [section 151B above].*[4]

(4) Subsection (5) below applies where, before the time when the dependant dies or ceases to be a relevant dependant, there have been one or more reductions of tax by virtue of the coming into force of a substitution of a new Table in Schedule 1 to this Act since the member's death.

(5) The rate or rates at which tax is charged under section 151B above is to be determined as if the new Table effecting the reduction of tax (or the most recent reduction of tax) [("the applicable Table") had been in force at the time of the member's death, but subject to subsections (6) and (9) below.][2]*]*[1]

[(6) The nil-rate band maximum in the applicable Table is to be treated for the purposes of this section as reduced by the used-up percentage of the difference between—

(a) that nil-rate band maximum, and

(b) the nil-rate band maximum which was actually in force at the time of the member's death.

(7) For the purposes of subsection (6) above "the used-up percentage" is—

$$100 - \left(\frac{E}{NRBM}\right) \times 100$$

where—

E is the amount by which M is greater than VT under section 8A(2) above in the case of the member; and

NRBM is the nil-rate band maximum at the time of the member's death.][2]

[(8) The following provisions apply where—

(a) tax is charged under section 151B above, and

(b) immediately before the member's death, the member had a spouse or civil partner ("the survivor").

(9) If the survivor died before the event giving rise to the charge, tax is charged as if the personal nil-rate band maximum of the member were appropriately reduced.

(10) In subsection (9) above—

"the personal nil-rate band maximum of the member" is the nil rate band maximum in the applicable Table, increased in accordance with section 8A above where that section effected an increase in that nil-rate band maximum in the case of the member (as a survivor of another deceased person), and "appropriately reduced" means reduced by the amount (if any) by which the amount on which tax was charged at the rate of nil per cent. on the death of the survivor was increased by reason of the operation of section 8A above by virtue of the position of the member.

(11) If the survivor did not die before the event giving rise to the charge, tax is to be charged on the death of the survivor as if the percentage referred to in section 8A(3) above in the case of the member were that specified in subsection (12) below.

(12) That percentage is—

$$\frac{AE}{ANRBM} \times 100$$

where—

AE is the adjusted excess, that is the amount by which M would be greater than VT under section 8A(2) above in the case of the member if—

(a) the taxable amount were included in the value transferred by the chargeable transfer made on the member's death, and

(b) the nil-rate band maximum at the time of the member's death were ANRBM; and

ANRBM is the adjusted nil-rate band maximum, that is the nil-rate band maximum in the applicable Table (as reduced under subsection (6) above where that subsection applies).][3], [5]

Amendments—[1] This section inserted by FA 2007 s 69, Sch 19 paras 19, 22, 29(8) with effect in relation to deaths, cases where scheme administrators become aware of deaths, and cessations of dependency occurring on or after 6 April 2007.

[2] Words in sub-s (5) substituted, and sub-ss (6), (7) inserted by FA 2008 s 10, Sch 4 paras 1, 4(2), (3) with effect in relation to deaths, cases where scheme administrators become aware of deaths and cessations of dependency occurring on or after 6 April 2008.

[3] Sub-ss (8)–(12) inserted by FA 2008 s 10, Sch 4 paras 1, 4(4) with effect in relation to cases where the survivor's death occurs on or after 9 October 2007.

[4] Words in sub-s (1), (3) substituted, and sub-s (2) repealed, by FA 2008 s 91 Sch 28 paras 6, 8 with effect in relation to deaths occurring on or after 6 April 2008.

[5] Sections 151A–151E repealed by FA 2011 s 65, Sch 16 para 48 with effect in relation to deaths occurring on or after 6 April 2011, subject to transitional provisions in FA 2011, Sch 16 Pt 3.

[151C Dependant dying with other pension fund

(1) This section applies where—

(a) a dependant of a member of a registered pension scheme has a dependant's alternatively secured pension fund in respect of an arrangement under the pension scheme immediately before his death, and

(b) section 151B above does not apply.

[(2) Tax shall be charged on the relevant amount as if it were part of the value transferred by the transfer of value made on the dependant's death at the rate or rates at which it would be charged if it formed the highest part of that value.][2]

(3) The relevant amount is—

(a) the aggregate of the amount of the sums and the value of the assets forming part of the dependant's alternatively secured pension fund immediately before his death [but reduced by the amount of any previously charged income tax][2]*, less*

(b) so much of sums forming part of the dependant's alternatively secured pension fund (or sums directly or indirectly deriving from sums or assets forming part of that fund) as are paid as a charity lump sum death benefit within the period of six months beginning with the end of the month in which his death occurs.

[(3A) In subsection (3)(a) above "the amount of any previously charged income tax" means the amount of any liability to income tax which (after the dependant's death but before the time when tax is charged on the transfer of value treated as made by the dependant on death) has arisen by virtue of the making of an unauthorised member payment under Part 4 of the Finance Act 2004 relating to the dependant's alternatively secured pension fund.][2]

[(3B) Subsection (3C) below applies where the maximum [amount that could be transferred by a chargeable transfer made (under section 4 above) on the dependant's death if it were to be wholly chargeable at the rate of nil per cent. (assuming, if necessary, that the value of the dependant's estate were sufficient but otherwise having regard to the circumstances of the dependant)][3] *exceeds—*

(a) the value actually transferred by [the chargeable transfer so made][3]*, less*

(b) any previously untaxed dependant's alternatively secured pension fund amount.][2]

[(3C) Where this subsection applies, tax is to be charged on the previously untaxed dependant's alternatively secured pension fund amount as if the nil rate band maximum were—

$$\frac{UNRB \times 100}{100 - MUPR}$$

where—

UNRB is the unused nil rate band, that is the excess mentioned in subsection (3B) above; and

MUPR is the maximum unauthorised payment rate, that is the maximum aggregate rate at which tax is chargeable under Part 4 of the Finance Act 2004 in respect of an unauthorised member payment.][2]

[(3D) The relevant amount is to be reduced by the aggregate of so much of the sums and the value of the assets of the dependant's alternatively secured pension fund as arises, or (directly or indirectly) derives, from sums or assets forming part of an alternatively secured pension fund of the member which were designated as available for the payment of—

(a) dependants' unsecured pension, or

(b) dependants' alternatively secured pension,

to the dependant under the arrangement.][2]

(4) In this section—

"charity lump sum death benefit" has the meaning given by paragraph 18 of Schedule 29 to the Finance Act 2004;

"dependant" has the meaning given by paragraph 15 of that Schedule 28 to that Act; . . .[2]

["dependants' alternatively secured pension" has the meaning given by paragraph 19 of that Schedule;][3]

"dependant's alternatively secured pension fund" has the same meaning as in Part 4 of that Act (see paragraph 25 of [that Schedule][3]);][1]

["dependants' unsecured pension" has the meaning given by paragraph 18 of that Schedule;][3]

["previously untaxed dependant's alternatively secured pension fund amount" means so much of the aggregate mentioned in subsection (3)(a) above as has not given rise to any liability to tax by virtue of Part 4 of the Finance Act 2004 before tax is charged on the transfer treated as made by the dependant on death.][2], [4]

Amendments—[1] Sections 151A–151C inserted by FA 2006 s 160, Sch 22 paras 1, 4. This amendment is deemed to have come into force on 6 April 2006.

[2] Sub-s (2) substituted, words in sub-s (3)(*a*) inserted, sub-ss (3A)–(3D) inserted, and in sub-s (4), word repealed and definition inserted, by FA 2007 ss 69, 114, Sch 19 paras 19, 23, 29(8), Sch 27 Pt 3(1) with effect in relation to deaths, cases where scheme administrators become aware of deaths and cessations of dependency occurring on or after 6 April 2007.

[3] Words in sub-s (3B) substituted and words in sub-s (4) inserted, by FA 2008 s 91 Sch 28 paras 6, 9 with effect from 21 July 2008.

[4] Sections 151A–151E repealed by FA 2011 s 65, Sch 16 para 48 with effect in relation to deaths occurring on or after 6 April 2011, subject to transitional provisions in FA 2011, Sch 16 Pt 3.

[151D Unauthorised payment where person dies over 75 with pension or annuity

(1) This section applies where—

(a) a member of a registered pension scheme, or a dependant of such a member, dies after reaching the age of 75;

(b) immediately before death the member or dependant has under the pension scheme an actual right to payments under a relevant pension or relevant annuity or a prospective right to payments under a relevant pension; and

(c) at any time after the death a relevant unauthorised payment is made by the pension scheme.

(2) Where this section applies tax shall be charged under this section.

(3) The amount on which tax is charged under this section shall be the difference between—

(a) the amount of the relevant unauthorised payment; and

(b) the amount of any liability to income tax which has arisen under Part 4 of the Finance Act 2004 by virtue of the making of the relevant unauthorised payment.

(4) In this section—

"dependant" has the meaning given by paragraph 15 of Schedule 28 to the Finance Act 2004;

"dependants' annuity" has the same meaning as in that Part of that Act (see paragraph 17 of that Schedule);

"dependants' scheme pension" has the same meaning as in that Part of that Act (see paragraph 16 of that Schedule);

"lifetime annuity" has the same meaning as in that Part of that Act (see paragraph 3 of that Schedule);

"relevant annuity" means a lifetime annuity or dependants' annuity purchased by the application of sums or assets held for the purposes of the pension scheme;

"relevant pension" means a scheme pension or dependants' scheme pension provided by the scheme administrator or as a result of the application of sums or assets held for the purposes of the pension scheme;

"relevant unauthorised payment" means an unauthorised payment (within the meaning of Part 4 of the Finance Act 2004: see section 160(5) of that Act) which—

(a) consists of the payment of a lump sum in respect of the dead member or dependant; or

(b) is treated as made by virtue of the operation of section 172B of that Act by reason of the death; and

"scheme pension" has the same meaning as in Part 4 of that Act (see paragraph 2 of Schedule 28 to that Act).][1], [2]

Amendments—[1] Sections 151D, 151E inserted by FA 2008 s 91, Sch 28 paras 6, 10 with effect in relation to deaths occurring on or after 6 April 2008.

[2] Sections 151A–151E repealed by FA 2011 s 65, Sch 16 para 48 with effect in relation to deaths occurring on or after 6 April 2011, subject to transitional provisions in FA 2011, Sch 16 Pt 3.

[151E Rate or rates of charge under section 151D

(1) Tax charged under section 151D above shall be charged at the rate or rates at which it would be charged if the amount on which it is charged, and any amount on which tax was previously charged under that section in relation to the death of the member or dependant, were part of the value transferred by the transfer of value made on the death of the member or dependant.

(2) The rate or rates at which tax is charged on that amount shall be determined as if that amount had formed the highest part of that value.

(3) Subsection (4) below applies where, before the time when the unauthorised payment is made, there have been one or more reductions of tax by virtue of the coming into force of a substitution of a new Table in Schedule 1 to this Act since the death of the member or dependant.

(4) The rate or rates at which tax is charged under section 151D above is to be determined as if the new Table effecting the reduction of tax (or the most recent reduction of tax) ("the applicable Table") had been in force at the time of the death of the member or dependant, but subject to subsections (5) and (8) below.
(5) The nil-rate band maximum in the applicable Table is to be treated for the purposes of this section as reduced by the used-up percentage of the difference between—
(a) that nil-rate band maximum, and
(b) the nil-rate band maximum which was actually in force at the time of the death of the member or dependant.
(6) For the purposes of subsection (5) above "the used-up percentage" is—

$$100 - \left(\frac{E}{NRBM} \times 100\right)$$

where—
E is the amount by which M is greater than VT under section 8A(2) above in the case of the member or dependant; and
NRBM is the nil-rate band maximum at the time of the death of the member or dependant.
(7) The following provisions apply where—
(a) tax is charged under section 151D above, and
(b) immediately before the death of the member or dependant, the member or dependant had a spouse or civil partner ("the survivor").
(8) If the survivor died before the time when the unauthorised payment is made, tax is charged as if the personal nil-rate band maximum of the member or dependant were appropriately reduced.
(9) In subsection (8) above—
"the personal nil-rate band maximum of the member or dependant" is the nil rate band maximum in the applicable Table, increased in accordance with section 8A above where that section effected an increase in that nil-rate band maximum in the case of the member or dependant (as a survivor of another deceased person), and
"appropriately reduced" means reduced by the amount (if any) by which the amount on which tax was charged at the rate of nil per cent. on the death of the survivor was increased by reason of the operation of section 8A above by virtue of the position of the member or dependant.
(10) If the survivor did not die before the time when the unauthorised payment is made, tax is to be charged on the death of the survivor as if the percentage referred to in section 8A(3) above in the case of the member or dependant were that specified in subsection (11) below.
(11) That percentage is—

$$\frac{AE}{ANRBM} \times 100$$

where—
AE is the adjusted excess, that is the amount by which M would be greater than VT under section 8A(2) above in the case of the member or dependant if—
(a) the amount on which tax is charged under section 151D above were included in the value transferred by the chargeable value made on the death of the member or dependant, and
(b) the nil-rate band maximum at the time of the death were ANRBM; and
ANRBM is the adjusted nil-rate band maximum, that is the nil-rate band maximum in the applicable Table (as reduced under subsection (5) above where that subsection applies).][1], [2]

Amendments—[1] Sections 151D, 151E inserted by FA 2008 s 91, Sch 28 paras 6, 10 with effect in relation to deaths occurring on or after 6 April 2008.
[2] Sections 151A–151E repealed by FA 2011 s 65, Sch 16 para 48 with effect in relation to deaths occurring on or after 6 April 2011, subject to transitional provisions in FA 2011, Sch 16 Pt 3.

152 Cash options

[Where on a person's death an annuity becomes payable under a registered pension scheme[, a qualifying non-UK pension scheme or a section][3] 615(3) scheme to a widow, widower[, surviving civil partner][2][, dependant or nominee][4] of that person and under the terms of the scheme][1] a sum of money might at his option have become payable instead to his personal representatives, he shall not, by virtue of section 5(2) above, be treated as having been beneficially entitled to that sum.

Commentary—*Simon's Taxes* **I4.125, I3.212**.
HMRC Manuals—Inheritance Tax Manual IHTM17053 (death benefits cash options).
Definitions—"The Board"; "personal representatives", s 272.
Amendments—[1] Words substituted by FA 2004 s 203(5) with effect from 6 April 2006. For transitional provisions and savings see FA 2004 Sch 36.
The text previously read as follows—

"Where—

[(*a*) under approved personal pension arrangements within the meaning of Chapter [IV of Part XIV of the Taxes Act 1988], or

(*b*) under a contract or trust scheme approved by the Board under section [620 or 621 of the Taxes Act 1988] or (before [6th April 1970]) under section 22 of the Finance Act 1956]

an annuity becomes payable on a person's death to a widow, widower[, surviving civil partner] or dependant of that person, and under the terms of the contract or scheme".

2 Words inserted by the Tax and Civil Partnership Regulations, SI 2005/3229 regs 175, 178 with effect from 6 April 2006.

3 Words substituted by FA 2008 s 92, Sch 29 para 18(1), (5). This amendment is treated as having come into force on 6 April 2006.

4 Words substituted by FA 2016 s 22, Sch 5 para 11. This amendment is treated as having come into force on 6 April 2015 and has effect where the person on whose death an annuity is payable dies on or after that date.

153 Overseas pensions

(1) In determining for the purposes of this Act the value of a person's estate immediately before his death there shall be left out of account any pension payable under the regulations or rules relating to any fund vested in Commissioners under section 273 of the Government of India Act 1935 or to any fund administered under a scheme made under section 2 of the Overseas Pensions Act 1973 which is certified by the Secretary of State for the purpose of this section to correspond to an Order in Council under subsection (1) of the said section 273.

(2) For the purposes of this Act—

(*a*) a pension paid under the authority of a scheme made under section 2 of the Overseas Pensions Act 1973 which is constituted by the Pensions (India, Pakistan and Burma) Act 1955 or is certified by the Secretary of State for the purposes of this section to correspond to the said Act of 1955 shall be treated as if it had been paid by the Government of India or the Government of Pakistan (according as the arrangements in pursuance of which the pension was first paid under the said Act of 1955 were made with the one or the other Government);

(*b*) a pension paid out of any fund established in the United Kingdom by the Government of any country which, at the time when the fund was established, was, or formed part of, a colony, protectorate, protected state or United Kingdom trust territory shall, if the fund was established for the sole purpose of providing pensions, whether contributory or not, payable in respect of service under the Government be treated as if it had been paid by the Government by which the fund was established;

(*c*) a pension paid out of the Central African Pension Fund established by section 24 of the Federation of Rhodesia and Nyasaland (Dissolution) Order in Council 1963 shall be treated as if it had been paid by the Government of a territory outside the United Kingdom; and

(*d*) so much of any pension paid to or in respect of any person under—

(i) the scheme which by virtue of subsection (3) of section 2 of the Overseas Pensions Act 1973 is constituted under that section by section 2 or subsection (2) of section 4 of the Overseas Service Act 1958 or

(ii) such other scheme made under section 2 of the Overseas Pensions Act 1973 as is certified by the Secretary of State for the purposes of the Taxes Act to correspond to section 2 or subsection (2) of section 4 of the Overseas Service Act 1958

as is certified by the Secretary of State to be attributable to service under the Government of an overseas territory shall be treated as if it had been paid by the Government of that territory.

(3) Subsection (1) above shall be construed as if contained in section 273 of the Government of India Act 1935; and for the purposes of subsection (2) above—

(*a*) "pension" includes a gratuity and any sum payable on or in respect of death, and a return of contributions with or without interest thereon or any other addition thereto;

(*b*) "United Kingdom trust territory" means a territory administered by the Government of the United Kingdom under the trusteeship system of the United Nations;

(*c*) "overseas territory" means any country or territory outside the United Kingdom;

(*d*) references to the Government of any such country or territory as is mentioned in paragraph (*b*) or (*d*) of that subsection include a Government constituted for two or more such countries or territories and any authority established for the purpose of providing or administering services which are common to, or relate to matters of common interest to, two or more such countries or territories.

(4) If, by reason of Her Majesty's Government in the United Kingdom having assumed responsibility for a pension, allowance or gratuity within the meaning of section 1 of the Overseas Pensions Act 1973 payments in respect of it are made under that section, this section shall apply in relation to the pension, allowance or gratuity, exclusive of so much (if any) of it as is paid by virtue of the application to it of any provisions of the Pensions (Increase) Act 1971 or any enactment repealed by that Act, as if it continued to be paid by the Government or other body or fund which had responsibility for it before that responsibility was assumed by Her Majesty's Government in the United Kingdom.

Commentary—*Simon's Taxes* **I4.126, I9.325.**
HMRC Manuals—Inheritance Tax Manual IHTM04390 (overseas pension).

[Payments to victims of persecution during Second World War era

153ZA Qualifying payments

(1) This section applies where a qualifying payment has at any time been received by a person ("P"), or by the personal representatives of P.

(2) The tax chargeable on the value transferred by the transfer made on P's death (the "value transferred") is to be reduced by an amount equal to—

(*a*) the relevant percentage of the amount of the qualifying payment, or

(*b*) if lower, the amount of tax that would, apart from this section, be chargeable on the value transferred.

(3) In subsection (2) "relevant percentage" means the percentage specified in the last row of the third column of the Table in Schedule 1.

(4) For the purposes of this section, a "qualifying payment" is a payment that meets Condition A, B or C.

(5) Condition A is that the payment—

(*a*) is of a kind specified in Part 1 of Schedule 5A, and

(*b*) is made to a person, or the personal representatives of a person, who was—

(i) a victim of National-Socialist persecution, or

(ii) the spouse or civil partner of a person within sub-paragraph (i).

(6) Condition B is that the payment is of a kind listed in Part 2 of Schedule 5A.

(7) Condition C is that the payment—

(*a*) is of a kind specified in regulations made by the Treasury, and

(*b*) is made to a person, or the personal representatives of a person, who was—

(i) held as a prisoner of war, or a civilian internee, during the Second World War, or

(ii) the spouse or civil partner of a person within sub-paragraph (i).

(8) The Treasury may by regulations add a payment of a specified kind to the list in Part 1 of Schedule 5A.

(9) Regulations under this section are to be made by statutory instrument.

(10) A statutory instrument containing regulations under this section is subject to annulment in pursuance of a resolution of the House of Commons.][1]

Commentary—*Simon's Taxes* **I4.129**.

Amendments—[1] Section 153ZA inserted by FA 2016 s 95(1) with effect in relation to deaths occurring on or after 1 January 2015.

[Emergency services

153A Death of emergency service personnel etc

(1) The reliefs in subsection (2) apply where a person—

(*a*) dies from an injury sustained, accident occurring or disease contracted at a time when that person was responding to emergency circumstances in that person's capacity as an emergency responder, or

(*b*) dies from a disease contracted at some previous time, the death being due to, or hastened by, the aggravation of the disease during a period when that person was responding to emergency circumstances in that person's capacity as an emergency responder.

(2) The reliefs are—

(*a*) that no potentially exempt transfer made by the person becomes a chargeable transfer under section 3A(4) because of the death,

(*b*) that section 4 (transfers on death) does not apply in relation to the death, and

(*c*) that no additional tax becomes due under section 7(4) because of a transfer made by the person within 7 years of the death.

(3) "Emergency circumstances" means circumstances which are present or imminent and are causing or likely to cause—

(*a*) the death of a person,

(*b*) serious injury to, or the serious illness of, a person,

(*c*) the death of an animal,

(*d*) serious injury to, or the serious illness of, an animal,

(*e*) serious harm to the environment (including the life and health of plants and animals),

(*f*) serious harm to any building or other property, or

(*g*) a worsening of any such injury, illness or harm.

(4) A person is "responding to emergency circumstances" if the person—

(*a*) is going anywhere for the purpose of dealing with emergency circumstances occurring there, or

(*b*) is dealing with emergency circumstances, preparing to do so imminently or dealing with the immediate aftermath of emergency circumstances.

(5) For the purposes of this section, circumstances to which a person is responding are to be taken to be emergency circumstances if the person believes and has reasonable grounds for believing they are or may be emergency circumstances.

(6) "Emergency responder" means—

(*a*) a person employed, or engaged, in connection with the provision of fire services or fire and rescue services,

(*b*) a person employed for the purposes of providing, or engaged to provide, search services or rescue services (or both),

(*c*) a person employed for the purposes of providing, or engaged to provide, medical, ambulance or paramedic services,

(*d*) a constable or a person employed for police purposes or engaged to provide services for police purposes,

(*e*) a person employed for the purposes of providing, or engaged to provide, services for the transportation of organs, blood, medical equipment or medical personnel, or

(*f*) a person employed, or engaged, by the government of a state or territory, an international organisation or a charity in connection with the provision of humanitarian assistance.

(7) For the purposes of subsection (6)—

(*a*) it is immaterial whether the employment or engagement is paid or unpaid, and

(*b*) "international organisation" means an organisation of which—

(i) two or more sovereign powers are members, or

(ii) the governments of two or more sovereign powers are members.

(8) The Treasury may, by regulations made by statutory instrument, extend the definition of "emergency responder" in subsection (6).

(9) Regulations under this section are subject to annulment in pursuance of a resolution of the House of Commons.][1]

Commentary—*Simon's Taxes* **I4.211**.

HMRC Manuals—Inheritance Tax Manual IHTM11291 (emergency service personnel responding to emergency circumstances).
IHTM11294 (meaning of responding to emergency circumstances).
IHTM11292 (emergency service personnel responding to emergency circumstances).
IHTM11282 (effect of the exemptiions).

Amendments—[1] Section 153A inserted by FA 2015 s 75(1), (2) with effect in relation to deaths occurring on or after 19 March 2014.

Armed forces

154 Death on active service, etc

(1) [The reliefs in subsection (1A) apply][2] in relation to the death of a person in whose case it is certified by the Defence Council or the Secretary of State—

(*a*) that he died from a wound inflicted, accident occurring or disease contracted at a time when the conditions specified in subsection (2) below were satisfied, or

(*b*) that he died from a disease contracted at some previous time, the death being due to or hastened by the aggravation of the disease during a period when those conditions were satisfied.

[(1A) The reliefs are—

(*a*) that no potentially exempt transfer made by the deceased becomes a chargeable transfer under section 3A(4) because of the death,

(*b*) that section 4 (transfers on death) does not apply in relation to the death, and

(*c*) that no additional tax becomes due under section 7(4) because of a transfer made by the deceased within 7 years of the death.][2]

(2) The conditions referred to in subsection (1) above are that the deceased was a member of any of the armed forces of the Crown or [a civilian subject to service discipline within the meaning of the Armed Forces Act 2006][1] and (in any case) was[2] . . . —

(*a*) on active service against an enemy, or

(*b*) on other service of a warlike nature or which in the opinion of the Treasury involved the same risks as service of a warlike nature [or

(*c*) responding to emergency circumstances in the course of the person's duties as a member of any of those armed forces or as a civilian subject to service discipline.][2]

[(2A) Section 153A(3) to (5) applies for the purposes of this section.][2]

(3) In relation to any time before 28th July 1981 (the date of the passing of the Armed Forces Act 1981), the reference in subsection (2) above to membership of the armed forces of the Crown shall include a reference to employment as a person of any of the descriptions specified in paragraph 1(3) of Schedule 7 to the Finance Act 1975 (women's services).

Commentary—*Simon's Taxes* **I4.209**.

HMRC Manuals—Inheritance Tax Manual IHTM11281–11293 (killed in war exemption).
IHTM11301 and 11302 (types of certificate).
IHTM11311–11313 (categories of service entitled to exemption).

Concessions F5—Deaths of members of the Royal Ulster Constabulary. (Obsolete following enactment of FA 2015 s 75.)

F13—Subsequent devolution's of property under the wills of persons dying before 12 March 1952 whose estates were wholly exempted from estate duty.

Amendments—[1] Words in sub-s (2) substituted by the Armed Forces Act 2006 s 378(1), Sch 16 para 99 with effect, for certain purposes, from 28 March 2009 (by virtue of SI 2009/812 art 3(*a*), (*b*)) and, for remaining purposes, from 31 October 2009 (by virtue of SI 2009/1167, art 4) For savings see SI 2009/1059, art 205, Sch 1, para 27.

[2] In sub-s (1), words substituted, sub-ss (1A), (2A) inserted, in sub-s (2), word repealed, and sub-s (2)(*c*) and preceding word inserted, by FA 2015 s 75(1), (3) with effect in relation to deaths occurring on or after 19 March 2014.

155 Visiting forces, etc

(1) Section 6 (4) above applies to—

(*a*) the emoluments paid by the Government of any designated country to a member of a visiting force of that country, not being a British citizen, a British Dependent Territories citizen [, a British National (Overseas)][1] or a British Overseas citizen, and

(*b*) any tangible movable property the presence of which in the United Kingdom is due solely to the presence in the United Kingdom of such a person while serving as a member of the force.

(2) A period during which any such member of a visiting force as is referred to in subsection (1) above is in the United Kingdom by reason solely of his being such a member shall not be treated for the purposes of this Act as a period of residence in the United Kingdom or as creating a change of his residence or domicile.

(3) References in subsections (1) and (2) above to a visiting force shall apply to a civilian component of a visiting force as they apply to the force itself, and those subsections shall be construed as one with Part I of the Visiting Forces Act 1952 but so that for the purposes of this section references to a designated country shall be substituted in that Act for references to a country to which a provision of that Act applies.

(4) For the purpose of conferring on persons attached to any designated [international military][2] headquarters the like benefits as are conferred by subsections (1) and (2) above on members of a visiting force or civilian component, any members of the armed forces of a designated country shall, while attached to any such headquarters, be deemed to constitute a visiting force of that country, and there shall be a corresponding extension of the class of persons who may be treated as members of a civilian component of such a visiting force.

(5) In the case of persons of any category for the time being agreed between Her Majesty's Government in the United Kingdom and the other members of the North Atlantic Council, employment by a designated allied headquarters shall be treated for the purposes of subsections (1)(*b*) and (2) above as if it were service as a member of a visiting force of a designated country.

[(5A) Section 6(4) also applies to—

(*a*) the emoluments paid by the Government of any designated country to a person belonging to the EU civilian staff, not being a British citizen, a British overseas territories citizen, a British National (Overseas) or a British Overseas citizen, and

(*b*) any tangible movable property the presence of which in the United Kingdom is due solely to the presence in the United Kingdom of such a person serving as part of that staff.

(5B) A period during which any such person belonging to the EU civilian staff as is referred to in subsection (5A) is in the United Kingdom by reason solely of that person belonging to that staff is not to be treated for the purposes of this Act as a period of residence in the United Kingdom or as creating a change of that person's residence or domicile.][2]

(6) For the purposes of this section—

"allied headquarters" means any international military headquarters established under the North Atlantic Council;

"designated" means designated for the purpose in question by or under any Order in Council made for giving effect to any international agreement.

["the EU civilian staff" means—

(a) civilian personnel seconded by a member State to an EU institution for the purposes of activities (including exercises) relating to the preparation for, and execution of, tasks mentioned in Article 43(1) of the Treaty on European Union (tasks relating to a common security and defence policy), as amended from time to time, and

(b) civilian personnel (other than locally hired personnel)—

(i) made available to the EU by a member State to work with designated international military headquarters or a force of a designated country, or

(ii) otherwise made available to the EU by a member State for the purposes of activities of the kind referred to in paragraph (*a*).][2]

(7) Any Order in Council made under section 73 of the Finance Act 1960 which is in force immediately before the passing of this Act shall have effect for the purposes of this section as if had also been made under this section, and may be varied or revoked accordingly.

Commentary—*Simon's Taxes* **19.328**.

HMRC Manuals—Inheritance Tax Manual IHTM27272–27275 (specific property of visiting forces and staff of Allied Headquarters).

Inheritance Tax Manual IHTM04322 (qualifying persons).

IHTM04321 (property of visiting forces).

IHTM04323 (protection of domicile and residence).

Regulations—Visiting Forces and Allied Headquarters (Inheritance Tax) (Designation) Order, SI 1998/1515; Visiting Forces (Inheritance Tax) (Designation) Order, SI 1998/1516.

Visiting Forces and International Military Headquarters (EU SOFA) (Tax Designation) Order, SI 2012/3070.

Visiting Forces and International Military Headquarters (NATO and PfP) (Tax Designation) Order, SI 2012/3071.

Amendments—[1] Words in sub-s (1)(*a*) inserted by the Hong Kong (British Nationality) Order, SI 1986/948 art 4, Schedule.

[2] Words in sub-s (4) substituted for word "allied", sub-ss (5A), (5B) inserted, and in sub-s (6) definition of "the EU civilian staff" inserted, by FA 2012 s 220, Sch 37 para 3 with effect from 17 July 2012.

[Constables and service personnel

155A Death of constables and service personnel targeted because of their status

(1) The reliefs in subsection (3) apply where a person—

(*a*) dies from an injury sustained or disease contracted in circumstances where the person was deliberately targeted by reason of his or her status as a constable or former constable, or

(*b*) dies from a disease contracted at some previous time, the death being due to, or hastened by, the aggravation of the disease by an injury sustained or disease contracted in circumstances mentioned in paragraph (*a*).

(2) The reliefs in subsection (3) apply where it is certified by the Defence Council or the Secretary of State that a person—

(*a*) died from an injury sustained or disease contracted in circumstances where the person was deliberately targeted by reason of his or her status as a service person or former service person, or

(*b*) died from a disease contracted at some previous time, the death being due to, or hastened by, the aggravation of the disease by an injury sustained or disease contracted in circumstances mentioned in paragraph (*a*).

(3) The reliefs are—

(*a*) that no potentially exempt transfer made by the person becomes a chargeable transfer under section 3A(4) because of the death,

(*b*) that section 4 (transfers on death) does not apply in relation to the death, and

(*c*) that no additional tax becomes due under section 7(4) because of a transfer made by the person within 7 years of the death.

(4) For the purposes of this section, it is immaterial whether a person who was a constable or service person at the time the injury was sustained or the disease was contracted was acting in the course of his or her duties as such at that time (and for this purpose ignore the references in subsections (1)(*b*) and (2)(*b*) to a disease contracted at some previous time).

(5) "Service person" means a person who is a member of the armed forces of the Crown or a civilian subject to service discipline (within the meaning of the Armed Forces Act 2006).

(6) This section does not apply where section 153A or 154 applies in relation to a person's death.][1]

Commentary—*Simon's Taxes* **I4.210**.

HMRC Manuals—Inheritance Tax Manual IHTM11311 (constables and service personnel targeted because of their job).

IHTM11282 (effect of the exemptiions).

IHTM11312 (meaning of constables and service personnel).

Amendments—[1] Section 155A inserted by FA 2015 s 75(1), (4) with effect in relation to deaths occurring on or after 19 March 2014.

Apsley House and Chevening Estate

156 Apsley House and Chevening Estate

This Act shall not apply in respect of—

(*a*) the rights conferred by section 3 of the Wellington Museum Act 1947 or

(*b*) property held on the trusts of the trust instrument set out in the Schedule to the Chevening Estate Act 1959.

Commentary—*Simon's Taxes* **I7.601, I7.602**.

HMRC Manuals—Inheritance Tax Manual IHTM04141 (provisions which exclude the inheritance tax act).

Non-residents' bank accounts

157 Non-residents' bank accounts

(1) In determining for the purposes of this Act the value of the estate immediately before his death of a person to whom this section applies there shall be left out of account the balance on—

(*a*) any qualifying foreign currency account of his, and

(*b*) subject to subsection (3) below, any qualifying foreign currency account of the trustees of settled property in which he is beneficially entitled to an interest in possession.

[(2) This section applies to a person who is not domiciled and not resident in the United Kingdom immediately before his death.][6]

(3) Subsection (1)(*b*) above does not apply in relation to settled property if the settlor was domiciled in the United Kingdom when he made the settlement, or if the trustees are domiciled [or resident][6] in the United Kingdom immediately before the beneficiary's death.

[(3A) This section is subject to paragraph 5 of Schedule A1 (non-excluded overseas property).][7]

(4) For the purposes of this section—

(*a*) the question whether a person is resident . . . [6] in the United Kingdom shall, subject to paragraph (*b*) below, be determined as for the purposes of income tax; but

(*b*) the trustees of a settlement shall be regarded as not resident . . . [6] in the United Kingdom unless the general administration of the settlement is ordinarily carried on in the United Kingdom and the trustees or a majority of them (and, where there is more than one class of trustees, a majority of each class) are resident . . . [6] there.

(5) In this section "qualifying foreign currency account" means a foreign currency account with [a bank . . . [4]][1]; and for this purpose—

(*a*) "foreign currency account" means any account other than one denominated in sterling, . . .

[(*b*) . . .][2]

[(6) In this section "bank" has the meaning given by [section 991 of the Income Tax Act 2007][5].][3]

Commentary—*Simon's Taxes* **I4.124, I9.323**.

HMRC Manuals—Inheritance Tax Manual IHTM04380 (foreign currency bank account).

Definitions—"Estate", s 272; "settlement", "settled property", s 43; "trustee", s 45.

Cross references—Postal Services Act 2000 (Consequential Modifications No 1) Order, SI 2001/1149 art 4(4) (the repeal of the words "or the Post Office" in sub-s (5) above by SI 2001/1149 does not apply in relation to determining the value of an estate by reference to a point in time before 26 March 2001).

Amendments—[1] Words in sub-s (5) substituted by FA 1996 Sch 37 para 12(1), (3) in relation to deaths occurring after 29 April 1996.

[2] Word in sub-s (5)(*a*) and whole of sub-s (5)(*b*) repealed by FA 1996 Sch 37 para 12(3), Sch 41 Pt VIII(2) in relation to deaths occurring on or after 29 April 1996.

[3] Sub-s (6) inserted by FA 1996 Sch 37 para 12(2), (3) in relation to deaths occurring on or after 29 April 1996.

[4] Words in sub-s (5) repealed by the Postal Services Act 2000 (Consequential Modifications No 1) Order, SI 2001/1149 art 3, Sch 2 with effect from 26 March 2001.

[5] Words in sub-s (6) substituted for the words "section 840A of the Taxes Act 1988" by ITA 2007 s 1027, Sch 1 paras 268, 269, with effect for income tax purposes from 6 April 2007, and corporation tax purposes for accounting periods ending after 5 April 2007.

[6] Sub-s (2) and words in sub-s (3) substituted, and words in sub-s (4)(*a*), (*b*) repealed, by FA 2013 s 219, Sch 46 para 118 with effect where the person dies on or after 6 April 2013.

[7] Sub-s (3A) inserted by F(No 2)A 2017 s 33, Sch 10 paras 2, 6 with effect in relation to times on or after 6 April 2017, subject to transitional provisions in Sch 10 paras 10, 11.

Double taxation relief

158 Double taxation conventions

(1) If Her Majesty by Order in Council declares—

(*a*) that arrangements specified in the Order have been made with the government of any territory outside the United Kingdom with a view to affording relief from double taxation in relation to capital transfer tax payable under the laws of the United Kingdom and any tax imposed under the laws of that territory which is of a similar character or is chargeable on or by reference to death or gifts inter vivos, and

(*b*) that it is expedient that those arrangements should have effect,

the arrangements shall, notwithstanding anything in this Act, have effect so far as they provide for relief from capital transfer tax, or for determining the place where any property is to be treated as situated for the purposes of the tax.

(1A) . . . [1]

(2) Any arrangements to which effect is given under this section may include provision for relief in cases occurring before the making of the arrangements and provisions as to property which is not itself subject to double taxation.

(3) Any Order in Council under this section which revokes an earlier Order may contain such transitional provisions as appear to Her Majesty to be necessary or expedient.

(4) An Order under this section shall not be submitted to Her Majesty in Council unless a draft of it has been laid before, and approved by resolution of, the House of Commons.

(5) Where any arrangements have effect by virtue of this section, no obligation as to secrecy shall prevent the Board or an authorised officer of the Board from disclosing to any authorised officer of the government with which the arrangements are made such information as is required to be disclosed under the arrangements.

(6) Where arrangements with the government of any territory outside the United Kingdom are specified under any Order in Council which—

(*a*) was made, or has effect as made, under section 54 of the Finance (No 2) Act 1945 or section 2 of the Finance Act (Northern Ireland) 1946, and

(*b*) had effect immediately before the passing of this Act,

the Order shall, notwithstanding the repeal of that section by the Finance Act 1975 remain in force and have effect as if any provision made by those arrangements in relation to estate duty extended to capital transfer tax chargeable by virtue of section 4 above; but the Order may be amended or revoked by an Order in Council made under this section.

Commentary—*Simon's Taxes* **F4.101A, F4.102**.

HMRC Manuals—Inheritance Tax Manual IHTM27161 (double taxation conventions).

Cross references—See FA 1986 s 100(1), (2) (after 24 July 1986 CTT to be known as inheritance tax; accordingly references in this section to CTT must be construed as references to inheritance tax after that date).

FA 2003 s 198(3) (any reference in arrangements made before the passing of FA 2003, or in any Order in Council under which such arrangements have effect, to information necessary for the carrying out of the tax laws of the United Kingdom or the territory to which the arrangements relate shall be read as including any information foreseeably relevant to the administration or enforcement of the tax laws of the United Kingdom or, as the case may be, of that territory).

FA 2006 s 173(10)(*b*) (application of this section in relation to international tax enforcement arrangements).

Amendments—[1] Sub-s (1A) repealed by FA 2006 s 178, Sch 26 Pt 8(2) with effect from 19 July 2006. Former sub-s (1A) read as follows—

"(1A) Without prejudice to the generality of subsection (1) above, if it appears to Her Majesty to be appropriate, the arrangements specified in an Order in Council under this section may include provisions with respect to the exchange of information [foreseeably relevant to the administration or enforcement of] the domestic laws of the United Kingdom and the laws of the territory to which the arrangements relate concerning taxes covered by the arrangements including, in particular, provisions about the prevention of fiscal evasion with respect to those taxes; and where arrangements do include any such provisions, the declaration in the Order in Council shall state that fact."

159 Unilateral relief

(1) Where the Board are satisfied that in any territory outside the United Kingdom (an "overseas territory") any amount of tax imposed by reason of any disposition or other event is attributable to the value of any property, then, if—

(*a*) that tax is of a character similar to that of capital transfer tax or is chargeable on or by reference to death or gifts inter vivos, and

(*b*) any capital transfer tax chargeable by reference to the same disposition or other event is also attributable to the value of that property,

they shall allow a credit in respect of that amount ("the overseas tax") against that capital transfer tax in accordance with the following provisions.

(2) Where the property is situated in the overseas territory and not in the United Kingdom, the credit shall be of an amount equal to the overseas tax.

(3) Where the property—

(*a*) is situated neither in the United Kingdom nor in the overseas territory, or

(*b*) is situated both in the United Kingdom and in the overseas territory,

the credit shall be of an amount calculated in accordance with the following formula—

$$\frac{A}{A+B} \times C$$

where A is the amount of the capital transfer tax, B is the overseas tax and C is whichever of A and B is the smaller.

(4) Where tax is imposed in two or more overseas territories in respect of property which—

(*a*) is situated neither in the United Kingdom nor in any of those territories, or

(*b*) is situated both in the United Kingdom and in each of those territories,

subsection (3) above shall apply as if, in the formula there set out, B were the aggregate of the overseas tax imposed in each of those territories and C were the aggregate of all, except the largest, of A and the overseas tax imposed in each of them.

(5) Where credit is allowed under subsection (2) above or section 158 above in respect of overseas tax imposed in one overseas territory, any credit under subsection (3) above in respect of overseas tax imposed in another shall be calculated as if the capital transfer tax were reduced by the credit allowed under subsection (2) or section 158; and where, in the case of any overseas territory mentioned in subsection (3) or (4) above, credit is allowed against the overseas tax for tax charged in a territory in which the property is situated, the overseas tax shall be treated for the purposes of those provisions as reduced by the credit.

(6) In this section references to tax imposed in an overseas territory are references to tax chargeable under the law of that territory and paid by the person liable to pay it.

(7) Where relief can be given both under this section and under section 158 above, relief shall be given under whichever section provides the greater relief.

Commentary—*Simon's Taxes* **F4.104, I4.161A**.

HMRC Manuals—Inheritance Tax Manual IHTM27161–27178 (double taxation conventions).

IHTM27181–27183 (double taxation relief where there is a double taxation convention).

IHTM27185–27189 (double taxation relief: procedure with non-convention countries – unilateral relief).

IHTM27190–27202 (procedures for relief).

Simon's Tax Cases—*Whittaker v IRC* [2001] STC (SCD) 61.

Definitions—"The Board"; "disposition"; s 272.

Cross references—See FA 1986 s 100(1), (2) (after 24 July 1986 CTT to be known as inheritance tax; accordingly references in this section to CTT must be construed as references to inheritance tax after that date).

PART VI
VALUATION

CHAPTER I
GENERAL

160 Market value

Except as otherwise provided by this Act, the value at any time of any property shall for the purposes of this Act be the price which the property might reasonably be expected to fetch if sold in the open market at that time; but that price shall not be assumed to be reduced on the ground that the whole property is to be placed on the market at one and the same time.

Commentary—*Simon's Taxes* **C2.120, I8.201**.
HMRC Manuals—Inheritance Tax Manual IHTM06033 and IHTM09703 (valuation of assets).
IHTM18091 (basis of valuation of quoted investments).
IHTM18131 (basis of valuation of unquoted shares).
IHTM19070 (capital debts due to the estate).
IHTM20231 (value of policy: general rule).
IHTM21041 (how HMRC values household goods).
IHTM23001 (valuing interests in land).
IHTM36275 (valuations of land).
Statement of Practice SP 18/80—Securities dealt in on the Stock Exchange Unlisted Securities Market: status and valuation.
Press releases etc—Law Society's Gazette 18-3-92 (valuation of agricultural tenancies: factors to be considered).
Simon's Tax Cases—*Alexander v IRC* [1991] STC 112*; *IRC v Stenhouse's Trustees* [1992] STC 103*; *Gray (surviving executor of Lady Fox, decd) v IRC* [1994] STC 360*; *Walton (Executor of Walton, decd) v IRC* [1996] STC 68*; *R&C Comrs v Bower and another (executors of Bower (dec'd))* [2009] STC 510.

161 Related property

(1) Where the value of any property comprised in a person's estate would be less than the appropriate portion of the value of the aggregate of that and any related property, it shall be the appropriate portion of the value of that aggregate.

(2) For the purposes of this section, property is related to the property comprised in a person's estate if—

(*a*) it is comprised in the estate of his spouse [or civil partner][3]; or
(*b*) it is or has within the preceding five years been—
  (i) the property of a charity, or held on trust for charitable purposes only, or
  (ii) the property of a body mentioned in section 24, [24A,][1] [or 25][2] above,

and became so on a transfer of value which was made by him or his spouse [or civil partner][3] after 15th April 1976 and was exempt to the extent that the value transferred was attributable to the property.

(3) The appropriate portion of the value of the aggregate mentioned in subsection (1) above is such portion thereof as would be attributable to the value of the first-mentioned property if the value of that aggregate were equal to the sums of the values of that and any related property, the value of each property being determined as if it did not form part of that aggregate.

(4) For the purposes of subsection (3) above the proportion which the value of a smaller number of shares of any class bears to the value of a greater number shall be taken to be that which the smaller number bears to the greater; and similarly with stock, debentures and units of any other description of property.

(5) Shares shall not be treated for the purposes of subsection (4) above as being of the same class unless they are so treated by the practice of a recognised stock exchange or would be so treated if dealt with on such a stock exchange.

Commentary—*Simon's Taxes* **I1.506, I8.241–I8.243D**.
HMRC Manuals—Inheritance Tax Manual IHTM09731–09739 (related property).
Inheritance Tax Manual IHTM23206 (special valuation matters: related property).
HMRC Interpretation RI 110—Valuation of assets at the date of death where value of asset not ascertained for IHT.
Press releases etc—HMRC Brief 71/07, 28-11-07 (HMRC will apply IHTA 1984 s 161(4) when valuing shares of land as related property in any inheritance tax case where the account is received by HMRC after 28 November 2007).
Definitions—"Charity", "charitable"; "disposition"; "estate", s 272.
Amendments—[1] Number in sub-s (2)(*b*)(ii) inserted by FA 1989 s 171(4).
[2] Amended by FA 1998 s 143(6) in relation to any property becoming the property of a body on a transfer of value made on or after 17 March 1998.
[3] Words in sub-s (2) inserted by Tax and Civil Partnership Regulations, SI 2005/3229 regs 3, 34, with effect from 5 December 2005.

162 Liabilities

(1) A liability in respect of which there is a right to reimbursement shall be taken into account only to the extent (if any) that reimbursement cannot reasonably be expected to be obtained.

(2) Subject to subsection (3) below, where a liability falls to be discharged after the time at which it is to be taken into account it shall be valued as at the time at which it is to be taken into account.

(3) In determining the value of a transferor's estate immediately after a transfer of value, his liability for capital transfer tax shall be computed—

(*a*) without making any allowance for the fact that the tax will not be due immediately, and

(*b*) as if any tax recovered otherwise than from the transferor (or a person liable for it under section 203(1) below) were paid in discharge of a liability in respect of which the transferor had a right to reimbursement.

(4) A liability which is an incumbrance on any property shall, so far as possible [and to the extent that it is not taken to reduce value in accordance with section 162B][1], be taken to reduce the value of that property.

(5) Where a liability taken into account is a liability to a person resident outside the United Kingdom which neither—

(*a*) falls to be discharged in the United Kingdom, nor

(*b*) is an incumbrance on property in the United Kingdom,

it shall, so far as possible [and to the extent that it is not taken to reduce value in accordance with section 162B][1], be taken to reduce the value of property outside the United Kingdom.

Commentary—*Simon's Taxes* **I3.232, I3.234, I3.237, I3.238, I3.523, I4.146, I8.227.**
HMRC Manuals—Inheritance Tax Manual IHTM14547 (authority for grossing up).
IHTM28110 (future debts).
IHTM28158 (income tax payable on the death of a partner in a business).
IHTM28171 (contingent inheritance tax liability).
IHTM28392 (deducting liabilities that are charged or fixed to specific property).
IHTM28381 (law relating to debts).
IHTM28354 (reimbursement of guaranteed debt).
Definitions—"Incumbrance", s 272.
Cross references—See FA 1986 s 100(1), (2) (after 24 July 1986 CTT to be known as inheritance tax; accordingly the reference to CTT in sub-s (3) above is a reference to inheritance tax after that date).
Amendments—[1] Words inserted in sub-ss (4), (5) by FA 2013 s 176, Sch 36 paras 1, 2 with effect in relation to transfers of value made, or treated as made, on or after 17 July 2013.

[162A Liabilities attributable to financing excluded property

(1) To the extent that a liability is attributable to financing (directly or indirectly)—

(*a*) the acquisition of any excluded property, or

(*b*) the maintenance, or an enhancement, of the value of any such property,

it may only be taken into account so far as permitted by subsections (2) to (4).

(2) Where the property mentioned in subsection (1) has been disposed of, in whole or in part, for full consideration in money or money's worth, the liability may be taken into account up to an amount equal to so much of that consideration as—

(*a*) is not excluded property, and

(*b*) has not been used—

(i) to finance (directly or indirectly) the acquisition of excluded property or the maintenance, or an enhancement, of the value of such property, or

(ii) to discharge (directly or indirectly) any other liability that, by virtue of this section, would not be taken into account.

(3) The liability may be taken into account up to an amount equal to the value of such of the property mentioned in subsection (1) as—

(*a*) has not been disposed of, and

(*b*) is no longer excluded property.

(4) To the extent that any remaining liability is greater than the value of such of the property mentioned in subsection (1) as—

(*a*) has not been disposed of, and

(*b*) is still excluded property,

it may be taken into account, but only so far as the remaining liability is not greater than that value for any of the reasons mentioned in subsection (7).

(5) Subsection (6) applies where—

(*a*) a liability or any part of a liability is attributable to financing (directly or indirectly)—

(i) the acquisition of property that was not excluded property, or

(ii) the maintenance, or an enhancement, of the value of such property, and

(*b*) the property or part of the property—

(i) has not been disposed of, and

(ii) has become excluded property.

(6) The liability or (as the case may be) the part may only be taken into account to the extent that it exceeds the value of the property, or the part of the property, that has become excluded property, but only so far as it does not exceed that value for any of the reasons mentioned in subsection (7).

(7) The reasons are—

(*a*) arrangements the main purpose, or one of the main purposes, of which is to secure a tax advantage, (*b*) an increase in the amount of the liability (whether due to the accrual of interest or otherwise), or

(*c*) a disposal, in whole or in part, of the property.

(8) In this section—

"arrangements" includes any scheme, transaction or series of transactions, agreement or understanding, whether or not legally enforceable, and any associated operations;

"remaining liability" means the liability mentioned in subsection (1) so far as subsections (2) and (3) do not permit it to be taken into account;

"tax advantage" means—

(*a*) the avoidance or reduction of a charge to tax, or

(*b*) the avoidance of a possible determination in respect of tax.][1]

Commentary—*Simon's Taxes* **I3.231, I3.242.**

HMRC Manuals—Inheritance Tax Manual IHTM28013 (meaning of 'indirectly').

IHTM28014 - 28018 (liabilities: restricted deductions: money borrowed to acquire excluded property).

Amendments—[1] Sections 162A–162C inserted by FA 2013 s 176, Sch 36 paras 1, 3 with effect in relation to transfers of value made, or treated as made, on or after 17 July 2013.

[162AA Liabilities attributable to financing non-residents' foreign currency accounts

(1) This section applies if—

(*a*) in determining the value of a person's estate immediately before death, a balance on any qualifying foreign currency account ("the relevant balance") is to be left out of account under section 157 (non-residents' bank accounts), and

(*b*) the person has a liability which is attributable, in whole or in part, to financing (directly or indirectly) the relevant balance.

(2) To the extent that the liability is attributable as mentioned in subsection (1)(*b*), it may only be taken into account in determining the value of the person's estate immediately before death so far as permitted by subsection (3).

(3) If the amount of the liability that is attributable as mentioned in subsection (1)(*b*) exceeds the value of the relevant balance, the excess may be taken into account, but only so far as the excess does not arise for either of the reasons mentioned in subsection (4).

(4) The reasons are—

(*a*) arrangements the main purpose, or one of the main purposes, of which is to secure a tax advantage, or

(*b*) an increase in the amount of the liability (whether due to the accrual of interest or otherwise).

(5) In subsection (4)(*a*)—

"arrangements" includes any scheme, transaction or series of transactions, agreement or understanding, whether or not legally enforceable, and any associated operations;

"tax advantage" means—

(*a*) the avoidance or reduction of a charge to tax, or

(*b*) the avoidance of a possible determination in respect of tax.][1]

Commentary—*Simon's Taxes* **I3.231, I4.149G.**

HMRC Manuals—Inheritance Tax Manual IHTM28011 (when the provisions apply).

IHTM28033 (borrowed money used to fund a foreign currency bank account).

Amendments—[1] Section 162AA inserted by FA 2014 s 117, Sch 25 paras 1, 3(1) with effect in relation to transfers of value made, or treated as made, on or after 17 July 2014.

[162B Liabilities attributable to financing certain relievable property

(1) Subsection (2) applies if—

(*a*) the whole or part of any value transferred by a transfer of value is to be treated as reduced, under section 104, by virtue of it being attributable to the value of relevant business property, and

(*b*) the transferor has a liability which is attributable, in whole or in part, to financing (directly or indirectly)—

(i) the acquisition of that property, or

(ii) the maintenance, or an enhancement, of its value.

(2) The liability is, so far as possible, to be taken to reduce the value attributable to the value of the relevant business property, before it is treated as reduced under section 104, but only to the extent that the liability—

(*a*) is attributable as mentioned in subsection (1)(*b*), and

(*b*) does not reduce the value of the relevant business property by virtue of section 110(*b*).

(3) Subsection (4) applies if—

(*a*) the whole or part of any value transferred by a transfer of value is to be treated as reduced, under section 116, by virtue of it being attributable to the agricultural value of agricultural property, and

(*b*) the transferor has a liability which is attributable, in whole or in part, to financing (directly or indirectly)—

(i) the acquisition of that property, or

IHT

(ii) the maintenance, or an enhancement, of its agricultural value.

(4) To the extent that the liability is attributable as mentioned in subsection (3)(*b*), it is, so far as possible, to be taken to reduce the value attributable to the agricultural value of the agricultural property, before it is treated as reduced under section 116.

(5) Subsection (6) applies if—

(*a*) part of the value of a person's estate immediately before death is attributable to the value of land on which trees or underwood are growing,

(*b*) the value of the trees or underwood is to be left out of account, under section 125(2)(*a*), in determining the value transferred by the chargeable transfer made on the person's death, and

(*c*) the person has a liability which is attributable, in whole or in part, to financing (directly or indirectly)—

(i) the acquisition of the land or trees or underwood,

(ii) planting the trees or underwood, or

(iii) the maintenance, or an enhancement, of the value of the trees or underwood.

(6) To the extent that the liability is attributable as mentioned in subsection (5)(*c*), it is, so far as possible, to be taken to reduce the value of the trees or underwood, before their value is left out of account.

(7) Subject to subsection (8), to the extent that a liability is, in accordance with this section, taken to reduce value in determining the value transferred by a chargeable transfer, that liability is not then to be taken into account in determining the value transferred by any subsequent transfer of value by the same transferor.

(8) Subsection (7) does not prevent a liability from being taken into account by reason only that the liability has previously been taken into account in determining the amount on which tax is chargeable under section 64.

(9) For the purposes of subsections (1) to (4) and (7), references to a transfer of value or chargeable transfer include references to an occasion on which tax is chargeable under Chapter 3 of Part 3 (apart from section 79) and—

(*a*) references to the value transferred by a transfer of value or chargeable transfer include references to the amount on which tax is then chargeable, and

(*b*) references to the transferor include references to the trustees of the settlement concerned.

(10) In this section—

"agricultural property" and "agricultural value" have the same meaning as in Chapter 2 of Part 5;

"relevant business property" has the same meaning as in Chapter 1 of Part 5.][1]

Commentary—*Simon's Taxes* **I3.231, I3.241, I3.242.**

HMRC Manuals—Inheritance Tax Manual IHTM28019 (relievable property assets that qualify for reliefs).
IHTM28020 (borrowed money used to acquire assets that qualify for business relief).
IHTM28021 (borrowed money used to acquire assets that qualify for agricultural relief).
IHTM28023 (borrowed money used to acquire assets that qualify for woodlands relief).
IHTM28024 (transfer of relievable assets where borrowed money is used to acquire assets that qualify for relief).

Amendments—[1] Sections 162A–162C inserted by FA 2013 s 176, Sch 36 paras 1, 3 with effect in relation to transfers of value made, or treated as made, on or after 17 July 2013. Section 162B only has effect in relation to liabilities incurred on or after 6 April 2013. For this purposes, where a liability is incurred under an agreement, if the agreement was varied so that the liability could be incurred under it, the liability is to be treated as having been incurred on the date of the variation, and in any other case, the liability is to be treated as having been incurred on the date the agreement was made (FA 2013 Sch 36 para 5(2), (3)).

[162C Sections 162A[, 162AA] and 162B: supplementary provision

(1) This section applies for the purposes of determining the extent to which a liability is attributable as mentioned in section 162A(1) or (5)[, 162AA(1)][2] or 162B(1)(*b*), (3)(*b*) or (5)(*c*).

[(1A) In a case in which the value of a person's estate immediately before death is to be determined, where a liability was discharged in part before that time—

(*a*) any part of the liability that, at the time of discharge, was not attributable as mentioned in subsection (1) is, so far as possible, to be taken to have been discharged first,

(*b*) any part of the liability that, at the time of discharge, was attributable as mentioned in section 162B(1)(*b*), (3)(*b*) or (5)(*c*) is, so far as possible, only to be taken to have been discharged after any part of the liability within paragraph (*a*) was discharged,

(*c*) any part of the liability that, at the time of discharge, was attributable as mentioned in section 162AA(1) is, so far as possible, only to be taken to have been discharged after any parts of the liability within paragraph (*a*) or (*b*) were discharged, and

(*d*) any part of the liability that, at the time of discharge, was attributable as mentioned in section 162A(1) or (5) is, so far as possible, only to be taken to have been discharged after any parts of the liability within paragraphs (*a*) to (*c*) were discharged.][2]

(2) [In any other case, where][2] a liability was discharged in part before the time in relation to which the question as to whether or how to take it into account arises—

(*a*) any part of the liability that, at the time of discharge, was not attributable as mentioned in [section 162A(1) or (5) or 162B(1)(*b*), (3)(*b*) or (5)(*c*)][2] is, so far as possible, to be taken to have been discharged first,

(*b*) any part of the liability that, at the time of discharge, was attributable as mentioned in section 162B(1)(*b*), (3)(*b*) or (5)(*c*) is, so far as possible, only to be taken to have been discharged after any part of the liability within paragraph (*a*) was discharged, and

(*c*) any part of the liability that, at the time of discharge, was attributable as mentioned in section 162A(1) or (5) is, so far as possible, only to be taken to have been discharged after any parts of the liability within paragraph (*a*) or (*b*) were discharged.][1]

Commentary—*Simon's Taxes* **I3.231, I4.149G**.
HMRC Manuals—Inheritance Tax Manual IHTM28026 (partial repayment of loan before tax charge arises).
Amendments—[1] Sections 162A–162C inserted by FA 2013 s 176, Sch 36 paras 1, 3 with effect in relation to transfers of value made, or treated as made, on or after 17 July 2013.
[2] In heading and sub-s (1), reference inserted, sub-s (1A) inserted, in sub-s (2), words substituted for word "Where", and in sub-s (2)(*a*), words substituted for words "subsection (1)", by FA 2014 s 117, Sch 25 paras 1, 3(2)–(6) with effect in relation to transfers of value made, or treated as made, on or after 17 July 2014.

163 Restriction on freedom to dispose

(1) Where, by a contract made at any time, the right to dispose of any property has been excluded or restricted, then, in determining the value of the property for the purpose of the first relevant event happening after that time—

(*a*) the exclusion or restriction shall be taken into account only to the extent (if any) that consideration in money or money's worth was given for it, but

(*b*) if the contract was a chargeable transfer or was part of associated operations which together were a chargeable transfer, an allowance shall be made for the value transferred thereby (calculated as if no tax had been chargeable on it) or for so much of the value transferred as is attributable to the exclusion or restriction.

(2) Where the contract was made before 27th March 1974 subsection (1) above applies only if the first relevant event is a transfer made on death.

(3) In this section "relevant event", in relation to any property, means—

(*a*) a chargeable transfer in the case of which the whole or part of the value transferred is attributable to the value of the property; and

(*b*) anything which would be such a chargeable transfer but for this section.

Commentary—*Simon's Taxes* **I8.231**.
HMRC Manuals—Inheritance Tax Manual IHTM09771–09777 (restrictions of the freedom to dispose of assets).
Definitions—"Associated operations", s 268.

164 Transferor's expenses

In determining the value transferred by a transfer of value, expenses incurred by the transferor in making the transfer (but not his liability for capital transfer tax)—

(*a*) shall, if borne by him, be left out of account;

(*b*) shall, if borne by a person benefiting from the transfer, be treated as reducing the value transferred.

Commentary—*Simon's Taxes* **I3.252**.
HMRC Manuals—Inheritance Tax Manual IHTM14013 (treatment of expenses).
Cross references—See FA 1986 s 100(1), (2) (after 24 July 1986 CTT to be known as inheritance tax; accordingly the reference to CTT in this section is a reference to inheritance tax after that date).

165 Tax on capital gains

(1) Where a chargeable transfer is or includes a disposal of an asset and on the disposal a gain accrues to the transferor for the purposes of the [1992 Act][1], then if—

(*a*) the whole or part of the gain is a chargeable gain or a development gain, and

(*b*) the whole or part of any capital gains tax or income tax chargeable on the gain is borne by the donee (within the meaning of section [282][1] of that Act),

the amount of the tax so borne shall be treated as reducing the value transferred by the chargeable transfer.

(2) Subsection (1) above shall not apply where the chargeable transfer is made under Part III of this Act and the gain accrues to the trustees of the settlement; but if in such a case any capital gains tax chargeable on the gain is borne by a person who becomes absolutely entitled to the settled property concerned, the amount of the tax so borne shall be treated as reducing the value transferred by the chargeable transfer.

(3) In any case where—

(*a*) payment of an amount of capital gains tax is postponed by virtue of Schedule 14 to the Finance Act 1984 and

(*b*) any of that capital gains tax becomes payable in accordance with paragraph 11 of that Schedule by reason of the receipt of a capital payment by a close relative of the beneficiary, as mentioned in sub-paragraph (3) of that paragraph, and

(*c*) all or part of the capital gains tax becoming so payable is paid by the close relative, the payment by the close relative shall be treated for the purposes of this Act as made in satisfaction of a liability of his.

Commentary—*Simon's Taxes* **I3.611, I3.231, I5.915, I5.228.**

HMRC Manuals—Inheritance Tax Manual IHTM42163 (CGT on dispositions from the trust)
IHTM14013 (basis of valuation: treatment of expenses).

Definitions—"Settlement", s 43; "trustee", s 45.

Amendments—[1] Words in sub-s (1) substituted by TCGA 1992 Sch 10 para 8(1), (8).

166 Creditors' rights

In determining the value of a right to receive a sum due under any obligation it shall be assumed that the obligation will be duly discharged, except if or to the extent that recovery of the sum is impossible or not reasonably practicable and has not become so by any act or omission of the person to whom the sum is due.

Commentary—*Simon's Taxes* **I8.372.**

HMRC Manuals—Inheritance Tax Manual IHTM19100 (legal background).

167 Life policies, etc

(1) In determining in connection with a transfer of value the value of a policy of insurance on a person's life or of a contract for an annuity payable on a person's death, that value shall be taken to be not less than—

(*a*) the total of the premiums or other consideration which, at any time before the transfer of value, has been paid under the policy or contract or any policy or contract for which it was directly or indirectly substituted, less

(*b*) any sum which, at any time before the transfer of value, has been paid under, or in consideration for the surrender of any right conferred by, the policy or contract or a policy or contract for which it was directly or indirectly substituted.

(2) Subsection (1) above shall not apply in the case of—

(*a*) the transfer of value which a person makes on his death, or

(*b*) any other transfer of value which does not result in the policy or contract ceasing to be part of the transferor's estate,

. . . [1]

(3) Subsection (1) above shall not apply where the policy is one—

(*a*) under which the sum assured becomes payable only if the person whose life is insured dies before the expiry of a specified term or both before the expiry of a specified term and during the life of a specified person, and

(*b*) which, if that specified term ends, or can, under the policy, be extended so as to end, more than three years after the making of the insurance, satisfies the condition that, if neither the person whose life is insured nor the specified person dies before the expiry of the specified term—

(i) the premiums are payable during at least two-thirds of that term and at yearly or shorter intervals, and

(ii) the premiums payable in any one period of twelve months are not more than twice the premiums payable in any other such period.

(4) Where the policy is one under which—

(*a*) the benefit secured is expressed in units the value of which is published and subject to fluctuation, and

(*b*) the payment of each premium secures the allocation to the policy of a specified number of such units,

then, if the value, at the time of the transfer of value, of the units allocated to the policy on the payment of premiums is less than the aggregate of what the respective values of those units were at the time of allocation, the value to be taken under subsection (1) above as a minimum shall be reduced by the amount of the difference.

(5) References in subsections (1) and (4) above to a transfer of value shall be construed as including references to an event on which there is a charge to tax under Chapter III of Part III of this Act (apart from section 79), other than an event on which tax is chargeable in respect of the policy or contract by reason only that its value (apart from this section) is reduced.

Commentary—*Simon's Taxes* **I8.375.**

HMRC Manuals—Inheritance Tax Manual IHTM20241 - IHTM20244 (special rule for the valuation of life policies, etc, and the exclusions and modifications to this rule).

Concession F11—Property chargeable on the ceasing of an annuity.

Press releases etc—IR 17-1-79 (as regards sub-s (1)(*b*) the premiums are taken net of any tax deducted at source under TA 1988 s 266(5)).

Amendments—[1] Words in sub-s (2) repealed by FA 1986 Sch 23 Pt X in view of the repeal of ss 148, 149 of this Act.

168 Unquoted shares and securities

(1) In determining the price which unquoted shares or [unquoted][1] securities might reasonably be expected to fetch if sold in the open market it shall be assumed that in that market there is available to any prospective purchaser of the shares or securities all the information which a prudent prospective purchaser might reasonably require if he were proposing to purchase them from a willing vendor by private treaty and at arm's length.

(2) . . . [2]

Commentary—*Simon's Taxes* **I8.311, I8.313.**

HMRC Manuals—Inheritance Tax Manual IHTM18131 (basis of valuation of unquoted shares).

Simon's Tax Cases—*IRC v Stenhouse's Trustees* [1992] STC 103*.

Definitions—"Purchaser", "unquoted", s 272.

Amendments—[1] Word in sub-s (1) inserted by FA 1987 Sch 8 para 12(1).

[2] Sub-s (2) repealed by FA 1987 Sch 8 para 12(2) and Sch 16 Pt IX in relation to transfers of value made after 16 March 1987.

169 Farm cottages

(1) In determining the value of agricultural property which includes cottages occupied by persons employed solely for agricultural purposes in connection with the property, no account shall be taken of any value attributable to the fact that the cottages are suitable for the residential purposes of persons not so employed.

(2) Expressions used in subsection (1) above and in Chapter II of Part V of this Act have the same meaning in that subsection as in that Chapter.

Commentary—*Simon's Taxes* **I8.365, I8.101.**

HMRC Manuals—Inheritance Tax Manual IHTM24165 (role of the district valuer).

Definitions—"Agricultural property", s 115.

Concession F16—Agricultural property and farm cottages.

170 Leases for life, etc

Where under section 43(3) above a lease of property is to be treated as a settlement, the value of the lessor's interest in the property shall be taken to be such part of the value of the property as bears to it the same proportion as the value of the consideration, at the time the lease was granted, bore to what would then have been the value of a full consideration in money or money's worth.

Commentary—*Simon's Taxes* **I5.215, I8.222, I5.714, I5.116.**

HMRC Manuals—Inheritance Tax Manual IHTM16191 (leases for life: introduction).

IHTM16192 (what happens if consideration was given?).

Definitions—"Settlement", s 43.

CHAPTER II

ESTATE ON DEATH

171 Changes occurring on death

(1) In determining the value of a person's estate immediately before his death changes in the value of his estate which have occurred by reason of the death and fall within subsection (2) below shall be taken into account as if they had occurred before the death.

(2) A change falls within this subsection if it is an addition to the property comprised in the estate or an increase or decrease of the value of any property so comprised, other than a decrease resulting from such an alteration as is mentioned in section 98(1) above; but the termination on the death of any interest or the passing of any interest by survivorship does not fall within this subsection.

Commentary—*Simon's Taxes* **I4.114, I6.232, I8.102.**

HMRC Manuals—Inheritance Tax Manual IHTM04046 (changes in value by reason of death with examples).

Definitions—"Estate", s 272.

172 Funeral expenses

In determining the value of a person's estate immediately before his death, allowance shall be made for reasonable funeral expenses.

Commentary—*Simon's Taxes* **I1.516, I4.142.**

HMRC Manuals—Inheritance Tax Manual IHTM10371 IHT400 (funeral expenses: introduction and general approach).

IHTM10375 IHT400 (mourning expenses).

Concession F1—Mourning.

Statement of Practice SP 7/87—Deduction for reasonable funeral expenses.

Definitions—"Estate", s 272.

173 Expenses incurred abroad

In determining the value of a person's estate immediately before his death, an allowance against the value of property situated outside the United Kingdom shall be made for any expense incurred in administering or realising the property which is shown to be attributable to the situation of the property, but the allowance shall not exceed 5 per cent of the value of the property.

Commentary—*Simon's Taxes* **I4.143, I9.122.**

HMRC Manuals—Inheritance Tax Manual IHTM27050 (deduction for administration of non-UK assets).

IHTM10693 IHT100 (foreign assets).

Definitions—"Estate", s 272.

174 Income tax and unpaid capital transfer tax

(1) In determining the value of a person's estate immediately before his death, allowance shall be made for—

(*a*) any liability for income tax in respect of an offshore income gain, within the meaning of [regulations made under section 41(1) of the Finance Act 2008, arising on a disposal which is deemed, under such regulations (see regulation 34 of the Offshore Funds (Tax) Regulations 2009 (SI 2009/3001)), to occur on the death][2]; and

(*b*) any liability to income tax arising under [Chapter 8 of Part 4 of the Income Tax (Trading and Other Income) Act 2005 (deeply discounted securities)][1] on a transfer which is treated as taking place by virtue of [section 437(2) of that Act][1].]

(2) Where in determining the value of a person's estate immediately before his death a liability for capital transfer tax is taken into account, then, if that tax or any part of it is not in the event paid out of the estate, the value of the estate immediately before his death shall be treated as increased by an amount equal to that tax or so much of it as is not so paid.

Commentary—*Simon's Taxes* **I4.144, I4.145, I4.201, I4.209**.

HMRC Manuals—Inheritance Tax Manual IHTM28154 (income tax on the disposal of an 'offshore fund').

IHTM28155 (income tax on the disposal of deep discount securities).

IHTM28171 (contingent inheritance tax liability).

Definitions—"Estate", s 272.

Cross references—See FA 1986 s 100(1), (2) (after 24 July 1986 CTT to be known as inheritance tax; accordingly references in this section to CTT are references to inheritance tax after that date).

Amendments—[1] Words in sub-s (1)(*b*) substituted by ITTOIA 2005 s 882(1), Sch 1 paras 393, 396 with effect from 6 April 2005. ITTOIA 2005 has effect—

(a) for income tax purposes, for 2005–06 and subsequent tax years, and

(b) for corporation tax purposes, for accounting periods ending after 5 April 2005: ITTOIA 2005 s 883(1).

[2] Words in sub-s (1)(*a*) substituted by the Offshore Funds (Tax) Regulations, SI 2009/3001 reg 125 with effect for the purposes of income tax for the tax year 2009–10 and subsequent tax years and for distributions made on or after 1 December 2009; for the purposes of corporation tax, on income, for accounting periods ending on or after 1 December 2009 and for distributions made on or after that date and, on chargeable gains, in relation to disposals made on or after 1 December 2009; and for the purposes of capital gains tax, in relation to disposals made on or after 1 December 2009.

175 Liability to make future payments, etc

Where in determining the value of a person's estate immediately before his death a liability to make payments or transfer assets under such a disposition as is mentioned in section 262 below is taken into account, the liability shall be computed as if the amount or value of the payments or assets were reduced by the chargeable portion (as defined in that section).

Commentary—*Simon's Taxes* **I3.256, I4.146**.

HMRC Manuals—Inheritance Tax Manual IHTM28120 (future payments incurred under S262).

Definitions—"Estate", "disposition", s 272.

[175A Discharge of liabilities after death

(1) In determining the value of a person's estate immediately before death, a liability may be taken into account to the extent that—

(*a*) it is discharged on or after death, out of the estate or from excluded property owned by the person immediately before death, in money or money's worth, and

(*b*) it is not otherwise prevented, under any provision of this Act, from being taken into account.

(2) Where the whole or any part of a liability is not discharged in accordance with paragraph (*a*) of subsection (1), the liability or (as the case may be) the part may only be taken into account for the purpose mentioned in that subsection to the extent that—

(*a*) there is a real commercial reason for the liability or the part not being discharged,

(*b*) securing a tax advantage is not the main purpose, or one of the main purposes, of leaving the liability or part undischarged, and

(*c*) the liability or the part is not otherwise prevented, under any provision of this Act, from being taken into account.

(3) For the purposes of subsection (2)(*a*) there is a real commercial reason for a liability, or part of a liability, not being discharged where it is shown that—

(*a*) the liability is to a person dealing at arm's length, or

(*b*) if the liability were to a person dealing at arm's length, that person would not require the liability to be discharged.

(4) Where, by virtue of this section, a liability is not taken into account in determining the value of a person's estate immediately before death, the liability is also not to be taken into account in determining the extent to which the estate of any spouse or civil partner of the person is increased for the purposes of section 18.

(5) In subsection (2)(*b*) "tax advantage" means—

(*a*) a relief from tax or increased relief from tax,

(*b*) a repayment of tax or increased repayment of tax,

(*c*) the avoidance, reduction or delay of a charge to tax or an assessment to tax, or

(*d*) the avoidance of a possible assessment to tax or determination in respect of tax.

(6) In subsection (5) "tax" includes income tax and capital gains tax.

(7) Where the liability is discharged as mentioned in subsection (1)(*a*) only in part—

(*a*) any part of the liability that is attributable as mentioned in section 162A(1) or (5) is, so far possible, taken to be discharged first,

[(*aa*) any part of the liability that is attributable as mentioned in section 162AA(1) is, so far as possible, taken to be discharged only after any part of the liability within paragraph (a) is discharged,][2]

(*b*) any part of the liability that is attributable as mentioned in section 162B(1)(*b*), (3)(*b*) or (5)(*c*) is, so far as possible, taken to be discharged only after any [parts][2] of the liability within paragraph [(*a*) or (*aa*) are][2] discharged, and

(*c*) the liability so far as it is not attributable as mentioned in [any of paragraphs (*a*) to (*b*)][2] is, so far as possible, taken to be discharged only after any parts of the liability within [any][2] of those paragraphs are discharged.][1]

Commentary—*Simon's Taxes* **I3.241, I4.114, I4.149F**.

HMRC Manuals—Inheritance Tax Manual IHTM28027 (repayment of liabilities deducted against the estate on death).

IHTM28028 (meaning of 'out of estate').

IHTM28029 (non-repayment of liabilities deducted against the estate on death).

IHTM28032 (partial repayment of liabilities after death).

Amendments—[1] Section 175A inserted by FA 2013 s 176, Sch 36 paras 1, 4 with effect in relation to transfers of value made, or treated as made, on or after 17 July 2013.

[2] Sub-s (7)(*aa*) inserted, in sub-s (7)(*b*), word substituted for word "part" and words substituted for words "(*a*) is", and in sub-s (7)(*c*), words substituted for words "paragraph (*a*) or (*b*)" and word substituted for word "either", by FA 2014 s 117, Sch 25 paras 1, 3(7) with effect in relation to transfers of value made, or treated as made, on or after 17 July 2014.

176 Related property, etc—sales

(1) This section has effect where, within three years after the death of any person, there is a qualifying sale of any property ("the property concerned") comprised in his estate immediately before his death and valued for the purposes of this Act—

(*a*) in accordance with section 161 above, or

(*b*) in conjunction with property which was also comprised in the estate but has not at any time since the death been vested in the vendors.

(2) If a claim is made for relief under this section the value of the property concerned immediately before the death shall be taken to be what it would have been if it had not been determined as mentioned in subsection (1) above.

(3) For the purposes of subsection (1) above a sale is a qualifying sale if—

(*a*) the vendors are the persons in whom the property concerned vested immediately after the death or the deceased's personal representatives; and

(*b*) it is at arm's length for a price freely negotiated at the time of the sale and is not made in conjunction with a sale of any of the related property taken into account as mentioned in subsection (1)(*a*) above or any of the property mentioned in subsection (1)(*b*) above; and

(*c*) no person concerned as vendor (or as having an interest in the proceeds of sale) is the same as or connected with any person concerned as purchaser (or as having an interest in the purchase); and

(*d*) neither the vendors nor any other person having an interest in the proceeds of sale obtain in connection with the sale a right to acquire the property sold or any interest in or created out of it.

(4) Subsection (2) above shall not apply unless the price obtained on the sale, with any adjustment needed to take account of any difference in circumstances at the date of the sale and at the date of the death, is less than the value which, apart from this section and apart from Chapter IV of this Part of this Act, would be the value of the property concerned determined as mentioned in subsection (1) above.

(5) Where the property concerned consists of shares in or securities of a close company, subsection (2) above shall not apply if at any time between the death and the qualifying sale the value of the shares or securities is reduced by more than 5 per cent as a result of an alteration in the company's share or loan capital or in any rights attaching to shares in or securities of the company; and for the purposes of this subsection—

"alteration" includes extinguishment, and

"close company" has the same meaning as in Part IV of this Act.

Commentary—*Simon's Taxes* **I4.321–I4.324, I8.244**.

HMRC Manuals—Inheritance Tax Manual IHTM09751–09763 (sales of related property).

IHTM24021 (sale within three years of death).

IHTM09731 (related property valuation: introduction).

Definitions—"close company", s 102(1); "estate", "purchaser", s 272.

177 Scottish agricultural leases

(1) Where any part of the value of a person's estate immediately before his death is attributable to the interest of a tenant in an unexpired portion of a lease for a fixed term of agricultural property in Scotland then, subject to subsection (3) below, there shall be left out of account in determining that value any value associated with any prospect of renewal of the lease by tacit relocation.

(2) Where any part of the value of a person's estate immediately before his death is attributable to the interest of a tenant of agricultural property in Scotland, being an interest which is—

(*a*) held by virtue of tacit relocation, and

(*b*) acquired on the death by a new tenant,

then, subject to subsection (3) below, the value of the interest shall be left out of account in determining the value of that estate.

(3) Subsections (1) and (2) above shall not apply unless the deceased had been tenant of the property in question continuously for a period of at least two years immediately preceding his death or had become tenant by succession.

(4) The value to be left out of account by virtue of subsection (2) above shall not include the value of any rights to compensation in respect of tenant's improvements.

Commentary—*Simon's Taxes* **I8.368, I4.123**.

Definitions—"Estate", s 272.

Cross references—See FA 1995 s 145(2), (3), (5) (the cultivation of short rotation coppice is regarded as agriculture for the inheritance tax purposes in relation to transfers of value and other events after 5 April 1995).

CHAPTER III

SALE OF SHARES ETC FROM DECEASED'S ESTATE

178 Preliminary

(1) In this Chapter—

"the appropriate person", in relation to any qualifying investments comprised in a person's estate immediately before his death, means the person liable for capital transfer tax attributable to the value of those investments or, if there is more than one such person, and one of them is in fact paying the tax, that person;

"the loss on sale" means the amount determined in accordance with section 179(1) below;

"qualifying investments" means (subject to subsection (2) below) shares or securities which [are quoted at the date of the death in question][1], holdings in a unit trust which at that date is an authorised unit trust[, shares in an open-ended investment company][5] . . . [6] and shares in any common investment fund established under [section 42 of the Administration of Justice Act 1982][5];

"relevant proportion", in relation to the investments to which a claim relates, or any of them, means the proportion by which the loss on sale is reduced under section 180 below;

"sale value", in relation to any qualifying investments, means their value for the purposes of section 179(1)(*b*) below;

"value on death", in relation to any qualifying investments, means their value for the purposes of section 179(1)(*a*) below.

(2) Shares or securities which are comprised in a person's estate immediately before his death and in respect of which [listing][4] on a recognised stock exchange [or dealing on the Unlisted Securities Market][2] is suspended at that time shall be qualifying investments for the purposes of this Chapter if they are again [so listed or dealt in][4] . . . [3] when they are sold as mentioned in section 179(1) below or exchanged as mentioned in section 184 below.

(3) Any reference in this Chapter to the investments to which a claim relates is a reference to all the qualifying investments which, on the making of the claim, are taken into account under section 179(1) below in determining the loss on sale.

(4) For the purposes of this Chapter—

(*a*) the personal representatives of the deceased, and

(*b*) the trustees of a settlement,

shall each be treated as a single and continuing body of persons (distinct from the persons who may from time to time be the personal representatives or trustees).

(5) In any case where, for the purposes of this Chapter, it is necessary to determine the price at which any investments were purchased or sold or the best consideration that could reasonably have been obtained on the sale of any investments, no account shall be taken of expenses (whether by way of commission, stamp duty or otherwise) which are incidental to the sale or purchase.

Commentary—*Simon's Taxes* **I4.301-I4.303**.

HMRC Manuals—Inheritance Tax Manual IHTM27024 (loss on sale of foreign shares).

IHTM34131 and 34132 (qualifying and non-qualifying investments).

IHTM34161–34164 (the "appropriate person").

Definitions—"authorised unit trust", "Personal representatives", "quoted", s 272; "settlement", s 43; "trustee", s 45.

Cross references—See FA 1986 s 100(1), (2) (after 24 July 1986 CTT to be known as inheritance tax; accordingly the reference in the definition of "the appropriate person" in sub-s (1) above to CTT is a reference to inheritance tax after that date).

Amendments—[1] Words in sub-s (1) substituted by FA 1987 s 58 and Sch 8 para 13 in relation to transfers of value or other events occurring after 16 March 1987.

[2] Words in sub-s (2) inserted by FA 1987 s 58 and Sch 8 para 13 in relation to transfers of value or other events occurring after 16 March 1987.

[3] Words in sub-s (2) repealed by FA 1987 s 58 and Sch 16 Pt IX in relation to transfers of value or other events occurring after 16 March 1987.

[4] Words in sub-s (2) substituted by FA 1996 Sch 38 para 4 in relation to investments sold, or treated as sold, after 31 March 1996.

[5] In sub-s (1), in the definition of "qualifying investments", words inserted, and words substituted by FA 2003 s 186(1), (4) with effect for transfers of value or other events occurring after 15 October 2002: FA 2003 s 186(8).

[6] In sub-s (1), in the definition of "qualifying investments", words "(as defined in section 468 of the Taxes Act 1988)" repealed by FA 2003 s 216, Sch 43 Pt 4(1) with effect for transfers of value and other events occurring after 15 October 2002.

179 The relief

(1) On a claim being made in that behalf by the appropriate person there shall be determined for the purposes of this Chapter the amount (if any) by which—

(*a*) the aggregate of the values which, apart from this Chapter, would be the values for the purposes of tax of all the qualifying investments comprised in a person's estate immediately before his death which are sold by the appropriate person within the period of twelve months immediately following the date of the death

exceeds

(*b*) the aggregate of the values of those investments at the time they were so sold, taking the value of any particular investments for this purpose as the price for which they were so sold or, if it is greater, the best consideration which could reasonably have been obtained for them at the time of the sale.

(2) Subject to the following provisions of this Chapter, in determining the tax chargeable on the death in question, the value of the investments to which the claim relates shall be treated as reduced by an amount equal to the loss on sale.

[(2A) A claim under this Chapter must be made not more than 4 years after the end of the period mentioned in subsection (1)(*a*)][1]

(3) A claim made by the appropriate person under this Chapter shall specify the capacity in which he makes the claim, and the reference in subsection (1) above to qualifying investments which are sold by him is a reference to investments which, immediately before their sale, were held by him in the capacity in which he makes the claim.

Commentary—*Simon's Taxes* **I4.302, I1.517, I4.301, I4.303.**

HMRC Manuals—Inheritance Tax Manual IHTM34133 (unlisted securities market shares).

IHTM34151 (the basic condition for relief).

IHTM34171–34177 (calculating the loss).

IHTM34011 (loss on sale of shares: basic conditions).

Definitions—"Appropriate person", s 178; "estate", s 272; "loss on sale", "qualifying investments", s 178.

Cross references—See IHTA 1984 s 186A (modification of this section where qualifying investments in a person's estate are cancelled within 12 months from date of his death and they are included in the calculation under sub-s (1) above).

IHTA 1984 s 186B (modification of this section where listed qualifying investments in a person's estate are suspended at end of 12 months from date of his death and they are included in calculation under sub-s (1) above.

Amendments—[1] Sub-s (2A) inserted by FA 2009 s 99, Sch 51 para 9 with effect from 1 April 2011 (by virtue of SI 2010/867 art 2(2)).

180 Effect of purchases

(1) If a claim is made under this Chapter and, at any time during the period beginning on the date of the death in question and ending two months after the date of the last sale made as mentioned in section 179(1)(*a*) above, the person making the claim purchases any qualifying investments in the same capacity as that in which he makes the claim, the loss on sale of the investments to which the claim relates shall be treated for the purposes of section 179(2) above as reduced by the proportion which the aggregate of the purchase prices of all the qualifying investments so purchased bears to the aggregate of the values referred to in section 179(1)(*b*) above (or, if the aggregate of those purchase prices equals or exceeds the aggregate of those values, the loss on sale shall be extinguished).

(2) If a claim is made under this Chapter by any person in a capacity other than that of personal representative or trustee—

(*a*) subsection (1) above shall have effect in his case as if for the words "in the same capacity as that in which he makes the claim" there were substituted the words "otherwise than in the capacity of personal representative or trustee", and

(*b*) no account shall be taken under that subsection of any qualifying investments purchased by him unless they are of the same description as one of the qualifying investments to which the claim relates.

(3) For the purposes of subsection (2) above, two investments, not being investments in an authorised unit trust or common investment fund, shall not be treated as of the same description if they are separately [listed][2] on a recognised stock exchange [or separately dealt in on the Unlisted

Securities Market][1], and an investment in one authorised unit trust or common investment fund shall not be treated as of the same description as an investment in another authorised unit trust or common investment fund.

Commentary—*Simon's Taxes* **I4.301, I4.302**.
HMRC Manuals—Inheritance Tax Manual IHTM34211–34230 (restrictions of relief for purchases).
Definitions—"authorised unit trust", "loss on sale", s 178; "personal representative", s 272; "qualifying investments", s 178; "trustee", s 45.
Amendments—[1] Words in sub-s (3) inserted by FA 1987 s 58 and Sch 8 para 14 in relation to transfers of value or other events occurring after 16 March 1987.
[2] Word in sub-s (3) substituted by FA 1996 Sch 38 para 3, with effect from 1 April 1996.

181 Capital receipts

(1) For the purposes of section 179(1)(*b*) above, if—

(*a*) at any time after the death in question (whether during or after the period of twelve months immediately following the date of the death) the appropriate person receives any capital payment or payments which is or are attributable to any qualifying investments comprised in the deceased's estate immediately before his death, and

(*b*) those investments are sold by him within that period,

the price for which those investments were sold or, as the case may be, the best consideration referred to in section 179(1)(*b*) shall be taken to be increased by an amount equal to the capital payment or, as the case may be, the aggregate of the capital payments, referred to in paragraph (*a*) above.

(2) If the appropriate person receives or becomes entitled to receive in respect of any qualifying investments a provisional allotment of shares in or debentures of a company and he disposes of his rights, the amount of the consideration for the disposal shall be treated for the purposes of this section as a capital payment attributable to those investments.

(3) In this section "capital payment", in relation to any investment, does not include the price paid on the sale of the investment but, subject to that, includes any money or money's worth which does not constitute income for the purposes of income tax.

Commentary—*Simon's Taxes* **I4.306**.
HMRC Manuals—Inheritance Tax Manual IHTM34177 (capital payments).
IHTM34188 (rights sold).
Definitions—"Appropriate person", s 178; "estate", s 272; "qualifying investments", s 178.

182 Payment of calls

For the purposes of section 179(1)(*a*) above, if—

(*a*) at any time after the death in question (whether during or after the period of twelve months immediately following the date of the death) the appropriate person pays an amount in pursuance of a call in respect of any qualifying investments comprised in the deceased's estate immediately before his death, and

(*b*) those investments are sold by the appropriate person within that period,

the value on death of those investments shall be the aggregate of the amount so paid and their value as determined apart from this Chapter.

Commentary—*Simon's Taxes* **I4.305**.
HMRC Manuals—Inheritance Tax Manual IHTM34173 (value on death).
IHTM34175 (calculating the loss - call).
Definitions—"Appropriate person", s 178; "estate", s 272; "qualifying investments", s 178.

183 Changes in holdings

(1) This section applies in any case where, within the period of twelve months immediately following the date of the death in question, there occurs in relation to any qualifying investments comprised in the deceased's estate immediately before his death (in this section referred to as "the original holding") a transaction to which section [127 of the 1992 Act][1] applies, that is to say—

(*a*) a reorganisation, within the meaning of section [126(1)][1] of that Act; or

(*b*) the conversion of securities within the meaning of section [132][1] of that Act; or

(*c*) the issue by a company of shares or debentures in exchange for shares in or debentures of another company in such circumstances that section [135][1] of that Act applies; or

(*d*) the issue by a company of shares or debentures under such an arrangement as is referred to in section [136][1] of that Act;

or any transaction relating to a unit trust scheme which corresponds to any of the transactions referred to in paragraphs (*a*) to (*d*) above and to which section [127][1] of that Act applies by virtue of section [99][1] of that Act.

(2) Where this section applies, the holding of investments which, as the result of the transaction, constitutes a new holding within the meaning of section [126(1) of the 1992 Act][1] shall be treated for the purposes of this Chapter as being the same as the original holding; and references in the following provisions of this section to the new holding shall be construed accordingly.

(3) If the appropriate person gives, or becomes liable to give, as part of or in connection with the transaction concerned, any consideration for the new holding or any part of it, then, for the purposes of subsection (5) below, the value on death of the new holding shall be treated as the aggregate of—

(*a*) the value on death of the original holding, and
(*b*) an amount equal to that consideration,

and in any other case the value on death of the new holding shall be taken to be the same as the value on death of the original holding.

(4) For the purposes of subsection (3) above, there shall not be treated as consideration given for the new holding or any part of it—

(*a*) any surrender, cancellation or other alteration of any of the investments comprised in the original holding or of the rights attached thereto, or
(*b*) any consideration consisting of any application, in paying up the new holding or any part of it, of assets of the company concerned or of any dividend or other distribution declared out of those assets but not made.

(5) If, within the period referred to in subsection (1) above, the appropriate person sells any investments comprised in the new holding, the value on death of those investments shall be determined by the formula—

$$\frac{Vs(H-S)}{(Vs+Vr)}$$

where—

Vs is the sale value of the investments,
Vr is the market value at the time of the sale of any investments remaining in the new holding after the sale,
H is the value on death of the new holding, and
S is the value on death of any investments which were originally comprised in the new holding but have been sold on a previous occasion or occasions.

(6) For the purposes of subsection (5) above the market value of any investments at any time means the value which they would (apart from this Chapter) have for the purposes of this Act if they were comprised in the estate of a person who died at that time.

Commentary—*Simon's Taxes* **I4.307**.
HMRC Manuals—Inheritance Tax Manual IHTM34154 (exchanges).
IHTM34181 (changes in the capitalisation of a company).
IHTM34182 and 34183 (date of death value).
IHTM34184 (investments forming part of the new holding).
IHTM34185 and 34186 (bonus issues).
IHTM34187–34192 (rights issues).
Definitions—"Appropriate person", s 178; "estate", s 272; "qualifying investments", "sale value", "value on death", s 178.
Amendments—[1] Words in sub-ss (1), (2) substituted by TCGA 1992 Sch 10 para 8(1), (9).

184 Exchanges

(1) If—

(*a*) within the period of twelve months immediately following the date of the death in question, the appropriate person exchanges (with or without any payment by way of equality of exchange) any qualifying investments comprised in the deceased's estate immediately before his death, and
(*b*) the market value of those investments is at the date of the exchange greater than their value on death,

then, regardless of the nature of the property taken in exchange, they shall be treated for the purposes of this Chapter as having been sold at the date of the exchange for a price equal to that market value.

(2) This section shall not apply in any case where the exchange falls within section 183(1) above; and section 183(6) shall apply for the purposes of subsection (1) above as it applies for the purposes of section 183(5).

Commentary—*Simon's Taxes* **I4.304**.
HMRC Manuals—Inheritance Tax Manual IHTM34154 (exchanges).
Definitions—"Appropriate person", s 178; "qualifying investments", "value on death", s 178.

185 Acquisition of like investments

(1) If, at any time within the period of twelve months immediately following the date of the death in question, the appropriate person sells any investments which form part of a holding of investments which are all of the same description and consist of—

(*a*) investments comprised in the deceased's estate immediately before his death, and
(*b*) investments acquired by the appropriate person, by purchase or otherwise, after the death but not in the circumstances in which section 183 above applies,

the investments so sold shall be apportioned for the purposes of this Chapter between those falling within paragraph (*a*) and those falling within paragraph (*b*) above in the same proportion as, immediately before the sale, the investments comprised in the holding and falling within paragraph (*a*) above bore to the investments so comprised and falling within paragraph (*b*) above.

(2) For the purposes of this section, if the appropriate person holds investments of any description in the capacity of personal representative or trustee, the investments shall not be treated as forming part of the same holding as investments which, though of the same description, are held by him otherwise than in that capacity.

(3) Section 180(3) above shall have effect for the purposes of this section as it has effect for the purposes of section 180(2).

Commentary—*Simon's Taxes* **I4.308**.

HMRC Manuals—Inheritance Tax Manual IHTM34193 (acquisitions prior to sale).

IHTM34215 (prior purchase of similar shares).

Definitions—"Appropriate person", s 178; "personal representative", s 272; "qualifying investments", s 178; "trustee", s 45.

186 Value of part of a fund

(1) In any case where—

(*a*) part only of a holding of qualifying investments is comprised in a person's estate, and

(*b*) investments included in that holding are sold by the appropriate person within the period of twelve months immediately following the date of the death,

this Chapter shall apply as if the entirety of the holding were comprised in the estate and, if a claim is made in respect of the investments referred to in paragraph (b) above, the taxable fraction of the value of the investments to which the claim relates, as determined under this Chapter, shall be the value of that part of those investments which is comprised in the estate.

(2) In subsection (1) above, "taxable fraction" means the fraction of which the numerator is the value, as determined apart from this Chapter, of the part of the holding referred to in paragraph (*a*) of that subsection and the denominator is the value, as so determined, of the entirety of that holding.

Commentary—*Simon's Taxes* **I4.303**.

HMRC Manuals—Inheritance Tax Manual IHTM34220 (part of holding only in the deceased's estate).

Definitions—"Appropriate person", s 178; "estate", s 272; "qualifying investments", s 178.

[186A Cancelled investments

(1) Where any qualifying investments comprised in a person's estate immediately before his death are—

(*a*) cancelled within the period of twelve months immediately following the date of the death without being replaced by other shares or securities, and

(*b*) held, immediately before cancellation, by the appropriate person,

they shall be treated for the purposes of this Chapter as having been sold by the appropriate person for a nominal consideration (one pound) immediately before cancellation.

(2) Where any qualifying investments are included in the calculation under section 179(1) above by virtue of this section, paragraph (*b*) of that subsection shall have effect, so far as relating to those investments, with the omission of the words from "or" to the end.]

Commentary—*Simon's Taxes* **I4.302**.

HMRC Manuals—Inheritance Tax Manual IHTM34157 (cancellation of shares).

IHTM34158 (deceased died on or after 22 February 2007 and on or before 21 February 2008).

Definitions—"Appropriate person", "qualifying investments", s 178.

Amendments—This section inserted by FA 1993 s 198 with effect in relation to deaths occurring after 15 March 1992.

[186B Suspended investments

(1) This section applies to any qualifying investments comprised in a person's estate immediately before his death in respect of which [listing][2] on a recognised stock exchange or dealing on the Unlisted Securities Market is suspended at the end of the period of twelve months immediately following the date of the death ("the relevant period").

(2) Where—

(*a*) any qualifying investments to which this section applies are, at the end of the relevant period, held by the appropriate person, and

(*b*) the value on death of those investments exceeds their value at the end of that period,

they shall be treated for the purposes of this Chapter as having been sold by the appropriate person immediately before the end of that period for a price equal to their value at that time.

(3) Where any qualifying investments are included in the calculation under section 179(1) above by virtue of this section, paragraph (*b*) of that subsection shall have effect, so far as relating to those investments, with the omission of the words from "or" to the end.][1]

Commentary—*Simon's Taxes* **I4.302**.

HMRC Manuals—Inheritance Tax Manual IHTM34156 (suspension of shares).

Definitions—"Appropriate person"; "qualifying investments", s 178.

Amendments—[1] This section inserted by FA 1993 s 198 with effect in relation to deaths occurring after 15 March 1992.

[2] Word in sub-s (1) substituted by FA 1996 Sch 38 para 4(2), (3) in relation to investments sold, or treated as sold, after 31 March 1996.

187 Attribution of values to specific investments

(1) This section shall have effect in determining the value for the purposes of this Act (and, accordingly, the market value for the purposes of capital gains tax under section [274 of the 1992 Act])[1] of any investment (in this section referred to as a "specific investment") which is included among the investments to which a claim relates.

(2) Subject to the following provisions of this section, the value of a specific investment shall be its sale value.

(3) Subject to the following provisions of this section, in a case where the calculation of the loss on sale of the investments to which a claim relates is affected by section 180 above—

(*a*) if the value on death of a specific investment exceeds its sale price, the value of that investment shall be the aggregate of its sale value and an amount equal to the relevant proportion of the difference between its sale price and its value on death; and

(*b*) if the sale price of a specific investment exceeds its value on death, the value of the investment shall be its sale value less an amount equal to the relevant proportion of the difference between its value on death and its sale price.

(4) For the purposes of subsections (2) and (3) above, the sale value of a specific investment in respect of which an amount has been paid in pursuance of a call, as mentioned in section 182 above, shall be reduced by the amount so paid in respect of that investment.

(5) In a case where, by virtue of subsection (3) of section 183 above, the value on death of the new holding, within the meaning of that section, includes an amount equal to the consideration referred to in that subsection, the sale value of any specific investment comprised in the new holding shall be reduced, for the purposes of subsections (2) and (3) above, by an amount which bears to that consideration the like proportion as the value on death of the specific investment sold bears to the value on death of the whole of the new holding.

(6) In subsection (3) above "sale price", in relation to a specific investment, means the price for which the investment was sold by the appropriate person or, if it is greater, the best consideration which could reasonably have been obtained for the specific investment at the time of the sale; and section 181 above shall apply for the purposes of this subsection as it applies for the purposes of section 179(1)(*b*).

Commentary—*Simon's Taxes* **I4.309**.
HMRC Manuals—Inheritance Tax Manual IHTM34241–34245 (attribution of values to specific investments).
Definitions—"Appropriate person"; "loss on sale"; "qualifying investments", "relevant proportion"; "sale value"; "value on death", s 178.
Amendments—[1] Words in sub-s (1) substituted by TCGA 1992 Sch 10 para 8(1), (10).

188 Limitation of loss on sale

In any case where, apart from this section, the loss on sale of any investments—

(*a*) in respect of which an amount has been paid in pursuance of a call as mentioned in section 182 above, or

(*b*) which are sold as mentioned in section 183(5) above,

would exceed their value as determined apart from this Chapter, their sale value shall be treated for the purposes of sections 179(2) and 187 above as being of such an amount that the loss on sale would be equal to their value as so determined.

Commentary—*Simon's Taxes* **I4.305, I4.307, I4.309, C4.109**.
HMRC Manuals—Inheritance Tax Manual IHTM34230 (loss on sale is greater than the original date of death value).
Definitions—"Loss on sale"; "sale value", s 178.

189 Date of sale or purchase

(1) Subject to subsection (2) below, for the purposes of this Chapter where any investments are sold or purchased by the appropriate person the date on which they are sold or purchased shall be taken to be the date on which he entered into a contract to sell or purchase them.

(2) If the sale or purchase of any investments by the appropriate person results from the exercise (whether by him or by any other person) of an option, then, for the purposes of this Chapter, the date on which the investments are sold or purchased shall be taken to be the date on which the option was granted.

Commentary—*Simon's Taxes* **I4.302, I4.303**.
HMRC Manuals—Inheritance Tax Manual IHTM34152 (sales: date of sale).

CHAPTER IV

SALE OF LAND FROM DECEASED'S ESTATE

190 Preliminary

(1) In this Chapter—

"the appropriate person", in relation to any interest in land comprised in a person's estate immediately before his death, means the person liable for capital transfer tax attributable to the value of that interest or, if there is more than one such person and one of them is in fact paying the tax, that person;

"interest in land" does not include any estate, interest or right by way of mortgage or other security;

"sale price", in relation to any interest in land, means the price for which it is sold or, if greater, the best consideration that could reasonably have been obtained for it at the time of the sale;

"sale value", in relation to any interest in land, means its sale price as increased or reduced under the following provisions of this Chapter;

"value on death", in relation to any interest in land comprised in a person's estate immediately before his death, means the value which, apart from this Chapter, (and apart from section 176 above) would be its value as part of that estate for the purposes of this Act.

(2) Any reference in this Chapter to the interests to which a claim relates is a reference to the interests to which section 191(1) below applies by virtue of the claim.

(3) For the purposes of this Chapter—

(*a*) the personal representatives of the deceased, and

(*b*) the trustees of a settlement,

shall each be treated as a single and continuing body of persons (distinct from the persons who may from time to time be the personal representatives or trustees).

(4) In any case where, for the purposes of this Chapter, it is necessary to determine the price at which any interest was purchased or sold or the best consideration that could reasonably have been obtained on the sale of any interest, no account shall be taken of expenses (whether by way of commission, stamp duty [or stamp duty land tax][1] or otherwise) which are incidental to the sale or purchase.

Commentary—*Simon's Taxes* **I4.311, I4.319, I8.361**.

HMRC Manuals—Inheritance Tax Manual IHTM27042 (loss on sale of foreign land).

IHTM33050 (meaning of "appropriate person").

IHTM33061 (meaning of "interest in land").

IHTM33011 (outline of the relief).

IHTM33072 (sale price).

IHTM33073 (sale value).

Simon's Tax Cases—*Stonor (exors of Dickinson, decd) v IRC* [2001] STC (SCD) 199.

Definitions—"Mortgage", "personal representatives", s 272; "settlement", s 43; "trustee", s 45.

Amendments—[1] Words inserted by FA 2003 s 123(1), Sch 18 para 2 with effect in accordance with FA 2003 s 124, Sch 19.

191 The relief

(1) Where—

(*a*) an interest in land is comprised in a person's estate immediately before his death and is sold by the appropriate person within the period of three years immediately following the date of the death, and

(*b*) the appropriate person makes a claim under this Chapter stating the capacity in which he makes it,

the value for the purposes of this Act of that interest and of any other interest in land comprised in that estate and sold within that period by the person making the claim acting in the same capacity shall, subject to the following provisions of this Chapter, be its sale value.

[(1A) A claim under this Chapter must be made not more than 4 years after the end of the period mentioned in subsection (1)(*a*)][2]

(2) Subsection (1) above shall not apply to an interest if its sale value would differ from its value on death by less than the lower of—

(*a*) £1,000, and

(*b*) 5 per cent of its value on death.

(3) Subsection (1) above shall not apply to an interest if its sale is—

(*a*) a sale by a personal representative or trustee to—

(i) a person who, at any time between the death and the sale, has been beneficially entitled to, or to an interest in possession in, property comprising the interest sold, or

(ii) the spouse [or civil partner][1]or a child or remoter descendant of a person within sub-paragraph (i) above, or

(iii) trustees of a settlement under which a person within sub-paragraph (i) or (ii) above has an interest in possession in property comprising the interest sold; or

(*b*) a sale in connection with which the vendor or any person within sub-paragraph (i), (ii) or (iii) of paragraph (*a*) above obtains a right to acquire the interest sold or any other interest in the same land;

and for the purposes of this subsection a person shall be treated as having in the property comprised in an unadministered estate (within the meaning of section 91(2) above) the same interest as he would have if the administration of the estate had been completed.

Commentary—*Simon's Taxes* **I4.312, I4.311, I4.316**.

HMRC Manuals—Inheritance Tax Manual IHTM33011 (outline of the relief and claiming the relief).

IHTM33081–33090 (sales excluded from relief).

IHTM33181 and 33182 (calculating the loss on a sale of joint property).

IHTM33012 (claiming the relief).

Definitions—"Appropriate person", "interest in land", "sale value", s 190; "settlement", s 43; "trustee", s 45.

Simon's Tax Cases—*Jones and anor (Balls' Administrators) v IRC* [1997] STC 358; *Stonor (exors of Dickinson, decd) v IRC* [2001] STC (SCD) 199.

Amendments—[1] Words in sub-s (3)(*a*)(ii) inserted by Tax and Civil Partnership Regulations, SI 2005/3229, regs 3, 35, with effect from 5 December 2005 (reg 1(1)).

[2] Sub-s (1A) inserted by FA 2009 s 99, Sch 51 para 10 with effect from 1 April 2011 (by virtue of SI 2010/867 art 2(2)).

192 Effect of purchases

(1) This section applies where a claim is made under this Chapter and, at any time during the period beginning on the date of the death and ending four months after the last of the sales referred to in section 191(1) above, the person making the claim purchases any interests in land in the same capacity as that in which he makes the claim.

(2) If the aggregate of the purchase prices of all the interests purchased as mentioned in subsection (1) above equals or exceeds the aggregate of the sale prices (as adjusted under sections 193 to 195 below) of all the interests to which the claim relates, this Chapter shall not apply in relation to the claim; but otherwise subsection (3) below shall have effect, and in that subsection "the appropriate fraction" means the fraction of which—

(*a*) the numerator is the aggregate of the said purchase prices, and

(*b*) the denominator is the aggregate of the said sale prices.

(3) Subject to subsection (4) below, where this subsection has effect an addition shall be made to the sale price of every interest to which the claim relates; and the amount of the addition shall be equal to the appropriate fraction of the difference between the value on death of the interest and its sale price (as adjusted under sections 193 to 196 below).

(4) Where the value on death of an interest is less than its sale price (as adjusted under sections 193 to 196 below) subsection (3) above shall apply as if it provided for a reduction instead of an increase in the sale price.

Commentary—*Simon's Taxes* **I4.317**.

HMRC Manuals—Inheritance Tax Manual IHTM33161–33163 (purchases).

Definitions—"Sale price", "value on death", s 190.

193 Changes between death and sale

(1) Where the conditions mentioned in subsection (2) below are not satisfied in relation to any interest to which the claim relates then, subject to subsections (3) and (4) below, an addition shall be made to the sale price of the interest; and the amount of the addition shall be equal to the difference between—

(*a*) the value on death of the interest, and

(*b*) what that value would have been if the circumstances prevailing at the date of the sale and by reason of which the conditions are not satisfied had prevailed immediately before the death.

(2) The conditions referred to in subsection (1) above are—

(*a*) that the interest was the same in all respects and with the same incidents at the date of the death and at the date of the sale; and

(*b*) that the land in which the interest subsists was in the same state and with the same incidents at the date of the death and at the date of the sale.

(3) If after the date of the death but before the date of the sale compensation becomes payable under any enactment to the appropriate person or any other person liable for tax attributable to the value of the interest—

(*a*) because of the imposition of a restriction on the use or development of the land in which the interest subsists,

or

(*b*) because the value of the interest is reduced for any other reason,

the imposition of the restriction or the other cause of the reduction in value shall be ignored for the purposes of subsections (1) and (2) above, but there shall be added to the sale price of the interest an amount equal to the amount of compensation.

(4) Where the value on death of an interest is less than it would have been as mentioned in subsection (1) above, that subsection shall apply as if, instead of providing for an addition to be made to the sale price, it provided for that price to be reduced to what it would have been if the change in circumstances by reason of which the conditions mentioned in subsection (2) above are not satisfied had not occurred.

Commentary—*Simon's Taxes* **I4.313**.

HMRC Manuals—Inheritance Tax Manual IHTM33121–33130 (changes in the interest or underlying land).

Definitions—"Sale price", "value on death", s 190.

194 Leases

(1) Where the claim relates to an interest which is the interest of a lessee under a lease the duration of which at the date of the death does not exceed fifty years, an addition shall be made to the sale price of the interest; and the amount of the addition shall be equal to the appropriate fraction of the value on death of the interest.

(2) In subsection (1) above, "the appropriate fraction" means the fraction—

$$\frac{P(1) - P(2)}{P(1)}$$

where—

P(1) is the percentage that would be derived from the Table in paragraph 1 of Schedule [8 to the 1992 Act][1] for the duration of the lease at the date of the death, and

P(2) is the percentage that would be so derived for the duration of the lease at the date of the sale.

Commentary—*Simon's Taxes* **I4.314.**
HMRC Manuals—Inheritance Tax Manual IHTM33131 (changes in the interest or underlying land: leases).
Definitions—"Sale price", "value on death", s 190.
Amendments—[1] Words in sub-s (2) substituted by TCGA 1992 Sch 10 para 8(1), (11).

195 Valuation by reference to other interests

If in determining the value on death of any interest to which the claim relates, any other interests, whether in the same or other land, were taken into account, an addition shall be made to the sale price of the interest; and the amount of the addition shall be equal to the difference between the value on death of the interest and the value which would have been the value on death if no other interests had been taken into account.

Commentary—*Simon's Taxes* **I4.315.**
HMRC Manuals—Inheritance Tax Manual IHTM33132 (valuation with, and sales without, other land).
Definitions—"Sale price", "value on death", s 190.

196 Sales to beneficiaries etc and exchanges

(1) This section applies where a person who makes a claim under this Chapter, acting in the same capacity as that in which he makes the claim—

(*a*) sells an interest to which section 191(1) would apply but for section 191(3), or

(*b*) within the period of three years immediately following the date of the death exchanges (with or without any payment by way of equality of exchange) any interest in land which was comprised in the deceased's estate immediately before his death,

and the sale price of the interest, or in the case of an exchange its market value at the date of the exchange, exceeds its value on death.

(2) Where this section applies, an addition shall be made to the sale price of any interest to which the claim relates; and the amount of the addition—

(*a*) if the claim relates to one interest only, shall be equal to the excess referred to in subsection (1) above, and

(*b*) if the claim relates to more than one interest, shall be equal to the appropriate fraction of that excess.

(3) In subsection (2) above "the appropriate fraction" in relation to any interest to which the claim relates is the fraction of which—

(*a*) the numerator is the difference between the value on death of that interest and its sale price (as adjusted under sections 193 to 195 above) and

(*b*) the denominator is the aggregate of that difference and the corresponding differences for all the other interests to which the claim relates;

and the aggregate referred to in paragraph (b) above shall be calculated without regard to which is the greater, in the case of any particular interest, of its value on death and its sale price.

Commentary—*Simon's Taxes* **I4.316.**
HMRC Manuals—Inheritance Tax Manual IHTM33141–33150 (non-qualifying sales).
Definitions—"Sale price", "value on death", s 190.

197 Compulsory acquisition more than three years after death

(1) If after the end of the period of three years immediately following the date of the death an interest in land is acquired from the appropriate person in pursuance of a notice to treat served before the death or within that period by an authority possessing powers of compulsory acquisition, this Chapter shall apply in relation to the interest as it applies in relation to interests sold within that period.

(2) Subsection (1) above shall not have effect in relation to an interest if its sale value would exceed its value on death.

(3) In determining the period referred to in section 192(1) above, no account shall be taken of the sale of an interest in relation to which subsection (1) above has effect; and if the claim relates only to such interests, section 192 shall not apply in relation to the claim.

Commentary—*Simon's Taxes* **I4.318, I4.317.**
HMRC Manuals—Inheritance Tax Manual IHTM33091 (compulsory purchase).
Definitions—"Interest in land", "sale value", "value on death", s 190.

[197A Sales in fourth year after death

(1) Where an interest in land—

(*a*) is comprised in a person's estate immediately before his death, and (*b*) is sold by the appropriate person in the fourth year immediately following the date of the death, otherwise than in circumstances in which section 197(1) above has effect,

the interest shall be treated, for the purposes of section 191(1) above, as having been sold within the period of three years immediately following the date of the death.

(2) Subsection (1) above shall not have effect in relation to an interest if its sale value would exceed its value on death.

(3) In determining the period referred to in section 192(1) above, no account shall be taken of the sale of an interest in relation to which subsection (1) above has effect; and if the claim relates only to such interests, section 192 shall not apply in relation to the claim.

(4) In applying section 196(1) above, no account shall be taken, for the purposes of paragraph (*a*) of that subsection, of an interest in relation to which subsection (1) above has effect.]

Commentary—*Simon's Taxes* **I4.312, I4.316.**
HMRC Manuals—Inheritance Tax Manual IHTM33074 (sales in the fourth year after death).
Definitions—"Interest in land", "sale value", "value on death", s 190.
Amendments—This section inserted by FA 1993 s 199 with effect in relation to deaths occurring after 15 March 1990.

198 Date of sale or purchase

(1) Subject to the following subsections, the date on which an interest in land is sold or purchased by the appropriate person shall for the purposes of this Chapter be taken to be the date on which he enters into a contract to sell or purchase it.

(2) If the sale or purchase of any interest by the appropriate person results from the exercise (whether by him or by any other person) of an option granted not more than six months earlier, the date on which the interest is sold or purchased shall be taken to be the date on which the option was granted.

(3) If an interest is acquired from the appropriate person in pursuance of a notice to treat served by an authority possessing powers of compulsory acquisition, the date on which the interest is sold shall, subject to subsection (4) below, be taken to be the date on which compensation for the acquisition is agreed or otherwise determined (variations on appeal being disregarded for this purpose) or, if earlier, the date when the authority enter on the land in pursuance of their powers.

(4) If an interest in land is acquired from the appropriate person—

(*a*) in England, Scotland or Wales by virtue of a general vesting declaration within the meaning of the Compulsory Purchase (Vesting Declarations) Act 1981 or, in Scotland, Schedule 24 to the Town and Country Planning (Scotland) Act 1972 or

(*b*) in Northern Ireland, by way of a vesting order,

the date on which it is sold by the appropriate person shall be taken to be the last day of the period specified in the declaration or, in Northern Ireland, the date on which the vesting order becomes operative.

Commentary—*Simon's Taxes* **I4.319**.
HMRC Manuals—Inheritance Tax Manual IHTM33071 (date of sale or purchase).
Inheritance Tax Manual IHTM33091 (sales excluded from relief: compulsary purchase).
Definitions—"Appropriate person", "interest in land", "value on death", s 190.

PART VII
LIABILITY
General rules

199 Dispositions by transferor

(1) The persons liable for the tax on the value transferred by a chargeable transfer made by a disposition (including any omission treated as a disposition under section 3(3) above) of the transferor are—

(*a*) the transferor;

(*b*) any person the value of whose estate is increased by the transfer;

(*c*) so far as the tax is attributable to the value of any property, any person in whom the property is vested (whether beneficially or otherwise) at any time after the transfer, or who at any such time is beneficially entitled to an interest in possession in the property;

(*d*) where by the chargeable transfer any property becomes comprised in a settlement, any person for whose benefit any of the property or income from it is applied.

[(2) Subsection (1)(*a*) above shall apply in relation to—

(*a*) the tax on the value transferred by a potentially exempt transfer; and

(*b*) so much of the tax on the value transferred by any other chargeable transfer made within seven years of the transferor's death as exceeds what it would have been had the transferor died more than seven years after the transfer,

with the substitution for the reference to the transferor of a reference to his personal representatives.][1]

(3) A purchaser of property, and a person deriving title from or under such a purchaser, shall not by virtue of subsection (1)(*c*) above be liable for tax attributable to the value of the property unless the property is subject to an Inland Revenue charge.

(4) For the purposes of this section—

(*a*) any person who takes possession of or intermeddles with, or otherwise acts in relation to, property so as to become liable as executor or trustee (or, in Scotland, any person who intromits with property or has become liable as a vitious intromitter), and

(*b*) any person to whom the management of property is entrusted on behalf of a person not of full legal capacity,

shall be treated as a person in whom the property is vested.

(5) References in this section to any property include references to any property directly or indirectly representing it.

Commentary—*Simon's Taxes* **I10.111**.

HMRC Manuals—Inheritance Tax Manual IHTM30041–30044 (liability on potentially exempt transfers).

IHTM30051–30054 (definition and extent of liability for potentially exempt transfers).

IHTM30061 and 30062 (liability on lifetime transfers chargeable when made).

Statement of Practice SP 1/82—Interaction of income tax and IHT on assets put into settlements.

Press releases etc—Law Society 13-3-91 (the CTO will not pursue personal representatives after they have obtained a certificate of discharge and distributed the estate provided that they made the "fullest enquiries that are reasonably practicable in the circumstances" to discover lifetime transfers).

Cross references—See FA 1986 Sch 19 para 40 (where a death or other event occurs after 17 March 1986, the amendment to this section by FA 1986 Sch 19 (see below) not to affect the tax chargeable on a transfer of value occurring before 18 March 1986).

Definitions—"Inland Revenue charge", "purchaser", s 272.

Amendments—[1] Sub-s (2) substituted by FA 1986 s 101(3) and Sch 19 para 26 with respect to transfers of value made after 17 March 1986.

200 Transfer on death

(1) The persons liable for the tax on the value transferred by a chargeable transfer made (under section 4 above) on the death of any person are[1] . . . —

(*a*) so far as the tax is attributable to the value of property which either—

(i) was not immediately before the death comprised in a settlement, or

(ii) was so comprised and consists of land in the United Kingdom which devolves upon or vests in the deceased's personal representatives,

the deceased's personal representatives;

(*b*) so far as the tax is attributable to the value of property which, immediately before the death, was comprised in a settlement, the trustees of the settlement;

(*c*) so far as the tax is attributable to the value of any property, any person in whom the property is vested (whether beneficially or otherwise) at any time after the death, or who at any such time is beneficially entitled to an interest in possession in the property;

(*d*) so far as the tax is attributable to the value of any property which, immediately before the death, was comprised in a settlement, any person for whose benefit any of the property or income from it is applied after the death.

(1A) . . . [1]

(2) A purchaser of property, and a person deriving title from or under such a purchaser, shall not by virtue of subsection (1)(*c*) above be liable for tax attributable to the value of the property unless the property is subject to an Inland Revenue charge.

(3) For the purposes of subsection (1) above a person entitled to part only of the income of any property shall, notwithstanding anything in section 50 above, be deemed to be entitled to an interest in the whole of the property.

(4) Subsections (4) and (5) of section 199 above shall have effect for the purposes of this section as they have effect for the purposes of that section.

Commentary—*Simon's Taxes* **I10.112**.

HMRC Manuals—Inheritance Tax Manual IHTM30021–30023 (persons liable on death transfers).

IHTM30035 and 30036 (persons liable, or excluded from liability, for the tax).

IHTM30083 and 30084 (liability for gifts with reservation).

Concession F6—Foreign assets.

Statement of Practice SP 1/82—Interaction of income tax and IHT on assets put into settlements.

Definitions—"Inland Revenue charge", "personal representatives", "purchaser", s 272.

Amendments—[1] In sub-s (1) words "(subject to subsection (1A) below)" repealed, and sub-s (1A) repealed, by FA 2011 s 65, Sch 16 paras 49, 52 with effect in relation to deaths occurring on or after 6 April 2011, subject to transitional provisions in FA 2011, Sch 16 Pt 3. Sub-s (1A) previously read as follows—

> "(1A) The person liable for tax chargeable by virtue of section 151A or 151C above in relation to any registered pension scheme is the scheme administrator of the pension scheme.".

201 Settled property

(1) The persons liable for the tax on the value transferred by a chargeable transfer made under Part III of this Act are—

(*a*) the trustees of the settlement;

(*b*) any person entitled (whether beneficially or not) to an interest in possession in the settled property;

(*c*) any person for whose benefit any of the settled property or income from it is applied at or after the time of the transfer;

(*d*) where the transfer is made during the life of the settlor and the trustees are not for the time being resident in the United Kingdom, the settlor.

(2) Where the chargeable transfer is made within [seven years][1] of the transferor's death [but is not a potentially exempt transfer][2], subsection (1)(*d*) above shall not apply in relation to so much of the tax as exceeds what it would have been had the transferor died more than [seven years][1] after the transfer.

(3) Subsection (1)(*d*) above shall not apply in relation to a settlement made before 11th December 1974 if the trustees were resident in the United Kingdom when the settlement was made, but have not been resident there at any time during the period between 10th December 1974 and the time of the transfer.

[(3A) Subsection (1)(*d*) above shall not apply in relation to the tax chargeable on the value transferred by a potentially exempt transfer which proves to be a chargeable transfer in a case where the settlement was made before 17th March 1987 if the trustees were resident in the United Kingdom when the settlement was made, but have not been resident there at any time between 16th March 1987 and the death of the transferor.][3]

(4) Where more than one person is a settlor in relation to a settlement and the circumstances so require, subsection (1)(*d*) above shall have effect in relation to it as if the settled property were comprised in separate settlements.

[(4A) Where—

(*a*) a charge to tax arises under or by virtue of section 74A, or

(*b*) in a case where paragraphs (*a*) to (*d*) of section 74A are satisfied, a charge to tax arises under section 64 or 65 in respect of the relevant settled property (within the meaning of section 74A),

subsection (1) of this section has effect as if the persons listed in that subsection included the individual mentioned in section 74A(1)(*b*)(i).][4]

(5) For the purposes of this section trustees of a settlement shall be regarded as not resident in the United Kingdom unless the general administration of the settlement is ordinarily carried on in the United Kingdom and the trustees or a majority of them (and, where there is more than one class of trustees, a majority of each class) are for the time being resident in the United Kingdom.

(6) References in this section to any property include references to any property directly or indirectly representing it.

Commentary—*Simon's Taxes* **I10.113**.

HMRC Manuals—Inheritance Tax Manual IHTM30091 (persons liable to tax on settled property).
IHTM30111 (liability: the settlor).
IHTM30112 (limitations on settlor's liability).
IHTM30114 (death charge on lifetime transfers chargeable when made).
IHTM30115 (settlement made before 11 december 1974).

Statement of Practice SP 1/82—Interaction of income tax and IHT on assets put into settlements.

Definitions—"Settled property", "settlement", s 43; "trustee", s 45.

Cross references—See FA 1986 Sch 19 para 40 (where a death or other event occurs after 17 March 1986, the amendment to this section by FA 1986 Sch 19 (see below) not to affect the tax chargeable on a transfer of value occurring before 18 March 1986).

Amendments—[1] Words in sub-s (2) substituted by FA 1986 s 101(3) and Sch 19 para 27 with respect to transfers of value made after 17 March 1986.

[2] Words in sub-s (2) inserted by F(No 2)A 1987 s 96(1), (6) and Sch 7 para 3(1), (2) with respect to transfers of value made after 16 March 1987.

[3] Sub-s (3A) inserted by F(No 2)A 1987 Sch 7 para 3(1), (3).

[4] Sub-s (4A) inserted by FA 2012 s 210(1), (4). This amendment is treated as having come into force on 20 June 2012 and has effect in relation to arrangements entered into on or after that day.

202 Close companies

(1) The persons liable for tax chargeable by virtue of section 94(1) or section 99(2) above are—

(*a*) the company making the transfer of value concerned, and

(*b*) so far as the tax remains unpaid after it ought to have been paid, the persons to whom any amounts have been apportioned under section 94 above and any individual (whether such a person or not) the value of whose estate is increased by the company's transfer.

(2) A person to whom not more than 5 per cent of the value transferred by the company's transfer is apportioned shall not as such be liable for any of the tax; and each of the other persons to whom any part of that value has been apportioned shall be so liable only for such part of the tax as corresponds to that part of that value.

(3) A person the value of whose estate is increased by the company's transfer shall not as such be liable for a greater amount than the amount of the increase.

(4) No person other than those liable under this section shall be liable for any tax chargeable by virtue of section 94(1) or section 99(2) above.

Commentary—*Simon's Taxes* **I6.129, I10.114**.

HMRC Manuals—Inheritance Tax Manual IHTM30124 (transfers by a close company).

203 Liability of spouse [or civil partner][1]

(1) Where—

(*a*) a transferor is liable for any tax on the value transferred by a chargeable transfer, and

(*b*) by another transfer of value made by him on or after 27th March 1974 ("the spouse [or civil partner][1] transfer") any property became the property of a person ("the transferee") who at the time of both transfers was his spouse [or civil partner][1],

the transferee is liable for so much of the tax as does not exceed the market value of the property at the time of the spouse [or civil partner][1] transfer or, in a case where subsection (2) below applies the lower market value mentioned in paragraph (c) of that subsection.

(2) This subsection applies where—

(*a*) the chargeable transfer is made after the spouse [or civil partner][1] transfer; and

(*b*) the property ("the transferred property") which became the property of the transferee either remains the transferee's property at the date of the chargeable transfer or has before that date been sold by the transferee by a qualifying sale; and

(*c*) the market value of the transferred property on the relevant date (that is to say, the date of the chargeable transfer or, as the case may be, of the qualifying sale) is lower than its market value at the time of the spouse transfer; and

(*d*) the transferred property is not tangible movable property.

(3) In this section "qualifying sale" has the same meaning as in section 131 above; and, subject to subsection (4) below, sections 133 to 140 above shall have effect for the purposes of this section as they have effect for the purposes of section 131.

(4) In their application by virtue of subsection (3) above, sections 133 to 140 above shall have effect as if—

(*a*) references to the chargeable transfer were references to the spouse [or civil partner][1] transfer,

(*b*) references to the transferee's spouse [or civil partner][1] were omitted, and

(*c*) references to section 131 above were references to this section.

Commentary—*Simon's Taxes* **I10.115**.

HMRC Manuals—Inheritance Tax Manual IHTM30073 (liability of spouse or civil partner of transferor).

Amendments—[1] Words in sub-ss (1), (2), (4), and words in heading, inserted by Tax and Civil Partnership Regulations, SI 2005/3229, regs 3, 36, with effect from 5 December 2005 (reg 1(1)).

204 Limitation of liability

(1) A person shall not be liable under section 200(1)(*a*) above for any tax as a personal representative of a deceased person, except to the extent of the following assets, namely—

(*a*) so far as the tax is attributable to the value of any property other than such as is mentioned in paragraph (*b*) below, the assets (other than property so mentioned) which he has received as personal representative or might have so received but for his own neglect or default; and

(*b*) so far as the tax is attributable to property which, immediately before the death, was comprised in a settlement and consists of land in the United Kingdom, so much of that property as is at any time available in his hands for the payment of the tax, or might have been so available but for his own neglect or default.

(2) A person shall not be liable for tax as trustee in relation to any property, except to the extent of—

(*a*) so much of the property as he has actually received or disposed of or as he has become liable to account for to the persons beneficially entitled thereto, and

(*b*) so much of any other property as is for the time being available in his hands as trustee for the payment of the tax or might have been so available but for his own neglect or default.

(3) A person not liable as mentioned in subsection (1) or (2) above but liable for tax as a person in whom property is vested or liable for tax as a person entitled to a beneficial interest in possession in any property shall not be liable for the tax except to the extent of that property.

(4) . . . [1]

(5) A person liable for tax as a person for whose benefit any settled property, or income from any settled property, is applied, shall not be liable for the tax except to the extent of the amount of the property or income (reduced in the case of income by the amount of any income tax borne by him in respect of it, and in the case of other property in respect of which he has borne income tax by virtue of [Chapter 2 of Part 13 of the Income Tax Act 2007][4] by the amount of that tax).

(6) Where a person is liable for any tax—

(*a*) under section 199 above otherwise than as transferor [or personal representative of the transferor][2], or

(*b*) under section 201 above otherwise than as trustee of the settlement,

he shall be liable only if the tax remains unpaid after it ought to have been paid and, in a case where any part of the value transferred is attributable to the tax on it, shall be liable to no greater extent than he would have been had the value transferred been reduced by the tax remaining unpaid.

[(7) Where the tax exceeds what it would have been had the transferor died more than seven years after the transfer, subsection (6) above shall not apply in relation to the excess.][3]

[(8) A person liable by virtue of section 199(2) above for any tax as personal representative of the transferor shall be liable only to the extent that either—

(*a*) in consequence of subsections (2), (3) and (5) above, no person falling within paragraphs (*b*) to (*d*) of section 199(1) above is liable for the tax, or

(*b*) the tax remains unpaid twelve months after the end of the month in which the death of the transferor occurs,

and, subject to that, shall be liable only to the extent of the assets mentioned in subsection (1) above.][3]

[(9) Where by virtue of subsection (3) of section 102 of the Finance Act 1986 the estate of a deceased person is treated as including property which would not apart from that subsection form part of his estate, a person shall be liable under section 200(1)(*a*) above as personal representative for tax attributable to the value of that property only if the tax remains unpaid twelve months after the end of the month in which the death occurs and, subject to that, only to the extent of the assets mentioned in subsection (1) above.][3]

Commentary—*Simon's Taxes* **I10.116**.

HMRC Manuals—Inheritance Tax Manual IHTM30032 and 30033 (extent and nature of a personal representative's liability).

IHTM30072 (extent of liability of persons secondarily liable).

IHTM30101–30104 (definition and extent of liability for settled property).

IHTM30112–30115 (further provisions regarding settlor's liability to tax).

Concession F6—Foreign assets.

Definitions—"Personal representative", s 272; "settlement", s 43; "trustee", s 45.

Cross references—See FA 1986 Sch 19 para 40 (where a death or other event occurs after 17 March 1986, the amendments to this section by FA 1986 Sch 19 (see below) not to affect the tax chargeable on a transfer of value occurring before 18 March 1986).

Amendments—[1] Sub-s (4) repealed by FA 1986 Sch 19 para 28 and Sch 23 Pt X with respect to transfers of value made after 17 March 1986.

[2] Words in sub-s (6)(*a*) inserted by FA 1986 Sch 19 para 28 with respect to transfers of value made after 17 March 1986.

[3] Sub-ss (7)–(9) substituted for sub-s (7) by FA 1986 Sch 19 para 28 with respect to transfers of value made after 17 March 1986.

[4] Words in sub-s (5) substituted for the words "section 739 or 740 of the Taxes Act 1988" by ITA 2007 s 1027, Sch 1 paras 268, 270, with effect for income tax purposes from 6 April 2007, and corporation tax purposes for accounting periods ending after 5 April 2007.

205 More than one person liable

Except as otherwise provided, where under this Act two or more persons are liable for the same tax, each of them shall be liable for the whole of it.

Commentary—*Simon's Taxes* **I10.117**.

HMRC Manuals—Inheritance Tax Manual IHTM30011 (liability).

Special cases

206 Gifts to political parties

Amendments—This section repealed by FA 1988 Sch 14 Pt X in relation to transfers of value made after 14 March 1988.

207 Conditional exemption, etc

(1) Where tax is chargeable under section 32 above on the occurrence of an event which is a chargeable event with respect to any property by virtue of subsection (2) or subsection (3)(*a*) of that section, the person liable for the tax is the person who, if the property were sold—

(*a*) in a case within subsection (2) of that section, at the time the tax becomes chargeable, and

(*b*) in a case within subsection (3)(*a*), immediately after the death,

would be entitled to receive (whether for his benefit or not) the proceeds of sale or any income arising from them.

(2) Where tax is chargeable under section 32 above on the occurrence of an event which is a chargeable event with respect to any property by virtue of subsection (3)(*b*) of that section, the person liable for the tax is the person by whom or for whose benefit the property is disposed of.

[(2A) Where tax is chargeable under section 32A above on the occurrence of an event which is a chargeable event with respect to any property by virtue of subsection (3) or subsection (4)(*a*) of that section, the person liable for the tax is the person who, if the property were sold—

(*a*) in a case within subsection (3) of that section, at the time the tax becomes chargeable, and

(*b*) in a case within subsection (4)(*a*), immediately after the death,

would be entitled to receive (whether for his benefit or not) the proceeds of sale or any income arising from them.][1]

[(2B) Where tax is chargeable under section 32A above on the occurrence of an event which is a chargeable event with respect to any property by virtue of subsection (4)(*b*) of that section, the person liable for the tax is the person by whom or for whose benefit the property is disposed of.][1]

(3) The persons liable for tax charged under [section 79(3A)][2] above are—

(*a*) the trustees of the settlement concerned, and

(*b*) any person for whose benefit any of the property or income from it is applied at or after the time of the event occasioning the charge.

(4) The person liable for tax chargeable under paragraph 1(1) or 3(1) of Schedule 5 to this Act is the person who, if the property were sold at the time the tax becomes chargeable, would be entitled to receive (whether for his benefit or not) the proceeds of sale or any income arising from them.
(5) The person liable for tax chargeable under paragraph 1(2) or 3(2) of Schedule 5 to this Act is the person by whom or for whose benefit the property is disposed of.

Commentary—*Simon's Taxes* **I7.513E, I10.122**.
HMRC Manuals—Inheritance Tax Manual IHTM30121 and 30122 (liability for heritage property).
Definitions—"Personal representatives", s 272; "settlement", s 43; "trustee", s 45.
Amendments—[1] Sub-ss (2A), (2B) inserted by FA 1985 Sch 26 para 10 in relation to events after 18 March 1985.
[2] In sub-s (3), words substituted for words "section 79(3)" by F(No 2)A 2015 s 12(8)(*a*) with effect in relation to occasions on which tax would (ignoring the effect of the amendments made by F(No 2)A 2015 s 12) fall to be charged under IHTA 1984 s 64 on or after 18 November 2015.

208 Woodlands

The person liable for tax chargeable under section 126 above in relation to a disposal is the person who is entitled to the proceeds of sale or would be so entitled if the disposal were a sale.

Commentary—*Simon's Taxes* **I7.404, I10.123**.
HMRC Manuals—Inheritance Tax Manual IHTM30123 (liability in special cases: woodlands).

209 Succession in Scotland

(1) A person shall not be liable under section 200(1)(*a*) above for tax attributable to the value of any heritable property in Scotland which is vested in him as executor in the circumstances and for the purposes mentioned in subsection (1) or (2) of section 18 of the Succession (Scotland) Act 1964.
(2) The persons liable for tax chargeable under section 147(4) above are the person who claims legitim [or rights under section 131 of the Civil Partnership Act 2004][1] and any person mentioned in section 200(1)(*c*) above.
(3) Section 200(1)(*a*) shall not apply in relation to tax chargeable under section 147(4) above, but section 204(1) shall apply in relation to the person who claims legitim [or rights under section 131 of the Civil Partnership Act 2004][1] as it applies in relation to the personal representatives of a deceased person.

Commentary—*Simon's Taxes* **I10.124**.
HMRC Manuals—Inheritance Tax Manual IHTM30024 (liability: succession in scotland).
Definitions—"Personal representatives", s 272.
Amendments—[1] Words in sub-ss (2), (3) inserted by Tax and Civil Partnership Regulations, SI 2005/3229, regs 3, 37, with effect from 5 December 2005 (reg 1(1)).

210 Pension rights, etc

[(1)] [1] Where any tax chargeable on a transfer of value is attributable to the value of an interest satisfying the conditions of paragraphs (*a*) and (*b*) of section 151(2) above, the persons liable for the tax shall not include the trustees of the scheme or fund concerned but shall, if the transfer is made on the death of the person entitled to the interest, include his personal representatives.
(2) . . . [2]
(3) . . . [2]

Commentary—*Simon's Taxes* **I10.125**.
HMRC Manuals—Inheritance Tax Manual IHTM30025 (liability on interests under superannuation schemes).
IHTM30101 (extent of iability (settled property) trustees).
Definitions—"Personal representatives", s 272.
Amendments—[1] Sub-s (1) numbered as such, and sub-s (2) inserted, by FA 2006 s 160, Sch 22 paras 1, 6. These amendments are deemed to have come into force on 6 April 2006.
[2] Sub-ss (2), (3) repealed by FA 2011 s 65, Sch 16 paras 49, 53 with effect in relation to deaths occurring on or after 6 April 2011, subject to transitional provisions in FA 2011, Sch 16 Pt 3. Sub-ss (2), (3) previously read as follows—

> "(2) The person liable for tax chargeable under section 151B above is the scheme administrator of the registered pension scheme.
> (3) The person liable for tax chargeable under section 151D—
> (a) if the tax is charged by reason of an unauthorised payment actually made by any person other than the scheme administrator of the pension scheme, that person, and
> (b) otherwise, the scheme administrator of the pension scheme.".

Burden of tax, etc

211 Burden of tax on death

(1) Where personal representatives are liable for tax on the value transferred by a chargeable transfer made on death, the tax shall be treated as part of the general testamentary and administration expenses of the estate, but only so far as it is attributable to the value of property in the United Kingdom which—
(*a*) vests in the deceased's personal representatives, and
(*b*) was not immediately before the death comprised in a settlement.
(2) Subsection (1) above shall have effect subject to any contrary intention shown by the deceased in his will.

(3) Where any amount of tax paid by personal representatives on the value transferred by a chargeable transfer made on death does not fall to be borne as part of the general testamentary and administration expenses of the estate, that amount shall, where occasion requires, be repaid to them by the person in whom the property to the value of which the tax is attributable is vested.
(4) References in this section to tax include references to interest on tax.

Commentary—*Simon's Taxes* **I10.201, 206**.
HMRC Manuals—Inheritance Tax Manual IHTM26124 (how to decide whether specific gifts out of the free estate bear their own tax).
IHTM26123 (the specific gifts you should gross up).
Definitions—"Personal representatives", s 272.

212 Powers to raise tax

(1) Where a person is liable, otherwise than as transferor, and otherwise than under section 203 above, for tax attributable to the value of any property he shall, for the purpose of paying the tax or raising the amount of it when paid, have power, whether or not the property is vested in him, to raise the amount of the tax by sale or mortgage of, or a terminable charge on, that property or any part of it.
(2) A person having a limited interest in any property who pays the tax attributable to the value of that property shall be entitled to the like charge as if the tax so attributable had been raised by means of a mortgage to him.
(3) Any money held on the trusts of a settlement may be expended in paying the tax attributable to the value of any property comprised in the settlement and held on the same trusts.
(4) References in this section to tax include references to interest on tax and to costs properly incurred in respect of tax.

Commentary—*Simon's Taxes* **I10.205, I11.406, I10.206**.
Definitions—"Mortgage", s 272; "settlement", s 43.

213 Refund by instalments

Where a person has paid to the Board any tax which is or might at his option have been payable by instalments and he is entitled to recover the whole or part of it from another person, that other person shall, unless otherwise agreed between them, be entitled to refund the tax or that part by the same instalments (with the same interest thereon) as those by which it might have been paid to the Board.

Commentary—*Simon's Taxes* **I10.207, I11.407**.
Definitions—"The Board", s 272.

214 Certificates of tax paid

(1) On an application being made in such form as the Board may prescribe by a person who has paid or borne the tax attributable to the value of any property, being tax for which he is not ultimately liable, the Board shall grant a certificate specifying the tax paid and the debts and incumbrances allowed in valuing the property.
(2) Except to the extent of any repayment which may be or become due from the Board, a certificate under subsection (1) above shall be conclusive as between any person by whom the tax specified in the certificate falls to be borne and the person seeking to recover the tax from him; and any repayment of the tax falling to be made by the Board shall be duly made if made to the person producing the certificate.
(3) References in this section to tax include references to interest on tax.

Commentary—*Simon's Taxes* **I10.208, I11.408**.
HMRC Manuals—Inheritance Tax Manual HTM40154 (certificate of tax paid).
Definitions—"The Board", "incumbrance", s 272.

PART VIII
ADMINISTRATION AND COLLECTION
Management

215 General

The tax shall be under the care and management of the Board.

Commentary—*Simon's Taxes* **I11.102**.
Definitions—"The Board", s 272.

Accounts and information

216 Delivery of accounts

(1) Except as otherwise provided by this section or by regulations under section 256 below, the personal representatives of a deceased person and every person who—
(*a*) is liable as transferor for tax on the value transferred by a chargeable transfer, or would be so liable if tax were chargeable on that value, or
(*b*) is liable as trustee of a settlement for tax on the value transferred by a transfer of value, or would be so liable if tax were chargeable on that value, or

[(*bb*) is liable under section 199(1)(*b*) above for tax on the value transferred by a potentially exempt transfer which proves to be a chargeable transfer, or would be so liable if tax were chargeable on that value, or][2]

[(*bc*) is liable under section 200(1)(*c*) above for tax on the value transferred by a chargeable transfer made on death, so far as the tax is attributable to the value of property which, apart from section 102(3) of the Finance Act 1986 would not form part of the deceased's estate, or would be so liable if tax were chargeable on the value transferred on the death, or][2]

(*bca*) . . . [5]

[(*bd*) is liable under section 201(1)(*b*), (*c*) or (*d*) above for tax on the value transferred by a potentially exempt transfer which is made under section 52 above and which proves to be a chargeable transfer, or would be so liable if tax were chargeable on that value, or][4]

(*c*) is liable as trustee of a settlement for tax on an occasion on which tax is chargeable under Chapter III of Part III of this Act (apart from section 79), or would be so liable if tax were chargeable on the occasion,

shall deliver to the Board an account specifying to the best of his knowledge and belief all appropriate property and the value of that property.

(2) Where in the case of the estate of a deceased person no grant of representation or confirmation has been obtained in the United Kingdom before the expiration of the period of twelve months from the end of the month in which the death occurred—

(*a*) every person in whom any of the property forming part of the estate vests (whether beneficially or otherwise) on or at any time after the deceased's death or who at any such time is beneficially entitled to an interest in possession in any such property, and

(*b*) where any of the property is at any such time comprised in a settlement and there is no person beneficially entitled to an interest in possession in that property, every person for whose benefit any of that property (or income from it) is applied at any such time,

shall deliver to the Board an account specifying to the best of his knowledge and belief the appropriate property vested in him, in which he has an interest or which (or income from which) is applicable for his benefit and the value of that property.

[(3) Subject to subsections (3A) and (3B) below, where an account is to be delivered by personal representatives (but not where it is to be delivered by a person who is an executor of the deceased only in respect of settled land in England and Wales), the appropriate property is—

(*a*) all property which formed part of the deceased's estate immediately before his death . . . [5], other than property which would not, apart from section 102(3) of the Finance Act 1986, form part of his estate; and

(*b*) all property to which was attributable the value transferred by any chargeable transfers made by the deceased within seven years of his death.][3]

[(3A) If the personal representatives, after making the fullest enquiries that are reasonably practicable in the circumstances, are unable to ascertain the exact value of any particular property, their account shall in the first instance be sufficient as regards that property if it contains—

(*a*) a statement to that effect;

(*b*) a provisional estimate of the value of the property; and

(*c*) an undertaking to deliver a further account of it as soon as its value is ascertained.][3]

[(3B) The Board may from time to time give such general or special directions as they think fit for restricting the property to be specified in pursuance of subsection (3) above by any class of personal representatives.][3]

(4) Where subsection (3) above does not apply the appropriate property is any property to the value of which the tax is or would be attributable . . . [5]

(5) Except in the case of an account to be delivered by personal representatives, a person shall not be required to deliver an account under this section with respect to any property if a full and proper account of the property, specifying its value, has already been delivered to the Board by some other person who—

(*a*) is or would be liable for the tax attributable to the value of the property, and

(*b*) is not or would not be liable with him jointly as trustee;

and a person within subsection (2) above shall not be required to deliver an account under that subsection if he or another person within that subsection has satisfied the Board that an account will in due course be delivered by the personal representatives.

(6) An account under the preceding provisions of this section shall be delivered—

(*a*) in the case of an account to be delivered by personal representatives, before the expiration of the period of twelve months from the end of the month in which the death occurs, or, if it expires later, the period of three months beginning with the date on which the personal representatives first act as such;

[(*aa*) in the case of an account to be delivered by a person within subsection (1)(*bb*) [or (*bd*)][4] above, before the expiration of the period of twelve months from the end of the month in which the death of the transferor occurs;][2]

[(*ab*) in the case of an account to be delivered by a person within subsection (1)(*bc*) above, before the expiration of the period of twelve months from the end of the month in which the death occurs;][2]

(*ac*) . . . [5]

[(*ad*) in the case of an account to be delivered by a person within subsection (1)(*c*) above, before the expiration of the period of six months from the end of the month in which the occasion concerned occurs;][8]

(*b*) in the case of an account to be delivered by a person within subsection (2) above, before the expiration of the period of three months from the time when he first has reason to believe that he is required to deliver an account under that subsection;

(*c*) in the case of an account to be delivered by any other person, before the expiration of the period of twelve months from the end of the month in which the transfer is made or, if it expires later, the period of three months beginning with the date on which he first becomes liable for tax.

(7) A person liable for tax under section 32, [32A,][1] 79 [or 126][5] above or under Schedule 5 to this Act shall deliver an account under this section before the expiration of the period of six months from the end of the month in which the event by reason of which the tax is chargeable occurs.

Commentary—*Simon's Taxes* **I11.201–I11.214**.

HMRC Manuals—Inheritance Tax Manual IHTM10814–10824 (transfers on death and lifetime transfers).
IHTM05043 (completing the account).
IHTM10831 (accountability: settled property: general rule on accountability when there is a qualifying interest in possession).
IHTM10833 (accountability: settled property: lifetime transfers).
IHTM10836 (accountability: settled property: relevant property settlements, including maintenance funds).

Press releases etc—Tax Journal 25-1-90 (accounts for a deceased's estate must be sent direct to the Inland Revenue, not to the probate registry).
IR 24-2-93 (use of simplified account form IHT 202/202N restricted to estates where gross value of estate does not exceed twice the IHT threshold at death).

Simon's Tax Cases—s 216(1), *Re Clore (decd) (No 3)* [1985] STC 394*.
s 216(3), (3A) *Robertson v IRC* [2002] STC (SCD) 182.

Definitions—"The Board", "personal representatives", s 272; "settlement", s 43.

Cross references—See IHT (Delivery of Accounts) Regulations, SI 1981/880, 881, 1440, 1441 (no accounts required for excepted estates or excepted transfers (covered by NIL rate band) unless Revenue give notice).
FA 1986 Sch 19 para 40 (where a death or other event occurs after 17 March 1986, the amendments to this section by FA 1986 Sch 19 (see below) not to affect the tax chargeable on a transfer of value occurring before 18 March 1986).
See IHTA 1984 s 245(1) (penalty for failing to deliver an account under this section).
The Inheritance Tax (Delivery of Accounts) (Excepted Transfers and Excepted Terminations) Regulations, SI 2008/605 reg 3(1) (requirement under this section to deliver an account of an excepted transfer or an excepted termination).
The Inheritance Tax (Delivery of Accounts) (Excepted Settlements) Regulations, SI 2008/606 reg 3(1) (no person is required to deliver an account under this section of the property comprised in an excepted settlement unless the Commissioners so require by notice in writing).
FA 2009 Sch 55 (penalty for failure to make returns etc).
FA 2009 Sch 56 (penalty for failure to make payments on time).
FA 2012 Sch 36 paras 22, 23 (inclusion in account of cleared assets under the agreement between the UK and Switzerland).
F(No 2)A 2017 Sch 18 para 8 (application of the penalties regime in F(No 2)A 2017 Sch 18 (failure to correct certain offshore tax non-compliance) in relation to accounts produced under this section).
F(No 2)A 2017 Sch 10 para 11 (application of sub-s (6) in connection with UK residential property held by a non-UK domiciled individual through an overseas structure).
F(No 2)A 2017 s 30(13), (14) (application of sub-s (1)(*c*), (6)(*ad*) in connection with deemed domicile for IHT purposes)

Amendments—[1] Words in sub-s (7) inserted by FA 1985 Sch 26 para 11.

[2] Sub-ss (1)(*bb*), (*bc*), (6)(*aa*), (*ab*) inserted by FA 1986 s 101(3) and Sch 19 para 29 with respect to transfers of value made, and other events occurring, after 17 March 1986.

[3] Sub-s (3) substituted and sub-ss (3A) and (3B) inserted by FA 1999 s 105 with effect in relation to deaths occurring after 8 March 1999.

[4] Sub-s (1)(*bd*) and words in sub-s (6)(*aa*) inserted by F(No 2)A 1987 s 96(1), (6) and Sch 7 para 4 with respect to transfers of value, and other events occurring, after 16 March 1987.

[5] Sub-ss (1)(*bca*), (6)(*ac*) repealed, in sub-s (3)(*a*) words "(or would do apart from section 151A(3)(*b*) or 151C(3)(*b*) above)" repealed, in sub-s (4) words "(or would be apart from section 151A(3)(*b*), 151C(3)(*b*) or 151B(4) above)" repealed, and words in sub-s (7) substituted for words ", 126 or 151D", by FA 2011 s 65, Sch 16 paras 49, 54 with effect in relation to deaths occurring on or after 6 April 2011, subject to transitional provisions in FA 2011, Sch 16 Pt 3. Sub-ss (1)(*bca*), (6)(*ac*) previously read as follows—

"(bca) is liable under section 200(1A) or 210(2) or (3) above for tax in respect of any amount, or would be so liable if tax were chargeable in respect of that amount, or".

"(ac) in the case of an account to be delivered by the scheme administrator of a registered pension scheme otherwise than by reason of a liability to tax under section 210(3), before the expiration of the period of twelve months from the end of the month in which the death occurs, the scheme administrator becomes aware of the death or the person ceases to be a relevant dependant of the member [(depending on which occasions the charge)".

[6] Words in sub-s (6)(*ac*) inserted by FA 2007 s 69, Sch 19 paras 19, 24, 29(8) with effect in relation to deaths, cases where scheme administrators become aware of deaths, and cessations of dependency occurring on or after 6 April 2007.

[7] Words in sub-s (1)(*bca*), (6)(*ac*) inserted, and in sub-s (7), words substituted for words "or 126", by FA 2008 s 91, Sch 28 paras 6, 12 with effect in relation to deaths occurring on or after 6 April 2008.

[8] Sub-s (6)(*ad*) inserted by FA 2014 s 117, Sch 25 paras 1, 5(1) with effect in relation to chargeable transfers made on or after 6 April 2014.

217 Defective accounts

If a person who has delivered an account under section 216 above discovers at any time that the account is defective in a material respect by reason of anything contained in or omitted from it he shall, within six months of that time, deliver to the Board a further account containing such information as may be necessary to remedy the defect.

Commentary—*Simon's Taxes* **I11.217**.

HMRC Manuals—Inheritance Tax Manual IHTM10805 (corrective accounts).

Cross references—See IHTA 1984 s 245(1) (penalty for failing to deliver an account under this section).

FA 2009 Sch 55 (penalty for failure to make returns etc).

FA 2009 Sch 56 (penalty for failure to make payments on time).

FA 2012 Sch 36 paras 22, 23 (inclusion in account of cleared assets under the agreement between the UK and Switzerland).

F(No 2)A 2017 Sch 18 para 8 (application of the penalties regime in F(No 2)A 2017 Sch 18 (failure to correct certain offshore tax non-compliance) in relation to accounts produced under this section).

218 Non-resident trustees

(1) Where any person, in the course of a trade or profession carried on by him, other than the profession of a barrister, has been concerned with the making of a settlement and knows or has reason to believe—

(*a*) that the settlor was domiciled in the United Kingdom, and

(*b*) that the trustees of the settlement are not or will not be resident in the United Kingdom,

he shall, within three months of the making of the settlement, make a return to the Board stating the names and addresses of the settlor and of the trustees of the settlement.

(2) A person shall not be required to make a return under this section in relation to—

(*a*) any settlement made by will, or

(*b*) any other settlement, if such a return in relation to that settlement has already been made by another person or if an account has been delivered in relation to it under section 216 above.

(3) For the purposes of this section trustees of a settlement shall be regarded as not resident in the United Kingdom unless the general administration of the settlement is ordinarily carried on in the United Kingdom and the trustees or a majority of them (and, where there is more than one class of trustees, a majority of each class) are for the time being resident in the United Kingdom.

Commentary—*Simon's Taxes* **I11.216**.

HMRC Manuals—Inheritance Tax Manual IHTM42604 (offshore trust declaration).

Definitions—"Barrister", "the Board", s 272; "settlement", s 43; "trustee", s 45.

Cross references—See IHTA 1984 s 245(1) (penalty for failure to make a return under this section).

[218A Instruments varying dispositions taking effect on death

(1) Where—

(*a*) an instrument is made varying any of the dispositions of the property comprised in the estate of a deceased person immediately before his death,

(*b*) the instrument contains a statement under subsection (2) of section 142 above, and

(*c*) the variation results in additional tax being payable,

the relevant persons (within the meaning of that subsection) shall, within six months after the day on which the instrument is made, deliver a copy of it to the Board and notify them of the amount of the additional tax.

(2) To the extent that any of the relevant persons comply with the requirements of this section, the others are discharged from the duty to comply with them.][1]

Commentary—*Simon's Taxes* **I4.411, I1.519**.

HMRC Manuals—Inheritance Tax Manual IHTM36091 and 36092 (penalties chargeable for failure to deliver an Instrument of Variation).

IHTM35029 (instruments of variation: calculation of additional tax).

IHTM10850 (accountability: instruments of variation executed on or after 1 august 2002).

Amendments—[1] This section inserted by FA 2002 s 120(2), (4) with effect for instruments made after 31 July 2002.

219 Power to require information

(1) The Board may by notice in writing require any person to furnish them within such time, not being less than thirty days, as may be specified in the notice with such information as the Board may require for the purposes of this Act.

[(1A) A notice under this section is not to be given except with the consent of [the tribunal][2] and the [tribunal is to give consent][2] only on being satisfied that in all the circumstances the Board are justified in proceeding under this section.][1]

(2) A notice under this section may be combined with one relating to income tax.

(3) Subject to subsection (4) below, a [relevant lawyer][3] shall not be obliged in pursuance of a notice under this section to disclose, without his client's consent, any information with respect to which a claim to professional privilege could be maintained.

(4) A [relevant lawyer][3] may be obliged in pursuance of a notice under this section to disclose the name and address of his client; and if his client is resident outside the United Kingdom and carries on outside the United Kingdom a business which includes the provision for persons in the United Kingdom of services or facilities relating to—

(a) the formation of companies outside the United Kingdom,

(b) the making of settlements outside the United Kingdom, or

(c) the securing of control over, or the management or administration of, such companies or settlements,

a [relevant lawyer][3] may also be so obliged to disclose the names and addresses of persons in the United Kingdom for whom such services or facilities have been provided in the course of that business.[4]

[(5) In this section "relevant lawyer" means a barrister, advocate, solicitor or other legal representative communications with whom may be the subject of a claim to professional privilege.][3]

Commentary—*Simon's Taxes* **I11.231**; *Foster* **L2.31**.

HMRC Manuals—Inheritance Tax Manual IHTM32131–32140 (failure to provide information by the agreed date).
IHTM32231–32233 (section 219 notices).

Definitions—"The Board", "the Tribunal", s 272.

Cross references—See IHTA 1984 s 245(1) (penalty for failure to comply with a notice under this section).
FA 1990 s 125(3), (4), (6) (extension of the Board's power to require information for tax authorities in other member States).

Amendments—[1] Sub-s (1A) inserted by FA 1990 s 124 with respect to notices given after 25 July 1990.

[2] In sub-s (1A), words substituted for words "a Special Commissioner" and "Commissioner is to give his consent" respectively, by the Transfer of Tribunal Functions and Revenue and Customs Appeals Order, SI 2009/56 art 3, Sch 1 paras 108, 112 with effect from 1 April 2009.

[3] In sub-ss (3), (4) words substituted, and sub-s (3) inserted, by the Legal Services Act 2007 s 208, Sch 21 para 62 with effect from 1 January 2010 (by virtue of SI 2009/3250 art 2(*h*)).

[4] Sections 219, 219A, 219B repealed by the Finance Act 2009, Section 96 and Schedule 48 (Appointed Day, Savings and Consequential Amendments) Order, SI 2009/3054 art 3, Schedule para 2 with effect from 1 April 2010. Note that, in relation to a notice given under s 219 or 219A before 1 April 2010, s 219B continues to have effect on and after 1 April 2010 despite this repeal, and s 245A applies on and after 1 April 2010 disregarding the amendments made by the Schedule to SI 2009/3054.

[219A Power to call for documents etc][1]

[(1) An officer of the Board may by notice in writing require any person who has delivered, or is liable to deliver, an account under section 216 or 217 above, within such time as may be specified in the notice—

(a) to produce to the officer such documents as are in the person's possession or power and as the officer may reasonably require for any of the purposes mentioned in subsection (2) below; and

(b) to furnish the officer with such accounts or particulars as he may reasonably require for any of those purposes.

(2) The purposes are—

(a) enquiring into an account under section 216 or 217 above (including any claim or election included in the account);

(b) determining whether and, if so, the extent to which such an account is incorrect or incomplete; and

(c) making a determination for the purposes of a notice under section 221 below.

(3) To comply with a notice under subsection (1) above, copies of documents may be produced instead of originals; but the copies must be photographic or otherwise by way of facsimile.

(4) If so required by a notice in writing given by the officer, in the case of any document specified in the notice, the original of any copy produced under subsection (3) above must be produced for inspection by him within such time as may be specified in the notice.

(5) The time specified in a notice under subsection (1) or (4) above shall not be less than thirty days.

(6) The officer may take copies of, or make extracts from, any document produced to him under subsection (1) or (4) above.

(7) A notice under subsection (1) above does not oblige a person to produce documents or furnish accounts or particulars relating to the conduct of any pending appeal by him.][1, 2]

Commentary—*Simon's Taxes* **I11.231**.

HMRC Manuals—Inheritance Tax Manual IHTM32131–32140 (failure to provide information by the agreed date).
IHTM32201–32206 (section 219A notices).
IHTM32211–32221 (appeals against s 219A notices).

Definitions—"The Board", s 272.

Amendments—[1] This section inserted by FA 1999 s 106 with effect from 27 July 1999.

[2] Sections 219, 219A, 219B repealed by the Finance Act 2009, Section 96 and Schedule 48 (Appointed Day, Savings and Consequential Amendments) Order, SI 2009/3054 art 3, Schedule para 2 with effect from 1 April 2010. Note that, in relation to a notice given under s 219 or 219A before 1 April 2010, s 219B continues to have effect on and after 1 April 2010 despite this repeal, and s 245A applies on and after 1 April 2010 disregarding the amendments made by the Schedule to SI 2009/3054.

[219B Appeal against requirement to produce documents etc][1]

[(1) An appeal may be brought against any requirement imposed by a notice under section 219A(1) above to produce any document or to furnish any accounts or particulars.

(2) Subject to the following provisions of this section, the provisions of this Act relating to appeals shall have effect in relation to an appeal under this section as they have effect in relation to an appeal against a determination specified in a notice under section 221 below.

(3) An appeal under this section must be brought within the period of thirty days beginning with the date on which the notice under section 219A(1) above is given.

(4) On an appeal under this section the [tribunal][2] *may—*

(a) if it appears . . . [2] *that the production of the document or the furnishing of the accounts or particulars was reasonably required by the officer of the Board for any of the purposes mentioned in section 219A(2) above, confirm the notice under section 219A(1) above so far as relating to the requirement; or*

(b) if it does not so appear . . . [2]*, set aside that notice so far as so relating.*

(5) Where, on an appeal under this section, the [tribunal confirms][2] *the notice under section 219A(1) above so far as relating to any requirement, the notice shall have effect in relation to that requirement as if it had specified thirty days beginning with the determination of the appeal.*

(6) Neither the person required to produce documents or furnish accounts or particulars nor the officer of the Board shall be entitled to appeal [under sections 11 or 13 of the TCEA 2007][2] *against the determination of an appeal under this section.]*[1, 3]

Commentary—*Simon's Taxes* **I11.231**.

Definitions—"The Board", "the Tribunal", s 272.

Amendments—[1] This section inserted by FA 1999 s 106 with effect from 27 July 1999.

[2] In sub-s (4), word substituted for words "Special Commissioners" and in paras (*a*), (*b*) words "to them" repealed, in sub-s (5), words substituted for words "Special Commissioners confirm", and in sub-s (6), words substituted for words "under section 225 below", by the Transfer of Tribunal Functions and Revenue and Customs Appeals Order, SI 2009/56 art 3, Sch 1 paras 108, 113 with effect from 1 April 2009.

[3] Sections 219, 219A, 219B repealed by the Finance Act 2009, Section 96 and Schedule 48 (Appointed Day, Savings and Consequential Amendments) Order, SI 2009/3054 art 3, Schedule para 2 with effect from 1 April 2010. Note that, in relation to a notice given under s 219 or 219A before 1 April 2010, s 219B continues to have effect on and after 1 April 2010 despite this repeal, and s 245A applies on and after 1 April 2010 disregarding the amendments made by the Schedule to SI 2009/3054.

220 Inspection of property

Amendments—This section repealed by the Finance Act 2009, Section 96 and Schedule 48 (Appointed Day, Savings and Consequential Amendments) Order, SI 2009/3054 art 3, Schedule para 2 with effect from 1 April 2010.

[220A Exchange of information with other countries

Amendments—This section repealed by FA 2006 s 178, Sch 26 Pt 8(2) with effect from 19 July 2006.

Determinations[, reviews] and appeals

Amendments—Word in heading inserted by the Transfer of Tribunal Functions and Revenue and Customs Appeals Order, SI 2009/56 art 3, Sch 1 paras 108, 114 with effect from 1 April 2009.

221 Notices of determination

(1) Where it appears to the Board that a transfer of value has been made or where a claim under this Act is made to the Board in connection with a transfer of value, the Board may give notice in writing to any person who appears to the Board to be the transferor or the claimant or to be liable for any of the tax chargeable on the value transferred, stating that they have determined the matters specified in the notice.

(2) The matters that may be specified in a notice under this section in relation to any transfer of value are all or any of the following—

(*a*) the date of the transfer;

(*b*) the value transferred and the value of any property to which the value transferred is wholly or partly attributable;

(*c*) the transferor;

(*d*) the tax chargeable (if any) and the persons who are liable for the whole or part of it;

(*e*) the amount of any payment made in excess of the tax for which a person is liable and the date from which and the rate at which tax or any repayment of tax overpaid carries interest; and

(*f*) any other matter that appears to the Board to be relevant for the purposes of this Act.

(3) A determination for the purposes of a notice under this section of any fact relating to a transfer of value—

(*a*) shall, if that fact has been stated in an account or return under this Part of this Act and the Board are satisfied that the account or return is correct, be made by the Board in accordance with that account or return, but

(*b*) may, in any other case, be made by the Board to the best of their judgment.

(4) A notice under this section shall state the time within which and the manner in which an appeal against any determination in it may be made.

(5) Subject to any variation by agreement in writing or on appeal, a determination in a notice under this section shall be conclusive for the purposes of this Act against the person on whom the notice is served; and if the notice is served on the transferor and specifies a determination of the value transferred by the transfer of value or previous transfers of value, the determination, so far as relevant to the tax chargeable in respect of later transfers of value (whether or not made by the transferor) shall be conclusive also against any other person, subject however to any adjustment under section 240 or 241 below.

(6) References in this section to transfers of value or to the values transferred by them shall be construed as including references to—

(*a*) chargeable events by reference to which tax is chargeable under section 32 [or 32A][1] of this Act,

(*b*) occasions on which tax is chargeable under Chapter III of Part III of this Act,

(*c*) disposals on which tax is chargeable under section 126 of this Act,

or to the amounts on which tax is then chargeable.

Commentary—*Simon's Taxes* **I11.301–I11.304**.

HMRC Manuals—Inheritance Tax Manual IHTM37001–37014 (notices of determination).

IHTM37051–37056 (land valuation cases).

IHTM37060–37080 (non-land valuation cases).

IHTM37091–37095 (example of notices of determination).

Definitions—"The Board", s 272.

Cross-references—FA 2013 s 210 (general anti-abuse rule: claim for consequential adjustments).

Simon's Tax Cases—*Gray (surviving executor of Lady Fox, decd) v IRC* [1994] STC 360*.

Amendments—[1] Words in sub-s (6)(*a*) inserted by FA 1985 Sch 26 para 5.

222 Appeals against determinations

(1) A person on whom a notice under section 221 above has been served may, within thirty days of the service, appeal against any determination specified in it by notice in writing given to the Board and specifying the grounds of appeal.

[(2) Sections 223D, 223G and 223H provide for notification of the appeal to the tribunal.][2]

(3) Where—

(*a*) it is so agreed between the appellant and the Board, or

(*b*) the High Court, on an application made by the appellant, is satisfied that the matters to be decided on the appeal are likely to be substantially confined to questions of law and gives leave for that purpose,

the appeal may be [notified][2] to the High Court.

[(4) An appeal on any question as to the value of land in the United Kingdom may be [notified][1] to the appropriate . . .[3] Tribunal.][1]

[(4ZA) The appeal may be notified under subsection (3) or (4) only if it could be notified to the tribunal under section 223D, 223G or 223H.][2]

[(4A) If and so far as the question in dispute on any appeal under this section which has been notified to the tribunal or the High Court is a question as to the value of land in the United Kingdom, the question shall be determined on a reference to the appropriate . . .[3].][2]

[(4B) In this section "the [appropriate tribunal[3]]" means—

(*a*) where the land is in England or Wales, the [Upper Tribunal][3];

(*b*) where the land is in Scotland, the Lands Tribunal for Scotland;

(*c*) where the land is in Northern Ireland, the Lands Tribunal for Northern Ireland.][1]

(5) In the application of this section to Scotland, for references to the High Court there shall be substituted references to the Court of Session.

Commentary—*Simon's Taxes* **I11.311, I11.313–I11.315**.

HMRC Manuals—Inheritance Tax Manual IHTM37013 (appeals).

Definitions—"The Board", "the Tribunal", s 272.

Simon's Tax Cases—*Alexander v IRC* [1991] STC 112*.

s 222(3)(*b*), *Bennett v IRC* [1995] STC 54.

Cross references—See FA 2014 s 203(*f*) (appeals under this section made against determinations in respect of a transfer of value when the transferor's return is under enquiry, do not constitute tax appeals for the purpose of FA 2014 Pt 4 (follower notices and accelerated payments).

Amendments—[1] Sub-ss (4), (4A), (4B) substituted for sub-s (4) by FA 1993 s 200(1), (3) in relation to any appeal made or heard after 26 July 1993.

[2] Sub-s (2) substituted, in sub-s (3), words inserted, sub-s (4ZA) inserted, and sub-s (4A) substituted, by the Transfer of Tribunal Functions and Revenue and Customs Appeals Order, SI 2009/56 art 3, Sch 1 paras 108, 115 with effect from 1 April 2009.

[3] In sub-ss (4), (4A), word "Lands" repealed, in sub-s (4B), words substituted for words "appropriate Lands tribunal" and "Lands Tribunal", by the Transfer of Tribunal Functions (Lands Tribunal and Miscellaneous Amendments) Order, SI 2009/1307 art 5(1), (3), Sch 1 para 167 with effect from 1 June 2009.

[223 Late notice of appeal

(1) This section applies in a case where—

(*a*) notice of appeal may be given to HMRC under section 222, but

(*b*) no notice is given before the relevant time limit.

(2) Notice may be given after the relevant time limit if—

(*a*) HMRC agree, or

(*b*) where HMRC do not agree, the tribunal gives permission.

(3) If the following conditions are met, HMRC shall agree to notice being given after the relevant time limit.

(4) Condition A is that the appellant has made a request in writing to HMRC to agree to the notice being given.

(5) Condition B is that HMRC are satisfied that there was reasonable excuse for not giving the notice before the relevant time limit.

(6) Condition C is that HMRC are satisfied that request under subsection (4) was made without unreasonable delay after the reasonable excuse ceased.

(7) If a request of the kind referred to in subsection (4) is made, HMRC must notify the appellant whether or not HMRC agree to the appellant giving notice of appeal after the relevant time limit.

(8) In this section "relevant time limit", in relation to notice of appeal, means the time before which the notice is to be given (but for this section).][1]

Commentary—*Simon's Taxes* **I11.312**.

HMRC Manuals—Inheritance Tax Manual IHTM37101 (appeals against appeals out of time).

Amendments—[1] This section substituted by the Transfer of Tribunal Functions and Revenue and Customs Appeals Order, SI 2009/56 art 3, Sch 1 paras 108, 116 with effect from 1 April 2009.

[223A Appeal: HMRC review or determination by tribunal

(1) This section applies if notice of appeal has been given to HMRC.

(2) In such a case—

(*a*) the appellant may notify HMRC that the appellant requires HMRC to review the matter in question (see section 223B),

(*b*) HMRC may notify the appellant of an offer to review the matter in question (see section 223C), or

(*c*) the appellant may notify the appeal to the tribunal (see section 223D).

(3) See sections 223G and 223H for provision about notifying appeals to the tribunal after a review has been required by the appellant or offered by HMRC.][1]

Commentary—*Simon's Taxes* **I11.312A**.

HMRC Manuals—Inheritance Tax Manual IHTM37100 (appeals against referral to the tribunal).

Amendments—[1] Sections 223A–223I inserted by the Transfer of Tribunal Functions and Revenue and Customs Appeals Order, SI 2009/56 art 3, Sch 1 paras 108, 117 with effect from 1 April 2009.

[223B Appellant requires review by HMRC

(1) Subsections (2) and (3) apply if the appellant notifies HMRC that the appellant requires HMRC to review the matter in question.

(2) HMRC must, within the relevant period, notify the appellant of HMRC's view of the matter in question.

(3) HMRC must review the matter in question in accordance with section 223E.

(4) The appellant may not notify HMRC that the appellant requires HMRC to review the matter in question and HMRC shall not be required to conduct a review if—

(*a*) the appellant has already given a notification under this section in relation to the matter in question,

(*b*) HMRC have given a notification under section 223C in relation to the matter in question, or

(*c*) the appellant has notified the appeal to the court under section 222(3), the appropriate Lands tribunal under section 222(4), or the tribunal under section 223D.

(5) In this section "relevant period" means—

(*a*) the period of 30 days beginning with the day on which HMRC receive the notification from the appellant, or

(*b*) such longer period as is reasonable.][1]

Commentary—*Simon's Taxes* **I11.312A**.

HMRC Manuals—Inheritance Tax Manual IHTM37110 (provision for statutory review).

Amendments—[1] Sections 223A–223I inserted by the Transfer of Tribunal Functions and Revenue and Customs Appeals Order, SI 2009/56 art 3, Sch 1 paras 108, 117 with effect from 1 April 2009.

[223C HMRC offer review

(1) Subsections (2) to (6) apply if HMRC notify the appellant of an offer to review the matter in question.

(2) When HMRC notify the appellant of the offer, HMRC must also notify the appellant of HMRC's view of the matter in question.

(3) If, within the acceptance period, the appellant notifies HMRC of acceptance of the offer, HMRC must review the matter in question in accordance with section 223E.

(4) If the appellant does not give HMRC such a notification within the acceptance period, HMRC's view of the matter in question shall be conclusive for the purposes of this Act.

(5) The same consequences shall follow for all purposes as would have followed if, on the date that HMRC gave notice of their view, the tribunal had determined the appeal in accordance with its terms.

(6) Subsection (4) does not apply to the matter in question if, or to the extent that, the appellant notifies the appeal to the tribunal under section 223H.
(7) HMRC may not notify the appellant of an offer to review the matter in question (and, accordingly, HMRC shall not be required to conduct a review) if—
(*a*) HMRC have already given a notification under this section in relation to the matter in question,
(*b*) the appellant has given a notification under section 223B in relation to the matter in question, or
(*c*) the appellant has notified the appeal to the court under section 222(3), the appropriate Lands tribunal under section 222(4) or the tribunal under section 223D.
(8) In this section "acceptance period" means the period of 30 days beginning with the date of the document by which HMRC notify the appellant of the offer to review the matter in question.][1]

Commentary—*Simon's Taxes* **I11.312A**.
HMRC Manuals—Inheritance Tax Manual IHTM37110 (provision for statutory review).
Amendments—[1] Sections 223A–223I inserted by the Transfer of Tribunal Functions and Revenue and Customs Appeals Order, SI 2009/56 art 3, Sch 1 paras 108, 117 with effect from 1 April 2009.

[223D Notifying appeal to the tribunal

(1) This section applies if notice of appeal has been given to HMRC.
(2) The appellant may notify the appeal to the tribunal.
(3) If the appellant notifies the appeal to the tribunal, the tribunal is to decide the matter in question.
(4) Subsections (2) and (3) do not apply in a case where—
(*a*) HMRC have given a notification of their view of the matter in question under section 223B, or
(*b*) HMRC have given a notification under section 223C in relation to the matter in question.
(5) In a case falling within subsection (4)(*a*) or (*b*), the appellant may notify the appeal to the tribunal, but only if permitted to do so by section 223G or 223H.][1]

Commentary—*Simon's Taxes* **I11.312A**.
HMRC Manuals—Inheritance Tax Manual IHTM37100 (appeals against referral to the tribunal).
Amendments—[1] Sections 223A–223I inserted by the Transfer of Tribunal Functions and Revenue and Customs Appeals Order, SI 2009/56 art 3, Sch 1 paras 108, 117 with effect from 1 April 2009.

[223E Nature of review etc

(1) This section applies if HMRC are required by section 223B or 223C to review the matter in question.
(2) The nature and extent of the review are to be such as appear appropriate to HMRC in the circumstances.
(3) For the purpose of subsection (2), HMRC must, in particular, have regard to steps taken before the beginning of the review—
(*a*) by HMRC in deciding the matter in question, and
(*b*) by any person in seeking to resolve disagreement about the matter in question.
(4) The review must take account of any representations made by the appellant at a stage which gives HMRC a reasonable opportunity to consider them.
(5) The review may conclude that HMRC's view of the matter in question is to be—
(*a*) upheld,
(*b*) varied, or
(*c*) cancelled.
(6) HMRC must notify the appellant of the conclusions of the review and their reasoning within—
(*a*) the period of 45 days beginning with the relevant day, or
(*b*) such other period as may be agreed.
(7) In subsection (6) "relevant day" means—
(*a*) in a case where the appellant required the review, the day when HMRC notified the appellant of HMRC's view of the matter in question,
(*b*) in a case where HMRC offered the review, the day when HMRC received notification of the appellant's acceptance of the offer.
(8) Where HMRC are required to undertake a review but do not give notice of the conclusions within the time period specified in subsection (6), the review is to be treated as having concluded that HMRC's view of the matter in question (see sections 223B(2) and 223C(2)) is upheld.
(9) If subsection (8) applies, HMRC must notify the appellant of the conclusion which the review is treated as having reached.][1]

Commentary—*Simon's Taxes* **I11.312B, I11.312C**.
HMRC Manuals—Inheritance Tax Manual IHTM37111 (conduct of review).
Amendments—[1] Sections 223A–223I inserted by the Transfer of Tribunal Functions and Revenue and Customs Appeals Order, SI 2009/56 art 3, Sch 1 paras 108, 117 with effect from 1 April 2009.

[223F Effect of conclusions of review

(1) This section applies if HMRC give notice of the conclusions of a review (see section 223E(6) and (9)).

(2) The conclusions of the review shall be conclusive for the purposes of this Act.

(3) Subsections (2) and (3) do not apply to the matter in question if, or to the extent that, the appellant notifies the appeal to the tribunal under section 223G.][1]

Commentary—*Simon's Taxes* **I11.312C**.

HMRC Manuals—Inheritance Tax Manual IHTM37111 (conduct of review).

Amendments—[1] Sections 223A–223I inserted by the Transfer of Tribunal Functions and Revenue and Customs Appeals Order, SI 2009/56 art 3, Sch 1 paras 108, 117 with effect from 1 April 2009.

[223G Notifying appeal to tribunal after review concluded

(1) This section applies if—

(*a*) HMRC have given notice of the conclusions of a review in accordance with section 223E, or

(*b*) the period specified in section 223E(6) has ended and HMRC have not given notice of the conclusions of the review.

(2) The appellant may notify the appeal to the tribunal within the post-review period.

(3) If the post-review period has ended, the appellant may notify the appeal to the tribunal only if the tribunal gives permission.

(4) If the appellant notifies the appeal to the tribunal, the tribunal is to determine the matter in question.

(5) The appellant may not notify the appeal to the tribunal under this section if the appeal has been notified to the court under section 222(3) or the appropriate Lands tribunal under section 222(4).

(6) In this section "post-review period" means—

(*a*) in a case falling within subsection (1)(*a*), the period of 30 days beginning with the date of the document in which HMRC give notice of the conclusions of the review in accordance with section 223E(6), or

(*b*) in a case falling within subsection (1)(*b*), the period that—

(i) begins with the day following the last day of the period specified in section 223E(6), and

(ii) ends 30 days after the date of the document in which HMRC give notice of the conclusion of the review in accordance with section 223E(9).][1]

Commentary—*Simon's Taxes* **I11.312C**.

Amendments—[1] Sections 223A–223I inserted by the Transfer of Tribunal Functions and Revenue and Customs Appeals Order, SI 2009/56 art 3, Sch 1 paras 108, 117 with effect from 1 April 2009.

[223H Notifying appeal to tribunal after review offered but not accepted

(1) This section applies if—

(*a*) HMRC have offered to review the matter in question (see section 223C), and

(*b*) the appellant has not accepted the offer.

(2) The appellant may notify the appeal to the tribunal within the acceptance period.

(3) But if the acceptance period has ended, the appellant may notify the appeal to the tribunal only if the tribunal gives permission.

(4) If the appellant notifies the appeal to the tribunal, the tribunal is to determine the matter in question.

(5) The appellant may not notify the appeal to the tribunal under this section if the appeal has been notified to the court under section 222(3) or the appropriate Lands tribunal under section 222(4).

(6) In this section "acceptance period" has the same meaning as in section 223C.][1]

Commentary—*Simon's Taxes* **I11.312A**.

Amendments—[1] Sections 223A–223I inserted by the Transfer of Tribunal Functions and Revenue and Customs Appeals Order, SI 2009/56 art 3, Sch 1 paras 108, 117 with effect from 1 April 2009.

[223I Interpretation of sections 223A to 223I

(1) In sections 223A to 223H—

(*a*) "matter in question" means the matter to which an appeal relates;

(*b*) a reference to a notification is a reference to a notification in writing.

(2) In sections 223A to 223H, a reference to the appellant includes a person acting on behalf of the appellant except in relation to—

(*a*) notification of HMRC's view under section 223B(2);

(*b*) notification by HMRC of an offer of review (and of their view of the matter) under section 223C;

(*c*) notification of the conclusions of a review under section 223E(6); and

(*d*) notification of the conclusions of a review under section 223E(9).

(3) But if a notification falling within any of the paragraphs of subsection (2) is given to the appellant, a copy of the notification may also be given to a person acting on behalf of the appellant.][1]

Amendments—[1] Sections 223A–223I inserted by the Transfer of Tribunal Functions and Revenue and Customs Appeals Order, SI 2009/56 art 3, Sch 1 paras 108, 117 with effect from 1 April 2009.

[224 Determination of appeal by tribunal

If an appeal is notified to the tribunal, the tribunal must confirm the determination appealed against (or that determination as varied on a review under section 223E) unless the tribunal is satisfied that it ought to be varied (or further varied) or quashed.][1]

IHT

Commentary—*Simon's Taxes* **I11.341**.

Amendments—[1] This section substituted by the Transfer of Tribunal Functions and Revenue and Customs Appeals Order, SI 2009/56 art 3, Sch 1 paras 108, 118 with effect from 1 April 2009.

225 Appeals from Special Commissioners

Amendments—This section repealed by the Transfer of Tribunal Functions and Revenue and Customs Appeals Order, SI 2009/56 art 3, Sch 1 paras 108, 119 with effect from 1 April 2009.

[225A Extension of regulation-making powers

Amendments—This section repealed by the Transfer of Tribunal Functions and Revenue and Customs Appeals Order, SI 2009/56 art 3, Sch 1 paras 108, 119 with effect from 1 April 2009.

Payment

226 Payment: general rules

(1) Except as otherwise provided by the following provisions of this Part of this Act, the tax on the value transferred by a chargeable transfer shall be due six months after the end of the month in which the chargeable transfer is made or, in the case of a transfer made after 5th April and before 1st October in any year otherwise than on death, at the end of April in the next year.

(2) Personal representatives shall, on delivery of their account, pay all the tax for which they are liable and may, on delivery of that account, also pay any part of the tax chargeable on the death for which they are not liable, if the persons liable for it request them to make the payment.

(3) So much of the tax chargeable on the value transferred by a chargeable transfer made within [seven years][2] . . . [4] of the death of the transferor as—

(*a*) exceeds what it would have been had the transferor died more than [seven years][2] after the transfer, . . . [5]

(*b*) . . . [5]

shall be due six months after the end of the month in which the death occurs.

[(3A) Without prejudice to subsection (3) above, the tax chargeable on the value transferred by a potentially exempt transfer which proves to be a chargeable transfer shall be due six months after the end of the month in which the transferor's death occurs.][3]

[(3B) So much (if any) of the tax chargeable on the value transferred by a chargeable transfer made under Chapter III of Part III of this Act within the period of seven years ending with the settlor's death as exceeds what it would have been had the settlor died more than seven years after the date of the transfer shall be due six months after the end of the month in which the death occurs.][3]

[(3C) Tax chargeable under Chapter 3 of Part 3 of this Act on the value transferred by a chargeable transfer, other than any for which the due date is given by subsection (3B) above, is due six months after the end of the month in which the chargeable transfer is made.][7]

(4) Tax chargeable under section 32, [32A,][1] 79 [or 126][6] above or under Schedule 5 to this Act . . . [6] shall be due six months after the end of the month in which the event by reason of which it is chargeable occurs.

(5) The Board may in the first instance, and without prejudice to the recovery of the remainder of the tax, accept or demand payment of an amount by reference to the value stated in an account delivered to the Board under section 216 or 217 above.

(6) Nothing in this section shall be taken to authorise the recovery from, or require the payment by, any person of tax in excess of his liability as limited by section 204 above.

Commentary—*Simon's Taxes* **I11.401–I11.404**.

HMRC Manuals—Inheritance Tax Manual IHTM30140–30159 (general payment rule).

Definitions—"The Board", "personal representatives", "the Tribunal", s 272.

Cross references—See FA 1986 Sch 19 para 40 (where a death or other event occurs after 17 March 1986, the amendments to this section by FA 1986 Sch 19 (see below) not to affect the tax chargeable on a transfer of value occurring before 18 March 1986).

FA 2009 Sch 56 (penalty for failure to make payments on time).

Amendments—[1] Words in sub-s (4) inserted by FA 1985 Sch 26 para 11.

[2] Words in sub-s (3) substituted by FA 1986 s 101(3) and Sch 19 para 30 with respect to transfers of value made after 17 March 1986.

[3] Sub-ss (3A), (3B) inserted by FA 1986 s 101(3) and Sch 19 para 30 with respect to transfers of value made after 17 March 1986.

[4] Words in sub-s (3) repealed by FA 1988 Sch 14 Part X with respect to transfers of value made after 14 March 1988.

[5] Sub-s (3)(*b*) and the word "or" preceding it repealed by FA 1988 Sch 14 Part X with respect to transfers of value made after 14 March 1988.

[6] In sub-s (4) words substituted for words ", 126, 151B or 151D" and words "or under section 151A above by virtue of subsection (6) of that section," repealed, by FA 2011 s 65, Sch 16 paras 49, 55 with effect in relation to deaths occurring on or after 6 April 2011, subject to transitional provisions in FA 2011, Sch 16 Pt 3.

[7] Sub-s (3C) inserted by FA 2014 s 117, Sch 25 paras 1, 5(2) with effect in relation to chargeable transfers made on or after 6 April 2014.

227 Payment by instalments—land, shares and businesses

(1) Where any of the tax payable on the value transferred by a chargeable transfer is attributable to the value of qualifying property and—

(*a*) the transfer is made on death, or

(*b*) the tax so attributable is borne by the person benefiting from the transfer, or
(*c*) the transfer is made under Part III of this Act and the property concerned continues to be comprised in the settlement,

the tax so attributable may, if the person paying it by notice in writing to the Board so elects, be paid by ten equal yearly instalments.

[(1A) Subsection (1) above does not apply to—
(*a*) tax payable on the value transferred by a potentially exempt transfer which proves to be a chargeable transfer, or
(*b*) additional tax becoming payable on the value transferred by any chargeable transfer by reason of the transferor's death within seven years of the transfer,

except to the extent that the tax is attributable to the value of property which satisfies one of the conditions specified in subsection (1C) below and, in the case of property consisting of unquoted shares or unquoted securities, the further condition specified in section 228(3A) below.][3]

[(1AA) In subsection (1A) above, "unquoted", in relation to any shares or securities, means not [listed][7] on a recognised stock exchange.][6]

[(1B) In [this section][4] "the transferee" means the person whose property the qualifying property became on the transfer or, where on the transfer the qualifying property became comprised in a settlement in which no qualifying interest in possession (within the meaning of Chapter III of Part III of this Act) subsists, the trustees of the settlement.][1]

[(1C) The conditions referred to in subsection (1A) above are—
(*a*) that the property was owned by the transferee throughout the period beginning with the date of the chargeable transfer and ending with the death of the transferor (or, if earlier, the death of the transferee), or
(*b*) that for the purposes of determining the tax, or additional tax, due by reason of the death of the transferor, the value of the property is reduced in accordance with the provisions of Chapter I or Chapter II of Part V of this Act by virtue of section 113B or section 124B above.][5]

(2) In this section "qualifying property" means—
(*a*) land of any description, wherever situated;
(*b*) shares or securities to which section 228 below applies;
(*c*) a business or an interest in a business.

(3) The first of the instalments referred to in subsection (1) above shall be payable—
(*a*) if the chargeable transfer was made on death, six months after the end of the month in which the death occurred, and
(*b*) in any other case, at the time when the tax would be due if it were not payable by instalments;

and interest under section 233 below on the unpaid portion of the tax shall be added to each instalment and paid accordingly, except as otherwise provided in section 234 below.

(4) Notwithstanding the making of an election under this section, the tax for the time being unpaid, with interest to the time of payment, may be paid at any time; and if at any time (whether before or after the date when the first instalment is payable) the whole or any part of the property concerned is sold, the tax unpaid (or, in the case of a sale of part, the proportionate part of that tax) shall become payable forthwith (or, if the sale precedes the date when the first instalment is payable, on that date) together with any interest accrued under section 233 below.

(5) References in subsection (4) above to the sale of property shall have effect—
(*a*) in a case within subsection (1)(*b*) above [other than a case within subsection (1A) above where the transferee dies before the transferor][2], as if they included references to any chargeable transfer in which the value transferred is wholly or partly attributable to the value of the property, other than a transfer made on death, and
(*b*) in a case within subsection (1)(*c*) above, as references to the property ceasing to be comprised in the settlement.

(6) For the purposes of subsection (4) above—
(*a*) the sale of an interest or part of an interest in a business shall be treated as a sale of part of the business, and
(*b*) the payment, under a partnership agreement or otherwise, of a sum in satisfaction of the whole or part of an interest in a business otherwise than on a sale shall be treated as a sale of the interest or part at the time of payment.

(7) For the purposes of this section—
(*a*) the value of a business or of an interest in a business shall be taken to be its net value;
(*b*) the net value of a business is the value of the assets used in the business (including goodwill) reduced by the aggregate amount of any liabilities incurred for the purposes of the business;
(*c*) in ascertaining the net value of an interest in a business, no regard shall be had to assets or liabilities other than those by reference to which the net value of the business would have fallen to be ascertained if the tax had been attributable to the entire business; and
(*d*) "business" includes a business carried on in the exercise of a profession or vocation, but does not include a business carried on otherwise than for gain.

Commentary—*Simon's Taxes* **I11.511–I11.514, I11.501.**
HMRC Manuals—Inheritance Tax Manual IHTM14541 (situations of grossing up where no instalments allowed).
IHTM26190 (apportioning the grossed up estate between instalment and non-instalment option property).
IHTM30191–30324 (details of instalment option).
IHTM25122 (valuing businesses and partnerships: installments).
Definitions—"qualifying interest in possession", s 59(1).
Cross references—See FA 1986 Sch 19 para 40 (where a death or other event occurs after 17 March 1986, the amendments to this section by FA 1986 Sch 19 para 31 not to affect the tax chargeable on a transfer of value occurring before 18 March 1986).
FA 2009 Sch 53 Part 2 (late payment interest start date).
FA 2009 Sch 56 (penalty for failure to make payments on time).
FA 2014 s 223 (due date for payment of DOTAS accelerated payment notice).
Amendments—[1] Sub-s (1B) inserted by FA 1986 s 101(3) and Sch 19 para 31 with respect to transfers of value made after 17 March 1986.
[2] Words in sub-s (5) inserted by FA 1986 s 101 and Sch 19 para 31 with respect to transfers of value made after 17 March 1986.
[3] Sub-s (1A) substituted by FA 1987 s 58 and Sch 8 para 15 with respect to transfers of value made after 16 March 1987.
[4] Words in sub-s (1B) substituted by FA 1987 s 58 and Sch 8 para 15 with respect to transfers of value made after 16 March 1987.
[5] Sub-s (1C) inserted by FA 1987 s 58 and Sch 8 para 15 with respect to transfers of value made after 16 March 1987.
[6] Sub-s (1AA) inserted by F(No 2)A 1992 Sch 14 paras 5, 8 in relation to transfers of value made and other events occurring after 9 March 1992.
[7] Word in sub-s (1AA) substituted by FA 1996 Sch 38 para 5 in relation to transfers of value occurring after 31 March 1996 and for the purposes of charging to tax any event after that date, in relation to which the transfer of value occurred before 1 April 1996.

228 Shares, etc within section 227

(1) This section applies—

(*a*) to shares or securities of a company which immediately before the chargeable transfer gave control of the company—

(i) in the case of a transfer on death, to the deceased,

(ii) in the case of a transfer under Chapter III of Part III of this Act, to the trustees, and

(iii) in any other case, to the transferor;

(*b*) to shares or securities of a company [which do not fall under paragraph (*a*) above and are unquoted][1], if the chargeable transfer is made on death and the condition stated in subsection (2) below is satisfied;

(*c*) to shares or securities of a company [which do not fall under paragraph (*a*) above and are unquoted][1], if the Board are satisfied that the tax attributable to their value cannot be paid in one sum without undue hardship (assuming, in the case of a chargeable transfer made otherwise than on death, that the shares or securities would be retained by the persons liable to pay the tax);

(*d*) to shares of a company [which do not fall under paragraph (*a*) above and are unquoted][1], if the conditions stated in subsection (3) below are satisfied.

(2) The condition mentioned in subsection (1)(*b*) above is that not less than 20 per cent of so much of the tax chargeable on the value transferred as is tax for which the person paying the tax attributable as mentioned in section 227(1) above is liable (in the same capacity) consists of tax attributable to the value of the shares or securities or such other tax (if any) as may by virtue of section 227 be paid by instalments.

(3) The conditions mentioned in subsection (1)(*d*) above are that so much of the value transferred (calculated, if the transfer is not made on death, as if no tax were chargeable on it) as is attributable to the shares exceeds £20,000, and that either—

(*a*) the nominal value of the shares is not less than 10 per cent of the nominal value of all the shares of the company at the time of the transfer, or

(*b*) the shares are ordinary shares and their nominal value is not less than 10 per cent of the nominal value of all ordinary shares of the company at that time.

[(3A) The further condition referred to in section 227(1A) above is that the shares or securities remained unquoted throughout the period beginning with the date of the chargeable transfer and ending with the death of the transferor (or, if earlier, the death of the transferee).][2]

(4) In this section "ordinary shares" means shares which carry either—

(*a*) a right to dividends not restricted to dividends at a fixed rate, or

(*b*) a right to conversion into shares carrying such a right as is mentioned in paragraph (*a*) above.

[(5) In this section "unquoted", in relation to any shares or securities, means not [listed][4] on a recognised stock exchange.][3]

Commentary—*Simon's Taxes* **I11.512, I11.513.**
HMRC Manuals—Inheritance Tax Manual IHTM30191–30324 (details of instalment option).
IHTM30219 (tranfer on death: unquoted shares - 20% tax test).
IHTM30254 (unquouted shares or securities - undue hardship).
IHTM42950 (dispositions by an individual: conditions).
Definitions—"unquoted", s 272.
Amendments—[1] Words in sub-s (1)(*b*), (*c*), (*d*) substituted by FA 1987 s 58 and Sch 8 para 16 in relation to transfers of value made or events occurring after 16 March 1987.

2 Sub-s (3A) inserted by FA 1987 s 58 and Sch 8 para 16 in relation to transfers of value made or events occurring after 16 March 1987.

3 Sub-s (5) added by F(No 2)A 1992 Sch 14 paras 6, 8 in relation to transfers of value made and other events occurring after 9 March 1992.

4 Word in sub-s (5) substituted by FA 1996 Sch 38 para 5 in relation to transfers of value occurring after 31 March 1996 and for the purposes of charging to tax any event after that date, in relation to which the transfer of value occurred before 1 April 1996.

229 Payment by instalments—woodlands

Tax chargeable on such a chargeable transfer as is mentioned in section 129 above may, if the person paying the tax by notice in writing to the Board so elects, be paid by ten equal yearly instalments, of which the first shall be payable six months after the end of the month in which the transfer is made.

Commentary—*Simon's Taxes* **I11.521**.
HMRC Manuals—Inheritance Tax Manual IHTM30300 (instalment option: woodlands).
Definitions—"The Board", s 272.
Cross references—FA 2009 Sch 53 Part 2 (late payment interest start date).
FA 2009 Sch 56 (penalty for failure to make payments on time).

230 Acceptance of property in satisfaction of tax

(1) The Board may, if they think fit and the [Secretary of State agrees][1], on the application of any person liable to pay tax or interest payable under section 233 below, accept in satisfaction of the whole or any part of it any property to which this section applies.

(2) This section applies to any such land as may be agreed upon between the Board and the person liable to pay tax.

(3) This section also applies to any objects which are or have been kept in any building—

(*a*) if the Board have determined to accept or have accepted that building in satisfaction or part satisfaction of tax or of estate duty, or

(*b*) if the building or any interest in it belongs to Her Majesty in right of the Crown or of the Duchy of Lancaster, or belongs to the Duchy of Cornwall or belongs to a Government department or is held for the purposes of a Government department, or

(*c*) if the building is one of which the Secretary of State is guardian under the Ancient Monuments and Archaeological Areas Act 1979 or of which the Department of the Environment for Northern Ireland is guardian under [the Historic Monuments and Archaeological Objects (Northern Ireland) Order 1995][3], or

(*d*) if the building belongs to any body within Schedule 3 to this Act,

in any case where it appears to the [Secretary of State][1] desirable for the objects to remain associated with the building.

(4) This section also applies to—

(*a*) any picture, print, book, manuscript, work of art, scientific object or other thing which the [Secretary of State is][1] satisfied is pre-eminent for its national, scientific, historic or artistic interest, and

(*b*) any collection or group of pictures, prints, books, manuscripts, works of art, scientific objects or other things if the [Secretary of State is][1] satisfied that the collection or group, taken as a whole, is pre-eminent for its national, scientific, historic or artistic interest.

(5) In this section—

. . . [2];

"national interest" includes interest within any part of the United Kingdom;

and in determining under subsection (4) above whether an object or collection or group of objects is pre-eminent, regard shall be had to any significant association of the object, collection or group with a particular place.

[(6) The functions of the Ministers under this section in relation to the acceptance, in satisfaction of tax, of property in which there is a Scottish interest may be exercised separately.

(7) For the purposes of subsection (6) a Scottish interest in the property exists—

(*a*) where the property is located in Scotland; or

(*b*) the person liable to pay the tax has expressed a wish or imposed a condition on his offer of the property in satisfaction of tax that it be displayed in Scotland or disposed of or transferred to a body or institution in Scotland.][4]

Commentary—*Simon's Taxes* **I11.541**.
HMRC Manuals—Inheritance Tax Manual IHTM30373 (property accepted in satisfaction of tax).
IHTM30185 (tax payable on taking out of grant: payment by transfer of land or chattels).
Statement of Practice SP 6/87—Acceptance of property in lieu of IHT, CTT and estate duty.
Press releases etc—Hansard 7-8-80 (guidelines on interpretation of "pre-eminent" in sub-ss (4), (5)).
Cross references—See the National Assembly for Wales (Transfer of Functions) Order, SI 2004/3044 for provision regarding the exercise by the National Assembly for Wales of statutory functions currently vested in Ministers of the Crown. By virtue of that Order, such functions under this section are exercisable by the Assembly. However, where there is both a Welsh interest and another interest in the property to which this section applies, it is directed that the functions of the Secretary of State shall be exercisable by the Assembly concurrently with the Secretary of State.
FA 2009 Sch 53 Part 2 (late payment interest start date).

Government of Wales Act 2006 Sch 3A para 1 (functions of the Secretary of State under this section, where there is both a Welsh interest and another interest in the property to which the section applies, exercisable concurrently with the Welsh Ministers; "Welsh interest" and "another interest" are defined in GOWA 2006 Sch 3A para 6).

Definitions—"The Board", "estate duty", "government department", s 272.

Amendments—[1] Words in sub-ss (1), (3), (4) substituted by the Transfer of Functions (National Heritage) Order SI 1992/1311 Sch 2 para 6 with effect from 3 July 1992.

[2] Definition of "the Ministers" in sub-s (5) repealed by the Transfer of Functions (National Heritage) Order SI 1992/1311 Sch 2 para 6 with effect from 3 July 1992.

[3] Words in sub-s (3)(*c*) substituted by the Historic Monuments and Archaeological Objects (Northern Ireland) Order SI 1995/1625 Sch 3 para 1.

[4] Sub-ss (6), (7) inserted by the Scotland Act 1998 (Modification of Functions) Order, SI 1999/1756 art 2, Schedule para 8. This amendment comes into force immediately before the principal appointed day, defined as 1 July 1999, by the Scotland Act 1998 (Commencement) Order, SI 1998/3178.

231 Powers to transfer property in satisfaction of tax

(1) Where a person has power to sell any property in order to raise money for the payment of tax, he may agree with the Board for the property to be accepted in satisfaction of that tax in pursuance of section 230 above; and, except as regards the nature of the consideration and its receipt and application, any such agreement shall be subject to the same provisions and shall be treated for all purposes as a sale made in the exercise of the said power, and any conveyance or transfer made or purporting to be made to give effect to such an agreement shall have effect accordingly.

(2) The references in subsection (1) above to tax include references to interest payable under section 233 below.

(3) This section shall not affect paragraph 1(4) or 3(4) of Schedule 5 to this Act.

Commentary—*Simon's Taxes* **I11.541**.

HMRC Manuals—Inheritance Tax Manual IHTM30203 (request to elect for instalments after tax paid in one sum).

Press releases etc—DES March 1977 (special purchase scheme for artistic objects: sale to public collections).

Definitions—"The Board", s 272.

232 Administration actions

Where proceedings are pending in any court for the administration of any property to the value of which any tax charged on the value transferred by a chargeable transfer is attributable, the court shall provide, out of any such property in the possession or control of the court, for the payment of any of the tax so attributable, or interest on it, which remains unpaid.

Commentary—*Simon's Taxes* **I11.415**.

Interest

233 Interest on unpaid tax

(1) If—

(*a*) an amount of tax charged on the value transferred by a chargeable transfer [not within paragraph (*aa*) below and][7] made after 5th April and before 1st October in any year and otherwise than on death remains unpaid after the end of the period ending with April in the next year, or

[(*aa*) an amount of tax charged under Chapter 3 of Part 3 of this Act on the value transferred by a chargeable transfer remains unpaid after the end of the period of six months beginning with the end of the month in which the chargeable transfer was made, or][7]

(*b*) an amount of tax charged on the value transferred by [a chargeable transfer not within paragraph (*a*) or (*aa*) above][7] remains unpaid after the end of the period of six months beginning with the end of the month in which the chargeable transfer was made, or

(*c*) an amount of tax chargeable under section 32, [32A][2], [79(3A)][8] [or 126][1] above or under Schedule 5 to this Act . . . [1] remains unpaid after the end of the period of six months beginning with the end of the month in which the event occasioning the charge occurs,

[then, subject to subsection (1A) below][3] it shall carry interest from the end of that period at the [rate applicable under section 178 of the Finance Act 1989].[5]

[(1A) If, under section 230 above, the Board agree to accept property in satisfaction of any tax on terms that the value to be attributed to the property for the purposes of that acceptance is determined as at a date earlier than that on which the property is actually accepted, the terms may provide that the amount of tax which is satisfied by the acceptance of the property shall not carry interest under this section from that date.][4]

(2) . . . [6]

(3) Interest payable under this section shall not be allowed as a deduction in computing any income, profits or losses for any tax purposes.

(4) . . . [6]

Commentary—*Simon's Taxes* **I11.405, I11.541**.

HMRC Manuals—Inheritance Tax Manual IHTM30341 (interest: introduction).

IHTM30373 (interest: special rules).

IHTM36253 (instalment offers: re-calculating the penalty).

Regulations—Taxes (Interest Rate) Regulations, SI 1989/1297.

Statement of Practice SP 6/87—Acceptance of property in lieu of IHT: interest on tax to cease to accrue from date of offer.

Note—FA 1989 s 178 and the Taxes (Interest Rate) Regulations SI 1989/1297 reg 4 which came into force on 18 August 1989 lay down the procedure and formula for calculating interest rate. Variations in rates as a result of the said procedure and formula are announced from time to time by Inland Revenue press releases. The rates as applicable for various periods may be obtained from *Simon's Taxes*, Binder 1, Tax compliance data.

Definitions—"The Board", s 272.

Cross references—See FA 1986 Sch 19 para 40 (where a death or other event occurs after 17 March 1986, the amendments to this section by FA 1986 Sch 19 (see below) not to affect the tax chargeable on a transfer of value occurring before 18 March 1986).

F(No 2)A 2017 Sch 10 para 10(1), (2) (application of sub-s (1) in connection with UK residential property held by a non-UK domiciled individual through an overseas structure).

F(No 2)A 2017 s 30(13), (14) (application of sub-s (1) in connection with deemed domicile for IHT purposes)

Amendments—[1] In sub-s (1)(*c*) words substituted for words ", 126, 151B or 151D", and words "or under section 151A above by virtue of subsection (6) of that section," repealed, by FA 2011 s 65, Sch 16 paras 49, 56 with effect in relation to deaths occurring on or after 6 April 2011, subject to transitional provisions in FA 2011, Sch 16 Pt 3.

[2] Words in sub-s (1)(*c*) inserted by FA 1985 Sch 26 para 11.

[3] Words in sub-s (1) inserted by FA 1987 s 60(1), (3) where the acceptance of property occurs after 16 March 1987.

[4] Sub-s (1A) inserted by FA 1987 s 60(2), (3) where the acceptance of property occurs after 16 March 1987.

[5] Words in sub-s (1) substituted by FA 1989 s 179(1)(*d*) with effect for periods beginning after 17 August 1989.

[6] Sub-ss (2), (4) repealed by FA 1989 Sch 17 Pt X with effect for periods beginning after 17 August 1989 by virtue of FA 1989 s 178(1) (Appointed Day No 1) Order, SI 1989/1298.

[7] Words in sub-s (1)(*a*) inserted, sub-s (1)(*aa*) inserted, and words in sub-s (1)(*b*) substituted by FA 2014 s 117, Sch 25 paras 1, 5(3) with effect in relation to chargeable transfers made on or after 6 April 2014.

[8] In sub-s (1)(*c*), reference substituted for reference "79(3)" by F(No 2)A 2015 s 12(8)(*b*) with effect in relation to occasions on which tax would (ignoring the effect of the amendments made by F(No 2)A 2015 s 12) fall to be charged under IHTA 1984 s 64 on or after 18 November 2015.

234 Interest on instalments

(1) Where tax payable on the value transferred by a chargeable transfer—

(*a*) is payable by instalments under section 227 above and is attributable to the value of any shares, securities, business or interest in a business, or to value treated as reduced under Chapter II of Part V of this Act, or

(*b*) is payable by instalments under section 229 above,

it shall, for the purposes of any interest to be added to each instalment, be treated as carrying interest from the date at which the instalment is payable.

(2) Subsection (1) above shall not apply to tax attributable to the value of shares or securities of a company falling within paragraph (*a*) of subsection (3) below (not being tax attributable to value treated as reduced under Chapter II of Part V of this Act) unless it also falls within paragraph (*b*) or (*c*) of that subsection.

(3) The companies referred to in subsection (2) above are—

(*a*) any company whose business consists wholly or mainly of one or more of the following, that is to say, dealing in securities, stocks or shares, land or buildings, or making or holding investments;

(*b*) any company whose business consists wholly or mainly in being a holding company ([as defined in section [1159 of and Schedule 6 to][5]][4] the [Companies Act [2006][5]][1]) of one or more companies not falling within paragraph (*a*) above;

[(*c*) any company—

(i) whose business is wholly that of a market maker or is that of a discount house and (in either case) is carried on in the United Kingdom, or

(ii) which is of a description set out in regulations under section 107(5) of the Finance Act 1986.][2]

[(4) In this section "market maker" means a person who—

(*a*) holds himself out at all normal times in compliance with the rules of The Stock Exchange as willing to buy and sell securities, stocks or shares at a price specified by him, and

(*b*) is recognised as doing so by the Council of The Stock Exchange.][3]

Commentary—*Simon's Taxes* **I11.531, I11.501**.

HMRC Manuals—Inheritance Tax Manual IHTM30363 (instalments with interest relief).

Regulations—FA 1986 s 107(4), (6), (8) empowers the Board to make Regulations to modify the definition of "market makers" in sub-s (4) above. The Inheritance Tax (Market Makers) Regulations, SI 1992/3181 regs 2, 3, 4 make such modification in relation to transfers of value made after 22 March 1992.

Cross-references—Inheritance Tax (Market Makers and Discount Houses) Regulations, SI 2012/2903 (Description of "business" and "company" for the purposes of ss 105(4A) and 234(3)(*c*)(ii)).

F(No 2)A 2017 Sch 10 para 10(1), (3) (application of sub-s (1) in connection with UK residential property held by a non-UK domiciled individual through an overseas structure).

F(No 2)A 2017 s 30(13), (14) (application of sub-s (1) in connection with deemed domicile for IHT purposes)

Amendments—[1] Words in sub-s (3)(*b*) substituted by the Companies Consolidation (Consequential Provisions) Act 1985 Sch 2 with effect from 1 July 1985.

[2] Sub-s (3)(*c*) substituted by the Inheritance Tax (Market Makers and Discount Houses) Regulations, SI 2012/2903 regs 3, 5 with effect from 31 December 2012. Also see cross-reference note above.

[3] Sub-s (4) inserted by FA 1986 s 107(2).

[4] Words in sub-s (3)(*b*) substituted by the Companies Act 1989 s 144(4), Sch 18 para 30(1), (4).

IHT

[5] In para (3)(*b*), words substituted for words "736 of" and "1985", by the Companies Act 2006 (Consequential Amendments) (Taxes and National Insurance) Order, SI 2009/1890 art 4(1)(*f*) with effect from 1 October 2009.

235 Interest on overpaid tax

(1) Any repayment of an amount paid in excess of a liability for tax or for interest on tax shall carry interest from the date on which the payment was made [until the order for repayment is issued][1] at [the rate applicable under section 178 of the Finance Act 1989][2].

(2) Interest paid under this section shall not constitute income for any tax purposes.

Commentary—*Simon's Taxes* **I11.411, I11.405.**

HMRC Manuals—Inheritance Tax Manual IHTM31665 (repayments: interest supplement).

Press releases etc—Law Society's Gazette 18-11-92 (Inland Revenue cheques are crossed "account payee only". If personal representatives or trustees want a refund to be made direct to another payee they must provide written authority).

Note—For rates of interest, see IHTA 1984 s 233 above.

Amendments—[1] Words in sub-s (1) inserted by FA 1989 s 180(4), (7) and deemed always to have had effect.

[2] In sub-s (1) words substituted for the words "the same rate as that at which the tax, if outstanding, would have carried interest" by FA 2009 s 105(4) with effect from 21 July 2009.

236 Special cases

(1) Section 233 above shall apply in relation to—

(*a*) the amount by which tax chargeable on the value transferred by a chargeable transfer made within [seven years][1] of the transferor's death exceeds what it would have been had the transferor died more than [seven years][1] after the transfer, . . . [4]

(*b*) . . . [4]

as if the chargeable transfer had been made on the death of the transferor.

[(1A) Section 233 above shall apply in relation to the amount (if any) by which—

(*a*) the tax chargeable on the value transferred by a chargeable transfer made under Chapter III of Part III of this Act within the period of seven years ending with the settlor's death,

exceeds

(*b*) what that tax would have been had the settlor died more than seven years after the date of the transfer,

as if the chargeable transfer had been made on the death of the settlor.][2]

(2) Tax overpaid or underpaid in consequence of—

(*a*) section 146(1) above, or section 19(1) of the Inheritance (Provision for Family and Dependants) Act 1975 or

(*b*) the corresponding provision of the Inheritance (Provision for Family and Dependants) (Northern Ireland) Order 1979,

shall not carry interest for any period before the order there mentioned is made.

(3) Tax repayable on a claim under section 146(2), . . . [3] or 150 above shall carry interest (which shall not constitute income for any tax purposes) at the [rate applicable under section 178 of the Finance Act 1989][5] from the date on which the claim is made.

(4) Tax repayable under section 147(2) above shall carry interest (which shall not constitute income for any tax purposes) at the [rate applicable under section 178 of the Finance Act 1989][5] from the date on which the tax was paid; and tax charged by virtue of section 147(4) above shall carry interest at that rate [from the end of the period mentioned in section 233(1)(*b*) above][5].

Commentary—*Simon's Taxes* **I11.405, I11.410, I11.411.**

HMRC Manuals—Inheritance Tax Manual IHTM30371 (interest: special rules: inheritance (provision for family & dependants) act 1975).

IHTM30374 (interest: special rules: scotland - legitim).

Regulations—See Taxes (Interest Rate) Regulations, SI 1989/1297.

Note—For the interest rate applicable under sub-ss (3), (4), see note under s 233 above.

Cross references—See FA 1986 Sch 19 para 40 (where a death or other event occurs after 17 March 1986, the amendments to this section by FA 1986 Sch 19 (see below) not to affect the tax chargeable on a transfer of value occurring before 18 March 1986).

Amendments—[1] Words in sub-s (1)(*a*) substituted by FA 1986 s 101(3) and Sch 19 para 33 with respect to transfers of value made after 17 March 1986.

[2] Sub-s (1A) inserted by FA 1986 s 101(3) and Sch 19 para 33 with respect to transfers of value made after 17 March 1986.

[3] Number "149" in sub-s (3) repealed by FA 1986 Sch 23 Pt X as a consequence of the repeal of s 149.

[4] Sub-s (1)(*b*) and the preceding word "and" repealed by FA 1988 Sch 14, Part X with respect to transfers of value made after 14 March 1988.

[5] Words in sub-ss (3), (4) substituted by FA 1989 s 179(1)(*e*), (3), (4).

Inland Revenue charge for unpaid tax

237 Imposition of charge

(1) Except as otherwise provided, where any tax charged on the value transferred by a chargeable transfer, or any interest on it, is for the time being unpaid a charge for the amount unpaid (to be known as an Inland Revenue charge) is by virtue of this section imposed in favour of the Board on—

(*a*) any property to the value of which the value transferred is wholly or partly attributable, and

(*b*) where the chargeable transfer is made by the making of a settlement or is made under Part III of this Act, any property comprised in the settlement.

(2) References in subsection (1) above to any property include references to any property directly or indirectly representing it.

[(2A) Where tax is charged by virtue of Schedule A1 on the value transferred by a chargeable transfer, the reference in subsection (1)(*a*) to property to the value of which the value transferred is wholly or partly attributable includes the UK residential property interest (within the meaning of that Schedule) to which the charge to tax relates.][6]

(3) Where the chargeable transfer is made on death, personal or movable property situated in the United Kingdom which was beneficially owned by the deceased immediately before his death and vests in his personal representatives is not subject to the Inland Revenue charge; and for this purpose ["personal property" does not include leaseholds[3]] . . . [2] and the question whether any property was beneficially owned by the deceased shall be determined without regard to section 49(1) above.

[(3A) In the case of a potentially exempt transfer which proves to be a chargeable transfer—

(*a*) property concerned, or an interest in property concerned, which has been disposed of to a purchaser before the transferor's death is not subject to the Inland Revenue charge, but

(*b*) property concerned which has been otherwise disposed of before the death and property which at the death represents any property or interest falling within paragraph (*a*) above shall be subject to the charge;

and in this subsection "property concerned" means property to the value of which the value transferred by the transfer is wholly or partly attributable.][1]

[(3B) Subsection (3C) below applies to any tax charged—

(*a*) under section 32, 32A [or 79(3A)][5] above in respect of any property,

(*b*) under paragraph 8 of Schedule 4 to this Act in respect of any property, or

(*c*) under paragraph 1 or 3 of Schedule 5 to this Act with respect to any object or property.][4]

[(3C) Where any tax to which this subsection applies, or any interest on it, is for the time being unpaid, a charge for the amount unpaid is also by virtue of this section imposed in favour of the Board—

(*a*) except where the event giving rise to the charge was a disposal to a purchaser of the property or object in question, on that property or object; and

(*b*) in the excepted case, on any property for the time being representing that property or object.][4]

(4) No heritable property situated in Scotland is subject to the Inland Revenue charge, but where such property is disposed of any other property for the time being representing it is subject to the charge to which the first-mentioned property would have been subject but for this subsection.

(5) The Inland Revenue charge imposed on any property shall take effect subject to any incumbrance on it which is allowable as a deduction in valuing that property for the purposes of the tax.

(6) Except as provided by section 238 below, a disposition of property subject to an Inland Revenue charge shall take effect subject to that charge.

Commentary—*Simon's Taxes* **I11.601, I11.602.**

HMRC Manuals—Inheritance Tax Manual IHTM30125 (liability in special cases: liabilityt of purchaser).

IHTM30464 (limitation of liability by lapse of time: property in the hands of purchasers).

Simon's Tax Cases—*Howarth's Executors v IRC* [1997] STC (SCD) 162.

Definitions—"The Board", "incumbrance", "personal representatives", "purchaser", s 272.

Cross references—See FA 1986 Sch 19 para 40 (where a death or other event occurs after 17 March 1986, the amendments to this section by FA 1986 Sch 19 (see below) not to affect the tax chargeable on a transfer of value occurring before 18 March 1986).

Amendments—[1] Sub-s (3A) inserted by FA 1986 s 101(3) and Sch 19 para 34 with respect to transfers of value made after 17 March 1986.

[2] Words "and undivided shares in land held on trust for sale, whether statutory or not," repealed by the Trusts of Land and Appointment of Trustees Act 1996 Sch 4 with effect from a day to be appointed.

[3] Words in sub-s (3) substituted by FA 1999 s 107(1) with effect in relation to deaths occurring after 8 March 1999.

[4] Sub-ss (3B) and (3C) inserted by FA 1999 s 107(2) with effect in relation to tax charged after 8 March 1999.

[5] In sub-s (3B)(*a*),words substituted for words "or 79(3)" by F(No 2)A 2015 s 12(8)(*c*) with effect in relation to occasions on which tax would (ignoring the effect of the amendments made by F(No 2)A 2015 s 12) fall to be charged under IHTA 1984 s 64 on or after 18 November 2015.

[6] Sub-s (2A) inserted by F(No 2)A 2017 s 33, Sch 10 paras 2, 7 with effect in relation to times on or after 6 April 2017, subject to transitional provisions in Sch 10 paras 10, 11.

238 Effect of purchases

(1) Where property subject to an Inland Revenue charge, or an interest in such property, is disposed of to a purchaser, then if at the time of the disposition—

(*a*) in the case of land in England and Wales, the charge was not registered as a land charge or, in the case of registered land, was not protected by notice on the register, or

(*b*) in the case of land in Northern Ireland the title to which is registered under the Land Registration Act (Northern Ireland) 1970, the charge was not entered as a burden on the appropriate register maintained under that Act or was not protected by a caution or inhibition under that Act or, in the case of other land in Northern Ireland, the purchaser had no notice of the facts giving rise to the charge, or (*c*) in the case of personal property situated in the United Kingdom other than such property as is mentioned in paragraph (*a*) or (*b*) above, and of any property situated outside the United Kingdom, the purchaser had no notice of the facts giving rise to the charge, or

(*d*) in the case of any property, a certificate of discharge had been given by the Board under section 239 below and the purchaser had no notice of any fact invalidating the certificate,

the property or interest shall then cease to be subject to the charge but the property for the time being representing it shall be subject to it.

(2) Where property subject to an Inland Revenue charge, or an interest in such property, is disposed of to a purchaser in circumstances where it does not then cease to be subject to the charge, it shall cease to be subject to it at the end of the period of six years beginning with the later of—

(*a*) the date on which the tax became due, and

(*b*) the date on which a full and proper account of the property was first delivered to the Board in connection with the chargeable transfer concerned.

(3) In this section "the time of the disposition" means—

[(*a*) in relation to registered land—

(i) if the disposition is required to be completed by registration, the time of registration, and

(ii) otherwise, the time of completion,][1] and

(*b*) in relation to other property, the time of completion.

Commentary—*Simon's Taxes* **I11.604**.

HMRC Manuals—Inheritance Tax Manual IHTM30125 (liability in special cases: liability of purchaser).

IHTM30464 (limitation of liability by lapse of time: property in the hands of purchasers).

Definitions—"Inland Revenue charge", "purchaser", s 237.

Amendments—[1] Sub-s (3)(*a*) substituted by the Land Registration Act 2002 s 133, Sch 11 para 17 with effect from 13 October 2003 (by virtue of SI 2003/1725).

Certificates of discharge

239 Certificates of discharge

(1) Where application is made to the Board by a person liable for any tax on the value transferred by a chargeable transfer which is attributable to the value of property specified in the application, the Board, on being satisfied that the tax so attributable has been or will be paid, may give a certificate to that effect, and shall do so if the chargeable transfer is one made on death or the transferor has died.

(2) Where tax is or may be chargeable on the value transferred by a transfer of value and—

(*a*) application is made to the Board after the expiration of two years from the transfer (or, if the Board think fit to entertain the application, at an earlier time) by a person who is or might be liable for the whole or part of the tax, and

(*b*) the applicant delivers to the Board, if the transfer is one made on death, a full statement to the best of his knowledge and belief of all property included in the estate of the deceased immediately before his death and, in any other case, a full and proper account under this Part of this Act,

the Board may, as the case requires, determine the amount of the tax or determine that no tax is chargeable; and subject to the payment of any tax so determined to be chargeable the Board may give a certificate of their determination, and shall do so if the transfer of value is one made on death or the transferor has died.

[(2A) An application under subsection (1) or (2) above with respect to tax which is or may become chargeable on the value transferred by a potentially exempt transfer may not be made before the expiration of two years from the death of the transferor (except where the Board think fit to entertain the application at an earlier time after the death).][1]

(3) Subject to subsection (4) below,—

(*a*) a certificate under subsection (1) above shall discharge the property shown in it from the Inland Revenue charge on its acquisition by a purchaser, and

(*b*) a certificate under subsection (2) above shall discharge all persons from any further claim for the tax on the value transferred by the chargeable transfer concerned and extinguish any Inland Revenue charge for that tax.

(4) A certificate under this section shall not discharge any person from tax in case of fraud or failure to disclose material facts and shall not affect any further tax—

(*a*) that may afterwards be shown to be payable by virtue of section 93, 142, 143, 144 or 145 above,

[(*aa*) that may afterwards be shown to be payable by reason of too great an increase having been made under section 8A(3) above,][2] or

(*b*) that may be payable if any further property is afterwards shown to have been included in the estate of a deceased person immediately before his death;

but in so far as the certificate shows any tax to be attributable to the value of any property it shall remain valid in favour of a purchaser of that property without notice of any fact invalidating the certificate.

(5) References in this section to a transfer of value, or to the value transferred by a transfer of value, shall be construed as including references to an occasion on which tax is chargeable under Chapter III of Part III of this Act (apart from section 79) or to the amount on which tax is then chargeable.

Commentary—*Simon's Taxes* **I11.413, I11.414**.

HMRC Manuals—Inheritance Tax Manual IHTM40010–40134 (details regarding clearance certificates).

Inheritance Tax Manual IHTM40141–40147 (changes after the issue of a clearance certificate).

IHTM40151–40154 (non-statutory assurances and other types of certificate).

Definitions—"The Board", s 272; "Inland Revenue charge", "purchaser", s 237.

Cross references—See FA 1986 Sch 19 para 40 (where a death or other event occurs after 17 March 1986, sub-s (2A) above not to affect the tax chargeable on a transfer of value occurring before 18 March 1986).

Amendments—[1] Sub-s (2A) inserted by FA 1986 s 101(3) and Sch 19 para 35 with respect to transfers of value made after 17 March 1986.

[2] Sub-s (4)(*aa*) inserted by FA 2008 s 10, Sch 4 paras 1, 5; this amendment is treated as having come into force on 9 October 2007.

Adjustments

240 Underpayments

(1) Where too little tax has been paid in respect of a chargeable transfer the tax underpaid shall be payable with interest under section 233 above, whether or not the amount that has been paid was that stated as payable in a notice under section 221 above; but subject to section 239 above and to the following provisions of this section.

(2) Where tax attributable to the value of any property is paid in accordance with an account duly delivered to the Board under this Part of this Act and the payment is made and accepted in full satisfaction of the tax so attributable, no proceedings shall be brought for the recovery of any additional tax so attributable after the end of the period of [four][1] years beginning with the later of—

(*a*) the date on which the payment (or in the case of tax paid by instalments the last payment) was made and accepted, and

(*b*) the date on which the tax or the last instalment became due;

and at the end of that period any liability for the additional tax and any Inland Revenue charge for that tax shall be extinguished.

[(3) Subsection (2) has effect subject to subsections (4) [to (5A)][2].

(4) Proceedings in a case involving a loss of tax brought about carelessly by a person liable for the tax (or a person acting on behalf of such a person) may be brought at any time not more than 6 years after the later of the dates in subsection (2)(*a*) and (*b*).

(5) Proceedings in a case involving a loss of tax brought about deliberately by a person liable for the tax (or a person acting on behalf of such a person) may be brought at any time not more than 20 years after the later of [the dates in subsection (2)(*a*) and (*b*)][2].

[(5A) Proceedings in a case involving a loss of tax attributable to arrangements which were expected to give rise to a tax advantage in respect of which a person liable for the tax was under an obligation to make a report under section 253 of the Finance Act 2014 (duty to notify Commissioners of promoter reference number) but failed to do so, may be brought at any time not more than 20 years after the later of the dates in subsection (2)(*a*) and (*b*).][2]

(6) Subsection (7) applies to any case not falling within subsection (2) where too little tax has been paid in respect of a chargeable transfer, provided that the case does not involve a loss of tax brought about deliberately by a person liable for the tax (or a person acting on behalf of such a person).

(7) Where this subsection applies—

(*a*) no proceedings are to be brought for the recovery of the tax after the end of the period of 20 years beginning with the date on which the chargeable transfer was made, and

(*b*) at the end of that period any liability for the tax and any Inland Revenue charge for that tax is extinguished.

(8) In relation to cases of tax chargeable under Chapter 3 of Part 3 of this Act (apart from section 79), the references in subsections (4)[to (6)][2] to a person liable for the tax are to be treated as including references to a person who is the settlor in relation to the settlement.][1]

Commentary—*Simon's Taxes* **I11.410**.

HMRC Manuals—Inheritance Tax Manual IHTM14595 (late reported transfers).

Inheritance Tax Manual IHTM30462 (time limits for recovery of unpaid tax).

Cross references—SI 2010/867 art 6 (in a case under sub-s (2) where the chargeable transfer took place on or before 31 March 2011, and a loss of tax was brought about deliberately by any person (or a person acting on behalf of such a person), the period within which proceedings may be brought is the period of six years beginning when the deliberate conduct comes to the knowledge of HMRC or the period of 20 years provided in sub-s (5), whichever ends soonest).

Amendments—[1] In sub-s (2) words substituted for the words "six years", and new sub-ss (3)–(8) substituted for previous sub-s (3), by FA 2009 s 99, Sch 51 para 11 with effect from 1 April 2011 (by virtue of SI 2010/867 art 2(2)).

[2] In sub-s (3), words substituted for words "and (5)", in sub-s (5), words substituted for words "those dates", sub-s (5A) inserted, and in sub-s (8), words substituted for words ", (5) and (6)", by FA 2014 s 277(3) with effect from 17 July 2014.

[240A Underpayments: supplementary

(1) This section applies for the purposes of section 240.

(2) A loss of tax is brought about carelessly by a person if the person fails to take reasonable care to avoid bringing about that loss.

(3) Where—

(*a*) information is provided to Her Majesty's Revenue and Customs,

(*b*) the person who provided the information, or the person on whose behalf the information was provided, discovers some time later that the information was inaccurate, and

(*c*) that person fails to take reasonable steps to inform Her Majesty's Revenue and Customs,

any loss of tax brought about by the inaccuracy is to be treated as having been brought about carelessly by that person.

(4) References to a loss of tax brought about deliberately by a person include a loss of tax brought about as a result of a deliberate inaccuracy in a document given to Her Majesty's Revenue and Customs by or on behalf of that person.]

Commentary—*Simon's Taxes* **I11.410**.

[241 Overpayments

(1) If it is proved to the satisfaction of the Board that too much tax has been paid on the value transferred by a chargeable transfer or on so much of that value as is attributable to any property, the Board shall repay the excess unless the claim for repayment was made more than [four][2] years after the date on which the payment or last payment of the tax was made.

(2) References in this section to tax include references to interest on tax.][1]

Commentary—*Simon's Taxes* **I11.411**.

HMRC Manuals—Inheritance Tax Manual IHTM30402 (adjustment of tax paid: repayments).

Note—Where an amount paid by way of IHT or interest on IHT is repayable as a result of the insertion of IHTA 1984 s 12A, sub-s (1) applies as if the last date for making a claim for repayment of the amount were 5 April 2020 if that is later than what would otherwise be the last date for that purpose (FA 2016 s 94(6)).

Statement of Practice SP 6/95—Legal entitlement and administrative practices.

Amendments—[1] Section 241 inserted by FA 2009 s 99, Sch 51 para 12 with effect from 1 April 2011 (by virtue of SI 2010/867 art 2(2))

[2] In sub-s (1) words substituted for words "six years" by FA 2009 s 99, Sch 51 para 13 with effect from 1 April 2011 (by virtue of SI 2010/867 art 2(2)).

Recovery of tax

242 Recovery of tax

(1) The Board shall not take any legal proceedings for the recovery of any amount of tax or of interest on tax which is due from any person unless the amount has been agreed in writing between that person and the Board or has been determined and specified in a notice under section 221 above.

(2) Where an amount has been so determined and specified but an appeal to which this subsection applies is pending against the determination the Board shall not take any legal proceedings to recover the amount determined except such part of it as may be agreed in writing or determined and specified in a further notice under section 221 above to be a part not in dispute.

(3) Subsection (2) above applies to any appeal under section 222 above but not to any further appeal; and section 222 above shall have effect, in relation to a determination made in pursuance of subsection (2) above, as if [subsections (4) to (4B)][1] of that section were omitted.

[(4) Where a person has been given an accelerated payment notice under Chapter 3 of Part 4 of the Finance Act 2014 and that notice has not been withdrawn, nothing in this section prevents legal proceedings being taken for the recovery of (as the case may be)—

(*a*) the understated tax to which the payment specified in the notice under section 220(2)(*b*) of that Act relates, or

(*b*) the disputed tax specified in the notice under section 221(2)(*b*) of that Act.][2]

Commentary—*Simon's Taxes* **I11.409, I11.321**.

Amendments—[1] Words in sub-s (3) substituted by FA 1993 s 200(2) in relation to any appeal which is made on or after 27 July 1993, or which is made, but has not begun to be heard, before that day.

[2] Sub-s (4) inserted by FA 2014 s 224(2) with effect from 17 July 2014.

243 Scotland: recovery of tax in sheriff court

In Scotland, tax and interest on tax may, without prejudice to any other remedy, and if the amount of the tax and interest does not exceed the sum for the time being specified in section 35(1)(*a*) of the Sheriff Courts (Scotland) Act 1971 be sued for and recovered in the sheriff court.

Commentary—*Simon's Taxes* **I11.321**.

244 Right to address court

An officer of the Board who is authorised by the Board to do so may address the court in any proceedings in a . . . [1] sheriff court for the recovery of tax or interest on tax.

Commentary—*Simon's Taxes* **I11.321**.

Definitions—"The Board", s 272.

Amendments—[1] Words "county court or" repealed by FA 2008 s 137(4) with effect from 21 July 2008. This amendment does not affect proceedings commenced or brought in the name of a collector or authorised officer before 21 July 2008 (FA 2008 s 137(7)).

Penalties

[245 Failure to deliver accounts][1]

[(1) This section applies where a person ("the taxpayer") fails to deliver an account under section 216 or 217 above.

(2) The taxpayer shall be liable—

(*a*) to a penalty [of][2] £100; and

(*b*) to a further penalty not exceeding £60 for every day after the day on which the failure has been declared by a court or the [tribunal][4] and before the day on which the account is delivered.

(3) If—

(*a*) proceedings in which the failure could be declared are not commenced before the end of the relevant period, and

(*b*) the taxpayer has not delivered the account by the end of that period,

he shall be liable to a further penalty [of][2] £100.

(4) In subsection (3) above "the relevant period" means the period of six months beginning immediately after the end of the period given by section 216(6) or (7) or section 217 above (whichever is applicable).

[(4A) Without prejudice to any penalties under subsections (2) and (3) above, if—

(*a*) the failure by the taxpayer to deliver the account continues after the anniversary of the end of the period given by section 216(6) or (7) (whichever is applicable), and

(*b*) there would have been a liability to tax shown in the account,

the taxpayer shall be liable to a penalty of an amount not exceeding £3,000.][3]

(5) If the taxpayer proves that his liability to tax does not exceed a particular amount, the penalty under subsection (2)(*a*) above, together with any penalty under subsection (3) above, shall not exceed that amount.

(6) A person shall not be liable to a penalty under subsection (2)(*b*) above if he delivers the account required by section 216 or 217 before proceedings in which the failure could be declared are commenced.

(7) A person who has a reasonable excuse for failing to deliver an account shall not be liable by reason of that failure to a penalty under this section, unless he fails to deliver the account without unreasonable delay after the excuse has ceased.][1]

Commentary—*Simon's Taxes* **I11.702.**

HMRC Manuals—Inheritance Tax Manual IHTM36022–36023 (accounts subject to a penalty and penalties chargeable). IHTM36061–36071 (reasonable excuse).

Cross-references—For penalties provisions generally, see FA 2007 Sch 24 (errors in returns), FA 2008 Sch 41 (failure to notify), FA 2009 Sch 55 (failure to make returns), Sch 56 (failure to pay tax).

Modifications—FA 2004 s 295 (6)(*b*) (modification of this section where there is a failure to deliver an account under IHTA 1984 s 216 where the period under IHTA 1984 ss 216(6) or (7) (whichever is applicable) expires on or before 22 July 2004.

Amendments—[1] This section substituted by FA 1999 s 108(1) with effect from 27 July 1999 subject to FA 1999 s 108(3).

[2] In sub-ss (2)(*a*), (3), words substituted for the words "not exceeding" by FA 2004 s 295 (2)(*a*). This amendment has effect in relation to a failure by any person to deliver an account under IHTA 1984 s 216 or 217, where the period under IHTA 1984 s 216(6) or (7) or 217 (whichever is applicable) within which the person is required to deliver the account, expires after six months from Royal Assent. Royal Assent was given on 22 July 2004.

[3] Sub-s (4A) inserted by FA 2004 s 295(2)(*b*) with effect in relation to a failure by any person to deliver an account under IHTA 1984 s 216 where the period under IHTA 1984 ss 216(6) or (7) (whichever is applicable), within which the person is required to deliver the account, expires after Royal Assent. In relation to such a failure to deliver such an account where that period expires on or before Royal Assent, see FA 2004 s 289(6)(*b*). Royal Assent was given on 22 July 2004.

[4] In sub-s (2)(*b*), word substituted for words "Special Commissioners", by the Transfer of Tribunal Functions and Revenue and Customs Appeals Order, SI 2009/56 art 3, Sch 1 paras 108, 120 with effect from 1 April 2009.

[245A Failure to provide information etc][1]

[(1) A person who fails to make a return under section 218 above shall be liable—

(*a*) to a penalty not exceeding £300; and

(*b*) to a further penalty not exceeding £60 for every day after the day on which the failure has been declared by a court or the [tribunal][5] and before the day on which the return is made.

[(1A) A person who fails to comply with the requirements of section 218A above shall be liable—

(*a*) to a penalty not exceeding £100; and

(*b*) to a further penalty not exceeding £60 for every day after the day on which the failure has been declared by a court or the [tribunal][5] and before the day on which the requirements are complied with.][2]

[(1B) Without prejudice to any penalties under subsection (1A) above, if a person continues to fail to comply with the requirements of section 218A after the anniversary of the end of the period of six months referred to in section 218A(1), he shall be liable to a penalty of an amount not exceeding £3,000.][3]

(2) A person who fails to comply with a notice under section 219 above shall be liable—

(a) to a penalty not exceeding £300; and

(b) to a further penalty not exceeding £60 for every day after the day on which the failure has been declared by a court or the [tribunal][5] and before the day on which the notice is complied with.[4]

(3) A person who fails to comply with a notice under section 219A(1) or (4) above shall be liable—

(a) to a penalty not exceeding £50; and

(b) to a further penalty not exceeding £30 for every day after the day on which the failure has been declared by a court or the [tribunal][5] and before the day on which the notice is complied with.[2]

(4) A person shall not be liable to a penalty under subsection (1)(*b*), [or (1A)(b)][2] above if—

(*a*) he makes the return required by section 218 above, [or][2]

[(*aa*) he complies with the requirements of section 218A above,][2]

(b) he complies with the notice under section 219 above, or[2]

(c) he complies with the notice under section 219A(1) or (4) above,[2]

before proceedings in which the failure could be declared are commenced.

(5) A person who has a reasonable excuse for failing to make a return [or to comply with the requirements of section 218A][2] shall not be liable by reason of that failure to a penalty under this section, unless he fails to make the return [or to comply with those requirements][2] without unreasonable delay after the excuse has ceased.][1]

Commentary—*Simon's Taxes* **I11.702**.

HMRC Manuals—Inheritance Tax Manual IHTM36092 (failure to deliver an instrument of variation: penalties chargeable).

IHTM36091 (failure to deliver an instrument of variation where additional tax payable: when can you seek a penalty).

Cross-references—For penalties provisions generally, see FA 2007 Sch 24 (errors in returns), FA 2008 Sch 41 (failure to notify), FA 2009 Sch 55 (failure to make returns), Sch 56 (failure to pay tax).

Modifications—FA 2004 s 295(7)(*b*) (modification of this section where there is a failure to comply with the requirements of IHTA 1984 s 218A where the period where the period of six months referred to in IHTA 1984 s 218A(1) expires on or before 22 July 2004.

Amendments—[1] This section inserted by FA 1999 s 108(1) with effect from 27 July 1999 subject to FA 1999 s 108(3).

[2] Sub-s (1A) inserted, and in sub-s (4) words inserted, and para (*aa*) inserted, by FA 2002 s 120(3), (4) with effect for instruments made after 31 July 2002.

[3] Sub-s (1B) inserted by FA 2004 s 295(3)(*a*) with effect in relation to a failure to comply with the requirements of IHTA 1984 s 218A where the period of six months referred to in IHTA 1984 s 218A(1) expires after 22 July 2004.

[4] Sub-ss (2), (3) repealed, in sub-s (4), words substituted for words ", (1A)(*b*), (2)(*b*) or (3)(*b*)", at end of para (*a*) word "or" inserted, and paras (*b*), (*c*) repealed, and in sub-s (5), words substituted for words ", to comply with the requirements of section 218A or to comply with a notice" and " to comply with the requirements of section 218A or to comply with the notice", by the Finance Act 2009, Section 96 and Schedule 48 (Appointed Day, Savings and Consequential Amendments) Order, SI 2009/3054 art 3, Schedule para 2(1), (4) with effect from 1 April 2010. Note that, in relation to a notice given under s 219 or 219A before 1 April 2010, s 219B continues to have effect on and after 1 April 2010 despite this repeal, and s 245A applies on and after 1 April 2010 disregarding the amendments made by the Schedule to SI 2009/3054.

[5] Word substituted, in each place, for words "Special Commissioners", by the Transfer of Tribunal Functions and Revenue and Customs Appeals Order, SI 2009/56 art 3, Sch 1 paras 108, 121 with effect from 1 April 2009.

246 Failure to appear before Special Commissioners, etc

. . . [1]

Amendments—[1] This section repealed by the General and Special Commissioners (Amendment of Enactments) Regulations SI 1994/1813 reg 2, Sch 1 paras 1, 20, Sch 2 Pt I with effect from 1 September 1994.

247 Provision of incorrect information

(1), (2) . . . [2]

(3) Any person not liable for tax on the value transferred by a chargeable transfer who fraudulently or negligently furnishes or produces to the Board any incorrect information or document in connection with the transfer shall be liable [to a penalty not exceeding £3,000][1].

(4) . . . [3].

Commentary—*Simon's Taxes* **I11.703**.

HMRC Manuals—Inheritance Tax Manual IHTM36101 (when is an account, information or document incorrect?).

IHTM36102 (types of penalty).

IHTM36103 (section 247(1) penalty).

IHTM36104 (section 247(3) penalty).

IHTM36105 (section 247(4) penalty).

IHTM36153 and 36154 (undervaluations).

IHTM36302 (who must you show to be negligent?).

Simon's Tax Cases—*Robertson v IRC* [2002] STC (SCD) 182.

Cross references—FA 2004 s 313(4) (disapplication of this section in respect of disclosure of tax avoidance scheme information; but see TMA 1970 s 98C).

For penalties provisions generally, see FA 2007 Sch 24 (errors in returns), FA 2008 Sch 41 (failure to notify), FA 2009 Sch 55 (failure to make returns), Sch 56 (failure to pay tax).

Amendments—[1] In sub-s (1), (3) words substituted by FA 2004 s 295(4) with effect in relation to incorrect accounts, information or documents delivered, furnished or produced after 22 July 2004.

[2] Sub-ss (1), (2) repealed by FA 2008 s 122, Sch 40 para 21(*c*) with effect from 1 April 2009 (by virtue of SI 2009/571 art 2).

[3] Sub-s (4) repealed by FA 2012 s 223, Sch 38 para 52 with effect from 1 April 2013 (by virtue of SI 2013/279 art 2).

248 Failure to remedy errors

(1) If after any . . . [1] information or document has been . . . [1] furnished or produced by any person without fraud or negligence it comes to his notice that it was incorrect in any material respect it shall be treated for the purposes of section 247 above as having been negligently . . . [1] furnished or produced unless the error is remedied without unreasonable delay.

(2) If after any account, information or document has been delivered, furnished or produced by any person in pursuance of this Part of this Act it comes to the notice of any other person that it contains an error whereby tax for which that other person is liable has been or might be underpaid, that other person shall inform the Board of the error; and if he fails to do so without unreasonable delay he shall be liable to the penalty to which he would be liable . . . [1] if the account, information or document had been delivered, furnished or produced by him and the case were one of negligence.

Commentary—*Simon's Taxes* **I11.703**.

HMRC Manuals—IHTM36106 (section 248(1) penalty).

IHTM36107 (section 248(2) penalty).

Cross-references—For penalties provisions generally, see FA 2007 Sch 24 (errors in returns), FA 2008 Sch 41 (failure to notify), FA 2009 Sch 55 (failure to make returns), Sch 56 (failure to pay tax).

Amendments—[1] In sub-s (1), words "account," and "delivered," (in both places), and in sub-s (2), words "under section 247 above", repealed by FA 2008 s 122, Sch 40 para 21(*c*) with effect from 1 April 2009 (by virtue of SI 2009/571 art 2).

249 Recovery of penalties

(1) All proceedings for the recovery of penalties under this Part of this Act shall be commenced by the Board or, in Scotland, by the Board or the Lord Advocate.

(2) Any such proceedings may be commenced either before the [First-tier Tribunal][1] or in the High Court or the Court of Session and shall, if brought in the High Court, be deemed to be civil proceedings by the Crown within the meaning of Part II of the Crown Proceedings Act 1947 or, as the case may be, that Part as for the time being in force in Northern Ireland.

[(3) Where any proceedings are brought before the First-tier Tribunal, in addition to any right of appeal on a point of law under section 11(2) of the TCEA 2007, the person liable to the penalty may appeal to the Upper Tribunal against the amount of a penalty which has been determined under this Part, but not against any decision which falls under section 11(5)(*d*) and (*e*) of the TCEA 2007 and was made in connection with the determination of the amount of the penalty.

(3A) Section 11(3) and (4) of the TCEA 2007 applies to the right of appeal under subsection (3) as it applies to the right of appeal under section 11(2) of the TCEA 2007.

(3B) On an appeal under this section the Upper Tribunal has the same powers as are conferred on the First-tier Tribunal by virtue of this section.][1]

[(4) The person liable to the penalty shall be a party to the proceedings.][1]

(5) References in this section to the Court of Session are references to that Court as the Court of Exchequer in Scotland.

Note—The functions of the Lord Advocate are hereby transferred to the Advocate General for Scotland by virtue of the Transfer of Functions (Lord Advocate and Advocate General for Scotland) Order, SI 1999/679.

Commentary—*Simon's Taxes* **I11.705**.

Cross-references—For penalties provisions generally, see FA 2007 Sch 24 (errors in returns), FA 2008 Sch 41 (failure to notify), FA 2009 Sch 55 (failure to make returns), Sch 56 (failure to pay tax).

Amendments—[1] In sub-s (2), words substituted for words "Special Commissioners", sub-ss (3)–(3B) substituted for previous sub-s (3), and sub-s (4) substituted, by the Transfer of Tribunal Functions and Revenue and Customs Appeals Order, SI 2009/56 art 3, Sch 1 paras 108, 122 with effect from 1 April 2009.

250 Time limit for recovery

(1) No proceedings for the recovery of a penalty under this Part of this Act shall be brought after the end of the period of three years beginning with the date on which the amount of the tax properly payable in respect of the chargeable transfer concerned was notified by the Board to the person or one of the persons liable for the tax or any part of it.

(2) . . . [1]

Commentary—*Simon's Taxes* **I11.705**.

HMRC Manuals—Inheritance Tax Manual IHTM36108 (time limit for seeking penalties).

Definitions—"Personal representatives", s 272.

Cross-references—For penalties provisions generally, see FA 2007 Sch 24 (errors in returns), FA 2008 Sch 41 (failure to notify), FA 2009 Sch 55 (failure to make returns), Sch 56 (failure to pay tax).

Amendments—[1] Sub-s (2) repealed by FA 2008 s 122, Sch 40 para 21(*c*) with effect from 1 April 2009 (by virtue of SI 2009/571 art 2).

251 Appeals against summary determination of penalties

Amendments—This section repealed by the Transfer of Tribunal Functions and Revenue and Customs Appeals Order, SI 2009/56 art 3, Sch 1 paras 108, 123 with effect from 1 April 2009.

252 Effect of award by [the tribunal][1]

Any penalty awarded by the [tribunal][1] shall be recoverable by the Board as a debt due to the Crown.

Commentary—*Simon's Taxes* **I11.705**.

Cross-references—For penalties provisions generally, see FA 2007 Sch 24 (errors in returns), FA 2008 Sch 41 (failure to notify), FA 2009 Sch 55 (failure to make returns), Sch 56 (failure to pay tax).

Amendments—[1] Words substituted for words "Special Commissioners" in both places, by the Transfer of Tribunal Functions and Revenue and Customs Appeals Order, SI 2009/56 art 3, Sch 1 paras 108, 124 with effect from 1 April 2009.

253 Mitigation of penalties

The Board may in their discretion mitigate any penalty, or stay or compound any proceedings for recovery of any penalty, and may also, after judgment, further mitigate or entirely remit the penalty.

Commentary—*Simon's Taxes* **I11.707**.

HMRC Manuals—Inheritance Tax Manual IHTM36171 (calculating the penalty: board's policy).

Cross-references—For penalties provisions generally, see FA 2007 Sch 24 (errors in returns), FA 2008 Sch 41 (failure to notify), FA 2009 Sch 55 (failure to make returns), Sch 56 (failure to pay tax).

Miscellaneous

254 Evidence

(1) For the purposes of the preceding provisions of this Part of this Act, a notice under section 221 above specifying any determination which can no longer be varied or quashed on appeal shall be sufficient evidence of the matters determined.

(2) . . . [1]

Commentary—*Simon's Taxes* **I11.706**.

Amendments—[1] Sub-s (2) repealed by FA 2008 s 138, Sch 44 para 3 with effect from 21 July 2008.

255 Determination of questions on previous view of law

Where any payment has been made and accepted in satisfaction of any liability for tax and on a view of the law then generally received or adopted in practice, any question whether too little or too much has been paid or what was the right amount of tax payable shall be determined on the same view, notwithstanding that it appears from a subsequent legal decision or otherwise that the view was or may have been wrong.

Commentary—*Simon's Taxes* **I11.412**.

HMRC Manuals—Inheritance Tax Manual IHTM30451–30457 (determination of questions on previous view of the law).

256 Regulations about accounts, etc

(1) The Board may make regulations—

(*a*) dispensing with the delivery of accounts under section 216 above in such cases as may be specified in [or determined under][1] the regulations;

[(*aa*) requiring persons who by virtue of regulations under paragraph (*a*) above are not required to deliver accounts under section 216 above to produce to the Board, in such manner as may be specified in or determined under the regulations, such information or documents as may be so specified or determined;][1]

(*b*) discharging, subject to such restrictions as may be so specified [or determined][1], property from an Inland Revenue charge and persons from further claims for tax in cases other than those mentioned in section 239 above;

(*c*) . . . [1]

(*d*) modifying section 264(8) below in cases where the delivery of an account has been dispensed with under the regulations.

[(1A) Regulations under subsection (1)(*aa*) may in particular—

(*a*) provide that information or documents must be produced to the Board by producing it or them to—

(i) a probate registry in England and Wales;

(ii) the sheriff in Scotland;

(iii) the Probate and Matrimonial Office in Northern Ireland;

(*b*) provide that information or documents produced as specified in paragraph (*a*) is or are to be treated for any or all purposes of this Act as produced to the Board;

(*c*) provide for the further transmission to the Board of information or documents produced as specified in paragraph (*a*).][1]

(2) . . . [1]

(3) Regulations under this section may contain such supplementary or incidental provisions as the Board think fit [and may make different provision for different cases][1].

[(3A) Regulations under this section may only be made—

(*a*) in relation to England and Wales, after consulting the Lord Chancellor;

(*b*) in relation to Scotland, after consulting the Scottish Ministers;

(*c*) in relation to Northern Ireland, after consulting the Lord Chief Justice of Northern Ireland.

(3B) The Lord Chief Justice of Northern Ireland may nominate any of the following to exercise his functions under subsection (3A)—

(*a*) the holder of one of the offices listed in Schedule 1 to the Justice (Northern Ireland) Act 2002;

(*b*) a Lord Justice of Appeal (as defined in section 88 of that Act).][2]

(4) The power to make regulations under this section shall be exercisable by statutory instrument, which shall be subject to annulment in pursuance of a resolution of the House of Commons.

Commentary—*Simon's Taxes* **I9.201, I11.212A**.

Cross-references—See the Finance Act 2008, Schedule 40 (Appointed Day, Transitional Provisions and Consequential Amendments) Order, SI 2009/571 arts 2, 3 (application of the penalties regime in FA 2007 Sch 4 in relation to relevant documents produced under regulations under this section).

F(No 2)A 2017 Sch 18 para 8 (application of the penalties regime in F(No 2)A 2017 Sch 18 (failure to correct certain offshore tax non-compliance) in relation to relevant documents produced under regulations under this section).

Regulations—Inheritance Tax (Delivery of Accounts) (Excepted Estates) Regulations, SI 2004/2543.

Inheritance Tax (Delivery of Accounts) (Excepted Transfers and Excepted Terminations) Regulations, SI 2008/605.

Inheritance Tax (Delivery of Accounts) (Excepted Settlements) Regulations, SI 2008/606.

Inheritance Tax (Delivery of Accounts) (Excepted Estates) (Amendment) Regulations, SI 2014/488.

Amendments—[1] In sub-s (1), words in paras (*a*), (*b*) inserted, para (*aa*) inserted, and para (*c*) repealed; sub-s (1A) inserted; sub-s (2) repealed; words in sub-s (3) inserted; by FA 2004 ss 293, 326, Sch 42 Pt 4(1) with effect from 22 July 2004.

[2] Sub-ss (3A), (3B) substituted for sub-s (3A) by the Constitutional Reform Act 2005 s 15, Sch 4 paras 175, 176 with effect from 3 April 2006 (SI 2006/1014, art 2(*a*), Sch 1 para 11).

257 Form etc of accounts

(1) All accounts and other documents required for the purposes of this Act shall be in such form and shall contain such particulars as may be prescribed by the Board.

(2) All accounts to be delivered to the Board under this Act shall be supported by such books, papers and other documents, and verified (whether on oath or otherwise) in such manner, as the Board may require.

(3) For the purposes of this Act, an account delivered to a probate registry pursuant to arrangements made between the President of the Family Division and the Board or delivered to the Probate and Matrimonial Office in Northern Ireland pursuant to arrangements made between the [Lord Chief Justice of Northern Ireland][1] and the Board shall be treated as an account delivered to the Board.

[(4) The Lord Chief Justice of Northern Ireland may nominate any of the following to exercise his functions under subsection (3)—

(*a*) the holder of one of the offices listed in Schedule 1 to the Justice (Northern Ireland) Act 2002;

(*b*) a Lord Justice of Appeal (as defined in section 88 of that Act).][1]

Commentary—*Simon's Taxes* **I11.201**.

Statements of Practice E15—Close companies—group transfers.

SP 2/93—Computer-produced facsimiles of accounts and forms: criteria for acceptance by the Board.

Amendments—[1] Words in sub-s (3) substituted, and sub-s (4) inserted, by the Constitutional Reform Act 2005 s 15, Sch 4 paras 175, 177 with effect from 3 April 2006 (SI 2006/1014, art 2(*a*), Sch 1 para 11).

258 Service of documents

A notice or other document which is to be served on a person under this Act may be delivered to him or left at his usual or last known place of residence or served by post, addressed to him at his usual or last known place of residence or his place of business or employment.

Commentary—*Simon's Taxes* **I11.371**.

259 Inspection of records

Section 16 of the Stamp Act 1891, section 56 of the Finance Act 1946 and section 27 of the Finance (No 2) Act (Northern Ireland) 1946 (inspection of public records and records of unit trusts) shall apply in relation to capital transfer tax as they apply in relation to stamp duties.

Commentary—*Simon's Taxes* **I11.233**.

Note—Stamp Act 1891, s 16 and FA 1946 s 56 are reproduced under Stamp Duties legislation, *post*.

Cross references—See FA 1986 s 100(1), (2) (with effect from 25 July 1986 CTT to be known as inheritance tax; accordingly the reference to CTT in this section to be read as a reference to inheritance tax with effect from that date);

FA 1990 s 93(9) (the application of FA 1946 s 56 by this section not affected notwithstanding its repeal by FA 1990).

260 Inland Revenue Regulation Act 1890

Sections 21, 22 and 35 of the Inland Revenue Regulation Act 1890 (proceedings for fines, etc) shall not apply in relation to capital transfer tax.

Cross references—See FA 1986 s 100(1), (2) (with effect from 25 July 1986 CTT to be known as inheritance tax; accordingly the reference to CTT in this section to be read as a reference to inheritance tax with effect from that date).

261 Scotland: inventories

In the application of this Part of this Act to Scotland, references to an account required to be delivered to the Board by the personal representatives of a deceased person, however expressed, shall be construed as references to such an inventory or additional inventory as is mentioned in section 38 of the Probate and Legacy Duties Act 1808 which has been duly exhibited as required by that section.

Commentary—*Simon's Taxes* **I11.201**.

PART IX
MISCELLANEOUS AND SUPPLEMENTARY

Miscellaneous

262 Tax chargeable in certain cases of future payments, etc

(1) Where a disposition made for a consideration in money or money's worth is a transfer of value and any payments made or assets transferred by the transferor in pursuance of the disposition are made or transferred more than one year after the disposition is made, tax (if any) shall be charged as if—

(*a*) any payment made or asset transferred in pursuance of the disposition were made or transferred in pursuance of a separate disposition made, without consideration, at the time the payment is made or the asset is transferred, and

(*b*) the amount of the payment made or the value of the asset transferred in pursuance of each of those separate dispositions were the chargeable portion of the payment or asset.

(2) For the purposes of this section the chargeable portion of any payment made or any asset transferred at any time shall be such portion of its value at that time as is found by applying to it the fraction of which—

(*a*) the numerator is the value actually transferred by the disposition first mentioned in subsection (1) above (calculated as if no tax were payable on it), and

(*b*) the denominator is the value, at the time of that disposition, of the aggregate of the payments made or to be made and assets transferred or to be transferred by the transferor in pursuance of it.

Commentary—*Simon's Taxes* I3.256.

HMRC Manuals—Inheritance Tax Manual IHTM14871–14874 (future payments).

IHTM28120 (future payments incurred under this section).

Definitions—"Disposition", s 272.

Cross reference—See IHTA 1984 s 175 (computation of liability to make future payments in determining value of deceased's estate).

263 Annuity purchased in conjunction with life policy

(1) Where—

(*a*) a policy of life insurance is issued in respect of an insurance made after 26th March 1974 or is after that date varied or substituted for an earlier policy, and

(*b*) at the time the insurance is made or at any earlier or later date an annuity on the life of the insured is purchased, and

(*c*) the benefit of the policy is vested in a person other than the person who purchased the annuity,

then, unless it is shown that the purchase of the annuity and the making of the insurance (or, as the case may be, the substitution or variation) were not associated operations, the person who purchased the annuity shall be treated as having made a transfer of value by a disposition made at the time the benefit of the policy became so vested (to the exclusion of any transfer of value which, apart from this section, he might have made as a result of the vesting, or of the purchase and the vesting being associated operations).

(2) The value transferred by that transfer of value shall be equal to whichever of the following is less, namely,—

(*a*) the aggregate of—

(i) the value of the consideration given for the annuity, and

(ii) any premium paid or other consideration given under the policy on or before the transfer; and

(*b*) the value of the greatest benefit capable of being conferred at any time by the policy, calculated as if that time were the date of the transfer.

(3) The preceding provisions of this section shall apply, with the necessary modifications, where a contract for an annuity payable on a person's death is after 26th March 1974 made or varied or substituted for or replaced by such a contract or a policy of life insurance as they apply where a policy of life insurance is issued, varied or substituted as mentioned in subsection (1) above.

Commentary—*Simon's Taxes* I3.118, I3.257.

HMRC Manuals—Inheritance Tax Manual IHTM20371–20377 (life policy linked with an annuity).

IHTM04065 (lifetime transfers: purchase of a policy linked with an annuity).

Statement of Practice E4—Associated operations.

Simon's Tax Cases—*Smith and others v R&C Comrs* [2008] STC 1649.

Definitions—"Associated operations", s 268.

264 Transfers reported late

(1) This section has effect where a person has made a transfer of value ("the earlier transfer") which—

(*a*) is not notified to the Board in an account under section 216 above or by information furnished under section 219 above before the expiration of the period specified in section 216 for the delivery of accounts, and

(*b*) is not discovered until after payment has been accepted by the Board in full satisfaction of the tax on the value transferred by another transfer of value ("the later transfer") made by him on or after the day on which he made the earlier transfer.

(2) Where the earlier transfer is made in the period of ten years ending with the date of the later transfer there shall be charged on the value transferred by the earlier transfer, in addition to any tax chargeable on it apart from this section, an amount of tax equal to the difference, if any, between—

(*a*) the tax which, having regard to the earlier transfer, was properly chargeable on the value transferred by the later transfer, and

(*b*) the payment accepted by the Board in full satisfaction of the tax chargeable on that value;

and any such difference shall not be chargeable on the value transferred by the later transfer.

(3) Where in the period mentioned in subsection (2) above there have been two or more earlier transfers the reference in paragraph (*a*) of that subsection to the earlier transfer shall be construed as a reference to both or all of those transfers, but the amount of tax chargeable under that subsection in respect of each of them shall, subject to subsection (4) below, be reduced in the proportion which the value transferred by it bears to the aggregate of the values transferred by it and the other or others.

(4) Where the earlier transfers mentioned in subsection (3) above include a settled transfer, that is to say, a transfer in the case of which an amount in full satisfaction of the tax chargeable in respect of it under subsection (2) above has been paid to and accepted by the Board before the discovery of one or more of the other earlier transfers,—

(*a*) no further tax shall be chargeable under subsection (2) above in respect of the settled transfer in consequence of regard being had under paragraph (*a*) of that subsection to the subsequently discovered transfer or transfers;

(*b*) the amount so paid and accepted shall reduce the amount chargeable under subsection (2) above in respect of the subsequently discovered transfer or transfers; and

(*c*) if there are two or more subsequently discovered transfers, the value transferred by the settled transfer shall be disregarded in calculating under subsection (3) above the reduction in the amount of tax chargeable in respect of each of them.

(5) Where the later transfer referred to in subsection (2) above is itself an earlier transfer in relation to another later transfer the references in paragraphs (*a*) and (*b*) of that subsection to tax chargeable on the value transferred by it are references to tax so chargeable apart from this section.

(6) Subsection (2) above shall not increase the amount in respect of which interest is payable under section 233 above in relation to the earlier transfer in respect of any period falling before the expiration of six months from the date on which it was discovered.

(7) Where, apart from this subsection, the earlier transfer would be wholly or partly exempt by reason of some or all of the value transferred by it falling within a limit applicable to an exemption, then, if tax has been accepted as mentioned in subsection (1)(*b*) above on the basis that the later transfer is partly exempt by reason of part of the value thereby transferred falling within that limit—

(*a*) tax shall not be chargeable on that part of the value transferred by the later transfer, but

(*b*) a corresponding part of the value transferred by the earlier transfer shall be treated as falling outside that limit.

(8) Subsection (1)(*b*) above shall apply to a transfer in respect of which no tax is chargeable because the rate of tax applicable under section 7 above is nil as if payment had been accepted when the transfer was notified in an account under section 216 above, and subsection (2)(*b*) above shall apply in relation to any such transfer as if the amount of the payment were nil.

(9) For the purposes of this section a transfer is discovered—

(*a*) if it is notified under the provisions mentioned in subsection (1)(*a*) above after the expiration of the period there mentioned, on the date on which it is so notified;

(*b*) in any other case, on the date on which the Board give notice of a determination in respect of the transfer under section 221 above.

Commentary—*Simon's Taxes* **I3.551–I3.554, I4.171**.

HMRC Manuals—Inheritance Tax Manual IHTM14595 (the charge to tax: the charge on late reported transfers).

Cross-reference—The Inheritance Tax (Delivery of Accounts) (Excepted Transfers and Excepted Terminations) Regulations, SI 2008/605 reg 8 (where no account of an excepted transfer is required by HMRC, an account of that transfer shall, for the purposes of this section, be treated as having been delivered 12 months after the end of the month in which that transfer is made).

265 Chargeable transfers affecting more than one property

Where the value transferred by a chargeable transfer is determined by reference to the values of more than one property the tax chargeable on the value transferred shall be attributed to the respective values in the proportions which they bear to their aggregate, but subject to [section 54B(3) above and to][1] any provision reducing the amount of tax attributable to the value of any particular property.

Commentary—*Simon's Taxes* **I3.524**.

Amendments—[1] Words inserted by F(No 2)A 1987 Sch 7 para 5 in relation to transfers of value made after 16 March 1987.

266 More than one chargeable transfer on one day

(1) Where the value transferred by more than one chargeable transfer made by the same person on the same day depends on the order in which the transfers are made, they shall be treated as made in the order which results in the lowest value chargeable.

(2) Subject to subsection (1) above, the rate at which the tax is charged on the values transferred by two or more chargeable transfers made by the same person on the same day shall be the effective rate at which tax would have been charged if those transfers had been a single chargeable transfer of the same total value.

(3) The chargeable transfers referred to in subsections (1) and (2) above do not include a transfer made on the death of the transferor.

(4) Chargeable transfers under Chapter III of Part III of this Act shall if they relate to the same settlement be treated for the purposes of subsections (1) and (2) above as made by the same person.

Commentary—*Simon's Taxes* **I3.525, I3.259.**

HMRC Manuals—Inheritance Tax Manual IHTM14591 (simultaneous and same day transfers).

267 Persons treated as domiciled in United Kingdom

(1) A person not domiciled in the United Kingdom at any time (in this section referred to as "the relevant time") shall be treated for the purposes of this Act as domiciled in the United Kingdom (and not elsewhere) at the relevant time if—

(*a*) he was domiciled in the United Kingdom within the three years immediately preceding the relevant time, . . .[3]

[(*aa*) he is a formerly domiciled resident for the tax year in which the relevant time falls ("the relevant tax year"), or][3]

[(*b*) he was resident in the United Kingdom—

(i) for at least fifteen of the twenty tax years immediately preceding the relevant tax year, and

(ii) for at least one of the four tax years ending with the relevant tax year.][3]

(2) Subsection (1) above shall not apply for the purposes of section 6(2) or (3) or 48(4) above and shall not affect the interpretation of any such provision as is mentioned in section 158(6) above.

(3) Paragraph (a) of subsection (1) above shall not apply in relation to a person who (apart from this section) has not been domiciled in the United Kingdom at any time since 9th December 1974, and paragraph (*b*) of that subsection shall not apply in relation to a person who has not been resident there at any time since that date; and that subsection shall be disregarded—

(a) in determining whether settled property which became comprised in the settlement on or before that date is excluded property,

(b) in determining the settlor's domicile for the purposes of section 65(8) above in relation to settled property which became comprised in the settlement on or before that date, and

(c) in determining for the purpose of section 65(8) above whether the condition in section 82(3) above is satisfied in relation to such settled property.[3]

(4) For the purposes of this section the question whether a person was resident in the United Kingdom [for any tax year][3] shall be determined as for the purposes of income tax, . . .[1].

[(5) In determining for the purposes of this section whether a person is, or at any time was, domiciled in the United Kingdom, sections 267ZA and 267ZB are to be ignored.][2]

Commentary—*Simon's Taxes* **I9.206, I9.332.**

HMRC Manuals—Inheritance Tax Manual IHTM13024 (deemed domicile).

IHTM10685 (claim for non UK domicile).

Statement of Practice E9—Excluded property.

Definitions—"Excluded property", s 272.

Amendments—[1] Words in sub-s (4) repealed by FA 1993 s 208(3), (5) and Sch 23 Pt V with effect for 1993–94 and subsequent years of assessment.

[2] Sub-s (5) inserted by FA 2013 s 177(1), (2) with effect from 17 July 2013.

[3] In sub-s (1)(*a*), word "or" repealed; sub-s (1)(*aa*) inserted; sub-s (1)(*b*) substituted; sub-s (3) repealed; and in sub-s (4), words substituted for words "in any year of assessment", by F(No 2)A 2017 s 30(1)–(3), with effect in relation to times after 5 April 2017, subject to transitional provisions in F(No 2)A 2017 s 30(10)–(12). Sub-s (1)(*b*) previously read as follows—

"(*b*) he was resident in the United Kingdom in not less than seventeen of the twenty years of assessment ending with the year of assessment in which the relevant time falls.".

[267ZA Election to be treated as domiciled in United Kingdom

(1) A person may, if condition A or B is met, elect to be treated for the purposes of this Act as domiciled in the United Kingdom (and not elsewhere).

(2) A person's personal representatives may, if condition B is met, elect for the person to be treated for the purposes of this Act as domiciled in the United Kingdom (and not elsewhere).

(3) Condition A is that, at any time on or after 6 April 2013 and during the period of 7 years ending with the date on which the election is made, the person had a spouse or civil partner who was domiciled in the United Kingdom.

(4) Condition B is that a person ("the deceased") dies and, at any time on or after 6 April 2013 and within the period of 7 years ending with the date of death, the deceased was—

(*a*) domiciled in the United Kingdom, and
(*b*) the spouse or civil partner of the person who would, by virtue of the election, be treated as domiciled in the United Kingdom.

(5) An election under this section does not affect a person's domicile for the purposes of section 6(2) or (3) or 48(4).

(6) An election under this section is to be ignored—
(*a*) in interpreting any such provision as is mentioned in section 158(6), and
(*b*) in determining the effect of any qualifying double taxation relief arrangements in relation to a transfer of value by the person making the election.

(7) For the purposes of subsection (6)(*b*) a qualifying double taxation relief arrangement is an arrangement which is specified in an Order in Council made under section 158 before the coming into force of this section (other than by way of amendment by an Order made on or after the coming into force of this section).

(8) In determining for the purposes of this section whether a person making an election under this section is or was domiciled in the United Kingdom, section 267 is to be ignored.][1]

Commentary—*Simon's Taxes* **I9.207, I9.201**.

HMRC Manuals—Inheritance Tax Manual IHTM13040 (domicile: election by non-UK domiciled spouse Or civil partner: introduction).

IHTM13042 (when can an election be made?).

Amendments—[1] Sections 267ZA, 267ZB inserted by FA 2013 s 177(1), (3) with effect from 17 July 2013.

[267ZB Section 267ZA: further provision about election

(1) For the purposes of this section—
(*a*) references to a lifetime election are to an election made by virtue of section 267ZA(3), and
(*b*) references to a death election are to an election made by virtue of section 267ZA(4).

(2) A lifetime or death election is to be made by notice in writing to HMRC.

(3) A lifetime or death election is treated as having taken effect on a date specified, in accordance with subsection (4), in the notice.

(4) The date specified in a notice under subsection (3) must—
(*a*) be 6 April 2013 or a later date,
(*b*) be within the period of 7 years ending with—
(i) in the case of a lifetime election, the date on which the election is made, or
(ii) in the case of a death election, the date of the deceased's death, and
(*c*) meet the condition in subsection (5).

(5) The condition in this subsection is met by a date if, on the date—
(*a*) in the case of a lifetime election—
(i) the person making the election was married to, or in a civil partnership with, the spouse or civil partner, and
(ii) the spouse or civil partner was domiciled in the United Kingdom, or
(*b*) in the case of a death election—
(i) the person who is, by virtue of the election, to be treated as domiciled in the United Kingdom was married to, or in a civil partnership with, the deceased, and
(ii) the deceased was domiciled in the United Kingdom.

(6) A death election may only be made within 2 years of the death of the deceased or such longer period as an officer of Revenue and Customs may in the particular case allow.

(7) Subsection (8) applies if—
(*a*) a lifetime or death election is made,
(*b*) a disposition is made, or another event occurs, during the period beginning with the time when the election is treated by virtue of subsection (3) as having taken effect and ending at the time when the election is made, and
(*c*) the effect of the election being treated as having taken effect at that time is that the disposition or event gives rise to a transfer of value.

(8) This Act applies with the following modifications in relation to the transfer of value—
(*a*) subsections (1) and (6)(*c*) of section 216 have effect as if the period specified in subsection (6)(*c*) of that section were the period of 12 months from the end of the month in which the election is made, and
(*b*) sections 226 and 233 have effect as if the transfer were made at the time when the election is made.

(9) A lifetime or death election cannot be revoked.

(10) If a person who made an election under section 267ZA(1) is not resident in the United Kingdom for the purposes of income tax for a period of four successive tax years beginning at any time after the election is made, the election ceases to have effect at the end of that period.][1]

Commentary—*Simon's Taxes* **I9.201, I9.207**.

HMRC Manuals—Inheritance Tax Manual IHTM13046 (domicile: election by non-uk domiciled spouse or civil partner: the date the election takes effect).

IHTM13048 (domicile: election by non-uk domiciled spouse or civil partner: delivery of accounts and payment of tax after making an election).

Amendments—[1] Sections 267ZA, 267ZB inserted by FA 2013 s 177(1), (3) with effect from 17 July 2013.

[267A Limited liability partnerships

For the purposes of this Act and any other enactments relating to inheritance tax—

(*a*) property to which a limited liability partnership is entitled, or which it occupies or uses, shall be treated as property to which its members are entitled, or which they occupy or use, as partners,

(*b*) any business carried on by a limited liability partnership shall be treated as carried on in partnership by its members,

(*c*) incorporation, change in membership or dissolution of a limited liability partnership shall be treated as formation, alteration or dissolution of a partnership, and

(*d*) any transfer of value made by or to a limited liability partnership shall be treated as made by or to its members in partnership (and not by or to the limited liability partnership as such).][1]

Commentary—*Simon's Taxes* **I6.201**.

HMRC Manuals—Inheritance Tax Manual IHTM25094 (valuing businesses and partnerships: what is a partnership: limited liability partnerships).

Amendments—[1] This section inserted by the Limited Liability Partnerships Act 2000 s 11 with effect from 6 April 2001 (by virtue of SI 2001/3316). For the full text of that Act, see *Halsbury's Statutes* (4th edn) PARTNERSHIP.

Interpretation

268 Associated operations

(1) In this Act "associated operations" means, subject to subsection (2) below, any two or more operations of any kind, being—

(*a*) operations which affect the same property, or one of which affects some property and the other or others of which affect property which represents, whether directly or indirectly, that property, or income arising from that property, or any property representing accumulations of any such income, or

(*b*) any two operations of which one is effected with reference to the other, or with a view to enabling the other to be effected or facilitating its being effected, and any further operation having a like relation to any of those two, and so on,

whether those operations are effected by the same person or different persons, and whether or not they are simultaneous; and "operation" includes an omission.

(2) The granting of a lease for full consideration in money or money's worth shall not be taken to be associated with any operation effected more than three years after the grant, and no operation effected on or after 27th March 1974 shall be taken to be associated with an operation effected before that date.

(3) Where a transfer of value is made by associated operations carried out at different times it shall be treated as made at the time of the last of them; but where any one or more of the earlier operations also constitute a transfer of value made by the same transferor, the value transferred by the earlier operations shall be treated as reducing the value transferred by all the operations taken together, except to the extent that the transfer constituted by the earlier operations but not that made by all the operations taken together is exempt under section 18 above.

Commentary—*Simon's Taxes* **I3.115, I3.132, I3.261–I3.267**.

HMRC Manuals—Inheritance Tax Manual IHTM14821–14836 (associated operations).

IHTM20375 (life policy linked with an annuity).

Statement of Practice E4—Associated operations.

Press releases etc—Hansard 10-3-75 (unconditional transfers between spouses not caught—reaffirmed in Revenue letter to ICAEW dated 20-9-85).

IR letter 1-3-78 (this section covers the sale of an asset where the consideration is left outstanding as a loan which is written off in annual instalments covered by annual exemption: it does not cover the case of a gift where the donee pays the tax in instalments and the donor makes further annual gifts to help pay the tax).

Simon's Tax Cases—s 268(1), *Reynaud v IRC* [1999] STC (SCD) 185; *Rysaffe Trustee Co (CI) Ltd v IRC* [2002] STC 872I, [2003] STC 536.

269 Control of company

(1) For the purposes of this Act a person has control of a company at any time if he then has the control of powers of voting on all questions affecting the company as a whole which if exercised would yield a majority of the votes capable of being exercised on them.

(2) For the purposes of this Act shares or securities shall be deemed to give a person control of a company if, together with any shares or securities which are related property within the meaning of section 161 above, they would be sufficient to give him control of the company (as defined in subsection (1) above).

(3) Where shares or securities are comprised in a settlement, any powers of voting which they give to the trustees of the settlement shall for the purposes of subsection (1) above be deemed to be given to the person beneficially entitled in possession to the shares or securities (except in a case where no individual is so entitled).

(4) Where a company has shares or securities of any class giving powers of voting limited to either or both of—

(*a*) the question of winding up the company, and

(*b*) any question primarily affecting shares or securities of that class,

the reference in subsection (1) above to all questions affecting the company as a whole shall have effect as a reference to all such questions except any in relation to which those powers are capable of being exercised.

Commentary—*Simon's Taxes* **I7.136, I7.335, I11.512.**

HMRC Manuals—Inheritance Tax Manual IHTM25224 (*Walding v IRC*: control for the purposes of business property relief).

Simon's Tax Cases—s 269(1), *Walding (Executors of Walding, decd) v IRC* [1996] STC 13, *Walker's Executors v IRC* [2001] STC (SCD) 86.

270 Connected persons

For the purposes of this Act any question whether a person is connected with another shall be determined as, for the purposes of the [1992 Act][1], it falls to be determined under section [286][1] of that Act, but as if in that section "relative" included uncle, aunt, nephew and niece and "settlement", "settlor" and "trustee" had the same meanings as in this Act.

Commentary—*Simon's Taxes* **I3.142.**

HMRC Manuals—Inheritance Tax Manual IHTM42962 (employee benefit trusts: dispositions by close companies: restriction of exemption - connected person).

Cross reference—See TCGA 1992 s 286 (interpretation of the term connected persons).

Amendments—[1] Words substituted by TCGA 1992 Sch 10 para 8(1), (12).

271 Property of corporations sole

References in this Act (except section 59) to property to which a person is beneficially entitled do not include references to property to which a person is entitled as a corporation sole.

Commentary—*Simon's Taxes* **I3.218, I4.128.**

HMRC Manuals—Inheritance Tax Manual IHTM04033 (structure of the charge: how the meaning of estate is restricted)

[271A Qualifying non-UK pension scheme

(1) For the purposes of this Act "qualifying non-UK pension scheme" means a pension scheme (other than a registered pension scheme) which—

(*a*) is established in a country or territory outside the United Kingdom, and

(*b*) satisfies any requirements prescribed for the purposes of this section by regulations made by the Commissioners for Her Majesty's Revenue and Customs.

(2) "Pension scheme" has the same meaning as in Part 4 of the Finance Act 2004 (see section 150 of that Act).

(3) Regulations under this section may include provision having effect in relation to times before the regulations are made if it does not increase any person's liability to tax.

(4) The power to make regulations under this section is exercisable by statutory instrument, which is subject to annulment in pursuance of a resolution of the House of Commons.][1]

HMRC Manuals—Inheritance Tax Manual IHTM17025 (pensions: types of pension scheme: qualifying non-uk pension schemes (QNUPS))

Regulations—Inheritance Tax (Qualifying Non-UK Pension Schemes) Regulations, SI 2010/51.

Amendments—[1] Section 271A inserted by FA 2008 s 92, Sch 29 para 18(1), (6). This amendment is treated as having come into force on 6 April 2006.

272 General interpretation

In this Act, except where the context otherwise requires,—

"amount" includes value;

["authorised unit trust" means a scheme which is a unit trust scheme for the purposes of [the Income Tax Acts (see section 1007 of the Income Tax Act 2007)][12] and in the case of which an order under section 243 of the Financial Services and Markets Act 2000 is in force;][7]

"barrister" includes a member of the Faculty of Advocates;

"the Board" means the Commissioners of Inland Revenue;

. . .[17]

"conditionally exempt transfer" shall be construed in accordance with section 30(2) above;

["disabled person's interest" has the meaning given by section 89B above;][11]

"disposition" includes a disposition effected by associated operations;

"estate" shall be construed in accordance with sections 5, 55 and 151(4) above;

"estate duty" includes estate duty under the law of Northern Ireland;

"excluded property" shall be construed in accordance with sections 6 and 48 above [and Schedule A1][18];

["foreign-owned", in relation to property at any time, means property—

(*a*) in the case of which the person beneficially entitled to it is at that time domiciled outside the United Kingdom, or

(*b*) if the property is comprised in a settlement, in the case of which the settlor—

(i) is not a formerly domiciled resident for the tax year in which that time falls, and

(ii) was domiciled outside the United Kingdom when the property became comprised in the settlement;][19]

["formerly domiciled resident", in relation to a tax year, means a person—

(*a*) who was born in the United Kingdom,

(*b*) whose domicile of origin was in the United Kingdom,

(*c*) who was resident in the United Kingdom for that tax year, and

(*d*) who was resident in the United Kingdom for at least one of the two tax years immediately preceding that tax year;][19]

"Government department" includes a Northern Ireland department;

"heritable security" means any security capable of being constituted over any interest in land by disposition or assignation of that interest in security of any debt and of being recorded in the General Register of Sasines;

["HMRC" means Her Majesty's Revenue and Customs;][14]

["immediate post-death interest" means an immediate post-death interest for the purposes of Chapter 2 of Part 3 (see section 49A above);][11]

"incumbrance" includes any heritable security, or other debt or payment secured upon heritage;

"Inland Revenue charge" means a charge imposed by virtue of section 237 above;

"land" does not include any estate, interest or right by way of mortgage or other security;

"local authority" has the meaning given by section [section 1130 of the Corporation Tax Act 2010][3];

["member", in relation to a registered pension scheme, has the same meaning as in Part 4 of the Finance Act 2004 (see section 151 of that Act);][10]

"mortgage" includes a heritable security and a security constituted over any interest in movable property;

["nil-rate band maximum" has the meaning given by section 8A(7);][13]

["open-ended investment company" means an open-ended investment company within the meaning given by section 236 of the Financial Services and Markets Act 2000 which is incorporated in the United Kingdom;][7]

"personal representatives" includes any person by whom or on whose behalf an application for a grant of administration or for the resealing of a grant made outside the United Kingdom is made, and any such person as mentioned in section 199(4)(*a*) above;

"property" includes rights and interests of any description [but does not include a settlement power][6];

["public display" means display to which the public are admitted, on payment or not, but does not include display with a view to sale;][15]

"purchaser" means a purchaser in good faith for consideration in money or money's worth other than a nominal consideration and includes a lessee, mortgagee or other person who for such consideration acquires an interest in the property in question;

["quoted", in relation to any shares or securities, means [listed][5] on a recognised stock exchange or dealt in on the Unlisted Securities Market and "unquoted", in relation to any shares or securities, means neither so [listed][5] nor so dealt in][1];

["registered pension scheme" has the same meaning as in Part 4 of the Finance Act 2004;][9]

"reversionary interest" has the meaning given by section 47 above;

16

["section 615(3) scheme" means a superannuation fund to which section 615(3)of the Taxes Act 1988 applies;][9]

"settlement" and "settled property" shall be construed in accordance with section 43 above;

["settlement power" has the meaning given by section 47A above;][6]

"settlor" shall be construed in accordance with section 44 above;

14

. . .

["step-child", in relation to a civil partner, shall be construed in accordance with section 246 of the Civil Partnership Act 2004;][8]

"tax" means capital transfer tax;

["the Taxes Act 1970" means the Income and Corporation Taxes Act 1970;][2]

["the Taxes Act 1988" means the Income and Corporation Taxes Act 1988;][2]

["the TCEA 2007" means the Tribunals, Courts and Enforcement Act 2007;][14]

["transitional serial interest" means a transitional serial interest for the purposes of Chapter 2 of Part 3 (see section 49B above);][11]

["the tribunal" means the First-tier Tribunal or, where determined by or under Tribunal Procedure Rules, the Upper Tribunal;][14]

"trustee" shall be construed in accordance with section 45 above [and

"the 1992 Act" means the Taxation of Chargeable Gains Act 1992.][4]

Commentary—*Simon's Taxes* **I3.115, I5.131, I9.330B.**

HMRC Manuals—Inheritance Tax Manual IHTM04023 (definition of "disposition").

IHTM04030 (meaning of "property").

IHTM11225 (meaning of "local authority").
IHTM11226 (meaning of "government department").
IHTM04262 (definition of 'authorised unit trust').
Statement of Practice SP 18/80—Securities dealt in on the Stock Exchange Unlisted Securities Market: status and valuation.
Simon's Tax Cases—*Reynaud v IRC* [1999] STC (SCD) 185, *Melville v IRC* [2001] STC 1271; *Rysaffe Trustee Co (CI) Ltd v IRC* [2002] STC 872, [2003] STC 536; *Daffodil (administrator of Daffodil, decd) v IRC* [2002] STC (SCD) 224; *Marquess of Linlithgow and anor v R&C Comrs* [2010] STC 1563.
Definitions—"Associated operations", s 268.
Cross references—See FA 1986 s 100(1)–(3) (modification of the definition of "tax" with effect from 25 July 1986).
Amendments—[1] Definition inserted by FA 1987 Sch 8 para 17.

[2] Definitions "the Taxes Act 1970" and "the Taxes Act 1988" substituted by TA 1988 Sch 29 para 32 Table.

[3] In definition of "local authority", words substituted for words "section 842A of the Taxes Act 1988" by the Tax Law Rewrite Acts (Amendment) Order, SI 2013/463 art 2(1) with effect from 1 April 2013.

[4] Definition of "the 1992 Act", and the word "and" at the end of the definition "trustee", inserted by TCGA 1992 Sch 10 para 8(1), (13).

[5] Words in definition of "quoted" substituted by FA 1996 Sch 38 para 2(1)(*b*), (2) in relation to transfers of value occurring after 31 March 1996 and for the purpose of charging to tax any event after that date, in relation to which the transfer of value occurred before 1 April 1996.

[6] Definition of "settlement power" inserted, and words in definition of "property" added, by FA 2002 s 119(1), (4), (6), (7) with effect for transfers of value after 16 April 2002. These amendments are also deemed always to have had effect (subject to and in accordance with the other provisions of IHTA 1984) for the purpose of determining the value, immediately before his death, of the estate of any person who died before 17 April 2002, for the purposes of the transfer of value which that person is treated by IHTA 1984 s 4(1) as having made immediately before his death.

[7] Definitions of "authorised unit trust" and "open-ended investment company" inserted by FA 2003 s 186(1), (5)–(7) with effect for transfers of value or other events occurring after 15 October 2002: FA 2003 s 186(8).

[8] Definition of "step-child" inserted by Tax and Civil Partnership Regulations, SI 2005/3229, regs 3, 38, with effect from 5 December 2005 (reg 1(1)).

[9] Definition of "registered pension scheme" and "section 615(3) scheme" inserted by FA 2004 s 203(6) with effect from 6 April 2006. For transitional provisions and savings see FA 2004 Sch 36.

[10] Definition of "member" and "scheme administrator" inserted by FA 2006 s 160, Sch 22 paras 1, 10. These amendments are deemed to have come into force on 6 April 2006.

[11] Definition of "disabled person's interest", "immediate post-death interest" and "transitional serial interest" inserted by FA 2006 s 156, Sch 20 paras 7, 28. These amendments are deemed to have come into force on 22 March 2006.

[12] Words in the definition of "authorised unit trust" substituted for the words "section 469 of the Taxes Act 1988 (see subsection (7) of that section)" by ITA 2007 s 1027, Sch 1 paras 268, 271, with effect for income tax purposes from 6 April 2007, and corporation tax purposes for accounting periods ending after 5 April 2007.

[13] Definition of "nil-rate band maximum" inserted by FA 2008 s 10, Sch 4 paras 1, 7; this amendment is treated as having come into force on 9 October 2007.

[14] Definition of "Special Commissioners" repealed, and definitions of "HMRC", "the TCEA 2007" and "the tribunal" inserted, by the Transfer of Tribunal Functions and Revenue and Customs Appeals Order, SI 2009/56 art 3, Sch 1 paras 108, 125 with effect from 1 April 2009.

[15] Definition of " "public display" inserted, by the Enactment of Extra-Statutory Concessions Order, SI 2009/730 art 13(1), (5) with effect in relation to deaths and ten-year anniversaries occurring on or after 6 April 2009.

[16] Definition of "scheme administrator" repealed by FA 2011 s 65, Sch 16 paras 49, 57 with effect in relation to deaths occurring on or after 6 April 2011, subject to transitional provisions in FA 2011, Sch 16 Pt 3. Definition previously read—

> ""scheme administrator", in relation to a registered pension scheme, has the same meaning as in Part 4 of the Finance Act 2004 (see sections 270 to 274 of that Act);".

[17] Definitions of "charity" and "charitable" repealed by FA 2010 s 30, Sch 6 para 10 with effect in relation to a transfer of value made on or after 1 April 2012 (SI 2012/736 art 5).

[18] In definition of "excluded property", words inserted by F(No 2)A 2017 s 33, Sch 10 paras 2, 8 with effect in relation to times on or after 6 April 2017, subject to transitional provisions in Sch 10 paras 10, 11.

[19] Definition of "foreign-owned" substituted, and definition of "formerly domiciled resident" inserted, by F(No 2)A 2017 s 30(8) with effect in relation to times after 5 April 2017, subject to transitional provisions in F(No 2)A 2017 s 30(10)–(12). Definition of "foreign-owned" previously read as follows—

> "["foreign-owned", in relation to property, means property in the case of which the person beneficially entitled to it is domiciled outside the United Kingdom or, if the property is comprised in a settlement, in the case of which the settlor was domiciled outside the United Kingdom when the property became comprised in the settlement;]".

Supplementary

273 Transition from estate duty

Schedule 6 to this Act shall have effect.

274 Commencement

(1) This Act shall come into force on 1st January 1985, but shall not apply to transfers of value made before that date or to other events before that date on which capital transfer tax is chargeable or would be chargeable but for an exemption, exception or relief.
(2) Subsection (1) above shall have effect subject to section 275 below, to Schedule 7 to this Act and to any other provision to the contrary.

275 Continuity, and construction of references to old and new law

(1) The continuity of the operation of the law relating to capital transfer tax shall not be affected by the substitution of this Act for the repealed enactments.

(2) Any reference, whether express or implied, in any enactment, instrument or document (including this Act and any enactment amended by Schedule 8 to this Act) to, or to things done or falling to be done under or for the purposes of, any provision of this Act shall, if and so far as the nature of the reference permits, be construed as including, in relation to the times, circumstances or purposes in relation to which the corresponding provision in the repealed enactments has or had effect, a reference to, or as the case may be, to things done or falling to be done under or for the purposes of, that corresponding provision.

(3) Any reference, whether express or implied, in any enactment, instrument or document (including the repealed enactments and enactments, instruments and documents passed or made after the passing of this Act) to, or to things done or falling to be done under or for the purposes of, any of the repealed enactments shall, if and so far as the nature of the reference permits, be construed as including, in relation to the times, circumstances or purposes in relation to which the corresponding provision of this Act has effect, a reference to, or as the case may be, to things done or falling to be done under or for the purposes of, that corresponding provision.

(4) Subsection (2) above shall have effect without prejudice to section 17(2) of the Interpretation Act 1978.

(5) In this section "the repealed enactments" means the enactments repealed by this Act.

Commentary—*Simon's Taxes* **I2.109**.

Cross references—See FA 1986 s 100(1)–(3) (with effect from 25 July 1986, CTT to be known as inheritance tax; accordingly the reference to CTT in this section to be read as a reference to inheritance tax with effect from that date).

276 Consequential amendments

Schedule 8 to this Act shall have effect.

277 Repeals

The enactments mentioned in Schedule 9 to this Act are hereby repealed to the extent specified in the third column of that Schedule.

278 Short title

This Act may be cited as the [Inheritance Tax Act 1984][1].

Cross references—See FA 1986 s 100(1)(*a*) (change of citation of this Act with effect from 25 July 1986).

Amendments—[1] Words substituted by virtue of FA 1986 s 100(1)(*a*).

SCHEDULES

[SCHEDULE A1

NON-EXCLUDED OVERSEAS PROPERTY]

Commentary—*Simon's Taxes* **I9.335**.

Amendments—Schedule A1 inserted by F(No 2)A 2017 s 33, Sch 10 para 1 with effect in relation to times on or after 6 April 2017, subject to transitional provisions in Sch 10 paras 10, 11.

[PART 1

OVERSEAS PROPERTY WITH VALUE ATTRIBUTABLE TO UK RESIDENTIAL PROPERTY]

Amendments—Schedule A1 inserted by F(No 2)A 2017 s 33, Sch 10 para 1 with effect in relation to times on or after 6 April 2017, subject to transitional provisions in Sch 10 paras 10, 11.

[Introductory

1 Property is not excluded property by virtue of section 6(1) or 48(3)(*a*) if and to the extent that paragraph 2 or 3 applies to it.][1]

Commentary—*Simon's Taxes* **I9.335**.

Amendments—[1] Schedule A1 inserted by F(No 2)A 2017 s 33, Sch 10 para 1 with effect in relation to times on or after 6 April 2017, subject to transitional provisions in Sch 10 paras 10, 11.

Close company and partnership interests

[**2** (1) This paragraph applies to an interest in a close company or in a partnership, if and to the extent that the interest meets the condition in sub-paragraph (2).

(2) The condition is that the value of the interest is—

- (*a*) directly attributable to a UK residential property interest, or
- (*b*) attributable to a UK residential property interest by virtue only of one or more of the following—
  - (i) an interest in a close company;
  - (ii) an interest in a partnership;
  - (iii) property to which paragraph 3 (loans) applies.

(3) For the purposes of sub-paragraphs (1) and (2) disregard—

(*a*) an interest in a close company, if the value of the interest is less than 5% of the total value of all the interests in the close company;

(*b*) an interest in a partnership, if the value of the interest is less than 5% of the total value of all the interests in the partnership.

(4) In determining under sub-paragraph (3) whether to disregard a person's interest in a close company or partnership, treat the value of the person's interest as increased by the value of any connected person's interest in the close company or partnership.

(5) In determining whether or to what extent the value of an interest in a close company or in a partnership is attributable to a UK residential property interest for the purposes of sub-paragraph (1), liabilities of a close company or partnership are to be attributed rateably to all of its property, whether or not they would otherwise be attributed to any particular property.][1]

Commentary—*Simon's Taxes* **I9.335**.

Amendments—[1] Schedule A1 inserted by F(No 2)A 2017 s 33, Sch 10 para 1 with effect in relation to times on or after 6 April 2017, subject to transitional provisions in Sch 10 paras 10, 11.

[Loans

3 This paragraph applies to—

(*a*) the rights of a creditor in respect of a loan which is a relevant loan (see paragraph 4), and

(*b*) money or money's worth held or otherwise made available as security, collateral or guarantee for a loan which is a relevant loan, to the extent that it does not exceed the value of the relevant loan.][1]

Commentary—*Simon's Taxes* **I9.335**.

Amendments—[1] Schedule A1 inserted by F(No 2)A 2017 s 33, Sch 10 para 1 with effect in relation to times on or after 6 April 2017, subject to transitional provisions in Sch 10 paras 10, 11.

[4 (1) For the purposes of this Schedule a loan is a relevant loan if and to the extent that money or money's worth made available under the loan is used to finance, directly or indirectly—

(*a*) the acquisition by an individual, a partnership or the trustees of a settlement of—

(i) a UK residential property interest, or

(ii) property to which paragraph 2 to any extent applies, or

(*b*) the acquisition by an individual, a partnership or the trustees of a settlement of an interest in a close company or a partnership ("the intermediary") and the acquisition by the intermediary of property within paragraph (*a*)(i) or (ii).

(2) In this paragraph references to money or money's worth made available under a loan or sale proceeds being used "indirectly" to finance the acquisition of something include the money or money's worth or sale proceeds being used to finance—

(*a*) the acquisition of any property the proceeds of sale of which are used directly or indirectly to finance the acquisition of that thing, or

(*b*) the making, or repayment, of a loan to finance the acquisition of that thing.

(3) In this paragraph references to the acquisition of a UK residential property interest by an individual, a partnership, the trustees of a settlement or a close company include the maintenance, or an enhancement, of the value of a UK residential property interest which is (as the case may be) the property of the individual, property comprised in the settlement or property of the partnership or close company.

(4) Where the UK residential property interest by virtue of which a loan is a relevant loan is disposed of, the loan ceases to be a relevant loan.

(5) Where a proportion of the UK residential property interest by virtue of which a loan is a relevant loan is disposed of, the loan ceases to be a relevant loan by the same proportion.

(6) In this Schedule, references to a loan include an acknowledgment of debt by a person or any other arrangement under which a debt arises; and in such a case references to money or money's worth made available under the loan are to the amount of the debt.][1]

Commentary—*Simon's Taxes* **I9.335**.

Amendments—[1] Schedule A1 inserted by F(No 2)A 2017 s 33, Sch 10 para 1 with effect in relation to times on or after 6 April 2017, subject to transitional provisions in Sch 10 paras 10, 11.

PART 2
[SUPPLEMENTARY]

Amendments—Schedule A1 inserted by F(No 2)A 2017 s 33, Sch 10 para 1 with effect in relation to times on or after 6 April 2017, subject to transitional provisions in Sch 10 paras 10, 11.

[Disposals and repayments

5 (1) This paragraph applies to—

(*a*) property which constitutes consideration in money or money's worth for the disposal of property to which paragraph 2 or paragraph 3(*a*) applies;

(*b*) any money or money's worth paid in respect of a creditor's rights falling within paragraph 3(*a*);

(*c*) any property directly or indirectly representing property within paragraph (*a*) or (*b*).

(2) If and to the extent that this paragraph applies to any property—

(*a*) for the two-year period it is not excluded property by virtue of section 6(1), (1A) or (2) or 48(3)(*a*), (3A) or (4), and

(*b*) if it is held in a qualifying foreign currency account within the meaning of section 157 (non-residents' bank accounts), that section does not apply to it for the two-year period.

(3) The two-year period is the period of two years beginning with the date of—

(*a*) the disposal referred to in sub-paragraph (1)(*a*), or

(*b*) the payment referred to in sub-paragraph (1)(*b*).

(4) The value of any property within sub-paragraph (1)(*c*) is to be treated as not exceeding the relevant amount.

(5) The relevant amount is—

(*a*) where the property within sub-paragraph (1)(*c*) directly or indirectly represents property within sub-paragraph (1)(*a*) ("the consideration"), the value of the consideration at the time of the disposal referred to in that sub-paragraph, and

(*b*) where the property within sub-paragraph (1)(*c*) directly or indirectly represents property within sub-paragraph (1)(*b*), the amount of the money or money's worth paid as mentioned in that sub-paragraph.][1]

Commentary—*Simon's Taxes* **I9.335**.

Amendments—[1] Schedule A1 inserted by F(No 2)A 2017 s 33, Sch 10 para 1 with effect in relation to times on or after 6 April 2017, subject to transitional provisions in Sch 10 paras 10, 11. Sub-para (1)(*a*) does not apply in relation to a disposal of property occurring before 6 April 2017, and sub-para (1)(*b*) does not apply in relation to a payment of money or money's worth occurring before 6 April 2017 (F(No 2)A 2017 Sch 10 para 9(2)).

[Tax avoidance arrangements

6 (1) In determining whether or to what extent property situated outside the United Kingdom is excluded property, no regard is to be had to any arrangements the purpose or one of the main purposes of which is to secure a tax advantage by avoiding or minimising the effect of paragraph 1 or 5.

(2) In this paragraph—

"tax advantage" has the meaning given in section 208 of the Finance Act 2013;

"arrangements" includes any scheme, transaction or series of transactions, agreement or understanding (whether or not legally enforceable and whenever entered into) and any associated operations.][1]

Commentary—*Simon's Taxes* **I9.335**.

Amendments—[1] Schedule A1 inserted by F(No 2)A 2017 s 33, Sch 10 para 1 with effect in relation to times on or after 6 April 2017, subject to transitional provisions in Sch 10 paras 10, 11.

Double taxation relief arrangements

[7 (1) Nothing in any double taxation relief arrangements made with the government of a territory outside the United Kingdom is to be read as preventing a person from being liable for any amount of inheritance tax by virtue of paragraph 1 or 5 in relation to any chargeable transfer if under the law of that territory—

(*a*) no tax of a character similar to inheritance tax is charged on that chargeable transfer, or

(*b*) a tax of a character similar to inheritance tax is charged in relation to that chargeable transfer at an effective rate of 0% (otherwise than by virtue of a relief or exemption).

(2) In this paragraph—

"double taxation relief arrangements" means arrangements having effect under section 158(1);

"effective rate" means the rate found by expressing the tax chargeable as a percentage of the amount by reference to which it is charged.][1]

Commentary—*Simon's Taxes* **I9.335**.

Amendments—[1] Schedule A1 inserted by F(No 2)A 2017 s 33, Sch 10 para 1 with effect in relation to times on or after 6 April 2017, subject to transitional provisions in Sch 10 paras 10, 11.

[PART 3
INTERPRETATION]

Amendments—Schedule A1 inserted by F(No 2)A 2017 s 33, Sch 10 para 1 with effect in relation to times on or after 6 April 2017, subject to transitional provisions in Sch 10 paras 10, 11.

[UK residential property interest

8 (1) In this Schedule "UK residential property interest" means an interest in UK land—

(*a*) where the land consists of a dwelling,

(*b*) where and to the extent that the land includes a dwelling, or

(*c*) where the interest subsists under a contract for an off-plan purchase.

(2) For the purposes of sub-paragraph (1)(*b*), the extent to which land includes a dwelling is to be determined on a just and reasonable basis.

(3) In this paragraph—

"interest in UK land" has the meaning given by paragraph 2 of Schedule B1 to the 1992 Act (and the power in sub-paragraph (5) of that paragraph applies for the purposes of this Schedule);

"the land", in relation to an interest in UK land which is an interest subsisting for the benefit of land, is a reference to the land for the benefit of which the interest subsists;

"dwelling" has the meaning given by paragraph 4 of Schedule B1 to the 1992 Act (and the power in paragraph 5 of that Schedule applies for the purposes of this Schedule);

"contract for an off-plan purchase" has the meaning given by paragraph 1(6) of Schedule B1 to the 1992 Act.][1]

Commentary—*Simon's Taxes* **I9.335**.

Amendments—[1] Schedule A1 inserted by F(No 2)A 2017 s 33, Sch 10 para 1 with effect in relation to times on or after 6 April 2017, subject to transitional provisions in Sch 10 paras 10, 11.

[Close companies

9 (1) In this Schedule—

"close company" means a company within the meaning of the Corporation Tax Acts which is (or would be if resident in the United Kingdom) a close company for the purposes of those Acts;

references to an interest in a close company are to the rights and interests that a participator in a close company has in that company.

(2) In this paragraph—

"participator", in relation to a close company, means any person who is (or would be if the company were resident in the United Kingdom) a participator in relation to that company within the meaning given by section 454 of the Corporation Tax Act 2010;

references to rights and interests in a close company include references to rights and interests in the assets of the company available for distribution among the participators in the event of a winding-up or in any other circumstances.][1]

Commentary—*Simon's Taxes* **I9.335**.

Amendments—[1] Schedule A1 inserted by F(No 2)A 2017 s 33, Sch 10 para 1 with effect in relation to times on or after 6 April 2017, subject to transitional provisions in Sch 10 paras 10, 11.

[Partnerships

10 In this Schedule "partnership" means—

(*a*) a partnership within the Partnership Act 1890,

(*b*) a limited partnership registered under the Limited Partnerships Act 1907,

(*c*) a limited liability partnership formed under the Limited Liability Partnerships Act 2000 or the Limited Liability Partnerships Act (Northern Ireland) 2002, or

(*d*) a firm or entity of a similar character to either of those mentioned in paragraph (*a*) or (*b*) formed under the law of a country or territory outside the United Kingdom.][1]

Commentary—*Simon's Taxes* **I9.335**.

Amendments—[1] Schedule A1 inserted by F(No 2)A 2017 s 33, Sch 10 para 1 with effect in relation to times on or after 6 April 2017, subject to transitional provisions in Sch 10 paras 10, 11.

SCHEDULE 1

[TABLE OF RATES OF TAX

Section 7

Portion of value		*Rate of tax*
Lower limit (£)	*Upper limit (£)*	*Per cent*
0	325,000	Nil
325,000		40][1]

Commentary—*Simon's Taxes* **I3.511**; *Foster* **C5.11**.

Notes—Table was to be substituted by FA 2007 s 4(1) with effect for chargeable transfers made on or after 6 April 2010. This substitution was repealed by FA 2010 s 8 and therefore never took effect. FA 2010 s 8 provides for the Table, as substituted by FA 2006 s 155(1)(*b*), (4) to have effect in relation to chargeable transfers made on or after 6 April 2010.

Amendments—[1] Table substituted by FA 2006 s 155(1)(*b*), (4). with effect for any chargeable transfer made on or after 6 April 2009.

[SCHEDULE 1A

GIFTS TO CHARITIES ETC: TAX CHARGED AT LOWER RATE]

Amendments—This Schedule inserted by FA 2012 s 209, Sch 33 para 1 with effect in cases where D's death occurs on or after 6 April 2012.

[Application of this Schedule

1—(1) This Schedule applies if—

(a) a chargeable transfer is made (under section 4) on the death of a person ("D"), and

(b) all or part of the value transferred by the chargeable transfer is chargeable to tax at a rate other than nil per cent.

(2) The part of the value transferred that is chargeable to tax at a rate other than nil per cent is referred to in this Schedule as "TP".][1]

Amendments—[1] This Schedule inserted by FA 2012 s 209, Sch 33 para 1 with effect in cases where D's death occurs on or after 6 April 2012.

[The relief

2—(1) If the charitable giving condition is met—

(a) the tax charged on the part of TP that qualifies for the lower rate of tax is to be charged at the lower rate of tax, and

(b) the tax charged on any remaining part of TP is to be charged at the rate at which it would (but for this Schedule) have been charged on the whole of TP in accordance with section 7.

(2) For the purposes of this paragraph, the charitable giving condition is met if, for one or more components of the estate (taking each component separately), the donated amount is at least 10% of the baseline amount.

(3) Paragraph 3 defines the components of the estate.

(4) Paragraphs 4 and 5 explain how to calculate the donated amount and the baseline amount for each component.

(5) The part of TP that "qualifies for the lower rate of tax" is the part attributable to all the property in each of the components for which the donated amount is at least 10% of the baseline amount.

(6) The lower rate of tax is 36%.][1]

Amendments—[1] This Schedule inserted by FA 2012 s 209, Sch 33 para 1 with effect in cases where D's death occurs on or after 6 April 2012.

[The components of the estate

3—(1) For the purposes of paragraph 2, the components of the estate are—

(a) the survivorship component,

(b) the settled property component, and

(c) the general component.

(2) The survivorship component is made up of all the property comprised in the estate that, immediately before D's death, was joint (or common) property liable to pass on D's death—

(a) by survivorship (in England and Wales or Northern Ireland),

(b) under a special destination (in Scotland), or

(c) by or under anything corresponding to survivorship or a special destination under the law of a country or territory outside the United Kingdom.

(3) The settled property component is made up of all the settled property comprised in the estate in which there subsisted, immediately before D's death, an interest in possession to which D was beneficially entitled immediately before death.

(4) The general component is made up of all the property comprised in the estate other than—

(a) property in the survivorship component,

(b) property in the settled property component, and

(c) property that forms part of the estate by virtue of section 102(3) of the Finance Act 1986 (gifts with reservation).][1]

Amendments—[1] This Schedule inserted by FA 2012 s 209, Sch 33 para 1 with effect in cases where D's death occurs on or after 6 April 2012.

[The donated amount

4—The donated amount, for a component of the estate, is so much of the value transferred by the relevant transfer as (in total) is attributable to property that—

(a) forms part of that component, and

(b) is property in relation to which section 23(1) applies.][1]

Amendments—[1] This Schedule inserted by FA 2012 s 209, Sch 33 para 1 with effect in cases where D's death occurs on or after 6 April 2012.

[The baseline amount

5—The baseline amount, for a component of the estate, is the amount calculated in accordance with the following steps—

Step 1

Determine the part of the value transferred by the chargeable transfer that is attributable to property in that component.

Step 2

Deduct from the amount determined under Step 1 the appropriate proportion of the available nil-rate band.

"The appropriate proportion" is a proportion equal to the proportion that the amount determined under Step 1 bears to the value transferred by the chargeable transfer as a whole.

"The available nil-rate band" is the amount (if any) by which—

(a) the nil-rate band maximum (increased, where applicable, in accordance with section 8A), exceeds

(b) the sum of the values transferred by previous chargeable transfers made by D in the period of 7 years ending with the date of the relevant transfer.

Step 3

Add to the amount determined under Step 2 an amount equal to so much of the value transferred by the relevant transfer as (in total) is attributable to property that—

(a) forms part of that component, and

(b) is property in relation to which section 23(1) applies.

The result is the baseline amount for that component.][1]

Amendments—[1] This Schedule inserted by FA 2012 s 209, Sch 33 para 1 with effect in cases where D's death occurs on or after 6 April 2012.

[Rules for determining whether charitable giving condition is met

6—(1) For the purpose of calculating the donated amount and the baseline amount, any amount to be arrived at in accordance with section 38(3) or (5) is to be arrived at assuming the rate of tax is the lower rate of tax (see paragraph 2(6)).

(2) For the purpose of calculating the donated amount, section 39A does not apply to a specific gift of property in relation to which section 23(1) applies (but that section does apply to such a gift for the purpose of calculating the baseline amount).

(3) Subject to sub-paragraphs (1) and (2), the provisions of this Act apply for the purpose of calculating the donated amount and the baseline amount as for the purpose of calculating the tax to be charged on the value transferred by the chargeable transfer.][1]

Amendments—[1] This Schedule inserted by FA 2012 s 209, Sch 33 para 1 with effect in cases where D's death occurs on or after 6 April 2012.

[Election to merge parts of the estate

7—(1) An election may be made under this paragraph if, for a component of the estate, the donated amount is at least 10% of the baseline amount.

(2) That component is referred to as "the qualifying component".

(3) The effect of the election is that the qualifying component and one or more eligible parts of the estate (as specified in the election) are to be treated for the purposes of this Schedule as if they were a single component.

(4) Accordingly, if the donated amount for that deemed single component is at least 10% of the baseline amount for it, the property in that component is to be included in the part of TP that qualifies for the lower rate of tax.

(5) In relation to the qualifying component—

(a) each one of the other two components of the estate is an "eligible part" of the estate, and

(b) all the property that forms part of the estate by virtue of section 102(3) of the Finance Act 1986 (gifts with reservation) is also an "eligible part" of the estate.

(6) The election must be made by all those who are appropriate persons with respect to the qualifying component and each of the eligible parts to be treated as a single component.

(7) "Appropriate persons" means—

(a) with respect to the survivorship component, all those to whom the property in that component passes on D's death (or, if they have subsequently died, their personal representatives),

(b) with respect to the settled property component, the trustees of all the settled property in that component,

(c) with respect to the general component, all the personal representatives of D or, if there are none, all those who are liable for the tax attributable to the property in that component, and

(d) with respect to property within paragraph (b) of subparagraph (5), all those in whom the property within that paragraph is vested when the election is to be made.][1]

Amendments—[1] This Schedule inserted by FA 2012 s 209, Sch 33 para 1 with effect in cases where D's death occurs on or after 6 April 2012.

[Opting out

8—(1) If an election is made under this paragraph in relation to a component of the estate, this Schedule is to apply as if the donated amount for that component were less than 10% of the baseline amount for it (whether or not it actually is).

(2) The election must be made by all those who are appropriate persons (as defined in paragraph 7(7)) with respect to the component.][1]

Amendments—[1] This Schedule inserted by FA 2012 s 209, Sch 33 para 1 with effect in cases where D's death occurs on or after 6 April 2012.

[Elections: procedure

9—(1) An election under this Schedule must be made by notice in writing to HMRC within two years after D's death.

(2) An election under this Schedule may be withdrawn by notice in writing to HMRC given—

(a) by all those who would be entitled to make such an election, and

(b) no later than the end of the period of two years and one month after D's death.

(3) An officer of Revenue and Customs may agree in a particular case to extend the time limit in sub-paragraph (1) or (2)(b) by such period as the officer may allow.][1]

Amendments—[1] This Schedule inserted by FA 2012 s 209, Sch 33 para 1 with effect in cases where D's death occurs on or after 6 April 2012.

[General interpretation

10—In this Schedule, in relation to D—

"the chargeable transfer" means the chargeable transfer mentioned in paragraph 1(1);

"the estate" means D's estate immediately before death;

"the relevant transfer" means the transfer of value that D is treated (under section 4) as having made immediately before death.][1]

Amendments—[1] This Schedule inserted by FA 2012 s 209, Sch 33 para 1 with effect in cases where D's death occurs on or after 6 April 2012.

SCHEDULE 2
PROVISIONS APPLYING ON REDUCTION OF TAX

Section 9

Interpretation

1 In this Schedule—

(*a*) references to a reduction are to a reduction of tax by the substitution of [a new Table][1] in Schedule 1 to this Act, and

(*b*) references to something happening before or after a reduction are to its happening before or, as the case may be, on or after the date on which [the Table][1] giving effect to the reduction [comes][1] into force.

Cross references—See FA 1986 Sch 19 para 40 (where a death or other event occurs after 17 March 1986, the amendments to this paragraph by FA 1986 Sch 19 (see below) not to affect tax chargeable on a transfer of value occurring before 18 March 1986).

Amendments—[1] Words substituted by FA 1986 Sch 19 para 37 in respect of transfers of value made after 17 March 1986.

[Death within seven years of potentially exempt transfer

1A Where a person who has made a potentially exempt transfer before a reduction dies after that reduction (or after that and one or more subsequent reductions) and within the period of seven years beginning with the date of the transfer, tax shall be chargeable by reason of the transfer proving to be a chargeable transfer only if, and to the extent that, it would have been so chargeable if the Table in Schedule 1 as substituted by that reduction (or by the most recent of those reductions) had applied to that transfer.][1]

Commentary—*Simon's Taxes* **I3.511**; *Foster* **C5.11.**

Cross references—See FA 1986 Sch 19 para 40 (where a death occurs after 17 March 1986, this paragraph not to affect tax chargeable on a transfer of value occurring before 18 March 1986).

Amendments—[1] This paragraph inserted by FA 1986 s 101(3) and Sch 19 para 37(3) in respect of transfers of value made after 17 March 1986.

Death within [seven years] of chargeable transfer

2 Where a person who has made a chargeable transfer [(other than a potentially exempt transfer)][1] before a reduction dies after that reduction (or after that and one or more subsequent reductions) and within [seven years][1] of the transfer, additional tax shall be chargeable by reason of his death only if, and to the extent that, it would have been so chargeable if . . . [1] [the Table][1] in Schedule 1 as substituted by that reduction (or by the most recent of those reductions) had applied to that transfer.

Commentary—*Simon's Taxes* **I3.532**; *Foster* **C5.32**.

Cross references—See FA 1986 Sch 19 para 40 (where a death occurs after 17 March 1986, the amendments to this paragraph by FA 1986 Sch 19 (see below) not to affect tax chargeable on a transfer of value occurring before 18 March 1986),

Sch 19 para 44 (modification of this paragraph in relation to a case where the chargeable transfer is made before 18 March 1986 but the death occurs on or after that date).

Amendments—[1] Words substituted, repealed and inserted by FA 1986 s 101 and Sch 19 para 37 in respect of transfers of value made after 17 March 1986.

Settlement without interest in possession

3 Where tax is chargeable under section 65 of this Act on any occasion after a reduction and the rate at which it is charged is determined under section 69 by reference to the rate that was (or would have been) charged under section 64 on an occasion before that reduction (or before that and one or more other reductions), the rate charged on the later occasion shall be determined as if . . . [1] [the Table][2] in Schedule 1 as substituted by that reduction (or by the most recent of those reductions) had been in force on the earlier occasion.

Commentary—*Simon's Taxes* **I5.441**; *Foster* **E4.41**.

Cross references—See FA 1986 Sch 19 para 40 (where a death occurs after 17 March 1986, the amendments to this paragraph by FA 1986 Sch 19 (see below) not to affect tax chargeable on a transfer of value occurring before 18 March 1986),

Sch 19 para 43(3) (modification of this paragraph in certain circumstances).

Amendments—[1] Words repealed by FA 1986 Sch 19 para 37 and Sch 23 Pt X in respect of transfers of value made after 17 March 1986.

[2] Words substituted by FA 1986 Sch 19 para 37 in respect of transfers of value made after 17 March 1986.

Disposal of trees etc following exemption on death

4 Where the value of any trees or underwood has been left out of account under Chapter III of Part V of this Act in determining the value transferred by the chargeable transfer made on a death before a reduction and tax is chargeable under section 126 on a disposal of the trees or underwood after that reduction (or after that and one or more subsequent reductions) the rate or rates mentioned in section 128 shall be determined as if . . . [1] [the Table][2] in Schedule 1 as substituted by that reduction (or by the most recent of those reductions) had applied to that transfer.

Commentary—*Simon's Taxes* **I7.405**; *Foster* **G4.05**.

Cross references—See FA 1986 Sch 19 para 40 (where a death occurs after 17 March 1986, the amendments to this paragraph by FA 1986 Sch 19 (see below) not to affect tax chargeable on a transfer of value occurring before 18 March 1986),

Sch 19 para 45 (modification of this paragraph in relation to a case where a disposal is made on or after 18 March 1986 but the death occurs before that date).

Amendments—[1] Words repealed by FA 1986 Sch 19 para 37 and Sch 23 Pt X in respect of transfers of value made after 17 March 1986.

[2] Words substituted by FA 1986 Sch 19 para 37.

Conditionally exempt transfers

5 Where tax is chargeable under section 32 [or 32A][1] of this Act by reason of a chargeable event occurring after a reduction and the rate or rates at which it is charged fall to be determined under the provisions of section 33(1)(*b*)(ii) by reference to a death which occurred before that reduction (or before that and one or more other reductions) those provisions shall apply as if [the Table][2] in Schedule 1 as substituted by that reduction (or by the most recent of those reductions) had been in force at the time of the death.

Commentary—*Simon's Taxes* **I7.514B**; *Foster* **G5.14B**.

Cross references—See FA 1986 Sch 19 para 40 (where a death occurs after 17 March 1986, the amendments to this paragraph by FA 1986 Sch 19 (see below) not to affect tax chargeable on a transfer of value occurring before 18 March 1986).

Amendments—[1] Words inserted by FA 1985 Sch 26 para 5.

[2] Words substituted by FA 1986 Sch 19 para 37 in respect of transfers of value made after 17 March 1986.

Maintenance funds for historic buildings

6 Where tax is chargeable under paragraph 8 of Schedule 4 to this Act on any occasion after a reduction and the rate at which it is charged falls to be determined under paragraph 14 of that Schedule by reference to a death which occurred before that reduction (or before that and one or more other reductions) paragraph 14 shall apply as if [the Table][1] in Schedule 1 as substituted by that reduction (or by the most recent of those reductions) had been in force at the time of the death.

Commentary—*Simon's Taxes* **I5.651, I7.545**; *Foster* **E6.51, G5.45**.

Cross references—See FA 1986 Sch 19 para 40 (where a death occurs after 17 March 1986, the amendment to this paragraph by FA 1986 Sch 19 para 37(1)(*b*) not to affect tax chargeable on a transfer of value occurring before 18 March 1986).

Amendments—[1] Words substituted by FA 1986 Sch 19 para 37(1)(*b*) in respect of transfers of value made after 17 March 1986.

[Relevant dependant with pension fund inherited from member over 75

6A . . .

Amendment—This paragraph repealed by FA 2007 ss 69, 114, Sch 19 paras 19, 27, 29(8), Sch 27 Pt 3(1) with effect in relation to deaths, cases where scheme administrators become aware of deaths and cessations of dependency occurring on or after 6 April 2007.

Mutual transfers

7 . . .

Amendments—This paragraph repealed by FA 1986 Sch 23 Pt X in a case where the donee's transfer is made after 17 March 1986.

SCHEDULE 3

GIFTS FOR NATIONAL PURPOSES, ETC

Sections 25, 32, 230 etc

The National Gallery.

The British Museum.

[The National Museums of Scotland.][1]

The National Museum of Wales.

The Ulster Museum.

Any other similar national institution which exists wholly or mainly for the purpose of preserving for the public benefit a collection of scientific, historic or artistic interest and which is approved for the purposes of this Schedule by the Treasury.

Any museum or art gallery in the United Kingdom which exists wholly or mainly for that purpose and is [or has been][5] maintained by a local authority or university in the United Kingdom.

Any library the main function of which is to serve the needs of teaching and research at a university in the United Kingdom.

The Historic Buildings and Monuments Commission for England.

The National Trust for Places of Historic Interest or Natural Beauty.

The National Trust for Scotland for Places of Historic Interest or Natural Beauty.

The National Art Collections Fund.

The Trustees of the National Heritage Memorial Fund.

. . . [9]

The Friends of the National Libraries.

The Historic Churches Preservation Trust.

[Nature Conservancy Council for England.][3]

[. . . [10]

Natural England.][6]

[Scottish Natural Heritage.][4]

[Countryside Council for Wales.][3]

[The Marine Management Organisation][8]

Any local authority.

Any Government department (including the National Debt Commissioners).

Any university or university college in the United Kingdom.

[A health service body, within the meaning of [section 986 of the Corporation Tax Act 2010][7].][2]

Commentary—*Simon's Taxes* **I4.218**; *Foster* **D2.18**.

NOTE—

The function of approval conferred by Sch 3, in the entry beginning "Any other similar national institution" (and which was initially conferred on the Treasury but, along with other functions, transferred to the Commissioners of Inland Revenue under FA 1985 s 95) is transferred to the Treasury with effect from 15 September 2016 (FA 2016 s 96(1), (2)). This does not affect any approval given under Sch 3 before 15 September 2016 (FA 2016 s 96(3)).

HMRC Manuals—Inheritance Tax Manual IHTM11224 (qualifying bodies for gifts for national purposes).

Cross references—See FA 1985 s 95 (transfer of Treasury functions under this Schedule to the Commissioners of Inland Revenue).

Definitions—"Government department", s 272; "local authority", s 272.

Amendments—[1] Words substituted by the National Heritage (Scotland) Act 1985 Sch 2 para 4 with effect from 1 October 1985 by virtue of the National Heritage (Scotland) Act 1985 Commencement Order, SI 1985/851 art 3 and Sch 2.

[2] Words added by the National Health Service and Community Care Act 1990 s 61(5) with effect from 17 September 1990 by virtue of the National Health Service and Community Care Act 1990 (Commencement No 1) Order, SI 1990/1329.

[3] Words substituted by the Environmental Protection Act 1990 Sch 6 para 25 with effect from 1 April 1991 by virtue of the Environment Protection Act 1990 (Commencement No 6 and Appointed Day) Order, SI 1991/685.

[4] Words substituted by the Natural Heritage (Scotland) Act 1991 Sch 2 para 9 with effect from 1 April 1992 by virtue of the Natural Heritage (Scotland) Act 1991 (Commencement No 2) Order, SI 1991/2633.

[5] In entry beginning "Any museum", words inserted by FA 2016 s 96(4) with effect from 15 September 2016.

[6] Entries "Commission for Rural Communities" and "Natural England" substituted for entry "English Nature" as originally enacted, by the Natural Environment and Rural Communities Act 2006 s 105(1), Sch 11 para 105 with effect for the purposes of entry "Natural England" from 2 May 2006 (SI 2006/1176 art 4) and for remaining purposes from 1 October 2006 (SI 2006/2541 art 2).

[7] In entry for "health service body", words substituted for words "section 519A of the Income and Corporation Taxes Act 1988" by CTA 2010 s 1177, Sch 1 para 192. CTA 2010 has effect for corporation tax purposes for accounting periods ending on or after 1 April 2010, and for income and capital gains tax purposes for the tax year 2010–11 and subsequent tax years.

[8] Entry inserted by the Marine and Coastal Access Act 2009, s 1(4), Sch 2, para 5 with effect from 12 January 2010 (by virtue of SI 2009/3345, art 2, Schedule, para 1).

[9] Entry "The National Endowment for Science, Technology and the Arts" repealed by the Public Bodies (Abolition of the National Endowment for Science, Technology and the Arts) Order, SI 2012/964 art 3(1), Schedule, with effect from 1 April 2012.

[10] Entry "Commission for Rural Communities" repealed by the Public Bodies (Abolition of the Commission for Rural Communities) Order, SI 2012/2654 art 4, Schedule, with effect from 1 April 2013.

SCHEDULE 4
MAINTENANCE FUNDS FOR HISTORIC BUILDINGS, ETC
Sections 27, 58, 77 etc

Cross references—See FA 1985 s 95 (transfer of Treasury functions under this Schedule to the Commissioners of Inland Revenue from 25 July 1985).

PART I
TREASURY DIRECTIONS
Giving of directions

1—(1) If the conditions mentioned in paragraph 2(1) below are fulfilled in respect of settled property, the Treasury shall, on a claim made for the purpose, give a direction under this paragraph in respect of the property.

(2) The Treasury may give a direction under this paragraph in respect of property proposed to be comprised in a settlement or to be held on particular trusts in any case where, if the property were already so comprised or held, they would be obliged to give the direction.

(3) Property comprised in a settlement by virtue of a transfer of value made before the coming into force of section 94 of the Finance Act 1982 and exempt under section 84 of the Finance Act 1976 shall be treated as property in respect of which a direction has been given under this paragraph.

Commentary—*Simon's Taxes* **I7.542, I7.543**; *Foster* **G5.42, 43**.

Definitions—"Settlement", "settled property", s 43.

Conditions

2—(1) The conditions referred to in paragraph 1 above are—

(*a*) that the Treasury are satisfied—

(i) that the trusts on which the property is held comply with the requirements mentioned in paragraph 3 below, and

(ii) that the property is of a character and amount appropriate for the purposes of those trusts; and

(*b*) that the trustees—

(i) are approved by the Treasury,

(ii) include a trust corporation, a solicitor, an accountant or a member of such other professional body as the Treasury may allow in the case of the property concerned, and

(iii) are, at the time the direction is given, resident in the United Kingdom.

(2) For the purposes of this paragraph trustees shall be regarded as resident in the United Kingdom if—

(*a*) the general administration of the trusts is ordinarily carried on in the United Kingdom, and

(*b*) the trustees or a majority of them (and, where there is more than one class of trustees, a majority of each class) are resident in the United Kingdom;

and where a trustee is a trust corporation, the question whether the trustee is resident in the United Kingdom shall, for the purposes of paragraph (b) above, be determined as for the purposes of corporation tax.

(3) In this paragraph—

"accountant" means a member of an incorporated society of accountants;

"trust corporation" means a person that is a trust corporation for the purposes of the Law of Property Act 1925 or for the purposes of Article 9 of the Administration of Estates (Northern Ireland) Order 1979.

Commentary—*Simon's Taxes* **I7.542, I7.543**; *Foster* **G5.42, 43**.
Definitions—"Trustee", s 45.

3—(1) The requirements referred to in paragraph 2(1)(*a*)(i) above are (subject to paragraph 4 below)—

(*a*) that none of the property held on the trusts can at any time in the period of six years beginning with the date on which it became so held be applied otherwise than—

(i) for the maintenance, repair or preservation of, or making provision for public access to, property which is for the time being qualifying property, for the maintenance, repair or preservation of property held on the trusts or for such improvement of property so held as is reasonable having regard to the purposes of the trusts, or for defraying the expenses of the trustees in relation to the property so held;

(ii) as respects income not so applied and not accumulated, for the benefit of a body within Schedule 3 to this Act or of a qualifying charity; and

(*b*) that none of the property can, on ceasing to be held on the trusts at any time in that period or, if the settlor dies in that period, at any time before his death, devolve otherwise than on any such body or charity; and

(*c*) that income arising from property held on the trusts cannot at any time after the end of that period be applied except as mentioned in paragraph (*a*)(i) or (ii) above.

(2) Property is qualifying property for the purposes of sub-paragraph (1) above if—

(*a*) it has been designated under section 34(1) of the Finance Act 1975 or section 77(1)(*b*), (*c*), (*d*) or (*e*) of the Finance Act 1976 or section 31(1)(*b*), (*c*), (*d*) or (*e*) of this Act; and

(*b*) the requisite undertaking has been given with respect to it under section 34 of the Finance Act 1975 or under section 76, 78(5)(*b*) or 82(3) of the Finance Act 1976 or under section 30, 32(5)(*b*) [, 32A(6), (8)(*b*) or (9)(*b*)][1] or 79(3) of this Act or paragraph 5 of Schedule 5 to this Act; and

(*c*) tax has not (since the last occasion on which such an undertaking was given) become chargeable with respect to it under the said section 34 or under section 78 or 82(3) of the Finance Act 1976 or under section 32 [, 32A][1] [or 79(3A)][4] of this Act or paragraph 3 of Schedule 5 to this Act.

(3) If it appears to the Treasury that provision is, or is to be, made by a settlement for the maintenance, repair or preservation of any such property as is mentioned in subsection (1)(*b*), (*c*), (*d*) or (*e*) of section 31 of this Act they may, on a claim made for the purpose—

(*a*) designate that property under this sub-paragraph, and

(*b*) accept with respect to it an undertaking such as is described in subsection (4) [, or (as the case may be) undertakings such as are described in subsections (4) and (4A),][1] of that section;

and, if they do so, sub-paragraph (2) above shall have effect as if the designation were under that section and the undertaking [or undertakings][1] under section 30 of this Act and as if the reference to tax becoming chargeable were a reference to the occurrence of an event on which tax would become chargeable under section 32 [or 32A][1] of this Act if there had been a conditionally exempt transfer of the property when the claim was made and the undertaking [or undertakings][1] had been given under section 30.

[(3A) Section 35A of this Act shall apply in relation to an undertaking given under sub-paragraph (3) above as it applies in relation to an undertaking given under section 30 of this Act.][3]

(4) A charity is a qualifying charity for the purposes of sub-paragraph (1) above if it exists wholly or mainly for maintaining, repairing or preserving for the public benefit buildings of historic or architectural interest, land of scenic, historic or scientific interest or objects of national, scientific, historic or artistic interest; and in this sub-paragraph "national interest" includes interest within any part of the United Kingdom.

(5) Designations, undertakings and acceptances made under section 84(6) of the Finance Act 1976 or section 94(3) of the Finance Act 1982 shall be treated as made under sub-paragraph (3) above.

[(5A) In the case of property which, if a direction is given under paragraph 1 above, will be property to which paragraph 15A below applies, sub-paragraph (1)(*b*) above shall have effect as if for the reference to the settlor there were substituted a reference to either the settlor or the person referred to in paragraph 15A(2).][2]

Commentary—*Simon's Taxes* **I7.542, I7.543**; *Foster* **G5.42, 43**.

Definitions—"Charity", s 272; "conditionally exempt transfer", s 30(2); "settlor", s 44.

Cross references—FA 2004 Sch 15 para 11 (exemptions from charge to tax under FA 2004 Sch 15 (benefits received by former owner of property) where this paragraph applies).

Amendments—[1] Words in sub-paras (2)(*b*), (*c*), (3) inserted by FA 1985 Sch 26 para 12 in relation to events after 18 March 1985.

[2] Sub-para (5A) added by FA 1987 Sch 9 paras 2, 5 in relation to directions given after 16 March 1987.

[3] Inserted by FA 1998 Sch 25 para 8 in relation to undertakings given on or after 31 July 1998.

[4] In sub-para (2)(*c*), words substituted for words "or 79(3)" by F(No 2)A 2015 s 12(8)(*d*) with effect in relation to occasions on which tax would (ignoring the effect of the amendments made by F(No 2)A 2015 s 12) fall to be charged under IHTA 1984 s 64 on or after 18 November 2015.

4—(1) Paragraphs (*a*) and (*b*) of paragraph 3(1) above do not apply to property which—

(*a*) was previously comprised in another settlement, and

(*b*) ceased to be comprised in that settlement and became comprised in the current settlement in circumstances such that by virtue of paragraph 9(1) below there was no charge (or, but for paragraph 9(4), there would have been no charge) to tax in respect of it;

and in relation to any such property paragraph 3(1)(c) above shall apply with the omission of the words "at any time after the end of that period".

(2) Sub-paragraph (1) above shall not have effect if the time when the property comprised in the previous settlement devolved otherwise than on any such body or charity as is mentioned in paragraph 3(1)(*a*) above fell before the expiration of the period of six years there mentioned; but in such a case paragraph 3(1) above shall apply to the current settlement as if for the references to that period of six years there were substituted references to the period beginning with the date on which the property became comprised in the current settlement and ending six years after the date on which it became held on the relevant trusts of the previous settlement (or, where this sub-paragraph has already had effect in relation to the property, the date on which it became held on the relevant trusts of the first settlement in the series).

Commentary—*Simon's Taxes* **I7.542, I7.543**; *Foster* **G5.42, 43**.

Definitions—"Charity", s 272; "settlement", s 43; "settlor", s 44.

Withdrawal

5 If in the Treasury's opinion the facts concerning any property or its administration cease to warrant the continuance of the effect of a direction given under paragraph 1 above in respect of the property, they may at any time by notice in writing to the trustees withdraw the direction on such grounds, and from such date, as may be specified in the notice; and the direction shall cease to have effect accordingly.

Information

6 Where a direction under paragraph 1 above has effect in respect of property, the trustees shall from time to time furnish the Treasury with such accounts and other information relating to the property as the Treasury may reasonably require.

Enforcement of trusts

7 Where a direction under paragraph 1 above has effect in respect of property, the trusts on which the property is held shall be enforceable at the suit of the Treasury and the Treasury shall, as respects the appointment, removal and retirement of trustees, have the rights and powers of a beneficiary.

Commentary—*Simon's Taxes* **I7.542, I7.543**; *Fosters* **G5.42, 43**.

PART II
PROPERTY LEAVING MAINTENANCE FUNDS

Charge to tax

8—(1) This paragraph applies to settled property which is held on trusts which comply with the requirements mentioned in paragraph 3(1) above, and in respect of which a direction given under paragraph 1 above has effect.

(2) Subject to paragraphs 9 and 10 below, there shall be a charge to tax under this paragraph—

(*a*) where settled property ceases to be property to which this paragraph applies, otherwise than by virtue of an application of the kind mentioned in paragraph 3(1)(*a*)(i) or (ii) above or by devolving on any such body or charity as is mentioned in paragraph 3(1)(*a*)(ii);

(*b*) in a case in which paragraph (*a*) above does not apply, where the trustees make a disposition (otherwise than by such an application) as a result of which the value of settled property to which this paragraph applies is less than it would be but for the disposition.

(3) Subsections (4), (5) and (10) of section 70 of this Act shall apply for the purposes of this paragraph as they apply for the purposes of that section (with the substitution of a reference to sub-paragraph (2)(*b*) above for the reference in section 70(4) to section 70(2)(*b*)).

(4) The rate at which tax is charged under this paragraph shall be determined in accordance with paragraphs 11 to 15 below.

(5) The devolution of property on a body or charity shall not be free from charge by virtue of sub-paragraph (2)(*a*) above if, at or before the time of devolution, an interest under the settlement in which the property was comprised immediately before the devolution is or has been acquired for a consideration in money or money's worth by that or another such body or charity; but for the purposes of this sub-paragraph any acquisition from another such body or charity shall be disregarded.

(6) For the purposes of sub-paragraph (5) above a body or charity shall be treated as acquiring an interest for a consideration in money or money's worth if it becomes entitled to the interest as a result of transactions which include a disposition for such consideration (whether to that body or charity or to another person) of that interest or of other property.

Commentary—*Simon's Taxes* **I5.651, I7.545**; *Foster* **E6.51, G5.45**.

Definitions—"Charity", s 272; "settled property", s 43.

Cross references—See FA 1986 Sch 19 para 42 (the new rates of tax substituted by FA 1986 Sch 19 para 36 and s 7 above as amended by FA 1986 to apply for tax chargeable under this paragraph in certain events occurring before 18 March 1986).

Exceptions from charge

9—(1) Tax shall not be charged under paragraph 8 above in respect of property which, within the permitted period after the occasion on which tax would be chargeable under that paragraph, becomes comprised in another settlement as a result of a transfer of value which is exempt under section 27 of this Act.

(2) In sub-paragraph (1) above "the permitted period" means the period of thirty days except in a case where the occasion referred to is the death of the settlor, and in such a case means the period of two years.

(3) Sub-paragraph (1) above shall not apply to any property if the person who makes the transfer of value has acquired it for a consideration in money or money's worth; and for the purposes of this sub-paragraph a person shall be treated as acquiring any property for such consideration if he becomes entitled to it as a result of transactions which include a disposition for such consideration (whether to him or another) of that or other property.

(4) If the amount on which tax would be charged apart from sub-paragraph (1) above in respect of any property exceeds the value of the property immediately after it becomes comprised in the other settlement (less the amount of any consideration for its transfer received by the person who makes the transfer of value), that sub-paragraph shall not apply but the amount on which tax is charged shall be equal to the excess.

(5) The reference in sub-paragraph (4) above to the amount on which tax would be charged is a reference to the amount on which it would be charged apart from—

(*a*) section 5(5)(*b*) of this Act (as applied by paragraph 8(3) above), and

(*b*) Chapters I and II of Part V of this Act;

and the reference in that sub-paragraph to the amount on which tax is charged is a reference to the amount on which it would be charged apart from section 70(5)(b) and those Chapters.

Commentary—*Simon's Taxes* **I7.545**; *Foster* **G5.45**.

10—(1) Tax shall not be charged under paragraph 8 above in respect of property which ceases to be property to which that paragraph applies on becoming—

(*a*) property to which the settlor or his spouse [or civil partner][1] is beneficially entitled, or

(*b*) property to which the settlor's widow or widower [or surviving civil partner][1] is beneficially entitled if the settlor has died in the two years preceding the time when it becomes such property.

(2) If the amount on which tax would be charged apart from sub-paragraph (1) above in respect of any property exceeds the value of the property immediately after it becomes property of a description specified in paragraph (*a*) or (*b*) of that sub-paragraph (less the amount of any consideration for its transfer received by the trustees), that sub-paragraph shall not apply but the amount on which tax is charged shall be equal to the excess.

(3) The reference in sub-paragraph (2) above to the amount on which tax would be charged is a reference to the amount on which it would be charged apart from—

(*a*) section 70(5)(*b*) of this Act (as applied by paragraph 8(3) above), and

(*b*) Chapters I and II of Part V of this Act;

and the reference in sub-paragraph (2) above to the amount on which tax is charged is a reference to the amount on which it would be charged apart from section 70(5)(b) and those Chapters.

(4) Sub-paragraph (1) above shall not apply in relation to any property if, at or before the time when it becomes property of a description specified in paragraph (*a*) or (*b*) of that sub-paragraph, an interest under the settlement in which the property was comprised immediately before it ceased to be property to which paragraph 8 above applies is or has been acquired for a consideration in money or money's worth by the person who becomes beneficially entitled.

(5) For the purposes of sub-paragraph (4) above a person shall be treated as acquiring an interest for a consideration in money or money's worth if he becomes entitled to the interest as a result of transactions which include a disposition for such consideration (whether to him or to another person) of that interest or of other property.

(6) Sub-paragraph (1) above shall not apply in respect of property if it was relevant property before it became (or last became) property to which paragraph 8 above applies and, by virtue of paragraph 16(1) or 17(1) below, tax was not chargeable (or, but for paragraph 16(2) or 17(4), would not have been chargeable) under section 65 of this Act in respect of its ceasing to be relevant property before becoming (or last becoming) property to which paragraph 8 above applies.

(7) Sub-paragraph (1) above shall not apply in respect of property if—

(*a*) before it last became property to which paragraph 8 above applies it was comprised in another settlement in which it was property to which that paragraph applies, and

(*b*) it ceased to be comprised in the other settlement and last became property to which that paragraph applies in circumstances such that by virtue of paragraph 9(1) above there was no charge (or, but for paragraph 9(4), there would have been no charge) to tax in respect of it.

(8) Sub-paragraph (1) above shall not apply unless the person who becomes beneficially entitled to the property is domiciled in the United Kingdom at the time when he becomes so entitled.

Commentary—*Simon's Taxes* **I5.651, I7.545**; *Foster* **E6.51, G5.45**.
Definitions—"relevant property", s 58(1).
Amendments—[1] Words in sub-para (1) inserted by Tax and Civil Partnership Regulations, SI 2005/3229, regs 3, 39(1), (2), with effect from 5 December 2005 (reg 1(1)).

Rates of charge

11—(1) This paragraph applies where tax is chargeable under paragraph 8 above and—

(*a*) the property in respect of which the tax is chargeable was relevant property before it became (or last became) property to which that paragraph applies, and

(*b*) by virtue of paragraph 16(1) or 17(1) below tax was not chargeable (or, but for paragraph 16(2) or 17(4), would not have been chargeable) under section 65 of this Act in respect of its ceasing to be relevant property on or before becoming (or last becoming) property to which paragraph 8 above applies.

(2) Where this paragraph applies, the rate at which the tax is charged shall be the aggregate of the following percentages—

(*a*) 0·25 per cent for each of the first forty complete successive quarters in the relevant period,

(*b*) 0·20 per cent for each of the next forty,

(*c*) 0·15 per cent for each of the next forty,

(*d*) 0·10 per cent for each of the next forty, and

(*e*) 0·05 per cent for each of the next forty.

(3) In sub-paragraph (2) above "the relevant period" means the period beginning with the latest of—

(*a*) the date of the last ten-year anniversary of the settlement in which the property was comprised before it ceased (or last ceased) to be relevant property,

(*b*) the day on which the property became (or last became) relevant property before it ceased (or last ceased) to be such property, and

(*c*) 13th March 1975,

and ending with the day before the event giving rise to the charge.

(4) Where the property in respect of which the tax is chargeable has at any time ceased to be and again become property to which paragraph 8 above applies in circumstances such that by virtue of paragraph 9(1) above there was no charge to tax in respect of it (or, but for paragraph 9(4), there would have been no charge), it shall for the purposes of this paragraph be treated as having been property to which paragraph 8 above applies throughout the period mentioned in paragraph 9(1).

Commentary—*Simon's Taxes* **I5.651, I7.545**; *Foster* **E6.51, G5.45**.
Definitions—"relevant property", s 58(1).

12—(1) This paragraph applies where tax is chargeable under paragraph 8 above and paragraph 11 above does not apply.

(2) Where this paragraph applies, the rate at which the tax is charged shall be the higher of—

(*a*) the first rate (as determined in accordance with paragraph 13 below), and

(*b*) the second rate (as determined in accordance with paragraph 14 below).

Commentary—*Simon's Taxes* **I5.651, I7.545**; *Foster* **E6.51, G5.45**.

13—(1) The first rate is the aggregate of the following percentages—

(*a*) 0·25 per cent for each of the first forty complete successive quarters in the relevant period,

(*b*) 0·20 per cent for each of the next forty,

(*c*) 0·15 per cent for each of the next forty,

(*d*) 0·10 per cent for each of the next forty, and

(*e*) 0·05 per cent for each of the next forty.

(2) In sub-paragraph (1) above "the relevant period" means the period beginning with the day on which the property in respect of which the tax is chargeable became (or first became) property to which paragraph 8 above applies, and ending with the day before the event giving rise to the charge.

(3) For the purposes of sub-paragraph (2) above, any occasion on which property became property to which paragraph 8 above applies, and which occurred before an occasion of charge to tax under that paragraph in respect of the property, shall be disregarded.

(4) The reference in sub-paragraph (3) above to an occasion of charge to tax under paragraph 8 does not include a reference to—

(*a*) the occasion by reference to which the rate is being determined in accordance with this Schedule, or

(*b*) an occasion which would not be an occasion of charge but for paragraph 9(4) above.

Commentary—*Simon's Taxes* **I5.651, I7.545**; *Foster* **E6.51, G5.45**.

14—(1) If the settlor is alive, the second rate is the effective rate at which tax would be charged, on the amount on which it is chargeable, [in accordance with the appropriate provision of section 7 of this Act][1] if the amount were the value transferred by a chargeable transfer made by him on the occasion on which the tax becomes chargeable.

[(1A) The rate or rates of tax determined under sub-paragraph (1) above in respect of any occasion shall not be affected by the death of the settlor after that occasion.][2]

(2) If the settlor is dead, the second rate is (subject to sub-paragraph (3) below) the effective rate at which tax would have been charged, on the amount on which it is chargeable, [in accordance with the appropriate provision of section 7 of this Act][1] if the amount had been added to the value transferred on his death and had formed the highest part of it.

[(2A) In determining for the purposes of sub-paragraph (2) the effective rate or rates at which tax would have been charged on the amount in accordance with section 7(1), the effect of Schedule 1A (if it would have applied) is to be disregarded.][4]

(3) If the settlor died before 13th March 1975, the second rate is the effective rate at which tax would have been charged, on the amount on which it is chargeable ("the chargeable amount"), [in accordance with the appropriate provision of section 7 of this Act][1] if the settlor had died when the event occasioning the charge under paragraph 8 above occurred, the value transferred on his death had been equal to the amount on which estate duty was chargeable when he in fact died, and the chargeable amount had been added to that value and had formed the highest part of it.

(4) Where, in the case of a settlement ("the current settlement"), tax is chargeable under paragraph 8 above in respect of property which—

(*a*) was previously comprised in another settlement, and

(*b*) ceased to be comprised in that settlement and became comprised in the current settlement in circumstances such that by virtue of paragraph 9(1) above there was no charge (or, but for paragraph 9(4), there would have been no charge) to tax in respect of it,

then, subject to sub-paragraph (5) below, references in sub-paragraphs (1) to (3) above to the settlor shall be construed as references to the person who was the settlor in relation to the settlement mentioned in paragraph (a) above (or, if the Board so determine, the person who was the settlor in relation to the current settlement).

(5) Where, in the case of a settlement ("the current settlement"), tax is chargeable under paragraph 8 above in respect of property which—

(*a*) was previously comprised at different times in other settlements ("the previous settlements"), and

(*b*) ceased to be comprised in each of them, and became comprised in another of them or in the current settlement, in circumstances such that by virtue of paragraph 9(1) above there was no charge (or, but for paragraph 9(4), there would have been no charge) to tax in respect of it,

references in sub-paragraphs (1) to (3) above to the settlor shall be construed as references to the person who was the settlor in relation to the previous settlement in which the property was first comprised (or, if the Board so determine, any person selected by them who was the settlor in relation to any of the other previous settlements or the current settlement).

(6) Sub-paragraph (7) below shall apply if—

(*a*) in the period of [seven years][1] preceding a charge under paragraph 8 above (the "current charge"), there has been another charge under that paragraph where tax was charged at the second rate, and (*b*) the person who is the settlor for the purposes of the current charge is the settlor for the purposes of the other charge (whether or not the settlements are the same and, if the settlor is dead, whether or not he has died since the other charge);

and in sub-paragraph (7) below the other charge is referred to as the "previous charge".

(7) Where this sub-paragraph applies, the amount on which tax was charged on the previous charge (or, if there have been more than one, the aggregate of the amounts on which tax was charged on each)—

(*a*) shall, for the purposes of calculating the rate of the current charge under sub-paragraph (1) above, be taken to be the value transferred by a chargeable transfer made by the settlor immediately before the occasion of the current charge, and

(*b*) shall, for the purposes of calculating the rate of the current charge under sub-paragraph (2) or (3) above, be taken to increase the value there mentioned by an amount equal to that amount (or aggregate).

(8) References in sub-paragraphs (1) to (3) above to the effective rate are to the rate found by expressing the tax chargeable as a percentage of the amount on which it is charged.

[(9) For the purposes of sub-paragraph (1) above the appropriate provision of section 7 of this Act is subsection (2), and for the purposes of sub-paragraphs (2) and (3) above it is (if the settlement was made on death) subsection (1) and (if not) subsection (2).][3]

Commentary—*Simon's Taxes* **I5.651, I7.545**; *Foster* **E6.51, G5.45**.

Definitions—"Estate duty", s 272; "settlor", s 44.

Cross references—See FA 1986 Sch 19 para 40 (where a death or other event occurs after 17 March 1986, the amendments to this paragraph by FA 1986 Sch 19 para 38 not to affect the tax chargeable on a transfer of value occurring before 18 March 1986),

Sch 19 para 42 (s 7 and Sch 1 above as amended by FA 1986 to apply in certain events occurring before 18 March 1986).

Amendments—[1] Words in sub-paras (1), (2), (3), (6)(*a*) substituted by FA 1986 s 101(3) and Sch 19 para 38 with respect to transfers of value made, and other events occurring after 17 March 1986.

[2] Sub-para (1A) inserted by FA 1986 s 101(3) and Sch 19 para 38 with respect to transfers of value made, and other events occurring after 17 March 1986.

[3] Sub-para (9) substituted by FA 1986 s 101(3) and Sch 19 para 38 with respect to transfers of value made, and other events occurring after 17 March 1986.

[4] Sub-para (2A) inserted by FA 2012 s 209, Sch 33 paras 2, 8 with effect in cases where D's death occurs on or after 6 April 2012.

15 Where property is, by virtue of paragraph 1(3) above, treated as property in respect of which a direction has been given under paragraph 1, it shall for the purposes of paragraphs 11 to 14 above be treated as having become property to which paragraph 8 above applies when the transfer of value mentioned in paragraph 1(3) was made.

Commentary—*Simon's Taxes* **I5.651, I7.545**; *Foster* **E6.51, G5.45**.

[Maintenance fund following interest in possession

15A—(1) In relation to settled property to which this paragraph applies, the provisions of this Part of this Schedule shall have effect with the modifications set out in the following sub-paragraphs.

(2) This paragraph applies to property which became property to which paragraph 8 above applies on the occasion of a transfer of value which was made by a person beneficially entitled to an interest in possession in the property, and which (so far as the value transferred by it was attributable to the property)—

(*a*) was an exempt transfer by virtue of the combined effect of either—

(i) sections 27 and 57(5) of this Act, or

(ii) sections 27 and 57A of this Act, and

(*b*) would but for those sections have been a chargeable transfer;

and in the following sub-paragraphs "the person entitled to the interest in possession" means the person above referred to.

(3) Paragraph 9(2) shall have effect as if for the reference to the settlor there were substituted a reference to either the settlor or the person entitled to the interest in possession.

(4) Paragraph 10 shall not apply if the person entitled to the interest in possession had died at or before the time when the property became property to which paragraph 8 above applies; and in any other case shall have effect with the substitution in sub-paragraph (1) of the following words for the words from "on becoming" onwards—

"(*a*) on becoming property to which the person entitled to the interest in possession is beneficially entitled, or

(*b*) on becoming—

(i) property to which that person's spouse [or civil partner][2] is beneficially entitled, or

(ii) property to which that person's widow or widower [or surviving civil partner][2] is beneficially entitled if that person has died in the two years preceding the time when it becomes such property;

but paragraph (b) above applies only where the [spouse or civil partner, or widow or widower or surviving civil partner,][2] would have become beneficially entitled to the property on the termination of the interest in possession had the property not then become property to which paragraph 8 above applies.".

(5) Paragraph 11 shall not apply.

(6) Sub-paragraphs (1) to (3) of paragraph 14 shall have effect as if for the references to the settlor there were substituted references to the person entitled to the interest in possession.

(7) Sub-paragraph (4) of paragraph 14 shall have effect with the insertion after paragraph (*b*) of the words "and

(*c*) was, in relation to either of those settlements, property to which paragraph 15A below applied,",

and with the substitution for the words from "settlor shall" onwards of the words "person entitled to the interest in possession shall, if the Board so determine, be construed as references to the person who was the settlor in relation to the current settlement.".

(8) Sub-paragraph (5) of paragraph 14 shall have effect with the insertion after paragraph (*b*) of the words "and

(*c*) was, in relation to any of those settlements, property to which paragraph 15A below applied,",

and with the substitution for the words from "settlor shall" onwards of the words "person entitled to the interest in possession shall, if the Board so determine, be construed as references to any person selected by them who was the settlor in relation to any of the previous settlements or the current settlement."

(9) Except in a case where the Board have made a determination under sub-paragraph (4) or (5) of paragraph 14, sub-paragraphs (6) and (7) of that paragraph shall have effect as if for the references to the settlor there were substituted references to the person entitled to the interest in possession.

(10) Sub-paragraph (9) of paragraph 14 shall have effect with the substitution for the words "(if the settlement was made on death)" of the words "(if the person entitled to the interest in possession had died at or before the time when the property became property to which paragraph 8 above applies).][1]

Commentary—*Simon's Taxes* **I7.544**; *Foster* **G5.44**.

Amendments—[1] This paragraph inserted by FA 1987 Sch 9 paras 3, 6 where the occasion of the charge or potential charge to tax under para 8 above falls after 16 March 1987.

[2] Words in sub-para (4) (in substituted para 10(1)) inserted and substituted by Tax and Civil Partnership Regulations, SI 2005/3229, regs 3, 39(1), (3), with effect from 5 December 2005 (reg 1(1)).

PART III
PROPERTY BECOMING COMPRISED IN MAINTENANCE FUNDS

16—(1) Tax shall not be charged under section 65 of this Act in respect of property which ceases to be relevant property on becoming property in respect of which a direction under paragraph 1 above then has effect.

(2) If the amount on which tax would be charged apart from sub-paragraph (1) above in respect of any property exceeds the value of the property immediately after it becomes property in respect of which the direction has effect (less the amount of any consideration for its transfer received by the trustees of the settlement in which it was comprised immediately before it ceased to be relevant property), that sub-paragraph shall not apply but the amount on which tax is charged shall be equal to the excess.

(3) Sub-paragraph (1) above shall not apply in relation to any property if, at or before the time when it becomes property in respect of which the direction has effect, an interest under the settlement in which it was comprised immediately before it ceased to be relevant property is or has been acquired for a consideration in money or money's worth by the trustees of the settlement in which it becomes comprised on ceasing to be relevant property.

(4) For the purposes of sub-paragraph (3) above trustees shall be treated as acquiring an interest for a consideration in money or money's worth if they become entitled to the interest as a result of transactions which include a disposition for such consideration (whether to them or to another person) of that interest or of other property.

Definitions—"relevant property", s 58(1); "trustee", s 45.

17—(1) Tax shall not be charged under section 65 of this Act in respect of property which ceases to be relevant property if within the permitted period an individual makes a transfer of value—

(*a*) which is exempt under section 27 of this Act, and

(*b*) the value transferred by which is attributable to that property.

(2) In sub-paragraph (1) above "the permitted period" means the period of thirty days beginning with the day on which the property ceases to be relevant property except in a case where it does so on the death of any person, and in such a case means the period of two years beginning with that day.

(3) Sub-paragraph (1) above shall not apply if the individual has acquired the property concerned for a consideration in money or money's worth; and for the purposes of this sub-paragraph an individual shall be treated as acquiring any property for such consideration if he becomes entitled to it as a result of transactions which include a disposition for such consideration (whether to him or another) of that or other property.

(4) If the amount on which tax would be charged apart from sub-paragraph (1) above in respect of any property exceeds the value of the property immediately after the transfer there referred to (less the amount of any consideration for its transfer received by the individual), that sub-paragraph shall not apply but the amount on which tax is charged shall be equal to the excess.

Definitions—"relevant property", s 58(1).

18 In paragraphs 16(2) and 17(4) above the references to the amount on which tax would be charged are references to the amount on which it would be charged apart from—

(*a*) paragraph (*b*) of section 65(2) of this Act, and

(*b*) Chapters I and II of Part V of this Act;

and the references to the amount on which tax is charged are references to the amount on which it would be charged apart from that paragraph and those Chapters.

Commentary—*Simon's Taxes* **I5.337, I7.544**; *Foster* **E3.37, G5.44**.

SCHEDULE 5

CONDITIONAL EXEMPTION: DEATHS BEFORE 7TH APRIL 1976

Section 35

HMRC Manuals—Inheritance Tax Manual IHTM20501–20512 (life policy linked with a loan and inheritance trusts).

Cross references—See FA 1985 s 95 (transfer of Treasury functions under this Schedule to the Commissioners of Inland Revenue from 25 July 1985).

FA 2012 Sch 14 para 33 (gifts to the nation).

Charge on failure of condition of exemption—objects

1—(1) Where, under section 31 of the Finance Act 1975 the value of an object has been left out of account and the Treasury are satisfied that at any time the undertaking given under that section or under paragraph 5 below with respect to the object has not been observed in a material respect, tax shall be chargeable with respect to the object in accordance with paragraph 2 below.

(2) Where, under section 31 of the Finance Act 1975 the value of any object has been left out of account and—

(*a*) sub-paragraph (1) above does not apply, but

(*b*) the object is disposed of, whether on sale or otherwise,

then, subject to the following provisions of this paragraph, tax shall be chargeable with respect to the object in accordance with paragraph 2 below; but where the value of an object has been so left out of account on the death of more than one person, the tax chargeable under this sub-paragraph shall be chargeable only by reference to the last death.

(3) Tax shall not be chargeable by virtue of sub-paragraph (2) above with respect to an object—

(*a*) on its being sold by private treaty to a body mentioned in Schedule 3 to this Act or on its being disposed of to such a body otherwise than by sale, or

(*b*) if it is disposed of otherwise than by sale and the undertaking previously given with respect to it is replaced by a further undertaking under paragraph 5 below.

(4) For the purposes of sub-paragraph (2) above, the acceptance of an object under section 230 of this Act shall not be treated as a disposal of the object.

Commentary—*Simon's Taxes* **I7.522**; *Foster* **G5.22**.

2—(1) The following provisions of this paragraph shall have effect where, under section 31 of the Finance Act 1975 the value of any object has been left out of account in determining the value transferred by the transfer of value made on the death of any person (in this paragraph referred to as the value transferred on death) and tax becomes chargeable with respect to the object under paragraph 1 above by reason of the disposal of the object or the non-observance of an undertaking (in this paragraph referred to as a chargeable event).

(2) The tax chargeable under paragraph 1 above with respect to an object shall be so much of the tax that would have been chargeable on the value transferred on death as would have been attributable to the value of the object if—

(*a*) section 31 of the Finance Act 1975 had not applied to the object, and (*b*) the value of the object at the time of the death had been equal to its value at the time of the chargeable event and, if the chargeable event was a disposal on sale complying with paragraph 6 below, that value had been equal to the proceeds of sale.

(3) Where—

(*a*) under section 31 of the Finance Act 1975 the value of two or more objects has been left out of account in determining the value transferred on death, and

(*b*) those objects formed a set at the time of the death, and

(*c*) tax becomes chargeable under paragraph 1 above with respect to two or more of the objects by reason of chargeable events occurring at different times,

the preceding provisions of this paragraph shall apply as if both or all the chargeable events had occurred at the time of the earlier or earliest one, and the tax chargeable with respect to the objects shall be adjusted accordingly on the occurrence of each of the subsequent chargeable events.

(4) Sub-paragraph (3) above shall not apply with respect to two or more chargeable events which are disposals to different persons who are neither acting in concert nor connected with each other.

Commentary—*Simon's Taxes* **I7.522**; *Foster* **G5.22**.

Press releases etc—IR 3-5-84 (taper relief under FA 1960 s 64 is not available in relation to a charge under these provisions).

Charge on failure of condition of exemption—buildings etc

3—(1) Where, under subsection (2) of section 34 of the Finance Act 1975 the value of any property has been left out of account and the Treasury are satisfied that at any time the undertaking given under that subsection or under paragraph 5 below in respect of that property has not been observed in a material respect, then, subject to sub-paragraph (3) below, tax shall be chargeable in accordance with paragraph 4 below with respect to the property and any property associated with it.

(2) Where, under section 34(2) of the Finance Act 1975 the value of any property has been left out of account in determining the value transferred on the death of any person and—

(*a*) sub-paragraph (1) above does not apply, but

(*b*) the property is disposed of, whether on sale or otherwise,

then, subject to sub-paragraphs (3) and (4) below, tax shall be chargeable in accordance with paragraph 4 below with respect to the property and any property associated with it; but where the value of the property has been left out of account on the death of more than one person, the tax chargeable under this sub-paragraph shall be chargeable only by reference to the last death.

(3) The Treasury may direct that the tax chargeable under this paragraph on a failure to observe an undertaking with respect to any property or on the disposal of any property shall be chargeable with respect only to that property, if it appears to them that the entity consisting of the building, land and objects concerned has not been materially affected.

(4) Tax shall not be chargeable under sub-paragraph (2) above with respect to any property—

(*a*) on its being sold by private treaty to a body mentioned in Schedule 3 to this Act or on its being disposed of to such a body otherwise than by sale, or

(*b*) if it is disposed of otherwise than by sale and the undertaking previously given with respect to it is replaced by a further undertaking under paragraph 5 below;

and for the purposes of sub-paragraph (2) above the acceptance of any property under section 230 of this Act shall not be treated as a disposal of the property.

(5) For the purposes of this paragraph, two or more properties are associated with each other if one of them is a building falling within subsection (1)(*b*) of section 34 of the Finance Act 1975 and the other or others such land or objects as, in relation to that building, fall within subsection (1)(*c*) or (*d*) of that section.

Commentary—*Simon's Taxes* **I7.522**; *Foster* **G5.22**.

4 The tax chargeable under paragraph 3 above with respect to any property shall be so much of the tax that would have been chargeable on the value transferred on the death as would have been attributable to the value of the property if—

(*a*) section 34 of the Finance Act 1975 had not applied to the property; and

(*b*) the value of the property at the time of the death had been equal to its value at the time the tax becomes chargeable and, if it becomes chargeable on a sale complying with paragraph 6 below, that value had been equal to the proceeds of sale.

Commentary—*Simon's Taxes* **I7.522**; *Foster* **G5.22**.

Further undertaking on disposal

[**5**—(1) The further undertaking referred to in paragraph 1 above is the requisite undertaking described in section 31(2) of this Act given with respect to the object in question by such person as the Board think appropriate in the circumstances of the case.

(2) Subsection (3) of section 31 of this Act shall apply in relation to documents which are designated as objects to which section 31 of the Finance Act 1975 applies as that subsection applies in relation to documents designated under section 31(1)(*a*) of this Act.

(3) The further undertaking referred to in paragraph 3 above is—

(*a*) the requisite undertaking described in subsection (4) of section 31 of this Act given with respect to the property in question by such person as the Board think appropriate in the circumstances of the case, or

(*b*) (where applicable) the requisite undertakings described in subsections (4) and (4A) of that section given with respect to the property in question by such person or persons as the Board think appropriate in the circumstances of the case.][1]

Commentary—*Simon's Taxes* **I7.521, I7.522**; *Foster* **G5.21, 22.**

Amendments—[1] Substituted by FA 1998 Sch 25 para 7 in relation to the giving of any undertaking on or after 31 July 1998.

Requirements of sale

6 A sale complies with this paragraph if—

(*a*) it was not intended to confer any gratuitous benefit on any person, and

(*b*) it was either a transaction at arm's length between persons not connected with each other or a transaction such as might be expected to be made at arm's length between persons not connected with each other.

Commentary—*Simon's Taxes* **I7.521, I7.522**; *Foster* **G5.21, 22.**

[SCHEDULE 5A

QUALIFYING PAYMENTS: VICTIMS OF PERSECUTION DURING SECOND WORLD WAR ERA

Section 153ZA

Amendments—Schedule 5A inserted by FA 2016 s 95(2) with effect in relation to deaths occurring on or after 1 January 2015.

PART 1
COMPENSATION PAYMENTS

Amendments—Schedule 5A inserted by FA 2016 s 95(2) with effect in relation to deaths occurring on or after 1 January 2015.

1 A payment of a fixed amount from the German foundation known as "Remembrance, Responsibility and Future" (*Stiftung EVZ*) in respect of a person who was a slave or forced labourer.

2 A payment of a fixed amount in accordance with the arrangements made under the Swiss Bank Settlement (Holocaust Victim Assets Litigation) in respect of the slave or forced labourers qualifying for compensation under the Remembrance, Responsibility and Future scheme.

3 A payment of a fixed amount from the Hardship Fund established by the Government of the Federal Republic of Germany.

4 A payment of a fixed amount from the National Fund of the Republic of Austria for Victims of National-Socialism under the terms of the scheme as at June 1995.

5 A payment of a fixed amount in respect of a slave or forced labourer from the Austrian Reconciliation Fund.

6 A payment of a fixed amount by the Swiss Refugee Programme in accordance with the arrangements made under the Swiss Bank Settlement (Holocaust Victim Assets Litigation) in respect of refugees.

7 A payment of a fixed amount under the foundation established in the Netherlands and known as the Dutch Maror Fund (*Stichting Maror-Gelden Overheid*).

8 A one-off payment of a fixed amount from the scheme established by the Government of the French Republic and known as the French Orphan Scheme.

9 A payment of a fixed amount from the Child Survivor Fund established by the Government of the Federal Republic of Germany.

PART 2
EX-GRATIA PAYMENTS

Amendments—Schedule 5A inserted by FA 2016 s 95(2) with effect in relation to deaths occurring on or after 1 January 2015.

10 A payment of a fixed amount made from the scheme established by the United Kingdom Government and known as the Far Eastern Prisoners of War Ex Gratia Scheme.][1]

Amendments—[1] Schedule 5A inserted by FA 2016 s 95(2) with effect in relation to deaths occurring on or after 1 January 2015.

SCHEDULE 6
TRANSITION FROM ESTATE DUTY
Section 273

General

1 References in any enactment, in any instrument made under any enactment, or in any document (whether executed before or after the passing of this Act) to estate duty or to death duties shall have effect, as far as may be, as if they included references to capital transfer tax chargeable under section 4 of this Act (or under section 22 of the Finance Act 1975).

Commentary—*Simon's Taxes* **I9.327, I10.211**; *Foster* **J3.27, K2.11.**
HMRC Manuals—Inheritance Tax Manual IHTM16233 (purchased or mortgaged reversions)
Definitions—"Estate duty", s 272.
Cross references—See FA 1986 s 100(1) (with effect from 25 July 1986 CTT to be known as inheritance tax; the reference to CTT in this paragraph to be construed accordingly).

Surviving spouse or former spouse

2 In determining for the purposes of this Act the value of the estate, immediately before his death, of a person whose spouse (or former spouse) died before 13th November 1974, there shall be left out of account the value of any property which, if estate duty were chargeable on the later death, would be excluded from the charge by section 5(2) of the Finance Act 1894 (relief on death of surviving spouse); and tax shall not be chargeable under section 52 of this Act on the coming to an end of an interest in possession in settled property if—

(*a*) the spouse (or former spouse) of the person beneficially entitled to the interest died before 13th November 1974, and

(*b*) the value of the property in which the interest subsists would by virtue of the preceding provisions of this paragraph have been left out of account in determining the value of the survivor's estate had he died immediately before the interest came to an end.

Commentary—*Simon's Taxes* **I5.921–I5.926**; *Foster* **E9.21–26.**
Definitions—"Estate duty", s 272.

Sales and mortgages of reversionary interests

3—(1) Where a reversionary interest in settled property was before 27th March 1974 sold or mortgaged for full consideration in money or money's worth, no greater amount of tax shall be payable by the purchaser or mortgagee when the interest falls into possession than the amounts of estate duty that would have been payable by him if none of the provisions of the Finance Act 1975 or this Act had been passed; and any tax which, by virtue of this paragraph, is not payable by the mortgagee but which is payable by the mortgagor shall rank as a charge subsequent to that of the mortgagee.

(2) Where the interest referred to in sub-paragraph (1) above was sold or mortgaged to a close company in relation to which the person entitled to the interest was a participator, sub-paragraph (1) above shall apply only to the extent that other persons had rights and interests in the company; and this sub-paragraph shall be construed as if contained in Part IV of this Act.

Commentary—*Simon's Taxes* **I5.285**; *Foster* **E2.85.**
Definitions—"close company", s 102(1); "mortgage", s 272; "participator", s 102(1); "purchaser", s 272; "reversionary interest", s 47.

Objects of national etc interest left out of account on death

4—(1) In its application to a sale which does not comply with paragraph 6 of Schedule 5 to this Act, subsection (2) of section 40 of the Finance Act 1930 shall have effect as if the reference to the proceeds of sale were a reference to the value of the objects on that date.

(2) Where there has been a death in relation to which the value of any property has been left out of account under section 40 of the Finance Act 1930 and, before any estate duty has become chargeable under the provisions of that section or of section 48 of the Finance Act 1950 there is a conditionally exempt transfer of that property, then, on the occurrence of a chargeable event in respect of that property—

[(*a*) tax shall be chargeable under section 32 or 32A of this Act (as the case may be), or

(*b*) estate duty shall be chargeable under those provisions,

as the Board may elect,][2]

and in this sub-paragraph "conditionally exempt transfer" includes a conditionally exempt occasion within the meaning of section 78(2) of this Act.

(3) In sections 33(7) [and (8)][1] and 79(1) of this Act, references to a conditionally exempt transfer of any property include references to a death in relation to which the value of any property has been left out of account under section 40 of the Finance Act 1930 and, in relation to such property, references to a chargeable event or to the tax chargeable in accordance with section 33 of this Act by reference to a chargeable event include references to an event on the occurrence of which estate duty becomes chargeable under section 40 of the Finance Act 1930 or section 48 of the Finance Act 1950 or to the estate duty so chargeable.

(4) In determining for the purposes of section 40(2) [or (2A)][2] of the Finance Act 1930 what is the last death on which the objects passed, there shall be disregarded any death after 6th April 1976.

(5) In the application of this paragraph to Northern Ireland for references to section 40 of the Finance Act 1930 and section 48 of the Finance Act 1950 there shall be substituted references to section 2 of the Finance Act (Northern Ireland) 1931 and Article 6 of the Finance (Northern Ireland) Order 1972 respectively.

Commentary—*Simon's Taxes* **I4.521**; *Foster* **D5.21**.
Cross-references—FA 2014 s 118 (gifts to the nation: estate duty).
Definitions—"Conditionally exempt transfer", s 30(2); "estate duty", s 272.
Amendments—[1] Words in sub-para (3) inserted by FA 1986 Sch 19 para 39 in relation to events after 17 March 1986.
[2] Sub-para (2)(*a*), (*b*) substituted, and words in sub-para (4) inserted, by FA 2016 s 97(7) with effect in relation to a chargeable event where the conditionally exempt transfer referred to in sub-s (2) or Sch 6 para 4(2) occurred after 16 March 2016. Those paras previously read as follows—

"(*a*) if there has been no conditionally exempt transfer of the property on death, either—
(i) tax shall be chargeable under section 32 or 32A of this Act (as the case may be), or
(ii) estate duty shall be chargeable under those provisions,
as the Board may elect, and
(*b*) if there has been such a conditionally exempt transfer, there shall be a charge under section 32 or 32A of this Act (as the case may be) and not under those provisions;".

SCHEDULE 7
COMMENCEMENT: SUPPLEMENTARY RULES
Section 274

1 In this Schedule "the repealed enactments" means the enactments repealed by this Act.

2 Sections 126 to 130 of this Act shall have effect (to the exclusion of the corresponding repealed enactments) in relation to any disposal after the end of 1984, whether the death in respect of which relief was given occurred before or after that time.

3 Where section 146 of this Act has effect in relation to a death after the end of 1984, it shall also have effect (to the exclusion of section 122 of the Finance Act 1976) in relation to any chargeable transfer of the kind referred to in section 146(2), whether made before or after that time.

4 Section 147 of this Act, so far as it relates to charges to tax in respect of claims to legitim made in the circumstances described in subsection (4) of that section, shall have effect (to the exclusion of the corresponding repealed enactments) in relation to claims made after the end of 1984, whether the testator died before or after that time.

5 Sections 148 and 149 of this Act shall have effect (to the exclusion of the corresponding repealed enactments) in any case where the donee's transfer is made after the end of 1984, whether the donor's transfer was made before or after that time.

6 Section 150 of this Act shall have effect (to the exclusion of section 88 of the Finance Act 1976) in relation to any claim made after the end of 1984.

7 Section 203 of this Act shall have effect (to the exclusion of the corresponding repealed enactments) in relation to any chargeable transfer made after the end of 1984 (whether the spouse transfer concerned was made before or after that time).

8 Section 218 of this Act, and section 245 so far as it relates to section 218, shall have effect in relation to settlements made after the end of 1984 to the exclusion of the corresponding repealed enactments, and those enactments shall continue to have effect in relation to settlements made before that time.

9 Section 219 of this Act, and section 245 so far as it relates to section 219, shall come into force on 1st January 1985 for all purposes to the exclusion of the corresponding repealed enactments, except that those enactments shall continue to have effect in relation to notices given before that time.

10 Section 220 of this Act shall come into force on 1st January 1985 for all purposes to the exclusion of the corresponding repealed enactments, except that those enactments shall continue to have effect in relation to authorisations given before that time.

11 Any order made under section 233 of this Act shall have effect in relation to interest chargeable (under the repealed enactments) in respect of chargeable transfers and other events before the end of 1984 as it has effect in relation to interest chargeable (under this Act) in respect of transfers and other events after that time.

12 Where payments are made or assets transferred after the end of 1984 in the circumstances described in section 262 of this Act, that section shall have effect (to the exclusion of the corresponding repealed enactments) whether the disposition first mentioned in that section was made before or after that time.

13 Section 264 of this Act shall have effect (to the exclusion of section 114 of the Finance Act 1976) in any case where the later transfer is made after the end of 1984, whether the earlier transfer was made before or after that date.

14 This Act shall not have effect in a case which would otherwise fall within paragraph 2(3) of Schedule 5 if the first chargeable event occurred before the end of 1984.

FINANCE ACT 1985

(1985 Chapter 54)

PART V

MISCELLANEOUS AND SUPPLEMENTARY

95 The national heritage: transfer of Treasury functions to Board

(1) The functions of the Treasury under—

(*a*) Part II, and section 76 of, and Schedules 3 to 5 to, the Capital Transfer Tax Act 1984 (exempt transfers);

(*b*) . . . ;[1]

(*c*) the enactments re-enacted by those provisions;

and the corresponding functions of the Treasury under any earlier enactments relating to capital transfer tax or estate duty, are hereby transferred to the Commissioners of Inland Revenue ("the Board").

(2) This section shall not affect the validity of anything done by or in relation to the Treasury before the passing of this Act; and anything which at that date is in the process of being done by or in relation to the Treasury may, if it relates to functions transferred by this section to the Board, be continued by or in relation to the Board.

(3) Any authorisation, designation, direction, approval, determination, or other thing given, made or done by the Treasury in connection with functions transferred by this section shall have effect as if given, made or done by the Board in so far as that is required for continuing its effect after the passing of this Act.

(4) Any enactment passed or instrument or other document made before the coming into operation of this section shall have effect, so far as may be necessary, for the purpose or in consequence of the transfer of functions effected by this section as if any reference to the Treasury were or included a reference to the Board.

Commentary—*Simon's Taxes* **I7.501**; *Foster* **G5.01**.

Cross references—See FA 1986 s 100(1)(*a*) (CTTA 1984 may be cited as Inheritance Tax Act 1984 with effect from 25 July 1986).

Amendments—[1] Sub-s (1)(*b*) repealed by TCGA 1992 s 290(3), Sch 12.

FINANCE ACT 1986

(1986 Chapter 41)

An Act to grant certain duties, to alter other duties, and to amend the law relating to the National Debt and the Public Revenue, and to make further provision in connection with Finance.

[25th July 1986]

PART V

INHERITANCE TAX

100 Capital transfer tax to be known as inheritance tax

(1) On and after the passing of this Act, the tax charged under the Capital Transfer Tax Act 1984 (in this Part of this Act referred to as "the 1984 Act") shall be known as inheritance tax and, accordingly, on and after that passing,—

(*a*) the 1984 Act may be cited as the Inheritance Tax Act 1984; and

(*b*) subject to subsection (2) below, any reference to capital transfer tax in the 1984 Act, in any other enactment passed before or in the same Session as this Act or in any document executed, made, served or issued on or before the passing of this Act or at any time thereafter shall have effect as a reference to inheritance tax.

(2) Subsection (1)(*b*) above does not apply where the reference to capital transfer tax relates to a liability to tax arising before the passing of this Act.

(3) In the following provisions of this Part of this Act, any reference to tax except where it is a reference to a named tax is a reference to inheritance tax and, in so far as it occurs in a provision which relates to a time before the passing of this Act, includes a reference to capital transfer tax.

Commentary—*Simon's Taxes* **I1.401**; *Foster* **A4.01**.

101 Lifetime transfers potentially exempt etc

(1) The 1984 Act shall have effect subject to the amendments in Part I of Schedule 19 to this Act, being amendments—

(*a*) removing liability for tax on certain transfers of value where the transfer occurs at least seven years before the transferor's death;

(*b*) providing for one Table of rates of tax;

(*c*) abolishing exemptions for mutual transfers;

(*d*) making provision with respect to the amounts of tax to be charged on transfers occurring before the death of the transferor;

(*e*) making provision with respect to the application of relief under Chapter I (business property) and Chapter II (agricultural property) of Part V of the 1984 Act to such transfers; and

(*f*) reducing the period during which the values transferred by chargeable transfers are aggregated from ten years to seven;

and amendments making provisions consequential on or incidental to the matters referred to above and to sections 102 and 103 below.

(2) . . .[1]

(3) Part I of Schedule 19 to this Act has effect, subject to Part II of that Schedule, with respect to transfers of value made, and other events occurring, on or after 18th March 1986.

(4) The transitional provisions in Part II of Schedule 19 to this Act shall have effect.

Commentary—*Simon's Taxes* See **Division I3**.

Amendments—[1] Sub-s (2), which amended FA 1980 s 79(5), (6)(*a*), repealed, with a saving by FA 1989 s 187(1), Sch 17 Pt VII, in relation to disposals on or after 14 March 1989.

102 Gifts with reservation

(1) Subject to subsections (5) and (6) below, this section applies where, on or after 18th March 1986, an individual disposes of any property by way of gift and either—

(*a*) possession and enjoyment of the property is not bona fide assumed by the donee at or before the beginning of the relevant period; or

(*b*) at any time in the relevant period the property is not enjoyed to the entire exclusion, or virtually to the entire exclusion, of the donor and of any benefit to him by contract or otherwise;

and in this section "the relevant period" means a period ending on the date of the donor's death and beginning seven years before that date or, if it is later, on the date of the gift.

(2) If and so long as—

(*a*) possession and enjoyment of any property is not bona fide assumed as mentioned in subsection (1)(*a*) above, or

(*b*) any property is not enjoyed as mentioned in subsection (1)(*b*) above,

the property is referred to (in relation to the gift and the donor) as property subject to a reservation.

(3) If, immediately before the death of the donor, there is any property which, in relation to him, is property subject to a reservation then, to the extent that the property would not, apart from this section, form part of the donor's estate immediately before his death, that property shall be treated for the purposes of the 1984 Act as property to which he was beneficially entitled immediately before his death.

(4) If, at a time before the end of the relevant period, any property ceases to be property subject to a reservation, the donor shall be treated for the purposes of the 1984 Act as having at that time made a disposition of the property by a disposition which is a potentially exempt transfer.

(5) This section does not apply if or, as the case may be, to the extent that the disposal of property by way of gift is an exempt transfer by virtue of any of the following provisions of Part II of the 1984 Act,—

- (*a*) section 18 (transfers between spouses [or civil partners][4])[, except as provided by subsections (5A) and (5B) below][3];
- (*b*) section 20 (small gifts);
- (*c*) section 22 (gifts in consideration of marriage [or civil partnership][4]);
- (*d*) section 23 (gifts to charities);
- (*e*) section 24 (gifts to political parties);
- [(*ee*) section 24A (gifts to housing associations);][1]
- (*f*) section 25 (gifts for national purposes, etc);
- (*g*) [. . .][2];
- (*h*) section 27 (maintenance funds for historic buildings); . . .[5]
- (*i*) section 28 (employee trusts)[; and
- (*j*) section 28A (employee-ownership trusts).][5]

[(5A) Subsection (5)(*a*) above does not prevent this section from applying if or, as the case may be, to the extent that—

- (*a*) the property becomes settled property by virtue of the gift,
- (*b*) by reason of the donor's spouse [or civil partner][4] ("the relevant beneficiary") becoming beneficially entitled to an interest in possession in the settled property, the disposal is or, as the case may be, is to any extent an exempt transfer by virtue of section 18 of the 1984 Act in consequence of the operation of section 49 of that Act (treatment of interests in possession),
- (*c*) at some time after the disposal, but before the death of the donor, the relevant beneficiary's interest in possession comes to an end, and
- (*d*) on the occasion on which that interest comes to an end, the relevant beneficiary does not become beneficially entitled to the settled property or to another interest in possession in the settled property.][3]

[(5B) If or, as the case may be, to the extent that this section applies by virtue of subsection (5A) above, it has effect as if the disposal by way of gift had been made immediately after the relevant beneficiary's interest in possession came to an end.][3]

[(5C) For the purposes of subsections (5A) and (5B) above—

- (*a*) section 51(1)(*b*) of the 1984 Act (disposal of interest in possession treated as coming to end of interest) applies as it applies for the purposes of Chapter 2 of Part 3 of that Act; and
- (*b*) references to any property or to an interest in any property include references to part of any property or interest.][3]

(6) This section does not apply if the disposal of property by way of gift is made under the terms of a policy issued in respect of an insurance made before 18th March 1986 unless the policy is varied on or after that date so as to increase the benefits secured or to extend the term of the insurance; and, for this purpose, any change in the terms of the policy which is made in pursuance of an option or other power conferred by the policy shall be deemed to be a variation of the policy.

(7) If a policy issued as mentioned in subsection (6) above confers an option or other power under which benefits and premiums may be increased to take account of increases in the retail prices index (as defined in section 8(3) of the 1984 Act) or any similar index specified in the policy, then, to the extent that the right to exercise that option or power would have been lost if it had not been exercised on or before 1st August 1986, the exercise of that option or power before that date shall be disregarded for the purposes of subsection (6) above.

(8) Schedule 20 to this Act has effect for supplementing this section.

Commentary—*Simon's Taxes* **I3.401–I3.416, I3.431, I3.432, I3.441–I3.454**; *Foster* **C4.01–16, 31, 32, 41–54**.

HMRC Manuals—Inheritance Tax Manual IHTM14301–14453 (gifts with reservation).

IHTM14301 (requirements for a gift with reservation).

IHTM14302 (identifying and investigating a gift with reservation).

IHTM14303 (devolution of gift with reservation property).

IHTM14311–14317 (the gift).

IHTM14318 and 14319 (exempt transfers).

IHTM14331 and 14332 (the reservation: requirements and possession and enjoyment).

IHTM14333–14335 (exclusion and non-exclusion of the donor and examples).

IHTM14336 (effect of consideration).

IHTM14337 (continuation of reasonable commercial arrangements).
IHTM14338 (benefit by associated operations).
IHTM14339 (benefit to donor's spouse or civil partner).
IHTM14340–14342 (when occupation is not reservation for gifts of land).
IHTM14343 (annual exemption where a reservation ceases).
IHTM14360 (interests in land).
IHTM14371–14374 (tracing gifts).
IHTM14391–14396 (settled property and gifts with reservation).
IHTM14401–14403 (tracing settled property).
IHTM14421–14453 (gift with reservation rules and insurance policies).
IHTM24194 (agricultural property at the time of the gift with reservation charge).

HMRC Interpretation RI 55—(i) Interpretation of the words "virtually to the entire exclusion" in sub-s (1)(*b*) above; (ii) Potentially exempt transfer cannot be reduced by the annual exemption in IHTA 1984 s 19.

Press releases etc—IR letter 19-2-87 (gift of shares: donor remaining director or employee of company: no reservation of benefit if remuneration package commercially justifiable).

IR letter 18-5-87 (1. Gift of share in house: donor retaining share: whether donor's occupation a reservation of benefit; 2. Gift involving family business or farm: donor remaining in the business on commercial terms not a reservation of benefit; 3. Gift into trust: settlor retaining reversionary interest is not a reservation of benefit).

Simon's Tax Cases—*Ingram (exors of the Estate of Lady Ingram, decd) v IRC* [1997] STC 1234; *R v IRC, ex p Newfields Developments Ltd* [1999] STC 37; *Essex and anor (exors of Somerset, decd) v IRC* [2002] STC (SCD) 39; *IRC v Eversden and anor (exors of Greenstock, decd)* [2002] STC 1109.

Cross references—See IHTA 1984 s 142(5) (the provision that a disclaimed benefit conferred by testamentary or other dispositions to be treated as never having been conferred not to apply to property to which a person is entitled by virtue of this section).

FA 2004 Sch 15 para 11 (exemptions from charge to tax under FA 2004 Sch 15 (benefits received by former owner of property) where any of paragraphs (*d*) to (*i*) of sub-s (5) of this section applies).

Amendments—[1] Sub-s (5)(*ee*) inserted by FA 1989, s 171(5), (6) with respect to transfers of value made after 13 March 1989.

[2] Sub-s (5)(*g*) repealed by FA 1998 Sch 27 Part IV with respect to any disposal made on or after 17 March 1998.

[3] Words in sub-s (5) inserted, and sub-ss (5A)–(5C) inserted, by FA 2003 s 185 with effect for disposals made after 19 June 2003.

[4] Words in sub-ss (5), (5A) inserted by Tax and Civil Partnership Regulations, SI 2005/3229, regs 43, 44, with effect from 5 December 2005 (reg 1(1)).

[5] In sub-s (5)(*h*), word repealed, and sub-s (5)(*j*) and preceding word inserted, by FA 2014 s 290, Sch 37 para 17 with effect in relation to disposals made on or after 6 April 2014.

[102ZA Gifts with reservation: termination of interests in possession

(1) Subsection (2) below applies where—

(*a*) an individual is beneficially entitled to an interest in possession in settled property,

(*b*) either—

(i) the individual became beneficially entitled to the interest in possession before 22nd March 2006, or

(ii) the individual became beneficially entitled to the interest in possession on or after 22nd March 2006 and the interest is an immediate post-death interest, a disabled person's interest or a transitional serial interest [or falls within section 5(1B) of the 1984 Act][2], and

(*c*) the interest in possession comes to an end during the individual's life.

(2) For the purposes of—

(*a*) section 102 above, and

(*b*) Schedule 20 to this Act,

the individual shall be taken (if, or so far as, he would not otherwise be) to dispose, on the coming to an end of the interest in possession, of the no-longer-possessed property by way of gift.

(3) In subsection (2) above "the no-longer-possessed property" means the property in which the interest in possession subsisted immediately before it came to an end, other than any of it to which the individual becomes absolutely and beneficially entitled in possession on the coming to an end of the interest in possession.][1]

Amendments—[1] This section inserted by FA 2006 s 156, Sch 20 para 33(1), (2), (4). This amendment is deemed to have come into force on 22 March 2006, but only in respect of cases where an interest in possession comes to an end on or after that day.

[2] In sub-s (1)(*b*)(ii) words inserted by FA 2010 s 53(1), (8) with effect in relation to an interest in possession to which a person is beneficially entitled if the person becomes beneficially entitled to it on or after 9 December 2009.

[102A Gifts with reservation: interest in land][1]

[(1) This section applies where an individual disposes of an interest in land by way of gift on or after 9th March 1999.

(2) At any time in the relevant period when the donor or his spouse [or civil partner][2] enjoys a significant right or interest, or is party to a significant arrangement, in relation to the land—

(*a*) the interest disposed of is referred to (in relation to the gift and the donor) as property subject to a reservation; and

(*b*) section 102(3) and (4) above shall apply.

(3) Subject to subsections (4) and (5) below, a right, interest or arrangement in relation to land is significant for the purposes of subsection (2) above if (and only if) it entitles or enables the donor to occupy all or part of the land, or to enjoy some right in relation to all or part of the land, otherwise than for full consideration in money or money's worth.

(4) A right, interest or arrangement is not significant for the purposes of subsection (2) above if—

(*a*) it does not and cannot prevent the enjoyment of the land to the entire exclusion, or virtually to the entire exclusion, of the donor; or

(*b*) it does not entitle or enable the donor to occupy all or part of the land immediately after the disposal, but would do so were it not for the interest disposed of.

(5) A right or interest is not significant for the purposes of subsection (2) above if it was granted or acquired before the period of seven years ending with the date of the gift.

(6) Where an individual disposes of more than one interest in land by way of gift, whether or not at the same time or to the same donee, this section shall apply separately in relation to each interest.][1]

Commentary—*Simon's Taxes* **I3.416–I3.418**.

HMRC Manuals—Inheritance Tax Manual IHTM14360 (gift with reservation: interests in land).

Amendments—[1] This section inserted by FA 1999 s 104 with effect from 27 July 1999 for disposals made after 8 March 1999.

[2] Words in sub-s (2) inserted by Tax and Civil Partnership regulations, SI 2005/3229, regs 43, 45, with effect from 5 December 2005 (reg 1(1)).

[102B Gifts with reservation: share of interest in land][1]

[(1) This section applies where an individual disposes, by way of gift on or after 9th March 1999, of an undivided share of an interest in land.

(2) At any time in the relevant period, except when subsection (3) or (4) below applies—

(*a*) the share disposed of is referred to (in relation to the gift and the donor) as property subject to a reservation; and

(*b*) section 102(3) and (4) above shall apply.

(3) This subsection applies when the donor—

(*a*) does not occupy the land; or

(*b*) occupies the land to the exclusion of the donee for full consideration in money or money's worth.

(4) This subsection applies when—

(*a*) the donor and the donee occupy the land; and

(*b*) the donor does not receive any benefit, other than a negligible one, which is provided by or at the expense of the donee for some reason connected with the gift.][1]

Commentary—*Simon's Taxes* **I3.416–I3.418, I3.737**.

HMRC Manuals—Inheritance Tax Manual IHTM14360 (gift with reservation: interests in land).

Cross references—FA 2004 Sch 15 para 11 (exemptions from charge to tax under FA 2004 Sch 15 (benefits received by former owner of property) where sub-s (4) of this section applies).

Amendments—[1] This section inserted by FA 1999 s 104 with effect from 27 July 1999 for disposals made after 8 March 1999.

[102C Sections 102A and 102B: supplemental][1]

[(1) In sections 102A and 102B above "the relevant period" has the same meaning as in section 102 above.

(2) An interest or share disposed of is not property subject to a reservation under section 102A(2) or 102B(2) above if or, as the case may be, to the extent that the disposal is an exempt transfer by virtue of any of the provisions listed in section 102(5) above.

(3) In applying sections 102A and 102B above no account shall be taken of—

(*a*) occupation of land by a donor, or

(*b*) an arrangement which enables land to be occupied by a donor,

in circumstances where the occupation, or occupation pursuant to the arrangement, would be disregarded in accordance with paragraph 6(1)(b) of Schedule 20 to this Act.

(4) The provisions of Schedule 20 to this Act, apart from paragraph 6, shall have effect for the purposes of sections 102A and 102B above as they have effect for the purposes of section 102 above; and any question which falls to be answered under section 102A or 102B above in relation to an interest in land shall be determined by reference to the interest which is at that time treated as property comprised in the gift.

(5) Where property other than an interest in land is treated by virtue of paragraph 2 of that Schedule as property comprised in a gift, the provisions of section 102 above shall apply to determine whether or not that property is property subject to a reservation.

(6) Sections 102 and 102A above shall not apply to a case to which section 102B above applies.

(7) Section 102A above shall not apply to a case to which section 102 above applies.][1]

Commentary—*Simon's Taxes* **I3.416–I3.418**.

HMRC Manuals—Inheritance Tax Manual IHTM14360 (gift with reservation: interests in land).

Cross references—FA 2004 Sch 15 para 11 (exemptions from charge to tax under FA 2004 Sch 15 (benefits received by former owner of property) where sub-s (3) of this section and FA 1986 Sch 20 para 6 apply).

Amendments—[1] This section inserted by FA 1999 s 104 with effect from 27 July 1999.

IHT

103 Treatment of certain debts and incumbrances

(1) Subject to subsection (2) below, if, in determining the value of a person's estate immediately before his death, account would be taken, apart from this subsection, of a liability consisting of a debt incurred by him or an incumbrance created by a disposition made by him, that liability shall be subject to abatement to an extent proportionate to the value of any of the consideration given for the debt or incumbrance which consisted of—

(*a*) property derived from the deceased; or

(*b*) consideration (not being property derived from the deceased) given by any person who was at any time entitled to, or amongst whose resources there was at any time included, any property derived from the deceased.

(2) If, in a case where the whole or a part of the consideration given for a debt or incumbrance consisted of such consideration as is mentioned in subsection (1)(*b*) above, it is shown that the value of the consideration given, or of that part thereof, as the case may be, exceeded that which could have been rendered available by application of all the property derived from the deceased, other than such (if any) of that property—

(*a*) as is included in the consideration given, or

(*b*) as to which it is shown that the disposition of which it, or the property which it represented, was the subject matter was not made with reference to, or with a view to enabling or facilitating, the giving of the consideration or the recoupment in any manner of the cost thereof,

no abatement shall be made under subsection (1) above in respect of the excess.

(3) In subsections (1) and (2) above "property derived from the deceased" means, subject to subsection (4) below, any property which was the subject matter of a disposition made by the deceased, either by himself alone or in concert or by arrangement with any other person or which represented any of the subject matter of such a disposition, whether directly or indirectly, and whether by virtue of one or more intermediate dispositions.

(4) If the disposition first-mentioned in subsection (3) above was not a transfer of value and it is shown that the disposition was not part of associated operations which included—

(*a*) a disposition by the deceased, either alone or in concert or by arrangement with any other person, otherwise than for full consideration in money or money's worth paid to the deceased for his own use or benefit; or

(*b*) a disposition by any other person operating to reduce the value of the property of the deceased,

that first-mentioned disposition shall be left out of account for the purposes of subsections (1) to (3) above.

(5) If, before a person's death but on or after 18th March 1986, money or money's worth, is paid or applied by him—

(*a*) in or towards the satisfaction or discharge of a debt or incumbrance in the case of which subsection (1) above would have effect on his death if the debt or incumbrance had not been satisfied or discharged, or

(*b*) in reduction of a debt or incumbrance in the case of which that subsection has effect on his death,

the 1984 Act shall have effect as if, at the time of the payment or application, the person concerned had made a transfer of value equal to the money or money's worth and that transfer were a potentially exempt transfer.

(6) Any reference in this section to a debt incurred is a reference to a debt incurred on or after 18th March 1986 and any reference to an incumbrance created by a disposition is a reference to an incumbrance created by a disposition made on or after that date; and in this section "subject matter" includes, in relation to any disposition, any annual or periodical payment made or payable under or by virtue of the disposition.

(7) In determining the value of a person's estate immediately before his death, no account shall be taken (by virtue of section 5 of the 1984 Act) of any liability arising under or in connection with a policy of life insurance issued in respect of an insurance made on or after 1st July 1986 unless the whole of the sums assured under that policy form part of that person's estate immediately before his death.

Commentary—*Simon's Taxes* **I3.544, I4.147, I4.151–I4.154**; *Foster* **C5.44, D1.47, 51–54.**

HMRC Manuals—Inheritance Tax Manual IHTM28361–28370 (section 103 liabilities).

IHTM14721 and 14722 (double charges relief and calculations).

IHTM20521 (legislation designed to counteract reverse loan scheme).

Cross reference—See IHTA 1984 s 5 (meaning of estate; a person's estate is the aggregate of all property to which he is beneficially entitled).

104 Regulations for avoiding double charges etc

(1) For the purposes of the 1984 Act the Board may by regulations make such provision as is mentioned in subsection (2) below with respect to transfers of value made, and other events occurring, on or after 18th March 1986 where—

(*a*) a potentially exempt transfer proves to be a chargeable transfer and, immediately before the death of the transferor, his estate includes property acquired by him from the transferee otherwise than for full consideration in money or money's worth;

(*b*) an individual disposes of property by a transfer of value which is or proves to be a chargeable transfer and the circumstances are such that subsection (3) or subsection (4) of section 102 above applies to the property as being or having been property subject to a reservation;

(*c*) in determining the value of a person's estate immediately before his death, a liability of his to any person is abated as mentioned in section 103 above and, before his death, the deceased made a transfer of value by virtue of which the estate of that other person was increased or by virtue of which property becomes comprised in a settlement of which that other person is a trustee; or

(*d*) the circumstances are such as may be specified in the regulations for the purposes of this subsection, being circumstances appearing to the Board to be similar to those referred to in paragraphs (*a*) to (*c*) above.

(2) The provision which may be made by regulations under this section is provision for either or both of the following,—

(*a*) treating the value transferred by a transfer of value as reduced by reference to the value transferred by another transfer of value; and

(*b*) treating the whole or any part of the tax paid or payable on the value transferred by a transfer of value as a credit against the tax payable on the value transferred by another transfer of value.

(3) The power to make regulations under this section shall be exercisable by statutory instrument subject to annulment in pursuance of a resolution of the Commons House of Parliament.

Commentary—*Simon's Taxes* **I3.502, I3.513, I3.534, I3.543, I3.545**; *Foster* **C5.02, 13, 34, 43, 45**.

HMRC Manuals—Inheritance Tax Manual IHTM14691–14732 (double charges relief).

Regulations—See IHT (Double Charges Relief) Regulations, SI 1987/1130; IHT (Double Charges Relief) Regulations, SI 2005/3441.

105 Application of business and agricultural relief where transfer partly exempt

(*inserts* IHTA 1984 s 39A).

106 Changes in financial institutions: business property

(1)–(3) (*substitute* sub-s (4)(*a*) *and insert* sub-s (7) in IHTA 1984 s 105.)

(4) The Board may by regulations provide that section 105(7) of the 1984 Act (as inserted by subsection (2) above) shall have effect—

(*a*) as if the reference to The Stock Exchange in paragraph (*a*) were to any recognised investment exchange (within the meaning [given by section 285(1)(*a*) of the Financial Services and Markets Act 2000][1]) or to any of those exchanges specified in the regulations, and

(*b*) as if the reference to the Council of The Stock Exchange in paragraph (*b*) were to the investment exchange concerned.

(5) The Board may by regulations amend section 105 of the 1984 Act so as to secure that section 105(3) does not apply to any property if the business concerned is of such a description as is set out in the regulations; and the regulations may include such incidental and consequential provisions as the Board think fit.

(6) Regulations under subsection (4) or (5) above shall apply in relation to transfers of value made, and other events occurring, on or after such day, after the day of The Stock Exchange reforms, as is specified in the regulations.

(7) The power to make regulations under subsection (4) or (5) above shall be exercisable by statutory instrument subject to annulment in pursuance of a resolution of the Commons House of Parliament.

(8) In this section "the day of The Stock Exchange reforms" means the day on which the rule of The Stock Exchange that prohibits a person from carrying on business as both a broker and a jobber is abolished.

Commentary—*Simon's Taxes* **I7.112, I7.123**; *Foster* **G1.12, 23**.

Regulations—Inheritance Tax (Market Makers) Regulations, SI 1992/3181.

Inheritance Tax (Market Makers and Discount Houses) Regulations, SI 2012/2903.

Cross references—See Inheritance Tax (Market Makers) Regulations, SI 1992/3181 reg 3 (the day specified in sub-s (6) above for the application of these Regulations is 23 March 1992).

Inheritance Tax (Market Makers and Discount Houses) Regulations, SI 2012/2903 reg 2 (the day specified in sub-s (6) above for the application of these Regulations is 31 December 2012).

Amendments—[1] Words in sub-s (4)(*a*) substituted by the Financial Services and Markets Act 2000 (Consequential Amendments) (Taxes) Order, SI 2001/3629 arts 6, 11 with effect from 1 December 2001, immediately after the coming into force of the Financial Services and Markets Act 2000 ss 411, 432(1), Sch 20.

107 Changes in financial institutions: interest

(1)–(3) . . .

(4) The Board may by regulations provide that section 234(4) of the 1984 Act (as inserted by subsection (2) above) shall have effect—

(*a*) as if the reference to The Stock Exchange in paragraph (*a*) were to any recognised investment exchange (within the meaning [given by section 285(1)(*a*) of the Financial Services and Markets Act 2000][1]) or to any of those exchanges specified in the regulations, and

(*b*) as if the reference to the Council of The Stock Exchange in paragraph (*b*) were to the investment exchange concerned.

(5) The Board may by regulations amend section 234 of the 1984 Act so as to secure that companies of a description set out in the regulations fall within section 234(3)(*c*); and the regulations may include such incidental and consequential provisions as the Board think fit.

(6) Regulations under subsection (4) or (5) above shall apply in relation to chargeable transfers made, and other events occurring, on or after such day, after the day of The Stock Exchange reforms, as is specified in the regulations.

(7) The power to make regulations under subsection (4) or (5) above shall be exercisable by statutory instrument subject to annulment in pursuance of a resolution of the Commons House of Parliament.

(8) In this section "the day of The Stock Exchange reforms" has the same meaning as in section 106 above.

Commentary—*Simon's Taxes* **I11.531**; *Foster* **L5.31**.

Regulations—Inheritance Tax (Market Makers) Regulations, SI 1992/3181.

Inheritance Tax (Market Makers and Discount Houses) Regulations, SI 2012/2903.

Note—Sub-ss (1)–(3) substitute sub-s (3)(*c*) and insert sub-s (4) in IHTA 1984 s 234.

Cross references—See Inheritance Tax (Market Makers) Regulations, SI 1992/3181 reg 3 (the day specified in sub-s (6) above for the application of these Regulations is 23 March 1992).

Inheritance Tax (Market Makers and Discount Houses) Regulations, SI 2012/2903 reg 2 (the day specified in sub-s (6) above for the application of these Regulations is 31 December 2012).

Amendments—[1] Words in sub-s (4)(*a*) substituted by the Financial Services and Markets Act 2000 (Consequential Amendments) (Taxes) Order, SI 2001/3629 arts 6, 11 with effect from 1 December 2001, immediately after the coming into force of the Financial Services and Markets Act 2000 ss 411, 432(1), Sch 20.

Prospective amendments—In sub-s (4), words "paragraph 7(8) of Schedule 53 to the Finance Act 2009 (late payment interest: inheritance tax payable by instalments)" to be substituted for words from "section 234(4)" to "above)", and in sub-s (5), words "set out one or more descriptions of company for the purposes of paragraph 7(7) of Schedule 53 to the Finance Act 2009" to be substituted for words from "amend" to "section 234(3)(*c*)" by F(No 2)A 2015 s 15(1) with effect from a date to be appointed.

PART VII
MISCELLANEOUS AND SUPPLEMENTARY

114 Short title, interpretation, construction and repeals

(1) This Act may be cited as the Finance Act 1986.

(2)–(4) . . .

(5) Part V of this Act, other than section 100, shall be construed as one with the Capital Transfer Tax Act 1984.

(6) The enactments and Orders specified in Schedule 23 to this Act are hereby repealed to the extent specified in the third column of that Schedule, but subject to any provision at the end of any Part of that Schedule.

Note—Sub-ss (2)–(4) are not relevant to CTT.

Cross references—See FA 1986 s 100(1)(*a*) (CTTA 1984 may be cited as Inheritance Tax Act 1984 with effect from 25 July 1986).

SCHEDULES
SCHEDULE 19
INHERITANCE TAX
Section 101

PART I
AMENDMENTS OF 1984 ACT

Note—The provisions of IHTA 1984 amended, substituted or inserted by this Part, which has been repealed in part by F(No 2)A 1987 Sch 9 Pt III, FA 1988 Sch 14 Pt X and FA 1989 Sch 17 Pt X, are—

ss 3A, 7, 8, 9, 19, 26A, 30, 31, 32, 32A, 33, 35, 38, 66, 67, 68, 78, 98, 113A, 113B, 124A, 124B, 131, 142, 148, 199, 201, 204, 216, 226, 227, 236, 237, 239.

Sch 1.

Sch 2, paras 1, 1A, 2, 3, 4.

Sch 4, para 14.

Sch 6, para 4.

PART II
TRANSITIONAL PROVISIONS

40—(1) Notwithstanding that Part I of this Schedule has effect with respect to events occurring on or after 18th March 1986, where a death or other event occurs on or after that date, nothing in that Part shall affect the tax chargeable on a transfer of value occurring before that date.

(2) Sub-paragraph (1) above does not authorise the making of a claim under section 149 of the 1984 Act where the donee's transfer, as defined in section 148 of that Act, occurs on or after 18th March 1986.

Commentary—*Simon's Taxes* **I3.705, I10.111, I10.116**; *Foster* **C7.05, K1.11, K1.16**.

41 Where tax is chargeable under section 32 or section 32A of the 1984 Act by reason of a chargeable event occurring on or after 18th March 1986 and the rate or rates at which it is charged fall to be determined under the provisions of section 33(1)(*b*) (ii) of the 1984 Act by reference to a death which occurred before that date, those provisions shall apply (subject to paragraph 5 of Schedule 2 to that Act) as if the amendments of section 7 of, and Schedule 1 to, that Act contained in Part I of this Schedule had been in force at the time of the death.

Commentary—*Simon's Taxes* **I7.514B**; *Foster* **G5.14B**.

42 Where tax is chargeable under paragraph 8 of Schedule 4 to the 1984 Act on any occasion on or after 18th March 1986 and the rate at which it is charged falls to be determined under paragraph 14 of that Schedule by reference to a death which occurred before that date, that paragraph shall apply (subject to paragraph 6 of Schedule 2 to the 1984 Act) as if the amendments of section 7 of, and Schedule 1 to, the 1984 Act contained in Part I of this Schedule had been in force at the time of the death.

Commentary—*Simon's Taxes* **I7.545**; *Foster* **G5.45**.

43—(1) This paragraph applies if, in the case of a settlement,—

(*a*) tax is charged under section 65 of the 1984 Act on an occasion falling on or after 18th March 1986; and

(*b*) the rate at which tax is so charged falls to be determined under section 69 of that Act (rate between ten-year anniversaries) by reference to the rate (in this paragraph referred to as "the last ten-year rate") at which tax was last charged under section 64 of that Act (or would have been charged apart from section 66(2) thereof); and

(*c*) the most recent ten-year anniversary fell before 18th March 1986.

(2) For the purpose of determining the rate at which tax is charged on the occasion referred to in sub-paragraph (1)(*a*) above, it shall be assumed that the last ten-year rate was what that rate would have been if, immediately before the ten-year anniversary referred to in sub-paragraph (1) (*c*) above, the amendments of sections 66 and 67 of the 1984 Act contained in Part I of this Schedule had been in force.

(3) Where this paragraph applies, paragraph 3 of Schedule 2 to the 1984 Act shall have effect as if—

(*a*) references to a reduction included references to a reduction by the substitution of a new Table in Schedule 1 to the 1984 Act; and

(*b*) in relation to a reduction resulting from the substitution of such a new Table, the reference to the second of the Tables in Schedule 1 to the 1984 Act were a reference to a Table in which the rates of tax were one-half of those specified in the new Table.

(4) In this paragraph "ten-year anniversary" has the same meaning as in Chapter III of Part III of the 1984 Act.

Commentary—*Simon's Taxes* **I5.441**; *Foster* **E4.41**.

44 In relation to a death on or after 18th March 1986, paragraph 2 of Schedule 2 to the 1984 Act (provisions applying on reduction of tax) shall have effect, in a case where the chargeable transfer in question was made before 18th March 1986, as if—

(*a*) references to a reduction included references to a reduction by the substitution of a new Table in Schedule 1 to the 1984 Act; and

(*b*) the Table in Schedule 1 to the Act was the first Table in that Schedule.

Commentary—*Simon's Taxes* **I3.705**; *Foster* **C7.05**.

45 In relation to a disposal of trees or underwood on or after 18th March 1986, paragraph 4 of Schedule 2 to the 1984 Act shall have effect, in a case where the death in question occurred before 18th March 1986, as mentioned in paragraphs (*a*) and (*b*) of paragraph 44 above.

Commentary—*Simon's Taxes* **I7.405**; *Foster* **G4.05**.

46 Notwithstanding anything in section 3A of the 1984 Act, a transfer of value which is made on or after 1st July 1986 and which, by virtue of subsection (4) of section 49 of the Finance Act 1975 (transitional provision relating to estate duty deferment in respect of timber etc), brings to an end the period during which estate duty is payable on the net moneys received from the sale of timber etc is not a potentially exempt transfer [to the extent that the value transferred is attributable to the land concerned][1].

Commentary—*Simon's Taxes* **I3.314**; *Foster* **C3.14**.

Concession F15—Restricts scope of this para to that part of the value transferred which is attributable to the woodlands subject to the deferred estate duty charge.

Cross reference—See IHTA 1984 s 3A (potentially exempt transfers).

Amendments—[1] Words inserted by the Enactment of Extra-Statutory Concessions Order, SI 2017/495 arts 2, 3 with effect in relation to transfers of value made on or after 6 April 2017.

SCHEDULE 20

GIFTS WITH RESERVATION

Section 102

Statement of Practice SP 10/86—Death benefits under superannuation arrangements.

Interpretation and application

1—(1) In this Schedule—

"the material date", in relation to any property means, in the case of property falling within subsection (3) of the principal section, the date of the donor's death and, in the case of property falling within subsection (4) of that section, the date on which the property ceases to be property subject to a reservation;

"the principal section" means section 102 of this Act; and

"property subject to a reservation" has the same meaning as in the principal section.

(2) Any reference in this Schedule to a disposal by way of gift is a reference to such a disposal which is made on or after 18th March 1986.

(3) This Schedule has effect for the purposes of the principal section and the 1984 Act.

Commentary—*Simon's Taxes* **I3.421–I3.429**; *Foster* **C4.21–29**.

Substitutions and accretions

2—(1) Where there is a disposal by way of gift and, at any time before the material date, the donee ceases to have the possession and enjoyment of any of the property comprised in the gift, then on and after that time the principal section and the following provisions of this Schedule shall apply as if the property, if any, received by the donee in substitution for that property had been comprised in the gift instead of that property (but in addition to any other property comprised in the gift).

(2) This paragraph does not apply if the property disposed of by the gift—

(*a*) becomes settled property by virtue of the gift; or

(*b*) is a sum of money in sterling or any other currency.

(3) In sub-paragraph (1) above the reference to property received by the donee in substitution for property comprised in the gift includes in particular—

(*a*) in relation to property sold, exchanged or otherwise disposed of by the donee, any benefit received by him by way of consideration for the sale, exchange or other disposition; and

(*b*) in relation to a debt or security, any benefit received by the donee in or towards the satisfaction or redemption thereof; and

(*c*) in relation to any right to acquire property, any property acquired in pursuance of that right.

(4) Where, at a time before the material date, the donee makes a gift of property comprised in the gift to him, or otherwise voluntarily divests himself of any such property otherwise than for a consideration in money or money's worth not less than the value of the property at that time, then, unless he does so in favour of the donor, he shall be treated for the purposes of the principal section and sub-paragraph (1) above as continuing to have the possession and enjoyment of that property.

(5) For the purposes of sub-paragraph (4) above—

(*a*) a disposition made by the donee by agreement shall not be deemed to be made voluntarily if it is made to any authority who, when the agreement is made, is authorised by, or is or can be authorised under, any enactment to acquire the property compulsorily; and

(*b*) a donee shall be treated as divesting himself, voluntarily and without consideration, of any interest in property which merges or is extinguished in another interest held or acquired by him in the same property.

(6) Where any shares in or debentures of a body corporate are comprised in a gift and the donee is, as the holder of those shares or debentures, issued with shares in or debentures of the same or any other body corporate, or granted any right to acquire any such shares or debentures, then, unless the issue or grant is made by way of exchange for the first-mentioned shares or debentures, the shares or debentures so issued, or the right granted, shall be treated for the purposes of the principal section and this Schedule as having been comprised in the gift in addition to any other property so comprised.

(7) In sub-paragraph (6) above the reference to an issue being made or right being granted to the donee as the holder of shares or debentures shall be taken to include any case in which an issue or grant is made to him as having been the holder of those shares or debentures, or is made to him in

pursuance of an offer or invitation made to him as being or having been the holder of those shares or debentures, or of an offer or invitation in connection with which any preference is given to him as being or having been the holder thereof.

Commentary—*Simon's Taxes* **I3.421–I3.427**; *Foster* **C4.21–27**.

HMRC Manuals—Inheritance Tax Manual IHTM14373 (tracing of absolute gifts of property).

3—(1) Where either sub-paragraph (3)(*c*) or sub-paragraph (6) of paragraph 2 above applies to determine, for the purposes of the principal section, the property comprised in a gift made by a donor—

(*a*) the value of any consideration in money or money's worth given by the donee for the acquisition in pursuance of the right referred to in the said sub-paragraph (3)(*c*) or for the issue or grant referred to in and said sub-paragraph (6), as the case may be, shall be allowed as a deduction in valuing the property comprised in the gift at any time after the consideration is given, but

(*b*) if any part (not being a sum of money) of that consideration consists of property comprised in the same or another gift from the donor and treated for the purposes of the 1984 Act as forming part of the donor's estate immediately before his death or as being attributable to the value transferred by a potentially exempt transfer made by him, no deduction shall be made in respect of it under this sub-paragraph.

(2) For the purposes of sub-paragraph (1) above, there shall be left out of account so much (if any) of the consideration for any shares in or debentures of a body corporate, or for the grant of any right to be issued with any such shares or debentures, as consists in the capitalisation of reserves of that body corporate, or in the retention by that body corporate, by way of set-off or otherwise, of any property distributable by it, or is otherwise provided directly or indirectly out of the assets or at the expense of that or any associated body corporate.

(3) For the purposes of sub-paragraph (2) above, two bodies corporate shall be deemed to be associated if one has control of the other or if another person has control of both.

Commentary—*Simon's Taxes* **I3.421, I3.423, I3.424, I3.427**; *Foster* **C4.21, 23, 24, 27**.

Donee predeceasing the material date

4 Where there is a disposal by way of gift and the donee dies before the date which is the material date in relation to any property comprised in the gift, paragraphs 2 and 3 above shall apply as if—

(*a*) he had not died and the acts of his personal representatives were his acts; and

(*b*) property taken by any person under his testamentary dispositions or his intestacy (or partial intestacy) were taken under a gift made by him at the time of his death.

Commentary—*Simon's Taxes* **I3.426**; *Foster* **C4.26**.

[Termination of interests in possession

4A—(1) This paragraph applies where—

(*a*) under section 102ZA of this Act, an individual ("D") is taken to dispose of property by way of gift, and

(*b*) the property continues to be settled property immediately after the disposal.

(2) Paragraphs 2 to 4 above shall not apply but, subject to the following provisions of this paragraph, the principal section and the following provisions of this Schedule shall apply as if the property comprised in the gift consisted of the property comprised in the settlement on the material date, except in so far as that property neither is, nor represents, nor is derived from, property originally comprised in the gift.

(3) Any property which—

(*a*) on the material date is comprised in the settlement, and

(*b*) is derived, directly or indirectly, from a loan made by D to the trustees of the settlement,

shall be treated for the purposes of sub-paragraph (2) above as derived from property originally comprised in the gift.

(4) If the settlement comes to an end at some time before the material date as respects all or any of the property which, if D had died immediately before that time, would be treated as comprised in the gift,—

(*a*) the property in question, other than property to which D then becomes absolutely and beneficially entitled in possession, and

(*b*) any consideration (not consisting of rights under the settlement) given by D for any of the property to which D so becomes entitled,

shall be treated as comprised in the gift (in addition to any other property so comprised).

(5) Where, under any trust or power relating to settled property, income arising from that property after the material date is accumulated, the accumulations shall not be treated for the purposes of sub-paragraph (2) above as derived from that property.][1]

Amendments—[1] This paragraph inserted by FA 2006 s 156, Sch 20 para 33(1), (3), (4). This amendment is deemed to have come into force on 22 March 2006, but only with respect to cases where an interest in possession comes to an end on or after that day.

Settled gifts

5—(1) Where there is a disposal by way of gift and the property comprised in the gift becomes settled property by virtue of the gift, paragraphs 2 to 4 above shall not apply but, subject to the following provisions of this paragraph, the principal section and the following provisions of this Schedule shall apply as if the property comprised in the gift consisted of the property comprised in the settlement on the material date, except in so far as that property neither is, nor represents, nor is derived from, property originally comprised in the gift.

(2) If the settlement comes to an end at some time before the material date as respects all or any of the property which, if the donor had died immediately before that time would be treated as comprised in the gift,—

(*a*) the property in question, other than property to which the donor then becomes absolutely and beneficially entitled in possession, and

(*b*) any consideration (not consisting of rights under the settlement) given by the donor for any of the property to which he so becomes entitled,

shall be treated as comprised in the gift (in addition to any other property so comprised).

(3) Where property comprised in a gift does not become settled property by virtue of the gift, but is before the material date settled by the donee, sub-paragraphs (1) and (2) above shall apply in relation to property comprised in the settlement as if the settlement had been made by the gift; and for this purpose property which becomes settled property under any testamentary disposition of the donee or on his intestacy (or partial intestacy) shall be treated as settled by him.

(4) Where property comprised in a gift becomes settled property either by virtue of the gift or as mentioned in sub-paragraph (3) above, any property which—

(*a*) on the material date is comprised in the settlement, and

(*b*) is derived, directly or indirectly, from a loan made by the donor to the trustees of the settlement,

shall be treated for the purposes of sub-paragraph (1) above as derived from property originally comprised in the gift.

(5) Where, under any trust or power relating to settled property, income arising from that property after the material date is accumulated, the accumulations shall not be treated for the purposes of sub-paragraph (1) above as derived from that property.

Commentary—*Simon's Taxes* **I3.429**, *Foster* **C4.29**.

HMRC Manuals—Inheritance Tax Manual IHTM14401 (the property comprised in the settled gift).

Exclusion of benefit

6—(1) In determining whether any property which is disposed of by way of gift is enjoyed to the entire exclusion, or virtually to the entire exclusion, of the donor and of any benefit to him by contract or otherwise—

(*a*) in the case of property which is an interest in land or a chattel, retention or assumption by the donor of actual occupation of the land or actual enjoyment of an incorporeal right over the land, or actual possession of the chattel shall be disregarded if it is for full consideration in money or money's worth;

(*b*) in the case of property which is an interest in land, any occupation by the donor of the whole or any part of the land shall be disregarded if—

(i) it results from a change in the circumstances of the donor since the time of the gift, being a change which was unforeseen at that time and was not brought about by the donor to receive the benefit of this provision; and

(ii) it occurs at a time when the donor has become unable to maintain himself through old age, infirmity or otherwise; and

(iii) it represents a reasonable provision by the donee for the care and maintenance of the donor; and

(iv) the donee is a relative of the donor or his spouse [or civil partner][1];

(*c*) a benefit which the donor obtained by virtue of any associated operations (as defined in section 268 of the 1984 Act) of which the disposal by way of gift is one shall be treated as a benefit to him by contract or otherwise.

(2) Any question whether any property comprised in a gift was at any time enjoyed to the entire exclusion, or virtually to the entire exclusion, of the donor and of any benefit to him shall (so far as that question depends upon the identity of the property) be determined by reference to the property which is at that time treated as property comprised in the gift.

(3) In the application of this paragraph to Scotland, references to a chattel shall be construed as references to a corporeal moveable.

Commentary—*Simon's Taxes* **I3.415, I3.421, I3.433, I3.434**; *Foster* **C4.15, 21, 33, 34**.
HMRC Manuals—Inheritance Tax Manual IHTM14335 (non–exclusion of donor need not be continuous).
IHTM14341 and 14342 (exclusions to gift with reservation treatment for land).
Cross reference—FA 2004 Sch 15 para 11 (exemptions from charge to tax under FA 2004 Sch 15 (benefits received by former owner of property) where this paragraph and FA 1986 s 102C(3) apply).
Amendments—[1] Words in sub-para (1)(*b*)(iv) inserted by Tax and Civil Partnership Regulations, SI 2005/3229, regs 43, 46, with effect from 5 December 2005 (reg 1(1)).

7—(1) Where arrangements are entered into under which—

(*a*) there is a disposal by way of gift which consists of or includes, or is made in connection with, a policy of insurance on the life of the donor or his spouse [or civil partner][1] or on their joint lives, and

(*b*) the benefits which will or may accrue to the donee as a result of the gift vary by reference to benefits accruing to the donor or his spouse [or civil partner][1] (or both of them) under that policy or under another policy (whether issued before, at the same time as or after that referred to in paragraph (*a*) above),

the property comprised in the gift shall be treated for the purposes of the principal section as not enjoyed to the entire exclusion, or virtually to the entire exclusion, of the donor.

(2) In sub-paragraph (1) above—

(*a*) the reference in paragraph (*a*) to a policy on the joint lives of the donor and his spouse [or civil partner][1] includes a reference to a policy on their joint lives and on the life of the survivor; and

(*b*) the reference in paragraph (*b*) to benefits accruing to the donor or his spouse [or civil partner][1] (or both of them) includes a reference to benefits which accrue by virtue of the exercise of rights conferred on either or both of them.

Commentary—*Simon's Taxes* **I3.414**; *Foster* **C4.14**.
HMRC Manuals—Inheritance Tax Manual IHTM14452 (special rules for policies with linked benefits).
IHTM14453 (examples of reservation rules applying to insurance policies).
Amendments—[1] Words in sub-paras (1), (2) inserted by Tax and Civil Partnership Regulations, SI 2005/3229, regs 43, 46, with effect from 5 December 2005 (reg 1(1)).

Agricultural property and business property

8—(1) [This paragraph applies where][1] there is a disposal by way of gift of property which, in relation to the donor, is at that time—

(*a*) relevant business property within the meaning of Chapter I of Part V of the 1984 Act, or

(*b*) agricultural property, within the meaning of Chapter II of that Part, to which section 116 of that Act applies, or

(*c*) shares or securities to which section 122(1) of that Act applies (agricultural property of companies),

and that property is property subject to a reservation . . . [2]

[(1A) Where this paragraph applies—

(*a*) any question whether, on the material transfer of value, any shares or securities fall [within paragraph (*b*), (*bb*) or (*cc*) of section 105(1) of the 1984 Act (certain shares or securities qualifying for relief)][4] shall be determined, subject to the following provisions of this paragraph, as if the shares or securities were owned by the donor and had been owned by him since the disposal by way of gift; and

(*b*) subject to paragraph (*a*) above, any question whether, on the material transfer of value, relief is available by virtue of Chapter I or Chapter II of Part V of the 1984 Act and, if relief is available by virtue of Chapter II, what is the appropriate percentage for that relief, shall be determined, subject to the following provisions of this paragraph, as if, so far as it is attributable to the property comprised in the gift, that transfer were a transfer of value by the donee.][3]

(2) For the purpose only of determining whether, on the transfer of value which, by virtue of [sub-paragraph (1A)(*b*)][1] above, the donee is assumed to make, the requirement of section 106 or, as the case may be, section 117 of the 1984 Act (minimum period of ownership or occupation) is fulfilled,—

(*a*) ownership by the donor prior to the disposal by way of gift shall be treated as ownership by the donee; and

(*b*) occupation by the donor prior to the disposal and any occupation by him after that disposal shall be treated as occupation by the donee.

(3) Where the property disposed of by the gift consists of shares or securities falling within paragraph (*c*) of sub-paragraph (1) above, [relief shall not be available by virtue of Chapter II of Part V of the 1984 Act on the material transfer of value][1] unless—

(*a*) section 116 of the 1984 Act applied in relation to the value transferred by the disposal, and (*b*) throughout the period beginning with the disposal and ending on the material date, the shares or securities are owned by the donee,

and for the purpose only of determining whether, on the transfer of value which, [by virtue of sub-paragraph (1A)(b) above][1], the donee is assumed to make, the requirements of subsection (1) of section 123 of the 1984 Act are fulfilled, it shall be assumed that the requirement in paragraph (b) of that subsection (as to the ownership of the shares or securities) is fulfilled.

(4) In this paragraph, "the material transfer of value" means, as the case may require,—

(*a*) the transfer of value under section 4 of the 1984 Act on the death of the donor; or

(*b*) the transfer of value under subsection (4) of the principal section on the property concerned ceasing to be subject to a reservation.

(5) If the donee dies before the material transfer of value, then, as respects any time after his death, any reference in the preceding provisions of this paragraph to the donee shall be construed as a reference to his personal representatives or, as the case may require, the person (if any) by whom the property, shares or securities concerned were taken under a testamentary disposition made by the donee or under his intestacy (or partial intestacy).

Commentary—*Simon's Taxes* **I7.192, I7.382**; *Foster* **G1.92, G3.82**.

HMRC Manuals—Inheritance Tax Manual IHTM24195–24199 (gift with reservation: agricultural property relief).
IHTM25381–25384 (gift with reservation: business property relief).

Amendments—[1] Words in sub-paras (1), (2), (3) substituted by FA 1987 s 58 and Sch 8 para 18 in relation to transfers of value made or other events occurring after 16 March 1987.

[2] Words in sub-para (1) repealed by FA 1987 s 58, Sch 8 para 18 and Sch 16 Pt IX in relation to transfers of value made or other events occurring after 16 March 1987.

[3] Sub-para (1A) inserted by FA 1987 s 58 and Sch 8 para 18 in relation to transfers of value made or other events occurring after 16 March 1987.

[4] Words in sub-para (1A)(*a*) substituted for the words "within paragraph (*b*) or paragraph (*bb*) of section 105(1) of the 1984 Act (which specify shares and securities qualifying for 50 per cent relief)" by F(No 2)A 1992 Sch 14 paras 7, 8 in relation to transfers of value and other events occurring after 9 March 1992 but subject to F(No 2)A 1992 Sch 14 para 9.

FINANCE ACT 1987

(1987 Chapter 16)

An Act to grant certain duties, to alter other duties, and to amend the law relating to the National Debt and the Public Revenue, and to make further provision in connection with Finance.

[15th May 1987]

PART IV

INHERITANCE TAX

58 Securities, other business property and agricultural property

(1) The 1984 Act and Schedule 20 to the Finance Act 1986 (gifts with reservation) shall have effect subject to the amendments in Schedule 8 to this Act, being amendments—

(*a*) making provision with respect to the treatment for the purposes of the 1984 Act of shares and securities dealt in on the Unlisted Securities Market;

(*b*) making other amendments of Chapter I of Part V of the 1984 Act (business property);

(*c*) making provision with respect to the application to certain transfers of relief under that Chapter and under Chapter II of that Part (agricultural property); and

(*d*) making provision with respect to the payment of tax by instalments.

(2) Subject to subsection (3) below, Schedule 8 to this Act shall have effect in relation to transfers of value made, and other events occurring, on or after 17th March 1987.

(3) The amendments of the 1984 Act made by Schedule 8 to this Act shall be disregarded in determining under section 113A(3) or section 113B(3) of the 1984 Act whether any property acquired by the transferee before 17th March 1987 would be relevant business property in relation to a notional transfer of value made on or after that date.

59 Maintenance funds for historic buildings etc

Schedule 9 to this Act shall have effect.

60 Acceptance in lieu; waiver of interest

(*Amends* IHTA 1984 s 233.)

PART VI

MISCELLANEOUS AND SUPPLEMENTARY

70 Arrangements specified in Orders in Council relating to double taxation relief etc

(*Amends* IHTA 1984 s 158 *and is repealed in part by* TA 1988 s 844(4), Sch 31 and FA 2006 s 178, Sch 26 Pt 8(2).)

72 Short title, interpretation, construction and repeals

(1) This Act may be cited as the Finance Act 1987.

(2)–(4) (*not relevant to IHT*).

(5) In Part IV of this Act "the 1984 Act" means the Inheritance Tax Act 1984.

(6) (*not relevant to IHT*).

(7) The enactments specified in Schedule 16 to this Act (which include enactments which are spent or otherwise unnecessary) are hereby repealed to the extent specified in the third column of that Schedule, but subject to any provision at the end of any Part of that Schedule.

SCHEDULE 8

SECURITIES, OTHER BUSINESS PROPERTY AND AGRICULTURAL PROPERTY

Section 58

Note—This Schedule amends IHTA 1984 ss 10, 98, 100, 104, 113A, 124A, 136, 140, 168, 180, 227, 228, 272 and FA 1986 Sch 20 para 8.

Paras 5–7 (which amend IHTA 1984 ss 105, 107(4) and insert IHTA 1984 s 109A respectively) are repealed by FA 1996 s 184(6)(*b*), Sch 41 Pt VI with effect for transfers of value occurring after 5 April 1996, and for the purpose of charging to tax any event after that date, in relation to which the transfer of value occurred before 6 April 1996.

SCHEDULE 9

MAINTENANCE FUNDS FOR HISTORIC BUILDINGS ETC

Section 59

Note—This Schedule amends IHTA 1984 s 57A, Sch 4 paras 3, 15A.

FINANCE (NO 2) ACT 1987

(1987 Chapter 51)

An Act to grant certain duties, to alter other duties, and to amend the law relating to the National Debt and the Public Revenue, and to make further provision in connection with Finance.

[23rd July 1987]

PART II

INHERITANCE TAX ETC

96 Interests in possession

(amended IHTA 1984 ss 3A, 49, 55 and introduces Sch 7 to this Act); *repealed in part* by FA 2010 s 53(1), (9).

97 Acceptance in lieu: capital transfer tax and estate duty

(1) If, under paragraph 17 of Schedule 4 to the Finance Act 1975 the Commissioners of Inland Revenue agree to accept property in satisfaction of an amount of capital transfer tax on terms that the value to be attributed to the property for the purposes of that acceptance is determined as at a date earlier than that on which the property is actually accepted, the terms may provide that the amount of capital transfer tax which is satisfied by the acceptance of that property shall not carry interest under paragraph 19 of that Schedule from that date.

(2) If, under any of the enactments set out in paragraphs (*a*) to (*c*) of subsection (3) of section 8 of the National Heritage Act 1980 the Commissioners of Inland Revenue agree to accept property in satisfaction of an amount of estate duty on terms that the value to be attributed to the property for the purposes of that acceptance is determined as at a date earlier than that on which the property is actually accepted, the terms may provide that the amount of estate duty which is satisfied by the acceptance of that property shall not carry interest under section 18 of the Finance Act 1896 from that date.

(3) Subsections (1) and (2) above apply in any case where the acceptance of the property in question occurs on or after 17th March 1987 and paragraph 19 of Schedule 4 to the Finance Act 1975 or, as the case may be, section 18 of the Finance Act 1896 shall have effect subject to any such terms as are referred to in subsection (1) or subsection (2) above.

(4) In this section "estate duty" and "property" have the meaning assigned by section 272 of the Inheritance Tax Act 1984.

Commentary—*Simon's Taxes* **I11.541**; *Foster* **L5.41**.

Statement of Practice SP 6/87—Acceptance of property in lieu of IHT, CTT and estate duty.

98 Personal pension schemes

(*amended* IHTA 1984 ss 12, 151, 152; *repealed* by FA 2004 s 326, Sch 42 Pt 3 with effect from 6 April 2006, but subject to FA 2004 Sch 36).

SCHEDULE 7

INHERITANCE TAX: INTERESTS IN POSSESSION

Section 96

Note—This Schedule inserts IHTA 1984 ss 54A, 54B, 201(3A), 216(1)(*bd*) and amends ss 56, 201, 216, 265.

FINANCE ACT 1989

(1989 Chapter 26)

An Act to grant certain duties, to alter other duties, and to amend the law relating to the National Debt and the Public Revenue, and to make further provision in connection with Finance.

[27th July 1989]

PART III

MISCELLANEOUS AND GENERAL

Inheritance tax

171 Gifts to housing associations

(*inserts* IHTA 1984 s 24A *and amends* ss 23(5), 29(5), 161(2)(*b*)(ii) *of that Act*).

172 Abatement of exemption where claim settled out of beneficiary's own resources

(*inserts* IHTA 1984 s 29A).

Interest etc

178 Setting of rates of interest

(1) The rate of interest applicable for the purposes of an enactment to which this section applies shall be the rate which for the purposes of that enactment is provided for by regulations made by the Treasury under this section.

(2) This section applies to—

[(*aa*) section 15A of the Stamp Act 1891;][12]

(*a*) section 8(9) of the Finance Act 1894,

(*b*) section 18 of the Finance Act 1896,

(*c*) section 61(5) of the Finance (1909–10) Act 1910,

(*d*) section 17(3) of the Law of Property Act 1925,

(*e*) . . . [20]

(*f*) [sections . . . [23] 86, 86A, 87, 87A, . . . [9] and [103A][10]][8] of the Taxes Management Act 1970,

(*g*) paragraph 3 of Schedule 16A to the Finance Act 1973,

[(*ga*) section 48(1) of the Finance Act 1975,][21]

[(*gg*) [paragraph 6 of Schedule 1 to the Social Security Contributions and Benefits Act 1992][4],][1]

[(*gh*) section 71(8A) of the Social Security Administration Act 1992, and section 69(8A) of the Social Security Administration (Northern Ireland) Act 1992, as they have effect in any case where the overpayment was made in respect of working families' tax credit or disabled person's tax credit;][15]

(*h*) paragraphs 15 and 16 of Schedule 2, and paragraph 8 of Schedule 5, to the Oil Taxation Act 1975,

[(*i*) section 283 of the Taxation of Chargeable Gains Act 1992;][5]

(*j*) paragraph 59 of Schedule 8 to the Development Land Tax Act 1976,

(*k*) sections 233[, 235(1)][21] and 236(3) and (4) of the Inheritance Tax Act 1984,

(*l*) section 92 of the Finance Act 1986, and

(*m*) sections . . . [16] *160*[17], 824, 825 [826 and 826A(1)(*b*)][11] of . . . ,[7] and paragraph 3 of Schedule 19A to, the Taxes Act 1988 [and][2].

[(*n*) . . .][6] [and][3]

[(*o*) section 14(4) of the Ports Act 1991][3]

[(*p*) paragraph 8 of Schedule 4 to the Tax Credits Act 1999][13] [, *and*[17]

[(*q*)][17] section 110 of the Finance Act][14][, and

[(*q*) paragraph 8 of Schedule 1 to the Employment Act 2002][18]

(*r*) Chapter 7 of Part 3 of the Income Tax (Earnings and Pensions) Act 2003][17]

[(*r*) sections 87, 88 and 89 of the Finance Act 2003][19] . . . [25]

(*u*) paragraph 11 of Schedule 35 to the Finance Act 2014][24][, and

[(*v*) section 79 of FA 2015.][25]

(3) Regulations under this section may—

(*a*) make different provision for different enactments or for different purposes of the same enactment,

(b) either themselves specify a rate of interest for the purposes of an enactment or make provision for any such rate to be determined by reference to such rate or the average of such rates as may be referred to in the regulations,
(c) provide for rates to be reduced below, or increased above, what they otherwise would be by specified amounts or by reference to specified formulae,
(d) provide for rates arrived at by reference to averages to be rounded up or down,
(e) provide for circumstances in which alteration of a rate of interest is or is not to take place, and
(f) provide that alterations of rates are to have effect for periods beginning on or after a day determined in accordance with the regulations in relation to interest running from before that day as well as from or from after that day.

(4) The power to make regulations under this section shall be exercisable by statutory instrument which shall be subject to annulment in pursuance of a resolution of the House of Commons.

(5) . . . [21]

(6) (amends TA 1988 s 828(2)).[22]

(7) Subsection (1) shall have effect for periods beginning on or after such day as the Treasury may by order made by statutory instrument appoint and shall have effect in relation to interest running from before that day as well as from or from after that day; and different days may be appointed for different enactments.

Commentary—*Simon's Taxes* **A4.621**.

Regulations—Taxes (Interest Rate) Regulations, SI 1989/1297.
Finance Act 1989, section 178(1), (Appointed Day No 1) Order, SI 1989/1298.
Finance Act 1989, section 178(1), (Appointed Day) Order, SI 1992/2073.
Finance Act 1989, section 178(1), (Appointed Day) Order, SI 1993/754.
Taxes (Interest Rate) (Amendment No 3) Regulations, SI 1993/2212.
Taxes (Interest Rate) (Amendment) Regulations, SI 1994/1307.
Taxes (Interest Rate) (Amendment No 4) Regulations, SI 1996/3187.
Taxes (Interest Rate) (Amendment No 2) Regulations, SI 1997/2707.
Finance Act 1989, section 178(1), (Appointed Day) Order, SI 1997/2708.
Taxes (Interest Rate) (Amendment) Regulations, SI 1998/310.
Finance Act 1989, section 178(1), (Appointed Day) Order, SI 1998/311.
Taxes (Interest Rate) (Amendment No 2) Regulations, SI 1998/3176.
Taxes (Interest Rate) (Amendment) Regulations, SI 1999/419.
Taxes (Interest Rate) (Amendment No 2) Regulations, SI 1999/1928.
Taxes (Interest Rate) (Amendment No 4) Regulations, SI 1999/2637.
Taxes (Interest Rate) (Amendment) Regulations, SI 2000/893.
Taxes (Interest Rate) (Amendment No 1) Regulations, SI 2001/204.
Finance Act 1989, Section 178(1), (Appointed Day) Order, SI 2001/253.
Taxes (Interest Rate) (Amendment) Regulations, SI 2005/2462.
Taxes (Interest Rate) (Amendment) Regulations, SI 2008/778.
Taxes and Duties (Interest Rate) (Amendment) Regulations, SI 2008/3234.
Taxes (Interest Rate) (Amendment) Regulations, SI 2009/199.
Taxes and Duties (Interest Rate) (Amendment) Regulations, SI 2009/2032.
Taxes (Interest Rate) (Amendment) Regulations, SI 2010/415.
Taxes (Interest Rate) (Amendment) Regulations, SI 2014/496.
Taxes (Interest Rate) (Amendment) Regulations, SI 2015/441.

Note—The appointed day for the purposes of all the enactments mentioned in sub-s (2) above (with such exceptions as mentioned in the **Amendments** note below) and appointed under sub-s (7) above is 18 August 1989; FA 1989 s 178(1) (Appointed Day No 1) Order, SI 1989/1298.

Amendments—[1] Sub-s (2)(*gg*) inserted by the Social Security Act 1990 s 17(10) with effect from 6 April 1992.
[2] Word "and" added by FA 1990 s 118(8) with effect from 26 July 1990.
[3] Sub-s (2)(*o*) and preceding word "and" added by the Ports Act 1991 s 14(5) with effect from 15 July 1991.
[4] Words in sub-s (2)(*gg*) substituted by the Social Security (Consequential Provisions) Act 1992 s 4, Sch 2 para 107 with effect from 1 July 1992.
[5] Sub-s (2)(*i*) substituted by TCGA 1992 Sch 10 para 19(4) with effect from the year 1992–93.
[6] Sub-s (2)(*n*) (inserted by FA 1990 s 118(8)) repealed by FA 1995 Sch 29 Pt XII.
[7] Words in sub-s (2)(*m*) repealed by FA 1996 Sch 7 para 30 and Sch 41 Pt V(2) with effect for income tax for the year 1996–97 and for corporation tax for accounting periods ending after 31 March 1996.
[8] Words in sub-s (2)(*f*) substituted by FA 1994 ss 196, 199 and Sch 19 para 44 with effect from the year 1996–97 in relation to income tax and capital gains tax and, in relation to corporation tax, for accounting periods ending after 30 June 1999 (by virtue of Finance Act 1994, Section 199, (Appointed Day) Order, SI 1998/3173 art 2).
[9] Word "88" in sub-s (2)(*f*) repealed by FA 1996 Sch 18 para 13 and Sch 41 Pt V(8) with effect for the year 1996–97, and in relation to any income tax or capital gains tax which is charged by an assessment made after 5 April 1998 which is for the year 1995–96 or any earlier year of assessment, and so far as relating to partnerships whose trades, professions or businesses were set up and commenced before 6 April 1994 from the year 1997–98 in relation to any income tax which is charged by an assessment made after 5 April 1998 which is for the year 1995–96 or any earlier year of assessment.
[10] The appointed day for the purposes of TMA 1970 ss 59C and 103A and appointed under sub-s (7) above is 9 March 1998; Finance Act 1989, section 178(1), (Appointed Day) Order 1998, SI 1998/311.
[11] Words substituted by FA 1998 Sch 4 para 1(3) with effect for accounting periods ending on or after 1 July 1999 (the date appointed under FA 1994 s 199, by virtue of SI 1998/3173, for the purposes of corporation tax self-assessment).
[12] Sub-s (2)(*aa*) inserted by FA 1999 s 109(2), (4) with effect for instruments executed after 30 September 1999.
[13] Sub-s (2)(*p*) inserted by Tax Credits Act 1999 Sch 4 para 8(1) with effect from 7 March 2001 (by virtue of SI 2001/253).

14 Sub-s (2)(*p*) and preceding word ", and" inserted by FA 1999 s 110(8), (9) with effect for instruments executed after 30 September 1999. It would appear that this paragraph has been incorrectly numbered.

15 Sub-s (2)(*gh*) inserted in relation to the transfer of functions concerning the working families' tax credit and the disabled person's tax credit by Tax Credits Act 1999 s 2(3), Sch 2 para 10(2) with effect from 5 October 1999.

16 Words in sub-s (2)(*m*) repealed by FA 2000 s 156, Sch 40 Pt II(17) with effect for relevant payments or receipts in relation to which the chargeable date for the purposes of TA 1988 Pt IV, Ch VIIA is after 31 March 2001.

17 In sub-s (2), in para (*m*), reference "160" repealed, in para (*p*), word in italics repealed, para (*q*) numbered as such, and para (*r*) and word preceding it inserted by ITEPA 2003 ss 722, 724, Sch 6 paras 156, 162, Sch 8 with effect, for income tax purposes, from 2003–04; and for corporation tax purposes, for accounting periods ending after 5 April 2003. For transitional provisions and savings see ITEPA 2003 s 723, Sch 7.

18 Sub-s (2)(*q*), which appears to have been numbered incorrectly, inserted by EmA 2002 ss 11, 12, Sch 1 para 8(1) with effect from 8 December 2002 (by virtue of SI 2002/2866).

19 Sub-s (2)(*r*) inserted by FA 2003 s 123(1), Sch 18 para 4 with effect in accordance with FA 2003 s 124, Sch 19. It would appear that this provision has been incorrectly numbered.

20 Sub-s (2)(*e*) repealed by the Land Registration Act 2002 ss 135, 136(2), Sch 13 with effect from 13 October 2003 (by virtue of SI 2003/1725).

21 Sub-s (2)(*ga*) and words in sub-s (2)(*k*) inserted, and sub-s (5) repealed, by FA 2009 s 105(5), (6)(a) with effect from 21 July 2009.

22 Sub-s (6) repealed by CTA 2010 s 1181, Sch 3 Pt 1. CTA 2010 has effect for corporation tax purposes for accounting periods ending on or after 1 April 2010, and for income and capital gains tax purposes for the tax year 2010–11 and subsequent tax years.

23 In sub-s (2)(*f*), reference "59C," repealed by the Finance Act 2009, Schedules 55 and 56 (Income Tax Self Assessment and Pension Schemes) (Appointed Days and Consequential and Savings Provisions) Order, SI 2011/702 art 12 with effect from 1 April 2011. This amendment has no effect in relation to a return or other document which is required to be made or delivered to HMRC or an amount of tax which is payable in relation to the tax year 2009–10 or any previous tax year (SI 2011/702 art 20).

24 Sub-s (2)(*u*) and preceding word "and" inserted by FA 2014 s 274, Sch 35 para 11 with effect from 17 July 2014.

25 In sub-s (2), word "and" previously preceding para (*u*) repealed, and para (*v*) and preceding word inserted, by FA 2015 s 115(4) with effect in relation to accounting periods beginning on or after 1 April 2015. For accounting periods that straddle that date, see FA 2015 s 116(2), (3).

179 Provisions consequential on section 178

(4) Any amendment made by subsection (1), . . . or (3) above shall have effect in relation to any period for which section 178(1) above has effect for the purposes of the enactment concerned.

Notes—Sub-s (1)(*d*) amends IHTA 1984 s 233(1).
Sub-s (1)(*e*) amends IHTA 1984 s 236(3), (4).
Sub-s (3) amends IHTA 1984 s 236(4).
Sub-ss (1)(*a*)–(*c*), (*f*)–(*g*), (2), (5) are not relevant to inheritance tax.

180 Repayment interest: period of accrual

(4) (*amends* FA 1975 Sch 4 para 19(3) and IHTA 1984 s 235(1)).

(7) The amendments made by this section shall be deemed always to have had effect.

Notes—Sub-ss (1)–(3), (5)–(6) are not relevant to inheritance tax.

Miscellaneous

182 Disclosure of information

(1) A person who discloses any information which he holds or has held in the exercise of tax functions[, tax credit functions][4][, child trust fund functions][6] [or social security functions][2] is guilty of an offence if it is information about any matter relevant, for the purposes of [any of those functions—

(*a*) to tax or duty in the case of any identifiable person,

[(*aa*) to a tax credit in respect of any identifiable person,][4]

[(*ab*) to a child trust fund of any identifiable person,][6]

(*b*) to contributions payable by or in respect of any identifiable person, or

(*c*) to statutory sick pay [, statutory maternity pay, [statutory paternity pay,][13] statutory adoption pay][5] [or statutory shared parental pay][15] in respect of any identifiable person.][2]

(2) In this section "tax functions" means functions relating to tax . . . —

(*a*) of . . . the Board and their officers,

(*b*) of any person carrying out the administrative work of [the First-tier Tribunal or Upper Tribunal][12], and

(*c*) of any other person providing, or employed in the provision of, services to any person mentioned in paragraph (*a*) or (*b*) above.

[(2ZA) In this section "tax credit functions" means the functions relating to tax credits—

(*a*) of the Board,

(*b*) of any person carrying out the administrative work of [the First-tier Tribunal or Upper Tribunal][12], and

(*c*) of any other person providing, or employed in the provision of, services to the Board or to any person mentioned in paragraph (*b*) above.][4]

[(2ZB) In this section "child trust fund functions" means the functions relating to child trust funds—

(*a*) of the Board and their officers,

(*b*) of any person carrying out the administrative work of [First-tier Tribunal or an appeal tribunal constituted under Chapter 1 of Part 2 of the Social Security (Northern Ireland) Order 1998][12], or

(*c*) of any person providing, or employed in the provision of, services to the Board or any person mentioned in paragraph (*b*) above.][6]

[(2A) In this section "social security functions" means—

(*a*) the functions relating to contributions, [child benefit, guardian's allowance,][3] statutory sick pay[, statutory maternity pay, [statutory paternity pay,][13] statutory adoption pay][5] [or statutory shared parental pay][15]

(i) of the Board and their officers,

(ii) of any person carrying out the administrative work of [the First-tier Tribunal or Upper Tribunal][12], and

(iii) of any other person providing, or employed in the provision of, services to any person mentioned in sub-paragraph (i) or (ii) above, and

(*b*) the functions under Part III of the Pension Schemes Act 1993 or Part III of the Pension Schemes (Northern Ireland) Act 1993 of the Board and their officers and any other person providing, or employed in the provision of, services to the Board or their officers.][2]

(3) The tribunals referred to in subsection (2)(b) above are—

(a) the General Commissioners and the Special Commissioners,

(b) . . .

(c) . . . [9] *and*

(d) any tribunal established under section 463 of the Taxes Act 1970 or section 706 of the Taxes Act 1988 [or section 704 of the Income Tax Act 2007][11],[12].

(4) A person who discloses any information which—

(*a*) he holds or has held in the exercise of functions—

(i) of the Comptroller and Auditor General[, of the National Audit Office and any member or employee of that Office or of any member of the staff of the National Audit Office that was established by section 3 of the National Audit Act 1983][14],

[(*ia*) of the Comptroller and Auditor General for Northern Ireland and any member of the staff of the Northern Ireland Audit Office,][14]

(ii) of the Parliamentary Commissioner for Administration and his officers,

[(iii) of the Auditor General for Wales and any member of his staff, . . .[7]

[(iv) of the Public Services Ombudsman for Wales and any member of his staff, or][10]]

(v) of the Scottish Public Services Ombudsman and any member of his staff,][7]

(*b*) is, or is derived from, information which was held by any person in the exercise of tax functions[, tax credit functions][4][, child trust fund functions][6] [or social security functions][2], and

(*c*) is information about any matter relevant, for the purposes of [tax functions[, tax credit functions][4][, child trust fund functions][6] or social security functions—

(i) to tax or duty in the case of any identifiable person,

[(ia) to a tax credit in respect of any identifiable person,][4]

[(ib) to a child trust fund of any identifiable person,][6]

(ii) to contributions payable by or in respect of any identifiable person, or

(iii) to [child benefit, guardian's allowance,][3] statutory sick pay [, statutory maternity pay, [statutory paternity pay,][13] statutory adoption pay][5] [or statutory shared parental pay][15] in respect of any identifiable person.][2]

is guilty of an offence.

(5) Subsections (1) and (4) above do not apply to any disclosure of information—

(*a*) with lawful authority,

(*b*) with the consent of any person in whose case the information is about a matter relevant to tax or duty[, to a tax credit or to a child trust fund][6] [or to contributions, statutory sick pay[, statutory maternity pay, [statutory paternity pay,][13] statutory adoption pay][5]][2] [or statutory shared parental pay][15], or

(*c*) which has been lawfully made available to the public before the disclosure is made.

(6) For the purposes of this section a disclosure of any information is made with lawful authority if, and only if, it is made—

(*a*) by a Crown servant in accordance with his official duty,

(*b*) by any other person for the purposes of the function in the exercise of which he holds the information and without contravening any restriction duly imposed by the person responsible,

(*c*) to, or in accordance with an authorisation duly given by, the person responsible,

(*d*) in pursuance of any enactment or of any order of a court, or

(*e*) in connection with the institution of or otherwise for the purposes of any proceedings relating to any matter within the general responsibility of the Commissioners or, as the case requires, the Board, and in this subsection "the person responsible" means . . . the Board, the Comptroller, [and Auditor General, the Comptroller and Auditor General for Northern Ireland,[14]] [the Parliamentary Commissioner, the Auditor General for Wales [the Public Services Ombudsman for Wales][10] [, or the Scottish Public Services Ombudsman][7]][1] as the case requires.

(7) It is a defence for a person charged with an offence under this section to prove that at the time of the alleged offence—

(*a*) he believed that he had lawful authority to make the disclosure in question and had no reasonable cause to believe otherwise, or

(*b*) he believed that the information in question had been lawfully made available to the public before the disclosure was made and had no reasonable cause to believe otherwise.

(8) A person guilty of an offence under this section is liable—

(*a*) on conviction on indictment, to imprisonment for a term not exceeding two years or a fine or both, and

(*b*) on summary conviction, to imprisonment for a term not exceeding six months or a fine not exceeding the statutory maximum or both.

(9) No prosecution for an offence under this section shall be instituted in England and Wales or in Northern Ireland except—

(*a*) by . . . the Board . . . or

(*b*) by or with the consent of the Director of Public Prosecutions or, in Northern Ireland, the Director of Public Prosecutions for Northern Ireland.

(10) In this section—

"the Board" means the Commissioners of Inland Revenue,

["child trust fund" has the same meaning as in the Child Trust Funds Act 2004,][6]

. . .

["contributions" means contributions under Part I of the Social Security Contributions and Benefits Act 1992 or Part I of the Social Security Contributions and Benefits (Northern Ireland) Act 1992;][2]

"Crown servant" has the same meaning as in the Official Secrets Act 1989,

["tax credit" means a tax credit under the Tax Credits Act 2002,][4] and

"tax . . . " means any tax . . . within the general responsibility of . . . the Board.

[(10A) In this section, in relation to the disclosure of information "identifiable person" means a person whose identity is specified in the disclosure or can be deduced from it.][8]

(11) In this section—

(*a*) . . . [14]

(*b*) . . . [14]

(*c*) references to the Parliamentary Commissioner for Administration include the Health Service Commissioner for England, . . . [10] . . . [7] the [Assembly, Ombudsman for Northern Ireland] and the Northern Ireland Commissioner for Complaints.

[(11A) In this section, references to [statutory paternity pay,][16] statutory adoption pay [or statutory shared parental pay][16] include statutory pay under Northern Ireland legislation corresponding to Part 12ZA[, Part 12ZB or Part 12ZC][16] of the Social Security Contributions and Benefits Act 1992 (c 4).][5]

(12) This section shall come into force on the repeal of section 2 of the Official Secrets Act 1911.

Notes—This section came into force on 1 March 1990 when the repeal of the Official Secrets Act 1911 came into effect by virtue of the Official Secrets Act Order, SI 1990/199.

Words omitted from this section are not relevant for the purposes of this publication.

Amendments—[1] Sub-s (4)(a)(iii) and (iv) inserted by, and words in sub-s (6) substituted by, the Government of Wales Act 1998 with effect from 1 February 1999 (by virtue of the Government of Wales Act 1998 (Commencement No 3) Order, SI 1999/118 art 2).

[2] Sub-ss (1), (4), (5), (10) amended, and sub-s (2A) inserted, by the Social Security Contributions (Transfer of Functions, etc) Act 1999 Sch 6 para 9 with effect from 1 April 1999 by virtue of the Social Security Contributions (Transfer of Functions, etc) Act 1999 (Commencement No 1 and Transitional Provisions) Order, SI 1999/527 art 2, Sch 2.

[3] Words in sub-ss (2A)(*a*), (4)(*c*)(iii) inserted by TCA 2002 s 59, Sch 5 para 11(1), (4) with effect for the purpose of making subordinate legislation, from 26 February 2003, and for remaining purposes, from 1 April 2003 (by virtue of SI 2003/392).

[4] Words in sub-ss (1), (4), (5)(*b*) inserted, sub-ss (1)(*aa*), (4)(*c*)(ia) substituted, sub-s (2ZA) substituted for sub-s (2AA), and in sub-s (10), definition of "tax credit" inserted, by TCA 2002 s 59, Sch 5 para 11(1), (2) with effect from 1 August 2002 (by virtue of SI 2002/1727).

[5] Words in sub-ss (1)(*c*), (2A)(*a*) substituted, and sub-s (11A) inserted, by the Employment Act 2002 s 53, Sch 7 para 1 with effect from 8 December 2002 (by virtue of SI 2002/2866).

[6] Words in sub-ss (1), (4) inserted, sub-ss (1)(*ab*), (2ZB), (4)(*c*)(ib) inserted, words in sub-s (5)(*b*) substituted, and definition of "child trust fund" inserted in sub-s (10), by the Child Trust Funds Act 2004 s 18 with effect from 1 January 2005 (by virtue of SI 2004/2422).

[7] Words in sub-ss (4)(*a*)(iii), (11)(*c*) repealed, sub-s (4)(*a*)(v) inserted, and words in sub-s (6) substituted, by the Scottish Public Services Ombudsman Act 2002 (Consequential Provisions and Modifications) Order, SI 2004/1823 art 10 with effect from 14 July 2004.

[8] Sub-s (10A) inserted by CRCA 2005 s 50, Sch 4 para 39 with effect from 18 April 2005 (by virtue of SI 2005/1126).

[9] Sub-s (3)(*c*) repealed by the Statute Law (Repeals) Act 2004.

[10] Words in sub-ss (4), (6) substituted, and words in sub-s (11) repealed, by the Public Services Ombudsman (Wales) Act 2005 s 39, Sch 6 para 22, Sch 7 with effect from 1 April 2006 (by virtue of SI 2005/2800). See SI 2005/2800 for further provisions about commencement.

[11] Words in sub-s (3)(*d*) inserted by ITA 2007 s 1027, Sch 1 paras 278, 282 with effect for income tax purposes from 6 April 2007, and corporation tax purposes for accounting periods ending after 5 April 2007.

[12] In sub-s (2)(*b*) words substituted for the words "any tribunal mentioned in subsection (3) below"; in sub-ss (2ZA)(*b*), (2ZB)(*b*) and (2A)(*a*)(ii) words substituted for the words "the General Commissioners or the Special Commissioners"; sub-s (3) repealed by the Transfer of Tribunal Functions and Revenue and Customs Appeals Order, SI 2009/56 art 3, Sch 1 para 167 with effect from 1 April 2009.

[13] In sub-ss (1)(*c*), (2A)(*a*), (4)(*c*)(iii) and (5)(*b*), words substituted for words "ordinary statutory paternity pay, additional statutory paternity pay or" by the Children and Families Act 2014 s 126, Sch 7 para 5(1), (2)(*a*), (3)(*a*), (4)(*a*), (5)(*a*) with effect from 5 April 2015 (by virtue of SI 2014/1640 art 7(*c*) and subject to transitional provisions in SI 2014/1640 art 17

[14] The following amendments made by the Budget Responsibility and National Audit Act 2011 s 26, Sch 5 para 14 with effect from 1 April 2012 (SI 2011/2576 art 5)—

– In sub-s (4)(*a*)(i), words substituted and sub-s (4)(*ia*) inserted;
– in sub-s (6), words inserted; and
– in sub-s (11)(*a*), (*b*) repealed.

[15] Words in sub-ss (1)(*c*), (2A)(*a*), (4)(*c*)(iii) and (5)(*b*) inserted by the Children and Families Act 2014 s 126, Sch 7 para 5(1), (2)(*b*), (3)(*b*), (4)(*b*), (5)(*b*) with effect from 1 December 2014 (by virtue of SI 2014/1640 art 5(2)).

[16] In sub-s (11A), words substituted and inserted by the Children and Families Act 2014 s 126, Sch 7 para 5(6) with effect from 15 March 2015 (by virtue of SI 2014/1640 art 8(*a*)) subject to transitional provisions in SI 2014/1640 art 18..

FINANCE ACT 1990

(1990 Chapter 29)

An Act to grant certain duties, to alter other duties, and to amend the law relating to the National Debt and the Public Revenue, and to make further provision in connection with Finance.

[26th July 1990]

PART IV
MISCELLANEOUS AND GENERAL

Miscellaneous

124 Inheritance tax: restriction on power to require information

Note—This section inserted IHTA 1984 s 219(1A). Repealed by the Finance Act 2009, Section 96 and Schedule 48 (Appointed Day, Savings and Consequential Amendments) Order, SI 2009/3054 art 3, Schedule para 16(*a*) with effect from 1 April 2010.

125 Information for tax authorities in other member States

(1) Subsections (1) to (8) and (8C) to (9) of section 20 of the Taxes Management Act 1970 (powers to call for information relevant to liability to income tax, corporation tax or capital gains tax) shall have effect as if the references in those provisions to tax liability included a reference to liability to a tax of a member State other than the United Kingdom which is a tax on income or on capital for the purposes of the Directive of the Council of the European Communities dated 19th December 1977 No 77/799/EEC.

(2) In their application by virtue of subsection (1) above those provisions shall have effect as if—

(a) the reference in section 20(7A) to any provision of the Taxes Acts were a reference to any provision of the law of the member State in accordance with which the tax in question is charged,

(b) the references in subsection (2) of section 20B to an appeal relating to tax were references to an appeal, review or similar proceedings under the law of the member State relating to the tax in question, and

(c) the reference in subsection (6) of that section to believing that tax has or may have been lost to the Crown were a reference to believing that the tax in question has or may have been lost to the member State.[2]

(3), (4) (*not relevant to this work*).

(5) . . . [1]

(6) . . . [3]

Commentary—*Simon's Taxes* **E6.455**.

Amendments—[1] Sub-s (5) repealed by FA 2003 s 216, Sch 43 Pt 5(1) with effect from 10 July 2003.

[2] Sub-ss (1), (2) repealed by FA 2008 s 113, Sch 36 para 83 with effect from 1 April 2009 (by virtue of SI 2009/404 art 2).

[3] Sub-s (6) repealed by Finance Act 2009 Schedule 47 (Consequential Amendments) Order, SI 2009/2035, Art 2 Schedule, para 26 with effect from 13 August 2009.

126 Pools payments for football ground improvements

Amendments—This section repealed by FA 2012 s 227, Sch 39 para 19(1) with effect in relation to payments made—

– for corporation tax purposes, on or after 1 April 2013; and
– for income tax purposes, on or after 6 April 2013, and

For inheritance tax purposes, this amendment comes into force on 6 April 2013 and has effect in relation to payments whenever made.

FINANCE (NO 2) ACT 1992

(1992 Chapter 48)

An Act to grant certain duties, to alter other duties, and to amend the law relating to the National Debt and the Public Revenue, and to make further provision in connection with Finance.

[16th July 1992]

PART III

MISCELLANEOUS AND GENERAL

Inheritance tax

72 Increase of rate bands

(*This section substituted Table of Rates in* IHTA 1984 Sch 1 *and is now spent*).

73 Business and agricultural property relief

Schedule 14 to this Act (which makes provision in relation to relief in respect of business property and agricultural property) shall have effect.

General

83 Short title

This Act may be cited as the Finance (No 2) Act 1992.

SCHEDULE 14

INHERITANCE TAX

Section 73

Business property

1 (*amends* IHTA 1984 s 104).

2 (*amends* IHTA 1984 s 105).

3 (*amends* IHTA 1984 s 113A).

Agricultural property

4 (*amends* IHTA 1984 s 116).

Payment by instalments

5 (*amends* IHTA 1984 s 227).

6 (*amends* IHTA 1984 s 228).

Gifts with reservation

7 (*amends* FA 1986 Sch 20 para 8(1A)(*a*)).

Commencement

8 Subject to paragraph 9 below, the amendments made by this Schedule shall have effect in relation to transfers of value made, and other events occurring, on or after 10th March 1992.

9—(1) This paragraph applies where by reason of a death occurring on or after 10th March 1992—

(*a*) a potentially exempt transfer made before that date proves to be a chargeable transfer, or

(*b*) additional tax falls to be calculated in respect of a chargeable transfer (other than a potentially exempt transfer) made before that date and within seven years of the death.

(2) Subject to sub-paragraph (3) below, for the purposes of sections 113A and 113B of the Inheritance Tax Act 1984 it shall be assumed—

(*a*) that the amendments made by this Schedule came into effect at the time the transfer was made, and

(*b*) (in a case within sub-paragraph (1)(*b*) above) that so much of the value transferred as would have been reduced in accordance with Chapter I of Part V of that Act as amended by this Schedule was so reduced.

(3) Where, disregarding the amendments made by this Schedule, any shares or securities transferred fell within section 105(1)(*b*) of that Act in relation to the transfer, those amendments shall be disregarded in determining whether section 113A(3A) applies to the shares or securities.

(4) This paragraph shall be construed as if it were contained in Chapter I of Part V of that Act.

Commentary—*Simon's Taxes* **I7.102, I7.191A, I7.304**; *Foster* **G1.02, 91A, G3.04**.

FINANCE ACT 1993

(1993 Chapter 34)

An Act to grant certain duties, to alter other duties, and to amend the law relating to the National Debt and the Public Revenue, and to make further provision in connection with Finance.

[27th July 1993]

PART IV
INHERITANCE TAX

196 Rate bands: no indexation in 1993

(*spent*).

197 Rate bands: indexation for 1994 onwards

(*amends* IHTA 1984 s 8).

198 Fall in value relief: qualifying investments

(*inserts* IHTA 1984 ss 186A, 186B).

199 Fall in value relief: interests in land

(*inserts* IHTA 1984 s 197A).

200 Appeals: questions as to value of land

(1) (*amends* IHTA 1984 s 222).

(2) (*amends* IHTA 1984 s 242).

(3) This section shall apply in relation to any appeal which—

(*a*) is made on or after the day on which this Act is passed, or

(*b*) is made, but has not begun to be heard, before that day.

FINANCE ACT 1994

(1994 Chapter 9)

An Act to grant certain duties, to alter other duties, and to amend the law relating to the National Debt and the Public Revenue, and to make further provision in connection with Finance.

[3rd May 1994]

PART VII
INHERITANCE TAX

246 Rate bands: no indexation in 1994

(*This section disapplied* IHTA 1984 s 8(1) *for the year beginning 6 April 1994 and amended the Table in* IHTA 1984 Sch 1).

247 Business and agricultural relief

(1) (*amends* IHTA 1984 s 113B(2)(*a*), (5)(*b*), (8)).

(2) (*amends* IHTA 1984 s 124B(2)(*a*), (5)(*b*), (8)).

(3) This section applies in relation to transfers of value made, and other events occurring, on or after 30th November 1993.

248 Corporate Lloyd's underwriters

(1) No property forming part of a premiums trust fund or ancillary trust fund of a corporate member shall be relevant property for the purposes of Chapter III of Part III of the Inheritance Tax Act 1984 (settlements without interests in possession).

(2) In this section "ancillary trust fund", "corporate member" and "premiums trust fund" have the same meanings as in Chapter V of Part IV of this Act (Lloyd's underwriters: corporations etc).

FINANCE ACT 1995

(1995 Chapter 4)

An Act to grant certain duties, to alter other duties, and to amend the law relating to the National Debt and the Public Revenue, and to make further provision in connection with Finance.

[1st May 1995]

PART VI
MISCELLANEOUS AND GENERAL

Miscellaneous

154 Short rotation coppice

(1) (*not relevant to IHT*).

(2) For the purposes of the Inheritance Tax Act 1984 the cultivation of short rotation coppice shall be regarded as agriculture; and accordingly for those purposes—

(*a*) land on which short rotation coppice is cultivated shall be regarded as agricultural land, and

(*b*) buildings used in connection with the cultivation of short rotation coppice shall be regarded as farm buildings.

(3) In subsections (1) and (2) "short rotation coppice" means a perennial crop of tree species planted at high density, the stems of which are harvested above ground level at intervals of less than ten years.

(4) (*not relevant to IHT*).

(5) Subsection (2) and subsection (3) so far as relating to subsection (2) shall have effect in relation to transfers of value or other events occurring on or after 6th April 1995.

Commentary—*Simon's Taxes* **I7.303**; *Foster* **G3.03**.

155 Inheritance tax: agricultural property

(1) (*amends* IHTA 1984 s 116(2)).

(2) (*inserts* IHTA 1984 s 116(2A), *which is repealed by* FA 1996 Sch 41 Pt VI *in any case where the death of the tenant, or the sole surviving tenant occurs after 31 August 1995*).

(3) Subsections (1) and (2) above shall apply in relation to transfers of value made, and other events occurring, on or after 1st September 1995.

Commentary—*Simon's Taxes* **I7.303, I7.304**; *Foster* **G3.03, 04**.

FINANCE ACT 1996

(1996 Chapter 8)

An Act to grant certain duties, to alter other duties, and to amend the law relating to the National Debt and the Public Revenue, and to make further provision in connection with Finance.

29th April 1996

PART V
INHERITANCE TAX

183 Rate bands

(*substitutes the Table in* IHTA 1984 Sch 1 *and disapplied* s 8 *of that Act as respects any difference between the RPI for September 1994 and that for September 1995*).

184 Business property relief

(1) The Inheritance Tax Act 1984 shall be amended as follows.

(2)–(5) (*amend* IHTA 1984 ss 105(1), 107(4), 113A(3A)(*b*) *and insert s* 113A(7A) *in that Act*).

(6) This section—

(*a*) so far is it inserts a new subsection (7A) in section 113A, has effect in relation to any transfer of value on or after 28th November 1995; and

(*b*) so far as it makes any other provision, has effect—

(i) in relation to any transfer of value on or after 6th April 1996, and

(ii) for the purposes of any charge to tax by reason of an event occurring on or after 6th April 1996, in relation to transfers of value before that date.

185 Agricultural property relief

(1) Chapter II of Part V of the Inheritance Tax Act 1984 (agricultural property) shall be amended as follows.

(2)–(4) (*inserts* IHTA 1984 s 116 (5A)–(5E), *repeals* 116(2A) *and inserts* 124A(7A) *of that Act*).

(5) Subsection (2) above—

(*a*) so far as relating to subsections (5A) to (5C) of section 116 of the Inheritance Tax Act 1984, has effect in any case where the death of the tenant or, as the case may be, the sole surviving tenant, occurs on or after 1st September 1995; and (*b*) so far as relating to subsections (5D) and (5E) of that section, has effect in any case where the death of the transferor occurs on or after 1st September 1995.

(6) Subsection (3) above has effect in any case where the death of the tenant or, as the case may be, the sole surviving tenant, occurs on or after 1st September 1995.

(7) Subsection (4) above has effect in relation to any transfer of value on or after 28th November 1995.

PART VII
MISCELLANEOUS AND SUPPLEMENTAL

Miscellaneous: direct taxation

198 Banks

Schedule 37 to this Act (which re-defines "bank" for certain purposes, and makes related amendments) shall have effect.

199 Quotation or listing of securities

Schedule 38 to this Act (which contains amendments of enactments referring to the quotation or listing of securities) shall have effect.

200 Domicile for tax purposes of overseas electors

(1) In determining—

(*a*) for the purposes of inheritance tax, *income tax* [2]or capital gains tax where a person is domiciled at any time on or after 6th April 1996, or

(*b*) for the purposes of section 267(1)(*a*) of the Inheritance Tax Act 1984 (deemed UK domicile for three years after ceasing to be so domiciled) where a person was domiciled at any time on or after 6th April 1993,

there shall be disregarded any relevant action taken by that person (whether before, on or after that date) in connection with electoral rights.

(2) Relevant action is taken by a person in connection with electoral rights where—

(*a*) he does anything with a view to, or in connection with, being registered as an overseas elector; or

(*b*) when registered as an overseas elector, he votes in any election at which he is entitled to vote by virtue of being so registered.

(3) For the purposes of this section, a person is registered as an overseas elector if he is—

(*a*) registered in any register [of parliamentary electors in pursuance of such a declaration as is mentioned in section 1(1)(*a*)][1] of the Representation of the People Act 1985 (extension of parliamentary franchise to certain non-resident British citizens); or

(*b*) registered under section 3 of that Act of 1985 (certain non-resident peers entitled to vote at European Parliamentary elections).

(4) Nothing in subsection (1) above prevents regard being had, in determining the domicile of a person at any time, to any relevant action taken by him in connection with electoral rights if—

(*a*) his domicile at that time falls to be determined for the purpose of ascertaining his or any other person's liability to [either][2] of the taxes mentioned in subsection (1)(*a*) above; and

(*b*) the person whose liability is being ascertained wishes regard to be had to that action;

and a person's domicile determined in accordance with any such wishes shall be taken to have been so determined for the purpose only of ascertaining the liability in question.

Amendments—[1] Words in sub-s (3) substituted by the Representation of People Act 2000 s 151, Sch 6 para 19 with effect from 16 February 2001 (except for the purposes of any election where the last day for the publication of the notice of election for that election is before that date) (by virtue of SI 2001/116).

[2] In sub-s (1)(*a*), words ", income tax" repealed, and in sub-s (4)(*a*), word substituted for word "any", by TIOPA 2010 ss 371, 378(1), Sch 7 paras 73, 74(1), (2), Sch 10, Pt 12. TIOPA 2010 has effect for corporation tax purposes for accounting periods ending on or after 1 April 2010, for income and capital gains tax purposes for the tax year 2010–11 and subsequent tax years, and for petroleum revenue tax purposes for chargeable periods beginning on or after 1 July 2010.

Miscellaneous: other matters

202 Gilt stripping

(1)–(4) (*not relevant to IHT*).

(5) The Treasury may by regulations make provision for securing that enactments and subordinate legislation which—

(*a*) apply in relation to government securities or to any description of such securities, or

(*b*) for any other purpose refer (in whatever terms) to such securities or to any description of them,

have effect with such modifications as the Treasury may think appropriate in consequence of the making of any provision or arrangements for, or in connection with, the issue or transfer of strips of government securities or the consolidation of such strips into other securities.

(6) Regulations under subsection (5) above may—

(*a*) impose a charge to income tax, corporation tax, capital gains tax, inheritance tax, stamp duty or stamp duty reserve tax;

(*b*) include provision applying generally to, or to any description of, enactments or subordinate legislation;

(*c*) make different provision for different cases; and

(*d*) contain such incidental, supplemental, consequential and transitional provision as the Treasury think appropriate.

(7) The power to make regulations under subsection (5) above shall be exercisable by statutory instrument subject to annulment in pursuance of a resolution of the House of Commons.

(8)–(9) (*not relevant to IHT*).

(10) In this section—

"government securities" means any securities included in Part I of Schedule 11 to the Finance Act 1942;

"modifications" includes amendments, additions and omissions; and

"subordinate legislation" has the same meaning as in the Interpretation Act 1978;

and expressions used in this section and in section 47 of the Finance Act 1942 have the same meanings in this section as in that section.

SCHEDULE 37
BANKS

Section 198

PART III
OTHER AMENDMENTS

Amendments of the Inheritance Tax Act 1984

12—(1) (*amends* IHTA 1984 s 157(5)).

(2) (*inserts* IHTA 1984 s 157 (6)).

(3) This paragraph applies in relation to deaths occurring on or after the day on which this Act is passed.

SCHEDULE 38
QUOTATION OR LISTING OF SECURITIES

Section 199

The Inheritance Tax Act 1984

2—(1) (*amends* IHTA 1984 ss 105(12A), 113A(3B), 272).

(2) This paragraph has effect—

(*a*) in relation to transfers of value on or after 1st April 1996; and

(*b*) for the purposes of any charge to tax by reason of an event occurring on or after 1st April 1996, in relation to transfers of value before that date.

3—(1) (*amends* IHTA 1984 s 180(3)).

(2) This paragraph has effect in relation to any time falling on or after 1st April 1996.

4—(1) (*amends* IHTA 1984 s 178(2)).

(2) (*amends* IHTA 1984 s 186B(1)).

(3) This paragraph has effect in relation to investments sold, or treated as sold, on or after 1st April 1996.

5—(1) (*amends* IHTA 1984 s 227(1AA), 228(5))

(2) This paragraph has effect—

(*a*) in relation to transfers of value on or after 1st April 1996; and

(*b*) for the purposes of any charge to tax by reason of an event occurring on or after 1st April 1996, in relation to transfers of value before that date.

FINANCE ACT 1997

(1997 Chapter 16)

An Act to grant certain duties, to alter other duties, and to amend the law relating to the National Debt and the Public Revenue, and to make further provision in connection with Finance.

[19th March 1997]

PART VI

INHERITANCE TAX

93 Rate bands

(1) (*Substitutes table in* IHTA 1984 Sch 1).

(2) Subsection (1) above shall apply to any chargeable transfer made on or after 6th April 1997; and section 8 of that Act (indexation of rate bands) shall not have effect as respects any difference between the retail prices index for the month of September 1995 and that for the month of September 1996.

94 Agricultural property relief

(*Inserts* IHTA 1984 s 124C).

FINANCE ACT 1998

(1998 Chapter 36)

An Act to grant certain duties, to alter other duties, and to amend the law relating to the National Debt and the Public Revenue, and to make further provision in connection with Finance.

[31 July 1998]

PART IV

INHERITANCE TAX ETC

142 Property of historic interest etc

Schedule 25 to this Act (which makes provision about the designation of property of historic interest, etc. and about undertakings in relation to such property) shall have effect.

143 Removal of exemption for gifts for public benefit

(1) Section 26 of the Inheritance Tax Act 1984 (gifts for public benefit) shall not apply to any transfer of value made on or after 17th March 1998.

(2) Accordingly, in that Act, in relation to any transfer of value made on or after 17th March 1998—

(*a*) (*amends* IHTA 1984 s 23(5), 29A(6)).

(*b*) (*amends* IHTA 1984 s 29(5)).

(3) (*amends* IHTA 1984 s 56(4)(7)).

(4) (*amends* IHTA 1984 s 76).

(5) Subsection (4) above has effect in relation to property which ceases to be relevant property, or to be property to which any of sections 70 to 74 of the Inheritance Tax Act 1984 or paragraph 8 of Schedule 4 to that Act applies, on or after 17th March 1998.

(6) (*amends* IHTA 1984 s 161(2)(*b*)).

(7) (*amends* TCGA 1992 s 258(2)).

144 Maintenance funds for historic buildings, etc

(1) (*amends* IHTA 1984 s 27(1), *inserts* IHTA 1984 s 27(1A)).

(2) This section has effect in relation to transfers of value made on or after 17th March 1998.

145 Accounting for property accepted in satisfaction of tax

Amendment—This section repealed by CRCA 2005 s 50, Sch 4 para 67 with effect from 18 April 2005 (by virtue of SI 2005/1126).

SCHEDULE 25

PROPERTY OF HISTORIC INTEREST ETC

Section 142

Meaning of "the 1984 Act"

1 In this Schedule "the 1984 Act" means the Inheritance Tax Act 1984.

Claims for designation

2—(1) (*inserts* IHTA 1984 s 30(3BA)).

(2) This paragraph has effect in relation to any transfer of value or death on or after 17th March 1998.

3—(1) (*inserts* IHTA 1984 s 78(1A)).
(2) This paragraph has effect in relation to transfers of property made, and other events occurring, on or after 17th March 1998.

Property capable of designation

4—(1) (*substitutes* IHTA 1984 s 31(1)(*a*)(*aa*)).
(2) (*amends* IHTA 1984 s 31(2)(3)).
(3) (*substitutes* IHTA 1984 s 31(5)).
(4) This paragraph has effect in relation to the making of any designation on a claim made on or after the day on which this Act is passed.

Access to designated property

5—(1) (*inserts* IHTA 1984 s 31(4F)).
(2) This paragraph has effect in relation to the giving of any undertaking on or after the day on which this Act is passed.

Publication of information about designated property

6—(1) (*inserts* IHTA 1984 s 31(4FB)).
(2) This paragraph has effect in relation to the giving of any undertaking on or after the day on which this Act is passed.

Undertakings on death, disposal of property, etc.

7—(1) (*amends* IHTA 1984 s 32(2)).
(2) (*substitutes* IHTA 1984 s 32(5)).
(3) (*inserts* IHTA 1984 s 32(5AA)).
(4) (*amends* IHTA 1984 s 32A(6)).
(5) (*substitutes* IHTA 1984 s 32A(8)(*b*)).
(6) (*inserts* IHTA 1984 s 32A(8A)).
(7) (*substitutes* IHTA 1984 s 32A(9)).
(8) (*substitutes* IHTA 1984 Sch 5 para 5).
(9) This paragraph has effect in relation to the giving of any undertaking on or after the day on which this Act is passed.

Variation of undertakings

8—(1) (*inserts* IHTA 1984 s 35A).
(2) (*inserts* IHTA 1984 s 79A).
(3) (*inserts* IHTA 1984 Sch 4 para 3(3A)).
(4) Subject to paragraph 10 below, this paragraph has effect in relation to undertakings given on or after the day on which this Act is passed.
9—(1) (*inserts* TCGA 1992 s 258(8A)).
(2) Subject to paragraph 10 below, this paragraph has effect in relation to undertakings given on or after the day on which this Act is passed.

10—(1) Section 35A of the 1984 Act applies in relation to a relevant undertaking given with respect to any property before the day on which this Act is passed except in a case where there has been a chargeable event with respect to that property at any time after the giving of the undertaking but before that day.
(2) In its application to such a relevant undertaking, section 35A of the 1984 Act applies with the modifications set out in sub-paragraphs (3) and (4) below.
(3) The first modification is the substitution, for paragraph (*a*) of subsection (2), of the following paragraph—

"(*a*) the Board have made a proposal to the person bound by such an undertaking for the undertaking to be varied so as to include (where it does not already do so) an extended access requirement or a publication requirement (or both those requirements),".

(4) The second modification is the insertion, after subsection (4), of the following subsections—

"(5) For the purposes of subsection (2)(*a*) above—

(*a*) an extended access requirement is a requirement for the taking of steps ensuring that the access to the public that is secured is not confined to access only where a prior appointment has been made; and

(*b*) a publication requirement is a requirement for the taking of steps involving the publication of any matter mentioned in paragraph (*a*) or (*b*) of section 31(4FB) above.

(6) In determining for the purposes of subsection (2)(*a*) above whether an undertaking already includes an extended access requirement, there shall be disregarded so much of the undertaking as includes provision for the property with respect to which the undertaking was given to be made available temporarily for the purposes of special exhibitions."

(5) In this paragraph "relevant undertaking" means any of the following—

(*a*) an undertaking given under section 30, 32, 32A, 78 or 79 of the 1984 Act;

(*b*) an undertaking given under paragraph 3(3) of Schedule 4 to the 1984 Act or paragraph 5(2) of Schedule 5 to that Act;

(*c*) an undertaking given under section 76, 78, 81 or 82 of the Finance Act 1976;

(*d*) an undertaking given under section 34(2) of the Finance Act 1975;

(*e*) an undertaking given under section 258 of the Taxation of Chargeable Gains Act 1992.

(6) In this paragraph "chargeable event", in relation to any property means—

(*a*) an event which under section 32 or 32A of the 1984 Act is a chargeable event with respect to that property; or

(*b*) an event which under either of those sections would be such an event if (where it is not the case) the undertaking in question had been given under section 30 of that Act.

HUMAN RIGHTS ACT 1998

(1998 Chapter 42)

An Act to give further effect to rights and freedoms guaranteed under the European Convention on Human Rights; to make provision with respect to holders of certain judicial offices who become judges of the European Court of Human Rights; and for connected purposes.

[9th November 1998]

Note—The relevant provisions of the Human Rights Act 1998 are reproduced in Part 1 of this publication.

FINANCE ACT 1999

(1999 Chapter 16)

An Act to grant certain duties, to alter other duties, and to amend the law relating to the National Debt and the Public Revenue, and to make further provision in connection with Finance.

[27 July 1999]

PART V
INHERITANCE TAX

104 Gifts

(*inserts* FA 1986 ss 102A, 102B, 102C).

105 Delivery of accounts

(1) (*substitutes* IHTA 1984 s 216(3)–(3B)).

(2) This section has effect in relation to deaths occurring on or after 9th March 1999.

106 Power to call for documents etc

(*inserted* IHTA 1984 ss 219A, 219B). Repealed by the Finance Act 2009, Section 96 and Schedule 48 (Appointed Day, Savings and Consequential Amendments) Order, SI 2009/3054 art 3, Schedule para 16(*d*) with effect from 1 April 2010.

107 Inland revenue charge

(1) In subsection (3) of section 237 of the Inheritance Tax Act 1984 (imposition of Inland Revenue charge), for " "personal property" includes leaseholds" there shall be substituted " "personal property" does not include leaseholds".

(2) (*inserts* IHTA 1984 s 237(3B), (3C)).

(3) Subsection (1) above has effect in relation to deaths occurring on or after 9th March 1999; and subsection (2) above has effect in relation to tax charged on or after that day.

Commentary—*Simon's Taxes* **I11.601, I11.602**.
Definitions—"Purchaser", s 272.

108 Penalties

(1) (*substitutes* IHTA 1984 ss 245, 245A).

(2) (amends IHTA 1984 s 247).[1]

(3) Subsection (1) above does not have effect in relation to a failure by any person—

(*a*) to deliver an account under section 216 or 217 of the Inheritance Tax Act 1984,

(*b*) to make a return under section 218 of that Act, or

(*c*) to comply with a notice under section 219 of that Act, where the period within which the person is required to perform the obligation in question expires before the day on which this Act is passed.

(4) Subsection (2) above has effect in relation to incorrect accounts, information or documents delivered, furnished or produced on or after the day on which this Act is passed.

Commentary—*Simon's Taxes* **I11.702, I11.703**.

Amendments—[1] Sub-s (2) repealed by FA 2008 s 122, Sch 40 para 21(*g*) with effect from 1 April 2009 (by virtue of SI 2009/571 art 2).

FINANCE ACT 2000

(2000 Chapter 17)

PART V

OTHER TAXES

Inheritance tax

138 Treatment of employee share ownership trusts

(1) The Inheritance Tax Act 1984 is amended as follows.

(2) (*Amends* IHTA 1984 s 13).

(3) In section 72 (property leaving employee trusts and newspaper trusts)—

(*a*) (*Amends* IHTA 1984 s 72(2)).

(*b*) (*inserts* IHTA 1984 s 72(4A)).

(4) (*Amends* IHTA 1984 s 86(3)).

Commentary—*Simon's Taxes* **I5.631, I3.156**.

PART VI

MISCELLANEOUS AND SUPPLEMENTARY PROVISIONS

Compliance

147 International exchange of information: inheritance tax

. . .

This section repealed by FA 2006 s 178 Sch 26 Pt 8(2) with effect from 19 July 2006.

FINANCE ACT 2001

(2001 Chapter 9)

An Act to grant certain duties, to alter other duties, and to amend the law relating to the National Debt and the Public Revenue, and to make further provision in connection with Finance.

[11 May 2001]

PART IV

OTHER TAXES

Inheritance tax

106 Transfers within group etc

(1) Section 97 of the Inheritance Tax Act 1984 (transfers within group etc) is amended as follows.

(2) (*substitutes* IHTA 1984 s 97(1)(*a*)).

(3) The amendment made by this section has effect, and shall be taken always to have had effect, in relation to disposals made, or transfers deemed to have been made, on or after 1st April 2000.

Commentary—*Simon's Taxes* **I6.124**.

FINANCE ACT 2002

(2002 Chapter 23)

An Act to grant certain duties, to alter other duties, and to amend the law relating to the National Debt and the Public Revenue, and to make further provision in connection with finance.

[24 July 2002]

PART 5

OTHER TAXES

Inheritance tax

118 IHT: rate bands

(1) (*substitutes* Table in IHTA 1984 Sch 1).

(2) Subsection (1) shall apply to any chargeable transfer made on or after 6th April 2002; and section 8(1) of that Act (indexation of rate bands) shall not have effect as respects any difference between the retail prices index for the month of September 2000 and that for the month of September 2001.

Commentary—*Simon's Taxes* **I3.511**.

119 IHT: powers over, or exercisable in relation to, settled property or a settlement

(1) The Inheritance Tax Act 1984 is amended in accordance with the following provisions of this section.
(2) (*inserts* IHTA 1984 s 47A).
(3) (*inserts* IHTA 1984 s 55A).
(4) (*inserts* definition of "settlement power" in IHTA 1884 s 272 and *amends* definition of "property").
(5) In consequence of the amendments made by this section, the title of Chapter 2 of Part 3 of the Inheritance Tax Act 1984 (c 51) becomes "Interests in possession, reversionary interests and settlement powers".
(6) The amendments made by this section have effect in relation to transfers of value on or after 17th April 2002.
(7) The amendments made by subsections (2) and (4) shall also be deemed always to have had effect (subject to and in accordance with the other provisions of the Inheritance Tax Act 1984) for the purpose of determining the value, immediately before his death, of the estate of any person who died before 17th April 2002, for the purposes of the transfer of value which that person is treated by section 4(1) of that Act as having made immediately before his death.

Commentary—*Simon's Taxes* **I3.211**.

120 IHT: variation of dispositions taking effect on death

(1) (*substitutes* IHTA 1984 s 142(2), (2A)).
(2) (*inserts* IHTA 1984 s 218A).
(3) (*inserts* IHTA 1984 s 245A(1A) and (4)(*aa*)).
(4) This section applies in relation to instruments made on or after 1st August 2002.

Commentary—*Simon's Taxes* **C1.206, I4.411, I4.421, I4.434, I4.444**.

FINANCE ACT 2003

(2003 Chapter 14)

An Act to grant certain duties, to alter other duties, and to amend the law relating to the National Debt and the Public Revenue, and to make further provision in connection with finance.

[10 July 2003]

PART 8
OTHER TAXES

Inheritance tax

185 Inheritance tax: Gifts with reservation

(1) Section 102 of the Finance Act 1986 (c 41) (gifts with reservation) is amended as follows.
(2) In subsection (5) (section not to apply where disposal is an exempt transfer by virtue of any of the provisions of the Inheritance Tax Act 1984 specified in the paragraphs of that subsection) at the end of paragraph (*a*) (section 18: transfers between spouses) insert ", except as provided by subsections (5A) and (5B) below".
(3) (*inserts* FA 1986 s 102(5A)–(5C)).
(4) The amendments made by this section have effect in relation to disposals made on or after 20th June 2003.

Commentary—*Simon's Taxes I3.431; Foster C4.31.*
Simon's Tax Cases—*IRC v Eversden* [2003] STC 822 (CA).

186 Authorised unit trusts, OEICs and common investment funds

(1) The Inheritance Tax Act 1984 (c 51) is amended as follows.
(2) (*inserts* IHTA 1984 s 6(1A))
(3) (*inserts* IHTA 1984 s 48(3A))
(4) (*amends* IHTA 1984 s 178(1), definition of "qualifying investments")
(5) Section 272 (general interpretation) is amended as follows.
(6), (7) (*insert* IHTA 1984 s 272, definitions "authorised unit trust", "open-ended investment company")
(8) This section has effect in relation to transfers of value or other events occurring on or after 16th October 2002.

Commentary—*Simon's Taxes I9.311, I9.401, I4.302; Foster J3.30A, 30B, 41.*

PART 9

MISCELLANEOUS AND SUPPLEMENTARY PROVISIONS

International matters

198 Arrangements for mutual exchange of tax information

Amendments—This section repealed by FA 2006 s 178, Sch 26 Pt 8(2) with effect from 19 July 2006.

FINANCE ACT 2004

(2004 Chapter 12)

An Act to Grant certain duties, to alter other duties, and to amend the law relating to the National Debt and the Public Revenue, and to make further provision in connection with finance.

[22 July 2004]

PART 4

PENSION SCHEMES ETC

CHAPTER 4

REGISTERED PENSION SCHEMES: TAX RELIEFS AND EXEMPTIONS

Inheritance tax exemptions

203 Inheritance tax exemptions

(1) The Inheritance Tax Act 1984 (c 51) is amended as follows.

(2) In section 12 (dispositions that are not transfers of value)—

(*a*) (*amends* IHTA 1984 s 12(2))

(*b*) (*repeals* IHTA 1984 s 12(3) and (4))

(3) (*substitutes* IHTA 1984 s 58(1)(*d*))

(4) In section 151 (treatment of pension rights etc)—

(*a*) (*repeals* IHTA 1984 s 151(1), (1A))

(*b*) (*amends* IHTA 1984 s 151(2), (4) and (5))

(*c*) (*amends* IHTA 1984 s 151(2)(*b*)

(5) (*amends* IHTA 1984 s 152; inserted text *amended* by the Tax and Civil Partnership Regulations, SI 2005/3229, regs 175, 178, with effect from 6 April 2006)

(6) (*amends* IHTA 1984 s 272)

Cross reference—Pension Protection Fund (Tax) Regulations 2006, SI 2006/575, regs 2–32 (this Part applies in relation to the Pension Protection Fund in the same way as it applies to a registered pension scheme for the period beginning on 6 April 2006).

CHAPTER 8

SUPPLEMENTARY

Other supplementary provisions

283 Transitionals and savings

(1) Schedule 36 contains miscellaneous transitional provisions and savings.

(2) The Treasury may by order make any other transitional provision which may appear appropriate in consequence of, or otherwise in connection with, this Part or the repeals made by this Act in consequence of this Part.

(3) An order under subsection (2) may, in particular, include savings from the effect of any amendment made by this Part or any repeal made by this Act in consequence of this Part.

[(3A) The Treasury may by order make any transitional provision which may appear appropriate in consequence of, or otherwise in connection with, any amendment (or repeal or revocation) made in this Part by any enactment contained in an Act passed after this Act (an "amending Act").][1]

[(3B) An order under subsection (3A) may, in particular, include savings from the effect of any amendment (or repeal or revocation) made by the amending Act.][1]

[(3C) An order under subsection (2) or (3A) may include provision having effect in relation to times before it is made if it does not increase any person's liability to tax.][1], [2]

(4) Nothing in Schedule 36 limits the power conferred by subsection (2) [or (3A)][1].

(5) Nothing in that Schedule or in any provision made by virtue of subsection (2) [or (3A)][1] prejudices the operation of sections 16 and 17 of the Interpretation Act 1978 (c 30) (effect of repeals).

Regulations—Taxation of Pension Schemes (Transitional Provisions) Order, SI 2006/572.

Pension Schemes (Transfers, Reorganisations and Winding Up) (Transitional Provisions) Order, SI 2006/573.

Cross references—See ITTOIA 2005 Sch 2 para 15(7) (the power of the Treasury to make an order under this section has effect as if FA 2004 Sch 35 contained an amendment substituting ITTOIA 2005 ss 38–44 for those sections as amended by ITTOIA 2005 Sch 2 para 15(2)–(6)).

ITTOIA 2005 Sch 2 para 57(3) (the power of the Treasury to make an order under this section has effect as if FA 2004 Sch 35 contained an amendment substituting ITTOIA 2005 s 232(4) for that subsection as amended by ITTOIA 2005 Sch 2 para 57(2)).

ITTOIA 2005 Sch 2 para 60(4) (the power of the Treasury to make an order under this section has effect as if FA 2004 Sch 35 contained an amendment substituting ITTOIA 2005 s 256 for that subsection as amended by ITTOIA 2005 Sch 2 para 60(2), (3)).

ITTOIA 2005 Sch 2 para 74(4) (the power of the Treasury to make an order under this section has effect as if FA 2004 Sch 35 contained an amendment substituting ITTOIA 2005 ss 322(2), 328(2) for those subsections as amended by ITTOIA 2005 Sch 2 para 74(2), (3)).

ITTOIA 2005 Sch 2 para 74(4) (the power of the Treasury to make an order under this section has effect as if FA 2004 Sch 35 contained an amendment substituting ITTOIA 2005 ss 322(2), 328(2) for those subsections as amended by ITTOIA 2005 Sch 2 para 74(2), (3)).

ITTOIA 2005 Sch 2 para 75(3) (the power of the Treasury to make an order under this section has effect as if FA 2004 Sch 35 contained an amendment substituting TA 1988 s 504A (as inserted by ITTOIA 2005 Sch 1) for that section as amended by ITTOIA 2005 Sch 2 para 75(2)).

ITTOIA 2005 Sch 2 para 86(4) (the power of the Treasury to make an order under this section has effect as if FA 2004 Sch 35 contained amendments substituting ITTOIA 2005 s 479 for that section as substituted by ITTOIA 2005 Sch 2 para 86(2), and substituting "non-registered occupational pension" for "sponsored superannuation" in ITTOIA 2005 s 486).

ITTOIA 2005 Sch 2 para 132(4) (the power of the Treasury to make an order under this section has effect as if FA 2004 Sch 35 contained an amendment substituting ITTOIA 2005 s 627 for that section as amended by ITTOIA 2005 Sch 2 para 132(2)).

ITTOIA 2005 Sch 2 para 156(3) (the power of the Treasury to make an order under this section has effect as if FA 2004 Sch 35 contained an amendment substituting ITTOIA 2005 s 866(5) for that subsection as amended by ITTOIA 2005 Sch 2 para 156(2)).

Taxation of Pensions Act 2014 s 1, Sch 1 para 69(2) (the amendment made under the Taxation of Pensions Act 2014 s 1, Sch 1 para 69(1) to the Taxation of Pension Schemes (Transitional Provisions) Order 2006, SI 2006/572 art 25C is to be treated as having been made by the Treasury under the powers to make orders conferred by sub-s (2))

Amendments—[1] Sub-ss (3A)–(3C) inserted, and words in sub-ss (4), (5) inserted, by FA 2006 s 161, Sch 23 paras 1, 35. These amendments are deemed to have come into force on 6 April 2006.

[2] Sub-s (3C) repealed by FA 2009 s 75(2)(*c*) with effect from 21 July 2009.

PART 6
OTHER TAXES

Inheritance tax

293 Delivery of accounts etc

(1) Section 256 of the Inheritance Tax Act 1984 (c. 51) (regulations about information to be furnished to the Board) is amended as follows.

(2)–(6) (*amend* sub-ss (1), (3) *insert* sub-ss (1A), (3A), *repeal* sub-s (2))

294 Grant of probate

(1) (*amends* the Supreme Court Act 1981 (now the Senior Courts Act 1981) s 109).

(2) (*amends* the Probate and Legacy Duties Act 1808 s 42).

(3) (*amends* the Administration of Estates (Northern Ireland) Order, SI 1979/1575 art 20).

(4) Subsection (1) shall come into force on such day as the Treasury may after consulting the Lord Chancellor by order made by statutory instrument appoint.

(5) Subsection (2) shall come into force on such day as the Treasury may after consulting the Scottish Ministers by order made by statutory instrument appoint.

(6) Subsection (3) shall come into force on such day as the Treasury may after consulting the Lord Chancellor by order made by statutory instrument appoint.

Order—FA 2004, Section 294 (Appointed Day) Order, SI 2004/2571 art 2 (the day appointed for the purposes of sub-ss (1)–(3) is 1 November 2004).

295 Amendments to penalty regime

(1) The Inheritance Tax Act 1984 (c. 51) is amended as specified in subsections (2) to (4).

(2) In section 245 (failure to deliver accounts)—

(*a*) (*amends* sub-ss (2)(*a*), (3)).

(*b*) (*inserts* sub-s (4A)).

(3) In section 245A (failure to provide information etc)—

(*a*) (*inserts* sub-s (1B)).

(*b*) (*amends* sub-s (5)).

(4) In section 247 (provision of incorrect information)—

(a) (amends sub-s (1)).[1]

(*b*) (*amends* sub-s (3)).

(5) Subsection (2)(*a*) above has effect in relation to a failure by any person to deliver an account under section 216 or 217 of the Inheritance Tax Act 1984 (c 51) where the period under section 216(6) or (7) or 217 of that Act (whichever is applicable) within which the person is required to deliver the account expires after six months from the day on which this Act is passed.

(6) Subsection (2)(*b*) above has effect—

(*a*) in relation to a failure by any person to deliver an account under section 216 of the Inheritance Tax Act 1984 where the period under section 216(6) or (7) of that Act (whichever is applicable) within which the person is required to deliver the account expires after the day on which this Act is passed; and (*b*) in relation to such a failure to deliver such an account where that period expires on or before the day on which this Act is passed, as if, in the subsection (4A) inserted in section 245 of that Act by subsection (2)(*b*) above, for the words "anniversary of the end of the period given by section 216(6) or (7) (whichever is applicable)" there were substituted "end of the period of twelve months beginning with the day on which the Finance Act 2004 is passed".

(7) Subsection (3)(*a*) above has effect—

(*a*) in relation to a failure to comply with the requirements of section 218A of the Inheritance Tax Act 1984 where the period of six months referred to in subsection (1) of that section expires after the day on which this Act is passed; and

(*b*) in relation to such a failure to comply with those requirements where that period expires on or before the day on which this Act is passed, as if, in the subsection (1B) inserted in section 245A of that Act by subsection (3)(*a*) above, for the words "anniversary of the end of the period of six months referred to in section 218A(1)" there were substituted "end of the period of twelve months beginning with the day on which the Finance Act 2004 is passed".

(8) Subsection (3)(*b*) above has effect in relation to a failure to comply with the requirements of section 218A of the Inheritance Tax Act 1984 where the period of six months referred to in subsection (1) of that section expires after the day on which this Act is passed.

(9) Subsection (4) above has effect in relation to incorrect accounts, information or documents delivered, furnished or produced after the day on which this Act is passed.

Amendments—[1] Sub-s (4)(*a*) repealed by FA 2008 s 122, Sch 40 para 21(*l*) with effect from 1 April 2009 (by virtue of SI 2009/571 art 2).

SCHEDULE 36

PENSION SCHEMES ETC: TRANSITIONAL PROVISIONS AND SAVINGS

Section 283

PART 4

OTHER PROVISIONS

Inheritance tax

56—(1) This paragraph applies in relation to a fund or scheme—

(*a*) which is not a registered pension scheme[, a qualifying non-UK pension scheme][1] or a superannuation fund to which section 615(3) of ICTA applies, but

(*b*) to which section 151 of the Inheritance Tax Act 1984 (c 51) (treatment of pension rights) applied immediately before 6th April 2006.

(2) If no contributions are made under the fund or scheme on or after that date—

(*a*) section 151 of the Inheritance Tax Act 1984 continues to apply to the fund or scheme on and after that date for all purposes of that Act, and

(*b*) property which is part of or held for the purposes of the fund or scheme does not constitute relevant property for the purposes of Chapter 3 of Part 3 of that Act (settlements without interest in possession).

(3) In any other case, paragraphs 57 and 58 apply to the fund or scheme on and after that date.

[(4) In this paragraph "qualifying non-UK pension scheme" has the same meaning as in the Inheritance Tax Act 1984 (see section 271A of that Act).][1]

Commentary—*Simon's Taxes* **E7.247**.

Amendments—[1] Words in sub-para (1) substituted, and sub-para (4) inserted. by FA 2008 s 92, Sch 29 para 18(1), (7). This amendment is treated as having come into force on 6 April 2006.

57—(1) The [percentage][1] of the assets of the fund or scheme which at any time is the protected proportion of those assets does not at that time constitute relevant property for the purposes of Chapter 3 of Part 3 of the Inheritance Tax Act 1984 (settlements without interest in possession).

(2) "The protected [percentage[1]]" of the assets of the fund or scheme at a time is—

$$\frac{ACV}{V} \times 100$$

where—

V is the market value of the assets of the fund or scheme at that time, and

ACV is the adjusted commencement value, that is an amount equal to the market value of the assets of the fund or scheme on 5th April 2006, but subject to the adjustments provided by sub-paragraph (3).

(3) The adjustments are—

(*a*) an increase by the percentage by which the retail prices index for the month of September immediately preceding the time in question is greater than that for April 2006, and (*b*) a reduction by the amount of any relevant payments made under the fund or scheme on or after 6th April 2006 and before that time.

(4) "Relevant payments" are payments other than—

(*a*) payments of costs or expenses, or

(*b*) payments which are (or will be) income of any person for any of the purposes of income tax.

Amendments—[1] In sub-paras (1), (2), word substituted by FA 2005 s 101, Sch 10 paras 58(2), 64(1) with effect from 6 April 2006.

58—(1) Section 151 of the Inheritance Tax Act 1984 (c 51) (treatment of pension rights) continues to apply to so much of the assets of the fund or scheme at any time as does not exceed the amount that is the protected amount at that time.

(2) But sub-paragraph (1) does not affect the operation of subsection (1)(*d*) of section 58 of that Act (because paragraph 57 makes provision about the extent to which the assets of the fund or scheme constitute relevant property within the meaning given by that section).

(3) If inheritance tax has not previously been chargeable (otherwise than only because of this paragraph) by reference to the value of the assets of the fund or scheme on or after 6th April 2006, the protected amount is an amount equal to the amount of the market value of the assets of the fund or scheme on 5th April 2006, but subject to the adjustments provided by sub-paragraph (4).

(4) The adjustments are—

(*a*) an increase by the percentage by which the retail prices index for the month of September immediately preceding the time in question is greater than that for April 2006, and

(*b*) a reduction by the amount of any relevant payments made under the fund or scheme on or after 6th April 2006 and before that time.

(5) If inheritance tax would (apart from this paragraph) have previously been chargeable by reference to the value of the assets of the fund or scheme on one or more occasions on or after 6th April 2006, the protected amount is what it was immediately before the occasion, or (where there has been more than one) the last occasion, on which inheritance tax would have been so chargeable ("the relevant tax occasion"), but—

(*a*) reduced by the value of the property on which inheritance tax would have been chargeable on the relevant tax occasion, and

(*b*) subject to the adjustments provided by sub-paragraph (6).

(6) The adjustments are—

(*a*) an increase by the percentage by which the retail prices index for the month of September immediately preceding the time in question is greater than that for the month in which the relevant tax occasion fell, and

(*b*) a reduction by the amount of any [relevant][1] payments made under the fund or scheme since the relevant tax occasion.

(7) "Relevant payments" are payments other than—

(*a*) payments of costs or expenses, or

(*b*) payments which are (or will be) income of any person for any of the purposes of income tax.

Amendments—[1] In sub-para (6)(*b*), word inserted by FA 2005 s 101, Sch 10 paras 58(3), 64(1) with effect from 6 April 2006.

FINANCE ACT 2005

(2005 Chapter 7)

An Act to Grant certain duties, to alter other duties, and to amend the law relating to the National Debt and the Public Revenue, and to make further provision in connection with finance.

[7 April 2005]

PART 4

OTHER TAXES

Inheritance tax

98 Rates and rate bands for the next three years

(1) (*substitutes* Table in IHTA 1984 Sch 1 in relation to the tax years 2005–06, 2006–07 and 2007–08).

COMMISSIONERS FOR REVENUE AND CUSTOMS ACT 2005

(2005 Chapter 11)

[7 April 2005]

Note—Please see Part 1 of this publication for the text of this Act.

FINANCE ACT 2006

(2006 Chapter 25)

An Act to Grant certain duties, to alter other duties, and to amend the law relating to the National Debt and the Public Revenue, and to make further provision in connection with finance.

[19 July 2006]

PART 6

INHERITANCE TAX

Future rates and bands

155 Rates and rate bands for 2008–09 and 2009–10

(1) For the Table in Schedule 1 to IHTA 1984 (rates and rate bands), as it has effect in relation to chargeable transfers made on or after 6th April 2008, there shall be successively substituted—

(*a*) the 2008–09 Table, which shall apply to any chargeable transfer made on or after 6th April 2008 (but before 6th April 2009), and

(*b*) the 2009–10 Table, which shall apply to any chargeable transfer made on or after 6th April 2009.

(2) Subsection (1)(*b*) is without prejudice to the application of section 8 of IHTA 1984 (indexation) by virtue of the difference between the retail prices index for the month of September in 2008 or any later year and that for the month of September in the following year.

(3) The 2008–09 Table is—

Table of rates of tax

Portion of value		*Rate of tax*
Lower limit (£)	Upper limit (£)	Per cent.
0	312,000	Nil
312,000	—	40

(4) The 2009–10 Table is—

Table of rates of tax

Portion of value		*Rate of tax*
Lower limit (£)	Upper limit (£)	Per cent.
0	325,000	Nil
325,000	—	40

(5) Section 8(1) of IHTA 1984 (indexation of rate bands) shall not have effect as respects any difference between the retail prices index—

(*a*) for the month of September 2006 and that for the month of September 2007, or

(*b*) for the month of September 2007 and that for the month of September 2008.

Trusts

156 Rules for trusts etc

(1) Schedule 20 contains—

(*a*) amendments of provisions of IHTA 1984 relating to settled property,

(*b*) amendments of provisions relating to property that, for purposes of that Act, is property subject to a reservation, and

(*c*) related amendments of provisions relating to chargeable gains.

(2) Those amendments have effect as mentioned in that Schedule.

157 Purchase of interests in foreign trusts

(1) Section 48 of IHTA 1984 (settled property: excluded property) is amended as follows.

(2) (*amends* IHTA 1984 s 48(3))

(3) (*amends* IHTA 1984 s 48(3A))

(4) (*inserts* IHTA 1984 s 48(3B)–(3C))

(5) If, in consequence of the amendments made by this section, an amount of inheritance tax would (but for this subsection) fall due before the day on which this Act is passed, that amount is to be treated instead as falling due at the end of the period of 14 days beginning with that day.

(6) This section is deemed to have come into force on 5th December 2005.

PART 7
PENSIONS

160 Inheritance tax

(1) Schedule 22 (provisions about inheritance tax in relation to registered pension schemes) has effect.

(2) This section and that Schedule are deemed to have come into force on 6th April 2006.

PART 10
SUPPLEMENTARY PROVISIONS

178 Repeals

(1) The enactments mentioned in Schedule 26 (which include provisions that are spent or of no practical utility) are repealed to the extent specified.

(2) The repeals specified in that Schedule have effect subject to the commencement provisions and savings contained or referred to in the notes set out in that Schedule.

SCHEDULES

SCHEDULE 20

INHERITANCE TAX: RULES FOR TRUSTS ETC

Section 156

PART 1

"TRUSTS FOR BEREAVED MINORS", "AGE 18-TO-25 TRUSTS" AND "ACCUMULATION AND MAINTENANCE" TRUSTS

Trusts for bereaved minors and Age 18-to-25 trusts

1—(1) (*inserts* IHTA 1984 ss 71A–71H)

(2) Sub-paragraph (1) shall be deemed to have come into force on 22nd March 2006.

Section 71 of IHTA 1984 not to apply to property settled on or after 22nd March 2006

2—(1) Section 71 of IHTA 1984 (accumulation and maintenance trusts) is amended as follows.

(2) (*amends* IHTA 1984 s 71(1))

(3) (*inserts* IHTA 1984 s 71(1A), (1B))

(4) Where a chargeable transfer to which section 54A of IHTA 1984 applies was made before 22nd March 2006, that section has effect in relation to that transfer as if references in that section to section 71 of IHTA 1984 were to section 71 of IHTA 1984 without the amendments made by sub-paragraphs (2) and (3).

(5) There is no charge to tax under section 71 of IHTA 1984 in a case where settled property ceases, by the operation of the subsection (1B) inserted into that section by this paragraph, to be property to which that section applies.

(6) Sub-paragraphs (1) to (5) shall be deemed to have come into force on 22nd March 2006.

Section 71 of IHTA 1984 to cease to apply to certain settled property from 6th April 2008

3—(1) In section 71(1)(*a*) of IHTA 1984 (section applies to settled property only if one or more persons will become beneficially entitled on or before reaching a specified age not exceeding 25)—

(*a*) for "twenty-five" substitute "eighteen", and

(*b*) omit "or to an interest in possession in it".

(2) Sub-paragraph (1) comes into force on 6th April 2008 but only for the purpose of determining whether, at a time on or after that day, section 71 of IHTA 1984 applies to settled property.

(3) There is no charge to tax under section 71 of IHTA 1984 in a case where—

(*a*) settled property ceases, on the coming into force of sub-paragraph (1), to be property to which that section applies, but

(*b*) that section would immediately after the coming into force of sub-paragraph (1) apply to the settled property but for the amendments made by sub-paragraph (1).

PART 2

INTERESTS IN POSSESSION: WHEN SETTLED PROPERTY IS PART OF BENEFICIARY'S ESTATE

Aggregation with person's estate of property in which interest in possession subsists

4—(1) (*inserts* IHTA 1984 s 49(1A), (1B))

(2) Sub-paragraph (1) shall be deemed to have come into force on 22nd March 2006.

"Immediate post-death interests" and "transitional serial interests"

5—(1) (*inserts* IHTA 1984 ss 49A–49E)
(2) Sub-paragraph (1) shall be deemed to have come into force on 22nd March 2006.

Disabled persons' trusts: meaning of "disabled person's interest" and "disabled person"

6—(1) (*inserts* IHTA 1984 ss 89A, 89B)
(2) (*inserts* IHTA 1984 s 89(5), (6))
(3) Sub-paragraph (1) shall be deemed to have come into force on 22nd March 2006.
(4) Sub-paragraph (2) shall be deemed to have come into force on 22nd March 2006, but only in respect of property transferred into settlement on or after that day.

PART 3
RELATED AMENDMENTS IN IHTA 1984

Commencement

7 The following paragraphs of this Part of this Schedule shall be deemed to have come into force on 22nd March 2006.

Deemed disposition where omission to exercise a right increases value of another person's estate or of settled property not aggregated with a person's estate

8 (*amends* IHTA 1984 s 3(3))

Potentially exempt transfers: provision in consequence of section 71 of IHTA 1984 not applying to property settled on or after 22nd March 2006

9—(1) Section 3A of IHTA 1984 (potentially exempt transfers) is amended as follows.
(2) (*amends* IHTA 1984 s 3A(1)(*a*))
(3) (*inserts* IHTA 1984 s 3A(1A), (1B))
(4) (*amends* IHTA 1984 s 3A(2))
(5) (*inserts* IHTA 1984 s 3A(3A), (3B))
(6) (*amends* IHTA 1984 s 3A(7))

Person's "estate" not to include certain interests in possession

10—(1) Section 5 of IHTA 1984 (meaning of "estate") is amended as follows.
(2) (*amends* IHTA 1984 s 5(1))
(3) (*inserts* IHTA 1984 s 5(1A))

Life assurance policies entered into before 22nd March 2006

11—(1) (*inserts* IHTA 1984 ss 46A, 46B)
(2) Sub-paragraph (1) shall be deemed to have come into force on 22nd March 2006.

Tax where interest in possession ends, or is treated as ending, during beneficiary's life

12 (*inserts* IHTA 1984 s 51(1A), (1B))

13—(1) Section 52 of IHTA 1984 (tax on termination of interest in possession) is amended as follows.
(2) (*inserts* IHTA 1984 s 52(2A))
(3) (*inserts* IHTA 1984 s 52(3A))

14—(1) Section 53 of IHTA 1984 (exceptions from tax charge under section 52) is amended as follows.
(2) (*inserts* IHTA 1984 s 53(1A))
(3) (*inserted* IHTA 1984 s 53(2A); *repealed* by FA 2008 s 141(2))

Non-aggregation with deceased person's estate of property in which he had interest in possession if property reverts to settlor or passes to settlor's spouse or civil partner etc

15—(1) Section 54 of IHTA 1984 (exceptions from charge on death) is amended as follows.
(2) (*inserts* IHTA 1984 s 54(2A), (2B))
(3) (*amends* IHTA 1984 s 54(3))

Rate of tax on ending of interest in possession in property settled during settlor's life

16—(1) Section 54A of IHTA 1984 (special rate of charge on coming to end of interest in possession in settled property affected by potentially exempt transfer) is amended as follows.

(2) (*inserts* IHTA 1984 s 54A(1A))
(3) (*amends* IHTA 1984 s 54A(2)(*c*), (*d*)(i))
(4) Where a chargeable transfer to which section 54A of IHTA 1984 applies was made before 22nd March 2006, that section has effect in relation to that transfer without the amendments made by sub-paragraph (3).

Property entering maintenance fund after death of person entitled to interest in possession

17 (*inserts* IHTA 1984 s 57A(1A))

"Relevant property" not to include property held on trust for a bereaved child

18 (*amends* IHTA 1984 s 58(1)(*b*))

"Relevant property" to include property held on employee trusts or newspaper trusts if certain interests in possession subsist in the property

19—(1) Section 58 of IHTA 1984 (meaning of "relevant property" in Chapter 3 of Part 3) is amended as follows.
(2) (*amends* IHTA 1984 s 58(1)(*b*))
(3) (*inserts* IHTA 1984 s 58(1A)–(1C))

Certain interests in possession to which a person becomes entitled on or after 22nd March 2006 not to be "qualifying interests in possession" for purposes of Chapter 3 of Part 3 of IHTA 1984

20—(1) Section 59 of IHTA 1984 (settlements without interests in possession: meaning of "qualifying interest in possession") is amended as follows.
(2) (*substitutes* IHTA 1984 s 59(1))
(3) (*inserts* IHTA 1984 s 59(2)(*c*))
(4) Where a chargeable transfer to which section 54A of IHTA 1984 applies was made before 22nd March 2006, that section has effect in relation to that transfer as if in that section "qualifying interest in possession" has the meaning it would have apart from sub-paragraphs (1) to (3).
(5) (*amends* heading to Chapter 3 of Part 3 of IHTA 1984)

New meaning of "qualifying interest in possession" not to apply in section 72 of IHTA 1984

21—(1) Section 72 of IHTA 1984 (property leaving employee trusts and newspaper trusts) is amended as follows.
(2) (*inserts* IHTA 1984 s 72(1)(*a*), (*b*))
(3) (*inserts* IHTA 1984 s 72(1A), (1B))

No charge under sections 71B, 71E etc where property held on trusts for bereaved child becomes held on trusts for charitable purposes etc

22 (*amends* IHTA 1984 s 76(1))

No postponement of commencement date of settlement where property settled on or after 22nd March 2006 unless settlor, or spouse or civil partner, has immediate post-death interest

23 (*inserts* IHTA 1984 s 80(4))

Protective trusts

24 (*inserts* IHTA 1984 s 88(3)–(6))

Alterations of capital etc of close company where participator holds shares etc in company as trustee of settled property in which an interest in possession subsists

25 (*inserts* IHTA 1984 s 100(1A))

Close company's interest in possession treated as interest of its participators

26 (*inserts* IHTA 1984 s 101(1A)–(1C))

Distributions within two years of person's death out of property settled by his will

27—(1) Section 144 of IHTA 1984 (distribution etc from property settled by will) is amended as follows.
(2) (*amends* IHTA 1984 s 144(1))
(3) (*inserts* IHTA 1984 s 144(1A))

(4) (*amends* IHTA 1984 s 144(2))
(5) (*inserts* IHTA 1984 s 144(3)–(6))

Interpretation of IHTA 1984

28 (*amends* IHTA 1984 s 272)

PART 4
RELATED AMENDMENTS IN TCGA 1992

29—(1) TCGA 1992 is amended in accordance with the following paragraphs of this Part of this Schedule.
(2) The following paragraphs of this Part of this Schedule shall be deemed to have come into force on 22nd March 2006.

30—(1) Section 72 (death of person entitled to an interest in possession) is amended as follows.
(2) (*inserts* TCGA 1992 s 72(1A)–(1C))
(3) (*inserts* TCGA 1992 s 72(2A))

31 (*inserts* TCGA 1992 s 73(2A))

32 (*inserts* TCGA 1992 s 260(2)(*da*), (*db*))

PART 5
PROPERTY SUBJECT TO A RESERVATION

33—(1) FA 1986 is amended as follows.
(2) (*inserts* FA 1986 s 102ZA)
(3) (*inserts* FA 1986 Sch 20 para 4A)
(4) Sub-paragraphs (1) to (3) shall be deemed to have come into force on 22nd March 2006, but only as respects cases where an interest in possession comes to an end on or after that day.

PART 6
CONDITIONAL EXEMPTION: RELIEF FROM CHARGES

34—(1) Section 79 of IHTA 1984 (subsection (3) of which provides for charges to tax where, in the case of settled property designated under section 31 on a claim under section 79, an event occurs that would be chargeable under section 32 or 32A if the claim had been under section 30) is amended as follows.
(2) (*inserts* IHTA 1984 s 79(5A))
(3) (*substitutes* IHTA 1984 s 79(7)–(7C))
(4) (*inserts* IHTA 1984 s 79(9A), (9B))

SCHEDULE 22

PENSION SCHEMES: INHERITANCE TAX

Section 160

Introductory

1 IHTA 1984 is amended as follows.

Dispositions

2 (*inserts* IHTA 1984 s 12(2A)–(2G) and *amends* s 12 heading)

Secured pension funds

3 (*amended* IHTA 1984 s 151(2); *repealed* by FA 2011 s 65, Sch 16 para 84(*b*)(i))

4 (*inserted* IHTA 1984 s 151A–151C; *repealed* by FA 2011 s 65, Sch 16 para 84(*b*)(i))

Liability

5 *(1) Section 200 (liability for tax: transfer on death) is amended as follows.*
(2) (amends IHTA 1984 s 200(1))
(3) (inserts IHTA 1984 s 200(1A))

Amendments—This para repealed by FA 2011 s 65, Sch 16 para 84(*b*)(i) with effect for the tax year 2011–12 and subsequent tax years, subject to transitional provisions in FA 2011 Sch 16 Pt 3.

6 (*inserted* IHTA 1984 s 210(2); *repealed* by FA 2011 s 65, Sch 16 para 84(*b*)(i))

Delivery of accounts

7 (1) Section 216 (delivery of accounts) is amended as follows.
(2) (inserts IHTA 1984 s 216(1)(*bca*))
(3) (amends IHTA 1984 s 216(3)(*a*))
(4) (amends IHTA 1984 s 216(4))
(5) (inserts IHTA 1984 s 216(6)(*ac*))

Amendments—This para repealed by FA 2011 s 65, Sch 16 para 84(*b*)(i) with effect for the tax year 2011–12 and subsequent tax years, subject to transitional provisions in FA 2011 Sch 16 Pt 3.

Payment

8 (*amended* IHTA 1984 s 226(4); *repealed* by FA 2011 s 65, Sch 16 para 84(*b*)(i))

Interest

9 (*amended* IHTA 1984 s 233(1)(*c*); *repealed* by FA 2011 s 65, Sch 16 para 84(*b*)(i))

Interpretation

10 (1) Section 272 (general interpretation) is amended as follows.
(2) (*amends* IHTA 1984 s 272)
(3) (*amended* IHTA 1984 s 272); *repealed* by FA 2011 s 65, Sch 16 para 84(*b*)(i)

Rates of tax

11 (*inserted* IHTA 1984 Sch 2 para 6A; *repealed* by FA 2007 s 114, Sch 27, Pt 3(1))

Transitional

12 The reference in section 12(2A) of IHTA 1984 (inserted by paragraph 2) to a member of a registered pension scheme having omitted to exercise pension rights under the pension scheme includes an omission before 6th April 2006 in relation to a pension scheme which on that date becomes a registered pension scheme.

Amendments—This para repealed by FA 2011 s 65, Sch 16 para 84(*b*)(i) with effect for the tax year 2011–12 and subsequent tax years, subject to transitional provisions in FA 2011 Sch 16 Pt 3.

SCHEDULE 26
REPEALS
Section 178

PART 6
INHERITANCE TAX

Short title and chapter	*Extent of repeal*
Inheritance Tax Act 1984 (c 51)	In section 3A(1), the words after paragraph (*c*). In section 54A(2), in paragraph (*c*), the words ", other than property to which section 71 below applies" and, in paragraph (*d*)(i), the words "or to which section 71 below applies". In section 71(1)(*a*), the words "or to an interest in possession in it".

1 The repeals in sections 3A(1) and 54A(2) of IHTA 1984 shall be deemed to have come into force on 22nd March 2006, but the repeal in section 54A(2) of IHTA 1984 is to be read with paragraph 16(4) of Schedule 20 to this Act.

2 The repeal in section 71(1)(*a*) of IHTA 1984 comes into force in accordance with paragraph 3(2) of Schedule 20 to this Act.

FINANCE ACT 2007

(2007 Chapter 11)

An Act to Grant certain duties, to alter other duties, and to amend the law relating to the National Debt and the Public Revenue, and to make further provision in connection with finance.

[19 July 2007]

PART 1

CHARGES, RATES, THRESHOLDS ETC

Inheritance tax

4 Rates and rate bands for 2010–11

Amendments—This section repealed by FA 2010 s 8(2)(*b*) with effect from 8 April 2010.

PART 4

PENSIONS

69 Alternatively secured pensions etc

Schedule 19 contains provisions about alternatively secured pensions and transfer lump sum death benefit etc.

PART 6

INVESTIGATION, ADMINISTRATION ETC

Other administration

97 Penalties for errors

(1) Schedule 24 contains provisions imposing penalties on taxpayers who—

(*a*) make errors in certain documents sent to HMRC, or

(*b*) unreasonably fail to report errors in assessments by HMRC.

(2) That Schedule comes into force in accordance with provision made by the Treasury by order.

(3) An order—

(*a*) may commence a provision generally or only for specified purposes,

(*b*) may make different provision for different purposes, and

(*c*) may include incidental, consequential or transitional provision.

(4) The power to make an order is exercisable by statutory instrument.

Orders—Finance Act 2007, Schedule 24 (Commencement and Transitional Provisions) Order 2008, SI 2008/568.

SCHEDULES

SCHEDULE 19

ALTERNATIVELY SECURED PENSIONS AND TRANSFER LUMP SUM DEATH BENEFIT ETC

Section 69

Inheritance tax

19 IHTA 1984 is amended as follows.

20—(1) Section 151A (person dying with alternatively secured pension fund) is amended as follows.

(2) (*substitutes* IHTA 1984 s 151A(2))

(3) (*amends* IHTA 1984 s 151A(3)(*a*))

(4) (*inserts* IHTA 1984 s 151A(4A)–(4C))

(5) (*inserts* definition into IHTA 1984 s 151A(5))—

(6) (*inserts* IHTA 1984 s 151A(6)–(7))

21—(1) Section 151B (relevant dependant with pension fund inherited from member over 75) is amended as follows.

(2) (*amends* IHTA 1984 s 151B(1)(*b*))

(3) (*repeals* IHTA 1984 s 151B(5))

22 (*inserts* IHTA 1984 s 151BA)

23—(1) Section 151C (dependant dying with other pension fund) is amended as follows.

(2) (*substitutes* IHTA 1984 s 151C(2))

(3) (*amends* IHTA 1984 s 151C(3)(*a*))

(4) (*repeals* IHTA 1984 s 151C(3A)–(3D))

(5) (*amends* IHTA 1984 s 151C(4))

24 (*amends* IHTA 1984 s 216(6)(*ac*))

25 (*amends* IHTA 1984 s 226(4))

26 (*amends* IHTA 1984 s 233(1)(*c*))

27 (*repeals* IHTA 2984 Sch 2 para 6A)

Consequential amendment

28—(*amended* ITEPA 2003 s 636A(1), (7); repealed in part by the Taxation of Pensions Act 2014 s 3, Sch 2 para 19(4)(*b*))

Commencement

29—(1) The amendments made by paragraphs 2(2) and 3 have effect in relation to deaths of members of registered pension schemes occurring on or after 6th April 2007.
(2) The amendments made by paragraphs 2(3), 4, 14 and 15 have effect for alternatively secured pension years beginning on or after 6th April 2007.
(3) The amendments made by paragraphs 5 to 10, 18(2) and (3) and 28 have effect in relation to lump sum death benefits paid in respect of members of schemes whose deaths occur on or after 6th April 2007.
(4) The amendments made by paragraphs 11, 12(5) and 16(2), (4) and (6) are deemed to have come into force on 6th April 2006.
(5) The amendments made by paragraphs 12(2) and 13 have effect in relation to members of registered pension schemes becoming entitled to alternatively secured rights on or after 6th April 2007 in respect of members whose deaths occur on or after that date.
(6) The amendments made by paragraph 16(3) and (5) have effect in relation to charity lump sum death benefits paid on or after 6th April 2007.
(7) The amendment made by paragraph 17 is deemed to have come into force on 6th April 2007.
(8) The amendments made by paragraphs 19 to 27 have effect in relation to deaths, cases where scheme administrators become aware of deaths and cessations of dependency occurring on or after 6th April 2007.

SCHEDULE 24

PENALTIES FOR ERRORS

Section 97

HMRC Manuals—Compliance Handbook Manual, CH81000–84974 (HMRC Compliance Handbook Manual chapter on penalties for inaccuracies).

Orders—The Finance Act 2007, Schedule 24 (Commencement And Transitional Provisions) Order, SI 2008/568: this Schedule has effect as follows—

(a) 1 April 2008 in relation to relevant documents relating to tax periods commencing on or after that date;
(b) 1 April 2008 in relation to assessments falling within Sch 24 para 2 for tax periods commencing on or after that date;
(c) 1 July 2008 in relation to relevant documents relating to claims under the Thirteenth Council Directive (arrangements for the refund of value added tax to persons not established in Community territory) for years commencing on or after that date;
(d) 1 January 2009 in relation to relevant documents relating to claims under the Eighth Council Directive (arrangements for the refund of value added tax to taxable persons not established in the territory of the country) for years commencing on or after that date;
(e) 1 April 2009 in relation to documents relating to all other claims for repayments of relevant tax made on or after 1 April 2009 which are not related to a tax period; and
(f) in any other case, 1 April 2009 in relation to documents given where a person's liability to pay relevant tax arises on or after that date.

Press releases etc—HMRC Compliance Checks Factsheet CC/FS7a—Compliance checks series—Penalties for inaccuracies in returns or documents.

HMRC Compliance Checks Factsheet CC/FS7b—Compliance checks series—Penalties for not telling us about an under-assessment.

HMRC Compliance Checks Factsheet CC/FS19—Compliance checks—Employer and Contractor returns and "old" penalty rules.

Cross-references—Small Charitable Donations Regulations, SI 2013/938 reg 15 (application of this Schedule, with modifications, in relation to small charitable donations under the Small Charitable Donations Act 2012).

FA 2014 ss 208–214, Sch 30 (follower notices: penalties).

FA 2014 Sch 35 para 13(*a*) (a person is not liable to a penalty under this Schedule by reason of any failure to include in any return or account a reference number required by FA 2014 s 253).

SSCBA 1992 s 11A (this Schedule applies with the necessary modifications, in relation to Class 2 contributions under SSCBA 1992 s 11(2) as if those contributions were income tax chargeable under ITTOIA 2005 Pt 2 Ch 2 in respect of profits of a trade, profession or vocation which is not carried on wholly outside the United Kingdom).

Education (Postgraduate Master's Degree Loans) Regulations, SI 2016/606 regs 24(3), 85 (application of this Schedule in relation to postgraduate master's degree loans).

FA 2017 Sch 9 paras 1(7), 2(4) (soft drinks industry levy: penalties)

F(No 2)A 2017 Sch 16 (enablers of defeated tax avoidance: penalties)

PART 1
LIABILITY FOR PENALTY

Error in taxpayer's document

1—(1) A penalty is payable by a person (P) where—

(*a*) P gives HMRC a document of a kind listed in the Table below, and

(*b*) Conditions 1 and 2 are satisfied.

(2) Condition 1 is that the document contains an inaccuracy which amounts to, or leads to—

(*a*) an understatement of [a][1] liability to tax,

(*b*) a false or inflated statement of a loss . . . [1], or

(*c*) a false or inflated claim to repayment of tax.

(3) Condition 2 is that the inaccuracy was [careless (within the meaning of paragraph 3) or deliberate on P's part][1].

(4) Where a document contains more than one inaccuracy, a penalty is payable for each inaccuracy.

Tax	*Document*
Income tax or capital gains tax	Return under section 8 of TMA 1970 (personal return).
Income tax or capital gains tax	Return under section 8A of TMA 1970 (trustee's return).
Income tax or capital gains tax	Return, statement or declaration in connection with a claim for an allowance, deduction or relief.
Income tax or capital gains tax	Accounts in connection with ascertaining liability to tax.
Income tax or capital gains tax	Partnership return.
Income tax or capital gains tax	Statement or declaration in connection with a partnership return.
Income tax or capital gains tax	Accounts in connection with a partnership return.
[Apprenticeship levy	Return under regulations under section 105 of FA 2016.][7]
[Capital gains tax	Return under section 12ZB of TMA 1970 (NRCGT return).][6]
[Income tax	Return under section 254 of FA 2004.][1]
Income tax	Return for the purposes of PAYE regulations.
Construction industry deductions	Return for the purposes of regulations under section 70(1)(a) of FA 2004 in connection with deductions on account of tax under the Construction Industry Scheme.
Corporation tax	Company tax return under paragraph 3 of Schedule 18 to FA 1998.
Corporation tax	Return, statement or declaration in connection with a claim for an allowance, deduction or relief.
Corporation tax	Accounts in connection with ascertaining liability to tax.
VAT	VAT return under regulations made under paragraph 2 of Schedule 11 to VATA 1994.
VAT	Return, statement or declaration in connection with a claim.
[VAT	Return under a special scheme.][5]
[Insurance premium tax	Return under regulations under section 54 of FA 1994.
Insurance premium tax	Return, statement or declaration in connection with a claim.
Inheritance tax	Account under section 216 or 217 of IHTA 1984.

Tax	*Document*
Inheritance tax	Information or document under regulations under section 256 of IHTA 1984.
Inheritance tax	Statement or declaration in connection with a deduction, exemption or relief.
Stamp duty land tax	Return under section 76 of FA 2003.
Stamp duty reserve tax	Return under regulations under section 98 of FA 1986.
[Annual tax on enveloped dwellings	Annual tax on enveloped dwellings return.
Annual tax on enveloped dwellings	Return of adjusted chargeable amount.][4]
Petroleum revenue tax	Return under paragraph 2 of Schedule 2 to the Oil Taxation Act 1975.
[Petroleum revenue tax	Statement or declaration in connection with a claim under paragraph 13A of Schedule 2 to the Oil Taxation Act 1975.][2]
Petroleum revenue tax	Statement or declaration in connection with a claim under Schedule 5, 6, 7 or 8 to the Oil Taxation Act 1975.
Petroleum revenue tax	Statement under section 1(1)(*a*) of the Petroleum Revenue Tax Act 1980.
Aggregates levy	Return under regulations under section 25 of FA 2001.
Climate change levy	Return under regulations under paragraph 41 of Schedule 6 to FA 2000.
Landfill tax	Return under regulations under section 49 of FA 1996.
Air passenger duty	Return under section 38 of FA 1994.
Alcoholic liquor duties	Return under regulations under section 13, 49, 56 or 62 of the Alcoholic Liquor Duties Act 1979.
Alcoholic liquor duties	Statement or declaration in connection with a claim for repayment of duty under section 4(4) of FA 1995.
Tobacco products duty	Return under regulations under section 7 of the Tobacco Products Duties Act 1979.
Hydrocarbon oil duties	Return under regulations under section 21 of the Hydrocarbon Oil Duties Act 1979.
Excise duties	Return under regulations under section 93 of CEMA 1979.
Excise duties	Return under regulations under section 100G or 100H of CEMA 1979.
Excise duties	Statement or declaration in connection with a claim.
General betting duty	Return under regulations under paragraph 2 of Schedule 1 to BGDA 1981.
Pool betting duty	Return under regulations under paragraph 2A of Schedule 1 to BGDA 1981.
Bingo duty	Return under regulations under paragraph 9 of Schedule 3 to BGDA 1981.
Lottery duty	Return under regulations under section 28(2) of FA 1993.
Gaming duty	Return under directions under paragraph 10 of Schedule 1 to FA 1997.
Remote gaming duty	Return under regulations under section 26K of BGDA 1981.][1]
[Machine games duty	Return under regulations under paragraph 18 of Schedule 24 to FA 2012.][3]
[Any of the taxes mentioned above][1]	Any document which is likely to be relied upon by HMRC to determine, without further inquiry, a question about—

Tax	*Document*
	(*a*) P's liability to tax, (*b*) payments by P by way of or in connection with tax, (*c*) any other payment by P (including penalties), or (*d*) repayments, or any other kind of payment or credit, to P.

[(4A) In this paragraph "return under a special scheme" means any of the following, so far as relating to supplies of services treated as made in the United Kingdom—

(*a*) a special accounting return under paragraph 11 of Schedule 3B;

(*b*) a value added tax return submitted under any provision of the law of a member State other than the United Kingdom which implements Article 364 of the VAT Directive (as substituted by Article 5(11) of the Amending Directive);

(*c*) a value added tax return submitted under any provision of the law of a member State other than the United Kingdom which implements Article 369f of the VAT Directive (as inserted by Article 5(15) of the Amending Directive).

(4B) A value added tax return mentioned in paragraph (*b*) or (*c*) of subparagraph (4A) is regarded for the purposes of sub-paragraph (1) as given to HMRC when it is submitted to the authority to whom it is required to be submitted.

(4C) In sub-paragraph (4A)—

"the VAT Directive" means Directive 2006/112/EC;

"the Amending Directive" means Council Directive 2008/8/EC.][5]

(5) In relation to a return under paragraph 2 of Schedule 2 to the Oil Taxation Act 1975 [or a statement or declaration under paragraph 13A of that Schedule][2], references in this Schedule to P include any person who, after the giving of the return for a taxable field (within the meaning of that Act), becomes the responsible person for the field (within the meaning of that Act).][1]

HMRC Manuals—Compliance Handbook Manual, CH81011–81013 (penalties for inaccuracies: commencement date for penalties).

CH81060 (penalties for inaccuracies: which documents do penalties for inaccuracies apply to).

CH81070 (conditions for penalty for inaccuracy).

Cross reference—FA 2009 s 94 (publishing details of deliberate tax defaulters).

FA 2015 Sch 21 (penalties in connection with offshore asset moves).

FA 2016 Sch 20 (penalties for enablers of offshore tax evasion or non-compliance).

FA 2016 Sch 22 (asset-based penalty for offshore inaccuracies and failures).

Modifications—FA 2007 Sch 24 has effect as if, in the Table in this para, the list of taxes included bank payroll tax and the list of documents included a bank payroll tax return (FA 2010 s 22, Sch 1 para 37(1)).

Simon's Tax Cases—*Harding v R&C Comrs* [2013] UKUT 575 (TCC), [2014] STC 891.

Amendments—[1] In sub-para (2), word substituted and words repealed, in sub-para (3), words substituted, in the table, entries inserted, in the last entry in column 1 words substituted, and sub-para (5) inserted, by FA 2008 s 122, Sch 40 paras 1, 2 with effect from 1 April 2009 (by virtue of SI 2009/571 art 2). In their application in relation to penalties payable under paras 1, 1A of this Schedule, the entries inserted in the table (by FA 2008 Sch 40 para 2(4), (5)) shall have effect in relation to—

(a) relevant documents—

(i) which relate to tax periods commencing on or after 1 April 2009, and

(ii) for which the filing date is on or after 1 April 2010;

(b) relevant documents relating to all claims for repayments of relevant tax made on or after 1 April 2010 which are not related to a tax period;

(c) relevant documents produced under regulations under IHTA 1984 s 256 where the date of death is on or after 1 April 2009; and

(d) in any other case, relevant documents given where a person's liability to pay relevant tax arises on or after 1 April 2010 (SI 2009/571 arts 3, 4).

In their application in relation to assessments falling within para 2 of this Schedule, the entries inserted in the table (by FA 2008 Sch 40 para 2(4), (5)) shall have effect in relation to tax periods commencing on or after 1 April 2009, where the filing date for the relevant document is on or after 1 April 2010 (SI 2009/571 art 5).

[2] In table, entry inserted, and in sub-para (5) words inserted, by F(No 3)A 2010 s 28, Sch 12 Pt 2 para 12 with effect in relation to claims made on or after 1 April 2011.

[3] In table, entry inserted by FA 2012 s 191, Sch 24 para 29 with effect in relation to the playing of machine games on or after 1 February 2013

[4] In table, entries inserted by FA 2013 s 164, Sch 34 para 6 with effect from 17 July 2013.

[5] In para 1, third entry for VAT inserted, and sub-paras (4A)–(4C) inserted, by FA 2014 s 103, Sch 22 para 19 with effect in relation to supplies made on or after 1 January 2015.

[6] In table, entry inserted by FA 2015 s 37, Sch 7 para 56(1), (2) with effect in relation to disposals made on or after 6 April 2015.

[7] In table, entry inserted by FA 2016 s 113(1), (2) with effect from 6 April 2017 (by virtue of SI 2017/355).

Prospective amendments—In table, entry relating to soft drinks industry to be inserted after entry relating to the statement under the Petroleum Revenue Tax Act 1980 s 1(1)(*a*) by FA 2017 s 56, Sch 11 para 3 with effect from a day to be appointed (FA 2017 s 61). Table entry as inserted to read as follows—

"Soft drinks industry levy	Return under regulations under section 52 of FA 2017".

[Error in taxpayer's document attributable to another person

1A—(1) A penalty is payable by a person (T) where—

(*a*) another person (P) gives HMRC a document of a kind listed in the Table in paragraph 1,

(*b*) the document contains a relevant inaccuracy, and

(*c*) the inaccuracy was attributable to T deliberately supplying false information to P (whether directly or indirectly), or to T deliberately withholding information from P, with the intention of the document containing the inaccuracy.

(2) A "relevant inaccuracy" is an inaccuracy which amounts to, or leads to—

(*a*) an understatement of a liability to tax,

(*b*) a false or inflated statement of a loss, or

(*c*) a false or inflated claim to repayment of tax.

(3) A penalty is payable under this paragraph in respect of an inaccuracy whether or not P is liable to a penalty under paragraph 1 in respect of the same inaccuracy.][1]

HMRC Manuals—Compliance Handbook Manual, CH81011–81013 (penalties for inaccuracies: commencement date for penalties).
CH84545 (other penalty issues: agent acting – inaccuracy attributable to another person).
CH81075 (penalties for inaccuracies: inaccuracy due to another person).
CH81165–81166 (inaccuracy attributable to another person).
CH81167–81168 (intentions of another person, with examples).
CH81110 (penalties for inaccuracies: the four types of inaccuracy).
Cross reference—FA 2009 s 94 (Publishing details of deliberate tax defaulters).
Amendment—[1] Paragraph 1A inserted by FA 2008 s 122, Sch 40 paras 1, 3 with effect from 1 April 2009 (by virtue of SI 2009/571 art 2).

Under-assessment by HMRC

2—(1) A penalty is payable by a person (P) where—

(*a*) an assessment issued to P by HMRC understates P's liability to [a relevant tax][1], and

(*b*) P has failed to take reasonable steps to notify HMRC, within the period of 30 days beginning with the date of the assessment, that it is an under-assessment.

(2) In deciding what steps (if any) were reasonable HMRC must consider—

(*a*) whether P knew, or should have known, about the under-assessment, and

(*b*) what steps would have been reasonable to take to notify HMRC.

[(3) In sub-paragraph (1) "relevant tax" means any tax mentioned in the Table in paragraph 1.][1]

[(4) In this paragraph (and in Part 2 of this Schedule so far as relating to this paragraph)—

(*a*) "assessment" includes determination, and

(*b*) accordingly, references to an under-assessment include an under-determination.][2]

HMRC Manuals—Compliance Handbook Manual, CH81011–81013 (penalties for inaccuracies: commencement date for penalties).
CH81090 (penalties for inaccuracies: under assessment by HMRC).
CH81170 (under assessment by HMRC).
Amendments—[1] In sub-para (1), words substituted, and sub-para (3) substituted, by FA 2008 s 122, Sch 40 paras 1, 4 with effect from 1 April 2009 (by virtue of SI 2009/571 art 2).
[2] Sub-para (4) inserted by FA 2009 s 109, Sch 57 para 2 with effect from 21 July 2009.

Degrees of culpability

3—(1) [For the purposes of a penalty under paragraph 1, inaccuracy in][1] a document given by P to HMRC is—

(*a*) "careless" if the inaccuracy is due to failure by P to take reasonable care,

(*b*) "deliberate but not concealed" if the inaccuracy is deliberate [on P's part][1] but P does not make arrangements to conceal it, and

(*c*) "deliberate and concealed" if the inaccuracy is deliberate [on P's part][1] and P makes arrangements to conceal it (for example, by submitting false evidence in support of an inaccurate figure).

(2) An inaccuracy in a document given by P to HMRC, which was neither careless nor deliberate [on P's part][1] when the document was given, is to be treated as careless if P—

(*a*) discovered the inaccuracy at some later time, and

(*b*) did not take reasonable steps to inform HMRC.

[(3) Paragraph 47 of Schedule 19 to FA 2016 (special measures for persistently unco-operative large businesses) provides for certain inaccuracies to be treated, for the purposes of this Schedule, as being due to a failure by P to take reasonable care.][2]

HMRC Manuals—Compliance Handbook Manual, CH81080 (penalties for inaccuracies: inaccuracy discovered after document sent to HMRC).
CH81120–81140 (what is reasonable care, with examples at CH81131).
CH81141–81142 (correction of errors for indirect taxes).
CH81145 (examples of careless inaccuracy).
CH81150–81151 (deliberate but not concealed inaccuracy, with examples).
CH81160–81161 (deliberate and concealed inaccuracy, with examples).
CH81110 (penalties for inaccuracies: the four types of inaccuracy).
Cross references—FA 2014 s 276 (for the purposes of sub-para (1)(*a*) above, reliance on legal advice provided by monitored promoter not to be regarded as taking reasonable care).
Simon's Tax Cases—*Harding v R&C Comrs* [2013] UKUT 575 (TCC), [2014] STC 891.
Amendments—[1] In sub-para (1), words substituted, and in sub-paras (1), (2), words inserted, by FA 2008 s 122, Sch 40 paras 1, 5 with effect from 1 April 2009 (by virtue of SI 2009/571 art 2).
[2] Sub-para (3) inserted by FA 2016 s 161, Sch 19 para 48 with effect in relation to financial years beginning on or after 15 September 2016.

[Errors related to avoidance arrangements

3A

(1) This paragraph applies where a document of a kind listed in the Table in paragraph 1 is given to HMRC by a person ("P") and the document contains an inaccuracy which—

(*a*) falls within paragraph 1(2), and

(*b*) arises because the document is submitted on the basis that particular avoidance arrangements (within the meaning of paragraph 3B) had an effect which in fact they did not have.

(2) It is to be presumed that the inaccuracy was careless, within the meaning of paragraph 3, unless—

(*a*) the inaccuracy was deliberate on P's part, or

(*b*) P satisfies HMRC or (on an appeal notified to the tribunal) the tribunal that P took reasonable care to avoid inaccuracy.

(3) In considering whether P took reasonable care to avoid inaccuracy, HMRC and (on an appeal notified to the tribunal) the tribunal must take no account of any evidence of any reliance by P on advice where the advice is disqualified.

(4) Advice is "disqualified" if any of the following applies—

(*a*) the advice was given to P by an interested person;

(*b*) the advice was given to P as a result of arrangements made between an interested person and the person who gave the advice;

(*c*) the person who gave the advice did not have appropriate expertise for giving the advice;

(*d*) the advice took no account of P's individual circumstances;

(*e*) the advice was addressed to, or given to, a person other than P;

but this is subject to sub-paragraphs (5) and (7).

(5) Where (but for this sub-paragraph) advice would be disqualified under any of paragraphs (*a*) to (*c*) of sub-paragraph (4), the advice is not disqualified under that paragraph if at the relevant time P—

(*a*) has taken reasonable steps to find out whether the advice falls within that paragraph, and

(*b*) reasonably believes that it does not.

(6) In sub-paragraph (4) "an interested person" means—

(*a*) a person, other than P, who participated in the avoidance arrangements or any transaction forming part of them, or

(*b*) a person who for any consideration (whether or not in money) facilitated P's entering into the avoidance arrangements.

(7) Where (but for this sub-paragraph) advice would be disqualified under paragraph (*a*) of sub-paragraph (4) because it was given by a person within sub-paragraph (6)(*b*), the advice is not disqualified under that paragraph if—

(*a*) the person giving the advice had appropriate expertise for giving it,

(*b*) the advice took account of P's individual circumstances, and

(*c*) at the time when the question whether the advice is disqualified arises—

(i) Condition E in paragraph 3B(5) is met in relation to the avoidance arrangements, but

(ii) none of Conditions A to D in paragraph 3B(5) is or has at any time been met in relation to them.

(8) If the document mentioned in sub-paragraph (1) is given to HMRC by P as a personal representative of a deceased person ("D")—

(*a*) sub-paragraph (4) is to be read as if—

(i) the references in paragraphs (*a*) and (*b*) to P were to P or D;

(ii) the reference in paragraph (*d*) to P were to D, and

(iii) the reference in paragraph (*e*) to a person other than P were to a person who is neither P nor D,

(*b*) sub-paragraph (6) is to be read as if—

(i) the reference in paragraph (*a*) to P were a reference to the person to whom the advice was given, and

(ii) the reference in paragraph (*b*) to P were to D (or, where P also participated in the avoidance arrangements, P or D), and

(*c*) sub-paragraph (7) is to be read as if the reference in paragraph (*b*) to P were to D.

(9) In this paragraph—

"arrangements" includes any agreement, understanding, scheme, transaction or series of transactions (whether or not legally enforceable);

"the relevant time" means the time when the document mentioned in sub-paragraph (1) is given to HMRC;

"the tribunal" has the same meaning as in paragraph 17 (see paragraph 17(5A)).][1]

Commentary—*Simon's Taxes* **A4.512**.

Amendments—[1] Paragraphs 3A, 3B inserted by F(No 2)A 2017 s 64(1), (2) with effect in relation to any document of a kind listed in the Table in FA 2007 Sch 24 para 1 which is given to HMRC on or after 16 November 2017 and which relates to a tax period beginning on or after 6 April 2017 and ending on or after 16 November 2017. "Tax period", and the reference to giving a document to HMRC have the same meaning as in FA 2007 Sch 24 para 28 (F(No 2)A 2017 s 64(6)).

[3B

(1) In paragraph 3A "avoidance arrangements" means, subject to sub-paragraph (3), arrangements which fall within sub-paragraph (2).

(2) Arrangements fall within this sub-paragraph if, having regard to all the circumstances, it would be reasonable to conclude that the obtaining of a tax advantage was the main purpose, or one of the main purposes, of the arrangements.

(3) Arrangements are not avoidance arrangements for the purposes of paragraph 3A if (although they fall within sub-paragraph (2))—

(*a*) they are arrangements which accord with established practice, and

(*b*) HMRC had, at the time the arrangements were entered into, indicated its acceptance of that practice.

(4) If, at any time, any of Conditions A to E is met in relation to particular arrangements—

(*a*) for the purposes of this Schedule the arrangements are to be taken to fall within (and always to have fallen within) sub-paragraph (2), and

(*b*) in relation to the arrangements, sub-paragraph (3) (and the reference to it in sub-paragraph (1)) are to be treated as omitted.

This does not prevent arrangements from falling within sub-paragraph (2) other than by reason of one or more of Conditions A to E being met.

(5) Conditions A to E are as follows—

(*a*) Condition A is that the arrangements are DOTAS arrangements within the meaning given by section 219(5) and (6) of FA 2014;

(*b*) Condition B is that the arrangements are disclosable VAT arrangements or disclosable indirect tax arrangements for the purposes of Schedule 18 to FA 2016 (see paragraphs 8A to 9A of that Schedule);

(*c*) Condition C is that both of the following apply—

(i) P has been given a notice under a provision mentioned in sub-paragraph (6) stating that a tax advantage arising from the arrangements is to be counteracted, and

(ii) that tax advantage has been counteracted under section 209 of FA 2013;

(*d*) Condition D is that a follower notice under section 204 of FA 2014 has been given to P by reference to the arrangements (and not withdrawn) and—

(i) the necessary corrective action for the purposes of section 208 of FA 2014 has been taken in respect of the denied advantage, or

(ii) the denied advantage has been counteracted otherwise than as mentioned in sub-paragraph (i);

(*e*) Condition E is that a tax advantage asserted by reference to the arrangements has been counteracted (by an assessment, an amendment of a return or claim, or otherwise) on the basis that an avoidance-related rule applies in relation to P's affairs.

(6) The provisions referred to in sub-paragraph (5)(*c*)(i) are—

(*a*) paragraph 12 of Schedule 43 to FA 2013 (general anti-abuse rule: notice of final decision);

(*b*) paragraph 8 or 9 of Schedule 43A to that Act (pooled or bound arrangements: notice of final decision);

(*c*) paragraph 8 of Schedule 43B to that Act (generic referrals: notice of final decision).

(7) In sub-paragraph (5)(*d*) the reference to giving a follower notice to P includes giving a partnership follower notice in respect of a partnership return in relation to which P is a relevant partner; and for the purposes of this sub-paragraph—

(*a*) "relevant partner" has the meaning given by paragraph 2(5) of Schedule 31 to FA 2014;

(*b*) a partnership follower notice is given "in respect of" the partnership return mentioned in paragraph 2(2)(*a*) or (*b*) of that Schedule.

(8) For the purposes of sub-paragraph (5)(*d*) it does not matter whether the denied advantage has been dealt with—

(*a*) wholly as mentioned in one or other of sub-paragraphs (i) and (ii) of sub-paragraph (5)(*d*), or

(*b*) partly as mentioned in one of those sub-paragraphs and partly as mentioned in the other;

and "the denied advantage" has the same meaning as in Chapter 2 of Part 4 of FA 2014 (see section 208(3) of and paragraph 4(3) of Schedule 31 to that Act).

(9) For the purposes of sub-paragraph (5)(*e*) a tax advantage has been "asserted by reference to" the arrangements if a return, claim or appeal has been made by P on the basis that the tax advantage results from the arrangements.

(10) In this paragraph—

"arrangements" has the same meaning as in paragraph 3A;

"avoidance-related rule" has the same meaning as in Part 4 of Schedule 18 to FA 2016 (see paragraph 25 of that Schedule);

a "tax advantage" includes—

(*a*) relief or increased relief from tax,

(*b*) repayment or increased repayment of tax,

(*c*) avoidance or reduction of a charge to tax or an assessment to tax,

(*d*) avoidance of a possible assessment to tax,

(*e*) deferral of a payment of tax or advancement of a repayment of tax,

(*f*) avoidance of an obligation to deduct or account for tax, and

(*g*) in relation to VAT, anything which is a tax advantage for the purposes of Schedule 18 to FA 2016 under paragraph 5 of that Schedule.][1]

Commentary—*Simon's Taxes* **A4.512.**

Amendments—[1] Paragraphs 3A, 3B inserted by F(No 2)A 2017 s 64(1), (2) with effect in relation to any document of a kind listed in the Table in FA 2007 Sch 24 para 1 which is given to HMRC on or after 16 November 2017 and which relates to a tax period beginning on or after 6 April 2017 and ending on or after 16 November 2017. "Tax period", and the reference to giving a document to HMRC have the same meaning as in FA 2007 Sch 24 para 28 (F(No 2)A 2017 s 64(6)).

PART 2
AMOUNT OF PENALTY

Standard amount

[4 (1) This paragraph sets out the penalty payable under paragraph 1.

(2) If the inaccuracy is in category 1, the penalty is—

(*a*) for careless action, 30% of the potential lost revenue,

(*b*) for deliberate but not concealed action, 70% of the potential lost revenue, and

(*c*) for deliberate and concealed action, 100% of the potential lost revenue.

(3) If the inaccuracy is in category 2, the penalty is—

(*a*) for careless action, 45% of the potential lost revenue,

(*b*) for deliberate but not concealed action, 105% of the potential lost revenue, and (*c*) for deliberate and concealed action, 150% of the potential lost revenue.

(4) If the inaccuracy is in category 3, the penalty is—

(*a*) for careless action, 60% of the potential lost revenue,

(*b*) for deliberate but not concealed action, 140% of the potential lost revenue, and

(*c*) for deliberate and concealed action, 200% of the potential lost revenue.

(5) Paragraph 4A explains the 3 categories of inaccuracy.][1]

HMRC Manuals—Compliance Handbook Manual, CH82120 (penalties for inaccuracies: introduction to amount of penalty).

Cross references—FA 2014 s 212 (application of this paragraph in calculation of aggregate penalties for failure to take corrective action in response to a follower notice).

Amendments—[1] Paras 4–4D substituted for previous para 4 by FA 2010 s 35 Sch 10 paras 1, 2 with effect from 6 April 2011 (by virtue of SI 2011/975 art 2(1)). Note that these changes do not have effect in relation to documents given to HMRC, and assessments issued by HMRC, in relation to a tax period commencing on or before 5 April 2011 (SI 2011/975 art 3).

Prospective amendments—Sub-para (1A) to be inserted, in sub-para (2), figures "37.5%" to be substituted for "30%", "87.5%" to be substituted for "70%" and "125%" to be substituted for "100%", and in sub-para (5), figure "4" to be substituted for figure "3", by FA 2015 s 120, Sch 20 paras 1, 2 with effect from a day to be appointed. Sub-para (1A) as inserted to read as follows—

"(1A) If the inaccuracy is in category 0, the penalty is—

(a) for careless action, 30% of the potential lost revenue,

(b) for deliberate but not concealed action, 70% of the potential lost revenue, and

(c) for deliberate and concealed action, 100% of the potential lost revenue.".

[4A (1) An inaccuracy is in category 1 if—

(*a*) it involves a domestic matter, or

(*b*) it involves an offshore matter and—

(i) the territory in question is a category 1 territory, or

(ii) the tax at stake is a tax other than income tax or capital gains tax.

(2) An inaccuracy is in category 2 if—

(*a*) it involves an offshore matter [or an offshore transfer][2],

(*b*) the territory in question is a category 2 territory, and

(*c*) the tax at stake is income tax[, capital gains tax or inheritance tax][2].

(3) An inaccuracy is in category 3 if—

(*a*) it involves an offshore matter [or an offshore transfer][2],

(*b*) the territory in question is a category 3 territory, and

(*c*) the tax at stake is income tax[, capital gains tax or inheritance tax][2].

(4) An inaccuracy "involves an offshore matter" if it results in a potential loss of revenue that is charged on or by reference to—

(*a*) income arising from a source in a territory outside the UK,

(*b*) assets situated or held in a territory outside the UK,

(*c*) activities carried on wholly or mainly in a territory outside the UK, or

(*d*) anything having effect as if it were income, assets or activities of a kind described above.

[(4A) Where the tax at stake is inheritance tax, assets are treated for the purposes of sub-paragraph (4) as situated or held in a territory outside the UK if they are so situated or held immediately after the transfer of value by reason of which inheritance tax becomes chargeable.

(4B) An inaccuracy "involves an offshore transfer" if—

(*a*) it does not involve an offshore matter,

(*b*) it is deliberate (whether or not concealed) and results in a potential loss of revenue,

(*c*) the tax at stake is income tax, capital gains tax or inheritance tax, and

(*d*) the applicable condition in paragraph 4AA is satisfied.][2]

(5) An inaccuracy "involves a domestic matter" if it results in a potential loss of revenue [and does not involve either an offshore matter or an offshore transfer][2].

(6) If a single inaccuracy is in more than one category (each referred to as a "relevant category")—

(*a*) it is to be treated for the purposes of this Schedule as if it were separate inaccuracies, one in each relevant category according to the matters [or transfers][2] that it involves, and

(*b*) the potential lost revenue is to be calculated separately in respect of each separate inaccuracy.

(7) "Category 1 territory", "category 2 territory" and "category 3 territory" are defined in paragraph 21A.

(8) "Assets" has the meaning given in section 21(1) of TCGA 1992, but also includes sterling.][1]

Amendments—[1] Paras 4–4D substituted for previous para 4 by FA 2010 s 35 Sch 10 paras 1, 2 with effect from 6 April 2011 (by virtue of SI 2011/975 art 2(1)). Note that these changes do not have effect in relation to documents given to HMRC, and assessments issued by HMRC, in relation to a tax period commencing on or before 5 April 2011 (SI 2011/975 art 3).

[2] In sub-paras (2)(*a*), (3)(*a*), (6)(*a*), words inserted, in sub-paras (2)(*c*). (3)(*c*), (5), words substituted, and sub-paras (4A), (4B) inserted by FA 2015 s 120, Sch 20 paras 1, 3(3)–(7) with effect from 1 April 2016 (by virtue of SI 2016/456 art 3) in relation to documents given to HMRC relating to—

– for the purposes of inheritance tax, a transfer of value made on or after that date; and

– for the purposes of income tax and capital gains tax, a tax year commencing on or after 6 April 2016).

Prospective amendments—The following amendments to be made by FA 2015 s 120, Sch 20 paras 1, 3(1), (2), (8) with effect from a day to be appointed—

– sub-paras (A1), (1) to be substituted for sub-para (1);

– in sub-para (7), words "“Category 0 territory”, “category 1” to be substituted for words "“Category 1”.

Sub-paragraphs (A1), (1) as substituted to read as follows—

"(A1) An inaccuracy is in category 0 if—

(a) it involves a domestic matter,

(b) it involves an offshore matter or an offshore transfer, the territory in question is a category 0 territory and the tax at stake is income tax, capital gains tax or inheritance tax, or

(c) it involves an offshore matter and the tax at stake is a tax other than income tax, capital gains tax or inheritance tax.

(1) An inaccuracy is in category 1 if—

(a) it involves an offshore matter or an offshore transfer,

(b) the territory in question is a category 1 territory, and

(c) the tax at stake is income tax, capital gains tax or inheritance tax.".

[4AA (1) This paragraph makes provision in relation to offshore transfers.

(2) Where the tax at stake is income tax, the applicable condition is satisfied if the income on or by reference to which the tax is charged, or any part of the income—

(*a*) is received in a territory outside the UK, or

(*b*) is transferred before the filing date to a territory outside the UK.

(3) Where the tax at stake is capital gains tax, the applicable condition is satisfied if the proceeds of the disposal on or by reference to which the tax is charged, or any part of the proceeds—

(*a*) are received in a territory outside the UK, or

(*b*) are transferred before the filing date to a territory outside the UK.

(4) Where the tax at stake is inheritance tax, the applicable condition is satisfied if—

(*a*) the disposition that gives rise to the transfer of value by reason of which the tax becomes chargeable involves a transfer of assets, and

(*b*) after that disposition but before the filing date the assets, or any part of the assets, are transferred to a territory outside the UK.

(5) In the case of a transfer falling within sub-paragraph (2)(*b*), (3)(*b*) or (4)(*b*), references to the income, proceeds or assets transferred are to be read as including references to any assets derived from or representing the income, proceeds or assets.

(6) In relation to an offshore transfer, the territory in question for the purposes of paragraph 4A is the highest category of territory by virtue of which the inaccuracy involves an offshore transfer.

(7) "Filing date" means the date when the document containing the inaccuracy is given to HMRC.

(8) "Assets" has the same meaning as in paragraph 4A.][1]

Amendments—[1] Paragraph 4AA inserted by FA 2015 s 120, Sch 20 paras 1, 4 with effect from 1 April 2016 (by virtue of SI 2016/456 art 3) in relation to documents given to HMRC relating to—

– for the purposes of inheritance tax, a transfer of value made on or after that date; and

– for the purposes of income tax and capital gains tax, a tax year commencing on or after 6 April 2016).

[4B The penalty payable under paragraph 1A is 100% of the potential lost revenue.][1]

Amendments—[1] Paras 4–4D substituted for previous para 4 by FA 2010 s 35 Sch 10 paras 1, 2 with effect from 6 April 2011 (by virtue of SI 2011/975 art 2(1)). Note that these changes do not have effect in relation to documents given to HMRC, and assessments issued by HMRC, in relation to a tax period commencing on or before 5 April 2011 (SI 2011/975 art 3).

[4C The penalty payable under paragraph 2 is 30% of the potential lost revenue.][1]

Amendments—[1] Paras 4–4D substituted for previous para 4 by FA 2010 s 35 Sch 10 paras 1, 2 with effect from 6 April 2011 (by virtue of SI 2011/975 art 2(1)). Note that these changes do not have effect in relation to documents given to HMRC, and assessments issued by HMRC, in relation to a tax period commencing on or before 5 April 2011 (SI 2011/975 art 3).

[4D Paragraphs 5 to 8 define "potential lost revenue".][1]

Amendments—[1] Paras 4–4D substituted for previous para 4 by FA 2010 s 35 Sch 10 paras 1, 2 with effect from 6 April 2011 (by virtue of SI 2011/975 art 2(1)). Note that these changes do not have effect in relation to documents given to HMRC, and assessments issued by HMRC, in relation to a tax period commencing on or before 5 April 2011 (SI 2011/975 art 3).

Potential lost revenue: normal rule

5—(1) "The potential lost revenue" in respect of an inaccuracy in a document [(including an inaccuracy attributable to a supply of false information or withholding of information)][1] or a failure to notify an under-assessment is the additional amount due or payable in respect of tax as a result of correcting the inaccuracy or assessment.

(2) The reference in sub-paragraph (1) to the additional amount due or payable includes a reference to—

(*a*) an amount payable to HMRC having been erroneously paid by way of repayment of tax, and (*b*) an amount which would have been repayable by HMRC had the inaccuracy or assessment not been corrected.

(3) In sub-paragraph (1) "tax" includes national insurance contributions.

(4) The following shall be ignored in calculating potential lost revenue under this paragraph—

(*a*) group relief, and

[(*b*) any relief under [section 458 of CTA 2010][3] (relief in respect of repayment etc of loan) which is deferred under [subsection (5)][3] of that section;][2]

(but this sub-paragraph does not prevent a penalty being charged in respect of an inaccurate claim for relief).

HMRC Manuals—Compliance Handbook Manual, CH82160–82161 (penalties for inaccuracies: single inaccuracy with examples of potential lost revenue).

CH82162 (examples of potential lost revenue for an under assessment).

Cross reference—FA 2009 s 94 (Publishing details of deliberate tax defaulters).

Amendments—[1] In sub-para (1), words inserted by FA 2008 s 122, Sch 40 paras 1, 7 with effect from 1 April 2009 (by virtue of SI 2009/571 art 2).

[2] Sub-para (4)(*b*) substituted by FA 2009 s 109, Sch 57 para 3 with effect from 21 July 2009.

[3] In sub-para (4)(*b*) words substituted by CTA 2010 s 1177, Sch 1 paras 573, 575. CTA 2010 has effect for corporation tax purposes for accounting periods ending on or after 1 April 2010, and for income and capital gains tax purposes for the tax year 2010–11 and subsequent tax years.

Potential lost revenue: multiple errors

6—(1) Where P is liable to a penalty [under paragraph 1][1] in respect of more than one inaccuracy, and the calculation of potential lost revenue under paragraph 5 in respect of each inaccuracy depends on the order in which they are corrected—

(*a*) careless inaccuracies shall be taken to be corrected before deliberate inaccuracies, and

(*b*) deliberate but not concealed inaccuracies shall be taken to be corrected before deliberate and concealed inaccuracies.

(2) In calculating potential lost revenue where P is liable to a penalty [under paragraph 1][1] in respect of one or more understatements in one or more documents relating to a tax period, account shall be taken of any overstatement in any document given by P which relates to the same tax period.

(3) In sub-paragraph (2)—

(*a*) "understatement" means an inaccuracy that satisfies Condition 1 of paragraph 1, and

(*b*) "overstatement" means an inaccuracy that does not satisfy that condition.

(4) For the purposes of sub-paragraph (2) overstatements shall be set against understatements in the following order—

(*a*) understatements in respect of which P is not liable to a penalty,

(*b*) careless understatements,

(*c*) deliberate but not concealed understatements, and

(*d*) deliberate and concealed understatements.

(5) In calculating [for the purposes of a penalty under paragraph 1][1] potential lost revenue in respect of a document given by or on behalf of P no account shall be taken of the fact that a potential loss of revenue from P is or may be balanced by a potential over-payment by another person (except to the extent that an enactment requires or permits a person's tax liability to be adjusted by reference to P's).

HMRC Manuals—Compliance Handbook Manual, CH82180–82250 (penalties for inaccuracies: more than one inaccuracy and when inaccuracies should or should not be grouped).

CH82260 (overstatements, with a worked example).

CH82270 (calculating potential lost revenue for multiple inaccuracies).

CH82271 (calculating potential lost revenue for multiple inaccuracies – employer and contractor issues).

CH82272 (example of allocating overstatements to potential lost revenue).

Cross reference—FA 2009 s 94 (Publishing details of deliberate tax defaulters).

Amendments—[1] In sub-paras (1), (2), (5) words inserted, by FA 2008 s 122, Sch 40 paras 1, 8 with effect from 1 April 2009 (by virtue of SI 2009/571 art 2).

Potential lost revenue: losses

7—(1) Where an inaccuracy has the result that a loss is wrongly recorded for purposes of direct tax and the loss has been wholly used to reduce the amount due or payable in respect of tax, the potential lost revenue is calculated in accordance with paragraph 5.

(2) Where an inaccuracy has the result that a loss is wrongly recorded for purposes of direct tax and the loss has not been wholly used to reduce the amount due or payable in respect of tax, the potential lost revenue is—

(*a*) the potential lost revenue calculated in accordance with paragraph 5 in respect of any part of the loss that has been used to reduce the amount due or payable in respect of tax, plus

(*b*) 10% of any part that has not.

(3) Sub-paragraphs (1) and (2) apply both—

(*a*) to a case where no loss would have been recorded but for the inaccuracy, and

(*b*) to a case where a loss of a different amount would have been recorded (but in that case sub-paragraphs (1) and (2) apply only to the difference between the amount recorded and the true amount).

(4) Where an inaccuracy has the effect of creating or increasing an aggregate loss recorded for a group of companies—

(*a*) the potential lost revenue shall be calculated in accordance with this paragraph, and

(*b*) in applying paragraph 5 in accordance with sub-paragraphs (1) and (2) above, group relief may be taken into account (despite paragraph 5(4)(*a*)).

(5) The potential lost revenue in respect of a loss is nil where, because of the nature of the loss or P's circumstances, there is no reasonable prospect of the loss being used to support a claim to reduce a tax liability (of any person).

HMRC Manuals—Compliance Handbook Manual, CH82310–82320 (calculating the penalty: losses used and not used).
CH82330 (losses available for potential lost revenue calculation).
CH82331 (losses available – income tax example).
CH82332 (losses available – capital gains tax example).
CH82333 (losses available – corporation tax example).
CH82340–82341 (aggregate group profits).
CH82342–82345 (worked examples of understatements and overstatements of profits creating or increasing and aggregate loss).
CH82350 (losses and when to assess a penalty).
CH82370–82371 (losses where there is no reasonable prospect of use, with example).
Cross reference—FA 2009 s 94 (Publishing details of deliberate tax defaulters).

Potential lost revenue: delayed tax

8—(1) Where an inaccuracy resulted in an amount of tax being declared later than it should have been ("the delayed tax"), the potential lost revenue is—

(*a*) 5% of the delayed tax for each year of the delay, or

(*b*) a percentage of the delayed tax, for each separate period of delay of less than a year, equating to 5% per year.

(2) This paragraph does not apply to a case to which paragraph 7 applies.

HMRC Manuals—Compliance Handbook Manual, CH82390 (calculating the penalty: delayed tax and potential lost revenue).
CH82395 and 82396 (examples of tax declared late).
CH82397 (capital allowances example of delayed tax).
Cross reference—FA 2009 s 94 (Publishing details of deliberate tax defaulters).

Reductions for disclosure

9—[(A1) Paragraph 10 provides for reductions in penalties—

(*a*) under paragraph 1 where a person discloses an inaccuracy that involves a domestic matter,

(*b*) under paragraph 1A where a person discloses a supply of false information or withholding of information, and

(*c*) under paragraph 2 where a person discloses a failure to disclose an under-assessment.

(A2) Paragraph 10A provides for reductions in penalties under paragraph 1 where a person discloses an inaccuracy that involves an offshore matter or an offshore transfer.

(A3) Sub-paragraph (1) applies where a person discloses—

(*a*) an inaccuracy that involves a domestic matter,

(*b*) a careless inaccuracy that involves an offshore matter,

(*c*) a supply of false information or withholding of information, or

(*d*) a failure to disclose an under-assessment.][3]

(1) A person discloses an inaccuracy[, a supply of false information or withholding of information,][1] or a failure to disclose an under-assessment by—

(*a*) telling HMRC about it,

(*b*) giving HMRC reasonable help in quantifying the inaccuracy[, the inaccuracy attributable to the [supply of false information][2] or withholding of information, or the][1] under-assessment, and

(*c*) allowing HMRC access to records for the purpose of ensuring that the inaccuracy[, the inaccuracy attributable to the [supply of false information][2] or withholding of information, or the][1] under-assessment is fully corrected.

[(1A) Sub-paragraph (1B) applies where a person discloses—

(*a*) a deliberate inaccuracy (whether concealed or not) that involves an offshore matter, or

(*b*) an inaccuracy that involves an offshore transfer.

(1B) A person discloses the inaccuracy by—

(*a*) telling HMRC about it,

(*b*) giving HMRC reasonable help in quantifying the inaccuracy, (*c*) allowing HMRC access to records for the purpose of ensuring that the inaccuracy is fully corrected, and

(*d*) providing HMRC with additional information.

(1C) The Treasury must make regulations setting out what is meant by "additional information" for the purposes of sub-paragraph (1B)(*d*).

(1D) Regulations under sub-paragraph (1C) are to be made by statutory instrument.

(1E) An instrument containing regulations under sub-paragraph (1C) is subject to annulment in pursuance of a resolution of the House of Commons.][3]

(2) Disclosure—

(*a*) is "unprompted" if made at a time when the person making it has no reason to believe that HMRC have discovered or are about to discover the inaccuracy[, the supply of false information or withholding of information, or the under-assessment][1], and

(*b*) otherwise, is "prompted".

(3) In relation to disclosure "quality" includes timing, nature and extent.

[(4) Paragraph 4A(4) to (5) applies to determine whether an inaccuracy involves an offshore matter, an offshore transfer or a domestic matter for the purposes of this paragraph.][3]

HMRC Manuals—Compliance Handbook Manual, CH82410 (calculating the penalty: penalty reductions for disclosure).
CH82420–82422 (unprompted and prompted disclosure, with examples).
CH82430–82431 (quality of disclosure).
CH82432 (calculating the reduction for disclosure example).
CH82440–82460 (quality of disclosure: telling, helping and giving access),
CH82470 (maximum and minimum penalties for each type of behaviour).

Regulations—Penalties Relating to Offshore Matters and Offshore Transfers (Additional Information) Regulations, SI 2017/345.

Cross-references—See VATA 1994 Sch 3B para 16M (correction of special scheme return which involves disclosure of inaccuracy, supply of false information or a withholding of information to the tax authority for the administering member State, regarded as disclosure to HMRC for the purposes of this para).
VATA 1994 Sch 3BA para 34 (correction of non-UK return which involves disclosure of inaccuracy, supply of false information or a withholding of information to the tax authority for the administering member State, regarded as disclosure to HMRC for the purposes of this para).

Amendments—[1] In sub-para (1), words inserted, in paras (*b*), (*c*), words substituted, and in sub-para (2)(*a*), words substituted, by FA 2008 s 122, Sch 40 paras 1, 9 with effect from 1 April 2009 (by virtue of SI 2009/571 art 2).
[2] In sub-para (1)(*b*), (*c*), words substituted by FA 2009 s 109, Sch 57 para 4 with effect from 21 July 2009.
[3] Sub-paras (A1)–(A3) substituted for sub-para (A1); in sub-para (1), words substituted; and sub-paras (1A)–(1E), (4) inserted, by FA 2016 s 163, Sch 21 paras 1, 2 with effect, by virtue of SI 2017/259 regs 2, 3—

– for inheritance tax purposes, in relation to transfers of value made on or after 1 April 2017;
– for income tax and capital gains tax purposes, in relation to any tax year commencing on or after 6 April 2016; and
– for the purpose of making regulations, from 8 March 2017.

[10—(1) If a person who would otherwise be liable to a penalty of a percentage shown in column 1 of the Table (a "standard percentage") has made a disclosure, HMRC must reduce the standard percentage to one that reflects the quality of the disclosure.

(2) But the standard percentage may not be reduced to a percentage that is below the minimum shown for it—

(*a*) in the case of a prompted disclosure, in column 2 of the Table, and

(*b*) in the case of an unprompted disclosure, in column 3 of the Table.

[Standard %	*Minimum % for prompted disclosure*	*Minimum % for unprompted disclosure*
30%	15%	0%
70%	35%	20%
100%	50%	30%][2].

HMRC Manuals—Compliance Handbook Manual, CH82500–82512 (calculating the penalty: how to calculate the penalty with examples).

Cross reference—FA 2009 s 94 (Publishing details of deliberate tax defaulters).

Amendments—[1] This para substituted by FA 2010 s 35 Sch 10 paras 1, 3 with effect from 6 April 2011 (by virtue of SI 2011/975 art 2(1)). Note that these changes do not have effect in relation to documents given to HMRC, and assessments issued by HMRC, in relation to a tax period commencing on or before 5 April 2011 (SI 2011/975 art 3).
[2] In sub-para (2), Table substituted by FA 2016 s 163, Sch 21 paras 1, 3 with effect, by virtue of SI 2017/259 regs 2, 3—

– for inheritance tax purposes, in relation to transfers of value made on or after 1 April 2017; and
– for income tax and capital gains tax purposes, in relation to any tax year commencing on or after 6 April 2016.

Prospective amendments—In sub-para (2), the following Table entries to be inserted at the appropriate places by FA 2015 s 120, Sch 20 paras 1, 5 with effect from a day to be appointed—

"37.5%	18.75%	0%"

"87.5%	43.75%	25%"
"125%	62.5%	40%".

[10A—(1) If a person who would otherwise be liable to a penalty of a percentage shown in column 1 of the Table (a "standard percentage") has made a disclosure, HMRC must reduce the standard percentage to one that reflects the quality of the disclosure.
(2) But the standard percentage may not be reduced to a percentage that is below the minimum shown for it—

(*a*) in the case of a prompted disclosure, in column 2 of the Table, and
(*b*) in the case of an unprompted disclosure, in column 3 of the Table.

Standard %	*Minimum % for prompted disclosure*	*Minimum % for unprompted disclosure*
30%	15%	0%
37.5%	18.75%	0%
45%	22.5%	0%
60%	30%	0%
70%	45%	30%
87.5%	53.75%	35%
100%	60%	40%
105%	62.5%	40%
125%	72.5%	50%
140%	80%	50%
150%	85%	55%
200%	110%	70%][1]

Amendments—[1] Paragraph 10A inserted by FA 2016 s 163, Sch 21 paras 1, 4 with effect, by virtue of SI 2017/259 regs 2, 3—
– for inheritance tax purposes, in relation to transfers of value made on or after 1 April 2017; and
– for income tax and capital gains tax purposes, in relation to any tax year commencing on or after 6 April 2016.

Special reduction

11—(1) If they think it right because of special circumstances, HMRC may reduce a penalty under paragraph 1[, 1A][1] or 2.
(2) In sub-paragraph (1) "special circumstances" does not include—

(*a*) ability to pay, or
(*b*) the fact that a potential loss of revenue from one taxpayer is balanced by a potential overpayment by another.

(3) In sub-paragraph (1) the reference to reducing a penalty includes a reference to—

(*a*) staying a penalty, and
(*b*) agreeing a compromise in relation to proceedings for a penalty.

HMRC Manuals—Compliance Handbook Manual, CH82490 (calculating the penalty: guidance regarding special reduction).
Amendments—[1] In sub-para (1) reference inserted, by FA 2008 s 122, Sch 40 paras 1, 10 with effect from 1 April 2009 (by virtue of SI 2009/571 art 2).

Interaction with other penalties [and late payment surcharges]

12—(1) The final entry in the Table in paragraph 1 excludes a document in respect of which a penalty is payable under section 98 of TMA 1970 (special returns).
(2) The amount of a penalty for which P is liable under paragraph 1 or 2 in respect of a document relating to a tax period shall be reduced by the amount of any other penalty [incurred by P, or any surcharge for late payment of tax imposed on P, if the amount of the penalty or surcharge is determined by reference to the same tax liability.][1]
[(2A) In sub-paragraph (2) "any other penalty" does not include a penalty under Part 4 of FA 2014 (penalty where corrective action not taken after follower notice etc).][3] [or Schedule 22 to FA 2016 (asset-based penalty)][4]
(3) In the application of section 97A of TMA 1970 (multiple penalties) no account shall be taken of a penalty under paragraph 1 or 2.

[(4) Where penalties are imposed under paragraphs 1 and 1A in respect of the same inaccuracy, the aggregate of the amounts of the penalties must not exceed the relevant percentage of the potential lost revenue.

(5) The relevant percentage is—

[(*za*) if the penalty imposed under paragraph 1 is for an inaccuracy in category 0, 100%,][5]

(*a*) if the penalty imposed under paragraph 1 is for an inaccuracy in category 1, [125%][5],

(*b*) if the penalty imposed under paragraph 1 is for an inaccuracy in category 2, 150%, and

(*c*) if the penalty imposed under paragraph 1 is for an inaccuracy in category 3, 200%.][2]

HMRC Manuals—Compliance Handbook Manual, CH84960 (interaction with other penalties: penalties for inaccurate documents other than returns).

CH84970–84972 (more than one penalty/surcharge on the same tax with examples).

Amendments—[1] In sub-para (2), words substituted, and words inserted at end of heading, by FA 2008 s 122, Sch 40 paras 1, 11 with effect from 1 April 2009 (by virtue of SI 2009/571 art 2).

[2] Sub-paras (4), (5) substituted for previous sub-para (4) by FA 2010 s 35 Sch 10 paras 1, 4 with effect from 6 April 2011 (by virtue of SI 2011/975 art 2(1)). Note that these changes do not have effect in relation to documents given to HMRC, and assessments issued by HMRC, in relation to a tax period commencing on or before 5 April 2011 (SI 2011/975 art 3).

[3] Sub-para (2A) inserted by FA 2014 s 233, Sch 33 para 3 with effect from 17 July 2014.

[4] Words in sub-para (2A) inserted by FA 2016 Sch 22 para 20 with effect from a date to be appointed.

[5] Sub-para (5)(*za*) inserted, and in sub-para (5)(*a*), figure "125%" substituted for "100%", by FA 2015 s 120, Sch 20 paras 1, 6 with effect —

– for inheritance tax purposes, in relation to transfers of value (within the meaning of IHTA 1984 s 3) made on or after that day; and

– for income tax and capital gains tax purposes, in relation to any tax year commencing on or after 6 April 2016.

PART 3
PROCEDURE

Assessment

13—(1) [Where a person][1] becomes liable for a penalty under paragraph 1[, 1A][1] or 2 HMRC shall—

(*a*) assess the penalty,

(*b*) [notify the person][1], and

(*c*) state in the notice a tax period in respect of which the penalty is assessed [(subject to sub-paragraph (1ZB))][3].

[(1ZA) Sub-paragraph (1ZB) applies where—

(*a*) a person is at any time liable for two or more penalties relating to PAYE returns, or for two or more penalties relating to CIS returns, [or for two or more penalties relating to apprenticeship levy returns,][4] and

(*b*) the penalties ("the relevant penalties") are assessed in respect of more than one tax period ("the relevant tax periods").

(1ZB) A notice under sub-paragraph (1) in respect of any of the relevant penalties may, instead of stating the tax period in respect of which the penalty is assessed, state the tax year or the part of a tax year to which the penalty relates.

(1ZC) For that purpose, a relevant penalty relates to the tax year or the part of a tax year in which the relevant tax periods fall.

(1ZD) For the purposes of sub-paragraph (1ZA)—

"a PAYE return" means a return for the purposes of PAYE regulations;

"a CIS return" means a return for the purposes of regulations under section 70(1)(*a*) of FA 2004 in connection with deductions on account of tax under the Construction Industry Scheme.][3]

["an apprenticeship levy return" means a return under regulations under section 105 of FA 2016;][4]

[(1A) A penalty under paragraph 1, 1A or 2 must be paid before the end of the period of 30 days beginning with the day on which notification of the penalty is issued.][1]

(2) An assessment—

(*a*) shall be treated for procedural purposes in the same way as an assessment to tax (except in respect of a matter expressly provided for by this Act),

(*b*) may be enforced as if it were an assessment to tax, and

(*c*) may be combined with an assessment to tax.

(3) An assessment of a penalty under paragraph 1[or 1A][1] must be made [before the end of the][1] period of 12 months beginning with—

(*a*) the end of the appeal period for the decision correcting the inaccuracy, or

(*b*) if there is no assessment [to the tax concerned][1] within paragraph (*a*), the date on which the inaccuracy is corrected.

(4) An assessment of a penalty under paragraph 2 must be made [before the end of the period of 12 months beginning with—

(*a*) the end of the appeal period for the assessment of tax which corrected the understatement, or

(*b*) if there is no assessment within paragraph (*a*), the date on which the understatement is corrected.][1]

(5) For the purpose of sub-paragraphs (3) and (4) a reference to an appeal period is a reference to the period during which—

(*a*) an appeal could be brought, or

(*b*) an appeal that has been brought has not been determined or withdrawn.

(6) Subject to sub-paragraphs (3) and (4), a supplementary assessment may be made in respect of a penalty if an earlier assessment operated by reference to an underestimate of potential lost revenue.

[(7) In this Part of this Schedule references to an assessment to tax, in relation to inheritance tax and stamp duty reserve tax, are to a determination.][2]

HMRC Manuals—Compliance Handbook Manual, CH83020–83030 (processing the penalty: penalty assessments and what they must include).

CH83040 (when you should assess a penalty).

CH83050 (supplementary penalties).

CH83060 (enforcement of penalties).

Amendments—[1] In sub-para (1), words substituted and words inserted, sub-para (1A) inserted, in sub-para (3), words inserted and words substituted , and in sub-para (4), words substituted, by FA 2008 s 122, Sch 40 paras 1, 12 with effect from 1 April 2009 (by virtue of SI 2009/571 art 2).

[2] Sub-s (7) inserted by FA 2009 s 109, Sch 57 para 5 with effect from 21 July 2009.

[3] Words in sub-para (1)(*c*) inserted, and sub-paras (1ZA)–(1ZD) inserted, by FA 2013 s 230, Sch 50 para 1 with effect in relation to any assessment of a penalty under this Schedule made on or after 17 July 2013.

[4] In sub-para (1ZA), words inserted, and in sub-para (1ZD), entry inserted by FA 2016 s 113(1), (3) with effect from 6 April 2017 (by virtue of SI 2017/355).

Suspension

14—(1) HMRC may suspend all or part of a penalty for a careless inaccuracy under paragraph 1 by notice in writing to P.

(2) A notice must specify—

(*a*) what part of the penalty is to be suspended,

(*b*) a period of suspension not exceeding two years, and

(*c*) conditions of suspension to be complied with by P.

(3) HMRC may suspend all or part of a penalty only if compliance with a condition of suspension would help P to avoid becoming liable to further penalties under paragraph 1 for careless inaccuracy.

(4) A condition of suspension may specify—

(*a*) action to be taken, and

(*b*) a period within which it must be taken.

(5) On the expiry of the period of suspension—

(*a*) if P satisfies HMRC that the conditions of suspension have been complied with, the suspended penalty or part is cancelled, and

(*b*) otherwise, the suspended penalty or part becomes payable.

(6) If, during the period of suspension of all or part of a penalty under paragraph 1, P becomes liable for another penalty under that paragraph, the suspended penalty or part becomes payable.

HMRC Manuals—Compliance Handbook Manual, CH83110–83120 (suspension of a penalty).

Appeal

15—(1) [A person may][1] appeal against a decision of HMRC that a penalty is payable [by the person][1].

(2) [A person may][1] appeal against a decision of HMRC as to the amount of a penalty payable [by the person][1].

(3) [A person may][1] appeal against a decision of HMRC not to suspend a penalty payable [by the person][1].

(4) [A person may][1] appeal against a decision of HMRC setting conditions of suspension of a penalty payable [by the person][1].

HMRC Manuals—Compliance Handbook Manual, CH84010–84020 (appeals against a penalty: types of appeal and entitlement to appeal).

Amendments—[1] Words substituted by FA 2008 s 122, Sch 40 paras 1, 13 with effect from 1 April 2009 (by virtue of SI 2009/571 art 2).

[**16**—(1) An appeal under this Part of this Schedule shall be treated in the same way as an appeal against an assessment to the tax concerned (including by the application of any provision about bringing the appeal by notice to HMRC, about HMRC review of the decision or about determination of the appeal by the First-tier Tribunal or Upper Tribunal).

[(2) Sub-paragraph (1) does not apply—

(*a*) so as to require P to pay a penalty before an appeal against the assessment of the penalty is determined, or (*b*) in respect of any other matter expressly provided for by this Act.][2]][1]

HMRC Manuals—Compliance Handbook Manual, CH84070 (appeals against a penalty: which Tribunal will hear the appeal and procedures).

Amendments—[1] Paragraph 16 substituted by the Transfer of Tribunal Functions and Revenue and Customs Appeals Order, SI 2009/56 art 3, Sch 1 para 466 with effect from 1 April 2009. The previous substitution made by FA 2008 therefore effectively never took place.

[2] Sub-para (2) substituted by FA 2009 s 109, Sch 57 para 6 with effect from 21 July 2009.

17—(1) On an appeal under paragraph 15(1) the . . . [1] tribunal may affirm or cancel HMRC's decision.

(2) On an appeal under paragraph 15(2) the . . . [1] tribunal may—

(*a*) affirm HMRC's decision, or

(*b*) substitute for HMRC's decision another decision that HMRC had power to make.

(3) If the . . . [1] tribunal substitutes its decision for HMRC's, the . . . [1] tribunal may rely on paragraph 11—

(*a*) to the same extent as HMRC (which may mean applying the same percentage reduction as HMRC to a different starting point), or

(*b*) to a different extent, but only if the . . . [1] tribunal thinks that HMRC's decision in respect of the application of paragraph 11 was flawed.

(4) On an appeal under paragraph 15(3)—

(*a*) the . . . [1] tribunal may order HMRC to suspend the penalty only if it thinks that HMRC's decision not to suspend was flawed, and

(*b*) if the . . . [1] tribunal orders HMRC to suspend the penalty—

(i) P may appeal [1] against a provision of the notice of suspension, and

(ii) the . . . [1] tribunal may order HMRC to amend the notice.

(5) On an appeal under paragraph 15(4) the . . . [1] tribunal—

(*a*) may affirm the conditions of suspension, or

(*b*) may vary the conditions of suspension, but only if the . . . [1] tribunal thinks that HMRC's decision in respect of the conditions was flawed.

[(5A) In this paragraph "tribunal" means the First-tier Tribunal or Upper Tribunal (as appropriate by virtue of paragraph 16(1)).][1]

(6) In sub-paragraphs (3)(*b*), (4)(*a*) and (5)(*b*) "flawed" means flawed when considered in the light of the principles applicable in proceedings for judicial review.

(7) Paragraph 14 (see in particular paragraph 14(3)) is subject to the possibility of an order under this paragraph.

HMRC Manuals—Compliance Handbook Manual, CH84030–84040 (appeals against a penalty: appeals against the imposition or amount of a penalty).

CH84050 (appeals against the decision not to suspend a penalty).

CH84060 (appeals against the conditions set for penalty suspension).

CH84080 (flawed decision).

Amendment—[1] In sub-paras (1), (2), (3), (4)(*a*), (4)(*b*) in the first place, (4)(*b*)(ii), (5) in each place, word "appellate" repealed, in para (4)(*b*) (i) words "to the appellate tribunal" repealed; sub-para (5A) inserted by the Transfer of Tribunal Functions and Revenue and Customs Appeals Order, SI 2009/56 art 3, Sch 1 para 467 with effect from 1 April 2009.

PART 4
MISCELLANEOUS

Agency

18—(1) P is liable under paragraph 1(1)(*a*) where a document which contains a careless inaccuracy (within the meaning of paragraph 3) is given to HMRC on P's behalf.

(2) In paragraph 2(1)(*b*) and (2)(*a*) a reference to P includes a reference to a person who acts on P's behalf in relation to tax.

(3) Despite sub-paragraphs (1) and (2), P is not liable to a penalty [under paragraph 1 or 2][1] in respect of anything done or omitted by P's agent where P satisfies HMRC that P took reasonable care to avoid inaccuracy (in relation to paragraph 1) or unreasonable failure (in relation to paragraph 2).

(4) In paragraph 3(1)(*a*) (whether in its application to a document given by P or, by virtue of sub-paragraph (1) above, in its application to a document given on P's behalf) a reference to P includes a reference to a person who acts on P's behalf in relation to tax.

(5) In paragraph 3(2) a reference to P includes a reference to a person who acts on P's behalf in relation to tax.

[(6) Paragraph 3A applies where a document is given to HMRC on behalf of P as it applies where a document is given to HMRC by P (and in paragraph 3B(9) the reference to P includes a person acting on behalf of P).][2]

HMRC Manuals—Compliance Handbook Manual, CH84520–84530 (other penalty issues: agent acting).

CH84540 (reliance on use of an agent to avoid an inaccuracy).

CH84545 (agent acting – inaccuracy attributable to another person).

Amendments—[1] In sub-para (3), words inserted by FA 2008 s 122, Sch 40 paras 1, 15 with effect from 1 April 2009 (by virtue of SI 2009/571 art 2).

[2] Sub-para (6) inserted by F(No 2)A 2017 s 64(1), (3) with effect in relation to any document of a kind listed in the Table in FA 2007 Sch 24 para 1 which is given to HMRC on or after 16 November 2017 and which relates to a tax period beginning on or after 6 April 2017 and ending on or after 16 November 2017. "Tax period", and the reference to giving a document to HMRC have the same meaning as in FA 2007 Sch 24 para 28 (F(No 2)A 2017 s 64(6)).

Companies: officers' liability

19—(1) Where a penalty under paragraph 1 is payable by a company for a deliberate inaccuracy which was attributable to an officer [of the company, the officer is liable to pay such portion of the penalty (which may be 100%) as HMRC][1] may specify by written notice to the officer.

(2) Sub-paragraph (1) does not allow HMRC to recover more than 100% of a penalty.

(3) In the application of sub-paragraph (1) to a body corporate [other than a limited liability partnership][2] "officer" means—

(*a*) a director (including a shadow director within the meaning of section 251 of the Companies Act 2006 (c 46)), . . . [2]

[(*aa*) a manager, and][2]

(*b*) a secretary.

[(3A) In the application of sub-paragraph (1) to a limited liability partnership, "officer" means a member.][2]

(4) In the application of sub-paragraph (1) in any other case "officer" means—

(*a*) a director,

(*b*) a manager,

(*c*) a secretary, and

(*d*) any other person managing or purporting to manage any of the company's affairs.

[(5) Where HMRC have specified a portion of a penalty in a notice given to an officer under sub-paragraph (1)—

(*a*) paragraph 11 applies to the specified portion as to a penalty,

(*b*) the officer must pay the specified portion before the end of the period of 30 days beginning with the day on which the notice is given,

(*c*) paragraph 13(2), (3) and (5) apply as if the notice were an assessment of a penalty,

(*d*) a further notice may be given in respect of a portion of any additional amount assessed in a supplementary assessment in respect of the penalty under paragraph 13(6),

(*e*) paragraphs 15(1) and (2), 16 and 17(1) to (3) and (6) apply as if HMRC had decided that a penalty of the amount of the specified portion is payable by the officer, and

(*f*) paragraph 21 applies as if the officer were liable to a penalty.][1]

[(6) In this paragraph "company" means any body corporate or unincorporated association, but does not include a partnership, a local authority or a local authority association.][2]

HMRC Manuals—Compliance Handbook Manual, CH84610 (company penalties: officer of a company liable to a penalty).
CH84611 (deliberate action by officer of the company).
CH84620 (what is a company).
CH84625 (who is an officer of the company).
CH84630 (notice of liability).
CH84640 (amount of officer's liability).
CH84650 (personal gain),
CH84660 (insolvency or imminent insolvency).

Amendments—[1] In sub-para (1), words substituted, and sub-para (5) substituted, by FA 2008 s 122, Sch 40 paras 1, 16 with effect from 1 April 2009 (by virtue of SI 2009/571 art 2).

[2] In sub-para (3) words inserted; word "or" repealed and para (*aa*) inserted; sub-paras (3A), (6) inserted, by FA 2009 s 109, Sch 57 para 7 with effect from 21 July 2009.

Partnerships

20—(1) This paragraph applies where P is liable to a penalty under paragraph 1 for an inaccuracy in or in connection with a partnership return.

(2) Where the inaccuracy affects the amount of tax due or payable by a partner of P, the partner is also liable to a penalty ("a partner's penalty").

(3) Paragraphs 4 to 13 and 19 shall apply in relation to a partner's penalty (for which purpose a reference to P shall be taken as a reference to the partner).

(4) Potential lost revenue shall be calculated separately for the purpose of P's penalty and any partner's penalty, by reference to the proportions of any tax liability that would be borne by each partner.

(5) Paragraph 14 shall apply jointly to P's penalty and any partner's penalties.

(6) P may bring an appeal under paragraph 15 in respect of a partner's penalty (in addition to any appeal that P may bring in connection with the penalty for which P is liable).

HMRC Manuals—Compliance Handbook Manual, CH84720 (partnership penalties: partnerships and self assessment).
CH84730 (liable partners).
CH84740–84741 (calculating potential lost revenue, with example for partnerships).
CH84750–84760 (suspended penalties and appeals against penalties).

Double jeopardy

21 [A person is][1] not liable to a penalty under paragraph 1[, 1A][1] or 2 in respect of an inaccuracy or failure in respect of which [the person has][1] been convicted of an offence.

HMRC Manuals—Compliance Handbook Manual, CH84900 (partnership penalties: double jeopardy).
Amendments—[1] Words substituted and reference inserted, by FA 2008 s 122, Sch 40 paras 1, 17 with effect from 1 April 2009 (by virtue of SI 2009/571 art 2).

[21ZA (1) A person is not liable to a penalty under paragraph 1 in respect of an inaccuracy if—

(*a*) the inaccuracy involves a claim by the person to exercise or rely on a VAT right (in relation to a supply) that has been denied or refused by HMRC as mentioned in subsection (4) of section 69C of VATA 1994, and

(*b*) the person has been assessed to a penalty under that section (and the assessment has not been successfully appealed against or withdrawn).

(2) In sub-paragraph (1)(*a*) "VAT right" has the same meaning as in section 69C of VATA 1994.][1]

Amendments—[1] Paragraph 21ZA inserted by F(No 2)A 2017 s 68(1), (6) with effect from 16 November 2017.

PART 5
GENERAL

[Classification of territories

21A—(1) A category 1 territory is a territory designated as a category 1 territory by order made by the Treasury.

(2) A category 2 territory is a territory that is neither—

(*a*) a category 1 territory, nor

(*b*) a category 3 territory.

(3) A category 3 territory is a territory designated as a category 3 territory by order made by the Treasury.

(4) In considering how to classify a territory for the purposes of this paragraph, the Treasury must have regard to—

(*a*) the existence of any arrangements between the UK and that territory for the exchange of information for tax enforcement purposes,

(*b*) the quality of any such arrangements (in particular, whether they provide for information to be exchanged automatically or on request), . . . [2]

(*c*) the benefit that the UK would be likely to obtain from receiving information from that territory, were such arrangements to exist with it,

(*d*) the existence of any other arrangements between the UK and that territory for co-operation in the area of taxation, and

(*e*) the quality of any such other arrangements (in particular, the extent to which the co-operation provided for in them assists or is likely to assist in the protection of revenue raised from taxation in the UK).][2]

(5) An order under this paragraph is to be made by statutory instrument.

(6) Subject to sub-paragraph (7), an instrument containing an order under this paragraph is subject to annulment in pursuance of a resolution of the House of Commons.

(7) If the order is—

(*a*) the first order to be made under sub-paragraph (1), or

(*b*) the first order to be made under sub-paragraph (3),

it may not be made unless a draft of the instrument containing it has been laid before, and approved by a resolution of, the House of Commons.

(8) An order under this paragraph does not apply to inaccuracies in a document given to HMRC (or, in a case within paragraph 3(2), inaccuracies discovered by P) before the date on which the order comes into force.][1]

Orders—Penalties, Offshore Income etc. (Designation of Territories) Order, SI 2011/976.
Penalties, Offshore Income etc. (Designation of Territories) (Amendment) Order, SI 2013/1618.

Amendments—[1] Paras 21A, 21B inserted by FA 2010 s 35 Sch 10 paras 1, 5 with effect from 6 April 2011 (by virtue of SI 2011/975 art 2(1)). Note that these changes do not have effect in relation to documents given to HMRC, and assessments issued by HMRC, in relation to a tax period commencing on or before 5 April 2011 (SI 2011/975 art 3).
[2] Word "and" at the end of sub-para (4)(*b*) repealed, and sub-para (4)(*d*), (*e*) inserted, by FA 2012 s 219 with effect from 17 July 2012.

Prospective amendments—Sub-para (A1) to be inserted before sub-para (1), and sub-paras (2), (7) to be substituted, by FA 2015 s 120, Sch 20 paras 1, 7 with effect from a day to be appointed. Sub-para (A1) as inserted to read as follows—

"(A1) A category 0 territory is a territory designated as a category 0 territory by order made by the Treasury.".

Sub-para (2) as substituted to read as follows—

"(2) A category 2 territory is a territory that is not any of the following—

(a) a category 0 territory;

(b) a category 1 territory;

(c) a category 3 territory.".

Sub-para (7) as substituted to read as follows—

"(7) An instrument containing (whether alone or with other provisions) the first order to be made under sub-paragraph (A1) may not be made unless a draft of the instrument has been laid before, and approved by a resolution of, the House of Commons.".

[Location of assets etc

21B—(1) The Treasury may by regulations make provision for determining for the purposes of paragraph 4A where—

(*a*) a source of income is located,

(*b*) an asset is situated or held, or

(*c*) activities are wholly or mainly carried on.

[(1A) The Treasury may by regulations make provision for determining for the purposes of paragraph 4AA where—

(*a*) income is received or transferred,

(*b*) the proceeds of a disposal are received or transferred, or

(*c*) assets are transferred.][2]

(2) Different provision may be made for different cases and for income tax[, capital gains tax and inheritance tax][2].

(3) Regulations under this paragraph are to be made by statutory instrument.

(4) An instrument containing regulations under this paragraph is subject to annulment in pursuance of a resolution of the House of Commons.][1]

Amendments—[1] Paras 21A, 21B inserted by FA 2010 s 35 Sch 10 paras 1, 5 with effect from 6 April 2011 (by virtue of SI 2011/975 art 2(1)). Note that these changes do not have effect in relation to documents given to HMRC, and assessments issued by HMRC, in relation to a tax period commencing on or before 5 April 2011 (SI 2011/975 art 3).

[2] Sub-para (1A) inserted, and in sub-para (2), words substituted by FA 2015 s 120, Sch 20 paras 1, 8 with effect from 1 April 2016 (by virtue of SI 2016/456 art 3) in relation to documents given to HMRC relating to—

– for the purposes of inheritance tax, a transfer of value made on or after that date; and

– for the purposes of income tax and capital gains tax, a tax year commencing on or after 6 April 2016.

[Treatment of certain payments on account of tax

21C In paragraphs 1(2) and 5 references to "tax" are to be interpreted as if amounts payable under section 59AA(2) of TMA 1970 (non-resident CGT disposals: payments on account of capital gains tax [and amounts payable on account of apprenticeship levy][2]) were tax.][1]

Amendments—[1] Paragraph 21C inserted by FA 2015 s 37, Sch 7 para 56(1), (3) with effect in relation to disposals made on or after 6 April 2015.

[2] Words inserted by FA 2016 s 113(1), (4) with effect from 6 April 2017 (by virtue of SI 2017/355).

Interpretation

22 Paragraphs 23 to [27][1] apply for the construction of this Schedule.

Amendments—[1] Reference substituted by FA 2008 s 122, Sch 40 paras 1, 18 with effect from 1 April 2009 (by virtue of SI 2009/571 art 2).

23 HMRC means Her Majesty's Revenue and Customs.

[23A "Tax", without more, includes duty.][1]

Amendments—[1] Paragraph 23A inserted by FA 2008 s 122, Sch 40 paras 1, 19 with effect from 1 April 2009 (by virtue of SI 2009/571 art 2).

[23B "UK" means the United Kingdom, including the territorial sea of the United Kingdom.][1]

Amendments—[1] This para inserted by FA 2010 s 35 Sch 10 paras 1, 6 with effect from 6 April 2011 (by virtue of SI 2011/975 art 2(1)). Note that these changes do not have effect in relation to documents given to HMRC, and assessments issued by HMRC, in relation to a tax period commencing on or before 5 April 2011 (SI 2011/975 art 3).

24 An expression used in relation to income tax has the same meaning as in the Income Tax Acts.

25 An expression used in relation to corporation tax has the same meaning as in the Corporation Tax Acts.

26 An expression used in relation to capital gains tax has the same meaning as in the enactments relating to that tax.

27 An expression used in relation to VAT has the same meaning as in VATA 1994.

28 In this Schedule—

(*a*) a reference to corporation tax includes a reference to tax or duty which by virtue of an enactment is assessable or chargeable as if it were corporation tax,

(*b*) a reference to tax includes a reference to construction industry deductions under Chapter 3 of Part 3 of FA 2004,

(*c*) "direct tax" means—

(i) income tax,

(ii) capital gains tax, . . . [1]

(iii) corporation tax, [and

(iv) petroleum revenue tax,][1]

(*d*) a reference to understating liability to VAT includes a reference to overstating entitlement to a VAT credit,

[(*da*) *references to an assessment to tax, in relation to inheritance tax, means a determination,*][1,3]

(*e*) a reference to a loss includes a reference to a charge, expense, deficit and any other amount which may be available for, or relied on to claim, a deduction or relief,

(*f*) a reference to repayment of tax includes a reference to allowing a credit [against tax or to a payment of a corporation tax credit][1],

[(*fa*) "corporation tax credit" means—

(i) an R&D tax credit under [Chapter 2 or 7 of Part 13 of CTA 2009][2],

[(ia) an R&D expenditure credit under Chapter 6A of Part 3 of CTA 2009,][4]

(ii) a land remediation tax credit or life assurance company tax credit under [Chapter 3 or 4 respectively of Part 14 of CTA 2009][2],

(iii) *a tax credit under Schedule 13 to FA 2002 (vaccine research etc),*[2]

(iv) a film tax credit under [Chapter 3 of Part 15 of CTA 2009][2], . . . [5]

[(iva) a television tax credit under Chapter 3 of Part 15A of that Act,

(ivb) a video game tax credit under Chapter 3 of Part 15B of that Act, . . . [6]][5]

[(ivc) a theatre tax credit under section 1217K of that Act, . . . [7]][6]

[(ivd) an orchestra tax credit under Chapter 3 of Part 15D of that Act, . . . [8]][7]

[(ive) a museums and galleries exhibition tax credit under Chapter 3 of Part 15E of that Act, or][8]

(v) a first-year tax credit under Schedule A1 to CAA 2001,][1]

(*g*) "tax period" means a tax year, accounting period or other period in respect of which tax is charged,

(*h*) a reference to giving a document to HMRC includes a reference to communicating information to HMRC in any form and by any method (whether by post, fax, email, telephone or otherwise),

(*i*) a reference to giving a document to HMRC includes a reference to making a statement or declaration in a document,

(*j*) a reference to making a return or doing anything in relation to a return includes a reference to amending a return or doing anything in relation to an amended return, and

(*k*) a reference to action includes a reference to omission.

HMRC Manuals—Compliance Handbook Manual, CH81050 (penalties for inaccuracies: what is meant by "giving a document").

CH81071 (what is a "repayment of tax").

Amendments—[1] In sub-para (*c*), word "and" after para (ii) repealed, after para (iii) word "and" inserted, and para (iv) inserted, sub-paras (*da*), (*fa*) inserted, and in sub-para (*f*), words inserted, by FA 2008 s 122, Sch 40 para 20 with effect from 1 April 2009 (by virtue of SI 2009/571 art 2).

[2] In sub-para (*fa*)(i), (ii), (iv), words substituted and sub-para (*fa*)(iii) repealed by CTA 2009 ss 1322, 1326, Sch 1 paras 722, 727, Sch 3 Part 1. CTA 2009 applies for accounting periods ending on or after 1 April 2009 (for corporation tax purposes) and for tax years 2009–10 onwards (for income and capital gains tax purposes).

[3] Sub-para (*da*) repealed by FA 2009 s 109, Sch 57 para 8 with effect from 21 July 2009.

[4] Sub-para (*fa*)(ia) inserted by FA 2013 s 35, Sch 15 para 8 with effect in relation to expenditure incurred on or after 1 April 2013.

[5] In sub-para (*fa*), word "or" at end of para (iv) repealed and paras (iva), (ivb) inserted, by FA 2013 s 36, Sch 18 para 7. The amendments made by Sch 18 come into force as follows—

– so far as relating to television tax relief on 19 July 2013 (by virtue of SI 2013/1817 art 2(2)); and

– so far as relating to video game development, with effect from 1 April 2014 (by virtue of SI 2014/1962 art 2(3)).

Those amendments have effect in relation to accounting periods beginning on or after the "relevant day", subject to transitional provisions. The "Relevant day" is defined as follows—.

– in the case of amendments relating to CTA 2009 Part 15A (as inserted by FA 2013 Sch 16), 1 April 2013, and

– in the case of amendments relating to CTA 2009 Part 15B (as inserted by FA 2013 Sch 17), 1 April 2014 (by virtue of SI 2014/1962 art 2(3)).).

See FA 2013 Sch 18 paras 22, 23 for commencement provisions.

6 In sub-para (*fa*), word "or" at the end of para (ivb) repealed, and para (ivc) inserted, by FA 2014 s 36, Sch 4 para 8 with effect in relation to accounting periods beginning on or after 1 September 2014, subject to transitional provisions for accounting periods straddling that date (FA 2014 Sch 4 para 17). SI 2014/2228 reg 2 provides that the amendments made by FA 2014 Sch 4 come into force on 22 August 2014 (other than the power to make regulations under Sch 4 para 16(1) which came into force on 17 July 2014).

7 In sub-para (*fa*), word "or" at the end of para (ivc) repealed, and para (ivd) inserted, by FA 2016 s 54, Sch 8 para 8 with effect in relation to accounting periods beginning on or after 1 April 2016, subject to transitional provisions for accounting periods straddling that date (FA 2016 Sch 8 para 17). Note that any power conferred on the Treasury by FA 2016 Sch 8 to make regulations came into force on 15 September 2016 (FA 2016 Sch 8 para 16).

8 In sub-para (*fa*), word "or" at end of para (ivd) repealed, and para (ive) inserted, by F(No 2)A 2017 s 21, Sch 6 para 8 with effect in relation to accounting periods beginning on or after 1 April 2017.

Consequential amendments

29 The following provisions are omitted—

(*a*) (*repeals* TMA 1970 ss 95, 95A, 97, 98A(4))

(*b*) (*repeals* TMA 1970 ss 100A(1), 103(2))

(*c*) (*repeals*FA 1998 Sch 18 paras 20, 89)

(*d*) (*repeals* VATA 1994 ss 60, 61, 63, 64)

Note—Notwithstanding sub-para (*d*), VATA 1994 ss 60, 61 shall continue to have effect with respect to conduct involving dishonesty which does not relate to an inaccuracy in a document or a failure to notify HMRC of an under-assessment by HMRC (SI 2009/571 art 7).

30 In [paragraphs 7 and 7B][1] of Schedule 1 to the Social Security Contributions and Benefits Act 1992 (c 4) (penalties) a reference to a provision of TMA 1970 shall be construed as a reference to this Schedule so far as is necessary to preserve its effect.

Amendments—[1] Words substituted by FA 2009 s 109, Sch 57 para 9 with effect from 21 July 2009.

31 In [paragraphs 7 and 7B][1] of Schedule 1 to the Social Security Contributions and Benefits (Northern Ireland) Act 1992 (c 7) (penalties) a reference to a provision of TMA 1970 shall be construed as a reference to this Schedule so far as is necessary to preserve its effect.

Amendments—[1] Words substituted by FA 2009 s 109, Sch 57 para 9 with effect from 21 July 2009.

FINANCE ACT 2008

(2008 Chapter 9)

An Act to Grant certain duties, to alter other duties, and to amend the law relating to the National Debt and the Public Revenue, and to make further provision in connection with finance.

[21 July 2008]

PART 1
CHARGES, RATES, ALLOWANCES, RELIEFS ETC

Inheritance tax

10 Transfer of unused nil-rate band etc

Schedule 4 contains provisions about the transfer of unused nil-rate band between spouses and civil partners for the purposes of the charge to inheritance tax etc.

PART 4
PENSIONS

91 Inheritance etc of tax-relieved pension savings

Schedule 28 contains provision about the inheritance etc of tax-relieved pension savings.

92 Pension schemes: further provision

Schedule 29 contains further provision about pension schemes.

PART 7
ADMINISTRATION

CHAPTER 1
INFORMATION ETC

New information etc powers

113 Information and inspection powers

(1) Schedule 36 contains provision about the powers of officers of Revenue and Customs to obtain information and to inspect businesses.

(2) That Schedule comes into force on such day as the Treasury may by order made by statutory instrument appoint.
(3) An order under subsection (2) may contain transitional provision and savings.

Orders—Finance Act 2008, Schedule 36 (Appointed Day and Savings) Order, SI 2009/404.

PART 8
MISCELLANEOUS
Inheritance tax

140 Charge on termination of interest in possession where new interest acquired
(1) (*substitutes* IHTA 1984 s 53(2A))
(2) The amendment made by subsection (1) is treated as having come into force on 22 March 2006 (so that paragraph 14(3) of Schedule 20 to FA 2006 is treated as never having had effect).

141 Interest in possession settlements: extension of transitional period
(1) (*amends* IHTA 1984 ss 49C–49E)
(2) The amendments made by subsection (1) are treated as having come into force on 6 April 2008.

SCHEDULES
SCHEDULE 4
INHERITANCE TAX: TRANSFER OF NIL-RATE BAND ETC
Section 10

Amendments of IHTA 1984

1 IHTA 1984 is amended as follows.

2 (*inserts* IHTA 1984 ss 8A–8C)

3 (*inserts* IHTA 1984 s 147(10))

4—(1) Section 151BA (rates of charge under section 151B) is amended as follows.
(2) (amends IHTA 1984 s 151BA(5))
(3) (inserts IHTA 1984 s 151BA(6), (7))
(4) (inserts IHTA 1984 s 151BA(8)–(12))

Amendments—This para repealed by FA 2011 s 65, Sch 16 para 84(*d*)(i) with effect for the tax year 2011–12 and subsequent tax years, subject to transitional provisions in FA 2011 Sch 16 Pt 3.

5 (*inserts* IHTA 1984 s 239(4)(*aa*))

6 (*amends* IHTA 1984 s 247(2))

7 (*amends* IHTA 1984 s 272)

Amendment of TCGA 1992

8 (*amends* TCGA 1992 s 274)

Commencement

9—(1) The amendments made by paragraphs 2, 3 and 4(4) have effect in relation to cases where the survivor's death occurs on or after 9 October 2007.
(2) The amendments made by paragraphs 4(2) and (3) have effect in relation to deaths, cases where scheme administrators become aware of deaths and cessations of dependency occurring on or after 6 April 2008.
(3) The amendments made by paragraphs 5 and 7 are to be treated as having come into force on 9 October 2007.
(4) The amendment made by paragraph 8 has effect in relation to any ascertainment of value made on or after 6 April 2008.

Amendments—Sub-para(2) repealed by FA 2011 s 65, Sch 16 para 84(*d*)(i) with effect for the tax year 2011–12 and subsequent tax years, subject to transitional provisions in FA 2011 Sch 16 Pt 3.

Modifications for cases where deceased person died before 25 July 1986

10—(1) Section 8A of IHTA 1984 (as inserted by paragraph 2) has effect in relation to cases where the deceased person died before 25 July 1986 (and the survivor dies on or after 9 October 2007) subject as follows.
(2) Where the deceased person died on or after 1 January 1985—
(*a*) the references in subsection (2) to a chargeable transfer made under section 4 of IHTA 1984 is to a chargeable transfer made under section 4 of CTTA 1984, and

(*b*) the reference in subsection (4) to the nil-rate band maximum is to the amount shown in the second column of the first row, and the first column of the second row, of the First Table in Schedule 1 to that Act.

(3) Where the deceased person died on or after 13 March 1975 and before 1 January 1985—

(*a*) the references in subsection (2) to a chargeable transfer made under section 4 of IHTA 1984 is to a chargeable transfer made under section 22 of FA 1975, and

(*b*) the reference in subsection (4) to the nil-rate band maximum is to the amount shown in the second column of the first row, and in the first column of the second row, of the First Table in section 37 of that Act.

(4) Where the deceased person died on or after 16 April 1969 and before 13 March 1975, section 8A applies as if—

(*a*) M were the amount specified in paragraph (*a*) in Part 1 of Schedule 17 to FA 1969 at the time of the deceased person's death,

(*b*) VT were the aggregate principal value of all property comprised in the estate of the deceased person for the purposes of estate duty, and

(*c*) the reference in subsection (4) to the nil-rate band maximum were to the amount mentioned in paragraph (*a*).

(5) Where the deceased person died before 16 April 1969, section 8A applies as if—

(*a*) M were the amount specified as the higher figure in the first line, and the lower figure in the second line, in the first column of the scale in section 17 of FA 1894 at the time of the deceased person's death,

(*b*) VT were the principal value of the estate of the deceased person for the purposes of estate duty, and

(*c*) the reference in subsection (4) to the nil-rate band maximum were to the figure mentioned in paragraph (*a*).

11—(1) Section 8C of IHTA 1984 (as inserted by paragraph 2) has effect in relation to cases where the deceased person died before 25 July 1986 but on or after 13 March 1975 (and the survivor dies on or after 9 October 2007) subject as follows.

(2) Where the deceased person died on or after 1 January 1985—

(*a*) the reference in subsection (1) to sections 32, 32A and 126 of IHTA 1984 includes sections 32, 32A and 126 of CTTA 1984,

(*b*) the reference in that subsection to section 4 of IHTA 1984 is to section 4 of CTTA 1984,

(*c*) the reference in subsection (2) to the nil-rate band maximum includes the amount shown in the second column of the first row, and the first column of the second row, of the First Table in Schedule 1 to that Act,

(*d*) the first reference in subsection (5) to the nil-rate band maximum is to that amount, and

(*e*) the reference in subsection (5) to Schedule 2 to IHTA 1984 includes Schedule 2 to CTTA 1984.

(3) Where the deceased person died on or after 7 April 1976 and before 1 January 1985—

(*a*) the reference in subsection (1) to sections 32, 32A and 126 of IHTA 1984 includes sections 32, 32A and 126 of CTTA 1984, section 78 of FA 1976 and paragraph 2 of Schedule 9 to FA 1975,

(*b*) the reference in that subsection to section 4 of IHTA is to section 22 of FA 1975,

(*c*) the reference in subsection (2) to the nil-rate band maximum includes the amount shown in the second column of the first row, and the first column of the second row, of the First Table in Schedule 1 to CTTA 1984 and the amount shown in the second column of the first row, and in the first column of the second row, of the First Table in section 37 of FA 1975,

(*d*) the first reference in subsection (5) to the nil-rate band maximum is to that amount, and

(*e*) the reference in subsection (5) to Schedule 2 to IHTA 1984 includes Schedule 2 to CTTA 1984, Schedule 15 to FA 1980 and section 62 of FA 1978;

but, if the event occasioning the charge occurred before 27 October 1977, the reference in subsection (4) to the personal nil-rate band maximum is to the amount shown in the second column of the first row, and in the first column of the second row, of the First Table in section 37 of FA 1975 at the time of the deceased person's death.

(4) Where the deceased person died on or after 13 March 1975 and before 7 April 1976—

(*a*) the reference in subsection (1) to sections 32, 32A and 126 of IHTA 1984 includes paragraph 1 of Schedule 5 to that Act, section 126 of CTTA 1984 and paragraph 2 of Schedule 9 to FA 1975,

(*b*) the reference in that subsection to section 4 of IHTA is to section 22 of FA 1975,

(*c*) the reference in subsection (2) to the nil-rate band maximum includes the amount shown in the second column of the first row, and the first column of the second row, of the First Table in Schedule 1 to CTTA 1984 and the amount shown in the second column of the first row, and in the first column of the second row, of the First Table in section 37 of FA 1975, and (*d*) the reference in subsection (4) to the personal nil-rate band maximum is to the amount shown in the second column of the first row, and in the first column of the second row, of the First Table in section 37 of FA 1975 at the time of the deceased person's death.

SCHEDULE 28

INHERITANCE OF TAX-RELIEVED PENSION SAVINGS

Section 91

Amendments of Part 4 of FA 2004

1 Part 4 of FA 2004 (pensions schemes etc) is amended as follows.

2—(1) Section 172 (assignment) is amended as follows.
(2) (*amends* FA 2004 s 172(3))

3—(1) Section 172A (surrender) is amended as follows.
(2) (*inserts* FA 2004 s 172A(1)(*aa*))
(3) (*amends* FA 2004 s 172A(3)(*a*))
(4) (*inserts* FA 2004 s 172A(5)(*ca*))
(5) (*inserts* FA 2004 s 172A(9A))

4—(1) Section 172B (increase in rights of connected person on death) is amended as follows.
(2) (*inserts* FA 2004 s 172B(2)(*aa*))
(3) (*amends* FA 2004 s 172B(3)(*a*), (7)(*b*))
(4) (*amends* FA 2004 s 172B(7))
(5) (*inserts* FA 2004 s 172B(7A), (7B))

5 (*amends* FA 2004 Sch 28 para 16(2))

Amendments of IHTA 1984

6 *IHTA 1984 is amended as follows.*

Amendments—This para repealed by FA 2011 s 65, Sch 16 para 84(*d*)(ii) with effect for the tax year 2011–12 and subsequent tax years, subject to transitional provisions in FA 2011 Sch 16 Pt 3.

***7**—(1) Section 151A (person dying with alternatively secured pension fund) is amended as follows.*
(2) (amends IHTA 1984 s 151A(2))
(3) (amends IHTA 1984 s 151A(4B))

Amendments—This para repealed by FA 2011 s 65, Sch 16 para 84(*d*)(ii) with effect for the tax year 2011–12 and subsequent tax years, subject to transitional provisions in FA 2011 Sch 16 Pt 3.

***8**—(1) Section 151BA (rate or rates of charge under section 151B) is amended as follows.*
(2) (amends IHTA 1984 s 151BA(1))
(3) (repeals IHTA 1984 s 151BA(2))
(4) (amends IHTA 1984 s 151BA(3))

Amendments—This para repealed by FA 2011 s 65, Sch 16 para 84(*d*)(ii) with effect for the tax year 2011–12 and subsequent tax years, subject to transitional provisions in FA 2011 Sch 16 Pt 3.

***9**—(1) Section 151C (dependant dying with alternatively secured pension fund where section 151B does not apply) is amended as follows.*
(2) (amends IHTA 1984 s 151C(3B))
(3) (amends IHTA 1984 s 151C(4))

Amendments—This para repealed by FA 2011 s 65, Sch 16 para 84(*d*)(ii) with effect for the tax year 2011–12 and subsequent tax years, subject to transitional provisions in FA 2011 Sch 16 Pt 3.

10 *(inserted* IHTA 1984 ss 151D, 151E; *repealed* by FA 2011 Sch 16 para 84(*d*)(ii))

11 *(inserted* IHTA 1984 s 210(3); *repealed* by FA 2011 Sch 16 para 84(*d*)(ii))

***12**—(1) Section 216 (delivery of accounts) is amended as follows.*
(2) (amends IHTA 1984 s 216(1)(*bca*))
(3) amends IHTA 1984 s 216(6)(*ac*))
(4) amends IHTA 1984 s 216(7))

Amendments—This para repealed by FA 2011 s 65, Sch 16 para 84(*d*)(ii) with effect for the tax year 2011–12 and subsequent tax years, subject to transitional provisions in FA 2011 Sch 16 Pt 3.

13 *(amended* IHTA 1984 s 226(4); *repealed* by FA 2011 Sch 16 para 84(*d*)(ii))

14 *(amended* IHTA 1984 s 233(1)(*c*); *repealed* by FA 2011 Sch 16 para 84(*d*)(ii))

Commencement

15 (1) The amendments made by paragraph 2 have effect in relation to assignments or agreements to assign made on or after 10 October 2007.
(2) The amendments made by paragraph 3 have effect in relation to surrenders and agreements to surrender made on or after that date.
(3) The amendments made by paragraphs 4, 7(2), 8, 10 and 11 to 14 have effect in relation to deaths occurring on or after 6 April 2008.

SCHEDULE 29

FURTHER PROVISION ABOUT PENSION SCHEMES

Section 92

Authorised member payments

1—(1) Part 4 of FA 2004 (pension schemes etc) is amended as follows.
(2) (*inserts* FA 2004 s 164(2))
(3) (*amends* FA 2004 s 216 table)

Transfer of lifetime annuities and dependants' annuities

2—(1) Schedule 28 to FA 2004 (authorised pensions etc) is amended as follows.
(2) (inserts FA 2004 Sch 28 para 2(2CA))
(3) (inserts FA 2004 Sch 28 para 17(4A))

Amendments—Para 2 repealed by FA 2009 s 75(3)(*b*) with effect from 21 July 2009.

Definition of investment-regulated pension schemes

3—(1) (*repeals* FA 2004 Sch 29A para 2(1)(*b*))
(2) The amendment made by sub-paragraph (1) is treated as having come into force on 6 April 2006.

Benefit crystallisation event 3

4 Part 4 of FA 2004 (pension schemes etc) is amended as follows.

5 (*amends* FA 2004 s 216 table)

6 Schedule 32 (benefit crystallisation events: supplementary) is amended as follows.

7 (*amends* FA 2004 Sch 32 para 10)
8 (*inserts* FA 2004 Sch 32 para 10A)

9—(1) Paragraph 11 (benefit crystallisation event 3: permitted margin) is amended as follows.
(2) (*amends* FA 2004 Sch 32 para 11(6))
(3) (*inserts* FA 2004 Sch 32 para 11(7A), (7B))

10 (*substitutes* FA 2004 Sch 32 para 13(2)–(2G))

11 In consequence of the amendment made by paragraph 7(3), in Schedule 10 to FA 2005, omit paragraph 44.

12—(1) The amendments made by paragraphs 9(2) and (3) come into force on 6 April 2008.
(2) The amendment made by paragraph 10 has effect for the purposes of any benefit crystallisation event 3 occurring on or after 10 October 2007 (including the calculation, for the purposes of such an event, of the amount of XP on any benefit crystallisation event occurring before that date).
(3) Subject to that, the amendments made by paragraphs 4 to 11 are treated as having come into force on 6 April 2006.

Transitional protection of lump sums

13—(1) (*amends* FA 2004 Sch 36 para 34)
(2) The amendments made by sub-paragraph (1) are treated as having come into force on 6 April 2006.

Miscellaneous provision about registered pension schemes

14—(*amends* FA 2004 ss 197, 199(2); ITTOIA 2005 Sch 1 para 648)

15 (*amends* FA 2004 s 215(4)(*a*))

16 *(amended* FA 2004 Sch 34 para 7ZA; *repealed* by FA 2011 s 65, Sch 16 para 84(*d*)(iii))

Employer contributions under exempt approved schemes

17—(1) This paragraph applies in relation to section 592 of ICTA (which before its repeal made provision about exempt approved pension schemes), where that section had effect as amended by the 2004 Order.

(2) Section 592 is to be treated as having had effect as if after subsection (4) (as substituted by the 2004 Order) there had been inserted—

"(4A) No sums other than contributions made by the employer to the pension scheme in respect of an individual—

(*a*) are deductible in computing the amount of the profits of the employer for the purposes of Part 2 of ITTOIA 2005 or Case I or II of Schedule D,

(*b*) are expenses of management for the purposes of section 75, or

(*c*) are to be brought into account at Step 1 in section 76(7),

in connection with the cost of providing benefits under the pension scheme."

(3) But the words "Part 2 of ITTOIA 2005 or" in subsection (4A)(*a*) are to be treated as having had effect only in relation to times in relation to which (by virtue of paragraph 253(3) of Schedule 1 to ITTOIA 2005) they had effect in section 592(4)(*a*).

(4) In this paragraph "the 2004 Order" means the Finance Act 2004, Sections 38 to 45 and Schedule 6 (Consequential Amendment of Enactments No. 2) Order 2004 (SI 2004/3269).

Inheritance tax treatment of non-UK pension schemes

18—(1) IHTA 1984 is amended as follows.

(2) (*amends* IHTA 1984 s 12(2))

(3) (*amends* IHTA 1984 s 58(1)(*d*), (2A)(*b*))

(4) (*amends* IHTA 1984 s 151(2), (4), (5))

(5) (*amends* IHTA 1984 s 152)

(6) (*inserts* IHTA 1984 s 271A)

(7) (*amends* FA 2004 Sch 36 para 56)

(8) The amendments made by this paragraph are treated as having come into force on 6 April 2006.

Application of charges to non-UK pension schemes

19—(1) Schedule 34 to FA 2004 (which applies certain charges to non-UK pension schemes) is amended as follows.

(2) (*amends* FA 2004 Sch 34 para 10(2))

(3) (*amends* FA 2004 Sch 34 para 11(2))

(4) The amendment made by sub-paragraph (2) has effect for the tax year 2008–09 and subsequent tax years.

(5) The amendment made by sub-paragraph (3) has effect—

(*a*) for the tax year 2007–08 in accordance with sub-paragraph (6), and

(*b*) for the tax year 2008–09 and subsequent tax years.

(6) For the tax year 2007–08, for the purposes of paragraph 11(1)(*b*) of Schedule 34 to FA 2004 the appropriate fraction of the contributions mentioned in that paragraph is the aggregate of—

(*a*) the appropriate fraction of so much of those contributions as are paid before 12 March 2008, calculated in accordance with paragraph 11(2) unamended by sub-paragraph (3), and

(*b*) the appropriate fraction of so much of those contributions as are paid on and after that date, calculated in accordance with paragraph 11(2) as amended by sub-paragraph (3).

SCHEDULE 36

INFORMATION AND INSPECTION POWERS

Section 113

Commentary—*Simon's Taxes* **A6.301A**.

Commencement—Finance Act 2008, Schedule 36 (Appointed Day and Savings) Order, SI 2009/404 art 2 (appointed day for the coming into force of Sch 36 is 1 April 2009).

HMRC Manuals—Compliance Handbook Manual, CH275000–285000 (HMRC inspection powers – compliance check).

CH20150–27200 (HMRC information and inspection powers).

Cross-references—See TIOPA 2010 Sch 7A Part 7 (interest restriction returns: HMRC powers to obtain information and documents).

the Small Charitable Donations Regulations, SI 2013/938 reg 5 (application of this Schedule regarding checking a charity's position in relation to a top-up claim or an overpayment for the purposes of small charitable donations).

Education (Postgraduate Master's Degree Loans) Regulations, SI 2016/606 regs 43, 77 (application of this Schedule, with modifications, to checking a person's tax position in relation to loans for postgraduate master's degree courses which begin on or after 1st August 2016).

Savings (Government Contributions) Act 2017 Schs 1, 2 (application of this Schedule to checking a person's tax position in relation to lifetime ISAs and Help-to-save accounts).

Modifications—See F(No 2)A 2017 Sch 16 para 41 (application of this Schedule in relation to penalties for enablers of defeated tax avoidance).

PART 1
POWERS TO OBTAIN INFORMATION AND DOCUMENTS

Power to obtain information and documents from taxpayer

1—(1) An officer of Revenue and Customs may by notice in writing require a person ("the taxpayer")—

(*a*) to provide information, or

(*b*) to produce a document,

if the information or document is reasonably required by the officer for the purpose of checking the taxpayer's tax position.

(2) In this Schedule, "taxpayer notice" means a notice under this paragraph.

Commentary—*Simon's Taxes* **A6.301A**.

Commencement—Finance Act 2008, Schedule 36 (Appointed Day and Savings) Order, SI 2009/404 art 2 (appointed day for the coming into force of Sch 36 is 1 April 2009).

HMRC Manuals—Compliance Handbook Manual, CH23060 and 23080 (HMRC inspection powers: three types of information notice and approval thereof).

CH23520 (HMRC inspection powers: specific rules regarding taxpayer notice).

CH221000–223200 (HMRC inspection powers – how to do a compliance check: taxpayer notice).

CH223400 (tribunal approval).

Cross references—FA 2014 Sch 34 para 10 (failure to comply with a notice under this section triggers threshold condition leading to consideration for a conduct notice).

Power to obtain information and documents from third party

2—(1) An officer of Revenue and Customs may by notice in writing require a person—

(*a*) to provide information, or

(*b*) to produce a document,

if the information or document is reasonably required by the officer for the purpose of checking the tax position of another person whose identity is known to the officer ("the taxpayer").

(2) A third party notice must name the taxpayer to whom it relates, unless the [tribunal][1] has approved the giving of the notice and disapplied this requirement under paragraph 3.

(3) In this Schedule, "third party notice" means a notice under this paragraph.

Commentary—*Simon's Taxes* **A6.301A**.

Commencement—Finance Act 2008, Schedule 36 (Appointed Day and Savings) Order, SI 2009/404 art 2 (appointed day for the coming into force of Sch 36 is 1 April 2009).

HMRC Manuals—Compliance Handbook Manual, CH23060 and 23080 (HMRC inspection powers: three types of information notice and approval thereof).

CH23620 (HMRC inspection powers: specific rules regarding third party notice).

CH225050 (HMRC inspection powers – how to do a compliance check: what is a third party notice).

CH225100 (persons on whom a third party notice can be served).

CH225150 (considerations prior to issue).

CH225200 (restrictions on third party notices).

Cross references—FA 2014 Sch 34 para 10 (failure to comply with a notice under this section triggers threshold condition leading to consideration for a conduct notice).

Amendments—[1] In sub-para (2) word substituted for the words "First-tier Tribunal" by the Transfer of Tribunal Functions and Revenue and Customs Appeals Order, SI 2009/56 art 3, Sch 1 para 471 with effect from 1 April 2009.

Simon's Tax Cases—*R (on the appn of Derrin Brother Properties Ltd and others) R&C Comrs (HSBC Bank plc and another, interested parties)* [2016] EWCA Civ 15, [2016] STC 1081.

Approval etc of taxpayer notices and third party notices

3—(1) An officer of Revenue and Customs may not give a third party notice without—

(*a*) the agreement of the taxpayer, or

(*b*) the approval of the [tribunal][1].

(2) An officer of Revenue and Customs may ask for the approval of the [tribunal][1] to the giving of any taxpayer notice or third party notice (and for the effect of obtaining such approval see paragraphs 29, 30 and 53 (appeals against notices and offence)).

[(2A) An application for approval under this paragraph may be made without notice (except as required under sub-paragraph (3)).][2]

(3) The [tribunal][1] may not approve the giving of a taxpayer notice or third party notice unless—

(*a*) an application for approval is made by, or with the agreement of, an authorised officer of Revenue and Customs,

(*b*) the [tribunal][1] is satisfied that, in the circumstances, the officer giving the notice is justified in doing so,

(*c*) the person to whom the notice is [to be][2] addressed has been told that the information or documents referred to in the notice are required and given a reasonable opportunity to make representations to an officer of Revenue and Customs,

(*d*) the [tribunal][1] has been given a summary of any representations made by that person, and

(*e*) in the case of a third party notice, the taxpayer has been given a summary of the reasons why an officer of Revenue and Customs requires the information and documents.

(4) Paragraphs (*c*) to (*e*) of sub-paragraph (3) do not apply to the extent that the [tribunal][1] is satisfied that taking the action specified in those paragraphs might prejudice the assessment or collection of tax.

(5) Where the [tribunal][1] approves the giving of a third party notice under this paragraph, it may also disapply the requirement to name the taxpayer in the notice if it is satisfied that the officer has reasonable grounds for believing that naming the taxpayer might seriously prejudice the assessment or collection of tax.

Commentary—*Simon's Taxes* **A6.301A**.

Commencement—Finance Act 2008, Schedule 36 (Appointed Day and Savings) Order, SI 2009/404 art 2 (appointed day for the coming into force of Sch 36 is 1 April 2009).

HMRC Manuals—Compliance Handbook Manual, CH23060 and 23080 (HMRC inspection powers: three types of information notice and approval thereof).

CH23520 (HMRC inspection powers: specific rules regarding taxpayer notice).

CH23620 (HMRC inspection powers: specific rules regarding third party notice).

CH24100 (HMRC inspection powers: the Tribunal).

CH24120–24180 (taxpayer and third party notices).

CH25450 (Tribunal approval).

CH225310–225320 (where no approval is required).

CH225410 (where approval is required).

CH225420 (taxpayer agreement).

CH225430–225440 (summary of reasons and reasons not be given).

CH225460 (opportunity letter requirements).

Amendments—[1] Word substituted for the words "First-tier Tribunal" in each place; in sub-para (4) word substituted for the word "Tribunal" by the Transfer of Tribunal Functions and Revenue and Customs Appeals Order, SI 2009/56 art 3, Sch 1 para 471 with effect from 1 April 2009.

[2] Sub-para (2A), and words in sub-para (3)(*c*), inserted, by FA 2009 s 95, Sch 47 para 2 with effect from 21 July 2009.

Simon's Tax Cases—*R (on the appn of Derrin Brother Properties Ltd and others) R&C Comrs (HSBC Bank plc and another, interested parties)* [2016] EWCA Civ 15, [2016] STC 1081.

Copying third party notice to taxpayer

4—(1) An officer of Revenue and Customs who gives a third party notice must give a copy of the notice to the taxpayer to whom it relates, unless the [tribunal][1] has disapplied this requirement.

(2) The [tribunal][1] may not disapply that requirement unless—

(*a*) an application for approval is made by, or with the agreement of, an authorised officer of Revenue and Customs, and

(*b*) the [tribunal][1] is satisfied that the officer has reasonable grounds for believing that giving a copy of the notice to the taxpayer might prejudice the assessment or collection of tax.

Commentary—*Simon's Taxes* **A6.301A**.

Commencement—Finance Act 2008, Schedule 36 (Appointed Day and Savings) Order, SI 2009/404 art 2 (appointed day for the coming into force of Sch 36 is 1 April 2009).

HMRC Manuals—Compliance Handbook Manual, CH23620 (HMRC inspection powers: specific rules regarding third party notice).

CH23640–23660 (HMRC inspection powers: copy of the notice to the named person).

CH225250 (HMRC inspection powers – how to do a compliance check: copying notice to taxpayer).

Amendments—[1] Word substituted for the words "First-tier Tribunal" in each place; in sub-para (2)(*b*) word substituted for the word "Tribunal" by the Transfer of Tribunal Functions and Revenue and Customs Appeals Order, SI 2009/56 art 3, Sch 1 para 471 with effect from 1 April 2009.

Power to obtain information and documents about persons whose identity is not known

5—(1) An authorised officer of Revenue and Customs may by notice in writing require a person—

(*a*) to provide information, or

(*b*) to produce a document,

if the condition in sub-paragraph (2) is met.

(2) That condition is that the information or document is reasonably required by the officer for the purpose of checking the . . . [4] tax position of—

(*a*) a person whose identity is not known to the officer, or (*b*) a class of persons whose individual identities are not known to the officer.

(3) An officer of Revenue and Customs may not give a notice under this paragraph without the approval of the [tribunal][1].

[(3A) An application for approval under this paragraph may be made without notice.][2]

(4) The [tribunal][1] may not [approve the giving of a notice under][2] this paragraph unless it is satisfied that—

(*a*) the notice would meet the condition in sub-paragraph (2),

(*b*) there are reasonable grounds for believing that the person or any of the class of persons to whom the notice relates may have failed or may fail to comply with any provision of [the law (including the law of a territory outside the United Kingdom) relating to tax,][4]][3],

(*c*) any such failure is likely to have led or to lead to serious prejudice to the assessment or collection of . . . [4] tax, and

(*d*) the information or document to which the notice relates is not readily available from another source.

(5) . . .[4]

Commentary—*Simon's Taxes* **A6.301A**.

Commencement—Finance Act 2008, Schedule 36 (Appointed Day and Savings) Order, SI 2009/404 art 2 (appointed day for the coming into force of Sch 36 is 1 April 2009).

HMRC Manuals—Compliance Handbook Manual, CH23900 (HMRC inspection powers: identity unknown notice).
CH24200 (HMRC inspection powers: Tribunal approval of identity unknown notice).
CH227100–227200 (HMRC inspection powers – how to do a compliance check: identity unknown notice).

Cross references—FA 2014 Sch 34 para 10 (failure to comply with a notice under this section triggers threshold condition leading to consideration for a conduct notice).

Amendments—[1] In sub-paras (3), (4) word substituted for the words "First-tier Tribunal" by the Transfer of Tribunal Functions and Revenue and Customs Appeals Order, SI 2009/56 art 3, Sch 1 para 471 with effect from 1 April 2009.

[2] Sub-para (3A) inserted, in sub-para (4) words substituted for words "give its approval for the purpose of", by FA 2009 s 95, Sch 47 para 3 with effect from 21 July 2009.

[3] In sub-para (4)(*b*) words substituted for words ", VATA 1994 or any other enactment relating to value added tax charged in accordance with that Act", by FA 2009 s 96, Sch 48 para 2 with effect from 1 April 2010 (by virtue of SI 2009/3054 art 2.

[4] In sub-paras (2), (4)*c*), word repealed, in sub-para (4)(*b*) words substituted, and sub-para (5) repealed, by FA 2011 s 86(2), Sch 24 paras 1, 2 with effect from 1 April 2012 and from then on in relation to tax regardless of when the tax became due (whether before, on or after that date).

[Power to obtain information about persons whose identity can be ascertained

5A—(1) An authorised officer of Revenue and Customs may by notice in writing require a person to provide relevant information about another person ("the taxpayer") if conditions A to D are met.

(2) Condition A is that the information is reasonably required by the officer for the purpose of checking the tax position of the taxpayer.

(3) Condition B is that—

(*a*) the taxpayer's identity is not known to the officer, but

(*b*) the officer holds information from which the taxpayer's identity can be ascertained.

(4) Condition C is that the officer has reason to believe that—

(*a*) the person will be able to ascertain the taxpayer's identity from the information held by the officer, and

(*b*) the person obtained relevant information about the taxpayer in the course of carrying on a business.

(5) Condition D is that the taxpayer's identity cannot readily be ascertained by other means from the information held by the officer.

(6) "Relevant information" means all or any of the following—

(*a*) name,

(*b*) last known address, and

(*c*) date of birth (in the case of an individual).

(7) This paragraph applies for the purpose of checking the tax position of a class of persons as for the purpose of checking the tax position of a single person (and references to "the taxpayer" are to be read accordingly).][1]

Cross references—FA 2014 Sch 34 para 10 (failure to comply with a notice under this section triggers threshold condition leading to consideration for a conduct notice).

Amendments—[1] This para inserted by FA 2012 s 224(1), (2) with effect for the purpose of checking the tax position of a taxpayer as regards periods or tax liabilities whenever arising (whether before, on or after 17 July 2012).

Notices

6—(1) In this Schedule, "information notice" means a notice under paragraph 1, 2[, 5 or 5A][3].

(2) An information notice may specify or describe the information or documents to be provided or produced.

(3) If an information notice is given with the approval of the [tribunal][1], it must state that it is given with that approval.

[(4) A decision of the tribunal under paragraph 3, 4 or 5 is final (despite the provisions of sections 11 and 13 of the Tribunals, Courts and Enforcement Act 2007).][2]

Commentary—*Simon's Taxes* **A6.301A**.

Commencement—Finance Act 2008, Schedule 36 (Appointed Day and Savings) Order, SI 2009/404 art 2 (appointed day for the coming into force of Sch 36 is 1 April 2009).

HMRC Manuals—Compliance Handbook Manual, CH229300–229900 (HMRC inspection powers – how to do a compliance check: rules that apply to all notices).

Amendments—[1] In sub-para (3) word substituted for the words "First-tier Tribunal" by the Transfer of Tribunal Functions and Revenue and Customs Appeals Order, SI 2009/56 art 3, Sch 1 para 471 with effect from 1 April 2009.

[2] Sub-para (4) inserted by FA 2009 s 95, Sch 47 para 4 with effect from 21 July 2009.

[3] In sub-para (1) words substituted by FA 2012 s 224(1), (3) with effect for the purpose of checking the tax position of a taxpayer as regards periods or tax liabilities whenever arising (whether before, on or after 17 July 2012).

Complying with notices

7—(1) Where a person is required by an information notice to provide information or produce a document, the person must do so—

(*a*) within such period, and

(*b*) at such time, by such means and in such form (if any),

as is reasonably specified or described in the notice.

(2) Where an information notice requires a person to produce a document, it must be produced for inspection—

(*a*) at a place agreed to by that person and an officer of Revenue and Customs, or

(*b*) at such place as an officer of Revenue and Customs may reasonably specify.

(3) An officer of Revenue and Customs must not specify a place that is used solely as a dwelling.

(4) The production of a document in compliance with an information notice is not to be regarded as breaking any lien claimed on the document.

Commencement—Finance Act 2008, Schedule 36 (Appointed Day and Savings) Order, SI 2009/404 art 2 (appointed day for the coming into force of Sch 36 is 1 April 2009).

HMRC Manuals—Compliance Handbook Manual, CH23220 (HMRC inspection powers: meaning or "provide information", with example).

CH23260 (meaning of "produce documents").

CH23420 (date by which information required).

CH23480 (complying with a notice).

Producing copies of documents

8—(1) Where an information notice requires a person to produce a document, the person may comply with the notice by producing a copy of the document, subject to any conditions or exceptions set out in regulations made by the Commissioners.

(2) Sub-paragraph (1) does not apply where—

(*a*) the notice requires the person to produce the original document, or

(*b*) an officer of Revenue and Customs subsequently makes a request in writing to the person for the original document.

(3) Where an officer of Revenue and Customs requests a document under sub-paragraph (2)(*b*), the person to whom the request is made must produce the document—

(*a*) within such period, and

(*b*) at such time and by such means (if any),

as is reasonably requested by the officer.

Commencement—Finance Act 2008, Schedule 36 (Appointed Day and Savings) Order, SI 2009/404 art 2 (appointed day for the coming into force of Sch 36 is 1 April 2009).

Restrictions and special cases

9 This Part of this Schedule has effect subject to Parts 4 and 6 of this Schedule.

Commencement—Finance Act 2008, Schedule 36 (Appointed Day and Savings) Order, SI 2009/404 art 2 (appointed day for the coming into force of Sch 36 is 1 April 2009).

PART 2

POWERS TO INSPECT [PREMISES AND OTHER PROPERTY][1]

Amendments—[1] Words in heading substituted for words "Businesses etc" by the Finance Act 2009, Section 96 and Schedule 48 (Appointed Day, Savings and Consequential Amendments) Order, SI 2009/3054 art 3, Schedule para 15 with effect from 1 April 2010.

Power to inspect business premises etc

10—(1) An officer of Revenue and Customs may enter a person's business premises and inspect—

(*a*) the premises,

(*b*) business assets that are on the premises, and

(*c*) business documents that are on the premises,

if the inspection is reasonably required for the purpose of checking that person's tax position.

(2) The powers under this paragraph do not include power to enter or inspect any part of the premises that is used solely as a dwelling.

(3) In this Schedule—

"business assets" means assets that an officer of Revenue and Customs has reason to believe are owned, leased or used in connection with the carrying on of a business by any person [(but see sub-paragraph (4))][1],

"business documents" means documents (or copies of documents)—

(*a*) that relate to the carrying on of a business by any person, and

(*b*) that form part of any person's statutory records, and

"business premises", in relation to a person, means premises (or any part of premises) that an officer of Revenue and Customs has reason to believe are (or is) used in connection with the carrying on of a business by or on behalf of the person.

[(4) For the purposes of this Schedule, "business assets" does not include documents, other than—

(*a*) documents that are trading stock for the purposes of Chapter 11A of Part 2 of ITTOIA 2005 (see section 172A of that Act), and

(*b*) documents that are plant for the purposes of Part 2 of CAA 2001.][1]

Commentary—*Simon's Taxes* **A6.301A**.

Commencement—Finance Act 2008, Schedule 36 (Appointed Day and Savings) Order, SI 2009/404 art 2 (appointed day for the coming into force of Sch 36 is 1 April 2009).

HMRC Manuals—Compliance Handbook Manual, CH25120 (HMRC inspection powers: meaning of "enter").

CH25140–25160 (meaning of "inspect" with examples).

CH25180 (meaning of "business premises").

CH25220–25240 (inspecting business premises that are a home).

CH25260 and 25280 (meaning of "business assets" and "business documents").

CH25420 (HMRC inspection powers: start and end of an inspection).

CH25460 (when to carry out an inspection).

CH25480 (HMRC inspection powers: announced and unannounced inspection).

CH25540 (Tribunal approval).

CH25560 (wording of inspection notices).

Amendments—[1] In sub-para (3) in the definition of "business assets" words substituted for words ", excluding documents", and sub-para (4) inserted by FA 2009 s 95, Sch 47 para 5 with effect from 21 July 2009.

Prospective amendments—Sub-para (5) to be inserted by FA 2017 s 56, Sch 11 para 1(1), (2) with effect from a date to be appointed. Once appointed, the charge to soft drinks industry levy will arise on chargeable events which occur on or after 6 April 2018 (FA 2017 s 31(1)). Sub-para (5) to read as follows—

"(5) In sub-paragraph (1), the reference to a person's tax position does not include a reference to a person's position as regards soft drinks industry levy.".

[Power to inspect business premises etc of involved third parties

10A—(1) An officer of Revenue and Customs may enter business premises of an involved third party (see paragraph 61A) and inspect—

(*a*) the premises,

(*b*) business assets that are on the premises, and

(*c*) relevant documents that are on the premises,

if the inspection is reasonably required by the officer for the purpose of checking the position of any person or class of persons as regards a relevant tax.

(2) The powers under this paragraph may be exercised whether or not the identity of that person is, or the individual identities of those persons are, known to the officer.

(3) The powers under this paragraph do not include power to enter or inspect any part of the premises that is used solely as a dwelling.

(4) In relation to an involved third party, "relevant documents" and "relevant tax" are defined in paragraph 61A.]

Modification—See FA 2016 Sch 20 para 21 (application of this para in relation to penalties for enablers of offshore tax evasion or non-compliance).

See F(No 2)A 2017 Sch 16 para 42(2) (application of this para in relation to penalties for enablers of defeated tax avoidance).

Amendments—Para 10A inserted by FA 2009 s 96, Sch 48 para 3 with effect from 1 April 2010 (by virtue of SI 2009/3054 art 2).

Power to inspect premises used in connection with taxable supplies etc

11—(1) This paragraph applies where an officer of Revenue and Customs has reason to believe that—

(*a*) premises are used in connection with the supply of goods under taxable supplies and goods to be so supplied [or documents relating to such goods][1] are on those premises, (*b*) premises are used in connection with the acquisition of goods from other member States under taxable acquisitions and goods to be so acquired [or documents relating to such goods][1] are on those premises, or

(*c*) premises are used as [or in connection with][1] a fiscal warehouse.

(2) An officer of Revenue and Customs may enter the premises and inspect—

(*a*) the premises,

(*b*) any goods that are on the premises, and

(*c*) any documents on the premises that appear to the officer to relate to [the supply of goods under taxable supplies, the acquisition of goods from other member States under taxable acquisitions or fiscal warehousing][1].

(3) The powers under this paragraph do not include power to enter or inspect any part of the premises that is used solely as a dwelling.

(4) Terms used both in [this paragraph][1] and in VATA 1994 have the same meaning [here][1] as they have in that Act.

Commentary—*Simon's Taxes* **A6.301A**.

Commencement—Finance Act 2008, Schedule 36 (Appointed Day and Savings) Order, SI 2009/404 art 2 (appointed day for the coming into force of Sch 36 is 1 April 2009).

HMRC Manuals—Compliance Handbook Manual, CH25420 (HMRC inspection powers: start and end of an inspection).
CH25460 (when to carry out an inspection).
CH25480 (HMRC inspection powers: announced and unannounced inspection).
CH25540 (Tribunal approval).
CH25560 (wording of inspection notices).

Amendments—[1] In sub-para (1)(*a*), (*b*), (*c*) words inserted; in sub-para (2)(*c*) words substituted for words "such goods"; in sub-para (4) words substituted in the first place for words "sub-paragraph (1)" and in the second place for words "in that sub-paragraph", by FA 2009 s 95, Sch 47 para 6 with effect from 21 July 2009.

Carrying out inspections [under paragraph 10, 10A or 11]

12—(1) An inspection under [paragraph 10, 10A or 11][3] may be carried out only—

(*a*) at a time agreed to by the occupier of the premises, or

(*b*) if sub-paragraph (2) is satisfied, at any reasonable time.

(2) This sub-paragraph is satisfied if—

(*a*) the occupier of the premises has been given at least 7 days' notice of the time of the inspection (whether in writing or otherwise), or

(*b*) the inspection is carried out by, or with the agreement of, an authorised officer of Revenue and Customs.

(3) An officer of Revenue and Customs seeking to carry out an inspection under sub-paragraph (2)(*b*) must provide a notice in writing as follows—

(*a*) if the occupier of the premises is present at the time the inspection is to begin, the notice must be provided to the occupier,

(*b*) if the occupier of the premises is not present but a person who appears to the officer to be in charge of the premises is present, the notice must be provided to that person, and

(*c*) in any other case, the notice must be left in a prominent place on the premises.

(4) The notice referred to in sub-paragraph (3) must state the possible consequences of obstructing the officer in the exercise of the power.

(5) If a notice referred to in sub-paragraph (3) is given [in respect of an inspection approved by][2] the [tribunal][1] (see paragraph 13), it must state that [the inspection has been so approved][2].

Commencement—Finance Act 2008, Schedule 36 (Appointed Day and Savings) Order, SI 2009/404 art 2 (appointed day for the coming into force of Sch 36 is 1 April 2009).

HMRC Manuals—Compliance Handbook Manual, CH25480 (HMRC inspection powers: announced and unannounced inspection).
CH25540 (Tribunal approval).
CH25560 (wording of inspection notices).
CH250000 (HMRC inspection powers – how to do a compliance check: visits to business premises).
CH254000 (how to do a compliance check: unannounced visits).
CH255500 (how to do a compliance check: during a visit).
CH255520 (how to do a compliance check: what to do if entry is refused).

Amendments—[1] In sub-para (5) word substituted for the words "First-tier Tribunal" by the Transfer of Tribunal Functions and Revenue and Customs Appeals Order, SI 2009/56 art 3, Sch 1 para 471 with effect from 1 April 2009.

[2] In sub-para (5) words substituted in the first place for the words "with the approval of" and in the second place for the words "it is given with that approval", by FA 2009 s 95, Sch 47 para 7 with effect from 21 July 2009.

[3] In heading words inserted, in sub-para (1) words substituted for words "this Part of this Schedule", by FA 2009 s 96, Sch 48 para 4 with effect from 1 April 2010 (by virtue of SI 2009/3054 art 2).

[Powers to inspect property for valuation etc

12A—(1) An officer of Revenue and Customs may enter and inspect premises for the purpose of valuing the premises if the valuation is reasonably required for the purpose of checking any person's position as regards income tax or corporation tax.

(2) An officer of Revenue and Customs may enter premises and inspect—

(*a*) the premises, and

(*b*) any other property on the premises,

for the purpose of valuing, measuring or determining the character of the premises or property.

(3) Sub-paragraph (2) only applies if the valuation, measurement or determination is reasonably required for the purpose of checking any person's position as regards—

(*a*) capital gains tax,

(*b*) corporation tax in respect of chargeable gains,

(*c*) inheritance tax,

(*d*) stamp duty land tax, . . . [2]

(*e*) stamp duty reserve tax[, or

(*f*) annual tax on enveloped dwellings.][2]

(4) A person who the officer considers is needed to assist with the valuation, measurement or determination may enter and inspect the premises or property with the officer.][1]

Amendments—[1] Paras 12A, 12B inserted by FA 2009 s 96, Sch 48 para 5 with effect from 1 April 2010 (by virtue of SI 2009/3054 art 2).

[2] In sub-para (3), word "or" in para (*d*) repealed, and para (*f*) and preceding word "or" inserted by FA 2013 s 164, Sch 34 paras 1, 2 with effect from 17 July 2013.

[Carrying out inspections under paragraph 12A

12B—(1) An inspection under paragraph 12A may be carried out only if condition A or B is satisfied.

(2) Condition A is that—

(*a*) the inspection is carried out at a time agreed to by a relevant person, and

(*b*) the relevant person has been given notice in writing of the agreed time of the inspection.

(3) "Relevant person" means—

(*a*) the occupier of the premises, or

(*b*) if the occupier cannot be identified or the premises are vacant, a person who controls the premises.

(4) Condition B is that—

(*a*) the inspection has been approved by the tribunal, and

(*b*) any relevant person specified by the tribunal has been given at least 7 days' notice in writing of the time of the inspection.

(5) A notice under sub-paragraph (4)(*b*) must state the possible consequences of obstructing the officer in the exercise of the power.

(6) If a notice is given under this paragraph in respect of an inspection approved by the tribunal (see paragraph 13), it must state that the inspection has been so approved.

(7) An officer of Revenue and Customs seeking to carry out an inspection under paragraph 12A must produce evidence of authority to carry out the inspection if asked to do so by—

(*a*) the occupier of the premises, or

(*b*) any other person who appears to the officer to be in charge of the premises or property.]

Amendments—Paras 12A, 12B inserted by FA 2009 s 96, Sch 48 para 5 with effect from 1 April 2010 (by virtue of SI 2009/3054 art 2).

Approval of [tribunal]

13—(1) An officer of Revenue and Customs may ask the [tribunal][1] to approve an inspection under this Part of this Schedule [(and for the effect of obtaining such approval see paragraph 39 (penalties))][3].

[(1A) An application for approval under this paragraph may be made without notice [(except as required under sub-paragraph (2A))][3].][2]

(2) The [tribunal][1] may not approve an inspection [under paragraph 10, 10A or 11][3] unless—

(*a*) an application for approval is made by, or with the agreement of, an authorised officer of Revenue and Customs, and

(*b*) the [tribunal][1] is satisfied that, in the circumstances, the inspection is justified.

[(2A) The tribunal may not approve an inspection under paragraph 12A unless—

(*a*) an application for approval is made by, or with the agreement of, an authorised officer of Revenue and Customs, (*b*) the person whose tax position is the subject of the proposed inspection has been given a reasonable opportunity to make representations to the officer of Revenue and Customs about that inspection,

(*c*) the occupier of the premises has been given a reasonable opportunity to make such representations,

(*d*) the tribunal has been given a summary of any representations made, and

(*e*) the tribunal is satisfied that, in the circumstances, the inspection is justified.

(2B) Paragraph (*c*) of sub-paragraph (2A) does not apply if the tribunal is satisfied that the occupier of the premises cannot be identified.][3]

[(3) A decision of the tribunal under this paragraph is final (despite the provisions of sections 11 and 13 of the Tribunals, Courts and Enforcement Act 2007).][2]

Commencement—Finance Act 2008, Schedule 36 (Appointed Day and Savings) Order, SI 2009/404 art 2 (appointed day for the coming into force of Sch 36 is 1 April 2009).

Amendments—[1] Word substituted for the words "First-tier Tribunal" in the heading and in each place; in sub-para (2)(*b*) word substituted for the word "Tribunal" by the Transfer of Tribunal Functions and Revenue and Customs Appeals Order, SI 2009/56 art 3, Sch 1 para 471 with effect from 1 April 2009.

[2] Sub-paras (1A), (3) inserted by FA 2009 s 95, Sch 47 para 8 with effect from 21 July 2009.

[3] In sub-paras (1), (1A), (2), words inserted, and whole of sub-paras (2A), (2B) inserted, by FA 2009 s 96, Sch 48 para 6 with effect from 1 April 2010 (by virtue of SI 2009/3054 art 2).

Restrictions and special cases

14 This Part of this Schedule has effect subject to Parts 4 and 6 of this Schedule.

Commencement—Finance Act 2008, Schedule 36 (Appointed Day and Savings) Order, SI 2009/404 art 2 (appointed day for the coming into force of Sch 36 is 1 April 2009).

HMRC Manuals—Compliance Handbook Manual, CH25300 (HMRC inspection powers: documents you cannot inspect).

PART 3
FURTHER POWERS

Power to copy documents

15 Where a document (or a copy of a document) is produced to, or inspected by, an officer of Revenue and Customs, such an officer may take copies of, or make extracts from, the document.

Commencement—Finance Act 2008, Schedule 36 (Appointed Day and Savings) Order, SI 2009/404 art 2 (appointed day for the coming into force of Sch 36 is 1 April 2009).

HMRC Manuals—Compliance Handbook Manual, CH23300 (HMRC inspection powers: copying or removing documents).
CH25320 (HMRC inspection powers: obtaining and recording information and copying documents).
CH255540 (HMRC inspection powers – how to do a compliance check: copying records).

Power to remove documents

16—(1) Where a document is produced to, or inspected by, an officer of Revenue and Customs, such an officer may—

(*a*) remove the document at a reasonable time, and

(*b*) retain it for a reasonable period,

if it appears to the officer to be necessary to do so.

(2) Where a document is removed in accordance with sub-paragraph (1), the person who produced the document may request—

(*a*) a receipt for the document, and

(*b*) if the document is reasonably required for any purpose, a copy of the document,

and an officer of Revenue and Customs must comply with such a request without charge.

(3) The removal of a document under this paragraph is not to be regarded as breaking any lien claimed on the document.

(4) Where a document removed under this paragraph is lost or damaged, the Commissioners are liable to compensate the owner of the document for any expenses reasonably incurred in replacing or repairing the document.

(5) In this paragraph references to a document include a copy of a document.

Commencement—Finance Act 2008, Schedule 36 (Appointed Day and Savings) Order, SI 2009/404 art 2 (appointed day for the coming into force of Sch 36 is 1 April 2009).

HMRC Manuals—Compliance Handbook Manual, CH23300 (HMRC inspection powers: copying or removing documents).
CH25320 (HMRC inspection powers: obtaining and recording information and copying documents).
CH255545–255555 (inspection powers – how to do a compliance check: removing, storing and returning records).

Power to mark assets and to record information

17 The powers under Part 2 of this Schedule include—

(*a*) power to mark business assets, and anything containing business assets, for the purpose of indicating that they have been inspected, and (*b*) power to obtain and record information (whether electronically or otherwise) relating to the premises, [property, goods,][1] assets and documents that have been inspected.

Commencement—Finance Act 2008, Schedule 36 (Appointed Day and Savings) Order, SI 2009/404 art 2 (appointed day for the coming into force of Sch 36 is 1 April 2009).

HMRC Manuals—Compliance Handbook Manual, CH25320 (HMRC inspection powers: obtaining and recording information and copying documents).
CH25340 (HMRC inspection powers: marking goods or assets).

Amendments—[1] In para (*b*) words inserted by FA 2009 s 96, Sch 48 para 7 with effect from 1 April 2010 (by virtue of SI 2009/3054 art 2).

PART 4
RESTRICTIONS ON POWERS

Documents not in person's possession or power

18 An information notice only requires a person to produce a document if it is in the person's possession or power.

Commentary—*Simon's Taxes* **A6.301A**.

Commencement—Finance Act 2008, Schedule 36 (Appointed Day and Savings) Order, SI 2009/404 art 2 (appointed day for the coming into force of Sch 36 is 1 April 2009).

HMRC Manuals—Compliance Handbook Manual, CH22120 (HMRC inspection powers: meaning of possession and power).

Modification—See FA 2016 Sch 20 para 19 (application of this para in relation to penalties for enablers of offshore tax evasion or non-compliance).

Types of information

19—(1) An information notice does not require a person to provide or produce—

(*a*) information that relates to the conduct of a pending appeal relating to tax or any part of a document containing such information, or

(*b*) journalistic material (as defined in section 13 of the Police and Criminal Evidence Act 1984 (c 60)) or information contained in such material.

(2) An information notice does not require a person to provide or produce personal records (as defined in section 12 of the Police and Criminal Evidence Act 1984) or information contained in such records, subject to sub-paragraph (3).

(3) An information notice may require a person—

(*a*) to produce documents, or copies of documents, that are personal records, omitting any information whose inclusion (whether alone or with other information) makes the original documents personal records ("personal information"), and

(*b*) to provide any information contained in such records that is not personal information.

Commentary—*Simon's Taxes* **A6.301A**.

Commencement—Finance Act 2008, Schedule 36 (Appointed Day and Savings) Order, SI 2009/404 art 2 (appointed day for the coming into force of Sch 36 is 1 April 2009).

HMRC Manuals—Compliance Handbook Manual, CH22160 (HMRC inspection powers: appeal material, with example).
CH22180 and 22200 (personal records, with example).

Prospective amendments—Sub-paras (4), (5) to be inserted by the Investigatory Powers Act 2016 s 12(1), Sch 2 para 10 with effect from a date to be appointed. Sub-paras (4), (5) as inserted to read as follows—

"(4) An information notice does not require a telecommunications operator or postal operator to provide or produce communications data.

(5) In sub-paragraph (4) "communications data", "postal operator" and "telecommunications operator" have the same meanings as in the Investigatory Powers Act 2016 (see sections 261 and 262 of that Act).".

Old documents

20 An information notice may not require a person to produce a document if the whole of the document originates more than 6 years before the date of the notice, unless the notice is given by, or with the agreement of, an authorised officer.

Commentary—*Simon's Taxes* **A6.301A**.

Commencement—Finance Act 2008, Schedule 36 (Appointed Day and Savings) Order, SI 2009/404 art 2 (appointed day for the coming into force of Sch 36 is 1 April 2009).

HMRC Manuals—Compliance Handbook Manual, CH22140 (HMRC inspection powers: old documents).

Taxpayer notices [following tax return]

21—(1) Where a person has made a tax return in respect of a chargeable period under section 8, 8A or 12AA of TMA 1970 (returns for purpose of income tax and capital gains tax), a taxpayer notice may not be given for the purpose of checking that person's income tax position or capital gains tax position in relation to the chargeable period.

(2) Where a person has made a tax return in respect of a chargeable period under paragraph 3 of Schedule 18 to FA 1998 (company tax returns), a taxpayer notice may not be given for the purpose of checking that person's corporation tax position in relation to the chargeable period.

(3) Sub-paragraphs (1) and (2) do not apply where, or to the extent that, any of conditions A to D is met.

(4) Condition A is that a notice of enquiry has been given in respect of—

(*a*) the return, or

(*b*) a claim or election (or an amendment of a claim or election) made by the person in relation to the chargeable period in respect of the tax (or one of the taxes) to which the return relates ("relevant tax"),

and the enquiry has not been completed [so far as relating to the matters to which the taxpayer notice relates][3].

(5) In sub-paragraph (4), "notice of enquiry" means a notice under—

(*a*) section 9A or 12AC of, or paragraph 5 of Schedule 1A to, TMA 1970, or

(*b*) paragraph 24 of Schedule 18 to FA 1998.

(6) Condition B is that an officer of Revenue and Customs has reason to suspect that[, as regards the person,][1]

(*a*) an amount that ought to have been assessed to relevant tax for the chargeable period may not have been assessed,

(*b*) an assessment to relevant tax for the chargeable period may be or have become insufficient, or

(*c*) relief from relevant tax given for the chargeable period may be or have become excessive.

(7) Condition C is that the notice is given for the purpose of obtaining any information or document that is also required for the purpose of checking [the][1] person's [position as regards any tax other than income tax, capital gains tax or corporation tax][2].

(8) Condition D is that the notice is given for the purpose of obtaining any information or document that is required (or also required) for the purpose of checking the person's position as regards any deductions or repayments [of tax or withholding of income][1] referred to in paragraph 64(2) [or (2A)][1] (PAYE etc).

[(9) In this paragraph, references to the person who made the return are only to that person in the capacity in which the return was made.][1]

Commencement—Finance Act 2008, Schedule 36 (Appointed Day and Savings) Order, SI 2009/404 art 2 (appointed day for the coming into force of Sch 36 is 1 April 2009).

Modification—See FA 2010 Sch 1 para 36 (modification of this para in relation to bank payroll tax).

HMRC Manuals—Compliance Handbook Manual, CH23520 (HMRC inspection powers: specific rules regarding taxpayer notice).

CH23540 (HMRC inspection powers: where self assessment return made).

CH23560 (meaning of "reason to suspect").

Amendments—[1] In sub-paras (6), (8) in both places, words inserted; in sub-para (7) word substituted for the word "that"; and sub-para (9) inserted, by FA 2009 s 95, Sch 47 para 9 with effect from 21 July 2009.

[2] In the cross-heading words inserted, and in sub-para (7) words substituted for words "VAT position", by FA 2009 s 95, Sch 48 para 8 with effect from 1 April 2010 (by virtue of SI 2009/3054 art 2).

[3] In sub-para (4), words inserted by F(No 2)A 2017 s 63, Sch 15 para 36 with effect in relation to an enquiry under TMA 1970 ss 9A, 12ZM or 12AC or FA 1998 Sch 18 where notice of the enquiry is given on or after 16 November 2017 or the enquiry is in progress immediately before that day.

Prospective amendments—In sub-para (1), words ", or regulations under paragraph 10 of Schedule A1 to," to be inserted after words "12AA of" by F(No 2)A 2017 s 61(1), Sch 14 para 38(1), (2) with effect from a day to be appointed.

[Taxpayer notices following NRCGT return

21ZA (1) Where a person has delivered an NRCGT return with respect to a non-resident CGT disposal, a taxpayer notice may not be given for the purpose of checking the person's capital gains tax position as regards the matters dealt with in that return.

(2) Sub-paragraph (1) does not apply where, or to the extent that, any of conditions A to C is met.

(3) Condition A is that notice of enquiry has been given in respect of—

(*a*) the return, or

(*b*) a claim (or an amendment of a claim) made by the person in relation to the chargeable period,

and the enquiry has not been completed [so far as relating to the matters to which the taxpayer notice relates][2].

(4) In sub-paragraph (3) "notice of enquiry" means a notice under section 12ZM of TMA 1970.

(5) Condition B is that an officer of Revenue and Customs has reason to suspect that—

(*a*) an amount that ought to have been assessed under section 12ZE of TMA 1970 as payable on account of the person's liability to capital gains tax for the tax year to which the return relates has not been so assessed by the filing date for the return, or (*b*) an assessment under section 12ZE of TMA 1970 of the amount payable on account of P's liability to capital gains tax for the tax year to which the return relates has become insufficient.

(6) Condition C is that the notice is given for the purpose of obtaining any information or document that is also required for the purpose of checking that person's position as regards a tax other than capital gains tax.

(7) In this paragraph—

"NRCGT return" has the meaning given by section 12ZB of TMA 1970;

"non-resident CGT disposal" has the meaning given by section 14B of TCGA 1992.][1]

Amendments—[1] Paragraph 21ZA inserted by FA 2015 s 37, Sch 7 para 57 with effect in relation to disposals made on or after 6 April 2015.

[2] In sub-para (3), words inserted by F(No 2)A 2017 s 63, Sch 15 para 36 with effect in relation to an enquiry under TMA 1970 ss 9A, 12ZM or 12AC or FA 1998 Sch 18 where notice of the enquiry is given on or after 16 November 2017 or the enquiry is in progress immediately before that day.

[Taxpayer notices following land transaction return

21A—(1) Where a person has delivered a land transaction return under section 76 of FA 2003 (returns for purposes of stamp duty land tax) in respect of a transaction, a taxpayer notice may not be given for the purpose of checking that person's stamp duty land tax position in relation to that transaction.

(2) Sub-paragraph (1) does not apply where, or to the extent that, any of conditions A to C is met.

(3) Condition A is that a notice of enquiry has been given in respect of—

(*a*) the return, or

(*b*) a claim (or an amendment of a claim) made by the person in connection with the transaction,

and the enquiry has not been completed.

(4) In sub-paragraph (3) "notice of enquiry" means a notice under paragraph 12 of Schedule 10, or paragraph 7 of Schedule 11A, to FA 2003.

(5) Condition B is that, as regards the person, an officer of Revenue and Customs has reason to suspect that—

(*a*) an amount that ought to have been assessed to stamp duty land tax in respect of the transaction may not have been assessed,

(*b*) an assessment to stamp duty land tax in respect of the transaction may be or have become insufficient, or

(*c*) relief from stamp duty land tax in respect of the transaction may be or have become excessive.

(6) Condition C is that the notice is given for the purpose of obtaining any information or document that is also required for the purpose of checking that person's position as regards a tax other than stamp duty land tax.]

Amendments—Para 21A inserted by FA 2009 s 96, Sch 48 para 9 with effect from 1 April 2010 (by virtue of SI 2009/3054 art 2).

[Annual tax on enveloped dwellings: taxpayer notices following return

21B—(1) Where a person has delivered, for a chargeable period with respect to a single-dwelling interest—

(*a*) an annual tax on enveloped dwellings return, or

(*b*) a return of the adjusted chargeable amount,

a taxpayer notice may not be given for the purpose of checking the person's annual tax on enveloped dwellings position as regards the matters dealt with in that return.

(2) Sub-paragraph (1) does not apply where, or to the extent that, any of conditions A to C is met.

(3) Condition A is that notice of enquiry has been given in respect of—

(*a*) the return, or

(*b*) a claim (or an amendment of a claim) made by the person in relation to the chargeable period,

and the enquiry has not been completed.

(4) In sub-paragraph (3) "notice of enquiry" means a notice under paragraph 8 of Schedule 33 to FA 2013 or paragraph 7 of Schedule 11A to FA 2003 (as applied by paragraphs 28(2) and 31(3) of Schedule 33 to FA 2013).

(5) Condition B is that, as regards the person, an officer of Revenue and Customs has reason to suspect that—

(*a*) an amount that ought to have been assessed to annual tax on enveloped dwellings for the chargeable period may not have been assessed,

(*b*) an assessment to annual tax on enveloped dwellings for the chargeable period may be or have become insufficient, or

(*c*) relief from annual tax on enveloped dwellings for the chargeable period may be or have become excessive.

(6) Condition C is that the notice is given for the purpose of obtaining any information or document that is also required for the purpose of checking that person's position as regards a tax other than annual tax on enveloped dwellings.

(7) In this Schedule references to a "single-dwelling interest" are to be read in accordance with section 108 of FA 2013.][1]

Amendments—[1] Para 21B inserted by FA 2013 s 164, Sch 34 paras 1, 3 with effect from 17 July 2013.

Deceased persons

22 An information notice given for the purpose of checking the tax position of a person who has died may not be given more than 4 years after the person's death.

Commencement—Finance Act 2008, Schedule 36 (Appointed Day and Savings) Order, SI 2009/404 art 2 (appointed day for the coming into force of Sch 36 is 1 April 2009).

HMRC Manuals—Compliance Handbook Manual, CH23620 (HMRC inspection powers: specific rules regarding third party notice).

Privileged communications between professional legal advisers and clients

23—(1) An information notice does not require a person—

(*a*) to provide privileged information, or

(*b*) to produce any part of a document that is privileged.

(2) For the purpose of this Schedule, information or a document is privileged if it is information or a document in respect of which a claim to legal professional privilege, or (in Scotland) to confidentiality of communications as between client and professional legal adviser, could be maintained in legal proceedings.

(3) The Commissioners may by regulations make provision for the resolution by the [tribunal][1] of disputes as to whether any information or document is privileged.

(4) The regulations may, in particular, make provision as to—

(*a*) the custody of a document while its status is being decided, . . . [1]

(*b*) . . . [1]

Commentary—*Simon's Taxes* **A6.301A**.

Commencement—Finance Act 2008, Schedule 36 (Appointed Day and Savings) Order, SI 2009/404 art 2 (appointed day for the coming into force of Sch 36 is 1 April 2009).

HMRC Manuals—Compliance Handbook Manual, CH22240 (HMRC restrictions on inspection powers: legal professional privilege).

Regulations—Information Notice: Resolution of Disputes as to Privileged Communications Regulations, SI 2009/1916.

Cross references—See FA 2012 Sch 38 para 17 (application of regulations made under this para to disputes as to whether a document is privileged).

Amendments—[1] In sub-para (3) word substituted for the words "First-tier Tribunal"; sub-para (4)(*b*) and the word "and" immediately preceding it repealed by the Transfer of Tribunal Functions and Revenue and Customs Appeals Order, SI 2009/56 art 3, Sch 1 para 471 with effect from 1 April 2009.

Auditors

24—(1) An information notice does not require a person who has been appointed as an auditor for the purpose of an enactment—

(*a*) to provide information held in connection with the performance of the person's functions under that enactment, or

(*b*) to produce documents which are that person's property and which were created by that person or on that person's behalf for or in connection with the performance of those functions.

(2) Sub-paragraph (1) has effect subject to paragraph 26.

Commentary—*Simon's Taxes* **A6.301A, A6.310**.

Commencement—Finance Act 2008, Schedule 36 (Appointed Day and Savings) Order, SI 2009/404 art 2 (appointed day for the coming into force of Sch 36 is 1 April 2009).

Modification—See FA 2016 Sch 20 para 20(*a*) (disapplication of this para in relation to penalties for enablers of offshore tax evasion or non-compliance).

Tax advisers

25—(1) An information notice does not require a tax adviser—

(*a*) to provide information about relevant communications, or

(*b*) to produce documents which are the tax adviser's property and consist of relevant communications.

(2) Sub-paragraph (1) has effect subject to paragraph 26.

(3) In this paragraph—

"relevant communications" means communications between the tax adviser and—

(*a*) a person in relation to whose tax affairs he has been appointed, or

(*b*) any other tax adviser of such a person,

the purpose of which is the giving or obtaining of advice about any of those tax affairs, and "tax adviser" means a person appointed to give advice about the tax affairs of another person (whether appointed directly by that person or by another tax adviser of that person).

Commentary—*Simon's Taxes* **A6.301A, A6.310**.

Commencement—Finance Act 2008, Schedule 36 (Appointed Day and Savings) Order, SI 2009/404 art 2 (appointed day for the coming into force of Sch 36 is 1 April 2009).

HMRC Manuals—Compliance Handbook Manual, CH22240 and 22320 (HMRC restrictions on inspection powers: tax advisers' papers).

Modification—See FA 2016 Sch 20 para 20(*b*) (disapplication of this para in relation to penalties for enablers of offshore tax evasion or non-compliance).

Auditors and tax advisers: supplementary

26—(1) Paragraphs 24(1) and 25(1) do not have effect in relation to—

(*a*) information explaining any information or document which the person to whom the notice is given has, as tax accountant, assisted any client in preparing for, or delivering to, HMRC, or

(*b*) a document which contains such information.

(2) In the case of a notice given under paragraph 5, paragraphs 24(1) and 25(1) do not have effect in relation to—

(*a*) any information giving the identity or address of a person to whom the notice relates or of a person who has acted on behalf of such a person, or

(*b*) a document which contains such information.

(3) Paragraphs 24(1) and 25(1) are not disapplied by sub-paragraph (1) or (2) if the information in question has already been provided, or a document containing the information in question has already been produced, to an officer of Revenue and Customs.

Commentary—*Simon's Taxes* **A6.301A, A6.310**.

Commencement—Finance Act 2008, Schedule 36 (Appointed Day and Savings) Order, SI 2009/404 art 2 (appointed day for the coming into force of Sch 36 is 1 April 2009).

HMRC Manuals—Compliance Handbook Manual, CH22340 (HMRC restrictions on inspection powers: exceptions for auditors' and tax advisers' papers).

Modification—See FA 2016 Sch 20 para 20(*c*) (disapplication of this para in relation to penalties for enablers of offshore tax evasion or non-compliance).

27—(1) This paragraph applies where paragraph 24(1) or 25(1) is disapplied in relation to a document by paragraph 26(1) or (2).

(2) An information notice that requires the document to be produced has effect as if it required any part or parts of the document containing the information mentioned in paragraph 26(1) or (2) to be produced.

Commencement—Finance Act 2008, Schedule 36 (Appointed Day and Savings) Order, SI 2009/404 art 2 (appointed day for the coming into force of Sch 36 is 1 April 2009).

HMRC Manuals—Compliance Handbook Manual, CH22340 (HMRC restrictions on inspection powers: exceptions for auditors' and tax advisers' papers).

Modification—See FA 2016 Sch 20 para 20(*c*) (disapplication of this para in relation to penalties for enablers of offshore tax evasion or non-compliance).

Corresponding restrictions on inspection of . . . documents[1]

28 An officer of Revenue and Customs may not inspect a business document under Part 2 of this Schedule if or to the extent that, by virtue of this Part of this Schedule, an information notice given at the time of the inspection to the occupier of the premises could not require the occupier to produce the document.

Commencement—Finance Act 2008, Schedule 36 (Appointed Day and Savings) Order, SI 2009/404 art 2 (appointed day for the coming into force of Sch 36 is 1 April 2009).

Amendments—[1] In the heading, word "business" repealed by FA 2009 s 96, Sch 48 para 10 with effect from 1 April 2010 (by virtue of SI 2009/3054 art 2).

PART 5
APPEALS AGAINST INFORMATION NOTICES

Right to appeal against taxpayer notice

29—(1) Where a taxpayer is given a taxpayer notice, the taxpayer may appeal . . . [1] against the notice or any requirement in the notice.

(2) Sub-paragraph (1) does not apply to a requirement in a taxpayer notice to provide any information, or produce any document, that forms part of the taxpayer's statutory records.

(3) Sub-paragraph (1) does not apply if the [tribunal][1] approved the giving of the notice in accordance with paragraph 3.

Commentary—*Simon's Taxes* **A6.301A**.

Commencement—Finance Act 2008, Schedule 36 (Appointed Day and Savings) Order, SI 2009/404 art 2 (appointed day for the coming into force of Sch 36 is 1 April 2009).

HMRC Manuals—Compliance Handbook Manual, CH23520 (HMRC inspection powers: specific rules regarding taxpayer notice).

CH24100 (HMRC inspection powers: appealing against a taxpayer notice).

Amendments—[1] In sub-para (1) words "to the First-tier Tribunal" repealed; in sub-para (3) word substituted for the words "First-tier Tribunal" by the Transfer of Tribunal Functions and Revenue and Customs Appeals Order, SI 2009/56 art 3, Sch 1 para 471 with effect from 1 April 2009.

Right to appeal against third party notice

30—(1) Where a person is given a third party notice, the person may appeal . . . [1] against the notice or any requirement in the notice on the ground that it would be unduly onerous to comply with the notice or requirement.

(2) Sub-paragraph (1) does not apply to a requirement in a third party notice to provide any information, or produce any document, that forms part of the taxpayer's statutory records.

(3) Sub-paragraph (1) does not apply if the [tribunal][1] approved the giving of the notice in accordance with paragraph 3.

Commentary—*Simon's Taxes* **A6.301A**.

Commencement—Finance Act 2008, Schedule 36 (Appointed Day and Savings) Order, SI 2009/404 art 2 (appointed day for the coming into force of Sch 36 is 1 April 2009).

HMRC Manuals—Compliance Handbook Manual, CH23620 (HMRC inspection powers: specific rules regarding third party notice).

CH24100 (HMRC inspection powers: appealing against a third party notice).

CH24420 (meaning of "unduly onerous").

Amendments—[1] In sub-para (1) words "to the First-tier Tribunal" repealed; in sub-para (3) word substituted for the words "First-tier Tribunal" by the Transfer of Tribunal Functions and Revenue and Customs Appeals Order, SI 2009/56 art 3, Sch 1 para 471 with effect from 1 April 2009.

Right to appeal against notice given under paragraph 5 [or 5A]

31 Where a person is given a notice under paragraph 5 [or 5A][2], the person may appeal . . . [1] against the notice or any requirement in the notice on the ground that it would be unduly onerous to comply with the notice or requirement.

Commencement—Finance Act 2008, Schedule 36 (Appointed Day and Savings) Order, SI 2009/404 art 2 (appointed day for the coming into force of Sch 36 is 1 April 2009).

HMRC Manuals—Compliance Handbook Manual, CH23900 (HMRC inspection powers: identity unknown notice).

CH24100 (HMRC inspection powers: appealing against an identity unknown notice).

Amendments—[1] In sub-para (1) words "to the First-tier Tribunal" repealed by the Transfer of Tribunal Functions and Revenue and Customs Appeals Order, SI 2009/56 art 3, Sch 1 para 471 with effect from 1 April 2009.

[2] Words inserted by FA 2012 s 224(1), (4), (5) with effect for the purpose of checking the tax position of a taxpayer as regards periods or tax liabilities whenever arising (whether before, on or after 17 July 2012).

Procedure

32—(1) Notice of an appeal under this Part of this Schedule must be given—

(*a*) in writing,

(*b*) before the end of the period of 30 days beginning with the date on which the information notice is given, and

(*c*) to the officer of Revenue and Customs by whom the information notice was given.

(2) Notice of an appeal under this Part of this Schedule must state the grounds of appeal.

(3) On an appeal the [that is notified to the tribunal, the tribunal][1] may—

(*a*) confirm the information notice or a requirement in the information notice,

(*b*) vary the information notice or such a requirement, or

(*c*) set aside the information notice or such a requirement.

(4) Where the [tribunal][1] confirms or varies the information notice or a requirement, the person to whom the information notice was given must comply with the notice or requirement—

(*a*) within such period as is specified by the [tribunal][1], or

(*b*) if the [tribunal][1] does not specify a period, within such period as is reasonably specified in writing by an officer of Revenue and Customs following the [tribunal's][1] decision.

[(5) Notwithstanding the provisions of sections 11 and 13 of the Tribunals, Courts and Enforcement Act 2007 a decision of the tribunal on an appeal under this Part of this Schedule is final.][1]

(6) Subject to this paragraph, the provisions of Part 5 of TMA 1970 relating to appeals have effect in relation to appeals under this Part of this Schedule as they have effect in relation to an appeal against an assessment to income tax.

Commentary—*Simon's Taxes* **A6.301A**.

Commencement—Finance Act 2008, Schedule 36 (Appointed Day and Savings) Order, SI 2009/404 art 2 (appointed day for the coming into force of Sch 36 is 1 April 2009).

Simon's Tax Cases—*Jordan v R&C Comrs* [2015] UKUT 218 (TCC), [2015] STC 2314.

HMRC Manuals—Compliance Handbook Manual, CH24340 (HMRC inspection powers: appeal procedures).
CH24440 (what the first-tier Tribunal can decide).

Amendments—[1] In sub-paras (3), (4) word substituted for the words "First-tier Tribunal"; in sub-para (4)(*a*), (*b*) word substituted for word "Tribunal" and "Tribunal's"; sub-para (5) substituted by the Transfer of Tribunal Functions and Revenue and Customs Appeals Order, SI 2009/56 art 3, Sch 1 para 471 with effect from 1 April 2009.

Special cases

33 This Part of this Schedule has effect subject to Part 6 of this Schedule.

Commencement—Finance Act 2008, Schedule 36 (Appointed Day and Savings) Order, SI 2009/404 art 2 (appointed day for the coming into force of Sch 36 is 1 April 2009).

PART 6
SPECIAL CASES

Supply of goods or services etc

34—(1) This paragraph applies to a taxpayer notice or third party notice that refers only to information or documents that form part of any person's statutory records and relate to—

(*a*) the supply of goods or services,

(*b*) the acquisition of goods from another member State, or

(*c*) the importation of goods from a place outside the member States in the course of carrying on a business.

(2) Paragraph 3(1) (requirement for consent to, or approval of, third party notice) does not apply to such a notice.

(3) Where a person is given such a notice, the person may not appeal . . . [1] against the notice or any requirement in the notice.

(4) Sections 5, 11 and 15 of, and Schedule 4 to, VATA 1994, and any orders made under those provisions, apply for the purposes of this paragraph as if it were part of that Act.

Commencement—Finance Act 2008, Schedule 36 (Appointed Day and Savings) Order, SI 2009/404 art 2 (appointed day for the coming into force of Sch 36 is 1 April 2009).

HMRC Manuals—Compliance Handbook Manual, CH23520 (HMRC inspection powers: specific rules regarding taxpayer notice).
CH23620 (HMRC inspection powers: specific rules regarding third party notice).

Amendments—[1] In sub-para (3) words "to the First-tier Tribunal" repealed by the Transfer of Tribunal Functions and Revenue and Customs Appeals Order, SI 2009/56 art 3, Sch 1 para 471 with effect from 1 April 2009.

[Involved third parties

***34A**—(1) This paragraph applies to a third party notice or a notice under paragraph 5 if—*

(a) it is given to an involved third party (see paragraph 61A),

(b) it is given for the purpose of checking the position of a person, or a class of persons, as regards the relevant tax, and

(c) it refers only to relevant information or relevant documents.

(2) In relation to such a third party notice—

(a) paragraph 3(1) (approval etc of third party notices) does not apply,

(b) paragraph 4(1) (copying third party notices to taxpayer) does not apply, and

(c) paragraph 30(1) (appeal) has effect as if it permitted an appeal on any grounds.

(3) In relation to such a notice under paragraph 5—

(a) sub-paragraphs (3) and (4) of that paragraph (approval of tribunal) have effect as if they permitted, but did not require, an authorised officer of Revenue and Customs to obtain the approval of the tribunal, and

(b) paragraph 31 (appeal) has effect as if it permitted an appeal on any grounds.

(4) The involved third party may not appeal against a requirement in the notice to provide any information, or produce any document, that forms part of the involved third party's statutory records.

(5) In relation to an involved third party, "relevant documents", "relevant information" and "relevant tax" are defined in paragraph 61A.][1, 2]

Amendments—[1] Paras 34A–34C inserted by FA 2009 s 96, Sch 48 para 11 with effect from 1 April 2010 (by virtue of SI 2009/3054 art 2).

[2] This para repealed by FA 2011 s 86(1), Sch 23 paras 60, 62(1), (2) with effect from 1 April 2012 in relation to relevant data with a bearing on any period (whether before, on or after 1 April 2012) subject to FA 2011 Sch 23 para 3(2). This para will continue to have effect in relation to notices given, or requests made, under any of the provisions repealed by FA 2011 Sch 23 Pt 6 before 1 April 2012 as if the repeal had not been made (FA 2011 Sch 23 para 65(2)).

[Registered pension schemes etc

34B—(1) This paragraph applies to a third party notice or a notice under paragraph 5 if it refers only to information or documents that relate to any pensions matter.

(2) "Pensions matter" means any matter relating to—

(*a*) a registered pension scheme,

(*b*) an annuity purchased with sums or assets held for the purposes of a registered pension scheme or a pre-2006 pension scheme, . . . [2]

(*c*) an employer-financed retirement benefits scheme,

[(*d*) a QROPS or former QROPS, or

(*e*) an annuity purchased with sums or assets held for the purposes of a QROPS or former QROPS.][2]

(3) In relation to such a third party notice—

(*a*) paragraph 3(1) (approval etc of third party notices) does not apply,

(*b*) paragraph 4(1) (copying third party notices to taxpayer) does not apply, and

(*c*) paragraph 30(1) (appeal) has effect as if it permitted an appeal on any grounds.

(4) In relation to such a notice under paragraph 5—

(*a*) sub-paragraphs (3) and (4) of that paragraph (approval of tribunal) have effect as if they permitted, but did not require, an authorised officer of Revenue and Customs to obtain the approval of the tribunal, and

(*b*) paragraph 31 (appeal) has effect as if it permitted an appeal on any grounds.

[(4A) In relation to a notice to which this paragraph applies that refers only to information or documents relating to a matter within sub-paragraph (2)(*d*) or (*e*), paragraph 20 (old documents) has effect as if the reference to 6 years were to 10 years.][2]

(5) A person may not appeal against a requirement in the notice to provide any information, or produce any document, that forms part of any person's statutory records.

(6) Where the notice relates to a matter within sub-paragraph (2)(*a*) or (*b*), the officer of Revenue and Customs who gives the notice must give a copy of the notice to the scheme administrator in relation to the pension scheme.

(7) Where the notice relates to a matter within sub-paragraph (2)(*c*), the officer of Revenue and Customs who gives the notice must give a copy of the notice to the responsible person in relation to the employer-financed retirement benefits scheme.

[(7A) Where the notice relates to a matter within sub-paragraph (2)(*d*) or (*e*), the officer of Revenue and Customs who gives the notice must give a copy of the notice to the scheme manager in relation to the pension scheme.][2]

(8) Sub-paragraphs (6) [to (7A)][2] do not apply if the notice is given to a person who, in relation to the scheme or annuity to which the notice relates, is a prescribed description of person.][1]

RegulationsRegistered Pension Schemes and Overseas Pension Schemes (Miscellaneous Amendments) Regulations 2013, SI 2013/2259.

Note—References in this para to a former QROPS include a scheme that ceased to be a QROPS before FA 2013 was passed (17 July 2013) (FA 2013 s 54(4)).

Amendments—[1] Paras 34A–34C inserted by FA 2009 s 96, Sch 48 para 11 with effect from 1 April 2010 (by virtue of SI 2009/3054 art 2).

[2] In sub-para (2), word "or" at end of para (*b*) repealed, and paras (*d*), (*e*) inserted; sub-paras (4A), (7A) inserted; and in sub-para (8), words substituted for words "and (7)"; by FA 2013 s 54(1), (2) with effect from 17 July 2013.

[Registered pension schemes etc: interpretation

34C In paragraph 34B—

"employer-financed retirement benefits scheme" has the same meaning as in Chapter 2 of Part 6 of ITEPA 2003 (see sections 393A and 393B of that Act);

"pension scheme" has the same meaning as in Part 4 of FA 2004;

"pre-2006 pension scheme" means a scheme that, at or in respect of any time before 6 April 2006, was—

(*a*) a retirement benefits scheme approved for the purposes of Chapter 1 of Part 14 of ICTA,

(*b*) a former approved superannuation fund (as defined in paragraph 1(3) of Schedule 36 to FA 2004),

(*c*) a relevant statutory scheme (as defined in section 611A of ICTA) or a pension scheme treated as if it were such a scheme, or

(*d*) a personal pension scheme approved under Chapter 4 of Part 14 of ICTA;

"prescribed" means prescribed by regulations made by the Commissioners;

["QROPS" and "former QROPS" have the meanings given by section 169(8) of FA 2004;][2]

"registered pension scheme" means a pension scheme that is or has been a registered pension scheme within the meaning of Part 4 of FA 2004 or in relation to which an application for registration under that Part of that Act has been made;

"responsible person", in relation to an employer-financed retirement benefits scheme, has the same meaning as in Chapter 2 of Part 6 of ITEPA 2003 (see section 399A of that Act);

"scheme administrator", in relation to a pension scheme, has the same meaning as in Part 4 of FA 2004 (see section 270 of that Act).

["scheme manager", in relation to a pension scheme, has the meaning given by section 169(3) of FA 2004.][2]][1]

Note—References in this para to a former QROPS include a scheme that ceased to be a QROPS before FA 2013 was passed (17 July 2013) (FA 2013 s 54(4)).

Amendments—[1] Paras 34A–34C inserted by FA 2009 s 96, Sch 48 para 11 with effect from 1 April 2010 (by virtue of SI 2009/3054 art 2).

[2] Definitions of "QROPS" and "former QROPS", and "scheme manager", inserted by FA 2013 s 54(1), (3) with effect from 17 July 2013.

Groups of undertakings

35—(1) This paragraph applies where an undertaking is a parent undertaking in relation to another undertaking (a subsidiary undertaking).

(2) Where a third party notice is given to any person for the purpose of checking the tax position of the parent undertaking and any of its subsidiary undertakings, [—

(*a*) paragraph 2(2)][1] only requires the notice to state this and name the parent undertaking[, and

(*b*) the references in paragraph 3(5) to naming the taxpayer are to making that statement and naming the parent undertaking][1].

(3) In relation to such a notice—

(*a*) in paragraphs 3 and 4 (approval etc of notices and copying third party notices to taxpayer), the references to the taxpayer have effect as if they were references to the parent undertaking, but

(*b*) in paragraph 30(2) (no appeal in relation to taxpayer's statutory records), the reference to the taxpayer has effect as if it were a reference to the parent undertaking and each of its subsidiary undertakings.

[(4) Where a third party notice is given to the parent undertaking for the purpose of checking the tax position of more than one subsidiary undertaking—

(*a*) paragraph 2(2) only requires the notice to state this, and

(*b*) the references in paragraph 3(5) to naming the taxpayer are to making that statement.

(4A) In relation to such a notice—

(*a*) in paragraph 3 (approval etc of notices), sub-paragraphs (1) and (3)(*e*) do not apply,

(*b*) paragraph 4(1) (copying third party notices to taxpayer) does not apply,

(*c*) [paragraphs 21 and 21A][2] (restrictions on giving taxpayer notice where taxpayer has made return) [apply][2] as if the notice was a taxpayer notice or taxpayer notices given to each subsidiary undertaking (or, if the notice names the subsidiary undertakings to which it relates, to each of those undertakings),

(*d*) paragraph 30(1) (appeal) has effect as if it permitted an appeal on any grounds, and

(*e*) in paragraph 30(2) (no appeal in relation to taxpayer's statutory records), the reference to the taxpayer has effect as if it were a reference to the parent undertaking or any of its subsidiary undertakings.][1]

(5) Where a notice is given under paragraph 5 to the parent undertaking for the purpose of checking the tax position of one or more subsidiary undertakings whose identities are not known to the officer giving the notice[—

(*a*) sub-paragraphs (3) and (4) of that paragraph (approval of tribunal) have effect as if they permitted, but did not require, the officer to obtain the approval of the tribunal, and

(*b*) paragraph 31 (appeal) has effect as if it permitted an appeal on any grounds, but the parent undertaking may not appeal against a requirement in the notice to produce any document that forms part of the statutory records of the parent undertaking or any of its subsidiary undertakings][1].

(6) Where a third party notice or a notice under paragraph 5 is given to the parent undertaking for the purpose of checking the tax position of one or more subsidiary undertakings, the parent undertaking may not appeal against a requirement in the notice to produce any document that forms part of the statutory records of the parent undertaking or any of its subsidiary undertakings.[1]

(7) In this paragraph "parent undertaking", "subsidiary undertaking" and "undertaking" have the same meaning as in the Companies Acts (see sections 1161 and 1162 of, and Schedule 7 to, the Companies Act 2006 (c 46)).

Commencement—Finance Act 2008, Schedule 36 (Appointed Day and Savings) Order, SI 2009/404 art 2 (appointed day for the coming into force of Sch 36 is 1 April 2009).

HMRC Manuals—Compliance Handbook Manual, CH23740 (HMRC inspection powers: groups of undertakings).
CH23760–23780 (notice about the parent and its subsidiaries).
CH23900 (HMRC inspection powers: identity unknown notice).
CH225510–225530 (HMRC inspection powers – how to do a compliance check: guidance on groups of undertakings).

Amendments—[1] In sub-para (2), words substituted for the words "paragraph 2" and words at the end inserted; sub-paras (4), (4A) substituted for previous sub-para (4); words in sub-para (5) substituted for the words ", sub-paragraph (3) of that paragraph (approval of tribunal) does not apply"; and sub-para (6) repealed, by FA 2009 s 95, Sch 47 para 10 with effect from 21 July 2009.

[2] In sub-para (4A)(*c*), words substituted for words "paragraph 21", and word substituted for word "applies", by FA 2009 s 96, Sch 48 para 12 with effect from 1 April 2010 (by virtue of SI 2009/3054 art 2).

Change of ownership of companies

36—(1) Sub-paragraph (2) applies where it appears to the Commissioners that—

(*a*) there has been a change in the ownership of a company, and

(*b*) in connection with that change a person ("the seller") may be or become liable to be assessed and charged to corporation tax under [section 710 or 713 of CTA 2010][1].

(2) Paragraph 21 (restrictions on giving taxpayer notice where taxpayer has made tax return) does not apply in relation to a taxpayer notice given to the seller.

(3) [Chapter 7 of Part 14 of CTA 2010][1] applies for the purposes of determining when there has been a change in the ownership of a company.

HMRC Manuals—Compliance Handbook Manual, CH23520 (HMRC inspection powers: specific rules regarding taxpayer notice).

Amendments—[1] In sub-para (1)(*b*) words "section 767A or 767AA of ICTA" substituted and in sub-para (3) words "Section 769 of ICTA" substituted by CTA 2010 s 1177, Sch 1 paras 576, 582(1), (2). CTA 2010 has effect for corporation tax purposes for accounting periods ending on or after 1 April 2010, and for income and capital gains tax purposes for the tax year 2010–11 and subsequent tax years.

Partnerships

37—(1) This paragraph applies where a business is carried on by two or more persons in partnership.

[(2) Where, in respect of a chargeable period, any of the partners has—

(*a*) made a tax return under section 12AA of TMA 1970 (partnership returns), or

(*b*) made a claim or election in accordance with section 42(6)(*b*) of TMA 1970 (partnership claims and elections),

paragraph 21 (restrictions where taxpayer has made tax return) has effect as if that return, claim or election had been made by each of the partners.][1]

[(2A) Where, in respect of a transaction entered into as purchaser by or on behalf of the members of the partnership, any of the partners has—

(*a*) delivered a land transaction return under Part 4 of FA 2003 (stamp duty land tax), or

(*b*) made a claim under that Part of that Act, paragraph 21A (restrictions where taxpayer has delivered land transaction return) has effect as if that return had been delivered, or that claim had been made, by each of the partners.][2]

[(2B) Where, in respect of a single-dwelling interest (see paragraph 21B(7)) to which one or more companies are or were entitled as members of a partnership, any member of the partnership has—

(*a*) delivered an annual tax on enveloped dwellings return or a return of the adjusted chargeable amount under Part 3 of FA 2013, or

(*b*) made a claim under that Part of that Act,

paragraph 21B (restrictions where taxpayer has delivered return) has effect as if that return had been delivered, or that claim had been made, by each member of the partnership.][4]

(3) Where a third party notice is given . . . [1] for the purpose of checking the tax position of more than one of the partners (in their capacity as such), [—

(*a*) ...[3]

(*b*) the references in paragraph 3(5) to naming the taxpayer are to making that statement and naming the partnership][1].

(4) In relation to such a notice [given to a person other than one of the partners][1]

(*a*) in paragraphs 3 and 4 (approval etc of notices and copying third party notices to taxpayer), the references to the taxpayer have effect as if they were references to at least one of the partners, and

(*b*) in paragraph 30(2) (no appeal in relation to taxpayer's statutory records), the reference to the taxpayer has effect as if it were a reference to [any of the partners in the partnership][1] [, or

(*c*) section 733 of CTA 2010 (company liable to counteraction of corporation tax advantage).][3]

[(5) In relation to a third party notice given to one of the partners for the purpose of checking the tax position of one or more of the other partners (in their capacity as such)—

(*a*) in paragraph 3 (approval etc of notices), sub-paragraphs (1) and (3)(*e*) do not apply,

(*b*) paragraph 4(1) (copying third party notices to taxpayer) does not apply,

(*c*) paragraph 30(1) (appeal) has effect as if it permitted an appeal on any grounds, and

(*d*) in paragraph 30(2) (no appeal in relation to taxpayer's statutory records), the reference to the taxpayer has effect as if it were a reference to any of the partners in the partnership.][1]

(6) Where a notice is given under paragraph 5 to one of the partners for the purpose of checking the tax position of one or more of the other partners whose identities are not known to the officer giving the notice[—

(*a*) sub-paragraphs (3) and (4) of that paragraph (approval of tribunal) have effect as if they permitted, but did not require, the officer to obtain the approval of the tribunal, and

(*b*) paragraph 31 (appeal) has effect as if it permitted an appeal on any grounds, but the partner to whom the notice is given may not appeal against a requirement in the notice to produce any document that forms part of that partner's statutory records.][1]

(7) Where a third party notice or a notice under paragraph 5 is given to one of the partners for the purpose of checking the tax position of one or more of the other partners, that partner may not appeal against a requirement in the notice to produce any document that forms part of that partner's statutory records.[1]

Commencement—Finance Act 2008, Schedule 36 (Appointed Day and Savings) Order, SI 2009/404 art 2 (appointed day for the coming into force of Sch 36 is 1 April 2009).

HMRC Manuals—Compliance Handbook Manual, CH23520 (HMRC inspection powers: specific rules regarding taxpayer notice).

CH23620 (HMRC inspection powers: specific rules regarding third party notice).

CH23680–23720 (HMRC inspection powers: notices given to partners).

CH23900 (HMRC inspection powers: identity unknown notice).

Amendments—[1] The following amendments made by FA 2009 s 95, Sch 47 para 11 with effect from 21 July 2009—

- sub-paras (2), (5) substituted;
- in sub-para (3) words "to any person (other than one of the partners)" repealed, words substituted for the words "paragraph 2", and para (*b*) and the preceding word "and" inserted;
- in sub-para (4) words inserted, and words substituted for the words "each of the partners";
- in sub-para (6) words substituted for the words ", sub-paragraph (3) of that paragraph (approval of tribunal) does not apply";
- sub-para (7) repealed.

[2] Sub-para (2A) inserted by FA 2009 s 96, Sch 48 para 13 with effect from 1 April 2010 (by virtue of SI 2009/3054 art 2).

[3] Sub-para (3)(*a*) repealed and (3)(*c*) inserted by CTA 2010 s 1177, Sch 1 paras 576, 582(1),(3), Sch 3 Pt 1. CTA 2010 has effect for corporation tax purposes for accounting periods ending on or after 1 April 2010, and for income and capital gains tax purposes for the tax year 2010–11 and subsequent tax years.

[4] Sub-para (2B) inserted by FA 2013 s 164, Sch 34 paras 1, 4 with effect from 17 July 2013.

Prospective amendments—In sub-para (2)(*a*), words ", or regulations under paragraph 10 of Schedule A1 to," to be inserted after words "section 12AA of" by F(No 2)A 2017 s 61(1), Sch 14 para 38(1), (3) with effect from a day to be appointed.

[Information in connection with herd basis election

37A—(1) This paragraph applies to a taxpayer notice given to a person carrying on a trade in relation to which a herd basis election is made if the notice refers only to information or documents that relate to—

(*a*) the animals kept for the purposes of the trade, or

(*b*) the products of those animals.

(2) Paragraph 21 (restrictions on giving taxpayer notice where taxpayer has made tax return) does not apply in relation to the notice.

(3) "Herd basis election" means an election under Chapter 8 of Part 2 of ITTOIA 2005 or Chapter 8 of Part 3 of CTA 2009.][1]

Amendments—[1] Paras 37A, 37B inserted by FA 2009 s 95, Sch 47 para 12 with effect from 21 July 2009.

[Information from persons liable to counteraction of tax advantage

37B—(1) This paragraph applies to a taxpayer notice given to a person if—

(*a*) it appears to an officer of Revenue and Customs that a counteraction provision may apply to the person by reason of one or more transactions, and

(*b*) the notice refers only to information or documents relating to the transaction (or, if there are two or more transactions, any of them).

(2) Paragraph 21 (restrictions on giving taxpayer notice where taxpayer has made tax return) does not apply in relation to the notice.

(3) "Counteraction provision" means—

(*a*) *section 703 of ICTA (company liable to counteraction of corporation tax advantage), or*[2]

(*b*) section 684 of ITA 2007 (person liable to counteraction of income tax advantage)][1] [, or

(*c*) section 733 of CTA 2010 (company liable to counteraction of corporation tax advantage).][2]

Amendments—[1] Paras 37A, 37B inserted by FA 2009 s 94, Sch 47 para 12 with effect from 21 July 2009.

[2] Sub-s (3)(*a*) repealed and sub-para (3)(*c*) inserted by CTA 2010 ss 1177, 1181, Sch 1 paras 576, 582 (1) ,(3), Sch 3 Pt 1. CTA 2010 has effect for corporation tax purposes for accounting periods ending on or after 1 April 2010, and for income and capital gains tax purposes for the tax year 2010–11 and subsequent tax years.

IHT

Application to the Crown

38 This Schedule (other than Part 8) applies to the Crown, but not to Her Majesty in Her private capacity (within the meaning of the Crown Proceedings Act 1947 (c 44)).

Commencement—Finance Act 2008, Schedule 36 (Appointed Day and Savings) Order, SI 2009/404 art 2 (appointed day for the coming into force of Sch 36 is 1 April 2009).
HMRC Manuals—Compliance Handbook Manual, CH21580 (HMRC inspection powers: meaning of "person").

PART 7
PENALTIES

. . . *Penalties [for failure to comply or obstruction]*

39—(1) This paragraph applies to a person who—

(*a*) fails to comply with an information notice, or

(*b*) deliberately obstructs an officer of Revenue and Customs in the course of an inspection under Part 2 of this Schedule that has been approved by the [tribunal][1].

(2) [The person][2] is liable to a penalty of £300.

(3) The reference in this paragraph to a person who fails to comply with an information notice includes a person who conceals, destroys or otherwise disposes of, or arranges for the concealment, destruction or disposal of, a document in breach of paragraph 42 or 43.

Commentary—*Simon's Taxes* **A6.301A**.
Commencement—Finance Act 2008, Schedule 36 (Appointed Day and Savings) Order, SI 2009/404 art 2 (appointed day for the coming into force of Sch 36 is 1 April 2009).
HMRC Manuals—Compliance Handbook Manual, CH25700 (HMRC inspection powers: information and deliberate obstruction of an inspection).
CH26220 (penalties: failure to comply with an information notice).
CH26240 (deliberate obstruction of a Tribunal approved inspection).
CH26260 (concealing, destroying or disposing of a document).
CH26640 (details of standard penalty).
CH26760 (HMRC inspection powers: two examples relating to penalties).
Cross-references—Recognised Overseas Pensions Schemes and Corresponding Relief) Regulations, SI 2006/208 reg 5 (application and modification of the penalty provisions in FA 2008 Sch 36 Pt 7 in respect of QROPS).
Amendments—[1] In sub-para (1)(*b*) word substituted for the words "First-tier Tribunal" by the Transfer of Tribunal Functions and Revenue and Customs Appeals Order, SI 2009/56 art 3, Sch 1 para 471 with effect from 1 April 2009.
[2] In heading, word "Standard" at the start repealed and words at the end inserted, and in sub-para (2) words substituted for the words "A person to whom this paragraph applies", by FA 2009 s 95, Sch 47 para 13 with effect from 21 July 2009.

Daily default penalties [for failure to comply or obstruction]

40—(1) This paragraph applies if the failure or obstruction mentioned in paragraph 39(1) continues after the date on which a penalty is imposed under that paragraph in respect of the failure or obstruction.

(2) The person is liable to a further penalty or penalties not exceeding £60 for each subsequent day on which the failure or obstruction continues.

Commentary—*Simon's Taxes* **A6.301A**.
Commencement—Finance Act 2008, Schedule 36 (Appointed Day and Savings) Order, SI 2009/404 art 2 (appointed day for the coming into force of Sch 36 is 1 April 2009).
HMRC Manuals—Compliance Handbook Manual, CH26660–26680 (HMRC inspection powers: details regarding daily penalties).
CH26760 (HMRC inspection powers: two examples relating to penalties).
Cross-references—Recognised Overseas Pensions Schemes and Corresponding Relief) Regulations, SI 2006/208 reg 5 (application and modification of the penalty provisions in FA 2008 Sch 36 Pt 7 in respect of QROPS).
Amendments—In heading words at the end inserted by FA 2009 s 95, Sch 47 para 14 with effect from 21 July 2009.

[Penalties for inaccurate information and documents

40A—(1) This paragraph applies if—

(*a*) in complying with an information notice, a person provides inaccurate information or produces a document that contains an inaccuracy, and

(*b*) condition [A, B or C][2] is met.

(2) Condition A is that the inaccuracy is careless or deliberate.

(3) An inaccuracy is careless if it is due to a failure by the person to take reasonable care.

[(3A) Condition B is that the person knows of the inaccuracy at the time the information is provided or the document produced but does not inform HMRC at that time.][2]

(4) Condition [C][2] is that the person—

(*a*) discovers the inaccuracy some time later, and

(*b*) fails to take reasonable steps to inform HMRC.

(5) The person is liable to a penalty not exceeding £3,000.

(6) Where the information or document contains more than one inaccuracy, a penalty is payable for each inaccuracy.][1]

Cross-references—Recognised Overseas Pensions Schemes and Corresponding Relief) Regulations, SI 2006/208 reg 5 (application and modification of the penalty provisions in FA 2008 Sch 36 Pt 7 in respect of QROPS).

Amendments—[1] Para 40A inserted by FA 2009 s 95, Sch 47 para 15 with effect from 21 July 2009.

[2] In sub-para (1)(*b*), words substituted, sub-para (3A) inserted, and in sub-para (4), letter substituted, by FA 2011 s 86(2), Sch 24 paras 1, 3 with effect in relation to any inaccuracy in information provided, or in documents produced, on or after 1 April 2012.

Power to change amount of . . . penalties

41—(1) If it appears to the Treasury that there has been a change in the value of money since the last relevant date, they may by regulations substitute for the sums for the time being specified in paragraphs 39(2)[, 40(2) and 40A(5)][1] such other sums as appear to them to be justified by the change.

(2) In sub-paragraph (1)[, in relation to a specified sum,][1] "relevant date" means—

(*a*) the date on which this Act is passed, and

(*b*) each date on which the power conferred by that sub-paragraph has been exercised [in relation to that sum][1].

(3) Regulations under this paragraph do not apply to[—

(*a*)] [1]any failure or obstruction which began before the date on which they come into force[, or

(*b*) an inaccuracy in any information or document provided to HMRC before that date.][1]

Commencement—Finance Act 2008, Schedule 36 (Appointed Day and Savings) Order, SI 2009/404 art 2 (appointed day for the coming into force of Sch 36 is 1 April 2009).

Cross-references—Recognised Overseas Pensions Schemes and Corresponding Relief) Regulations, SI 2006/208 reg 5 (application and modification of the penalty provisions in FA 2008 Sch 36 Pt 7 in respect of QROPS).

Amendments—[1] In cross-heading words "standard and daily default" repealed; in sub-para (1) words substituted for the words "and 40(2)"; in sub-para (2) words inserted in both places; in sub-para (3) words inserted, and para (*b*) and the preceding word "or" inserted; by FA 2009 s 95, Sch 47 para 16 with effect from 21 July 2009.

Concealing, destroying etc documents following information notice

42—(1) A person must not conceal, destroy or otherwise dispose of, or arrange for the concealment, destruction or disposal of, a document that is the subject of an information notice addressed to the person (subject to sub-paragraphs (2) and (3)).

(2) Sub-paragraph (1) does not apply if the person acts after the document has been produced to an officer of Revenue and Customs in accordance with the information notice, unless an officer of Revenue and Customs has notified the person in writing that the document must continue to be available for inspection (and has not withdrawn the notification).

(3) Sub-paragraph (1) does not apply, in a case to which paragraph 8(1) applies, if the person acts after the expiry of the period of 6 months beginning with the day on which a copy of the document was produced in accordance with that paragraph unless, before the expiry of that period, an officer of Revenue and Customs made a request for the original document under paragraph 8(2)(*b*).

Commencement—Finance Act 2008, Schedule 36 (Appointed Day and Savings) Order, SI 2009/404 art 2 (appointed day for the coming into force of Sch 36 is 1 April 2009).

Cross-references—Recognised Overseas Pensions Schemes and Corresponding Relief) Regulations, SI 2006/208 reg 5 (application and modification of the penalty provisions in FA 2008 Sch 36 Pt 7 in respect of QROPS).

Concealing, destroying etc documents following informal notification

43—(1) A person must not conceal, destroy or otherwise dispose of, or arrange for the concealment, destruction or disposal of, a document if an officer of Revenue and Customs has informed the person that the document is, or is likely, to be the subject of an information notice addressed to that person (subject to sub-paragraph (2)).

(2) Sub-paragraph (1) does not apply if the person acts after—

(*a*) at least 6 months has expired since the person was, or was last, so informed, or

(*b*) an information notice has been given to the person requiring the document to be produced.

Commencement—Finance Act 2008, Schedule 36 (Appointed Day and Savings) Order, SI 2009/404 art 2 (appointed day for the coming into force of Sch 36 is 1 April 2009).

Cross-references—Recognised Overseas Pensions Schemes and Corresponding Relief) Regulations, SI 2006/208 reg 5 (application and modification of the penalty provisions in FA 2008 Sch 36 Pt 7 in respect of QROPS).

Failure to comply with time limit

44 A failure by a person to do anything required to be done within a limited period of time does not give rise to liability to a penalty under paragraph 39 or 40 if the person did it within such further time, if any, as an officer of Revenue and Customs may have allowed.

Commencement—Finance Act 2008, Schedule 36 (Appointed Day and Savings) Order, SI 2009/404 art 2 (appointed day for the coming into force of Sch 36 is 1 April 2009).

Commentary—*Simon's Taxes* **A6.301A**.

Cross-references—Recognised Overseas Pensions Schemes and Corresponding Relief) Regulations, SI 2006/208 reg 5 (application and modification of the penalty provisions in FA 2008 Sch 36 Pt 7 in respect of QROPS).

Reasonable excuse

45—(1) Liability to a penalty under paragraph 39 or 40 does not arise if the person satisfies HMRC or [(on an appeal notified to the tribunal) the tribunal][1] that there is a reasonable excuse for the failure or the obstruction of an officer of Revenue and Customs.

(2) For the purposes of this paragraph—

(*a*) an insufficiency of funds is not a reasonable excuse unless attributable to events outside the person's control,

(*b*) where the person relies on any other person to do anything, that is not a reasonable excuse unless the first person took reasonable care to avoid the failure or obstruction, and

(*c*) where the person had a reasonable excuse for the failure or obstruction but the excuse has ceased, the person is to be treated as having continued to have the excuse if the failure is remedied, or the obstruction stops, without unreasonable delay after the excuse ceased.

Commentary—*Simon's Taxes* **A6.301A**.

Commencement—Finance Act 2008, Schedule 36 (Appointed Day and Savings) Order, SI 2009/404 art 2 (appointed day for the coming into force of Sch 36 is 1 April 2009).

HMRC Manuals—Compliance Handbook Manual, CH26320–26440 (HMRC inspection powers: what is and is not a reasonable excuse, with example at CH26420).

Cross-references—Recognised Overseas Pensions Schemes and Corresponding Relief) Regulations, SI 2006/208 reg 5 (application and modification of the penalty provisions in FA 2008 Sch 36 Pt 7 in respect of QROPS).

Amendments—[1] In sub-para (1) words substituted for the words "(on appeal) the First-tier Tribunal" by the Transfer of Tribunal Functions and Revenue and Customs Appeals Order, SI 2009/56 art 3, Sch 1 para 471 with effect from 1 April 2009.

Assessment of . . . penalty

46—(1) Where a person becomes liable for a penalty under paragraph 39[, 40 or 40A][1], . . . [1]

(*a*) [HMRC may][1] assess the penalty, and

(*b*) [if they do so, they must][1] notify the person.

(2) An assessment of a penalty under paragraph 39 or 40 must be made [within the period of 12 months beginning with the date on which the person became liable to the penalty, subject to sub-paragraph (3)][1].

[(3) In a case involving an information notice against which a person may appeal, an assessment of a penalty under paragraph 39 or 40 must be made within the period of 12 months beginning with the latest of the following—

(*a*) the date on which the person became liable to the penalty,

(*b*) the end of the period in which notice of an appeal against the information notice could have been given, and

(*c*) if notice of such an appeal is given, the date on which the appeal is determined or withdrawn.

(4) An assessment of a penalty under paragraph 40A must be made—

(*a*) within the period of 12 months beginning with the date on which the inaccuracy first came to the attention of an officer of Revenue and Customs, and

(*b*) within the period of 6 years beginning with the date on which the person became liable to the penalty.][1]

Commencement—Finance Act 2008, Schedule 36 (Appointed Day and Savings) Order, SI 2009/404 art 2 (appointed day for the coming into force of Sch 36 is 1 April 2009).

HMRC Manuals—Compliance Handbook Manual, CH26840 (HMRC inspection powers: what the penalty assessment must include).

CH26860 (when to issue a penalty assessment).

Cross-references—Recognised Overseas Pensions Schemes and Corresponding Relief) Regulations, SI 2006/208 reg 5 (application and modification of the penalty provisions in FA 2008 Sch 36 Pt 7 in respect of QROPS).

Amendments—[1] In the cross-heading, words "standard penalty or daily default" repealed; in sub-para (1) words substituted for the words "or 40"; words "HMRC may" repealed and words at the beginning of paras (*a*), (*b*) inserted; in sub-para (2), words substituted for the words "within 12 months of the relevant date"; and sub-paras (3), (4) substituted for previous sub-para (3), by FA 2009 s 95, Sch 47 para 17 with effect from 21 July 2009.

Right to appeal against . . . penalty

47 A person may appeal . . . [1] against any of the following decisions of an officer of Revenue and Customs—

(*a*) a decision that a penalty is payable by that person under paragraph 39[, 40 or 40A][2], or

(*b*) a decision as to the amount of such a penalty.

Commentary—*Simon's Taxes* **A6.301A**.

Commencement—Finance Act 2008, Schedule 36 (Appointed Day and Savings) Order, SI 2009/404 art 2 (appointed day for the coming into force of Sch 36 is 1 April 2009).

HMRC Manuals—Compliance Handbook Manual, CH26900 (HMRC inspection powers (penalties): types of appeal and procedures).

Cross-references—Recognised Overseas Pensions Schemes and Corresponding Relief) Regulations, SI 2006/208 reg 5 (application and modification of the penalty provisions in FA 2008 Sch 36 Pt 7 in respect of QROPS).

Modification—See F(No 2)A 2017 Sch 16 para 42(3) (application of this para in relation to penalties for enablers of defeated tax avoidance).

Amendments—[1] Words "to the First-tier Tribunal" repealed by the Transfer of Tribunal Functions and Revenue and Customs Appeals Order, SI 2009/56 art 3, Sch 1 para 471 with effect from 1 April 2009.

[2] In the cross-heading, words "standard penalty or daily default" repealed, in sub-para (*a*) words substituted for the words "or 40", by FA 2009 s 95, Sch 47 para 18 with effect from 21 July 2009.

Procedure on appeal against . . . penalty

48—(1) Notice of an appeal under paragraph 47 must be given—

(*a*) in writing,

(*b*) before the end of the period of 30 days beginning with the date on which the notification under paragraph 46 was issued, and

(*c*) to HMRC.

(2) Notice of an appeal under paragraph 47 must state the grounds of appeal.

(3) On an appeal under paragraph 47(*a*), [that is notified to the tribunal, the tribunal][1] may confirm or cancel the decision.

(4) On an appeal under paragraph 47(*b*), [that is notified to the tribunal, the tribunal][1] may—

(*a*) confirm the decision, or

(*b*) substitute for the decision another decision that the officer of Revenue and Customs had power to make.

(5) Subject to this paragraph and paragraph 49, the provisions of Part 5 of TMA 1970 relating to appeals have effect in relation to appeals under this Part of this Schedule as they have effect in relation to an appeal against an assessment to income tax.

Commencement—Finance Act 2008, Schedule 36 (Appointed Day and Savings) Order, SI 2009/404 art 2 (appointed day for the coming into force of Sch 36 is 1 April 2009).

HMRC Manuals—Compliance Handbook Manual, CH26900 (HMRC inspection powers (penalties): types of appeal and procedures).

Cross-references—Recognised Overseas Pensions Schemes and Corresponding Relief) Regulations, SI 2006/208 reg 5 (application and modification of the penalty provisions in FA 2008 Sch 36 Pt 7 in respect of QROPS).

Amendments—In the heading, words "standard penalty or daily default" repealed by FA 2009 s 95, Sch 47 para 19 with effect from 21 July 2009.

[1] In sub-paras (3), 4) words substituted for the words "First-tier Tribunal" by the Transfer of Tribunal Functions and Revenue and Customs Appeals Order, SI 2009/56 art 3, Sch 1 para 471 with effect from 1 April 2009.

Enforcement of . . . penalty

49—(1) A penalty under paragraph 39[, 40 or 40A][1] must be paid—

(*a*) before the end of the period of 30 days beginning with the date on which the notification under paragraph 46 was issued, or

(*b*) if a notice of an appeal against the penalty is given, before the end of the period of 30 days beginning with the date on which the appeal is determined or withdrawn.

(2) A penalty under paragraph 39[, 40 or 40A][1] may be enforced as if it were income tax charged in an assessment and due and payable.

Commentary—*Simon's Taxes* **A6.301A**.

Commencement—Finance Act 2008, Schedule 36 (Appointed Day and Savings) Order, SI 2009/404 art 2 (appointed day for the coming into force of Sch 36 is 1 April 2009).

HMRC Manuals—Compliance Handbook Manual, CH26880 (HMRC inspection powers: when is the penalty payable).

Cross-references—Recognised Overseas Pensions Schemes and Corresponding Relief) Regulations, SI 2006/208 reg 5 (application and modification of the penalty provisions in FA 2008 Sch 36 Pt 7 in respect of QROPS).

Amendments—[1] In the heading, words "standard penalty or daily default" repealed, in sub-paras (1), (2) words substituted for the words "or 40", by FA 2009 s 95, Sch 47 para 20 with effect from 21 July 2009.

[Increased daily default penalty

49A (1) This paragraph applies if—

(*a*) a penalty under paragraph 40 is assessed under paragraph 46 in respect of a person's failure to comply with a notice under paragraph 5,

(*b*) the failure continues for more than 30 days beginning with the date on which notification of that assessment was issued, and

(*c*) the person has been told that an application may be made under this paragraph for an increased daily penalty to be imposed.

(2) If this paragraph applies, an officer of Revenue and Customs may make an application to the tribunal for an increased daily penalty to be imposed on the person.

(3) If the tribunal decides that an increased daily penalty should be imposed, then for each applicable day (see paragraph 49B) on which the failure continues—

(*a*) the person is not liable to a penalty under paragraph 40 in respect of the failure, and

(*b*) the person is liable instead to a penalty under this paragraph of an amount determined by the tribunal.

(4) The tribunal may not determine an amount exceeding £1,000 for each applicable day.

(5) But subject to that, in determining the amount the tribunal must have regard to—

(*a*) the likely cost to the person of complying with the notice,

(*b*) any benefits to the person of not complying with it, and

(*c*) any benefits to anyone else resulting from the person's non-compliance.

(6) Paragraph 41 applies in relation to the sum specified in sub-paragraph (4) as it applies in relation to the sums mentioned in paragraph 41(1).][1]

Cross-references—Recognised Overseas Pensions Schemes and Corresponding Relief) Regulations, SI 2006/208 reg 5 (application and modification of the penalty provisions in FA 2008 Sch 36 Pt 7 in respect of QROPS).

Modification—See F(No 2)A 2017 Sch 16 para 42(4) (application of this para in relation to penalties for enablers of defeated tax avoidance).

Amendments—[1] Paras 49A–49C inserted by FA 2011 s 86(2), Sch 24 paras 1, 4 with effect in relation to failures to comply with a notice under FA 2008 Sch 36 para 5 that begin on or after 1 April 2012.

[49B (1) If a person becomes liable to a penalty under paragraph 49A, HMRC must notify the person.

(2) The notification must specify the day from which the increased penalty is to apply.

(3) That day and any subsequent day is an "applicable day" for the purposes of paragraph 49A(3).][1]

Cross-references—Recognised Overseas Pensions Schemes and Corresponding Relief) Regulations, SI 2006/208 reg 5 (application and modification of the penalty provisions in FA 2008 Sch 36 Pt 7 in respect of QROPS).

Modification—See F(No 2)A 2017 Sch 16 para 42(5) (application of this para in relation to penalties for enablers of defeated tax avoidance).

Amendments—[1] Paras 49A–49C inserted by FA 2011 s 86(2), Sch 24 paras 1, 4 with effect in relation to failures to comply with a notice under FA 2008 Sch 36 para 5 that begin on or after 1 April 2012.

[49C (1) A penalty under paragraph 49A must be paid before the end of the period of 30 days beginning with the date on which the notification under paragraph 49B is issued.

(2) A penalty under paragraph 49A may be enforced as if it were income tax charged in an assessment and due and payable.][1]

Cross-references—Recognised Overseas Pensions Schemes and Corresponding Relief) Regulations, SI 2006/208 reg 5 (application and modification of the penalty provisions in FA 2008 Sch 36 Pt 7 in respect of QROPS).

Modification—See F(No 2)A 2017 Sch 16 para 42(6) (disapplication of this para in relation to penalties for enablers of defeated tax avoidance).

Amendments—[1] Paras 49A–49C inserted by FA 2011 s 86(2), Sch 24 paras 1, 4 with effect in relation to failures to comply with a notice under FA 2008 Sch 36 para 5 that begin on or after 1 April 2012.

Tax-related penalty

50—(1) This paragraph applies where—

(*a*) a person becomes liable to a penalty under paragraph 39,

(*b*) the failure or obstruction continues after a penalty is imposed under that paragraph,

(*c*) an officer of Revenue and Customs has reason to believe that, as a result of the failure or obstruction, the amount of tax that the person has paid, or is likely to pay, is significantly less than it would otherwise have been,

(*d*) before the end of the period of 12 months beginning with the relevant date . . . [1], an officer of Revenue and Customs makes an application to the Upper Tribunal for an additional penalty to be imposed on the person, and

(*e*) the Upper Tribunal decides that it is appropriate for an additional penalty to be imposed.

(2) The person is liable to a penalty of an amount decided by the Upper Tribunal.

(3) In deciding the amount of the penalty, the Upper Tribunal must have regard to the amount of tax which has not been, or is not likely to be, paid by the person.

(4) Where a person becomes liable to a penalty under this paragraph, HMRC must notify the person.

(5) Any penalty under this paragraph is in addition to the penalty or penalties under paragraph 39 or 40.

(6) In the application of the following provisions, no account shall be taken of a penalty under this paragraph—

(*a*) section 97A of TMA 1970 (multiple penalties),

(*b*) paragraph 12(2) of Schedule 24 to FA 2007 (interaction with other penalties), and

(*c*) paragraph 15(1) of Schedule 41 (interaction with other penalties).

[(7) In sub-paragraph (1)(*d*) "the relevant date" means—

(*a*) in a case involving an information notice against which a person may appeal, the latest of—

(i) the date on which the person became liable to the penalty under paragraph 39,

(ii) the end of the period in which notice of an appeal against the information notice could have been given, and

(iii) if notice of such an appeal is given, the date on which the appeal is determined or withdrawn, and

(*b*) in any other case, the date on which the person became liable to the penalty under paragraph 39.][1]

Commentary—*Simon's Taxes* **A6.301A**.

Commencement—Finance Act 2008, Schedule 36 (Appointed Day and Savings) Order, SI 2009/404 art 2 (appointed day for the coming into force of Sch 36 is 1 April 2009).

HMRC Manuals—Compliance Handbook Manual, CH26720 (HMRC inspection powers: details regarding tax related penalty). CH26760 (HMRC inspection powers: two examples relating to penalties).

Cross-references—Recognised Overseas Pensions Schemes and Corresponding Relief) Regulations, SI 2006/208 reg 5 (application and modification of the penalty provisions in FA 2008 Sch 36 Pt 7 in respect of QROPS).

Modification—See FA 2016 Sch 20 para 20(*d*) (disapplication of this para in relation to penalties for enablers of offshore tax evasion or non-compliance).

See F(No 2)A 2017 Sch 16 para 43 (disapplication of this para in relation to penalties for enablers of defeated tax avoidance).

Amendments—[1] In sub-para (1)(*d*) words "(within the meaning of paragraph 46)" repealed, and sub-para (7) inserted, by FA 2011 s 86(2), Sch 24 paras 1, 5(1)–(3) with effect where a person becomes liable to a penalty under FA 2008 Sch 36 para 39 on or after 19 July 2011.

Simon's Tax Cases—*R&C Comrs v Tager and another* [2015] UKUT 40 (TCC), [2015] STC 1687.

Enforcement of tax-related penalty

51—(1) A penalty under paragraph 50 must be paid before the end of the period of 30 days beginning with the date on which the notification of the penalty is issued.

(2) A penalty under paragraph 50 may be enforced as if it were income tax charged in an assessment and due and payable.

Commentary—*Simon's Taxes* **A6.301A**.

Commencement—Finance Act 2008, Schedule 36 (Appointed Day and Savings) Order, SI 2009/404 art 2 (appointed day for the coming into force of Sch 36 is 1 April 2009).

Cross-references—Recognised Overseas Pensions Schemes and Corresponding Relief) Regulations, SI 2006/208 reg 5 (application and modification of the penalty provisions in FA 2008 Sch 36 Pt 7 in respect of QROPS).

Modification—See FA 2016 Sch 20 para 20(*d*) (disapplication of this para in relation to penalties for enablers of offshore tax evasion or non-compliance).

See F(No 2)A 2017 Sch 16 para 43 (disapplication of this para in relation to penalties for enablers of defeated tax avoidance).

Double jeopardy

52 A person is not liable to a penalty under this Schedule in respect of anything in respect of which the person has been convicted of an offence.

Commentary—*Simon's Taxes* **A6.301A**.

Commencement—Finance Act 2008, Schedule 36 (Appointed Day and Savings) Order, SI 2009/404 art 2 (appointed day for the coming into force of Sch 36 is 1 April 2009).

Cross-references—Recognised Overseas Pensions Schemes and Corresponding Relief) Regulations, SI 2006/208 reg 5 (application and modification of the penalty provisions in FA 2008 Sch 36 Pt 7 in respect of QROPS).

PART 8
OFFENCE

Concealing etc documents following information notice

53—(1) A person is guilty of an offence (subject to sub-paragraphs (2) and (3)) if—

(*a*) the person is required to produce a document by an information notice,

(*b*) the [tribunal][1] approved the giving of the notice in accordance with paragraph 3 or 5, and

(*c*) the person conceals, destroys or otherwise disposes of, or arranges for the concealment, destruction or disposal of, that document.

(2) Sub-paragraph (1) does not apply if the person acts after the document has been produced to an officer of Revenue and Customs in accordance with the information notice, unless an officer of Revenue and Customs has notified the person in writing that the document must continue to be available for inspection (and has not withdrawn the notification).

(3) Sub-paragraph (1) does not apply, in a case to which paragraph 8(1) applies, if the person acts after the expiry of the period of 6 months beginning with the day on which a copy of the document was so produced unless, before the expiry of that period, an officer of Revenue and Customs made a request for the original document under paragraph 8(2)(*b*).

Commencement—Finance Act 2008, Schedule 36 (Appointed Day and Savings) Order, SI 2009/404 art 2 (appointed day for the coming into force of Sch 36 is 1 April 2009).

HMRC Manuals—Compliance Handbook Manual, CH27200 (HMRC inspection powers (penalties): criminal proceedings for concealing, destroying or disposing of a document).

Amendments—[1] In sub-para (1)(*b*) word substituted for the words "First-tier Tribunal" by the Transfer of Tribunal Functions and Revenue and Customs Appeals Order, SI 2009/56 art 3, Sch 1 para 471 with effect from 1 April 2009.

Concealing etc documents following informal notification

54—(1) A person is also guilty of an offence (subject to sub-paragraph (2)) if the person conceals, destroys or otherwise disposes of, or arranges for the concealment, destruction or disposal of a document after the person has been informed by an officer of Revenue and Customs in writing that—

(*a*) the document is, or is likely, to be the subject of an information notice addressed to that person, and

(*b*) an officer of Revenue and Customs intends to seek the approval of the [tribunal][1] to the giving of the notice under paragraph 3 or 5 in respect of the document.

(2) A person is not guilty of an offence under this paragraph if the person acts after—

(*a*) at least 6 months has expired since the person was, or was last, so informed, or

(*b*) an information notice has been given to the person requiring the document to be produced.

Commencement—Finance Act 2008, Schedule 36 (Appointed Day and Savings) Order, SI 2009/404 art 2 (appointed day for the coming into force of Sch 36 is 1 April 2009).

Amendments—[1] In sub-para (1)(*b*) word substituted for the words "First-tier Tribunal" by the Transfer of Tribunal Functions and Revenue and Customs Appeals Order, SI 2009/56 art 3, Sch 1 para 471 with effect from 1 April 2009.

Fine or imprisonment

55 A person who is guilty of an offence under this Part of this Schedule is liable—

(*a*) on summary conviction, to a fine not exceeding the statutory maximum, and

(*b*) on conviction on indictment, to imprisonment for a term not exceeding 2 years or to a fine, or both.

Commencement—Finance Act 2008, Schedule 36 (Appointed Day and Savings) Order, SI 2009/404 art 2 (appointed day for the coming into force of Sch 36 is 1 April 2009).

PART 9

MISCELLANEOUS PROVISIONS AND INTERPRETATION

Application of provisions of TMA 1970

56 Subject to the provisions of this Schedule, the following provisions of TMA 1970 apply for the purposes of this Schedule as they apply for the purposes of the Taxes Acts—

(*a*) section 108 (responsibility of company officers),

(*b*) section 114 (want of form), and

(*c*) section 115 (delivery and service of documents).

Commencement—Finance Act 2008, Schedule 36 (Appointed Day and Savings) Order, SI 2009/404 art 2 (appointed day for the coming into force of Sch 36 is 1 April 2009).

HMRC Manuals—Compliance Handbook Manual, CH23440 (HMRC inspection powers: serving notices).
CH23460 (mistakes in a notice).

Regulations under this Schedule

57—(1) Regulations made by the Commissioners or the Treasury under this Schedule are to be made by statutory instrument.

(2) A statutory instrument containing regulations under this Schedule is subject to annulment in pursuance of a resolution of the House of Commons.

Commencement—Finance Act 2008, Schedule 36 (Appointed Day and Savings) Order, SI 2009/404 art 2 (appointed day for the coming into force of Sch 36 is 1 April 2009).

General interpretation

58 In this Schedule—

"checking" includes carrying out an investigation or enquiry of any kind,

"the Commissioners" means the Commissioners for Her Majesty's Revenue and Customs,

"document" includes a part of a document (except where the context otherwise requires),

"enactment" includes subordinate legislation (within the meaning of the Interpretation Act 1978 (c 30)),

"HMRC" means Her Majesty's Revenue and Customs,

"premises" includes—

(*a*) any building or structure,

(*b*) any land, and

(*c*) any means of transport,

"the Taxes Acts" means—

(*a*) TMA 1970,

(*b*) the Tax Acts, and

(*c*) TCGA 1992 and all other enactments relating to capital gains tax, . . . [1]

"taxpayer", in relation to a taxpayer notice or a third party notice, has the meaning given in paragraph 1(1) or 2(1) (as appropriate) [and][1]

["tribunal" means the First-tier Tribunal or, where determined by or under Tribunal Procedure Rules, the Upper Tribunal.][1]

Commencement—Finance Act 2008, Schedule 36 (Appointed Day and Savings) Order, SI 2009/404 art 2 (appointed day for the coming into force of Sch 36 is 1 April 2009).

HMRC Manuals—Compliance Handbook Manual, CH21660 (HMRC inspection powers: checks).

CH23320–23360 (HMRC inspection powers: what is a "document", part of a document or electronic document).

Amendments—[1] In sub-para (*c*) in the definition of "the Taxes Acts" word "and" at the end repealed; definition of "tribunal" and the preceding word "and" inserted by the Transfer of Tribunal Functions and Revenue and Customs Appeals Order, SI 2009/56 art 3, Sch 1 para 471 with effect from 1 April 2009.

Authorised officer of Revenue and Customs

59 A reference in a provision of this Schedule to an authorised officer of Revenue and Customs is a reference to an officer of Revenue and Customs who is, or is a member of a class of officers who are, authorised by the Commissioners for the purpose of that provision.

Commencement—Finance Act 2008, Schedule 36 (Appointed Day and Savings) Order, SI 2009/404 art 2 (appointed day for the coming into force of Sch 36 is 1 April 2009).

HMRC Manuals—Compliance Handbook Manual, CH260000 (HMRC inspection powers – how to do a compliance check: authorisation levels).

CH21720 (HMRC inspection powers: authorised officer).

Business

60—(1) In this Schedule (subject to regulations under this paragraph), references to carrying on a business include—

(*a*) the letting of property,

(*b*) the activities of a charity, and

(*c*) the activities of a government department, a local authority, a local authority association and any other public authority.

(2) In sub-paragraph (1)—

. . . [1]

"local authority" has the meaning given in section 999 of ITA 2007, and

"local authority association" has the meaning given in section 1000 of that Act.

(3) The Commissioners may by regulations provide that for the purposes of this Schedule—

(*a*) the carrying on of an activity specified in the regulations, or

(*b*) the carrying on of such an activity (or any activity) by a person specified in the regulations,

is or is not to be treated as the carrying on of a business.

Commencement—Finance Act 2008, Schedule 36 (Appointed Day and Savings) Order, SI 2009/404 art 2 (appointed day for the coming into force of Sch 36 is 1 April 2009).

HMRC Manuals—Compliance Handbook Manual, CH25200 (HMRC inspection powers: meaning of "carrying on a business").

Amendments—[1] In sub-s (2) definition of "charity" repealed by FA 2010 s 30, Sch 6 para 24 with effect from 1 April 2012 (SI 2012/736 art 19).

Chargeable period

61 In this Schedule "chargeable period" means—

(*a*) in relation to income tax or capital gains tax, a tax year, and

(*b*) in relation to corporation tax, an accounting period.

Commencement—Finance Act 2008, Schedule 36 (Appointed Day and Savings) Order, SI 2009/404 art 2 (appointed day for the coming into force of Sch 36 is 1 April 2009).

[Involved third parties

61A—(1) In this Schedule, "involved third party" means a person described in the first column of the Table below.

(2) In this Schedule, in relation to an involved third party, . . . [3] "relevant document" and "relevant tax" have the meaning given in the corresponding entries in that Table.

	Involved third party	*Relevant . . .* [3] *documents*	*Relevant tax*
1	A body approved by an officer of Revenue and Customs for the purpose of paying donations within the meaning of Part 12 of ITEPA 2003 (donations to charity: payroll giving) (see section 714 of that Act)	[Documents][3] relating to the donations	Income tax
2	A plan manager (see section 696 of ITTOIA 2005 (managers of individual investment plans))	[Documents][3] relating to the plan, including investments which are or have been held under the plan	Income tax
3	An account provider in relation to a child trust fund (as defined in section 3 of the Child Trust Funds Act 2004)	[Documents][3] relating to the fund, including investments which are or have been held under the fund	Income tax
4	A person who is or has been registered as a managing agent at Lloyd's in relation to a syndicate of underwriting members of Lloyd's	[Documents][3] relating to, and to the activities of, the syndicate	Income tax Capital gains tax Corporation tax
5	A person involved (in any capacity) in an insurance business (as defined for the purposes of Part 3 of FA 1994)	[Documents][3] relating to contracts of insurance entered into in the course of the business	Insurance premium tax
6	A person who makes arrangements for persons to enter into contracts of insurance	[Documents][3] relating to the contracts	Insurance premium tax
7	A person who— (*a*) is concerned in a business that is not an insurance business (as defined for the purposes of Part 3 of FA 1994), and (*b*) has been involved in the entry into a contract of insurance providing cover for any matter associated with that business	[Documents][3] relating to the contracts	Insurance premium tax
8	A person who, in relation to a charge to stamp duty reserve tax on an agreement, transfer, issue, appropriation or surrender, is an accountable person (as defined in regulation 2 of the Stamp Duty Reserve Tax Regulations SI 1986/1711 (as amended from time to time))	[Documents][3] relating to the agreement, transfer, issue, appropriation or surrender	Stamp duty reserve tax
9	A responsible person in relation to an oil field (as defined for the purposes of Part 1 of OTA 1975)	[Documents][3] relating to the oil field	Petroleum revenue tax
10	A person involved (in any capacity) in subjecting aggregate to exploitation in the United Kingdom (as defined for the purposes of Part 2 of FA 2001) or in connected activities	[Documents][3] relating to matters in which the person is or has been involved	Aggregates levy

	Involved third party	*Relevant . . .*[3] *documents*	*Relevant tax*
11	A person involved (in any capacity) in making or receiving [supplies of][2] taxable commodities (as defined for the purposes of Schedule 6 to FA 2000) or in connected activities	[Documents][3] relating to matters in which the person is or has been involved	Climate change levy
12	A person involved (in any capacity) with any landfill disposal (as defined for the purposes of Part 3 of FA 1996)	[Documents][3] relating to the disposal	Landfill tax][1]

Amendments—[1] Para 61A inserted by FA 2009 s 96, Sch 48 para 14 with effect from 1 April 2010 (by virtue of SI 2009/3054 art 2).

[2] In Table, words in item 11 inserted by FA 2011 s 86(2), Sch 24 paras 1, 6 with effect from 19 July 2011.

[3] In sub-para (2) words ""relevant information"," repealed, in each in entry in second column of the Table word substituted for words "Information and documents", and in heading of that column words "information and relevant" repealed, by FA 2011 s 86(1), Sch 23 paras 60, 62(1), (3) with effect from 1 April 2012 in relation to relevant data with a bearing on any period (whether before, on or after 1 April 2012) subject to FA 2011 Sch 23 para 3(2). This para will continue to have effect in relation to notices given, or requests made, under any of the provisions repealed by FA 2011 Sch 23 Pt 6 before 1 April 2012 as if the amendments had not been made (FA 2011 Sch 23 para 65(2)).

Statutory records

62— (1) For the purposes of this Schedule, information or a document forms part of a person's statutory records if it is information or a document which the person is required to keep and preserve under or by virtue of—

(*a*) the Taxes Acts, or

[(*b*) any other enactment relating to a tax,][1]

subject to the following provisions of this paragraph.

(2) To the extent that any information or document that is required to be kept and preserved under or by virtue of the Taxes Acts—

(*a*) does not relate to the carrying on of a business, and

(*b*) is not also required to be kept or preserved under or by virtue of [any other enactment relating to a tax][1],

it only forms part of a person's statutory records to the extent that the chargeable period or periods to which it relates has or have ended.

(3) Information and documents cease to form part of a person's statutory records when the period for which they are required to be preserved by the enactments mentioned in sub-paragraph (1) has expired.

Commencement—Finance Act 2008, Schedule 36 (Appointed Day and Savings) Order, SI 2009/404 art 2 (appointed day for the coming into force of Sch 36 is 1 April 2009).

HMRC Manuals—Compliance Handbook Manual, CH21700 (HMRC inspection powers: statutory records).

Amendments—[1] Sub-para (1)(*b*) substituted, and in sub-para (2) words substituted for words "VATA 1994 or any other enactment relating to value added tax", by FA 2009 s 95, Sch 48 para 15 with effect from 1 April 2010 (by virtue of SI 2009/3054 art 2).

Tax

63—(1) In this Schedule, except where the context otherwise requires, "tax" means all or any of the following—

(*a*) income tax,

(*b*) capital gains tax,

(*c*) corporation tax,

[(*ca*) diverted profits tax,][5]

[(*cb*) apprenticeship levy,][6]

(*d*) VAT, and

[(*e*) insurance premium tax,

(*f*) inheritance tax,

(*g*) stamp duty land tax,

(*h*) stamp duty reserve tax,

[(*ha*) annual tax on enveloped dwellings,][3]

(*i*) petroleum revenue tax,

(*j*) aggregates levy,

(*k*) climate change levy,
(*l*) landfill tax, and
(*m*) relevant foreign tax,][2]
and references to "a tax" are to be interpreted accordingly.
(2) In this Schedule "corporation tax" includes any amount assessable or chargeable as if it were corporation tax.
(3) In this Schedule "VAT" means—
(*a*) value added tax charged in accordance with VATA 1994, . . . [1]
(*b*) value added tax charged in accordance with the law of another member State, [and
(*c*) amounts listed in sub-paragraph (3A).][1]
[(3A) Those amounts are—
(*a*) any amount that is recoverable under paragraph 5(2) of Schedule 11 to VATA 1994 (amounts shown on invoices as VAT), and
(*b*) any amount that is treated as VAT by virtue of regulations under section 54 of VATA 1994 (farmers etc).][1]
(4) In this Schedule "relevant foreign tax" means—
(*a*) a tax of a member State, other than the United Kingdom, which is covered by the provisions for the exchange of information under [Council Directive 2011/16/EU of 15 February 2011 on administrative cooperation in the field of taxation][4] (as amended from time to time), and
(*b*) any tax or duty which is imposed under the law of a territory in relation to which arrangements having effect by virtue of section 173 of FA 2006 (international tax enforcement arrangements) have been made and which is covered by the arrangements.

Commencement—Finance Act 2008, Schedule 36 (Appointed Day and Savings) Order, SI 2009/404 art 2 (appointed day for the coming into force of Sch 36 is 1 April 2009).
Modification—See FA 2010 Sch 1 para 36 (modification of this para in relation to bank payroll tax).
HMRC Manuals—Compliance Handbook Manual, CH21540 (HMRC inspection powers: tax position).
CH21560 (meaning of relevant foreign tax).
Amendments—[1] In sub-para (3)(*a*) word "and" repealed, sub-para (3)(*c*) and the preceding word "and" substituted for the words "and includes any amount that is recoverable under paragraph 5(2) of Schedule 11 to VATA 1994 (amounts shown on invoices as VAT)", and sub-para (3A) inserted, by FA 2009 s 95, Sch 47 para 21 with effect from 21 July 2009.
[2] In sub-para (1), paras (*e*)–(*m*) substituted for previous para (*e*) and preceding word "and" by FA 2009 s 96(1) with effect from 1 April 2010 (by virtue of SI 2009/3054 art 2).
[3] Sub-para (1)(*ha*) inserted by FA 2013 s 164, Sch 34 paras 1, 5 with effect from 17 July 2013.
[4] In sub-para (4)(*a*), words substituted by the European Administrative Co-operation (Taxation) Regulations, SI 2012/3062 reg 6 with effect from 1 January 2013.
[5] Sub-para (1)(*ca*) inserted by FA 2015 s 105(2) with effect in relation to accounting periods beginning on or after 1 April 2015. For accounting periods that straddle that date, see FA 2015 s 116(2).
[6] Sub-para (1)(*cb*) inserted by FA 2016 s 112 with effect from 15 September 2016. The apprenticeship levy applies in relation to 2017–18 and subsequent tax years.
Prospective amendments—Sub-para (1)(*ia*) to be inserted by FA 2017 s 56, Sch 11 para 1(1), (3) with effect from a date to be appointed. Once appointed, the charge to soft drinks industry levy will arise on chargeable events which occur on or after 6 April 2018 (FA 2017 s 31(1)). Sub-para (1)(*ia*) to read as follows—

"(*ia*) soft drinks industry levy,".

Tax position

64—(1) In this Schedule, except as otherwise provided, "tax position", in relation to a person, means the person's position as regards any tax, including the person's position as regards—
(*a*) past, present and future liability to pay any tax,
(*b*) penalties and other amounts that have been paid, or are or may be payable, by or to the person in connection with any tax, and
(*c*) claims, elections, applications and notices that have been or may be made or given in connection with [the person's liability to pay][1] any tax,
and references to a person's position as regards a particular tax (however expressed) are to be interpreted accordingly.
(2) References in this Schedule to a person's tax position include, where appropriate, a reference to the person's position as regards any deductions or repayments of tax, or of sums representing tax, that the person is required to make—
(*a*) under PAYE regulations,
(*b*) under Chapter 3 of Part 3 of FA 2004 or regulations made under that Chapter (construction industry scheme), or
(*c*) by or under any other provision of the Taxes Acts.
[(2A) References in this Schedule to a person's tax position also include, where appropriate, a reference to the person's position as regards the withholding by the person of another person's PAYE income (as defined in section 683 of ITEPA 2003).][1]

(3) References in this Schedule to the tax position of a person include the tax position of—

(*a*) a company that has ceased to exist, and

(*b*) an individual who has died.

(4) References in this Schedule to a person's tax position are to the person's tax position at any time or in relation to any period, unless otherwise stated.

Commencement—Finance Act 2008, Schedule 36 (Appointed Day and Savings) Order, SI 2009/404 art 2 (appointed day for the coming into force of Sch 36 is 1 April 2009).

Amendments—[1] In sub-para (1)(*c*) words inserted, and sub-para (2A) inserted, by FA 2009 s 95, Sch 47 para 22 with effect from 21 July 2009.

PART 10
CONSEQUENTIAL PROVISIONS

Commencement—Finance Act 2008, Schedule 36 (Appointed Day and Savings) Order, SI 2009/404 art 2 (appointed day for the coming into force of Sch 36 is 1 April 2009).

TMA 1970

65 TMA 1970 is amended as follows.

66 Omit section 19A (power to call for documents for purposes of enquiries).

67 Omit section 20 (power to call for documents of taxpayer and others).

68—(1) Section 20B (restrictions on powers to call for documents under ss 20 and 20A) is amended as follows.

(2) In the heading, for "**ss 20 and**" substitute "**section**".

(3) In subsection (1)—

(*a*) omit "under section 20(1), (3) or (8A), or",

(*b*) omit "(or, in the case of section 20(3), to deliver or make available)",

(*c*) omit ", or to furnish the particulars in question", and

(*d*) omit "section 20(7) or (8A) or, as the case may be,".

(4) Omit subsections (1A) and (1B).

(5) In subsection (2), omit from the beginning to "taxpayer; and".

(6) In subsection (3)—

(*a*) omit "under section 20(1) or (3) or", and

(*b*) omit "section 20(3) and (4) and".

(7) In subsection (4)—

(*a*) omit "section 20(1) or", and

(*b*) omit ", and as an alternative to delivering documents to comply with a notice under section 20(3) or (8A)".

(8) Omit subsections (5), (6) and (7).

(9) In subsection (8), omit "section 20(3) or (8A) or".

(10) Omit subsections (9) to (14).

69—(1) Section 20BB (falsification etc of documents) is amended as follows.

(2) In subsection (1)(*a*), omit "20 or".

(3) In subsection (2)(*b*), omit "or, in a case within section 20(3) or (8A) above, inspected".

70—(1) Section 20D (interpretation) is amended as follows.

(2) In subsection (2), for "sections 20 and" substitute "section".

(3) Omit subsection (3).

71 In section 29(6)(*c*) (assessment where loss of tax discovered), omit ", whether in pursuance of a notice under section 19A of this Act or otherwise".

72 Omit section 97AA (failure to produce documents under section 19A).

73 In section 98 (penalties), in the Table—

(*a*) in the first column, omit the entry for section 767C of ICTA, and

(*b*) in the second column, omit the entry for section 28(2) of F(No 2)A 1992.

74 *In section 100(2) (exclusions from provisions relating to determination of penalties under the Taxes Acts), insert at the end "or*

(g) Schedule 36 to the Finance Act 2008."

Amendments—Para 74 repealed by FA 2009 s 109, Sch 57 para 14(*a*) with effect from 21 July 2009.

75 (1) Section 107A (relevant trustees) is amended as follows.

(2) In subsection (2)(*a*), for ", 95 or 97AA" substitute 'or 95'.

(3) In subsection (3)(*a*), omit "or 97AA(1)(*b*)".

76 In section 118 (interpretation), in the definition of "tax", omit "20,".

77 In Schedule 1A (claims etc not included in returns), omit paragraphs 6 and 6A (power to call for documents for purposes of enquiries and power to appeal against notice to produce documents).

National Savings Bank Act 1971 (c 29)

78 In section 12(3) (secrecy), for the words from "and of section 20(3)" to the end substitute "and of Schedule 36 to the Finance Act 2008 (powers of officers of Revenue and Customs to obtain information and documents and inspect business premises)".

ICTA

79 ICTA is amended as follows.

80 *In section 767B (change of company ownership: supplementary), in subsection (4), for "767AA and 767C" substitute "and 767AA".*[1]

Amendments—[1] This para repealed by CTA 2010 s 1181, Sch 3 Pt 1. CTA 2010 has effect for corporation tax purposes for accounting periods ending on or after 1 April 2010, and for income and capital gains tax purposes for the tax year 2010–11 and subsequent tax years.

81 Omit section 767C (change in company ownership: information).

82 *In section 769 (rules for ascertaining change in ownership of company)—*

(*a*) *in subsections (1) and (5), omit ", 767C", and*

(*b*) *in subsections (2A) and (9), for "767AA or 767C" substitute "or 767AA".*[1]

Amendments—[1] This para repealed by CTA 2010 s 1181, Sch 3 Pt 1. CTA 2010 has effect for corporation tax purposes for accounting periods ending on or after 1 April 2010, and for income and capital gains tax purposes for the tax year 2010–11 and subsequent tax years.

FA 1990

83 In section 125 of FA 1990 (information for tax authorities in other member States)—

(*a*) omit subsections (1) and (2),

(*b*) *in subsection (3), for "the Directive mentioned in subsection (1) above" substitute "the Directive of the Council of the European Communities dated 19 December 1977 No 77/799/EEC (the "1977 Directive")",*[1]

(c) in subsection (4), for "such as is mentioned in subsection (1) above" substitute "which is covered by the provisions for the exchange of information under the 1977 Directive", and[1]

(d) in subsection (6), omit the words from the beginning to "passed,".[1]

Amendments—[1] Sub-paras (*b*)–(*d*) repealed by Finance Act 2009 Schedule 47 (Consequential Amendments) Order, SI 2009/2035, Art 2 Schedule, para 60(*p*) with effect from 13 August 2009.

Social Security Administration Act 1992 (c 5)

84 In section 110ZA of the Social Security Administration Act 1992 (Class 1, 1A, 1B or 2 contributions: powers to call for documents etc), for subsections (1) and (2) substitute—

"(1) Schedule 36 to the Finance Act 2008 (information and inspection powers) applies for the purpose of checking a person's position as regards relevant contributions as it applies for the purpose of checking a person's tax position, subject to the modifications in subsection (2).

(2) That Schedule applies as if—

(*a*) references to any provision of the Taxes Acts were to any provision of this Act or the Contributions and Benefits Act relating to relevant contributions,

(*b*) references to prejudice to the assessment or collection of tax were to prejudice to the assessment of liability for, and payment of, relevant contributions,

(*c*) the reference to information relating to the conduct of a pending appeal relating to tax were a reference to information relating to the conduct of a pending appeal relating to relevant contributions, and

(*d*) paragraphs 21, 35(4)(*b*), 36 and 37(2) of that Schedule (restrictions on giving taxpayer notice where taxpayer has made tax return) were omitted."

Social Security Administration (Northern Ireland) Act 1992 (c 8)

85 In section 104ZA of the Social Security Administration (Northern Ireland) Act 1992 (Class 1, 1A, 1B or 2 contributions: powers to call for documents etc), for subsections (1) and (2) substitute—

"(1) Schedule 36 to the Finance Act 2008 (information and inspection powers) applies for the purpose of checking a person's position as regards relevant contributions as it applies for the purpose of checking a person's tax position, subject to the modifications in subsection (2).

(2) That Schedule applies as if—

(*a*) references to any provision of the Taxes Acts were to any provision of this Act or the Contributions and Benefits Act relating to relevant contributions,

(*b*) references to prejudice to the assessment or collection of tax were to prejudice to the assessment of liability for, and payment of, relevant contributions,

(*c*) the reference to information relating to the conduct of a pending appeal relating to tax were a reference to information relating to the conduct of a pending appeal relating to relevant contributions, and

(*d*) paragraphs 21, 35(4)(*b*), 36 and 37(2) of that Schedule (restrictions on giving taxpayer notice where taxpayer has made tax return) were omitted."

F(No 2)A 1992

86 Omit section 28(1) to (3) (powers of inspection).

VATA 1994

87 (*amends* VATA 1994 Sch 11)

FA 1998

88 In Schedule 18 to FA 1998 (company tax returns), omit paragraphs 27, 28 and 29 (notice to produce documents etc for purposes of enquiry into company tax return, power to appeal against such notices and penalty for failure to produce documents etc).

FA 1999

89 In section 13(5) (gold), omit paragraph (*c*).

Tax Credits Act 2002 (c 21)

90 In section 25 of the Tax Credits Act 2002 (payments of working tax credit by employers), omit subsections (3) and (4).

FA 2006

91 Omit section 174 of FA 2006 (international tax enforcement arrangements: information powers).

Other repeals

92 In consequence of the preceding provisions of this Part of this Schedule, omit the following—

(*a*) section 126 of FA 1988,

(*b*) sections 142(2), (3), (4), (6)(*a*), (7), (8) and (9) and 144(3), (5) and (7) of FA 1989,

(*c*) sections 187 and 255 of, and paragraph 29 of Schedule 19 to, FA 1994,

(*d*) paragraph 6 of Schedule 1 to the Civil Evidence Act 1995 (c 38),

(*e*) paragraph 17 of Schedule 3, paragraph 3 of Schedule 19 and paragraph 2 of Schedule 22 to FA 1996,

(*f*) paragraph 17 of Schedule 3, paragraph 3 of Schedule 19 and paragraph 2 of Schedule 22 to FA 1996,

(*g*) section 115 of, and paragraphs 36 and 42(6) and (7) of Schedule 19 to, FA 1998,

(*h*) section 15(3) of FA 1999,

(*i*) paragraphs 21 and 38(4) of Schedule 29 to FA 2001,

(*j*) section 20 of FA 2006, and

(*k*) paragraph 350 of Schedule 1 to ITA 2007.

SCHEDULE 40

PENALTIES: AMENDMENTS OF SCHEDULE 24 TO FA 2007

Note—*Please see Yellow Tax Handbook Part 1 for the text of this Schedule.*

SCHEDULE 41

PENALTIES: FAILURE TO NOTIFY AND CERTAIN VAT AND EXCISE WRONGDOING

Note—*Please see Yellow Tax Handbook Part 1 for the text of this Schedule.*

FINANCE ACT 2009

(2009 Chapter 10)

An Act to Grant certain duties, to alter other duties, and to amend the law relating to the National Debt and the Public Revenue, and to make further provision in connection with finance.

[21 July 2009]

Assessments, claims etc

99 Time limits for assessments, claims etc

(1) Schedule 51 contains provision about time limits for assessments, claims etc

(2) The amendments made by that Schedule come into force on such day as the Treasury may by order made by statutory instrument appoint.

(3) An order under subsection (2)—

(*a*) may make different provision for different purposes, and

(*b*) may include transitional provision and savings.

Commencement—Finance Act 2009, Schedule 51 (Time Limits for Assessments, Claims, etc) (Appointed Days and Transitional Provisions) Order 2010, SI 2010/867 (appointed days for the purposes of amendments made by Sch 51 are—

(a) 1 April 2010 for amendments made by paras 1 to 4 and 27 to 43 (insurance premium tax, aggregates levy, climate change levy, landfill tax and minor and consequential provision); and

(b) 1 April 2011 for amendments made by paragraphs 5 to 26 (inheritance tax, stamp duty land tax and petroleum revenue tax.))

Interest

101 Late payment interest on sums due to HMRC

(1) This section applies to any amount that is payable by a person to HMRC under or by virtue of an enactment.

(2) But this section does not apply to—

(*a*) an amount of corporation tax,

(*b*) an amount of petroleum revenue tax, or

(*c*) an amount of any description specified in an order made by the Treasury.

(3) An amount to which this section applies carries interest at the late payment interest rate from the late payment interest start date until the date of payment.

(4) The late payment interest start date in respect of any amount is the date on which that amount becomes due and payable.

(5) In Schedule 53—

(*a*) Part 1 makes special provision as to the amount on which late payment interest is calculated,

(*b*) Part 2 makes special provision as to the late payment interest start date,

(*c*) Part 3 makes special provision as to the date to which late payment interest runs, and

(*d*) Part 4 makes provision about the effect that the giving of a relief has on late payment interest.

(6) Subsection (3) applies even if the late payment interest start date is a non-business day within the meaning of section 92 of the Bills of Exchange Act 1882.

(7) Late payment interest is to be paid without any deduction of income tax.

(8) Late payment interest is not payable on late payment interest.

(9) For the purposes of this section any reference to the payment of an amount to HMRC includes a reference to its being set off against an amount payable by HMRC (and, accordingly, the reference to the date on which an amount is paid includes a reference to the date from which the set-off takes effect).

[(10) The reference in subsection (1) to amounts payable to HMRC includes—

(*a*) amounts of UK VAT payable under a non-UK special scheme;

(*b*) amounts of UK VAT payable under a special scheme;

and references in Schedule 53 to amounts due or payable to HMRC are to be read accordingly.

(11) In subsection (10)—

(*a*) expressions used in paragraph (a) have the meaning given by paragraph 23(1) of Schedule 3B to VATA 1994 (non- Union scheme);

(*b*) expressions used in paragraph (b) have the meaning given by paragraph 38(1) of Schedule 3BA to VATA 1994 (Union scheme).][1]

Commentary—*Simon's Taxes* **A4.620.**

Commencement—Finance Act 2009, Sections 101 to 103 (Appointed Day and Supplemental Provision) Order, SI 2010/1878 (day appointed as the day on which FA 2009 ss 101–103 come into force for the purposes of bank payroll tax (including any penalties assessed in relation to that tax) is 31 August 2010).

Finance Act 2009, Sections 101 to 103 (Income Tax Self Assessment) (Appointed Days and Transitional and Consequential Provisions) Order, SI 2011/701 (for the purposes of any self–assessment amount payable by a person to HMRC, ss 101 and 103 come into force on 31 October 2011; for the purposes of any self-assessment amount payable or repayable by HMRC to any person, ss 102 and 103 come into force on 31 October 2011).

Finance (No 3) Act 2010, Schedule 10 and the Finance Act 2009, Schedule 55 and Sections 101 to 103 (Appointed Day, etc) (Construction Industry Scheme) Order, SI 2011/2391 (the day appointed for the coming into force of ss 101–103 is 6 October 2011, but only in relation to a penalty under Sch 55 paras 7–13 (Construction Industry Scheme).

Finance Act 2009, Sections 101 and 102 (Machine Games Duty) (Appointed Day) Order, SI 2013/67 (the day appointed for the coming into force of ss 101 and 102 is 1 February 2013 for the purposes of machine games duty, including any penalties assessed in relation to that duty).

Finance Act 2009, Section 101 (Tax Agents: Dishonest Conduct) (Appointed Day) Order, SI 2013/280 (the day appointed for the coming into force of s 101 is 1 April 2013 for the purposes of penalties assessed under FA 2012 Sch 38 Parts 3–5 (penalties for dishonest conduct or for failure to comply with a file access notice).

Finance Act 2009, Sections 101 and 102 (Annual Tax on Enveloped Dwellings) (Appointed Day) Order, SI 2013/2472 (the day appointed for the coming into force of ss 101 and 102 for the purposes of the annual tax on enveloped dwellings and penalties assessed in relation to that tax is 1 October 2013).

Finance Act 2009, Sections 101 and 102 (Interest on Late Payments and Repayments), Appointed Days and Consequential Provisions Order, SI 2014/992 (the day appointed for the coming into force of ss 101 and 102 is 6 May 2014 for the purposes of PAYE and Class 1 contributions payable by, or repayable by HMRC to, an employer, and any CIS amount either payable by, or repayable by HMRC to, a contractor).

Finance Act 2009, Schedules 55 and 56 and Sections 101 and 102 (Stamp Duty Reserve Tax) (Appointed Days, Consequential and Transitional Provision) Order, SI 2014/3269 art 4 (the day appointed as the day on which ss 101 and 102 come into force for the purposes of stamp duty reserve tax (including any penalties assessed in relation to that tax) is 1 January 2015. This only applies to a charge with a due and payable date falling after 31 December 2014.).

Finance Act 2009, Sections 101 and 102 (Remote Gambling Taxes) (Appointed Day) Order, SI 2014/3324 art 3 (the day appointed as the day on which ss 101 and 102 come into force for the purposes of remote gambling taxes is 1 January 2015).

Finance Act 2009, Sections 101 and 102 (Diverted Profits Tax) (Appointed Day) Order, SI 2015/974 (the day appointed for the coming into force of ss 101, 102 for the purposes of diverted profits tax and penalties assessed in relation to that tax is 1 April 2015).

Regulations—Taxes and Duties, etc (Interest Rate) Regulations, SI 2011/2446 (formula for calculating late payment interest rate for the purposes of this section).

Cross-references—See FA 2014 s 176 in relation to interest charged under s 101 in relation to general betting duty, pool betting duty and remote gaming duty (outside the scope of this work).

SSCBA 1992 s 11A (this section applies with the necessary modifications, in relation to Class 2 contributions under SSCBA 1992 s 11(2) as if those contributions were income tax chargeable under ITTOIA 2005 Pt 2 Ch 2 in respect of profits of a trade, profession or vocation which is not carried on wholly outside the United Kingdom).

Education (Postgraduate Master's Degree Loans) Regulations, SI 2016/606 regs 49, 68, 80 (application of this section to loans for postgraduate master's degree courses which begin on or after 1 August 2016).

Amendments—[1] Sub-ss (10), (11) inserted by FA 2014 s 103, Sch 22 para 20(1), (2) with effect from 17 July 2014.

Prospective amendment—Sub-s (2)(*a*), (*b*) to be repealed by F(No 3)A 2010 s 25, Sch 9 Pt 1 paras 1, 2, Pt 2 paras 13, 14 with effect from a day to be appointed by Treasury order (F(No 3)A 2010 s 25).

102 Repayment interest on sums to be paid by HMRC

(1) This section applies to—

(*a*) any amount that is payable by HMRC to any person under or by virtue of an enactment, and

(*b*) a relevant amount paid by a person to HMRC that is repaid by HMRC to that person or to another person.

(2) But this section does not apply to—

(*a*) an amount constituting a repayment of corporation tax,

(*b*) an amount constituting a repayment of petroleum revenue tax, or

(*c*) an amount of any description specified in an order made by the Treasury.

(3) An amount to which this section applies carries interest at the repayment interest rate from the repayment interest start date until the date on which the payment or repayment is made.

(4) In Schedule 54—

(*a*) Parts 1 and 2 define the repayment interest start date, and

(*b*) Part 3 makes supplementary provision.

(5) Subsection (3) applies even if the repayment interest start date is a non-business day within the meaning of section 92 of the Bills of Exchange Act 1882.

(6) Repayment interest is not payable on an amount payable in consequence of an order or judgment of a court having power to allow interest on the amount.

(7) Repayment interest is not payable on repayment interest.

(8) For the purposes of this section—

(*a*) "relevant amount" means any sum that was paid in connection with any liability (including any purported or anticipated liability) to make a payment to HMRC under or by virtue of an enactment, and

(*b*) any reference to the payment or repayment of an amount by HMRC includes a reference to its being set off against an amount owed to HMRC (and, accordingly, the reference to the date on which an amount is paid or repaid by HMRC includes a reference to the date from which the set-off takes effect).

Commentary—*Simon's Taxes* **A4.629.**

Commencement—Finance Act 2009, Sections 101 to 103 (Appointed Day and Supplemental Provision) Order, SI 2010/1878 (day appointed as the day on which FA 2009 ss 101–103 come into force for the purposes of bank payroll tax (including any penalties assessed in relation to that tax) is 31 August 2010).

Finance Act 2009, Sections 101 to 103 (Income Tax Self Assessment) (Appointed Days and Transitional and Consequential Provisions) Order, SI 2011/701 (for the purposes of any self-assessment amount payable by a person to HMRC, ss 101 and 103 come into force on 31 October 2011; for the purposes of any self-assessment amount payable or repayable by HMRC to any person, ss 102 and 103 come into force on 31 October 2011).

Finance (No 3) Act 2010, Schedule 10 and the Finance Act 2009, Schedule 55 and Sections 101 to 103 (Appointed Day, etc) (Construction Industry Scheme) Order, SI 2011/2391 (the day appointed for the coming into force of ss 101–103 is 6 October 2011, but only in relation to a penalty under Sch 55 paras 7–13 (Construction Industry Scheme).

Finance Act 2009, Sections 101 and 102 (Machine Games Duty) (Appointed Day) Order, SI 2013/67 (the day appointed for the coming into force of ss 101 and 102 is 1 February 2013 for the purposes of machine games duty, including any penalties assessed in relation to that duty).

Finance Act 2009, Sections 101 and 102 (Annual Tax on Enveloped Dwellings) (Appointed Day) Order, SI 2013/2472 (the day appointed for the coming into force of ss 101 and 102 for the purposes of the annual tax on enveloped dwellings and penalties assessed in relation to that tax is 1 October 2013).

Finance Act 2009, Sections 101 and 102 (Interest on Late Payments and Repayments), Appointed Days and Consequential Provisions Order, SI 2014/992 (the day appointed for the coming into force of ss 101 and 102 is 6 May 2014 for the purposes of PAYE and Class 1 contributions payable by, or repayable by HMRC to, an employer, and any CIS amount either payable by, or repayable by HMRC to, a contractor).

Finance Act 2009, Schedules 55 and 56 and Sections 101 and 102 (Stamp Duty Reserve Tax) (Appointed Days, Consequential and Transitional Provision) Order, SI 2014/3269 art 4 (the day appointed as the day on which ss 101 and 102 come into force for the purposes of stamp duty reserve tax (including any penalties assessed in relation to that tax) is 1 January 2015. This only applies to a charge with a due and payable date falling after 31 December 2014.).

Finance Act 2009, Sections 101 and 102 (Remote Gambling Taxes) (Appointed Day) Order, SI 2014/3324 art 3 (the day appointed as the day on which ss 101 and 102 come into force for the purposes of remote gambling taxes is 1 January 2015).

Finance Act 2009, Sections 101 and 102 (Diverted Profits Tax) (Appointed Day) Order, SI 2015/974 art 2 (the day appointed for the coming into force of ss 101, 102 for the purposes of diverted profits tax and penalties assessed in relation to that tax is 1 April 2015).

Cross-references—See SSCBA 1992 s 11A (this section applies with the necessary modifications, in relation to Class 2 contributions under SSCBA 1992 s 11(2) as if those contributions were income tax chargeable under ITTOIA 2005 Pt 2 Ch 2 in respect of profits of a trade, profession or vocation which is not carried on wholly outside the United Kingdom).

Regulations—Taxes and Duties, etc (Interest Rate) Regulations, SI 2011/2446 (formula for calculating repayment payment interest rate for the purposes of this section).

Prospective amendment—Sub-s (2)(*a*), (*b*) to be repealed, and sub-s (4)(*za*) to be inserted before sub-s (4)(*a*), by F(No 3)A 2010 s 25, Sch 9 Pt 1 paras 1, 3, Pt 2 paras 13, 15 with effect from a day to be appointed by Treasury order (F(No 3)A 2010 s 25). Sub-s (4)(*za*) as inserted to read—

"(*za*) Part A1 makes special provision as to the amount of corporation tax on which repayment interest is calculated,".

103 Rates of interest

(1) The late payment interest rate is the rate provided for in regulations made by the Treasury under this subsection.

(2) The repayment interest rate is the rate provided for in regulations made by the Treasury under this subsection.

(3) Regulations under subsection (1) or (2)—

- (*a*) may make different provision for different purposes,
- (*b*) may either themselves specify a rate of interest or make provision for such a rate to be determined (and to change from time to time) by reference to such rate, or the average of such rates, as may be referred to in the regulations,
- (*c*) may provide for rates to be reduced below, or increased above, what they otherwise would be by specified amounts or by reference to specified formulae,
- (*d*) may provide for rates arrived at by reference to averages to be rounded up or down,
- (*e*) may provide for circumstances in which alteration of a rate of interest is or is not to be take place, and
- (*f*) may provide that alterations of rates are to have effect for periods beginning on or after a day determined in accordance with the regulations in relation to interest running from before that day as well as from or from after that day.

Commencement—Finance Act 2009, Sections 101 to 103 (Appointed Day and Supplemental Provision) Order, SI 2010/1878 (day appointed as the day on which FA 2009 ss 101–103 come into force for the purposes of bank payroll tax (including any penalties assessed in relation to that tax) is 31 August 2010).

Finance Act 2009, Sections 101 to 103 (Income Tax Self Assessment) (Appointed Days and Transitional and Consequential Provisions) Order, SI 2011/701 (for the purposes of any self-assessment amount payable by a person to HMRC, ss 101 and 103 come into force on 31 October 2011; for the purposes of any self-assessment amount payable or repayable by HMRC to any person, ss 102 and 103 come into force on 31 October 2011).

Finance (No 3) Act 2010, Schedule 10 and the Finance Act 2009, Schedule 55 and Sections 101 to 103 (Appointed Day, etc) (Construction Industry Scheme) Order, SI 2011/2391 (the day appointed for the coming into force of ss 101–103 is 6 October 2011, but only in relation to a penalty under Sch 55 paras 7–13 (Construction Industry Scheme).

Finance Act 2009, Section 103 (Appointed Day) Order, SI 2011/2401 (the day appointed as the day on which s 103 comes into force generally is 6 October 2011).

Regulations—Taxes and Duties, etc (Interest Rate) Regulations, SI 2011/2446.

Penalties

106 Penalties for failure to make returns etc

(1) Schedule 55 contains provision for imposing penalties on persons in respect of failures to make returns and other documents relating to liabilities for tax.

(2) That Schedule comes into force on such day as the Treasury may by order appoint.

(3) An order under subsection (2)—

(*a*) may commence a provision generally or only for specified purposes, and

(*b*) may appoint different days for different provisions or for different purposes.

(4) The Treasury may by order make any incidental, supplemental, consequential, transitional, transitory or saving provision which may appear appropriate in consequence of, or otherwise in connection with, Schedule 55.

(5) An order under subsection (4) may include provision amending, repealing or revoking any provision of any Act or subordinate legislation whenever passed or made (including this Act and any Act amended by it).

(6) An order under subsection (4) may make different provision for different purposes.

(7) An order under this section is to be made by statutory instrument.

(8) A statutory instrument containing an order under subsection (4) which includes provision amending or repealing any provision of an Act is subject to annulment in pursuance of a resolution of the House of Commons.

Commentary—*Simon's Taxes* **E4.11122.**

Orders—Finance Act 2009, Schedules 55 and 56 (Income Tax Self Assessment and Pension Schemes) (Appointed Days and Consequential and Savings Provisions) Order, SI 2011/702.

Finance Act 2009, Schedule 55 (Penalties for failure to make returns) (Appointed Days and Consequential Provision) Order, SI 2014/2395.

Finance Act 2009, Schedules 55 and 56 and Sections 101 and 102 (Stamp Duty Reserve Tax) (Appointed Days, Consequential and Transitional Provision) (Amendment) Order, SI 2014/3346.

Cross references—See FA 2016 s 113(17) (in sub-ss (2) and (4), references to Sch 55 have effect as references to that Schedule as amended by FA 2016 s 113(5)–(8)).

FA 2017 Sch 11 para 4(4) (in sub-ss (2) and (4), references to Sch 55 have effect as references to that Schedule as amended by FA 2017 Sch 11 para 4).

107 Penalties for failure to pay tax

(1) Schedule 56 contains provision for imposing penalties on persons in respect of failures to comply with obligations to pay tax.

(2) That Schedule comes into force on such day as the Treasury may by order appoint.

(3) An order under subsection (2)—

(*a*) may commence a provision generally or only for specified purposes, and

(*b*) may appoint different days for different provisions or for different purposes.

(4) The Treasury may by order make any incidental, supplemental, consequential, transitional, transitory or saving provision which may appear appropriate in consequence of, or otherwise in connection with, Schedule 56.

(5) An order under subsection (4) may include provision amending, repealing or revoking any provision of any Act or subordinate legislation whenever passed or made (including this Act and any Act amended by it).

(6) An order under subsection (4) may make different provision for different purposes.

(7) An order under this section is to be made by statutory instrument.

(8) A statutory instrument containing an order under subsection (4) which includes provision amending or repealing any provision of an Act is subject to annulment in pursuance of a resolution of the House of Commons.

Commentary—*Simon's Taxes* **E4.11119.**

Orders—Finance Act 2009, Schedule 56 (Appointed Day and Consequential Provisions) Order, SI 2010/466.

Finance Act 2009, Schedules 55 and 56 (Income Tax Self Assessment and Pension Schemes) (Appointed Days and Consequential and Savings Provisions) Order, SI 2011/702.

Finance Act 2009, Schedules 55 and 56 and Sections 101 and 102 (Stamp Duty Reserve Tax) (Appointed Days, Consequential and Transitional Provision) (Amendment) Order, SI 2014/3346.

Cross references—See FA 2017 Sch 11 para 5(3) (in sub-ss (2) and (4), references to Sch 56 have effect as references to that Schedule as amended by FA 2017 Sch 11 para 5).

PART 8
MISCELLANEOUS
Other matters

122 Inheritance tax: agricultural property and woodlands relief for EEA land

(1) Part 5 of IHTA 1984 (miscellaneous reliefs) is amended as follows.

(2) In section 115 (agricultural property relief: preliminary), in subsection (3), insert at the end "(or, in the case of property outside the United Kingdom, the Channel Islands and the Isle of Man, if it were subject to provisions equivalent in effect to such a covenant)."

(3) (*inserts* IHTA 1984 s 115(5))

(4) (*inserts* IHTA 1984 s 116(8))

(5) In section 125 (woodlands relief), in paragraph (*a*) of subsection (1), omit "in the United Kingdom".

(6) (*inserts* IHTA 1984 s 125(1A))

(7) The amendments made by this section have effect in relation to transfers of value where the tax payable but for this section (or, in the case of tax payable by instalments, the last instalment of that tax)—

(*a*) would have been due on or after 22 April 2009, or

(*b*) was paid or due on or after 23 April 2003.

(8) Where tax falling within subsection (7) has been paid, Her Majesty's Revenue and Customs must repay the tax (together with interest under section 235(1) of IHTA 1984) if, but only if, a claim for repayment is made on or before—

(*a*) the date determined under section 241(1) of that Act as the last date on which the claim may be made, or

(*b*) 21 April 2010,

whichever is later.

(9) Where, by virtue of the amendments made by subsections (5) and (6), an election is made under section 125 of IHTA 1984, that election must be made on or before—

(*a*) the date determined under section 125(3) as the last date on which the election may be made, or

(*b*) 21 April 2010,

whichever is later.

SCHEDULES

SCHEDULE 51

TIME LIMITS FOR ASSESSMENTS, CLAIMS ETC

Section 99

Inheritance tax

5 IHTA 1984 is amended as follows.

Commencement—Finance Act 2009, Schedule 51 (Time Limits for Assessments, Claims, etc) (Appointed Days and Transitional Provisions) Order, SI 2010/867 art 2(2) (day appointed as the day on which the amendments made by paras 5 to 26 (inheritance tax, stamp duty land tax and petroleum revenue tax) come into force is 1 April 2011).

6 In section 131 (transfers within 7 years before death: the relief), after subsection (2) insert—

"(2ZA) A claim under subsection (2)(*b*) must be made not more than 4 years after the transferor's death."

Commencement—Finance Act 2009, Schedule 51 (Time Limits for Assessments, Claims, etc) (Appointed Days and Transitional Provisions) Order, SI 2010/867 art 2(2) (day appointed as the day on which the amendments made by paras 5 to 26 (inheritance tax, stamp duty land tax and petroleum revenue tax) come into force is 1 April 2011).

7 In section 146(2)(*a*) (Inheritance (Provision for Family and Dependants) Act 1975), after "claim for the purpose" insert "not more than 4 years after the date on which the order is made".

Commencement—Finance Act 2009, Schedule 51 (Time Limits for Assessments, Claims, etc) (Appointed Days and Transitional Provisions) Order, SI 2010/867 art 2(2) (day appointed as the day on which the amendments made by paras 5 to 26 (inheritance tax, stamp duty land tax and petroleum revenue tax) come into force is 1 April 2011).

8 In section 150 (voidable transfers), insert at the end—

"(3) A claim under this section must be made not more than 4 years after the claimant knew, or ought reasonably to have known, that the relevant transfer has been set aside."

Commencement—Finance Act 2009, Schedule 51 (Time Limits for Assessments, Claims, etc) (Appointed Days and Transitional Provisions) Order, SI 2010/867 art 2(2) (day appointed as the day on which the amendments made by paras 5 to 26 (inheritance tax, stamp duty land tax and petroleum revenue tax) come into force is 1 April 2011).

9 In section 179 (sale of shares etc from deceased's estate: the relief), after subsection (2) insert—

"(2A) A claim under this Chapter must be made not more than 4 years after the end of the period mentioned in subsection (1)(*a*)."

Commencement—Finance Act 2009, Schedule 51 (Time Limits for Assessments, Claims, etc) (Appointed Days and Transitional Provisions) Order, SI 2010/867 art 2(2) (day appointed as the day on which the amendments made by paras 5 to 26 (inheritance tax, stamp duty land tax and petroleum revenue tax) come into force is 1 April 2011).

10 In section 191 (sale of land from deceased's estate: the relief), after subsection (1) insert—

"(1A) A claim under this Chapter must be made not more than 4 years after the end of the period mentioned in subsection (1)(*a*)."

Commencement—Finance Act 2009, Schedule 51 (Time Limits for Assessments, Claims, etc) (Appointed Days and Transitional Provisions) Order, SI 2010/867 art 2(2) (day appointed as the day on which the amendments made by paras 5 to 26 (inheritance tax, stamp duty land tax and petroleum revenue tax) come into force is 1 April 2011).

11—(1) Section 240 (underpayments) is amended as follows.

(2) In subsection (2), for "six years" substitute "4 years".

(3) For subsection (3) substitute—

"(3) Subsection (2) has effect subject to subsections (4) and (5).

(4) Proceedings in a case involving a loss of tax brought about carelessly by a person liable for the tax (or a person acting on behalf of such a person) may be brought at any time not more than 6 years after the later of the dates in subsection (2)(*a*) and (*b*).

(5) Proceedings in a case involving a loss of tax brought about deliberately by a person liable for the tax (or a person acting on behalf of such a person) may be brought at any time not more than 20 years after the later of those dates.

(6) Subsection (7) applies to any case not falling within subsection (2) where too little tax has been paid in respect of a chargeable transfer, provided that the case does not involve a loss of tax brought about deliberately by a person liable for the tax (or a person acting on behalf of such a person).

(7) Where this subsection applies—

(*a*) no proceedings are to be brought for the recovery of the tax after the end of the period of 20 years beginning with the date on which the chargeable transfer was made, and

(*b*) at the end of that period any liability for the tax and any Inland Revenue charge for that tax is extinguished.

(8) In relation to cases of tax chargeable under Chapter 3 of Part 3 of this Act (apart from section 79), the references in subsections (4), (5) and (6) to a person liable for the tax are to be treated as including references to a person who is the settlor in relation to the settlement."

Commencement—Finance Act 2009, Schedule 51 (Time Limits for Assessments, Claims, etc) (Appointed Days and Transitional Provisions) Order, SI 2010/867 art 2(2) (day appointed as the day on which the amendments made by paras 5 to 26 (inheritance tax, stamp duty land tax and petroleum revenue tax) come into force is 1 April 2011).

12 After that section insert—

"240A Underpayments: supplementary

(1) This section applies for the purposes of section 240.

(2) A loss of tax is brought about carelessly by a person if the person fails to take reasonable care to avoid bringing about that loss.

(3) Where—

(*a*) information is provided to Her Majesty's Revenue and Customs,

(*b*) the person who provided the information, or the person on whose behalf the information was provided, discovers some time later that the information was inaccurate, and

(*c*) that person fails to take reasonable steps to inform Her Majesty's Revenue and Customs,

any loss of tax brought about by the inaccuracy is to be treated as having been brought about carelessly by that person.

(4) References to a loss of tax brought about deliberately by a person include a loss of tax brought about as a result of a deliberate inaccuracy in a document given to Her Majesty's Revenue and Customs by or on behalf of that person."

Commencement—Finance Act 2009, Schedule 51 (Time Limits for Assessments, Claims, etc) (Appointed Days and Transitional Provisions) Order, SI 2010/867 art 2(2) (day appointed as the day on which the amendments made by paras 5 to 26 (inheritance tax, stamp duty land tax and petroleum revenue tax) come into force is 1 April 2011).

13 In section 241(1) (overpayments), for "six years" substitute "4 years".

Commencement—Finance Act 2009, Schedule 51 (Time Limits for Assessments, Claims, etc) (Appointed Days and Transitional Provisions) Order, SI 2010/867 art 2(2) (day appointed as the day on which the amendments made by paras 5 to 26 (inheritance tax, stamp duty land tax and petroleum revenue tax) come into force is 1 April 2011).

SCHEDULE 53

LATE PAYMENT INTEREST

Section 101

PART 2

SPECIAL PROVISION: LATE PAYMENT INTEREST START DATE

. . .

Inheritance tax payable by instalments

7—(1) The late payment interest start date for each instalment of an amount to which this paragraph applies is the date on which that instalment is to be paid.

(2) This paragraph applies to any amount of inheritance tax which is payable by instalments under section 229 of IHTA 1984.

(3) This paragraph also applies to any amount of inheritance tax which is payable by instalments under section 227 of IHTA 1984 if the value on which the amount is payable is attributable to—

(*a*) the value of qualifying property within subsection (2)(*b*) or (*c*) of that section (shares or securities, or business or interest in a business), or

(*b*) value treated as reduced under Chapter 2 of Part 5 of that Act.

(4) But this paragraph does not apply to an amount by virtue of sub-paragraph (3)(*a*) if the qualifying property is shares or securities of a company which—

(*a*) falls within sub-paragraph (5), but

(*b*) does not fall within sub-paragraph (6) or (7).

(5) A company falls within this sub-paragraph if its business consists wholly or mainly of one or more of the following—

(*a*) dealing in securities, stocks or shares, land or buildings, or

(*b*) making or holding investments.

(6) A company falls within this sub-paragraph if its business consists wholly or mainly in being a holding company (as defined in section 1159 of the Companies Act 2006) of one or more companies not falling within sub-paragraph (5).

(7) A company falls within this sub-paragraph if its business is carried on in the United Kingdom and is—

(*a*) wholly that of a market maker, or

(*b*) that of a discount house.

(8) A company is a market maker if—

(*a*) it holds itself out at all normal times in compliance with the rules of The Stock Exchange as willing to buy and sell securities, stocks or shares at a price specified by it, and

(*b*) it is recognised as doing so by the Council of The Stock Exchange.

Prospective amendments—Para (7) to be substituted by F(No 2)A 2015 s 15(2)(*a*) with effect from a date to be appointed. Para (7) as substituted to read as follows—

"(7) A company falls within this sub-paragraph if—

(*a*) its business is carried on in the United Kingdom and is—

(i) wholly that of a market maker, or

(ii) that of a discount house, or

(*b*) it is of a description set out in regulations under section 107(5) of FA 1986.",

Certain other amounts of inheritance tax

8 An amount of inheritance tax which is underpaid in consequence of any of the following provisions—

(*a*) section 146(1) of IHTA 1984,

(*b*) section 19 of the Inheritance (Provision for Family and Dependants) Act 1975, or

(*c*) Article 21 of the Inheritance (Provision for Family and Dependants) (Northern Ireland) Order 1979, does not carry late payment interest before the order mentioned in that provision is made.

9 In the case of an amount which is payable under section 147(4) of IHTA 1984, the late payment interest start date is the day after the end of the period of 6 months beginning with the date of the testator's death.

Prospective amendments—Words "end of the month in which the testator died" to be substituted for words "date of the testator's death" by F(No 2)A 2015 s 15(2)(*b*) with effect from a date to be appointed.

PART 3
SPECIAL PROVISION: DATE TO WHICH LATE PAYMENT INTEREST RUNS

. . .

Property accepted in lieu of inheritance tax

14 If, in the case of any amount of inheritance tax—

(*a*) HMRC agree under section 230 of IHTA 1984 to accept property in satisfaction of the amount, and

(*b*) under terms of that acceptance the value to be attributed to the property for the purposes of the acceptance is determined as at a date earlier than that on which the property is actually accepted,

the terms may provide that the amount of tax which is satisfied by the acceptance of the property does not carry late payment interest after that date.

SCHEDULE 54
REPAYMENT INTEREST
Section 102

PART 2
SPECIAL PROVISION AS TO REPAYMENT INTEREST START DATE

. . .

Certain amounts of inheritance tax

10 An amount of inheritance tax which is overpaid in consequence of any of the following provisions—

(*a*) section 146(1) of IHTA 1984,

(*b*) section 19 of the Inheritance (Provision for Family and Dependants) Act 1975, or

(*c*) Article 21 of the Inheritance (Provision for Family and Dependants) (Northern Ireland) Order 1979, does not carry repayment interest before the order mentioned in that provision is made.

11 In the case of an amount which is repayable on a claim under section 146(2) or 150 of IHTA 1984, the repayment interest start date is the date on which the claim is made.

12 In the case of an amount which is repayable under section 147(2) of IHTA 1984, the repayment interest start date is the date on which the tax was paid.

SCHEDULE 55
PENALTY FOR FAILURE TO MAKE RETURNS ETC
Section 106

Commencement—Finance Act 2009, Schedules 55 and 56 (Income Tax Self Assessment and Pension Schemes) (Appointed Days and Consequential and Savings Provisions) Order, SI 2011/702 art 2 (appointed day for the coming into force of Sch 55 is 6 April 2011 in relation to a return or other document which is required to be made or delivered to HMRC in relation to the tax year 2010–11 or any subsequent tax year and falls within item 1, 2 or 3 of the Table in para 1).

Finance (No 3) Act 2010, Schedule 10 and the Finance Act 2009, Schedule 55 and Sections 101 to 103 (Appointed Day, etc) (Construction Industry Scheme) Order, SI 2011/2391 (the day appointed for the coming into force of the following paras of Sch 55 is 6 October 2011, with effect only in relation to a return within item 6 of Sch 55 para 1(5), and for which the filing date for the purposes of Sch 55 is after 19 October 2011—

– para 1 (but only in relation to item 6 in the Table in para 1(5);
– paras 7–13; and
– 14–24, 26, and 27(1)–(4) but only as relevant to paras 7–13).

FA 2013 Sch 34 para 7(2) (Sch 55, as amended by FA 2013 Sch 34 para 7(1), is taken to have come into force for the purposes of annual tax on enveloped dwellings on 17 July 2013).

Finance Act 2009, Schedule 55 (Penalties for failure to make returns) (Appointed Days and Consequential Provision) Order, SI 2014/2395 (appoints various days for the coming into force of Sch 55 in relation to a return falling within item 4 of the Table in para 1). The effect of SI 2014/2395, along with SI 2014/2396, is to bring into force the penalties for late returns of in-year PAYE information under the real time information regime with effect from 6 October 2014 for existing large RTI employers (50 or more employees), and 6 March 2015 for remaining employers.

Finance Act 2009, Schedules 55 and 56 and Sections 101 and 102 (Stamp Duty Reserve Tax) (Appointed Days, Consequential and Transitional Provision) Order, SI 2014/3269 art 2 (the day appointed for the coming into force of Sch 55 is 1 January 2015 in relation to a charge to tax which is specified in item 11 of the Table in para 1 (SDRT)).

FA 2015 Sch 7 para 59 (Sch 55, as amended by FA 2015 Sch 7 para 59(2), is taken to have come into force for the purposes of NRCGT returns on 26 March 2015).

Cross-references—See FA 2014 ss 208–214, Sch 30 (follower notices: penalties).

SSCBA 1992 s 11A (this Schedule applies with the necessary modifications, in relation to Class 2 contributions under SSCBA 1992 s 11(2) as if those contributions were income tax chargeable under ITTOIA 2005 Pt 2 Ch 2 in respect of profits of a trade, profession or vocation which is not carried on wholly outside the United Kingdom).

Education (Postgraduate Master's Degree Loans) Regulations, SI 2016/606 reg 50 (this schedule applies to failure to disclose required information about loans for postgraduate master's degree courses which begin on or after 1 August 2016).

Penalty for failure to make returns etc'

1—(1) A penalty is payable by a person ("P") where P fails to make or deliver a return, or to deliver any other document, specified in the Table below on or before the filing date.

(2) Paragraphs 2 to 13 set out—

(*a*) the circumstances in which a penalty is payable, and

(*b*) subject to paragraphs 14 to 17, the amount of the penalty.

(3) If P's failure falls within more than one paragraph of this Schedule, P is liable to a penalty under each of those paragraphs (but this is subject to paragraph 17(3)).

(4) In this Schedule—

"filing date", in relation to a return or other document, means the date by which it is required to be made or delivered to HMRC;

"penalty date", in relation to a return or other document [falling within any of items 1 to 3 and 5 to 13 in the Table][3], means the date on which a penalty is first payable for failing to make or deliver it (that is to say, the day after the filing date).

[(4A) The Treasury may by order make such amendments to item 4 in the Table as they think fit in consequence of any amendment, revocation or re-enactment of the regulations mentioned in that item.][3]

(5) In the provisions of this Schedule which follow the Table—

(*a*) any reference to a return includes a reference to any other document specified in the Table, and

(*b*) any reference to making a return includes a reference to delivering a return or to delivering any such document.

	Tax to which return etc relates	*Return or other document*
1	Income tax or capital gains tax	(a) Return under section 8(1)(a) of TMA 1970 (b) Accounts, statement or document required under section 8(1)(b) of TMA 1970
2	Income tax or capital gains tax	(a) Return under section 8A(1)(a) of TMA 1970 (b) Accounts, statement or document required under section 8A(1)(b) of TMA 1970
[2A	Capital gains tax	NRCGT return under section 12ZB of TMA 1970][4]
3	Income tax or corporation tax	(a) Return under section 12AA(2)(a) or (3)(a) of TMA 1970 (b) Accounts, statement or document required under section 12AA(2)(b) or (3)(b) of TMA 1970
4	Income tax	[Return under any of the following provisions of the Income Tax (PAYE) Regulations 2003 (SI 2003/2682)— (a) regulation 67B (real time returns) (b) regulation 67D (exceptions to regulation 67B)][3]
[4A	Apprenticeship levy	Return under regulations under section 105 of FA 2016][6]
5	Income tax	Return under section 254 of FA 2004 (pension schemes)
6	Deductions on account of tax under Chapter 3 of Part 3 of FA 2004 (construction industry scheme)	Return under regulations under section 70 of FA 2004
7	Corporation tax	Company tax return under paragraph 3 of Schedule 18 to FA 1998
8	Inheritance tax	Account under section 216 or 217 of IHTA 1984
9	Stamp duty land tax	Land transaction return under section 76 of FA 2003 or further return under section 81 of that Act
10	Stamp duty land tax	Return under paragraph 3, 4 or 8 of Schedule 17A to FA 2003
11	Stamp duty reserve tax	Notice of charge to tax under regulations under section 98 of FA 1986
[11A	Annual tax on enveloped dwellings	Annual tax on enveloped dwellings return under section 157 of FA 2013

	Tax to which return etc relates	*Return or other document*
11B	Annual tax on enveloped dwellings	Return of adjusted chargeable amount under section 158 of FA 2013][2]
12	Petroleum revenue tax	Return under paragraph 2 of Schedule 2 to OTA 1975
13	Petroleum revenue tax	Statement under section 1(1)(a) of PRTA 1980
[20A	Excise duties	Return under regulations under section 60A of the Customs and Excise Management Act 1979][5]
[29	Machine games duty	Return under regulations under paragraph 18 of Schedule 24 to FA 2012][1]

Commencement—Finance Act 2009, Schedules 55 and 56 (Income Tax Self Assessment and Pension Schemes) (Appointed Days and Consequential and Savings Provisions) Order, SI 2011/702 art 2 (appointed day for the coming into force of Sch 55 is 6 April 2011 in relation to a return or other document which is required to be made or delivered to HMRC in relation to the tax year 2010–11 or any subsequent tax year and falls within item 1, 2 or 3 of the Table in para 1).

Finance (No 3) Act 2010, Schedule 10 and the Finance Act 2009, Schedule 55 and Sections 101 to 103 (Appointed Day, etc) (Construction Industry Scheme) Order, SI 2011/2391 (the day appointed for the coming into force of the following paras of Sch 55 is 6 October 2011, with effect only in relation to a return within item 6 of Sch 55 para 1(5), and for which the filing date for the purposes of Sch 55 is after 19 October 2011—

- para 1 (but only in relation to item 6 in the Table in para 1(5);
- paras 7–13; and
- 14–24, 26, and 27(1)–(4) but only as relevant to paras 7–13).

Finance Act 2009, Schedule 55 (Penalties for failure to make returns) (Appointed Days and Consequential Provision) Order, SI 2014/2395 provides dates for the coming into force of Sch 55 in relation to returns falling within item 4 of the table (PAYE returns), as follows—

- **11 September 2014:** powers to make regulations in relation to quanta of RTI late-filing penalties in para 6C(5), (7), (8), (9), (11) (see also SI 2014/2396).
- **6 October 2014:** provisions of Sch 55 relating to failures to make returns under the PAYE Regulations (SI 2003/2682) regs 67B and 67D where the employer is a large existing employer (an employer which as at 6 October 2014 employs at least 50 employees). Affected returns are those required to be made or delivered to HMRC on or after 6 October 2014.
- **6 March 2015:** provisions of Sch 55 relating to failures to make returns under regs 67B and 67D where the employer is a small existing employer (an employer which as at 6 October 2014 employs no more than 49 employees) or is a new employer. Affected returns are those required to be made or delivered to HMRC on or after 6 March 2015.

Cross references See FA 2016 s 91 (this para does not apply to a NRCGT return made under TMA 1970 s 12ZBA).

Modifications—FA 2009 Sch 55 has effect as if a bank payroll tax return were specified in the Table in this para (and bank payroll tax were specified in relation to it) (FA 2010 s 22, Sch 1 para 38(1)(*a*)).

Amendments—[1] Item 29 inserted by FA 2012 s 191, Sch 24 para 31 with effect in relation to the playing of machine games on or after 1 February 2013 (and Schs 55, 56, as amended by FA 2012 Sch 24 Part 1, are taken to have come into force for the purposes of machine games duty on that date).

[2] In table, entries inserted by FA 2013 s 164, Sch 34 para 7 with effect from 17 July 2013. Note that Sch 55 is taken to have come into force for the purposes of annual tax on enveloped dwellings on 17 July 2013 (FA 2013 Sch 34 para 7(2)).

[3] In sub-para (4), in definition of "penalty date" words inserted, sub-para (4A) inserted, and in Table, in item 4, words in the third column substituted, by FA 2013 s 230, Sch 50 paras 2–4, with effect for the tax year 2014–15 and subsequent tax years in relation to failures to make returns with a filing date (as defined in FA 2009 Sch 55 para 1(4)) on or after 6 April 2014.

[4] In table, entry inserted by FA 2015 s 37, Sch 7 para 59 with effect for the purposes of NRCGT returns from 26 March 2015.

[5] In Table, item 20A inserted by FA 2014 s 101, Sch 21 para 7 with effect from 1 April 2015 (by virtue of SI 2015/812 art 2).

[6] In Table, item 4A inserted by FA 2016 s 113(5), (6) with effect from 15 September 2016.

Prospective amendments—In sub-para (2), figure"13J" to be substituted for figure "13", in sub-para (4), in the definition of "filing date" at the end, words "(or, in the case of a return mentioned in item 7AA or 7AB of the Table, to the tax authorities to whom the return is required to be delivered)" to be inserted, and in the table, entries to be inserted after item 7, by F(No 3)A 2010 s 26, Sch 10 paras 1, 2 (as amended by FA 2014 s 103, Sch 22 para 21) with effect from a day to be appointed by Treasury order. Note that entries 23, 24 and 28 are amended by FA 2014 s 196, Sch 28 paras 28, 29 with effect from a date to be appointed). Entries as inserted to read as follows—

"7A	Value added tax	Return under regulations under paragraph 2 of Schedule 11 to VATA 1994
7AA	Value added tax	Relevant non-UK return (as defined in paragraph 20(3) of Schedule 3BA to VATA 1994)
7AB	Value added tax	Relevant special scheme return (as defined in paragraph 16(3) of Schedule 3B to VATA 1994)
7B	Insurance premium tax	Return under regulations under section 54 of FA 1994".

and

"14	Aggregates levy	Return under regulations under section 25 of FA 2001
15	Climate change levy	Return under regulations under paragraph 41 of Schedule 6 to FA 2000
16	Landfill tax	Return under regulations under section 49 of FA 1996
17	Air passenger duty	Return under regulations under section 38 of FA 1994
18	Alcoholic liquor duties	Return under regulations under section 13, 49, 56 or 62 of ALDA 1979
19	Tobacco products duty	Return under regulations under section 7 of TPDA 1979
20	Hydrocarbon oil duties	Return under regulations under section 21 of HODA 1979
21	Excise duties	Return under regulations under section 93 of the Customs and Excise Management Act 1979
22	Excise duties	Return under regulations under section 100G or 100H of the Customs and Excise Management Act 1979
23	General betting duty	Return under regulations under [section 166 of FA 2014]
24	Pool betting duty	Return under regulations under [section 166 of FA 2014]
25	Bingo duty	Return under regulations under paragraph 9 of Schedule 3 to BGDA 1981
26	Lottery duty	Return under regulations under section 28(2) of FA 1993
27	Gaming duty	Return under directions under paragraph 10 of Schedule 1 to FA 1997
28	Remote gaming duty	Return under regulations under [166 of FA 2014]".

In sub-para (4), in definition of "penalty date", "13A" to be substituted for "13", and in table, entry 13A to be inserted, by FA 2017 s 56, Sch 11 para 4(1)–(3) with effect from a date to be appointed. Once appointed, the charge to soft drinks industry levy will arise on chargeable events which occur on or after 6 April 2018 (FA 2017 s 31(1)). Entry 13A to read as follows—

"13A	Soft drinks industry levy	Return under regulations under section 52 of FA 2017".

Amount of penalty: occasional returns and annual returns

2 Paragraphs 3 to 6 apply in the case of a return falling within any of items [1 to 3, 5][1] and 7 to 13 in the Table.

Commencement—Finance Act 2009, Schedules 55 and 56 (Income Tax Self Assessment and Pension Schemes) (Appointed Days and Consequential and Savings Provisions) Order, SI 2011/702 art 2 (appointed day for the coming into force of Sch 55 is 6 April 2011 in relation to a return or other document which is required to be made or delivered to HMRC in relation to the tax year 2010–11 or any subsequent tax year and falls within item 1, 2 or 3 of the Table in para 1).

Modifications—FA 2009 Sch 55 has effect as if the reference in this para to a return falling within certain items in the Table included a reference to a bank payroll tax return (FA 2010 s 22, Sch 1 para 38(1)(*b*)).

Amendments—[1] Words substituted by FA 2013 s 230, Sch 50 paras 2, 5, with effect for the tax year 2014–15 and subsequent tax years in relation to failures to make returns with a filing date (as defined in FA 2009 Sch 55 para 1(4)) on or after 6 April 2014.

Prospective amendments—This para and preceding cross-head to be substituted by F(No 3)A 2010 s 26, Sch 10 paras 1, 3 with effect from a day to be appointed by Treasury order. This para as substituted to read—

"Amount of penalty: occasional returns and returns for periods of 6 months or more

(1) Paragraphs 3 to 6 apply in the case of—

(a) a return falling within any of items 1 to 5, 7 and 8 to 13 in the Table,

(b) a return falling within any of items 7A, 7B and 14 to 28 which relates to a period of 6 months or more, and

(c) a return falling within item 7A which relates to a transitional period for the purposes of the annual accounting scheme.

(2) In sub-paragraph (1)(*c*), a transitional period for the purposes of the annual accounting scheme is a prescribed accounting period (within the meaning of section 25(1) of VATA 1994) which—

(a) ends on the day immediately preceding the date indicated by the Commissioners for Her Majesty's Revenue and Customs in a notification of authorisation under regulation 50 of the Value Added Tax Regulations 1995 (SI 1995/2518) (admission to annual accounting scheme), or

(b) begins on the day immediately following the end of the last period of 12 months for which such an authorisation has effect.".

In sub-para (1)(*b*) (as substituted), "29" to be substituted for "28", by FA 2012 s 191, Sch 24 para 32(*a*), with effect in relation to the playing of machine games on or after 1 February 2013 (and Schs 55, 56, as amended by FA 2012 Sch 24 Part 1, are taken to have come into force for the purposes of machine games duty on that date).

3 P is liable to a penalty under this paragraph of £100.

Commencement—Finance Act 2009, Schedules 55 and 56 (Income Tax Self Assessment and Pension Schemes) (Appointed Days and Consequential and Savings Provisions) Order, SI 2011/702 art 2 (appointed day for the coming into force of Sch 55 is 6 April 2011 in relation to a return or other document which is required to be made or delivered to HMRC in relation to the tax year 2010–11 or any subsequent tax year and falls within item 1, 2 or 3 of the Table in para 1).

4—(1) P is liable to a penalty under this paragraph if (and only if)—

(*a*) P's failure continues after the end of the period of 3 months beginning with the penalty date,

(*b*) HMRC decide that such a penalty should be payable, and

(*c*) HMRC give notice to P specifying the date from which the penalty is payable.

(2) The penalty under this paragraph is £10 for each day that the failure continues during the period of 90 days beginning with the date specified in the notice given under sub-paragraph (1)(*c*).

(3) The date specified in the notice under sub-paragraph (1)(*c*)—

(*a*) may be earlier than the date on which the notice is given, but

(*b*) may not be earlier than the end of the period mentioned in sub-paragraph (1)(*a*).

Commencement—Finance Act 2009, Schedules 55 and 56 (Income Tax Self Assessment and Pension Schemes) (Appointed Days and Consequential and Savings Provisions) Order, SI 2011/702 art 2 (appointed day for the coming into force of Sch 55 is 6 April 2011 in relation to a return or other document which is required to be made or delivered to HMRC in relation to the tax year 2010–11 or any subsequent tax year and falls within item 1, 2 or 3 of the Table in para 1).

Simon's Tax Cases—*R&C Comrs v Donaldson* [2014] UKUT 536 (TCC), [2015] STC 689; *R&C Comrs v Donaldson* [2016] EWCA Civ 761, [2016] STC 2511.

5—(1) P is liable to a penalty under this paragraph if (and only if) P's failure continues after the end of the period of 6 months beginning with the penalty date.

(2) The penalty under this paragraph is the greater of—

(*a*) 5% of any liability to tax which would have been shown in the return in question, and

(*b*) £300.

Commencement—Finance Act 2009, Schedules 55 and 56 (Income Tax Self Assessment and Pension Schemes) (Appointed Days and Consequential and Savings Provisions) Order, SI 2011/702 art 2 (appointed day for the coming into force of Sch 55 is 6 April 2011 in relation to a return or other document which is required to be made or delivered to HMRC in relation to the tax year 2010–11 or any subsequent tax year and falls within item 1, 2 or 3 of the Table in para 1).

Cross references—FA 2014 s 212 (application of this paragraph in calculation of aggregate penalties for failure to take corrective action in response to a follower notice).

6—(1) P is liable to a penalty under this paragraph if (and only if) P's failure continues after the end of the period of 12 months beginning with the penalty date.

(2) Where, by failing to make the return, P [deliberately][1] withholds information which would enable or assist HMRC to assess P's liability to tax, the penalty under this paragraph is determined in accordance with sub-paragraphs (3) and (4).

(3) If the withholding of the information is deliberate and concealed, the penalty is the greater of—

(*a*) [the relevant percentage][2] of any liability to tax which would have been shown in the return in question, and

(*b*) £300.

[(3A) For the purposes of sub-paragraph (3)(*a*), the relevant percentage is—

(*a*) for the withholding of category 1 information, 100%,

(*b*) for the withholding of category 2 information, 150%, and

(*c*) for the withholding of category 3 information, 200%.][2]

(4) If the withholding of the information is deliberate but not concealed, the penalty is the greater of—

(*a*) [the relevant percentage][2] of any liability to tax which would have been shown in the return in question, and

(*b*) £300.

[(4A) For the purposes of sub-paragraph (4)(*a*), the relevant percentage is—

(*a*) for the withholding of category 1 information, 70%,

(*b*) for the withholding of category 2 information, 105%, and

(*c*) for the withholding of category 3 information, 140%.][2]

(5) In [any case not falling within sub-paragraph (2)][1], the penalty under this paragraph is the greater of—

(*a*) 5% of any liability to tax which would have been shown in the return in question, and

(*b*) £300.

[(6) Paragraph 6A explains the 3 categories of information.][2]

Commencement—Finance Act 2009, Schedules 55 and 56 (Income Tax Self Assessment and Pension Schemes) (Appointed Days and Consequential and Savings Provisions) Order, SI 2011/702 art 2 (appointed day for the coming into force of Sch 55 is 6 April 2011 in relation to a return or other document which is required to be made or delivered to HMRC in relation to the tax year 2010–11 or any subsequent tax year and falls within item 1, 2 or 3 of the Table in para 1).

Cross references—FA 2014 s 212 (application of this paragraph in calculation of aggregate penalties for failure to take corrective action in response to a follower notice).

FA 2015 Sch 21 (penalties in connection with offshore asset moves).

FA 2016 Sch 20 (penalties for enablers of offshore tax evasion or non-compliance).

FA 2016 Sch 22 (asset-based penalty for offshore inaccuracies and failures).

Amendments—[1] In sub-para (2) word inserted, and in sub-para (5) words substituted, by F(No 3)A 2010 s 26, Sch 10 paras 1, 4 with effect as follows (by virtue of SI 2011/703)—

– from 6 April 2011 in relation to a return or other document which is required to be made or delivered to HMRC in relation to the tax year 2010–11 or any subsequent tax year, and falls within item 1, 2 or 3 of the Table in Sch 55 para 1; and
– from 1 April 2011 in relation to a return under FA 2004 s 254 to be made in respect of a return period ending on or after 31 March 2011.

[2] In sub-parsa (3)(*a*), (4)(*a*), words substituted, and sub-paras (3A), (4A), (6) inserted, by FA 2010 s 35, Sch 10 paras 10, 11 with effect from 6 April 2011 in relation to a return or other document which is required to be made or delivered to HMRC in relation to the tax year 2011–12 or any subsequent tax year, and falls within item 1, 2 or 3 of the Table in FA 2009 Sch 55 para 1. Note that these changes do not have effect in relation to Sch 55 in relation to a return or other document which is required to be made or delivered to HMRC in relation to the tax year 2010–11 or any previous tax year (SI 2011/975 art 5).

Prospective amendments—Sub-paras (3A)(*za*), (4A)(*za*) to be inserted before sub-paras (3A)(*a*), (4A)(*a*), in sub-para (3A)(*a*), figure "125%" to be substituted for "100%", in sub-para (4A)(*a*), figure "87.5%" to be substituted for "70%", and in sub-para (6), figure "4" to be substituted for figure "3" by FA 2015 s 120, Sch 20 paras 14, 15 with effect from a day to be appointed. Sub-para (3A)(*za*) as inserted to read as follows—

"(za) for the withholding of category 0 information, 100%,".

Sub-para (4A)(*za*) as inserted to read as follows—

"(za) for the withholding of category 0 information, 70%,".

[6A (1) Information is category 1 information if—

(*a*) it involves a domestic matter, or

(*b*) it involves an offshore matter and—

(i) the territory in question is a category 1 territory, or

(ii) it is information which would enable or assist HMRC to assess P's liability to a tax other than income tax or capital gains tax.

(2) Information is category 2 information if—

(*a*) it involves an offshore matter [or an offshore transfer][2],

(*b*) the territory in question is a category 2 territory, and

(*c*) it is information which would enable or assist HMRC to assess P's liability to income tax[, capital gains tax or inheritance tax][2].

(3) Information is category 3 information if—

(*a*) it involves an offshore matter [or an offshore transfer][2],

(*b*) the territory in question is a category 3 territory, and

(*c*) it is information which would enable or assist HMRC to assess P's liability to income tax[, capital gains tax or inheritance tax][2].

(4) Information "involves an offshore matter" if the liability to tax which would have been shown in the return includes a liability to tax charged on or by reference to—

(*a*) income arising from a source in a territory outside the UK,

(*b*) assets situated or held in a territory outside the UK,

(*c*) activities carried on wholly or mainly in a territory outside the UK, or

(*d*) anything having effect as if it were income, assets or activities of a kind described above.

[(4A) If the liability to tax which would have been shown in the return is a liability to inheritance tax, assets are treated for the purposes of sub-paragraph (4) as situated or held in a territory outside the UK if they are so situated or held immediately after the transfer of value by reason of which inheritance tax becomes chargeable.

(4B) Information "involves an offshore transfer" if—

(*a*) it does not involve an offshore matter,

(*b*) it is information which would enable or assist HMRC to assess P's liability to income tax, capital gains tax or inheritance tax,

(*c*) by failing to make the return, P deliberately withholds the information (whether or not the withholding of the information is also concealed), and

(*d*) the applicable condition in paragraph 6AA is satisfied.][2]

(5) Information "involves a domestic matter" if [it does not involve an offshore matter or an offshore transfer][2].

(6) If the information which P withholds falls into more than one category—

(*a*) P's failure to make the return is to be treated for the purposes of this Schedule as if it were separate failures, one for each category of information according to the matters [or transfers][2] which the information involves, and

(*b*) for each separate failure, the liability to tax which would have been shown in the return in question is taken to be such share of the liability to tax which would have been shown in the return mentioned in paragraph (*a*) as is just and reasonable.

(7) For the purposes of this Schedule—

(*a*) paragraph 21A of Schedule 24 to FA 2007 (classification of territories) has effect, but

(*b*) an order under that paragraph does not apply to a failure if the filing date is before the date on which the order comes into force.

(8) . . . [2]

(9) In this paragraph [and paragraph 6AA[2]]—

"assets" has the meaning given in section 21(1) of TCGA 1992, but also includes sterling;

"UK" means the United Kingdom, including the territorial sea of the United Kingdom.][1]

Commencement—Finance Act 2009, Schedules 55 and 56 (Income Tax Self Assessment and Pension Schemes) (Appointed Days and Consequential and Savings Provisions) Order, SI 2011/702 art 2 (appointed day for the coming into force of Sch 55 is 6 April 2011 in relation to a return or other document which is required to be made or delivered to HMRC in relation to the tax year 2010–11 or any subsequent tax year and falls within item 1, 2 or 3 of the Table in para 1).

Amendments—[1] Para 6A inserted by FA 2010 s 35, Sch 10 paras 10, 12 with effect from 6 April 2011 in relation to a return or other document which is required to be made or delivered to HMRC in relation to the tax year 2011–12 or any subsequent tax year, and falls within item 1, 2 or 3 of the Table in FA 2009 Sch 55 para 1. Note that these changes do not have effect in relation to Sch 55 in relation to a return or other document which is required to be made or delivered to HMRC in relation to the tax year 2010–11 or any previous tax year (SI 2011/975 art 5).

[2] In sub-paras (2)(*a*), (3)(*a*), (6)(*a*), (9), words inserted, in sub-paras (2)(*c*). (3)(*c*), (5), words substituted, sub-paras (4A), (4B) inserted, and sub-para (8) repealed by FA 2015 s 120, Sch 20 paras 14, 16(3)–(9) with effect from 6 April 2016 (by virtue of SI 2016/456 art 5) in relation to a return or other document which—

- is required to be made or delivered to HMRC in relation to a tax year commencing on or after that date; and
- falls within item 1, 2 or 3 of the Table in FA 2009 Sch 55 para 1(5)).

Prospective amendments—Sub-paras (A1), (1) to be substituted for sub-para (1) by FA 2015 s 120, Sch 20 paras 14, 16 with effect from a day to be appointed. Sub-paragraphs (A1), (1) as substituted to read as follows—

"(A1) Information is category 0 information if—

(a) it involves a domestic matter,

(b) it involves an offshore matter or an offshore transfer, the territory in question is a category 0 territory and it is information which would enable or assist HMRC to assess P's liability to income tax, capital gains tax or inheritance tax, or

(c) it involves an offshore matter and it is information which would enable or assist HMRC to assess P's liability to a tax other than income tax, capital gains tax or inheritance tax.

(1) Information is category 1 information if—

(a) it involves an offshore matter or an offshore transfer,

(b) the territory in question is a category 1 territory, and

(c) it is information which would enable or assist HMRC to assess P's liability to income tax, capital gains tax or inheritance tax.".

[6AA (1) This paragraph makes provision in relation to offshore transfers.

(2) Where the liability to tax which would have been shown in the return is a liability to income tax, the applicable condition is satisfied if the income on or by reference to which the tax is charged, or any part of the income—

(*a*) is received in a territory outside the UK, or

(*b*) is transferred before the relevant date to a territory outside the UK.

(3) Where the liability to tax which would have been shown in the return is a liability to capital gains tax, the applicable condition is satisfied if the proceeds of the disposal on or by reference to which the tax is charged, or any part of the proceeds—

(*a*) are received in a territory outside the UK, or

(*b*) are transferred before the relevant date to a territory outside the UK.

(4) Where the liability to tax which would have been shown in the return is a liability to inheritance tax, the applicable condition is satisfied if—

(*a*) the disposition that gives rise to the transfer of value by reason of which the tax becomes chargeable involves a transfer of assets, and

(*b*) after that disposition but before the relevant date the assets, or any part of the assets, are transferred to a territory outside the UK.

(5) In the case of a transfer falling within sub-paragraph (2)(*b*), (3)(*b*) or (4)(*b*), references to the income, proceeds or assets transferred are to be read as including references to any assets derived from or representing the income, proceeds or assets.
(6) In relation to an offshore transfer, the territory in question for the purposes of paragraph 6A is the highest category of territory by virtue of which the information involves an offshore transfer.
(7) "Relevant date" means the date on which P becomes liable to a penalty under paragraph 6.][1]

Amendments—[1] Paragraphs 6AA, 6AB inserted by FA 2015 s 120, Sch 20 paras 14, 17 with effect from 6 April 2016 (by virtue of SI 2016/456 art 5) in relation to a return or other document which—
- is required to be made or delivered to HMRC in relation to a tax year commencing on or after that date; and
- falls within item 1, 2 or 3 of the Table in FA 2009 Sch 55 para 1(5)).

[6AB Regulations under paragraph 21B of Schedule 24 to FA 2007 (location of assets etc) apply for the purposes of paragraphs 6A and 6AA of this Schedule as they apply for the purposes of paragraphs 4A and 4AA of that Schedule.][1]

Amendments—[1] Paragraphs 6AA, 6AB inserted by FA 2015 s 120, Sch 20 paras 14, 17 with effect from 6 April 2016 (by virtue of SI 2016/456 art 5) in relation to a return or other document which—
- is required to be made or delivered to HMRC in relation to a tax year commencing on or after that date; and
- falls within item 1, 2 or 3 of the Table in FA 2009 Sch 55 para 1(5)).

[Amount of penalty: real time information for PAYE [and apprenticeship levy]

6B Paragraphs 6C and 6D apply in the case of a return falling within item 4 [or 4A][2] in the Table.][1]

Commencement—Finance Act 2009, Schedule 55 (Penalties for failure to make returns) (Appointed Days and Consequential Provision) Order, SI 2014/2395 provides dates for the coming into force of Sch 55 in relation to returns falling within item 4 of the table in para 1 above (PAYE returns), as follows—
- **11 September 2014:** powers to make regulations in relation to quanta of RTI late-filing penalties in para 6C(5), (7), (8), (9), (11) (see also SI 2014/2396).
- for paras 1, 6B, 6C(1)–(4), (6), (10), 6D, 16–24, 26, 27 (relating to failures to make returns under the PAYE Regulations (SI 2003/2682) regs 67B and 67D):
  - (a) **6 October 2014:** where the employer is a large existing employer (an employer which as at 6 October 2014 employs at least 50 employees). Affected returns are those required to be made or delivered to HMRC on or after 6 October 2014.
  - (b) **6 March 2015:** where the employer is a small existing employer (an employer which as at 6 October 2014 employs no more than 49 employees) or is a new employer. Affected returns are those required to be made or delivered to HMRC on or after 6 March 2015.

Amendments—[1] Paragraphs 6B–6D and preceding cross-head inserted by FA 2013 s 230, Sch 50 paras 2, 6 with effect for the tax year 2014–15 and subsequent tax years in relation to failures to make returns with a filing date (as defined in FA 2009 Sch 55 para 1(4)) on or after 6 April 2014.
[2] Words inserted by FA 2016 s 113(5), (7), (8) with effect from 15 September 2016 in relation to the apprenticeship levy which applies for 2017–18 and subsequent tax years.

[6C—(1) If P fails during a tax month to make a return on or before the filing date, P is liable to a penalty under this paragraph in respect of that month.
(2) But this is subject to sub-paragraphs (3) and (4).
(3) P is not liable to a penalty under this paragraph in respect of a tax month as a result of any failure to make a return on or before the filing date which occurs during the initial period.
(4) P is not liable to a penalty under this paragraph in respect of a tax month falling in a tax year if the month is the first tax month in that tax year during which P fails to make a return on or before the filing date (disregarding for this purpose any failure which occurs during the initial period).
(5) In sub-paragraphs (3) and (4) "the initial period" means the period which—
(*a*) begins with the day in the first tax year on which P is first required to make a return, and
(*b*) is of such duration as is specified in regulations made by the Commissioners,
and for this purpose "the first tax year" means the first tax year in which P is required to make returns.
(6) P may be liable under this paragraph to no more than one penalty in respect of each tax month.
(7) The penalty under this paragraph is to be calculated in accordance with regulations made by the Commissioners.
(8) Regulations under sub-paragraph (7) may provide for a penalty under this paragraph in respect of a tax month to be calculated by reference to either or both of the following matters—
(*a*) the number of persons employed by P, or treated as employed by P for the purposes of PAYE regulations;
(*b*) the number of previous penalties incurred by P under this paragraph in the same tax year.
(9) The Commissioners may by regulations disapply sub-paragraph (3) or (4) in such circumstances as are specified in the regulations.
(10) If P has elected under PAYE regulations to be treated as different employers in relation to different groups of employees, this paragraph applies to P as if—
(*a*) in respect of each group P were a different person, and
(*b*) each group constituted all of P's employees.

(11) Regulations made by the Commissioners under this paragraph may—

(*a*) make different provision for different cases, and

(*b*) include incidental, consequential and supplementary provision.][1]

Commencement—Finance Act 2009, Schedule 55 (Penalties for failure to make returns) (Appointed Days and Consequential Provision) Order, SI 2014/2395 provides dates for the coming into force of Sch 55 in relation to returns falling within item 4 of the table in para 1 above (PAYE returns), as follows—

– **11 September 2014:** powers to make regulations in relation to quanta of RTI late-filing penalties in para 6C(5), (7), (8), (9), (11) (see also SI 2014/2396).

– for paras 1, 6B, 6C(1)–(4), (6), (10), 6D, 16–24, 26, 27 (relating to failures to make returns under the PAYE Regulations (SI 2003/2682) regs 67B and 67D):

(a) **6 October 2014:** where the employer is a large existing employer (an employer which as at 6 October 2014 employs at least 50 employees). Affected returns are those required to be made or delivered to HMRC on or after 6 October 2014.

(b) **6 March 2015:** where the employer is a small existing employer (an employer which as at 6 October 2014 employs no more than 49 employees) or is a new employer. Affected returns are those required to be made or delivered to HMRC on or after 6 March 2015.

Regulations—Income Tax (Pay As You Earn) (Amendment No 3) Regulations, SI 2014/2396 (inserting regs 67I–67K into the PAYE Regulations (SI 2003/2682)).

Cross-references—See Income Tax (Pay As You Earn) Regulations, SI 2003/2682 regs 67I–67K (amount of penalties for employers who fail to file a return by the relevant filing date).

Amendments—[1] Paragraphs 6B–6D and preceding cross-head inserted by FA 2013 s 230, Sch 50 paras 2, 6 with effect for the tax year 2014–15 and subsequent tax years in relation to failures to make returns with a filing date (as defined in FA 2009 Sch 55 para 1(4)) on or after 6 April 2014.

[6D—(1) P may be liable to one or more penalties under this paragraph in respect of extended failures.

(2) In this paragraph an "extended failure" means a failure to make a return on or before the filing date which continues after the end of the period of 3 months beginning with the day after the filing date.

(3) P is liable to a penalty or penalties under this paragraph if (and only if)—

(*a*) HMRC decide at any time that such a penalty or penalties should be payable in accordance with sub-paragraph (4) or (6), and

(*b*) HMRC give notice to P specifying the date from which the penalty, or each penalty, is payable.

(4) HMRC may decide under sub-paragraph (3)(*a*) that a separate penalty should be payable in respect of each unpenalised extended failure in the tax year to date.

(5) In that case the amount of the penalty in respect of each failure is 5% of any liability to make payments which would have been shown in the return in question.

(6) HMRC may decide under sub-paragraph (3)(*a*) that a single penalty should be payable in respect of all the unpenalised extended failures in the tax year to date.

(7) In that case the amount of the penalty in respect of those failures is 5% of the sum of the liabilities to make payments which would have been shown in each of the returns in question.

(8) For the purposes of this paragraph, an extended failure is unpenalised if a penalty has not already been imposed in respect of it under this paragraph (whether in accordance with subparagraph (4) or (6)).

(9) The date specified in the notice under sub-paragraph (3)(*b*) in relation to a penalty—

(*a*) may be earlier than the date on which the notice is given, but

(*b*) may not be earlier than the end of the period mentioned in sub-paragraph (2) in relation to the relevant extended failure.

(10) In sub-paragraph (9)(*b*) "the relevant extended failure" means—

(*a*) the extended failure in respect of which the penalty is payable, or

(*b*) if the penalty is payable in respect of more than one extended failure (in accordance with sub-paragraph (6)), the extended failure with the latest filing date.][1]

Commencement—Finance Act 2009, Schedule 55 (Penalties for failure to make returns) (Appointed Days and Consequential Provision) Order, SI 2014/2395 provides dates for the coming into force of Sch 55 in relation to returns falling within item 4 of the table in para 1 above (PAYE returns), as follows—

– **11 September 2014:** powers to make regulations in relation to quanta of RTI late-filing penalties in para 6C(5), (7), (8), (9), (11) (see also SI 2014/2396).

– for paras 1, 6B, 6C(1)–(4), (6), (10), 6D, 16–24, 26, 27 (relating to failures to make returns under the PAYE Regulations (SI 2003/2682) regs 67B and 67D):

(a) **6 October 2014:** where the employer is a large existing employer (an employer which as at 6 October 2014 employs at least 50 employees). Affected returns are those required to be made or delivered to HMRC on or after 6 October 2014.

(b) **6 March 2015:** where the employer is a small existing employer (an employer which as at 6 October 2014 employs no more than 49 employees) or is a new employer. Affected returns are those required to be made or delivered to HMRC on or after 6 March 2015.

Amendments—[1] Paragraphs 6B–6D and preceding cross-head inserted by FA 2013 s 230, Sch 50 paras 2, 6 with effect for the tax year 2014–15 and subsequent tax years in relation to failures to make returns with a filing date (as defined in FA 2009 Sch 55 para 1(4)) on or after 6 April 2014.

Amount of penalty: CIS returns

7 Paragraphs 8 to 13 apply in the case of a return falling within item 6 in the Table.

Commencement—Finance Act 2009, Schedules 55 and 56 (Income Tax Self Assessment and Pension Schemes) (Appointed Days and Consequential and Savings Provisions) Order, SI 2011/702 art 2 (appointed day for the coming into force of Sch 55 is 6 April 2011 in relation to a return or other document which is required to be made or delivered to HMRC in relation to the tax year 2010–11 or any subsequent tax year and falls within item 1, 2 or 3 of the Table in para 1).

Finance (No 3) Act 2010, Schedule 10 and the Finance Act 2009, Schedule 55 and Sections 101 to 103 (Appointed Day, etc) (Construction Industry Scheme) Order, SI 2011/2391 (the day appointed for the coming into force of the following paras of Sch 55 is 6 October 2011, with effect only in relation to a return within item 6 of Sch 55 para 1(5), and for which the filing date for the purposes of Sch 55 is after 19 October 2011—

- para 1 (but only in relation to item 6 in the Table in para 1(5);
- paras 7–13; and
- 14–24, 26, and 27(1)–(4) but only as relevant to paras 7–13).

8 P is liable to a penalty under this paragraph of £100.

Commencement—Finance Act 2009, Schedules 55 and 56 (Income Tax Self Assessment and Pension Schemes) (Appointed Days and Consequential and Savings Provisions) Order, SI 2011/702 art 2 (appointed day for the coming into force of Sch 55 is 6 April 2011 in relation to a return or other document which is required to be made or delivered to HMRC in relation to the tax year 2010–11 or any subsequent tax year and falls within item 1, 2 or 3 of the Table in para 1).

Finance (No 3) Act 2010, Schedule 10 and the Finance Act 2009, Schedule 55 and Sections 101 to 103 (Appointed Day, etc) (Construction Industry Scheme) Order, SI 2011/2391 (the day appointed for the coming into force of the following paras of Sch 55 is 6 October 2011, with effect only in relation to a return within item 6 of Sch 55 para 1(5), and for which the filing date for the purposes of Sch 55 is after 19 October 2011—

- para 1 (but only in relation to item 6 in the Table in para 1(5);
- paras 7–13; and
- 14–24, 26, and 27(1)–(4) but only as relevant to paras 7–13).

9—(1) P is liable to a penalty under this paragraph if (and only if) P's failure continues after the end of the period of 2 months beginning with the penalty date.

(2) The penalty under this paragraph is £200.

Commencement—Finance Act 2009, Schedules 55 and 56 (Income Tax Self Assessment and Pension Schemes) (Appointed Days and Consequential and Savings Provisions) Order, SI 2011/702 art 2 (appointed day for the coming into force of Sch 55 is 6 April 2011 in relation to a return or other document which is required to be made or delivered to HMRC in relation to the tax year 2010–11 or any subsequent tax year and falls within item 1, 2 or 3 of the Table in para 1).

Finance (No 3) Act 2010, Schedule 10 and the Finance Act 2009, Schedule 55 and Sections 101 to 103 (Appointed Day, etc) (Construction Industry Scheme) Order, SI 2011/2391 (the day appointed for the coming into force of the following paras of Sch 55 is 6 October 2011, with effect only in relation to a return within item 6 of Sch 55 para 1(5), and for which the filing date for the purposes of Sch 55 is after 19 October 2011—

- para 1 (but only in relation to item 6 in the Table in para 1(5);
- paras 7–13; and
- 14–24, 26, and 27(1)–(4) but only as relevant to paras 7–13).

10—(1) P is liable to a penalty under this paragraph if (and only if) P's failure continues after the end of the period of 6 months beginning with the penalty date.

(2) The penalty under this paragraph is the greater of—

(*a*) 5% of any liability to make payments which would have been shown in the return in question, and

(*b*) £300.

Commencement—Finance Act 2009, Schedules 55 and 56 (Income Tax Self Assessment and Pension Schemes) (Appointed Days and Consequential and Savings Provisions) Order, SI 2011/702 art 2 (appointed day for the coming into force of Sch 55 is 6 April 2011 in relation to a return or other document which is required to be made or delivered to HMRC in relation to the tax year 2010–11 or any subsequent tax year and falls within item 1, 2 or 3 of the Table in para 1).

Finance (No 3) Act 2010, Schedule 10 and the Finance Act 2009, Schedule 55 and Sections 101 to 103 (Appointed Day, etc) (Construction Industry Scheme) Order, SI 2011/2391 (the day appointed for the coming into force of the following paras of Sch 55 is 6 October 2011, with effect only in relation to a return within item 6 of Sch 55 para 1(5), and for which the filing date for the purposes of Sch 55 is after 19 October 2011—

- para 1 (but only in relation to item 6 in the Table in para 1(5);
- paras 7–13; and
- 14–24, 26, and 27(1)–(4) but only as relevant to paras 7–13).

11—(1) P is liable to a penalty under this paragraph if (and only if) P's failure continues after the end of the period of 12 months beginning with the penalty date.

(2) Where, by failing to make the return, P [deliberately][1] withholds information which would enable or assist HMRC to assess the amount that P is liable to pay to HMRC in accordance with Chapter 3 of Part 3 of FA 2004, the penalty under this paragraph is determined in accordance with sub-paragraphs (3) and (4).

(3) If the withholding of the information is deliberate and concealed, the penalty is the greater of—

(*a*) 100% of any liability to make payments which would have been shown in the return in question, and

(*b*) £3,000.

(4) If the withholding of the information is deliberate but not concealed, the penalty is the greater of—

(*a*) 70% of any liability to make payments which would have been shown in the return in question, and

(*b*) £1,500.

(5) In [any case not falling within sub-paragraph (2)][1], the penalty under this paragraph is the greater of—

(*a*) 5% of any liability to make payments which would have been shown in the return in question, and

(*b*) £300.

Commencement—Finance Act 2009, Schedules 55 and 56 (Income Tax Self Assessment and Pension Schemes) (Appointed Days and Consequential and Savings Provisions) Order, SI 2011/702 art 2 (appointed day for the coming into force of Sch 55 is 6 April 2011 in relation to a return or other document which is required to be made or delivered to HMRC in relation to the tax year 2010–11 or any subsequent tax year and falls within item 1, 2 or 3 of the Table in para 1).

Finance (No 3) Act 2010, Schedule 10 and the Finance Act 2009, Schedule 55 and Sections 101 to 103 (Appointed Day, etc) (Construction Industry Scheme) Order, SI 2011/2391 (the day appointed for the coming into force of the following paras of Sch 55 is 6 October 2011, with effect only in relation to a return within item 6 of Sch 55 para 1(5), and for which the filing date for the purposes of Sch 55 is after 19 October 2011—

– para 1 (but only in relation to item 6 in the Table in para 1(5);
– paras 7–13; and
– 14–24, 26, and 27(1)–(4) but only as relevant to paras 7–13).

Amendments—[1] In sub-para (2) word inserted, and in sub-para (5) words substituted for words "any other case", by F(No 3)A 2010 s 26, Sch 10 paras 1, 5 with effect from 6 October 2011 (by virtue of SI 2011/2391). These amendments have effect in relation to a return within item 6 of Sch 55 para 1(5), and for which the filing date for the purposes of Sch 55 is after 19 October 2011 (SI 2011/2391 art 3(1)).

12—(1) P is liable to a penalty under this paragraph if (and only if)—

(*a*) P's failure continues after the end of the period of 12 months beginning with the penalty date, and

(*b*) the information required in the return relates only to persons registered for gross payment (within the meaning of Chapter 3 of Part 3 of FA 2004).

(2) Where, by failing to make the return, P [deliberately][1] withholds information which relates to such persons, the penalty under this paragraph is—

(*a*) if the withholding of the information is deliberate and concealed, £3,000, and

(*b*) if the withholding of the information is deliberate but not concealed, £1,500.

Commencement—Finance Act 2009, Schedules 55 and 56 (Income Tax Self Assessment and Pension Schemes) (Appointed Days and Consequential and Savings Provisions) Order, SI 2011/702 art 2 (appointed day for the coming into force of Sch 55 is 6 April 2011 in relation to a return or other document which is required to be made or delivered to HMRC in relation to the tax year 2010–11 or any subsequent tax year and falls within item 1, 2 or 3 of the Table in para 1).

Finance (No 3) Act 2010, Schedule 10 and the Finance Act 2009, Schedule 55 and Sections 101 to 103 (Appointed Day, etc) (Construction Industry Scheme) Order, SI 2011/2391 (the day appointed for the coming into force of the following paras of Sch 55 is 6 October 2011, with effect only in relation to a return within item 6 of Sch 55 para 1(5), and for which the filing date for the purposes of Sch 55 is after 19 October 2011—

– para 1 (but only in relation to item 6 in the Table in para 1(5);
– paras 7–13; and
– 14–24, 26, and 27(1)–(4) but only as relevant to paras 7–13).

Amendments—[1] In sub-para (2) word inserted by F(No 3)A 2010 s 26, Sch 10 paras 1, 6 with effect from 6 October 2011 (by virtue of SI 2011/2391). This amendment has effect in relation to a return within item 6 of Sch 55 para 1(5), and for which the filing date for the purposes of Sch 55 is after 19 October 2011 (SI 2011/2391 art 3(1)).

13—(1) This paragraph applies—

(*a*) at any time before P first makes a return falling within item 6 in the Table, to any return falling within that item, and

(*b*) at any time after P first makes a return falling within that item, to that return and any earlier return.

(2) In respect of any return or returns to which this paragraph applies—

(*a*) paragraphs 10(2)(*b*) and 11(5)(*b*) do not apply, and

(*b*) P is not liable to penalties under paragraphs 8 and 9 which exceed, in total, £3,000.

(3) In sub-paragraph (1)(*b*) "earlier return" means any return falling within item 6 which has a filing date earlier than the date on which P first made a return.

Commencement—Finance Act 2009, Schedules 55 and 56 (Income Tax Self Assessment and Pension Schemes) (Appointed Days and Consequential and Savings Provisions) Order, SI 2011/702 art 2 (appointed day for the coming into force of Sch 55 is

6 April 2011 in relation to a return or other document which is required to be made or delivered to HMRC in relation to the tax year 2010–11 or any subsequent tax year and falls within item 1, 2 or 3 of the Table in para 1).

Finance (No 3) Act 2010, Schedule 10 and the Finance Act 2009, Schedule 55 and Sections 101 to 103 (Appointed Day, etc) (Construction Industry Scheme) Order, SI 2011/2391 (the day appointed for the coming into force of the following paras of Sch 55 is 6 October 2011, with effect only in relation to a return within item 6 of Sch 55 para 1(5), and for which the filing date for the purposes of Sch 55 is after 19 October 2011—

- para 1 (but only in relation to item 6 in the Table in para 1(5);
- paras 7–13; and
- 14–24, 26, and 27(1)-(4) but only as relevant to paras 7–13).

[Amount of penalty: returns for periods of between 2 and 6 months

13A—*(1) Paragraphs 13B to 13E apply in the case of a return falling within any of items 7A to 7B and 14 to [29][1] in the Table which relates to a period of less than 6 months but more than 2 months.*
(2) But those paragraphs do not apply in the case of a return mentioned in paragraph 2(1)(c).]

Commencement—Finance Act 2009, Schedules 55 and 56 (Income Tax Self Assessment and Pension Schemes) (Appointed Days and Consequential and Savings Provisions) Order, SI 2011/702 art 2 (appointed day for the coming into force of Sch 55 is 6 April 2011 in relation to a return or other document which is required to be made or delivered to HMRC in relation to the tax year 2010–11 or any subsequent tax year and falls within item 1, 2 or 3 of the Table in para 1).

Amendments—[1] In sub-para (1) figure substituted by FA 2012 s 191, Sch 24 para 32(*b*), with effect in relation to the playing of machine games on or after 1 February 2013 (and Schs 55, 56, as amended by FA 2012 Sch 24 Part 1, are taken to have come into force for the purposes of machine games duty on that date).

Prospective amendments—Paras 13A–13J and preceding cross-heads to be inserted by F(No 3)A 2010 s 26, Sch 10 paras 1, 7 (as amended by FA 2014 s 103, Sch 22 para 21) with effect from a day to be appointed by Treasury order.

[13B—*(1) P is liable to a penalty under this paragraph of £100.*
(2) In addition, a penalty period begins to run on the penalty date for the return.
(3) The penalty period ends with the day 12 months after the filing date for the return, unless it is extended under paragraph 13C(2)(c) or *13H(2)(c).]*

Commencement—Finance Act 2009, Schedules 55 and 56 (Income Tax Self Assessment and Pension Schemes) (Appointed Days and Consequential and Savings Provisions) Order, SI 2011/702 art 2 (appointed day for the coming into force of Sch 55 is 6 April 2011 in relation to a return or other document which is required to be made or delivered to HMRC in relation to the tax year 2010–11 or any subsequent tax year and falls within item 1, 2 or 3 of the Table in para 1).

Prospective amendment—Paras 13A–13J and preceding cross-heads to be inserted by F(No 3)A 2010 s 26, Sch 10 paras 1, 7 with effect from a day to be appointed by Treasury order.

[13C—(1) This paragraph applies if—

(*a*) a penalty period has begun under paragraph 13B or 13G because P has failed to make a return ("return A"), and

(*b*) before the end of the period, P fails to make another return ("return B") falling within the same item in the Table as return A.

(2) In such a case—

(*a*) paragraph 13B(1) and (2) do not apply to the failure to make return B, but

(*b*) P is liable to a penalty under this paragraph for that failure, and

(*c*) the penalty period that has begun is extended so that it ends with the day 12 months after the filing date for return B.

(3) The amount of the penalty under this paragraph is determined by reference to the number of returns that P has failed to make during the penalty period.

(4) If the failure to make return B is P's first failure to make a return during the penalty period, P is liable, at the time of the failure, to a penalty of £200.

(5) If the failure to make return B is P's second failure to make a return during the penalty period, P is liable, at the time of the failure, to a penalty of £300.

(6) If the failure to make return B is P's third or a subsequent failure to make a return during the penalty period, P is liable, at the time of the failure, to a penalty of £400.

(7) For the purposes of this paragraph—

(*a*) in accordance with sub-paragraph (1)(*b*), the references in sub-paragraphs (3) to (6) to a return are references to a return falling within the same item in the Table as returns A and B, and

(*b*) a failure to make a return counts for the purposes of those sub-paragraphs if (but only if) the return relates to a period of less than 6 months.

(8) A penalty period may be extended more than once under sub-paragraph (2)(*c*).

Commencement—Finance Act 2009, Schedules 55 and 56 (Income Tax Self Assessment and Pension Schemes) (Appointed Days and Consequential and Savings Provisions) Order, SI 2011/702 art 2 (appointed day for the coming into force of Sch 55 is 6 April 2011 in relation to a return or other document which is required to be made or delivered to HMRC in relation to the tax year 2010–11 or any subsequent tax year and falls within item 1, 2 or 3 of the Table in para 1).

Prospective amendment—Paras 13A–13J and preceding cross-heads to be inserted by F(No 3)A 2010 s 26, Sch 10 paras 1, 7 with effect from a day to be appointed by Treasury order.

[13D—(1) P is liable to a penalty under this paragraph if (and only if) P's failure continues after the end of the period of 6 months beginning with the penalty date.

(2) The penalty under this paragraph is the greater of—

(*a*) 5% of any liability to tax which would have been shown in the return in question, and

(*b*) £300.]

Commencement—Finance Act 2009, Schedules 55 and 56 (Income Tax Self Assessment and Pension Schemes) (Appointed Days and Consequential and Savings Provisions) Order, SI 2011/702 art 2 (appointed day for the coming into force of Sch 55 is 6 April 2011 in relation to a return or other document which is required to be made or delivered to HMRC in relation to the tax year 2010–11 or any subsequent tax year and falls within item 1, 2 or 3 of the Table in para 1).

Prospective amendment—Paras 13A–13J and preceding cross-heads to be inserted by F(No 3)A 2010 s 26, Sch 10 paras 1, 7 with effect from a day to be appointed by Treasury order.

[13E—(1) P is liable to a penalty under this paragraph if (and only if) P's failure continues after the end of the period of 12 months beginning with the penalty date.

(2) Where, by failing to make the return, P deliberately withholds information which would enable or assist HMRC to assess P's liability to tax, the penalty under this paragraph is determined in accordance with sub-paragraphs (3) and (4).

(3) If the withholding of the information is deliberate and concealed, the penalty is the greater of—

(*a*) 100% of any liability to tax which would have been shown in the return in question, and

(*b*) £300.

(4) If the withholding of the information is deliberate but not concealed, the penalty is the greater of—

(*a*) 70% of any liability to tax which would have been shown in the return in question, and

(*b*) £300.

(5) In any case not falling within sub-paragraph (2), the penalty under this paragraph is the greater of—

(*a*) 5% of any liability to tax which would have been shown in the return in question, and

(*b*) £300.]

Commencement—Finance Act 2009, Schedules 55 and 56 (Income Tax Self Assessment and Pension Schemes) (Appointed Days and Consequential and Savings Provisions) Order, SI 2011/702 art 2 (appointed day for the coming into force of Sch 55 is 6 April 2011 in relation to a return or other document which is required to be made or delivered to HMRC in relation to the tax year 2010–11 or any subsequent tax year and falls within item 1, 2 or 3 of the Table in para 1).

Prospective amendment—Paras 13A–13J and preceding cross-heads to be inserted by F(No 3)A 2010 s 26, Sch 10 paras 1, 7 with effect from a day to be appointed by Treasury order.

[Amount of penalty: returns for periods of 2 months or less

13F (1) Paragraphs 13G to 13J apply in the case of a return falling within any of items 7A, 7B and 14 to [29][1] in the Table which relates to a period of 2 months or less.

(2) But those paragraphs do not apply in the case of a return mentioned in paragraph 2(1)(*c*).]

Commencement—Finance Act 2009, Schedules 55 and 56 (Income Tax Self Assessment and Pension Schemes) (Appointed Days and Consequential and Savings Provisions) Order, SI 2011/702 art 2 (appointed day for the coming into force of Sch 55 is 6 April 2011 in relation to a return or other document which is required to be made or delivered to HMRC in relation to the tax year 2010–11 or any subsequent tax year and falls within item 1, 2 or 3 of the Table in para 1).

Amendments—[1] In sub-para (1), "29" substituted for "28", by FA 2012 s 191, Sch 24 para 32(*a*), with effect in relation to the playing of machine games on or after 1 February 2013 (and Schs 55, 56, as amended by FA 2012 Sch 24 Part 1, are taken to have come into force for the purposes of machine games duty on that date).

Prospective amendments—Paras 13A–13J and preceding cross-heads to be inserted by F(No 3)A 2010 s 26, Sch 10 paras 1, 7 with effect from a day to be appointed by Treasury order.

[13G—(1) P is liable to a penalty under this paragraph of £100.

(2) In addition, a penalty period begins to run on the penalty date for the return.

(3) The penalty period ends with the day 12 months after the filing date for the return, unless it is extended under paragraph 13C(2)(*c*) or 13H(2)(*c*).]

Commencement—Finance Act 2009, Schedules 55 and 56 (Income Tax Self Assessment and Pension Schemes) (Appointed Days and Consequential and Savings Provisions) Order, SI 2011/702 art 2 (appointed day for the coming into force of Sch 55 is 6 April 2011 in relation to a return or other document which is required to be made or delivered to HMRC in relation to the tax year 2010–11 or any subsequent tax year and falls within item 1, 2 or 3 of the Table in para 1).

Prospective amendment—Paras 13A–13J and preceding cross-heads to be inserted by F(No 3)A 2010 s 26, Sch 10 paras 1, 7 with effect from a day to be appointed by Treasury order.

[13H—(1) This paragraph applies if—

(*a*) a penalty period has begun under paragraph 13B or 13G because P has failed to make a return ("return A"), and

(*b*) before the end of the period, P fails to make another return ("return B") falling within the same item in the Table as return A.

(2) In such a case—

(*a*) paragraph 13G(1) and (2) do not apply to the failure to make return B, but (*b*) P is liable to a penalty under this paragraph for that failure, and

(*c*) the penalty period that has begun is extended so that it ends with the day 12 months after the filing date for return B.

(3) The amount of the penalty under this paragraph is determined by reference to the number of returns that P has failed to make during the penalty period.

(4) If the failure to make return B is P's first, second, third, fourth or fifth failure to make a return during the penalty period, P is liable, at the time of the failure, to a penalty of £100.

(5) If the failure to make return B is P's sixth or a subsequent failure to make a return during the penalty period, P is liable, at the time of the failure, to a penalty of £200.

(6) For the purposes of this paragraph—

(*a*) in accordance with sub-paragraph (1)(*b*), the references in sub-paragraphs (3) to (5) to a return are references to a return falling within the same item in the Table as returns A and B, and

(*b*) a failure to make a return counts for the purposes of those sub-paragraphs if (but only if) the return relates to a period of less than 6 months.

(7) A penalty period may be extended more than once under sub-paragraph (2)(*c*).]

Commencement—Finance Act 2009, Schedules 55 and 56 (Income Tax Self Assessment and Pension Schemes) (Appointed Days and Consequential and Savings Provisions) Order, SI 2011/702 art 2 (appointed day for the coming into force of Sch 55 is 6 April 2011 in relation to a return or other document which is required to be made or delivered to HMRC in relation to the tax year 2010–11 or any subsequent tax year and falls within item 1, 2 or 3 of the Table in para 1).

Prospective amendment—Paras 13A–13J and preceding cross-heads to be inserted by F(No 3)A 2010 s 26, Sch 10 paras 1, 7 with effect from a day to be appointed by Treasury order.

[13I—(1) P is liable to a penalty under this paragraph if (and only if) P's failure continues after the end of the period of 6 months beginning with the penalty date.

(2) The penalty under this paragraph is the greater of—

(*a*) 5% of any liability to tax which would have been shown in the return in question, and

(*b*) £300.]

Commencement—Finance Act 2009, Schedules 55 and 56 (Income Tax Self Assessment and Pension Schemes) (Appointed Days and Consequential and Savings Provisions) Order, SI 2011/702 art 2 (appointed day for the coming into force of Sch 55 is 6 April 2011 in relation to a return or other document which is required to be made or delivered to HMRC in relation to the tax year 2010–11 or any subsequent tax year and falls within item 1, 2 or 3 of the Table in para 1).

Prospective amendment—Paras 13A–13J and preceding cross-heads to be inserted by F(No 3)A 2010 s 26, Sch 10 paras 1, 7 with effect from a day to be appointed by Treasury order.

[13J—(1) P is liable to a penalty under this paragraph if (and only if) P's failure continues after the end of the period of 12 months beginning with the penalty date.

(2) Where, by failing to make the return, P deliberately withholds information which would enable or assist HMRC to assess P's liability to tax, the penalty under this paragraph is determined in accordance with sub-paragraphs (3) and (4).

(3) If the withholding of the information is deliberate and concealed, the penalty is the greater of—

(*a*) 100% of any liability to tax which would have been shown in the return in question, and

(*b*) £300.

(4) If the withholding of the information is deliberate but not concealed, the penalty is the greater of—

(*a*) 70% of any liability to tax which would have been shown in the return in question, and

(*b*) £300.

(5) In any case not falling within sub-paragraph (2), the penalty under this paragraph is the greater of—

(*a*) 5% of any liability to tax which would have been shown in the return in question, and

(*b*) £300.]

Commencement—Finance Act 2009, Schedules 55 and 56 (Income Tax Self Assessment and Pension Schemes) (Appointed Days and Consequential and Savings Provisions) Order, SI 2011/702 art 2 (appointed day for the coming into force of Sch 55 is 6 April 2011 in relation to a return or other document which is required to be made or delivered to HMRC in relation to the tax year 2010–11 or any subsequent tax year and falls within item 1, 2 or 3 of the Table in para 1).

Prospective amendment—Paras 13A–13J and preceding cross-heads to be inserted by F(No 3)A 2010 s 26, Sch 10 paras 1, 7 with effect from a day to be appointed by Treasury order.

Reductions for disclosure

14—[(A1) In this paragraph, "relevant information" means information which has been withheld by a failure to make a return.][1]

(1) Paragraph 15 provides for reductions in the penalty under paragraph 6(3) or (4) [where P discloses relevant information that involves a domestic matter][1] or 11(3) or (4) where P discloses [relevant information][1].

[(1A) Paragraph 15A provides for reductions in the penalty under paragraph 6(3) or (4) where P discloses relevant information that involves an offshore matter or an offshore transfer.

(1B) Sub-paragraph (2) applies where—

(*a*) P is liable to a penalty under paragraph 6(3) or (4) and P discloses relevant information that involves a domestic matter, or

(*b*) P is liable to a penalty under any of the other provisions mentioned in sub-paragraph (1) and P discloses relevant information.][1]

(2) P discloses relevant information by—

(*a*) telling HMRC about it,

(*b*) giving HMRC reasonable help in quantifying any tax unpaid by reason of its having been withheld, and

(*c*) allowing HMRC access to records for the purpose of checking how much tax is so unpaid.

[(2A) Sub-paragraph (2B) applies where P is liable to a penalty under paragraph 6(3) or (4) and P discloses relevant information that involves an offshore matter or an offshore transfer.

(2B) P discloses relevant information by—

(*a*) telling HMRC about it,

(*b*) giving HMRC reasonable help in quantifying any tax unpaid by reason of its having been withheld,

(*c*) allowing HMRC access to records for the purpose of checking how much tax is so unpaid, and

(*d*) providing HMRC with additional information.][1]

(2C) The Treasury must make regulations setting out what is meant by "additional information" for the purposes of sub-paragraph (2B)(*d*).

(2D) Regulations under sub-paragraph (2C) are to be made by statutory instrument.

(2E) An instrument containing regulations under sub-paragraph (2C) is subject to annulment in pursuance of a resolution of the House of Commons.][1]

(3) Disclosure of relevant information—

(*a*) is "unprompted" if made at a time when P has no reason to believe that HMRC have discovered or are about to discover the relevant information, and

(*b*) otherwise, is "prompted".

(4) In relation to disclosure "quality" includes timing, nature and extent.

[(5) Paragraph 6A(4) to (5) applies to determine whether relevant information involves an offshore matter, an offshore transfer or a domestic matter for the purposes of this paragraph.][1]

Commencement—Finance Act 2009, Schedules 55 and 56 (Income Tax Self Assessment and Pension Schemes) (Appointed Days and Consequential and Savings Provisions) Order, SI 2011/702 art 2 (appointed day for the coming into force of Sch 55 is 6 April 2011 in relation to a return or other document which is required to be made or delivered to HMRC in relation to the tax year 2010–11 or any subsequent tax year and falls within item 1, 2 or 3 of the Table in para 1).

Finance (No 3) Act 2010, Schedule 10 and the Finance Act 2009, Schedule 55 and Sections 101 to 103 (Appointed Day, etc) (Construction Industry Scheme) Order, SI 2011/2391 (the day appointed for the coming into force of the following paras of Sch 55 is 6 October 2011, with effect only in relation to a return within item 6 of Sch 55 para 1(5), and for which the filing date for the purposes of Sch 55 is after 19 October 2011—

– para 1 (but only in relation to item 6 in the Table in para 1(5);
– paras 7–13; and
– 14–24, 26, and 27(1)-(4) but only as relevant to paras 7–13).

Regulations—
Penalties Relating to Offshore Matters and Offshore Transfers (Additional Information) Regulations, SI 2017/345.

Amendments—[1] Sub-paras (A1), (1A), (1B) (2A)–(2E), (5) inserted, and in sub-para (1), words inserted and words substituted, by FA 2016 s 163, Sch 21 paras 9, 10 with effect, by virtue of SI 2017/259 regs 2, 3—

– for inheritance tax purposes, in relation to transfers of value made on or after 1 April 2017;
– for income tax and capital gains tax purposes, in relation to any tax year commencing on or after 6 April 2016; and
– for the purpose of making regulations, from 8 March 2017.

Prospective amendments—In sub-para (1), words ", 11(3) or (4), 13E(3) or (4) or 13J(3) or (4)" to be substituted for words "or 11(3) or (4)" by F(No 3)A 2010 s 26, Sch 10 paras 1, 8 with effect from a day to be appointed by Treasury order.

15—[(1) If a person who would otherwise be liable to a penalty of a percentage shown in column 1 of the Table (a "standard percentage") has made a disclosure, HMRC must reduce the standard percentage to one that reflects the quality of the disclosure.

(2) But the standard percentage may not be reduced to a percentage that is below the minimum shown for it—

(*a*) in the case of a prompted disclosure, in column 2 of the Table, and

(*b*) in the case of an unprompted disclosure, in column 3 of the Table.

[Standard %	*Minimum % for prompted disclosure*	*Minimum % for unprompted disclosure*
70%	35%	20%

100%	50%	30%][2]

(3) . . . [1]

(4) . . . [1]

(5) But HMRC must not under this paragraph—

(*a*) reduce a penalty under paragraph 6(3) or (4) below £300, or

(*b*) reduce a penalty under paragraph 11(3) or (4) below the amount set by paragraph 11(3)(*b*) or (4)(*b*) (as the case may be).

Commencement—Finance Act 2009, Schedules 55 and 56 (Income Tax Self Assessment and Pension Schemes) (Appointed Days and Consequential and Savings Provisions) Order, SI 2011/702 art 2 (appointed day for the coming into force of Sch 55 is 6 April 2011 in relation to a return or other document which is required to be made or delivered to HMRC in relation to the tax year 2010–11 or any subsequent tax year and falls within item 1, 2 or 3 of the Table in para 1).

Finance (No 3) Act 2010, Schedule 10 and the Finance Act 2009, Schedule 55 and Sections 101 to 103 (Appointed Day, etc) (Construction Industry Scheme) Order, SI 2011/2391 (the day appointed for the coming into force of the following paras of Sch 55 is 6 October 2011, with effect only in relation to a return within item 6 of Sch 55 para 1(5), and for which the filing date for the purposes of Sch 55 is after 19 October 2011—

– para 1 (but only in relation to item 6 in the Table in para 1(5);
– paras 7–13; and
– 14–24, 26, and 27(1)-(4) but only as relevant to paras 7–13).

Amendments—[1] Sub-paras (1), (2) substituted, and sub-paras (3), (4) repealed, by FA 2010 s 35, Sch 10 paras 10, 13 with effect from 6 April 2011 in relation to a return or other document which is required to be made or delivered to HMRC in relation to the tax year 2011–12 or any subsequent tax year, and falls within item 1, 2 or 3 of the Table in FA 2009 Sch 55 para 1. Note that these changes do not have effect in relation to Sch 55 in relation to a return or other document which is required to be made or delivered to HMRC in relation to the tax year 2010–11 or any previous tax year (SI 2011/975 art 5).

[2] In sub-para (2), Table substituted by FA 2016 s 163, Sch 21 paras 9, 11 with effect, by virtue of SI 2017/259 regs 2, 3—

– for inheritance tax purposes, in relation to transfers of value made on or after 1 April 2017; and
– for income tax and capital gains tax purposes, in relation to any tax year commencing on or after 6 April 2016.

Prospective amendments—In sub-para (5), words "sub-paragraph (3) or (4) of any of paragraphs 11, 13E and 13J" to be substituted for words "paragraph 11(3) or (4)", and words "paragraph (*b*) of that sub-paragraph" to be substituted for words "paragraph 11(3)(*b*) or (4)(*b*) (as the case may be)", by F(No 3)A 2010 s 26, Sch 10 paras 1, 9 with effect from a day to be appointed by Treasury order.

In sub-para (2), the following Table entries to be inserted at the appropriate places by FA 2015 s 120, Sch 20 paras 14, 18 with effect from a day to be appointed—

"87.5%	43.75%	25%"
"125%	62.5%	40%".

[15A—(1) If a person who would otherwise be liable to a penalty of a percentage shown in column 1 of the Table (a "standard percentage") has made a disclosure, HMRC must reduce the standard percentage to one that reflects the quality of the disclosure.

(2) But the standard percentage may not be reduced to a percentage that is below the minimum shown for it—

(*a*) in the case of a prompted disclosure, in column 2 of the Table, and

(*b*) in the case of an unprompted disclosure, in column 3 of the Table.

Standard %	*Minimum % for prompted disclosure*	*Minimum % for unprompted disclosure*
70%	45%	30%
87.5%	53.75%	35%
100%	60%	40%
105%	62.5%	40%
125%	72.5%	50%
140%	80%	50%
150%	85%	55%
200%	110%	70%

(3) But HMRC must not under this paragraph reduce a penalty below £300.][1]

Amendments—[1] Paragraph 15A inserted by FA 2016 s 163, Sch 21 paras 9, 12 with effect, by virtue of SI 2017/259 regs 2, 3—

– for inheritance tax purposes, in relation to transfers of value made on or after 1 April 2017; and
– for income tax and capital gains tax purposes, in relation to any tax year commencing on or after 6 April 2016.

IHT

Special reduction

16—(1) If HMRC think it right because of special circumstances, they may reduce a penalty under any paragraph of this Schedule.

(2) In sub-paragraph (1) "special circumstances" does not include—

(*a*) ability to pay, or

(*b*) the fact that a potential loss of revenue from one taxpayer is balanced by a potential overpayment by another.

(3) In sub-paragraph (1) the reference to reducing a penalty includes a reference to—

(*a*) staying a penalty, and

(*b*) agreeing a compromise in relation to proceedings for a penalty.

Commencement—Finance Act 2009, Schedules 55 and 56 (Income Tax Self Assessment and Pension Schemes) (Appointed Days and Consequential and Savings Provisions) Order, SI 2011/702 art 2 (appointed day for the coming into force of Sch 55 is 6 April 2011 in relation to a return or other document which is required to be made or delivered to HMRC in relation to the tax year 2010–11 or any subsequent tax year and falls within item 1, 2 or 3 of the Table in para 1).

Finance (No 3) Act 2010, Schedule 10 and the Finance Act 2009, Schedule 55 and Sections 101 to 103 (Appointed Day, etc) (Construction Industry Scheme) Order, SI 2011/2391 (the day appointed for the coming into force of the following paras of Sch 55 is 6 October 2011, with effect only in relation to a return within item 6 of Sch 55 para 1(5), and for which the filing date for the purposes of Sch 55 is after 19 October 2011—

– para 1 (but only in relation to item 6 in the Table in para 1(5);
– paras 7–13; and
– 14–24, 26, and 27(1)–(4) but only as relevant to paras 7–13).

Finance Act 2009, Schedule 55 (Penalties for failure to make returns) (Appointed Days and Consequential Provision) Order, SI 2014/2395 provides dates for the coming into force of Sch 55 in relation to returns falling within item 4 of the table in para 1 above (PAYE returns), as follows—

– **11 September 2014:** powers to make regulations in relation to quanta of RTI late-filing penalties in para 6C(5), (7), (8), (9), (11) (see also SI 2014/2396).
– for paras 1, 6B, 6C(1)–(4), (6), (10), 6D, 16–24, 26, 27 (relating to failures to make returns under the PAYE Regulations (SI 2003/2682) regs 67B and 67D):
  (a) **6 October 2014:** where the employer is a large existing employer (an employer which as at 6 October 2014 employs at least 50 employees). Affected returns are those required to be made or delivered to HMRC on or after 6 October 2014.
  (b) **6 March 2015:** where the employer is a small existing employer (an employer which as at 6 October 2014 employs no more than 49 employees) or is a new employer. Affected returns are those required to be made or delivered to HMRC on or after 6 March 2015.

Interaction with other penalties and late payment surcharges

17—(1) Where P is liable for a penalty under any paragraph of this Schedule which is determined by reference to a liability to tax, the amount of that penalty is to be reduced by the amount of any other penalty incurred by P, if the amount of the penalty is determined by reference to the same liability to tax.

(2) In sub-paragraph (1) the reference to "any other penalty" does not include—

(*a*) a penalty under any other paragraph of this Schedule, or

(*b*) a penalty under Schedule 56 (penalty for late payment of tax)[, or

(*c*) a penalty under Part 4 of FA 2014 (penalty where corrective action not taken after follower notice etc)[, or][2]

(*d*) a penalty under Schedule 22 to FA 2016 (asset-based penalty).][3]

(3) Where P is liable for a penalty under more than one paragraph of this Schedule which is determined by reference to a liability to tax, the aggregate of the amounts of those penalties must not exceed [the relevant percentage][1] of the liability to tax.

[(4) The relevant percentage is—

(*a*) if one of the penalties is a penalty under paragraph 6(3) or (4) and the information withheld is category 3 information, 200%,

(*b*) if one of the penalties is a penalty under paragraph 6(3) or (4) and the information withheld is category 2 information, 150%, and

(*c*) in all other cases, 100%.][1]

Commencement—Finance Act 2009, Schedules 55 and 56 (Income Tax Self Assessment and Pension Schemes) (Appointed Days and Consequential and Savings Provisions) Order, SI 2011/702 art 2 (appointed day for the coming into force of Sch 55 is 6 April 2011 in relation to a return or other document which is required to be made or delivered to HMRC in relation to the tax year 2010–11 or any subsequent tax year and falls within item 1, 2 or 3 of the Table in para 1).

Finance (No 3) Act 2010, Schedule 10 and the Finance Act 2009, Schedule 55 and Sections 101 to 103 (Appointed Day, etc) (Construction Industry Scheme) Order, SI 2011/2391 (the day appointed for the coming into force of the following paras of Sch 55 is 6 October 2011, with effect only in relation to a return within item 6 of Sch 55 para 1(5), and for which the filing date for the purposes of Sch 55 is after 19 October 2011—

– para 1 (but only in relation to item 6 in the Table in para 1(5);
– paras 7–13; and
– 14–24, 26, and 27(1)–(4) but only as relevant to paras 7–13).

Finance Act 2009, Schedule 55 (Penalties for failure to make returns) (Appointed Days and Consequential Provision) Order, SI 2014/2395 provides dates for the coming into force of Sch 55 in relation to returns falling within item 4 of the table in para 1 above (PAYE returns), as follows—

– **11 September 2014:** powers to make regulations in relation to quanta of RTI late-filing penalties in para 6C(5), (7), (8), (9), (11) (see also SI 2014/2396).

– for paras 1, 6B, 6C(1)–(4), (6), (10), 6D, 16–24, 26, 27 (relating to failures to make returns under the PAYE Regulations (SI 2003/2682) regs 67B and 67D):

(a) **6 October 2014:** where the employer is a large existing employer (an employer which as at 6 October 2014 employs at least 50 employees). Affected returns are those required to be made or delivered to HMRC on or after 6 October 2014.

(b) **6 March 2015:** where the employer is a small existing employer (an employer which as at 6 October 2014 employs no more than 49 employees) or is a new employer. Affected returns are those required to be made or delivered to HMRC on or after 6 March 2015.

Amendments—[1] In sub-para (3) words substituted for figure "100%", and sub-s (4) inserted, by FA 2010 s 35, Sch 10 paras 10, 14 with effect from 6 April 2011 in relation to a return or other document which is required to be made or delivered to HMRC in relation to the tax year 2011–12 or any subsequent tax year, and falls within item 1, 2 or 3 of the Table in FA 2009 Sch 55 para 1. Note that these changes do not have effect in relation to Sch 55 in relation to a return or other document which is required to be made or delivered to HMRC in relation to the tax year 2010–11 or any previous tax year (SI 2011/975 art 5).

[2] Sub-para (2)(*c*) and preceding word "or" inserted by FA 2014 s 233, Sch 33 para 5 with effect from 17 July 2014.

[3] Sub-para (2)(*d*) and preceding word "or" inserted by FA 2016 Sch 22 para 20(5) with effect—

– for inheritance tax purposes, in relation to transfers of value (within the meaning of IHTA 1984 s 3) made on or after that day; and

– for income tax and capital gains tax purposes, in relation to any tax year commencing on or after 6 April 2016.

Prospective amendments—Para 17(4)(*ba*) to be inserted by FA 2015 s 120, Sch 20 paras 14, 19 with effect from a day to be appointed. Para 17(4)(*ba*) as inserted to read as follows—

"(*ba*) if one of the penalties is a penalty under paragraph 6(3) or (4) and the information withheld is category 1 information, 125%, and".

[Cancellation of penalty

17A—(1) This paragraph applies where—

(*a*) P is liable for a penalty under any paragraph of this Schedule in relation to a failure to make a return falling within item 1 or 2 in the Table, and

(*b*) [HMRC decide to give P a notice under section 8B withdrawing][2] a notice under section 8 or 8A of that Act.

(2) The notice under section 8B of TMA 1970 may include provision under this paragraph cancelling liability to the penalty from the date specified in the notice.][1]

Commencement—Finance Act 2009, Schedule 55 (Penalties for failure to make returns) (Appointed Days and Consequential Provision) Order, SI 2014/2395 provides dates for the coming into force of Sch 55 in relation to returns falling within item 4 of the table in para 1 above (PAYE returns), as follows—

– **11 September 2014:** powers to make regulations in relation to quanta of RTI late-filing penalties in para 6C(5), (7), (8), (9), (11) (see also SI 2014/2396).

– for paras 1, 6B, 6C(1)–(4), (6), (10), 6D, 16–24, 26, 27 (relating to failures to make returns under the PAYE Regulations (SI 2003/2682) regs 67B and 67D):

(a) **6 October 2014:** where the employer is a large existing employer (an employer which as at 6 October 2014 employs at least 50 employees). Affected returns are those required to be made or delivered to HMRC on or after 6 October 2014.

(b) **6 March 2015:** where the employer is a small existing employer (an employer which as at 6 October 2014 employs no more than 49 employees) or is a new employer. Affected returns are those required to be made or delivered to HMRC on or after 6 March 2015.

Amendments—[1] Paragraphs 17A, 17B and preceding cross-head inserted by FA 2013 s 233, Sch 51 para 8 with effect in relation to a return—

(a) under TMA 1970 s 12AA for a partnership which includes one or more companies, for a relevant period beginning on or after 6 April 2012; and

(b) under TMA 1970 s 12AA for any other partnership, or a return under TMA 1970 s 8 or s 8A, for a year of assessment beginning on or after 6 April 2012.

A "relevant period" means a period in respect of which a return is required: FA 2013 Sch 51 para 9(2).

[2] In sub-para (1)(*b*), words substituted by FA 2016 s 169(1), (6) with effect in relation to any notice under TMA 1970 s 8 or s 8A given in relation to the tax year 2014–15 or any subsequent year. It is immaterial whether the notice was given before or after 15 September 2016.

[**17B—**(1) This paragraph applies where—

(*a*) P is liable for a penalty under any paragraph of this Schedule in relation to a failure to make a return falling within item 3 in the Table, and

(*b*) a request is made under section 12AAA of TMA 1970 for HMRC to withdraw a notice under section 12AA of that Act.

(2) The notice under section 12AAA of TMA 1970 may include provision under this paragraph cancelling liability to the penalty from the date specified in the notice.][1]

Commencement—Finance Act 2009, Schedule 55 (Penalties for failure to make returns) (Appointed Days and Consequential Provision) Order, SI 2014/2395 provides dates for the coming into force of Sch 55 in relation to returns falling within item 4 of the table in para 1 above (PAYE returns), as follows—

- **11 September 2014:** powers to make regulations in relation to quanta of RTI late-filing penalties in para 6C(5), (7), (8), (9), (11) (see also SI 2014/2396).
- for paras 1, 6B, 6C(1)–(4), (6), (10), 6D, 16–24, 26, 27 (relating to failures to make returns under the PAYE Regulations (SI 2003/2682) regs 67B and 67D):
  - (a) **6 October 2014:** where the employer is a large existing employer (an employer which as at 6 October 2014 employs at least 50 employees). Affected returns are those required to be made or delivered to HMRC on or after 6 October 2014.
  - (b) **6 March 2015:** where the employer is a small existing employer (an employer which as at 6 October 2014 employs no more than 49 employees) or is a new employer. Affected returns are those required to be made or delivered to HMRC on or after 6 March 2015.

Amendments—[1] Paragraphs 17A, 17B and preceding cross-head inserted by FA 2013 s 233, Sch 51 para 8 with effect in relation to a return—

- (a) under TMA 1970 s 12AA for a partnership which includes one or more companies, for a relevant period beginning on or after 6 April 2012; and
- (b) under TMA 1970 s 12AA for any other partnership, or a return under TMA 1970 s 8 or s 8A, for a year of assessment beginning on or after 6 April 2012.

A "relevant period" means a period in respect of which a return is required: FA 2013 Sch 51 para 9(2).

Assessment

18—(1) Where P is liable for a penalty under any paragraph of this Schedule HMRC must—

(*a*) assess the penalty,

(*b*) notify P, and

(*c*) state in the notice the period in respect of which the penalty is assessed.

(2) A penalty under any paragraph of this Schedule must be paid before the end of the period of 30 days beginning with the day on which notification of the penalty is issued.

(3) An assessment of a penalty under any paragraph of this Schedule—

(*a*) is to be treated for procedural purposes in the same way as an assessment to tax (except in respect of a matter expressly provided for by this Schedule),

(*b*) may be enforced as if it were an assessment to tax, and

(*c*) may be combined with an assessment to tax.

(4) A supplementary assessment may be made in respect of a penalty if an earlier assessment operated by reference to an underestimate of the liability to tax which would have been shown in a return.

[(5) Sub-paragraph (6) applies if—

(*a*) an assessment in respect of a penalty is based on a liability to tax that would have been shown in a return, and

(*b*) that liability is found by HMRC to be excessive.

(6) HMRC may by notice to P amend the assessment so that it is based upon the correct amount.

(7) An amendment under sub-paragraph (6)—

(*a*) does not affect when the penalty must be paid;

(*b*) may be made after the last day on which the assessment in question could have been made under paragraph 19.][1]

Commencement—Finance Act 2009, Schedules 55 and 56 (Income Tax Self Assessment and Pension Schemes) (Appointed Days and Consequential and Savings Provisions) Order, SI 2011/702 art 2 (appointed day for the coming into force of Sch 55 is 6 April 2011 in relation to a return or other document which is required to be made or delivered to HMRC in relation to the tax year 2010–11 or any subsequent tax year and falls within item 1, 2 or 3 of the Table in para 1).

Finance (No 3) Act 2010, Schedule 10 and the Finance Act 2009, Schedule 55 and Sections 101 to 103 (Appointed Day, etc) (Construction Industry Scheme) Order, SI 2011/2391 (the day appointed for the coming into force of the following paras of Sch 55 is 6 October 2011, with effect only in relation to a return within item 6 of Sch 55 para 1(5), and for which the filing date for the purposes of Sch 55 is after 19 October 2011—

- para 1 (but only in relation to item 6 in the Table in para 1(5);
- paras 7–13; and
- 14–24, 26, and 27(1)–(4) but only as relevant to paras 7–13).

Finance Act 2009, Schedule 55 (Penalties for failure to make returns) (Appointed Days and Consequential Provision) Order, SI 2014/2395 provides dates for the coming into force of Sch 55 in relation to returns falling within item 4 of the table in para 1 above (PAYE returns), as follows—

- **11 September 2014:** powers to make regulations in relation to quanta of RTI late-filing penalties in para 6C(5), (7), (8), (9), (11) (see also SI 2014/2396).
- for paras 1, 6B, 6C(1)–(4), (6), (10), 6D, 16–24, 26, 27 (relating to failures to make returns under the PAYE Regulations (SI 2003/2682) regs 67B and 67D):
  - (a) **6 October 2014:** where the employer is a large existing employer (an employer which as at 6 October 2014 employs at least 50 employees). Affected returns are those required to be made or delivered to HMRC on or after 6 October 2014.

(b) **6 March 2015:** where the employer is a small existing employer (an employer which as at 6 October 2014 employs no more than 49 employees) or is a new employer. Affected returns are those required to be made or delivered to HMRC on or after 6 March 2015.

Amendments—[1] Sub-paras (5)–(7) substituted for sub-para (5) by FA 2013 s 230, Sch 50 paras 2, 7 with effect for the tax year 2014–15 and subsequent tax years in relation to failures to make returns with a filing date (as defined in FA 2009 Sch 55 para 1(4)) on or after 6 April 2014.

19—(1) An assessment of a penalty under any paragraph of this Schedule in respect of any amount must be made on or before the later of date A and (where it applies) date B.

(2) Date A is[—

(*a*) in the case of an assessment of a penalty under paragraph 6C, the last day of the period of 2 years beginning with the end of the tax month in respect of which the penalty is payable,

(*b*) in the case of an assessment of a penalty under paragraph 6D, the last day of the period of 2 years beginning with the filing date for the relevant extended failure (as defined in paragraph 6D(10)), and

(*c*) in any other case,][1] the last day of the period of 2 years beginning with the filing date.

(3) Date B is the last day of the period of 12 months beginning with—

(*a*) the end of the appeal period for the assessment of the liability to tax which would have been shown in the return, [or returns (as the case may be in relation to penalties under section 6C or 6D)][1] or

(*b*) if there is no such assessment, the date on which that liability is ascertained or it is ascertained that the liability is nil.

(4) In sub-paragraph (3)(*a*) "appeal period" means the period during which—

(*a*) an appeal could be brought, or

(*b*) an appeal that has been brought has not been determined or withdrawn.

(5) Sub-paragraph (1) does not apply to a re-assessment under paragraph 24(2)(*b*).

Commencement—Finance Act 2009, Schedules 55 and 56 (Income Tax Self Assessment and Pension Schemes) (Appointed Days and Consequential and Savings Provisions) Order, SI 2011/702 art 2 (appointed day for the coming into force of Sch 55 is 6 April 2011 in relation to a return or other document which is required to be made or delivered to HMRC in relation to the tax year 2010–11 or any subsequent tax year and falls within item 1, 2 or 3 of the Table in para 1).

Finance (No 3) Act 2010, Schedule 10 and the Finance Act 2009, Schedule 55 and Sections 101 to 103 (Appointed Day, etc) (Construction Industry Scheme) Order, SI 2011/2391 (the day appointed for the coming into force of the following paras of Sch 55 is 6 October 2011, with effect only in relation to a return within item 6 of Sch 55 para 1(5), and for which the filing date for the purposes of Sch 55 is after 19 October 2011—

– para 1 (but only in relation to item 6 in the Table in para 1(5);
– paras 7–13; and
– 14–24, 26, and 27(1)–(4) but only as relevant to paras 7–13).

Finance Act 2009, Schedule 55 (Penalties for failure to make returns) (Appointed Days and Consequential Provision) Order, SI 2014/2395 provides dates for the coming into force of Sch 55 in relation to returns falling within item 4 of the table in para 1 above (PAYE returns), as follows—

– **11 September 2014:** powers to make regulations in relation to quanta of RTI late-filing penalties in para 6C(5), (7), (8), (9), (11) (see also SI 2014/2396).
– for paras 1, 6B, 6C(1)–(4), (6), (10), 6D, 16–24, 26, 27 (relating to failures to make returns under the PAYE Regulations (SI 2003/2682) regs 67B and 67D):
  (a) **6 October 2014:** where the employer is a large existing employer (an employer which as at 6 October 2014 employs at least 50 employees). Affected returns are those required to be made or delivered to HMRC on or after 6 October 2014.
  (b) **6 March 2015:** where the employer is a small existing employer (an employer which as at 6 October 2014 employs no more than 49 employees) or is a new employer. Affected returns are those required to be made or delivered to HMRC on or after 6 March 2015.

Amendments—[1] In sub-paras (2), 3(*a*) words inserted by FA 2013 s 230, Sch 50 paras 2, 8 with effect for the tax year 2014–15 and subsequent tax years in relation to failures to make returns with a filing date (as defined in FA 2009 Sch 55 para 1(4)) on or after 6 April 2014.

Appeal

20—(1) P may appeal against a decision of HMRC that a penalty is payable by P.

(2) P may appeal against a decision of HMRC as to the amount of a penalty payable by P.

Commencement—Finance Act 2009, Schedules 55 and 56 (Income Tax Self Assessment and Pension Schemes) (Appointed Days and Consequential and Savings Provisions) Order, SI 2011/702 art 2 (appointed day for the coming into force of Sch 55 is 6 April 2011 in relation to a return or other document which is required to be made or delivered to HMRC in relation to the tax year 2010–11 or any subsequent tax year and falls within item 1, 2 or 3 of the Table in para 1).

Finance (No 3) Act 2010, Schedule 10 and the Finance Act 2009, Schedule 55 and Sections 101 to 103 (Appointed Day, etc) (Construction Industry Scheme) Order, SI 2011/2391 (the day appointed for the coming into force of the following paras of Sch 55 is 6 October 2011, with effect only in relation to a return within item 6 of Sch 55 para 1(5), and for which the filing date for the purposes of Sch 55 is after 19 October 2011—

– para 1 (but only in relation to item 6 in the Table in para 1(5);
– paras 7–13; and
– 14–24, 26, and 27(1)–(4) but only as relevant to paras 7–13).

Finance Act 2009, Schedule 55 (Penalties for failure to make returns) (Appointed Days and Consequential Provision) Order, SI 2014/2395 provides dates for the coming into force of Sch 55 in relation to returns falling within item 4 of the table in para 1 above (PAYE returns), as follows—

- **11 September 2014:** powers to make regulations in relation to quanta of RTI late-filing penalties in para 6C(5), (7), (8), (9), (11) (see also SI 2014/2396).
- for paras 1, 6B, 6C(1)–(4), (6), (10), 6D, 16–24, 26, 27 (relating to failures to make returns under the PAYE Regulations (SI 2003/2682) regs 67B and 67D):
  - (a) **6 October 2014:** where the employer is a large existing employer (an employer which as at 6 October 2014 employs at least 50 employees). Affected returns are those required to be made or delivered to HMRC on or after 6 October 2014.
  - (b) **6 March 2015:** where the employer is a small existing employer (an employer which as at 6 October 2014 employs no more than 49 employees) or is a new employer. Affected returns are those required to be made or delivered to HMRC on or after 6 March 2015.

21—(1) An appeal under paragraph 20 is to be treated in the same way as an appeal against an assessment to the tax concerned (including by the application of any provision about bringing the appeal by notice to HMRC, about HMRC review of the decision or about determination of the appeal by the First-tier Tribunal or Upper Tribunal).

(2) Sub-paragraph (1) does not apply—

(*a*) so as to require P to pay a penalty before an appeal against the assessment of the penalty is determined, or

(*b*) in respect of any other matter expressly provided for by this Act.

Commencement—Finance Act 2009, Schedules 55 and 56 (Income Tax Self Assessment and Pension Schemes) (Appointed Days and Consequential and Savings Provisions) Order, SI 2011/702 art 2 (appointed day for the coming into force of Sch 55 is 6 April 2011 in relation to a return or other document which is required to be made or delivered to HMRC in relation to the tax year 2010–11 or any subsequent tax year and falls within item 1, 2 or 3 of the Table in para 1).

Finance (No 3) Act 2010, Schedule 10 and the Finance Act 2009, Schedule 55 and Sections 101 to 103 (Appointed Day, etc) (Construction Industry Scheme) Order, SI 2011/2391 (the day appointed for the coming into force of the following paras of Sch 55 is 6 October 2011, with effect only in relation to a return within item 6 of Sch 55 para 1(5), and for which the filing date for the purposes of Sch 55 is after 19 October 2011—

- para 1 (but only in relation to item 6 in the Table in para 1(5);
- paras 7–13; and
- 14–24, 26, and 27(1)–(4) but only as relevant to paras 7–13).

Finance Act 2009, Schedule 55 (Penalties for failure to make returns) (Appointed Days and Consequential Provision) Order, SI 2014/2395 provides dates for the coming into force of Sch 55 in relation to returns falling within item 4 of the table in para 1 above (PAYE returns), as follows—

- **11 September 2014:** powers to make regulations in relation to quanta of RTI late-filing penalties in para 6C(5), (7), (8), (9), (11) (see also SI 2014/2396).
- for paras 1, 6B, 6C(1)–(4), (6), (10), 6D, 16–24, 26, 27 (relating to failures to make returns under the PAYE Regulations (SI 2003/2682) regs 67B and 67D):
  - (a) **6 October 2014:** where the employer is a large existing employer (an employer which as at 6 October 2014 employs at least 50 employees). Affected returns are those required to be made or delivered to HMRC on or after 6 October 2014.
  - (b) **6 March 2015:** where the employer is a small existing employer (an employer which as at 6 October 2014 employs no more than 49 employees) or is a new employer. Affected returns are those required to be made or delivered to HMRC on or after 6 March 2015.

22—(1) On an appeal under paragraph 20(1) that is notified to the tribunal, the tribunal may affirm or cancel HMRC's decision.

(2) On an appeal under paragraph 20(2) that is notified to the tribunal, the tribunal may—

(*a*) affirm HMRC's decision, or

(*b*) substitute for HMRC's decision another decision that HMRC had power to make.

(3) If the tribunal substitutes its decision for HMRC's, the tribunal may rely on paragraph 16—

(*a*) to the same extent as HMRC (which may mean applying the same percentage reduction as HMRC to a different starting point), or

(*b*) to a different extent, but only if the tribunal thinks that HMRC's decision in respect of the application of paragraph 16 was flawed.

(4) In sub-paragraph (3)(*b*) "flawed" means flawed when considered in the light of the principles applicable in proceedings for judicial review.

(5) In this paragraph "tribunal" means the First-tier Tribunal or Upper Tribunal (as appropriate by virtue of paragraph 21(1)).

Commencement—Finance Act 2009, Schedules 55 and 56 (Income Tax Self Assessment and Pension Schemes) (Appointed Days and Consequential and Savings Provisions) Order, SI 2011/702 art 2 (appointed day for the coming into force of Sch 55 is 6 April 2011 in relation to a return or other document which is required to be made or delivered to HMRC in relation to the tax year 2010–11 or any subsequent tax year and falls within item 1, 2 or 3 of the Table in para 1).

Finance (No 3) Act 2010, Schedule 10 and the Finance Act 2009, Schedule 55 and Sections 101 to 103 (Appointed Day, etc) (Construction Industry Scheme) Order, SI 2011/2391 (the day appointed for the coming into force of the following paras of Sch 55 is 6 October 2011, with effect only in relation to a return within item 6 of Sch 55 para 1(5), and for which the filing date for the purposes of Sch 55 is after 19 October 2011—

- para 1 (but only in relation to item 6 in the Table in para 1(5);
- paras 7–13; and
- 14–24, 26, and 27(1)–(4) but only as relevant to paras 7–13).

Finance Act 2009, Schedule 55 (Penalties for failure to make returns) (Appointed Days and Consequential Provision) Order, SI 2014/2395 provides dates for the coming into force of Sch 55 in relation to returns falling within item 4 of the table in para 1 above (PAYE returns), as follows—

- **11 September 2014:** powers to make regulations in relation to quanta of RTI late-filing penalties in para 6C(5), (7), (8), (9), (11) (see also SI 2014/2396).
- for paras 1, 6B, 6C(1)–(4), (6), (10), 6D, 16–24, 26, 27 (relating to failures to make returns under the PAYE Regulations (SI 2003/2682) regs 67B and 67D):
  - (a) **6 October 2014:** where the employer is a large existing employer (an employer which as at 6 October 2014 employs at least 50 employees). Affected returns are those required to be made or delivered to HMRC on or after 6 October 2014.
  - (b) **6 March 2015:** where the employer is a small existing employer (an employer which as at 6 October 2014 employs no more than 49 employees) or is a new employer. Affected returns are those required to be made or delivered to HMRC on or after 6 March 2015.

Reasonable excuse

23—(1) Liability to a penalty under any paragraph of this Schedule does not arise in relation to a failure to make a return if P satisfies HMRC or (on appeal) the First-tier Tribunal or Upper Tribunal that there is a reasonable excuse for the failure.

(2) For the purposes of sub-paragraph (1)—

(*a*) an insufficiency of funds is not a reasonable excuse, unless attributable to events outside P's control,

(*b*) where P relies on any other person to do anything, that is not a reasonable excuse unless P took reasonable care to avoid the failure, and

(*c*) where P had a reasonable excuse for the failure but the excuse has ceased, P is to be treated as having continued to have the excuse if the failure is remedied without unreasonable delay after the excuse ceased.

Commencement—Finance Act 2009, Schedules 55 and 56 (Income Tax Self Assessment and Pension Schemes) (Appointed Days and Consequential and Savings Provisions) Order, SI 2011/702 art 2 (appointed day for the coming into force of Sch 55 is 6 April 2011 in relation to a return or other document which is required to be made or delivered to HMRC in relation to the tax year 2010–11 or any subsequent tax year and falls within item 1, 2 or 3 of the Table in para 1).

Finance (No 3) Act 2010, Schedule 10 and the Finance Act 2009, Schedule 55 and Sections 101 to 103 (Appointed Day, etc) (Construction Industry Scheme) Order, SI 2011/2391 (the day appointed for the coming into force of the following paras of Sch 55 is 6 October 2011, with effect only in relation to a return within item 6 of Sch 55 para 1(5), and for which the filing date for the purposes of Sch 55 is after 19 October 2011—

- para 1 (but only in relation to item 6 in the Table in para 1(5);
- paras 7–13; and
- 14–24, 26, and 27(1)–(4) but only as relevant to paras 7–13).

Finance Act 2009, Schedule 55 (Penalties for failure to make returns) (Appointed Days and Consequential Provision) Order, SI 2014/2395 provides dates for the coming into force of Sch 55 in relation to returns falling within item 4 of the table in para 1 above (PAYE returns), as follows—

- **11 September 2014:** powers to make regulations in relation to quanta of RTI late-filing penalties in para 6C(5), (7), (8), (9), (11) (see also SI 2014/2396).
- for paras 1, 6B, 6C(1)–(4), (6), (10), 6D, 16–24, 26, 27 (relating to failures to make returns under the PAYE Regulations (SI 2003/2682) regs 67B and 67D):
  - (a) **6 October 2014:** where the employer is a large existing employer (an employer which as at 6 October 2014 employs at least 50 employees). Affected returns are those required to be made or delivered to HMRC on or after 6 October 2014.
  - (b) **6 March 2015:** where the employer is a small existing employer (an employer which as at 6 October 2014 employs no more than 49 employees) or is a new employer. Affected returns are those required to be made or delivered to HMRC on or after 6 March 2015.

Prospective amendment—Sub-para (1) to be substituted by F(No 3)A 2010 s 26, Sch 10 paras 1, 11 with effect from a day to be appointed by Treasury order. Sub-para (1) as substituted to read as follows—

"(1) If P satisfies HMRC or (on appeal) the First-tier Tribunal or Upper Tribunal that there is a reasonable excuse for a failure to make a return—

(a) liability to a penalty under any paragraph of this Schedule does not arise in relation to that failure, and

(b) the failure does not count for the purposes of paragraphs 13B(2), 13C, 13G(2) and 13H.".

Determination of penalty geared to tax liability where no return made

24—(1) References to a liability to tax which would have been shown in a return are references to the amount which, if a complete and accurate return had been delivered on the filing date, would have been shown to be due or payable by the taxpayer in respect of the tax concerned for the period to which the return relates.

(2) In the case of a penalty which is assessed at a time before P makes the return to which the penalty relates—

(*a*) HMRC is to determine the amount mentioned in sub-paragraph (1) to the best of HMRC's information and belief, and

(*b*) if P subsequently makes a return, the penalty must be re-assessed by reference to the amount of tax shown to be due and payable in that return (but subject to any amendments or corrections to the return).

(3) In calculating a liability to tax which would have been shown in a return, no account is to be taken of any relief under [section 458 of CTA 2010][1] (relief in respect of repayment etc of loan) which is deferred under [subsection (5)][1] of that section.

Commencement—Finance Act 2009, Schedules 55 and 56 (Income Tax Self Assessment and Pension Schemes) (Appointed Days and Consequential and Savings Provisions) Order, SI 2011/702 art 2 (appointed day for the coming into force of Sch 55 is 6 April 2011 in relation to a return or other document which is required to be made or delivered to HMRC in relation to the tax year 2010–11 or any subsequent tax year and falls within item 1, 2 or 3 of the Table in para 1).

Finance (No 3) Act 2010, Schedule 10 and the Finance Act 2009, Schedule 55 and Sections 101 to 103 (Appointed Day, etc) (Construction Industry Scheme) Order, SI 2011/2391 (the day appointed for the coming into force of the following paras of Sch 55 is 6 October 2011, with effect only in relation to a return within item 6 of Sch 55 para 1(5), and for which the filing date for the purposes of Sch 55 is after 19 October 2011—

– para 1 (but only in relation to item 6 in the Table in para 1(5);
– paras 7–13; and
– 14–24, 26, and 27(1)–(4) but only as relevant to paras 7–13).

Finance Act 2009, Schedule 55 (Penalties for failure to make returns) (Appointed Days and Consequential Provision) Order, SI 2014/2395 provides dates for the coming into force of Sch 55 in relation to returns falling within item 4 of the table in para 1 above (PAYE returns), as follows—

– **11 September 2014:** powers to make regulations in relation to quanta of RTI late-filing penalties in para 6C(5), (7), (8), (9), (11) (see also SI 2014/2396).
– for paras 1, 6B, 6C(1)–(4), (6), (10), 6D, 16–24, 26, 27 (relating to failures to make returns under the PAYE Regulations (SI 2003/2682) regs 67B and 67D):
  (a) **6 October 2014:** where the employer is a large existing employer (an employer which as at 6 October 2014 employs at least 50 employees). Affected returns are those required to be made or delivered to HMRC on or after 6 October 2014.
  (b) **6 March 2015:** where the employer is a small existing employer (an employer which as at 6 October 2014 employs no more than 49 employees) or is a new employer. Affected returns are those required to be made or delivered to HMRC on or after 6 March 2015.

Amendments—[1] In sub-para (3) words substituted for words "subsection (4) of section 419 of ICTA" and "subsection (4A)" by CTA 2010 s 1177, Sch 1 paras 706, 723. CTA 2010 has effect for corporation tax purposes for accounting periods ending on or after 1 April 2010, and for income and capital gains tax purposes for the tax year 2010–11 and subsequent tax years.

Partnerships

25—(1) This paragraph applies where—

(*a*) the representative partner, or

(*b*) a successor of the representative partner,

fails to make a return falling within item 3 in the Table (partnership returns).

(2) A penalty in respect of the failure is payable by every relevant partner.

(3) In accordance with sub-paragraph (2), any reference in this Schedule to P is to be read as including a reference to a relevant partner.

(4) An appeal under paragraph 20 in connection with a penalty payable by virtue of this paragraph may be brought only by—

(*a*) the representative partner, or

(*b*) a successor of the representative partner.

(5) Where such an appeal is brought in connection with a penalty payable in respect of a failure, the appeal is to treated as if it were an appeal in connection with every penalty payable in respect of that failure.

(6) In this paragraph—

"relevant partner" means a person who was a partner in the partnership to which the return relates at any time during the period in respect of which the return was required;

"representative partner" means a person who has been required by a notice served under or for the purposes of section 12AA(2) or (3) of TMA 1970 to deliver any return;

"successor" has the meaning given by section 12AA(11) of TMA 1970.

Commencement—Finance Act 2009, Schedules 55 and 56 (Income Tax Self Assessment and Pension Schemes) (Appointed Days and Consequential and Savings Provisions) Order, SI 2011/702 art 2 (appointed day for the coming into force of Sch 55 is 6 April 2011 in relation to a return or other document which is required to be made or delivered to HMRC in relation to the tax year 2010–11 or any subsequent tax year and falls within item 1, 2 or 3 of the Table in para 1).

Double jeopardy

26 P is not liable to a penalty under any paragraph of this Schedule in respect of a failure or action in respect of which P has been convicted of an offence.

Commencement—Finance Act 2009, Schedules 55 and 56 (Income Tax Self Assessment and Pension Schemes) (Appointed Days and Consequential and Savings Provisions) Order, SI 2011/702 art 2 (appointed day for the coming into force of Sch 55 is 6 April 2011 in relation to a return or other document which is required to be made or delivered to HMRC in relation to the tax year 2010–11 or any subsequent tax year and falls within item 1, 2 or 3 of the Table in para 1).

Finance (No 3) Act 2010, Schedule 10 and the Finance Act 2009, Schedule 55 and Sections 101 to 103 (Appointed Day, etc) (Construction Industry Scheme) Order, SI 2011/2391 (the day appointed for the coming into force of the following paras of Sch 55 is 6 October 2011, with effect only in relation to a return within item 6 of Sch 55 para 1(5), and for which the filing date for the purposes of Sch 55 is after 19 October 2011—

- para 1 (but only in relation to item 6 in the Table in para 1(5);
- paras 7–13; and
- 14–24, 26, and 27(1)–(4) but only as relevant to paras 7–13).

Finance Act 2009, Schedule 55 (Penalties for failure to make returns) (Appointed Days and Consequential Provision) Order, SI 2014/2395 provides dates for the coming into force of Sch 55 in relation to returns falling within item 4 of the table in para 1 above (PAYE returns), as follows—

- **11 September 2014:** powers to make regulations in relation to quanta of RTI late-filing penalties in para 6C(5), (7), (8), (9), (11) (see also SI 2014/2396).
- for paras 1, 6B, 6C(1)–(4), (6), (10), 6D, 16–24, 26, 27 (relating to failures to make returns under the PAYE Regulations (SI 2003/2682) regs 67B and 67D):
  (a) **6 October 2014:** where the employer is a large existing employer (an employer which as at 6 October 2014 employs at least 50 employees). Affected returns are those required to be made or delivered to HMRC on or after 6 October 2014.
  (b) **6 March 2015:** where the employer is a small existing employer (an employer which as at 6 October 2014 employs no more than 49 employees) or is a new employer. Affected returns are those required to be made or delivered to HMRC on or after 6 March 2015.

Interpretation

27—(1) This paragraph applies for the construction of this Schedule.

(2) The withholding of information by P is—

(*a*) "deliberate and concealed" if P deliberately withholds the information and makes arrangements to conceal the fact that the information has been withheld, and

(*b*) "deliberate but not concealed" if P deliberately withholds the information but does not make arrangements to conceal the fact that the information has been withheld.

[(2A) "The Commissioners" means the Commissioners for Her Majesty's Revenue and Customs.][1]

(3) "HMRC" means Her Majesty's Revenue and Customs.

[(3A) "Tax month" means the period beginning with the 6th day of a month and ending with the 5th day of the following month.][1]

(4) References to a liability to tax, in relation to a return falling within item 6 in the Table (construction industry scheme), are to a liability to make payments in accordance with Chapter 3 of Part 3 of FA 2004.

(5) References to an assessment to tax, in relation to inheritance tax and stamp duty reserve tax, are to a determination.

Commencement—Finance Act 2009, Schedules 55 and 56 (Income Tax Self Assessment and Pension Schemes) (Appointed Days and Consequential and Savings Provisions) Order, SI 2011/702 art 2 (appointed day for the coming into force of Sch 55 is 6 April 2011 in relation to a return or other document which is required to be made or delivered to HMRC in relation to the tax year 2010–11 or any subsequent tax year and falls within item 1, 2 or 3 of the Table in para 1).

Finance (No 3) Act 2010, Schedule 10 and the Finance Act 2009, Schedule 55 and Sections 101 to 103 (Appointed Day, etc) (Construction Industry Scheme) Order, SI 2011/2391 (the day appointed for the coming into force of the following paras of Sch 55 is 6 October 2011, with effect only in relation to a return within item 6 of Sch 55 para 1(5), and for which the filing date for the purposes of Sch 55 is after 19 October 2011—

- para 1 (but only in relation to item 6 in the Table in para 1(5);
- paras 7–13; and
- 14–24, 26, and 27(1)–(4) but only as relevant to paras 7–13).

Finance Act 2009, Schedule 55 (Penalties for failure to make returns) (Appointed Days and Consequential Provision) Order, SI 2014/2395 provides dates for the coming into force of Sch 55 in relation to returns falling within item 4 of the table in para 1 above (PAYE returns), as follows—

- **11 September 2014:** powers to make regulations in relation to quanta of RTI late-filing penalties in para 6C(5), (7), (8), (9), (11) (see also SI 2014/2396).
- for paras 1, 6B, 6C(1)–(4), (6), (10), 6D, 16–24, 26, 27 (relating to failures to make returns under the PAYE Regulations (SI 2003/2682) regs 67B and 67D):
  (a) **6 October 2014:** where the employer is a large existing employer (an employer which as at 6 October 2014 employs at least 50 employees). Affected returns are those required to be made or delivered to HMRC on or after 6 October 2014.
  (b) **6 March 2015:** where the employer is a small existing employer (an employer which as at 6 October 2014 employs no more than 49 employees) or is a new employer. Affected returns are those required to be made or delivered to HMRC on or after 6 March 2015.

Amendments—[1] Sub-paras (2A), (3A) inserted by FA 2013 s 230, Sch 50 paras 2, 9 with effect for the tax year 2014–15 and subsequent tax years in relation to failures to make returns with a filing date (as defined in FA 2009 Sch 55 para 1(4)) on or after 6 April 2014.

SCHEDULE 56

PENALTY FOR FAILURE TO MAKE PAYMENTS ON TIME

Section 107

Commencement—Finance Act 2009, Schedule 56 (Appointed Day and Consequential Provisions) Order, SI 2010/466 (6 April 2010 appointed as day on which Sch 56 comes into force for certain purposes).

Finance Act 2009, Schedules 55 and 56 (Income Tax Self Assessment and Pension Schemes) (Appointed Days and Consequential and Savings Provisions) Order, SI 2011/702 art 2 (appointed day for the coming into force of Sch 56 is 6 April 2011 in relation to an amount of tax which is payable in relation to the tax year 2010–11 or any subsequent tax year and falls within item 1, 12, 18 or 19 of the Table in para 1, or in so far as the tax falls within item 1 of that Table, item 17, 23 or 24 of that Table).

FA 2013 Sch 34 para 12 (Sch 56, as amended by FA 2013 Sch 34 para 9, is taken to have come into force for the purposes of the annual tax on enveloped dwellings on 17 July 2013).

Finance Act 2009, Schedules 55 and 56 and Sections 101 and 102 (Stamp Duty Reserve Tax) (Appointed Days, Consequential and Transitional Provision) Order, SI 2014/3269 art 3 (the day appointed for the coming into force of Sch 56 is 1 January 2015 in relation to an amount of SDRT which is in item 10, 17, 23 or 24 of the Table in para 1).

Finance Act 2016 s 113(18) (for the purposes of apprenticeship levy, Sch 56 as amended by FA 2016 s 113 is taken to come into force on 15 September 2016).

Cross-references—See SSCBA 1992 s 11A (this Schedule applies with the necessary modifications, in relation to Class 2 contributions under SSCBA 1992 s 11(2) as if those contributions were income tax chargeable under ITTOIA 2005 Pt 2 Ch 2 in respect of profits of a trade, profession or vocation which is not carried on wholly outside the United Kingdom).

Education (Postgraduate Master's Degree Loans) Regulations, SI 2016/606 regs 46, 85 (this schedule applies to loans for postgraduate master's degree courses which begin on or after 1 August 2016).

Penalty for failure to pay tax

1—(1) A penalty is payable by a person ("P") where P fails to pay an amount of tax specified in column 3 of the Table below on or before the date specified in column 4.

(2) Paragraphs 3 to 8 set out—

(*a*) the circumstances in which a penalty is payable, and

(*b*) subject to paragraph 9, the amount of the penalty.

(3) If P's failure falls within more than one provision of this Schedule, P is liable to a penalty under each of those provisions.

(4) In the following provisions of this Schedule, the "penalty date", in relation to an amount of tax, means [the day after the date specified in or for the purposes of column 4 of the Table in relation to that amount.][5]

	Tax to which payment relates	*Amount of tax payable*	*Date after which penalty is incurred*
PRINCIPAL AMOUNTS			
1	Income tax or capital gains tax	Amount payable under section 59B(3) or (4) of TMA 1970	The date falling 30 days after the date specified in section 59B(3) or (4) of TMA 1970 as the date by which the amount must be paid
2	Income tax	Amount payable under PAYE regulations . . . [1]	The date determined by or under PAYE regulations as the date by which the amount must be paid
3	Income tax	Amount shown in return under section 254(1) of FA 2004	The date falling 30 days after the date specified in section 254(5) of FA 2004 as the date by which the amount must be paid
[3A	Income tax	Amount payable under regulations under section 244L(2)(*a*) of FA 2004	The date falling 30 days after the due date determined by or under the regulations][10]
[4A	Apprenticeship levy	Amount payable under regulations under section 105 of FA 2016	The date determined by or under regulations under section 105 of FA 2016][9]

	Tax to which payment relates	*Amount of tax payable*	*Date after which penalty is incurred*
4	Deductions on account of tax under Chapter 3 of Part 3 of FA 2004 (construction industry scheme)	Amount payable under section 62 of FA 2004 (except an amount falling within item 17, 23 or 24)	The date determined by or under regulations under [section 71][1] of FA 2004 as the date by which the amount must be paid
5	Corporation tax	Amount shown in company tax return under paragraph 3 of Schedule 18 to FA 1998	The filing date for the company tax return for the accounting period for which the tax is due (see paragraph 14 of Schedule 18 to FA 1998)
6	Corporation tax	Amount payable under regulations under section 59E of TMA 1970 (except an amount falling within item 17, 23 or 24)	The filing date for the company tax return for the accounting period for which the tax is due (see paragraph 14 of Schedule 18 to FA 1998)
[6ZZA	Corporation tax	Amount payable under section 357YQ of CTA 2010	The end of the period within which, in accordance with section 357YQ(5), the amount must be paid.][8]
[6ZA	Corporation tax	Amount payable under an exit charge payment plan entered into in accordance with Schedule 3ZB to TMA 1970	The later of— (*a*) the first day after the period of 12 months beginning immediately after the migration accounting period (as defined in Part 1 or 2 of Schedule 3ZB to TMA 1970, as the case may be), and (*b*) the date on which the amount is payable under the plan.][3]
[6ZB	Diverted profits tax	Amount of diverted profits tax payable under Part 3 of FA 2015	The date when, in accordance with section 98(2) of FA 2015, the amount must be paid][7]
7	Inheritance tax	Amount payable under section 226 of IHTA 1984 (except an amount falling within item 14 or 21)	The filing date (determined under section 216 of IHTA 1984) for the account in respect of the liability for that amount
8	Inheritance tax	Amount payable under section 227 or 229 of IHTA 1984 (except an amount falling within item 14 or 21)	For the first instalment, the filing date (determined under section 216 of IHTA 1984) for the account in respect of the liability for that amount For any later instalment, the date falling 30 days after the date determined under section 227 or 229 of IHTA 1984 as the date by which the instalment must be paid
9	Stamp duty land tax	Amount payable under section 86(1) or (2) of FA 2003	The date falling 30 days after the date specified in section 86(1) or (2) of FA 2003 as the date by which the amount must be paid
10	Stamp duty reserve tax	Amount payable under section 87, 93 or 96 of FA 1986 or Schedule 19 to FA 1999 (except an amount falling within item 17, 23 or 24)	The date falling 30 days after the date determined by or under regulations under section 98 of FA 1986 as the date by which the amount must be paid

	Tax to which payment relates	*Amount of tax payable*	*Date after which penalty is incurred*
[10A	Annual tax on enveloped dwellings	Amount payable under section 161(1) or (2) of FA 2013 (except an amount falling within item 23).	The date falling 30 days after the date specified in section 161(1) or (2) of FA 2013 as the date by which the amount must be paid][4]
11	Petroleum revenue tax	Amount charged in an assessment under paragraph 11(1) of Schedule 2 to OTA 1975	The date falling 30 days after the date determined in accordance with paragraph 13 of Schedule 2 to OTA 1975 as the date by which the amount must be paid
[11GA	Excise duties	Amount payable under regulations under section 60A of the Customs and Excise Management Act 1979 (except an amount falling within item 17A, 23 or 24).	The date determined by or under regulations under section 60A of the Customs and Excise Management Act 1979 as the date by which the amount must be paid][6]
[11N	Machine games duty	Amount payable under paragraph 6 of Schedule 24 to FA 2012 (except an amount falling within item 17A, 23 or 24)	The date determined by or under regulations under paragraph 19 of Schedule 24 to FA 2012 as the date by which the amount must be paid][2]
AMOUNTS PAYABLE IN DEFAULT OF A RETURN BEING MADE			
12	Income tax or capital gains tax	Amount payable under section 59B(5A) of TMA 1970	The date falling 30 days after the date specified in section 59B(5A) of TMA 1970 as the date by which the amount must be paid
13	Corporation tax	Amount shown in determination under paragraph 36 or 37 of Schedule 18 to FA 1998	The filing date for the company tax return for the accounting period for which the tax is due (see paragraph 14 of Schedule 18 to FA 1998)
14	Inheritance tax	Amount shown in a determination made by HMRC in the circumstances set out in paragraph 2	The filing date (determined under section 216 of IHTA 1984) for the account in respect of the liability for that amount
15	Stamp duty land tax	Amount shown in determination under paragraph 25 of Schedule 10 to FA 2003 (including that paragraph as applied by section 81(3) of that Act)	The date falling 30 days after the filing date for the return in question
[15A	Annual tax on enveloped dwellings	Amount shown in determination under paragraph 18 of Schedule 31 to FA 2013	The date falling 30 days after the filing date for the return in question][4]
16	Petroleum revenue tax	Amount charged in an assessment made where participator fails to deliver return for a chargeable period	The date falling 6 months and 30 days after the end of the chargeable period
17	Tax falling within any of items 1 to 6, 9[, 10 or 10A][3]	Amount (not falling within any of items 12 to [15A][3]) which is shown in an assessment or determination made by HMRC in the circumstances set out in paragraph 2	The date falling 30 days after the date by which the amount would have been required to be paid if it had been shown in the return in question
AMOUNT SHOWN TO BE DUE IN OTHER ASSESSMENTS, DETERMINATIONS, ETC			

	Tax to which payment relates	*Amount of tax payable*	*Date after which penalty is incurred*
18	Income tax or capital gains tax	Amount payable under section 55 of TMA 1970	The date falling 30 days after the date determined in accordance with section 55(3), (4), (6) or (9) of TMA 1970 as the date by which the amount must be paid
19	Income tax or capital gains tax	Amount payable under section 59B(5) or (6) of TMA 1970	The date falling 30 days after the date specified in section 59B(5) or (6) of TMA 1970 as the date by which the amount must be paid
20	. . . [1]		
21	Inheritance tax	Amount shown in— (*a*) an amendment or correction of a return showing an amount falling within item 7 or 8, or (*b*) a determination made by HMRC in circumstances other than those set out in paragraph 2	The later of— (*a*) the filing date (determined under section 216 of IHTA 1984) for the account in respect of the liability for that amount, and (*b*) the date falling 30 days after the date on which the amendment, correction, assessment or determination is made
22	Petroleum revenue tax	Amount charged in an assessment, or an amendment of an assessment, made in circumstances other than those set out in items 11 and 16	The date falling 30 days after— (*a*) the date by which the amount must be paid, or (*b*) the date on which the assessment or amendment is made, whichever is later
23	Tax falling within any of items 1 to 6, 9 or 10	Amount (not falling within any of items 18 to 20) shown in an amendment or correction of a return showing an amount falling within any of items 1 to 6, 9 or 10	The date falling 30 days after— (*a*) the date by which the amount must be paid, or (*b*) the date on which the amendment or correction is made, whichever is later
24	Tax falling within any of items 1 to 6, 9 or 10	Amount (not falling within any of items 18 to 20) shown in an assessment or determination made by HMRC in circumstances other than those set out in paragraph 2	The date falling 30 days after— (*a*) the date by which the amount must be paid, or (*b*) the date on which the assessment or determination is made, whichever is later

[(5) Sub-paragraph (4) is subject to paragraph 2A.][1]

Commentary—*Simon's Taxes* **A4.560**.

Modifications—FA 2009 Sch 56 has effect as if the Table in this para included references to bank payroll tax (FA 2010 s 22, Sch 1 para 39 (1)–(4)).

FA 2013 Sch 34 para 10(1) (until F(No 3)A 2010 Sch 11 para 2(13)(*a*), (14)(*a*) come into force, this para has effect as if—

- in item 23 the references in the second and third columns to items 1 to 6, 9 or 10 included item 10A, and
- in item 24 the reference in the second column to items 1 to 6, 9 or 10 included item 10A.

Commencement—Finance Act 2009, Schedule 56 (Appointed Day and Consequential Provisions) Order, SI 2010/466: 6 April 2010 appointed as day on which Sch 56 comes into force for the following amounts specified in column 3 of the Table—items 2–4, and items 17, 23 and 24 but only in so far as the tax falls within any of items 2, 3 or 4 (see SI 2010/466 art 3).

Finance Act 2009, Schedules 55 and 56 (Income Tax Self Assessment and Pension Schemes) (Appointed Days and Consequential and Savings Provisions) Order, SI 2011/702 art 2 (appointed day for the coming into force of Sch 56 is 6 April 2011 in relation to an amount of tax which is payable in relation to the tax year 2010–11 or any subsequent tax year and falls within item 1, 12, 18 or 19 of the Table in para 1, or in so far as the tax falls within item 1 of that Table, item 17, 23 or 24 of that Table).

FA 2009 Sch 56, as amended by FA 2013 Sch 34 para 9, is taken to have come into force for the purposes of the annual tax on enveloped dwellings on 17 July 2013 (FA 2013 Sch 34 para 12).

Amendments—[1] Sub-para (5) inserted; in Table, in item 2 column 3, words "(except an amount falling within item 20)" repealed, in item 4 column 4, words substituted for words "section 62", and item 20 repealed, by F(No 3)A 2010 s 27, Sch 11 paras 1, 2(1), (3), (5), (6), (12) with effect from 25 January 2011 (by virtue of SI 2011/132 art 2(*a*)).

[2] Item 11N inserted, and in items 17A, 23, 24 (as to be inserted by F(No 3)A 2010: see prospective amendment note below) reference "11N" to be substituted for reference "11M" by FA 2012 s 191, Sch 24 paras 33, 34 with effect in relation to the playing of machine games on or after 1 February 2013 (and Schs 55, 56, as amended by FA 2012 Sch 24 Part 1, are taken to have come into force for the purposes of machine games duty on that date).

[3] In sub-para (4), in Table, item 6ZA inserted by FA 2013 s 229, Sch 49 paras 1, 7. This amendment is treated as having come into force on 11 December 2012 in relation to an accounting period if the relevant day in relation to that period falls on or after 11 December 2012, subject to transitional provisions where the relevant day falls between 11 December 2012 and 31 March 2013 (inclusive): FA 2013 Sch 49 para 8(3).

The relevant day, in relation to an accounting period, means the first day after the period of 9 months beginning immediately after the accounting period: FA 2013 Sch 49 para 8(2).

[4] In Table, items 10A, 15A inserted, and in item 17, in second column words substituted for words "or 10", and in third column reference substituted for reference "15", by FA 2013 s 164, Sch 34 paras 8, 9 with effect from 17 July 2013.

[5] In sub-para (4), words substituted by FA 2013 s 230, Sch 50 paras 10, 11 with effect for defaults made in relation to the tax year 2014–15 and subsequent tax years (see FA 2009 Sch 56 para 6(2), as amended by FA 2013 Sch 50 para 12(3), as to when a default is made in relation to a tax year).

[6] In Table, item 11GA inserted by FA 2014 s 101, Sch 21 para 8 with effect from 1 April 2015 (by virtue of SI 2015/812).

[7] In Table, item 6ZB inserted by FA 2015 s 104(1), (2) with effect in relation to accounting periods beginning on or after 1 April 2015. For accounting periods that straddle that date, see FA 2015 s 116(2).

[8] In Table, item 6ZZA inserted by F(No 2)A 2015 s 38(6), (7) with effect in relation to payments of restitution interest in respect of awards that are finally determined on or after 21 October 2015, whether the interest arose before, on or after that date. HMRC must deduct tax from a payment of restitution interest made on or after 26 October 2015 (see F(No 2)A 2015 s 38(10)). Note however that this Schedule is not yet in force except to the extent specified: see Commencement note above.

[9] In Table, item 4A inserted by FA 2016 s 113(9), (10) with effect from 15 September 2016. Note that Sch 56, as amended by FA 2016 s 113, is taken to come into force for the purposes of apprenticeship levy on 15 September 2016 (FA 2016 s 113(18)).

[10] In Table, item 3A inserted by FA 2017 s 10, Sch 4 para 20 with effect in relation to transfers made on or after 9 March 2017.

[11] In Table, entry inserted by FA 2017 s 56, Sch 11 para 5(1), (2) with effect from 27 April 2017.

Prospective amendments—The following amendments are to be made by F(No 3)A 2010 s 27, Sch 11 paras 1, 2 (as amended by FA 2014 s 103, Sch 22 para 22(1)–(5)) with effect from a date to be appointed by Treasury order.

Note that the inserted text is amended by FA 2012 Sch 24 para 34 with effect in relation to the playing of machine games on or after 1 February 2013, as per the above footnote. See also the modification note above in relation to the application of this para until the coming into force of F(No 3)A 2010 Sch 11 para 2(13)(*a*), (14)(*a*)

Note that the inserted text is also amended by FA 2014 s 196, Sch 28 paras 28, 30 with effect from a date to be appointed. The FA 2014 amendments substitute items 11H, 11I and 11M; these changes are accounted for in the text below—

- in sub-para (2) figure "8J" to be substituted for figure "8";
- in Table—
  - entries to be inserted after items 6, 11, 13, 16 and 17;
  - item 20 to be repealed;
  - in item 23 columns 2, 3, item 24 column 2, words "items 1 to 6A, 6BA, 6BB, 6C, 9, 10 or 11A to 11M" to be substituted for words "items 1 to 6, 9 or 10";
  - in items 23, 24 column 3, words "item 18 or 19" to be substituted for words "any of items 18 to 20".

Table entries as inserted to read as follows—

"6A	Value added tax	Amount payable under section 25(1) of VATA 1994 (except an amount falling within item 6B, 13A, 23 or 24)	The date determined— (*a*) by or under regulations under section 25 of VATA 1994, or (*b*) in accordance with an order under section 28 of that Act,

			as the date by which the amount must be paid
6B	Value added tax	Amount payable under section 25(1) of VATA 1994 which is an instalment of an amount due in respect of a period of 9 months or more ("amount A")	The date on or before which P must pay any balancing payment or other outstanding payment due in respect of amount A
6BA	Value added tax	Amount payable under relevant special scheme return (as defined in paragraph 16(3) of Schedule 3B to VATA 1994) (except an amount falling within item 13A, 13AA, 13AB, 23 or 24)	The date by which the amount must be paid under the law of the member State which has established the special scheme
6BB	Value added tax	Amount payable under relevant non-UK return (as defined in paragraph 20(3) of Schedule 3BA to VATA 1994) (except an amount falling within item 13A, 13AA, 13AB, 23 or 24)	The date by which the amount must be paid under the law of the member State which has established the non-UK special scheme
6C	Insurance premium tax	Amount payable under regulations under section 54 of FA 1994 (except an amount falling within item 13B, 23 or 24)	The date determined by or under regulations under section 54 of FA 1994 as the date by which the amount must be paid".

"11A	Aggregates levy	Amount payable under regulations under section 25 of FA 2001 (except an amount falling within item 16A, 23 or 24)	The date determined by or under regulations under section 25 of FA 2001 as the date by which the amount must be paid
11B	Climate change levy	Amount payable under regulations under paragraph 41 of Schedule 6 to FA 2000 (except an amount falling within item 16B, 23 or 24)	The date determined by or under regulations under paragraph 41 of Schedule 6 to FA 2000 as the date by which the amount must be paid
11C	Landfill tax	Amount payable under regulations under section 49 of FA 1996 (except an amount falling within item 16C, 23 or 24)	The date determined by or under regulations under section 49 of FA 1996 as the date by which the amount must be paid
11D	Air passenger duty	Amount payable under regulations under section 38 of FA 1994 (except an amount falling within item 17A, 23 or 24)	The date determined by or under regulations under section 38 of FA 1994 as the date by which the amount must be paid
11E	Alcoholic liquor duties	Amount payable under regulations under section 13, 49, 56 or 62 of ALDA 1979 (except an amount falling within item 17A, 23 or 24)	The date determined by or under regulations under section 13, 49, 56 or 62 of ALDA 1979 as the date by which the amount must be paid
11F	Tobacco products duty	Amount payable under regulations under section 7 of TPDA 1979 (except an amount falling within item 17A, 23 or 24)	The date determined by or under regulations under section 7 of TPDA 1979 as the date by which the amount must be paid

11G	Hydrocarbon oil duties	Amount payable under regulations under section 21 or 24 of HODA 1979 (except an amount falling within item 17A, 23 or 24)	The date determined by or under regulations under section 21 or 24 of HODA 1979 as the date by which the amount must be paid
[11H	General betting duty	Amount payable under section 142 of FA 2014	The date determined— (*a*) under section 142 of FA 2014, or (*b*) by or under regulations under section 163 or 167 of that Act, as the date by which the amount must be paid
11I	Pool betting duty	Amount payable under section 151 of FA 2014	The date determined— (*a*) under section 151 of FA 2014, or (*b*) by or under regulations under section 163 or 167 of that Act, as the date by which the amount must be paid]
11J	Bingo duty	Amount payable under regulations under paragraph 9 of Schedule 3 to BGDA 1981 (except an amount falling within item 17A, 23 or 24)	The date determined by or under regulations under paragraph 9 of Schedule 3 to BGDA 1981 as the date by which the amount must be paid
11K	Lottery duty	Amount payable under section 26 of FA 1993 (except an amount falling within item 17A, 23 or 24)	The date determined — (*a*) by section 26 of FA 1993, or (*b*) by or under regulations under that section, as the date by which the amount must be paid
11L	Gaming duty	Amount payable under section 12 of FA 1997 (except an amount falling within item 17A, 23 or 24)	The date determined by or under regulations under — (*a*) section 12 of FA 1997, or (*b*) paragraph 11 of Schedule 1 to that Act, as the date by which the amount must be paid
[11M	Remote gaming duty	Amount payable under section 162 of FA 2014	The date determined by or under regulations under section 163 or 167 of FA 2014 as the date by which the amount must be paid]".

"13A	Value added tax	Amount assessed under section 73(1) of VATA 1994 in the absence of a return	The date by which the amount would have been required to be paid if it had been shown in the return

13AA	Value added tax	Amount assessed under section 73(1) of VATA 1994, by virtue of paragraph 16 of Schedule 3B to that Act, in the absence of a value added tax return (as defined in paragraph 23(1) of that Schedule)	The date by which the amount would have been required to be paid under the law of the member State under whose law the return was required
13AB	Value added tax	Amount assessed under section 73(1) of VATA 1994, by virtue of paragraph 20 of Schedule 3BA to that Act, in the absence of a relevant non-UK return (as defined in paragraph 38(1) of that Schedule)	The date by which the amount would have been required to be paid under the law of the member State under whose law the return was required
13B	Insurance premium tax	Amount assessed under section 56(1) of FA 1994 in the absence of a return	The date by which the amount would have been required to be paid if it had been shown in the return".

"16A	Aggregates levy	Amount assessed under paragraph 2 or 3 of Schedule 5 to FA 2001 in the absence of a return	The date by which the amount would have been required to be paid if it had been shown in the return
16B	Climate change levy	Amount assessed under paragraph 78 or 79 of Schedule 6 to FA 2000 in the absence of a return	The date by which the amount would have been required to be paid if it had been shown in the return
16C	Landfill tax	Amount assessed under section 50(1) of FA 1996 in the absence of a return	The date by which the amount would have been required to be paid if it had been shown in the return".

"17A	Tax falling within any of items 11D to 11M	Amount assessed under section 12(1) of FA 1994 in the absence of a return	The date by which the amount would have been required to be paid if it had been shown in the return".

In items 17A, 23 and 24 (as inserted), "11N" to be substituted for "11M" by FA 2012 s 191, Sch 24 para 34(*a*) with effect in relation to the playing of machine games on or after 1 February 2013 (and Schs 55, 56, as amended by FA 2012 Sch 24 Part 1, are taken to have come into force for the purposes of machine games duty on that date).

The following amendments to be made by FA 2013 Sch 34 para 10(2) with effect from the coming into force of F(No 3)A 2010 Sch 11 para 2(13)(*a*), (14)(*a*)—

– in item 23, in the second and third columns, for "9, 10" substitute "9 to 10A"; and
– in item 24, in the second column, for "9, 10" substitute "9 to 10A".

In para 1, Table entry to be inserted by FA 2016 s 167, Sch 23 para 9(1), (2) with effect from a day to be appointed. Table entry as inserted to read as follows—

"1A	Income tax or capital gains tax	Amount payable under section 59BA(4) or (5) of TMA 1970	The date falling 30 days after the date specified in section 59BA(4) or (5) of TMA 1970 as the date by which the amount must be paid.".

In para 1, Table entry to be inserted by FA 2017 s 56, Sch 11 para 5(1), (2) with effect from a date to be appointed. Once appointed, the charge to soft drinks industry levy will arise on chargeable events which occur on or after 6 April 2018 (FA 2017 s 31(1)). Table entry as inserted to read as follows—

"11ZA	Soft drinks industry levy	Amount payable under regulations under section 52 of FA 2017 or paragraphs 6 or 14 of Schedule 8 to that Act	The date determined by or under regulations under section 52 of FA 2017".

Assessments and determinations in default of return

2 The circumstances referred to in items 14, 17, 21 and 24 are where—

(*a*) P or another person is required to make or deliver a return falling within any item in the Table in Schedule 55,

(*b*) that person fails to make or deliver the return on or before the date by which it is required to be made or delivered, and

(*c*) if the return had been made or delivered as required, the return would have shown that an amount falling within any of items 1 to 10 was due and payable.

Modifications—FA 2009 Sch 56 has effect as if the reference to a return in this para included a reference to a bank payroll tax return (FA 2010 s 22, Sch 1 para 39(1), (5)).

Until F(No 3)A 2010 Sch 11 para 3 comes into force, para 2(*c*) has effect as if the reference in that para to items 1 to 10 were to items 1 to 10A (FA 2013 Sch 34 para 11).

Commencement—Finance Act 2009, Schedule 56 (Appointed Day and Consequential Provisions) Order, SI 2010/466: 6 April 2010 appointed as day on which Sch 56 comes into force for the following amounts specified in column 3 of the Table—items 2–4, and items 17, 23 and 24 but only in so far as the tax falls within any of items 2, 3 or 4 (see SI 2010/466 art 3).

Finance Act 2009, Schedules 55 and 56 (Income Tax Self Assessment and Pension Schemes) (Appointed Days and Consequential and Savings Provisions) Order, SI 2011/702 art 2 (appointed day for the coming into force of Sch 56 is 6 April 2011 in relation to an amount of tax which is payable in relation to the tax year 2010–11 or any subsequent tax year and falls within item 1, 12, 18 or 19 of the Table in para 1, or in so far as the tax falls within item 1 of that Table, item 17, 23 or 24 of that Table).

Prospective amendments—In sub-para (*c*) figure "11M" to be substituted for figure "10" by F(No 3)A 2010 s 27, Sch 11 paras 1, 3 with effect from a date to be appointed by Treasury order. Also see Modification note above.

In sub-para (*c*) "11N" substituted for "11M" (as prospectively substituted by F(No 3)A 2010) by FA 2012 s 191, Sch 24 para 34(*b*) with effect in relation to the playing of machine games on or after 1 February 2013 (and Schs 55, 56, as amended by FA 2012 Sch 24 Part 1, are taken to have come into force for the purposes of machine games duty on that date).

[Different penalty date for certain PAYE payments

2A—(1) PAYE regulations may provide that, in relation to specified payments of tax falling within item 2, the penalty date is a specified date later than that determined in accordance with column 4 of the Table.

(2) In sub-paragraph (1) "specified" means specified in the regulations.][1]

Commencement—Finance Act 2009, Schedules 55 and 56 (Income Tax Self Assessment and Pension Schemes) (Appointed Days and Consequential and Savings Provisions) Order, SI 2011/702 art 2 (appointed day for the coming into force of Sch 56 is 6 April 2011 in relation to an amount of tax which is payable in relation to the tax year 2010–11 or any subsequent tax year and falls within item 1, 12, 18 or 19 of the Table in para 1, or in so far as the tax falls within item 1 of that Table, item 17, 23 or 24 of that Table).

Amendments—[1] This para and preceding cross-head inserted by F(No 3)A 2010 s 27, Sch 11 paras 1, 4 with effect from 25 January 2011 (by virtue of SI 2011/132 art 2(*b*)).

Amount of penalty: occasional amounts and amounts in respect of periods of 6 months or more

3—(1) This paragraph applies in the case of—

(*a*) a payment of tax falling within any of items 1, 3 and 7 to 24 in the Table,

[(*aa*) a payment of tax falling within [item 4A or][2] item 6ZB in the Table,][1]

(*b*) a payment of tax falling within item 2 or 4 which relates to a period of 6 months or more, and

(*c*) a payment of tax falling within item 2 which is payable under regulations under section 688A of ITEPA 2003 (recovery from other persons of amounts due from managed service companies).

[(*ca*) an amount in respect of apprenticeship levy falling within item 4A which is payable by virtue of regulations under section 106 of FA 2016 (recovery from third parties).][2]

(2) P is liable to a penalty of 5% of the unpaid tax.

(3) If any amount of the tax is unpaid after the end of the period of 5 months beginning with the penalty date, P is liable to a penalty of 5% of that amount.

(4) If any amount of the tax is unpaid after the end of the period of 11 months beginning with the penalty date, P is liable to a penalty of 5% of that amount.

Modifications—FA 2009 Sch 56 has effect as if sub-para (1)(*a*) included a reference to a payment of bank payroll tax (FA 2010 s 22, Sch 1 para 39(1), (6)).

Commencement—Finance Act 2009, Schedule 56 (Appointed Day and Consequential Provisions) Order, SI 2010/466: 6 April 2010 appointed as day on which Sch 56 comes into force for the following amounts specified in column 3 of the Table—items 2–4, and items 17, 23 and 24 but only in so far as the tax falls within any of items 2, 3 or 4 (see SI 2010/466 art 3).

Finance Act 2009, Schedules 55 and 56 (Income Tax Self Assessment and Pension Schemes) (Appointed Days and Consequential and Savings Provisions) Order, SI 2011/702 art 2 (appointed day for the coming into force of Sch 56 is 6 April 2011 in relation to an amount of tax which is payable in relation to the tax year 2010–11 or any subsequent tax year and falls within item 1, 12, 18 or 19 of the Table in para 1, or in so far as the tax falls within item 1 of that Table, item 17, 23 or 24 of that Table).

Amendments—[1] Sub-para (1)(*aa*) inserted by FA 2015 s 104(1), (3) with effect in relation to accounting periods beginning on or after 1 April 2015. For accounting periods that straddle that date, see FA 2015 s 116(2).

[2] Words in sub-para (1)(*b*) inserted, and sub-para (1)(*ca*) inserted by FA 2016 s 113(9), (11) with effect from 15 September 2016.

Prospective amendments—In sub-para (1)(*a*) words "items 1, 3, 6B, 7 to 11 and 12 to 24" to be substituted for words "items 1, 3 and 7 to 24", in sub-para (1)(*b*) words "any of items 2, 4, 6A, 6C and 11A to 11M" to be substituted for words "item 2 or 4" and word "and" at the end to be repealed, and sub-paras (1)(*d*) and preceding word "and", and (1A) to be inserted, by F(No 3)A 2010 s 27, Sch 11 paras 1, 5 with effect from a date to be appointed by Treasury order. Sub-paras (1)(*d*), (1A) as inserted to read—

"(*d*) a payment of tax falling within item 6A which relates to a transitional period for the purposes of the annual accounting scheme.".

"(1A) In sub-paragraph (1)(*d*), a transitional period for the purposes of the annual accounting scheme is a prescribed accounting period (within the meaning of section 25(1) of VATA 1994) which—

(a) ends on the day immediately preceding the date indicated by the Commissioners for Her Majesty's Revenue and Customs in a notification of authorisation under regulation 50 of the Value Added Tax Regulations 1995 (SI 1995/2518) (admission to annual accounting scheme), or

(b) begins on the day immediately following the end of the last period of 12 months for which such an authorisation has effect.".

In sub-para (1)(*b*) "11N" to be substituted for "11M" by FA 2012 s 191, Sch 24 para 34(*c*) with effect in relation to the playing of machine games on or after 1 February 2013 (and Schs 55, 56, as amended by FA 2012 Sch 24 Part 1, are taken to have come into force for the purposes of machine games duty on that date).

In sub-para (1)(*a*), words "1A," to be inserted after words "items 1," by FA 2016 s 167, Sch 23 para 9(1), (3) with effect from a day to be appointed.

4—(1) This paragraph applies in the case of a payment of tax falling within item 5[, 6 or 6ZZA][1] in the Table.

(2) P is liable to a penalty of 5% of the unpaid tax.

(3) If any amount of the tax is unpaid after the end of the period of 3 months beginning with the penalty date, P is liable to a penalty of 5% of that amount.

(4) If any amount of the tax is unpaid after the end of the period of 9 months beginning with the penalty date, P is liable to a penalty of 5% of that amount.

Commencement—Finance Act 2009, Schedules 55 and 56 (Income Tax Self Assessment and Pension Schemes) (Appointed Days and Consequential and Savings Provisions) Order, SI 2011/702 art 2 (appointed day for the coming into force of Sch 56 is 6 April 2011 in relation to an amount of tax which is payable in relation to the tax year 2010–11 or any subsequent tax year and falls within item 1, 12, 18 or 19 of the Table in para 1, or in so far as the tax falls within item 1 of that Table, item 17, 23 or 24 of that Table).

Amendments—[1] In sub-para (1), words substituted for words "or 6" by F(No 2)A 2015 s 38(6), (8) with effect in relation to payments of restitution interest in respect of awards that are finally determined on or after 21 October 2015, whether the interest arose before, on or after that date. HMRC must deduct tax from a payment of restitution interest made on or after 26 October 2015 (see F(No 2)A 2015 s 38(10)). Note however that this Schedule is not yet in force except to the extent specified: see Commencement note above.

Amount of penalty: PAYE and CIS amounts [etc.]

5—(1) Paragraphs 6 to 8 apply in the case of a payment of tax falling within item 2[, 4 or 4A][1] in the Table.

(2) But those paragraphs do not apply in the case of a payment mentioned in paragraph 3(1)(*b*) [, (*c*) or (*ca*).][1]

Commencement—Finance Act 2009, Schedule 56 (Appointed Day and Consequential Provisions) Order, SI 2010/466: 6 April 2010 appointed as day on which Sch 56 comes into force for the following amounts specified in column 3 of the Table—items 2–4, and items 17, 23 and 24 but only in so far as the tax falls within any of items 2, 3 or 4 (see SI 2010/466 art 3).

Finance Act 2009, Schedules 55 and 56 (Income Tax Self Assessment and Pension Schemes) (Appointed Days and Consequential and Savings Provisions) Order, SI 2011/702 art 2 (appointed day for the coming into force of Sch 56 is 6 April 2011 in relation to an amount of tax which is payable in relation to the tax year 2010–11 or any subsequent tax year and falls within item 1, 12, 18 or 19 of the Table in para 1, or in so far as the tax falls within item 1 of that Table, item 17, 23 or 24 of that Table).

Amendments—[1] Word in heading inserted, words in sub-para (1) substituted for words "or 4", and words in sub-para (2) substituted for words "or (*c*)", by FA 2016 s 113(9), (12), (13), (15) with effect from 15 September 2016.

[**6**—[(1) P is liable to a penalty under this paragraph, in relation to each tax, each time that P makes a default in relation to a tax year.][2]

(2) For the purposes of this paragraph, P makes a default [in relation to a tax year][2] when P fails to make one of the following payments (or to pay an amount comprising two or more of those payments) in full on or before the date on which it becomes due and payable—

(*a*) a payment under PAYE regulations [of tax payable in relation to the tax year][2];

(*b*) a payment of earnings-related contributions within the meaning of the Social Security (Contributions) Regulations 2001 (SI 2001/1004) [payable in relation to the tax year][2];

[(*ba*) a payment under regulations under section 105 of FA 2016 of an amount in respect of apprenticeship levy payable in relation to the tax year;][2]

(*c*) a payment due under the Income Tax (Construction Industry Scheme) Regulations 2005 (SI 2005/2045) [payable in relation to the tax year][2];

(*d*) a repayment in respect of a student loan due under the Education (Student Loans) (Repayments) Regulations 2009 (SI 2009/470) or the Education (Student Loans) (Repayments) Regulations (Northern Ireland) 2000 (S.R. 2000 No 121) [and due for the tax year][2].

[(3) But where a failure to make one of those payments (or to pay an amount comprising two or more of those payments) would, apart from this sub-paragraph, constitute the first default in relation to a tax year, that failure does not count as a default in relation to that year for the purposes of a penalty under this paragraph.

(4) The amount of the penalty for a default made in relation to a tax year is determined by reference to—

(*a*) the amount of the tax comprised in the default, and

(*b*) the number of previous defaults that P has made in relation to the same tax year.

(5) If the default is P's 1st, 2nd or 3rd default in relation to the tax year, P is liable, at the time of the default, to a penalty of 1% of the amount of tax comprised in the default.

(6) If the default is P's 4th, 5th or 6th default in relation to the tax year, P is liable, at the time of the default, to a penalty of 2% of the amount of tax comprised in the default.

(7) If the default is P's 7th, 8th or 9th default in relation to the tax year, P is liable, at the time of the default, to a penalty of 3% of the amount of tax comprised in the default.

(7A) If the default is P's 10th or subsequent default in relation to the tax year, P is liable, at the time of the default, to a penalty of 4% of the amount of tax comprised in the default.][2]

(8) For the purposes of this paragraph—

(*a*) the amount of a tax comprised in a default is the amount of that tax comprised in the payment which P fails to make;

[(*b*) a previous default counts for the purposes of subparagraphs (5) to (7A) even if it is remedied before the time of the default giving rise to the penalty.][2]

[(8A) Regulations made by the Commissioners for Her Majesty's Revenue and Customs may specify—

(*a*) circumstances in which, for the purposes of sub-paragraph (2), a payment of less than the full amount may be treated as a payment in full;

(*b*) circumstances in which sub-paragraph (3) is not to apply.

(8B) Regulations under sub-paragraph (8A) may—

(*a*) make different provision for different cases, and

(*b*) include incidental, consequential and supplementary provision.][2]

(9) The Treasury may by order made by statutory instrument make such amendments to sub-paragraph (2) as they think fit in consequence of any amendment, revocation or re-enactment of the regulations mentioned in that sub-paragraph.][1]

Commencement—Finance Act 2009, Schedule 56 (Appointed Day and Consequential Provisions) Order, SI 2010/466: 6 April 2010 appointed as day on which Sch 56 comes into force for the following amounts specified in column 3 of the Table—items 2–4, and items 17, 23 and 24 but only in so far as the tax falls within any of items 2, 3 or 4 (see SI 2010/466 art 3).

Finance Act 2009, Schedules 55 and 56 (Income Tax Self Assessment and Pension Schemes) (Appointed Days and Consequential and Savings Provisions) Order, SI 2011/702 art 2 (appointed day for the coming into force of Sch 56 is 6 April 2011 in relation to an amount of tax which is payable in relation to the tax year 2010–11 or any subsequent tax year and falls within item 1, 12, 18 or 19 of the Table in para 1, or in so far as the tax falls within item 1 of that Table, item 17, 23 or 24 of that Table).

Regulations—Income Tax (Pay As You Earn) and the Income Tax (Construction Industry Scheme) (Amendment) Regulations, SI 2014/472.

Amendments—[1] This para substituted by F(No 3)A 2010 s 27, Sch 11 paras 1, 6 with effect from 25 January 2011 (by virtue of SI 2011/132 art 2(*b*)).

[2] Sub-paras (1), (8)(*b*) substituted, sub-paras (3)–(7A) substituted for sub-paras (3)–(7), in sub-para (2), (2)(*a*)–(*d*), words inserted, and sub-paras (8A), (8B) inserted, by FA 2013 s 230, Sch 50 paras 10, 12 with effect for defaults made in relation to the tax year 2014–15 and subsequent tax years (see FA 2009 Sch 56 para 6(2), as amended by FA 2013 Sch 50 para 12(3), as to when a default is made in relation to a tax year)—

7 If any amount of the tax is unpaid after the end of the period of 6 months beginning with the penalty date, P is liable to a penalty of 5% of that amount.

Commencement—Finance Act 2009, Schedule 56 (Appointed Day and Consequential Provisions) Order, SI 2010/466: 6 April 2010 appointed as day on which Sch 56 comes into force for the following amounts specified in column 3 of the Table—items 2–4, and items 17, 23 and 24 but only in so far as the tax falls within any of items 2, 3 or 4 (see SI 2010/466 art 3).

Finance Act 2009, Schedules 55 and 56 (Income Tax Self Assessment and Pension Schemes) (Appointed Days and Consequential and Savings Provisions) Order, SI 2011/702 art 2 (appointed day for the coming into force of Sch 56 is 6 April 2011 in relation to an amount of tax which is payable in relation to the tax year 2010–11 or any subsequent tax year and falls within item 1, 12, 18 or 19 of the Table in para 1, or in so far as the tax falls within item 1 of that Table, item 17, 23 or 24 of that Table).

8 If any amount of the tax is unpaid after the end of the period of 12 months beginning with the penalty date, P is liable to a penalty of 5% of that amount.

Commencement—Finance Act 2009, Schedule 56 (Appointed Day and Consequential Provisions) Order, SI 2010/466: 6 April 2010 appointed as day on which Sch 56 comes into force for the following amounts specified in column 3 of the Table—items 2–4, and items 17, 23 and 24 but only in so far as the tax falls within any of items 2, 3 or 4 (see SI 2010/466 art 3).

Finance Act 2009, Schedules 55 and 56 (Income Tax Self Assessment and Pension Schemes) (Appointed Days and Consequential and Savings Provisions) Order, SI 2011/702 art 2 (appointed day for the coming into force of Sch 56 is 6 April 2011 in relation to an amount of tax which is payable in relation to the tax year 2010–11 or any subsequent tax year and falls within item 1, 12, 18 or 19 of the Table in para 1, or in so far as the tax falls within item 1 of that Table, item 17, 23 or 24 of that Table).

[Amount of penalty: amounts in respect of periods of between 2 and 6 months

8A—(1) Paragraphs 8B to 8E apply in the case of a payment of tax falling within any of items 6A, 6BA, 6BB, 6C and 11A to [11N] in the Table which relates to a period of less than 6 months but more than 2 months.

(2) But those paragraphs do not apply in the case of a payment mentioned in paragraph 3(1)(*d*).

(3) Paragraph 8K sets out how payments on account of VAT (item 6A) are to be treated for the purposes of paragraphs 8B to 8E.]

Commencement—Finance Act 2009, Schedules 55 and 56 (Income Tax Self Assessment and Pension Schemes) (Appointed Days and Consequential and Savings Provisions) Order, SI 2011/702 art 2 (appointed day for the coming into force of Sch 56 is 6 April 2011 in relation to an amount of tax which is payable in relation to the tax year 2010–11 or any subsequent tax year and falls within item 1, 12, 18 or 19 of the Table in para 1, or in so far as the tax falls within item 1 of that Table, item 17, 23 or 24 of that Table).

Prospective amendments—Paras 8A–8J and preceding cross-heads to be inserted by F(No 3)A 2010 s 27, Sch 11 paras 1, 7 (as amended by FA 2014 s 103, Sch 22 para 22(6)) with effect from a date to be appointed by Treasury order.

In sub-para (1) "11N" substituted for "11M" by FA 2012 s 191, Sch 24 para 34(*d*) with effect in relation to the playing of machine games on or after 1 February 2013 (and Schs 55, 56, as amended by FA 2012 Sch 24 Part 1, are taken to have come into force for the purposes of machine games duty on that date).

[**8B**—(1) A penalty period begins to run on the penalty date for the payment of tax.

(2) The penalty period ends with the day 12 months after the date specified in or for the purposes of column 4 for the payment, unless it is extended under paragraph 8C(2)(*c*) or 8H(2)(*c*).]

Commencement—Finance Act 2009, Schedules 55 and 56 (Income Tax Self Assessment and Pension Schemes) (Appointed Days and Consequential and Savings Provisions) Order, SI 2011/702 art 2 (appointed day for the coming into force of Sch 56 is 6 April 2011 in relation to an amount of tax which is payable in relation to the tax year 2010–11 or any subsequent tax year and falls within item 1, 12, 18 or 19 of the Table in para 1, or in so far as the tax falls within item 1 of that Table, item 17, 23 or 24 of that Table).

Prospective amendments—Paras 8A–8J and preceding cross-heads to be inserted by F(No 3)A 2010 s 27, Sch 11 paras 1, 7 with effect from a date to be appointed by Treasury order.

[**8C**—(1) This paragraph applies if—

(*a*) a penalty period has begun under paragraph 8B or 8G because P has failed to make a payment ("payment A"), and

(*b*) before the end of the period, P fails to make another payment ("payment B") falling within the same item in the Table as payment A.

(2) In such a case—

(*a*) paragraph 8B(1) does not apply to the failure to make payment B,

(*b*) P is liable to a penalty under this paragraph for that failure, And

(*c*) the penalty period that has begun is extended so that it ends with the day 12 months after the date specified in or for the purposes of column 4 for payment B.

(3) The amount of the penalty under this paragraph is determined by reference to the number of defaults that P has made during the penalty period.

(4) If the default is P's first default during the penalty period, P is liable, at the time of the default, to a penalty of 2% of the amount of the default.

(5) If the default is P's second default during the penalty period, P is liable, at the time of the default, to a penalty of 3% of the amount of the default.

(6) If the default is P's third or a subsequent default during the penalty period, P is liable, at the time of the default, to a penalty of 4% of the amount of the default.

(7) For the purposes of this paragraph—

(*a*) P makes a default when P fails to pay an amount of tax in full on or before the date on which it becomes due and payable;

(*b*) in accordance with sub-paragraph (1)(*b*), the references in sub-paragraphs (3) to (6) to a default are references to a default in relation to the tax to which payments A and B relate;

(*c*) a default counts for the purposes of those sub-paragraphs if (but only if) the period to which the payment relates is less than 6 months;

(*d*) the amount of a default is the amount which P fails to pay.

(8) A penalty period may be extended more than once under subparagraph (2)(*c*).]

Commencement—Finance Act 2009, Schedules 55 and 56 (Income Tax Self Assessment and Pension Schemes) (Appointed Days and Consequential and Savings Provisions) Order, SI 2011/702 art 2 (appointed day for the coming into force of Sch 56 is 6 April 2011 in relation to an amount of tax which is payable in relation to the tax year 2010–11 or any subsequent tax year and falls within item 1, 12, 18 or 19 of the Table in para 1, or in so far as the tax falls within item 1 of that Table, item 17, 23 or 24 of that Table).

Prospective amendments—Paras 8A–8J and preceding cross-heads to be inserted by F(No 3)A 2010 s 27, Sch 11 paras 1, 7 with effect from a date to be appointed by Treasury order.

[8D If any amount of the tax is unpaid after the end of the period of 6 months beginning with the penalty date, P is liable to a penalty of 5% of that amount.]

Commencement—Finance Act 2009, Schedules 55 and 56 (Income Tax Self Assessment and Pension Schemes) (Appointed Days and Consequential and Savings Provisions) Order, SI 2011/702 art 2 (appointed day for the coming into force of Sch 56 is 6 April 2011 in relation to an amount of tax which is payable in relation to the tax year 2010–11 or any subsequent tax year and falls within item 1, 12, 18 or 19 of the Table in para 1, or in so far as the tax falls within item 1 of that Table, item 17, 23 or 24 of that Table).

Prospective amendments—Paras 8A–8J and preceding cross-heads to be inserted by F(No 3)A 2010 s 27, Sch 11 paras 1, 7 with effect from a date to be appointed by Treasury order.

[8E If any amount of the tax is unpaid after the end of the period of 12 months beginning with the penalty date, P is liable to a penalty of 5% of that amount.]

Commencement—Finance Act 2009, Schedules 55 and 56 (Income Tax Self Assessment and Pension Schemes) (Appointed Days and Consequential and Savings Provisions) Order, SI 2011/702 art 2 (appointed day for the coming into force of Sch 56 is 6 April 2011 in relation to an amount of tax which is payable in relation to the tax year 2010–11 or any subsequent tax year and falls within item 1, 12, 18 or 19 of the Table in para 1, or in so far as the tax falls within item 1 of that Table, item 17, 23 or 24 of that Table).

Prospective amendments—Paras 8A–8J and preceding cross-heads to be inserted by F(No 3)A 2010 s 27, Sch 11 paras 1, 7 with effect from a date to be appointed by Treasury order.

[Amount of penalty: amounts in respect of periods of 2 months or less

8F—(1) Paragraphs 8G to 8J apply in the case of a payment of tax falling within any of items 6A, 6C and 11A to [11N] in the Table which relates to a period of 2 months or less.

(2) But those paragraphs do not apply in the case of a payment mentioned in paragraph 3(1)(*d*).]

Commencement—Finance Act 2009, Schedules 55 and 56 (Income Tax Self Assessment and Pension Schemes) (Appointed Days and Consequential and Savings Provisions) Order, SI 2011/702 art 2 (appointed day for the coming into force of Sch 56 is 6 April 2011 in relation to an amount of tax which is payable in relation to the tax year 2010–11 or any subsequent tax year and falls within item 1, 12, 18 or 19 of the Table in para 1, or in so far as the tax falls within item 1 of that Table, item 17, 23 or 24 of that Table).

Prospective amendments—Paras 8A–8J and preceding cross-heads to be inserted by F(No 3)A 2010 s 27, Sch 11 paras 1, 7 with effect from a date to be appointed by Treasury order.

In sub-para (1) "11N" substituted for "11M" by FA 2012 s 191, Sch 24 para 34(*e*) with effect in relation to the playing of machine games on or after 1 February 2013 (and Schs 55, 56, as amended by FA 2012 Sch 24 Part 1, are taken to have come into force for the purposes of machine games duty on that date).

[8G—(1) A penalty period begins to run on the penalty date for the payment of tax.

(2) The penalty period ends with the day 12 months after the date specified in or for the purposes of column 4 for the payment, unless it is extended under paragraph 8C(2)(*c*) or 8H(2)(*c*).]

Commencement—Finance Act 2009, Schedules 55 and 56 (Income Tax Self Assessment and Pension Schemes) (Appointed Days and Consequential and Savings Provisions) Order, SI 2011/702 art 2 (appointed day for the coming into force of Sch 56 is 6 April 2011 in relation to an amount of tax which is payable in relation to the tax year 2010–11 or any subsequent tax year and falls within item 1, 12, 18 or 19 of the Table in para 1, or in so far as the tax falls within item 1 of that Table, item 17, 23 or 24 of that Table).

Prospective amendments—Paras 8A–8J and preceding cross-heads to be inserted by F(No 3)A 2010 s 27, Sch 11 paras 1, 7 with effect from a date to be appointed by Treasury order.

[8H—(1) This paragraph applies if—

(*a*) a penalty period has begun under paragraph 8B or 8G because P has failed to make a payment ("payment A"), and

(*b*) before the end of the period, P fails to make another payment ("payment B") falling within the same item in the Table as payment A.

(2) In such a case—

(*a*) paragraph 8G(1) does not apply to the failure to make payment B,

(*b*) P is liable to a penalty under this paragraph for that failure, and

(*c*) the penalty period that has begun is extended so that it ends with the day 12 months after the date specified in or for the purposes of column 4 for payment B.

(3) The amount of the penalty under this paragraph is determined by reference to the number of defaults that P has made during the penalty period.

(4) If the default is P's first, second or third default during the penalty period, P is liable, at the time of the default, to a penalty of 1% of the amount of the default.

(5) If the default is P's fourth, fifth or sixth default during the penalty period, P is liable, at the time of the default, to a penalty of 2% of the amount of the default.

(6) If the default is P's seventh, eighth or ninth default during the penalty period, P is liable, at the time of the default, to a penalty of 3% of the amount of the default.
(7) If the default is P's tenth or a subsequent default during the penalty period, P is liable, at the time of the default, to a penalty of 4% of the amount of the default.
(8) For the purposes of this paragraph—
(*a*) P makes a default when P fails to pay an amount of tax in full on or before the date on which it becomes due and payable;
(*b*) in accordance with sub-paragraph (1)(*b*), the references in sub-paragraphs (3) to (7) to a default are references to a default in relation to the tax to which payments A and B relate;
(*c*) a default counts for the purposes of those sub-paragraphs if (but only if) the period to which the payment relates is less than 6 months;
(*d*) the amount of a default is the amount which P fails to pay.
(9) A penalty period may be extended more than once under subparagraph (2)(*c*).]

Commencement—Finance Act 2009, Schedules 55 and 56 (Income Tax Self Assessment and Pension Schemes) (Appointed Days and Consequential and Savings Provisions) Order, SI 2011/702 art 2 (appointed day for the coming into force of Sch 56 is 6 April 2011 in relation to an amount of tax which is payable in relation to the tax year 2010–11 or any subsequent tax year and falls within item 1, 12, 18 or 19 of the Table in para 1, or in so far as the tax falls within item 1 of that Table, item 17, 23 or 24 of that Table).

Prospective amendments—Paras 8A–8J and preceding cross-heads to be inserted by F(No 3)A 2010 s 27, Sch 11 paras 1, 7 with effect from a date to be appointed by Treasury order.

[8I If any amount of the tax is unpaid after the end of the period of 6 months beginning with the penalty date, P is liable to a penalty of 5% of that amount.]

Commencement—Finance Act 2009, Schedules 55 and 56 (Income Tax Self Assessment and Pension Schemes) (Appointed Days and Consequential and Savings Provisions) Order, SI 2011/702 art 2 (appointed day for the coming into force of Sch 56 is 6 April 2011 in relation to an amount of tax which is payable in relation to the tax year 2010–11 or any subsequent tax year and falls within item 1, 12, 18 or 19 of the Table in para 1, or in so far as the tax falls within item 1 of that Table, item 17, 23 or 24 of that Table).

Prospective amendments—Paras 8A–8J and preceding cross-heads to be inserted by F(No 3)A 2010 s 27, Sch 11 paras 1, 7 with effect from a date to be appointed by Treasury order.

[8J If any amount of the tax is unpaid after the end of the period of 12 months beginning with the penalty date, P is liable to a penalty of 5% of that amount.]

Commencement—Finance Act 2009, Schedules 55 and 56 (Income Tax Self Assessment and Pension Schemes) (Appointed Days and Consequential and Savings Provisions) Order, SI 2011/702 art 2 (appointed day for the coming into force of Sch 56 is 6 April 2011 in relation to an amount of tax which is payable in relation to the tax year 2010–11 or any subsequent tax year and falls within item 1, 12, 18 or 19 of the Table in para 1, or in so far as the tax falls within item 1 of that Table, item 17, 23 or 24 of that Table).

Prospective amendments—Paras 8A–8J and preceding cross-heads to be inserted by F(No 3)A 2010 s 27, Sch 11 paras 1, 7 with effect from a date to be appointed by Treasury order.

[Calculation of unpaid VAT: treatment of payments on account

8K—(1) Where P is required, by virtue of an order under section 28 of VATA 1994, to make any payment on account of VAT—
(*a*) each payment is to be treated for the purposes of this Schedule as relating to the prescribed accounting period in respect of which it is to be paid (and not as relating to the interval between the dates on which payments on account are required to be made), and
(*b*) the amount of tax unpaid in respect of the prescribed accounting period is the total of the amounts produced by paragraphs (*a*) and (*b*) of sub-paragraph (3).
(2) In determining that total—
(*a*) if there is more than one amount of POAD or POAT, those amounts are to be added together, and
(*b*) if the amount produced by sub-paragraph (3)(*b*) is less than zero, that amount is to be disregarded.
(3) The amounts are—
(*a*) POAD – POAT, and
(*b*) BPD – BPT.
(4) In this paragraph—
POAD is the amount of any payment on account due in respect of the prescribed accounting period,
POAT is the amount of any payment on account paid on time (that is, on or before the date on which it was required to be made),
BPD (which is the balancing payment due in respect of the prescribed accounting period) is equal to PAPD – POAD, and
BPT (which is the amount paid on time in satisfaction of any liability to pay BPD) is equal to PAPP – POAP.

(5) In sub-paragraph (4)—

PAPD is the amount of VAT due in respect of the prescribed accounting period,

PAPP is the total amount paid, on or before the last day on which P is required to make payments in respect of that period, in satisfaction of any liability to pay PAPD, and

POAP is the total amount paid, on or before that day (but whether or not paid on time), in satisfaction of any liability to pay POAD.]

Commencement—Finance Act 2009, Schedules 55 and 56 (Income Tax Self Assessment and Pension Schemes) (Appointed Days and Consequential and Savings Provisions) Order, SI 2011/702 art 2 (appointed day for the coming into force of Sch 56 is 6 April 2011 in relation to an amount of tax which is payable in relation to the tax year 2010–11 or any subsequent tax year and falls within item 1, 12, 18 or 19 of the Table in para 1, or in so far as the tax falls within item 1 of that Table, item 17, 23 or 24 of that Table).

Prospective amendments—Para 8K and preceding cross-head to be inserted by F(No 3)A 2010 s 27, Sch 11 paras 1, 8 with effect from a date to be appointed by Treasury order.

Special reduction

9—(1) If HMRC think it right because of special circumstances, they may reduce a penalty under any paragraph of this Schedule.

(2) In sub-paragraph (1) "special circumstances" does not include—

(*a*) ability to pay, or

(*b*) the fact that a potential loss of revenue from one taxpayer is balanced by a potential overpayment by another.

(3) In sub-paragraph (1) the reference to reducing a penalty includes a reference to—

(*a*) staying a penalty, and

(*b*) agreeing a compromise in relation to proceedings for a penalty.

Commencement—Finance Act 2009, Schedule 56 (Appointed Day and Consequential Provisions) Order, SI 2010/466: 6 April 2010 appointed as day on which Sch 56 comes into force for the following amounts specified in column 3 of the Table—items 2–4, and items 17, 23 and 24 but only in so far as the tax falls within any of items 2, 3 or 4 (see SI 2010/466 art 3).

Finance Act 2009, Schedules 55 and 56 (Income Tax Self Assessment and Pension Schemes) (Appointed Days and Consequential and Savings Provisions) Order, SI 2011/702 art 2 (appointed day for the coming into force of Sch 56 is 6 April 2011 in relation to an amount of tax which is payable in relation to the tax year 2010–11 or any subsequent tax year and falls within item 1, 12, 18 or 19 of the Table in para 1, or in so far as the tax falls within item 1 of that Table, item 17, 23 or 24 of that Table).

Cross-references—See FA 2014 s 226(7) (application of paras 9–18 of this Schedule, with any necessary modifications, to penalties for failure to pay accelerated payment).

[Interaction with other penalties and late payment surcharges

9A In the application of the following provisions, no account shall be taken of a penalty under this Schedule—

(*a*) section 97A of TMA 1970 (multiple penalties),

(*b*) paragraph 12(2) of Schedule 24 to FA 2007 (interaction with other penalties), and

(*c*) paragraph 15(1) of Schedule 41 to FA 2008 (interaction with other penalties).][1]

Cross-references—See FA 2014 s 226(7) (application of paras 9–18 of this Schedule, with any necessary modifications, to penalties for failure to pay accelerated payment).

Amendments—[1] Paragraph 9A and preceding cross-head inserted by FA 2013 s 230, Sch 50 paras 10, 13 with effect for defaults made in relation to the tax year 2014–15 and subsequent tax years (see FA 2009 Sch 56 para 6(2), as amended by FA 2013 Sch 50 para 12(3), as to when a default is made in relation to a tax year).

Suspension of penalty during currency of agreement for deferred payment

10—(1) This paragraph applies if—

(*a*) P fails to pay an amount of tax when it becomes due and payable,

(*b*) P makes a request to HMRC that payment of the amount of tax be deferred, and

(*c*) HMRC agrees that payment of that amount may be deferred for a period ("the deferral period").

(2) If P would (apart from this sub-paragraph) become liable, between the date on which P makes the request and the end of the deferral period, to a penalty under any paragraph of this Schedule for failing to pay that amount, P is not liable to that penalty.

(3) But if—

(*a*) P breaks the agreement (see sub-paragraph (4)), and

(*b*) HMRC serves on P a notice specifying any penalty to which P would become liable apart from sub-paragraph (2),

P becomes liable, at the date of the notice, to that penalty.

(4) P breaks an agreement if—

(*a*) P fails to pay the amount of tax in question when the deferral period ends, or

(*b*) the deferral is subject to P complying with a condition (including a condition that part of the amount be paid during the deferral period) and P fails to comply with it.

(5) If the agreement mentioned in sub-paragraph (1)(*c*) is varied at any time by a further agreement between P and HMRC, this paragraph applies from that time to the agreement as varied.

Commencement—Finance Act 2009, Schedule 56 (Appointed Day and Consequential Provisions) Order, SI 2010/466: 6 April 2010 appointed as day on which Sch 56 comes into force for the following amounts specified in column 3 of the Table—items 2–4, and items 17, 23 and 24 but only in so far as the tax falls within any of items 2, 3 or 4 (see SI 2010/466 art 3).

Finance Act 2009, Schedules 55 and 56 (Income Tax Self Assessment and Pension Schemes) (Appointed Days and Consequential and Savings Provisions) Order, SI 2011/702 art 2 (appointed day for the coming into force of Sch 56 is 6 April 2011 in relation to an amount of tax which is payable in relation to the tax year 2010–11 or any subsequent tax year and falls within item 1, 12, 18 or 19 of the Table in para 1, or in so far as the tax falls within item 1 of that Table, item 17, 23 or 24 of that Table).

Cross-references—See FA 2014 s 226(7) (application of paras 9–18 of this Schedule, with any necessary modifications, to penalties for failure to pay accelerated payment).

Assessment

11—(1) Where P is liable for a penalty under any paragraph of this Schedule HMRC must—

(*a*) assess the penalty,

(*b*) notify P, and

(*c*) state in the notice the period in respect of which the penalty is assessed.

(2) A penalty under any paragraph of this Schedule must be paid before the end of the period of 30 days beginning with the day on which notice of the assessment of the penalty is issued.

(3) An assessment of a penalty under any paragraph of this Schedule—

(*a*) is to be treated for procedural purposes in the same way as an assessment to tax (except in respect of a matter expressly provided for by this Schedule),

(*b*) may be enforced as if it were an assessment to tax, and

(*c*) may be combined with an assessment to tax.

(4) A supplementary assessment may be made in respect of a penalty if an earlier assessment operated by reference to an underestimate of an amount of [tax which was due or payable][1].

[(4A) If an assessment in respect of a penalty is based on an amount of tax due or payable that is found by HMRC to be excessive, HMRC may by notice to P amend the assessment so that it is based upon the correct amount.

(4B) An amendment made under sub-paragraph (4A)—

(*a*) does not affect when the penalty must be paid;

(*b*) may be made after the last day on which the assessment in question could have been made under paragraph 12.][2]

(5) . . . [2]

Commencement—Finance Act 2009, Schedule 56 (Appointed Day and Consequential Provisions) Order, SI 2010/466: 6 April 2010 appointed as day on which Sch 56 comes into force for the following amounts specified in column 3 of the Table—items 2–4, and items 17, 23 and 24 but only in so far as the tax falls within any of items 2, 3 or 4 (see SI 2010/466 art 3).

Finance Act 2009, Schedules 55 and 56 (Income Tax Self Assessment and Pension Schemes) (Appointed Days and Consequential and Savings Provisions) Order, SI 2011/702 art 2 (appointed day for the coming into force of Sch 56 is 6 April 2011 in relation to an amount of tax which is payable in relation to the tax year 2010–11 or any subsequent tax year and falls within item 1, 12, 18 or 19 of the Table in para 1, or in so far as the tax falls within item 1 of that Table, item 17, 23 or 24 of that Table).

Cross-references—See FA 2014 s 226(7) (application of paras 9–18 of this Schedule, with any necessary modifications, to penalties for failure to pay accelerated payment).

Amendments—[1] In sub-para (4) words substituted for words "unpaid tax", and sub-para (4A) inserted, by (F(No 3)A 2010 s 27, Sch 11 paras 1, 9 with effect from 6 April 2011 in relation to an amount of tax which is payable in relation to the tax year 2010–11 or any subsequent tax year, and falls within item 1, 12, 18 or 19 of the Table in FA 2009 Sch 56 para 1, or insofar as the tax falls within item 1 of that Table, item 17, 23 or 24 of that Table (by virtue of SI 2011/703 art 3).

[2] Sub-paras (4A), (4B) substituted for sub-para (4A), and sub-para (5) repealed, by FA 2013 s 230, Sch 50 paras 10, 14 with effect for defaults made in relation to the tax year 2014–15 and subsequent tax years (see FA 2009 Sch 56 para 6(2), as amended by FA 2013 Sch 50 para 12(3), as to when a default is made in relation to a tax year).

12—(1) An assessment of a penalty under any paragraph of this Schedule in respect of any amount must be made on or before the later of date A and (where it applies) date B.

(2) Date A is the last day of the period of 2 years beginning with the date specified in or for the purposes of column 4 of the Table (that is to say, the last date on which payment may be made without incurring a penalty).

(3) Date B is the last day of the period of 12 months beginning with—

(*a*) the end of the appeal period for the assessment of the amount of tax in respect of which the penalty is assessed, or

(*b*) if there is no such assessment, the date on which that amount of tax is ascertained.

(4) In sub-paragraph (3)(*a*) "appeal period" means the period during which—

(*a*) an appeal could be brought, or

(*b*) an appeal that has been brought has not been determined or withdrawn.

Commencement—Finance Act 2009, Schedule 56 (Appointed Day and Consequential Provisions) Order, SI 2010/466: 6 April 2010 appointed as day on which Sch 56 comes into force for the following amounts specified in column 3 of the Table—items 2–4, and items 17, 23 and 24 but only in so far as the tax falls within any of items 2, 3 or 4 (see SI 2010/466 art 3).

Finance Act 2009, Schedules 55 and 56 (Income Tax Self Assessment and Pension Schemes) (Appointed Days and Consequential and Savings Provisions) Order, SI 2011/702 art 2 (appointed day for the coming into force of Sch 56 is 6 April 2011 in relation to an amount of tax which is payable in relation to the tax year 2010–11 or any subsequent tax year and falls within item 1, 12, 18 or 19 of the Table in para 1, or in so far as the tax falls within item 1 of that Table, item 17, 23 or 24 of that Table).

Cross-references—See FA 2014 s 226(7) (application of paras 9–18 of this Schedule, with any necessary modifications, to penalties for failure to pay accelerated payment).

Appeal

13—(1) P may appeal against a decision of HMRC that a penalty is payable by P.

(2) P may appeal against a decision of HMRC as to the amount of a penalty payable by P.

Commencement—Finance Act 2009, Schedule 56 (Appointed Day and Consequential Provisions) Order, SI 2010/466: 6 April 2010 appointed as day on which Sch 56 comes into force for the following amounts specified in column 3 of the Table—items 2–4, and items 17, 23 and 24 but only in so far as the tax falls within any of items 2, 3 or 4 (see SI 2010/466 art 3).

Finance Act 2009, Schedules 55 and 56 (Income Tax Self Assessment and Pension Schemes) (Appointed Days and Consequential and Savings Provisions) Order, SI 2011/702 art 2 (appointed day for the coming into force of Sch 56 is 6 April 2011 in relation to an amount of tax which is payable in relation to the tax year 2010–11 or any subsequent tax year and falls within item 1, 12, 18 or 19 of the Table in para 1, or in so far as the tax falls within item 1 of that Table, item 17, 23 or 24 of that Table).

Cross-references—See FA 2014 s 226(7) (application of paras 9–18 of this Schedule, with any necessary modifications, to penalties for failure to pay accelerated payment).

14—(1) An appeal under paragraph 13 is to be treated in the same way as an appeal against an assessment to the tax concerned (including by the application of any provision about bringing the appeal by notice to HMRC, about HMRC review of the decision or about determination of the appeal by the First-tier Tribunal or Upper Tribunal).

(2) Sub-paragraph (1) does not apply—

(*a*) so as to require P to pay a penalty before an appeal against the assessment of the penalty is determined, or

(*b*) in respect of any other matter expressly provided for by this Act.

Commencement—Finance Act 2009, Schedule 56 (Appointed Day and Consequential Provisions) Order, SI 2010/466: 6 April 2010 appointed as day on which Sch 56 comes into force for the following amounts specified in column 3 of the Table—items 2–4, and items 17, 23 and 24 but only in so far as the tax falls within any of items 2, 3 or 4 (see SI 2010/466 art 3).

Finance Act 2009, Schedules 55 and 56 (Income Tax Self Assessment and Pension Schemes) (Appointed Days and Consequential and Savings Provisions) Order, SI 2011/702 art 2 (appointed day for the coming into force of Sch 56 is 6 April 2011 in relation to an amount of tax which is payable in relation to the tax year 2010–11 or any subsequent tax year and falls within item 1, 12, 18 or 19 of the Table in para 1, or in so far as the tax falls within item 1 of that Table, item 17, 23 or 24 of that Table).

Cross-references—See FA 2014 s 226(7) (application of paras 9–18 of this Schedule, with any necessary modifications, to penalties for failure to pay accelerated payment).

15—(1) On an appeal under paragraph 13(1) that is notified to the tribunal, the tribunal may affirm or cancel HMRC's decision.

(2) On an appeal under paragraph 13(2) that is notified to the tribunal, the tribunal may—

(*a*) affirm HMRC's decision, or

(*b*) substitute for HMRC's decision another decision that HMRC had power to make.

(3) If the tribunal substitutes its decision for HMRC's, the tribunal may rely on paragraph 9—

(*a*) to the same extent as HMRC (which may mean applying the same percentage reduction as HMRC to a different starting point), or

(*b*) to a different extent, but only if the tribunal thinks that HMRC's decision in respect of the application of paragraph 9 was flawed.

(4) In sub-paragraph (3)(*b*) "flawed" means flawed when considered in the light of the principles applicable in proceedings for judicial review.

(5) In this paragraph "tribunal" means the First-tier Tribunal or Upper Tribunal (as appropriate by virtue of paragraph 14(1)).

Commencement—Finance Act 2009, Schedule 56 (Appointed Day and Consequential Provisions) Order, SI 2010/466: 6 April 2010 appointed as day on which Sch 56 comes into force for the following amounts specified in column 3 of the Table—items 2–4, and items 17, 23 and 24 but only in so far as the tax falls within any of items 2, 3 or 4 (see SI 2010/466 art 3).

Finance Act 2009, Schedules 55 and 56 (Income Tax Self Assessment and Pension Schemes) (Appointed Days and Consequential and Savings Provisions) Order, SI 2011/702 art 2 (appointed day for the coming into force of Sch 56 is 6 April 2011 in relation to an amount of tax which is payable in relation to the tax year 2010–11 or any subsequent tax year and falls within item 1, 12, 18 or 19 of the Table in para 1, or in so far as the tax falls within item 1 of that Table, item 17, 23 or 24 of that Table).

Cross-references—See FA 2014 s 226(7) (application of paras 9–18 of this Schedule, with any necessary modifications, to penalties for failure to pay accelerated payment).

Reasonable excuse

16—(1) Liability to a penalty under any paragraph of this Schedule does not arise in relation to a failure to make a payment if P satisfies HMRC or (on appeal) the First-tier Tribunal or Upper Tribunal that there is a reasonable excuse for the failure.

(2) For the purposes of sub-paragraph (1)—

(*a*) an insufficiency of funds is not a reasonable excuse unless attributable to events outside P's control,

(*b*) where P relies on any other person to do anything, that is not a reasonable excuse unless P took reasonable care to avoid the failure, and

(*c*) where P had a reasonable excuse for the failure but the excuse has ceased, P is to be treated as having continued to have the excuse if the failure is remedied without unreasonable delay after the excuse ceased.

Commencement—Finance Act 2009, Schedule 56 (Appointed Day and Consequential Provisions) Order, SI 2010/466: 6 April 2010 appointed as day on which Sch 56 comes into force for the following amounts specified in column 3 of the Table—items 2–4, and items 17, 23 and 24 but only in so far as the tax falls within any of items 2, 3 or 4 (see SI 2010/466 art 3).

Finance Act 2009, Schedules 55 and 56 (Income Tax Self Assessment and Pension Schemes) (Appointed Days and Consequential and Savings Provisions) Order, SI 2011/702 art 2 (appointed day for the coming into force of Sch 56 is 6 April 2011 in relation to an amount of tax which is payable in relation to the tax year 2010–11 or any subsequent tax year and falls within item 1, 12, 18 or 19 of the Table in para 1, or in so far as the tax falls within item 1 of that Table, item 17, 23 or 24 of that Table).

Cross-references—See FA 2014 s 226(7) (application of paras 9–18 of this Schedule, with any necessary modifications, to penalties for failure to pay accelerated payment).

Amendments—Sub-para (1) substituted by F(No 3)A 2010 s 27, Sch 11 paras 1, 10 with effect as follows—

– from 25 January 2011 in respect of the following amounts of tax specified in column 3 of the Table in Sch 56 para 1—
  – item 2 (PAYE regulations);
  – item 3 (returns under FA 2004 s 254(1));
  – item 4 (FA 2004 s 62); and
  – items 17, 23 and 24 but only insofar as the tax falls within any of items 2, 3 or 4.

for remaining purposes from a date to be appointed by Treasury order.

Sub-para (1) as substituted reads as follows—

"(1) If P satisfies HMRC or (on appeal) the First-tier Tribunal or Upper Tribunal that there is a reasonable excuse for a failure to make a payment—

(a) liability to a penalty under any paragraph of this Schedule does not arise in relation to that failure, and

(b) the failure does not count as a default for the purposes of paragraphs 6, 8B, 8C, 8G and 8H.".

Double jeopardy

17 P is not liable to a penalty under any paragraph of this Schedule in respect of a failure or action in respect of which P has been convicted of an offence.

Commencement—Finance Act 2009, Schedule 56 (Appointed Day and Consequential Provisions) Order, SI 2010/466: 6 April 2010 appointed as day on which Sch 56 comes into force for the following amounts specified in column 3 of the Table—items 2–4, and items 17, 23 and 24 but only in so far as the tax falls within any of items 2, 3 or 4 (see SI 2010/466 art 3).

Finance Act 2009, Schedules 55 and 56 (Income Tax Self Assessment and Pension Schemes) (Appointed Days and Consequential and Savings Provisions) Order, SI 2011/702 art 2 (appointed day for the coming into force of Sch 56 is 6 April 2011 in relation to an amount of tax which is payable in relation to the tax year 2010–11 or any subsequent tax year and falls within item 1, 12, 18 or 19 of the Table in para 1, or in so far as the tax falls within item 1 of that Table, item 17, 23 or 24 of that Table).

Cross-references—See FA 2014 s 226(7) (application of paras 9–18 of this Schedule, with any necessary modifications, to penalties for failure to pay accelerated payment).

Interpretation

18—(1) This paragraph applies for the construction of this Schedule.

(2) "HMRC" means Her Majesty's Revenue and Customs.

(3) References to tax include construction industry deductions under Chapter 3 of Part 3 of FA 2004.

(4) References to a determination, in relation to an amount payable under PAYE regulations or under Chapter 3 of Part 3 of FA 2004, include a certificate.

(5) References to an assessment to tax, in relation to inheritance tax and stamp duty reserve tax, are to a determination.

Commencement—Finance Act 2009, Schedule 56 (Appointed Day and Consequential Provisions) Order, SI 2010/466: 6 April 2010 appointed as day on which Sch 56 comes into force for the following amounts specified in column 3 of the Table—items 2–4, and items 17, 23 and 24 but only in so far as the tax falls within any of items 2, 3 or 4 (see SI 2010/466 art 3).

Finance Act 2009, Schedules 55 and 56 (Income Tax Self Assessment and Pension Schemes) (Appointed Days and Consequential and Savings Provisions) Order, SI 2011/702 art 2 (appointed day for the coming into force of Sch 56 is 6 April 2011 in relation to an amount of tax which is payable in relation to the tax year 2010–11 or any subsequent tax year and falls within item 1, 12, 18 or 19 of the Table in para 1, or in so far as the tax falls within item 1 of that Table, item 17, 23 or 24 of that Table).

Cross-references—See FA 2014 s 226(7) (application of paras 9–18 of this Schedule, with any necessary modifications, to penalties for failure to pay accelerated payment).

FINANCE ACT 2010

(2010 Chapter 13)

[8 April 2010]

PART 1
CHARGES, RATES ETC

Inheritance tax

8 Rate bands

(1) The Table substituted in Schedule 1 to IHTA 1984 by section 155(1)(*b*) and (4) of FA 2006 (which provides for a rate of nil per cent on such portion of the value concerned as does not exceed £325,000 and a rate of 40 per cent on such portion as exceeds that amount) has effect in relation to chargeable transfers made on or after 6 April 2010.

(2) Accordingly, omit—

(*a*) in IHTA 1984, the Table substituted in Schedule 1 in relation to chargeable transfers made on or after that date (which provided for a rate of nil per cent on such portion of the value concerned as does not exceed £350,000 and a rate of 40 per cent on such portion as exceeds that amount), and

(*b*) in FA 2007, section 4 (which substituted it).

(3) Section 8 of IHTA 1984 (indexation) does not have effect by virtue of any difference between the retail prices index for the month of September in 2010, 2011, 2012 or 2013 and the previous September.

PART 2
ANTI-AVOIDANCE AND REVENUE PROTECTION

Inheritance tax

52 Reversionary interests of purchaser or settlor etc in relevant property

(1) In IHTA 1984, after section 81 insert—

"81A Reversionary interests in relevant property

(1) Where a reversionary interest in relevant property to which—

(*a*) a person who acquired it for a consideration in money or money's worth, or

(*b*) the settlor or the spouse or civil partner of the settlor,

(a "relevant reversioner") is beneficially entitled comes to an end by reason of the relevant reversioner becoming entitled to an interest in possession in the relevant property, the relevant reversioner is to be treated as having made a disposition of the reversionary interest at that time.

(2) A transfer of value of a reversionary interest in relevant property to which a relevant reversioner is beneficially entitled is to be taken to be a transfer which is not a potentially exempt transfer."

(2) The amendment made by subsection (1) has effect in relation to reversionary interests to which a relevant reversioner becomes beneficially entitled on or after 9 December 2009.

53 Interests in possession

(1) IHTA 1984 is amended as follows.

(2) In section 3A (potentially exempt transfers)—

(*a*) in subsection (6), omit "other than section 52", and

(*b*) after that subsection insert—

"(6A) The reference in subsection (6) above to any provision of this Act does not include section 52 below except where the transfer of value treated as made by that section is one treated as made on the coming to an end of an interest which falls within section 5(1B) below."

(3) In section 5 (meaning of estate)—

(*a*) in subsection (1)(*a*)(ii), after "below" insert "unless it falls within subsection (1B) below", and

(*b*) after subsection (1A) insert—

"(1B) An interest in possession falls within this subsection if the person—

(*a*) was domiciled in the United Kingdom on becoming beneficially entitled to it, and

(*b*) became beneficially entitled to it by virtue of a disposition which was prevented from being a transfer of value by section 10 below."

(4) In—

(*a*) section 49(1A) (treatment of interests in possession),

(*b*) section 51(1A) (disposal of interest in possession), and

(*c*) section 52(2A) and (3A) (charge on termination of interest in possession),

insert at the end (not as part of paragraph (c))—

"or falls within section 5(1B) above."

(5) In section 57A(1A) (relief where property enters maintenance fund), insert at the end (not as part of paragraph (*c*))—

"or fell within section 5(1B) above."

(6) In section 100(1A) (alterations of capital etc where participators are trustees), insert at the end (not as part of paragraph (*c*))—

"or falls within section 5(1B) above."

(7) In section 101(1A) (companies' interests in settled property), insert at the end (not as part of paragraph (*b*))—

"or falls within section 5(1B) above."

(8) In section 102ZA(1)(*b*)(ii) of FA 1986 (gifts with reservation: termination of interests in possession), after "serial interest" insert "or falls within section 5(1B) of the 1984 Act".

(9) In F(No 2)A 1987, omit section 96(2)(*c*).

(10) The amendments made by this section have effect in relation to an interest in possession to which a person is beneficially entitled if the person becomes beneficially entitled to it on or after 9 December 2009.

SCHEDULE 6

CHARITIES AND COMMUNITY AMATEUR SPORTS CLUBS: DEFINITIONS

Section 30

PART 1

DEFINITION OF "CHARITY", "CHARITABLE COMPANY" AND "CHARITABLE TRUST"

Definition of "charity" etc

1 (1) For the purposes of the enactments to which this Part applies "charity" means a body of persons or trust that—

(*a*) is established for charitable purposes only,

(*b*) meets the jurisdiction condition (see paragraph 2),

(*c*) meets the registration condition (see paragraph 3), and

(*d*) meets the management condition (see paragraph 4).

(2) For the purposes of the enactments to which this Part applies—

"charitable company" means a charity that is a body of persons;

"charitable trust" means a charity that is a trust.

(3) Sub-paragraphs (1) and (2) are subject to any express provision to the contrary.

(4) For the meaning of "charitable purpose", see [section 2 of the Charities Act 2011][1] (which—

(*a*) applies regardless of where the body of persons or trust in question is established, and

(*b*) for this purpose forms part of the law of each part of the United Kingdom [(see sections 7 and 8 of that Act)][1]).

Cross-reference—Finance Act 2010, Schedule 6, Part 1 (Further Consequential and Incidental Provision etc) Order, SI 2012/735, arts 5, 6 (definition of "charity" in Part 1 of this Schedule applies for the purposes of enactments relating to value added tax, and capital gains tax).

FA 2015 s 123 (in the enactments to which FA 2010 Sch 6 Part 1 applies, any reference to a charity includes —

(a) the Commonwealth War Graves Commission, and

(b) the Imperial War Graves Endowment Fund Trustees.)

Amendments—[1] In sub-para (4) words substituted by the Charities Act 2011 s 354, Sch 7 para 143(1), (2) with effect from 14 March 2012.

Jurisdiction condition

2 (1) A body of persons or trust meets the jurisdiction condition if it falls to be subject to the control of—

(*a*) a relevant UK court in the exercise of its jurisdiction with respect to charities, or

(*b*) any other court in the exercise of a corresponding jurisdiction under the law of a relevant territory.

(2) In sub-paragraph (1)(*a*) "a relevant UK court" means—

(*a*) the High Court,

(*b*) the Court of Session, or

(*c*) the High Court in Northern Ireland.

[(and, for enactments relating to value added tax, includes the High Court of the Isle of Man).][1]

(3) In sub-paragraph (1)(*b*) "a relevant territory" means—

(*a*) a member State other than the United Kingdom, or

(*b*) a territory specified in regulations made by the Commissioners for Her Majesty's Revenue and Customs.

(4) Regulations under this paragraph are to be made by statutory instrument.

(5) A statutory instrument containing regulations under this paragraph is subject to annulment in pursuance of a resolution of the House of Commons.

Regulations—Taxes (Definition of Charity) (Relevant Territories) Regulations, SI 2010/1904 (the Republic of Iceland and the Kingdom of Norway specified as "relevant territories" for the purposes of the meaning of a relevant territory in sub-para (3)).
Taxes (Definition of Charity) (Relevant Territories) Regulations, SI 2014/1807 (the Principality of Liechtenstein specified as a "relevant territory" for the purposes of the meaning of a relevant territory in sub-para (3)).

Cross-reference—Finance Act 2010, Schedule 6, Part 1 (Further Consequential and Incidental Provision etc) Order, SI 2012/735, arts 5, 6 (definition of "charity" in Part 1 of this Schedule applies for the purposes of enactments relating to value added tax, and capital gains tax).
FA 2015 s 123 (in the enactments to which FA 2010 Sch 6 Part 1 applies, any reference to a charity includes —

(a) the Commonwealth War Graves Commission, and
(b) the Imperial War Graves Endowment Fund Trustees.)

Amendments[1] Para 2(2): words in square brackets inserted by FA 2016 s 125 with effect from 15 September 2016.

Registration condition

3 (1) A body of persons or trust meets the registration condition if—

(*a*) in the case of a body of persons or trust that is a charity [within the meaning of section 10 the Charities Act 2011][1], condition A is met, and
(*b*) in the case of any other body of persons or trust, condition B is met.

(2) Condition A is that the body of persons or trust has complied with any requirement to be registered in the register of charities kept under [section 29 of the Charities Act 2011][1].

(3) Condition B is that the body of persons or trust has complied with any requirement under the law of a territory outside England and Wales to be registered in a register corresponding to that mentioned in sub-paragraph (2).

Cross-reference—Finance Act 2010, Schedule 6, Part 1 (Further Consequential and Incidental Provision etc) Order, SI 2012/735, arts 5, 6 (definition of "charity" in Part 1 of this Schedule applies for the purposes of enactments relating to value added tax, and capital gains tax).
FA 2015 s 123 (in the enactments to which FA 2010 Sch 6 Part 1 applies, any reference to a charity includes —

(a) the Commonwealth War Graves Commission, and
(b) the Imperial War Graves Endowment Fund Trustees.)

Amendments—[1] In sub-paras (1)(*a*), (2) words substituted by the Charities Act 2011 s 354, Sch 7 para 143(1), (3), (4) with effect from 14 March 2012.

Management condition

4 (1) A body of persons or trust meets the management condition if its managers are fit and proper persons to be managers of the body or trust.

(2) In this paragraph "managers", in relation to a body of persons or trust, means the persons having the general control and management of the administration of the body or trust.

Cross-reference—Finance Act 2010, Schedule 6, Part 1 (Further Consequential and Incidental Provision etc) Order, SI 2012/735, arts 5, 6 (definition of "charity" in Part 1 of this Schedule applies for the purposes of enactments relating to value added tax, and capital gains tax).
FA 2015 s 123 (in the enactments to which FA 2010 Sch 6 Part 1 applies, any reference to a charity includes —

(a) the Commonwealth War Graves Commission, and
(b) the Imperial War Graves Endowment Fund Trustees.)

Periods over which management condition treated as met

5 (1) This paragraph applies in relation to any period throughout which the management condition is not met.

(2) The management condition is treated as met throughout the period if the Commissioners for Her Majesty's Revenue and Customs consider that—

(*a*) the failure to meet the management condition has not prejudiced the charitable purposes of the body or trust, or
(*b*) it is just and reasonable in all the circumstances for the condition to be treated as met throughout the period.

Cross-reference—Finance Act 2010, Schedule 6, Part 1 (Further Consequential and Incidental Provision etc) Order, SI 2012/735, arts 5, 6 (definition of "charity" in Part 1 of this Schedule applies for the purposes of enactments relating to value added tax, and capital gains tax).
FA 2015 s 123 (in the enactments to which FA 2010 Sch 6 Part 1 applies, any reference to a charity includes —

(a) the Commonwealth War Graves Commission, and
(b) the Imperial War Graves Endowment Fund Trustees.)

Publication of names and addresses of bodies or trusts regarded by HMRC as charities

6 Her Majesty's Revenue and Customs may publish the name and address of any body of persons or trust that appears to them to meet, or at any time to have met, the definition of a charity in paragraph 1.

Cross-reference—Finance Act 2010, Schedule 6, Part 1 (Further Consequential and Incidental Provision etc) Order, SI 2012/735, arts 5, 6 (definition of "charity" in Part 1 of this Schedule applies for the purposes of enactments relating to value added tax, and capital gains tax).

FA 2015 s 123 (in the enactments to which FA 2010 Sch 6 Part 1 applies, any reference to a charity includes —

(a) the Commonwealth War Graves Commission, and

(b) the Imperial War Graves Endowment Fund Trustees.)

Enactments to which this Part applies

7 The enactments to which this Part applies are the enactments relating to—

(*a*) income tax

(*b*) capital gains tax,

(*c*) corporation tax,

(*d*) value added tax,

(*e*) inheritance tax,

(*f*) stamp duty,

(*g*) stamp duty land tax, . . . [1]

(*h*) stamp duty reserve tax[, . . . [2]

(*i*) annual tax on enveloped dwellings][1][, and

[(*j*) diverted profits tax.][2]

Amendments—[1] Word "and" in para (*g*) repealed, and para (*i*) inserted, by FA 2013 s 168, Sch 35 para 3 with effect from 17 July 2013.

[2] Word "and" in para (*h*) repealed, and para (*j*) inserted, by FA 2015 s 115(2) with effect in relation to accounting periods beginning on or after 1 April 2015. For accounting periods that straddle that date, see FA 2015 s 116(2), (3).

Cross-reference—Finance Act 2010, Schedule 6, Part 1 (Further Consequential and Incidental Provision etc) Order, SI 2012/735, arts 5, 6 (definition of "charity" in Part 1 of this Schedule applies for the purposes of enactments relating to value added tax, and capital gains tax).

FA 2015 s 123 (in the enactments to which FA 2010 Sch 6 Part 1 applies, any reference to a charity includes —

(a) the Commonwealth War Graves Commission, and

(b) the Imperial War Graves Endowment Fund Trustees.)

PART 2
REPEALS OF SUPERSEDED DEFINITIONS AND OTHER CONSEQUENTIAL AMENDMENTS

FA 1982

8 (*amends* FA 1982 s 129(1))

Commencement—Finance Act 2010, Schedule 6, Part 2 (Commencement) Order, SI 2012/736 art 3 (para 8 comes into force in relation to any conveyance, transfer or lease made or agreed to be made on or after 1 April 2012).

FA 1983

9 (*amends* FA 1983 s 46(3))

Commencement—Finance Act 2010, Schedule 6, Part 2 (Commencement) Order, SI 2012/736 art 4 (para 9 comes into force on 1 April 2012).

IHTA 1984

10 (*amends* IHTA 1984 s 272)

Commencement—Finance Act 2010, Schedule 6, Part 2 (Commencement) Order, SI 2012/736 art 5 (para 10 comes into force in respect of transfers of value made on or after 1 April 2012).

FA 1986

11 (*amends* FA 1986 s 90(7))

Commencement—Finance Act 2010, Schedule 6, Part 2 (Commencement) Order, SI 2012/736 art 6 (para 11 comes into force in relation to any agreement to transfer securities made on or after 1 April 2012).

FA 1989

12 (*repeals* FA 1989 Sch 5 para 4(10)).

Commencement—Finance Act 2010, Schedule 6, Part 2 (Commencement) Order, SI 2012/736 art 7 (para 12 comes into force in relation to trusts established on or after 1 April 2012).

TCGA 1992

13 (1) TCGA 1992 is amended as follows.

(2) (*amends* TCGA 1992 s 222(8B)(*b*)(*iii*).

(3) (*repeals* TCGA 1992 s 256(6), (8))
(4) (*repeals* TCGA 1992 s 256C(6))
(5) (*repeals*TCGA 1992 s 256D(7)).

Commencement—Finance Act 2010, Schedule 6, Part 2 (Commencement) Order, SI 2012/736 arts 8, 9 (the amendments made by para 13 come into force as follows:

- sub-para (2): in relation to living accommodation provided for a director on or after 6 April 2012 if that accommodation was not already provided for the director immediately before that date;
- sub-paras (3)–(5): for corporation tax purposes, for accounting periods beginning on or after 1 April 2012 and, for capital gains tax purposes, for the tax year 2012–13 and subsequent tax years.

F(No 2)A 1997

14 ...

Amendments—This para repealed by FA 2011 s 91, Sch 26 para 1(1), (2)(*b*)(ii) with effect from 19 July 2011.

FA 1999

15 (1) Schedule 19 to FA 1999 (stamp duty and stamp duty reserve tax: unit trusts) is amended as follows.
(2) (*amends* para 6(3))
(3) (*amends* para 15(*c*))

Commencement—Finance Act 2010, Schedule 6, Part 2 (Commencement) Order, SI 2012/736 arts 10, 11 (para 15(2) comes into force in relation to surrenders occurring on or after 1 April 2012; para 15(3) comes into force on 1 April 2012).

CAA 2001

16 (*amends* CAA 2001 s 63(2))

Commencement—Finance Act 2010, Schedule 6, Part 2 (Commencement) Order, SI 2012/736 art 12 (para 16 comes into force, for corporation tax purposes, for accounting periods beginning on or after 1 April 2012 and, for income tax purposes, for 2012–13 and subsequent tax years).

ITEPA 2003

17 (1) ITEPA 2003 is amended as follows.
(2) (*amends* ITEPA 2003 s 99(3)(*b*)(ii))
(3) (*amends* ITEPA 2003 s 216(3)(*b*))
(4) (*amends*ITEPA 2003 s 223(7)(*b*)(ii))
(5) I(*amends*ITEPA 2003 s 290(5))
(6) (*repeals* ITEPA 2003 s 351(5))
(7) (*amends* ITEPA 2003 s 714(2))

Commencement—Finance Act 2010, Schedule 6, Part 2 (Commencement) Order, SI 2012/736 art 13 (para 17 comes into effect for the tax year 2012–13 and subsequent tax years).

FA 2003

18 Schedule 8 to FA 2003 (SDLT: charities relief) is amended as follows.

Commencement—Finance Act 2010, Schedule 6, Part 2 (Commencement) Order, SI 2012/736 art 14 (para 18 comes into force in relation to a land transaction of which the effective date is on or after 1 April 2012).

19 (*repeals* FA 2003 Sch 8 para 1(4))

Commencement—Finance Act 2010, Schedule 6, Part 2 (Commencement) Order, SI 2012/736 art 14 (para 19 comes into force in relation to a land transaction of which the effective date is on or after 1 April 2012).

20 (*amends* FA 2003 Sch 8 para 4(2))

Commencement—Finance Act 2010, Schedule 6, Part 2 (Commencement) Order, SI 2012/736 art 14 (para 20 comes into force in relation to a land transaction of which the effective date is on or after 1 April 2012).

ITTOIA 2005

21 (1) ITTOIA 2005 is amended as follows.
(2) (*amends* ITTOIA 2005 s 410(3)(*b*))
(3) (*amends* ITTOIA 2005 s 545(1))
(4) (*amended*ITTOIA 2005 s 568(3); *repealed* by FA 2013 s 28, Sch 12 para 17)
(5) (*amends* ITTOIA 2005 Sch 4 Pt 2)

Commencement—Finance Act 2010, Schedule 6, Part 2 (Commencement) Order, SI 2012/736 art 15 (these amendments come into force for the tax year 2012–13 and subsequent tax years, subject to the following:

- the amendment made by sub-para (3) comes into force in relation to insurances and contracts made on or after 6 April 2012; and
- the amendment made by sub-para (5) comes into force in relation to insurances and contracts made on or after 6 April 2012, so far as the amendment applies in relation to ITTOIA 2005 Part 4 Chapter 9).

F(No 2)A 2005

22 (*amends* F(No 2)A s 18(3)(*b*)(i))

Commencement—Finance Act 2010, Schedule 6, Part 2 (Commencement) Order, SI 2012/736 art 16 (para 22 comes into force on 1 April 2012).

ITA 2007

23 (1) ITA 2007 is amended as follows.
(2) (*amends* ITA 2007 s 479(1)(*b*))
(3) (*amends* ITA 2007 s 481(1)(*c*))
(4) (*repeals* ITA 2007 s 519)
(5) (*amends*ITA 2007, s 873(2)(*a*), (*b*))
(6) (*amends* ITA 2007 s 989)
(7) (*amends* ITA 2007 Sch 4)

Commencement—Finance Act 2010, Schedule 6, Part 2 (Commencement) Order, SI 2012/736 arts 17, 18 (sub-paras (2)–(5), (7) come into force for the tax year 2012–13 and subsequent tax years; sub-para (6), so far as it applies for purposes other than those of ITA 2007 Part 8 Chapter 2, comes into force for the tax year 2012–13 and subsequent tax years).

FA 2008

24 (*amends* FA 2008 Sch 36 para 60(2))

Commencement—Finance Act 2010, Schedule 6, Part 2 (Commencement) Order, SI 2012/736 art 19 (para 24 comes into force on 1 April 2012).

CTA 2009

25 (1) CTA 2009 is amended as follows.
(2) In section 1319 (other definitions), omit the definition of "charity".
(3) In Schedule 4 (index of defined expressions), in the entry for "charity", for "section 1319" substitute "paragraph 1 of Schedule 6 to FA 2010".

FA 2009

26 (*amends* FA 2009 Sch 49 para 8)

Commencement—Finance Act 2010, Schedule 6, Part 2 (Commencement) Order, SI 2012/736 art 20 (para 26 comes into force on 1 April 2012).

CTA 2010

27 (1) CTA 2010 is amended as follows.
(2) (*amends* CTA 2010 s 202)
(3) (*amends* CTA 2010 s 217)
(4) (*repeals* CTA 2010 s 467)
(5) (*amends*CTA 2010 s 610(2)(*a*))
(6) (*amends* CTA 2010 s 1119)
(7) (*amends* CTA 2010 Sch 4)

Commencement—Finance Act 2010, Schedule 6, Part 2 (Commencement) Order, SI 2012/736 art 21 (para 27 comes into force as follows: for corporation tax purposes, for accounting periods beginning on or after 1 April 2012 and, for income tax purposes, for the tax year 2012-13 and subsequent tax years).

TIOPA 2010

28 (*amends* TIOPA 2010 s 326(3))

Commencement—Finance Act 2010, Schedule 6, Part 2 (Commencement) Order, SI 2012/736 art 22 (para 28 comes into force for accounting periods beginning on or after 1 April 2012).

Power to make further consequential provision

29 (1) The Commissioners for Her Majesty's Revenue and Customs may by order make such further consequential, incidental, supplemental, transitional or transitory provision or saving as appears appropriate in consequence of, or otherwise in connection with, Part 1.
(2) An order under this paragraph may—
   (*a*) make different provision for different purposes, and
   (*b*) make provision repealing, revoking or otherwise amending any enactment or instrument (whenever passed or made).
(3) An order under this paragraph is to be made by statutory instrument.
(4) A statutory instrument containing an order under this paragraph is subject to annulment in pursuance of an order of the House of Commons.

Regulations—Finance Act 2010, Schedule 6, Part 1 (Further Consequential and Incidental Provision etc) Order, SI 2012/735.

PART 3
MEANING OF "COMMUNITY AMATEUR SPORTS CLUB"

30 Chapter 9 of Part 13 of CTA 2010 (community amateur sports clubs) is amended as follows.

31 (*amended* CTA 2010 s 658; *repealed by* FA 2012 s 52(2))

32 (*inserts* CTA 2010 s 661A–661C)

PART 4
COMMENCEMENT

Commencement of Part 1

33 (1) Part 1 is treated as having come into force on 6 April 2010.
(2) But the definitions of "charity", "charitable company" and "charitable trust" in that Part do not apply for the purposes of an enactment in relation to which, on that date, another definition applies until such time as that other definition ceases to have effect on the coming into force of provision made by or under Part 2.
(3) For provision about the coming into force of provision made by that Part, see paragraph 34.

Cross-reference—Finance Act 2010, Schedule 6, Part 1 (Further Consequential and Incidental Provision etc) Order, SI 2012/735, arts 5, 6 (definition of "charity" in Part 1 of this Schedule applies for the purposes of enactments relating to value added tax, and capital gains tax).

FA 2015 s 123 (in the enactments to which FA 2010 Sch 6 Part 1 applies, any reference to a charity includes —

(a) the Commonwealth War Graves Commission, and
(b) the Imperial War Graves Endowment Fund Trustees.)

Commencement of Part 2

34 (1) The repeal of the definition of "charity" in section 989 of ITA 2007 made by paragraph 23(6) above has effect—

(*a*) so far as it applies for the purposes of Chapter 2 of Part 8 of that Act (gift aid), in relation to gifts made on or after 6 April 2010, and
(*b*) so far as it applies for other purposes, in accordance with such provision as the Treasury may make by order.

(2) The other amendments made by Part 2 come into force in accordance with such provision as the Treasury may make by order.
(3) An order under this paragraph may—

(*a*) make different provision for different purposes, and
(*b*) include transitional provision and savings.

(4) An order under this paragraph is to be made by statutory instrument.

Orders—Finance Act 2010, Schedule 6, Part 2 (Commencement) Order, SI 2012/736.

Commencement of Part 3

35 The amendments made by Part 3 are treated as having come into force on 6 April 2010.

FINANCE (NO 3) ACT 2010
(2010 Chapter 33)

An ACT TO Grant certain duties, to alter other duties, and to amend the law relating to the National Debt and the Public Revenue, and to make further provision in connection with finance.

[16 December 2010]

PART 4
MISCELLANEOUS PROVISIONS

31 Asbestos compensation settlements

Schedule 14 contains provision about the taxation of settlements the purpose of which is to make compensation payments to or in respect of individuals affected by an asbestos-related condition.

SCHEDULE 14
ASBESTOS COMPENSATION SETTLEMENTS
Section 31

Inheritance tax

1 (1) Section 58 of IHTA 1984 (relevant property) is amended as follows.
(2) (*amends* IHTA 1984 s 58(1))
(3) (*inserts* IHTA 1984 s 58(4), (5))
(4) The amendments made by this paragraph are treated as having come into force on 6 April 2006.

POSTAL SERVICES ACT 2011

(2011 Chapter 5)

An Act to make provision for the restructuring of the Royal Mail group and about the Royal Mail Pension Plan; to make new provision about the regulation of postal services, including provision for a special administration regime; and for connected purposes.

[13th June 2011]

Commencement—1 October 2011: see SI 2011/2329, art 3(1).

BE IT ENACTED by the Queen's most Excellent Majesty, by and with the advice and consent of the Lords Spiritual and Temporal, and Commons, in this present Parliament assembled, and by the authority of the same, as follows:—

PART 2
ROYAL MAIL PENSION PLAN

Supplementary provisions

23 Taxation

(1) The Treasury may by regulations make provision for varying the way in which any relevant tax would, apart from the regulations, have effect in relation to—
  (a) a new public scheme,
  (b) members of a new public scheme, or
  (c) a fund within section 21(1)(c).
(2) Regulations under subsection (1) may include provision for treating a new public scheme as a registered pension scheme.
(3) The Treasury may by regulations make provision for varying the way in which any relevant tax would, apart from the regulations, have effect in relation to, or in connection with, anything done in relation to—
  (a) the RMPP, or
  (b) any members of the RMPP,
by or under, or in consequence of, an order made under this Part.
(4) Regulations under subsection (1) or (3) may include provision for any of the following—
  (a) a tax provision not to apply or to apply with modifications,
  (b) anything done to have or not to have a specified consequence for the purposes of a tax provision, and
  (c) the withdrawal of relief and the charging of a relevant tax.
(5) Provision made by regulations under subsection (1) or (3), other than provision withdrawing a relief or charging a relevant tax, may have retrospective effect.
(6) The Treasury may by regulations make provision, in relation to qualifying accounting periods, for extinguishing such losses made in a trade as they consider are attributable to deductions made for, or in connection with, contributions in respect of qualifying members of the RMPP.
(7) A "qualifying" accounting period is one beginning on or after the date ("the trigger date") on which an order under section 17 is made establishing a new public scheme or transferring qualifying accrued rights to a new public scheme.
(8) Regulations under subsection (6) have effect only if the company whose losses are extinguished is wholly owned by the Crown (within the meaning of Part 1) on the day before the trigger date.
(9) In this section—
  "relevant tax" means—
    (a) income tax,
    (b) capital gains tax,
    (c) corporation tax,
    (d) inheritance tax,
    (e) stamp duty and stamp duty reserve tax, and

(f) stamp duty land tax,

"registered pension scheme" has the same meaning as in Part 4 of the Finance Act 2004,

"tax provision" means any provision made by or under an enactment relating to a relevant tax.

Regulations—Postal Services Act 2011 (Taxation) Regulations, SI 2012/764.

FINANCE ACT 2011

(2011 Chapter 11)

[19 July 2011]

PART 2

INCOME TAX, CORPORATION TAX AND CAPITAL GAINS TAX

Chargeable gains

45 Company ceasing to be member of a group

Schedule 10 contains provision about the consequences, for the purposes of corporation tax on chargeable gains, of a company ceasing to be a member of a group.

PART 4

PENSIONS

65 Benefits under pension schemes

Schedule 16 contains provision about the benefits available under pension schemes and related matters.

70 Power to make further provision about section 67 pension scheme

(1) The Treasury may by regulations make provision for and in connection with—

(*a*) the application of the relevant taxes in relation to a pension scheme established under section 67 of the Pensions Act 2008, and

(*b*) the application of the relevant taxes in relation to any person in connection with such a pension scheme.

(2) The provision that may be made by regulations under this section includes provision imposing any of the relevant taxes (as well as provisions for exemptions or reliefs).

(3) The relevant taxes are—

(*a*) income tax,

(*b*) capital gains tax,

(*c*) corporation tax, and

(*d*) inheritance tax.

(4) Regulations under this section may include provision having effect in relation to any time before they are made if the provision does not increase any person's liability to tax.

(5) Regulations under this section may include—

(*a*) provision amending any enactment or instrument, and

(*b*) consequential, supplementary and transitional provision.

(6) Regulations under this section are to be made by statutory instrument.

(7) A statutory instrument containing regulations under this section is subject to annulment in pursuance of a resolution of the House of Commons.

Regulations—Finance Act 2004, Section 180(5) (Modification) Regulations, SI 2012/1258.

71 Tax provision consequential on Part 1 of Pensions Act 2008 etc

(1) The Treasury may by regulations make provision in relation to any of the relevant taxes in consequence of Part 1 of the Pensions Act 2008 or Part 1 of the Pensions (No 2) Act (Northern Ireland) 2008.

(2) The provision that may be made by regulations under this section includes provision imposing any of the relevant taxes (as well as provisions for exemptions or reliefs).

(3) The relevant taxes are—

(*a*) income tax,

(*b*) capital gains tax,

(*c*) corporation tax,

(*d*) inheritance tax,

(*e*) value added tax,

(*f*) stamp duty land tax,

(*g*) stamp duty, and

(*h*) stamp duty reserve tax.

(4) Regulations under this section may include provision having effect in relation to any time before they are made if the provision does not increase any person's liability to tax.

(5) Regulations under this section may make different provision for different cases.

(6) Regulations under this section may include—

(*a*) provision amending any enactment or instrument, and

(*b*) consequential, supplementary and transitional provision.

(7) Regulations under this section are to be made by statutory instrument.

(8) A statutory instrument containing regulations under this section is subject to annulment in pursuance of a resolution of the House of Commons.

PART 7

ADMINISTRATION ETC

86 Data-gathering powers

(1) Schedule 23 contains provision for officers of Revenue and Customs to obtain data from data-holders.

(2) . . .

SCHEDULE 10

COMPANY CEASING TO BE MEMBER OF GROUP

Section 45

Consequential repeals

8 In consequence of the repeals made by paragraph 5, the following are also repealed—

(*a*) in IHTA 1984, section 97(1)(*a*)(iii) and the "or" before it,

(*b*) . . .

(*c*) . . .

(*d*) . . .

Commencement

9 (1) The amendments made by paragraphs 1 to 5 and 8 have effect in relation to any disposal of an asset by one company ("company B") to another company ("company A") made at a time when company B is a member of a group, if—

(*a*) company A ceases to be a member of the group on or after the passing of this Act, or

(*b*) where company A ceased to be such a member before the passing of this Act in circumstances where section 179(6) to (8) of TCGA 1992 applied, company A ceases to satisfy the conditions in section 179(7) of that Act on or after the passing of this Act.

(2) The amendments made by paragraph 6 have effect in relation to disposals of shares made on or after the passing of this Act.

(3) The amendments made by paragraph 7 have effect in relation to any disposal of an asset by one company ("company B") to another company ("company A") made at a time when company B is a member of a group, if—

(*a*) company A ceases to be a member of the group on or after the passing of this Act, or

(*b*) where company A ceased to be such a member before the passing of this Act in circumstances where section 783 of CTA 2009 applied, company A ceases to be a member of another group on or after the passing of this Act.

(4) But where an early commencement election is made in relation to a group—

(*a*) sub-paragraphs (1) and (3) apply in relation to that group as if the references in those sub-paragraphs to the passing of this Act were references to 1 April 2011, and

(*b*) sub-paragraph (2) applies in relation to any disposal of shares by a member of that group as if the reference in that sub-paragraph to the passing of this Act were a reference to 1 April 2011.

(5) An early commencement election in relation to a group means an election made for the purposes of this paragraph by the principal company of the group.

(6) If a company ceases to be a member of a group in the period which begins with 1 April 2011 and ends with the passing of this Act, an early commencement election may be made or revoked in relation to the group only with the consent of that company contained in a notice which accompanies the election or revocation.

(7) Where an early commencement election is revoked, the election is treated as never having had effect.

(8) An early commencement election may not be made or revoked after 31 March 2012 (and paragraph 3(1)(*b*) of Schedule 1A to the Management Act (amendment of elections etc) does not apply in relation to an early commencement election).

SCHEDULE 16
BENEFITS UNDER PENSION SCHEMES
Section 65

PART 1
CHANGES TO BENEFITS AVAILABLE UNDER PENSION SCHEMES ETC

Removal of certain charges to inheritance tax in respect of pension schemes

46 IHTA 1984 is amended as follows.

47 (1) Section 12 (dispositions allowable for income tax or conferring benefits under pension scheme) is amended as follows.
(2) (*inserts* IHTA 1984 s 12(2ZA))
(3) (*repeals* IHTA 1984 s 12((2A)–(2E))

48 (*repeals* IHTA 1984 ss 151A–151E)

PART 2
CONSEQUENTIAL AMENDMENTS

Inheritance Tax Act 1984

49 IHTA 1984 is amended as follows.

50 (1) Section 12 (dispositions allowable for income tax or conferring benefits under pension scheme) is amended as follows.
(2), (*repeals* IHTA 1984 s 12(2F)(*b*))
(3) (*amends* IHTA 1984 s 12(2G))

51 (*amends* IHTA 1984 s 151(2))

52 In section 200 (transfer on death)—
(*a*) (*amends* IHTA 1984 s 200(1))
(*b*) (*repeals* IHTA 1984 s 200(1A))

53 (*repeals* IHTA 1984 s 210(2), (3))

54 (*amends* IHTA 1984 s 216(1), (3)(*a*), (4), (6), (7))

55 (*amends* IHTA 1984 s 226(4))

56 (*amends* IHTA 1984 s 233 (interest on unpaid tax)(1)(*c*))

57 (*amends* IHTA 1984 s 272)

Consequential repeals

84 In consequence of the amendments made by this Schedule, omit the following provisions—
(*a*) . . .
(*b*) in FA 2006—
(i) (*repeals* FA 2006 Sch 22 paras 3–9, 10(3), 12)
(ii) (*repeals* FA 2006 Sch 23 para 29)
(*c*) . . .
(*d*) in FA 2008—
(i) (*repeals* FA 2008 Sch 4, paras 4, 9(2))
(ii) (*repeals* FA 2008 Sch 28, paras 6–14)
(iii) (*repeals* FA 2008 Sch 29, para 16)
(*e*) . . .

PART 3
COMMENCEMENT AND TRANSITIONAL PROVISION

Inheritance tax

105 The amendments made by paragraphs 47 and 50 have effect in relation to dispositions made (or treated as made) on or after 6 April 2011.

106 The amendments made by paragraphs 48 and 51 to 57 have effect in relation to deaths occurring on or after 6 April 2011.

Consequential repeals

107 Any repeal in paragraph 84 has effect to the same extent as the provision of this Schedule to which the repeal relates.

SCHEDULE 23
DATA-GATHERING POWERS
Section 86(1)

Commentary—*Simon's Taxes* **A4.150**.
HMRC Manuals—Compliance Handbook, CH271400 (amount of penalty).

PART 1
POWER TO OBTAIN DATA

Power to give notice

1 (1) An officer of Revenue and Customs may by notice in writing require a relevant data-holder to provide relevant data.
(2) Part 2 of this Schedule sets out who is a relevant data-holder.
(3) In relation to a relevant data-holder, "relevant data" means data of a kind specified for that type of data-holder in regulations made by the Treasury.
(4) The data that a relevant data-holder may be required to provide—
(*a*) may be general data or data relating to particular persons or matters, and
(*b*) may include personal data (such as names and addresses of individuals).
(5) A notice under this paragraph is referred to as a data-holder notice.

Regulations—Data-gathering Powers (Relevant Data) Regulations, SI 2012/847.
Data-gathering Powers (Relevant Data) (Amendment) Regulations, SI 2015/672.
Data-gathering Powers (Relevant Data) (Amendment) Regulations, SI 2016/979.

Purpose of power

2 (1) The power in paragraph 1(1) is exercisable to assist with the efficient and effective discharge of HMRC's tax functions—
(*a*) whether a particular function or more generally, and
(*b*) whether involving a particular taxpayer or taxpayers generally.
(2) It is additional to and is not limited by other powers that HMRC may have to obtain data (for example, in Schedule 36 to FA 2008).
(3) But it may not be used (in place of the power in paragraph 1 of that Schedule) to obtain data required for the purpose of checking the relevant data-holder's own tax position.
(4) Sub-paragraph (3) does not prevent use of the power in paragraph 1(1) of this Schedule to obtain data about a matter mentioned in paragraph 14(3)(*a*) (beneficial ownership of certain payments etc).
(5) Nothing in this paragraph limits the use that may be made of data that have been obtained under this Schedule (see section 17(1) of CRCA 2005).

Specifying relevant data

3 (1) A data-holder notice must specify the relevant data to be provided.
(2) Relevant data may not be specified in a data-holder notice unless an officer of Revenue and Customs has reason to believe that the data could have a bearing on chargeable or other periods ending on or after the applicable day.
(3) The applicable day is the first day of the period of 4 years ending with the day on which the notice is given.

Compliance

4 (1) Relevant data specified in a data-holder notice must be provided by such means and in such form as is reasonably specified in the notice.
(2) If the notice specifies that the data are to be provided by sending them somewhere, the data must be sent to such address and within such period as is reasonably specified in the notice.
(3) If the notice specifies that the data are to be provided by making documents available for inspection somewhere, the documents must be made available for inspection at such place and time as is—
(*a*) reasonably specified in the notice, or
(*b*) agreed between an officer of Revenue and Customs and the data-holder.
(4) A place used solely as a dwelling may not be specified under sub-paragraph (3)(a).
(5) A data-holder notice requiring the provision of specified documents requires the documents to be provided only if they are in the data-holder's possession or power.

(6) A power in this paragraph to specify something in a notice includes power to specify it in a document referred to in the notice.

Approval by tribunal

5 (1) An officer of Revenue and Customs may ask for the approval of the tribunal before giving a data-holder notice.
(2) This does not require an officer to do so (but see paragraph 28(3) for the effect of obtaining approval).
(3) An application for approval under this paragraph may be made without notice (except as required under sub-paragraph (4)).
(4) The tribunal may not approve the giving of a data-holder notice unless—
- (*a*) the application for approval is made by, or with the agreement of, an authorised officer,
- (*b*) the tribunal is satisfied that, in the circumstances, the officer giving the notice is justified in doing so,
- (*c*) the data-holder has been told that the data are to be required and given a reasonable opportunity to make representations to an officer of Revenue and Customs, and
- (*d*) the tribunal has been given a summary of any representations made by the data-holder.

(5) Paragraphs (*c*) and (*d*) of sub-paragraph (4) do not apply to the extent that the tribunal is satisfied that taking the action specified in those paragraphs might prejudice any purpose for which the data are required.
(6) A decision by the tribunal under this paragraph is final (despite the provisions of sections 11 and 13 of the Tribunals, Courts and Enforcement Act 2007).
(7) "Authorised officer" means an officer of Revenue and Customs who is, or is a member of a class of officers who are, authorised by the Commissioners for the purposes of this paragraph.

Power to copy documents

6 An officer of Revenue and Customs may take copies of or make extracts from any document provided pursuant to a data-holder notice.

Power to retain documents

7 (1) If an officer of Revenue and Customs thinks it reasonable to do so, HMRC may retain documents provided pursuant to a data-holder notice for a reasonable period.
(2) While a document is being retained, the data-holder may, if the document is reasonably required for any purpose, request a copy of it.
(3) The retention of a document under this paragraph is not to be regarded as breaking any lien claimed on the document.
(4) If a document retained under this paragraph is lost or damaged, the Commissioners are liable to compensate the owner of the document for any expenses reasonably incurred in replacing or repairing the document.

PART 2
RELEVANT DATA-HOLDERS

Introduction

8 (1) This Part of this Schedule sets out who is a relevant data-holder for the purposes of this Schedule.
(2) Descriptions of the various types of data-holder are to be read as including anyone who was previously of such a description.

Salaries, fees, commission etc

9 (1) Each of the following is a relevant data-holder—
- (*a*) an employer,
- (*b*) a person who is concerned in making payments to or in respect of another person's employees with respect to their employment with that other person,
- (*c*) an approved agent within the meaning of section 714 of ITEPA 2003 (which relates to payroll giving), and
- (*d*) a person who carries on a business in connection with which relevant payments are or are likely to be made.

(2) Relevant payments are—
- (*a*) payments for or in connection with services provided by persons who are not employed in the business, or
- (*b*) periodical or lump sum payments in respect of any copyright, public lending right, right in a registered design or design right.

(3) Payments are taken to be made in connection with a business if they are made—

(*a*) in the course of carrying on the business or a part of it, or

(*b*) in connection with the formation, acquisition, development or disposal of the business or a part of it.

(4) Sub-paragraph (1)(*d*) applies to the carrying on of any other kind of activity as it applies to the carrying on of a business, but only if the activity is being carried on by a body of persons (and references in sub-paragraphs (2) and (3) to the business are to be read accordingly).

(5) A reference in this paragraph to the making of payments includes—

(*a*) the provision of benefits, and

(*b*) the giving of any other valuable consideration.

Cross-references—See Data-gathering Powers (Relevant Data) Regulations, SI 2012/847 reg 3 (relevant data for data-holders under this para).

10 (1) This paragraph applies if—

(*a*) services that an individual provides or is obliged to provide under an agency contract are treated under section 44(2) of ITEPA 2003 as the duties of an employment held by the individual with the agency, or

(*b*) remuneration receivable under or in consequence of arrangements falling within section 45 of that Act is treated as earnings from an employment held by an individual with the agency.

(2) For the purposes of paragraph 9—

(*a*) the individual is treated as being employed by the agency, and

(*b*) payments made to the individual under or in consequence of the agency contract, or treated as earnings under section 45 of ITEPA 2003, do not count as "relevant payments".

(3) "Agency contract" and "remuneration" have the same meaning as in Chapter 7 of Part 2 of ITEPA 2003.

11 (1) This paragraph applies if—

(*a*) a person ("A") performs in the United Kingdom duties of an employment,

(*b*) the employment is under or with a person resident outside and not resident in the United Kingdom,

(*c*) the duties performed in the United Kingdom are performed for a continuous period of not less than 30 days, and

(*d*) those duties are performed for the benefit of a person ("B") resident or carrying on a trade, profession or vocation in the United Kingdom.

(2) For the purposes of paragraph 9—

(*a*) B is treated as if B were an employer, but

(*b*) only the name and place of residence of A may be specified for a relevant data-holder of B's type in regulations made under paragraph 1(3).

Cross-references—See Data-gathering Powers (Relevant Data) Regulations, SI 2012/847 reg 4 (relevant data for data-holders under this para).

Interest etc

12 (1) A person by or through whom interest is paid or credited is a relevant data-holder.

(2) For the purposes of this paragraph, the following are to be treated as interest—

(*a*) a dividend in respect of a share in a building society,

(*b*) an amount to which a person holding a deeply discounted security is entitled on the redemption of that security,

(*c*) a foreign dividend, and

(*d*) an alternative finance return.

(3) In sub-paragraph (2)—

"alternative finance return" means—

(*a*) an alternative finance return within the meaning of Part 10A of ITA 2007, and

(*b*) an alternative finance return within the meaning of Part 6 of CTA 2009;

"building society" means a building society within the meaning of the Building Societies Act 1986;

"deeply discounted security" has the same meaning as in Chapter 8 of Part 4 of ITTOIA 2005;

"foreign dividend" means any annual payment, interest or dividend payable out of, or in respect of the funds or securities of—

(*a*) a body of persons that is not resident in the United Kingdom, or

(*b*) a government or public or local authority in a country outside the United Kingdom.

Cross-references—See Data-gathering Powers (Relevant Data) Regulations, SI 2012/847 regs 5–7 (relevant data for data-holders under this para).

Income, assets etc belonging to others

13 A person who (in whatever capacity) is in receipt of money or value of or belonging to another is a relevant data-holder.

Cross–references—See Data-gathering Powers (Relevant Data) Regulations, SI 2012/847 reg 11 (relevant data for data-holders under this para).

[Merchant acquirers etc

13A—(1) A person who has a contractual obligation to make payments to retailers in settlement of payment card transactions is a relevant data-holder.

(2) In this paragraph—

"payment card" includes a credit card, a charge card and a debit card;

"payment card transaction" means any transaction in which a payment card is accepted as payment;

"retailer" means a person who accepts a payment card as payment for any transaction.

(3) In this paragraph any reference to a payment card being accepted as payment includes a reference to any account number or other indicators associated with a payment card being accepted as payment.][1]

Amendments—[1] Para 13A inserted by FA 2013 s 228 with effect in relation to relevant data with a bearing on any period (whether before, on or after 17 July 2013).

[Providers of electronic stored-value payment services

13B (1) A person who provides electronic stored-value payment services is a relevant data-holder.

(2) In this paragraph "electronic stored-value payment services" means services by means of which monetary value is stored electronically for the purpose of payments being made in respect of transactions to which the provider of those services is not a party.][1]

Amendments—[1] Paragraphs 13B, 13C inserted by FA 2016 s 176 with effect in relation to relevant data with a bearing on any period (whether before, on or after 15 September 2016).

[Business intermediaries

13C (1) A person who—

(*a*) provides services to enable or facilitate transactions between suppliers and their customers or clients (other than services provided solely to enable payments to be made), and

(*b*) receives information about such transactions in the course of doing so,

is a relevant data-holder.

(2) In this paragraph "suppliers" means persons supplying goods or services in the course of business.

(3) For the purposes of this paragraph, information about transactions includes information that is capable of indicating the likely quantity or value of transactions.][1]

Amendments—[1] Paragraphs 13B, 13C inserted by FA 2016 s 176 with effect in relation to relevant data with a bearing on any period (whether before, on or after 15 September 2016).

[Money service businesses

13D (1) A person is a relevant data-holder if the person—

(*a*) carries on any of the activities in sub-paragraph (2) by way of business,

(*b*) is a relevant person within the meaning of regulation 8(1) of the Money Laundering, Terrorist Financing and Transfer of Funds (Information on the Payer) Regulations 2017 (SI 2017/692), and

(*c*) is not an excluded credit institution.

(2) The activities referred to in sub-paragraph (1)(*a*) are—

(*a*) operating a currency exchange office;

(*b*) transmitting money (or any representation of monetary value) by any means;

(*c*) cashing cheques which are made payable to customers.

(3) An excluded credit institution is a credit institution which has permission to carry on the regulated activity of accepting deposits—

(*a*) under Part 4A of the Financial Services and Markets Act 2000 (permission to carry on regulated activities), or

(*b*) resulting from Part 2 of Schedule 3 to that Act (exercise of passport rights by EEA firms).

(4) Sub-paragraph (3) is to be read with section 22 of and Schedule 2 to the Financial Services and Markets Act 2000, and any order under that section (classes of regulated activities).

(5) In this paragraph "credit institution" has the meaning given by Article 4.1(1) of Regulation (EU) No 575/2013 of the European Parliament and of the Council of 26 June 2013 on prudential requirements for credit institutions and investment firms.][1]

Amendments—[1] Paragraph 13D inserted by F(No 2)A 2017 s 69 with effect in relation to relevant data with a bearing on any period (whether before, on or after 16 November 2017).

Payments derived from securities

14 (1) Each of the following is a relevant data-holder—

(*a*) a person who is the registered or inscribed holder of securities,

(*b*) a person who receives a payment derived from securities or would be entitled to do so if a payment were made,

(*c*) a person who receives a payment treated by the company that makes it as a payment to which section 1033 of CTA 2010 applies (purchase by unquoted trading company of own shares), and

(*d*) a person who receives a chargeable payment within the meaning of Chapter 5 of Part 23 of CTA 2010 (company distributions: demergers).

(2) But, for a relevant data-holder of a type described in this paragraph, data may only be specified in regulations under paragraph 1(3) if the data concern a matter mentioned in sub-paragraph (3).

(3) The matters are—

(*a*) whether the relevant data-holder is the beneficial owner (or sole beneficial owner) of the securities or payment in question,

(*b*) if not—

(i) details of the beneficial owner (or other beneficial owners), and

(ii) if those details are not known or if different, details of the person for whom the securities are held or to whom the payment is or may be paid on, and

(*c*) if there is more than one beneficial owner or more than one person of the kind mentioned in paragraph (*b*)(ii), their respective interests in the securities or payment.

(4) "Payment derived from securities" includes in particular—

(*a*) an amount (whether of income or capital) that is payable out of or in respect of securities or rights attaching to securities, and

(*b*) a payment that is representative of any such amount.

Cross–references—See Data-gathering Powers (Relevant Data) Regulations, SI 2012/847 reg 12 (relevant data for data-holders under this para).

15 (1) A person who makes a payment derived from securities that has been received from or is paid on behalf of another is a relevant data-holder.

(2) "Payment derived from securities" has the same meaning as in paragraph 14.

Cross–references—See Data-gathering Powers (Relevant Data) Regulations, SI 2012/847 reg 13 (relevant data for data-holders under this para).

Grants and subsidies out of public funds

16 (1) A person by whom a payment out of public funds is made by way of grant or subsidy is a relevant data-holder.

(2) For these purposes, a payment is a payment out of public funds if it is provided directly or indirectly by—

(*a*) the Crown,

(*b*) any government, public or local authority whether in the United Kingdom or elsewhere, or

(*c*) any EU institution.

Cross–references—See Data-gathering Powers (Relevant Data) Regulations, SI 2012/847 reg 14 (relevant data for data-holders under this para).

Licences, approvals etc

17 (1) A person by whom licences or approvals are issued or a register is maintained is a relevant data-holder.

(2) "Register" includes—

(*a*) any record or list that a local authority maintains, and

(*b*) any record or list that any other person is required or permitted to maintain by or under an enactment.

Cross–references—See Data-gathering Powers (Relevant Data) Regulations, SI 2012/847 reg 15 (relevant data for data-holders under this para).

Rent and other payments arising from land

18 (1) Each of the following is a relevant data-holder—

(*a*) a lessee (or successor in title of a lessee),

(*b*) an occupier of land,

(*c*) a person having the use of land, and
(*d*) a person who, as agent, manages land or is in receipt of rent or other payments arising from land.

(2) The reference to a person who manages land includes a person who markets property to potential tenants, searches for tenants or provides similar services.

Cross-references—See Data-gathering Powers (Relevant Data) Regulations, SI 2012/847 reg 16 (relevant data for data-holders under this para).

Dealing etc in securities

19 (1) Each of the following is a relevant data-holder—
(*a*) a person who effects or is a party to securities transactions wholly or partly on behalf of others (whether as agent or principal),
(*b*) a person who, in the course of business, acts as registrar or administrator in respect of securities transactions (including a person who manages a clearing house for any terminal market in securities),
(*c*) a person who makes a payment derived from securities to anyone other than the registered or inscribed holder of the securities,
(*d*) a person who makes a payment derived from bearer securities, and
(*e*) an accountable person within the meaning of the Stamp Duty Reserve Tax Regulations 1986 (S.I. 1986/1711).

(2) "Payment derived from securities" has the same meaning as in paragraph 14 (and "payment derived from bearer securities" is to be read accordingly).

(3) "Securities transactions" means—
(*a*) transactions in securities,
(*b*) transactions under which a representative payment has been, is to be or may be made, or
(*c*) the making or receipt of a representative payment.

(4) In sub-paragraph (3)—

"representative payment" means a payment that is representative of an amount payable out of or in respect of securities or rights attaching to securities;

"transactions in securities" means transactions, of whatever description, relating to securities, and includes in particular—
(*a*) the purchase, sale or exchange of securities,
(*b*) issuing or securing the issue of new securities,
(*c*) applying or subscribing for new securities, and
(*d*) altering or securing the alteration of rights attached to securities.

Cross-references—See Data-gathering Powers (Relevant Data) Regulations, SI 2012/847 reg 17 (relevant data for data-holders under this para).

Dealing in other property

20 Each of the following is a relevant data-holder—
(*a*) the committee or other person or body of persons responsible for managing a clearing house for any terminal market in commodities,
(*b*) an auctioneer,
(*c*) a person carrying on a business of dealing in any description of tangible movable property, and
(*d*) a person carrying on a business of acting as an agent or intermediary in dealings in any description of tangible movable property.

Cross-references—See Data-gathering Powers (Relevant Data) Regulations, SI 2012/847 reg 18 (relevant data for data-holders under this para).

Lloyd's

21 A person who is registered as managing agent at Lloyd's in relation to a syndicate of underwriting members of Lloyd's is a relevant data-holder.

Cross-references—See Data-gathering Powers (Relevant Data) Regulations, SI 2012/847 reg 19 (relevant data for data-holders under this para).

Investment plans etc

22 Each of the following is a relevant data-holder—
(*a*) a plan manager (see section 696 of ITTOIA 2005), and
(*b*) an account provider in relation to a child trust fund (as defined in section 3 of the Child Trust Funds Act 2004).

Cross–references—See Data-gathering Powers (Relevant Data) Regulations, SI 2012/847 reg 20 (relevant data for data-holders under this para).

Petroleum activities

23 Each of the following is a relevant data-holder—

(*a*) the holder of a licence granted under Part 1 of the Petroleum Act 1998, and

(*b*) the responsible person in relation to an oil field (within the meaning of Part 1 of OTA 1975).

Cross–references—See Data-gathering Powers (Relevant Data) Regulations, SI 2012/847 reg 21 (relevant data for data-holders under this para).

Insurance activities

24 Each of the following is a relevant data-holder—

(*a*) a person who is involved (in any capacity) in an insurance business (as defined for the purposes of Part 3 of FA 1994),

(*b*) a person who makes arrangements for persons to enter into contracts of insurance, and

(*c*) a person who is concerned in a business that is not an insurance business and who has been involved in the entering into of a contract of insurance that provides cover for any matter associated with the business.

Cross–references—See Data-gathering Powers (Relevant Data) Regulations, SI 2012/847 reg 22 (relevant data for data-holders under this para).

[Chargeable soft drinks

24A (1) A person who is involved (in any capacity) in any of the following activities is a relevant data-holder—

(*a*) producing chargeable soft drinks;

(*b*) packaging chargeable soft drinks;

(*c*) carrying on a business involving the sale of chargeable soft drinks.

(2) For the purposes of sub-paragraph (1), "chargeable soft drinks", "producing" and "packaging" have the same meaning as in Part 3 of FA 2017.]

Prospective amendments—Paragraph 24A and preceding cross-head to be inserted by FA 2017 s 56, Sch 11 para 6(1), (2) with effect from a date to be appointed. Once appointed, the charge to soft drinks industry levy will arise on chargeable events which occur on or after 6 April 2018 (FA 2017 s 31(1)).

Environmental activities

25 A person who is involved (in any capacity) in any of the following activities is a relevant data-holder—

(*a*) subjecting aggregate to exploitation in the United Kingdom (as defined for the purposes of Part 2 of FA 2001) or connected activities,

(*b*) making or receiving supplies of taxable commodities (as defined for the purposes of Schedule 6 to FA 2000) or connected activities, and

(*c*) landfill disposal (as defined for the purposes of Part 3 of FA 1996).

Cross–references—See Data-gathering Powers (Relevant Data) Regulations, SI 2012/847 reg 23 (relevant data for data-holders under this para).

Prospective amendments—In para (*a*), words "England, Wales or Northern Ireland" to be substituted for words "the United Kingdom" by the Scotland Act 2016 s 18(3), Sch 1 para 13 with effect from a date to be announced.

Settlements

26 (1) Each of the following is a relevant data-holder—

(*a*) a person who makes a settlement,

(*b*) the trustees of a settlement,

(*c*) a beneficiary under a settlement, and

(*d*) any other person to whom income is payable under a settlement.

(2) Section 620 of ITTOIA 2005 (meaning of "settlement" etc) applies for the purposes of this paragraph.

Cross–references—See Data-gathering Powers (Relevant Data) Regulations, SI 2012/847 reg 24 (relevant data for data-holders under this para).

Charities

27 A charity is a relevant data-holder.

Cross–references—See Data-gathering Powers (Relevant Data) Regulations, SI 2012/847 reg 25 (relevant data for data-holders under this para).

PART 3
APPEALS AGAINST DATA-HOLDER NOTICES

Right of appeal

28 (1) The data-holder may appeal against a data-holder notice, or any requirement in such a notice, on any of the following grounds—

(*a*) it is unduly onerous to comply with the notice or requirement,

(*b*) the data-holder is not a relevant data-holder, or

(*c*) data specified in the notice are not relevant data.

(2) Sub-paragraph (1)(*a*) does not apply to a requirement to provide data that form part of the data-holder's statutory records.

(3) Sub-paragraph (1) does not apply if the tribunal approved the giving of the notice in accordance with paragraph 5.

Procedure for appeal

29 (1) Notice of an appeal under paragraph 28 must be given—

(*a*) in writing,

(*b*) before the end of the period of 30 days beginning with the date on which the data-holder notice was given, and

(*c*) to the officer of Revenue and Customs by whom the data-holder notice was given.

(2) It must state the grounds of appeal.

(3) On an appeal that is notified to the tribunal, the tribunal may confirm, vary or set aside the data-holder notice or a requirement in it.

(4) If the tribunal confirms or varies the notice or a requirement in it, the data-holder must comply with the notice or requirement—

(*a*) within such period as is specified by the tribunal, or

(*b*) if the tribunal does not specify a period, within such period as is reasonably specified in writing by an officer of Revenue and Customs following the tribunal's decision.

(5) A decision by the tribunal under this Part is final (despite the provisions of sections 11 and 13 of the Tribunals, Courts and Enforcement Act 2007).

(6) Subject to this paragraph, the provisions of Part 5 of TMA 1970 relating to appeals have effect in relation to appeals under paragraph 28 as they have effect in relation to an appeal against an assessment to income tax.

PART 4
PENALTIES

Penalties for failure to comply

30 (1) If the data-holder fails to comply with a data-holder notice, the data-holder is liable to a penalty of £300.

(2) A reference in this Schedule to failing to comply with a data-holder notice includes—

(*a*) concealing, destroying or otherwise disposing of a material document, or

(*b*) arranging for any such concealment, destruction or disposal.

(3) A document is a material document if, at the time when the data-holder acts—

(*a*) the data-holder has received a data-holder notice requiring the data-holder to provide the document or data contained in the document, or

(*b*) the data-holder has not received such a notice but has been informed by an officer of Revenue and Customs that the data-holder will do so or is likely to do so.

(4) A document is not a material document by virtue of sub-paragraph (3)(*a*) if the data-holder notice has already been complied with, unless—

(*a*) the data-holder has been notified in writing by an officer of Revenue and Customs that the data-holder must continue to preserve the document, and

(*b*) the notification has not been withdrawn.

(5) A document is not a material document by virtue of sub-paragraph (3)(b) if more than 6 months have elapsed since the data-holder was (or was last) informed.

Daily default penalties for failure to comply

31 If—

(*a*) a penalty under paragraph 30 is assessed, and

(*b*) the failure in question continues after the data-holder has been notified of the assessment,

the data-holder is liable to a further penalty, for each subsequent day on which the failure continues, of an amount not exceeding £60 for each such day.

Penalties for inaccurate information or documents

32 (1) This paragraph applies if—

(*a*) in complying with a data-holder notice, the data-holder provides inaccurate data, and

(*b*) condition A, B or C is met.

(2) Condition A is that the inaccuracy is—

(*a*) due to a failure by the data-holder to take reasonable care, or

(*b*) deliberate on the data-holder's part.

(3) Condition B is that the data-holder knows of the inaccuracy at the time the data are provided but does not inform HMRC at that time.

(4) Condition C is that the data-holder—

(*a*) discovers the inaccuracy some time later, and

(*b*) fails to take reasonable steps to inform HMRC.

(5) If this paragraph applies, the data-holder is liable to a penalty not exceeding £3,000.

Failure to comply with time limit

33 A failure to do anything required to be done within a limited period of time does not give rise to liability under paragraph 30 or 31 if the thing was done within such further time (if any) as an officer of Revenue and Customs may have allowed.

Reasonable excuse

34 (1) Liability to a penalty under paragraph 30 or 31 does not arise if the data-holder satisfies HMRC or (on an appeal notified to the tribunal) the tribunal that there is a reasonable excuse for the failure.

(2) For the purposes of this paragraph—

(*a*) an insufficiency of funds is not a reasonable excuse unless attributable to events outside the data-holder's control,

(*b*) if the data-holder relies on another person to do anything, that is not a reasonable excuse unless the data-holder took reasonable care to avoid the failure,

(*c*) if the data-holder had a reasonable excuse for the failure but the excuse has ceased, the data-holder is to be treated as having continued to have the excuse if the failure is remedied without unreasonable delay after the excuse ceased.

Assessment of penalties

35 (1) If the data-holder becomes liable to a penalty under paragraph 30, 31 or 32, HMRC may assess the penalty.

(2) If they do so, they must notify the data-holder.

(3) An assessment of a penalty under paragraph 30 or 31 must be made within the period of 12 months beginning with the latest of the following—

(*a*) the date on which the data-holder became liable to the penalty,

(*b*) the end of the period in which notice of an appeal against the data-holder notice (or a requirement in it) could have been given, and

(*c*) if notice of such an appeal is given, the date on which the appeal is determined or withdrawn.

(4) An assessment of a penalty under paragraph 32 must be made—

(*a*) within the period of 12 months beginning with the date on which the inaccuracy first came to the attention of an officer of Revenue and Customs, and

(*b*) within the period of 6 years beginning with the date on which the data-holder became liable to the penalty.

Right to appeal against penalty

36 [(1)] The data-holder may appeal against a decision by an officer of Revenue and Customs—

(*a*) that a penalty is payable under paragraph 30, 31 or 32, or

(*b*) as to the amount of such a penalty.

[(2) But sub-paragraph (1)(*b*) does not give a right of appeal against the amount of an increased daily penalty payable by virtue of paragraph 38.][2]

Amendments—[1] Sub-s (1) numbered as such, and sub-s (2) inserted, by FA 2016 s 177(1), (5) with effect from 15 September 2016.

Procedure on appeal against penalty

37 (1) Notice of an appeal under paragraph 36 must be given—

(*a*) in writing,

(*b*) before the end of the period of 30 days beginning with the date on which notification under paragraph 35 was given, and

(*c*) to HMRC.

(2) It must state the grounds of appeal.

(3) On an appeal under paragraph 36(*a*) that is notified to the tribunal, the tribunal may confirm or cancel the decision.

(4) On an appeal under paragraph 36(*b*) that is notified to the tribunal, the tribunal may—

(*a*) confirm the decision, or

(*b*) substitute for the decision another decision that the officer of Revenue and Customs had power to make.

(5) Subject to this paragraph and paragraph 40, the provisions of Part 5 of TMA 1970 relating to appeals have effect in relation to appeals under paragraph 36 as they have effect in relation to an appeal against an assessment to income tax.

Increased daily default penalty

38 (1) This paragraph applies if—

(*a*) a penalty under paragraph 31 is assessed under paragraph 35,

(*b*) the failure in respect of which that assessment is made continues for more than 30 days beginning with the date on which notification of that assessment is given, and

(*c*) the data-holder has been told that an application may be made under this paragraph for an increased daily penalty to be [assessable][1].

(2) If this paragraph applies, an officer of Revenue and Customs may make an application to the tribunal for an increased daily penalty to be [assessable][1] on the data-holder.

[(3) If the tribunal decides that an increased daily penalty should be assessable—

(*a*) the tribunal must determine the day from which the increased daily penalty is to apply and the maximum amount of that penalty ("the new maximum amount");

(*b*) from that day, paragraph 31 has effect in the data-holder's case as if "the new maximum amount" were substituted for "£60".

(4) The new maximum amount may not be more than £1,000.][1]

(5) But subject to that, in determining [the new maximum amount][1] the tribunal must have regard to—

(*a*) the likely cost to the data-holder of complying with the data-holder notice,

(*b*) any benefits to the data-holder of not complying with it, and

(*c*) any benefits to anyone else resulting from the data-holder's non-compliance.

Amendments—[1] In sub-paras (1)(*c*), (2), word substituted for word "imposed", sub-paras (3), (4) substituted, and in sub-para (5), words substituted for words "the amount", by FA 2016 s 177(1), (2) with effect from 15 September 2016. Sub-paras (3), (4) previously read as follows—

"(3) If the tribunal decides that an increased daily penalty should be imposed, then for each applicable day (see paragraph 39) on which the failure continues—

(*a*) the data-holder is not liable to a penalty under paragraph 31 in respect of the failure, and

(*b*) the data-holder is liable instead to a penalty under this paragraph of an amount determined by the tribunal.

(4) The tribunal may not determine an amount exceeding £1,000 for each applicable day.".

39 (1) If [the tribunal makes a determination][1] under paragraph 38, HMRC must notify the data-holder.

(2) The notification must specify [new maximum amount and the day from which it applies][1].

(3) . . . [1]

Amendments—[1] In sub-para (1), words substituted for words "a data-holder becomes liable to a penalty", in sub-para (2), words substituted for words "the day from which the increased penalty is to apply", and sub-para (3) repealed, by FA 2016 s 177(1), (3) with effect from 15 September 2016. Sub-para (3) previously read as follows—

"(3) That day and any subsequent day is an "applicable day" for the purposes of paragraph 38(3).".

Enforcement of penalties

40 (1) A penalty under this Schedule must be paid before the end of the period of 30 days beginning with the date mentioned in sub-paragraph (2).

(2) That date is—

(*a*) the date on which notification under paragraph 35 . . . [1] is given in respect of the penalty, or

(*b*) if (in the case of a penalty under paragraph 30, 31 or 32) a notice of appeal under paragraph 36 is given, the date on which the appeal is finally determined or withdrawn.

(3) A penalty under this Schedule may be enforced as if it were income tax charged in an assessment and due and payable.

Amendments—[1] In sub-para (2)(*a*), words "or 39" repealed by FA 2016 s 177(1), (4) with effect from 15 September 2016.

Power to change amount of penalties

41 (1) If it appears to the Treasury that there has been a change in the value of money since the last relevant date, they may by regulations substitute for the sums for the time being specified in paragraphs 30(1), 31, 32(5) and 38(4) such other sums as appear to them to be justified by the change.

(2) "Relevant date", in relation to a specified sum, means—

(*a*) the day on which this Act is passed, and

(*b*) each date on which the power conferred by sub-paragraph (1) has been exercised in relation to that sum.

(3) Regulations under this paragraph do not apply to—

(*a*) a failure which began before the date on which they come into force, or

(*b*) an inaccuracy in any data or document provided to HMRC before that date.

Double jeopardy

42 The data-holder is not liable to a penalty under this Schedule in respect of anything in respect of which the data-holder has been convicted of an offence.

PART 5

MISCELLANEOUS PROVISION AND INTERPRETATION

Application of provisions of TMA 1970

43 Subject to the provisions of this Schedule, the following provisions of TMA 1970 apply for the purposes of this Schedule as they apply for the purposes of the Taxes Acts—

(*a*) section 108 (responsibility of company officers),

(*b*) section 114 (want of form), and

(*c*) section 115 (delivery and service of documents).

Regulations

44 (1) Regulations under this Schedule are to be made by statutory instrument.

(2) The first regulations to be made under paragraph 1(3) may not be made unless the instrument containing them has been laid in draft before, and approved by a resolution of, the House of Commons.

(3) Subject to sub-paragraph (2), a statutory instrument containing regulations under this Schedule is subject to annulment in pursuance of a resolution of the House of Commons.

Tax

45 (1) In this Schedule "tax" means any or all of the following—

(*a*) income tax,

(*b*) capital gains tax,

(*c*) corporation tax,

[(*ca*) diverted profits tax,][2]

(*d*) VAT,

(*e*) insurance premium tax,

(*f*) inheritance tax,

(*g*) stamp duty land tax,

(*h*) stamp duty reserve tax,

(*i*) petroleum revenue tax,

(*j*) aggregates levy,

(*k*) climate change levy,

(*l*) landfill tax, and

(*m*) relevant foreign tax.

(2) "Corporation tax" includes any amount assessable or chargeable as if it were corporation tax.

(3) "VAT" means—

(*a*) value added tax charged in accordance with VATA 1994, and

(*b*) value added tax charged in accordance with the law of another member State,

and includes any amount that is recoverable under paragraph 5(2) of Schedule 11 to VATA 1994 (amounts shown on invoices as VAT).

(4) "Relevant foreign tax" means—

(*a*) a tax of a member State, other than the United Kingdom, which is covered by the provisions for the exchange of information under the [Council Directive 2011/16/EU of 15 February 2011 on administrative cooperation in the field of taxation][1] (as amended from time to time), and

(*b*) any tax or duty which is imposed under the law of a territory in relation to which arrangements having effect by virtue of section 173 of FA 2006 (international tax enforcement arrangements) have been made and which is covered by the arrangements.

Amendments—[1] In sub-para (4), words substituted by the European Administrative Co-operation (Taxation) Regulations, SI 2012/3062 reg 6(2) with effect from 1 January 2013.

[2] Sub-para (1)(*ca*) inserted by FA 2015 s 105(1) with effect in relation to accounting periods beginning on or after 1 April 2015. For accounting periods that straddle that date, see FA 2015 s 116(2).

Prospective amendments—Sub-para (1)(*ia*) to be inserted by FA 2017 s 56, Sch 11 para 6(1), (3) with effect from a date to be appointed. Once appointed, the charge to soft drinks industry levy will arise on chargeable events which occur on or after 6 April 2018 (FA 2017 s 31(1)).Sub-para (1)(*ia*) as inserted to read as follows—

"(*ia*) soft drinks industry levy,".

Statutory records

46 (1) For the purposes of this Schedule data form part of a data-holder's statutory records if they are data that the data-holder is required to keep and preserve under or by virtue of any enactment relating to tax.

(2) Data cease to form part of a data-holder's statutory records when the period for which the data are required to be preserved under or by virtue of that enactment has expired.

General interpretation

47 In this Schedule—

"address" includes an electronic address;

"body of persons" has the same meaning as in TMA 1970;

"chargeable period" means a tax year, accounting period or other period for which a tax is charged;

"charity" has the meaning given by paragraph 1(1) of Schedule 6 to FA 2010;

"the Commissioners" means the Commissioners for Her Majesty's Revenue and Customs;

"company" has the meaning given by section 288(1) of TCGA 1992;

"data" includes information held in any form;

"the data-holder", in relation to a data-holder notice, means the person to whom the notice is addressed;

"data-holder notice" is defined in paragraph 1;

"dividend" includes any kind of distribution;

"document" includes a copy of a document (see also section 114 of FA 2008);

"employment", "employee" and "employer" have the same meaning as in Parts 2 to 7 of ITEPA 2003 (see, in particular, sections 4 and 5 of that Act);

"HMRC" means Her Majesty's Revenue and Customs;

"local authority" has the meaning given in section 999 of ITA 2007;

"provide" includes make available for inspection;

"specify" includes describe;

"securities" includes—

(*a*) shares and stock,

(*b*) debentures, including debenture stock, loan stock, bonds, certificates of deposit and other instruments creating or acknowledging indebtedness, and

(*c*) warrants or other instruments entitling the holder to subscribe for or otherwise acquire anything within paragraph (*a*) or (*b*),

issued by or on behalf of a person resident in, or a government or public or local authority of, any country (including a country outside the United Kingdom);

"shares" is to be construed in accordance with sections 99 and 103A of TCGA 1992;

"tax functions" means functions relating to tax;

"the tribunal" means the First-tier Tribunal or, where determined by or under the Tribunal Procedure Rules, the Upper Tribunal.

48 A reference in this Schedule to providing data includes—

(*a*) preparing and delivering a return, statement or declaration, and

(*b*) providing documents.

49 (1) A reference in this Schedule to the carrying on of a business also includes—
(*a*) the letting of property,
(*b*) the activities of a charity, and
(*c*) the activities of a government department, a local authority, a local authority association or any other public authority.
(2) "Local authority association" has the meaning given in section 1000 of ITA 2007.

Crown application

50 This Schedule applies to the Crown but not to Her Majesty in Her private capacity (within the meaning of the Crown Proceedings Act 1947).

PART 6
CONSEQUENTIAL PROVISIONS

TMA 1970

51 (1) TMA 1970 is amended as follows.
(2) (*repeals* TMA 1970 ss 13–19, 21, 23–27, 76, 77I)
(3), (4) (*amend* TMA 1970 s 98, Table)
(5) (*inserts* TMA 1970 s 103ZA(*f*))

FA 1973

52 (*repeals* FA 1973 Sch 15 para 2)

FA 1974

53 (1) (*amends* FA 1974 s 24)
(2) Sub-paragraph (1) applies so far as section 24 of FA 1974 continues to have effect (see section 381 of TIOPA 2010).

Note—TIOPA 2010 s 381 was renumbered as s 506 by F(No 2)A 2017 Sch 5 para 10(3)(*h*).

FA 1986

54 (*repeals* FA 1986 Sch 18 para 8(4), (5))

ICTA

55 (*repeals* TA 1988 ss 42(7), 217(4), 226(4), 768(9), 816(3))

FA 1989

56 (*repeals* FA 1989 Sch 12 para 3)

ITTOIA 2005

57 (*repeals* ITTOIA 2005 ss 302B(3), (4), 647)

FA 2005

58 (*repeals* FA 2005 Sch 2 para 2)

CRCA 2005

59 (*repeals* CRCA 2005 Sch 2 para 2)

FA 2008

60 FA 2008 is amended as follows.

61 (*repeals* FA 2008 s 39(1)(*a*))

62 (1) Schedule 36 (information and inspection powers) is amended as follows.
(2) (*repeals* FA 2008 Sch 36 para 34A)
(3) (*amends* FA 2008 Sch 36 para 61A)

CTA 2009

63 (*repeals* CTA 2009 s 241(3), (4))

CTA 2010

64 (1), (2) (*repeal* CTA 2010 ss 31(1), 465(1), 728, 1046(5)–(7), 1097, 1102(2))
(3) (*amended* CTA 2010 s 1109; *repealed* by FA 2016 s 5, Sch 1 para 69(*a*))

PART 7
APPLICATION OF THIS SCHEDULE

65 (1) This Schedule—

(*a*) comes into force on 1 April 2012, and
(*b*) applies from then on to relevant data with a bearing on any period (whether before, on or after that date), subject to paragraph 3(2).

(2) The provisions repealed or otherwise amended by Part 6 of this Schedule continue to have effect in relation to notices given, or requests made, pursuant to any of the repealed provisions before 1 April 2012 as if the repeals and other amendments had not been made.

FINANCE ACT 2012

(2012 Chapter 14)

CONTENTS

An Act to grant certain duties, to alter other duties, and to amend the law relating to the National Debt and the Public Revenue, and to make further provision in connection with finance.

[17 July 2012]

PART 1
INCOME TAX, CORPORATION TAX AND CAPITAL GAINS TAX

CHAPTER 5
MISCELLANEOUS

Charitable giving etc

49 Gifts to the nation

Schedule 14 contains provision for a person's tax liability to be reduced in return for giving pre-eminent property to the nation.

Commentary—*Simon's Taxes* **C1.417**.

PART 8
OTHER TAXES

Inheritance tax

208 Indexation of rate bands

(1) Section 8 of IHTA 1984 (indexation of rate bands) is amended as follows.

(2) In subsection (1), for "retail prices index for the month of September in 1993 or any later year" substitute "consumer prices index for the month of September in any year".

(3) In subsection (2), for "retail prices index" substitute "consumer prices index".

(4) For subsection (3) substitute—

"(3) In this section, "consumer prices index" means the all items consumer prices index published by the Statistics Board."

(5) The amendments made by this section have effect for the purposes of chargeable transfers made on or after 6 April 2015.

209 Gifts to charities etc

Schedule 33 contains provision for a lower rate of inheritance tax to be charged on transfers made on death that include sufficient gifts to charities or registered clubs.

210 Settled property: effect of certain arrangements

(1) IHTA 1984 is amended as follows.

(2) In section 48 (settled property: excluded property)—

(a) in subsection (1), after paragraph (c) insert "or,

(d) in a case where paragraphs (a), (b) and (d) of section 74A(1) are satisfied—

(i) it is a reversionary interest, in the relevant settled property, to which the individual is beneficially entitled, and

(ii) the individual has or is able to acquire (directly or indirectly) another interest in that relevant settled property.

Terms used in paragraph (d) have the same meaning as in section 74A.",

(b) in subsection (3), for "subsection (3B)" substitute "subsections (3B) and (3D)", and

(c) after subsection (3C) insert—

"(3D) Where paragraphs (a) to (d) of section 74A(1) are satisfied, subsection (3)(a) above does not apply at the time they are first satisfied or any later time to make the relevant settled property (within the meaning of section 74A) excluded property."

(3) After section 74 insert—

"74A Arrangements involving acquisition of interest in settled property etc

(1) This section applies where—

(a) one or more persons enter into arrangements,

(b) in the course of the arrangements—

(i) an individual ("the individual") domiciled in the United Kingdom acquires or becomes able to acquire (directly or indirectly) an interest in property comprised in a settlement ("the relevant settled property"), and

(ii) consideration in money or money's worth is given by one or more of the persons mentioned in paragraph (a) (whether or not in connection with the acquisition of that interest or the individual becoming able to acquire it),

(c) there is a relevant reduction in the value of the individual's estate, and

(d) condition A or condition B is met.

(2) Condition A is that—

(a) the settlor was not domiciled in the United Kingdom at the time the settlement was made, and

(b) the relevant settled property is situated outside the United Kingdom at any time during the course of the arrangements.

(3) Condition B is that—

(a) the settlor was not an individual or a close company at the time the settlement was made, and

(b) condition A is not met.

(4) Subsection (6) applies if all or a part of a relevant reduction ("amount A") is attributable to the value of the individual's section 49(1) property being less than it would have been in the absence of the arrangements.

(5) "The individual's section 49(1) property" means settled property to which the individual is treated as beneficially entitled under section 49(1) by reason of the individual being beneficially entitled to an interest in possession in the property.

(6) Where this subsection applies—

(a) a part of that interest in possession is deemed, for the purposes of section 52, to come to an end at the relevant time, and

(b) that section applies in relation to the coming to an end of that part as if the reference in subsection (4)(a) of that section to a corresponding part of the whole value of the property in which the interest in possession subsists were a reference to amount A.

(7) Subsection (8) applies to so much (if any) of a relevant reduction as is not amount A ("amount B").

(8) Tax is to be charged as if the individual had made a transfer of value at the relevant time and the value transferred by it had been equal to amount B.

74B Section 74A: supplementary provision

(1) A transfer of value arising by virtue of section 74A is to be taken to be a transfer which is not a potentially exempt transfer.

(2) For the purposes of section 74A—

(a) when determining the value transferred by a transfer of value arising by virtue of that section, no account is to be taken of section 3(2),

(b) nothing in section 10(1) applies to prevent such a transfer, and

(c) nothing in sections 102 to 102C of the Finance Act 1986 applies in relation to such a transfer.

(3) Where, ignoring this subsection, a transfer of value would arise by virtue of section 74A ("the current transfer"), the value transferred by a relevant related transfer is to be treated as reducing the value transferred by the current transfer.

But this subsection does not apply if and to the extent that the relevant related transfer has already been applied to reduce another transfer of value arising by virtue of that section.

(4) "Relevant related transfer" means—

(a) where the arrangements consist of a series of operations, any transfer of value constituted by one or more of those operations which occur before or at the same time as the current transfer, other than a transfer of value arising by virtue of section 74A, and

(b) where the arrangements consist of a single operation, any transfer of value which arises from that operation, other than a transfer of value arising by virtue of section 74A.

(5) Section 268(3) does not apply to a transfer of value arising by virtue of section 74A.

(6) Where—

(a) a transfer of value has arisen by virtue of section 74A,

(b) in the course of the arrangements the individual acquires an interest in possession in settled property, and

(c) section 5(1B) applies to the interest in possession so that it forms part of the individual's estate,

this Act has effect as if that transfer of value had never arisen.

74C Interpretation of sections 74A and 74B

(1) Subsections (2) to (4) have effect for the purposes of sections 74A and 74B.

(2) An individual has an interest in property comprised in a settlement if—

(a) the property, or any derived property, is or will or may become payable to, or applicable for the benefit of—

(i) the individual,

(ii) the individual's spouse or civil partner, or

(iii) a close company in relation to which the individual or the individual's spouse or civil partner is a participator or a company which is a 51% subsidiary of such a close company,

in any circumstances whatsoever, or

(b) a person within sub-paragraph (i), (ii) or (iii) of paragraph (a) enjoys a benefit deriving (directly or indirectly) from the property or any derived property.

(3) A "relevant reduction" in the value of the individual's estate occurs—

(a) if and when the value of the individual's estate first becomes less than it would have been in the absence of the arrangements, and

(b) on each subsequent occasion when the value of that estate becomes less than it would have been in the absence of the arrangements and that difference in value is greater than the sum of any previous relevant reductions.

(4) The amount of a relevant reduction is—

(a) in the case of a reduction within subsection (3)(a), the difference between the value of the estate and its value in the absence of the arrangements, and

(b) in the case of a reduction within subsection (3)(b), the amount by which the difference in value mentioned in that provision exceeds the sum of any previous relevant reductions.

(5) In sections 74A and 74B and this section—

"arrangements" includes any scheme, transaction or series of transactions, agreement or understanding, whether or not legally enforceable, and any associated operations;

"close company" has the meaning given in section 102;

"derived property", in relation to any property, means—

(a) income from that property,

(b) property directly or indirectly representing—

(i) proceeds of that property, or

(ii) proceeds of income from that property, or

(c) income from property which is derived property by virtue of paragraph (b);

"operation" includes an omission;

"participator" has the meaning given in section 102;

"the relevant time" means—

(a) the time the relevant reduction occurs, or

(b) if later, the time section 74A first applied;

"51% subsidiary" has the same meaning as in the Corporation Tax Acts (see Chapter 3 of Part 24 of the Corporation Tax Act 2010)."

(4) In section 201 (liability for tax: settled property), after subsection (4) insert—

"(4A) Where—

(a) a charge to tax arises under or by virtue of section 74A, or

(b) in a case where paragraphs (a) to (d) of section 74A are satisfied, a charge to tax arises under section 64 or 65 in respect of the relevant settled property (within the meaning of section 74A),

subsection (1) of this section has effect as if the persons listed in that subsection included the individual mentioned in section 74A(1)(b)(i)."

(5) The amendments made by this section are treated as having come into force on 20 June 2012 and have effect in relation to arrangements entered into on or after that day.

PART 9
MISCELLANEOUS MATTERS

International matters

218 Agreement between UK and Switzerland

(1) Schedule 36 contains provision giving effect to—
(a) an agreement signed on 6 October 2011 between the United Kingdom and the Swiss Confederation on co-operation in the area of taxation, as amended by a protocol signed by them on 20 March 2012 and by a mutual agreement signed by them on 18 April 2012 implementing article XVIII of that protocol, and
(b) the joint declaration (concerning a tax finality payment) forming an integral part of that protocol.

(2) Schedule 36 comes into force on the day on which the agreement of 6 October 2011 enters into force.

(3) In section 23 of the Constitutional Reform and Governance Act 2010, after subsection (2A) insert—

"(2B) Section 20 does not apply to any treaty referred to in section 218(1) of the Finance Act 2012."

220 International military headquarters, EU forces, etc

Schedule 37 contains provision about the tax treatment of international military headquarters, EU forces, etc.

Administration

223 Tax agents: dishonest conduct

(1) Schedule 38 contains provision about tax agents who engage in dishonest conduct.
(2) That Schedule comes into force on such day as the Treasury may by order appoint.
(3) An order under subsection (2)—
(a) may make different provision for different purposes, and
(b) may include transitional provision and savings.
(4) The Treasury may by order make any incidental, supplemental, consequential, transitional or saving provision in consequence of Schedule 38.
(5) An order under subsection (4) may—
(a) make different provision for different purposes, and
(b) make provision amending, repealing or revoking any provision made by or under an Act (whenever passed or made).
(6) An order under this section is to be made by statutory instrument.
(7) A statutory instrument containing an order under subsection (4) is subject to annulment in pursuance of a resolution of the House of Commons.

Orders—Finance Act 2012, Schedule 38 (Tax Agents: Dishonest Conduct) (Appointed Day and Savings) Order, SI 2013/279.
Commentary—*Simon's Taxes* **I11.703**.

Miscellaneous reliefs etc

227 Repeals of miscellaneous reliefs etc

Schedule 39 contains repeals of miscellaneous reliefs etc.

PART 10
FINAL PROVISIONS

228 Interpretation

(1) In this Act—
"ALDA 1979" means the Alcoholic Liquor Duties Act 1979,
"BGDA 1981" means the Betting and Gaming Duties Act 1981,
"CAA 2001" means the Capital Allowances Act 2001,
"CEMA 1979" means the Customs and Excise Management Act 1979,
"CRCA 2005" means the Commissioners for Revenue and Customs Act 2005,
"CTA 2009" means the Corporation Tax Act 2009,
"CTA 2010" means the Corporation Tax Act 2010,
"F(No 3)A 2010" means the Finance (No 3) Act 2010,
"HODA 1979" means the Hydrocarbon Oil Duties Act 1979,
"ICTA" means the Income and Corporation Taxes Act 1988,
"IHTA 1984" means the Inheritance Tax Act 1984,
"ITA 2007" means the Income Tax Act 2007,
"ITEPA 2003" means the Income Tax (Earnings and Pensions) Act 2003,
"ITTOIA 2005" means the Income Tax (Trading and Other Income) Act 2005,
"OTA 1975" means the Oil Taxation Act 1975,
"PRTA 1980" means the Petroleum Revenue Tax Act 1980,
"TCGA 1992" means the Taxation of Chargeable Gains Act 1992,

"TIOPA 2010" means the Taxation (International and Other Provisions) Act 2010,
"TMA 1970" means the Taxes Management Act 1970,
"TPDA 1979" means the Tobacco Products Duty Act 1979,
"VATA 1994" means the Value Added Tax Act 1994, and
"VERA 1994" means the Vehicle Excise and Registration Act 1994.

(2) In this Act—
"FA", followed by a year, means the Finance Act of that year;
"F(No 2)A", followed by a year, means the Finance (No 2) Act of that year.

229 Short title

This Act may be cited as the Finance Act 2012.

SCHEDULE 14

GIFTS TO THE NATION

Commentary—*Simon's Taxes* **C1.417, D1.356, E1.815**.

Section 49

PART 5
RELATED CHANGES

IHTA 1984

26 IHTA 1984 is amended as follows.

27 In section 25 (gifts for national purposes etc), after subsection (2) insert—

"(3) A transfer of value is an exempt transfer to the extent that the value transferred by it is attributable to property that is being transferred in the circumstances described in paragraph 1 of Schedule 14 to the Finance Act 2012 (gifts to the nation)."

28 In section 26A (potentially exempt transfer of property subsequently held for national purposes etc), in paragraph (b), after "below" insert "or in the circumstances described in paragraph 1 of Schedule 14 to the Finance Act 2012 (gifts to the nation)".

29 (1) Section 32 (conditionally exempt transfers: chargeable events) is amended as follows.

(2) In subsection (3), for "subsections (4) and (5)" substitute "subsections (4), (4A) and (5)".

(3) After subsection (4) insert—

"(4A) A death or disposal is not a chargeable event with respect to any property if—

(a) in the case of a death, a person who became beneficially entitled to the property on the death disposes of it in the circumstances described in paragraph 1 of Schedule 14 to the Finance Act 2012 (gifts to the nation) within 3 years of the death, or

(b) in the case of a disposal, the disposal is made in the circumstances described in paragraph 1 of that Schedule, and a death or disposal of the property after such a disposal as is mentioned in paragraph (a) or (b) is not a chargeable event with respect to the property unless there has again been a conditionally exempt transfer of it after that disposal."

30 (1) Section 32A (associated properties) is amended as follows.

(2) After subsection (5) insert—

"(5A) The death of a person beneficially entitled to property, or the disposal of property, is not a chargeable event if—

(a) in the case of a death, a person who became beneficially entitled to the property on the death disposes of it in the circumstances described in paragraph 1 of Schedule 14 to the Finance Act 2012 (gifts to the nation) within 3 years of the death, or

(b) in the case of a disposal, the disposal is made in the circumstances described in paragraph 1 of that Schedule."

(3) In subsection (7), after "(5)(a) or (b)" insert "or (5A)(a) or (b)".

31 In section 33 (amount of charge under section 32), in subsection (6)—

(a) for "section 32(4)" substitute "section 32(4) or (4A)", and

(b) for "section 32A(5)", in both places it appears, substitute "section 32A(5) or (5A)".

32 In section 34 (reinstatement of transferor's cumulative total), in subsection (4)—

(a) for "section 32(4)" substitute "section 32(4) or (4A)", and

(b) for "section 32A(5)", in both places it appears, substitute "section 32A(5) or (5A)".

Estate duty etc

[32A—(1) This paragraph applies where a person ("the donor") makes a qualifying gift of an object in circumstances where, had the donor instead sold the object to an individual at market value, a charge to estate duty would have arisen under section 40 of FA 1930 on the proceeds of sale.
(2) At the time when the gift is made, estate duty becomes chargeable under that section as if the gift were such a sale (subject to any limitation imposed by paragraph 33(2)).
(3) In the application of this paragraph to Northern Ireland, the references to section 40 of FA 1930 are to be read as references to section 2 of the Finance Act (Northern Ireland) 1931.][1]

Amendments—[1] Para 32A inserted by FA 2014 s 118(1) with effect from 17 July 2014.

33 (1) This paragraph applies if a person makes a qualifying gift and as a result—
- (a) estate duty becomes chargeable under section 40 of FA 1930 (exemption from death duties of objects of national etc interest), or
- (b) tax becomes chargeable under Schedule 5 to IHTA 1984 (conditional exemption: deaths before 7 April 1976).

(2) Despite any other enactment, the amount of duty or tax that becomes so chargeable as a result of the gift is to be limited to the amount (if any) by which A exceeds B.
(3) For these purposes—
"A" is the amount of duty or tax that becomes so chargeable as a result of the gift (absent this paragraph), and
"B" is what that amount would be if the effective rate at which the duty or tax is charged were the highest rate specified in column 3 of the Table in Schedule 1 to IHTA 1984.
(4) References in this paragraph to the amount of duty or tax that becomes so chargeable are to the amount before applying any credit allowable against it under section 33(7) of IHTA 1984.
(5) Nothing in this paragraph entitles a person to any repayment of inheritance tax if the amount of any such credit exceeds the amount (if any) chargeable in accordance with sub-paragraph (2).
(6) In the application of this paragraph to Northern Ireland, for the reference to section 40 of FA 1930 substitute a reference to section 2 of the Finance Act (Northern Ireland) 1931.

TCGA 1992

34 (*amends* TCGA 1992 s 258(1A))

ITA 2007

35 (*amends* ITA 2007 s 809YE)

PART 6
COMMENCEMENT

36 (1) Parts 2 and 3 of this Schedule have effect in relation to liabilities for tax years and accounting periods beginning on or after such day as the Treasury may by order appoint.
(2) The power of the Treasury under sub-paragraph (1) includes power to appoint a day that is earlier than the day on which the order is made, but no earlier than 1 April 2012.
(3) An order under this paragraph is to be made by statutory instrument.

SCHEDULE 16
PART 2: MINOR AND CONSEQUENTIAL AMENDMENTS

Section 146

PART 3
AMENDMENTS OF OTHER ACTS

Inheritance Tax Act 1984

68 IHTA 1984 is amended as follows.

69 In section 59(3)(b) (qualifying interest in possession), for "Chapter I of Part XII of the Taxes Act 1988" substitute "Part 2 of the Finance Act 2012".

SCHEDULE 33
INHERITANCE TAX: GIFTS TO CHARITIES ETC

Section 209

Reduced rate of inheritance tax

1 After Schedule 1 to IHTA 1984 insert—

SCHEDULE 1A

GIFTS TO CHARITIES ETC: TAX CHARGED AT LOWER RATE

Application of this Schedule

1

(1) This Schedule applies if—

(a) a chargeable transfer is made (under section 4) on the death of a person ("D"), and

(b) all or part of the value transferred by the chargeable transfer is chargeable to tax at a rate other than nil per cent.

(2) The part of the value transferred that is chargeable to tax at a rate other than nil per cent is referred to in this Schedule as "TP".

The relief

2

(1) If the charitable giving condition is met—

(a) the tax charged on the part of TP that qualifies for the lower rate of tax is to be charged at the lower rate of tax, and

(b) the tax charged on any remaining part of TP is to be charged at the rate at which it would (but for this Schedule) have been charged on the whole of TP in accordance with section 7.

(2) For the purposes of this paragraph, the charitable giving condition is met if, for one or more components of the estate (taking each component separately), the donated amount is at least 10% of the baseline amount.

(3) Paragraph 3 defines the components of the estate.

(4) Paragraphs 4 and 5 explain how to calculate the donated amount and the baseline amount for each component.

(5) The part of TP that "qualifies for the lower rate of tax" is the part attributable to all the property in each of the components for which the donated amount is at least 10% of the baseline amount.

(6) The lower rate of tax is 36%.

The components of the estate

3

(1) For the purposes of paragraph 2, the components of the estate are—

(a) the survivorship component,

(b) the settled property component, and

(c) the general component.

(2) The survivorship component is made up of all the property comprised in the estate that, immediately before D's death, was joint (or common) property liable to pass on D's death—

(a) by survivorship (in England and Wales or Northern Ireland),

(b) under a special destination (in Scotland), or

(c) by or under anything corresponding to survivorship or a special destination under the law of a country or territory outside the United Kingdom.

(3) The settled property component is made up of all the settled property comprised in the estate in which there subsisted, immediately before D's death, an interest in possession to which D was beneficially entitled immediately before death.

(4) The general component is made up of all the property comprised in the estate other than—

(a) property in the survivorship component,

(b) property in the settled property component, and

(c) property that forms part of the estate by virtue of section 102(3) of the Finance Act 1986 (gifts with reservation).

The donated amount

4

The donated amount, for a component of the estate, is so much of the value transferred by the relevant transfer as (in total) is attributable to property that—

(a) forms part of that component, and

(b) is property in relation to which section 23(1) applies.

The baseline amount

5

The baseline amount, for a component of the estate, is the amount calculated in accordance with the following steps—

Step 1

Determine the part of the value transferred by the chargeable transfer that is attributable to property in that component.

Step 2

Deduct from the amount determined under Step 1 the appropriate proportion of the available nil-rate band.

"The appropriate proportion" is a proportion equal to the proportion that the amount determined under Step 1 bears to the value transferred by the chargeable transfer as a whole.

"The available nil-rate band" is the amount (if any) by which—

(a) the nil-rate band maximum (increased, where applicable, in accordance with section 8A), exceeds

(b) the sum of the values transferred by previous chargeable transfers made by D in the period of 7 years ending with the date of the relevant transfer.

Step 3

Add to the amount determined under Step 2 an amount equal to so much of the value transferred by the relevant transfer as (in total) is attributable to property that—

(a) forms part of that component, and

(b) is property in relation to which section 23(1) applies.

The result is the baseline amount for that component.

Rules for determining whether charitable giving condition is met

6

(1) For the purpose of calculating the donated amount and the baseline amount, any amount to be arrived at in accordance with section 38(3) or (5) is to be arrived at assuming the rate of tax is the lower rate of tax (see paragraph 2(6)).

(2) For the purpose of calculating the donated amount, section 39A does not apply to a specific gift of property in relation to which section 23(1) applies (but that section does apply to such a gift for the purpose of calculating the baseline amount).

(3) Subject to sub-paragraphs (1) and (2), the provisions of this Act apply for the purpose of calculating the donated amount and the baseline amount as for the purpose of calculating the tax to be charged on the value transferred by the chargeable transfer.

Election to merge parts of the estate

7

(1) An election may be made under this paragraph if, for a component of the estate, the donated amount is at least 10% of the baseline amount.

(2) That component is referred to as "the qualifying component".

(3) The effect of the election is that the qualifying component and one or more eligible parts of the estate (as specified in the election) are to be treated for the purposes of this Schedule as if they were a single component.

(4) Accordingly, if the donated amount for that deemed single component is at least 10% of the baseline amount for it, the property in that component is to be included in the part of TP that

qualifies for the lower rate of tax.

(5) In relation to the qualifying component—

(a) each one of the other two components of the estate is an "eligible part" of the estate, and

(b) all the property that forms part of the estate by virtue of section 102(3) of the Finance Act 1986 (gifts with reservation) is also an "eligible part" of the estate.

(6) The election must be made by all those who are appropriate persons with respect to the qualifying component and each of the eligible parts to be treated as a single component.

(7) "Appropriate persons" means—

(a) with respect to the survivorship component, all those to whom the property in that component passes on D's death (or, if they have subsequently died, their personal representatives),

(b) with respect to the settled property component, the trustees of all the settled property in that component,

(c) with respect to the general component, all the personal representatives of D or, if there are none, all those who are liable for the tax attributable to the property in that component, and

(d) with respect to property within paragraph (b) of subparagraph

(5) , all those in whom the property within that paragraph is vested when the election is to be made.

Opting out

8

(1) If an election is made under this paragraph in relation to a component of the estate, this Schedule is to apply as if the donated amount for that component were less than 10% of the baseline amount for it (whether or not it actually is).

(2) The election must be made by all those who are appropriate persons (as defined in paragraph 7(7)) with respect to the component.

Elections: procedure

9

(1) An election under this Schedule must be made by notice in writing to HMRC within two years after D's death.

(2) An election under this Schedule may be withdrawn by notice in writing to HMRC given—

(a) by all those who would be entitled to make such an election, and

(b) no later than the end of the period of two years and one month after D's death.

(3) An officer of Revenue and Customs may agree in a particular case to extend the time limit in sub-paragraph (1) or (2)(b) by such period as the officer may allow.

General interpretation

10

In this Schedule, in relation to D—

"the chargeable transfer" means the chargeable transfer mentioned in paragraph 1(1);

"the estate" means D's estate immediately before death;

"the relevant transfer" means the transfer of value that D is treated (under section 4) as having made immediately before death."

Consequential amendments

2 IHTA 1984 is amended as follows in consequence of paragraph 1.

3 In section 7 (rates), in subsection (1), after "(4) and (5) below" insert "and to Schedule 1A".

4 In section 33 (amount of charge under section 32), after subsection (2) insert—

"(2ZA) In determining for the purposes of subsection (1)(b)(ii) the rate or rates that would have applied in accordance with subsection (1) of section 7, the effect of Schedule 1A (if it would have applied) is to be disregarded."

5 In section 78 (conditionally exempt occasion), in subsection (3), for "33(3)" substitute "33(2ZA)".

6 In section 128 (rate of charge: woodlands)—

(a) the existing provisions become subsection (1) of that section, and

(b) after that subsection insert—

"(2) In determining for the purposes of subsection (1) the rate or rates at which tax would have been charged on the amount determined under section 127, the effect of Schedule 1A (if it would have applied) is to be disregarded."

7 After section 141 insert—

"141A Apportionment of relief under section 141

(1) This section applies if any part of the value transferred by the later transfer qualifies for the lower rate of tax in accordance with Schedule 1A.

(2) The amount of the reduction made under section 141(1) is to be apportioned in accordance with this section.

(3) For each qualifying component, the tax chargeable on so much of the value transferred by the later transfer as is attributable to property in that component ("the relevant part of the tax") is to be reduced by the appropriate proportion of the amount calculated in accordance with section 141(3).

(4) "The appropriate proportion" is a proportion equal to the proportion that—

(a) the relevant part of the tax, bears to

(b) the tax chargeable on the value transferred by the later transfer as a whole.

(5) If parts of an estate are treated under Schedule 1A as a single component, subsection (3) applies to the single component (and not to individual components forming part of the deemed single component).

(6) If, after making the reductions required by subsection (3), there remains any part of the tax chargeable on the value transferred by the later transfer that has not been reduced, the remaining part of the tax is to be reduced by so much of the amount calculated in accordance with section 141(3) as has not been used up for the purposes of making the reductions required by subsection (3).

(7) In this section—

"component" means a component of the estate, as defined in paragraph 3 of Schedule 1A;

"the later transfer" has the meaning given in section 141(1);

"qualifying component" means a component (or deemed single component) for which the donated amount is at least 10% of the baseline amount, as determined in accordance with Schedule 1A."

8 In Schedule 4 (maintenance funds for historic buildings etc), in paragraph 14, after sub-paragraph (2) insert—

"(2A) In determining for the purposes of sub-paragraph (2) the effective rate or rates at which tax would have been charged on the amount in accordance with section 7(1), the effect of Schedule 1A (if it would have applied) is to be disregarded."

Instruments of variation to be notified to charities etc

9 In section 142 of IHTA 1984 (alteration of dispositions taking effect on death), after subsection (3) insert—

"(3A) Subsection (1) does not apply to a variation by virtue of which any property comprised in the estate immediately before the person's death becomes property in relation to which section 23(1) applies unless it is shown that the appropriate person has been notified of the existence of the instrument of variation.

(3B) For the purposes of subsection (3A) "the appropriate person" is—

(a) the charity or registered club to which the property is given, or

(b) if the property is to be held on trust for charitable purposes or for the purposes of registered clubs, the trustees in question."

Commencement

10 (1) The Schedule inserted by paragraph 1 has effect in cases where D's death occurs on or after 6 April 2012 (and the amendments made by paragraphs 3 to 8 are to be read accordingly).

(2) The amendment made by paragraph 9 has effect in cases where the person's death occurs on or after 6 April 2012.

SCHEDULE 36
AGREEMENT BETWEEN UK AND SWITZERLAND

Section 218

Commentary—*Simon's Taxes* **A6.1216**.

PART 1
INTRODUCTION

The Agreement and the Joint Declaration

1 In this Schedule—

(a) "the Agreement" means the agreement signed on 6 October 2011 between the United Kingdom and the Swiss Confederation on co-operation in the area of taxation, as amended by a protocol signed by them on 20 March 2012 and by a mutual agreement signed by them on 18 April 2012 implementing article XVIII of that protocol,

(b) "the Joint Declaration" means the joint declaration (concerning a tax finality payment) forming an integral part of that protocol,

(c) "the start date" is the date on which the Agreement enters into force in accordance with its terms (see Article 44), and

(d) references to a numbered Article are to the Article of that number in the Agreement.

Commentary—*Simon's Taxes* **A6.1216**.

PART 2
THE PAST

Taxes affected

2 (1) The taxes affected by this Part are—

(a) income tax,

(b) capital gains tax,

(c) inheritance tax, and

(d) VAT.

(2) Accordingly, this Part affects—

(a) amounts of income on which income tax is charged,

(b) chargeable gains,

(c) the value of property forming part of the value transferred by a chargeable transfer, and

(d) the value of supplies on which VAT is charged.

(3) An amount falling within one (or more) of those descriptions is referred to as a "taxable amount" and, in relation to such an amount, "tax" means whichever of the taxes mentioned in sub-paragraph (1) is (or are) charged on it.

Commentary—*Simon's Taxes* **A6.1216**.

Application of this Part

3 (1) This Part applies if—

(a) a one-off payment is levied in accordance with Part 2 of the Agreement,

(b) a certificate is issued under Article 9(4) to a person ("P") in respect of that payment, and

(c) the certificate is approved by P or considered approved by virtue of that Article.

(2) The certificate is referred to in this Part as "the Part 2 certificate".

Commentary—*Simon's Taxes* **A6.1216**.

Qualifying amounts

4 (1) The Part 2 certificate applies to taxable amounts in respect of which the conditions in sub-paragraph (2) are met.

(2) The conditions are—

(a) P is liable to tax on the amount,

(b) the amount is untaxed,

(c) the taxable event took place before the start date, and

(d) the necessary link with the certificate can be demonstrated.

(3) The necessary link is—

(a) in a case falling within Article 9(3) (non-UK domiciled individuals opting for self-assessment method), that the amount is included in the omitted taxable base by reference to which the one-off payment was calculated, and

(b) in any other case, that the amount forms part of or is represented by the assets comprised in the relevant capital by reference to which the one-off payment was calculated (referred to in the Agreement as C_r).

(4) For the purposes of sub-paragraph (3)(b), amounts are assumed to be attributed to assets in the way that produces the most beneficial outcome for P.

(5) Paragraph 11 makes further provision about the interpretation of subparagraph (2).

(6) Amounts to which the Part 2 certificate applies in accordance with this paragraph are referred to in this Part as "qualifying amounts".

Commentary—*Simon's Taxes* **A6.1216**.

Eligibility for clearance

5 (1) The effect of the Part 2 certificate depends on whether P is eligible for clearance.

(2) P is "eligible for clearance" if—

(a) none of the circumstances listed in Article 9(13)(a) to (e) apply (tax investigations etc), and

(b) Article 12(1) does not apply (wrongful behaviour in relation to non-UK domiciled status).

(3) Otherwise, P is "not eligible for clearance".

Commentary—*Simon's Taxes* **A6.1216**.

Effect if P eligible for clearance

6 (1) This paragraph sets out the effect of the Part 2 certificate if P is eligible for clearance.

(2) P ceases to be liable to tax on qualifying amounts.

(3) Sub-paragraph (2) does not apply to a qualifying amount if—

(a) the amount was held in the United Kingdom,

(b) at some point during the period beginning with 6 October 2011 and ending immediately before the start date, it ceased to be held in the United Kingdom, and

(c) after that point (but before the start date) it began to be held in Switzerland.

(4) Instead, such part of the one-off payment as is attributable (on a just and reasonable basis) to the qualifying amount is to be treated as if it were a credit allowable against the tax due from P taking account of that amount.

(5) The meaning of tax due "taking account of" an amount is explained in Part 5 of this Schedule.

(6) The form in which a qualifying amount was held in the United Kingdom is irrelevant (so references in sub-paragraph (3) to the amount include an asset representing the amount).

(7) The total qualifying amounts to which sub-paragraphs (2) and (4) can apply as a result of the Part 2 certificate is limited to X.

(8) If the total exceeds X, the particular qualifying amounts to which those subparagraphs apply are assumed to be those that would produce the most beneficial outcome for P.

(9) X is—

(a) in a case falling within Article 9(3), the value of the omitted taxable base by reference to which the one-off payment was calculated, and

(b) in any other case, the value shown in the Part 2 certificate as the value of the relevant capital (C_r).

Commentary—*Simon's Taxes* **A6.1216**.

Ceasing to be liable to tax

7 (1) The result of "ceasing to be liable" to tax on a qualifying amount depends on the tax (or taxes) in respect of which the amount is untaxed.

(2) For income tax or capital gains tax, the result is that the amount is no longer liable to be brought into account in assessing the income tax or capital gains tax due from P for the tax year in which the amount would otherwise be liable to be brought into account.

(3) For inheritance tax, the result is that any inheritance tax due from P in respect of the chargeable transfer and attributable to the property whose value is included in the amount is no longer due from P.

(4) For VAT, the result is that P is no longer required to account for output tax on the amount in determining the VAT payable by P for the prescribed accounting period in which P would otherwise be required to account for output tax on the amount.

(5) But—

(a) ceasing to be liable to tax on a qualifying amount does not affect P's liability to tax on any other amount, and

(b) P's liability to tax on any other amount remains what it would have been, had the qualifying amount been brought into account in calculating that liability.

(6) Accordingly, if the qualifying amount were ever to be brought into account and it were found that the tax assessed on any other amount should have been higher as a result, P would remain liable for the extra tax due on that other amount and for any associated ancillary charge.

(7) For the purposes of sub-paragraphs (5) and (6), the qualifying amount is assumed to form the top slice of the total sum on which P is liable to tax.

Commentary—*Simon's Taxes* **A6.1216**.

Effect if P not eligible for clearance

8 (1) This paragraph sets out the effect of the Part 2 certificate if P is not eligible for clearance.

(2) The one-off payment is to be treated as if it were a credit allowable against the tax due from P taking account of qualifying amounts.

(3) The one-off payment is to be applied for the purposes of sub-paragraph (2)—

(a) in the order specified in sub-paragraph (4), and

(b) subject to that, in the way that produces the most beneficial outcome for P.

(4) The order is—

(a) first, for VAT,

(b) then, for income tax,

(c) then, for capital gains tax, and

(d) finally, for inheritance tax.

Commentary—*Simon's Taxes* **A6.1216**.

Interest, penalties etc

9 (1) Where, by virtue of this Part, P ceases to be liable to tax on a qualifying amount, P also ceases to be liable to any ancillary charge directly connected with that amount.

(2) Where, by virtue of this Part, all or part of a one-off payment is treated as if it were a credit allowable against the tax due from P taking account of a qualifying amount, the credit may also be used to offset any ancillary charge directly connected with that amount.

(3) Sub-paragraph (4) applies in the case of a qualifying amount that is part only of—

(a) an amount of income on which income tax is charged,

(b) a chargeable gain,

(c) the value of property forming part of the value transferred by a chargeable transfer, or

(d) the value of a supply on which VAT is charged.

(4) The amount of any ancillary charge directly connected with that qualifying amount is determined by apportioning the ancillary charge directly connected with the income, gain or value on a just and reasonable basis.

Commentary—*Simon's Taxes* **A6.1216**.

Repayments

10 Nothing in this Part entitles any person to a repayment or refund of tax, save for any repayment or refund to which P may be entitled by virtue of paragraph 6(4) or 8(2) if the credit allowable under that paragraph exceeds the total amount of tax against which the credit is allowable.

Commentary—*Simon's Taxes* **A6.1216**.

Paragraph 4: supplementary provision

11 (1) This paragraph explains how paragraph 4(2) is to be read for each description of taxable amount.

(2) For income and chargeable gains—

(a) the reference to P being "liable to tax" includes a case where P would be so liable if the income or gain were to be remitted to the United Kingdom,

(b) "the taxable event" takes place when the income arises or the gain accrues (whether or not, in a remittance basis case, it is remitted to the United Kingdom), and

(c) the income or gain is "untaxed" if it has not been brought into account in an assessment to income tax or, as the case may be, capital gains tax for the tax year in which it is required to be brought into account.

(3) For the value of property forming part of the value transferred by a chargeable transfer—

(a) "the taxable event" takes place when the chargeable transfer is made (or, in the case of a potentially exempt transfer, when death occurs), and

(b) the value of the property is "untaxed" if it has not been brought into account in determining the value transferred by the chargeable transfer.

(4) For the value of supplies on which VAT is charged—

(a) "the taxable event" takes place when P makes the supply, and

(b) the value of the supply is "untaxed" if output tax on the supply has not been accounted for in determining the VAT payable by P for the prescribed accounting period in which P is required to account for output tax on the supply.

(5) Paragraph 4(2)(a) is not satisfied in a case where P is liable to tax only because the liability has been transferred to P as a result of action taken by HMRC (for example, as a result of a notice given under section 77A of VATA 1994 or a direction given under regulation 81 of the Income Tax (PAYE) Regulations 2003 (SI 2003/2682)).

Commentary—*Simon's Taxes* A6.1216.

Refund of one-off payment

12 If a one-off payment is refunded by HMRC in accordance with Article 15(3), this Part ceases to apply with respect to that payment.

Commentary—*Simon's Taxes* A6.1216.

PART 3

THE FUTURE: INCOME TAX AND CAPITAL GAINS TAX

Taxes affected

13 The taxes affected by this Part are—

(a) income tax, and

(b) capital gains tax.

Commentary—*Simon's Taxes* A6.1216.

Application of this Part

14 (1) This Part applies if—

(a) a sum is levied under Article 19 on an amount of income or a gain of a person, and

(b) a certificate is issued to the person under Article 30(1) in respect of the levying of that sum (or sums that include that sum).

(2) This Part also applies if—

(a) a retention is made under EUSA from an amount of income or a gain of a person,

(b) a tax finality payment, as contemplated by the Joint Declaration, is made on the same income or gain, and

(c) a certificate is issued to the person under the Joint Declaration in respect of the making of that payment (or payments that include that payment).

(3) In this Part—

(a) the person is referred to as "P",

(b) the certificate is referred to as "the relevant certificate",

(c) the amount of income, or the gain, is referred to as "the cleared amount",

(d) the account or deposit (within the meaning of the Agreement) to which the certificate relates (or to which certificates relate that include the certificate) is referred to as "the underlying account", and

(e) the sum levied under Article 19 on the cleared amount or, as the case may be, the tax finality payment made on it is referred to as "the transferred sum".

Commentary—*Simon's Taxes* A6.1216.

Effect of relevant certificate

15 (1) The effect of the relevant certificate depends on whether P makes an election under paragraph 16 in respect of the underlying account for the applicable year.

(2) "The applicable year" is the tax year for which P is liable to income tax or, as the case may be, capital gains tax on the cleared amount.

(3) If P makes an election, the transferred sum is to be treated as if it were a credit allowable against the income tax or, as the case may be, capital gains tax due from P for the applicable year.

(4) If P does not make an election, P ceases to be liable to income tax or, as the case may be, capital gains tax on the cleared amount.

(5) Sub-paragraph (4) is to be read in accordance with paragraph 7.

(6) Where P ceases to be liable to tax on the cleared amount, P also ceases to be liable to any ancillary charge directly connected with that amount.

Commentary—*Simon's Taxes* A6.1216.

Election

16 (1) P may make an election under this paragraph in respect of the underlying account for a tax year if all the affected amounts are included in full in a return (or amended return) made by P under Part 2 of TMA 1970 for that tax year.

(2) In relation to a tax year, an amount is an "affected amount" if—

(a) a certificate is issued to P under Article 30(1) or the Joint Declaration in respect of the levying of a sum, or the making of a tax finality payment, on that amount,

(b) the account or deposit to which the certificate relates is the underlying account, and

(c) the amount is required to be brought into account in assessing the income tax or capital gains tax due from P for that tax year.

(3) An election under this paragraph must be made in the return or amended return in which the affected amounts are included.

(4) An election may only be made under this paragraph if it is accompanied by all the relevant certificates relating to the underlying account.

(5) For the purposes of paragraph 15, P is treated as making an election under this paragraph in respect of the underlying account for a tax year if a claim is made under Part 3 of TIOPA 2010 (double taxation relief for special withholding tax) in relation to any of the affected amounts.

(6) Section 143 of TIOPA 2010 (taking account of special withholding tax in calculating income or gains) applies with any necessary modifications in relation to a tax finality payment as it applies in relation to special withholding tax.

Commentary—*Simon's Taxes* **A6.1216**.

Other credits to be allowed first

17 Other than a credit allowed under Part 3 of TIOPA 2010, any credit for foreign tax allowed under that Act against the income tax or, as the case may be, capital gains tax due from P for the applicable year is to be allowed before effect is given to paragraph 15(3).

Commentary—*Simon's Taxes* **A6.1216**.

Repayments

18 (1) Sub-paragraph (2) applies if the amount of a credit allowable under paragraph 15(3) exceeds the amount of income tax or, as the case may be, capital gains tax due from P for the applicable year (before set-off).

(2) The excess is to be set against any amount of the other tax (income tax or capital gains tax) due from P for that year.

(3) Nothing in this Part entitles any person to a repayment or refund of tax, save for any repayment to which P may be entitled as a result of paragraph 15(3) if, in relation to a credit allowable under that paragraph, there is any remaining balance after applying—

(a) sub-paragraph (2), and

(b) section 138(4)(a) or 140(5)(a) of TIOPA 2010, if applicable to the cleared amount.

Commentary—*Simon's Taxes* **A6.1216**.

Relationship with special withholding tax rules

19 The Joint Declaration does not count for the purposes of section 136(6)(b) of TIOPA 2010 (definition of "special withholding tax") as a corresponding provision of international arrangements.

Commentary—*Simon's Taxes* **A6.1216**.

PART 4
THE FUTURE: INHERITANCE TAX

Taxes affected

20 This Part affects inheritance tax.

Application of this Part

21 (1) This Part applies if—

(a) an amount is withheld under Article 32(2) in respect of relevant assets of a deceased person ("P"), and

(b) a certificate is issued under Article 32(6) in respect of the withholding of that amount.

(2) The certificate is referred to in this Part as "the Article 32 certificate".

(3) The relevant assets in relation to which the Article 32 certificate is issued are referred to as "the cleared assets".

(4) Any reference in this Part to "the chargeable transfer" is to the transfer made (under section 4 of IHTA 1984) on P's death.

Commentary—*Simon's Taxes* **A6.1216**.

Effect of Article 32 certificate

22 (1) The cleared assets are to be treated as if they were excluded property in determining the value of P's estate immediately before P's death.

(2) As a result, any ancillary charge directly connected with those assets is also extinguished.
(3) But—

(a) treating the cleared assets as if they were excluded property does not affect any liability to inheritance tax on the rest of P's estate, and
(b) that liability remains what it would have been, had the cleared assets not been treated as excluded property.

(4) Accordingly, if the cleared assets were ever to be included in an account or further account under section 216 or 217 of IHTA 1984 in respect of the chargeable transfer and it were found that the inheritance tax charged on the value of the property in P's estate other than the cleared assets should have been higher, the extra tax charged on the value of that other property remains due, together with any associated ancillary charge.
(5) For the purposes of sub-paragraphs (3) and (4), the value of the cleared assets is assumed to form the highest part of the value transferred by the chargeable transfer.

Commentary—*Simon's Taxes* **A6.1216**.

Election in respect of Article 32 certificates

23 (1) This paragraph applies if the cleared assets for each of the Article 32 certificates issued in respect of P's death are included in full in an account or further account delivered in respect of P's death under section 216 or 217 of IHTA 1984 within the time permitted for delivering such an account or further account.
(2) The person who delivers the account or further account may elect to disapply paragraph 22.
(3) An election under this paragraph must be made in writing at the same time as the account or further account in which all the cleared assets are included, and signed by each person delivering the account or further account.
(4) An election may only be made under this paragraph if it is accompanied by each of the Article 32 certificates.
(5) If an election is made under this paragraph—

(a) paragraph 22 does not apply to the cleared assets for any of the Article 32 certificates issued in respect of P's death, and
(b) the amounts withheld under Article 32(2) are instead to be treated as if they were credits allowable against the inheritance tax due on the value transferred by the chargeable transfer (calculated with the value of all those cleared assets brought into account).

Commentary—*Simon's Taxes* **A6.1216**.

Repayments

24 Nothing in this Part entitles any person to a repayment or refund of tax, save for any repayment to which a person may be entitled as a result of paragraph 23 if the credit allowable under that paragraph exceeds the inheritance tax due from the person on the value transferred by the chargeable transfer.

Commentary—*Simon's Taxes* **A6.1216**.

PART 5
GENERAL PROVISIONS

Information exchange

25 No obligation of secrecy (whether imposed by statute or otherwise) prevents HMRC from disclosing information pursuant to a request made by virtue of Article 36 (reciprocity measures of the United Kingdom).

Commentary—*Simon's Taxes* **A6.1216**.

Amounts recoverable as if they were VAT

26 (1) Part 2 of this Schedule applies to amounts otherwise recoverable under paragraph 5(3) of Schedule 11 to VATA 1994 as a debt due to the Crown (amounts shown on invoices as VAT etc) in the same way as it applies to VAT.
(2) But in the application of Part 2 to such amounts—

(a) a reference to the value of a supply on which VAT is charged is a reference to the value of the supply shown in the invoice mentioned in paragraph 5(2) of that Schedule,
(b) "the taxable event" takes place when the invoice is issued,
(c) the value of the supply shown in the invoice is "untaxed" if the amount otherwise recoverable under paragraph 5(3) of that Schedule has not been recovered, and
(d) "ceasing to be liable" to tax on the value of that supply means that the amount otherwise recoverable is no longer recoverable.

Commentary—*Simon's Taxes* **A6.1216.**

[Transfers to HMRC under Agreement

26A—(1) Income or chargeable gains of a person are to be treated as not remitted to the United Kingdom if conditions A to D are met.

(2) Condition A is that (but for sub-paragraph (1)) the income or gains would be regarded as remitted to the United Kingdom by virtue of the bringing of money to the United Kingdom.

(3) Condition B is that the money is brought to the United Kingdom pursuant to a transfer made to HMRC in accordance with the Agreement.

(4) Condition C (which applies only if the money brought to the United Kingdom is a sum levied under Article 19(2)(*b*)) is that the sum was levied within the period of 45 days beginning with the day on which the amount derived from the income or gain in question was remitted as mentioned in Article 19(2)(*b*).

(5) Condition D is that the transfer is made in relation to a tax year in which section 809B, 809D or 809E of ITA 2007 (application of remittance basis) applies to the person.

(6) Sub-paragraph (1) does not apply in relation to money brought to the United Kingdom if or to the extent that—

(*a*) paragraph 18(2), or section 138(4)(*a*) or 140(5)(*a*) of TIOPA 2010, is applied in relation to it (set-off against other tax liabilities), or

(*b*) it is repaid or refunded by HMRC.][1]

Amendments—[1] Paras 26A, 26B and preceding heading inserted by FA 2013 s 221. This amendment is treated as having come into force on 1 January 2013.

[**26B**—(1) This paragraph applies if—

(*a*) but for paragraph 26A(1), income or chargeable gains would have been regarded as remitted to the United Kingdom by virtue of the bringing of money to the United Kingdom, and

(*b*) section 809Q of ITA 2007 (transfers from mixed funds) would have applied in determining the amount that would have been so remitted.

(2) The bringing of the money to the United Kingdom counts as an offshore transfer for the purposes of section 809R(4) of ITA 2007 (composition of mixed fund).][1]

Amendments—[1] Paras 26A, 26B preceding heading inserted by FA 2013 s 221. This amendment is treated as having come into force on 1 January 2013.

General interpretation

27 (1) In this Schedule—

"ancillary charge" means any interest, penalty, surcharge or other ancillary charge;

"assessment", in relation to a tax, includes a determination and also includes an amended assessment or determination (and "assess" is to be read accordingly);

"chargeable gain" means a gain that is a chargeable gain for the purposes of TCGA 1992;

"chargeable transfer" has the meaning given in section 2 of IHTA 1984;

"EUSA" means the agreement dated 26 October 2004 between the European Community and the Swiss Confederation providing for measures equivalent to those laid down in Council Directive 2003/ 48/EC on taxation on savings income in the form of interest payments;

"HMRC" means Her Majesty's Revenue and Customs;

"qualifying amount" is defined in paragraph 4;

"remitted to the United Kingdom" means remitted to the United Kingdom within the meaning of Chapter A1 of Part 14 of ITA 2007;

"the value transferred", in relation to a chargeable transfer, has the meaning given in section 3 of IHTA 1984;

"taxable amount" is defined in paragraph 2;

"VAT" means value added tax charged in accordance with VATA 1994.

(2) An expression used in relation to a tax has the same meaning as in enactments relating to that tax.

(3) A reference to a person being "liable" includes being liable jointly with others.

(4) A reference to the most beneficial outcome for P is a reference to the most beneficial outcome for P with respect to P's liability to tax.

(5) A reference to the tax due "taking account of" a qualifying amount is—

(a) if the amount is an amount of income or a chargeable gain, a reference to the income tax or capital gains tax due for the tax year in which the amount is required to be brought into account (calculated with that amount brought into account),

(b) if the amount is the value of property forming part of the value transferred by a chargeable transfer, a reference to the inheritance tax due on the value transferred by the chargeable transfer (calculated with that amount brought into account),

(c) if the amount is the value of a supply on which VAT is charged, a reference to the VAT payable for the prescribed accounting period in which output tax on the supply is required to be brought into account (calculated with that output tax brought into account), and

(d) if the amount is the value of a supply to which Part 2 applies by virtue of paragraph 26, a reference to the amount otherwise recoverable under paragraph 5(3) of Schedule 11 to VATA 1994 in respect of that supply.

Commentary—*Simon's Taxes* **A6.1216**.

SCHEDULE 38

TAX AGENTS: DISHONEST CONDUCT

Section 223

Commentary—*Simon's Taxes* **A6.321**.

HMRC Manuals—Compliance Handbook, CH186240 (Human Rights Act and Data Protection Act).

Commencement—Finance Act 2012, Schedule 38 (Tax Agents: Dishonest Conduct) (Appointed Day and Savings) Order, SI 2013/279 (1 April 2013 appointed as the day on which Sch 38 comes into force).

Cross-references—See the Small Charitable Donations Regulations, SI 2013/938 reg 6 (modification of Parts 1–6 of this Schedule in relation to an individual who, in the course of business, assists a charity in connection with a top-up claim, a top-up payment or an overpayment under the Small Charitable Donations Act 2012).

Social Security (Contributions) (Amendment and Application of Schedule 38 to the Finance Act 2012) Regulations SI 2013/622 (application of this Schedule in relation to Class 1, Class 1A, Class 1B and Class 2 National Insurance contributions as in relation to tax to the extent that they do not already apply.

PART 1

INTRODUCTION

Overview

1 This Schedule is arranged as follows—

(a) this Part explains who is a tax agent and what it means to engage in dishonest conduct,

(b) Part 2 sets out the process for establishing whether someone is engaging in or has engaged in dishonest conduct,

(c) Part 3 confers power on HMRC to obtain relevant documents,

(d) Part 4 sets out sanctions for engaging in dishonest conduct,

(e) Part 5 provides for assessment of and appeals against penalties, and

(f) Parts 6 and 7 contain miscellaneous provisions and consequential amendments.

Commentary—*Simon's Taxes* **A6.321**.

Commencement—Finance Act 2012, Schedule 38 (Tax Agents: Dishonest Conduct) (Appointed Day and Savings) Order, SI 2013/279 (1 April 2013 appointed as the day on which Sch 38 comes into force).

Tax agent

2 (1) A "tax agent" is an individual who, in the course of business, assists other persons ("clients") with their tax affairs.

(2) Individuals can be tax agents even if they (or the organisations for which they work) are appointed—

(a) indirectly, or

(b) at the request of someone other than the client.

(3) Assistance with a client's tax affairs includes—

(a) advising a client in relation to tax, and

(b) acting or purporting to act as agent on behalf of a client in relation to tax.

(4) Assistance with a client's tax affairs also includes assistance with any document that is likely to be relied on by HMRC to determine a client's tax position.

(5) Assistance given for non-tax purposes counts as assistance with a client's tax affairs if it is given in the knowledge that it will be, or is likely to be, used by a client in connection with the client's tax affairs.

Commentary—*Simon's Taxes* **A6.321**.

Commencement—Finance Act 2012, Schedule 38 (Tax Agents: Dishonest Conduct) (Appointed Day and Savings) Order, SI 2013/279 (1 April 2013 appointed as the day on which Sch 38 comes into force).

Dishonest conduct

3 (1) An individual "engages in dishonest conduct" if, in the course of acting as a tax agent, the individual does something dishonest with a view to bringing about a loss of tax revenue.

(2) It does not matter whether a loss is actually brought about.

(3) Nor does it matter whether the individual is acting on the instruction of clients.

(4) A loss of tax revenue would be brought about for these purposes if clients were to—

(a) account for less tax than they are required to account for by law,
(b) obtain more tax relief than they are entitled to obtain by law,
(c) account for tax later than they are required to account for it by law, or
(d) obtain tax relief earlier than they are entitled to obtain it by law.

(5) "Tax" is defined in Part 6 of this Schedule.

(6) "Tax relief" includes—
(a) any exemption from or deduction or credit against or in respect of tax, and
(b) any repayment of tax.

(7) A reference in this paragraph to doing something dishonest includes—
(a) dishonestly omitting to do something, and
(b) advising or assisting a client to do something that the individual knows to be dishonest.

Commentary—*Simon's Taxes* **A6.322**.

Commencement—Finance Act 2012, Schedule 38 (Tax Agents: Dishonest Conduct) (Appointed Day and Savings) Order, SI 2013/279 (1 April 2013 appointed as the day on which Sch 38 comes into force).

PART 2
ESTABLISHING DISHONEST CONDUCT

Conduct notice

4 (1) This paragraph applies if HMRC determine that an individual is engaging in or has engaged in dishonest conduct.

(2) An authorised officer (or an officer of Revenue and Customs with the approval of an authorised officer) may notify the individual of that determination.

(3) The notice must state the grounds on which the determination was made.

(4) For the effect of notifying the individual, see paragraphs 7(2) and 29(2).

(5) A notice under this paragraph is referred to as a "conduct notice".

(6) In relation to a conduct notice, a reference to "the determination" is to the determination forming the subject of the notice.

Commentary—*Simon's Taxes* **A6.322**.

Commencement—Finance Act 2012, Schedule 38 (Tax Agents: Dishonest Conduct) (Appointed Day and Savings) Order, SI 2013/279 (1 April 2013 appointed as the day on which Sch 38 comes into force).

Cross references—See FA 2014 Sch 34 para 4 (application of this para in relation to the issue of conduct notices to promoters of tax avoidance schemes).

Appeal against determination

5 (1) An individual to whom a conduct notice is given may appeal against the determination.

(2) Notice of appeal must be given—
(a) in writing to the officer who gave the conduct notice, and
(b) within the period of 30 days beginning with the day on which the conduct notice was given.

(3) It must state the grounds of appeal.

(4) On an appeal that is notified to the tribunal, the tribunal may confirm or set aside the determination.

(5) Subject to this paragraph, the provisions of Part 5 of TMA 1970 relating to appeals have effect in relation to an appeal under this paragraph as they have effect in relation to an appeal against an assessment to income tax.

(6) Setting aside a determination does not prevent a further conduct notice being given in respect of the same conduct if further evidence emerges.

Commentary—*Simon's Taxes* **A6.322**.

Commencement—Finance Act 2012, Schedule 38 (Tax Agents: Dishonest Conduct) (Appointed Day and Savings) Order, SI 2013/279 (1 April 2013 appointed as the day on which Sch 38 comes into force).

Offence of concealment etc in connection with conduct notice

6 (1) A person ("P") commits an offence if, after a relevant event has occurred, P—
(a) conceals, destroys or otherwise disposes of a material document, or
(b) arranges for the concealment, destruction or disposal of a material document.

(2) A "relevant event" occurs if—
(a) a conduct notice is given to an individual, or
(b) an individual is informed by an officer of Revenue and Customs that a conduct notice will be or is likely to be given to the individual.

(3) A "material document" is any document that could be sought under paragraph 8 as a result of the giving of the conduct notice.

(4) If P acts after the event described in sub-paragraph (2)(a), no offence is committed if P acts—
(a) after the determination has been set aside,

(b) more than 4 years after the conduct notice was given, or

(c) without knowledge of that event.

(5) If P acts before that event but after the event described in sub-paragraph (2)(b), no offence is committed if P acts—

(a) more than 2 years after the individual was, or was last, so informed, or

(b) without knowledge of the event described in sub-paragraph (2)(b).

(6) P acts without knowledge of an event if P—

(a) is not the individual with respect to whom the event has occurred, and

(b) does not know, and could not reasonably be expected to know, that the event has occurred.

(7) A person guilty of an offence under this paragraph is liable—

(a) on summary conviction, to a fine not exceeding the statutory maximum, and

(b) on conviction on indictment, to imprisonment for a term not exceeding 2 years or to a fine, or both.

Commentary—*Simon's Taxes* **A6.322**.

Commencement—Finance Act 2012, Schedule 38 (Tax Agents: Dishonest Conduct) (Appointed Day and Savings) Order, SI 2013/279 (1 April 2013 appointed as the day on which Sch 38 comes into force).

PART 3
POWER TO OBTAIN TAX AGENT'S FILES ETC

Circumstances in which power is exercisable

7 (1) The power in paragraph 8 is exercisable only in case A or case B and only with the approval of the tribunal.

(2) Case A is where a conduct notice has been given to an individual and either—

(a) the time allowed for giving notice of appeal against the determination has expired without any such notice being given, or

(b) notice of appeal against the determination was given within that time, but the appeal has been withdrawn or the determination confirmed.

(3) Case B is where—

(a) an individual has been convicted of an offence relating to tax that involves fraud or dishonesty,

(b) the offence was committed after the individual became a tax agent (whether or not the individual was still a tax agent when it was committed and regardless of the capacity in which it was committed),

(c) either—

(i) the time allowed for appealing against the conviction has expired without any such appeal being brought, or

(ii) an appeal against the conviction was brought within that time, but the appeal has been withdrawn or the conviction upheld, and

(d) no more than 12 months have elapsed since the date on which paragraph (c) was satisfied.

(4) For the purposes of this paragraph, a determination or conviction that is appealed is not considered to have been confirmed or upheld until—

(a) the time allowed for bringing any further appeal has expired, or

(b) if a further appeal is brought within that time, that further appeal has been withdrawn or determined.

(5) In this Schedule, a reference to "the tax agent" is—

(a) in a case falling within case A, a reference to the individual mentioned in sub-paragraph (2), and

(b) in a case falling within case B, a reference to the individual mentioned in sub-paragraph (3).

(6) It does not matter whether the individual is still a tax agent when the power in paragraph 8 is to be exercised.

Commentary—*Simon's Taxes* **A6.323**.

Commencement—Finance Act 2012, Schedule 38 (Tax Agents: Dishonest Conduct) (Appointed Day and Savings) Order, SI 2013/279 (1 April 2013 appointed as the day on which Sch 38 comes into force).

Cross-references—See Finance Act 2009, Section 101 (Tax Agents: Dishonest Conduct) (Appointed Day) Order, SI 2013/280 (the day appointed for the coming into force of FA 2009 s 101 is 1 April 2013 for the purposes of penalties assessed under FA 2012 Sch 38 Parts 3–5.

File access notice

8 (1) Subject to paragraph 7, an officer of Revenue and Customs may by notice in writing require any person mentioned in sub-paragraph (2) to provide relevant documents.

(2) The persons are—

(a) the tax agent, and

(b) any other person the officer believes may hold relevant documents.

(3) "Relevant documents" is defined in paragraph 9.

(4) A notice under this paragraph is referred to as a "file access notice".

(5) The person to whom a file access notice is given is referred to as "the document-holder".

Commentary—*Simon's Taxes* **A6.323**.

Commencement—Finance Act 2012, Schedule 38 (Tax Agents: Dishonest Conduct) (Appointed Day and Savings) Order, SI 2013/279 (1 April 2013 appointed as the day on which Sch 38 comes into force).

Cross-references—See Finance Act 2009, Section 101 (Tax Agents: Dishonest Conduct) (Appointed Day) Order, SI 2013/280 (the day appointed for the coming into force of FA 2009 s 101 is 1 April 2013 for the purposes of penalties assessed under FA 2012 Sch 38 Parts 3–5.

Relevant documents

9 (1) "Relevant documents" means the tax agent's working papers (whenever acting as a tax agent) and any other documents received, created, prepared or used by the tax agent for the purposes of or in the course of assisting clients with their tax affairs.

(2) It does not matter who owns the papers or other documents.

(3) The reference in sub-paragraph (1) to clients—

(a) includes former clients, and

(b) is not limited to the clients with respect to whom the tax agent is engaging in or has engaged in dishonest conduct.

Commentary—*Simon's Taxes* **A6.323**.

Commencement—Finance Act 2012, Schedule 38 (Tax Agents: Dishonest Conduct) (Appointed Day and Savings) Order, SI 2013/279 (1 April 2013 appointed as the day on which Sch 38 comes into force).

Cross-references—See Finance Act 2009, Section 101 (Tax Agents: Dishonest Conduct) (Appointed Day) Order, SI 2013/280 (the day appointed for the coming into force of FA 2009 s 101 is 1 April 2013 for the purposes of penalties assessed under FA 2012 Sch 38 Parts 3–5.

Content of notice

10 (1) A file access notice may require the provision of—

(a) particular relevant documents specified in the notice, or

(b) all relevant documents in the document-holder's possession or power.

(2) A file access notice does not need to identify the clients of the tax agent.

(3) A file access notice addressed to anyone other than the tax agent must name the tax agent.

Commentary—*Simon's Taxes* **A6.323**.

Commencement—Finance Act 2012, Schedule 38 (Tax Agents: Dishonest Conduct) (Appointed Day and Savings) Order, SI 2013/279 (1 April 2013 appointed as the day on which Sch 38 comes into force).

Cross-references—See Finance Act 2009, Section 101 (Tax Agents: Dishonest Conduct) (Appointed Day) Order, SI 2013/280 (the day appointed for the coming into force of FA 2009 s 101 is 1 April 2013 for the purposes of penalties assessed under FA 2012 Sch 38 Parts 3–5.

Compliance

11 A file access notice may require documents to be provided—

(a) within such period,

(b) by such means and in such form, and

(c) to such person and at such place,

as is reasonably specified in the notice or in a document referred to in the notice.

Commentary—*Simon's Taxes* **A6.323**.

Commencement—Finance Act 2012, Schedule 38 (Tax Agents: Dishonest Conduct) (Appointed Day and Savings) Order, SI 2013/279 (1 April 2013 appointed as the day on which Sch 38 comes into force).

Cross-references—See Finance Act 2009, Section 101 (Tax Agents: Dishonest Conduct) (Appointed Day) Order, SI 2013/280 (the day appointed for the coming into force of FA 2009 s 101 is 1 April 2013 for the purposes of penalties assessed under FA 2012 Sch 38 Parts 3–5.

12 Unless otherwise specified in the notice, a file access notice may be complied with by providing copies of the relevant documents.

Commentary—*Simon's Taxes* **A6.323**.

Commencement—Finance Act 2012, Schedule 38 (Tax Agents: Dishonest Conduct) (Appointed Day and Savings) Order, SI 2013/279 (1 April 2013 appointed as the day on which Sch 38 comes into force).

Cross-references—See Finance Act 2009, Section 101 (Tax Agents: Dishonest Conduct) (Appointed Day) Order, SI 2013/280 (the day appointed for the coming into force of FA 2009 s 101 is 1 April 2013 for the purposes of penalties assessed under FA 2012 Sch 38 Parts 3–5.

Approval by tribunal

13 (1) The tribunal may not approve the giving of a file access notice unless—

(a) the application for approval is made by or with the agreement of an authorised officer,

(b) the tribunal is satisfied that the case falls within case A or case B (see paragraph 7),
(c) the tribunal is satisfied that, in the circumstances, the officer giving the notice is justified in doing so,
(d) the document-holder and (where different) the tax agent have been told that relevant documents are to be required and given a reasonable opportunity to make representations to an officer of Revenue and Customs, and
(e) the tribunal has been given a summary of any representations so made.

(2) Nothing in sub-paragraph (1) requires the tribunal to determine whether an individual is engaging in or has engaged in dishonest conduct.

(3) A decision by the tribunal under this paragraph is final (despite the provisions of sections 11 and 13 of the Tribunals, Courts and Enforcement Act 2007).

Commentary—*Simon's Taxes* **A6.323**.

Commencement—Finance Act 2012, Schedule 38 (Tax Agents: Dishonest Conduct) (Appointed Day and Savings) Order, SI 2013/279 (1 April 2013 appointed as the day on which Sch 38 comes into force).

Cross-references—See Finance Act 2009, Section 101 (Tax Agents: Dishonest Conduct) (Appointed Day) Order, SI 2013/280 (the day appointed for the coming into force of FA 2009 s 101 is 1 April 2013 for the purposes of penalties assessed under FA 2012 Sch 38 Parts 3–5.

Documents not in person's possession or power

14 A file access notice only requires the document-holder to provide a document if it is in the document-holder's possession or power.

Commentary—*Simon's Taxes* **A6.323**.

Commencement—Finance Act 2012, Schedule 38 (Tax Agents: Dishonest Conduct) (Appointed Day and Savings) Order, SI 2013/279 (1 April 2013 appointed as the day on which Sch 38 comes into force).

Cross-references—See Finance Act 2009, Section 101 (Tax Agents: Dishonest Conduct) (Appointed Day) Order, SI 2013/280 (the day appointed for the coming into force of FA 2009 s 101 is 1 April 2013 for the purposes of penalties assessed under FA 2012 Sch 38 Parts 3–5.

Types of information

15 (1) A file access notice does not require the document-holder to provide—
(a) parts of a document that contain information relating to the conduct of a pending appeal relating to tax, or
(b) journalistic material (as defined in section 13 of the Police and Criminal Evidence Act 1984).

(2) A file access notice does not require the document-holder to provide personal records (as defined in section 12 of the Police and Criminal Evidence Act 1984).

(3) But a file access notice may require the document-holder to provide documents that are personal records, omitting any information whose inclusion (whether alone or with other information) makes the original documents personal records.

Commentary—*Simon's Taxes* **A6.323**.

Commencement—Finance Act 2012, Schedule 38 (Tax Agents: Dishonest Conduct) (Appointed Day and Savings) Order, SI 2013/279 (1 April 2013 appointed as the day on which Sch 38 comes into force).

Cross-references—See Finance Act 2009, Section 101 (Tax Agents: Dishonest Conduct) (Appointed Day) Order, SI 2013/280 (the day appointed for the coming into force of FA 2009 s 101 is 1 April 2013 for the purposes of penalties assessed under FA 2012 Sch 38 Parts 3–5.

Old documents

16 (1) A file access notice does not require the document-holder to provide a relevant document if—
(a) the whole of the document originated before the back-stop day, and
(b) no part of it has a bearing on tax periods ending on or after that day.

(2) "The back-stop day" is the first day of the period of 20 years ending with the day on which the file access notice is given.

Commentary—*Simon's Taxes* **A6.323**.

Commencement—Finance Act 2012, Schedule 38 (Tax Agents: Dishonest Conduct) (Appointed Day and Savings) Order, SI 2013/279 (1 April 2013 appointed as the day on which Sch 38 comes into force).

Cross-references—See Finance Act 2009, Section 101 (Tax Agents: Dishonest Conduct) (Appointed Day) Order, SI 2013/280 (the day appointed for the coming into force of FA 2009 s 101 is 1 April 2013 for the purposes of penalties assessed under FA 2012 Sch 38 Parts 3–5.

Privileged communications between professional legal advisers and clients

17 (1) A file access notice does not require the document-holder to provide any part of a document that is privileged.

(2) For the purposes of this paragraph a document is privileged if it is a document in respect of which a claim to legal professional privilege, or (in Scotland) to confidentiality of communications between client and professional legal adviser, could be maintained in legal proceedings.

(3) Regulations under paragraph 23 of Schedule 36 to FA 2008 (information powers: privileged communications) apply (with any necessary modifications) to disputes under this paragraph as to whether a document is privileged.

Commentary—*Simon's Taxes* **A6.323**.

Commencement—Finance Act 2012, Schedule 38 (Tax Agents: Dishonest Conduct) (Appointed Day and Savings) Order, SI 2013/279 (1 April 2013 appointed as the day on which Sch 38 comes into force).

Cross-references—See Finance Act 2009, Section 101 (Tax Agents: Dishonest Conduct) (Appointed Day) Order, SI 2013/280 (the day appointed for the coming into force of FA 2009 s 101 is 1 April 2013 for the purposes of penalties assessed under FA 2012 Sch 38 Parts 3–5.

Power to copy documents

18 If a document is provided pursuant to a file access notice, an officer of Revenue and Customs may take copies of or make extracts from the document.

Commentary—*Simon's Taxes* **A6.323**.

Commencement—Finance Act 2012, Schedule 38 (Tax Agents: Dishonest Conduct) (Appointed Day and Savings) Order, SI 2013/279 (1 April 2013 appointed as the day on which Sch 38 comes into force).

Cross-references—See Finance Act 2009, Section 101 (Tax Agents: Dishonest Conduct) (Appointed Day) Order, SI 2013/280 (the day appointed for the coming into force of FA 2009 s 101 is 1 April 2013 for the purposes of penalties assessed under FA 2012 Sch 38 Parts 3–5.

Power to retain documents

19 (1) If a document is provided pursuant to a file access notice, HMRC may retain the document for a reasonable period if an officer of Revenue and Customs thinks it necessary to do so.

(2) While a document is retained—

(a) the document-holder may, if the document is reasonably required for any purpose, request a copy of it, and

(b) an officer of Revenue and Customs must comply with such a request without charge.

(3) The retention of a document under this paragraph is not to be regarded as breaking any lien claimed on the document.

(4) If a document retained under this paragraph is lost or damaged, the Commissioners are liable to compensate the owner of the document for any expenses reasonably incurred in replacing or repairing the document.

Commentary—*Simon's Taxes* **A6.323**.

Commencement—Finance Act 2012, Schedule 38 (Tax Agents: Dishonest Conduct) (Appointed Day and Savings) Order, SI 2013/279 (1 April 2013 appointed as the day on which Sch 38 comes into force).

Cross-references—See Finance Act 2009, Section 101 (Tax Agents: Dishonest Conduct) (Appointed Day) Order, SI 2013/280 (the day appointed for the coming into force of FA 2009 s 101 is 1 April 2013 for the purposes of penalties assessed under FA 2012 Sch 38 Parts 3–5.

Appeal against file access notice

20 (1) If the document-holder is a person other than the tax agent, the document-holder may appeal against the file access notice, or any requirement in it, on the ground that it would be unduly onerous to comply with the notice or requirement.

(2) Notice of appeal must be given—

(a) in writing to the officer by whom the file access notice was given, and

(b) within the period of 30 days beginning with the day on which the file access notice was given.

(3) It must state the grounds of appeal.

(4) On an appeal that is notified to the tribunal, the tribunal may confirm, vary or set aside the file access notice or a requirement in it.

(5) If the tribunal confirms or varies the notice or a requirement in it, the document-holder must comply with the notice or requirement—

(a) within such period as is specified by the tribunal, or

(b) if the tribunal does not specify a period, within such period as is reasonably specified in writing by an officer of Revenue and Customs following the tribunal's decision.

(6) A decision by the tribunal under this paragraph is final (despite the provisions of sections 11 and 13 of the Tribunals, Courts and Enforcement Act 2007).

(7) Subject to this paragraph, the provisions of Part 5 of TMA 1970 relating to appeals have effect in relation to an appeal under this paragraph as they have effect in relation to an appeal against an assessment to income tax.

Commentary—*Simon's Taxes* **A6.323**.

Commencement—Finance Act 2012, Schedule 38 (Tax Agents: Dishonest Conduct) (Appointed Day and Savings) Order, SI 2013/279 (1 April 2013 appointed as the day on which Sch 38 comes into force).

Cross-references—See Finance Act 2009, Section 101 (Tax Agents: Dishonest Conduct) (Appointed Day) Order, SI 2013/280 (the day appointed for the coming into force of FA 2009 s 101 is 1 April 2013 for the purposes of penalties assessed under FA 2012 Sch 38 Parts 3–5.

Offence of concealment etc in connection with file access notice

21 (1) A person ("P") commits an offence if P—

(a) conceals, destroys or otherwise disposes of a required document, or

(b) arranges for the concealment, destruction or disposal of a required document.

(2) A "required document" is a document within sub-paragraph (3) or subparagraph (4).

(3) A document is within this sub-paragraph if at the time when P acts—

(a) P is required to provide the document by a file access notice, and

(b) either—

(i) the notice has not been complied with, or

(ii) it has been complied with, but P has been notified in writing by an officer of Revenue and Customs that P must continue to preserve the document (and the notification has not been withdrawn).

(4) A document is within this sub-paragraph if at the time when P acts—

(a) P is not required to provide the document by a file access notice,

(b) P has been informed by an officer of Revenue and Customs that P will be or is likely to be so required, and

(c) no more than 6 months have elapsed since P was, or was last, so informed.

(5) A person guilty of an offence under this paragraph is liable—

(a) on summary conviction, to a fine not exceeding the statutory maximum, and

(b) on conviction on indictment, to imprisonment for a term not exceeding 2 years or to a fine, or both.

Commentary—*Simon's Taxes* **A6.323**.

Commencement—Finance Act 2012, Schedule 38 (Tax Agents: Dishonest Conduct) (Appointed Day and Savings) Order, SI 2013/279 (1 April 2013 appointed as the day on which Sch 38 comes into force).

Cross-references—See Finance Act 2009, Section 101 (Tax Agents: Dishonest Conduct) (Appointed Day) Order, SI 2013/280 (the day appointed for the coming into force of FA 2009 s 101 is 1 April 2013 for the purposes of penalties assessed under FA 2012 Sch 38 Parts 3–5.

Penalty for failure to comply

22 (1) A person who fails to comply with a file access notice is liable to a penalty of £300.

(2) Failing to comply with a file access notice also includes—

(a) concealing, destroying or otherwise disposing of a required document, or

(b) arranging for any such concealment, destruction or disposal.

(3) "Required document" has the same meaning as in paragraph 21.

Commentary—*Simon's Taxes* **A4.595**.

Commencement—Finance Act 2012, Schedule 38 (Tax Agents: Dishonest Conduct) (Appointed Day and Savings) Order, SI 2013/279 (1 April 2013 appointed as the day on which Sch 38 comes into force).

Cross-references—See Finance Act 2009, Section 101 (Tax Agents: Dishonest Conduct) (Appointed Day) Order, SI 2013/280 (the day appointed for the coming into force of FA 2009 s 101 is 1 April 2013 for the purposes of penalties assessed under FA 2012 Sch 38 Parts 3–5.

Daily penalty for failure to comply

23 If the failure continues after notification of a penalty under paragraph 22 has been issued, the person is liable to a further penalty, for each subsequent day on which the failure continues, of an amount not exceeding £60 for each such day.

Commentary—*Simon's Taxes* **A4.595**.

Commencement—Finance Act 2012, Schedule 38 (Tax Agents: Dishonest Conduct) (Appointed Day and Savings) Order, SI 2013/279 (1 April 2013 appointed as the day on which Sch 38 comes into force).

Cross-references—See Finance Act 2009, Section 101 (Tax Agents: Dishonest Conduct) (Appointed Day) Order, SI 2013/280 (the day appointed for the coming into force of FA 2009 s 101 is 1 April 2013 for the purposes of penalties assessed under FA 2012 Sch 38 Parts 3–5.

Failure to comply with time limit

24 A failure to do anything required to be done within a limited period of time does not give rise to liability to a penalty under paragraph 22 or 23 if the thing was done within such further time (if any) as an officer of Revenue and Customs may have allowed.

Commentary—*Simon's Taxes* **A4.595**.

Commencement—Finance Act 2012, Schedule 38 (Tax Agents: Dishonest Conduct) (Appointed Day and Savings) Order, SI 2013/279 (1 April 2013 appointed as the day on which Sch 38 comes into force).

Cross-references—See Finance Act 2009, Section 101 (Tax Agents: Dishonest Conduct) (Appointed Day) Order, SI 2013/280 (the day appointed for the coming into force of FA 2009 s 101 is 1 April 2013 for the purposes of penalties assessed under FA 2012 Sch 38 Parts 3–5.

Reasonable excuse

25 (1) Liability to a penalty under paragraph 22 or 23 does not arise if the person satisfies HMRC or (on an appeal notified to the tribunal) the tribunal that there is a reasonable excuse for the failure.

(2) For the purposes of this paragraph—

- (a) an insufficiency of funds is not a reasonable excuse unless attributable to events outside the person's control,
- (b) if the person relies on another person to do anything, that is not a reasonable excuse unless the first person took reasonable care to avoid the failure,
- (c) if the person had a reasonable excuse for the failure but the excuse has ceased, the person is to be treated as having continued to have the excuse if the failure is remedied without unreasonable delay after the excuse ceased.

Commentary—*Simon's Taxes* **A4.595**.

Commencement—Finance Act 2012, Schedule 38 (Tax Agents: Dishonest Conduct) (Appointed Day and Savings) Order, SI 2013/279 (1 April 2013 appointed as the day on which Sch 38 comes into force).

Cross-references—See Finance Act 2009, Section 101 (Tax Agents: Dishonest Conduct) (Appointed Day) Order, SI 2013/280 (the day appointed for the coming into force of FA 2009 s 101 is 1 April 2013 for the purposes of penalties assessed under FA 2012 Sch 38 Parts 3–5.

PART 4
SANCTIONS FOR DISHONEST CONDUCT

Penalty for dishonest conduct

26 (1) An individual who engages in dishonest conduct is liable to a penalty.

(2) Subject to paragraph 27, the penalty to which the individual is liable is to be—

- (a) no less than £5,000, and
- (b) no more than £50,000.

(3) In assessing the amount of the penalty, regard must be had to—

- (a) whether the individual disclosed the dishonest conduct,
- (b) whether that disclosure was prompted or unprompted,
- (c) the quality of that disclosure, and
- (d) the quality of the individual's compliance with any file access notice in connection with the dishonest conduct.

(4) An individual "discloses" dishonest conduct by—

- (a) telling HMRC about it,
- (b) giving HMRC reasonable help in identifying the client or clients concerned and in quantifying the loss of tax revenue (if any) brought about by it, and
- (c) allowing HMRC access to records for the purpose of ensuring that any such loss is recovered or otherwise properly accounted for.

(5) A disclosure is "unprompted" if it is made at a time when the individual has no reason to believe that HMRC have discovered or are about to discover the dishonest conduct.

(6) Otherwise, a disclosure is "prompted".

(7) In relation to disclosure or compliance, "quality" includes timing, nature and extent.

Commentary—*Simon's Taxes* **A4.595**.

Commencement—Finance Act 2012, Schedule 38 (Tax Agents: Dishonest Conduct) (Appointed Day and Savings) Order, SI 2013/279 (1 April 2013 appointed as the day on which Sch 38 comes into force).

Cross-references—See Finance Act 2009, Section 101 (Tax Agents: Dishonest Conduct) (Appointed Day) Order, SI 2013/280 (the day appointed for the coming into force of FA 2009 s 101 is 1 April 2013 for the purposes of penalties assessed under FA 2012 Sch 38 Parts 3–5.

Special reduction

27 (1) This paragraph applies if HMRC propose to assess an individual to a penalty under paragraph 26 of £5,000.

(2) If they think it right because of special circumstances, HMRC may take one or more of the following steps—

- (a) reduce the penalty to an amount below £5,000 (which may be nil),
- (b) stay the penalty, or
- (c) agree a compromise in relation to proceedings for the penalty.

(3) "Special circumstances" does not include—

- (a) ability to pay, or
- (b) the fact that a loss of tax revenue from a client is balanced by an overpayment by another person (whether or not a client).

Commentary—*Simon's Taxes* **A4.595**.

Commencement—Finance Act 2012, Schedule 38 (Tax Agents: Dishonest Conduct) (Appointed Day and Savings) Order, SI 2013/279 (1 April 2013 appointed as the day on which Sch 38 comes into force).

Cross-references—See Finance Act 2009, Section 101 (Tax Agents: Dishonest Conduct) (Appointed Day) Order, SI 2013/280 (the day appointed for the coming into force of FA 2009 s 101 is 1 April 2013 for the purposes of penalties assessed under FA 2012 Sch 38 Parts 3–5.

Power to publish details

28 (1) The Commissioners may publish information about an individual if the individual incurs a penalty under paragraph 26.

(2) The information that may be published is—

(a) the individual's name (including any trading name, previous name or pseudonym),
(b) the individual's address,
(c) the nature of any business carried on by the individual,
(d) the amount of the penalty,
(e) the periods or times to which the dishonest conduct relates,
(f) any other information the Commissioners consider it appropriate to publish in order to make clear the individual's identity, and
(g) the link (if there is one) between the dishonest conduct and any inaccuracy, failure or action as a result of which information is published under section 94 of FA 2009 (which relates to deliberate tax defaulters).

(3) No information may be published under this paragraph if the penalty incurred by the individual is £5,000 or less.

(4) Subsections (5) to (9) and (11) of section 94 of FA 2009 apply to publishing information about an individual under this paragraph as they apply to publishing information about a person under that section.

(5) If, in acting as a tax agent, the individual works or worked for an organisation, sub-paragraph (2)(f) includes power to publish such information about that organisation as the Commissioners consider appropriate in order to make clear the individual's identity.

(6) Before publishing information about the organisation, the Commissioners must—

(a) inform the organisation that they are considering doing so, and
(b) afford the organisation reasonable opportunity to make representations about whether it should be published.

Commentary—*Simon's Taxes* **A4.587**.

Commencement—Finance Act 2012, Schedule 38 (Tax Agents: Dishonest Conduct) (Appointed Day and Savings) Order, SI 2013/279 (1 April 2013 appointed as the day on which Sch 38 comes into force).

Cross-references—See Finance Act 2009, Section 101 (Tax Agents: Dishonest Conduct) (Appointed Day) Order, SI 2013/280 (the day appointed for the coming into force of FA 2009 s 101 is 1 April 2013 for the purposes of penalties assessed under FA 2012 Sch 38 Parts 3–5.

PART 5

PENALTIES: ASSESSMENT ETC

Assessment of penalties

29 (1) If a person becomes liable to a penalty under Part 3 or 4 of this Schedule, HMRC may assess the penalty.

(2) But, in the case of a penalty under Part 4, they may only do so if a conduct notice has been given to the person and either—

(a) the time allowed for giving notice of appeal against the determination has expired without notice of appeal being given, or
(b) notice of appeal against the determination was given within the time allowed, but the appeal has been withdrawn or the determination confirmed.

(3) Paragraph 7(4) applies for the purposes of sub-paragraph (2)(b).

(4) If HMRC assess a penalty, they must notify the person.

Commentary—*Simon's Taxes* **A4.595**.

Commencement—Finance Act 2012, Schedule 38 (Tax Agents: Dishonest Conduct) (Appointed Day and Savings) Order, SI 2013/279 (1 April 2013 appointed as the day on which Sch 38 comes into force).

Cross-references—See Finance Act 2009, Section 101 (Tax Agents: Dishonest Conduct) (Appointed Day) Order, SI 2013/280 (the day appointed for the coming into force of FA 2009 s 101 is 1 April 2013 for the purposes of penalties assessed under FA 2012 Sch 38 Parts 3–5.

30 (1) HMRC may not assess a penalty under this Schedule after the applicable deadline.

(2) For a penalty under Part 3, the applicable deadline is the end of the period of 12 months beginning with the day on which the person became liable to the penalty.

(3) For a penalty under Part 4, the applicable deadline is the end of the period of 12 months beginning with the later of—

(a) the first day on which HMRC may assess the penalty (see paragraph 29(2)), and

(b) day X.

(4) If a loss of tax revenue is brought about by the dishonest conduct, day X is—

(a) the day immediately following the end of the appeal period for the assessment or determination of the tax revenue lost (or, if more than one client is involved, the end of the last such period), or

(b) if there is no such assessment or determination, the day on which the amount of tax revenue lost is ascertained.

(5) Otherwise, day X is the day on which HMRC ascertain that no loss of tax revenue has been brought about by the dishonest conduct.

(6) In sub-paragraph (4), "appeal period" means the period during which—

(a) an appeal could be brought, or

(b) an appeal that has been brought has not been withdrawn or determined.

Commentary—*Simon's Taxes* **A4.595**.

Commencement—Finance Act 2012, Schedule 38 (Tax Agents: Dishonest Conduct) (Appointed Day and Savings) Order, SI 2013/279 (1 April 2013 appointed as the day on which Sch 38 comes into force).

Cross-references—See Finance Act 2009, Section 101 (Tax Agents: Dishonest Conduct) (Appointed Day) Order, SI 2013/280 (the day appointed for the coming into force of FA 2009 s 101 is 1 April 2013 for the purposes of penalties assessed under FA 2012 Sch 38 Parts 3–5.

Appeal against penalty

31 (1) A person may appeal against a decision of HMRC—

(a) that a penalty is payable under Part 3 of this Schedule, or

(b) as to the amount of a penalty payable under Part 3 or 4 of this Schedule.

(2) Notice of appeal must be given—

(a) in writing to HMRC, and

(b) before the end of the period of 30 days beginning with the day on which notification of the penalty was issued.

(3) It must state the grounds of appeal.

(4) On an appeal under sub-paragraph (1)(a) that is notified to the tribunal, the tribunal may confirm or cancel the decision.

(5) On an appeal under sub-paragraph (1)(b) that is notified to the tribunal, the tribunal may—

(a) confirm the decision, or

(b) substitute for the decision another decision that HMRC had power to make.

(6) If, in the case of an appeal against a penalty under Part 4, the tribunal substitutes its decision for HMRC's, the tribunal may rely on paragraph 27 (special reduction)—

(a) to the same extent as HMRC (which may mean applying the same reduction as HMRC to a different starting point), or

(b) to a different extent, but only if the tribunal thinks that HMRC's decision in respect of the application of that paragraph was flawed (when considered in the light of the principles applicable in proceedings for judicial review).

(7) Subject to this paragraph and paragraph 32, the provisions of Part 5 of TMA 1970 relating to appeals have effect in relation to an appeal under this paragraph as they have effect in relation to an appeal against an assessment to income tax.

Commentary—*Simon's Taxes* **A4.595**.

Commencement—Finance Act 2012, Schedule 38 (Tax Agents: Dishonest Conduct) (Appointed Day and Savings) Order, SI 2013/279 (1 April 2013 appointed as the day on which Sch 38 comes into force).

Cross-references—See Finance Act 2009, Section 101 (Tax Agents: Dishonest Conduct) (Appointed Day) Order, SI 2013/280 (the day appointed for the coming into force of FA 2009 s 101 is 1 April 2013 for the purposes of penalties assessed under FA 2012 Sch 38 Parts 3–5.

Enforcement of penalty

32 (1) A penalty under this Schedule must be paid—

(a) before the end of the period of 30 days beginning with the day on which notification of the penalty was issued, or

(b) if a notice of appeal under paragraph 31 is given, before the end of the period of 30 days beginning with the day on which the appeal is withdrawn or determined.

(2) A penalty under this Schedule may be enforced as if it were income tax charged in an assessment and due and payable.

Commentary—*Simon's Taxes* **A4.595**.

Commencement—Finance Act 2012, Schedule 38 (Tax Agents: Dishonest Conduct) (Appointed Day and Savings) Order, SI 2013/279 (1 April 2013 appointed as the day on which Sch 38 comes into force).

Cross-references—See Finance Act 2009, Section 101 (Tax Agents: Dishonest Conduct) (Appointed Day) Order, SI 2013/280 (the day appointed for the coming into force of FA 2009 s 101 is 1 April 2013 for the purposes of penalties assessed under FA 2012 Sch 38 Parts 3–5.

Double jeopardy

33 A person is not liable to a penalty under this Schedule in respect of anything in respect of which the person has been convicted of an offence.

Commentary—*Simon's Taxes* **A4.595**.

Commencement—Finance Act 2012, Schedule 38 (Tax Agents: Dishonest Conduct) (Appointed Day and Savings) Order, SI 2013/279 (1 April 2013 appointed as the day on which Sch 38 comes into force).

Cross-references—See Finance Act 2009, Section 101 (Tax Agents: Dishonest Conduct) (Appointed Day) Order, SI 2013/280 (the day appointed for the coming into force of FA 2009 s 101 is 1 April 2013 for the purposes of penalties assessed under FA 2012 Sch 38 Parts 3–5.

34 (1) A person is not liable to a penalty under this Schedule in respect of anything in respect of which the person is personally liable to a penalty under—

(a) Schedule 24 to FA 2007 (penalties for errors),

(b) Schedule 41 to FA 2008 (penalties for failure to notify etc), or

(c) Schedule 55 to FA 2009 (penalties for failure to make a return etc).

(2) Sub-paragraph (1) applies where, for example, the person is personally liable by virtue of section 48(3) of VATA 1994 (VAT representatives).

Commentary—*Simon's Taxes* **A4.595**.

Commencement—Finance Act 2012, Schedule 38 (Tax Agents: Dishonest Conduct) (Appointed Day and Savings) Order, SI 2013/279 (1 April 2013 appointed as the day on which Sch 38 comes into force).

Cross-references—See Finance Act 2009, Section 101 (Tax Agents: Dishonest Conduct) (Appointed Day) Order, SI 2013/280 (the day appointed for the coming into force of FA 2009 s 101 is 1 April 2013 for the purposes of penalties assessed under FA 2012 Sch 38 Parts 3–5.

Power to change amount of penalties

35 (1) If it appears to the Treasury that there has been a change in the value of money since the last relevant day, they may by regulations substitute for the sums for the time being specified in paragraphs 22(1), 23, 26(2), 27(1) and (2)(a) and 28(3) such other sums as appear to them to be justified by the change.

(2) "Relevant day", in relation to a specified sum, means—

(a) the day on which this Act is passed, and

(b) each day on which the power conferred by sub-paragraph (1) has been exercised in relation to that sum.

(3) Regulations under this paragraph do not apply to a failure or conduct that began before the day on which they come into force.

(4) The power to make regulations under this paragraph is exercisable by statutory instrument.

(5) A statutory instrument containing regulations under this paragraph is subject to annulment in pursuance of a resolution of the House of Commons.

Commentary—*Simon's Taxes* **A4.595**.

Commencement—Finance Act 2012, Schedule 38 (Tax Agents: Dishonest Conduct) (Appointed Day and Savings) Order, SI 2013/279 (1 April 2013 appointed as the day on which Sch 38 comes into force).

Cross-references—See Finance Act 2009, Section 101 (Tax Agents: Dishonest Conduct) (Appointed Day) Order, SI 2013/280 (the day appointed for the coming into force of FA 2009 s 101 is 1 April 2013 for the purposes of penalties assessed under FA 2012 Sch 38 Parts 3–5.

PART 6
MISCELLANEOUS PROVISION AND INTERPRETATION

Application of provisions of TMA 1970

36 Subject to the provisions of this Schedule, the following provisions of TMA 1970 apply for the purposes of this Schedule as they apply for the purposes of the Taxes Acts—

(a) section 108 (responsibility of company officers),

(b) section 114 (want of form), and

(c) section 115 (delivery and service of documents).

Commentary—*Simon's Taxes* **A4.595**.

Commencement—Finance Act 2012, Schedule 38 (Tax Agents: Dishonest Conduct) (Appointed Day and Savings) Order, SI 2013/279 (1 April 2013 appointed as the day on which Sch 38 comes into force).

Tax

37 (1) "Tax" means—

(a) income tax,

(b) capital gains tax,

(c) corporation tax,

(d) construction industry deductions,

(e) VAT,
(f) insurance premium tax,
(g) inheritance tax,
(h) stamp duty land tax,
(i) stamp duty reserve tax,
(j) petroleum revenue tax,
(k) aggregates levy,
(l) climate change levy,
[(la) apprenticeship levy,][1]
(m) landfill tax, and
(n) any duty of excise other than vehicle excise duty.

(2) "Construction industry deductions" means construction industry deductions under Chapter 3 of Part 3 of FA 2004.

(3) "Corporation tax" includes an amount assessable or chargeable as if it were corporation tax.

(4) "VAT" means—

(a) value added tax charged in accordance with VATA 1994,
(b) amounts recoverable under paragraph 5(2) of Schedule 11 to that Act (amounts shown on invoices as VAT), and
(c) amounts treated as VAT by virtue of regulations under section 54 of that Act (farmers etc).

Commencement—Finance Act 2012, Schedule 38 (Tax Agents: Dishonest Conduct) (Appointed Day and Savings) Order, SI 2013/279 (1 April 2013 appointed as the day on which Sch 38 comes into force).

Amendments—[1] Sub-para (1)(*la*) inserted by FA 2016 s 115 with effect from 15 September 2016. The apprenticeship levy applies in relation to 2017–18 and subsequent tax years.

General interpretation

38 In this Schedule—

"appointed" includes engaged;

"client" (except in paragraph 17)—

(a) has the meaning given in paragraph 2(1), and
(b) in relation to a particular tax agent, means a client of that tax agent;

"the Commissioners" means the Commissioners for Her Majesty's Revenue and Customs;

"conduct notice" has the meaning given in paragraph 4;

"the document-holder" has the meaning given in paragraph 8;

"document" includes a copy of a document (see also section 114 of FA 2008);

"file access notice" has the meaning given in paragraph 8;

"HMRC" means Her Majesty's Revenue and Customs;

"organisation" includes any person or firm carrying on a business;

"specify" includes describe;

"tax period" means a tax year, accounting period or other period in respect of which tax is charged;

"the tribunal" means the First-tier Tribunal or, where determined by or under the Tribunal Procedure Rules, the Upper Tribunal.

Commencement—Finance Act 2012, Schedule 38 (Tax Agents: Dishonest Conduct) (Appointed Day and Savings) Order, SI 2013/279 (1 April 2013 appointed as the day on which Sch 38 comes into force).

39 (1) A reference in this Schedule to clients of a tax agent (or to a tax agent's clients) is a reference to the persons whom the agent assists with their tax affairs.

(2) Sub-paragraph (1) applies even if—

(a) the agent works for an organisation, and
(b) it is the organisation that is appointed to give the assistance.

Commencement—Finance Act 2012, Schedule 38 (Tax Agents: Dishonest Conduct) (Appointed Day and Savings) Order, SI 2013/279 (1 April 2013 appointed as the day on which Sch 38 comes into force).

40 A loss of tax revenue is taken for the purposes of this Schedule to be (or to be capable of being) brought about by dishonest conduct despite the fact that the loss can be recovered or properly accounted for (following discovery of the conduct or otherwise).

Commencement—Finance Act 2012, Schedule 38 (Tax Agents: Dishonest Conduct) (Appointed Day and Savings) Order, SI 2013/279 (1 April 2013 appointed as the day on which Sch 38 comes into force).

41 A reference in this Schedule to working for an organisation includes being a partner or member of an organisation.

Commencement—Finance Act 2012, Schedule 38 (Tax Agents: Dishonest Conduct) (Appointed Day and Savings) Order, SI 2013/279 (1 April 2013 appointed as the day on which Sch 38 comes into force).

42 A reference in a provision of this Schedule to an authorised officer is to an officer of Revenue and Customs who is, or is a member of a class of officers who are, authorised by the Commissioners for the purposes of that provision.

Commencement—Finance Act 2012, Schedule 38 (Tax Agents: Dishonest Conduct) (Appointed Day and Savings) Order, SI 2013/279 (1 April 2013 appointed as the day on which Sch 38 comes into force).

Relationship with other enactments

43 Nothing in this Schedule limits—

(a) any liability a person may have under any other enactment in respect of conduct in respect of which a person is liable to a penalty under this Schedule, or

(b) any power a person may have under any other enactment to obtain relevant documents.

Commencement—Finance Act 2012, Schedule 38 (Tax Agents: Dishonest Conduct) (Appointed Day and Savings) Order, SI 2013/279 (1 April 2013 appointed as the day on which Sch 38 comes into force).

PART 7
CONSEQUENTIAL PROVISIONS

TMA 1970

44 TMA 1970 is amended as follows.

Commencement—Finance Act 2012, Schedule 38 (Tax Agents: Dishonest Conduct) (Appointed Day and Savings) Order, SI 2013/279 (1 April 2013 appointed as the day on which Sch 38 comes into force).

Cross-reference—See Finance Act 2012, Schedule 38 (Tax Agents: Dishonest Conduct) (Appointed Day and Savings) Order, SI 2013/279 art 3 (where a notice is given under TMA 1970 s 20A, on or before 31 March 2013, for the purposes of that notice the amendments made by paras 44–47 of this Schedule shall be disregarded).

45 (*repeals* TMA 1970 ss 20A, 20B, 99)

Commencement—Finance Act 2012, Schedule 38 (Tax Agents: Dishonest Conduct) (Appointed Day and Savings) Order, SI 2013/279 (1 April 2013 appointed as the day on which Sch 38 comes into force).

Cross-reference—See Finance Act 2012, Schedule 38 (Tax Agents: Dishonest Conduct) (Appointed Day and Savings) Order, SI 2013/279 art 3 (where a notice is given under TMA 1970 s 20A, on or before 31 March 2013, for the purposes of that notice the amendments made by paras 44–47 of this Schedule shall be disregarded).

46 (1) Section 20BB (falsification etc of documents) is amended as follows.

(2)–(5) (*amend* TMA 1970 s 20BB(1)–(4))

Commencement—Finance Act 2012, Schedule 38 (Tax Agents: Dishonest Conduct) (Appointed Day and Savings) Order, SI 2013/279 (1 April 2013 appointed as the day on which Sch 38 comes into force).

Cross-reference—See Finance Act 2012, Schedule 38 (Tax Agents: Dishonest Conduct) (Appointed Day and Savings) Order, SI 2013/279 art 3 (where a notice is given under TMA 1970 s 20A, on or before 31 March 2013, for the purposes of that notice the amendments made by paras 44–47 of this Schedule shall be disregarded).

47 (*amends* TMA 1970 s 20D(1), (2))

Commencement—Finance Act 2012, Schedule 38 (Tax Agents: Dishonest Conduct) (Appointed Day and Savings) Order, SI 2013/279 (1 April 2013 appointed as the day on which Sch 38 comes into force).

Cross-reference—See Finance Act 2012, Schedule 38 (Tax Agents: Dishonest Conduct) (Appointed Day and Savings) Order, SI 2013/279 art 3 (where a notice is given under TMA 1970 s 20A, on or before 31 March 2013, for the purposes of that notice the amendments made by paras 44–47 of this Schedule shall be disregarded).

48 (*amends* TMA 1970 s 103(3), (4))

Commencement—Finance Act 2012, Schedule 38 (Tax Agents: Dishonest Conduct) (Appointed Day and Savings) Order, SI 2013/279 (1 April 2013 appointed as the day on which Sch 38 comes into force).

49 (*inserts* TMA 1970 s 103ZA(*g*))

Commencement—Finance Act 2012, Schedule 38 (Tax Agents: Dishonest Conduct) (Appointed Day and Savings) Order, SI 2013/279 (1 April 2013 appointed as the day on which Sch 38 comes into force).

50 (*amends* TMA 1970 s 118)

Commencement—Finance Act 2012, Schedule 38 (Tax Agents: Dishonest Conduct) (Appointed Day and Savings) Order, SI 2013/279 (1 April 2013 appointed as the day on which Sch 38 comes into force).

OTA 1975

51 (*amends* OTA 1975 Sch 2, Table, para 1(1))

Commencement—Finance Act 2012, Schedule 38 (Tax Agents: Dishonest Conduct) (Appointed Day and Savings) Order, SI 2013/279 (1 April 2013 appointed as the day on which Sch 38 comes into force).

IHTA 1984

52 (*repeals* IHTA 1984 s 247(4))

Commencement—Finance Act 2012, Schedule 38 (Tax Agents: Dishonest Conduct) (Appointed Day and Savings) Order, SI 2013/279 (1 April 2013 appointed as the day on which Sch 38 comes into force).

Social Security Contributions and Benefits Act 1992

53 (*amends* SSCBA 1992 s 16(1)(*c*))

Commencement—Finance Act 2012, Schedule 38 (Tax Agents: Dishonest Conduct) (Appointed Day and Savings) Order, SI 2013/279 (1 April 2013 appointed as the day on which Sch 38 comes into force).

54 (*amends* SSCBA 1992 Sch 1 para 7B(5A))

Commencement—Finance Act 2012, Schedule 38 (Tax Agents: Dishonest Conduct) (Appointed Day and Savings) Order, SI 2013/279 (1 April 2013 appointed as the day on which Sch 38 comes into force).

Social Security Contributions and Benefits (Northern Ireland) Act 1992

55 (*amends* SSCB(NI)A 1992 Sch 1 para 7B(5A))

Commencement—Finance Act 2012, Schedule 38 (Tax Agents: Dishonest Conduct) (Appointed Day and Savings) Order, SI 2013/279 (1 April 2013 appointed as the day on which Sch 38 comes into force).

Social Security Administration Act 1992

56 (*inserts* SSAA 1992 s 110ZA(2A))

Commencement—Finance Act 2012, Schedule 38 (Tax Agents: Dishonest Conduct) (Appointed Day and Savings) Order, SI 2013/279 (1 April 2013 appointed as the day on which Sch 38 comes into force).

Social Security Administration (Northern Ireland) Act 1992

57 (*inserts* SSA(NI)A 1992 s 110ZA(2A))

Commencement—Finance Act 2012, Schedule 38 (Tax Agents: Dishonest Conduct) (Appointed Day and Savings) Order, SI 2013/279 (1 April 2013 appointed as the day on which Sch 38 comes into force).

FA 2003

58 (1) FA 2003 is amended as follows.

(2) (*amends* FA 2003 s 93(2), (3)–(6))

(3) (*repeals* FA 2003 s 96)

(4) In Schedule 13 (stamp duty land tax: information powers)—

(a) (*repeals* FA 2003 Sch 13 Pts 3, 4)

(b) (*substitutes* FA 2003 Sch 13 para 53)

Commencement—Finance Act 2012, Schedule 38 (Tax Agents: Dishonest Conduct) (Appointed Day and Savings) Order, SI 2013/279 (1 April 2013 appointed as the day on which Sch 38 comes into force).

SCHEDULE 39
REPEAL OF MISCELLANEOUS RELIEFS ETC

Section 227

PART 3
PAYMENTS RELATING TO REDUCTIONS IN POOL BETTING DUTY

19 (1) Section 126 of FA 1990 (capital allowances and IHT: pools payments for football ground improvements) is repealed.

(2) Accordingly, the following are also repealed—

(a) paragraph 72 of Schedule 2 to CAA 2001;

(b) paragraph 416 of Schedule 1 to ITTOIA 2005.

(3) The repeals made by this paragraph—

(a) for corporation tax purposes, have effect in relation to payments made on or after 1 April 2013,

(b) for income tax purposes, have effect in relation to payments made on or after 6 April 2013, and

(c) for inheritance tax purposes, come into force on 6 April 2013 (and have effect in relation to payments whenever made).

20 (1) Section 121 of FA 1991 (inheritance tax: pools payments to support games etc) is repealed.

(2) The repeal made by this paragraph comes into force on 6 April 2013 (and has effect in relation to payments whenever made).

21 (1) In ITTOIA 2005, the following provisions are repealed—

(a) section 162 (deductions in respect of payments by persons liable to pool betting duty);

(b) section 748 (exemption for payments by persons liable to pool betting duty).

(2) Accordingly, section 683(4)(g) of that Act is also repealed.

(3) The repeals made by this paragraph have effect in relation to payments made on or after 6 April 2013.

Commentary—*Simon's Taxes* **B2.472, B5.666.**

22 (1) In CTA 2009, the following provisions are repealed—

(a) section 138 (deductions in respect of payments by companies liable to pool betting duty);

(b) section 978 (exemption for payments by persons liable to pool betting duty).

(2) Accordingly, section 976(1)(b) of that Act (and the "and" before it) are also repealed.

(3) The repeals made by this paragraph have effect in relation to payments made on or after 1 April 2013.

Commentary—*Simon's Taxes* **B2.472.**

FINANCE ACT 2013

(2013 Chapter 29)

AN ACT TO Grant certain duties, to alter other duties, and to amend the law relating to the National Debt and the Public Revenue, and to make further provision in connection with finance.

[17 July 2013]

CONTENTS

PART 2
OIL

Decommissioning security settlements

86 Removal of IHT charges in respect of decommissioning security settlements

(1) In Chapter 3 of Part 3 of IHTA 1984 (settled property: settlements without interests in possession etc), section 58 (relevant property) is amended as follows.

(2) In subsection (1), omit the "and" at the end of paragraph (ea) and before paragraph (*f*) insert—

"(eb) property comprised in a decommissioning security settlement; and".

(3) At the end insert—

"(6) For the purposes of subsection (1)(eb) above a settlement is a "decommissioning security settlement" if the sole or main purpose of the settlement is to provide security for the performance of obligations under an abandonment programme.

(7) In subsection (6)—

"abandonment programme" means an abandonment programme approved under Part 4 of the Petroleum Act 1998 (including such a programme as revised);

"security" has the same meaning as in section 38A of that Act."

(4) This section is treated as having come into force on 20 March 1993.

(5) For the purposes of section 58 of IHTA 1984—

(*a*) any reference in that section to Part 4 of the Petroleum Act 1998 has effect, in relation to any period before the coming into force of that Part, as a reference to Part 1 of the Petroleum Act 1987, and

(*b*) section 38A of the Petroleum Act 1998 is to be treated as having come into force at the same time as this section.

(6) There is to be no charge to tax under section 65 of IHTA 1984 if the only reason for such a charge would be that property ceases to be relevant property by virtue of the coming into force of this section.

PART 3
ANNUAL TAX ON ENVELOPED DWELLINGS

Exemptions

155 Dwelling conditionally exempt from inheritance tax

(1) Subsection (2) applies to a single-dwelling interest if—

(*a*) the whole or part of the dwelling has been designated under section 31 of IHTA 1984 (buildings of outstanding historic or architectural interest etc),
(*b*) an undertaking has been made with respect to the dwelling under section 30 of that Act (conditionally exempt transfers), and
(*c*) a transfer of value is exempt from inheritance tax by virtue of that designation and that undertaking.

(2) The taxable value of the single-dwelling interest on any day is taken to be zero if no chargeable event has occurred with respect to the dwelling in the time between the transfer of value and the beginning of that day.

(3) Subsection (4) applies to a single-dwelling interest if—
(*a*) the whole or part of the dwelling has been designated under section 31 of IHTA 1984,
(*b*) an undertaking has been made with respect to the dwelling under section 78 of that Act (settled property: conditionally exempt occasions), and
(*c*) a transfer of property or other event is a conditionally exempt occasion by virtue of that designation and that undertaking.

(4) The taxable value of the single-dwelling interest on any day is taken to be zero if no chargeable event has occurred with respect to the dwelling in the time between the conditionally exempt occasion and the beginning of that day.

(5) In this section—
"chargeable event" means an event which is a chargeable event under section 32 of IHTA 1984;
"conditionally exempt occasion" is to be read in accordance with section 78(2) of that Act;
"transfer of value" has the same meaning as in that Act.

Commentary—*Simon's Taxes* **B6.762**.

PART 4

EXCISE DUTIES AND OTHER TAXES

Inheritance tax

175 Open-ended investment companies and authorised unit trusts

(1) In section 65 of IHTA 1984 (settlements without interests in possession etc: charge when property ceases to be relevant property etc), after subsection (7) insert—

"(7A) Tax shall not be charged under this section by reason only that property comprised in a settlement becomes excluded property by virtue of section 48(3A)(*a*) (holding in an authorised unit trust or a share in an open-ended investment company is excluded property unless settlor domiciled in UK when settlement made)."

(2) The amendment made by this section is treated as having come into force on 16 October 2002.

176 Treatment of liabilities for inheritance tax purposes

Schedule 36 makes provision in relation to the treatment of liabilities for the purposes of inheritance tax.

177 Election to be treated as domiciled in United Kingdom

(1) IHTA 1984 is amended as follows.

(2) In section 267 (persons treated as domiciled in United Kingdom), at the end insert—

"(5) In determining for the purposes of this section whether a person is, or at any time was, domiciled in the United Kingdom, sections 267ZA and 267ZB are to be ignored."

(3) After that section insert—

"267ZA Election to be treated as domiciled in United Kingdom

(1) A person may, if condition A or B is met, elect to be treated for the purposes of this Act as domiciled in the United Kingdom (and not elsewhere).

(2) A person's personal representatives may, if condition B is met, elect for the person to be treated for the purposes of this Act as domiciled in the United Kingdom (and not elsewhere).

(3) Condition A is that, at any time on or after 6 April 2013 and during the period of 7 years ending with the date on which the election is made, the person had a spouse or civil partner who was domiciled in the United Kingdom.

(4) Condition B is that a person ("the deceased") dies and, at any time on or after 6 April 2013 and within the period of 7 years ending with the date of death, the deceased was—
(*a*) domiciled in the United Kingdom, and
(*b*) the spouse or civil partner of the person who would, by virtue of the election, be treated as domiciled in the United Kingdom.

(5) An election under this section does not affect a person's domicile for the purposes of section 6(2) or (3) or 48(4).

(6) An election under this section is to be ignored—
(*a*) in interpreting any such provision as is mentioned in section 158(6), and

(*b*) in determining the effect of any qualifying double taxation relief arrangements in relation to a transfer of value by the person making the election.

(7) For the purposes of subsection (6)(*b*) a qualifying double taxation relief arrangement is an arrangement which is specified in an Order in Council made under section 158 before the coming into force of this section (other than by way of amendment by an Order made on or after the coming into force of this section).

(8) In determining for the purposes of this section whether a person making an election under this section is or was domiciled in the United Kingdom, section 267 is to be ignored.

267ZB Section 267ZA: further provision about election

(1) For the purposes of this section—

(*a*) references to a lifetime election are to an election made by virtue of section 267ZA(3), and

(*b*) references to a death election are to an election made by virtue of section 267ZA(4).

(2) A lifetime or death election is to be made by notice in writing to HMRC.

(3) A lifetime or death election is treated as having taken effect on a date specified, in accordance with subsection (4), in the notice.

(4) The date specified in a notice under subsection (3) must—

(*a*) be 6 April 2013 or a later date,

(*b*) be within the period of 7 years ending with—

(i) in the case of a lifetime election, the date on which the election is made, or

(ii) in the case of a death election, the date of the deceased's death, and

(*c*) meet the condition in subsection (5).

(5) The condition in this subsection is met by a date if, on the date—

(*a*) in the case of a lifetime election—

(i) the person making the election was married to, or in a civil partnership with, the spouse or civil partner, and

(ii) the spouse or civil partner was domiciled in the United Kingdom, or

(*b*) in the case of a death election—

(i) the person who is, by virtue of the election, to be treated as domiciled in the United Kingdom was married to, or in a civil partnership with, the deceased, and

(ii) the deceased was domiciled in the United Kingdom.

(6) A death election may only be made within 2 years of the death of the deceased or such longer period as an officer of Revenue and Customs may in the particular case allow.

(7) Subsection (8) applies if—

(*a*) a lifetime or death election is made,

(*b*) a disposition is made, or another event occurs, during the period beginning with the time when the election is treated by virtue of subsection (3) as having taken effect and ending at the time when the election is made, and

(*c*) the effect of the election being treated as having taken effect at that time is that the disposition or event gives rise to a transfer of value.

(8) This Act applies with the following modifications in relation to the transfer of value—

(*a*) subsections (1) and (6)(*c*) of section 216 have effect as if the period specified in subsection (6)(*c*) of that section were the period of 12 months from the end of the month in which the election is made, and

(*b*) sections 226 and 233 have effect as if the transfer were made at the time when the election is made.

(9) A lifetime or death election cannot be revoked.

(10) If a person who made an election under section 267ZA(1) is not resident in the United Kingdom for the purposes of income tax for a period of four successive tax years beginning at any time after the election is made, the election ceases to have effect at the end of that period."

178 Transfer to spouse or civil partner not domiciled in United Kingdom

(1) Section 18 of IHTA 1984 (transfers between spouses or civil partners) is amended as follows.

(2) In subsection (2) (transfer to spouse or civil partner not domiciled in United Kingdom), for "£55,000" substitute "the exemption limit at the time of the transfer,".

(3) After subsection (2) insert—

"(2A) For the purposes of subsection (2), the exemption limit is the amount shown in the second column of the first row of the Table in Schedule 1 (upper limit of portion of value charged at rate of nil per cent)."

(4) The amendments made by this section have effect in relation to transfers of value made on or after 6 April 2013.

PART 5

GENERAL ANTI-ABUSE RULE

Note—In Part 5, references to tax, other than references to particular taxes, include National Insurance contributions, and references to a charge to tax include a liability to pay National Insurance contributions (NICs Act 2014 s 10(1)).

Cross-references—See NICs Act 2014 s 11 (power of the Treasury to modify application of the GAAR rules in relation to NICs).

206 General anti-abuse rule

(1) This Part has effect for the purpose of counteracting tax advantages arising from tax arrangements that are abusive.

(2) The rules of this Part are collectively to be known as "the general anti-abuse rule".

(3) The general anti-abuse rule applies to the following taxes—

(*a*) income tax,

(*b*) corporation tax, including any amount chargeable as if it were corporation tax or treated as if it were corporation tax,

(*c*) capital gains tax,

(*d*) petroleum revenue tax,

[(*da*) diverted profits tax,][1]

[(*db*) apprenticeship levy,][2]

(*e*) inheritance tax,

(*f*) stamp duty land tax, and

(*g*) annual tax on enveloped dwellings.

Commentary—*Simon's Taxes* **A2.125**.

Modification—Sub-s (3) has effect as if it included a reference to National Insurance contributions, with effect from 13 March 2014 (NICs Act 2014 s 10(2)).

Press releases etc—HMRC Notice: General Anti-Abuse Rule (GAAR) Advisory Panel (see *SWTI 2013, Issue 22*).

HMRC Official Guidance (approved by the Advisory Panel with effect from 15 April 2013): www.hmrc.gov.uk/avoidance/gaar.htm.

Amendments—[1] Sub-s (3)(*da*) inserted by FA 2015 s 115(1) with effect in relation to accounting periods beginning on or after 1 April 2015. For accounting periods that straddle that date, see FA 2015 s 116(2), (3).

[2] Sub-s (3)(*db*) inserted by FA 2016 s 104(2) with effect from 15 September 2016.

207 Meaning of "tax arrangements" and "abusive"

(1) Arrangements are "tax arrangements" if, having regard to all the circumstances, it would be reasonable to conclude that the obtaining of a tax advantage was the main purpose, or one of the main purposes, of the arrangements.

(2) Tax arrangements are "abusive" if they are arrangements the entering into or carrying out of which cannot reasonably be regarded as a reasonable course of action in relation to the relevant tax provisions, having regard to all the circumstances including—

(*a*) whether the substantive results of the arrangements are consistent with any principles on which those provisions are based (whether express or implied) and the policy objectives of those provisions,

(*b*) whether the means of achieving those results involves one or more contrived or abnormal steps, and

(*c*) whether the arrangements are intended to exploit any shortcomings in those provisions.

(3) Where the tax arrangements form part of any other arrangements regard must also be had to those other arrangements.

(4) Each of the following is an example of something which might indicate that tax arrangements are abusive—

(*a*) the arrangements result in an amount of income, profits or gains for tax purposes that is significantly less than the amount for economic purposes,

(*b*) the arrangements result in deductions or losses of an amount for tax purposes that is significantly greater than the amount for economic purposes, and

(*c*) the arrangements result in a claim for the repayment or crediting of tax (including foreign tax) that has not been, and is unlikely to be, paid,

but in each case only if it is reasonable to assume that such a result was not the anticipated result when the relevant tax provisions were enacted.

(5) The fact that tax arrangements accord with established practice, and HMRC had, at the time the arrangements were entered into, indicated its acceptance of that practice, is an example of something which might indicate that the arrangements are not abusive.

(6) The examples given in subsections (4) and (5) are not exhaustive.

Commentary—*Simon's Taxes* **A2.125**.

Cross-references—See NICs Act 2014 s 10(8)–(10) (tax arrangements that would not have been tax arrangements but for the modification of the GAAR rules in relation to NICs by the NICs Act 2014 s 10).

Modification—This section has effect as if, in sub-s (4)(*a*), after "income," there were inserted "earnings (within the meaning of Part 1 of the Social Security Contributions and Benefits Act 1992 or Part 1 of the Social Security Contributions and Benefits (Northern Ireland) Act 1992),", with effect from 13 March 2014 (NICs Act 2014 s 10(3)).

208 Meaning of "tax advantage"

A "tax advantage" includes—

(*a*) relief or increased relief from tax,
(*b*) repayment or increased repayment of tax,
(*c*) avoidance or reduction of a charge to tax or an assessment to tax,
(*d*) avoidance of a possible assessment to tax,
(*e*) deferral of a payment of tax or advancement of a repayment of tax, and
(*f*) avoidance of an obligation to deduct or account for tax.

Commentary—*Simon's Taxes* **A2.125**.

209 Counteracting the tax advantages

(1) If there are tax arrangements that are abusive, the tax advantages that would (ignoring this Part) arise from the arrangements are to be counteracted by the making of adjustments.

(2) The adjustments required to be made to counteract the tax advantages are such as are just and reasonable.

(3) The adjustments may be made in respect of the tax in question or any other tax to which the general anti-abuse rule applies.

(4) The adjustments that may be made include those that impose or increase a liability to tax in any case where (ignoring this Part) there would be no liability or a smaller liability, and tax is to be charged in accordance with any such adjustment.

(5) Any adjustments required to be made under this section (whether by an officer of Revenue and Customs or the person to whom the tax advantage would arise) may be made by way of an assessment, the modification of an assessment, amendment or disallowance of a claim, or otherwise.

(6) But—

(*a*) no steps may be taken by an officer of Revenue and Customs by virtue of this section unless the procedural requirements of Schedule 43[, 43A or 43B][1] have been complied with, and
(*b*) the power to make adjustments by virtue of this section is subject to any time limit imposed by or under any enactment other than this Part.

(7) Any adjustments made under this section have effect for all purposes.

[(8) Where a matter is referred to the GAAR Advisory Panel under paragraph 5 or 6 of Schedule 43, the taxpayer (as defined in paragraph 3 of that Schedule) must not make any GAAR-related adjustments in relation to the taxpayer's tax affairs in the period (the "closed period") which—

(*a*) begins with the 31st day after the end of the 45 day period mentioned in paragraph 4(1) of that Schedule, and
(*b*) ends immediately before the day on which the taxpayer is given the notice under paragraph 12 of Schedule 43 (notice of final decision after considering opinion of GAAR Advisory Panel).

(9) Where a person has been given a pooling notice or a notice of binding under Schedule 43A in relation to any tax arrangements, the person must not make any GAAR-related adjustments in the period ("the closed period") that—

(*a*) begins with the 31st day after that on which that notice is given, and
(*b*) ends—
  (i) in the case of a pooling notice, immediately before the day on which the person is given a notice under paragraph 8(2) or 9(2) of Schedule 43A, or a notice under paragraph 8(2) of Schedule 43B, in relation to the tax arrangements (notice of final decision after considering opinion of GAAR Advisory Panel), or
  (ii) in the case of a notice of binding, with the 30th day after the day on which the notice is given.

(10) In this section "GAAR-related adjustments" means—

(*a*) for the purposes of subsection (8), adjustments which give effect (wholly or in part) to the proposed counteraction set out in the notice under paragraph 3 of Schedule 43;
(*b*) for the purposes of subsection (9), adjustments which give effect (wholly or partly) to the proposed counteraction set out in the notice of pooling or binding (as the case may be).][2]

Commentary—*Simon's Taxes* **A2.125**.

Note—Adjustments to be made in respect of NICs under this section may be made by a notice given under FA 2013 Sch 43 para 12 (NICs Act 2014 s 10(4)).

Amendments—[1] In sub-s (6)(*a*), words inserted by FA 2016 s 157(1), (4) with effect in relation to tax arrangements (within the meaning of FA 201 Pt 5) entered into at any time (whether before or on or after 15 September 2016).

[2] Sub-ss (8)–(10) inserted by FA 2016 s 158(1), (4) with effect in relation to tax arrangements (within the meaning of FA 2013 Pt 4) entered into on or after 15 September 2016.

[209A Effect of adjustments specified in a provisional counteraction notice

(1) Adjustments made by an officer of Revenue and Customs which—

(*a*) are specified in a provisional counteraction notice given to a person by the officer (and have not been cancelled: see sections 209B to 209E),
(*b*) are made in respect of a tax advantage that would (ignoring this Part) arise from tax arrangements that are abusive, and
(*c*) but for section 209(6)(*a*), would have effected a valid counteraction of that tax advantage under section 209,

are treated for all purposes as effecting a valid counteraction of the tax advantage under that section.

(2) A "provisional counteraction notice" is a notice which—
(*a*) specifies adjustments (the "notified adjustments") which the officer reasonably believes may be required under section 209(1) to counteract a tax advantage that would (ignoring this Part) arise to the person from tax arrangements;
(*b*) specifies the arrangements and the tax advantage concerned, and
(*c*) notifies the person of the person's rights of appeal with respect to the notified adjustments (when made) and contains a statement that if an appeal is made against the making of the adjustments—
(i) no steps may be taken in relation to the appeal unless and until the person is given a notice referred to in section 209F(2), and
(ii) the notified adjustments will be cancelled if HMRC fails to take at least one of the actions mentioned in section 209B(4) within the period specified in section 209B(2).

(3) It does not matter whether the notice is given before or at the same time as the making of the adjustments.

(4) In this section "adjustments" includes adjustments made in any way permitted by section 209(5).][1]

Amendments—[1] Sections 209A–209F inserted by FA 2016 s 156(1) with effect in relation to tax arrangements (within the meaning of FA 2013 Pt 5) entered into at any time (whether before, on or after 15 September 2016).

[209B Notified adjustments: 12 month period for taking action if appeal made

(1) This section applies where a person (the "taxpayer") to whom a provisional counteraction notice has been given appeals against the making of the notified adjustments.

(2) The notified adjustments are to be treated as cancelled with effect from the end of the period of 12 months beginning with the day on which the provisional counteraction notice is given unless an action mentioned in subsection (4) is taken before that time.

(3) For the purposes of subsection (2) it does not matter whether the action mentioned in subsection (4)(*c*), (*d*) or (*e*) is taken before or after the provisional counteraction notice is given (but if that action is taken before the provisional counteraction notice is given subsection (5) does not have effect).

(4) The actions are—
(*a*) an officer of Revenue and Customs notifying the taxpayer that the notified adjustments are cancelled;
(*b*) an officer of Revenue and Customs giving the taxpayer written notice of the withdrawal of the provisional counteraction notice (without cancelling the notified adjustments);
(*c*) a designated HMRC officer giving the taxpayer a notice under paragraph 3 of Schedule 43 which—
(i) specifies the arrangements and the tax advantage which are specified in the provisional counteraction notice, and
(ii) specifies the notified adjustments (or lesser adjustments) as the counteraction that the officer considers ought to be taken (see paragraph 3(2)(*c*) of that Schedule);
(*d*) a designated HMRC officer giving the taxpayer a pooling notice or a notice of binding under Schedule 43A which—
(i) specifies the arrangements and the tax advantage which are specified in the provisional counteraction notice, and
(ii) specifies the notified adjustments (or lesser adjustments) as the counteraction that the officer considers ought to be taken;
(*e*) a designated HMRC officer giving the taxpayer a notice under paragraph 1(2) of Schedule 43B which—
(i) specifies the arrangements and the tax advantage which are specified in the provisional counteraction notice, and
(ii) specifies the notified adjustments (or lesser adjustments) as the counteraction that the officer considers ought to be taken.

(5) In a case within subsection (4)(*c*), (*d*) or (*e*), if—
(*a*) the notice under paragraph 3 of Schedule 43, or
(*b*) the pooling notice or notice of binding, or
(*c*) the notice under paragraph 1(2) of Schedule 43B,

(as the case may be) specifies lesser adjustments the officer must modify the notified adjustments accordingly.

(6) The officer may not take the action in subsection (4)(*b*) unless the officer was authorised to make the notified adjustments otherwise than under this Part.

(7) In this section "lesser adjustments" means adjustments which assume a smaller tax advantage than was assumed in the provisional counteraction notice.][1]

Amendments—[1] Sections 209A–209F inserted by FA 2016 s 156(1) with effect in relation to tax arrangements (within the meaning of FA 2013 Pt 5) entered into at any time (whether before, on or after 15 September 2016).

[209C Notified adjustments: case within section 209B(4)(*c*)

(1) This section applies if the action in section 209B(4)(*c*) (notice to taxpayer of proposed counteraction of tax advantage) is taken.

(2) If the matter is not referred to the GAAR Advisory Panel, the notified adjustments are to be treated as cancelled with effect from the date of the designated HMRC officer's decision under paragraph 6(2) of Schedule 43 unless the notice under paragraph 6(3) of Schedule 43 states that the adjustments are not to be treated as cancelled under this section.

(3) A notice under paragraph 6(3) of Schedule 43 may not contain the statement referred to in subsection (2) unless HMRC would have been authorised to make the adjustments if the general anti-abuse rule did not have effect.

(4) If the taxpayer is given a notice under paragraph 12 of Schedule 43 which states that the specified tax advantage is not to be counteracted under the general anti-abuse rule, the notified adjustments are to be treated as cancelled unless that notice states that those adjustments are not to be treated as cancelled under this section.

(5) A notice under paragraph 12 of Schedule 43 may not contain the statement referred to in subsection (4) unless HMRC would have been authorised to make the adjustments if the general anti-abuse rule did not have effect.

(6) If the taxpayer is given a notice under paragraph 12 of Schedule 43 stating that the specified tax advantage is to be counteracted—

(*a*) the notified adjustments are confirmed only so far as they are specified in that notice as adjustments required to give effect to the counteraction, and

(*b*) so far as they are not confirmed, the notified adjustments are to be treated as cancelled.][1]

Amendments—[1] Sections 209A–209F inserted by FA 2016 s 156(1) with effect in relation to tax arrangements (within the meaning of FA 2013 Pt 5) entered into at any time (whether before, on or after 15 September 2016).

[209D Notified adjustments: case within section 209B(4)(*d*)

(1) This section applies if the action in section 209B(4)(*d*) (pooling notice or notice of binding) is taken.

(2) If the taxpayer is given a notice under paragraph 8(2) or 9(2) of Schedule 43A which states that the specified tax advantage is not to be counteracted under the general anti-abuse rule, the notified adjustments are to be treated as cancelled, unless that notice states that those adjustments are not to be treated as cancelled under this section.

(3) A notice under paragraph 8(2) or 9(2) of Schedule 43A may not contain the statement referred to in subsection (2) unless HMRC would have been authorised to make the adjustments if the general anti-abuse rule did not have effect.

(4) If the taxpayer is given a notice under paragraph 8(2) or 9(2) of Schedule 43A stating that the specified tax advantage is to be counteracted—

(*a*) the notified adjustments are confirmed only so far as they are specified in that notice as adjustments required to give effect to the counteraction, and

(*b*) so far as they are not confirmed, the notified adjustments are to be treated as cancelled.][1]

Amendments—[1] Sections 209A–209F inserted by FA 2016 s 156(1) with effect in relation to tax arrangements (within the meaning of FA 2013 Pt 5) entered into at any time (whether before, on or after 15 September 2016).

[209E Notified adjustments: case within section 209B(4)(*e*)

(1) This section applies if the action in section 209B(4)(*e*) (notice of proposal to make generic referral) is taken.

(2) If the notice under paragraph 1(2) of Schedule 43B is withdrawn, the notified adjustments are to be treated as cancelled unless the notice of withdrawal states that the adjustments are not to be treated as cancelled under this section.

(3) The notice of withdrawal may not contain the statement referred to in subsection (2) unless HMRC was authorised to make the notified adjustments otherwise than under this Part.

(4) If the taxpayer is given a notice under paragraph 8(2) of Schedule 43B, which states that the specified tax advantage is not to be counteracted under the general anti-abuse rule, the notified adjustments are to be treated as cancelled, unless that notice states that those adjustments are not to be treated as cancelled under this section.

(5) A notice under paragraph 8(2) of Schedule 43B may not contain the statement referred to in subsection (4) unless HMRC was authorised to make the adjustments otherwise than under this Part.

(6) If the taxpayer is given a notice under paragraph 8(2) of Schedule 43B stating that the specified tax advantage is to be counteracted—

(*a*) the notified adjustments are confirmed only so far as they are specified in that notice as adjustments required to give effect to the counteraction, and

(*b*) so far as they are not confirmed, the notified adjustments are to be treated as cancelled.][1]

Amendments—[1] Sections 209A–209F inserted by FA 2016 s 156(1) with effect in relation to tax arrangements (within the meaning of FA 2013 Pt 5) entered into at any time (whether before, on or after 15 September 2016).

[209F Appeals against provisional counteractions: further provision

(1) Subsections (2) to (5) have effect in relation to an appeal by a person ("the taxpayer") against the making of adjustments which are specified in a provisional counteraction notice.

(2) No steps after the initial notice of appeal are to be taken in relation to the appeal unless and until the taxpayer is given—

(*a*) a notice under section 209B(4)(*b*),

(*b*) a notice under paragraph 6(3) of Schedule 43 (notice of decision not to refer matter to GAAR advisory panel) containing the statement described in section 209C(2) (statement that adjustments are not to be treated as cancelled),

(*c*) a notice under paragraph 12 of Schedule 43,

(*d*) a notice under paragraph 8(2) or 9(2) of Schedule 43A, or

(*e*) a notice under paragraph 8 of Schedule 43B,

in respect of the tax arrangements concerned.

(3) The taxpayer has until the end of the period mentioned in subsection (4) to comply with any requirement to specify the grounds of appeal.

(4) The period mentioned in subsection (3) is the 30 days beginning with the day on which the taxpayer receives the notice mentioned in subsection (2).

(5) In subsection (2) the reference to "steps" does not include the withdrawal of the appeal.][1]

Amendments—[1] Sections 209A–209F inserted by FA 2016 s 156(1) with effect in relation to tax arrangements (within the meaning of FA 2013 Pt 5) entered into at any time (whether before on or after 15 September 2016).

210 Consequential relieving adjustments

(1) This section applies where—

(*a*) the counteraction of a tax advantage under section 209 is final, and

(*b*) if the case is not one in which notice of the counteraction was given under paragraph 12 of Schedule 43, [paragraph 8 or 9 of Schedule 43A or paragraph 8 of Schedule 43B,][1] HMRC have been notified of the counteraction by the taxpayer.

(2) A person has 12 months, beginning with the day on which the counteraction becomes final, to make a claim for one or more consequential adjustments to be made in respect of any tax to which the general anti-abuse rule applies.

(3) On a claim under this section, an officer of Revenue and Customs must make such of the consequential adjustments claimed (if any) as are just and reasonable.

(4) Consequential adjustments—

(*a*) may be made in respect of any period, and

(*b*) may affect any person (whether or not a party to the tax arrangements).

(5) But nothing in this section requires or permits an officer to make a consequential adjustment the effect of which is to increase a person's liability to any tax.

(6) For the purposes of this section—

(*a*) if the claim relates to income tax or capital gains tax, Schedule 1A to TMA 1970 applies to it;

(*b*) if the claim relates to corporation tax, Schedule 1A to TMA 1970 (and not Schedule 18 to FA 1998) applies to it;

(*c*) if the claim relates to petroleum revenue tax, Schedule 1A to TMA 1970 applies to it, but as if the reference in paragraph 2A(4) of that Schedule to a year of assessment included a reference to a chargeable period within the meaning of OTA 1975 (see section 1(3) and (4) of that Act);

(*d*) if the claim relates to inheritance tax it must be made in writing to HMRC and section 221 of IHTA 1984 applies as if the claim were a claim under that Act;

(*e*) if the claim relates to stamp duty land tax or annual tax on enveloped dwellings, Schedule 11A to FA 2003 applies to it as if it were a claim to which paragraph 1 of that Schedule applies.

(7) Where an officer of Revenue and Customs makes a consequential adjustment under this section, the officer must give the person who made the claim written notice describing the adjustment which has been made.

(8) For the purposes of this section the counteraction of a tax advantage is final when the adjustments made to effect the counteraction, and any amounts arising as a result of those adjustments, can no longer be varied, on appeal or otherwise.

(9) Any adjustments required to be made under this section may be made—

(*a*) by way of an assessment, the modification of an assessment, the amendment of a claim, or otherwise, and

(*b*) despite any time limit imposed by or under any enactment other than this Part.

(10) In this section "the taxpayer", in relation to a counteraction of a tax advantage under section 209, means the person to whom the tax advantage would have arisen.

Commentary—*Simon's Taxes* **A2.125**.

Note—For the purposes of this section, if a claim under this section relates to Class 4 NICs, TMA 1970 Sch 1A (as that Schedule applies in relation to such contributions) applies to it, and if a claim under this section relates to any other class of NICs, it must be made in such form and manner, and contain such information, as HMRC may require (NICs Act 2014 s 10(6)). Adjustments to be made in respect of NICs under this section may be made by a notice given under sub-s (7) above (NICs Act 2014 s 10(7)).

Amendments—[1] In sub-s (1)(*b*), words inserted by FA 2016 s 157(1), (5) with effect in relation to tax arrangements (within the meaning of FA 201 Pt 5) entered into at any time (whether before on or after 15 September 2016).

211 Proceedings before a court or tribunal

(1) In proceedings before a court or tribunal in connection with the general anti-abuse rule, HMRC must show—

(*a*) that there are tax arrangements that are abusive, and

(*b*) that the adjustments made to counteract the tax advantages arising from the arrangements are just and reasonable.

(2) In determining any issue in connection with the general anti-abuse rule, a court or tribunal must take into account—

(*a*) HMRC's guidance about the general anti-abuse rule that was approved by the GAAR Advisory Panel at the time the tax arrangements were entered into, and

(*b*) any opinion of the GAAR Advisory [Panel given—.

(i) under paragraph 11 of Schedule 43 about the arrangements or any tax arrangements which are, as a result of a notice under paragraph 1 or 2 of Schedule 43A, the referred or (as the case may be) counteracted arrangements in relation to the arrangements, or

(ii) under paragraph 6 of Schedule 43B in respect of a generic referral of the arrangements.][1]

(3) In determining any issue in connection with the general anti-abuse rule, a court or tribunal may take into account—

(*a*) guidance, statements or other material (whether of HMRC, a Minister of the Crown or anyone else) that was in the public domain at the time the arrangements were entered into, and

(*b*) evidence of established practice at that time.

Commentary—*Simon's Taxes* **A2.125**.

Amendments—[1] In sub-s (2)(*b*) words substituted for words "Panel about the arrangements (see paragraph 11 of Schedule 43)" by FA 2016 s 157(1), (6) with effect in relation to tax arrangements (within the meaning of FA 201 Pt 5) entered into at any time (whether before on or after 15 September 2016).

212 Relationship between the GAAR and priority rules

(1) Any priority rule has effect subject to the general anti-abuse rule (despite the terms of the priority rule).

(2) A "priority rule" means a rule (however expressed) to the effect that particular provisions have effect to the exclusion of, or otherwise in priority to, anything else.

(3) Examples of priority rules are—

(*a*) the rule in section 464, 699 or 906 of CTA 2009 (priority of loan relationships rules, derivative contracts rules and intangible fixed assets rules for corporation tax purposes), and

(*b*) the rule in section 6(1) of TIOPA 2010 (effect to be given to double taxation arrangements despite anything in any enactment).

[212A Penalty

(1) A person (P) is liable to pay a penalty if—

(*a*) P has been given a notice under—

(i) paragraph 12 of Schedule 43,

(ii) paragraph 8 or 9 of Schedule 43A, or

(iii) paragraph 8 of Schedule 43B,

stating that a tax advantage arising from particular tax arrangements is to be counteracted,

(*b*) a tax document has been given to HMRC on the basis that the tax advantage arises to P from those arrangements,

(*c*) that document was given to HMRC—

(i) by P, or

(ii) by another person in circumstances where P knew, or ought to have known, that the other person gave the document on the basis mentioned in paragraph (*c*), and

(*d*) the tax advantage has been counteracted by the making of adjustments under section 209.

(2) The penalty is 60% of the value of the counteracted advantage.

(3) Schedule 43C—

(*a*) gives the meaning of "the value of the counteracted advantage", and

(*b*) makes other provision in relation to penalties under this section.

(4) In this section "tax document" means any return, claim or other document submitted in compliance (or purported compliance) with any provision of, or made under, an Act.
(5) In this section the reference to giving a tax document to HMRC is to be interpreted in accordance with paragraph 11(*g*) and (*h*) of Schedule 43C.][1]

Cross-references—See FA 2016 Sch 18 para 40(1), (2) (penalty under FA 2016 Sch 18 para 30 not to be reduced by penalty under this section where determined by reference to the same tax liability).

Amendments—[1] Section 212A inserted by FA 2016 s 158(1), (2) with effect in relation to tax arrangements (within the meaning of FA 2013 Pt 5) entered into on or after 15 September 2016.

213 Consequential amendment

(1) Section 42 of TMA 1970 (procedure for making claims etc) is amended as follows.
(2), (3) (*amend* TMA 1970 s 42(2) and *insert* TMA 1970 s 42(3ZC))

214 Interpretation of Part 5

[(1)] [2]In this Part—

"abusive", in relation to tax arrangements, has the meaning given by section 207(2) to (6);
"arrangements" includes any agreement, understanding, scheme, transaction or series of transactions (whether or not legally enforceable);
"the Commissioners" means the Commissioners for Her Majesty's Revenue and Customs;
["designated HMRC officer" has the meaning given by paragraph 2 of Schedule 43;][2]
"the GAAR Advisory Panel" has the meaning given by paragraph 1 of Schedule 43;
"the general anti-abuse rule" has the meaning given by section 206;
"HMRC" means Her Majesty's Revenue and Customs;
["notice of binding" has the meaning given by paragraph 2(2) of Schedule 43A;][2]
["notified adjustments", in relation to a provisional counteraction notice, has the meaning given by section 209A(2);][1]
["pooling notice" has the meaning given by paragraph 1(4) of Schedule 43A;][2]
["provisional counteraction notice" has the meaning given by section 209A(2);][1]
"tax advantage" has the meaning given by section 208;
["tax appeal" has the meaning given by paragraph 1A of Schedule 43;][2]
"tax arrangements" has the meaning given by section 207(1).
["tax enquiry" has the meaning given by section 202(2) of FA 2014.][2]

[(2) In this Part references to any "opinion of the GAAR Advisory Panel" about any tax arrangements are to be interpreted in accordance with paragraph 11(5) of Schedule 43.
(3) In this Part references to tax arrangements which are "equivalent" to one another are to be interpreted in accordance with paragraph 11 of Schedule 43A.][2]

Commentary—*Simon's Taxes* **A2.125**.

Amendments—[1] Definitions of "notified adjustments" and "provisional counteraction notice" inserted by FA 2016 s 156(1), (2) with effect in relation to tax arrangements (within the meaning of FA 2013 Pt 5) entered into at any time (whether before on or after 15 September 2016).

[2] Sub-s (1) numbered as such, definitions of "designated HMRC officer", "notice of binding", "pooling notice", "tax appeal", "tax enquiry" inserted, and sub-ss (2), (3) inserted by FA 2016 s 157(1), (7)–(10) with effect in relation to tax arrangements (within the meaning of FA 201 Pt 5) entered into at any time (whether before on or after 15 September 2016).

215 Commencement and transitional provision

(1) The general anti-abuse rule has effect in relation to any tax arrangements entered into on or after the day on which this Act is passed.
(2) Where the tax arrangements form part of any other arrangements entered into before that day those other arrangements are to be ignored for the purposes of section 207(3), subject to subsection (3).
(3) Account is to be taken of those other arrangements for the purposes of section 207(3) if, as a result, the tax arrangements would not be abusive.

Commentary—*Simon's Taxes* **A2.125**.

PART 6
OTHER PROVISIONS

Trusts

216 Trusts with vulnerable beneficiary

Schedule 44 contains provision about trusts which have a vulnerable beneficiary.

Residence

218 Statutory residence test

(1) Schedule 45 contains—
(*a*) provision for determining whether individuals are resident in the United Kingdom for the purposes of income tax, capital gains tax and (where relevant) inheritance tax and corporation tax,
(*b*) provision about split years, and
(*c*) provision about periods when individuals are temporarily non-resident.

(2) The Treasury may by order make any incidental, supplemental, consequential, transitional or saving provision in consequence of Schedule 45.

(3) An order under subsection (2) may—

(*a*) make different provision for different purposes, and

(*b*) make provision amending, repealing or revoking any provision made by or under an Act (whenever passed or made).

(4) An order under subsection (2) is to be made by statutory instrument.

(5) A statutory instrument containing an order under subsection (2) is subject to annulment in pursuance of a resolution of the House of Commons.

219 Ordinary residence

(1) Schedule 46 contains provision removing or replacing rules relating to ordinary residence.

(2) The Treasury may by order make further provision removing or replacing rules relating to ordinary residence with respect to—

(*a*) income tax,

(*b*) capital gains tax, and

(*c*) (so far as the ordinary residence status of individuals is relevant to them) inheritance tax and corporation tax.

(3) An order under subsection (2) may take effect from the start of the tax year in which the order is made.

(4) The Treasury may by order make any incidental, supplemental, consequential, transitional or saving provision in consequence of Schedule 46 or in consequence of any further provision made under subsection (2).

(5) An order under this section may—

(*a*) make different provision for different purposes, and

(*b*) make provision amending, repealing or revoking any provision made by or under an Act (whenever passed or made).

(6) An order under this section is to be made by statutory instrument.

(7) A statutory instrument containing an order under subsection (2) (whether alone or with other provisions) may not be made unless a draft of the instrument has been laid before, and approved by a resolution of, the House of Commons.

(8) Subject to subsection (7), a statutory instrument containing an order under this section is subject to annulment in pursuance of a resolution of the House of Commons.

Commentary—*Simon's Taxes* **I3.612**.

ORDERS—

Income Tax (Removal of Ordinary Residence) Order, SI 2014/3062.

International matters

221 Agreement between UK and Switzerland

(1) (*inserts* FA 2012 Sch 36 paras 26A, 26B)

(2) The amendment made by this section is to be treated as having come into force on 1 January 2013.

Commentary—*Simon's Taxes* **E6.327**.

Disclosure

223 Disclosure of tax avoidance schemes

(Please see Yellow Tax Handbook Part 1)

Powers

228 Data-gathering from merchant acquirers etc

(1) (*inserts* FA 2011 Sch 23 para 13A)

(2) This section applies in relation to relevant data with a bearing on any period (whether before, on or after the day on which this Act is passed).

Commentary—*Simon's Taxes* **A6.337**.

Interim remedies

234 Restrictions on interim payments in proceedings relating to taxation matters

(1) This section applies to an application for an interim remedy (however described), made in any court proceedings relating to a taxation matter, if the application is founded (wholly or in part) on a point of law which has yet to be finally determined in the proceedings.

(2) Any power of a court to grant an interim remedy (however described) requiring the Commissioners for Her Majesty's Revenue and Customs, or an officer of Revenue and Customs, to pay any sum to any claimant (however described) in the proceedings is restricted as follows.

(3) The court may grant the interim remedy only if it is shown to the satisfaction of the court—

(*a*) that, taking account of all sources of funding (including borrowing) reasonably likely to be available to fund the proceedings, the payment of the sum is necessary to enable the proceedings to continue, or (*b*) that the circumstances of the claimant are exceptional and such that the granting of the remedy is necessary in the interests of justice.

(4) The powers restricted by this section include (for example)—

(*a*) powers under rule 25 of the Civil Procedure Rules 1998 (S.I. 1998/3132);

(*b*) powers under Part II of Rule 29 of the Rules of the Court of Judicature (Northern Ireland) (Revision) 1980 (S.R. 1980 No.346).

(5) This section applies in relation to proceedings whenever commenced, but only in relation to applications made in those proceedings on or after 26 June 2013.

(6) This section applies on and after 26 June 2013.

(7) Subsection (8) applies where, on or after 26 June 2013 but before the passing of this Act, an interim remedy was granted by a court using a power which, because of subsection (6), is to be taken to have been restricted by this section.

(8) Unless it is shown to the satisfaction of the court that paragraph (*a*) or (*b*) of subsection (3) applied at the time the interim remedy was granted, the court must, on an application made to it under this subsection—

(*a*) revoke or modify the interim remedy so as to secure compliance with this section, and

(*b*) if the Commissioners have, or an officer of Revenue and Customs has, paid any sum as originally required by the interim remedy, order the repayment of the sum or any part of the sum as appropriate (with interest from the date of payment).

(9) For the purposes of this section, proceedings on appeal are to be treated as part of the original proceedings from which the appeal lies.

(10) In this section "taxation matter" means anything, other than national insurance contributions, the collection and management of which is the responsibility of the Commissioners for Her Majesty's Revenue and Customs (or was the responsibility of the Commissioners of Inland Revenue or Commissioners of Customs and Excise).

PART 7

FINAL PROVISIONS

235 Interpretation

(1) In this Act—

"ALDA 1979" means the Alcoholic Liquor Duties Act 1979,

"BGDA 1981" means the Betting and Gaming Duties Act 1981,

"CAA 2001" means the Capital Allowances Act 2001,

"CEMA 1979" means the Customs and Excise Management Act 1979,

"CRCA 2005" means the Commissioners for Revenue and Customs Act 2005,

"CTA 2009" means the Corporation Tax Act 2009,

"CTA 2010" means the Corporation Tax Act 2010,

"F(No.3)A 2010" means the Finance (No. 3) Act 2010,

"HODA 1979" means the Hydrocarbon Oil Duties Act 1979,

"ICTA" means the Income and Corporation Taxes Act 1988,

"IHTA 1984" means the Inheritance Tax Act 1984,

"ITA 2007" means the Income Tax Act 2007,

"ITEPA 2003" means the Income Tax (Earnings and Pensions) Act 2003,

"ITTOIA 2005" means the Income Tax (Trading and Other Income) Act 2005,

"OTA 1975" means the Oil Taxation Act 1975,

"TCGA 1992" means the Taxation of Chargeable Gains Act 1992,

"TIOPA 2010" means the Taxation (International and Other Provisions) Act 2010,

"TMA 1970" means the Taxes Management Act 1970,

"TPDA 1979" means the Tobacco Products Duty Act 1979,

"VATA 1994" means the Value Added Tax Act 1994, and

"VERA 1994" means the Vehicle Excise and Registration Act 1994.

(2) In this Act—

"FA", followed by a year, means the Finance Act of that year;

"F(No.2)A", followed by a year, means the Finance (No. 2) Act of that year.

236 Short title

This Act may be cited as the Finance Act 2013.

SCHEDULE 36

TREATMENT OF LIABILITIES FOR INHERITANCE TAX PURPOSES

Section 176

IHTA 1984

1 IHTA 1984 is amended as follows.

2 (1) Section 162 (liabilities) is amended as follows.
(2) In subsection (4), after "possible" insert "and to the extent that it is not taken to reduce value in accordance with section 162B".
(3) In subsection (5), after "possible" insert "and to the extent that it is not taken to reduce value in accordance with section 162B".

3 After section 162 insert—

"162A Liabilities attributable to financing excluded property

(1) To the extent that a liability is attributable to financing (directly or indirectly)—

(*a*) the acquisition of any excluded property, or

(*b*) the maintenance, or an enhancement, of the value of any such property,

it may only be taken into account so far as permitted by subsections (2) to (4).

(2) Where the property mentioned in subsection (1) has been disposed of, in whole or in part, for full consideration in money or money's worth, the liability may be taken into account up to an amount equal to so much of that consideration as—

(*a*) is not excluded property, and

(*b*) has not been used—

(i) to finance (directly or indirectly) the acquisition of excluded property or the maintenance, or an enhancement, of the value of such property, or

(ii) to discharge (directly or indirectly) any other liability that, by virtue of this section, would not be taken into account.

(3) The liability may be taken into account up to an amount equal to the value of such of the property mentioned in subsection (1) as—

(*a*) has not been disposed of, and

(*b*) is no longer excluded property.

(4) To the extent that any remaining liability is greater than the value of such of the property mentioned in subsection (1) as—

(*a*) has not been disposed of, and

(*b*) is still excluded property,

it may be taken into account, but only so far as the remaining liability is not greater than that value for any of the reasons mentioned in subsection (7).

(5) Subsection (6) applies where—

(*a*) a liability or any part of a liability is attributable to financing (directly or indirectly)—

(i) the acquisition of property that was not excluded property, or

(ii) the maintenance, or an enhancement, of the value of such property, and

(*b*) the property or part of the property—

(i) has not been disposed of, and

(ii) has become excluded property.

(6) The liability or (as the case may be) the part may only be taken into account to the extent that it exceeds the value of the property, or the part of the property, that has become excluded property, but only so far as it does not exceed that value for any of the reasons mentioned in subsection (7).

(7) The reasons are—

(*a*) arrangements the main purpose, or one of the main purposes, of which is to secure a tax advantage,

(*b*) an increase in the amount of the liability (whether due to the accrual of interest or otherwise), or

(*c*) a disposal, in whole or in part, of the property.

(8) In this section—

"arrangements" includes any scheme, transaction or series of transactions, agreement or understanding, whether or not legally enforceable, and any associated operations;

"remaining liability" means the liability mentioned in subsection (1) so far as subsections (2) and (3) do not permit it to be taken into account;

"tax advantage" means—

(*a*) the avoidance or reduction of a charge to tax, or

(*b*) the avoidance of a possible determination in respect of tax.

162B Liabilities attributable to financing certain relievable property

(1) Subsection (2) applies if—

(*a*) the whole or part of any value transferred by a transfer of value is to be treated as reduced, under section 104, by virtue of it being attributable to the value of relevant business property, and

(*b*) the transferor has a liability which is attributable, in whole or in part, to financing (directly or indirectly)—

(i) the acquisition of that property, or

(ii) the maintenance, or an enhancement, of its value.

(2) The liability is, so far as possible, to be taken to reduce the value attributable to the value of the relevant business property, before it is treated as reduced under section 104, but only to the extent that the liability—

(*a*) is attributable as mentioned in subsection (1)(*b*), and

(*b*) does not reduce the value of the relevant business property by virtue of section 110(*b*).

(3) Subsection (4) applies if—

(*a*) the whole or part of any value transferred by a transfer of value is to be treated as reduced, under section 116, by virtue of it being attributable to the agricultural value of agricultural property, and

(*b*) the transferor has a liability which is attributable, in whole or in part, to financing (directly or indirectly)—

(i) the acquisition of that property, or

(ii) the maintenance, or an enhancement, of its agricultural value.

(4) To the extent that the liability is attributable as mentioned in subsection (3)(*b*), it is, so far as possible, to be taken to reduce the value attributable to the agricultural value of the agricultural property, before it is treated as reduced under section 116.

(5) Subsection (6) applies if—

(*a*) part of the value of a person's estate immediately before death is attributable to the value of land on which trees or underwood are growing,

(*b*) the value of the trees or underwood is to be left out of account, under section 125(2)(*a*), in determining the value transferred by the chargeable transfer made on the person's death, and

(*c*) the person has a liability which is attributable, in whole or in part, to financing (directly or indirectly)—

(i) the acquisition of the land or trees or underwood,

(ii) planting the trees or underwood, or

(iii) the maintenance, or an enhancement, of the value of the trees or underwood.

(6) To the extent that the liability is attributable as mentioned in subsection (5)(*c*), it is, so far as possible, to be taken to reduce the value of the trees or underwood, before their value is left out of account.

(7) Subject to subsection (8), to the extent that a liability is, in accordance with this section, taken to reduce value in determining the value transferred by a chargeable transfer, that liability is not then to be taken into account in determining the value transferred by any subsequent transfer of value by the same transferor.

(8) Subsection (7) does not prevent a liability from being taken into account by reason only that the liability has previously been taken into account in determining the amount on which tax is chargeable under section 64.

(9) For the purposes of subsections (1) to (4) and (7), references to a transfer of value or chargeable transfer include references to an occasion on which tax is chargeable under Chapter 3 of Part 3 (apart from section 79) and—

(*a*) references to the value transferred by a transfer of value or chargeable transfer include references to the amount on which tax is then chargeable, and

(*b*) references to the transferor include references to the trustees of the settlement concerned.

(10) In this section—

"agricultural property" and "agricultural value" have the same meaning as in Chapter 2 of Part 5;

"relevant business property" has the same meaning as in Chapter 1 of Part 5.

162C Sections 162A and 162B: supplementary provision

(1) This section applies for the purposes of determining the extent to which a liability is attributable as mentioned in section 162A(1) or (5) or 162B(1)(*b*), (3)(*b*) or (5)(*c*).

(2) Where a liability was discharged in part before the time in relation to which the question as to whether or how to take it into account arises—

(*a*) any part of the liability that, at the time of discharge, was not attributable as mentioned in subsection (1) is, so far as possible, to be taken to have been discharged first,

(*b*) any part of the liability that, at the time of discharge, was attributable as mentioned in section 162B(1)(*b*), (3)(*b*) or (5)(*c*) is, so far as possible, only to be taken to have been discharged after any part of the liability within paragraph (*a*) was discharged, and

(*c*) any part of the liability that, at the time of discharge, was attributable as mentioned in section 162A(1) or (5) is, so far as possible, only to be taken to have been discharged after any parts of the liability within paragraph (*a*) or (*b*) were discharged."

4 After section 175 (estate on death: liability to make future payments etc) insert—

"175A Discharge of liabilities after death

(1) In determining the value of a person's estate immediately before death, a liability may be taken into account to the extent that—

(*a*) it is discharged on or after death, out of the estate or from excluded property owned by the person immediately before death, in money or money's worth, and

(*b*) it is not otherwise prevented, under any provision of this Act, from being taken into account.

(2) Where the whole or any part of a liability is not discharged in accordance with paragraph (*a*) of subsection (1), the liability or (as the case may be) the part may only be taken into account for the purpose mentioned in that subsection to the extent that—

(*a*) there is a real commercial reason for the liability or the part not being discharged,

(*b*) securing a tax advantage is not the main purpose, or one of the main purposes, of leaving the liability or part undischarged, and

(*c*) the liability or the part is not otherwise prevented, under any provision of this Act, from being taken into account.

(3) For the purposes of subsection (2)(*a*) there is a real commercial reason for a liability, or part of a liability, not being discharged where it is shown that—

(*a*) the liability is to a person dealing at arm's length, or

(*b*) if the liability were to a person dealing at arm's length, that person would not require the liability to be discharged.

(4) Where, by virtue of this section, a liability is not taken into account in determining the value of a person's estate immediately before death, the liability is also not to be taken into account in determining the extent to which the estate of any spouse or civil partner of the person is increased for the purposes of section 18.

(5) In subsection (2)(*b*) "tax advantage" means—

(*a*) a relief from tax or increased relief from tax,

(*b*) a repayment of tax or increased repayment of tax,

(*c*) the avoidance, reduction or delay of a charge to tax or an assessment to tax, or

(*d*) the avoidance of a possible assessment to tax or determination in respect of tax.

(6) In subsection (5) "tax" includes income tax and capital gains tax.

(7) Where the liability is discharged as mentioned in subsection (1)(*a*) only in part—

(*a*) any part of the liability that is attributable as mentioned in section 162A(1) or (5) is, so far possible, taken to be discharged first,

(*b*) any part of the liability that is attributable as mentioned in section 162B(1)(*b*), (3)(*b*) or (5)(*c*) is, so far as possible, taken to be discharged only after any part of the liability within paragraph (*a*) is discharged, and

(*c*) the liability so far as it is not attributable as mentioned in paragraph (*a*) or (*b*) is, so far as possible, taken to be discharged only after any parts of the liability within either of those paragraphs are discharged."

Commencement

5 (1) Subject to sub-paragraph (2), the amendments made by this Schedule have effect in relation to transfers of value made, or treated as made, on or after the day on which this Act is passed.

(2) Section 162B of IHTA 1984 (inserted by paragraph 3) only has effect in relation to liabilities incurred on or after 6 April 2013.

(3) For the purposes of sub-paragraph (2), where a liability is incurred under an agreement—

(*a*) if the agreement was varied so that the liability could be incurred under it, the liability is to be treated as having been incurred on the date of the variation, and

(*b*) in any other case, the liability is to be treated as having been incurred on the date the agreement was made.

SCHEDULE 43

GENERAL ANTI-ABUSE RULE: PROCEDURAL REQUIREMENTS

Section 209

Commentary—*Simon's Taxes* **A2.125**.

Cross references—See FA 2014 Pt 4, Ch 3 (DOTAS accelerated payments).

FA 2014 Pt 5 (promoters of tax avoidance schemes).

The GAAR Advisory Panel

1 (1) In this Part "the GAAR Advisory Panel" means the panel of persons established by the Commissioners for the purposes of the general anti-abuse rule.

(2) In this Schedule "the Chair" means any member of the GAAR Advisory Panel appointed by the Commissioners to chair it.

[Meaning of "tax appeal"

1A In this Part "tax appeal" means—

(*a*) an appeal under section 31 of TMA 1970 (income tax: appeals against amendments of self-assessment, amendments made by closure notices under section 28A or 28B of that Act, etc), including an appeal under that section by virtue of regulations under Part 11 of ITEPA 2003 (PAYE),

(*b*) an appeal under paragraph 9 of Schedule 1A to TMA 1970 (income tax: appeals against amendments made by closure notices under paragraph 7(2) of that Schedule, etc),

(*c*) an appeal under section 705 of ITA 2007 (income tax: appeals against counteraction notices),

(*d*) an appeal under paragraph 34(3) or 48 of Schedule 18 to FA 1998 (corporation tax: appeals against amendment of a company's return made by closure notice, assessments other than self-assessments, etc),

(*e*) an appeal under section 750 of CTA 2010 (corporation tax: appeals against counteraction notices),

(*f*) an appeal under section 222 of IHTA 1984 (appeals against HMRC determinations) other than an appeal made by a person against a determination in respect of a transfer of value at a time when a tax enquiry is in progress in respect of a return made by that person in respect of that transfer,

(*g*) an appeal under paragraph 35 of Schedule 10 to FA 2003 (stamp duty land tax: appeals against amendment of self-assessment, discovery assessments, etc),

(*h*) an appeal under paragraph 35 of Schedule 33 to FA 2013 (annual tax on enveloped dwellings: appeals against amendment of self-assessment, discovery assessments, etc),

(*i*) an appeal under paragraph 14 of Schedule 2 to the Oil Taxation Act 1975 (petroleum revenue tax: appeal against assessment, determination etc),

(*j*) an appeal under section 102 of FA 2015 (diverted profits tax: appeal against charging notice etc),

(*k*) an appeal under section 114 of FA 2016 (apprenticeship levy: appeal against an assessment), or

(*l*) an appeal against any determination of—

(i) an appeal within paragraphs (*a*) to (*k*), or

(ii) an appeal within this paragraph.][1]

Amendments—[1] Paragraph (1A) inserted by FA 2016 s 158(5), (6) with effect in relation to tax arrangements (within the meaning of FA 2013 Pt 5) entered into on or after 15 September 2016.

Meaning of "designated HMRC officer"

2 In this Schedule a "designated HMRC officer" means an officer of Revenue and Customs who has been designated by the Commissioners for the purposes of the general anti-abuse rule.

Notice to taxpayer of proposed counteraction of tax advantage

3 (1) If a designated HMRC officer considers—

(*a*) that a tax advantage has arisen to a person ("the taxpayer") from tax arrangements that are abusive, and

(*b*) that the advantage ought to be counteracted under section 209, the officer must give the taxpayer a written notice to that effect.

(2) The notice must—

(*a*) specify the arrangements and the tax advantage,

(*b*) explain why the officer considers that a tax advantage has arisen to the taxpayer from tax arrangements that are abusive,

(*c*) set out the counteraction that the officer considers ought to be taken,

(*d*) inform the taxpayer of the period under paragraph 4 for making representations, and

(*e*) explain the effect [of—

(i) paragraphs 5 and 6, and

(ii) sections 209(8) and (9) and 212A.][1]

(3) The notice may set out steps that the taxpayer may take to avoid the proposed counteraction.

Amendments—[1] In sub-para (2)(*e*), words substituted for words "of paragraphs 5 and 6" by FA 2016 s 158(5), (7) with effect in relation to tax arrangements (within the meaning of FA 2013 Pt 5) entered into on or after 15 September 2016.

4 (1) If a notice is given to the taxpayer under paragraph 3, the taxpayer has 45 days beginning with the day on which the notice is given to send written representations in response to the notice to the designated HMRC officer.

(2) The designated officer may, on a written request made by the taxpayer, extend the period during which representations may be made.

[Corrective action by taxpayer

4A (1) If the taxpayer takes the relevant corrective action before the beginning of the closed period mentioned in section 209(8), the matter is not to be referred to the GAAR Advisory Panel.

(2) For the purposes of this Schedule the "relevant corrective action" is taken if (and only if) the taxpayer takes the steps set out in sub-paragraphs (3) and (4).

(3) The first step is that—

(*a*) the taxpayer amends a return or claim to counteract the tax advantage specified in the notice under paragraph 3, or

(*b*) if the taxpayer has made a tax appeal (by notifying HMRC or otherwise) on the basis that the tax advantage specified in the notice under paragraph 3 arises from the tax arrangements specified in that notice, the taxpayer takes all necessary action to enter into an agreement with HMRC (in writing) for the purpose of relinquishing that advantage.

(4) The second step is that the taxpayer notifies HMRC—

(*a*) that the taxpayer has taken the first step, and

(*b*) of any additional amount which has or will become due and payable in respect of tax by reason of the first step being taken.

(5) Where the taxpayer takes the first step described in sub-paragraph (3)(*b*), HMRC may proceed as if the taxpayer had not taken the relevant corrective action if the taxpayer fails to enter into the written agreement.

(6) In determining the additional amount which has or will become due and payable in respect of tax for the purposes of sub-paragraph (4)(*b*), it is to be assumed that, where the taxpayer takes the necessary action as mentioned in sub-paragraph (3)(*b*), the agreement is then entered into.

(7) No enactment limiting the time during which amendments may be made to returns or claims operates to prevent the taxpayer taking the first step mentioned in sub-paragraph (3)(*a*) before the tax enquiry is closed (whether or not before the specified time).

(8) No appeal may be brought, by virtue of a provision mentioned in sub-paragraph (9), against an amendment made by a closure notice in respect of a tax enquiry to the extent that the amendment takes into account an amendment made by the taxpayer to a return or claim in taking the first step mentioned in sub-paragraph (3)(*a*).

(9) The provisions are—

(*a*) section 31(1)(*b*) or (*c*) of TMA 1970,

(*b*) paragraph 9 of Schedule 1A to TMA 1970,

(*c*) paragraph 34(3) of Schedule 18 to FA 1998,

(*d*) paragraph 35(1)(*b*) of Schedule 10 to FA 2003, and

(*e*) paragraph 35(1)(*b*) of Schedule 33 to FA 2013.][1]

Amendments—[1] Paragraph 4A inserted by FA 2016 s 158(5), (8) with effect in relation to tax arrangements (within the meaning of FA 2013 Pt 5) entered into on or after 15 September 2016.

Referral to GAAR Advisory Panel

[4B Paragraphs 5 and 6 apply if the taxpayer does not take the relevant corrective action (see paragraph 4A) by the beginning of the closed period mentioned in section 209(8).][1]

Amendments—[1] Paragraph 4B inserted by FA 2016 s 158(1), (9) with effect in relation to tax arrangements (within the meaning of FA 2013 Pt 5) entered into on or after 15 September 2016.

5 If no representations are made in accordance with paragraph 4, a designated HMRC officer must refer the matter to the GAAR Advisory Panel.

6 (1) If representations are made in accordance with paragraph 4, a designated HMRC officer must consider them.
(2) If, after considering them, the designated HMRC officer considers that the tax advantage ought to be counteracted under section 209, the officer must refer the matter to the GAAR Advisory Panel.
[(3) The officer must, as soon as reasonably practicable after deciding whether or not the matter is to be referred to the GAAR Advisory Panel, give the taxpayer written notice of the decision.][1]

Amendments—[1] Sub-para (3) inserted by FA 2016 s 157(1), (11) with effect in relation to tax arrangements (within the meaning of FA 2013 Pt 5) entered into at any time (whether before on or after 15 September 2016).

7 If the matter is referred to the GAAR Advisory Panel, the designated HMRC officer must at the same time provide it with—
(*a*) a copy of the notice given to the taxpayer under paragraph 3,
(*b*) a copy of any representations made in accordance with paragraph 4 and any comments that the officer has on those representations, and
(*c*) a copy of the notice given to the taxpayer under paragraph 8.

8 If the matter is referred to the GAAR Advisory Panel, the designated HMRC officer must at the same time give the taxpayer a notice which—
(*a*) specifies that the matter is being referred,
(*b*) is accompanied by a copy of any comments provided to the GAAR Advisory Panel under paragraph 7(*b*), and
(*c*) informs the taxpayer of the period under paragraph 9 for making representations, and of the requirement under that paragraph to send any representations to the officer.

9 (1) The taxpayer has 21 days beginning with the day on which a notice is given under paragraph 8 to send the GAAR Advisory Panel written representations about—
(*a*) the notice given to the taxpayer under paragraph 3, or
(*b*) any comments provided under paragraph 7(*b*).
(2) The GAAR Advisory Panel may, on a written request made by the taxpayer, extend the period during which representations may be made.
(3) The taxpayer must send a copy of any representations to the designated HMRC officer at the same time as the representations are sent to the GAAR Advisory Panel.
(4) If no representations were made in accordance with paragraph 4, the designated HMRC officer—
(*a*) may provide the GAAR Advisory Panel with comments on any representations made under this paragraph, and
(*b*) if comments are provided, must at the same time send a copy of them to the taxpayer.

Decision of GAAR Advisory Panel and opinion notices

10 (1) If the matter is referred to the GAAR Advisory Panel, the Chair must arrange for a sub-panel consisting of 3 members of the GAAR Advisory Panel (one of whom may be the Chair) to consider it.
(2) The sub-panel may invite the taxpayer or the designated HMRC officer (or both) to supply the sub-panel with further information within a period specified in the invitation.
(3) Invitations must explain the effect of sub-paragraph (4) or (5) (as appropriate).
(4) If the taxpayer supplies information to the sub-panel under this paragraph, the taxpayer must at the same time send a copy of the information to the designated HMRC officer.
(5) If the designated HMRC officer supplies information to the sub-panel under this paragraph, the officer must at the same time send a copy of the information to the taxpayer.

11 (1) Where the matter is referred to the GAAR Advisory Panel, the sub-panel must produce—
(*a*) one opinion notice stating the joint opinion of all the members of the sub-panel, or
(*b*) two or three opinion notices which taken together state the opinions of all the members.
(2) The sub-panel must give a copy of the opinion notice or notices to—
(*a*) the designated HMRC officer, and
(*b*) the taxpayer.
(3) An opinion notice is a notice which states that in the opinion of the members of the sub-panel, or one or more of those members—
(*a*) the entering into and carrying out of the tax arrangements is a reasonable course of action in relation to the relevant tax provisions—

(i) having regard to all the circumstances (including the matters mentioned in subsections (2)(*a*) to (*c*) and (3) of section 207), and

(ii) taking account of subsections (4) to (6) of that section, or

(*b*) the entering into or carrying out of the tax arrangements is not a reasonable course of action in relation to the relevant tax provisions having regard to those circumstances and taking account of those subsections, or

(*c*) it is not possible, on the information available, to reach a view on that matter,

and the reasons for that opinion.

(4) For the purposes of the giving of an opinion under this paragraph, the arrangements are to be assumed to be tax arrangements.

(5) In this Part, a reference to any opinion of the GAAR Advisory Panel about any tax arrangements is a reference to the contents of any opinion notice about the arrangements.

Cross references—FA 2014 Sch 34 para 7 (application of sub-para (3)(*b*) above in relation to the issue of conduct notices to promoters of tax avoidance schemes).

Notice of final decision after considering opinion of GAAR Advisory Panel

12 (1) A designated HMRC officer who has received a notice or notices under paragraph 11 must, having considered any opinion of the GAAR Advisory Panel about the tax arrangements, give the taxpayer a written notice setting out whether the tax advantage arising from the arrangements is to be counteracted under the general anti-abuse rule.

(2) If the notice states that a tax advantage is to be counteracted, it must also set out—

(*a*) the adjustments required to give effect to the counteraction, and

(*b*) if relevant, any steps that the taxpayer is required to take to give effect to it.

Commentary—*Simon's Taxes* **A2.125**.

Note—Adjustments to be made in respect of NICs under FA 2013 s 209 may be made by a notice of final decision given under this para (NICA 2014 s 10(4)).

Cross references—See FA 2014 Pt 4, Ch 3 (DOTAS accelerated payments).

Notices may be given on assumption that tax advantage does arise

13 (1) A designated HMRC officer may give a notice, or do anything else, under this Schedule where the officer considers that a tax advantage might have arisen to the taxpayer.

(2) Accordingly, any notice given by a designated HMRC officer under this Schedule may be expressed to be given on the assumption that the tax advantage does arise (without agreeing that it does).

[SCHEDULE 43A

PROCEDURAL REQUIREMENTS: POOLING NOTICES AND NOTICES OF BINDING]

Amendments—Schedule 43A inserted by FA 2016 s 157(1), (2) with effect in relation to tax arrangements (within the meaning of FA 2013 Pt 5) entered into at any time (whether before, on or after 15 September 2016).

[Pooling notices

1 (1) This paragraph applies where a person has been given a notice under paragraph 3 of Schedule 43 in relation to any tax arrangements (the "lead arrangements") and the condition in sub-paragraph (2) is met.

(2) The condition is that the period of 45 days mentioned in paragraph 4(1) of Schedule 43 has expired but no notice under paragraph 12 of Schedule 43 or paragraph 8 of Schedule 43B has yet been given in respect of the matter.

(3) If a designated HMRC officer considers—

(*a*) that a tax advantage has arisen to another person ("R") from tax arrangements that are abusive,

(*b*) that those tax arrangements ("R's arrangements") are equivalent to the lead arrangements, and

(*c*) that the advantage ought to be counteracted under section 209,

the officer may give R a notice (a "pooling notice") which places R's arrangements in a pool with the lead arrangements.

(4) There is one pool for any lead arrangements, so all tax arrangements placed in a pool with the lead arrangements (as well as the lead arrangements themselves) are in one and the same pool.

(5) Tax arrangements which have been placed in a pool do not cease to be in the pool except where that is expressly provided for by this Schedule (regardless of whether or not the lead arrangements or any other tax arrangements remain in the pool).

(6) The officer may not give R a pooling notice if R has been given in respect of R's arrangements a notice under paragraph 3 of Schedule 43.][1]

Amendments—[1] Schedule 43A inserted by FA 2016 s 157(1), (2) with effect in relation to tax arrangements (within the meaning of FA 2013 Pt 5) entered into at any time (whether before, on or after 15 September 2016).

[Notice of proposal to bind arrangements to counteracted arrangements

2 (1) This paragraph applies where a counteraction notice has been given to a person in relation to any tax arrangements (the "counteracted arrangements") which are in a pool created under paragraph 1.

(2) If a designated HMRC officer considers—

(*a*) that a tax advantage has arisen to another person ("R") from tax arrangements that are abusive,

(*b*) that those tax arrangements ("R's arrangements") are equivalent to the counteracted arrangements, and

(*c*) that the advantage ought to be counteracted under section 209,

the officer may give R a notice (a "notice of binding") in relation to R's arrangements.

(3) The officer may not give R a notice of binding if R has been given in respect of R's arrangements a notice under—

(*a*) paragraph 1, or

(*b*) paragraph 3 of Schedule 43.

(4) In this paragraph "counteraction notice" means a notice such as is mentioned in sub-paragraph (2) of paragraph 12 of Schedule 43 or sub-paragraph (3) of paragraph 8 of Schedule 43B (notice of final decision to counteract).

3 (1) The decision whether or not to give R a pooling notice or notice of binding must be taken, and any notice must be given, as soon as is reasonably practicable after HMRC becomes aware of the relevant facts.

(2) A pooling notice or notice of binding must—

(*a*) specify the tax arrangements in relation to which the notice is given and the tax advantage,

(*b*) explain why the officer considers R's arrangements to be equivalent to the lead arrangements or the counteracted arrangements (as the case may be),

(*c*) explain why the officer considers that a tax advantage has arisen to R from tax arrangements that are abusive,

(*d*) set out the counteraction that the officer considers ought to be taken, and

(*e*) explain the effect of—

(i) paragraphs 4 to 10,

(ii) subsection (9) of section 209, and

(iii) section 212A.

(3) A pooling notice or notice of binding may set out steps that R may (subject to subsection (9) of section 209) take to avoid the proposed counteraction.][1]

Amendments—[1] Schedule 43A inserted by FA 2016 s 157(1), (2) with effect in relation to tax arrangements (within the meaning of FA 2013 Pt 5) entered into at any time (whether before, on or after 15 September 2016).

[Corrective action by a notified taxpayer

4 (1) If a person to whom a pooling notice or notice of binding has been given takes the relevant corrective action in relation to the tax arrangements and tax advantage specified in the notice before the beginning of the closed period mentioned in section 209(9), the person is to be treated for the purposes of paragraphs 8 and 9 and Schedule 43B (generic referral of tax arrangements) as not having been given the notice in question (and accordingly the tax arrangements in question are no longer in the pool).

(2) For the purposes of this Schedule the "relevant corrective action" is taken if (and only if) the person takes the steps set out in sub-paragraphs (3) and (4).

(3) The first step is that—

(*a*) the person amends a return or claim to counteract the tax advantage specified in the pooling notice or notice of binding, or

(*b*) if the person has made a tax appeal (by notifying HMRC or otherwise) on the basis that the tax advantage specified in the pooling notice or notice of binding arises from the tax arrangements specified in that notice, the person takes all necessary action to enter into an agreement with HMRC (in writing) for the purpose of relinquishing that advantage.

(4) The second step is that the person notifies HMRC—

(*a*) that the first step has been taken, and

(*b*) of any additional amount which has or will become due and payable in respect of tax by reason of the first step being taken.

(5) Where a person takes the first step described in sub-paragraph (3)(*b*), HMRC may proceed as if the person had not taken the relevant corrective action if the person fails to enter into the written agreement.

(6) In determining the additional amount which has or will become due and payable in respect of tax for the purposes of sub-paragraph (4)(*b*), it is to be assumed that, where the person takes the necessary action as mentioned in sub-paragraph (3)(*b*), the agreement is then entered into.
(7) No enactment limiting the time during which amendments may be made to returns or claims operates to prevent the person taking the first step mentioned in sub-paragraph (3)(*a*) before the tax enquiry is closed.
(8) No appeal may be brought, by virtue of a provision mentioned in sub-paragraph (9), against an amendment made by a closure notice in respect of a tax enquiry to the extent that the amendment takes into account an amendment made by the taxpayer to a return or claim in taking the first step mentioned in sub-paragraph (3)(*a*).
(9) The provisions are—

(*a*) paragraph 35(1)(*b*) of Schedule 33,
(*b*) section 31(1)(*b*) or (*c*) of TMA 1970,
(*c*) paragraph 9 of Schedule 1A to TMA 1970,
(*d*) paragraph 34(3) of Schedule 18 to FA 1998, and
(*e*) paragraph 35(1)(*b*) of Schedule 10 to FA 2003.][1]

Amendments—[1] Schedule 43A inserted by FA 2016 s 157(1), (2) with effect in relation to tax arrangements (within the meaning of FA 2013 Pt 5) entered into at any time (whether before, on or after 15 September 2016).

[Corrective action by lead taxpayer

5 If the person mentioned in paragraph 1(1) takes the relevant corrective action (as defined in paragraph 4A of Schedule 43) before the end of the period of 75 days beginning with the day on which the notice mentioned in paragraph 1(1) was given to that person, the lead arrangements are treated as ceasing to be in the pool.][1]

Amendments—[1] Schedule 43A inserted by FA 2016 s 157(1), (2) with effect in relation to tax arrangements (within the meaning of FA 2013 Pt 5) entered into at any time (whether before, on or after 15 September 2016).

[Opinion notices and right to make representations

6 (1) Sub-paragraph (2) applies where—

(*a*) a pooling notice is given to a person in relation to any tax arrangements, and
(*b*) an opinion notice (or opinion notices) under paragraph 11(2) of Schedule 43 about another set of tax arrangements in the pool ("the referred arrangements") is subsequently given to a designated HMRC officer.

(2) The officer must give the person a pooled arrangements opinion notice.
(3) No more than one pooled arrangements opinion notice may be given to a person in respect of the same tax arrangements.
(4) Where a designated HMRC officer gives a person a notice of binding, the officer must, at the same time, give the person a bound arrangements opinion notice.][1]

Amendments—[1] Schedule 43A inserted by FA 2016 s 157(1), (2) with effect in relation to tax arrangements (within the meaning of FA 2013 Pt 5) entered into at any time (whether before, on or after 15 September 2016).

[7 (1) In relation to a person who is, or has been, given a pooling notice, "pooled arrangements opinion notice" means a written notice which—

(*a*) sets out a report prepared by HMRC of any opinion of the GAAR Advisory Panel about the referred arrangements,
(*b*) explains the person's right to make representations falling within sub-paragraph (3), and
(*c*) sets out the period in which those representations may be made.

(2) In relation to a person who is given a notice of binding "bound arrangements opinion notice" means a written notice which—

(*a*) sets out a report prepared by HMRC of any opinion of the GAAR Advisory Panel about the counteracted arrangements (see paragraph 2(1)),
(*b*) explains the person's right to make representations falling within sub-paragraph (3), and
(*c*) sets out the period in which those representations may be made.

(3) A person who is given a pooled arrangements opinion notice or a bound arrangements opinion notice has 30 days beginning with the day on which the notice is given to make representations in any of the following categories—

(*a*) representations that no tax advantage has arisen to the person from the arrangements to which the notice relates;
(*b*) representations as to why the arrangements to which the notice relates are or may be materially different from—
   (i) the referred arrangements (in the case of a pooled arrangements opinion notice), or
   (ii) the counteracted arrangements (in the case of a bound arrangements opinion notice).

(4) In sub-paragraph (3)(*b*) references to "arrangements" include any circumstances which would be relevant in accordance with section 207 to a determination of whether the tax arrangements in question are abusive.][1]

Amendments—[1] Schedule 43A inserted by FA 2016 s 157(1), (2) with effect in relation to tax arrangements (within the meaning of FA 2013 Pt 5) entered into at any time (whether before, on or after 15 September 2016).

[Notice of final decision

8 (1) This paragraph applies where—

(*a*) any tax arrangements have been placed in a pool by a notice given to a person under paragraph 1, and

(*b*) a designated HMRC officer has given a notice under paragraph 12 of Schedule 43 in relation to any other arrangements in the pool (the "referred arrangements").

(2) The officer must, having considered any opinion of the GAAR Advisory Panel about the referred arrangements and any representations made under paragraph 7(3) in relation to the arrangements mentioned in sub-paragraph (1)(*a*), give the person a written notice setting out whether the tax advantage arising from those arrangements is to be counteracted under the general anti-abuse rule.][1]

Amendments—[1] Schedule 43A inserted by FA 2016 s 157(1), (2) with effect in relation to tax arrangements (within the meaning of FA 2013 Pt 5) entered into at any time (whether before, on or after 15 September 2016).

[9 (1) This paragraph applies where—

(*a*) a person has been given a notice of binding under paragraph 2, and

(*b*) the period of 30 days for making representations under paragraph 7(3) has expired.

(2) A designated HMRC officer must, having considered any opinion of the GAAR Advisory Panel about the counteracted arrangements and any representations made under paragraph 7(3) in relation to the arrangements specified in the notice of binding, give the person a written notice setting out whether the tax advantage arising from the arrangements specified in the notice of binding is to be counteracted under the general anti-abuse rule.][1]

Amendments—[1] Schedule 43A inserted by FA 2016 s 157(1), (2) with effect in relation to tax arrangements (within the meaning of FA 2013 Pt 5) entered into at any time (whether before, on or after 15 September 2016).

[10 If a notice under paragraph 8(2) or 9(2) states that a tax advantage is to be counteracted, it must also set out—

(*a*) the adjustments required to give effect to the counteraction, and

(*b*) if relevant, any steps the person concerned is required to take to give effect to it.][1]

Amendments—[1] Schedule 43A inserted by FA 2016 s 157(1), (2) with effect in relation to tax arrangements (within the meaning of FA 2013 Pt 5) entered into at any time (whether before, on or after 15 September 2016).

["Equivalent arrangements"

11 (1) For the purposes of paragraph 1, tax arrangements are "equivalent" to one another if they are substantially the same as one another having regard to—

(*a*) their substantive results,

(*b*) the means of achieving those results, and

(*c*) the characteristics on the basis of which it could reasonably be argued, in each case, that the arrangements are abusive tax arrangements under which a tax advantage has arisen to a person.][1]

Amendments—[1] Schedule 43A inserted by FA 2016 s 157(1), (2) with effect in relation to tax arrangements (within the meaning of FA 2013 Pt 5) entered into at any time (whether before, on or after 15 September 2016).

[Notices may be given on assumption that tax advantage does arise

12 (1) A designated HMRC officer may give a notice, or do anything else, under this Schedule where the officer considers that a tax advantage might have arisen to the person concerned.

(2) Accordingly, any notice given by a designated HMRC officer under this Schedule may be expressed to be given on the assumption that a tax advantage does arise (without conceding that it does).][1]

Amendments—[1] Schedule 43A inserted by FA 2016 s 157(1), (2) with effect in relation to tax arrangements (within the meaning of FA 2013 Pt 5) entered into at any time (whether before, on or after 15 September 2016).

[Power to amend

13 (1) The Treasury may by regulations amend this Schedule (apart from this paragraph).

(2) Regulations under sub-paragraph (1) may include—

(*a*) any amendment of this Part that is appropriate in consequence of an amendment by virtue of sub-paragraph (1);

(*b*) transitional provision.

(3) Regulations under sub-paragraph (1) are to be made by statutory instrument.

(4) A statutory instrument containing regulations under sub-paragraph (1) is subject to annulment in pursuance of a resolution of the House of Commons.][1]

Amendments—[1] Schedule 43A inserted by FA 2016 s 157(1), (2) with effect in relation to tax arrangements (within the meaning of FA 2013 Pt 5) entered into at any time (whether before, on or after 15 September 2016).

[SCHEDULE 43B

PROCEDURAL REQUIREMENTS: GENERIC REFERRAL OF TAX ARRANGEMENTS]

Amendments—[1] Schedule 43B inserted by FA 2016 s 157(1), (3) with effect in relation to tax arrangements (within the meaning of FA 2013 Pt 5) entered into at any time (whether before, on or after 15 September 2016).

[Notice of proposal to make generic referral of tax arrangements

1 (1) Sub-paragraph (2) applies if—

(*a*) pooling notices given under paragraph 1 of Schedule 43A have placed one or more sets of tax arrangements in a pool with the lead arrangements,

(*b*) the lead arrangements (see paragraph 1(1) of Schedule 43A) have ceased to be in the pool, and

(*c*) no referral under paragraph 5 or 6 of Schedule 43 has been made in respect of any arrangements in the pool.

(2) A designated HMRC officer may determine that, in respect of each of the tax arrangements that are in the pool, there is to be given (to the person to whom the pooling notice in question was given) a written notice of a proposal to make a generic referral to the GAAR Advisory Panel in respect of the arrangements in the pool.

(3) Only one determination under sub-paragraph (2) may be made in relation to any one pool.

(4) The persons to whom those notices are given are "the notified taxpayers".

(5) A notice given to a person ("T") under sub-paragraph (2) must—

(*a*) specify the arrangements (the "specified arrangements") and the tax advantage (the "specified advantage") to which the notice relates,

(*b*) inform T of the period under paragraph 2 for making a proposal.][1]

Amendments—[1] Schedule 43B inserted by FA 2016 s 157(1), (3) with effect in relation to tax arrangements (within the meaning of FA 2013 Pt 5) entered into at any time (whether before, on or after 15 September 2016).

[2 (1) T has 30 days beginning with the day on which the notice under paragraph 1 is given to propose to HMRC that it—

(*a*) should give T a notice under paragraph 3 of Schedule 43 in respect of the arrangements to which the notice under paragraph 1 relates, and

(*b*) should not proceed with the proposal to make a generic referral to the GAAR Advisory Panel in respect of those arrangements.

(2) If a proposal is made in accordance with sub-paragraph (1) a designated HMRC officer must consider it.][1]

Amendments—[1] Schedule 43B inserted by FA 2016 s 157(1), (3) with effect in relation to tax arrangements (within the meaning of FA 2013 Pt 5) entered into at any time (whether before, on or after 15 September 2016).

[Generic referral

3 (1) This paragraph applies where a designated HMRC officer has given notices to the notified taxpayers in accordance with paragraph 1(2).

(2) If none of the notified taxpayers has made a proposal under paragraph 2 by the end of the 30 day period mentioned in that paragraph, the officer must make a referral to the GAAR Advisory Panel in respect of the notified taxpayers and the arrangements which are specified arrangements in relation to them.

(3) If at least one of the notified taxpayers makes a proposal in accordance with paragraph 2, the designated HMRC officer must, after the end of that 30 day period, decide whether to—

(*a*) give a notice under paragraph 3 of Schedule 43 in respect of one set of tax arrangements in the relevant pool, or

(*b*) make a referral to the GAAR Advisory Panel in respect of the tax arrangements in the relevant pool.

(4) A referral under this paragraph is a "generic referral".][1]

Amendments—[1] Schedule 43B inserted by FA 2016 s 157(1), (3) with effect in relation to tax arrangements (within the meaning of FA 2013 Pt 5) entered into at any time (whether before, on or after 15 September 2016).

[4 (1) If a generic referral is made to the GAAR Advisory Panel, the designated HMRC officer must at the same time provide it with—

(*a*) a general statement of the material characteristics of the specified arrangements, and

(*b*) a declaration that—

(i) the statement under paragraph (*a*) is applicable to all the specified arrangements, and

(ii) as far as HMRC is aware, nothing which is material to the GAAR Advisory Panel's consideration of the matter has been omitted.

(2) The general statement under sub-paragraph (1)(*a*) must—

(*a*) contain a factual description of the tax arrangements;

(*b*) set out HMRC's view as to whether the tax arrangements accord with established practice (when the arrangements were entered into);

(*c*) explain why it is the designated HMRC officer's view that a tax advantage of the nature described in the statement and arising from tax arrangements having the characteristics described in the statement would be a tax advantage arising from arrangements that are abusive;

(*d*) set out any matters the designated officer is aware of which may suggest that any view of HMRC or the designated HMRC officer expressed in the general statement is not correct;

(*e*) set out any other matters which the designated officer considers are required for the purposes of the exercise of the GAAR Advisory Panel's functions under paragraph 6.][1]

Amendments—[1] Schedule 43B inserted by FA 2016 s 157(1), (3) with effect in relation to tax arrangements (within the meaning of FA 2013 Pt 5) entered into at any time (whether before, on or after 15 September 2016).

[5 If a generic referral is made the designated HMRC officer must at the same time give each of the notified taxpayers a notice which—

(*a*) specifies that a generic referral is being made, and

(*b*) is accompanied by a copy of the statement given to the GAAR Advisory Panel in accordance with paragraph 4(1)(*a*).][1]

Amendments—[1] Schedule 43B inserted by FA 2016 s 157(1), (3) with effect in relation to tax arrangements (within the meaning of FA 2013 Pt 5) entered into at any time (whether before, on or after 15 September 2016).

[Decision of GAAR Advisory Panel and opinion notices

6 (1) If a generic referral is made to the GAAR Advisory Panel under paragraph 3, the Chair must arrange for a sub-panel consisting of 3 members of the GAAR Advisory Panel (one of whom may be the Chair) to consider it.

(2) The sub-panel must produce—

(*a*) one opinion notice stating the joint opinion of all the members of the sub-panel, or

(*b*) two or three opinion notices which taken together state the opinions of all the members.

(3) The sub-panel must give a copy of the opinion notice or notices to the designated HMRC officer.

(4) An opinion notice is a notice which states that in the opinion of the members of the sub-panel, or one or more of those members—

(*a*) the entering into and carrying out of tax arrangements such as are described in the general statement under paragraph 4(1)(*a*) is a reasonable course of action in relation to the relevant tax provisions,

(*b*) the entering into or carrying out of such tax arrangements is not a reasonable course of action in relation to the relevant tax provisions, or

(*c*) it is not possible, on the information available, to reach a view on that matter,

and the reasons for that opinion.

(5) In forming their opinions for the purposes of sub-paragraph (4) members of the sub-panel must—

(*a*) have regard to all the matters set out in the statement under paragraph 4(1)(*a*),

(*b*) assume (unless the contrary is stated in the statement under paragraph 4(1)(*a*)) that the tax arrangements do not form part of any other arrangements,

(*c*) have regard to the matters mentioned in paragraphs (*a*) to (*c*) of section 207(2), and

(*d*) take account of subsections (4) to (6) of section 207.

(6) For the purposes of the giving of an opinion under this paragraph, the arrangements are to be assumed to be tax arrangements.

(7) In this Part, a reference to any opinion of the GAAR Advisory Panel in respect of a generic referral of any tax arrangements is a reference to the contents of any opinion notice given in relation to a generic referral in respect of the arrangements.][1]

Amendments—[1] Schedule 43B inserted by FA 2016 s 157(1), (3) with effect in relation to tax arrangements (within the meaning of FA 2013 Pt 5) entered into at any time (whether before, on or after 15 September 2016).

[Notice of right to make representations

7 (1) Where a designated HMRC officer is given an opinion notice (or opinion notices) under paragraph 6, the officer must give each of the notified taxpayers a copy of the opinion notice (or notices) and a written notice which—

(*a*) explains the notified taxpayer's right to make representations falling within sub-paragraph (2), and

(*b*) sets out the period in which those representations may be made.

(2) A notified taxpayer ("T") who is given a notice under sub-paragraph (1) has 30 days beginning with the day on which the notice is given to make representations in any of the following categories—

(*a*) representations that no tax advantage has arisen from the specified arrangements;

(*b*) representations that T has already been given a notice under paragraph 6 of Schedule 43A in relation to the specified arrangements;

(*c*) representations that any matter set out in the statement under paragraph 4(1)(*a*) is materially inaccurate as regards the specified arrangements (having regard to all circumstances which would be relevant in accordance with section 207 to a determination of whether the tax arrangements in question are abusive).][1]

Amendments—[1] Schedule 43B inserted by FA 2016 s 157(1), (3) with effect in relation to tax arrangements (within the meaning of FA 2013 Pt 5) entered into at any time (whether before, on or after 15 September 2016).

[Notice of final decision after considering opinion of GAAR Advisory Panel

8 (1) A designated HMRC officer who has received a copy of a notice or notices under paragraph 6(3) in respect of a generic referral must consider the case of each notified taxpayer in accordance with sub-paragraph (2).

(2) The officer must, having considered—

(*a*) any opinion of the GAAR Advisory Panel about the matters referred to it, and

(*b*) any representations made by the notified taxpayer under paragraph 7,

give to the notified taxpayer a written notice setting out whether the specified advantage is to be counteracted under the general anti-abuse rule.

(3) If the notice states that a tax advantage is to be counteracted, it must also set out—

(*a*) the adjustments required to give effect to the counteraction, and

(*b*) if relevant, any steps that the taxpayer is required to take to give effect to it.][1]

Amendments—[1] Schedule 43B inserted by FA 2016 s 157(1), (3) with effect in relation to tax arrangements (within the meaning of FA 2013 Pt 5) entered into at any time (whether before, on or after 15 September 2016).

[Notices may be given on assumption that tax advantage does arise

9 (1) A designated HMRC officer may give a notice, or do anything else, under this Schedule where the officer considers that a tax advantage might have arisen to the person concerned.

(2) Accordingly, any notice given by a designated HMRC officer under this Schedule may be expressed to be given on the assumption that a tax advantage does arise (without conceding that it does).][1]

Amendments—[1] Schedule 43B inserted by FA 2016 s 157(1), (3) with effect in relation to tax arrangements (within the meaning of FA 2013 Pt 5) entered into at any time (whether before, on or after 15 September 2016).

[Power to amend

10 (1) The Treasury may by regulations amend this Schedule (apart from this paragraph).

(2) Regulations under sub-paragraph (1) may include—

(*a*) any amendment of this Part that is appropriate in consequence of an amendment by virtue of sub-paragraph (1);

(*b*) transitional provision.

(3) Regulations under sub-paragraph (1) are to be made by statutory instrument.

(4) A statutory instrument containing regulations under sub-paragraph (1) is subject to annulment in pursuance of a resolution of the House of Commons.][1]

Amendments—[1] Schedule 43B inserted by FA 2016 s 157(1), (3) with effect in relation to tax arrangements (within the meaning of FA 2013 Pt 5) entered into at any time (whether before, on or after 15 September 2016).

[SCHEDULE 43C

PENALTY UNDER SECTION 212A: SUPPLEMENTARY PROVISION]

Amendments—[1] Schedule 43C inserted by FA 2016 s 158(1), (3) with effect in relation to tax arrangements (within the meaning of of FA 2013 Pt 5) entered into on or after 15 September 2016.

[Value of the counteracted advantage: introduction

1 Paragraphs 2 to 4 set out how to calculate the "value of the counteracted advantage" for the purposes of section 212A.][1]

Amendments—[1] Schedule 43C inserted by FA 2016 s 158(1), (3) with effect in relation to tax arrangements (within the meaning of of FA 2013 Pt 5) entered into on or after 15 September 2016.

[Value of the counteracted advantage: basic rule

2 (1) The "value of the counteracted advantage" is the additional amount due or payable in respect of tax as a result of the counteraction mentioned in section 212A(1)(*c*).

(2) The reference in sub-paragraph (1) to the additional amount due and payable includes a reference to—

(*a*) an amount payable to HMRC having erroneously been paid by way of repayment of tax, and

(*b*) an amount which would be repayable by HMRC if the counteraction were not made.

(3) The following are ignored in calculating the value of the counteracted advantage—

(*a*) group relief, and

(*b*) any relief under section 458 of CTA 2010 (relief in respect of repayment etc of loan) which is deferred under subsection (5) of that section.

(4) For the purposes of this paragraph consequential adjustments under section 210 are regarded as part of the counteraction in question.

(5) If the counteraction affects the person's liability to two or more taxes, the taxes concerned are to be considered together for the purpose of determining the value of the counteracted advantage.

(6) This paragraph is subject to paragraphs 3 and 4.][1]

Amendments—[1] Schedule 43C inserted by FA 2016 s 158(1), (3) with effect in relation to tax arrangements (within the meaning of of FA 2013 Pt 5) entered into on or after 15 September 2016.

[Value of counteracted advantage: losses

3 (1) To the extent that the tax advantage mentioned in section 212A(1)(*b*) ("the tax advantage") resulted in the wrong recording of a loss for the purposes of direct tax and the loss has been wholly used to reduce the amount due or payable in respect of tax, the value of the counteracted advantage is determined in accordance with paragraph 2.

(2) To the extent that the tax advantage resulted in the wrong recording of a loss for purposes of direct tax and the loss has not been wholly used to reduce the amount due or payable in respect of tax, the value of the counteracted advantage is—

(*a*) the value under paragraph 2 of so much of the tax advantage as results (or would in the absence of the counteraction result) from the part (if any) of the loss which was used to reduce the amount due or payable in respect of tax, plus

(*b*) 10% of the part of the loss not so used.

(3) Sub-paragraphs (1) and (2) apply both—

(*a*) to a case where no loss would have been recorded but for the tax advantage, and

(*b*) to a case where a loss of a different amount would have been recorded (but in that case sub-paragraphs (1) and (2) apply only to the difference between the amount recorded and the true amount).

(4) To the extent that the tax advantage creates or increases (or would in the absence of the counteraction create or increase) an aggregate loss recorded for a group of companies—

(*a*) the value of the counteracted advantage is calculated in accordance with this paragraph, and

(*b*) in applying paragraph 2 in accordance with sub-paragraphs (1) and (2), group relief may be taken into account (despite paragraph 2(3)).

(5) To the extent that the tax advantage results (or would in the absence of the counteraction result) in a loss, the value of it is nil where, because of the nature of the loss or the person's circumstances, there was no reasonable prospect of the loss being used to support a claim to reduce a tax liability (of any person).][1]

Amendments—[1] Schedule 43C inserted by FA 2016 s 158(1), (3) with effect in relation to tax arrangements (within the meaning of of FA 2013 Pt 5) entered into on or after 15 September 2016.

[Value of counteracted advantage: deferred tax

4 (1) To the extent that the tax advantage mentioned in section 212A is a deferral of tax, the value of the counteracted advantage is—

(*a*) 25% of the amount of the deferred tax for each year of the deferral, or

(*b*) a percentage of the amount of the deferred tax, for each separate period of deferral of less than a year, equating to 25% per year,

or, if less, 100% of the amount of the deferred tax.

(2) This paragraph does not apply to a case to the extent that paragraph 3 applies.][1]

Amendments—[1] Schedule 43C inserted by FA 2016 s 158(1), (3) with effect in relation to tax arrangements (within the meaning of of FA 2013 Pt 5) entered into on or after 15 September 2016.

[Assessment of penalty

5 (1) Where a person is liable for a penalty under section 212A, HMRC must assess the penalty.

(2) Where HMRC assess the penalty, HMRC must—

(*a*) notify the person who is liable for the penalty, and

(*b*) state in the notice a tax period in respect of which the penalty is assessed.

(3) A penalty under this paragraph must be paid before the end of the period of 30 days beginning with the day on which notification of the penalty is issued.

(4) An assessment—

(*a*) is to be treated for procedural purposes as if it were an assessment to tax,

(*b*) may be enforced as if it were an assessment to tax, and

(*c*) may be combined with an assessment to tax.

(5) An assessment of a penalty under this paragraph must be made before the end of the period of 12 months beginning with—

(*a*) the end of the appeal period for the assessment which gave effect to the counteraction mentioned in section 212A(1)(*b*), or

(*b*) if there is no assessment within paragraph (*a*), the date (or the latest of the dates) on which that counteraction becomes final.

(6) The reference in sub-paragraph (5)(*b*) to the counteraction becoming final is to be interpreted in accordance with section 210(8).][1]

Amendments—[1] Schedule 43C inserted by FA 2016 s 158(1), (3) with effect in relation to tax arrangements (within the meaning of of FA 2013 Pt 5) entered into on or after 15 September 2016.

[Alteration of assessment of penalty

6 (1) After notification of an assessment has been given to a person under paragraph 5(2), the assessment may not be altered except in accordance with this paragraph or paragraph 7, or on appeal.

(2) A supplementary assessment may be made in respect of a penalty if an earlier assessment operated by reference to an underestimate of the value of the counteracted advantage.

(3) An assessment may be revised as necessary if it operated by reference to an overestimate of the value of the counteracted advantage.][1]

Amendments—[1] Schedule 43C inserted by FA 2016 s 158(1), (3) with effect in relation to tax arrangements (within the meaning of of FA 2013 Pt 5) entered into on or after 15 September 2016.

[Revision of assessment following consequential relieving adjustment

7 (1) Sub-paragraph (2) applies where a person—

(*a*) is notified under section 210(7) of a consequential adjustment relating to a counteraction under section 209, and

(*b*) an assessment to a penalty in respect of that counteraction of which the person has been notified under paragraph 5(2) does not take account of that consequential adjustment.

(2) HMRC must make any alterations of the assessment that appear to HMRC to be just and reasonable in connection with the consequential amendment.

(3) Alterations under this paragraph may be made despite any time limit imposed by or under an enactment.][1]

Amendments—[1] Schedule 43C inserted by FA 2016 s 158(1), (3) with effect in relation to tax arrangements (within the meaning of of FA 2013 Pt 5) entered into on or after 15 September 2016.

[Aggregate penalties

8 (1) Sub-paragraph (3) applies where—

(*a*) two or more penalties are incurred by the same person and fall to be determined by reference to an amount of tax to which that person is chargeable,

(*b*) one of those penalties is incurred under section 212A, and

(*c*) one or more of the other penalties are incurred under a relevant penalty provision.

(2) But sub-paragraph (3) does not apply if section 212(2) of FA 2014 (follower notices: aggregate penalties) applies in relation to the amount of tax in question.

(3) The aggregate of the amounts of the penalties mentioned in subsection (1)(*b*) and (*c*), so far as determined by reference to that amount of tax, must not exceed—

(*a*) the relevant percentage of that amount, or

(*b*) in a case where at least one of the penalties is under paragraph 5(2)(*b*) of, or sub-paragraph (3)(*b*), (4)(*b*) or (5)(*b*) of paragraph 6 of, Schedule 55 to FA 2009, £300 (if greater).

(4) In the application of section 97A of TMA 1970 (multiple penalties) no account shall be taken of a penalty under section 212A.

(5) "Relevant penalty provision" means—

(*a*) Schedule 24 to FA 2007 (penalties for errors),

(*b*) Schedule 41 to FA 2008 (penalties: failure to notify etc),

(*c*) Schedule 55 to FA 2009 (penalties for failure to make returns etc), or

(*d*) Part 5 of Schedule 18 to FA 2016 (penalty under serial tax avoidance regime).

(6) "The relevant percentage" means—

(*a*) 200% in a case where at least one of the penalties is determined by reference to the percentage in—

(i) paragraph 4(4)(*c*) of Schedule 24 to FA 2007,

(ii) paragraph 6(4)(*a*) of Schedule 41 to FA 2008, or
(iii) paragraph 6(3A)(*c*) of Schedule 55 to FA 2009,

(*b*) 150% in a case where paragraph (*a*) does not apply and at least one of the penalties is determined by reference to the percentage in—
(i) paragraph 4(3)(*c*) of Schedule 24 to FA 2007,
(ii) paragraph 6(3)(*a*) of Schedule 41 to FA 2008, or
(iii) paragraph 6(3A)(*b*) of Schedule 55 to FA 2009,

[(*ba*) 125% in a case where neither paragraph (*a*) nor paragraph (*b*) applies and at least one of the penalties is determined by reference to the percentage in—
(i) paragraph 4(2)(*c*) of Schedule 24 to FA 2007,
(ii) paragraph 6(2)(*a*) of Schedule 41 to FA 2008,
(iii) paragraph 6(3A)(*a*) of Schedule 55 to FA 2009,][2]

(*c*) 140% in a case where [none of paragraphs (*a*) to (*ba*) applies][2] and at least one of the penalties is determined by reference to the percentage in—
(i) paragraph 4(4)(*b*) of Schedule 24 to FA 2007,
(ii) paragraph 6(4)(*b*) of Schedule 41 to FA 2008, or
(iii) paragraph 6(4A)(*c*) of Schedule 55 to FA 2009,

(*d*) 105% in a case where at [none of paragraphs (*a*) to (*c*) applies][2] and at least one of the penalties is determined by reference to the percentage in—
(i) paragraph 4(3)(*b*) of Schedule 24 to FA 2007,
(ii) paragraph 6(3)(*b*) of Schedule 41 to FA 2008, or
(iii) paragraph 6(4A)(*b*) of Schedule 55 to FA 2009, and

(*e*) in any other case, 100%.][1]

Amendments—[1] Schedule 43C inserted by FA 2016 s 158(1), (3) with effect in relation to tax arrangements (within the meaning of of FA 2013 Pt 5) entered into on or after 15 September 2016.

[2] Sub-para (6)(*ba*) inserted, in sub-para (6), (*c*), words substituted for words "neither paragraph (*a*) nor paragraph (*b*) applies", and in sub-para (6)(*d*), words substituted for words "none of paragraphs (*a*), (*b*) and (*c*) applies" by FA 2015 Sch 20 para 20, as inserted by FA 2016 s 158(14), with effect in relation to tax arrangements (within the meaning of of FA 2013 Pt 5) entered into on or after 15 September 2016.

[Appeal against penalty

9 (1) A person may appeal against—

(*a*) the imposition of a penalty under section 212A, or

(*b*) the amount assessed under paragraph 5.

(2) An appeal under sub-paragraph (1)(*a*) may only be made on the grounds that the arrangements were not abusive or there was no tax advantage to be counteracted.

(3) An appeal under sub-paragraph (1)(*b*) may only be made on the grounds that the assessment was based on an overestimate of the value of the counteracted advantage (whether because the estimate was made by reference to adjustments which were not just and reasonable or for any other reason).

(4) An appeal under this paragraph must be made within the period of 30 days beginning with the day on which notification of the penalty is given under paragraph 5(2).

(5) An appeal under this paragraph is to be treated in the same way as an appeal against an assessment to the tax concerned (including by the application of any provision about bringing the appeal by notice to HMRC, about HMRC's review of the decision or about determination of the appeal by the First-tier Tribunal or Upper Tribunal).

(6) Sub-paragraph (5) does not apply—

(*a*) so as to require a person to pay a penalty before an appeal against the assessment of the penalty is determined, or

(*b*) in respect of any other matter expressly provided for by this Part.

(7) On an appeal against the penalty the tribunal may affirm or cancel HMRC's decision.

(8) On an appeal against the amount of the penalty the tribunal may—

(*a*) affirm HMRC's decision, or

(*b*) substitute for HMRC's decision another decision that HMRC has power to make.

(9) In this paragraph "tribunal" means the First-tier Tribunal or Upper Tribunal (as appropriate by virtue of sub-paragraph (5)).][1]

Amendments—[1] Schedule 43C inserted by FA 2016 s 158(1), (3) with effect in relation to tax arrangements (within the meaning of of FA 2013 Pt 5) entered into on or after 15 September 2016.

[Mitigation of penalties

10 (1) The Commissioners may in their discretion mitigate a penalty under section 212A, or stay or compound any proceedings for such a penalty.

(2) They may also, after judgment, further mitigate or entirely remit the penalty.][1]

Amendments—[1] Schedule 43C inserted by FA 2016 s 158(1), (3) with effect in relation to tax arrangements (within the meaning of of FA 2013 Pt 5) entered into on or after 15 September 2016.

[Interpretation

11 In this Schedule—

(*a*) a reference to an "assessment" to tax is to be interpreted, in relation to inheritance tax, as a reference to a determination;

(*b*) "direct tax" means—

(i) income tax,

(ii) capital gains tax,

(iii) corporation tax (including any amount chargeable as if it were corporation tax or treated as corporation tax),

(iv) petroleum revenue tax, and

(v) diverted profits tax;

(*c*) a reference to a loss includes a reference to a charge, expense, deficit and any other amount which may be available for, or relied on to claim, a deduction or relief;

(*d*) a reference to a repayment of tax includes a reference to allowing a credit against tax or to a payment of a corporation tax credit;

(*e*) "corporation tax credit" means—

(i) an R&D tax credit under Chapter 2 or 7 of Part 13 of CTA 2009,

(ii) an R&D expenditure credit under Chapter 6A of Part 3 of CTA 2009,

(iii) a land remediation tax credit or life assurance company tax credit under Chapter 3 or 4 respectively of Part 14 of CTA 2009,

(iv) a film tax credit under Chapter 3 of Part 15 of CTA 2009,

(v) a television tax credit under Chapter 3 of Part 15A of CTA 2009,

(vi) a video game tax credit under Chapter 3 of Part 15B of CTA 2009,

(vii) a theatre tax credit under section 1217K of CTA 2009,

(viii) an orchestra tax credit under Chapter 3 of Part 15D of CTA 2009, or

(ix) a first-year tax credit under Schedule A1 to CAA 2001;

(*f*) "tax period" means a tax year, accounting period or other period in respect of which tax is charged;

(*g*) a reference to giving a document to HMRC includes a reference to communicating information to HMRC in any form and by any method (whether by post, fax, email, telephone or otherwise),

(*h*) a reference to giving a document to HMRC includes a reference to making a statement or declaration in a document.][1]

Amendments—[1] Schedule 43C inserted by FA 2016 s 158(1), (3) with effect in relation to tax arrangements (within the meaning of of FA 2013 Pt 5) entered into on or after 15 September 2016.

SCHEDULE 44

TRUSTS WITH VULNERABLE BENEFICIARY

Section 216

Commentary—*Simon's Taxes* **C4.259**.

Inheritance Tax Act 1984

1 IHTA 1984 is amended as follows.

2 (1) Section 71A (trusts for bereaved minors) is amended as follows.

(2) (*substitutes* IHTA 1984 s 71A(3)(*c*)(ii))

(3), (4) (*insert* IHTA 1984 s 71A(4)(*za*), (4A)–(4E))

3 (1) Section 71B (charge to tax on property to which section 71A applies) is amended as follows.

(2) (*amends* IHTA 1984 s 71B(1))

(3) (*inserts* IHTA 1984 s 71B(2A), (2B))

4 (1) Section 71D (age 18-to-25 trusts) is amended as follows.

(2) (*substitutes* IHTA 1984 s 71D(6)(*c*)(ii))

(3)–(5) (*insert* IHTA 1984 s 71D(6A), (7)(*za*), (7A)–(7E))

5 (1) Section 71E (charge to tax on property to which section 71D applies) is amended as follows.

(2) (*amends* IHTA 1984 s 71E(1))

(3) (*inserts* IHTA 1984 s 71E(4A))

6 (1) Section 89 (trusts for disabled persons) is amended as follows.

(2), (3), (5) (*substitute* IHTA 1984 s 89(1)(*b*), (3), (5), (6))

(4) (*amends* IHTA 1984 s 89(4))

7 (1) Section 89A (self-settlement by person with condition expected to lead to disability) is amended as follows.
(2), (3), (7) (*amend* IHTA 1984 s 89A(1)(*b*), (2) and section heading)
(4), (6) (*substitute* IHTA 1984 s 89A(5), (6), (8))
(5) (*inserts* IHTA 1984 s 89A(6A)–(6F))

8 (1) Section 89B (meaning of "disabled person's interest") is amended as follows.
(2) (*substitutes* IHTA 1984 s 89B(2))
(3) (*inserts* IHTA 1984 s 89B(2A))

9 (1) The amendments made by paragraphs 2 to 8 have effect in relation to property transferred into settlement on or after 8 April 2013.
(2) Nothing in paragraphs 6 to 8 is to be read as preventing property transferred into a relevant settlement on or after 8 April 2013 from being property to which section 89 or 89A of IHTA 1984 applies.

10 (1) In section 89B (meaning of "disabled person's interest"), in subsection (1)(*c*) after "2006" insert "if the trusts on which the settled property is held secure that, if any of the settled property is applied during the disabled person's life for the benefit of a beneficiary, it is applied for the benefit of the disabled person".
(2) (*inserts* IHTA 1984 s 89C)
(3) The amendments made by this paragraph have effect in relation to property transferred into settlement on or after the day on which this Act is passed.
(4) Nothing in this paragraph is to be read as preventing property transferred into a settlement to which sub-paragraph (5) applies from being settled property for the purposes of section 89B(1)(*c*) or (*d*) of IHTA 1984.
(5) This sub-paragraph applies to a settlement—
- (*a*) created before the day on which this Act is passed the trusts of which have not been altered on or after that day, or
- (*b*) arising on or after the day on which this Act is passed under the will of a testator, if—
  - (i) the will was executed before the day on which this Act is passed and its provisions, so far as relating to the settlement, have not been altered on or after that day, or
  - (ii) the will was executed or confirmed on or after the day on which this Act is passed and its provisions, so far as relating to the settlement, are in the same terms as those contained in a will executed by the same testator before that day.

Taxation of Chargeable Gains Act 1992

11 TCGA 1992 is amended as follows.

12 (1) Section 169D (exceptions to rules on gifts to settlor-interested settlements etc) is amended as follows.
(2), (4) (*substitute* TCGA 1992 s 167D(3), (7)–(9))
(3) (*inserts* TCGA 1992 s 167D(4A)–(4F))
(5) (*repeals* TCGA 1992 s 167D(10))
(6) The amendments made by this paragraph have effect in relation to disposals to the trustees of a settlement on or after 8 April 2013.
(7) But if the settlement is a relevant settlement, nothing in this paragraph is to be read as preventing section 169D(2) of TCGA 1992 from applying in relation to the disposal.

13 (1) Paragraph 1 of Schedule 1 (application of exempt amount and reporting limits in cases involving settled property) is amended as follows.
(2), (4), (5) (*amend* TCGA 1992 Sch 1 para 1(1), (2), (6))
(3) (*inserts* TCGA 1992 Sch 1 para 1(1A)–(1E))
(6) The amendments made by this paragraph have effect in relation to the tax year 2013–14 and subsequent tax years.
(7) But if the settlement is a relevant settlement, nothing in this paragraph is to be read as preventing sections 3(1) to (5C) and 3A of TCGA 1992 from applying in relation to the settlement as provided by paragraph 1(1) of Schedule 1 to that Act.

Finance Act 2005

14 FA 2005 is amended as follows.

15 (1) Section 34 (disabled persons) is amended as follows.
(2), (3) (*substitute* FA 2005 s 34(2)(*b*), (3))

16 (1) Section 35 (relevant minors) is amended as follows.
(2), (3) (*substitute* FA 2005 s 35(3)(*c*)(ii), (4))

17 (*substitutes* FA 2005 s 38)

18 The amendments made by paragraphs 15 to 17 have effect for the tax year 2013–14 and subsequent tax years.

19 (*inserts* FA 2005 Sch 1A)

Interpretation: relevant settlement

20 (1) In this Schedule, "relevant settlement" means—
(*a*) a settlement created before 8 April 2013 the trusts of which have not been altered on or after that date, or
(*b*) a settlement arising on or after 8 April 2013 under the will of a testator, if—
(i) the will was executed before 8 April 2013 and its provisions, so far as relating to the settlement, have not been altered on or after that date, or
(ii) the will was executed or confirmed on or after 8 April 2013 and its provisions, so far as relating to the settlement, are in the same terms as those contained in a will executed by the same testator before that date.
(2) In this Schedule a reference to a will includes a reference to a codicil.

SCHEDULE 45
STATUTORY RESIDENCE TEST
Section 218

PART 1
THE RULES

Press releases etc—HMRC Notice: Statutory Residence Test and Overseas Workday Relief—revised guidance (see *SWTI 2013, Issue 19*).

Commentary—*Simon's Taxes* **E6.103**.

Introduction

1 (1) This Part of this Schedule sets out the rules for determining for the purposes of relevant tax whether individuals are resident or not resident in the UK.
(2) The rules are referred to collectively as "the statutory residence test".
(3) The rules do not apply in determining for the purposes of relevant tax whether individuals are resident or not resident in England, Wales, Scotland or Northern Ireland specifically (rather than in the UK as a whole).
(4) "Relevant tax" means—
(*a*) income tax,
(*b*) capital gains tax, and
(*c*) (so far as the residence status of individuals is relevant to them) inheritance tax and corporation tax.
(5) Key concepts used in the rules are defined in Part 2 of this Schedule.

Interpretation of enactments

2 (1) In enactments relating to relevant tax, a reference to being resident (or not resident) in the UK is, in the case of individuals, a reference to being resident (or not resident) in the UK in accordance with the statutory residence test.
(2) Sub-paragraph (1) applies even if the reference relates to the tax liability of an actual or deemed person that is not an individual (for example, where the liability of another person depends on the residence status of an individual).
(3) An individual who, in accordance with the statutory residence test, is resident (or not resident) in the UK "for" a tax year is taken for the purposes of any enactment relating to relevant tax to be resident (or not resident) there at all times in that tax year.
(4) But see Part 3 of this Schedule (split year treatment) for cases where the effect of sub-paragraph (3) is relaxed in certain circumstances.
(5) This Schedule has effect subject to any express provision to the contrary in (or falling to be recognised and acknowledged in law by virtue of) any enactment.

The basic rule

3 An individual ("P") is resident in the UK for a tax year ("year X") if—
(*a*) the automatic residence test is met for that year, or

(*b*) the sufficient ties test is met for that year.

4 If neither of those tests is met for that year, P is not resident in the UK for that year.

The automatic residence test

5 The automatic residence test is met for year X if P meets—

(*a*) at least one of the automatic UK tests, and

(*b*) none of the automatic overseas tests.

The automatic UK tests

6 There are 4 automatic UK tests.

7 The first automatic UK test is that P spends at least 183 days in the UK in year X.

8 (1) The second automatic UK test is that—

(*a*) P has a home in the UK during all or part of year X,

(*b*) that home is one where P spends a sufficient amount of time in year X, and

(*c*) there is at least one period of 91 (consecutive) days in respect of which the following conditions are met—

(i) the 91-day period in question occurs while P has that home,

(ii) at least 30 days of that 91-day period fall within year X, and

(iii) throughout that 91-day period, condition A or condition B is met or a combination of those conditions is met.

(2) Condition A is that P has no home overseas.

(3) Condition B is that—

(*a*) P has one or more homes overseas, but

(*b*) each of those homes is a home where P spends no more than a permitted amount of time in year X.

(4) In relation to a home of P's in the UK, P "spends a sufficient amount of time" there in year X if there are at least 30 days in year X when P is present there on that day for at least some of the time (no matter how short a time).

(5) In relation to a home of P's overseas, P "spends no more than a permitted amount of time" there in year X if there are fewer than 30 days in year X when P is present there on that day for at least some of the time (no matter how short a time).

(6) In sub-paragraphs (4) and (5)—

(*a*) a reference to 30 days is to 30 days in aggregate, whether the days are consecutive or intermittent, and

(*b*) a reference to P being present at the home is to P being present there at a time when it is a home of P's (so presence there on any other occasion, for example to look round the property with a view to buying it, is to be disregarded).

(7) Sub-paragraph (1)(*c*) is satisfied so long as there is a period of 91 days in respect of which the conditions described there are met, even if those conditions are in fact met for longer than that.

(8) If P has more than one home in the UK—

(*a*) each of those homes must be looked at separately to see if the second automatic UK test is met, and

(*b*) the second automatic UK test is then met so long as it is met in relation to at least one of those homes.

9 (1) The third automatic UK test is that—

(*a*) P works sufficient hours in the UK, as assessed over a period of 365 days,

(*b*) during that period, there are no significant breaks from UK work,

(*c*) all or part of that period falls within year X,

(*d*) more than 75% of the total number of days in the 365-day period on which P does more than 3 hours' work are days on which P does more than 3 hours' work in the UK, and

(*e*) at least one day which falls in both that period and year X is a day on which P does more than 3 hours' work in the UK.

(2) Take the following steps to work out, for any given period of 365 days, whether P works "sufficient hours in the UK" as assessed over that period—

Step 1

Identify any days in the period on which P does more than 3 hours' work overseas, including ones on which P also does work in the UK on the same day.

The days so identified are referred to as "disregarded days".

Step 2
Add up (for all employments held and trades carried on by P) the total number of hours that P works in the UK during the period, but ignoring any hours that P works in the UK on disregarded days. The result is referred to as P's "net UK hours".
Step 3
Subtract from 365—
(*a*) the total number of disregarded days, and
(*b*) any days that are allowed to be subtracted, in accordance with the rules in paragraph 28 of this Schedule, to take account of periods of leave and gaps between employments.
The result is referred to as the "reference period".
Step 4
Divide the reference period by 7. If the answer is more than 1 and is not a whole number, round down to the nearest whole number. If the answer is less than 1, round up to 1.
Step 5
Divide P's net UK hours by the number resulting from step 4.
If the answer is 35 or more, P is considered to work "sufficient hours in the UK" as assessed over the 365-day period in question.
(3) This paragraph does not apply to P if—
(*a*) P has a relevant job on board a vehicle, aircraft or ship at any time in year X, and
(*b*) at least 6 of the trips that P makes in year X as part of that job are cross-border trips that either begin in the UK, end in the UK or begin and end in the UK.

10 (1) The fourth automatic UK test is that—
(*a*) P dies in year X,
(*b*) for each of the previous 3 tax years, P was resident in the UK by virtue of meeting the automatic residence test,
(*c*) even assuming P were not resident in the UK for year X, the tax year preceding year X would not be a split year as respects P (see Part 3 of this Schedule),
(*d*) when P died, either—
(i) P's home was in the UK, or
(ii) P had more than one home and at least one of them was in the UK, and
(*e*) if P had a home overseas during all or part of year X, P did not spend a sufficient amount of time there in year X.
(2) In relation to a home of P's overseas, P "spent a sufficient amount of time" there in year X if—
(*a*) there were at least 30 days in year X when P was present there on that day for at least some of the time (no matter how short a time), or
(*b*) P was present there for at least some of the time (no matter how short a time) on each day of year X up to and including the day on which P died.
(3) In sub-paragraph (2)—
(*a*) the reference to 30 days is to 30 days in aggregate, whether the days were consecutive or intermittent, and
(*b*) the reference to P being present at the home is to P being present there at a time when it was a home of P's.
(4) If P had more than one home overseas—
(*a*) each of those homes must be looked at separately to see if the requirement of sub-paragraph (1)(*e*) is met, and
(*b*) that requirement is then met so long as it is met in relation to each of them.

Modifications—FA 2013 Sch 45 para 154 (modification of the application of para 10(b) in relation to a pre-commencement tax year).

The automatic overseas tests

11 There are 5 automatic overseas tests.

12 The first automatic overseas test is that—
(*a*) P was resident in the UK for one or more of the 3 tax years preceding year X,
(*b*) the number of days in year X that P spends in the UK is less than 16, and
(*c*) P does not die in year X.

13 The second automatic overseas test is that—
(*a*) P was resident in the UK for none of the 3 tax years preceding year X, and
(*b*) the number of days that P spends in the UK in year X is less than 46.

14 (1) The third automatic overseas test is that—
(*a*) P works sufficient hours overseas, as assessed over year X,

(*b*) during year X, there are no significant breaks from overseas work,

(*c*) the number of days in year X on which P does more than 3 hours' work in the UK is less than 31, and

(*d*) the number of days in year X falling within sub-paragraph (2) is less than 91.

(2) A day falls within this sub-paragraph if—

(*a*) it is a day spent by P in the UK, but

(*b*) it is not a day that is treated under paragraph 23(4) as a day spent by P in the UK.

(3) Take the following steps to work out whether P works "sufficient hours overseas" as assessed over year X—

Step 1

Identify any days in year X on which P does more than 3 hours' work in the UK, including ones on which P also does work overseas on the same day.

The days so identified are referred to as "disregarded days".

Step 2

Add up (for all employments held and trades carried on by P) the total number of hours that P works overseas in year X, but ignoring any hours that P works overseas on disregarded days.

The result is referred to as P's "net overseas hours".

Step 3

Subtract from 365 (or 366 if year X includes 29 February)—

(*a*) the total number of disregarded days, and

(*b*) any days that are allowed to be subtracted, in accordance with the rules in paragraph 28 of this Schedule, to take account of periods of leave and gaps between employments.

The result is referred to as the "reference period".

Step 4

Divide the reference period by 7. If the answer is more than 1 and is not a whole number, round down to the nearest whole number. If the answer is less than 1, round up to 1.

Step 5

Divide P's net overseas hours by the number resulting from step 4.

If the answer is 35 or more, P is considered to work "sufficient hours overseas" as assessed over year X.

(4) This paragraph does not apply to P if—

(*a*) P has a relevant job on board a vehicle, aircraft or ship at any time in year X, and

(*b*) at least 6 of the trips that P makes in year X as part of that job are cross-border trips that either begin in the UK, end in the UK or begin and end in the UK.

15 (1) The fourth automatic overseas test is that—

(*a*) P dies in year X,

(*b*) P was resident in the UK for neither of the 2 tax years preceding year X or, alternatively, P's case falls within sub-paragraph (2), and

(*c*) the number of days that P spends in the UK in year X is less than 46.

(2) P's case falls within this sub-paragraph if—

(*a*) P was not resident in the UK for the tax year preceding year X, and

(*b*) the tax year before that was a split year as respects P because the circumstances of the case fell within Case 1, Case 2 or Case 3 (see Part 3 of this Schedule).

16 (1) The fifth automatic overseas test is that—

(*a*) P dies in year X,

(*b*) P was resident in the UK for neither of the 2 tax years preceding year X because P met the third automatic overseas test for each of those years or, alternatively, P's case falls within sub-paragraph (2), and

(*c*) P would meet the third automatic overseas test for year X if paragraph 14 were read with the relevant modifications.

(2) P's case falls within this sub-paragraph if—

(*a*) P was not resident in the UK for the tax year preceding year X because P met the third automatic overseas test for that year, and

(*b*) the tax year before that was a split year as respects P because the circumstances of the case fell within Case 1 (see Part 3 of this Schedule).

(3) The relevant modifications of paragraph 14 are—

(*a*) in sub-paragraph (1)(*a*) and (*b*) and sub-paragraph (3), for "year X" read "the period from the start of year X up to and including the day before the day of P's death", and

(*b*) in step 3 of sub-paragraph (3), for "365 (or 366 if year X includes 29 February)" read "the number of days in the period from the start of year X up to and including the day before the day of P's death".

Modifications—FA 2013 Sch 45 para 154 (modification of the application of this para in relation to a pre-commencement tax year).

The sufficient ties test

17 (1) The sufficient ties test is met for year X if—

(*a*) P meets none of the automatic UK tests and none of the automatic overseas tests, but

(*b*) P has sufficient UK ties for that year.

(2) "UK ties" is defined in Part 2 of this Schedule.

(3) Whether P has "sufficient" UK ties for year X will depend on—

(*a*) whether P was resident in the UK for any of the previous 3 tax years, and

(*b*) the number of days that P spends in the UK in year X.

(4) The Tables in paragraphs 18 and 19 show how many ties are sufficient in each case.

Sufficient UK ties

18 The Table below shows how many UK ties are sufficient in a case where P was resident in the UK for one or more of the 3 tax years preceding year X—

Days spent by P in the UK in year X	*Number of ties that are sufficient*
More than 15 but not more than 45	At least 4
More than 45 but not more than 90	At least 3
More than 90 but not more than 120	At least 2
More than 120	At least 1

19 The Table below shows how many UK ties are sufficient in a case where P was resident in the UK for none of the 3 tax years preceding year X—

Days spent by P in the UK in year X	*Number of ties that are sufficient*
More than 45 but not more than 90	All 4
More than 90 but not more than 120	At least 3
More than 120	At least 2

20 (1) If P dies in year X, paragraph 18 has effect as if the words "More than 15 but" were omitted from the first column of the Table.

(2) In addition to that modification, if the death occurs before 1 March in year X, paragraphs 18 and 19 have effect as if each number of days mentioned in the first column of the Table were reduced by the appropriate number.

(3) The appropriate number is found by multiplying the number of days, in each case, by—

$A / 12$

where "A" is the number of whole months in year X after the month in which P dies.

(4) If, for any number of days, the appropriate number is not a whole number, the appropriate number is to be rounded up or down as follows—

(*a*) if the first figure after the decimal point is 5 or more, round the appropriate number up to the nearest whole number,

(*b*) otherwise, round it down to the nearest whole number.

PART 2

KEY CONCEPTS

Introduction

21 This Part of this Schedule defines some key concepts for the purposes of this Schedule.

Days spent

22 (1) If P is present in the UK at the end of a day, that day counts as a day spent by P in the UK.

(2) But it does not do so in the following two cases.

(3) The first case is where—

(*a*) P only arrives in the UK as a passenger on that day,

(*b*) P leaves the UK the next day, and

(*c*) between arrival and departure, P does not engage in activities that are to a substantial extent unrelated to P's passage through the UK.

(4) The second case is where—

(*a*) P would not be present in the UK at the end of that day but for exceptional circumstances beyond P's control that prevent P from leaving the UK, and

(*b*) P intends to leave the UK as soon as those circumstances permit.

(5) Examples of circumstances that may be "exceptional" are—

(*a*) national or local emergencies such as war, civil unrest or natural disasters, and

(*b*) a sudden or life-threatening illness or injury.

(6) For a tax year—

(*a*) the maximum number of days to which sub-paragraph (2) may apply in reliance on sub-paragraph (4) is limited to 60, and

(*b*) accordingly, once the number of days within sub-paragraph (4) reaches 60 (counting forward from the start of the tax year), any subsequent days within that sub-paragraph, whether involving the same or different exceptional circumstances, will count as days spent by P in the UK.

23 (1) If P is not present in the UK at the end of a day, that day does not count as a day spent by P in the UK.

(2) This is subject to the deeming rule.

(3) The deeming rule applies if—

(*a*) P has at least 3 UK ties for a tax year,

(*b*) the number of days in that tax year when P is present in the UK at some point in the day but not at the end of the day ("qualifying days") is more than 30, and

(*c*) P was resident in the UK for at least one of the 3 tax years preceding that tax year.

(4) The deeming rule is that, once the number of qualifying days in the tax year reaches 30 (counting forward from the start of the tax year), each subsequent qualifying day in the tax year is to be treated as a day spent by P in the UK.

(5) The deeming rule does not apply for the purposes of sub-paragraph (3)(*a*) (so, in deciding for those purposes whether P has a 90-day tie, qualifying days in excess of 30 are not to be treated as days spent by P in the UK).

Days spent "in" a period

24 Any reference to a number of days spent in the UK "in" a given period is a reference to the total number of days spent there (in aggregate) in that period, whether continuously or intermittently.

Home

25 (1) A person's home could be a building or part of a building or, for example, a vehicle, vessel or structure of any kind.

(2) Whether, for a given building, vehicle, vessel, structure or the like, there is a sufficient degree of permanence or stability about P's arrangements there for the place to count as P's home (or one of P's homes) will depend on all the circumstances of the case.

(3) But somewhere that P uses periodically as nothing more than a holiday home or temporary retreat (or something similar) does not count as a home of P's.

(4) A place may count as a home of P's whether or not P holds any estate or interest in it (and references to "having" a home are to be read accordingly).

(5) Somewhere that was P's home does not continue to count as such merely because P continues to hold an estate or interest in it after P has moved out (for example, if P is in the process of selling it or has let or sub-let it, having set up home elsewhere).

Work

26 (1) P is considered to be "working" (or doing "work") at any time when P is doing something—

(*a*) in the performance of duties of an employment held by P, or

(*b*) in the course of a trade carried on by P (alone or in partnership).

(2) In deciding whether something is being done in the performance of duties of an employment, regard must be had to whether, if value were received by P for doing the thing, it would fall within the definition of employment income in section 7 of ITEPA 2003.

(3) In deciding whether something is being done in the course of a trade, regard must be had to whether, if expenses were incurred by P in doing the thing, the expenses could be deducted in calculating the profits of the trade for income tax purposes.

(4) Time spent travelling counts as time spent working—

(*a*) if the cost of the journey could, if it were incurred by P, be deducted in calculating P's earnings from that employment under section 337, 338, 340 or 342 of ITEPA 2003 or, as the case may be, in calculating the profits of the trade under ITTOIA 2005, or

(*b*) to the extent that P does something else during the journey that would itself count as work in accordance with this paragraph.

(5) Time spent undertaking training counts as time spent working if—

(*a*) in the case of an employment held by P, the training is provided or paid for by the employer and is undertaken to help P in performing duties of the employment, and

(*b*) in the case of a trade carried on by P, the cost of the training could be deducted in calculating the profits of the trade for income tax purposes.

(6) Sub-paragraphs (4) and (5) have effect without prejudice to the generality of sub-paragraphs (2) and (3).

(7) Assume for the purposes of sub-paragraphs (2) to (5) that P is someone who is chargeable to income tax under ITEPA 2003 or ITTOIA 2005.

(8) A voluntary post for which P has no contract of service does not count as an employment for the purposes of this Schedule.

Location of work

27 (1) Work is done where it is actually done, regardless of where the employment is held or the trade is carried on by P.

(2) But work done by way of or in the course of travelling to or from the UK by air or sea or via a tunnel under the sea is assumed to be done overseas even during the part of the journey in or over the UK.

(3) For these purposes, travelling to or from the UK is taken to—

(*a*) begin when P boards the aircraft, ship or train that is bound for a destination in the UK or (as the case may be) overseas, and

(*b*) end when P disembarks from that aircraft, ship or train.

(4) This paragraph is subject to express provisions in this Schedule about the location of work done by people with relevant jobs on board vehicles, aircraft or ships.

Rules for calculating the reference period

28 (1) This paragraph applies in calculating the "reference period" (which is a step taken in determining whether P works "sufficient hours in the UK" or "sufficient hours overseas" as assessed over a given period of days).

(2) The number of days in the given period may be reduced to take account of—

(*a*) reasonable amounts of annual leave or parenting leave taken by P during the period (for all employments held and trades carried on by P during the period, whether in the UK or overseas),

(*b*) absences from work at times during the period when P is on sick leave and cannot reasonably be expected to work as a result of the illness or injury in question, and

(*c*) non-working days embedded within a block of leave for which a reduction is made under paragraph (*a*) or (*b*).

(3) But no reduction may be made in respect of any day that is a "disregarded day" (see paragraphs 9(2) and 14(3) in Part 1 of this Schedule).

(4) For any particular employment or trade, "reasonable" amounts of annual leave or parenting leave are to be assessed having regard to (among other things)—

(*a*) the nature of the work, and

(*b*) the country or countries where P is working.

(5) Non-working days are "embedded within" a block of leave only if there are, as part of that block of leave—

(*a*) at least 3 consecutive days of leave taken before the non-working day or series of non-working days in question, and

(*b*) at least 3 consecutive days of leave taken after the non-working day or series of non-working days in question.

(6) A "non-working day" is any day of the week, month or year on which P—

(*a*) is not normally expected to work (according to P's contract of employment or usual pattern of work), and

(*b*) does not in fact work.

(7) In calculating the reductions to be made under sub-paragraph (2)—

(*a*) if it turns out, after applying sub-paragraph (3), that the reasonable amounts of annual leave or parenting leave or, as the case may be, the absences from work on sick leave do not add up (across the period) to a whole number of days, the number in that case is to be rounded down to the nearest whole number, but

(*b*) any such rounding is to be ignored for the purposes of subparagraph (2)(*c*).

(8) If—

(*a*) P changes employment during the given period,

(*b*) there is a gap between the two employments, and

(*c*) P does not work at all at any time between the two employments, the number of days in the given period may be reduced by the number of days in that gap.

(9) But—

(*a*) if the gap lasts for more than 15 days, only 15 days may be subtracted, and

(*b*) if there is more than one change of employment during the period, the maximum number of days that may be subtracted under subparagraph (8) for all the gaps in total is 30.

Significant breaks from UK or overseas work

29 (1) There is a "significant break from UK work" if at least 31 days go by and not one of those days is—

(*a*) a day on which P does more than 3 hours' work in the UK, or

(*b*) a day on which P would have done more than 3 hours' work in the UK but for being on annual leave, sick leave or parenting leave.

(2) There is a "significant break from overseas work" if at least 31 days go by and not one of those days is—

(*a*) a day on which P does more than 3 hours' work overseas, or

(*b*) a day on which P would have done more than 3 hours' work overseas but for being on annual leave, sick leave or parenting leave.

Relevant jobs on board vehicles, aircraft or ships

30 (1) P has a "relevant" job on board a vehicle, aircraft or ship if condition A and condition B are met.

(2) Condition A is that P either—

(*a*) holds an employment, the duties of which consist of duties to be performed on board a vehicle, aircraft or ship while it is travelling, or

(*b*) carries on a trade, the activities of which consist of work to be done or services to be provided on board a vehicle, aircraft or ship while it is travelling.

(3) Condition B is that substantially all of the trips made in performing those duties or carrying on those activities are ones that involve crossing an international boundary at sea, in the air or on land (referred to as "cross-border trips").

(4) Sub-paragraph (2)(*b*) is not satisfied unless, in order to do the work or provide the services, P has to be present (in person) on board the vehicle, aircraft or ship while it is travelling.

(5) Duties or activities of a purely incidental nature are to be ignored in deciding whether the duties of an employment or the activities of a trade consist of duties or activities of a kind described in sub-paragraph (2)(*a*) or (*b*).

UK ties

31 (1) What counts as a "UK tie" depends on whether P was resident in the UK for one or more of the 3 tax years preceding year X.

(2) If P was resident in the UK for one or more of those 3 tax years, each of the following types of tie counts as a UK tie—

(*a*) a family tie,

(*b*) an accommodation tie,

(*c*) a work tie,

(*d*) a 90-day tie, and

(*e*) a country tie.

(3) Otherwise, each of the following types of tie counts as a UK tie—

(*a*) a family tie,

(*b*) an accommodation tie,

(*c*) a work tie, and

(*d*) a 90-day tie.

(4) In order to have the requisite number of UK ties for year X, each tie of P's must be of a different type.

Family tie

32 (1) P has a family tie for year X if—

(*a*) in year X, a relevant relationship exists at any time between P and another person, and

(*b*) that other person is someone who is resident in the UK for year X.

(2) A relevant relationship exists at any time between P and another person if at the time—

(*a*) P and the other person are husband and wife or civil partners and, in either case, are not separated, (*b*) P and the other person are living together as husband and wife or, if they are of the same sex, as if they were civil partners, or

(*c*) the other person is a child of P's and is under the age of 18.

(3) P does not have a family tie for year X by virtue of sub-paragraph (2)(*c*) if P sees the child in the UK on fewer than 61 days (in total) in—

(*a*) year X, or

(*b*) if the child turns 18 during year X, the part of year X before the day on which the child turns 18.

(4) A day counts as a day on which P sees the child if P sees the child in person for all or part of the day.

(5) "Separated" means separated—

(*a*) under an order of a court of competent jurisdiction,

(*b*) by deed of separation, or

(*c*) in circumstances where the separation is likely to be permanent.

33 (1) This paragraph applies in deciding for the purposes (only) of paragraph 32(1)(*b*) whether a person with whom P has a relevant relationship (a "family member") is someone who is resident in the UK for year X.

(2) A family tie based on the fact that a family member has, by the same token, a relevant relationship with P is to be disregarded in deciding whether that family member is someone who is resident in the UK for year X.

(3) A family member falling within sub-paragraph (4) is to be treated as being not resident in the UK for year X if the number of days that he or she spends in the UK in the part of year X outside term-time is less than 21.

(4) A family member falls within this sub-paragraph if he or she—

(*a*) is a child of P's who is under the age of 18,

(*b*) is in full-time education in the UK at any time in year X, and

(*c*) is resident in the UK for year X but would not be so resident if the time spent in full-time education in the UK in that year were disregarded.

(5) In sub-paragraph (4)—

(*a*) references to full-time education in the UK are to full-time education at a university, college, school or other educational establishment in the UK, and

(*b*) the reference to the time spent in full-time education in the UK is to the time spent there during term-time.

(6) For the purposes of this paragraph, half-term breaks and other breaks when teaching is not provided during a term are considered to form part of "term-time".

Accommodation tie

34 (1) P has an accommodation tie for year X if—

(*a*) P has a place to live in the UK,

(*b*) that place is available to P during year X for a continuous period of at least 91 days, and

(*c*) P spends at least one night at that place in that year.

(2) If there is a gap of fewer than 16 days between periods in year X when a particular place is available to P, that place is to be treated as continuing to be available to P during the gap.

(3) P is considered to have a "place to live" in the UK if—

(*a*) P's home or at least one of P's homes (if P has more than one) is in the UK, or

(*b*) P has a holiday home or temporary retreat (or something similar) in the UK, or

(*c*) accommodation is otherwise available to P where P can live when P is in the UK.

(4) Accommodation may be "available" to P even if P holds no estate or interest in it and even if P has no legal right to occupy it.

(5) If the accommodation is the home of a close relative of P's, sub-paragraph (1)(*c*) has effect as if for "at least one night" there were substituted "a total of at least 16 nights".

(6) A "close relative" is—

(*a*) a parent or grandparent,

(*b*) a brother or sister,

(*c*) a child aged 18 or over, or

(*d*) a grandchild aged 18 or over,

in each case, including by half-blood or by marriage or civil partnership.

Work tie

35 (1) P has a work tie for year X if P works in the UK for at least 40 days (whether continuously or intermittently) in year X.

(2) For these purposes, P works in the UK for a day if P does more than 3 hours' work in the UK on that day.

36 (1) This paragraph applies for the purposes of paragraph 35.

(2) It applies in cases where P has a relevant job on board a vehicle, aircraft or ship.

(3) When making a cross-border trip as part of that job—

(*a*) if the trip begins in the UK, P is assumed to do more than 3 hours' work in the UK on the day on which it begins,

(*b*) if the trip ends in the UK, P is assumed to do fewer than 3 hours' work in the UK on the day on which it ends.

(4) Those assumptions apply regardless of how late in the day the trip begins or ends (even if it begins or ends just before midnight).

(5) For the purposes of sub-paragraph (3)(*a*), it does not matter whether the trip ends on that same day.

(6) A day that falls within both paragraph (*a*) and paragraph (*b*) of subparagraph (3) is to be treated as if it fell only within paragraph (*a*).

(7) In the case of a cross-border trip to or from the UK that is undertaken in stages—

(*a*) the day on which the trip begins or, as the case may be, ends is the day on which the stage of the trip that involves crossing the UK border begins or ends, and

(*b*) accordingly, any day on which a stage is undertaken by P solely within the UK must (if it lasts for more than 3 hours) be counted separately as a day on which P does more than 3 hours' work in the UK.

90-day tie

37 P has a 90-day tie for year X if P has spent more than 90 days in the UK in—

(*a*) the tax year preceding year X,

(*b*) the tax year preceding that tax year, or

(*c*) each of those tax years separately.

Country tie

38 (1) P has a country tie for year X if the country in which P meets the midnight test for the greatest number of days in year X is the UK.

(2) If—

(*a*) P meets the midnight test for the same number of days in year X in two or more countries, and

(*b*) that number is the greatest number of days for which P meets the midnight test in any country in year X, P has a country tie for year X if one of those countries is the UK.

(3) P meets the "midnight test" in a country for a day if P is present in that country at the end of that day.

PART 3
SPLIT YEAR TREATMENT

Commentary—*Simon's Taxes* **E6.123**.

Introduction

39 This Part of this Schedule—

(*a*) explains when, as respects an individual, a tax year is a split year,

(*b*) defines the overseas part and the UK part of a split year, and

(*c*) amends certain enactments to provide for special charging rules in cases involving split years.

40 (1) The effect of a tax year being a split year is to relax the effect of paragraph 2(3) (which treats individuals who are UK resident "for" a tax year as being UK resident at all times in that year).

(2) When and how the effect of paragraph 2(3) is relaxed is defined in the special charging rules introduced by the amendments made by this Part.

(3) Subject to those special charging rules (and any other special charging rules for split years that may be introduced in the future), nothing in this Part alters an individual's residence status for a tax year or affects his or her liability to tax.

41 This Part—

(*a*) does not apply in determining the residence status of personal representatives, and

(*b*) applies to only a limited extent in determining the residence status of the trustees of a settlement (see section 475 of ITA 2007 and section 69 of TCGA 1992, as amended by this Part).

42 The existence of special charging rules for cases involving split years is not intended to affect any question as to whether an individual would fall to be regarded under double taxation arrangements as a resident of the UK.

Definition of a "split year"

43 (1) As respects an individual, a tax year is a "split year" if—

(*a*) the individual is resident in the UK for that year, and

(*b*) the circumstances of the case fall within—

(i) Case 1, Case 2 or Case 3 (cases involving actual or deemed departure from the UK), or

(ii) Case 4, Case 5, Case 6, Case 7 or Case 8 (cases involving actual or deemed arrival in the UK).

(2) The 8 Cases are described in paragraphs 44 to 51.

(3) In those paragraphs, the individual is referred to as "the taxpayer" and the tax year as "the relevant year".

(4) In applying Part 2 of this Schedule to those paragraphs, for "P" read "the taxpayer".

Case 1: starting full-time work overseas

44 (1) The circumstances of a case fall within Case 1 if they are as described in subparagraphs (2) to (4).

(2) The taxpayer was resident in the UK for the previous tax year (whether or not it was a split year).

(3) There is at least one period (consisting of one or more days) that—

(*a*) begins with a day that—

(i) falls within the relevant year, and

(ii) is a day on which the taxpayer does more than 3 hours' work overseas,

(*b*) ends with the last day of the relevant year, and

(*c*) satisfies the overseas work criteria.

(4) The taxpayer is not resident in the UK for the next tax year because the taxpayer meets the third automatic overseas test for that year (see paragraph 14).

(5) A period "satisfies the overseas work criteria" if—

(*a*) the taxpayer works sufficient hours overseas, as assessed over that period,

(*b*) during that period, there are no significant breaks from overseas work,

(*c*) the number of days in that period on which the taxpayer does more than 3 hours' work in the UK does not exceed the permitted limit, and

(*d*) the number of days in that period falling within sub-paragraph (6) does not exceed the permitted limit.

(6) A day falls within this sub-paragraph if—

(*a*) it is a day spent by the taxpayer in the UK, but

(*b*) it is not a day that is treated under paragraph 23(4) as a day spent by the taxpayer in the UK.

(7) To work out whether the taxpayer works "sufficient hours overseas" as assessed over a given period, apply paragraph 14(3) but with the following modifications—

(*a*) for "P" read "the taxpayer",

(*b*) for "year X" read "the period under consideration",

(*c*) for "365 (or 366 if year X includes 29 February)" read "the number of days in the period under consideration", and

(*d*) in paragraph 28(9)(*b*), as it applies for the purposes of step 3, for "30" read "the permitted limit".

(8) The permitted limit is—

(*a*) for sub-paragraphs (5)(*c*) and (7)(*d*), the number found by reducing 30 by the appropriate number, and

(*b*) for sub-paragraph (5)(*d*), the number found by reducing 90 by the appropriate number.

(9) The appropriate number is the result of—

A x (B / 12)

where—

"A" is—

(*a*) 30, for sub-paragraphs (5)(*c*) and (7)(*d*), or

(*b*) 90, for sub-paragraph (5)(*d*), and

"B" is the number of whole months in the part of the relevant year before the day mentioned in sub-paragraph (3)(*a*).

Case 2: the partner of someone starting full-time work overseas

45 (1) The circumstances of a case fall within Case 2 if they are as described in subparagraphs (2) to (6).

(2) The taxpayer was resident in the UK for the previous tax year (whether or not it was a split year).
(3) The taxpayer has a partner whose circumstances fall within Case 1 for—

(*a*) the relevant year, or

(*b*) the previous tax year.

(4) On a day in the relevant year, the taxpayer moves overseas so the taxpayer and the partner can continue to live together while the partner is working overseas.
(5) In the part of the relevant year beginning with the deemed departure day—

(*a*) the taxpayer has no home in the UK at any time, or has homes in both the UK and overseas but spends the greater part of the time living in the overseas home, and

(*b*) the number of days that the taxpayer spends in the UK does not exceed the permitted limit.

(6) The taxpayer is not resident in the UK for the next tax year.
(7) If sub-paragraph (3)(*a*) applies, the "deemed departure day" is the later of—

(*a*) the day mentioned in sub-paragraph (4), and

(*b*) the first day of what is, for the partner, the overseas part of the relevant year as defined for Case 1 (see paragraph 53).

(8) If sub-paragraph (3)(*b*) applies, the "deemed departure day" is the day mentioned in sub-paragraph (4).
(9) The permitted limit is the number found by reducing 90 by the appropriate number.
(10) The appropriate number is the result of—
A x (B / 12)
where—

"A" is 90, and

"B" is the number of whole months in the part of the relevant year before the deemed departure day.

Case 3: ceasing to have a home in the UK

46 (1) The circumstances of a case fall within Case 3 if they are as described in subparagraphs (2) to (6).
(2) The taxpayer was resident in the UK for the previous tax year (whether or not it was a split year).
(3) At the start of the relevant year the taxpayer had one or more homes in the UK but—

(*a*) there comes a day in the relevant year when P ceases to have any home in the UK, and

(*b*) from then on, P has no home in the UK for the rest of that year.

(4) In the part of the relevant year beginning with the day mentioned in subparagraph (3)(*a*), the taxpayer spends fewer than 16 days in the UK.
(5) The taxpayer is not resident in the UK for the next tax year.
(6) At the end of the period of 6 months beginning with the day mentioned in sub-paragraph (3)(*a*), the taxpayer has a sufficient link with a country overseas.
(7) The taxpayer has a "sufficient link" with a country overseas if and only if—

(*a*) the taxpayer is considered for tax purposes to be a resident of that country in accordance with its domestic laws, or

(*b*) the taxpayer has been present in that country (in person) at the end of each day of the 6-month period mentioned in sub-paragraph (6), or

(*c*) the taxpayer's only home is in that country or, if the taxpayer has more than one home, they are all in that country.

Case 4: starting to have a home in the UK only

47 (1) The circumstances of a case fall within Case 4 if they are as described in subparagraphs (2) to (4).
(2) The taxpayer was not resident in the UK for the previous tax year.
(3) At the start of the relevant year, the taxpayer did not meet the only home test, but there comes a day in the relevant year when that ceases to be the case and the taxpayer then continues to meet the only home test for the rest of that year.
(4) For the part of the relevant year before that day, the taxpayer does not have sufficient UK ties.
(5) The "only home test" is met if—

(*a*) the taxpayer has only one home and that home is in the UK, or

(*b*) the taxpayer has more than one home and all of them are in the UK.

(6) Paragraphs 17 to 20 (and Part 2 of this Schedule so far as it relates to those paragraphs) apply for the purposes of sub-paragraph (4) with the following adjustments—

(*a*) references in those paragraphs and that Part to year X are to be read as references to the part of the relevant year mentioned in subparagraph (4), and

(*b*) each number of days mentioned in the first column of the Table in paragraphs 18 and 19 is to be reduced by the appropriate number.

(7) The appropriate number is found by multiplying the number of days, in each case, by—

A / 12

where "A" is the number of whole months in the part of the relevant year beginning with the day mentioned in sub-paragraph (3).

(8) Sub-paragraph (6)(*a*) does not apply to the references to year X in paragraphs 32(1)(*b*) and 33 of this Schedule (which relate to the residence status of family members) so those references must continue to be read as references to year X.

Case 5: starting full-time work in the UK

48 (1) The circumstances of a case fall within Case 5 if they are as described in subparagraphs (2) and (3).

(2) The taxpayer was not resident in the UK for the previous tax year.

(3) There is at least one period of 365 days in respect of which the following conditions are met—

- (*a*) the period begins with a day that—
  - (i) falls within the relevant year, and
  - (ii) is a day on which the taxpayer does more than 3 hours' work in the UK,
- (*b*) in the part of the relevant year before the period begins, the taxpayer does not have sufficient UK ties,
- (*c*) the taxpayer works sufficient hours in the UK, as assessed over the period,
- (*d*) during the period, there are no significant breaks from UK work, and
- (*e*) at least 75% of the total number of days in the period on which the taxpayer does more than 3 hours' work are days on which the taxpayer does more than 3 hours' work in the UK.

(4) To work out whether the taxpayer works "sufficient hours in the UK" as assessed over a given period, apply paragraph 9(2) but for "P" read "the taxpayer".

(5) Paragraphs 17 to 20 (and Part 2 of this Schedule so far as it relates to those paragraphs) apply for the purposes of sub-paragraph (3)(*b*) with the following adjustments—

- (*a*) references in those paragraphs and that Part to year X are to be read as references to the part of the relevant year mentioned in subparagraph (3)(*b*), and
- (*b*) each number of days mentioned in the first column of the Table in paragraphs 18 and 19 is to be reduced by the appropriate number.

(6) The appropriate number is found by multiplying the number of days, in each case, by—

A / 12

where "A" is the number of whole months in the part of the relevant year beginning with the day on which the 365-day period in question begins.

(7) Sub-paragraph (5)(*a*) does not apply to the references to year X in paragraphs 32(1)(*b*) and 33 of this Schedule (which relate to the residence status of family members) so those references must continue to be read as references to year X.

Case 6: ceasing full-time work overseas

49 (1) The circumstances of a case fall within Case 6 if they are as described in subparagraphs (2) to (4).

(2) The taxpayer—

- (*a*) was not resident in the UK for the previous tax year because the taxpayer met the third automatic overseas test for that year (see paragraph 14), but
- (*b*) was resident in the UK for one or more of the 4 tax years immediately preceding that year.

(3) There is at least one period (consisting of one or more days) that—

- (*a*) begins with the first day of the relevant year,
- (*b*) ends with a day that—
  - (i) falls within the relevant year, and
  - (ii) is a day on which the taxpayer does more than 3 hours' work overseas, and
- (*c*) satisfies the overseas work criteria.

(4) The taxpayer is resident in the UK for the next tax year (whether or not it is a split year).

(5) A period "satisfies the overseas work criteria" if—

- (*a*) the taxpayer works sufficient hours overseas, as assessed over that period,
- (*b*) during that period, there are no significant breaks from overseas work,
- (*c*) the number of days in that period on which the taxpayer does more than 3 hours' work in the UK does not exceed the permitted limit, and
- (*d*) the number of days in that period falling within sub-paragraph (6) does not exceed the permitted limit.

(6) A day falls within this sub-paragraph if—

- (*a*) it is a day spent by the taxpayer in the UK, but
- (*b*) it is not a day that is treated under paragraph 23(4) as a day spent by the taxpayer in the UK.

(7) To work out whether the taxpayer works "sufficient hours overseas" as assessed over a given period, apply paragraph 14(3) but with the following modifications—

(*a*) for "P" read "the taxpayer",

(*b*) for "year X" read "the period under consideration",

(*c*) for "365 (or 366 if year X includes 29 February)" read "the number of days in the period under consideration", and

(*d*) in paragraph 28(9)(*b*), as it applies for the purposes of step 3, for "30" read "the permitted limit".

(8) The permitted limit is—

(*a*) for sub-paragraphs (5)(*c*) and (7)(*d*), the number found by reducing 30 by the appropriate number, and

(*b*) for sub-paragraph (5)(*d*), the number found by reducing 90 by the appropriate number.

(9) The appropriate number is the result of—

A x (B / 12)

where—

"A" is—

(*a*) 30, for sub-paragraphs (5)(*c*) and (7)(*d*), or

(*b*) 90, for sub-paragraph (5)(*d*), and

"B" is the number of whole months in the part of the relevant year after the 365-day period in question ends.

Modifications—FA 2013 Sch 45 para 154 (modification of the application of this para in relation to a pre-commencement tax year).

Case 7: the partner of someone ceasing full-time work overseas

50 (1) The circumstances of a case fall within Case 7 if they are as described in subparagraphs (2) to (6).

(2) The taxpayer was not resident in the UK for the previous tax year.

(3) The taxpayer has a partner whose circumstances fall within Case 6 for—

(*a*) the relevant year, or

(*b*) the previous tax year.

(4) On a day in the relevant year, the taxpayer moves to the UK so the taxpayer and the partner can continue to live together on the partner's return or relocation to the UK.

(5) In the part of the relevant year before the deemed arrival day—

(*a*) the taxpayer has no home in the UK at any time, or has homes in both the UK and overseas but spends the greater part of the time living in the overseas home, and

(*b*) the number of days that the taxpayer spends in the UK does not exceed the permitted limit.

(6) The taxpayer is resident in the UK for the next tax year (whether or not it is a split year).

(7) If sub-paragraph (3)(*a*) applies, the "deemed arrival day" is the later of—

(*a*) the day mentioned in sub-paragraph (4), and

(*b*) the first day of what is, for the partner, the UK part of the relevant year as defined for Case 6 (see paragraph 54).

(8) If sub-paragraph (3)(*b*) applies, the "deemed arrival day" is the day mentioned in sub-paragraph (4).

(9) The permitted limit is the number found by reducing 90 by the appropriate number.

(10) The appropriate number is the result of—

A x (B / 12)

where—

"A" is 90, and

"B" is the number of whole months in the part of the relevant year beginning with the deemed arrival day.

Cross–referencesFA 2013 Sch 45 para 156 (determining whether the tax year in question was a split tax year).

Case 8: starting to have a home in the UK

51 (1) The circumstances of a case fall within Case 8 if they are as described in subparagraphs (2) to (5).

(2) The taxpayer was not resident in the UK for the previous tax year.

(3) At the start of the relevant year, the taxpayer had no home in the UK but—

(*a*) there comes a day when, for the first time in that year, the taxpayer does have a home in the UK, and

(*b*) from then on, the taxpayer continues to have a home in the UK for the rest of that year and for the whole of the next tax year.

(4) For the part of the relevant year before the day mentioned in sub-paragraph (3)(*a*), the taxpayer does not have sufficient UK ties.

(5) The taxpayer is resident in the UK for the next tax year and that tax year is not a split year as respects the taxpayer.

(6) Paragraphs 17 to 20 (and Part 2 of this Schedule so far as it relates to those paragraphs) apply for the purposes of sub-paragraph (4) with the following adjustments—

(*a*) references in those paragraphs and that Part to year X are to be read as references to the part of the relevant year mentioned in subparagraph (4), and

(*b*) each number of days mentioned in the first column of the Table in paragraphs 18 and 19 is to be reduced by the appropriate number.

(7) The appropriate number is found by multiplying the number of days, in each case, by—

A / 12

where "A" is the number of whole months in the part of the relevant year beginning with the day mentioned in sub-paragraph (3)(*a*).

(8) Sub-paragraph (6)(*a*) does not apply to the references to year X in paragraphs 32(1)(*b*) and 33 of this Schedule (which relate to the residence status of family members) so those references must continue to be read as references to year X.

General rules for construing Cases 1 to 8

52 (1) This paragraph applies for the purposes of paragraphs 44 to 51.

(2) A reference to "the previous tax year" is to the tax year preceding the relevant year.

(3) A reference to "the next tax year" is to the tax year following the relevant year.

(4) "Partner", in relation to the taxpayer, means—

(*a*) a husband or wife or civil partner,

(*b*) if the taxpayer and another person are living together as husband and wife, that other person, or

(*c*) if the taxpayer and another person of the same sex are living together as if they were civil partners, that other person.

(5) If calculation of the appropriate number results in a number of days that is not a whole number, the appropriate number is to be rounded up or down as follows—

(*a*) if the first figure after the decimal point is 5 or more, round the appropriate number up to the nearest whole number,

(*b*) otherwise, round it down to the nearest whole number.

The overseas part

53 (1) "The overseas part" of a split year is the part of that year defined below—

(*a*) for the Case in question, or

(*b*) if the taxpayer's circumstances fall within more than one Case, for the Case which has priority (see paragraphs 54 and 55).

(2) For Case 1, the overseas part is—

(*a*) if there is only one period falling within paragraph 44(3), the part beginning with the first day of that period, and

(*b*) if there is more than one such period, the part beginning with the first day of the longest of those periods.

(3) For Case 2, the overseas part is the part beginning with the deemed departure day as defined in paragraph 45(7) and (8).

(4) For Case 3, the overseas part is the part beginning with the day mentioned in paragraph 46(3)(*a*).

(5) For Case 4, the overseas part is the part before the day mentioned in paragraph 47(3).

(6) For Case 5, the overseas part is—

(*a*) if there is only one period falling within paragraph 48(3), the part before that period begins, and

(*b*) if there is more than one such period, the part before the first of those periods begins.

(7) For Case 6, the overseas part is—

(*a*) if there is only one period falling within paragraph 49(3), the part ending with the last day of that period, and

(*b*) if there is more than one such period, the part ending with the last day of the longest of those periods.

(8) For Case 7, the overseas part is the part before the deemed arrival day as defined in paragraph 50(7) and (8).

(9) For Case 8, the overseas part is the part before the day mentioned in paragraph 51(3)(*a*).

Priority between Cases 1 to 3

54 (1) This paragraph applies to determine which Case has priority where the taxpayer's circumstances for the relevant year fall within two or all of the following—

Case 1 (starting full-time work overseas);

Case 2 (the partner of someone starting full-time work overseas);

Case 3 (ceasing to have a home in the UK).

(2) Case 1 has priority over Case 2 and Case 3.

(3) Case 2 has priority over Case 3.

Priority between Cases 4 to 8

55 (1) This paragraph applies to determine which Case has priority where the taxpayer's circumstances for the relevant year fall within two or more of the following—

Case 4 (starting to have a home in the UK only);

Case 5 (starting full-time work in the UK);

Case 6 (ceasing full-time work overseas);

Case 7 (the partner of someone ceasing full-time work overseas);

Case 8 (starting to have a home in the UK).

(2) In this paragraph "the split year date" in relation to a Case means the final day of the part of the relevant year defined in paragraph 53(5) to (9) for that Case.

(3) If Case 6 applies—

(*a*) if Case 5 also applies and the split year date in relation to Case 5 is earlier than the split year date in relation to Case 6, Case 5 has priority;

(*b*) otherwise, Case 6 has priority.

(4) If Case 7 (but not Case 6) applies—

(*a*) if Case 5 also applies and the split year date in relation to Case 5 is earlier than the split year date in relation to Case 7, Case 5 has priority;

(*b*) otherwise, Case 7 has priority

(5) If two or all of Cases 4, 5 and 8 apply (but neither Case 6 nor Case 7), the Case which has priority is the one with the earliest split year date.

(6) But if, in a case to which sub-paragraph (5) applies, two or all of the Cases which apply share the same split year date and that date is the only, or earlier, split year date of the Cases which apply, the Cases with that split year date are to be treated as having priority.

The UK part

56 "The UK part" of a split year is the part of that year that is not the overseas part.

Special charging rules for employment income

57 ITEPA 2003 is amended as follows.

58 (1) (*substitutes* ITEPA 2003 s 15(1))
(2) (*inserts* ITEPA 2003 s 15(4)–(6))

59 (*substitutes* ITEPA 2003 s 22(7))

60 (1) Section 23 (calculation of "chargeable overseas earnings") is amended as follows.
(2), (3) (*amend* ITEPA 2003 s 23(3))
(4) (*inserts* ITEPA 2003 s 23(4))

61 (1) Section 24 (limit on chargeable overseas earnings where duties of associated employment performed in UK) is amended as follows.
(2), (3) (*insert* ITEPA 2003 s 24(2A), (3A))

62 (1) Section 26 (foreign earnings for year when remittance basis applies and employee meets section 26A requirement) is amended as follows.
(2) (*amends* ITEPA 2003 s 26(1))
(3) (*inserts* ITEPA 2003 s 26(5A))
(4) (*substitutes* ITEPA 2003 s 26(6))

63 (*inserts* ITEPA 2003 s 232(6A))

64 (1) Section 329 (deduction from earnings not to exceed earnings) is amended as follows.
(2) (*inserts* ITEPA 2003 s 329(1A))
(3), (4) (*amend* ITEPA 2003 s 329(2), (3))

65 (1) Section 394 (charge on employer-financed retirement benefits) is amended as follows.
(2) (*inserts* ITEPA 2003 s 394(4C)(*ba*))

(3) (*substitutes* ITEPA 2003 s 394(4C)(*c*))

66 (1) Section 421E (income relating to securities: exclusions about residence etc) is amended as follows.
(2) (*substitutes* ITEPA 2003 s 421E(1))
(3) (*inserts* ITEPA 2003 s 421E(2A))

67 (*substitutes* ITEPA 2003 s 474(1))

68 (1) Section 554Z4 (residence issues) is amended as follows.
(2) (*substitutes* ITEPA 2003 s 554Z4(3)–(5))
(3) (*inserts* ITEPA 2003 s 554Z4(5A), (5B))

69

(*amends* ITEPA 2003 s 554Z6(1)(*a*))

70 (*amends* ITEPA 2003 s 554Z9(5)(*b*), (*c*))

71 (1) Section 554Z10 (remittance basis: A is not ordinarily resident) is amended as follows.
(2), (3), (6) (*substitute* ITEPA 2003 s 554Z10(1)(*a*), (2), (4))
(4) (*inserts* ITEPA 2003 s 554Z10(2A), (2B))
(5) (*amends* ITEPA 2003 s 554Z10(3))

Special charging rules for pension income

72 (1) Section 575 of ITEPA 2003 (foreign pensions: taxable pension income) is amended as follows.
(2), (4) (*amend* ITEPA 2003 s 575(1), (2); sub-para (4) *repealed* by FA 2017 s 9, Sch 3 para 2(4)(*d*))
(3) (*inserts* ITEPA 2003 s 575(1A))

PAYE income

73 (1) Section 690 of ITEPA 2003 (employee non-residents etc) is amended as follows.
(2) (*amends* ITEPA 2003 s 690(1))
(3) (*inserts* ITEPA 2003 s 690(1A))

Special charging rules for trading income

74 ITTOIA 2005 is amended as follows.

75 (*inserts* ITTOIA 2005 s 6(2A))

76 (1) Section 17 (effect of becoming or ceasing to be UK resident) is amended as follows.
(2) (*substitutes* ITTOIA 2005 s 17(1))
(3) (*amends* ITTOIA 2005 s 17(2))

77 (*inserts* ITTOIA 2005 s 243(6))

78 (*inserts* ITTOIA 2005 s 849(3A))

79 (1) Section 852 (carrying on by partner of notional trade) is amended as follows.
(2) (*substitutes* ITTOIA 2005 s 852(6))
(3) (*inserts* ITTOIA 2005 s 852(8))

80 (1) Section 854 (carrying on by partner of notional business) is amended as follows.
(2) (*substitutes* ITTOIA 2005 s 854(5))
(3) (*inserts* ITTOIA 2005 s 854(5A))

Special charging rules for property income

81 (*inserts* ITTOIA 2005 s 270(3)–(5))

Special charging rules for savings and investment income

82 Part 4 of ITTOIA 2005 (savings and investment income) is amended as follows.

83 (*inserts* ITTOIA 2005 s 368(2A))

84 (*inserts* ITTOIA 2005 s 465(1A))

85 (*inserts* ITTOIA 2005 s 467(4)(*aa*))

86 (1) Section 528 (reduction in amount charged under Chapter 9 of Part 4: non-UK resident policy holders) is amended as follows.

(2) The amendments made by sub-paragraphs (3) to (6) apply to section 528 as substituted by paragraph 3 of Schedule 8 to this Act, and have effect in relation to policies and contracts in relation to which that section as so substituted has effect.
(3), (5), (6) (*amend* ITTOIA 2005 s 528(1)(*b*), (3), (8))
(4) (*inserts* ITTOIA 2005 s 528(1A))
(7) The amendments made by sub-paragraphs (8) to (10) apply to section 528 as in force immediately before the substitution mentioned in sub-paragraph (2) so far as that section as so in force continues to have effect after the substitution.
(8), (10) (*amend* ITTOIA 2005 s 528(1), (3))
(9) (*inserts* ITTOIA 2005 s 528(1A))

87 (1) Section 528A (reduction in amount charged on basis of non-UK residence of deceased person), as inserted by paragraph 3 of Schedule 8 to this Act, is amended as follows.
(2), (3), (5), (6) (*amend* ITTOIA 2005 s 528A(1)(*b*), (2), (4), (8))
(4) (*inserts* ITTOIA 2005 s 528A(2A))

88 (1) Section 536 (top slicing relieved liability: one chargeable event) is amended as follows.
(2) The amendment made by sub-paragraph (3) applies to section 536 as amended by paragraph 5 of Schedule 8 to this Act, and has effect in accordance with paragraph 7 of that Schedule.
(3) (*substitutes* ITTOIA 2005 s 536(7))
(4) The amendment made by sub-paragraph (5) applies to section 536 as in force immediately before it is amended by paragraph 5 of Schedule 8 to this Act, so far as that section as so in force continues to have effect after it is so amended.
(5) (*substitutes* ITTOIA 2005 s 536(7))

Special charging rules for miscellaneous income

89 (*inserts* ITTOIA 2005 s 577(2A))

Special charging rules for relevant foreign income charged on remittance basis

90 (*substitutes* ITTOIA 2005 s 832(2))

91 (1) Chapter 2 of Part 13 of ITA 2007 (transfer of assets abroad) is amended as follows in consequence of the amendment made by the preceding paragraph.
(2) (*inserts* ITA 2007 s 726(5))
(3) (*inserts* ITA 2007 s 730(5))
(4) (*inserts* ITA 2007 s 735(5))

Special charging rules for capital gains

92 TCGA 1992 is amended as follows.

93 (1) Section 2 (persons and gains chargeable to capital gains tax, and allowable losses) is amended as follows.
(2) (*inserts* TCGA 1992 s 2(1B), (1C))
(3) (*amends* TCGA 1992 s 2(2))

94 (1) Section 3A (reporting limits) is amended as follows.
(2), (3) (*amend* TCGA 1992 s 3A(1)(*a*), (*b*), (2))

95 (1) Section 12 (non-UK domiciled individuals to whom remittance basis applies) is amended as follows.
(2) (*inserts* TCGA 1992 s 12(2A))
(3) (*amend* TCGA 1992 s 12(3))

96 (*inserts* TCGA 1992 s 13(3A))

97 (*inserts* TCGA 1992 s 16(3A))

98 (*amends* TCGA 1992 s 16ZB(1)(*c*))

99 (1) Section 16ZC (individual who has made election under section 16ZA and to whom remittance basis applies) is amended as follows.
(2), (3) (*amend* TCGA 1992 s 16ZC(3)(*a*), (*b*), (7))

100 (*amends* TCGA 1992 s 86(4)(*a*))

101 (*inserts* TCGA 1992 s 87(7))

Trustees of a settlement

102 (*inserts* TCGA 1992 s 69(2DA), (2DB))

103 (*inserts* ITA 2007 s 475(7)–(9))

Definitions in enactments relating to income tax and CGT

104 (1) Section 288 of TCGA 1992 (interpretation) is amended as follows.
(2) (*amends* TCGA 1992 s 288(1))
(3) (*inserts* TCGA 1992 s 288(1ZB))

105 (*amends* ITEPA 2003 Sch 1 Pt 2)

106 (*amends* ITTOIA 2005 Sch 4 Pt 2)

107 (*amends* ITA 2007 s 989)

108 (*amends* ITA 2007 Sch 4)

PART 4
ANTI-AVOIDANCE

Commentary—*Simon's Taxes* **E6.103A**.

Introduction

109 This Part of this Schedule—
(*a*) explains when an individual is to be regarded for the purposes of certain enactments as temporarily non-resident,
(*b*) defines the year of departure and the period of return for the purposes of those enactments,
(*c*) makes consequential amendments to certain enactments containing special rules for temporary non-residents, and
(*d*) inserts some more special rules for temporary non-residents in certain cases.

Meaning of temporarily non-resident

110 (1) An individual is to be regarded as "temporarily non-resident" if—
(*a*) the individual has sole UK residence for a residence period,
(*b*) immediately following that period (referred to as "period A"), one or more residence periods occur for which the individual does not have sole UK residence,
(*c*) at least 4 out of the 7 tax years immediately preceding the year of departure were either—
(i) a tax year for which the individual had sole UK residence, or
(ii) a split year that included a residence period for which the individual had sole UK residence, and
(*d*) the temporary period of non-residence is 5 years or less.
(2) Terms used in sub-paragraph (1) are defined below.

Cross-referencesFA 2013 Sch 45 para 157 (application of temporary non-residence rules in relation to pre-commencement years for which the concept of sole UK residence does not apply).

Residence periods

111 In relation to an individual, a "residence period" is—
(*a*) a tax year that, as respects the individual, is not a split year, or
(*b*) the overseas part or the UK part of a tax year that, as respects the individual, is a split year.

Sole UK residence

112 (1) An individual has "sole UK residence" for a residence period consisting of an entire tax year if—
(*a*) the individual is resident in the UK for that year, and
(*b*) there is no time in that year when the individual is Treaty non-resident.
(2) An individual has "sole UK residence" for a residence period consisting of part of a split year if—
(*a*) the residence period is the UK part of that year, and
(*b*) there is no time in that part of the year when the individual is Treaty non-resident.
(3) An individual is "Treaty non-resident" at any time if at the time the individual falls to be regarded as resident in a country outside the UK for the purposes of double taxation arrangements having effect at the time.

Temporary period of non-residence

113 In relation to an individual, "the temporary period of non-residence" is the period between—

(*a*) the end of period A, and
(*b*) the start of the next residence period after period A for which the individual has sole UK residence.

Year of departure

114 "The year of departure" is the tax year consisting of or including period A.

Period of return

115 "The period of return" is the first residence period after period A for which the individual has sole UK residence.

Consequential amendments: income tax

116 (*substitutes* ITEPA 2003 s 576A)

Commentary—*Simon's Taxes* **E6.105A**.

117 (*substitutes* ITEPA 2003 s 579CA)

Commentary—*Simon's Taxes* **E6.105A**.

118 (*substitutes* ITTOIA 2005 s 832A)

Consequential amendments: capital gains tax

119 (*substitutes* TCGA 1992 s 10A)

120 (*substitutes* TCGA 1992 s 86A)

121 (*amends* TCGA 1992 s 96(9A))

122 (1) Section 279B (deferred unascertainable consideration: supplementary provisions) is amended as follows.
(2), (3) (*amend* TCGA 1992 s 279B(7), (8)(*a*), (*b*))

123 (1) Schedule 4C (transfers of value: attribution of gains to beneficiaries) is amended as follows.
(2) (*amends* TCGA 1992 Sch 4C para 6(1)(*b*))
(3)–(4) (*amend* TCGA 1992 Sch 4C para 12(1), (2))
(5) (*amends* TCGA 1992 Sch 4C para 12A(1))

New special rule: lump sum payments under pension schemes etc

124 ITEPA 2003 is amended as follows.

125 (*inserts* ITEPA 2003 s 394A)

126 (*inserts* ITEPA 2003 s 554Z4A)

127 (*inserts* ITEPA 2003 s 554Z11A)

128 (*inserts* ITEPA 2003 s 554Z12(9), (10))

129 (*inserts* ITEPA 2003 s 572A)

130 (1) In Chapter 1 of Part 11 (pay as you earn: introduction), section 683 is amended as follows.
(2) (*inserts* ITEPA 2003 s 683(3ZA))
(3) (*substitutes* ITEPA 2003 s 683(3B))

New special rule: distributions to participators in close companies etc

131 Part 4 of ITTOIA 2005 (savings and investment income) is amended as follows.

132 (*inserts* ITTOIA 2005 s 368A)

133 (*inserts* ITTOIA 2005 s 401C)

134 (*inserts* ITTOIA 2005 s 408A)

135 (*inserts* ITTOIA 2005 s 413A)

136 (*inserts* ITTOIA 2005 s 420A)

137 (*inserts* ITTOIA 2005 s 689A)

138 (*inserts* ITA 2007 s 812A)

New special rule: chargeable event gains

139 Chapter 9 of Part 4 of ITTOIA 2005 (gains from contracts for life insurance etc) is amended as follows.

140 (*inserts* ITTOIA 2005 s 465B)

141 (*inserts* ITTOIA 2005 s 468(7))

142 (*inserts* ITTOIA 2005 s 514(4A))

143 (*amends* ITTOIA 2005 s 541(4)(*b*))

144 (*amends* TA 1988 s 552(13))

PART 5
MISCELLANEOUS

Interpretation

145 In this Schedule—

"corporation tax" includes any amount assessable or chargeable as if it were corporation tax;

"country" includes a state or territory;

"cross-border trip" is defined in paragraph 30;

"double taxation arrangements" means arrangements that have effect under section 2(1) of TIOPA 2010;

"employment"—

(*a*) has the meaning given in section 4 of ITEPA 2003, and

(*b*) includes an office within the meaning of section 5(3) of that Act;

"enactment" means an enactment whenever passed (including this Act) and includes—

(*a*) an Act of the Scottish Parliament,

(*b*) a Measure or Act of the National Assembly for Wales,

(*c*) any Northern Ireland legislation as defined by section 24(5) of the Interpretation Act 1978, and

(*d*) any Orders in Council, orders, rules, regulations, schemes warrants, byelaws and other instruments made under an enactment (including anything mentioned in paragraphs (*a*) to (*c*) of this definition);

"home" is to be construed in accordance with paragraph 25;

"individual" means an individual acting in any capacity (including as trustee or personal representative);

"overseas" means anywhere outside the UK;

"parenting leave" means maternity leave, paternity leave, adoption leave or parental leave (whether statutory or otherwise);

"relevant job on board a vehicle, aircraft or ship" is defined in paragraph 30;

"ship" includes any kind of vessel (including a hovercraft);

"significant break from overseas work" is defined in paragraph 29;

"significant break from UK work" is defined in paragraph 29;

"split year", as respects an individual, means a tax year that is, as respects that individual, a split year within the meaning of Part 3 of this Schedule;

"trade" also includes—

(*a*) a profession or vocation,

(*b*) anything that is treated as a trade for income tax purposes, and

(*c*) the commercial occupation of woodlands (within the meaning of section 11(2) of ITTOIA 2005);

"work" is defined in paragraph 26;

"UK" means the United Kingdom, including the territorial sea of the United Kingdom;

"UK tie" is defined in paragraph 31;

"whole month" means the whole of January, the whole of February and so on, except that the period from the start of a tax year to the end of April is to count as a whole month.

146 In relation to an individual who carries on a trade—

(*a*) a reference in this Schedule to annual leave or parenting leave is to reasonable amounts of time off from work for the same purposes as the purposes for which annual leave or parenting leave is taken, and (*b*) what are "reasonable amounts" is to be assessed having regard to the annual leave or parenting leave to which an employee might reasonably expect to be entitled if doing similar work.

147 A reference in this Schedule to a number of days being less than a specified number includes a case where the number of days is zero.

Consequential amendments

148 (1) TCGA 1992 is amended as follows.
(2) (*repeals* TCGA 1992 s 9)
(3) (*amends* TCGA 1992 s 288(1), (8))

149 (*amends* ITEPA 2003 s 27(1))

150 (*amends* ITTOIA 2005 s 465(1))

151 (1) Chapter 4 of Part 2 of FA 2005 (trusts with vulnerable beneficiary) is amended as follows.
(2) (*substitutes* FA 2005 s 28)
(3) In section 30 (qualifying trusts gains: special capital gains tax treatment)—
(*a*) (*amends* FA 2005 s 30(2)(*a*), *b*))
(*b*) (*repeals* FA 2005 s 30(5))
(4) (*amends* FA 2005 s 31(1))
(5) (*amends* FA 2005 s 32(1))
(6) In section 41—
(*a*) (*amends* FA 2005 s 41(1))
(*b*) (*repeals* FA 2005 s 41(2))

152 (1) ITA 2007 is amended as follows.
(2) (*amends* ITA 2007 s 809B(1)(*a*))
(3) (*amends* ITA 2007 s 809D(1)(*a*))
(4) (*amends* ITA 2007 s 809E(1)(*a*))
(5) (*inserts* ITA 2007 s 810(4))
(6) (*repeals* ITA 2007 ss 829–832)

Commencement

153 (1) Parts 1 and 2 of this Schedule have effect for determining whether individuals are resident or not resident in the UK for the tax year 2013–14 or any subsequent tax year.
(2) Part 3 of this Schedule has effect in calculating an individual's liability to income tax or capital gains tax for the tax year 2013–14 or any subsequent tax year.
(3) Part 4 of this Schedule has effect if the year of departure (as defined in that Part) is the tax year 2013–14 or a subsequent tax year.

Transitional and saving provision

154 (1) This paragraph applies if—
(*a*) year X or, in Part 3 of this Schedule, the relevant year is the tax year 2013–14, 2014–15, 2015–16, 2016–17 or 2017–18, and
(*b*) it is necessary to determine under this Schedule whether an individual was resident or not resident in the UK for a tax year before the tax year 2013–14 (a "pre-commencement tax year").
(2) The question under this Schedule is to be determined in accordance with the rules in force for determining an individual's residence for that pre-commencement tax year (and not in accordance with the statutory residence test).
(3) But an individual may by notice in writing to Her Majesty's Revenue and Customs elect, as respects one or more pre-commencement tax years, for the question under this Schedule to be determined instead in accordance with the statutory residence test.
(4) A notice under sub-paragraph (3)—
(*a*) must be given no later than the first anniversary of the end of year X or, in a Part 3 case, the relevant year, and
(*b*) is irrevocable.
(5) Unless, in relation to a pre-commencement tax year, an election is made under sub-paragraph (3) as respects that year—
(*a*) paragraph 10(*b*) of this Schedule has effect in relation to that year as if the words "by virtue of meeting the automatic residence test" were omitted,
(*b*) paragraph 16 of this Schedule has effect in relation to that year as if—
(i) in sub-paragraph (1)(*b*), the words "because P met the third automatic overseas test for each of those years" were omitted, and

(ii) in sub-paragraph (2)(*a*), the words "because P met the third automatic overseas test for that year" were omitted, and

(*c*) paragraph 49 of this Schedule has effect in relation to that year as if in sub-paragraph (2)(*a*) for the words from "because" to the end there were substituted "in circumstances where the taxpayer was working overseas full-time for the whole of that year."

155 (1) This paragraph applies if—

(*a*) year X or, for Part 3 of this Schedule, the tax year for which an individual's liability to tax is being calculated is the tax year 2013–14 or a subsequent tax year, and

(*b*) it is necessary to determine under a provision of this Schedule, or a provision inserted by Part 3 of this Schedule, whether a tax year before the tax year 2013–14 (a "pre-commencement tax year") was a split year as respects the individual.

(2) The provision is to have effect as if—

(*a*) the reference to a split year were to a tax year to which the relevant ESC applied, and

(*b*) any reference to the UK part or the overseas part of such a year were to the part corresponding as far as possible, in accordance with the terms of the relevant ESC, to the UK part or the overseas part of a split year.

(3) Where the provision also refers to cases involving actual or deemed departure from the UK, the reference is to be read and given effect so far as possible in accordance with the terms of the relevant ESC.

(4) "The relevant ESC" means whichever of the extra-statutory concessions to which effect is given by Part 3 of this Schedule is relevant in the individual's case.

156 (1) Sub-paragraph (2) applies in determining whether the test in paragraph 50(3) is met where the relevant year is the tax year 2013–14.

(2) The circumstances of a partner of the taxpayer are to be treated as falling within Case 6 for the previous tax year if the partner was eligible for split year treatment in relation to that tax year under the relevant ESC on the grounds that he or she returned to the United Kingdom after a period working overseas full-time.

(3) Where the circumstances of a partner are treated as falling within Case 6 under sub-paragraph (2), the reference in paragraph 50(7)(*b*) to the UK part of the relevant year as defined for Case 6 is a reference to the part corresponding, so far as possible, in accordance with the terms of the relevant ESC, to the UK part of that year.

(4) "The relevant ESC" means whichever of the extra-statutory concessions to which effect is given by Part 3 of this Schedule is relevant in the partner's case.

157 (1) This paragraph applies in determining whether the test in paragraph 110(1)(*c*) is met in relation to a tax year before the tax year 2013–14 (a "pre-commencement tax year").

(2) Paragraph 110(1) is to have effect as if for paragraph (*c*) there were substituted—

"(*c*) at least 4 out of the 7 tax years immediately preceding the year of departure was a tax year meeting the following conditions—

(i) the individual was resident in the UK for that year, and

(ii) there was no time in that year when the individual was Treaty non-resident (see paragraph 112(3))."

(3) Whether an individual was resident in the UK for a pre-commencement tax year is to be determined in accordance with the rules in force for determining an individual's residence for that pre-commencement tax year (and not in accordance with the statutory residence test).

158 (1) The existing temporary non-resident provisions, as in force immediately before the day on which this Act is passed, continue to have effect on and after that day in any case where the year of departure (as defined in Part 4 of this Schedule) is a tax year before the tax year 2013–14.

(2) Where those provisions continue to have effect by virtue of sub-paragraph (1)—

(*a*) the question of whether a person is or is not resident in the UK for the tax year 2013–14 or a subsequent tax year is to be determined for the purposes of those provisions in accordance with Part 1 of this Schedule, but

(*b*) the effect of Part 3 is to be ignored.

(3) The existing temporary non-resident provisions are—

(*a*) section 10A of TCGA 1992 (chargeable gains),

(*b*) section 576A of ITEPA 2003 (income withdrawals under certain foreign pensions),

(*c*) section 579CA of that Act (income withdrawals under registered pension schemes), and

(*d*) section 832A of ITTOIA (relevant foreign income charged on remittance basis).

159 Section 13 of FA 2012 (Champions League final 2013) is to be read and given effect, on and after the day on which this Act is passed, as if section 218 and this Schedule had not been enacted.

SCHEDULE 46

ORDINARY RESIDENCE

Section 219

Commentary—*Simon's Taxes* **E6.109**.

PART 1

INCOME TAX AND CAPITAL GAINS TAX: REMITTANCE BASIS OF TAXATION

Remittance basis restricted to non-doms

1 Chapter A1 of Part 14 of ITA 2007 (remittance basis) is amended as follows.

2 (*amends* ITA 2007 s 809A)

3 In section 809B (claim for remittance basis to apply)—

(*a*) (*amends* ITA 2007 s 809B(1)(*b*))

(*b*) (*repeals* ITA 2007 s 809B(2))

4 (*amends* ITA 2007 s 809D(1)(*b*), (1A))

5 (*amends* ITA 2007 s 809E(1)(*b*))

Treatment of relevant foreign earnings

6 ITEPA 2003 is amended as follows.

7 (1) (*substitutes* ITEPA 2003 s 22(*b*))

(2) (*amends* ITEPA 2003 s 22 section heading and preceding crosshead)

8 (*substitutes* ITEPA 2003 s 23(2)(*aa*))

9 (*amends* ITEPA 2003 s 26(1), section heading and preceding crosshead)

10 (*inserts* ITEPA 2003 s 26A)

11 (1) Section 41C (foreign securities income) is amended as follows.

(2), (3) (*substitute* ITEPA 2003 s 41C(4)(*b*), (6)(*b*))

12 (*amends* ITEPA 2003 s 271(2)(*a*), (*b*))

13 (1) (*substitutes* ITEPA 2003 s 554Z9(1)(*c*))

(2) (*amends* heading to ITEPA 2003 s 554Z9)

14 (1) (*substitutes* ITEPA 2003 s 554Z10(1)(*c*))

(2) (*amends* heading to ITEPA 2003 s 554Z10)

15 (1) Section 690 (employee non-resident etc) is amended as follows.

(2) (*substitutes* ITEPA 2003 s 690(1)(*a*))

(3) (*amends* ITEPA 2003 s 690(2A))

Consequential amendments

16 (*amends* TA 1988 s 266A(8)(*a*), (*b*))

17 (*substitutes* TCGA 1992 s 12(1))

18 (*amends* TCGA 1992 s 87B(1))

19 (*substitutes* ITA 2007 s 726(1))

20 (*substitutes* ITA 2007 s 730(1))

21 (*substitutes* ITA 2007 s 735(1))

22 (*amends* ITA 2007 s 809F(4))

23 (*amends* ITA 2007 s 809YD(3))

24 (*amends* ITA 2007 s 809Z7(2)(*d*), (3)(*a*))

Commencement

25 The amendments made by this Part of this Schedule have effect in relation to an individual's foreign income and gains for the tax year 2013–14 or any subsequent tax year.

Savings

26 (1) This paragraph applies to an individual who—

(*a*) was resident in the United Kingdom for the tax year 2012-13, but

(*b*) was not ordinarily resident there at the end of the tax year 2012–13.

(2) Enactments relating to income tax or capital gains tax have effect, in relation to any eligible foreign income and gains of the individual, as if the amendments made by this Part of this Schedule had not been made.

(3) "Eligible foreign income and gains" means—

(*a*) if the individual was resident in the United Kingdom for the tax year 2010–11 and the tax year 2011–12, foreign income and gains for the tax year 2013–14,

(*b*) if the individual was not resident in the United Kingdom for the tax year 2010–11 but was resident in the United Kingdom for the tax year 2011–12, foreign income and gains for the tax year 2013–14 and the tax year 2014–15, and

(*c*) if the individual was not resident in the United Kingdom for the tax year 2011–12, foreign income and gains for the tax year 2013–14, the tax year 2014–15 and the tax year 2015–16.

(4) Where, by virtue of this paragraph, it is necessary to determine whether an individual is (or is not) ordinarily resident in the United Kingdom at a time on or after 6 April 2013, the question is to be determined as it would have been in the absence of this Schedule.

Interpretation

27 References in this Part of this Schedule to an individual's "foreign income and gains" for a tax year are to be read in accordance with section 809Z7 of ITA 2007 (interpretation of remittance basis rules).

PART 2
INCOME TAX: ARISING BASIS OF TAXATION

ICTA

28 (*amends* TA 1988 s 614(4), (5))

ITEPA 2003

29 ITEPA 2003 is amended as follows.

30 In section 56 (application of Income Tax Acts in relation to deemed employment), in subsection (5)—

(*a*) (*substitutes* ITEPA 2003 s 56(5)(*a*))

(*b*) (*amends* ITEPA 2003 s 56(5)(*b*))

31 In section 61G (application of Income Tax Acts in relation to deemed employment), in subsection (5)—

(*a*) (*substitutes* ITEPA 2003 s 61G(5)(*a*))

(*b*) (*amends* ITEPA 2003 s 61G(5)(*b*))

32 (*amends* ITEPA 2003 s 328(5))

33 (*amends* ITEPA 2003 s 341(3))

34 (*amends* ITEPA 2003 s 342(6))

35 (*amends* ITEPA 2003 s 370(6))

36 (*amends* ITEPA 2003 s 376(1)(*b*))

37 (1) Section 378 (deductions from seafarers' earnings: eligibility) is amended as follows.

(2) (*amends* ITEPA 2003 s 378(1))

(3) (*substitutes* ITEPA 2003 s 378(5))

(4) (*repeals* ITEPA 2003 s 378(6))

38 (1) Section 413 (exception in certain cases of foreign service) is amended as follows.

(2), (4) (*amend* ITEPA 2003 s 413(2), (3))

(3), (5) (*insert* ITEPA 2003 s 413(2A), (3ZA))

39 (1) (*substitutes* ITEPA 2003 s 681A(4))

(2) The amendment made by this paragraph does not apply to a person who became a consular officer or employee in the United Kingdom before 6 April 2013.

40 (1) (*repeals* ITEPA 2003 Sch 2 para 8(2)(*b*))

(2) The amendments made by this paragraph do not apply to plans that have been approved before the day on which this Act is passed.

41 (1) (*repeals* ITEPA 2003 Sch 3 para 6(2)(*ca*))
(2) The amendments made by this paragraph do not apply to schemes that have been approved before the day on which this Act is passed.

42 (*amends* ITEPA 2003 Sch 5 para 27(3)(*b*))

ITTOIA 2005

43 ITTOIA 2005 is amended as follows.

44 (*amends* ITTOIA 2005 s 154A(1)(*a*))

45 (*amends* ITTOIA 2005 s 459(2))

46 (*substitutes* ITTOIA 2005 s 468(2))

47 (*amends* ITTOIA 2005 s 569(2))

48 (1) (*amends* ITTOIA 2005 s 636(2)(*b*))
(2) The amendment made by this paragraph does not apply in calculating income arising under a settlement in tax years ending before 6 April 2013.

49 (*amends* ITTOIA 2005 s 648(1)(*b*))

50 (*amends* ITTOIA 2005 s 651(3))

51 (*amends* ITTOIA 2005 s 664(2)(*b*)(i))

52 (1) Section 715 (interest from FOTRA securities held on trust) is amended as follows.
(2), (3) (*amend* ITTOIA 2005 s 715(1)(*b*), (2))
(4) In relation to a FOTRA security issued before 6 April 2013, the amendments made by this paragraph apply only if the security was acquired by the trust on or after that date.

53 (1) (*substitutes* ITTOIA 2005 s 771(4))
(2) The amendment made by this paragraph does not apply to a person who became a consular officer or employee in the United Kingdom before 6 April 2013.

ITA 2007

54 ITA 2007 is amended as follows.

55 (*amends* ITA 2007 s 465(4))

56 (1) Section 475 (residence of trustees) is amended as follows.
(2) (*substitutes* ITA 2007 s 475(1))
(3), (4) (*amend* ITA 2007 s 475(2))

57 (1) Section 476 (how to work out whether settlor meets condition C) is amended as follows.
(2), (3) (*amend* ITA 2007 s 476(2)(*b*), (3)(*b*))
(4) The amendment made by sub-paragraph (2) does not apply if the person died before 6 April 2013.
(5) The amendment made by sub-paragraph (3) does not apply if the settlement was made before 6 April 2013.

58 (*amends* ITA 2007 s 643(1))

59 (*amends* ITA 2007 s 718 (2)(*b*))

60 (*amends* ITA 2007 s 720(1))

61 (1) Section 721 (individuals with power to enjoy income as a result of relevant transactions) is amended as follows.
(2) (*amends* ITA 2007 s 721(1))
(3) (*inserts* ITA 2007 s 721(3A))
(4) (*substitutes* ITA 2007 s 721(5)(*b*))

62 (*amends* ITA 2007 s 727(1))

63 (1) Section 728 (individuals receiving capital sums as a result of relevant transactions) is amended as follows.
(2) (*inserts* ITA 2007 s 728(1)(*c*))
(3) (*substitutes* ITA 2007 s 728(3)(*b*))

64 (*amends* ITA 2007 s 732(1)(*b*))

65 (1) (*amends* ITA 2007 s 749(2))
(2) The amendment made by this paragraph applies only if the transfer is made or, in the case of an associated operation, the transfer is made and the associated operation is effected on or after 6 April 2013.

66 (*amends* ITA 2007 s 812(1)(*a*))

67 (1) (*amends* ITA 2007 s 834(3))
(2) The amendment made by this paragraph does not apply if D died before 6 April 2013.

68 (1) (*amends* ITA 2007 s 858(3)(*a*), (4); *partly repealed by* FA 2016 s 39, Sch 6 para 25(*c*)(i))
(2) The amendments made by this paragraph apply to the making of declarations on or after 6 April 2014, and any declarations made before that date continue to have effect in respect of interest paid on or after that date as if those amendments had not been made.

69 (1) (*amends* ITA 2007 s 859(3), (4); *partly repealed by* FA 2016 s 39, Sch 6 para 25(*c*)(ii))
(2) The amendments made by this paragraph apply to the making of declarations on or after 6 April 2014, and any declarations made before that date continue to have effect in respect of interest paid on or after that date as if those amendments had not been made.

70 (1) (*amended* ITA 2007 s 860(3); *repealed by* FA 2016 s 39, Sch 6 para 25(*c*)(iii))
(2) The amendment made by this paragraph applies only if the deceased died on or after 6 April 2014.

71 (1) Section 861 (declarations of non-UK residence: settlements) is amended as follows.
(2), (3) (*amend* ITA 2007 s 861(3)(*b*)(i), (iii), (4) (*b*), (*d*), (*f*); sub-para (3) *partly repealed by* FA 2016 s 39, Sch 6 para 25(*c*)(iv))
(4) The amendments made by this paragraph apply to the making of declarations on or after 6 April 2014, and any declarations made before that date continue to have effect in respect of interest paid on or after that date as if those amendments had not been made.

Commencement

72 (1) The amendments made by this Part of this Schedule have effect for the purposes of a person's liability to income tax for the tax year 2013–14 or any subsequent tax year.
(2) Sub-paragraph (1) is without prejudice to any provision in this Part of the Schedule about the application of a particular amendment.

Savings

73 (1) This paragraph applies to an individual who—
(*a*) was resident in the United Kingdom for the tax year 2012–13, but
(*b*) was not ordinarily resident there at the end of the tax year 2012–13.
(2) The provisions listed in sub-paragraph (3) have effect, in relation to such an individual and a qualifying tax year, as if the amendments made to or with respect to those provisions by this Part of this Schedule had not been made.
(3) The provisions are—
(*a*) section 413 of ITEPA 2003 (exception for payments and benefits on termination of employment etc in certain cases involving foreign service),
(*b*) section 414 of that Act (reduction in other cases of foreign service), and
(*c*) Chapter 2 of Part 13 of ITA 2007 (transfer of assets abroad).
(4) But, in the case of provisions within paragraph (*a*) or (*b*) of sub-paragraph (3), this paragraph applies only if service in the employment in question began before the start of the tax year 2013–14.
(5) The meaning of "qualifying tax year" depends on the individual's residence status—
(*a*) if the individual was resident in the United Kingdom for the tax year 2010–11 and the tax year 2011–12, "qualifying tax year" means the tax year 2013–14,
(*b*) if the individual was not resident in the United Kingdom for the tax year 2010–11 but was resident in the United Kingdom for the tax year 2011–12, "qualifying tax year" means each of the tax year 2013–14 and the tax year 2014–15, and
(*c*) if the individual was not resident in the United Kingdom for the tax year 2011–12, "qualifying tax year" means each of the tax year 2013–14, the tax year 2014–15 and the tax year 2015–16.
(6) Where, by virtue of this paragraph, it is necessary to determine whether an individual is (or is not) ordinarily resident in the United Kingdom at a time on or after 6 April 2013, the question is to be determined as it would have been in the absence of this Schedule.

PART 3
CAPITAL GAINS TAX: ACCRUALS BASIS OF TAXATION
TCGA 1992

74 TCGA 1992 is amended as follows.

75 (1) Section 2 (persons and gains chargeable to capital gains tax, and allowable losses) is amended as follows.
(2) (*amends* TCGA 1992 s 2(1))
(3) (*inserts* TCGA 1992 s 2(1A))

76 (*amends* TCGA 1992 s 10(1))

77 (1) Section 13 (attribution of gains to members of non-resident companies) is amended as follows.
(2)–(4) (*amend* TCGA 1992 s 13(2), (10), (13)(*b*))

78 (*amends* TCGA 1992 s 16(3))

79 (*amends* TCGA 1992 s 62(3))

80 (*amends* TCGA 1992 s 65(3)(*b*))

81 (*amends* TCGA 1992 s 67(6)(*a*))

82 (1) Section 69 (trustees of settlements) is amended as follows.
(2)–(4) (*amend* TCGA 1992 s 69(2), (2B)(*c*), (2E))

83 (*amends* TCGA 1992 s 76(1B)(*a*))

84 (*amends* TCGA 1992 s 80(1))

85 (1) Section 81 (death of trustee: special rules) is amended as follows.
(2)–(5) (*amend* TCGA 1992 s 81(1)(*b*), (3)(*b*), (4)(*b*), (5)(*a*))

86 (*amends* TCGA 1992 s 82(3)(*b*))

87 (*amends* TCGA 1992 s 83(1))

88 (1) Section 83A (trustees both resident and non-resident in a year of assessment) is amended as follows.
(2), (3) (*amend* TCGA 1992 s 83A(3)(*a*), (4)(*a*), (*b*))

89 (*amends* TCGA 1992 s 84(1)(*b*))

90 (*amends* TCGA 1992 s 85(1))

91 (1) Section 86 (attribution of gains to settlors with interest in non-resident or dual resident settlements) is amended as follows.
(2), (4) (*amend* TCGA 1992 s 86(1)(*c*), (3))
(3) (*substitutes* TCGA 1992 s 86(2))

92 (1) Section 87 (non-UK resident settlements: attribution of gains to beneficiaries) is amended as follows.
(2), (3) (*amend* TCGA 1992 s 87(1), (4)(*a*))

93 (*amends* TCGA 1992 s 88(1) (*a*), (*b*))

94 (1) Section 96 (payments by and to companies) is amended as follows.
(2)–(4) (*amend* TCGA 1992 s 96(3), (4)(*a*), (*b*), (5)(*b*))

95 (*amends* TCGA 1992 s 97(1)(*a*))

96 (*amends* TCGA 1992 s 99(1)(*c*))

97 (*amends* TCGA 1992 s 106A(5A)(*a*), (*b*))

98 (1) Section 159 (non-residents: roll-over relief) is amended as follows.
(2), (3) (*amend* TCGA 1992 s 159(2)(*b*), (5))

99 (1) Section 166 (gifts to non-residents) is amended as follows.
(2), (3) (*amend* TCGA 1992 s 166(1), (2)(*a*))

100 (1) Section 167 (gifts to foreign-controlled companies) is amended as follows.
(2), (3) (*amend* TCGA 1992 s 167(2)(*a*), (3))

101 (1) Section 168 (emigration of donee) is amended as follows.
(2)–(4) (*amend* TCGA 1992 s 168(1)(*b*), (4), (5)(*a*), (*b*))

102 (*amends* TCGA 1992 s 169(3)(*a*))

103 (*amends* TCGA 1992 s 199(2))

104 (1) Section 261 (section 260 relief: gifts to non-residents) is amended as follows.
(2), (3) (*amend* TCGA 1992 s 261(1), (2)(*a*))

105 (*amends* TCGA 1992 Sch 1 para 2(7)(*a*))

106 (1) Schedule 4A (disposal of interest in settled property: deemed disposal of underlying assets) is amended as follows.
(2), (3) (*amend* TCGA 1992 Sch 4A paras 5(1), (2), (6)(1))
(4) If any of the previous 5 years of assessment mentioned in paragraph 6(1) of Schedule 4A ends before 6 April 2013, the test in that paragraph is to be applied, as respects any such year ending before that date, as if that paragraph had not been amended by sub-paragraph (3).

107 (1) Schedule 4C (transfers of value: attribution of gains to beneficiaries) is amended as follows.
(2) (*amends* TCGA 1992 Sch 4C para 1A(3))
(3) (*amends* TCGA 1992 Sch 4C para 4(1), (2))
(4) (*amends* TCGA 1992 Sch 4C para 5(1)(*a*), (*b*))
(5) (*amends* TCGA 1992 Sch 4C para 9(3)(*a*)(i))
(6) (*amends* TCGA 1992 Sch 4C para 10(1))

108 (1) Schedule 5 (attribution of gains to settlors with interest in non-resident or dual resident settlement) is amended as follows.
(2) (*amends* TCGA 1992 Sch 5 para 2A(4)(*a*), (*b*))
(3) (*amends* TCGA 1992 Sch 5 para 9(4) (*a*), (*b*))
(4) The amendments made by this paragraph apply to changes in the residence status of trustees on or after 6 April 2013.

109 (1) Schedule 5A (settlements with foreign element: information) is amended as follows.
(2) (*amends* TCGA 1992 Sch 5A para 2(1)(*c*), (*d*))
(3) (*amends* TCGA 1992 Sch 5A para 3(1)(*a*), (*b*), (3))
(4) (*amends* TCGA 1992 Sch 5A para 4(1)(*a*), (*b*), (3))
(5) (*amends* TCGA 1992 Sch 5A para 5(1)(*a*), (*b*))
(6) The amendments made by this paragraph apply as follows—

(*a*) the amendments made by sub-paragraph (2) apply in relation to transfers of property made on or after 6 April 2013,

(*b*) the amendments made by sub-paragraphs (3) and (4) apply in relation to settlements created on or after that date, and

(*c*) the amendments made by sub-paragraph (5) apply to changes in the residence status of trustees on or after that date.

110 (1) Schedule 5B (enterprise investment scheme: re-investment) is amended as follows.
(2) (*amends* TCGA 1992 Sch 5B para 1(1)(*d*), (4)(*a*))
(3) (*amends* TCGA 1992 Sch 5B para 3(3)(*b*))
(4) (*amends* TCGA 1992 Sch 5B para 19(1))
(5) The amendments made by this paragraph apply in cases where the accrual time is on or after 6 April 2013 (even if the qualifying investment was made before that date).

111 (*substitutes* TCGA 1992 Sch 7C para 8(*a*))

Commencement

112 (1) The amendments made by this Part of this Schedule have effect in relation to a person's liability to capital gains tax for the tax year 2013–14 or any subsequent tax year.
(2) Sub-paragraph (1) is without prejudice to any provision in this Part of this Schedule about the application of a particular amendment.

PART 4
OTHER AMENDMENTS

FA 1916

113 (*repeals* FA 1916 s 63)

F(No 2)A 1931

114 (1) (*amends* F(No 2)A 1931 s 22(1)(*a*))
(2) Nothing in sub-paragraph (1) limits the power conferred by section 60(1) of FA 1940.
(3) Subject to sub-paragraph (5), the amendment made by sub-paragraph (1) does not affect a pre-commencement security (nor the availability of the relevant exemption).
(4) Sub-paragraph (5) applies to a person who becomes the beneficial owner of a pre-commencement security (or an interest in such a security) on or after 6 April 2013.
(5) If obtaining the relevant exemption is conditional on being not ordinarily resident in the United Kingdom, any enactment conferring the exemption is to have effect (in relation to a person to whom this sub-paragraph applies) as if obtaining the exemption were conditional instead on being not resident in the United Kingdom.
(6) In this paragraph—

"pre-commencement security" means a FOTRA security (as defined in section 713 of ITTOIA 2005) issued before the day on which this Act is passed;

"the relevant exemption", in relation to a pre-commencement security, means the exemption for which provision is made in the exemption condition (as defined in that section).

TMA 1970

115 TMA 1970 is amended as follows.

116 (1) (*amends* TMA 1970 s 98(4E)(*d*))
(2) The amendment made by this paragraph takes effect on the coming into force of regulations made under section 17(3) of F(No 2)A 2005 (authorised investment funds) by virtue of the amendment made by paragraph 136.

117 (*amends* TMA 1970 Sch 1A para 2(6))

IHTA 1984

118 (1) Section 157 of IHTA 1984 (non-residents' bank accounts) is amended as follows.
(2) (*substitutes* IHTA 1984 s 157(2))
(3), (4) *amend* IHTA 1984 s 157(3), (4)(*a*), (*b*))
(5) The amendments made by this paragraph do not apply if the person dies before 6 April 2013.

FA 2004

119 Part 4 of FA 2004 (pension schemes etc) is amended as follows.

120 (*amends* FA 2004 s 185G(3)(*a*))

121 (*amends* FA 2004 s 205(3))

122 (*amends* FA 2004 s 205A(3))

123 (*amends* FA 2004 s 206(3))

124 (*amends* FA 2004 s 207(3))

125 (*amends* FA 2004 s 208(4))

126 (*amends* FA 2004 s 209(5))

127 (*amends* FA 2004 s 217(5))

128 (*amends* FA 2004 s 237A(2))

129 (*amends* FA 2004 s 237B(8))

130 (*amends* FA 2004 s 239(4))

131 (*amends* FA 2004 s 242(3))

132 The amendments of Part 4 of FA 2004 made by this Part of this Schedule have effect in relation to the tax year 2013–14 and any subsequent tax year.

FA 2005

133 (1) (*substitutes* FA 2005 s 30(1)(*c*))
(2) The amendment made by this paragraph has effect in relation to the tax year 2013–14 and any subsequent tax year.

F(No 2)A 2005

134 F(No 2)A 2005 is amended as follows.

135 (1) (*amends* F(No 2)A 2005 s 7(3))
(2) The amendment made by this paragraph has effect in relation to the tax year 2013–14 and any subsequent tax year.

136 (*amends* F(No 2)A 2005 s 18(1)(*f*), (*g*))

CTA 2009

137 CTA 2009 is amended as follows.

138 (1) (*amends* CTA 2009 s 900(2))
(2) The amendment made by this paragraph applies in relation to gains accruing or treated as accruing on or after 6 April 2013.

139 (1) (*amends* CTA 2009 s 936(3))
(2) The amendment made by this paragraph applies if the tax year in question begins on or after 6 April 2013.

140 (1) (*amends* CTA 2009 s 947(2)(*b*)(i))
(2) The amendment made by this paragraph applies if the tax year in question begins on or after 6 April 2013.

141 (1) (*amends* CTA 2009 s 1009(5)(*a*))
(2) The amendment made by this paragraph applies in relation to shares acquired on or after 6 April 2013.

142 (1) (*amends* CTA 2009 s 1017(4)(*a*))
(2) The amendment made by this paragraph applies in relation to options obtained on or after 6 April 2013.

143 (1) (*amends* CTA 2009 s 1025(5)(*a*))
(2) The amendment made by this paragraph applies in relation to restricted shares acquired on or after 6 April 2013.

144 (1) (*amends* CTA 2009 s 1032(5)(*a*))
(2) The amendment made by this paragraph applies in relation to convertible shares acquired on or after 6 April 2013.

CTA 2010

145 (1) Section 1034 of CTA 2010 (purchase by unquoted trading company of own shares: requirements as to residence) is amended as follows.
(2), (3) (*amend* CTA 2010 s 1034(1)–(3))
(4) (*repeals* CTA 2010 s 1034(4))
(5) The amendments made by this paragraph do not apply in relation to a purchase by an unquoted trading company of its own shares if the purchase takes place before 6 April 2013.

TIOPA 2010

146 (*amends* TIOPA 2010 s 363A(3))

Constitutional Reform and Governance Act 2010

147 (1) (*amends* the Constitutional Reform and Governance Act 2010 s 41(2))
(2) The amendment made by this paragraph has effect for the purposes of a member's liability to income tax or capital gains tax for the tax year 2013–14 or any subsequent tax year.

SCHEDULE 50

PENALTIES: LATE FILING, LATE PAYMENT AND ERRORS

Section 230

Note—(*Please see Yellow Tax Handbook Part 1*)

FINANCE ACT 2014

(2014 Chapter 26)

AN ACT TO Grant certain duties, to alter other duties, and to amend the law relating to the National Debt and the Public Revenue, and to make further provision in connection with finance.

[17 July 2014]

CONTENTS

CHAPTER 3

ACCELERATED PAYMENT

Accelerated payment notices

PART 2
EXCISE DUTIES AND OTHER TAXES

Inheritance tax

117 Inheritance tax

Schedule 25 contains provision about inheritance tax.

Estate duty

118 Gifts to the nation: estate duty

(1) In Schedule 14 to FA 2012 (gifts to the nation), before paragraph 33 insert—

"**32A**

(1) This paragraph applies where a person ("the donor") makes a qualifying gift of an object in circumstances where, had the donor instead sold the object to an individual at market value, a charge to estate duty would have arisen under section 40 of FA 1930 on the proceeds of sale.

(2) At the time when the gift is made, estate duty becomes chargeable under that section as if the gift were such a sale (subject to any limitation imposed by paragraph 33(2)).

(3) In the application of this paragraph to Northern Ireland, the references to section 40 of FA 1930 are to be read as references to section 2 of the Finance Act (Northern Ireland) 1931."

(2) Subsection (3) applies where a person ("the donor") has, before the day on which this Act is passed, made a qualifying gift of an object in circumstances where, had the donor instead sold the object to an individual at market value, a charge to estate duty would have arisen under section 40 of FA 1930 on the proceeds of sale.

(3) No liability to estate duty under section 40 of FA 1930 arises in respect of the object on or after the day on which this Act is passed.

(4) In subsection (2) "qualifying gift" has the same meaning as in Schedule 14 to FA 2012.

(5) In the application of subsections (2) and (3) to Northern Ireland, the references to section 40 of FA 1930 are to be read as references to section 2 of the Finance Act (Northern Ireland) 1931.

PART 4
FOLLOWER NOTICES AND ACCELERATED PAYMENTS

CHAPTER 1
INTRODUCTION

Press releases etc—Tackling marketed tax avoidance—summary of responses to the consultation on extension of "accelerated payments": HMRC Notice 28 March 2014 (see *SWTI 2014, Issue 13*).

HMRC publishes list of avoidance schemes facing accelerated payments: HMRC Notice 15 July 2014 (see *SWTI 2014, Issue 29*).

Cross-references—See SSCBA 1992 s 11A (Parts 4 and 5 of FA 2014 apply with the necessary modifications, in relation to Class 2 contributions under SSCBA 1992 s 11(2) as if those contributions were income tax chargeable under ITTOIA 2005 Pt 2 Ch 2 in respect of profits of a trade, profession or vocation which is not carried on wholly outside the United Kingdom).

NICA 2015 Sch 2 Part 1 (Part 4 has effect with certain modifications for NICs purposes with effect from 12 April 2015; *see Part 3 of the Yellow Tax Handbook*).

FA 2016 Sch 18 para 40(1), (2) (penalty under FA 2016 Sch 18 para 30 not to be reduced by penalty under Part 4 where determined by reference to the same tax liability).

Overview

199 Overview of Part 4

In this Part—

(a) sections 200 to 203 set out the main defined terms used in the Part,

(b) Chapter 2 makes provision for follower notices and for penalties if account is not taken of judicial rulings which lay down principles or give reasoning relevant to tax cases,

(c) Chapter 3 makes—

(i) provision for accelerated payments to be made on account of tax,

(ii) provision restricting the circumstances in which payments of tax can be postponed pending an appeal, . . .[1]

(iii) provision to enable a court to prevent repayment of tax, for the purpose of protecting the public revenue[, and

(iv) provision restricting the surrender of losses and other amounts for the purposes of group relief.][1]

(d) Chapter 4—

(i) makes special provision about the application of this Part in relation to stamp duty land tax and annual tax for enveloped dwellings,

(ii) confers a power to extend the provisions of this Part to other taxes, and

(iii) makes amendments consequential on this Part.

Amendments—[1] Word "and" at the end of para (*c*)(ii) repealed, and para (*c*)(iv) and preceding word inserted, by FA 2015 s 118, Sch 18 paras 1, 2 with effect from 26 March 2015.

Main definitions

200 "Relevant tax"

In this Part, "relevant tax" means—

(a) income tax,

(b) capital gains tax,

(c) corporation tax, including any amount chargeable as if it were corporation tax or treated as if it were corporation tax,

[(ca) apprenticeship levy,][1]

(d) inheritance tax,

(e) stamp duty land tax, and

(f) annual tax on enveloped dwellings.

Cross-references—FA 2014 s 232 (Treasury power to amend s 200 to extend follower notices and accelerated payments provisions to any other tax).

Amendments[1] Para (*ca*) inserted by FA 2016 s 104(3), (4) with effect from 15 September 2016.

201 "Tax advantage" and "tax arrangements"

(1) This section applies for the purposes of this Part.

(2) "Tax advantage" includes—

(a) relief or increased relief from tax,

(b) repayment or increased repayment of tax,

(c) avoidance or reduction of a charge to tax or an assessment to tax,

(d) avoidance of a possible assessment to tax,

(e) deferral of a payment of tax or advancement of a repayment of tax, and

(f) avoidance of an obligation to deduct or account for tax.

(3) Arrangements are "tax arrangements" if, having regard to all the circumstances, it would be reasonable to conclude that the obtaining of a tax advantage was the main purpose, or one of the main purposes, of the arrangements.

(4) "Arrangements" includes any agreement, understanding, scheme, transaction or series of transactions (whether or not legally enforceable).

202 "Tax enquiry" and "return"

(1) This section applies for the purposes of this Part.

(2) "Tax enquiry" means—

(a) an enquiry under section 9A or 12AC of TMA 1970 (enquiries into self-assessment returns for income tax and capital gains tax), including an enquiry by virtue of notice being deemed to be given under section 9A of that Act by virtue of section 12AC(6) of that Act,

(b) an enquiry under paragraph 5 of Schedule 1A to that Act (enquiry into claims made otherwise than by being included in a return),

(c) an enquiry under paragraph 24 of Schedule 18 to FA 1998 (enquiry into company tax return for corporation tax etc), including an enquiry by virtue of notice being deemed to be given under that paragraph by virtue of section 12AC(6) of TMA 1970,

(d) an enquiry under paragraph 12 of Schedule 10 to FA 2003 (enquiries into SDLT returns),

(e) an enquiry under paragraph 8 of Schedule 33 to FA 2013 (enquiries into annual tax for enveloped dwellings returns), or

(f) a deemed enquiry under subsection (6).

(3) The period during which an enquiry is in progress—

(a) begins with the day on which notice of enquiry is given, and

(b) ends with the day on which the enquiry is completed.

(4) Subsection (3) is subject to subsection (6).

(5) In the case of inheritance tax, each of the following is to be treated as a return—

(a) an account delivered by a person under section 216 or 217 of IHTA 1984 (including an account delivered in accordance with regulations under section 256 of that Act);

(b) a statement or declaration which amends or is otherwise connected with such an account produced by the person who delivered the account;

(c) information or a document provided by a person in accordance with regulations under section 256 of that Act;

and such a return is to be treated as made by the person in question.

(6) An enquiry is deemed to be in progress, in relation to a return to which subsection (5) applies, during the period which—

(a) begins with the time the account is delivered or (as the case may be) the statement, declaration, information or document is produced, and

(b) ends when the person is issued with a certificate of discharge under section 239 of that Act, or is discharged by virtue of section 256(1)(b) of that Act, in respect of the return (at which point the enquiry is to be treated as completed).

203 "Tax appeal"

In this Part "tax appeal" means—

(a) an appeal under section 31 of TMA 1970 (income tax: appeals against amendments of self-assessment, amendments made by closure notices under section 28A or 28B of that Act, etc), including an appeal under that section by virtue of regulations under Part 11 of ITEPA 2003 (PAYE),

(b) an appeal under paragraph 9 of Schedule 1A to TMA 1970 (income tax: appeals against amendments made by closure notices under paragraph 7(2) of that Schedule, etc),

(c) an appeal under section 705 of ITA 2007 (income tax: appeals against counteraction notices),

(d) an appeal under paragraph 34(3) or 48 of Schedule 18 to FA 1998 (corporation tax: appeals against amendment of a company's return made by closure notice, assessments other than self-assessments, etc),

(e) an appeal under section 750 of CTA 2010 (corporation tax: appeals against counteraction notices),

[(ea) an appeal under section 114 of FA 2016 (apprenticeship levy: appeal against an assessment),][1]

(f) an appeal under section 222 of IHTA 1984 (appeals against HMRC determinations) other than an appeal made by a person against a determination in respect of a transfer of value at a time when a tax enquiry is in progress in respect of a return made by that person in respect of that transfer,

(g) an appeal under paragraph 35 of Schedule 10 to FA 2003 (stamp duty land tax: appeals against amendment of self-assessment, discovery assessments, etc),

(h) an appeal under paragraph 35 of Schedule 33 to FA 2013 (annual tax on enveloped dwellings: appeals against amendment of self-assessment, discovery assessments, etc), or

(i) an appeal against any determination of—

(i) an appeal within paragraphs (a) to (h), or

(ii) an appeal within this paragraph.

Commentary—*Simon's Taxes* **A7.247**.

Amendments[1] Para *(ea)* inserted by FA 2016 s 104(3), (5) with effect from 15 September 2016.

CHAPTER 2

FOLLOWER NOTICES

Giving of follower notices

204 Circumstances in which a follower notice may be given

(1) HMRC may give a notice (a "follower notice") to a person ("P") if Conditions A to D are met.

(2) Condition A is that—

(a) a tax enquiry is in progress into a return or claim made by P in relation to a relevant tax, or

(b) P has made a tax appeal (by notifying HMRC or otherwise) in relation to a relevant tax, but that appeal has not yet been—

(i) determined by the tribunal or court to which it is addressed, or

(ii) abandoned or otherwise disposed of.

(3) Condition B is that the return or claim or, as the case may be, appeal is made on the basis that a particular tax advantage ("the asserted advantage") results from particular tax arrangements ("the chosen arrangements").
(4) Condition C is that HMRC is of the opinion that there is a judicial ruling which is relevant to the chosen arrangements.
(5) Condition D is that no previous follower notice has been given to the same person (and not withdrawn) by reference to the same tax advantage, tax arrangements, judicial ruling and tax period.
(6) A follower notice may not be given after the end of the period of 12 months beginning with the later of—
- (a) the day on which the judicial ruling mentioned in Condition C is made, and
- (b) the day the return or claim to which subsection (2)(a) refers was received by HMRC or (as the case may be) the day the tax appeal to which subsection (2)(b) refers was made.

Cross-references—FA 2014 s 217 (transitional provision in relation to judicial rulings made before Royal Assent).
FA 2014 Sch 31 para 3 (follower notices in relation to partnership returns).

205 "Judicial ruling" and circumstances in which a ruling is "relevant"

(1) This section applies for the purposes of this Chapter.
(2) "Judicial ruling" means a ruling of a court or tribunal on one or more issues.
(3) A judicial ruling is "relevant" to the chosen arrangements if—
- (a) it relates to tax arrangements,
- (b) the principles laid down, or reasoning given, in the ruling would, if applied to the chosen arrangements, deny the asserted advantage or a part of that advantage, and
- (c) it is a final ruling.

(4) A judicial ruling is a "final ruling" if it is—
- (a) a ruling of the Supreme Court, or
- (b) a ruling of any other court or tribunal in circumstances where—
  - (i) no appeal may be made against the ruling,
  - (ii) if an appeal may be made against the ruling with permission, the time limit for applications has expired and either no application has been made or permission has been refused,
  - (iii) if such permission to appeal against the ruling has been granted or is not required, no appeal has been made within the time limit for appeals, or
  - (iv) if an appeal was made, it was abandoned or otherwise disposed of before it was determined by the court or tribunal to which it was addressed.

(5) Where a judicial ruling is final by virtue of sub-paragraph (ii), (iii) or (iv) of subsection (4)(b), the ruling is treated as made at the time when the sub-paragraph in question is first satisfied.

206 Content of a follower notice

A follower notice must—
- (a) identify the judicial ruling in respect of which Condition C in section 204 is met,
- (b) explain why HMRC considers that the ruling meets the requirements of section 205(3), and
- (c) explain the effects of sections 207 to 210.

Representations

207 Representations about a follower notice

(1) Where a follower notice is given under section 204, P has 90 days beginning with the day that notice is given to send written representations to HMRC objecting to the notice on the grounds that—
- (a) Condition A, B or D in section 204 was not met,
- (b) the judicial ruling specified in the notice is not one which is relevant to the chosen arrangements, or
- (c) the notice was not given within the period specified in subsection (6) of that section.

(2) HMRC must consider any representations made in accordance with subsection (1).
(3) Having considered the representations, HMRC must determine whether to—
- (a) confirm the follower notice (with or without amendment), or
- (b) withdraw the follower notice, and notify P accordingly.

Cross-references—FA 2014 s 231(6) (annual tax on enveloped dwellings: where follower notice or accelerated payment notice is given to more than one person, power conferred on P by this section is exercisable by each of those persons separately or by two or more jointly).

Penalties

208 Penalty if corrective action not taken in response to follower notice

(1) This section applies where a follower notice is given to P (and not withdrawn).
(2) P is liable to pay a penalty if the necessary corrective action is not taken in respect of the denied advantage (if any) before the specified time.

(3) In this Chapter "the denied advantage" means so much of the asserted advantage (see section 204(3)) as is denied by the application of the principles laid down, or reasoning given, in the judicial ruling identified in the follower notice under section 206(a).

(4) The necessary corrective action is taken in respect of the denied advantage if (and only if) P takes the steps set out in subsections (5) and (6).

(5) The first step is that—

(a) in the case of a follower notice given by virtue of section 204(2)(a), P amends a return or claim to counteract the denied advantage;

(b) in the case of a follower notice given by virtue of section 204(2)(b), P takes all necessary action to enter into an agreement with HMRC (in writing) for the purpose of relinquishing the denied advantage.

(6) The second step is that P notifies HMRC—

(a) that P has taken the first step, and

(b) of the denied advantage and (where different) the additional amount which has or will become due and payable in respect of tax by reason of the first step being taken.

(7) In determining the additional amount which has or will become due and payable in respect of tax for the purposes of subsection (6)(b), it is to be assumed that, where P takes the necessary action as mentioned in subsection (5)(b), the agreement is then entered into.

(8) In this Chapter—

"the specified time" means—

(a) if no representations objecting to the follower notice were made by P in accordance with subsection (1) of section 207, the end of the 90 day post-notice period;

(b) if such representations were made and the notice is confirmed under that section (with or without amendment), the later of—

(i) the end of the 90 day post-notice period, and

(ii) the end of the 30 day post-representations period;

"the 90 day post-notice period" means the period of 90 days beginning with the day on which the follower notice is given;

"the 30 day post-representations period" means the period of 30 days beginning with the day on which P is notified of HMRC's determination under section 207.

(9) No enactment limiting the time during which amendments may be made to returns or claims operates to prevent P taking the first step mentioned in subsection (5)(a) before the tax enquiry is closed (whether or not before the specified time).

(10) No appeal may be brought, by virtue of a provision mentioned in subsection (11), against an amendment made by a closure notice in respect of a tax enquiry to the extent that the amendment takes into account an amendment made by P to a return or claim in taking the first step mentioned in subsection (5)(a) (whether or not that amendment was made before the specified time).

(11) The provisions are—

(a) section 31(1)(b) or (c) of TMA 1970,

(b) paragraph 9 of Schedule 1A to TMA 1970,

(c) paragraph 34(3) of Schedule 18 to FA 1998,

(d) paragraph 35(1)(b) of Schedule 10 to FA 2003, and

(e) paragraph 35(1)(b) of Schedule 33 to FA 2013.

Definitions—"denied advantage" in relation to partnerships, FA 2014 Sch 31 para 4(3).

Modifications—FA 2014 Sch 31 para 4(2), (4) (in relation to a partnership follower notice, sub-s (2) applies as if reference to P were to each relevant partner; in sub-s (6)(*b*), words from "and (where different)" to the end to be ignored and sub-s (7) not to apply).

Cross-references—See FA 2014 Sch 31 para 4 (penalty for failure to take corrective action in response to partnership follower notice).

209 Amount of a section 208 penalty

(1) The penalty under section 208 is 50% of the value of the denied advantage.

(2) Schedule 30 contains provision about how the denied advantage is valued for the purposes of calculating penalties under this section.

(3) Where P before the specified time—

(a) amends a return or claim to counteract part of the denied advantage only, or

(b) takes all necessary action to enter into an agreement with HMRC (in writing) for the purposes of relinquishing part of the denied advantage only,

in subsections (1) and (2) the references to the denied advantage are to be read as references to the remainder of the denied advantage.

Modifications—FA 2014 Sch 31 para 5(2): in relation to a partnership follower notice, this section applies with the following modifications—

– the total amount of the penalties under s 208(2) for which the relevant partners are liable is 20% of the value of the denied advantage;

– the amount of the penalty for which each relevant partner is liable is that partner's appropriate share of that total amount; and

– the value of the denied advantage for the purposes of calculating the total amount of the penalties is: (i) in the case of a notice given under s 204(2)(*a*), the net amount of the amendments required to be made to the partnership return to counteract the denied advantage, and (ii) in the case of a notice given under s 204(2)(*b*), the net amount of the amendments that have been made to the partnership return to counteract the denied advantage, (and Sch 30 does not apply).

The Treasury has the power to vary the percentage rate (FA 2014 Sch 31 para 5(11)).

210 Reduction of a section 208 penalty for co-operation

(1) Where—

(a) P is liable to pay a penalty under section 208 of the amount specified in section 209(1),

(b) the penalty has not yet been assessed, and

(c) P has co-operated with HMRC,

HMRC may reduce the amount of that penalty to reflect the quality of that cooperation.

(2) In relation to co-operation, "quality" includes timing, nature and extent.

(3) P has co-operated with HMRC only if P has done one or more of the following—

(a) provided reasonable assistance to HMRC in quantifying the tax advantage;

(b) counteracted the denied advantage;

(c) provided HMRC with information enabling corrective action to be taken by HMRC;

(d) provided HMRC with information enabling HMRC to enter an agreement with P for the purpose of counteracting the denied advantage;

(e) allowed HMRC to access tax records for the purpose of ensuring that the denied advantage is fully counteracted.

(4) But nothing in this section permits HMRC to reduce a penalty to less than 10% of the value of the denied advantage.

Modifications—FA 2014 Sch 31 para 5(4), (5): in relation to a partnership follower notice, where—

– the relevant partners are liable to pay a penalty under s 208(2) as modified (see modification note following s 208),

– the penalties have not yet been assessed, and

– P has co-operated with HMRC,

sub-s (1) does not apply, but HMRC may reduce the total amount of the penalties determined in accordance with Sch 31 para 5(2)(*a*) to reflect the quality of that co-operation.

For these purposes—

– sub-ss (2), (3) apply in relation to the quality of co-operation, and

– HMRC may not reduce the total amount of the penalties to less than 4% of the value of the denied advantage.

The Treasury has the power to vary the minimum percentage (FA 2014 Sch 31 para 5(11)).

211 Assessment of a section 208 penalty

(1) Where a person is liable for a penalty under section 208, HMRC may assess the penalty.

(2) Where HMRC assess the penalty, HMRC must—

(a) notify the person who is liable for the penalty, and

(b) state in the notice a tax period in respect of which the penalty is assessed.

(3) A penalty under section 208 must be paid before the end of the period of 30 days beginning with the day on which the person is notified of the penalty under subsection (2).

(4) An assessment—

(a) is to be treated for procedural purposes in the same way as an assessment to tax (except in respect of a matter expressly provided for by this Chapter),

(b) may be enforced as if it were an assessment to tax, and

(c) may be combined with an assessment to tax.

(5) No penalty under section 208 may be notified under subsection (2) later than—

(a) in the case of a follower notice given by virtue of section 204(2)(a) (tax enquiry in progress), the end of the period of 90 days beginning with the day the tax enquiry is completed, and

(b) in the case of a follower notice given by virtue of section 204(2)(b) (tax appeal pending), the end of the period of 90 days beginning with the earliest of—

(i) the day on which P takes the necessary corrective action (within the meaning of section 208(4)),

(ii) the day on which a ruling is made on the tax appeal by P, or any further appeal in that case, which is a final ruling (see section 205(4)), and

(iii) the day on which that appeal, or any further appeal, is abandoned or otherwise disposed of before it is determined by the court or tribunal to which it is addressed.

(6) In this section a reference to an assessment to tax, in relation to inheritance tax, is to a determination.

212 Aggregate penalties

(1) Subsection (2) applies where—

(a) two or more penalties are incurred by the same person and fall to be determined by reference to an amount of tax to which that person is chargeable,

(b) one of those penalties is incurred under section 208, and

(c) one or more of the other penalties are incurred under a relevant penalty provision.

(2) The aggregate of the amounts of the penalties mentioned in subsection (1)(b) and (c), so far as determined by reference to that amount of tax, must not exceed—

(a) the relevant percentage of that amount, or

(b) in a case where at least one of the penalties is under paragraph 5(2)(b) or 6(3)(b), (4)(b) or (5)(b) of Schedule 55 to FA 2009, £300 (if greater).

(3) In the application of section 97A of TMA 1970 (multiple penalties), no account is to be taken of a penalty under section 208.

(4) "Relevant penalty provision" means—

(a) Schedule 24 to FA 2007 (penalties for errors),

(b) Schedule 41 to FA 2008 (penalties: failure to notify etc), . . . [1]

(c) Schedule 55 to FA 2009 (penalties for failure to make returns etc)[, ...[2]

(*d*) Part 5 of Schedule 18 to FA 2016 (serial tax avoidance)[,or][1]

(*e*) section 212A of FA 2013 (general anti-abuse rule).][2]

(5) "The relevant percentage" means—

(a) 200% in a case where at least one of the penalties is determined by reference to the percentage in—

(i) paragraph 4(4)(c) of Schedule 24 to FA 2007,

(ii) paragraph 6(4)(a) of Schedule 41 to FA 2008, or

(iii) paragraph 6(3A)(c) of Schedule 55 to FA 2009,

(b) 150% in a case where paragraph (a) does not apply and at least one of the penalties is determined by reference to the percentage in—

(i) paragraph 4(3)(c) of Schedule 24 to FA 2007,

(ii) paragraph 6(3)(a) of Schedule 41 to FA 2008, or

(iii) paragraph 6(3A)(b) of Schedule 55 to FA 2009,

(c) 140% in a case where neither paragraph (a) nor paragraph (b) applies and at least one the penalties is determined by reference to the percentage in—

(i) paragraph 4(4)(b) of Schedule 24 to FA 2007,

(ii) paragraph 6(4)(b) of Schedule 41 to FA 2008,

(iii) paragraph 6(4A)(c) of Schedule 55 to FA 2009,

(d) 105% in a case where none of paragraphs (a), (b) and (c) applies and at least one of the penalties is determined by reference to the percentage in—

(i) paragraph 4(3)(b) of Schedule 24 to FA 2007,

(ii) paragraph 6(3)(b) of Schedule 41 to FA 2008,

(iii) paragraph 6(4A)(b) of Schedule 55 to FA 2009, and

(e) in any other case, 100%.

Cross-references—See FA 2014 Sch 31 para 5(6): for the purposes of this section, a penalty imposed on a relevant partner by virtue of FA 2014 Sch 31 para 4(2) is to be treated as if it were determined by reference to such additional amount of tax as is due and payable by the relevant partner as a result of the counteraction of the denied advantage.

Amendments—[1] In sub-s (4)(*b*) word "or" at the end repealed, and para (*d*) and preceding word inserted, by FA 2016 Sch 18 para 60 with effect in relation to relevant defeats incurred after 15 September 2016 subject to FA 2016 Sch 18 para 64 (relevant defeats to be disregarded).

[2] In sub-s (4)(*c*), word "or" at the end repealed, and para (*e*) and preceding word inserted, by FA 2016 s 158(11) with effect in relation to tax arrangements (within the meaning of FA 2013 Pt 5) entered into on or after 15 September 2016.

213 Alteration of assessment of a section 208 penalty

(1) After notification of an assessment has been given to a person under section 211(2), the assessment may not be altered except in accordance with this section or on appeal.

(2) A supplementary assessment may be made in respect of a penalty if an earlier assessment operated by reference to an underestimate of the value of the denied advantage.

(3) An assessment or supplementary assessment may be revised as necessary if it operated by reference to an overestimate of the denied advantage; and, where more than the resulting assessed penalty has already been paid by the person to HMRC, the excess must be repaid.

214 Appeal against a section 208 penalty

(1) P may appeal against a decision of HMRC that a penalty is payable by P under section 208.

(2) P may appeal against a decision of HMRC as to the amount of a penalty payable by P under section 208.

(3) The grounds on which an appeal under subsection (1) may be made include in particular—

(a) that Condition A, B or D in section 204 was not met in relation to the follower notice,

(b) that the judicial ruling specified in the notice is not one which is relevant to the chosen arrangements,

(c) that the notice was not given within the period specified in subsection (6) of that section, or

(d) that it was reasonable in all the circumstances for P not to have taken the necessary corrective action (see section 208(4)) in respect of the denied advantage.

(4) An appeal under this section must be made within the period of 30 days beginning with the day on which notification of the penalty is given under section 211.

(5) An appeal under this section is to be treated in the same way as an appeal against an assessment to the tax concerned (including by the application of any provision about bringing the appeal by notice to HMRC, about HMRC's review of the decision or about determination of the appeal by the First-tier Tribunal or Upper Tribunal).

(6) Subsection (5) does not apply—

(a) so as to require a person to pay a penalty before an appeal against the assessment of the penalty is determined, or

(b) in respect of any other matter expressly provided for by this Part.

(7) In this section a reference to an assessment to tax, in relation to inheritance tax, is to a determination.

(8) On an appeal under subsection (1), the tribunal may affirm or cancel HMRC's decision.

(9) On an appeal under subsection (2), the tribunal may—

(a) affirm HMRC's decision, or

(b) substitute for HMRC's decision another decision that HMRC had power to make.

(10) The cancellation under subsection (8) of HMRC's decision on the ground specified in subsection (3)(d) does not affect the validity of the follower notice, or of any accelerated payment notice or partner payment notice under Chapter 3 related to the follower notice.

(11) In this section "tribunal" means the First-tier Tribunal or Upper Tribunal (as appropriate by virtue of subsection (5)).

Cross-references—See FA 2014 Sch 31 para 5(7)–(9): the right of appeal under this section extends to—

- a decision that penalties are payable by the relevant partners by virtue of Sch 31 para 5, and
- a decision as to the total amount of those penalties payable by those partners, but not to a decision as to the appropriate share of, or the amount of a penalty payable by, a relevant partner.

Such an appeal may be brought only by the representative partner or, if that partner is no longer available, the person who is for the time being the successor of that partner.

Partners and partnerships

215 Follower notices: treatment of partners and partnerships

Schedule 31 makes provision about the application of this Chapter in relation to partners and partnerships.

Appeals out of time

216 Late appeal against final judicial ruling

(1) This section applies where a final judicial ruling ("the original ruling") is the subject of an appeal by reason of a court or tribunal granting leave to appeal out of time.

(2) If a follower notice has been given identifying the original ruling under section 206(a), the notice is suspended until such time as HMRC notify P that—

(a) the appeal has resulted in a judicial ruling which is a final ruling, or

(b) the appeal has been abandoned or otherwise disposed of (before it was determined).

(3) Accordingly the period during which the notice is suspended does not count towards the periods mentioned in section 208(8).

(4) When a follower notice is suspended under subsection (2), HMRC must notify P as soon as reasonably practicable.

(5) If the new final ruling resulting from the appeal is not a judicial ruling which is relevant to the chosen arrangements (see section 205), the follower notice ceases to have effect at the end of the period of suspension.

(6) In any other case, the follower notice continues to have effect after the end of the period of suspension and, in a case within subsection (2)(a), is treated as if it were in respect of the new final ruling resulting from the appeal.

(7) The notice given under subsection (2) must—

(a) state whether subsection (5) or (6) applies, and

(b) where subsection (6) applies in a case within subsection (2)(a), make any amendments to the follower notice required to reflect the new final ruling.

(8) No new follower notice may be given in respect of the original ruling unless the appeal has been abandoned or otherwise disposed of before it is determined by the court or tribunal to which it is addressed.

(9) Nothing in this section prevents a follower notice being given in respect of a new final ruling resulting from the appeal.

(10) Where the appeal is abandoned or otherwise disposed of before it is determined by the court or tribunal to which it is addressed, for the purposes of the original ruling the period beginning when leave to appeal out of time was granted, and ending when the appeal is disposed of, does not count towards the period of 12 months mentioned in section 204(6).

Cross-references—FA 2014 s 217 (transitional provision in relation to judicial rulings made before Royal Assent).

Transitional provision

217 Transitional provision

(1) In the case of judicial rulings made before the day on which this Act is passed, this Chapter has effect as if for section 204(6) there were substituted—

"(6) A follower notice may not be given after—

(a) the end of the period of 24 months beginning with the day on which this Act is passed, or

(b) the end of the period of 12 months beginning with the day the return or claim to which subsection (2)(a) refers was received by HMRC or (as the case may be) with the day the tax appeal to which subsection (2)(b) refers was made,

whichever is later."

(2) Accordingly, the reference in section 216(10) to the period of 12 months includes a reference to the period of 24 months mentioned in the version of section 204(6) set out in subsection (1) above.

Defined terms

218 Defined terms used in Chapter 2

For the purposes of this Chapter—

"arrangements" has the meaning given by section 201(4);

"the asserted advantage" has the meaning given by section 204(3);

"the chosen arrangements" has the meaning given by section 204(3);

"the denied advantage" has the meaning given by section 208(3);

"follower notice" has the meaning given by section 204(1);

"HMRC" means Her Majesty's Revenue and Customs;

"judicial ruling", and "relevant" in relation to a judicial ruling and the chosen arrangements, have the meaning given by section 205;

"relevant tax" has the meaning given by section 200;

"the specified time" has the meaning given by section 208(8);

"tax advantage" has the meaning given by section 201(2);

"tax appeal" has the meaning given by section 203;

"tax arrangements" has the meaning given by section 201(3);

"tax enquiry" has the meaning given by section 202(2);

"tax period" means a tax year, accounting period or other period in respect of which tax is charged;

"P" has the meaning given by section 204(1);

"the 30 day post-representations period" has the meaning given by section 208(8);

"the 90 day post-notice period" has the meaning given by section 208(8).

Press releases etc—Tackling marketed tax avoidance—summary of responses to the consultation on extension of "accelerated payments": HMRC Notice 28 March 2014 (see *SWTI 2014, Issue 13*).

HMRC publishes list of avoidance schemes facing accelerated payments: HMRC Notice 15 July 2014 (see *SWTI 2014, Issue 29*).

Commentary—*Simon's Taxes* **A4.230**.

CHAPTER 3

ACCELERATED PAYMENT

Accelerated payment notices

219 Circumstances in which an accelerated payment notice may be given

(1) HMRC may give a notice (an "accelerated payment notice") to a person ("P") if Conditions A to C are met.

(2) Condition A is that—

(a) a tax enquiry is in progress into a return or claim made by P in relation to a relevant tax, or

(b) P has made a tax appeal (by notifying HMRC or otherwise) in relation to a relevant tax but that appeal has not yet been—

(i) determined by the tribunal or court to which it is addressed, or

(ii) abandoned or otherwise disposed of.

(3) Condition B is that the return or claim or, as the case may be, appeal is made on the basis that a particular tax advantage ("the asserted advantage") results from particular arrangements ("the chosen arrangements").

(4) Condition C is that one or more of the following requirements are met—

(a) HMRC has given (or, at the same time as giving the accelerated payment notice, gives) P a follower notice under Chapter 2—

(i) in relation to the same return or claim or, as the case may be, appeal, and

(ii) by reason of the same tax advantage and the chosen arrangements;

(b) the chosen arrangements are DOTAS arrangements;

(c) a GAAR counteraction notice has been given in relation to the asserted advantage or part of it and the chosen arrangements (or is so given at the same time as the accelerated payment notice) in a case where the stated opinion of at least two of the members of the sub-panel of the GAAR Advisory Panel which considered the matter under paragraph 10 of Schedule 43 to FA 2013 was as set out in paragraph 11(3)(b) of that Schedule (entering into tax arrangements not reasonable course of action etc).

[(*d*) a notice has been given under paragraph 8(2) or 9(2) of Schedule 43A to FA 2013 (notice of final decision after considering Panel's opinion about referred or counteracted arrangements) in relation to the asserted advantage or part of it and the chosen arrangements (or is so given at the same time as the accelerated payment notice) in a case where the stated opinion of at least two of the members of the sub-panel of the GAAR Advisory Panel about the other arrangements (see subsection (8)) was as set out in paragraph 11(3)(*b*) of Schedule 43 to FA 2013;

(*e*) a notice under paragraph 8(2) of Schedule 43B to FA 2013 (GAAR: generic referral of tax arrangements) has been given in relation to the asserted advantage or part of it and the chosen arrangements (or is so given at the same time as the accelerated payment notice) in a case where the stated opinion of at least two of the members of the sub-panel of the GAAR Advisory Panel which considered the generic referral in respect of those arrangements under paragraph 6 of Schedule 43B to FA 2013 was as set out in paragraph 6(4)(*b*) of that Schedule.][1]

(5) "DOTAS arrangements" means—

(a) notifiable arrangements to which HMRC has allocated a reference number under section 311 of FA 2004,

(b) notifiable arrangements implementing a notifiable proposal where HMRC has allocated a reference number under that section to the proposed notifiable arrangements, or

(c) arrangements in respect of which the promoter must provide prescribed information under section 312(2) of that Act by reason of the arrangements being substantially the same as notifiable arrangements within paragraph (a) or (b).

(6) But the notifiable arrangements within subsection (5) do not include arrangements in relation to which HMRC has given notice under section 312(6) of FA 2004 (notice that promoters not under duty imposed to notify client of reference number).

(7) "GAAR counteraction notice" means a notice under paragraph 12 of Schedule 43 to FA 2013 (notice of final decision to counteract under the general anti-abuse rule).

[(8) In subsection (4)(*d*) "other arrangements" means—

(*a*) in relation to a notice under paragraph 8(2) of Schedule 43A to FA 2013, the referred arrangements (as defined in that paragraph);

(*b*) in relation to a notice under paragraph 9(2) of that Schedule, the counteracted arrangements (as defined in paragraph 2 of that Schedule).][1]

Modifications—Where HMRC have issued a notice that a company may not surrender a specified amount by way of group relief, and the company has already claimed an amount, the company must amend its return to reflect any amounts already surrendered. Where such amendment cannot take effect because there is an open enquiry into the return, FA 2014 s 225A(7), (8) modifies s 219 to allow HMRC to issue the APN.

Simon's Tax Cases—*R (on the appn of Walapu) v R&C Comrs* [2016] EWHC 658 (Admin), [2016] STC 1682.

Amendments—[1] Sub-ss (4)(*d*), (*e*), (8) inserted by FA 2016 s 157(18)–(20) with effect in relation to tax arrangements (within the meaning of FA 2013 Pt 5) entered into at any time (whether before on or after 15 September 2016).

220 Content of notice given while a tax enquiry is in progress

(1) This section applies where an accelerated payment notice is given by virtue of section 219(2)(a) (notice given while a tax enquiry is in progress).

(2) The notice must—

(a) specify the paragraph or paragraphs of section 219(4) by virtue of which the notice is given,

(b) specify the payment [(if any)][1] required to be made under section 223 and the requirements of that section, . . . [1]

(c) explain the effect of sections 222 and 226, and of the amendments made by sections 224 and 225 (so far as relating to the relevant tax in relation to which the accelerated payment notice is given)[, and

(*d*) if the denied advantage consists of or includes an asserted surrenderable amount, specify that amount and any action which is required to be taken in respect of it under section 225A.][1]

(3) The payment required to be made under section 223 is an amount equal to the amount which a designated HMRC officer determines, to the best of that officer's information and belief, as the understated tax.

(4) "The understated tax" means the additional amount that would be due and payable in respect of tax if—

(a) in the case of a notice given by virtue of section 219(4)(a) (cases where a follower notice is given)—

(i) it were assumed that the explanation given in the follower notice in question under section 206(b) is correct, and

(ii) the necessary corrective action were taken under section 208 in respect of what the designated HMRC officer determines, to the best of that officer's information and belief, as the denied advantage;

(b) in the case of a notice given by virtue of section 219(4)(b) (cases where the DOTAS requirements are met), such adjustments were made as are required to counteract what the designated HMRC officer determines, to the best of that officer's information and belief, as the denied advantage;

(c) in the case of a notice given by virtue of section 219(4)(c)[, (*d*) or (*e*)][2] (cases involving counteraction under the general anti-abuse rule), such of the adjustments set out in the GAAR counteraction notice as have effect to counteract the denied advantage were made.

[(4A) "Asserted surrenderable amount" means so much of a surrenderable loss as a designated HMRC officer determines, to the best of that officer's information and belief, to be an amount—

(*a*) which would not be a surrenderable loss of P if the position were as stated in paragraphs (*a*), (*b*) or (*c*) of subsection (4), and

(*b*) which is not the subject of a claim by P for relief from corporation tax reflected in the understated tax amount (and hence in the payment required to be made under section 223).

(4B) "Surrenderable loss" means a loss or other amount within section 99(1) of CTA 2010 (or part of such a loss or other amount).][1]

(5) "The denied advantage"—

(a) in the case of a notice given by virtue of section 219(4)(a), has the meaning given by section 208(3),

(b) in the case of a notice given by virtue of section 219(4)(b), means so much of the asserted advantage as is not a tax advantage which results from the chosen arrangements or otherwise, and

(c) in the case of a notice given by virtue of section 219(4)(c)[, (*d*) or (*e*)][2], means so much of the asserted advantage as would be counteracted by making the adjustments set out in the GAAR counteraction notice.

(6) If a notice is given by reason of two or all of the requirements in section 219(4) being met, [any payment specified under subsection (2)(*b*) or amount specified under subsection (2)(*d*)][1] is to be determined as if the notice were given by virtue of such one of them as is stated in the notice as being used for this purpose.

(7) "The GAAR counteraction notice" means the notice [under—

(*a*) paragraph 12 of Schedule 43 to FA 2013,

(*b*) paragraph 8 or 9 of Schedule 43A to that Act, or

(*c*) paragraph 8 of Schedule 43B to that Act,

as the case may be.][2]

Amendments—[1] In sub-s (2)(*b*), words inserted and word "and" repealed, sub-s (2)(*d*) and preceding word inserted, sub-ss (4A), (4B) inserted, and in sub-s (6), words substituted, by FA 2015 s 118, Sch 18 paras 1, 3 with effect from 26 March 2015.

[2] In sub-ss (4)(*c*), (5)(*c*), words inserted, and in sub-s (7), words substituted for words "under paragraph 12 of Schedule 43 to FA 2013 (notice of final decision to counteract under the general anti-abuse rule)." by FA 2016 s 157(21) with effect in relation to tax arrangements (within the meaning of FA 2013 Pt 5) entered into at any time (whether before on or after 15 September 2016).

221 Content of notice given pending an appeal

(1) This section applies where an accelerated payment notice is given by virtue of section 219(2)(b) (notice given pending an appeal).

(2) The notice must—

(a) specify the paragraph or paragraphs of section 219(4) by virtue of which the notice is given,

(b) specify the disputed tax [(if any)][1], . . . [1]

(c) explain the effect of section 222 and of the amendments made by sections 224 and 225 so far as relating to the relevant tax in relation to which the accelerated payment notice is given[, and

(*d*) if the denied advantage consists of or includes an asserted surrenderable amount (within the meaning of section 220(4A)), specify that amount and any action which is required to be taken in respect of it under section 225A.][1]

(3) "The disputed tax" means so much of the amount of the charge to tax arising in consequence of—

(a) the amendment or assessment to tax appealed against, or

(b) where the appeal is against a conclusion stated by a closure notice, that conclusion,

as a designated HMRC officer determines, to the best of the officer's information and belief, as the amount required to ensure the counteraction of what that officer so determines as the denied advantage.

(4) "The denied advantage" has the same meaning as in section 220(5).

(5) If a notice is given by reason of two or all of the requirements in section 219(4) being met, the denied advantage is to be determined as if the notice were given by virtue of such one of them as is stated in the notice as being used for this purpose.

(6) In this section a reference to an assessment to tax, in relation to inheritance tax, is to a determination.

Cross-references—F(No 2)A 2015 Sch 8 para 2(3)(*c*) (disputed tax specified in a notice under sub-s (2)(*b*) are relevant sums for the purposes of scheme for enforcement by deduction from accounts (direct recovery of debts)).

Amendments—[1] In sub-s (2)(*b*), words inserted and word "and" repealed, and sub-s (2)(*d*) and preceding word inserted, by FA 2015 s 118, Sch 18 paras 1, 4 with effect from 26 March 2015.

222 Representations about a notice

(1) This section applies where an accelerated payment notice has been given under section 219 (and not withdrawn).

(2) P has 90 days beginning with the day that notice is given to send written representations to HMRC—

(a) objecting to the notice on the grounds that Condition A, B or C in section 219 was not met, . . . [1]

(b) objecting to the amount specified in the notice under section 220(2)(b) or section 221(2)(b)[, or

(*c*) objecting to the amount specified in the notice under section 220(2)(*d*) or section 221(2)(*d*).][1]

(3) HMRC must consider any representations made in accordance with subsection (2).

(4) Having considered the representations, HMRC must—

(a) if representations were made under subsection (2)(a), determine whether—

(i) to confirm the accelerated payment notice (with or without amendment), or

(ii) to withdraw the accelerated payment notice, . . . [1]

(b) if representations were made under subsection (2)(b) (and the notice is not withdrawn under paragraph (a)), determine whether a different amount [(or no amount)][1] ought to have been specified under section 220(2)(b) or section 221(2)(b), and then—

(i) confirm the amount specified in the notice, . . . [1]

(ii) amend the notice to specify a different amount[, or

(iii) remove from the notice the provision made under section 220(2)(*b*) or section 221(2)(*b*), and

(*c*) if representations were made under subsection (2)(*c*) (and the notice is not withdrawn under paragraph (*a*)), determine whether a different amount (or no amount) ought to have been specified under section 220(2)(*d*) or 221(2)(*d*), and then—

(i) confirm the amount specified in the notice,

(ii) amend the notice to specify a different amount, or

(iii) remove from the notice the provision made under section 220(2)(*d*) or section 221(2)(*d*),][1]

and notify P accordingly.

Cross-references—FA 2014 s 231(6) (annual tax on enveloped dwellings: where follower notice or accelerated payment notice is given to more than one person, power conferred on P by this section is exercisable by each of those persons separately or by two or more jointly).

Amendments—[1] In sub-ss (2)(*a*), (4)(*a*)(ii), (*b*)(i), word repealed, sub-s (2)(*c*) and preceding word inserted, in sub-s (4)(*b*), words inserted, and sub-s (4)(*b*)(iii), (*c*) inserted, by FA 2015 s 118, Sch 18 paras 1, 5 with effect from 26 March 2015.

Forms of accelerated payment

223 Effect of notice given while tax enquiry is in progress[: accelerated payment]

[(1) This section applies where—

(*a*) an accelerated payment notice is given by virtue of section 219(2)(*a*) (notice given while a tax enquiry is in progress) (and not withdrawn), and

(*b*) an amount is stated in the notice in accordance with section 220(2)(*b*).][1]

(2) P must make a payment ("the accelerated payment") to HMRC of [that amount][1].

(3) The accelerated payment is to be treated as a payment on account of the understated tax (see section 220).

(4) The accelerated payment must be made before the end of the payment period.

(5) "The payment period" means—

(a) if P made no representations under section 222, the period of 90 days beginning with the day on which the accelerated payment notice is given, and

(b) if P made such representations, whichever of the following periods ends later—

(i) the 90 day period mentioned in paragraph (a);

(ii) the period of 30 days beginning with the day on which P is notified under section 222 of HMRC's determination.

(6) But where the understated tax would be payable by instalments by virtue of an election made under section 227 of IHTA 1984, to the extent that the accelerated payment relates to tax payable by an instalment which falls to be paid at a time after the payment period, the accelerated payment must be made no later than that time.
(7) If P pays any part of the understated tax before the accelerated payment in respect of it, the accelerated payment is treated to that extent as having been paid at the same time.
(8) Any tax enactment which relates to the recovery of a relevant tax applies to an amount to be paid on account of the relevant tax under this section in the same manner as it applies to an amount of the relevant tax.
(9) "Tax enactment" means provisions of or made under—
(a) the Tax Acts,
(b) any enactment relating to capital gains tax,
(c) IHTA 1984 or any other enactment relating to inheritance tax,
(d) Part 4 of FA 2003 or any other enactment relating to stamp duty land tax, or
(e) Part 3 of FA 2013 or any other enactment relating to annual tax on enveloped dwellings.

Cross-references—See FA 2014 s 226 (where sub-s (6) applies to require an amount of the accelerated payment to be paid before a later time than the end of the payment period, references in sub-ss (2) and (5) to the end of that period are to be read, in relation to that amount, as references to that later time).
F(No 2)A 2015 Sch 8 para 2(3)(*b*) (sums due under this section are relevant sums for the purposes of scheme for enforcement by deduction from accounts (direct recovery of debts)).

Amendments—[1] In heading, words inserted, sub-s (1) substituted, and words in sub-s (2) substituted, by FA 2015 s 118, Sch 18 paras 1, 6 with effect from 26 March 2015.

224 Restriction on powers to postpone tax payments pending initial appeal
(1) (*inserts* TMA 1970 s 55(8B)–(8D))
(2) (*inserts* IHTA 1984 s 242(4))
(3) (*inserts* FA 2003 Sch 10 para 39(9)–(11))
(4) (*inserts* FA 2003 Sch 10 para 40(4))
(5) (*inserts* FA 2013 Sch 33 para 48(8A)–(8C))
(6) (*inserts* FA 2013 Sch 33 para 49(4))

225 Protection of the revenue pending further appeals
(1) (*inserts* TMA 1970 s 56(4)–(6))
(2) (*inserts* FA 2003 Sch 10 para 43(3)–(5))
(3) (*inserts* FA 2013 Sch 33 para 53(3)–(5))

[Prevention of surrender of losses

225A Effect of notice: surrender of losses ineffective, etc
(1) This section applies where—
(*a*) an accelerated payment notice is given (and not withdrawn), and
(*b*) an amount is specified in the notice in accordance with section 220(2)(*d*) or 221(2)(*d*).
(2) P may not consent to any claim for group relief in respect of the amount so specified.
(3) Subject to subsection (2), paragraph 75 (other than sub-paragraphs (7) and (8)) of Schedule 18 to FA 1998 (reduction in amount available for surrender) has effect as if the amount so specified ceased to be an amount available for surrender at the time the notice was given to P.
(4) For the purposes of subsection (3), paragraph 75 of that Schedule has effect as if, in sub-paragraph (2) of that paragraph for "within 30 days" there were substituted "before the end of the payment period (within the meaning of section 223(5) of the Finance Act 2014)".
(5) The time limits otherwise applicable to amendment of a company tax return do not prevent an amendment being made in accordance with paragraph 75(6) of Schedule 18 to FA 1998 where, pursuant to subsection (3), a claimant company receives—
(*a*) notice of the withdrawal of consent under paragraph 75(3) of that Schedule, or
(*b*) a copy of a notice containing directions under paragraph 75(4) of that Schedule.
(6) Subsection (7) applies where—
(*a*) a company makes such an amendment to its company tax return at a time when an enquiry is in progress into the return, and
(*b*) paragraph 31(3) of that Schedule prevents the amendment from taking effect until the enquiry is completed.
(7) Section 219 (circumstances in which an accelerated payment notice may be given) has effect, in its application to that company in a case where section 219(2)(*a*) applies (tax enquiry in progress), as if—
(*a*) for the purposes of section 219(3), that amendment to the return had not been made,
(*b*) in section 219(4), after paragraph (*c*) there were inserted—
"(*d*) P has amended its company tax return, in accordance with paragraph 75(6) of Schedule 18 to FA 1998, in circumstances where pursuant to section 225A(3), P has received—

(i) notice of the withdrawal of consent under paragraph 75(3) of that Schedule, or

(ii) a copy of a notice containing directions under paragraph 75(4) of that Schedule,

but paragraph 31(3) of that Schedule prevents that amendment having effect.",

(*c*) in section 220(4), after paragraph (*c*) there were inserted—

"(*d*) in the case of a notice given by virtue of section 219(4)(*d*) (cases involving withdrawal of consent for losses claimed), it were assumed that P had never made the claim to group relief to which the amendment to its company tax return relates.", and

(*d*) in section 227(10), for "or (*c*)" there were substituted ", (*c*) or (*d*)".

(8) Subsections (2) and (3) are subject to—

(*a*) section 227(14) to (16) (provision about claims for group relief, and consents to claims, following amendment or withdrawal of an accelerated payment notice), and

(*b*) section 227A (provision about claims for group relief, and consents to claims, once tax position finally determined).][1]

Amendments—[1] Section 225A and preceding crosshead inserted by FA 2015 s 118, Sch 18 paras 1, 7 with effect from 26 March 2015. Subsection (3) has effect in relation to an amount specified in a notice in accordance with FA 2014 s 220(2)(*d*) or s 221(2)(*d*), whether the consent to a claim for group relief was given, or the claim itself was made, before or on or after 26 March 2015.

Penalties

226 Penalty for failure to pay accelerated payment

(1) This section applies where an accelerated payment notice is given by virtue of section 219(2)(a) (notice given while tax enquiry is in progress) (and not withdrawn).

(2) If any amount of the accelerated payment is unpaid at the end of the payment period, P is liable to a penalty of 5% of that amount.

(3) If any amount of the accelerated payment is unpaid after the end of the period of 5 months beginning with the penalty day, P is liable to a penalty of 5% of that amount.

(4) If any amount of the accelerated payment is unpaid after the end of the period of 11 months beginning with the penalty day, P is liable to a penalty of 5% of that amount.

(5) "The penalty day" means the day immediately following the end of the payment period.

(6) Where section 223(6) (accelerated payment payable by instalments when it relates to inheritance tax payable by instalments) applies to require an amount of the accelerated payment to be paid before a later time than the end of the payment period, references in subsections (2) and (5) to the end of that period are to be read, in relation to that amount, as references to that later time.

(7) Paragraphs 9 to 18 (other than paragraph 11(5)) of Schedule 56 to FA 2009 (provisions which apply to penalties for failures to make payments of tax on time) apply, with any necessary modifications, to a penalty under this section in relation to a failure by P to pay an amount of the accelerated payment as they apply to a penalty under that Schedule in relation to a failure by a person to pay an amount of tax.

Cross-references—See FA 2014 Sch 32 para 7 (application of this section in relation to accelerated partner payments).

FA 2014 s 231 (annual tax on enveloped dwellings: joint and several liability in respect of accelerated payment or penalty under this section).

Withdrawal etc of accelerated payment notice

227 Withdrawal, modification or suspension of accelerated payment notice

(1) In this section a "Condition C requirement" means one of the requirements set out in Condition C in section 219.

(2) Where an accelerated payment notice has been given, HMRC may, at any time, by notice given to P—

(a) withdraw the notice,

(b) where the notice is given by virtue of more than one Condition C requirement being met, withdraw it to the extent it is given by virtue of one of those requirements (leaving the notice effective to the extent that it was also given by virtue of any other Condition C requirement and has not been withdrawn), . . . [1]

(c) reduce the amount specified in the accelerated payment notice under section 220(2)(b) or 221(2)(b)[, or

(*d*) reduce the amount specified in the accelerated payment notice under section 220(2)(*d*) or 221(2)(*d*).][1]

(3) Where—

(a) an accelerated payment notice is given by virtue of the Condition C requirement in section 219(4)(a), and

(b) the follower notice to which it relates is withdrawn,

HMRC must withdraw the accelerated payment notice to the extent it was given by virtue of that requirement.

(4) Where—

(a) an accelerated payment notice is given by virtue of the Condition C requirement in section 219(4)(a), and

(b) the follower notice to which it relates is amended under section 216(7)(b) (cases where there is a new relevant final judicial ruling following a late appeal),

HMRC may by notice given to P make consequential amendments (whether under subsection (2)(c) [or (d)][1] or otherwise) to the accelerated payment notice.

(5) Where—

(a) an accelerated payment notice is given by virtue of the Condition C requirement in section 219(4)(b), and

(b) HMRC give notice under section 312(6) of FA 2004 with the result that promoters are no longer under the duty in section 312(2) of that Act in relation to the chosen arrangements,

HMRC must withdraw the notice to the extent it was given by virtue of that requirement.

(6) Subsection (7) applies where—

(a) an accelerated payment notice is withdrawn to the extent that it was given by virtue of a Condition C requirement,

(b) that requirement is the one stated in the notice for the purposes of section 220(6) or 221(5) (calculation of amount of the accelerated payment or of the denied advantage [etc][1]), and

(c) the notice remains effective to the extent that it was also given by virtue of any other Condition C requirement.

(7) HMRC must, by notice given to P—

(a) modify the accelerated payment notice so as to state the remaining, or one of the remaining, Condition C requirements for the purposes of section 220(6) or 221(5), . . .[1]

(b) if the amount of the accelerated payment or (as the case may be) the amount of the disputed tax determined on the basis of the substituted Condition C requirement is less than the amount specified in the notice, amend that notice under subsection (2)(c) to substitute the lower amount[, and

(*c*) if the amount of the asserted surrenderable amount is less than the amount specified in the notice, amend the notice under subsection (2)(*d*) to substitute the lower amount.][1]

(8) If a follower notice is suspended under section 216 (appeals against final rulings made out of time) for any period, an accelerated payment notice in respect of the follower notice is also suspended for that period.

(9) Accordingly, the period during which the accelerated payment notice is suspended does not count towards the periods mentioned in the following provisions—

(a) section 223;

(b) section 55(8D) of TMA 1970;

(c) paragraph 39(11) of Schedule 10 to FA 2003;

(d) paragraph 48(8C) of Schedule 33 to FA 2013.

(10) But the accelerated payment notice is not suspended under subsection (8) if it was also given by virtue of section 219(4)(b) or (c) and has not, to that extent, been withdrawn.

(11) In a case within subsection (10), subsections (6) and (7) apply as they would apply were the notice withdrawn to the extent that it was given by virtue of section 219(4)(a), except that any change made to the notice under subsection (7) has effect during the period of suspension only.

(12) Where an accelerated payment notice is withdrawn, it is to be treated as never having had effect (and any accelerated payment made in accordance with, or penalties paid by virtue of, the notice are to be repaid).

[(12A) Where, as a result of an accelerated payment notice specifying an amount under section 220(2)(*d*) or 221(2)(*d*), a notice of consent by P to a claim for group relief in respect of the amount specified (or part of it) became ineffective by virtue of section 225A(3), nothing in subsection (12) operates to revive that notice.][1]

(13) If, as a result of a modification made under subsection (2)(c), more than the resulting amount of the accelerated payment has already been paid by P, the excess must be repaid.

[(14) If the accelerated payment notice is amended under subsection (2)(*d*) or withdrawn—

(*a*) section 225A(2) and (3) (which prevents consent being given to group relief claims) cease to apply in relation to the released amount, and

(*b*) a claim for group relief may be made in respect of any part of the released amount within the period of 30 days after the day on which the notice is amended or withdrawn.

(15) The time limits otherwise applicable to amendment of a company tax return do not apply to the extent that it makes a claim for group relief within the time allowed by subsection (14).

(16) "The released amount" means—

(*a*) in a case where the accelerated payment notice is amended under subsection (2)(*d*), the amount represented by the reduction, and

(*b*) in a case where the accelerated payment notice is withdrawn, the amount specified under section 220(2)(*d*) or 221(2)(*d*).][1]

Cross-references—See FA 2014 Sch 32 para 8 (application of this section in relation to accelerated partner payment notices).

Amendments—[1] The following amendments made by FA 2015 s 118, Sch 18 paras 1, 8 with effect from 26 March 2015—

- in sub-ss (2)(*b*), (7)(*a*), words repealed;
- sub-ss (2)(*d*), (7)(*c*) and preceding words inserted;
- in sub-ss (4), (6)(*b*), word inserted; and
- sub-ss (12A), (14)–(16) inserted.

[Group relief claims after accelerated payment notices

227A Group relief claims after accelerated payment notices

(1) This section applies where as a result of an accelerated payment notice given to P—

(*a*) P was prevented from consenting to a claim for group relief in respect of an amount under section 225A(2), or

(*b*) pursuant to section 225A(3), a consent given by P to a claim for group relief in respect of an amount was ineffective.

(2) If a final determination establishes that the amount P has available to surrender consists of or includes the amount referred to in subsection (1)(*a*) or (*b*) or a part of it ("the allowed amount")—

(*a*) section 225A(2) and (3) (which prevents consent being given to group relief claims) ceases to apply in relation to the allowed amount, and

(*b*) a claim for group relief in respect of any part of the allowed amount may be made within the period of 30 days after the relevant time.

(3) The time limits otherwise applicable to amendment of a company tax return do not apply to an amendment to the extent that it makes a claim for group relief in respect of any part of the allowed amount within the time limit allowed by subsection (2)(*b*).

(4) In this section—

"final determination" means—

(*a*) a conclusion stated in a closure notice under paragraph 34 of Schedule 18 to FA 1998 against which no appeal is made;

(*b*) the final determination of a tax appeal within paragraph (*d*) or (*e*) of section 203;

"relevant time" means—

(*a*) in a case within paragraph (*a*) above, the end of the period during which the appeal could have been made;

(*b*) in the case within paragraph (*b*) above, the end of the day on which the final determination occurs.][1]

Amendments—[1] Section 227A and preceding crosshead inserted by FA 2015 s 118, Sch 18 paras 1, 9 with effect from 26 March 2015.

Partners and partnerships

228 Accelerated partner payments

Schedule 32 makes provision for accelerated partner payments and modifies this Chapter in relation to partnerships.

Defined terms

229 Defined terms used in Chapter 3

In this Chapter—

"the accelerated payment" has the meaning given by section 223(2);

"accelerated payment notice" has the meaning given by section 219(1);

"arrangements" has the meaning given by section 201(4);

"the asserted advantage" has the meaning given by section 219(3);

"the chosen arrangements" has the meaning given by section 219(3), except in Schedule 32 where it has the meaning given by paragraph 3(3) of that Schedule;

"the denied advantage" has the meaning given by section 220(5), except in paragraph 4 of Schedule 32 where it has the meaning given by paragraph 4(4) of that Schedule;

"designated HMRC officer" means an officer of Revenue and Customs who has been designated by the Commissioners for the purposes of this Part;

"follower notice" has the meaning given by section 204(1);

"HMRC" means Her Majesty's Revenue and Customs;

"P" has the meaning given by section 219(1);

"partner payment notice" has the meaning given by paragraph 3 of Schedule 32;

"relevant tax" has the meaning given by section 200;

"tax advantage" has the meaning given by section 201(2);

"tax appeal" has the meaning given by section 203;

"tax enquiry" has the meaning given by section 202(2).

CHAPTER 4
MISCELLANEOUS AND GENERAL PROVISION

Stamp duty land tax and annual tax on enveloped dwellings

230 Special case: stamp duty land tax

(1) This section applies to modify the application of this Part in the case of—
- (a) a return or claim in respect of stamp duty land tax, or
- (b) a tax appeal within section 203(g), or any appeal within section 203(i) which derives from such an appeal.

(2) If two or more persons acting jointly are the purchasers in respect of the land transaction—
- (a) anything required or authorised by this Part to be done in relation to P must be done in relation to all of those persons, and
- (b) any liability of P in respect of an accelerated payment, or a penalty under this Part, is a joint and several liability of all of those persons.

(3) Subsection (2) is subject to subsections (4) to (8).

(4) If the land transaction was entered into by or on behalf of the members of a partnership—
- (a) anything required or authorised to be done under this Part in relation to P is required or authorised to be done in relation to all the responsible partners, and
- (b) any liability of P in respect of an accelerated payment, or a penalty under this Part, is a joint and several liability of the responsible partners.

(5) But nothing in subsection (4) enables—
- (a) an accelerated payment to be recovered from a person who did not become a responsible partner until after the effective date of the transaction in respect of which the tax to which the accelerated payment relates is payable, or
- (b) a penalty under this Part to be recovered from a person who did not become a responsible partner until after the time when the omission occurred that caused the penalty to become payable.

(6) Where the trustees of a settlement are liable to pay an accelerated payment or a penalty under this Part, the payment or penalty may be recovered (but only once) from any one or more of the responsible trustees.

(7) But nothing in subsection (6) enables a penalty to be recovered from a person who did not become a responsible trustee until after the time when the omission occurred that caused the penalty to become payable.

(8) Where a follower notice or accelerated payment notice is given to more than one person, the power conferred on P by section 207 or 222 is exercisable by each of those persons separately or by two or more of them jointly.

(9) In this section—

"the accelerated payment" has the meaning given by section 223(2);

"accelerated payment notice" has the meaning given by section 219(1);

"effective date", in relation to a land transaction, has the meaning given by section 119 of FA 2003;

"follower notice" has the meaning given by section 204(1);

"the responsible partners", in relation to a land transaction, has the meaning given by paragraph 6(2) of Schedule 15 to that Act;

"the responsible trustees" has the meaning given by paragraph 5(3) of Schedule 16 to that Act;

"P"—
- (a) in relation to Chapter 2, has the meaning given by section 204(1);
- (b) in relation to Chapter 3, has the meaning given by section 219.

231 Special case: annual tax on enveloped dwellings

(1) This section applies to modify the application of this Part in the case of—
- (a) a return or claim in respect of annual tax on enveloped dwellings, or
- (b) a tax appeal within section 203(h), or any appeal within section 203(i) which derives from such an appeal.

(2) If the responsible partners of a partnership are the chargeable person in relation to the tax to which the return or claim or appeal relates—
- (a) anything required or authorised by this Part to be done in relation to P must be done in relation to all of those partners, and
- (b) any liability of P in respect of an accelerated payment, or a penalty under this Part, is a joint and several liability of all of those persons.

(3) Where—
- (a) a follower notice is given by virtue of a tax enquiry into the return or claim or the appeal, and
- (b) by virtue of section 97 or 98 of FA 2013, two or more persons would have been jointly and severally liable for an additional amount of tax had the necessary corrective action been taken before the specified time for the purposes of section 208,

any liability of P in respect of a penalty under that section is a joint and several liability of all of them.

(4) Where—

(a) an accelerated payment notice is given by virtue of a tax enquiry into the return or claim or the appeal, and

(b) two or more persons would, by virtue of section 97 or 98 of FA 2013, be jointly and severally liable for the understated tax relating to the accelerated payment specified in the notice or (as the case may be) the disputed tax specified in the notice,

any liability of P in respect of the accelerated payment or a penalty under section 226 is a joint and several liability of all of them.

(5) Accordingly—

(a) where a follower notice is given in a case where subsection (3) applies, or

(b) an accelerated payment notice is given in a case to which subsection (4) applies,

HMRC must also give a copy of the notice to any other person who would be jointly and severally liable for a penalty or payment, in relation to the notice, by virtue of this section.

(6) Where a follower notice or accelerated payment notice is given to more than one person, the power conferred on P by section 207 or 222 is exercisable by each of those persons separately or by two or more of them jointly.

(7) In this section—

"the accelerated payment" has the meaning given by section 223(2);

"accelerated payment notice" has the meaning given by section 219(1);

"the chargeable person" has the same meaning as in Part 3 of FA 2013 (annual tax on enveloped dwellings);

"follower notice" has the same meaning as in Chapter 2;

"P"—

(a) in relation to Chapter 2, has the meaning given by section 204(1);

(b) in relation to Chapter 3, has the meaning given by section 219;

"the responsible partners" has the same meaning as in Part 3 of FA 2013 (annual tax on enveloped dwellings).

Extension of Part by order

232 Extension of this Part by order

(1) The Treasury may by order amend section 200 (definition of "relevant tax") so as to extend this Part to any other tax.

(2) An order under this section may include—

(a) provision in respect of that other tax corresponding to the provision made by sections 224 and 225,

(b) consequential and supplemental provision, and

(c) transitional and transitory provision and savings.

(3) For the purposes of subsection (1) or (2) an order under this section may amend this Part (other than this section) or any other enactment whenever passed or made.

(4) The power to make orders under this section is exercisable by statutory instrument.

(5) An order under this section may only be made if a draft of the instrument containing the order has been laid before and approved by a resolution of the House of Commons.

(6) In this section "tax" includes duty.

Consequential amendments

233 Consequential amendments

Schedule 33 contains consequential amendments.

PART 5

PROMOTERS OF TAX AVOIDANCE SCHEMES

Commentary—*Simon's Taxes* **A7.250**.

Cross-references—See SSCBA 1992 s 11A (Parts 4 and 5 of FA 2014 apply with the necessary modifications, in relation to Class 2 contributions under SSCBA 1992 s 11(2) as if those contributions were income tax chargeable under ITTOIA 2005 Pt 2 Ch 2 in respect of profits of a trade, profession or vocation which is not carried on wholly outside the United Kingdom).

NICA 2015 Sch 2 Part 2 (Part 5 has effect with certain modifications for NICs purposes with effect from 12 April 2015; *see Part 3 of the Yellow Tax Handbook*).

Introduction

234 Meaning of "relevant proposal" and "relevant arrangements"

(1) "Relevant proposal" means a proposal for arrangements which (if entered into) would be relevant arrangements (whether the proposal relates to a particular person or to any person who may seek to take advantage of it).

(2) Arrangements are "relevant arrangements" if—

(a) they enable, or might be expected to enable, any person to obtain a tax advantage, and
(b) the main benefit, or one of the main benefits, that might be expected to arise from the arrangements is the obtaining of that advantage.

(3) "Tax advantage" includes—
(a) relief or increased relief from tax,
(b) repayment or increased repayment of tax,
(c) avoidance or reduction of a charge to tax or an assessment to tax,
(d) avoidance of a possible assessment to tax,
(e) deferral of a payment of tax or advancement of a repayment of tax, and
(f) avoidance of an obligation to deduct or account for tax.

(4) "Arrangements" includes any agreement, scheme, arrangement or understanding of any kind, whether or not legally enforceable, involving a single transaction or two or more transactions.

235 Carrying on a business "as a promoter"

(1) A person carrying on a business in the course of which the person is, or has been, a promoter in relation to a relevant proposal or relevant arrangements carries on that business "as a promoter".

(2) A person is a "promoter" in relation to a relevant proposal if the person—
(a) is to any extent responsible for the design of the proposed arrangements,
(b) makes a firm approach to another person in relation to the relevant proposal with a view to making the proposal available for implementation by that person or any other person, or
(c) makes the relevant proposal available for implementation by other persons.

(3) A person is a "promoter" in relation to relevant arrangements if the person—
(a) is by virtue of subsection (2)(b) or (c), a promoter in relation to a relevant proposal which is implemented by the arrangements, or
(b) is responsible to any extent for the design, organisation or management of the arrangements.

(4) For the purposes of this Part a person makes a firm approach to another person in relation to a relevant proposal if—
(a) the person communicates information about the relevant proposal to the other person at a time when the proposed arrangements have been substantially designed,
(b) the communication is made with a view to that other person or any other person entering into transactions forming part of the proposed arrangements, and
(c) the information communicated includes an explanation of the tax advantage that might be expected to be obtained from the proposed arrangements.

(5) For the purposes of subsection (4) proposed arrangements have been substantially designed at any time if by that time the nature of the transactions to form them (or part of them) has been sufficiently developed for it to be reasonable to believe that a person who wished to obtain the tax advantage mentioned in subsection (4)(c) might enter into—
(a) transactions of the nature developed, or
(b) transactions not substantially different from transactions of that nature.

(6) A person is not a promoter in relation to a relevant proposal or relevant arrangements by reason of anything done in prescribed circumstances.

(7) Regulations under subsection (6) may contain provision having retrospective effect.

Regulations—Promoters of Tax Avoidance Schemes (Prescribed Circumstances under Section 235) Regulations, SI 2015/130.

236 Meaning of "intermediary"

For the purposes of this Part a person ("A") is an intermediary in relation to a relevant proposal if—
(a) A communicates information about the relevant proposal to another person in the course of a business,
(b) the communication is made with a view to that other person, or any other person, entering into transactions forming part of the proposed arrangements, and
(c) A is not a promoter in relation to the relevant proposal.

Conduct notices

237 Duty to give conduct notice

(1) Subsections (5) to (9) apply if an authorised officer becomes aware at any time that a person ("P") who is carrying on a business as a promoter—
(a) has, in the period of 3 years ending with that time, met one or more threshold conditions, and
(b) was carrying on a business as a promoter when P met that condition.

[(1A) Subsections (5) to (9) also apply if an authorised officer becomes aware at any time ("the relevant time") that—
(*a*) a person has, in the period of 3 years ending with the relevant time, met one or more threshold conditions,
(*b*) at the relevant time another person ("P") meets one or more of those conditions by virtue of Part 2 of Schedule 34 (meeting the threshold conditions: bodies corporate and partnerships), and
(*c*) P is, at the relevant time, carrying on a business as a promoter.][1]

(2) Part 1 of Schedule 34 sets out the threshold conditions and describes how they are met.
(3) Part 2 of that Schedule contains provision about [when a person is treated as meeting a threshold condition][1].
(4) See also Schedule 36 (which contains provision about the meeting of threshold conditions and other conditions by partnerships).
[(5) The authorised officer must determine—
(*a*) in a case within subsection (1), whether or not P's meeting of the condition mentioned in subsection (1)(*a*) (or, if more than one condition is met, the meeting of all of those conditions, taken together) should be regarded as significant in view of the purposes of this Part, or
(*b*) in a case within subsection (1A), whether or not—
(i) the meeting of the condition by the person as mentioned in subsection (1A)(*a*) (or, if more than one condition is met, the meeting of all of those conditions, taken together), and
(ii) P's meeting of the condition (or conditions) as mentioned in subsection (1A)(*b*),
should be regarded as significant in view of those purposes.][1]
(6) Subsection (5) does not apply if a conduct notice or a monitoring notice already has effect in relation to P.
(7) If the authorised officer determines under [subsection (5)(*a*)][1] that P's meeting of the condition or conditions in question should be regarded as significant, the officer must give P a conduct notice, unless subsection (8) applies.
[(7A) If the authorised officer determines under subsection (5)(*b*) that both—
(*a*) the meeting of the condition or conditions by the person as mentioned in subsection (1A)(*a*), and
(*b*) P's meeting of the condition or conditions as mentioned in subsection (1A)(*b*),
should be regarded as significant, the officer must give P a conduct notice, unless subsection (8) applies.][1]
(8) This subsection applies if the authorised officer determines that, having regard to the extent of the impact that P's activities as a promoter are likely to have on the collection of tax, it is inappropriate to give P a conduct notice.
(9) The authorised officer must determine under subsection (5) that the meeting of the condition (or all the conditions) . . . [1] should be regarded as significant if the condition (or any of the conditions) is in any of the following paragraphs of Schedule 34—
(a) paragraph 2 (deliberate tax defaulters);
(b) paragraph 3 (breach of Banking Code of Practice);
(c) paragraph 4 (dishonest tax agents);
(d) paragraph 6 (persons charged with certain offences);
(e) paragraph 7 (opinion notice of GAAR Advisory Panel).
[(10) If, as a result of subsection (1A), subsections (5) to (9) apply to a person, this does not prevent the giving of a conduct notice to the person mentioned in subsection (1A)(*a*).][1]

Press releases etc—Queen's Speech 2014—Bills with tax implications (including NICs Bill proposals which would mirror the Finance Act 2014 conduct notices and monitoring provisions for NICs purposes) (see *SWTI 2014, Issue 23*)
Definitions—"authorised officer" (for the purposes of Part 5), s 283(2); "threshold condition", Sch 34 paras 2–12.
Cross-references—See FA 2014 Sch 32 paras 5, 6 (conduct notices and monitoring notices given to partnerships).
Amendments—[1] Sub-ss (1A), (7A), (10) inserted, sub-s (5) substituted, words in sub-ss (3), (7) substituted, and in sub-s (9), words repealed, by FA 2015 s 119, Sch 19 paras 1, 2 with effect for the purposes of determining whether a person meets a threshold condition in a period of three years ending on or after 26 March 2015.

[237A Duty to give conduct notice: defeat of promoted arrangements
(1) If an authorised officer becomes aware at any time ("the relevant time") that a person ("P") who is carrying on a business as a promoter meets any of the conditions in subsections (11) to (13), the officer must determine whether or not P's meeting of that condition should be regarded as significant in view of the purposes of this Part.
But see also subsection (14).
(2) An authorised officer must make the determination set out in subsection (3) if the officer becomes aware at any time ("the section 237A(2) relevant time") that—
(*a*) a person meets a condition in subsection (11), (12) or (13), and
(*b*) at the section 237A(2) relevant time another person ("P"), who is carrying on a business as a promoter, meets that condition by virtue of Part 4 of Schedule 34A (meeting the section 237A conditions: bodies corporate and partnerships).
(3) The authorised officer must determine whether or not—
(*a*) the meeting of the condition by the person as mentioned in subsection (2)(*a*), and
(*b*) P's meeting of the condition as mentioned in subsection (2)(*b*),
should be regarded as significant in view of the purposes of this Part.
(4) Subsections (1) and (2) do not apply if a conduct notice or monitoring notice already has effect in relation to P.

(5) Subsection (1) does not apply if, at the relevant time, an authorised officer is under a duty to make a determination under section 237(5) in relation to P.
(6) Subsection (2) does not apply if, at the section 237A(2) relevant time, an authorised officer is under a duty to make a determination under section 237(5) in relation to P.
(7) But in a case where subsection (1) does not apply because of subsection (5), or subsection (2) does not apply because of subsection (6), subsection (5) of section 237 has effect as if—
- (*a*) the references in paragraph (*a*) of that subsection to "subsection (1)", and "subsection (1)(*a*)" included subsection (1) of this section, and
- (*b*) in paragraph (*b*) of that subsection the reference to "subsection (1A)(*a*)" included a reference to subsection (2)(*a*) of this section and the reference to subsection (1A)(*b*) included a reference to subsection (2)(*b*) of this section.

(8) If the authorised officer determines under subsection (1) that P's meeting of the condition in question should be regarded as significant, the officer must give P a conduct notice, unless subsection (10) applies.
(9) If the authorised officer determines under subsection (3) that—
- (*a*) the meeting of the condition by the person as mentioned in subsection (2)(*a*), and
- (*b*) P's meeting of the condition as mentioned in subsection (2)(*b*), should be regarded as significant in view of the purposes of this Part, the officer must give P a conduct notice, unless subsection (10) applies.

(10) This subsection applies if the authorised officer determines that, having regard to the extent of the impact that P's activities as a promoter are likely to have on the collection of tax, it is inappropriate to give P a conduct notice.
(11) The condition in this subsection is that in the period of 3 years ending with the relevant time at least 3 relevant defeats have occurred in relation to P.
(12) The condition in this subsection is that at least two relevant defeats have occurred in relation to P at times when a single defeat notice under section 241A(2) or (6) had effect in relation to P.
(13) The condition in this subsection is that at least one relevant defeat has occurred in relation to P at a time when a double defeat notice under section 241A(3) had effect in relation to P.
(14) A determination that the condition in subsection (12) or (13) is met cannot be made unless—
- (*a*) the defeat notice in question still has effect when the determination is made, or
- (*b*) the determination is made on or before the 90th day after the day on which the defeat notice in question ceased to have effect.

(15) Schedule 34A sets out the circumstances in which a "relevant defeat" occurs in relation to a person and includes provision limiting what can amount to a further relevant defeat in relation to a person (see paragraph 6).][1]

Cross-references—See FA 2016 s 160(20)–(25) (circumstances in which defeats are treated for the purposes of this section as not having occurred).
Amendments—[1] Sections 237A–237D inserted by FA 2016 s 160(1), (2) with effect from 15 September 2016.

[237B Duty to give further conduct notice where provisional notice not complied with
(1) An authorised officer must give a conduct notice to a person ("P") who is carrying on a business as a promoter if—
- (*a*) a conduct notice given to P under section 237A(8)—
  - (i) has ceased to have effect otherwise than as a result of section 237D(2) or 241(3) or (4), and
  - (ii) was provisional immediately before it ceased to have effect,
- (*b*) the officer determines that P had failed to comply with one or more conditions in the conduct notice,
- (*c*) the conduct notice relied on a Case 3 relevant defeat,
- (*d*) since the time when the conduct notice ceased to have effect, one or more relevant defeats falling within subsection (2) have occurred in relation to—
  - (i) P, and
  - (ii) any arrangements to which the Case 3 relevant defeat also relates, and
- (*e*) had that relevant defeat or (as the case may be) those relevant defeats, occurred before the conduct notice ceased to have effect, an authorised officer would have been required to notify the person under section 237C(3) that the notice was no longer provisional.

(2) A relevant defeat falls within this subsection if it occurs by virtue of Case 1 or Case 2 in Schedule 34A.
(3) Subsection (1) does not apply if the authorised officer determines that, having regard to the extent of the impact that the person's activities as a promoter are likely to have on the collection of tax, it is inappropriate to give the person a conduct notice.
(4) Subsection (1) does not apply if a conduct notice or monitoring notice already has effect in relation to the person.
(5) For the purposes of this Part a conduct notice "relies on a Case 3 relevant defeat" if it could not have been given under the following condition.

The condition is that paragraph 9 of Schedule 34A had effect with the substitution of "100% of the tested arrangements" for "75% of the tested arrangements".][1]

Amendments—[1] Sections 237A–237D inserted by FA 2016 s 160(1), (2) with effect from 15 September 2016.

[237C When a conduct notice given under section 237A(8) is "provisional"

(1) This section applies to a conduct notice which—

(*a*) is given to a person under section 237A(8), and

(*b*) relies on a Case 3 relevant defeat.

(2) The notice is "provisional" at all times when it has effect, unless an authorised officer notifies the person that the notice is no longer provisional.

(3) An authorised officer must notify the person that the notice is no longer provisional if subsection (4) or (5) applies.

(4) This subsection applies if—

(*a*) the condition in subsection (5)(*a*) is not met, and

(*b*) a full relevant defeat occurs in relation to P.

(5) This subsection applies if—

(*a*) two, or all three, of the relevant defeats by reference to which the conduct notice is given would not have been relevant defeats if paragraph 9 of Schedule 34A had effect with the substitution of "100% of the tested arrangements" for "75% of the tested arrangements", and

(*b*) the same number of full relevant defeats occur in relation to P.

(6) A "full relevant defeat" occurs in relation to P if—

(*a*) a relevant defeat occurs in relation to P otherwise than by virtue of Case 3 in paragraph 9 of Schedule 34A, or

(*b*) circumstances arise which would be a relevant defeat in relation to P by virtue of paragraph 9 of Schedule 34A if that paragraph had effect with the substitution of "100% of the tested arrangements" for "75% of the tested arrangements".

(7) In determining under subsection (6) whether a full relevant defeat has occurred in relation to P, assume that in paragraph 6 of Schedule 34A (provision limiting what can amount to a further relevant defeat in relation to a person) the first reference to a "relevant defeat" does not include a relevant defeat by virtue of Case 3 in paragraph 9 of Schedule 34A.][1]

Amendments—[1] Sections 237A–237D inserted by FA 2016 s 160(1), (2) with effect from 15 September 2016.

[237D Judicial ruling upholding asserted tax advantage: effect on conduct notice which is provisional

(1) Subsection (2) applies if at any time—

(*a*) a conduct notice which relies on a Case 3 relevant defeat (see section 237B(5)) is provisional, and

(*b*) a court or tribunal upholds a corresponding tax advantage which has been asserted in connection with any of the related arrangements to which that relevant defeat relates (see paragraph 5(2) of Schedule 34A).

(2) The conduct notice ceases to have effect when that judicial ruling becomes final.

(3) An authorised officer must give the person to whom the conduct notice was given a written notice stating that the conduct notice has ceased to have effect.

(4) For the purposes of this section, a tax advantage is "asserted" in connection with any arrangements if a person makes a return, claim or election on the basis that the tax advantage arises from those arrangements.

In relation to the arrangements mentioned in paragraph (*b*) of subsection (1) "corresponding tax advantage" means a tax advantage corresponding to any tax advantage the counteraction of which contributed to the relevant defeat mentioned in that paragraph.

(5) For the purposes of this section a court or tribunal "upholds" a tax advantage if—

(*a*) the court or tribunal makes a ruling to the effect that no part of the tax advantage is to be counteracted, and

(*b*) that judicial ruling is final.

(6) For the purposes of this Part a judicial ruling is "final" if it is—

(*a*) a ruling of the Supreme Court, or

(*b*) a ruling of any other court or tribunal in circumstances where—

(i) no appeal may be made against the ruling,

(ii) if an appeal may be made against the ruling with permission, the time limit for applications has expired and either no application has been made or permission has been refused,

(iii) if such permission to appeal against the ruling has been granted or is not required, no appeal has been made within the time limit for appeals, or

(iv) if an appeal was made, it was abandoned or otherwise disposed of before it was determined by the court or tribunal to which it was addressed.

(7) In this section references to "counteraction" include anything referred to as a counteraction in any of Conditions A to F in paragraphs 11 to 16 of Schedule 34A.][1]

Note—In this section, "tax" includes VAT, and "tax advantage" has the meaning given by s 234(3) and also includes a tax advantage as defined in VATA 1994 Sch 11A para 1.

Amendments—[1] Sections 237A–237D inserted by FA 2016 s 160(1), (2) with effect from 15 September 2016.

238 Contents of a conduct notice

(1) A conduct notice is a notice requiring the person to whom it has been given ("the recipient") to comply with conditions specified in the notice.

(2) Before deciding on the terms of a conduct notice, the authorised officer must give the person to whom the notice is to be given an opportunity to comment on the proposed terms of the notice.

(3) A notice may include only conditions that it is reasonable to impose for any of the following purposes—

(a) to ensure that the recipient provides adequate information to its clients about relevant proposals, and relevant arrangements, in relation to which the recipient is a promoter;

(b) to ensure that the recipient provides adequate information about relevant proposals in relation to which it is a promoter to persons who are intermediaries in relation to those proposals;

(c) to ensure that the recipient does not fail to comply with any duty under a specified disclosure provision;

(d) to ensure that the recipient does not discourage others from complying with any obligation to disclose to HMRC information of a description specified in the notice;

(e) to ensure that the recipient does not enter into an agreement with another person ("C") which relates to a relevant proposal or relevant arrangements in relation to which the recipient is a promoter, on terms which—

(i) impose a contractual obligation on C which falls within paragraph 11(2) or (3) of Schedule 34 (contractual terms restricting disclosure), or

(ii) impose on C obligations within both paragraph 11(4) and (5) of that Schedule (contractual terms requiring contribution to fighting funds and restricting settlement of proceedings);

(f) to ensure that the recipient does not promote relevant proposals or relevant arrangements which rely on, or involve a proposal to rely on, one or more contrived or abnormal steps to produce a tax advantage;

(g) to ensure that the recipient does not fail to comply with any stop notice which has effect under paragraph 12 of Schedule 34.

(4) References in subsection (3) to ensuring that adequate information is provided about proposals or arrangements include—

(a) ensuring the adequacy of the description of the arrangements or proposed arrangements;

(b) ensuring that the information includes an adequate assessment of the risk that the arrangements or proposed arrangements will fail;

(c) ensuring that the information does not falsely state, and is not likely to create a false impression, that HMRC have (formally or informally) considered, approved or expressed a particular opinion in relation to the proposal or arrangements.

(5) In subsection (3)(c) "specified disclosure provision" means a disclosure provision that is specified in the notice; and for this purpose "disclosure provision" means any of the following—

(a) section 308 of FA 2004 (disclosure of tax avoidance schemes: duties of promoter);

(b) section 312 of FA 2004 (duty of promoter to notify client of number);

(c) sections 313ZA and 313ZB of FA 2004 (duties to provide details of clients and certain others);

(d) Part 1 of Schedule 36 to FA 2008 (duties to provide information and produce documents).

(6) In subsection (4)(b) "fail", in relation to arrangements or proposed arrangements, means not result in a tax advantage which the arrangements or (as the case may be) proposed arrangements might be expected to result in.

(7) The Treasury may by regulations amend the definition of "disclosure provision" in subsection (5).

Definitions—"authorised officer" (for the purposes of Part 5), s 283(2).

Cross-references—See FA 2014 Sch 32 paras 5, 6 (conduct notices and monitoring notices given to partnerships).

239 Section 238: supplementary

(1) In section 238 the following expressions are to be interpreted as follows.

(2) "Adequate" means adequate having regard to what it might be reasonable for a client or (as the case may be) an intermediary to expect; and "adequacy" is to be interpreted accordingly.

(3) A person ("C") is a "client" of a promoter, if at any time when a conduct notice has effect, the promoter—

(a) makes a firm approach to C in relation to a relevant proposal with a view to the promoter making the proposal available for implementation by C or another person;

(b) makes a relevant proposal available for implementation by C;

(c) takes part in the organisation or management of relevant arrangements entered into by C.

(4) The recipient of a conduct notice "promotes" a relevant proposal if it—

(a) takes part in designing the proposal,

(b) makes a firm approach to a person in relation to the proposal with a view to making the proposal available for implementation by that person or another person, or

(c) makes the proposal available for implementation by persons (other than the recipient).

(5) The recipient of a conduct notice "promotes" relevant arrangements if it takes part in designing, organising or managing the arrangements.

240 Amendment or withdrawal of conduct notice

(1) This section applies where a conduct notice has been given to a person.

(2) An authorised officer may at any time amend the notice.

(3) An authorised officer—

(a) may withdraw the notice if the officer thinks it is not necessary for it to continue to have effect, and

(b) in considering whether or not that is necessary must take into account the person's record of compliance, or failure to comply, with the conditions in the notice.

Definitions—"authorised officer" (for the purposes of Part 5), s 283(2).

241 Duration of conduct notice

(1) A conduct notice has effect from the date specified in it as its commencement date.

(2) A conduct notice ceases to have effect—

(a) at the end of the period of two years beginning with its commencement date, or

(b) if an earlier date is specified in it as its termination date, at the end of that day.

(3) A conduct notice ceases to have effect if withdrawn by an authorised officer under section 240.

(4) A conduct notice ceases to have effect in relation to a person when a monitoring notice takes effect in relation to that person.

[(5) See also section 237D(2) (provisional conduct notice affected by judicial ruling).][1]

Definitions—"authorised officer" (for the purposes of Part 5), s 283(2).

Amendments—[1] Sub-s (5) inserted by FA 2016 s 160(6) with effect from 15 September 2016.

[Defeat notices

241A Defeat notices

(1) This section applies in relation to a person ("P") only if P is carrying on a business as a promoter.

(2) An authorised officer, or an officer of Revenue and Customs with the approval of an authorised officer, may give P a notice if the officer concerned has become aware of one (and only one) relevant defeat which has occurred in relation to P in the period of 3 years ending with the day on which the notice is given.

(3) An authorised officer, or an officer of Revenue and Customs with the approval of an authorised officer, may give P a notice if the officer concerned has become aware of two (but not more than two) relevant defeats which have occurred in relation to P in the period of 3 years ending with the day on which the notice is given.

(4) A notice under this section must be given by the end of the 90 days beginning with the day on which the matters mentioned in subsection (2) or (as the case may be) (3) come to the attention of HMRC.

(5) Subsection (6) applies if—

(*a*) a single defeat notice which had been given to P (under subsection (2) or (6)) ceases to have effect as a result of section 241B(1), and

(*b*) in the period when the defeat notice had effect a relevant defeat ("the further relevant defeat") occurred in relation to P.

(6) An authorised officer or an officer of Revenue and Customs with the approval of an authorised officer may give P a notice in respect of the further relevant defeat (regardless of whether or not it occurred in the period of 3 years ending with the day on which the notice is given).

(7) In this Part—

(*a*) "single defeat notice" means a notice under subsection (2) or (6);

(*b*) "double defeat notice" means a notice under subsection (3);

(*c*) "defeat notice" means a single defeat notice or a double defeat notice.

(8) A defeat notice must—

(*a*) set out the dates on which the look-forward period for the notice begins and ends;

(*b*) in the case of a single defeat notice, explain the effect of section 237A(12);

(*c*) in the case of a double defeat notice, explain the effect of section 237A(13).

(9) HMRC may specify what further information must be included in a defeat notice.

(10) "Look-forward period"—

(*a*) in relation to a defeat notice under subsection (2) or (3), means the period of 5 years beginning with the day after the day on which the notice is given;

(*b*) in relation to a defeat notice under subsection (6), means the period beginning with the day after the day on which the notice is given and ending at the end of the period of 5 years beginning with the day on which the further relevant defeat mentioned in subsection (6) occurred in relation to P.

(11) A defeat notice has effect throughout its look-forward period unless it ceases to have effect earlier in accordance with section 241B(1) or (4).][1]

Cross-references—See FA 2016 s 160(20)–(25) (circumstances in which defeats are treated for the purposes of this section as not having occurred).

Amendments—[1] Sections 241A, 241B and preceding crosshead inserted by FA 2016 s 160(1), (3) with effect from 15 September 2016.

[241B Judicial ruling upholding asserted tax advantage: effect on defeat notice

(1) If the relevant defeat to which a single defeat notice relates is overturned (see subsection (5)), the notice has no further effect on and after the day on which it is overturned.

(2) Subsection (3) applies if one (and only one) of the relevant defeats in respect of which a double defeat notice was given is overturned.

(3) The notice is to be treated for the purposes of this Part (including this section) as if it had always been a single defeat notice given (in respect of the other of the two relevant defeats) on the date on which the notice was in fact given.

The look-forward period for the notice is accordingly unchanged.

(4) If both the relevant defeats to which a double defeat notice relates are overturned (on the same date), that notice has no further effect on and after that date.

(5) A relevant defeat specified in a defeat notice is "overturned" if—

(*a*) the notice could not have specified that relevant defeat if paragraph 9 of Schedule 34A had effect with the substitution of "100% of the tested arrangements" for "75% of the tested arrangements", and

(*b*) at a time when the notice has effect a court or tribunal upholds a corresponding tax advantage which has been asserted in connection with any of the related arrangements to which the relevant defeat relates (see paragraph 5(2) of Schedule 34A).

Accordingly the relevant defeat is overturned on the day on which the judicial ruling mentioned in paragraph (*b*) becomes final.

(6) If a defeat notice ceases to have effect as a result of subsection (1) or (4) an authorised officer, or an officer of Revenue and Customs with the approval of an authorised officer, must notify the person to whom the notice was given that it has ceased to have effect.

(7) If subsection (3) has effect in relation to a defeat notice, an authorised officer, or an officer of Revenue and Customs with the approval of an authorised officer, must notify the person of the effect of that subsection.

(8) For the purposes of this section, a tax advantage is "asserted" in connection with any arrangements if a person makes a return, claim or election on the basis that the tax advantage arises from those arrangements.

(9) In relation to the arrangements mentioned in paragraph (*b*) of subsection (5) "corresponding tax advantage" means a tax advantage corresponding to any tax advantage the counteraction of which contributed to the relevant defeat mentioned in that paragraph.

(10) For the purposes of this section a court or tribunal "upholds" a tax advantage if—

(*a*) the court or tribunal makes a ruling to the effect that no part of the tax advantage is to be counteracted, and

(*b*) that judicial ruling is final.

(11) In this section references to "counteraction" include anything referred to as a counteraction in any of Conditions A to F in paragraphs 11 to 16 of Schedule 34A.][1]

Note—In this section, "tax" includes VAT, and "tax advantage" has the meaning given by s 234(3) and also includes a tax advantage as defined in VATA 1994 Sch 11A para 1.

Amendments—[1] Sections 241A, 241B and preceding crosshead inserted by FA 2016 s 160(1), (3) with effect from 15 September 2016.

Monitoring notices: procedure and publication

242 Monitoring notices: duty to apply to tribunal

(1) If—

(a) a conduct notice has effect in relation to a person who is carrying on a business as a promoter, and

(b) an authorised officer determines that the person has failed to comply with one or more conditions in the notice,

the authorised officer must apply to the tribunal for approval to give the person a monitoring notice.

(2) An application under subsection (1) must include a draft of the monitoring notice.

(3) Subsection (1) does not apply if—

(a) the condition (or all the conditions) mentioned in subsection (1)(b) were imposed under subsection (3)(a), (b) or (c) of section 238, and

(b) the authorised officer considers that the failure to comply with the condition (or all the conditions, taken together) is such a minor matter that it should be disregarded for the purposes of this section.

(4) Where an authorised officer makes an application to the tribunal under subsection (1), the officer must at the same time give notice to the person to whom the application relates.

(5) The notice under subsection (4) must state which condition (or conditions) the authorised officer has determined under subsection (1)(b) that the person has failed to comply with and the reasons for that determination.

[(6) At a time when a notice given under section 237A is provisional, no determination is to be made under subsection (1) in respect of the notice.

(7) If a promoter fails to comply with conditions in a conduct notice at a time when the conduct notice is provisional, nothing in subsection (6) prevents those failures from being taken into account under subsection (1) at any subsequent time when the conduct notice is not provisional.][1]

Definitions—"authorised officer" (for the purposes of Part 5), s 283(2).

Cross-references—See FA 2014 Sch 32 paras 5, 6 (conduct notices and monitoring notices given to partnerships).

Amendments—[1] Sub-ss (6), (7) inserted by FA 2016 s 160(1), (4) with effect from 15 September 2016.

243 Monitoring notices: tribunal approval

(1) On an application under section 242, the tribunal may approve the giving of a monitoring notice only if—

(a) the tribunal is satisfied that, in the circumstances, the authorised officer would be justified in giving the monitoring notice, and

(b) the person to whom the monitoring notice is to be given ("the affected person") has been given a reasonable opportunity to make representations to the tribunal.

(2) The tribunal may amend the draft notice included with the application under section 242.

(3) If the representations that the affected person makes to the tribunal include a statement that in the affected person's view it was not reasonable to include the condition mentioned in section 242(1)(b) in the conduct notice, the tribunal must refuse to approve the giving of the monitoring notice if it is satisfied that it was not reasonable to include that condition (but see subsection (4)).

(4) If the representations made to the tribunal include the statement described in subsection (3) and the determination under section 242(1)(b) is a determination that there has been a failure to comply with more than one condition in the conduct notice—

(a) subsection (3) does not apply, but

(b) in deciding whether or not to approve the giving of the monitoring notice, the tribunal is to assume, in the case of any condition that the tribunal considers it was not reasonable to include in the conduct notice, that there has been no failure to comply with that condition.

Definitions—"authorised officer" (for the purposes of Part 5), s 283(2).

244 Monitoring notices: content and issuing

(1) Where the tribunal has approved the giving of a monitoring notice, the authorised officer must give the notice to the person to whom it relates.

(2) A monitoring notice given under subsection (1) or paragraph 9 or 10 of Schedule 36 must—

(a) explain the effect of the monitoring notice and specify the date from which it takes effect;

(b) inform the recipient of the right to request the withdrawal of the monitoring notice under section 245.

(3) In addition, a monitoring notice must—

(a) if given under subsection (1), state which condition (or conditions) it has been determined the person has failed to comply with and the reasons for that determination;

(b) if given under paragraph 9 or 10 of Schedule 36, state the date of the original monitoring notice and name the partnership to which that notice was given.

(4) The date specified under subsection (2)(a) must not be earlier than the date on which the monitoring notice is given.

(5) In this Part, a person in relation to whom a monitoring notice has effect is called a "monitored promoter".

Definitions—"authorised officer" (for the purposes of Part 5), s 283(2).

245 Withdrawal of monitoring notice

(1) A person in relation to whom a monitoring notice has effect may, at any time after the end of the period of 12 months beginning with the end of the appeal period, request that the notice should cease to have effect.

(2) The "appeal period" means—

(a) the period during which an appeal could be brought against the approval by the tribunal of the giving of the monitoring notice, or

(b) where an appeal mentioned in paragraph (a) has been brought, the period during which that appeal has not been finally determined, withdrawn or otherwise disposed of.

(3) A request under this section is to be made in writing to an authorised officer.

(4) Where a request is made under this section, an authorised officer must within 30 days beginning with the day on which the request is received determine either—

(a) that the monitoring notice is to cease to have effect, or

(b) that the request is to be refused.

(5) The matters to be taken into account by an authorised officer in making a determination under subsection (4) include—

(a) whether or not the person subject to the monitoring notice has, since the time when the notice took effect, engaged in behaviour of a sort that conditions included in a conduct notice in accordance with section 238(3) could be used to regulate;

(b) whether or not it appears likely that the person will in the future engage in such behaviour;

(c) the person's record of compliance, or failure to comply, with obligations imposed on it under this Part, since the time when the monitoring notice took effect.

(6) An authorised officer—

(a) may withdraw a monitoring notice if the officer thinks it is not necessary for it to continue to have effect, and

(b) in considering whether or not that is necessary, the officer must take into account the matters in paragraphs (a) to (c) of subsection (5).

(7) If the authorised officer makes a determination under subsection (4)(a), or decides to withdraw a monitoring notice under subsection (6), the officer must also determine that the person is, or is not, to be given a follow-on conduct notice.

(8) "Follow-on conduct notice" means a conduct notice taking effect immediately after the monitoring notice ceases to have effect.

(9) Where the monitoring notice mentioned in subsection (1) is a replacement monitoring notice—

(a) in subsection (1) the reference to the end of the appeal period is to be read as a reference to whichever is the later of the end of the appeal period for the original monitoring notice and the date the replacement monitoring notice takes effect, and

(b) in subsection (5)(a) and (c) the time referred to is to be read as the time when the original monitoring notice (see paragraph 11(2) of Schedule 36) took effect.

Definitions—"authorised officer" (for the purposes of Part 5), s 283(2).

246 Notification of determination under section 245

(1) Where an authorised officer makes a determination under section 245(4), that officer, or an officer of Revenue and Customs with that officer's approval, must notify the person who made the request of the determination.

(2) If the determination is that the monitoring notice is to cease to have effect, the notice must—

(a) specify the date from which the monitoring notice is to cease to have effect, and

(b) inform the person of the determination made under section 245(7).

(3) If the determination is that the request is to be refused, the notice must inform the person who made the request—

(a) of the reasons for the refusal, and

(b) of the right to appeal under section 247.

Definitions—"authorised officer" (for the purposes of Part 5), s 283(2).

247 Appeal against refusal to withdraw monitoring notice

(1) A person may appeal against a refusal by an authorised officer of a request that a monitoring notice should cease to have effect.

(2) Notice of appeal must be given—

(a) in writing to the officer who gave the notice of the refusal under section 245, and

(b) within the period of 30 days beginning with the day on which notice of the refusal was given.

(3) The notice of appeal must state the grounds of appeal.

(4) On an appeal that is notified to the tribunal, the tribunal may—

(a) confirm the refusal, or

(b) direct that the monitoring notice is to cease to have effect.

(5) Subject to this section, the provisions of Part 5 of TMA 1970 relating to appeals have effect in relation to an appeal under this section.

Definitions—"authorised officer" (for the purposes of Part 5), s 283(2).

248 Publication by HMRC

(1) An authorised officer may publish the fact that a person is a monitored promoter.

(2) Publication under subsection (1) may also include the following information about the monitored promoter—

(a) its name;

(b) its business address or registered office;

(c) the nature of the business mentioned in section 242(1)(a);

(d) any other information that the authorised officer considers it appropriate to publish in order to make clear the monitored promoter's identity.

(3) The reference in subsection (2)(a) to the monitored promoter's name includes any name under which it carries on a business as a promoter and any previous name or pseudonym.

(4) Publication under subsection (1) may also include a statement of which of the conditions in a conduct notice it has been determined that the person (or, in the case of a replacement monitoring notice, the person to whom the original monitoring notice was given) has failed to comply with.

(5) Publication may not take place before the end of the appeal period (or, in the case of a replacement monitoring notice, the appeal period for the original monitoring notice).

(6) The "appeal period", in relation to a monitoring notice, means—

(a) the period during which an appeal could be brought against the approval by the tribunal of the giving of the notice, or

(b) where an appeal mentioned in paragraph (a) has been brought, the period during which that appeal has not been finally determined, withdrawn or otherwise disposed of.

(7) Publication under this section is to be in such manner as the authorised officer thinks fit; but see subsection (8).

(8) If an authorised officer publishes the fact that a person is a monitored promoter and the monitoring notice is withdrawn, the officer must publish the fact of the withdrawal in the same way as the officer published the fact that the person was a monitored promoter.

Definitions—"authorised officer" (for the purposes of Part 5), s 283(2).

Cross-references—See FA 2014 Sch 36 para 14 (where the monitored promoter referred to in sub-s (2) above is a partnership, paras (*a*), (*b*) and (*d*) of that subsection are to be read as referring to details of the partnership, not to details of particular partners).

249 Publication by monitored promoter

(1) A person who is given a monitoring notice ("the monitored promoter") must give the persons mentioned in subsection (6) a notice stating—

(a) that it is a monitored promoter, and

(b) which of the conditions in a conduct notice it has been determined that it (or, if the monitoring notice is a replacement monitoring notice, the person to whom that notice was given) has failed to comply with.

(2) If the monitoring notice is a replacement monitoring notice, the notice under subsection (1) must also identify the original monitoring notice.

(3) If regulations made by the Commissioners so require, the monitored promoter must publish on the internet—

(a) the information mentioned in paragraph (a) and (b) of subsection (1), and

(b) its promoter reference number (see section 250).

(4) Subsection (1) and any duty imposed under subsection (3) or (10) do not apply until the end of the period of 10 days beginning with the end of the appeal period (and also see subsection (9)).

(5) The "appeal period" means—

(a) the period during which an appeal could be brought against the approval by the tribunal of the giving of the monitoring notice, or

(b) where an appeal mentioned in paragraph (a) has been brought, the period during which that appeal has not been finally determined, withdrawn or otherwise disposed of.

(6) The notice under subsection (1) must be given—

(a) to any person who becomes a client of the monitored promoter while the monitoring notice has effect, and

(b) (except in a case where the monitoring notice is a replacement monitoring notice) any person who is a client of the monitored promoter at the time the monitoring notice takes effect.

(7) A person ("C") is a client of a monitored promoter at the time a monitoring notice takes effect if during the period beginning with the date the conduct notice mentioned in subsection (1)(b) takes effect and ending with that time the promoter—

(a) made a firm approach to C in relation to a relevant proposal with a view to the promoter making the proposal available for implementation by C or another person;

(b) made a relevant proposal available for implementation by C;

(c) took part in the organisation or management of relevant arrangements entered into by C.

(8) A person becomes a client of a monitored promoter if the promoter does any of the things mentioned in paragraph (a) to (c) of subsection (7) in relation to that person.

(9) In the case of a person falling within subsection (6)(a), notice under subsection (1) may be given within the period of 10 days beginning with the day on which the person first became a client of the monitored promoter if that period would expire at a later date than the date on which notification would otherwise be required by virtue of subsection (4).

(10) A monitored promoter must also include in any prescribed publication or prescribed correspondence—

(a) the information mentioned in paragraph (a) and (b) of subsection (1), and

(b) its promoter reference number (see section 250).

(11) Notification under subsection (1), publication under subsection (3) or inclusion of the information required by subsection (10) is to be in such form and manner as is prescribed.

(12) Where the monitoring notice mentioned in subsection (1) is a replacement monitoring notice, the reference in subsection (4) to the end of the appeal period is to be read as a reference to whichever is the later of the end of the appeal period for the original monitoring notice and the date the replacement monitoring notice takes effect.

Definitions—"authorised officer" (for the purposes of Part 5), s 283(2).

Cross-references—See FA 2014 Sch 35 (penalties for failure to comply with duties under this section)

Allocation and distribution of promoter reference number

250 Allocation of promoter reference number

(1) Where a monitoring notice is given to a person ("the monitored promoter") HMRC must as soon as practicable after the end of the appeal period—

(a) allocate the monitored promoter a reference number, and

(b) notify the relevant persons of that number.

(2) "Relevant persons" means—

(a) the monitored promoter, and

(b) if the monitored promoter is resident outside the United Kingdom, any person who HMRC know is an intermediary in relation to a relevant proposal of the monitored promoter.

(3) The "appeal period" means—

(a) the period during which an appeal could be brought against the approval by the tribunal of the giving of the monitoring notice, or

(b) where an appeal mentioned in paragraph (a) has been brought, the period during which that appeal has not been finally determined, withdrawn or otherwise disposed of.

(4) The duty in subsection (1) does not apply if the monitoring notice is set aside following an appeal.

(5) A number allocated to a person under this section is referred to in this Part as a "promoter reference number".

(6) Where the monitoring notice mentioned in subsection (1) is a replacement monitoring notice—

(a) in subsection (1) the reference to the end of the appeal period is to be read as a reference to whichever is the later of the end of the appeal period for the original monitoring notice and the date the replacement monitoring notice takes effect, and

(b) in subsection (4) the reference to the monitoring notice is to be read as a reference to the original monitoring notice.

251 Duty of monitored promoter to notify clients and intermediaries of number

(1) This section applies where a person who is a monitored promoter ("the monitored promoter") is notified under section 250 of a promoter reference number.

(2) The monitored promoter must, within the relevant period, notify the promoter reference number to—

(a) any person who has become its client at any time in the period beginning with the day on which the monitoring notice in relation to the monitored promoter took effect and ending with the day on which the monitored promoter was notified of that number,

(b) any person who becomes its client after the end of the period mentioned in paragraph (a) but while the monitoring notice has effect,

(c) any person who the monitored promoter could reasonably be expected to know falls within subsection (4), and

(d) any person who the monitored promoter could reasonably be expected to know is a relevant intermediary in relation to a relevant proposal of the monitored promoter.

(3) A person ("C") becomes a client of a monitored promoter if the promoter does any of the following in relation to C—

(a) makes a firm approach to C in relation to a relevant proposal with a view to the promoter making the proposal available for implementation by C or another person;

(b) makes a relevant proposal available for implementation by C;

(c) takes part in the organisation or management of relevant arrangements entered into by C.

(4) A person falls within this subsection if during the period beginning with the date the conduct notice took effect and ending with the date on which the monitoring notice took effect the person has entered into transactions forming part of relevant arrangements and those arrangements—

(a) enable, or are likely to enable, the person to obtain a tax advantage during the time a monitoring notice has effect, and

(b) are either relevant arrangements in relation to which the monitored promoter is or was a promoter or implement a relevant proposal in relation to which the monitored promoter was a promoter.

(5) A person is a relevant intermediary in relation to a relevant proposal of a monitored promoter if the person meets the conditions in section 236(a) to (c) (meaning of "intermediary") at any time while the monitoring notice in relation to the monitored promoter has effect.

(6) The "relevant period" means—

(a) in the case of a person falling within subsection (2)(a), the period of 30 days beginning with the day of the notification mentioned in subsection (1),

(b) in the case of a person falling within subsection (2)(b), the period of 30 days beginning with the day on which the person first became a client in relation to the monitored promoter,

(c) in the case of a person falling within subsection (2)(c), the period of 30 days beginning with the later of the day of the notification mentioned in subsection (1) and the first day on which the monitored promoter could reasonably be expected to know that the person fell within subsection (4), and

(d) in the case of a person falling within subsection (2)(d), the period of 30 days beginning with the later of the day of the notification mentioned in subsection (1) and the first day on which the monitored promoter could reasonably be expected to know that the person was a relevant intermediary in relation to a relevant proposal of the monitored promoter.

(7) In this section "the conduct notice" means the conduct notice that the monitored promoter failed to comply with which resulted in the monitoring notice being given to the monitored promoter.

(8) Subsection (2)(c) is to be ignored in a case where the monitoring notice is a replacement monitoring notice.

Cross-references—See FA 2014 Sch 35 (penalties for failure to comply with duties under this section)

252 Duty of those notified to notify others of promoter's number

(1) In this section "notified client" means—

(a) a person who is notified of a promoter reference number under section 250 by reason of being a person falling within subsection (2)(b) of that section, and

(b) a person who is notified of a promoter reference number under section 251.

(2) A notified client must, within 30 days of being notified as described in subsection (1), provide the promoter reference number to any other person who the notified client might reasonably be expected to know has become, or is likely to have become, a client in relation to the monitored promoter concerned at a time when the monitoring notice in relation to that monitored promoter had effect.

(3) A person ("C") becomes a client of a monitored promoter if the promoter does any of the following in relation to C—

(a) makes a firm approach to C in relation to a relevant proposal with a view to the promoter making the proposal available for implementation by C or another person;

(b) makes a relevant proposal available for implementation by C;

(c) takes part in the organisation or management of relevant arrangements entered into by C.

(4) Where the notified client is an intermediary in relation to a relevant proposal of the monitored promoter concerned, the notified client must also, within 30 days, provide the promoter reference number to—

(a) any person to whom the notified client has, since the monitoring notice in relation to the monitored promoter concerned took effect, communicated in the course of a business information about a relevant proposal of the monitored promoter, and

(b) any person who the notified client might reasonably be expected to know has, since that monitoring notice took effect, entered into, or is likely to enter into, transactions forming part of relevant arrangements in relation to which that monitored promoter is a promoter.

(5) Subsection (2) or (4) does not impose a duty on a notified client to notify a person of a promoter reference number if the notified client reasonably believes that the person has already been notified of the promoter reference number (whether as a result of a duty under this section or as a result of any of the other provision of this Part).

Cross-references—See FA 2014 Sch 35 (penalties for failure to comply with duties under this section)

253 Duty of persons to notify the Commissioners

(1) If a person ("N") is notified of a promoter reference number under section 250, 251 or 252, N must report the number to the Commissioners if N expects to obtain a tax advantage from relevant arrangements in relation to which the monitored promoter to whom the reference number relates (whether that is N or another person) is the promoter.

(2) A report under this section—

(a) must be made in (or, if prescribed circumstances exist, submitted with) each tax return made by N for a period that is or includes a period for which the arrangements enable N to obtain a tax advantage (whether in relation to the tax to which the return relates or another tax);

(b) if no tax return falls within paragraph (a), or in the case mentioned in subsection (3), must contain such information, and be made in such form and manner and within such time, as is prescribed.

(3) The case is that the tax return in which the report would (apart from this subsection) have been made is not submitted—

(a) by the filing date, or

(b) if there is no filing date in relation to the tax return concerned, by such other time that the tax return is required to be submitted by or under any enactment.

(4) Where N expects to obtain the tax advantage referred to in subsection (1) in respect of inheritance tax, stamp duty land tax, stamp duty reserve tax or petroleum revenue tax—

(a) subsection (2) does not apply in relation to that tax advantage, and

(b) a report under this section in respect of that tax must be in such form and manner and contain such information and be made within such time as is prescribed.

(5) Where the relevant arrangements referred to in subsection (1) give rise to N making a claim under section 261B of TCGA 1992 (treating trade loss as CGT loss) or for loss relief under Part 4 of ITA 2007 and that claim is not contained in a tax return, a report under this section must also be made in that claim.

(6) In this section "tax return" means any of the following—

(a) a return under section 8 of TMA 1970 (income tax and capital gains tax: personal return);

(b) a return under section 8A of TMA 1970 (income tax and capital gains tax: trustee's return);

(c) a return under section 12AA of TMA 1970 (income tax and corporation tax: partnership return);

(d) a company tax return under paragraph 3 of Schedule 18 to the FA 1998 (company tax return);

[(da) a return under regulations made under section 105 of FA 2016 (apprenticeship levy)][1]

(e) a return under section 159 or 160 of FA 2013 (returns and further returns for annual tax on enveloped dwellings).

Cross-references—See FA 2014 Sch 35 (penalties for failure to comply with duties under this section)

Amendments[1] Sub-s (6)(*da*) inserted by FA 2016 s 104(6), (7) with effect from 15 September 2016.

Prospective amendments—In sub-s (6)(*c*), words ", or regulations under paragraph 10 of Schedule A1 to," to be inserted after words "section 12AA of" by F(No 2)A 2017 s 61(1), Sch 14 paras 43, 44 with effect from a day to be appointed.

Obtaining information and documents

254 Meaning of "monitored proposal" and "monitored arrangements"

(1) For the purposes of this Part a relevant proposal in relation to which a person ("P") is a promoter is a "monitored proposal" in relation to P if any of the following dates fell on or after the date on which a monitoring notice took effect—

(a) the date on which P first made a firm approach to another person in relation to the relevant proposal;

(b) the date on which P first made the relevant proposal available for implementation by any other person;

(c) the date on which P first became aware of any transaction forming part of the proposed arrangements being entered into by any person.

(2) For the purposes of this Part relevant arrangements in relation to which a person ("P") is a promoter are "monitored arrangements" in relation to P if—

(a) P was by virtue of section 235(2)(b) or (c) a promoter in relation to a relevant proposal which was implemented by the arrangements and any of the following fell on or after the date on which the monitoring notice took effect—

(i) the date on which P first made a firm approach to another person in relation to the relevant proposal;

(ii) the date on which P first made the relevant proposal available for implementation by any other person;

(iii) the date on which P first became aware of any transaction forming part of the proposed arrangements being entered into by any person,

(b) the date on which P first took part in designing, organising or managing the arrangements fell on or after the date on which a monitoring notice took effect, or

(c) the arrangements enable, or are likely to enable, the person who has entered into transactions forming them to obtain the tax advantage by reason of which they are relevant arrangements, at any time on or after the date on which a monitoring notice took effect.

255 Power to obtain information and documents

(1) An authorised officer, or an officer of Revenue and Customs with the approval of an authorised officer, may by notice in writing require any person ("P") to whom this section applies—

(a) to provide information, or

(b) to produce a document,

if the information or document is reasonably required by the officer for any of the purposes in subsection (3).

(2) This section applies to—

(a) any person who is a monitored promoter, and

(b) any person who is a relevant intermediary in relation to a monitored proposal of a monitored promoter,

and in either case that monitored promoter is referred to below as "the relevant monitored promoter".

(3) The purposes mentioned in subsection (1) are—

(a) considering the possible consequences of implementing a monitored proposal of the relevant monitored promoter for the tax position of persons implementing the proposal,

(b) checking the tax position of any person who the officer reasonably believes has implemented a monitored proposal of the relevant monitored promoter, or

(c) checking the tax position of any person who the officer reasonably believes has entered into transactions forming monitored arrangements of the relevant monitored promoter.

(4) A person is a "relevant intermediary" in relation to a monitored proposal if the person meets the conditions in section 236(a) to (c) (meaning of "intermediary") in relation to the proposal at any time after the person has been notified of a promoter reference number of a person who is a promoter in relation to the proposal.

(5) In this section "checking" includes carrying out an investigation or enquiry of any kind.

(6) In this section "tax position", in relation to a person, means the person's position as regards any tax, including the person's position as regards—

- (a) past, present and future liability to pay any tax,
- (b) penalties and other amounts that have been paid, or are or may be payable, by or to the person in connection with any tax,
- (c) claims, elections, applications and notices that have been or may be made or given in connection with the person's liability to pay any tax,
- (d) deductions or repayments of tax, or of sums representing tax, that the person is required to make—
  - (i) under PAYE regulations, or
  - (ii) by or under any other provision of the Taxes Acts, and
- (e) the withholding by the person of another person's PAYE income (as defined in section 683 of ITEPA 2003).

(7) In this section the reference to the tax position of a person—

- (a) includes the tax position of a company that has ceased to exist and an individual who has died, and
- (b) is to the person's tax position at any time or in relation to any period.

(8) A notice under subsection (1) which is given for the purpose of checking the tax position of a person mentioned in subsection (3)(b) or (c) may not be given more than 4 years after the person's death.

(9) A notice under subsection (1) may specify or describe the information or documents to be provided or produced.

(10) Information or a document required as a result of a notice under subsection (1) must be provided or produced within—

- (a) the period of 10 days beginning with the day on which the notice was given, or
- (b) such longer period as the officer who gives the notice may direct.

Definitions—"authorised officer" (for the purposes of Part 5), s 283(2).

Cross-references—See FA 2014 s 264 (power to apply to tribunal to require promoter to provide information or documents where reasonable grounds to suspect not all information or documents have been provided by promoter).

FA 2014 s 266 (right of appeal against notice imposing information etc requirements).

FA 2014 s 267 (form and manner of providing information).

FA 2014 s 268 (compliance with requirement to produce documents by producing copies).

FA 2014 ss 278, 279 (offence of concealing documents).

FA 2014 Sch 35 (penalties for failure to comply with duties under this section)

256 Tribunal approval for certain uses of power under section 255

(1) An officer of Revenue and Customs may not, without the approval of the tribunal, give a notice under section 255 requiring a person ("A") to provide information or produce a document which relates (in whole or in part) to a person who is neither A nor an undertaking in relation to which A is a parent undertaking.

(2) An officer of Revenue and Customs may apply to the tribunal for the approval required by subsection (1); and an application for approval may be made without notice.

(3) The tribunal may approve the giving of the notice only if—

- (a) the application for approval is made by, or with the agreement of, an authorised officer,
- (b) the tribunal is satisfied that, in the circumstances, the officer giving the notice is justified in doing so,
- (c) the person to whom the notice is to be given has been informed that the information or documents referred to in the notice are required and given a reasonable opportunity to make representations to an officer of Revenue and Customs, and
- (d) the tribunal has been given a summary of any representations made by that person.

(4) Where a notice is given under section 255 with the approval of the tribunal, it must state that it is given with that approval.

(5) Paragraphs (c) and (d) of subsection (3) do not apply to the extent that the tribunal is satisfied that taking the action specified in those paragraphs might prejudice the assessment or collection of tax.

(6) In subsection (1) "parent undertaking" and "undertaking" have the same meaning as in the Companies Acts (see section 1161 and 1162 of, and Schedule 7 to, the Companies Act 2006).

(7) A decision of the tribunal under this section is final (despite the provisions of sections 11 and 13 of the Tribunals, Courts and Enforcement Act 2007).

Definitions—"authorised officer" (for the purposes of Part 5), s 283(2).

Cross-references—See FA 2014 s 278 (offence of concealing documents).

257 Ongoing duty to provide information following HMRC notice

(1) An authorised officer, or an officer of Revenue and Customs with the approval of an authorised officer, may give a notice to a person ("P") in relation to whom a monitoring notice has effect.

(2) A person to whom a notice is given under subsection (1) must provide prescribed information and produce prescribed documents relating to—

(a) all the monitored proposals and all the monitored arrangements in relation to which the person is a promoter at the time of the notice, and

(b) all the monitored proposals and all the monitored arrangements in relation to which the person becomes a promoter after that time.

(3) The duty under subsection (2)(b) does not apply in relation to any proposals or arrangements in relation to which the person first becomes a promoter after the monitoring notice ceases to have effect.

(4) A notice under subsection (1) must specify the time within which information must be provided or a document produced and different times may be specified for different cases.

Definitions—"authorised officer" (for the purposes of Part 5), s 283(2).

Cross-references—See FA 2014 s 264 (power to apply to tribunal to require promoter to provide information or documents where reasonable grounds to suspect not all information or documents have been provided by promoter).

FA 2014 s 266 (right of appeal against notice imposing information etc requirements).

FA 2014 s 268 (compliance with requirement to produce documents by producing copies).

FA 2014 Sch 35 (penalties for failure to comply with duties under this section)

258 Duty of person dealing with non-resident monitored promoter

(1) This section applies where a monitored promoter who is resident outside the United Kingdom has failed to comply with a duty under section 255 or 257 to provide information about a monitored proposal or monitored arrangements.

(2) An authorised officer, or an officer of Revenue and Customs with the approval of an authorised officer, may give a notice to a relevant person which—

(a) specifies or describes the information which the monitored promoter has failed to provide, and

(b) requires the person to provide the information.

(3) A "relevant person" means—

(a) any person who is an intermediary in relation to the monitored proposal concerned, and

(b) any person ("A") to whom the monitored promoter has made a firm approach in relation to the monitored proposal concerned with a view to making the proposal available for implementation by a person other than A.

(4) If an authorised officer is not aware of any person to whom a notice could be given under subsection (2) the authorised officer, or an officer of Revenue and Customs with the approval of the authorised officer, may give a notice to any person who has implemented the proposal which—

(a) specifies or describes the information which the monitored promoter has failed to provide, and

(b) requires the person to provide the information.

(5) If the duty mentioned in subsection (1) relates to monitored arrangements an authorised officer, or an officer of Revenue and Customs with the approval of an authorised officer, may give a notice to any person who has entered into any transaction forming part of the monitored arrangements concerned which—

(a) specifies or describes the information which the monitored promoter has failed to provide, and

(b) requires the person to provide the information.

(6) A notice under this section may be given only if the officer giving the notice reasonably believes that the person to whom the notice is given is able to provide the information requested.

(7) Information required as a result of a notice under this section must be provided within—

(a) the period of 10 days beginning with the day on which the notice was given, or

(b) such longer period as the officer who gives the notice may direct.

Definitions—"authorised officer" (for the purposes of Part 5), s 283(2).

Cross-references—See FA 2014 s 264 (power to apply to tribunal to require promoter to provide information or documents where reasonable grounds to suspect not all information or documents have been provided by promoter).

FA 2014 s 266 (right of appeal against notice imposing information etc requirements).

FA 2014 s 272 (notice given under sub-s (4) or (5) to tax adviser).

FA 2014 Sch 35 (penalties for failure to comply with duties under this section)

259 Monitored promoters: duty to provide information about clients

(1) An authorised officer, or an officer of Revenue and Customs with the approval of an authorised officer, may give notice to a person in relation to whom a monitoring notice has effect ("the monitored promoter").

(2) A person to whom a notice is given under subsection (1) must, for each relevant period, give the officer who gave the notice the information set out in subsection (9) in respect of each person who was its client with reference to that relevant period (see subsections (5) to (8)).

(3) Each of the following is a "relevant period"—

(a) the calendar quarter in which the notice under subsection (1) was given but not including any time before the monitoring notice takes effect,
(b) the period (if any) beginning with the date the monitoring notice takes effect and ending immediately before the beginning of the period described in paragraph (a), and
(c) each calendar quarter after the period described in paragraph (a) but not including any time after the monitoring notice ceases to have effect.

(4) Information required as a result of a notice under subsection (1) must be given—
(a) within the period of 30 days beginning with the end of the relevant period concerned, or
(b) in the case of a relevant period within subsection (3)(b), within the period of 30 days beginning with the day on which the notice under subsection (1) was given if that period would expire at a later time than the period given by paragraph (a).

(5) A person ("C") is a client of the monitored promoter with reference to a relevant period if—
(a) the promoter did any of the things mentioned in subsection (6) in relation to C at any time during that period, or
(b) the person falls within subsection (7).

(6) Those things are that the monitored promoter—
(a) made a firm approach to C in relation to a relevant proposal with a view to the promoter making the proposal available for implementation by C or another person;
(b) made a relevant proposal available for implementation by C;
(c) took part in the organisation or management of relevant arrangements entered into by C.

(7) A person falls within this subsection if the person has entered into transactions forming part of relevant arrangements and those arrangements—
(a) enable the person to obtain a tax advantage either in that relevant period or a later relevant period, and
(b) are either relevant arrangements in relation to which the monitored promoter is or was a promoter, or implement a relevant proposal in relation to which the monitored promoter was a promoter.

(8) But a person is not a client of the monitored promoter with reference to a relevant period if—
(a) the person has previously been a client of the monitored promoter with reference to a different relevant period,
(b) the promoter complied with the duty in subsection (2) in respect of the person for that relevant period, and
(c) the information provided as a result of complying with that duty remains accurate.

(9) The information mentioned in subsection (2) is—
(a) the person's name and address, and
(b) such other information about the person as may be prescribed.

(10) Where the monitoring notice mentioned in subsection (1) is a replacement monitoring notice, subsection (5)(b) does not impose a duty on the monitored promoter concerned to provide information about a person who has entered into transactions forming part of relevant arrangements (as described in subsection (7)) if the monitored promoter reasonably believes that information about that person has, in relation to those arrangements, already been provided under the original monitoring notice.

Definitions—"authorised officer" (for the purposes of Part 5), s 283(2).

Cross-references—See FA 2014 s 264 (power to apply to tribunal to require promoter to provide information or documents where reasonable grounds to suspect not all information or documents have been provided by promoter).
FA 2014 s 266 (right of appeal against notice imposing information etc requirements).
FA 2014 Sch 35 (penalties for failure to comply with duties under this section)

260 Intermediaries: duty to provide information about clients

(1) An authorised officer, or an officer of Revenue and Customs with the approval of an authorised officer, may give notice to a person ("the intermediary") who is an intermediary in relation to a relevant proposal which is a monitored proposal of a person in relation to whom a monitoring notice has effect ("the monitored promoter").

(2) A person to whom a notice is given under subsection (1) must, for each relevant period, give the officer who gave the notice the information set out in subsection (7) in respect of each person who was its client with reference to that relevant period (see subsections (5) to (6)).

(3) Each of the following is a "relevant period"—
(a) the calendar quarter in which the notice under subsection (1) was given but not including any time before the intermediary was first notified under section 250, 251 or 252 of the promoter reference number of the monitored promoter,
(b) the period (if any) beginning with the date of the notification under section 250, 251 or 252 and ending immediately before the beginning of the period described in paragraph (a), and
(c) each calendar quarter after the period described in paragraph (a) but not including any time after the monitoring notice mentioned in subsection (1) ceases to have effect.

(4) Information required as a result of a notice under subsection (1) must be given—
(a) within the period of 30 days beginning with the end of the relevant period concerned, or

(b) in the case of a relevant period within subsection (3)(b), within the period of 30 days beginning with the day on which the notice under subsection (1) was given if that period would expire at a later time than the period given by paragraph (a).

(5) A person ("C") is a client of the intermediary with reference to a relevant period if during that period—

(a) the intermediary communicated information to C about a monitored proposal in the course of a business, and

(b) the communication was made with a view to C, or any other person, entering into transactions forming part of the proposed arrangements.

(6) But a person is not a client of the intermediary with reference to a relevant period if—

(a) the person has previously been a client of the intermediary with reference to a different relevant period,

(b) the intermediary complied with the duty in subsection (2) in respect of the person for that relevant period, and

(c) the information provided as a result of complying with that duty remains accurate.

(7) The information mentioned in subsection (2) is—

(a) the person's name and address, and

(b) such other information about the person as may be prescribed.

Definitions—"authorised officer" (for the purposes of Part 5), s 283(2).

Cross-references—See FA 2014 s 264 (power to apply to tribunal to require promoter to provide information or documents where reasonable grounds to suspect not all information or documents have been provided by promoter).

FA 2014 s 266 (right of appeal against notice imposing information etc requirements).

FA 2014 Sch 35 (penalties for failure to comply with duties under this section)

261 Enquiry following provision of client information

(1) This section applies where—

(a) a person ("the notifying person") has provided information under section 259 or 260 about a person who was a client of the notifying person with reference to a relevant period (within the meaning of the section concerned) in connection with a particular relevant proposal or particular relevant arrangements, and

(b) an authorised officer suspects that a person in respect of whom information has not been provided under section 259 or 260—

(i) has at any time been, or is likely to be, a party to transactions implementing the proposal, or

(ii) is a party to a transaction forming (in whole or in part) particular relevant arrangements.

(2) The authorised officer may by notice in writing require the notifying person to provide prescribed information in relation to any person whom the notifying person might reasonably be expected to know—

(a) has been, or is likely to be, a party to transactions implementing the proposal, or

(b) is a party to a transaction forming (in whole or in part) the relevant arrangements.

(3) But a notice under subsection (2) does not impose a requirement on the notifying person to provide information which the notifying person has already provided to an authorised officer under section 259 or 260.

(4) The notifying person must comply with a requirement under subsection (2) within—

(a) 10 days of the notice, or

(b) such longer period as the authorised officer may direct.

Definitions—"authorised officer" (for the purposes of Part 5), s 283(2).

Cross-references—See FA 2014 s 264 (power to apply to tribunal to require promoter to provide information or documents where reasonable grounds to suspect not all information or documents have been provided by promoter).

FA 2014 s 266 (right of appeal against notice imposing information etc requirements).

FA 2014 Sch 35 (penalties for failure to comply with duties under this section)

262 Information required for monitoring compliance with conduct notice

(1) This section applies where a conduct notice has effect in relation to a person.

(2) An authorised officer, or an officer of Revenue and Customs with the approval of an authorised officer, may (as often as is necessary for the purpose mentioned below) by notice in writing require the person—

(a) to provide information, or

(b) to produce a document,

if the information or document is reasonably required for the purpose of monitoring whether and to what extent the person is complying with the conditions in the conduct notice.

Definitions—"authorised officer" (for the purposes of Part 5), s 283(2).

Cross-references—See FA 2014 s 264 (power to apply to tribunal to require promoter to provide information or documents where reasonable grounds to suspect not all information or documents have been provided by promoter).

FA 2014 s 266 (right of appeal against notice imposing information etc requirements).

FA 2014 s 268 (compliance with requirement to produce documents by producing copies).

FA 2014 Sch 35 (penalties for failure to comply with duties under this section)

263 Duty to notify HMRC of address

If, on the last day of a calendar quarter, a monitoring notice has effect in relation to a person ("the monitored promoter") the monitored promoter must within 30 days of the end of the calendar quarter inform an authorised officer of its current address.

Definitions—"authorised officer" (for the purposes of Part 5), s 283(2).

Cross-references—See FA 2014 Sch 35 (penalties for failure to comply with duties under this section)

264 Failure to provide information: application to tribunal

(1) This section applies where—

(a) a person ("P") has provided information or produced a document in purported compliance with section 255, 257, 258, 259, 260, 261 or 262, but

(b) an authorised officer suspects that P has not provided all the information or produced all the documents required under the section concerned.

(2) The authorised officer, or an officer of Revenue and Customs with the approval of the authorised officer, may apply to the tribunal for an order requiring P to—

(a) provide specified information about persons who are its clients for the purposes of the section to which the application relates,

(b) provide specified information, or information of a specified description, about a monitored proposal or monitored arrangements,

(c) produce specified documents relating to a monitored proposal or monitored arrangements.

(3) The tribunal may make an order under subsection (2) in respect of information or documents only if satisfied that the officer has reasonable grounds for suspecting that the information or documents—

(a) are required under section 255, 257, 258, 259, 260, 261 or 262 (as the case may be), or

(b) will support or explain information required under the section concerned.

(4) A requirement by virtue of an order under subsection (2) is to be treated as part of P's duty under section 255, 257, 258, 259, 260, 261 or 262 (as the case may be).

(5) Information or a document required as a result of subsection (2) must be provided, or the document produced, within the period of 10 days beginning with the day on which the order under subsection (2) was made.

(6) An authorised officer may, by direction, extend the 10 day period mentioned in subsection (5).

Definitions—"authorised officer" (for the purposes of Part 5), s 283(2).

Cross-references—FA 2014 s 267 (form and manner of providing information).

265 Duty to provide information to monitored promoter

(1) This section applies where a person has been notified of a promoter reference number—

(a) under section 250 by reason of being a person falling within subsection (2)(b) of that section, or

(b) under section 251 or 252.

(2) The person notified ("C") must within 10 days notify the person whose promoter reference number it is of—

(a) C's national insurance number (if C has one), and

(b) C's unique tax reference number (if C has one).

(3) If C has neither a national insurance number nor a unique tax reference number, C must within 10 days inform the person whose promoter reference number it is of that fact.

(4) A unique tax reference number is an identification number allocated to a person by HMRC.

(5) Subsection (2) or (3) does not impose a duty on C to provide information which C has already provided to the person whose promoter reference number it is.

Cross-references—See FA 2014 Sch 35 (penalties for failure to comply with duties under this section)

Obtaining information and documents: appeals

266 Appeals against notices imposing information etc requirements

(1) This section applies where a person is given a notice under section 255, 257, 258, 259, 260, 261 or 262.

(2) The person to whom the notice is given may appeal against the notice or any requirement under the notice.

(3) Subsection (2) does not apply—

(a) to a requirement to provide any information or produce any document that forms part of the person's statutory records, or

(b) if the tribunal has approved the giving of the notice under section 256.

(4) For the purposes of this section, information or a document forms part of a person's statutory records if it is information or a document which the person is required to keep and preserve under or by virtue of—

(a) the Taxes Acts, or

(b) any other enactment relating to a tax.

(5) Information and documents cease to form part of a person's statutory records when the period for which they are required to be preserved by the enactments mentioned in subsection (4) has expired.

(6) Notice of appeal must be given—

(a) in writing to the officer who gave the notice, and

(b) within the period of 30 days beginning with the day on which the notice was given.

(7) The notice of appeal must state the grounds of the appeal.

(8) On an appeal that is notified to the tribunal, the tribunal may—

(a) confirm the notice or a requirement under the notice,

(b) vary the notice or such a requirement, or

(c) set aside the notice or such a requirement.

(9) Where the tribunal confirms or varies the notice or a requirement, the person to whom the notice was given must comply with the notice or requirement—

(a) within such period as is specified by the tribunal, or

(b) if the tribunal does not specify a period, within such period as is reasonably specified in writing by an officer of Revenue and Customs following the tribunal's decision.

(10) A decision of the tribunal on an appeal under this section is final (despite the provisions of sections 11 and 13 of the Tribunals, Courts and Enforcement Act 2007).

(11) Subject to this section, the provisions of Part 5 of TMA 1970 relating to appeals have effect in relation to an appeal under this section.

Obtaining information and documents: supplementary

267 Form and manner of providing information

(1) The Commissioners may specify the form and manner in which information required to be provided or documents required to be produced by sections 255 to 264 must be provided or produced if the provision is to be complied with.

(2) The Commissioners may specify that a document must be produced for inspection—

(a) at a place agreed between the person and an officer of Revenue and Customs, or

(b) at such place (which must not be a place used solely as a dwelling) as an officer of Revenue and Customs may reasonably specify.

(3) The production of a document in compliance with a notice under this Part is not to be regarded as breaking any lien claimed on the document.

268 Production of documents: compliance

(1) Where the effect of a notice under section 255, 257 or 262 is to require a person to produce a document, the person may comply with the requirement by producing a copy of the document, subject to any conditions or exceptions that may be prescribed.

(2) Subsection (1) does not apply where—

(a) the effect of the notice is to require the person to produce the original document, or

(b) an authorised officer, or an officer of Revenue and Customs with the approval of an authorised officer, subsequently makes a request in writing to the person for the original document.

(3) Where an officer requests a document under subsection (2)(b), the person to whom the request is made must produce the document—

(a) within such period, and

(b) at such time and by such means,

as is reasonably requested by the officer.

Definitions—"authorised officer" (for the purposes of Part 5), s 283(2).

Cross-references—See FA 2014 s 278 (offence of concealing documents: exception in cases where sub-s (1) above applies).

269 Exception for certain documents or information

(1) Nothing in this Part requires a person to provide or produce—

(a) information that relates to the conduct of a pending appeal relating to tax or any part of a document containing such information,

(b) journalistic material (as defined in section 13 of the Police and Criminal Evidence Act 1984) or information contained in such material, or

(c) personal records (as defined in section 12 of the Police and Criminal Evidence Act 1984) or information contained in such records (but see subsection (2)).

(2) A notice under this Part may require a person—

(a) to produce documents, or copies of documents, that are personal records, omitting any information whose inclusion (whether alone or with other information) makes the original documents personal records ("personal information"), and

(b) to provide any information contained in such records that is not personal information.

270 Limitation on duty to produce documents

Nothing in this Part requires a person to produce a document—

(a) which is not in the possession or power of that person, or

(b) if the whole of the document originates more than 6 years before the requirement to produce it would, if it were not for this section, arise.

271 Legal professional privilege

(1) Nothing in this Part requires any person to disclose to HMRC any privileged information.

(2) "Privileged information" means information with respect to which a claim to legal professional privilege by the person who would (ignoring the effect of this section) be required to disclose it, could be maintained in legal proceedings.

(3) In the case of legal proceedings in Scotland, the reference in subsection (2) to legal professional privilege is to be read as a reference to confidentiality of communications.

272 Tax advisers

(1) This section applies where a notice is given under section 258(4) or (5) and the person to whom the notice is given is a tax adviser.

(2) The notice does not require a tax adviser—

(a) to provide information about relevant communications, or

(b) to produce documents which are the tax adviser's property and consist of relevant communications.

(3) Subsection (2) does not have effect in relation to—

(a) information explaining any information or document which the person to whom the notice is given has, as tax accountant, assisted any person in preparing for, or delivering to, HMRC, or

(b) a document which contains such information.

(4) But subsection (2) is not disapplied by subsection (3) if the information in question has already been provided, or a document containing the information has already been produced, to an officer of Revenue and Customs.

(5) In this section—

"relevant communications" means communications between the tax adviser and—

(a) a person in relation to whose tax affairs the tax adviser has been appointed, or

(b) any other tax adviser of such a person,

the purpose of which is the giving or obtaining of advice about any of those tax affairs, and

"tax adviser" means a person appointed to give advice about the tax affairs of another person (whether appointed directly by that person or by another tax adviser of that person).

273 Confidentiality

(1) No duty of confidentiality or other restriction on disclosure (however imposed) prevents the voluntary disclosure by a relevant client or a relevant intermediary to HMRC of information or documents about—

(a) a monitored promoter, or

(b) relevant proposals or relevant arrangements in relation to which a monitored promoter is a promoter.

(2) "Relevant client" means a person in relation to whom the monitored promoter mentioned in subsection (1)(a) or (b)—

(a) has made a firm approach in relation to a relevant proposal with a view to making the proposal available for implementation by that person or another person;

(b) has made a relevant proposal available for implementation by that person;

(c) took part in the organisation or management of relevant arrangements entered into by that person.

(3) "Relevant intermediary" means a person who is an intermediary in relation to a relevant proposal in relation to which the monitored promoter mentioned in subsection (1)(a) or (b) is a promoter.

(4) The relevant proposal or relevant arrangements mentioned in subsection (2) or (3) need not be the relevant proposals or relevant arrangements to which the disclosure relates.

Penalties

274 Penalties

Schedule 35 contains provision about penalties for failure to comply with provisions of this Part.

275 Failure to comply with Part 7 of the Finance Act 2004

(*inserts* TMA 1970 s 98C(2EA), (2EB))

276 Limitation of defence of reasonable care

(1) Subsection (2) applies where—

(a) *a person gives HMRC a document of a kind listed in the Table in paragraph 1 of Schedule 24 to FA 2007 (penalties for providing inaccurate documents to HMRC), and*

(b) *the document contains an inaccuracy.*

(2) In determining whether or not the inaccuracy was careless for the purposes of paragraph 3(1)(a) of Schedule 24 to FA 2007, reliance by the person on legal advice relating to relevant arrangements in relation to which a monitored promoter is a promoter is to be disregarded if the advice was given or procured by a person who was a monitored promoter in relation to the arrangements.

Amendments—This section repealed by F(No 2)A 2017 s 64(1), (4) with effect in relation to any document of a kind listed in the Table in FA 2007 Sch 24 para 1 which is given to HMRC on or after 16 November 2017 and which relates to a tax period beginning on or after 6 April 2017 and ending on or after 16 November 2017. "Tax period", and the reference to giving a document to HMRC have the same meaning as in FA 2007 Sch 24 para 28 (F(No 2)A 2017 s 64(6)).

277 Extended time limit for assessment

(1) (*amends* TMA 1970 s 36(1A))

(2) (*amends* OTA 1975 Sch 2 para 12B(1), (5), (6) and *inserts* OTA 1975 Sch 2 para 12B(2A))

(3) (*amends* IHTA 1984 s 240(3), (5), (8) and *inserts* IHTA 1984 s 240(5A))

(4) (*amends* FA 1998 Sch 18 para 46(2A))

(5) (*amends* FA 2003 Sch 10 para 31(2A))

(6) (*amends* FA 2013 Sch 33 para 25(4))

Offences

278 Offence of concealing etc documents

(1) A person is guilty of an offence if—

(a) the person is required to produce a document by a notice given under section 255,

(b) the tribunal approved the giving of the notice under section 256, and

(c) the person conceals, destroys or otherwise disposes of, or arranges for the concealment, destruction or disposal of, that document.

(2) Subsection (1) does not apply if the person acts after the document has been produced to an officer of Revenue and Customs in accordance with section 255, unless the officer has notified the person in writing that the document must continue to be available for inspection (and has not withdrawn the notification).

(3) Subsection (1) does not apply, in a case to which section 268(1) applies, if the person acts after the end of the expiry of 6 months beginning with the day on which a copy of the document was produced in accordance with that section unless, before the expiry of that period, an officer of Revenue and Customs makes a request for the original document under section 268(2)(b).

Cross-references—See FA 2014 s 280 (penalties for offences under ss 278 or 279).

279 Offence of concealing etc documents following informal notification

(1) A person is guilty of an offence if the person conceals, destroys or otherwise disposes of, or arranges for the concealment, destruction or disposal of, a document after an officer of Revenue and Customs has informed the person in writing that—

(a) the document is, or is likely, to be the subject of a notice under section 255, and

(b) the officer of Revenue and Customs intends to seek the approval of the tribunal to the giving of the notice.

(2) A person is not guilty of an offence under this section if the person acts after—

(a) at least 6 months has expired since the person was, or was last, informed as described in subsection (1), or

(b) a notice has been given to the person under section 255, requiring the document to be produced.

Cross-references—See FA 2014 s 280 (penalties for offences under ss 278 or 279).

280 Penalties for offences

(1) A person who is guilty of an offence under section 278 or 279 is liable—

(a) on summary conviction, to—

(i) in England and Wales, a fine, or

(ii) in Scotland or Northern Ireland, a fine not exceeding the statutory maximum, or

(b) on conviction on indictment, to imprisonment for a term not exceeding 2 years or to a fine or both.

(2) In relation to an offence committed before section 85(1) of the Legal Aid, Sentencing and Punishment of Offenders Act 2012 comes into force, subsection (1)(a)(i) has effect as if the reference to "a fine" were a reference to "a fine not exceeding the statutory maximum".

Supplemental

281 Partnerships

Schedule 36 contains provision about the application of this Part to partnerships.

[281A VAT [and other indirect taxes]

(1) In the provisions mentioned in subsection (2)—

(*a*) "tax" includes value added tax [and other indirect taxes]^2, and

(*b*) "tax advantage" has the meaning given by section 234(3) and also includes a tax advantage as defined [for VAT in paragraph 6, and for other indirect taxes in paragraph 7, of Schedule 17 to FA 2017 (disclosure of tax avoidance schemes: VAT and other indirect taxes)."]^2

(2) Those provisions are—

(*a*) section 237D;

(*b*) section 241B;

(*c*) Schedule 34A.

(3) Other references in this Part to "tax" are to be read as including value added tax [or other indirect taxes][2] so far as that is necessary for the purposes of sections 237A to 237D, 241A and 241B and Schedule 34A; but "tax" does not include value added tax [or other indirect taxes][2] in section 237A(10) or 237B(3).

[(4) In this section "indirect tax" has the same meaning as in Schedule 17 to FA 2017.][2]][1]

Amendments—[1] Section 281A inserted by FA 2016 s 160(7) with effect from 15 September 2016.

[2] The following amendments made by F(No 2)A 2017 s 66, Sch 17 paras 52, 53 with effect from 1 January 2018—

- in heading, sub-ss (1)(*a*), (3) (in both places), words inserted;
- in sub-s (1)(*b*), words substituted for words "in paragraph 1 of Schedule 11A to VATA 1994."; and
- sub-s (4) inserted.

282 Regulations under this Part

(1) Regulations under this Part are to be made by statutory instrument.

(2) Apart from an instrument to which subsection (3) applies, a statutory instrument containing regulations made under this Part is subject to annulment in pursuance of a resolution of the House of Commons.

(3) A statutory instrument containing (whether alone or with other provision) regulations made under—

(a) section 238(7),

(b) paragraph 14 of Schedule 34,

[(*ba*) paragraph 31 of Schedule 34A,][1]

(c) paragraph 5(1) of Schedule 35, or

(d) paragraph 21 of Schedule 36,

may not be made unless a draft of the instrument has been laid before and approved by a resolution of the House of Commons.

(4) Regulations under this Part—

(a) may make different provision for different purposes;

(b) may include transitional provision and savings.

Amendments—[1] Sub-s (3)(*ba*) inserted by FA 2016 s 160(8) with effect from 15 September 2016.

283 Interpretation of this Part

(1) In this Part—

"arrangements" has the meaning given by section 234(4);

"the Commissioners" means the Commissioners for Her Majesty's Revenue and Customs;

"calendar quarter" means a period of 3 months beginning with 1 January, 1 April, 1 July or 1 October;

"conduct notice" means a notice of the description in section 238 that is given under—

(a) section 237(7) [or (7A)][1],

[(*aa*) section 237A(8),

(*ab*) section 237B(1),][2]

(b) section 245(7), or

(c) paragraph 8(2) or (3) or 10(3)(a) or (4)(a) of Schedule 36;

["contract settlement" means an agreement in connection with a person's liability to make a payment to the Commissioners under or by virtue of an enactment;][2]

["defeat", in relation to arrangements, has the meaning given by paragraph 10 of Schedule 34A;][2]

["defeat notice" has the meaning given by section 241A(7);][2]

["double defeat notice" has the meaning given by section 241A(7);][2]

["final", in relation to a judicial ruling, is to be interpreted in accordance with section 237D(6);][1]

"firm approach" has the meaning given by section 235(4);

"HMRC" means Her Majesty's Revenue and Customs;

["judicial ruling" means a ruling of a court or tribunal on one or more issues;][2]

["look-forward period", in relation to a defeat notice, has the meaning given by section 241A(10);][2]

"monitored promoter" has the meaning given by section 244(5);

"monitored proposal" and "monitored arrangements" have the meaning given by section 254;

"monitoring notice" means a notice given under section 244(1) or paragraph 9(2) or (3) or 10(3)(b) or (4)(b) of Schedule 36;

"the original monitoring notice" has the meaning given by paragraph 11(2) of Schedule 36;

"prescribed" means prescribed, or of a description prescribed, in regulations made by the Commissioners;

"promoter reference number" has the meaning given by section 250(5);

["provisional", in relation to a conduct notice given under section 237A(8), is to be interpreted in accordance with section 237C;][2]

["related", in relation to arrangements, is to be interpreted in accordance with paragraph 2 of Schedule 34A;][2]

"relevant arrangements" has the meaning given by section 234(2);

["relevant defeat", in relation to a person, is to be interpreted in accordance with Schedule 34A;][2]

"relevant proposal" has the meaning given by section 234(1);

["relies on a Case 3 relevant defeat" is to be interpreted in accordance section 237B(5);][2]

"replacement conduct notice" has the meaning given by paragraph 11(1) of Schedule 36;

"replacement monitoring notice" has the meaning given by paragraph 11(1) of Schedule 36;

["single defeat notice" has the meaning given by section 241A(7).][2]

"tax" [(except in provisions to which section 281A applies)][2] means—

(a) income tax,

(b) capital gains tax,

(c) corporation tax,

(d) petroleum revenue tax,

[(da) apprenticeship levy,][3]

(e) inheritance tax,

(f) stamp duty land tax,

(g) stamp duty reserve tax, or

(h) annual tax on enveloped dwellings;

"tax advantage" has the meaning given by section 234(3) [(but see also section 281A)][2];

"Taxes Acts" has the same meaning as in TMA 1970 (see section 118(1) of that Act);

"the tribunal" means the First-tier Tribunal or, where determined by or under Tribunal Procedure Rules, the Upper Tribunal.

(2) A reference in a provision of this Part to an authorised officer is to an officer of Revenue and Customs who is, or is a member of a class of officers who are, authorised by the Commissioners for the purposes of that provision.

(3) A reference in a provision of this Part to meeting a threshold condition is to meeting one of the conditions described in paragraphs 2 to 12 of Schedule 34.

Regulations—Promoters of Tax Avoidance Schemes (Prescribed Circumstances under Section 235) Regulations, SI 2015/130.

Definitions—"threshold condition", Sch 34 paras 2–12.

Amendments—[1] In definition of "conduct notice", words inserted by FA 2015 s 119, Sch 19 paras 1, 3 with effect for the purposes of determining whether a person meets a threshold condition in a period of three years ending on or after 26 March 2015.

[2] In sub-s (1), in definition of "conduct notice", sub-paras (*aa*), (*ab*) inserted, in definitions of "tax" and "tax advantage", words inserted, and definitions inserted, by FA 2016 s 160(9) with effect from 15 September 2016.

[3] In sub-s (1), in definition of "tax", para (*da* inserted by FA 2016 s 104(6), (8) with effect from 15 September 2016.

PART 6
OTHER PROVISIONS

Employee-ownership trusts

290 Companies owned by employee-ownership trusts

Schedule 37 contains provision about tax reliefs in connection with companies owned by employee-ownership trusts.

Trusts

291 Trusts with vulnerable beneficiary: meaning of "disabled person"

(1) Schedule 1A to FA 2005 (meaning of "disabled person") is amended as follows.

(2) In paragraph 1—

(a) for paragraph (c) substitute—

"(c) a person in receipt of a disability living allowance by virtue of entitlement to—

(i) the care component at the highest or middle rate, or

(ii) the mobility component at the higher rate,", and

(b) in paragraph (d), omit "by virtue of entitlement to the daily living component".

(3) In paragraph 3, after "rate" insert ", or to the mobility component at the higher rate,".

(4) In paragraph 4, omit "by virtue of entitlement to the daily living component".

(5) The amendments made by this section have effect—

(a) for the purposes of sections 89, 89A and 89B of IHTA 1984, in relation to property transferred into settlement on or after 6 April 2014, and

(b) for all other purposes, for the tax year 2014–15 and subsequent tax years.

Commentary—*Simon's Taxes* **C4.259**.

PART 7
FINAL PROVISIONS

301 Power to update indexes of defined terms

(1) The Treasury may by order amend any index of defined expressions contained in an Act relating to taxation, so as to make amendments consequential on any enactment.

(2) In this section—

"enactment" means any provision made by or under an Act (whether before or after the passing of this Act);

"index of defined expressions" means a provision contained in an Act relating to taxation which lists where expressions used in the Act, or in a particular part of the Act, are defined or otherwise explained.

(3) The power to make an order under this section is exercisable by statutory instrument.

Commentary—*Simon's Taxes* **A1.150**.

(4) An order under this section is subject to annulment in pursuance of a resolution of the House of Commons.

302 Interpretation

(1) In this Act—

"ALDA 1979" means the Alcoholic Liquor Duties Act 1979,
"BGDA 1981" means the Betting and Gaming Duties Act 1981,
"CAA 2001" means the Capital Allowances Act 2001,
"CEMA 1979" means the Customs and Excise Management Act 1979,
"CRCA 2005" means the Commissioners for Revenue and Customs Act 2005,
"CTA 2009" means the Corporation Tax Act 2009,
"CTA 2010" means the Corporation Tax Act 2010,
"F(No 3)A 2010" means the Finance (No 3) Act 2010,
"IHTA 1984" means the Inheritance Tax Act 1984,
"ITA 2007" means the Income Tax Act 2007,
"ITEPA 2003" means the Income Tax (Earnings and Pensions) Act 2003,
"ITTOIA 2005" means the Income Tax (Trading and Other Income) Act 2005,
"OTA 1975" means the Oil Taxation Act 1975,
"TCGA 1992" means the Taxation of Chargeable Gains Act 1992,
"TIOPA 2010" means the Taxation (International and Other Provisions) Act 2010,
"TMA 1970" means the Taxes Management Act 1970,
"TPDA 1979" means the Tobacco Products Duty Act 1979,
"VATA 1994" means the Value Added Tax Act 1994, and
"VERA 1994" means the Vehicle Excise and Registration Act 1994.

(2) In this Act—

"FA", followed by a year, means the Finance Act of that year, and
"F(No 2)A", followed by a year, means the Finance (No 2) Act of that year.

303 Short title

This Act may be cited as the Finance Act 2014.

SCHEDULE 25
INHERITANCE TAX
Section 117

Introductory

1 IHTA 1984 is amended as follows.

Rate bands for tax years 2015–16, 2016-17 and 2017-18

2 Section 8 (indexation) does not have effect by virtue of any difference between the consumer prices index for the month of September in 2014, 2015 or 2016 and the previous September.

Treatment of certain liabilities

3 (1) After section 162A (liabilities attributable to financing excluded property) insert—

"162AA Liabilities attributable to financing non-residents' foreign currency accounts

(1) This section applies if—

(a) in determining the value of a person's estate immediately before death, a balance on any qualifying foreign currency account ("the relevant balance") is to be left out of account under section 157 (non-residents' bank accounts), and

(b) the person has a liability which is attributable, in whole or in part, to financing (directly or indirectly) the relevant balance.

(2) To the extent that the liability is attributable as mentioned in subsection (1)(b), it may only be taken into account in determining the value of the person's estate immediately before death so far as permitted by subsection (3).

(3) If the amount of the liability that is attributable as mentioned in subsection (1)(b) exceeds the value of the relevant balance, the excess may be taken into account, but only so far as the excess does not arise for either of the reasons mentioned in subsection (4).

(4) The reasons are—

(a) arrangements the main purpose, or one of the main purposes, of which is to secure a tax advantage, or

(b) an increase in the amount of the liability (whether due to the accrual of interest or otherwise).

(5) In subsection (4)(a)—

"arrangements" includes any scheme, transaction or series of transactions, agreement or understanding, whether or not legally enforceable, and any associated operations;

"tax advantage" means—

(a) the avoidance or reduction of a charge to tax, or

(b) the avoidance of a possible determination in respect of tax."

(2) Section 162C (sections 162A and 162B: supplementary provision) is amended as follows.

(3) In the heading, after "162A" insert ", 162AA".

(4) In subsection (1), after "162A(1) or (5)" insert ", 162AA(1)".

(5) After subsection (1) insert—

"(1A) In a case in which the value of a person's estate immediately before death is to be determined, where a liability was discharged in part before that time—

(a) any part of the liability that, at the time of discharge, was not attributable as mentioned in subsection (1) is, so far as possible, to be taken to have been discharged first,

(b) any part of the liability that, at the time of discharge, was attributable as mentioned in section 162B(1)(b), (3)(b) or (5)(c) is, so far as possible, only to be taken to have been discharged after any part of the liability within paragraph (a) was discharged,

(c) any part of the liability that, at the time of discharge, was attributable as mentioned in section 162AA(1) is, so far as possible, only to be taken to have been discharged after any parts of the liability within paragraph (a) or (b) were discharged, and

(d) any part of the liability that, at the time of discharge, was attributable as mentioned in section 162A(1) or (5) is, so far as possible, only to be taken to have been discharged after any parts of the liability within paragraphs (a) to (c) were discharged."

(6) In subsection (2)—

(a) for "Where" substitute "In any other case, where", and

(b) in paragraph (a), for "subsection (1)" substitute "section 162A(1) or (5) or 162B(1)(b), (3)(b) or (5)(c)".

(7) In section 175A (discharge of liabilities after death), in subsection (7)—

(a) after paragraph (a) insert—

"(aa) any part of the liability that is attributable as mentioned in section 162AA(1) is, so far as possible, taken to be discharged only after any part of the liability within paragraph (a) is discharged,",

(b) in paragraph (b)—

(i) for "part", in the second place it appears, substitute "parts", and

(ii) for "(a) is" substitute "(a) or (aa) are",

(c) in paragraph (c)—

(i) for "paragraph (a) or (b)" substitute "any of paragraphs (a) to (b)", and

(ii) for "either" substitute "any".

(8) The amendments made by this paragraph have effect in relation to transfers of value made, or treated as made, on or after the day on which this Act is passed.

Commentary—*Simon's Taxes* **I3.321, I4.146**.

Ten-year anniversary charge

4 (1) In section 64 (charge at ten-year anniversary), after subsection (1) insert—

"(1A) For the purposes of subsection (1) above, property held by the trustees of a settlement immediately before a ten-year anniversary is to be regarded as relevant property comprised in the settlement at that time if—

(a) it is income of the settlement,

(b) the income arose before the start of the five years ending immediately before the ten-year anniversary,

(c) the income arose (directly or indirectly) from property comprised in the settlement that, when the income arose, was relevant property, and

(d) when the income arose, no person was beneficially entitled to an interest in possession in the property from which the income arose.

(1B) Where the settlor of a settlement was not domiciled in the United Kingdom at the time the settlement was made, income of the settlement is not to be regarded as relevant property comprised in the settlement as a result of subsection (1A) above so far as the income—

(a) is situated outside the United Kingdom, or

(b) is represented by a holding in an authorised unit trust or a share in an open-ended investment company.

(1C) Income of the settlement is not to be regarded as relevant property comprised in the settlement as a result of subsection (1A) above so far as the income—

(a) is represented by securities issued by the Treasury subject to a condition of the kind mentioned in subsection (2) of section 6 above, and

(b) it is shown that all known persons for whose benefit the settled property or income from it has been or might be applied, or who are or might become beneficially entitled to an interest in possession in it, are persons of a description specified in the condition in question."

(2) In section 66 (rate of ten-yearly charge), after subsection (2) insert—

"(2A) Subsection (2) above does not apply to property which is regarded as relevant property as a result of section 64(1A) (and accordingly that property is charged to tax at the rate given by subsection (1) above)."

(3) The amendments made by this paragraph have effect in relation to occasions on which tax falls to be charged under section 64 of IHTA 1984 on or after 6 April 2014.

Delivery of account and payment of tax

5 (1) In section 216(6) (time for delivery of accounts), before paragraph (b) insert—

"(ad) in the case of an account to be delivered by a person within subsection (1)(c) above, before the expiration of the period of six months from the end of the month in which the occasion concerned occurs;".

(2) In section 226 (payment of tax: general rules), after subsection (3B) insert—

"(3C) Tax chargeable under Chapter 3 of Part 3 of this Act on the value transferred by a chargeable transfer, other than any for which the due date is given by subsection (3B) above, is due six months after the end of the month in which the chargeable transfer is made."

(3) In section 233 (interest on unpaid tax)—

(a) in subsection (1)(a), after "transfer" insert "not within paragraph (aa) below and",

(b) after subsection (1)(a) insert—

"(aa) an amount of tax charged under Chapter 3 of Part 3 of this Act on the value transferred by a chargeable transfer remains unpaid after the end of the period of six months beginning with the end of the month in which the chargeable transfer was made, or", and

(c) in subsection (1)(b), for "any other chargeable transfer" substitute "a chargeable transfer not within paragraph (a) or (aa) above".

(4) The amendments made by this paragraph have effect in relation to chargeable transfers made on or after 6 April 2014.

SCHEDULE 30

SECTION 208 PENALTY: VALUE OF THE DENIED ADVANTAGE

Section 209

Commentary—*Simon's Taxes* **A7.247**.

Introduction

1 This Schedule applies for the purposes of calculating penalties under section 209.

Value of denied advantage: normal rule

2 (1) The value of the denied advantage is the additional amount due or payable in respect of tax as a result of counteracting the denied advantage.

(2) The reference in sub-paragraph (1) to the additional amount due or payable includes a reference to—

(a) an amount payable to HMRC having erroneously been paid by way of repayment of tax, and

(b) an amount which would be repayable by HMRC if the denied advantage were not counteracted.

(3) The following are ignored in calculating the value of the denied advantage—

(a) group relief, and

(b) any relief under section 458 of CTA 2010 (relief in respect of repayment etc of loan) which is deferred under subsection (5) of that section.

(4) This paragraph is subject to paragraphs 3 and 4.

Value of denied advantage: losses

3 (1) To the extent that the denied advantage has the result that a loss is wrongly recorded for purposes of direct tax and the loss has been wholly used to reduce the amount due or payable in respect of tax, the value of the denied advantage is determined in accordance with paragraph 2.

(2) To the extent that the denied advantage has the result that a loss is wrongly recorded for purposes of direct tax and the loss has not been wholly used to reduce the amount due or payable in respect of tax, the value of the denied advantage is—

(a) the value under paragraph 2 of so much of the denied advantage as results from the part (if any) of the loss which is used to reduce the amount due or payable in respect of tax, plus

(b) 10% of the part of the loss not so used.

(3) Sub-paragraphs (1) and (2) apply both—

(a) to a case where no loss would have been recorded but for the denied advantage, and

(b) to a case where a loss of a different amount would have been recorded (but in that case sub-paragraphs (1) and (2) apply only to the difference between the amount recorded and the true amount).

(4) To the extent that a denied advantage creates or increases an aggregate loss recorded for a group of companies—

(a) the value of the denied advantage is calculated in accordance with this paragraph, and

(b) in applying paragraph 2 in accordance with sub-paragraphs (1) and (2), group relief may be taken into account (despite paragraph 2(3)).

(5) To the extent that the denied advantage results in a loss, the value of it is nil where, because of the nature of the loss or P's circumstances, there is no reasonable prospect of the loss being used to support a claim to reduce a tax liability (of any person).

Value of denied advantage: deferred tax

4 (1) To the extent that the denied advantage is a deferral of tax, the value of that advantage is—

(a) 25% of the amount of the deferred tax for each year of the deferral, or

(b) a percentage of the amount of the deferred tax, for each separate period of deferral of less than a year, equating to 25% per year,

or, if less, 100% of the amount of the deferred tax.

(2) This paragraph does not apply to a case to the extent that paragraph 3 applies.

SCHEDULE 31

FOLLOWER NOTICES AND PARTNERSHIPS

Section 215

Commentary—*Simon's Taxes* **A7.247**.

Introduction

1 This Schedule makes special provision about the application of Chapter 2 to partners and partnerships.

Interpretation

2 (1) This paragraph applies for the purposes of this Schedule.

(2) "Partnership follower notice" means a follower notice given by reason of—

(a) a tax enquiry being in progress into a partnership return, or

(b) an appeal having been made in relation to an amendment of a partnership return or against a conclusion stated by a closure notice in relation to a tax enquiry into a partnership return.

(3) "Partnership return" means a return in pursuance of a notice under section 12AA(2) or (3) of TMA 1970.
(4) "The representative partner", in relation to a partnership return, means the person who was required by a notice served under or for the purposes of section 12AA(2) or (3) of TMA 1970 to deliver the return.
(5) "Relevant partner", in relation to a partnership return, means a person who was a partner in the partnership to which the return relates at any time during the period in respect of which the return was required.
(6) References to a "successor", in relation to the representative partner are to be construed in accordance with section 12AA(11) of TMA 1970.

Prospective amendments—The following amendments to be made by F(No 2)A 2017 s 61(1), Sch 14 paras 43, 45(1), (2) with effect from a day to be appointed—

- in sub-para (3), words from "in pursuance" to the end to be numbered as para (*a*), in that para, words "(a "section 12AA partnership return"), or" to be inserted at the end, and sub-para (3)(*b*) to be inserted;
- in sub-para (4), words "section 12AA" to be inserted after words "in relation to a"; and
- sub-para (4A) to be inserted.

Sub-para (3)(*b*) as inserted to read as follows—

"(*b*) required by regulations under paragraph 10 of Schedule A1 to TMA 1970 (a "Schedule A1 partnership return").".

Sub-para (4A) as inserted to read as follows—

"(4A) "The nominated partner", in relation to a Schedule A1 partnership return, has the meaning given by paragraph 5 of Schedule A1 to TMA 1970.".

Giving of follower notices in relation to partnership returns

3 (1) If the representative partner in relation to a partnership return is no longer available, then, for the purposes of section 204 the return, or an appeal in respect of the return, is to be regarded as made by the person who is for the time being the successor of that partner (if that would not otherwise be the case).
(2) Where, at any time after a partnership follower notice is given to P, P is no longer available, any reference in this Chapter (other than section 204 and this sub-paragraph) to P is to be read as a reference to the person who is, for the time being, the successor of the representative partner.
(3) For the purposes of Condition B in section 204 a partnership return, or appeal in respect of a partnership return, is made on the basis that a particular tax advantage results from particular tax arrangements if—
(a) it is made on the basis that an increase or reduction in one or more of the amounts mentioned in section 12AB(1) of TMA 1970 (amounts in the partnership statement in a partnership return) results from those tax arrangements, and
(b) that increase or reduction results in that tax advantage for one or more of the relevant partners.
(4) For the purposes of Condition D in section 204—
(a) a notice given to a person in the person's capacity as the representative partner of a partnership, or a successor of that partner, and a notice given to that person otherwise than in that capacity are not to be treated as given to the same person, and
(b) all notices given to the representative partner and successors of that partner, in that capacity, are to be treated as given to the same person.
(5) In this paragraph references to a person being "no longer available" have the same meaning as in section 12AA(11) of TMA 1970.

Prospective amendments—The following amendments to be made by F(No 2)A 2017 s 61(1), Sch 14 paras 43, 45(1), (3) with effect from a day to be appointed—

- in sub-para (1), words "section 12AA" to be inserted after words "in relation to a";
- sub-para (1A) to be inserted.
- in sub-para (2), words ", or the nominated partner (as the case may be)." to be inserted at the end;
- in sub-para (4)(*a*), words "or as the nominated partner of a partnership," to be inserted after words "or a successor of that partner,"; and
- in sub-para (4)(*b*), words "or to a nominated partner" to be inserted after words "successors of that partner".

Sub-para (1A) as inserted to read as follows—

"(1A) For the purposes of section 204 a Schedule A1 partnership return, or an appeal in respect of the return, is to be regarded as made by the person who is for the time being the nominated partner (if that would not otherwise be the case).".

Penalty if corrective action not taken in response to partnership follower notice

4 (1) Section 208 applies, in relation to a partnership follower notice, in accordance with this paragraph.
(2) Subsection (2) applies as if the reference to P were to each relevant partner.

(3) References to the denied advantage are to be read as references to the increase or reduction in an amount in the partnership statement mentioned in paragraph 3(3) which is denied by the application of the principles laid down or the reasoning given in the judicial ruling identified in the partnership follower notice under section 206(a) or, if only part of any increase or reduction is so denied, that part.

(4) In subsection (6)(b) the words from "and (where different)" to the end are to be ignored, and accordingly subsection (7) does not apply.

Calculation of penalty etc

5 (1) This paragraph applies in relation to a partnership follower notice.

(2) Section 209 applies subject to the following modifications—

(a) the total amount of the penalties under section 208(2) for which the relevant partners are liable is 20% of the value of the denied advantage,

(b) the amount of the penalty for which each relevant partner is liable is that partner's appropriate share of that total amount, and

(c) the value of the denied advantage for the purposes of calculating the total amount of the penalties is—

(i) in the case of a notice given under section 204(2)(a), the net amount of the amendments required to be made to the partnership return to counteract the denied advantage, and

(ii) in the case of a notice given under section 204(2)(b), the net amount of the amendments that have been made to the partnership return to counteract the denied advantage,

(and, accordingly, Schedule 30 does not apply).

(3) For the purposes of sub-paragraph (2), a relevant partner's appropriate share is—

(a) the same share as the share in which any profits or loss for the period to which the return relates would be apportioned to that partner in accordance with the firm's profit-sharing arrangements, or

(b) if HMRC do not have sufficient information from P to establish that share, such share as is determined for the purposes of this paragraph by an officer of HMRC.

(4) Where—

(a) the relevant partners are liable to pay a penalty under section 208(2) (as modified by this paragraph),

(b) the penalties have not yet been assessed, and

(c) P has co-operated with HMRC,

section 210(1) does not apply, but HMRC may reduce the total amount of the penalties determined in accordance with sub-paragraph (2)(a) to reflect the quality of that co-operation.

Section 210(2) and (3) apply for the purposes of this sub-paragraph.

(5) Nothing in sub-paragraph (4) permits HMRC to reduce the total amount of the penalties to less than 4% of the value of the denied advantage (as determined in accordance with sub-paragraph (2)(c)).

(6) For the purposes of section 212, a penalty imposed on a relevant partner by virtue of paragraph 4(2) is to be treated as if it were determined by reference to such additional amount of tax as is due and payable by the relevant partner as a result of the counteraction of the denied advantage.

(7) The right of appeal under section 214 extends to—

(a) a decision that penalties are payable by the relevant partners by virtue of this paragraph, and

(b) a decision as to the total amount of those penalties payable by those partners,

but not to a decision as to the appropriate share of, or the amount of a penalty payable by, a relevant partner.

(8) Section 214(3) applies to an appeal by virtue of sub-paragraph (7)(a) as it applies to an appeal under section 214(1).

(9) Section 214(8) applies to an appeal by virtue of sub-paragraph (7)(a), and section 214(9) to an appeal by virtue of sub-paragraph (7)(b).

(10) An appeal by virtue of sub-paragraph (7) may be brought only by the representative partner or, if that partner is no longer available, the person who is for the time being the successor of that partner.

(11) The Treasury may by order made by statutory instrument vary the rates for the time being specified in sub-paragraphs (2)(a) and (5).

(12) Any statutory instrument containing an order under sub-paragraph (11) is subject to annulment in pursuance of a resolution of the House of Commons.

Prospective amendments—In sub-para (10), words from "the representative partner" to the end to be numbered as para (*a*), in that para, words "(in relation to a section 12AA partnership return), or" to be inserted at the end, and sub-para (10)(*b*) to be inserted, by F(No 2)A 2017 s 61(1), Sch 14 paras 43, 45(1), (4) with effect from a day to be appointed. Sub-para (10)(*b*) as inserted to read as follows—

"(*b*) the nominated partner (in relation to a Schedule A1 partnership return).".

SCHEDULE 32

ACCELERATED PAYMENTS AND PARTNERSHIPS

Section 228

Commentary—*Simon's Taxes* **A4.233**.

Simon's Tax Cases—*R (on the appn of Sword Services Ltd and ors) v R&C Comrs* [2016] EWHC 1473 (Admin), [2017] STC 596.

Interpretation

1 (1) This paragraph applies for the purposes of this Schedule.

(2) "Partnership return" means a return in pursuance of a notice under section 12AA(2) or (3) of TMA 1970.

(3) "The representative partner", in relation to a partnership return, means the person who was required by a notice served under or for the purposes of section 12AA(2) or (3) of TMA 1970 to deliver the return.

(4) "Relevant partner", in relation to a partnership return, means a person who was a partner in the partnership to which the return relates at any time during the period in respect of which the return was required.

(5) References to a "successor", in relation to the representative partner, are to be construed in accordance with section 12AA(11) of TMA 1970.

Prospective amendments—The following amendments to be made by F(No 2)A 2017 s 61(1), Sch 14 paras 43, 46(1), (2) with effect from a day to be appointed—

– in sub-para (2), words from "in pursuance" to the end to be numbered as para (*a*), in that para, words "(a "section 12AA partnership return"), or" to be inserted at the end, and sub-para (2)(*b*) to be inserted;
– in sub-para (3), words "section 12AA" to be inserted after words "in relation to a"; and
– sub-para (3A) to be inserted.

Sub-para (2)(*b*) as inserted to read as follows—

"(*b*) required by regulations under paragraph 10 of Schedule A1 to TMA 1970 (a "Schedule A1 partnership return")".

Sub-para (4A) as inserted to read as follows—

"(4A) "The nominated partner", in relation to a Schedule A1 partnership return, has the meaning given by paragraph 5 of Schedule A1 to TMA 1970.".

Restriction on circumstances when accelerated payment notices can be given

2 (1) This paragraph applies where—

(a) a tax enquiry is in progress in relation to a partnership return, or

(b) an appeal has been made in relation to an amendment of such a return or against a conclusion stated by a closure notice in relation to a tax enquiry into such a return.

(2) No accelerated payment notice may be given to the representative partner of the partnership, or a successor of that partner, by reason of that enquiry or appeal.

(3) But this Schedule makes provision for partner payment notices and accelerated partner payments in such cases.

Prospective amendments—In sub-para (2), words "(in relation to a section 12AA partnership return), or to the nominated partner of the partnership (in relation to a Schedule A1 partnership return)" to be inserted after words "a successor of that partner" by F(No 2)A 2017 s 61(1), Sch 14 paras 43, 46(1), (3) with effect from a day to be appointed.

Circumstances in which partner payment notices may be given

3 (1) Where a partnership return has been made in respect of a partnership, HMRC may give a notice (a "partner payment notice") to each relevant partner of the partnership if Conditions A to C are met.

(2) Condition A is that—

(a) a tax enquiry is in progress in relation to the partnership return, or

(b) an appeal has been made in relation to an amendment of the return or against a conclusion stated by a closure notice in relation to a tax enquiry into the return.

(3) Condition B is that the return or, as the case may be, appeal is made on the basis that a particular tax advantage ("the asserted advantage") results from particular arrangements ("the chosen arrangements").

(4) Paragraph 3(3) of Schedule 31 applies for the purposes of sub-paragraph (3) as it applies for the purposes of Condition B in section 204(3).

(5) Condition C is that one or more of the following requirements are met—

(a) HMRC has given (or, at the same time as giving the partner payment notice, gives) the representative partner, or a successor of that partner, a follower notice under Chapter 2—

(i) in relation to the same return or, as the case may be, appeal, and

(ii) by reason of the same tax advantage and the chosen arrangements;

(b) the chosen arrangements are DOTAS arrangements (within the meaning of section 219(5) and (6));

(c) the relevant partner in question has been given a GAAR counteraction notice in respect of any tax advantage resulting from the asserted advantage or part of it and the chosen arrangements (or is given such a notice at the same time as the partner payment notice) in a case where the stated opinion of at least two of the members of the sub-panel of the GAAR Advisory Panel which considered the matter under paragraph 10 of Schedule 43 to FA 2013 was as set out in paragraph 11(3)(b) of that Schedule (entering into tax arrangements not reasonable course of action etc).

[(d) the relevant partner in question has been given a notice under paragraph 8(2) or 9(2) of Schedule 43A to FA 2013 (notice of final decision after considering Panel's opinion about referred or counteracted arrangements) in respect of any tax advantage resulting from the asserted advantage or part of it and the chosen arrangements (or is given such a notice at the same time as the partner payment notice) in a case where the stated opinion of at least two of the members of the sub-panel of the GAAR Advisory Panel about the other arrangements (see sub-paragraph (7)) was as set out in paragraph 11(3)(*b*) of Schedule 43 to FA 2013;

(e) the relevant partner in question has been given a notice under paragraph 8(2) of Schedule 43B to FA 2013 (GAAR: generic referral of arrangements) in respect of any tax advantage resulting from the asserted advantage or part of it and the chosen arrangements (or is given such a notice at the same time as the partner payment notice) in a case where the stated opinion of at least two of the members of the sub-panel of the GAAR Advisory Panel which considered the generic referral in respect of those arrangements was as set out in paragraph 6(4)(*b*) of that Schedule.][1]

(6) "GAAR counteraction notice" has the meaning given by section 219(7).

[(7) "Other arrangements" means—

(a) in relation to a notice under paragraph 8(2) of Schedule 43A to FA 2013, the referred arrangements (as defined in that paragraph);

(b) in relation to a notice under paragraph 9(2) of that Schedule, the counteracted arrangements (as defined in paragraph 2 of that Schedule).][1]

Amendments—[1] Sub-paras (5)(*d*), (*e*), (7) inserted by FA 2016 s 157(26)–(28) with effect in relation to tax arrangements (within the meaning of FA 2013 Pt 5) entered into at any time (whether before on or after 15 September 2016.

Prospective amendments—In sub-para (5)(*a*), words "(in relation to a section 12AA partnership return), or to the nominated partner (in relation to a Schedule A1 partnership return)" to be inserted after words "or a successor of that partner" by F(No 2)A 2017 s 61(1), Sch 14 paras 43, 46(1), (4) with effect from a day to be appointed.

Content of partner payment notices

4 (1) The partner payment notice given to a relevant partner must—

(a) specify the paragraph or paragraphs of paragraph 3(5) by virtue of which the notice is given,

(b) specify the payment [(if any)][1] required to be made under paragraph 6, . . . [1]

(c) explain the effect of paragraphs 5 and 6, and of the amendments made by sections 224 and 225 (so far as relating to the relevant tax in relation to which the partner payment notice is given)[, and

(*d*) if the denied advantage consists of or includes an asserted surrenderable amount, specify that amount and any action which is required to be taken in respect of it under paragraph 6A.][1]

(2) The payment required to be made under paragraph 6 is an amount equal to the amount which a designated HMRC officer determines, to the best of the officer's information and belief, as the understated partner tax.

(3) "The understated partner tax" means the additional amount that would become due and payable by the relevant partner in respect of tax if—

(a) in the case of a notice given by virtue of paragraph 3(5)(a) (case where a partnership follower notice is given)—

(i) it were assumed that the explanation given in the follower notice in question under section 206(b) is correct, and

(ii) what the officer may determine to the best of the officer's information and belief as the denied advantage is counteracted to the extent that it is reflected in a return or claim of the relevant partner;

(b) in the case of a notice given by virtue of paragraph 3(5)(b) (cases where the DOTAS arrangements are met), such adjustments were made as are required to counteract so much of what the designated HMRC officer so determines as the denied advantage as is reflected in a return or claim of the relevant partner;

(c) in the case of a notice given by virtue of paragraph 3(5)(c) (cases involving counteraction under the general anti-abuse rule), such of the adjustments set out in the GAAR counteraction notice are made as have effect to counteract so much of the denied advantage as is reflected in a return or claim of the relevant partner.

(4) "The denied advantage"—

(a) in the case of the notice given by virtue of paragraph 3(5)(a), has the meaning given by paragraph 4(3) of Schedule 31,

(b) in the case of a notice given by virtue of paragraph 3(5)(b), means so much of the asserted advantage as is not a tax advantage which results from the chosen arrangements or otherwise, and

(c) in the case of a notice given by virtue of paragraph 3(5)(c), means so much of the asserted advantage as would be counteracted by making the adjustments set out in the GAAR counteraction notice.

[(4A) "Asserted surrenderable amount" means so much of a surrenderable loss which the relevant partner asserts to have as a designated HMRC officer determines, to the best of that officer's information and belief, to be an amount—

(*a*) which would not be a surrenderable loss of that partner if the position were as stated in paragraphs (*a*), (*b*) or (*c*) of sub-paragraph (3), and

(*b*) which is not the subject of a claim by the relevant partner to relief from corporation tax which is reflected in the amount of the understated partner tax of that partner (and hence in the payment required to be made under paragraph 6).

(4B) "Surrenderable loss" means a loss or other amount within section 99(1) of CTA 2010 (or part of such a loss or other amount).][1]

(5) If a notice is given by reason of two or all of the requirements of paragraph 3(5) being met, [any payment specified under sub-paragraph (1)(*b*) or amount specified under sub-paragraph (1)(*d*)][1] is to be determined as if the notice were given by virtue of such one of them as is stated in the notice as being used for this purpose.

Amendments—[1] In sub-para (1)(*b*), words inserted and word repealed, sub-para (4)(*d*) and preceding word inserted, sub-paras (4A), (4B) inserted, and in sub-para (5), words substituted, by FA 2015 s 118, Sch 18 paras 1, 10(1), (2) with effect from 26 March 2015.

Representations about a partner payment notice

5 (1) This paragraph applies where a partner payment notice has been given to a relevant partner under paragraph 3 (and not withdrawn).

(2) The relevant partner has 90 days beginning with the day that notice is given to send written representations to HMRC—

(a) objecting to the notice on the grounds that Condition A, B or C in that paragraph was not met, . . . [1]

(b) objecting to the amount specified in the notice under paragraph 4(1)(b)[, or

(*c*) objecting to the amount specified in the notice under paragraph 4(1)(*d*).][1]

(3) HMRC must consider any representations made in accordance with sub-paragraph (2).

(4) Having considered the representations, HMRC must—

(a) if representations were made under sub-paragraph (2)(a), determine whether—

(i) to confirm the partner payment notice (with or without amendment), or

(ii) to withdraw the partner payment notice, . . . [1]

(b) if representations were made under sub-paragraph (2)(b) (and the notice is not withdrawn under paragraph (a)), determine whether a different amount [(or no amount)][1] ought to have been specified as the understated partner tax, and then—

(i) confirm the amount specified in the notice, . . . [1]

(ii) amend the notice to specify a different amount[, or

(iii) remove from the notice the provision made under paragraph 4(1)(*b*),][1] [and

(*c*) if representations were made under sub-paragraph (2)(*c*) (and the notice is not withdrawn under paragraph (*a*)), determine whether a different amount (or no amount) ought to have been specified under paragraph 4(1)(*d*), and then—

(i) confirm the amount specified in the notice,

(ii) amend the notice to specify a different amount, or

(iii) remove from the notice the provision made under paragraph 4(1)(*d*),][1]

and notify P accordingly.

Amendments—[1] In sub-paras (2)(*a*), (4)(*a*), (*b*)(i), word repealed, sub-paras (2)(*c*), (4)(*b*) (iii), (*c*) and preceding words inserted, and in sub-para (4)(*b*), words inserted, by FA 2015 s 118, Sch 18 paras 1, 10(1), (3) with effect from 26 March 2015.

Effect of partner payment notice

6 [(1) This paragraph applies where—

(*a*) a partner payment notice has been given to a relevant partner (and not withdrawn), and

(*b*) an amount is stated in the notice in accordance with paragraph 4(1)(*b*).][1]

(2) The relevant partner must make a payment ("the accelerated partner payment") to HMRC of [that amount][1].

(3) The accelerated partner payment is to be treated as a payment on account of the understated partner tax (see paragraph 4).

(4) The accelerated partner payment must be made before the end of the payment period.

(5) "The payment period" means—

(a) if the relevant partner made no representations under paragraph 5, the period of 90 days beginning with the day on which the partner payment notice is given;

(b) if the relevant partner made such representations, whichever of the following ends later—

(i) the 90 day period mentioned in paragraph (a);

(ii) the period of 30 days beginning with the day on which the relevant partner is notified under paragraph 5 of HMRC's determination.

(6) If the relevant partner pays any part of the understated partner tax before the accelerated partner payment in respect of it, the accelerated partner payment is treated to that extent as having been paid at the same time.

(7) Subsections (8) and (9) of section 223 apply in relation to a payment under this paragraph as they apply to a payment under that section.

Cross-references—F(No 2)A 2015 Sch 8 para 2(3)(*b*) (sums due under this para are relevant sums for the purposes of scheme for enforcement by deduction from accounts (direct recovery of debts)).

Amendments—[1] Sub-para (1) substituted, and words in sub-para (2) substituted, by FA 2015 s 118, Sch 18 paras 1, 10(1), (4) with effect from 26 March 2015.

[6A (1) This paragraph applies where—

(*a*) an accelerated payment notice is given (and not withdrawn), and

(*b*) an amount is specified in the notice in accordance with paragraph 4(1)(*d*).

(2) The relevant partner may not at any time when the notice has effect consent to any claim for group relief in respect of the amount so specified.

(3) Subject to sub-paragraph (2), paragraph 75 (other than sub-paragraphs (7) and (8)) of Schedule 18 to FA 1998 (reduction in amount available for surrender) has effect at any time when the notice has effect as if that specified amount ceased to be an amount available for surrender at the time the notice was given to the relevant partner.

(4) For the purposes of sub-paragraph (3), paragraph 75 of that Schedule has effect as if, in sub-paragraph (2) of that paragraph for "within 30 days" there were substituted "before the end of the payment period (within the meaning of paragraph 6(5) of Schedule 32 to the Finance Act 2014)".

(5) The time limits otherwise applicable to amendment of a company tax return do not prevent an amendment being made in accordance with paragraph 75(6) of Schedule 18 to FA 1998 where the relevant partner withdraws consent by virtue of sub-paragraph (3).][1]

Amendments—[1] Paragraph 6A inserted by FA 2015 s 118, Sch 18 paras 1, 10(1), (5) with effect from 26 March 2015. Sub-para (3) has effect in relation to an amount specified in a notice in accordance with FA 2014 Sch 32 para 4(1)(*d*) whether the consent to a claim for group relief was given, or the claim itself was made, before or on or after 26 March 2015 (FA 2015 Sch 18 para 12(2)).

Penalty for failure to comply with partner payment notice

7 Section 226 (penalty for failure to make accelerated payment on time) applies to accelerated partner payments as if—

(a) references in that section to the accelerated payment were to the accelerated partner payment,

(b) references to P were to the relevant partner, and

(c) "the payment period" had the meaning given by paragraph 6(5).

Withdrawal, suspension or modification of partner payment notices

8 (1) Section 227 (withdrawal, modification or suspension of accelerated payment notice) applies in relation to a relevant partner, a partner payment notice, Condition C in paragraph 3 and an accelerated partner payment as it applies in relation to P, an accelerated payment notice, Condition C in section 219 and an accelerated payment.

(2) Accordingly, for this purpose—

[(*za*) section 227(2)(*d*), (12A) and (16) has effect as if the references to section 220(2)(*d*) or 221(2)(*d*) were to paragraph 4(1)(*d*) of this Schedule,][1]

(a) section 227(6)(b) and (7)(a) has effect as if the references to section 220(6) were to paragraph 4(5) of this Schedule, . . . [1]

(b) the provisions listed in section 227(9) are to be read as including paragraph 6(5) of this Schedule[, or (*c*) section 227(12A) has effect as if the reference to section 225A(3) were to paragraph 6A(3) of this Schedule.][1]

Amendments—[1] Sub-para (2)(*za*) inserted, in sub-para (2)(*a*), word repealed, and sub-para (2)(*c*) and preceding word inserted, by FA 2015 s 118, Sch 18 paras 1, 10(1), (6) with effect from 26 March 2015.

SCHEDULE 33

PART 4: CONSEQUENTIAL AMENDMENTS

Section 233

Taxes Management Act 1970

1 (*amends* TMA 1970 s 9B(1))

2 (*inserts* TMA 1970 s 103ZA(h))

Finance Act 2007

3 (*inserts* FA 2007 Sch 24 para 12(2A))

Finance Act 2008

4 (*inserts* FA 2008 Sch 41 para 15(1A))

Finance Act 2009

5 (*inserts* FA 2009 Sch 55 para 17(2)(c))

SCHEDULE 34

PROMOTERS OF TAX AVOIDANCE SCHEMES: THRESHOLD CONDITIONS

Section 237

Commentary—*Simon's Taxes* **A7.252**.

PART 1

MEETING THE THRESHOLD CONDITIONS: GENERAL

Meaning of "threshold condition"

1 Each of the conditions described in paragraphs 2 to 12 is a "threshold condition".

Deliberate tax defaulters

2 A person meets this condition if the Commissioners publish information about the person in reliance on section 94 of FA 2009 (publishing details of deliberate tax defaulters).

Breach of the Banking Code of Practice

3 A person meets this condition if the person is named in a report under section 285 as a result of the Commissioners determining that the person breached the Code of Practice on Taxation for Banks by reason of promoting arrangements which the person cannot have reasonably believed achieved a tax result which was intended by Parliament.

Dishonest tax agents

4 A person meets this condition if the person is given a conduct notice under paragraph 4 of Schedule 38 to FA 2012 (tax agents: dishonest conduct) and either—

(a) the time period during which a notice of appeal may be given in relation to the notice has expired, or

(b) an appeal against the notice has been made and the tribunal has confirmed the determination referred to in sub-paragraph (1) of paragraph 4 of that Schedule.

Non-compliance with Part 7 of FA 2004

5 (1) A person meets this condition if the person fails to comply with any of the following provisions of Part 7 of FA 2004 (disclosure of tax avoidance schemes)—

(a) section 308(1) and (3) (duty of promoter in relation to notifiable proposals and notifiable arrangements);

(b) section 309(1) (duty of person dealing with promoter outside the United Kingdom);

(c) section 310 (duty of parties to notifiable arrangements not involving promoter);

(d) section 313ZA (duty of promoter to provide details of clients).

[(2) For the purposes of sub-paragraph (1), a person ("P") fails to comply with a provision mentioned in that sub-paragraph if and only if any of conditions A to C are met.

(3) Condition A is met if—

(*a*) the tribunal has determined that P has failed to comply with the provision concerned,

(*b*) the appeal period has ended, and

(*c*) the determination has not been overturned on appeal.

(4) Condition B is met if—

(*a*) the tribunal has determined for the purposes of section 118(2) of TMA 1970 that P is to be deemed not to have failed to comply with the provision concerned as P had a reasonable excuse for not doing the thing required to be done,

(*b*) the appeal period has ended, and

(*c*) the determination has not been overturned on appeal.

(5) Condition C is met if P has admitted in writing to HMRC that P has failed to comply with the provision concerned.

(6) The "appeal period" means—

(*a*) the period during which an appeal could be brought against the determination of the tribunal, or

(*b*) where an appeal mentioned in paragraph (*a*) has been brought, the period during which that appeal has not been finally determined, withdrawn or otherwise disposed of.][1]

Amendments—[1] Sub-paras (2)–(6) substituted for previous sub-para (2) by FA 2015 s 119, Sch 19 para 6 with effect for the purposes of determining whether a person meets a threshold condition in a period of three years ending on or after 26 March 2015.

Criminal offences

6 (1) A person meets this condition if the person is charged with a relevant offence.

(2) The fact that a person has been charged with an offence is disregarded for the purposes of this paragraph if—

(a) the person has been acquitted of the offence, or

(b) the charge has been dismissed or the proceedings have been discontinued.

(3) An acquittal is not taken into account for the purposes of sub-paragraph (2) if an appeal has been brought against the acquittal and has not yet been disposed of.

(4) "Relevant offence" means any of the following—

(a) an offence at common law of cheating in relation to the public revenue;

(b) in Scotland, an offence at common law of—

(i) fraud;

(ii) uttering;

(c) an offence under section 17(1) of the Theft Act 1968 or section 17 of the Theft Act (Northern Ireland) 1969 (c. 16 (NI)) (false accounting);

(d) an offence under section 106A of TMA 1970 (fraudulent evasion of income tax);

(e) an offence under section 107 of TMA 1970 (false statements: Scotland);

(f) an offence under any of the following provisions of CEMA 1979—

(i) section 50(2) (improper importation of goods with intent to defraud or evade duty);

(ii) section 167 (untrue declarations etc);

(iii) section 168 (counterfeiting documents etc);

(iv) section 170 (fraudulent evasion of duty);

(v) section 170B (taking steps for the fraudulent evasion of duty);

(g) an offence under any of the following provisions of VATA 1994—

(i) section 72(1) (being knowingly concerned in the evasion of VAT);

(ii) section 72(3) (false statement etc);

(iii) section 72(8) (conduct involving commission of other offence under section 72);

(h) an offence under section 1 of the Fraud Act 2006 (fraud);

(i) an offence under any of the following provisions of CRCA 2005—

(i) section 30 (impersonating a Commissioner or officer of Revenue and Customs);

(ii) section 31 (obstruction of officer of Revenue and Customs etc);

(iii) section 32 (assault of officer of Revenue and Customs);

(j) an offence under [regulation 86(1) of the Money Laundering, Terrorist Financing and Transfer of Funds (Information on the Payer) Regulations 2017][1];

(k) an offence under section 49(1) of the Criminal Justice and Licensing (Scotland) Act 2010 (asp 13) (possession of articles for use in fraud).

Amendments—[1] In sub-para (4)(j), words substituted for words "regulation 45(1) of the Money Laundering Regulations 2007 (SI 2007/2157)" by the Money Laundering, Terrorist Financing and Transfer of Funds (Information on the Payer) Regulations, SI 2017/692 reg 109, Sch 7 para 10 with effect from 26 June 2017.

Opinion notice of GAAR Advisory Panel

7 A person meets this condition if—

(a) arrangements in relation to which the person is a promoter[—

(i) have been referred to the GAAR Advisory Panel under Schedule 43 to FA 2013 (referrals of single schemes),

(ii) are in a pool in respect of which a referral has been made to that Panel under Schedule 43B to that Act (generic referrals), or

(iii) have been referred to that Panel under paragraph 26 of Schedule 16 to F(No. 2)A 2017 (referrals in relation to penalties for enablers of defeated tax avoidance),][2]

(b) one or more opinion notices are given [in respect of the referral][1] [under (as the case may be)—

(i) paragraph 11(3)(*b*) of Schedule 43 to FA 2013,

(ii) paragraph 6(4)(*b*) of Schedule 43B to that Act, or

(iii) paragraph 34(3)(*b*) of Schedule 16 to F(No. 2)A 2017,

(opinion of sub-panel of GAAR Advisory Panel that arrangements are not reasonable), and][2]

(c) the notice, or the notices taken together, either—

(i) state the joint opinion of all the members of the sub-panel arranged under ...[1] that Schedule, or

(ii) state the opinion of two or more members of that sub-panel.

Amendments—[1] In paras (*a*), (*b*), words inserted, in para (*b*), words substituted for words "in relation to the arrangements", and in para (*c*), words "paragraph 10 of" repealed, by FA 2016 s 157(29) with effect in relation to tax arrangements (within the meaning of FA 2013 Pt 5) entered into at any time (whether before on or after 15 September 2016).

[2] In para (*a*), words substituted for words "have been referred to the GAAR Advisory Panel under Schedule 43 to FA 2013, (referrals of single schemes) or are in a pool in respect of which a referral has been made to that Panel under Schedule 43B to that Act (generic referrals),", and in para (b), words substituted for words "under paragraph 11(3)(b) or (as the case may be) 6(4)(*b*) of that Schedule (opinion of sub-panel of GAAR Advisory Panel that arrangements are not reasonable), and", by F(No 2)A 2017 s 65, Sch 16 para 61 with effect in relation to arrangements entered into on or after 16 November 2017. In determining in relation to any particular arrangements whether a person is a person who enabled the arrangements, any action of the person carried out before 16 November 2017 is to be disregarded, and these amendments do not apply in relation to a person who is a promoter in relation to arrangements if that person is not a person who enabled the arrangements (F(No 2)A 2017 Sch 16 para 62(2), (3)).

Disciplinary action [against a member of a trade or profession]

8 [(1) A person who carries on a trade or profession that is regulated by a professional body meets this condition if all of the following conditions are met—

(*a*) the person is found guilty of misconduct of a prescribed kind,

(*b*) action of a prescribed kind is taken against the person in relation to that misconduct, and

(*c*) a penalty of a prescribed kind is imposed on the person as a result of that misconduct.][1]

(2) Misconduct may only be prescribed for the purposes of sub-paragraph (1)(a) if it is misconduct other than misconduct in matters (such as the payment of fees) that relate solely or mainly to the person's relationship with the professional body.

(3) A "professional body" means—

(a) the Institute of Chartered Accountants in England and Wales;

(b) the Institute of Chartered Accountants of Scotland;

(c) the General Council of the Bar;

(d) the Faculty of Advocates;

(e) the General Council of the Bar of Northern Ireland;

(f) the Law Society;

(g) the Law Society of Scotland;

(h) the Law Society [of][1] Northern Ireland;

(i) the Association of Accounting Technicians;

(j) the Association of Chartered Certified Accountants;

(k) the Association of Taxation Technicians;

(l) any other prescribed body with functions relating to the regulation of a trade or profession.

Amendments—[1] Sub-para (1) substituted, and words in heading and word in sub-para (3)(*h*) substituted, by FA 2015 s 119, Sch 19 para 7 with effect for the purposes of determining whether a person meets a threshold condition in a period of three years ending on or after 26 March 2015.

Disciplinary action by a regulatory authority

9 (1) A person meets this condition if a regulatory authority imposes a relevant sanction on the person.

(2) A "relevant sanction" is a sanction which is—

(a) imposed in relation to misconduct other than misconduct in matters (such as the payment of fees) that relate solely or mainly to the person's relationship with the regulatory authority, and

(b) prescribed.

(3) The following are regulatory authorities for the purposes of this paragraph—

(a) the Financial Conduct Authority;

(b) the Financial Services Authority;

(c) any other authority that may be prescribed.

(4) Only authorities that have functions relating to the regulation of financial institutions may be prescribed under sub-paragraph (3)(c).

Exercise of information powers

10 (1) A person meets this condition if the person fails to comply with an information notice given under any of paragraphs 1, 2, 5 and 5A of Schedule 36 to FA 2008.

(2) For the purposes of section 237, the failure to comply is taken to occur when the period within which the person is required to comply with the notice expires (without the person having complied with it).

Restrictive contractual terms

11 (1) A person ("P") meets this condition if P enters into an agreement with another person ("C") which relates to a relevant proposal or relevant arrangements in relation to which P is a promoter, on terms which—

(a) impose a contractual obligation on C which falls within sub-paragraph (2) or (3), or

(b) impose on C both obligations within sub-paragraph (4) and obligations within sub-paragraph (5).

(2) A contractual obligation falls within this sub-paragraph if it prevents or restricts the disclosure by C to HMRC of information relating to the proposals or arrangements, whether or not by referring to a wider class of persons.

(3) A contractual obligation falls within this sub-paragraph if it requires C to impose on any tax adviser to whom C discloses information relating to the proposals or arrangements a contractual obligation which prevents or restricts the disclosure of that information to HMRC by the adviser.

(4) A contractual obligation falls within this sub-paragraph if it requires C to—

(a) meet (in whole or in part) the costs of, or contribute to a fund to be used to meet the costs of, any proceedings relating to arrangements in relation to which P is a promoter (whether or not implemented by C), or

(b) take out an insurance policy which insures against the risk of having to meet the costs connected with proceedings relating to arrangements which C has implemented and in relation to which P is a promoter.

(5) A contractual obligation falls within this paragraph if it requires C to obtain the consent of P before—

(a) entering into any agreement with HMRC regarding arrangements which C has implemented and in relation to which P is a promoter, or

(b) withdrawing or discontinuing any appeal against any decision regarding such arrangements.

(6) In sub-paragraph (5)(b), the reference to withdrawing or discontinuing an appeal includes any action or inaction which results in an appeal being discontinued.

(7) In this paragraph—

"proceedings" includes any sort of proceedings for resolving disputes (and not just proceedings in court), whether commenced or contemplated;

"tax adviser" means a person appointed to give advice about the tax affairs of another person (whether appointed directly by that person or by another tax adviser of that person).

Continuing to promote certain arrangements

12 (1) A person ("P") meets this condition if P has been given a stop notice and after the end of the notice period P—

(a) makes a firm approach to another person ("C") in relation to an affected proposal with a view to making the affected proposal available for implementation by C or another person, or

(b) makes an affected proposal available for implementation by other persons.

(2) "Affected proposal" means a relevant proposal that is in substance the same as the relevant proposal specified in the stop notice in accordance with sub-paragraph (4)(c).

(3) An authorised officer may give a person ("P") a notice (a "stop notice") if each of these conditions is met—

(a) a person has been given a follower notice under section 204 (circumstances in which a follower notice may be given) in relation to particular relevant arrangements;

(b) P is a promoter in relation to a relevant proposal that is implemented by those arrangements;

(c) 90 days have elapsed since the follower notice was given and—

(i) the follower notice has not been withdrawn, and

(ii) if representations objecting to the follower notice were made under section 207 (representations about a follower notice), HMRC have confirmed the follower notice.

(4) A stop notice must—

(a) specify the arrangements which are the subject of the follower notice mentioned in sub-paragraph (3)(a),

(b) specify the judicial ruling identified in that follower notice,

(c) specify a relevant proposal in relation to which the condition in sub-paragraph (3)(b) is met, and

(d) explain the effect of the stop notice.

(5) An authorised officer may determine that a stop notice given to a person is to cease to have effect.

(6) If an authorised officer makes a determination under sub-paragraph (5) the officer must give the person written notice of the determination.

(7) The notice must specify the date from which it takes effect, which may be earlier than the date on which the notice is given.

(8) In this paragraph—

"the notice period" means the period of 30 days beginning with the day on which a stop notice is given;

"judicial ruling" means a ruling of a court or tribunal.

PART 2
MEETING THE THRESHOLD CONDITIONS: BODIES CORPORATE [AND PARTNERSHIPS]

Amendments—In heading, words inserted by FA 2015 s 119, Sch 19 para 4(1), (2) with effect for the purposes of determining whether a person meets a threshold condition in a period of three years ending on or after 26 March 2015.

[Interpretation

13A (1) This paragraph contains definitions for the purposes of this Part of this Schedule.

(2) Each of the following is a "relevant body"—

(*a*) a body corporate, and

(*b*) a partnership.

(3) "Relevant time" means the time referred to in section 237(1A) (duty to give conduct notice to person treated as meeting threshold condition).

(4) "Relevant threshold condition" means a threshold condition specified in any of the following paragraphs of this Schedule—

(*a*) paragraph 2 (deliberate tax defaulters);

(*b*) paragraph 4 (dishonest tax agents);

(*c*) paragraph 6 (criminal offences);

(*d*) paragraph 7 (opinion notice of GAAR advisory panel);

(*e*) paragraph 8 (disciplinary action against a member of a trade or profession);

(*f*) paragraph 9 (disciplinary action by regulatory authority);

(*g*) paragraph 10 (failure to comply with information notice).

(5) A person controls a body corporate if the person has power to secure that the affairs of the body corporate are conducted in accordance with the person's wishes—

(*a*) by means of the holding of shares or the possession of voting power in relation to the body corporate or any other relevant body,

(*b*) as a result of any powers conferred by the articles of association or other document regulating the body corporate or any other relevant body, or

(*c*) by means of controlling a partnership.

[(6) Two or more persons together control a body corporate if together they have the power to secure that the affairs of the body corporate are conducted in accordance with their wishes in any way specified in sub-paragraph (5)(*a*) to (*c*).

(7) A person controls a partnership if the person is a member of the partnership and—

(*a*) has the right to a share of more than half the assets, or more than half the income, of the partnership, or

(*b*) directs, or is on a day-to-day level in control of, the management of the business of the partnership.

(8) Two or more persons together control a partnership if they are members of the partnership and together they—

(*a*) have the right to a share of more than half the assets, or of more than half the income, of the partnership, or

(*b*) direct, or are on a day-to-day level in control of, the management of the business of the partnership.

(9) Paragraph 19(2) to (5) of Schedule 36 (connected persons etc) applies to a person referred to in sub-paragraph (7) or (8) as if references to "P" were to that person.

(10) A person has significant influence over a body corporate or partnership if the person—

(*a*) does not control the body corporate or partnership, but

(*b*) is able to, or actually does, exercise significant influence over it (whether or not as the result of a legal entitlement).

(11) Two or more persons together have significant influence over a body corporate or partnership if together those persons—

(*a*) do not control the body corporate or partnership, but

(*b*) are able to, or actually do, exercise significant influence over it (whether or not as the result of a legal entitlement).

(12) References to a person being a promoter are to the person carrying on business as a promoter.][2]][1]

Commentary—*Simon's Taxes* **A7.251, A7.252A, A7.259** .

Press releases etc—HMRC TIIN (Budget 2017), "Promoters of Tax Avoidance Schemes—associated and successor entities rules", 8 March 2017 (see *SWTI 2017, Budget Edition*).

Amendments—[1] Paragraphs 13A–13D substituted for previous para 13 by FA 2015 s 119, Sch 19 para 4(1), (3) with effect for the purposes of determining whether a person meets a threshold condition in a period of three years ending on or after 26 March 2015.

[2] Sub-paras (6)–(12) substituted for previous sub-paras (6)–(8) by FA 2017 s 24(1) with effect for the purposes of determining whether a person meets a threshold condition in a period of three years ending on or after 8 March 2017.

[Relevant bodies controlled etc by other persons treated as meeting a threshold condition

13B (1) A relevant body is treated as meeting a threshold condition at the relevant time if any of Conditions A to C is met.

(2) Condition A is that—

(*a*) a person met the threshold condition at a time when the person was a promoter, and

(*b*) the person controls or has significant influence over the relevant body at the relevant time.

(3) Condition B is that—

(*a*) a person met the threshold condition at a time when the person controlled or had significant influence over the relevant body,

(*b*) the relevant body was a promoter at that time, and

(*c*) the person controls or has significant influence over the relevant body at the relevant time.

(4) Condition C is that—

(*a*) two or more persons together controlled or had significant influence over the relevant body at a time when one of those persons met the threshold condition,

(*b*) the relevant body was a promoter at that time, and

(*c*) those persons together control or have significant influence over the relevant body at the relevant time.

(5) Where the person referred to in sub-paragraph (2)(*a*) or (3)(*a*) or (4)(*a*) as meeting a threshold condition is an individual, sub-paragraph (1) only applies if the threshold condition is a relevant threshold condition.

(6) For the purposes of sub-paragraph (2) it does not matter whether the relevant body existed at the time referred to in sub-paragraph (2)(*a*).][1]

Commentary—*Simon's Taxes* **A7.259** .

Press releases etc—HMRC TIIN (Budget 2017), "Promoters of Tax Avoidance Schemes—associated and successor entities rules", 8 March 2017 (see *SWTI 2017, Budget Edition*).

Amendments—[1] Paragraphs 13B–13D substituted by FA 2017 s 24(2) with effect for the purposes of determining whether a person meets a threshold condition in a period of three years ending on or after 8 March 2017.

[Persons who control etc a relevant body treated as meeting a threshold condition

13C (1) If at a time when a person controlled or had significant influence over a relevant body—

(*a*) the relevant body met a threshold condition, and

(*b*) the relevant body, or another relevant body which the person controlled or had significant influence over, was a promoter,

the person is treated as meeting the threshold condition at the relevant time.

(2) It does not matter whether any relevant body referred to sub-paragraph (1) exists at the relevant time.][1]

Commentary—*Simon's Taxes* **A7.259** .

Press releases etc—HMRC TIIN (Budget 2017), "Promoters of Tax Avoidance Schemes—associated and successor entities rules", 8 March 2017 (see *SWTI 2017, Budget Edition*).

Amendments—[1] Paragraphs 13B–13D substituted by FA 2017 s 24(2) with effect for the purposes of determining whether a person meets a threshold condition in a period of three years ending on or after 8 March 2017.

[Relevant bodies controlled etc by the same person treated as meeting a threshold condition

13D (1) If—

(*a*) a person controlled or had significant influence over a relevant body at a time when it met a threshold condition, and

(*b*) at that time that body, or another relevant body which the person controlled or had significant influence over, was a promoter,

any relevant body which the person controls or has significant influence over at the relevant time is treated as meeting the threshold condition at the relevant time.

(2) If—

(*a*) two or more persons together controlled or had significant influence over a relevant body at a time when it met a threshold condition, and

(*b*) at that time that body, or another relevant body which those persons together controlled or had significant influence over, was a promoter,

any relevant body which those persons together control or have significant influence over at the relevant time is treated as meeting the threshold condition at the relevant time.

(3) It does not matter whether—

(*a*) a relevant body referred to in sub-paragraph (1)(*a*) or (*b*) or (2)(*a*) or (*b*) exists at the relevant time, or

(*b*) a relevant body existing at the relevant time existed at the time referred to in sub-paragraph (1)(*a*) or (2)(*a*).][1]

Commentary—*Simon's Taxes* **A7.259** .

Press releases etc—HMRC TIIN (Budget 2017), "Promoters of Tax Avoidance Schemes—associated and successor entities rules", 8 March 2017 (see *SWTI 2017, Budget Edition*).

Amendments—[1] Paragraphs 13B–13D substituted by FA 2017 s 24(2) with effect for the purposes of determining whether a person meets a threshold condition in a period of three years ending on or after 8 March 2017.

PART 3
POWER TO AMEND

14 (1) The Treasury may by regulations amend this Schedule.

(2) An amendment made by virtue of sub-paragraph (1) may, in particular—

(a) vary or remove any of the conditions set out in paragraphs 2 to 12;

(b) add new conditions;

[(*c*) vary any of the circumstances described in paragraphs 13B to 13D in which a person is treated as meeting a threshold condition (including by amending paragraph 13A);

(*d*) add new circumstances in which a person will be so treated.][1]

(3) Regulations under sub-paragraph (1) may include any amendment of this Part of this Act that is appropriate in consequence of an amendment made by virtue of sub-paragraph (1).

Amendments—[1] Sub-para (2)(*c*), (*d*) inserted by FA 2015 s 119, Sch 19 para 8 with effect from 26 March 2015.

[SCHEDULE 34A

PROMOTERS OF TAX AVOIDANCE SCHEMES: DEFEATED ARRANGEMENTS

Note—In this Schedule, "tax" includes VAT, and "tax advantage" has the meaning given by s 234(3) and also includes a tax advantage as defined in VATA 1994 Sch 11A para 1.

Amendments—Schedule 34A inserted by FA 2016 s 160(1), (5) with effect from 15 September 2016.

PART 1
INTRODUCTION]

Amendments—Schedule 34A inserted by FA 2016 s 160(1), (5) with effect from 15 September 2016.

[**1** In this Schedule—

(*a*) Part 2 is about the meaning of "relevant defeat";

(*b*) Part 3 contains provision about when a relevant defeat is treated as occurring in relation to a person;

(*c*) Part 4 contains provision about when a person is treated as meeting a condition in subsection (11), (12) or (13) of section 237A;

(*d*) Part 5 contains definitions and other supplementary provisions.][1]

Amendments—[1] Schedule 34A inserted by FA 2016 s 160(1), (5) with effect from 15 September 2016.

[PART 2
MEANING OF "RELEVANT DEFEAT"

"Related" arrangements

2 (1) For the purposes of this Part of this Act, separate arrangements which persons have entered into are "related" to one another if (and only if) they are substantially the same.
(2) Sub-paragraphs (3) to (6) set out cases in which arrangements are to be treated as being "substantially the same" (if they would not otherwise be so treated under sub-paragraph (1)).
(3) Arrangements to which the same reference number has been allocated under Part 7 of FA 2004 (disclosure of tax avoidance schemes) are treated as being substantially the same. For this purpose arrangements in relation to which information relating to a reference number has been provided in compliance with section 312 of FA 2004 are treated as arrangements to which that reference number has been allocated under Part 7 of that Act.
(4) Arrangements to which the same reference number has been allocated under paragraph 9 of Schedule 11A to VATA 1994 (disclosure of avoidance schemes) [or paragraph 22 of Schedule 17 to FA 2017 (disclosure of avoidance schemes: VAT and other indirect taxes)][2] are treated as being substantially the same.
(5) Any two or more sets of arrangements which are the subject of follower notices given by reference to the same judicial ruling are treated as being substantially the same.
(6) Where a notice of binding has been given in relation to any arrangements ("the bound arrangements") on the basis that they are, for the purposes of Schedule 43A to FA 2013, equivalent arrangements in relation to another set of arrangements (the "lead arrangements")—
- (*a*) the bound arrangements and the lead arrangements are treated as being substantially the same, and
- (*b*) the bound arrangements are treated as being substantially the same as any other arrangements which, as a result of this sub-paragraph, are treated as substantially the same as the lead arrangements.][1]

Amendments—[1] Schedule 34A inserted by FA 2016 s 160(1), (5) with effect from 15 September 2016.
[2] In sub-para (4), words inserted by F(No 2)A 2017 s 66, Sch 17 paras 52, 54(1), (2) with effect from 1 January 2018.

["Promoted arrangements"

3 (1) For the purposes of this Schedule arrangements are "promoted arrangements" in relation to a person if—
- (*a*) they are relevant arrangements or would be relevant arrangements under the condition stated in sub-paragraph (2), and
- (*b*) the person is carrying on a business as a promoter and—
  - (i) the person is or has been a promoter in relation to the arrangements, or
  - (ii) that would be the case if the condition in subparagraph (2) were met.

(2) That condition is that the definition of "tax" in section 283 includes, and has always included, value added tax.][1]

Amendments—[1] Schedule 34A inserted by FA 2016 s 160(1), (5) with effect from 15 September 2016.

[Relevant defeat of single arrangements

4 (1) A defeat of arrangements (entered into by any person) which are promoted arrangements in relation to a person ("the promoter") is a "relevant defeat" in relation to the promoter if the condition in subparagraph (2) is met.
(2) The condition is that the arrangements are not related to any other arrangements which are promoted arrangements in relation to the promoter.
(3) For the meaning of "defeat" see paragraphs 10 to 16.][1]

Amendments—[1] Schedule 34A inserted by FA 2016 s 160(1), (5) with effect from 15 September 2016.

[Relevant defeat of related arrangements

5 (1) This paragraph applies if arrangements (entered into by any person) ("Set A")—
- (*a*) are promoted arrangements in relation to a person ("P"), and
- (*b*) are related to other arrangements which are promoted arrangements in relation to P.

(2) If Case 1, 2 or 3 applies (see paragraphs 7 to 9) a relevant defeat occurs in relation to P and each of the related arrangements.
(3) "The related arrangements" means Set A and the arrangements mentioned in sub-paragraph (1)(*b*).][1]

Amendments—[1] Schedule 34A inserted by FA 2016 s 160(1), (5) with effect from 15 September 2016.

[Limit on number of separate relevant defeats in relation to the same, or related, arrangements

6 In relation to a person, if there has been a relevant defeat of arrangements (whether under paragraph 4 or 5) there cannot be a further relevant defeat of—

(*a*) those particular arrangements, or

(*b*) arrangements which are related to those arrangements.][1]

Amendments—[1] Schedule 34A inserted by FA 2016 s 160(1), (5) with effect from 15 September 2016.

[Case 1: counteraction upheld by judicial ruling

7 (1) Case 1 applies if—

(*a*) any of Conditions A to E is met in relation to any of the related arrangements, and

(*b*) in the case of those arrangements the decision to make the relevant counteraction has been upheld by a judicial ruling (which is final).

(2) In sub-paragraph (1) "the relevant counteraction" means the counteraction mentioned in paragraph 11(*d*), 12(1)(*b*), 13(1)(*d*), 14(1)(*d*) or 15(1)(*d*) (as the case requires).][1]

Amendments—[1] Schedule 34A inserted by FA 2016 s 160(1), (5) with effect from 15 September 2016.

[Case 2: judicial ruling that avoidance-related rule applies

8 Case 2 applies if Condition F is met in relation to any of the related arrangements.][1]

Amendments—[1] Schedule 34A inserted by FA 2016 s 160(1), (5) with effect from 15 September 2016.

[Case 3: proportion-based relevant defeat

9 (1) Case 3 applies if—

(*a*) at least 75% of the tested arrangements have been defeated, and

(*b*) no final judicial ruling in relation to any of the related arrangements has upheld a corresponding tax advantage which has been asserted in connection with any of the related arrangements.

(2) In this paragraph "the tested arrangements" means so many of the related arrangements (as defined in paragraph 5(3)) as meet the condition in sub-paragraph (3) or (4).

(3) Particular arrangements meet this condition if a person has made a return, claim or election on the basis that a tax advantage results from those arrangements and—

(*a*) there has been an enquiry or investigation by HMRC into the return, claim or election, or

(*b*) HMRC assesses the person to tax on the basis that the tax advantage (or any part of it) does not arise, or

(*c*) a GAAR counteraction notice has been given in relation to the tax advantage or part of it and the arrangements.

(4) Particular arrangements meet this condition if HMRC takes other action on the basis that a tax advantage which might be expected to arise from those arrangements, or is asserted in connection with them, does not arise.

(5) For the purposes of this paragraph a tax advantage has been "asserted" in connection with particular arrangements if a person has made a return, claim or election on the basis that the tax advantage arises from those arrangements.

(6) In sub-paragraph (1)(*b*) "corresponding tax advantage" means a tax advantage corresponding to any tax advantage the counteraction of which is taken into account by HMRC for the purposes of subparagraph (1)(*a*).

(7) For the purposes of this paragraph a court or tribunal "upholds" a tax advantage if—

(*a*) the court or tribunal makes a ruling to the effect that no part of the tax advantage is to be counteracted, and

(*b*) that judicial ruling is final.

(8) In this paragraph references to "counteraction" include anything referred to as a counteraction in any of Conditions A to F in paragraphs 11 to 16.

(9) In this paragraph "GAAR counteraction notice" means—

(*a*) a notice such as is mentioned in sub-paragraph (2) of paragraph 12 of Schedule 43 to FA 2013 (notice of final decision to counteract),

(*b*) a notice under paragraph 8(2) or 9(2) of Schedule 43A to that Act (pooling or binding of arrangements) stating that the tax advantage is to be counteracted under the general anti-abuse rule, or

(*c*) a notice under paragraph 8(2) of Schedule 43B to that Act (generic referrals) stating that the tax advantage is to be counteracted under the general anti-abuse rule.][1]

Amendments—[1] Schedule 34A inserted by FA 2016 s 160(1), (5) with effect from 15 September 2016.

["Defeat" of arrangements

10 For the purposes of this Part of this Act a "defeat" of arrangements occurs if any of Conditions A to F (in paragraphs 11 to 16) is met in relation to the arrangements.][1]

Amendments—[1] Schedule 34A inserted by FA 2016 s 160(1), (5) with effect from 15 September 2016.

[**11** Condition A is that—

(*a*) a person has made a return, claim or election on the basis that a tax advantage arises from the arrangements,

(*b*) a notice given to the person under paragraph 12 of Schedule 43 to, paragraph 8(2) or 9(2) of Schedule 43A to or paragraph 8(2) of Schedule 43B to FA 2013 stated that the tax advantage was to be counteracted under the general anti-abuse rule,

(*c*) the tax advantage has been counteracted (in whole or in part) under the general anti-abuse rule, and

(*d*) the counteraction is final.][1]

Amendments—[1] Schedule 34A inserted by FA 2016 s 160(1), (5) with effect from 15 September 2016.

[**12** (1) Condition B is that a follower notice has been given to a person by reference to the arrangements (and not withdrawn) and—

(*a*) the person has complied with subsection (2) of section 208 of FA 2014 by taking the action specified in subsections (4) to (6) of that section in respect of the denied tax advantage (or part of it), or

(*b*) the denied tax advantage has been counteracted (in whole or in part) otherwise than as mentioned in paragraph (*a*) and the counteraction is final.

(2) In this paragraph "the denied tax advantage" is to be interpreted in accordance with section 208(3) of FA 2014.

(3) In this Schedule "follower notice" means a follower notice under Chapter 2 of Part 4 of FA 2014.][1]

Amendments—[1] Schedule 34A inserted by FA 2016 s 160(1), (5) with effect from 15 September 2016.

[**13** (1) Condition C is that—

(*a*) the arrangements are DOTAS arrangements,

(*b*) a person ("the taxpayer") has made a return, claim or election on the basis that a relevant tax advantage arises,

(*c*) the relevant tax advantage has been counteracted, and

(*d*) the counteraction is final.

(2) For the purposes of sub-paragraph (1) "relevant tax advantage" means a tax advantage which the arrangements might be expected to enable the taxpayer to obtain.

(3) For the purposes of this paragraph the relevant tax advantage is "counteracted" if adjustments are made in respect of the taxpayer's tax position on the basis that the whole or part of that tax advantage does not arise.][1]

Amendments—[1] Schedule 34A inserted by FA 2016 s 160(1), (5) with effect from 15 September 2016.

[**14** (1) Condition D is that—

(*a*) the arrangements are disclosable VAT [or other indirect tax][2] arrangements to which a . . . [2] person is a party,

(*b*) the . . . [2] person has made a return or claim on the basis that a relevant tax advantage arises,

(*c*) the relevant tax advantage has been counteracted, and

(*d*) the counteraction is final.

(2) For the purposes of sub-paragraph (1) "relevant tax advantage" means a tax advantage which the arrangements might be expected to enable the . . . [2] person to obtain.

(3) For the purposes of this paragraph the relevant tax advantage is "counteracted" if adjustments are made in respect of the . . . [2] person's tax position on the basis that the whole or part of that tax advantage does not arise.][1]

Amendments—[1] Schedule 34A inserted by FA 2016 s 160(1), (5) with effect from 15 September 2016.

[2] In sub-para (1)(*a*), words inserted, and in sub-paras (1)(*a*), (*b*), (2), (3), word "taxable" repealed, by F(No 2)A 2017 s 66, Sch 17 paras 52, 54(1), (3) with effect from 1 January 2018.

[**15** (1) Condition E is that the arrangements are disclosable VAT arrangements to which a taxable person ("T") is a party and—

(*a*) the arrangements relate to the position with respect to VAT of a person other than T ("S") who has made supplies of goods or services to T,

(*b*) the arrangements might be expected to enable T to obtain a tax advantage in connection with those supplies of goods or services,

(*c*) the arrangements have been counteracted, and

(*d*) the counteraction is final.

(2) For the purposes of this paragraph the arrangements are "counteracted" if—

(*a*) HMRC assess S to tax or take any other action on a basis which prevents T from obtaining (or obtaining the whole of) the tax advantage in question, or

(*b*) adjustments are made on a basis such as is mentioned in paragraph (*a*).][1]

Amendments—[1] Schedule 34A inserted by FA 2016 s 160(1), (5) with effect from 15 September 2016.

[16 (1) Condition F is that—

(*a*) a person has made a return, claim or election on the basis that a relevant tax advantage arises,

(*b*) the tax advantage, or part of the tax advantage would not arise if a particular avoidance-related rule (see paragraph 25) applies in relation to the person's tax affairs,

(*c*) it is held in a judicial ruling that the relevant avoidance-related rule applies in relation to the person's tax affairs, and

(*d*) the judicial ruling is final.

(2) For the purposes of sub-paragraph (1) "relevant tax advantage" means a tax advantage which the arrangements might be expected to enable the person to obtain.][1]

Amendments—[1] Schedule 34A inserted by FA 2016 s 160(1), (5) with effect from 15 September 2016.

[PART 3

RELEVANT DEFEATS: ASSOCIATED PERSONS

Attribution of relevant defeats

17 (1) Sub-paragraph (2) applies if—

(*a*) there is (or has been) a person ("Q"),

(*b*) arrangements ("the defeated arrangements") have been entered into,

(*c*) an event occurs such that either—

(i) there is a relevant defeat in relation to Q and the defeated arrangements, or

(ii) the condition in sub-paragraph (i) would be met if Q had not ceased to exist,

(*d*) at the time of that event a person ("P") is carrying on a business as a promoter (or is carrying on what would be such a business under the condition in paragraph 3(2)), and

(*e*) Condition 1 or 2 is met in relation to Q and P.

(2) The event is treated for all purposes of this Part of this Act as a relevant defeat in relation to P and the defeated arrangements (whether or not it is also a relevant defeat in relation to Q, and regardless of whether or not P existed at any time when those arrangements were promoted arrangements in relation to Q).

(3) Condition 1 is that—

(*a*) P is not an individual,

(*b*) at a time when the defeated arrangements were promoted arrangements in relation to Q—

(i) P was a relevant body controlled by Q, or

(ii) Q was a relevant body controlled by P, and

(*c*) at the time of the event mentioned in sub-paragraph (1)(*c*)—

(i) Q is a relevant body controlled by P,

(ii) P is a relevant body controlled by Q, or

(iii) P and Q are relevant bodies controlled by a third person.

(4) Condition 2 is that—

(*a*) P and Q are relevant bodies,

(*b*) at a time when the defeated arrangements were promoted arrangements in relation to Q, a third person ("C") controlled Q, and

(*c*) C controls P at the time of the event mentioned in subparagraph (1)(*c*).

(5) For the purposes of sub-paragraphs (3)(*b*) and (4)(*b*), the question whether arrangements are promoted arrangements in relation to Q at any time is to be determined on the assumption that the reference to "design" in paragraph (*b*) of section 235(3) (definition of "promoter" in relation to relevant arrangements) is omitted.][1]

Amendments—[1] Schedule 34A inserted by FA 2016 s 160(1), (5) with effect from 15 September 2016.

[Deemed defeat notices

18 (1) This paragraph applies if—

(*a*) an authorised officer becomes aware at any time ("the relevant time") that a relevant defeat has occurred in relation to a person ("P") who is carrying on a business as a promoter,

(*b*) there have occurred, more than 3 years before the relevant time—

(i) one third party defeat, or

(ii) two third party defeats, and

(*c*) conditions A1 and B1 (in a case within paragraph (*b*)(i)), or conditions A2 and B2 (in a case within paragraph (*b*)(ii)), are met.

(2) Where this paragraph applies by virtue of sub-paragraph (1)(*b*)(i), this Part of this Act has effect as if an authorised officer had (with due authority), at the time of the time of the third party defeat, given P a single defeat notice under section 241A(2) in respect of it.

(3) Where this paragraph applies by virtue of sub-paragraph (1)(*b*)(ii), this Part of this Act has effect as if an authorised officer had (with due authority), at the time of the second of the two third party defeats, given P a double defeat notice under section 241A(3) in respect of the two third party defeats.

(4) Section 241A(8) has no effect in relation to a notice treated as given as mentioned in sub-paragraph (2) or (3).

(5) Condition A1 is that—

(*a*) a conduct notice or a single or double defeat notice has been given to the other person (see sub-paragraph (9)) in respect of the third party defeat,

(*b*) at the time of the third party defeat an authorised officer would have had power by virtue of paragraph 17 to give P a defeat notice in respect of the third party defeat, had the officer been aware that it was a relevant defeat in relation to P, and

(*c*) so far as the authorised officer mentioned in sub-paragraph (1)(*a*) is aware, the conditions for giving P a defeat notice in respect of the third party defeat have never been met (ignoring this paragraph).

(6) Condition A2 is that—

(*a*) a conduct notice or a single or double defeat notice has been given to the other person (see sub-paragraph (9)) in respect of each, or both, of the third party defeats,

(*b*) at the time of the second third party defeat an authorised officer would have had power by virtue of paragraph 17 to give P a double defeat notice in respect of the third party defeats, had the officer been aware that either of the third party defeats was a relevant defeat in relation to P, and

(*c*) so far as the authorised officer mentioned in sub-paragraph(1)(*a*) is aware, the conditions for giving P a defeat notice in respect of those third party defeats (or either of them) have never been met (ignoring this paragraph).

(7) Condition B1 is that, had an authorised officer given P a defeat notice in respect of the third party defeat at the time of that relevant defeat, that defeat notice would still have effect at the relevant time (see subparagraph (1)).

(8) Condition B2 is that, had an authorised officer given P a defeat notice in respect of the two third party defeats at the time of the second of those relevant defeats, that defeat notice would still have effect at the relevant time.

(9) In this paragraph "third party defeat" means a relevant defeat which has occurred in relation to a person other than P.][1]

Amendments—[1] Schedule 34A inserted by FA 2016 s 160(1), (5) with effect from 15 September 2016.

[Meaning of "relevant body" and "control"

19 (1) In this Part of this Schedule "relevant body" means—

(*a*) a body corporate, or

(*b*) a partnership.

(2) For the purposes of this Part of this Schedule a person controls a body corporate if the person has power to secure that the affairs of the body corporate are conducted in accordance with the person's wishes—

(*a*) by means of the holding of shares or the possession of voting power in relation to the body corporate or any other relevant body,

(*b*) as a result of any powers conferred by the articles of association or other document regulating the body corporate or any other relevant body, or

(*c*) by means of controlling a partnership.

(3) For the purposes of this Part of this Schedule a person controls a partnership if the person is a controlling member or the managing partner of the partnership.

(4) In this paragraph "controlling member" has the same meaning as in Schedule 36 (partnerships).

(5) In this paragraph "managing partner", in relation to a partnership, means the member of the partnership who directs, or is on a day-today level in control of, the management of the business of the partnership.][1]

Amendments—[1] Schedule 34A inserted by FA 2016 s 160(1), (5) with effect from 15 September 2016.

[PART 4
MEETING SECTION 237A CONDITIONS: BODIES CORPORATE AND PARTNERSHIPS

[Relevant bodies controlled etc by other persons treated as meeting section 237A condition

20 (1) A relevant body is treated as meeting a section 237A condition at the section 237A(2) relevant time if any of Conditions A to C is met.

(2) Condition A is that—

(*a*) a person met the section 237A condition at a time when the person was a promoter, and

(*b*) the person controls or has significant influence over the relevant body at the section 237A(2) relevant time.

(3) Condition B is that—

(*a*) a person met the section 237A condition at a time when the person controlled or had significant influence over the relevant body,

(*b*) the relevant body was a promoter at that time, and

(*c*) the person controls or has significant influence over the relevant body at the section 237A(2) relevant time.

(4) Condition C is that—

(*a*) two or more persons together controlled or had significant influence over the relevant body at a time when one of those persons met the section 237A condition,

(*b*) the relevant body was a promoter at that time, and

(*c*) those persons together control or have significant influence over the relevant body at the section 237A(2) relevant time.

(5) Sub-paragraph (1) does not apply where the person referred to in sub-paragraph (2)(*a*), (3)(*a*), or (4)(*a*) as meeting a section 237A condition is an individual.

(6) For the purposes of sub-paragraph (2) it does not matter whether the relevant body existed at the time referred to in sub-paragraph (2)(*a*).][2]][1]

Commentary—*Simon's Taxes* **A7.252A**.

Press releases etc—HMRC TIIN (Budget 2017), "Promoters of Tax Avoidance Schemes—associated and successor entities rules", 8 March 2017 (see *SWTI 2017, Budget Edition*).

Amendments—[1] Schedule 34A inserted by FA 2016 s 160(1), (5) with effect from 15 September 2016.

[2] Paras 20–22 substituted by FA 2017 s 24(2) with effect for the purposes of determining whether a person meets a section 237A condition in a period of three years ending on or after 8 March 2017.

[Persons who control etc a relevant body treated as meeting a section 237A condition

21 (1) If at a time when a person controlled or had significant influence over a relevant body—

(*a*) the relevant body met a section 237A condition, and

(*b*) the relevant body, or another relevant body which the person controlled or had significant influence over, was a promoter,

the person is treated as meeting the section 237A condition at the section 237A(2) relevant time.

(2) It does not matter whether any relevant body referred to in sub-paragraph (1) exists at the section 237A(2) relevant time.][1]

Commentary—*Simon's Taxes* **A7.252A**.

Press releases etc—HMRC TIIN (Budget 2017), "Promoters of Tax Avoidance Schemes—associated and successor entities rules", 8 March 2017 (see *SWTI 2017, Budget Edition*).

Amendments—[1] Paras 20–22 substituted by FA 2017 s 24(2) with effect for the purposes of determining whether a person meets a section 237A condition in a period of three years ending on or after 8 March 2017.

[Relevant bodies controlled etc by the same person treated as meeting a section 237A condition

22 (1) If—

(*a*) a person controlled or had significant influence over a relevant body at a time when it met a section 237A condition, and

(*b*) at that time that body, or another relevant body which the person controlled or had significant influence over, was a promoter,

any relevant body which the person controls or has significant influence over at the section 237A(2) relevant time is treated as meeting the section 237A condition at the section 237A(2) relevant time.

(2) If—

(*a*) two or more persons together controlled or had significant influence over a relevant body at a time when it met a section 237A condition, and

(*b*) at that time that body, or another relevant body which those persons together controlled or had significant influence over, was a promoter,

any relevant body which those persons together control or have significant influence over at the section 237A(2) relevant time is treated as meeting the section 237A condition at the section 237A(2) relevant time.

(3) It does not matter whether—

(*a*) a relevant body referred to in sub-paragraph (1)(*a*) or (*b*) or (2)(*a*) or (*b*) exists at the section 237A(2) relevant time, or

(*b*) a relevant body existing at the section 237A(2) relevant time existed at the time referred to in sub-paragraph (1)(*a*) or (2)(*a*).][1]

Commentary—*Simon's Taxes* **A7.252A**.

Press releases etc—HMRC TIIN (Budget 2017), "Promoters of Tax Avoidance Schemes—associated and successor entities rules", 8 March 2017 (see *SWTI 2017, Budget Edition*).

Amendments—[1] Paras 20–22 substituted by FA 2017 s 24(2) with effect for the purposes of determining whether a person meets a section 237A condition in a period of three years ending on or after 8 March 2017.

[Interpretation

23 (1) In this Part of this Schedule—

["control" and "significant influence" have the same meanings as in Part 4 of Schedule 34 (see paragraph 13A(5) to (11));

references to a person being a promoter are to the person carrying on business as a promoter;][2]

"relevant body" has the same meaning as in Part 3 of this Schedule;

"section 237A(2) relevant time" means the time referred to in section 237A(2);

"section 237A condition" means any of the conditions in section 237A(11), (12) and (13).

(2) For the purposes of paragraphs [20 to 22][2], the condition in section 237A(11) (occurrence of 3 relevant defeats in the 3 years ending with the relevant time) is taken to have been met by a person at any time if at least 3 relevant defeats have occurred in relation to the person in the period of 3 years ending with that time.][1]

Commentary—*Simon's Taxes* **A7.252A**.

Press releases etc—HMRC TIIN (Budget 2017), "Promoters of Tax Avoidance Schemes—associated and successor entities rules", 8 March 2017 (see *SWTI 2017, Budget Edition*).

Amendments—[1] Schedule 34A inserted by FA 2016 s 160(1), (5) with effect from 15 September 2016.

[2] In sub-para (1), definition of "control" substituted, and in sub-para (2), words substituted, by FA 2017 s 24(4) with effect for the purposes of determining whether a person meets a section 237A condition in a period of three years ending on or after 8 March 2017.

[PART 5
SUPPLEMENTARY

"Adjustments"

24 In this Schedule "adjustments" means any adjustments, whether by way of an assessment, the modification of an assessment or return, the amendment or disallowance of a claim, the entering into of a contract settlement or otherwise (and references to "making" adjustments accordingly include securing that adjustments are made by entering into a contract settlement).][1]

Amendments—[1] Schedule 34A inserted by FA 2016 s 160(1), (5) with effect from 15 September 2016.

[Meaning of "avoidance-related rule"

25 (1) In this Schedule "avoidance-related rule" means a rule in Category 1 or 2.

(2) A rule is in Category 1 if—

(*a*) it refers (in whatever terms) to the purpose or main purpose or purposes of a transaction, arrangements or any other action or matter, and

(*b*) to whether or not the purpose in question is or involves the avoidance of tax or the obtaining of any advantage in relation to tax (however described).

(3) A rule is also in Category 1 if it refers (in whatever terms) to—

(*a*) expectations as to what are, or may be, the expected benefits of a transaction, arrangements or any other action or matter, and

(*b*) whether or not the avoidance of tax or the obtaining of any advantage in relation to tax (however described) is such a benefit.

For the purposes of paragraph (*b*) it does not matter whether the reference is (for instance) to the "sole or main benefit" or "one of the main benefits" or any other reference to a benefit.

(4) A rule falls within Category 2 if as a result of the rule a person may be treated differently for tax purposes depending on whether or not purposes referred to in the rule (for instance the purposes of an actual or contemplated action or enterprise) are (or are shown to be) commercial purposes.

(5) For example, a rule in the following form would fall within Category 1 and within Category 2—

"Example rule

Section X does not apply to a company in respect of a transaction if the company shows that the transaction meets Condition A or B.

Condition A is that the transaction is effected—

(*a*) for genuine commercial reasons, or

(*b*) in the ordinary course of managing investments.

Condition B is that the avoidance of tax is not the main object or one of the main objects of the transaction."][1]

Amendments—[1] Schedule 34A inserted by FA 2016 s 160(1), (5) with effect from 15 September 2016.

["DOTAS arrangements"

26 (1) For the purposes of this Schedule arrangements are "DOTAS arrangements" at any time if at that time a person—

(*a*) has provided, information in relation to the arrangements under section 308(3), 309 or 310 of FA 2004, or

(*b*) has failed to comply with any of those provisions in relation to the arrangements.

(2) But for the purposes of this Schedule "DOTAS arrangements" does not include arrangements in respect of which HMRC has given notice under section 312(6) of FA 2004 (notice that promoters not under duty to notify client of reference number).

(3) For the purposes of sub-paragraph (1) a person who would be required to provide information under subsection (3) of section 308 of FA 2004—

(*a*) but for the fact that the arrangements implement a proposal in respect of which notice has been given under subsection (1) of that section, or

(*b*) but for subsection (4A), (4C) or (5) of that section,

is treated as providing the information at the end of the period referred to in subsection (3) of that section.][1]

Amendments—[1] Schedule 34A inserted by FA 2016 s 160(1), (5) with effect from 15 September 2016.

[Disclosable VAT or other indirect tax arrangements"

26A (1) For the purposes of this Schedule arrangements are "disclosable VAT or other indirect tax arrangements" at any time if at that time—

(*a*) the arrangements are disclosable Schedule 11A arrangements, or

(*b*) sub-paragraph (2) applies.

(2) This sub-paragraph applies if a person—

(*a*) has provided information in relation to the arrangements under paragraph 12(1), 17(2) or 18(2) of Schedule 17 to FA 2017, or

(*b*) has failed to comply with any of those provisions in relation to the arrangements.

(3) But for the purposes of this Schedule arrangements in respect of which HMRC have given notice under paragraph 23(6) of that Schedule (notice that promoters not under duty to notify client of reference number) are not to be regarded as disclosable VAT or other indirect tax arrangements.

(4) For the purposes of sub-paragraph (2) a person who would be required to provide information under paragraph 12(1) of that Schedule—

(*a*) but for the fact that the arrangements implement a proposal in respect of which notice has been given under paragraph 11(1) of that Schedule, or

(*b*) but for paragraph 13, 14 or 15 of that Schedule,

is treated as providing the information at the end of the period referred to in paragraph 12(1).][1]

Amendments—[1] Paragraph 26A inserted by F(No 2)A 2017 s 66, Sch 17 paras 52, 54(1), (4) with effect from 1 January 2018.

["Disclosable [Schedule 11A] VAT arrangements"

27 For the purposes of [paragraph 26A][2] arrangements are "disclosable [Schedule 11A][2] VAT arrangements" at any time if at that time—

(*a*) a person has complied with paragraph 6 of Schedule 11A to VATA 1994 in relation to the arrangements (duty to notify Commissioners),

(*b*) a person under a duty to comply with that paragraph in relation to the arrangements has failed to do so, or

(*c*) a reference number has been allocated to the scheme under paragraph 9 of that Schedule (voluntary notification of avoidance scheme which is not a designated scheme).][1]

Amendments—[1] Schedule 34A inserted by FA 2016 s 160(1), (5) with effect from 15 September 2016.

[2] In heading, words inserted, and in opening words, words inserted and words substituted for words "this Schedule", by F(No 2)A 2017 s 66, Sch 17 paras 52, 54(1), (5), (6) with effect from 1 January 2018.

[Paragraphs 26 [to 27]: supplementary

28 (1) A person "fails to comply" with any provision mentioned in paragraph 26(1)(*a*) [26A(2)(*a*)][2] or 27(*b*) if and only if any of the conditions in subparagraphs (2) to (4) is met.

(2) The condition in this sub-paragraph is that—

(*a*) the tribunal has determined that the person has failed to comply with the provision concerned,
(*b*) the appeal period has ended, and
(*c*) the determination has not been overturned on appeal.
(3) The condition in this sub-paragraph is that—
(*a*) the tribunal has determined for the purposes of section 118(2) of TMA 1970 that the person is to be deemed not to have failed to comply with the provision concerned as the person had a reasonable excuse for not doing the thing required to be done,
(*b*) the appeal period has ended, and
(*c*) the determination has not been overturned on appeal.
(4) The condition in this sub-paragraph is that the person admitted in writing to HMRC that the person has failed to comply with the provision concerned.
(5) In this paragraph "the appeal period" means—
(*a*) the period during which an appeal could be brought against the determination of the tribunal, or
(*b*) where an appeal mentioned in paragraph (*a*) has been brought, the period during which that appeal has not been finally determined, withdrawn or otherwise disposed of.][1]

Amendments—[1] Schedule 34A inserted by FA 2016 s 160(1), (5) with effect from 15 September 2016.
[2] In heading, words substituted for words "and 27", and in sub-para (1), words inserted, by F(No 2)A 2017 s 66, Sch 17 paras 52, 54(1), (7), (8) with effect from 1 January 2018.

["Final" counteraction

29 For the purposes of this Schedule the counteraction of a tax advantage or of arrangements is "final" when the assessment or adjustments made to effect the counteraction, and any amounts arising as a result of the assessment or adjustments, can no longer be varied, on appeal or otherwise.][1]

Amendments—[1] Schedule 34A inserted by FA 2016 s 160(1), (5) with effect from 15 September 2016.

[Inheritance tax, stamp duty reserve tax, VAT and petroleum revenue tax

30 (1) In this Schedule, in relation to inheritance tax, each of the following is treated as a return—
(*a*) an account delivered by a person under section 216 or 217 of IHTA 1984 (including an account delivered in accordance with regulations under section 256 of that Act);
(*b*) a statement or declaration which amends or is otherwise connected with such an account produced by the person who delivered the account;
(*c*) information or a document provided by a person in accordance with regulations under section 256 of that Act;
and such a return is treated as made by the person in question.
(2) In this Schedule references to an assessment to tax, in relation to inheritance tax, stamp duty reserve tax and petroleum revenue tax, include a determination.
(3) In this Schedule an expression used in relation to VAT has the same meaning as in VATA 1994.][1]

Amendments—[1] Schedule 34A inserted by FA 2016 s 160(1), (5) with effect from 15 September 2016.

[Power to amend

31 (1) The Treasury may by regulations amend this Schedule (apart from this paragraph).
(2) An amendment by virtue of sub-paragraph (1) may, in particular, add, vary or remove conditions or categories (or otherwise vary the meaning of "avoidance-related rule").
(3) Regulations under sub-paragraph (1) may include any amendment of this Part of this Act that is appropriate in consequence of an amendment made by virtue of sub-paragraph (1).][1]

Amendments—[1] Schedule 34A inserted by FA 2016 s 160(1), (5) with effect from 15 September 2016.

SCHEDULE 35

PROMOTERS OF TAX AVOIDANCE SCHEMES: PENALTIES

Section 274

Commentary—*Simon's Taxes* **A7.264.**

Introduction

1 In this Schedule a reference to an "information duty" is to a duty arising under any of the following provisions to provide information or produce a document—
(a) section 255 (duty to provide information or produce document);
(b) section 257 (ongoing duty to provide information);
(c) section 258 (duty of person dealing with non-resident promoter);
(d) section 259 (monitored promoter: duty to provide information about clients);
(e) section 260 (intermediaries: duty to provide information about clients);

(f) section 261 (duty to provide information about clients following enquiry);
(g) section 262 (information required for monitoring compliance with conduct notice);
(h) section 263 (information about monitored promoter's address).

Penalties for failure to comply

2 (1) A person who fails to comply with a duty imposed by or under this Part mentioned in column 1 of the Table is liable to a penalty not exceeding the amount shown in relation to that provision in column 2 of the Table.

Table

Column 1 *Provision*	*Column 2* *Maximum penalty (£)*
Section 249(1) (duty to notify clients of monitoring notice)	5,000
Section 249(3) (duty to publicise monitoring notice)	1,000,000
Section 249(10) (duty to include information on correspondence etc)	1,000,000
Section 251 (duty of promoter to notify clients and intermediaries of reference number)	5,000
Section 252 (duty of those notified to notify others of promoter's number)	5,000
Section 253 (duty to notify HMRC of reference number)	the relevant amount (see sub-paragraph (3))
Section 255 (duty to provide information or produce document)	1,000,000
Section 257 (ongoing duty to provide information or produce document)	1,000,000
Section 258 (duty of person dealing with non-resident promoter)	1,000,000
Section 259 (monitored promoter: duty to provide information about clients)	5,000
Section 260 (intermediaries: duty to provide information about clients)	5,000
Section 261 (duty to provide information about clients following an enquiry)	10,000
Section 262 (duty to provide information required to monitor compliance with conduct notice)	5,000
Section 263 (duty to provide information about address)	5,000
Section 265 (duty to provide information to promoter)	5,000

(2) In relation to a failure to comply with section 249(1), 251, 252, 259 or 260 the maximum penalty specified in column 2 of the Table is a maximum penalty which may be imposed in respect of each person to whom the failure relates.

(3) In relation to a failure to comply with section 253, the "relevant amount" is—

(a) £5,000, unless paragraph (b) or (c) applies;
(b) £7,500, where a person has previously failed to comply with section 253 on one (and only one) occasion during the period of 36 months ending with the date on which the current failure occurred;
(c) £10,000, where a person has previously failed to comply with section 253 on two or more occasions during the period mentioned in paragraph (b).

(4) The amount of a penalty imposed under sub-paragraph (1) is to be arrived at after taking account of all relevant considerations, including the desirability of setting it at a level which appears appropriate for deterring the person, or other persons, from similar failures to comply on future occasions having regard (in particular)—

(a) in the case of a penalty imposed for a failure to comply with section 255 or 257, to the amount of fees received, or likely to have been received, by the person in connection with the monitored proposal, arrangements implementing the monitored proposal or monitored arrangements to which the information or document required as a result of section 255 or 257 relates,

(b) in the case of a penalty imposed in relation to a failure to comply with section 258(4) or (5), to the amount of any tax advantage gained, or sought to be gained, by the person in relation to the monitored arrangements or the arrangements implementing the monitored proposal.

Daily default penalties for failure to comply

3 (1) If the failure to comply with an information duty continues after a penalty is imposed under paragraph 2(1), the person is liable to a further penalty or penalties not exceeding the relevant sum for each day on which the failure continues after the day on which the penalty under paragraph 2(1) was imposed.

(2) In sub-paragraph (1) "the relevant sum" means—

(a) £10,000, in a case where the maximum penalty which could have been imposed for the failure was £1,000,000;

(b) £600, in cases not falling within paragraph (a).

Penalties for inaccurate information and documents

4 (1) If—

(a) in complying with an information duty, a person provides inaccurate information or produces a document that contains an inaccuracy, and

(b) condition A, B or C is met,

the person is liable to a penalty not exceeding the relevant sum.

(2) Condition A is that the inaccuracy is careless or deliberate.

(3) An inaccuracy is careless if it is due to a failure by the person to take reasonable care.

(4) For the purpose of determining whether or not a person who is a monitored promoter took reasonable care, reliance on legal advice is to be disregarded if either—

(a) the advice was not based on a full and accurate description of the facts, or

(b) the conclusions in the advice that the person relied on were unreasonable.

(5) For the purpose of determining whether or not a person who complies with a duty under section 258 took reasonable care, reliance on legal advice is to be disregarded if the advice was given or procured by the monitored promoter mentioned in subsection (1) of that section.

(6) Condition B is that the person knows of the inaccuracy at the time the information is provided or the document produced but does not inform HMRC at that time.

(7) Condition C is that the person—

(a) discovers the inaccuracy some time later, and

(b) fails to take reasonable steps to inform HMRC.

(8) The "relevant sum" means—

(a) £1,000,000, where the information is provided or document produced in compliance with a duty under section 255, 257 or 258;

(b) £10,000, where the information is provided in compliance with a duty under section 261;

(c) £5,000, where the information is provided or document produced in compliance with a duty under section 259, 260, 262 or 263.

(9) If the information or document contains more than one inaccuracy, one penalty is payable under this paragraph whatever the number of inaccuracies.

Power to change amount of penalties

5 (1) If it appears to the Treasury that there has been a change in the value of money since the last relevant date, they may by regulations substitute for the sums for the time being specified in paragraph 2, 3 or 4 such other sums as appear to them to be justified by the change.

(2) Regulations under sub-paragraph (1) may include any amendment of paragraph 10(b) that is appropriate in consequence of an amendment made by virtue of sub-paragraph (1).

(3) The "relevant date", in relation to a specified sum, means—

(a) the date on which this Act is passed, and

(b) each date on which the power conferred by sub-paragraph (1) has been exercised in relation to that sum.

Concealing, destroying etc documents following imposition of a duty to provide information

6 (1) A person must not conceal, destroy or otherwise dispose of, or arrange for the concealment, destruction or disposal of, a document which is subject to a duty under section 255, 257 or 262.

(2) Sub-paragraph (1) does not apply if the person acts after the document has been produced to an officer of Revenue and Customs in accordance with the duty, unless the officer has notified the person in writing that the document must continue to be available for inspection (and has not withdrawn the notification).

(3) Sub-paragraph (1) does not apply, in a case to which section 268(1) applies, if the person acts after the expiry of the period of 6 months beginning with the day on which a copy of the document was produced in accordance with that section unless, before the expiry of that period, an officer of Revenue and Customs makes a request for the original document under section 268(2)(b).

(4) A person who conceals, destroys or otherwise disposes of, or arranges for the concealment, destruction or disposal of, a document in breach of sub-paragraph (1), is taken to have failed to comply with the duty to produce the document under the provision concerned (but see sub-paragraph (5)).

(5) If a person conceals, destroys or otherwise disposes of, or arranges for the concealment, destruction or disposal of, a document which is subject to a duty under more than one of the provisions mentioned in sub-paragraph (1) then—

(a) in a case where a duty under section 255 applies, the person will be taken to have failed to comply only with that provision, or

(b) in a case where a duty under section 255 does not apply, the person will be taken to have failed to comply only with section 257.

Concealing, destroying etc documents following informal notification

7 (1) A person must not conceal, destroy or otherwise dispose of, or arrange for the concealment, destruction or disposal of, a document if an officer of Revenue and Customs has informed the person in writing that the person is, or is likely, to be given a notice under 255, 257 or 262 the effect of which will, or is likely to, require the production of the document.

(2) Sub-paragraph (1) does not apply if the person acts—

(a) at least 6 months after the person was, or was last, informed as described in sub-paragraph (1), or

(b) after the person becomes subject to a duty under 255, 257 or 262 which requires the document to be produced.

(3) A person who conceals, destroys or otherwise disposes of, or arranges for the concealment, destruction or disposal of, a document in breach of sub-paragraph (1), is taken to have failed to comply with the duty to produce the document under the provision concerned (but see sub-paragraph (4)).

(4) If a person conceals, destroys or otherwise disposes of, or arranges for the concealment, destruction or disposal of, a document which is subject to a duty under more than one of the provisions mentioned in sub-paragraph (1) then—

(a) in a case where a duty under section 255 applies, the person will be taken to have failed to comply only with that provision, or

(b) in a case where a duty under section 255 does not apply, the person will be taken to have failed to comply only with section 257.

Failure to comply with time limit

8 A failure to do anything required to be done within a limited period of time does not give rise to liability to a penalty under this Schedule if the person did it within such further time, if any, as an officer of Revenue and Customs or the tribunal may have allowed.

Reasonable excuse

9 (1) Liability to a penalty under this Schedule does not arise if there is a reasonable excuse for the failure.

(2) For the purposes of this paragraph—

(a) an insufficiency of funds is not a reasonable excuse unless attributable to events outside the person's control,

(b) if the person relies on any other person to do anything, that is not a reasonable excuse unless the first person took reasonable care to avoid the failure,

(c) if the person had a reasonable excuse for the failure but the excuse has ceased, the person is to be treated as having continued to have the excuse if the failure is remedied without unreasonable delay after the excuse ceased,

(d) reliance on legal advice is to be taken automatically not to constitute a reasonable excuse where the person is a monitored promoter if either—

(i) the advice was not based on a full and accurate description of the facts, or

(ii) the conclusions in the advice that the person relied on were unreasonable, and

(e) reliance on legal advice is to be taken automatically not to constitute a reasonable excuse in the case of a penalty for failure to comply with section 258, if the advice was given or procured by the monitored promoter mentioned in subsection (1) of that section.

Assessment of penalty and appeals

10 Part 10 of TMA 1970 (penalties, etc) has effect as if—

(a) the reference in section 100(1) to the Taxes Acts were read as a reference to the Taxes Acts and this Schedule,

(b) in subsection (2) of section 100, there were inserted a reference to a penalty under this Schedule, other than a penalty under paragraph 3 of this Schedule in respect of which the relevant sum is £600.

Interest on penalties

11 (1) A penalty under this Schedule is to carry interest at the rate applicable under section 178 of FA 1989 from the date it is determined until payment.

(2) (*inserts* FA 1989 s 178(2)(u))

Double jeopardy

12 A person is not liable to a penalty under this Schedule in respect of anything in respect of which the person has been convicted of an offence.

Overlapping penalties

13 A person is not liable to a penalty under—

(a) Schedule 24 to the FA 2007 (penalties for errors),

(b) Part 7 of FA 2004, or

(c) any other provision which is prescribed,

by reason of any failure to include in any return or account a reference number required by section 253.

SCHEDULE 37

COMPANIES OWNED BY EMPLOYEE-OWNERSHIP TRUSTS

Section 290

PART 3

INHERITANCE TAX RELIEF

Commentary—*Simon's Taxes* **I5.136A**.

9 IHTA 1984 is amended as follows.

10 (1) After section 13 insert—

"13A Dispositions by close companies to employee-ownership trusts

(1) A disposition of property made to trustees by a close company ("C") whereby the property is to be held on trusts of the description specified in section 86(1) is not a transfer of value if—

(a) C meets the trading requirement,

(b) the trusts are of a settlement which meets the all-employee benefit requirement, and

(c) the settlement does not meet the controlling interest requirement immediately before the beginning of the tax year in which the disposition of property occurs but does meet it at the end of that year.

(2) Sections 236I, 236J, 236K, 236M and 236T (but not 236L) of the 1992 Act apply to determine whether—

(a) C meets the trading requirement;

(b) the settlement meets the all-employee benefit requirement;

(c) the settlement meets the controlling interest requirement;

with references in those sections to "C" being read accordingly.

(3) In this section—

"close company" has the same meaning as in Part 4 of this Act;

"tax year" means a year beginning on 6 April and ending on the following 5 April."

(2) The amendment made by this paragraph has effect in relation to dispositions of property made on or after 6 April 2014.

11 (1) After section 28 insert—

"28A Employee-ownership trusts

(1) A transfer of value made by an individual who is beneficially entitled to shares in a company ("C") is an exempt transfer to the extent that the value transferred is attributable to shares in or securities of C which become comprised in a settlement if—

(a) C meets the trading requirement,

(b) the settlement meets the all-employee benefit requirement, and

(c) the settlement does not meet the controlling interest requirement immediately before the beginning of the tax year in which the transfer of value is made but does meet it at the end of that year.

(2) Sections 236I, 236J, 236K, 236M and 236T (but not 236L) of the 1992 Act apply to determine whether—

(a) C meets the trading requirement;

(b) the settlement meets the all-employee benefit requirement;

(c) the settlement meets the controlling interest requirement;

with references in those sections to "C" being read accordingly.

(3) In this section "tax year" means a year beginning on 6 April and ending on the following 5 April."

(2) The amendment made by this paragraph has effect in relation to transfers of value made on or after 6 April 2014.

12 (1) In section 29A (abatement of exemption where claim settled out of beneficiary's own resources), in subsection (6)—

(a) for "to 28" substitute "to 28A", and

(b) for "or 28" substitute ", 28 or 28A".

(2) The amendment made by this paragraph has effect in relation to transfers of value made on or after 6 April 2014.

13 (1) Section 72 (property leaving employee trusts and newspaper trusts) is amended as follows.

(2) In subsection (2), after "Subject to subsections" insert "(3A),".

(3) After subsection (3) insert—

"(3A) Where settled property ceases to be property to which this section applies because paragraph (d) of section 86(3) no longer applies, tax is not chargeable under this section by virtue of subsection (2)(a) if the only reason that paragraph no longer applies is that one or both of the trading requirement and the controlling interest requirement mentioned in that paragraph are no longer met with respect to the company so mentioned."

(4) The amendments made by this paragraph are treated as having come into force on 6 April 2014.

14 (1) After section 75 insert—

"75A Property becoming subject to employee-ownership trust

(1) Tax is not charged under section 65 in respect of shares in or securities of a company ("C") which cease to be relevant property on becoming held on trusts of the description specified in section 86(1) if the conditions in subsection (2) are satisfied.

(2) The conditions referred to in subsection (1) are—

(a) that C meets the trading requirement,

(b) that the trusts are of a settlement which meets the all-employee benefit requirement, and

(c) that the settlement does not meet the controlling interest requirement immediately before the beginning of the tax year in which the shares or securities cease to be relevant property but does meet it at the end of that year.

(3) Sections 236I, 236J, 236K, 236M and 236T (but not 236L) of the 1992 Act apply to determine whether—

(a) C meets the trading requirement;

(b) the settlement meets the all-employee benefit requirement;

(c) the settlement meets the controlling interest requirement;

with references in those sections to "C" being read accordingly.

(4) In this section "tax year" means a year beginning on 6 April and ending on the following 5 April."

(2) The amendment made by this paragraph is treated as having come into force on 6 April 2014.

15 (1) Section 86 (trusts for benefit of employees) is amended as follows.

(2) In subsection (3), after paragraph (c) insert ", or

(d) the settled property consists of or includes ordinary share capital of a company which meets the trading requirement and the trusts on which the settled property is held are those of a settlement which—

(i) meets the controlling interest requirement with respect to the company, and

(ii) meets the all-employee benefit requirement with respect to the company."

(3) After that subsection insert—

"(3A) For the purpose of determining whether subsection (3)(d) is satisfied in relation to settled property which consists of or includes ordinary share capital of a company—

(a) section 236I of the 1992 Act applies to determine whether the company meets the trading requirement (with references to "C" being read as references to that company),

(b) sections 236J, 236K, 236M and 236T (but not 236L) of the 1992 Act apply to determine whether the settlement meets the all-employee benefit requirement and the controlling interest requirement (with references in those sections to "C" being read as references to that company), and

(c) "ordinary share capital" has the meaning given by section 1119 of the Corporation Tax Act 2010."

(4) The amendments made by this paragraph are treated as having come into force on 6 April 2014.

16 (1) In section 144 (distribution etc from property settled by will), in subsection (1)(b), after "section 75" insert ", 75A".

(2) The amendment made by this section is treated as having come into force on 6 April 2014.

PART 4

MISCELLANEOUS AMENDMENTS

Finance Act 1986

17 (1) In section 102 of FA 1986 (gifts with reservation), in subsection (5) omit the "and" after paragraph (h) and after paragraph (i) insert "; and

(j) section 28A (employee-ownership trusts)."

(2) The amendment made by this paragraph has effect in relation to disposals made on or after 6 April 2014.

FINANCE ACT 2015

2015 Chapter 11

An Act to grant certain duties, to alter other duties, and to amend the law relating to the National Debt and the Public Revenue, and to make further provision in connection with finance.

26 March 2015

CONTENTS

PART 2

EXCISE DUTIES AND OTHER TAXES

Inheritance tax

PART 4

OTHER PROVISIONS

Anti-avoidance

(*SEE YELLOW TAX HANDBOOK PART 1*)

WE, Your Majesty's most dutiful and loyal subjects, the Commons of the United Kingdom in Parliament assembled, towards raising the necessary supplies to defray Your Majesty's public expenses, and making an addition to the public revenue, have freely and voluntarily resolved to give and to grant unto Your Majesty the several duties hereinafter mentioned; and do therefore most humbly beseech Your Majesty that it may be enacted, and be it enacted by the Queen's most Excellent Majesty, by and with the advice and consent of the Lords Spiritual and Temporal, and Commons, in this present Parliament assembled, and by the authority of the same, as follows:—

PART 2

EXCISE DUTIES AND OTHER TAXES

Inheritance Tax

74 Inheritance tax: exemption for decorations and other awards

(1) In section 6 of IHTA 1984 (excluded property), for subsection (1B) substitute—

"(1B) A relevant decoration or award is excluded property if it has never been the subject of a disposition for a consideration in money or money's worth.

(1BA) In subsection (1B) "relevant decoration or award" means a decoration or other similar award—

(*a*) that is designed to be worn to denote membership of—

(i) an Order that is, or has been, specified in the Order of Wear published in the London Gazette ("the Order of Wear"), or

(ii) an Order of a country or territory outside the United Kingdom,

(*b*) that is, or has been, specified in the Order of Wear,

(*c*) that was awarded for valour or gallant conduct,

(*d*) that was awarded for, or in connection with, a person being, or having been, a member of, or employed or engaged in connection with, the armed forces of any country or territory,

(*e*) that was awarded for, or in connection with, a person being, or having been, an emergency responder within the meaning of section 153A (death of emergency service personnel etc), or

(*f*) that was awarded by the Crown or a country or territory outside the United Kingdom for, or in connection with, public service or achievement in public life."

(2) The amendment made by subsection (1) has effect in relation to transfers of value made, or treated as made, on or after 3 December 2014.

75 Inheritance tax: exemption for emergency service personnel etc

(1) IHTA 1984 is amended as follows.

(2) After section 153 insert—

"*Emergency services*

153A Death of emergency service personnel etc

(1) The reliefs in subsection (2) apply where a person—

(*a*) dies from an injury sustained, accident occurring or disease contracted at a time when that person was responding to emergency circumstances in that person's capacity as an emergency responder, or

(*b*) dies from a disease contracted at some previous time, the death being due to, or hastened by, the aggravation of the disease during a period when that person was responding to emergency circumstances in that person's capacity as an emergency responder.

(2) The reliefs are—

(*a*) that no potentially exempt transfer made by the person becomes a chargeable transfer under section 3A(4) because of the death,

(*b*) that section 4 (transfers on death) does not apply in relation to the death, and

(*c*) that no additional tax becomes due under section 7(4) because of a transfer made by the person within 7 years of the death.

(3) "Emergency circumstances" means circumstances which are present or imminent and are causing or likely to cause—

(*a*) the death of a person,

(*b*) serious injury to, or the serious illness of, a person,

(*c*) the death of an animal,

(*d*) serious injury to, or the serious illness of, an animal,

(*e*) serious harm to the environment (including the life and health of plants and animals),

(*f*) serious harm to any building or other property, or

(*g*) a worsening of any such injury, illness or harm.

(4) A person is "responding to emergency circumstances" if the person—

(*a*) is going anywhere for the purpose of dealing with emergency circumstances occurring there, or

(*b*) is dealing with emergency circumstances, preparing to do so imminently or dealing with the immediate aftermath of emergency circumstances.

(5) For the purposes of this section, circumstances to which a person is responding are to be taken to be emergency circumstances if the person believes and has reasonable grounds for believing they are or may be emergency circumstances.

(6) "Emergency responder" means—

(*a*) a person employed, or engaged, in connection with the provision of fire services or fire and rescue services,

(*b*) a person employed for the purposes of providing, or engaged to provide, search services or rescue services (or both),

(*c*) a person employed for the purposes of providing, or engaged to provide, medical, ambulance or paramedic services,

(*d*) a constable or a person employed for police purposes or engaged to provide services for police purposes,

(*e*) a person employed for the purposes of providing, or engaged to provide, services for the transportation of organs, blood, medical equipment or medical personnel, or

(*f*) a person employed, or engaged, by the government of a state or territory, an international organisation or a charity in connection with the provision of humanitarian assistance.

(7) For the purposes of subsection (6)—

(*a*) it is immaterial whether the employment or engagement is paid or unpaid, and

(*b*) "international organisation" means an organisation of which—

(i) two or more sovereign powers are members, or

(ii) the governments of two or more sovereign powers are members.

(8) The Treasury may, by regulations made by statutory instrument, extend the definition of "emergency responder" in subsection (6).

(9) Regulations under this section are subject to annulment in pursuance of a resolution of the House of Commons."

(3) In section 154 (death on active service)—

(*a*) in subsection (1), for "Section 4 shall not apply" substitute "The reliefs in subsection (1A) apply",

(*b*) after that subsection insert—

"(1A) The reliefs are—

(*a*) that no potentially exempt transfer made by the deceased becomes a chargeable transfer under section 3A(4) because of the death,

(*b*) that section 4 (transfers on death) does not apply in relation to the death, and

(*c*) that no additional tax becomes due under section 7(4) because of a transfer made by the deceased within 7 years of the death.",

(*c*) in subsection (2) omit "either" and after paragraph (*b*) insert "or

(*c*) responding to emergency circumstances in the course of the person's duties as a member of any of those armed forces or as a civilian subject to service discipline.", and

(*d*) after that subsection insert—

"(2A) Section 153A(3) to (5) applies for the purposes of this section."

(4) After section 155 insert—

"Constables and service personnel

155A Death of constables and service personnel targeted because of their status

(1) The reliefs in subsection (3) apply where a person—

(*a*) dies from an injury sustained or disease contracted in circumstances where the person was deliberately targeted by reason of his or her status as a constable or former constable, or

(*b*) dies from a disease contracted at some previous time, the death being due to, or hastened by, the aggravation of the disease by an injury sustained or disease contracted in circumstances mentioned in paragraph (*a*).

(2) The reliefs in subsection (3) apply where it is certified by the Defence Council or the Secretary of State that a person—

(*a*) died from an injury sustained or disease contracted in circumstances where the person was deliberately targeted by reason of his or her status as a service person or former service person, or

(*b*) died from a disease contracted at some previous time, the death being due to, or hastened by, the aggravation of the disease by an injury sustained or disease contracted in circumstances mentioned in paragraph (*a*).

(3) The reliefs are—

(*a*) that no potentially exempt transfer made by the person becomes a chargeable transfer under section 3A(4) because of the death,

(*b*) that section 4 (transfers on death) does not apply in relation to the death, and

(*c*) that no additional tax becomes due under section 7(4) because of a transfer made by the person within 7 years of the death.

(4) For the purposes of this section, it is immaterial whether a person who was a constable or service person at the time the injury was sustained or the disease was contracted was acting in the course of his or her duties as such at that time (and for this purpose ignore the references in subsections (1)(*b*) and (2)(*b*) to a disease contracted at some previous time).

(5) "Service person" means a person who is a member of the armed forces of the Crown or a civilian subject to service discipline (within the meaning of the Armed Forces Act 2006).

(6) This section does not apply where section 153A or 154 applies in relation to a person's death."

(5) The amendments made by this section have effect in relation to deaths occurring on or after 19 March 2014.

PART 4

OTHER PROVISIONS

Anti-Avoidance

121 Penalties in connection with offshore asset moves

Schedule 21 contains provision for imposing an additional penalty in cases where—

(*a*) a person is liable for a penalty for a failure to comply with an obligation or provide a document, or for providing an inaccurate document, relating to income tax, capital gains tax or inheritance tax, and

(*b*) there is a related transfer of, or change in the ownership arrangements for, an asset situated or held outside the United Kingdom.

SCHEDULE 17

DISCLOSURE OF TAX AVOIDANCE SCHEMES

Section 117

Requirement to update DOTAS information

Cross-references—See the Tax Avoidance Schemes (Information) (Amendment) Regulations, SI 2015/948 (information that employers must provide to employees and to HMRC in relation to avoidance involving their employees and changes to prescribed information that introducers must provide to HMRC in relation to avoidance to include information relating to persons with whom an introducer has made a marketing contact).

1 After section 310B of FA 2004 insert—

"310C Duty of promoters to provide updated information

(1) This section applies where—

(*a*) information has been provided under section 308 about any notifiable arrangements, or proposed notifiable arrangements, to which a reference number is allocated under section 311, and

(*b*) after the provision of the information, there is a change in relation to the arrangements of a kind mentioned in subsection (2).

(2) The changes referred to in subsection (1)(*b*) are—

(*a*) a change in the name by which the notifiable arrangements, or proposed notifiable arrangements, are known;

(*b*) a change in the name or address of any person who is a promoter in relation to the notifiable arrangements or, in the case of proposed notifiable arrangements, the notifiable proposal.

(3) A person who is a promoter in relation to the notifiable arrangements or, in the case of proposed notifiable arrangements, the notifiable proposal must inform HMRC of the change mentioned in subsection (1)(*b*) within 30 days after it is made.

(4) Subsections (5) and (6) apply for the purposes of subsection (3) where there is more than one person who is a promoter in relation to the notifiable arrangements or proposal.

(5) If the change in question is a change in the name or address of a person who is a promoter in relation to the notifiable arrangements or proposal, it is the duty of that person to comply with subsection (3).

(6) If a person provides information in compliance with subsection (3), the duty imposed by that subsection on any other person, so far as relating to the provision of that information, is discharged."

2 In section 316 of that Act (information to be provided in form and manner specified by HMRC), in subsection (2), after "310A," insert "310C,".

3 In section 98C of TMA 1970 (notification under Part 7 of FA 2004), in subsection (2), after paragraph (ca) insert—

"(cb) section 310C (duty of promoters to provide updated information),".

Arrangements to be given reference number

4 In section 311(1)(*a*) of FA 2004 (period for allocation of reference number to arrangements) for "30 days" substitute "90 days".

Notification of employees

5 (1) Section 312A of FA 2004 (duty of client to notify parties of number) is amended as follows.

(2) After subsection (2) insert—

"(2A) Where the client—

(*a*) is an employer, and

(*b*) by reason of the arrangements or proposed arrangements, receives or might reasonably be expected to receive an advantage, in relation to any relevant tax, in relation to the employment of one or more of the client's employees,

the client must, within the prescribed period, provide to each of the client's relevant employees prescribed information relating to the reference number."

(3) For subsection (3) substitute—

"(3) For the purposes of this section—

(*a*) a tax is a "relevant tax", in relation to arrangements or arrangements proposed in a proposal of any description, if it is prescribed in relation to arrangements or proposals of that description by regulations under section 306;

(*b*) "relevant employee" means an employee in relation to whose employment the client receives or might reasonably be expected to receive the advantage mentioned in subsection (2A);

(*c*) "employee" includes a former employee;

(*d*) a reference to employment includes holding an office (and references to "employee" and "employer" are to be construed accordingly)."

(4) In subsection (4), for "the duty under subsection (2)" substitute "one or both of the duties under this section".

(5) In subsection (5), after "subsection (2)" insert "or (2A)".

6 In section 313 of that Act (duty of parties to notifiable arrangements to notify Board of number, etc), after subsection (5) insert—

"(6) The duty under subsection (1) does not apply in prescribed circumstances."

7 In section 316 of that Act (information to be provided in form and manner specified by HMRC), in subsection (2), after "312A(2)" insert "and (2A)".

8 In section 98C of TMA 1970 (notification under Part 7 of FA 2004), in subsection (2), in paragraph (da), after "312A(2)" insert "and (2A)".

Employers' duty of disclosure

9 After section 313ZB of FA 2004 insert—

"313ZC Duty of employer to notify HMRC of details of employees etc

(1) This section applies if conditions A, B and C are met.

(2) Condition A is that a person who is a promoter in relation to notifiable arrangements or a notifiable proposal is providing (or has provided) services in connection with the notifiable arrangements or notifiable proposal to a person ("the client").

(3) Condition B is that the client receives information under section 312(2) or as mentioned in section 312(5).

(4) Condition C is that the client is an employer in circumstances where, as a result of the notifiable arrangement or proposed notifiable arrangement—

(*a*) one or more of the client's employees receive, or might reasonably be expected to receive, in relation to their employment, an advantage in relation to any relevant tax, or

(*b*) the client receives or might reasonably be expected to receive such an advantage in relation to the employment of one or more of the client's employees.

(5) Where an employee is within subsection (4)(*a*), or is an employee mentioned in subsection (4)(*b*), the client must provide HMRC with prescribed information relating to the employee at the prescribed time or times.

(6) The client need not comply with subsection (5) in relation to any notifiable arrangements at any time after HMRC have given notice under section 312(6) or 313(5) in relation to the notifiable arrangements.

(7) The duty under subsection (5) does not apply in prescribed circumstances.

(8) Section 312A(3) applies for the purposes of this section as it applies for the purposes of that section."

10 In section 316 of that Act (information to be provided in form and manner specified by HMRC), in subsection (2), for "and 313ZA(3)" substitute ", 313ZA(3) and 313ZC(5)".

11 In section 98C of TMA 1970 (notification under Part 7 of FA 2004), in subsection (2), after paragraph (dc) insert—

"(dca) section 313ZC (duty of employer to provide details of employees etc),".

Identifying scheme users

12 (1) Section 313C of FA 2004 (information provided to introducers) is amended as follows.

(2) For subsection (1) substitute—

"(1) This section applies where HMRC suspect—

(*a*) that a person ("P") is an introducer in relation to a proposal, and

(*b*) that the proposal may be notifiable.

(1A) HMRC may by written notice require P to provide HMRC with one or both of the following—

(*a*) prescribed information in relation to each person who has provided P with any information relating to the proposal;

(*b*) prescribed information in relation to each person with whom P has made a marketing contact in relation to the proposal."

(3) In subsection (3), for "or by virtue of subsection (1)" substitute "subsection (1A)".

(4) For the heading substitute "Provision of information to HMRC by introducers".

13 In section 98C of TMA 1970 (notification under Part 7 of FA 2004: penalties), in subsection (2)(*f*) after "information" insert "or have been provided with information".

Additional information

14 After section 316 of FA 2004 insert—

"316A Duty to provide additional information

(1) This section applies where a person is required to provide information under section 312(2) or 312A(2) or (2A).

(2) HMRC may specify additional information which must be provided by that person to the recipients under section 312(2) or 312A(2) or (2A) at the same time as the information referred to in subsection (1).

(3) HMRC may specify the form and manner in which the additional information is to be provided.

(4) For the purposes of this section "additional information" means information supplied by HMRC which relates to notifiable proposals or notifiable arrangements in general."

15 In section 98C of TMA 1970 (notification under Part 7 of FA 2004), in subsection (2), omit the "and" at the end of paragraph (*e*) and after paragraph (*f*) insert ", and

(*g*) section 316A (duty to provide additional information)."

Protection of persons making voluntary disclosures

16 After section 316A of FA 2004 insert—

"316B Confidentiality

No duty of confidentiality or other restriction on disclosure (however imposed) prevents the voluntary disclosure by any person to HMRC of information or documents which the person has reasonable grounds for suspecting will assist HMRC in determining whether there has been a breach of any requirement imposed by or under this Part."

Publication of DOTAS information

17 After section 316B of FA 2004 insert—

"316C Publication by HMRC

(1) HMRC may publish information about—

(*a*) any notifiable arrangements, or proposed notifiable arrangements, to which a reference number is allocated under section 311;

(*b*) any person who is a promoter in relation to the notifiable arrangements or, in the case of proposed notifiable arrangements, the notifiable proposal.

(2) The information that may be published is (subject to subsection (4))—

(*a*) any information relating to arrangements within subsection (1)(*a*), or a person within subsection (1)(*b*), that is prescribed information for the purposes of section 308, 309 or 310;

(*b*) any ruling of a court or tribunal relating to any such arrangements or person (in that person's capacity as a promoter in relation to a notifiable proposal or arrangements);

(*c*) the number of persons in any period who enter into transactions forming part of notifiable arrangements within subsection (1)(*a*);

(*d*) whether arrangements within subsection (1)(*a*) are APN relevant (see subsection (7));

(*e*) any other information that HMRC considers it appropriate to publish for the purpose of identifying arrangements within subsection (1)(*a*) or a person within subsection (1)(*b*).

(3) The information may be published in any manner that HMRC considers appropriate.

(4) No information may be published under this section that identifies a person who enters into a transaction forming part of notifiable arrangements within subsection (1)(*a*).

(5) But where a person who is a promoter within subsection (1)(*b*) is also a person mentioned in subsection (4), nothing in subsection (4) is to be taken as preventing the publication under this section of information so far as relating to the person's activities as a promoter.

(6) Before publishing any information under this section that identifies a person as a promoter within subsection (1)(*b*), HMRC must—

(*a*) inform the person that they are considering doing so, and

(*b*) give the person reasonable opportunity to make representations about whether it should be published.

(7) Arrangements are "APN relevant" for the purposes of subsection (2)(*d*) if HMRC has indicated in a publication that it may exercise (or has exercised) its power under section 219 of the Finance Act 2014 (accelerated payment notices) by virtue of the arrangements being DOTAS arrangements within the meaning of that section.

316D Section 316C: subsequent judicial rulings

(1) This section applies if—

(*a*) information about notifiable arrangements, or proposed notifiable arrangements, is published under section 316C,

(*b*) at any time after the information is published, a ruling of a court or tribunal is made in relation to tax arrangements, and

(*c*) HMRC is of the opinion that the ruling is relevant to the arrangements mentioned in paragraph (*a*).

(2) A ruling is "relevant" to the arrangements if—

(*a*) the principles laid down, or reasoning given, in the ruling would, if applied to the arrangements, allow the purported advantage arising from the arrangements in relation to tax, and

(*b*) the ruling is final.

(3) HMRC must publish information about the ruling.

(4) The information must be published in the same manner as HMRC published the information mentioned in subsection (1)(*a*) (and may also be published in any other manner that HMRC considers appropriate).

(5) A ruling is "final" if it is—

(*a*) a ruling of the Supreme Court, or

(*b*) a ruling of any other court or tribunal in circumstances where—

(i) no appeal may be made against the ruling,

(ii) if an appeal may be made against the ruling with permission, the time limit for applications has expired and either no application has been made or permission has been refused,

(iii) if such permission to appeal against the ruling has been granted or is not required, no appeal has been made within the time limit for appeals, or

(iv) if an appeal was made, it was abandoned or otherwise disposed of before it was determined by the court or tribunal to which it was addressed.

(6) Where a ruling is final by virtue of sub-paragraph (ii), (iii) or (iv) of subsection (5)(*b*), the ruling is to be treated as made at the time when the sub-paragraph in question is first satisfied.

(7) In this section "tax arrangements" means arrangements in respect of which it would be reasonable to conclude (having regard to all the circumstances) that the obtaining of an advantage in relation to tax was the main purpose, or one of the main purposes."

Increase in penalties for failure to comply with section 313 of FA 2004

18 In section 98C of TMA 1970 (notification under Part 7 of FA 2004)—

(*a*) in subsection (3) for "penalty of the relevant sum" substitute "penalty not exceeding the relevant sum", and

(*b*) in subsection (4)—

(i) in paragraph (*a*) for "£100" substitute "£5,000",

(ii) in paragraph (*b*) for "£500" substitute "£7,500", and

(iii) in paragraph (*c*) for "£1,000" substitute "£10,000".

Commentary—*Simon's Taxes* **A4.573**.

Transitional provisions

19 (1) Section 310C of FA 2004 applies in relation to notifiable arrangements, or proposed notifiable arrangements, only if a reference number under section 311 of that Act is allocated to the arrangements on or after the day on which this Act is passed.

(2) But section 310C of FA 2004 does not apply in relation to notifiable arrangements, or proposed notifiable arrangements, where prescribed information relating to the arrangements was provided to HMRC before that day in compliance with section 308 of that Act.

20 Any notice given by HMRC under section 312A(4) of FA 2004 (notice that section 312A(2) duty does not apply) before the day on which this Act is passed is treated on and after that day as given also in relation to the duty under section 312A(2A) of that Act.

21 (1) Section 316C of FA 2004 applies in relation to notifiable arrangements, or proposed notifiable arrangements, only if a reference number under section 311 of that Act is allocated to the arrangements on or after the day on which this Act is passed.

(2) But section 316C of FA 2004 does not apply in relation to notifiable arrangements, or proposed notifiable arrangements, where prescribed information relating to the arrangements was provided to HMRC before that day in compliance with section 308, 309 or 310 of that Act.

(3) Section 316C(2)(*b*) of FA 2004 applies in relation to a ruling of a court or tribunal only if the ruling is given on or after the day on which this Act is passed.

SCHEDULE 19

PROMOTERS OF TAX AVOIDANCE SCHEMES

Section 119

1 Part 5 of FA 2014 (promoters of tax avoidance schemes) is amended as follows.

Treating persons as meeting a threshold condition

2 (1) Section 237 (duty to give conduct notice) is amended as follows.

(2) After subsection (1) insert—

"(1A) Subsections (5) to (9) also apply if an authorised officer becomes aware at any time ("the relevant time") that—

(*a*) a person has, in the period of 3 years ending with the relevant time, met one or more threshold conditions,

(*b*) at the relevant time another person ("P") meets one or more of those conditions by virtue of Part 2 of Schedule 34 (meeting the threshold conditions: bodies corporate and partnerships), and

(*c*) P is, at the relevant time, carrying on a business as a promoter."

(3) In subsection (3), for the words from "the" to the end substitute "when a person is treated as meeting a threshold condition".

(4) For subsection (5) substitute—

"(5) The authorised officer must determine—

(*a*) in a case within subsection (1), whether or not P's meeting of the condition mentioned in subsection (1)(*a*) (or, if more than one condition is met, the meeting of all of those conditions, taken together) should be regarded as significant in view of the purposes of this Part, or

(*b*) in a case within subsection (1A), whether or not—

(i) the meeting of the condition by the person as mentioned in subsection (1A)(*a*) (or, if more than one condition is met, the meeting of all of those conditions, taken together), and

(ii) P's meeting of the condition (or conditions) as mentioned in subsection (1A)(*b*),

should be regarded as significant in view of those purposes."

(5) In subsection (7), for "subsection (5)" substitute "subsection (5)(*a*)".

(6) After subsection (7) insert—

"(7A) If the authorised officer determines under subsection (5)(*b*) that both—

(*a*) the meeting of the condition or conditions by the person as mentioned in subsection (1A)(*a*), and

(*b*) P's meeting of the condition or conditions as mentioned in subsection (1A)(*b*),

should be regarded as significant, the officer must give P a conduct notice, unless subsection (8) applies."

(7) In subsection (9), omit "mentioned in subsection (1)(*a*)".

(8) After subsection (9) insert—

"(10) If, as a result of subsection (1A), subsections (5) to (9) apply to a person, this does not prevent the giving of a conduct notice to the person mentioned in subsection (1A)(*a*)."

3 In section 283 (interpretation of Part 5), in the definition of "conduct notice", after "section 237(7)" insert "or (7A)".

4 (1) Part 2 of Schedule 34 (meeting the threshold conditions) is amended as follows.

(2) In the heading, at the end insert "AND PARTNERSHIPS".

(3) For paragraph 13 substitute—

"Interpretation

13A

(1) This paragraph contains definitions for the purposes of this Part of this Schedule.

(2) Each of the following is a "relevant body"—

(*a*) a body corporate, and

(*b*) a partnership.

(3) "Relevant time" means the time referred to in section 237(1A) (duty to give conduct notice to person treated as meeting threshold condition).

(4) "Relevant threshold condition" means a threshold condition specified in any of the following paragraphs of this Schedule—

(*a*) paragraph 2 (deliberate tax defaulters);

(*b*) paragraph 4 (dishonest tax agents);

(*c*) paragraph 6 (criminal offences);

(*d*) paragraph 7 (opinion notice of GAAR advisory panel);

(*e*) paragraph 8 (disciplinary action against a member of a trade or profession);

(*f*) paragraph 9 (disciplinary action by regulatory authority);

(*g*) paragraph 10 (failure to comply with information notice).

(5) A person controls a body corporate if the person has power to secure that the affairs of the body corporate are conducted in accordance with the person's wishes—

(*a*) by means of the holding of shares or the possession of voting power in relation to the body corporate or any other relevant body,

(*b*) as a result of any powers conferred by the articles of association or other document regulating the body corporate or any other relevant body, or

(*c*) by means of controlling a partnership.

(6) A person controls a partnership if the person is a controlling member or the managing partner of the partnership.

(7) "Controlling member" has the same meaning as in Schedule 36 (partnerships).

(8) "Managing partner", in relation to a partnership, means the member of the partnership who directs, or is on a day-to-day level in control of, the management of the business of the partnership.

Treating persons under another's control as meeting a threshold condition

13B

(1) A relevant body ("RB") is treated as meeting a threshold condition at the relevant time if—

(*a*) the threshold condition was met by a person ("C") at a time when—

(i) C was carrying on a business as a promoter, or

(ii) RB was carrying on a business as a promoter and C controlled RB, and

(*b*) RB is controlled by C at the relevant time.

(2) Where C is an individual sub-paragraph (1) applies only if the threshold condition mentioned in sub-paragraph (1)(*a*) is a relevant threshold condition.

(3) For the purposes of determining whether the requirements of sub-paragraph (1) are met by reason of meeting the requirement in sub-paragraph (1)(*a*)(i), it does not matter whether RB existed at the time when the threshold condition was met by C.

Treating persons in control of others as meeting a threshold condition

13C

(1) A person other than an individual is treated as meeting a threshold condition at the relevant time if—

(*a*) a relevant body ("A") met the threshold condition at a time when A was controlled by the person, and

(*b*) at the time mentioned in paragraph (*a*) A, or another relevant body ("B") which was also at that time controlled by the person, carried on a business as a promoter.

(2) For the purposes of determining whether the requirements of sub-paragraph (1) are met it does not matter whether A or B (or neither) exists at the relevant time.

Treating persons controlled by the same person as meeting a threshold condition

13D

(1) A relevant body ("RB") is treated as meeting a threshold condition at the relevant time if—

(*a*) RB or another relevant body met the threshold condition at a time ("time T") when it was controlled by a person ("C"),

(*b*) at time T, there was a relevant body controlled by C which carried on a business as a promoter, and

(*c*) RB is controlled by C at the relevant time.

(2) For the purposes of determining whether the requirements of sub-paragraph (1) are met it does not matter whether—

(*a*) RB existed at time T, or

(*b*) any relevant body (other than RB) by reason of which the requirements of sub-paragraph (1) are met exists at the relevant time."

Commentary—*Simon's Taxes* **A7.252A, A7.259**.

5 In Schedule 36 (partnerships)—

(*a*) omit paragraph 4 (threshold conditions: actions of partners in a personal capacity) and the italic heading before it,

(*b*) omit paragraph 20 (definition of "managing partner") and the italic heading before it, and

(*c*) in paragraph 21 (power to amend definitions) omit "or 20".

Failure to comply with Part 7 of FA 2004

6 In Schedule 34 (threshold conditions), in paragraph 5 (non-compliance with Part 7 of FA 2004), for sub-paragraph (2) substitute—

"(2) For the purposes of sub-paragraph (1), a person ("P") fails to comply with a provision mentioned in that sub-paragraph if and only if any of conditions A to C are met.

(3) Condition A is met if—

(*a*) the tribunal has determined that P has failed to comply with the provision concerned,

(*b*) the appeal period has ended, and

(*c*) the determination has not been overturned on appeal.

(4) Condition B is met if—

(*a*) the tribunal has determined for the purposes of section 118(2) of TMA 1970 that P is to be deemed not to have failed to comply with the provision concerned as P had a reasonable excuse for not doing the thing required to be done,

(*b*) the appeal period has ended, and

(*c*) the determination has not been overturned on appeal.

(5) Condition C is met if P has admitted in writing to HMRC that P has failed to comply with the provision concerned.

(6) The "appeal period" means—

(*a*) the period during which an appeal could be brought against the determination of the tribunal, or

(*b*) where an appeal mentioned in paragraph (*a*) has been brought, the period during which that appeal has not been finally determined, withdrawn or otherwise disposed of."

Disciplinary action in relation to professionals etc

7 (1) In Schedule 34 (threshold conditions), paragraph 8 (disciplinary action: professionals etc) is amended as follows.

(2) For sub-paragraph (1) substitute—

"(1) A person who carries on a trade or profession that is regulated by a professional body meets this condition if all of the following conditions are met—

(*a*) the person is found guilty of misconduct of a prescribed kind,

(*b*) action of a prescribed kind is taken against the person in relation to that misconduct, and

(*c*) a penalty of a prescribed kind is imposed on the person as a result of that misconduct."

(3) In the heading, for "*by a professional body*" substitute "*against a member of a trade or profession*".

(4) In sub-paragraph (3), in paragraph (*h*), for "for" substitute "of".

Power to amend Schedule 34

8 In Part 3 of Schedule 34 (power to amend), at the end of paragraph 14(2) insert—

"(*c*) vary any of the circumstances described in paragraphs 13B to 13D in which a person is treated as meeting a threshold condition (including by amending paragraph 13A);

(*d*) add new circumstances in which a person will be so treated."

Commencement

9 The amendments made by paragraphs 2 to 7 have effect for the purposes of determining whether a person meets a threshold condition in a period of three years ending on or after the day on which this Act is passed.

SCHEDULE 20

PENALTIES IN CONNECTION WITH OFFSHORE MATTERS AND OFFSHORE TRANSFERS

Section 120

Penalties for errors

1 Schedule 24 to FA 2007 is amended as follows.

2 (1) Paragraph 4 (penalties payable under paragraph 1) is amended as follows.
(2) After sub-paragraph (1) insert—
"(1A) If the inaccuracy is in category 0, the penalty is—
(*a*) for careless action, 30% of the potential lost revenue,
(*b*) for deliberate but not concealed action, 70% of the potential lost revenue, and
(*c*) for deliberate and concealed action, 100% of the potential lost revenue."
(3) In sub-paragraph (2)—
(*a*) in paragraph (*a*), for "30%" substitute "37.5%",
(*b*) in paragraph (*b*), for "70%" substitute "87.5%", and
(*c*) in paragraph (*c*), for "100%" substitute "125%".
(4) In sub-paragraph (5), for "3" substitute "4".

Commentary—*Simon's Taxes* **A4.522**.

3 (1) Paragraph 4A (categorisation of inaccuracies) is amended as follows.
(2) For sub-paragraph (1) substitute—
"(A1) An inaccuracy is in category 0 if—
(*a*) it involves a domestic matter,
(*b*) it involves an offshore matter or an offshore transfer, the territory in question is a category 0 territory and the tax at stake is income tax, capital gains tax or inheritance tax, or
(*c*) it involves an offshore matter and the tax at stake is a tax other than income tax, capital gains tax or inheritance tax.
(1) An inaccuracy is in category 1 if—
(*a*) it involves an offshore matter or an offshore transfer,
(*b*) the territory in question is a category 1 territory, and
(*c*) the tax at stake is income tax, capital gains tax or inheritance tax."
(3) In sub-paragraph (2)—
(*a*) in paragraph (*a*), after "matter" insert "or an offshore transfer", and
(*b*) in paragraph (*c*), for "or capital gains tax" substitute ", capital gains tax or inheritance tax".
(4) In sub-paragraph (3)—
(*a*) in paragraph (*a*), after "matter" insert "or an offshore transfer", and
(*b*) in paragraph (*c*), for "or capital gains tax" substitute ", capital gains tax or inheritance tax".
(5) After sub-paragraph (4) insert—
"(4A) Where the tax at stake is inheritance tax, assets are treated for the purposes of sub-paragraph (4) as situated or held in a territory outside the UK if they are so situated or held immediately after the transfer of value by reason of which inheritance tax becomes chargeable.
(4B) An inaccuracy "involves an offshore transfer" if—
(*a*) it does not involve an offshore matter,
(*b*) it is deliberate (whether or not concealed) and results in a potential loss of revenue,
(*c*) the tax at stake is income tax, capital gains tax or inheritance tax, and
(*d*) the applicable condition in paragraph 4AA is satisfied."
(6) In sub-paragraph (5), for the words following "revenue" substitute "and does not involve either an offshore matter or an offshore transfer".
(7) In sub-paragraph (6)(*a*), after "matters" insert "or transfers".
(8) In sub-paragraph (7), for ""Category 1" substitute ""Category 0 territory", "category 1".

Commencement—Finance Act 2015, Schedule 20 (Appointed Days) Order, SI 2016/456 (appointed day for the coming into force of sub-paras (3)–(7) is 1 April 2016 with effect in relation to documents given to HMRC relating to—
– a transfer of value made on or after that date for the purposes of inheritance tax; and
– a tax year commencing on or after 6 April 2016 for the purposes of income tax and capital gains tax).

Commentary—*Simon's Taxes* **A4.522**.

4 After paragraph 4A insert—
"4AA
(1) This paragraph makes provision in relation to offshore transfers.
(2) Where the tax at stake is income tax, the applicable condition is satisfied if the income on or by reference to which the tax is charged, or any part of the income—
(*a*) is received in a territory outside the UK, or
(*b*) is transferred before the filing date to a territory outside the UK.
(3) Where the tax at stake is capital gains tax, the applicable condition is satisfied if the proceeds of the disposal on or by reference to which the tax is charged, or any part of the proceeds—

(*a*) are received in a territory outside the UK, or

(*b*) are transferred before the filing date to a territory outside the UK.

(4) Where the tax at stake is inheritance tax, the applicable condition is satisfied if—

(*a*) the disposition that gives rise to the transfer of value by reason of which the tax becomes chargeable involves a transfer of assets, and

(*b*) after that disposition but before the filing date the assets, or any part of the assets, are transferred to a territory outside the UK.

(5) In the case of a transfer falling within sub-paragraph (2)(*b*), (3)(*b*) or (4)(*b*), references to the income, proceeds or assets transferred are to be read as including references to any assets derived from or representing the income, proceeds or assets.

(6) In relation to an offshore transfer, the territory in question for the purposes of paragraph 4A is the highest category of territory by virtue of which the inaccuracy involves an offshore transfer.

(7) "Filing date" means the date when the document containing the inaccuracy is given to HMRC.

(8) "Assets" has the same meaning as in paragraph 4A."

Commencement—Finance Act 2015, Schedule 20 (Appointed Days) Order, SI 2016/456 (appointed day for the coming into force of this para is 1 April 2016 with effect in relation to documents given to HMRC relating to—

– a transfer of value made on or after that date for the purposes of inheritance tax; and

– a tax year commencing on or after 6 April 2016 for the purposes of income tax and capital gains tax).

Commentary—*Simon's Taxes* **A4.522**.

5 In paragraph 10 (standard percentage reductions for disclosure), in the Table in sub-paragraph (2), at the appropriate places insert—

"37.5%	18.75%	0%"
"87.5%	43.75%	25%"
""125%	62.5%	40%"

6 In paragraph 12(5) (interaction with other penalties and late payment surcharges: the relevant percentage)—

(*a*) before paragraph (*a*) insert—

"(za) if the penalty imposed under paragraph 1 is for an inaccuracy in category 0, 100%,", and

(*b*) in paragraph (*a*), for "100%" substitute "125%".

7 (1) Paragraph 21A (classification of territories) is amended as follows.

(2) Before sub-paragraph (1) insert—

"(A1) A category 0 territory is a territory designated as a category 0 territory by order made by the Treasury."

(3) For sub-paragraph (2) substitute—

"(2) A category 2 territory is a territory that is not any of the following—

(*a*) a category 0 territory;

(*b*) a category 1 territory;

(*c*) a category 3 territory."

(4) For sub-paragraph (7) substitute—

"(7) An instrument containing (whether alone or with other provisions) the first order to be made under sub-paragraph (A1) may not be made unless a draft of the instrument has been laid before, and approved by a resolution of, the House of Commons."

8 (1) Paragraph 21B (location of assets etc) is amended as follows.

(2) After sub-paragraph (1) insert—

"(1A) The Treasury may by regulations make provision for determining for the purposes of paragraph 4AA where—

(*a*) income is received or transferred,

(*b*) the proceeds of a disposal are received or transferred, or

(*c*) assets are transferred."

(3) In sub-paragraph (2), for "and capital gains tax" substitute ", capital gains tax and inheritance tax".

Commencement—Finance Act 2015, Schedule 20 (Appointed Days) Order, SI 2016/456 (appointed day for the coming into force of this para is 1 April 2016 with effect in relation to documents given to HMRC relating to—

- a transfer of value made on or after that date for the purposes of inheritance tax; and
- a tax year commencing on or after 6 April 2016 for the purposes of income tax and capital gains tax).

Penalties for failure to notify

9 Schedule 41 to FA 2008 is amended as follows.

10 (1) Paragraph 6 (amount of penalty: standard amount) is amended as follows.
(2) After sub-paragraph (1) insert—

"(1A) If the failure is in category 0, the penalty is—

(*a*) for a deliberate and concealed failure, 100% of the potential lost revenue,

(*b*) for a deliberate but not concealed failure, 70% of the potential lost revenue, and

(*c*) for any other case, 30% of the potential lost revenue."

(3) In sub-paragraph (2)—

(*a*) in paragraph (*a*), for "100%" substitute "125%",

(*b*) in paragraph (*b*), for "70%" substitute "87.5%", and

(*c*) in paragraph (*c*), for "30%" substitute "37.5%".

(4) In sub-paragraph (5), for "3" substitute "4".

Commentary—*Simon's Taxes* **A4.522**.

11 (1) Paragraph 6A (categorisation of failures) is amended as follows.
(2) For sub-paragraph (1) substitute—

"(A1) A failure is in category 0 if—

(*a*) it involves a domestic matter,

(*b*) it involves an offshore matter or an offshore transfer, the territory in question is a category 0 territory and the tax at stake is income tax or capital gains tax, or

(*c*) it involves an offshore matter and the tax at stake is a tax other than income tax or capital gains tax.

(1) A failure is in category 1 if—

(*a*) it involves an offshore matter or an offshore transfer,

(*b*) the territory in question is a category 1 territory, and

(*c*) the tax at stake is income tax or capital gains tax."

(3) In sub-paragraph (2)(*a*), after "matter" insert "or an offshore transfer".
(4) In sub-paragraph (3)(*a*), after "matter" insert "or an offshore transfer".
(5) After sub-paragraph (4) insert—

"(4A) A failure "involves an offshore transfer" if—

(*a*) it does not involve an offshore matter,

(*b*) it is deliberate (whether or not concealed) and results in a potential loss of revenue,

(*c*) the tax at stake is income tax or capital gains tax, and

(*d*) the applicable condition in paragraph 6AA is satisfied."

(6) In sub-paragraph (5), for the words following "revenue" substitute "and does not involve either an offshore matter or an offshore transfer".
(7) In sub-paragraph (6)(*a*), after "matters" insert "or transfers".
(8) Omit sub-paragraph (8).
(9) In sub-paragraph (9), after "paragraph" insert "and paragraph 6AA".

Commencement—Finance Act 2015, Schedule 20 (Appointed Days) Order, SI 2016/456 (appointed day for the coming into force of sub-paras (3)–(9) is 6 April 2016 with effect in relation to an obligation arising under TMA 1970 s 7 in respect of a tax year commencing on or after that date).

12 After paragraph 6A insert—

"6AA

(1) This paragraph makes provision in relation to offshore transfers.

(2) Where the tax at stake is income tax, the applicable condition is satisfied if the income on or by reference to which the tax is charged, or any part of the income—

(*a*) is received in a territory outside the UK, or

(*b*) is transferred before the calculation date to a territory outside the UK.

(3) Where the tax at stake is capital gains tax, the applicable condition is satisfied if the proceeds of the disposal on or by reference to which the tax is charged, or any part of the proceeds—

(*a*) are received in a territory outside the UK, or

(*b*) are transferred before the calculation date to a territory outside the UK.

(4) In the case of a transfer falling within sub-paragraph (2)(*b*) or (3)(*b*), references to the income or proceeds transferred are to be read as including references to any assets derived from or representing the income or proceeds.

(5) In relation to an offshore transfer, the territory in question for the purposes of paragraph 6A is the highest category of territory by virtue of which the failure involves an offshore transfer.

(6) In this paragraph "calculation date" means the date by reference to which the potential lost revenue is to be calculated (see paragraph 7).

6AB

Regulations under paragraph 21B of Schedule 24 to FA 2007 (location of assets etc) apply for the purposes of paragraphs 6A and 6AA of this Schedule as they apply for the purposes of paragraphs 4A and 4AA of that Schedule."

Commencement—Finance Act 2015, Schedule 20 (Appointed Days) Order, SI 2016/456 (appointed day for the coming into force of this para is 6 April 2016 with effect in relation to an obligation arising under TMA 1970 s 7 in respect of a tax year commencing on or after that date).

13 In paragraph 13 (standard percentage reductions for disclosure), in the Table in sub-paragraph (3), at the appropriate places insert—

"37.5%	case A: 12.5% case B: 25%	case A: 0% case B: 12.5%"
"87.5%	43.75%	25%"
"125%	62.5%	40%"

Commentary—*Simon's Taxes* **A4.522**.

Penalties for failure to make returns etc

14 Schedule 55 to FA 2009 is amended as follows.

15 (1) Paragraph 6 (penalty for failure continuing 12 months after penalty date) is amended as follows.

(2) In sub-paragraph (3A)—

(*a*) before paragraph (*a*) insert—

"(za) for the withholding of category 0 information, 100%,", and

(*b*) in paragraph (*a*), for "100%" substitute "125%".

(3) In sub-paragraph (4A)—

(*a*) before paragraph (*a*) insert—

"(za) for the withholding of category 0 information, 70%,", and

(*b*) in paragraph (*a*), for "70%" substitute "87.5%".

(4) In sub-paragraph (6), for "3" substitute "4".

Commentary—*Simon's Taxes* **A4.522**.

16 (1) Paragraph 6A (categorisation of information) is amended as follows.

(2) For sub-paragraph (1) substitute—

"(A1) Information is category 0 information if—

(*a*) it involves a domestic matter,

(*b*) it involves an offshore matter or an offshore transfer, the territory in question is a category 0 territory and it is information which would enable or assist HMRC to assess P's liability to income tax, capital gains tax or inheritance tax, or

(*c*) it involves an offshore matter and it is information which would enable or assist HMRC to assess P's liability to a tax other than income tax, capital gains tax or inheritance tax.

(1) Information is category 1 information if—

(*a*) it involves an offshore matter or an offshore transfer,

(*b*) the territory in question is a category 1 territory, and

(*c*) it is information which would enable or assist HMRC to assess P's liability to income tax, capital gains tax or inheritance tax."

(3) In sub-paragraph (2)—

(*a*) in paragraph (*a*), after "matter" insert "or an offshore transfer", and

(*b*) in paragraph (*c*), for "or capital gains tax" substitute ", capital gains tax or inheritance tax".

(4) In sub-paragraph (3)—

(*a*) in paragraph (*a*), after "matter" insert "or an offshore transfer", and

(*b*) in paragraph (*c*), for "or capital gains tax" substitute ", capital gains tax or inheritance tax".

(5) After sub-paragraph (4) insert—

"(4A) If the liability to tax which would have been shown in the return is a liability to inheritance tax, assets are treated for the purposes of sub-paragraph (4) as situated or held in a territory outside the UK if they are so situated or held immediately after the transfer of value by reason of which inheritance tax becomes chargeable.

(4B) Information "involves an offshore transfer" if—

(*a*) it does not involve an offshore matter,

(*b*) it is information which would enable or assist HMRC to assess P's liability to income tax, capital gains tax or inheritance tax,

(*c*) by failing to make the return, P deliberately withholds the information (whether or not the withholding of the information is also concealed), and

(*d*) the applicable condition in paragraph 6AA is satisfied."

(6) In sub-paragraph (5), for the words following "if" substitute "it does not involve an offshore matter or an offshore transfer".

(7) In sub-paragraph (6)(*a*), after "matters" insert "or transfers".

(8) Omit sub-paragraph (8).

(9) In sub-paragraph (9), after "paragraph" insert "and paragraph 6AA".

Commencement—Finance Act 2015, Schedule 20 (Appointed Days) Order, SI 2016/456 (appointed day for the coming into force of sub-paras (3)–(9) is 6 April 2016 with effect in relation to a return or other document which—

– is required to be made or delivered to HMRC in relation to a tax year commencing on or after that date; and
– falls within item 1, 2 or 3 of the Table in FA 2009 Sch 55 para 1(5)).

17 After paragraph 6A insert—

"6AA

(1) This paragraph makes provision in relation to offshore transfers.

(2) Where the liability to tax which would have been shown in the return is a liability to income tax, the applicable condition is satisfied if the income on or by reference to which the tax is charged, or any part of the income—

(*a*) is received in a territory outside the UK, or

(*b*) is transferred before the relevant date to a territory outside the UK.

(3) Where the liability to tax which would have been shown in the return is a liability to capital gains tax, the applicable condition is satisfied if the proceeds of the disposal on or by reference to which the tax is charged, or any part of the proceeds—

(*a*) are received in a territory outside the UK, or

(*b*) are transferred before the relevant date to a territory outside the UK.

(4) Where the liability to tax which would have been shown in the return is a liability to inheritance tax, the applicable condition is satisfied if—

(*a*) the disposition that gives rise to the transfer of value by reason of which the tax becomes chargeable involves a transfer of assets, and

(*b*) after that disposition but before the relevant date the assets, or any part of the assets, are transferred to a territory outside the UK.

(5) In the case of a transfer falling within sub-paragraph (2)(*b*), (3)(*b*) or (4)(*b*), references to the income, proceeds or assets transferred are to be read as including references to any assets derived from or representing the income, proceeds or assets.

(6) In relation to an offshore transfer, the territory in question for the purposes of paragraph 6A is the highest category of territory by virtue of which the information involves an offshore transfer.

(7) "Relevant date" means the date on which P becomes liable to a penalty under paragraph 6.

6AB

Regulations under paragraph 21B of Schedule 24 to FA 2007 (location of assets etc) apply for the purposes of paragraphs 6A and 6AA of this Schedule as they apply for the purposes of paragraphs 4A and 4AA of that Schedule."

18 In paragraph 15 (standard percentage reductions for disclosure), in the Table in sub-paragraph (2), at the appropriate places insert—

"87.5%	43.75%	25%"
"125%	62.5%	40%"

Commentary—*Simon's Taxes* **A4.522**.

19 In paragraph 17(4) (interaction with other penalties and late payment surcharges), omit the "and" at the end of paragraph (*b*) and after that paragraph insert—

"(*ba*) if one of the penalties is a penalty under paragraph 6(3) or (4) and the information withheld is category 1 information, 125%, and".

[General anti-abuse rule: aggregate penalties

20 (1) In Schedule 43C to FA 2013 (general anti-abuse rule: supplementary provision about penalty), sub-paragraph (6) of paragraph 8 is amended as follows.

(2) After paragraph (*b*) insert—

"(*ba*) 125% in a case where neither paragraph (*a*) nor paragraph (*b*) applies and at least one of the penalties is determined by reference to the percentage in—
(i) paragraph 4(2)(*c*) of Schedule 24 to FA 2007,
(ii) paragraph 6(2)(*a*) of Schedule 41 to FA 2008,
(iii) paragraph 6(3A)(*a*) of Schedule 55 to FA 2009,".

(3) In sub-paragraph (*c*) for "neither paragraph (*a*) nor paragraph (*b*) applies" substitute "none of paragraphs (*a*) to (*ba*) applies".

(4) In sub-paragraph (*d*) for "none of paragraphs (*a*), (*b*) and (*c*) applies" substitute "none of paragraphs (*a*) to (*c*) applies".][1].

Amendment—[1] Paragraph 20 inserted by FA 2016 s 158(12), (14) with effect in relation to tax arrangements (within the meaning of Part 5 of FA 2013) entered into on or after 15 September 2016.

SCHEDULE 21

PENALTIES IN CONNECTION WITH OFFSHORE ASSET MOVES

Section 121

Penalty linked to offshore asset moves

1 (1) A penalty is payable by a person ("P") where Conditions A, B and C are met.

(2) Condition A is that—

(*a*) P is liable for a penalty specified in paragraph 2 ("the original penalty"), and

(*b*) the original penalty is for a deliberate failure (see paragraph 3).

(3) Condition B is that there is a relevant offshore asset move (see paragraph 4) which occurs after the relevant time (see paragraph 5).

(4) Condition C is that—

(*a*) the main purpose, or one of the main purposes, of the relevant offshore asset move is to prevent or delay the discovery by Her Majesty's Revenue and Customs ("HMRC") of a potential loss of revenue, and

(*b*) the original penalty relates to an inaccuracy or failure which relates to the same potential loss of revenue.

Cross-references See FA 2016 Sch 20 (penalties for enablers of offshore tax evasion or non-compliance).

Original penalties triggering penalties under this Schedule

2 The penalties referred to in paragraph 1(2) are—

(*a*) a penalty under paragraph 1 of Schedule 24 to FA 2007 (penalty for error in taxpayer's document) in relation to an inaccuracy in a document of a kind listed in the Table in paragraph 1 of that Schedule, where the tax at stake is income tax, capital gains tax or inheritance tax,

(*b*) a penalty under paragraph 1 of Schedule 41 to FA 2008 (penalty for failure to notify etc) in relation to the obligation under section 7 of TMA 1970 (obligation to give notice of liability to income tax or capital gains tax), . . . [1]

(*c*) a penalty under paragraph 6 of Schedule 55 to FA 2009 (penalty for failures to make return etc where failure continues after 12 months), where the tax at stake is income tax, capital gains tax or inheritance tax[, and

(*d*) a penalty under paragraph 1 of Schedule 18 to FA 2017 (requirement to correct relevant offshore tax non-compliance).][1]

Commentary—*Simon's Taxes* **A4.522**.

Amendments—[1] In sub-para (*b*), word "and" repealed, and sub-para (*d*) and preceding word "and" inserted, by F(No 2)A 2017 s 67, Sch 18 para 27(1), (2) with effect from 16 November 2017. A penalty under Sch 18 is payable by a person who has any relevant offshore tax non-compliance to correct at the end of the tax year 2016–17 and fails to correct that non-compliance within the period beginning with 6 April 2017 and ending with 30 September 2018 ("the RTC period").

"Deliberate failure"

3 The original penalty is for a "deliberate failure" if—

(*a*) in the case of a penalty within paragraph 2(*a*), the inaccuracy to which it relates was deliberate on P's part (whether or not concealed);

(*b*) in the case of a penalty within paragraph 2(*b*), the failure by P was deliberate (whether or not concealed);

(*c*) in the case of a penalty within paragraph 2(*c*), the withholding of the information, resulting from the failure to make the return, is deliberate (whether or not concealed);

[(*d*) in the case of a penalty within paragraph 2(*d*), P was aware at any time during the RTC period that at the end of the 2016–17 tax year P had relevant offshore tax non-compliance to correct;

and terms used in paragraph (*d*) have the same meaning as in Schedule 18 to FA 2017.][1]

Amendments—[1] Sub-para (*d*) inserted by F(No 2)A 2017 s 67, Sch 18 para 27(1), (3) with effect from 16 November 2017. A penalty under Sch 18 is payable by a person who has any relevant offshore tax non-compliance to correct at the end of the tax year 2016–17 and fails to correct that non-compliance within the period beginning with 6 April 2017 and ending with 30 September 2018 ("the RTC period").

"Relevant offshore asset move"

4 (1) There is a "relevant offshore asset move" if, at a time when P is the beneficial owner of an asset ("the qualifying time")—

(*a*) the asset ceases to be situated or held in a specified territory and becomes situated or held in a non-specified territory,

(*b*) the person who holds the asset ceases to be resident in a specified territory and becomes resident in a non-specified territory, or

(*c*) there is a change in the arrangements for the ownership of the asset,

and P remains the beneficial owner of the asset, or any part of it, immediately after the qualifying time.

(2) Whether a territory is a "specified territory" or "non-specified territory" is to be determined, for the purposes of sub-paragraph (1), as at the qualifying time.

(3) Where—

(*a*) an asset of which P is the beneficial owner ("the original asset") is disposed of, and

(*b*) all or part of any proceeds from the sale of the asset are (directly or indirectly) reinvested in another asset of which P is also the beneficial owner ("the new asset"),

the original asset and the new asset are to be treated as the same asset for the purposes of determining whether there is a relevant offshore asset move.

(4) "Asset" has the meaning given in section 21(1) of TCGA 1992, but also includes sterling.

(5) "Specified territory" means a territory specified in regulations made by the Treasury by statutory instrument; and references to "non-specified territory" are to be construed accordingly.

(6) Regulations under sub-paragraph (5) are subject to annulment in pursuance of a resolution of the House of Commons.

Regulations—Offshore Asset Moves Penalty (Specified Territories) Regulations, SI 2015/866.
Offshore Asset Moves Penalty (Specified Territories) (Amendment) Regulations, SI 2017/989.

"Relevant time"

5 (1) "The relevant time" has the meaning given by this paragraph.

(2) Where the original penalty is under Schedule 24 to FA 2007, the relevant time is—

(*a*) if the tax at stake as a result of the inaccuracy is income tax or capital gains tax, the beginning of the tax year to which the document containing the inaccuracy relates, and

(*b*) if the tax at stake as a result of the inaccuracy is inheritance tax, the time when liability to the tax first arises.

(3) Where the original penalty is for a failure to comply with an obligation specified in the table in paragraph 1 of Schedule 41 of FA 2008, the relevant time is the beginning of the tax year to which that obligation relates.

(4) Where the original penalty is for a failure to make a return or deliver a document specified in the table in paragraph 1 of Schedule 55 to FA 2009, the relevant time is—

(*a*) if the tax at stake is income tax or capital gains tax, the beginning of the tax year to which the return or document relates, and

(*b*) if the tax at stake is inheritance tax, the time when liability to the tax first arises.

[(5) Where the original penalty is under paragraph 1 of Schedule 18 to FA 2017, the relevant time is the time when that Schedule comes into force.][1]

Commentary—*Simon's Taxes* **A4.522.**

Amendments—[1] Sub-para (5) inserted by F(No 2)A 2017 s 67, Sch 18 para 27(1), (4) with effect from 16 November 2017. A penalty under Sch 18 is payable by a person who has any relevant offshore tax non-compliance to correct at the end of the tax year 2016–17 and fails to correct that non-compliance within the period beginning with 6 April 2017 and ending with 30 September 2018 ("the RTC period").

Amount of the penalty

6 (1) The penalty payable under paragraph 1(1) is 50% of the amount of the original penalty payable by P.

(2) The penalty payable under paragraph 1(1) is not a penalty determined by reference to a liability to tax (despite the fact that the original penalty by reference to which it is calculated may be such a penalty).

Commentary—*Simon's Taxes* **A4.522.**

Assessment

7 (1) Where a person becomes liable for a penalty under paragraph 1(1), HMRC must—

(*a*) assess the penalty,

(*b*) notify the person, and

(*c*) state in the notice the tax period in respect of which the penalty is assessed.

(2) A penalty under paragraph 1(1) must be paid before the end of the period of 30 days beginning with the day on which notification of the penalty is issued.

(3) An assessment—

(*a*) is to be treated for procedural purposes in the same way as an assessment to tax (except in respect of a matter expressly provided for by this Schedule),

(*b*) may be enforced as if it were an assessment to tax, and

(*c*) may be combined with an assessment to tax.

(4) An assessment of a penalty under paragraph 1(1) must be made within the same period as that allowed for the assessment of the original penalty.

(5) If, after an assessment of a penalty is made under this paragraph, HMRC amends the assessment, or makes a supplementary assessment, in respect of the original penalty, it must also at the same time amend the assessment, or make a supplementary assessment, in respect of the penalty under paragraph 1(1) to ensure that it is based on the correct amount of the original penalty.

(6) In this paragraph—

(*a*) a reference to an assessment to tax, in relation to inheritance tax, is to a determination, and

(*b*) "tax period" means a tax year, accounting period or other period in respect of which tax is charged.

Commentary—*Simon's Taxes* **A4.522.**

Appeal

8 (1) A person may appeal against a decision of HMRC that a penalty is payable by the person.

(2) An appeal under this paragraph is to be treated in the same way as an appeal against an assessment to, or determination of, the tax concerned (including by the application of any provision about bringing the appeal by notice to HMRC, about HMRC review of the decision or about determination of the appeal by the First-tier Tribunal or Upper Tribunal).

(3) Sub-paragraph (2) does not apply in respect of a matter expressly provided for by this Schedule.

(4) On an appeal under this paragraph, the tribunal may affirm or cancel HMRC's decision.

Commentary—*Simon's Taxes* **A4.522.**

Commencement and transitionals

9 (1) This Schedule has effect in relation to relevant offshore asset moves occurring after the day on which this Act is passed.

(2) For the purposes of this Schedule, it does not matter if liability for the original penalty first arose on or before that day, unless the case is one to which sub-paragraph (3) applies.

(3) The original penalty is to be ignored if P's liability for it for arose before the day on which this Act is passed and before that day—

(*a*) if the original penalty was under Schedule 24 to FA 2007, any tax which was unpaid as a result of the inaccuracy has been assessed or determined;

(*b*) if the original penalty was under Schedule 41 to FA 2008 or Schedule 55 to FA 2009, the failure to which it related was remedied and any tax which was unpaid as a result of the failure has been assessed or determined.

Commentary—*Simon's Taxes* **A4.522**.

FINANCE (NO 2) ACT 2015

2015 Chapter 33

An Act to grant certain duties, to alter other duties, and to amend the law relating to the National Debt and the Public Revenue, and to make further provision in connection with finance.

18 November 2015

CONTENTS

PART 2
INHERITANCE TAX

Rate bands

9 Increased nil-rate band where home inherited by descendants

(1) IHTA 1984 is amended as follows.

(2) In section 7(1) (rates at which inheritance tax charged on the value transferred by a chargeable transfer) after "Subject to subsections (2), (4) and (5) below and to" insert "section 8D and".

(3) In section 8A(2) (test for whether person has unused nil-rate band on death), in the definition of M (maximum amount transferable at 0%), after "were sufficient but" insert "that the maximum amount chargeable at nil per cent. under section 8D(2) is equal to the person's residence nil-rate amount and".

(4) After section 8C insert—

"8D Extra nil-rate band on death if interest in home goes to descendants etc

(1) Subsections (2) and (3) apply for the purpose of calculating the amount of the charge to tax under section 4 on a person's death if the person dies on or after 6 April 2017.

(2) If the person's residence nil-rate amount is greater than nil, the portion of VT that does not exceed the person's residence nil-rate amount is charged at the rate of 0%.

(3) References in section 7(1) to the value transferred by the chargeable transfer under section 4 on the person's death are to be read as references to the remainder (if any) of VT.

(4) The person's residence nil-rate amount is calculated in accordance with sections 8E to 8G.

(5) For the purposes of those sections and this section—

(*a*) the "residential enhancement" is—

(i) £100,000 for the tax year 2017–18,

(ii) £125,000 for the tax year 2018–19,

(iii) £150,000 for the tax year 2019–20, and

(iv) £175,000 for the tax year 2020–21 and subsequent tax years,

but this is subject to subsections (6) and (7),

(*b*) the "taper threshold" is £2,000,000 for the tax year 2017–18 and subsequent tax years, but this is subject to subsections (6) and (7),

(*c*) TT is the taper threshold at the person's death,

(*d*) E is the value of the person's estate immediately before the person's death,

(*e*) VT is the value transferred by the chargeable transfer under section 4 on the person's death,

(*f*) the person's "default allowance" is the total of—

(i) the residential enhancement at the person's death, and

(ii) the person's brought-forward allowance (see section 8G), and

(*g*) the person's "adjusted allowance" is—

(i) the person's default allowance, less

(ii) the amount given by—

$$\frac{E - TT}{2}$$

but is nil if that amount is greater than the person's default allowance.

(6) Subsection (7) applies if—

(*a*) the consumer prices index for the month of September in any tax year ("the prior tax year") is higher than it was for the previous September, and

(*b*) the prior tax year is the tax year 2020–21 or a later tax year.

(7) Unless Parliament otherwise determines, the amount of each of—

(*a*) the residential enhancement for the tax year following the prior tax year, and

(*b*) the taper threshold for that following tax year,

is its amount for the prior tax year increased by the same percentage as the percentage increase in the index and, if the result is not a multiple of £1,000, rounded up to the nearest amount which is such a multiple.

(8) The Treasury must before 6 April 2021 and each subsequent 6 April make an order specifying the amounts that in accordance with subsections (6) and (7) are the residential enhancement and taper threshold for the tax year beginning on that date; and any such order is to be made by statutory instrument.

(9) In this section—

"tax year" means a year beginning on 6 April and ending on the following 5 April, and

"the tax year 2017–18" means the tax year beginning on 6 April 2017 (and any corresponding expression in which two years are similarly mentioned is to be read in the same way).

8E Residence nil-rate amount: interest in home goes to descendants etc

(1) Subsections (2) to (7) apply if—

(*a*) the person's estate immediately before the person's death includes a qualifying residential interest, and

(*b*) N% of the interest is closely inherited, where N is a number—

(i) greater than 0, and

(ii) less than or equal to 100,

and in those subsections "NV/100" means N% of so much (if any) of the value transferred by the transfer of value under section 4 as is attributable to the interest.

(2) Where—

(*a*) E is less than or equal to TT, and

(*b*) NV/100 is less than the person's default allowance,

the person's residence nil-rate amount is equal to NV/100 and an amount, equal to the difference between NV/100 and the person's default allowance, is available for carry-forward.

(3) Where—

(*a*) E is less than or equal to TT, and

(*b*) NV/100 is greater than or equal to the person's default allowance,

the person's residence nil-rate amount is equal to the person's default allowance (and no amount is available for carry-forward).

(4) Where—

(*a*) E is greater than TT, and

(*b*) NV/100 is less than the person's adjusted allowance,

the person's residence nil-rate amount is equal to NV/100 and an amount, equal to the difference between NV/100 and the person's adjusted allowance, is available for carry-forward.

(5) Where—

(*a*) E is greater than TT, and

(*b*) NV/100 is greater than or equal to the person's adjusted allowance,

the person's residence nil-rate amount is equal to the person's adjusted allowance (and no amount is available for carry-forward).

(6) Subsections (2) to (5) have effect subject to subsection (7).

(7) Where the person's residence nil-rate amount as calculated under subsections (2) to (5) without applying this subsection is greater than VT—

(*a*) subsections (2) to (5) have effect as if each reference in them to NV/100 were a reference to VT,

(*b*) each of subsections (3) and (5) has effect as if it provided that the person's residence nil-rate amount were equal to VT (rather than the person's default allowance or, as the case may be, the person's adjusted allowance).

(8) See also—

section 8H (meaning of "qualifying residential interest"),
section 8J (meaning of "inherit"),
section 8K (meaning of "closely inherited"), and
section 8M (cases involving conditional exemption).

8F Residence nil-rate amount: no interest in home goes to descendants etc

(1) Subsections (2) and (3) apply if the person's estate immediately before the person's death—

(*a*) does not include a qualifying residential interest, or

(*b*) includes a qualifying residential interest but none of the interest is closely inherited.

(2) The person's residence nil-rate amount is nil.

(3) An amount—

(*a*) equal to the person's default allowance, or

(*b*) if E is greater than TT, equal to the person's adjusted allowance,

is available for carry-forward.

(4) See also—

section 8H (meaning of "qualifying residential interest"),
section 8J (meaning of "inherit"),
section 8K (meaning of "closely inherited"), and
section 8M (cases involving conditional exemption).

8G Meaning of "brought-forward allowance"

(1) This section is about the amount of the brought-forward allowance (see section 8D(5)(*f*)) for a person ("P") who dies on or after 6 April 2017.

(2) In this section "related person" means a person other than P where—

(*a*) the other person dies before P, and

(*b*) immediately before the other person dies, P is the other person's spouse or civil partner.

(3) P's brought-forward allowance is calculated as follows—

(*a*) identify each amount available for carry-forward from the death of a related person (see sections 8E and 8F, and subsections (4) and (5)),

(*b*) express each such amount as a percentage of the residential enhancement at the death of the related person concerned,

(*c*) calculate the percentage that is the total of those percentages, and

(*d*) the amount that is that total percentage of the residential enhancement at P's death is P's brought-forward allowance or, if that total percentage is greater than 100%, P's brought-forward allowance is the amount of the residential enhancement at P's death,

but P's brought-forward allowance is nil if no claim for it is made under section 8L.

(4) Where the death of a related person occurs before 6 April 2017—

(*a*) an amount equal to £100,000 is treated for the purposes of subsection (3) as being the amount available for carry-forward from the related person's death, but this is subject to subsection (5), and

(*b*) the residential enhancement at the related person's death is treated for those purposes as being £100,000.

(5) If the value ("RPE") of the related person's estate immediately before the related person's death is greater than £2,000,000, the amount treated under subsection (4)(*a*) as available for carry-forward is reduced (but not below nil) by—

$$\frac{RPE - £2,000,000}{2}$$

8H Meaning of "qualifying residential interest"

(1) This section applies for the purposes of sections 8E and 8F.

(2) In this section "residential property interest", in relation to a person, means an interest in a dwelling-house which has been the person's residence at a time when the person's estate included that, or any other, interest in the dwelling-house.

(3) Where a person's estate immediately before the person's death includes residential property interests in just one dwelling-house, the person's interests in that dwelling-house are a qualifying residential interest in relation to the person.

(4) Where—

(*a*) a person's estate immediately before the person's death includes residential property interests in each of two or more dwelling-houses, and

(*b*) the person's personal representatives nominate one (and only one) of those dwelling-houses,

the person's interests in the nominated dwelling-house are a qualifying residential interest in relation to the person.

(5) A reference in this section to a dwelling-house—

(*a*) includes any land occupied and enjoyed with it as its garden or grounds, but

(*b*) does not include, in the case of any particular person, any trees or underwood in relation to which an election is made under section 125 as it applies in relation to that person's death.

(6) If at any time when a person's estate includes an interest in a dwelling-house, the person—

(*a*) resides in living accommodation which for the person is job-related, and

(*b*) intends in due course to occupy the dwelling-house as the person's residence,

this section applies as if the dwelling-house were at that time occupied by the person as a residence.

(7) Section 222(8A) to (8D) of the 1992 Act (meaning of "job-related"), but not section 222(9) of that Act, apply for the purposes of subsection (6).

8J Meaning of "inherited"

(1) This section explains for the purposes of sections 8E and 8F whether a person ("B") inherits, from a person who has died ("D"), property which forms part of D's estate immediately before D's death.

(2) B inherits the property if there is a disposition of it (whether effected by will, under the law relating to intestacy or otherwise) to B.

(3) Subsection (2) does not apply if—

(*a*) the property becomes comprised in a settlement on D's death, or

(*b*) immediately before D's death, the property was settled property in which D was beneficially entitled to an interest in possession.

(4) Where the property becomes comprised in a settlement on D's death, B inherits the property if—

(*a*) B becomes beneficially entitled on D's death to an interest in possession in the property, and that interest in possession is an immediate post-death interest or a disabled person's interest, or

(*b*) the property becomes, on D's death, settled property—

(i) to which section 71A or 71D applies, and

(ii) held on trusts for the benefit of B.

(5) Where, immediately before D's death, the property was settled property in which D was beneficially entitled to an interest in possession, B inherits the property if B becomes beneficially entitled to it on D's death.

(6) Where the property forms part of D's estate immediately before D's death as a result of the operation of section 102(3) of the Finance Act 1986 (gifts with reservation) in relation to a disposal of the property made by D by way of gift, B inherits the property if B is the person to whom the disposal was made.

8K Meaning of "closely inherited"

(1) In relation to the death of a person ("D"), something is "closely inherited" for the purposes of sections 8E and 8F if it is inherited for those purposes (see section 8J) by—

(*a*) a lineal descendant of D,

(*b*) a person who, at the time of D's death, is the spouse or civil partner of a lineal descendant of D, or

(*c*) a person who—

(i) at the time of the death of a lineal descendant of D who died no later than D, was the spouse or civil partner of the lineal descendant, and

(ii) has not, in the period beginning with the lineal descendant's death and ending with D's death, become anyone's spouse or civil partner.

(2) The rules in subsections (3) to (8) apply for the interpretation of subsection (1).

(3) A person who is at any time a step-child of another person is to be treated, at that and all subsequent times, as if the person was that other person's child.

(4) Any rule of law, so far as it requires an adopted person to be treated as not being the child of a natural parent of the person, is to be disregarded (but this is without prejudice to any rule of law requiring an adopted person to be treated as the child of an adopter of the person).

(5) A person who is at any time fostered by a foster parent is to be treated, at that and all subsequent times, as if the person was the foster parent's child.

(6) Where—

(*a*) an individual ("G") is appointed (or is treated by law as having been appointed) under section 5 of the Children Act 1989, or under corresponding law having effect in Scotland or Northern Ireland or any country or territory outside the United Kingdom, as guardian (however styled) of another person, and

(*b*) the appointment takes effect at a time when the other person ("C") is under the age of 18 years,

C is to be treated, at all times after the appointment takes effect, as if C was G's child.

(7) Where—

(*a*) an individual ("SG") is appointed as a special guardian (however styled) of another person ("C") by an order of a court—

(i) that is a special guardianship order as defined by section 14A of the Children Act 1989, or

(ii) that is a corresponding order under legislation having effect in Scotland or Northern Ireland or any country or territory outside the United Kingdom, and

(*b*) the appointment takes effect at a time when C is under the age of 18 years,

C is to be treated, at all times after the appointment takes effect, as if C was SG's child.

(8) In particular, where under any of subsections (3) to (7) one person is to be treated at any time as the child of another person, that first person's lineal descendants (even if born before that time) are accordingly to be treated at that time (and all subsequent times) as lineal descendants of that other person.

(9) In subsection (4) "adopted person" means—

(*a*) an adopted person within the meaning of Chapter 4 of Part 1 of the Adoption and Children Act 2002, or

(*b*) a person who would be an adopted person within the meaning of that Chapter if, in section 66(1)(*e*) of that Act and section 38(1)(*e*) of the Adoption Act 1976, the reference to the law of England and Wales were a reference to the law of any part of the United Kingdom.

(10) In subsection (5) "foster parent" means—

(*a*) someone who is approved as a local authority foster parent in accordance with regulations made by virtue of paragraph 12F of Schedule 2 to the Children Act 1989,

(*b*) a foster parent with whom the person is placed by a voluntary organisation under section 59(1)(*a*) that Act,

(*c*) someone who looks after the person in circumstances in which the person is a privately fostered child as defined by section 66 of that Act, or

(*d*) someone who, under legislation having effect in Scotland or Northern Ireland or any country or territory outside the United Kingdom, is a foster parent (however styled) corresponding to a foster parent within paragraph (*a*) or (*b*).

8L Claims for brought-forward allowance

(1) A claim for brought-forward allowance for a person (see section 8G) may be made—

(*a*) by the person's personal representatives within the permitted period, or

(*b*) (if no claim is so made) by any other person liable to the tax chargeable on the person's death within such later period as an officer of Revenue and Customs may in the particular case allow.

(2) In subsection (1)(*a*) "the permitted period" means—

(*a*) the period of 2 years from the end of the month in which the person dies or (if it ends later) the period of 3 months beginning with the date on which the personal representatives first act as such, or

(*b*) such longer period as an officer of Revenue and Customs may in the particular case allow.

(3) A claim under subsection (1) made within either of the periods mentioned in subsection (2)(*a*) may be withdrawn no later than one month after the end of the period concerned.

(4) Subsection (5) applies if—

(*a*) no claim under this section has been made for brought-forward allowance for a person ("P"),

(*b*) the amount of the charge to tax under section 4 on the death of another person ("A") would be different if a claim under subsection (1) had been made for brought-forward allowance for P, and

(*c*) the amount of the charge to tax under section 4 on the death of P, and the amount of the charge to tax under section 4 on the death of any person who is neither P nor A, would not have been different if a claim under subsection (1) had been made for brought-forward allowance for P.

(5) A claim for brought-forward allowance for P may be made—

(*a*) by A's personal representatives within the allowed period, or

(*b*) (if no claim is so made) by any other person liable to the tax chargeable on A's death within such later period as an officer of Revenue and Customs may in the particular case allow.

(6) In subsection (5)(*a*) "the allowed period" means—

(*a*) the period of 2 years from the end of the month in which A dies or (if it ends later) the period of 3 months beginning with the date on which the personal representatives first act as such, or

(*b*) such longer period as an officer of Revenue and Customs may in the particular case allow.

(7) A claim under subsection (5) made within either of the periods mentioned in subsection (6)(*a*) may be withdrawn no later than one month after the end of the period concerned.

8M Residence nil-rate amount: cases involving conditional exemption

(1) This section applies where—

(*a*) the estate of a person ("D") immediately before D's death includes a qualifying residential interest,

(*b*) D dies on or after 6 April 2017, and

(*c*) some or all of the transfer of value under section 4 on D's death is a conditionally exempt transfer of property consisting of, or including, some or all of the qualifying residential interest.

(2) For the purposes of sections 8E and 8F, but subject to subsection (3), the exempt percentage of the qualifying residential interest is treated as being not closely inherited; and for this purpose "the exempt percentage" is given by—

$$\frac{X}{QRI} \times 100$$

where—

X is the attributable portion of the value transferred by the conditionally exempt transfer,

QRI is the attributable portion of the value transferred by the transfer under section 4, and

"the attributable portion" means the portion (which may be the whole) attributable to the qualifying residential interest.

(3) For the purposes of calculating tax chargeable under section 32 or 32A by reference to a chargeable event related to the qualifying residential interest where D is the relevant person for the purposes of section 33—

(*a*) in subsection (2), X is calculated as if the property forming the subject-matter of the conditionally exempt transfer had not included the property on which the tax is chargeable,

(*b*) section 33 has effect as if for subsection (1)(*b*)(ii) there were substituted—

"(ii) if the relevant person is dead, the rate or rates that would have applied to that amount in accordance with section 8D(2) and (3) above and the appropriate provision of section 7 above if—

(*a*) that amount had been added to the value transferred on the relevant person's death, and

(*b*) the unrelieved portion of that amount had formed the highest part of that value.", and

(*c*) for the purposes of that substituted section 33(1)(*b*)(ii) "the unrelieved portion" of the amount on which tax is chargeable is that amount itself less the amount (if any) by which—

(i) D's residence nil-rate amount for the purposes of the particular calculation under section 33, exceeds

(ii) D's residence nil-rate amount for the purposes of the charge to tax under section 4 on D's death.

(4) The following provisions of this section apply if immediately before D's death there is a person ("P") who is D's spouse or civil partner.

(5) For the purposes of calculating tax chargeable under section 32 or 32A by reference to a chargeable event related to the qualifying residential interest which occurs after P's death, the amount that would otherwise be D's residence nil-rate amount for those purposes is reduced by the amount (if any) by which P's residence nil-rate amount, or the residence nil-rate amount of any person who dies after P but before the chargeable event occurs, was increased by reason of an amount being available for carry-forward from D's death.

(6) Where tax is chargeable under section 32 or 32A by reference to a chargeable event related to the qualifying residential interest which occurs before P's death, section 8G(3) has effect for the purpose of calculating P's brought-forward allowance as if—

(*a*) before the "and" at the end of paragraph (*c*) there were inserted—

"(*ca*) reduce that total (but not below nil) by deducting from it the recapture percentage,",

(*b*) in paragraph (*d*), before "total", in both places, there were inserted "reduced", and

(*c*) the reference to the recapture percentage were to the percentage given by—

$$\frac{TA}{REE} \times 100$$

where—

REE is the residential enhancement at the time of the chargeable event, and

TA is the amount on which tax is chargeable under section 32 or 32A.

(7) If subsection (6) has applied by reason of a previous event or events related to the qualifying residential interest, the reference in subsection (6)(*c*) to the fraction—

$$\frac{TA}{REE}$$

is to the aggregate of that fraction in respect of the current event and the previous event (or each of the previous events)."

10 Rate bands for tax years 2018–19, 2019–20 and 2020–21

Section 8 of IHTA 1984 (indexation) does not have effect by virtue of any difference between—

(*a*) the consumer prices index for the month of September in 2017, 2018 or 2019, and

(*b*) that index for the previous September.

Settlements

11 Calculation of rate of inheritance tax on settled property

Schedule 1 contains provision about calculating the rate at which inheritance tax is charged under Chapter 3 of Part 3 of IHTA 1984.

12 Exemption from ten-yearly charge for heritage property

(1) Section 79 of IHTA 1984 (exemption from ten-yearly charge) is amended as follows.

(2) In subsection (3)—

(*a*) for "then, if" substitute "subsection (3A) below applies if",

(*b*) in paragraph (*a*), for "has, on a claim made for the purpose, been" substitute "is, on a claim made for the purpose,",
(*c*) after that paragraph insert—
"(*aa*) that claim is made during the period beginning with the date of a ten-year anniversary of the settlement ("the relevant ten-year anniversary") and ending—
(i) two years after that date, or
(ii) on such later date as the Board may allow,",
(*d*) in paragraph (*b*)—
(i) for "that section has been given" substitute "section 31 is given", and
(ii) for "have been given" substitute "are given", and
(*e*) omit the words from "section 64" to the end.

(3) After that subsection insert—

"(3A) Tax is not chargeable under section 64 above in relation to the property by reference to the relevant ten-year anniversary concerned or any subsequent ten-year anniversaries; but on the first occurrence of an event which, if there had been a conditionally exempt transfer of the property immediately before that relevant ten-year anniversary, would be a chargeable event with respect to the property—
(*a*) there is a charge to tax under this subsection, and
(*b*) on any ten-year anniversary falling after that event, tax is chargeable under section 64 above in relation to the property."

(4) In subsection (4), for the words from "subsection (3)" to "mentioned" substitute "subsection (3A) above in respect of property if, after the occasion mentioned in subsection (3) above and before the occurrence mentioned in subsection (3A)".

(5) In subsections (5), (5A), (6), (8)(*a*) and (9A)(*a*) for "subsection (3)" substitute "subsection (3A)".

(6) In subsection (7A), in paragraph (*c*), for the words from "day" to "section" substitute "relevant ten-year anniversary".

(7) In subsection (8)—
(*a*) in paragraph (*a*), for the words from "on the first" to the end substitute "by reference to the relevant ten-year anniversary of the settlement", and
(*b*) in paragraph (*c*), omit ", and the claim was made and the undertaking was given,".

(8) Accordingly, in that Act—
(*a*) in section 207 (liability: conditional exemption), in subsection (3), for "section 79(3)" substitute "section 79(3A)",
(*b*) in section 233 (interest on unpaid tax), in subsection (1)(*c*), for "79(3)" substitute "79(3A)",
(*c*) in section 237 (imposition of charge), in subsection (3B)(*a*), for "or 79(3)" substitute "or 79(3A)", and
(*d*) in Schedule 4 (maintenance funds for historic buildings), in paragraph 3(2)(*c*), for "or 79(3)" substitute "or 79(3A)".

(9) The amendments made by this section have effect in relation to occasions on which tax would (ignoring the effect of the amendments) fall to be charged under section 64 of IHTA 1984 on or after the day on which this Act is passed.

13 Settlements with initial interest in possession

(1) In section 80 of IHTA 1984 (initial interest of settlor or spouse or civil partner), for "an interest in possession", in each place it appears, substitute "a qualifying interest in possession".

(2) The amendments made by this section come into force on the day after the day on which this Act is passed subject to the saving provision in subsections (3) to (7).

(3) Subsections (4) to (7) apply where—
(*a*) the occasion first referred to in subsection (1) of section 80 of IHTA 1984 occurred before 22 March 2006,
(*b*) on that occasion the settlor, or the settlor's spouse or civil partner, became beneficially entitled to an interest in possession in property which, as a result of that subsection, was treated as not becoming comprised in a settlement for the purposes of Chapter 3 of Part 3 of IHTA 1984 on that occasion, and
(*c*) at all times in the relevant period that property, or some particular part of it, has been property in which the settlor, or the settlor's spouse or civil partner, has been beneficially entitled to an interest in possession,

and in subsections (4) to (7) "the protected property" means that property or, as the case may be, that particular part of it.

(4) The amendments made by subsection (1) do not have effect in relation to any particular part of the protected property for so long as the subsisting interest in possession continues to subsist in that part (but see subsections (5) and (6) for what happens afterwards).

(5) As from immediately before the time when the subsisting interest in possession comes to an end so far as subsisting in any particular part of the protected property (whether or not it also comes to an end at the same time so far as subsisting in some or all of the rest of the protected property), section 80(1) of IHTA 1984 has effect in relation to that part as if the second appearance of "an interest in possession" were "a qualifying interest in possession".
(6) If (ignoring this subsection), subsection (5) would have the consequence that a particular part of the protected property is treated as becoming comprised in a separate settlement at a time earlier than the time at which the subsisting interest in possession comes to an end so far as subsisting in that part, that part is to be treated as becoming comprised in a separate settlement at that later time.
(7) In this section—
(*a*) "the relevant period" means the period beginning with the occasion first mentioned in section 80(1) of IHTA 1984 and ending with the day on which this Act is passed,
(*b*) "qualifying interest in possession" has the same meaning as in section 80(1) of IHTA 1984,
(*c*) "subsisting interest in possession", in relation to a part of the protected property, means the interest in possession which subsisted in that part immediately before the end of the relevant period, and
(*d*) the reference in subsection (3)(*c*) to the spouse or civil partner of a settlor includes a reference to the widow or widower or surviving civil partner of the settlor.

14 Distributions etc from property settled by will
(1) In section 144 of IHTA 1984 (distributions etc from property settled by will), in subsection (1)(*b*), after "section" insert "65(4),".
(2) The amendment made by this section has effect in cases where the testator's death occurs on or after 10 December 2014.

Interest

15 Inheritance tax: interest
(1) In section 107 of FA 1986 (changes in financial institutions: interest)—
(*a*) in subsection (4), for the words from "section 234(4)" to "above)" substitute "paragraph 7(8) of Schedule 53 to the Finance Act 2009 (late payment interest: inheritance tax payable by instalments)";
(*b*) in subsection (5), for the words from "amend" to "section 234(3)(*c*)" substitute "set out one or more descriptions of company for the purposes of paragraph 7(7) of Schedule 53 to the Finance Act 2009".
(2) In Schedule 53 to FA 2009 (special provision: late payment interest start date)—
(*a*) in paragraph 7 (inheritance tax payable by instalments) for subparagraph (7) substitute—
"(7) A company falls within this sub-paragraph if—
(*a*) its business is carried on in the United Kingdom and is—
(i) wholly that of a market maker, or
(ii) that of a discount house, or
(*b*) it is of a description set out in regulations under section 107(5) of FA 1986.";
(*b*) in paragraph 9 (certain other amounts of inheritance tax), for "date of the testator's death" substitute "end of the month in which the testator died".
(3) The amendments made by this section come into force on such day or days as the Treasury may by regulations made by statutory instrument appoint.
(4) Regulations under subsection (3) may—
(*a*) appoint different days for different purposes;
(*b*) make transitional or saving provision.

PART 6

ADMINISTRATION AND ENFORCEMENT

51 Enforcement by deduction from accounts
(1) Schedule 8 contains provision about the enforcement of debts owed to the Commissioners for Her Majesty's Revenue and Customs by making deductions from accounts held with deposit-takers.
(2) The Treasury may, by regulations made by statutory instrument, make consequential, incidental or supplementary provision in connection with any provision made by that Schedule.
(3) Regulations under subsection (2) may amend, repeal or revoke any enactment (whenever passed or made).
(4) "Enactment" includes an enactment contained in subordinate legislation within the meaning of the Interpretation Act 1978.
(5) A statutory instrument containing (whether alone or with other provision) provision amending or repealing an Act may not be made unless a draft of the instrument has been laid before and approved by a resolution of the House of Commons.

(6) Any other statutory instrument containing regulations under subsection (2) is subject to annulment in pursuance of a resolution of the House of Commons.

52 Rate of interest applicable to judgment debts etc in taxation matters

(1) This section applies if a sum payable to or by the Commissioners under a judgment or order given or made in any court proceedings relating to a taxation matter (a "tax-related judgment debt") carries interest as a result of a relevant enactment.

(2) The "relevant enactments" are—

(*a*) section 17 of the Judgments Act 1838 (judgment debts to carry interest), and

(*b*) any order under section 74 of the County Courts Act 1984 (interest on judgment debts etc).

(3) The relevant enactment is to have effect in relation to the tax-related judgment debt as if for the rate specified in section 17(1) of the Judgments Act 1838 and any other rate specified in an order under section 74 of the County Courts Act 1984 there were substituted—

(*a*) in the case of a sum payable to the Commissioners, the late payment interest rate provided for in regulations made by the Treasury under section 103(1) of FA 2009, and

(*b*) in the case of a sum payable by the Commissioners, the special repayment rate.

(4) Subsection (3) does not affect any power of the court under the relevant enactment to prevent any sum from carrying interest or to provide for a rate of interest which is lower than (and incapable of exceeding) that for which the subsection provides.

(5) If section 44A of the Administration of Justice Act 1970 (interest on judgment debts expressed otherwise than in sterling), or any corresponding provision made under section 74 of the County Courts Act 1984 in relation to the county court, applies to a tax-related judgment debt—

(*a*) subsection (3) does not apply, but

(*b*) the court may not specify in an order under section 44A of the Administration of Justice Act 1970, or under any provision corresponding to that section which has effect under section 74 of the County Courts Act 1984, an interest rate which exceeds (or is capable of exceeding)—

(i) in the case of a sum payable to the Commissioners, the rate mentioned in subsection (3)(*a*), or

(ii) in the case of a sum payable by the Commissioners, the special repayment rate.

(6) The "special repayment rate" is the percentage per annum given by the formula—

BR + 2

where BR is the official Bank rate determined by the Bank of England Monetary Policy Committee at the operative meeting.

(7) "The operative meeting", in relation to the special repayment rate applicable in respect of any day, means the most recent meeting of the Bank of England Monetary Policy Committee apart from any meeting later than the 13th working day before that day.

(8) The Treasury may by regulations made by statutory instrument—

(*a*) repeal subsections (6) and (7), and

(*b*) provide that the "special repayment rate" for the purposes of this section is the rate provided for in the regulations.

(9) Regulations under subsection (8)—

(*a*) may make different provision for different purposes,

(*b*) may either themselves specify a rate of interest or make provision for such a rate to be determined (and to change from time to time) by reference to such rate, or the average of such rates, as may be referred to in the regulations,

(*c*) may provide for rates to be reduced below, or increased above, what they would otherwise be by specified amounts or by reference to specified formulae,

(*d*) may provide for rates arrived at by reference to averages to be rounded up or down,

(*e*) may provide for circumstances in which the alteration of a rate of interest is or is not to take place, and

(*f*) may provide that alterations of rates are to have effect for periods beginning on or after a day determined in accordance with the regulations ("the effective date") regardless of—

(i) the date of the judgment or order in question, and

(ii) whether interest begins to run on or after the effective date, or began to run before that date.

(10) A statutory instrument containing regulations under subsection (8) is subject to annulment in pursuance of a resolution of the House of Commons.

(11) To the extent that a tax-related judgment debt consists of an award of costs to or against the Commissioners, the reference in section 24(2) of the Crown Proceedings Act 1947 (which relates to interest on costs awarded to or against the Crown) to the rate at which interest is payable upon judgment debts due from or to the Crown is to be read as a reference to the rate at which interest is payable upon tax-related judgment debts.

(12) This section has effect in relation to interest for periods beginning on or after 8 July 2015, regardless of—

(*a*) the date of the judgment or order in question, and

(*b*) whether interest begins to run on or after 8 July 2015, or began to run before that date.

(13) Subsection (14) applies where, at any time during the period beginning with 8 July 2015 and ending immediately before the day on which this Act is passed ("the relevant period")—

(*a*) a payment is made in satisfaction of a tax-related judgment debt, and

(*b*) the payment includes interest under a relevant enactment in respect of any part of the relevant period.

(14) The court by which the judgment or order in question was given or made must, on an application made to it under this subsection by the person who made the payment, order the repayment of the amount by which the interest paid under the relevant enactment in respect of days falling within the relevant period exceeds the interest payable under the relevant enactment in respect of those days in accordance with the provisions of this section.

(15) In this section—

"the Commissioners" means the Commissioners for Her Majesty's Revenue and Customs;

"taxation matter" means anything . . . [1] the collection and management of which is the responsibility of the Commissioners (or was the responsibility of the Commissioners of Inland Revenue or Commissioners of Customs and Excise);

"working day" means any day other than a non-business day as defined in section 92 of the Bills of Exchange Act 1882.

(16) This section extends to England and Wales only.

Amendments—[1] In sub-s (15), in definition of "taxation matter", words ", other than national insurance contributions," repealed by FA 2016 s 172 with effect in relation to interest for periods beginning on or after 15 September 2016, regardless of—

– the date of the judgment or order in question; and

– whether interest begins to run on or after 15 September 2016, or began to run before that date.

This amendment extends to England and Wales only.

SCHEDULE 1

RATE OF TAX CHARGED UNDER CHAPTER 3 OF PART 3 IHTA 1984

Section 11

1 IHTA 1984 is amended as follows.

2 After section 62 insert—

"62A Same-day additions

(1) For the purposes of this Chapter, there is a "same-day addition", in relation to a settlement ("settlement A"), if—

(*a*) there is a transfer of value by a person as a result of which the value immediately afterwards of the property comprised in settlement A is greater than the value immediately before,

(*b*) as a result of the same transfer of value, or as a result of another transfer of value made by that person on the same day, the value immediately afterwards of the property comprised in another settlement ("settlement B") is greater than the value immediately before,

(*c*) that person is the settlor of settlement A and settlement B,

(*d*) at any point in the relevant period, all or any part of the property comprised in settlement A was relevant property, and

(*e*) at that point, or at any other point in the relevant period, all or any part of the property comprised in settlement B was relevant property.

For exceptions, see section 62B.

(2) Where there is a same-day addition, references in this Chapter to its value are to the difference between the two values mentioned in subsection (1)(*b*).

(3) "The relevant period" means—

(*a*) in the case of settlement A, the period beginning with the commencement of settlement A and ending immediately after the transfer of value mentioned in subsection (1)(*a*), and

(*b*) in the case of settlement B, the period beginning with the commencement of settlement B and ending immediately after the transfer of value mentioned in subsection (1)(*b*)).

(4) The transfer or transfers of value mentioned in subsection (1) include a transfer or transfers of value as a result of which property first becomes comprised in settlement A or settlement B; but not if settlements A and B are related settlements.

(5) For the purposes of subsection (1) above, it is immaterial whether the amount of the property comprised in settlement A or settlement B (or neither) was increased as a result of the transfer or transfers of value mentioned in that subsection.

62B Same day additions: exceptions

(1) There is not a same-day addition for the purposes of this Chapter if any of the following conditions is met—

(*a*) immediately after the transfer of value mentioned in section 62A(1)(*a*) all the property comprised in settlement A was held for charitable purposes only without limit of time (defined by a date or otherwise),

(*b*) immediately after the transfer of value mentioned in section 62A(1)(*b*) all the property comprised in settlement B was so held,

(*c*) either or each of settlement A and settlement B is a protected settlement (see section 62C), and

(*d*) the transfer of value, or either or each of the transfers of value, mentioned in section 62A(1)(*a*) and (*b*)—

(i) results from the payment of a premium under a contract of life insurance the terms of which provide for premiums to be due at regular intervals of one year or less throughout the contract term, or

(ii) is made to fund such a payment.

(2) If the transfer of value, or each of the transfers of value, mentioned in section 62A(1) is not the transfer of value under section 4 on the settlor's death, there is a same-day addition for the purposes of this Chapter only if conditions A and B are met.

(3) Condition A is that—

(*a*) the difference between the two values mentioned in section 62A(1)(*a*) exceeds £5,000, or

(*b*) in a case where there has been more than one transfer of value within section 62A(1)(*a*) on the same day, the difference between—

(i) the value of the property comprised in settlement A immediately before the first of those transfers, and

(ii) the value of the property comprised in settlement A immediately after the last of those transfers,

exceeds £5,000.

(4) Condition B is that—

(*a*) the difference between the two values mentioned in section 62A(1)(*b*) exceeds £5,000, or

(*b*) in a case where there has been more than one transfer of value within section 62A(1)(*b*), the difference between—

(i) the value of the property comprised in settlement B immediately before the first of those transfers, and

(ii) the value of the property comprised in settlement B immediately after the last of those transfers,

exceeds £5,000.

62C Protected settlements

(1) For the purposes of this Chapter, a settlement is a "protected settlement" if it commenced before 10 December 2014 and either condition A or condition B is met.

(2) Condition A is met if there have been no transfers of value by the settlor on or after 10 December 2014 as a result of which the value of the property comprised in the settlement was increased.

(3) Condition B is met if—

(*a*) there has been a transfer of value by the settlor on or after 10 December 2014 as a result of which the value of the property comprised in the settlement was increased, and

(*b*) that transfer of value was the transfer of value under section 4 on the settlor's death before 6 April 2017 and it had the result mentioned by reason of a protected testamentary disposition.

(4) In subsection (3)(*b*) "protected testamentary disposition" means a disposition effected by provisions of the settlor's will that at the settlor's death are, in substance, the same as they were immediately before 10 December 2014."

3 (1) Section 66 (rate of ten-yearly charge) is amended as follows.

(2) In subsection (4)—

(*a*) omit paragraph (*b*) and the "and" following it,

(*b*) in paragraph (*c*), before "property" insert "relevant", and (*c*) at the end of paragraph (*c*) insert—

"(*d*) the value of any same-day addition; and

(*e*) where—

(i) an increase in the value of the property comprised in another settlement is represented by the value of a same-day addition aggregated under paragraph (*d*) above, and

(ii) that other settlement is not a related settlement,

the value immediately after that other settlement commenced of the relevant property then comprised in that other settlement;".

(3) In subsection (6)(*a*), for "paragraphs (*b*) and (*c*)" substitute "paragraphs (*c*) to (*e*)".

4 In section 68 (rate before ten-year anniversary), in subsection (5)—

(*a*) in paragraphs (*a*) and (*b*), before "property" insert "relevant",

(*b*) omit the "and" following paragraph (*b*), and

(*c*) for paragraph (*c*) substitute—

"(*c*) the value, immediately after it became comprised in the settlement, of property which—

(i) became comprised in the settlement after the settlement commenced and before the occasion of the charge under section 65 above, and

(ii) was relevant property immediately after it became so comprised,

whether or not the property has remained relevant property comprised in the settlement;

(*d*) the value, at the time it became (or last became) relevant property, of property which—

(i) was comprised in the settlement immediately after the settlement commenced and was not then relevant property but became relevant property before the occasion of the charge under section 65 above, or

(ii) became comprised in the settlement after the settlement commenced and before the occasion of the charge under section 65 above, and was not relevant property immediately after it became comprised in the settlement, but became relevant property before the occasion of the charge under that section,

whether or not the property has remained relevant property comprised in the settlement;

(*e*) the value of any same-day addition; and

(*f*) where—

(i) an increase in the value of the property comprised in another settlement is represented by the value of a same-day addition aggregated under paragraph (*e*) above, and

(ii) that other settlement is not a related settlement,

the value immediately after that other settlement commenced of the relevant property then comprised in that other settlement."

5 (1) Section 69 (rate between ten-year anniversaries) is amended as follows.

(2) In subsection (1), for "subsection (2)" substitute "subsection (2A)".

(3) For subsection (2) substitute—

"(2) Subsection (2A) below applies—

(*a*) if, at any time in the period beginning with the most recent ten-year anniversary and ending immediately before the occasion of the charge under section 65 above (the "relevant period"), property has become comprised in the settlement which was relevant property immediately after it became so comprised, or

(*b*) if—

(i) at any time in the relevant period, property has become comprised in the settlement which was not relevant property immediately after it became so comprised, and

(ii) at a later time in the relevant period, that property has become relevant property, or

(*c*) if property which was comprised in the settlement immediately before the relevant period, but was not then relevant property, has at any time during the relevant period become relevant property.

(2A) Whether or not all of the property within any of paragraphs (*a*) to (*c*) of subsection (2) above has remained relevant property comprised in the settlement, the rate at which tax is charged under section 65 is to be the appropriate fraction of the rate at which it would last have been charged under section 64 above (apart from section 66(2) above) if—

(*a*) immediately before the most recent ten-year anniversary, all of that property had been relevant property comprised in the settlement with a value determined in accordance with subsection (3) below, and

(*b*) any same-day addition made on or after the most recent ten-year anniversary had been made immediately before that anniversary."

(4) In subsection (3)—

(*a*) omit the words from "which either" to the end of paragraph (*b*), and

(*b*) for "purposes of subsection (2)" substitute "purposes of subsection (2A)".

6 In section 71F (calculation of settlement rate in order to calculate the tax charged under section 71E), in subsection (9)(*b*), after "in it" insert "which was property to which section 71D above applied".

7 The amendments made by this Schedule have effect in relation to occasions on which tax falls to be charged under Chapter 3 of Part 3 of IHTA 1984 on or after the day on which this Act is passed.

SCHEDULE 8

ENFORCEMENT BY DEDUCTION FROM ACCOUNTS

Section 51

PART 1

SCHEME FOR ENFORCEMENT BY DEDUCTION FROM ACCOUNTS

Introduction

1 This Part of this Schedule contains provision about the collection of amounts due and payable to the Commissioners by the making of deductions from accounts held with deposit-takers.

Commentary—*Simon's Taxes* **A4.615**

"Relevant sum"

2 (1) In this Part of this Schedule "relevant sum", in relation to a person, means a sum that is due and payable by the person to the Commissioners—

(*a*) under or by virtue of an enactment, or

(*b*) under a contract settlement, and in relation to which Conditions A to C are met.

(2) Condition A is that the sum is at least £1,000.

(3) Condition B is that the sum is—

(*a*) an established debt (see sub-paragraph (5)),

(*b*) due under section 223 of, or paragraph 6 of Schedule 32 to, FA 2014 (accelerated payment notice or partner payment notice), or

(*c*) the disputed tax specified in a notice under section 221(2)(*b*) of FA 2014 (accelerated payment of tax: notice given pending appeal).

(4) Condition C is that HMRC is satisfied that the person is aware that the sum is due and payable by the person to the Commissioners.

(5) A sum that is due and payable to the Commissioners is an "established debt" if there is no possibility that the sum, or any part of it, will cease to be due and payable to the Commissioners on appeal.

(6) For the purposes of sub-paragraph (5) it does not matter whether the reason that there is no such possibility is—

(*a*) that there is no right of appeal in relation to the sum,

(*b*) that a period for bringing an appeal has expired without an appeal having been brought, or

(*c*) that an appeal which was brought has been finally determined or withdrawn;

and any power to grant permission to appeal out of time is to be disregarded.

Commentary—*Simon's Taxes* **A4.616**

Press releases etc—HMRC Direct Recovery of Debts Issue Briefing, 5 August 2015, see *SWTI 2015, Issue 32*.

Information notice

3 (1) This paragraph applies if it appears to HMRC that—

(*a*) a person has failed to pay a relevant sum, and

(*b*) that person holds one or more accounts with a deposit-taker.

(2) HMRC may give the deposit-taker a notice under this paragraph (an "information notice") requiring the deposit-taker to provide HMRC with—

(*a*) prescribed information about accounts held by the person with the deposit-taker,

(*b*) in relation to any joint account held by the person with the deposit-taker, prescribed information about the other holder or holders of the account, and

(*c*) any other prescribed information.

(3) HMRC may exercise the power under sub-paragraph (2) only for the purposes of determining whether to give a hold notice to the deposit-taker in respect of the person concerned (see paragraph 4).

(4) Where a deposit-taker is given an information notice, it must comply with the notice as soon as reasonably practicable and, in any event, within the period of 10 working days beginning with the day on which the notice is given to it.

(5) An information notice must explain the effect of—

(*a*) sub-paragraph (4), and

(*b*) paragraph 14 (penalties).

Commentary—*Simon's Taxes* **A4.617**

Regulations—Enforcement by Deduction from Accounts (Prescribed Information) Regulations, SI 2015/1986.

Cross-references—See the Enforcement by Deduction from Accounts (Prescribed Information) Regulations, SI 2015/1986 reg 4: the following information is prescribed for the purposes of sub-para (2)—

– account details for each account P holds with the deposit-taker; and

– specified information in relation to P.

SI 2015/1986 reg 2 provides the following definitions in relation to the above.

"Account details" in respect of an account held by P means—

(a) any account number;

(b) any roll number;

(c) any sort code;

(d) the type of account, including whether or not it is a joint account;

(e) the account balance (in the currency in which the account is held);

(f) whether interest is payable in respect of amounts standing to the credit of the account and, if so, the rate of interest payable;

(g) any minimum balance required to keep the account open;

(h) any contractual term by virtue of which an account holder or interested third party may suffer economic loss where a hold notice or deduction notice is, or has been, given;

(i) specified information about (i) any account holder other than P; (ii) any person (not falling within (i)) who is an interested third party in relation to the account; and any person who, in respect of the account, has power of attorney.

"specified information" in respect of a person means—

(a) name and address;

(b) national insurance number;

(c) all email addresses;

(d) all telephone numbers;

(e) in respect of an account which is a joint account, the proportion of the balance of that joint account to which the person is entitled.

Hold notice

4 (1) If it appears to HMRC that—

(*a*) a person ("P") has failed to pay a relevant sum, and

(*b*) P holds one or more accounts with a deposit-taker, HMRC may give the deposit-taker a notice under this paragraph (a "hold notice").

(2) The hold notice must—

(*a*) specify P's name and last known address,

(*b*) specify as the "specified amount" an amount that meets the conditions in sub-paragraph (4),

(*c*) specify as the "safeguarded amount" an amount that meets the requirements set out in sub-paragraphs (6) to (8),

(*d*) set out any rules which are to apply for the purposes of paragraph 7(5)(*b*) (priority of accounts subject to a hold notice),

(*e*) explain the effect of—

(i) paragraphs 6 to 13 (effect of hold notice, duty to notify account holders etc),

(ii) paragraph 14 (penalties), and

(iii) any regulations under paragraph 20(2)(*c*) or (*d*) (powers to restrict the accounts or amounts in relation to which a hold notice may have effect, in addition to the powers to make provision in the hold notice under sub-paragraph (3)(*b*) and (*c*)), and

(*f*) contain a statement about HMRC's compliance with paragraph 5 in relation to the notice.

For provision about the particular relevant sums to which a hold notice relates see paragraph 8(6)(*a*)(ii) and (7) (notice to be given by HMRC to P).

(3) The hold notice may—

(*a*) specify any other information which HMRC considers might assist the deposit-taker in identifying accounts which P holds with it;

(*b*) specify an account, or description of account, which is to be treated for the purposes of the hold notice and this Part of this Schedule as not being an account held by P with the deposit-taker;

(*c*) require that an amount specified in the notice is to be treated for the purposes of the hold notice and this Part of this Schedule as if it were not an amount standing to the credit of a specified account held by P.

(4) The amount specified as the specified amount in the hold notice ("the current hold notice") must not exceed so much of the notified sum (see paragraph 8(6) to (8)) as remains after deducting—

(*a*) the amount specified as the "specified amount" in any hold notice which relates to the same debts as the current hold notice (see subparagraph (5)) and is given to another deposit-taker on the same day as that notice, and

(*b*) the amount specified as the "specified amount" in any hold notice which relates to the same debts as the current hold notice and is given to a deposit-taker on an earlier day, (unless HMRC has received a notification under paragraph 8(4) in relation to that earlier hold notice).

(5) For the purposes of this paragraph, any two hold notices given in respect of the same person "relate to the same debts" if at least one relevant sum specified in relation to one of those notices by virtue of paragraph 8(7)(*a*) is the same debt as a relevant sum so specified in relation to the other notice.

(6) The amount specified in the hold notice as the safeguarded amount must be at least £5,000; but this is qualified by sub-paragraphs (7) and (8).

(7) The safeguarded amount must be nil if—

(*a*) HMRC has previously given a deposit-taker a hold notice ("the earlier hold notice") relating to the same debts as the hold notice mentioned in sub-paragraph (2) ("the new hold notice"), and

(*b*) within the period of 30 days ending with the day on which the new hold notice is given to the deposit-taker, HMRC has received a notice under paragraph 8 which states that there is a held amount as a result of the earlier hold notice.

(8) HMRC may (in a case not falling within sub-paragraph (7)) determine that an amount less than £5,000 (which may be nil) is to be the safeguarded amount if HMRC considers it appropriate to do so having regard to the value (or aggregate value) in sterling at the relevant time of any amounts which at that time stand to the credit of a qualifying non-sterling account or accounts.

(9) In sub-paragraph (8) "qualifying non-sterling account" means an account which, but for paragraph 6(6)(*b*) (account not denominated in sterling), would be a relevant account in relation to the hold notice.

(10) For the purposes of sub-paragraph (8), the value in sterling of any amount is to be determined in the prescribed manner; and regulations for the purposes of this sub-paragraph may specify circumstances in which the exchange rate is to be determined in accordance with a notice published by the Commissioners.

(11) In sub-paragraph (8) "the relevant time" means the time when the Commissioners determine the amount to be specified as the "safeguarded amount" under sub-paragraph (2)(*c*).

(12) HMRC must not on any one day give to a single deposit-taker more than one hold notice relating to the same debts.

Commentary—*Simon's Taxes* **A4.618**

Persons at a particular disadvantage in dealing with Revenue and Customs affairs

5 (1) Before deciding whether or not to exercise the power under paragraph 3(2) or 4(1) in relation to a person, HMRC must consider whether or not, to the best of HMRC's knowledge, there are any matters as a result of which the person is, or may be, at a particular disadvantage in dealing with the person's Revenue and Customs affairs.

(2) If HMRC determines that there are any such matters, HMRC must take those matters into account in deciding whether or not to exercise the power concerned in relation to the person.

(3) The Commissioners must publish guidance as to the factors which are relevant to determining whether or not a person is at a particular disadvantage in dealing with the person's Revenue and Customs affairs for the purposes of this Schedule.

(4) In this paragraph "Revenue and Customs affairs", in relation to a person by whom a relevant sum is payable, means any affairs of the person which relate to the relevant sum.

Commentary—*Simon's Taxes* **A4.615**

Effect of hold notice

6 (1) A deposit-taker to whom a hold notice is given under paragraph 4 must, for each relevant account (see sub-paragraph (6))—

(*a*) determine whether or not there is a held amount (greater than nil) in relation to that account, and

(*b*) if there is such a held amount in relation to that account, take the first or second type of action (see sub-paragraph (3)) in respect of that account.

See paragraph 7 for how to determine the held amount in relation to any relevant account.

(2) The deposit-taker must comply with sub-paragraph (1) as soon as is reasonably practicable and, in any event, within the period of 5 working days beginning with the day on which the hold notice is given.

(3) In relation to each affected account (see sub-paragraph (7))—

(*a*) the first type of action is to put in place such arrangements as are necessary to ensure that the deposit-taker does not do anything, or permit anything to be done, that would reduce the amount standing to the credit of that account below the held amount in relation to that account;

(*b*) the second type of action is to—

(i) transfer an amount equal to the held amount from the affected account into an account created by the deposit-taker for the sole purpose of containing that transferred amount (a "suspense account"), and

(ii) put in place such arrangements as are necessary to ensure that the deposit-taker does not do anything, or permit anything to be done, that would reduce the amount standing to the credit of that suspense account below the amount that is the held amount in relation to the affected account.

(4) The deposit-taker must maintain any arrangements made under subparagraph (3) until the hold notice ceases to be in force.

(5) A hold notice ceases to be in force when—

(*a*) the deposit-taker is given a notice cancelling it under paragraph 9(1) or 11 or the hold notice is cancelled under paragraph 12, or

(*b*) the deposit-taker is given a deduction notice in relation to the hold notice (see paragraph 13).

(6) In this Part of this Schedule "relevant account", in relation to a hold notice, means an account held with the deposit-taker by P, but not including—

(*a*) an account excluded under paragraph 4(3)(*b*) or by regulations under paragraph 20(2)(*c*),

(*b*) an account not denominated in sterling, or

(*c*) any suspense account.

(7) For the purposes of this Part of this Schedule, a relevant account is an "affected account" if, as a result of the hold notice, an amount is the held amount in relation to that account (see paragraph 7(1) and (2)).

Commentary—*Simon's Taxes* **A4.618A**

Determination of held amounts

7 (1) If there is only one relevant account (see paragraph 6(6)) in existence at the time the deposit-taker complies with paragraph 6(1), "the held amount" in relation to that account is—

(*a*) if the available amount in respect of the account (see sub-paragraph (3)) exceeds the safeguarded amount, so much of the amount of the excess as does not exceed the specified amount, and

(*b*) if the available amount does not exceed the safeguarded amount, nil.

For the meaning of "the safeguarded amount" and "the specified amount" see paragraph 23(1).

(2) If there is more than one relevant account in existence at the time the deposit-taker complies with paragraph 6(1), "the held amount" in relation to each relevant account is determined as follows—

Step 1

Determine the available amount in respect of each relevant account.

Step 2

Determine the total of the available amounts in respect of all of the relevant accounts. If that total does not exceed the safeguarded amount, the held amount in relation to each relevant account is nil (and no further steps are to be taken). In any other case, go to Step 3.

Step 3

Match the safeguarded amount against the available amounts in respect of the relevant accounts, taking those accounts in reverse priority order (see sub-paragraph (6)).

Step 4

Match the specified amount against what remains of the available amounts in respect of the relevant accounts by taking each relevant account in priority order (see sub-paragraph (5)) and matching the specified amount (or, as the case may be, what remains of the specified amount) against the available amount for each account until either—

(*a*) the specified amount has been fully matched, or

(*b*) what remains of the available amounts is exhausted.

Where this sub-paragraph applies, "the held amount", in relation to a relevant account—

(i) is so much of the amount standing to the credit of the account as is matched against the specified amount under Step 4, and

(ii) accordingly, is nil if no amount standing to the credit of the account is so matched against the specified amount.

(3) In this paragraph "the available amount" means—

(*a*) in the case of an account other than a joint account, the amount standing to the credit of that account at the time the deposit-taker complies with paragraph 6(1), or

(*b*) in the case of a joint account, the appropriate fraction of the amount standing to the credit of that account at that time;

so, if no amount stands to the credit of an account at that time, "the available amount" is nil.

(4) In this paragraph "the appropriate fraction", in relation to a joint account, means—

$$\frac{1}{N}$$

where N is the number of persons who together hold the joint account.

(5) In this paragraph "priority order" means such order as the deposit-taker considers appropriate, but the deposit-taker must ensure—

(*a*) that accounts other than joint accounts always have a higher priority than joint accounts, and

(*b*) subject to paragraph (*a*), that any rule set out in the hold notice under paragraph 4(2)(*d*) is adhered to.

(6) In this paragraph "reverse priority order" means the reverse of the order determined under sub-paragraph (5).

(7) In this paragraph references to an amount standing to the credit of an account are to be read subject to any regulations under paragraph 20(2)(*d*).

Commentary—*Simon's Taxes* **A4.618A**

Duty to notify HMRC and account holders etc

8 (1) This paragraph applies where a deposit-taker receives a hold notice.

(2) If the deposit-taker determines that there are one or more affected accounts (see paragraph 6(7)) as a result of the hold notice, the deposit-taker must give HMRC a notice which sets out—

(*a*) prescribed information about each of the affected accounts held by P,

(*b*) the amount of the held amount in relation to each such account,

(*c*) if any of the affected accounts is a joint account held by P and one or more other persons, prescribed information about the other person or persons, and

(*d*) any other prescribed information.

(3) The notice under sub-paragraph (2) must be given within the period of 5 working days beginning with the day on which the deposit-taker complies with paragraph 6(1).

(4) If the deposit-taker determines that there are no affected accounts as a result of the hold notice, it must give HMRC a notice which—

(*a*) states that this is the case, and

(*b*) sets out any other prescribed information.

(5) The notice under sub-paragraph (4) must be given within the period of 5 working days beginning with the day on which the deposit-taker makes that determination.

(6) If HMRC receives a notice under sub-paragraph (2) it must as soon as reasonably practicable—

(*a*) give P—

(i) a copy of the hold notice, and

(ii) a notice under sub-paragraph (7), and

(*b*) in relation to each affected account, give a notice to each person within sub-paragraph (9) explaining that a hold notice has been given in respect of the account, the effect of the hold notice so far as it relates to the account and the effect of paragraphs 10 to 12.

(7) A notice under this sub-paragraph must comply with the following requirements—

(*a*) the notice must specify the particular relevant sums (see paragraph 2) to which the hold notice relates;

(*b*) the details given for that purpose must include a statement, to the best of HMRC's knowledge, of the amount of each of those sums (that is, the unpaid amount) at the date of the notice;

(*c*) the notice must state the total of the amounts stated under paragraph (*b*) (if more than one), and

(*d*) the notice must state that the notified sum for the purposes of the hold notice (see paragraph 4(4)) is equal to—
   (i) the total amount specified under paragraph (*c*) or,
   (ii) if paragraph (*c*) is not applicable, the amount specified under paragraph (*b*) as the amount of the relevant sum to which the hold notice relates.

(8) In this Part of this Schedule "the notified sum", in relation to a hold notice, means the amount identified as such (or that is to be identified as such) in the notice under sub-paragraph (7).

(9) The persons mentioned in sub-paragraph (6)(*b*) are—
(*a*) in the case of a joint account, any holder of the account other than P, and
(*b*) any person (not falling within paragraph (*a*)) who is an interested third party in relation to the affected account, in respect of whom prescribed information has been provided under subparagraph (2)(*c*) or sufficient information has otherwise been given in the notice under sub-paragraph (2) to enable HMRC to give a notice.

(10) After the deposit-taker has complied with paragraph 6(1), the deposit-taker may, in relation to any affected account, give a notice to—
(*a*) P,
(*b*) if the account is a joint account, any other holder of the account, and
(*c*) any person (not falling within paragraph (*b*)) who is an interested third party in relation to the account,

which states that a hold notice has been received by the deposit-taker in respect of the account and the effect of that notice so far as it relates to that account.

(11) In this Part of this Schedule "interested third party", in relation to a relevant account, means a person other than P who has a beneficial interest in—
(*a*) an amount standing to the credit of the account, or
(*b*) an amount which has been transferred from that account to a suspense account.

(12) But, in relation to a hold notice, an interest which comes into existence after any arrangements under paragraph 6(3) have been put into place is treated as not being a beneficial interest for the purposes of sub-paragraph (11).

Commentary—*Simon's Taxes* **A4.618A**

Regulations—Enforcement by Deduction from Accounts (Prescribed Information) Regulations, SI 2015/1986.

Cross-references—See the Enforcement by Deduction from Accounts (Prescribed Information) Regulations, SI 2015/1986 reg 5: the following information is prescribed for the purposes of sub-para (2)—
- account details for each account P holds with the deposit-taker; and
- specified information in relation to P.
- confirmation of which of the accounts that P holds with the deposit-taker is an affected account;
- the date on which the deposit-taker complied with para 6(1) of this Schedule (effect of hold notice);
- confirmation that the deposit-taker understands the effect of para 14(1)(*g*) of this Schedule (penalties);
- the total of all held amounts notified by the deposit-taker under para 8(2)(*b*) of this Schedule in response to a hold notice;
- in respect of each account which P holds with the deposit-taker, the amount standing to the credit of the account which is not subject to action taken by the deposit-taker under para 6(3) of this Schedule; and
- a description of any economic loss suffered by an account holder or interested third party as a result of any contractual term specified in the definition of "account details" in SI 2015/1986 reg 2(*h*).

For the purposes of the above, "held amounts" is to be read in accordance with para 7 of this Schedule.

For the definitions of "account details" in respect of an account held by P, and "specified information" in respect of a person, see SI 2015/1986 reg 2, and the note to para 3 of this Schedule above.

For the purposes of sub-para (4)(*b*), the information prescribed is the information which the deposit-taker has taken into account to determine that there are no affected accounts (SI 2015/1986 reg 6).

Cancellation or variation of effects of hold notice

9 (1) Where a hold notice has been given to a deposit-taker HMRC may, by a notice given to the deposit-taker (a "notice of cancellation or variation")—
(*a*) cancel the hold notice,
(*b*) cancel the effect of the hold notice in relation to one or more accounts, or
(*c*) cancel the effect of the hold notice in relation to any part of the held amount standing to the credit of a particular account or accounts.

In this sub-paragraph references to the effect of a hold notice are to its effect by virtue of paragraph 6(4).

(2) Where HMRC gives a notice under sub-paragraph (1) it must give a copy of that notice to—
(*a*) P, and
(*b*) any other person who HMRC considers is affected by the giving of the notice of cancellation or variation and is—
   (i) a person who holds a relevant account of which P is also a holder and in respect of whom prescribed information is provided under paragraph 8(2)(*c*), or

(ii) an interested third party in relation to a relevant account in respect of whom sufficient information has been given in the notice under paragraph 8(2) to enable HMRC to give a notice.

(3) Where the deposit-taker is given a notice under sub-paragraph (1), it must as soon as reasonably practicable and, in any event, within the period of 5 working days beginning with the day the notice is given—

(*a*) if the notice is given under sub-paragraph (1)(*a*), cancel the arrangements made under paragraph 6(3) as a result of the notice, and

(*b*) if the notice is given under sub-paragraph (1)(*b*) or (*c*), make such adjustments to those arrangements as are necessary to give effect to the notice.

Commentary—*Simon's Taxes* **A4.618A, A4.618B**

Making objections to hold notice

10 (1) Where a hold notice is given to a deposit-taker, a person within subparagraph (2) may by a notice given to HMRC (a "notice of objection") object against the hold notice.

(2) The persons who may object are—

(*a*) P,

(*b*) any interested third party in relation to an affected account, and

(*c*) any person (not falling within paragraph (*a*) or (*b*)) who is a holder of an affected account which is a joint account,

but only P may object on the ground in sub-paragraph (3)(*a*).

(3) An objection may only be made on one or more of the following grounds—

(*a*) that the debts to which the hold notice relates (see paragraph 8(7)(*a*)) have been wholly or partly paid,

(*b*) that at the time when the hold notice was given, either there was no sum that was a relevant sum in relation to P or P did not hold any account with the deposit-taker,

(*c*) that the hold notice is causing or will cause exceptional hardship to the person making the objection or another person, or

(*d*) that there is an interested third party in relation to one or more of the affected accounts.

(4) A notice of objection must state the grounds of the objection.

(5) Objections under this paragraph may only be made within the period of 30 days beginning with—

(*a*) in the case of—

(i) P, or

(ii) a person within sub-paragraph (2)(*b*) or (*c*) who has not been given a notice under paragraph 8(6)(*b*),

the day on which a copy of the hold notice is given to P under paragraph 8(6)(*a*), and

(*b*) in the case of a person given a notice under paragraph 8(6)(*b*), the day on which that notice is given.

(6) Sub-paragraph (5) does not apply if HMRC agree to the notice of objection being given after the end of the period mentioned in that sub-paragraph.

(7) HMRC must agree to a notice of objection being given after the end of that period if the following conditions are met—

(*a*) the person seeking to make the objection has made a request in writing to HMRC to agree to the notice of objection being given;

(*b*) HMRC is satisfied that there was reasonable excuse for not giving the notice before the relevant time limit, and

(*c*) HMRC is satisfied that the person complied with paragraph (*a*) without unreasonable delay after the reasonable excuse ceased.

(8) If a request of the kind referred to in sub-paragraph (7)(*a*) is made, HMRC must by a notice inform the person making the request whether or not HMRC agrees to the request.

(9) Nothing in Part 5 of TMA 1970 (appeals and other proceedings) applies to an objection under this paragraph.

Commentary—*Simon's Taxes* **A4.618B**

Consideration of objections

11 (1) HMRC must consider any objections made under paragraph 10 within 30 working days of being given the notice of objection.

(2) Having considered the objections, HMRC must decide whether—

(*a*) to cancel the hold notice,

(*b*) to cancel the effect of the hold notice in relation to the held amount, or any part of the held amount, in respect of a particular account or accounts, or (*c*) to dismiss the objection.

(3) HMRC must give a notice stating its decision to—

(*a*) P,

(*b*) each person other than P who objected, and

(*c*) any other person who HMRC considers is affected by the decision and is—

(i) a person who holds a relevant account of which P is also a holder and in respect of whom prescribed information is provided under paragraph 8(2)(*c*), or

(ii) an interested third party in relation to a relevant account in respect of whom sufficient information has been given in the notice under paragraph 8(2) to enable HMRC to give a notice.

(4) HMRC must, by a notice to the deposit-taker—

(*a*) if it makes a decision under sub-paragraph (2)(*a*), cancel the hold notice;

(*b*) if it makes a decision under sub-paragraph (2)(*b*), cancel the effect of the hold notice in relation to the accounts or amounts in question.

(5) HMRC must give each person to whom HMRC is required to give a notice under sub-paragraph (3) a copy of any notice given to the deposit-taker under sub-paragraph (4).

(6) Where the deposit-taker is given a notice under sub-paragraph (4), it must as soon as reasonably practicable and, in any event, within the period of 5 working days beginning with the day the notice is given—

(*a*) if the notice is given under sub-paragraph (4)(*a*), cancel the arrangements mentioned in paragraph 6(3), or

(*b*) if the notice is given under sub-paragraph (4)(*b*), make such adjustments to those arrangements as are necessary to give effect to the notice.

(7) In this paragraph references to the effect of a hold notice are to its effect by virtue of paragraph 6(4).

Commentary—*Simon's Taxes* **A4.618B**

Appeals

12 (1) Where HMRC makes a decision under paragraph (*b*) or (*c*) of paragraph 11(2), a person within sub-paragraph (2) may appeal against the hold notice.

(2) The persons who may appeal are—

(*a*) P,

(*b*) any interested third party in relation to an affected account, and

(*c*) any person not falling within paragraph (*a*) or (*b*) who is a holder of an affected account which is a joint account.

(3) An appeal may only be made on one or more of the grounds set out in paragraph 10(3) (and for this purpose the reference in paragraph 10(3)(*c*) to "the objection" is to be read as a reference to the appeal).

(4) An appeal under sub-paragraph (1) must be made—

(*a*) in England and Wales, to the county court, and

(*b*) in Northern Ireland, to a county court.

(5) An appeal under this paragraph may only be made within the period of 30 days beginning—

(*a*) in the case of a person given a notice of HMRC's decision under paragraph 11(3), with the day on which that notice is given to that person, and

(*b*) in the case of any person within sub-paragraph (2)(*b*) or (*c*) to whom such a notice has not been given, the day on which P is given such a notice.

(6) A notice of appeal must state the grounds of appeal.

(7) On an appeal under this paragraph, the court may—

(*a*) cancel the hold notice,

(*b*) cancel the effect of the hold notice in relation to the held amount, or any part of the held amount, in respect of a particular account or accounts, or

(*c*) dismiss the appeal.

(8) Where the deposit-taker is served with an order made by the court under sub-paragraph (7)(*a*) or (*b*), the deposit-taker must as soon as reasonably practicable and, in any event, within the period of 5 working days beginning with the day the notice is given take such steps as are necessary to give effect to the order.

(9) Where an appeal on the ground that the hold notice is causing or will cause the person making the appeal or another person exceptional hardship (or a further appeal following such an appeal) is pending, the court to which the appeal is made may, on an application made by the person who made the appeal—

(*a*) suspend the effect of the hold notice if adequate security is provided in respect of so much of the notified sum as remains unpaid, (*b*) suspend the effect of the hold notice in relation to a particular account if adequate security is provided in respect of the held amount in relation to that account, or

(*c*) suspend the effect of the hold notice in relation to any part of the held amount standing to the credit of a particular account, if adequate security is provided in respect of that part.

(10) In this paragraph references to the effect of a hold notice are to its effect by virtue of paragraph 6(4).

(11) Nothing in Part 5 of TMA 1970 (appeals and other proceedings) applies to an appeal under this paragraph.

Commentary—*Simon's Taxes* **A4.618B**

Deduction notice

13 (1) If it appears to HMRC that a person in respect of whom a hold notice given to a deposit-taker is in force—

(*a*) has failed to pay a relevant sum, and

(*b*) holds an account (or more than one account) with the deposit-taker in respect of which there is a held amount in relation to that sum,

HMRC may give the deposit-taker a deduction notice in respect of that person.

(2) A "deduction notice" is a notice which—

(*a*) specifies the name of the person concerned,

(*b*) specifies one or more affected accounts held by that person with the deposit-taker, and

(*c*) in relation to each such specified account requires the deposit-taker to deduct and pay a qualifying amount (see sub-paragraph (6)) to the Commissioners by a day specified in the notice.

(3) Where a deduction notice specifies a particular affected account—

(*a*) the deduction required to be made in relation to that account by virtue of sub-paragraph (2)(*c*) must be made from the appropriate account, that is to say—

(i) if the deposit-taker has by virtue of the hold notice transferred an amount from the specified account into a suspense account, that suspense account, or

(ii) otherwise, the specified account, and

(*b*) the deposit-taker must not during the period in which the deduction notice is in force do anything, or permit anything to be done (except in accordance with paragraph (*a*)) that would reduce the amount standing to the credit of the appropriate account below the balance required for the purpose of making that deduction.

(4) A deduction notice must explain the effect of sub-paragraph (3)(*b*) and paragraph 14 (penalties).

(5) A deduction notice may not be given in respect of an account unless—

(*a*) the period for making an objection under paragraph 10 has expired and either no objections were made or any objection made has been decided or withdrawn, and

(*b*) if objections were made and decided, the period for appealing under paragraph 12 has expired and any appeal or further appeal has been finally determined.

(6) In this paragraph "qualifying amount", in relation to an affected account, means an amount not exceeding the held amount in relation to that account (as modified, where applicable, under paragraph 9(3)(*b*), 11(6)(*b*) or 12(7)(*b*)).

(7) The total of the qualifying amounts specified in the deduction notice must not exceed the unpaid amount of the notified sum (see paragraph 8(8)).

(8) HMRC must—

(*a*) give a copy of the deduction notice to the person in respect of whom it is given, and

(*b*) in the case of each account in respect of which the notice is given, give a notice to each person within sub-paragraph (9) explaining that a deduction notice has been given in respect of that account and the effect of the deduction notice so far as it relates to that account.

(9) The persons mentioned in sub-paragraph (8)(*b*) are—

(*a*) if the account is a joint account, each person other than P who is a holder of the account, and

(*b*) any person (not falling within paragraph (*a*))—

(i) who is an interested third party in relation to the account whom HMRC knows will be affected by the deduction notice, and

(ii) about whom HMRC has sufficient information to enable it to give the notice under sub-paragraph (8)(*b*).

(10) HMRC may, by a notice given to the deposit-taker, amend or cancel the deduction notice, and where it does so it must—

(*a*) give a copy of the notice under this sub-paragraph to the person in respect of whom the deduction notice was given, and

(*b*) in the case of each account affected by the amendment or cancellation, give a notice to each person within sub-paragraph (9) explaining the effect of the amendment or cancellation so far as it relates to that account.

(11) The deduction notice—

(*a*) comes into force at the time it is given to the deposit-taker, and

(*b*) ceases to be in force at the time—

(i) the deposit-taker is given a notice cancelling it under subparagraph (10), or

(ii) the deposit-taker makes the final payment required by virtue of sub-paragraph (2)(*c*).

Commentary—*Simon's Taxes* **A4.618B**

Cross-references—See the Enforcement by Deduction from Accounts (Imposition of Charges by Deposit-takers) Regulations, SI 2016/44 (conditions for administration fee to be charged by deposit-taker on account holder in respect of administration costs relating to obligations under the direct recovery provisions; and cap on that fee at lower of actual reasonably incurred costs and £55).

Penalties

14 (1) This paragraph applies to a deposit-taker who—

(*a*) fails to comply with an information notice,

(*b*) fails to comply with a hold notice or a deduction notice,

(*c*) fails to comply with an obligation under paragraph 8(2) in accordance with paragraph 8(3) (obligation to notify HMRC of effects of hold notice),

(*d*) fails to comply with an obligation under paragraph 8(4) in accordance with paragraph 8(5) (obligation to notify HMRC if no affected accounts),

(*e*) fails to comply with an obligation under paragraph 9(3) (obligation to cancel or modify effects of hold notice),

(*f*) fails to comply with an obligation under paragraph 11(6) (obligation to cancel or adjust arrangements to give effect to HMRC's decision of objection), or

(*g*) following receipt of an information notice or hold notice in relation to an account or accounts held with the deposit-taker by a person ("the affected person"), makes a disclosure of information to the affected person or any other person in circumstances where that disclosure is likely to prejudice HMRC's ability to use the provisions of this Part of this Schedule to recover a relevant sum owed by the affected person.

(2) In sub-paragraph (1)(*g*), the reference to a disclosure of information does not include the giving of a notice in accordance with paragraph 8(10) to the affected person in respect of a hold notice.

(3) The deposit-taker is liable to a penalty of £300.

(4) If a failure within sub-paragraph (1)(*a*) to (*f*) continues after the day on which notice is given under paragraph 15(1) of a penalty in respect of the failure, the deposit-taker is liable to a further penalty or penalties not exceeding £60 for each subsequent day on which the failure continues.

(5) A failure by a deposit-taker to do anything required to be done within a limited period of time does not give rise to liability to a penalty under this paragraph if the deposit-taker did it within such further time, if any, as HMRC may have allowed.

(6) Liability to a penalty under this paragraph does not arise if the person satisfies HMRC or (on an appeal notified to the tribunal) the tribunal that there is a reasonable excuse for the failure or (as the case may be) disclosure.

(7) For the purposes of this paragraph—

(*a*) where the deposit-taker relies on any other person to do anything, that is not a reasonable excuse unless the deposit-taker took reasonable care to avoid the failure or disclosure, and

(*b*) where the deposit-taker had a reasonable excuse for the failure but the excuse has ceased, the deposit-taker is to be treated as having continued to have the excuse if the failure is remedied without unreasonable delay after the excuse ceased.

Commentary—*Simon's Taxes* **A4.619**

Assessment of penalty

15 (1) Where a deposit-taker becomes liable to a penalty under paragraph 14—

(*a*) HMRC must assess the penalty, and

(*b*) if HMRC does so, it must notify the deposit-taker in writing.

(2) An assessment of a penalty by virtue of paragraph (*a*) of paragraph 14(1) must be made within the period of 12 months beginning with the day on which the deposit-taker becomes liable to the penalty.

(3) An assessment of a penalty under any of paragraphs (*b*) to (*g*) of paragraph 14(1) must be made within the period of 12 months beginning with the latest of the following—

(*a*) the day on which the deposit-taker became liable to the penalty,

(*b*) the end of the period in which notice of an appeal in respect of the hold notice could have been given, and

(*c*) if notice of such an appeal is given, the day on which the appeal is finally determined or withdrawn.

Commentary—*Simon's Taxes* **A4.619**

Appeal against penalty

16 (1) A deposit-taker may appeal against—

(*a*) a decision that a penalty is payable by the deposit-taker under paragraph 14, or

(*b*) a decision as to the amount of such a penalty.

(2) Notice of an appeal must be given to HMRC before the end of the period of 30 days beginning with the day on which the notification under paragraph 15 was given.

(3) Notice of an appeal must state the grounds of appeal.

(4) On an appeal under sub-paragraph (1)(*a*) that is notified to the tribunal (in accordance with Part 5 of TMA 1970: see below) the tribunal may confirm or cancel the decision.

(5) On an appeal under sub-paragraph (1)(*b*) that is notified to the tribunal, the tribunal may—

(*a*) confirm the decision, or

(*b*) substitute for the decision another decision that HMRC had power to make.

(6) Subject to this paragraph and paragraph 17, the provisions of Part 5 of TMA 1970 relating to appeals have effect in relation to appeals under this paragraph as they have effect in relation to an appeal against an assessment to income tax.

Commentary—*Simon's Taxes* **A4.619**

Enforcement of penalty

17 (1) A penalty under paragraph 14 must be paid—

(*a*) before the end of the period of 30 days beginning with the day on which the notification under paragraph 15 was given, or

(*b*) if notice of an appeal against the penalty is given, before the end of the period of 30 days beginning with the day on which the appeal is finally determined or withdrawn.

(2) A penalty under paragraph 14 may be enforced as if it were income tax charged in an assessment and due and payable.

Commentary—*Simon's Taxes* **A4.619**

Protection of deposit-takers acting in good faith

18 A deposit-taker is not liable for damages in respect of anything done in good faith for the purposes of complying with a hold notice or a deduction notice.

Power to modify amounts and time limits

19 (1) The Commissioners may by regulations amend any of the following provisions by substituting a different amount for the amount for the time being specified there—

(*a*) paragraph 2(2) (requirement that relevant sum is a minimum amount);

(*b*) paragraph 4(6) and (8) (threshold for safeguarded amount);

(*c*) paragraph 14(3) or (4) (level of penalties).

(2) The Commissioners may by regulations amend any of the following provisions by substituting a different period for the period for the time being specified there—

(*a*) paragraph 3(4) (time limit for complying with information notices);

(*b*) paragraph 6(2) (time limit for complying with hold notices);

(*c*) paragraph 8(3) or (5) (time limit for notifying HMRC of effects of hold notice);

(*d*) paragraph 9(3) (cancellation etc of hold notice: time limit for cancelling or adjusting arrangements);

(*e*) paragraph 10(5) (time limit for making objections);

(*f*) paragraph 11(1) (time limit for consideration of objections);

(*g*) paragraph 11(6) (consideration of objections: time limit for cancelling or adjusting arrangements);

(*h*) paragraph 12(8) (appeals: time limit for compliance with court order).

Power to make further provision

20 (1) The Commissioners may by regulations make provision supplementing this Part of this Schedule.

(2) The regulations may, in particular, make provision—

(*a*) about the manner in which a notice or a copy of a notice is to be given under this Part of this Schedule, or the circumstances in which a notice or a copy of a notice is to be treated as given, for the purposes of this Part of this Schedule;

(*b*) specifying circumstances in which a notice under this Part of this Schedule may not be given;

(*c*) specifying descriptions of account in respect of which a hold notice or deduction notice has no effect;

(*d*) specifying circumstances in which amounts standing to the credit of an account are to be treated as not standing to the credit of the account for the purposes of a hold notice or deduction notice;

(*e*) about fees a deposit-taker may charge a person in respect of whom a notice is given under this Part of this Schedule towards administrative costs in complying with that notice;

(*f*) with respect to priority as between a notice under this Part of this Schedule and—

(i) any other such notice, or

(ii) any notice or order under any other enactment.

Regulations—Enforcement by Deduction from Accounts (Imposition of Charges by Deposit-takers) Regulations, SI 2016/44.

Regulations

21 (1) Regulations under this Part of this Schedule may—

(*a*) make different provision for different purposes,

(*b*) include supplementary, incidental and consequential provision, or

(*c*) make transitional provision and savings.

(2) Regulations under this Part of this Schedule are to be made by statutory instrument.

(3) A statutory instrument containing only regulations within sub-paragraph (4) is subject to annulment in pursuance of a resolution of the House of Commons.

(4) The regulations within this sub-paragraph are—

(*a*) regulations which prescribe information for the purposes of paragraph 3(2) or any provision of paragraph 8,

(*b*) regulations under paragraph 4(10),

(*c*) regulations under paragraph (*a*), (*b*), (*c*), (*d*), (*g*) or (*h*) of paragraph 19(2), or

(*d*) regulations under paragraph 20(2).

(5) Any other statutory instrument containing regulations under this Part of this Schedule may not be made unless a draft of the instrument has been laid before, and approved by a resolution of, the House of Commons.

Joint accounts

22 In this Part of this Schedule a reference to an account held by a person includes a reference to a joint account held by that person and one or more other persons.

Defined terms

23 (1) In this Part of this Schedule—

"affected account" has the meaning given by paragraph 6(7);

"the Commissioners" means the Commissioners for Her Majesty's Revenue and Customs;

"contract settlement" means an agreement made in connection with any person's liability to make a payment to the Commissioners under or by virtue of an enactment;

"deduction notice" has the meaning given by paragraph 13;

"deposit-taker" means a person who may lawfully accept deposits in the United Kingdom in the course of a business (see sub-paragraph (2));

"HMRC" means Her Majesty's Revenue and Customs;

"hold notice" has the meaning given by paragraph 4;

"information notice" has the meaning given by paragraph 3;

"interested third party", in relation to a relevant account, has the meaning given by paragraph 8(11);

"joint account", in relation to a person, means an account held by the person and one or more other persons;

"notice" means notice in writing;

"notified sum", in relation to a hold notice, has the meaning given by paragraph 8(8);

"prescribed" means prescribed by regulations made by the Commissioners;

"relevant account" (in relation to a hold notice) has the meaning given by paragraph 6(6);

"relevant sum", in relation to a person, has the meaning given by paragraph 2(1);

"the safeguarded amount" (in relation to a hold notice) means the amount specified as the safeguarded amount in the notice (see paragraph 4(2)(*c*));

"the specified amount" (in relation to a hold notice) means the amount specified as such in the notice (see paragraph 4(2)(*b*));

"suspense account" has the meaning given by paragraph 6(3)(*b*)(i);

"the tribunal" means the First-tier Tribunal;

"working day" means a day other than—

(*a*) Saturday or Sunday,
(*b*) Christmas Eve, Christmas Day or Good Friday, or
(*c*) a day which is a bank holiday under the Banking and Financial Dealings Act 1971 in England and Wales or Northern Ireland.

(2) The definition of "deposit-taker" in sub-paragraph (1) is to be read with—
(*a*) section 22 of the Financial Services and Markets Act 2000 (regulated activities),
(*b*) any relevant order under that section, and
(*c*) Schedule 2 to that Act.

Commentary—*Simon's Taxes* **A4.617**
Regulations—Enforcement by Deduction from Accounts (Prescribed Information) Regulations, SI 2015/1986.

Extent

24 This Part of this Schedule extends to England and Wales and Northern Ireland.

Commentary—*Simon's Taxes* **A4.615**

PART 2
MISCELLANEOUS AMENDMENTS

TMA 1970

25 In section 28C of TMA 1970 (determination of tax where no return delivered), after subsection (4) insert—

"(4A) Where—
(*a*) action is being taken under Part 1 of Schedule 8 to the Finance (No. 2) Act 2015 (enforcement by deduction from accounts) for the recovery of an amount ("the original amount") of tax charged by a determination under this section, and
(*b*) before that action is concluded, the determination is superseded by such a self-assessment as is mentioned in subsection (3),

that action may be continued as if it were action for the purposes of the recovery of so much of the tax charged by the self-assessment as is due and payable, has not been paid and does not exceed the original amount."

Insolvency Act 1986

26 The Insolvency Act 1986 is amended as follows.

27 In section 126 (power to stay or restrain proceedings against company), after subsection (2) insert—

"(3) Subsection (1) applies in relation to any action being taken in respect of the company under Part 1 of Schedule 8 to the Finance (No. 2) Act 2015 (enforcement by deduction from accounts) as it applies in relation to any action or proceeding mentioned in paragraph (*b*) of that subsection."

28 In section 128 (avoidance of attachments, etc), after subsection (2) insert—

"(3) In subsection (1) "attachment" includes a hold notice or a deduction notice under Part 1 of Schedule 8 to the Finance (No. 2) Act 2015 (enforcement by deduction from accounts) and, if subsection (1) has effect in relation to a deduction notice, it also has effect in relation to the hold notice to which the deduction notice relates (whenever the hold notice was given)."

29 In section 130 (consequences of winding-up order), after subsection (3) insert—

"(3A) In subsections (2) and (3), the reference to an action or proceeding includes action in respect of the company under Part 1 of Schedule 8 to the Finance (No. 2) Act 2015 (enforcement by deduction from accounts)."

30 (1) Section 176 (preferential charge on goods distrained) is amended as follows.

(2) For subsection (2) substitute—

"(2) Subsection (2A) applies where—
(*a*) any person (whether or not a landlord or person entitled to rent) has distrained upon the goods or effects of the company, or
(*b*) Her Majesty's Revenue and Customs has been paid any amount from an account of the company under Part 1 of Schedule 8 to the Finance (No. 2) Act 2015 (enforcement by deduction from accounts),

in the period of 3 months ending with the date of the winding-up order.

(2A) Where this subsection applies—

(*a*) in a case within subsection (2)(*a*), the goods or effects, or the proceeds of their sale, and

(*b*) in a case within subsection (2)(*b*), the amount in question, is charged for the benefit of the company with the preferential debts of the company to the extent that the company's property is for the time being insufficient for meeting those debts."

(3) In subsection (3) for "(2)" substitute "(2A)".

(4) Accordingly, in the heading for the section, after "distrained" insert ", etc".

31 In section 183 (effect of execution or attachment (England and Wales)), after subsection (4) insert—

"(4A) For the purposes of this section, Her Majesty's Revenue and Customs is to be regarded as having attached a debt due to a company if it has taken action under Part 1 of Schedule 8 to the Finance (No. 2) Act 2015 (enforcement by deduction for accounts) as a result of which an amount standing to the credit of an account held by the company is—

(*a*) subject to arrangements made under paragraph 6(3) of that Schedule, or

(*b*) the subject of a deduction notice under paragraph 13 of that Schedule."

32 In section 346 (enforcement procedures), after subsection (1) insert—

"(1A) For the purposes of this section, Her Majesty's Revenue and Customs is to be regarded as having attached a debt due to a person if it has taken action under Part 1 of Schedule 8 to the Finance (No. 2) Act 2015 (enforcement by deduction from accounts) as a result of which an amount standing to the credit of an account held by that person is—

(*a*) subject to arrangements made under paragraph 6(3) of that Schedule, or

(*b*) the subject of a deduction notice under paragraph 13 of that Schedule."

33 (1) In section 347 (distress, etc)—

(*a*) for subsection (3) substitute—

"(3) Subsection (3A) applies where—

(*a*) any person (whether or not a landlord or person entitled to rent) has distrained upon the goods or effects of an individual who is adjudged bankrupt before the end of the period of 3 months beginning with the distraint, or

(*b*) Her Majesty's Revenue and Customs has been paid any amount from an account of an individual under Part 1 of Schedule 8 to the Finance (No. 2) Act 2015 (enforcement by deduction from accounts) and the individual is adjudged bankrupt before the end of the period of 3 months beginning with the payment.

(3A) Where this subsection applies—

(*a*) in a case within subsection (3)(*a*), the goods or effects, or the proceeds of their sale, and

(*b*) in a case within subsection (3)(*b*), the amount in question,

is charged for the benefit of the bankrupt's estate with the preferential debts of the bankrupt to the extent that the bankrupt's estate is for the time being insufficient for meeting them.";

(*b*) in subsection (4), for "(3)" substitute "(3A)".

(2) In paragraph 40(3) of Schedule 19 to the Enterprise and Regulatory Reform Act 2013 (which amends section 347(3) of the Insolvency Act 1986 to substitute "made" for "adjudged"), the reference to subsection (3) of section 347 is to be read as a reference to the version of subsection (3) substituted by sub-paragraph (1) of this paragraph.

Insolvency (Northern Ireland) Order 1989

34 The Insolvency (Northern Ireland) Order 1989 (S.I. 1989/2405 (N.I. 19) is amended as follows.

35 In Article 106 (power to stay or restrain proceedings against company), after paragraph (2) insert—

"(3) Paragraph (1) applies in relation to any action being taken in respect of the company under Part 1 of Schedule 8 to the Finance (No. 2) Act 2015 (enforcement by deduction from accounts) as it applies in relation to any action or proceeding mentioned in sub-paragraph (*b*) of that paragraph."

36 In Article 108 (avoidance of sequestration or distress)—

(*a*) the existing text becomes paragraph (1), and

(*b*) after that paragraph insert—

"(2) In paragraph (1) the reference to "sequestration or distress" includes a hold notice or a deduction notice under Part 1 of Schedule 8 to the Finance (No. 2) Act 2015 (enforcement by deduction from accounts) and, if paragraph (1) has effect in relation to a deduction notice, it also has effect in relation to the hold notice to which it relates (whenever the hold notice was given)."

37 In Article 110 (consequences of winding-up order), after paragraph (3) insert—

"(3A) In paragraphs (2) and (3), the reference to an action or proceeding includes action in respect of the company under Part 1 of Schedule 8 to the Finance (No. 2) Act 2015 (enforcement by deduction from accounts)."

38 (1) Article 150 (preferential charge on goods distrained) is amended as follows.

(2) For paragraph (2) substitute—

"(2) Paragraph (2A) applies where—

(*a*) any person has distrained upon the goods or effects of the company, or

(*b*) Her Majesty's Revenue and Customs has been paid any amount from an account of the company under Part 1 of Schedule 8 to the Finance (No. 2) Act 2015 (enforcement by deduction from accounts),

within the 3 months immediately preceding the date of the winding-up order.

(2A) Where this paragraph applies—

(*a*) in a case within paragraph (2)(*a*), the goods or effects, or the proceeds of their sale, and

(*b*) in a case within paragraph (2)(*b*), the amount in question,

is charged for the benefit of the company with the preferential debts of the company to the extent that the company's property is for the time being insufficient for meeting those debts."

(3) In paragraph (3) for "(2)" substitute "(2A)".

(4) Accordingly, in the heading for the Article after "distrained" insert ", etc".

39 (1) Article 301 (preferential charge on goods distrained) is amended as follows.

(2) For paragraph (1) substitute—

"(1) Paragraph (1A) applies where—

(*a*) any person has distrained upon the goods or effects of an individual who is adjudged bankrupt within 3 months from the distraint, or

(*b*) Her Majesty's Revenue and Customs has been paid any amount from an account of an individual under Part 1 of Schedule 8 to the Finance (No. 2) Act 2015 (enforcement by deduction from accounts) and the individual is adjudged bankrupt within 3 months from the payment.

(1A) Where this paragraph applies—

(*a*) in a case within paragraph (1)(*a*), the goods or effects, or the proceeds of their sale, and

(*b*) in a case within paragraph (1)(*b*), the amount in question,

is charged for the benefit of the bankrupt's estate with the preferential debts of the bankrupt to the extent that the bankrupt's estate is for the time being insufficient for meeting them."

(3) In paragraph (2) for "(1)" substitute "(1A)".

FA 1998

40 In Schedule 18 to FA 1998 (company tax returns, assessments etc), in paragraph 40, after sub-paragraph (4) insert—

"(5) Where—

(*a*) action is being taken under Part 1 of Schedule 8 to the Finance (No. 2) Act 2015 (enforcement of deduction from accounts) for the recovery of an amount ("the original amount") of any tax charged by a determination under paragraph 36 or 37, and

(*b*) before that action is concluded, the determination is superseded by a self-assessment,

that action may be continued as if it were action for the purposes of the recovery of so much of the tax charged by the self-assessment as is due and payable, has not been paid and does not exceed the original amount."

FA 2003

41 In Schedule 10 to FA 2003 (stamp duty land tax: returns etc), in paragraph 27, after sub-paragraph (3) insert—

"(4) Where—

(*a*) action is being taken under Part 1 of Schedule 8 to the Finance (No. 2) Act 2015 (enforcement of deduction from accounts) for the recovery of an amount ("the original amount") of tax charged by a Revenue determination, and

(*b*) before that action is concluded, the determination is superseded by a self-assessment,

that action may be continued as if it were action for the purposes of the recovery of so much of the tax charged by the self-assessment as is due and payable, has not yet been paid and does not exceed the original amount."

FA 2013

42 In Schedule 33 to FA 2013 (annual tax on enveloped dwellings: returns etc), in paragraph 20, after sub-paragraph (3) insert—

"(4) Where—

(*a*) action is being taken under Part 1 of Schedule 8 to the Finance (No. 2) Act 2015 (enforcement of deduction from accounts) for the recovery of an amount ("the original amount") of tax charged by an HMRC determination, and

(*b*) before that action is concluded, the determination is superseded by a self-assessment,

that action may be continued as if it were action for the purposes of the recovery of so much of the tax charged by the self-assessment as is due and payable, has not yet been paid and does not exceed the original amount."

FINANCE ACT 2016

2016 Chapter 24

An Act to grant certain duties, to alter other duties, and to amend the law relating to the National Debt and the Public Revenue, and to make further provision in connection with finance.

15 September 2016

CONTENTS

PART 5
INHERITANCE TAX ETC

93 Inheritance tax: increased nil-rate band

Schedule 15 contains provision in connection with the increased nil-rate band provided for by section 8D of IHTA 1984 (extra nil-rate band on death if interest in home goes to descendants etc).

94 Inheritance tax: pension drawdown funds

(1) IHTA 1984 is amended as follows.

(2) In the italic heading before section 10, at the end insert "(and omissions that do not give rise to deemed dispositions)".

(3) In section 12(2G) (interpretation of section 12(2ZA)), in the definition of "entitled", for "166(2)" substitute "167(1A), or section 166(2),".

(4) After section 12 insert—

"12A Pension drawdown fund not used up: no deemed disposition

(1) Where a person has a drawdown fund, section 3(3) above does not apply in relation to any omission that results in the fund not being used up in the person's lifetime.

(2) For the purposes of subsection (1) above, a person has a drawdown fund if the person has—

(*a*) a member's drawdown pension fund,
(*b*) a member's flexi-access drawdown fund,
(*c*) a dependant's drawdown pension fund,
(*d*) a dependant's flexi-access drawdown fund,
(*e*) a nominee's flexi-access drawdown fund, or
(*f*) a successor's flexi-access drawdown fund, and

in respect of a money purchase arrangement under a registered pension scheme.

(3) For the purposes of subsection (1) above, a person also has a drawdown fund if sums or assets held for the purposes of a money purchase arrangement under a corresponding scheme would, if that scheme were a registered pension scheme, be the person's—

(*a*) member's drawdown pension fund,
(*b*) member's flexi-access drawdown fund,
(*c*) dependant's drawdown pension fund,
(*d*) dependant's flexi-access drawdown fund,
(*e*) nominee's flexi-access drawdown fund, or
(*f*) successor's flexi-access drawdown fund,

in respect of the arrangement.

(4) In this section—

"corresponding scheme" means—

(*a*) a qualifying non-UK pension scheme (see section 271A below), or
(*b*) a section 615(3) scheme that is not a registered pension scheme;

"money purchase arrangement" has the same meaning as in Part 4 of the Finance Act 2004 (see section 152 of that Act);

"member's drawdown pension fund", "member's flexi-access drawdown fund", "dependant's drawdown pension fund", "dependant's flexi-access drawdown fund", "nominee's flexi-access drawdown fund" and "successor's flexi-access drawdown fund" have the meaning given, respectively, by paragraphs 8, 8A, 22, 22A, 27E and 27K of Schedule 28 to that Act."

(5) The amendment made by subsection (4)—

(*a*) so far as relating to a fund within the new section 12A(2)(*a*) or (*c*) (drawdown pension funds), or to a fund within the new section 12A(3) that corresponds to a fund within the new section 12A(2)(*a*) or (*c*)—

(i) has effect where the person who has the fund dies on or after 6 April 2011, and

(ii) is to be treated as having come into force on 6 April 2011, and

(*b*) so far as relating to a fund mentioned in the new section 12A(2)(*b*), (*d*), (*e*) or (*f*) (flexi-access drawdown funds), or to a fund within the new section 12A(3) that corresponds to a fund within the new section 12A(2)(*b*), (*d*), (*e*) or (*f*)—

(i) has effect where the person who has the fund dies on or after 6 April 2015, and

(ii) is to be treated as having come into force on 6 April 2015.

(6) Where an amount paid by way of—

(*a*) inheritance tax, or

(*b*) interest on inheritance tax,

is repayable as a result of the amendment made by subsection (4), section 241(1) of IHTA 1984 applies as if the last date for making a claim for repayment of the amount were 5 April 2020 if that is later than what would otherwise be the last date for that purpose.

95 Inheritance tax: victims of persecution during Second World War era

(1) After section 153 of IHTA 1984 insert—

"Payments to victims of persecution during Second World War era

153ZA Qualifying payments

(1) This section applies where a qualifying payment has at any time been received by a person ("P"), or by the personal representatives of P.

(2) The tax chargeable on the value transferred by the transfer made on P's death (the "value transferred") is to be reduced by an amount equal to—

(*a*) the relevant percentage of the amount of the qualifying payment, or

(*b*) if lower, the amount of tax that would, apart from this section, be chargeable on the value transferred.

(3) In subsection (2) "relevant percentage" means the percentage specified in the last row of the third column of the Table in Schedule 1.

(4) For the purposes of this section, a "qualifying payment" is a payment that meets Condition A, B or C.

(5) Condition A is that the payment—

(*a*) is of a kind specified in Part 1 of Schedule 5A, and

(*b*) is made to a person, or the personal representatives of a person, who was—

(i) a victim of National-Socialist persecution, or

(ii) the spouse or civil partner of a person within sub-paragraph (i).

(6) Condition B is that the payment is of a kind listed in Part 2 of Schedule 5A.

(7) Condition C is that the payment—

(*a*) is of a kind specified in regulations made by the Treasury, and

(*b*) is made to a person, or the personal representatives of a person, who was—

(i) held as a prisoner of war, or a civilian internee, during the Second World War, or

(ii) the spouse or civil partner of a person within sub-paragraph (i).

(8) The Treasury may by regulations add a payment of a specified kind to the list in Part 1 of Schedule 5A.

(9) Regulations under this section are to be made by statutory instrument.

(10) A statutory instrument containing regulations under this section is subject to annulment in pursuance of a resolution of the House of Commons."

(2) After Schedule 5 to IHTA 1984 insert—

"SCHEDULE 5A

QUALIFYING PAYMENTS: VICTIMS OF PERSECUTION DURING SECOND WORLD WAR ERA

Section 153ZA

PART 1

COMPENSATION PAYMENTS

1 *A payment of a fixed amount from the German foundation known as "Remembrance, Responsibility and Future" (Stiftung EVZ)* in respect of a person who was a slave or forced labourer.

2 *A payment of a fixed amount in accordance with the arrangements made under the Swiss Bank Settlement (Holocaust Victim Assets Litigation) in respect of the slave or forced labourers qualifying for compensation under the Remembrance, Responsibility and Future scheme.*

3 *A payment of a fixed amount from the Hardship Fund established by the Government of the Federal Republic of Germany.*

4 *A payment of a fixed amount from the National Fund of the Republic of Austria for Victims of National-Socialism under the terms of the scheme as at June 1995.*

5 *A payment of a fixed amount in respect of a slave or forced labourer from the Austrian Reconciliation Fund.*

6 *A payment of a fixed amount by the Swiss Refugee Programme in accordance with the arrangements made under the Swiss Bank Settlement (Holocaust Victim Assets Litigation) in respect of refugees.*

7 *A payment of a fixed amount under the foundation established in the Netherlands and known as the Dutch Maror Fund (Stichting Maror-Gelden Overheid).*

8 *A one-off payment of a fixed amount from the scheme established by the Government of the French Republic and known as the French Orphan Scheme.*

9 *A payment of a fixed amount from the Child Survivor Fund established by the Government of the Federal Republic of Germany.*

PART 2

EX-GRATIA PAYMENTS

10 *A payment of a fixed amount made from the scheme established by the United Kingdom Government and known as the Far Eastern Prisoners of War Ex Gratia Scheme."*

(3) The amendments made by this section have effect in relation to deaths occurring on or after 1 January 2015.

96 Inheritance tax: gifts for national purposes etc

(1) The Schedule 3 IHTA approval function is transferred to the Treasury.

(2) The "Schedule 3 IHTA approval function" is the function of approval conferred by Schedule 3 to IHTA 1984 in the entry beginning "Any other similar national institution" (and which was initially conferred on the Treasury but, along with other functions, transferred to the Commissioners of Inland Revenue under section 95 of FA 1985).

(3) Subsection (1) does not affect any approval given under Schedule 3 to IHTA 1984 before this Act is passed.

(4) In Schedule 3 to IHTA 1984 (gifts for national purposes, etc), in the entry beginning "Any museum", after "and is" insert "or has been".

97 Estate duty: objects of national, scientific, historic or artistic interest

(1) Section 40 of FA 1930 and section 2 of the Finance Act (Northern Ireland) 1931 (exemption from death duties of objects of national etc interest), so far as continuing to have effect, have effect as if after subsection (2) there were inserted—

"(2A) In the event of the loss of any objects to which this section applies, estate duty shall become chargeable on the value of those objects in respect of the last death on which the objects passed at the rate appropriate to the principal value of the estate passing on that death upon which estate duty is leviable, and with which the objects would have been aggregated if they had not been objects to which this section applies.

(2B) Where subsection (2A) applies, any owner of the objects—

(*a*) shall be accountable for the estate duty, and

(*b*) shall deliver an account for the purposes thereof.

(2C) The account under subsection (2B)(*b*) must be delivered within the period of one month beginning with—

(*a*) in the case of a loss occurring before the coming into force of subsection (2A)—

(i) the coming into force of subsection (2A), or

(ii) if later, the date when the owner became aware of the loss;

(*b*) in the case of a loss occurring after the coming into force of subsection (2A)—

(i) the date of the loss, or

(ii) if later, the date when the owner became aware of the loss.

This is subject to subsection (2E).

(2D) Subsection (2E) applies if—

(*a*) no account has been delivered under subsection (2B),

(*b*) the Commissioners for Her Majesty's Revenue and Customs have by notice required an owner of the objects to confirm that the objects have not been lost,

(*c*) the owner has not so confirmed by the end of—

(i) the period of three months beginning with the day on which the notice was sent, or

(ii) such longer period as the Commissioners may allow, and

(*d*) the Commissioners are satisfied that the objects are lost.

(2E) Where this subsection applies—

(*a*) the objects are to be treated as lost for the purposes of subsection (2A) on the day on which the Commissioners are satisfied as specified in subsection (2D)(*d*), and

(*b*) the account under subsection (2B)(*b*) must be delivered within the period of one month beginning with that date.

(2F) The reference in subsection (2A) to the value of objects is to their value at the time they are lost (or treated as lost).

(2G) Subsection (2A) does not apply in relation to a loss notified to the Commissioners before the coming into force of that subsection.

(2H) In this section "owner", in relation to any objects, means a person who, if the objects were sold, would be entitled to receive (whether for their own benefit or not) the proceeds of sale or any income arising therefrom.

(2I) In this section references to the loss of objects include their theft or destruction; but do not include a loss which the Commissioners are satisfied was outside the owner's control."

(2) Section 48 of FA 1950, so far as continuing to have effect, has effect as if—

(*a*) after subsection (3) there were inserted—

"(3A) But where the value of any objects is chargeable with estate duty under subsection (2A) of the said section forty (loss of objects), no estate duty shall be chargeable under this section on that value.";

(*b*) after subsection (4) there were inserted—

"(5) Where any objects are lost (within the meaning of the said section forty) after becoming chargeable with estate duty under this section in respect of any death, the value of those objects shall not be chargeable with estate duty under subsection (2A) of the said section forty."

(3) Section 39 of FA 1969, so far as continuing to have effect, has effect as if—

(*a*) in subsection (1)—

(i) after "subsection (2)" there were inserted "or (2A)";

(ii) after "other disposal" there were inserted "or loss";

(*b*) in subsection (2), after "subsection (2)" there were inserted ", (2A)";

(*c*) in subsection (3)—

(i) after "subsection (2)" there were inserted ", (2A)";

(ii) for the words from "the amount" to the end there were substituted "the amount in respect of which estate duty is chargeable under the said subsection".

(4) Section 6 of the Finance Act (Northern Ireland) 1969, so far as continuing to have effect as originally enacted, has effect as if—

(*a*) in subsection (1)—

(i) after "subsection (2)" there were inserted "or (2A)";

(ii) after "sale" there were inserted "or loss";

(*b*) in subsection (2)—

(i) for "sale" there were substituted "event";

(ii) after "subsection (2)" there were inserted "or (2A)";

(*c*) in subsection (3)—

(i) for "sale" there were substituted "event";

(ii) after "subsection (2)" there were inserted "or (2A)";

(iii) for "the amount of the proceeds of sale" there were substituted "the amount in respect of which estate duty is chargeable under the said subsection".

(5) Section 6 of the Finance Act (Northern Ireland) 1969, so far as continuing to have effect as amended by Article 7 of the Finance (Northern Ireland) Order 1972 (SI 1972/1100 (NI11)) (deaths occurring after the making of that Order), has effect as if—

(*a*) in subsection (1)—

(i) after "subsection (2)" there were inserted "or (2A)";

(ii) after "sale" there were inserted "or loss";

(*b*) in subsection (2), after "subsection (2)" there were inserted "or (2A)";

(*c*) in subsection (3)—

(i) in the opening words, after "subsection (2)" there were inserted "or (2A)";

(ii) in paragraphs (*a*) and (*b*), after "otherwise than on sale" there were inserted "or at the time of the loss".

(6) In section 35 of IHTA 1984 (conditional exemption on death before 7th April 1976), in subsection (2), for paragraphs (*a*) and (*b*) substitute—

"(*a*) tax shall be chargeable under section 32 or 32A (as the case may be), or

(*b*) tax shall be chargeable under Schedule 5, as the Board may elect,".

(7) In Schedule 6 to IHTA 1984 (transition from estate duty), in paragraph 4 (objects of national etc interest left out of account on death)—

(*a*) in sub-paragraph (2), for paragraphs (*a*) and (*b*) substitute—

"(*a*) tax shall be chargeable under section 32 or 32A of this Act (as the case may be), or

(*b*) estate duty shall be chargeable under those provisions,

as the Board may elect,", and

(*b*) in sub-paragraph (4), after "40(2)" insert "or (2A)".

(8) Subsections (6) and (7) have effect in relation to a chargeable event where the conditionally exempt transfer referred to in section 35(2) of or paragraph 4(2) of Schedule 6 to IHTA 1984 occurred after 16 March 2016.

PART 10
TAX AVOIDANCE AND EVASION

General anti-abuse rule

156 General anti-abuse rule: provisional counteractions

(1) In Part 5 of FA 2013 (general anti-abuse rule), after section 209 insert—

"209A Effect of adjustments specified in a provisional counteraction notice

(1) Adjustments made by an officer of Revenue and Customs which—

(*a*) are specified in a provisional counteraction notice given to a person by the officer (and have not been cancelled: see sections 209B to 209E),

(*b*) are made in respect of a tax advantage that would (ignoring this Part) arise from tax arrangements that are abusive, and

(*c*) but for section 209(6)(*a*), would have effected a valid counteraction of that tax advantage under section 209,

are treated for all purposes as effecting a valid counteraction of the tax advantage under that section.

(2) A "provisional counteraction notice" is a notice which—

(*a*) specifies adjustments (the "notified adjustments") which the officer reasonably believes may be required under section 209(1) to counteract a tax advantage that would (ignoring this Part) arise to the person from tax arrangements;

(*b*) specifies the arrangements and the tax advantage concerned, and

(*c*) notifies the person of the person's rights of appeal with respect to the notified adjustments (when made) and contains a statement that if an appeal is made against the making of the adjustments—

(i) no steps may be taken in relation to the appeal unless and until the person is given a notice referred to in section 209F(2), and

(ii) the notified adjustments will be cancelled if HMRC fails to take at least one of the actions mentioned in section 209B(4) within the period specified in section 209B(2).

(3) It does not matter whether the notice is given before or at the same time as the making of the adjustments.

(4) In this section "adjustments" includes adjustments made in any way permitted by section 209(5).

209B Notified adjustments: 12 month period for taking action if appeal made

(1) This section applies where a person (the "taxpayer") to whom a provisional counteraction notice has been given appeals against the making of the notified adjustments.

(2) The notified adjustments are to be treated as cancelled with effect from the end of the period of 12 months beginning with the day on which the provisional counteraction notice is given unless an action mentioned in subsection (4) is taken before that time.

(3) For the purposes of subsection (2) it does not matter whether the action mentioned in subsection (4)(*c*), (*d*) or (*e*) is taken before or after the provisional counteraction notice is given (but if that action is taken before the provisional counteraction notice is given subsection (5) does not have effect).

(4) The actions are—

(*a*) an officer of Revenue and Customs notifying the taxpayer that the notified adjustments are cancelled;

(*b*) an officer of Revenue and Customs giving the taxpayer written notice of the withdrawal of the provisional counteraction notice (without cancelling the notified adjustments);

(*c*) a designated HMRC officer giving the taxpayer a notice under paragraph 3 of Schedule 43 which—

(i) specifies the arrangements and the tax advantage which are specified in the provisional counteraction notice, and

(ii) specifies the notified adjustments (or lesser adjustments) as the counteraction that the officer considers ought to be taken (see paragraph 3(2)(*c*) of that Schedule);

(*d*) a designated HMRC officer giving the taxpayer a pooling notice or a notice of binding under Schedule 43A which—

(i) specifies the arrangements and the tax advantage which are specified in the provisional counteraction notice, and

(ii) specifies the notified adjustments (or lesser adjustments) as the counteraction that the officer considers ought to be taken;

(*e*) a designated HMRC officer giving the taxpayer a notice under paragraph 1(2) of Schedule 43B which—

(i) specifies the arrangements and the tax advantage which are specified in the provisional counteraction notice, and

(ii) specifies the notified adjustments (or lesser adjustments) as the counteraction that the officer considers ought to be taken.

(5) In a case within subsection (4)(*c*), (*d*) or (*e*), if—

(*a*) the notice under paragraph 3 of Schedule 43, or

(*b*) the pooling notice or notice of binding, or

(*c*) the notice under paragraph 1(2) of Schedule 43B,

(as the case may be) specifies lesser adjustments the officer must modify the notified adjustments accordingly.

(6) The officer may not take the action in subsection (4)(*b*) unless the officer was authorised to make the notified adjustments otherwise than under this Part.

(7) In this section "lesser adjustments" means adjustments which assume a smaller tax advantage than was assumed in the provisional counteraction notice.

209C Notified adjustments: case within section 209B(4)(*c*)

(1) This section applies if the action in section 209B(4)(*c*) (notice to taxpayer of proposed counteraction of tax advantage) is taken.

(2) If the matter is not referred to the GAAR Advisory Panel, the notified adjustments are to be treated as cancelled with effect from the date of the designated HMRC officer's decision under paragraph 6(2) of Schedule 43 unless the notice under paragraph 6(3) of Schedule 43 states that the adjustments are not to be treated as cancelled under this section.

(3) A notice under paragraph 6(3) of Schedule 43 may not contain the statement referred to in subsection (2) unless HMRC would have been authorised to make the adjustments if the general anti-abuse rule did not have effect.

(4) If the taxpayer is given a notice under paragraph 12 of Schedule 43 which states that the specified tax advantage is not to be counteracted under the general anti-abuse rule, the notified adjustments are to be treated as cancelled unless that notice states that those adjustments are not to be treated as cancelled under this section.

(5) A notice under paragraph 12 of Schedule 43 may not contain the statement referred to in subsection (4) unless HMRC would have been authorised to make the adjustments if the general anti-abuse rule did not have effect.

(6) If the taxpayer is given a notice under paragraph 12 of Schedule 43 stating that the specified tax advantage is to be counteracted—

(*a*) the notified adjustments are confirmed only so far as they are specified in that notice as adjustments required to give effect to the counteraction, and

(*b*) so far as they are not confirmed, the notified adjustments are to be treated as cancelled.

209D Notified adjustments: case within section 209B(4)(*d*)

(1) This section applies if the action in section 209B(4)(*d*) (pooling notice or notice of binding) is taken.

(2) If the taxpayer is given a notice under paragraph 8(2) or 9(2) of Schedule 43A which states that the specified tax advantage is not to be counteracted under the general anti-abuse rule, the notified adjustments are to be treated as cancelled, unless that notice states that those adjustments are not to be treated as cancelled under this section.

(3) A notice under paragraph 8(2) or 9(2) of Schedule 43A may not contain the statement referred to in subsection (2) unless HMRC would have been authorised to make the adjustments if the general anti-abuse rule did not have effect.

(4) If the taxpayer is given a notice under paragraph 8(2) or 9(2) of Schedule 43A stating that the specified tax advantage is to be counteracted—

(*a*) the notified adjustments are confirmed only so far as they are specified in that notice as adjustments required to give effect to the counteraction, and

(*b*) so far as they are not confirmed, the notified adjustments are to be treated as cancelled.

209E Notified adjustments: case within section 209B(4)(*e*)

(1) This section applies if the action in section 209B(4)(*e*) (notice of proposal to make generic referral) is taken.

(2) If the notice under paragraph 1(2) of Schedule 43B is withdrawn, the notified adjustments are to be treated as cancelled unless the notice of withdrawal states that the adjustments are not to be treated as cancelled under this section.

(3) The notice of withdrawal may not contain the statement referred to in subsection (2) unless HMRC was authorised to make the notified adjustments otherwise than under this Part.

(4) If the taxpayer is given a notice under paragraph 8(2) of Schedule 43B, which states that the specified tax advantage is not to be counteracted under the general anti-abuse rule, the notified adjustments are to be treated as cancelled, unless that notice states that those adjustments are not to be treated as cancelled under this section.

(5) A notice under paragraph 8(2) of Schedule 43B may not contain the statement referred to in subsection (4) unless HMRC was authorised to make the adjustments otherwise than under this Part.

(6) If the taxpayer is given a notice under paragraph 8(2) of Schedule 43B stating that the specified tax advantage is to be counteracted—

(*a*) the notified adjustments are confirmed only so far as they are specified in that notice as adjustments required to give effect to the counteraction, and

(*b*) so far as they are not confirmed, the notified adjustments are to be treated as cancelled.

209F Appeals against provisional counteractions: further provision

(1) Subsections (2) to (5) have effect in relation to an appeal by a person ("the taxpayer") against the making of adjustments which are specified in a provisional counteraction notice.

(2) No steps after the initial notice of appeal are to be taken in relation to the appeal unless and until the taxpayer is given—

(*a*) a notice under section 209B(4)(*b*),

(*b*) a notice under paragraph 6(3) of Schedule 43 (notice of decision not to refer matter to GAAR advisory panel) containing the statement described in section 209C(2) (statement that adjustments are not to be treated as cancelled),

(*c*) a notice under paragraph 12 of Schedule 43,

(*d*) a notice under paragraph 8(2) or 9(2) of Schedule 43A, or

(*e*) a notice under paragraph 8 of Schedule 43B,

in respect of the tax arrangements concerned.

(3) The taxpayer has until the end of the period mentioned in subsection (4) to comply with any requirement to specify the grounds of appeal.

(4) The period mentioned in subsection (3) is the 30 days beginning with the day on which the taxpayer receives the notice mentioned in subsection (2).

(5) In subsection (2) the reference to "steps" does not include the withdrawal of the appeal."

(2) In section 214(1) of FA 2013 (interpretation of Part 5), at the appropriate place insert—

""notified adjustments", in relation to a provisional counteraction notice, has the meaning given by section 209A(2);"

""provisional counteraction notice" has the meaning given by section 209A(2);".

(3) The amendments made by this section have effect in relation to tax arrangements (within the meaning of Part 5 of FA 2013) entered into at any time (whether before or on or after the day on which this Act is passed).

157 General anti-abuse rule: binding of tax arrangements to lead arrangements

(1) Part 5 of FA 2013 (general anti-abuse rule) is amended in accordance with subsections (2) to (11).

(2) After Schedule 43 insert—

"SCHEDULE 43A

PROCEDURAL REQUIREMENTS: POOLING NOTICES AND NOTICES OF BINDING

Pooling notices

1 (1) This paragraph applies where a person has been given a notice under paragraph 3 of Schedule 43 in relation to any tax arrangements (the "lead arrangements") and the condition in sub-paragraph (2) is met.

(2) The condition is that the period of 45 days mentioned in paragraph 4(1) of Schedule 43 has expired but no notice under paragraph 12 of Schedule 43 or paragraph 8 of Schedule 43B has yet been given in respect of the matter.

(3) If a designated HMRC officer considers—

(*a*) that a tax advantage has arisen to another person ("R") from tax arrangements that are abusive,

(*b*) that those tax arrangements ("R's arrangements") are equivalent to the lead arrangements, and

(*c*) that the advantage ought to be counteracted under section 209,

the officer may give R a notice (a "pooling notice") which places R's arrangements in a pool with the lead arrangements.

(4) There is one pool for any lead arrangements, so all tax arrangements placed in a pool with the lead arrangements (as well as the lead arrangements themselves) are in one and the same pool.

(5) Tax arrangements which have been placed in a pool do not cease to be in the pool except where that is expressly provided for by this Schedule (regardless of whether or not the lead arrangements or any other tax arrangements remain in the pool).

(6) The officer may not give R a pooling notice if R has been given in respect of R's arrangements a notice under paragraph 3 of Schedule 43.

Notice of proposal to bind arrangements to counteracted arrangements

2 (1) This paragraph applies where a counteraction notice has been given to a person in relation to any tax arrangements (the "counteracted arrangements") which are in a pool created under paragraph 1.

(2) If a designated HMRC officer considers—

(*a*) that a tax advantage has arisen to another person ("R") from tax arrangements that are abusive,

(*b*) that those tax arrangements ("R's arrangements") are equivalent to the counteracted arrangements, and

(*c*) that the advantage ought to be counteracted under section 209,

the officer may give R a notice (a "notice of binding") in relation to R's arrangements.

(3) The officer may not give R a notice of binding if R has been given in respect of R's arrangements a notice under—

(*a*) paragraph 1, or

(*b*) paragraph 3 of Schedule 43.

(4) In this paragraph "counteraction notice" means a notice such as is mentioned in sub-paragraph (2) of paragraph 12 of Schedule 43 or sub-paragraph (3) of paragraph 8 of Schedule 43B (notice of final decision to counteract).

3 (1) The decision whether or not to give R a pooling notice or notice of binding must be taken, and any notice must be given, as soon as is reasonably practicable after HMRC becomes aware of the relevant facts.

(2) A pooling notice or notice of binding must—

(*a*) specify the tax arrangements in relation to which the notice is given and the tax advantage,

(*b*) explain why the officer considers R's arrangements to be equivalent to the lead arrangements or the counteracted arrangements (as the case may be),

(*c*) explain why the officer considers that a tax advantage has arisen to R from tax arrangements that are abusive,

(*d*) set out the counteraction that the officer considers ought to be taken, and

(*e*) explain the effect of—

(i) paragraphs 4 to 10,

(ii) subsection (9) of section 209, and

(iii) section 212A.

(3) A pooling notice or notice of binding may set out steps that R may (subject to subsection (9) of section 209) take to avoid the proposed counteraction.

Corrective action by a notified taxpayer

4 (1) If a person to whom a pooling notice or notice of binding has been given takes the relevant corrective action in relation to the tax arrangements and tax advantage specified in the notice before the beginning of the closed period mentioned in section 209(9), the person is to be treated for the purposes of paragraphs 8 and 9 and Schedule 43B (generic referral of tax arrangements) as not having been given the notice in question (and accordingly the tax arrangements in question are no longer in the pool).

(2) For the purposes of this Schedule the "relevant corrective action" is taken if (and only if) the person takes the steps set out in sub-paragraphs (3) and (4).

(3) The first step is that—

(*a*) the person amends a return or claim to counteract the tax advantage specified in the pooling notice or notice of binding, or

(*b*) if the person has made a tax appeal (by notifying HMRC or otherwise) on the basis that the tax advantage specified in the pooling notice or notice of binding arises from the tax arrangements specified in that notice, the person takes all necessary action to enter into an agreement with HMRC (in writing) for the purpose of relinquishing that advantage.

(4) The second step is that the person notifies HMRC—

(*a*) that the first step has been taken, and

(*b*) of any additional amount which has or will become due and payable in respect of tax by reason of the first step being taken.

(5) Where a person takes the first step described in sub-paragraph (3)(*b*), HMRC may proceed as if the person had not taken the relevant corrective action if the person fails to enter into the written agreement.

(6) In determining the additional amount which has or will become due and payable in respect of tax for the purposes of sub-paragraph (4)(*b*), it is to be assumed that, where the person takes the necessary action as mentioned in sub-paragraph (3)(*b*), the agreement is then entered into.

(7) No enactment limiting the time during which amendments may be made to returns or claims operates to prevent the person taking the first step mentioned in sub-paragraph (3)(*a*) before the tax enquiry is closed.

(8) No appeal may be brought, by virtue of a provision mentioned in sub-paragraph (9), against an amendment made by a closure notice in respect of a tax enquiry to the extent that the amendment takes into account an amendment made by the taxpayer to a return or claim in taking the first step mentioned in sub-paragraph (3)(*a*).

(9) The provisions are—

(*a*) paragraph 35(1)(*b*) of Schedule 33,

(*b*) section 31(1)(*b*) or (*c*) of TMA 1970,
(*c*) paragraph 9 of Schedule 1A to TMA 1970,
(*d*) paragraph 34(3) of Schedule 18 to FA 1998, and
(*e*) paragraph 35(1)(*b*) of Schedule 10 to FA 2003.

Corrective action by lead taxpayer

5 If the person mentioned in paragraph 1(1) takes the relevant corrective action (as defined in paragraph 4A of Schedule 43) before the end of the period of 75 days beginning with the day on which the notice mentioned in paragraph 1(1) was given to that person, the lead arrangements are treated as ceasing to be in the pool.

Opinion notices and right to make representations

6 (1) Sub-paragraph (2) applies where—
(*a*) a pooling notice is given to a person in relation to any tax arrangements, and
(*b*) an opinion notice (or opinion notices) under paragraph 11(2) of Schedule 43 about another set of tax arrangements in the pool ("the referred arrangements") is subsequently given to a designated HMRC officer.

(2) The officer must give the person a pooled arrangements opinion notice.

(3) No more than one pooled arrangements opinion notice may be given to a person in respect of the same tax arrangements.

(4) Where a designated HMRC officer gives a person a notice of binding, the officer must, at the same time, give the person a bound arrangements opinion notice.

7 (1) In relation to a person who is, or has been, given a pooling notice, "pooled arrangements opinion notice" means a written notice which—
(*a*) sets out a report prepared by HMRC of any opinion of the GAAR Advisory Panel about the referred arrangements,
(*b*) explains the person's right to make representations falling within sub-paragraph (3), and
(*c*) sets out the period in which those representations may be made.

(2) In relation to a person who is given a notice of binding "bound arrangements opinion notice" means a written notice which—
(*a*) sets out a report prepared by HMRC of any opinion of the GAAR Advisory Panel about the counteracted arrangements (see paragraph 2(1)),
(*b*) explains the person's right to make representations falling within sub-paragraph (3), and
(*c*) sets out the period in which those representations may be made.

(3) A person who is given a pooled arrangements opinion notice or a bound arrangements opinion notice has 30 days beginning with the day on which the notice is given to make representations in any of the following categories—
(*a*) representations that no tax advantage has arisen to the person from the arrangements to which the notice relates;
(*b*) representations as to why the arrangements to which the notice relates are or may be materially different from—
(i) the referred arrangements (in the case of a pooled arrangements opinion notice), or
(ii) the counteracted arrangements (in the case of a bound arrangements opinion notice).

(4) In sub-paragraph (3)(*b*) references to "arrangements" include any circumstances which would be relevant in accordance with section 207 to a determination of whether the tax arrangements in question are abusive.

Notice of final decision

8 (1) This paragraph applies where—
(*a*) any tax arrangements have been placed in a pool by a notice given to a person under paragraph 1, and
(*b*) a designated HMRC officer has given a notice under paragraph 12 of Schedule 43 in

relation to any other arrangements in the pool (the "referred arrangements").(2) The officer must, having considered any opinion of the GAAR Advisory Panel about the referred arrangements and any representations made under paragraph 7(3) in relation to the arrangements mentioned in sub-paragraph (1)(*a*), give the person a written notice setting out whether the tax advantage arising from those arrangements is to be counteracted under the general anti-abuse rule.

9 (1) This paragraph applies where—

(*a*) a person has been given a notice of binding under paragraph 2, and

(*b*) the period of 30 days for making representations under paragraph 7(3) has expired.

(2) A designated HMRC officer must, having considered any opinion of the GAAR Advisory Panel about the counteracted arrangements and any representations made under paragraph 7(3) in relation to the arrangements specified in the notice of binding, give the person a written notice setting out whether the tax advantage arising from the arrangements specified in the notice of binding is to be counteracted under the general anti-abuse rule.

10 *If a notice under paragraph 8(2) or 9(2) states that a tax advantage is to be counteracted, it must also set out—*

(*a*) the adjustments required to give effect to the counteraction, and

(*b*) if relevant, any steps the person concerned is required to take to give effect to it.

"Equivalent arrangements"

11 (1) For the purposes of paragraph 1, tax arrangements are "equivalent" to one another if they are substantially the same as one another having regard to—

(*a*) their substantive results,

(*b*) the means of achieving those results, and

(*c*) the characteristics on the basis of which it could reasonably be argued, in each case, that the arrangements are abusive tax arrangements under which a tax advantage has arisen to a person.

Notices may be given on assumption that tax advantage does arise

12 (1) A designated HMRC officer may give a notice, or do anything else, under this Schedule where the officer considers that a tax advantage might have arisen to the person concerned.

(2) Accordingly, any notice given by a designated HMRC officer under this Schedule may be expressed to be given on the assumption that a tax advantage does arise (without conceding that it does).

Power to amend

13 (1) The Treasury may by regulations amend this Schedule (apart from this paragraph).

(2) Regulations under sub-paragraph (1) may include—

(*a*) any amendment of this Part that is appropriate in consequence of an amendment by virtue of sub-paragraph (1);

(*b*) transitional provision.

(3) Regulations under sub-paragraph (1) are to be made by statutory instrument.

(4) A statutory instrument containing regulations under sub-paragraph (1) is subject to annulment in pursuance of a resolution of the House of Commons."

(3) After Schedule 43A insert—

"SCHEDULE 43B

PROCEDURAL REQUIREMENTS: GENERIC REFERRAL OF TAX ARRANGEMENTS

Notice of proposal to make generic referral of tax arrangements

1 (1) Sub-paragraph (2) applies if—

(*a*) pooling notices given under paragraph 1 of Schedule 43A have placed one or more sets of tax arrangements in a pool with the lead arrangements,

(*b*) the lead arrangements (see paragraph 1(1) of Schedule 43A) have ceased to be in the pool, and (*c*) no referral under paragraph 5 or 6 of Schedule 43 has been made in respect of any arrangements in the pool.

(2) A designated HMRC officer may determine that, in respect of each of the tax arrangements that are in the pool, there is to be given (to the person to whom the pooling notice in question was given) a written notice of a proposal to make a generic referral to the GAAR Advisory Panel in respect of the arrangements in the pool.

(3) Only one determination under sub-paragraph (2) may be made in relation to any one pool.

(4) The persons to whom those notices are given are "the notified taxpayers".

(5) A notice given to a person ("T") under sub-paragraph (2) must—

(*a*) specify the arrangements (the "specified arrangements") and the tax advantage (the "specified advantage") to which the notice relates,

(*b*) inform T of the period under paragraph 2 for making a proposal.

2 (1) T has 30 days beginning with the day on which the notice under paragraph 1 is given to propose to HMRC that it—

(*a*) should give T a notice under paragraph 3 of Schedule 43 in respect of the arrangements to which the notice under paragraph 1 relates, and

(*b*) should not proceed with the proposal to make a generic referral to the GAAR Advisory Panel in respect of those arrangements.

(2) If a proposal is made in accordance with sub-paragraph (1) a designated HMRC officer must consider it.

Generic referral

3 (1) This paragraph applies where a designated HMRC officer has given notices to the notified taxpayers in accordance with paragraph 1(2).

(2) If none of the notified taxpayers has made a proposal under paragraph 2 by the end of the 30 day period mentioned in that paragraph, the officer must make a referral to the GAAR Advisory Panel in respect of the notified taxpayers and the arrangements which are specified arrangements in relation to them.

(3) If at least one of the notified taxpayers makes a proposal in accordance with paragraph 2, the designated HMRC officer must, after the end of that 30 day period, decide whether to—

(*a*) give a notice under paragraph 3 of Schedule 43 in respect of one set of tax arrangements in the relevant pool, or

(*b*) make a referral to the GAAR Advisory Panel in respect of the tax arrangements in the relevant pool.

(4) A referral under this paragraph is a "generic referral".

4 (1) If a generic referral is made to the GAAR Advisory Panel, the designated HMRC officer must at the same time provide it with—

(*a*) a general statement of the material characteristics of the specified arrangements, and

(*b*) a declaration that—

(i) the statement under paragraph (*a*) is applicable to all the specified arrangements, and

(ii) as far as HMRC is aware, nothing which is material to the GAAR Advisory Panel's consideration of the matter has been omitted.

(2) The general statement under sub-paragraph (1)(*a*) must—

(*a*) contain a factual description of the tax arrangements;

(*b*) set out HMRC's view as to whether the tax arrangements accord with established practice (when the arrangements were entered into);

(*c*) explain why it is the designated HMRC officer's view that a tax advantage of the nature described in the statement and arising from tax arrangements having the characteristics described in the statement would be a tax advantage arising from arrangements that are abusive;

(*d*) set out any matters the designated officer is aware of which may suggest that any view of HMRC or the designated HMRC officer expressed in the general statement is not correct;

(*e*) set out any other matters which the designated officer considers are required for the purposes of the exercise of the GAAR Advisory Panel's functions under paragraph 6.

5 If a generic referral is made the designated HMRC officer must at the same time give each of the notified taxpayers a notice which—

(*a*) specifies that a generic referral is being made, and

(*b*) is accompanied by a copy of the statement given to the GAAR Advisory Panel in accordance with paragraph 4(1)(*a*).

Decision of GAAR Advisory Panel and opinion notices

6 (1) If a generic referral is made to the GAAR Advisory Panel under paragraph 3, the Chair must arrange for a sub-panel consisting of 3 members of the GAAR Advisory Panel (one of whom may be the Chair) to consider it.

(2) The sub-panel must produce—

(*a*) one opinion notice stating the joint opinion of all the members of the sub-panel, or

(*b*) two or three opinion notices which taken together state the opinions of all the members.

(3) The sub-panel must give a copy of the opinion notice or notices to the designated HMRC officer.

(4) An opinion notice is a notice which states that in the opinion of the members of the sub-panel, or one or more of those members—

(*a*) the entering into and carrying out of tax arrangements such as are described in the general statement under paragraph 4(1)(*a*) is a reasonable course of action in relation to the relevant tax provisions,

(*b*) the entering into or carrying out of such tax arrangements is not a reasonable course of action in relation to the relevant tax provisions, or

(*c*) it is not possible, on the information available, to reach a view on that matter,

and the reasons for that opinion.

(5) In forming their opinions for the purposes of sub-paragraph (4) members of the sub-panel must—

(*a*) have regard to all the matters set out in the statement under paragraph 4(1)(*a*),

(*b*) assume (unless the contrary is stated in the statement under paragraph 4(1)(*a*)) that the tax arrangements do not form part of any other arrangements,

(*c*) have regard to the matters mentioned in paragraphs (*a*) to (*c*) of section 207(2), and

(*d*) take account of subsections (4) to (6) of section 207.

(6) For the purposes of the giving of an opinion under this paragraph, the arrangements are to be assumed to be tax arrangements.

(7) In this Part, a reference to any opinion of the GAAR Advisory Panel in respect of a generic referral of any tax arrangements is a reference to the contents of any opinion notice given in relation to a generic referral in respect of the arrangements.

Notice of right to make representations

7 (1) Where a designated HMRC officer is given an opinion notice (or opinion notices) under paragraph 6, the officer must give each of the notified taxpayers a copy of the opinion notice (or notices) and a written notice which—

(*a*) explains the notified taxpayer's right to make representations falling within sub-paragraph (2), and

(*b*) sets out the period in which those representations may be made.

(2) A notified taxpayer ("T") who is given a notice under sub-paragraph (1) has 30 days beginning with the day on which the notice is given to make representations in any of the following categories—

(*a*) representations that no tax advantage has arisen from the specified arrangements;

(*b*) representations that T has already been given a notice under paragraph 6 of Schedule 43A in relation to the specified arrangements;

(*c*) representations that any matter set out in the statement under paragraph 4(1)(*a*) is materially inaccurate as regards the specified arrangements (having regard to all circumstances which would be relevant in accordance with section 207 to a determination of whether the tax arrangements in question are abusive).

Notice of final decision after considering opinion of GAAR Advisory Panel

8 (1) A designated HMRC officer who has received a copy of a notice or notices under paragraph 6(3) in respect of a generic referral must consider the case of each notified taxpayer in accordance with sub-paragraph (2).

(2) The officer must, having considered—

(*a*) any opinion of the GAAR Advisory Panel about the matters referred to it, and

(*b*) any representations made by the notified taxpayer under paragraph 7,

give to the notified taxpayer a written notice setting out whether the specified advantage is to be counteracted under the general anti-abuse rule.

(3) If the notice states that a tax advantage is to be counteracted, it must also set out—

(*a*) the adjustments required to give effect to the counteraction, and

(*b*) if relevant, any steps that the taxpayer is required to take to give effect to it.

Notices may be given on assumption that tax advantage does arise

9 (1) A designated HMRC officer may give a notice, or do anything else, under this Schedule where the officer considers that a tax advantage might have arisen to the person concerned.

(2) Accordingly, any notice given by a designated HMRC officer under this Schedule may be expressed to be given on the assumption that a tax advantage does arise (without conceding that it does).

Power to amend

10 (1) The Treasury may by regulations amend this Schedule (apart from this paragraph).

(2) Regulations under sub-paragraph (1) may include—

(*a*) any amendment of this Part that is appropriate in consequence of an amendment by virtue of sub-paragraph (1);

(*b*) transitional provision.

(3) Regulations under sub-paragraph (1) are to be made by statutory instrument.

(4) A statutory instrument containing regulations under sub-paragraph (1) is subject to annulment in pursuance of a resolution of the House of Commons."

(4) In section 209 (counteracting tax advantages), in subsection (6)(*a*), after "Schedule 43" insert ", 43A or 43B".

(5) In section 210 (consequential relieving adjustments), in subsection (1)(*b*), after "Schedule 43," insert "paragraph 8 or 9 of Schedule 43A or paragraph 8 of Schedule 43B,".

(6) In section 211 (proceedings before a court or tribunal), in subsection (2)(*b*), for the words from "Panel" to the end substitute "Panel given—

(i) under paragraph 11 of Schedule 43 about the arrangements or any tax arrangements which are, as a result of a notice under paragraph 1 or 2 of Schedule 43A, the referred or (as the case may be) counteracted arrangements in relation to the arrangements, or

(ii) under paragraph 6 of Schedule 43B in respect of a generic referral of the arrangements."

(7) Section 214 (interpretation of Part 5) is amended in accordance with subsections (8) to (10).

(8) Renumber section 214 as subsection (1) of section 214.

(9) In subsection (1) (as renumbered), at the appropriate places insert—

""designated HMRC officer" has the meaning given by paragraph 2 of Schedule 43;".

""notice of binding" has the meaning given by paragraph 2(2) of Schedule 43A;

""pooling notice" has the meaning given by paragraph 1(4) of Schedule 43A;"

""tax appeal" has the meaning given by paragraph 1A of Schedule 43;"

""tax enquiry" has the meaning given by section 202(2) of FA 2014."

(10) After subsection (1) insert—

"(2) In this Part references to any "opinion of the GAAR Advisory Panel" about any tax arrangements are to be interpreted in accordance with paragraph 11(5) of Schedule 43.

(3) In this Part references to tax arrangements which are "equivalent" to one another are to be interpreted in accordance with paragraph 11 of Schedule 43A."

(11) In Schedule 43 (general anti-abuse rule: procedural requirements), in paragraph 6, after sub-paragraph (2) insert—

"(3) The officer must, as soon as reasonably practicable after deciding whether or not the matter is to be referred to the GAAR Advisory Panel, give the taxpayer written notice of the decision."

(12) Section 10 of the National Insurance Contributions Act 2014 (GAAR to apply to national insurance contributions) is amended in accordance with subsections (13) to (16).

(13) In subsection (4), at the end insert ", paragraph 8 or 9 of Schedule 43A to that Act (pooling of tax arrangements: notice of final decision) or paragraph 8 of Schedule 43B to that Act (generic referral of arrangements: notice of final decision)".

(14) After subsection (6) insert—

"(6A) Where, by virtue of this section, a case falls within paragraph 4A of Schedule 43 to the Finance Act 2013 (referrals of single schemes: relevant corrective action) or paragraph 4 of Schedule 43A to that Act (pooled schemes: relevant corrective action)—

(*a*) the person ("P") mentioned in sub-paragraph (1) of that paragraph takes the "relevant corrective action" for the purposes of that paragraph if (and only if)—

(i) in a case in which the tax advantage in question can be counteracted by making a payment to HMRC, P makes that payment and notifies HMRC that P has done so, or

(ii) in any case, P takes all necessary action to enter into an agreement in writing with HMRC for the purpose of relinquishing the tax advantage, and

(*b*) accordingly, sub-paragraphs (2) to (8) of that paragraph do not apply."

(15) In subsection (11)—

(*a*) for "and HMRC" substitute ", "HMRC" and "tax advantage"";

(*b*) after "2013" insert "(as modified by this section)".

(16) After subsection (11) insert—

"(12) See section 10A for further modifications of Part 5 of the Finance Act 2013."

(17) After section 10 of the National Insurance Contributions Act 2014 insert—

"10A Application of GAAR in relation to penalties

(1) For the purposes of this section a penalty under section 212A of the Finance Act 2013 is a "relevant NICs-related penalty" so far as the penalty relates to a tax advantage in respect of relevant contributions.

(2) A relevant NICs-related penalty may be recovered as if it were an amount of relevant contributions which is due and payable.

(3) Section 117A of the Social Security Administration Act 1992 or (as the case may be) section 111A of the Social Security Administration (Northern Ireland) Act 1992 (issues arising in proceedings: contributions etc) has effect in relation to proceedings before a court for recovery of a relevant NICs-related penalty as if the assessment of the penalty were a NICs decision as to whether the person is liable for the penalty.

(4) Accordingly, paragraph 5(4)(*b*) of Schedule 43C to the Finance Act 2013 (assessment of penalty to be enforced as if it were an assessment to tax) does not apply in relation to a relevant NICs-related penalty.

(5) In the application of Schedule 43C to the Finance Act 2013 in relation to a relevant NICs-related penalty, paragraph 9(5) has effect as if the reference to an appeal against an assessment to the tax concerned were to an appeal against a NICs decision.

(6) In paragraph 8 of that Schedule (aggregate penalties), references to a "relevant penalty provision" include—

(*a*) any provision mentioned in sub-paragraph (5) of that paragraph, as applied in relation to any class of national insurance contributions by regulations (whenever made);

(*b*) section 98A of the Taxes Management Act 1970, as applied in relation to any class of national insurance contributions by regulations (whenever made);

(*c*) any provision in regulations made by the Treasury under which a penalty can be imposed in respect of any class of national insurance contributions.

(7) The Treasury may by regulations—

(*a*) disapply, or modify the effect of, subsection (6)(*a*) or (*b*);

(*b*) modify paragraph 8 of Schedule 43C to the Finance Act 2013 as it has effect in relation to a relevant penalty provision by virtue of subsection (6)(*b*) or (*c*).

(8) Section 175(3) to (5) of SSCBA 1992 (various supplementary powers) applies to a power to make regulations conferred by subsection (7).

(9) Regulations under subsection (7) must be made by statutory instrument.

(10) A statutory instrument containing regulations under subsection (7) is subject to annulment in pursuance of a resolution of either House of Parliament.

(11) In this section "NICs decision" means a decision under section 8 of the Social Security Contributions (Transfer of Functions, etc) Act 1999 or Article 7 of the Social Security Contributions (Transfer of Functions, etc) (Northern Ireland) Order 1999 (SI 1999/671).

(12) In this section "relevant contributions" means the following contributions under Part 1 of SSCBA 1992 or Part 1 of SSCB(NI)A 1992—

(*a*) Class 1 contributions;

(*b*) Class 1A contributions;

(*c*) Class 1B contributions;

(*d*) Class 2 contributions which must be paid but in relation to which section 11A of the Act in question (application of certain provisions of the Income Tax Acts in relation to Class 2 contributions under section 11(2) of that Act) does not apply."

(18) Section 219 of FA 2014 (circumstances in which an accelerated payment notice may be given) is amended in accordance with subsections (19) and (20).

(19) In subsection (4), after paragraph (*c*) insert—

"(*d*) a notice has been given under paragraph 8(2) or 9(2) of Schedule 43A to FA 2013 (notice of final decision after considering Panel's opinion about referred or counteracted arrangements) in relation to the asserted advantage or part of it and the chosen arrangements (or is so given at the same time as the accelerated payment notice) in a case where the stated opinion of at least two of the members of the sub-panel of the GAAR Advisory Panel about the other arrangements (see subsection (8)) was as set out in paragraph 11(3)(*b*) of Schedule 43 to FA 2013;

(*e*) a notice under paragraph 8(2) of Schedule 43B to FA 2013 (GAAR: generic referral of tax arrangements) has been given in relation to the asserted advantage or part of it and the chosen arrangements (or is so given at the same time as the accelerated payment notice) in a case where the stated opinion of at least two of the members of the sub-panel of the GAAR Advisory Panel which considered the generic referral in respect of those arrangements under paragraph 6 of Schedule 43B to FA 2013 was as set out in paragraph 6(4)(*b*) of that Schedule."

(20) After subsection (7) insert—

"(8) In subsection (4)(*d*) "other arrangements" means—

(*a*) in relation to a notice under paragraph 8(2) of Schedule 43A to FA 2013, the referred arrangements (as defined in that paragraph);

(*b*) in relation to a notice under paragraph 9(2) of that Schedule, the counteracted arrangements (as defined in paragraph 2 of that Schedule).

(21) In section 220 of FA 2014 (content of notice given while a tax enquiry is in progress)—

(*a*) in subsection (4)(*c*), after "219(4)(*c*)" insert ", (*d*) or (*e*)";

(*b*) in subsection (5)(*c*), after "219(4)(*c*)" insert ", (*d*) or (*e*)";

(*c*) in subsection (7), for the words from "under" to the end substitute "under—

(*a*) paragraph 12 of Schedule 43 to FA 2013,

(*b*) paragraph 8 or 9 of Schedule 43A to that Act, or

(*c*) paragraph 8 of Schedule 43B to that Act,

as the case may be."

(22) Section 287 of FA 2014 (Code of Practice on Taxation for Banks) is amended in accordance with subsections (23) to (25).

(23) In subsection (4), after "(5)" insert "or (5A)".

(24) In subsection (5)(*b*), after "Schedule" insert "or paragraph 8 or 9 of Schedule 43A to that Act".

(25) After subsection (5) insert—

"(5A) This subsection applies to any conduct—

(*a*) in relation to which there has been given—

(i) an opinion notice under paragraph 6(4)(*b*) of Schedule 43B to FA 2013 (GAAR advisory panel: opinion that such conduct unreasonable) stating the joint opinion of all the members of a sub-panel arranged under that paragraph, or

(ii) one or more such notices stating the opinions of at least two members of such a sub-panel, and

(*b*) in relation to which there has been given a notice under paragraph 8 of that Schedule (HMRC final decision on tax advantage) stating that a tax advantage is to be counteracted.

(5B) For the purposes of subsection (5), any opinions of members of the GAAR advisory panel which must be considered before a notice is given under paragraph 8 or 9 of Schedule 43A to FA 2013 (opinions about the lead arrangements) are taken to relate to the conduct to which the notice relates."

(26) In Schedule 32 to FA 2014 (accelerated payments and partnerships), paragraph 3 is amended in accordance with subsections (27) and (28).

(27) In sub-paragraph (5), after paragraph (*c*) insert—

"(*d*) the relevant partner in question has been given a notice under paragraph 8(2) or 9(2) of Schedule 43A to FA 2013 (notice of final decision after considering Panel's opinion about referred or counteracted arrangements) in respect of any tax advantage resulting from the asserted advantage or part of it and the chosen arrangements (or is given such a notice at the same time as the partner payment notice) in a case where the stated opinion of at least two of the members of the sub-panel of the GAAR Advisory Panel about the other arrangements (see sub-paragraph (7)) was as set out in paragraph 11(3)(*b*) of Schedule 43 to FA 2013;

(*e*) the relevant partner in question has been given a notice under paragraph 8(2) of Schedule 43B to FA 2013 (GAAR: generic referral of arrangements) in respect of any tax advantage resulting from the asserted advantage or part of it and the chosen arrangements (or is given such a notice at the same time as the partner payment notice) in a case where the stated opinion of at least two of the members of the sub-panel of the GAAR Advisory Panel which considered the generic referral in respect of those arrangements was as set out in paragraph 6(4)(*b*) of that Schedule."

(28) After sub-paragraph (6) insert—

"(7) "Other arrangements" means—

(*a*) in relation to a notice under paragraph 8(2) of Schedule 43A to FA 2013, the referred arrangements (as defined in that paragraph);

(*b*) in relation to a notice under paragraph 9(2) of that Schedule, the counteracted arrangements (as defined in paragraph 2 of that Schedule)."

(29) In Schedule 34 to FA 2014 (promoters of tax avoidance schemes: threshold conditions), in paragraph 7—

(*a*) in paragraph (*a*), at the end insert "(referrals of single schemes) or are in a pool in respect of which a referral has been made to that Panel under Schedule 43B to that Act (generic referrals),";

(*b*) in paragraph (*b*)—

(i) for "in relation to the arrangements" substitute "in respect of the referral";

(ii) after "11(3)(*b*)" insert "or (as the case may be) 6(4)(*b*)";

(*c*) in paragraph (*c*)(i) omit "paragraph 10 of".

(30) The amendments made by this section have effect in relation to tax arrangements (within the meaning of Part 5 of FA 2013) entered into at any time (whether before or on or after the day on which this Act is passed).

158 General anti-abuse rule: penalty

(1) Part 5 of FA 2013 (general anti-abuse rule) is amended as follows.

(2) After section 212 insert—

"212A Penalty

(1) A person (P) is liable to pay a penalty if—

(*a*) P has been given a notice under—

(i) paragraph 12 of Schedule 43,

(ii) paragraph 8 or 9 of Schedule 43A, or

(iii) paragraph 8 of Schedule 43B,

stating that a tax advantage arising from particular tax arrangements is to be counteracted,

(*b*) a tax document has been given to HMRC on the basis that the tax advantage arises to P from those arrangements,

(*c*) that document was given to HMRC—

(i) by P, or

(ii) by another person in circumstances where P knew, or ought to have known, that the other person gave the document on the basis mentioned in paragraph (*c*), and

(*d*) the tax advantage has been counteracted by the making of adjustments under section 209.

(2) The penalty is 60% of the value of the counteracted advantage.

(3) Schedule 43C—

(*a*) gives the meaning of "the value of the counteracted advantage", and

(*b*) makes other provision in relation to penalties under this section.

(4) In this section "tax document" means any return, claim or other document submitted in compliance (or purported compliance) with any provision of, or made under, an Act.

(5) In this section the reference to giving a tax document to HMRC is to be interpreted in accordance with paragraph 11(*g*) and (*h*) of Schedule 43C.

(3) After Schedule 43B insert—

"SCHEDULE 43C

PENALTY UNDER SECTION 212A: SUPPLEMENTARY PROVISION

Value of the counteracted advantage: introduction

1 *Paragraphs 2 to 4 set out how to calculate the "value of the counteracted advantage" for the purposes of section 212A.*

Value of the counteracted advantage: basic rule

2 (1) The "value of the counteracted advantage" is the additional amount due or payable in respect of tax as a result of the counteraction mentioned in section 212A(1)(*c*).

(2) The reference in sub-paragraph (1) to the additional amount due and payable includes a reference to—

(*a*) an amount payable to HMRC having erroneously been paid by way of repayment of tax, and

(*b*) an amount which would be repayable by HMRC if the counteraction were not made.

(3) The following are ignored in calculating the value of the counteracted advantage—

(*a*) group relief, and

(*b*) any relief under section 458 of CTA 2010 (relief in respect of repayment etc of loan) which is deferred under subsection (5) of that section.

(4) For the purposes of this paragraph consequential adjustments under section 210 are regarded as part of the counteraction in question.

(5) If the counteraction affects the person's liability to two or more taxes, the taxes concerned are to be considered together for the purpose of determining the value of the counteracted advantage.

(6) This paragraph is subject to paragraphs 3 and 4.

Value of counteracted advantage: losses

3 (1) To the extent that the tax advantage mentioned in section 212A(1)(*b*) ("the tax advantage") resulted in the wrong recording of a loss for the purposes of direct tax and the loss has been wholly used to reduce the amount due or payable in respect of tax, the value of the counteracted advantage is determined in accordance with paragraph 2.

(2) To the extent that the tax advantage resulted in the wrong recording of a loss for purposes of direct tax and the loss has not been wholly used to reduce the amount due or payable in respect of tax, the value of the counteracted advantage is—

(*a*) the value under paragraph 2 of so much of the tax advantage as results (or would in the absence of the counteraction result) from the part (if any) of the loss which was used to reduce the amount due or payable in respect of tax, plus

(*b*) 10% of the part of the loss not so used.

(3) Sub-paragraphs (1) and (2) apply both—

(*a*) to a case where no loss would have been recorded but for the tax advantage, and

(*b*) to a case where a loss of a different amount would have been recorded (but in that case sub-paragraphs (1) and (2) apply only to the difference between the amount recorded and the true amount).

(4) To the extent that the tax advantage creates or increases (or would in the absence of the counteraction create or increase) an aggregate loss recorded for a group of companies—

(*a*) the value of the counteracted advantage is calculated in accordance with this paragraph, and

(*b*) in applying paragraph 2 in accordance with sub-paragraphs (1) and (2), group relief may be taken into account (despite paragraph 2(3)).

(5) To the extent that the tax advantage results (or would in the absence of the counteraction result) in a loss, the value of it is nil where, because of the nature of the loss or the person's circumstances, there was no reasonable prospect of the loss being used to support a claim to reduce a tax liability (of any person).

Value of counteracted advantage: deferred tax

4 (1) To the extent that the tax advantage mentioned in section 212A is a deferral of tax, the value of the counteracted advantage is—

(*a*) 25% of the amount of the deferred tax for each year of the deferral, or

(*b*) a percentage of the amount of the deferred tax, for each separate period of deferral of less than a year, equating to 25% per year,

or, if less, 100% of the amount of the deferred tax.

(2) This paragraph does not apply to a case to the extent that paragraph 3 applies.

Assessment of penalty

5 (1) Where a person is liable for a penalty under section 212A, HMRC must assess the penalty.

(2) Where HMRC assess the penalty, HMRC must—

(*a*) notify the person who is liable for the penalty, and

(*b*) state in the notice a tax period in respect of which the penalty is assessed.

(3) A penalty under this paragraph must be paid before the end of the period of 30 days beginning with the day on which notification of the penalty is issued.

(4) An assessment—

(*a*) is to be treated for procedural purposes as if it were an assessment to tax,

(*b*) may be enforced as if it were an assessment to tax, and

(*c*) may be combined with an assessment to tax.

(5) An assessment of a penalty under this paragraph must be made before the end of the period of 12 months beginning with—

(*a*) the end of the appeal period for the assessment which gave effect to the counteraction mentioned in section 212A(1)(*b*), or

(*b*) if there is no assessment within paragraph (*a*), the date (or the latest of the dates) on which that counteraction becomes final.

(6) The reference in sub-paragraph (5)(*b*) to the counteraction becoming final is to be interpreted in accordance with section 210(8).

Alteration of assessment of penalty

6 (1) After notification of an assessment has been given to a person under paragraph 5(2), the assessment may not be altered except in accordance with this paragraph or paragraph 7, or on appeal.

(2) A supplementary assessment may be made in respect of a penalty if an earlier assessment operated by reference to an underestimate of the value of the counteracted advantage.

(3) An assessment may be revised as necessary if it operated by reference to an overestimate of the value of the counteracted advantage.

Revision of assessment following consequential relieving adjustment

7 (1) Sub-paragraph (2) applies where a person—

(*a*) is notified under section 210(7) of a consequential adjustment relating to a counteraction under section 209, and

(*b*) an assessment to a penalty in respect of that counteraction of which the person has been notified under paragraph 5(2) does not take account of that consequential adjustment.

(2) HMRC must make any alterations of the assessment that appear to HMRC to be just and reasonable in connection with the consequential amendment.

(3) Alterations under this paragraph may be made despite any time limit imposed by or under an enactment.

Aggregate penalties

8 (1) Sub-paragraph (3) applies where—

(*a*) two or more penalties are incurred by the same person and fall to be determined by reference to an amount of tax to which that person is chargeable,

(*b*) one of those penalties is incurred under section 212A, and

(*c*) one or more of the other penalties are incurred under a relevant penalty provision.

(2) But sub-paragraph (3) does not apply if section 212(2) of FA 2014 (follower notices: aggregate penalties) applies in relation to the amount of tax in question.

(3) The aggregate of the amounts of the penalties mentioned in subsection (1)(*b*) and (*c*), so far as determined by reference to that amount of tax, must not exceed—

(*a*) the relevant percentage of that amount, or

(*b*) in a case where at least one of the penalties is under paragraph 5(2)(*b*) of, or sub-paragraph (3)(*b*), (4)(*b*) or (5)(*b*) of paragraph 6 of, Schedule 55 to FA 2009, £300 (if greater).

(4) In the application of section 97A of TMA 1970 (multiple penalties) no account shall be taken of a penalty under section 212A.

(5) "Relevant penalty provision" means—

(*a*) Schedule 24 to FA 2007 (penalties for errors),

(*b*) Schedule 41 to FA 2008 (penalties: failure to notify etc),

(*c*) Schedule 55 to FA 2009 (penalties for failure to make returns etc), or

(*d*) Part 5 of Schedule 18 to FA 2016 (penalty under serial tax avoidance regime).

(6) "The relevant percentage" means—

(*a*) 200% in a case where at least one of the penalties is determined by reference to the percentage in—

(i) paragraph 4(4)(*c*) of Schedule 24 to FA 2007,

(ii) paragraph 6(4)(*a*) of Schedule 41 to FA 2008, or

(iii) paragraph 6(3A)(*c*) of Schedule 55 to FA 2009,

(*b*) 150% in a case where paragraph (*a*) does not apply and at least one of the penalties is determined by reference to the percentage in—

(i) paragraph 4(3)(*c*) of Schedule 24 to FA 2007,

(ii) paragraph 6(3)(*a*) of Schedule 41 to FA 2008, or

(iii) paragraph 6(3A)(*b*) of Schedule 55 to FA 2009,

(*c*) 140% in a case where neither paragraph (*a*) nor paragraph (*b*) applies and at least one of the penalties is determined by reference to the percentage in—

(i) paragraph 4(4)(*b*) of Schedule 24 to FA 2007,

(ii) paragraph 6(4)(*b*) of Schedule 41 to FA 2008, or

(iii) paragraph 6(4A)(*c*) of Schedule 55 to FA 2009,

(*d*) 105% in a case where at none of paragraphs (*a*), (*b*) and (*c*) applies and at least one of the penalties is determined by reference to the percentage in—

(i) paragraph 4(3)(*b*) of Schedule 24 to FA 2007,

(ii) paragraph 6(3)(*b*) of Schedule 41 to FA 2008, or

(iii) paragraph 6(4A)(*b*) of Schedule 55 to FA 2009, and

(*e*) in any other case, 100%.

Appeal against penalty

9 (1) A person may appeal against—

(*a*) the imposition of a penalty under section 212A, or

(*b*) the amount assessed under paragraph 5.

(2) An appeal under sub-paragraph (1)(*a*) may only be made on the grounds that the arrangements were not abusive or there was no tax advantage to be counteracted.

(3) An appeal under sub-paragraph (1)(*b*) may only be made on the grounds that the assessment was based on an overestimate of the value of the counteracted advantage (whether because the estimate was made by reference to adjustments which were not just and reasonable or for any other reason).

(4) An appeal under this paragraph must be made within the period of 30 days beginning with the day on which notification of the penalty is given under paragraph 5(2).

(5) An appeal under this paragraph is to be treated in the same way as an appeal against an assessment to the tax concerned (including by the application of any provision about bringing the appeal by notice to HMRC, about HMRC's review of the decision or about determination of the appeal by the First-tier Tribunal or Upper Tribunal).

(6) Sub-paragraph (5) does not apply—

(*a*) so as to require a person to pay a penalty before an appeal against the assessment of the penalty is determined, or

(*b*) in respect of any other matter expressly provided for by this Part.

(7) On an appeal against the penalty the tribunal may affirm or cancel HMRC's decision.

(8) On an appeal against the amount of the penalty the tribunal may—

(*a*) affirm HMRC's decision, or

(*b*) substitute for HMRC's decision another decision that HMRC has power to make.

(9) In this paragraph "tribunal" means the First-tier Tribunal or Upper Tribunal (as appropriate by virtue of sub-paragraph (5)).

Mitigation of penalties

10 (1) The Commissioners may in their discretion mitigate a penalty under section 212A, or stay or compound any proceedings for such a penalty.

(2) They may also, after judgment, further mitigate or entirely remit the penalty.

Interpretation

11 *In this Schedule*—

(*a*) a reference to an "assessment" to tax is to be interpreted, in relation to inheritance tax, as a reference to a determination;

(*b*) "direct tax" means—

(i) income tax,

(ii) capital gains tax,

(iii) corporation tax (including any amount chargeable as if it were corporation tax or treated as corporation tax),

(iv) petroleum revenue tax, and

(v) diverted profits tax;

(*c*) a reference to a loss includes a reference to a charge, expense, deficit and any other amount which may be available for, or relied on to claim, a deduction or relief;

(*d*) a reference to a repayment of tax includes a reference to allowing a credit against tax or to a payment of a corporation tax credit;

(*e*) "corporation tax credit" means—

(i) an R&D tax credit under Chapter 2 or 7 of Part 13 of CTA 2009,

(ii) an R&D expenditure credit under Chapter 6A of Part 3 of CTA 2009,

(iii) a land remediation tax credit or life assurance company tax credit under Chapter 3 or 4 respectively of Part 14 of CTA 2009,

(iv) a film tax credit under Chapter 3 of Part 15 of CTA 2009,

(v) a television tax credit under Chapter 3 of Part 15A of CTA 2009,

(vi) a video game tax credit under Chapter 3 of Part 15B of CTA 2009,

(vii) a theatre tax credit under section 1217K of CTA 2009,

(viii) an orchestra tax credit under Chapter 3 of Part 15D of CTA 2009, or

(ix) a first-year tax credit under Schedule A1 to CAA 2001;

(*f*) "tax period" means a tax year, accounting period or other period in respect of which tax is charged;

(*g*) a reference to giving a document to HMRC includes a reference to communicating information to HMRC in any form and by any method (whether by post, fax, email, telephone or otherwise),

(*h*) a reference to giving a document to HMRC includes a reference to making a statement or declaration in a document."

(4) In section 209 (counteracting the tax advantages), after subsection (7) insert—

"(8) Where a matter is referred to the GAAR Advisory Panel under paragraph 5 or 6 of Schedule 43, the taxpayer (as defined in paragraph 3 of that Schedule) must not make any GAAR-related adjustments in relation to the taxpayer's tax affairs in the period (the "closed period") which—

(*a*) begins with the 31st day after the end of the 45 day period mentioned in paragraph 4(1) of that Schedule, and

(*b*) ends immediately before the day on which the taxpayer is given the notice under paragraph 12 of Schedule 43 (notice of final decision after considering opinion of GAAR Advisory Panel).

(9) Where a person has been given a pooling notice or a notice of binding under Schedule 43A in relation to any tax arrangements, the person must not make any GAAR-related adjustments in the period ("the closed period") that—

(*a*) begins with the 31st day after that on which that notice is given, and

(*b*) ends—

(i) in the case of a pooling notice, immediately before the day on which the person is given a notice under paragraph 8(2) or 9(2) of Schedule 43A, or a notice under paragraph 8(2) of Schedule 43B, in relation to the tax arrangements (notice of final decision after considering opinion of GAAR Advisory Panel), or

(ii) in the case of a notice of binding, with the 30th day after the day on which the notice is given.

(10) In this section "GAAR-related adjustments" means—

(*a*) for the purposes of subsection (8), adjustments which give effect (wholly or in part) to the proposed counteraction set out in the notice under paragraph 3 of Schedule 43;

(*b*) for the purposes of subsection (9), adjustments which give effect (wholly or partly) to the proposed counteraction set out in the notice of pooling or binding (as the case may be)."

(5) Schedule 43 (general anti-abuse rule: procedural requirements) is amended in accordance with subsections (6) to (9).

(6) After paragraph 1 insert—

"Meaning of "tax appeal"

1A

In this Part "tax appeal" means—

(*a*) an appeal under section 31 of TMA 1970 (income tax: appeals against amendments of self-assessment, amendments made by closure notices under section 28A or 28B of that Act, etc), including an appeal under that section by virtue of regulations under Part 11 of ITEPA 2003 (PAYE),

(*b*) an appeal under paragraph 9 of Schedule 1A to TMA 1970 (income tax: appeals against amendments made by closure notices under paragraph 7(2) of that Schedule, etc),

(*c*) an appeal under section 705 of ITA 2007 (income tax: appeals against counteraction notices),

(*d*) an appeal under paragraph 34(3) or 48 of Schedule 18 to FA 1998 (corporation tax: appeals against amendment of a company's return made by closure notice, assessments other than self-assessments, etc),

(*e*) an appeal under section 750 of CTA 2010 (corporation tax: appeals against counteraction notices),

(*f*) an appeal under section 222 of IHTA 1984 (appeals against HMRC determinations) other than an appeal made by a person against a determination in respect of a transfer of value at a time when a tax enquiry is in progress in respect of a return made by that person in respect of that transfer,

(*g*) an appeal under paragraph 35 of Schedule 10 to FA 2003 (stamp duty land tax: appeals against amendment of self-assessment, discovery assessments, etc),

(*h*) an appeal under paragraph 35 of Schedule 33 to FA 2013 (annual tax on enveloped dwellings: appeals against amendment of self-assessment, discovery assessments, etc),

(*i*) an appeal under paragraph 14 of Schedule 2 to the Oil Taxation Act 1975 (petroleum revenue tax: appeal against assessment, determination etc), (*j*) an appeal under section 102 of FA 2015 (diverted profits tax: appeal against charging notice etc),

(*k*) an appeal under section 114 of FA 2016 (apprenticeship levy: appeal against an assessment), or

(*l*) an appeal against any determination of—

(i) an appeal within paragraphs (*a*) to (*k*), or

(ii) an appeal within this paragraph."

(7) In paragraph 3(2)(*e*), for "of paragraphs 5 and 6" substitute "of—

(i) paragraphs 5 and 6, and

(ii) sections 209(8) and (9) and 212A."

(8) After paragraph 4 insert—

"Corrective action by taxpayer

4A

(1) If the taxpayer takes the relevant corrective action before the beginning of the closed period mentioned in section 209(8), the matter is not to be referred to the GAAR Advisory Panel.

(2) For the purposes of this Schedule the "relevant corrective action" is taken if (and only if) the taxpayer takes the steps set out in sub-paragraphs (3) and (4).

(3) The first step is that—

(*a*) the taxpayer amends a return or claim to counteract the tax advantage specified in the notice under paragraph 3, or

(*b*) if the taxpayer has made a tax appeal (by notifying HMRC or otherwise) on the basis that the tax advantage specified in the notice under paragraph 3 arises from the tax arrangements specified in that notice, the taxpayer takes all necessary action to enter into an agreement with HMRC (in writing) for the purpose of relinquishing that advantage.

(4) The second step is that the taxpayer notifies HMRC—

(*a*) that the taxpayer has taken the first step, and

(*b*) of any additional amount which has or will become due and payable in respect of tax by reason of the first step being taken.

(5) Where the taxpayer takes the first step described in sub-paragraph (3)(*b*), HMRC may proceed as if the taxpayer had not taken the relevant corrective action if the taxpayer fails to enter into the written agreement.

(6) In determining the additional amount which has or will become due and payable in respect of tax for the purposes of sub-paragraph (4)(*b*), it is to be assumed that, where the taxpayer takes the necessary action as mentioned in sub-paragraph (3)(*b*), the agreement is then entered into.

(7) No enactment limiting the time during which amendments may be made to returns or claims operates to prevent the taxpayer taking the first step mentioned in sub-paragraph (3)(*a*) before the tax enquiry is closed (whether or not before the specified time).

(8) No appeal may be brought, by virtue of a provision mentioned in sub-paragraph (9), against an amendment made by a closure notice in respect of a tax enquiry to the extent that the amendment takes into account an amendment made by the taxpayer to a return or claim in taking the first step mentioned in sub-paragraph (3)(*a*).

(9) The provisions are—

(*a*) section 31(1)(*b*) or (*c*) of TMA 1970,

(*b*) paragraph 9 of Schedule 1A to TMA 1970,

(*c*) paragraph 34(3) of Schedule 18 to FA 1998,

(*d*) paragraph 35(1)(*b*) of Schedule 10 to FA 2003, and

(*e*) paragraph 35(1)(*b*) of Schedule 33 to FA 2013."

(9) Before paragraph 5 (but after the heading "Referral to GAAR Advisory Panel") insert—

"4B Paragraphs 5 and 6 apply if the taxpayer does not take the relevant corrective action (see paragraph 4A) by the beginning of the closed period mentioned in section 209(8)."

(10) In section 103ZA of TMA 1970 (disapplication of sections 100 to 103 in the case of certain penalties)—

(*a*) omit "or" at the end of paragraph (*g*), and

(*b*) after paragraph (*g*) insert

"(*ga*) section 212A of the Finance Act 2013 (general anti-abuse rule), or"

(11) In section 212 of FA 2014 (follower notices: aggregate penalties) (as amended by Schedule 18), in subsection (4)—

(*a*) omit "or" at the end of paragraph (*c*), and

(*b*) after paragraph (*d*) insert ", or

(*e*) section 212A of FA 2013 (general anti-abuse rule)."

(12) FA 2015 is amended in accordance with subsections (13) and (14).

(13) In section 120 (penalties in connection with offshore matters and offshore transfers), in subsection (1), omit "and" before paragraph (*c*) and after paragraph (*c*) insert— ", and

(*d*) Schedule 43C to FA 2013 (as amended by FA 2016)."

(14) In Schedule 20 to that Act, after paragraph 19 insert—

"General anti-abuse rule: aggregate penalties

20

(1) In Schedule 43C to FA 2013 (general anti-abuse rule: supplementary provision about penalty), sub-paragraph (6) of paragraph 8 is amended as follows.

(2) After paragraph (*b*) insert—

"(*ba*) 125% in a case where neither paragraph (*a*) nor paragraph (*b*) applies and at least one of the penalties is determined by reference to the percentage in—

(i) paragraph 4(2)(*c*) of Schedule 24 to FA 2007,

(ii) paragraph 6(2)(*a*) of Schedule 41 to FA 2008,

(iii) paragraph 6(3A)(*a*) of Schedule 55 to FA 2009,".

(3) In sub-paragraph (*c*) for "neither paragraph (*a*) nor paragraph (*b*) applies" substitute "none of paragraphs (*a*) to (*ba*) applies.

(4) In sub-paragraph (*d*) for "none of paragraphs (*a*), (*b*) and (*c*) applies" substitute "none of paragraphs (*a*) to (*c*) applies".

(15) The amendments made by this section have effect in relation to tax arrangements (within the meaning of Part 5 of FA 2013) entered into on or after the day on which this Act is passed.

Tackling frequent avoidance

159 Serial tax avoidance

Schedule 18 contains provision about the issue of warning notices to, and further sanctions for, persons who incur a relevant defeat in relation to arrangements.

160 Promoters of tax avoidance schemes

(1) Part 5 of FA 2014 (promoters of tax avoidance schemes) is amended as follows.

(2) After section 237 insert—

"237A Duty to give conduct notice: defeat of promoted arrangements

(1) If an authorised officer becomes aware at any time ("the relevant time") that a person ("P") who is carrying on a business as a promoter meets any of the conditions in subsections (11) to (13), the officer must determine whether or not P's meeting of that condition should be regarded as significant in view of the purposes of this Part. But see also subsection (14).

(2) An authorised officer must make the determination set out in subsection (3) if the officer becomes aware at any time ("the section 237A(2) relevant time") that—

(*a*) a person meets a condition in subsection (11), (12) or (13), and

(*b*) at the section 237A(2) relevant time another person ("P"), who is carrying on a business as a promoter, meets that condition by virtue of Part 4 of Schedule 34A (meeting the section 237A conditions: bodies corporate and partnerships).

(3) The authorised officer must determine whether or not—

(*a*) the meeting of the condition by the person as mentioned in subsection (2)(*a*), and

(*b*) P's meeting of the condition as mentioned in subsection (2)(*b*),

should be regarded as significant in view of the purposes of this Part.

(4) Subsections (1) and (2) do not apply if a conduct notice or monitoring notice already has effect in relation to P.

(5) Subsection (1) does not apply if, at the relevant time, an authorised officer is under a duty to make a determination under section 237(5) in relation to P.

(6) Subsection (2) does not apply if, at the section 237A(2) relevant time, an authorised officer is under a duty to make a determination under section 237(5) in relation to P.

(7) But in a case where subsection (1) does not apply because of subsection (5), or subsection (2) does not apply because of subsection (6), subsection (5) of section 237 has effect as if—

(*a*) the references in paragraph (*a*) of that subsection to "subsection (1)", and "subsection (1)(*a*)" included subsection (1) of this section, and (*b*) in paragraph (*b*) of that subsection the reference to "subsection (1A)(*a*)" included a reference to subsection (2)(*a*) of this section and the reference to subsection (1A)(*b*) included a reference to subsection (2)(*b*) of this section.

(8) If the authorised officer determines under subsection (1) that P's meeting of the condition in question should be regarded as significant, the officer must give P a conduct notice, unless subsection (10) applies.

(9) If the authorised officer determines under subsection (3) that—

(*a*) the meeting of the condition by the person as mentioned in subsection (2)(*a*), and

(*b*) P's meeting of the condition as mentioned in subsection (2)(*b*), should be regarded as significant in view of the purposes of this Part, the officer must give P a conduct notice, unless subsection (10) applies.

(10) This subsection applies if the authorised officer determines that, having regard to the extent of the impact that P's activities as a promoter are likely to have on the collection of tax, it is inappropriate to give P a conduct notice.

(11) The condition in this subsection is that in the period of 3 years ending with the relevant time at least 3 relevant defeats have occurred in relation to P.

(12) The condition in this subsection is that at least two relevant defeats have occurred in relation to P at times when a single defeat notice under section 241A(2) or (6) had effect in relation to P.

(13) The condition in this subsection is that at least one relevant defeat has occurred in relation to P at a time when a double defeat notice under section 241A(3) had effect in relation to P.

(14) A determination that the condition in subsection (12) or (13) is met cannot be made unless—

(*a*) the defeat notice in question still has effect when the determination is made, or

(*b*) the determination is made on or before the 90th day after the day on which the defeat notice in question ceased to have effect.

(15) Schedule 34A sets out the circumstances in which a "relevant defeat" occurs in relation to a person and includes provision limiting what can amount to a further relevant defeat in relation to a person (see paragraph 6).

237B Duty to give further conduct notice where provisional notice not complied with

(1) An authorised officer must give a conduct notice to a person ("P") who is carrying on a business as a promoter if—

(*a*) a conduct notice given to P under section 237A(8)—

(i) has ceased to have effect otherwise than as a result of section 237D(2) or 241(3) or (4), and

(ii) was provisional immediately before it ceased to have effect,

(*b*) the officer determines that P had failed to comply with one or more conditions in the conduct notice,

(*c*) the conduct notice relied on a Case 3 relevant defeat,

(*d*) since the time when the conduct notice ceased to have effect, one or more relevant defeats falling within subsection (2) have occurred in relation to—

(i) P, and

(ii) any arrangements to which the Case 3 relevant defeat also relates, and

(*e*) had that relevant defeat or (as the case may be) those relevant defeats, occurred before the conduct notice ceased to have effect, an authorised officer would have been required to notify the person under section 237C(3) that the notice was no longer provisional.

(2) A relevant defeat falls within this subsection if it occurs by virtue of Case 1 or Case 2 in Schedule 34A.

(3) Subsection (1) does not apply if the authorised officer determines that, having regard to the extent of the impact that the person's activities as a promoter are likely to have on the collection of tax, it is inappropriate to give the person a conduct notice.

(4) Subsection (1) does not apply if a conduct notice or monitoring notice already has effect in relation to the person.

(5) For the purposes of this Part a conduct notice "relies on a Case 3 relevant defeat" if it could not have been given under the following condition.

The condition is that paragraph 9 of Schedule 34A had effect with the substitution of "100% of the tested arrangements" for "75% of the tested arrangements".

237C When a conduct notice given under section 237A(8) is "provisional"

(1) This section applies to a conduct notice which—

(*a*) is given to a person under section 237A(8), and

(*b*) relies on a Case 3 relevant defeat.

(2) The notice is "provisional" at all times when it has effect, unless an authorised officer notifies the person that the notice is no longer provisional.

(3) An authorised officer must notify the person that the notice is no longer provisional if subsection (4) or (5) applies.

(4) This subsection applies if—

(*a*) the condition in subsection (5)(*a*) is not met, and

(*b*) a full relevant defeat occurs in relation to P.

(5) This subsection applies if—

(*a*) two, or all three, of the relevant defeats by reference to which the conduct notice is given would not have been relevant defeats if paragraph 9 of Schedule 34A had effect with the substitution of "100% of the tested arrangements" for "75% of the tested arrangements", and

(*b*) the same number of full relevant defeats occur in relation to P.

(6) A "full relevant defeat" occurs in relation to P if—

(*a*) a relevant defeat occurs in relation to P otherwise than by virtue of Case 3 in paragraph 9 of Schedule 34A, or

(*b*) circumstances arise which would be a relevant defeat in relation to P by virtue of paragraph 9 of Schedule 34A if that paragraph had effect with the substitution of "100% of the tested arrangements" for "75% of the tested arrangements".

(7) In determining under subsection (6) whether a full relevant defeat has occurred in relation to P, assume that in paragraph 6 of Schedule 34A (provision limiting what can amount to a further relevant defeat in relation to a person) the first reference to a "relevant defeat" does not include a relevant defeat by virtue of Case 3 in paragraph 9 of Schedule 34A.

237D Judicial ruling upholding asserted tax advantage: effect on conduct notice which is provisional

(1) Subsection (2) applies if at any time—

(*a*) a conduct notice which relies on a Case 3 relevant defeat (see section 237B(5)) is provisional, and

(*b*) a court or tribunal upholds a corresponding tax advantage which has been asserted in connection with any of the related arrangements to which that relevant defeat relates (see paragraph 5(2) of Schedule 34A).

(2) The conduct notice ceases to have effect when that judicial ruling becomes final.

(3) An authorised officer must give the person to whom the conduct notice was given a written notice stating that the conduct notice has ceased to have effect.

(4) For the purposes of this section, a tax advantage is "asserted" in connection with any arrangements if a person makes a return, claim or election on the basis that the tax advantage arises from those arrangements.

In relation to the arrangements mentioned in paragraph (*b*) of subsection (1) "corresponding tax advantage" means a tax advantage corresponding to any tax advantage the counteraction of which contributed to the relevant defeat mentioned in that paragraph.

(5) For the purposes of this section a court or tribunal "upholds" a tax advantage if—

(*a*) the court or tribunal makes a ruling to the effect that no part of the tax advantage is to be counteracted, and

(*b*) that judicial ruling is final.

(6) For the purposes of this Part a judicial ruling is "final" if it is—

(*a*) a ruling of the Supreme Court, or

(*b*) a ruling of any other court or tribunal in circumstances where—

(i) no appeal may be made against the ruling,

(ii) if an appeal may be made against the ruling with permission, the time limit for applications has expired and either no application has been made or permission has been refused,

(iii) if such permission to appeal against the ruling has been granted or is not required, no appeal has been made within the time limit for appeals, or

(iv) if an appeal was made, it was abandoned or otherwise disposed of before it was determined by the court or tribunal to which it was addressed.

(7) In this section references to "counteraction" include anything referred to as a counteraction in any of Conditions A to F in paragraphs 11 to 16 of Schedule 34A."

(3) After section 241 insert—

"Defeat notices

241A Defeat notices

(1) This section applies in relation to a person ("P") only if P is carrying on a business as a promoter.

(2) An authorised officer, or an officer of Revenue and Customs with the approval of an authorised officer, may give P a notice if the officer concerned has become aware of one (and only one) relevant defeat which has occurred in relation to P in the period of 3 years ending with the day on which the notice is given.

(3) An authorised officer, or an officer of Revenue and Customs with the approval of an authorised officer, may give P a notice if the officer concerned has become aware of two (but not more than two) relevant defeats which have occurred in relation to P in the period of 3 years ending with the day on which the notice is given.

(4) A notice under this section must be given by the end of the 90 days beginning with the day on which the matters mentioned in subsection (2) or (as the case may be) (3) come to the attention of HMRC.

(5) Subsection (6) applies if—

(*a*) a single defeat notice which had been given to P (under subsection (2) or (6)) ceases to have effect as a result of section 241B(1), and

(*b*) in the period when the defeat notice had effect a relevant defeat ("the further relevant defeat") occurred in relation to P.

(6) An authorised officer or an officer of Revenue and Customs with the approval of an authorised officer may give P a notice in respect of the further relevant defeat (regardless of whether or not it occurred in the period of 3 years ending with the day on which the notice is given).

(7) In this Part—

(*a*) "single defeat notice" means a notice under subsection (2) or (6);

(*b*) "double defeat notice" means a notice under subsection (3);

(*c*) "defeat notice" means a single defeat notice or a double defeat notice.

(8) A defeat notice must—

(*a*) set out the dates on which the look-forward period for the notice begins and ends;

(*b*) in the case of a single defeat notice, explain the effect of section 237A(12);

(*c*) in the case of a double defeat notice, explain the effect of section 237A(13).

(9) HMRC may specify what further information must be included in a defeat notice.

(10) "Look-forward period"—

(*a*) in relation to a defeat notice under subsection (2) or (3), means the period of 5 years beginning with the day after the day on which the notice is given;

(*b*) in relation to a defeat notice under subsection (6), means the period beginning with the day after the day on which the notice is given and ending at the end of the period of 5 years beginning with the day on which the further relevant defeat mentioned in subsection (6) occurred in relation to P.

(11) A defeat notice has effect throughout its look-forward period unless it ceases to have effect earlier in accordance with section 241B(1) or (4).

241B Judicial ruling upholding asserted tax advantage: effect on defeat notice

(1) If the relevant defeat to which a single defeat notice relates is overturned (see subsection (5)), the notice has no further effect on and after the day on which it is overturned.

(2) Subsection (3) applies if one (and only one) of the relevant defeats in respect of which a double defeat notice was given is overturned.

(3) The notice is to be treated for the purposes of this Part (including this section) as if it had always been a single defeat notice given (in respect of the other of the two relevant defeats) on the date on which the notice was in fact given.

The look-forward period for the notice is accordingly unchanged.

(4) If both the relevant defeats to which a double defeat notice relates are overturned (on the same date), that notice has no further effect on and after that date.

(5) A relevant defeat specified in a defeat notice is "overturned" if—

(*a*) the notice could not have specified that relevant defeat if paragraph 9 of Schedule 34A had effect with the substitution of "100% of the tested arrangements" for "75% of the tested arrangements", and (*b*) at a time when the notice has effect a court or tribunal upholds a corresponding tax advantage which has been asserted in connection with any of the related arrangements to which the relevant defeat relates (see paragraph 5(2) of Schedule 34A).

Accordingly the relevant defeat is overturned on the day on which the judicial ruling mentioned in paragraph (*b*) becomes final.

(6) If a defeat notice ceases to have effect as a result of subsection (1) or (4) an authorised officer, or an officer of Revenue and Customs with the approval of an authorised officer, must notify the person to whom the notice was given that it has ceased to have effect.

(7) If subsection (3) has effect in relation to a defeat notice, an authorised officer, or an officer of Revenue and Customs with the approval of an authorised officer, must notify the person of the effect of that subsection.

(8) For the purposes of this section, a tax advantage is "asserted" in connection with any arrangements if a person makes a return, claim or election on the basis that the tax advantage arises from those arrangements.

(9) In relation to the arrangements mentioned in paragraph (*b*) of subsection (5) "corresponding tax advantage" means a tax advantage corresponding to any tax advantage the counteraction of which contributed to the relevant defeat mentioned in that paragraph.

(10) For the purposes of this section a court or tribunal "upholds" a tax advantage if—

(*a*) the court or tribunal makes a ruling to the effect that no part of the tax advantage is to be counteracted, and

(*b*) that judicial ruling is final.

(11) In this section references to "counteraction" include anything referred to as a counteraction in any of Conditions A to F in paragraphs 11 to 16 of Schedule 34A."

(4) In section 242 (monitoring notices: duty to apply to tribunal), after subsection (5) insert—

"(6) At a time when a notice given under section 237A is provisional, no determination is to be made under subsection (1) in respect of the notice.

(7) If a promoter fails to comply with conditions in a conduct notice at a time when the conduct notice is provisional, nothing in subsection (6) prevents those failures from being taken into account under subsection (1) at any subsequent time when the conduct notice is not provisional."

(5) After Schedule 34 insert—

"SCHEDULE 34A
PROMOTERS OF TAX AVOIDANCE SCHEMES: DEFEATED ARRANGEMENTS

PART 1
INTRODUCTION

1 *In this Schedule—*

(*a*) Part 2 is about the meaning of "relevant defeat";

(*b*) Part 3 contains provision about when a relevant defeat is treated as occurring in relation to a person;

(*c*) Part 4 contains provision about when a person is treated as meeting a condition in subsection (11), (12) or (13) of section 237A;

(*d*) Part 5 contains definitions and other supplementary provisions.

PART 2
MEANING OF "RELEVANT DEFEAT"

"Related" arrangements

2 (1) For the purposes of this Part of this Act, separate arrangements which persons have entered into are "related" to one another if (and only if) they are substantially the same.

(2) Sub-paragraphs (3) to (6) set out cases in which arrangements are to be treated as being "substantially the same" (if they would not otherwise be so treated under sub-paragraph (1)).

(3) Arrangements to which the same reference number has been allocated under Part 7 of FA 2004 (disclosure of tax avoidance schemes) are treated as being substantially the same. For this purpose arrangements in relation to which information relating to a reference number has been provided in compliance with section 312 of FA 2004 are treated as arrangements to which that reference number has been allocated under Part 7 of that Act.

(4) Arrangements to which the same reference number has been allocated under paragraph 9 of Schedule 11A to VATA 1994 (disclosure of avoidance schemes) are treated as being substantially the same.

(5) Any two or more sets of arrangements which are the subject of follower notices given by reference to the same judicial ruling are treated as being substantially the same.

(6) Where a notice of binding has been given in relation to any arrangements ("the bound arrangements") on the basis that they are, for the purposes of Schedule 43A to FA 2013, equivalent arrangements in relation to another set of arrangements (the "lead arrangements")—

(*a*) the bound arrangements and the lead arrangements are treated as being substantially the same, and

(*b*) the bound arrangements are treated as being substantially the same as any other arrangements which, as a result of this sub-paragraph, are treated as substantially the same as the lead arrangements.

"Promoted arrangements"

3 (1) For the purposes of this Schedule arrangements are "promoted arrangements" in relation to a person if—

(*a*) they are relevant arrangements or would be relevant arrangements under the condition stated in sub-paragraph (2), and

(*b*) the person is carrying on a business as a promoter and—

(i) the person is or has been a promoter in relation to the arrangements, or

(ii) that would be the case if the condition in subparagraph (2) were met.

(2) That condition is that the definition of "tax" in section 283 includes, and has always included, value added tax.

Relevant defeat of single arrangements

4 (1) A defeat of arrangements (entered into by any person) which are promoted arrangements in relation to a person ("the promoter") is a "relevant defeat" in relation to the promoter if the condition in subparagraph (2) is met.

(2) The condition is that the arrangements are not related to any other arrangements which are promoted arrangements in relation to the promoter.

(3) For the meaning of "defeat" see paragraphs 10 to 16.

Relevant defeat of related arrangements

5 (1) This paragraph applies if arrangements (entered into by any person) ("Set A")—

(*a*) are promoted arrangements in relation to a person ("P"), and

(*b*) are related to other arrangements which are promoted arrangements in relation to P.

(2) If Case 1, 2 or 3 applies (see paragraphs 7 to 9) a relevant defeat occurs in relation to P and each of the related arrangements.

(3) "The related arrangements" means Set A and the arrangements mentioned in sub-paragraph (1)(*b*).

Limit on number of separate relevant defeats in relation to the same, or related, arrangements

6 In relation to a person, if there has been a relevant defeat of arrangements (whether under paragraph 4 or 5) there cannot be a further relevant defeat of—

(*a*) those particular arrangements, or

(*b*) arrangements which are related to those arrangements.

Case 1: counteraction upheld by judicial ruling

7 (1) Case 1 applies if—

(*a*) any of Conditions A to E is met in relation to any of the related arrangements, and

(*b*) in the case of those arrangements the decision to make the relevant counteraction has been upheld by a judicial ruling (which is final).

(2) In sub-paragraph (1) "the relevant counteraction" means the counteraction mentioned in paragraph 11(*d*), 12(1)(*b*), 13(1)(*d*), 14(1)(*d*) or 15(1)(*d*) (as the case requires).

Case 2: judicial ruling that avoidance-related rule applies

8 *Case 2 applies if Condition F is met in relation to any of the related arrangements.*

Case 3: proportion-based relevant defeat

9 (1) Case 3 applies if—

(*a*) at least 75% of the tested arrangements have been defeated, and

(*b*) no final judicial ruling in relation to any of the related arrangements has upheld a corresponding tax advantage which has been asserted in connection with any of the related arrangements.

(2) In this paragraph "the tested arrangements" means so many of the related arrangements (as defined in paragraph 5(3)) as meet the condition in sub-paragraph (3) or (4).

(3) Particular arrangements meet this condition if a person has made a return, claim or election on the basis that a tax advantage results from those arrangements and—

(*a*) there has been an enquiry or investigation by HMRC into the return, claim or election, or

(*b*) HMRC assesses the person to tax on the basis that the tax advantage (or any part of it) does not arise, or

(*c*) a GAAR counteraction notice has been given in relation to the tax advantage or part of it and the arrangements.

(4) Particular arrangements meet this condition if HMRC takes other action on the basis that a tax advantage which might be expected to arise from those arrangements, or is asserted in connection with them, does not arise.

(5) For the purposes of this paragraph a tax advantage has been "asserted" in connection with particular arrangements if a person has made a return, claim or election on the basis that the tax advantage arises from those arrangements.

(6) In sub-paragraph (1)(*b*) "corresponding tax advantage" means a tax advantage corresponding to any tax advantage the counteraction of which is taken into account by HMRC for the purposes of subparagraph (1)(*a*).

(7) For the purposes of this paragraph a court or tribunal "upholds" a tax advantage if—

(*a*) the court or tribunal makes a ruling to the effect that no part of the tax advantage is to be counteracted, and

(*b*) that judicial ruling is final.

(8) In this paragraph references to "counteraction" include anything referred to as a counteraction in any of Conditions A to F in paragraphs 11 to 16.

(9) In this paragraph "GAAR counteraction notice" means—

(*a*) a notice such as is mentioned in sub-paragraph (2) of paragraph 12 of Schedule 43 to FA 2013 (notice of final decision to counteract),

(*b*) a notice under paragraph 8(2) or 9(2) of Schedule 43A to that Act (pooling or binding of arrangements) stating that the tax advantage is to be counteracted under the general anti-abuse rule, or

(*c*) a notice under paragraph 8(2) of Schedule 43B to that Act (generic referrals) stating that the tax advantage is to be counteracted under the general anti-abuse rule.

"Defeat" of arrangements

10 *For the purposes of this Part of this Act a "defeat" of arrangements occurs if any of Conditions A to F (in paragraphs 11 to 16) is met in relation to the arrangements.*

11 *Condition A is that—*

(*a*) a person has made a return, claim or election on the basis that a tax advantage arises from the arrangements,

(*b*) a notice given to the person under paragraph 12 of Schedule 43 to, paragraph 8(2) or 9(2) of Schedule 43A to or paragraph 8(2) of Schedule 43B to FA 2013 stated that the tax advantage was to be counteracted under the general anti-abuse rule, (*c*) the tax advantage has been counteracted (in whole or in part) under the general anti-abuse rule, and

(*d*) the counteraction is final.

12 (1) Condition B is that a follower notice has been given to a person by reference to the arrangements (and not withdrawn) and—

(*a*) the person has complied with subsection (2) of section 208 of FA 2014 by taking the action specified in subsections (4) to (6) of that section in respect of the denied tax advantage (or part of it), or

(*b*) the denied tax advantage has been counteracted (in whole or in part) otherwise than as mentioned in paragraph (*a*) and the counteraction is final.

(2) In this paragraph "the denied tax advantage" is to be interpreted in accordance with section 208(3) of FA 2014.

(3) In this Schedule "follower notice" means a follower notice under Chapter 2 of Part 4 of FA 2014.

13 (1) Condition C is that—

(*a*) the arrangements are DOTAS arrangements,

(*b*) a person ("the taxpayer") has made a return, claim or election on the basis that a relevant tax advantage arises,

(*c*) the relevant tax advantage has been counteracted, and

(*d*) the counteraction is final.

(2) For the purposes of sub-paragraph (1) "relevant tax advantage" means a tax advantage which the arrangements might be expected to enable the taxpayer to obtain.

(3) For the purposes of this paragraph the relevant tax advantage is "counteracted" if adjustments are made in respect of the taxpayer's tax position on the basis that the whole or part of that tax advantage does not arise.

14 (1) Condition D is that—

(*a*) the arrangements are disclosable VAT arrangements to which a taxable person is a party,

(*b*) the taxable person has made a return or claim on the basis that a relevant tax advantage arises,

(*c*) the relevant tax advantage has been counteracted, and

(*d*) the counteraction is final.

(2) For the purposes of sub-paragraph (1) "relevant tax advantage" means a tax advantage which the arrangements might be expected to enable the taxable person to obtain.

(3) For the purposes of this paragraph the relevant tax advantage is "counteracted" if adjustments are made in respect of the taxable person's tax position on the basis that the whole or part of that tax advantage does not arise.

15 (1) Condition E is that the arrangements are disclosable VAT arrangements to which a taxable person ("T") is a party and—

(*a*) the arrangements relate to the position with respect to VAT of a person other than T ("S") who has made supplies of goods or services to T,

(*b*) the arrangements might be expected to enable T to obtain a tax advantage in connection with those supplies of goods or services,

(*c*) the arrangements have been counteracted, and

(*d*) the counteraction is final.

(2) For the purposes of this paragraph the arrangements are "counteracted" if—

(*a*) HMRC assess S to tax or take any other action on a basis which prevents T from obtaining (or obtaining the whole of) the tax advantage in question, or

(*b*) adjustments are made on a basis such as is mentioned in paragraph (*a*).

16 (1) Condition F is that—

(*a*) a person has made a return, claim or election on the basis that a relevant tax advantage arises,

(*b*) the tax advantage, or part of the tax advantage would not arise if a particular avoidance-related rule (see paragraph 25) applies in relation to the person's tax affairs,

(*c*) it is held in a judicial ruling that the relevant avoidance-related rule applies in relation to the person's tax affairs, and (*d*) the judicial ruling is final.

(2) For the purposes of sub-paragraph (1) "relevant tax advantage" means a tax advantage which the arrangements might be expected to enable the person to obtain.

PART 3

RELEVANT DEFEATS: ASSOCIATED PERSONS

Attribution of relevant defeats

17 (1) Sub-paragraph (2) applies if—

(*a*) there is (or has been) a person ("Q"),

(*b*) arrangements ("the defeated arrangements") have been entered into,

(*c*) an event occurs such that either—

(i) there is a relevant defeat in relation to Q and the defeated arrangements, or

(ii) the condition in sub-paragraph (i) would be met if Q had not ceased to exist,

(*d*) at the time of that event a person ("P") is carrying on a business as a promoter (or is carrying on what would be such a business under the condition in paragraph 3(2)), and

(*e*) Condition 1 or 2 is met in relation to Q and P.

(2) The event is treated for all purposes of this Part of this Act as a relevant defeat in relation to P and the defeated arrangements (whether or not it is also a relevant defeat in relation to Q, and regardless of whether or not P existed at any time when those arrangements were promoted arrangements in relation to Q).

(3) Condition 1 is that—

(*a*) P is not an individual,

(*b*) at a time when the defeated arrangements were promoted arrangements in relation to Q—

(i) P was a relevant body controlled by Q, or

(ii) Q was a relevant body controlled by P, and

(*c*) at the time of the event mentioned in sub-paragraph (1)(*c*)—

(i) Q is a relevant body controlled by P,

(ii) P is a relevant body controlled by Q, or

(iii) P and Q are relevant bodies controlled by a third person.

(4) Condition 2 is that—

(*a*) P and Q are relevant bodies,

(*b*) at a time when the defeated arrangements were promoted arrangements in relation to Q, a third person ("C") controlled Q, and

(*c*) C controls P at the time of the event mentioned in subparagraph (1)(*c*).

(5) For the purposes of sub-paragraphs (3)(*b*) and (4)(*b*), the question whether arrangements are promoted arrangements in relation to Q at any time is to be determined on the assumption that the reference to "design" in paragraph (*b*) of section 235(3) (definition of "promoter" in relation to relevant arrangements) is omitted.

Deemed defeat notices

18 (1) This paragraph applies if—

(*a*) an authorised officer becomes aware at any time ("the relevant time") that a relevant defeat has occurred in relation to a person ("P") who is carrying on a business as a promoter,

(*b*) there have occurred, more than 3 years before the relevant time—

(i) one third party defeat, or

(ii) two third party defeats, and

(*c*) conditions A1 and B1 (in a case within paragraph (*b*)(i)), or conditions A2 and B2 (in a case within paragraph (*b*)(ii)), are met.

(2) Where this paragraph applies by virtue of sub-paragraph (1)(*b*)(i), this Part of this Act has effect as if an authorised officer had (with due authority), at the time of the time of the third party defeat, given P a single defeat notice under section 241A(2) in respect of it.

(3) Where this paragraph applies by virtue of sub-paragraph (1)(*b*)(ii), this Part of this Act has effect as if an authorised officer had (with due authority), at the time of the second of the two third party defeats, given P a double defeat notice under section 241A(3) in respect of the two third party defeats.

(4) Section 241A(8) has no effect in relation to a notice treated as given as mentioned in sub-paragraph (2) or (3).

(5) Condition A1 is that—

(*a*) a conduct notice or a single or double defeat notice has been given to the other person (see sub-paragraph (9)) in respect of the third party defeat,

(*b*) at the time of the third party defeat an authorised officer would have had power by virtue of paragraph 17 to give P a defeat notice in respect of the third party defeat, had the officer been aware that it was a relevant defeat in relation to P, and

(*c*) so far as the authorised officer mentioned in sub-paragraph (1)(*a*) is aware, the conditions for giving P a defeat notice in respect of the third party defeat have never been met (ignoring this paragraph).

(6) Condition A2 is that—

(*a*) a conduct notice or a single or double defeat notice has been given to the other person (see sub-paragraph (9)) in respect of each, or both, of the third party defeats,

(*b*) at the time of the second third party defeat an authorised officer would have had power by virtue of paragraph 17 to give P a double defeat notice in respect of the third party defeats, had the officer been aware that either of the third party defeats was a relevant defeat in relation to P, and

(*c*) so far as the authorised officer mentioned in sub-paragraph(1)(*a*) is aware, the conditions for giving P a defeat notice in respect of those third party defeats (or either of them) have never been met (ignoring this paragraph).

(7) Condition B1 is that, had an authorised officer given P a defeat notice in respect of the third party defeat at the time of that relevant defeat, that defeat notice would still have effect at the relevant time (see subparagraph (1)).

(8) Condition B2 is that, had an authorised officer given P a defeat notice in respect of the two third party defeats at the time of the second of those relevant defeats, that defeat notice would still have effect at the relevant time.

(9) In this paragraph "third party defeat" means a relevant defeat which has occurred in relation to a person other than P.

Meaning of "relevant body" and "control"

19 (1) In this Part of this Schedule "relevant body" means—

(*a*) a body corporate, or

(*b*) a partnership.

(2) For the purposes of this Part of this Schedule a person controls a body corporate if the person has power to secure that the affairs of the body corporate are conducted in accordance with the person's wishes—

(*a*) by means of the holding of shares or the possession of voting power in relation to the body corporate or any other relevant body,

(*b*) as a result of any powers conferred by the articles of association or other document regulating the body corporate or any other relevant body, or

(*c*) by means of controlling a partnership.

(3) For the purposes of this Part of this Schedule a person controls a partnership if the person is a controlling member or the managing partner of the partnership.

(4) In this paragraph "controlling member" has the same meaning as in Schedule 36 (partnerships).

(5) In this paragraph "managing partner", in relation to a partnership, means the member of the partnership who directs, or is on a day-today level in control of, the management of the business of the partnership.

PART 4

MEETING SECTION 237A CONDITIONS: BODIES CORPORATE AND PARTNERSHIPS

Treating persons under another's control as meeting section 237A condition

20 (1) A relevant body ("RB") is treated as meeting a section 237A condition at the section 237A(2) relevant time if—

(*a*) that condition was met by a person ("C") at a time when—

(i) C was carrying on a business as a promoter, or

(ii) RB was carrying on a business as a promoter and C controlled RB, and

(*b*) RB is controlled by C at the section 237A(2) relevant time.

(2) Sub-paragraph (1) does not apply if C is an individual.

(3) For the purposes of determining whether the requirements of subparagraph (1) are met by reason of meeting the requirement in subparagraph (1)(*a*)(i), it does not matter whether RB existed at the time when C met the section 237A condition.

Treating persons in control of others as meeting section 237A condition

21 (1) A person other than an individual is treated as meeting a section 237A condition at the section 237A(2) relevant time if—

(*a*) a relevant body ("A") met the condition at a time when A was controlled by the person, and

(*b*) at the time mentioned in paragraph (*a*) A, or another relevant body ("B") which was also at that time controlled by the person, carried on a business as a promoter.

(2) For the purposes of determining whether the requirements of subparagraph (1) are met it does not matter whether A or B (or neither) exists at the section 237A(2) relevant time.

Treating persons controlled by the same person as meeting section 237A condition

22 (1) A relevant body ("RB") is treated as meeting a section 237A condition at the section 237A(2) relevant time if—

(*a*) another relevant body met that condition at a time ("time T") when it was controlled by a person ("C"),

(*b*) at time T, there was a relevant body controlled by C which carried on a business as a promoter, and

(*c*) RB is controlled by C at the section 237A(2) relevant time.

(2) For the purposes of determining whether the requirements of subparagraph (1) are met it does not matter whether—

(*a*) RB existed at time T, or

(*b*) any relevant body (other than RB) by reason of which the requirements of sub-paragraph (1) are met exists at the section 237A(2) relevant time.

Interpretation

23 (1) In this Part of this Schedule—

"control" has the same meaning as in Part 3 of this Schedule;

"relevant body" has the same meaning as in Part 3 of this Schedule;

"section 237A(2) relevant time" means the time referred to in section 237A(2);

"section 237A condition" means any of the conditions in section 237A(11), (12) and (13).

(2) For the purposes of paragraphs 20(1)(*a*), 21(1)(*a*) and 22(1)(*a*), the condition in section 237A(11) (occurrence of 3 relevant defeats in the 3 years ending with the relevant time) is taken to have been met by a person at any time if at least 3 relevant defeats have occurred in relation to the person in the period of 3 years ending with that time.

PART 5
SUPPLEMENTARY

"Adjustments"

24 *In this Schedule "adjustments" means any adjustments, whether by way of an assessment, the modification of an assessment or return, the amendment or disallowance of a claim, the entering into of a contract settlement or otherwise (and references to "making" adjustments accordingly include securing that adjustments are made by entering into a contract settlement).*

Meaning of "avoidance-related rule"

25 (1) In this Schedule "avoidance-related rule" means a rule in Category 1 or 2.

(2) A rule is in Category 1 if—

(*a*) it refers (in whatever terms) to the purpose or main purpose or purposes of a transaction, arrangements or any other action or matter, and

(*b*) to whether or not the purpose in question is or involves the avoidance of tax or the obtaining of any advantage in relation to tax (however described).

(3) A rule is also in Category 1 if it refers (in whatever terms) to—

(*a*) expectations as to what are, or may be, the expected benefits of a transaction, arrangements or any other action or matter, and

(*b*) whether or not the avoidance of tax or the obtaining of any advantage in relation to tax (however described) is such a benefit.

For the purposes of paragraph (*b*) it does not matter whether the reference is (for instance) to the "sole or main benefit" or "one of the main benefits" or any other reference to a benefit.

(4) A rule falls within Category 2 if as a result of the rule a person may be treated differently for tax purposes depending on whether or not purposes referred to in the rule (for instance the purposes of an actual or contemplated action or enterprise) are (or are shown to be) commercial purposes.

(5) For example, a rule in the following form would fall within Category 1 and within Category 2—

"Example rule

Section X does not apply to a company in respect of a transaction if the company shows that the transaction meets Condition A or B.

Condition A is that the transaction is effected—

(*a*) for genuine commercial reasons, or

(*b*) in the ordinary course of managing investments.

Condition B is that the avoidance of tax is not the main object or one of the main objects of the transaction."

"DOTAS arrangements"

26 (1) For the purposes of this Schedule arrangements are "DOTAS arrangements" at any time if at that time a person—

(*a*) has provided, information in relation to the arrangements under section 308(3), 309 or 310 of FA 2004, or

(*b*) has failed to comply with any of those provisions in relation to the arrangements.

(2) But for the purposes of this Schedule "DOTAS arrangements" does not include arrangements in respect of which HMRC has given notice under section 312(6) of FA 2004 (notice that promoters not under duty to notify client of reference number).

(3) For the purposes of sub-paragraph (1) a person who would be required to provide information under subsection (3) of section 308 of FA 2004—

(*a*) but for the fact that the arrangements implement a proposal in respect of which notice has been given under subsection (1) of that section, or

(*b*) but for subsection (4A), (4C) or (5) of that section,

is treated as providing the information at the end of the period referred to in subsection (3) of that section.

"Disclosable VAT arrangements"

27 *For the purposes of this Schedule arrangements are "disclosable VAT arrangements" at any time if at that time—*

(*a*) a person has complied with paragraph 6 of Schedule 11A to VATA 1994 in relation to the arrangements (duty to notify Commissioners),

(*b*) a person under a duty to comply with that paragraph in relation to the arrangements has failed to do so, or

(*c*) a reference number has been allocated to the scheme under paragraph 9 of that Schedule (voluntary notification of avoidance scheme which is not a designated scheme).

Paragraphs 26 and 27: supplementary

28 (1) A person "fails to comply" with any provision mentioned in paragraph 26(1)(*a*) or 27(*b*) if and only if any of the conditions in subparagraphs (2) to (4) is met.

(2) The condition in this sub-paragraph is that—

(*a*) the tribunal has determined that the person has failed to comply with the provision concerned,

(*b*) the appeal period has ended, and

(*c*) the determination has not been overturned on appeal.

(3) The condition in this sub-paragraph is that—

(*a*) the tribunal has determined for the purposes of section 118(2) of TMA 1970 that the person is to be deemed not to have failed to comply with the provision concerned as the person had a reasonable excuse for not doing the thing required to be done,

(*b*) the appeal period has ended, and

(*c*) the determination has not been overturned on appeal.

(4) The condition in this sub-paragraph is that the person admitted in writing to HMRC that the person has failed to comply with the provision concerned.

(5) In this paragraph "the appeal period" means—

(*a*) the period during which an appeal could be brought against the determination of the tribunal, or

(*b*) where an appeal mentioned in paragraph (*a*) has been brought, the period during which that appeal has not been finally determined, withdrawn or otherwise disposed of.

"Final" counteraction

29 *For the purposes of this Schedule the counteraction of a tax advantage or of arrangements is "final" when the assessment or adjustments made to effect the counteraction, and any amounts arising as a result of the assessment or adjustments, can no longer be varied, on appeal or otherwise.*

Inheritance tax, stamp duty reserve tax, VAT and petroleum revenue tax

30 (1) In this Schedule, in relation to inheritance tax, each of the following is treated as a return—

(*a*) an account delivered by a person under section 216 or 217 of IHTA 1984 (including an account delivered in accordance with regulations under section 256 of that Act);

(*b*) a statement or declaration which amends or is otherwise connected with such an account produced by the person who delivered the account;

(*c*) information or a document provided by a person in accordance with regulations under section 256 of that Act;

and such a return is treated as made by the person in question.

(2) In this Schedule references to an assessment to tax, in relation to inheritance tax, stamp duty reserve tax and petroleum revenue tax, include a determination.

(3) In this Schedule an expression used in relation to VAT has the same meaning as in VATA 1994.

Power to amend

31 (1) The Treasury may by regulations amend this Schedule (apart from this paragraph).

(2) An amendment by virtue of sub-paragraph (1) may, in particular, add, vary or remove conditions or categories (or otherwise vary the meaning of "avoidance-related rule").

(3) Regulations under sub-paragraph (1) may include any amendment of this Part of this Act that is appropriate in consequence of an amendment made by virtue of sub-paragraph (1)."

(6) In section 241 (duration of conduct notice), after subsection (4) insert—

"(5) See also section 237D(2) (provisional conduct notice affected by judicial ruling)."

(7) After section 281 insert—

"281A VAT

(1) In the provisions mentioned in subsection (2)—

(*a*) "tax" includes value added tax, and

(*b*) "tax advantage" has the meaning given by section 234(3) and also includes a tax advantage as defined in paragraph 1 of Schedule 11A to VATA 1994.

(2) Those provisions are—

(*a*) section 237D;

(*b*) section 241B;

(*c*) Schedule 34A.

(3) Other references in this Part to "tax" are to be read as including value added tax so far as that is necessary for the purposes of sections 237A to 237D, 241A and 241B and Schedule 34A; but "tax" does not include value added tax in section 237A(10) or 237B(3)."

(8) In section 282 (regulations), in subsection (3), after paragraph (*b*) insert—

"(*ba*) paragraph 31 of Schedule 34A,".

(9) In section 283(1) (interpretation of Part 5)—

(*a*) in the definition of "conduct notice", after paragraph (*a*) insert—

"(*aa*) section 237A(8),

(*ab*) section 237B(1),";

(*b*) in the definition of "tax", after ""tax"" insert "(except in provisions to which section 281A applies)";

(*c*) in the definition of ""tax advantage"", after "234(3)" insert "(but see also section 281A)";

(*d*) at the appropriate places insert—

""contract settlement" means an agreement in connection with a person's liability to make a payment to the Commissioners under or by virtue of an enactment;"

""defeat", in relation to arrangements, has the meaning given by paragraph 10 of Schedule 34A;"

""defeat notice" has the meaning given by section 241A(7);"

""double defeat notice" has the meaning given by section 241A(7);"

""final", in relation to a judicial ruling, is to be interpreted in accordance with section 237D(6);"

""judicial ruling" means a ruling of a court or tribunal on one or more issues;"

""look-forward period, in relation to a defeat notice, has the meaning given by section 241A(10);"

""provisional", in relation to a conduct notice given under section 237A(8), is to be interpreted in accordance with section 237C;"

""relevant defeat", in relation to a person, is to be interpreted in accordance with Schedule 34A;"

""related", in relation to arrangements, is to be interpreted in accordance with paragraph 2 of Schedule 34A;"

""relies on a Case 3 relevant defeat" is to be interpreted in accordance section 237B(5);"

""single defeat notice" has the meaning given by section 241A(7)."

(10) Schedule 36 (promoters of tax avoidance schemes: partnerships) is amended in accordance with subsections (11) to (16).

(11) In Part 2, before paragraph 5 insert—

"Defeat notices

4A

A defeat notice that is given to a partnership must state that it is a partnership defeat notice.".

(12) In paragraph 7(1)(*b*) after "a" insert "defeat notice,".

(13) In paragraph 7(2) after "the" insert "defeat notice,".
(14) After paragraph 7 insert—

"Persons leaving partnership: defeat notices

7A

(1) Sub-paragraphs (2) and (3) apply where—

(*a*) a person ("P") who was a controlling member of a partnership at the time when a defeat notice ("the original notice") was given to the partnership has ceased to be a member of the partnership,

(*b*) the defeat notice had effect in relation to the partnership at the time of that cessation, and

(*c*) P is carrying on a business as a promoter.

(2) An authorised officer may give P a defeat notice.

(3) If P is carrying on a business as a promoter in partnership with one or more other persons and is a controlling member of that partnership ("the new partnership"), an authorised officer may give a defeat notice to the new partnership.

(4) A defeat notice given under sub-paragraph (3) ceases to have effect if P ceases to be a member of the new partnership.

(5) A notice under sub-paragraph (2) or (3) may not be given after the original notice has ceased to have effect.

(6) A defeat notice given under sub-paragraph (2) or (3) is given in respect of the relevant defeat or relevant defeats to which the original notice relates."

(15) In paragraph 10—

(*a*) in sub-paragraph (1)(*b*) for "conduct notice or a" substitute ", defeat notice, conduct notice or";

(*b*) in sub-paragraph (3), after "partner—" insert—

"(*za*) a defeat notice (if the original notice is a defeat notice);".

(*c*) in sub-paragraph (4), after "("the new partnership")—" insert—

"(*za*) a defeat notice (if the original notice is a defeat notice);".

(*d*) after sub-paragraph (5) insert—

"(5A) A notice under sub-paragraph (3)(*za*) or (4)(*za*) may not be given after the end of the look-forward period of the original notice."

(16) After paragraph 11 insert—

11A

The look-forward period for a notice under paragraph 7A(2) or (3) or 10(3)(*za*) or (4)(*za*)—

(*a*) begins on the day after the day on which the notice is given, and

(*b*) continues to the end of the look-forward period for the original notice (as defined in paragraph 7A(1)(*a*) or 10(2), as the case may be).

(17) Part 2 of Schedule 2 to the National Insurance Contributions Act 2015 (application of Part 5 of FA 2014 to national insurance contributions) is amended in accordance with subsections (18) and (19).

(18) After paragraph 30 insert—

"Threshold conditions

30A

(1) In paragraph 5 of Schedule 34 (non-compliance with Part 7 of FA 2004), in sub-paragraph (4)—

(*a*) paragraph (*a*) includes a reference to a decision having been made for corresponding NICs purposes that P is to be deemed not to have failed to comply with the provision concerned as P had a reasonable excuse for not doing the thing required to be done, and

(*b*) the reference in paragraph (*c*) to a determination is to be read accordingly.

(2) In this paragraph "corresponding NICs purposes" means the purposes of any provision of regulations under section 132A of SSAA 1992.

Relevant defeats

30B

(1) Schedule 34A (promoters of tax avoidance schemes: defeated arrangements) has effect with the following modifications.

(2) References to an assessment (or an assessment to tax) include a NICs decision relating to a person's liability for relevant contributions.

(3) References to adjustments include a payment in respect of a liability to pay relevant contributions (and the definition of "adjustments" in paragraph 24 accordingly has effect as if such payments were included in it).

(4) In paragraph 9(3) the reference to an enquiry into a return includes a relevant contributions dispute (as defined in paragraph 6 of this Schedule).

(5) In paragraph 28(3)—

(*a*) paragraph (*a*) includes a reference to a decision having been made for corresponding NICs purposes that the person is to be deemed not to have failed to comply with the provision concerned as the person had a reasonable excuse for not doing the thing required to be done, and

(*b*) the reference in paragraph (*c*) to a determination is to be read accordingly.

"Corresponding NICs purposes" means the purposes of any provision of regulations under section 132A of SSAA 1992."

(19) In paragraph 31 (interpretation)—

(*a*) before paragraph (*a*) insert—

"(*za*) "NICs decision" means a decision under section 8 of SSC(TF)A 1999 or Article 7 of the Social Security Contributions (Transfer of Functions, etc) (Northern Ireland) Order 1999 (SI 1999/671);"

(*b*) in paragraph (*b*), for "are to sections of" substitute "or Schedules are to sections of, or Schedules to".

(20) For the purposes of sections 237A and 241A of FA 2014, a defeat (by virtue of any of Conditions A to F in Schedule 34A to that Act) of arrangements is treated as not having occurred if—

(*a*) there has been a final judicial ruling on or before the day on which this Act is passed as a result of which the counteraction referred to in paragraph 11(*d*), 12(1)(*b*), 13(1)(*d*), 14(1)(*d*) or 15(1)(*d*) (as the case may be) is final for the purposes of Schedule 34A of that Act, or

(*b*) (in the case of a defeat by virtue of Condition F in Schedule 34A) the judicial ruling mentioned in paragraph 16(1)(*d*) of that Schedule becomes final on or before the day on which this Act is passed.

(21) Subsection (20) does not apply in relation to a person (who is carrying on a business as a promoter) if at any time after 17 July 2014 that person or an associated person takes action as a result of which the person taking the action—

(*a*) becomes a promoter in relation to the arrangements, or arrangements related to those arrangements, or

(*b*) would have become a promoter in relation to arrangements mentioned in paragraph (*a*) had the person not already been a promoter in relation to those arrangements.

(22) For the purposes of sections 237A and 241A of FA 2014, a defeat of arrangements is treated as not having occurred if it would (ignoring this subparagraph) have occurred—

(*a*) on or before the first anniversary of the day on which this Act is passed, and

(*b*) by virtue of any of Conditions A to E in Schedule 34A to FA 2014, but otherwise than as a result of a final judicial ruling.

(23) For the purposes of subsection (21) a person ("Q") is an "associated person" in relation to another person ("P") at any time when any of the following conditions is met—

(*a*) P is a relevant body which is controlled by Q;

(*b*) Q is a relevant body, P is not an individual and Q is controlled by P;

(*c*) P and Q are relevant bodies and a third person controls P and Q.

(24) In subsection (23) "relevant body" and "control" are to be interpreted in accordance with paragraph 19 of Schedule 34A to FA 2014.

(25) In subsections (20) to (22) expressions used in Part 5 of FA 2014 (as amended by this section) have the same meaning as in that Part.

Offshore activities

162 Penalties for enablers of offshore tax evasion or non-compliance

(1) Schedule 20 makes provision for penalties for persons who enable offshore tax evasion or non-compliance by other persons.

(2) Subsection (1) and that Schedule come into force on such day as the Treasury may appoint by regulations made by statutory instrument.

(3) Regulations under this section may—

(*a*) commence a provision generally or only for specified purposes,

(*b*) appoint different days for different purposes, and

(*c*) make supplemental, incidental and transitional provision in connection with the coming into force of any provision of the Schedule.

Commencement—Finance Act 2016, Section 162(1) and Schedule 20 (Appointed Day) Regulations, SI 2016/1249 (the appointed day for the purposes of s 162(1) is 1 January 2017 with effect in relation to acts or omissions occurring on or after that day which encourage, assist or otherwise facilitate conduct constituting offshore tax evasion or non-compliance within FA 2016 Sch 20 para 1(2)).

165 Asset-based penalties for offshore inaccuracies and failures

(1) Schedule 22 contains provision imposing asset-based penalties on certain taxpayers who have been charged a penalty for deliberate offshore inaccuracies and failures.

(2) That Schedule comes into force on such day as the Treasury may by regulations made by statutory instrument appoint.

(3) Regulations under subsection (2) may—

(*a*) commence a provision generally or only for specified purposes,

(*b*) appoint different days for different provisions or for different purposes, and

(*c*) make supplemental, incidental and transitional provision.

Regulations—Finance Act 2016, Schedule 22 (Appointed Day) Regulations, SI 2017/277.

PART 11

ADMINISTRATION, ENFORCEMENT AND SUPPLEMENTARY POWERS

Enforcement powers

176 Data-gathering powers: providers of payment or intermediary services

(1) In Part 2 of Schedule 23 to FA 2011 (data-gathering powers: relevant data-holders), after paragraph 13A insert—

"Providers of electronic stored-value payment services

13B

(1) A person who provides electronic stored-value payment services is a relevant data-holder.

(2) In this paragraph "electronic stored-value payment services" means services by means of which monetary value is stored electronically for the purpose of payments being made in respect of transactions to which the provider of those services is not a party.

Business intermediaries

13C

(1) A person who—

(*a*) provides services to enable or facilitate transactions between suppliers and their customers or clients (other than services provided solely to enable payments to be made), and

(*b*) receives information about such transactions in the course of doing so,

is a relevant data-holder.

(2) In this paragraph "suppliers" means persons supplying goods or services in the course of business.

(3) For the purposes of this paragraph, information about transactions includes information that is capable of indicating the likely quantity or value of transactions."

(2) This section applies in relation to relevant data with a bearing on any period (whether before, on or after the day on which this Act is passed).

177 Data-gathering powers: daily penalties for extended default

(1) Part 4 of Schedule 23 to FA 2011 (data-gathering powers: penalties) is amended as follows.

(2) In paragraph 38 (increased daily default penalty)—

(*a*) in sub-paragraphs (1)(*c*) and (2), for "imposed" substitute "assessable";

(*b*) for sub-paragraphs (3) and (4) substitute—

"(3) If the tribunal decides that an increased daily penalty should be assessable—

(*a*) the tribunal must determine the day from which the increased daily penalty is to apply and the maximum amount of that penalty ("the new maximum amount");

(*b*) from that day, paragraph 31 has effect in the data-holder's case as if "the new maximum amount" were substituted for "£60".

(4) The new maximum amount may not be more than £1,000.";

(*c*) in sub-paragraph (5), for "the amount" substitute "the new maximum amount".

(3) In paragraph 39—

(*a*) in sub-paragraph (1), for "a data-holder becomes liable to a penalty" substitute "the tribunal makes a determination";

(*b*) in sub-paragraph (2), for "the day from which the increased penalty is to apply" substitute "new maximum amount and the day from which it applies";

(*c*) omit sub-paragraph (3).

(4) In paragraph 40 (enforcement of penalties), in sub-paragraph (2)(*a*) omit "or 39".

(5) At the end of paragraph 36 (right to appeal against penalty), the existing text of which becomes sub-paragraph (1), insert—

"(2) But sub-paragraph (1)(*b*) does not give a right of appeal against the amount of an increased daily penalty payable by virtue of paragraph 38."

SCHEDULE 15

INHERITANCE TAX: INCREASED NIL-RATE BAND

Section 93

1 IHTA 1984 is amended as follows.

2 (1) Section 8D (extra nil-rate band on death if interest in home goes to descendants etc) is amended as follows.

(2) In subsection (4), after "8G" insert "(and see also section 8M)".

(3) In subsection (9), before the definition of "tax year" insert—

""consumer prices index" means the all items consumer prices index published by the Statistics Board,".

3 (1) Section 8E (residence nil-rate amount: interest in home goes to descendants etc) is amended as follows.

(2) In subsection (6), after "(7)" insert "and sections 8FC and 8M(2B) to (2E)".

(3) In subsection (7), for paragraphs (a) and (b) substitute—

"(a) the person's residence nil-rate amount is equal to VT,

(b) where E is less than or equal to TT, an amount, equal to the difference between VT and the person's default allowance, is available for carry-forward, and

(c) where E is greater than TT, an amount, equal to the difference between VT and the person's adjusted allowance, is available for carry-forward."

(4) In subsection (8)—

(a) before the entry for section 8H insert—

"section 8FC (modifications of this section where there is entitlement to a downsizing addition),", and

(b) in the entry for section 8H, after ""qualifying residential interest"" insert ", "qualifying former residential interest" and "residential property interest"".

4 In section 8F(4) (list of other relevant sections)—

(a) before the entry for section 8H insert—

"section 8FD (which applies instead of this section where there is entitlement to a downsizing addition),", and

(b) in the entry for section 8H, after ""qualifying residential interest"" insert ", "qualifying former residential interest" and "residential property interest"".

5 After section 8F insert—

"8FA Downsizing addition: entitlement: low-value death interest in home

(1) There is entitlement to a downsizing addition in calculating the person's residence nil-rate amount if each of conditions A to F is met (see subsection (8) for the amount of the addition).

(2) Condition A is that—

(a) the person's residence nil-rate amount is given by section 8E(2) or (4), or

(b) the person's estate immediately before the person's death includes a qualifying residential interest but none of the interest is closely inherited, and—

(i) where E is less than or equal to TT, so much of VT as is attributable to the person's qualifying residential interest is less than the person's default allowance, or

(ii) where E is greater than TT, so much of VT as is attributable to the person's qualifying residential interest is less than the person's adjusted allowance.

Section 8E(6) and (7) do not apply, and any entitlement to a downsizing addition is to be ignored, when deciding whether paragraph (a) of condition A is met.

(3) Condition B is that not all of VT is attributable to the person's qualifying residential interest.

(4) Condition C is that there is a qualifying former residential interest in relation to the person (see sections 8H(4A) to (4F) and 8HA).

(5) Condition D is that the value of the qualifying former residential interest exceeds so much of VT as is attributable to the person's qualifying residential interest.

Section 8FE(2) explains what is meant by the value of the qualifying former residential interest.

(6) Condition E is that at least some of the remainder is closely inherited, where "the remainder" means everything included in the person's estate immediately before the person's death other than the person's qualifying residential interest.

(7) Condition F is that a claim is made for the addition in accordance with section 8L(1) to (3).

(8) Where there is entitlement as a result of this section, the addition—

(a) is equal to the lost relievable amount (see section 8FE) if that amount is less than so much of VT as is attributable to so much of the remainder as is closely inherited, and

(b) otherwise is equal to so much of VT as is attributable to so much of the remainder as is closely inherited.

(9) Subsection (8) has effect subject to section 8M(2G) (reduction of downsizing addition in certain cases involving conditional exemption).

(10) See also—

section 8FC (effect of an addition: section 8E case),

section 8FD (effect of an addition: section 8F case),

section 8H (meaning of "qualifying residential interest", "qualifying former residential interest" and "residential property interest"),

section 8J (meaning of "inherit"),

section 8K (meaning of "closely inherited"), and

section 8M (cases involving conditional exemption).

8FB Downsizing addition: entitlement: no residential interest at death

(1) There is also entitlement to a downsizing addition in calculating the person's residence nil-rate amount if each of conditions G to K is met (see subsection (7) for the amount of the addition).

(2) Condition G is that the person's estate immediately before the person's death ("the estate") does not include a residential property interest.

(3) Condition H is that VT is greater than nil.

(4) Condition I is that there is a qualifying former residential interest in relation to the person (see sections 8H(4A) to (4F) and 8HA).

(5) Condition J is that at least some of the estate is closely inherited.

(6) Condition K is that a claim is made for the addition in accordance with section 8L(1) to (3).

(7) Where there is entitlement as a result of this section, the addition—

(a) is equal to the lost relievable amount (see section 8FE) if that amount is less than so much of VT as is attributable to so much of the estate as is closely inherited, and

(b) otherwise is equal to so much of VT as is attributable to so much of the estate as is closely inherited.

(8) Subsection (7) has effect subject to section 8M(2G) (reduction of downsizing addition in certain cases involving conditional exemption).

(9) See also—

section 8FD (effect of an addition: section 8F case),

section 8H (meaning of "qualifying residential interest", "qualifying former residential interest" and "residential property interest"),

section 8J (meaning of "inherit"),

section 8K (meaning of "closely inherited"), and

section 8M (cases involving conditional exemption).

8FC Downsizing addition: effect: section 8E case

(1) Subsection (2) applies if—

(a) as a result of section 8FA, there is entitlement to a downsizing addition in calculating the person's residence nil-rate amount, and

(b) the person's residence nil-rate amount is given by section 8E.

(2) Section 8E has effect as if, in subsections (2) to (5) of that section, each reference to NV/100 were a reference to the total of—

(a) NV/100, and
(b) the downsizing addition.

8FD Downsizing addition: effect: section 8F case

(1) This section applies if—

(a) as a result of section 8FA or 8FB, there is entitlement to a downsizing addition in calculating the person's residence nil-rate amount, and
(b) apart from this section, the person's residence nil-rate amount is given by section 8F.

(2) Subsections (3) to (6) apply instead of section 8F.

(3) The person's residence nil-rate amount is equal to the downsizing addition.

(4) Where—

(a) E is less than or equal to TT, and the downsizing addition is equal to the person's default allowance, or
(b) E is greater than TT, and the downsizing addition is equal to the person's adjusted allowance,

no amount is available for carry-forward.

(5) Where—

(a) E is less than or equal to TT, and
(b) the downsizing addition is less than the person's default allowance,

an amount, equal to the difference between the downsizing addition and the person's default allowance, is available for carry-forward.

(6) Where—

(a) E is greater than TT, and
(b) the downsizing addition is less than the person's adjusted allowance,

an amount, equal to the difference between the downsizing addition and the person's adjusted allowance, is available for carry-forward.

8FE Calculation of lost relievable amount

(1) This section is about how to calculate the person's lost relievable amount for the purposes of sections 8FA(8) and 8FB(7).

(2) For the purposes of this section and section 8FA(5), the value of the person's qualifying former residential interest is the value of the interest at the time of completion of the disposal of the interest.

(3) In this section, the person's "former allowance" is the total of—

(a) the residential enhancement at the time of completion of the disposal of the qualifying former residential interest,
(b) any brought-forward allowance that the person would have had if the person had died at that time, having regard to the circumstances of the person at that time (see section 8G as applied by subsection (4)), and
(c) if the person's allowance on death includes an amount of brought-forward allowance which is greater than the amount of brought-forward allowance given by paragraph (b), the difference between those two amounts.

(4) For the purposes of calculating any brought-forward allowance that the person ("P") would have had as mentioned in subsection (3)(b)—

(a) section 8G (brought-forward allowance) applies, but as if references to the residential enhancement at P's death were references to the residential enhancement at the time of completion of the disposal of the qualifying former residential interest, and
(b) assume that a claim for brought-forward allowance was made in relation to an amount available for carry-forward from a related person's death if, on P's death, a claim was in fact made in relation to the amount.

(5) For the purposes of subsection (3)(c), where the person's allowance on death is equal to the person's adjusted allowance, the amount of brought-forward allowance included in the person's allowance on death is calculated as follows.

Step 1

Express the person's brought-forward allowance as a percentage of the person's default allowance.

Step 2

Multiply—

(E - TT) / 2

by the percentage given by step 1.

Step 3

Reduce the person's brought-forward allowance by the amount given by step 2.

The result is the amount of brought-forward allowance included in the person's allowance on death.

(6) If completion of the disposal of the qualifying former residential interest occurs before 6 April 2017—

(a) for the purposes of subsection (3)(a), the residential enhancement at the time of completion of the disposal is treated as being £100,000, and

(b) for the purposes of subsection (3)(b), the amount of brought-forward allowance that the person would have had at that time is treated as being nil.

(7) In this section, the person's "allowance on death" means—

(a) where E is less than or equal to TT, the person's default allowance, or

(b) where E is greater than TT, the person's adjusted allowance.

(8) For the purposes of this section, "completion" of the disposal of a residential property interest occurs at the time of the disposal or, if the disposal is under a contract which is completed by a conveyance, at the time when the interest is conveyed.

(9) Where, as a result of section 8FA, there is entitlement to a downsizing addition in calculating the person's residence nil-rate amount, take the following steps to calculate the person's lost relievable amount.

Step 1

Express the value of the person's qualifying former residential interest as a percentage of the person's former allowance, but take that percentage to be 100% if it would otherwise be higher.

Step 2

Express QRI as a percentage of the person's allowance on death, where QRI is so much of VT as is attributable to the person's qualifying residential interest, but take that percentage to be 100% if it would otherwise be higher.

Step 3

Subtract the percentage given by step 2 from the percentage given by step 1, but take the result to be 0% if it would otherwise be negative.

The result is P%.

Step 4

The person's lost relievable amount is equal to P% of the person's allowance on death.

(10) Where, as a result of section 8FB, there is entitlement to a downsizing addition in calculating the person's residence nil-rate amount, take the following steps to calculate the person's lost relievable amount.

Step 1

Express the value of the person's qualifying former residential interest as a percentage of the person's former allowance, but take that percentage to be 100% if it would otherwise be higher.

Step 2

Calculate that percentage of the person's allowance on death.

The result is the person's lost relievable amount."

6 In section 8G (meaning of "brought-forward allowance"), in subsection (3)(a), for "and 8F" substitute ", 8F and 8FD".

7 (1) Section 8H (meaning of "qualifying residential interest") is amended as follows.

(2) In the heading, at the end insert ", "qualifying former residential interest" and "residential property interest"".

(3) In subsection (1), for "and 8F" substitute "to 8FE and section 8M".

(4) In subsection (2), for "In this section" substitute "A".

(5) After subsection (4) insert—

"(4A) Subsection (4B) or (4C) applies where—

(a) a person disposes of a residential property interest in a dwelling-house on or after 8 July 2015 (and before the person dies), and

(b) the person's personal representatives nominate—

(i) where there is only one such dwelling-house, that dwelling-house, or

(ii) where there are two or more such dwelling-houses, one (and only one) of those dwelling-houses.

(4B) Where—

(a) the person—

(i) disposes of a residential property interest in the nominated dwelling-house at a post-occupation time, or

(ii) disposes of two or more residential property interests in the nominated dwelling-house at the same post-occupation time or at post-occupation times on the same day, and

(b) the person does not otherwise dispose of residential property interests in the nominated dwelling-house at post-occupation times,

the interest disposed of is, or the interests disposed of are, a qualifying former residential interest in relation to the person.

(4C) Where—

(a) the person disposes of residential property interests in the nominated dwelling-house at post-occupation times on two or more days, and

(b) the person's personal representatives nominate one (and only one) of those days,

the interest or interests disposed of at post-occupation times on the nominated day is or are a qualifying former residential interest in relation to the person.

(4D) For the purposes of subsections (4A) to (4C)—

(a) a person is to be treated as not disposing of a residential property interest in a dwelling-house where the person disposes of an interest in the dwelling-house by way of gift and the interest is, in relation to the gift and the donor, property subject to a reservation within the meaning of section 102 of the Finance Act 1986 (gifts with reservation), and

(b) a person is to be treated as disposing of a residential property interest in a dwelling-house if the person is treated as making a potentially exempt transfer of the interest as a result of the operation of section 102(4) of that Act (property ceasing to be subject to a reservation).

(4E) Where—

(a) a transfer of value by a person is a conditionally exempt transfer of a residential property interest, and

(b) at the time of the person's death, no chargeable event has occurred with respect to that interest,

that interest may not be, or be included in, a qualifying former residential interest in relation to the person.

(4F) In subsections (4B) and (4C) "post-occupation time" means a time—

(a) on or after 8 July 2015,

(b) after the nominated dwelling-house first became the person's residence, and

(c) before the person dies.

(4G) For the purposes of subsections (4A) to (4C), if the disposal is under a contract which is completed by a conveyance, the disposal occurs at the time when the interest is conveyed."

8 After section 8H insert—

"8HA Qualifying former residential interest": interests in possession

(1) This section applies for the purposes of determining whether certain interests may be, or be included in, a qualifying former residential interest in relation to a person (see section 8H(4A) to (4C)).

(2) This section applies where—

(a) a person ("P") is beneficially entitled to an interest in possession in settled property, and

(b) the settled property consists of, or includes, an interest in a dwelling-house.

(3) Subsection (4) applies where—

(a) the trustees of the settlement dispose of the interest in the dwelling-house to a person other than P,

(b) P's interest in possession in the settled property subsists immediately before the disposal, and

(c) P's interest in possession—

(i) falls within subsection (7) throughout the period beginning with P becoming beneficially entitled to it and ending with the disposal, or

(ii) falls within subsection (8).

(4) The disposal is to be treated as a disposal by P of the interest in the dwelling-house to which P is beneficially entitled as a result of the operation of section 49(1).

(5) Subsection (6) applies where—

(a) P disposes of the interest in possession in the settled property, or P's interest in possession in the settled property comes to an end in P's lifetime,

(b) the interest in the dwelling-house is, or is part of, the settled property immediately before the time when that happens, and

(c) P's interest in possession—

(i) falls within subsection (7) throughout the period beginning with P becoming beneficially entitled to it and ending with the time mentioned in paragraph (b), or

(ii) falls within subsection (8).

(6) The disposal, or (as the case may be) the coming to an end of P's interest in possession, is to be treated as a disposal by P of the interest in the dwelling-house to which P is beneficially entitled as a result of the operation of section 49(1).

(7) An interest in possession falls within this subsection if—

(a) P became beneficially entitled to it before 22 March 2006 and section 71A does not apply to the settled property; or

(b) P becomes beneficially entitled to it on or after 22 March 2006 and the interest is—

(i) an immediate post-death interest,

(ii) a disabled person's interest, or

(iii) a transitional serial interest.

(8) An interest in possession falls within this subsection if P becomes beneficially entitled to it on or after 22 March 2006 and it falls within section 5(1B)."

9 In section 8J (meaning of "inherited"), in subsection (1), for "and 8F" substitute ", 8F, 8FA, 8FB and 8M".

10 In section 8K (meaning of "closely inherited"), in subsection (1), for "and 8F" substitute ", 8F, 8FA, 8FB and 8M".

11 In section 8L (claims for brought-forward allowance)—

(a) in the heading, at the end insert "and downsizing addition", and

(b) in subsection (1), after "(see section 8G)" insert "or for a downsizing addition for a person (see sections 8FA to 8FD)".

12 (1) Section 8M (residence nil-rate amount: cases involving conditional exemption) is amended as follows.

(2) For subsections (1) and (2) substitute—

"(1) This section applies where—

(a) a person ("D") dies on or after 6 April 2017,

(b) ignoring the application of this section, D's residence nil-rate amount is greater than nil, and

(c) some or all of the transfer of value under section 4 on D's death is a conditionally exempt transfer of property consisting of, or including, any of the following—

(i) some or all of a qualifying residential interest;

(ii) some or all of a residential property interest, at least some portion of which is closely inherited, and which is not, and is not included in, a qualifying residential interest;

(iii) one or more closely inherited assets that are not residential property interests.

(2) Subsections (2B) to (2E) apply for the purposes of sections 8E to 8FD if—

(a) ignoring the application of this section, D's residence nil-rate amount is given by section 8E, and

(b) some or all of the transfer of value under section 4 is a conditionally exempt transfer of property mentioned in subsection (1)(c)(i).

(2A) In subsections (2B) to (2E), but subject to subsection (3)(a), "the exempt percentage of the QRI" is given by—

(X / QRI) x 100

where—

X is the attributable portion of the value transferred by the conditionally exempt transfer,

QRI is the attributable portion of the value transferred by the transfer of value under section 4, and

"the attributable portion" means the portion (which may be the whole) attributable to the qualifying residential interest.

(2B) If—

(a) the exempt percentage of the QRI is 100%, and

(b) D has no entitlement to a downsizing addition,

D's residence nil-rate amount and amount available for carry-forward are given by section 8F(2) and (3) (instead of section 8E).

(2C) If—

(a) the exempt percentage of the QRI is 100%, and

(b) D has an entitlement to a downsizing addition,

D's residence nil-rate amount and amount available for carry-forward are given by section 8FD(3) to (6) (instead of section 8E as modified by section 8FC(2)).

See also subsection (2G).

(2D) If—

(a) the exempt percentage of the QRI is less than 100%, and

(b) D has no entitlement to a downsizing addition,

D's residence nil-rate amount and amount available for carry-forward are given by section 8E but as if, in subsections (2) to (5) of that section, each reference to NV/100 were a reference to NV/100 multiplied by the percentage that is the difference between 100% and the exempt percentage of the QRI.

(2E) If—

(a) the exempt percentage of the QRI is less than 100%, and

(b) D has an entitlement to a downsizing addition,

D's residence nil-rate amount and amount available for carry-forward are given by section 8E as modified by section 8FC(2), but as if the reference to NV/100 in section 8FC(2)(a) were a reference to NV/100 multiplied by the percentage that is the difference between 100% and the exempt percentage of the QRI.

See also subsection (2G).

(2F) Subsection (2G) applies for the purposes of sections 8FA to 8FD if—

(a) some or all of the transfer of value under section 4 is a conditionally exempt transfer of property mentioned in subsection (1)(c)(ii) or (iii) (or both),

(b) D has an entitlement to a downsizing addition, and

(c) DA exceeds Y (see subsection (2H)).

(2G) Subject to subsection (3)(aa) and (ab), the amount of the downsizing addition is treated as reduced by whichever is the smaller of—

(a) the difference between DA and Y, and

(b) Z.

(2H) In subsections (2F) and (2G)—

DA is the amount of the downsizing addition to which D has an entitlement (ignoring the application of subsection (2G));

Y is so much (if any) of the value transferred by the transfer of value under section 4 as—

(a) is not transferred by a conditionally exempt transfer, and

(b) is attributable to—

(i) the closely inherited portion (which may be the whole) of any residential property interests that are not, and are not included in, a qualifying residential interest, or

(ii) closely inherited assets that are not residential property interests;

Z is the total of—

(a) the closely inherited conditionally exempt values of all residential property interests mentioned in subsection (1)(c)(ii), and

(b) so much of the value transferred by the conditionally exempt transfer as is attributable to property mentioned in subsection (1)(c)(iii).

(2I) For the purposes of the definition of "Z", "the closely inherited conditionally exempt value" of a residential property interest means—

(a) so much of the value transferred by the conditionally exempt transfer as is attributable to the interest, multiplied by

(b) the percentage of the interest which is closely inherited."

(3) In subsection (3), for the words before paragraph (b) substitute—

"(3) For the purposes of calculating tax chargeable under section 32 or 32A by reference to a chargeable event related to property forming the subject-matter of the conditionally exempt transfer where D is the relevant person for the purposes of section 33—

(a) where subsections (2B) to (2E) apply and the chargeable event relates to property mentioned in subsection (1)(c)(i), in calculating the exempt percentage of the QRI, X is calculated as if the attributable portion of the value transferred by the conditionally exempt transfer had not included the portion (which may be the whole) of the qualifying residential interest on which the tax is chargeable,

(aa) where subsection (2G) applies and the chargeable event relates to property mentioned in subsection (1)(c)(ii), Z is calculated as if it had not included the portion (which may be the whole) of the closely inherited conditionally exempt value of the residential property interest on which the tax is chargeable,

(ab) where subsection (2G) applies and the chargeable event relates to an asset mentioned in subsection (1)(c)(iii) ("the taxable asset"), Z is calculated as if it had not included so much of the value transferred by the conditionally exempt transfer as is attributable to the taxable asset,".

(4) In subsection (3)—

(a) at the beginning of paragraph (b) insert "in the cases mentioned in paragraphs (a), (aa) and (ab),",

(b) at the end of paragraph (b) omit "and",

(c) in paragraph (c), for "less" substitute "reduced (but not below nil) by", and

(d) after paragraph (c) insert ", and

(d) where the chargeable event relates to property mentioned in subsection (1)(c)(i) and subsections (2B) to (2E) do not apply, section 33 has effect as if in subsection (1)(b)(ii) after "in accordance with" there were inserted "section 8D(2) and (3) above and"."

(5) In subsection (5), for "the qualifying residential interest which" substitute "property which forms the subject-matter of the conditionally exempt transfer where the chargeable event".

(6) In subsection (6), for "the qualifying residential interest which" substitute "property which forms the subject-matter of the conditionally exempt transfer and the chargeable event".

(7) In subsection (7), for "the qualifying residential interest" substitute "property which forms the subject-matter of the conditionally exempt transfer".

SCHEDULE 18

SERIAL TAX AVOIDANCE

Section 159

PART 1

CONTENTS OF SCHEDULE

1 In this Schedule—

(*a*) Part 2 provides for HMRC to give warning notices to persons who incur relevant defeats and includes—

(i) provision about the duration of warning periods under warning notices (see paragraph 3), and

(ii) definitions of "relevant defeat" and other key terms;

(*b*) Part 3 contains provisions about persons to whom a warning notice has been given, and in particular—

(i) imposes a duty to give information notices, and

(ii) allows the Commissioners to publish information about such persons in certain cases involving repeated relevant defeats;

(*c*) Part 4 contains provision about the restriction of reliefs;

(*d*) Part 5 imposes liability to penalties on persons who incur relevant defeats in relation to arrangements used in warning periods;

(*e*) Part 6 contains provisions about corporate groups, associated persons and partnerships;

(*f*) Part 7 contains definitions and other supplementary provisions.

PART 2

ENTRY INTO THE REGIME AND BASIC CONCEPTS

Duty to give warning notice

2 (1) This paragraph applies where a person incurs a relevant defeat in relation to any arrangements.

(2) HMRC must give the person a written notice (a "warning notice").

(3) The notice must be given within the period of 90 days beginning with the day on which the relevant defeat is incurred.

(4) The notice must—

(*a*) set out when the warning period begins and ends (see paragraph 3),

(*b*) specify the relevant defeat to which the notice relates, and

(*c*) explain the effect of paragraphs 3 and 17 to 46.

(5) A warning notice given by virtue of paragraph 49 must also explain the effect of paragraph 51 (information in certain cases involving partnerships).

(6) In this Schedule "arrangements" includes any agreement, understanding, scheme, transaction or series of transactions (whether or not legally enforceable).

(7) For the meaning of "relevant defeat" and provision about when a relevant defeat is incurred see paragraph 11.

Warning period

3 (1) If a person is given a warning notice with respect to a relevant defeat (and sub-paragraph (2) does not apply) the period of 5 years beginning with the day after the day on which the notice is given is a "warning period" in relation to that person.

(2) If a person incurs a relevant defeat in relation to arrangements during a period which is a warning period in relation to that person, the warning period is extended to the end of the 5 years beginning with the day after the day on which the relevant defeat occurs.

(3) In relation to a warning period which has been extended under this Schedule, references in this Schedule (including this paragraph) to the warning period are to be read as references to the warning period as extended.

Meaning of "tax"

4 [(1)] [1]In this Schedule "tax" includes any of the following taxes—

(*a*) income tax,

(*b*) corporation tax, including any amount chargeable as if it were corporation tax or treated as if it were corporation tax,

(*c*) capital gains tax,

(*d*) petroleum revenue tax,

(*e*) diverted profits tax,

(*f*) apprenticeship levy,

(*g*) inheritance tax,

(*h*) stamp duty land tax,

(*i*) annual tax on enveloped dwellings,

(*j*) VAT [and indirect taxes][1], and

(*k*) national insurance contributions.

[(2) For the purposes of this Schedule "indirect tax" means any of the following—

insurance premium tax
general betting duty
pool betting duty
remote gaming duty
machine games duty
gaming duty
lottery duty
bingo duty
air passenger duty
hydrocarbon oils duty
tobacco products duty
duties on spirits, beer, wine, made-wine and cider
soft drinks industry levy
aggregates levy
landfill tax
climate change levy
customs duties.][1]

Amendments—[1] Sub-para (1) numbered as such, in sub-para (1)(*j*), words inserted, and sub-para (2) inserted, by F(No 2)A 2017 s 66, Sch 17 para 55(1), (2) with effect from 1 January 2018.

Meaning of "tax advantage" in relation to VAT

5 (1) In this Schedule "tax advantage", in relation to VAT, is to be read in accordance with sub-paragraphs (2) to (4).

(2) A taxable person obtains a tax advantage if—

(*a*) in any prescribed accounting period, the amount by which the output tax accounted for by the person exceeds the input tax deducted by the person is less than it would otherwise be,

(*b*) the person obtains a VAT credit when the person would not otherwise do so, or obtains a larger VAT credit or obtains a VAT credit earlier than would otherwise be the case,

(*c*) in a case where the person recovers input tax as a recipient of a supply before the supplier accounts for the output tax, the period between the time when the input tax is recovered and the time when the output tax is accounted for is greater than would otherwise be the case, or

(*d*) in any prescribed accounting period, the amount of the person's non-deductible tax is less than it would otherwise be.

(3) A person who is not a taxable person obtains a tax advantage if the person's non-refundable tax is less than it otherwise would be.

(4) In sub-paragraph (3) "non-refundable tax", in relation to a person who is not a taxable person, means—

(*a*) VAT on the supply to the person of any goods or services,

(*b*) VAT on the acquisition by the person from another member State of any goods, and

(*c*) VAT paid or payable by the person on the importation of any goods from a place outside the member States,

but excluding (in each case) any VAT in respect of which the person is entitled to a refund from the Commissioners by virtue of any provision of VATA 1994.

Meaning of "non-deductible tax"

6 (1) In this Schedule "non-deductible tax", in relation to a taxable person, means—

(*a*) input tax for which the person is not entitled to credit under section 25 of VATA 1994, and

(*b*) any VAT incurred by the person which is not input tax and in respect of which the person is not entitled to a refund from the Commissioners by virtue of any provision of VATA 1994.

(2) For the purposes of sub-paragraph (1)(*b*), the VAT "incurred" by a taxable person is—

(*a*) VAT on the supply to the person of any goods or services,

(*b*) VAT on the acquisition by the person from another member State of any goods, and

(*c*) VAT paid or payable by the person on the importation of any goods from a place outside the member States.

"Tax advantage": other taxes

7 In relation to taxes other than VAT, "tax advantage" includes—

(*a*) relief or increased relief from tax,

(*b*) repayment or increased repayment of tax,

(*c*) receipt, or advancement of a receipt, of a tax credit,

(*d*) avoidance or reduction of a charge to tax, an assessment of tax or a liability to pay tax,

(*e*) avoidance of a possible assessment to tax or liability to pay tax,

(*f*) deferral of a payment of tax or advancement of a repayment of tax, and

(*g*) avoidance of an obligation to deduct or account for tax.

"DOTAS arrangements"

8 (1) For the purposes of this Schedule arrangements are "DOTAS arrangements" at any time if they are notifiable arrangements at the time in question and a person—

(*a*) has provided information in relation to the arrangements under section 308(3), 309 or 310 of FA 2004, or

(*b*) has failed to comply with any of those provisions in relation to the arrangements.

(2) But for the purposes of this Schedule "DOTAS arrangements" does not include arrangements in respect of which HMRC has given notice under section 312(6) of FA 2004 (notice that promoters not under duty to notify client of reference number).

(3) For the purposes of sub-paragraph (1) a person who would be required to provide information under subsection (3) of section 308 of FA 2004—

(*a*) but for the fact that the arrangements implement a proposal in respect of which notice has been given under subsection (1) of that section, or

(*b*) but for subsection (4A), (4C) or (5) of that section,

is treated as providing the information at the end of the period referred to in subsection (3) of that section.

(4) In this paragraph "notifiable arrangements" has the same meaning as in Part 7 of FA 2004.

[8A (1) For the purposes of this Schedule arrangements are "disclosable VAT arrangements" at any time if at that time sub-paragraph (2) or (3) applies.

(2) This sub-paragraph applies if the arrangements are disclosable Schedule 11A VAT arrangements (see paragraph 9).

(3) This paragraph applies if—

(*a*) the arrangements are notifiable arrangements for the purposes of Schedule 17 to FA 2017,

(*b*) the main benefit, or one of the main benefits that might be expected to arise from the arrangements is the obtaining of a tax advantage in relation to VAT (within the meaning of paragraph 6 of that Schedule), and

(*c*) a person—

(i) has provided information about the arrangements under paragraph 12(1), 17(2) or 18(2) of that Schedule, or

(ii) has failed to comply with any of those provisions in relation to the arrangements.

(4) But for the purposes of this Schedule arrangements in respect of which HMRC have given notice under paragraph 23(6) of Schedule 17 (notice that promoters not under duty to notify client of reference number) are not to be regarded as "disclosable VAT arrangements".

(5) For the purposes of sub-paragraph (3)(*c*) a person who would be required to provide information under paragraph 12(1) of Schedule 17 to FA 2017—

(*a*) but for the fact that the arrangements implement a proposal in respect of which notice has been given under paragraph 11(1) of that Schedule, or

(*b*) but for paragraph 13, 14 or 15 of that Schedule,

is treated as providing the information at the end of the period referred to in paragraph 12(1).][1]

Amendments—[1] Paragraph 8A inserted by F(No 2)A 2017 s 66, Sch 17 para 55(1), (3) with effect from 1 January 2018.

"Disclosable [Schedule 11A] VAT arrangements"

9 For the purposes of [paragraph 8A][1] arrangements are "disclosable [Schedule 11A][1] VAT arrangements" at any time if at that time—

(*a*) a person has complied with paragraph 6 of Schedule 11A to VATA 1994 in relation to the arrangements (duty to notify Commissioners),

(*b*) a person under a duty to comply with that paragraph in relation to the arrangements has failed to do so, or

(*c*) a reference number has been allocated to the scheme under paragraph 9 of that Schedule (voluntary notification of avoidance scheme which is not a designated scheme).

Amendments—[1] In heading, words inserted, and in opening words, words substituted for words "this Schedule", and words inserted, by F(No 2)A 2017 s 66, Sch 17 para 55(1), (4), (5) with effect from 1 January 2018.

["Disclosable indirect tax arrangements"

9A (1) For the purposes of this Schedule arrangements are "disclosable indirect tax arrangements" at any time if at that time—

(*a*) the arrangements are notifiable arrangements for the purposes of Schedule 17 to FA 2017,

(*b*) the main benefit, or one of the main benefits that might be expected to arise from the arrangements is the obtaining of a tax advantage in relation to an indirect tax other than VAT (within the meaning of paragraph 7 of that Schedule), and

(*c*) a person—

(i) has provided information about the arrangements under paragraph 12(1), 17(2) or 18(2) of that Schedule, or

(ii) has failed to comply with any of those provisions in relation to the arrangements.

(2) But for the purposes of this Schedule arrangements in respect of which HMRC have given notice under paragraph 23(6) of Schedule 17 to FA 2016 (notice that promoters not under duty to notify client of reference number) are not to be regarded as "disclosable indirect tax arrangements".

(3) For the purposes of sub-paragraph (1)(*c*) a person who would be required to provide information under paragraph 12(1) of Schedule 17—

(*a*) but for the fact that the arrangements implement a proposal in respect of which notice has been given under paragraph 11(1) of that Schedule, or

(*b*) but for paragraph 13, 14 or 15 of that Schedule,

is treated as providing the information at the end of the period referred to in paragraph 12(1).][1]

Amendments—[1] Paragraph 9A inserted by F(No 2)A 2017 s 66, Sch 17 para 55(1), (6) with effect from 1 January 2018.

Paragraphs 8 [to 9A]: "failure to comply"

10 (1) A person "fails to comply" with any provision mentioned in paragraph 8(1)[, 8A(2)(*c*), 9(*a*) or 9A(1)(*c*)][1] if and only if any of the conditions in sub-paragraphs (2) to (4) is met.

(2) The condition in this sub-paragraph is that—

(*a*) the tribunal has determined that the person has failed to comply with the provision concerned,

(*b*) the appeal period has ended, and

(*c*) the determination has not been overturned on appeal.

(3) The condition in this sub-paragraph is that—

(*a*) the tribunal has determined for the purposes of section 118(2) of TMA 1970 that the person is to be deemed not to have failed to comply with the provision concerned as the person had a reasonable excuse for not doing the thing required to be done,

(*b*) the appeal period has ended, and

(*c*) the determination has not been overturned on appeal.

(4) The condition in this sub-paragraph is that the person admitted in writing to HMRC that the person has failed to comply with the provision concerned.

(5) In this paragraph "the appeal period" means—

(*a*) the period during which an appeal could be brought against the determination of the tribunal, or

(*b*) where an appeal mentioned in paragraph (*a*) has been brought, the period during which that appeal has not been finally determined, withdrawn or otherwise disposed of.

(6) In this paragraph "the tribunal" means the First-tier tribunal or, where determined by or under Tribunal Procedure Rules, the Upper Tribunal.

Amendments—[1] In heading, words substituted for words "and 9", and in sub-para (1), words substituted for words "or 9(*a*)", by F(No 2)A 2017 s 66, Sch 17 para 55(1), (7), (8) with effect from 1 January 2018.

"Relevant defeat"

11 (1) A person ("P") incurs a "relevant defeat" in relation to arrangements if any of Conditions A to E is met in relation to P and the arrangements.

(2) The relevant defeat is incurred when the condition in question is first met.

Amendments—[1] In sub-para (1), letter substituted for letter "E" by F(No 2)A 2017 s 66, Sch 17 para 55(1), (9) with effect from 1 January 2018.

Condition A

12 (1) Condition A is that—

(*a*) P has been given a notice under paragraph 12 of Schedule 43 to FA 2013 (general anti-abuse rule: notice of final decision), paragraph 8 or 9 of Schedule 43A to that Act (pooling and binding of arrangements: notice of final decision) or paragraph 8 of Schedule 43B to that Act (generic referrals: notice of final decision) stating that a tax advantage arising from the arrangements is to be counteracted,

(*b*) that tax advantage has been counteracted under section 209 of FA 2013, and

(*c*) the counteraction is final.

(2) For the purposes of this paragraph the counteraction of a tax advantage is "final" when the adjustments made to effect the counteraction, and any amounts arising as a result of those adjustments, can no longer be varied, on appeal or otherwise.

Condition B

13 (1) Condition B is that (in a case not falling within Condition A above) a follower notice has been given to P by reference to the arrangements (and not withdrawn) and—

(*a*) the necessary corrective action for the purposes of section 208 of FA 2014 has been taken in respect of the denied advantage, or

(*b*) the denied advantage has been counteracted otherwise than as mentioned in paragraph (*a*) and the counteraction of the denied advantage is final.

(2) In sub-paragraph (1) the reference to giving a follower notice to P includes a reference to giving a partnership follower notice in respect of a partnership return in relation to which P is a relevant partner (as defined in paragraph 2(5) of Schedule 31 to FA 2014).

(3) For the purposes of this paragraph it does not matter whether the denied advantage has been dealt with—

(*a*) wholly as mentioned in one or other of paragraphs (*a*) and (*b*) of sub-paragraph (1), or

(*b*) partly as mentioned in one and partly as mentioned in the other of those paragraphs.

(4) In this paragraph "the denied advantage" has the same meaning as in Chapter 2 of Part 4 of FA 2014 (see section 208(3) of and paragraph 4(3) of Schedule 31 to that Act).

(5) For the purposes of this paragraph the counteraction of a tax advantage is "final" when the adjustments made to effect the counteraction, and any amounts arising as a result of those adjustments, can no longer be varied, on appeal or otherwise.

(6) In this Schedule "follower notice" means a follower notice under Chapter 2 of Part 4 of FA 2014.

(7) For the purposes of this paragraph a partnership follower notice is given "in respect of" the partnership return mentioned in paragraph (*a*) or (*b*) of paragraph 2(2) of Schedule 31 to FA 2014.

Condition C

14 (1) Condition C is that (in a case not falling within Condition A or B)—

(*a*) the arrangements are DOTAS arrangements,

(*b*) P has relied on the arrangements (see sub-paragraph (2))—

(*c*) the arrangements have been counteracted, and

(*d*) the counteraction is final.

(2) For the purposes of sub-paragraph (1), P "relies on the arrangements" if—

(*a*) P makes a return, claim or election, or a partnership return is made, on the basis that a relevant tax advantage arises, or

(*b*) P fails to discharge a relevant obligation ("the disputed obligation") and there is reason to believe that P's failure to discharge that obligation is connected with the arrangements.

(3) For the purposes of sub-paragraph (2) "relevant tax advantage" means a tax advantage which the arrangements might be expected to enable P to obtain.

(4) For the purposes of sub-paragraph (2) an obligation is a "relevant obligation" if the arrangements might be expected to have the result that the obligation does not arise.

(5) For the purposes of this paragraph the arrangements are "counteracted" if—

(*a*) adjustments, other than taxpayer emendations, are made in respect of P's tax position—

(i) on the basis that the whole or part of the relevant tax advantage mentioned in sub-paragraph (2)(*a*) does not arise, or

(ii) on the basis that the disputed obligation does (or did) arise, or

(*b*) an assessment to tax other than a self-assessment is made, or any other action is taken by HMRC, on the basis mentioned in paragraph (*a*)(i) or (ii) (otherwise than by way of an adjustment).

(6) For the purposes of this paragraph a counteraction is "final" when the assessment, adjustments or action in question, and any amounts arising from the assessment, adjustments or action, can no longer be varied, on appeal or otherwise.

(7) For the purposes of sub-paragraph (1) the time at which it falls to be determined whether or not the arrangements are DOTAS arrangements is when the counteraction becomes final.

(8) The following are "taxpayer emendations" for the purposes of sub-paragraph (5)—

(*a*) an adjustment made by P at a time when P had no reason to believe that HMRC had begun or were about to begin enquiries into P's affairs relating to the tax in question;

(*b*) an adjustment (by way of an assessment or otherwise) made by HMRC with respect to P's tax position as a result of a disclosure made by P which meets the conditions in sub-paragraph (9).

For the purposes of paragraph (*a*) a payment in respect of a liability to pay national insurance contributions is not an adjustment unless it is a payment in full.

(9) The conditions are that the disclosure—

(*a*) is a full and explicit disclosure of an inaccuracy in a return or other document or of a failure to comply with an obligation, and

(*b*) was made at a time when P had no reason to believe that HMRC were about to begin enquiries into P's affairs relating to the tax in question.

(10) For the purposes of this paragraph a contract settlement which HMRC enters into with P is treated as an assessment to tax (other than a self-assessment); and in relation to contract settlements references in sub-paragraph (5) to the basis on which any assessment or adjustments are made, or any other action is taken, are to be read with any necessary modifications.

Condition D

15 (1) Condition D is that—

(*a*) P is a taxable person;

(*b*) the arrangements are disclosable VAT arrangements to which P is a party,

(*c*) P has relied on the arrangements (see sub-paragraph (2));

(*d*) the arrangements have been counteracted, and

(*e*) the counteraction is final.

(2) For the purposes of sub-paragraph (1) P "relies on the arrangements" if—

(*a*) P makes a return or claim on the basis that a relevant tax advantage arises, or

b) P fails to discharge a relevant obligation ("the disputed obligation") and there is reason to believe that P's failure to discharge that obligation is connected with those arrangements.

(3) For the purposes of sub-paragraph (2) "relevant tax advantage" means a tax advantage which the arrangements might be expected to enable P to obtain.

(4) For the purposes of sub-paragraph (2) an obligation is a "relevant obligation" if the arrangements might be expected to have the result that the obligation does not arise.

(5) For the purposes of this paragraph the arrangements are "counteracted" if—

(*a*) adjustments, other than taxpayer emendations, are made in respect of P's tax position—

(i) on the basis that the whole or part of the relevant tax advantage mentioned in sub-paragraph (2)(*a*) does not arise, or

(ii) on the basis that the disputed obligation does (or did) arise, or

(*b*) an assessment to tax is made, or any other action is taken by HMRC, on the basis mentioned in paragraph (*a*)(i) or (ii) (otherwise than by way of an adjustment).

(6) For the purposes of this paragraph a counteraction is "final" when the assessment, adjustments or action in question, and any amounts arising from the assessment, adjustments or action, can no longer be varied, on appeal or otherwise.

(7) For the purposes of sub-paragraph (1) the time at which it falls to be determined whether or not the arrangements are disclosable VAT arrangements is when the counteraction becomes final.

(8) The following are "taxpayer emendations" for the purposes of sub-paragraph (5)—

(*a*) an adjustment made by P at a time when P had no reason to believe that HMRC had begun or were about to begin enquiries into P's affairs relating to VAT;

(*b*) an adjustment made by HMRC with respect to P's tax position (by way of an assessment or otherwise) as a result of a disclosure made by P which meets the conditions in sub-paragraph (9).

(9) The conditions are that the disclosure—

(*a*) is a full and explicit disclosure of an inaccuracy in a return or other document or of a failure to comply with an obligation, and

(*b*) was made at a time when P had no reason to believe that HMRC were about to begin enquiries into P's affairs relating to VAT.

Condition E

16 (1) Condition E is that the arrangements are disclosable VAT arrangements to which P is a party and—

(*a*) the arrangements relate to the position with respect to VAT of a person other than P ("S") who has made supplies of goods or services to P,

(*b*) the arrangements might be expected to enable P to obtain a tax advantage in connection with those supplies of goods or services,

(*c*) the arrangements have been counteracted, and

(*d*) the counteraction is final.

(2) For the purposes of this paragraph the arrangements are "counteracted" if—

(*a*) HMRC assess S to tax or take any other action on a basis which prevents P from obtaining (or obtaining the whole of) the tax advantage in question, or

(*b*) adjustments, other than taxpayer emendations, are made in relation to S's VAT affairs on a basis such as is mentioned in paragraph (*a*).

(3) For the purposes of this paragraph a counteraction is "final" when the assessment, adjustments or action in question, and any amounts arising from the assessment, adjustments or action, can no longer be varied, on appeal or otherwise.

(4) For the purposes of sub-paragraph (1) the time when it falls to be determined whether or not the arrangements are disclosable VAT arrangements is when the counteraction becomes final.

(5) The following are "taxpayer emendations" for the purposes of sub-paragraph (2)—

(*a*) an adjustment made by S at a time when neither P nor S had reason to believe that HMRC had begun or were about to begin enquiries into the affairs of S or P relating to VAT;

(*b*) an adjustment (by way of an assessment or otherwise) made by HMRC with respect to S's tax position as a result of a disclosure made by S which meets the conditions in sub-paragraph (6).

(6) The conditions are that the disclosure—

(*a*) is a full and explicit disclosure of an inaccuracy in a return or other document or of a failure to comply with an obligation, and

(*b*) was made at a time when neither S nor P had reason to believe that HMRC were about to begin enquiries into the affairs of S or P relating to VAT.

[Condition F

16A (1) Condition F is that—

(*a*) the arrangements are indirect tax arrangements,

(*b*) P has relied on the arrangements (see sub-paragraph (2),

(*c*) the arrangements have been counteracted, and

(*d*) the counteraction is final.

(2) For the purpose of sub-paragraph (1) P relies on the arrangements if—

(*a*) P makes a return, claim, declaration or application for approval on the basis that a relevant tax advantage arises, or (*b*) P fails to discharge a relevant obligation ("the disputed obligation") and there is reason to believe that P's failure to discharge that obligation is connected with the arrangements.

(3) For the purposes of sub-paragraph (2) "relevant tax advantage" means a tax advantage which the arrangements might be expected to enable P to obtain.

(4) For the purposes of sub-paragraph (2) an obligation is a relevant obligation if the arrangements might be expected to have the result that the obligation does not arise.

(5) For the purposes of this paragraph the arrangements are "counteracted" if—

(*a*) adjustments, other than taxpayer emendations, are made in respect of P's tax position —

(i) on the basis that the whole or part of the relevant tax advantage mentioned in sub-paragraph (2)(*a*) does not arise, or

(ii) on the basis that the disputed obligation does (or did) arise, or

(*b*) an assessment to tax is made, or any other action is taken by HMRC, on the basis mentioned in paragraph (*a*)(i) or (ii) (otherwise than by way of an adjustment).

(6) For the purposes of this paragraph a "counteraction" is final when the adjustments, assessment or action in question, and any amounts arising from the adjustments, assessment or action, can no longer be varied, on appeal or otherwise.

(7) For the purposes of sub-paragraph (1) the time at which it falls to be determined whether or not the arrangements are disclosable indirect tax arrangements is when the counteraction becomes final.

(8) The following are "taxpayer emendations" for the purposes of sub-paragraph (5)—

(*a*) an adjustment made by P at a time when P had no reason to believe that HMRC had begun or were about to begin enquiries into P's affairs in relation to the tax in question;

(*b*) an adjustment made by HMRC with respect to P's tax position (whether by way of an assessment or otherwise) as a result of a disclosure by P which meets the conditions in sub-paragraph (9).

(9) The conditions are that the disclosure—

(*a*) is a full and explicit disclosure of an inaccuracy in a return or other document or of a failure to comply with an obligation, and

(*b*) was made at a time when P had no reason to believe that HMRC were about to begin enquiries into P's affairs in relation to the tax in question.][1]

Amendments—[1] Paragraph 16A inserted by F(No 2)A 2017 s 66, Sch 17 para 55(1), (10) with effect from 1 January 2018.

PART 3

ANNUAL INFORMATION NOTICES AND NAMING

Annual information notices

17 (1) A person ("P") who has been given a warning notice under this Schedule must give HMRC a written notice (an "information notice") in respect of each reporting period in the warning period (see sub-paragraph (11)).

(2) An information notice must be given not later than the 30th day after the end of the reporting period to which it relates.

(3) An information notice must state whether or not P—

(*a*) has in the reporting period delivered a return, or made a claim[, election, declaration or application for approval,][1] on the basis that a relevant tax advantage arises, or has since the end of the reporting period delivered on that basis a return which P was required to deliver before the end of that period,

(*b*) has in the reporting period failed to take action which P would be required to take under or by virtue of an enactment relating to tax but for particular [disclosable][1] arrangements to which P is a party,

(*c*) has in the reporting period become a party to arrangements which—

(i) relate to the position with respect to VAT of another person ("S") who has made supplies of goods or services to P, and

(ii) might be expected to enable P to obtain a relevant tax advantage ("the expected tax advantage") in connection with those supplies of goods or services,

(*d*) has failed to deliver a return which P was required to deliver by a date falling in the reporting period.

(4) In this paragraph "relevant tax advantage" means a tax advantage which particular [disclosable][1] arrangements enable, or might be expected to enable, P to obtain.

(5) If P has, in the reporting period concerned, made a return, claim[, election, declaration or application for approval,][1] on the basis mentioned in sub-paragraph (3)(*a*) or failed to take action as mentioned in sub-paragraph (3)(*b*) the information notice must—

(*a*) explain (on the assumptions made by P in so acting or failing to act) how the [disclosable][1] arrangements enable P to obtain the tax advantage, or (as the case may be) have the result that P is not required to take the action in question, and (*b*) state (on the same assumptions) the amount of the relevant tax advantage mentioned in sub-paragraph (3)(*a*) or (as the case may be) the amount of any tax advantage which arises in connection with the absence of a requirement to take the action mentioned in sub-paragraph (3)(*b*).

(6) If P has, in the reporting period, become a party to arrangements such as are mentioned in sub-paragraph (3)(*c*), the information notice—

(*a*) must state whether or not it is P's view that the expected tax advantage arises to P, and

(*b*) if that is P's view, must explain how the arrangements enable P to obtain the tax advantage and state the amount of the tax advantage.

(7) If the time by which P must deliver a return falls within a reporting period and P fails to deliver the return by that time, HMRC may require P to give HMRC a written notice (a "supplementary information notice") setting out any matters which P would have been required to set out in an information notice had P delivered the return in that reporting period.

(8) A requirement under sub-paragraph (7) must be made by a written notice which states the period within which P must comply with the notice.

(9) If P fails to comply with a requirement of (or imposed under) this paragraph HMRC may by written notice extend the warning period to the end of the period of 5 years beginning with—

(*a*) the day by which the information notice or supplementary information notice should have been given (see sub-paragraphs (2) and (8)) or, as the case requires,

(*b*) the day on which P gave the defective information notice or supplementary information notice to HMRC,

or, if earlier, the time when the warning period would have expired but for the extension.

(10) HMRC may permit information notices given by members of the same group of companies (as defined in paragraph 46(9)) to be combined.

(11) For the purposes of this paragraph—

(*a*) the first reporting period in any warning period begins with the first day of the warning period and ends with a day specified by HMRC ("the specified day"),

(*b*) the remainder of the warning period is divided into further reporting periods each of which begins immediately after the end of the preceding reporting period and is twelve months long or (if that would be shorter) ends at the end of the warning period.

[(12) In this paragraph "disclosable arrangements" means any of the following—

(*a*) DOTAS arrangements,

(*b*) disclosable VAT arrangements, and

(*c*) disclosable indirect tax arrangements.][1]

Amendments—[1] In sub-paras (3)(*a*), (5), words substituted for words "or election", in sub-paras (3)(*b*), (4), (5)(*a*), word substituted for words "DOTAS arrangements or VAT", and sub-para 12 inserted, by F(No 2)A 2017 s 66, Sch 17 para 55(1), (11) with effect from 1 January 2018.

Naming

18 (1) The Commissioners may publish information about a person if the person—

(*a*) incurs a relevant defeat in relation to arrangements which the person has used in a warning period, and

(*b*) has been given at least two warning notices in respect of other defeats of arrangements which were used in the same warning period.

(2) Information published for the first time under sub-paragraph (1) must be published within the 12 months beginning with the day on which the most recent of the warning notices falling within that sub-paragraph has been given to the person.

(3) No information may be published (or continue to be published) after the end of the period of 12 months beginning with the day on which it is first published.

(4) The information that may be published is—

(*a*) the person's name (including any trading name, previous name or pseudonym),

(*b*) the person's address (or registered office),

(*c*) the nature of any business carried on by the person,

(*d*) information about the fiscal effect of the defeated arrangements (had they not been defeated), for instance information about total amounts of tax understated or total amounts by which claims, or statements of losses, have been adjusted,

(*e*) the amount of any penalty to which the person is liable under paragraph 30 in respect of the relevant defeat of any defeated arrangements,

(*f*) the periods in which or times when the defeated arrangements were used, and

(*g*) any other information the Commissioners may consider it appropriate to publish in order to make clear the person's identity.

(5) If the person mentioned in sub-paragraph (1) is a member of a group of companies (as defined in paragraph 46(9)), the information which may be published also includes—

(*a*) any trading name of the group, and

(*b*) information about other members of the group of the kind described in sub-paragraph (4)(*a*), (*b*) or (*c*).

(6) If the person mentioned in sub-paragraph (1) is a person carrying on a trade or business in partnership, the information which may be published also includes—

(*a*) any trading name of the partnership, and

(*b*) information about other members of the partnership of the kind described in sub-paragraph (4)(*a*) or (*b*).

(7) The information may be published in any manner the Commissioners may consider appropriate.

(8) Before publishing any information the Commissioners—

(*a*) must inform the person that they are considering doing so, and

(*b*) afford the person reasonable opportunity to make representations about whether or not it should be published.

(9) Arrangements are "defeated arrangements" for the purposes of sub-paragraph (4) if the person used them in the warning period mentioned in sub-paragraph (1) and a warning notice specifying the defeat of those arrangements has been given to the person before the information is published.

(10) If a person has been given a single warning notice in relation to two or more relevant defeats, the person is treated for the purposes of this paragraph as having been given a separate warning notice in relation to each of those relevant defeats.

(11) Nothing in this paragraph prevents the power under sub-paragraph (1) from being exercised on a subsequent occasion in relation to arrangements used by the person in a different warning period.

PART 4
RESTRICTION OF RELIEFS

Duty to give a restriction relief notice

19 (1) HMRC must give a person a written notice (a "restriction of relief notice") if—

(*a*) the person incurs a relevant defeat in relation to arrangements which the person has used in a warning period,

(*b*) the person has been given at least two warning notices in respect of other relevant defeats of arrangements which were used in that same warning period, and

(*c*) the defeats mentioned in paragraphs (*a*) and (*b*) meet the conditions in sub-paragraph (2).

(2) The conditions are—

(*a*) that each of the relevant defeats is by virtue of Condition A, B or C,

(*b*) that each of the relevant defeats relates to the misuse of a relief (see sub-paragraph (5)), and

(*c*) in the case of each of the relevant defeats, either—

(i) that the relevant counteraction (see sub-paragraph (7)) was made on the basis that a particular avoidance-related rule applies in relation to a person's affairs, or

(ii) that the misused relief is a loss relief.

(3) In sub-paragraph (2)(*c*)—

(*a*) the "misused relief" means the relief mentioned in sub-paragraph (5), and

(*b*) "loss relief" means any relief under Part 4 of ITA 2007 or Part 4 or 5 of CTA 2010.

(4) A restriction of relief notice must—

(*a*) explain the effect of paragraphs 20, 21 and 22, and

(*b*) set out when the restricted period is to begin and end.

(5) For the purposes of this Part of this Schedule, a relevant defeat by virtue of Condition A, B or C "relates to the misuse of a relief" if—

(*a*) the tax advantage in question, or part of the tax advantage in question, is or results from (or would but for the counteraction be or result from) a relief or increased relief from tax, or

(*b*) it is reasonable to conclude that the making of a particular claim for relief, or the use of a particular relief, is a significant component of the arrangements in question.

(6) In sub-paragraph (5) "the tax advantage in question" means—

(*a*) in relation to a defeat by virtue of Condition A, the tax advantage mentioned in paragraph 12(1)(*a*),

(*b*) in relation to a defeat by virtue of Condition B, the denied advantage (as defined in paragraph 13(4)), or

(*c*) in relation to a defeat by virtue of Condition C—

(i) the tax advantage mentioned in paragraph 14(2)(*a*), or, as the case requires,

(ii) the absence of the relevant obligation (as defined in paragraph 14(4)).

(7) In this paragraph "the relevant counteraction", in relation to a relevant defeat means—

(*a*) in the case of a defeat by virtue of Condition A, the counteraction referred to in paragraph 12(1)(*c*);

(*b*) in the case of a defeat by virtue of Condition B, the action referred to in paragraph 13(1);

(*c*) in the case of a defeat by virtue of Condition C, the counteraction referred to in paragraph 14(1)(*d*).

(8) If a person has been given a single warning notice in relation to two or more relevant defeats, the person is treated for the purposes of this paragraph as having been given a separate warning notice in relation to each of those relevant defeats.

Restriction of relief

20 (1) Sub-paragraphs (2) to (15) have effect in relation to a person to whom a relief restriction notice has been given.

(2) The person may not, in the restricted period, make any claim for relief.

(3) Sub-paragraph (2) does not have effect in relation to—

(*a*) a claim for relief under Schedule 8 to FA 2003 (stamp duty land tax: charities relief);

(*b*) a claim for relief under Chapter 3 of Part 8 of ITA 2007 (gifts of shares, securities and real property to charities etc);

(*c*) a claim for relief under Part 10 of ITA 2007 (special rules about charitable trusts etc);

(*d*) a claim for relief under double taxation arrangements;

(*e*) an election under section 426 of ITA 2007 (gift aid: election to treat gift as made in previous year).

(4) Claims under the following provisions in Part 4 of FA 2004 (registered pension schemes: tax reliefs etc) do not count as claims for relief for the purposes of this paragraph—

section 192(4) (increase of basic rate limit and higher rate limit);

section 193(4) (net pay arrangements: excess relief);

section 194(1) (relief on making of a claim).

(5) The person may not, in the restricted period, surrender group relief under Part 5 of CTA 2010.

(6) No deduction is to be made under section 83 of ITA 2007 (carry forward against subsequent trade profits) in calculating the person's net income for a relevant tax year.

(7) No deduction is to be made under section 118 of ITA 2007 (carry-forward property loss relief) in calculating the person's net income for a relevant tax year.

(8) The person is not entitled to relief under section 448 (annual payments: relief for individuals) or 449 (annual payments: relief for other persons) of ITA 2007 for any payment made in the restricted period.

(9) No deduction of expenses referable to a relevant accounting period is to be made under section 1219(1) of CTA 2009 (expenses of management of a company's investment business).

(10) No reduction is to be made under section 45(4) of CTA 2010 (carry-forward of trade loss relief) in calculating the profits for a relevant accounting period of a trade carried on by the person.

(11) In calculating the total amount of chargeable gains accruing to a person in a relevant tax year (or part of a relevant tax year), no losses are to be deducted under subsections (2) to (2B) of section 2 of TCGA 1992 (persons and gains chargeable to capital gains tax, and allowable losses).

(12) In calculating the total amount of ATED-related chargeable gains accruing to a person in a relevant tax year, no losses are to be deducted under subsection (3) of section 2B of TCGA 1992 (persons chargeable to capital gains tax on ATED-related gains).

(13) In calculating the total amount of chargeable NRCGT gains accruing to a person in a relevant tax year on relevant high value disposals, no losses are to be deducted under subsection (2) of section 14D of TCGA 1992 (persons chargeable to capital gains tax on NRCGT gains).

(14) If the person is a company, no deduction is to be made under section 62 of CTA 2010 (relief for losses made in UK property business) from the company's total profits of a relevant accounting period.

(15) No deduction is to be made under regulation 18 of the Unauthorised Unit Trusts (Tax) Regulations 2013 (S.I. 2013/2819) (relief for deemed payments by trustees of an exempt unauthorised unit trust) in calculating the person's net income for a relevant tax year.

(16) In this paragraph "relevant tax year" means any tax year the first day of which is in the restricted period.

(17) In this paragraph "relevant accounting period" means an accounting period the first day of which is in the restricted period.

(18) In this paragraph "double taxation arrangements" means arrangements which have effect under section 2(1) of TIOPA 2010 (double taxation relief by agreement with territories outside the UK).

The restricted period

21 (1) In paragraphs 19 and 20 (and this paragraph) "the restricted period" means the period of 3 years beginning with the day on which the relief restriction notice is given.

(2) If during the restricted period (or the restricted period as extended under this sub-paragraph) the person to whom a relief restriction notice has been given incurs a further relevant defeat meeting the conditions in sub-paragraph (4), HMRC must give the person a written notice (a "restricted period extension notice").

(3) A restricted period extension notice extends the restricted period to the end of the period of 3 years beginning with the day on which the further relevant defeat occurs.

(4) The conditions mentioned in sub-paragraph (2) are that—

(*a*) the relevant defeat is incurred by virtue of Condition A, B or C in relation to arrangements which the person used in the warning period mentioned in paragraph 19(1)(*a*), and

(*b*) the warning notice given to the person in respect of the relevant defeat relates to the misuse of a relief.

(5) If the person to whom a relief restriction notice has been given incurs a relevant defeat which meets the conditions in sub-paragraph (4) after the restricted period has expired but before the end of a concurrent warning period, HMRC must give the person a restriction of relief notice.

(6) In sub-paragraph (5) "concurrent warning period" means a warning period which at some time ran concurrently with the restricted period.

Reasonable excuse

22 (1) If a person who has incurred a relevant defeat satisfies HMRC or, on an appeal under paragraph 24, the First-tier Tribunal or Upper Tribunal that the person had a reasonable excuse for the matters to which that relevant defeat relates, then—

(*a*) for the purposes of paragraph 19(1)(*a*) and 21(2) and (5), the person is treated as not having incurred that relevant defeat, and

(*b*) for the purposes of paragraph 19(1)(*b*) and (*c*) any warning notice given to the person which relates to that relevant defeat is treated as not having been given to the person.

(2) For the purposes of this paragraph, in the case of a person ("P")—

(*a*) an insufficiency of funds is not a reasonable excuse unless attributable to events outside P's control,

(*b*) where P relies on another person to do anything, that is not a reasonable excuse unless P took reasonable care to avoid the relevant failure, and

(*c*) where P had reasonable excuse for the relevant failure but the excuse had ceased, P is to be treated as having continued to have the excuse if the failure is remedied without unreasonable delay after the excuse ceased.

(3) In determining for the purposes of this paragraph whether or not a person ("P") had a reasonable excuse for any action, failure or inaccuracy, reliance on advice is to be taken automatically not to constitute a reasonable excuse if the advice is addressed to, or was given to, a person other than P or takes no account of P's individual circumstances.

(4) In this paragraph "relevant failure", in relation to a relevant defeat, is to be interpreted in accordance with sub-paragraphs (2) to (7) of paragraph 43.

Mitigation of restriction of relief

23 (1) The Commissioners may mitigate the effects of paragraph 20 in relation to a person ("P") so far as it appears to them that there are exceptional circumstances such that the operation of that paragraph would otherwise have an unduly serious impact with respect to the tax affairs of P or another person.

(2) For the purposes of sub-paragraph (1) the Commissioners may modify the effects of paragraph 20 in any way they think appropriate, including by allowing P access to the whole or part of a relief to which P would otherwise not be entitled as a result of paragraph 20.

Appeal

24 (1) A person may appeal against—

(*a*) a relief restriction notice, or

(*b*) a restricted period extension notice.

(2) An appeal under this paragraph must be made within the period of 30 days beginning with the day on which the notice is given.

(3) An appeal under this paragraph is to be treated in the same way as an appeal against an assessment to income tax (including by the application of any provision about bringing the appeal by notice to HMRC, about HMRC's review of the decision or about determination of the appeal by the First-tier Tribunal or Upper Tribunal).

(4) On an appeal the tribunal may—

(*a*) cancel HMRC's decision, or

(*b*) affirm that decision with or without any modifications in accordance with sub-paragraph (5).

(5) On an appeal the tribunal may rely on paragraph 23 (mitigation of restriction of relief)—

(*a*) to the same extent as HMRC (which may mean applying the same mitigation as HMRC to a different starting point), or

(*b*) to a different extent, but only if the tribunal thinks that HMRC's decision in respect of the application of paragraph 23 was flawed.

(6) In this paragraph "tribunal" means the First-tier Tribunal or Upper Tribunal (as appropriate by virtue of sub-paragraph (3)).

Meaning of "avoidance-related rule"

25 (1) In this Part of this Schedule "avoidance-related rule" means a rule in Category 1 or 2.

(2) A rule is in Category 1 if it refers (in whatever terms)—

(*a*) to the purpose or main purpose or purposes of a transaction, arrangements or any other action or matter, and

(*b*) to whether or not the purpose in question is or involves the avoidance of tax or the obtaining of any advantage in relation to tax (however described).

(3) A rule is also in Category 1 if it refers (in whatever terms) to—

(*a*) expectations as to what are, or may be, the expected benefits of a transaction, arrangements or any other action or matter, and

(*b*) whether or not the avoidance of tax or the obtaining of any advantage in relation to tax (however described) is such a benefit.

For the purposes of paragraph (*b*) it does not matter whether the reference is (for instance) to the "sole or main benefit" or "one of the main benefits" or any other reference to a benefit.

(4) A rule falls within Category 2 if as a result of the rule a person may be treated differently for tax purposes depending on whether or not purposes referred to in the rule (for instance the purposes of an actual or contemplated action or enterprise) are (or are shown to be) commercial purposes.

(5) For example, a rule in the following form would fall within Category 1 and within Category 2—

"Example rule

Section X does not apply to a company in respect of a transaction if the company shows that the transaction meets Condition A or B.

Condition A is that the transaction is effected—

(*a*) for genuine commercial reasons, or

(*b*) in the ordinary course of managing investments.

Condition B is that the avoidance of tax is not the main object or one of the main objects of the transaction."

Meaning of "relief"

26 The following are "reliefs" for the purposes of this Part of this Schedule—

(*a*) any relief from tax (however described) which must be claimed, or which is not available without making an election,

(*b*) relief under section 1219 of CTA 2009 (expenses of management of a company's investment business),

(*c*) any relief (not falling within paragraph (*a*)) under Part 4 of ITA 2007 (loss relief) or Part 4 or 5 of CTA 2010 (loss relief and group relief), and

(*d*) any relief (not falling within paragraph (*a*) or (*b*)) under a provision listed in section 24 of ITA 2007 (reliefs deductible at Step 2 of the calculation of income tax liability).

"Claim" for relief

27 In this Part of this Schedule "claim for relief" includes any election or other similar action which is in substance a claim for relief.

VAT [and indirect taxes]

28 In this Part of this Schedule "tax" does not include VAT [or any other indirect tax][1].

Amendments—[1] In heading and text, words inserted by F(No 2)A 2017 s 66, Sch 17 para 55(1), (12), (13) with effect from 1 January 2018.

Power to amend

29 (1) The Treasury may by regulations—

(*a*) amend paragraph 20;

(*b*) amend paragraph 26.

(2) Regulations under sub-paragraph (1)(*a*) may, in particular, alter the application of paragraph 20 in relation to any relief, exclude any relief from its application or extend its application to further reliefs.

(3) Regulations under sub-paragraph (1)(*b*) may amend the meaning of "relief" in any way (including by extending or limiting the meaning).

(4) Regulations under this paragraph may—

(*a*) make supplementary, incidental and consequential provision;

(*b*) make transitional provision.

(5) Regulations under this paragraph are to be made by statutory instrument.

(6) A statutory instrument containing regulations under this paragraph may not be made unless a draft of the instrument has been laid before and approved by a resolution of the House of Commons.

PART 5
PENALTY

Penalty

30 (1) A person is liable to pay a penalty if the person incurs a relevant defeat in relation to any arrangements which the person has used in a warning period.

(2) The penalty is 20% of the value of the counteracted advantage if neither sub-paragraph (3) nor sub-paragraph (4) applies.

(3) The penalty is 40% of the value of the counteracted advantage if before the relevant defeat is incurred the person has been given, or become liable to be given, one (but not more than one) relevant prior warning notice.

(4) The penalty is 60% of the value of the counteracted advantage if before the current defeat is incurred the person has been given, or become liable to be given, two or more relevant prior warning notices.

(5) In this paragraph "relevant prior warning notice" means a warning notice in relation to the defeat of arrangements which the person has used in the warning period mentioned in sub-paragraph (1).

(6) For the meaning of "the value of the counteracted advantage" see paragraphs 32 to 37.

Simultaneous defeats etc

31 (1) If a person incurs simultaneously two or more relevant defeats in relation to different arrangements, sub-paragraphs (2) to (4) of paragraph 30 have effect as if the relevant defeat with the lowest value was incurred last, the relevant defeat with the next lowest value immediately before it, and so on.

(2) For this purpose the "value" of a relevant defeat is taken to be equal to the value of the counteracted advantage.

(3) If a person has been given a single warning notice in relation to two or more relevant defeats, the person is treated for the purposes of paragraph 30 as having been given a separate warning notice in relation to each of those relevant defeats.

Value of the counteracted advantage: basic rule for taxes other than VAT

32 (1) In relation to a relevant defeat incurred by virtue of Condition A, B[, C or F][1], the "value of the counteracted advantage" is—

(*a*) in the case of a relevant defeat incurred by virtue of Condition A, the additional amount due or payable in respect of tax as a result of the counteraction mentioned in paragraph 12(1)(*c*);

(*b*) in the case of a relevant defeat incurred by virtue of Condition B, the additional amount due or payable in respect of tax as a result of the action mentioned in paragraph 13(1);

(*c*) in the case of a relevant defeat incurred by virtue of Condition C, the additional amount due or payable in respect of tax as a result of the counteraction mentioned in paragraph 14(1)(*d*).

[(*d*) in the case of a relevant defeat incurred by virtue of Condition F, the additional amount due or payable in respect of tax as a result of the counteraction mentioned in paragraph 16A(1)(*d*).][1]

(2) The reference in sub-paragraph (1) to the additional amount due and payable includes a reference to—

(*a*) an amount payable to HMRC having erroneously been paid by way of repayment of tax, and

(*b*) an amount which would be repayable by HMRC if the counteraction mentioned in paragraph (*a*)[, (*c*) or (*d*)][1] of sub-paragraph (1) were not made or the action mentioned in paragraph (*b*) of that sub-paragraph were not taken (as the case may be).

(3) The following are ignored in calculating the value of the counteracted advantage—

(*a*) group relief, and

(*b*) any relief under section 458 of CTA 2010 (relief in respect of repayment etc of loan) which is deferred under subsection (5) of that section.

(4) This paragraph is subject to paragraphs 33 and 34.

Amendments—[1] In sub-para (1), words substituted for words "or C", sub-para (1)(*d*) inserted, and in sub-para (2)(*b*), words substituted for words "or c" by F(No 2)A 2017 s 66, Sch 17 para 55(1), (14) with effect from 1 January 2018.

Value of counteracted advantage: losses for purposes of direct tax

33 (1) This paragraph has effect in relation to relevant defeats incurred by virtue of Condition A, B or C.

(2) To the extent that the counteracted advantage (see paragraph 35) has the result that a loss is wrongly recorded for the purposes of direct tax and the loss has been wholly used to reduce the amount due or payable in respect of tax, the value of the counteracted advantage is determined in accordance with paragraph 32.

(3) To the extent that the counteracted advantage has the result that a loss is wrongly recorded for purposes of direct tax and the loss has not been wholly used to reduce the amount due or payable in respect of tax, the value of the counteracted advantage is—

- (*a*) the value under paragraph 32 of so much of the counteracted advantage as results from the part (if any) of the loss which is used to reduce the amount due or payable in respect of tax, plus
- (*b*) 10% of the part of the loss not so used.

(4) Sub-paragraphs (2) and (3) apply both—

- (*a*) to a case where no loss would have been recorded but for the counteracted advantage, and
- (*b*) to a case where a loss of a different amount would have been recorded (but in that case sub-paragraphs (2) and (3) apply only to the difference between the amount recorded and the true amount).

(5) To the extent that a counteracted advantage creates or increases an aggregate loss recorded for a group of companies—

- (*a*) the value of the counteracted advantage is calculated in accordance with this paragraph, and
- (*b*) in applying paragraph 32 in accordance with sub-paragraphs (2) and (3), group relief may be taken into account (despite paragraph 32(3)).

(6) To the extent that the counteracted advantage results in a loss, the value of it is nil where, because of the nature of the loss or the person's circumstances, there is no reasonable prospect of the loss being used to support a claim to reduce a tax liability (of any person).

Value of counteracted advantage: deferred tax

34 (1) To the extent that the counteracted advantage (see paragraph 35) is a deferral of tax (other than VAT), the value of that advantage is—

- (*a*) 25% of the amount of the deferred tax for each year of the deferral, or
- (*b*) a percentage of the amount of the deferred tax, for each separate period of deferral of less than a year, equating to 25% per year,

or, if less, 100% of the amount of the deferred tax.

(2) This paragraph does not apply to a case to the extent that paragraph 33 applies.

Meaning of "the counteracted advantage" in paragraphs 33 and 34

35 (1) In paragraphs 33 and 34 "the counteracted advantage" means—

- (*a*) in relation to a relevant defeat incurred by virtue of Condition A, the tax advantage mentioned in paragraph 12(1)(*b*);
- (*b*) in relation to a relevant defeat incurred by virtue of Condition B, the denied advantage in relation to which the action mentioned in paragraph 13(1) is taken;
- (*c*) in relation to a relevant defeat incurred by virtue of Condition C, means any tax advantage in respect of which the counteraction mentioned in paragraph 14(1)(*c*) is made.
- [(*d*) in relation to a relevant defeat incurred by virtue of Condition F, means any tax advantage in respect of which the counteraction mentioned in paragraph 16A(1)(*c*) is made.][1]

(2) In sub-paragraph (1)(*c*) "counteraction" is to be interpreted in accordance with paragraph 14(5).

Amendments—[1] Sub-para (1)(*d*) inserted by F(No 2)A 2017 s 66, Sch 17 para 55(1), (15) with effect from 1 January 2018.

Value of the counteracted advantage: Conditions D and E

36 (1) In relation to a relevant defeat incurred by a person by virtue of Condition D or E, the "value of the counteracted advantage" is equal to the sum of any counteracted tax advantages determined under sub-paragraphs (3) to (6). But see also paragraph 37.

(2) In this paragraph "the counteraction" means the counteraction mentioned in paragraph 15(1) or 16(1) (as the case may be).

(3) If the amount of VAT due or payable by the person in respect of any prescribed accounting period (X) exceeds the amount (Y) that would have been so payable but for the counteraction, the amount by which X exceeds Y is a counteracted tax advantage.

(4) If the person obtains no VAT credit for a particular prescribed accounting period, the amount of any VAT credit which the person would have obtained for that period but for the counteraction is a counteracted tax advantage.

(5) If for a prescribed accounting period the person obtains a VAT credit of an amount (Y) which is less than the amount (X) of the VAT credit which the person would have obtained but for the counteraction, the amount by which X exceeds Y is a counteracted tax advantage.

(6) If the amount (X) of the person's non-deductible tax for any prescribed accounting period is greater than Y, where Y is what would be the amount of the person's non-deductible tax for that period but for the counteraction, then the amount by which X exceeds Y is a counteracted tax advantage, but only to the extent that amount is not represented by a corresponding amount which is the whole or part of a counteracted tax advantage by virtue of sub-paragraphs (3) to(5).

(7) In this paragraph "non-deductible tax", in relation to the person who incurred the relevant defeat, means—

(*a*) input tax for which the person is not entitled to credit under section 25 of VATA 1994, and

(*b*) any VAT incurred by the person which is not input tax and in respect of which the person is not entitled to a refund from the Commissioners by virtue of any provision of VATA 1994.

(8) For the purposes of sub-paragraph (7)(*b*) the VAT "incurred" by a taxable person is—

(*a*) VAT on the supply to the person of any goods or services,

(*b*) VAT on the acquisition by the person from another member State of any goods;

(*c*) VAT on the importation of any goods from a place outside the member States.

(9) References in sub-paragraph (3) to amounts due and payable by the person in respect of a prescribed accounting period include references to—

(*a*) amounts payable to HMRC having erroneously been paid by way of repayment of tax, and

(*b*) amounts which would be repayable by HMRC if the counteraction mentioned in sub-paragraph (3) were not made.

Value of counteracted advantage: delayed VAT

37 (1) Sub-paragraph (3) of paragraph 36 has effect as follows so far as the tax advantage which is counteracted as mentioned in that sub-paragraph is in the nature of a delay in relation to the person's obligations with respect to VAT.

(2) That sub-paragraph has effect as if for "the amount by which X exceeds Y is a counteracted tax advantage" there were substituted, "there is a counteracted tax advantage of—

(*d*) 25% of the amount of the delayed VAT for each year of the delay, or

(*e*) a percentage of the amount of the delayed VAT, for each separate period of delay of less than a year, equating to 25% per year,

or, if less, 100% of the amount of the delayed VAT".

Assessment of penalty

38 (1) Where a person is liable for a penalty under paragraph 30, HMRC must assess the penalty.

(2) Where HMRC assess the penalty, HMRC must—

(*a*) notify the person who is liable for the penalty, and

(*b*) state in the notice a tax period in respect of which the penalty is assessed.

(3) A penalty under this paragraph must be paid before the end of the period of 30 days beginning with the day on which the person is notified of the penalty under sub-paragraph (2).

(4) An assessment—

(*a*) is to be treated for procedural purposes as if it were an assessment to tax,

(*b*) may be enforced as if it were an assessment to tax, and

(*c*) may be combined with an assessment to tax.

(5) An assessment of a penalty under this paragraph must be made before the end of the period of 12 months beginning with the date of the defeat mentioned in paragraph 30(1).

Alteration of assessment of penalty

39 (1) After notification of an assessment has been given to a person under paragraph 38(2), the assessment may not be altered except in accordance with this paragraph or on appeal.

(2) A supplementary assessment may be made in respect of a penalty if an earlier assessment operated by reference to an underestimate of the value of the counteracted advantage.

(3) An assessment may be revised as necessary if operated by reference to an overestimate of the value of the counteracted advantage.

Aggregate penalties

40 (1) The amount of a penalty for which a person is liable under paragraph 30 is to be reduced by the amount of any other penalty incurred by the person, or any surcharge for late payment of tax imposed on the person, if the amount of the penalty or surcharge is determined by reference to the same tax liability.

(2) In sub-paragraph (1) "any other penalty" does not include a penalty under section 212A of FA 2013 (GAAR penalty) or Part 4 of FA 2014 (penalty where corrective action not taken after follower notice etc).

(3) In the application of section 97A of TMA 1970 (multiple penalties) no account shall be taken of a penalty under paragraph 30.

Appeal against penalty

41 (1) A person may appeal against a decision of HMRC that a penalty is payable under paragraph 30.

(2) A person may appeal against a decision of HMRC as to the amount of a penalty payable by P under paragraph 30.

(3) An appeal under this paragraph must be made within the period of 30 days beginning with the day on which notification of the penalty is given under paragraph 38.

(4) An appeal under this paragraph is to be treated in the same way as an appeal against an assessment to the tax concerned (including by the application of any provision about bringing the appeal by notice to HMRC, about HMRC's review of the decision or about determination of the appeal by the First-tier Tribunal or Upper Tribunal).

(5) Sub-paragraph (4) does not apply—

(*a*) so as to require a person to pay a penalty before an appeal against the assessment of the penalty is determined, or

(*b*) in respect of any other matter expressly provided for by this Part of this Schedule.

(6) On an appeal under sub-paragraph (1) or (2) the tribunal may—

(*a*) affirm HMRC's decision, or

(*b*) substitute for HMRC's decision another decision that HMRC has power to make.

(7) In this paragraph "tribunal" means the First-tier Tribunal or Upper Tribunal (as appropriate by virtue of sub-paragraph (4)).

Penalties: reasonable excuse

42 (1) A person is not liable to a penalty under paragraph 30 in respect of a relevant defeat if the person satisfies HMRC or (on appeal) the First-tier Tribunal or Upper Tribunal that the person had a reasonable excuse for the relevant failure to which that relevant defeat relates (see paragraph 43).

(2) Sub-paragraph (3) applies if—

(*a*) a person has incurred a relevant defeat in respect of which the person is liable to a penalty under paragraph 30, and

(*b*) before incurring that defeat the person had been given, or become liable to be given, an excepted warning notice.

(3) The person is treated for the purposes of sub-paragraphs (2) to (4) of paragraph 30 (rate of penalty) as not having been given, and not having become liable to be given, the excepted notice (so far as it relates to the relevant defeat in respect of which the person had a reasonable excuse).

(4) A warning notice is "excepted" for the purposes of this paragraph if the person was not liable to a penalty in respect of the defeat specified in it because the person had a reasonable excuse for the relevant failure in question.

(5) For the purposes of this paragraph, in the case of a person ("P")—

(*a*) an insufficiency of funds is not a reasonable excuse unless attributable to events outside P's control,

(*b*) where P relies on another person to do anything, that is not a reasonable excuse unless P took reasonable care to avoid the relevant failure, and

(*c*) where P had a reasonable excuse for the relevant failure but the excuse had ceased, P is to be treated as having continued to have the excuse if the failure is remedied without unreasonable delay after the excuse ceased.

(6) In determining for the purposes of this paragraph whether or not a person ("P") had a reasonable excuse for any action, failure or inaccuracy, reliance on advice is to be taken automatically not to constitute a reasonable excuse if the advice is addressed to, or was given to, a person other than P or takes no account of P's individual circumstances.

Paragraph 42: meaning of "the relevant failure"

43 (1) In paragraph 42 "the relevant failure", in relation to a relevant defeat, is to be interpreted in accordance with sub-paragraphs (2) to (7).

(2) In relation to a relevant defeat incurred by virtue of Condition A, "the relevant failure" means the failures or inaccuracies as a result of which the counteraction under section 209 of FA 2013 was necessary

(3) In relation to a relevant defeat incurred by virtue of Condition B, "the relevant failure" means the failures or inaccuracies in respect of which the action mentioned in paragraph 13(1) was taken.

(4) In relation to a relevant defeat incurred by virtue of Condition C, "the relevant failure" means the failures of inaccuracies as a result of which the adjustments, assessments, or other action mentioned in paragraph 14(5) are required.

(5) In relation to a relevant defeat incurred by virtue of Condition D, "the relevant failure" means the failures or inaccuracies as a result of which the adjustments, assessments or other action mentioned in paragraph 15(5) are required.

(6) In relation to a relevant defeat incurred by virtue of Condition E, "the relevant failure" means P's actions (and failures to act), so far as they are connected with matters in respect of which the counteraction mentioned in paragraph 16(1) is required.

(7) In sub-paragraph (6) "counteraction" is to be interpreted in accordance with paragraph 16(2).

[(8) In relation to a relevant defeat incurred by virtue of Condition F, "the relevant failure" means the failures or inaccuracies as a result of which the adjustments, assessments, or other actions mentioned in paragraph 16A(5) are required.][1]

Amendments—[1] Sub-para (8) inserted by F(No 2)A 2017 s 66, Sch 17 para 55(1), (16) with effect from 1 January 2018.

Mitigation of penalties

44 (1) The Commissioners may in their discretion mitigate a penalty under paragraph 30, or stay or compound any proceedings for such a penalty.

(2) They may also, after judgment, further mitigate or entirely remit the penalty.

PART 6

CORPORATE GROUPS, ASSOCIATED PERSONS AND PARTNERSHIPS

Representative member of a VAT group

45 (1) Where a body corporate ("R") is the representative member of a group (and accordingly is treated for the purposes of this Schedule as mentioned in section 43(1) of VATA 1994), anything which has been done by or in relation to another body corporate ("B") in B's capacity as representative member of that group is treated for the purposes of this Schedule as having been done by or in relation to R in R's capacity as representative member of the group. Accordingly paragraph 3 (warning period) operates as if the successive representative members of a group were a single person.

(2) This Schedule has effect as if the representative member of a group, so far as acting in its capacity as such, were a different person from that body corporate so far as acting in any other capacity.

(3) In this paragraph the reference to a "group" is to be interpreted in accordance with sections 43A to 43D of VATA 1994.

Corporate groups

46 (1) Sub-paragraphs (2) and (3) apply if HMRC has a duty under paragraph 2 to give a warning notice to a company ("C") which is a member of a group.

(2) That duty has effect as a duty to give a warning notice to each current group member (see sub-paragraph (8)).

(3) Any warning notice which has been given (or is treated as having been given) previously to any current group member is treated as having been given to each current group member (and any provision in this Schedule which refers to a "warning period" in relation to a person is to be interpreted accordingly).

But see sub-paragraphs (4) and (5).

(4) In relation to a company which incurs a relevant defeat, paragraph 19(1) (duty to give relief restriction notice) does not have effect unless the warning period mentioned in that sub-paragraph would be a warning period in relation to the company regardless of sub-paragraph (3).

(5) A company which incurs a relevant defeat is not liable to pay a penalty under paragraph 30 unless the warning period mentioned in sub-paragraph (1) of that paragraph would be a warning period in relation to the company regardless of sub-paragraph (3).

(6) HMRC may discharge any duty to give a warning notice to a current group member in accordance with sub-paragraph (2) by delivering the notice to C (and if it does so may combine one or more warning notices in a single notice).

(7) If a company ceases to be a member of a group, and—

- (*a*) immediately before it ceases to be a member of the group, a warning period has effect in relation to the company, but
- (*b*) no warning period would have effect in relation to the company at that time but for sub-paragraph (2) or (3),

that warning period ceases to have effect in relation to the company when it ceases to be a member of that group.

(8) In this paragraph "current group member" means a company which is a member of the group concerned at the time when the warning notice mentioned in sub-paragraph (1) is given.

(9) For the purposes of this paragraph two companies are members of the same group of companies if—

- (*a*) one is a 75% subsidiary of the other, or
- (*b*) both are 75% subsidiaries of a third company.

(10) In this paragraph "75% subsidiary" has the meaning given by section 1154 of CTA 2010.

(11) In this paragraph "company" has the same meaning as in the Corporation Tax Acts (see section 1121 of CTA 2010).

Associated persons treated as incurring relevant defeats

47 (1) Sub-paragraph (2) applies if a person ("P") incurs a relevant defeat in relation to any arrangements (otherwise than by virtue of this paragraph).

(2) Any person ("S") who is associated with P at the relevant time is also treated for the purposes of paragraphs 2 (duty to give warning notice) and 3(2) (warning period) as having incurred that relevant defeat in relation to those arrangements (but see sub-paragraph (3)).

For the meaning of "associated" see paragraph 48.

(3) Sub-paragraph (2) does not apply if P and S are members of the same group of companies (as defined in paragraph 46(9)).

(4) In relation to a warning notice given to S by virtue of sub-paragraph (2), paragraph 2(4)(*c*) (certain information to be included in warning notice) is to be read as referring only to paragraphs 3, 17 and 18.

(5) A warning notice which is given to a person by virtue of sub-paragraph (2) is treated for the purposes of paragraphs 19(1) (duty to give relief restriction notice) and 30 (penalty) as not having been given to that person.

(6) In sub-paragraph (2) "the relevant time" means the time when P is given a warning notice in respect of the relevant defeat.

Meaning of "associated"

48 (1) For the purposes of paragraph 47 two persons are associated with one another if—

(*a*) one of them is a body corporate which is controlled by the other, or

(*b*) they are bodies corporate under common control.

(2) Two bodies corporate are under common control if both are controlled—

(*a*) by one person,

(*b*) by two or more, but fewer than six, individuals, or

(*c*) by any number of individuals carrying on business in partnership.

(3) For the purposes of this section a body corporate ("H") is taken to control another body corporate ("B") if—

(*a*) H is empowered by statute to control B's activities, or

(*b*) H is B's holding company within the meaning of section 1159 of and Schedule 6 to the Companies Act 2006.

(4) For the purposes of this section an individual or individuals are taken to control a body corporate ("B") if the individual or individuals, were they a body corporate, would be B's holding company within the meaning of those provisions.

Partners treated as incurring relevant defeats

49 (1) Where paragraph 50 applies in relation to a partnership return, each relevant partner is treated for the purposes of this Schedule as having incurred the relevant defeat mentioned in paragraph 50(1)(*b*), (2) or (3)(*b*) (as the case may be).

(2) In this paragraph "relevant partner" means any person who was a partner in the partnership at any time during the relevant reporting period (but see sub-paragraph (3)).

(3) The "relevant partners" do not include—

(*a*) the person mentioned in sub-paragraph (1)(*b*), (2) or (3)(*b*) (as the case may be) of paragraph 50, or

(*b*) any other person who would, apart from this paragraph, incur a relevant defeat in connection with the subject matter of the partnership return mentioned in sub-paragraph (1).

(4) In this paragraph the "relevant reporting period" means the period in respect of which the partnership return mentioned in sub-paragraph (1), (2) or (3) of paragraph 50 was required.

Partnership returns to which this paragraph applies

50 (1) This paragraph applies in relation to a partnership return if—

(*a*) that return has been made on the basis that a tax advantage arises to a partner from any arrangements, and

(*b*) that person has incurred, in relation to that tax advantage and those arrangements, a relevant defeat by virtue of Condition A (final counteraction of tax advantage under general anti-abuse rule).

(2) Where a person has incurred a relevant defeat by virtue of sub-paragraph (2) of paragraph 13 (Condition B: case involving partnership follower notice) this paragraph applies in relation to the partnership return mentioned in that sub-paragraph.

(3) This paragraph applies in relation to a partnership return if—

(*a*) that return has been made on the basis that a tax advantage arises to a partner from any arrangements, and

(*b*) that person has incurred, in relation to that tax advantage and those arrangements, a relevant defeat by virtue of Condition C (return, claim or election made in reliance on DOTAS arrangements).

(4) The references in this paragraph to a relevant defeat do not include a relevant defeat incurred by virtue of paragraph 47(2).

Partnerships: information

51 (1) If paragraph 50 applies in relation to a partnership return, the appropriate partner must give HMRC a written notice (a "partnership information notice") in respect of each sub-period in the information period.

(2) The "information period" is the period of 5 years beginning with the day after the day of the relevant defeat mentioned in paragraph 50.

(3) If, in the case of a partnership, a new information period (relating to another partnership return) begins during an existing information period, those periods are treated for the purposes of this paragraph as a single period (which includes all times that would otherwise fall within either period).

(4) An information period under this paragraph ends if the partnership ceases.

(5) A partnership information notice must be given not later than the 30th day after the end of the sub-period to which it relates.

(6) A partnership information notice must state—

(*a*) whether or not any relevant partnership return which was, or was required to be, delivered in the sub-period has been made on the basis that a relevant tax advantage arises, and

(*b*) whether or not there has been a failure to deliver a relevant partnership return in the sub-period.

(7) In this paragraph—

(*a*) "relevant partnership return" means a partnership return in respect of the partnership's trade, profession or business;

(*b*) "relevant tax advantage" means a tax advantage which particular DOTAS arrangements enable, or might be expected to enable, a person who is or has been a partner in the partnership to obtain.

(8) If a partnership information notice states that a relevant partnership return has been made on the basis mentioned in sub-paragraph (6)(*a*) the notice must—

(*a*) explain (on the assumptions made for the purposes of the return) how the DOTAS arrangements enable the tax advantage concerned to be obtained, and

(*b*) describe any variation in the amounts required to be stated in the return under section 12AB(1) of TMA 1970 which results from those arrangements.

(9) HMRC may require the appropriate partner to give HMRC a notice (a "supplementary information notice") setting out further information in relation to a partnership information notice. In relation to a partnership information notice "further information" means information which would have been required to be set out in the notice by virtue of sub-paragraph (6)(*a*) or (8) had there not been a failure to deliver a relevant partnership return.

(10) A requirement under sub-paragraph (9) must be made by a written notice and the notice must state the period within which the notice must be complied with.

(11) If a person fails to comply with a requirement of (or imposed under) this paragraph, HMRC may by written notice extend the information period concerned to the end of the period of 5 years beginning with—

(*a*) the day by which the partnership information notice or supplementary information notice was required to be given to HMRC or, as the case requires,

(*b*) the day on which the person gave the defective notice to HMRC,

or, if earlier, the time when the information period would have expired but for the extension.

(12) For the purposes of this paragraph—

(*a*) the first sub-period in an information period begins with the first day of the information period and ends with a day specified by HMRC,

(*b*) the remainder of the information period is divided into further sub-periods each of which begins immediately after the end of the preceding sub-period and is twelve months long or (if that would be shorter) ends at the end of the information period.

(13) In this paragraph "the appropriate partner" means the partner in the partnership who is for the time being nominated by HMRC for the purposes of this paragraph.

Prospective amendments—In sub-para (8)(*b*), words ", or under equivalent provision made by regulations under paragraph 10 of Schedule A1 to that Act," to be inserted after words "TMA 1970" by F(No 2)A 2017 s 61(1), Sch 14 paras 47, 48(1), (2) with effect from a day to be appointed.

Partnerships: special provision about taxpayer emendations

52 (1) Sub-paragraph (2) applies if a partnership return is amended at any time under section 12ABA of TMA 1970 (amendment of partnership return by representative partner etc) on a basis that—

(*a*) results in an increase or decrease in, or

(*b*) otherwise affects the calculation of,

any amount stated under subsection (1)(*b*) of section 12AB of that Act (partnership statement) as a partner's share of any income, loss, consideration, tax or credit for any period.

(2) For the purposes of paragraph 14 (Condition C: counteraction of DOTAS arrangements), the partner is treated as having at that time amended—

(*a*) the partner's return under section 8 or 8A of TMA 1970, or

(*b*) the partner's company tax return,

so as to give effect to the amendments of the partnership return.

(3) Sub-paragraph (4) applies if a partnership return is amended at any time by HMRC as a result of a disclosure made by the representative partner or that person's successor on a basis that—

(*a*) results in an increase or decrease in, or

(*b*) otherwise affects the calculation of,

any amount stated under subsection (1)(*b*) of section 12AB of TMA 1970 (partnership statement) as the share of a particular partner (P) of any income, loss, consideration, tax or credit for any period.

(4) If the conditions in sub-paragraph (5) are met, P is treated for the purposes of paragraph 14 as having at that time amended—

(*a*) P's return under section 8 or 8A of TMA 1970, or

(*b*) P's company tax return,

so as to give effect to the amendments of the partnership return.

(5) The conditions are that the disclosure—

(*a*) is a full and explicit disclosure of an inaccuracy in the partnership return, and

(*b*) was made at a time when neither the person making the disclosure nor P had reason to believe that HMRC was about to begin enquiries into the partnership return.

Prospective amendments—The following amendments to be made by F(No 2)A 2017 s 61(1), Sch 14 paras 47, 48(1), (3) with effect from a day to be appointed—

– in sub-para (1), words "section 12AB(1)(*b*) of that Act or under equivalent provision made by regulations under paragraph 10 of Schedule A1 to that Act (partnership statement)" to be substituted for words "subsection (1)(*b*) of section 12AB of that Act (partnership statement)"; and

– in sub-para (3), in words at the beginning, words "(in the case of a section 12AA partnership return) or the nominated partner (in the case of a Schedule A1 partnership return)" to be inserted after words "that person's successor", and in words at the end, words "section 12AB(1)(*b*) of TMA 1970 or under equivalent provision made by regulations under paragraph 10 of Schedule A1 to that Act (partnership statement)" to be substituted for words "subsection (1)(*b*) of section 12AB of TMA 1970 (partnership statement)".

Supplementary provision relating to partnerships

53 (1) In paragraphs 49 to 52 and this paragraph—

"partnership" is to be interpreted in accordance with section 12AA of TMA 1970 (and includes a limited liability partnership);

"the representative partner", in relation to a partnership return, means the person who was required by a notice served under or for the purposes of section 12AA(2) or (3) of TMA 1970 to deliver the return;

"successor", in relation to a person who is the representative partner in the case of a partnership return, has the same meaning as in TMA 1970 (see section 118(1) of that Act).

(2) For the purposes of this Part of this Schedule a partnership is treated as the same partnership notwithstanding a change in membership if any person who was a member before the change remains a member after the change.

Prospective amendments—In sub-s (1), in definition of "the representative partner", words "section 12AA" to be inserted after words "in relation to a", and definition of "the nominated partner" to be inserted after definition of "successor", by F(No 2)A 2017 s 61(1), Sch 14 paras 47, 48(1), (4) with effect from a day to be appointed. Definition as inserted to read as follows—

""the nominated partner", in relation to a Schedule A1 partnership return, has the meaning given by paragraph 5 of Schedule A1 to TMA 1970.".

PART 7
SUPPLEMENTAL

Meaning of "adjustments"

54 (1) In this Schedule "adjustments" means any adjustments, whether by way of an assessment, the modification of an assessment or return, amendment or disallowance of a claim, a payment, the entering into of a contract settlement, or otherwise (and references to "making" adjustments accordingly include securing that adjustments are made by entering into a contract settlement).
(2) "Adjustments" also includes a payment in respect of a liability to pay national insurance contributions.

Time of "use" of defeated arrangements

55 (1) With reference to a particular relevant defeat incurred by a person in relation to arrangements, the person is treated as having "used" the arrangements on the dates set out in this paragraph.
(2) If the person incurs the relevant defeat by virtue of Condition A, the person is treated as having "used" the arrangements on the following dates—
(*a*) the filing date of any return made by the person on the basis that the tax advantage mentioned in paragraph 12(1)(*a*) arises from the arrangements;
(*b*) the date on which the person makes any claim or election on that basis;
(*c*) the date of any relevant failure by the person to comply with an obligation.
(3) For the purposes of sub-paragraph (2) a failure to comply with an obligation is a "relevant failure" if the whole or part of the tax advantage mentioned in paragraph 12(1)(*b*) arose as a result of, or in connection with, that failure.
(4) If the person incurs the relevant defeat by virtue of Condition B, the person is treated as having "used" the arrangements on the following dates—
(*a*) the filing date of any return made by the person on the basis that the asserted advantage (see section 204(3) of FA 2014) results from the arrangements,
(*b*) the date on which any claim is made by the person on that basis,
(*c*) the date of any failure by the person to comply with a relevant obligation.
In this sub-paragraph "relevant obligation" means an obligation which would not have fallen on the person (or might have been expected not to do so), had the denied advantage arisen (see section 208(3) of FA 2014).
(5) If the person incurs the relevant defeat by virtue of Condition C, the person is treated as having "used" the arrangements on the following dates—
(*a*) the filing date of any return made by the person on the basis mentioned in paragraph 14(2)(*a*);
(*b*) the date on which the person makes any claim or election on that basis;
(*c*) the date of any failure by the person to comply with a relevant obligation (as defined in paragraph 14(4)).
(6) If the person incurs the relevant defeat by virtue of Condition D, the person is treated as having "used" the arrangements on the following dates—
(*a*) the filing date of any return made by the person on the basis mentioned in paragraph 15(2)(*a*);
(*b*) the date on which the person makes any claim on that basis;
(*c*) the date of any failure by the person to comply with a relevant obligation (as defined in paragraph 15(4)).
(7) If the person incurs the relevant defeat by virtue of Condition E, the person is treated as having "used" the arrangements on the following dates—
(*a*) the filing date of any return made by S to which the counteraction mentioned in paragraph 16(1)(*c*) relates;
(*b*) the date on which S made any claim to which that counteraction relates;
(*c*) the date of any relevant failure by S to which that counteraction relates.
(8) In sub-paragraph (7) "relevant failure" means a failure to comply with an obligation relating to VAT.
[(8A) If the person incurs the relevant defeat by virtue of Condition F, the person is treated as having "used" the arrangements on the following dates—
(*a*) the filing date of any return made by the person on the basis mentioned in paragraph 16A(2)(*a*);
(*b*) the date on which the person makes any claim, declaration or application for approval;
(*c*) the date of any failure by the person to comply with a relevant obligation (as defined in paragraph 16A(4)).][1]
(9) In this paragraph "filing date", in relation to a return, means the earlier of—
(*a*) the day on which the return is delivered, or
(*b*) the last day of the period within which the return must be delivered.

(10) References in this paragraph to the date on which a person fails to comply with an obligation are to the date on which the person is first in breach of the obligation.

Amendments—[1] Sub-para (8A) inserted by F(No 2)A 2017 s 66, Sch 17 para 55(1), (17) with effect from 1 January 2018.

Inheritance tax

56 (1) In the case of inheritance tax, each of the following is treated as a return for the purposes of this Schedule—

(*a*) an account delivered by a person under section 216 or 217 of IHTA 1984 (including an account delivered in accordance with regulations under section 256 of that Act);

(*b*) a statement or declaration which amends or is otherwise connected with such an account produced by the person who delivered the account;

(*c*) information or a document provided by a person in accordance with regulations under section 256 of that Act;

and such a return is treated as made by the person in question.

(2) In this Schedule (except where the context requires otherwise) "assessment", in relation to inheritance tax, includes a determination.

National insurance contributions

57 (1) In this Schedule references to an assessment to tax include a NICs decision relating to a person's liability for relevant contributions.

(2) In this Schedule a reference to a provision of Part 7 of FA 2004 (disclosure of tax avoidance schemes) (a "DOTAS provision") includes a reference to—

(*a*) that DOTAS provision as applied by regulations under section 132A of the Social Security Administration Act 1992 (disclosure of contributions avoidance arrangements);

(*b*) any provision of regulations under that section that corresponds to that DOTAS provision,

whenever the regulations are made.

(3) Regulations under section 132A of that Act may disapply, or modify the effect of, sub-paragraph (2).

(4) In this paragraph "NICs decision" means a decision under section 8 of the Social Security Contributions (Transfer of Functions, etc) Act 1999 or Article 7 of the Social Security Contributions (Transfer of Functions, etc) (Northern Ireland) Order 1999 (S.I. 1999/671).

General interpretation

58 (1) In this Schedule—

"arrangements" has the meaning given by paragraph 2(6);

"the Commissioners" means the Commissioners for Her Majesty's Revenue and Customs;

"contract settlement" means an agreement in connection with a person's liability to make a payment to the Commissioners under or by virtue of an enactment;

["disclosable indirect tax arrangements" is to be interpreted in accordance with paragraph 9A;

"disclosable Schedule 11A VAT arrangements" is to be interpreted in accordance with paragraph 9;][1]

"disclosable VAT arrangements" is to be interpreted in accordance with paragraph [8A][1];

"DOTAS arrangements" is to be interpreted in accordance with paragraph 8 (and see also paragraph 57(2));

"follower notice" has the meaning given by paragraph 13(6);

"HMRC" means Her Majesty's Revenue and Customs;

["indirect tax" has the meaning given by paragraph 4(2);][1]

"national insurance contributions" means contributions under Part 1 of the Social Security Contributions and Benefits Act 1992 or Part 1 of the Social Security Contributions and Benefits (Northern Ireland) Act 1992;

"net income" has the meaning given by section 23 of ITA 2007 (see Step 2 of that section);

"partnership follower notice" has the meaning given by paragraph 2(2) of Schedule 31 to FA 2014;

"partnership return" means a return under section 12AA of TMA 1970;

"relevant contributions" means the following contributions under Part 1 of the Social Security Contributions and Benefits Act 1992 or Part 1 of the Social Security Contributions and Benefits (Northern Ireland) Act 1992—

(*a*) Class 1 contributions;

(*b*) Class 1A contributions;

(*c*) Class 1B contributions;

(*d*) Class 2 contributions which must be paid but in relation to which section 11A of the Act in question (application of certain provisions of the Income Tax Acts in relation to Class 2 contributions under section 11(2) of that Act) does not apply;

"relevant defeat" is to be interpreted in accordance with paragraph 11;

"tax" has the meaning given by paragraph [4(1)][1];

"tax advantage" has the meaning given by paragraph 7;

"warning notice" has the meaning given by paragraph 2.

(2) In this Schedule an expression used in relation to VAT has the same meaning as in VATA 1994.

(3) In this Schedule (except where the context requires otherwise) references, however expressed, to a person's affairs in relation to tax include the person's position as regards deductions or repayments of, or of sums representing, tax that the person is required to make by or under an enactment.

(4) For the purposes of this Schedule a partnership return is regarded as made on the basis that a particular tax advantage arises to a person from particular arrangements if—

(*a*) it is made on the basis that an increase or reduction in one or more of the amounts mentioned in section 12AB(1) of TMA 1970 (amounts in the partnership statement in a partnership return) results from those arrangements, and

(*b*) that increase or reduction results in that tax advantage for the person.

Amendments—[1] In sub-para (1), definitions of "disclosable indirect tax arrangements", "disclosable Schedule 11A VAT arrangements" and "indirect tax" inserted; in definition of "disclosable VAT arrangements", reference substituted for reference "9"; and in definition of "tax", reference substituted for reference "4", by F(No 2)A 2017 s 66, Sch 17 para 55(1), (18) with effect from 1 January 2018.

Prospective amendments—In sub-s (1), definition of "partnership return" to be substituted by F(No 2)A 2017 s 61(1), Sch 14 paras 47, 48(1), (5) with effect from a day to be appointed. Definition as substituted to read as follows—

""partnership return" means a return—

(a) under section 12AA of TMA 1970 (a "section 12AA partnership return"), or

(b) required by regulations made under paragraph 10 of Schedule A1 to TMA 1970 (a "Schedule A1 partnership return");".

Consequential amendments

59 In section 103ZA of TMA 1970 (disapplication of sections 100 to 103 in the case of certain penalties)—

(*a*) omit "or" at the end of paragraph (ga), and

(*b*) after paragraph (*h*) insert "or

(i) Part 5 of Schedule 18 to the Finance Act 2016 (serial tax avoidance)."

60 In section 212 of FA 2014 (follower notices: aggregate penalties), in subsection (4)—

(*a*) omit "or" at the end of paragraph (*b*), and

(*b*) after paragraph (*c*) insert ", or

(*d*) Part 5 of Schedule 18 to FA 2016 (serial tax avoidance)."

61 (1) The Social Security Contributions and Benefits Act 1992 is amended as follows.

(2) In section 11A (application of certain provisions of the Income Tax Acts in relation to Class 2 contributions under section 11(2)), in subsection (1), at the end of paragraph (*e*) insert—

"(*ea*) the provisions of Schedule 18 to the Finance Act 2016 (serial tax avoidance);".

(3) In section 16 (application of Income Tax Acts and destination of Class 4 contributions), in subsection (1), at the end of paragraph (*d*) insert "and

"(*e*) the provisions of Schedule 18 to the Finance Act 2016 (serial tax avoidance),".

62 In the Social Security Contributions and Benefits (Northern Ireland) Act 1992, in section 11A (application of certain provisions of the Income Tax Acts in relation to Class 2 contributions under section 11(2)), in subsection (1), at the end of paragraph (*e*) insert—

"(*ea*) the provisions of Schedule 18 to the Finance Act 2016 (serial tax avoidance);".

Commencement

63 Subject to paragraphs 64 and 65, paragraphs 1 to 62 of this Schedule have effect in relation to relevant defeats incurred after the day on which this Act is passed.

64 (1) A relevant defeat is to be disregarded for the purposes of this Schedule if it is incurred before 6 April 2017 in relation to arrangements which the person has entered into before the day on which this Act is passed.

(2) A relevant defeat incurred on or after 6 April 2017 is to be disregarded for the purposes of this Schedule if—

(*a*) the person entered into the arrangements concerned before the day on which this Act is passed, and (*b*) before 6 April 2017—

(i) the person incurring the defeat fully discloses to HMRC the matters to which the relevant counteraction relates, or

(ii) that person gives HMRC notice of a firm intention to make a full disclosure of those matters and makes such a full disclosure within any time limit set by HMRC.

(3) In sub-paragraph (2) "the relevant counteraction" means—

(*a*) in a case within Condition A, the counteraction mentioned in paragraph 12(1)(*c*);

(*b*) in a case within Condition B, the action mentioned in paragraph 13(1);

(*c*) in a case within Condition C, the counteraction mentioned in paragraph 14(1)(*c*);

(*d*) in a case within Condition D, the counteraction mentioned in paragraph 15(1)(*d*);

(*e*) in a case within Condition E, the counteraction mentioned in paragraph 16(1)(*c*).

(4) In sub-paragraph (3)—

(*a*) in paragraph (*c*) "counteraction" is to be interpreted in accordance with paragraph 14(5);

(*b*) in paragraph (*d*) "counteraction" is to be interpreted in accordance with paragraph 15(5);

(*c*) in paragraph (*e*) "counteraction" is to be interpreted in accordance with paragraph 16(2).

(5) See paragraph 11(2) for provision about when a relevant defeat is incurred. 65 (1) A warning notice given to a person is to be disregarded for the purposes of—

(*a*) paragraph 18 (naming), and

(*b*) Part 4 of this Schedule (restriction of reliefs), if the relevant defeat specified in the notice relates to arrangements which the person has entered into before the day on which this Act is passed.

(2) Where a person has entered into any arrangements before the day on which this Act is passed—

(*a*) a relevant defeat incurred by a person in relation to the arrangements, and

(*b*) any warning notice specifying such a relevant defeat, is to be disregarded for the purposes of paragraph 30 (penalty).

65 (1) A warning notice given to a person is to be disregarded for the purposes of—

(*a*) paragraph 18 (naming), and

(*b*) Part 4 of this Schedule (restriction of reliefs),

if the relevant defeat specified in the notice relates to arrangements which the person has entered into before the day on which this Act is passed.

(2) Where a person has entered into any arrangements before the day on which this Act is passed—

(*a*) a relevant defeat incurred by a person in relation to the arrangements, and

(*b*) any warning notice specifying such a relevant defeat,

is to be disregarded for the purposes of paragraph 30 (penalty).

SCHEDULE 20

PENALTIES FOR ENABLERS OF OFFSHORE TAX EVASION OR NON-COMPLIANCE

Section 162

Commencement—Finance Act 2016, Section 162(1) and Schedule 20 (Appointed Day) Regulations 2016 (the appointed day for the purposes of this Schedule is 1 January 2017 with effect in relation to acts or omissions occurring on or after that day which encourage, assist or otherwise facilitate conduct constituting offshore tax evasion or non-compliance within para 1(2)).

PART 1
LIABILITY FOR PENALTY

Commencement—Finance Act 2016, Section 162(1) and Schedule 20 (Appointed Day) Regulations, SI 2016/1249 (the appointed day for the purposes of this Schedule is 1 January 2017 with effect in relation to acts or omissions occurring on or after that day which encourage, assist or otherwise facilitate conduct constituting offshore tax evasion or non-compliance within para 1(2)).

Liability for penalty

1 (1) A penalty is payable by a person (P) who has enabled another person (Q) to carry out offshore tax evasion or non-compliance, where conditions A and B are met.

(2) For the purposes of this Schedule—

(*a*) Q carries out "offshore tax evasion or non-compliance" by—

(i) committing a relevant offence, or

(ii) engaging in conduct that makes Q liable (if the applicable conditions are met) to a relevant civil penalty,

where the tax at stake is income tax, capital gains tax or inheritance tax, and

(*b*) P "has enabled" Q to carry out offshore tax evasion or noncompliance if P has encouraged, assisted or otherwise facilitated conduct by Q that constitutes offshore tax evasion or noncompliance.

(3) The relevant offences are—

(*a*) an offence of cheating the public revenue involving offshore activity, or

(*b*) an offence under section 106A of TMA 1970 (fraudulent evasion of income tax) involving offshore activity,

(*c*) an offence under section 106B, 106C or 106D of TMA 1970 (offences relating to certain failures to comply with section 7 or 8 by a taxpayer chargeable to income tax or capital gains tax on or by reference to offshore income, assets or liabilities).

(4) The relevant civil penalties are—

(*a*) a penalty under paragraph 1 of Schedule 24 to FA 2007 (errors in taxpayer's document) involving an offshore matter or an offshore transfer (within the meaning of that Schedule),

(*b*) a penalty under paragraph 1 of Schedule 41 to FA 2008 (failure to notify etc) in relation to a failure to comply with section 7(1) of TMA 1970 involving offshore activity,

(*c*) a penalty under paragraph 6 of Schedule 55 to FA 2009 (failure to make return for 12 months) involving offshore activity,

(*d*) a penalty under paragraph 1 of Schedule 21 to FA 2015 (penalties in connection with relevant offshore asset moves).

(5) Condition A is that P knew when P's actions were carried out that they enabled, or were likely to enable, Q to carry out offshore tax evasion or noncompliance.

(6) Condition B is that—

(*a*) in the case of offshore tax evasion or non-compliance consisting of the commission of a relevant offence, Q has been convicted of the offence and the conviction is final, or

(*b*) in the case of offshore tax evasion or non-compliance consisting of conduct that makes Q liable to a relevant penalty—

(i) Q has been found to be liable to such a penalty, assessed and notified, and the penalty is final, or

(ii) a contract has been made between the Commissioners for Her Majesty's Revenue and Customs and Q under which the Commissioners undertake not to assess the penalty or (if it has been assessed) not to take proceedings to recover it.

(7) For the purposes of sub-paragraph (6)(*a*)—

(*a*) "convicted of the offence" means convicted of the full offence (and not for example of an attempt), and

(*b*) a conviction becomes final when the time allowed for bringing an appeal against it expires or, if later, when any appeal against conviction has been determined.

(8) For the purposes of sub-paragraph (6)(*b*)(i) a penalty becomes final when the time allowed for any appeal or further appeal relating to it expires or, if later, any appeal or final appeal relating to it is determined.

(9) It is immaterial for the purposes of condition B that—

(*a*) any offence of which Q was convicted, or

(*b*) any penalty for which Q was found to be liable,

relates also to other tax evasion or non-compliance by Q.

(10) In this Schedule "other tax evasion or non-compliance by Q" means conduct by Q that—

(*a*) constitutes an offence of cheating the public revenue or an offence of fraudulent evasion of tax, or

(*b*) makes Q liable to a penalty under any provision of the Taxes Acts,

but does not constitute offshore tax evasion or non-compliance.

(11) Nothing in condition B affects the law of evidence as to the relevance if any of a conviction, assessment of a penalty or contract mentioned in subparagraph (6) for the purpose of proving that condition A is met in relation to P.

(12) In this Schedule "conduct" includes a failure to act.

Commencement—Finance Act 2016, Section 162(1) and Schedule 20 (Appointed Day) Regulations, SI 2016/1249 (the appointed day for the purposes of this Schedule is 1 January 2017 with effect in relation to acts or omissions occurring on or after that day which encourage, assist or otherwise facilitate conduct constituting offshore tax evasion or non-compliance within para 1(2)).

Meaning of "involving offshore activity" and related expressions

2 (1) This paragraph has effect for the purposes of this Schedule.

(2) Conduct involves offshore activity if it involves—

(*a*) an offshore matter,

(*b*) an offshore transfer, or

(*c*) a relevant offshore asset move.

(3) Conduct involves an offshore matter if it results in a potential loss of revenue that is charged on or by reference to—

(*a*) income arising from a source in a territory outside the United Kingdom,

(*b*) assets situated or held in a territory outside the United Kingdom, (*c*) activities carried on wholly or mainly in a territory outside the United Kingdom, or

(*d*) anything having effect as if it were income, assets or activities of the kind described above.

(4) Where the tax at stake is inheritance tax, assets are treated for the purposes of sub-paragraph (3) as situated or held in a territory outside the United Kingdom if they are so held or situated immediately after the transfer of value by reason of which inheritance tax becomes chargeable.

(5) Conduct involves an offshore transfer if—

(*a*) it does not involve an offshore matter,

(*b*) it is deliberate (whether or not concealed) and results in a potential loss of revenue,

(*c*) the condition set out in paragraph 4AA of Schedule 24 to FA 2007 is satisfied.

(6) Conduct involves a relevant offshore asset move if at a time when Q is the beneficial owner of an asset ("the qualifying time")—

(*a*) the asset ceases to be situated or held in a specified territory and becomes situated or held in a non-specified territory,

(*b*) the person who holds the asset ceases to be resident in a specified territory and becomes resident in a non-specified territory, or

(*c*) there is a change in the arrangements for the ownership of the asset,

and Q remains the beneficial owner of the asset, or any part of it, immediately after the qualifying time.

(7) Paragraphs 4(2) to (4) of Schedule 21 to FA 2015 apply for the purposes of sub-paragraph (6) above as they apply for purposes of paragraph 4 of that Schedule.

(8) In sub-paragraph (6) above, "specified territory" has the same meaning as in paragraph 4(5) of Schedule 21 to FA 2015.

Commencement—Finance Act 2016, Section 162(1) and Schedule 20 (Appointed Day) Regulations, SI 2016/1249 (the appointed day for the purposes of this Schedule is 1 January 2017 with effect in relation to acts or omissions occurring on or after that day which encourage, assist or otherwise facilitate conduct constituting offshore tax evasion or non-compliance within para 1(2)).

Amount of penalty

3 (1) The penalty payable under paragraph 1 is (except in a case mentioned in sub-paragraph (2)) the higher of—

(*a*) 100% of the potential lost revenue, or

(*b*) £3,000.

(2) In a case where P has enabled Q to engage in conduct which makes Q liable to a penalty under paragraph 1 of Schedule 21 to FA 2015, the penalty payable under paragraph 1 is the higher of—

(*a*) 50% of the potential lost revenue in respect of the original tax non-compliance, and

(*b*) £3,000.

(3) In sub-paragraph (2)(*a*) "the original tax non-compliance" means the conduct that incurred the original penalty and "the potential lost revenue" (in respect of that non-compliance) is—

(*a*) the potential lost revenue under Schedule 24 to FA 2007,

(*b*) the potential lost revenue under Schedule 41 to FA 2008, or

(*c*) the liability to tax which would have been shown on the return (within the meaning of Schedule 55 to FA 2009),

according to whether the original penalty was incurred under paragraph 1 of Schedule 24, paragraph 1 of Schedule 41 or paragraph 6 of Schedule 55.

Commencement—Finance Act 2016, Section 162(1) and Schedule 20 (Appointed Day) Regulations, SI 2016/1249 (the appointed day for the purposes of this Schedule is 1 January 2017 with effect in relation to acts or omissions occurring on or after that day which encourage, assist or otherwise facilitate conduct constituting offshore tax evasion or non-compliance within para 1(2)).

Potential lost revenue: enabling Q to commit relevant offence

4 (1) The potential lost revenue in a case where P is liable to a penalty under paragraph 1 for enabling Q to commit a relevant offence is the same amount as the potential lost revenue applicable for the purposes of the corresponding relevant civil penalty (determined in accordance with the relevant sub-paragraph of paragraph 5).

(2) Where Q's offending conduct is—

(*a*) an offence of cheating the public revenue involving offshore activity, or

(*b*) an offence under section 106A of TMA 1970 involving offshore activity,

the corresponding relevant civil penalty is the penalty which Q is liable for as a result of that offending conduct.

(3) Where Q's offending conduct is an offence under section 106B, 106C or 106D of TMA 1970, the corresponding relevant civil penalty is—

(*a*) for an offence under section 106B of TMA 1970, a penalty under paragraph 1 of Schedule 41 to FA 2008,

(*b*) for an offence under section 106C of TMA 1970, a penalty under paragraph 6 of Schedule 55 to FA 2009, and (*c*) for an offence under section 106D of TMA 1970, a penalty under paragraph 1 of Schedule 24 to FA 2007.

(4) In determining any amount of potential lost revenue for the purposes of this paragraph, the fact Q has been prosecuted for the offending conduct is to be disregarded.

Commencement—Finance Act 2016, Section 162(1) and Schedule 20 (Appointed Day) Regulations, SI 2016/1249 (the appointed day for the purposes of this Schedule is 1 January 2017 with effect in relation to acts or omissions occurring on or after that day which encourage, assist or otherwise facilitate conduct constituting offshore tax evasion or non-compliance within para 1(2)).

Potential lost revenue: enabling Q to engage in conduct incurring relevant civil penalty

5 (1) The potential lost revenue in a case where P is liable to a penalty under paragraph 1 for enabling Q to engage in conduct that makes Q liable (if the applicable conditions are met) to a relevant civil penalty is to be determined as follows.

(2) In the case of a penalty under paragraph 1 of Schedule 24 to FA 2007 involving an offshore matter or an offshore transfer, the potential lost revenue is the amount that under that Schedule is the potential lost revenue in respect of Q's conduct.

(3) In the case of a penalty under paragraph 1 of Schedule 41 to FA 2008 in relation to a failure to comply with section 7(1) of TMA 1970 involving offshore activity, the potential lost revenue is the amount that under that Schedule is the potential lost revenue in respect of Q's conduct.

(4) In the case of a penalty under paragraph 6 of Schedule 55 to FA 2009 involving offshore activity, the potential lost revenue is the liability to tax which would have been shown in the return in question (within the meaning of that Schedule).

Commencement—Finance Act 2016, Section 162(1) and Schedule 20 (Appointed Day) Regulations, SI 2016/1249 (the appointed day for the purposes of this Schedule is 1 January 2017 with effect in relation to acts or omissions occurring on or after that day which encourage, assist or otherwise facilitate conduct constituting offshore tax evasion or non-compliance within para 1(2)).

Treatment of potential lost revenue attributable to both offshore tax evasion or non-compliance and other tax evasion or non-compliance

6 (1) This paragraph applies where any amount of potential lost revenue in a case falling within paragraph 4 or 5 is attributable not only to Q's offshore tax evasion or non-compliance but also to any other tax evasion or noncompliance by Q.

(2) In that case the potential lost revenue in respect of Q's offshore tax evasion or non-compliance is to be taken for the purposes of assessing the penalty to which P is liable as being or (as the case may be) including such share as is just and reasonable of the amount mentioned in sub-paragraph (1).

Commencement—Finance Act 2016, Section 162(1) and Schedule 20 (Appointed Day) Regulations, SI 2016/1249 (the appointed day for the purposes of this Schedule is 1 January 2017 with effect in relation to acts or omissions occurring on or after that day which encourage, assist or otherwise facilitate conduct constituting offshore tax evasion or non-compliance within para 1(2)).

Reduction of penalty for disclosure etc by P

7 (1) If P (who would otherwise be liable to a penalty under paragraph 1)—

(*a*) makes a disclosure to HMRC of—

(i) a matter relating to an inaccuracy in a document, a supply of false information or a failure to disclose an under-assessment,

(ii) P's enabling of actions by Q that constituted (or might constitute) a relevant offence or that made (or might make) Q liable to a relevant penalty, or

(iii) any other matter HMRC regard as assisting them in relation to the assessment of P's liability to a penalty under paragraph 1, or

(*b*) assists HMRC in any investigation leading to Q being charged with a relevant offence or found liable to a relevant penalty,

HMRC must reduce the penalty to one that reflects the quality of the disclosure or assistance.

(2) But the penalty may not be reduced—

(*a*) in the case of unprompted disclosure or assistance, below whichever is the higher of—

(i) 10% of the potential lost revenue, or

(ii) £1,000, or

(*b*) in the case of prompted disclosure or assistance, below whichever is the higher of—

(i) 30% of the potential lost revenue, or

(ii) £3,000.

Commencement—Finance Act 2016, Section 162(1) and Schedule 20 (Appointed Day) Regulations, SI 2016/1249 (the appointed day for the purposes of this Schedule is 1 January 2017 with effect in relation to acts or omissions occurring on or after that day which encourage, assist or otherwise facilitate conduct constituting offshore tax evasion or non-compliance within para 1(2)).

8 (1) This paragraph applies for the purposes of paragraph 7.

(2) P discloses a matter by—

(*a*) telling HMRC about it,

(*b*) giving HMRC reasonable help in relation to the matter (for example by quantifying an inaccuracy in a document, an inaccuracy attributable to the supply of false information or withholding of information or an under-assessment), and

(*c*) allowing HMRC access to records for any reasonable purpose connected with resolving the matter (for example for the purpose of ensuring that an inaccuracy in a document, an inaccuracy attributable to the supply of false information or withholding of information or an under-assessment is fully corrected).

(3) P assists HMRC in relation to an investigation leading to Q being charged with a relevant offence or found liable to a relevant penalty by—

(*a*) assisting or encouraging Q to disclose all relevant facts to HMRC,

(*b*) allowing HMRC access to records, or

(*c*) any other conduct which HMRC considers assisted them in investigating or assessing Q's liability to such a penalty.

(4) Disclosure or assistance by P—

(*a*) is "unprompted" if made at a time when P has no reason to believe that HMRC have discovered or are about to discover Q's offshore tax evasion or non-compliance (including any inaccuracy in a document, supply of false information or withholding of information, or under-assessment), and

(*b*) otherwise is "prompted".

(5) In relation to disclosure or assistance, "quality" includes timing, nature and extent.

Commencement—Finance Act 2016, Section 162(1) and Schedule 20 (Appointed Day) Regulations, SI 2016/1249 (the appointed day for the purposes of this Schedule is 1 January 2017 with effect in relation to acts or omissions occurring on or after that day which encourage, assist or otherwise facilitate conduct constituting offshore tax evasion or non-compliance within para 1(2)).

9 (1) If they think it right because of special circumstances, HMRC may reduce a penalty under paragraph 1.

(2) In sub-paragraph 1 "special circumstances" does not include—

(*a*) ability to pay, or

(*b*) the fact that a potential loss of revenue from one taxpayer is balanced by a potential overpayment by another.

(3) In sub-paragraph (1) the reference to reducing a penalty includes a reference to—

(*a*) staying a penalty, or

(*b*) agreeing a compromise in relation to proceedings for a penalty.

Commencement—Finance Act 2016, Section 162(1) and Schedule 20 (Appointed Day) Regulations, SI 2016/1249 (the appointed day for the purposes of this Schedule is 1 January 2017 with effect in relation to acts or omissions occurring on or after that day which encourage, assist or otherwise facilitate conduct constituting offshore tax evasion or non-compliance within para 1(2)).

Procedure for assessing penalty, etc

10 (1) Where a person is found liable for a penalty under paragraph 1 HMRC must—

(*a*) assess the penalty,

(*b*) notify the person, and

(*c*) state in the notice the period in respect of which the penalty is assessed.

(2) A penalty must be paid before the end of the period of 30 days beginning with the day on which notification of the penalty is issued.

(3) An assessment of a penalty—

(*a*) is to be treated for procedural purposes in the same way as an assessment to tax (except in respect of a matter expressly provided for by this Schedule), and

(*b*) may be enforced as if it were an assessment to tax.

(4) A supplementary assessment may be made in respect of a penalty if an earlier assessment operated by reference to an underestimate of the liability to tax that would have been shown in a return.

(5) Sub-paragraph (6) applies if—

(*a*) an assessment in respect of a penalty is based on a liability to tax that would have been shown on a return, and

(*b*) that liability is found by HMRC to have been excessive.

(6) HMRC may amend the assessment so that it is based upon the correct amount.

(7) But an amendment under sub-paragraph (6)—

(*a*) does not affect when the penalty must be paid, and

(*b*) may be made after the last day on which the assessment in question could have been made under paragraph 11.

Commencement—Finance Act 2016, Section 162(1) and Schedule 20 (Appointed Day) Regulations, SI 2016/1249 (the appointed day for the purposes of this Schedule is 1 January 2017 with effect in relation to acts or omissions occurring on or after that day which encourage, assist or otherwise facilitate conduct constituting offshore tax evasion or non-compliance within para 1(2)).

11 An assessment of a person as liable to a penalty under paragraph 1 may not take place more than 2 years after the fulfilment of the conditions mentioned in paragraph 1(1) (in relation to that person) first came to the attention of an officer of Revenue and Customs.

Commencement—Finance Act 2016, Section 162(1) and Schedule 20 (Appointed Day) Regulations, SI 2016/1249 (the appointed day for the purposes of this Schedule is 1 January 2017 with effect in relation to acts or omissions occurring on or after that day which encourage, assist or otherwise facilitate conduct constituting offshore tax evasion or non-compliance within para 1(2)).

Appeals

12 A person may appeal against—

(*a*) a decision of HMRC that a penalty under paragraph 1 is payable by that person, or

(*b*) a decision of HMRC as to the amount of a penalty under paragraph 1 payable by the person.

Commencement—Finance Act 2016, Section 162(1) and Schedule 20 (Appointed Day) Regulations, SI 2016/1249 (the appointed day for the purposes of this Schedule is 1 January 2017 with effect in relation to acts or omissions occurring on or after that day which encourage, assist or otherwise facilitate conduct constituting offshore tax evasion or non-compliance within para 1(2)).

13 (1) An appeal under paragraph 12 is to be treated in the same way as an appeal against an assessment to the tax at stake (including by the application of any provision about bringing the appeal by notice to HMRC, about HMRC review of the decision or about determination of the appeal by the First-tier Tribunal or Upper Tribunal).

(2) Sub-paragraph (1) does not apply—

(*a*) so as to require the person bringing the appeal to pay a penalty before an appeal against the assessment of the penalty is determined,

(*b*) in respect of any other matter expressly provided for by this Schedule.

Commencement—Finance Act 2016, Section 162(1) and Schedule 20 (Appointed Day) Regulations, SI 2016/1249 (the appointed day for the purposes of this Schedule is 1 January 2017 with effect in relation to acts or omissions occurring on or after that day which encourage, assist or otherwise facilitate conduct constituting offshore tax evasion or non-compliance within para 1(2)).

14 (1) On an appeal under paragraph 12(*a*) that is notified to the tribunal, the tribunal may affirm or cancel HMRC's decision.

(2) On an appeal under paragraph 12(*b*) that is notified to the tribunal, the tribunal may—

(*a*) affirm HMRC's decision, or

(*b*) substitute for that decision another decision that HMRC had power to make.

(3) If the tribunal substitutes its own decision for HMRC's, the tribunal may rely on paragraph 7 or 9 (or both)—

(*a*) to the same extent as HMRC (which may mean applying the same percentage reduction as HMRC to a different starting point),

(*b*) to a different extent, but only if the tribunal thinks that HMRC's decision in respect of the application of that paragraph was flawed.

(4) In sub-paragraph (3)(*b*) "flawed" means flawed when considered in the light of the principles applicable in proceedings for judicial review.

(5) In this paragraph "tribunal" means the First-tier Tribunal or Upper Tribunal (as appropriate by virtue of paragraph 13(1).

Commencement—Finance Act 2016, Section 162(1) and Schedule 20 (Appointed Day) Regulations, SI 2016/1249 (the appointed day for the purposes of this Schedule is 1 January 2017 with effect in relation to acts or omissions occurring on or after that day which encourage, assist or otherwise facilitate conduct constituting offshore tax evasion or non-compliance within para 1(2)).

Double jeopardy

15 A person is not liable to a penalty under paragraph 1 in respect of conduct for which the person—

(*a*) has been convicted of an offence, or

(*b*) has been assessed to a penalty under any provision other than paragraph 1.

Commencement—Finance Act 2016, Section 162(1) and Schedule 20 (Appointed Day) Regulations, SI 2016/1249 (the appointed day for the purposes of this Schedule is 1 January 2017 with effect in relation to acts or omissions occurring on or after that day which encourage, assist or otherwise facilitate conduct constituting offshore tax evasion or non-compliance within para 1(2)).

Application of provisions of TMA 1970

16 Subject to the provisions of this Part of this Schedule, the following provisions of TMA 1970 apply for the purposes of this Part of this Schedule as they apply for the purposes of the Taxes Acts—

(*a*) section 108 (responsibility of company officers),

(*b*) section 114 (want of form), and

(*c*) section 115 (delivery and service of documents).

Commencement—Finance Act 2016, Section 162(1) and Schedule 20 (Appointed Day) Regulations, SI 2016/1249 (the appointed day for the purposes of this Schedule is 1 January 2017 with effect in relation to acts or omissions occurring on or after that day which encourage, assist or otherwise facilitate conduct constituting offshore tax evasion or non-compliance within para 1(2)).

Interpretation of Part 1

17 (1) This paragraph applies for the purposes of this Schedule.
(2) References to an assessment to tax, in relation to inheritance tax, are to a determination.

Commencement—Finance Act 2016, Section 162(1) and Schedule 20 (Appointed Day) Regulations, SI 2016/1249 (the appointed day for the purposes of this Schedule is 1 January 2017 with effect in relation to acts or omissions occurring on or after that day which encourage, assist or otherwise facilitate conduct constituting offshore tax evasion or non-compliance within para 1(2)).

PART 2
APPLICATION OF SCHEDULE 36 TO FA 2008: INFORMATION POWERS

Commencement—Finance Act 2016, Section 162(1) and Schedule 20 (Appointed Day) Regulations, SI 2016/1249 (the appointed day for the purposes of this Schedule is 1 January 2017 with effect in relation to acts or omissions occurring on or after that day which encourage, assist or otherwise facilitate conduct constituting offshore tax evasion or non-compliance within para 1(2)).

General application of information and inspection powers to suspected enablers

18 (1) Schedule 36 to FA 2008 (information and inspection powers) applies for the purpose of checking a relevant person's position as regards liability for a penalty under paragraph 1 as it applies for checking a person's tax position, subject to the modifications in paragraphs 19 to 21.
(2) In this Part of this Schedule "relevant person" means a person an officer of Revenue and Customs has reason to suspect has or may have enabled offshore tax evasion or non-compliance by another person so as to be liable to a penalty under paragraph 1.

Commencement—Finance Act 2016, Section 162(1) and Schedule 20 (Appointed Day) Regulations, SI 2016/1249 (the appointed day for the purposes of this Schedule is 1 January 2017 with effect in relation to acts or omissions occurring on or after that day which encourage, assist or otherwise facilitate conduct constituting offshore tax evasion or non-compliance within para 1(2)).

General modifications

19 In its application for the purpose mentioned in paragraph 18(1) Schedule 36 to FA 2008 has effect as if—

(*a*) any provisions which can have no application for that purpose, or are specifically excluded by paragraph 20, were omitted,
(*b*) references to "the taxpayer" were references to the relevant person whose position as regards liability for a penalty under paragraph 1 is to be checked, and references to "a taxpayer" were references to a relevant person,
(*c*) references to a person's "tax position" are to the relevant person's position as regards liability for a penalty under paragraph 1,
(*d*) references to prejudice to the assessment or collection of tax included a reference to prejudice to the investigation of the relevant person's position as regards liability for a penalty under paragraph 1,
(*e*) references to information relating to the conduct of a pending appeal relating to tax were references to information relating to the conduct of a pending appeal relating to an assessment of liability for a penalty under paragraph 1.

Commencement—Finance Act 2016, Section 162(1) and Schedule 20 (Appointed Day) Regulations, SI 2016/1249 (the appointed day for the purposes of this Schedule is 1 January 2017 with effect in relation to acts or omissions occurring on or after that day which encourage, assist or otherwise facilitate conduct constituting offshore tax evasion or non-compliance within para 1(2)).

Specific modifications

20 The following provisions are excluded from the application of Schedule 36 to FA 2008 for the purpose mentioned in paragraph 18(1)—

(*a*) paragraph 24 (exception for auditors),
(*b*) paragraph 25 (exception for tax advisers),
(*c*) paragraphs 26 and 27 (provisions supplementary to paragraphs 24 and 25),
(*d*) paragraphs 50 and 51 (tax-related penalty).

Commencement—Finance Act 2016, Section 162(1) and Schedule 20 (Appointed Day) Regulations, SI 2016/1249 (the appointed day for the purposes of this Schedule is 1 January 2017 with effect in relation to acts or omissions occurring on or after that day which encourage, assist or otherwise facilitate conduct constituting offshore tax evasion or non-compliance within para 1(2)).

21 In the application of Schedule 36 to FA 2008 for the purpose mentioned in paragraph 18(1), paragraph 10A (power to inspect business premises of involved third parties) has effect as if the reference in sub-paragraph (1) to the position of any person or class of persons as regards a relevant tax were a reference to the position of a relevant person as regards liability for a penalty under paragraph 1.

Commencement—Finance Act 2016, Section 162(1) and Schedule 20 (Appointed Day) Regulations, SI 2016/1249 (the appointed day for the purposes of this Schedule is 1 January 2017 with effect in relation to acts or omissions occurring on or after that day which encourage, assist or otherwise facilitate conduct constituting offshore tax evasion or non-compliance within para 1(2)).

PART 3
PUBLISHING DETAILS OF PERSONS FOUND LIABLE TO PENALTIES

Naming etc of persons assessed to penalty or penalties under paragraph 1

Commencement—Finance Act 2016, Section 162(1) and Schedule 20 (Appointed Day) Regulations, SI 2016/1249 (the appointed day for the purposes of this Schedule is 1 January 2017 with effect in relation to acts or omissions occurring on or after that day which encourage, assist or otherwise facilitate conduct constituting offshore tax evasion or non-compliance within para 1(2)).

22 (1) The Commissioners for Her Majesty's Revenue and Customs ("the Commissioners") may publish information about a person if—

(*a*) in consequence of an investigation the person has been found to have incurred one or more penalties under paragraph 1 (and has been assessed or is the subject of a contract settlement), and

(*b*) the potential lost revenue in relation to the penalty (or the aggregate of the potential lost revenue in relation to each of the penalties) exceeds £25,000.

(2) The Commissioners may also publish information about a person if the person has been found to have incurred 5 or more penalties under paragraph 1 in any 5 year period.

(3) The information that may be published is—

(*a*) the person's name (including any trading name, previous name or pseudonym),

(*b*) the person's address (or registered office),

(*c*) the nature of any business carried on by the person,

(*d*) the amount of the penalty or penalties in question,

(*e*) the periods or times to which the actions giving rise to the penalty or penalties relate,

(*f*) any other information that the Commissioners consider it appropriate to publish in order to make clear the person's identity.

(4) The information may be published in any manner that the Commissioners consider appropriate.

(5) Before publishing any information the Commissioners must—

(*a*) inform the person that they are considering doing so, and

(*b*) afford the person the opportunity to make representations about whether it should be published.

(6) No information may be published before the day on which the penalty becomes final or, where more than one penalty is involved, the latest day on which any of the penalties becomes final.

(7) No information may be published for the first time after the end of the period of one year beginning with that day.

(8) No information may be published if the amount of the penalty—

(*a*) is reduced under paragraph 7 to—

(i) 10% of the potential lost revenue (in a case of unprompted disclosure or assistance), or

(ii) 30% of potential lost revenue (in a case of prompted disclosure or assistance),

(*b*) would have been reduced to 10% or 30% of potential lost revenue but for the imposition of the minimum penalty,

(*c*) is reduced under paragraph 9 to nil or stayed.

(9) For the purposes of this paragraph a penalty becomes final—

(*a*) if it has been assessed, when the time for any appeal or further appeal relating to it expires or, if later, any appeal or final appeal relating to it is finally determined, and

(*b*) if a contract settlement has been made, at the time when the contract is made.

(10) In this paragraph "contract settlement", in relation to a penalty, means a contract between the Commissioners and the person under which the Commissioners undertake not to assess the penalty or (if it has been assessed) not to take proceedings to recover it.

Commencement—Finance Act 2016, Section 162(1) and Schedule 20 (Appointed Day) Regulations, SI 2016/1249 (the appointed day for the purposes of this Schedule is 1 January 2017 with effect in relation to acts or omissions occurring on or after that day which encourage, assist or otherwise facilitate conduct constituting offshore tax evasion or non-compliance within para 1(2)).

23 (1) The Treasury may by regulations amend paragraph 22(1) to vary the amount for the time being specified in paragraph (*b*).

(2) Regulations under this paragraph are to be made by statutory instrument.

(3) A statutory instrument under this paragraph is subject to annulment in pursuance of a resolution of the House of Commons.

Commencement—Finance Act 2016, Section 162(1) and Schedule 20 (Appointed Day) Regulations, SI 2016/1249 (the appointed day for the purposes of this Schedule is 1 January 2017 with effect in relation to acts or omissions occurring on or after that day which encourage, assist or otherwise facilitate conduct constituting offshore tax evasion or non-compliance within para 1(2)).

SCHEDULE 22

ASSET-BASED PENALTY FOR OFFSHORE INACCURACIES AND FAILURES

Section 165

Commencement—Finance Act 2016, Schedule 22 (Appointed Days) Regulations, SI 2017/277 reg 2 (the appointed day for the coming into force of Sch 22 is 1 April 2017 for all purposes, except the making of regulations, with effect—

- for inheritance tax purposes, in relation to transfers of value (within the meaning of IHTA 1984 s 3) made on or after that day; and
- for income tax and capital gains tax purposes, in relation to any tax year commencing on or after 6 April 2016.

The appointed day for the purpose of making regulations under Sch 22 para 8 is 8 March 2017).

PART 1

LIABILITY FOR PENALTY

Commencement—Finance Act 2016, Schedule 22 (Appointed Days) Regulations, SI 2017/277 reg 2 (the appointed day for the coming into force of Sch 22 is 1 April 2017 for all purposes, except the making of regulations, with effect—

- for inheritance tax purposes, in relation to transfers of value (within the meaning of IHTA 1984 s 3) made on or after that day; and
- for income tax and capital gains tax purposes, in relation to any tax year commencing on or after 6 April 2016.

The appointed day for the purpose of making regulations under Sch 22 para 8 is 8 March 2017).

Circumstances in which asset-based penalty is payable

1 (1) An asset-based penalty is payable by a person (P) where—

(*a*) one or more standard offshore tax penalties have been imposed on P in relation to a tax year (see paragraphs 2 and 3), and

(*b*) the potential lost revenue threshold is met in relation to that tax year (see paragraph 4).

(2) But this is subject to paragraph 6 (restriction on imposition of multiple asset-based penalties in relation to the same asset).

Commencement—Finance Act 2016, Schedule 22 (Appointed Days) Regulations, SI 2017/277 reg 2 (the appointed day for the coming into force of Sch 22 is 1 April 2017 for all purposes, except the making of regulations, with effect—

- for inheritance tax purposes, in relation to transfers of value (within the meaning of IHTA 1984 s 3) made on or after that day; and
- for income tax and capital gains tax purposes, in relation to any tax year commencing on or after 6 April 2016.

The appointed day for the purpose of making regulations under Sch 22 para 8 is 8 March 2017).

Meaning of standard offshore tax penalty

2 (1) A standard offshore tax penalty is a penalty that falls within sub-paragraph (2), (3)[, (4) or (4A)][1].

(2) A penalty falls within this sub-paragraph if—

(*a*) it is imposed under paragraph 1 of Schedule 24 to FA 2007 (inaccuracy in taxpayer's document),

(*b*) the inaccuracy for which the penalty is imposed involves an offshore matter or an offshore transfer,

(*c*) it is imposed for deliberate action (whether concealed or not), and

(*d*) the tax at stake is (or includes) capital gains tax, inheritance tax or asset-based income tax.

(3) A penalty falls within this sub-paragraph if—

(*a*) it is imposed under paragraph 1 of Schedule 41 to FA 2008 (penalty for failure to notify),

(*b*) the failure for which the penalty is imposed involves an offshore matter or an offshore transfer,

(*c*) it is imposed for a deliberate failure (whether concealed or not), and

(*d*) the tax at stake is (or includes) capital gains tax or asset-based income tax.

(4) A penalty falls within this sub-paragraph if—

(*a*) it is imposed under paragraph 6 of Schedule 55 to FA 2009 (penalty for failure to make return more than 12 months after filing date),

(*b*) it is imposed for the withholding of information involving an offshore matter or an offshore transfer,

(*c*) it is imposed for a deliberate withholding of information (whether concealed or not), and

(*d*) the tax at stake is (or includes) capital gains tax, inheritance tax or asset-based income tax.

[(4A) A penalty falls within this paragraph if—

(*a*) it is imposed on a person under paragraph 1 of Schedule 18 to FA 2017 (requirement to correct relevant offshore tax non-compliance),

(*b*) the person was aware at any time during the RTC period that at the end of the 2016–17 tax year P had relevant offshore tax non-compliance to correct, and (*c*) the tax at stake is (or includes) capital gains tax, inheritance tax or asset-based income tax.][1]

(5) In a case where the inaccuracy, failure or withholding of information for which a penalty is imposed involves both an offshore matter or an offshore transfer and a domestic matter, the standard offshore tax penalty is only that part of the penalty that involves the offshore matter or offshore transfer.

[(5A) Sub-paragraph (5) does not apply to a penalty imposed under paragraph 1 of Schedule 18 to FA 2017.][1]

(6) In a case where the tax at stake in relation to a penalty includes a tax other than capital gains tax, inheritance tax or asset-based income tax, the standard offshore tax penalty is only that part of the penalty which relates to capital gains tax, inheritance tax or asset-based income tax.

(7) "Asset-based income tax" means income tax that is charged under any of the provisions mentioned in column 1 of the table in paragraph 13(2).

Commencement—Finance Act 2016, Schedule 22 (Appointed Days) Regulations, SI 2017/277 reg 2 (the appointed day for the coming into force of Sch 22 is 1 April 2017 for all purposes, except the making of regulations, with effect—

- for inheritance tax purposes, in relation to transfers of value (within the meaning of IHTA 1984 s 3) made on or after that day; and
- for income tax and capital gains tax purposes, in relation to any tax year commencing on or after 6 April 2016.

The appointed day for the purpose of making regulations under Sch 22 para 8 is 8 March 2017).

Amendments—[1] In sub-para (1), words substituted for words "or (4)", and sub-paras (4A), (5A) inserted, by F(No 2)A 2017 s 67, Sch 18 para 28(1), (2) with effect from 16 November 2017. A penalty under Sch 18 is payable by a person who has any relevant offshore tax non-compliance to correct at the end of the tax year 2016–17 and fails to correct that non-compliance within the period beginning with 6 April 2017 and ending with 30 September 2018 ("the RTC period").

Tax year to which standard offshore tax penalty relates

3 (1) Where a standard offshore tax penalty is imposed under paragraph 1 of Schedule 24 to FA 2007, the tax year to which that penalty relates is—

(*a*) if the tax at stake as a result of the inaccuracy is income tax or capital gains tax, the tax year to which the document containing the inaccuracy relates;

(*b*) if the tax at stake as a result of the inaccuracy is inheritance tax, the year, beginning on 6 April and ending on the following 5 April, in which the liability to tax first arose.

(2) Where a standard offshore tax penalty is imposed under paragraph 1 of Schedule 41 to FA 2008 for a failure to comply with an obligation specified in the table in that paragraph, the tax year to which that penalty relates is the tax year to which the obligation relates.

(3) Where a standard offshore tax penalty is imposed under paragraph 6 of Schedule 55 to FA 2009 for a failure to make a return or deliver a document specified in the table of paragraph 1 of that Schedule, the tax year to which that penalty relates is—

(*a*) if the tax at stake is income tax or capital gains tax, the tax year to which the return or document relates;

(*b*) if the tax at stake is inheritance tax, the year, beginning on 6 April and ending on the following 5 April, in which the liability to tax first arose.

[(4) Where a standard offshore penalty is imposed under paragraph 1 of Schedule 18 to FA 2017, the tax year to which that penalty relates is—

(*a*) if the tax at stake in relation to the uncorrected relevant offshore tax non-compliance is income tax or capital gains tax, the tax year or years to which the failure or inaccuracy constituting the relevant offshore tax non-compliance in question relates;

(*b*) if the tax at stake in relation to the uncorrected relevant offshore tax non-compliance is inheritance tax, the year, beginning on 6 April and ending on the following 5 April, in which the liability to tax first arose.

(5) In sub-paragraph (4) references to uncorrected relevant offshore tax non-compliance are to the relevant offshore tax non-compliance in respect of which the standard offshore penalty is imposed.][1]

Commencement—Finance Act 2016, Schedule 22 (Appointed Days) Regulations, SI 2017/277 reg 2 (the appointed day for the coming into force of Sch 22 is 1 April 2017 for all purposes, except the making of regulations, with effect—

- for inheritance tax purposes, in relation to transfers of value (within the meaning of IHTA 1984 s 3) made on or after that day; and
- for income tax and capital gains tax purposes, in relation to any tax year commencing on or after 6 April 2016.

The appointed day for the purpose of making regulations under Sch 22 para 8 is 8 March 2017).

Amendments—[1] Sub-paras (4), (5) inserted by F(No 2)A 2017 s 67, Sch 18 para 28(1), (3) with effect from 16 November 2017. A penalty under Sch 18 is payable by a person who has any relevant offshore tax non-compliance to correct at the end of the tax year 2016–17 and fails to correct that non-compliance within the period beginning with 6 April 2017 and ending with 30 September 2018 ("the RTC period").

Potential lost revenue threshold

4 (1) The potential lost revenue threshold is reached where the offshore PLR in relation to a tax year exceeds £25,000.

(2) The Treasury may by regulations change the figure for the time being specified in sub-paragraph (1).

(3) Regulations under sub-paragraph (2) are to be made by statutory instrument.

(4) A statutory instrument containing regulations under sub-paragraph (2) is subject to annulment in pursuance of a resolution of the House of Commons.

(5) Regulations under sub-paragraph (2)—

(*a*) may make different provision for different purposes;

(*b*) may contain supplemental, incidental, consequential, transitional and transitory provision.

Commencement—Finance Act 2016, Schedule 22 (Appointed Days) Regulations, SI 2017/277 reg 2 (the appointed day for the coming into force of Sch 22 is 1 April 2017 for all purposes, except the making of regulations, with effect—

– for inheritance tax purposes, in relation to transfers of value (within the meaning of IHTA 1984 s 3) made on or after that day; and

– for income tax and capital gains tax purposes, in relation to any tax year commencing on or after 6 April 2016.

The appointed day for the purpose of making regulations under Sch 22 para 8 is 8 March 2017).

Offshore PLR

5 (1) The offshore PLR, in relation to a tax year, is the total of—

(*a*) the potential lost revenue (in the case of a standard offshore tax penalty imposed under Schedule 24 to FA 2007 or Schedule 41 to FA 2008[or Schedule 18 to FA 2017][1]), and

(*b*) the liability to tax (in the case of a standard offshore tax penalty imposed under Schedule 55 to FA 2009),

by reference to which all of the standard offshore tax penalties imposed on P in relation to the tax year are assessed.

(2) Sub-paragraphs (3) to (5) apply where—

(*a*) a penalty is imposed on P under paragraph 1 of Schedule 24 to FA 2007, paragraph 1 of Schedule 41 to FA 2008 or paragraph 6 of Schedule 55 to FA 2009, and

(*b*) the potential lost revenue or liability to tax by reference to which the penalty is assessed relates to a standard offshore tax penalty and one or more other penalties.

In this paragraph, such a penalty is referred to as a "combined penalty".

(3) Only the potential lost revenue or liability to tax relating to the standard offshore tax penalty is to be taken into account in calculating the offshore PLR.

(4) Where the calculation of the potential lost revenue or liability to tax by reference to which a combined penalty is assessed depends on the order in which income or gains are treated as having been taxed, for the purposes of calculating the offshore PLR—

(*a*) income and gains relating to domestic matters are to be taken to have been taxed before income and gains relating to offshore matters and offshore transfers;

(*b*) income and gains relating to taxes that are not capital gains tax, inheritance tax or asset-based income tax are to be taken to have been taxed before income and gains relating to capital gains tax, inheritance tax and asset-based income tax.

(5) In a case where it cannot be determined—

(*a*) whether income or gains relate to an offshore matter or offshore transfer or to a domestic matter, or

(*b*) whether income or gains relate to capital gains tax, asset-based income tax or inheritance tax or not,

for the purposes of calculating the offshore PLR, the potential lost revenue or liability to tax relating to the standard offshore tax penalty is to be taken to be such share of the total potential lost revenue or liability to tax by reference to which the combined penalty was calculated as is just and reasonable.

(6) Sub-paragraph (7) applies where—

(*a*) a standard offshore tax penalty or a combined penalty is imposed on P, and

(*b*) there are two or more taxes at stake, including capital gains tax and asset-based income tax.

(7) Where the calculation of the potential lost revenue or liability to tax by reference to which the penalty is assessed depends on the order in which income or gains are treated as having been taxed, for the purposes of calculating the offshore PLR, income and gains relating to asset-based income tax are to be taken to have been taxed before income and gains relating to capital gains tax.

Commencement—Finance Act 2016, Schedule 22 (Appointed Days) Regulations, SI 2017/277 reg 2 (the appointed day for the coming into force of Sch 22 is 1 April 2017 for all purposes, except the making of regulations, with effect—

– for inheritance tax purposes, in relation to transfers of value (within the meaning of IHTA 1984 s 3) made on or after that day; and

– for income tax and capital gains tax purposes, in relation to any tax year commencing on or after 6 April 2016.

The appointed day for the purpose of making regulations under Sch 22 para 8 is 8 March 2017).

Amendments—[1] In sub-para (1)(*a*), words inserted by F(No 2)A 2017 s 67, Sch 18 para 28(1), (4) with effect from 16 November 2017. A penalty under Sch 18 is payable by a person who has any relevant offshore tax non-compliance to correct at the end of the tax year 2016–17 and fails to correct that non-compliance within the period beginning with 6 April 2017 and ending with 30 September 2018 ("the RTC period").

Restriction on imposition of multiple asset-based penalties in relation to the same asset

6 (1) Sub-paragraphs (2) and (3) apply where—

(*a*) a standard offshore tax penalty [(other than one imposed under paragraph 1 of Schedule 18 to FA 2017)][1] has been imposed on P, and

(*b*) the potential lost revenue threshold is met,

in relation to more than one tax year falling within the same investigation period.

(2) Only one asset-based penalty is payable by P in the investigation period in relation to any given asset.

(3) The asset-based penalty is to be charged by reference to the tax year in the investigation period with the highest offshore PLR.

(4) An "investigation period" is—

(*a*) the period starting with the day on which this Schedule comes into force and ending with the last day of the last tax year before P was notified of an asset-based penalty in respect of an asset, and

(*b*) subsequent periods beginning with the day after the previous period ended and ending with the last day of the last tax year before P is notified of a subsequent asset-based penalty in respect of the asset,

and different investigation periods may apply in relation to different assets.

Commencement—Finance Act 2016, Schedule 22 (Appointed Days) Regulations, SI 2017/277 reg 2 (the appointed day for the coming into force of Sch 22 is 1 April 2017 for all purposes, except the making of regulations, with effect—

– for inheritance tax purposes, in relation to transfers of value (within the meaning of IHTA 1984 s 3) made on or after that day; and

– for income tax and capital gains tax purposes, in relation to any tax year commencing on or after 6 April 2016.

The appointed day for the purpose of making regulations under Sch 22 para 8 is 8 March 2017).

Amendments—[1] In sub-para (1)(*a*), words inserted by F(No 2)A 2017 s 67, Sch 18 para 28(1), (5) with effect from 16 November 2017. A penalty under Sch 18 is payable by a person who has any relevant offshore tax non-compliance to correct at the end of the tax year 2016–17 and fails to correct that non-compliance within the period beginning with 6 April 2017 and ending with 30 September 2018 ("the RTC period").

[6A Where—

(*a*) a penalty has been imposed on a person under paragraph 1 of Schedule 18 to FA 2017, and

(*b*) the potential loss of revenue threshold has been met,

only one asset-based penalty is payable by the person in relation to any given asset.][1]

Amendments—[1] Paragraph 6A inserted by F(No 2)A 2017 s 67, Sch 18 para 28(1), (6) with effect from 16 November 2017. A penalty under Sch 18 is payable by a person who has any relevant offshore tax non-compliance to correct at the end of the tax year 2016–17 and fails to correct that non-compliance within the period beginning with 6 April 2017 and ending with 30 September 2018 ("the RTC period").

PART 2
AMOUNT OF PENALTY

Commencement—Finance Act 2016, Schedule 22 (Appointed Days) Regulations, SI 2017/277 reg 2 (the appointed day for the coming into force of Sch 22 is 1 April 2017 for all purposes, except the making of regulations, with effect—

– for inheritance tax purposes, in relation to transfers of value (within the meaning of IHTA 1984 s 3) made on or after that day; and

– for income tax and capital gains tax purposes, in relation to any tax year commencing on or after 6 April 2016.

The appointed day for the purpose of making regulations under Sch 22 para 8 is 8 March 2017).

Standard amount of asset-based penalty

7 (1) The standard amount of the asset-based penalty is the lower of—

(*a*) 10% of the value of the asset, and

(*b*) offshore PLR x 10.

(2) See also—

(*a*) paragraphs 8 and 9, which provide for reductions in the standard amount, and

(*b*) Part 3, which makes provision about the identification and valuation of the asset.

Commencement—Finance Act 2016, Schedule 22 (Appointed Days) Regulations, SI 2017/277 reg 2 (the appointed day for the coming into force of Sch 22 is 1 April 2017 for all purposes, except the making of regulations, with effect—

– for inheritance tax purposes, in relation to transfers of value (within the meaning of IHTA 1984 s 3) made on or after that day; and

– for income tax and capital gains tax purposes, in relation to any tax year commencing on or after 6 April 2016.

The appointed day for the purpose of making regulations under Sch 22 para 8 is 8 March 2017).

Reductions for disclosure and co-operation

8 (1) HMRC must reduce the standard amount of the asset-based penalty where P does all of the following things—

(*a*) makes a disclosure of the inaccuracy or failure relating to the standard offshore tax penalty;

(*b*) provides HMRC with a reasonable valuation of the asset;

(*c*) provides HMRC with information or access to records that HMRC requires from P for the purposes of valuing the asset.

(2) A reduction under sub-paragraph (1) must reflect the quality of the disclosure, valuation and information provided (and for these purposes "quality" includes timing, nature and extent).

(3) The Treasury must make regulations setting out the maximum amount of the penalty reduction under sub-paragraph (1).

(4) The maximum amount may differ according to whether the case involves only unprompted disclosures or involves prompted disclosures.

(5) A case involves only unprompted disclosures where—

(*a*) in a case where the asset-based penalty relates to only one standard offshore tax penalty, that standard offshore tax penalty was reduced on the basis of an unprompted disclosure, or

(*b*) in a case where the asset-based penalty relates to more than one standard offshore tax penalty, all of those standard offshore tax penalties were reduced on the basis of unprompted disclosures.

(6) A case involves prompted disclosures where any of the standard offshore tax penalties to which the asset-based penalty relates was reduced on the basis of a prompted disclosure.

(7) Regulations under sub-paragraph (3) are to be made by statutory instrument.

(8) A statutory instrument containing regulations under sub-paragraph (3) is subject to annulment in pursuance of a resolution of the House of Commons.

(9) Regulations under sub-paragraph (3)—

(*a*) may make different provision for different purposes;

(*b*) may contain supplemental, incidental, consequential, transitional and transitory provision.

Commencement—Finance Act 2016, Schedule 22 (Appointed Days) Regulations, SI 2017/277 reg 2 (the appointed day for the coming into force of Sch 22 is 1 April 2017 for all purposes, except the making of regulations, with effect—

– for inheritance tax purposes, in relation to transfers of value (within the meaning of IHTA 1984 s 3) made on or after that day; and

– for income tax and capital gains tax purposes, in relation to any tax year commencing on or after 6 April 2016.

The appointed day for the purpose of making regulations under Sch 22 para 8 is 8 March 2017).

Regulations—Asset-based Penalty for Offshore Inaccuracies and Failures (Reductions for Disclosure and Co-operation) Regulations, SI 2017/334.

Special reduction

9 (1) If HMRC think it right because of special circumstances, they may reduce the standard amount of the asset-based penalty.

(2) In sub-paragraph (1) "special circumstances" does not include—

(*a*) ability to pay, or

(*b*) the fact that a potential loss of revenue from one taxpayer is balanced by a potential over-payment by another.

(3) In sub-paragraph (1) the reference to reducing a penalty includes a reference to—

(*a*) staying a penalty, and

(*b*) agreeing a compromise in relation to proceedings for a penalty.

Commencement—Finance Act 2016, Schedule 22 (Appointed Days) Regulations, SI 2017/277 reg 2 (the appointed day for the coming into force of Sch 22 is 1 April 2017 for all purposes, except the making of regulations, with effect—

– for inheritance tax purposes, in relation to transfers of value (within the meaning of IHTA 1984 s 3) made on or after that day; and

– for income tax and capital gains tax purposes, in relation to any tax year commencing on or after 6 April 2016.

The appointed day for the purpose of making regulations under Sch 22 para 8 is 8 March 2017).

PART 3
IDENTIFICATION AND VALUATION OF ASSETS

Commencement—Finance Act 2016, Schedule 22 (Appointed Days) Regulations, SI 2017/277 reg 2 (the appointed day for the coming into force of Sch 22 is 1 April 2017 for all purposes, except the making of regulations, with effect—

– for inheritance tax purposes, in relation to transfers of value (within the meaning of IHTA 1984 s 3) made on or after that day; and

– for income tax and capital gains tax purposes, in relation to any tax year commencing on or after 6 April 2016.

The appointed day for the purpose of making regulations under Sch 22 para 8 is 8 March 2017).

Introduction

10 (1) This Part makes provision about the identification and valuation of the asset for the purposes of calculating the amount of the asset-based penalty.

(2) An asset-based penalty may relate to more than one asset.

(3) The identification and valuation of the asset is to be determined—

(*a*) under paragraph 11 where the principal tax at stake is capital gains tax,

(*b*) under paragraph 12 where the principal tax at stake is inheritance tax, and

(*c*) under paragraph 13 where the principal tax at stake is asset-based income tax.

See also paragraph 14 (jointly held assets).

(4) The principal tax at stake—

(*a*) in a case where the standard offshore tax penalty (or penalties) relates to only one type of tax, is the tax to which that standard offshore tax penalty (or penalties) relates;

(*b*) in a case where the standard offshore tax penalty (or penalties) relate to more than one type of tax, is the tax which gives rise to the highest offshore PLR value.

(5) The offshore PLR value, in relation to a type of tax, is the potential lost revenue or liability to tax by reference to which the part of the penalty relating to that type of tax was assessed.

(6) The rules in paragraph 5(2) to (7) apply for the purposes of calculating the offshore PLR value, in relation to a type of tax, as they apply for the purposes of calculating the offshore PLR.

Commencement—Finance Act 2016, Schedule 22 (Appointed Days) Regulations, SI 2017/277 reg 2 (the appointed day for the coming into force of Sch 22 is 1 April 2017 for all purposes, except the making of regulations, with effect—

– for inheritance tax purposes, in relation to transfers of value (within the meaning of IHTA 1984 s 3) made on or after that day; and

– for income tax and capital gains tax purposes, in relation to any tax year commencing on or after 6 April 2016.

The appointed day for the purpose of making regulations under Sch 22 para 8 is 8 March 2017).

Capital gains tax

11 (1) This paragraph applies where the principal tax at stake is capital gains tax.

(2) The asset is the asset that is the subject of the disposal (or deemed disposal) on or by reference to which the capital gains tax to which the standard offshore penalty relates is charged.

(3) For the purposes of calculating the amount of the asset-based penalty, the value of the asset is to be taken to be the consideration for the disposal of the asset that would be used in the computation of the gain under TCGA 1992 (other than in a case where sub-paragraph (4) applies).

(4) In a case where the disposal on or by reference to which the capital gains tax is charged is a part disposal of an asset, the asset-based penalty is to be calculated by reference to the full market value of the asset immediately before the part disposal took place.

(5) Terms used in this paragraph have the same meaning as in TCGA 1992.

Commencement—Finance Act 2016, Schedule 22 (Appointed Days) Regulations, SI 2017/277 reg 2 (the appointed day for the coming into force of Sch 22 is 1 April 2017 for all purposes, except the making of regulations, with effect—

– for inheritance tax purposes, in relation to transfers of value (within the meaning of IHTA 1984 s 3) made on or after that day; and

– for income tax and capital gains tax purposes, in relation to any tax year commencing on or after 6 April 2016.

The appointed day for the purpose of making regulations under Sch 22 para 8 is 8 March 2017).

Inheritance tax

12 (1) This paragraph applies where the principal tax at stake is inheritance tax.

(2) The asset is the property the disposition of which gave rise to the transfer of value by reason of which the inheritance tax to which the standard offshore penalty relates became chargeable.

(3) For the purposes of calculating the amount of the asset-based penalty, the value of the property is to be the value of the property used by HMRC in assessing the liability to inheritance tax.

(4) Terms used in this paragraph have the same meaning as in IHTA 1984.

Commencement—Finance Act 2016, Schedule 22 (Appointed Days) Regulations, SI 2017/277 reg 2 (the appointed day for the coming into force of Sch 22 is 1 April 2017 for all purposes, except the making of regulations, with effect—

– for inheritance tax purposes, in relation to transfers of value (within the meaning of IHTA 1984 s 3) made on or after that day; and

– for income tax and capital gains tax purposes, in relation to any tax year commencing on or after 6 April 2016.

The appointed day for the purpose of making regulations under Sch 22 para 8 is 8 March 2017).

Asset-based income tax

13 (1) This paragraph applies where the principal tax at stake is asset-based income tax.

(2) Where the standard offshore tax penalty relates to income tax charged under a provision shown in column 1 of the Table, the asset is the asset mentioned in column 2 of the Table.

Provision under which income tax is charged	*Asset*
Chapters 3, 7 and 10 of Part 3 of ITTOIA 2005 (property businesses)	The estate, interest or right in or over the land that generates the income for the business (see sections 264 to 266 of ITTOIA 2005)
Chapter 8 of Part 3 of ITTOIA 2005 (rent receivable in connection with a s.12(4) concern)	The estate, interest or right in or over the land that generates the rent receivable in connection with a UK section 12(4) concern (see sections 335 and 336 of ITTOIA 2005)
Chapters 2 and 2A of Part 4 of ITTOIA 2005 (interest and disguised interest)	The asset that generates the interest
Chapters 3 to 5 of Part 4 of ITTOIA 2005 (dividends etc)	The shares or other securities in relation to which the dividend or distribution is paid
Chapter 7 of Part 4 of ITTOIA 2005 (purchased life annuity payments)	The annuity that gives rise to the payments
Chapter 8 of Part 4 of ITTOIA 2005 (profits from deeply discounted securities)	The deeply discounted securities that are disposed of (see sections 427 to 430 of ITTOIA 2005)
Chapter 9 of Part 4 of ITTOIA 2005 (gains from contracts for life insurance etc)	The policy or contract from which the gain is treated as arising
Chapter 11 of Part 4 of ITTOIA 2005 (transactions in deposits)	The deposit right which is disposed of (see sections 551 and 552 of ITTOIA 2005)
Chapter 2 of Part 5 of ITTOIA 2005 (receipts from intellectual property)	The intellectual property, knowhow or patent rights which generate the income (see sections 579, 583 and 587 of ITTOIA 2005)
Chapter 4 of Part 5 of ITTOIA 2005 (certain telecommunication rights: non-trading income)	The relevant telecommunication right from which the income derives (see section 614 of ITTOIA 2005)
Chapter 5 of Part 5 of ITTOIA 2005 (settlements: amounts treated as income of settlor)	The settlement which gives rise to the income or capital sums treated as income of a settlor

[(2A) In relation to cases where the standard offshore penalty is a penalty falling within paragraph 2(4A), each reference to provisions of ITTOIA 2005 in column 1 of the Table in sub-paragraph (2) includes a reference—

(*a*) to the corresponding provisions of the legislation in force immediately before those provisions of ITTOIA 2005 came into force (and to any previous text of those corresponding provisions), and

(*b*) to any other provision that had the same purpose as, or a similar purpose to, any of those corresponding provisions (or any earlier text mentioned in paragraph (*a*)), if and so far as that other provision was in force—

(i) on or after 6 April 1997, but

(ii) before the corresponding provisions (or the earlier text mentioned in paragraph (*a*)) came into force.][1]

(3) For the purposes of calculating the amount of the asset-based penalty, the asset is to be valued as follows.

(4) In a case where the charge to income tax was triggered by a disposal of the asset, the value of the asset is to be taken as its market value on the date of disposal (and in the case of a part disposal, the value of the asset is to be taken as its full market value immediately before the part disposal took place).

(5) In any other case—

(*a*) where P still owns the asset on the last day of the tax year to which the standard offshore tax penalty relates, the value of the asset is to be taken as its market value on that day;

(*b*) where P disposed of the asset during the course of the tax year to which the standard offshore tax penalty relates, the value of the asset is to be taken as its market value on the date of disposal;

(*c*) where P disposed of part of the asset during the course of the tax year to which the standard offshore tax penalty relates, the value of the asset is to be taken as the market value of the part disposed on the date (or dates) of disposal plus the market value of the part still owned by the person on the last day of that tax year.

(6) But if the value of the asset, as determined in accordance with subparagraphs (4) and (5), does not appear to HMRC to be a fair and reasonable value, then HMRC may value the asset for the purposes of this Schedule in any other way which appears to them to be fair and reasonable.

(7) For the purposes of sub-paragraph (5)—

(*a*) P owns an asset if P is liable to asset-based income tax in relation to that asset;

IHT

(*b*) references to a disposal (and related expressions) have the same meaning as in TCGA 1992.

(8) In this paragraph "market value" has the same meaning as in TCGA 1992 (see section 272 of that Act).

(9) Other terms used in this paragraph have the same meaning as in ITTOIA 2005.

Commencement—Finance Act 2016, Schedule 22 (Appointed Days) Regulations, SI 2017/277 reg 2 (the appointed day for the coming into force of Sch 22 is 1 April 2017 for all purposes, except the making of regulations, with effect—

– for inheritance tax purposes, in relation to transfers of value (within the meaning of IHTA 1984 s 3) made on or after that day; and
– for income tax and capital gains tax purposes, in relation to any tax year commencing on or after 6 April 2016.

The appointed day for the purpose of making regulations under Sch 22 para 8 is 8 March 2017).

Amendments—[1] Sub-para (2A) inserted by F(No 2)A 2017 s 67, Sch 18 para 28(1), (7) with effect from 16 November 2017. A penalty under Sch 18 is payable by a person who has any relevant offshore tax non-compliance to correct at the end of the tax year 2016–17 and fails to correct that non-compliance within the period beginning with 6 April 2017 and ending with 30 September 2018 ("the RTC period").

Jointly held assets

14 (1) This paragraph applies where an asset-based penalty is chargeable in relation to an asset that is jointly held by P and another person (*a*).

(2) The value of the asset is to be taken to be the value of P's share of the asset.

(3) In a case where P and A—

(*a*) are married to, or are civil partners of, each other, and

(*b*) live together,

the asset is to be taken to be jointly owned by P and A in equal shares, unless it appears to HMRC that this is not the case.

Commencement—Finance Act 2016, Schedule 22 (Appointed Days) Regulations, SI 2017/277 reg 2 (the appointed day for the coming into force of Sch 22 is 1 April 2017 for all purposes, except the making of regulations, with effect—

– for inheritance tax purposes, in relation to transfers of value (within the meaning of IHTA 1984 s 3) made on or after that day; and
– for income tax and capital gains tax purposes, in relation to any tax year commencing on or after 6 April 2016.

The appointed day for the purpose of making regulations under Sch 22 para 8 is 8 March 2017).

PART 4
PROCEDURE

Commencement—Finance Act 2016, Schedule 22 (Appointed Days) Regulations, SI 2017/277 reg 2 (the appointed day for the coming into force of Sch 22 is 1 April 2017 for all purposes, except the making of regulations, with effect—

– for inheritance tax purposes, in relation to transfers of value (within the meaning of IHTA 1984 s 3) made on or after that day; and
– for income tax and capital gains tax purposes, in relation to any tax year commencing on or after 6 April 2016.

The appointed day for the purpose of making regulations under Sch 22 para 8 is 8 March 2017).

Assessment

15 (1) Where a person (P) becomes liable for an asset-based penalty under paragraph 1, HMRC must—

(*a*) assess the penalty,

(*b*) notify P, and

(*c*) state in the notice—

(i) the tax year to which the penalty relates, and

(ii) the investigation period within which that tax year falls (see paragraph 6).

(2) A penalty under paragraph 1 must be paid before the end of the period of 30 days beginning with the day on which notification of the penalty is issued.

(3) An assessment—

(*a*) is to be treated for procedural purposes in the same way as an assessment to tax (except in respect of a matter expressly provided for by this Schedule),

(*b*) may be enforced as if it were an assessment to tax, and

(*c*) may be combined with an assessment to tax.

(4) An assessment of an asset-based penalty under paragraph 1 must be made within the period allowed for making an assessment of the standard offshore tax penalty to which the asset-based penalty relates (and where an asset-based penalty relates to more than one standard offshore tax penalty, the assessment must be made within the latest of those periods).

(5) In this Part of this Schedule references to an assessment to tax, in relation to inheritance tax, are to a determination.

Commencement—Finance Act 2016, Schedule 22 (Appointed Days) Regulations, SI 2017/277 reg 2 (the appointed day for the coming into force of Sch 22 is 1 April 2017 for all purposes, except the making of regulations, with effect—

– for inheritance tax purposes, in relation to transfers of value (within the meaning of IHTA 1984 s 3) made on or after that day; and
– for income tax and capital gains tax purposes, in relation to any tax year commencing on or after 6 April 2016.

The appointed day for the purpose of making regulations under Sch 22 para 8 is 8 March 2017).

Appeal

16 (1) P may appeal against a decision of HMRC that a penalty is payable by P.

(2) P may appeal against a decision of HMRC as to the amount of a penalty payable by P.

Commencement—Finance Act 2016, Schedule 22 (Appointed Days) Regulations, SI 2017/277 reg 2 (the appointed day for the coming into force of Sch 22 is 1 April 2017 for all purposes, except the making of regulations, with effect—

– for inheritance tax purposes, in relation to transfers of value (within the meaning of IHTA 1984 s 3) made on or after that day; and
– for income tax and capital gains tax purposes, in relation to any tax year commencing on or after 6 April 2016.

The appointed day for the purpose of making regulations under Sch 22 para 8 is 8 March 2017).

17 (1) An appeal is to be treated in the same way as an appeal against an assessment to the tax concerned (including by the application of any provision about bringing the appeal by notice to HMRC, about HMRC review of the decision or about determination of the appeal by the First-tier Tribunal or the Upper Tribunal).

(2) Sub-paragraph (1) does not apply—

(*a*) so as to require P to pay a penalty before an appeal against the assessment of the penalty is determined, or

(*b*) in respect of any other matter expressly provided for by this Schedule.

Commencement—Finance Act 2016, Schedule 22 (Appointed Days) Regulations, SI 2017/277 reg 2 (the appointed day for the coming into force of Sch 22 is 1 April 2017 for all purposes, except the making of regulations, with effect—

– for inheritance tax purposes, in relation to transfers of value (within the meaning of IHTA 1984 s 3) made on or after that day; and
– for income tax and capital gains tax purposes, in relation to any tax year commencing on or after 6 April 2016.

The appointed day for the purpose of making regulations under Sch 22 para 8 is 8 March 2017).

18 (1) On an appeal under paragraph 16(1), the tribunal may affirm or cancel HMRC's decision.

(2) On an appeal under paragraph 16(2), the tribunal may—

(*a*) affirm HMRC's decision, or

(*b*) substitute for HMRC's decision another decision that HMRC had power to make.

(3) If the tribunal substitutes its decision for HMRC's, the tribunal may rely on paragraph 9—

(*a*) to the same extent as HMRC (which may mean applying the same percentage reduction as HMRC to a different starting point), or

(*b*) to a different extent, but only if the tribunal thinks that HMRC's decision in respect of the application of paragraph 9 was flawed.

(4) In sub-paragraph (3), "flawed" means flawed when considered in the light of the principles applied in proceedings for judicial review.

(5) In this paragraph "tribunal" means the First-tier Tribunal or the Upper Tribunal (as appropriate by virtue of paragraph 17(1)).

Commencement—Finance Act 2016, Schedule 22 (Appointed Days) Regulations, SI 2017/277 reg 2 (the appointed day for the coming into force of Sch 22 is 1 April 2017 for all purposes, except the making of regulations, with effect—

– for inheritance tax purposes, in relation to transfers of value (within the meaning of IHTA 1984 s 3) made on or after that day; and
– for income tax and capital gains tax purposes, in relation to any tax year commencing on or after 6 April 2016.

The appointed day for the purpose of making regulations under Sch 22 para 8 is 8 March 2017).

PART 5
GENERAL

Commencement—Finance Act 2016, Schedule 22 (Appointed Days) Regulations, SI 2017/277 reg 2 (the appointed day for the coming into force of Sch 22 is 1 April 2017 for all purposes, except the making of regulations, with effect—

– for inheritance tax purposes, in relation to transfers of value (within the meaning of IHTA 1984 s 3) made on or after that day; and
– for income tax and capital gains tax purposes, in relation to any tax year commencing on or after 6 April 2016.

The appointed day for the purpose of making regulations under Sch 22 para 8 is 8 March 2017).

Interpretation

19 (1) In this Schedule—

"asset" has the same meaning as in TCGA 1992 (but also includes currency in sterling);

"asset-based income tax" has the meaning given in paragraph 2(7);

"HMRC" means Her Majesty's Revenue and Customs;

"investigation period" has the meaning given in paragraph 6(4);

"offshore PLR" has the meaning given in paragraph 5;

"standard amount of the asset-based penalty" has the meaning given in paragraph 7;

"standard offshore tax penalty" has the meaning given in paragraph 2.

(2) Terms used in relation to a penalty imposed under Schedule 24 to FA 2007, Schedule 41 to FA 2008[, Schedule 55 to FA 2009 or Part 1 of Schedule 18 to FA 2017][1] have the same meaning as in the Schedule under which the penalty was imposed.

(3) References in this Schedule to capital gains tax do not include capital gains tax payable by companies in respect of chargeable gains accruing to them to the extent that those gains are NRCGT gains in respect of which the companies are chargeable to capital gains tax under section 14D or 188D of TCGA 1992 (see section 1(2A)(*b*) of that Act).

Commencement—Finance Act 2016, Schedule 22 (Appointed Days) Regulations, SI 2017/277 reg 2 (the appointed day for the coming into force of Sch 22 is 1 April 2017 for all purposes, except the making of regulations, with effect—

- for inheritance tax purposes, in relation to transfers of value (within the meaning of IHTA 1984 s 3) made on or after that day; and
- for income tax and capital gains tax purposes, in relation to any tax year commencing on or after 6 April 2016.

The appointed day for the purpose of making regulations under Sch 22 para 8 is 8 March 2017).

Amendments—[1] In sub-para (2), words substituted for words "or Schedule 55 to FA 2009" by F(No 2)A 2017 s 67, Sch 18 para 28(1), (8) with effect from 16 November 2017. A penalty under Sch 18 is payable by a person who has any relevant offshore tax non-compliance to correct at the end of the tax year 2016–17 and fails to correct that non-compliance within the period beginning with 6 April 2017 and ending with 30 September 2018 ("the RTC period").

Consequential amendments etc

20 (1) In section 103ZA to TMA 1970 (disapplication of sections 100 to 103 in case of certain penalties), omit the "or" at the end of paragraph (*h*), and at the end insert ", or

(*j*) Schedule 22 to the Finance Act 2016 (asset-based penalty)".

(2) In section 107A of that Act (relevant trustees)—

(*a*) in subsection (2)(*a*), after "Schedule 55 to the Finance Act 2009" insert "or Schedule 22 to the Finance Act 2016";

(*b*) after subsection (3)(*a*) insert—

"(*aa*) in relation to a penalty under Schedule 22 to the Finance Act 2016, or to interest under section 101 of the Finance Act 2009 on such a penalty, the time when the relevant act or omission occurred;";

(*c*) in the words after paragraph (*c*), after "paragraph" insert "(*aa*) and".

(3) In Schedule 24 to FA 2007 (penalties for errors), in paragraph 12 (interaction with other penalties etc), in sub-paragraph (2A) at the end insert "or Schedule 22 to FA 2016 (asset-based penalty)".

(4) In Schedule 41 to FA 2008 (penalties for failure to notify), in paragraph 15 (interaction with other penalties etc), in sub-paragraph (1A) at the end insert "or Schedule 22 to FA 2016 (asset-based penalty)."

(5) In Schedule 55 to FA 2009 (penalty for failure to make return etc), in paragraph 17 (interaction with other penalties etc), in sub-paragraph (2), at the end insert ", or

(*d*) a penalty under Schedule 22 to FA 2016 (asset-based penalty)."

Commencement—Finance Act 2016, Schedule 22 (Appointed Days) Regulations, SI 2017/277 reg 2 (the appointed day for the coming into force of Sch 22 is 1 April 2017 for all purposes, except the making of regulations, with effect—

- for inheritance tax purposes, in relation to transfers of value (within the meaning of IHTA 1984 s 3) made on or after that day; and
- for income tax and capital gains tax purposes, in relation to any tax year commencing on or after 6 April 2016.

The appointed day for the purpose of making regulations under Sch 22 para 8 is 8 March 2017).

21 Section 97A of TMA 1970 (two or more tax-geared penalties in respect of same tax) does not apply in relation to an asset-based penalty imposed under this Schedule.

Commencement—Finance Act 2016, Schedule 22 (Appointed Days) Regulations, SI 2017/277 reg 2 (the appointed day for the coming into force of Sch 22 is 1 April 2017 for all purposes, except the making of regulations, with effect—

- for inheritance tax purposes, in relation to transfers of value (within the meaning of IHTA 1984 s 3) made on or after that day; and
- for income tax and capital gains tax purposes, in relation to any tax year commencing on or after 6 April 2016.

The appointed day for the purpose of making regulations under Sch 22 para 8 is 8 March 2017).

FINANCE (NO 2) ACT 2017

16 November 2017

An Act To Grant certain duties, to alter other duties, and to amend the law relating to the national debt and the public revenue, and to make further provision in connection with finance.

CONTENTS

PART 1
DIRECT TAXES

Domicile, overseas property etc

30 Deemed domicile: inheritance tax

(1) In section 267 of IHTA 1984 (persons treated as domiciled in the United Kingdom), in subsection (1)—

(*a*) in paragraph (*a*), omit the final "or";

(*b*) after that paragraph insert—

"(*aa*) he is a formerly domiciled resident for the tax year in which the relevant time falls ("the relevant tax year"), or";

(*c*) for paragraph (*b*) substitute—

"(*b*) he was resident in the United Kingdom—

(i) for at least fifteen of the twenty tax years immediately preceding the relevant tax year, and

(ii) for at least one of the four tax years ending with the relevant tax year."

(2) In that section, omit subsection (3).

(3) In that section, in subsection (4), for "in any year of assessment" substitute "for any tax year".

(4) In section 48 of that Act (settlements: excluded property)—

(*a*) in subsection (3)(*b*), for "and (3D)" substitute "to (3E)";

(*b*) in subsection (3A)(*b*), for "subsection (3B)" substitute "subsections (3B) and (3E)";

(*c*) after subsection (3D) insert—

"(3E) In a case where the settlor of property comprised in a settlement is not domiciled in the United Kingdom at the time the settlement is made, the property is not excluded property by virtue of subsection (3) or (3A) above at any time in a tax year if the settlor was a formerly domiciled resident for that tax year."

(5) In section 64 of that Act (charge at ten-year anniversary), in subsection (1B), after "was made" insert "and is not a formerly domiciled resident for the tax year in which the ten-year anniversary falls".

(6) In section 65 of that Act (charge at other times), after subsection (7A) insert—

"(7B) Tax shall not be charged under this section by reason only that property comprised in a settlement becomes excluded property by virtue of section 48(3E) ceasing to apply in relation to it."

(7) In section 82 of that Act (excluded property)—

(*a*) for subsection (1) substitute—

"(1) In a case where, apart from this section, property to which section 80 or 81 applies would be excluded property by virtue of section 48(3)(*a*) above, that property shall not be taken to be excluded property at any time ("the relevant time") for the purposes of this Chapter (except sections 78 and 79) unless Conditions A and B are satisfied.";

(*b*) in subsection (2), for "the condition in subsection (3) below" substitute "Condition A";

(*c*) in subsection (3), for "The condition" substitute "Condition A";

(*d*) after subsection (3) insert—

"(4) Condition B referred to in subsection (1) above is—

(*a*) in the case of property to which section 80 above applies, that the person who is the settlor in relation to the settlement first mentioned in that section, and

(*b*) in the case of property to which subsection (1) or (2) of section 81 above applies, that the person who is the settlor in relation to the first or second of the settlements mentioned in that subsection,

was not a formerly domiciled resident for the tax year in which the relevant time falls."

(8) In section 272 of that Act (interpretation)—

(*a*) for the definition of "foreign-owned" substitute—

""foreign-owned", in relation to property at any time, means property—

(*a*) in the case of which the person beneficially entitled to it is at that time domiciled outside the United Kingdom, or

(*b*) if the property is comprised in a settlement, in the case of which the settlor—

(i) is not a formerly domiciled resident for the tax year in which that time falls, and

(ii) was domiciled outside the United Kingdom when the property became comprised in the settlement;";

(*b*) at the appropriate place insert—

""formerly domiciled resident", in relation to a tax year, means a person—

(*a*) who was born in the United Kingdom,

(*b*) whose domicile of origin was in the United Kingdom,

(*c*) who was resident in the United Kingdom for that tax year, and

(*d*) who was resident in the United Kingdom for at least one of the two tax years immediately preceding that tax year;".

(9) The amendments made by this section have effect in relation to times after 5 April 2017, subject to subsections (10) to (12).

(10) The amendment to section 267(1) of IHTA 1984 made by subsection (1)(*c*) does not have effect in relation to a person if—

(*a*) the person is not resident in the United Kingdom for the relevant tax year, and

(*b*) there is no tax year beginning after 5 April 2017 and preceding the relevant tax year in which the person was resident in the United Kingdom.

In this subsection "relevant tax year" is to be construed in accordance with section 267(1) of IHTA 1984 as amended by subsection (1).

(11) The amendment to section 267(1) of IHTA 1984 made by subsection (1)(*c*) also does not have effect in determining—

(*a*) whether settled property which became comprised in the settlement on or before that date is excluded property for the purposes of IHTA 1984;

(*b*) the settlor's domicile for the purposes of section 65(8) of that Act in relation to settled property which became comprised in the settlement on or before that date;

(*c*) whether, for the purpose of section 65(8) of that Act, the condition in section 82(3) of that Act is satisfied in relation to such settled property.

(12) Despite subsection (2), section 267(1) of IHTA 1984, as originally enacted, shall continue to be disregarded in determining—

(*a*) whether settled property which became comprised in the settlement on or before 9 December 1974 is excluded property for the purposes of IHTA 1984;

(*b*) the settlor's domicile for the purposes of section 65(8) of that Act in relation to settled property which became comprised in the settlement on or before that date;

(*c*) whether, for the purpose of section 65(8) of that Act, the condition in section 82(3) of that Act is satisfied in relation to such settled property.

(13) Subsections (14) and (15) apply if an amount of inheritance tax—

(*a*) would not be charged but for the amendments made by this section, or

(*b*) is, because of those amendments, greater than it would otherwise have been.

(14) Section 233 of IHTA 1984 (interest on unpaid inheritance tax) applies in relation to the amount of inheritance tax as if the reference, in the closing words of subsection (1) of that section, to the end of the period mentioned in paragraph (*a*), (*aa*), (*b*) or (*c*) of that subsection were a reference to—

(*a*) the end of that period, or

(*b*) if later, the end of the month immediately following the month in which this Act is passed.

(15) Subsection (1) of section 234 of IHTA 1984 (cases where inheritance tax payable by instalments carries interest only from instalment dates) applies in relation to the amount of inheritance tax as if the reference, in the closing words of that subsection, to the date at which an instalment is payable were a reference to—

(*a*) the date at which the instalment is payable, or

(*b*) if later, the end of the month immediately following the month in which this Act is passed.

(16) Subsection (17) applies if—

(*a*) a person is liable as mentioned in section 216(1)(*c*) of IHTA 1984 (trustee liable on 10-year anniversary, and other trust cases) for an amount of inheritance tax charged on an occasion, and

(*b*) but for the amendments made by this section—

(i) no inheritance tax would be charged on that occasion, or

(ii) a lesser amount of inheritance tax would be charged on that occasion.

(17) Section 216(6)(ad) of IHTA 1984 (delivery date for accounts required by section 216(1)(*c*)) applies in relation to the account to be delivered in connection with the occasion as if the reference to the expiration of the period of 6 months from the end of the month in which the occasion occurs were a reference to—

(*a*) the expiration of that period, or

(*b*) if later, the end of the month immediately following the month in which this Act is passed.

33 Inheritance tax on overseas property representing UK residential property

Schedule 10 makes provision about the extent to which overseas property is excluded property for the purposes of inheritance tax, in cases where the value of the overseas property is attributable to residential property in the United Kingdom.

PART 4

ADMINISTRATION, AVOIDANCE AND ENFORCEMENT

Avoidance etc

65 Penalties for enablers of defeated tax avoidance

Schedule 16 makes provision for penalties for persons who enable tax avoidance which is defeated.

67 Requirement to correct certain offshore tax non-compliance

Schedule 18 makes provision for and in connection with requiring persons to correct any offshore tax non-compliance subsisting on 6 April 2017.

Information

69 Data-gathering from money service businesses

(1) In Part 2 of Schedule 23 to FA 2011 (data-gathering powers: relevant data-holders), after paragraph 13C insert—

"*Money service businesses*

13D

(1) A person is a relevant data-holder if the person—

(*a*) carries on any of the activities in sub-paragraph (2) by way of business,

(*b*) is a relevant person within the meaning of regulation 8(1) of the Money Laundering, Terrorist Financing and Transfer of Funds (Information on the Payer) Regulations 2017 (S.I. 2017/692), and

(*c*) is not an excluded credit institution.

(2) The activities referred to in sub-paragraph (1)(*a*) are—

(*a*) operating a currency exchange office;

(*b*) transmitting money (or any representation of monetary value) by any means;

(*c*) cashing cheques which are made payable to customers.

(3) An excluded credit institution is a credit institution which has permission to carry on the regulated activity of accepting deposits—

(*a*) under Part 4A of the Financial Services and Markets Act 2000 (permission to carry on regulated activities), or

(*b*) resulting from Part 2 of Schedule 3 to that Act (exercise of passport rights by EEA firms).

(4) Sub-paragraph (3) is to be read with section 22 of and Schedule 2 to the Financial Services and Markets Act 2000, and any order under that section (classes of regulated activities).

(5) In this paragraph "credit institution" has the meaning given by Article 4.1(1) of Regulation (EU) No 575/2013 of the European Parliament and of the Council of 26 June 2013 on prudential requirements for credit institutions and investment firms."

(2) This section applies in relation to relevant data with a bearing on any period (whether before, on or after the day on which this Act is passed).

Commentary—*Simon's Taxes* **A6.332C**.

SCHEDULE 10
INHERITANCE TAX ON OVERSEAS PROPERTY REPRESENTING UK RESIDENTIAL PROPERTY

Section 33

Non-excluded overseas property

1 In IHTA 1984, before Schedule 1 insert—

"SCHEDULE A1
NON-EXCLUDED OVERSEAS PROPERTY

PART 1
OVERSEAS PROPERTY WITH VALUE ATTRIBUTABLE TO UK RESIDENTIAL PROPERTY

Introductory

1

Property is not excluded property by virtue of section 6(1) or 48(3)(a) if and to the extent that paragraph 2 or 3 applies to it.

Close company and partnership interests

2

(1) This paragraph applies to an interest in a close company or in a partnership, if and to the extent that the interest meets the condition in sub-paragraph (2).

(2) The condition is that the value of the interest is—

(*a*) directly attributable to a UK residential property interest, or

(*b*) attributable to a UK residential property interest by virtue only of one or more of the following—

(i) an interest in a close company;

(ii) an interest in a partnership;

(iii) property to which paragraph 3 (loans) applies.

(3) For the purposes of sub-paragraphs (1) and (2) disregard—

(*a*) an interest in a close company, if the value of the interest is less than 5% of the total value of all the interests in the close company;

(*b*) an interest in a partnership, if the value of the interest is less than 5% of the total value of all the interests in the partnership.

(4) In determining under sub-paragraph (3) whether to disregard a person's interest in a close company or partnership, treat the value of the person's interest as increased by the value of any connected person's interest in the close company or partnership.

(5) In determining whether or to what extent the value of an interest in a close company or in a partnership is attributable to a UK residential property interest for the purposes of sub-paragraph (1), liabilities of a close company or partnership are to be attributed rateably to all of its property, whether or not they would otherwise be attributed to any particular property.

Loans

3

This paragraph applies to—

(*a*) the rights of a creditor in respect of a loan which is a relevant loan (see paragraph 4), and

(*b*) money or money's worth held or otherwise made available as security, collateral or guarantee for a loan which is a relevant loan, to the extent that it does not exceed the value of the relevant loan.

4

(1) For the purposes of this Schedule a loan is a relevant loan if and to the extent that money or money's worth made available under the loan is used to finance, directly or indirectly—

(*a*) the acquisition by an individual, a partnership or the trustees of a settlement of—

(i) a UK residential property interest, or

(ii) property to which paragraph 2 to any extent applies, or

(*b*) the acquisition by an individual, a partnership or the trustees of a settlement of an interest in a close company or a partnership ("the intermediary") and the acquisition by the intermediary of property within paragraph (*a*)(i) or (ii).

(2) In this paragraph references to money or money's worth made available under a loan or sale proceeds being used "indirectly" to finance the acquisition of something include the money or money's worth or sale proceeds being used to finance—

(*a*) the acquisition of any property the proceeds of sale of which are used directly or indirectly to finance the acquisition of that thing, or

(*b*) the making, or repayment, of a loan to finance the acquisition of that thing.

(3) In this paragraph references to the acquisition of a UK residential property interest by an individual, a partnership, the trustees of a settlement or a close company include the maintenance, or an enhancement, of the value of a UK residential property interest which is (as the case may be) the property of the individual, property comprised in the settlement or property of the partnership or close company.

(4) Where the UK residential property interest by virtue of which a loan is a relevant loan is disposed of, the loan ceases to be a relevant loan.

(5) Where a proportion of the UK residential property interest by virtue of which a loan is a relevant loan is disposed of, the loan ceases to be a relevant loan by the same proportion.

(6) In this Schedule, references to a loan include an acknowledgment of debt by a person or any other arrangement under which a debt arises; and in such a case references to money or money's worth made available under the loan are to the amount of the debt.

PART 2
SUPPLEMENTARY

Disposals and repayments

5

(1) This paragraph applies to—

(*a*) property which constitutes consideration in money or money's worth for the disposal of property to which paragraph 2 or paragraph 3(*a*) applies;

(*b*) any money or money's worth paid in respect of a creditor's rights falling within paragraph 3(*a*);

(*c*) any property directly or indirectly representing property within paragraph (*a*) or (*b*).

(2) If and to the extent that this paragraph applies to any property—

(*a*) for the two-year period it is not excluded property by virtue of section 6(1), (1A) or (2) or 48(3)(*a*), (3A) or (4), and (*b*) if it is held in a qualifying foreign currency account within the meaning of section 157 (non-residents' bank accounts), that section does not apply to it for the two-year period.

(3) The two-year period is the period of two years beginning with the date of—

(*a*) the disposal referred to in sub-paragraph (1)(*a*), or

(*b*) the payment referred to in sub-paragraph (1)(*b*).

(4) The value of any property within sub-paragraph (1)(*c*) is to be treated as not exceeding the relevant amount.

(5) The relevant amount is—

(*a*) where the property within sub-paragraph (1)(*c*) directly or indirectly represents property within sub-paragraph (1)(*a*) ("the consideration"), the value of the consideration at the time of the disposal referred to in that sub-paragraph, and

(*b*) where the property within sub-paragraph (1)(*c*) directly or indirectly represents property within sub-paragraph (1)(*b*), the amount of the money or money's worth paid as mentioned in that sub-paragraph.

Tax avoidance arrangements

6

(1) In determining whether or to what extent property situated outside the United Kingdom is excluded property, no regard is to be had to any arrangements the purpose or one of the main purposes of which is to secure a tax advantage by avoiding or minimising the effect of paragraph 1 or 5.

(2) In this paragraph—

"tax advantage" has the meaning given in section 208 of the Finance Act 2013;

"arrangements" includes any scheme, transaction or series of transactions, agreement or understanding (whether or not legally enforceable and whenever entered into) and any associated operations.

Double taxation relief arrangements

7

(1) Nothing in any double taxation relief arrangements made with the government of a territory outside the United Kingdom is to be read as preventing a person from being liable for any amount of inheritance tax by virtue of paragraph 1 or 5 in relation to any chargeable transfer if under the law of that territory—

(*a*) no tax of a character similar to inheritance tax is charged on that chargeable transfer, or

(*b*) a tax of a character similar to inheritance tax is charged in relation to that chargeable transfer at an effective rate of 0% (otherwise than by virtue of a relief or exemption).

(2) In this paragraph—

"double taxation relief arrangements" means arrangements having effect under section 158(1);

"effective rate" means the rate found by expressing the tax chargeable as a percentage of the amount by reference to which it is charged.

PART 3
INTERPRETATION

UK residential property interest

8

(1) In this Schedule "UK residential property interest" means an interest in UK land—

(*a*) where the land consists of a dwelling,

(*b*) where and to the extent that the land includes a dwelling, or

(*c*) where the interest subsists under a contract for an off-plan purchase.

(2) For the purposes of sub-paragraph (1)(*b*), the extent to which land includes a dwelling is to be determined on a just and reasonable basis.

(3) In this paragraph—

"interest in UK land" has the meaning given by paragraph 2 of Schedule B1 to the 1992 Act (and the power in sub-paragraph (5) of that paragraph applies for the purposes of this Schedule);

"the land", in relation to an interest in UK land which is an interest subsisting for the benefit of land, is a reference to the land for the benefit of which the interest subsists;

"dwelling" has the meaning given by paragraph 4 of Schedule B1 to the 1992 Act (and the power in paragraph 5 of that Schedule applies for the purposes of this Schedule);

"contract for an off-plan purchase" has the meaning given by paragraph 1(6) of Schedule B1 to the 1992 Act.

Close companies

9

(1) In this Schedule—

"close company" means a company within the meaning of the Corporation Tax Acts which is (or would be if resident in the United Kingdom) a close company for the purposes of those Acts;

references to an interest in a close company are to the rights and interests that a participator in a close company has in that company.

(2) In this paragraph—

"participator", in relation to a close company, means any person who is (or would be if the company were resident in the United Kingdom) a participator in relation to that company within the meaning given by section 454 of the Corporation Tax Act 2010;

references to rights and interests in a close company include references to rights and interests in the assets of the company available for distribution among the participators in the event of a winding-up or in any other circumstances.

Partnerships

10

In this Schedule "partnership" means—

(*a*) a partnership within the Partnership Act 1890,

(*b*) a limited partnership registered under the Limited Partnerships Act 1907,

(*c*) a limited liability partnership formed under the Limited Liability Partnerships Act 2000 or the Limited Liability Partnerships Act (Northern Ireland) 2002, or

(*d*) a firm or entity of a similar character to either of those mentioned in paragraph (*a*) or (*b*) formed under the law of a country or territory outside the United Kingdom."

Commentary—*Simon's Taxes* **I9.335**.

Consequential and supplementary amendments

2 IHTA 1984 is amended as follows.

3 In section 6 (excluded property), at the end insert—

"(5) This section is subject to Schedule A1 (non-excluded overseas property)."

4 In section 48 (excluded property)—

(*a*) in subsections (3) and (3A), at the end insert "and to Schedule A1";

(*b*) in subsection (4), at the end (but on a new line) insert "This subsection is subject to Schedule A1."

5 In section 65 (charge at other times), after subsection (7B) (as inserted by section 30) insert—

"(7C) Tax shall not be charged under this section by reason only that property comprised in a settlement ceases to any extent to be property to which paragraph 2 or 3 of Schedule A1 applies and thereby becomes excluded property by virtue of section 48(3)(*a*) above.

(7D) Tax shall not be charged under this section where property comprised in a settlement or any part of that property—

(*a*) is, by virtue of paragraph 5(2)(*a*) of Schedule A1, not excluded property for the two year period referred to in that paragraph, but

(*b*) becomes excluded property at the end of that period."

6 In section 157 (non-residents' bank accounts), after subsection (3) insert—

"(3A) This section is subject to paragraph 5 of Schedule A1 (non-excluded overseas property)."

7 In section 237 (imposition of charge), after subsection (2) insert—

"(2A) Where tax is charged by virtue of Schedule A1 on the value transferred by a chargeable transfer, the reference in subsection (1)(*a*) to property to the value of which the value transferred is wholly or partly attributable includes the UK residential property interest (within the meaning of that Schedule) to which the charge to tax relates."

8 In section 272 (general interpretation), in the definition of "excluded property", after "above" insert "and Schedule A1".

Commencement

9 (1) The amendments made by this Schedule have effect in relation to times on or after 6 April 2017.

(2) But for the purposes of paragraph 5(1) of Schedule A1 to IHTA 1984 as inserted by this Schedule—

(*a*) paragraph (*a*) of that paragraph does not apply in relation to a disposal of property occurring before 6 April 2017, and

(*b*) paragraph (*b*) of that paragraph does not apply in relation to a payment of money or money's worth occurring before 6 April 2017.

Transitional provision

10 (1) Sub-paragraphs (2) and (3) apply if an amount of inheritance tax—

(*a*) would not be charged but for the amendments made by this Schedule, or

(*b*) is, because of those amendments, greater than it would otherwise have been.

(2) Section 233 of IHTA 1984 (interest on unpaid inheritance tax) applies in relation to the amount of inheritance tax as if the reference, in the closing words of subsection (1) of that section, to the end of the period mentioned in paragraph (*a*), (*aa*), (*b*) or (*c*) of that subsection were a reference to—

(*a*) the end of that period, or

(*b*) if later, the end of the month immediately following the month in which this Act is passed.

(3) Subsection (1) of section 234 of IHTA 1984 (cases where inheritance tax payable by instalments carries interest only from instalment dates) applies in relation to the amount of inheritance tax as if the reference, in the closing words of that subsection, to the date at which an instalment is payable were a reference to—

(*a*) the date at which the instalment is payable, or

(*b*) if later, the end of the month immediately following the month in which this Act is passed.

11 (1) Sub-paragraph (2) applies if—

(*a*) a person is liable as mentioned in section 216(1)(*c*) of IHTA 1984 (trustee liable on 10-year anniversary, and other trust cases) for an amount of inheritance tax charged on an occasion, and

(*b*) but for the amendments made by this Schedule—

(i) no inheritance tax would be charged on that occasion, or

(ii) a lesser amount of inheritance tax would be charged on that occasion.

(2) Section 216(6)(ad) of IHTA 1984 (delivery date for accounts required by section 216(1)(*c*)) applies in relation to the account to be delivered in connection with the occasion as if the reference to the expiration of the period of 6 months from the end of the month in which the occasion occurs were a reference to—

(*a*) the expiration of that period, or

(*b*) if later, the end of the month immediately following the month in which this Act is passed.

SCHEDULE 16

PENALTIES FOR ENABLERS OF DEFEATED TAX AVOIDANCE

Section 65

PART 1

LIABILITY TO PENALTY

1 Where—

(*a*) a person ("T") has entered into abusive tax arrangements, and

(*b*) T incurs a defeat in respect of the arrangements,

a penalty is payable by each person who enabled the arrangements.

Commentary—*Simon's Taxes* **A4.573A**.

2 (1) Parts 2 to 4 of this Schedule define—

"abusive tax arrangements";

a "defeat in respect of the arrangements";
a "person who enabled the arrangements".

(2) The other Parts of this Schedule make provision supplementing paragraph 1 as follows—

(*a*) Part 5 makes provision about the amount of a penalty;

(*b*) Parts 6 to 8 provide for the assessment of penalties, referrals to the GAAR Advisory Panel and appeals against assessments;

(*c*) Part 9 applies information and inspection powers, and makes provision about declarations relating to legally privileged communications;

(*d*) Part 10 confers power to publish details of persons who have incurred penalties;

(*e*) Parts 11 and 12 contain miscellaneous and general provisions.

Commentary—*Simon's Taxes* **A4.573A**.

PART 2
"ABUSIVE" AND "TAX ARRANGEMENTS": MEANING

3 (1) Arrangements are "tax arrangements" for the purposes of this Schedule if, having regard to all the circumstances, it would be reasonable to conclude that the obtaining of a tax advantage was the main purpose, or one of the main purposes, of the arrangements.

(2) Tax arrangements are "abusive" for the purposes of this Schedule if they are arrangements the entering into or carrying out of which cannot reasonably be regarded as a reasonable course of action in relation to the relevant tax provisions, having regard to all the circumstances.

(3) The circumstances to which regard must be had under sub-paragraph (2) include—

(*a*) whether the substantive results, or the intended substantive results, of the arrangements are consistent with any principles on which the relevant tax provisions are based (whether express or implied) and the policy objectives of those provisions,

(*b*) whether the means of achieving those results involves one or more contrived or abnormal steps, and

(*c*) whether the arrangements are intended to exploit any shortcomings in those provisions.

(4) Where the tax arrangements form part of any other arrangements regard must also be had to those other arrangements.

(5) Each of the following is an example of something which might indicate that tax arrangements are abusive—

(*a*) the arrangements result in an amount of income, profits or gains for tax purposes that is significantly less than the amount for economic purposes;

(*b*) the arrangements result in deductions or losses of an amount for tax purposes that is significantly greater than the amount for economic purposes;

(*c*) the arrangements result in a claim for the repayment or crediting of tax (including foreign tax) that has not been, and is unlikely to be, paid;

but a result mentioned in paragraph (*a*), (*b*) or (*c*) is to be taken to be such an example only if it is reasonable to assume that such a result was not the anticipated result when the relevant tax provisions were enacted.

(6) The fact that tax arrangements accord with established practice, and HMRC had, at the time the arrangements were entered into, indicated their acceptance of that practice, is an example of something which might indicate that the arrangements are not abusive.

(7) The examples given in sub-paragraphs (5) and (6) are not exhaustive.

(8) In sub-paragraph (5) the reference to income includes earnings, within the meaning of Part 1 of the Social Security Contributions and Benefits Act 1992 or Part 1 of the Social Security Contributions and Benefits (Northern Ireland) Act 1992.

Commentary—*Simon's Taxes* **A4.573A**.

PART 3
"DEFEAT" IN RESPECT OF ABUSIVE TAX ARRANGEMENTS

"Defeat" in respect of abusive tax arrangements

4 T (within the meaning of paragraph 1) incurs a "defeat" in respect of abusive tax arrangements entered into by T ("the arrangements concerned") if—

(*a*) Condition A (in paragraph 5) is met, or

(*b*) Condition B (in paragraph 6) is met.

Commentary—*Simon's Taxes* **A4.573A**.

Condition A

5 (1) Condition A is that—

(*a*) T, or a person on behalf of T, has given HMRC a document of a kind listed in the Table in paragraph 1 of Schedule 24 to FA 2007 (returns etc),

(*b*) the document was submitted on the basis that a tax advantage ("the relevant tax advantage") arose from the arrangements concerned,

(*c*) the relevant tax advantage has been counteracted, and

(*d*) the counteraction is final.

(2) For the purposes of this paragraph the relevant tax advantage has been "counteracted" if adjustments have been made in respect of T's tax position on the basis that the whole or part of the relevant tax advantage does not arise.

(3) For the purposes of this paragraph a counteraction is "final" when the adjustments in question, and any amounts arising from the adjustments, can no longer be varied, on appeal or otherwise.

(4) In this paragraph "adjustments" means any adjustments, whether by way of an assessment, the modification of an assessment or return, the amendment or disallowance of a claim, a payment, the entering into of a contract settlement or otherwise.

Accordingly, references to "making" adjustments include securing that adjustments are made by entering into a contract settlement.

(5) Any reference in this paragraph to giving HMRC a document includes—

(*a*) communicating information to HMRC in any form and by any method;

(*b*) making a statement or declaration in a document.

(6) Any reference in this paragraph to a document of a kind listed in the Table in paragraph 1 of Schedule 24 to FA 2007 includes—

(*a*) a document amending a document of a kind so listed, and

(*b*) a document which—

(i) relates to national insurance contributions, and

(ii) is a document in relation to which that Schedule applies.

Commentary—*Simon's Taxes* **A4.573A**.

Condition B

6 (1) Condition B is that (in a case not falling within Condition A)—

(*a*) HMRC have made an assessment in relation to tax,

(*b*) the assessment counteracts a tax advantage that it is reasonable to assume T expected to obtain from the arrangements concerned ("the expected tax advantage"), and

(*c*) the counteraction is final.

(2) For the purposes of this paragraph an assessment "counteracts" the expected tax advantage if the assessment is on a basis which prevents T from obtaining (or obtaining the whole of) the expected tax advantage.

(3) For the purposes of this paragraph a counteraction is "final"—

(*a*) when a relevant contract settlement is made, or

(*b*) if no contract settlement has been made, when the assessment in question and any amounts arising from the assessment can no longer be varied, on appeal or otherwise.

(4) In sub-paragraph (3) a "relevant contract settlement" means a contract settlement on a basis which prevents T from obtaining (or obtaining the whole of) the expected tax advantage.

Commentary—*Simon's Taxes* **A4.573A**.

PART 4
PERSONS WHO "ENABLED" THE ARRANGEMENTS

Persons who "enabled" the arrangements

7 (1) A person is a person who "enabled" the arrangements mentioned in paragraph 1 if that person is—

(*a*) a designer of the arrangements (see paragraph 8),

(*b*) a manager of the arrangements (see paragraph 9),

(*c*) a person who marketed the arrangements to T (see paragraph 10),

(*d*) an enabling participant in the arrangements (see paragraph 11), or

(*e*) a financial enabler in relation to the arrangements (see paragraph 12).

(2) This paragraph is subject to paragraph 13 (excluded persons).

Commentary—*Simon's Taxes* **A4.573A**.

Designers of arrangements

8 (1) For the purposes of paragraph 7 a person is a "designer" of the arrangements if that person was, in the course of a business carried on by that person, to any extent responsible for the design of—

(*a*) the arrangements, or
(*b*) a proposal which was implemented by the arrangements;
but this is subject to sub-paragraph (2).

(2) Where a person would (in the absence of this sub-paragraph) fall within sub-paragraph (1) because of having provided advice which was used in the design of the arrangements or of a proposal, that person does not because of that advice fall within that sub-paragraph unless—
(*a*) the advice is relevant advice, and
(*b*) the knowledge condition is met.

(3) Advice is "relevant advice" if—
(*a*) the advice or any part of it suggests arrangements or an alteration of proposed arrangements, and
(*b*) it is reasonable to assume that the suggestion was made with a view to arrangements being designed in such a way that a tax advantage (or a greater tax advantage) might be expected to arise from them.

(4) The knowledge condition is that, when the advice was provided, the person providing it knew or could reasonably be expected to know—
(*a*) that the advice would be used in the design of abusive tax arrangements or of a proposal for such arrangements, or
(*b*) that it was likely that the advice would be so used.

(5) For the purposes of sub-paragraph (3), advice is not to be taken to "suggest" anything—
(*a*) which is put forward by the advice for consideration, but
(*b*) which the advice can reasonably be read as recommending against.

(6) In sub-paragraph (3)—
(*a*) the reference in paragraph (*a*) to arrangements or an alteration of proposed arrangements includes a proposal for arrangements or an alteration of a proposal for arrangements, and
(*b*) the reference in paragraph (*b*) to arrangements includes arrangements proposed by a proposal.

(7) For the purposes of this paragraph—
(*a*) references to advice include an opinion;
(*b*) advice is "used" in a design if the advice is taken account of in that design.

Commentary—*Simon's Taxes* **A4.573A**.

Managers of arrangements

9 (1) For the purposes of paragraph 7 a person is a "manager" of the arrangements if that person—
(*a*) was, in the course of a business carried on by that person, to any extent responsible for the organisation or management of the arrangements, and
(*b*) when carrying out any functions in relation to the organisation or management of the arrangements, knew or could reasonably be expected to know that the arrangements involved were abusive tax arrangements.

(2) Where—
(*a*) a person is, in the course of a business carried on by the person, to any extent responsible for facilitating T's withdrawal from the arrangements, and
(*b*) it is reasonable to assume that the obtaining of a tax advantage is not T's purpose (or one of T's purposes) in withdrawing from the arrangements,
that person is not because of anything done in the course of facilitating that withdrawal to be regarded as to any extent responsible for the organisation or management of the arrangements.

Commentary—*Simon's Taxes* **A4.573A**.

Marketers of arrangements

10 For the purposes of paragraph 7 a person "marketed" the arrangements to T if, in the course of a business carried on by that person—
(*a*) that person made available for implementation by T a proposal which has since been implemented, in relation to T, by the arrangements, or
(*b*) that person—
(i) communicated information to T or another person about a proposal which has since been implemented, in relation to T, by the arrangements, and
(ii) did so with a view to T entering into the arrangements or transactions forming part of the arrangements.

Commentary—*Simon's Taxes* **A4.573A**.

Enabling participants

11 For the purposes of paragraph 7 a person is "an enabling participant" in the arrangements if—

(*a*) that person is a person (other than T) who enters into the arrangements or a transaction forming part of the arrangements,

(*b*) without that person's participation in the arrangements or transaction (or the participation of another person in the arrangements or transaction in the same capacity as that person), the arrangements could not be expected to result in a tax advantage for T, and

(*c*) when that person entered into the arrangements or transaction, that person knew or could reasonably be expected to know that what was being entered into was abusive tax arrangements or a transaction forming part of such arrangements.

Commentary—*Simon's Taxes* **A4.573A**.

Financial enablers

12 (1) For the purposes of paragraph 7 a person is a "financial enabler" in relation to the arrangements if—

(*a*) in the course of a business carried on by that person, that person provided a financial product (directly or indirectly) to a relevant party,

(*b*) it is reasonable to assume that the purpose (or a purpose) of the relevant party in obtaining the financial product was to participate in the arrangements, and

(*c*) when the financial product was provided, the person providing it knew or could reasonably be expected to know that the purpose (or a purpose) of obtaining it was to participate in abusive tax arrangements.

(2) In this paragraph "a relevant party" means T or an enabling participant in the arrangements within the meaning given by paragraph 11.

(3) Any reference in this paragraph to a person's providing a financial product to a relevant party includes (but is not limited to) the person's doing any of the following—

(*a*) providing a loan to a relevant party;

(*b*) issuing or transferring a share to a relevant party;

(*c*) entering into arrangements with a relevant party such that—

(i) the person becomes a party to a relevant contract within the meaning of section 577 of CTA 2009 (derivative contracts);

(ii) there is a repo in respect of securities within the meaning of section 263A(A1) of TCGA 1992;

(iii) the person or the relevant party has a creditor repo, creditor quasi-repo, debtor repo or debtor quasi-repo within the meaning of sections 543, 544, 548 and 549 of CTA 2009;

(*d*) entering into a stock lending arrangement, within the meaning of section 263B(1) of TCGA 1992, with a relevant party;

(*e*) entering into an alternative finance arrangement, within the meaning of Chapter 6 of Part 6 of CTA 2009 or Part 10A of ITA 2007, with a relevant party;

(*f*) entering into a contract with a relevant party which, whether alone or in combination with one or more other contracts—

(i) is in accordance with generally accepted accounting practice required to be treated as a loan, deposit or other financial asset or obligation, or

(ii) would be required to be so treated by the person if the person were a company to which the Companies Act 2006 applies;

and references to obtaining a financial product are to be read accordingly.

(4) The Treasury may by regulations amend sub-paragraph (3).

Commentary—*Simon's Taxes* **A4.573A**.

Excluded persons

13 (1) A person who—

(*a*) would (in the absence of this paragraph) be regarded for the purposes of this Schedule as having enabled particular arrangements mentioned in paragraph 1, but

(*b*) is a person within sub-paragraph (2),

is not to be regarded as having enabled those arrangements.

(2) The persons within this sub-paragraph are—

(*a*) T;

(*b*) where T is a company, any company in the same group as T.

Commentary—*Simon's Taxes* **A4.573A**.

Powers to add categories of enabler and to provide exceptions

14 (1) The Treasury may by regulations add to the categories of persons who, in relation to arrangements mentioned in paragraph 1, are for the purposes of this Schedule persons who enabled the arrangements.

(2) The Treasury may by regulations provide that a person who would otherwise be regarded for the purposes of this Schedule as having enabled arrangements is not to be so regarded where conditions prescribed by the regulations are met.

(3) Regulations under this paragraph may—

(*a*) amend this Part of this Schedule;

(*b*) make supplementary, incidental, and consequential provision, including provision amending any other Part of this Schedule;

(*c*) make transitional provision.

Commentary—*Simon's Taxes* **A4.573A**.

PART 5
AMOUNT OF PENALTY

Amount of penalty

15 (1) For each person who enabled the arrangements mentioned in paragraph 1, the penalty payable under paragraph 1 is the total amount or value of all the relevant consideration received or receivable by that person ("the person in question").

(2) Particular consideration is "relevant" for the purposes of this paragraph if—

(*a*) it is consideration for anything done by the person in question which enabled the arrangements mentioned in paragraph 1, and

(*b*) it has not previously been taken into account in calculating the amount of a penalty payable under paragraph 1.

(3) For the purposes of this paragraph a thing done by a person "enabled" the arrangements mentioned in paragraph 1 if, by doing that thing (alone or with anything else), the person fell within the definition in Part 4 of this Schedule of a person who enabled those arrangements.

Commentary—*Simon's Taxes* **A4.573A**.

16 (1) This paragraph applies for the purposes of paragraph 15.

(2) Where consideration for anything done by a person ("A") is, under any arrangements with A, paid or payable to a person other than A, it is to be taken to be received or receivable by A.

(3) The "consideration" for anything done by a person does not include any amount charged by that person in respect of value added tax.

(4) Consideration attributable to two or more transactions is to be apportioned on a just and reasonable basis.

(5) Any consideration given for what is in substance one bargain is to be treated as attributable to all elements of the bargain, even though—

(*a*) separate consideration is, or purports to be, given for different elements of the bargain, or

(*b*) there are, or purport to be, separate transactions in respect of different elements of the bargain.

Commentary—*Simon's Taxes* **A4.573A**.

Reduction of penalty where other penalties incurred

17 (1) The amount of a penalty for which a person is liable under paragraph 1 is to be reduced by the amount of any other penalty incurred by the person in respect of conduct for which the person is liable to the penalty under paragraph 1.

(2) In this paragraph "any other penalty" means a penalty—

(*a*) which is a penalty under a provision other than paragraph 1, and

(*b*) which has been assessed.

Commentary—*Simon's Taxes* **A4.573A**.

Mitigation of penalty

18 (1) HMRC may in their discretion reduce a penalty under paragraph 1.

(2) In this paragraph the reference to reducing a penalty includes a reference to—

(*a*) entirely remitting the penalty, or

(*b*) staying, or agreeing a compromise in relation to, proceedings for the recovery of a penalty.

Commentary—*Simon's Taxes* **A4.573A**.

PART 6
ASSESSMENT OF PENALTY

Assessment of penalty

19 (1) Where a person is liable for a penalty under paragraph 1 HMRC must—

(*a*) assess the penalty, and

(*b*) notify the person.

(2) If—

(*a*) HMRC do not have all the information required to determine the amount or value of the relevant consideration within the meaning of paragraph 15, and

(*b*) HMRC have taken all reasonable steps to obtain that information,

HMRC may assess the penalty on the basis of a reasonable estimate by HMRC of that consideration.

(3) This paragraph is subject to—

(*a*) paragraphs 21 and 22 (limits on when penalty may be assessed); and

(*b*) Part 7 of this Schedule (requirement for opinion of GAAR Advisory Panel before penalty may be assessed).

Commentary—*Simon's Taxes* **A4.573A.**

20 (1) A penalty under paragraph 1 must be paid before the end of the period of 30 days beginning with the day on which notification of the penalty is issued.

(2) An assessment of a penalty under paragraph 1—

(*a*) is to be treated for procedural purposes in the same way as an assessment to tax (except in respect of a matter expressly provided for by this Schedule), and

(*b*) may be enforced as if it were an assessment to tax.

Commentary—*Simon's Taxes* **A4.573A.**

Special provision about assessment for multi-user schemes

21 (1) This paragraph applies where—

(*a*) a proposal for arrangements is implemented more than once, by a number of tax arrangements which are substantially the same as each other ("related arrangements"),

(*b*) paragraph 1 applies in relation to particular arrangements ("the arrangements concerned") which are one of the number of related arrangements implementing the proposal, and

(*c*) at the time when the person who entered into the arrangements concerned incurs a defeat in respect of them, the required percentage of relevant defeats has not been reached.

(2) HMRC may not assess any penalty payable under paragraph 1 in respect of the arrangements concerned until the required percentage of relevant defeats is reached.

(3) For the purposes of this paragraph the "required percentage of relevant defeats" is reached when HMRC reasonably believe that defeats have been incurred in the case of more than 50% of the related arrangements implementing the proposal.

(4) Sub-paragraph (2) does not apply in relation to a penalty if the person liable to the penalty requests assessment of the penalty sooner than the time allowed by sub-paragraph (2).

Commentary—*Simon's Taxes* **A4.573A.**

Time limit for assessment

22 (1) An assessment of a person as liable to a penalty under paragraph 1 may not take place after the relevant time.

(2) In this paragraph "the relevant time" means, subject to sub-paragraphs (3) to (6)—

(*a*) where a GAAR final decision notice within the meaning of paragraph 24(1) has been given in relation to the arrangements to which the penalty relates, the end of 12 months beginning with the date on which T incurs the defeat mentioned in paragraph 1;

(*b*) where a notice under paragraph 25 has been given to the person mentioned in sub-paragraph (1) above in respect of the arrangements to which the penalty relates, the end of 12 months beginning with the end of the time allowed for making representations in respect of that notice;

(*c*) where—

(i) a referral has been made under paragraph 26 in respect of the arrangements to which the penalty relates, and

(ii) paragraph (*d*) does not apply,

the end of 12 months beginning with the date on which the opinion of the GAAR Advisory Panel is given on the referral (within the meaning given by paragraph 34(6));

(*d*) where a notice under paragraph 35 has been given to the person mentioned in sub-paragraph (1) above in respect of the arrangements to which the penalty relates, the end of 12 months beginning with the end of the time allowed for making representations in respect of that notice.

(3) Where—

(*a*) paragraph 21 prevented a penalty from being assessed before the required percentage of relevant defeats was reached, and (*b*) the required percentage of relevant defeats (within the meaning of paragraph 21) has been reached,

the relevant time in relation to that penalty is whichever is the later of—

(i) the relevant time given by sub-paragraph (2), and

(ii) the end of 12 months beginning with the date on which that required percentage was reached.

(4) Where under paragraph 21(4) a person requests assessment of a penalty, the relevant time in relation to that penalty is whichever is the later of—

(*a*) the relevant time given by sub-paragraph (2), and

(*b*) the end of 12 months beginning with the date on which the request is made,

and sub-paragraph (3) does not apply to the penalty even if the required percentage of relevant defeats is reached.

(5) Sub-paragraph (6) applies where—

(*a*) at any time a declaration has been made under paragraph 44 for the purposes of any determination of whether a person is liable to a penalty under paragraph 1 in relation to particular arrangements ("the arrangements concerned"), and

(*b*) subsequently, facts that in the Commissioners' opinion are sufficient to indicate that the declaration contains a material inaccuracy have come to the Commissioners' knowledge.

(6) The relevant time in respect of any penalty under paragraph 1 payable by that person in relation to the arrangements concerned is whichever is the later of—

(*a*) the relevant time given by the preceding provisions of this paragraph, and

(*b*) the end of 12 months beginning with the date on which such facts came to the Commissioners' knowledge.

Commentary—*Simon's Taxes* **A4.573A**.

PART 7
GAAR ADVISORY PANEL OPINION, AND REPRESENTATIONS

Requirement for opinion of GAAR Advisory Panel

23 (1) A penalty under paragraph 1 may not be assessed unless—

(*a*) the decision that it should be assessed is taken by a designated HMRC officer, and

(*b*) either the condition in sub-paragraph (2) or the condition in sub-paragraph (3) is met.

(2) The condition in this sub-paragraph is that, when the assessment is made—

(*a*) a GAAR final decision notice has been given in relation to—

(i) the arrangements to which the penalty relates ("the relevant arrangements"), or

(ii) arrangements that are equivalent to the relevant arrangements,

(*b*) where a notice is required by paragraph 25 to be given to the person liable to the penalty, that notice has been given and the time allowed for making representations under that paragraph has expired, and

(*c*) a designated HMRC officer has, in deciding whether the penalty should be assessed, considered—

(i) the opinion of the GAAR Advisory Panel which was considered by HMRC in preparing that GAAR final decision notice, and

(ii) any representations made under paragraph 25.

(3) The condition in this sub-paragraph is that, when the assessment is made—

(*a*) an opinion of the GAAR Advisory Panel which applies to the relevant arrangements has been given on a referral under paragraph 26,

(*b*) where a notice is required by paragraph 35 to be given to the person liable to the penalty, that notice has been given and the time allowed for making representations under that paragraph has expired, and

(*c*) a designated HMRC officer has, in deciding whether the penalty should be assessed, considered—

(i) that opinion of the GAAR Advisory Panel, and

(ii) any representations made under paragraph 35.

(4) Where a notification of a penalty under paragraph 1 is given, the notification must be accompanied by a report prepared by HMRC of—

(*a*) if the condition in sub-paragraph (2) is met, the opinion of the GAAR Advisory Panel which was considered by HMRC in preparing the GAAR final decision notice;

(*b*) if the condition in sub-paragraph (3) is met, the opinion of the GAAR advisory panel mentioned in that sub-paragraph.

(5) Paragraph 24 contains definitions of terms used in this paragraph.

Commentary—*Simon's Taxes* **A4.573A**.

24 (1) In this Schedule a "GAAR final decision notice" means a notice under—

(*a*) paragraph 12 of Schedule 43 to FA 2013 (notice of final decision after considering opinion of GAAR Advisory Panel on referral under Schedule 43),
(*b*) paragraph 8 or 9 of Schedule 43A to FA 2013 (notice of final decision after considering opinion of GAAR Advisory Panel), or
(*c*) paragraph 8 of Schedule 43B to FA 2013 (notice of final decision after considering opinion of GAAR Advisory Panel on referral under Schedule 43B).

(2) For the purposes of this Part of this Schedule, where the GAAR Advisory Panel gives an opinion on a referral under paragraph 26 the arrangements to which the opinion "applies" are—
(*a*) the arrangements in respect of which the referral was made (that is, "the arrangements in question" within the meaning given by paragraph 26(1)), and
(*b*) any arrangements that are equivalent to those arrangements.

(3) For the purposes of this Part of this Schedule, arrangements are "equivalent" to one another if they are substantially the same as one another having regard to—
(*a*) their substantive results or intended substantive results,
(*b*) the means of achieving those results, and
(*c*) the characteristics on the basis of which it could reasonably be argued, in each case, that the arrangements are abusive tax arrangements.

Commentary—*Simon's Taxes* **A4.573A**.

Notice where Panel opinion already obtained in relation to equivalent arrangements

25 (1) This paragraph applies where a designated HMRC officer is of the view that—
(*a*) a person is liable to a penalty under paragraph 1 in relation to particular arrangements ("the arrangements concerned"),
(*b*) no GAAR final decision notice has been given in relation to those arrangements, but those arrangements are equivalent to arrangements in relation to which a GAAR final decision notice has been given ("the GAAR decision arrangements"), and
(*c*) accordingly, the opinion of the GAAR Advisory Panel which was considered by HMRC in preparing that GAAR final decision notice is relevant to the arrangements concerned.

(2) A designated HMRC officer must give the person mentioned in sub-paragraph (1) a notice in writing—
(*a*) explaining that the officer is of the view mentioned there,
(*b*) specifying the arrangements concerned,
(*c*) describing the material characteristics of the GAAR decision arrangements,
(*d*) setting out a report prepared by HMRC of the opinion of the GAAR Advisory Panel which was considered by HMRC in preparing the GAAR final decision notice, and
(*e*) explaining the effect of sub-paragraphs (3) and (4).

(3) A person to whom a notice under this paragraph is given has 30 days, beginning with the day on which the notice is given, to send to the designated HMRC officer (in writing) any representations that that person wishes to make as to why the arrangements concerned are not equivalent to the GAAR decision arrangements.

(4) A designated HMRC officer may, on a written request by that person, extend the period during which representations may be made by that person.

(5) Paragraph 24 contains definitions of the following terms used in this paragraph—
"GAAR final decision notice";
"equivalent", in relation to arrangements.

Commentary—*Simon's Taxes* **A4.573A**.

Referral to GAAR Advisory Panel

26 (1) A designated HMRC officer may make a referral under this paragraph if—
(*a*) the officer considers that a person is liable to a penalty under paragraph 1 in relation to particular arrangements ("the arrangements in question"), and
(*b*) the requirements of paragraph 28 (procedure before making of referral) have been complied with.

(2) But a referral may not be made under this paragraph if a GAAR final decision notice (within the meaning of paragraph 24(1)) has already been given in relation to—
(*a*) the arrangements in question, or
(*b*) arrangements that are equivalent to those arrangements.

(3) A referral under this paragraph is a referral to the GAAR Advisory Panel of the question whether the entering into and carrying out of tax arrangements such as are described in the referral statement (see paragraph 27) is a reasonable course of action in relation to the relevant tax provisions.

Commentary—*Simon's Taxes* **A4.573A**.

27 (1) In this Part of this Schedule "the referral statement", in relation to a referral under paragraph 26, means a statement made by a designated HMRC officer which—

(*a*) accompanies the referral,

(*b*) is a general statement of the material characteristics of the arrangements in question (within the meaning given by paragraph 26(1)), and

(*c*) complies with sub-paragraph (2).

(2) A statement under this paragraph must—

(*a*) contain a factual description of the arrangements in question,

(*b*) set out HMRC's view as to whether those arrangements accord with established practice (as it stood when those arrangements were entered into),

(*c*) explain why it is the designated HMRC officer's view that a tax advantage of the nature described in the statement and arising from tax arrangements having the characteristics described in the statement would be a tax advantage arising from arrangements that are abusive,

(*d*) set out any matters the designated HMRC officer is aware of which may suggest that any view of HMRC or the designated HMRC officer expressed in the statement is not correct, and

(*e*) set out any other matters which the designated HMRC officer considers are required for the purposes of the exercise of the GAAR Advisory Panel's functions under paragraphs 33 and 34.

Commentary—*Simon's Taxes* **A4.573A**.

Notice before decision whether to refer

28 (1) A referral must not be made under paragraph 26 unless—

(*a*) a designated HMRC officer has given each relevant person a notice under this paragraph,

(*b*) in the case of each relevant person, the time allowed for making representations has expired, and

(*c*) in deciding whether to make the referral, a designated HMRC officer has considered any representations made by a relevant person within the time allowed.

(2) In this paragraph a "relevant person" means any person who at the time of the referral is considered by the officer making the referral to be liable to a penalty under paragraph 1 in relation to the arrangements in question (within the meaning given by paragraph 26(1)).

(3) A notice under this paragraph is a notice in writing which—

(*a*) explains that the officer giving the notice considers that the person to whom the notice is given is liable to a penalty under paragraph 1 in relation to the arrangements in question (specifying those arrangements),

(*b*) explains why the officer considers those arrangements to be abusive tax arrangements,

(*c*) explains that HMRC are proposing to make a referral under paragraph 26 of the question whether the entering into and carrying out of tax arrangements that have the characteristics of the arrangements in question is a reasonable course of action in relation to the relevant tax provisions, and

(*d*) explains the effect of sub-paragraphs (4) and (5).

(4) Each person to whom a notice under this paragraph is given has 45 days, beginning with the day on which the notice is given to that person, to send written representations to the designated HMRC officer in response to the notice.

(5) A designated HMRC officer may, on a written request by a person to whom a notice is given, extend the period during which representations may be made by that person.

Commentary—*Simon's Taxes* **A4.573A**.

Notice of decision whether to refer

29 Where a designated HMRC officer decides whether to make a referral under paragraph 26, the officer must, as soon as reasonably practicable, give written notice of that decision to each person to whom notice under paragraph 28 was given.

Commentary—*Simon's Taxes* **A4.573A**.

Information to accompany referral

30 A referral under paragraph 26 must (as well as being accompanied by the referral statement under paragraph 27) be accompanied by—

(*a*) a declaration that, as far as HMRC are aware, nothing which is material to the GAAR Advisory Panel's consideration of the matter has been omitted from that statement,

(*b*) a copy of each notice given under paragraph 28 by HMRC in relation to the referral,

(*c*) a copy of any representations received under paragraph 28 and any comments that HMRC wish to make in respect of those representations, and (*d*) a copy of each notice given under paragraph 31 by HMRC.

Commentary—*Simon's Taxes* **A4.573A**.

Notice on making of referral

31 (1) Where a referral is made under paragraph 26, a designated HMRC officer must at the same time give to each relevant person a notice in writing which—

(*a*) notifies the person of the referral,

(*b*) is accompanied by a copy of the referral statement,

(*c*) is accompanied by a copy of any comments provided to the GAAR Advisory Panel under paragraph 30(*c*) in respect of representations made by the person,

(*d*) notifies the person of the period under paragraph 32 for making representations, and

(*e*) notifies the person of the requirement under that paragraph to send any representations to the officer.

(2) In this paragraph "relevant person" has the same meaning as in paragraph 28 (see sub-paragraph (2) of that paragraph).

Commentary—*Simon's Taxes* **A4.573A**.

Right to make representations to GAAR Advisory Panel

32 (1) A person who has received a notice under paragraph 31 has 21 days, beginning with the day on which that notice is given, to send to the GAAR Advisory Panel written representations about—

(*a*) the notice given to the person under paragraph 28, or

(*b*) any comments provided to the GAAR Advisory Panel under paragraph 30(*c*) in respect of representations made by the person.

(2) The GAAR Advisory Panel may, on a written request made by the person, extend the period during which representations may be made.

(3) If a person sends representations to the GAAR Advisory Panel under this paragraph, the person must at the same time send a copy of the representations to the designated HMRC officer.

(4) If a person sends representations to the GAAR Advisory Panel under this paragraph and that person made no representations under paragraph 28, a designated HMRC officer—

(*a*) may provide the GAAR Advisory Panel with comments on that person's representations under this paragraph, and

(*b*) if such comments are provided, must at the same time send a copy of them to that person.

Commentary—*Simon's Taxes* **A4.573A**.

Decision of GAAR Advisory Panel and opinion notices

33 (1) Where a referral is made to the GAAR Advisory Panel under paragraph 26, the Chair must arrange for a sub-panel consisting of 3 members of the GAAR Advisory Panel (one of whom may be the Chair) to consider it.

(2) The sub-panel may invite—

(*a*) any person to whom notice under paragraph 28 was given, or

(*b*) the designated HMRC officer,

(or both) to supply the sub-panel with further information within a period specified in the invitation.

(3) Invitations must explain the effect of sub-paragraph (4) or (5) (as appropriate).

(4) If a person invited under sub-paragraph (2)(*a*) supplies information to the sub-panel under this paragraph, that person must at the same time send a copy of the information to the designated HMRC officer.

(5) If a designated HMRC officer supplies information to the sub-panel under this paragraph, the officer must at the same time send a copy of the information to each person to whom notice under paragraph 28 was given.

Commentary—*Simon's Taxes* **A4.573A**.

34 (1) The sub-panel must produce—

(*a*) one opinion notice stating the joint opinion of all the members of the sub-panel, or

(*b*) two or three opinion notices which taken together state the opinions of all the members.

(2) The sub-panel must give a copy of the opinion notice or notices to the designated HMRC officer.

(3) An opinion notice is a notice which states that in the opinion of the members of the sub-panel, or one or more of those members—

(*a*) the entering into and carrying out of tax arrangements such as are described in the referral statement is a reasonable course of action in relation to the relevant tax provisions,

(*b*) the entering into or carrying out of such tax arrangements is not a reasonable course of action in relation to the relevant tax provisions, or

(*c*) it is not possible, on the information available, to reach a view on that matter,

and the reasons for that opinion.

(4) In forming their opinions for the purposes of sub-paragraph (3) members of the sub-panel must—

(*a*) have regard to all the matters set out in the referral statement,

(*b*) have regard to the matters mentioned in paragraphs (*a*) to (*c*) of paragraph 3(3) and paragraph 3(4), and

(*c*) take account of paragraph 3(5) to (7).

(5) For the purposes of the giving of an opinion under this paragraph, the arrangements are to be assumed to be tax arrangements.

(6) For the purposes of this Schedule—

(*a*) an opinion of the GAAR Advisory Panel is to be treated as having been given on a referral under paragraph 26 when an opinion notice (or notices) has been given under this paragraph in respect of the referral, and

(*b*) any requirement to consider the opinion of the GAAR Advisory Panel given on such a referral is a requirement to consider the contents of the opinion notice (or notices) given on the referral.

Commentary—*Simon's Taxes* **A4.573A**.

Notice before deciding that arrangements are ones to which Panel opinion applies

35 (1) This paragraph applies where—

(*a*) an opinion of the GAAR Advisory Panel has been given on a referral under paragraph 26,

(*b*) a designated HMRC officer is of the view that a person is liable to a penalty under paragraph 1 in relation to particular arrangements ("the arrangements concerned") and that that opinion of the GAAR Advisory Panel applies to those arrangements, and

(*c*) that person is not a person to whom notice under paragraph 28 was given in connection with the referral.

(2) A designated HMRC officer must give the person mentioned in sub-paragraph (1)(*b*) a notice in writing—

(*a*) explaining that the officer is of the view mentioned in that paragraph,

(*b*) specifying the arrangements concerned,

(*c*) setting out a report prepared by HMRC of the opinion mentioned in sub-paragraph (1)(*a*), and

(*d*) explaining the effect of sub-paragraphs (3) and (4).

(3) A person to whom a notice under this paragraph is given has 30 days, beginning with the day on which the notice is given, to send the designated HMRC officer (in writing) any representations as to why the opinion does not apply to the arrangements concerned.

(4) A designated HMRC officer may, on a written request by that person, extend the period during which representations may be made by that person.

(5) Paragraph 24(2) defines the arrangements that an opinion given on a referral under paragraph 26 "applies to".

Commentary—*Simon's Taxes* **A4.573A**.

Requirement for court or tribunal to take Panel opinion into account

36 (1) In this paragraph "enabler penalty proceedings" means proceedings before a court or tribunal in connection with a penalty under paragraph 1.

(2) In determining in enabler penalty proceedings any question whether tax arrangements to which the penalty relates were abusive, the court or tribunal—

(*a*) must take into account the relevant Panel opinion, and

(*b*) may also take into account any matter mentioned in sub-paragraph (4).

(3) In sub-paragraph (2)(*a*) "the relevant Panel opinion" means the opinion of the GAAR Advisory Panel which under this Part of this Schedule was required to be considered by a designated HMRC officer in deciding whether the penalty should be assessed.

(4) The matters mentioned in sub-paragraph (2)(*b*) are—

(*a*) guidance, statements or other material (whether of HMRC, a Minister of the Crown or anyone else) that was in the public domain at the time the arrangements were entered into, and

(*b*) evidence of established practice at that time.

Commentary—*Simon's Taxes* **A4.573A**.

PART 8

APPEALS

37 A person may appeal against—

(*a*) a decision of HMRC that a penalty under paragraph 1 is payable by that person, or

(*b*) a decision of HMRC as to the amount of a penalty under paragraph 1 payable by the person.

Commentary—*Simon's Taxes* **A4.573A**.

38 (1) An appeal under paragraph 37 is to be treated in the same way as an appeal against an assessment to the tax to which the arrangements concerned relate (including by the application of any provision about bringing the appeal by notice to HMRC, about HMRC review of the decision or about determination of the appeal by the First-tier Tribunal or Upper Tribunal).

(2) Sub-paragraph (1) does not apply—

(*a*) so as to require a person to pay a penalty under paragraph 1 before an appeal against the assessment of the penalty is determined;

(*b*) in respect of any other matter expressly provided for by this Schedule.

(3) In this paragraph "the arrangements concerned" means the arrangements to which the penalty relates.

Commentary—*Simon's Taxes* **A4.573A**.

39 (1) On an appeal under paragraph 37(*a*) that is notified to the tribunal, the tribunal may affirm or cancel HMRC's decision.

(2) On an appeal under paragraph 37(*b*) that is notified to the tribunal, the tribunal may—

(*a*) affirm HMRC's decision, or

(*b*) substitute for that decision another decision that HMRC had power to make.

(3) If the tribunal substitutes its decision for HMRC's, the tribunal may rely on paragraph 18—

(*a*) to the same extent as HMRC (which may mean applying the same percentage reduction as HMRC to a different starting point), or

(*b*) to a different extent, but only if the tribunal thinks that HMRC's decision in respect of the application of paragraph 18 was flawed.

(4) In sub-paragraph (3)(*b*) "flawed" means flawed when considered in the light of the principles applicable in proceedings for judicial review.

(5) In this paragraph "tribunal" means the First-tier Tribunal or Upper Tribunal (as appropriate by virtue of paragraph 38(1)).

Commentary—*Simon's Taxes* **A4.573A**.

PART 9
INFORMATION

Information and inspection powers: application of Schedule 36 to FA 2008

40 (1) Schedule 36 to FA 2008 (information and inspection powers) applies for the purpose of checking a relevant person's position as regards liability for a penalty under paragraph 1 as it applies for checking a person's tax position, subject to the modifications in paragraphs 41 to 43.

(2) In this paragraph and paragraphs 41 to 43—

"relevant person" means a person an officer of Revenue and Customs has reason to suspect is or may be liable to a penalty under paragraph 1;

"the Schedule" means Schedule 36 to FA 2008.

Commentary—*Simon's Taxes* **A4.573A**.

General modifications of Schedule 36 to FA 2008 as applied

41 In its application for the purpose mentioned in paragraph 40(1) above, the Schedule has effect as if—

(*a*) any provisions which can have no application for that purpose were omitted,

(*b*) references to "the taxpayer" were references to the relevant person whose position as regards liability for a penalty under paragraph 1 is to be checked, and references to "a taxpayer" were references to a relevant person,

(*c*) references to a person's "tax position" were to the relevant person's position as regards liability for a penalty under paragraph 1,

(*d*) references to prejudice to the assessment or collection of tax included prejudice to the investigation of the relevant person's position as regards liability for a penalty under paragraph 1, and

(*e*) references to a pending appeal relating to tax were to a pending appeal relating to an assessment of liability for a penalty under paragraph 1.

Commentary—*Simon's Taxes* **A4.573A**.

Specific modifications of Schedule 36 to FA 2008 as applied

42 (1) The Schedule as it applies for the purpose mentioned in paragraph 40(1) above has effect with the modifications in sub-paragraphs (2) to (6).

(2) Paragraph 10A (power to inspect business premises of involved third parties) has effect as if the reference in sub-paragraph (1) to the position of any person or class of persons as regards a relevant tax were to the position of a relevant person as regards liability for a penalty under paragraph 1.

(3) Paragraph 47 (right to appeal against penalties under the Schedule) has effect as if after paragraph (*b*) (but not as part of that paragraph) there were inserted the words "but paragraph (*b*) does not give a right of appeal against the amount of an increased daily penalty payable by virtue of paragraph 49A."

(4) Paragraph 49A (increased daily default penalty) has effect as if—

(*a*) in sub-paragraphs (1)(*c*) and (2) for "imposed" there were substituted "assessable";

(*b*) for sub-paragraphs (3) and (4) there were substituted—

"(3) If the tribunal decides that an increased daily penalty should be assessable—

(*a*) the tribunal must determine the day from which the increased daily penalty is to apply and the maximum amount of that penalty ("the new maximum amount");

(*b*) from that day, paragraph 40 has effect in the person's case as if "the new maximum amount" were substituted for "£60".

(4) The new maximum amount may not be more than £1,000.";

(*c*) in sub-paragraph (5) for "the amount" there were substituted "the new maximum amount".

(5) Paragraph 49B (notification of increased daily default penalty) has effect as if—

(*a*) in sub-paragraph (1) for "a person becomes liable to a penalty" there were substituted "the tribunal makes a determination";

(*b*) in sub-paragraph (2) for "the day from which the increased penalty is to apply" there were substituted "the new maximum amount and the day from which it applies";

(*c*) sub-paragraph (3) were omitted.

(6) Paragraph 49C is treated as omitted.

Commentary—*Simon's Taxes* **A4.573A**.

43 Paragraphs 50 and 51 are excluded from the application of the Schedule for the purpose mentioned in paragraph 40(1) above.

Commentary—*Simon's Taxes* **A4.573A**.

Declarations about contents of legally privileged communications

44 (1) Subject to sub-paragraph (5), a declaration under this paragraph is to be treated by—

(*a*) HMRC, or

(*b*) in any proceedings before a court or tribunal in connection with a penalty under paragraph 1, the court or tribunal,

as conclusive evidence of the things stated in the declaration.

(2) A declaration under this paragraph is a declaration which—

(*a*) is made by a relevant lawyer,

(*b*) relates to one or more communications falling within sub-paragraph (3), and

(*c*) meets such requirements as may be prescribed by regulations under sub-paragraph (4).

(3) A communication falls within this sub-paragraph if—

(*a*) it was made by a relevant lawyer (whether or not the one making the declaration),

(*b*) it is legally privileged, and

(*c*) if it were not legally privileged, it would be relied on by a person for the purpose of establishing that that person is not liable to a penalty under paragraph 1 (whether or not that person is the person who made the communication or is making the declaration).

(4) The Treasury may by regulations impose requirements as to the form and contents of declarations under this paragraph.

(5) Sub-paragraph (1) does not apply where HMRC or (as the case may be) the court or tribunal is satisfied that the declaration contains information which is incorrect.

(6) In this paragraph "a relevant lawyer" means a barrister, advocate, solicitor or other legal representative communications with whom may be the subject of a claim to legal professional privilege or, in Scotland, protected from disclosure in legal proceedings on the grounds of confidentiality of communication.

(7) For the purpose of this paragraph, a communication is "legally privileged" if it is a communication in respect of which a claim to legal professional privilege, or (in Scotland) to confidentiality of communications as between client and professional legal adviser, could be maintained in legal proceedings.

Commentary—*Simon's Taxes* **A4.573A**.

45 (1) Where a person carelessly or deliberately gives any incorrect information in a declaration under paragraph 44, the person is liable to a penalty not exceeding £5,000.

(2) For the purposes of this paragraph, incorrect information is carelessly given by a person if the information is incorrect because of a failure by the person to take reasonable care.

(3) Paragraphs 19(1), 20, 22(1), 37, 38 and 39(1), (2) and (5) apply in relation to a penalty under this paragraph as they apply in relation to a penalty under paragraph 1, subject to the modifications in sub-paragraphs (4) and (5).
(4) In its application to a penalty under this paragraph, paragraph 22(1) has effect as if for "the relevant time" there were substituted "the end of 12 months beginning with the date on which facts sufficient to indicate that the person is liable to the penalty came to the Commissioners' knowledge".
(5) In its application to a penalty under this paragraph, paragraph 38(3) has effect as if the reference to the arrangements to which the penalty relates were to the arrangements to which the declaration under paragraph 44 relates.
(6) In paragraph 44 any reference to a penalty under paragraph 1 includes a reference to a penalty under this paragraph.

Commentary—*Simon's Taxes* **A4.573A**.

PART 10
PUBLISHING DETAILS OF PERSONS WHO HAVE INCURRED PENALTIES
Power to publish details

46 (1) The Commissioners may publish information about a person where—
- (*a*) the person has incurred a penalty under paragraph 1,
- (*b*) the penalty has become final, and
- (*c*) either the condition in sub-paragraph (2) or the condition in sub-paragraph (3) is met.

(2) The condition in this sub-paragraph is that, at the time when the penalty mentioned in sub-paragraph (1) becomes final, 50 or more other penalties which are reckonable penalties have been incurred by the person.
(3) The condition in this sub-paragraph is that—
- (*a*) the amount of the penalty mentioned in sub-paragraph (1), or
- (*b*) the total amount of that penalty and any other penalties incurred by that person which are reckonable penalties,

is more than £25,000.
(4) The information that may be published under this paragraph is—
- (*a*) the person's name (including any trading name, previous name or pseudonym),
- (*b*) the person's address (or registered office),
- (*c*) the nature of any business carried on by the person,
- (*d*) the total number of the penalties in question (that is, the penalty mentioned in sub-paragraph (1) and any penalties that are reckonable penalties in relation to that penalty),
- (*e*) the total amount of the penalties in question, and
- (*f*) any other information that the Commissioners consider it appropriate to publish in order to make clear the person's identity.

(5) The information may be published in any way that the Commissioners consider appropriate.
(6) For the purposes of this Part of this Schedule a penalty becomes "final"—
- (*a*) if the penalty has been assessed and paragraph (*b*) does not apply, at the time when the period for any appeal or further appeal relating to the penalty expires or, if later, when any appeal or final appeal relating to it is finally determined;
- (*b*) if a contract settlement has been made in relation to the penalty, at the time when the contract is made;

and "contract settlement" here means a contract between the Commissioners and the person under which the Commissioners undertake not to assess the penalty or (if it has been assessed) not to take proceedings to recover it.
(7) "Reckonable penalty" has the meaning given by paragraph 47.
(8) This paragraph is subject to paragraphs 48 to 50.

Commentary—*Simon's Taxes* **A4.573A**.

47 (1) A penalty is a "reckonable penalty" for the purposes of paragraph 46 if—
- (*a*) it is a penalty under paragraph 1 which becomes final at the same time as, or before, the penalty mentioned in paragraph 46(1),
- (*b*) its entry date and the entry date of the penalty mentioned in paragraph 46(1) are not more than 12 months apart, and
- (*c*) it is not a penalty which under paragraph 48(1) is to be disregarded.

(2) For the purposes of this paragraph the "entry date" of a penalty under paragraph 1 is the date (or, if more than one, the latest date) on which the arrangements concerned or any agreement or transaction forming part of those arrangements was entered into by the taxpayer.
(3) In sub-paragraph (2)—

"the arrangements concerned" means the arrangements to which the penalty relates, and "the taxpayer" means the person whose defeat in respect of those arrangements resulted in the penalty being payable.

(4) For the purposes of this paragraph, the entry date of a penalty is not more than 12 months apart from the entry date of another penalty if—

(*a*) the entry dates of those penalties are the same, or

(*b*) the period beginning with whichever of the entry dates is the earlier and ending with whichever of the entry dates is the later is 12 months or less.

Commentary—*Simon's Taxes* **A4.573A**.

Restrictions on power

48 (1) In determining at any time whether or what information may be published in relation to a person under paragraph 46, the following penalties incurred by the person are to be disregarded—

(*a*) a penalty which has been reduced to nil or stayed;

(*b*) a penalty by reference to which information has previously been published under paragraph 46;

(*c*) a penalty where—

(i) the arrangements to which the penalty relates ("the arrangements concerned") are related to other arrangements, and

(ii) the condition in sub-paragraph (3) is not met;

(*d*) a penalty that relates to arrangements which are related to arrangements that have already been dealt with (within the meaning given by sub-paragraph (4)).

(2) For the purposes of sub-paragraph (1)(*c*) and (*d*) arrangements are "related to" each other if they—

(*a*) implement the same proposal for tax arrangements, and

(*b*) are substantially the same as each other.

(3) The condition referred to in sub-paragraph (1)(*c*) is that HMRC reasonably believe that—

(*a*) defeats have been incurred in the case of all the arrangements that are related to the arrangements concerned ("the related arrangements"), and

(*b*) each penalty under paragraph 1 which relates to the arrangements concerned or to any of the related arrangements has become final.

(4) For the purposes of sub-paragraph (1)(*d*) arrangements have "already been dealt with" if information about the person has already been published under paragraph 46 by reference to a penalty that relates to those arrangements.

Commentary—*Simon's Taxes* **A4.573A**.

49 (1) Publication of information under paragraph 46 on the basis of a penalty or penalties incurred by a person may not take place after the relevant time.

(2) In this paragraph "the relevant time" means the end of 12 months beginning with the date on which the penalty became final or, where more than one penalty is involved, the latest date on which any of them became final.

(3) Sub-paragraph (1) is not to be taken to prevent the re-publishing, or continued publishing, after the relevant time of a set of information published under paragraph 46 before that time.

(4) Information published under paragraph 46 may not be re-published, or continue to be published, after the end of 12 months beginning with the date on which it was first published.

(5) Nothing in paragraph 48 applies in relation to determining whether to re-publish (or continue to publish) a set of information already published under paragraph 46.

Commentary—*Simon's Taxes* **A4.573A**.

50 Before publishing information under paragraph 46 the Commissioners must—

(*a*) inform the person that they are considering doing so, and

(*b*) afford the person the opportunity to make representations about whether it should be published.

Commentary—*Simon's Taxes* **A4.573A**.

Power to amend

51 The Treasury may by regulations amend this Part of this Schedule so as to alter any of the following—

(*a*) the figure for the time being specified in paragraph 46(2);

(*b*) the sum for the time being specified in paragraph 46(3);

(*c*) any period for the time being specified in paragraph 47(1)(*b*) or (4).

PART 11
MISCELLANEOUS

Double jeopardy

52 A person is not liable to a penalty under paragraph 1 in respect of conduct for which the person has been convicted of an offence.

Commentary—*Simon's Taxes* **A4.573A**.

Application of provisions of TMA 1970

53 Subject to the provisions of this Schedule, the following provisions of TMA 1970 apply for the purposes of this Schedule as they apply for the purposes of the Taxes Acts—

(*a*) section 108 (responsibility of company officers),
(*b*) section 114 (want of form), and
(*c*) section 115 (delivery and service of documents).

PART 12
GENERAL

Meaning of "tax"

54 (1) In this Schedule "tax" includes any of the following taxes—

(*a*) income tax,
(*b*) corporation tax, including any amount chargeable as if it were corporation tax or treated as if it were corporation tax,
(*c*) capital gains tax,
(*d*) petroleum revenue tax,
(*e*) diverted profits tax,
(*f*) apprenticeship levy,
(*g*) inheritance tax,
(*h*) stamp duty land tax, and
(*i*) annual tax on enveloped dwellings,

and also includes national insurance contributions.

(2) The Treasury may by regulations amend sub-paragraph (1) so as to—

(*a*) add a tax to the list of taxes for the time being set out in that sub-paragraph;
(*b*) remove a tax for the time being set out in that sub-paragraph;
(*c*) remove the reference to national insurance contributions;
(*d*) substitute for that reference a reference to national insurance contributions of a particular class or classes;
(*e*) where provision has been made under paragraph (*d*)—
  (i) add a class or classes of national insurance contributions to those for the time being specified in that sub-paragraph;
  (ii) remove a class or classes of national insurance contributions for the time being so specified.

(3) Regulations under this paragraph may—

(*a*) make supplementary, incidental, and consequential provision, including provision amending or repealing any provision of this Schedule;
(*b*) make transitional provision.

Meaning of "tax advantage"

55 In this Schedule "tax advantage" includes—

(*a*) relief or increased relief from tax,
(*b*) repayment or increased repayment of tax,
(*c*) receipt, or advancement of a receipt, of a tax credit,
(*d*) avoidance or reduction of a charge to tax, an assessment of tax or a liability to pay tax,
(*e*) avoidance of a possible assessment to tax or liability to pay tax,
(*f*) deferral of a payment of tax or advancement of a repayment of tax, and
(*g*) avoidance of an obligation to deduct or account for tax.

Other definitions

56 (1) In this Schedule—

"abusive tax arrangements" has the meaning given by paragraph 3;

"arrangements" includes any agreement, understanding, scheme, transaction or series of transactions (whether or not legally enforceable);

"business" includes any trade or profession;

"the Commissioners" means the Commissioners for Her Majesty's Revenue and Customs;

"company" has the same meaning as in the Corporation Tax Acts (see section 1121 of CTA 2010);

"contract settlement" (except in paragraph 46(6)) means an agreement in connection with a person's liability to make a payment to the Commissioners under or by virtue of an enactment;

"a defeat", in relation to arrangements, is to be read in accordance with paragraph 4;

a "designated HMRC officer" means an officer of Revenue and Customs who has been designated by the Commissioners for the purposes of this Schedule;

"the GAAR Advisory Panel" has the meaning given by paragraph 1 of Schedule 43 to FA 2013;

"group" is to be read in accordance with sub-paragraph (2);

"HMRC" means Her Majesty's Revenue and Customs;

"national insurance contributions" means contributions under Part 1 of the Social Security Contributions and Benefits Act 1992 or Part 1 of the Social Security Contributions and Benefits (Northern Ireland) Act 1992;

a "NICs decision" means a decision under section 8 of the Social Security Contributions (Transfer of Functions, etc.) Act 1999 or Article 7 of the Social Security Contributions (Transfer of Functions, etc.) (Northern Ireland) Order 1999 (SI 1999/671) relating to a person's liability for relevant contributions;

"relevant contributions" means any of the following contributions under Part 1 of the Social Security Contributions and Benefits Act 1992 or Part 1 of the Social Security Contributions and Benefits (Northern Ireland) Act 1992—

(*a*) Class 1 contributions;

(*b*) Class 1A contributions;

(*c*) Class 1B contributions;

(*d*) Class 2 contributions which must be paid but in relation to which section 11A of the Act in question (application of certain provisions of the Income Tax Acts) does not apply;

"tax" is to be read in accordance with paragraph 54;

"tax advantage" is to be read in accordance with paragraph 55.

(2) For the purposes of this Schedule two companies are members of the same group if—

(*a*) one is a 75% subsidiary of the other, or

(*b*) both are 75% subsidiaries of a third company;

and in this paragraph "75% subsidiary" has, subject to sub-paragraph (3), the meaning given by section 1154 of CTA 2010.

(3) So far as relating to 75% subsidiaries, section 151(4) of CTA 2010 (requirements relating to beneficial ownership) applies for the purposes of this Schedule as it applies for the purposes of Part 5 of that Act.

(4) In this Schedule references to an assessment to tax, however expressed—

(*a*) in relation to inheritance tax and petroleum revenue tax, include a determination;

(*b*) in relation to relevant contributions, include a NICs decision.

Regulations

57 (1) Any regulations under this Schedule must be made by statutory instrument.

(2) A statutory instrument which contains (alone or with other provision) any regulations within sub-paragraph (3) may not be made unless a draft of the instrument has been laid before, and approved by a resolution of, the House of Commons.

(3) Regulations within this sub-paragraph are—

(*a*) regulations under paragraph 12;

(*b*) regulations under paragraph 14(1);

(*c*) regulations under paragraph 14(2) which amend or repeal any provision of this Schedule;

(*d*) regulations under paragraph 51;

(*e*) regulations under paragraph 54.

(4) A statutory instrument containing only—

(*a*) regulations under paragraph 14(2) which do not amend or repeal any provision of this Schedule, or

(*b*) regulations under paragraph 44,

is subject to annulment in pursuance of a resolution of the House of Commons.

Consequential amendments

58 In section 103ZA of TMA 1970 (disapplication of sections 100 to 103 of that Act in the case of certain penalties)—

(*a*) omit "or" at the end of paragraph (i), and

(*b*) after paragraph (*j*) insert "or

"(*k*) paragraph 1 or 45 of Schedule 16 to the Finance (No. 2) Act 2017 (enablers of defeated tax avoidance etc)."

59 In section 54 of ITTOIA 2005 (no deduction allowed for certain penalties etc) at the end of the table in subsection (2) insert—

"Penalty under Schedule 16 to F(No. 2)A 2017	Various taxes"

60 In section 1303 of CTA 2009 (no deduction allowed for certain penalties etc) at the end of the table in subsection (2) insert—

"Penalty under Schedule 16 to F(No. 2)A 2017	Various taxes"

61 In Schedule 34 to FA 2014 (promoters of tax avoidance schemes: threshold conditions), in paragraph 7—

(*a*) in paragraph (*a*), for the words after "promoter" substitute "—

(i) have been referred to the GAAR Advisory Panel under Schedule 43 to FA 2013 (referrals of single schemes),

(ii) are in a pool in respect of which a referral has been made to that Panel under Schedule 43B to that Act (generic referrals), or

(iii) have been referred to that Panel under paragraph 26 of Schedule 16 to F(No. 2)A 2017 (referrals in relation to penalties for enablers of defeated tax avoidance),";

(*b*) in paragraph (*b*), for the words after "referral" substitute "under (as the case may be)—

(i) paragraph 11(3)(*b*) of Schedule 43 to FA 2013,

(ii) paragraph 6(4)(*b*) of Schedule 43B to that Act, or

(iii) paragraph 34(3)(*b*) of Schedule 16 to F(No. 2)A 2017,

(opinion of sub-panel of GAAR Advisory Panel that arrangements are not reasonable), and".

Commencement

62 (1) Subject to sub-paragraphs (2) and (3), paragraphs 1 to 61 of this Schedule have effect in relation to arrangements entered into on or after the day on which this Act is passed.

(2) In determining in relation to any particular arrangements whether a person is a person who enabled the arrangements, any action of the person carried out before the day on which this Act is passed is to be disregarded.

(3) The amendments made by paragraph 61 do not apply in relation to a person who is a promoter in relation to arrangements if by virtue of sub-paragraph (2) above that person is not a person who enabled the arrangements.

SCHEDULE 18

REQUIREMENT TO CORRECT CERTAIN OFFSHORE TAX NON-COMPLIANCE

Section 67

PART 1

LIABILITY FOR PENALTY FOR FAILURE TO CORRECT

Failure to correct relevant offshore tax non-compliance

1 A penalty is payable by a person who—

(*a*) has any relevant offshore tax non-compliance to correct at the end of the tax year 2016-17, and (*b*) fails to correct the relevant offshore tax non-compliance within the period beginning with 6 April 2017 and ending with 30 September 2018 (referred to in this Schedule as "the RTC period").

Commentary—*Simon's Taxes* **A4.575B–A4.575D**.

Main definitions: general

2 Paragraphs 3 to 13 have effect for the purposes of this Schedule.

"Relevant offshore tax non-compliance"

3 (1) At the end of the 2016-17 tax year a person has "relevant offshore tax non-compliance" to correct if—

(*a*) Conditions A and B are satisfied in respect of any offshore tax non-compliance committed by that person on or before 5 April 2017 ("the original offshore tax non-compliance"), and

(*b*) Condition C will be satisfied on the relevant date (see paragraph 6).

(2) Where the original offshore tax non-compliance committed by a person has been corrected in part by the end of the tax year 2016-17, the person's "relevant offshore tax non-compliance" is the uncorrected part of the original offshore tax non-compliance.

Commentary—*Simon's Taxes* **A4.575B–A4.575D**.

4 Condition A is that the original offshore tax non-compliance has not been fully corrected before the end of the tax year 2016-17 (see paragraph 13).

Commentary—*Simon's Taxes* **A4.575B–A4.575D**.

5 Condition B is that—

(*a*) the original offshore tax non-compliance involved a potential loss of revenue when it was committed, and

(*b*) if the original offshore tax non-compliance has been corrected in part by the end of the tax year 2016-17, the uncorrected part at that time involved a potential loss of revenue.

Commentary—*Simon's Taxes* **A4.575B–A4.575D**.

6 (1) Condition C is that on the relevant date it is lawful, on the assumptions set out in sub-paragraph (2), for HMRC to assess the person concerned to any tax the liability to which would have been disclosed to or discovered by HMRC if on that date—

(*a*) where none of the original offshore tax non-compliance was corrected before the end of the 2016-17 tax year, HMRC were aware of the information missing as a result of the failure to correct that tax non-compliance, or

(*b*) where the original offshore tax non compliance was corrected in part before that time, HMRC were aware of the information missing as a result of the failure to correct the rest of that tax non-compliance.

(2) The assumptions are—

(*a*) that paragraph 26 is to be disregarded, and

(*b*) where the tax at stake is inheritance tax, that the relevant offshore tax non-compliance is not corrected before the relevant date

(3) In this paragraph "the relevant date" is—

(*a*) where the tax at stake is income tax or capital gains tax, 6 April 2017, and

(*b*) where the tax at stake is inheritance tax, the day after the day on which this Act is passed.

Commentary—*Simon's Taxes* **A4.575B–A4.575D**.

"Offshore tax-non compliance" etc

7 (1) "Offshore tax non-compliance" means tax non-compliance which involves an offshore matter or an offshore transfer, whether or not it also involves an onshore matter.

(2) Tax non-compliance "involves an onshore matter" if and to the extent that it does not involve an offshore matter or an offshore transfer.

(3) For the meaning of "involves an offshore matter or an offshore transfer" (in relation to the different descriptions of tax non-compliance) see paragraphs 9 to 11.

Commentary—*Simon's Taxes* **A4.575B–A4.575D**.

"Tax non-compliance"

8 (1) "Tax non-compliance" means any of the following—

(*a*) a failure to comply on or before the filing date with an obligation under section 7 of TMA 1970 to give notice of chargeability to income tax or capital gains tax,

(*b*) a failure to comply on or before the filing date with an obligation to deliver to HMRC a return or other document which is listed in sub-paragraph (3), or

(*c*) delivering to HMRC a return or other document which is listed in sub-paragraph (3) or (4) and contains an inaccuracy which amounts to, or leads to—
  (i) an understatement of a liability to tax,
  (ii) a false or inflated statement of a loss, or
  (iii) a false or inflated claim to repayment of tax.

(2) In sub-paragraph (1)—
(*a*) "filing date", in relation to a notice of chargeability or a return or other document, means the date by which it is required to be given, made or delivered to HMRC,
(*b*) "loss" includes a charge, expense, deficit and any other amount which may be available for, or relied on to claim, a deduction or relief, and
(*c*) "repayment of tax" includes a reference to allowing a credit against tax.

(3) The documents relevant for the purposes of both of paragraphs (*b*) and (*c*) of sub-paragraph (1) are (so far as they relate to the tax or taxes shown in the first column)—

Tax to which document relates	Document
Income tax or capital gains tax	Return, accounts, statement or document required under section 8(1) of TMA 1970 (personal return)
Income tax or capital gains tax	Return, accounts, statement or document required under section 8A(1) of TMA 1970 (trustee's return)
Income tax	Return, accounts, statement or document required under section 12AA(2) or (3) of TMA 1970 (partnership return)
Income tax	Return under section 254 of FA 2004 (pension schemes)
Income tax	Particulars or documents required under regulation 12 of the Retirement Benefits Schemes (Information Powers) Regulations 1995 (SI 1995/3101) (information relating to pension schemes)
Capital gains tax	NRCGT return under section 12ZB of TMA 1970
Inheritance tax	Account under section 216 or 217 of IHTA 1984.

(4) The documents relevant for the purposes only of paragraph (*c*) of sub-paragraph (1) are (so far as they relate to the tax or taxes shown in the first column)—

Tax to which document relates	Document
Income tax or capital gains tax	Return, statement or declaration in connection with a claim for an allowance, deduction or relief
Income tax or capital gains tax	Accounts in connection with ascertaining liability to tax
Income tax or capital gains tax	Statement or declaration in connection with a partnership return
Income tax or capital gains tax	Accounts in connection with a partnership return
Inheritance tax	Information or document under regulations under section 256 of IHTA 1984
Inheritance tax	Statement or declaration in connection with a deduction, exemption or relief.

Income tax, capital gains tax or inheritance tax	Any other document given to HMRC by a person ("P") which is likely to be relied on by HMRC to determine, without further inquiry, a question about— (*a*) P's liability to tax; (*b*) payments by P by way of or in connection with tax; (*c*) any other payment by P (including penalties); (*d*) repayments, or any other kind of payment or credit, to P.

Commentary—*Simon's Taxes* **A4.575B–A4.575D**.

"Involves an offshore matter" and "involves an offshore transfer"

9 (1) This paragraph applies to any tax non-compliance consisting of a failure to comply with an obligation under section 7 of TMA 1970 to notify chargeability to income tax or capital gains tax.

(2) The tax non-compliance "involves an offshore matter" if the potential loss of revenue is charged on or by reference to—

(*a*) income arising from a source in a territory outside the UK,

(*b*) assets situated or held in a territory outside the UK,

(*c*) activities carried on wholly or mainly in a territory outside the UK, or

(*d*) anything having effect as if it were income, assets or activities of a kind described above.

(3) The tax non-compliance "involves an offshore transfer" if—

(*a*) it does not involve an offshore matter, and

(*b*) the applicable condition is satisfied (see sub-paragraphs (4) and (5)).

(4) Where the tax at stake is income tax the applicable condition is satisfied if the income on or by reference to which tax is charged, or any part of the income—

(*a*) was received in a territory outside the UK, or

(*b*) was transferred on or before 5 April 2017 to a territory outside the UK.

(5) Where the tax at stake is capital gains tax, the applicable condition is satisfied if the proceeds of the disposal on or by reference to which the tax is charged, or any part of the proceeds—

(*a*) were received in a territory outside the UK, or

(*b*) were transferred on or before 5 April 2017 to a territory outside the UK.

(6) In the case of a transfer falling within sub-paragraph (4)(*b*) or (5)(*b*), references to the income or proceeds transferred are to be read as including references to any assets derived from or representing the income or proceeds.

(7) In this paragraph and paragraphs 10 and 11 "assets" has the meaning given in section 21(1) of TCGA 1992, but also includes sterling.

Commentary—*Simon's Taxes* **A4.575B–A4.575D**.

10 (1) This paragraph applies where—

(*a*) any tax non-compliance by a person consists of a failure to comply with an obligation to deliver a return or other document, and

(*b*) a complete and accurate return or other document would have included information that would have enabled or assisted HMRC to assess the person's liability to tax.

(2) The tax non-compliance "involves an offshore matter" if the liability to tax that would have been shown in the return or other document is or includes a liability to tax charged on or by reference to—

(*a*) income arising from a source in a territory outside the UK,

(*b*) assets situated or held in a territory outside the UK,

(*c*) activities carried on wholly or mainly in a territory outside the UK, or

(*d*) anything having effect as if it were income, assets or activities of a kind described above.

(3) Where the tax at stake is inheritance tax, assets are treated for the purposes of sub-paragraph (2) as situated or held in a territory outside the UK if they are so situated or held immediately after the transfer of value by reason of which inheritance tax becomes chargeable.

(4) The tax non-compliance "involves an offshore transfer" if—

(*a*) it does not involve an offshore matter, and

(*b*) the applicable condition is satisfied in respect of the liability to tax that would have been shown by the return or other document (see sub-paragraphs (5) to (7)).

(5) Where the tax at stake is income tax the applicable condition is satisfied if the income on or by reference to which tax is charged, or any part of the income—

(*a*) was received in a territory outside the UK, or

(*b*) was transferred on or before 5 April 2017 to a territory outside the UK.

(6) Where the tax at stake is capital gains tax, the applicable condition is satisfied if the proceeds of the disposal on or by reference to which the tax is charged, or any part of the proceeds—

(*a*) was received in a territory outside the UK, or

(*b*) was transferred on or before 5 April 2017 to a territory outside the UK.

(7) Where the liability to tax which would have been shown in the document is a liability to inheritance tax, the applicable condition is satisfied if—

(*a*) the disposition that gives rise to the transfer of value by reason of which the tax becomes chargeable involves a transfer of assets, and

(*b*) after that disposition but on or before 5 April 2017 the assets, or any part of the assets, are transferred to a territory outside the UK.

(8) In the case of a transfer falling within sub-paragraph (5)(*b*), (6)(*b*) or (7)(*b*), references to the income or proceeds transferred are to be read as including references to any assets derived from or representing the income or proceeds.

Commentary—*Simon's Taxes* **A4.575B–A4.575D**.

11 (1) This paragraph applies to any tax non-compliance by a person if—

(*a*) the tax non-compliance consists of delivering or giving HMRC a return or other document which contains an inaccuracy, and

(*b*) the inaccuracy relates to information that would have enabled or assisted HMRC to assess the person's liability to tax.

(2) The tax non-compliance to which this paragraph applies "involves an offshore matter" if the information that should have been given in the tax document relates to—

(*a*) income arising from a source in a territory outside the UK,

(*b*) assets situated or held in a territory outside the UK,

(*c*) activities carried on wholly or mainly in a territory outside the UK, or

(*d*) anything having effect as if it were income, assets or activities of a kind described above.

(3) Where the tax at stake is inheritance tax, assets are treated for the purposes of sub-paragraph (2) as situated or held in a territory outside the UK if they are so situated or held immediately after the transfer of value by reason of which inheritance tax becomes chargeable.

(4) Tax non-compliance to which this paragraph applies "involves an offshore transfer" if—

(*a*) it does not involve an offshore matter, and

(*b*) the applicable condition is satisfied in respect of the liability to tax that would have been shown by the return or other document (see sub-paragraphs (5) to (7)).

(5) Where the tax at stake is income tax the applicable condition is satisfied if the income on or by reference to which the tax is charged, or any part of the income—

(*a*) was received in a territory outside the UK, or

(*b*) was transferred on or before 5 April 2017 to a territory outside the UK.

(6) Where the tax at stake is capital gains tax, the applicable condition is satisfied if—

(*a*) the information that should have been given in the tax document relates to the proceeds of the disposal on or by reference to which the tax is charged, and

(*b*) the proceeds, or any part of the proceeds—

(i) were received in a territory outside the UK, or

(ii) were transferred on or before 5 April 2017 to a territory outside the UK.

(7) Where the tax at stake is inheritance tax, the applicable condition is satisfied if—

(*a*) the information that should have been given in the tax document relates to the disposition that gives rise to the transfer of value by reason of which the tax becomes payable relates to a transfer of assets, and

(*b*) after that disposition but on or before 5 April 2017 the assets or any part of the assets are transferred to a territory outside the UK.

(8) In the case of a transfer falling within sub-paragraph (5)(*b*), (6)(*b*) or (7)(*b*), references to the income, proceeds or assets transferred are to be read as including references to any assets derived from or representing the income, proceeds or assets.

Commentary—*Simon's Taxes* **A4.575B–A4.575D**.

"Tax"

12 (1) References to "tax" are (unless in the context the reference is more specific) to income tax, capital gains tax or inheritance tax.

(2) References to "capital gains tax" do not include capital gains tax payable by companies in respect of chargeable gains accruing to them to the extent that those gains are NRCGT gains in respect of which the companies are chargeable to capital gains tax under section 14D or 188D of TCGA 1992 (see section 1(2A)(*b*) of that Act).

(3) In sub-paragraph (2) "company" has the same meaning as in TCGA 1992.

Commentary—*Simon's Taxes* **A4.575B–A4.575D**.

Correcting offshore tax non-compliance

13 (1) This paragraph sets out how offshore tax non-compliance may be corrected.

(2) References to the correction of offshore tax non-compliance of any description are to the taking of any action specified in this paragraph as a means of correcting offshore tax non-compliance of that description.

(3) Offshore tax non-compliance consisting of a failure to notify chargeability may be corrected by—

(*a*) giving the requisite notice to HMRC (unless before doing so the person has received a notice requiring the person to make and deliver a tax return) and giving HMRC the relevant information by any means mentioned in paragraph (*b*),

(*b*) giving HMRC the relevant information—

(i) by making and delivering a tax return,

(ii) using the digital disclosure service or any other service provided by HMRC as a means of correcting tax non-compliance,

(iii) communicating it to an officer of Revenue and Customs in the course of an enquiry into the person's tax affairs, or

(iv) using a method agreed with an officer of Revenue and Customs.

(4) In sub-paragraph (3) "relevant information" means information relating to offshore tax that—

(*a*) had the requisite notice been given in time and the person given a notice to make and deliver a tax return, would have been required to be included in the tax return, and

(*b*) would have enabled or assisted HMRC to calculate the offshore tax due.

(5) Offshore tax non-compliance consisting of a failure to make or deliver a return or other document may be corrected by giving HMRC the relevant information by—

(*a*) making or delivering the requisite return or document,

(*b*) using the digital disclosure service or any other service provided by HMRC as a means of correcting tax non-compliance,

(*c*) communicating it to an officer of Revenue and Customs in the course of an enquiry into the person's tax affairs, or

(*d*) using a method agreed with an officer of Revenue and Customs.

(6) In subsection (5) "relevant information" means information relating to offshore tax that—

(*a*) should have been included in the return or other document, and

(*b*) would have enabled or assisted HMRC to calculate the offshore tax due.

(7) Offshore tax non-compliance consisting of making and delivering a return or other document containing an inaccuracy may be corrected by giving HMRC the relevant information by—

(*a*) in the case of an inaccurate tax document, amending the document or delivering a new document,

(*b*) using the digital disclosure service or any other service provided by HMRC as a means of correcting tax non-compliance,

(*c*) communicating it to an officer of Revenue and Customs in the course of an enquiry into the person's tax affairs, or

(*d*) using a method agreed with an officer of Revenue and Customs.

(8) In sub-paragraph (7) "relevant information" means information relating to offshore tax that—

(*a*) should have been included in the return but was not (whether due to an omission or the giving of inaccurate information), and

(*b*) would have enabled or assisted HMRC to calculate the offshore tax due.

(9) In this paragraph "offshore tax", in relation to any offshore tax non-compliance, means tax corresponding to the offshore PLR in respect of the non-compliance.

Commentary—*Simon's Taxes* **A4.575B–A4.575D**.

PART 2
AMOUNT OF PENALTY

Amount of penalty

14 (1) The penalty payable under paragraph 1 is 200% of the offshore PLR attributable to the uncorrected offshore tax non-compliance (subject to any reduction under a provision of this Part of this Schedule).

(2) In this Part of this Schedule "the uncorrected offshore tax non-compliance" means—

(*a*) the relevant offshore tax non-compliance, in a case where none of it is corrected within the RTC period, or

(*b*) so much of the relevant offshore tax non-compliance as has not been corrected within the RTC period, in a case where part of it is corrected within that period.

Commentary—*Simon's Taxes* **A4.575B–A4.575D**.

Offshore PLR

15 (1) In this Schedule "offshore PLR", in relation to any offshore tax non-compliance means the potential loss of revenue attributable to that non-compliance, to be determined as follows.

(2) The potential lost revenue attributable to any offshore tax non-compliance is (subject to sub-paragraphs (5) and (6)) —

(*a*) if the non-compliance is a failure to notify chargeability, the potential lost revenue under the applicable provisions of paragraph 7 of Schedule 41 to FA 2008 (or, where the original offshore tax non-compliance took place before 1 April 2010, the amount referred to in section 7(8) of TMA 1970),

(*b*) if the non-compliance is a failure to deliver a return or other document, the amount of the liability to tax under the applicable provisions of paragraph 24 of Schedule 55 to FA 2009 (or, where the original offshore tax non-compliance took place before 1 April 2011, the amount of liability to tax that would have been shown in the return as defined in section 93(9) of TMA 1970), and

(*c*) if the non-compliance is delivering a return or other document containing an inaccuracy, the potential lost revenue under the applicable provisions of paragraphs 5 to 8 of Schedule 24 to FA 2007 (or, where the original offshore tax non-compliance took place before 1 April 2008, the difference described in section 95(2) of TMA 1970).

(3) In its application for the purposes of sub-paragraph (2)(*c*) above, paragraph 6 of Schedule 24 to FA 2007 has effect as if—

(*a*) for sub-paragraph (1) there were substituted—

"(1) Where—

(*a*) P is liable to a penalty in respect of two or more inaccuracies (each being an inaccuracy in a return or other document listed in paragraph 8(3) or (4) of Schedule 18) to F(No 2)A 2017) in relation to a tax year or, in the case of inheritance tax, a single transfer of value,

(*b*) in relation to any one (or more than one) of those inaccuracies, the delivery of the return or other document containing it constitutes offshore tax non-compliance, and

(*c*) the calculation of potential lost revenue attributable to each of those inaccuracies depends on the order in which they are corrected,

the potential lost revenue attributable to any offshore tax non-compliance constituted by any one of those inaccuracies is to be taken to be such amount as is just and reasonable.

(1A) In sub-paragraph (1) "offshore tax non-compliance" has the same meaning as in Schedule 18 to F(No2)A 2017."; and

(*b*) in sub-paragraph (4), for paragraphs (*b*) to (*d*) there were substituted—

"(*b*) other understatements."

(4) In sub-paragraphs (5) and (6) "combined tax non-compliance" is tax non-compliance that—

(*a*) involves an offshore matter or an offshore transfer, but

(*b*) also involves an onshore matter.

(5) Any combined tax non-compliance is to be treated for the purposes of this Schedule as if it were two separate acts of tax non-compliance, namely—

(*a*) the combined tax non-compliance so far as it involves an offshore matter or an offshore transfer (which is then offshore tax non-compliance within the meaning of this Schedule), and

(*b*) the combined tax non-compliance so far as it involves an onshore matter.

(6) The potential lost revenue attributable to the offshore tax non-compliance referred to in sub-paragraph (5)(*a*) is to be taken to be such share of the potential lost revenue attributable to the combined tax non-compliance as is just and reasonable.

Commentary—*Simon's Taxes* **A4.575B–A4.575D**.

Reduction of penalty for disclosure etc by person liable to penalty

16 (1) This paragraph provides for a reduction in a penalty under paragraph 1 for any uncorrected relevant offshore tax non-compliance if the person ("P") who is liable to the penalty discloses any matter mentioned in sub-paragraph (2) that is relevant to the non-compliance or its correction or to the assessment or enforcement of the offshore tax attributable to it.

(2) The matters are—

(*a*) chargeability to income tax or capital gains tax (where the tax non-compliance is a failure to notify chargeability),

(*b*) a missing tax return,

(*c*) an inaccuracy in a document,

(*d*) a supply of false information or a withholding of information, or

(*e*) a failure to disclose an under-assessment.

(3) A person discloses a matter for the purposes of this paragraph only by—

(*a*) telling HMRC about it,

(*b*) giving HMRC reasonable help in relation to the matter (for example by quantifying an inaccuracy in a document),

(*c*) informing HMRC of any person who acted as an enabler of the relevant offshore tax non-compliance or the failure to correct it, and

(*d*) allowing HMRC access to records—

(i) for any reasonable purpose connected with resolving the matter (for example for the purpose of ensuring that an inaccuracy in a document is fully corrected), and

(ii) for the purpose of ensuring that HMRC can identify all persons who may have acted as an enabler of the relevant offshore tax non-compliance or the failure to correct it.

(4) Where a person liable to a penalty under paragraph 1 discloses a matter HMRC must reduce the penalty to one that reflects the quality of the disclosure.

(5) But the penalty may not be reduced below 100% of the offshore PLR.

(6) In relation to disclosure or assistance, "quality" includes timing, nature and extent.

(7) For the purposes of sub-paragraph (3) a person "acted as an enabler" of relevant offshore tax non-compliance by another if the person encouraged, assisted or otherwise facilitated the conduct by the other person that constituted the offshore tax non-compliance.

Commentary—*Simon's Taxes* **A4.575B–A4.575D**.

17 (1) If they think it right because of special circumstances, HMRC may reduce a penalty under paragraph 1.

(2) In sub-paragraph (1) "special circumstances" does not include—

(*a*) ability to pay, or

(*b*) the fact that a potential loss of revenue from one taxpayer is balanced by a potential overpayment by another.

(3) In sub-paragraph (1) the reference to reducing a penalty includes a reference to—

(*a*) staying a penalty, or

(*b*) agreeing a compromise in relation to proceedings for a penalty.

Commentary—*Simon's Taxes* **A4.575B–A4.575D**.

Procedure for assessing penalty, etc

18 (1) Where a person is found liable for a penalty under paragraph 1 HMRC must—

(*a*) assess the penalty,

(*b*) notify the person, and

(*c*) state in the notice—

(i) the uncorrected relevant offshore tax non-compliance to which the penalty relates, and

(ii) the tax period to which that offshore tax non-compliance relates.

(2) A penalty must be paid before the end of the period of 30 days beginning with the day on which notification of the penalty is issued.

(3) An assessment of a penalty—

(*a*) is to be treated for procedural purposes in the same way as an assessment to tax (except in respect of a matter expressly provided for by this Schedule),

(*b*) may be enforced as if it were an assessment to tax, and

(*c*) may be combined with an assessment to tax.

(4) A supplementary assessment may be made in respect of a penalty if an earlier assessment operated by reference to an underestimate of the liability to tax that would have been shown in a return.

(5) Sub-paragraph (6) applies if—

(*a*) an assessment in respect of a penalty is based on a liability to offshore tax that would have been shown on a return, and

(*b*) that liability is found by HMRC to have been excessive.

(6) HMRC may amend the assessment so that it is based upon the correct amount.

(7) But an amendment under sub-paragraph (6)—

(*a*) does not affect when the penalty must be paid, and

(*b*) may be made after the last day on which the assessment in question could have been made under paragraph 19.

Commentary—*Simon's Taxes* **A4.575B–A4.575D**.

19 (1) An assessment of a penalty under paragraph 1 in respect of uncorrected relevant offshore tax non-compliance must be made before the end of the relevant period for that non-compliance.

(2) If the non-compliance consists of a failure to notify chargeability, the relevant period is the period of 12 months beginning with—

(*a*) the end of the appeal period for the assessment of tax unpaid by reason of the failure, or (*b*) if there is no such assessment, the date on which the amount of tax unpaid by reason of the failure is ascertained.

(3) If the non-compliance consists of a failure to submit a return or other document, the relevant period is the period of 12 months beginning with—

(*a*) the end of the appeal period for the assessment of the liability to tax which would have been shown in the return, or

(*b*) if there is no such assessment, the date on which that liability is ascertained.

(4) If the non-compliance consists of making and delivering a tax document containing an inaccuracy, the relevant period is the period of 12 months beginning with—

(*a*) the end of the appeal period for the decision correcting the inaccuracy, or

(*b*) if there is no assessment to the tax concerned within paragraph (*a*), the date on which the inaccuracy is corrected.

(5) In this paragraph references to the appeal period are to the period during which—

(*a*) an appeal could be brought, or

(*b*) an appeal that has been brought has not been finally determined or withdrawn.

Commentary—*Simon's Taxes* **A4.575B–A4.575D**.

Appeals

20 A person may appeal against—

(*a*) a decision of HMRC that a penalty under paragraph 1 is payable by that person, or

(*b*) a decision of HMRC as to the amount of a penalty under paragraph 1 payable by the person.

Commentary—*Simon's Taxes* **A4.575B–A4.575D**.

21 (1) An appeal under paragraph 20 is to be treated in the same way as an appeal against an assessment to the tax at stake (including by the application of any provision about bringing the appeal by notice to HMRC, about HMRC review of the decision or about determination of the appeal by the First-tier Tribunal or Upper Tribunal).

(2) Sub-paragraph (1) does not apply—

(*a*) so as to require the person bringing the appeal to pay a penalty before an appeal against the assessment of the penalty is determined,

(*b*) in respect of any other matter expressly provided for by this Schedule.

Commentary—*Simon's Taxes* **A4.575B–A4.575D**.

22 (1) On an appeal under paragraph 20(*a*) that is notified to the tribunal, the tribunal may affirm or cancel HMRC's decision.

(2) On an appeal under paragraph 20(*b*) that is notified to the tribunal, the tribunal may—

(*a*) affirm HMRC's decision, or

(*b*) substitute for that decision another decision that HMRC had power to make.

(3) If the tribunal substitutes its own decision for HMRC's, the tribunal may rely on paragraph 16 or 17 (or both)—

(*a*) to the same extent as HMRC (which may mean applying the same percentage reduction as HMRC to a different starting point),

(*b*) to a different extent, but only if the tribunal thinks that HMRC's decision in respect of the application of that paragraph was flawed.

(4) In sub-paragraph (3)(*b*) "flawed" means flawed when considered in the light of the principles applicable in proceedings for judicial review.

(5) In this paragraph "tribunal" means the First-tier Tribunal or Upper Tribunal (as appropriate by virtue of paragraph 21(1)).

Commentary—*Simon's Taxes* **A4.575B–A4.575D**.

Reasonable excuse

23 (1) Liability to a penalty under paragraph 1 does not arise in relation to a particular failure to correct any relevant offshore tax non-compliance within the RTC period if the person concerned (P) satisfies HMRC or the relevant tribunal (as the case may be) that there is a reasonable excuse for the failure.

(2) For this purpose—

(*a*) an insufficiency of funds is not a reasonable excuse, unless attributable to events outside P's control,

(*b*) where P relied on any other person to do anything, that cannot be a reasonable excuse unless P took reasonable care to avoid the failure,

(*c*) where P had a reasonable excuse but the excuse has ceased, P is to be treated as continuing to have the excuse if the failure is remedied without unreasonable delay after the excuse ceased, and (*d*) reliance on advice is to be taken automatically not to be a reasonable excuse if it is disqualified under sub-paragraph (3).

(3) Advice is disqualified (subject to sub-paragraph (4)) if—

(*a*) the advice was given to P by an interested person,

(*b*) the advice was given to P as a result of arrangements made between an interested person and the person who gave the advice,

(*c*) the person who gave the advice did not have appropriate expertise for giving the advice,

(*d*) the advice failed to take account of all P's individual circumstances (so far as relevant to the matters to which the advice relates), or

(*e*) the advice was addressed to, or was given to, a person other than P.

(4) Where advice would otherwise be disqualified under any of paragraphs (*a*) to (*d*) of sub-paragraph (3) the advice is not disqualified if at the end of the RTC period P—

(*a*) has taken reasonable steps to find out whether or not the advice falls within that paragraph, and

(*b*) reasonably believes that it does not.

(5) In sub-paragraph (3) "an interested person" means, in relation to any relevant offshore tax non-compliance—

(*a*) a person (other than P) who participated in relevant avoidance arrangements or any transaction forming part of them, or

(*b*) a person who for any consideration (whether or not in money) facilitated P's entering into relevant avoidance arrangements.

(6) In this paragraph "avoidance arrangements" means arrangements as respects which, in all the circumstances, it would be reasonable to conclude that their main purpose, or one of their main purposes, is the obtaining of a tax advantage.

(7) But arrangements are not avoidance arrangements for the purposes of this paragraph if (although they fall within sub-paragraph (6))—

(*a*) they are arrangements which accord with established practice, and

(*b*) HMRC had, at the time the arrangements were entered into, indicated its acceptance of that practice.

(8) Where any relevant offshore tax non-compliance arose originally because information was submitted to HMRC on the basis that particular avoidance arrangements had an effect which they did not have, those avoidance arrangements are "relevant avoidance arrangements" in relation to that tax non-compliance.

(9) In sub-paragraph (6)—

(*a*) "arrangements" includes any agreement, understanding, scheme, transaction or series of transactions (whether or not legally enforceable), and

(*b*) a "tax advantage" includes—

(i) relief or increased relief from tax,

(ii) repayment or increased repayment of tax,

(iii) avoidance or reduction of a charge to tax or an assessment to tax,

(iv) avoidance of a possible assessment to tax,

(v) deferral of a payment of tax or advancement of a repayment of tax.

Commentary—*Simon's Taxes* **A4.575B–A4.575D**.

Double jeopardy

24 (1) Where by reason of any conduct a person—

(*a*) has been convicted of an offence, or

(*b*) is liable to a penalty otherwise than under paragraph 1 for which the person has been assessed (and the assessment has not been successfully appealed against or withdrawn),

that conduct does not give rise to liability to a penalty under paragraph 1.

(2) In sub-paragraph (1) the reference to a penalty otherwise than under paragraph 1—

(*a*) includes a penalty under paragraph 6 of Schedule 55 to FA 2009, but does not include penalties under any other provision of that Schedule, and

(*b*) includes a penalty under subsection (5) of section 93 of TMA 1970 but, does not include penalties under any other provision of that section.

(3) But the aggregate of—

(*a*) the amount of a penalty under paragraph 1, and

(*b*) the amount of a penalty under paragraph 5 of Schedule 55 which is determined by reference to a liability to tax,

must not exceed 200% of that liability to tax.

(4) In sub-paragraph (1) "conduct" includes a failure to act.

Commentary—*Simon's Taxes* **A4.575B–A4.575D**.

Application of provisions of TMA 1970

25 Subject to the provisions of this Part of this Schedule, the following provisions of TMA 1970 apply for the purposes of this Part of this Schedule as they apply for the purposes of the Taxes Acts—

(*a*) section 108 (responsibility of company officers),

(*b*) section 114 (want of form), and

(*c*) section 115 (delivery and service of documents).

Commentary—*Simon's Taxes* **A4.575B–A4.575D**.

PART 3

FURTHER PROVISIONS RELATING TO THE REQUIREMENT TO CORRECT

Extension of period for assessment etc of offshore tax

26 (1) This paragraph applies where—

(*a*) at the end of the tax year 2016-17 a person has relevant offshore tax non-compliance to correct, and

(*b*) the last day on which it would (disregarding this paragraph) be lawful for HMRC to assess the person to any offshore tax falls within the period beginning with 6 April 2017 and ending with 4 April 2021.

(2) The period in which it is lawful for HMRC to assess the person to the offshore tax is extended by virtue of this paragraph to end with 5 April 2021.

(3) In this paragraph "offshore tax", in relation to any relevant offshore tax non-compliance, means tax corresponding to the offshore PLR in respect of the non-compliance.

Commentary—*Simon's Taxes* **A4.575B–A4.575D**.

Further penalty in connection with offshore asset moves

27 (1) Schedule 21 to FA 2015 (penalties in connection with offshore asset moves) is amended as follows.

(2) In paragraph 2 (original penalties triggering penalties under Schedule 21) omit "and" after paragraph (*b*) and after paragraph (*c*) insert ", and

"(*d*) a penalty under paragraph 1 of Schedule 18 to FA 2017 (requirement to correct relevant offshore tax non-compliance)."

(3) In paragraph 3 (meaning of deliberate failure) after paragraph (*c*) insert—

"(*d*) in the case of a penalty within paragraph 2(*d*), P was aware at any time during the RTC period that at the end of the 2016-17 tax year P had relevant offshore tax non-compliance to correct;

and terms used in paragraph (*d*) have the same meaning as in Schedule 18 to FA 2017."

(4) In paragraph 5 (meaning of "relevant time") after sub-paragraph (4) insert—

"(5) Where the original penalty is under paragraph 1 of Schedule 18 to FA 2017, the relevant time is the time when that Schedule comes into force."

Commentary—*Simon's Taxes* **A4.575B–A4.575D**.

Asset-based penalty in addition to penalty under paragraph 1

28 (1) Schedule 22 to FA 2016 (asset-based penalty for offshore inaccuracies and failures) is amended as follows.

(2) In paragraph 2 (meaning of standard offshore penalty)—

(*a*) in sub-paragraph (1) for "or (4)" substitute "(4) or (4A)",

(*b*) after sub-paragraph (4) insert—

"(4A) A penalty falls within this paragraph if—

(*a*) it is imposed on a person under paragraph 1 of Schedule 18 to FA 2017 (requirement to correct relevant offshore tax non-compliance),

(*b*) the person was aware at any time during the RTC period that at the end of the 2016-17 tax year P had relevant offshore tax non-compliance to correct, and

(*c*) the tax at stake is (or includes) capital gains tax, inheritance tax or asset-based income tax.", and

(*c*) after sub-paragraph (5) insert—

"(5A) Sub-paragraph (5) does not apply to a penalty imposed under paragraph 1 of Schedule 18 to FA 2017."

(3) In paragraph 3 (tax year to which standard offshore penalty relates) after sub-paragraph (3) insert—

"(4) Where a standard offshore penalty is imposed under paragraph 1 of Schedule 18 to FA 2017, the tax year to which that penalty relates is—

(*a*) if the tax at stake in relation to the uncorrected relevant offshore tax non-compliance is income tax or capital gains tax, the tax year or years to which the failure or inaccuracy constituting the relevant offshore tax non-compliance in question relates;

(*b*) if the tax at stake in relation to the uncorrected relevant offshore tax non-compliance is inheritance tax, the year, beginning on 6 April and ending on the following 5 April, in which the liability to tax first arose.

(5) In sub-paragraph (4) references to uncorrected relevant offshore tax non-compliance are to the relevant offshore tax non-compliance in respect of which the standard offshore penalty is imposed."

(4) In paragraph 5 (meaning of offshore PLR), in sub-paragraph (1)(*a*) after "FA 2008" insert "or Schedule 18 to FA 2017".

(5) In paragraph 6 (restriction on imposition of multiple asset-based penalties for same asset), in sub-paragraph (1)(*a*) after "penalty" insert "(other than one imposed under paragraph 1 of Schedule 18 to FA 2017)".

(6) After paragraph 6 insert—

"6A

Where—

(*a*) a penalty has been imposed on a person under paragraph 1 of Schedule 18 to FA 2017, and

(*b*) the potential loss of revenue threshold has been met,

only one asset-based penalty is payable by the person in relation to any given asset."

(7) In paragraph 13 (asset-based income tax) after sub-paragraph (2) insert—

"(2A) In relation to cases where the standard offshore penalty is a penalty falling within paragraph 2(4A), each reference to provisions of ITTOIA 2005 in column 1 of the Table in sub-paragraph (2) includes a reference—

(*a*) to the corresponding provisions of the legislation in force immediately before those provisions of ITTOIA 2005 came into force (and to any previous text of those corresponding provisions), and

(*b*) to any other provision that had the same purpose as, or a similar purpose to, any of those corresponding provisions (or any earlier text mentioned in paragraph (*a*)), if and so far as that other provision was in force—

(i) on or after 6 April 1997, but

(ii) before the corresponding provisions (or the earlier text mentioned in paragraph (*a*)) came into force.""

(8) In paragraph 19(2) (interpretation: incorporation of definitions from other legislation for "or Schedule 55 to FA 2009" substitute "Schedule 55 to FA 2009 or Part 1 of Schedule 18 to FA 2017".

Commentary—*Simon's Taxes* **A4.575B–A4.575D.**

29 (1) TMA 1970 is amended as follows.

(2) In section 103ZA (disapplication of sections 100 to 103 in the case of certain penalties) omit the "or" after paragraph (*j*) and after paragraph (*k*) insert ", or

(*l*) Schedule 18 to the Finance Act 2017."

(3) In section 107A (relevant trustees)—

(*a*) in subsection (2)(*a*) after "Finance Act 2009" insert or Schedule 18 to the Finance Act 2017", and

(*b*) in subsection (3), after paragraph (*c*) insert—

"(*d*) in relation to—

(i) a penalty under Schedule 18 to the Finance Act 2017, or

(ii) interest under section 101 of the Finance Act 2009 on a penalty within sub-paragraph (i),

the end of the RTC period (within the meaning of Schedule 18 to the Finance Act 2017);".

Commentary—*Simon's Taxes* **A4.575B–A4.575D.**

Publishing details of persons assessed to penalty or penalties under paragraph 1

30 (1) The Commissioners for Her Majesty's Revenue and Customs ("the Commissioners") may publish information about a person (P) if in consequence of an investigation they consider that sub-paragraph (2) or (3) applies in relation to P.

(2) This sub-paragraph applies if—

(*a*) P has been found to have incurred one or more relevant penalties under paragraph 1 (and has been assessed or is the subject of a contract settlement), and (*b*) the offshore potential lost revenue in relation to the penalty, or the aggregate of the offshore potential lost revenue in relation to each of the penalties, exceeds £25,000.

(3) This sub-paragraph applies if P has been found to have incurred 5 or more relevant penalties under paragraph 1.

(4) A penalty incurred by P under paragraph 1 is "relevant" if —

(*a*) P was aware at any time during the RTC period that at the end of the 2016-17 tax year the person had relevant offshore tax non-compliance to correct, and

(*b*) the penalty relates to the failure to correct that non-compliance.

(5) The information that may be published is—

(*a*) P's name (including any trading name, previous name or pseudonym),

(*b*) P's address (or registered office),

(*c*) the nature of any business carried on by P,

(*d*) the amount of the penalty or penalties,

(*e*) the offshore potential lost revenue in relation to the penalty or the aggregate of the offshore potential lost revenue in relation to each of the penalties,

(*f*) the periods or times to which the uncorrected relevant offshore tax non-compliance relates,

(*g*) any other information that the Commissioners consider it appropriate to publish in order to make clear the person's identity.

(6) In sub-paragraph (5)(*f*) the reference to the uncorrected relevant offshore tax non-compliance is to so much of P's relevant offshore tax non-compliance at the end of the 2016-17 tax year as P failed to correct within the RTC period.

(7) The information may be published in any manner that the Commissioners consider appropriate.

(8) Before publishing any information the Commissioners must—

(*a*) inform P that they are considering doing so, and

(*b*) afford P the opportunity to make representations about whether it should be published.

(9) No information may be published before the day on which the penalty becomes final or, where more than one penalty is involved, the latest day on which any of the penalties becomes final.

(10) No information may be published for the first time after the end of the period of one year beginning with that day.

(11) No information may be published (or continue to be published) after the end of the period of one year beginning with the day on which it is first published.

(12) No information may be published if the amount of the penalty—

(*a*) is reduced under paragraph 16 to the minimum permitted amount (being 100% of the offshore PLR), or

(*b*) is reduced under paragraph 17 to nil or stayed.

(13) For the purposes of this paragraph a penalty becomes final—

(*a*) if it has been assessed, when the time for any appeal or further appeal relating to it expires or, if later, any appeal or final appeal relating to it is finally determined, and

(*b*) if a contract settlement has been made, at the time when the contract is made.

(14) In this paragraph "contract settlement", in relation to a penalty, means a contract between the Commissioners and the person under which the Commissioners undertake not to assess the penalty or (if it has been assessed) not to take proceedings to recover it.

Commentary—*Simon's Taxes* **A4.575B–A4.575D**.

31 (1) The Treasury may by regulations amend paragraph 30(2) to vary the amount for the time being specified in paragraph (*b*).

(2) Regulations under this paragraph are to be made by statutory instrument.

(3) A statutory instrument under this paragraph is subject to annulment in pursuance of a resolution of the House of Commons.

Commentary—*Simon's Taxes* **A4.575B–A4.575D**.

PART 4
SUPPLEMENTARY

Interpretation: minor

32 (1) In this Schedule (apart from the amendments made by Part 3)—

"HMRC" means Her Majesty's Revenue and Customs;

"tax period" means a tax year or other period in respect of which tax is charged (or in the case of inheritance tax, the year beginning with 6 April and ending on the following 5 April in which the liability to tax first arose);

"tax year", in relation to inheritance tax, means a period of 12 months beginning on 6 April and ending on the following 5 April;

"UK" means the United Kingdom, including its territorial sea.

(2) A reference to making a return or doing anything in relation to a return includes a reference to amending a return or doing anything in relation to an amended return.
(3) References to delivery (of a document) include giving, sending and any other similar expressions.
(4) A reference to delivering a document to HMRC includes—
 (*a*) a reference to communicating information to HMRC in any form and by any method (whether by post, fax, email, telephone or otherwise, and
 (*b*) a reference to making a statement or declaration in a document.
(5) References to an assessment to tax, in relation to inheritance tax, are to a determination.
(6) An expression used in relation to income tax has the same meaning as in the Income Tax Acts.
(7) An expression used in relation to capital gains tax has the same meaning as in the enactments relating to that tax.
(8) An expression used in relation to inheritance tax has the same meaning as in IHTA 1984.

Terms defined or explained for purposes of more than one paragraph of this Schedule

Term	Paragraph
assets (in paragraphs 8 to 10)	paragraph 9(7)
capital gains tax	paragraph 12(2)
HMRC	paragraph 32(1)
involves an offshore matter (in relation to failure to notify chargeability)	paragraph 9(2)
involves an offshore matter (in relation to failure to deliver a return or other document)	paragraph 10(2) and (3)
involves an offshore matter (in relation to delivery of a return or other document containing an inaccuracy)	paragraph 11(2) and (3)
involves an offshore transfer (in relation to failure to notify chargeability)	paragraph 9(3) to (6)
involves an offshore transfer (in relation to failure to deliver a return or other document)	paragraph 10(4) to (8)
involves an offshore transfer (in relation to delivery of a return or other document containing an inaccuracy)	paragraph 11(4) to (8)
involves an onshore matter (in relation to any tax non-compliance)	paragraph 7(2)
offshore tax non-compliance	paragraph 7(1)
offshore PLR	paragraph 15(1)
potential lost revenue	paragraph 15(2)
RTC period	paragraph 1(*b*)
relevant offshore tax non-compliance	paragraph 3
tax non-compliance	paragraph 8(1)
tax period	paragraph 32(1)
tax year (in relation to inheritance tax)	paragraph 32(1)
tax	paragraph 12(1)
UK	paragraph 32(1)
uncorrected offshore tax non-compliance (in Part 2)	paragraph 14(2)

Statutory Instruments

Contents

Chronological list of printed statutory instruments

Chronological list of statutory instruments

SI 2010/51 Inheritance Tax (Qualifying Non-UK Pension Schemes) Regulations 2010
SI 2010/867 Finance Act 2009, Schedule 51 (Time Limits for Assessments, Claims, etc) (Appointed Days and Transitional Provisions) Order 2010
SI 2010/1879 Taxes and Duties (Interest Rate) Regulations 2010 (revoked by SI 2011/2446)
SI 2011/170 Inheritance Tax Avoidance Schemes (Prescribed Descriptions of Arrangements) Regulation 2011
SI 2011/1502 Taxation of Equitable Life (Payments) Order 2011
SI 2011/2446 Taxes and Duties, etc (Interest Rate) Regulations 2011
SI 2012/847 Data-gathering Powers (Relevant Data) Regulations 2012
SI 2012/1836 Tax Avoidance Schemes (Information) Regulations 2012
SI 2012/2903 Inheritance Tax (Market Makers and Discount Houses) Regulations 2012
SI 2012/3070 Visiting Forces and International Military Headquarters (EU SOFA) (Tax Designation) Order 2012
SI 2012/3071 Visiting Forces and International Military Headquarters (NATO and PfP) (Tax Designation) Order 2012
SI 2013/279 Finance Act 2012, Schedule 38 (Tax Agents: Dishonest Conduct) (Appointed Day and Savings) Order 2013
SI 2013/1811 Data-gathering Powers (Relevant Data) (Amendment) Regulations 2013
SI 2014/488 Inheritance Tax (Delivery of Accounts) (Excepted Estates) (Amendment) Regulations 2014
SI 2015/623 National Savings Regulations 2015
SI 2015/624 National Savings (No 2) Regulations 2015
SI 2015/866 Offshore Asset Moves Penalty (Specified Territories) Regulations 2015
SI 2015/1378 Inheritance Tax (Electronic Communications) Regulations 2015
SI 2017/259 Finance Act 2016, Schedule 21 (Appointed Days) Regulations 2017
SI 2017/277 Finance Act 2016, Schedule 22 (Appointed Day) Regulations 2017
SI 2017/345 Penalties Relating to Offshore Matters and Offshore Transfers (Additional Information) Regulations 2017
SI 2017/355 Finance Act 2016, Section 113(1) to (4) (Commencement) Regulations 2017
SI 2017/495 Enactment of Extra-Statutory Concessions Order 2017

1980/1000

CAPITAL TRANSFER TAX (SETTLED PROPERTY INCOME YIELD) ORDER 1980

Made . . . . 16 July 1980

Laid before the House of Commons . . . . 16 July 1980

Coming into Operation . . . . 15 August 1980

Note—With effect from 25 July 1986, capital transfer tax is renamed as inheritance tax by FA 1986 s 100(1), (2). For transfers of value made after 17 February 2000 see the Inheritance Tax (Settled Property Income Yield) Order, SI 2000/174.

1—(1) This Order may be cited as the Capital Transfer Tax (Settled Property Income Yield) Order 1980.

(2) This Order shall have effect in relation to transfers of value made on or after 15th August 1980.

2 In this Order references to the "indices" are to the indices compiled jointly by the Financial Times, the Institute of Actuaries and the Faculty of Actuaries, and known as the "FT—Actuaries Shares Indices".

3—*(1) For the purposes of paragraph 3 of Schedule 5 to the Finance Act 1975, the higher and lower rates referred to in sub-paragraph (4) of that paragraph shall be the rates per annum equal to the designated rates of yield in the indices compiled for the date as at which the value in question is to be determined (or, if no indices are compiled for that date, in the indices for the latest earlier date for which indices are compiled).*

(2) For the purposes of paragraph (1) above the designated rates of yield are—

(a) for the higher rate, the Irredeemables' yield of the Fixed Interest Yields, and

(b) for the lower rate, the gross dividend yield of the All-Share Index.

Note—Finance Act 1975, Sch 5 para 3: repealed; see now the Inheritance Tax Act 1984, s 50(3).

1981/880

CAPITAL TRANSFER TAX (DELIVERY OF ACCOUNTS) REGULATIONS 1981

Note—With effect from 25 July 1986, capital transfer tax is renamed inheritance tax by FA 1986 s 100(1), (2). These Regulations were revoked by the Inheritance Tax (Delivery of Accounts) (Excepted Estates) Regulations, SI 2002/1733 reg 9, Schedule with effect from 1 August 2002 for deaths occurring after 5 April 2002.

1981/881

CAPITAL TRANSFER TAX (DELIVERY OF ACCOUNTS) (SCOTLAND) REGULATIONS 1981

Note—With effect from 25 July 1986, capital transfer tax is renamed as inheritance tax by FA 1986 s 100(1), (2). These Regulations were revoked by the Inheritance Tax (Delivery of Accounts) (Excepted Estates) Regulations, SI 2002/1733 reg 9, Schedule with effect from 1 August 2002 for deaths occurring after 5 April 2002.

1981/1440

CAPITAL TRANSFER TAX (DELIVERY OF ACCOUNTS) (NO 2) REGULATIONS 1981

Note—With effect from 25 July 1986, capital transfer tax is renamed as inheritance tax by FA 1986 s 100(1), (2). These Regulations were revoked by the Inheritance Tax (Delivery of Accounts) (Excepted Transfers and Excepted Terminations) Regulations, SI 2002/1731 reg 8 with effect from 1 August 2002.

1981/1441

CAPITAL TRANSFER TAX (DELIVERY OF ACCOUNTS) (NORTHERN IRELAND) REGULATIONS 1981

Note—These Regulations were revoked by the Inheritance Tax (Delivery of Accounts) (Excepted Estates) Regulations, SI 2002/1733 reg 9, Schedule with effect from 1 August 2002 for deaths occurring after 5 April 2002.

1987/1130

INHERITANCE TAX (DOUBLE CHARGES RELIEF) REGULATIONS 1987

Made . . . .*30 June 1987*
Laid before the House of Commons . . . .*1 July 1987*
Coming into force . . . .*22 July 1987*

HMRC Manuals—Inheritance Tax Manual IHTM14691–14732 (double charges relief).

1 Citation and commencement

These Regulations may be cited as the Inheritance Tax (Double Charges Relief) Regulations 1987 and shall come into force on 22nd July 1987.

2 Interpretation

In these Regulations unless the context otherwise requires—
"PET" means potentially exempt transfer;
"property" includes part of any property;
"the 1984 Act" means the Inheritance Tax Act 1984;
"the 1986 Act" means Part V of the Finance Act 1986;
"section" means section of the 1984 Act.

3 Introductory

These Regulations provide for the avoidance, to the extent specified, of double charges to tax arising with respect to specified transfers of value made, and other events occurring, on or after 18th March 1986.

4 Double charges—potentially exempt transfers and death

(1) This regulation applies in the circumstances to which paragraph (*a*) of section 104(1) of the 1986 Act refers where the conditions ("specified conditions") of paragraph (2) are fulfilled.
(2) The specified conditions to which paragraph (1) refers are—
(*a*) an individual ("the deceased") makes a transfer of value to a person ("the transferee") which is a PET,
(*b*) the transfer is made on or after 18th March 1986,
(*c*) the transfer proves to be a chargeable transfer, and
(*d*) the deceased immediately before his death was beneficially entitled to property to which paragraph (3) refers.
(3) The property to which paragraph (2)(*d*) refers is property—
(*a*) which the deceased, after making the PET to which paragraph (2)(*a*) refers, acquired from the transferee otherwise than for full consideration in money or money's worth,
(*b*) which is property which was transferred to the transferee by the PET to which paragraph (2)(*a*) refers or which is property directly or indirectly representing that property, and
(*c*) which is property comprised in the estate of the deceased immediately before his death (within the meaning of section 5(1)), value attributable to which is transferred by a chargeable transfer (under section 4).
(4) Where the specified conditions are fulfilled there shall be calculated, separately in accordance with sub-paragraphs (*a*) and (*b*), the total tax chargeable as a consequence of the death of the deceased—
(*a*) disregarding so much of the value transferred by the PET to which paragraph (2)(*a*) refers as is attributable to the property, value of which is transferred by the chargeable transfer to which paragraph (3)(*c*) refers, and
(*b*) disregarding so much of the value transferred by the chargeable transfer to which paragraph (3)(*c*) refers as is attributable to the property, value of which is transferred by the PET to which paragraph (2)(*a*) refers.
(5)
(*a*) Whichever of the two amounts of tax calculated under paragraph (4)(*a*) or (*b*) is the lower amount shall be treated as reduced to nil but, subject to sub-paragraph (*b*), the higher amount shall be payable,
(*b*) where the amount calculated under paragraph (4)(*a*) is higher than the amount calculated under paragraph (4)(*b*)—
(i) so much of the tax chargeable on the value transferred by the chargeable transfer to which paragraph (2)(*c*) refers as is attributable to the amount of that value which falls to be disregarded by virtue of paragraph (ii) shall be treated as a nil amount, and
(ii) for all the purposes of the 1984 Act so much of the value transferred by the PET to which paragraph (2)(*a*) refers as is attributable to the property to which paragraph (3)(*c*) refers shall be disregarded.

(6) Part I of the Schedule to these Regulations provides an example of the operation of this regulation.

5 Double charges—gifts with reservation and death

(1) This regulation applies in the circumstances to which paragraph (*b*) of section 104(1) of the 1986 Act refers where the conditions ("specified conditions") of paragraph (2) are fulfilled.

(2) The specified conditions to which paragraph (1) refers are—

(*a*) an individual ("the deceased") makes a transfer of value by way of gift of property,

(*b*) the transfer is made on or after 18th March 1986,

(*c*) the transfer is or proves to be a chargeable transfer,

(*d*) the deceased dies on or after 18th March 1986,

(*e*) the property in relation to the gift and the deceased is property subject to a reservation (within the meaning of section 102 of the 1986 Act),

(*f*)

(i) the property is by virtue of section 102(3) of the 1986 Act treated for the purposes of the 1984 Act as property to which the deceased was beneficially entitled immediately before his death, or,

(ii) the property ceases to be property subject to a reservation and is the subject of a PET by virtue of section 102(4) of the 1986 Act, and

(*g*)

(i) the property is comprised in the estate of the deceased immediately before his death (within the meaning of section 5(1)) and value attributable to it is transferred by a chargeable transfer (under section 4), or

(ii) the property is property transferred by the PET to which sub-paragraph (*f*)(ii) refers, value attributable to which is transferred by a chargeable transfer.

(3) Where the specified conditions are fulfilled there shall be calculated, separately in accordance with sub-paragraphs (*a*) and (*b*), the total tax chargeable as a consequence of the death of the deceased—

(*a*) disregarding so much of the value transferred by the transfer of value to which paragraph (2)(*a*) refers as is attributable to property to which paragraph (2)(*g*) refers, and

(*b*) disregarding so much of the value of property to which paragraph (2)(*g*) refers as is attributable to property to which paragraph (2)(*a*) refers.

(4) Where the amount calculated under paragraph (3)(*a*) is higher than the amount calculated under paragraph (3)(*b*)—

(*a*) only so much of that higher amount shall be payable as remains after deducting, as a credit, from the amount comprised in that higher amount which is attributable to the value of the property to which paragraph (2)(*g*) refers, a sum (not exceeding the amount so attributable) equal to so much of the tax paid—

(i) as became payable before the death of the deceased, and

(ii) as is attributable to the value disregarded under paragraph (3)(*a*), and

(*b*) so much of the value transferred by the transfer of value to which paragraph (2)(*a*) refers as is attributable to the property to which paragraph (2)(*g*) refers shall (except in relation to chargeable transfers which were chargeable to tax, when made by the deceased, for the purposes of an occasion which occurred before the death of the deceased on which tax was chargeable under section 64 or 65) be treated as reduced to a nil amount for all the purposes of the 1984 Act.

(5) Where the amount calculated under paragraph (3)(*a*) is less than the amount calculated under paragraph (3)(*b*) the value of the property to which paragraph (2)(*g*) refers shall be reduced to nil for all the purposes of the 1984 Act.

(6) For the purposes of the interpretation and application of this regulation section 102 of and Schedule 20 to the 1986 Act shall apply.

(7) Part II of the Schedule to these Regulations provides examples of the operation of this regulation.

6 Double charges—liabilities subject to abatement and death

(1) This regulation applies in the circumstances to which paragraph (*c*) of section 104(1) of the 1986 Act refers where the conditions ("specified conditions") of paragraph (2) are fulfilled.

(2) The specified conditions to which paragraph (1) refers are—

(*a*) a transfer of value which is or proves to be a chargeable transfer ("the transfer") is made on or after 18th March 1986 by an individual ("the deceased") by virtue of which the estate of the transferee is increased or by virtue of which property becomes comprised in a settlement of which the transferee is a trustee, and

(*b*) at any time before his death the deceased incurs a liability to the transferee ("the liability") which is a liability subject to abatement under the provisions of section 103 of the 1986 Act in determining the value transferred by a chargeable transfer (under section 4).

(3) Where the specified conditions are fulfilled there shall be calculated, separately in accordance with sub-paragraphs (*a*) and (*b*), the total tax chargeable as a consequence of the death of the deceased—

(*a*) disregarding so much of the value transferred by the transfer—

(i) as is attributable to the property by reference to which the liability falls to be abated, and

(ii) as is equal to the amount of the abatement of the liability, and

(*b*) taking account both of the value transferred by the transfer and of the liability.

(4)

(*a*) Whichever of the two amounts of tax calculated under paragraph (3)(*a*) or (*b*) is the lower amount shall be treated as reduced to nil but, subject to sub-paragraph (*b*), the higher amount shall be payable,

(*b*) where the amount calculated under paragraph (3)(*a*) is higher than the amount calculated under paragraph (3)(*b*)—

(i) only so much of that higher amount shall be payable as remains after deducting, as a credit, from that amount a sum equal to so much of the tax paid—

(*a*) as became payable before the death of the deceased, and

(*b*) as is attributable to the value disregarded under paragraph (3)(*a*), and

(*c*) as does not exceed the difference between the amount of tax calculated under paragraph (3)(*a*) and the amount of tax that would have fallen to be calculated under paragraph (3)(*b*) if the liability had been taken into account, and

(ii) so much of the value transferred by the transfer to which paragraph (2)(*a*) refers—

(*a*) as is attributable to property by reference to which the liability is abated, and

(*b*) as is equal to the amount of the abatement of the liability,

shall (except in relation to chargeable transfers which were chargeable to tax, when made by the deceased, for the purposes of an occasion which occurred before the death of the deceased on which tax was chargeable under section 64 or 65) be treated as reduced to a nil amount for all the purposes of the 1984 Act.

(5) Where there is a number of transfers made by the deceased which are relevant to the liability to which paragraph (2)(*b*) applies the provisions of this regulation shall apply to those transfers taking them in reverse order of their making, that is to say, taking the latest first and the earliest last, but only to the extent that in aggregate the value of those transfers does not exceed the amount of the abatement to which paragraph (2)(*b*) refers.

(6) Part III of the Schedule to these Regulations provides examples of the operation of this regulation.

7 Double charges—chargeable transfers and death

(1) This regulation applies in the circumstances specified (by this regulation) for the purposes of paragraph (*d*) of section 104(1) of the 1986 Act (being circumstances which appear to the Board to be similar to those referred to in paragraphs (*a*) to (*c*) of that subsection) where the conditions ("specified conditions") of paragraph (2) are fulfilled.

(2) The specified conditions to which paragraph (1) refers are—

(*a*) an individual ("the deceased") makes a transfer of value to a person ("the transferee") which is a chargeable transfer,

(*b*) the transfer is made on or after 18th March 1986,

(*c*) the deceased dies within 7 years after that chargeable transfer is made, and

(*d*) the deceased immediately before his death was beneficially entitled to property to which paragraph (3) refers.

(3) The property to which paragraph (2)(*d*) refers is property—

(*a*) which the deceased, after making the chargeable transfer to which paragraph (2)(*a*) refers, acquired from the transferee otherwise than for full consideration in money or money's worth,

(*b*) which was transferred to the transferee by the chargeable transfer to which paragraph (2)(*a*) refers or which is property directly or indirectly representing that property, and

(*c*) which is property comprised in the estate of the deceased immediately before his death (within the meaning of section 5(1)), value attributable to which is transferred by a chargeable transfer (under section 4).

(4) Where the specified conditions are fulfilled there shall be calculated, separately in accordance with sub-paragraphs (*a*) and (*b*), the total tax chargeable as a consequence of the death of the deceased—

(*a*) disregarding so much of the value transferred by the chargeable transfer to which paragraph (2)(*a*) refers as is attributable to the property, value of which is transferred by the chargeable transfer to which paragraph (3)(*c*) refers, and

(*b*) disregarding so much of the value transferred by the chargeable transfer to which paragraph (3)(*c*) refers as is attributable to the property, value of which is transferred by the chargeable transfer to which paragraph (2)(*a*) refers.

(5)

(*a*) Whichever of the two amounts of tax calculated under paragraph (4)(*a*) or (*b*) is the lower amount shall be treated as reduced to nil but, subject to sub-paragraph (*b*), the higher amount shall be payable,

(*b*) where the amount calculated under paragraph (4)(*a*) is higher than the amount calculated under paragraph (4)(*b*)—

(i) only so much of that higher amount shall be payable as remains after deducting, as a credit, from the amount comprised in that higher amount which is attributable to the value of the property to which paragraph (2)(*d*) refers, a sum (not exceeding the amount so attributable) equal to so much of the tax paid—

(*a*) as became payable before the death of the deceased, and

(*b*) as is attributable to the value disregarded under paragraph (4)(*a*), and

(ii) so much of the value transferred by the chargeable transfer to which paragraph (2)(*a*) refers as is attributable to the property to which paragraph (3)(*c*) refers shall (except for the purposes of an occasion which occurred before the death of the deceased on which tax was chargeable under section 64 or 65) be treated as reduced to a nil amount for all the purposes of the 1984 Act.

(6) Part IV of the Schedule to these Regulations provides an example of the operation of this regulation.

8 Equal calculations of tax—special rule

Where the total tax chargeable as a consequence of death under the two separate calculations provided for by any of regulation 4(4), 5(3), 6(3) or 7(4) is equal in amount the first of those calculations shall be treated as producing a higher amount for the purposes of the regulation concerned.

9 Schedule and saving

The Schedule to these Regulations shall have effect only for providing examples of the operation of these Regulations and, in the event of any conflict between the Schedule and the Regulations, the Regulations shall prevail.

SCHEDULE

Regulation 9

INTRODUCTORY

1 This Schedule provides examples of the operation of the Regulations.

2 In this Schedule—

"cumulation" means the inclusion of the total chargeable transfers made by the transferor in the 7 years preceding the current transfer;

"GWR" means gift with reservation;

"taper relief" means the reduction in tax provided under section 7(4) of the 1984 Act, inserted by paragraph 2(4) of Schedule 19 to the 1986 Act.

3 Except where otherwise stated, the examples assume that—

– tax rates and bands remain as at 18th March 1987;

– the transferor has made no other transfers than those shown in the examples;

– no exemptions (including annual exemption) or reliefs apply to the value transferred by the relevant transfer; and

– "grossing up" does not apply in determining any lifetime tax (the tax is not borne by the transferor).

PART I

REGULATION 4: EXAMPLE

Jul. 1987	A makes PET of £100,000 to B	
Jul. 1988	A makes gift into discretionary trust of £95,000	Tax paid £750
Jan. 1989	A makes further gift into same trust of £45,000	Tax paid £6,750
Jan. 1990	B dies and the 1987 PET returns to A	
Apr. 1991	A dies. His death estate of £300,000 includes the 1987 PET returned to him in 1990, which is still worth £100,000	

First calculation under reg 4(4)(a)

Charge the returned PET in A's death estate and ignore the PET made in 1987.

		Tax
Jul. 1987	PET £100,000 ignored	NIL
Jul. 1988	Gift £95,000	
	Tax £1,500 less £750 already paid	£750
Jan. 1989	Gift £45,000 as top slice of £140,000	
	Tax £13,500 less £6,750 already paid	£6,750
Apr. 1991	Death estate £300,000 as top slice of £440,000	£153,000 *
	Total tax due as result of A's death	£160,500

* In first calculation the tax of £153,000 on death estate does not allow for any successive charges relief (under s 141, IHTA 1984) that might be due in respect of "the returned PET" by reference to any tax charged on that "PET" in connection with B's death.

Second calculation under reg 4(4)(b)

Charge the 1987 PET and ignore the value of the returned PET in A's death estate.

		Tax
Jul. 1987	PET £100,000. Tax with taper relief	£2,400
Jul. 1988	Gift £95,000 as top slice of £195,000	
	Tax £34,000 less £750 already paid	£33,250
Jan. 1989	Gift £45,000 as top slice of £240,000	
	Tax £20,000 less £6,750 already paid	£13,250
Apr. 1991	Death estate £200,000 as top slice of £440,000	£111,000
	Total tax due as result of A's death	£159,900

*Result**

First calculation gives higher amount of tax. So PET reduced to nil and tax on other transfers is as in first calculation.

* If, after allowing any successive charges relief, the second calculation gives higher amount of tax, 1987 PET will be charged and tax on other transfers will be as in second calculation.

PART II

REGULATION 5: EXAMPLE 1

Jan. 1988	A makes PET of £150,000 to B	
Mar. 1992	A makes gift of land worth £200,000 into a discretionary trust of which he is a potential beneficiary. The gift is a "GWR"	Tax paid £19,500
Feb. 1995	A dies without having released his interest in the trust. His death estate valued at £400,000, includes the GWR land currently worth £300,000	

First calculation under reg 5(3)(a)

Charge the GWR land in A's death estate and ignore the GWR.

		Tax
Jan. 1988	PET (now exempt)	NIL
Mar. 1992	GWR ignored	NIL
Feb. 1995	Death estate £400,000	
	Tax £144,000 less £19,500 already paid on GWR*	£124,500
	Total tax due as result of A's death	£124,500

* Credit for the tax already paid cannot exceed the amount of the death tax attributable to the value of the GWR property. In this example the tax so attributable is £108,000, ie—

$$\frac{144,000}{400,000} \times 300,000$$

So credit is given for the full amount of £19,500

Second calculation under reg 5(3)(b)

Charge the GWR and ignore the GWR land in the death estate.

		Tax
Jan. 1988	PET (now exempt)	NIL
Mar. 1992	GWR £200,000	
	Tax £39,000 less £19,500 already paid	£19,500
Feb. 1995	Death estate £100,000 (ignoring GWR property) as top slice of £300,000	£48,000
	Total tax due as result of A's death	£67,500

Result

First calculation yields higher amount of tax. So the value of the GWR transfer is reduced to nil and tax on death is charged as in first calculation with credit for the tax already paid.

PART II
REGULATION 5: EXAMPLE 2

Apr. 1987	A makes gift into discretionary trust of £150,000	Tax paid £9,500
Jan. 1988	A makes further gift into same trust of £50,000	Tax paid £10,000
Mar. 1993	A makes PET of shares valued at £150,000 to B	
Feb. 1996	A dies. He had continued to enjoy the income of the shares he had given to B (the 1993 PET is a GWR). His death estate, valued at £300,000, includes those shares currently worth £200,000	

First calculation under reg 5(3)(a)

Charge the GWR shares in the death estate and ignore the PET.

		Tax
Apr. 1987	Gift £150,000. No adjustment to tax as gift made more than 7 years before death	NIL
Jan. 1988	Gift £50,000. No adjustment to tax as gift made more than 7 years before death	NIL
Mar. 1993	PET £150,000 now reduced to NIL	NIL
Feb. 1996	Death estate including GWR shares £300,000	
	No previous cumulation	£87,000
	Total tax due as result of A's death	£87,000

Second calculation under reg 5(3)(b)

Charge the PET and ignore the value of the GWR shares in the death estate.

		Tax
Apr. 1987	Gift £150,000. No adjustment to tax as gift made more than 7 years before death	NIL
Jan. 1988	Gift £50,000. No adjustment to tax as gift made more than 7 years before death	NIL

		Tax
Mar. 1993	GWR £150,000 as top slice of £350,000 (ie previous gifts totalling £200,000+£150,000)	£75,000
Feb. 1996	Death estate (excluding GWR shares) £100,000 as top slice of £250,000 (the 1987 and 1988 gifts drop out of cumulation)	£43,000
	Total tax due as result of A's death	£118,000

Result

Second calculation yields higher amount of tax. So tax is charged by reference to the PET and the value of the GWR shares in the death estate is reduced to NIL.

PART III
REGULATION 6: EXAMPLE 1

Nov. 1987	X makes a PET of cash of £95,000 to Y
Dec. 1987	Y makes a loan to X of £95,000
May 1988	X makes a gift into discretionary trust of £20,000
Apr. 1993	X dies. His death estate is worth £182,000. A deduction of £95,000 is claimed for the loan from Y.

First calculation under reg 6(3)(a)

No charge on November 1987 gift, and no deduction against death estate.

		Tax
Nov. 1987	PET ignored	NIL
May 1988	Gift £20,000	NIL
Apr. 1993	Death estate £182,000 as top slice of £202,000	£39,800
	Total tax due as result of X's death	£39,800

Second calculation under reg 6(3)(b)

Charge the November 1987 PET, and allow the deduction against the death estate.

		Tax
Nov. 1987	PET £95,000. Tax with taper relief	£600
May 1988	Gift £20,000 as top slice of £115,000. Tax with taper relief	£3,600
Apr. 1993	Death estate (£182,000–loan of £95,000) £87,000 as top slice of £202,000	£32,300
	Total tax due as result of X's death	£36,500

Result

First calculation gives higher amount of tax. So debt is disallowed against death estate, but PET of £95,000 is not charged.

PART III
REGULATION 6: EXAMPLE 2

Aug. 1988	P makes a PET of cash of £100,000 to Q	
Sept. 1988	Q makes a loan to P of £100,000	
Oct. 1989	P makes gift into discretionary trust of £98,000	Tax paid £1,200
Nov. 1992	P dies. Death estate £110,000 less allowable liabilities of £80,000 (which do not include the debt of £100,000 owed to Q)	

First calculation under reg 6(3)(a)

No charge on August 1988 PET, and no deduction against death estate for the £100,000 owed to Q.

		Tax
Aug. 1988	PET ignored	NIL
Oct. 1989	Gift £98,000	
	Tax (with taper relief) £1,920 less £1,200 already paid	£720
Nov. 1992	Death estate £30,000 as top slice of £128,000	£9,000
	Total tax due as result of P's death	£9,720

Second calculation under reg 6(3)(b)

Charge the August 1988 PET, and allow deduction against death estate for the £100,000 owed to Q.

		Tax
Aug. 1988	PET £100,000. Tax with taper relief	£1,800
Oct. 1989	Gift £98,000 as top slice of £198,000	
	Tax (with taper relief) £28,100 less £1,200 already paid	£26,960
Nov. 1992	Death estate £30,000–£100,000 (owed to Q)	NIL
	Total tax due as result of P's death	£28,760

Result

Second calculation gives higher amount of tax. So the PET to Q is charged, and deduction is allowed against death estate for the debt to Q.

PART III

REGULATION 6: EXAMPLE 3

1 May 1987	A makes PET to B of £95,000	
1 Jan. 1988	A makes PET to B of £40,000	
1 Jul. 1988	A makes gift into discretionary trust of £100,000	Tax paid £1,500
1 Jan. 1989	A makes PET to B of £30,000	
1 Jul. 1989	B makes a loan to A of £100,000	
1 Dec. 1990	A dies. Death estate £200,000, against which deduction is claimed for debt of £100,000 due to B	

First calculation under reg 6(3)(a)

Disallow the debt and ignore corresponding amounts (£100,000) of PETs from A to B, starting with the latest PET.

		Tax
1 May 1987	PET now reduced to £65,000	NIL
1 Jan. 1988	PET now reduced to NIL	NIL
1 Jul. 1988	Gift into trust £100,000 as top slice of £165,000	
	Tax £25,000 less £1,500 already paid	£23,500
1 Jan. 1989	PET now reduced to NIL	NIL
1 Dec. 1990	Death estate £200,000 as top slice of £365,000	£98,000
	Total tax due as result of A's death	£121,500

Second calculation under reg 6(3)(b)

Allow the debt and charge PETs to B in full

		Tax
1 May 1987	PET £95,000. Tax with taper relief	£1,200
1 Jan. 1988	PET £40,000 as top slice of £135,000	£12,000
1 Jul. 1988	Gift into trust £100,000 as top slice of £235,000.	
	Tax £41,000 less £1,500 already paid	£39,500
1 Jan. 1989	PET £30,000 as top slice of £265,000	£15,000
1 Dec. 1990	Death estate £100,000 as top slice of £365,000	£53,500
	Total tax due as result of A's death	£121,200

Result

First calculation yields higher amount of tax. So the debt is disallowed and corresponding amounts of PETs to B are ignored in determining the tax due as a result of the death.

PART III
REGULATION 6: EXAMPLE 4

1 Apr. 1987	A makes gift into discretionary trust of £100,000	Tax paid £1,500
1 Jan. 1990	A makes PET to B of £60,000	
1 Jan. 1991	A makes further gift into same trust of £50,000	Tax paid £8,000
1 Jan. 1992	Same trust makes a loan to A of £120,000	
1 Jun. 1994	A dies. Death estate is £220,000 against which deduction is claimed for debt of £120,000 due to the trust	

First calculation under reg 6(3)(a)

Disallow the debt and ignore corresponding amount (£120,000) of gifts from A to trust, starting with the latest gift.

		Tax
1 Apr. 1987	Gift now reduced to £30,000. No adjustment to tax already paid as gift made more than 7 years before death	NIL
1 Jan. 1990	PET £60,000 as top slice of £90,000	NIL
1 Jan. 1991	Gift now reduced to NIL. No adjustment to tax already paid	NIL
1 Jun. 1994	Death estate £220,000 as top slice of £280,000 (the 1987 gift at £30,000 drops out of cumulation)	£77,000
		£77,000
	Less credit for tax already paid £1,500+£8,000	£9,500
	Total tax due as result of A's death	£67,500

Second calculation under reg 6(3)(b)

Allow the debt and no adjustment to gifts into the trust.

		Tax
1 Apr. 1987	Gift £100,000. No adjustment to tax already paid as gift made more than 7 years before death	NIL
1 Jan. 1990	PET £60,000 as top slice of £160,000. Tax with taper relief	£12,000
1 Jan. 1991	Gift £50,000 as top slice of £210,000	
	Tax (with taper relief) £16,000 less £8,000 already paid	£8,000
1 Jun. 1994	Death estate £100,000 as top slice of £210,000. (The 1987 gift drops out of cumulation. No credit for tax paid on that gift.)	£37,000

	Tax
Total tax due as result of A's death	£57,000

Result

First calculation yields higher amount of tax. So the debt is disallowed and corresponding amounts of gifts into trust are ignored in determining the tax due as a result of the death.

PART IV

REGULATION 7: EXAMPLE

May 1986	S transfers into discretionary trust property worth £150,000. Immediate charge at the rates then in force	Tax paid £13,750
Oct. 1986	S gives T a life interest in shares worth £85,000. Immediate charge at the rates then in force	Tax paid £19,500
Jan. 1991	S makes a PET to R of £20,000	
Dec. 1992	T dies, and the settled shares return to S who is the settlor and therefore no tax charge on the shares on T's death	
Aug. 1993	S dies. His death estate includes the shares returned from T which are currently worth £75,000, and other assets worth £144,000	

First calculation under reg 7(4)(a)

Charge the returned shares in the death estate and ignore the October 1986 gift. Tax rates and bands are those in force at the date of S's death.

		Tax
May 1986	Gift into trust made more than 7 years before death. So no adjustment to tax already paid but the gift cumulates in calculating tax on other gifts	NIL
Oct. 1986	Gift ignored and no adjustment to tax already paid	NIL
Jan. 1991	PET of £20,000 as top slice of (£150,000+£20,000) £170,000	£8,000
Nov. 1993	Death estate £219,000 as top slice of £239,000 Tax £56,000 less £19,350 (part of tax already paid)*	£37,150
	Total tax due as result of S's death	£45,150

* £19,350 represents the amount of the death tax attributable to the value of the returned shares, and is lower than the amount of the lifetime tax charged on those shares. So credit against the death charge for the tax already paid is restricted to the lower amount.

Second calculation under reg 7(4)(b)

Charge the October 1986 gift and ignore the returned shares in the death estate. Tax rates and bands are those in force at the date of S's death.

		Tax
May 1986	Gift into trust made more than 7 years before death. So no adjustment to tax already paid but the gift is taken into account in calculating the tax on the other gifts	NIL
Oct. 1986	Gift of £85,000 as top slice of £235,000 Tax (with taper relief) £7,100 less £19,500 already paid	NIL*
Jan. 1991	PET of £20,000 as top slice of £225,000	£10,000
Aug. 1993	Death estate (excluding the returned shares) £144,000 as top slice of £249,000 (£85,000+£20,000+£144,000)	£57,000
	Total tax due as a result of S's death	£67,000

* Credit for the tax already paid restricted to the (lower) amount of tax payable as result of the death. No repayment of the excess.

IHT

Result

Second calculation gives higher amount of tax. So tax is charged as in second calculation by excluding the shares from the death estate.

Commentary—*Simon's Taxes* **I3.502, I3.513, I3.534, I3.543, I3.545;** *Foster* **C5.02, 13, 34, 43, 45.**

1989/1297

TAXES (INTEREST RATE) REGULATIONS 1989

Made . . . . *27 July 1989*

Laid before the House of Commons . . . . *28 July 1989*

Coming into force . . . . *18 August 1989*

1 Citation and commencement

These Regulations may be cited as the Taxes (Interest Rate) Regulations 1989 and shall come into force on 18th August 1989.

2 Interpretation

(1) In these Regulations unless the context otherwise requires—

["the 1998 Regulations" means the Corporation Tax (Instalment Payments Regulations 1998;][1]

"established rate" means—

(*a*) on the coming into force of these Regulations, 14 per cent per annum; and

(*b*) in relation to any date after the first reference date after the coming into force of these Regulations, the reference rate found on the immediately preceding reference date;

["operative date" means—

(*a*) the [twelfth][3] working day after the reference date, or

(*b*) where regulation 3ZA or 3BA applies—

(i) where the reference date is the first Tuesday, the day which is the Monday next following the first Tuesday, or

(ii) where the reference date is the second Tuesday, the day which is the Monday next following the second Tuesday;][2]

["reference date" means—

(*a*) the . . . [3] working day following the day on which the most recent meeting of the Monetary Policy Committee of the Bank of England took place, or

(*b*) where regulation 3ZA or 3BA applies—

(i) the day which is the Tuesday next following the day on which that meeting took place ("the first Tuesday"), and

(ii) the day which is the Tuesday ("the second Tuesday") occurring two weeks after the first Tuesday;][2]

"section 178" means section 178 of the Finance Act 1989;

"working day" means any day other than a non-business day within the meaning of section 92 of the Bills of Exchange Act 1882.

[(2) In these Regulations the reference rate found on a reference date is the official bank rate determined by the most recent meeting of the Monetary Policy Committee of the Bank of England.][3]

Amendments—[1] Words in para (1) inserted by the Taxes (Interest Rate) (Amendment No 2) Regulations, SI 1998/3176 reg 3 with effect for accounting periods ending on or after 1 July 1999 by virtue of the Finance Act 1994, Section 199 (Appointed Day) Order, SI 1998/3173 art 2.

[2] In para (1), definitions of "operative date" and "reference date" substituted by the Taxes and Duties (Interest Rate) (Amendment) Regulations, SI 2008/3234 reg 2 with effect from 7 January 2009.

[3] In definition of "operative date" word substituted, in definition of "reference date" word revoked, and para (2) substituted, by the Taxes and Duties (Interest Rate) (Amendment) Regulations, SI 2009/2032 regs 2, 3 with effect from 12 August 2009.

2A Applicable rate of interest equal to zero

Amendments—This reg revoked by the Taxes and Duties (Interest Rate) (Amendment) Regulations, SI 2009/2032 regs 2, 4 with effect from 12 August 2009.

3, 3AA, 3AB, 3AC Applicable rate of interest on unpaid tax, tax repaid and repayment supplement

Note—These regulations are not relevant to IHT.

3A, 3ZA, 3ZB Applicable rate of interest on overdue corporation tax

Note—These regulations are not relevant to IHT.

3B, 3BA, 3BB Applicable rate of interest on tax overpaid

. . .

Note—These regulations are not relevant to IHT.

4 Applicable rate of interest on unpaid inheritance tax, capital transfer tax and estate duty

(1) For the purposes of—

(*a*) –(*e*) . . .

(*f*) sections 233 and . . . [1] of the Inheritance Tax Act 1984;

[(*g*) section 236(4) of the Inheritance Tax Act 1984 so far as it relates to tax charged by virtue of section 147(4) of that Act.][1]

the rate applicable under section 178 shall, subject to paragraph (2), be 11 per cent per annum.

(2) Where, on a reference date after the coming into force of these Regulations, the reference rate found on that date differs from the established rate, the rate applicable under section 178 for the purposes of the enactment's referred to in paragraph (1) shall, on and after the next operative date, be the percentage per annum found by applying the formula specified in paragraph (3) . . . [1].

[(3) The formula specified in this paragraph is—

RR + 2.5,

where RR is the reference rate referred to in paragraph (2).][1]

Note—Sub-paras (1)(*a*)–(*e*) are not relevant to IHT.

Amendments—[1] In para (1), in sub-paras (*f*),(2), words revoked, sub-para (*g*) inserted, and para (3) substituted, by the Taxes and Duties (Interest Rate) (Amendment) Regulations, SI 2009/2032 regs 2, 12 with effect from 12 August 2009.

5 Applicable rate of official rate of interest

. . .

Note—This Regulation is not relevant to IHT.

6 Effect of change in applicable rate

Where the rate applicable under section 178 for the purpose of any of the enactments referred to in [these Regulations][1] changes on an operative date by virtue of these Regulations, that change shall have effect for periods beginning on or after the operative date in relation to interest running from before that date as well as from or from after that date.

Amendments—[1] Words substituted by the Taxes and Duties (Interest Rate) (Amendment) Regulations, SI 2009/2032 regs 2, 14 with effect from 12 August 2009.

1992/3181

INHERITANCE TAX (MARKET MAKERS) REGULATIONS 1992

Made . . . . *11 December 1992*

Coming into force . . . . *6 January 1993*

1 Citation and commencement

These Regulations may be cited as the Inheritance Tax (Market Makers) Regulations 1992 and shall come into force on 6th January 1993.

2 Interpretation

In these Regulations "subsection (7)" and "subsection (4)" means subsection (7) of section 105 and subsection (4) of section 234 respectively of the Inheritance Tax Act 1984.

3 Application of Regulations

The day specified for the application of these Regulations in accordance with sections 106(6) and 107(7) of the Finance Act 1986 is 23rd March 1992.

4 Modification of subsection (7) and subsection (4)

Subsection (7) and subsection (4) shall have effect as if—

(*a*) the reference to The Stock Exchange in paragraph (*a*) of each of those subsections were a reference to either of The Stock Exchange and LIFFE (Administration and Management) (both being recognised investment exchanges within the meaning [given by section 285(1)(a) of the Financial Services and Markets Act 2000][1], and

(*b*) the references to the Council of The Stock Exchange in paragraph (*b*) of each of those subsections were a reference to the investment exchange concerned.

Commentary—*Simon's Taxes* **I7.112, I7.123, I11.531**; *Foster* **G1.12, 23, L5.31**.

Amendments—[1] Words in para (4)(*a*) substituted by the Financial Services and Markets Act 2000 (Consequential Amendments) (Taxes) Order, SI 2001/3629 art 135 with effect from 1 December 2001, immediately after the coming into force of SI 2001/3629 Pts 1 and 2.

1998/1515

VISITING FORCES AND ALLIED HEADQUARTERS (INHERITANCE TAX) (DESIGNATION) ORDER 1998

Made . . . . *24 June 1998*

Coming into force . . . . *24 June 1998*

Revocation—These Regulations revoked by the Visiting Forces and International Military Headquarters (NATO and PfP) (Tax Designation) Order, SI 2012/3071 art 2, Sch 1 with effect from 13 December 2012.

1998/1516

VISITING FORCES (INHERITANCE TAX) (DESIGNATION) ORDER 1998

Made . . . .*24 June 1998*

Coming into force in relation to each country specified in article 2, the date determined in accordance with . . . .*article 1(2)*

Revocation—These Regulations revoked by the Visiting Forces and International Military Headquarters (NATO and PfP) (Tax Designation) Order, SI 2012/3071 art 2, Sch 1 with effect from 13 December 2012.

2000/174

INHERITANCE TAX (SETTLED PROPERTY INCOME YIELD) ORDER 2000

Made . . . .*27 January 2000*

Laid before the House of Commons . . . .*28 January 2000*

Coming into force . . . .*18 February 2000*

Note—For transfers of value made before 18 February 2000 see Capital Transfer Tax (Settled Property Income Yield) Order 1980, SI 1980/1000.

The Treasury in exercise of the powers conferred on them by section 50(3) of the Inheritance Tax Act 1984 hereby make the following Order:

1—(1) This Order may be cited as the Inheritance Tax (Settled Property Income Yield) Order 2000 and shall come into force on 18th February 2000.

(2) This Order shall have effect in relation to transfers of value made on or after 18th February 2000.

2 In this Order references to "indices" are to the indices which are published in the Financial Times and produced in conjunction with the Institute of Actuaries and the Faculty of Actuaries.

3 The rate prescribed as the higher rate for the purposes of section 50 of the Inheritance Tax Act 1984 is the rate that is equal to the rate of the Irredeemables' yield shown in the indices which are known as the "FTSE Actuaries Government Securities UK Indices" and which are produced either—

(*a*) for the date on which the value in question is to be determined, or, if those indices are not produced for that date,

(*b*) for the latest date preceding that date for which those indices are produced.

4 The rate prescribed as the lower rate for the purposes of section 50 of the Inheritance Tax Act 1984 is the rate that is equal to the rate of the All-Share actual dividend yield shown in the indices which are known as the "FTSE Actuaries Share Indices" and which are produced either—

(*a*) for the date on which the value in question is to be determined, or, if those indices are not produced for that date,

(*b*) for the latest date preceding that date for which those indices are produced.

Commentary—*Simon's Taxes* **I5.213**.

2002/1731

INHERITANCE TAX (DELIVERY OF ACCOUNTS) (EXCEPTED TRANSFERS AND EXCEPTED TERMINATIONS) REGULATIONS 2002

Made by the Commissioners of Inland Revenue under IHTA 1984 s 256(1)(*a*)

Revocation—These Regulations revoked by the Inheritance Tax (Delivery of Accounts) (Excepted Transfers and Excepted Terminations) Regulations, SI 2008/605 reg 8 with effect in relation to any excepted transfer or excepted termination made on or after 6 April 2007: SI 2008/605 regs 1, 9.

2002/1732

INHERITANCE TAX (DELIVERY OF ACCOUNTS) (EXCEPTED SETTLEMENTS) REGULATIONS 2002

Revocation—These Regulations revoked by the Inheritance Tax (Delivery of Accounts) (Excepted Settlements) Regulations, SI 2008/606 reg 8 with effect in relation to chargeable events occurring on or after 6 April 2007: SI 2008/606 reg 1.

2002/1733

INHERITANCE TAX (DELIVERY OF ACCOUNTS) (EXCEPTED ESTATES) REGULATIONS 2002

Made by the Commissioners of Inland Revenue under IHTA 1984 s 256(1)(*a*)

Made . . . . *5 July 2002*
Laid before the House of Commons . . . . *8 July 2002*
Coming into force . . . . *1 August 2002*

Note—These Regulations revoked by the Inheritance Tax (Delivery of Accounts) (Excepted Estates) Regulations, SI 2004/2543 reg 11 with effect from 1 November 2004 for deaths occurring after 5 April 2004.

2004/1864

TAX AVOIDANCE SCHEMES (INFORMATION) REGULATIONS 2004

Made by the Treasury under FA 1999 s 132, FA 2002 s 135, FA 2004 ss 308(1), (3), 309(1), 310, 312, 313(1), (3), (4)(*g*), 317(2), 318(1)

Made . . . . *22 July 2004*
Laid before the House of Commons . . . . *22 July 2004*
Coming into force . . . . *1 August 2004*

Revocation—These Regulations are revoked by the Tax Avoidance Schemes (Information) Regulations, SI 2012/1836 reg 3, Schedule, with effect from 1 September 2012.

Note that, anything begun under or for the purpose of these Regulations shall be continued under or, as the case may be, for the purpose of the corresponding provision of SI 2012/1836. Where any document refers to a provision of a regulation revoked by SI 2012/1836, such reference shall, unless the context otherwise requires, be construed as a reference to the corresponding provision of SI 2012/1836 (see SI 2012/1836 reg 3(2), (3)).

Modification—NIC (Application of Part 7 of the Finance Act 2004) Regulations, SI 2007/785 reg 17 (for the purposes of NIC avoidance schemes and proposals, any reference in these Regulations to FA 2004 ss 306–313 shall be construed as a reference to the corresponding provisions of the 2007 Regulations; see SI 2007/785 reg 4(2)).

1 Citation, commencement and effect

(1) These Regulations may be cited as the Tax Avoidance Schemes (Information) Regulations 2004 and shall come into force on 1st August 2004.

(2) These Regulations do not have effect in respect of proposals or arrangements (as the case may be) which are notifiable by virtue of any of the provisions of Part 2 of the Schedule to the Arrangements Regulations—

(*a*) for the purposes of section 308(1), if the relevant date in relation to a proposal falls before 22nd June 2004;

(*b*) for the purposes of section 308(3), if the date on which the promoter first becomes aware of any transaction forming part of arrangements falls before that date;

(*c*) for the purposes of sections 309 and 310, if the date on which any transaction forming part of arrangements is entered into falls before that date.

Modification—NIC (Application of Part 7 of the Finance Act 2004) Regulations, SI 2007/785 reg 17 (modification of this regulation for the purposes of NIC avoidance schemes and proposals).

2 Interpretation

In the Regulations—

"the Act" means the Finance Act 2004, and a reference to a numbered section (without more) is a reference to the section of the Act which is so numbered;

"the Arrangements Regulations" means the Tax Avoidance Schemes (Prescribed Descriptions of Arrangements) [Regulations 2006][2];

["the IHT Arrangements Regulations" means the Inheritance Tax Avoidance Schemes (Prescribed Descriptions of Arrangements) Regulations 2011;][3]

["the SDLT Arrangements Regulations" means the Stamp Duty Land Tax Avoidance Schemes (Prescribed Descriptions of Arrangements) Regulations 2005;][1]

"corporation tax" shall be construed in accordance with section 318(1);

"employment" has the same meaning as it has for the purposes of the employment income Parts of the Income Tax (Earnings and Pensions) Act 2003 (see section 4 of that Act) and includes offices to which the provisions of those Parts that are expressed to apply to employments apply equally (see section 5 of that Act); and "employee" and "employer" have corresponding meanings;

"notifiable arrangements" has the meaning given by section 306(1);

"notifiable proposal" has the meaning given by section 306(2);

"promoter" has the meaning given by section 307;

"the prescribed taxes" means capital gains tax, corporation tax[, income tax[, inheritance tax][3] and stamp duty land tax][1];

"the relevant date" has the meaning given by section 308(2).

Modification—NIC (Application of Part 7 of the Finance Act 2004) Regulations, SI 2007/785 reg 17 (modification of this regulation for the purposes of NIC avoidance schemes and proposals).

Amendments—[1] Definition of "the SDLT Arrangements Regulations" inserted, and words in the definition of "the prescribed taxes" substituted, by the Tax Avoidance Schemes (Information) (Amendment) Regulations, SI 2005/1869 regs 2, 3 with effect from 1 August 2005.

However, these amendments do not have effect in respect of proposals or arrangements (as the case may be) which are notifiable by virtue of the Stamp Duty Land Tax Avoidance Schemes (Prescribed Descriptions of Arrangements) Regulations, SI 2005/1868—

(a) for the purposes of FA 2004 s 308(1), if the relevant date in relation to a proposal falls before 1 August 2005;

(b) for the purposes of FA 2004 s 308(3), if the date on which the promoter first becomes aware of any transaction forming part of the arrangements falls before that date;

(c) for the purposes of FA 2004 s 309 or 310, the date on which any transaction forming part of the arrangements is entered into falls before that date: SI 2005/1869 reg 1.

[2] Words in the definition of "the Arrangements Regulations" substituted by the Tax Avoidance Schemes (Information) (Amendment) Regulations, SI 2006/1544 regs 2, 3 with effect from 1 August 2006.

[3] Definition of "the IHT Arrangements Regulations", and words in definition of "the prescribed taxes", inserted, by the Tax Avoidance Schemes (Information) (Amendment) Regulations, SI 2011/171 regs 2, 3 with effect from 6 April 2011.

3 Prescribed information in respect of notifiable proposals and arrangements

(1) The information which must be provided to the Board by a promoter under section 308(1) in respect of a notifiable proposal is sufficient information as might reasonably be expected to enable an officer of the Board to comprehend the manner in which the proposal is intended to operate, including—

(*a*) the promoter's name and address;

(*b*) details of the provision of the Arrangements Regulations[, the IHT Arrangements Regulations][2] [or the SDLT Arrangement Regulations][1] by virtue of which the proposal is notifiable;

(*c*) a summary of the proposal and the name (if any) by which it is known;

(*d*) information explaining each element of the proposed arrangements (including the way in which they are structured) from which the tax advantage expected to be obtained under those arrangements arises; and

(*e*) the statutory provisions, relating to any of the prescribed taxes, on which that tax advantage is based.

(2) The information which must be provided to the Board by a promoter under section 308(3) in respect of notifiable arrangements is sufficient information as might reasonably be expected to enable an officer of the Board to comprehend the manner in which the arrangements are intended to operate, including—

(*a*) the promoter's name and address;

(*b*) details of the provision of the Arrangements Regulations[, the IHT Arrangements Regulations][2] [or the SDLT Arrangement Regulations][1] by virtue of which the arrangements are notifiable;

(*c*) a summary of the arrangements and the name (if any) by which they are known;

(*d*) information explaining each element of the arrangements (including the way in which they are structured) from which the tax advantage expected to be obtained under the arrangements arises; and

(*e*) the statutory provisions, relating to any of the prescribed taxes, on which that tax advantage is based.

(3) The information which must be provided to the Board by a client under section 309 (duty of person dealing with promoter outside the United Kingdom) in respect of notifiable arrangements is sufficient information as might reasonably be expected to enable an officer of the Board to comprehend the manner in which the arrangements are intended to operate, including—

(*a*) the client's name and address;

(*b*) the name and address of the promoter;

(*c*) details of the provision of the Arrangements Regulations[, the IHT Arrangements Regulations][2] [or the SDLT Arrangement Regulations][1] by virtue of which the arrangements are notifiable;

(*d*) a summary of the arrangements, and the name (if any) by which they are known;

(*e*) information explaining each element of the arrangements (including the way in which they are structured) from which the tax advantage expected to be obtained under the arrangements arises; and

(*f*) the statutory provisions, relating to any of the prescribed taxes, on which that tax advantage is based.

(4) The information which must be provided to the Board by a person obliged to do so by section 310 (duty of parties to notifiable arrangements not involving promoter) is sufficient information as might reasonably be expected to enable an officer of the Board to comprehend the manner in which the arrangements of which that transaction forms part are intended to operate, including—

(*a*) the name and address of the person entering into the transaction;

(*b*) details of the provision of the Arrangements Regulations[, the IHT Arrangements Regulations][2] [or the SDLT Arrangement Regulations][1] by virtue of which the arrangements are notifiable;

(*c*) a summary of the arrangements and the name (if any) by which they are known;

(*d*) information explaining each element of the arrangements (including the way in which they are structured) from which the tax advantage expected to be obtained under the arrangements arises; and

(*e*) the statutory provisions, relating to any of the prescribed taxes, on which that tax advantage is based.

[(5) If, but for this paragraph—

(*a*) a person would be obliged to provide information in relation to two or more notifiable arrangements,

(*b*) those arrangements are substantially the same (whether they relate to the same parties or different parties), and

(*c*) he has already provided information under paragraph (4) in relation to any of the other arrangements, he need not provide further information under paragraph (4).][1]

Commentary—*Simon's Taxes* **A7.230, A7.232.**

Modification—NIC (Application of Part 7 of the Finance Act 2004) Regulations, SI 2007/785 reg 17 (modification of this regulation for the purposes of NIC avoidance schemes and proposals).

Amendments—[1] Words inserted, and para (5) inserted, by the Tax Avoidance Schemes (Information) (Amendment) Regulations, SI 2005/1869 regs 2, 4 with effect from 1 August 2005.

However, these amendments do not have effect in respect of proposals or arrangements (as the case may be) which are notifiable by virtue of the Stamp Duty Land Tax Avoidance Schemes (Prescribed Descriptions of Arrangements) Regulations, SI 2005/1868—

(a) for the purposes of FA 2004 s 308(1), if the relevant date in relation to a proposal falls before 1 August 2005;

(b) for the purposes of FA 2004 s 308(3), if the date on which the promoter first becomes aware of any transaction forming part of the arrangements falls before that date;

(c) for the purposes of FA 2004 s 309 or 310, the date on which any transaction forming part of the arrangements is entered into falls before that date: SI 2005/1869 reg 1.

[2] In paras (1)(*b*), (2)(*b*), (3)(*c*), (4)(*b*), words inserted by the Tax Avoidance Schemes (Information) (Amendment) Regulations, SI 2011/171 regs 2, 4 with effect from 6 April 2011.

4 [Time for providing information under section 308, 308A, 309 or 310]

(1) The period or time (as the case may be) [within which—

(*a*) the prescribed information under section 308, 309 or 310, and

(*b*) the information or documents which will support or explain the prescribed information under section 308A,][4]

must be provided to the Board is found in accordance with the following paragraphs of this regulation.

[(1A) Where a proposal or arrangements (not being otherwise notifiable) is or are treated as notifiable by virtue of an order under section 306A(1), the prescribed period is the period of 10 days beginning on the day after that on which the order is made.][4]

(2) In the case of a notification under section 308(1), the prescribed period is the period of 5 days beginning with the day after the relevant date.

(3) In the case of a notification under section 308(3), the prescribed period is the period of 5 days beginning with the day after that on which the promoter first becomes aware of any transaction forming part of arrangements to which that subsection applies.

[(3A) Neither paragraph (2) nor (3) applies in a case falling within paragraph (1A) or (3B).

(3B) In the case of a requirement to provide specified information about, or documents relating to, the notifiable proposal or arrangements which arises by virtue of an order under section 308A(2), the prescribed period is the period of 10 days beginning on the day after that on which the order is made.][4]

(4) In the case of a notification under section 309(1), the prescribed period is the period of 5 days beginning with the day after that on which the client enters into the first transaction forming part of notifiable arrangements to which that subsection applies.

(5) In the case of a notification under section 310 the prescribed time is any time [during the period of 30 days beginning with the day after that on which the person enters into the first transaction forming part of the notifiable arrangements.][3]

[This is subject to [paragraph (5A)][2].][1]

(5ZA) . . .

[(5A) In the case of a notification under section 310 which arises by virtue of the application of regulation 6 of the Tax Avoidance Schemes (Promoters and Prescribed Circumstances) Regulations 2004 (persons not to be treated as promoters: legal professional privilege), the prescribed time is any time during the period of 5 days beginning with the day after [that on][4] which the person enters into the first transaction forming part of the notifiable arrangements.][1]
(6) In reckoning any period under this regulation or regulation 5 any day which is a non-business day within the meaning of section 92 of the Bills of Exchange Act 1882 shall be disregarded.
(7) Where paragraph (2), (3) or (4) applies, if the prescribed period referred to in that paragraph would otherwise end before 30th September 2004, it shall instead end upon that date.
(8) This regulation is subject to regulations 5 (statutory clearances) and 6 (transitional provisions).

Commentary—*Simon's Taxes* **A7.213, A7.231**.

Amendments—[1] Words in para (5) inserted, and para (5A) inserted, by the Tax Avoidance Schemes (Promoters, Prescribed Circumstances and Information) (Amendment) Regulations, SI 2004/2613 reg 3 with effect from 14 October 2004. However, in any case where the latest time at which a person would by virtue of para (5A) above, be required to provide information to the Board under FA 2004 s 310 would be earlier than 19 November 2004, the latest time at which that information shall be required to be provided shall instead be 19 November 2004: SI 2004/2613 reg 1.

[2] Words in para (5) substituted, and para (5ZA) revoked, by the Tax Avoidance Schemes (Information) (Amendment) Regulations, SI 2010/410, regs 2, 3, with effect from 1 April 2010.

[3] Words in para (5) substituted by the Tax Avoidance Schemes (Information) (Amendment) Regulations, SI 2006/1544 regs 2, 4 with effect from 1 August 2006.

[4] Heading, and words in paras (1), (5ZA), (5A), substituted, and paras (1A), (3A) inserted, by the Tax Avoidance Schemes (Information) (Amendment) Regulations, SI 2007/2153 regs 2, 3 with effect from 1 September 2007: SI 2007/2153 reg 1.

5 Statutory clearances

(1) If—

(*a*) a promoter must provide information under subsection (1) of section 308;
(*b*) the relevant date by reference to which he must provide that information is that referred to in subsection (2)(*a*) of that section; and
(*c*) he reasonably expects to make an application on behalf of a client under any of the provisions listed in paragraph (3) ("a clearance application");

the prescribed period is that beginning with the day after the relevant date and ending with the applicable date.
(2) The applicable date is—

(*a*) the date on which the first transaction occurs in pursuance of the arrangements, or
(*b*) if the promoter ceases to hold the reasonable expectation referred to in paragraph (1)(*c*) 5 days after he ceases to hold it.

(3) The provisions are—

(*a*) sections 215, 225, 444A and 707 of the Income and Corporation Taxes Act 1988; and
(*b*) sections 138, 139, 140B and 140D of the Taxation of Chargeable Gains Act 1992.

Commentary—*Simon's Taxes* **A7.231**.

Modification—NIC (Application of Part 7 of the Finance Act 2004) Regulations, SI 2007/785 reg 17 (modification of this regulation for the purposes of NIC avoidance schemes and proposals).

6 Time for providing information under section 308, 309 or 310: transitional provisions

. . .

Commentary—*Simon's Taxes* **A7.228**.

Amendment—This regulation revoked by the Tax Avoidance Schemes (Information) (Amendment) Regulations, SI 2006/1544 regs 2, 5 with effect from 1 August 2006.

[7 [Prescribed information under sections 312 and 312A]

For the purposes of sections 312(2) and (5) (duty of promoter to notify client of number) and 312A(2) (duty of client to notify parties of number) the prescribed information is—

(*a*) the name and address of the promoter;
(*b*) the name, or a brief description of the notifiable arrangements or proposal;
(*c*) the reference number (or if more than one, any one reference number) allocated under the provisions of section 311; and
(*d*) the date that the reference number was—
(i) sent by the promoter to the client; or (as the case may be)
(ii) sent to any other person by the client under section 312A(2).][1]

Commentary—*Simon's Taxes* **A7.233**.

Amendments—Regulation heading substituted by the Tax Avoidance Schemes (Information) (Amendment) Regulations, SI 2008/1947 regs 2, 3 with effect from 1 November 2008.

[1] This regulation substituted by the Tax Avoidance Schemes (Information) (Amendment) Regulations, SI 2009/611 regs 2, 3 with effect in relation to duties under FA 2004 ss 312 or 312A which arise on or after 1 April 2009.

7A [Time for providing information under 312A

In the case of a notification under section 312A the prescribed period is the period of 30 days beginning with—

(*a*) the day on which the client first becomes aware of any transaction forming part of notifiable arrangements or proposed notifiable arrangements; or, if later,

(*b*) the day on which the prescribed information is notified to the client by the promoter under section 312.][1]

Amendments—[1] Regulations 7A, 7B inserted by the Tax Avoidance Schemes (Information) (Amendment) Regulations, SI 2008/1947 regs 2, 4 with effect from 1 November 2008.

7B [Exemption from duty under section 312A

The duty of a client to notify other persons under section 312A does not apply to an employer of an employee where the employee by reason of employment receives or expects to receive a tax advantage in respect of income tax or capital gains tax as a result of notifiable arrangements or proposed notifiable arrangements.][1]

Amendments—[1] Regulations 7A, 7B inserted by the Tax Avoidance Schemes (Information) (Amendment) Regulations, SI 2008/1947 regs 2, 4 with effect from 1 November 2008.

[8 Prescribed information under section 313: timing and manner of delivery

(1) For the purposes of section 313(1) (duty of parties to notifiable arrangements to notify HMRC of number etc) the prescribed information is that specified in whichever of paragraphs (4)[, (5) or (5A)][2] is applicable.

(2) For the purposes of section 313(3)(*a*) (cases in which the prescribed information is to be included in returns) the prescribed cases are those specified at paragraphs (6) to [(8A)][3].

(3) For the purposes of section 313(3)(*b*) (cases in which the prescribed information is to be provided separately)—

(*a*) the prescribed cases are those specified at paragraphs (10) to [(14A)][2]; and

(*b*) the prescribed times are those specified at paragraph (15).

(4) In the cases prescribed at paragraphs (6) to [(8A)][3] the prescribed information is—

(*a*) the reference number allocated by HMRC under section 311 to the notifiable arrangements or proposed notifiable arrangements; and

(*b*) the year of assessment, tax year or accounting period (as the case may be) in which, or the date on which, the person providing the information expects a tax advantage to be obtained.

(5) In the cases prescribed at paragraphs (10) to (14) the prescribed information is—

(*a*) the name and address of the person providing it;

(*b*) any National Insurance number, tax reference number, PAYE reference number or other personal identifier allocated by HMRC to the person to whom the information relates;

(*c*) the reference number allocated to the scheme by HMRC under section 311 to the notifiable arrangements or proposed notifiable arrangements;

(*d*) the year of assessment, tax year or accounting period (as the case may be) in which, or the date on which, the person providing the information or, in the case of paragraph (10), an employee of that person, expects to obtain a tax advantage by virtue of the notifiable arrangements;

(*e*) the name of the person providing the declaration as to the accuracy and completeness of the notification; and

(*f*) the capacity in which the person mentioned in sub-paragraph (*e*) is acting.

[(5A) In the case prescribed at paragraph (14A) the prescribed information is—

(*a*) the name and address of the purchaser;

(*b*) the reference number (or, if more than one, any one reference number) allocated under the provisions of section 311;

(*c*) the address of the property forming the subject of the arrangements ("the property");

(*d*) the title number of the property (if any is allocated);

(*e*) the unique transaction reference number(if a land transaction return has been submitted to HMRC at the time the prescribed information is provided);

(*f*) the market value of the property, taking into account all chargeable interests in the property held by the same person or connected persons;

(*g*) the effective date of the first land transaction which forms part of the arrangements;

(*h*) the name of the person providing the declaration as to the accuracy and completeness of the notification; and

(i) the capacity in which that person is acting.][2]

(6) Subject to paragraphs (10), (12) and (13), in the case of a person who—

(*a*) expects an advantage to arise in respect of his liability to pay, entitlement to a repayment of, or to a deferment of his liability to pay, income tax or capital gains tax as a result of notifiable arrangements; and

(*b*) is required to make a return to HMRC by a notice under section 8 or 8A of the Taxes Management Act 1970 (income tax and capital gains tax: personal return and trustee's return), in respect of income tax or capital gains tax,

the prescribed information shall be included in the return under that section which relates to the year of assessment in which the person first enters into a transaction forming part of the notifiable arrangements and in the return for each subsequent year of assessment until the advantage ceases to apply to that person.

This paragraph does not apply if the advantage arises in respect of a partner's share of partnership profits or gains.

(7) Subject to paragraphs (10), (12) and (13), in the case of a company which—

(*a*) expects a tax advantage to arise in respect of its liability to pay, entitlement to a repayment of, or to a deferment of its liability to pay, corporation tax as a result of notifiable arrangements; and

(*b*) is required to make a return to HMRC by a notice under paragraph 3 of Schedule 18 to the Finance Act 1998 (company tax return), in respect of corporation tax,

the prescribed information shall be notified to HMRC in the return under that paragraph covering the period in which the company first enters into a transaction forming part of the notifiable arrangements and in the return covering each subsequent period until the tax advantage ceases to apply to the company.

This paragraph does not apply if the advantage arises in respect of a partner's share of partnership profits or gains.

(8) Subject to paragraphs (10) to (13) [and (14A)][2], in the case of a partnership—

(*a*) which expects an advantage to arise in respect of a partner's liability to pay, entitlement to a repayment of, or to a deferment of the partner's liability to pay any of the prescribed taxes in respect of partnership profits or gains as a result of notifiable arrangements; and

(*b*) in respect of which a return is required to be made to the Board by virtue of a notice under section 12AA of the Taxes Management Act 1970 (partnership return) in respect of any of the prescribed taxes,

the prescribed information shall be included in the returns specified in paragraph (9) covering the period in which the partnership first enters into a transaction forming part of the notifiable arrangements and in the returns covering each subsequent period until the tax advantage ceases to apply to the partner in question.

[(8A) Subject to paragraphs (11A), (12) and (13) in the case of a person who—

(*a*) is a party to notifiable arrangements which are prescribed by the Inheritance Tax Avoidance Schemes (Prescribed Descriptions of Arrangements) Regulations 2011; and

(*b*) is required to make a return to HMRC under section 216 of the Inheritance Tax Act 1984 in respect of a transaction forming part of the notifiable arrangements,

the prescribed information shall be notified to HMRC in the return under that section.][3]

(9) The returns referred to in paragraph (8) are—

(*a*) the partnership's return under section 12AA of the Taxes Management Act 1970; and

(*b*) the return under section 8 or 8A of that Act, or under paragraph 3 of Schedule 18 to the Finance Act 1998, of the partner in respect of whom an advantage is expected.

(10) In the case of a person who is the employer of an employee, by reason of whose employment a tax advantage is expected to arise to any person in respect of income tax, corporation tax or capital gains tax as a result of notifiable arrangements—

(*a*) paragraphs (6) to (8) shall not apply; and

(*b*) the prescribed information shall be provided separately to HMRC in such form and manner as they may specify by the time in paragraph (15).

(11) In the case of a person who would be obliged to comply with a duty under paragraphs (6) to (8), but is not required, in respect of a year of assessment, accounting period or tax year—

(*a*) in the case of notifiable arrangements to which paragraph (6) applies, to make a return under either of the provisions mentioned in paragraph (6)(*b*);

(*b*) in the case of notifiable arrangements to which paragraph (7) applies, to make a return under the provision referred to in paragraph (7)(b); or

(*c*) in the case of notifiable arrangements to which paragraph (8) applies, to make a return under any of the provisions in paragraph (9);

the person must provide the information specified in paragraph (5) separately to HMRC in such form and manner as they may specify by the time in paragraph (15).

[(11A) In the case of a person who—

(*a*) is a party to notifiable arrangements which are prescribed by the Inheritance Tax Avoidance Schemes (Prescribed Descriptions of Arrangements) Regulations 2011; and

(*b*) is not required to make a return to HMRC under section 216 of the Inheritance Tax Act 1984 in respect of a transaction forming part of the notifiable arrangements within a period of 12 months of the end of the month in which the first transaction forming part of the arrangements is entered into,

the prescribed information shall be provided separately to HMRC in such form and manner as they may specify.][3]

(12) In a case of a person who is obliged to comply with a duty under paragraphs (6) to [(8A)][3] and—

(a) the relevant return is not delivered by the filing date; or

(b) the relevant return is delivered by the filing date but does not include the prescribed information;

paragraphs (6) to [(8A)][3] shall not apply and the prescribed information shall be provided separately to HMRC in such form and manner as they may specify by the time in paragraph (15).

(13) In a case where—

(a) a person is required to provide information relating to more than one reference number;

(b) the information is included in a return under paragraphs (6) to [(8A)][3]; and

(c) the number of reference numbers in relation to which information is required exceeds the number of spaces allocated to the information on the return form;

the information relating to so many of the reference numbers as exceeds the number of allocated spaces shall be provided separately to HMRC in such form and manner as they may specify by the time in paragraph (15).

(14) In addition to the duty under any other paragraph above, in a case where the arrangements give rise to a claim submitted separately from the return under—

(a) section 261B of the Taxation of Chargeable Gains Act 1992 (treating trade loss etc as CGT loss); or

(b) Part 4 of the Income Tax Act 2007 (loss relief);

the prescribed information shall be provided separately to HMRC in such form and manner as they may specify at the time in paragraph (15).

[(14A) In a case where a purchaser expects an advantage to arise in respect of his liability to pay, entitlement to a repayment of, or to a deferment of his liability to pay stamp duty land tax as a result of notifiable arrangements the prescribed information shall be provided separately to HMRC in such form and manner as they may specify by the time in paragraph (15).

(14B) If paragraph 14A applies in relation to a land transaction entered into as purchaser by or on behalf of a partnership notification of the prescribed information by or in relation to the responsible partners may instead be done by or in relation to a representative partner or partners.][2]

(15) The prescribed times for providing information separately under paragraphs (10) to [(14A)][2] are—

(a) in the case of paragraph (10), any time during the period ending on the date on which—

(i) the return under regulation 73 of the Income Tax (Pay As You Earn) Regulations 2003 is or would be due in respect of the tax year in which the employer first enters into a transaction forming part of the notifiable arrangements; and

(ii) the return for each subsequent year is or would be due until an advantage ceases to apply to any person;

(b) in the case of paragraph (11)—

(i) for sub-paragraph (a), any time during the period ending on 31st January next following the end of the year of assessment in question;

(ii) for sub-paragraph (b), any time during the period ending on the date defined as the filing date for the purposes of paragraph 14 of Schedule 18 to the Finance Act 1998 in respect of the period of account in question;

(iii) for sub-paragraph (c), any time during the period ending on the earliest date by which the person in question could be required to file a return under section 12AA of the Taxes Management Act 1970, determined in accordance with whichever of subsections (4) and (5) of that section is applicable;

[(ba) in the case of paragraph (11A), any time during the period of 12 months of the end of the month in which the first transaction forming part of the arrangement is entered into.][3]

(c) in the case of paragraphs (12) and (13), any time during the period ending on the filing date for the relevant return;

(d) in the case of paragraph (14), the time that the claim is made;

[(e) in the case of paragraph (14A) no later than 30 days following the later of—

(i) the effective date of the first land transaction which forms part of the arrangements; or

(ii) the receipt of the reference number allocated under the provisions of section 311.][2]

(16) For the purposes of paragraph (15)(c) "the filing date" is whichever date in paragraph (i) to (iii) of paragraph (15)(b) applies to the relevant return.

[(16A) In paragraphs (5A), (14A), (14B) and (15), expressions which are used in Part 4 of the Finance Act 2003 have the same meaning as in that Part.][2]

(17) This regulation does not apply to information provided in respect of the SDLT Arrangement Regulations.[2]][1]

Commentary—*Simon's Taxes* **A7.233.**

Amendments—[1] This regulation substituted by the Tax Avoidance Schemes (Information) (Amendment) Regulations, SI 2009/611 regs 2, 4 with effect in relation to—

(a) reference numbers notified to a person under FA 2004 ss 311, 312 or 312A on or after 1 April 2009, where that person has a duty under FA 2004 s 313; and

(b) claims under either of the provisions mentioned in para (14) of the substituted reg 8 above, made on or after 1 April 2009 (SI 2009/611 reg 1(3)).

2 Words in paras (1), (3)(*a*), (15) substituted, words in para (8), and paras (5A), (14A), (14B), (16A) inserted, and para (17) revoked, by the Tax Avoidance Schemes (Information) (Amendment) Regulations, SI 2010/410, regs 2, 3, with effect from 1 April 2010.

3 In paras (2), (4), (12), (13)(*b*), reference substituted for reference "(8)", and paras (8A), (11A) and (15)(*b*) inserted, by the Tax Avoidance Schemes (Information) (Amendment) Regulations, SI 2011/171 regs 2, 5 with effect from 6 April 2011.

8ZA [Prescribed information under section 313ZA: information and timing

(1) For the purposes of section 313ZA(3) (duty of promoter to provide client lists)—

(*a*) the prescribed period is 30 days;

(*b*) the prescribed information is—

(i) any reference number allocated by HMRC under section 311 to the arrangements (or to a proposal for them) to which the information provided relates;

(ii) the name and address of each client in relation to whom the relevant date occurs in the relevant period in relation to which the information is being provided;

(ii) the promoter's name and address; and

(iv) the end date of the relevant period in relation to which the information is being provided.

(*c*) in sub-paragraph (*b*)(ii) the address of the client is the address to which the promoter has sent or would have sent the prescribed information under section 312.

(2) For the purposes of section 313ZA(4) the relevant period is each calendar quarter.][1]

Amendments—[1] Reg 8ZA inserted by the Tax Avoidance Schemes (Information) (Amendment) (No 2) Regulations, SI 2010/2928 regs 2, 3 with effect from 1 January 2011.

8A [Time for providing information under section 313A and 313B

(1) In the case of a requirement under or by virtue of section 313A(1), the prescribed period is the period of 10 days beginning on the day after that on which the notice is issued.

(2) In the case of a requirement under or by virtue of section 313B(1), the prescribed period is the period of 14 days beginning on the day after that on which the order is made.][1]

Amendments—[1] This reg inserted by the Tax Avoidance Schemes (Information) (Amendment) Regulations, SI 2007/2153 regs 2, 4 with effect from 1 September 2007: SI 2007/2153 reg 1.

8B [Higher rate of penalty following a failure to comply with an order under section 306A or 314A

(1) For the purposes of section 98C(2A) of the Taxes Management Act 1970 (higher rate of penalty after the making of an order under section 306A) the prescribed period is the period of 10 days beginning on the date on which the order is made.

(2) For the purposes of section 98C(2B) of the Taxes Management Act 1970 (higher rate of penalty after the making of an order under section 314A) the prescribed period is the period of 10 days beginning on the date on which the order is made.][1]

Amendments—[1] This reg substituted by the Tax Avoidance Schemes (Information) (Amendment) (No 2) Regulations, SI 2010/2928 regs 2, 4 with effect from 1 January 2011.

8C [Prescribed information under section 313C: information and timing

(1) For the purposes of section 313C(1) (information provided to introducers) the prescribed information is—

(*a*) P's name and address; and

(*b*) the name and address of each person who has provided P with any information relating to the proposal.

(2) For the purposes of section 313C(3)(a) the prescribed period is 10 days.][1]

Amendments—[1] This reg inserted by the Tax Avoidance Schemes (Information) (Amendment) (No 2) Regulations, SI 2010/2928 regs 2, 5 with effect from 1 January 2011.

9 Exemption from liability for penalty

For the purposes of section 313(4)(*g*) (exemption from liability to penalty under other provisions about returns in respect of duty to notify Board of reference number for notifiable arrangements) section 98A(4) of the Taxes Management Act 1970 is prescribed.

10 Electronic delivery of information

(1) Information required to be delivered to the Board or to any other person by virtue of these Regulations may be delivered in such form and by such means of electronic communications as are for the time being authorised for that purpose.

(2) The use of a particular means of electronic communications is authorised for the purposes of paragraph (1) only if—

(*a*) it is authorised by directions given by the Board under section 132(5) of the Finance Act 1999 (voluntary filing by electronic means of returns and other documents); and

(*b*) the user complies with any conditions imposed by the Board under that section.

(3) Nothing in this regulation prevents the delivery of information by electronic communications if the information is contained in a return which is—

(a) authorised to be delivered electronically by virtue of regulations under section 132 of the Finance Act 1999; or

(b) required to be so delivered by virtue of regulations under section 135 of the Finance Act 2002 (mandatory e-filing).

Modification—NIC (Application of Part 7 of the Finance Act 2004) Regulations, SI 2007/785 reg 17 (modification of this regulation for the purposes of NIC avoidance schemes and proposals).

2004/2543

INHERITANCE TAX (DELIVERY OF ACCOUNTS) (EXCEPTED ESTATES) REGULATIONS 2004

Made by the Commissioners of Inland Revenue under IHTA 1984 s 256(1)

Made .... *27 September 2004*
Laid before the House of Commons .... *28 September 2004*
Coming into force .... *1 November 2004*

1 Citation, commencement and effect

These Regulations may be cited as the Inheritance Tax (Delivery of Accounts) (Excepted Estates) Regulations 2004, shall come into force on 1st November 2004 and shall have effect in relation to deaths occurring on or after 6th April 2004.

2 Interpretation

In these Regulations—

"the Board" means the [Commissioners for Her Majesty's Revenue and Customs][2];

"the 1984 Act" means the Inheritance Tax Act 1984;

"an excepted estate" has the meaning given in regulation 4;

["IHT threshold" has the meaning given in regulation 5A;][3]

"the prescribed period" in relation to any person is the period beginning with that person's death and ending—

(a) in England, Wales and Northern Ireland, 35 days after the making of the first grant of representation in respect of that person (not being a grant limited in duration, in respect of property or to any special purpose); or

(b) in Scotland, 60 days after the date on which confirmation to that person's estate was first issued;

["section 131 rights" means the rights of issue under section 131(2) of the Civil Partnership Act 2004;][1]

"spouse[, civil partner][1] and charity transfer" has the meaning given in regulation 5;

"value" means value for the purpose of tax.

Amendments—[1] Definition of "section 131 rights" inserted, and words in definition of "spouse and charity transfer" inserted by Tax and Civil Partnership (No 2) Regulations, SI 2005/3230, reg 15(1), (2), with effect from 5 December 2005 (reg 1).

[2] Words in definition of "the Board" substituted by Inheritance Tax (Delivery of Accounts) (Excepted Estates) (Amendment) Regulations, SI 2006/2141, regs 2, 3, with effect in relation to deaths occurring on or after 1 September 2006.

[3] Definition of "IHT threshold" substituted by the Inheritance Tax (Delivery of Accounts) (Excepted Estates) (Amendment) Regulations, SI 2011/214 reg 2 with effect in relation to deaths occurring on or after 6 April 2010 (reg 1(3)).

3 Accounts

(1) No person is required to deliver an account under section 216 of the 1984 Act of the property comprised in an excepted estate.

(2) If in reliance on these Regulations a person has not delivered an account paragraphs (3) and (4) apply.

(3) If it is discovered at any time that the estate is not an excepted estate, the delivery to the Board within six months of that time of an account of the property comprised in that estate shall satisfy any requirement to deliver an account.

(4) If the estate is no longer an excepted estate following an alteration of the dispositions taking effect on death within section 142 of the 1984 Act, the delivery to the Board within six months of the date of the instrument of variation of an account of the property comprised in that estate shall satisfy any requirement to deliver an account.

4 Excepted estates

(1) An excepted estate means the estate of a person immediately before his death in the circumstances prescribed by paragraphs (2), (3) or [(5)][2].

(2) The circumstances prescribed by this paragraph are that—

(a) the person died on or after 6th April 2004, domiciled in the United Kingdom;

(b) the value of that person's estate is attributable wholly to property passing—

(i) under his will or intestacy,

(ii) under a nomination of an asset taking effect on death,

(iii) under a single settlement in which he was entitled to an interest in possession in settled property, or

(iv) by survivorship in a beneficial joint tenancy or, in Scotland, by survivorship in a special destination;

(*c*) of that property —

(i) not more than [£150,000][2] represented value attributable to property which, immediately before that person's death, was settled property; and

(ii) not more than [£100,000][2] represented value attributable to property which, immediately before that person's death, was situated outside the United Kingdom;

[(*ca*) that person was not a person by reason of whose death one of the alternatively secured pension fund provisions applies;][2]

(*d*) [subject to paragraph (7A),][3] that person died without having made any chargeable transfers during the period of seven years ending with his death other than specified transfers where, subject to paragraph (7), the aggregate value transferred did not exceed [£150,000][2]; and

(*e*) the aggregate of—

(i) the gross value of that person's estate,

(ii) subject to paragraph (7), the value transferred by any specified transfers made by that person, and

(iii) the value transferred by any specified exempt transfers made by that person,

did not exceed the IHT threshold.

(3) The circumstances prescribed by this paragraph are that—

(*a*) the person died on or after 6th April 2004, domiciled in the United Kingdom;

(*b*) the value of that person's estate is attributable wholly to property passing—

(i) under his will or intestacy,

(ii) under a nomination of an asset taking effect on death,

(iii) under a single settlement in which he was entitled to an interest in possession in settled property, or

(iv) by survivorship in a beneficial joint tenancy or, in Scotland, by survivorship in a special destination;

(*c*) of that property—

(i) subject to paragraph (8), not more than [£150,000][2] represented value attributable to property which, immediately before that person's death, was settled property; and

(ii) not more than [£100,000][2] represented value attributable to property which, immediately before that person's death, was situated outside the United Kingdom;

[(*ca*) that person was not a person by reason of whose death one of the alternatively secured pension fund provisions applies;][2]

(*d*) [subject to paragraph (7A),][3] that person died without having made any chargeable transfers during the period of seven years ending with his death other than specified transfers where, subject to paragraph (7), the aggregate value transferred did not exceed [£150,000][2];

(*e*) the aggregate of—

(i) the gross value of that person's estate,

(ii) subject to paragraph (7), the value transferred by any specified transfers made by that person, and

(iii) the value transferred by any specified exempt transfers made by that person, did not exceed £1,000,000; . . . [3]

[(*ea*) the total value transferred on that person's death by a spouse, civil partner or charity transfer is greater than nil; and][3]

(*f*) the aggregate of—

$$A-(B+C)$$

does not exceed the IHT threshold, where—

A is the aggregate of the values in sub-paragraph (*e*),

B, subject to paragraph (4), is the total value transferred on that person's death by a spouse[, civil partner][1] or charity transfer, and

C[, subject to paragraph (7B),][5] is the total liabilities of the estate.

[(4) In Scotland, if legitim or section 131 rights could be claimed which would reduce the value of the spouse, civil partner or charity transfer, the value of B is reduced—

(*a*) to take account of any legitim or section 131 rights claimed, and

(*b*) on the basis that any part of the remaining legitim fund, which has been neither claimed nor renounced at the time of the application for confirmation, will be claimed in full, and

(*c*) on the basis that all section 131 rights, which have been neither claimed nor renounced at the time of the application for confirmation, will be claimed in full.][1]

(5) The circumstances prescribed by this paragraph are that—

(*a*) the person died on or after 6th April 2004;

[(*b*) that person was never domiciled in the United Kingdom or treated as domiciled in the United Kingdom by section 267 of the 1984 Act;

(*ba*) that person was not a person by reason of whose death one of the alternatively secured pension fund provisions applies; and][2]

(*c*) the value of that person's estate situated in the United Kingdom is wholly attributable to cash or quoted shares or securities passing under his will or intestacy or by survivorship in a beneficial joint tenancy or, in Scotland, by survivorship in a special destination, the gross value of which does not exceed [£150,000][2].

(6) For the purposes of paragraphs (2) and (3)—

"specified transfers"[, subject to paragraph (7A),][3] means chargeable transfers made by a person during the period of seven years ending with that person's death where the value transferred is attributable to—

(*a*) cash;

(*b*) personal chattels or corporeal moveable property;

(*c*) quoted shares or securities; or

(*d*) an interest in or over land, save to the extent that sections 102 and 102A(2) of the Finance Act 1986 apply to that transfer or the land became settled property on that transfer;

"specified exempt transfers" means transfers of value made by a person during the period of seven years ending with that person's death which are exempt transfers only by reason of—

(*a*) section 18 (transfers between spouses [or civil partners][1]),

(*b*) section 23 (gifts to charities),

(*c*) section 24 (gifts to political parties),

(*d*) section 24A (gifts to housing associations),

(*e*) section 27 (maintenance funds for historic buildings, etc), or

(*f*) section 28 (employee trusts) of the 1984 Act.

(7) For the purpose of paragraphs (2)(*d*) and (*e*) and (3)(*d*) and (*e*), sections 104 (business property relief) and 116 (agricultural property relief) of the 1984 Act shall not apply in determining the value transferred by a chargeable transfer.

[(7A) For the purpose of paragraphs (2)(*d*) and (*e*), (3)(*d*) and (*e*) and (6) any transfers of value made by that person in any period from 6th April in any year until and including the following 5th April which—

(i) are exempt transfers by virtue of section 21 (normal expenditure out of income) of the 1984 Act,

(ii) are made less than seven years prior to the death of that person, and

(iii) are in total more than £3,000,

shall be treated as chargeable transfers.][3]

[(7B) For the purpose of paragraph (3)(*f*) "the total liabilities of the estate" do not include liabilities of the estate to the extent that they—

(*a*) are not discharged as mentioned in section 175A(1)(*a*) of the 1984 Act (discharge of liabilities after death);

(*b*) are prevented from being taken into account as mentioned in section 175A(1)(b) of the 1984 Act (discharge of liabilities after death); or

(*c*) are attributable as mentioned in section 162A(1)(a) or (b), or section 162A(5), of the 1984 Act (liabilities attributable to financing excluded property).][5]

(8) Paragraph (3)(*c*)(i) does not apply to property which immediately before the person's death was settled property, to the extent that the property is transferred on that person's death by a spouse[, civil partner][1] or charity transfer.

[(9) In this regulation "the alternatively secured pension fund provisions" means the following sections of the 1984 Act—

(*a*) section 151A (person dying with alternatively secured pension fund);

(*b*) section 151B (relevant dependant with pension fund inherited from member over 75); and

(*c*) section 151C (dependant dying with other pension fund).][2]

[(10) Paragraphs (2)(*ca*), (3)(*ca*) and (5)(*ba*) shall not have effect in relation to deaths occurring on or after 6th April 2011.][4]

Amendments—[1] In para (3)(*f*), in the definition B, words inserted; in para (6), in sub-para (*a*) of the definition of "specified exempt transfers", words inserted; in para (8) words inserted; and para (4) substituted, by the Tax and Civil Partnership (No 2) Regulations, SI 2005/3230, reg 15(1), (3), with effect from 5 December 2005.

[2] In paras (1), (2)(*c*)(i), (ii), (*d*), (3)(*c*)(i), (ii), (*d*), (5)(*c*) figures substituted; paras (5)(*b*), (*ba*) substituted for original para (5)(*b*); and paras (2)(*ca*), (3)(*ca*), (9) inserted, by Inheritance Tax (Delivery of Accounts) (Excepted Estates) (Amendment) Regulations, SI 2006/2141, regs 2, 4, with effect in relation to deaths occurring on or after 1 September 2006.

[3] In paras (2)(*d*), (6) words inserted, in para (3) words in sub-para (*d*) inserted, word "and" in sub-para (*e*) revoked, and sub-para (*ea*) inserted, and para (7A) inserted, by the Inheritance Tax (Delivery of Accounts) (Excepted Estates) (Amendment) Regulations, SI 2011/214 reg 3 with effect in relation to deaths occurring on or after 1 March 2011.

[4] Para (10) inserted by the Inheritance Tax (Delivery of Accounts) (Excepted Estates) (Amendment) (No 2) Regulations, SI 2011/2226 reg 2 with effect from 1 October 2011.

[5] Words in para (3)(*f*), and whole of para (7B), inserted, by the Inheritance Tax (Delivery of Accounts) (Excepted Estates) (Amendment) Regulations, SI 2014/488 reg 2 with effect in relation to deaths occurring on or after 1 April 2014.

5 Spouse[, civil partner] and charity transfers

(1) For the purposes of these Regulations, a spouse[, civil partner][1] or charity transfer means any disposition (whether effected by will, under the law relating to intestacy or otherwise) of property comprised in a person's estate—

(*a*) subject to paragraph (2), to the person's spouse [or civil partner][1] within section 18(1) of the 1984 Act; and

(*b*) subject to paragraph (3), to a charity within section 23(1) of the 1984 Act or for national purposes within section 25(1) of the 1984 Act.

(2) A transfer is not a spouse [or civil partner][1] transfer within paragraph (1)(*a*) if either spouse [or civil partner][1] was not domiciled in the United Kingdom at any time prior to the transfer.

(3) A transfer is not a charity transfer within paragraph (1)(*b*) if the property becomes comprised in a settlement as a result of the disposition.

Amendments—[1] In heading and paras (1), (2), words inserted by the Tax and Civil Partnership (No 2) Regulations, SI 2005/3230, reg 15(1), (4), with effect from 5 December 2005.

5A [IHT threshold

(1) Subject to paragraph (2), for the purposes of these Regulations "IHT threshold" means the amount shown in the second column in the first row of the Table in Schedule 1 to the 1984 Act (upper limit of portion of value charged at rate of nil per cent) and in the first column in the second row of that Table (lower limit of portion charged at next rate) applicable to—

(*a*) chargeable transfers made in the year before that in which a person's death occurred if—

(i) that person died on or after 6th April and before 6th August, and

(ii) an application for a grant of representation or, in Scotland, an application for confirmation, is made before 6th August in that year; or

(*b*) chargeable transfers made in the year in which a person's death occurred in any other case,

and for this purpose "year" means a period of twelve months ending with 5th April.

(2) Where the criteria specified in paragraphs (3) and (4) are met "IHT threshold" means the IHT threshold as defined in paragraph (1) as increased by 100 per cent.

(3) The criteria specified in this paragraph are as follows—

(*a*) immediately before the death of a person (referred to for the purposes of this paragraph and paragraphs (4), (5) and (6), as a "first deceased person") that first deceased person was the spouse or civil partner of the person specified in regulation 4(2) or (3) (referred to for the purposes of this paragraph as "the survivor");

(*b*) the survivor survived the first deceased person;

(*c*) either—

(i) in a case where the first deceased person was the spouse of the survivor, the first deceased person died on or after 13th November 1974, or

(ii) in a case where the first deceased person was the civil partner of the survivor, the first deceased person died on or after 5th December 2005; and

(*d*) a claim is made pursuant to section 8A of the 1984 Act—

(i) by virtue of which the nil-rate band maximum at the time of the survivor's death is treated, for the purpose of the charge to tax on the death of the survivor, as increased by 100 per cent, and

(ii) which is made in respect of not more than one first deceased person.

(4) The criteria specified in this paragraph are as follows—

(*a*) the first deceased person died domiciled in the United Kingdom;

(*b*) the value of the first deceased person's estate is attributable wholly to property passing—

(i) under the first deceased person's will or intestacy, or

(ii) by survivorship in a beneficial joint tenancy or, in Scotland, by survivorship in a special destination;

(*c*) of that property, not more than £100,000 represented value attributable to property which immediately before the first deceased person's death was situated outside the United Kingdom;

(*d*) the first deceased person was not a person by reason of whose death one of the alternatively secured pension fund provisions applies;

(*e*) the first deceased person died without having made any chargeable transfers during the period of seven years ending with the first deceased person's death; and (*f*) the value transferred by any chargeable transfer made on the death of the first deceased person was not reduced by virtue of section 104 (business property relief) or section 116 (agricultural property relief) of the 1984 Act.

(5) For the purpose of paragraph 4(*e*), sections 104 (business property relief) and 116 (agricultural property relief) of the 1984 Act shall not apply in determining whether the first deceased person has made a chargeable transfer.

(6) Subject to paragraph [(8)(*a*)][1], for the purpose of paragraph (4)(*e*) any transfers of value made by the first deceased person in any period from 6th April in any year until and including the following 5th April which—

(i) are exempt transfers by virtue of section 21 (normal expenditure out of income) of the 1984 Act,

(ii) are made less than seven years prior to the death of that person, and

(iii) are in total more than £3,000,

shall be treated as chargeable transfers.

[(7) In this regulation "the alternatively secured pension fund provisions" means the following sections of the 1984 Act—

(*a*) section 151A (person dying with alternatively secured pension fund);

(*b*) section 151B (relevant dependant with pension fund inherited from member over 75); and

(*c*) section 151C (dependant dying with other pension fund).

(8) In this regulation—

(*a*) paragraph (6) shall have effect in relation to deaths occurring on or after 1st March 2011; and

(*b*) paragraph (7) shall have effect in relation to deaths occurring on or after 6th April 2010.][1]

Amendments—[1] Reg 5A inserted by the Inheritance Tax (Delivery of Accounts) (Excepted Estates) (Amendment) Regulations, SI 2011/214 reg 4 with effect in relation to deaths occurring on or after 6 April 2010 (reg 1(3)).

6 Production of information

[(1) Subject to [paragraphs (3) and (4)][3], a person who by virtue of these Regulations is not required to deliver to the Board an account under section 216 of the 1984 Act of the property comprised in an excepted estate, must produce the information specified in paragraph (2) and, where the criteria specified in regulation 5A(3) and (4) are met, paragraph (2A), to the Board in such form as the Board may prescribe.][2]

(2) The information specified for the purpose of paragraph (1) is—

(*a*) the following details in relation to the deceased—

(i) full name;

(ii) date of death;

(iii) marital [or civil partnership][1] status;

(iv) occupation;

(v) any surviving spouse [or civil partner][1], parent, brother or sister;

(vi) he number of surviving children, step-children, adopted children or grandchildren;

(vii) national insurance number, tax district and tax reference;

(viii) if the deceased was not domiciled in the United Kingdom at his date of death, his domicile and address;

(*b*) details of all property to which the deceased was beneficially entitled and the value of that property;

(*c*) details of any specified transfers, specified exempt transfers and the value of those transfers;

(*d*) the liabilities of the estate; and

(*e*) any spouse[, civil partner][1] or charity transfers and the value of those transfers.

[(2A) The information specified for the purpose of paragraph (1) is—

(*a*) the full name of the first deceased person,

(*b*) the last known address of the first deceased person,

(*c*) the date of death of the first deceased person,

(*d*) the date and place of the marriage or civil partnership (as the case may be) between the first deceased person and the survivor, and

(*e*) either—

(i) a statement specifying whether a grant of probate, grant of letters of administration or grant of confirmation was issued in relation to the estate of the first deceased person and the date and place of issue of such grant, or

(ii) a statement specifying that no grant of probate, grant of letters of administration or grant of confirmation was issued in relation to the estate of the first deceased person.

(2B) In paragraph (2A) "first deceased person" and "survivor" shall have the meaning given to them in regulation 5A(3)(*a*).][2]

(3) Paragraph (1) does not apply [to the extent that the information][2] specified in paragraph (2) [and, where applicable, paragraph (2A)][2] has been produced in an account under section 216 of the 1984 Act of the property comprised in the excepted estate that has been delivered to the Board.

[(4) Paragraph (2)(*a*)(v) and (vi) shall not have effect in relation to information produced to the Board pursuant to paragraph (1) of this regulation on or after 1st March 2011.][3]

Amendments—[1] In para (2) words inserted by the Tax and Civil Partnership (No 2) Regulations, SI 2005/3230, reg 15(1), (5), with effect from 5 December 2005.

[2] Para (1) substituted, paras (2A), (2B) inserted, and in para (3) words substituted and words inserted, by the Inheritance Tax (Delivery of Accounts) (Excepted Estates) (Amendment) Regulations, SI 2011/214 reg 5 with effect in relation to deaths occurring on or after 6 April 2010 (reg 1(3)).

[3] In para (1), words substituted, and para (4) inserted, by the Inheritance Tax (Delivery of Accounts) (Excepted Estates) (Amendment) (No 2) Regulations, SI 2011/2226 reg 4 with effect from 1 October 2011.

7—(1) The information specified in regulation 6(2) [and (2A)][1] must be produced to the Board by producing it to—

(*a*) a probate registry in England and Wales;
(*b*) the sheriff in Scotland;
(*c*) the Probate and Matrimonial Office in Northern Ireland.

(2) Information produced in accordance with paragraph (1) is to be treated for all purposes of the 1984 Act as produced to the Board.

(3) The person or body specified in paragraph (1) must transmit the information produced to them to the Board within one week of the issue of the grant of probate or confirmation.

Amendments—[1] In para (1), words inserted by the Inheritance Tax (Delivery of Accounts) (Excepted Estates) (Amendment) Regulations, SI 2011/214 reg 6 with effect in relation to deaths occurring on or after 6 April 2010 (reg 1(3)).

8 Discharge of persons and property from tax

(1) Subject to paragraph (2) and regulation 9, if the information specified in regulation 6 has been produced in accordance with these Regulations, all persons shall on the expiration of the prescribed period be discharged from any claim for tax on the value transferred by the chargeable transfer made on the deceased's death and attributable to the value of the property comprised in an excepted estate and any Inland Revenue charge for that tax shall then be extinguished.

(2) Paragraph (1) shall not apply if within the prescribed period the Board issue a notice to—

(*a*) the person or persons who would apart from these Regulations be required to deliver an account under section 216 of the 1984 Act, or
(*b*) the solicitor or agent of that person or those persons who produced the specified information pursuant to regulation 6, requiring additional information or documents to be produced in relation to the specified information produced pursuant to regulation 6.

9 Regulation [8][1] shall not discharge any person from tax in the case of fraud or failure to disclose material facts and shall not affect any tax that may be payable if further property is later shown to form part of the estate and, in consequence of that property, the estate is not an excepted estate.

Amendments—[1] Figure substituted by Inheritance Tax (Delivery of Accounts) (Excepted Estates) (Amendment) Regulations, SI 2006/2141, regs 2, 5, with effect in relation to deaths occurring on or after 1 September 2006.

10 Transfers reported late

An account of an excepted estate shall, for the purposes of section 264(8) of the 1984 Act (delivery of account to be treated as payment where tax rate nil), be treated as having been delivered on the last day of the prescribed period in relation to that person.

11 Revocation

The Inheritance Tax (Delivery of Accounts) (Excepted Estates) Regulations 2002 and the Inheritance Tax (Delivery of Accounts) (Excepted Estates) (Amendment) Regulations 2003 are revoked in relation to deaths occurring on or after 6th April 2004.

2005/3441

INHERITANCE TAX (DOUBLE CHARGES RELIEF) REGULATIONS 2005

Made by the Commissioners for Her Majesty's Revenue and Customs under FA 1986 s 104

Made . . . . *14 December 2005*
Laid before the House of Commons . . . . *14 December 2005*
Coming into force . . . . *4 January 2006*

1 Citation, commencement and interpretation

(1) These Regulations may be cited as the Inheritance Tax (Double Charges Relief) Regulations 2005, and shall come into force on 4th January 2006.

(2) In these Regulations—

"the Commissioners" means the Commissioners for Her Majesty's Revenue and Customs;
"the debt" means the debt mentioned in regulation 3(2);
"the relevant property" has the meaning given in regulation 3(6).

2 General

(1) These Regulations apply in the circumstances specified in regulation 3.

(2) They apply for the purposes of paragraph (*d*) of section 104(1) of the Finance Act 1986 (which refers to circumstances appearing to the Commissioners to be circumstances similar to those referred to in paragraphs (*a*) to (*c*) of that provision).

(3) To the extent specified in regulation 4, these Regulations apply for the avoidance of double charges to tax.

3 Circumstances in which these Regulations apply

(1) These Regulations apply where conditions A to D are met.

(2) Condition A is that an individual ("the deceased") enters into arrangements ("the arrangements") under which—

(*a*) the disposal condition or the contribution condition is met as respects the relevant property, and

(*b*) the deceased makes a transfer of value as a result of which a third party becomes entitled to the benefit of a debt ("the debt") owed to the deceased.

(3) Condition B is that, before the deceased's death, any outstanding part of the debt is wholly written off, waived or released, and the write-off, waiver or release is made otherwise than for full consideration in money or money's worth.

(4) Condition C is that the deceased dies on or after 6th April 2005.

(5) Condition D is that—

(*a*) on the deceased's death, the transfer of value treated as made immediately before the deceased's death included the relevant property (or any property then representing the relevant property), and

(*b*) as a result of the deceased's death, the transfer of value referred to in paragraph (2)(*b*) has become a chargeable transfer.

(6) In these Regulations "the relevant property" means property which, immediately after the carrying out of the arrangements, falls within the definition of "the relevant property" given in paragraph 11(9) of Schedule 15 to the Finance Act 2004.

(7) In paragraph (2)(*a*) "the disposal condition" and "the contribution condition" are to be construed in accordance with Schedule 15 to the Finance Act 2004.

4 Avoidance of double charge: amounts to be calculated

(1) Where these Regulations apply, amounts A and B must be calculated separately.

(2) Amount A is the total tax chargeable as a consequence of the death of the deceased, but disregarding the value transferred represented by the relevant property (or by any property which, at the time of the death, represents the relevant property).

(3) Amount B is the total tax chargeable as a consequence of the death of the deceased, but disregarding the value transferred by the transfer of value specified in regulation 3(2)(*b*).

(4) The total tax chargeable is reduced to amount A or to amount B (whichever is the greater).

2008/605

INHERITANCE TAX (DELIVERY OF ACCOUNTS) (EXCEPTED TRANSFERS AND EXCEPTED TERMINATIONS) REGULATIONS 2008

Made by the Commissioners for Her Majesty's Revenue and Customs under IHTA 1984 s 256(1)(*a*), after consultation with the Lord Chancellor, the Scottish Ministers and the Lord Chief Justice of Northern Ireland in accordance with IHTA 1984 s 256(3A).

Made . . . . 6 *March 2008*
Laid before the House of Commons . . . . . . 6 *March 2008*
Coming into force . . . . 6 *April 2008*

Commentary—*Simon's Taxes* **I11.211**.

1 Citation, commencement and effect

These Regulations may be cited as the Inheritance Tax (Delivery of Accounts) (Excepted Transfers and Excepted Terminations) Regulations 2008 and shall come into force on 6th April 2008.

2 Interpretation

(1) In these Regulations—

"the Commissioners" means the Commissioners for Her Majesty's Revenue and Customs;

"the 1984 Act" means the Inheritance Tax Act 1984;

"the IHT threshold" means the lower limit shown in the Table in Schedule 1 to the 1984 Act applicable in the year in which the chargeable transfer is made by the transferor;

"the net IHT threshold" means the IHT threshold less the aggregate of the values transferred by all previous chargeable transfers made by the transferor during the seven years preceding the chargeable transfer;

"a specified trust" means one of the following—

(*a*) a trust of settled property where a person became beneficially entitled to an interest in possession before 22nd March 2006;

(*b*) a trust for a bereaved minor within section 71A;

(*c*) a trust in which there is an immediate post-death interest within section 49A;

(*d*) a trust for a disabled person within section 89, a self-settlement within section 89A or a disabled person's interest within section 89B;

(*e*) a trust in which there is a transitional serial interest within sections 49B to 49E;

"value" means value for the purpose of tax.

(2) In these Regulations, a reference to a section is a reference to the section of the 1984 Act bearing that number.

3 Accounts

(1) Save as provided in paragraph (2), no person is required under section 216 to deliver an account of an excepted transfer or an excepted termination unless the Commissioners so require by notice in writing issued to that person.

(2) Paragraph (1) does not apply to—

(*a*) The duty on trustees to deliver an account under section 216(1)(*b*) where the transferor dies within seven years of the chargeable transfer;

(*b*) The duty on trustees and persons to deliver an account under section 216(1)(*bb*) and (*bd*).

(3) If any person who has not delivered an account in reliance on paragraph (1) discovers at any time that the transfer is not an excepted transfer, or that the termination is not an excepted termination, the delivery to the Commissioners within six months of that time of an account of that transfer or termination shall satisfy any requirement to deliver an account imposed on that person.

4 Excepted transfers

(1) For the purposes of regulation 3 an excepted transfer means a chargeable transfer made on or after 6th April 2007 which is a disposition made by an individual in the circumstances in paragraph (2) or (3), but not any other transaction that is treated as a disposition for the purposes of inheritance tax.

(2) The circumstances are that—

(*a*) the value transferred by the chargeable transfer is attributable to either—

(i) cash; or

(ii) quoted shares or securities; and

(*b*) the value transferred by the chargeable transfer, together with the values transferred by any previous chargeable transfers made by the transferor during the seven years preceding the transfer does not exceed the IHT threshold.

(3) The circumstances are that—

(*a*) the value transferred by the chargeable transfer, together with the values transferred by any previous chargeable transfers made by the transferor during the seven years preceding the transfer does not exceed 80% of the IHT threshold, and

(*b*) the value transferred by the transfer of value giving rise to the chargeable transfer does not exceed the net IHT threshold.

(4) For the purpose of paragraph (3)(*b*), sections 104 (business property relief) and 116 (agricultural property relief) shall not apply in determining the value transferred by the chargeable transfer.

5 Excepted terminations

(1) An excepted termination is the termination of an interest in possession in the settled property of a specified trust in any of the following circumstances.

(2) The circumstances are that—

(*a*) the transferor has, in connection with the termination, given to the trustees of the settlement a notice under section 57(3) informing them of the availability of the exemption; and

(*b*) the value transferred in consequence of the termination does not exceed the amount of the exemption specified in the notice.

(3) The circumstances are that—

(*a*) the value of the property in which the interest subsisted is attributable to either—

(i) cash; or

(ii) quoted shares or securities; and

(*b*) the value transferred in consequence of the termination, together with the values transferred by any previous chargeable transfers made by the transferor during the seven years preceding the transfer does not exceed the IHT threshold.

(4) The circumstances are that—

(*a*) the value transferred in consequence of the termination, together with the values transferred by any previous chargeable transfers made by the transferor during the seven years preceding the termination does not exceed 80% of the IHT threshold; and

(*b*) the value transferred in consequence of the termination does not exceed the net IHT threshold.

(5) For the purpose of paragraph (4)(*b*), sections 104 (business property relief) and 116 (agricultural property relief) shall not apply in determining the value transferred in consequence of the termination.

6 Discharge of trustees from tax

(1) This regulation applies to an excepted termination within regulation 5(2).

(2) The trustees of the settlement shall, at the expiration of the period of six months beginning with the date of the excepted termination, be discharged from any claim for tax attributable to the value of the property in which the interest subsisted unless, within that period, the Commissioners issue a notice requiring an account of that property.

(3) This regulation is subject to regulation 7.

7 Regulation 6 does not—

(*a*) discharge any person from tax in the case of fraud or failure to disclose material facts; or

(*b*) affect the liability to tax of any person other than the trustees of the settlement, or tax on any property other than that in which the interest subsisted.

8 Transfers reported late

Where no account of an excepted transfer is required by the Commissioners, an account of that transfer shall, for the purposes of section 264(8) (delivery of account to be treated as payment where tax rate nil), be treated as having been delivered twelve months after the end of the month in which that transfer is made.

9 Revocation

The Inheritance Tax (Delivery of Accounts) (Excepted Transfers and Terminations) Regulations 2002 are revoked in relation to any excepted transfer or excepted termination made on or after 6th April 2007.

2008/606

INHERITANCE TAX (DELIVERY OF ACCOUNTS) (EXCEPTED SETTLEMENTS) REGULATIONS 2008

Made by the Commissioners for Her Majesty's Revenue and Customs under IHTA 1984 s 256(1)(*a*), after consultation with the Lord Chancellor, the Scottish Ministers and the Lord Chief Justice of Northern Ireland in accordance with section 256(3A).

Made . . . . *6 March 2008*

Laid before the House of Commons . . . . *6 March 2008*

Coming into force . . . . *6 April 2008*

Commentary—*Simon's Taxes* **I11.213**.

1 Citation, commencement and effect

These Regulations may be cited as the Inheritance Tax (Delivery of Accounts) (Excepted Settlements) Regulations 2008, shall come into force on 6th April 2008 and shall have effect in relation to chargeable events occurring on or after 6th April 2007.

2 Interpretation

(1) In these Regulations—

"the 1984 Act" means the Inheritance Tax Act 1984;

"the Commissioners" means the Commissioners for Her Majesty's Revenue and Customs;

"a chargeable event" means an occasion on which tax is chargeable under section 64 (charge at ten-year anniversary), section 65 (charge at other times) or section 71E (charge to tax on property to which section 71D applies);

"an excepted settlement" has the meaning given in regulation 4;

"the IHT threshold" means the lower limit shown in the Table in Schedule 1 to the 1984 Act applicable on the occasion of the chargeable event;

"qualifying interest in possession" has the meaning given in section 59;

"related settlement" has the meaning given in section 62;

"settlement" has the meaning given in section 43;

"settlor" has the meaning given in section 44;

"trustee" has the meaning given in section 45;

"value" means value for the purposes of tax.

(2) In these Regulations, a reference to a section is a reference to the section of the 1984 Act bearing that number.

3 Accounts

(1) No person is required to deliver an account under section 216 of the property comprised in an excepted settlement unless the Commissioners so require by notice in writing addressed to that person.

(2) If in reliance on these Regulations a person has not delivered an account and it is discovered at any time that the settlement is not an excepted settlement, the delivery to the Commissioners within six months of that time of an account of the property comprised in that settlement shall satisfy any requirement to deliver an account imposed on that person.

4 Excepted settlement

(1) An excepted settlement means a settlement in which no qualifying interest in possession subsists on an occasion of a chargeable event on or after 6th April 2007 in the circumstances in paragraph (2) or (3).

(2) The circumstances are that—

- (*a*) throughout the existence of the settlement, cash is the only property comprised in the settlement;
- (*b*) after making the settlement, the settlor provided no further property which became comprised in the settlement;
- (*c*) the trustees of the settlement are resident in the United Kingdom throughout the existence of the settlement;
- (*d*) the gross value of the settled property throughout the existence of the settlement does not exceed £1,000; and
- (*e*) there are no related settlements.

(3) The circumstances are that—

- (*a*) the settlor is domiciled in the United Kingdom at the time the settlement was made and throughout the existence of the settlement until either the chargeable event or the death of the settlor, whichever is earlier;
- (*b*) the trustees of the settlement are resident in the United Kingdom throughout the existence of the settlement;
- (*c*) there are no related settlements; and
- (*d*) the relevant condition contained in paragraph (4), (6), (7) or (8) is met.

(4) On the occasion of a chargeable event under section 64, the condition is that the value transferred by a chargeable transfer of the description specified in section 66(3) does not exceed 80% of the IHT threshold.

(5) Where, in reliance on these Regulations, no person was required to deliver an account under section 216 of the property comprised in the settlement on an occasion of a chargeable event under section 65 in respect of the settlement in the ten years before the chargeable event in paragraph (4), the amounts on which any charges to tax were imposed under section 65 shall, for the purpose of determining the value transferred by a chargeable transfer of the description specified in section 66(3), be without deduction for liabilities or reliefs contained in the 1984 Act.

(6) On the occasion of a chargeable event under section 65 preceding the first ten-year anniversary after the settlement's commencement, the condition is that the value transferred by a chargeable transfer of the description specified in section 68(4) does not exceed 80% of the IHT threshold.

(7) On the occasion of a chargeable event under section 65 following one or more ten-year anniversaries after the settlement's commencement, the condition is that the value transferred by a chargeable transfer of the description specified in section 66(3), taking into account section 69, does not exceed 80% of the IHT threshold.

(8) On the occasion of a chargeable event under section 71E by reason of the happening of an event within section 71F(2), the condition is that the value transferred by a chargeable transfer of the description specified in section 71F(8) does not exceed 80% of the IHT threshold.

(9) For the purposes of this regulation—

- (*a*) trustees of a settlement shall be regarded as resident in the United Kingdom if the general administration of the settlement is ordinarily carried on in the United Kingdom and the trustees or a majority of them (and, where there is more than one class of trustees, a majority of each class) are for the time being resident in the United Kingdom; and
- (*b*) in determining value for the purposes of paragraph (4), (6), (7) or (8) disregard any liabilities or reliefs contained in the 1984 Act.

5 Discharge of trustees and property from tax

(1) Paragraph (2) shall apply to an excepted settlement within regulation 4(2).

(2) The trustees of the settlement shall, on the expiration of the period of six months beginning with the date of the chargeable event, be discharged from any claim for tax on the occasion of the chargeable event and attributable to the value of the property comprised in the excepted settlement and any Inland Revenue charge for that tax shall then be extinguished unless, within that period, the Commissioners issue a notice requiring an account of that property.

(3) This regulation is subject to regulation 6.

6 Regulation 5 does not—

(*a*) discharge any person from tax in the case of fraud or failure to disclose material facts; or

(*b*) affect the liability to tax of any persons other than the trustees of the settlement, or any tax that may be payable if the settlement is not an excepted settlement.

7 Transfers reported late

Where no account of an excepted settlement is required by the Commissioners, an account of that settlement shall, for the purposes of section 264(8) (delivery of account to be treated as payment where tax rate nil), be treated as having been delivered twelve months after the end of the month in which the chargeable event occurred.

8 Revocation

The Inheritance Tax (Delivery of Accounts) (Excepted Settlements) Regulations 2002 are revoked in relation to an occasion of a chargeable event on or after 6th April 2007.

2009/571

FINANCE ACT 2008, SCHEDULE 40 (APPOINTED DAY, TRANSITIONAL PROVISIONS AND CONSEQUENTIAL AMENDMENTS) ORDER 2009

Made by the Treasury under FA 2008 s 122

Made . . . .*9 March 2009*
Laid before the House of Commons . . . .*10 March 2009*
Coming into force . . . .*1 April 2009*

1 Citation and interpretation

(1) This Order may be cited as the Finance Act 2008, Schedule 40 (Appointed Day, Transitional Provisions and Consequential Amendments) Order 2009 and comes into force on 1st April 2009.

(2) In this Order a reference to a paragraph (without more) is a reference to that paragraph of Schedule 40 to the Finance Act 2008.

(3) In this Order—

"filing date", in relation to a relevant document, means—

(i) where the document is required to be given to HMRC, the date by which it is required to be given, and

(ii) where the document is not required to be given to HMRC, the date on which it is given;

"HMRC" means Her Majesty's Revenue and Customs;

"relevant documents" means documents given to HMRC of a kind inserted in the Table in paragraph 1 of Schedule 24 by paragraph 2(4) or (5);

"relevant tax" means any tax inserted in the Table in paragraph 1 of Schedule 24 by paragraph 2(4) or (5);

"Schedule 24" means Schedule 24 to the Finance Act 2007; and

"tax period" has the meaning given in paragraph 28(*g*) of Schedule 24.

2 Appointed day

The day appointed for the coming into force of Schedule 40 to the Finance Act 2008 is 1st April 2009.

3 In their application in relation to penalties payable under paragraph 1 of Schedule 24 (error in taxpayer's document), the entries inserted by paragraph 2(4) and (5) shall have effect in relation to—

(*a*) relevant documents—

(i) which relate to tax periods commencing on or after 1st April 2009, and

(ii) for which the filing date is on or after 1st April 2010;

(*b*) relevant documents relating to all claims for repayments of relevant tax made on or after 1st April 2010 which are not related to a tax period;

(*c*) relevant documents produced under regulations under section 256 of the Inheritance Tax Act 1984 ("IHTA 1984") (regulations about accounts, etc), where the date of death is on or after 1st April 2009; and

(*d*) in any other case, relevant documents given where a person's liability to pay relevant tax arises on or after 1st April 2010.

4 In their application in relation to penalties payable under paragraph 1A of Schedule 24 (error in taxpayer's document attributable to another person), the entries inserted by paragraph 2(4) and (5) shall have effect in relation to—

(*a*) relevant documents—

(i) which relate to tax periods commencing on or after 1st April 2009, and
(ii) for which the filing date is on or after 1st April 2010;

(*b*) relevant documents relating to all claims for repayments of relevant tax made on or after 1st April 2010 which are not related to a tax period;

(*c*) relevant documents produced under regulations under section 256 of IHTA 1984 (regulations about accounts, etc) where the date of death is on or after 1st April 2009; and

(*d*) in any other case, relevant documents given where a person's liability to pay relevant tax arises on or after 1st April 2010.

5 In their application in relation to assessments falling within paragraph 2 of Schedule 24 (under-assessment by HMRC), the entries inserted by paragraph 2(4) and (5) shall have effect in relation to tax periods commencing on or after 1st April 2009, where the filing date for the relevant document is on or after 1st April 2010.

6 Transitional provisions

(1) Paragraph 21 (consequential repeals) repeals the provisions listed in paragraph (2) only in so far as those provisions relate to conduct involving dishonesty which relates to—

(*a*) an inaccuracy in a document, or

(*b*) a failure to notify HMRC of an under-assessment by HMRC.

(2) The provisions referred to in paragraph (1) are—

(*a*) in the Finance Act 1994—

(i) section 8 (penalty for evasion of excise duty), and
(ii) paragraphs 12 and 13 of Schedule 7 (insurance premium tax: civil penalties),

(*b*) paragraphs 18 and 19 of Schedule 5 to the Finance Act 1996 (landfill tax: civil penalties: evasion and misdeclaration or neglect),

(*c*) paragraphs 98 and 99 of Schedule 6 to the Finance Act 2000 (climate change levy: civil penalties: evasion, liability of directors and misdeclaration or neglect),

(*d*) in Schedule 6 to the Finance Act 2001—

(i) paragraphs 7 and 8 (aggregates levy: civil penalties: evasion, liability of directors and misdeclaration or neglect), and
(ii) paragraph 9A(5)(*b*) (penalty under paragraph 7 above),

(*e*) section 133(2) to (4) of the Finance Act 2002 (aggregates levy: amendments to provisions about civil penalties).

7 Notwithstanding paragraph 29(*d*) of Schedule 24 (consequential amendments), sections 60 and 61 of the Value Added Tax Act 1994 (VAT evasion) shall continue to have effect with respect to conduct involving dishonesty which does not relate to an inaccuracy in a document or a failure to notify HMRC of an under-assessment by HMRC.

8 Consequential amendments to enactments

Schedule 1 contains amendments of enactments in consequence of the provisions omitted by paragraph 21 and by paragraph 29 of Schedule 24.

9 Schedule 2 contains consequential amendments to secondary legislation.

SCHEDULE 1

CONSEQUENTIAL AMENDMENTS—PRIMARY LEGISLATION

Article 8

TAXES MANAGEMENT ACT 1970

10–13(*amend* TMA 1970 ss 59C(4), 100B(1), 107A)

14 Betting and Gaming Duties Act 1981

15 The Betting and Gaming Duties Act 1981 is amended as follows.

16 In paragraph 15(1)(*a*)(ii) of Schedule 1 after "section 8 of the Finance Act 1994 (penalty for evasion)" insert "or a penalty for a deliberate inaccuracy under paragraph 1 of Schedule 24 to the Finance Act 2007 (penalties for errors)".

FINANCE ACT 1982

17, 18 (*amend* FA 1982 Sch 18 para 10)

INCOME AND CORPORATION TAXES ACT 1988

19, 20 (*amend* TA 1988 s 827)

FINANCE ACT 1994

21 (*amends* FA 1994 Sch 7 (IPT))

VALUE ADDED TAX ACT 1994

22–27 (*amend* VATA 1994)

FINANCE ACT 1996

28, 29 (*amend* FA 1996 Sch 5 (landfill tax))

FINANCE ACT 2000

30 (*amends* FA 2000 Sch 6 (climate change levy))

FINANCE ACT 2001

31–35 (*amend* FA 2001 ss 25(5), 45(3), Sch 4, Sch 7)

FINANCE ACT 2004

36 (*amends* FA 2004 s 313)

INCOME TAX (TRADING AND OTHER INCOME) ACT 2005

37–39 (*amend* ITTOIA 2005 ss 54(2), 869(4))

SCHEDULE 2

CONSEQUENTIAL AMENDMENTS—SECONDARY LEGISLATION

Article 9

(*amends* the Registered Pension Schemes (Relief at Source) Regulations 2005 and the Duty Stamps Regulations 2006)

2010/51

INHERITANCE TAX (QUALIFYING NON-UK PENSION SCHEMES) REGULATIONS 2010

Made. . . . .*12 January 2010*
Laid before the House of Commons . . . .*14 January 2010*
Coming into force. . . . .*15 February 2010*

The Commissioners for Her Majesty's Revenue and Customs make the following Regulations in exercise of the powers conferred by section 271A of the Inheritance Tax Act 1984.

1 Citation, commencement and effect

(1) These Regulations may be cited as the Inheritance Tax (Qualifying Non-UK Pension Schemes) Regulations 2010 and shall come into force on 15th February 2010.

(2) These Regulations shall have effect from 6th April 2006.

2 Interpretation

In these Regulations—

"pension rule 1" means pension rule 1 in section 165 of the Finance Act 2004;

"relevant scheme funds" means any sums and assets held under a pension scheme—

(*a*) to which these Regulations apply, and

(*b*) which would be subject to inheritance tax if the scheme did not meet the requirements for a qualifying non-UK pension scheme.

3 Scope of these Regulations

These Regulations apply to pension schemes which are established in a country or territory outside the United Kingdom.

4 Requirements for qualifying non-UK pension schemes

(1) For the purposes of section 271A of the Inheritance Tax Act 1984 (qualifying non-UK pension scheme) a pension scheme must—

(*a*) be recognised for tax purposes under the tax legislation of the country or territory in which it is established (see regulation 5) and satisfy regulation 6; or

(*b*) be established by an international organisation for the purpose of providing benefits for, or in respect of, past service as an employee of the organisation and satisfy regulation 7.

(2) In this regulation "international organisation" means an organisation to which section 1 of the International Organisations Act 1968 applies by virtue of an Order in Council under subsection (1) of that section.

5 Recognition for tax purposes

(1) A scheme is recognised for tax purposes under the tax legislation of a country or territory in which it is established if it meets both Primary Condition 1 and Primary Condition 2 and either Condition A or Condition B.

Primary Condition 1

The scheme is open to persons resident in the country or territory in which it is established.

Primary Condition 2

The scheme is established in a country or territory where there is a system of taxation of personal income under which tax relief is available in respect of pensions and—

(*a*) tax relief is not available to the member on contributions made to the scheme by the member or, if the member is an employee, by their employer, in respect of earnings to which benefits under the scheme relate;

(*b*) the scheme is liable to taxation on its income and gains and is of a kind specified in the Schedule to these Regulations; or

(*c*) all or most of the benefits paid by the scheme to members who are not in serious ill-health are subject to taxation.

For the purposes of this condition "tax relief" includes the grant of an exemption from tax.

Condition A

(2) The scheme is approved or recognised by, or registered with, the relevant tax authorities as a pension scheme in the country or territory in which it is established.

Condition B

(3) If no system applies for the approval or recognition by, or registration with, relevant tax authorities of pension schemes in the country or territory in which it is established—

(*a*) the scheme must be resident there;

(*b*) the scheme rules must provide that at least 70% of a member's relevant scheme funds will be designated by the scheme manager for the purpose of providing the member with an income for life, or, in the case of a member who has died, so provided immediately before the member's death; and

(*c*) the pension benefits payable to the member under the scheme (and any lump sum associated with those benefits) must be payable no earlier than they would be if pension rule 1 applied.

6 Requirements for schemes recognised for tax purposes

(1) This regulation is satisfied if paragraph (2), (3) or (4) applies.

(2) This paragraph applies if the scheme is an occupational pension scheme and there is a body in the country or territory in which it is established—

(*a*) which regulates occupational pension schemes; and

(*b*) which regulates the scheme in question.

(3) This paragraph applies if the scheme is not an occupational scheme and there is a body in the country or territory in which it is established—

(*a*) which regulates pension schemes other than occupational pension schemes; and

(*b*) which regulates the scheme in question.

(4) This paragraph applies if neither paragraph (2) nor (3) applies by reason only that no such regulatory body exists in the country or territory and—

(*a*) the scheme is established in another member State, Norway, Iceland or Liechtenstein; or

(*b*) the scheme is one where—

(i) the scheme rules provide that at least 70% of a member's relevant scheme funds will be designated by the scheme manager for the purpose of providing the member with an income for life, or, in the case of a member who has died, so provided immediately before the member's death, and

(ii) the pension benefits payable to the member under the scheme (and any lump sum associated with those benefits) are payable no earlier than they would be if pension rule 1 applied.

(5) In this regulation "occupational pension scheme" has the meaning given by section 150(5) of the Finance Act 2004.

7 Requirements for schemes established by international organisations

This regulation is satisfied if—

(*a*) the scheme rules provide that at least 70% of a member's relevant scheme funds will be designated by the scheme manager for the purpose of providing the member with an income for life, or, in the case of a member who has died, so provided immediately before the member's death, and

(*b*) the pension benefits payable to the member under the scheme (and any lump sum associated with those benefits) are payable no earlier than they would be if pension rule 1 applied.

SCHEDULE

SPECIFIED SCHEMES

Regulation 5

A complying superannuation plan as defined in section 995-1 (definitions) of the Income Tax Assessment Act 1997 of Australia (as amended by the Tax Law Amendment (Simplified Superannuation) Act 2007 of Australia).

2010/867

FINANCE ACT 2009, SCHEDULE 51 (TIME LIMITS FOR ASSESSMENTS, CLAIMS, ETC) (APPOINTED DAYS AND TRANSITIONAL PROVISIONS) ORDER 2010

Made . . . . *18 March 2010*

The Treasury make the following Order in exercise of the powers conferred by sections 99(2) and 99(3) of the Finance Act 2009.

PART 1

APPOINTED DAYS AND PRELIMINARY PROVISIONS

1 Citation and interpretation

(1) This Order may be cited as the Finance Act 2009, Schedule 51 (Time Limits for Assessments, Claims, etc) (Appointed Days and Transitional Provisions) Order 2010.

(2) In this Order a reference to a paragraph (without more) is a reference to that paragraph of Schedule 51 to the Finance Act 2009.

(3) In this Order—

"The Commissioners" means the Commissioners for Her Majesty's Revenue and Customs;

"FA", followed by a year, means the Finance Act of that year.

"IHTA 1984" means the Inheritance Tax Act 1984;

2 Appointed days

(1) The day appointed as the day on which the amendments made by paragraphs 1 to 4 and 27 to 43 (insurance premium tax, aggregates levy, climate change levy, landfill tax and minor and consequential provision) come into force is 1st April 2010.

(2) The day appointed as the day on which the amendments made by paragraphs 5 to 26 (inheritance tax, stamp duty land tax and petroleum revenue tax) come into force is 1st April 2011.

PART 2

TRANSITIONAL PROVISION

3–5 (not relevant to IHT)

6 Inheritance tax: underpayments

In a case under section 240(2) IHTA 1984, where—

(*a*) the chargeable transfer took place on or before 31st March 2011, and

(*b*) a loss of tax was brought about deliberately by any person (or a person acting on behalf of such a person),

the period within which proceedings may be brought is the period of 6 years beginning when the deliberate conduct comes to the knowledge of Her Majesty's Revenue and Customs or the period of 20 years provided in section 240(5) IHTA 1984, whichever ends soonest.

7–28 (not relevant to IHT)

2010/1904

TAXES (DEFINITION OF CHARITY) (RELEVANT TERRITORIES) REGULATIONS 2010

Made . . . . *23 July 2010*

Laid before the House of Commons . . . . *26 July 2010*

Coming into force . . . . *20 August 2010*

The Commissioners for Her Majesty's Revenue and Customs make the following Regulations in exercise of the powers conferred by paragraph 2 of Schedule 6 to the Finance Act 2010:

1 These Regulations may be cited as the Taxes (Definition of Charity) (Relevant Territories) Regulations 2010 and come into force on 20th August 2010.

2 The territories specified in the Schedule to these Regulations are relevant territories for the purposes of the meaning of a relevant territory in paragraph 2(3) of Schedule 6 to the Finance Act 2010 (the jurisdiction condition of the definition of "charity" in paragraph 1 of Schedule 6 to the Finance Act 2010).

SCHEDULE

Regulation 2

[The Republic of Iceland

The Kingdom of Norway][1]

[The Principality of Liechtenstein][2]

Amendments—[1] Entries inserted by the Taxes (Definition of Charity) (Relevant Territories) (Amendment) Regulations, SI 2010/1904 reg 2, Schedule with effect from 20 August 2010.

[2] Entry inserted by the Taxes (Definition of Charity) (Relevant Territories) (Amendment) Regulations, SI 2014/1807 reg 2 with effect from 31 July 2014.

2011/170

INHERITANCE TAX AVOIDANCE SCHEMES (PRESCRIBED DESCRIPTIONS OF ARRANGEMENTS) REGULATIONS 2011

Made . . . . 1 February 2011

Laid before House of Commons . . . . 2 February 2011

Coming into force . . . . 6 April 2011

The Treasury make the following Regulations in accordance with the powers conferred by FA 2004 s 306(1)(*a*) and (*b*).

1 Citation and commencement

These Regulations may be cited as the Inheritance Tax Avoidance Schemes (Prescribed Descriptions of Arrangements) Regulations 2011 and come into force on 6th April 2011.

2 Prescribed description of arrangements in relation to inheritance tax

(1) For the purposes of Part 7 of the Finance Act 2004 (disclosure of tax avoidance schemes) the arrangements specified in paragraph (2) are prescribed in relation to inheritance tax.

(2) Arrangements are prescribed if—

(*a*) as a result of any element of the arrangements property becomes relevant property; and

(*b*) a main benefit of the arrangements is that an advantage is obtained in relation to a relevant property entry charge.

(3) In this regulation—

"property" shall be construed in accordance with section 272 of the Inheritance Tax Act 1984;

"relevant property" has the meaning given by section 58(1) of the Inheritance Tax Act 1984 ;

"relevant property entry charge" means the charge to inheritance tax which arises on a transfer of value made by an individual during that individual's life as a result of which property becomes relevant property;

"transfer of value" has the meaning given by section 3(1) of the Inheritance Tax Act 1984.

3 Arrangements are excepted from disclosure under these Regulations if they are of the same, or substantially the same, description as arrangements—

(*a*) which were first made available for implementation before 6th April 2011; or

(*b*) in relation to which the date of any transaction forming part of the arrangements falls before 6th April 2011; or

(*c*) in relation to which a promoter first made a firm approach to another person before 6th April 2011.

2011/1502

TAXATION OF EQUITABLE LIFE (PAYMENTS) ORDER 2011

Made . . . . 15 June 2011

Coming into force in accordance with article 1(1)

The Treasury make the following Order in exercise of the powers conferred by section 1(3) and (4) of the Equitable Life (Payments) Act 2010

In accordance with section 1(5) of that Act, a draft of this Order was laid before Parliament and approved by a resolution of each House of Parliament.

1 Citation, commencement, effect and interpretation

(1) This Order may be cited as the Taxation of Equitable Life (Payments) Order 2011 and shall come into force on the day after the day on which it is made.

(2) This Order has effect in relation to authorised payments made after the day on which this Order is made.

(3) In this Order "authorised payment" means a payment to which section 1 of the Equitable Life (Payments) Act 2010 applies.

2 Capital gains tax

An authorised payment shall be disregarded for the purposes of capital gains tax.

3 Corporation tax

An authorised payment shall be disregarded for the purposes of the Corporation Tax Acts.

4 Income tax

An authorised payment shall be disregarded for the purposes of the Income Tax Acts.

5 Inheritance tax

(1) For the purposes of the Inheritance Tax Act 1984—

(*a*) in determining the value of a person's estate immediately before that person's death, no account shall be taken of any value attributable to a right to, or interest in, an authorised payment made after that person's death; and

(*b*) in determining the value of relevant property immediately before a ten-year anniversary for the purposes of the charge under section 64 of the Inheritance Tax Act 1984, no account shall be taken of any value attributable to a right to, or interest in, an authorised payment made on or after that ten-year anniversary.

(2) In this article—

"estate" has the meaning given by section 272 of the Inheritance Tax Act 1984;

"relevant property" has the meaning given by section 58 of that Act; and

"ten-year anniversary" has the meaning given by section 61 of that Act.

6 Tax Credits

In calculating investment income in accordance with regulation 10 of the Tax Credits (Definition and Calculation of Income) Regulations 2002, an authorised payment shall be disregarded.

2011/2446

TAXES AND DUTIES, ETC (INTEREST RATE) REGULATIONS 2011

Made . . . . 10 October 2011

Laid before the House of Commons . . . . 10 October 2011

Coming into force . . . . 31 October 2011

The Treasury make the following Regulations in exercise of the powers conferred by section 103 of the Finance Act 2009.

1 Citation and commencement

These Regulations may be cited as the Taxes and Duties, etc (Interest Rate) Regulations 2011 and come into force on 31st October 2011.

2 Interpretation

In these Regulations—

"Bank of England rate" means the official bank rate as announced at the relevant meeting;

"operative date" means the 13th working day following the relevant meeting;

"relevant meeting" means the most recent meeting of the Bank of England Monetary Policy Committee;

"working day" means any day other than a non-business day within the meaning of section 92 of the Bills of Exchange Act 1882.

3 Late payment interest rate

(1) Except where regulation 5 applies, the late payment interest rate for the purposes of section 101 of the Finance Act 2009 (late payment interest on sums due to HMRC), is the percentage per annum found by applying the following formula—

Bank of England rate + 2.5.

(2) The interest rate found under paragraph (1) applies on and after the operative date.

4 Repayment interest rate

(1) Except where regulation 5 applies, the repayment interest rate for the purposes of section 102 of the Finance Act 2009 (repayment interest on sums to be paid by HMRC), is the higher of—

(*a*) 0.5% per annum; and

(*b*) the percentage per annum found by applying the following formula—

Bank of England rate – 1.

(2) The interest rate found under paragraph (1) applies on and after the operative date.

5 Initial rates of interest

(1) This regulation applies immediately on the coming into force of these Regulations until the first operative date after the coming into force of these Regulations.

(2) The late payment interest rate and repayment interest rate shall be the respective percentages per annum found by applying regulation 3(1) and regulation 4(1) as if the references in those regulations to the Bank of England rate were references to the official bank rate announced at the meeting of the Bank of England Monetary Policy Committee on, or most recently before, the 13th working day before the coming into force of these Regulations.

6 Effect of change in rates of interest

Where the late payment interest rate or repayment interest rate changes in accordance with these Regulations with effect from an operative date, the change has effect in respect of interest running from before that date as well as interest running from or after that date.

7 Earlier instrument revoked

The Taxes and Duties (Interest Rate) Regulations 2010 are revoked.

2012/847

DATA-GATHERING POWERS (RELEVANT DATA) REGULATIONS 2012

Made . . . . *14 March 2012*

Coming into force . . . . *1 April 2012*

A draft of these Regulations was laid before, and approved by a resolution of, the House of Commons under paragraph 44(2) of Schedule 23 to the Finance Act 2011.

Accordingly the Treasury make the following Regulations in exercise of the power conferred by paragraph 1(3) of Schedule 23 to the Finance Act 2011.

1 Citation, commencement and interpretation

These Regulations may be cited as the Data-gathering Powers (Relevant Data) Regulations 2012 and come into force on 1st April 2012.

2 In these Regulations "Schedule 23" means Schedule 23 to the Finance Act 2011.

3 Salaries, fees, commission etc

(1) The relevant data for a data-holder of the type described in paragraph 9(1)(a) of Schedule 23 are information relating to all payments made by the employer that relate to the employment (referred to in this regulation as "employment related payments").

(2) The relevant data for a data-holder of the type described in paragraph 9(1)(b) are information relating to payments by any other person who has made employment related payments to the employer's employees or to the employees of another person.

(3) Information relating to apportioned expenses incurred partly in respect of employment related payments and partly in, or in connection with, other matters are relevant data for the purposes of paragraph 9(1)(*a*) and 9(1)(*b*).

(4) The relevant data for a data-holder of the type described in paragraph 9(1)(c) are information and documents relating to the donations made under Part 12 of the Income Tax (Earnings and Pensions) Act 2003 (payroll giving).

(5) For the purposes of paragraph 9(1)(*d*) and, where relevant, paragraph 9(4)—

(a) the relevant data are information relating to relevant payments made in connection with a business, or a part of a business;

(b) particulars of the following payments are not relevant data—

(i) payments from which income tax is deductible; and

(ii) payments made to any one person where the total of those payments, particulars of which would otherwise fall to be provided, does not exceed £500.

4 The relevant data for a data-holder of the type described in paragraph 11 of Schedule 23 are the data described in paragraph 11(2)(*b*).

5 Interest etc

(1) The relevant data for a data-holder of the type described in paragraph 12 of Schedule 23 are information and documents relating to accounts or sums on which relevant interest is payable, including but not limited to the data in regulations 8, 9 and 10.

(2) "Relevant interest" means interest paid or credited—

(*a*) on money received or retained in the United Kingdom; and (*b*) either without deduction of income tax or after deduction of income tax.

6 Information relating to the following payments is not relevant data for the purposes of a data-holder of the type described in paragraph 12—

(*a*) a payment in respect of a certificate of deposit within the meaning given by section 1019 of the Income Tax Act 2007;

(*b*) a payment in respect of an investment or a deposit held by a branch of a person to whom a data-holder notice is issued, where the branch is situated in a territory other than the United Kingdom;

(*c*) . . . [1]

(*d*) a payment in respect of an investment under a plan provided for by regulations made under Chapter 3 of Part 6 of the Income Tax (Trading and Other Income) Act 2005;

(*e*) a payment to or a receipt for a person other than an individual (in whatever capacity the individual is acting), except where the case falls within regulation 9(*c*) or 10(*d*) [or where the relevant dataholder is carrying on a trade or business and, in the ordinary course of the operations thereof, receives or retains money in such circumstances that interest becomes payable thereon][1];

(*f*) any other payment not falling within any of paragraphs (*a*) to (*e*) which is specified in the data-holder notice as being a payment in respect of which information is not required.

Amendments—[1] Para (*c*) revoked and in para (*e*), words inserted by the Data-gathering Powers (Relevant Data) (Amendment) Regulations, SI 2013/1811 regs 2–4 with effect from 1 September 2013.

7 (1) Information is not relevant data for the purposes of a data-holder of the type described in paragraph 12 if it is in respect of a relevant dormant account before the balance of the account is paid out to the account-holder following a repayment claim (such payment being referred to in this regulation as the repayment claim being "settled").

(2) Where a repayment claim to the balance of a dormant account is settled, all interest paid, credited or included in the balance of the account, during and at the end of the relevant dormant period, is relevant data for the purposes of paragraph 12 and shall be treated—

(*a*) as paid at the time the repayment claim is settled; and

(*b*) as if the bank or building society in question had retained the balance of the account, in the ordinary course of the operations of its trade or business.

(3) If the data-holder notice specifies the year of assessment in which the relevant dormant period for any account ends, the notice shall (unless it states otherwise) be deemed to require as relevant data the inclusion of information for all relevant dormant accounts, in respect of which repayment claims were settled in that year.

(4) Information in respect of a relevant dormant account which, at the time it first became a relevant dormant account, was a plan provided for by regulations made under Chapter 3 of Part 6 of the Income Tax (Trading and Other Income) Act 2005 (individual investment plans) is not relevant data for the purpose of paragraph 12.

(5) In this regulation—

"relevant dormant account" has the meaning in section 39(2) of the Finance Act 2008;

"relevant dormant period" means the period between the time when a dormant account becomes a relevant dormant account and the time at which a repayment claim is settled; and

"repayment claim" means a repayment claim mentioned in section 5(6) of the Dormant Bank and Building Society Accounts Act 2008 ("the Dormant Accounts Act").

Other terms used have the same meaning as in the Dormant Accounts Act.

8 If a payment is made in circumstances in which a certificate has been supplied under regulation 4 of the Income Tax (Deposit-takers and Building Societies) (Interest Payments) Regulations 2008 . . . [1] the relevant data are—

(*a*) the name and address of the person or persons by or on behalf of whom a certificate has been given in connection with the payment ("the beneficiary") if other than the person or persons to whom the payment was made;

(*b*) the date of birth of the beneficiary;

(*c*) the national insurance number or tax identification number of the beneficiary (or confirmation that a national insurance number or tax identification number is not held) for any account in respect of which the payment was made opened on or after 6th April 2013, and for any account opened earlier if such number is provided to the deposit-taker or building society;

(*d*) notification of the fact that the account in respect of which the payment was made is or was one in connection with which a certificate or certificates had been given which had not ceased to be valid at the 5th April in the year in which the payment was made or at the date of closure of the account, if earlier in that year;

(*e*) the reference number of the account referred to in paragraph (*d*) and, where necessary for identifying the account, the branch of the payer where the account is held;

(*f*) where the payment was made to two or more account-holders each of whom was beneficially entitled to the payment, notification of that fact and, if known, the number of such persons;

(*g*) the national insurance numbers or tax identification numbers of persons referred to in paragraph (*f*) other than the beneficiary referred to in paragraphs (*b*) and (*c*) (or confirmation that a national insurance number or tax identification number is not held) for any account opened on or after 6th April 2013, and for any account opened earlier if such number is provided to the deposit-taker or building society;

(*h*) where a certificate was given by or on behalf of one, or more, but not all, of the persons referred to in paragraph (*f*) and had not ceased to be valid at the 5th April in the year in which the payment was made or at the date of closure of the account, if earlier in that year, notification of those facts;

(*i*) where the payment was the first payment made in respect of an account, notification of that fact;

(*j*) where the payment was in a currency other than sterling and the amount of the payment is recorded in that currency in the data provided under a data-holder notice notification of the fact that the amount is so recorded and the specification of the currency concerned.

Amendments—[1] Words revoked by the Data-gathering Powers (Relevant Data) (Amendment) Regulations, SI 2015/672 reg 2 with effect from 1 April 2015.

9 In cases to which regulation 8 does not apply, the relevant data relating to payments in respect of deposits are—

(*a*) the reference number of the account in respect of which a payment was made and, where necessary for identifying the account, the branch of the payer where the account is held;

(*b*) where a payment was made to two or more account holders, notification of that fact and, if known, the number of such persons;

(*c*) where the payment was made without deduction of tax by virtue of a declaration made after 5th April 2001 under section 858, 859, 860 or 861 of the Income Tax Act 2007—

(i) the name and principal residential address of the individual beneficially entitled to the payment or, if more than one, of each individual entitled to the payment; or

(ii) where the person beneficially entitled to the payment is a Scottish partnership, all the partners in which are individuals, the name and principal residential address of each of the partners;

(*d*) in a case falling within paragraph (*c*) notification of the fact that the account in respect of which the payment was made was one in respect of which a declaration had been made as mentioned in that paragraph;

(*e*) the national insurance number or tax identification number (or confirmation that a national insurance number or tax identification number is not held) of the person or, where paragraph (*b*) applies, each person to whom a payment was made for any account opened on or after 6th April 2013, and for any account opened earlier if such number is provided to the deposit-taker or building society;

(*f*) where a payment made in the course of the year was the first payment in respect of an account, notification of that fact;

(*g*) where a payment was in a currency other than sterling and the amount of the payment is recorded in that currency in the data provided under a data-holder notice notification of the fact that the amount is so recorded and the specification of the currency concerned.

10 In cases to which regulation 8 does not apply, the relevant data relating to payments and receipts of interest other than payments in respect of deposits are—

(*a*) identification of the security or investment in respect of which the payment was made or received;

(*b*) where a payment or receipt was in a currency other than sterling and the amount of the payment is recorded in that currency in the data provided under a data-holder notice notification of the fact that the amount is so recorded and the specification of the currency concerned;

(*c*) where a payment was made to, or the receipt was for, two or more persons, notification of that fact and, if known, the number of such persons;

(*d*) where a payment was made without deduction of tax by virtue of a declaration made under regulation 31 of the Authorised Investment Funds (Tax) Regulations 2006, the name and principal residential address of the person beneficially entitled to the payment, or if more than one, of each person beneficially entitled to the payment;

(*e*) in a case falling within paragraph (*d*), notification of the fact that the account in respect of which the payment was made was one in respect of which the declaration had been made.

11 Income, assets etc belonging to others

The relevant data for a data-holder of the type described in paragraph 13 of Schedule 23 are—

(*a*) information relating to the money or value received; and
(*b*) the name and address of the beneficial owner of the money or value.

[11A Merchant acquirers etc

(1) The relevant data for a data-holder of the type described in paragraph 13A of Schedule 23 are—

(*a*) in relation to a retailer, information relating to payment card transactions recorded against a merchant account, including the currency these payment card transactions were made in;
(*b*) the reference number of the account into which payments are made by the relevant data-holder to the retailer and, where necessary for identifying the account, the branch where the account is held;
(*c*) any unique identifier which has been allocated to a retailer, for the purposes of identifying the retailer, as part of the business arrangement between the relevant data-holder and the retailer;
(*d*) any identifier which has been allocated to a retailer, for the purposes of classifying the trade of the retailer, as part of the business arrangement between the relevant data-holder and the retailer;
(*e*) any unique identifier which has been allocated to a retailer's merchant account, for the purposes of identifying this merchant account, as part of the business arrangement between the relevant data-holder and the retailer;
(*f*) the name, address, telephone number, e-mail address, website address and VAT number ("relevant details") of a retailer and, if different, the relevant details associated with a merchant account.

(2) In this regulation—

"merchant account" means an account held by a retailer with the relevant data-holder, by reference to which the amount due to be paid by the relevant data-holder to the retailer in settlement of payment card transactions is calculated; and

"VAT number" means ""registration number" for the purposes of paragraph (1) of regulation 2 of the Value Added Tax Regulations 1995.][1]

Amendments—[1] Regulation 11A inserted by the Data-gathering Powers (Relevant Data) (Amendment) Regulations, SI 2013/1811 regs 2, 5 with effect from 1 September 2013.

12 Payments derived from securities

The relevant data for a data-holder of the type described in paragraph 14 of Schedule 23 are—

(*a*) whether the relevant data-holder is the beneficial owner (or sole beneficial owner) of the securities or payment in question;
(*b*) if not—
  (i) details of the beneficial owner (or other beneficial owners); and
  (ii) if those details are not known or if different, details of the person for whom the securities are held or to whom the payment is or may be paid on; and
(*c*) if there is more than one beneficial owner or more than one person of the kind mentioned in paragraph (*b*)(ii), their respective interests in the securities or payment.

13 The relevant data for a data-holder of the type described in paragraph 15 of Schedule 23 are details of the amounts paid that were received from or paid on behalf of another person including the name and address of each such person.

14 Grants and subsidies out of public funds

The relevant data for a data-holder of the type described in paragraph 16 of Schedule 23 are—

(*a*) the name and address of the person to whom the payment has been made or on whose behalf the payment has been received;
(*b*) the amount of the payment so made or received; and
(*c*) the address of any property in respect of which the payment has been made.

15 Licences, approvals etc

The relevant data for a data-holder of the type described in paragraph 17 of Schedule 23 are—

(*a*) the name and address of anyone who is or has been the holder of a licence or approval or to whom an entry in the register relates or related;
(*b*) particulars of the licence, approval or entry;
(*c*) information relating to any application for such a licence or approval or for entry on that register.

16 Rent and other payments arising from land

(1) The relevant data for a data-holder of the type described in paragraph 18 of Schedule 23 are—

(*a*) information relating to the terms applying to the lease, occupation or use of land;
(*b*) information relating to any consideration given for the grant or assignment of the tenancy;

(*c*) information relating to any person on whose behalf the land is managed or the payments received, including particulars of payments arising from the land.

(2) In this regulation—

(*a*) "lease" includes an agreement for a lease, and any tenancy, but does not include a mortgage or heritable security;

(*b*) "lessee" includes a successor in title of a lease; and

(*c*) in relation to Scotland, "assignment" means an assignation.

17 Dealing etc in securities

(1) The relevant data for a data-holder of the type described in paragraph 19 of Schedule 23 are—

(*a*) information and documents relating to securities transactions in respect of which that person is a relevant data-holder; and

(*b*) in relation to a person who carries on a business of effecting public issues or placings or otherwise effects public issues or placings, information relating to the issue, allotment or placing of the public issues or placings.

(2) In this regulation—

(*a*) "placing" means a placing of shares or securities in a company; and

(*b*) "public issue" means a public issue of shares or securities in a company.

18 Dealing in other property

The relevant data for a data-holder of the type described in paragraph 20 of Schedule 23 are—

(*a*) particulars of any transactions effected through a clearing house;

(*b*) particulars of any transaction which meets the following conditions—

(i) the transaction is effected by or through that person;

(ii) in the transaction, an asset which is tangible moveable property is disposed of; and

(iii) the amount or value of the consideration for the disposal exceeds, in the hands of the recipient, £6,000.

19 Lloyd's

The relevant data for a data-holder of the type described in paragraph 21 of Schedule 23 are information and documents relating to, and to the activities of, the syndicate of underwriting members of Lloyd's.

20 Investment plans etc

The relevant data for a data-holder of the type described in paragraph 22 of Schedule 23 are—

(*a*) information and documents relating to the plan, including investments which are or have been held under the plan;

(*b*) information and documents relating to the child trust fund including investments which are or have been held under the fund.

21 Petroleum activities

The relevant data for a data-holder of the type described in paragraph 23 of Schedule 23 are—

(*a*) particulars of transactions in connection with any activities authorised by a petroleum licence as a result of which any person is or might be liable to tax by virtue of section 276 of the Taxation of Chargeable Gains Act 1992, section 1313 of the Corporation Tax Act 2009 or section 874 of the Income Tax (Trading and Other Income) Act 2005;

(*b*) particulars of earnings or money treated as earnings, which constitute employment income (see section 7(2)(*a*) or (*b*) of the Income Tax (Earnings and Pensions) Act 2003) or other payments paid or payable in respect of duties or services performed in an area in which those activities may be carried on under the petroleum licence;

(*c*) particulars of the persons to whom such earnings, money or other payments were paid and are payable;

(*d*) information and documents relating to the oil field.

22 Insurance activities

The relevant data for a data-holder of the type described in paragraph 24 of Schedule 23 are—

(*a*) information and documents relating to contracts of insurance entered into in the course of an insurance business;

(*b*) if paragraph 24(*b*) or (*c*) applies, information and documents relating to the contracts of insurance.

23 Environmental activities

The relevant data for a data-holder of the type described in paragraph 25 of Schedule 23 are—

(*a*) information and documents relating to aggregates levy matters in which the person is or has been involved;
(*b*) information and documents relating to climate change levy matters in which the person is or has been involved;
(*c*) information and documents relating to any landfill disposal.

24 Settlements

The relevant data for a data-holder of the type described in paragraph 26 of Schedule 23 are information and documents relating to the settlement in question and to income or gains arising to the settlement.

25 Charities

The relevant data for a data-holder of the type described in paragraph 27 of Schedule 23 are information relating to donations to the charity that are eligible for tax relief under any of the following provisions—

(*a*) section 257 of the Taxation of Chargeable Gains Act 1992 (gifts to charities etc);
(*b*) section 63(2)(*a*) or (*aa*) of the Capital Allowances Act 2001(cases in which disposal value is nil);
(*c*) Part 12 of the Income Tax (Earnings and Pensions) Act 2003 (payroll giving);
(*d*) section 108 of the Income Tax (Trading and Other Income) Act 2005 (gifts of trading stock to charities etc);
(*e*) Chapter 2 or 3 of Part 8 of the Income Tax Act 2007 (gift aid, gifts of shares, securities and real property to charities etc);
(*f*) section 105 of the Corporation Tax Act 2009 (gifts of trading stock to charities etc); and
(*g*) Part 6 of the Corporation Tax Act 2010 (charitable donations relief).

2012/1836

TAX AVOIDANCE SCHEMES (INFORMATION) REGULATIONS 2012

Made . . . . *12 July 2012*
Laid before the House of Commons . . . . *13 July 2012*
Coming into force . . . . *1 September 2012*

The Commissioners for Her Majesty's Revenue and Customs in exercise of the powers conferred by section 98C(2A),(2B) and (2C)(b) of the Taxes Management Act 1970, section 132 of the Finance Act 1999, section 135 of the Finance Act 2002 and sections 306A(6), 307(5), 308(1) and (3), 308A(5) and (6)(*a*), 309(1), 310, 312(2) and (5), 312A(2) and (5), 313(1) and (3), 313ZA(3) and (4), 313A(4)(*a*), 313B(2)(*a*), 313C(1) and (3)(*a*), 317(2) and 318(1) of the Finance Act 2004, make the following Regulations:

Note—NIC (Application of Part 7 of the Finance Act 2004) Regulations, SI 2012/1868 reg 26(1) (any reference in these Regulations to FA 2004 ss 306–313C and s 314A shall be construed as a reference to the corresponding provision of the NIC (Application of Part 7 of the Finance Act 2004) Regulations, SI 2012/1868, and any reference in these Regulations to TMA 1970 s 98C shall be construed as a reference to SI 2012/1868 reg 22.)

Press releases—HMRC Issue Briefing—Tackling tax avoidance. 6 September 2012 (see Simon's Weekly Tax Intelligence 2012, Issue 36).

1 Citation and commencement

These Regulations may be cited as the Tax Avoidance Schemes (Information) Regulations 2012 and shall come into force on 1st September 2012.

2 Interpretation

(1) In these Regulations a reference to a numbered section (without more) is a reference to the section of the Finance Act 2004 which is so numbered.

(2) In these Regulations—

"employment" has the same meaning as it has for the purposes of the employment income Parts of the Income Tax (Earnings and Pensions) Act 2003 (see section 4 of that Act) and includes offices to which the provisions of those Parts that are expressed to apply to employments apply equally (see section 5 of that Act); and "employee" and "employer" have corresponding meanings;

"the filing date" is—

(*a*) whichever date in regulation 12(4)(*a*) to (*c*) applies to the relevant return or in the case of inheritance tax the last day of the period mentioned in regulation 9(5)(b); or
(*b*) in the case of regulation 10(7) the date by which the relevant return is required to be delivered;

["the prescribed taxes" means capital gains tax, corporation tax, income tax, inheritance tax, stamp duty land tax and annual tax on enveloped dwellings.][1]

(3) In reckoning any period under regulation 5 (apart from paragraph (8)), or regulations [8A, 13A,][2] 14, 15 and 16, any day which is a non-business day within the meaning of section 92 of the Bills of Exchange Act 1882 (computation of time) shall be disregarded.

(4) In regulations 10(2) and (3), 11(4) and 12(2) expressions which are used in Part 4 of the Finance Act 2003 have the same meaning as in that Part.

Modifications—See the National Insurance Contributions (Application of Part 7 of the Finance Act 2004) Regulations, SI 2012/1868 reg 26(1), (2) for the modification of this regulation is its applications to notifiable contribution arrangements and notifiable contribution proposals.

Amendments—[1] In para (2), definition of "the prescribed taxes" substituted by the Tax Avoidance Schemes (Information) (Amendment, etc) Regulations, SI 2013/2592 regs 3, 4 with effect from 4 November 2013.

[2] Words in para (3) inserted by the Tax Avoidance Schemes (Information) (Amendment, etc) Regulations, SI 2013/2592 regs 3, 15 with effect from 4 November 2013.

3 Revocations

(1) The Regulations described in the Schedule to these Regulations are revoked.

(2) Anything begun under or for the purpose of any Regulations revoked by these Regulations shall be continued under or, as the case may be, for the purpose of the corresponding provision of these Regulations.

(3) Where any document refers to a provision of a regulation revoked by these Regulations, such reference shall, unless the context otherwise requires, be construed as a reference to the corresponding provision of these Regulations.

4 Prescribed information in respect of notifiable proposals and arrangements

(1) The information which must be provided to HMRC by a promoter under section 308(1) or (3) (duties of promoter) in respect of a notifiable proposal or notifiable arrangements is sufficient information as might reasonably be expected to enable an officer of HMRC to comprehend the manner in which the proposal or arrangements are intended to operate, including—

(*a*) the promoter's name and address;

(*b*) details of the provision of the Arrangements Regulations, [the ATED Arrangements Regulations,][1] the IHT Arrangements Regulations or the SDLT Arrangements Regulations by virtue of which the arrangements or the proposed arrangements are notifiable;

(*c*) a summary of the arrangements or proposed arrangements and the name (if any) by which they are known;

(*d*) information explaining each element of the arrangements or proposed arrangements (including the way in which they are structured) from which the tax advantage expected to be obtained under those arrangements arises; and

(*e*) the statutory provisions, relating to any of the prescribed taxes, on which that tax advantage is based.

(2) The information which must be provided to HMRC by a client under section 309 (duty of person dealing with promoter outside the United Kingdom) in respect of notifiable arrangements is sufficient information as might reasonably be expected to enable an officer of HMRC to comprehend the manner in which the arrangements are intended to operate, including—

(*a*) the client's name and address;

(*b*) the name and address of the promoter;

(*c*) details of the provision of the Arrangements Regulations, [the ATED Arrangements Regulations,][1] the IHT Arrangements Regulations or the SDLT Arrangements Regulations by virtue of which the arrangements are notifiable;

(*d*) a summary of the arrangements, and the name (if any) by which they are known;

(*e*) information explaining each element of the arrangements (including the way in which they are structured) from which the tax advantage expected to be obtained under the arrangements arises; and

(*f*) the statutory provisions, relating to any of the prescribed taxes, on which that tax advantage is based.

(3) The information which must be provided to HMRC by a person obliged to do so by section 310 (duty of parties to notifiable arrangements not involving promoter) is sufficient information as might reasonably be expected to enable an officer of HMRC to comprehend the manner in which the arrangements of which that transaction forms part are intended to operate, including—

(*a*) the name and address of the person entering into the transaction;

(*b*) details of the provision of the Arrangements Regulations, [the ATED Arrangements Regulations,][1] the IHT Arrangements Regulations or the SDLT Arrangements Regulations by virtue of which the arrangements are notifiable;

(*c*) a summary of the arrangements and the name (if any) by which they are known;

(*d*) information explaining each element of the arrangements (including the way in which they are structured) from which the tax advantage expected to be obtained under the arrangements arises; and

(*e*) the statutory provisions, relating to any of the prescribed taxes, on which that tax advantage is based.

(4) If, but for this paragraph—

(*a*) a person would be obliged to provide information in relation to two or more notifiable arrangements,

(*b*) those arrangements are substantially the same (whether they relate to the same parties or different parties), and

(*c*) the person has already provided information under paragraph (2) or (3) in relation to any of the other arrangements,

the person need not provide further information under paragraph (2) or (3).

(5) In this regulation—

"the Arrangements Regulations" means the Tax Avoidance Schemes (Prescribed Descriptions of Arrangements) Regulations 2006;

["the ATED Arrangements Regulations" means the Annual Tax on Enveloped Dwellings Avoidance Schemes (Prescribed Descriptions of Arrangements) Regulations 2013;][1]

"the IHT Arrangements Regulations" means the Inheritance Tax Avoidance Schemes (Prescribed Descriptions of Arrangements) Regulations 2011;

"the SDLT Arrangements Regulations" means the Stamp Duty Land Tax Avoidance Schemes (Prescribed Descriptions of Arrangements) Regulations 2005.

Modifications—See the National Insurance Contributions (Application of Part 7 of the Finance Act 2004) Regulations, SI 2012/1868 reg 26(1), (3) for the modification of this regulation is its applications to notifiable contribution arrangements and notifiable contribution proposals.

Amendments—[1] In paras (1)(*b*), (2)(*c*), (3)(*b*), words inserted, and in para (5) definition of "the ATED Arrangements Regulations" inserted, by the Tax Avoidance Schemes (Information) (Amendment, etc) Regulations, SI 2013/2592 regs 3, 5–8 with effect from 4 November 2013.

5 Time for providing information under section 308, 308A, 309 or 310

(1) The period or time (as the case may be) within which—

(*a*) the prescribed information under section 308, 309 or 310, and

(*b*) the information or documents which will support or explain the prescribed information under section 308A (supplemental information),

must be provided to HMRC is found in accordance with the following paragraphs of this regulation.

(2) Where a proposal or arrangements (not being otherwise notifiable) is or are treated as notifiable by virtue of an order under section 306A(1) (doubt as to notifiability) the prescribed period is the period of 10 days beginning on the day after that on which the order is made.

(3) In the case of a requirement to provide specified information about, or documents relating to, the notifiable proposal or arrangements which arises by virtue of an order under section 308A(2), the prescribed period is the period of 10 days beginning on the day after that on which the order is made.

(4) In any other case of a notification under section 308(1), the prescribed period is the period of 5 days beginning on the day after the relevant date.

(5) In any other case of a notification under section 308(3), the prescribed period is the period of 5 days beginning on the day after that on which the promoter first becomes aware of any transaction forming part of arrangements to which that subsection applies.

(6) In the case of a notification under section 309(1), the prescribed period is the period of 5 days beginning on the day after that on which the client enters into the first transaction forming part of notifiable arrangements to which that subsection applies.

(7) In the case of a notification under section 310 which arises by virtue of the application of regulation 6 of the Tax Avoidance Schemes (Promoters and Prescribed Circumstances) Regulations 2004 (persons not to be treated as promoters: legal professional privilege), the prescribed time is any time during the period of 5 days beginning on the day after that on which the person enters into the first transaction forming part of the notifiable arrangements.

(8) In any other case of a notification under section 310 the prescribed time is any time during the period of 30 days beginning on the day after that on which the person enters into the first transaction forming part of the notifiable arrangements.

Modifications—NIC (Application of Part 7 of the Finance Act 2004) Regulations, SI 2012/1868 reg 26(4) (this reg modified in relation to NIC avoidance schemes and proposals).

The Tax Avoidance Schemes (Information) (Amendment, etc) Regulations, SI 2013/2592 reg 2. In respect of proposals or arrangements that are notifiable by virtue of the Annual Tax on Enveloped Dwellings Avoidance Schemes (Prescribed Descriptions of Arrangements) Regulations, SI 2013/2571 reg 4, where—

- for the purposes of FA 2004 s 308(1) the relevant date in relation to a proposal falls within the period beginning with 31 January 2013 and ending on 3 November 2013, or
- for the purposes of FA 2004 s 308(3) the date on which the promoter first becomes aware of any transaction forming part of the arrangements falls within the period beginning with 31 January 2013 and ending on 3 November 2013,

the period, or time, to be found in accordance with this regulation shall end on 17 January 2014 instead of the day on which it would otherwise end by virtue of this regulation.

6 Prescribed information under sections 312 and 312A

For the purposes of sections 312(2) and (5) (duty of promoter to notify client of number) and 312A(2) [and (2A) (duty of client to provide information to parties)][1] the prescribed information is—

(*a*) the name and address of the promoter;

(*b*) the name, or a brief description of the notifiable arrangements or proposal;
(*c*) the reference number (or if more than one, any one reference number) allocated by HMRC under section 311 (arrangements to be given reference number) to the notifiable arrangements or proposed notifiable arrangements;
(*d*) the date that the reference number was—
(i) sent by the promoter to the client; or (as the case may be)
(ii) sent to any other person by the client under section 312A(2) [or (2A)][1].

Amendments—[1] Words substituted, and in para (*d*)(ii), words inserted by the Tax Avoidance Schemes (Information) (Amendment) Regulations, SI 2015/948 regs 2, 3 with effect from 16 April 2015.

7 Time for providing information under section 312A

In the case of a notification under section 312A(2) [or (2A)][1] the prescribed period is the period of 30 days beginning on—
(*a*) the day on which the client first becomes aware of any transaction forming part of notifiable arrangements or proposed notifiable arrangements; or, if later,
(*b*) the day on which the prescribed information is notified to the client by the promoter under section 312.

Modification—NIC (Application of Part 7 of the Finance Act 2004) Regulations, SI 2012/1868 reg 26(5) (this reg modified in relation to NIC avoidance schemes and proposals).

Amendments—[1] Words inserted by the Tax Avoidance Schemes (Information) (Amendment) Regulations, SI 2015/948 regs 2, 4 with effect from 16 April 2015.

8 Exemption from duty under section 312A

Amendments—Regulation 8 revoked by the Tax Avoidance Schemes (Information) (Amendment) Regulations, SI 2015/948 regs 2, 5 with effect from 16 April 2015.

[8A Prescribed information under section 312B: information and timing

(1) For the purposes of section 312B (duty of client to provide information to promoter)—
(*a*) the prescribed period is 10 days from the later of the date that the client receives the reference number allocated by HMRC under section 311 to the notifiable arrangements, and the date the client first enters into a transaction which forms part of the notifiable arrangements; and
(*b*) the prescribed information is—
(i) any identification number allocated to the client by HMRC ("unique taxpayer number") and the client's national insurance number; or
(ii) confirmation that the client does not have a unique taxpayer number or a national insurance number or has neither number.][1]

Amendments—[1] Reg 8A inserted by the Tax Avoidance Schemes (Information) (Amendment, etc) Regulations, SI 2013/2592 regs 3, 16 with effect from 4 November 2013.

[8B Exemption from duty under section 313

Where an employee receives prescribed information from an employer under section 312A(2) or (2A) in circumstances where the employer has a duty to notify HMRC under section 313ZC in respect of that employee, then no duty arises under section 313(1) in respect of that employee.][1]

Amendments—[1] Regulation 8B inserted by the Tax Avoidance Schemes (Information) (Amendment) Regulations, SI 2015/948 regs 2, 6 with effect from 16 April 2015.

9 Prescribed cases under section 313(3)(a)

(1) The prescribed cases for the purposes of section 313(3)(a) (cases in which the information is to be included in returns) are as follows.

(2) Subject to regulation [10(7)][2] and (8), in the case of a person who—
(*a*) expects an advantage to arise in respect of that person's liability to pay, entitlement to a repayment of, or to a deferment of the liability to pay, income tax or capital gains tax as a result of notifiable arrangements; and
(*b*) is required to make a return to HMRC by a notice under section 8 or 8A of the Taxes Management Act 1970 (income tax and capital gains tax: personal return and trustee's return), in respect of income tax or capital gains tax,

the prescribed information shall be included in the return (under the section which applies) which relates to the year of assessment in which the person first enters into a transaction forming part of the notifiable arrangements and in the return for each subsequent year of assessment until the advantage ceases to apply to that person.

(3) Subject to regulation [10(7)][2] and (8) in the case of a company which—
(*a*) expects a tax advantage to arise in respect of its liability to pay, entitlement to a repayment of, or to a deferment of its liability to pay, corporation tax as a result of notifiable arrangements; and
(*b*) is required to make a return to HMRC by a notice under paragraph 3 of Schedule 18 to the Finance Act 1998 (company tax return), in respect of corporation tax,

the prescribed information shall be included in the return under that paragraph covering the period in which the company first enters into a transaction forming part of the notifiable arrangements and in the return covering each subsequent period until the tax advantage ceases to apply to the company.

(4) Subject to regulation [10(7)][2] and (8) in the case of a partnership—

(*a*) which expects an advantage to arise in respect of a partner's liability to pay, entitlement to a repayment of, or to a deferment of the liability to pay income tax, capital gains tax or corporation tax in respect of partnership profits or gains as a result of notifiable arrangements; and

(*b*) in respect of which a return is required to be made to HMRC by virtue of a notice under section 12AA of the Taxes Management Act 1970 (partnership return) in respect of income tax, capital gains tax or corporation tax,

in addition to any duty under paragraph (2) or (3) the prescribed information shall be included in the return under that section covering the period in which the partnership first enters into a transaction forming part of the notifiable arrangements and in the returns covering each subsequent period until the tax advantage ceases to apply to the partner in question.

(5) Subject to regulation 10(7) and (8) in the case of a person who—

(*a*) expects an advantage to arise in respect of that person's liability to pay, entitlement to a repayment of, or to a deferment of the liability to pay inheritance tax as a result of notifiable arrangements; and

(*b*) is required to make a return to HMRC under section 216 of the Inheritance Tax Act 1984 (accounts and information) in respect of a transaction forming part of the notifiable arrangements within a period of 12 months from the end of the month in which the first transaction forming part of the arrangements is entered into,

the prescribed information shall be included in the return under that section.

[(6) Subject to regulation 10(7) and (8) in the case of a person who—

(*a*) expects an advantage to arise in respect of that person's liability to pay, entitlement to a repayment of, or deferment of the liability to pay, annual tax on enveloped dwellings as a result of notifiable arrangements; and

(*b*) is required to make a return to HMRC under section 159 of the Finance Act 2013 in respect of annual tax on enveloped dwellings;

the prescribed information shall be included in the return under that section.][1]

Modifications—See the National Insurance Contributions (Application of Part 7 of the Finance Act 2004) Regulations, SI 2012/1868 reg 26(1), (7) for the modification of this regulation is its applications to notifiable contribution arrangements and notifiable contribution proposals.

Amendments—[1] Para (6) inserted by the Tax Avoidance Schemes (Information) (Amendment, etc) Regulations, SI 2013/2592 regs 3, 9 with effect from 4 November 2013.

[2] In paras (2), (3), (4), reference substituted by the Tax Avoidance Schemes (Information) (Amendment) Regulations, SI 2015/948 regs 2, 7 with effect from 16 April 2015.

10 Prescribed cases under section 313(3)(*b*)

(1) The prescribed cases for the purposes of section 313(3)(*b*) (cases in which the information is to be provided separately) are as follows.

(2) In a case where a purchaser expects an advantage to arise in respect of that person's liability to pay, entitlement to a repayment of, or to a deferment of the liability to pay stamp duty land tax as a result of notifiable arrangements the prescribed information shall be provided separately to HMRC in such form and manner as they may specify.

(3) If paragraph (2) applies in relation to a land transaction entered into as purchaser by or on behalf of a partnership notification of the prescribed information by or in relation to the responsible partners may instead be done by or in relation to a representative partner or partners.

(4) . . . [2]

(5) In the case of a person who would be obliged to comply with a duty under regulation 9(2) to (4), but is not required, in respect of a year of assessment, accounting period or tax year—

(a) in the case of notifiable arrangements to which regulation 9(2) applies, to make a return under either of the provisions referred to in regulation 9(2)(*b*);

(*b*) in the case of notifiable arrangements to which regulation 9(3) applies, to make a return under the provision referred to in regulation 9(3)(*b*); or

(*c*) in the case of notifiable arrangements to which regulation 9(4) applies, to make a return under the provision referred to in regulation 9(4)(*b*);

the prescribed information shall be provided separately to HMRC in such form and manner as they may specify.

(6) In the case of a person who—

(*a*) expects an advantage to arise in respect of that person's liability to pay, entitlement to a repayment of, or to a deferment of the liability to pay inheritance tax as a result of notifiable arrangements; and

(*b*) is not required to make a return to HMRC under section 216 of the Inheritance Tax Act 1984 in respect of a transaction forming part of the notifiable arrangements within a period of 12 months from the end of the month in which the first transaction forming part of the arrangements is entered into, the prescribed information shall be provided separately to HMRC in such form and manner as they may specify.

[(6A) In the case of a person who—

(*a*) expects an advantage to arise in respect of that person's liability to pay, entitlement to a repayment of, or deferment of the liability to pay, annual tax on enveloped dwellings as a result of notifiable arrangements; and

(*b*) is not required to make a return to HMRC under section 159 of the Finance Act 2013 in respect of a transaction forming part of the notifiable arrangements within a period of 30 days beginning with the later of—

(i) the effective date of the first transaction which forms part of the arrangements; or

(ii) the date of the receipt of the reference number allocated under the provisions of section 311;

the prescribed information shall be provided separately to HMRC.][1]

(7) In a case of a person who would, but for this paragraph, be obliged to comply with a duty under regulation 9 and—

(*a*) the relevant return is not delivered by the filing date; or

(*b*) the relevant return is delivered by the filing date but does not include the prescribed information;

the prescribed information shall be provided separately to HMRC in such form and manner as they may specify.

(8) In a case where—

(*a*) a person is required to provide information relating to more than one reference number;

(*b*) the information is included in a return under regulation 9; and

(*c*) the number of reference numbers in relation to which information is required exceeds the number of spaces allocated to the information on the return form;

the information relating to so many of the reference numbers as exceeds the number of allocated spaces shall be provided separately to HMRC in such form and manner as they may specify.

(9) In addition to the duty under any other paragraph above, or regulation 9, in a case where the arrangements give rise to a claim submitted separately from the return under—

(*a*) section 261B of the Taxation of Chargeable Gains Act 1992 (treating trade loss etc as CGT loss); or

(*b*) Part 4 of the Income Tax Act 2007 (loss relief);

the prescribed information shall be provided separately to HMRC in such form and manner as they may specify.

Modifications—See the National Insurance Contributions (Application of Part 7 of the Finance Act 2004) Regulations, SI 2012/1868 reg 26(1), (8) for the modification of this regulation is its applications to notifiable contribution arrangements and notifiable contribution proposals.

Amendments—[1] Para (6A) inserted by the Tax Avoidance Schemes (Information) (Amendment, etc) Regulations, SI 2013/2592 regs 3, 10 with effect from 4 November 2013.

[2] Para (4) revoked by the Tax Avoidance Schemes (Information) (Amendment) Regulations, SI 2015/948 regs 2, 8 with effect from 16 April 2015.

11 Prescribed information under section 313(1)

(1) For the purposes of section 313(1) (duty of parties to notifiable arrangements to notify Board of number, etc) the prescribed information is that specified in whichever of paragraph (2), (3) or (4) is applicable.

(2) In cases prescribed in regulation 9 the prescribed information is—

(*a*) the reference number (or if more than one, any one reference number) allocated by HMRC under section 311 to the notifiable arrangements or proposed notifiable arrangements; and

(*b*) the year of assessment, tax year or accounting period (as the case may be) in which, or the date on which, the person providing the information expects a tax advantage to be obtained.

(3) In the cases prescribed in regulation 10 (apart from paragraph (2) [and any case relating to annual tax on enveloped dwellings][1]) the prescribed information is—

(*a*) the name and address of the person providing it;

(*b*) any National Insurance number, tax reference number, PAYE reference number or other personal identifier allocated by HMRC to the person to whom the information relates;

(*c*) the reference number (or if more than one, any one reference number) allocated by HMRC under section 311 to the notifiable arrangements or proposed notifiable arrangements;

(*d*) the year of assessment, tax year or accounting period (as the case may be) in which, or the date on which, the person providing the information . . . [2] expects to obtain a tax advantage by virtue of the notifiable arrangements;

(*e*) the name of the person providing the declaration as to the accuracy and completeness of the notification; and

(*f*) the capacity in which the person mentioned in sub-paragraph (*e*) is acting.

(4) In the case prescribed at regulation 10(2) the prescribed information is—

(*a*) the name and address of the purchaser;
(*b*) the reference number (or if more than one, any one reference number) allocated by HMRC under section 311 to the notifiable arrangements or proposed notifiable arrangements;
(*c*) the address of the property forming the subject of the arrangements ("the property");
(*d*) the title number of the property (if any is allocated);
(*e*) the unique transaction reference number(if a land transaction return has been submitted to HMRC at the time the prescribed information is provided);
(*f*) the market value of the property, taking into account all chargeable interests in the property held by the same person or connected persons;
(*g*) the effective date of the first land transaction which forms part of the arrangements;
(*h*) the name of the person providing the declaration as to the accuracy and completeness of the notification; and
(*i*) the capacity in which that person is acting.

[(5) In the cases prescribed in regulation 10(6A), (7) and (8), where they relate to annual tax on enveloped dwellings, the prescribed information is—
(*a*) the name and address of the person providing the information;
(*b*) any tax reference number or other personal identifier allocated by HMRC or a foreign tax authority to the person to whom the information relates;
(*c*) where a foreign tax authority has allocated a personal identifier, the name of the country on behalf of which that foreign tax authority acts;
(*d*) the reference number (or if more than one, any one reference number) allocated by HMRC under section 311 to the notifiable arrangements or proposed notifiable arrangements;
(*e*) the address of the property forming the subject of the arrangements ("the property");
(*f*) the title number of the property (if any is allocated);
(*g*) the first chargeable period (within the meaning of section 94(8) of the Finance Act 2013) in which the person providing the information expects to obtain a tax advantage by virtue of the notifable arrangements;
(*h*) the name of the person providing the declaration as to the accuracy and completeness of the notification, where different from information provided under sub-paragraph (*a*); and
(*i*) the capacity in which the person mentioned in sub-paragraph (*h*) is acting.][1]

Modifications—See the National Insurance Contributions (Application of Part 7 of the Finance Act 2004) Regulations, SI 2012/1868 reg 26(1), (9) for the modification of this regulation is its applications to notifiable contribution arrangements and notifiable contribution proposals.

Amendments—[1] Words in para (3), and whole of para (5), inserted, by the Tax Avoidance Schemes (Information) (Amendment, etc) Regulations, SI 2013/2592 regs 3, 11, 12 with effect from 4 November 2013.
[2] In para (3)(*d*), words revoked by the Tax Avoidance Schemes (Information) (Amendment) Regulations, SI 2015/948 regs 2, 9 with effect from 16 April 2015.

12 Time for providing information under section 313(3)(*b*)

(1) The prescribed times for providing information in the cases prescribed in regulation 10 are as follows.

(2) In the case of regulation 10(2) any time during the period of 30 days beginning with the later of—
(*a*) the effective date of the first land transaction which forms part of the arrangements; or
(*b*) the date of the receipt of the reference number allocated under the provisions of section 311.

(3) . . . [2]

(4) In the case of regulation 10(5)—
(*a*) for regulation 10(5)(*a*), any time during the period ending on 31st January next following the end of the year of assessment in question;
(*b*) for regulation 10(5)(*b*), any time during the period ending on the date defined as the filing date for the purposes of paragraph 14 of Schedule 18 to the Finance Act 1998 in respect of the period of account in question;
(*c*) for regulation 10(5)(*c*), any time during the period ending on the earliest date by which the person in question could be required to file a return under section 12AA of the Taxes Management Act 1970, determined in accordance with whichever of subsections (4) and (5) of that section is applicable.

(5) In the case of regulation 10(6) any time during the period of 12 months from the end of the month in which the first transaction forming part of the arrangements is entered into.

[(5A) In the cases of regulation 10(6A), (7) and (8), where it relates to annual tax on enveloped dwellings, any time during the period of 30 days beginning with the later of—
(*a*) the effective date of the first transaction which forms part of the arrangements; or
(*b*) the date of the receipt of the reference number allocated under the provisions of section 311.][1]

(6) In the case of regulation 10(7) and (8)[, except where they relate to annual tax on enveloped dwellings,][1] any time during the period ending on the filing date for the relevant return.

(7) In the case of regulation 10(9) the time that the claim is made.

Modifications—See the National Insurance Contributions (Application of Part 7 of the Finance Act 2004) Regulations, SI 2012/1868 reg 26(1), (9) for the modification of this regulation is its applications to notifiable contribution arrangements and notifiable contribution proposals.

Amendments—[1] Para (5A), and words in para (6), inserted, by the Tax Avoidance Schemes (Information) (Amendment, etc) Regulations, SI 2013/2592 regs 3, 13 with effect from 4 November 2013.

[2] Para (3) revoked by the Tax Avoidance Schemes (Information) (Amendment) Regulations, SI 2015/948 regs 2, 10 with effect from 16 April 2015.

13 Prescribed information under section 313ZA: information and timing

(1) For the purposes of section 313ZA(3) (duty of promoter to provide client lists)-

[(*a*) the prescribed period is—

(i) 30 days; or

(ii) where the circumstances in sub-paragraph (*d*)(iii) apply, 60 days in respect of the information prescribed under sub-paragraph (*b*)(iii) only.][1]

(*b*) the prescribed information is—

(i) any reference number allocated by HMRC under section 311 to the arrangements (or to a proposal for them) to which the information provided relates;

(ii) the name and address of each client in relation to whom the relevant date (within the meaning of section 312(3)) occurs in the relevant period in relation to which the information is being provided;

[(iii) any identification number allocated by HMRC ("unique taxpayer number") and national insurance number for each client in relation to whom the relevant date (within the meaning of section 312(3)) occurs in the relevant period in relation to which the information is being provided;

(iv) the promoter's name and address; and

(v) the end date of the relevant period in relation to which the information is being provided.][1]

(*c*) in sub-paragraph (*b*)(ii) the address of the client is the address to which the promoter has sent or would have sent the prescribed information under section 312.

[(*d*) at the end of the prescribed period under sub-paragraph (*a*)(i), where the promoter is unable to provide any unique taxpayer number or national insurance number, the prescribed information under sub-paragraph (*b*) must include confirmation that one of the following applies—

(i) the client has complied with section 312B and does not have a unique taxpayer number or national insurance number or has neither number;

(ii) the client has not complied with section 312B;

(iii) on the sixteenth day after the end of the relevant period, the prescribed period under regulation 8A(1)(*a*) had not yet expired;

(e) at the end of the prescribed period under sub-paragraph (*a*)(ii), where the promoter is unable to provide any unique taxpayer number or national insurance number, the prescribed information under sub-paragraph (*b*) must include confirmation that either sub-paragraph (*d*)(i) or sub-paragraph (*d*)(ii) applies.][1]

(2) For the purposes of section 313ZA(4) the relevant period is each calendar quarter.

Modifications—See the National Insurance Contributions (Application of Part 7 of the Finance Act 2004) Regulations, SI 2012/1868 reg 26(1), (10) for the modification of this regulation is its applications to notifiable contribution arrangements and notifiable contribution proposals.

Amendments—[1] Para (1)(*a*) substituted, paras (1)(*b*)(iii)–(v) substituted for previous paras (1)(*b*)(iii), (iv), and paras (1)(*d*), (*e*) inserted, by the Tax Avoidance Schemes (Information) (Amendment, etc) Regulations, SI 2013/2592 regs 3, 17–19 with effect from 4 November 2013.

[13A Prescribed information under section 313ZB: information and timing

(1) For the purposes of section 313ZB (further information from promoters)—

(*a*) the prescribed period is 10 days from the date that the promoter receives the written notice under section 313ZB; and

(*b*) the prescribed information is—

(i) the name and address of any person described in section 313ZB(2) (but only those who will, or are likely to, either sell the arrangements to another person, or achieve a tax advantage by implementing the arrangements);

(ii) any identification number allocated by HMRC to any person mentioned at sub-paragraph (*b*)(i); and

(iii) sufficient information as might reasonably be expected to enable an officer of HMRC to comprehend the manner in which any person mentioned at sub-paragraph (*b*)(i) is involved in the arrangements.

(2) Paragraph (1)(*b*) only extends to information held by the promoter at the time of receipt of a written notice under section 313ZB(2).][1]

Amendments—[1] Reg 13A inserted by the Tax Avoidance Schemes (Information) (Amendment, etc) Regulations, SI 2013/2592 regs 3, 20 with effect from 4 November 2013.

[13B Prescribed information under section 313ZC: information and timing

(1) For the purposes of section 313ZC (duty of employer to notify HMRC of details of employees etc) the prescribed time for providing prescribed information is 14 days after the end of the final tax period in respect of the tax year in which any person first enters into a transaction forming part of the notifiable arrangements and on the same date in each subsequent year until an advantage ceases to apply to the employee and the employer.

In this paragraph, "tax period" has the meaning given in regulation 2(1) (interpretation) of the Income Tax (Pay As You Earn) Regulations 2003.

(2) For the purposes of section 313ZC the prescribed information is—

(*a*) the name, address and reference number of the employer;

(*b*) the name and any National Insurance Number of the employee;

(*c*) the reference number (or, if more than one, any one reference number) allocated by HMRC under section 311 (arrangements to be given reference number) to the notifiable arrangements or proposed notifiable arrangements;

(*d*) where the employee obtains or might reasonably be expected to obtain a tax advantage by virtue of the notifiable arrangements, the tax year in which the employee obtains or expects to obtain the tax advantage;

(*e*) where a tax advantage is obtained or might reasonably be expected to be obtained only by a person other than the employee by virtue of the notifiable arrangements, confirmation that the employee's tax advantage is expected to be nil; and

(*f*) the name and address of the promoter, and any name given to the notifiable arrangement when it was notified.][1]

Amendments—[1] Regulation 13B inserted by the Tax Avoidance Schemes (Information) (Amendment) Regulations, SI 2015/948 regs 2, 11 with effect from 16 April 2015.

14 Time for providing information under section 313A and 313B

(1) In the case of a requirement under or by virtue of section 313A(1) (pre-disclosure enquiry), the prescribed period is the period of 10 days beginning on the day after that on which the notice is issued.

(2) In the case of a requirement under or by virtue of section 313B(1) (reasons for non-disclosure: supporting information), the prescribed period is the period of 14 days beginning on the day after that on which the order is made.

15 Prescribed information under section 313C: information and timing

(1) For the purposes of section 313C(1) (information provided to introducers) the prescribed information is—

(*a*) P's name and address; . . . [1]

(*b*) the name and address of each person who has provided P with any information relating to the proposal[; and

(*c*) the name and address of each person with whom P has made a marketing contact.][1]

(2) For the purposes of section 313C(3)(*a*) the prescribed period is 10 days.

Modification—NIC (Application of Part 7 of the Finance Act 2004) Regulations, SI 2012/1868 reg 26(11) (this reg modified in relation to NIC avoidance schemes and proposals).

Amendments—[1] Word at the end of para (1)(*a*) revoked, and para (1)(*c*) and preceding word inserted by the Tax Avoidance Schemes (Information) (Amendment) Regulations, SI 2015/948 regs 2, 12 with effect from 16 April 2015.

16 Higher rate of penalty following a failure to comply with an order under section 306A or 314A

(1) For the purposes of section 98C(2A) of the Taxes Management Act 1970 (higher rate of penalty after the making of an order under section 306A) the prescribed period is the period of 10 days beginning on the date on which the order is made.

(2) For the purposes of section 98C(2B) of the Taxes Management Act 1970 (higher rate of penalty after the making of an order under section 314A) the prescribed period is the period of 10 days beginning on the date on which the order is made.

17 Electronic delivery of information

(1) Information required to be delivered to HMRC or to any other person by virtue of these Regulations may be delivered in such form and by such means of electronic communications as are for the time being authorised for that purpose.

(2) The use of a particular means of electronic communications is authorised for the purposes of paragraph (1) only if—

(*a*) it is authorised by directions given by HMRC under section 132(5) of the Finance Act 1999 (voluntary filing by electronic means of returns and other documents); and

(*b*) the user complies with any conditions imposed by HMRC under that section.

(3) Nothing in this regulation prevents the delivery of information by electronic communications if the information is contained in a return which is—

(*a*) authorised to be delivered electronically by virtue of regulations under section 132 of the Finance Act 1999; or

(*b*) required to be so delivered by virtue of regulations under section 135 of the Finance Act 2002 (mandatory e-filing).

Modification—NIC (Application of Part 7 of the Finance Act 2004) Regulations, SI 2012/1868 reg 26(12) (this reg modified in relation to NIC avoidance schemes and proposals).

18 Amendment of the Tax Avoidance Schemes (Promoters and Prescribed Circumstances) Regulations 2004

In regulation 6 of the Tax Avoidance Schemes (Promoters and Prescribed Circumstances) Regulations 2004(1) for "paragraph (1) or (2) (as the case may be) of regulation 3 of the Tax Avoidance Schemes (Information) Regulations 2004" substitute "regulation 4(1) of the Tax Avoidance Schemes (Information) Regulations 2012".

Modification—NIC (Application of Part 7 of the Finance Act 2004) Regulations, SI 2012/1868 reg 26(13) (this reg revoked in relation to NIC avoidance schemes and proposals).

SCHEDULE
REVOCATIONS

Regulation 3

Statutory Instrument Number	Title of Regulations	Extent of revocation
SI 2004/1864	The Tax Avoidance Schemes (Information) Regulations 2004	The whole regulations
SI 2004/2613	The Tax Avoidance Schemes (Promoters, Prescribed Circumstances and Information) (Amendment) Regulations 2004	Regulation 3
SI 2005/1869	The Tax Avoidance Schemes (Information) (Amendment) Regulations 2005	The whole regulations
SI 2006/1544	The Tax Avoidance Schemes (Information) (Amendment) Regulations 2006	The whole regulations
SI 2007/2153	The Tax Avoidance Schemes (Information) (Amendment) Regulations 2007	The whole regulations
SI 2007/3103	The Tax Avoidance Schemes (Information) (Amendment) (No 2) Regulations 2007	The whole regulations
SI 2008/1947	The Tax Avoidance Schemes (Information) (Amendment) Regulations 2008	The whole regulations
SI 2009/611	The Tax Avoidance Schemes (Information) (Amendment) Regulations 2009	The whole regulations
SI 2010/410	The Tax Avoidance Schemes (Information) (Amendment) Regulations 2010	The whole regulations
SI 2010/2928	The Tax Avoidance Schemes (Information) (Amendment) Regulations (No 2) 2010	The whole regulations
SI 2011/171	The Tax Avoidance Schemes (Information) (Amendment) Regulations 2011	The whole regulations

2012/2903

INHERITANCE TAX (MARKET MAKERS AND DISCOUNT HOUSES) REGULATIONS 2012

Made . . . .*19 November 2012*
Laid before the House of Commons . . . .*21 November 2012*
Coming into force . . . .*31 December 2012*

The Commissioners for Her Majesty's Revenue and Customs make the following Regulations in exercise of powers conferred by sections 106(5) and 107(5) of the Finance Act 1986 and now exercisable by them.

1 Citation and commencement

These Regulations may be cited as the Inheritance Tax (Market Makers and Discount Houses) Regulations 2012 and come into force on 31st December 2012.

2 Application of these Regulations

The day specified for the purposes of sections 106(6) and 107(6) of the Finance Act 1986 for the application of these Regulations is 31st December 2012.

3 Amendment of the Inheritance Tax Act 1984

The Inheritance Tax Act 1984 is amended as follows.

4 (*inserts IHTA 1984 s 105(4A)*)

5 (*substitutes IHTA 1984 s 234(3)(c)*)

6 Description for the purposes of sections 105(4A) and 234(3)(*c*)(ii) of the Inheritance Tax Act 1984

For the purposes of section 105(4A) of the Inheritance Tax Act 1984 the description of a business is a business in an EEA State other than the United Kingdom which—

(*a*) holds itself out at all normal times, in compliance with the rules of a regulated market which has been notified to the European Commission, as willing to buy and sell securities, stocks and shares at a price specified by it, and

(*b*) is recognised as doing so by that regulated market.

7 For the purposes of section 234(3)(*c*)(ii) of the Inheritance Tax Act 1984 the description of a company is a company in an EEA State other than the United Kingdom which—

(*a*) holds itself out at all normal times, in compliance with the rules of a regulated market which has been notified to the European Commission, as willing to buy and sell securities, stocks and shares at a price specified by it, and

(*b*) is recognised as doing so by that regulated market.

2012/3070

VISITING FORCES AND INTERNATIONAL MILITARY HEADQUARTERS (EU SOFA) (TAX DESIGNATION) ORDER 2012

Made . . . .*12 December 2012*
Coming into force in accordance with Article 1(2)

At the Court at Buckingham Palace, the 12th day of December 2012

Present,

The Queen's Most Excellent Majesty in Council

Her Majesty, in exercise of the powers conferred upon Her by section 303 of the Income Tax (Earnings and Pensions) Act 2003, section 833 of the Income Tax Act 2007, section 155 of the Inheritance Tax Act 1984, by and with the advice of Her Privy Council, makes the following Order—

1 Citation and commencement

(1) This Order may be cited as the Visiting Forces and International Military Headquarters (EU SOFA) (Tax Designation) Order 2012.

(2) This Order shall come into force immediately after the coming into force of the EU SOFA in respect of the United Kingdom.

2 Interpretation

In this Order—

"the EU SOFA" means the Agreement between the member states of the European Union concerning the status of military and civilian staff seconded to the institutions of the European Union, of the headquarters and forces which may be made available to the European Union in the context of the preparation and execution of the tasks referred to in Article 17(2) of the Treaty on European Union, including exercises, and of the military and civilian staff of the member states put at the disposal of the European Union to act in this context;

"the Treaty on European Union" means the Treaty on European Union signed at Maastricht on 7 February 1992 (as amended by the Treaty of Lisbon).

3 Designation

For the purpose of giving effect to Article 16 of the EU SOFA, each of the countries specified in the First Schedule to this Order, and the international military headquarters specified in the Second Schedule to this Order, are hereby designated for the purposes of—

(a) section 303 of the Income Tax (Earnings and Pensions) Act 2003;

(b) section 833 of the Income Tax Act 2007; and

(c) section 155 of the Inheritance Tax Act 1984.

SCHEDULE 1

DESIGNATED COUNTRIES

Article 3

Austria, Belgium, Bulgaria, Cyprus, Czech Republic, Denmark, Estonia, Finland, France, Germany, Greece, Hungary, Ireland, Italy, Latvia, Lithuania, Luxembourg, Malta, Netherlands, Poland, Portugal, Romania, Slovakia, Slovenia, Spain, Sweden.

SCHEDULE 2

DESIGNATED INTERNATIONAL MILITARY HEADQUARTERS

Article 3

The European Union Operational Headquarters at Northwood.

2012/3071

VISITING FORCES AND INTERNATIONAL MILITARY HEADQUARTERS (NATO AND PFP) (TAX DESIGNATION) ORDER 2012

Made . . . . 12 December 2012

Coming into force in accordance with Article 1(2)

At the Court at Buckingham Palace, the 12th day of December 2012

Present,

The Queen's Most Excellent Majesty in Council

Her Majesty, in exercise of the powers conferred upon Her by section 74A of the Finance Act 1960, section 155 of the Inheritance Tax Act 1984, section 303 of the Income Tax (Earnings and Pensions) Act 2003 and section 833 of the Income Tax Act 2007, by and with the advice of Her Privy Council, makes the following Order—

1 Citation and commencement

(1) This Order may be cited as the Visiting Forces and International Military Headquarters (NATO and PfP) (Tax Designation) Order 2012.

(2) This Order shall come into force on the day after the date on which it is made.

2 Revocations

The Orders in Schedule 1 are revoked.

3 Interpretation

In this Order—

"NATO" means the North Atlantic Treaty Organisation based on the North Atlantic Treaty dated 4th April 1949;

"the NATO SOFA" means the Agreement regarding the Status of Forces of Parties to the North Atlantic Treaty dated 19th June 1951;

"the Paris Protocol" means the Protocol on the Status of International Military Headquarters set up pursuant to the North Atlantic Treaty dated 28th August 1952;

"PfP" means the Partnership for Peace programme of practical bilateral cooperation between individual Partner countries and NATO;

"the PfP SOFA" means the Agreement among the State Parties to the North Atlantic Treaty and the Other States Participating in the Partnership for Peace regarding the Status of their Forces dated 19th June 1995.

4 NATO designation

For the purpose of giving effect to Article X of the NATO SOFA and Article VII of the Paris Protocol each of the countries specified in the Second Schedule to this Order, and each of the headquarters specified in the Fourth Schedule to this Order, is hereby designated for the purposes of section 74A of the Finance Act 1960, section 155 of the Inheritance Tax Act 1984, section 303 of the Income Tax (Earnings and Pensions) Act 2003 and section 833 of the Income Tax Act 2007.

5 PfP designation

For the purpose of giving effect to Article I of the PfP SOFA each of the countries specified in the Third Schedule to this Order is hereby designated for the purposes of section 74A of the Finance Act 1960, section 155 of the Inheritance Tax Act 1984, section 303 of the Income Tax (Earnings and Pensions) Act 2003 and section 833 of the Income Tax Act 2007.

SCHEDULE 1

Article 2

Designation Orders revoked

Orders revoked	*References*
The Visiting Forces and Allied Headquarters (Income Tax and Death Duties) (Designation) Order 1961	SI 1961/580
The Visiting Forces and Allied Headquarters (Stamp Duties) (Designation) Order 1961	SI 1960/581
The Visiting Forces and Allied Headquarters (Income Tax and Capital Gains Tax) (Designation) Order 1998	SI 1998/1513
The Visiting Forces (Income Tax and Capital Gains Tax) (Designation) Order 1998	SI 1998/1514
The Visiting Forces and Allied Headquarters (Inheritance Tax) (Designation) Order 1998	SI 1998/1515
The Visiting Forces (Inheritance Tax) (Designation) Order 1998	SI 1998/1516
The Visiting Forces and Allied Headquarters (Stamp Duties) (Designation) Order 1998	SI 1998/1517
The Visiting Forces (Stamp Duties) (Designation) Order 1998	SI 1998/1518

SCHEDULE 2

DESIGNATED NATO COUNTRIES

Article 4

Albania, Belgium, Bulgaria, Canada, Croatia, Czech Republic, Denmark, Estonia, France, Germany, Greece, Hungary, Iceland, Italy, Latvia, Lithuania, Luxembourg, Netherlands, Norway, Poland, Portugal, Romania, Slovakia, Slovenia, Spain, Turkey, United States of America.

SCHEDULE 3

DESIGNATED PFP COUNTRIES

Article 5

Armenia, Austria, Azerbaijan, Belarus, Bosnia and Herzegovina, Finland, Georgia, Ireland, Kazakhstan, Kyrgyz Republic, Malta, Moldova, Montenegro, Russia, Serbia, Sweden, Switzerland, Tajikistan, the former Yugoslav Republic of Macedonia, Turkmenistan, Ukraine, Uzbekistan.

SCHEDULE 4

DESIGNATED HEADQUARTERS

Article 4

Headquarters of the Supreme Allied Commander Transformation (HQ SACT)

Supreme Headquarters Allied Powers Europe (SHAPE)

Maritime Component Command Headquarters Northwood (CC-MAR HQ Northwood)
Commander Submarines Allied Naval Forces North (COMSUBNORTH)
NATO Airborne Early Warning and Control Force (NAEW&CF)
NATO Joint Electronic Warfare Core Staff (NATO JEWCS)
Headquarters United Kingdom—Netherlands Amphibious Force (UKNLAF)
Headquarters United Kingdom—Netherlands Landing Force (UKNLLF)
The European Air Group (EAG)
The Intelligence Fusion Centre (IFC)
Headquarters Allied Rapid Reaction Corps (HQ ARRC)

2015/623

NATIONAL SAVINGS REGULATIONS 2015

Made . . . . 10 March 2015
Laid before Parliament . . . . 13 March 2015
Coming into force . . . . 6 April 2015

The Treasury in exercise of the powers conferred by sections 2, 3(2), 4, 6(1), 7(2), 8, 9(1) and 15(3) of the National Savings Bank Act 1971, section 33 of the Finance Act 1962, sections 426 and 427 of the Financial Services and Markets Act 2000 and section 140(2) of the Finance Act 2002 make the following Regulations:

PART 3
GENERAL PROVISIONS

CHAPTER 4

DEATH OF DEPOSITORS AND HOLDERS

53 Law applicable on the death of a depositor

On the death of a depositor the Director of Savings may make a payment for the purposes of these Regulations in accordance with the law of the place where the depositor or holder resided at the date of death, unless the Director of Savings has received notice in writing that the depositor or holder was at the date of death domiciled elsewhere.

54 Payment without a grant of representation

(1) Where, on the death of a depositor the amount held in the depositor's name does not exceed £5,000 and no probate of the will or letters of administration to the estate are produced to the Director of Savings within what is considered by the Director of Savings to be a reasonable period, the Director of Savings may, for the purposes of these Regulations, pay the amount (or any part of it) in accordance with paragraph (2).

(2) The Director of Savings may pay the amount—

(*a*) to a person appearing to the Director of Savings to be entitled to take out probate of the will or letters of administration to the estate;

(*b*) where the deceased has left a will in relation to which the Director of Savings is satisfied that probate or letters of administration would be granted, to a person to whom the amount (or any part of it) would be payable under the will (as appears to the Director of Savings), if probate or letters of administration were granted;

(*c*) to a person who satisfies the Director of Savings of their entitlement to receive the amount (or any part of it), being—

(i) a person who has paid the funeral expenses of the deceased;

(ii) a creditor of the deceased; or

(iii) a person who has a beneficial interest in the estate of the deceased;

(*d*) if the deceased was a British citizen and the next of kin appears to the Director of Savings to reside outside the United Kingdom, the Isle of Man and the Channel Islands, to any officer or authority who, as appears to the Director of Savings, may be entrusted with distributing the amount properly;

(*e*) if the deceased was a seaman of a foreign country, being a country with which a treaty has been made in relation to the payment of money due to seamen, to the consular authority of that country;

(*f*) if the deceased was a foreign subject, not being a seaman to whom sub-paragraph (*e*) applies, to the consular authority of the country to which the deceased belonged, or to any authority who, as appears to the Director of Savings, may be entrusted with distributing the amount properly;

(*g*) in a case where the estate of the deceased appears to the Director of Savings to have devolved upon the Crown, the Duchy of Lancaster or the Duchy of Cornwall, to the Treasury Solicitor, the Solicitor for the affairs of the Duchy of Lancaster, or the Solicitor for the affairs of the Duchy of Cornwall respectively,

but where a person to whom an amount may be paid under subparagraph (*b*) or (*c*) has died before payment, the amount (or any part of it) may be paid to a person to whom it would be paid as if the first mentioned person was, immediately before death, a person in paragraph (1).

(3) Despite any legal requirement to the contrary, a person to whom an amount may be paid under paragraph (2)(*b*) or (*c*) (or under the proviso to paragraph (2)) may, if having attained the age of sixteen years, give a receipt for the payment in an approved manner and the receipt shall be valid without the signature of another person; but if that person by reason of age or for any other reason may not accept payment, the Director of Savings may pay the amount to a person who the Director of Savings is satisfied will apply it for the maintenance or otherwise for the benefit of that person.

(4) Subject to paragraph (3), the Director of Savings in making a payment under paragraph (2)(*b*) or (*c*) (or under the proviso to paragraph (2)) must have regard to legal requirements relating to the distribution of the estates of deceased persons, but the Director of Savings may depart from those requirements to the extent it is considered by the Director of Savings that they would cause hardship or inconvenience.

(5) In this regulation "will" includes a codicil.

(6) Nothing in this regulation affects the operation of a nomination made under these Regulations.

55 Death duties or inheritance tax chargeable on death of depositors

(1) This regulation applies on the death of a depositor where the aggregate value of the specified assets exceeds £50,000.

(2) The Director of Savings must, before paying or transferring deposits held in the name of the depositor (either alone or jointly with another depositor) for the purposes of these Regulations, seek a statement from the Commissioners of Her Majesty's Revenue and Customs confirming that death duties, or inheritance or capital transfer tax (being inheritance or capital transfer tax chargeable on the death of the depositor or holder) either are not payable, or have been paid.

(3) A statement under paragraph (2) is not required—

(*a*) where the payment or transfer is made to or on the direction of—

(i) the deceased's legal personal representative acting under probate or letters of administration granted by a court in the United Kingdom; or

(ii) the Public Trustee, the Official Receiver, or the trustee in bankruptcy of the estate of the deceased;

(*b*) where the deceased was at the time of death domiciled in the Isle of Man or the Channel Islands;

(*c*) where the beneficial interest in the deposit has passed to the spouse or civil partner of the deceased in circumstances in which death duties or inheritance or capital transfer tax are not payable.

(4) In this regulation "the specified assets" means the following assets (not being assets in relation to which the deceased was a trustee) at the date of death—

(*a*) the total amount (including interest) held in all accounts in the deceased's name alone, or jointly with another person, in the National Savings Bank;

(*b*) the total amount which would have been repayable (had repayment been demanded) in relation to all certificates recorded in the deceased's name alone, or jointly with another person;

(*c*) the total amount repayable and any other amount payable in relation to all bonds recorded in the deceased's name;

(*d*) the total amount (including any bonus or interest) which would have been repayable (had repayment been demanded) in relation to all savings contracts entered into by the deceased and registered by the Director of Savings under a contractual savings scheme certified by the Treasury in accordance with section 326(2) of the Income and Corporation Taxes Act 1988;

(*e*)

(i) in relation to a deceased depositor or holder of a certificate, all stock and securities registered in the National Savings Stock Register in the sole name of the depositor or holder, or in the depositor or holder's name jointly with any other person;

(ii) in relation to a deceased holder of stock, all stock registered in the register in the deceased's name alone or jointly with any other person; and

(*f*) in relation to a deceased holder of a certificate, the total amount (including interest) which would have been repayable (had repayment been demanded) in relation to all agreements entered into or certificates held by the deceased in accordance with the Savings Certificates (Yearly Plan) Regulations 1984.

(5) The value of stock or securities referred to in paragraph (4)(*e*) shall be—

(*a*) in the case of stock which is of a description corresponding to stock or securities transferable in the registers kept by the Registrar of Government Stock in accordance with regulations under section 47 of the Finance Act 1942 (see regulation 7 (registers of stock and stockholders) of the Government Stock Regulations 2004), the market value; or

(*b*) in all other cases, the capital value.

2015/624

NATIONAL SAVINGS (NO 2) REGULATIONS 2015

Made . . . .*10 March 2015*

Laid before Parliament. . . . .*13 March 2015*

Coming into force. . . . .*6 April 2015*

The Treasury in exercise of the powers conferred by sections 3 and 11 of the National Debt Act 1972 make the following Regulations:

PART 6
COMMON PROVISIONS

CHAPTER 4
DEATH OF DEPOSITORS AND HOLDERS

87 Law applicable on the death of a holder of a bond, stock or certificate

On the death of a holder of—

(*a*) a bond;

(*b*) stock;

(*c*) a certificate; or

(*d*) a children's certificate,

the Director of Savings may make a payment for the purposes of these Regulations in accordance with the law of the place where the depositor or holder resided at the date of death, unless the Director of Savings has received notice in writing that the depositor or holder was at the date of death domiciled elsewhere.

88 Payments under grant of representation in relation to bonds and certificates

(1) In the event of the death of the holder of a bond, a certificate, or a children's certificate, the production of probate or letters of administration (or of a certified copy) granted, or having effect as if granted, in relation to personal estate including those things by a court in the United Kingdom, the Isle of Man or the Channel Islands, is sufficient authority for the Director of Savings to pay the amount repayable (or any other amount payable), or make a transfer (if applicable) for the purposes of these Regulations, to the person to whom the grant was made, or as directed by that person.

(2) Where a payment or transfer is made under this Regulation, the payment or transfer shall, despite the invalidity of, or any defect in, the probate or letters of administration, be deemed to have been lawfully made.

89 Payment without a grant of representation

(1) Where, on the death of a person—

(*a*) the amount repayable, or any other amount payable, to a holder of a bond does not exceed £5,000;

(*b*) the value of stock held solely by a person does not exceed in the aggregate £5,000 (or if death occurred before 12th August 1975, £500);

(*c*) the amount repayable in relation to certificates held solely by a person does not exceed in the aggregate £5,000; or

(*d*) the amount repayable to a holder of a children's certificate does not exceed in the aggregate £5,000,

and no probate of the will or letters of administration to the estate are produced to the Director of Savings within what is considered by the Director of Savings to be a reasonable period, the Director of Savings may for the purposes of these Regulations pay the amount (or any part of it) in accordance with paragraph (2).

(2) The Director of Savings may pay the amount—

(*a*) to a person appearing to the Director of Savings to be entitled to take out probate of the will or letters of administration to the estate;

(*b*) where the deceased has left a will in relation to which the Director of Savings is satisfied that probate or letters of administration would be granted, to a person to whom the amount (or any part of it) would be payable under the will (as appears to the Director of Savings), if probate or letters of administration were granted;

(*c*) to a person who satisfies the Director of Savings of their entitlement to receive the amount (or any part of it), being—

(i) a person who has paid the funeral expenses of the deceased;

(ii) a creditor of the deceased; or

(iii) a person who has a beneficial interest in the estate of the deceased;

(*d*) if the deceased was a British citizen and the next of kin appears to the Director of Savings to reside outside the United Kingdom, the Isle of Man and the Channel Islands, to any officer or authority who, as appears to the Director of Savings, may be entrusted with distributing the amount properly;

(*e*) if the deceased was a seaman of a foreign country, being a country with which a treaty has been made in relation to the payment of money due to seamen, to the consular authority of that country;

(*f*) if the deceased was a foreign subject, not being a seaman to whom sub-paragraph (*e*) applies, to the consular authority of the country to which the deceased belonged, or to any authority who, as appears to the Director of Savings, may be entrusted with distributing the amount properly;

(*g*) in a case where the estate of the deceased appears to the Director of Savings to have devolved upon the Crown, the Duchy of Lancaster or the Duchy of Cornwall, to the Treasury Solicitor, the Solicitor for the affairs of the Duchy of Lancaster, or the Solicitor for the affairs of the Duchy of Cornwall respectively,

but where a person to whom an amount may be paid under subparagraph (*b*) or (*c*) has died before payment, the amount (or any part of it) may be paid to a person to whom it would be paid as if the first mentioned person was, immediately before death, a person in paragraph (1).

(3) Despite any legal requirement to the contrary, a person to whom an amount may be paid under paragraph (2)(*b*) or (*c*) (or under the proviso to paragraph (2)) may, if having attained the age of sixteen years, give a receipt for the payment in an approved manner and the receipt shall be valid without the signature of another person; but if that person by reason of age or for any other reason may not accept payment, the Director of Savings may pay the amount to a person who the Director of Savings is satisfied will apply it for the maintenance or otherwise for the benefit of that person.

(4) Subject to paragraph (3), the Director of Savings in making a payment under paragraph (2)(*b*) or (*c*) (or under the proviso to paragraph (2)) must have regard to legal requirements relating to the distribution of the estates of deceased persons, but the Director of Savings may depart from those requirements to the extent it is considered by the Director of Savings that they would cause hardship or inconvenience.

(5) In relation to stock, where a payment may be made to a person under paragraphs (1) or (2), the Director of Savings may, instead of making a payment, register the person (or another person as directed by that person), as the holder of the stock or a part of it.

(6) In relation to stock, the value of stock shall be—

(*a*) in the case of stock which is of a description corresponding to stock or securities transferable in the registers kept by the Registrar of Government Stock in accordance with regulations under section 47 of the Finance Act 1942 (see regulation 7 (registers of stock and stockholders) of the Government Stock Regulations 2004), the market value; and

(*b*) in all other cases, the capital value.

(7) In this regulation "will" includes a codicil.

(8) Nothing in this regulation affects the operation of a nomination made under these Regulations.

90 Death duties or inheritance tax chargeable on death of holders of stock or certificates

(1) This regulation applies on the death of a holder of stock or certificates (not being stock or certificates in relation to which the Director of Savings is satisfied that the deceased holder had no interest otherwise than as a trustee), where the aggregate value of the specified assets exceeds £50,000.

(2) The Director of Savings must, before—

(*a*) making a payment in relation to the stock or registering it in the name of another person; or

(*b*) making a payment in relation to, or transferring, a certificate,

for the purposes of these Regulations, seek a statement from the Commissioners of Her Majesty's Revenue and Customs confirming that death duties, or inheritance or capital transfer tax (being inheritance or capital transfer tax chargeable on the death of the depositor or holder) either are not payable, or have been paid.

(3) A statement under paragraph (2) is not required—

(*a*) where the payment or transfer is made to or on the direction of, or the stock is registered in the name of any person on the direction of—

(i) the deceased's legal personal representative acting under probate or letters of administration granted by a court in the United Kingdom; or

(ii) the Public Trustee, the Official Receiver, or the trustee in bankruptcy of the estate of the deceased;

(*b*)

(i) in relation to a deceased holder of a certificate, where the deceased was at the time of death domiciled in the Isle of Man or the Channel Islands;

(ii) in relation to a deceased holder of stock, where—

(*aa*) the stock is not of a description corresponding to stock or securities transferable in the registers kept by the Registrar of Government Stock in accordance with regulations under section 47 of the Finance Act 1942 (see regulation 7 (registers of stock and stockholders) of the Government Stock Regulations 2004); and

(*bb*) the deceased was at the time of death domiciled in, and any certificates or subscription books relating to the stock were situated in, the Isle of Man or the Channel Islands; or

(*c*) where the beneficial interest in the stock or certificate has passed to the spouse or civil partner of the deceased in circumstances in which death duties or inheritance or capital transfer tax are not payable.

(4) In this regulation "the specified assets" means the following assets (not being assets in relation to which the deceased was a trustee) at the date of death—

(*a*) the total amount (including interest) held in all accounts in the deceased's name alone, or jointly with another person, in the National Savings Bank;

(*b*) the total amount which would have been repayable (had repayment been demanded) in relation to all certificates recorded in the deceased's name alone, or jointly with another person;

(*c*) the total amount repayable and any other amount payable in relation to all bonds recorded in the deceased's name;

(*d*) the total amount (including any bonus or interest) which would have been repayable (had repayment been demanded) in relation to all savings contracts entered into by the deceased and registered by the Director of Savings under a contractual savings scheme certified by the Treasury in accordance with section 326(2) of the Income and Corporation Taxes Act 1988;

(*e*)

(i) in relation to a deceased depositor or holder of a certificate, all stock and securities registered in the National Savings Stock Register in the sole name of the depositor or holder, or in the depositor or holder's name jointly with any other person;

(ii) in relation to a deceased holder of stock, all stock registered in the register in the deceased's name alone or jointly with any other person; and

(*f*) in relation to a deceased holder of a certificate, the total amount (including interest) which would have been repayable (had repayment been demanded) in relation to all agreements entered into or certificates held by the deceased in accordance with the Savings Certificates (Yearly Plan) Regulations 1984.

(5) The value of stock or securities referred to in paragraph (4)(*e*) shall be—

(*a*) in the case of stock which is of a description corresponding to stock or securities transferable in the registers kept by the Registrar of Government Stock in accordance with regulations under section 47 of the Finance Act 1942 (see regulation 7 (registers of stock and stockholders) of the Government Stock Regulations 2004), the market value; or

(*b*) in all other cases, the capital value.

2015/866

OFFSHORE ASSET MOVES PENALTY (SPECIFIED TERRITORIES) REGULATIONS 2015

Made . . . . .at 5.20 pm on 26 March 2015
Coming into force . . . . .27 March 2015
Laid before the House of Commons . . . . . . at 12.30 pm on 27 March 2015

The Treasury make the following Regulations in exercise of the powers conferred by paragraph 4(5) of Schedule 21 to the Finance Act 2015.

1 Citation and commencement

These Regulations may be cited as the Offshore Asset Moves Penalty (Specified Territories) Regulations 2015 and come into force on 27th March 2015.

2 Territories specified

The territories listed in the Schedule to these Regulations are specified for the purposes of Schedule 21 to the Finance Act 2015.

SCHEDULE

Regulation 2

Territories specified

Albania, Andorra, Anguilla, Antigua and Barbuda, Argentina, Aruba, Australia, Austria, The Bahamas, Barbados, Belgium, Belize, Bermuda, Brazil, British Virgin Islands, Brunei Darussalam, Bulgaria, Canada, Cayman Islands, Chile, China, Colombia, Costa Rica, Croatia, Curaçao, Cyprus, Czech Republic, Denmark, Dominica, Estonia, Faroe Islands, Finland, France, Germany, Gibraltar, Greece, Greenland, Grenada, Guernsey, Hong Kong, Hungary, Iceland, India, Indonesia, Ireland, Isle of Man, Israel, Italy, Japan, Jersey, Korea (South), Latvia, Liechtenstein, Lithuania, Luxembourg, Macau, Malaysia, Malta, Marshall Islands, Mauritius, Mexico, Monaco, Montserrat, Netherlands (including Bonaire, Sint Eustatius and Saba) New Zealand (not including Tokelau), Niue, Norway, Poland, Portugal, Qatar, Romania, Russia, Saint Kitts and Nevis, Saint Lucia, Saint Vincent and the Grenadines, Samoa, San Marino, Saudi Arabia, Seychelles, Singapore, Sint Maarten, Slovak Republic, Slovenia, South Africa, Spain, Sweden, Switzerland, Trinidad and Tobago, Turkey, Turks and Caicos Islands, United Arab Emirates, United States of America (not including overseas territories and possessions), Uruguay.

2015/1378

INHERITANCE TAX (ELECTRONIC COMMUNICATIONS) REGULATIONS 2015

Made . . . . *9 June 2015*

Laid before the House of Commons . . . . *11 June 2015*

Coming into force . . . . *6 July 2015*

The Commissioners for Her Majesty's Revenue and Customs make the following Regulations in exercise of the powers conferred by section 132 of the Finance Act 1999 and now exercisable by them:

1 Citation, commencement and interpretation

(1) These Regulations may be cited as the Inheritance Tax (Electronic Communications) Regulations 2015 and come into force on 6th July 2015.

(2) In these Regulations—

"approved" means approved, for the purposes of these Regulations and for the time being, by means of a general or specific direction given by HMRC;

"HMRC" means the Commissioners for Her Majesty's Revenue and Customs;

"IHTA 1984" means the Inheritance Tax Act 1984;

"information delivered by means of electronic communications" includes information delivered to a secure mailbox; and

"official computer system" means a computer system maintained by or on behalf of HMRC—

(*a*) to send or receive information or payments; or

(*b*) to process or store information.

(3) In paragraph (2) "secure mailbox" means a facility or feature which—

(*a*) forms part of an official computer system; and

(*b*) can be accessed by an individual permitted to use electronic communications by an authorisation given by means of a direction by HMRC.

(4) References in these Regulations to information and to the delivery of information shall be construed in accordance with section 132(8) of the Finance Act 1999.

2 Scope of these Regulations

(1) Subject to paragraph (2), these Regulations apply to—

(*a*) the delivery of information, to or by HMRC, the delivery of which is authorised or required by or under IHTA 1984; and

(*b*) the making of any payment or repayment of tax or other sums in connection with the operation of IHTA 1984.

(2) These Regulations do not apply to the delivery of information which is authorised or required by or under sections 222 to 223I of IHTA 1984.

3 Use of electronic communications

(1) HMRC may only use electronic communications in connection with the matters referred to in regulation 2(1) if—

(*a*) the recipient has consented to HMRC using electronic communications in connection with those matters; and

(*b*) HMRC have not been notified that the consent has been withdrawn.

(2) HMRC may specify by specific or general direction the manner in which the consent may be provided and withdrawn, including the time from which the consent and withdrawal is to take effect.

(3) A person other than HMRC may only use electronic communications in connection with the matters referred to in regulation 2(1) if the conditions specified in paragraphs (4) to (7) are satisfied.

(4) The first condition is that the person is for the time being permitted to use electronic communications for the purpose in question by an authorisation given by means of a direction given by HMRC.

(5) The second condition is that the person uses—

(*a*) an approved method for authenticating the identity of the sender of the communication;

(*b*) an approved method of electronic communications; and

(*c*) an approved method for authenticating any information delivered by means of electronic communications.

(6) The third condition is that any information or payment sent by means of electronic communications is in a form approved for the purpose of these Regulations, and Extensible Business Reporting Language (XBRL), Inline XBRL and other electronic data handling techniques are among the forms that may be so approved.

Here "form" includes the manner in which the information is presented.

(7) The fourth condition is that the person maintains such records in written or electronic form as may be specified in a general or specific direction given by HMRC.

Directions—HMRC issued the following revised Directions on 6 May 2016.

These statutory directions revise the approved method of authenticating the sender's identity for IHT online to reflect two-step authentication, and update the postal address for withdrawing consent to using the service. The revisions have effect from 9 May 2016. Direction 2 of the July 2015 directions and direction 1 of the October 2015 directions are revoked.

Directions under regulation 3(2) and (5) of the Inheritance Tax (Electronic Communications) Regulations 2015 (SI 2015/1378)

(Authenticating sender's identity and withdrawing consent to use IHT online)

The Commissioners for Her Majesty's Revenue and Customs (the Commissioners) make the following Directions under regulation 3(2) and (5) of the Inheritance Tax (Electronic Communications) Regulations 2015 in relation to the delivery of information referred to in regulation 2(1)(a) of those Regulations.

These Directions have effect from 9 May 2016.

1 Authenticating the identity of the sender

The method approved for authenticating the identity of the person sending information to HMRC is that the person—

(i) enters a User ID and password issued by the Government Gateway service;

(ii) enters an access code sent to the person's mobile phone; and

(iii) on first registration only, answers a series of identity verification questions.

2 Withdrawing consent

(a) A person may withdraw consent to the Commissioners using electronic communications to deliver information, by writing to HMRC Inheritance Tax, Trusts and Pensions, Ferrers House, Castle Meadow Road, Nottingham NG2 1BB giving notice of the withdrawal of consent.

(b) Withdrawal of consent will take effect 5 days after the day on which HMRC receives the notice.

3 Revocation of previous directions

The following Directions shall cease to have effect from 9 May 2016—

(a) Direction 2 of the Directions under regulations 3(2), (4) to (7) and 9(3) of the Inheritance Tax (Electronic Communications) Regulations 2015 made on 31 July 2015;

(b) Direction 1 of the Directions under regulations 3(5) and 9(3) of the Inheritance Tax (Electronic Communications) Regulations 2015 made on 26 October 2015.

Commentary—*Simon's Taxes* **I11.216A**, **I11.401**.

4 Use of intermediaries

HMRC may use intermediaries in connection with—

(*a*) the delivery of information or the making of payments or repayments by means of electronic communications in connection with the matters referred to in regulation 2(1), and

(*b*) the authentication or security of anything transmitted by such means,

and may require other persons to use intermediaries in connection with those matters.

5 Effect of delivering information by means of electronic communications

(1) Information to which these Regulations apply, and which is delivered by means of electronic communications, shall be treated as having been delivered, in the manner or form required by or under IHTA 1984 if, but only if, all the conditions imposed by—

(*a*) these Regulations,

(*b*) any other applicable enactment (except to the extent that the condition thereby imposed is incompatible with these Regulations), and

(*c*) any specific or general direction given by HMRC,

are satisfied.

(2) Information delivered by means of electronic communications shall be treated as having been delivered on the day on which the last of the conditions imposed as mentioned in paragraph (1) is satisfied.

This is subject to paragraphs (3) and (4).

(3) HMRC may by a general or specific direction provide for information to be treated as delivered upon a different date (whether earlier or later) than that given by paragraph (2).

(4) Information shall not be taken to have been delivered to an official computer system by means of electronic communications unless it is accepted by the system to which it is delivered.

6 Proof of content

(1) A document certified by an officer of HMRC to be a printed-out version of any information delivered by means of electronic communications under these Regulations on any occasion shall be evidence, unless the contrary is proved, that that information—

(*a*) was delivered by means of electronic communications on that occasion; and

(*b*) constitutes the entirety of what was delivered on that occasion.

(2) A document purporting to be a certificate given in accordance with paragraph (1) shall be presumed to be such a certificate unless the contrary is proved.

7 Proof of sender or recipient

The identity of—

(*a*) the sender of any information delivered to an official computer system by means of electronic communications under these Regulations, or

(*b*) the recipient of any information delivered by means of electronic communications from an official computer system,

shall be presumed, unless the contrary is proved, to be the person recorded as such on an official computer system.

8 Information delivered electronically on another's behalf

Any information delivered by an approved method of electronic communications on behalf of any person ("P") shall be deemed to have been delivered by P unless P proves that it was delivered without P's knowledge or connivance.

9 Information delivered jointly by more than one person

(1) Where an enactment to which these Regulations apply permits or requires information to be delivered jointly by more than one person ("the relevant persons") any one of the relevant persons may deliver the information by means of electronic communications also on behalf of one or more other relevant persons but only if the condition in paragraph (2) is met.

(2) The condition is that the relevant person delivering the information has prescribed authorisation from each of the other relevant persons on whose behalf he is delivering that information.

(3) In this regulation "prescribed authorisation" means authorisation prescribed for this purpose by means of a specific or general direction given by HMRC.

10 Proof of delivery of information and payments

(1) The use of an approved method of electronic communications shall be presumed, unless the contrary is proved, to have resulted in the making of a payment or the delivery of information—

(*a*) in the case of information falling to be delivered, or a payment falling to be made, to HMRC, if the making of the payment or the delivery of the information has been recorded on an official computer system; and

(*b*) in the case of information falling to be delivered, or a payment falling to be made, by HMRC, if the despatch of that payment or information has been recorded on an official computer system.

(2) The use of an approved method of electronic communications shall be presumed, unless the contrary is proved, not to have resulted in the making of a payment, or the delivery of information—

(*a*) in the case of information falling to be delivered, or a payment falling to be made, to HMRC, if the making of the payment or the delivery of the information has not been recorded on an official computer system; and

(*b*) in the case of information falling to be delivered, or a payment falling to be made, by HMRC, if the despatch of that payment or information has not been recorded on an official computer system.

(3) The time of receipt of any information or payment sent by an approved means of electronic communications shall be presumed, unless the contrary is proved, to be that recorded on an official computer system.

11 Use of unauthorised methods of electronic communications

(1) Paragraph (2) applies to information which is permitted or required to be delivered to HMRC in connection with the matters mentioned in regulation 2(1).

(2) The use of a means of electronic communication, for the purpose of delivering any information to which this paragraph applies, shall be conclusively presumed not to have resulted in the delivery of that information, unless—

(*a*) that means of electronic communications is for the time being approved for the delivery of information of that kind; and

(*b*) the sender is approved, if necessary, for the use of that means of electronic communications in relation to information of that kind.

2017/345

PENALTIES RELATING TO OFFSHORE MATTERS AND OFFSHORE TRANSFERS (ADDITIONAL INFORMATION) REGULATIONS 2017

Made . . . . *9 March 2017*
Laid before the House of Commons . . . . *10 March 2017*
Coming into force . . . . *1 April 2017*

The Treasury make the following Regulations in exercise of the powers conferred by paragraph 9(1C) of Schedule 24 to the Finance Act 2007, paragraph 12(2C) of Schedule 41 to the Finance Act 2008 and paragraph 14(2C) of Schedule 55 to the Finance Act 2009:

1 Citation and commencement

These Regulations may be cited as the Penalties Relating to Offshore Matters and Offshore Transfers (Additional Information) Regulations 2017 and come into force on 1st April 2017.

2 Interpretation

In these Regulations—

"asset" has the meaning given in section 21(1) of the Taxation of Capital Gains Act 1992, but also includes sterling;

"document" includes part of a document.

3 Additional information for the purposes of paragraph 9(1B)(*d*) of Schedule 24 to the Finance Act 2007, paragraph 12(2B)(*d*) of Schedule 41 to the Finance Act 2008 and paragraph 14(2B)(*d*) of Schedule 55 to the Finance Act 2009

The additional information required for the purposes of paragraph 9(1B)(*d*) of Schedule 24 to the Finance Act 2007, paragraph 12(2B)(*d*) of Schedule 41 to the Finance Act 2008 and paragraph 14(2B)(*d*) of Schedule 55 to the Finance Act 2009, is that a person ("P") must—

(*a*) tell HMRC whether or not regulations 4 or 5 (or both) apply to P; and

(*b*) provide HMRC with the information specified in relation to those regulations set out in regulations 6 and 7 (as appropriate).

4 This regulation applies to P if there is a person ("the enabler") who encouraged, assisted or otherwise facilitated the conduct by P giving rise to the penalty in question.

5 This regulation applies to P if—

(*a*) P is the sole or a joint beneficial owner of an asset ("the asset") situated or held in a territory outside the United Kingdom; and

(*b*) the person holding the asset ("the asset holder") is not P.

6 Additional information to be provided to HMRC where regulation 4 applies to P

The additional information to be provided to HMRC where regulation 4 applies to P is—

(*a*) the name and address of the enabler;

(*b*) a description of the enabler's conduct that encouraged, assisted or otherwise facilitated the conduct by P giving rise to the penalty in question;

(*c*) a description of how the first contact between P and the enabler was made and how the contact was maintained during the times when the enabler's conduct encouraged, assisted or otherwise facilitated the conduct by P giving rise to the penalty in question; and

(*d*) a description of all documents held by P relating to the enabler's conduct that encouraged, assisted or otherwise facilitated the conduct by P giving rise to the penalty in question.

7 Additional information to be provided to HMRC where regulation 5 applies to P

The additional information to be provided to HMRC where regulation 5 applies to P is—

(*a*) the name and address of any other joint beneficial owner of the asset;

(*b*) the extent of P's share of the beneficial ownership of the asset;

(*c*) a description of all documents of title or other documents indicating P's beneficial ownership of the asset;

(*d*) details of where the asset is situated or held;

(*e*) details of when and how P became a beneficial owner of the asset (including a description of all documents held by P relating to the acquisition of P's beneficial ownership of the asset);
(*f*) a description of all changes in the arrangements for the ownership of the asset since P became a beneficial owner of it (including the date of any change in the arrangements and a description of all documents held by P relating to such changes);
(*g*) the names and last known addresses of all persons who have been asset holders of the asset during P's beneficial ownership of it; and
(*h*) in relation to an asset holder who is not an individual, the name and business address (if known) of any director, senior manager, employee or agent of the asset holder who has advised or assisted P in relation to P's beneficial ownership of the asset.

8 (1) A description of a document provided in accordance with regulations 6 or 7 must (as far as it is reasonably practicable to do so) state in relation to the document—
(*a*) the latest of the date when the document was made, prepared or, if appropriate, signed or executed;
(*b*) the person who made or prepared it (and the person on whose behalf it was made or prepared if different);
(*c*) the person who signed or executed the document (if appropriate);
(*d*) the person to whom the document was given or sent (if appropriate);
(*e*) a summary of its contents or the information recorded in the document;
(*f*) the location of the document or where it may be inspected.
(2) The requirement to provide a description of a document in accordance with regulations 6 or 7 may be met by the provision of the document in question to HMRC or a suitable copy of it.
(3) The provision of a document (or a copy of it) to HMRC as described in paragraph (2) is without prejudice to any requirement to produce the document in question to HMRC or power of HMRC to require the production of the document.

Extra-Statutory Concessions

Notes—Please note that references to the 'Inland Revenue' should now be considered as referring to 'HM Revenue and Customs' and references to the 'Board of the Inland Revenue' should be read as the 'Commissioners for HM Revenue and Customs'.

Contents

Inheritance Tax (and Capital Transfer Tax)

F6 BLOCKED FOREIGN ASSETS

Where, because of restrictions imposed by the foreign government, executors who intend to transfer to this country sufficient of the deceased's foreign assets for the payment of the inheritance tax attributable to them cannot do so immediately, they are given the option of deferring payment until the transfer can be effected. If the amount in sterling that the executors finally succeed in bringing to this country is less than this tax, the balance is waived.

Commentary—*Simon's Taxes* **I8.226**; *Foster* **H2.26.**
Note—The text of this concession is as it appears at 6 April 2016.

F10 PARTNERSHIP ASSURANCE POLICIES

A partnership assurance scheme under which each partner effects a policy on his own life in trust for the other partners is not regarded as a settlement for inheritance tax purposes if the following conditions are fulfilled.

(a) The premiums paid on the policy fall within IHTA 1984, Section 10 (exemption for dispositions not intended to confer a gratuitous benefit to any person);
(b) the policy was effected prior to 15 September 1976 and has not been varied on or after that date (but the exercise of a power of appointment under a 'discretionary' trust policy would not be regarded as a variation for this purpose); and
(c) the trusts of the policy are governed by English law or by Scots law, provided that in the latter case the policy does not directly or indirectly involve a partnership itself as a separate persona.

Commentary—*Simon's Taxes* **I5.117**; *Foster* **E1.17.**
Note—The text of this concession is as it appears at 6 April 2016.

F13 SUBSEQUENT DEVOLUTIONS OF PROPERTY UNDER THE WILLS OF PERSONS DYING BEFORE 12 MARCH 1952 WHOSE ESTATES WERE WHOLLY EXEMPTED FROM ESTATE DUTY UNDER FA 1894 S 8(1)

Where a person died before 12 March 1952 and his estate was wholly exempted from estate duty as the property of a common seaman, marine or soldier who died in the service of the Crown and under his will he left a limited interest to someone who dies on or after 12 March 1975, inheritance tax is not charged on any property exempted on the original death which passes under the terms of the will on the termination of the limited interest.

Commentary—*Simon's Taxes* **I5.923**; *Foster* **E9.23.**
Note—The text of this concession is as it appears at 6 April 2016.

F15 WOODLANDS

FA 1986 Sch 19 para 46 denies potentially exempt transfer treatment for inheritance tax purposes to all property comprised in a single transfer any part of which, however small, is woodlands subject to a deferred estate duty charge. By concession the scope of this paragraph will henceforth be restricted solely to that part of the value transferred which is attributable to the woodlands which are the subject of the deferred charge.

Commentary—*Simon's Taxes* **I3.314, I3.622**; *Foster* **C3.14, C6.22.**
Note—The text of this concession is as it appears at 6 April 2016.

F16 AGRICULTURAL PROPERTY AND FARM COTTAGES

On a transfer of agricultural property which includes a cottage occupied by a retired farm employee or their widow (er), the condition in sections 117 and 169 of IHTA 1984 concerning occupation for agricultural purposes is regarded as satisfied with respect to the cottage if either—

- the occupier is a statutorily protected tenant, or
- the occupation is under a lease granted to the farm employee for his/her life and that of any surviving spouse as part of the employee's contract of employment by the landlord for agricultural purposes.

Commentary—*Simon's Taxes* **I7.311, I8.365**; *Foster* **G3.02, 03.**

Cross reference—See IHTA 1984 s 117 (minimum period of occupation or ownership); IHTA 1984 s 169 (farm cottages).

Note—The text of this concession is as it appears at 6 April 2016.

F17 RELIEF FOR AGRICULTURAL PROPERTY

On a transfer of tenanted agricultural land, the condition in section 116(2)(a) of IHTA 1984 is regarded as satisfied where the transferor's interest in the property either carries a right to vacant possession within 24 months of the date of the transfer, or is, notwithstanding the terms of the tenancy, valued at an amount broadly equivalent to the vacant possession value of the property.

Commentary—*Simon's Taxes* **I7.304**; *Foster* **G3.02, 04.**

Cross reference—See IHTA 1984 s 116 (agricultural property—the relief).

Note—The text of this concession is as it appears at 6 April 2016.

F20 LATE COMPENSATION FOR WORLD WAR II CLAIMS

Commentary—*Simon's Taxes* **I4.201.**

Note—This concession is obsolete – enacted in FA 2016 s 95.

Statements of Practice

Notes—Following a review of their methods of publishing information on administrative practice with a view to making it available to the public in a uniform, accessible and more readily identifiable way, the Revenue introduced a new series of Statements of Practice on 18 July 1978.

Before 18 July 1978 information on administrative practice was disseminated in a variety of ways including Statements in Parliament, Written Parliamentary Answers (often reproduced in Revenue Press Releases), letters to professional bodies and to journals, etc.

Civil Partnership Act—The Civil Partnership Act (CPA) received Royal Assent on 18-11-04 and became effective from 5 December 2005. The Government's commitment is that, for all tax purposes, same-sex couples who form a civil partnership will be treated the same as married couples.

As part of this commitment to tax parity, from 5 December 2005 all Statements of Practice should be taken as extended to apply equally to civil partners and married couples.

Contents

Statements issued before 18 July 1978

Accumulation and maintenance settlements

E1 POWERS OF APPOINTMENT

1. It is not necessary for the interests of individual beneficiaries to be defined. They can for instance be subject to powers of appointment. In any particular case the exemption will depend on the precise terms of the trust and power concerned, and on the facts to which they apply. In general, however, the official view is that the conditions do not restrict the application of IHTA 1984 s 71 to settlements where the interests of individual beneficiaries are defined and indefeasible.

2. The requirement of IHTA 1984 s 71(1)(*a*) is that one or more persons will, on or before attaining a specified age not exceeding twenty five, become beneficially entitled to, or to an interest in possession in, the settled property or part of it. It is considered that settled property would meet this condition if at the relevant time it must vest for an interest in possession in some member of an existing class of potential beneficiaries on or before that member attains 25. The existence of a special power of appointment would not of itself exclude section 71 if neither the exercise nor the release of the power could break the condition. To achieve this effect might, however, require careful drafting.

3. The inclusion of issue as possible objects of a special power of appointment would exclude a settlement from the benefit of section 71 if the power would allow the trustees to prevent any interest in possession in the settled property from commencing before the beneficiary concerned attained the age specified. It would depend on the precise words of the settlement and the facts to which they had to be applied whether a particular settlement satisfied the conditions of s 71(1). In many cases the rules against perpetuity and accumulations would operate to prevent an effective appointment outside those conditions. However the application of s 71 is not a matter for a once-for-all decision. It is a question that needs to be kept in mind at all times when there is settled property in which no interest in possession subsists.

4. Also, a trust which otherwise satisfies the requirement of s 71(1)(*a*) would not be disqualified by the existence of a power to vary or determine the respective shares of members of the class (even to the extent of excluding some members altogether) provided the power is exercisable only in favour of a person under 25 who is a member of the class.

ANNEX TO SP E1

Practical illustrations of IHTA 1984 s 71. The examples set out below are based on a settlement for the children of X contingently on attaining 25, the trustees being required to accumulate the income so far as it is not applied for the maintenance of X's children.

Example A

The settlement was made on X's marriage and he has as yet no children.

IHTA 1984 s 71 will not apply until a child is born and that event will give rise to a charge for tax under IHTA 1984 s 65.

Example B

The trustees have power to apply income for the benefit of X's unmarried sister.

IHTA 1984 s 71 does not apply because the conditions of subsection (1)(*b*) are not met.

Example C

X has power to appoint the capital not only among his children but also among his remoter issue.

IHTA 1984 s 71 does not apply (unless the power can be exercised only in favour of persons who would thereby acquire interests in possession on or before attaining age 25). A release of the disqualifying power would give rise to a charge for tax under IHTA 1984 s 65. Its exercise would also give rise to a charge under IHTA 1984 s 65.

Example D

The trustees have an overriding power of appointment in favour of other persons.

IHTA 1984 s 71 does not apply (unless the power can be exercised only in favour of persons who would thereby acquire interests in possession on or before attaining age 25). A release of the disqualifying power would give rise to a charge for tax under IHTA 1984 s 65. Its exercise would also give rise to a charge under IHTA 1984 s 65.

Example E

The settled property has been revocably appointed to one of the children contingently on his attaining 25 and the appointment is now made irrevocable.

If the power to revoke prevents IHTA 1984 s 71 from applying, (as it would for example, if the property thereby became subject to a power of appointment as at C or D above), tax will be chargeable under IHTA 1984 s 65 when the appointment is made irrevocable.

Example F

The trust to accumulate income is expressed to be during the life of the settlor.

As the settlor may live beyond the 25th birthday of any of his children, the trust does not satisfy the condition in subsection (1)(*a*) and IHTA 1984 s 71 does not apply.

Commentary—*Simon's Taxes* **I5.513**; *Foster* **E5.13**.
First publication—*Law Society's Gazette* 11 June 1975.

Superannuation, life insurance and accident schemes

E3 SUPERANNUATION SCHEMES

1. This Statement clarifies the IHT liability of benefits payable under pension schemes.

2. No liability to IHT arises in respect of benefits payable on a person's death under a normal pension scheme except in the circumstances explained immediately below. Nor does a charge to IHT arise on payments made by the trustees of a superannuation scheme within IHTA 1984 s 151 in direct exercise of discretion to pay a lump sum death benefit to any one or more of a member's dependants. It is not considered that pending the exercise of the discretion the benefit should normally be regarded as relevant property comprised in a settlement so as to bring it within the scope of IHTA 1984 Part III. The protection of IHTA 1984 s 151 would not of course extend further if the trustees themselves then settled the property so paid.

3. Benefits are liable to IHT if—

(a) they form part of the freely disposable property passing under the will or intestacy of a deceased person – this applies only if the executors or administrators have a legally enforceable claim to the benefits, if they were payable to them only at the discretion of the trustees of the pension fund or some similar persons they are not liable to IHT; or

(b) the deceased had the power, immediately before the death, to nominate or appoint the benefits to any person including his dependants.

4. In these cases the benefits should be included in the personal representatives' account (schedule of the deceased's assets) which has to be completed when applying for a grant of probate or letters of administration. The IHT (if any) which is assessed on the personal representatives' account has to be paid before the grant can be obtained.

5. On some events other than the death of a member information should be given to the appropriate office of HMRC Capital Taxes. Those events are—

(i) the payment of contributions to a scheme which has not been approved for income tax purposes;

(ii) the making of an irrevocable nomination or the disposal of a benefit by a member in their lifetime (otherwise than in favour of a spouse) which reduces the value of their estate (eg the surrender of part of the pension or lump sum benefit in exchange for a pension for the life of another);

(iii) the decision by a member to postpone the realisation of any of their retirement benefits.

6. If IHT proves to be payable the HMRC Capital Taxes will communicate with the persons liable to pay the tax.

7. See also Statement of Practice 10/86 and Tax Bulletin No 2 of February 1992, the article "Inheritance tax—retirement benefits under private pension contracts: IHTA 1984 s 3(3).".

Commentary—*Simon's Taxes* **I5.637**; *Foster* **D1.25, E6.37**.

Interests in possession settlements

E5 CLOSE COMPANIES

The Commissioners for HMRC consider that the general intention of IHTA 1984 s 101 is to treat the participators as beneficial owners for all the purposes of that Act. Consequently, the conditions of IHTA 1984 ss 52(2), 53(2) are regarded as satisfied where it is the company that in fact becomes entitled to the property or disposes of the interest.

Commentary—*Simon's Taxes* **I5.226, 251, I6.31**; *Foster* **E2.26, 51, F1.31.**

E6 POWER TO AUGMENT INCOME

This statement sets out the effect for IHT of the exercise by trustees of a power to augment a beneficiary's income out of capital.

In the normal case, where the beneficiary concerned is life tenant of the settled property this will have no immediate consequences for IHT. The life tenant already has an interest in possession and under the provisions of IHTA 1984 s 49(1) is treated as beneficially entitled to the property. The enlargement of that interest to an absolute interest does not change this position (IHTA 1984 s 53(2)) and it is not affected by the relationship of the beneficiary to the testator.

In the exceptional case, where the beneficiary is not the life tenant, or in which there is no subsisting interest in possession, the exercise of the power would give rise to a charge for tax under IHTA 1984 s 52(1), although on or after 17 March 1987 this may be a potentially exempt transfer, or a charge under IHTA 1984 s 65(1)(*a*). But if the life tenant is the surviving spouse of a testator who died before 13 November 1974, exemption might be available under IHTA 1984 Sch 6 para 2.

The exercise of the power would be regarded as distributing the settled property rather than as reducing its value, so that IHTA 1984 s 52(3) and s 65(1)(*b*) would not be in point.

Commentary—*Simon's Taxes* **I5.260**; *Foster* **E2.60.**

E7 PROTECTIVE TRUSTS

In the Commissioners for HMRC's view, the reference to trusts "to the like effect as those specified in section 33(1) of the Trustee Act 1925"—contained in IHTA 1984 ss 73 and 88—is a reference to trusts which are not materially different in their tax consequences.

The Commissioners for HMRC would not wish to distinguish a trust by reason of a minor variation or additional administrative duties or powers. The extension of the list of potential beneficiaries to, for example, brothers and sisters is *not* regarded as a minor variation.

Commentary—*Simon's Taxes* **I5.621**; *Foster* **E6.21.**

Settled property: miscellaneous

E9 EXCLUDED PROPERTY

Property is regarded, for the purposes of IHTA 1984 s 48(3), as becoming comprised in a settlement when it, or other property which it represents, is introduced by the settlor.

Commentary—*Simon's Taxes* **I9.332**; *Foster* **J3.32.**

Non-settled property: miscellaneous

E13 CHARITIES

1. IHTA 1984 ss 23 and 24 exempt from IHT certain gifts to charities and political parties to the extent that the value transferred is attributable to property given to a charity etc. IHTA 1984 s 25 exempts certain gifts for national purposes and for the public benefit.

2. Where the value transferred (ie the loss to transferor's estate as a result of the disposition) exceeds the value of the gift in the hands of a charity, etc, the Commissioners for HMRC take the view that the exemption extends to the whole value transferred.

Commentary—*Simon's Taxes* **I4.215, I8.242**; *Foster* **D2.15, H2.42.**
First publication—Revenue Press Release dated 15 April 1976.
Note—This statement was amended by IR 131 Supplement (November 1998).

E14 POOLS, ETC SYNDICATES

No liability to IHT arises on winnings by a football pool, National Lottery or similar syndicate provided that the winnings are paid out in accordance with the terms of an agreement drawn up before the win.

Where for example football winnings are paid out, in accordance with a pre-existing enforceable arrangement, among the members of a syndicate in proportion to the share of the stake money each has provided, each member of the syndicate receives what already belongs to him or her. There is therefore no "gift" or "chargeable transfer" by the person who, on behalf of the members, receives the winnings from the pools promoter.

Members of a pool syndicate may think it wise to record in a written, signed and dated statement, the existence and terms of the agreement between them. But HMRC cannot advise on the wording or legal effect of such a statement, nor do they wish copies of such statements to be sent to them for approval or registration. Where following a pools win the terms of an agreement are varied or part of the winnings are distributed to persons who are not members of the syndicate, an IHT liability may be incurred. The same principles apply to premium bonds syndicates and other similar arrangements.

Commentary—*Simon's Taxes* **I3.148**; *Foster* **C1.48.**
First publication—Revenue Press Release dated 16 September 1977.

E15 CLOSE COMPANIES—GROUP TRANSFERS

This statement clarifies the position concerning dividend payments and transfers of assets from a subsidiary company to a parent or sister company as appropriate.

Whether or not a disposition is a transfer of value for CTT or IHT purposes has to be determined by reference to IHTA 1984 s 3(1), (2) and s 10 provides that a disposition is not a transfer of value if it was not intended to confer any gratuitous benefit on any person, subject to the other provisions of that subsection.

In the Commissioners for HMRC's view, the effect is that a dividend paid by a subsidiary company to its parent is not a transfer of value and so IHTA 1984 s 94 does not start to operate in relation to such dividends. Nor do the Commissioners feel that they can justifiably treat a transfer of assets between a wholly-owned subsidiary and its parent or between two wholly-owned subsidiaries as a transfer of value.

Commentary—*Simon's Taxes* **I6.122**; *Foster* **F1.22.**
First publication—British Tax Review 1975 p 139.

E18 PARTIAL DISCLAIMERS OF RESIDUE

Under Scots law there are certain circumstances in which a residuary legatee can make a partial disclaimer. Where this is possible the Commissioners for HMRC accept that the provisions of IHTA 1984 s 142 which deal with disclaimers, apply.

Commentary—*Simon's Taxes* **I4.416**; *Foster* **D4.16.**

Statements issued after 17 July 1978

SP 10/79 (15 AUGUST 1979) POWER FOR TRUSTEES TO ALLOW A BENEFICIARY TO OCCUPY A DWELLING-HOUSE

Many wills and settlements contain a clause empowering the trustees to permit a beneficiary to occupy a dwelling-house which forms part of trust property on such terms as they think fit. The Commissioners for HMRC do not regard the existence of such a power as excluding any interest in possession of the property.

When there is no interest in possession in the property in question, the Commissioners for HMRC do not regard the exercise of the power as creating one if the effect is merely to allow non-exclusive occupation or to create a contractual tenancy for full consideration. The Commissioners for HMRC also take the view that no interest in possession arises on the creation of a lease for a term or a periodic tenancy for less than full consideration, though this will normally give rise to a charge for tax under IHTA 1984 s 65(1)(*b*). On the other hand, if the power is drawn in terms wide enough to cover the creation of an exclusive or joint residence, albeit revocable, for a definite or indefinite period, and is exercised with the intention of providing a particular beneficiary with a permanent home, HMRC will normally regard the exercise of the power as creating an interest in possession. And if the trustees in exercise of their powers grant a lease for life for less than full consideration, this will be regarded as creating an interest in possession in view of IHTA 1984 ss 43(3), 50(6).

A similar view will be taken where the power is exercised over property in which another beneficiary had an interest in possession up to the time of the exercise.

Press releases etc—IR 6-8-75 (grant by trustees of a non-commercial lease could also bring about a charge under IHTA 1984 s 52(3), (4)).

SP 12/80 (13 OCTOBER 1980) BUSINESS PROPERTY RELIEF: "BUY AND SELL" AGREEMENTS

The Commissioners for HMRC understand that it is sometimes the practice for partners or shareholder directors of companies to enter into an agreement (known as a "Buy and Sell" Agreement) whereby, in the event of the death before retirement of one of them, the deceased's personal representatives are obliged to sell and the survivors are obliged to purchase the deceased's business interests or shares, funds for the purchase being frequently provided by means of appropriate life assurance policies.

In the Commissioners for HMRC's view such an agreement, requiring as it does a sale and purchase and not merely conferring an option to sell or buy, is a binding contract for sale within IHTA 1984 s 113. As a result the inheritance tax business property relief will not be due on the business interest or shares. (IHTA 1984 s 113 provides that where any property would be relevant business property for the purpose of business property relief in relation to a transfer of value but a binding contract for its sale has been entered into at the time of the transfer, it is not relevant business property in relation to that transfer.)

Press releases etc—ICAEW TR557 19-9-84 (partnerships: death of partner: availability of business property relief: whether affected by provisions of partnership agreement: examples).

SP 1/82 (6 APRIL 1981) THE INTERACTION OF INCOME TAX AND INHERITANCE TAX ON ASSETS PUT INTO SETTLEMENTS

1. For many years the tax code has contained legislation to prevent a person avoiding higher rate income tax by making a settlement, while still retaining some rights to enjoy the income or capital of the settlement. This legislation, which is embodied in TA 1988 Part XV (from 6 April 2005, ITTOIA 2005 Pt 5 Ch 5), provides in general terms that the income of a settlement shall, for income tax purposes, be treated as that of the settlor in all circumstances where the settlor might benefit directly or indirectly from the settlement.

2. If the trustees have power to pay or do in fact pay inheritance tax due on assets which the settlor puts into the settlement HMRC have taken the view that the settlor has thereby an interest in the income or property of the settlement, and that the income of the settlement should be treated as his for income tax purposes under TA 1988 Part XV (from 6 April 2005, ITTOIA 2005 Pt 5 Ch 5).

3. The inheritance tax legislation (IHTA 1984 s 199) however, provides that *both* the settlor *and* the trustees are liable for any inheritance tax payable when a settlor puts assets into a settlement. The Commissioners for HMRC have therefore decided that they will no longer, in these circumstances, treat the income of the settlement as that of the settlor for income tax purposes solely because the trustees have power to pay or do in fact pay inheritance tax on assets put into settlements.

4. This change of practice applies to settlement income for 1981–82, et seq.

Commentary—*Simon's Taxes* **C4.325.**

SP 11/84 ESTATE DUTY: CALCULATION OF DUTY PAYABLE ON A CHARGEABLE EVENT AFFECTING HERITAGE OBJECTS PREVIOUSLY GRANTED CONDITIONAL EXEMPTION

Under the estate duty provisions, an object which in the opinion of the Treasury was of national, scientific, historic or artistic interest could be exempt from duty if undertakings were given to preserve it and keep it in the United Kingdom. If an object which had been exempted from duty was subsequently sold (unless the purchaser was a national institution or similar body), or if the undertaking was broken, duty became chargeable, generally either on the sale proceeds or on the value of the object at the date of the charge. These "clawback" charges may still apply now in relation to objects which have previously been exempted from estate duty.

Estate duty applied not only to property passing on death but also to property given away by the deceased within a certain period before his death. In these latter cases the duty chargeable could be reduced by a taper relief (FA 1960 s 64). The exemption described in the preceding paragraph could also apply to an object which came within the charge to duty because it was the subject of an inter vivos gift. The Commissioners for HMRC have been advised that in these circumstances taper relief under s 64 is not available to reduce the amount liable to the clawback charge, and that the amount chargeable to duty is the full value or sale proceeds.

SP 8/86 (9 JULY 1986) TREATMENT OF INCOME OF DISCRETIONARY TRUSTS

This statement sets out the Commissioners for HMRC's practice concerning the IHT/CTT treatment of income of discretionary trusts.

The Commissioners for HMRC take the view that—

- undistributed and unaccumulated income should not be treated as a taxable trust asset; and
- for the purpose of determining the rate of charge on accumulated income, the income should be treated as becoming a taxable asset of the trust on the date when the accumulation is made.

This practice applies from 10 November 1986 to all new cases and to existing cases where the tax liability has not been settled.

Commentary—*Simon's Taxes* **I5.321.**

SP 10/86 (9 JULY 1986) DEATH BENEFITS UNDER SUPERANNUATION ARRANGEMENTS

The Commissioners for HMRC confirm that their previous practice (see SP E3) of not charging capital transfer tax on death benefits that are payable from tax-approved occupational pension and retirement annuity schemes under discretionary trusts also applies to inheritance tax.

The practice extends to tax under the "gifts with reservation" rules as well as to tax under the ordinary inheritance tax rules.

SP 6/87 (8 APRIL 1987) ACCEPTANCE OF PROPERTY IN LIEU OF INHERITANCE TAX, CAPITAL TRANSFER TAX AND ESTATE DUTY

1. The Commissioners for HMRC, with the agreement of the Secretary of State for Culture, Media and Sport (and, where appropriate, other ministers), accept heritage property in whole or part satisfaction of an inheritance tax, capital transfer tax or estate duty debt and any interest payable on the tax.

2. No capital tax is payable on property that is accepted in lieu of tax. The amount of tax satisfied is determined by agreeing a special price. This price is found by establishing an agreed value for the item and deducting a proportion of the tax given up on the item itself, using an arrangement known as the "douceur". The terms on which property is accepted are a matter for negotiation.

3. FA 1987 s 60 and F(No 2)A 1987 s 97 provide that, where the special price is based on the value of the item at a date earlier than the date on which it is accepted, interest on the tax which is being satisfied may cease to accrue from that earlier date.

4. The persons liable for the tax which is to be satisfied by an acceptance in lieu can choose between having the special price calculated from the value of the item when they offer it or when the Commissioners for HMRC accept it. Since most offers are made initially on the basis of the current value of the item, HMRC consider them on the basis of the value at the "offer date", unless the offeror notifies them that he wishes to adopt the "acceptance date" basis of valuation. The offeror's option will normally remain open until the item is formally accepted. But this will be subject to review if more than two years elapse from the date of the offer without the terms being settled. The Commissioners for HMRC may then give six months notice that they will no longer be prepared to accept the item on the "offer date" basis.

5. Where the "offer date" option remains open and is chosen, interest on the tax to be satisfied by the item will cease to accrue from that date.

Note—This statement was amended by IR 131 (January 2000).

SP 7/87 (15 JULY 1987) DEDUCTION FOR REASONABLE FUNERAL EXPENSES

The Commissioners for HMRC take the view that the term "funeral expenses" in IHTA 1984 s 172 allows a deduction from the value of a deceased's estate for the cost of a tombstone or gravestone.

SP 2/93 (13 JANUARY 1993) INHERITANCE TAX: THE USE OF SUBSTITUTE FORMS

INTRODUCTION

1. This statement explains the Commissioners for HMRC's approach towards the acceptance of facsimiles of inheritance tax forms as substitutes for officially produced printed forms.

LEGISLATIVE CONTEXT

2. IHTA 1984 s 257(1) says that all accounts and other documents required for the purposes of the Act shall be in such form and shall contain such particulars as the Commissioners for HMRC may prescribe. The Commissioners for HMRC are satisfied that an accurate facsimile of an official Account or other required document will satisfy the requirements of the section.

WHAT WILL BE CONSIDERED AN ACCURATE FACSIMILE?

3. For any substitute inheritance tax form to be acceptable, it must show clearly to the taxpayer the information which the Commissioners for HMRC have determined shall be before them when they sign the declaration that the form is correct and complete to the best of his or her knowledge. In other words, the facsimile must accurately reproduce the words and layout of the official form. It need not, however, be colour printed.

4. The facsimile must also be readily recognisable as an inheritance tax form when it is received by HMRC Capital Taxes, and the entries must be distinguishable from the background text. Where a facsimile is submitted instead of a previously supplied official form it is important that it bears the same reference as appeared on the official form. It is equally important that if no official form was supplied the taxpayer's reference should be inserted on the facsimile.

5. Advances in printing technology now mean that accurate facsimile forms can be produced. The Commissioners for HMRC will accept such forms if approval by the Capital Taxes Offices of their wording and design has been obtained before they are used. Any substitute which is produced with approval will need to bear an agreed unique imprint so that its source can be readily identified at all times.

APPLICATIONS FOR APPROVAL

6. Applications for approval should be made to—

In England, Wales and Northern Ireland: The Customer Service Manager, HMRC Capital Taxes Office, Ferrers House, PO Box 38, Castle Meadow Road, Nottingham NG2 1BB or DX 701201 Nottingham 4; or in Scotland: The Customer Service Manager, HMRC, Mulberry House, 16 Picardy Place, Edinburgh EH1 3NB or DX ED305 Edin 1.

All applications will be considered as quickly as possible.

FURTHER INFORMATION AVAILABLE

7. A set of guidelines giving further details on the production of substitute forms is available on application to the appropriate office at the above address.

Note—This statement was updated in IR 131 (August 2002).

SP 6/95 (31 MARCH 1995) LEGAL ENTITLEMENT AND ADMINISTRATIVE PRACTICES

Where an assessment has been made and this shows a repayment due to the taxpayer, repayment is invariably made of the full amount. In self-assessment where any amount is repayable it will be repaid in full on request. Where the end of the year check applied to Schedule E taxpayers who have not had a tax return for the year in question shows an overpayment of £10 or less, the repayment is not made automatically.

As regards payment of tax assessed, where a payment to the Accounts Offices exceeds the amount due and the discrepancy is not noted before the payment has been processed, the excess is not repaid routinely by the computer system unless it exceeds £0.99, or where clerical intervention is required, unless it exceeds £9.99.

For inheritance tax (and capital transfer tax), assessments that lead to repayments of sums overpaid are not initiated automatically by the Capital Taxes Offices if the amount involved is £25 or less.

The aim of these tolerances is to minimise work which is highly cost-effective; they cannot operate to deny repayment to a taxpayer who claims it.

Note—This statement supersedes Statement of Practice SP 1/80.

HMRC Interpretations

Notes—These Interpretations were published in HMRC's *Tax Bulletin*. HMRC state that the Interpretations will normally be applied in relevant cases, but that this is subject to a number of qualifications. Particular cases may turn on their own facts or context and there may be circumstances in which an interpretation will not apply. There may also be circumstances in which the Board would find it necessary to argue for a different Interpretation in appeal proceedings.

The texts of the following Interpretations are Crown copyright.

The number before each interpretation (eg RI 55) does not appear in the official publications. It has been added by the publishers to facilitate identification for the purpose of cross references.

Please note that references to the "Inland Revenue" should now be considered as referring to "HM Revenue and Customs" and references to the "Board of the Inland Revenue" should be read as the "Commissioners for HM Revenue and Customs".

List of Interpretations

HMRC Interpretations: IHT

RI 55 (NOVEMBER 1993) INHERITANCE TAX—GIFTS WITH RESERVATION

Under FA 1986 s 102, any property given away on or after 18 March 1986 subject to a reservation is, on the death of the donor, treated as forming part of the donor's estate immediately before his death. Gifts with reservation (GWRs) are defined as gifts where either—

- the donee does not assume bona fide possession and enjoyment of the property at the date of the gift or seven years before the donor's death, if later; or
- at any time in the period ending with the donor's death and beginning seven years before that date or, if later, from the date of gift, the property is not enjoyed to the entire exclusion or virtually to the entire exclusion of the donor.

This note provides some guidance on the Revenue's interpretation of the *de minimis* rule which is expressed as "virtually to the entire exclusion" and comments on the exclusion from the GWR provisions where the donor pays full consideration for any use of the property. The note also clarifies the position of the annual exemption under IHTA 1984 s 19 where a reservation of benefit ceases.

INTERPRETATION OF DE MINIMIS RULE

The word "virtually" in the *de minimis* rule in FA 1986 s 102(1)(*b*) is not defined and the statute does not give any express guidance about its meaning. However, the shorter Oxford English Dictionary defines it as, amongst other things, "to all intents" and "as good as". Our interpretation of "virtually to the entire exclusion" is that it covers cases in which the benefit to the donor is insignificant in relation to the gifted property.

It is not possible to reduce this test to a single crisp proposition. Each case turns on its own unique circumstances and the questions are likely to be ones of fact and degree. We do not operate s 102(1)(*b*) in such a way that donors are unreasonably prevented from having limited access to property they have given away and a measure of flexibility is adopted in applying the test.

Some examples of situations in which we consider that FA 1986 s 102(1)(*b*) permits limited benefit to the donor without bringing the GWR provisions into play are given below to illustrate how we apply the *de minimis* test—

- a house which becomes the donee's residence but where the donor subsequently—
  - stays, in the absence of the donee, for not more than two weeks each year, or
  - stays with the donee for less than one month each year;
- social visits, excluding overnight stays made by a donor as a guest of the donee, to a house which he had given away. The extent of the social visits should be no greater than the visits which the donor might be expected to make to the donee's house in the absence of any gift by the donor;
- a temporary stay for some short term purpose in a house the donor had previously given away, for example—
  - while the donor convalesces after medical treatment;
  - while the donor looks after a donee convalescing after medical treatment;
  - while the donor's own home is being redecorated;
- visits to a house for domestic reasons, for example baby-sitting by the donor for the donee's children;
- a house together with a library of books which the donor visits less than five times in any year to consult or borrow a book;
- a motor car which the donee uses to give occasional (ie less than three times a month) lifts to the donor;
- land which the donor uses to walk his dogs or for horse riding provided this does not restrict the donee's use of the land.

It follows, of course, that if the benefit to the donor is, or becomes, more significant, the GWR provisions are likely to apply. Examples of this include gifts of—

- a house in which the donor then stays most weekends, or for a month or more each year;
- a second home or holiday home which the donor and the donee both then use on an occasional basis;
- a house with a library in which the donor continues to keep his own books, or which the donor uses on a regular basis, for example because it is necessary for his work;
- a motor car which the donee uses every day to take the donor to work.

EXCLUSION OF BENEFIT WHERE FULL CONSIDERATION PAID FOR USE OF PROPERTY

The GWR provisions do not apply where an interest in land is given away and the donor pays full consideration for future use of the property (FA 1986 Sch 20 para 6(1)(*a*)). While we take the view that such full consideration is required throughout the relevant period—and therefore consider that the rent paid should be reviewed at appropriate intervals to reflect market changes—we do recognise that there is no single value at which consideration can be fixed as "full". Rather, we accept that what constitutes full consideration in any case lies within a range of values reflecting normal valuation tolerances, and that any amount within that range can be accepted as satisfying the para 6(1)(*a*) test.

TERMINATION OF RESERVED BENEFITS AND THE ANNUAL EXEMPTION

Where a reservation ceases, the donor is treated by FA 1986 s 102(4) as having made a potentially exempt transfer (PET) at that time. In that event the PET will only be taxable if the donor dies within the next seven years but the value of the PET cannot be reduced by any available annual exemption under IHTA 1984 s 19. The statement in para 3.4 of the IHT1 booklet, which indicates that the annual exemption may apply if the reservation ceases to exist in the donor's lifetime and a PET is treated as made at that time, is incorrect. This will be corrected in IHT1 when it is next updated.

A typical outright gift to an individual of an amount exceeding the available annual exemption is partly exempt, with the balance above the available annual exemption being a PET. But a PET itself cannot qualify for the annual exemption. The reason is that a PET is a transfer which, but for the provisions of IHTA 1984 s 3A, would be an immediately chargeable transfer. By definition a chargeable transfer is a transfer of value which is not an exempt transfer—IHTA 1984 s 2(1). So a PET cannot be an exempt transfer at the time it is made. The PET will, of course, escape a charge to IHT if the donor survives the statutory period after making it.

The annual exemption is not necessarily lost by the taxpayer. For example, suppose he makes a gift of his home in August 1991 but continues to reside there. In May 1992 he finally leaves the gifted house and the reservation ceases. In October 1992 he makes a gift into a discretionary trust (an immediately chargeable transfer). He is treated as making a PET of his residence in May 1992—the annual £3,000 exemption does not reduce its value. But the £3,000 exemption is available for setting off against the immediately chargeable transfer in October, and so is any unused exemption carried forward from the previous year.

RI 95 (DECEMBER 1994) INHERITANCE TAX—BUSINESS AND AGRICULTURAL RELIEF

The inheritance tax (IHT) legislation provides relief for transfers of agricultural property and for business property. We have been asked for our views on the availability of relief—

- where agricultural property is replaced by business property (or vice versa) shortly before the owner's death; and
- on the donor's death, where the donee of a potentially exempt transfer of agricultural property has sold it and reinvested the proceeds in a non-agricultural business (or vice versa).

A "potentially exempt transfer" (PET) is a lifetime transfer which only becomes chargeable to IHT if the donor dies within seven years of the transfer.

All statutory references in this article are to the Inheritance Tax Act (IHTA) 1984.

IHT business and agricultural relief reduces the value of relevant business property, or the agricultural value of agricultural property, by either 50 or 100 per cent. The rate of relief depends on the nature of the property and interest held.

The qualifying conditions for the relief include requirements of a minimum period of ownership and, in the case of agricultural property, of occupation of the property for agricultural purposes immediately before the transfer. If, and to the extent that, the same property may qualify for relief as both agricultural property and business property, s 114 prevents double relief.

There are also rules which allow for the sale and replacement of qualifying property. The replacement is qualifying property only if it, and the original qualifying property, have together been owned (and, in the case of agricultural property, occupied) for a combined minimum period.

In the Revenue's view, where agricultural property which is a farming business is replaced by non-agricultural business property, the period of ownership of the original property will be relevant for applying the minimum ownership condition to the replacement property. Business property relief will be available on the replacement if all the conditions for that relief are satisfied. Where non-agricultural business property is replaced by a farming business, and the latter is not eligible for agricultural property relief, s 114(1) does not exclude business property relief if the conditions for that relief are satisfied.

There could be cases where, for example, agricultural land is not part of a farming business, so any replacement could only qualify for business property relief if it satisfied the minimum ownership conditions in its own right. However, our experience suggests such cases are likely to be exceptional.

Where the donee of a PET of a farming business sells the business, and replaces it with a non-agricultural business, the effect of s 124A(1) is to deny agricultural property relief on the value transferred by the PET. Consequently, s 114(1) does not exclude business property relief if the conditions for that relief are satisfied; and, in the reverse situation, the farming business acquired by the donee can be "relevant business property" for the purposes of s 113B(3)(*c*).

[IHTA 1984 Pt V Ch I, II as amended by F(No 2)A 1992 s 73 and FA 1994 s 247.]

Commentary—*Simon's Taxes* **I7.114.**
HMRC interpretation RI 121—Relief for tenanted agricultural land.

RI 101 (FEBRUARY 1995) VARIATION OF INHERITANCES FOLLOWING A DEATH

The beneficiaries of a deceased person's estate may wish to alter their entitlements under the estate, by changing the terms under which the original inheritance arose, whether by the deceased's will, the laws of intestacy or otherwise. For example, a daughter inheriting under her father's will may want to pass the inheritance on to her own child.

Not surprisingly everyone who would lose out as a result of the change—called a variation—must agree to it.

There are special rules concerning the consequences of variations in inheritance tax IHTA 1984 s 142. The main ones are set out below.

If a variation is made [by the parties affected by it]—

- in a written instrument [that includes a statement that IHTA 1984 s 142 is to apply to the variation]; and
- within two years of the relevant death; and
- where the variation means that additional inheritance tax is payable, the personal representatives of the deceased [are also parties to the instrument],

then the estate will be taxed as if the variation had been made by the deceased at the time of his/her death. In other words inheritance tax will be calculated on the basis of the varied entitlements, not the original ones.

We have recently been asked for guidance in two areas relating to inheritance tax and instruments of variation.

MARSHALL V KERR

In June 1994 the House of Lords, in the case of *Marshall v Kerr* [1994] 2 All ER 106, found that those provisions of TCGA 1992 s 62 which apply where there is a variation and election, did not mean that the variation of the terms of a deceased person's will was to be treated for all purposes of capital gains tax as made by the deceased. We have been asked whether variations which meet the conditions in IHTA 1984 s 142 will still be treated for inheritance tax purposes as made by the deceased and not by the beneficiary or beneficiaries.

Our view is that, as the relevant inheritance tax legislation differs from the capital gains tax provisions which were considered in *Marshall v Kerr*, that decision has no application to inheritance tax. Variations which meet all the statutory conditions will continue to be treated for inheritance tax purposes as having been made by the deceased.

VARIATION OF INHERITANCES FOLLOWING THE DEATH OF AN ORIGINAL BENEFICIARY WITHIN THE STATUTORY TWO-YEAR PERIOD

As explained above, for IHTA 1984 s 142 to apply, all the beneficiaries affected by the variation must join in a written [instrument effecting the variation]. We have been asked how this requirement should be interpreted when one of the beneficiaries dies before a variation is made.

Our view is that the legal personal representatives of a beneficiary (the second deceased) may enter into a variation and sign an election.

If the variation will reduce the entitlements of the beneficiaries of the second deceased then they, as well as the legal personal representatives of the second deceased, must agree to the variation. The Revenue will require evidence of the consent of the beneficiaries of the second deceased to the variation. If they are not themselves parties to the variation other written evidence of their consent will be sought.

This view applies for capital gains tax purposes also [IHTA 1084 s 142; TCGA 1992 s 62].

Commentary—*Simon's Taxes* **I4.411.**

Note—This interpretation was amended in Tax Bulletin 74 (December 2004).

RI 110 (APRIL 1995) INHERITANCE TAX—VALUATION OF ASSETS AT THE DATE OF DEATH

Where the value of an asset is ascertained for Inheritance Tax (IHT) purposes on the owner's death, this is also taken as the beneficiary's acquisition value for capital gains tax (CGT) purposes. [The Revenue] have been asked to say whether [they] will ascertain the value of the estate assets using the IHT principles, where either—

– the asset is wholly exempt or relieved from IHT; or
– no IHT is payable on the deceased's estate,

in order to provide a value for any other Revenue purpose, in particular the CGT acquisition value.

The value of an asset for IHT purposes is usually the price it would realise if sold in the open market. In certain circumstances special rules may apply to give a different value. For example, under the related property provisions of IHTA 1984 s 161, property held jointly by husband and wife is treated as a single unit in arriving at the value of their respective interests.

IHT is charged on the assets in a person's estate on death if their value together with the value of any chargeable lifetime gifts exceeds the IHT "threshold" (£154,000 for deaths and other chargeable events occurring on or after 6 April 1995). There are various exemptions and reliefs. These include the exemption for assets given to a surviving spouse and up to 100 per cent relief for agricultural or business property.

If an asset is wholly exempt or relieved from IHT, neither the personal representatives of the deceased nor the Revenue can require the value of that asset to be ascertained for IHT purposes.

Where it is evident that any possible increase or decrease in the value of the chargeable assets of the estate, as included in an Inland Revenue Account, will leave the total value of the estate below the IHT threshold, it will not be necessary to ascertain the value of all the individual assets for IHT purposes. In some cases, particularly where the estate is close to the threshold, values may be considered but not necessarily "ascertained".

For example, the value included in the Inland Revenue Account for a holding of shares in an unquoted company might appear to the Revenue's Shares Valuation Division (SVD) to be too high. In this situation, as no IHT is at stake, SVD is unlikely to negotiate an ascertained value for IHT. On the other hand if the value included seems, on the face of it, too low, SVD may negotiate an ascertained value if the likely amount of IHT at stake warrants this.

If the value of an asset is not ascertained for IHT, the normal rules of TCGA 1992 s 272 will apply to determine the CGT acquisition value of the beneficiary.

[The Revenue] have also been asked how [they] will approach the valuation of a holding of shares in an unquoted company where not all of the company's assets qualify for IHT business property relief, so that the shares are not wholly relieved. Again, SVD's approach will depend very much upon whether in any event IHT is payable and, if so, the amount of tax involved. SVD is unlikely to negotiate an ascertained value for the holding if very little or no tax is at stake.

Commentary—*Simon's Taxes* **I4.114.**

RI 121 (AUGUST 1995) INHERITANCE TAX—RELIEF FOR TENANTED AGRICULTURAL LAND

INHERITANCE TAX—RELIEF FOR TENANTED AGRICULTURAL LAND—FA 1995 S 155

FA 1995 s 155 increased the rate of the inheritance tax relief for transfers of tenanted agricultural land from 50 per cent to 100 per cent. The full relief applies to transfers, made on or after 1 September 1995, of agricultural land which is let on a tenancy starting on or after that date. The purpose of the full relief is, as indicated in the [Revenue] Press Release of 27 January 1995, to boost the Government's reforms of the law on agricultural tenancies, now contained in the Agricultural Tenancies Act 1995. ATA 1995 applies to England and Wales, and not to Northern Ireland or Scotland.

APPLICATION OF INHERITANCE TAX RELIEF

[The Revenue] have received enquiries asking whether the increased relief will only apply where the tenancy in question is within the provisions of ATA 1995.

The relief will apply to all agricultural tenancies, throughout the UK, starting on or after 1 September 1995, provided that all the statutory conditions for relief are met. In particular, a tenancy starting on or after that date by reason of statutory succession to an existing tenancy is not excluded from the full relief.

Commentary—*Simon's Taxes* **I7.302–I7.304.**
HMRC interpretation RI 95—Business and agricultural relief.
Note—This interpretation superseded by IHTM 24240.

RI 127 (OCTOBER 1995) POST-DEATH VARIATION OF INHERITANCE BY SURVIVORSHIP

Beneficiaries of the estate of a deceased person—whether under the will, rules relating to intestacy or otherwise—may wish to change their inheritances. There are special inheritance tax rules for changes or variations made within two years after the deceased's death.

If a variation made within the two-year period satisfies certain other conditions, inheritance tax is charged on the death as though the deceased person had made the variation and the beneficiaries do not have to pay tax on any gift of their inheritance. The main conditions are that the variation is made in writing and that [the variation contains a statement that] the inheritance tax rules [are intended] to apply.

Similar rules apply for certain purposes of capital gains tax.

Recently, [the Revenue] have seen suggestions that these rules do not apply to a variation of the deceased's interest in jointly held assets, which passed on the death to the surviving joint owner(s).

For example, the family home was owned by a mother and her son as beneficial joint tenants and on the mother's death, her interest passed by survivorship to the son who then became the sole owner of the property. It has been suggested that, in this example, the son cannot, for inheritance tax/capital gains tax purposes, vary his inheritance of his mother's interest by redirecting it to his children.

[The Revenue] do not share this view.

Both inheritance tax and capital gains tax rules apply not only to dispositions/inheritances arising under will or the law of intestacy but also those effected "otherwise". In [The Revenue's] view, the words "or otherwise" bring within the rules the automatic inheritance of a deceased owner's interest in jointly held assets by the surviving joint owner(s).

Commentary—*Simon's Taxes* **I4.411.**

Note—This Interpretation was amended in Tax Bulletin 74 (December 2004).

RI 166 (FEBRUARY 1997) EXCLUDED PROPERTY SETTLEMENTS BY PEOPLE DOMICILED OVERSEAS

EXCLUDED PROPERTY SETTLEMENTS BY PEOPLE DOMICILED OVERSEAS—IHTA 1984 SS 43, 44, 48

[The Revenue] have been asked how the IHT provisions on excluded property apply to the assets of a settlement made by a person domiciled overseas where—

– all, or only some, of the settled assets are situated outside the UK when a chargeable event occurs; or
– a person domiciled in the UK has also provided property or funds for the purposes of that settlement.

References in this article are to sections of the Inheritance Tax Act 1984.

EXCLUDED PROPERTY

For persons domiciled abroad, IHT generally applies only to their UK assets; it treats their overseas assets as excluded property, that is; not within the charge to IHT—s 6(1). For assets owned outright, it is the owner's domicile at the time of a tax charge that is relevant in deciding whether or not the assets are excluded property.

Slightly different rules apply to property held in settlement. An asset is excluded property if it is situated abroad when a chargeable event occurs and if the settlor (defined in s 44) was domiciled outside the UK *at the time the settlement was made*—s 48(3).

However, an "excluded" asset is not always completely irrelevant for the purposes of IHT. So—

– an "excluded" asset in a person's estate may still affect the valuation of another asset in the estate, for example, an "excluded" holding of shares in an unquoted company may affect the value of a similar holding in the estate which is not "excluded";
– the value of an "excluded" asset at the time the asset becomes comprised in a settlement may be relevant in determining the rate of any tax charge arising in respect of the settlement under the IHT rules concerning trusts without interests in possession—ss 68(5), 66(4) and 69(3).

Domicile is a concept of general law but, in certain circumstances (s 267), a person with a general law domicile abroad can be treated as having a UK domicile for IHT purposes.

SETTLOR ADDS ASSETS TO HIS/HER EXISTING SETTLEMENTS

In the light of the definitions of "settlement" and "settled property" in s 43, [the Revenue's] view is that a settlement in relation to any particular asset is made at the time when that asset is transferred to the settlement trustees to hold on the declared trusts. Thus, assets added to a settlor's own settlement made at an earlier time when the settlor was domiciled abroad will not be "excluded", wherever they may be situated, if the settlor has a UK domicile at the time of making the addition.

In determining the tax treatment of particular assets held in the same settlement it may, therefore, be necessary to consider the settlor's domicile at times other than when the settlement was first made. And if assets added at different times have become mixed, any dealings with the settled fund after the addition(s) may also need to be considered.

SEVERAL PERSONS CONTRIBUTE TO A SINGLE SETTLEMENT

There are rules (s 44(2)) which provide that assets contributed to a "single" settlement by more than one settlor are to be treated as comprised in separate settlements for IHT purposes if "the circumstances so require". There is no definition of "required circumstances" or statutory guidance on how the assets in the single, actual settlement are to be attributed to the deemed separate settlements.

However, the provision is similar in terms to FA 1975 Sch 5 para 1(8), which was considered by Chadwick J in *Hatton v IRC* [1992] STC 140. In the light of the decision in that case [the Revenue] take the view

- that the determination of the extent to which overseas assets in a settlement are excluded property by reason of the settlor's domicile is a relevant "required circumstance"; and
- that
  - where a clear, or reasonably sensible, attribution of settled property between the contributions made by several settlors is possible, there will be a separate settlement, with its own attributed assets, for each contributor for IHT purposes;
  - if such an attribution is not feasible, each separate settlement will comprise all the assets of the single, actual settlement.

TRUST RECORDS

It follows from the comments above that the trustees of a settlement should keep adequate records to enable any necessary attribution of the settled property to be made if either—

- the settlor has added further assets to the settlement after it was made; or
- two or more persons have contributed funds for the purposes of the settlement.

Commentary—*Simon's Taxes* **I5.181.**

RI 210 (OCTOBER 1999) BOOKMAKERS' PITCHES AND CAPITAL GAINS TAX

BACKGROUND

Up until October 1998, the pitch committee of the appropriate Bookmakers' Protection Association (BPA) allocated pitches at each horse racecourse on behalf of the racecourse authorities. BPAs covered all courses between them and combined formed the National Association of Bookmakers. On-course bookmakers obtained a "pitch"—a specified position in Tattersall's or the Silver Ring on which they erected a stand and traded. In each enclosure the pitches were arranged in rows, the front rows being regarded as the best from which to attract the most custom and the largest bets.

A bookmaker could only have one pitch at a racecourse at a time. A pitch was deemed to fall vacant if the occupant failed to regularly attend the course meetings. When a pitch fell vacant, the bookmaker with the longest satisfactory attendance in the ring concerned was given preference if they applied for it, except that in certain circumstances a member of the previous holder's family could obtain it.

Fundamental changes to the administration of on-course bookmakers and the allocation of pitches were introduced with effect from 8 October 1998, when the National Association of Bookmakers lost its control of racecourse betting rings to the National Joint Pitch Council, which is in turn administered by the Horse Race Betting Levy Board. Under the new regime, a number of changes to existing practices were introduced including the fact that although the seniority system used to determine pitch positions in the betting ring is maintained, transferring seniority by auction is now permitted. In addition, inherited seniority alone is no longer sufficient for a bookmaker to retain a ring position.

. . .

INHERITED PITCHES

Where a pitch has been acquired by inheritance after the October 1998 changes to the rules came into effect, however, we consider that the position will be different. TCGA 1992 s 62(1) provides that—

"The assets of which a deceased person was competent to dispose—

(*a*) shall be deemed to be acquired on his death by the personal representatives or other persons on whom they devolve for a consideration equal to their market value at the date of death."

Clearly a particular pitch will now have a market value and as it was an asset "of which the deceased was competent to dispose" would fall within s 62(1).

A pitch will also be "property to which (the deceased) is beneficially entitled", IHTA 1984 s 5(1), and where it formed part of the deceased's business, its value may qualify for inheritance tax business property relief at 100% if the statutory conditions are met, IHTA 1984 ss 103–114.

If a member of the family acquires a pitch through inheritance then where its value has been "ascertained" for inheritance tax purposes, this will also be their acquisition cost, TCGA 1992 s 274.

. . . .

Commentary—*Simon's Taxes* **Division I7.1.**
Note—Words omitted are not relevant to IHT.

Press Releases etc

IHT

Contents

List of Press Releases etc

Press releases

CTT—ASSOCIATED OPERATIONS

10 March 1975. *Hansard*

The Chief Secretary to the Treasury (Mr Joel Barnett)

I want to explain the reason for the clause [now IHTA 1984 s 268]. As I said in Committee, it is reasonable for a husband to share capital with his wife when she has no means of her own. If she chooses to make gifts out of the money she has received from her husband, there will be no question of using the associated operation provisions to treat them as gifts made by the husband and taxable as such.

In a blatant case, where a transfer by a husband to a wife was made on condition that the wife should at once use the money to make gifts to others, a charge on a gift by the husband might arise under the clause. The Hon Gentleman fairly recognised that.

I want to give an example of certain circumstances that could mean the clause having to be invoked. There are complex situations involving transactions between husband and wife and others where, for example, a controlling shareholder with a 60 per cent holding in a company wished to transfer his holding to his son. If he gave half to his son, having first transferred half to his wife, and later his wife transferred her half share to the son, the effect would be to pass a controlling shareholding from father to son. The Revenue would then use the associated operations provisions to ensure that the value of a controlling holding was taxed.

There are ordinary, perfectly innocent transfers between husband and wife. For example, where a husband has the money and the wife has no money—or the other way round, which happens from time to time—and the one with the money gives something to the other to enable the spouse to make a gift to a son or a daughter on marriage, that transaction would not be caught by the clause. It would be a reasonable thing to do. I have made that clear in Committee upstairs, and I make it clear again now.

HC Deb, 10 March 1975, Vol. 888, col 56.

POWER TO ALLOW BENEFICIARY TO OCCUPY HOUSE

6 August 1975. *Inland Revenue*

"Commonly such a power is ancillary to a primary trust created by the will and we should not regard its presence as affecting any interest in possession existing under that trust. If there is no such interest it could perhaps be argued that the exercise of the power might create one, but in the ordinary case we should not take this view unless the trustees were empowered to, and did, grant a lease for life within the terms of FA 1975 Sch 5 para 1(3) [now IHTA 1984 s 43(3)].

If the exercise of the power reduces the value of the settled property, as it would if the trustees could and did grant a lease for a fixed term at less than a rack rent, we should in practice seek the alternative charge given by para 6 (3) [repealed 1982] or 4 (9) [now IHTA 1984 s 52 (3),(4)] of the Schedule."

Statement of Practice SP 10/79—Power for trustees to allow a beneficiary to occupy dwelling house.

ACCUMULATION AND MAINTENANCE SETTLEMENTS: POWERS OF APPOINTMENT

8 October 1975. *Inland Revenue letter*

The inclusion of issue as possible objects of a special power of appointment would exclude a settlement from the benefit of FA 1975 Sch 5 para 15 [repealed 1982] if the power would allow the trustees to prevent any interest in possession in the settled property from commencing before the beneficiary concerned attained the age specified. It would depend on the precise words of the settlement and the facts to which they had to be applied whether a particular settlement satisfied the conditions of para 15(1). In many cases the rules against perpetuity and accumulations would operate to prevent an effective appointment outside those conditions. Perhaps I should add that the application of para 15 is not a matter for a once-for-all decision. It is a question that needs to be kept in mind at all times when there is settled property in which no interest in possession subsists.

I am afraid that I do not understand why Mr . . . should think inequality between the beneficiaries fatal to the application of para 15. There is nothing in that paragraph requiring the "beneficiaries" to be identified or their interests to be quantified, much less equal. (Letter from the Inland Revenue quoted in Law Society's Gazette, October 1975.)

Cross reference—See IHTA 1984 s 71.

PAYMENTS TO EMPLOYEES UNDER ACCIDENT INSURANCE SCHEMES—CTT/IHT LIABILITY (FA 1975 S 20(4) [NOW IHTA 1984 S 10])

6 January 1976. *Inland Revenue*

The Board of Inland Revenue understand that there is uncertainty about the capital transfer tax position of payments by an employer to an employee or his dependants following a claim by the employer under the terms of an accident insurance policy effected by the employer under the terms of which the benefits are payable to him absolutely.

The Board wish to make it clear that FA 1975 s 20(4) provides that there will not be a "transfer of value" where the employer and employee are at arm's length and not connected with each other and where there is no intention to confer a gratuitous benefit. Where the employer and employee are connected there will be no liability if the payment was such as might reasonably be expected between non-connected persons.

In many cases the payment will be covered by the exemption in FA 1975 Sch 6 para 9 as being allowable as a deduction in computing the taxable profits of a trade, profession or vocation, so that no question of a capital transfer tax liability can arise. If a payment not covered by FA 1975 Sch 6 para 9 [repealed] is allowable for income tax or corporation tax purposes, eg under the TA 1970 ss 72, 304 provisions, the Board will accept that this of itself establishes that the requirements of s 20(4) are met.

Commentary—*Simon's Taxes* **I3.148**; *Foster* **C1.48.**

REVERSIONARY INTERESTS

4 February 1976. *Inland Revenue letter*

"A reversionary interest is excluded property if—

(*a*) Wherever it is situated it has not been acquired for consideration and it is not expectant on the determination of a lease for life etc granted otherwise than for full consideration, or

(*b*) if the interest itself is situated outside the UK and is either

(i) in the actual beneficial ownership of someone domiciled outside the UK or

(ii) itself settled property comprised in a settlement made by someone who was domiciled outside the UK when he made the settlement."

Letter from the Inland Revenue, Law Society's Gazette, 4 February 1976.

IHT: SETTLED PROPERTY—INTEREST IN POSSESSION

12 February 1976. *Inland Revenue*

The Board of Inland Revenue are aware that doubts have been expressed in the legal press and elsewhere concerning the precise scope of the term "interest in possession" as used in the Inheritance Tax Act 1984 and in particular about its application where an interest in settled property is subject to a discretion or power to accumulate the income of property or to divert it elsewhere.

The Board therefore feel it appropriate, in view of the importance of the expression in IHTA 1984 Pt III to make known their understanding of the meaning of the expression. This is that an interest in possession in settled property exists where the person having the interest has the immediate entitlement (subject to any prior claim by the trustees for expenses or other outgoings properly payable out of income) to any income produced by that property as the income arises; but that a discretion or power, in whatever form, which can be exercised after income arises so as to withhold it from that person negatives the existence of an interest in possession. For this purpose a power to accumulate income is regarded as a power to withhold it, unless any accumulations must be held solely for the person having the interest or his personal representatives.

On the other hand the existence of a mere power of revocation or appointment, the exercise of which would determine the interest wholly or in part (but which, so long as it remains unexercised, does not affect the beneficiary's immediate entitlement to income) does not in the Board's view prevent the interest from being an interest in possession.

Commentary—*Simon's Taxes* **I5.141**; *Foster* **E1.41**.

REVERSIONARY INTERESTS, CREATED ON PURCHASE

3 March 1976. *Inland Revenue letter*

"In your letter of 15 October you asked about the protection from capital transfer tax of bona fide purchasers of reversionary interests.

You were concerned in particular with the situation in which a settlement is created by the sale of a reversionary interest in property wholly owned by the vendor. In that situation, FA 1894, s 3 would normally have excluded any claim for estate duty on the death of the vendor to the extent that the purchase price represented full consideration for the interest purchased.

I confirm that where such an interest was purchased by the reversioner before 27 March 1974, FA 1975 Sch 5 para 23(1) [now IHTA 1984 Sch 6 para 3] will protect the purchaser from any capital transfer tax in excess of the estate duty which he would have had to pay had that Act not been passed. Thus, if the purchaser had paid the full actuarial value of the interest concerned he would not have to pay any tax on the death of the vendor. The interest itself when purchased is not 'excluded property' for capital transfer tax and must be taken into account in the estate of the purchaser."

Letter from the Inland Revenue, Law Society's Gazette, 3 March 1976.

CTT: PENSION SCHEMES (FA 1975 SCH 5 PARA 16 [NOW IHTA 1984 SS 151, 210])

7 May 1976. *Inland Revenue*

1. This note has been prepared at the request of The National Association of Pension Funds primarily to enable the administrators of pension schemes to answer enquiries about the capital transfer tax liability of benefits payable under such schemes.

2. No liability to capital transfer tax arises in respect of benefits payable on a person's death under a normal pension scheme except in the circumstances explained below.

3. Such benefits are liable to capital transfer tax if:

(a) they form part of his freely disposable property passing under his will or intestacy. (This applies only if his executors or administrators have a legally enforceable claim to the benefits: if they were payable to them only at the discretion of the trustees of the pension fund or some similar persons they are not liable to capital transfer tax.), or

(b) he had the power, immediately before his death, to nominate or appoint the benefits to anyone he pleased.

In these cases the benefits should be included in the personal representatives' account (schedule of the deceased's assets) which has to be completed when applying for a grant of probate or letters of administration. The capital transfer tax (if any) which is assessed on the personal representatives' account has to be paid before the grant can be obtained.

4. On some events other than the death of a member information should be given to the appropriate Estate Duty Office. These are:

(a) the payment of contributions to a scheme which has not been approved for income tax purposes;

(b) the making of an irrevocable nomination or the disposal of a benefit by a member in his lifetime (otherwise than in favour of his spouse) which reduces the value of his estate (*eg* the surrender of part of his pension or his lump sum benefit in exchange for a pension for the life of another).

If capital transfer tax proves to be payable the Estate Duty Office will communicate with the persons liable to pay the tax.

Commentary—*Simon's Taxes* **I4.125, I5.637**; *Foster* **D1.25, E6.37**.
Statement of Practice SP 10/86—Death benefits under superannuation arrangements.

NORMAL EXPENDITURE OUT OF INCOME (IHTA 1984 S 21)

9 June 1976. *Inland Revenue letter*

"The statute does not lay down a precise definition of income for the purposes of this exemption. We would therefore take the view that the word has to be interpreted in accordance with normal accountancy rules. This implies taking income net of tax; as regards taking into account the tax on a wife's income, I think it implies adopting a factual test—ie looking to see what tax is actually borne by the spouse concerned. Of course this is an area in which it is difficult to lay down an inflexible rule, and the circumstances of individual cases will doubtless be diverse."

Letter from Inland Revenue, Law Society's Gazette, 9 June 1976.

THE TAX POSITION OF GIFTS TO THE ARTS AND SALES OF ARTISTIC OBJECTS

March 1977. *Department of Education and Science*

. . .

CTT AND CGT

4. Many bodies in the arts field are registered as charities. Gifts of money or objects to charities are exempt from CTT without limit if they are made more than one year before the donor's death. Gifts made to charities on death or within one year before death are exempt up to a cumulative total of £100,000 per donor. The tax is not charged either on gifts or bequests to certain national institutions concerned with the preservation of the national heritage (or similar bodies approved by the Treasury), for example the National Gallery or the British Museum. [IHTA 1984 Sch 3] sets out the relevant national heritage bodies. Gifts to charities and to these national heritage bodies are not charged with CGT.

5. Gifts to non-profit-making bodies of works of art and other objects which in the opinion of the Treasury are of national, historic, artistic or scientific interest may be conditionally exempt from CTT and CGT if the Treasury so direct. The conditions are that the property is given to a body approved by the Treasury as appropriate for its preservation, and that suitable undertakings are given regarding the use or disposal of the property, its preservation, and reasonable access to the public.

ACCEPTANCE OF WORKS OF ART AND OTHER OBJECTS IN LIEU OF CTT

6. Objects or collections of objects may be accepted in lieu of CTT if the Treasury are satisfied that they are of pre-eminent national, scientific, historic or artistic interest. This also applies to objects which are not pre-eminent if they have been kept in a building which is itself accepted in lieu of tax or is owned by the Crown or by one of the bodies covered by [IHTA 1984 Sch 3], provided that in the opinion of the Treasury the objects should remain associated with the building.

ARTISTIC OBJECTS IN PRIVATE HANDS: CTT

7. An object of national, scientific, historic or artistic interest (referred to in the following paragraphs as an "object") may be conditionally exempted from CTT on the owner's death, even though it continues to be held in private ownership. It may also be similarly exempted from CTT on a lifetime gift if the donor, or his spouse, has owned it for at least 6 years before the gift or if he inherited it on a death on which it was conditionally exempt from estate duty or from CTT. Objects held on trust can qualify for exemption on broadly similar lines.

8. The objects covered include pictures, prints, books, manuscripts, works of art, and scientific collections. The qualifying test for exemption is whether the object would be good

enough to be displayed in a public collection, whether national, local authority or university. The exemption is subject to the giving of certain undertakings as set out in the legislation (eg reasonable access for the public). It is withdrawn if there is a breach of the undertakings or if the object is sold, other than by private treaty to one of the bodies covered by [IHTA 1984 Sch 3]. Exemption is not withdrawn if the object is accepted in lieu of all or part of a CTT liability.

9. If an exemption is withdrawn as a result of an open market sale or a breach of the undertakings, CTT is then charged, generally on the sale proceeds or the current market value of the object. The precise way in which the tax is calculated, under the rules in [IHTA 1984 s 35, Sch 5], will depend on whether the last exempt transfer of the object took place before 7 April 1976.

THE SPECIAL PURCHASE SCHEME FOR ARTISTIC OBJECTS

11. The combined liability to CTT and CGT on an open market sale of an exempt object can be very substantial. The owner may decide instead to take advantage of the special purchase scheme and give a public collection of his choice the opportunity to acquire the object by private treaty. The first step is to reach agreement on a valuation accepted by both parties as a fair assessment of the market price. It is for the owner to propose the valuation, which is then considered by the body's expert advisers. Once the valuation has been agreed the next step is to calculate the special private treaty sale price.

12. To enable the special sale price to be calculated the agreed valuation is split into two components—

(i) The potential liability to CTT and CGT on what is mutually agreed would be the sale proceeds of the object on the open market;

(ii) The net proceeds which would accrue to the owner from an open market sale (*ie* the gross valuation minus (i))

If the approved body paid the owner an amount equivalent to (ii), the owner would be no better or worse off than under an open market sale. To encourage sales to these approved bodies, however, the special sale price is calculated as (ii) plus 25 per cent of (i). By taking advantage of the special purchase scheme the owner is thus increasing his net proceeds from the sale by 25 per cent of the tax due on an open market sale.

Cross references—See IHTA 1984 ss 230, 231 (powers to accept and transfer property in satisfaction of tax).
See Capital Taxation and Works of Art, *post*.

ASSOCIATED OPERATIONS

1 March 1978. *Inland Revenue letter*

"You wrote on 7 November to say that you had received enquiries about the applications of FA 1975 s 44 [now IHTA 1984 s 268] (associated operations) to what I may perhaps loosely describe as schemes designed to maximise the advantage of the capital transfer tax £2,000 annual exemption. I am sorry I have not been able to reply earlier.

Your first example concerned the case where A sold an asset to B but left the price outstanding on loan, part of which was written-off each year. We will obviously need to consider any actual case of this kind in the light of the full facts but on the facts as given in the example it seems clear that the sale of the asset and the writing-off of the loans are associated with each other as a single arrangement and, prima facie, we would consider s 44 relevant, whether or not interest was payable on the loan. If section 44 does apply it may well follow that under s 44(3) we would have to look at the value of the asset at the date of the release of the last part of the debt.

Your second example involved a gift of shares on terms that the son would pay the CTT by instalments, the father subsequently making further gifts of cash to the son. In this case we agree that s 44 does not apply; the mere fact that the father made later gifts within the annual exemption to enable the son to pay the tax would not therefore require the value transferred by the original gift to be reviewed."

INLAND REVENUE ANSWER TO ACCOUNTANTS' COMPLAINTS ON ACCOUNTS EXAMINATION PROCEDURES (TA 1970 S 115)

4 October 1978. *CCAB TR. 309*

INTRODUCTION

1. In March 1977 the accountancy bodies held a meeting with the Inland Revenue to consider the selective examination of business accounts by Inspectors of Taxes introduced in 1977. The opportunity was also taken to clarify a number of other operational matters which had been causing difficulty . . .

2. It was considered to be to the mutual advantage of both the Revenue and the CCAB to hold a further meeting to review the selective system which had now been working almost eighteen months. As well as discussing the examination of business accounts the opportunity was taken to discuss a number of other matters.

3. These are the agreed notes of the meeting held on 1 June 1978 and, for this purpose, includes notes relating to some matters which were on the agenda but covered separately by correspondence.

. . .

VALUATION OF UNQUOTED SHARES BY VALUATION DIVISION

23. The CCAB pointed out a common difficulty where separate negotiations took place for valuations for stamp duty, capital gains tax and capital transfer tax. It was suggested that all valuations required should be agreed at the same time.

24. The value for stamp duty purposes was usually required very quickly after the transaction and if the other values were negotiated at the same time (often on a different basis) then there could be inconvenient delay in the stamp duty valuation. The Revenue promised to refer the points to its Technical Division to see if the processes could be streamlined but it was stressed that nobody wanted a solution which would cause delays in the stamp duty valuations. They have since written as follows—

"The Technical Division can offer no other solution to that given at our meetings, *ie* the parties request the Capital Taxes Office or Tax District soon after the transaction to start the valuation procedure. It is insisted that the facts to determine the value for CTT and CGT purposes are not usually available at the stamp duty valuation stage and without them Shares Valuation Division can make no progress.

Technical Division suggest that if the history of specific cases were instanced they could then identify where the material delays arose and perhaps see if there is anything basically wrong with the system."

LIFE ASSURANCE PREMIUMS: MEASURE OF VALUE FOR PURPOSE OF CTT (FA 1975 SCH 10 PARA 11 [NOW IHTA 1984 S 167])

17 January 1979. *Inland Revenue*

Where a person pays a life assurance premium for the benefit of someone else (for example where the policy is held in trust for another person) this may constitute a transfer of value for the purposes of capital transfer tax. From 6 April 1979 there will be a right in many cases for the payer to make a deduction from the premium in accordance with the system of relief introduced by FA 1976 s 34. The Board of Inland Revenue take the view that where the payment of a premium on a life assurance policy is a transfer of value for the purposes of capital transfer tax, the amount of the transfer is:

(a) the net amount of the premium after any deduction made under the authority of FA 1976 Sch 4, para 5;

(b) the gross premium where the premium is paid without deduction.

Commentary—*Simon's Taxes* **I3.114, 251**; *Foster* **C1.14, C2.51**.

DOMICILE: EFFECT OF DOMICILE AND MATRIMONIAL PROCEEDINGS ACT 1973 (IHTA 1984 S 267)

31 December 1979. *BTR 398*

In the course of an action for a declaration as to the validity of a marriage it was contended that the effect of the Domicile and Matrimonial Proceedings Act 1973 was that a married woman could avoid taking a dependent domicile if she did not want it but that she could still take it if she wished. Sir George Baker P. held that the effect of the Act was that dependent domicile had been abolished. If for example an English girl married an American she would not acquire an American domicile unless and until she went to America. "Of course, a marriage as normally understood would be strong evidence that a woman had acquired the same domicile as her husband, for example, when a foreign woman comes here and marries an Englishman and they settle down as a married couple, have children and so on; but it is only one factor in her choice." *Puttick v Attorney-General*, 8 May 1979, [1979] 3 WLR 542; [1979] 3 All ER 463.

CTT: SETTLED PROPERTY INCOME YIELDS

25 July 1980. *Inland Revenue*

1. An Order (SI 1980/1000) has today been laid before the House of Commons to replace an earlier Statutory Instrument (SI 1975/610) relating to capital transfer tax and settled property. This notice explains the effect of the new Order, which comes into effect on 15 August 1980, and invites application from taxpayers who feel that they may have been prejudiced by the Inland Revenue's treatment of cases since 16 May 1977, when the earlier Order became inoperative in part.

THE PURPOSE OF THE ORDER

2. Under FA 1975 Sch 5 para 3 [now IHTA 1984 s 49(1)] a person who has a beneficial entitlement to the income of settled property is treated for capital transfer tax purposes as being beneficially entitled to the property itself. Thus someone who has a life interest in property is treated as owning that property absolutely, so that on his death there is a charge to tax on the value of the property. But if a person's entitlement to income from settled property is expressed as a specified amount (ie typically if he has an annuity), special rules are needed to determine the proportion of the value of the settled property which is to be attributed to the annuitant or, conversely, to the person who has the right to receive the balance of the income after the annuity has been paid.

3. The rule for cases of this kind is contained in Sch 5, para 3(3) [now IHTA 1984 s 50(2)] which provides that the value of the annuitant's share or of the balance is to be found by reference to the income yield of the property in the settlement. Thus if, at the date when the interest has to be valued, settled property worth £5,000 is producing an income yield of 10 per cent per annum, and an annuity of £100 is payable, the annuitant will be treated as owning one-fifth of the settled property (ie £1,000) since he is entitled to one-fifth of the income; a person entitled to the balance will be treated as owning the remaining four-fifths.

4. The legislation recognises that taxpayers could take undue advantage of the rule by switching to high or low yielding investments shortly before the termination of one or other of the interests in the settled property. Sch 5, para 3(4) [now s 50(3)] therefore provides that the Treasury may prescribe upper and lower limits to the income yield that can be used for the calculation of the value of either portion. This was done in 1975 by an Order (SI 1975/610) which prescribed rates appearing in the FT-Actuaries Shares Indices compiled by the Financial Times, the Institute of Actuaries and the Faculty of Actuaries, and published in the Financial Times. The yield from 21/2 per cent Consols was designated as the higher rate, and the gross dividend yield of the All-Share Index as the lower rate.

5. The constituents of the FT-Actuaries Share Indices were changed on 16 May 1977; since then they have not contained a separate entry for the yield of 2½ per cent Consols. The yield continued, however, to be published elsewhere and the Capital Taxes Office has since that date used the 2½ per cent Consols yield derived from other sources as the higher rate limit. But following legal advice that there is no authority for this practice, it has been decided to provide a new higher rate by the making of a new Order.

THE NEW ORDER

6. The new Order retains the yield from the All-Shares Index as the measure of the lower rate but provides that the higher designated rate is to be that shown in the FT-Actuaries Share Indices for British Government Stocks ("Irredeemables"), a category which subsumes the

former $2^1/_2$ per cent Consols listing and responding to market conditions in very much the same way. It applies to transfers of value taking place on or after 15 August 1980.

Commentary—*Simon's Taxes* **I5.213**; *Foster* **E2.13**.

OBJECTS IN LIEU OF TAX

7 August 1980. *Hansard*

The Rt. Hon. Norman St. John-Stevas, MP, Chancellor of the Duchy of Lancaster and Minister for the Arts announced today that the present system of obtaining expert advice on the pre-eminence of objects offered in satisfaction of tax should be revised. The Chancellor of the Duchy has also issued new detailed guidelines on the interpretation of pre-eminence.

Replying to a Written Parliamentary Question from Mr Andrew Faulds, MP (Warley, East), who asked whether the Chancellor of the Duchy would make a statement on the interpretation of pre-eminence of works of art and museum objects accepted in satisfaction of capital transfer tax, he said:

"Following consultations with the national museums and galleries and the relevant advisory bodies, I have decided that the present system of obtaining expert advice on the pre-eminence of objects offered in satisfaction of tax should be revised and detailed guidelines issued on the interpretation of pre-eminence [reproduced below]. I shall continue to rely on the directors of the national museums and galleries as my principal source of advice but shall expect them usually to consult widely, particularly where an object has local significance or could be of especial interest within a local context, before formulating their advice. In cases of doubt they will be expected to consult the Standing Commission on Museums and Galleries or the Royal Commission on Historical Manuscripts who will then, if necessary, convene an informal panel of independent advisers which may include a representative of the relevant Historic Buildings Council. The new procedure will be kept under review."

(HC Written Ans. 7 Aug. 1980, col 274).

GUIDELINES ON THE INTERPRETATION OF PRE-EMINENCE IN RESPECT OF OBJECTS OFFERED IN SATISFACTION OF TAX

The following guidelines are intended as a framework of reference for the expert advisers (who are chosen from the directors of the relevant national museums and galleries), to help them in formulating their advice on whether an item is pre-eminent.

(i) Does the object have an especially close association with our history and national life?

This category includes foreign as well as British works, for example, gifts that foreign sovereigns or governments have made, and objects that have been acquired abroad in circumstances closely associated with our history. It includes objects closely associated with some part of the United Kingdom, or with the development of its institutions and industries. Some objects which fall under this category will be of such national importance that they deserve to enter a national museum or gallery. Others may well be of a lesser degree of national importance, though they will be nonetheless significant in a local context. This category will also include works which derive their significance from a local connection, and which may therefore qualify as pre-eminent only in a local or university museum.

(ii) Is the object of especial artistic or art-historical interest?

This category, like (iii) below, includes objects deserving of entering a national museum or gallery as well as other objects which may not be pre-eminent in a national museum or gallery in London, Edinburgh or Cardiff, but will be pre-eminent in museums or galleries elsewhere which do not already possess items of a similar genre or a similar quality.

(iii) Is the object of especial importance for the study of some particular form of art, learning or history?

This category includes a wide variety of objects, not restricted to works of art, which are of especial importance for the study of, say, a particular scientific development. The category also includes objects forming part of a historical unity, series or collection either in one place or in the country as a whole. Without a particular object or group of objects both a unity and a series may be impaired.

iv) Does the object have an especially close association with a particular historic setting?

This category will include primarily works of art, manuscripts, furniture or other items which have an especially close association with an important historic building. They will fall to be considered pre-eminent by virtue of the specific contribution they make to the understanding of an outstanding historic building. Thus, the category may include paintings or furniture specially commissioned for a particular house or a group of paintings having an association with a particular location.

Statement of Practice SP 6/87—Acceptance of heritage property.
Cross references—See IHTA 1984 ss 230, 231 (acceptance and transfer of property in satisfaction of tax).
See Capital Taxation and Works of Art, *post.*

ASSOCIATION FOR BUSINESS SPONSORSHIP OF THE ARTS

9 March 1981. *Hansard*

CAPITAL TRANSFER TAX

10. Gifts made in sponsorship of the arts may qualify for certain exemptions from the charge to capital transfer tax on gratuitous transfers of property by individuals and close companies.

11. There is a general exemption for the first [£3,000] of gifts by an individual in any one tax year and, in addition, gifts by an individual to any one person in one tax year are exempt up to a value of £250. Outright gifts to charity are exempt from capital transfer tax, whatever their value, if they are made more than one year before the death of the donor; if the gift takes place on or within one year of the donor's death they are exempt up to a cumulative total of £200,000 for each donor. (Prior to 26 March 1980 the limit was £100,000).

12. There is an unlimited exemption for gifts or bequests to certain national institutions concerned with the preservation of the national heritage (for example, the British Museum or the National Trust) or to certain bodies specified in FA 1975 Sch 6 para 12 [now IHTA 1984 Sch 3] such as universities and local authorities. There is also an exemption under Sch 6 para 13 [now IHTA 1984 s 26] (matched by a corresponding exemption from capital gains tax) for gifts or bequests of certain national heritage property (outstanding land and historic buildings, works of art etc of national, scientific, historic or artistic interest, and property given as a source of income for the upkeep of such items) to non-profit-making bodies approved by the Treasury. Under FA 1976 s 84 [repealed 1982] exemption may be claimed for transfers of property to, or capital distributions from, a special trust fund approved by the Treasury and devoted to the maintenance and preservation of buildings outstanding for their historic or architectural interest, together with their historically associated contents and amenity land; such a fund would also be exempt from the periodic charge to tax on discretionary trusts. FA 1976 s 55 [now CGTA 1979 s 148] "rolls over" for CGT purposes any accrued gain arising on the disposal of assets to such a trust fund.

13. Transfers by close companies may give rise to capital transfer tax. The liability is calculated by apportioning the value transferred among the participators of the company making the transfer, and the [£3,000] annual exemption applies to the value allocated to each individual participator. So far as the company's transfer of value relates to property given to charity or to the national institutions or bodies mentioned above, then the exemptions for gifts to those bodies extend to the amounts apportioned to the individual participators. Capital transfer tax does not apply to gifts by incorporated bodies other than close companies.

14. Capital transfer tax is not charged on dispositions which are allowed for income tax or corporation tax purposes.

BLOODSTOCK INDUSTRY (TAXATION)

2 November 1983. *Hansard*

Mr Latham asked the Chancellor of the Exchequer on what authority the capital taxes office indicated that horse owners and breeders will not be permitted 50 [now 100] per cent agricultural relief on capital transfer tax and also, in certain circumstances, not be permitted 50 [now 100] per cent business relief; and if he will instruct the office to reverse this decision.

Mr Moore: Under the provisions of the capital transfer tax, agricultural relief is given for agricultural property occupied for agricultural purposes. Business relief is given if the business is carried on for gain. Whether any particular property qualifies under these provisions is a matter of the proper interpretation of the law in relation to the fact of the particular case. If the taxpayer does not accept the view of the Inland Revenue he may appeal.

HC, 2 November 1983, Vol. 47, col 380.

Cross reference—See IHTA 1984 ss 103, 115 (business and agricultural property relief).

ESTATE DUTY: CALCULATION OF DUTY PAYABLE ON A CHARGEABLE EVENT AFFECTING HERITAGE OBJECTS PREVIOUSLY GRANTED CONDITIONAL EXEMPTION

3 May 1984. *Inland Revenue*

Under the estate duty provisions, an object which in the opinion of the Treasury was of national, scientific, historic or artistic interest could be exempt from duty if undertakings were given to preserve it and keep it in the UK. If an object which had been exempted from duty was subsequently sold (unless the purchaser was a national institution or similar body), or if the undertaking was broken, duty became chargeable, generally either on the sale proceeds or on the value of the object at the date of the charge. These "clawback" charges may still apply now in relation to objects which have previously been exempted from estate duty.

Estate duty applied not only to property passing on death but also to property given away by the deceased within a certain period before his death. In these latter cases the duty chargeable could be reduced by a taper relief (FA 1960 s 64). The exemption described in the preceding paragraph could also apply to an object which came within the charge to duty because it was the subject of an inter vivos gift. The Board have been advised that in these circumstances taper relief under s 64 is not available to reduce the amount liable to the clawback charge, and that the amount chargeable to duty is the full value or sale proceeds. The Board understand that the Capital Taxes Office have in the past applied taper relief to reduce the amount liable to the clawback charge. Assessments made on that basis before the date of this notice will not be reopened.

NOTE

Estate duty applied broadly to the value of all property passing on death. In addition, property given away by the deceased within a certain period before his death (latterly 7 years) was treated as passing on death. Depending on the period between the gift and the death a "taper relief " applied to reduce the value chargeable to duty by varying percentages.

The exemption from duty available—as now from capital transfer tax which superseded estate duty in 1975—for objects of national, scientific, historic or artistic interest could also apply to objects which became liable to duty because they were the subject of a lifetime gift. This notice explains how estate duty charges are to be calculated in future when objects of this kind are sold.

Commentary—*Simon's Taxes* **I4.521**; *Foster* **D5.21.**

Cross reference—See IHTA 1984 s 35, Sch 5 para 2 (value of property left out of account in determining value transferred on death before 7 April 1976).

MEMORANDUM TR 557: CTT: "BUY AND SELL" AGREEMENTS

19 September 1984. *ICAEW*

INTRODUCTION

1. This guidance note reproduces correspondence between the Inland Revenue and the accountancy bodies regarding the availability of business relief under FA 1976 Sch 10 para 3(4) [now IHTA 1984 s 113], where, on the death before retirement of a member of a partnership, the deceased's interest is to, or may, pass to the surviving partners.

2. In October 1980 the Inland Revenue issued a Statement of Practice (SP 12/80) entitled "Capital transfer tax—business relief from capital transfer tax: 'buy and sell' agreements".

3. In its issue of 6 May 1981 the Law Society's Gazette published a table which summarises the position in various circumstances. It is emphasised that although the Revenue have agreed that this table outlines the general position regard must be had to the construction of the particular agreement and the correct conclusion on the availability of business relief can only be drawn after careful scrutiny of the agreement in each individual case.

EXTRACTS FROM CORRESPONDENCE

4. Extracts from the correspondence referred to in paragraph 1 are set out in paragraphs 5 to 8 below.

5. Letter dated 10 May 1982 from the accountancy bodies to the Inland Revenue.

The Inland Revenue Statement of Practice SP 12/80 dated 13 October 1980 sets out the views of the Board as to the effect of FA 1976 Sch 10 para 3(4) [now IHTA 1984 s 113] on agreements between partners or shareholder directors whereby, in the event of death before retirement, the deceased's personal representatives must sell, and the survivors must buy, the deceased's interest in the business.

Paragraph 3(4) [s 113] denies relief where business property is the subject of a binding contract of sale which has been entered into at the time of transfer, and the Statement of Practice states that agreements of the type referred to above, commonly known as "buy and sell" agreements, fall within this definition.

It has generally been assumed that paragraph 3(4) [s 113] was intended to deny relief where the transferor had decided to cease trading, had entered into a binding contract for the sale of his business, and had subsequently died or given away his interest before completion of the sale. In the words of *Dymond's Capital Taxes*, "There is no point in giving business relief where the property is, in effect, cash realised on the sale of a business" [(para 24.733)].

However, the Statement of Practice extends the application of paragraph 3(4) [s 113] to situations where the sale is to take place only in the event of death before retirement. By inference it is assumed that business relief will also be denied in such circumstances to lifetime transfers, even though there was no intention to cease trading and the sale on death might be expected to be many years away. We consider this practice to be contrary to the intention of the legislation and to give rise to many anomalies because business relief will depend upon the form of words used rather than the substance. The following are examples of various forms of partnership provisions and the apparent effect on the availability of business relief.

Partnership provision	*Apparent effect*
(a) On the death in service or retirement of a partner the surviving partners shall purchase his share in the partnership for £X.	If a partner gives away part of his partnership share in his lifetime, or dies in service, business relief will presumably not be available.
(b) On the death in service or retirement of a partner the surviving partners have an option to buy and the retiring partner (or his personal representatives) have an option to sell his share in the partnership.	If a partner gives away part of his partnership share in his lifetime, or dies in service, 50% business relief will be available as an option is not a binding contract for sale.
(c) There is no provision for the purchase of a partner's share. By his will a partner directs that if he dies in service his partnership interest is to be sold.	If he gives away part of his partnership share in his lifetime or dies in service, 50% business relief will be available as there is no binding contract for sale.
(d) On the death in service or retirement of a partner his share is to accrue to the surviving partners who shall pay an annuity to the partner or his widow as appropriate.	If a partner gives away part of his partnership share in his lifetime, or dies in service, is this to be constituted as a binding contract for sale?

We are aware that an article appeared on this subject in the *Law Society's Gazette* of 6 May 1981 . . . but it is not clear whether this interpretation has the approval of the Revenue.

6. Reply from the Inland Revenue dated 5 July 1982.

The purpose of paragraph 3(4) [s 113] was to limit business relief to transfers of business property. To that end paragraph 3(4) [s 113] denies relief when—because of a binding contract for sale—what the transferor passes to the transferee is in effect an entitlement to the sale consideration rather than the right to a continuing business interest. While in principle therefore relief is not available on a transfer of business property which is bound by a contract for sale, the decision in any case involving the transfer of an interest in a partnership will depend on the terms of the partnership agreement. It was this situation which our Statement of Practice SP 12/80 was designed to illuminate (its purpose was not to—nor, of course, could it—extend the scope of paragraph 3(4) [s 113]).

In your examples (*b*) and (*c*) business relief will be available, but taking example (*a*) against this background it is clear that business relief will not be available on a partner's death in service or retirement. But if the contract for sale is not operative in his lifetime so that he can give his interest away—and it continues as a business interest in the hands of the recipient—then business relief will be available. Similarly in example (*d*) business relief will be available on a lifetime transfer of a partner's interest if the accrual clause and annuity provision does not then come into operation; but if it does, spouse exemption may be due to the extent of the value of the annuity. On death in service there would again be no business relief, but exemption would be due on the widow's annuity. In the case of example (*d*) the capital gains tax Statement of Practice of 17 January 1975 may also be in point. Any chargeable gains accruing to a retired partner would be computed by comparing the consideration received (including the capitalised value of the annuity) with the capital gains tax "cost", or the market value at the date of death for the personal representatives of a deceased partner.

While I accept that this is not a straightforward area, the effect does not seem to me to be contrary to the intention of the legislation, nor would there appear to be anomalies. The substance of the agreement is different in the different examples so it is not surprising that the tax consequences are also different.

Finally, for the sake of completeness, the article in the *Law Society's Gazette* for 6 May 1981 correctly states the general position since it is only in the final case that a binding contract for sale exists before the death of the partner.

7. Letter dated 19 January 1983 from the accountancy bodies to the Inland Revenue.

We think it would be helpful to publish our substantive correspondence, but before doing so it would be useful to clarify one point, which relates to FA 1976 Sch 10 para 3(4) [now IHTA 1984 s 113], and the view expressed in SP 12/80. This Statement of Practice states that a "buy and sell" agreement as outlined therein, is a binding contract for sale within paragraph 3(4) [s 113] so that it is not relevant business property and therefore business relief will not be due.

The argument against this view is that tax is charged on the death of any person "as if, *immediately before his death*, he had made a transfer of value and the value transferred by it had been equal to the value of his estate immediately before his death, but subject to the following provisions of this section". (FA 1975 s 22(1) [now IHTA 1984 s 4(1)].) The deemed transfer of value is, by definition, treated as made at a time when the deceased was alive. Paragraph 3(4), [s 113] provides:

"Where any property would be relevant business property in relation to a transfer of value but a binding contract for its sale has been entered into *at the time of the transfer*, it is not relevant business property in relation to the transfer . . .".

At the time of the deemed transfer value, the terms of the "buy and sell" agreement will not have been operative. In the case of a partnership, the agreement is conditional upon the death of a partner.

We suggest that the view in SP 12/80 ignores the effect of section 22 (1) [now s 4 (1)], and treats the transfer as taking place on, or immediately after, the death of the partner. On a strict construction (and if the Revenue are to withhold the relief, a strict construction is called for) it is submitted that the Revenue view is incorrect.

It should be added, for the avoidance of doubt, that FA 1975 Sch 10 para 9 [now IHTA 1984 s 171(1)] is not applicable in these circumstances. That paragraph [subsection] is relevant only for the purposes of determining changes in the value of a person's estate occurring by reason of his death. This has no bearing on the question of the availability of relief in respect of the value of property comprised in a person's estate.

8. Reply from the Inland Revenue dated 8 February 1983.

Thank you for your letter of 19 January. It brings into focus the cause of our differing views on the application of paragraph 3(4) [s 113].

It is common ground that paragraph 3(4) [s 113] excludes from the CTT business relief property which is subject to a binding contract for sale at "the time of the transfer". You argue that FA 1975 s 22(1) [IHTA 1984 s 4(1)] is authority for the view that for the purposes of the tax the time of a transfer on death is immediately before the death. A buy and sell agreement in a partnership deed which comes into operation only at the moment of death cannot be taken to fetter a partner's interest immediately before his death. Hence on this view it could not amount to a binding contract for sale at the time of the transfer and the partner's interest would qualify for business relief.

We consider however that this approach overlooks the complementary effect of FA 1975 s 51(2) [now IHTA 1984 s 3(4)]. Section 22(1) [s 4(1)] provides that an event—namely death—shall be an occasion of charge and requires a valuation to be made by reference to a hypothetical transfer before death. Section 51(2) [s 3(4)] effectively provides that the "event", ie the death, is itself a transfer of value. It follows therefore that when a binding contract for sale exists at the date of death, ie at the time of the statutory transfer of value within section 51(2) [s 3(4)], paragraph 3(4) [s 113] operates to exclude business relief.

I do not consider this to be an unreasonably strict interpretation of the legislation. It is consistent with the scheme of the tax to charge on death the value of the property which is transferred and a partner whose interest is bound by a buy and sell agreement which becomes effective at the moment of his death can only transfer his interest subject to that agreement. It is equally consistent with the scheme of business relief to deny relief in circumstances in which the deceased partner's estate receives, and is taxed on, a sum of money.

I have not commented on your penultimate paragraph since, as you will see, our construction does not rely on Sch 10, para 9 [s 171(1)].

TR 588: FURNISS V DAWSON

25 September 1985. *ICAEW*

Guidance note TR588 was issued in September 1985 by the Institute of Chartered Accountants in England and Wales, comprising—

- Text of a letter dated 8 July 1985 to the Inland Revenue following a meeting between representatives of the Institute of Chartered Accountants in England and Wales, The Law Society and the Inland Revenue.
- Text of a reply dated 20 September 1985 from the Board of Inland Revenue.

The Revenue reply is reproduced in full below, following the corresponding paragraphs from the Institute's letter.

From the text of a letter dated 8 July 1985 from the Institute of Chartered Accountants in England and Wales—

FURNISS V DAWSON

We are grateful to you and your colleagues for meeting representatives of the Institute and The Law Society on 10 June 1985.

INTRODUCTION

1. The meeting can conveniently be divided into two parts: the need for short-term guidance and the longer-term aspects. As explained at the meeting, although both we and The Law Society are concerned with both aspects it was felt appropriate for us to concern ourselves primarily with the former and for The Law Society to cover the latter aspect. We identified certain areas which are of immediate concern, although as stated at the meeting this is by no means intended to be exhaustive.

2. We agreed to write further on certain aspects of the matters to which we referred and, for the sake of completeness, all of the areas which we mentioned are set out in paragraphs 4–21 below. We have also referred to the need for clarification as to the instructions given to inspectors.

3. As we mentioned at our meeting the areas which we have identified below arise from no more than a quick review of topics which have been raised following the *Furniss v Dawson* decision ([1984] STC 153, HL). The fact that they have been raised is indicative of their importance but, as stated at the meeting, the list is not exhaustive and further areas might need to be covered in due course . . .

NOTE

The rest of this letter (paras 4–29) is reproduced below, before the corresponding paragraphs of the Revenue's reply.

From the text of a reply dated 20 September 1985 from the Board of Inland Revenue

I am writing in reply to your letter of 8 July.

As you know, the Board very much welcomed the recent opportunity to discuss with the Institute of Chartered Accountants and The Law Society the implications of the judgements handed down by the House of Lords in the cases of Ramsay, Burmah and Dawson.

Clearly, the interpretation of the Ramsay and Dawson judgements is a matter for the courts. It will be for the courts, not for officials, to determine the law. However, you have explained that, meanwhile, there are a number of points on which practitioners and businesses would find it helpful to have a note of how the Revenue understands the position, and in this letter I try to respond accordingly.

We start with much common ground between us. Perhaps the shortest and simplest explanation of the "new approach" was given by Lord Wilberforce, when he said that "legislation cannot be required . . . to enable the courts to arrive at a conclusion which corresponds with the parties' own intentions". I think many of us accept that this "new approach" brings interpretation of the law in this area closer to the reality, or if you like the substance, of the transactions with which it has to deal. We are also conscious that it has also brought with it a measure of uncertainty: partly because by its nature it requires us all to take a rather broader view of the legal implications of a transaction or series of transactions; but partly also because the approach is "new" and (as the House of Lords themselves have emphasised) will no doubt be refined further, as the courts come to consider more cases.

I do not want to get this out of proportion. It is commonplace that the courts in North America and a number of European countries have been following somewhat similar approaches for many years. And even in this country a number of fundamental questions for tax purposes—for example, the existence of a "partnership", of "employment", of "income" itself—have always been left undefined in the taxing statutes: there is such a wide and complex variety of facts and real-life relationships that, accepting some inevitable uncertainty at the margin, the tax code does not attempt to capture them in a mechanical formula but leaves them to be determined in the last resort by the courts, having regard to the actual facts of the particular case. Having said that, we are all agreed that the line of reasoning in Ramsay and subsequent cases represents a new and important development. When we discussed these issues with the Institute and the Society, we in the Revenue confirmed our readiness to co-operate with you in reducing uncertainties of this kind and (where possible) removing them. Taxpayers should not be burdened by unnecessary uncertainty in judging the likely tax consequences of their actions; and I might add that uncertainty of this kind can also make more difficult the work of those who are responsible for administering the Taxes Acts.

On your side, the Institute recognised that, whilst we could try to help with guidance and clarification of the Revenue's attitude in the normal or more straightforward case, we are not in a position to give categorical assurances. In particular, we might well take one view of a transaction standing on its own; we might take another view—and I think this follows necessarily from the approach described by Lord Wilberforce—where a similar transaction was one step in a series of transactions apparently designed to avoid tax. You have therefore said that the Institute appreciates that any response which we are able to give must be subject to the caveat that, even where it is agreed that the Revenue would not as a rule seek to invoke the Ramsay and Dawson principle, there may well be individual cases where, because of the circumstances, the Revenue would nevertheless feel it was obliged to follow the Ramsay and Dawson approach. In particular, we may need to look at all the facts of the case in order to establish the nature and legal implications of the transaction. What follows is to be read in that spirit.

I thought that it would be helpful to spell out all this, even at the cost of some length. And it is against this background that I now try to give you as positive and helpful a response as we can, at this stage, to the 10 specific questions which the Institute has raised with us . . .

CAPITAL TRANSFER TAX

11.

(a) The CTT regime contains anti-avoidance legislation of a wide-ranging nature relating to associated operations, basically IHTA 1984 s 268, under which gifts are to include other associated transactions affecting the same property. The doctrine arising from *Furniss v*

Dawson makes for additional uncertainty and it would be helpful to have an assurance that where, as in this case, specific anti-avoidance legislation exists, an attempt will not be made to extend it.

(b) We understand that, in response to our enquiry at the meeting, you agreed that the Revenue would not seek to disturb existing practice under which taxpayers arrange their affairs so as to take advantage of the exemption for inter-spouse transfers.

(c) We sought confirmation that the *Furniss v Dawson* principle would not apply to inheritance trusts.

Revenue response: You suggest it would be helpful to have an assurance that where specific anti-avoidance legislation like IHTA 1984 s 286 exists no attempt will be made to extend it by using a Ramsay approach. You will recall that the question of the relationship between the emerging principle in Ramsay and anti-avoidance provisions was considered in the Ramsay case. Lord Wilberforce said—

"I have a full respect for the principles which have been stated but I do not consider that they should exclude the approach for which the Crown contends. That does not introduce a new principle: it would be to apply to new and sophisticated legal devices the undoubted power and duty of the courts to determine their nature in law and to relate them to existing legislation. While the techniques of tax avoidance progress and are technically improved, the courts are not obliged to stand still. Such immobility must result either in loss of tax, to the prejudice of other taxpayers, or to Parliamentary congestion or (most likely) to both."

It is our understanding, therefore, that the Ramsay approach is applicable in the context of specific anti-avoidance legislation and outside it, depending upon the facts of the case.

I can confirm that we would not seek to disturb existing practices in relation to inter-spouse transfers. It should, however, be borne in mind that the circumstances of such transfers always need to be carefully examined to ensure, among other things, that the transaction has substance as well as form. (For example, an understanding between the spouses on the ultimate destination of the assets would be important in this connection.) In general the terms of the Press Release of 8 April 1975 (see Simon's Tax Intelligence 1975, p 180) remain valid as a description of the practice in this area.

The wide-ranging nature of the term "inheritance trusts" makes it difficult to give the confirmation you seek. The term can be used rather loosely in the context of insurance schemes and, while some of these may be regarded as not open to challenge, others are; and cases will be going to the Special Commissioners in due course.

ASSETS USED FOR LIFE TENANT'S BUSINESS: BUSINESS PROPERTY RELIEF

21 April 1986. *Law Society's Gazette*

Under the code in IHTA 1984 ss 103 to 114, business property relief is given at either [50] per cent or [100] per cent by adjusting the valuation of "relevant business property" as defined in s 105. In *Featherstonehaugh v IRC* [1984] STC 261, it was decided that relief at what is now the [100] per cent rate was available for land on which a sole trader was life tenant and on which he had carried on a farming business prior to the transfer on his death.

The Inland Revenue's understanding of this decision is that, where there is a transfer of value of a life tenant's business or interest in a business (including assets of which he was life tenant which were used in that business), the case falls within IHTA 1984 s 105 (1)(*a*) and the [100] per cent relief is available. Where, by contrast, the transfer of value is only of any land, building, machinery or plant, used wholly or mainly for the purposes of a business carried on by the life tenant and in which he had an interest in possession under a settlement, the relief is only available at the rate of [50] per cent if the transfer takes place in circumstances in which the business itself is not being disposed of.

Thus, if land in a settlement has been used for the purpose of the life tenant's business, the [100] per cent relief is only available if the transfer of value is one of his business as a whole (or an interest in it), including the property in which he has a life interest.

Cross reference—See IHTA 1984 s 105(1)(*e*) (meaning of relevant business property).

IHT/CTT TREATMENT OF INCOME OF DISCRETIONARY TRUSTS

10 November 1986. *Inland Revenue*

1. Following legal advice the Revenue today announced a change in the way that income of discretionary trusts is treated in determining the liability to IHT/CTT.

2. The change in practice means that:

(a) income which has neither been distributed to beneficiaries of the trust nor been accumulated—ie added to the trust—will be excluded from the tax charge on discretionary trusts; and

(b) accumulated income will be treated as an asset of the trust separate from the original property from which it derives, in calculating the rate of charge on that income.

3. Statement of Practice (SP 8/86) contains details of the change.

NOTE

1. A discretionary trust is one under which no particular individual has the right to receive the income arising from the trust assets—for example, where the income can be distributed at the trustees' discretion—or where the trustees can or must accumulate the income.

2. All the assets held in a discretionary trust immediately before each 10-year anniversary of the trust are taxed at 10-yearly intervals.

3. Property leaving the discretionary regime is liable to a proportionate charge—a time-based fraction of the 10-yearly charge.

4. The rate of tax is reduced for any property that has not been in the discretionary trust regime throughout the period for which the charge applies.

5. Up to now, income from trust property which has been neither distributed to beneficiaries nor accumulated has been treated as a chargeable asset. Undistributed income (whether or not accumulated) has been regarded as being in the trust for as long as the property from which it derives.

6. For all the new cases—as well as existing cases where the tax liability is yet to be settled—undistributed and unaccumulated income will not be brought into the tax charge. The rate of tax on accumulated income will be reduced according to the date on which the property from which that income derives was put into the trust.

Commentary—*Simon's Taxes* **I5.321**; *Foster* **E3.21.**

IHT—GIFTS WITH RESERVATION (FA 1986 S 102)

10 December 1986. *Law Society's Gazette*

The following exchange of correspondence between Vic Washtell of Touche Ross on 29 August 1986 and the Controller of the Capital Taxes Office on 29 October 1986 was published in The Law Society's Gazette on 10 December 1986.

Could you please let us know whether the Inland Revenue intends to issue a statement of practice regarding the Revenue's view on various types of gift which they would treat as gifts with reservation under the new inheritance tax legislation. If not, could you please let us know whether or not the Revenue would regard gifts in the following situations as gifts with reservation.

As you will doubtless appreciate, any question about the existence and/or extent of any future liability to tax can be determined only in accordance with the particular facts on the basis of the law as it is understood to be. However, in order to be as helpful to you as I can at this stage, I would offer the following comments on the situations outlined in your letter.

1. A transfers assets into a discretionary settlement. The class of beneficiaries includes A's wife at the trustees' discretion on a regular basis.

The mere fact that the donor's spouse is a member of the class of potential beneficiaries would not suffice to bring the gift within the provisions of FA 1986 s 102, [gifts with reservation]. I should, however, draw your attention to Sch 20 para 6(1)(c) and 7 [associated operations and certain life assurance arrangements].

2. B transfers assets into a discretionary settlement under which he is not included in the class of beneficiaries (including B) to the class of beneficiaries in future.

As you probably know the inclusion of the settlor among the class of beneficiaries subject to powers contained in his trust is considered to be sufficient to constitute his gift as a gift with reservation. Where there is a possibility of the settlor becoming included in the class of beneficiaries by exercise of a power in the settlement, it is considered likely that this would again constitute a gift with reservation.

3. C buys a house and puts it into the name of himself and his wife as tenants in common. On the death of the wife her share of the house passes to the son absolutely. C remains in occupation of the property. On the death of C is the whole or only C's half of the property treated as part of his estate for inheritance tax purposes?

Having regard to FA 1986 s 102(5)(a), [exempt transfers between spouses] it is not considered that the original gift to C's wife would constitute a gift with reservation. However, the death of C might give rise to a claim for tax on other grounds but this would fall for consideration in the light of the precise facts as they were shown to be at that time.

4. D owns freehold property and grants a lease to himself and his wife for twenty years at a peppercorn. D then gifts the reversionary interest in the property to his son.

If the true construction of the transactions here is that the gift to the son is of the reversionary interest only in the property then the gift would not constitute a gift with reservation.

5. E gifts all of his shares in his family company into an accumulation and maintenance settlement for his children under which E is a trustee.

The mere fact that E is a trustee of an accumulation and maintenance settlement for his children would not of itself involve a reservation to him.

6. F owns a home and some adjacent land. F gifts the land but retains the house.

If the situation is such that the subject matter of the gift is the land only, I do not see that this constitutes a gift with reservation.

7. G, a non-domiciliary, gifts excluded property into a discretionary settlement under which he is in the class of beneficiaries. G dies domiciled in the UK. Are the "excluded property" assets in the settlement treated as part of G's estate?

Here it seems to me that the settled property would be "property subject to a reservation" in relation to the settlor. Accordingly it would fall within FA 1986 s 102(3) to be treated as property to which he was beneficially entitled immediately before his death. The effect would be to lock the property into the settlor's estate within the meaning of CTTA/IHTA 1984 s 5(1), which is subject to the exception for "excluded property". It would follow that in the case of settled property, relief for foreign assets could continue to be available under ibid, s 48(3) provided that the settlor was domiciled outside the UK at the time the settlement was made.

8. Kindly confirm that Statement of Practice E10 will apply for inheritance tax purposes [vendor retaining a lease for life].

As you will know SP E10 applies in the context of the FA 1975 Sch 5 now para 1(3), CTTA/IHTA 1984 [lease for life treated as a settlement]. In the context of gifts with reservation, I might perhaps draw your attention to FA 1986 Sch 20 para 6(1)(a) [occupation, enjoyment or possession by the donor to be disregarded if for full consideration].

THE CONTROLLER'S LETTER CONCLUDES:

I would emphasise that each case must be looked at in the light of its own particular facts. Too much should not be read, therefore, into general comments on the bare situations outlined in your letter which may not, in the event, be found to apply to the facts of an individual case.

In a separate development, the Revenue has confirmed to the Association of British Insurers that the following do **not** constitute gifts with reservation:

(a) A whole life policy effected by the life assured in trusts for X should X survive the life assured, but otherwise for the life assured.

(b) An endowment effected by the life assured in trust for X if living at the death of the life assured before the maturity date but otherwise for the life assured.

Also, the Revenue has confirmed that if a gift with reservation is made into a pre-Budget day trust, this will **not** "taint" the whole trust fund so as to make the funds settled before Budget day liable to inheritance tax.

Note—Statement of practice E10 is obsolete (IR 131 1994).

CTT: HERITAGE PROPERTY

9 February 1987. *Hansard*

Mr David Clark asked the Chancellor of the Exchequer what machinery he has established about publicising landscape schemes offset against capital transfer tax under FA 1976.

Mr Norman Lamont: Publicity about public access to heritage property which has been conditionally exempted from capital tax is incorporated in the terms of the management agreement which is negotiated to give effect to the undertakings about preservation and public access that are required as a precondition of exemption. Requirements will differ from case to case but, outstanding chattels apart (for which different arrangements apply), these will normally comprise some or all of the following:

(a) Owner to inform the British Tourist Authority (the Scottish Tourist Board and the Highlands and Islands Development Board in Scotland) of the opening arrangements and subsequent changes.

(b) Owner to advertise the opening arrangements in one or more suitable publications with national circulation.

(c) Owner to display a notice outside the property giving details of the opening arrangements.

(d) Owner to agree that the advisory body or bodies (or its/or their agents), which confirmed the property's eligible quality and with whom the terms of the detailed management agreement will have been negotiated, can divulge the access arrangements to anyone who enquires about them.

(e) Owner to agree to such other publicity as the advisory body, or bodies, consider to be appropriate. This could include displaying a notice in some public place in the locality (eg the local post office, local library, local tourist office or town hall) or in a local preservation society's newsletter.

The management agreement would also normally provide scope for additional measures to be agreed, if appropriate, between the owner and the advisory body or bodies at a later stage.

Cross reference—See IHTA 1984 s 31 (Treasury's powers to designate property).

GIFTS WITH RESERVATION: DIRECTOR'S REMUNERATION

19 February 1987. *Inland Revenue letter*

You are concerned about the possible effects of the provisions concerning gifts with reservation in the case where a company director or employee makes a gift of shares in his company, but stays in the company as a director or employee in return for a salary and other benefits that are no greater than what might reasonably be provided under an arm's length deal between unconnected parties. The application or otherwise of these provisions to any given arrangement would, as you know, be a matter for determination in the light of the relevant facts and law at the date of the donor's death.

That said, I am pleased to tell you that the Revenue would accept that the continuation of reasonable commercial arrangements in the form of remuneration and other benefits for the donor's services to the business entered into prior to the gift would not, by itself, amount to a reservation provided that the benefits were in no way linked to or affected by the gift. For completeness, I might add that if in your example the gift of shares was into trust and the settlor was also a trustee of that trust and a director or employee of the company, the fact that the terms of the trust empowered trustees to retain directors' fees would not, of itself, amount to a reservation of benefit. In this context too, the Revenue will need to be satisfied that the remuneration and other benefits were on a reasonable commercial basis. What is "reasonable" will of course depend on the facts of the case.

Where, however, as part of the overall transaction, including the gift, new arrangements are made, it will be necessary to examine all the relevant facts to determine whether the remuneration package amounts to a reservation of benefit to the donor "by contract or otherwise".

GIFTS WITH RESERVATION: DIRECTOR'S REMUNERATION

5 March 1987. *Inland Revenue letter*

I confirm that a downward adjustment made at the time of the gift to a director's pre-existing remuneration to bring the arrangement into line with a level no higher than would be commercially justifiable will not be regarded as giving rise to a reservation of benefit.

IHT: GIFTS WITH RESERVATION

18 May 1987. *Inland Revenue letter*

I am now able to write to you about the points concerning the provisions on gifts with reservation.

It does not seem realistic to think in terms of precise and comprehensive guidance on how the gifts with reservation provisions will be interpreted and applied since so much will turn on the particular facts of individual cases. However, as the provisions are similar to those adopted for estate duty, the relevant estate duty case law and practice provide a helpful guide to the interpretation and application of the IHT legislation. That said, may I turn to your specific concerns.

GIFTS OF LAND

1. Consistent with the assurance given last year by the Minister of State in Standing Committee G (Hansard, 10 June 1986, col 425) the estate duty practice on the treatment of gifts involving a share in a house where the gifted property is occupied by all the joint owners including the donor will apply. The donor's retention of a share in the property will not by itself amount to a reservation. If, and for so long as, all the joint owners remain in occupation, the donor's occupation will not be treated as a reservation provided the gift is itself unconditional and there is no collateral benefit to the donor. The payment by the donee of the donor's share of the running costs, for example, might be such a benefit. An arrangement will not necessarily be jeopardised merely because it involves a gift of an unequal share in a house.

2. In other cases the donor's occupation or enjoyment of the gifted land will only be disregarded if the occupation is for full consideration in money or money's worth as provided in FA 1986 Sch 20 para 6 (1)(a) (or if it is by way of a reasonable "care and maintenance" provision within para 6(1)(b)). Whether an arrangement is for full consideration will of course depend on the precise facts. But among the attributes of an acceptable arrangement would be the existence of a bargain negotiated at arm's length by parties who were independently advised and which followed the normal commercial criteria in force at the time it was negotiated.

3. You raised the possibility that a donor might give his house subject to a prior lease created in his own favour. Consistent with the principles established in the case of *Munro v Commissioners of Stamp Duties (New South Wales)* [1934] AC 61, we would not normally expect the donor's retention of the lease to constitute a reservation, assuming that the creation of the lease and the subsequent gift of the property subject to that lease are independent transactions. The application or otherwise of the decision in *Re Nichols* [1975] 1 WLR 534 concerning a (donee) landlord's covenants would be a matter for determination in the light of all the facts at the time of the donor's death.

GIFTS INVOLVING FAMILY BUSINESSES OR FARMS

4. A gift involving a family business or farm will not necessarily amount to a gift with reservation merely because the donor remains in the business, perhaps as a director or a partner. For example, where the gift is of shares of a company, the continuation of reasonable commercial arrangements in the form of remuneration for the donor's ongoing services to the company entered into before the gift will not of itself amount to a reservation provided the remuneration is in no way linked to or beneficially affected by the gift. Similar considerations will apply in the case where the gift is into trust which empowered a trustee, who may be the donor, to retain director's fees etc for his own benefit.

5. The "Munro" principle will also be relevant in determining the tax treatment of gifts affecting family farms where the donor and the donee continue to farm the land in pursuance of arrangements entered into prior to and independently of the gift. In cases where this principle does not apply, the test of "full consideration" for the purposes of para 6(1)(a) will need to be satisfied with regard to the donor's occupation of the land. In applying that test we shall take account of all the circumstances surrounding the arrangement including the sharing of profits and losses, the donor's and the donee's interests in the land, and their respective commitment and expertise.

GIFTS OF CHATTELS

6. You referred to potential difficulties in determining what amounts to "full consideration" for the donor's continued enjoyment of gifted chattels, particularly pictures and paintings, for the purposes of Sch 20, para 6. These may not be insuperable, as appears from the recent case of *IR Comrs v Macpherson* [[1987] STC 73], and in any event it would be difficult to overturn an arm's length, commercial arrangement entered into by parties who were independently advised.

SETTLOR'S RETENTION OF REVERSION

7. In the case where a gift is made into trust, the retention by the settlor (donor) of a reversionary interest under the trust is not considered to constitute a reservation, whether the retained interest arises under the express terms of the trust or it arises by operation of general law eg a resulting trust.

IHT AND FAMILY COMPANIES

17 March 1988. *Hansard*

Viscount Mackintosh of Halifax asked whether, given their stated aim of creating a climate where family companies can flourish, it is their intention that clearance under [TA 1988 s 219(2)] will in all cases be refused on the death of a controlling shareholder where sufficient dividends can be voted by the executors to enable the inheritance tax liability to be met by instalments on the basis that hardship would not arise as the executors control the company and thus control the flow of dividends.

Lord Brabazon of Tara: I understand that there have been very few cases of the kind in question. However, where the company has surplus funds sufficient to discharge the inheritance tax liability, the Revenue take the view that there would be no hardship since the liability could be met by dividend payments from the company.

HL Written Answer, Vol. 494, col 1349

IHT: CHANGES IN REVENUE PRACTICE

9 May 1990. *The Law Society*

In a recent letter to the Law Society (published in the Law Society's Gazette, 9 May 1990) the Revenue notified two changes of inheritance tax practice as follows.

PARTLY EXEMPT TRANSFERS

IHTA 1984 s 40 directs that "where gifts taking effect on a transfer of value take effect separately out of different funds"—for example where on a death there are gifts out of the free estate and out of settlements—then each fund is to be considered separately for the purpose of the allocation of exemptions under Ch III, including the grossing-up of the gifts. The rate of tax used by the Capital Taxes Office to gross-up separate gifts out of different funds has until now been the rate applicable to the total value of all property chargeable on the testator's death. The Board now accepts that the rate of tax to be used for grossing-up should be found by looking at each fund separately and in isolation.

COMING TO AN END OF AN INTEREST IN POSSESSION IN SETTLED PROPERTY

When an interest in possession in settled property comes to an end during the lifetime of the person entitled to it, IHTA 1984 s 52(1) states that the value for inheritance tax purposes is ". . . equal to the value of the property in which his interest subsisted". Until now this value has been determined as a rateable proportion of the aggregate value of that settled property and other property of a similar kind in the person's estate. The Board now take the view that, in these circumstances, settled property in which the interest subsisted should be valued in isolation without reference to any similar property.

These statements of the Board's position are made without prejudice to the application in an appropriate case of the Ramsay principle or the provisions of IHTA 1984 relating to associated operations. The changes of view will be applied to all new cases and to existing cases where the tax liability has not been settled.

IHT: WOODLANDS—NEW EXTRA-STATUTORY CONCESSION

5 December 1990. *Inland Revenue*

The Revenue today announced an extra-statutory concession dealing with the transfer of property which includes woodlands subject to a deferred estate duty charge. In future, the deferred charge will only affect the inheritance tax treatment of that part of the transfer which consists of woodlands subject to the deferred charge. The concession will apply with effect from today.

[For the text of the concession see Concession F15.]

DETAILS

1. Transfers made during a person's lifetime are not normally liable to inheritance tax if the person lives for more than seven years after making the transfer. Until the seven years expire, such transfers are known as potentially exempt transfers, and once seven years have passed they fall out of account for inheritance tax purposes. But in the case of transfers of woodlands subject to a deferred estate duty charge, the position is different.

2. Under the old estate duty rules it was possible with woodlands to defer the charge due on the death of the owner until the heir felled and/or sold the timber. If the heir died before the timber was sold, the estate duty charge on his or her death superseded the earlier deferred estate duty charge. Estate duty was replaced in 1975 by capital transfer tax, which was in turn replaced in 1986 by inheritance tax. Under the inheritance tax rules, where somebody transfers a woodland subject to a deferred estate duty charge the transfer is immediately chargeable to inheritance tax, and the deferred estate duty charge is regarded as being discharged. Bringing the transfer immediately into account for inheritance tax, rather than treating it as a potentially exempt transfer, ensures that the deferred estate duty charge is not lost without a compensatory inheritance tax charge if the person making the transfer survives for at least seven years.

3. As the rules are presently written, all property comprised in a single transfer of which any part, however small, consists of woodlands subject to a deferred estate duty charge is excluded from being treated as a potentially exempt transfer for inheritance tax. The legislation therefore goes beyond simply preventing the deferred estate duty charge from falling out of account without a compensatory inheritance tax charge.

4. The extra-statutory concession announced today will remove this anomaly by ensuring that only that part of a transfer which consists of woodlands subject to a deferred charge is prevented from being a potentially exempt transfer.

INHERITANCE TAX—DISPOSITIONS BY TRANSFERORS

13 March 1991. *The Law Society*

In a letter to the Law Society (published in the Law Society's Gazette, 13 March 1991) the Director of the Inland Revenue's Capital and Valuation Division sets out the Revenue practice in regard to the liability of personal representatives for tax on transfers made by the deceased in the seven years before his death (IHTA 1984 s 199). The practice is stated in the following terms.

"The capital taxes offices will not usually pursue for inheritance tax personal representatives who—

- after making the fullest enquiries that are reasonably practicable in the circumstances to discover lifetime transfers, and so
- having done all in their powers to make full disclosure of them to the Board of Inland Revenue

have obtained a certificate of discharge and distributed the estate before a chargeable lifetime transfer comes to light.

This statement of the Board's position is made without prejudice to the application in an appropriate case of IHTA 1984 s 199(2)."

RETIREMENT ANNUITIES UNDER TRUST—IHTA 1984 S 3(3)

5 June 1991. *Capital Taxes Office to the Association of British Insurers*

1. You wrote to the Controller on 31 January enclosing a paper setting out the Association's views on this subject. He has asked me to reply and I would like to say at once how much we appreciate the detailed exposition of the issues set out in your Memorandum.

2. I am sorry for the delay in responding, but as you are aware we and our Head Office colleagues have been considering the various issues very carefully. We do understand the concern which has been expressed by the pensions industry about the application of IHTA 1984 s 3(3) to retirement benefits. Our conclusion is that while a s 3(3) claim may be appropriate in particular limited circumstances genuine pension arrangements should not be affected. Our purpose in this letter is—

(a) to clarify the basis for the claim and the very limited circumstances in which we might raise one;
(b) to reassure you that your fears of wider repercussions are misplaced; and so
(c) to remove uncertainty as far as possible about what our approach will be.

The annex deals point by point with the technical arguments advanced in your Memorandum [not reproduced].

THE SCOPE FOR A CLAIM UNDER IHTA 1984 S 3(3)

3. It is worth emphasising that, in practice, we expect to see very few cases where a claim would even be considered. First, the vast majority of policyholders exercise their right to take an annuity during their lifetime or survive to the age beyond which deferment cannot be made. All these cases fall outside the scope of the potential claim.

4. Second, the field is further restricted in practice to those policyholders whose chargeable estate exceeds the inheritance tax threshold. If no tax is actually payable we would obviously not pursue a claim.

5. Third, we would generally expect any claims that do arise to be limited to retirement annuity contracts or personal pension schemes. Only exceptionally would claims involve occupational pension schemes.

6. Fourth, there is no question of a claim being raised in cases of genuine pensions arrangements, ie where it is clear that the policyholder's primary intention is to provide for his or her own retirement benefits.

7. We would consider raising a claim in such cases as remain only where there was prima facie evidence that the policy holder's intention in failing to take up retirement benefits was to increase the estate of somebody else (the beneficiaries of the death benefit) rather than benefit himself or herself.

8. To this end, we would look closely at pensions arrangements where the policy holder became aware that he or she was suffering from a terminal illness or was in such poor health that his or her life was uninsurable and at or after that time the policy holder—

– took out a new policy and assigned the death benefit on trust; or
– assigned on trust the death benefit of an existing policy; or
– paid further contributions to a single premium policy or enhanced contributions to a regular premium policy where the death benefit had been previously assigned on trust[; or
– deferred the date for taking retirement benefits].

9. In these circumstances it would be difficult to argue that the actions of the policy holder were intended to make provision for his or her own retirement given the prospect of an early death. Even then we would not pursue the claim where the death benefit was paid to the policy holder's spouse and/or dependants (that is, any individuals financially dependent on the policyholder). In addition, a claim would not normally be pursued where the policyholder survived for two years or more after making any of these arrangements but the CTO reserve the right to examine each case individually.

For the avoidance of doubt, CTO would adopt a similar approach in cases involving—

– personal pension schemes set up under deed poll under the Superannuation Funds Office or Integrated Model rules; or
– buy-out policies under trust, approved under TA 1988 s 591(2)(*g*) (commonly known as "Section 32 policies" after the original legislation).

10. Our firm view is that this approach will give rise to only a small number of s 3(3) claims; the overwhelming majority of pensions arrangements will be unaffected.

11. I hope you find this explanation both helpful and reassuring.

Note: the additions in paras 8 and 9 appeared in IR Tax Bulletin, Issue 2, p 12, where the CTO summarised their view.

[This letter was referred to in ICAEW TR 854 on 2 December 1991 as follows:]

PERSONAL PENSION PLANS

13. IHTA 1984 s 151 generally prevents inheritance tax being charged on benefits from pension schemes etc but only on death. Where the death benefit under a personal pension policy or retirement annuity policy is payable outside the estate pursuant to the terms of a discretionary trust, and the policyholder fails to exercise his right to take pension benefits during his lifetime, it could be said that there had been an omission to exercise a right (IHTA 1984 s 3(3)). Clarification is sought as to whether the Revenue view this as an occasion of charge to inheritance tax.

REVENUE RESPONSE

You may not be aware that this matter is the subject of correspondence and discussion between the Association of British Insurers and the Capital Taxes Office (CTO).

I attach a copy of a letter from CTO to the Association which clarifies the circumstances in which a claim under IHTA 1984 s 3(3) might arise [not reproduced]. You will see that the CTO expects very few claims and that the overwhelming majority of pensions arrangements will be unaffected. The Association has welcomed this clarification.

INHERITANCE TAX ACT 1984 S 98(1)—DEFERRED SHARES

11 September 1991. *Law Society's Gazette*

Following recent legal advice, the Revenue's interpretation of IHTA 1984 s 98 has changed.

Until now the Capital Taxes Offices have taken the view that when deferred shares came to rank equally with another class of shares there would be no alteration in the rights of the shares within the meaning of IHTA 1984 s 98(1)(*b*). But there would be an alteration in the company's share capital within the meaning of IHTA 1984 s 98(1)(*a*).

The Board of Inland Revenue has now been advised that an alteration of rights, within the meaning of IHTA 1984 s 98(1)(*b*), occurs when deferred shares come to rank equally with another class of shares. Accordingly, claims for inheritance tax will be raised where deferred shares, issued after 5 August 1991, subsequently come to rank equally, or become merged, with shares of another class.

INHERITANCE TAX: WAIVER OF LOANS

18 December 1991. *Law Society's Gazette*

It has recently been brought to the attention of the Society's Revenue Law Committee that the Capital Taxes Office will not accept that a loan made between individuals has been waived by the lender, so the estate of the lender is reduced, for inheritance tax purposes, by the amount of the loan released—unless the waiver was effected by deed.

Letters and circumstantial evidence clearly indicating an intention to absolve the beneficiary of the loan from any liability to repay will be insufficient.

The Revenue has quoted in support of its contention that a waiver is ineffective unless made by deed Pinnell (1602) 5 Co Rep 117a, and *Edwards v Walters* (1896) 2 Ch D 157 CA.

In the Revenue Law Committee's view, although the Revenue's contention is not unassailable, unless and until the contention is confirmed or rejected by judicial authority, it must be prudent to advise all clients that any inheritance tax planning strategy involving the making of a loan, and subsequent waiver, should be effected by deed in order to ensure the estate of the lender is reduced accordingly.

For alterations of dispositions taking effect on death, IHTA 1984 s 142 does not require execution of a deed, but simply "an instrument in writing", though in practice as a prudent precaution, a deed is normally used.

VALUATION OF AGRICULTURAL TENANCIES

18 March 1992. *Law Society's Gazette*

The following is an agreed summary of a meeting between representatives of the Law Society of England and Wales, the Law Society of Scotland and the Inland Revenue held on 3 February 1992 to discuss the specific issue of valuation of agricultural tenancies.

For the purposes of the meeting there was a common acceptance by both Law Societies and the Inland Revenue (including the Valuation Office Agency) that under the existing law, the principles of Crossman [[1937] AC 26; [1936] 1 All ER 762] apply in general to valuation exercises where an asset is subject to restrictions on its disposition.

In valuing an agricultural tenancy, there are several special factors which need to be considered—

- the benefits attaching to the tenancy, eg residential accommodation, rights of compensation for disturbance, waygoing (Scotland), dilapidation's claims, improvements, manurial rights, and the fact that the rent might currently be less than the market rent;
- the principle that there should be no automatic presumption that the value of a tenancy could be arrived at by a method based upon a standard percentage of the vacant possession premium or value;
- the consideration of who might be in the hypothetical market for the tenancy; and
- the weight to attach to the various factors relevant in valuing the tenancy, which would be a matter of fact and for negotiation in each case.

In principle it appeared that there was only one area of dispute between the two sides, namely had the Revenue been correct to use as a starting point for valuing tenancies a percentage of the vacant possession value of the land or the vacant possession premium? It was very difficult for the Revenue to depart from this position since it obviously had a responsibility to both the Exchequer and the Government. If it started from a point which was lower than the final value which might be agreed upon, it would be open to the criticism that it had not carried out its duty properly.

It was open to the taxpayer to adduce evidence at an early stage if the character of the landlord was to be a factor in determining the value, namely that there was evidence that the landlord was likely to make a bid for vacant possession of the land, or not, as the case might be. If the issue had arisen, for example, on the death of a tenant farmer within seven years of transferring his tenancy, such evidence could be submitted at the same time as the accounts for the estate were sent in. The Revenue would then be on notice from the outset that the question of a bid by the landlord was a matter that the taxpayer believed was not a factor to take into account.

The Law Societies agreed that if taxpayers were given an opportunity to adduce such evidence, this would resolve many difficulties. However, there was the practical problem of a sizeable backlog of cases, where it had been impossible to agree a value for transfers which had taken place several years ago and it would clearly not be viable to take advantage of the opportunity to adduce evidence "at an early stage". For cases which were open and where it was still possible to adduce evidence as to the landlord's intention, would the Revenue consider such evidence if now submitted and give due weight to it as a factor?

Mr Cayley [for the Inland Revenue] said that he would have no objection in principle to this. However, he emphasised that by agreeing to give due weight to evidence of a landlord's intention, the Revenue would be unable to guarantee that it would always modify its approach to the valuation. The Law Societies understood this.

Cross reference—See IHTA 1984 s 160 (meaning of "market value").

GUIDANCE NOTE—NON-RESIDENT SETTLEMENTS (TAX 20/92)

14 December 1992. *ICAEW*

INTRODUCTION

1. FA 1991 ss 83–92, Sch 16–18 introduced new rules for capital gains of certain offshore trusts. The relevant legislation is now in TCGA 1992 ss 80–98, Sch 5.

2. In January 1992 the Inland Revenue invited various professional bodies to comment on a draft statement of practice explaining the practice to be followed in applying the new rules. Comments on the draft statement of practice were submitted by the Tax Faculty in February 1992 following which the statement of practice (SP 5/92) and two new extra-statutory concessions (D40 and D41) were issued in May 1992 [see Part 2 of this publication for SP 5/92 and ESC D40 and D41].

3. This guidance note sets out the text of some of the correspondence between the Tax Faculty and the Inland Revenue in respect of the statement of practice in both draft and final form. Correspondence quoted has been confined to matters which have not been clarified in the statement of practice or the extra-statutory concessions and has been amended to refer to the final version of statement of practice SP 5/92 and to TCGA 1992 a consolidating Act which came into force on 6 April 1992.

4. The paragraphs which follow are set out under the relevant headings and paragraph numbers in statement of practice SP 5/92. The point made by the Tax Faculty is followed by the Inland Revenue response.

PARAGRAPHS IN THE STATEMENT OF PRACTICE

IV Charge on the settlor: settlor's right to repayment from the trustees

Paragraph 9

6. As regards para 9 of SP 5/92, we note that a claim under IHTA 1984 s 3(3) may arise if the settlor does not exercise his right of reimbursement. The drop in value in the settlor's estate will occur when the right to reimbursement expires. We shall therefore be grateful for guidance as to when the right expires.

Revenue response: The duration of the settlor's right to reimbursement is governed by the general law Limitation Act, which prescribes a six-year limit (unless the settlor indicates to the trustees before the expiration of this period that he does not intend to exercise his right to reimbursement, at which point the right would expire). The six-year period would begin when the settlor pays the tax.

V Charge on the settlor: trusts created before 19 March 1991

(g) TCGA 1992 Sch 5 para 9(3): administrative expenses

Paragraph 2

20. May we have confirmation that, where such a power exists and is exercised, then the Revenue will not regard the exercise as removing a qualifying interest in possession for inheritance tax purposes.

Revenue response: If the trust deed contains a power to pay capital expenses out of income, exercise of this power will not cause the trust to lose interest in possession status for inheritance tax purposes.

MILK QUOTA

February 1993. *Inland Revenue Technical Bulletin*

For inheritance tax purposes, where agricultural land, or an interest in agricultural land, is valued and the valuation of the land reflects the benefit of milk quota, agricultural relief is given on that value.

Where milk quota is valued separately, it will normally constitute an asset used in the business, within IHTA 1984 s 110, so that business relief under IHTA 1984 s 105(1)(*a*) may be available.

LEASEHOLD ENFRANCHISEMENT OF CONDITIONALLY EXEMPT PROPERTY

7 May 1993. *Inland Revenue*

The Financial Secretary to the Treasury, Stephen Dorrell MP, today announced that the government propose there should be no review of designation of a conditionally exempt property where part of the property is sold under the leasehold enfranchisement provisions in the Housing and Urban Development Bill.

In a written reply to a Parliamentary Question, Mr Dorrell said—

"Where there is a disposal of part of a property which is conditionally exempt from inheritance tax, the conditional exemption designation of the whole property is reviewed. If the disposal has not materially affected the heritage entity, the designation for the remainder remains in force and the inheritance tax charge is limited to the part disposal.

Following consideration of representations received, the government proposes that, where a part disposal results solely from leasehold enfranchisement under the Housing and Urban Development Bill (or Leasehold Reform Act 1967) and there is no breach of undertakings in respect of the retained property, there should be no review of designation of the retained property. In these circumstances, the inheritance tax charge will be limited to the part disposal.

A new clause to the Finance (No 2) Bill 1993 will be tabled shortly on this proposal."

DETAILS

1. Conditional exemption from inheritance tax may be granted for buildings which are of outstanding historic or architectural interest, their essential amenity land and historically associated chattels. In return for conditional exemption, the owner has to undertake to maintain, repair and preserve the property and allow reasonable public access to it. If there is a disposal of the property or a breach of undertakings, inheritance tax will be charged on the market value of the property at the time of the disposal or breach.

2. Where there is a disposal of or breach of undertakings in respect of part of a conditionally exempt property, there will be an inheritance tax charge on the whole property. But, where the disposal has not materially affected the heritage entity, the inheritance tax charge will be restricted to the part disposal and the remainder of the property will remain conditionally exempt.

3. Under the Housing and Urban Development Bill which is currently before Parliament, leaseholders of long lease flats and houses will, subject to the eligibility criteria in the Bill, be able to purchase collectively the freehold of their building. If the property is conditionally exempt this disposal will be chargeable to inheritance tax.

4. Some concern has been expressed about the impact of these leasehold enfranchisement provisions on conditionally exempt property. During the debate on the Bill in the House of Lords on 9 March 1993, the government agreed to consider these concerns further. As a result, the government is proposing that, where there is a disposal of part of a conditionally exempt property which is solely attributable to leasehold enfranchisement under this Bill or earlier leasehold reform legislation, the inheritance tax charge will be limited to the property which is sold. Details of the government's proposals will be tabled as a Finance (No 2) Bill new clause shortly [not in fact tabled].

INHERITANCE TAX—GIFTS WITH RESERVATION

November 1993. *Tax Bulletin Issue 9*

Under FA 1986 s 102, any property given away on or after 18 March 1986 subject to a reservation is, on the death of the donor, treated as forming part of the donor's estate immediately before his death. Gifts with reservations (GWRs) are defined as gifts where either—

- the donee does not assume *bona fide* possession and enjoyment of the property at the date of the gift or seven years before the donor's death, if later; or
- at any time in the period ending with the donor's death and beginning seven years before that date or, if later, from the date of gift, the property is not enjoyed to the entire exclusion or virtually to the entire exclusion of the donor.

This note provides some guidance on the Revenue's interpretation of the *de minimis* rule which is expressed as "virtually to the entire exclusion" and comments on the exclusion from the GWR provisions where the donor pays full consideration for any use of the property. The note also clarifies the position of the annual exemption under IHTA 1984 s 19 where a reservation of benefit ceases.

INTERPRETATION OF DE MINIMIS RULE

The word "virtually" in the *de minimis* rule in IHTA 1984 s 102(1)(b) is not defined and the statute does not give any express guidance about its meaning. However, the shorter Oxford

English Dictionary defines it as, amongst other things, "to all intents" and "as good as". Our interpretation of "virtually to the entire exclusion" is that it covers cases in which the benefit to the donor is insignificant in relation to the gifted property.

It is not possible to reduce this test to a single crisp proposition. Each case turns on its own unique circumstances and the questions are likely to be ones of fact and degree. We do not operate s 102(1)(b) in such a way that donors are unreasonably prevented from having limited access to property they have given away and a measure of flexibility is adopted in applying the test. Some examples of situations in which we consider that IHTA 1984 s 102(1)(b) permits limited benefit to the donor without bringing the GWR provisions into play are given below to illustrate how we apply the *de minimis* test—

- a house which becomes the donee's residence but where the donor subsequently—
  - stays, in the absence of the donee, for not more than two weeks each year, or
  - stays with the donee for less than one month each year;
- social visits, excluding overnight stays made by a donor as a guest of the donee, to a house which he had given away. The extent of the social visits should be no greater than the visits which the donor might be expected to make to the donee's house in the absence of any gift by the donor;
- a temporary stay for some short-term purpose in a house the donor had previously given away, for example—
  - while the donor convalesces after medical treatment;
  - while the donor looks after a donee convalescing after medical treatment;
  - while the donor's own home is being redecorated;
  - visits to a house for domestic reasons, for example baby-sitting by the donor for the donee's children;
- a house together with a library of books which the donor visits less than five times in any year to consult or borrow a book;
- a motor car which the donee uses to give occasional (ie less than three times a month) lifts to the donor;
- land which the donor uses to walk his dogs or for horse riding provided this does not restrict the donee's use of the land.

It follows, of course, that if the benefit to the donor is, or becomes, more significant, the GWR provisions are likely to apply. Examples of this include gifts of—

- a house in which the donor then stays most weekends, or for a month or more each year;
- a second home or holiday home which the donor and the donee both then use on an occasional basis;
- a house with a library in which the donor continues to keep his own books, or which the donor uses on a regular basis, for example because it is necessary for his work;
- a motor car which the donee uses every day to take the donor to work.

Exclusion of benefit where full consideration paid for use of property

The GWR provisions do not apply where an interest in land is given away and the donor pays full consideration for future use of the property (FA 1986 Sch 20 para 6 (1)(*a*)). While we take the view that such full consideration is required throughout the relevant period—and therefore consider that the rent paid should be reviewed at appropriate intervals to reflect market changes—we do recognise that there is no single value at which consideration can be fixed as "full". Rather, we accept that what constitutes full consideration in any case lies within a range of values reflecting normal valuation tolerances, and that any amount within that range can be accepted as satisfying the para 6(1)(*a*) test.

TERMINATION OF RESERVED BENEFITS AND THE ANNUAL EXEMPTION

Where a reservation ceases, the donor is treated by FA 1986 s 102 (4) as having made a potentially exempt transfer (PET) at that time. In that event the PET will only be taxable if the donor dies within the next seven years but the value of the PET cannot be reduced by any available annual exemption under IHTA 1984 s 19. The statement in para 3.4 of the IHT1 booklet, which indicates that the annual exemption may apply if the reservation ceases to exist in the donor's lifetime and a PET is treated as made at that time, is incorrect. This will be corrected in IHT1 when it is next updated.

A typical outright gift to an individual of an amount exceeding the available annual exemption is partly exempt, with the balance above the available annual exemption being a PET. But a PET itself cannot qualify for the annual exemption. The reason is that a PET is a transfer which, but for the provisions of IHTA 1984 s 3A, would be an immediately chargeable transfer. By definition a chargeable transfer is a transfer of value which is not an exempt transfer—IHTA 1984 s 2(1). So a PET cannot be an exempt transfer at the time it is made. The PET will, of course, escape a charge to IHT if the donor survives the statutory period after making it.

The annual exemption is not necessarily lost by the taxpayer. For example, suppose he makes a gift of his home in August 1991 but continues to reside there. In May 1992 he finally leaves the gifted house and the reservation ceases. In October 1992 he makes a gift into a discretionary trust (an immediately chargeable transfer). He is treated as making a PET of his residence in May 1992—the annual £3,000 exemption does not reduce its value. But the £3,000 exemption is available for setting off against the immediately chargeable transfer in October, and so is any unused exemption carried forward from the previous year.

"HERITAGE PROPERTY": IHTA 1984 S 30

December 1995. *Inland Revenue*

The Capital Taxes Office (CTO) no longer requires to see, at the pre-grant stage, Inland Revenue Accounts in which a claim for conditional exemption is made.

Inheritance tax is essentially a self-assessed tax and legal personal representatives should be able to justify their claim during the post-grant examination of the account. It will assist the CTO if the following question is answered when the account is complete—

"Did the deceased own or have an interest in possession in any 'heritage' property which was given exemption from Capital Taxes on an earlier chargeable occasion for IHT/CTT/ED/CGT? If so, please provide full details and the CTO reference, if known."

(This question will be incorporated in future versions of Accounts.)

INHERITANCE TAX—THE REGISTER OF CONDITIONALLY EXEMPT WORKS OF ART

16 January 1996. *Inland Revenue*

The Inland Revenue have today issued a revised register of conditionally exempt works of art which are available for viewing by appointment with the owners. This is the tenth in a series of quarterly updates of the new computerised register.

Since August 1995 the number of items on the register has increased by 244 to 14,687. The more noteworthy additions to the list include—

- painting by Richard Wilson RA, of Tabley House and lake;
- watercolour by J M W Turner RA, of Walton Bridges;
- painting by Robert Bevan, "The Hay Harvest";
- a large Derby Botanical dessert service painted in colours in the manner of John Brewer with specimen flowers named on the reverse.

The computerised register can be consulted at the Victoria and Albert Museum (London), National Library of Scotland (Edinburgh), National Museum of Wales (Cardiff) and Ulster Museum (Belfast).

Copies of the register in computer-readable format may also be purchased from the Capital Taxes Office of the Inland Revenue for £10.

See Capital Taxation and Works of Art below.

LAW OF DOMICILE (REFORM)

16 January 1996. *Hansard*

Mr Hendry asked the Parliamentary Secretary, Lord Chancellor's Department whether the Government intend to bring forward legislation to give effect to the reforms of the law of domicile recommended by the Law Commission in its recent report on this subject (Law Com 168, Scot Law Com/107).

Mr Jonathan Evans: The Government have decided not to take forward these reforms on the basis that, although they are desirable in themselves, they do not contain sufficient practical benefits to outweigh the risks of proceeding with them and to justify disturbing the present long-established body of case law on this subject.

HC Written Answer. 16 January 1996, Vol. 269 cols. 488, 489.

INHERITANCE TAX: INLAND REVENUE ACCOUNT—REDUCED ACCOUNT FOR EXEMPT ESTATES

25 September 2000. *Inland Revenue*

Two separate but related measures concerning the administration of inheritance tax (IHT) are effective from today.

. . .

The second measure applies to England, Wales and Northern Ireland as well as to Scotland. It allows taxpayers to deliver a reduced Inland Revenue account where, because of exemptions, most or all of an estate is free from IHT. This relaxation will benefit around 10,000 estates each year.

The CTO has written to the Law Society, the Society of Trust and Estate Practitioners and other representative bodies setting out the circumstances when a reduced account may be delivered. The letter is reproduced here as an annex.

. . .

ANNEX

Inland Revenue letter to representative bodies

b In the light of representations received from both practitioners and taxpayers, it has been agreed that where the conditions detailed below are met, the personal representatives may deliver a reduced account of the deceased's estate.

2. The conditions are that—

- the deceased was domiciled in the UK at the date of death, and
- – most or all of the property passing by will or under intestacy passes to an "exempt beneficiary" either—
  - absolutely, or through an interest in possession trust, to the surviving spouse, who must also be domiciled in the UK, or
  - so as immediately to become the property of a body listed in IHTA 1984 Sch 3, or
  - so as immediately to become the property of a charity registered in the UK, or held on trusts established in the UK for charitable purposes only, and
- the *gross* value of property passing by will or under intestacy to beneficiaries other than exempt beneficiaries together with the value of other property chargeable on death and the *chargeable* value of any gifts made in the seven years prior to death do not, in total, exceed the IHT threshold.

(The *gross* value of an asset is the value *before* deducting liabilities, reliefs or exemptions. The *chargeable* value of any gifts is the gross value of the gifts *after* deducting any liabilities, reliefs or exemptions that are due.)

3. Other property chargeable on death includes—

- joint property passing by survivorship to someone other than the deceased's spouse (assuming that he or she was domiciled in the UK);
- settled property in which the deceased had a life interest, other than settled property which then devolves to the deceased's spouse, to a body listed in Sch 3, or to a charity registered in the UK;
- property that the deceased had given away but in which they reserved a benefit that either continued until death or ceased within seven years of death;
- property situated outside the UK which does not devolve under the UK will or intestacy.

4. Where the conditions in para 2 are met, the requirement to deliver an account containing all appropriate property and the value of that property is relaxed where indicated in the

following paragraphs. However, the account must still be delivered on form IHT200 and the declarations on page 8 still apply to the account other than to any estimated values permitted by para 7 below.

The reduced account

5. All the questions on page 2 of form IHT200 must still be answered and—

- if the answer to any of the questions D1–D6 is "Yes", the relevant supplementary page must be completed, but
- even if the answer to any of the questions D7–D16 is "Yes", the relevant supplementary page need not be completed if *all* the property concerned passes to an exempt beneficiary. Similarly, details of items passing to exempt beneficiaries need not be listed on D17.

Except in Scotland, form D18 (probate summary) must always be completed.

6. For the avoidance of doubt, where the conditions in para 2 are met but a percentage or fractional share of residue is left to an exempt beneficiary, a reduced account is *not* appropriate and a full account must be delivered.

The values to include

7. The value of property passing by will or under intestacy must be included in form IHT200 ss F, G. But where the property is passing to an exempt beneficiary, the personal representatives' own estimate of the open market value of that property may be used. So, for example, they need not incur the expense of a professional valuation where they might otherwise have done so. Similarly, their own estimate of value may be given for any property included on supplementary pages D1–D6 that passes to an exempt beneficiary. Nominal values must not be used.

8. Where an estimated value is given because property passes to an exempt beneficiary, the item should not be listed in box L3 on page 8 of form IHT200 and the personal representatives do not need to report any changes in value to that property.

Changes to the estate

9. Where an estate is subsequently found not to meet the conditions under which a reduced account may be delivered, or where an instrument of variation (IOV) is signed and an election made so that assets that were exempt from IHT become chargeable, any supplementary page(s) that apply to the chargeable or redirected assets must then be completed.

10. Whether or not an estimate of the open market value was included for those assets in form IHT200, a corrective account, signed by the personal representatives and containing the open market value of the assets concerned must also be delivered. The corrective account and any supplementary page(s) should be sent to CTO with the IOV and election.

11. In Scotland, a corrective inventory may be used instead of a corrective account.

Commentary?*Simon's Taxes* **I11.212.**

SIMPLER PAYMENT SCHEME FOR INHERITANCE TAX

27 March 2003. *Inland Revenue*

A streamlined new approach to paying inheritance tax and obtaining the grant of probate will start on Monday 31 March, Paymaster General, Dawn Primarolo announced today.

Electronic transfer from participating financial institutions direct to the Revenue will do away with the need for administrators to obtain funds from outside the estate in order to secure a grant.

The move follows agreement between the Revenue, the British Bankers' Association and the Building Societies' Association.

Ms Primarolo said—

"I am delighted that the close collaboration of the British Bankers' Association, Building Societies' Association and Government has had such a successful outcome. For a long time personal representatives have wanted access to funds already held in the deceased's account to pay the IHT bill. Financial institutions in turn have had concerns about releasing funds without appropriate authority. This new scheme addresses both these issues and is fully endorsed by Government. It will be widely welcomed and we hope to see maximum take up."

DETAILS

1 From Monday 31 March, participating institutions will accept instructions from personal representatives to make the initial payment of IHT by electronic transfer. The amount of the payment from the institution concerned will be limited to the lesser of the amount due and the net credit balance in the deceased's account(s) at the date of death. The scheme is voluntary on the part of the institutions and some will want to carry on with their existing informal arrangements and make such payments by cheque.

2 The arrangements are straightforward and intended to work with the minimum of bureaucracy. Personal representatives will get the necessary forms and guidance as part of their basic package of material for the IHT amount (IHT200). If they want to take advantage of the direct payment facility they will initiate it as part of the process of completing the account.

3 Broadly the scheme works as follows. Personal representatives will need to check with the institution(s) holding the deceased's funds to see if they are taking part. If so, the personal representatives will then contact us, in writing or by telephone (see below for details), for the IHT reference number allocated to the estate. When the personal representatives are ready to apply for a grant they will send the form(s) of authority to the relevant institution(s). They in turn will transfer the funds and pay the tax electronically. Once we have received the payment(s) we will, as we do now, provide the personal representatives with a receipt for the total amount paid for presentation to the Court Service to obtain the grant.

NOTES

1 The work on this issue was first mooted last summer in proceedings in the Committee on the Finance Bill (2002). A progress update was given by the Paymaster General in her written statement to the House of Commons on this topic on 21 January. The new scheme starts on 31 March.

2 Generally IHT has to be paid before executors can get access to the assets of the estate. Often they have to borrow the necessary money before probate (confirmation in Scotland) goes through. Up to now, understandably, many banks and building societies have been unwilling to release funds in advance of legal formalities being settled for fear of paying to unauthorised persons.

3 Only about 4 per cent of all estates, about 25,000, pay IHT.

4 Our contact details are as follows—telephone—0845 30 20 900; fax—0115 974 2526; or write to IR Capital Taxes, Ferrers House, PO Box 38, Castle Meadow Road, Nottingham NG2 1BB.

5 Copies of the new forms and guidance notes are obtainable on the internet at www.inland-revenue.gov.uk. Alternatively they can be obtained by contacting our Orderline as follows—telephone 0845 234 1000; fax 0845 234 1010; or email ir.purchasing@gtnet.gov.uk.

Commentary—*Simon's Taxes* **I11.403.**

MATTERS ON WHICH HMRC VIEW IS SOUGHT IN RELATION TO PRE-OWNED ASSETS INCOME TAX. PAPER SUBMITTED ON BEHALF OF STEP, CIOT AND LITRG.

14 July 2005. *STEP, CIOT, LITRG questions to HMRC.*

Note—The questions were submitted by the Society of Trust and Estate Practitioners, the Chartered Institute of Taxation and the Low Income Tax Reform Group on 14 July 2005. Where replies have been received from HMRC they are included. Answers as revised on 12/3/06.

SUMMARY OF QUESTIONS

Valuation issues

(1) Moving properties.
(2) Calculation of POAT on home loan schemes.
(3) Reduction of debt on home loan scheme.
(4) Calculation of POAT charge where mix of intangibles/house on home loan schemes.
(5) Discounts on DV.
(6) Commercial group life policies.
(7) Partnership life policies.
(8) Pension life policies.

(9) Pre-1986 life policies.
(10) Scope of Reg 6: election and home loan schemes/double charges.

Home Loan Schemes

(11) 11. Assigning debt back to settlor
(12) Valuing the excluded liability.
(13) Commercial borrowing by trust.
(14) Reservation of benefit on loan. Does POA apply?
(15) Which home loan schemes work?

Election

(16) Election by one spouse only.
(17) Effect of election on home loan schemes and s102(4).
(18) Spouse exemption and home loan schemes.
(19) New elections on change of property.
(20) Life interest settlor interested trusts and para 8.
(21) Elections on home loan schemes – whole house or only on debt part.
(22) Elections where only part of gifted property caught.
(23) Late elections.
(24) Wrong payment of income tax.

Equity release.

(25) Regulation 5 and part disposals. Promissory estoppel.
(26) Definition of RCAs
(27) Sales of whole.
(28) Carving out a lease.

Reversionary leases.

(29) Paying rent under legal obligation.
(30) HMRC policy on reversionary leases.

Miscellaneous

(31) 31. Disposal and contribution conditions.
(32) Meaning of "provision" and loans. The contribution condition.
(33) Occupation of house owned by company funded by loan.
(34) Overdrawn discounts.
(35) "Outright gift to another person" – para 10(2)(c).
(36) Partnerships and POAT.
(37) Annual exemption.
(38) Interaction of ROB/POAT and full consideration.
(39) Para 10(3). Spousal interest in possession. Spouse becomes absolutely entitled.
(40) Meaning of occupation.
(41) Non-exempt sales.

Foreign domiciliaries

(42) Interaction of paras 12(3) and 11.

Para 8 charge

(43) Reverter to settlor trusts holding intangibles.
(44) Intangibles and the election.

In this paper we raise a number of questions of principle illustrated by a specific example. For ease of reference we number the questions on which a specific response is sought.

1. **Valuation issues**

1.1 Regulation 4 provides that in relation to land and chattels the valuation is by reference to the first valuation date and this valuation is used for a period of 5 tax years. This is favourable to taxpayers where the gifted land increases in value. For instance, in relation to existing Ingram and reversionary lease schemes, one takes the value of the gifted property as at 6th April 2005 even though the gifted interest (the DV) is likely to increase in value over the next 5 years.

However, the position is unclear where the property is sold and the taxpayer moves to a smaller house.

Example 1

A gave £300,000 to his son in April 2000. Son later uses all the cash to purchase a house and contributes none of his own funds. A goes into occupation of house in April 2002. He falls within the contribution condition and is subject to the POA charge from 6th April 2005. The house is worth £1 million on 6th April 2005. He pays income tax in 2005/6 by reference to the rental value of the house.

In 2007 Son sells house and buys a new one for £500,000 into which A moves. In these circumstances there seems to be no mechanism for assessing A to income tax on the rental value of the new house.

Does A continue to pay income tax on a hypothetical rental value of the original £1 million house until 2010?

Similar problems can arise if A moves into a discrete part of the house and only occupies that part, letting the remainder. If he has not done this by 6th April 2005 it would appear that his charge is not reduced for the next 5 years.

Question 1

Do HMRC interpret the legislation in this restrictive way or do they take the view that the relevant land for the purposes of para 4(5) is the land that the taxpayer actually occupies and therefore a new valuation is done when the taxpayer first occupies the smaller property or the smaller part? This is on the basis that a new taxable period then starts in which that property or part is the relevant property. The Regulations would then apply on the basis that the first day of such occupation is the first day of the taxable period.

HMRC answer to question 1

The "relevant land" for the purposes of paragraph 4(5) is the land currently occupied by the chargeable person. A new valuation should be done when the occupation of that property starts, and we would intend that the new valuation should then be used for the remainder of that 5-year cycle.

1.2 Particular valuation problems arise in relation to the double trust or home loan schemes.

Example 2

B sells his house to a trust in which he retains an interest in possession ("the property trust") and the purchase price of £900,000 is left outstanding as a debt. B gives away the debt. Assume that B is caught by POA and that the debt is an excluded liability. The house is worth £1 million on 6th April 2005 and the debt is £900,000. Based on HMRC's example in the Appendix of the Guidance Notes, B pays income tax on 9/10 of the rental value attributable to the house.

Question 2

Can HMRC confirm that this is the view taken? ie that where the debt is only a percentage of the value of the house the taxpayer pays income tax on the same percentage of the rental value?

There seems no express provision in para 11 to allow for a percentage reduction in the charge in the event that the property is subject to a debt but has some excess value. We assume from the example in the Appendix that HMRC interpret the interaction of paras 11(6) and (1) and in particular the words "to the extent that" to mean that if the value of the property exceeds the excluded liability by 10% there is a 10% reduction in the charge under para 4.

HMRC answer to question 2

We confirm that, where, as in Example 2, the debt is only a percentage of the value of the chargeable property, income tax is payable on the same percentage of the rental value. As you suggest, this follows from the interaction of paras. 11(6) and (1). As far as subsequent valuation cycles are concerned, we would adjust the proportion of the rental value charged to reflect any adjustment to the value of the chargeable property.

1.3 If the debt was reduced to £500,000 (by partial repayment or by writing off) then it would appear that B would pay income tax from that date on half the rental value of the property and that Regulation 4 does *not* prevent a reduction in the income tax charge on repayment of the debt even if this is done half way through the five year period. Half the value of the property is now deemed to be comprised in the person's estate under para 11(1) and there is no charge on this part.

Question 3

Can HMRC confirm that if the debt "affecting" the property is reduced for any reason the income tax charge reduces by the same proportion even if this reduction occurs during the five year period?

Suppose in the above example the home loan scheme had been effected by a married couple H and W but only H later added the £500,000 to the property trust to enable the property trustees to repay part of the loan. Are we correct to assume that the loan is pro rated so that the excluded liability is reduced for H and W by £250,000 each rather than the repayment just reducing H's share of the excluded liability?

HMRC answer to question 3

We confirm that the income tax charge would be reduced by the same proportion by which the debt affecting the property was reduced. In view of the reference in paragraph 11(6) to "at any time", we confirm that the charge would be reduced even if the reduction of the debt occurred during the 5-year period.

Where the scheme had been effected by a married couple, H & W, we assume that the answer would depend on the precise terms of the property trust. But, assuming that the property is held by H & W equally, the addition by H of £500,000 to the trust would diminish his estate by £250,000 (an exempt transfer to W). On that basis, we would agree that the excluded liability for H & W would be reduced by £250,000 each.

1.4 Suppose that the house is sold by the property trust and the trustees then purchase a smaller property for say £600,000. The debt of £900,000 is not repaid but left outstanding and the spare cash of £400,000 is invested in intangibles to produce an income for B. On a literal reading of Regulation 4 it would appear that B still pays income tax on the market rental of the original property as at the April 2005 valuation (reduced by one tenth).

Question 4

We assume that HMRC consider that once a smaller property is purchased during the five year period, what is valued for the purposes of the POA charge under para 4 is indeed that smaller property. Please confirm.

HMRC answer to question 4

Assuming that the intangibles are held on the original trusts and that the debt of £900,000 is left outstanding, we agree that the smaller property would be within the charge under paragraph 4 and that the intangibles would come within paragraph 8.

In line with the answer to Q1, we would suggest that the paragraph 4 computation should be based on the value of the newer, smaller property with the intangible property being charged under paragraph 8. The parts chargeable under paragraphs 3 (as quantified in accordance with paragraph 4) and 8 should then be arrived at by apportioning the loan rateably between the two components. However if the loan was originally secured specifically on the land, one would calculate the paragraph 3 charge simply by reference to the value of the new, smaller property with the balance of the loan being charged under paragraph 8.

1.5 Suppose husband has given away his 50% share in the home originally owned jointly with his wife. The gift was into an Eversden settlement and is now caught by POA. In these circumstances, professional surveyors consider that the 50% share should be discounted and hence "the DV" figure be reduced.

Questions of valuation are not specifically addressed in the Guidance Notes but we assume that HMRC accept that, if professionally so advised, a discount for joint ownership would be appropriate for the DV figure.

Question 5

Can a standard percentage discount be agreed with HMRC in relation to jointly held interests?

HMRC answer to question 5

We agree that the 50% share of the house chargeable under POA should be valued on normal open market principles for the purposes of ascertaining DV. This would imply a discount, but not sure that we can agree a standard discount in advance, any more than we would do for "normal" IHT purposes.

1.6 There are difficulties in valuing settled insurance policies caught by para 8. For example, in their Guidance Notes HMRC take the view that life policies settled on a commercial basis by partners or shareholders for each other will be caught under POA if the settlor retains an interest. The settlor will often retain such an interest since there is usually a provision that the life policy will revert to the business owner if he leaves the business before death.

Question 6

In these circumstances how does one value the intangible property?

Would it be based on the surrender value of the life policy?

HMRC answer to question 6

Our current view is that a group policy taken out for the partners or shareholders is within the scope of the paragraph 8 charge, because each partner, as settlor, is not excluded from benefit. This appears to be the case whether or not each partner can benefit on leaving the partnership and whether or not the only benefits that can accrue to a partner are those arising on the death of a partner. As far as valuation is concerned, we would expect the value of the policy to be its open market value at the relevant time, not its surrender value.

1.7 The comments on life policies taken out by partnerships and other businesses contained at the end of the revised Guidance Notes seem to go directly against Government policy which is to encourage such arrangements (as illustrated by the relieving legislation introduced in FA 2003 s 539A for income tax purposes).

Question 7

Are HMRC considering an extra statutory concession to relieve such arrangements from the POA charge?

This would appear to be appropriate given that such arrangements are commercial with no donative intent and therefore outside the reservation of benefit provisions.

If the only interest of the settlor in the trust is that the life policy reverts to the settlor if he leaves the business before his death, do HMRC agree that the settlor's interest under such arrangement can be regarded as similar to his interest under discounted gift schemes and therefore outside the POA charge – see 8.1?

HMRC answer to question 7

An Extra Statutory Concession is not in view, as far as we are aware, and we do not think it is for us to comment on whether one would be appropriate. As far as the settlor's interest in the policy is concerned, We are doubtful that there is an exact analogy with Discounted Gift Schemes as you suggest. While this would depend on the terms of the policy concerned, it is not clear to us that the value of the settlor's contingent interest and the value of the interests of the surviving partners can be sufficiently distinguished in the way that we have agreed they can be for Discounted Gifts.

1.8 We should be grateful for some clarification of HMRC policy in respect of pension policies (whether retirement annuity or personal pension policies and whether approved or unapproved). Typically such policies provide that retirement benefits and other lifetime benefits such as a payment on demutualization are held for the absolute benefit of the individual member with death benefits being held on discretionary trusts.

Question 8

Do HMRC take the view that the analysis on such policies is similar to discounted gift schemes and that the retirement benefits represent separate unsettled property? See 8.1. Can HMRC confirm that the POA Regime does not apply to such pension arrangements? Does their view change if the individual member can benefit from the discretionary trust over the death benefits?

HMRC answer to question 8

(a) As a general rule, the pension and other lifetime benefits for the scheme member and the benefits paid on death are mutually exclusive. On this basis, we would agree that an analogy can be drawn with discounted gift schemes so that the pension benefits would either represent unsettled property or a trust separate from that on which the death benefits are held.

(b) On the basis of the above, we would agree that the POA regime would generally not apply to pension arrangements, where the individual scheme member was not able to benefit from the discretionary trust governing the death benefits.

1.9 Valuation problems arise where a settlor takes out a life policy and writes it on trust pre-18 March 1986. The reservation of benefit rules did not apply then and so he is often a potential beneficiary. Suppose that for the last 20 years he has been paying the premiums on such policy. Section 102(6) FA 1986 provides an exemption from reservation of benefit in respect of premiums paid post 17 March 1986 where the policy was taken out before 18 March and the premiums increase at a pre-arranged rate. However, there has been concern that premiums paid post 17 March 1986 would appear to be within the POA Regime.

Question 9

Do HMRC consider that such policies are caught? We would suggest that premiums paid since 17 March 1986 are not themselves additions to the settled property if paid direct to the insurance company but merely maintain the value of the settled property and therefore are not strictly within the wording of para 8.

We understand from correspondence in Taxation that HMRC believe POA does apply and apportion the premiums between pre 18 and post 17 March 1986.

In the light of the comment in (a) above will HMRC reconsider their views in respect of payments on such policies?

HMRC answer to question 9

In our view, it is correct to regard premiums paid after 17 March 1986 in respect of settled policies as additions to the settled property and so within paragraph 8 if the settlor is a potential beneficiary. As you suggest, the proportion of the settled property chargeable under paragraph 8 is arrived at by apportioning the premiums between those paid pre- 18 and post-17 March 1986.

2. **Home loan or double trust schemes**

We have a number of specific queries on home loan schemes and would welcome clarification with regard to the following points.

2.1 We welcome the provision for the avoidance of a double charge in the event of the GWR election being made. However, as discussed below, the election still has a number of uncertainties. Furthermore Regulation 6 is defective in a number of respects.

Firstly, it should not be limited to gifts into settlements (see Regulation 6(a)(ii)) since in some cases the gift of the debt was outright to a child rather than into trust.

2.2 Secondly, Regulation 6 should not be limited to a gift of property representing "the proceeds of the disposal of relevant property".

Many schemes proceeded on the basis of taxpayers lending money to the trustees by a loan agreement and the trustees then using that money to buy the house. The loan does not represent the proceeds of the house. There should be relief in these circumstances.

Question 10

Will HMRC in practice apply Regulation 6 to relieve all home loan schemes from a potential double charge where the donor has died having made an election or is Regulation 6 being amended to cover the above points?

HMRC answer to question 10

We note your view that Regulation 6 of SI 2005/724 is not wide enough to cover all cases where a double charge may arise after the taxpayer has elected. At this stage, we cannot give an assurance that we will apply the regulation more widely than its terms indicate, but we will pass on your views on this point.

2.3 One of the ways that taxpayers are unravelling home loan schemes is to appoint the debt to the children who then assign it back to the settlor thus losing all inheritance tax benefits but at least ensuring (provided that the children took interests in possession under the original trust) that if the settlor dies within 7 years of the original PET, there is relief under the Double Charges Regulations. (This course is often preferable unless double charges relief is to be given for the release of a debt.)

Although there is still an excluded liability in existence, the excluded liability does not appear to be relevant any longer in that it does not reduce the value of the parents' estates under paragraph 11(6) albeit it affects the value of the house. The wording in para 11(6) refers "to the value of the person's estate" and we assume that this means the value of someone's total estate for inheritance tax purposes.

Therefore the fact that the loan continues to reduce the value of the house does not mean that the loan is caught under para 11(6).

Question 11

Is the analysis in 2.4 correct (a) in stating that there is relief under the Double Charges Regulations if the children assign the debt back to the settlor and the settlor dies within 7 years of the original gift of the debt and (b) that para 11(6) is no longer in point once the assignment has been effected back to them because the debt no longer reduces the value of their estates?

HMRC answer to question 11

We agree with your analysis in paragraph 2.4(a): the circumstances you have in mind seem to be covered by Regulation 4 of SI 1987/1130. As far as paragraph 2.4(b) is concerned, we agree that paragraph 11(6) would no longer be in point.

2.4 Para 11(6) refers to "the amount of the excluded liability". We seek clarification as to whether this is the face value of the debt (including any rolled up interest or accrued indexation) or the commercial value of the debt.

Example 3

C entered into a home loan scheme. The house is worth £2 million and the debt is repayable on C's death, is linked to the RPI and has a face value of £1.9 million. Its commercial value is discounted due to the fact that it is not repayable until C's death. Allowing for the fact that the debt is linked to the RPI, its market value would be, say, £1.2 million but increasing.

In these circumstances the question is, whether the excess value which is treated as part of C's estate and therefore protected from the POA charge under para 11(1) is:

(i) £100,000

(ii) £800,000 or

some other figure such as £100,000 less accrued indexation?

Question 12

What is HMRC's view regarding the amount of the excluded liability in the above scenario?

It would appear that the correct view is to take the commercial value of the debt as reducing the person's estate because in reality the property is "affected" by this amount of debt. Obviously the POA charge would become higher as the commercial value of the debt increased towards the end of the donor's lifetime and hence less property exceeded the value of the debt.

HMRC answer to question 12

In our view, the fact that paragraph 11(6) refers to the "amount" of the excluded liability indicates that it is the face value of the debt, including any rolled-up interest or accrued indexation, that is relevant. In practice, we would only seek to adjust the value of the debt to take account of interest and indexation at the 5-yearly valuation dates, though we would be prepared to allow any reduction of the debt resulting from any repayment be taken account as it occurred and to be reflected in a revised computation of tax in the relevant year and subsequently.

2.5 A common scenario (both for foreign and UK domiciliaries) is where cash is settled into an interest in possession trust for the donor life tenant. The trustees then buy a house for the donor to live in using the gifted cash plus third party borrowings. Although not a home loan scheme, the legislation appears to affect such arrangements.

Example 4

E settles cash of £200,000 into an interest in possession trust for himself in 2003. The trustees purchase a property worth £500,000, borrowing £300,000 from a bank. There are other assets in the trust which can fund the interest but the borrowing is secured on the house which E then occupies.

In these circumstances, one would not expect a POA charge. There is no inheritance tax scheme since the property is part of E's estate and the borrowing is not internal. One would argue that E's estate still includes the house and therefore protection is available under para 11(1). The difficulty is that on one view the loan is an excluded liability within para 11(7) reducing E's estate, albeit it is a loan on commercial terms with a bank.

We would argue that the relevant property for the purposes of para 11 is simply the value of the property net of the commercial borrowing. As this is part of E's estate there is no POA charge.

Question 13

Is the above analysis correct?

HMRC answer to question 13

We agree with your analysis in paragraph 2.6.

2.6 In those home loan schemes where HMRC consider that there is a reservation of benefit in the debt, it would appear that the taxpayer can still face a POA charge – because he has made a disposal of land which is subject to an excluded liability. The fact that he has reserved a benefit in the debt does not make the debt part of his estate such that the excluded liability can be ignored.

Question 14

Where there is a reservation of benefit in respect of the loan can HMRC confirm that they would not expect the taxpayer to pay both POA and IHT and that the inheritance tax charge would take priority?

HMRC answer to question 14

We agree with the analysis at 2.6. (Even if there is a reservation of benefit in the loan for IHT purposes, it is the land, not the loan, which is the relevant property for POA purposes and para 11, Sch 15 in particular. And although the loan may be property subject to a reservation for IHT purposes, it remains an excluded liability within paras 11(6) and (7), Sch 15 for the purposes of the POA charge.) As matters currently stand, there is no provision to disapply the charge that may arise under Sch 15.

Question 15

Will any statement be issued by HMRC as to which home loan schemes of the various types seen they consider do not work for inheritance tax purposes?

Otherwise taxpayers may self-assess and pay the income tax charge, thinking to preserve the inheritance tax savings but be unaware of HMRC's view.

HMRC answer to question 15

We will shortly be issuing updated technical guidance that will include material to identify the circumstances in which we consider a reservation of benefit in the loan exists. Hopefully, this will give some indication to providers of schemes affected whether or not we consider their scheme to be one where a reservation of benefit in the loan exists. This in turn may make it easier for providers to help any clients (or ex-clients) who seek their assistance over completion of their tax return.

3. **The effect of the Election**

3.1 In the case of a married couple who have sold their jointly owned house to the property trust and given the debt to a second trust, it is assumed that one of them can elect to come within the gift with reservation rules and one can choose not to elect: i.e. it is not necessary for both to make the election.

Question 16

Will HMRC please confirm this point?

HMRC answer to question 16

As far as we can see, it is possible for one spouse and not the other to elect under paragraph 21.

3.2 There is some uncertainty about the effect of the election because para 21 does not as such deem there to be a gift for inheritance tax purposes but simply states that the property is treated as property subject to a reservation.

Furthermore in para 21(2)(b)(ii) it is stated that only sections 102(3) and (4) are to apply and not specifically section 102(8) which brings in Schedule 20.

We assume that the wording in para 21(2)(b)(i) referring to the property being treated as property subject to a reservation of benefit for the purposes of the 1986 Act does not limit the scope of the reservation of benefit provisions so that only sections 102(3) and (4) apply.

Example 5

D effected a home loan scheme. He elects into reservation of benefit and then in April 2010 starts to pay full consideration for the use of his house. Has he made a deemed PET at that point (under s102(4)) and is he protected from a reservation of benefit charge provided he continues to pay a market rent? We assume that HMRC take the view that para 21(2)(b)(ii) does not narrow the effect of 21(2)(b)(i) and the let-outs in para 6 Schedule 20 apply.

Question 17

Please confirm that on making an election there is a reservation of benefit in the house and not the debt in respect of the home loan scheme and that, once an election is made, all the provisions relating to reservation of benefit in FA 1986 and in particular Schedule 20 apply?

Please also confirm the position on deemed PETs in the example above where the person who elects is already paying full consideration.

Suppose A elects into GWR in respect of his home. The house is then appointed back to him absolutely (i.e. the arrangement eg. a home loan scheme, is unscrambled). In these circumstances the reservation of benefit has ceased but the house is back in their estates anyway. Is there a deemed PET under section 102(4) FA 1986?

HMRC answer to question 17

We confirm that on making an election under paragraph 21, there would be a reservation of benefit in the house, not the debt in respect of the home loan scheme. In our view, the reference to section 102(4) Finance Act 1986 in paragraph 21(2)(b)(ii) envisages circumstances in which the property ceases to be subject to a reservation and there is nothing to suggest that these would not include circumstances in which the provisions of paragraph 6, Schedule 20 Finance Act 1986 would be in point.

By analogy with the view we have taken for "actual" gifts with reservation, we believe that the tax treatment for the purposes of Sch 15 would depend on whether or not the taxpayer starts to pay full consideration for the continued use of the house or chattel immediately on making an election or after a period of time. We think it would only be in the latter case that there would be a deemed PET under section 102(4) FA 1986.

In our view, the provisions of s 102(4) do, in terms, apply, by virtue of para 21(2)(b)(ii), when the taxable property is appointed back to the chargeable person. But the value of A's estate would not be decreased by this deemed PET. On that basis we do not regard the deemed PET by A has having any practical consequences for A, because it would have no value.

3.3 We seek clarification of the position on home loan schemes when both spouses elect and one then dies.

Example 6

H and W have effected a home loan scheme. They both elect. On H's death his share in the house is worth £400,000 but is perhaps entirely subject to debt. His share passes to W but the value of her estate is not increased because H's share is subject to the debt. Hence the concern is that the effect of the election is to make H's share taxable immediately on his death by virtue of s 102(3) as to £400,000.

In our view it would appear that the spouse exemption is available on the first death since the deceased's share in the house passes to the surviving spouse under the terms of the property trust or otherwise becomes comprised in the survivor's estate as IHTA 1984 requires. This is so even if the value of the debt equals or exceeds that of the house.

Question 18

(a) Do HMRC agree with this interpretation? (See also Statement of Practice E13.)

(b) Is HMRC's view that:

—full spouse exemption is available even if the debt equals the value of the house; or

—full spouse exemption is available provided the spouse's estate is increased by even a small amount; or

—spouse exemption is only available to the extent the value of the house exceeds the debt?

HMRC answer to question 18

In the circumstances outlined in Example 6, the starting point is the disposals of property that H & W have each made in order to effect a home loan scheme. If then they elect under paragraph 21 and H then dies, we think the effect would indeed be to bring £400,000 into H's estate immediately before his death for IHT purposes by virtue of section 102(3) Finance Act 1986. As far as we can see, there is no scope for spouse exemption as regards this chargeable item as the property disposed of by H in setting up the home loan scheme did not become comprised in the estate of W. Nor, having regard to paragraph 21(3) can we see any scope for reducing the amount charged under section 102(3) FA 1986 by the amount of the debt. Of course, H's estate for IHT purposes will also include his interest in possession in the property trust. We imagine this would consist of his share in the house, subject to the debt. Undoubtedly spouse exemption would be available, but only to the extent that the value of H's share in the house exceeded the debt.

3.4 As noted in 1.5 above there are technical difficulties if the property is sold after an election. Assume that a smaller replacement property is acquired by the trustees but the debt is not repaid. Accepting that the replacement property will be within the para 3 land charge, what of the surplus cash which has been invested in intangibles?

Example 7

Suppose the taxpayer moves out of the home and has made an election. He purchases a smaller replacement house a week later. The balance of the proceeds are invested and he enjoys the income as life tenant.

Question 19

Does a new election need to be made at that point under para 22 in relation to the intangibles part and/or under para 21 in relation to the smaller home?

What happens if the time limits for making the election on the original property have passed?

HMRC answer to question 19

Para 21(2)(a) states that when an election has been made the income tax charge won't apply to the taxpayer's enjoyment of the relevant property "or of any property which has been substituted for the relevant property". From the "any property" we take that to include not only property in the form of land and chattels but also intangible property even though that is subject to a separate paragraph for the election. The equivalent measure in Para 22(2)(a) uses the phrase "or any property which represents or is derived from the relevant property". We think this difference is necessary as it may not be possible to "substitute" intangible property for other intangible property.

But we assume you can convert intangible property into something different and we think an election under Para 22 would similarly cover cases where intangible property is converted into land or chattels and would otherwise be subject to an election under Para 21. So as the paragraphs cover substitutions/derivations, we do not think we require a fresh election when the underlying property changes. In any event, if the taxpayer apparently has an interest in possession in the intangible property, would not paragraph 11(1) be in point assuming a home loan scheme was not involved? As we would not be looking for a fresh election, we assume part (b) of the question is not relevant.

3.5 It may be said that the deeming provision in section 660A(1) TA 1988 (now s 624 ITTOIA 2005) is irrelevant to interest in possession trusts where the settlor is life tenant given that there is no question of the income being taxed as that of any other person as envisaged in that provision.

Question 20

Does the para 8 charge apply to cash held in such a trust on the basis that this is a settlor interested trust to which section 660A TA 1988 (now s 624 ITTOIA 2005) is therefore applicable or does the fact that the settlor is the life tenant of this trust preclude the application of section 660A? This would obviously affect the election mechanism. This is relevant to home loan trusts now holding intangibles.

HMRC answer to question 20

We are not sure that we can see how the application of section 624 ITTOIA 2005, and therefore paragraph 8 is explicitly precluded per se.

3.6 **Question 21**

When an election is made on a double trust scheme, is this election in respect of the entire land or just the part subject to the debt? Can HMRC confirm the former is correct given that in para 21(3) the DV/V formulation would mean that the entire value of the land equals DV?

HMRC answer to question 21

It seems to us that the relevant property in terms of Schedule 15 generally and specifically for the purposes of the election would be the land in its entirety.

3.7 The election mechanism does not satisfactorily deal with the position where part of the original gifted property is not within the Regime and part is.

Example 8

Andrew gives his house on interest in possession trusts for spouse Emma in 2000. Her interest in possession is terminated in all but 20% of the fund. Hence the gift ceases to be an excluded disposal in relation to 80%.

Andrew decides to make an election rather than to pay the income tax charge. In these circumstances is the chargeable proportion 100% (being the DV/V figure) or 80%?

It is assumed the latter on the basis that Andrew is chargeable only by reference to his enjoyment of the 80% not by reference to his enjoyment of 100% (see wording in para 21(1)(a)). Hence "the relevant property" on which he can elect is only 80%.

Question 22

Do HMRC agree with this analysis?

HMRC answer to question 22

We would agree that, in the circumstances set out in Example 8, the "relevant property" would be 80% of it. The use of the formula DV/V, as ordained in paragraph 21(3), would simply mean that all of the 80% would be treated as the chargeable proportion.

3.8 Where a taxpayer is doubtful as to whether he is caught by the Regime in the first place he can put full details of his arguments on the additional information pages of the return and presumably would then be treated as having made full disclosure and be protected from a discovery assessment. Of course, even if a taxpayer does obtain finality in one tax year, this will not prevent HMRC raising an enquiry in later years if the taxpayer continued to self assess on the basis that the Regime does not apply to him.

Suppose HMRC do not enquire into the taxpayer's return for 2005/6. In 2006/7 he continues to self assess on the basis that he is outside the Regime; HMRC make an enquiry and it is established that the taxpayer was wrong to self assess on the basis that no income tax was due under the Regime. Possibly a court case clarifies the position or there is a change in legislation which is deemed to have always had effect.

In these circumstances the taxpayer will have missed the deadline for making the election (he first became chargeable under the Regime in 2005 and therefore needed to elect by January 31, 2007) and will have to pay income tax going forward or else try to unravel the arrangement.

Question 23

Will the taxpayer be able to make a late election in these circumstances?

HMRC answer to question 23

Whether the taxpayer is protected from a discovery assessment in the circumstances described will depend on whether the argument he presents is tenable and if not whether he could then be considered negligent in submitting an insufficient self assessment. Tenability would need to be judged against the practice generally prevailing at the time the return was made. We would consider that the taxpayer was bound by the time limit for that year of assessment for making an election regardless of whether HMRC made an enquiry relating to that year or a later year. It would be for the taxpayer to demonstrate that he had a reasonable excuse for failing to make an election in time.

In a situation where a court decision overturns the previous practice or legislation makes changes which is deemed to have always had effect, then the taxpayer would be protected for earlier years and he would be chargeable only from the time the change in practice or legislation was made. It would not be unreasonable to assume he would then have until the deadline for that year of assessment to make an election.

3.9 Another difficulty arises if the taxpayer wrongly pays income tax on the basis that he was within the Regime when in fact he was not. This is particularly pertinent in relation to home loan schemes where HMRC appear to accept that some work and some do not.

Question 24

What position will be taken by HMRC in these circumstances? Will the taxpayer (or his personal representatives) be able to make a claim for repayment of the tax paid under a mistake of law for 6 years from the date of overpayment?

HMRC answer to question 24

Providers of certain home loan or double trust schemes are already aware that HMRC takes the view that the gifts with reservation of benefit legislation applies to them. We will include in our guidance information about the circumstances in which we consider the GWR legislation applies.

If the taxpayer has made an excessive self assessment by virtue of error or mistake in his return then he can claim relief under section 33 of the Taxes Management Act 1970. The time limit for doing so is 5 years from the 31 January following the year of assessment to which the erroneous return relates.

4. **Regulation 5 and para 10(1)(a) – Equity Release Schemes**

4.1 The relief given in Regulation 5 seems unnecessarily restrictive as a matter of principle and we do not fully understand the Ministerial Statement or the Guidance Notes on this. It is suggested that where a child moves into the house to care for an aged parent and acquires an equitable interest in the shared home in consideration for providing caring services, the parent is protected from a POA charge under Regulation 5(b). However, such a disposal does not seem to be by way of a *transaction* at *arm's length* between persons not connected with each other. These are not normal commercial arrangements. It is difficult to put a value in advance or even retrospectively on what the services to be provided will actually be worth in terms of a share in the house.

Question 25

What evidence is required to satisfy Regulation 5(b)? It will be difficult to establish what would be regarded as an arms length transaction without a court hearing which would generally only occur in the event of a dispute.

HMRC answer to question 25

In considering whether regulation 5(b) was satisfied, we would need information about how the essential elements of the transaction had been arrived at. We do recognise that there is a substantial body of case law dealing with the circumstances in which an interest in a house is acquired in consequence of a person acting to his detriment. The Ministerial Statement had these sorts of situations in mind and we would interpret Regulation 5 accordingly. In particular, we accept that the requirement that "the disposal was by a transaction such as might be expected to be made at arm's length between persons not connected with each other" would be interpreted with such cases in mind. We would not therefore expect the parties to have sought separate advice and acted upon it or to have obtained a court order confirming the property entitlement. We recognise that detriment that the acquirer can demonstrate he has suffered can provide consideration for the acquisition of the interest and prevent the transaction from being gratuitous.

4.2 Suppose that something that had not been a readily convertible asset and was therefore protected under para 5(1)(b) subsequently became a RCA under ITEPA. We are concerned that a transaction that was previously protected could now lose such protection.

Question 26

What happens if the definition of readily convertible asset in ITEPA 2003 changes?

HMRC answer to question 26

If the definition of "readily convertible asset" in ITEPA 2003 were to change, I think we would need to review the appropriateness of Regulation 5(2). We are not aware that any such alteration is in prospect, however.

4.3 There are difficulties where land is held under one title but is physically discrete — for example, two fields. Suppose father sells one of the two fields to his son for full value and continues to farm in partnership over that field. Does father have a pre-owned assets problem.

Question 27

Is the father protected under para 10(1)(a)? Can it be treated as a sale of whole if son becomes beneficially and legally entitled to the entire field even though father is selling only one of the fields?

HMRC answer to question 27

The first issue is what constitutes "the property" for the purposes of paragraph 10(1)(a). We think it would be possible to regard each of the two discrete fields as "the property", so the disposal of one of them would be a disposal of the whole interest in that asset. As far as your example is concerned, a sale by father to son would be within paragraph 10(1)(a)(ii) on the basis that father receives a full open market price for his land.

4.4 It is not uncommon for taxpayers to enter into transactions whereby they carve out a lease for themselves and sell the freehold reversion at full market value. Indeed some commercial equity release schemes are structured along these lines. In earlier informal discussions HMRC appeared to agree that the wording in para 10(1)(a) did cover such arrangements but the Guidance Notes suggest there has to be a disposal of the taxpayer's entire interest without any reservation of a lease. The provisions on non-exempt sales of course use a different wording.

Question 28

Can HMRC confirm that a disposal of a taxpayer's whole interest in the property "except for any right expressly reserved by him over the property" as set out in para 10(1)(a) is intended to cover a transaction where F has carved out a lease for himself and sold the encumbered freehold reversion for full market value to his son? If so, will the Guidance Notes be amended to confirm this?

HMRC answer to question 28

In our view, paragraph 10(1)(a) does cover the scenario you envisage in 4.4. We will amend the Guidance Notes.

5. **Reversionary lease arrangements**

5.1 In the case of reversionary lease arrangements, the taxpayer retains the freehold interest giving away a long lease which vests in possession in (say) 20 years time. Assuming that he is within para 3 ie that the arrangement does not involve a reservation of benefit, the taxpayer may wish to pay a full rent for his use of the land so as to avoid a POA charge: see Schedule 15 para 4(1). The difficulty is that the owner of the relevant land in this case appears to be himself and he cannot pay rent to himself.

Question 29

Does this mean that in the context of reversionary leases this part of the legislation is meaningless? To obtain relief under para 4, will the taxpayer have to transfer his freehold to an interest in possession trust for himself and pay rent to the trustees?

HMRC answer to question 29

We agree that it would be difficult for the taxpayer to pay rent to himself in order to avoid a charge under Schedule 15. But, as you suggest, it would be possible to overcome the difficulty.

5.2 The Guidance Notes state that reversionary lease arrangements effected post 8 March 1999 are not caught because they are subject to a reservation of benefit. You will be aware that many advisers do not agree with this view. On the basis of HMRC's current advice there is no requirement for a taxpayer to self assess and pay the pre-owned asset income tax charge. If, however, it turns out that HMRC are wrong in their view that post 8 March 1999 reversionary lease schemes are caught by the reservation of benefit rules, pre-owned assets income tax would have been due.

Question 30

If HMRC's views are successfully challenged in the courts will the taxpayer be subject to back tax, interest and penalties?

We would hope that HMRC would not in these circumstances seek to collect income tax (and interest) in respect of past years but only in respect of future years.

Will it be a requirement for all taxpayers who have done a reversionary lease scheme post March 1999 to put this on their tax return in the white space and explain why they are not paying income tax?

HMRC answer to question 30

Our view on the IHT treatment of reversionary leases and, in particular, the application of section 102A Finance Act 1986 to them is under review at the moment. We will be issuing guidance as soon as we can.

6. **Miscellaneous problems**

6.1 There are difficulties in determining whether both contribution and disposal conditions have been met in a single transaction and this can be relevant when applying the exclusions in para 10 and the exemptions in para 11.

Para 3(2) provides that the disposal condition is met if the chargeable person owned an interest in the relevant land or "*in other property the proceeds of the disposal of which were directly or indirectly applied by another person towards the acquisition of an interest in the relevant land.*"

Para 3(3) refers to the contribution condition being met where the chargeable person "*has directly or indirectly provided, otherwise than by an excluded transaction, any of the consideration given by another person for the acquisition of an interest in the relevant land or an interest in any other property the proceeds of the disposal of which were directly or indirectly applied by another person towards the acquisition of an interest in the relevant land.*"

Question 31

Is the correct analysis of the interaction between the disposal condition and the contribution condition as follows?

1. If the transferred property is itself the relevant land (i.e. is occupied by the donor) only the disposal condition is met.

2. If the transferred property is cash and that cash is used by the donee to buy the relevant land occupied by the donor, only the contribution condition is met. If HMRC agree with this can the Guidance Notes be amended at 1.2.1 which suggest (we think wrongly) that the disposal not the contribution condition is breached if cash is given to the donee who then purchases a property for occupation by the donor.

3. If the transferred property is an asset other than cash, and the donee then sells that asset and uses the proceeds to buy the relevant land, both the disposal and the contribution conditions are met.

4. In such a case Sch 15 para 11(9)(a)(ii) means the relevant land is the relevant property for the purposes of para 11, so that the para 11 exemptions can apply if the other conditions in para 11 are met.

HMRC answer to question 31

Taking your four questions in turn:

If the property disposed of by the chargeable person is the relevant land, we agree that only the disposal condition in paragraph 3(2) is in point.

If the chargeable person transfers cash, which is then used by the donee to acquire relevant land, we agree that it is the contribution condition in paragraph 3(3) that is in point, not the disposal condition. As you suggest, our guidance at paragraph 1.2.1 needs revising on this point.

We agree that the contribution condition contemplates circumstances in which a chargeable person has indirectly provided consideration by way of a disposal of assets other than cash. Such a disposal might also meet the disposal condition, as you suggest.

Paragraph 3 makes it clear that, for the purposes of either the disposal or the contribution conditions, the "relevant land" is the land occupied by the chargeable person. In a case where the contribution condition (paragraphs 3(3) or 6(3), as appropriate) is in point, the "relevant property" for the purposes of the exemptions in paragraph 11 is the "property representing the consideration directly or indirectly provided": We think this must mean provided by the chargeable person. Whether this is the "relevant land must, we think, depend on whether paragraph 3(3)(a) or 3(3)(b) apply.

6.2 The meaning of the "provision" of "consideration" in the context of the contribution condition needs to be clarified. On the basis of the case law the word provided suggests some element of bounty.

On this basis our view is that if there is a transfer of Whiteacre by A (or another asset) to his son at full market value which is then sold by son and the sale proceeds used to purchase Blackacre for A to occupy this is a breach of the disposal but not the contribution condition because it lacks the necessary element of bounty.

Similarly the provision of a loan on commercial terms by A to his son to enable son to purchase a house which A then occupies in our view does not fall within the contribution condition.

Question 32

Do HMRC agree with this analysis?

HMRC answer to question 32

In our view, it is arguable that the contribution condition does not depend on a degree of bounty for its application. If, on the contrary, a degree of bounty was necessary, might not the operation of the contribution condition provisions in paragraphs 3(3) and 6(3) of Schedule 15 be circumvented by the relatively simple expedient of A, in your example, providing the wherewithal for the purchase of a house by his son by way of a loan, ostensibly on commercial terms, which is then left outstanding indefinitely?

Having said that, we have considered further the sort of case where a loan is made **and operated** on commercial terms eg a commercial rate of interest is specified and paid and there are provisions for repayment of the loan over the sort of period one would expect to find in a truly commercial loan. Having regard to paragraphs 4(2)(c) or 7(2)(c) of Schedule 15, the chargeable amount would depend on the value of DV in R (or N) × DV/V: that's to say on "such part of the value of the land/chattel as can reasonably be attributed to the consideration provided by the chargeable person." In the case where the loan is on truly commercial terms and conducted in a truly commercial way, we would accept that the attributable amount is nil or de minimis.

In determining "reasonable attribution" for the purposes of para. 4(2)(c), it is the terms on which the loan is made and operated that are relevant, as indicated above. In that context, the period over which the loan is repaid as well as whether a commercial rate of interest is charged is relevant.

Thus, where an interest-free loan is repaid over a typical "commercial" period, it would be reasonable to regard the interest foregone as attributable to the consideration provided by the chargeable person. In cases where the principal of the loan was left outstanding indefinitely, such principal could reasonably be regarded as attributable to the consideration provided.

[Following further CIOT representations to HMRC this HMRC response is now accepted to be wrong – see guidance notes issued on 30 May and para 1.2.1 "HMRC do not regard the contribution condition set out in Schedule 15 para 3(3) as being met where a lender resides in property purchased by another with money loaned to him by the lender. Our view is that since the outstanding debt will form part of his estate for IHT purposes it would not be reasonable to consider that the loan falls within the contribution condition even where the loan was interest free."]

6.3 Clarification is requested on the position where a house is owned by a company but the company is funded by way of loan. The concern is over paras 11(1)(b) and 11(3)(b).

Example 9

B owns 100 £1 shares in X Limited and otherwise funds it by shareholder loan. (Or the house is owned by a company held within an interest in possession trust for B and again the funding for the purchase comes by way of loan from trustees to company.) X Limited buys the house in which B lives. B *prima facie* falls within the para 3 charge. It would appear that para 11(1) protects him. The shares are not themselves property which derive much value from the house because they are worth substantially less than the house (see para 11(1)(b)(ii)) but the shares and the loan together are comprised in B's estate and between them indirectly derive their value from the house. On that basis para 11(1) does offer full protection.

Question 33

Do HMRC agree with this analysis or do they consider that the loan derives its value from the contractual undertakings that oblige the borrowing company to repay?

It would be odd if there is a POA problem when the company is funded by way of loan but not if it is funded by way of share capital.

HMRC answer to question 33

In our view, the loan, albeit an asset of B's estate, is not property that derives its value from the relevant property. However, our response to Q32 above would no doubt be applicable here in appropriate circumstances.

6.4 How is the charge computed under para 9 when the settled property comprises say a deposit account but also an overdrawn current account at 6 April in the relevant year? Is the POA tax charge based simply on the value of the deposit account without deducting the overdraft?

The definition of relevant property is property which is or represents property which the chargeable person settled. If A settles cash into trust retaining a remainder interest and then the trust invests that cash unwisely e.g. in a hedge fund incurring losses which require the trustees to borrow to settle, is it the net or gross value of the trust fund that is taken in computing the POA charge?

Question 34

Can HMRC clarify the above?

HMRC answer to question 34

In our view, it is the net value of the trust fund as at 6 April in the relevant year that should form the basis of the computation under paragraph 9.

6.5 The excluded transaction provision in para 10(2)(c) refers to an outright gift "to the other person" whereas the wording in para 10(2)(e) refers expressly to an outright gift to an individual. The word person must include trusts and companies. In our view para 10(2)(c) applies to settled gifts *and* gifts to individuals although of course cash gifts *into trust* will be caught by the tracing rules in schedule 20 and are therefore generally gifts with reservation if the donor can benefit from the trust and protected anyway under para 11(3).

Question 35

Do HMRC agree with this analysis?

HMRC answer to question 35

We think the "other person" referred to in paragraph 10(2)(c) must be the person referred to in paragraphs 3(3) and 6(3) as acquiring an interest in the relevant land etc. We agree that such a person need not necessarily be an individual. But we are more doubtful that an "outright" gift of money could include a gift to be held on trusts.

6.6 Partnership issues

The Guidance Notes suggest that a partnership is transparent for inheritance tax purposes. While this is true for capital gains tax purposes, as a matter of law a gift of a partnership interest is not a gift of the underlying assets within the partnership.

We therefore do not understand the example given in Appendix 1 which refers to C who gives his son D an interest in the partnership in return for D taking on the day to day running. In these circumstances why is there a disposal of land or chattels at all? There is a fundamental distinction between a firm's capital on the one hand and its individual assets on the other. C's proportionate interest in the capital may be equal to the value of the land or chattels but it is not an interest in the land or chattels itself and therefore he cannot dispose of that land (or the chattels) when he makes the gift of the partnership interest. See *Lindley on Partnerships* 17th Edn.

Question 36

Are HMRC treating partnerships as transparent for POA income tax purposes?

HMRC answer to question 36

We do not intend to treat partnerships as transparent for the purposes of Schedule 15. We will amend the example in Appendix 1 of the Guidance that you refer to.

6.7 Certain questions arise in relation to the annual exemption.

Example 10

X carried out a home loan scheme. In June 2005 he dismantles the scheme. The benefit enjoyed for POA purposes from April to June is £4,000.

Question 37

Will HMRC confirm that:

where the *de minimis* exemption under para 13 is not exceeded it is not possible for the transferor to make an election because he is not "chargeable to income tax"?

the £5,000 exemption is not pro-rated when a taxpayer is chargeable for only part of the year?

HMRC answer to question 37

We confirm both (a) and (b) are correct.

6.8 In a number of circumstances it is possible for (say) the husband to be caught by POA charge because he has made a disposal but not a gift and the wife to be caught potentially by gift with reservation.

In these circumstances do they each have to pay full consideration to escape their respective charges?

Example 11

In 1998 H transfers some properties into a company he wholly owns in consideration of the issue of shares. He has breached the disposal condition. He gives the shares to his wife. In 2003 W gives the company shares to her sons and later both of them occupy one of the properties owned by the company. H and W are not directors of the company.

In these circumstances H might wish to pay rent under paragraph 4 and W might want to pay full consideration under para 6 Schedule 20 in order respectively to avoid a pre-owned assets tax charge and a reservation of benefit situation.

Question 38

Is it sufficient that they pay such rent under an assured shorthold tenancy from their joint account and are jointly and severally liable for the rent?

Or does each person have to pay the full consideration separately?

HMRC answer to question 38

It seems to us that Example 11 is dealing with concurrent charges under two separate regimes: Schedule 15, and section 102 Finance Act 1986. In our view, it is arguable that H and W each has to pay full consideration separately in order to meet the separate requirements of paragraph 4(1) Schedule 15 and paragraph 6 Schedule 20 Finance Act 1986.

6.9 In 1.3.1 of the Guidance Notes under the bullet points relating to the spouse having to take an interest in possession from the outset it is not clear whether, if the interest in possession of the spouse or former spouse has come to an end other than on their death, the transaction is not an excluded transaction from the outset or whether it becomes so from the time the interest in possession terminates. It must surely cease to be an excluded transaction only from the time the interest in possession terminates.

Question 39

Will HMRC please clarify this point and confirm that the transaction only ceases to be an excluded transaction from the date the spousal interest terminates and therefore it is only from that point onwards there is a POA charge. Furthermore para 10(3) states that a disposal is not an excluded transaction if the interest in possession of the spouse comes to an end otherwise than on death of the spouse. Suppose a spouse becomes beneficially entitled to the property absolutely e.g. if the trustees advance the property outright to her so she becomes absolutely entitled. In these circumstances does the excluded transaction protection end? Her interest in possession has ended but only because she has become absolutely entitled to the property.

HMRC answer to question 39

In view of the way in which paragraph 10(3) is drafted, it is clear that the transaction ceases to be an excluded transaction only from the time that the interest in possession comes to an end otherwise than on the death of the (former) spouse.

As far as para 10(3) is concerned, we can see how it might be said that, where a spouse becomes absolutely entitled, the protection afforded by paras 10(1)(c) or 10(2)(b) is no longer available, particularly as the property in question would no longer be settled property. That would be a less than satisfactory result in our view, particularly bearing in mind the related provisions in paras 10(1)(b) and (2)(a). A more satisfactory approach might be to regard the interest in possession, which is not limited in terms to settled property as far as the reference in para 10(3) is concerned, as not coming to an end in these circumstances.

6.10 4.6 of the Guidance Notes give some examples of what HMRC consider constitutes occupation and the helpful letter from Mr McNicol dated 22 April 2005 gives further explanation. However, we do not fully understand HMRC's comments in this area. Please could the following common scenarios be clarified so that the taxpayer can self-assess appropriately. This is particularly relevant in relation to holiday homes.

Question 40

If there is a right to use a property throughout the year but it is not in fact used by the chargeable person, is it correct that there is no POA charge?

If there is a right to use a property throughout the year and the chargeable person uses the property but it falls within the de minimis limits set out in the guidance notes, is it correct that there is no POA charge?

If there is a right to use a property throughout the year and the chargeable person uses the property for say 3 months of the year there is a POA charge based on the whole year, even though others may have the right to use the property during that period (we are thinking particularly here of holiday homes)?

If there is a right to or actual storage of items in the relevant property but the chargeable person never lives there and the property is occupied by someone else, is it correct that there is no occupation of land within schedule 15?

Would the position of HMRC differ in (d) above if the property remained empty?

HMRC answer to question 40

Before dealing with your individual questions, we think it is worth reminding you of our view that occupation and use should be construed widely and are not confined to physical occupation.

If there is a right to use, but no occupation or use (in the wider sense) by the chargeable person in the year, it is unlikely that there would be a Schedule 15 charge.

We are not sure we can confirm that no Schedule 15 charge would arise in these circumstances. The examples of *de minimis* use given in paragraph 4.6 of the Guidance Notes do not contemplate (or, at least, do not assume) a right to use in the hands of the chargeable person for the rest of the year. If there is a right to use the property with even a small amount of use, the issue of how in fact the property was used for the rest of the year would need to be considered and whether this use also constituted use by the chargeable person.

We would agree that a Schedule 15 charge based on the whole year would arise.

We think it is difficult to give an assurance that there is no occupation of land under Schedule 15 by the chargeable person, if he is actually storing assets in the property. Particularly if he might have a right of access to these items, the circumstances might suggest that both the chargeable person and the person living in the property were using it.

By saying that the property remains empty, we assume you are envisaging that no-one is living in it. On that basis, if the chargeable person is storing items there, it seems clear that he is using the property for the purposes of Schedule 15.

6.11 The position on non-exempt sales is unclear. It is our view that there is no POA charge because the cash element paid is excluded under the computation in para 4 and the undervalue element is a reservation of benefit anyway and therefore exempted from POA under para 11(3).

If there is a part exchange at an undervalue with a cash adjustment, i.e. Y transfers Whiteacre worth £800,000 to X in exchange for Greenacre worth £200,000 and X also pays Y cash of £500,000, if at 6/4/05 Whiteacre is worth £800,000 (i.e. total consideration is paid by X of £700,000) we assume that POA is payable only on £200,000. The cash element is excluded under para 4 and the undervalue element is excluded under the reservation of benefit provisions.

Question 41

Is the above analysis correct?

HMRC answer to question 41

We broadly agree with this analysis. (We have assumed that, in order for this question to arise at all, Y continues to occupy Whiteacre after the transfer.)

In more detail, we would regard Y's disposition as one partly by way of gift (as to £100,000) and partly by way of sale (as to the remaining £700,000). In the circumstances envisaged, the proportion of the value of Whiteacre disposed of by way of gift would be treated as property subject to a reservation, thus remaining in Y's estate for IHT purposes and so, by virtue of paragraph 11(3), disapplying paragraph 3 to that extent. And, again in the circumstances envisaged, the disposition by way of sale would not be an excluded transaction and thus would be a non-exempt sale for the purposes of paragraphs 4(2) and (4).

We then need to apply this analysis to the provisions of paragraph 4 that determine how the chargeable amount is to be calculated and, in particular the R × DV/V formula in paragraph 4(2). First, we assume that, in this example, the relevant land would consist of 7/8ths of Whiteacre and, for any taxable period, V, in paragraph 4(2), would be the value of 7/8ths of Whiteacre at the appropriate valuation date. Looking at DV, we agree that, in applying the formula at paragraph 4(4) to arrive at the "appropriate proportion", P would be limited to the cash element of the consideration. Thus, in your example, (MV – P)/MV would be (£700,000 – £500,000) / £700,000, or 2/7.

In order to calculate the chargeable amount for a taxable period, let us assume that at the valuation date 7/8 of Whiteacre is worth £875,000 (the whole being worth £1,000,000) and the rental value (R) is £38,500. The appropriate rental value, as prescribed in para 4(4) would therefore be £38,500 × (2/7 × £875,000) / £875,000: in other words, £11,000.

(More simply, the calculation is £38,500 × 2/7.)

7. **Foreign domiciliaries**

7.1 Paragraph 12(3) states that no regard is to be had to excluded property. In a case where a trust settled by a foreign domiciliary) owns a UK house through a foreign registered company the shares in the company (and any loan to the company) are excluded property. Concern has been expressed that since para 12(3) says that no regard is to be had to these assets, this in turn means that the shares and loan have to be ignored in applying para 11 and in particular cannot be taken into account in determining whether there is derived property which is in the taxpayer's estate or GWR property in relation to him (which the shares and loans otherwise are). We think that this argument is misconceived but it has been advanced.

Question 42

Can HMRC confirm that they agree para 12(3) does not operate in this way and that para 11 can still work to protect the UK house or underlying assets owned by the offshore company in these circumstances?

HMRC answer to question 42

We agree with what you say in paragraph 7.1 about the interaction between paragraphs 12(3) and 11.

8. **Scope of the para 8 charge**

8.1 In addition to the points raised on valuation, we note that on insurance schemes involving for example quantitative carve outs (for example where the settlor taxpayer is the remainderman in the settlement as in a reverter to settlor trust) the settlor is treated as being outside the POA charge. This is on the basis that his interest in the trust property is either held on bare trust or on a separate trust.

Question 43

Will HMRC confirm that reverter to settlor trusts holding other assets are also outside the para 8 charge?

HMRC answer to question 43

If you are suggesting that reverter to settlor trusts are outside the scope of sections 624 and 625 ITTOIA 2005, we would be interested to see the reasoning put forward in support of this proposition. In the insurance schemes you mention, which we have agreed do not fall within the said sections 624 and 625 and therefore are outside the scope of paragraph 8, the interests held on trust for the settlor are, as you suggest, carved out of the gift and retained by him. In our view, such schemes are not analogous with reverter to settlor trusts.

Question 44

There is a potential problem about the wording in para 22(3): if income is treated as income of the chargeable person by virtue of section 660A then due to paragraph 22(3)(b) it shall be treated as property subject to a reservation. Income could be taxed under s 660A (now s624 ITTOIA) if only a spouse could benefit and that would not normally bring para 8 into play in the first place although this exclusion is not carried forward once an election is made.

So if someone elects on intangibles and then he but not his wife is excluded from benefiting under the settlement does this mean that the conditions in para 22(3) are satisfied and hence that he is still treated as having a reservation of benefit? Or does paragraph 22(2)(b)(ii) (which says sections 102(3) and (4) shall apply) mean that if he ceases to reserve a benefit in the property himself the effect of the election falls away so that there is a deemed PET then, even if the conditions in para 22(3) are prima facie satisfied because his wife can still benefit?

HMRC answer to question 44

We lean towards your first interpretation of the effect of para 22(3)(b). If someone is in a position to make an election under para 22(2), he or she must be someone who is (or would be) chargeable under para 8 for that year of assessment. Clearly, the condition in para 22(3)(b) would also be met at that time. It does seem that this condition would continue to be met until such time that both the chargeable person and his or her spouse (or civil partner) were excluded from benefit. At that point, a PET would be deemed to have arisen by virtue of para 22(2)(b)(ii).

FINANCE BILL—IHT AND PENSIONS

25 May 2006. *Chartered Institute of Taxation*

The Finance Bill, at Sch 22, includes provisions to impose an IHT charge on Alternatively Secured Pensions (ASP). Where the ASP is passed to a relevant dependant, such as the spouse, no IHT is due at that point.

Instead, IHT is calculated on cessation of the dependant's pension benefits, as the top slice of the estate of the late scheme member by reference to the rates of IHT applying at that time. (If, however, the left-over funds on the dependant's death are paid to charity then no IHT is payable.)

CIOT asked HMRC how this would work in practice, and they have agreed with us the following text containing four useful worked examples

EXAMPLE OF TOP SLICING CALCULATION (NEW S 151B—FINANCE BILL 2006 SCH 22)

Scheme member dies in 2006, with an estate of £450,000. He had an ASP fund worth £100,000 all of which was paid to his spouse. At the date of scheme member's death, the IHT threshold was £285,000, tax rate 40%.

When the dependant died in 2010, the left-over ASP fund was worth £80,000, the IHT threshold was £325,000 and the rate was 40%.

1 Assuming the scheme member had left the whole of estate to his spouse, the estate would have qualified for spouse/civil partner exemption and the chargeable value would have been £0. On the dependant's death, £80,000 is added to £0 = £80,000. As this is below the tax threshold (on the dependant's death) of £325,000; there is no tax to pay.

2 Assuming in this example that the scheme member had left £220,000 to his children and the remainder to his spouse, the chargeable value on his death would have been £220,000. On the dependant's death, £80,000 is added to £220,000 = £300,000. Again, as this is below the tax threshold of £325,000; there is no tax to pay.

3 In this example it is assumed that the scheme member had left £300,000 to his children with the remainder to his spouse so the chargeable value on his death would have been £300,000 and tax of £6,000 would have been paid on the £15,000 over the tax-free threshold (ie £300,000 less £285,000). On the dependant's death, £80,000 is added to £300,000 = £380,000. After deduction of the (then current) tax threshold of £325,000, tax of £22,000 would be due (as opposed to £32,000 had the rates of tax in force at the scheme member's death applied).

4 In this example it is assumed that the scheme member had left £250,000 to his children with the remainder to his spouse so the chargeable value on his death would have been £250,000 and no tax would have been paid (because below the IHT threshold £285,000). On the dependant's death, £80,000 is added to £250,000 = £330,000. After deduction of the (then current) tax threshold of £325,000, tax on £5,000 would be due.

Commentary—*Simon's Direct Tax Service* **E7.224.**

PRE-OWNED ASSETS AND ELECTION

13 October 2006. *Letter to HMRC Capital Taxes from STEP Technical/CIOT Capital Taxes*

There is some uncertainty about the actual effect of the election because para 21 does not as such deem there to be a gift for Inheritance Tax purposes but simply states that the property is treated as property subject to a reservation. Schedule 15 provides for what happens if the person ceases to benefit from the elected property but does not provide for what happens if the property actually comes back into a person's estate.

In the COP 10 letter we asked (at question 17) what happens if A makes the election in respect of his home on a home loan scheme (or indeed any other type of Inheritance Tax Scheme). The house is then appointed back to him absolutely i.e. the arrangements are unscrambled. The reservation of benefit has ceased because the house is back in his estate and you confirmed that even if there was a deemed PET under Section 102 (4) FA 1986, appointing the property back to A would have no immediate practical inheritance tax consequences because it is back in his estate anyway. This accords with how the reservation of benefit rules on actual gifts work. (See answer to question 17).

As you will be aware, many people are unravelling schemes but also wish to make the election in order to avoid an income tax charge from 6th April 2005. If once the property is back in their estates the effect of the election ceases to apply for all inheritance tax purposes (in the same way that a reservation of benefit on gifted property would cease if it was transferred back to the donor) then spouse (and charities) exemption is available. If the election is made and the scheme is not unravelled, spouse exemption is not available.

I am therefore requesting confirmation that HMRC apply the Schedule 15 FA 2004 legislation on elections in the same way as the reservation of benefit legislation on an actual gift. So even though HMRC would produce the election on any death, on being shown evidence that the property had been appointed back and the scheme entirely unravelled, the election would then be ignored for inheritance tax purposes. Spouse exemption is then available. If that approach is indeed the one HMRC adopt, does it matter if the election is made before or after the scheme is unravelled?

RESPONSE FROM HMRC CAPITAL TAXES NOTTINGHAM TECHNICAL DIVISION

[20 October 2006]

Pre-owned assets and elections

Thank you for your letter of 13 October.

I can confirm that we do believe that the Schedule 15 FA 2004 legislation on elections should be applied in the same way as the reservation of benefit legislation on an actual gift. As I suggested when you originally raised this question with me on the phone, section 102(3) Finance Act 1986 only has practical force in relation to property that is subject to a reservation immediately before death and only to the extent that it would not form part of the estate in any event.

On that basis, if evidence is produced that property, in respect of which an election under the Schedule 15 legislation had been made, has been appointed back to the estate, we would ignore the existence of the election for the purpose of determining the IHT estate on death.

On your supplementary question, we do not consider the timing of the election to be material. Even if it were made after the unscrambling, the chargeable person would still have been chargeable for the period up to the unscrambling, thus enabling the requirements of paragraphs 21(1) or 22(1), as appropriate, to be met.

PRE-OWNED ASSETS INCOME TAX – FA 2006 S 80

December 2006. *Correspondence between HMRC and STEP/CIOT from September to December 2006*

QUESTIONS FROM STEP/CIOT

Section 80 amends FA 2004 Sch 15 para 11. The amendments apply where the relevant property is comprised in a person's estate for the purposes of IHTA 1984 s 49 and previously one of two conditions has been met. These conditions are set out in new para 11(11) as follows—

(a) The relevant property has ceased to be comprised in the person's estate for inheritance tax purposes or

(b) The person has directly or indirectly provided any consideration for the acquisition of the relevant property.

If at any subsequent time the relevant property or derived property is in his estate for the purposes of s49 IHTA then the effect of s 80 is to provide that for POAT purposes (but for no other) the settlor is not treated as having an interest in possession or having reserved a benefit in the property.

The potential difficulty with paras 11(11) and 11(12) is that they do not distinguish between reverter to settler trusts and any trust set up between March 1986 and 22 March 2006 where the settlor has a qualifying interest in possession and would in that event be subject to inheritance tax on his death.

These difficulties arise because paras 11(11) and 11(12) catch not only those transactions where land has been given away and ceased to be comprised in the settlor's estate and then comes back into his estate (condition a above). They also catch transactions where a settlor contributed funds or property to a trust and the trust (or an underlying company) has then used those funds or property representing them to buy the relevant property i.e. the land which is now occupied (condition b above). There is nothing in the words about "any subsequent time" which suggests that under (b) the property had first to cease to be comprised in his estate before being caught by this provision. Indeed if that was the case the words in (a) would be redundant.

Are the following cases caught by POAT from 5th December 2005 (the date the change came into effect):

(1) In 1987, A sets up an interest in possession trust for himself into which he gifts his house. If the house is still held by the trustees now there is no POAT charge because nothing has left his estate. However assume that the house has since been sold but he retains an interest in possession. The trust holds a mixture of investments and another house that A occupies. Is para 11(11)(*b*) satisfied on the basis that A has provided consideration for the acquisition of the land which land has subsequently become comprised in his estate.

(2) A would then have to pay POAT on all the investments from 5th December 2005 for the foreseeable future even though they are prima facie chargeable to IHT in the event of his death. POAT may be due on the new house as well.

(3) B is a foreign domiciliary (not deemed domiciled) who before 22 March 2006 set up a discretionary trust into which he transferred cash. He remains a beneficiary of the trust. The trust then funds a company which buys a house or possibly holds UK investments (and B will pay income tax under s 739 in respect of any UK income). The trust was before 22 March 2006 converted into an interest in possession trust. If there is UK property or there are UK chattels occupied or used by B which are held by the trustees through the company within the interest in possession structure he is now subject to POAT on such property or chattels. (If B is deemed domiciled here then the charge would also apply to non-UK property or chattels occupied or used by him). Even if one reads "subsequent time" to mean some time must elapse between the date when the gift is made and the date the property comes back into B's estate this would still not protect B in this example because the trust was originally discretionary.

(4) In June 2006, C, a disabled person, sets up a trust for himself that qualifies as a disabled person's interest within s 89B. C puts in cash and the trustees invest in equities or a house that C occupies. C will pay POAT.

A simple amendment that would deal with the problem is to state that section 80 should not apply where the person with the qualifying interest in possession is the settlor. Is this in contemplation?

HMRC RESPONSE

As I understand your concern, it is that the new paragraph 11(11)(*b*) in Schedule 15 FA 2004 will catch someone who has settled, say, cash on interest in possession trusts for themselves (either before 22 March 2006, or afterwards if it is a "disabled person's interest") and subsequently occupies property bought by the trustees; or where the property they settled initially has been sold and replaced by other property, while the settlor has retained their interest in possession.

The new paragraph refers to the chargeable person "directly or indirectly [providing] any consideration for the acquisition of the relevant property", and goes on to require that, "at any subsequent time", the relevant property is comprised in the settlor's IHT estate by virtue of their having an interest in possession in it.

In our view, the words "at any subsequent time" should be read as meaning that a POA charge will arise where the consideration leaves the donor's estate, as a result of which that estate is reduced, and later property acquired with such consideration becomes comprised in it again because of their interest in possession. This is consistent with the reasons for Schedule 15.

We do not, therefore, consider that there will be a charge in the scenarios numbered 1 and 3 in your letters, because the assets transferred into trust and any derived assets have always been in the settlor's estate for IHT purposes. We believe that also applies if, in your second scenario, B set up an interest in possession trust from the outset before Budget Day. The taxpayer should self-assess on the basis that no POAT is due and there is therefore no need to put anything about POAT on the tax return or for him to make the election where the settlor has retained an interest in possession throughout and settled the cash or property directly into trust himself (rather than through any other funding vehicle such as another trust). This is because no POAT charge arises under s80 FA 2006.

In summary we do not consider that s.80 has any implications for:

- a settlement of cash on interest in possession trusts for oneself made before 22 March 2006, or made by a disabled person on or after that date, after which the trustees purchase a property in which the settlor resides; or
- the settlement of a house in the same way, which is subsequently sold by the trustees and replaced by other investments or another property.

That remains our view, on the basis that the words "at any subsequent time" mean that new paragraph 11(11)(*b*) Schedule 15 FA 2004 will only be relevant where:

- the consideration in question leaves the donor's estate, as a result of which that estate is reduced; and
- later, property acquired with such consideration becomes comprised in the estate once more by virtue of an interest in possession.

We do not agree that this interpretation makes paragraph 11(11)(*a*) redundant, since that relates to cases where the disposal condition is met and paragraph 11(11)(*b*) to cases where the contribution condition is met.

We accept that a POA charge may arise where someone set up a discretionary trust that has subsequently been converted into an interest in possession trust for the benefit of the settlor. (scenario 2 in your example). However, it remains possible in those circumstances to elect out of the charge. So, take the following example:

- H settles a property on discretionary trusts before 22 March 2006;
- also before that date, the trust is converted into an interest in possession trust for H's benefit, with remainder to his wife, W;
- a POA charge therefore arises because of s.80 but H elects.

As we see it, the effects of the election are:

- the chargeable proportion of the property will be treated as subject to a reservation, but only so far as H is not beneficially entitled to an interest in possession in the property (paragraph 21(2)(*b*)(i), Schedule 15 FA 2004) – ie not at all;
- section 102(3) and (4) FA 1986 will apply, but only so far as H is not beneficially entitled to an interest in possession in the property (paragraph 21(2)(*b*)(ii)) – ie not at all; and
- the reverter-to-settlor exemptions in s 53(3) and (4) and s 54 IHTA 1984 will not apply to the actual interest in possession (paragraph 21(2)(*b*)(iii)).

We do not, therefore, consider that the election affects the availability of spouse exemption on H's interest in possession on his death – or on its termination during his lifetime. That is because, as we have just noted, the election will not cause s 102(3) and (4) FA 1986 to apply because of H's interest in possession, so there will be no deemed PET.

CIOT/STEP COMMENT

In the light of the above it will be necessary for practitioners to review urgently all those trusts where the following conditions are satisfied:

(1) they were funded between March 1986 and March 2006
(2) at the date of funding, the settlor settled funds or property on discretionary trusts or on interest in possession trusts for someone else but before 22 March 2006 he acquired an interest in possession in the settled property.

In these circumstances the UK resident and UK domiciled person (domiciled in the UK under general law) will need to elect by 31 January 2007 but on HMRC's analysis there is no additional inheritance tax payable and the same reliefs and exemptions will be available as would have been due prior to the election.

If the conditions at 1 and 2 above are satisfied, the foreign domiciliary (whether or not deemed domiciled here now) who is resident in the UK and established his trust before he became domiciled here will need to elect by 31 January 2007 if the trust holds directly any UK situated intangibles or the trust directly or through a company holds UK real property that he occupies or UK chattels that he uses and he does not want to pay POAT. (An excluded property trust that holds intangibles through an offshore company structure will not be caught by s 80 in any event because para 8 does not apply to the underlying assets of a company and para 12(3) protects the offshore company shares). The settlor who is deemed domiciled here but was not domiciled here when he set up the trust will also need to consider an election on foreign situated land or chattels occupied or used by him where this is held in an offshore company owned by a trust assuming he does not want to pay POAT. However, there are a number of complexities.

Specialist advice should be sought as to the inheritance tax effects of such an election. In general terms an election will increase a foreign domiciliary's inheritance tax bill on his death where the UK situated property is owned by a company and he has an interest in possession in the shares. Otherwise the effect of making an election on UK situated property is likely to be broadly neutral.

FINANCE ACT 2006 S 80: NEED FOR POAT ELECTION

10 January 2007. *CIOT Note*

FA 2006 s 80 amended the income tax charge imposed by the 2004 Finance Act on preowned assets. Unfortunately a drafting error means it has a wider impact than was intended.

The section 80 amendment took effect when it was announced on 5th December 2005. PBRO5 on that date is headed "pre-owned assets and reverter-to-settlor trusts". The text of PBRO5 makes it clear that reverter to settlor trusts are those where the trust property reverts to the settlor or his spouse after termination of another beneficiary's interest in possession. Sections 53 and 54 of the Inheritance Tax Act 1984 are specifically referred to, those being the sections which exempt the trust from the Inheritance Tax otherwise payable on the termination of the beneficiary's interest in possession. For ease of reference it is convenient to refer to that beneficiary as the life tenant and his interest as the life interest.

The drafting error is that the amendment made by s 80 applies not only to trusts where the life tenant is another beneficiary but *also to those where the life tenant is the settlor himself*.

Where section 80 applies it removes the exemption from the preowned asset charge otherwise applicable where the taxpayer is treated as beneficially entitled to the relevant property for the purposes of Inheritance Tax. Loss of the exemption is thus in point in any case where the life interest vested in the settlor arose before 22nd March 2006 or where the settlor takes an interest in possession after 21 March 2006 and is disabled within the meaning of s 89 IHTA 1984. The effect, on the widest view, is that any such life interest exposes the settlor to pre-owned assets tax. Strictly this is only avoided where the asset was settled land or chattels which have at all times subsequently been retained in the trust.

As will be apparent this is an absurd result. The whole point of preowned assets tax is to tax assets which a settlor or donor enjoys despite them not being in his estate for Inheritance Tax purposes. By definition it is not a tax on property to which a settlor or donor is treated as beneficially entitled as such property is fully subject to Inheritance Tax in his hands.

As will be seen from the attached correspondence HMRC contend that s 80 does not apply if the life-interest of the settlor has subsisted **at all times** since the inception of the trust. Please note though that there is an exception to this point mentioned below. They have said that this view will be included in revised POAT guidance. On this basis, the difficulties identified above only arise where the initial trusts were discretionary or conferred interests in possession on other beneficiaries. But such scenarios are by no means uncommon, particularly in relation to non domiciliaries who are resident in the UK. A typical case where a non domiciliary would be caught would be where before 22 March 2006 he became entitled to an interest in possession in a UK house owned by a discretionary trust which he had created. Such interest could have arisen either by express appointment prior to the purchase of the house or as a result of SP 10/79.

HMRC have confirmed that the effect of s 80 can be removed by making an election, and that the cost of making the election is merely to disapply the reverter to settlor reliefs in ss 53 and 54 of the Inheritance Tax Act 1984. It is true that s 80 has conferred the right to make an election and it is also the case that in most cases the sole effect of the election is indeed to disapply ss 53 and 54. *For this reason an election should be considered urgently in all cases where the settlor did not have an interest in possession when the trust was created but has been appointed one subsequently.*

The purpose of this note is to draw attention to the fact that if an election is to be made, then subject to the de minimis exemption mentioned below, it must be made on or before 31 January 2007, ie the end of this month. STEP and CIOT are pressing HMRC to introduce amendments to reverse the unintended effect of s 80 as described above. But there is no certainty such amendments will be introduced and an election should therefore be seriously considered.

As the amendments made by s 80 took effect only on 5 December 2005, the amount potentially chargeable to POAT for 2005–06 may be modest. Should the taxable benefit fall within the de minimis exemption, which is £5,000 per taxpayer, no tax is due for 2005–06 and an election will only be needed for 2006-07. It is not possible to make an election on 31 January 2007 if the taxable benefit is under £5000. However, this gives the taxpayer another year to consider his options. An election would then need to be made by 31 January 2008 (assuming the de minimis charge does not also apply for the full year 2006–07).

An election may not be appropriate where the settlor is non domiciled and the asset giving rise to the pre-owned asset charge is land or chattels owned through an offshore company. In such cases an election could expose the land and chattels, and assets representing them to IHT. Specialist advice should therefore be sought. Such cases are comparatively rare because, as indicated above, on HMRC's view s 80 is only in issue if the settlor did not have an interest in possession when the trust was created but only acquired one subsequently. But if the settlor has by now acquired a deemed UK domicile, s 80 potentially impacts on such cases where the land or chattels owned by the company are foreign situs as well as where they are UK situs. (Where the foreign situated land or chattels are owned direct by the trustees then they should be protected from POAT under para 12(3) even if the trust was initially discretionary.)

As a final point, it should be born in mind that on one scenario s 80 can impact on a trust in which the settlor has had a life interest since inception. This is where the trust has been funded by an advance from another trust of which he was settlor but has not at all times had an interest in possession. In those cases too, election should be considered.

Correspondence between CIOT/STEP and HMRC on this point is attached to this note.

QUESTIONS BY STEP/CIOT AND ANSWERS FROM HMRC TO FA 2006 SCH 20

4 April 2007. *STEP/CIOT*

Note—These questions were submitted to HMRC by the Chartered Institute of Taxation and The Society of Trust and Estate Practitioners on 7 September 2006. The responses were received from HMRC on 3 November 2006 (as amended on 12 December 2006, January 2007 and April 2007). The answer to question 33 was added on 4 April 2007 based on a letter from HMRC dated 23 March 2007.

A. TRANSITIONAL SERIAL INTERESTS (TSI)

1. Condition 1 contains the requirement that "immediately before 22 March 2006, the property then comprised in the settlement was property in which B, or some other person, was beneficially entitled to an interest in possession ("the prior interest")".

2. Can it be confirmed that this requirement will be satisfied where B, or some other person, has a beneficial interest in possession in some of the property then comprised in the settlement but not all the property so comprised.

Example 1

Under a trust there are two funds. In Fund A, Mr Smith has an interest in possession. In Fund B, Mr Jones has an interest in possession.

Question 1

Will Condition 1 be satisfied separately in relation to Fund A and/or Fund B?

HMRC Answer

We can confirm that condition 1 can be satisfied separately in relation to both funds.

The new s 49C starts from the point of the view of the "current interest"—a beneficial interest in settled property. Given the wide definition of that term in s 43 IHTA, it seems that the beneficial IIP referred to in s 49C(1) can quite easily be in a fund or in property that was previously part of a larger disposition or settlement—and there is nothing to suggest that there must have been a single beneficiary.

Moreover, there is no requirement that the settlement must have been wholly IIP in nature (question 2 below) or that it must have come to an end in its entirety (question 3).

If one can then accept that the property referred to in s 49C(1) is also the property referred to in s 49C(2), and in which the "prior interest" (s 49C(2) & (3)) existed, the concerns raised in questions 1 to 4 fall away.

Question 2

Can it be confirmed that Condition 1 will be satisfied in relation to Fund A where Fund B is held not on trusts giving Mr Jones an interest in possession but on discretionary trusts? There is nothing in the wording of s 49C to suggest that the pre-Budget interest in possession must subsist in the entire fund.

HMRC Answer

We agree.

3. Section 49C(3) provides that Condition 2 requires the prior interest to come to an end at a time on or after 22 March 2006 but before 6 April 2008.

Question 3

Will Condition 2 be satisfied where the prior interest comes to an end in that period in part only of the settled property in which that interest subsists?

HMRC Answer

Yes—see the response to question 1 above.

EXAMPLE 2

In the example given above, if Mr Smith's interest in possession in Fund A comes to an end in 60% of Fund A and is replaced by an interest in possession in favour of Mr Smith's daughter, but Mr Smith's interest in possession continues in relation to the remaining 40% of Fund A, can it be confirmed that the interest in possession in favour of the daughter will be a transitional serial interest?

HMRC Answer

We can confirm this—for the reasons given immediately below.

While it has been suggested that Condition 2 requires that the prior interest comes to an end in all the property in which the interest subsists, Condition 2 does not state this and given the definition of current interest it appears that Condition 2 must be construed as referring to the prior interest coming to an end in the settled property concerned in which B takes a current interest but not necessarily in all the settled property of a particular settlement. The "current interest" is merely defined as an interest in possession in settled property and does not in any way require all the settled property comprised in the settlement to be a current interest.

Question 4

Please also confirm that the remaining 40% of Fund A continues to satisfy Condition 1 so that a transitional serial interest could be created in that 40% prior to 6th April 2008.

HMRC Answer

We can confirm this.

Question 5(1)

Please also confirm that in the above example if 40% of Mr Smith's pre-Budget interest in possession is ended as to half for his daughter and half for his son, both son and daughter take transitional serial interests in their respective shares.

HMRC Answer

We can confirm this.

Question 5(2)

If later the trustees wished to appropriate assets between the two funds for son and daughter and the assets were of the same value as the assets previously contained in each fund, do HMRC accept that such appropriation does not represent the termination of any qualifying interest in possession and therefore does not result in an inheritance tax charge?

HMRC Answer

We agree.

4. We would be grateful for your views on the circumstances in which the prior interest would be considered to have come to an end and have been replaced by a current interest. This is relevant because if a prior interest is considered to have come to an end and have been replaced by a current interest (in favour of the same beneficiary) there will be no possibility of the interest being replaced by a transitional serial interest later and the point is particularly important in relation to spousal relief because spouse exemption will not be available if a spouse of a life tenant who already has a transitional serial interest takes an interest in possession on the death of that life tenant.

EXAMPLE 3

Under a pre-Budget 2006 trust a beneficiary A is entitled to the capital contingently on attaining the age of 30 years. A was 21 on 22 March 2006 and had been entitled to an interest in possession under section 31 of the Trustee Act 1925 from the age of 18. The interest is therefore an interest in possession which subsisted on 22 March 2006. Before 2008 the trustees exercise their [enlarged] powers of advancement under section 32 of the Trustee Act 1925 to defer the vesting of the capital from the age of 30 to the age of 45 and A's interest in possession in the fund will therefore continue until age 45.

Clearly A reaches 30 after 2008 in the above example.

Question 6

There are two possible interpretations of the above and we should be grateful if HMRC could confirm which view they take.

Option 1. The exercise of the trustees' powers in this way creates a new interest in possession for A immediately on exercise of the power of advancement which therefore takes effect as the "current interest" or "transitional serial interest". Any successive interest in possession after A's interest in possession has ended cannot then be a transitional serial interest. The property will be taxed as part of A's estate on his death if he dies with the transitional serial interest. He continues to have a transitional serial interest until termination at 45 or earlier death.

Option 2: A's new interest only arises when A attains the age of 30. Until then he has a pre-Budget qualifying interest in possession.

The new interest cannot take effect as a transitional serial interest at all since on the above facts it will arise after April 2008. Until 30 A will have a pre-Budget interest in possession on the basis that nothing has changed until he reaches 30. Only from 30 will he take a new non-qualifying interest so the settled property will then become relevant property. There will not be an entry charge for A at 30 of 20% due to s 53(2) IHTA.

If A dies before reaching 30, then on this analysis his pre-Budget interest will not previously have ended and therefore if his spouse takes an interest in possession this is a transitional serial interest or if his children take interests in possession before 2008 these will be transitional serial interests.

Does the answer to whether option 1 or option 2 applies depend on whether the advancement is drafted in such a way that it extends the interest in possession from 30 without restating A's existing interest in possession until then? Or would any variation of A's interest in possession be regarded as a transitional serial interest from the date of the variation even if the variation only took effect in the future.

HMRC Answer

We consider that A's original IIP (until 30) will have "come to an end" when the trustees exercised their power of advancement and been replaced by a new IIP (until 45), which will therefore qualify as a TSI. A's interest is expressed as an entitlement to capital contingent on his attaining 30. It seems reasonable to regard the exercise of the s 32 Trustee Act power as immediately bringing this interest to an end and replacing it with a new one.

NB: As regards HMRC's view on whether a charge arises on the creation of the TSI (or other interest in possession) in these circumstances see warning posted on STEP website on 24th September 2007 and see also section 140 of Finance Act 2008 which has now removed any suggestion that there could be a charge where A is given a new IIP before October 2008.

5. An interest in possession might also subsist as follows:

EXAMPLE 4

Under a trust A has a life interest with remainder to his children. The trustees have a power of advancement and exercise such a power to provide that subject to A's existing life interest A's spouse takes a life interest on A's death with remainder to the children at the age of 25. A's interest in possession is not in any way altered.

Question 7

Can HMRC please confirm that the exercise of a power of advancement to create an interest in possession for the spouse, which is expressly made subject to A's existing life interest and does not in any way alter that interest but merely comes into effect on his death, will be a transitional serial interest. Similarly, if spouse predeceases A and the advancement on interest in possession trusts for A's children is made subject to A's interest and takes effect before 2008 (eg A surrenders his interest) presumably these trusts could also be transitional serial interests.

HMRC Answer

Assuming that A's present IIP existed before 22 March 2006, we can confirm that the spouse's IIP—whether or not it arises before or after 6 April 2008—will qualify as a TSI provided that it arises on the *death* of A and that A is at the date of his death still entitled to a pre-budget interest in possession. Any IIP taken by A's children on the death or earlier termination of A's IIP will also be a transitional serial interest provided that this occurs before 6 April 2008. If A's pre-Budget interest in possession terminates inter vivos in favour of the spouse then the spouse will only take a TSI if this termination occurs before 6th April 2008.

If, however, A's interest was in any way amended (eg the trustees exercised powers of revocation and reappointment restating A's interest in possession albeit in the same terms and then declaring interests in possession for A's spouse or for children if she has predeceased), presumably the interests for spouse and children could never be transitional serial interests because A's interest is a transitional serial interest?

HMRC Answer

We agree.

6. Can it be confirmed that an interest in possession can be a transitional serial interest where the interest arises under a different settlement to that in which the original interest subsisted?

EXAMPLE 5

Under Trust A Mr Smith has an interest in possession and subject to that, the capital passes to Mr Jones absolutely. Mr Jones on 30 December 2006 assigns his reversionary interest into Trust B set up in December 2006 under which his children have interests in possession. Mr Smith's interest in possession then comes to an end on 30 November 2007 at which time the settled property in Trust A passes to Trust B.

Question 8

Will the interest in possession of Mr Jones' children qualify as a transitional serial interest bearing in mind that the interests arise in relation to the same settled property even though not under the trusts of the original settlement? A similar situation could arise where there is technically a different settlement under which the successive life interest arises due to the exercise of the trustees' powers of appointment in the wider form (as referred to in *Bond v Pickford* 1983 STC 517).

HMRC Answer

Taken with question 9 below.

Question 9

If the difficulty is that Condition 1 is not satisfied because the second settlement is "made" post Budget does it make any difference if the second settlement was made pre-Budget and the interests in the first settlement fall into the second settlement before 2008 to be held on interest in possession trusts. This is a very common situation where there are "trusts over" and there appears nothing in the conditions to prevent this.

HMRC Answer

We do not consider that the IIPs of Mr Jones's children will qualify as TSIs whether the second settlement was made before or after Budget 2006.

As we said earlier, s 49C begins from the point of view of the "current interest". Condition 1 requires that "the settlement" in which that interest subsists "commenced" before 22 March 2006.

It goes on to require that, immediately before that date, the property "then comprised" in the settlement—ie the same settlement—was subject to the "prior interest".

The IIPs of Mr Jones's children arise under a different settlement (albeit one which happens to hold, following Mr Smith's death, the property that comprised the earlier one) and will not, therefore, qualify as TSIs—and it will make no difference when the settlement was made.

For the same reasons, the exercise of powers of appointment in such a way that assets are removed from one settlement and subjected to the trusts of another will not give rise to TSIs.

Note: where the second settlement was set up prior to 22 March 2006 and the reversionary interest of Mr Jones was assigned into an IIP trust prior to that date STEP/CIOT do not accept that on the death of the life tenant Mr Smith the property then comprised in the second trust (formerly the reversionary interest and now the settled property originally in trust 1) is not subject to a qualifying pre March 2006 IIP. It is however accepted that a TSI cannot arise if property is appointed from one IIP trust to another whenever they were set up.

7. Question 10

What is the position if the beneficiary holding the pre-Budget interest in possession assigns that interest in possession to another person? Does the assignee's interest qualify as a transitional serial interest? The concern here is that the original interest in possession is not "terminated" by virtue of the assignment, and so the precise terms of the legislation do not appear to have been met.

HMRC Answer

We consider that the assignee's interest can be a TSI in this case because the assignor's IIP will have "come to an end" for the purposes of s 49C(3). (The interest will be in the original settlement, so the problem outlined in our response to question 9 will not be an issue).

B ADMINISTRATION OF ESTATES

8. Question 11

Can it be confirmed that where a will provides that a beneficiary has an interest in possession in residue, that interest in possession will be treated as commencing on the date of death of the deceased and not only when the administration of the estate is completed. This appears to be the case by virtue of Section 91 IHTA 1984.

HMRC Answer

We can confirm this.

9. Question 12

Can it be confirmed that the position will be the same as in Question 11 above where the interest in possession is in a settled legacy of specific assets not forming part of residue. It seems that this should be the case: *IRC v Hawley* [1929] 1 KB 578.

HMRC Answer

We agree.

This is important for two reasons:

- in order for an interest in possession to satisfy Condition 2 in section 49A for an Immediate Post-Death Interest (IPDI), L must have become beneficially entitled to the interest on the death of the testator or intestate;
- in determining whether an interest in possession is one which subsisted prior to 22 March 2006 where the deceased died before 22 March 2006 but the completion of the administration of the estate was on or after 22 March 2006 there would be difficulties if the pre-Budget interest in possession was not regarded as commencing on the death of the deceased.

10. Question 13

Many wills include a provision which provides that a beneficiary will only take if he survives the testator by a period of time. Please confirm that such a provision would not by itself prevent an IPDI arising.

HMRC Answer

We can confirm this. We consider that s 92 IHTA removes any doubt here.

C IPDIS GENERALLY

11. Question 14

Can it be confirmed that if on the death of X a discretionary trust set up in his Will (eg a nil rate band legacy trust) is funded by a share in property, and the trustees allow the surviving spouse L to occupy it on an exclusive basis albeit at their discretion along the lines that occurred in *Judge & anor (Representatives of Walden deceased)* Sp C 506, this will not automatically be an IPDI but it will depend on the terms on which she occupies.

HMRC Answer

We agree.

There is a 3 month requirement for reading back under s 144 in respect of appointments of absolute interests but this does not apply to appointments of IPDIs. Therefore if the trustees immediately on the death of X or subsequently, conferred exclusive rights of occupation on L this could indeed be an IPDI.

HMRC Answer

We agree.

It appears to us unlikely that mere exclusivity of occupation could in itself be a problem because as Judge confirms a person can occupy exclusively but not have rights which constitute an interest in possession. Indeed if the surviving spouse merely continued in occupation on the same terms as before X's death without the trustees' doing anything positive either way to affect her occupation it would appear they have not exercised their powers so as to give her any IPDI anyway.

HMRC Answer

We agree.

(Indeed it is doubtful that they have any ability under the Trusts of Land and Appointment of Trustees Act 1996 to disturb her occupation if she already owns a half share in the property personally and therefore the trustees have not exercised any power to confer her a present right to present enjoyment which could constitute an immediate post death interest.)

It would be helpful (given how common this situation is) if HMRC could give some guidance on the various scenarios in which they would or would not regard the surviving spouse as taking an IPDI in a property left on nil rate band discretionary trusts in the will if she is already in occupation.

HMRC Answer

This will depend on the precise terms of the testator's will or any deed of appointment exercised by the trustees after the testator's death, and we will continue to examine each case on its particular facts.

12. Question 15

Can it be confirmed that where a settlement (including a settlement created by will) includes a general power of appointment and that power is exercised by will giving an immediate interest in possession, the interest created over the trust property will qualify as an IPDI?

HMRC Answer

We can confirm this.

13. Question 16

Can it be confirmed that HMRC takes the view that if an individual (I) leaves by will a gift to a person's estate, when the assets in the estate are held on trusts which qualify as trusts for bereaved minors or age 18-to-25 trusts, the property added pursuant to I's will would also be treated as being held on trusts which qualify as trusts for bereaved minors or 18-to-25 trusts.

HMRC Answer

We have assumed that the scenario envisaged here is: I dies leaving a legacy in their will to P; P dies after I but before the legacy has been paid; P's estate is held on trusts that meet s 71A or s 71D. We agree that, in those circumstances, the legacy from I's estate would qualify under those provisions, also.

EXAMPLE 6

I leaves his estate to his widow for life with remainder to his son S if alive at I's death. S survives I but predeceases the widow leaving a will under which his estate passes to his children on trusts which qualify as trusts for bereaved minors. The widow dies when the children are aged 10 and

12, so that I's estate falls to be held on the trusts of S's will. Will the property in I's estate benefit from trusts for bereaved minors status? I is the grandparent but the property is passing according to S's will.

HMRC Answer

We consider that the property added pursuant to I's will in this example would also fall within s 71A.

14. Question 17

If a property is left outright to someone by a will and they disclaim within two years of the deceased's death such that an interest in possession trust takes effect, can HMRC confirm that the trust will qualify as an IPDI?

HMRC Answer

We can confirm this.

15. Question 18

Can it be confirmed whether, when a will leaves property to an existing settlement (whether funded or unfunded) and under that settlement a beneficiary takes an immediate interest in possession, that interest will qualify as an IPDI. Such arrangements are common for US and other foreign domiciliaries in order to avoid complex probate issues. It might be argued that the interest in possession in the existing settlement does not arise under the will of the deceased. However, there are two arguments against this.

First, HMRC's own analysis is that additions by individuals to existing settlements should be treated as new settlements. Hence the addition by will to an existing settlement is a new settlement set up by virtue of the will.

Secondly, the wording in section 49A Condition 1 refers to "the settlement was effected by will or under the law of intestacy". The question though is what "the settlement" refers to. It would seem that it refers not as such to "the settlement" in the sense of a document but rather to the settlement into trust of the settled property which certainly is effected by will. The same wording is used on deeds of variation under section 142 IHTA and HMRC have always accepted that where property is added by will to a pre-existing settlement there is no reason why the beneficiary of that settlement cannot vary his entitlement.

HMRC Answer

We can confirm that the IIP in this scenario would qualify as an IPDI. We agree that "settlement" in this context relates to the contribution of property into the settlement rather than the document under which it will become held.

D TRUSTS FOR BEREAVED MINORS, 18-25 TRUSTS AND MODIFIED SECTION 71 TRUSTS: SECTION 71A AND SECTION 71D

16. Question 19

Can it be confirmed that trusts otherwise satisfying the requirements of section 71A or section 71D will be regarded as satisfying those conditions where the trusts were appointed under powers contained in the will and were not provided in the will itself at the outset.

HMRC Answer

We can confirm this—where the trusts are set up as a result of the exercise of a special power of appointment. We consider the position is different with general powers, on the basis, broadly speaking, that having a general power of appointment is tantamount to owning the property.

EXAMPLE 7

H dies in 2007. His will leaves an IPDI for his surviving spouse and subject thereto on discretionary trusts for issue of H. The trustees exercise their overriding powers of appointment to create s 71A trusts for the children of H. It would appear that the s 71A provisions do not need to be incorporated within the will trust from the start to qualify for relief but it would be helpful to have this confirmed. Presumably the presence of overriding powers of appointment over capital in favour of surviving spouse would not be treated as breaching the s 71A conditions while the s 71A interest was a remainder interest.

HMRC Answer

We agree (subject to our comments at question 19).

17. Question 20

Can it be further confirmed that the analysis in 16 above will apply both where the prior interest in possession is an IPDI and also where there is an interest in possession arising under the will of a person who died prior to 22 March 2006 where the interests will, by definition, not be an IPDI although in all other respects identical to an IPDI.

HMRC Answer

We can confirm this.

18. Question 21

Can it be confirmed that, where a will contains a gift "to such of my children as reach 18 and if more than one in equal shares" or "to such of my children as reach 25 and if more than one in equal shares" all the interests will qualify as trusts for bereaved minors (or as age 18-to-25 trusts) even though one or more of the children might die after the testator but before the capital vests (so that their shares are divided between their siblings).

HMRC Answer

We can confirm this. We consider that each child while alive and under 18/25 has a presumptive share that is held for his or her benefit, and one can apply s 71A or s 71D child by child and presumptive share by presumptive share.

Question 21A

On conversion of an existing pre-Budget A&M trust to s 71D status does the class need to close *ab initio* from the date the trust was converted or is it sufficient to say that until someone else is born, the trusts for "B" do qualify as s 71D trusts but not actually close the class?

HMRC Answer

We consider that a trust in the position where anyone (whether unborn or not) who is not currently benefiting can nevertheless become entitled would not meet the requirements of s 71D(6), since it could not be said for certain that 'B' will become absolutely entitled to the settled property etc. in due course or that no income will be applied for any other person in the meantime. So we take the view that it will be necessary to close the class of beneficiaries for s 71D to apply.

19. Question 22

Can it be confirmed that the answer to Question 21 is not affected by a gift over provision that substitutes the children (if any) of a deceased child who attain a certain age, so that the increase of the siblings' shares is dependent upon whether the child dies childless.

HMRC Answer

We can confirm this: the siblings' presumptive shares simply increase (or not) when one of their number dies, depending on whether or not the deceased child had any children of their own.

20. Question 23

Can it be confirmed that agricultural property relief (apr) and business property relief (bpr) will apply to charges arising under section 71E. It would appear that these reliefs should be applicable as the charges under section 71D (by reference to section 71E) are charges under Chapter III or Part III IHTA and the reliefs are expressly extended to events of charge under this Chapter (section 103(1) IHTA in relation to bpr and section 115(1) in relation to apr). Further, the formula for calculating the charge under section 71F is similar, in principle, to the charges as calculated under section 65 and section 68 IHTA in relation to exit charges for relevant property generally. Can HMRC confirm this analysis is agreed?

HMRC Answer

We agree—for the reasons given.

21. Question 24

Section 71E(4) provides that there will be no event of charge where a transaction is entered into by trustees as a result of which the assets held subject to the 18-to-25 trusts are diminished in value, where the disposition by the trustees would not have been a transfer of value under section 10 or section 16 IHTA if they had been beneficially entitled to the trust assets. There is a further exemption in section 71E(3). There are no similar provisions in relation to actions by trustees concerning assets which are held on trusts qualifying under section 71A. Can it be confirmed that in practice HMRC would apply similar principles in relation to events of charge under section 71B for section 71A trusts?

HMRC Answer

The provisions in s 71E that the question refers to are not reproduced in s 71B because the charge there arises under s 70—and s 70 already includes identical provisions at subsections (3) and (4). S 71B(3) says: "Subsections (3) to (8) and (10) of section 70 apply for the purposes of this section as they apply for the purposes of that section . . . "

22. Question 25

Can HMRC confirm that trusts which are held for beneficiaries as a class (eg on trust for such of my children as attain the age of 25 and if more than one in equal shares) will qualify as age 18-to-25 trusts under section 71D(3) and (4) notwithstanding that the class could be diminished by reason of the death of members of the class under the age of 25. While it might be said that the class gift does not fall within the strict wording of section 71D(6)(a) it might be said that nonetheless the assets are held on trust, for the time being, for each child being under the age of 25. HMRC are requested to confirm their view in relation to the continued application of 71D to class gifts where a beneficiary (B) dies before reaching 25 and the assets pass to the other beneficiaries under 25 on s 71D trusts. (This is a separate point from the situation where in relation to existing inter vivos A&M trusts the class increases as a result of future beneficiaries being born before the eldest reaches 25.)

HMRC Answer

We can confirm this. CIOT/STEP note: further queries were raised with HMRC on the class closing rules and the application of s 71D generally and these were posted on the websites separately.

23. Question 26

HMRC is asked to confirm that section 71A and section 71D will apply to trusts for a class of children whether or not the assets have been appropriated to each child's share.

HMRC Answer

We can confirm this.

24. Question 27

There will be a number of circumstances where different sets of beneficiaries under one accumulation and maintenance settlement may require to be treated differently (for example, a settlement for grandchildren where they differ widely in age). Can HMRC please confirm that trusts will qualify as 18-25 trusts or modified section 71 trusts (capital vesting at age 18) if those trusts exist in only part of the settled property. Thus, a settlement might be divided into two sub-funds, one for A's children who are approaching adulthood and for whom an 18-25 trust is appropriate and another for B's children who are very young and where the trustees value retaining flexibility so that that sub-fund will be allowed to fall within the relevant property regime with effect from 6 April 2008 (or be converted into an 18 trust).

HMRC Answer

We can confirm this.

25. Question 28

There has been some confusion about the interaction of s 71D(3) and (4) with s 71D(1) and (2). Please confirm that existing A&M trusts set up before the Budget where the settlor may still be alive (and the beneficiary's parent has not died) can qualify for 18-25 status if converted before April 2008 if this occurs immediately after the funds cease to qualify under s 71.

HMRC Answer

We can confirm that s 71D can apply to existing A&M trusts if the conversion occurs *before* the funds cease to qualify under s 71—for the reasons set out in example 8 below.

Further that there is no inheritance tax charge on conversion of an existing accumulation and maintenance trust to a s 71D trust; ie that para 3(3) schedule 20 protects all pre-Budget accumulation and maintenance trusts so that there is no inheritance tax entry charge either under s 71 or otherwise, at the point the trust starts to qualify for s 71D status (or indeed enters the relevant property regime).

HMRC Answer

We can confirm this.

EXAMPLE 8

U sets up an accumulation and maintenance trust for his two nieces S and T in 1999. On 22 March 2006 neither has an interest in possession. Currently the nieces take capital at 30 and income at 21. S becomes 21 in January 2007. T becomes 21 in January 2011.

The trustees exercise their powers to ensure that the trusts qualify for 18-25 status in February 2007 ie after S has attained entitlement to income (albeit this is not a qualifying interest in possession post Budget). They provide that each child takes capital outright at 25 in a fixed half share. In these circumstances it would appear that S's share cannot qualify for 18-25 status because immediately after the property ceased to be subject to s71 it did not then fall within s 71D. T's interest could however qualify under s 71D. There is no inheritance tax charge in February 2007 on S's part although there would be a ten year charge in 2009 on her share because this share is now within the relevant property regime and there would be an exit charge when she reaches 25. There are no ten year or entry or exit charges on T's interest until she reaches 25 at which point her share is subject to tax at 4.2%. (This assumes that she does not die before reaching 25).

It would be helpful if this could be spelt out in the guidance notes because trustees need to be aware of the requirement to act swiftly if beneficiaries are about to take entitlement to income. It would also be helpful if examples could be given as to how 18-25 trusts work in practice and their main advantages ie to avoid the ten year anniversary charge.

HMRC Answer

We agree with the consequences set out in the example and will incorporate them in guidance.

26. Question 29

It would appear that on the death of a child before 18 on a bereaved minor trust or on an 18-25 trust there is no inheritance tax charge even if they are entitled to income (albeit there is a base cost capital gains tax uplift if they are entitled to income).

HMRC Answer

We agree—by virtue of s 71B(2)(b) or s 71E(2)(b) and new s 5(1)(a)(i).

It would appear that after a child reaches 18 there is an exit charge on an 18-25 trust if the property ceases to be held on 18-25 trusts but no base cost uplift for capital gains tax purposes whether or not the child has a right to income. Please confirm.

HMRC Answer

We can confirm this.

Question 30

It would appear that, if a child reaches 18 and on his death his share of the trust fund remains on 18-25 trusts for his siblings under cross-accruer provisions, there will be no exit charge at that time. Please confirm.

HMRC Answer

We can confirm this.

27. Question 31

In the HMRC Customer Guide to Inheritance Tax recently published, HMRC state under the heading of "What is an age 18 to 25 trust?":

"If the terms of the trust are not rewritten before 6 April 2008 and the trust has not come to an end then existing accumulation and maintenance trusts will automatically become relevant property trusts on the 18th birthday of the beneficiary."

What is the statutory justification for this view. First it is surely the case that an existing A&M trust can become subject to the relevant property regime before 6th April 2008 if a beneficiary takes a post-Budget interest in possession.

HMRC Answer

We agree and will amend the Customer Guide.

Second our understanding is that such trusts will become relevant property trusts on the 6th April 2008 or the beneficiary becoming entitled to an interest in possession before that date unless the trust meets the requirements of a s 71D trust. If nothing has been done by April 2008 and a beneficiary is not entitled to an interest in possession then the trust falls within the relevant property regime from that date whether or not the beneficiary is a minor. This point needs to be clarified urgently and the information amended.

HMRC Answer

We agree. Section 71D(5)(b) provides that s 71D does not apply to property to which s 71 applies. A&M treatment will therefore continue up to an including 5 April 2008 if the trusts of the settlement meet s 71, and will fall away on 6 April 2008. If the trusts provide for absolute entitlement at 18 or 25, the settlement will then fall within s 71A or s 71D as appropriate; if they do not, the settlement will be "relevant property" from that date.

28. Question 32

Please also confirm whether or not hold over relief will be available if assets are distributed within 3 months of a beneficiary's 18th birthday under an 18-25 trust. There will be no inheritance tax charge as there will be no complete quarters since the 18th birthday. In these circumstances is hold over relief denied?

HMRC Answer

No. The distribution is still an occasion on which IHT is chargeable—it is just that the charge will be nil. There is no provision in s 71F along the lines of s 65(4).

E ABSOLUTE INTERESTS

29. Where assets are held by a person on bare trusts for minor children section 31 of the Trustee Act is implied in most cases without express reference and will apply unless expressly excluded.

30. It might be said that the application of the section will cause the property concerned to be settled property within section 43(2)(b) in view of the provisions for the accumulation of income under section 31(2) of the Trustee Act. However, the contrary argument is that the accumulations of income are held for the absolute benefit for the minor concerned and would pass to his estate if he died under 18 (the minor not being able to give a good receipt) and the assets are therefore not held in any real sense subject to any contingency or provision for the diversion of income from the minor. This latter view seems to be in line with the analysis in the IHT Manual which contemplates that section 43(2)(b) deals with the position where there is relevant property held on discretionary trusts (paragraph 4602). The statement in the Inland Revenue letter of 12 February 1976 where, in the last sentence of the second paragraph, it is stated that a provision to accumulate income will not prevent there being an interest in possession if the accumulations are held for the absolute benefit of the beneficiary, supports the view that section 31 of the Trustee Act will not in these circumstances cause the relevant property regime to apply.

31. Question 33

Can HMRC confirm that the application of section 31 of the Trustee Act 1925 to assets held on a bare trust for a minor will not result in the assets being settled property within the meaning of section 43 IHTA?

HMRC Answer

We confirm that our view is that where assets are held on an absolute trust (ie a bare trust) for a minor the assets so held will not be settled property within the meaning of section 43 IHTA 1984 and that this will be the case whether or not the provisions of section 31 Trustee Act 1925 have been excluded.

32. There appear to be new and unforeseen capital gains tax problems now where *Crowe v Appleby* [1975] STC 502 applies on settled property. The position is complex albeit common and can best be illustrated by example.

EXAMPLE 9

In February 2006 Andrew set up a trust for his children Charlotte and Luke. They each become entitled to one half of the income and capital on reaching 25. Charlotte becomes 25 in 2007 and Luke becomes 25 in 2009. They do not take interests in possession until reaching 25. The trust only holds one piece of land.

When Charlotte reaches 25 in 2007 she becomes absolutely entitled for inheritance tax purposes since *Crowe v Appleby* has no application for IHT purposes. The trusts over her share end for inheritance tax purposes before April 6 2008 so there is no exit charge since she is within the transitional regime. She is treated from 2007 as entitled to the half share in the property and if she died after that date it would form part of her estate for inheritance tax purposes and hence be potentially taxable.

There is a further problem. For capital gains tax purposes Charlotte does not become absolutely entitled to one half of the land. Until the land is sold or Luke reaches 25 and becomes absolutely entitled (whichever is the earlier) there is no disposal made by the trustees.

There is no inheritance tax change on 6 April 2008 but from that date Luke's share is no longer within A&M trust protection but is taxed as an 18-25 trust. There is no ten year anniversary charge before Luke reaches 25 but if he dies before then there is an inheritance tax charge (likely to be less than 4.2%). As noted above, there is no base cost uplift for capital gains tax purposes.

On Luke reaching 25 in 2009 there is an exit charge on Luke's share of 4.2%.

HMRC Answer

(Note: we do not consider this is quite right. We assume that the 4.2% is referred to on the basis of 7/10ths × 6%. However, the charge will not be based on the 7 years from Luke's 18th birthday. Section 71F(5)(a) provides that the starting date for calculating the relevant fraction is his 18th birthday "or, if later, the day on which the property became property to which section 71D above applies"—in this case, 6 April 2008).

If the land has not yet been sold there will at that point be a disposal of all the land by the trustees for capital gains tax purposes because both beneficiaries become absolutely entitled. Hold over relief is available on Luke's part under s 260 TCGA 1992 but not on Charlotte's part since there is no exit charge. In summary, the trustees will have to pay capital gains tax on any gain on Charlotte's share in 2009 and cannot hold over the gain on that share.

Question 34

Prior to the Finance Act 2006, Charlotte would have been treated as having a qualifying interest in possession in her share of the trust assets. If she died before Luke reached 25, there would have been a charge to inheritance tax on her death but because she had a qualifying interest in possession, for capital gains tax purposes, there would be an uplift in base cost on her share of the land under s 72(1) TCGA 1992.

Post the Finance Act 2006, if Charlotte dies before Luke reaches 25 there will be a charge to inheritance tax but s 72(1) TCGA 1992 does not seem to be applicable because Charlotte does not appear to have a qualifying interest in possession which qualifies her for the uplift. Hence she is subject to inheritance tax on her death with no uplift for capital gains tax.

Will HMRC regard her as having a qualifying interest in possession within section 72 for these purposes?

HMRC Answer

No—with the result, as stated, that there would be no CGT uplift under s 72(1) TCGA.

Question 35

If Charlotte attained 25 in say June 2015 and Luke only reached 25 in 2017 there would be an exit charge on both Luke and Charlotte's shares when each becomes 25 (rate = 4.2%) but hold-over relief is only available on Luke's share when the disposal of the land takes place for capital gains tax purposes.

Prior to the Finance Act 2006 there would have been no exit charge when Charlotte reached 25. However, the effect of the new rules is that on reaching 25 Charlotte will now suffer an exit charge but without any entitlement to hold over the gain which arises when the land is distributed to her when Luke reaches 25. Will HMRC in these circumstances allow hold over relief on both shares?

HMRC Answer

No—hold-over relief will be due on Luke's share only.

F DISABLED TRUSTS

33. Section 89A(2) appears to conflict with s 89A(3). Condition 1 states that if any of the settled property is applied for A it is applied for the benefit of A but Condition 2 envisages that capital *could* be paid to A or another person on the termination of A's interest during his life provided that the other person became absolutely entitled.

Question 36

Is HMRC's view that capital can be appointed to someone else on the termination of the trust only if it can be demonstrated that it is for the benefit of A?

HMRC Answer

No—we do not consider that that condition is in point.

Otherwise why does s 89A(3) Condition 2 refer to other persons at all?

HMRC Answer

We do not agree with the proposition that there is a conflict between s 89A(2) and (3). Condition 1 refers to the application of "settled property"—ie to property that is held on the trusts referred to in s 89A(1)(c). Condition 2, however, is applying conditions that are effective in the event of such trusts being brought to an end.

G GENERAL POINTS

34. Question 37(1)

New sections 46A(4) and 46B(5) provide that additions (by way of payment of further premiums) to a pre-Budget interest in possession or A&M trust which holds an insurance policy would not result either in a chargeable transfer or in any part of the trust falling within the relevant property regime.

It is understood that HMRC believe that additions of cash or other property to existing pre-Budget interest in possession settlements are subject to the new rules in Schedule 20.

There are other payments which are often made by settlors or beneficiaries on behalf of a trust. For example, buildings insurance premiums and general maintenance costs, payments to cover trust, administration and taxation expenses.

It is noted that for the purposes of TCGA 1992 Sch 5 para 9(3) the payment of expenses relating to administration and taxation of a trust are not be treated as the addition of property to the trust. In SP 5/92 the costs of acquiring, enhancing and disposing of a trust asset are not regarded as expenses relating to administration but other property expenses appear to fall within the definition and therefore are not treated as the addition of property to the trust. Would HMRC maintain that the addition of cash or other property to a settlement which may be used either to enhance trust property (eg payment of costs relating to the building of an extension to property) or to purchase other property will be treated as additions but accept that the payment of other trustee expenses (eg trustee fees, buildings insurance premiums and general maintenance costs) will not be treated as chargeable additions?

HMRC Answer

Schedule 5 TCGA is a statutory provision relating to certain, specific circumstances. There is no legal basis on which payments of "other trustee expenses" should not be treated as chargeable additions for IHT purposes.

Question 37(2)

If any of the additions do bring the trust within the new rules, what property within the trust will be caught and how will it be valued? For example, if an addition of cash was made which was then spent by the trustees and HMRC regard this addition as within the relevant property regime (eg an addition to pay expenses or improve properties), how would the proportion of the settled property subject to the new rules be calculated? Would a valuation be needed of the property before and after the improvement? In HMRC's view, do all subsequent post Budget additions need to be kept physically segregated?

HMRC Answer

[If a payment of cash was made and then spent immediately on, say, a tax liability or another administration expense, then that short period will be the extent of its time as "relevant property" and there will be no question of having to consider what proportion of the existing settled property represents it going forward.

If a payment was made towards the improvement of a property, then this would appear to require "with" and "without" valuations when there is a chargeable event.] *Note added 6 August 2008: HMRC have indicated that they are actively reconsidering this response with a view to producing further guidance shortly.*

It is clearly up to trustees to decide whether to keep post-Budget additions separate from the rest of the trust fund. We think that it may be sensible to do so—or, at least, to keep good records of additions. (The trustees of discretionary trusts already need to do this, of course, in order for the 10-year anniversary value of each addition to be identified correctly in light of the relief in s 66(2) IHTA for property that has not been "relevant property" for a full 10-year period).

35. Question 38

It is understood that additions to a trust which fall within the normal expenditure out of income exemption will not need to be reported as and when they are made as, following the normal rules, it is not necessary to report exempt transactions? Please confirm.

HMRC Answer

We can confirm this.

36. Question 39

It is not unknown for wills to include a gift of an annuity. Some wills give the executors sufficient powers to enable them to choose how best to satisfy the annuity. In such a case there are typically four methods which executors may use to deal with an annuity.

- Pay the annuity out of residue. In such a case the executors delay the completion of the administration of the estate until the annuitant dies.
- Create an appropriated annuity fund. In such a case the executors appropriate a capital fund of sufficient size to pay the annuity.
- Purchase an annuity. The executors purchase an annuity from an insurance office or life company.
- Commute the annuity. The executors pay the annuitant a cash sum sufficient to allow him to purchase the annuity personally.

The first two options create settled property. Will HMRC confirm that a provision in a will conferring the payment of an annuity upon a person (eg to make a gift of an annuity of £x for life) which the executors satisfy by one of the first two options outlined above will be treated as the creation of an IPDI in favour of the annuitant?

HMRC Answer

We can confirm this.

Under s 50(2), where a person is entitled to a specified amount (such as an annuity) for any period his interest is taken to subsist in that part of the property that produces that amount in that period. The property in which his interest subsists may therefore vary over time.

EXAMPLE 10

Say A is entitled to an annuity of £1,000 and the executors set aside a fund of £40,000 to pay this annuity. In year 1 the income from the £40,000 is £2,000 and half is paid to the annuitant. In year 2 the income from the £40,000 is £1,000 and all the income is paid to A. In year 3 (the year in which the annuitant dies) the income from the £40,000 is £4,000 and a quarter is paid to A. Please could HMRC confirm what property would fall within A's estate on his death (assuming he is treated as having an IPDI) and the basis upon which this has been calculated?

HMRC Answer

We would follow the existing principles set out in s 50(2) to s 50(5) IHTA at the date of A's death. (As Dymond, at 16.611, points out, s 50(2) does not give any guidance as to the period over which the income of the settled property should be computed. But the learned authors suggest that looking at the income in the year immediately before the chargeable occasion would normally be a reasonable approach and we would agree.)

H DEEDS OF VARIATION

Questions have arisen as to the effect of deeds of variation post-Budget.

37. Example 11

Testator dies pre-Budget leaving everything outright to X. His will is varied by X and an election made under s 142 to treat the variation as made by the will.

Question 40

Any trust established by the variation will be treated as having been established pre-Budget whether or not the variation is actually made pre- or post-Budget. If an interest in possession trust is established under such a variation by X, we assume it will be a qualifying interest in possession given it is deemed to be set up prior to the Budget by the deceased and not by X for inheritance tax purposes and further that it will be possible to create a transitional serial interest in relation to this trust before April 2008. Please confirm.

HMRC Answer

We can confirm this.

38. Example 12

Testator dies post-Budget leaving everything outright to Y. His will is varied to establish ongoing trusts and an election made under s 142 to read the variation back into the will.

Question 41

Assuming that the terms of the trusts are appropriate, it is possible to establish IPDIs, 18-25 trusts and BMTs by way of such a variation made by Y. Please confirm. As in question 40 it is assumed that for inheritance tax purposes the settlor is the deceased rather than Y.

HMRC Answer

We can confirm this.

39. Example 13

The testator is not domiciled in the UK at his death leaving everything outright to Z. His will dealing with property outside the UK is varied to establish trusts and an election made under s 142 to read the variation back into the will.

Question 42

Any trusts established by the variation holding non-UK property will be excluded property trusts whatever the domicile status of Z (the beneficiary making the variation) and whatever the terms of the new trusts. This will be the case whether or not the testator died pre- or post-Budget. Please confirm.

HMRC Answer

We can confirm this.

40. Section 54A IHTA contains certain anti-avoidance provisions that arise where a settlor settles assets into a qualifying interest in possession trust by PET and then the life interest is terminated so that discretionary trusts arise within 7 years. In effect the settlor rather than the life tenant can be treated as having made the chargeable transfer if this yields more tax. Section 54A(1A) states that where a person becomes beneficially entitled on or after 22 March 2006 to a disabled person's interest or a TSI, s 54(1)(b) applies. So if the disabled person or the holder of the TSI dies and relevant property trusts arise, the anti-avoidance provision potentially applies. Nothing is said though in respect of inter vivos terminations of the TSI or disabled person's interest when relevant property trusts arise and the termination occurs within 7 years of the original PET made by the settlor.

Question 43

Is it intended that s 54A should only apply to interests in possession arising on or after 22 March 2006 if the disabled person's interest or TSI terminates on death rather than inter vivos?

HMRC Answer

Section 54A applies both to lifetime terminations of a TSI or disabled person's interest where the other conditions of s 54A are satisfied as well as a termination on the death of the life tenant. The fact that s 54A(1)(A) refers expressly to death and not to lifetime terminations does not mean that s 54A did not cover both scenarios because s 54A(1) covered lifetime terminations. We believe s 54A can apply to both inter vivos and terminations on death because s 54A(1)(a) refers back to s 52, where s 52(2A) already provides that, where the person becomes beneficially entitled to the interest in possession on or after 22 March 2006, there will only be a charge under s 52(1)—and so s 54A will only potentially apply—if the interest is:

– an immediate post-death interest,
– a disabled person's interest, or
– a transitional serial interest.

DISCOUNTED GIFT SCHEMES (DGSS)

1 May 2007. *HMRC Technical Note*

BACKGROUND

Following recent press interest, this is an opportune moment to set out HMRC's approach to Discounted Gift Schemes (DGS) and their interaction with the Inheritance Tax (IHT) legislation. This note is particularly about valuation of lifetime transfers and the underlying valuation methodology. We are also taking this opportunity to set out the approach we will adopt in joint settlor cases, which, in some cases, will be more precise than that adopted up to now. It is emphasised that this note sets out HMRC's practice and is not seeking to prescribe the approach that must be taken to establish the chargeable value for IHT. Alternative approaches may be used to arrive at broadly similar results and HMRC continue to be open to considering and agreeing alternative valuation bases that achieve that aim.

HMRC has not made any fundamental change to its overall approach towards DGSs. But, as indicated at the end of this note, we are proposing to make a change to one element of the basis of valuation that we use to reflect current market conditions.

IHT TREATMENT OF DGSS

Essentially a DGS involves a gift of a bond from which a set of rights are retained, typically withdrawals or a set of successively maturing reversions. The retained rights are sufficiently well defined to preclude the gift being regarded as a gift with reservation (GWR) for IHT purposes.

The gift is a transfer of value for IHT purposes whose value is determined by the loss to the estate principle. This is set out in IHTA 1984 s 3(1), and quantified by the difference between the amount invested by the settlor and the open market value (OMV), IHTA 1984 s 160 refers, of the retained rights.

VALUATION ISSUES

The OMV of the retained rights will depend on, inter alia, the settlor's sex, age, health and thereby insurability, as at the gift date. If the settlor were to be uninsurable, for any reason, as at the gift date the OMV of the retained rights would be nominal and the gift would be close to the whole amount invested by the settlor. This is because IHTA 1984 s 160 provides that, in valuing the retained rights, we assume that a sale of them takes place.

The logic behind that premise is based upon sound open market evidence and fully endorsed by leading counsel from whom HMRC has taken advice. We have looked for evidence to sales of assets similar in nature to the retained rights, for example life interests or contingent reversions which are dependent upon the survival of the relevant life to a series of predetermined dates. This indicates that such rights are not saleable unless life assurance can be effected on that life by the open market purchaser (OMP) or it comes as part of the sale. If it cannot be effected market evidence shows that those assets will not sell. Without life cover being in place the OMP is at risk of anything up to the total loss of his investment should an early death of the settlor occur. We consider it to be fundamental that the open market valuation of the retained rights should be carried out having regard to what market evidence is available. Additionally we have been unable to find any evidence that it is possible to effect cover on lives older than 90 next birthday. HMRC therefore regard lives older than that, true or equivalent (mortality rated), as being uninsurable with the resultant ramifications in respect of the gift value.

POSITION WHERE THERE ARE JOINT SETTLORS

To date HMRC has taken a pragmatic approach to calculating the value transferred where there are joint settlors, usually husband and wife or civil partners. This approach has been to value the retained rights in their entirety and deduct this amount from the total sum invested. The value of the transfer has then been apportioned between the settlors in the proportions in which they provided the sum invested.

Example of HMRC's "old" approach—

> Husband (H) aged 80 and wife (W) aged 80 invest £100,000 equally in a DGS with monthly withdrawals of £416.67 payable until the death of the last to die of H and W.
> Open market value (OMV) of the retained rights calculated as £46,300.
> Transfer of value calculated as £100,000 – £46,300 = £53,700
> Of this, £26,850 is attributable to H and £26,850 attributable to W.

In practice, where the joint settlors are of similar ages and in similar states of health the results of this pragmatic approach do not differ dramatically from the results where the value of each settlor's retained rights are considered individually.

Following the changes brought about by the FA 2006, HMRC has seen a number of cases where DGSs have been taken out where there is a significant age difference between the joint settlors or where one of the joint settlors is in very poor health or even uninsurable. In such cases the pragmatic approach does not achieve a reasonable result. We have also been asked to clarify the correct method of valuation in these circumstances as different providers are calculating the transfer values using different methods, resulting in a lack of consistency. This also means that taxpayers and their advisers are unclear as to which approach is correct. In the light of this uncertainty we are setting out below what we consider to be the correct valuation approach. We intend to follow this approach for all DGSs where the transfer takes place after 1 June 2007. We will also use this method where a transfer has taken place before that date and the pragmatic approach would provide an unreasonable valuation of the settlor's retained rights and substantial sums are involved.

In HMRC's view, the correct approach is to value the retained rights in their entirety and to apportion this value between the joint settlors by reference to the OMV of each settlor's retained rights. In the case of joint settlors who are married or in a civil partnership, the related property provisions of s. 161 IHTA are to be taken into account in this valuation. The application of s. 161 IHTA has been considered in some detail in *Arkwright and anor v IRC* [2004] EWHC 1720 (Ch) STC 2004 p1323.

The impact of this on the above example is as follows—

OMV of H's retained rights = £16,400
OMV of W's retained rights = £19,900
OMV of the total retained rights = £46,300
(The calculations of retained rights reflect the age, state of health and insurability of H and W respectively.)
The OMV of H's retained rights, calculated in accordance with IHTA 1984 s 161 is—
£16,400 / (£16,400 + £19,900) × £46,300 = £20,900
The OMV of W's retained rights, calculated in accordance with IHTA 1984 s 161 is—
£19,900 / (£16,400 + £19,900) × £46,300 = £25,400
So the values transferred by H and W are—
Value transferred by H = £50,000—£20,900 = £29,100
So the values transferred by H and W are—
Value transferred by H = £50,000—£20,900 = £29,100
Value transferred by W = £50,000—£25,400 = £24,600

It is recognised that where there are significant differences in the ages of the settlors (whether their actual ages or their effective ages for insurance purposes) it is technically possible for the value of the retained rights to be calculated as a negative amount using the above approach. It is also technically possible to calculate the value of the retained rights as exceeding the contribution of the settlor. The value of the lifetime transfer is calculated, in accordance with IHTA 1984 s 3(1), as the loss to the transferor's estate. If the value of the retained rights is negative the loss to the transferor's estate cannot exceed the amount contributed, i.e. there cannot be a negative "discount". If the value of the retained rights exceeds the settlor's contribution, there would be no loss to the estate and therefore no transfer of value.

We do not propose to re-open cases where the values transferred have been accepted in accordance with our previously adopted approach.

UNDERWRITING APPROACH

As far as DGS contracts are concerned, it is clear that insurance companies adopt differing practices with regard to underwriting the settlor's life ranging from no underwriting through the so-called "sealed-envelope" to full underwriting. HMRC's preference is that full underwriting should be carried out prior to the DGS being effected.

The open-market based valuation method requires that evidence of the settlor's health exists at the transfer date that is sufficient for the settlor's life to be underwritten to the standards required for whole of life assurance. If no evidence of health has been obtained at the outset, HMRC take the view that a discount is not justified unless medical evidence sufficient to underwrite the settlor's life to the standards required for whole of life assurance was already in existence and can be produced, should it be necessary to quantify the gift at a later date.

HMRC adopt this stance because problems can and do arise if no evidence of health has been obtained at the outset and therefore is not reflected in the estimate of the value of the gift. On the death of a settlor, for example, where no evidence has been obtained HMRC will often need to ask the settlor's personal representatives to obtain evidence about the settlor's health at the time the gift was made. We recognise that this is undesirable as the surviving family may face intrusive and upsetting enquiries at a difficult time. This can be avoided if the information is obtained in advance. Problems also arise where medical evidence is not collected until after the transfer occurs and it then becomes apparent that up to date medical details are not held. This would be insufficient evidence on which to underwrite to the standards required for whole of life assurance and would therefore result in no discount. Additionally survivors may not have been party to the transaction entered into by the settlor. They may feel entitled to particular treatment based on expectations given by financial advisors and then feel aggrieved when HMRC begin investigating.

HMRC'S CURRENT BASIS OF VALUATION

The retained rights fall to be valued on an open market basis in accordance with IHTA 1984 s 160. In investing in the retained rights the open market purchaser (OMP) will need to take account of the rate of return he requires and the cost of insuring the settlor(s) life.

The annual amount to be paid under the retained rights, net of any income tax liability that the purchaser may suffer, is multiplied by a purchase factor generated from a suitable formula eg a Jellicoe formula (see for example "Actuarial Valuations of Interests in Settled Property" Beard FIA & Prevett FIA Institute of Actuaries 1973 page 15).

$1 - p / p + i$ where—
p is the annual premium expressed as a decimal; and
i is the OMP's rate of return also expressed as a decimal.

The present value of the retained rights is arrived at from the product of the net annual amount of the retained rights and the purchase factor. The OMV is 97% of that present value (rounded to the nearest £50) to reflect the OMP's costs of say 3%.

As mentioned at the start of this note, the aim is to set out HMRC's practice, not to prescribe the approach that must be taken to establish the chargeable value for IHT. Alternative approaches may be used to arrive at broadly similar results and HMRC continue to be open to considering and agreeing alternative valuation bases that achieve that aim. HMRC's current mortality and interest rate basis is—

– Mortality: 70% of AM / AF 80 Mortality (reflecting the improvement over the table for assured lives for males and females published by the Continuous Mortality Investigation Bureau in 1990 reference CMIR 10)
– Interest rate: 5.25% pa
– Open market purchaser's costs: 3% (as a deduction from the present value of the retained rights).

HMRC has recently reviewed its interest rate basis. In the light of recent rises in interest rates, HMRC are proposing to change that basis with effect from 1 June 2007 when a valuation rate of interest of 6% pa will be adopted [see note below]. Our analysis indicates clearly that such a rise in that rate is warranted and reintroduces the differential over base rate and corresponds to a 1% differential over short term Gilts as at 2 April 2007. The valuation basis is kept under review to ensure that it continues to reflect open market conditions. It is our intention to publish details of any future changes to our valuation basis on the HMRC website.

Any enquiries concerning this note should be directed to—

– Ian Hempstead, Assistant Actuarial Officer—Charity, Assets & Residence Actuarial Group, Ferrers House, PO Box 38, Castle Meadow Road, Nottingham, NG2 1BB. Telephone 0115 974 2939
– P Oxlade, Board's Actuarial Officer—Charity, Assets & Residence Actuarial Group, Ferrers House, PO Box 38, Castle Meadow Road, Nottingham, NG2 1BB. Telephone 0115 974 2950.

Note—HMRC have since announced (on 20 July 2007) a proposal to increase the valuation rate of interest used in connection with valuing the retained rights under discounted gift schemes to 6.75% from 1st September 2007. This returns the differential over short term Gilts to 1% as at 13th July 2007.

FINANCE ACT 2006 SCHEDULE 20: PRE-EXISTING INTERESTS IN POSSESSION AND RELATED MATTERS

8 May 2007. *CIOT/STEP letter.*

(*Response received from HMRC on 29 May 2007. This exchange represents HMRC's further views on the transitional serial interest regime*).

We are writing about a number of situations (set out in the questions below) where a person (A) was beneficially entitled to an interest in possession in settled property before 22 March 2006. Doubt has been expressed as to whether section 49(1) of the Inheritance Tax Act 1984 will continue to apply in the future, notwithstanding that A will throughout be entitled to the income of the settled property. We consider that, in all those situations, section 49(1) will continue to apply, notwithstanding section 49(1A) which (with exceptions) disapplies that sub-section where the interest in possession is one to which a person becomes beneficially entitled on or after 22 March 2006.

It has been suggested that A will, after that date, become entitled to a different proprietary interest in the settled property. As the Revenue argued in *Pearson v IRC* [1981] AC 753, and all the members of the House of Lords appear to have accepted, for inheritance tax purposes the expression "interest in possession" must be construed as a single phrase. Pearson decided that it means a present right to present enjoyment of the settled property, ie the right to the income from that property as it arises. And in each of the relevant situations, A became entitled to that right before 22 March 2006. Section 49(1A) does not, therefore, in our view, apply.

If we are right about this, then it means that the IHT treatment of the relevant situations will not depend on the accident of the particular drafting technique adopted, with settlements being treated differently notwithstanding that A's rights are the same and without any possible policy justification that we have been able to identify.

We would emphasise that, in each of the examples below, the trustees have not exercised any dispositive powers post-March 2006: the interest taken by A remains throughout merely an entitlement to income and, moreover, an entitlement which is defined under the terms of the settlement prior to March 2006.

We hope that you will be able to confirm that section 49(1) will continue to apply and, therefore, that the same pre-Budget interest in possession will continue to subsist in each of the following examples.

EXAMPLE 1

(1) Settled property is held on trust to pay the income to A for life contingently on A attaining the age of 25. The trust carries the intermediate income.

(2) A attained the age of 18 on 1 January 2006 and thereupon became entitled to an interest in possession by virtue of section 31 of the Trustee Act 1925. Section 49(1) applies.

In our view, it will continue to apply after age 25, when the express trust to pay income to him comes into effect. On any footing, A has only one interest, being the present right to present enjoyment, brought into possession earlier than would otherwise be the case by section 31.

Question 1 – do HMRC agree?

HMRC Answer to Question 1 – yes

EXAMPLE 2

(1) Under a pre-Budget 2006 trust, A is entitled to capital contingently on attaining the age of 25 years. The clause goes on to provide that the trusts carry the intermediate income and section 31 of the Trustee Act is to apply.

(2) The same clause provides that the capital should not vest absolutely on A attaining the age of 25 but should be retained on trust:
   (a) to pay the income to A for life, and then
   (b) for A's children after A's death,

(3) A attained the age of 18 on 1 January 2006. Section 49(1) applies.

In our view, it will continue to apply after A attains the age of 25 on 1 January 2013, when the "engrafted" trust to pay income to A comes into effect.

Question 2 – do HMRC agree?

HMRC Answer to Question 2 – yes

EXAMPLE 3

The facts are the same as example 3, except that the engrafted trusts are contained in a separate clause. In our view, the position is the same, and section 49(1) will continue to apply after A attains the age of 25.

Question 3 – do HMRC agree?

HMRC Answer to Question 3 – yes

EXAMPLE 4

(1) A became entitled to income at 25 in January 2006 and section 49(1) applies.

(2) A is contingently entitled to capital at the age of 35, but the trustees retain overriding powers of appointment exercisable during his lifetime. He therefore attains only a defeasible interest in capital in 2016, and the capital remains settled property until his death.

(3) In our view, section 49(1) will continue to apply after A attains the age of 35, notwithstanding that his contingent interest in capital is replaced by a vested but defeasible interest in capital.

Question 4 – do HMRC agree?

HMRC Answer to question 4 – yes

EXAMPLE 5

Presumably, where a transitional serial interest (TSI) arose after 21 March 2006 but before 6 April 2008 (eg a pre-22 March 06 Budget life tenant's interest was ended in 2007 and A the new life tenant takes an immediate interest in possession and capital at 35 but that capital entitlement is defeasible being subject to any exercise of the overriding powers), HMRC would agree that section 49C continues to apply to A after he attains the age of 35 for the same reasons, ie that his transitional serial interest entitlement continues following his 35th birthday.

Question 5 – do HMRC agree?

HMRC Answer to Question 5 – yes

In all the above examples, A's interest arises under the terms of the Settlement, and not from the exercise of the trustees' powers. We think these examples can be distinguished from the case where a beneficiary is absolutely entitled to capital on reaching a specified age and the trustees positively exercise their powers to defer that absolute entitlement and maintain the interest in possession, where we understand that different issues may arise as set out in the previous reply to queries on Schedule 20 – see questions revised in April 2007 and in particular Question 6

HMRC Answer — agreed

INTEREST IN POSSESSION WHICH CONTINUES AFTER DEATH OF LIFE TENANT

In some circumstances, an interest in possession may continue after the death of the person entitled to the interest up until their death. HMRC have confirmed that a lifetime assignment of an interest in possession will qualify as a TSI (assuming the other requirements are satisfied — Question 10 of Schedule 20 letter) on the basis that the interest in possession will have "come to an end" within the meaning of section 49C(3), presumably on the basis of IHTA section 51(1). There is no equivalent provision to IHTA section 51(1) in relation to transfers on death of an autre vie, but the entitlement of the prior beneficiary who is holding an interest pur autre vie will have come to an end, even though the interest itself will not have done so. This may arise, for example, where the will of the deceased life tenant leaves their residuary estate, which would include their remaining entitlement to the interest pur autre vie, to their surviving spouse.

Question 6

Do HMRC consider that, when a pre-Budget interest in possession beneficiary who holds the pur autre vie dies, any interest in possession in such property then taken by his spouse (or any other person if that occurs before 6 April 2008) will qualify as a transitional serial interest?

HMRC Answer to Question 6—Yes. In the circumstances outlined, it would seem that the death of the beneficiary holding a pur autre vie interest must bring "the prior interest" within the terms of s 49C IHTA to an end.

IHTA 1984 SECTION 46B

We should be grateful if you would confirm your view in relation to pre-Budget 2006 settled life policies, where a policy is held on section 71 accumulation and maintenance trusts and the trusts are then converted into trusts within section 71D IHTA. Insurance premiums continue to be paid on the policy.

It is clear that the continued payment of the insurance premiums will be potentially exempt transfers under section 46B(5).

Question 7

Are the added rights arising from the payment of the premiums settled property within section 71D, or are they separate settled property which is within the relevant property regime?

There is no equivalent provision in relation to section 71D trusts to section 46B(2), which applies for section 71 trusts where premiums continue to be paid on or after 22 March 2006. Section 46B(2) provides that the rights arising by reference to the payment of the further premiums shall also be within section 71 if they would be but for section 71(1A).

The rights arising from the payment of premiums on policies held on trusts where the payments are made after such trust has been converted to section 71D status do not appear to be strictly within section 71D(3), which is necessary for those rights to be held on trusts within section 71D. Section 46B(1) in relation to section 71 trusts refers to sections 46B(2) and (5), but section 46B(3) in relation to section 71D trusts only refers to section 46B(5).

Do HMRC accept that the policy held on section 71D trusts is, in reality, the same asset as that previously held on section 71 trusts and that, in effect, no new rights become comprised in the settlement so that all the policy and its proceeds would be within section 71D?

We would be grateful for HMRC's views on this.

HMRC Answer to question 7 – we do accept that any added rights from the payment of additional premiums would constitute settled property within s 71D. If a premium paid once the policy has become property to which s 71D applies gives rise to an addition to the settled property the addition will, in our view, automatically become property to which s 71D applies.

SECTION 200

Finally, we note that, under section 200(1)(c), a person with a non-qualifying interest in possession can become personally liable for the tax charged on death, with his liability limited only by reference to the value of the settled property (not the value of his actuarial interest). This seems a somewhat draconian provision, given that the beneficiary is no longer treated as beneficially entitled to the capital. Surely the liability should be limited to the property or income he actually receives? Similarly, in section 201(1)(*b*), the liability seems anomalous, given that most interests in possession will now be non-qualifying. Why should a beneficiary with a non-qualifying interest in possession have a greater personal liability than a discretionary beneficiary? Can we press for these sections to be reviewed?

HMRC Answer – we do not accept that there is an anomaly here. Although an IIP holder whose interest arose before 22.3.06 has been regarded as owning the underlying property for inheritance tax purposes, in reality he has only ever owned a limited interest. The FA 2006 changes do not alter the IIP owner's real position.

GUIDANCE ON TRANSFER OF NIL-RATE BAND

12 October 2007. *HMRC Guidance Note*

1. In his Pre-Budget Report, the Chancellor of the Exchequer announced that from 9th October 2007, it will be possible for spouses and civil partners to transfer their nil-rate band allowances so that any part of the nil-rate band that was not used when the first spouse or civil partner died can be transferred to the individual's surviving spouse or civil partner for use on their death.

2. HMRC will issue more detailed guidance shortly; what follows explains the basics of the scheme. Detailed guidance on other aspects of the IHT rules is available from the HMRC website as usual and should be read in conjunction with this document.

COMMENCEMENT

3. The transferable allowance will be available to all survivors of a marriage or civil partnership who die on or after 9th October 2007, no matter when the first partner died/dies.

4. The claim to transfer unused nil-rate band must be made by the accountable persons when the surviving spouse or civil partner dies and not when the first spouse or civil partner dies. So if you are dealing with the estate of the first spouse or civil partner to die, there is nothing you need do now in terms of making a claim. However you will need to record the proportion of the nil-rate band that goes unused, and the detailed guidance will explain what sort of records will need to be kept in order to support a claim when the surviving spouse or civil partner dies.

5. If you are dealing with the estate of the surviving spouse or civil partner, you can make a claim to transfer the unused nil-rate band from the estate of the first spouse or civil partner to die. To make a claim, you will need to fill in a claim form, which will be available from the HMRC website shortly.

6. The form will ask for information about the estate of the first spouse or civil partner to die that is necessary to calculate the amount of the nil-rate band that was unused. You can then calculate the extent to which the nil-rate band available to the survivor may be increased (see paragraph 9 below) and use that revised nil-rate band to calculate the inheritance tax payable on the survivor's estate.

7. You should send the form to HMRC, together with the documents requested (for example, the death certificate of the first spouse or civil partner to die, a copy of their Will and the marriage certificate) at the same time as you send form IHT200 for the estate of the survivor to HMRC.

8. The increased nil-rate band does not replace the single nil-rate band available to the survivor that determines whether or not their estate is an excepted estate (see paragraph 17 below).

HOW THE TRANSFER WILL WORK

9. Where a valid claim to transfer unused nil-rate band is made, the nil-rate band that is available when the surviving spouse or civil partner dies will be increased by the proportion of the nil-rate band unused on the first death. For example, if on the first death the chargeable estate is £150,000 and the nil-rate band is £300,000, 50% of the nil-rate band would be unused. If the nil-rate band when the survivor dies is £325,000, then that would be increased by 50% to £487,500.

10. The amount of the nil-rate band that can be transferred does not depend on the value of the first spouse or civil partner's estate. Whatever proportion of the nil-rate band is unused on the first death is available for transfer to the survivor.

11. It is important to remember that even if all the assets passing under the Will are left to the surviving spouse or civil partner, there may be other components of the aggregate chargeable "estate" on death for IHT purposes (such as assets in trust, or gifts to other people made within 7 years of death). If present, these may use up some or all of the nil-rate band in the normal way, and so reduce the amount of unused nil-rate band that may be available for transfer.

12. The rules apply in the same way whether the first spouse or civil partner to die leaves a Will or dies intestate.

13. The rules allow unused nil-rate band to be transferred from more than one deceased spouse or civil partner, up to a limit of one additional nil-rate band. So if someone has survived more than one spouse or civil partner, then on their death the accountable persons may be able to claim additional nil-rate band from more than one of the relevant estates. A separate claim form should be completed for each spouse or civil partner who died before the deceased. However the total additional nil-rate band accumulated for this purpose is limited to a maximum of the amount of the nil-rate band in force at the relevant time. Below are some examples showing how the scheme works.

EXISTING WILLS

14. The new rules will not change the effect of existing Wills. So people who have, for example, a nil-rate band trust written into their Will do not have to take any action as a result of this

measure. But if someone wants to change their Will to take account of the new rules, that change can usually be made by a Codicil, rather than having to rewrite the Will.

15. Where someone dies after 9th October 2007 with a nil-rate band discretionary trust in their Will, an appointment of the trust assets in favour of the surviving spouse or civil partner (before the second anniversary of the death, but not within the three months immediately following the death) would normally be treated for IHT purposes as if the assets had simply been left to the surviving spouse or civil partner outright. Ending the trust in this way would mean that the nil-rate band was not used on the first death, and so the amount available for eventual transfer to the surviving spouse or civil partner would be increased accordingly.

IMMEDIATE POST DEATH INTERESTS

16. Where individuals leave assets on trust with a life interest for their surviving spouse or civil partner, with the remainder passing on their spouse or civil partner's death to someone else (for example their children), there is no IHT to pay on the first death because spouse or civil partner exemption applies. So if the entire estate is left in trust to the surviving spouse or civil partner, the nil-rate band would be available for transfer to the estate of the survivor on their eventual death in the same way as if the estate had been left to them absolutely.

LINK WITH REPORTING "EXCEPTED ESTATES"

17. Any additional nil-rate band is only relevant in establishing whether or not any tax is payable on the estate of the survivor – it does not replace the individual nil-rate band amount that determines the excepted estate limit for reporting purposes. If when the survivor dies, their gross estate exceeds the individual nil-rate band amount applicable at the time of their death, the estate cannot qualify as an excepted estate. The accountable persons will still need to deliver form IHT200 and make their claim for the transferable nil-rate band on the death of the survivor.

FIRST DEATH BEFORE 18 MARCH 1986

18. Inheritance tax was introduced with effect from 18 March 1986, but before this date other estate taxes (Capital Transfer Tax and Estate Duty) applied. Where a surviving spouse dies on or after 9 October 2007 and their spouse died before the introduction of the current inheritance tax provisions, a claim may still be made for the nil-rate band of the surviving spouse to be increased by reference to unused allowances of their spouse.

19. Where the first spouse died between 13 March 1975 and18 March 1986 then the estate would have been subject to Capital Transfer Tax. Any transfers to the spouse would have been exempt from tax in the same way as the under the current rules. The transfer of nil-rate band provisions will operate in these cases in the same way as it works for inheritance tax. So that if on the death of the first spouse all their estate was transferred to their surviving spouse, then a claim may be made on the death of the surviving spouse to in-crease the nil-rate band by 100%.

20. Before 13 March 1975 Estate Duty applied. Under Estate Duty there was no tax-free transfer permitted between spouses until 21 March 1972 when a tax-free transfer between spouses of up to £15,000 was introduced.

21. Where the first spouse died between 21 March 1972 and 13 March 1975 a claim to transfer the nil-rate band to the surviving spouse will be based on the amount of the tax-free band that was unused on the death of the first spouse. For example, a husband died in 1973 and left an estate valued at £10,000, which was all transferred to his wife. As this was all within the spouse's exemption, the individual tax-free band was unused. In this case the full amount of that allowance may be transferred, and a claim may be made on the death of the surviving spouse to increase the nil-rate band by 100%.

22. Where any part of the first spouse's individual tax-free band was used then there will be a proportionate reduction in the amount by which the nil-rate band of the surviving spouse may be increased.

23. Similarly, where the first spouse died before 21 March 1972 the transfer of nil-rate band will be based on the proportion of the individual tax-free band that was unused on the death of the first spouse. However, as there was no relief from Estate Duty for transfers to spouses, any transfer made on the death of the first spouse will use up part of the tax-free band and so reduce the amount by which the nil-rate band of the surviving spouse may be increased.

24. HMRC will shortly publish details of the tax-free bands that applied for Estate Duty and Capital Transfer Taxes. But if you need this information in the meantime, please contact the Inheritance Tax & Probate Helpline on 0845 3020900.

25. Examples of how the new rules will work:

A. A dies on 14 April 2007 with an estate of £400,000, which he leaves entirely to his spouse, B. B dies on 17 June 2009 leaving an estate of £600,000 equally between her two children. When B dies the nil-rate band is £325,000. As 100% of A's nil-rate band was unused, the nil-rate band on B's death is doubled to £650,000. As B's estate is £600,000 there is no IHT to pay on B's death.
B. J dies on 27 May 2007, with an estate of £300,000. She leaves legacies of £40,000 to each of her three children with the remainder to her spouse K. The nil-rate band when J dies is £300,000. K dies on 15 September 2009 leaving his estate of £500,000 equally to his three children; the nil-rate band when K dies is £325,000. J used up 40% of her nil-rate band when she died, which means 60% is available to transfer to K on his death. So K's nil-rate band of £325,000 is increased by 60% to £520,000. As K's estate is only £500,000 there is no IHT to pay on K's death.
C. R dies on 14 April 2007 with an estate of £450,000, which he leaves entirely to his spouse, S. S dies on 17 June 2009 leaving an estate of £675,000 which she leaves equally between her two children. When S dies the nil-rate band is £325,000. As 100% of R's nil-rate band was unused, the nil-rate band on S's death is doubled to £650,000. This leaves £25,000 chargeable to IHT on S's death.
D. X dies on 14 April 2007 with an estate of £250,000, leaving £120,000 to his son Y and the remainder to his spouse Z. The nil-rate band when X dies is £300,000 so 60% of his nil-rate band is unused. Z later marries W who dies on 14 May 2008 and also leaves 60% of his nil-rate band unused. Z dies on 14 June 2009 with an estate of £700,000 when the individual nil-rate band is £325,000. Z's nil-rate band is increased to reflect the transfer from X and W, but the amount of increase is limited to 100% of the nil-rate band in force at the time. So Z's nil-rate band is £650,000, leaving £50,000 chargeable to IHT on Z's death.

INHERITANCE TAX AND THE VALUATION OF PROPERTY OWNED JOINTLY BY SPOUSES OR CIVIL PARTNERS

28 November 2007. *HMRC Brief 71/07*

BACKGROUND

In general terms Section 161 Inheritance Tax Act 1984 provides that, when valuing a share of property for inheritance tax where the spouse or civil partner also has an interest in the same property, the spouse's or civil partner's interest is taken into account. The effect is broadly to reduce the level of discount that smaller, un-aggregated shares of property can attract when valued. The precise basis on which this is done was the subject of litigation during 2004 and resulted in the High Court decision *Arkwright and another v IRC* [2004] EWHC 1720 (Ch).

The appeal had earlier been considered by the Special Commissioners who found that the Revenue could not rely on section 161(4) in the case of incorporeal shares of land. Section 161(4) requires the aggregate value to be apportioned in accordance with the proportion the smaller number of shares are held to the total held by both spouses/civil partners. The Special Commissioner found that whilst the measure could apply to property which had a distinct or individual existence as a unit, such as unit trusts or a set of furniture (for example twelve dining chairs), it did not apply to fractions of units. The Revenue did not pursue this point when its appeal was heard by the High Court.

HMRC TREATMENT OF EXISTING AND FUTURE CASES

The High Court decided that the question of the open market valuation was, in the absence of agreement between HMRC and the personal representatives, a matter for the Lands Tribunal.

In the course of seeking to reach agreement HMRC has received legal advice that section 161(4) may, in fact, apply to fractional shares of units.

Future cases

Accordingly, HMRC will apply section 161(4) when valuing shares of land as related property in any inheritance tax case where the account is received by HMRC after the publication date of this Brief. We will consider litigation in appropriate cases.

Existing cases

It is now not possible to have further judicial consideration of the section 161(4) point in the context of the Arkwright decision. Any existing cases in which section 161(4) is considered in point will therefore be dealt with on the basis of the Special Commissioners' decision in the Arkwright case as it relates to the interpretation of section 161(4).

HMRC will, when so requested, also reconsider any cases involving land valuations which were concluded after the Arkwright decision was handed down on 16 July 2004 and determined on the basis that section 161(4) applied.

If you believe a valuation was concluded on this basis and wish to have the matter reconsidered, you should write to—

HMRC Inheritance Tax
Ferrers House
PO Box 38
Castle Meadow Road
Nottingham NG2 1BB

Please state the name of the deceased, transferor or settlement and quote the official reference. To assist us, please also refer to this Brief in the heading to your letter.

DISCOUNTED GIFTS SCHEMES

We will review the guidance we give about valuation of joint settlor schemes in the Technical Note and make appropriate changes in the light of any future developments. Until then we will continue to value schemes on the basis of the guidance in the note.

Commentary—*Simon's Taxes* **I8.242A.**

INHERITANCE TAX AND VALUATION OF GIFTS INVOLVING A DISCOUNTED GIFT SCHEME

11 April 2008. *HMRC Brief 23/08*

HM Revenue & Customs (HMRC) has given notice of appeal to the High Court against the decision of Special Commissioner in the case of the Executors of the Estate of Mrs Marjorie Edna Bower (deceased) and the Commissioners for HMRC (SpC 665).

This brief sets out how, pending the outcome of the appeal, HMRC will deal with cases involving a gift for Inheritance Tax (IHT) purposes involving a Discounted Gift Scheme (DGS) where the settlor is older than 90 next birthday (actual or deemed) or is considered to be uninsurable as at the date of the gift. HMRC published a Technical Note in May 2007 confirming its long held practice.

When an IHT chargeable event arises, the value of any gift element of a DGS is considered by the Actuarial Team of HMRC. Open cases already being considered by the Actuarial Team will remain under review pending the outcome of the current litigation.

New cases will continue to be dealt with in accordance with the May 2007 Technical Note. Where the Actuarial Team consider (in calculating the value of the gift element) that the value of retained rights is only nominal (because of age of the donor or because the donor is considered to be uninsurable) we will advise those liable for the IHT accordingly, explain that we will not press for payment of the additional IHT for the time being, and suggest they consider putting an appropriate sum on account to stop (further) interest accruing on any IHT due.

This will enable cases to be progressed as far as possible pending the final outcome of the litigation, while safeguarding the position of taxpayers.

If you have any questions related to this matter please refer them to:

Phil Oxlade
Board's Actuarial Officer
Charity, Assets and Residency Actuarial Group
Ferrers House
PO Box 38
Castle Meadow Road Nottingham NG2 1BB
Tel 0115 974 2950

Note—See HMRC Brief 21/09, 2-4-09 (High Court finds in HMRC's favour at appeal on 5 November 2008).

EXTENSION OF NON-STATUTORY CLEARANCES SERVICE FOR HMRC BUSINESS CUSTOMERS

1 May 2008. *HMRC Brief 25/08*

WHO SHOULD READ THIS BUSINESS BRIEF?

All businesses, business owners and those acting on behalf of business.

BACKGROUND

At Budget 2006, the Chancellor of the Exchequer announced a review, led by Sir David Varney, of the relationship between large business and HMRC.

The review team consulted with over 140 large businesses and trade and representative bodies and identified four key outcomes that would benefit both large business and HMRC:

- greater certainty;
- an efficient risk based approach to dealing with tax matters;
- speedy resolution of issues;
- clarity through effective consultation and dialogue.

The "Review of Links with Large Business" report published in November 2006 outlined 14 key proposals that would together deliver these outcomes.

One of the proposals related to non-statutory clearances. A non-statutory clearance is written confirmation of our view of the application of tax law to a specific transaction or event.

At Pre-Budget Report 2007, we announced an extension of the non-statutory clearances we provide to all our business customers from April 2008. Further details on the extended non-statutory clearances service that was implemented on 1 April 2008 can be found in HMRC Brief 20/08.

Today we start a trial of a further extension of the non-statutory clearances we provide to business owners in the area of inheritance tax business property relief.

CHANGES AFFECTING BUSINESS AND BUSINESS OWNERS

From 1 May 2008, for a trial period of six months, clearances will be provided to business owners on the availability of inheritance tax business property relief (IHT-BPR) where there is material uncertainty over the interpretation of the law. For inheritance tax legislation older than the last four Finance Acts, there is a further requirement that the uncertainty relates to a commercially significant issue.

We will aim to respond to clearance applications within 28 calendar days, though in complex cases this may take longer.

As part of the extended clearances service from 1 May 2008, we will publish new guidance on IHT-BPR clearances for business owners on the HMRC website.

Guidance for businesses seeking clearances on issues other than IHT-BPR can be found on the HMRC website.

WHO DO I CONTACT?

All business owners and those acting on their behalf should send their applications relating to inheritance tax business property relief to:

IHT-BPR Clearances Team
Ferrers House
Castle Meadow Road
Nottingham NG2 1BB
Email: IHT-BPR Clearances Team

Other business clearance applications should continue to be sent to a Client Relationship Manager or the HMRC Clearances Team as set out in HMRC Brief 20/08.

Comments on the guidance and the extended service can be sent to:

Emma Bailey
Tax Administration Policy
Central Policy
100 Parliament Street SW1A 2BQ

OTHER GUIDANCE ON INFORMATION AND ADVICE

Code of Practice 10 (COP10) and Notice 700/6 "VAT rulings" will remain in place for our customers who are not covered by the new clearances process to provide guidance on how to seek information and advice from HMRC. We will be reviewing these documents over the next year to provide more consistent guidance on the information and advice available to our customers.

INHERITANCE TAX AND VALUATION OF DISCOUNTED GIFT SCHEMES

31 December 2008. *HMRC Brief 65/08*

Notice is given that the valuation rate of interest (the discount rate) will be reduced from 6.75 per cent per annum to 5.25 per cent per annum, with effect from 1 February 2009.

If you have any questions relating to this matter please refer them to:

Phil Oxlade, Board's Actuarial Officer
Charity Assets & Residence
Actuarial Group
Ferrers House
PO Box 38
Castle Meadow Road
Nottingham NG2 1BB

Commentary—*Simon's Taxes* **I8.375**.

INHERITANCE TAX AND VALUATION OF GIFTS INVOLVING DISCOUNTED GIFT SCHEMES (DGS)

2 April 2009. *HMRC Brief 21/09*

The appeal referred to in Revenue & Customs Brief 23/08 was heard on 5 November 2008. In its decision (2008) EWHC 3105 (Ch) reported at [2009] STC 510, the High Court found in favour of HM Revenue & Customs (HMRC) and the appeal is now final. The decision therefore confirms as correct the basis on which HMRC values the retained rights in DGS where the settlor is older than 90 next birthday (actual age or deemed age following underwriting) or where the settlor is considered to be uninsurable per se as at the transfer date. This means that only a nominal value is to be attributed to the retained rights and the value transferred by the gift (ie the amount given by the settlor less the nominal value of the retained rights) will extend to a sum adjacent to the whole amount invested in the scheme. Furthermore there is nothing in the Inheritance Tax legislation which allows any withdrawals actually taken between the gift date and the date of death of the settlor to be offset against the sum invested.

Now that the above case has been settled HMRC will begin to process those cases which have been on hold, as explained in Revenue & Customs Brief 23/08. In some cases, no tax has been paid, whereas in others tax has been paid on account to prevent interest accruing.

HMRC will be contacting executors and/or their agents in the near future in order to bring matters to a conclusion. Where (correct) sums have been placed on account no further Inheritance Tax should be payable and if there are no other outstanding matters clearance letters can be issued. Where no such payment on account has been made an Inheritance Tax calculation will be issued for payment of additional Inheritance Tax and interest. New cases will be dealt with in accordance with the Inheritance Tax Technical Note [see HMRC website] published in May 2007 in the light of the High Court decision.

Any questions related to this brief should be sent to:

Phil Oxlade
Board's Actuarial Officer
Charity, Assets and Residency Actuarial Group
Ferrers House
PO Box 38
Castle Meadow Road Nottingham NG2 1BB
Tel 0115 974 2950
Tel: 0115 974 2950

Commentary—*Simon's Taxes* **I8.375.**

BRADFORD & BINGLEY SHARES: INHERITANCE TAX RELIEF: Q&AS

2 April 2009. *HMRC Guidance Note*

Where an individual died in the period 29 September 2007 to 28 September 2008 (inclusive) owning shares in Bradford & Bingley, and the shares were subsequently taken into public ownership before they were either sold by the personal representatives or transferred to the person(s) entitled under the deceased's will or in-testacy, then for the purposes only of section 186A Inheritance Tax Act 1984 the shares will be treated as if they had been cancelled as at 29 September 2008. And provided the other conditions of s 186A are met, a claim to relief under those provisions may be made by the appropriate person.

More information about this is given in a question and answer section.

QUESTIONS AND ANSWERS

Q. Who does this apply to?

A. It applies potentially to the personal representatives of estates where

- The deceased died in the 12 months prior to 29 September 2008; and
- The deceased owned shares in Bradford & Bingley when they died; and
- The personal representatives still held the shares when they were taken into public ownership on 29 September 2008.

Q. How am I, as executor of such an estate, affected?

A. The treatment effectively means that for the purpose of making a claim for IHT "loss on sale" relief, a holding of Bradford & Bingley shares can be treated as if they had been sold for £1.

Q. Does that mean I'm due a refund of IHT?

A. That depends on whether there is a net loss from all the sales of qualifying shares (ie shares listed on a recognised stock exchange) by the personal representatives including the deemed loss on transfer of the Bradford & Bingley shares.

Q. How does the "loss on sale" relief work?

A. If qualifying shares (shares listed on a recognised stock exchange) are sold (or can be treated as sold) within one year of the date of death for less than the value on which IHT was paid, you may be able to claim relief for loss on sale of shares using form IHT35 (www.hmrc.gov.uk/cto/forms/iht35.pdf). Full instructions for making the claim are given on the form.

Q. The concessionary treatment would have applied except that I actually sold the Bradford & Bingley shares before 29 September 2008: can I substitute the £1 deemed sale proceeds for the actual sale proceeds?

A. No. If you had already sold the shares before 29 September 2008, you must use the actual sale proceeds when you are completing the IHT35 claim form.

Q. Why does the concessionary treatment apply only where the deceased died within the 12 months prior to 29 September 2008?

A. Where the deceased died more than 12 months before 29 September 2008, the full 12 month period during which the "loss on sale" relief applies will have expired before Bradford & Bingley shares were taken into public ownership. And where the deceased died on or after 29 September 2008, the estate of the deceased will not include shares in Bradford & Bingley, but a right to compensation.

Q. Will the IHT "loss on sale" relief calculation be revised once the Bradford & Bingley compensation has been fixed?

A. No.

Q. Will HMRC be reviewing their records to ascertain which estates contained holdings of Bradford & Bingley shares?

A. HMRC's records do not enable estates that included a holding of Bradford & Bingley shares to be identified. So Personal Representatives will need to apply for relief on form IHT 35, as stated above.

Q. I have already claimed "loss on sale" relief for sales of other qualifying shares and received an IHT refund. Can I now make a claim for the Bradford & Bingley shares?

A. Yes (assuming of course that the Bradford & Bingley shares were still held by the personal representatives immediately before 29 September 2008). You should use the IHT 35, as stated above.

Q. Following the Treasury's acquisition of Bradford & Bingley shares, I made a claim for relief, which HMRC rejected because the shares had not actually been sold. Will HMRC automatically review my case?

A. HMRC's records do not enable cases where a claim may have been made in respect of Bradford & Bingley shares, and rejected, to be identified. So you should write to the HMRC Inheritance Tax office that dealt with the original claim and ask for the claim to be reviewed.

If you have any further queries, you should contact the IHT and Probate helpline on 0845 30 20 900.

INHERITANCE TAX ON CONTRIBUTIONS TO EMPLOYEE BENEFIT TRUSTS

14 August 2009 *HMRC Brief 61/09*

The purpose of this note is to set out HM Revenue & Customs (HMRC) current view on the inheritance tax position in relation to contributions to an Employee Benefit Trust. Although the same principles apply where an individual makes a contribution to an Employee Benefit Trust the main thrust of this note is aimed at the more common scenario where the contribution is made by a close company as defined in s 102(1). All statutory references are to IHTA 1984 unless otherwise stated.

Employee Benefit Trust within s 86

For the purposes of this note it is assumed that the Employee Benefit Trust satisfies the provisions of s 86 that is, essentially the trust is one where the funds are held at the trustees' discretion to be applied for the benefit of "all or most of the persons employed by or holding office with the body concerned" (s 86(3)(a)).

Impact of section 13 on whether the contribution is a transfer of value

The effect of s 13 is that an inheritance tax charge arises under s 94 on contributions to an Employee Benefit Trust made by a close company where:

- the contribution is to an Employee Benefit Trust which satisfies s 86;
- the participators (as defined in s 102(1)) in that company and any person connected with them are not excluded from benefit under the terms of the Employee Benefit Trust (so that s 13(2) disapplies s 13(1)); and
- the contributions are not allowable in computing the company's profits for Corporation Tax purposes (s 12) and/or it is not shown for the purposes of s10 that the contributions are made in arms-length transactions not intended to confer a gratuitous benefit.

Participators excluded from benefit

Where the trust deed specifically purports to exclude the participators from benefit but nevertheless the participators do benefit in fact for example:

- by payment to them of loans; or
- by assigning funds from the Employee Benefit Trust on sub-trusts for their benefit and that of their family.

Then HMRC take the view that s 13(2) disapplies s 13(1) and the inheritance tax charge under s 94 arises because the funds have been applied for the benefit of the participators.

Impact of MacDonald (HMIT) v Dextra ("Dextra") [2005] STC 1111

This decision applies to contributions made before 27 November 2002. In that case, the trust deed gave the trustee wide discretion to pay money and other benefits to beneficiaries and power to lend them money. The potential beneficiaries of the trust included past present and future employees and officers of the participating companies in the Dextra group and their close relatives and dependants. The trustee did not make payments of emoluments out of the funds in the Employee Benefit Trust during the periods concerned, instead the trustee made loans to various individuals who were beneficiaries under the terms of the Employee Benefit Trust.

The point at issue was whether the company's contributions to the Employee Benefit Trust were "potential emoluments" within the meaning of FA 1989 s 43(11)(a) being amounts "held by an intermediary with a view to their becoming relevant emoluments".

The House of Lords held that the contributions by the company to the Employee Benefit Trust were potential emoluments as there was a "realistic possibility" that the trustee would use the trust funds to pay emoluments. This meant that the company's deductions were restricted. The company could only have a deduction for the amount of emoluments paid by the trustee within nine months of the end of the period of account for which the deduction would otherwise be due. Instead relief for the amount disallowed would be given in the period of accounting in which emoluments were paid.

Sch 24 FA 2003

This statute applies to contributions made after 27 November 2002.

Section 143 and Schedule 24 Finance Act 2003 prevents a deduction for Corporation Tax purposes until the contribution made for employee benefits is spent by a payment that has been subjected to both PAYE and National Insurance contributions. Thus the position already established in Dextra is therefore effectively formalised by legislation for events on or after 27 November 2002.

Dispositions allowable in computing profits for corporation tax purposes – S 12

HMRC take the view that there is nothing in s 12 that enables its relieving effect to be given provisionally while waiting to see whether the contribution will become allowable for corporation tax purposes. A deduction in the corporation tax accounts can be permanently disallowed by the following:

- capital expenditure disallowed by s 74(1)(f) ICTA1988.
- expenditure not wholly and exclusively incurred by s 74(1)(a) ICTA.

Also the timing of a deduction can be deferred to a later period by the following:

- generally accepted accounting practice (UITF13 and UITF32) which capitalises Employee Benefit Trust contributions by showing them as an asset on the company's balance sheet until and to the extent that the assets transferred to the intermediary vest unconditionally in identified beneficiaries;
- expenditure subject to s 43 FA 1989 that is, the Dextra decision – see above;
- and post 27 November 2002 expenditure subject to Sch 24 FA 2003 – see above.

It is HMRC's view that if expenditure is not allowable for any of these reasons then relief under s12 is not available. The effect of this for inheritance tax purposes is that the contribution to the Employee Benefit Trust is a chargeable transfer under s 94, assuming that participators are not excluded from benefit (s 13(2)).

Relief from the inheritance tax charge is only available under s 12(1) IHTA 1984 to the extent that a deduction is allowable to the company for the tax year in which the contribution is made.

Inheritance tax provisions on due date for tax and interest

Where, on HMRC's view of the matter, a charge to inheritance tax arises under s 94, any tax payable is due six months after the end of the month in which the contribution is made or at the end of April in the year following a contribution made between 6 April and 30 September inclusive. Interest is charged on any unpaid tax from the due date.

Does s 10 IHTA provide protection from the inheritance tax charge?

The s 10 test is a stringent one and in the view of HMRC it must be shown inter alia that there was no intent to confer any gratuitous benefit on any person. The possibility of the slightest benefit suffices to infringe the requirement. HMRC note that:

– by its very nature an Employee Benefit Trust is a discretionary trust;
– to satisfy the conditions of s 86 the trustees' absolute discretion must remain unfettered;
– the potential "beneficiaries" normally include the participators themselves, former employees and the wives husbands widows widowers and children and step children under the age of 18 of such employees and former employees contributions to an Employee Benefit Trust will often confer a gratuitous benefit on the participators.

In these circumstances, HMRC think it will normally be difficult to show that s 10 is satisfied at the date the contributions were made to the trust. HMRC take the view that it is the possibility of gratuitous intent at the date the contribution is made that we have to consider.

Charge on participators under s 94

Where a disposition is not prevented by s 13 from being a transfer of value, a charge arises under s 94 and the transfer of value is apportioned between the individual participators according to their respective rights and interest in the company immediately before the contribution to the Employee Benefit Trust giving rise to the transfer of value.

Summary

This sets out HMRC's current view. Pending the resolution of any legal challenge to this view, existing cases will be pursued by HMRC on this basis.

Corporation tax

For accounting periods ending on or after 1 April 2009:

– references to Schedule 24 Finance Act 2003 should be taken to be references to Sections 1290 to 1297 Corporation Tax Act 2009;
– references to s 74(1)(*a*) ICTA 1988 should be taken to be references to s 54 Corporation Tax Act 2009;
– references to s 74(1)(*f*) ICTA 1988 should be taken to be references to s 53 Corporation Tax Act 2009.

Income tax

For tax years 2005–06 onwards:

– references to Schedule 24 Finance Act 2003 should be taken to be references to Section 38 to 44 Income Tax (Trading and Other Income) Act 2005;
– references to s 74(1)(*a*) ICTA 1988 should be taken to be references to s 34 Income Tax (Trading and Other Income) Act 2005;
– references to s 74(1)(*f*) ICTA 1988 should be taken to be references to s 33 Income Tax (Trading and Other Income) Act 2005.

Commentary—*Simon's Taxes* **E4.1217, I6.102**.

DOMICILE AND INHERITANCE TAX

24 August 2010 *HMRC Brief 34/10*

HMRC has made changes to the circumstances in which it will consider an individual's domicile and decide whether to make a determination of inheritance tax based on that.

This Revenue & Customs Brief details changes to the circumstances in which HM Revenue & Customs (HMRC) will consider an individual's domicile and decide whether to make a determination of Inheritance Tax based on that. These changes are being made because in

HMRC experience the existing guidelines were not working well for the customer and HMRC. In future, by adopting a wider risk-based approach HMRC will ensure that resources are deployed in the most cost effective way.

Revenue & Customs Brief 17/09 issued on 25 March 2009 [see Part 2 of this publication] described changes to procedures following the changes to the remittance basis rules and the residence rules made by the Finance Act 2008. The relevant sections are in Appendix A below and these are superseded by the revised guidance below.

REVISED GUIDANCE

The revised guidance applies to dispositions made after the issue of this Revenue & Customs Brief.

In future HMRC will consider opening an enquiry where domicile could be an issue, or making a determination of Inheritance Tax in such cases, only where there is a significant risk of loss of UK tax.

The significance of the risk will be assessed by HMRC using a wide range of factors. The factors will depend very much on the individual case but will include, for example:

– a review of the information available to HMRC about the individual on HMRC databases
– whether there is a significant amount of tax (all taxes and duties not just Inheritance Tax) at risk

HMRC does not consider it appropriate to state an amount of tax that would be considered significant, as the amount of tax at stake is only one factor. It should be borne in mind that HMRC will take into account the potential costs involved in pursuing an enquiry, and also those of potential litigation should the enquiry not result in agreement between HMRC and the individual; clearly such costs can be substantial.

Where HMRC does open an Inheritance Tax enquiry in any of these cases, it will keep the factors in view and may stop the enquiry at any stage if it considers the continuation of the enquiry is not cost effective. The outcome of such an enquiry may be that HMRC does not consider it appropriate to make a determination of the Inheritance Tax.

Individuals should also bear in mind that enquiries into domicile involve a detailed inquiry into all of the relevant facts and HMRC is likely to require considerable personal information and extensive documentary evidence about the taxpayer and the taxpayer's close family.

APPENDIX A

> "Where an individual who is not domiciled in the UK settles non-UK assets into a non-UK resident trust then assets in that trust will not be subject to Inheritance Tax. Following the release of the new HMRC guidance on domicile most settlors should now be able to decide for themselves whether or not they are UK domiciled."

> "An individual setting up a non-resident trust who, having taken account of the new HMRC guidance, considers they are non-UK domiciled is not obliged to submit an Inheritance Tax account to HMRC. If the settlor is non-UK domiciled then no Inheritance Tax is due. But if an Inheritance Tax account is submitted in these circumstances, HMRC will continue its existing practice and only open an enquiry into that return if the amounts of Inheritance Tax at stake make such an enquiry cost effective to carry out. At present that limit is £10,000."

Commentary—*Simon's Taxes* **I9.201**.

EMPLOYEE BENEFIT TRUSTS: IHT & INCOME TAX ISSUES

4 April 2011. *HMRC Brief 18/11*

ABSTRACT

This brief sets out HMRC's current view on IHT issues associated with employee benefit trusts, including on matters not previously addressed such as the ongoing IHT liabilities of a trust and any sub-trusts it created and the taxation of income arising in offshore employee benefit trusts.

FULL TEXT

INTRODUCTION

Employment Benefit Trusts are discretionary trusts which seek to reward employees by making payments that favour employees or their families.

This brief sets out HM Revenue & Customs' (HMRC's) current view on Inheritance Tax issues associated with Employee Benefit Trusts. It supersedes and amplifies Revenue & Customs Brief 61/2009.

It also includes material on various matters not previously addressed including ongoing Inheritance Tax liabilities of the trust and any sub-trusts it created and the taxation of income arising in offshore Employee Benefit Trusts.

This brief is aimed at agents advising on the Inheritance Tax and trust taxation liabilities of Employee Benefit Trusts.

Existing cases will be taken forward by HMRC on the basis of the views set out in this brief.

All statutory references are to Inheritance Tax Act 1984 unless otherwise stated.

Contents

PART 1—ENTRY CHARGES PAYABLE BY A CLOSE COMPANY WHEN IT MAKES A CONTRIBUTION TO A S86 EMPLOYEE BENEFIT TRUST

1.1 EMPLOYEE BENEFIT TRUST

This part of the brief assumes that the Employee Benefit Trust qualifies as a s 86 Employee Benefit Trust in that it is a trust where the funds are held at the trustees' discretion to be applied for the benefit of "all or most of the persons employed or holding office with the body concerned" (s 86(3)(a)).

1.2 CHARGE ON PARTICIPATORS (S 94)

Where a Close Company (s 102(1)) makes a transfer of value (s 3) to an Employee Benefit Trust an Inheritance Tax charge arises under s94 unless, broadly, the disposition:

– is not a transfer of value under sections 10, 12 or 13
– is eligible for relief

1.3 TRANSFERS OF VALUE

Where there is a transfer of value it is apportioned between the individual participators according to their respective rights and interest in the company immediately before the contribution to the Employee Benefit Trust is made. There is an immediate charge of 20 per cent on the value transferred (the contribution) in excess of the participator's unused nil rate band.

The liability for the charge to Inheritance Tax that arises under s 94 is the company's or, so far as the tax remains unpaid, the participator's (s 202).

Inheritance Tax arising under s 94 is due six months after the end of the month in which the contribution is made or at the end of April in the year following a contribution made between 6 April and 30 September inclusive. Interest is charged on any unpaid tax from the due date.

1.3.1 DISPOSITIONS NOT INTENDED TO CONFER GRATUITOUS BENEFIT (S 10)

A disposition is not a transfer of value when the terms of s 10 are met. There is both a subjective test and an objective test; and both tests must be met to satisfy section 10.

1.3.1.1 SUBJECTIVE TEST—NO INTENTION TO CONFER GRATUITOUS INTENT

The test is not met if there is the slightest possibility of gratuitous intent at the date the contribution is made.

1.3.1.2 OBJECTIVE TEST—ARM'S LENGTH TRANSACTION

To meet the terms of s 10 the transaction must either:

– have been made at arm's length between persons not connected with each other (as defined in s 270)
– was such as might be expected to be made in a transaction at arm's length between persons not connected with each other

An Employee Benefit Trust is a discretionary trust and to satisfy the conditions of s 86 the trustees' discretion must remain unfettered. Given that the potential beneficiaries under an Employee Benefit Trust normally include the participators themselves; the employees or former employees; and/or the wives, husbands, civil partners, widows, widowers, surviving civil partners and children and step children under the age of 18 of such employees and former employees; it will normally be difficult to show that the conditions of s 10 are met.

1.3.2 DISPOSITIONS ALLOWABLE IN COMPUTING PROFITS FOR CORPORATION TAX (S 12)

1.3.2.1 OVERVIEW

A disposition by a person is not a transfer of value when the terms of s 12 are met: broadly, that the disposition is allowable for the purposes of calculating that person's Corporation Tax.

The relieving effect cannot be given provisionally while waiting to see whether the contribution will become allowable for Corporation Tax purposes; and is only available to the extent that a deduction is allowable to the company for the tax year in which the contribution is made.

A deduction in the Corporation Tax accounts can be permanently disallowed by the following:

– capital expenditure disallowed by ICTA 1988, s 74(1)(f)/CTA 2009, s 53
– expenditure not wholly and exclusively incurred under ICTA 1988, s 74(1)(a)/CTA 2009, s 54

Also the timing of a deduction can be deferred to a later period by the following:

– generally accepted accounting practice (UITF32) which capitalises Employee Benefit Trust contributions by showing them as an asset on the company's balance sheet until and to the extent that the assets transferred to the intermediary vest unconditionally in identified beneficiaries
– expenditure subject to FA 1989, s 43 (the Dextra decision) — see below
– post 27 November 2002 expenditure subject to FA 2003, Sch 24/CTA 2009, s 1290(2), (3) — see below

If expenditure is not allowable for any of these reasons then s 12 does not apply.

1.3.2.2 IMPACT OF *MACDONALD (HMIT) V DEXTRA* [2005] UKHL 47 ("DEXTRA")

The *Dextra* decision applies to contributions made before 27 November 2002.

In that case, the trust deed gave the trustee wide discretion to pay money and other benefits to beneficiaries and power to lend them money. The potential beneficiaries of the trust included past, present and future employees and officers of the participating companies in the Dextra group and their close relatives and dependants. The trustee did not make payments of emoluments out of the funds in the Employee Benefit Trust during the periods concerned. Instead the trustee made loans to various individuals who were beneficiaries under the terms of the Employee Benefit Trust.

The point at issue was whether the company's contributions to the Employee Benefit Trust were "potential emoluments" within the meaning of FA 1989, s 43(11)(*a*), being amounts "held by an intermediary with a view to their becoming relevant emoluments".

The House of Lords held that the contributions by the company to the Employee Benefit Trust were potential emoluments as there was a "realistic possibility" that the trustee would use the trust funds to pay emoluments. This meant that the company's deductions were restricted. The company could only have a deduction for the amount of emoluments paid by the trustee within nine months of the end of the period of account for which the deduction would otherwise be due. Relief for the amount disallowed would be given in the period of accounting in which emoluments were paid.

1.3.2.3 RESTRICTION OF DEDUCTIONS FOR EMPLOYEE BENEFIT CONTRIBUTIONS (FA 2003, SCH 24)

Section 143 and Schedule 24 to the Finance Act 2003 applies to contributions made after 27 November 2002 and prevents a deduction for Corporation Tax purposes until the contribution made for employee benefits is spent by a payment that has been subjected to both PAYE and National Insurance contributions. The position already established in Dextra is therefore effectively formalised by legislation for events on or after 27 November 2002.

1.3.3 DISPOSITIONS BY CLOSE COMPANIES FOR BENEFIT OF EMPLOYEES (S 13)

A disposition is not a transfer of value when the terms of section 13 are met.

However, this exclusion does not apply where (amongst other things):

- the contributions by the Close Company are made to an Employee Benefit Trust that does not satisfy section 86
- the participators (s 102(1)) in the company and any person connected with them are not excluded from benefit under the terms of the Employee Benefit Trust and so s 13(2) applies

1.4 RELIEF FROM INHERITANCE TAX—BUSINESS PROPERTY RELIEF (S 104)

Usually, sections 10, 12 or 13 will not be met and the contribution by the Close Company will be a transfer of value as a result of a reduction in the value of its estate — the aggregate of the property beneficially owned by the company.

Relief from Inheritance Tax may, however, be available where the value transferred is attributable to relevant business property (s 105).

The company's estate is capable of being relevant business property if it is "property consisting of a business" (s 105(1)(a)). However, the availability of business property relief is conditional on whether the transfer meets all the other requirements in Part V, Chapter 1. This means, in particular that:

- the business is not an excluded one, for example a company the business of which consists wholly or mainly of making or holding investments (s 105(3))
- the value of the relevant business property transferred is not attributable to any excepted assets (s 112)

Business property relief will, Therefore, not apply on a transfer of value made by a Close Company that is an investment company.

PART 2—FLAT RATE EXIT CHARGE (S 72) WHEN PROPERTY LEAVES A S 86 EMPLOYEE BENEFIT TRUST

This part describes charges to Inheritance Tax that can arise in any s 86 Employee Benefit Trust; *even where the original disposition into the trust was not made by a Close Company or individual.*

The charge arises where a payment is made from the Employee Benefit Trust into a sub-trust that is not itself a qualifying s 86 Employee Benefit Trust (as outlined at 1.1 above). The charge is a flat rate charge and is dependant on the length of time the property was held subject to the terms of the s 86 Employee Benefit Trust. Business property relief will not apply to the flat rate exit charge in these circumstances.

In addition, where there is a non-commercial loan to a participator then an exit charge may arise under s 72(2)(b).

PART 3—TEN YEAR AND EXIT CHARGES IN RESPECT OF ANY SUB-TRUSTS

In general, sub-trusts are not s 86 Employee Benefit Trusts and are, therefore, relevant property trusts for Inheritance Tax purposes (s 58). (Full details of "relevant property trusts" can be found in the Inheritance Tax Manual at page IHTM 42001+.)

Relevant property trusts pay Inheritance Tax on two key occasions:

- on the ten year anniversary of the commencement of the trust (s 64) (and every subsequent ten year anniversary)
- when property leaves the relevant property trust or when it ceases to be relevant property (s 65)

For both of these occasions a calculation is required in order to establish the Inheritance Tax liability but this charge will not exceed 6 per cent of the value of the trust assets concerned.

For the purposes of the ten year anniversary charge, the anniversary is calculated from the date on which the property became settled (s 81), that is, the date the s 86 Employee Benefit Trust commenced. However, property can only be treated as relevant property when it leaves the qualifying Employee Benefit Trust.

Where the trustees of a sub-trust decide to bring the trust to an end an exit charge will arise under s 65.

The basis of valuation for a charge arising under either s 64 or s 65 will be an open market value (s 160) and will include the value of loans and any accrued interest.

PART 4—PAYMENT OF ONGOING INHERITANCE TAX LIABILITIES

Section 201(1) (Settled Property) outlines the persons liable for Inheritance Tax on chargeable transfers arising in respect of trusts, including proportionate charges (s 65) and ten year anniversary charges (s 64) as well as the flat rate charge (s 72) (property leaving employee trusts). Where the transfer is made during the life of the settlor and the trustees are not resident in the UK then the settlor is liable for the ongoing trust Inheritance Tax liabilities (s 201(1)(d)).

The settlor of an Employee Benefit Trust will usually be the company, whether or not it is a Close Company.

In addition, where a participator has benefited then s 201(1)(c) means that they are liable for the ongoing trust Inheritance Tax liabilities.

PART 5—INCOME TAX ASSESSABLE UNDER THE TRANSFER OF ASSET (TOA) LEGISLATION ON INCOME ARISING IN OFFSHORE EMPLOYEE BENEFIT TRUSTS

5.1 OVERVIEW

It is common for the trust vehicle used as the Employee Benefit Trust to be situated in an offshore jurisdiction and this will potentially give rise to additional liabilities where income arises within the trust.

The ToA legislation was amended by FA 2006 and the legislation applicable following this amendment can be found at ITA 2007, s 714, onwards. It came into effect from 6 April 2007. The pre-FA 2006 legislation is contained in ICTA 1988, s 739, onwards. There are two potential charges that arise under the ToA legislation — the so-called "income charge" (ICTA 1988, s 739/ITA 2007, s 720) and the "benefits charge" (ICTA 1988, s 740/ITA 2007, s 732). Each of these are considered in turn.

5.1.1 INCOME CHARGE

The income charge provisions apply to prevent the avoidance of a liability to Income Tax by individuals who are ordinarily resident in the UK where the following conditions apply:

- there is a transfer of assets by virtue or in consequence of which, either alone or in conjunction with associated operations, income becomes payable to a person abroad

– the transferor has the power to enjoy the income

For the income charge provisions to apply the individual on whom the charge arises must be the person who transfers the assets or procures the transfer. If the offshore Employee Benefit Trust is a normal commercial arrangement by a company to reward its employees, the transferor is the employer company; and in such circumstances the income charge is unlikely to be applicable as the transferor and beneficiaries are different people. However, it may be that the employee has transferred a right to receive a bonus into the offshore Employee Benefit Trust and is therefore the transferor. If this is the case the ToA legislation may apply and the employee will be liable to tax on any income arising in the trust.

If the employer company is controlled by its shareholder/directors and the offshore Employee Benefit Trust was formed solely for their benefit, the director/shareholders may have procured the transfer into the offshore Employee Benefit Trust and could be considered transferors for the purposes of the income charge. Whether or not the ToA income charge is then applied will depend on the facts of each case.

5.1.2 BENEFIT CHARGE

Where the company, not the employee is the transferor the benefit charge may apply. The benefit charge matches any income arising within the Employee Benefit Trust with any benefits received by the employee. The test is effectively the same as ICTA 1988, s 739/ITA 2007, s 720 in that where by virtue or in consequence of a transfer income becomes payable to a person abroad, ICTA 1988, s 740(1)(b)/ITA 2007, s 732(1)(d) applies the charge to individuals not liable to tax under the income charge. If a person receives a benefit provided out of assets available for the purpose as a consequence of the transfer, and the trustees are in receipt of income, any benefit provided to a beneficiary is potentially chargeable. The amount of the benefit charged to tax is up to the maximum of either the income or benefit. The benefit charge could, therefore, catch any income arising in the offshore Employee Benefit Trust if it is not caught by the income charge and there are actual distributions by the trustees which are not otherwise chargeable to Income Tax.

PART 6—INCOME TAX IN RELATION TO UK SOURCE INCOME OF OFFSHORE EMPLOYMENT BENEFIT TRUSTS

If an offshore Employment Benefit Trust receives UK source income then, subject to ITA 2007, s 811, the income will be chargeable to tax in the UK and the trustees should make a return of this income to HMRC. ITA 2007, s 811 limits the scope of the liability to Income Tax of a non-UK resident trust provided that none of the trust's beneficiaries are resident in the UK. As Employee Benefit Trusts are discretionary trusts the trustees will be chargeable to tax at the trust rate under ITA 2007, s 479. If the trustees make a discretionary payment out of the trust income to a beneficiary this is treated as untaxed income of the UK resident beneficiary. It does not matter that the trustees have suffered tax on the trust income. The beneficiary returns the income received and can claim relief under Extra Statutory Concession B18.

The trustees of the offshore Employee Benefit Trust or sub-trusts may have advanced interest bearing loans to beneficiaries. If the beneficiaries are resident in the UK then depending on the particular circumstances of each beneficiary the interest will be UK source income in the hands of the trustees and should be reported as such. It is also likely that in such circumstances tax should be deducted at source by the beneficiary paying the interest under ITA 2007, s 874.

Where it is contended that the interest is not UK source income, the circumstances surrounding the payment of interest will be closely examined by HMRC.

If the beneficiary does not pay the interest, but the interest is rolled up by the trustees, no immediate tax charge will arise; however, if the interest is subsequently paid or capitalised it is likely that an Income Tax charge will accrue on payment or capitalisation.

PART 7—PAYMENT OF ONGOING TRUST INCOME TAX LIABILITIES

To the extent that income continues to arise within an offshore Employee Benefit Trust and is caught by the transfer of assets legislation the income charge and benefits charge will continue to apply. Likewise if the trustees continue to receive UK source income they will have an ongoing liability to Income Tax and should continue to complete Trust Returns.

PART 8—CONTACT DETAILS AND LEGAL REFERENCES

8.1 CONTACT DETAILS

If you wish to notify the Trusts and Estates business within HMRC of the existence of an Employee Benefit Trust; or, if you wish to discuss settlement of any Inheritance Tax and non-resident trust liabilities that have arisen in respect of an Employee Benefit Trust, then please contact HMRC Trusts & Estates via this link ebtiht.settlementmailbox@hmrc.gsi.gov.uk.

Further information can be obtained by contacting the Helpline on Tel 0845 30 20 900.

8.2 LEGAL REFERENCES

CORPORATION TAX

For accounting periods ending on or after 1 April 2009:

- references to Finance Act 2003, Sch 24 should be taken to be references to Corporation Tax Act 2009, sections 1290–1297
- references to ICTA 1988, s 74(1)(a) should be taken to be references to Corporation Tax Act 2009, s 54
- references to ICTA 1988, s 74(1)(f) should be taken to be references to Corporation Tax Act 2009, s 53

INCOME TAX

For tax years 2005–06 onwards:

- references to Finance Act 2003, Sch 24 should be taken to be references to Income Tax (Trading and Other Income) Act 2005, sections 38–44
- references to ICTA 1988, s 74(1)(a) should be taken to be references to Income Tax (Trading and Other Income) Act 2005, s 34
- references to ICTA 1988, s 74(1)(f) should be taken to be references to Income Tax (Trading and Other Income) Act 2005, s 33
- reference to ICTA 1988, s 739 should be taken to be references to ITA 2007, s 720
- reference to ICTA 1988, s 740 should be taken to be references to ITA 2007, s 731

THE EQUITABLE LIFE PAYMENT SCHEME: TAX AND TAX CREDIT IMPLICATIONS

27 July 2011. *HMRC Brief 26/11*

ABSTRACT

This HMRC brief explains the impact for taxes and tax credits of payments under the Equitable Life Payment Scheme, covering: the background to the scheme; how ELPS will work; and tax and the effect of tax credit, including reporting requirements.

FULL TEXT

WHAT THIS BRIEF COVERS

This brief explains the impact for taxes and tax credits of payments under the Equitable Life Payment Scheme (ELPS). It covers:

- background to the scheme
- how ELPS will work
- tax and tax credit effects, including reporting requirements

BACKGROUND

The Coalition's Programme for Government issued in May 2010 promised to implement the Parliamentary Ombudsman's recommendation to make fair and transparent payments to Equitable Life policy holders, through an independent payment scheme, for their relative loss as a consequence of regulatory failure. On 20 October 2010 the Financial Secretary, Mark

Hoban, announced in a written ministerial statement that £1.5 billion will be available for payment under ELPS. He also announced that the payments will be free of tax.

On 16 December 2010 the Equitable Life (Payments) Act 2010 came into force. The Act authorises the Treasury to incur expenditure when making ELPS payments and enables those payments to be made by National Savings and Investments (on the Treasury's behalf). The Act also allows the Treasury to make an order to provide for ELPS payments to be free of tax and to disregard them for tax credit purposes.

A Statutory Instrument, the Taxation of Equitable Life (Payments) Order 2011, SI 2011 No 1502 (the SI), makes the necessary provision to exempt authorised payments under ELPS. The SI was made on 15 June 2011 and came into force the following day. The SI can be found by following the link below.

HOW ELPS WILL WORK

The Treasury published full scheme design documentation on 16 May. A link to the full document ca be found by following the link below.

Equitable Life Payment Scheme - important next steps: www.hm-treasury.gov.uk/fin_equitable-_life.htm

In outline, the ELPS will work as follows:

– Payments will be made to individuals who have suffered relative loss as a result of Government maladministration in the regulation of Equitable Life.
– Relative loss is the difference between the actual returns received, or expected to be received, from Equitable Life and the assumed returns that the policyholder would have received, if they had invested the same amount in a similar product in a comparable company. Policyholders with With Profits Annuities (WPAs) will receive payments covering 100 per cent of their loss. Those with Accumulation With Profits (AWP), Conventional With Profits (CWP), or group scheme policies, will receive lump sum payments of 22.4 per cent of their loss, subject to a £10 de minimis on payments.
– First payments will be made by the end of June 2011. Payments to traceable AWP, CWP group scheme policyholders should be made over the first three years of the scheme. WPAs will receive their payments on an ongoing annual basis.

TAX AND TAX CREDIT EFFECTS

SI 2011/1502 provides that authorised payments under ELPS are disregarded for the purposes of:

– Income Tax
– calculating investment income for tax credits
– Capital Gains Tax
– Corporation

The SI also ensures that Inheritance Tax is not chargeable on the value of any right to receive an ELPS payment.

All direct payments from the scheme to payees as identified in the scheme documentation are authorised payments.

Payments from trusts to beneficiaries of trust will retain their tax free status where the beneficiary is entitled as of right to receive the payment under the terms of the trust.

Payments made by trustees in exercise of a power or discretion given to them by the trust deed are not authorised payments as they do not flow directly from the receipt of the payment. They will therefore be subject to the usual tax treatment for such payments.

The main practical effects of the exemptions under the SI are as follows.

INCOME TAX AND CORPORATION TAX ON INCOME

Payments under ELPS to individuals and companies are free of Income Tax and should be excluded from Self Assessment tax returns or claims for repayment of tax on form R40.

The position for trustees of pension schemes is set out below. In other cases, if the trust is a bare trust or interest in possession trust it is the beneficiary of the trust who is potentially liable to tax on the trust income. The position is therefore as in the previous paragraph: payments are free of Income Tax and should be excluded from tax returns or claims for repayment of tax. Trustees of accumulation or discretionary trusts are also exempt from Income Tax on payments made to them under ELPS and should exclude the payments from the Trust and Estate tax return.

PAYMENTS INVOLVING REGISTERED PENSION SCHEMES

"Authorised payment" and "trustee" in this context mean a payment as authorised by the ELPS and the recipient of that payment under the Equitable Life (Payments) Act 2010. An authorised payment under this Act is not the same as an authorised payment under the Registered Pension Schemes tax legislation in Finance Act 2004.

DIRECT PAYMENTS TO INDIVIDUALS

In a registered pension scheme case the authorised payment will generally be made to the member to whom the policy relates. All payments to individual payees will be free of tax. However, in certain circumstances, the payee will not be the individual member of the scheme. In these cases the principles for identifying the payee are shown below.

PAYMENTS IN GROUP PENSION SCHEMES

Payments will be made to group pension schemes in three ways:

- Payments will be made to group pension schemes in three ways:
- In some cases payments will be made to the trustee and they will be asked to distribute payments amongst their members. (For example, this will happen when the pension scheme has a single policy, which represents the investment of a number of members, for whom Equitable Life will not have contact details.) The trustee will receive the payment from the ELPS as their paying agent and will then pass the payment on to members. These payments will not be held as part of the pension scheme and will not be treated as payments from the pension scheme.
- Where the policy has been held by a defined benefits scheme (for example, a final salary scheme), payments will be made directly to the trustee as it is the scheme that has suffered the loss.

In all these cases, payments will remain free of tax to the final recipient, whether that is an individual scheme member, or the pension scheme trustee.

RETURNS AND REPORTING

In all pension cases the payments should be excluded from tax returns. The payments should not be included in any returns or reports made by a registered pension scheme administrator, for example event report, Pension Scheme Return.

NON-PENSION LIFE INSURANCE POLICIES/ANNUITY CONTRACTS

Payments under ELPS are disregarded for the purpose of Income Tax when calculating gains under the chargeable event gain regime. The payments will not be included in chargeable event certificates issued to policyholders by Equitable Life when gains arise. They do not have to be included in the parts of tax returns dealing with life insurance gains for persons liable to Income Tax on the gains, whether individuals, trustees or personal representatives.

Payments under ELPS are also disregarded for the purpose of Corporation Tax in the application of the loan relationships rules to investment life assurance contracts to which a company is a party.

TAX CREDITS

Authorised payments are disregarded as investment income for the purposes of the child and working tax credits and will not affect eligibility for such support. Consequently, authorised payments will not have to be reported by tax credit claimants as part of their annual income.

CAPITAL GAINS TAX AND CORPORATION TAX ON CHARGEABLE GAINS

Payments under ELPS to Equitable Life policy holders are disregarded for the purposes of Capital Gains Tax and Corporation Tax on chargeable gains. This treatment applies whether the payment is received by an individual, trustee, personal representative or company. The payments do not have to be shown on the capital gains pages of the recipient's tax return or otherwise reported to HMRC. They do not represent a disposal or part disposal of the policy for tax purposes, so any allowable cost of the policy is unaffected going forward.

INHERITANCE TAX

Where a payment is made to the estate of someone who has already died, the right to receive the payment is disregarded in establishing the value of the estate for Inheritance Tax purposes. There is no need to tell HMRC Trusts and Estates that the executors have received such a payment. A payment that is made to someone whilst they are alive, however, forms part of their estate and will be subject to Inheritance Tax in the normal way.

A similar treatment applies where the trustees of a "relevant property" trust receive a payment. "Relevant property" has the meaning given by section 58 of the Inheritance Tax Act 1984. The right to receive the payment should be disregarded in determining the value of relevant property that is subject to a 10 year charge. Again, there is no need to tell HMRC Trusts and Estates that the trustees have received such a payment after a 10 year charge has fallen due. Once the trustees have received the payment, however, it forms part of the assets of the trust and will be subject to Inheritance Tax in the normal way.

DISCOUNTED GIFT SCHEMES - UPDATED GUIDANCE ON IHT VALUATIONS

5 August 2013. *HMRC Brief 22/13*

ABSTRACT

This brief sets out HMRC's view on how to calculate the value subject to IHT for a Discounted Gift Scheme held in a relevant property trust when the ten-year anniversary charge arises for the trust. It also provides updated guidance on how the transfer value is to be calculated when a Discounted Gift Scheme is effected.

FULL TEXT

DISCOUNTED GIFT SCHEMES: TEN YEAR ANNIVERSARY VALUES FOR INHERITANCE TAX AND UPDATED GUIDANCE ON THE CALCULATION OF TRANSFER VALUES WHEN DISCOUNTED GIFT SCHEMES ARE EFFECTED

This brief sets out HM Revenue & Customs' (HMRC's) view on how to calculate the value that will be subject to Inheritance Tax for a Discounted Gift Scheme held in a relevant property trust when the ten year anniversary charge arises for the trust. It also provides updated guidance on how the transfer value is to be calculated when a Discounted Gift Scheme is effected including providing clarification and revisions to the assumptions underlying the valuation.

This brief is aimed at the trustees of a relevant property trust which holds a Discounted Gift Scheme and who are responsible for delivering an Inheritance Tax account for the ten year anniversary. It is also aimed at the providers of Discounted Gift Schemes who may wish to provide relevant values to their customers both when a Discounted Gift Scheme is effected and at subsequent Ten Year Anniversaries.

The intention of this brief is to provide certainty for taxpayers and Discounted Gift Scheme providers in that a valuation prepared in accordance with this brief will be acceptable to HMRC.

All statutory references are to Inheritance Tax Act 1984 unless otherwise stated.

1. THE TEN YEAR ANNIVERSARY CHARGE

Following changes to the taxation of trusts for Inheritance Tax purposes in the Finance Act 2006, most types of trust used for Discounted Gift Schemes created on or after 22 March 2006 are relevant property trusts and subject to Inheritance Tax under Part III, Chapter III Inheritance Tax Act 1984. Under s 64 a charge to Inheritance Tax arises on the value of the relevant property held in the trust every ten years at which time the trustees are required to report the value of the relevant property to HMRC.

1.1 VALUATION

Under a Discounted Gift Scheme the settlor will typically have settled a bond or a series of policies from which they have retained the right to either pre-determined regular withdrawals or to a succession of maturing reversions. The bond or policies are relevant property. However, the settlor's retained rights are normally held on bare trust for the settlor and as such, these rights are not relevant property for Inheritance Tax purposes. At the ten year anniversary, the value of the relevant property needs to be established for the purpose of calculating the charge that arises under s 64. The value of the relevant property is its open market value as required by s 160, but it does not include the value of the rights retained by the settlor.

The open market purchaser of the relevant property would be purchasing the right to receive the whole value of the underlying bond following the death of the settlor. The open market purchaser will take account of the fund value at the valuation date and will have to allow for

- the expected withdrawals to be received by the settlor between the valuation date and the settlor's date of death, and
- the expected delay between the valuation date and the eventual death of the settlor.

The closest equivalent asset which is sold in the open market is considered to be an interest in reversion. In the case of the purchase of an interest in reversion, analysis of sales indicates that open market purchasers take a prudent approach and they do not factor in any growth in the capital value of the asset. In addition, analysis indicates that an open market purchaser of a reversion takes no account of the interim income payable to the life tenant.

However, under a Discounted Gift Scheme the rights retained by the settlor are not precisely identical to the rights of a life tenant entitled to income. The retained benefits are not limited to any income produced by, or growth on, the fund. It is possible for the settlor's retained rights to exceed the growth generated by the fund itself so that the fund is depleted over time. Equally the growth on the fund may exceed the sums due to the settlor under the retained rights, so that the fund value increases over time. HMRC takes the view that an open market purchaser would take a prudent approach when taking these possibilities into account in the price he or she is prepared to pay.

1.2 VALUATION METHODOLOGY

The asset to be valued is the total fund, less the value of the rights retained by the settlor, payable on the death of the settlor. The actual valuation will be slightly different depending on whether the retained rights are structured as a series of withdrawals of pre-determined amounts or are based on the value of a series of funds payable on fixed future dates. In either case it is considered that the open market purchaser would not allow for any growth in the fund value, but would discount the current value to account for the delay until the fund will be available, being on the death of the settlor.

Where the retained rights are of pre-determined regular withdrawals, the total fund value is discounted to the expected date of death of the settlor. From this value is to be deducted the present value of the expected future withdrawals to be taken by the settlor based on their life expectancy and discounting those payments to the date that each payment is to be made.

Where the retained rights are based on the value of a series of funds payable on fixed future dates the value of the funds that are expected to mature after the death of the settlor are discounted to the expected date of death of the settlor.

There are a number of approaches that can be taken to these calculations that will produce virtually the same values, provided the same mortality and interest rate assumptions are used.

1.3 HEALTH OF THE SETTLOR AT THE TEN YEAR ANNIVERSARY

The open market purchaser of an interest payable only on the death of an individual, such as a reversion, will assume normal life expectancy for the life of that individual unless there is clear evidence that they are terminally ill, for example in the viatical market for life policies. The risk to the open market purchaser is that if the individual survives longer than expected the purchaser has to wait longer to realise his or her investment. This open market practice leads to the view that the age to be used in the valuation is the age next birthday of the settlor with no adjustment for their state of health.

This approach would, however, understate the value, possibly substantially, in cases where the settlor was terminally ill at the date of the ten year anniversary. The rate of tax payable at the ten year anniversary, which is dependent on the value of the relevant property at that date, determines the tax payable under s 65 on property in the settlement which ceases to be relevant property, for example on the distribution of the funds following the death of the settlor. There is therefore a risk that tax will be lost if the valuation at the ten year anniversary is based on the actual age next birthday of the settlor where, in fact, the settlor was terminally ill.

Three options to overcome this risk are:

- To obtain evidence of the settlor's state of health at the ten year anniversary in all cases. This would add both an administrative and a financial burden on the trustees and would require an assessment of the medical evidence obtained, presumably by the provider preparing the valuation, adding to their costs. In most cases the outcome would be that the settlor was not terminally ill and therefore that the valuation should be based on the actual age next birthday of the settlor. The advantage of this approach, however, is that there would be certainty for the trustees that the value at the ten year anniversary was finalised and it would remove the risk to HMRC of loss of tax on any distributions in the following ten years.
- To complete the valuation at the ten year anniversary on the basis of the settlor's actual age next birthday but, where the settlor dies within two years of the ten year anniversary, for HMRC to review the position at the ten year anniversary to satisfy itself as to whether the value needs revision. This would reduce the administrative burden at the ten year anniversary, but would not provide certainty for the trustees that the tax position was settled. There would also be practical difficulties in some cases in obtaining the relevant evidence of the settlor's state of health at the ten year anniversary retrospectively.
- To complete the valuation at the ten year anniversary on the basis of the settlor's rated age next birthday when the Discounted Gift Scheme was effected, plus an addition of 10 years for each ten year anniversary. This has the advantage of simplicity. The settlor's life will, in almost all cases, have been fully underwritten at the outset and no further medical evidence will be required. It would also provide certainty to the trustees that the tax position at the ten year anniversary was finalised and that HMRC would not review that position in the event that the settlor died within the next two years.

HMRC consider that the third option provides a practical approach to the valuation. It places the minimum administrative burden on trustees or product providers whilst at the same time protecting HMRC from potential loss of tax. The majority of settlors effecting Discounted Gift Schemes have no rating added to their age based on medical underwriting when the Discounted Gift Scheme is set up and therefore they would continue to have no rating applied at each ten year anniversary.

Where no underwriting was completed on the original transfer it may be necessary for HMRC to review the original transfer value if this has not previously been reported. Alternatively it may be necessary to obtain evidence of the settlor's state of health at the ten year anniversary to complete the valuation.

1.4 VALUATION BASIS

The valuation is required to be carried out on an open market basis in accordance with s 160 and it is not possible to predict what open market practice will be by the time these valuations are required, with the first valuations expected to be required in March 2016. The open market valuation would need to reflect current market practice on the mortality assumptions being applied to reversionary interests as well as the rates of return then required by purchasers.

In order to provide some certainty as to the valuations that will be acceptable, HMRC will accept valuations that are calculated using the same mortality basis as is then in use in valuing the transfer when a Discounted Gift Scheme is effected, replacing select with ultimate mortality. This does not preclude the use of alternative valuation approaches to establish open market values, but is intended to provide certainty for valuations provided in accordance with this approach. HMRC will publish any changes to its valuation basis at least three months before the changes are to take effect to give providers time to update their systems.

1.5 EXAMPLE

The examples below show how the value of the relevant property is calculated. The mortality and interest rate basis used is that set out in paragraph 2.2 below.

1.5.1 EXAMPLE 1

The first example assumes that the settlor was a woman aged 75 next birthday when the Discounted Gift Scheme was effected with no addition to age based on medical underwriting. At the ten year anniversary the underlying value of the bond is £1,000,000. The withdrawals retained by the settlor are equal to 5% of the original £500,000 investment, payable monthly in arrears.

CALCULATION

The open market value equals

The fund value at the ten year anniversary x $\bar{A}_x$, less

The annual rate of withdrawals x $a^{(p)}_x$, where

$\bar{A}_x$ is an immediate assurance factor, payable immediately on the death of a life aged x next birthday, and

$a^{(p)}_x$ is an annuity factor for an annuity payable in arrears at a frequency of p times per year for the term of a life aged x next birthday.

A deduction is made from this value to represent the purchaser's costs associated with the legal formalities connected with completing the purchase. The figures are:

£1,000,000 × $\bar{A}_{85}$	= £1,000,000 × 0.70301	= £703,010, less
£25,000 × $a^{(12)}_{85}$	= £25,000 × 6.710	= £167,750

Which gives a value of £535,260.

From this value a deduction of approximately £1,000 is made in respect of the purchaser's costs, to give a net value of £534,260.

1.5.2 EXAMPLE 2

The facts are as in example 1, except that an age addition of 4 years was made based on medical underwriting when the Discounted Gift Scheme was effected

CALCULATION

As the settlor was aged 75 next birthday when the Discounted Gift Scheme was effected and an age addition of 4 years was applied, the effective age to be used at the ten year anniversary is 89 next birthday. The calculations become:

£1,000,000 × $\bar{A}_{89}$	= £1,000,000 × 0.76160	= £761,600, less
£25,000 × $a^{(12)}_{89}$	= £25,000 × 5.379	= £134,475

Which gives a value of £627,125.

From this value a deduction of approximately £1,000 is made in respect of the purchaser's costs, to give a net value of £626,125.

1.5.3 EXAMPLE 3

The facts are as example 1, except that the settlor was a man aged 83 when the Discounted Gift Scheme was effected. No age addition was made as a result of medical underwriting.

CALCULATION

As the settlor was aged 83 next birthday when the Discounted Gift Scheme was effected, the calculations are based on an age next birthday of 93 at the ten year anniversary. The calculations are:

£1,000,000 × $\bar{A}_{93}$	= £1,000,000 × 0.81385	= £813,850, less
£25,000 × $a^{(12)}_{93}$	= £25,000 × 4.192	= £104,800

Which gives a value of £709,050.

From this value a deduction of approximately £1,000 is made in respect of the purchaser's costs, to give a net value of £708,050.

1.6 JOINTLY EFFECTED DISCOUNTED GIFT SCHEMES

Many Discounted Gift Schemes are effected jointly by two settlors with the retained rights payable until the death of the survivor of both settlors. Section 44(2) provides that where more than one person is the settlor in relation to a settlement then, for purposes including a ten year anniversary charge, the property is treated as being comprised in separate settlements. The value of the fund will be divided between the separate settlements in the proportion that the original funds were provided by each settlor, usually equally. The valuation of the fund needs to take into account that the fund will not be available to the open market purchaser until after the death of both settlors. The valuation of the expected withdrawals will need to take into account whether or not the full payments continue until the death of the survivor of both settlors.

1.6.1 EXAMPLE

A husband age 78 and his wife aged 75 each put £500,000 into a Discounted Gift Scheme from which withdrawals of £50,000 per year, paid monthly in arrears, are to be made until the death of the survivor. At the ten year anniversary the fund is worth £2,000,000.

The overall settlement will be treated as two separate settlements in view of s.44(2). The £2,000,000 is apportioned equally between the two settlements. For each settlement the calculations are:

£1,000,000 × $\bar{A}_{\overline{88:85}}$	= £1,000,000 x 0.63642	= £636,420, less
£25,000 × $a^{(12)}_{\overline{88:85}}$	= £25,000 × 8.223	= £205,575

Which gives a value of £430,845.

From this value a deduction of approximately £1,000 is made in respect of the purchaser's costs, to give a net value of £429,845.

1.7 TEN YEAR ANNIVERSARY REPORTING REQUIREMENTS

An account is required to be submitted to HMRC by the trustees of a relevant property settlement where a charge to tax arises under Part III, Chapter III of the Inheritance Tax Act 1984. The reporting requirements are relaxed in connection with Excepted Settlements, the definition of which are set out in the Inheritance Tax (Delivery of Accounts) (Excepted Settlements) Regulations 2008, SI 2008/606. For the purpose of establishing whether the transfer exceeds the 80% limit specified in Regulation 4(4), it is the value of the relevant property calculated in accordance with this brief that should be used.

2. UPDATED GUIDANCE ON THE CALCULATION OF TRANSFER VALUES WHEN A DISCOUNTED GIFT SCHEME IS EFFECTED

In May 2007 HMRC issued a Technical Note setting out the inheritance tax treatment of Discounted Gift Schemes (www.hmrc.gov.uk/cto/dgs-tech-note.pdf). That note dealt with the transfer of value that arises when a Discounted Gift Scheme is effected. It also set out the valuation basis that HMRC considered appropriate in establishing the value transferred. Subsequent to that note amendments to the valuation rate of interest have been made which are summarised in the inheritance tax manual at IHTM 20656 (www.hmrc.gov.uk/manuals/ihtmanual/IHTM20656.htm).

Following a European Court of Justice decision in March 2011 (the '*Test-Achats*' case) the use of gender as a factor in setting insurance premiums is no longer permissible from 21 December 2012. As one of the main factors used to establish the value transferred when a Discounted Gift Scheme is effected is the cost of insuring the life of the individual who has effected the Scheme, the valuation basis needs to be changed to reflect this significant change in how life assurance premiums are calculated.

The position at the date of a Ten Year Anniversary is somewhat different. At a Ten Year Anniversary the open market purchaser would not be concerned to insure the life of the settlor. Rather the purchaser's concern would be in establishing the settlor's life expectancy. This would be affected by the settlor's age, gender and state of health at that time and would use a different valuation basis from that used for valuing the retained rights when a Discounted Gift Scheme is effected.

In order to try to minimise the administrative burden around providing Discounted Gift Scheme valuations, HMRC will accept Ten Year Anniversary valuations which are calculated using the same mortality and interest rate basis as is then in force for calculating the transfer value when a Discounted Gift Scheme is effected. This is set out in paragraph 2.2 below. This does not preclude valuations being submitted using alternative methods or valuation assumptions, but is intended to provide assurance that valuations calculated in accordance with this brief will be accepted by HMRC.

2.1 VALUATION BASIS OF THE RETAINED RIGHTS

As set out in the 2007 Technical Note, the value transferred is calculated as the difference between the total amount invested in the Discounted Gift Scheme and the open market value of the retained rights. The formula used to calculate the open market value of the retained rights is

$$(1-p)+(p+i)$$

where

p is an annual whole life premium per £1 sum assured, expressed as a decimal, and

i is the open market purchaser's required rate of return on his investment.

2.2 MORTALITY AND INTEREST RATE BASIS

Following the removal of gender as a factor in setting life assurance premiums the mortality basis used by HMRC needs to be altered to reflect this change in open market premium rates.

At the same time it is an appropriate time to reconsider the current interest rate assumption within the calculation. The revised mortality and interest rate basis is

Mortality: 80% of AFC00 select mortality (Permanent assurances for females, combined rates from Continuous Mortality Investigation table "00" series published in the CMI Working Papers number 21 on 1 August 2006)

Interest rate of 4.5% p.a.

This revised basis will be applied to all transfers or Ten Year Anniversaries which occur on or after 1 December 2013.

2.3 FURTHER CLARIFICATION – WITHDRAWALS IN EXCESS OF 5% PER YEAR

HMRC has been asked to clarify the valuation approach it takes when withdrawals under a Discounted Gift Scheme exceed 5% per year.

Where the retained rights under a Discounted Gift Scheme derived from regular partial withdrawals from an investment bond do not exceed 5% per year, no personal income tax liabilities are taken into account in the valuation of those retained rights. Where the withdrawals in such circumstances exceed 5% per year, or where the cumulative 5% allowances are exhausted, the personal income tax liabilities of the open market purchaser need to be factored in to the valuation of the retained rights. In HMRC's view the open market purchaser of the retained rights will account for income tax at 40% on the excess over 5% per year. Where the bonds are onshore the assumption is that a 20% non-refundable tax credit will be taken into account so that the excess over 5% per year is reduced by 20% net rather than by 40% for offshore bonds.

EC MEASURES TO TACKLE CROSS-BORDER INHERITANCE TAX PROBLEMS

11 July 2014. *European Commission press release*

ABSTRACT

In December 2011, the European Commission published a package of recommendations on ways for member states to avoid the incidence of double taxation and discriminatory tax rates in relation to inheritance taxation. In July 2014, the tax profession's European body, the CFE, published an opinion statement on specific instances encountered by its members. The Commission proposes to follow up its recommendations with an evaluation report at the end of this year, to assess whether further measures are needed.

FULL TEXT

Brussels, 15 December 2011 - EU citizens that inherit foreign property are frequently faced with a tax bill from more than one Member State. In fact, in extreme cases the total value of a cross-border inherited asset might even have to be paid in tax, because several Member States may claim taxing rights on the same inheritance or tax foreign inheritances more heavily than local inheritances. Citizens may be forced to sell inherited assets, just to cover the taxes, and small businesses may face transfer difficulties on the death of their owners. To tackle these problems, the Commission today adopted a comprehensive package on inheritance taxation. Through a Communication, Recommendation and Working Paper, the Commission analyses the problems and presents solutions related to cross-border inheritance tax in the EU. Algirdas Šemeta, Commissioner for Taxation, Customs, Anti-fraud and Audit, commented:

> "Benjamin Franklin once said that nothing is certain except death and taxes. Unfortunately, when you put the two together, a huge amount of uncertainty seems to arise. The burden of cross-border inheritance tax can be crippling for citizens, due to discrimination and double taxation. Small changes in Member States' rules to make them more coherent with each other could deliver real benefits for hundreds of thousands of people across Europe. This is what we aim to achieve."

BACKGROUND

Today's Communication points out that there are two main problems when it comes to cross-border inheritance tax in the EU:

The first is double or multiple taxation, where more than one Member State claims the right to tax the same inheritance. Divergent national rules, a shortage of bilateral inheritance tax conventions, and inadequate national double tax relief measures can result in citizens being taxed twice or more on the same inheritance. Member States are free to apply national inheritance rules as they see fit once they are in line with EU rules on non-discrimination and free movement. The Commission is not proposing any harmonisation of Member States' inheritance tax rules. Instead it is recommending a broader and more flexible application of national double taxation relief measures so as to provide a pragmatic, speedy and cost-effective solution to the significant tax burdens facing many citizens. The Recommendation in today's Package suggests how Member States could improve existing national measures to ensure that there is adequate double tax relief. It sets out solutions for cases in which several Member States have taxing rights. The Commission invites Member States to introduce the appropriate solutions into national legislation or administrative practices.

The second inheritance tax problem that citizens can encounter is discrimination. Some Member States apply a higher tax rate if the assets, the deceased and/or the heir are located outside their territory. In such cases, EU law is clear: Member States are obliged to respect the basic principles of non-discrimination and free movement set out in the Treaties. The Working Paper published today sets out the principles on non-discriminatory inheritance and gift tax, using case-law to illustrate them. This will help Member States to bring their provisions into line with EU law, while also raising citizens' awareness of the rules which Member States must respect.

Although cross-border inheritance tax problems may seriously affect individuals, revenues from domestic and cross-border inheritances taxes account for a very small share - less than 0.5% - of total tax revenues in Member States. Cross-border cases alone must account for far less than that figure.

NEXT STEPS

The Commission will launch discussions with Member States to ensure appropriate follow up to the Recommendation. In addition, it is ready to assist all Member States in bringing their inheritance laws into line with EU law. In 3 years time, the Commission will present an evaluation report showing how the situation has evolved, and decide on this basis whether further measures are necessary at national or EU level. Meanwhile, the Commission, as guardian of the Treaties, is continuing to take the necessary steps to act against discriminatory features of Member States taxation rules.

For the full texts of the Communication, Recommendation and Staff Working Paper, see: ec.europa.eu/taxation_customs/taxation/personal_tax/inheritance/index_en.htm

For more information, see MEMO/11/917: europa.eu/rapid/press-release_MEMO-11-917_en.htm

NON-DOMICILED PERSONS IHT CHANGES ANNOUNCED AT SUMMER BUDGET 2015

8 July 2015. *HMRC Notice*

ABSTRACT

The government intends to legislate in Finance Bill 2016 to bring forward the point at which individuals are treated as deemed domiciled in the UK for IHT purposes to include where they have been resident in the UK for more than 15 out of the past 20 tax years, with effect from April 2017. A detailed consultation document will be published after the Summer recess.

FULL TEXT

www.gov.uk/government/publications/technical-briefing-on-foreign-domiciled-persons-changes-announced-at-summer-budget-2015

This note provides further detail on the proposals outlined at the Summer Budget on 8 July 2015 on new deemed domicile rules. It is written for practitioners advising foreign domiciliaries whether UK resident or non-UK resident and trustees of excluded property trusts.

INTRODUCTION

1. On July 8th 2015 the government announced a number of reforms to the taxation of foreign domiciled persons ("non-doms"). These changes will affect non-doms (i.e. those not domiciled in the UK under general law) who are resident in the UK for lengthy periods. In addition, changes will also be made to the qualifying rules governing those who have a UK domicile at birth (known as a UK domicile of origin).

2. This note sets out the detail of these proposals. A detailed consultation document will be published after summer recess to seek views on the best way to deliver these reforms, and a further consultation will follow on the draft legislation which is intended to form part of the 2016 Finance Bill. This note sets out the detailed parameters of the proposed changes and signals some of the areas that will be explored in consultation.

3. Individuals who are resident and domiciled in the UK are taxed on their worldwide income and gains. Non-doms are able to claim the remittance basis of taxation, which does not tax foreign income and gains as long as they are not brought ("remitted") to the UK. To access the remittance basis, longer term UK resident non-doms need to pay an annual remittance basis charge.

4. Individuals who are domiciled in the UK are subject to inheritance tax on gifts and on death on their worldwide assets. If they emigrate and settle permanently in another country, thus acquiring a foreign domicile under general law, nevertheless they remain deemed domiciled for inheritance tax purposes in the UK until 3 years after they have lost their UK domicile under general law ("the 3 year rule") even if they have been non-UK resident for many years. Non-domiciled individuals pay IHT only in respect of their UK assets. However, an individual who is not domiciled in the UK can become deemed-UK domiciled for IHT purposes in certain circumstances e.g. if they have been resident in the UK for 17 out of the last 20 tax years. Then they pay UK IHT on their worldwide assets. Once they have become deemed domiciled here for IHT purposes, they can only lose that deemed domicile by being non-UK resident for 4 tax years ("the 4 year rule").

5. The non-dom regime has been criticised by those concerned that a small group of very wealthy people have benefited from non-dom status in circumstances that have not looked fair to people who are not able to make the claim. These claims tend to be made in respect of people who have been here for lengthy periods of time and who therefore appear to have a settled presence in the UK. These criticisms have brought into question the fairness of the wider regime, which is intended to make the UK an attractive destination for people from overseas who come to live here for a period of time but who intend to leave at some point in the future. The government remains committed to a competitive tax regime that attracts talent and investment into the UK. The vast majority of those who claim non-dom status stay in the UK for less than 15 years but there are a small number who stay for much longer periods and are long-term residents of the UK.

WHAT THE GOVERNMENT INTENDS TO ACHIEVE

6. The government believes that long term UK resident non-doms should pay UK tax on their personal worldwide income and gains, regardless of whether the amounts are received in the UK or overseas.

7. The government also believes that those who have a strong connection with the UK having a UK domicile of origin at birth should not be able to access the remittance basis regime if they return and become UK resident here, even if they have lost that UK domicile as a matter of law.

8. From April 2017, those who have been resident in the UK for more than 15 out of the past 20 tax years will therefore be treated as deemed UK domiciled for all tax purposes. This will mean that they will no longer be able to use the remittance basis and they will be deemed domiciled for inheritance tax purposes. In addition, those who had a domicile in the UK at the date of their birth will revert to having a UK domicile for tax purposes whenever they are resident in the UK, even if under general law they have acquired a domicile in another country.

9. This is part of a package of reforms to the rules that affect non-doms including a proposal to ensure that UK inheritance tax (IHT) is paid on UK residential property, even when the property is held indirectly through an offshore company or similar structure. Details of these IHT reforms are provided in a separate paper.

10. These reforms mean that the £90,000 remittance basis charge payable by those who have been resident for 17 out of 20 years will be redundant as such persons will be taxable on an

arising basis after 15 years. The £30,000 and £60,000 remittance basis charges remain unchanged. The government will consult on the need to retain a de minimis exemption beyond 15 years where total unremitted foreign income and gains are less than £2,000 pa (ITA 2007 s809D(2)).

REFORMING THE NON-DOM REGIME

11. The government is proposing two changes which will restrict non-doms from being able to claim non-dom status for an indefinite period of time. These two rules are respectively referred to as:

a. the deemed domicile rule for long term resident non-doms ("15 year rule") and

b. the returning UK dom rule.

These proposals are explained further below.

LONG TERM RESIDENT NON DOMS – THE 15 YEAR RULE.

12. This introduces a "deemed-domicile" rule for long-term residents who nevertheless remain foreign domiciled under general law. The 15 year rule will not affect their domicile position under general law, only the UK tax treatment. Nor will it affect the domicile of the individual's children whose domicile under general law and deemed domicile for tax purposes will be tested separately by reference to the child's own individual circumstances.

Detail

13. Individuals who have been UK resident for more than 15 of the past 20 tax years but are foreign domiciled under general law will be deemed domiciled for all tax purposes in the UK. The government will consult on whether split years of UK residence count towards the 15 years for this purpose or whether complete tax years of UK residence are required.

14. This will mean that from their 16th tax year of UK residence long term residents will no longer be able to access the remittance basis and will be subject to tax on an arising basis on their worldwide personal income and gains.

15. At this point inheritance tax will also be paid on worldwide personal assets.

16. The new rules will be effective from 6 April 2017 irrespective of when someone arrived in the UK. There will be no special grandfathering rules for those already in the UK. For those who leave the UK before 6 April 2017 but would nevertheless be deemed domiciled under the 15 year rule on 6 April 2017 the present rules will apply.

17. Once the non-dom who has become deemed domiciled under the 15 year rule leaves the UK and spends more than five tax years outside the UK they will at that point lose their deemed tax domicile ("the five year rule"). In practice once they cease to be UK resident, their deemed tax domicile is likely only to be relevant for inheritance tax purposes. There will therefore be a longer "inheritance tax tail" for non-doms who leave the UK than at present for IHT purposes where as noted at paragraph 3 above a 4 year rule currently applies. The government will consult on whether other provisions need to be changed such as IHTA 1984 s267ZA (spousal election to be domiciled in the UK) and the effect of the change in relation to certain old estate duty treaties.

18. In order to have parity of treatment between UK doms and non doms, UK doms who leave after 5 April 2017 having been here for over 15 years will also be subject to the five year rule even if they intend to emigrate permanently and settle in a particular place on the day of their departure. The government will consult on the detail of the various interactions between the new five year rule and the existing three year and four year rules outlined at paragraph 3 above.

19. If at a later date (having spent more than five tax years abroad) the non-dom returns to the UK for a period but still intends eventually to leave the UK and therefore remains foreign domiciled under general law they will be able to spend another 15 years as a resident for tax purposes before becoming deemed domiciled again. (This will not apply to returning UK doms who are subject to different rules set out below).

20. The deemed domicile of the long term resident non-dom has no effect on the domicile status of the children, whose actual and deemed domicile position is looked at independently. Thus

they will take their father's domicile under general law at the date of their birth and if they are long term residents within the new rules will become deemed domiciled here. But they do not become deemed domiciled here simply because either parent is deemed domiciled here nor do they lose deemed domicile just because a parent does.

21. Once deemed domiciled here under the 15 year rule, non-doms will not be able to claim reliefs such as the remittance basis for overseas chargeable earnings under ITEPA 2003 s22. There will be consultation on the employment-related securities provisions.

22. Non doms who have set up an offshore trust before they become deemed domiciled here under the 15 year rule will not be taxed on trust income and gains that are retained in the trust and such excluded property trusts will have the same IHT treatment as at present (subject to the announcement made at Budget 2015 on UK residential property held through offshore companies and similar vehicles). However, such long term residents will, from April 2017 be taxed on any benefits, capital or income received from any trusts on a worldwide basis. The government will consult on the necessary changes to the transfer of assets regime and capital gains tax trust provisions. The government recognises that this is a significant change to the current rules and that changes to trust taxation are complex and will need to be considered carefully.

23. Certain transitional provisions relating to trusts were introduced for non-doms in 2008 (in particular rebasing). The interaction of these rules with the new regime after the non-dom becomes deemed domiciled here will be subject to consultation.

THE UK DOMICILIARY ("THE RETURNING UK DOM")

24. The government wishes to make it harder for individuals who have a UK domicile at the date of their birth to claim non-dom status if they leave the UK and acquire a domicile of choice in another country but subsequently return here.

25. Some individuals who have a UK domicile at the date of their birth (i.e. a UK domicile of origin) may emigrate. They may successfully be able to show that under general law they have acquired a domicile of choice overseas as they intend to settle in the foreign country. Under current rules and in particular the 3 year rule in IHTA s267(1)(a) referred to in paragraph 3 above, they will remain UK deemed domiciled for IHT purposes for at least 3 years after they have formed the intention to settle permanently (and do settle) in the foreign country even if they have been non-UK resident for many years before reaching that decision. Once they have lost their UK domicile and deemed domicile for IHT purposes they can set up trusts and obtain favourable treatment for excluded property trusts and their worldwide estate will fall outside IHT. These rules will not change except that UK doms who leave after 5 April 2017 will also be subject to the five year rule set out in paragraph 17 above.

26. However some of these individuals later return to the UK for some years and still maintain they have a foreign domicile of choice. In these circumstances, the new rules will mean that they are taxed as UK domiciled for tax purposes on their return irrespective of their domicile status under general law.

27. Irrespective of their actual intentions, such an individual (the returning UK dom) will become UK domiciled for tax purposes once they become UK resident. In addition, while UK resident after their return here, the returning UK domiciliary will not benefit from any favourable tax treatment in respect of trusts set up while not domiciled here (whether inheritance tax treatment or otherwise). The government will consult on the detail of these proposals.

28. On departure the returning UK dom can lose their UK tax domicile in the tax year after departure but only if both the following conditions are satisfied:

(a) they have not spent more than 15 tax years here and

(b) they have not acquired an actual domicile in the UK under general law during their return.

If (a) applies but not (b) they are subject to the five year rule in paragraph 17 above which requires five years' non-UK residence.

If (b) applies but not (a) they are subject to the three year rule in paragraph 3 and will remain UK domiciled for IHT purposes until more than 3 years after they have acquired (or reacquired) a foreign domicile of choice as a matter of law.

If both (a) and (b) apply they are subject to both the five year and three year rules and can lose UK tax domicile only on the later of those events.

29. This measure will affect all returning UK doms from 6 April 2017, including those who returned prior to April 2017. The five year rule will affect UK doms leaving after 5 April 2017. It will also affect trusts set up while such individuals were not UK domiciled if they are UK resident on or after 6 April 2017. In these circumstances, an individual will be taxed on all income and gains arising in such trusts under the same rules as any other UK domiciliary. The IHT treatment of such trusts will also be the same as for UK tax payers who have never lost a UK domicile.

30. The government intends to consult further on the interaction of the various deemed domicile rules for both UK doms and non doms and also in relation to the tax treatment of trusts.

WHEN WILL THE CHANGES BE INTRODUCED?

31. The government will consult widely with stakeholders and interested parties on the detail of these measures. This consultation will be published after the summer recess. The changes will be legislated in Finance Bill 2016 and introduced from 6 April 2017.

NON-DOMICILED PERSONS IHT RESIDENTIAL PROPERTY CHANGES ANNOUNCED AT SUMMER BUDGET 2015

8 July 2015. *HMRC Notice*

ABSTRACT

The government intends to legislate in Finance Bill 2017, with effect from April 2017, to ensure that IHT is payable on all UK residential property owned by non-domiciles, regardless of their residence status for tax purposes, including property held indirectly through an offshore structure. A full consultation will follow later this year.

FULL TEXT

http://www.gov.uk/government/publications/technical-briefing-on-foreign-domiciled-personsinheritance-tax-residential-property-changes

This note provides further detail on the proposals outlined at the Summer Budget on 8 July 2015 on new IHT rules on UK residential property held indirectly by non-UK domiciled individuals or by excluded property trusts. It is published alongside a separate technical briefing note on broader changes to the taxation of non-domiciles. The paper is provided for practitioners advising (a) foreign domiciled persons whether UK resident or non-UK resident; (b) trustees of excluded property trusts where in either case UK residential property is beneficially owned through foreign companies* or other opaque structures.

* The foreign incorporated company is sometimes based in an offshore jurisdiction; references in this Technical Note to offshore companies should be taken to include all foreign incorporated companies.

INTRODUCTION

1. The government announced on July 8th 2015 that, from April 2017, it intends to bring all UK residential property held directly or indirectly by foreign domiciled persons into charge for inheritance tax (IHT) purposes, even when the property is owned through an indirect structure such as an offshore company or partnership.

2. This note sets out some of the detail of these proposals. A consultation document will be published after summer recess to seek views on the best way to deliver these reforms and a further consultation will follow on the draft legislation which it is intended will form part of the 2017 Finance Bill.

3. Individuals who are domiciled in the UK are subject to IHT on all their worldwide assets, subject to reliefs and exemptions. However, individuals who are neither UK domiciled nor deemed domiciled for IHT purposes ("non-doms") are only subject to IHT on assets they own in the UK. Foreign assets owned by non-doms are excluded from the scope of IHT – such assets are referred to as "excluded property".

UK RESIDENTIAL PROPERTY – THE INDIVIDUAL

4. If a non-dom individual dies owning UK property directly, their personal representatives or the beneficiaries of their estate are liable to IHT at 40% on the value of the UK property subject to the usual exemptions. It is irrelevant whether the deceased was resident in the UK or not.

5. However, as IHT is only charged on UK property directly held by non-doms, it is relatively easy for a non-dom to own such property through an offshore vehicle so as to secure an IHT advantage on UK property in a way not available to a person domiciled in the UK. This is referred to as "enveloping" the property: the offshore company owns the UK property beneficially and the individual owns the shares of the company.

UK RESIDENTIAL PROPERTY – THE TRUST

6. Once a non-dom becomes UK domiciled or deemed domiciled for IHT purposes, their worldwide assets are subject to UK IHT unless they have been settled into an "excluded property trust" prior to the individual becoming domiciled or deemed domiciled here.

7. No IHT is charged on the transfer of foreign assets into the trust or at any later date in the life of the trust provided the trust is funded before the non-dom becomes deemed domiciled and the trust does not at any relevant time hold any UK assets directly. Excluded property trusts therefore tend to hold UK property through an offshore company. The settled property is then the foreign shares not the UK property. There is no provision in the IHT legislation to "look-through" the company and charge IHT on the underlying UK property.

PROPOSAL

8. The government intends to amend the rules on excluded property so that trusts or individuals owning UK residential property through an offshore company, partnership or other opaque vehicle, will pay IHT on the value of such UK property in the same way as UK domiciled individuals. The measure will apply to all UK residential property whether it is occupied or let and of whatever value.

9. The government does not intend to change the IHT position for non-doms or exclude property trusts in relation to UK assets other than residential property, or for non-UK assets. Nor will these reforms affect people who are domiciled in the UK.

POLICY DESIGN

10. The IHT charge on indirectly held UK property will be based on the Annual Tax on Enveloped Dwellings (ATED) rules, though these proposals will go further than ATED. ATED is limited to properties with a value of £1m and over (reducing to £500,000 and over from April 2016) and is not charged on properties held by offshore companies (and by certain other entities) that are let at arms' length to unconnected parties. The scope of the IHT charge will have no such minimum threshold and the various ATED reliefs will not be applicable here.

11. The intention is that broadly the same properties currently covered by the non-residents CGT legislation introduced in Finance Act 2015 will be subject to IHT. The definitions of UK residential property and the definition for persons chargeable as enacted in FA 2015 for non-residents CGT will be used as a starting point for these reforms with any necessary adaptions where appropriate. As with non-residents CGT, diversely held vehicles that hold UK residential property will not be within the scope of the IHT charge but any closely controlled offshore company, partnership or similar structure will be within the new provisions.

12. IHT will therefore be imposed on the value of UK residential property owned by the offshore company on the occasion of any chargeable event. This would include:

a. the death of the individual wherever resident who owns the company shares,

b. a gift of the company shares into trust,

c. the ten year anniversary of the trust,

d. distribution of the company shares out of trust,

e. the death of the donor within 7 years of having given the company that holds the UK property away to an individual or

f. the death of the donor or settlor where he benefits from the gifted UK property or shares within 7 years prior to his death. The reservation of benefit rules will apply to the shares of a company owning UK property in the same way as the rules currently apply to UK property held by foreign doms and generally to UK doms.

13. This will require a change in the legislation to provide that shares of offshore companies or similar structures are not excluded property to the extent that they derive their value directly or indirectly from UK residential property (as defined for non-residents CGT) or to the extent that the value of those shares is otherwise attributable to UK residential property. There will be no change to the taxation of UK property held by corporate structures which are owned by UK domiciled individuals or trusts that are not excluded property. The relevant property regime will also need to be amended in certain respects.

14. UK residential property may not be the only asset owned by the offshore company. The company may beneficially own non UK assets such as foreign land or equities or own UK commercial property which is not subject to the change. Moreover offshore companies holding UK land may be held in more complex structures involving groups. Further complications will arise where the non-dom individual or excluded property trust does not wholly own the company.

15. The government will consult on the details of these proposals so as to ensure that it is only the value of the UK residential property that is subject to tax (less any borrowings taken out to purchase such UK property).

16. It is intended that the same reliefs and charges will apply as if the property was held directly by the owner of the company. Hence a deceased individual who owned the company shares directly will have the benefit of spouse exemption if the company shares are left to a spouse. However, spouse exemption will not generally be available if the offshore company shares are held by trusts other than qualifying interest in possession trusts and the settlor is taxed on death under the reservation of benefit provisions.

ENFORCEMENT AND AVOIDANCE

17. Certain amendments will be made to the IHT legislation to ensure that liability, reporting and enforcement issues are addressed adequately in relation to offshore companies and non-residents generally. Further details will be given in the consultation.

18. HMRC are aware of a number of ways in which foreign domiciled individuals and trusts may seek to avoid IHT by manipulation of the rules involving excluded property. The anti-avoidance legislation will therefore be targeted and reviewed very carefully to stop this. Such arrangements may also be within the proposed extension of the DOTAS regulations in relation to IHT.

ENVELOPED PROPERTIES – DE-ENVELOPING

19. Properties held in companies or other envelopes can be 'sold' by transferring the shares of that company. Such a transaction is not subject to any Stamp Duty Land Tax (SDLT). ATED was introduced in Finance Act 2013 to ensure that people enveloping residential property in corporate vehicles pay a price for that privilege by a higher SDLT rate on entry into the corporate structure and ATED. ATED is targeted only at residential property held through a company where it is occupied rather than let out to an unconnected person. Properties let to unconnected parties qualify for relief and are therefore exempt from the ATED charge.

20. HMRC's research suggests that the most common reason for enveloping properties is IHT planning undertaken by non-doms. Under the present IHT regime many non-doms would not consider de-enveloping primarily because the cost of ATED does not outweigh the current benefits of the envelope and in the case of let property ATED does not apply anyway.

21. The proposed changes to the IHT rules will change the IHT treatment, so some non-doms and trusts may wish to remove the envelope and move into a simpler more straightforward structure outside the scope of future ATED charges, ATED reporting or ATED-related CGT. If the property is mortgaged or has increased in value since 2013 there may however, be significant costs in de-enveloping.

22. The government will consider the costs associated with de-enveloping and any other concerns stakeholders may have during the course of the consultation regarding de-enveloping.

NEXT STEPS

23. A consultation will be published towards the end of the summer inviting views and representations from interested parties and stakeholders. It is envisaged that legislation will be included in Finance Bill 2017 with the changes being effective on or after 6 April 2017.

SUMMER BUDGET 2015 TIIN: IHT MAIN RESIDENCE NIL-RATE BAND AND THE EXISTING NIL-RATE BAND

8 July 2015. *HMRC Notice*

ABSTRACT

Legislation in Summer Finance Bill 2015 will provide for an additional nil-rate band when a residence is passed on death to a direct descendant. This will be £100,000 in 2017/18, £125,000 in 2018/19, £150,000 in 2019/20, and £175,000 in 2020/21, increasing thereafter in line with the CPI. Any unused nil-rate band will be transferred to a surviving spouse or civil partner. Legislation in Finance Bill 2016 will allow that part of the main residence nil-rate band which might otherwise be lost when a person downsizes or ceases to own a home on or after 8 July 2015 to pass on death to direct descendants. There will be a tapered withdrawal of the additional nil-rate band for estates with a net value of more than £2m. The existing nil-rate band will remain at £325,000 from 2018/19 until the end of 2020/21.

FULL TEXT

www.gov.uk/government/publications/inheritance-tax-main-residence-nil-rate-band-and-the-existing-nil-rate-band

WHO IS LIKELY TO BE AFFECTED?

Individuals with direct descendants who have an estate (including a main residence) with total assets above the inheritance tax threshold (or nil-rate band) of £325,000 and personal representatives of deceased persons.

GENERAL DESCRIPTION OF THE MEASURE

This measure introduces an additional nil-rate band when a residence is passed on death to a direct descendant. This will be £100,000 in 2017-18, £125,000 in 2018-19, £150,000 in 2019-20, and £175,000 in 2020-21. It will then increase in line with Consumer Prices Index (CPI) from 2021-22 onwards. Any unused nil-rate band will be able to be transferred to a surviving spouse or civil partner.

The additional nil-rate band will also be available when a person downsizes or ceases to own a home on or after 8 July 2015 and assets of an equivalent value, up to the value of the additional nil-rate band, are passed on death to direct descendants.

There will be a tapered withdrawal of the additional nil-rate band for estates with a net value of more than £2m. This will be at a withdrawal rate of £1 for every £2 over this threshold.

The existing nil-rate band will remain at £325,000 from 2018-19 until the end of 2020-21.

POLICY OBJECTIVE

This measure will reduce the burden of inheritance tax for most families by making it easier to pass on the family home to direct descendants without a tax charge.

BACKGROUND TO THE MEASURE

The measure was announced at Summer Budget 2015.

Operative date

The measure will take effect for relevant transfers on death on or after 6 April 2017. It will apply to reduce the tax payable by an estate on death; it will not apply to reduce the tax payable on lifetime transfers that are chargeable as a result of death.

The main residence nil-rate band will be transferable where the second spouse or civil partner of a couple dies on or after 6 April 2017 irrespective of when the first of the couple died.

The nil-rate band will continue to be £325,000 from 2018-19 until the end of 2020-21.

Current law

Section 7 of the Inheritance Tax Act 1984 (IHTA) provides for the rates of inheritance tax to be as set out in the table in Schedule 1 to that Act. The current table provides that the nil-rate band is £325,000.

Inheritance tax is charged at a rate of 40% on the chargeable value of an estate, above the nil-rate band, after taking into account the value of any chargeable lifetime transfers. The chargeable value is the value after deducting any liabilities, reliefs and exemptions that apply.

Where an estate qualifies for spouse or civil partner exemption, the unused proportion of the nil-rate band when the first of the couple dies can be transferred to the estate of the surviving spouse or civil partner, sections 8A-C IHTA. The nil-rate band can be transferred when the surviving spouse or civil partner dies on or after 9 October 2007, irrespective of when the first of the couple died, so that the nil-rate band can be up to £650,000.

There is currently no specific exemption for a residence, or for assets being transferred to children and other direct descendants.

Section 8(3) to Finance Act 2010 provides for the nil-rate band to be frozen at £325,000 up to and including 2014-15. Section 117 and paragraph 2 of Schedule 25 to Finance Act 2014 extends the freeze on the nil-rate band until the end of 2017-18.

Proposed revisions

Legislation will be introduced in Summer Finance Bill 2015 to provide for an additional main residence nil-rate band for an estate if the deceased's interest in a residential property, which has been their residence at some point and is included in their estate, is left to one or more direct descendants on death.

The value of the main residence nil-rate band for an estate will be the lower of the net value of the interest in the residential property (after deducting any liabilities such a mortgage) or the maximum amount of the band. The maximum amount will be will be phased in so that it is £100,000 for 2017-18, £125,000 for 2018-19, £150,000 for 2019-20, and £175,000 for 2020-21. It will then increase in line with CPI for subsequent years.

The qualifying residential interest will be limited to one residential property but personal representatives will be able to nominate which residential property should qualify if there is more than one in the estate. A property which was never a residence of the deceased, such as a buy-to-let property, will not qualify.

A direct descendant will be a child (including a step-child, adopted child or foster child) of the deceased and their lineal descendants.

A claim will have to be made on the death of a person's surviving spouse or civil partner to transfer any unused proportion of the additional nil-rate band unused by the person on their death, in the same way that the existing nil-rate band can be transferred.

If the net value of the estate (after deducting any liabilities but before reliefs and exemptions) is above £2 million, the additional nil-rate band will be tapered away by £1 for every £2 that the net value exceeds that amount. The taper threshold at which the additional nil-rate band is gradually withdrawn will rise in line with CPI from 2021-22 onwards.

The legislation will also extend the current freeze of the existing nil-rate band at £325,000 until the end of 2020-21.

In addition, legislation in Finance Bill 2016 will provide that where part of the main residence nil-rate band might be lost because the deceased had downsized to a less valuable residence or had ceased to own a residence on or after 8 July 2015, that part will still be available provided the deceased left that smaller residence, or assets of equivalent value, to direct descendants. However, the total amount available will not exceed the maximum available residence nil-rate band. The technical details of how the additional nil-rate band will be enhanced to support those who have downsized or ceased to own their home will be the subject of a consultation to be published in September 2015 ahead of the draft Finance Bill 2016.

HOW DOWNSIZING, SELLING OR GIFTING A HOME AFFECTS THE ADDITIONAL INHERITANCE TAX THRESHOLD

11 August 2017. *HMRC Guidance Note*

ABSTRACT

When someone's sold, given away or downsized to a less valuable home before they die, their estate may be able to get an extra Inheritance Tax threshold. This is known as a downsizing addition, and all these conditions must apply—

– the person sold, gave away or downsized to a less valuable home, on or after 8 July 2015
– the former home would have qualified for the additional threshold if they'd kept it until they died
– their direct descendants inherit at least some of the estate

The downsizing rules are complicated.

This guide explains the basic rules, but it can't cover the more complex situations, for example, where trusts are involved. You might want to get professional advice about how to work out the additional threshold in these situations.

FULL TEXT

The amount of the downsizing addition will usually be the same as the additional threshold that's been lost when the former home is no longer in the estate.

It will also depend on the value of the other assets left to direct descendants. But the downsizing addition can't be more than the maximum amount of additional threshold that would have been available if the sale or downsizing hadn't happened.

The estate's personal representative must make a claim for the downsizing addition within 2 years of the end of the month that the person dies. HM Revenue and Customs (HMRC) can extend this time limit in some circumstances.

You don't have to tell HMRC when the downsizing move, sale or gift of the former home happens. The estate's personal representative makes a claim for the additional threshold and any downsizing addition when filling in the Inheritance Tax returns. But, keep the details of the move, gift or sale so that the estate's personal representative can get that information when they make the claim.

Only one move, sale or other disposal of a former home can be taken into account for the downsizing addition. If the person that died downsized more than once, or sold or gave away more than one home between 8 July 2015 and the date they died, the estate's personal representative can choose which to use to calculate the downsizing addition.

WORKING OUT THE LOST ADDITIONAL THRESHOLD

There are 5 steps to work out how much additional threshold has been lost:

Step 1. Work out the additional threshold that would have been available when the former home was sold or given away or when the move happened. This figure is made up of the maximum additional threshold due at that date (or £100,000 if it was before 6 April 2017) and any transferred additional threshold available when the person dies.

Step 2. Divide the value of the former home at the date of the move or when it was sold or given away by the figure in step 1, and multiply the result by 100 to get a percentage. If the value of the former home is greater than the figure in step 1 the percentage will be limited to 100%. If the value of the home sold is less than the figure in step 1, the percentage will be between 0% and 100%.

Step 3. If there's a home in the estate, divide the value of the home by the additional threshold that would be available at the date the person dies (including any transferred additional threshold). Multiply the result by 100 to get a percentage (again this percentage can't be more than 100%). If there's no home in the estate at the time the person dies this percentage will be 0%.

Step 4. Deduct the percentage in step 3 from the percentage in step 2.

Step 5. Multiply the additional threshold that would be available at the time the person died by the figure from step 4. This gives the amount of the lost additional threshold.

EXAMPLE

Katherine's a widow. She sold a home worth £195,000 in June 2018. The maximum additional threshold when she sold the home (in the tax year 2018 to 2019) is £125,000.

She died in August 2020 with no home in her estate. The maximum additional threshold in the tax year 2020 to 2021 is £175,000.

Her estate is also entitled to the transferred additional threshold of £175,000 from her late husband's estate.

To calculate the lost additional threshold:

Step 1. The maximum additional threshold when the home was sold was £125,000. Katherine's estate is also entitled to the transferred additional threshold of £175,000. So the total additional threshold that could have been available when the home was sold is £300,000 (£125,000 + £175,000).

Step 2. The home was worth £195,000 when it was sold. Divide this by the value at step 1 (£300,000) to give a percentage of 65%.

Step 3. There's no home in the estate when Katherine dies, so the percentage is 0%.

Step 4. Taking 0% from 65% gives a percentage of 65%.

Step 5. When Katherine dies, the maximum additional threshold is £175,000. Her estate is also entitled to the transferred additional threshold of £175,000, so the maximum additional threshold for her estate is £350,000. The "lost" additional threshold is £227,500 (65% of £350,000).

Although the lost additional threshold is £227,500, the amount of the downsizing addition available to her estate depends on the value of any other assets she leaves to her direct descendants.

The effect of step 3 is that there'll be a different amount of lost additional threshold depending on whether the person that's died has either—

- downsized to a less valuable home
- sold or given away a home

If the percentage in step 3 is the same or greater than the percentage in step 2, there's no loss of additional threshold and there'll be no downsizing addition.

DOWNSIZING TO A LESS VALUABLE HOME

There may be some lost additional threshold when someone downsizes to a less valuable home but still has a home in their estate when they die. This will only happen when the value of the new home is less than the maximum additional threshold available to the estate.

The downsizing rules won't apply if either—

- there's no loss of the additional threshold because the value of any new home is the same, or more than the maximum available additional threshold when they die
- the additional threshold isn't available because although there's a home in the estate it's not left to a direct descendant

To see if the downsizing addition applies, you don't just look at whether the estate qualifies for the maximum additional threshold. Instead you have to work out whether the value of any home still in the estate is too low to qualify for the maximum additional threshold if it was left to direct descendants.

EXAMPLE

Lillian downsized in 2018 from a house worth £450,000 to a bungalow. The maximum additional threshold in the tax year 2018 to 2019 is £125,000.

Lillian dies in the tax year 2020 to 2021 when her estate is worth £700,000. She leaves the bungalow worth £200,000 to her sister.

She leaves other assets worth £500,000 to her children.

The maximum additional threshold in the tax year 2020 to 2021 is £175,000.

There's no entitlement to the transferred additional threshold when Lillian dies.

Step 1. The maximum additional threshold when the house was sold was £125,000.

Step 2. The house was worth £450,000 when she sold it. Divide this by the figure at step 1 to give a percentage of 360%. But as the value of the house is more than the figure at step 1, the percentage is limited to 100%.

Step 3. When Lillian died, the bungalow was worth £200,000. Divide this by the maximum additional threshold available at death (£175,000). This would be 114•3%, but again is limited to 100%.

Step 4. Take away the percentage at step 3 (100%) from the percentage at step 2 (100%). This gives a percentage of 0%.

Step 5. Multiply the maximum additional threshold (£175,000) by the percentage at step 4 (0%), to give a total of lost additional threshold of £0.

As the percentage at step 4 is 0%, there's no lost additional threshold and so there's no downsizing addition.

CALCULATING THE ADDITIONAL THRESHOLD

When someone downsized and still had a home when they died, the additional threshold for the estate will be made up of both—

- the additional threshold on the home included in the estate
- any downsizing addition due for the former home

The downsizing addition will usually be the lower of—

- the amount of additional threshold that's been lost as a result of the downsizing move
- the value of the other assets in the estate left to direct descendants

EXAMPLE

In May 2018 Michael downsized from a large house worth £500,000 to a small flat. The maximum additional threshold in the tax year 2018 to 2019 is £125,000.

Michael dies in September 2020. He leaves the flat worth £105,000 to his son, and the rest of his estate worth £200,000 to his 2 daughters.

The maximum additional threshold in the tax year 2020 to 2021 is £175,000.

There's no entitlement to the transferred additional threshold when Michael dies.

Step 1. The maximum additional threshold when he downsized was £125,000.

Step 2. The house was worth £500,000 when he sold it. Divide this by the figure at step 1, but limit the percentage to 100%.

Step 3. The flat is worth £105,000 when Michael dies. Divide this by the maximum additional threshold available at that time (£175,000). This gives a percentage of 60%.

Step 4. Take away the percentage at step 3 (60%) from the percentage at step 2 (100%) to give a percentage of 40%.

Step 5. Multiply the maximum additional threshold when Michael dies (£175,000) by the percentage at step 4 (40%) to give a total of lost additional threshold of £70,000.

The actual amount of the downsizing addition depends on the value of other assets that are left to Michael's children.

As he leaves more than £70,000 worth of other assets to his daughters, the downsizing addition of £70,000 is added to the additional threshold due for the flat of £105,000 left to his son. This gives a total additional threshold for the estate of £175,000.

If instead he'd left the flat to his son, some assets worth £50,000 to his daughters, and the rest of his estate to his wife, the downsizing addition would be restricted to £50,000. This is because that's the value of other assets he left to his daughters.

The total additional threshold in that case would be £155,000 (£105,000 + £50,000).

LEAVING PART OF THE HOME TO DIRECT DESCENDANTS

If only part of the home in the estate is left to direct descendants, that part is used to work out the additional threshold. This may also affect the total additional threshold for the estate in downsizing situations.

EXAMPLE

Nigel downsized in February 2019 from a house worth £400,000 to a bungalow. The maximum additional threshold in the tax year 2018 to 2019 is £125,000.

When Nigel dies in September 2020, he leaves the bungalow, worth £105,000, in equal shares to his wife and son.

He leaves the other assets in his estate worth £150,000 to his daughter.

The maximum additional threshold in the tax year 2020 to 2021 is £175,000.

There's no entitlement to the transferred additional threshold when Nigel dies.

Step 1. The maximum additional threshold at the date of downsizing was £125,000.

Step 2. The house was worth £400,000 when it was sold. Divide this by the figure at step 1, but limit the percentage to 100%.

Step 3. When Nigel dies, the bungalow is worth £105,000. Divide this by the maximum additional threshold available at that time (£175,000). This gives a percentage of 60%.

Step 4. Take away the percentage at step 3 (60%) from the percentage at step 2 (100%). This gives a percentage of 40%.

Step 5. Multiply the maximum additional threshold (£175,000) by the percentage at step 4 (40%), to give a total of lost additional threshold of £70,000.

Nigel only leaves half of the bungalow to his son. So you reduce the additional threshold due for that home to £52,500 (50% of £105,000).

As he leaves other assets of £150,000 to his daughter, the downsizing addition is £70,000 (the lower of the lost additional threshold of £70,000 and £150,000). You add this to the additional threshold due for the bungalow of £52,500, to give a total of £122,500 (£52,500 + £70,000). The maximum available additional threshold is £175,000, but Nigel's estate can only use £122,500. So there's unused additional threshold of £52,500 that can be transferred to his wife's estate.

If the assets left to his daughter were worth only £20,000, the downsizing addition would be restricted to £20,000. So the total additional threshold for the estate would be £72,500 (£52,500 + £20,000).

There'd be unused additional threshold of £102,500 available for transfer.

DOWNSIZING BEFORE 6 APRIL 2017

Where the downsizing occurs before 6 April 2017, you treat the maximum available additional threshold at that time as £100,000.

If someone downsized but had never lived in the less valuable property, that property is not a home for additional threshold purpose. This means that the position is the same as if the former home had been sold or given away.

EXAMPLE

Oliver and his wife Karen downsized to an apartment in March 2016 from a house they owned jointly, worth £300,000. As the move happened before 6 April 2017 you treat the maximum additional threshold in March 2016 as £100,000.

When Karen dies in December 2019, she leaves her half share of the apartment, worth £105,000, to Oliver. She leaves other assets in her estate worth £80,000 to their daughter.

The maximum additional threshold in the tax year 2019 to 2020 is £150,000.

There's no entitlement to the transferred additional threshold when Karen dies.

Step 1. The maximum additional threshold at the date of sale is £100,000 because the downsizing happened before 6 April 2017.

Step 2. Karen's share of the house was worth £150,000 when it was sold. Divide this by the figure at step 1, but limit the percentage to 100%.

Step 3. The apartment is worth £105,000 when Karen dies. Divide this by the maximum additional threshold at that time (£150,000) to give a percentage of 70%.

Step 4. Take away the percentage at step 3 (70%) from the percentage at step 2 (100%) to give a percentage of 30%.

Step 5. Multiply the maximum additional threshold (£150,000) by the percentage at step 4 (30%) to give a total of lost additional threshold of £45,000.

Because the apartment was left to Oliver there's no additional threshold due for the share in that home.

The downsizing addition is the lower of the lost additional threshold (£45,000) or the amount of other assets left to their daughter (£80,000). So the downsizing addition is £45,000 in this case.

The total additional threshold for the estate is £45,000 due to the downsizing addition.

Karen's estate had a maximum available additional threshold of £150,000, but it can only use £45,000. So there's unused additional threshold of £105,000 that can be transferred to Oliver's estate.

If the value of the assets left to their daughter had only been £10,000, the downsizing addition would be reduced to £10,000. So the total additional threshold for the estate would be £10,000. In that case the unused amount available for transfer would be £140,000.

SELLING OR GIVING AWAY A HOME

When someone sells or gives away (disposes of) a former home so that there's no longer any home in their estate when they die, the additional threshold for the estate will be equal to the downsizing addition for the former home.

You calculate the downsizing allowance in these situations slightly differently because there's no home in the estate that could qualify for any additional threshold.

When you work out the lost additional threshold, the percentage at step 3 will always be 0% and the result at step 4 will always be the same as the figure at step 2. So, steps 3 and 4 can be missed out.

The amount of additional threshold that's been lost will depend on what the former property was worth, and the maximum additional threshold at the time of the disposal. Again, if the sale took place on or after 8 July 2015 but before 6 April 2017, you treat the maximum additional threshold available as £100,000.

HOMES WORTH MORE THAN THE ADDITIONAL THRESHOLD

If the value of the former home is the same or more than the maximum available additional threshold at the time of the disposal, you treat the lost additional threshold as 100% of the maximum additional threshold available when the person died.

When there's no home in the estate, the downsizing addition will be the lower of—

– the amount of additional threshold that's been lost as a result of the sale
– the value of the other assets in the estate that the direct descendants inherit

EXAMPLE

Pauline sold her home for £285,000 in October 2018 to go into residential care.

The maximum additional threshold in the tax year 2018 to 2019 is £125,000.

She dies in March 2021 with an estate worth £500,000.

She leaves half of her estate to her son and half to her nephew.

The maximum additional threshold in the tax year 2020 to 2021 is £175,000.

There's no entitlement to the transferred additional threshold when Pauline dies.

Step 1. The maximum additional threshold at the date of sale was £125,000.

Step 2. The house was sold for £285,000. Divide this by the figure at step 1, but limit the percentage to 100%.

Step 3. There's no home in the estate so the percentage here is 0%.

Step 4. Take away the percentage at step 3 (0%) from the percentage at step 2 (100%). The percentage at step 2 stays at 100%.

Step 5. Multiply the maximum additional threshold (£175,000) by 100%, so the total lost additional threshold is £175,000.

The value of the home at the time of the sale is more than the maximum additional threshold at that time so the whole of the additional threshold has been lost.

Before she downsized, Pauline's estate could have qualified for the maximum additional threshold at that time. So, when she dies, the lost additional threshold as a result of the downsizing is £175,000.

The downsizing addition is the lower of the value of other assets that are left to a direct descendant and the lost additional threshold.

As Pauline leaves £250,000 of other assets to her son, a downsizing addition of £175,000 is due.

If instead she'd only left £100,000 to her son and the rest of her estate to her nephew, the downsizing addition would be restricted to £100,000.

HOMES WORTH LESS THAN THE ADDITIONAL THRESHOLD

If the value of the home in the person's estate was less than the maximum additional threshold when they sold or gave it away, the lost additional threshold is worked out as a percentage of that maximum additional threshold. You then apply that percentage to the maximum additional threshold when the person dies.

EXAMPLE

Robert had a flat that he sold for £90,000 in May 2019. He moved in with his daughter. The maximum additional threshold in the tax year 2019 to 2020 is £150,000.

Robert dies in January 2021 with an estate worth £600,000. He leaves all of it to his daughter. The maximum additional threshold in the tax year 2020 to 2021 is £175,000.

There's no entitlement to the transferred additional threshold when Robert dies.

Step 1. The maximum additional threshold at the date of sale was £150,000.

Step 2. The flat was worth £90,000 when Robert sold it. Divide this by the figure at step 1, to give a percentage of 60%.

Step 3. There's no home in the estate so the percentage here is 0%.

Step 4. Take away the percentage at step 3 (0%) from the percentage at step 2 (60%). The percentage at step 2 is still 60%.

Step 5. Multiply the maximum additional threshold (£175,000) by 60%, so the total lost additional threshold is £105,000.

The actual amount of the downsizing addition is the lower of the lost additional threshold (£105,000) and the value of other assets left to a direct descendant.

As Robert leaves £600,000 of other assets to his daughter, a downsizing addition of £105,000 is due.

DOWNSIZING WHEN THERE'S TRANSFERRED ADDITIONAL THRESHOLD

When an additional threshold is transferred following the death of a husband, wife or civil partner, you calculate the downsizing allowance in the same way. The difference is that the maximum additional threshold available at both the date someone dies and the date they sell or give away their home is increased to include the amount of the transferred additional threshold.

EXAMPLE

Ruth sold her home for £285,000 in October 2018 to go into residential care. The maximum additional threshold in the tax year 2018 to 2019 is £125,000.

She dies in March 2021 with an estate worth £500,000.

She leaves half of her estate to her son and half to her nephew. The maximum additional threshold in the tax year 2020 to 2021 is £175,000.

Ruth's estate is entitled to the transferred additional threshold of £175,000.

Step 1. The maximum additional threshold at the date of sale was £125,000. There's also an entitlement to the transferred additional threshold of £175,000. So the total value at step 1 is £300,000 (£125,000 + £175,000).

Step 2. The house was sold for £285,000. Divide this by the figure at step 1 to give a percentage of 95%.

Step 3. There's no home in the estate when Ruth dies so the percentage here is 0%.

Step 4. Deduct the percentage at step 3 (0%) from the percentage at step 2 (95%). So the percentage at step 2 stays as 95%.

Step 5. The maximum additional threshold when Ruth dies is £175,000. There's also an entitlement to the transferred additional threshold of £175,000, so the maximum for Ruth's estate is £350,000. Multiply this by 95% to give total lost additional threshold of £332,500.

The actual amount of the downsizing addition is the lower of the value of other assets left to a direct descendant and the lost additional threshold. As she left £250,000 of other assets to her son, her estate is due a downsizing addition of £250,000.

DOWNSIZING AND TRUSTS

The downsizing rules apply where a person sells or gives away a home that's included in their estate. Property held in certain trusts is included within a person's estate for Inheritance Tax purposes and so the downsizing rules apply in these circumstances too.

When a home is held in such a trust, the trustees might be able to dispose of it or they may change it to a less valuable one. This is treated the same as if the person that died had downsized, sold or gave away the home themselves. Where a person's right to occupy a home held in a trust stops, for example on re-marriage, this is also treated as a disposal for the purposes of the downsizing rules.

A person can have more than one interest in the same home. For example, they may own half of a house outright while the other half is held in a trust for their benefit. These would be two separate interests in the same home.

If a person sells or gives away more than one interest in a single home at the same time, for example, because they sell the whole house, all those interests can be taken into account for downsizing purposes. But, if a person disposes of different interests at different times, the estate's personal representative can only nominate one of those disposals to be taken into account to work out any downsizing addition.

Commentary—*Simon's Taxes* **I4.164**.

INHERITANCE TAX—TRANSFERRING UNUSED TAX-FREE THRESHOLDS

11 August 2017. *HMRC Guidance Note*

OVERVIEW

If there are any thresholds that haven't been fully used when the first person in a marriage or civil partnership dies, the unused part can be transferred to the estate of the surviving husband, wife or civil partner when they die.

THE BASIC TAX-FREE THRESHOLD

The basic tax-free threshold available when a wife, husband or civil partner dies can be increased to as much as £650,000 if none of the £325,000 threshold was used when the first of the couple died.

The basic threshold that's available to their estate is increased by the percentage of the threshold that wasn't used when the first partner died.

EXAMPLE

Paul dies leaving legacies totalling £600,000. He leaves £130,000 to his children and the rest to his wife. The available threshold at the time was £325,000.

The legacies to the children would use up 40% (£130,000 ÷ £325,000 x 100) of the threshold, leaving 60% unused.

When his wife dies, the threshold is still £325,000, so their available threshold would be increased by the unused percentage (60%) to £520,000.

If his wife's estate isn't worth more than £520,000 there'll be no Inheritance Tax to pay when she dies. If it's worth more, Inheritance Tax should be paid on anything above £520,000.

TRANSFERRING ANY UNUSED BASIC THRESHOLD

The estate's executors must claim to transfer the unused basic threshold when the husband, wife or civil partner dies.

UNUSED ADDITIONAL THRESHOLD

Any additional threshold that's not used when someone dies can be transferred to their husband, wife or civil partner's estate when they die. This can also be done if the first of the couple died before 6 April 2017, even though the additional threshold wasn't available at that time.

The additional threshold and any transferred additional threshold is available if the surviving husband, wife or civil partner—

- leaves a home to their direct descendants
- includes the home in their estate

The home that the surviving husband, wife or civil partner leaves to their direct descendants doesn't have to be the same home that they lived in with their partner to either qualify for the additional threshold or to transfer it.

The surviving husband, wife or civil partner doesn't have to have previously owned the home with their late partner, or inherited it from them. It can be any home as long as the surviving spouse or civil partner lived in it at some stage before they died and the home is included in their estate.

If the surviving husband, wife or civil partner sold or gave away their home on or after 8 July 2015 and they leave other assets to their direct descendants when they die, the additional threshold may still be available under the downsizing rules.

Couples who aren't married or in a civil partnership, or who've divorced, will still be able to benefit from the additional threshold individually if they leave a home to their direct descendants. But they won't be able to transfer any unused additional threshold to each other.

Where the first of the couple died before 6 April 2017 their estate wouldn't have used any of the additional threshold as it wasn't available. So 100% of the additional threshold will be available for transfer unless their estate was worth more than £2 million and the additional threshold is tapered away.

It's the unused percentage of the additional threshold that's transferred, not the unused amount. This makes sure that if the maximum amount of additional threshold increases over time, the survivor's estate will benefit from the increase.

You calculate the actual amount that's transferred to the surviving spouse or civil partner's estate in 2 steps:

Step 1. Work out the percentage of additional threshold that wasn't used when the first of the couple died. You do this by dividing the unused amount of additional threshold by the total additional threshold that was available when the first of the couple died and multiplying the result by 100. If the person died before 6 April 2017 the unused additional threshold and total available additional threshold are both deemed to be £100,000 so the unused percentage is 100%.

Step 2. Multiply the percentage of additional threshold that was unused when the first of the couple died by the maximum additional threshold available at the time of the survivor's death. This gives you the sum available to transfer.

EXAMPLE

Philip died in 2015 and left his entire estate to his wife. This was before the additional threshold was available.

So, when he died, the additional threshold couldn't have been used. That means 100% is available to transfer to his wife's estate.

His wife dies on 30 July 2019 and leaves all her estate, including a home worth £400,000 to her daughter.

When she dies in the tax year 2019 to 2020, the maximum available additional threshold is £150,000.

Her executor makes a claim to transfer the unused additional threshold from Philip's estate.

So the total available additional threshold for Philip's wife's estate will be £300,000 (£150,000 + (transfer of 100% x £150,000)).

TRANSFERRING ANY UNUSED ADDITIONAL THRESHOLD

The estate's personal representative will need to give details of the amount due and supporting information on the Inheritance Tax return.

They'll make a claim to transfer any unused additional threshold from the estate of a late husband, wife or civil partner. They'll also need to make a claim for any additional threshold as a result of downsizing selling or giving away of the home before the person died.

As the additional threshold and basic Inheritance Tax threshold aren't linked, the percentages transferred can be different. This means that even if all of the basic Inheritance Tax threshold was used when the first of the couple died, you can still transfer the unused additional threshold.

The percentage of transferred additional threshold will be limited to 100%. This means that if an individual has had more than one spouse or civil partner and they make a claim to transfer the unused additional threshold from each one, the total transferred additional threshold can't be more than 100% of the maximum available amount.

Commentary—*Simon's Taxes* **I4.161A**.

HMRC'S TRUST REGISTRATION SERVICE GOES LIVE FOR AGENTS

18 October 2017. *CIOT press release*

ABSTRACT

The new online Trust Registration Service finally became available to agents on 17 October. HMRC launched the service for trustees in July and has extended the penalty deadline for first-time registrations by two months from 5 October until 5 December 2017. For certain trusts, beneficial ownership information will need to be submitted by 31 January 2018. Agents will have to set up a new "agent services account" as part of gaining full access to the system. The CIOT has passed on the latest update from HMRC.

www.tax.org.uk/policy-technical/technical-news/trust-registration-service-goes-live-agents

We are advised that a new Agent Services Account (ASA) will need to be set up as part of the process to access the TRS. The new ASA is being developed as part of Making Tax Digital for Business and ultimately it is envisaged all HMRC services will be provided via this portal. Whereas agents may have a number of Government Gateways, there will only be one ASA per agency. ASAs will also be secured by 2 Step Verification. This means that, in addition to a username and password, agents will need to associate a mobile, landline or HMRC app with their ASA to which security codes can be sent. Agents can then set up delegate access for individual staff members to access the main ASA for the firm.

Agents registering for TRS will need to think carefully about who should set up this account, as an ASA created during registration for TRS will become the sole access point to other HMRC services in the future. It is therefore unlikely that the trust department will be best placed to set this up for the firm.

Both the ATT and CIOT are seeking further guidance on the interaction of ASAs and the TRS. There is limited guidance on ASA at present – members may find an HMRC Talking Points from earlier this year helpful as an overview of Agent Services.

UPDATE FROM HMRC:

"From 17 October, the Trust Registration Service (TRS) is available to agents filing on behalf of trustees. Please see the following link for further details on how to gain access to the TRS.

The new TRS allows agents, acting on behalf of trustees, to register trusts and complex estates online and to provide information on the beneficial owners of those trusts or complex estates. The new service, which was launched in July 2017 for lead trustees, replaces the 41G (Trust) paper form, which was withdrawn at the end of April 2017. This is now the only way that trusts and complex estates can obtain their SA Unique Taxpayer Reference. As part of this online process, agents will be taken through the steps to create an Agent Services account before they can register on behalf of trustees.

In this first year of TRS, to allow sufficient time to complete the registration of a trust or complex estate for SA and provide beneficial ownership information, there will be no penalty imposed where registration is completed after 5 October 2017 but before 5 December 2017.

For both UK and non-UK express trusts which are either already registered for SA or do not require SA registration, but incur a liability to relevant UK taxes, the trustees are required to provide beneficial ownership information about the trust, using the TRS, by 31 January following the end of tax year. This means, if the trustees of a UK or non-UK express trust incurred a liability to any of the relevant UK taxes in tax year 2016–17, in relation to trust income or assets, then the trustees or their agent need to register that trust on TRS by no later than 31 January 2018.

The relevant taxes are—

- income tax
- capital gains tax
- inheritance tax
- stamp duty land tax
- stamp duty reserve tax
- land and buildings transaction tax (Scotland).

The new service will provide a single online service for trusts to comply with their registration obligations. This will improve the processes for the administration of trusts and allow HMRC to collect, hold and retrieve information in a central electronic register.

More information is available in the September's Trusts & Estates Newsletter.

Finally, we published on Monday 9 October our guidance in the form of a FAQ note to help our customers understand the TRS requirements. Here is a link to that guidance."

HMRC EXTENDS TRS DEADLINE FOR NEW TRUSTS

9 November 2017. *HMRC Notice*

ABSTRACT

HMRC has agreed to extend the trust registration service deadline for new trusts until 5 January 2018. The registration and reporting deadline for existing trusts remains 31 January 2018. HMRC had previously extended the penalty deadline for new trust registrations from 5 October until 5 December 2017. The service launched in July, but only became available to agents in October.

www.gov.uk/government/news/trusts-registration-service-registration-deadline-for-new-trusts-extended

Following feedback from agents and stakeholders we are pleased to announce the Trust Registration Service (TRS) deadline for new trusts has been extended further from 5 October 2017 to 5 January 2018.

Trusts which have incurred a liability to income tax or capital gains tax for the first time in the tax year 2016 to 2017 will need to complete registration on the TRS by no later than 5 January 2018. This extension is only for the first year of the TRS.

The deadline for existing trusts to register on the TRS will remain unchanged at 31 January 2018.

The TRS online service replaces the 41G (Trust) paper form, which was withdrawn at the end of April 2017. This is now the only way trusts and complex estates can obtain their Self-Assessment Unique Taxpayer Reference.

The service will provide a single online service for trusts to comply with their registration obligations.

Inheritance tax index

Defined words and phrases are listed separately at the end.

B

E

F

N

O

P

S

W

Words and phrases

Words in brackets indicate the context in which the word or phrase is used.

National Insurance Contributions

NIC

Contents

Statutes

NIC

Contents

SOCIAL SECURITY PENSIONS ACT 1975

(1975 Chapter 60)

ARRANGEMENT OF SECTIONS

PART V
GENERAL

An Act to provide for relating the rates of social security retirement pensions and certain other benefits to the earnings on which contributions have been paid; to enable employed earners to be contracted-out of full social security contributions and benefits where the requisite benefits are provided by an occupational pension scheme; to make provision for securing that men and women are afforded equal access to occupational pension schemes; and to make other amendments in the law relating to social security (including an amendment of Part II of the Social Security Act 1975 introducing a new non-contributory benefit called "mobility allowance"); and to make other provision about occupational pensions

[7th August 1975]

Cross references—See Social Security Administration Act 1992 s 110(8)(*d*) (appointment of inspectors and inspectors' powers of search, etc for the purposes of offences under this Act),
SSAA 1992 s 113 (offences in consequence of breach of regulations made under this Act);
SS(CP)A 1992, Sch 3 para 5 (continuing powers to make transitional etc regulations).

PART V
GENERAL

61 Consultation about regulations

Amendment—This section repealed by the Statute Law (Repeals) Act 2004 with effect from 22 July 2004.

[61B Orders and regulations (general provisions)

(1) Powers under this Act to make regulations or orders, . . . [2], are exercisable by statutory instrument.

(2) Except in so far as this Act otherwise provides, any power conferred thereby to make regulations or an order may be exercised—

(*a*) either in relation to all cases to which the power extends, or in relation to those cases subject to specified exceptions, or in relation to any specified cases or classes of case;

(*b*) so as to make, as respects the cases in relation to which it is exercised—

(i) the full provision to which the power extends or any less provision (whether by way of exception or otherwise),

(ii) the same provision for all cases in relation to which the power is exercised, or different provision for different cases or different classes of case or different provision as respects the same case or class of case for different purposes of this Act,

(iii) any such provision either unconditionally or subject to any specified condition;

and where such a power is expressed to be exercisable for alternative purposes it may be exercised in relation to the same case for any or all of those purposes; and powers to make regulations or an order for the purposes of any one provision of this Act are without prejudice to powers to make regulations or an order for the purposes of any other provision.

(3) Without prejudice to any specific provision in this Act, a power conferred by this Act to make regulations or an order includes power to make thereby such incidental, supplementary, consequential or transitional provision as appears to the authority making the regulations or order to be expedient for the purposes of the regulations or order.

(4) Without prejudice to any specific provisions in this Act, a power conferred by this Act to make regulations or an order includes power to provide for a person to exercise a discretion in dealing with any matter.

(5) A power conferred on the Secretary of State to make any regulations or order, where the power is not expressed to be exercisable with the consent of the Treasury, shall if the Treasury so direct be exercisable only in conjunction with them.][1]

Cross reference—See SSA 1986 s 83(1) (powers to make orders and regulations (general provisions)).

Amendments—[1] This section inserted by SS(CP)A 1992, Sch 2 paras 19, 37.

[2] Words omitted in sub-s (1) repealed by the Pensions Act 1995 ss 151, 171 Sch 5 para 6(2) and Sch 7 Pt III with effect from 6 Apr 1997 (by virtue of the Pensions Act 1995 (Commencement No 10) Order, SI 1997/664).

62 Other provisions about regulations and orders

[(1) . . . [3]][1]

[(2) A statutory instrument—

(*a*) which contains (whether alone or with other provisions) any order or regulations made under this Act by the Secretary of State, other than an order which, under any provision of this Act, is required to be laid before Parliament after being made; and

(*b*) which is not subject to any requirement that a draft of the instrument shall be laid before and approved by a resolution of each House of Parliament,

shall be subject to annulment in pursuance of a resolution of either House of Parliament.][2]

(3) . . . [3]

(4) . . . [4]

Amendments—[1] Sub-s (1) substituted by SSA 1990 s 21(1), Sch 6 para 8(2), with effect from 13 July 1990.

[2] Sub-s (2) substituted by SS(CP)A 1992 ss 4, 7(2) and Sch 2 paras 19, 38 with effect from 1 July 1992.

[3] Sub-ss (1), (3) repealed by SS(CP)A 1992 ss 3, 5, 7(2) and Sch 1 with effect from 1 July 1992.

[4] Sub-s (4) repealed by PSA 1993 s 188(1), Sch 5 Pt I.

67 Commencement

Amendment–This section repealed by the Statute Law (Repeals) Act 2004 with effect from 22 July 2004.

68 Short title, citation and extent

(1) This Act may be cited as the Social Security Pensions Act 1975.

(2) The Social Security Act 1975 and this Act may be cited together as the Social Security Acts 1975.

(3) The following provisions of this Act have the same extent as the Pensions (Increase) Act 1971—

(*a*) [Sections 59 and 59A][1];

(*b*) paragraph 18 of Schedule 4;

(*c*) Schedule 5, so far as it repeals provisions of that Act.

(4) . . . [2] This Act extends to Northern Ireland so far as it—

(*a*), (*b*) . . . [2]

(*c*) repeals Part III and section 89(3)(*c*) and (4) of that Act, and Schedules 18 to 20 to that Act;

(*d*) by section 65(2) and Part II of Schedule 4 amends the Social Security (Northern Ireland) Act 1975 and the Social Security (Consequential Provisions) Act 1975 and reinstates paragraph 1 of Schedule 5 to the Social Security Benefits Act 1975;

(*e*) repeals paragraphs 47 and (in part) 58 of Schedule 2 to the Social Security (Consequential Provisions) Act 1975;

(*f*) . . . [3]

(*g*) . . . [3]

(*h*) repeals provisions of the Public Records Act 1958, the Superannuation Act 1972, the Parliamentary and other Pensions Act 1972, the Pensions (Increase) Act 1974 and the House of Commons Disqualification Act 1975;

but subject to the foregoing provisions of this subsection and to subsection (3) above, this Act does not extend to Northern Ireland.

Amendments—[1] Words in sub-s (3) substituted by SSA 1979 s 21(4), Sch 3 para 22.

[2] Sub-s (4)(*a*), (*b*) and the words in sub-s (4) repealed by PSA 1993 s 188(1), Sch 5 Pt I.

[3] Sub-s (4)(*f*), (*g*) repealed by the Statute Law (Repeals) Act 2004 with effect from 22 July 2004.

SOCIAL SECURITY (MISCELLANEOUS PROVISIONS) ACT 1977

(1977 Chapter 5)

An Act to amend the law relating to social security and to regulate the manner of providing for certain benefits connected with service in the armed forces

[30th March 1977]

General

24 Supplemental

(1) In this Act, except where the context otherwise requires (and in particular except in a provision inserted by this Act into another Act)—

"modifications" includes additions, omissions and amendments;

. . . [2]

"the Pensions Act" means the Social Security Pensions Act 1975;

"prescribed" means prescribed by regulations;

"the principal Act" means the Social Security Act 1975; and

"regulations" means regulations made by the Secretary of State under this Act.

(2) . . . [2]

(3) [Subsections (3) to (6) and (9) of section 189 of the Social Security Administration Act 1992][1] (which contain general provisions relating to orders and regulations under that Act) shall have effect as if references to that Act included references to this Act and as if, in relation to powers to make

Orders in Council conferred by section 12 of this Act, [subsections (4) to (6) of that section][1] extended to Northern Ireland; [and a power under any of sections 116 to 120 of the Social Security Contributions and Benefits Act 1992 or 177 to 179 of the Social Security Administration Act 1992 to make provision by regulations or Order in Council for modifications or adaptations of those Acts shall be exercisable in relation to any enactment contained in this Act][1].

(4) . . . [2]

(5) Any statutory instrument—

[(*a*) which contains (whether alone or with other provisions) any regulations, and

(*b*) which is not subject to any requirement that a draft of the instrument be laid before and approved by a resolution of each House of Parliament,][3]

shall be subject to annulment in pursuance of a resolution of either House of Parliament.

(6) The enactments mentioned in the first and second columns of Schedule 2 to this Act are hereby repealed to the extent specified in the third column of that Schedule.

Amendments—[1] Words in sub-s (3) substituted by SS(CP)A 1992 ss 4, 7(2) and Sch 2 para 46 with effect from 1 July 1992.

[2] Definition omitted from sub-s (1) and sub-ss (2), (4) repealed by SS(CP)A 1992 ss 3, 5, 7(2) and Sch 1 with effect from 1 July 1992.

[3] Sub-s (5)(*a*), (*b*) substituted by SSA 1990 s 21(1), Sch 6 para 8(4).

25 Citation, commencement and extent

(1) This Act may be cited as the Social Security (Miscellaneous Provisions) Act 1977 and this Act, the principal Act and the Pensions Act may be cited together as the Social Security Acts 1975 to 1977.

(2)–(4) . . .

(5) The following provisions only of this Act shall extend to Northern Ireland, namely—

(*a*) this section and sections 12, 20(3) and (4) and 22(15);

(*b*) section 24(3) so far as it applies section 166(2) to (4) of the principal Act to powers conferred by section 12 of this Act; and

(*c*) section 24(6) and Schedule 2 so far as they relate to the Tribunals and Inquiries Act 1971 and the Social Security (Northern Ireland) Act 1975.

Note—Sub-ss (2), (4) are not relevant to this work. Sub-s (3) became spent on the repeal of the enactments brought into force thereby.

SOCIAL SECURITY ACT 1980

(1980 Chapter 30)

Commissioners

12 Change of title of National Insurance Commissioners

National Insurance Commissioners shall, instead of being so called, be called Social Security Commissioners; and accordingly—

(*a*) any enactment or instrument passed or made before the coming into force of this section shall have effect, so far as may be necessary in consequence of the change of title made by this section, as if for any reference to a Chief or other National Insurance Commissioner there were substituted respectively a reference to a Chief or other Social Security Commissioner; and

(*b*) documents and forms printed or duplicated for use in connection with functions of National Insurance Commissioners may be used notwithstanding that they contain references to such Commissioners and those references shall be construed as references to Social Security Commissioners.

General

21 Supplemental

(1) This Act may be cited as the Social Security Act 1980 and this Act and the Social Security Acts 1975 to 1979 may be cited together as the Social Security Acts 1975 to 1980.

(2) In this Act "the principal Act" means the Social Security Act 1975 and "the Pensions Act" means the Social Security Pensions Act 1975.

(3) [Section 175(3) and (4) of the Social Security Contributions and Benefits Act 1992][1] (which among other things make provision about the extent of powers to make regulations and orders) shall apply to powers to make regulations and orders conferred by sections 8 and 20(2) of this Act and by subsection (5) of this section as extended by the said sections 8 and 20(2) as they apply to powers to make regulations and orders conferred by that Act but as if for references to that Act there were substituted references to the said sections 8 and 20(2) and the said subsection (5) as so extended.

(4) . . .

(5) The following provisions of this Act, namely, section 6 (except subsection (4)) and sections 7 to 10, 14 and 15, Part I and paragraphs 10 and 14 of Schedule 1, Schedules 2 to 4 and Part II of Schedule 5, shall come into force on such day as the Secretary of State may appoint by order made by statutory instrument, and different days may be appointed in pursuance of this subsection for different provisions of this Act; and accordingly the other provisions of this Act come into force on the passing of this Act.

(6) The following provisions only of this Act shall extend to Northern Ireland, namely—

sections 9 to 16, except sections 11, 13(6) and 15;

. . .

this section;

Schedule 3; and

. . .

Note—Sub-s (4) and words omitted from sub-s (6) are outside the scope of this work.

Amendments—[1] Words in sub-s (3) substituted by SS(CP)A 1992 s 4, Sch 2 para 59 with effect from 1 July 1992.

INSOLVENCY ACT 1986

(1986 Chapter 45)

Note—This Act received Royal Assent on 25 July 1986. By virtue of s 443 of this Act and SI 1986/1924, art 3 it has effect from 29 December 1986.

Modification

The Legal Services Act 2007 (Designation as a Licensing Authority) (No. 2) order, SI 2011/2866 art 8 (modification of the whole Act for purposes specified in art 8(2)).

PART IV

WINDING UP OF COMPANIES REGISTERED UNDER THE COMPANIES ACTS

CHAPTER VIII

PROVISIONS OF GENERAL APPLICATION IN WINDING UP

Preferential debts

175 Preferential debts (general provision)

(1) In a winding up the company's preferential debts . . . [1] shall be paid in priority to all other debts.

[(1A) Ordinary preferential debts rank equally among themselves after the expenses of the winding up and shall be paid in full, unless the assets are insufficient to meet them, in which case they abate in equal proportions.

(1B) Secondary preferential debts rank equally among themselves after the ordinary preferential debts and shall be paid in full, unless the assets are insufficient to meet them, in which case they abate in equal proportions.][1]

(2) Preferential debts—

(*a*) . . . [1]

(*b*) so far as the assets of the company available for payment of general creditors are insufficient to meet them, have priority over the claims of holders of debentures secured by, or holders of, any floating charge created by the company, and shall be paid accordingly out of any property comprised in or subject to that charge.

[(3) In this section "preferential debts", "ordinary preferential debts" and "secondary preferential debts" each has the meaning given in section 386 in Part 12.][1]

AMENDMENTS—

[1] In sub-s (1), words revoked, sub-ss (1A), (1B), (3) inserted, and sub-s(2)(*a*) revoked, by the Banks and Building Societies (Depositor Preference and Priorities) Order, SI 2014/3486 art 5 with effect from 1 January 2015.

PART IX

BANKRUPTCY

CHAPTER IV

ADMINISTRATION BY TRUSTEE

Distribution of bankrupt's estate

328 Priority of debts

(1) In the distribution of the bankrupt's estate, his preferential debts . . . [1] shall be paid in priority to other debts.

[(1A) Ordinary preferential debts rank equally among themselves after the expenses of the bankruptcy and shall be paid in full, unless the bankrupt's estate is insufficient to meet them, in which case they abate in equal proportions between themselves.

(1B) Secondary preferential debts rank equally among themselves after the ordinary preferential debts and shall be paid in full, unless the bankrupt's estate is insufficient to meet them, in which case they abate in equal proportions between themselves.][1]

(2) . . . [1]

(3) Debts which are neither preferential debts nor debts to which the next section applies also rank equally between themselves and, after the preferential debts, shall be paid in full unless the bankrupt's estate is insufficient for meeting them, in which case they abate in equal proportions between themselves.

(4) Any surplus remaining after the payment of the debts that are preferential or rank equally under subsection (3) shall be applied in paying interest on those debts in respect of the periods during which they have been outstanding since the commencement of the bankruptcy; and interest on preferential debts ranks equally with interest on debts other than preferential debts.

(5) The rate of interest payable under subsection (4) in respect of any debt is whichever is the greater of the following—

(*a*) the rate specified in section 17 of the Judgments Act 1838 at the commencement of the bankruptcy, and

(*b*) the rate applicable to that debt apart from the bankruptcy.

(6) This section and the next are without prejudice to any provision of this Act or any other Act under which the payment of any debt or the making of any other payment is, in the event of bankruptcy, to have a particular priority or to be postponed.

[(7) In this section "preferential debts", "ordinary preferential debts" and "secondary preferential debts" each has the meaning given in section 386 in Part 12.][1]

Amendments—[1] In sub-s (1), words revoked, sub-ss (1A), (1B), (7) inserted, and sub-s (2) revoked, by the Banks and Building Societies (Depositor Preference and Priorities) Order, SI 2014/3486 art 7 with effect from 1 January 2015.

PART XII
PREFERENTIAL DEBTS IN COMPANY AND INDIVIDUAL INSOLVENCY

386 Categories of preferential debts

(1) A reference in this Act to the preferential debts of a company or an individual is to the debts listed in Schedule 6 to this Act [(contributions to occupational pension schemes; remuneration, &c of employees; levies on coal and steel production[; debts owed to the Financial Services Compensation Scheme][5])][2][; deposits covered by Financial Services Compensation Scheme][3][; other deposits][4] and references to preferential creditors are to be read accordingly.

[(1A) A reference in this Act to the "ordinary preferential debts" of a company or an individual is to the preferential debts listed in any of paragraphs 8 to 15B of Schedule 6 to this Act.

(1B) A reference in this Act to the "secondary preferential debts" of a company or an individual is to the preferential debts listed in paragraph 15BA or 15BB of Schedule 6 to this Act.][4]

(2) In [Schedule 6][4] "the debtor" means the company or the individual concerned.

(3) Schedule 6 is to be read with [Schedule 4 to the Pension Schemes Act 1993][1] (occupational pension scheme contributions).

Amendments—[1] Words in sub-s (3) substituted by the Pension Schemes Act 1993 s 190, Sch 8 para 18 with effect from 7 February 1994.

[2] Words in sub-s (1) substituted by the Enterprise Act 2002 ss 251(3), 279 with effect from 15 September 2003, subject to transitional provisions (by virtue of SI 2003/2093).

[3] In sub-s (1), words inserted by the Financial Services (Banking Reform) Act 2013 s 13(1) with effect from 31 December 2014 (by virtue of SI 2014/3160).

[4] In sub-s (1), words inserted, sub-ss (1A), (1B) inserted, and in sub-s (2), words substituted , by the Banks and Building Societies (Depositor Preference and Priorities) Order, SI 2014/3486 art 8 with effect from 1 January 2015.

[5] In sub-s (1), words inserted by the Deposit Guarantee Scheme Regulations, SI 2015/486 reg 14 (1), (2) with effect from 25 March 2015.

387 "The relevant date"

(1) This section explains references in Schedule 6 to the relevant date (being the date which determines the existence and amount of a preferential debt).

(2) For the purposes of section 4 in Part I ([consideration of][4] company voluntary arrangement), the relevant date in relation to a company which is not being wound up is—

[(*a*) if the company is in administration, the date on which it entered administration, and][3]

[(*b*) if the company is not in administration, the date on which the voluntary arrangement takes effect][3].

[(2A) For the purposes of paragraph 31 of Schedule A1 (meetings to consider company voluntary arrangement where a moratorium under section 1A is in force), the relevant date in relation to a company is the date of filing.][2]

(3) In relation to a company which is being wound up, the following applies—

(*a*) if the winding up is by the court, and the winding-up order was made immediately upon the discharge of an administration order, the relevant date is [the date on which the company entered administration][3];

[(*aa*) if the winding up is by the court and the winding-up order was made following conversion of administration into winding up by virtue of [Article 51 of the EU Regulation][6], the relevant date is [the date on which the company entered administration][3]][1]

[(*ab*) if the company is deemed to have passed a resolution for voluntary winding up by virtue of an order following conversion of administration into winding up under [Article 51 of the EU Regulation][6], the relevant date is [the date on which the company entered administration][3]][1]

(*b*) if the case does not fall within paragraph (*a*)[, (*aa*) or (*ab*)][1] and the company—

(i) is being wound up by the court, and

(ii) had not commenced to be wound up voluntarily before the date of the making of the winding-up order,

the relevant date is the date of the appointment (or first appointment) of a provisional liquidator or, if no such appointment has been made, the date of the winding-up order;

[(*ba*) if the case does not fall within paragraph (*a*), (*aa*), (*ab*) or (*b*) and the company is being wound up following administration pursuant to paragraph 83 of Schedule B1, the relevant date is the date on which the company entered administration;][3]

(*c*) if the case does not fall within [paragraph (*a*), (*aa*), (*ab*), (*b*) or (*ba*)][3], the relevant date is the date of the passing of the resolution for the winding up of the company.

[(3A) In relation to a company which is in administration (and to which no other provision of this section applies) the relevant date is the date on which the company enters administration.][3]

(4) In relation to a company in receivership (where section 40 or, as the case may be, section 59 applies), the relevant date is—

(*a*) in England and Wales, the date of the appointment of the receiver by debenture-holders, and

(*b*) in Scotland, the date of the appointment of the receiver under section 53(6) or (as the case may be) 54(5).

(5) For the purposes of section 258 in Part VIII (individual voluntary arrangements), the relevant date is, in relation to a debtor who is not an undischarged bankrupt—

[(*a*) where an interim order has been made under section 252 with respect to his proposal, the date of that order, and

(*b*) in any other case, the date on which the voluntary arrangement takes effect.][2]

(6) In relation to a bankrupt, the following applies—

(*a*) where at the time the bankruptcy order was made there was an interim receiver appointed under section 286, the relevant date is the date on which the interim receiver was first appointed after [the making of the bankruptcy application or (as the case may be)][5] the presentation of the bankruptcy petition;

(*b*) otherwise, the relevant date is the date of the making of the bankruptcy order.

Amendments—[1] In sub-s (3), paras (*aa*), (*ab*) inserted, words in para (*b*) inserted, and in para (*c*), words substituted; by the Insolvency Act 1986 (Amendment) (No 2) Regulations, SI 2002/1240 regs 3, 16 with effect from 31 May 2002.

[2] Words in sub-s (2)(*b*) substituted, sub-s (2A) inserted, and sub-s (5)(*a*), (*b*) substituted, by the Insolvency Act 2000 ss 1–3, Sch 1 paras 1, 9, Sch 2 paras 1, 11, Sch 3 para 15 with effect from 1 January 2003 (by virtue of SI 2002/2711).

[3] Sub-s (2)(*a*), (*b*) substituted; in sub-s (3), words substituted; and para (*ba*) inserted; and sub-s (3A) inserted; by the Enterprise Act 2002 ss 248, 279 Sch 17 paras 9, 34 with effect from 15 September 2003, subject to transitional provisions (by virtue of SI 2003/2093).

[4] In sub-s (2), words substituted for words "meetings to consider" by the Small Business, Enterprise and Employment Act 2015 s 126, Sch 9 paras 1, 55 with effect from 26 May 2015 for certain purposes and with effect from 6 April 2017 for remaining purposes (by virtue of SI 2016/1020), subject to transitional arrangements where a creditors' or contributories' meeting is held after that date as a result of a notice issued before that date: SI 2016/1020 reg 5.

[5] In sub-s (6)(*a*), words inserted by the Enterprise and Regulatory Reform Act 2013 s 71(3), Sch 19 para 55 with effect from 6 April 2016 (by virtue of SI 2016/191, art 2).

[6] In sib-s (3)(*aa*), (*ab*), words substituted for words "Article 37 of the EC Regulation" by the Insolvency Amendment (EU 2015/848) Regulations, SI 2017/702 reg 2, Schedule para 22 with effect from 26 June 2017.

PART XVII
MISCELLANEOUS AND GENERAL

434 Crown application

For the avoidance of doubt it is hereby declared that provisions of this Act which derive from the Insolvency Act 1985 bind the Crown so far as affecting or relating to the following matters, namely—

(*a*) . . .

(*b*) priorities of debts;

(*c*)–(*e*) . . .

Note—Paras (*a*) and (*c*)–(*e*) are not relevant to this work.

PART XIX

FINAL PROVISIONS

440 Extent (Scotland)

(1) . . . Provisions of this Act contained in the first Group of Parts extend to Scotland except where otherwise stated.

(2) The following provisions of this Act do not extend to Scotland—

(*a*) . . .

(*b*) the second Group of Parts;

(*c*)–(*d*) . . .

Note—Words omitted in sub-s (1), and sub-s (2)(*a*), (*c*) and (*d*), are not relevant to this work.

441 Extent (Northern Ireland)

(1) . . .

(2) Subject . . . to any provision expressly relating to companies incorporated elsewhere than in Great Britain, nothing in this Act extends to Northern Ireland or applies to or in relation to companies registered or incorporated in Northern Ireland.

Note—Sub-s (1), and words omitted in sub-s (2), are not relevant to this work.

442 Extent (other territories)

Her Majesty may, by Order in Council, direct that such of the provisions of this Act as are specified in the Order, being provisions formerly contained in the Insolvency Act 1985 shall extend to any of the Channel Islands or any colony with such modifications as may be so specified.

443 Commencement

This Act comes into force on the day appointed under section 236(2) of the Insolvency Act 1985 for the coming into force of Part III of that Act (individual insolvency and bankruptcy), immediately after that Part of that Act comes into force for England and Wales.

444 Citation

This Act may be cited as the Insolvency Act 1986.

SOCIAL SECURITY ACT 1986

(1986 Chapter 50)

ARRANGEMENT OF SECTIONS

PART VI

COMMON PROVISIONS

Administration

PART VII

MISCELLANEOUS, GENERAL AND SUPPLEMENTARY

Supplementary

An Act to make provision in relation to personal pension schemes, to amend the law relating to social security, occupational pension schemes and the provision of refreshments for school pupils, to abolish maternity pay under the Employment Protection (Consolidation) Act 1978 and provide for the winding-up of the Maternity Pay Fund, to empower the Secretary of State to pay the travelling expenses of certain persons, and for connected purposes

[25th July 1986]

Note—Amendments and modifications made to this Act in respect of disability living and working allowances by the Disability Living Allowance and Disability Working Allowance Act 1991 being outside the scope of this division of the Publication, are not included.

NIC

PART VI
COMMON PROVISIONS

Administration

54 Breach of regulations

(1) Regulations under any of the benefit Acts may provide for contravention of, or failure to comply with, any provision contained in regulations made under that Act to be an offence under that Act and for the recovery, on summary conviction of any such offence, of penalties not exceeding—

(*a*) for any one offence, level 3 on the standard scale; or

(*b*) for an offence of continuing any such contravention or failure after conviction, £40 for each day on which it is so continued.

(2) . . . [1]

Note—This section came into force on 6 April 1987 by virtue of SSA 1986 (Commencement No 4) Order, SI 1986/1959.

Amendments—[1] Sub-s (2) repealed by SS(CP)A 1992 s 3, Sch 1.

56 Legal proceedings

(1) Any person authorised by the Secretary of State in that behalf may conduct any proceedings under the benefit Acts before a magistrates' court . . . [4].

(2) Notwithstanding anything in any Act—

(*a*) proceedings for an offence under the benefit Acts . . . [2] may be begun at any time within the period of three months from the date on which evidence, sufficient in the opinion of the Secretary of State to justify a prosecution for the offence, comes to his knowledge or within a period of twelve months from the commission of the offence, whichever period last expires; . . . [3]

(*b*) . . . [3]

(3) For the purposes of subsection (2) above—

(*a*) a certificate purporting to be signed by or on behalf of the Secretary of State as to the date on which such evidence as is mentioned in paragraph (*a*) of that subsection came to his knowledge shall be conclusive evidence of that date; . . .

(*b*) . . .

(4)–(4B) . . . [3]

(5) In the application of this section to Scotland, the following provisions shall have effect in substitution for subsections (1) to [(4A)][1] above—

(*a*) proceedings for an offence under the benefit Acts may, notwithstanding anything in section 331 of the Criminal Procedure (Scotland) Act 1975 be commenced at any time within the period of three months from the date on which evidence sufficient in the opinion of the Lord Advocate to justify proceedings comes to his knowledge, or within the period of twelve months from the commission of the offence, whichever period last expires;

(*b*) for the purposes of this subsection—

(i) a certificate purporting to be signed by or on behalf of the Lord Advocate as to the date on which such evidence as is mentioned above came to his knowledge shall be conclusive evidence thereof;

(ii) subsection (3) of section 331 of the said Act of 1975 (date of commencement of proceedings) shall have effect as it has effect for the purposes of that section.

Note—This section came into force on 6 April 1987 by virtue of SSA 1986 (Commencement No 4) Order, SI 1986/1959.

Amendments—[1] Words in sub-s (5) substituted by the Local Government Finance Act 1988 s 135, Sch 10 paras 1, 9(1), (2), (5).

[2] Words in sub-s (2)(*a*) repealed by SS(CP)A 1992 ss 3, 5, 7(2) and Sch 1 with effect from 1 July 1992.

[3] Words in sub-s (2)(*b*) and the word "and" immediately preceding it, sub-s (3)(*b*) and the word "and" immediately preceding it and sub-ss (4), (4A), (4B), repealed by SS(CP)A 1992, s 3, Sch 1 with effect from 1 July 1992.

[4] In sub-s (1), words repealed by the Legal Services Act 2007 ss 208, 210, Sch 21 para 68, Sch 23, with effect from 1 January 2010 (by virtue of SI 2009/3250 art 9(*h*)).

57 Offences by bodies corporate

(1) Where an offence under any of the benefit Acts which has been committed by a body corporate is proved to have been committed with the consent or connivance of, or to be attributable to any neglect on the part of, a director, manager, secretary or other similar officer of the body corporate, or any person who was purporting to act in any such capacity, he, as well as the body corporate, shall be guilty of that offence and be liable to be proceeded against accordingly.

(2) Where the affairs of a body corporate are managed by its members, subsection (1) above applies in relation to the acts and defaults of a member in connection with his functions of management as if he were a director of the body corporate.

Note—This section came into force on 6 April 1987 by virtue of SSA 1986 (Commencement No 4) Order, SI 1986/1959.

Cross references—See SSAA 1992 s 115 (offences by bodies corporate).

PART VII
MISCELLANEOUS, GENERAL AND SUPPLEMENTARY

Supplementary

83 Orders and regulations (general provisions)

(1) [Section 61B(1) to (4) of the Social Security Pensions Act 1975][2] (extent of powers) shall apply to powers conferred by this Act to make regulations or orders as they apply to any power to make regulations or orders conferred by that Act but as if for references to that Act there were substituted references to this Act.

(2) . . . [3]

(3) . . . [4]

[(4) A statutory instrument—

(*a*) which contains (whether alone or with other provisions) orders or regulations under this Act, other than orders under section 88 below, and

(*b*) which is not subject to any requirement that a draft of the instrument be laid before and approved by a resolution of each House of Parliament,

shall be subject to annulment in pursuance of a resolution of either House of Parliament.][1]

(5) . . .

(6) A power conferred by this Act to make any regulations or order, where the power is not expressed to be exercisable with the consent of the Treasury, shall if the Treasury so direct be exercisable only in conjunction with them.

Note—Sub-s (5) is not relevant to this work.

Amendments—[1] Sub-s (4) substituted by SSA 1990 s 21(1), Sch 6 para 8(9), with effect from 13 July 1990.

[2] Words in sub-s (1) substituted by SS(CP)A 1992 ss 4, 7(2) and Sch 2, paras 75, 84 with effect from 1 July 1992.

[3] Sub-s (2), (3)(*b*)–(*e*), (5) (in part) repealed by SS(CP)A 1992 ss 3, 5, 7(2) and Sch 1 with effect from 1 July 1992.

[4] Sub-s (3) repealed by PSA 1993 s 188(1), Sch 5 Pt I with effect from 7 February 1994.

84 General interpretation

(1) In this Act, unless the context otherwise requires,—

. . .

"the benefit Acts" means—

(*a*) the Social Security Act 1973;

(*b*) [the Social Security Acts 1975 to 1991];[3]

. . . [4]

. . . [2]

. . .

"modifications" includes additions, omissions and amendments, and related expressions shall be construed accordingly;

. . .

"prescribed" means specified in or determined in accordance with regulations;

. . . [1];

. . .

"regulations" means regulations made by the Secretary of State under this Act;

. . . [2]

(2) . . . [2]

(3) . . . [1]

(4) In this Act—

(*a*) references to the United Kingdom include references to the territorial waters of the United Kingdom; and

(*b*) references to Great Britain include references to the territorial waters of the United Kingdom adjacent to Great Britain.

Note—Definitions omitted from sub-s (1) are not relevant to this work.

Amendments—[1] Definitions of "Primary Class 1 contributions" and "secondary Class 1 contributions" in sub-s (1) and sub-s (3) repealed by SS(CP)A 1992 ss 3, 5, 7(2) and Sch 1 with effect from 1 July 1992.

[2] Definitions of "contract of service", "employed earner", "employee", "employer", "tax exemption", "tax approval" and "tax year" and sub-s (2) repealed by PSA 1993 s 188(1), Sch 5 Pt I.

[3] The words "the Social Security Acts 1975 to 1991" substituted by Statutory Sick Pay Act 1991 ss 3(1), 4(2) with effect from 12 February 1991.

[4] Paras (*c*) and (*d*) of the definition of "the benefit Acts" repealed by SS(CP)A 1992 s 3, Sch 1 with effect from 1 July 1994.

87 Extent

(1) The following provisions of this Act extend to Northern Ireland—

(*a*) . . . [1]

(*b*) section 61 above;

(*c*) section 66 above, so far as relating to paragraph 3(6) of Schedule 6;

(*d*) section 81 above;

NIC

(*e*) sections 83 to 86 above;
(*f*) this section;
(*g*) sections 88 to 90 below.

(2) Section 82 above (with Schedule 9) extends to Northern Ireland only.

(3) . . .

(4) Where any enactment repealed or amended by this Act extends to any part of the United Kingdom, the repeal or amendment extends to that part.

(5) Except as provided by this section, this Act extends to England and Wales and Scotland, but not to Northern Ireland.

Note—Sub-s (3) is not relevant to this work.

Amendments—[1] Sub-s (1)(*a*) repealed by PSA 1993 s 188(1), Sch 5 Pt I with effect from 7 February 1994.

88 Commencement

(1) Subject to the following provisions of this section, the provisions of this Act shall come into force on such day as the Secretary of State may by order made by statutory instrument appoint, and different days may be appointed in pursuance of this section for different provisions or different purposes of the same provision.

(2) In relation to section 52 above (including Schedule 5) and section 82 above (including Schedule 9) for the reference to the Secretary of State in subsection (1) above there shall be substituted a reference to the Lord Chancellor and the Secretary of State, acting jointly.

(3)–(4) . . .

(5) The following provisions of this Act—

. . .
section 61;
. . .
section 74;
. . .
section 81;
sections 83 to 85;
section 86(1) so far as relating to paragraphs . . . 98, 99, 106 and 107 of Schedule 10;
section 86(2) so far as relating—

. . .
(*d*) to section 10 of the Social Security Act 1980; and
. . . ;

section 87;
this section; and
sections 89 and 90;

shall come into force on the day this Act is passed.

Note—Sub-ss (3), (4) and words omitted in sub-s (5) are not relevant to this work.

Orders—See SSA 1986 (Commencement) Orders, SI 1986 Nos 1609, 1719, 1958, 1959, SI 1987 Nos 354, 543, 1096, 1853, SI 1988/567.

89 Transitional

(1) Regulations may make such transitional and consequential provision (including provision modifying any enactment contained in this or any other Act) or saving as the Secretary of State considers necessary or expedient in preparation for or in connection with the coming into force of any provision of this Act or the operation of any enactment which is repealed or amended by a provision of this Act during any period when the repeal or amendment is not wholly in force.

[(1A) Without prejudice to any other powers conferred on him, the Secretary of State—

(*a*) may, for the purpose of making provision with respect to persons falling within subsection (1B) below, modify or revoke any regulations made under this section if he considers it necessary or expedient to do so in consequence of, or otherwise in connection with, provisions of Acts, schemes, arrangements or other instruments coming into force after the passing of this Act; and

(*b*) may, for the purpose of consolidation, revoke and re-enact, with any modifications which he considers necessary or desirable, any regulations under this section.

(1B) The persons referred to in subsection (1A)(*a*) above are any persons—

(*a*) to whom regulations under subsection (1) above apply; or

(*b*) to whom regulations made under Part II of this Act relating to income support applied at any time before the passing of the Social Security Act 1989.][1]

(2) The reference to regulations in subsection (1) above includes a reference—

(*a*) to regulations made by the Lord Chancellor; and

(*b*) to regulations made by the Lord Chancellor and the Secretary of State, acting jointly.

Amendments—[1] Sub-ss (1A), (1B) inserted by SSA 1989 s 31(1), Sch 8 para 10(2), with effect from 21 July 1989.

90 Citation

(1) This Act may be cited as the Social Security Act 1986.

(2) This Act . . . may be cited together with the Social Security Acts 1975 to 1985 as the Social Security Acts 1975 to 1986.

Note—Words omitted in sub-s (2) are not relevant to this work.

SOCIAL SECURITY ACT 1989

(1989 Chapter 24)

29 Regulations and orders: general provisions

(1) Subject to the following provisions of this section, [section 175(2) to (5) of the Social Security Contributions and Benefits Act 1992][2] shall apply in relation to any power conferred by any provision of this Act to make regulations or an order as they apply in relation to any power conferred by that Act to make regulations or an order, but as if for references to that Act there were substituted references to this Act.

(2) . . . [2]

[(3) A statutory instrument—

(*a*) which contains (whether alone or with other provisions) any regulations or orders under this Act, other than orders under section 33 below, and

(*b*) which is not subject to any requirement that a draft of the instrument be laid before and approved by a resolution of each House of Parliament,

shall be subject to annulment in pursuance of a resolution of either House of Parliament.][1]

(4) . . . [1]

(5) . . . [2]

(6) A power conferred by this Act to make any regulations or order, where the power is not expressed to be exercisable with the consent of the Treasury, shall if the Treasury so direct be exercisable only in conjunction with them.

(7) . . .

Note—Sub-s (7) is outside the scope of this work.

Amendments—[1] Sub-s (3) was substituted and sub-s (4) was repealed by SSA 1990 s 21, Sch 6 para 8(12), Sch 7.

[2] Words in sub-s (1) were substituted and sub-ss (2), (5) were repealed by SS(CP)A 1992 ss 3(1), 4, Sch 1, Sch 2 para 106.

30 Interpretation

(1) In this Act, unless the context otherwise requires—

. . .

"regulations" means regulations made by the Secretary of State.

(2) . . .

Note—Words omitted from sub-s (1) and sub-s (2) are outside the scope of this work.

31 Minor and consequential amendments, repeals and transitional provisions

(1) . . .

(2) . . .

(3) The Secretary of State may by regulations make—

(*a*) such transitional provision,

(*b*) such consequential provision, or

(*c*) such savings,

as he considers necessary or expedient in preparation for or in connection with the coming into force of any provision of this Act or the operation of any enactment repealed or amended by a provision of this Act during any period when the repeal or amendment is not wholly in force.

Note—Sub-ss (1), (2) are outside the scope of this work.

33 Short title, commencement and extent

(1) This Act may be cited as the Social Security Act 1989; and this Act, other than section 25, and the Social Security Acts 1975 to 1988 may be cited together as the Social Security Acts 1975 to 1989.

(2) Apart from the provisions specified in subsection (3) below, this Act shall come into force on such day as the Secretary of State may by order appoint; and different days may be so appointed for different provisions or different purposes of the same provision.

(3) The provisions referred to in subsection (2) above are the following—

(*a*) sections 2, 3, 4, 6, 14 to 20, 28, 29, 30, 31(3), 32 and this section;

(*b*)–(*g*) . . .

(4) Where any enactment repealed or amended by this Act extends to any part of the United Kingdom, the repeal or amendment extends to that part.

(5) . . .

(6) Sections 25, 31(3), 32 and this section, and paragraph 20A of Schedule 4][1] extend to Northern Ireland.

(7) Except as provided by this section this Act does not extend to Northern Ireland.

Note—Sub-ss (3)(*b*)–(*g*), (5) are outside the scope of this work.

Amendments—[1] Words in sub-s (6) inserted by SSA 1990 s 7, Sch 1 para 5(3) with effect from 13 July 1990.

NIC

FINANCE ACT 1989

(1989 Chapter 26)

PART III

MISCELLANEOUS AND GENERAL

Interest etc

178 Setting of rates of interest

(1) The rate of interest applicable for the purposes of an enactment to which this section applies shall be the rate which for the purposes of that enactment is provided for by regulations made by the Treasury under this section.

(2) This section applies to—

[(*aa*) section 15A of the Stamp Act 1891;][12]

(*a*) section 8(9) of the Finance Act 1894,

(*b*) section 18 of the Finance Act 1896,

(*c*) section 61(5) of the Finance (1909–10) Act 1910,

(*d*) section 17(3) of the Law of Property Act 1925,

(*e*) . . . [20]

(*f*) [sections . . . [23] 86, 86A, 87, 87A, . . . [9] and [103A][10]][8] of the Taxes Management Act 1970,

(*g*) paragraph 3 of Schedule 16A to the Finance Act 1973,

[(*ga*) section 48(1) of the Finance Act 1975,][21]

[(*gg*) [paragraph 6 of Schedule 1 to the Social Security Contributions and Benefits Act 1992][4],][1]

[(*gh*) section 71(8A) of the Social Security Administration Act 1992, and section 69(8A) of the Social Security Administration (Northern Ireland) Act 1992, as they have effect in any case where the overpayment was made in respect of working families' tax credit or disabled person's tax credit;][15]

(*h*) paragraphs 15 and 16 of Schedule 2, and paragraph 8 of Schedule 5, to the Oil Taxation Act 1975,

[(*i*) section 283 of the Taxation of Chargeable Gains Act 1992;][5]

(*j*) paragraph 59 of Schedule 8 to the Development Land Tax Act 1976,

(*k*) sections 233[, 235(1)][21] and 236(3) and (4) of the Inheritance Tax Act 1984,

(*l*) section 92 of the Finance Act 1986, and

(*m*) sections . . . [16] *160*[17], 824, 825 [826 and 826A(1)(*b*)][11] of . . . ,[7] and paragraph 3 of Schedule 19A to, the Taxes Act 1988 [and][2].

[(*n*) . . .][6] [and][3]

[(*o*) section 14(4) of the Ports Act 1991][3]

[(*p*) paragraph 8 of Schedule 4 to the Tax Credits Act 1999][13] [, *and*[17]

[(*q*)] [17] section 110 of the Finance Act][14][, and

[(*q*) paragraph 8 of Schedule 1 to the Employment Act 2002][18]

(*r*) Chapter 7 of Part 3 of the Income Tax (Earnings and Pensions) Act 2003][17]

[(*r*) sections 87, 88 and 89 of the Finance Act 2003][19] . . . [25]

(*u*) paragraph 11 of Schedule 35 to the Finance Act 2014][24][, and

[(*v*) section 79 of FA 2015.][25]

(3) Regulations under this section may—

(*a*) make different provision for different enactments or for different purposes of the same enactment,

(*b*) either themselves specify a rate of interest for the purposes of an enactment or make provision for any such rate to be determined by reference to such rate or the average of such rates as may be referred to in the regulations,

(*c*) provide for rates to be reduced below, or increased above, what they otherwise would be by specified amounts or by reference to specified formulae,

(*d*) provide for rates arrived at by reference to averages to be rounded up or down,

(*e*) provide for circumstances in which alteration of a rate of interest is or is not to take place, and

(*f*) provide that alterations of rates are to have effect for periods beginning on or after a day determined in accordance with the regulations in relation to interest running from before that day as well as from or from after that day.

(4) The power to make regulations under this section shall be exercisable by statutory instrument which shall be subject to annulment in pursuance of a resolution of the House of Commons.

(5) Where—

(a) *the rate provided for by regulations under this section as the rate applicable for the purposes of any enactment is changed, and*

(*b*) *the new rate is not specified in the regulations,*

the Board shall by order specify the new rate and the day from which it has effect.[21]

(6) (amends TA 1988 s 828(2)).[22]

(7) Subsection (1) shall have effect for periods beginning on or after such day as the Treasury may by order made by statutory instrument appoint and shall have effect in relation to interest running from before that day as well as from or from after that day; and different days may be appointed for different enactments.

Commentary—*Simon's Taxes* **A4.621**.
Regulations—Taxes (Interest Rate) Regulations, SI 1989/1297.
Finance Act 1989, section 178(1), (Appointed Day No 1) Order, SI 1989/1298.
Finance Act 1989, section 178(1), (Appointed Day) Order, SI 1992/2073.
Finance Act 1989, section 178(1), (Appointed Day) Order, SI 1993/754.
Taxes (Interest Rate) (Amendment No 3) Regulations, SI 1993/2212.
Taxes (Interest Rate) (Amendment) Regulations, SI 1994/1307.
Taxes (Interest Rate) (Amendment No 4) Regulations, SI 1996/3187.
Taxes (Interest Rate) (Amendment No 2) Regulations, SI 1997/2707.
Finance Act 1989, section 178(1), (Appointed Day) Order, SI 1997/2708.
Taxes (Interest Rate) (Amendment) Regulations, SI 1998/310.
Finance Act 1989, section 178(1), (Appointed Day) Order, SI 1998/311.
Taxes (Interest Rate) (Amendment No 2) Regulations, SI 1998/3176.
Taxes (Interest Rate) (Amendment) Regulations, SI 1999/419.
Taxes (Interest Rate) (Amendment No 2) Regulations, SI 1999/1928.
Taxes (Interest Rate) (Amendment No 4) Regulations, SI 1999/2637.
Taxes (Interest Rate) (Amendment) Regulations, SI 2000/893.
Taxes (Interest Rate) (Amendment No 1) Regulations, SI 2001/204.
Finance Act 1989, Section 178(1), (Appointed Day) Order, SI 2001/253.
Taxes (Interest Rate) (Amendment) Regulations, SI 2005/2462.
Taxes (Interest Rate) (Amendment) Regulations, SI 2008/778.
Taxes and Duties (Interest Rate) (Amendment) Regulations, SI 2008/3234.
Taxes (Interest Rate) (Amendment) Regulations, SI 2009/199.
Taxes and Duties (Interest Rate) (Amendment) Regulations, SI 2009/2032.
Taxes (Interest Rate) (Amendment) Regulations, SI 2010/415.
Taxes (Interest Rate) (Amendment) Regulations, SI 2014/496.
Taxes (Interest Rate) (Amendment) Regulations, SI 2015/441.

Note—The appointed day for the purposes of all the enactments mentioned in sub-s (2) above (with such exceptions as mentioned in the **Amendments** note below) and appointed under sub-s (7) above is 18 August 1989; FA 1989 s 178(1) (Appointed Day No 1) Order, SI 1989/1298.

Amendments—[1] Sub-s (2)(*gg*) inserted by the Social Security Act 1990 s 17(10) with effect from 6 April 1992.

[2] Word "and" added by FA 1990 s 118(8) with effect from 26 July 1990.

[3] Sub-s (2)(*o*) and preceding word "and" added by the Ports Act 1991 s 14(5) with effect from 15 July 1991.

[4] Words in sub-s (2)(*gg*) substituted by the Social Security (Consequential Provisions) Act 1992 s 4, Sch 2 para 107 with effect from 1 July 1992.

[5] Sub-s (2)(*i*) substituted by TCGA 1992 Sch 10 para 19(4) with effect from the year 1992–93.

[6] Sub-s (2)(*n*) (inserted by FA 1990 s 118(8)) repealed by FA 1995 Sch 29 Pt XII.

[7] Words in sub-s (2)(*m*) repealed by FA 1996 Sch 7 para 30 and Sch 41 Pt V(2) with effect for income tax for the year 1996–97 and for corporation tax for accounting periods ending after 31 March 1996.

[8] Words in sub-s (2)(*f*) substituted by FA 1994 ss 196, 199 and Sch 19 para 44 with effect from the year 1996–97 in relation to income tax and capital gains tax and, in relation to corporation tax, for accounting periods ending after 30 June 1999 (by virtue of Finance Act 1994, Section 199, (Appointed Day) Order, SI 1998/3173 art 2).

[9] Word "88" in sub-s (2)(*f*) repealed by FA 1996 Sch 18 para 13 and Sch 41 Pt V(8) with effect for the year 1996–97, and in relation to any income tax or capital gains tax which is charged by an assessment made after 5 April 1998 which is for the year 1995–96 or any earlier year of assessment, and so far as relating to partnerships whose trades, professions or businesses were set up and commenced before 6 April 1994 from the year 1997–98 in relation to any income tax which is charged by an assessment made after 5 April 1998 which is for the year 1995–96 or any earlier year of assessment.

[10] The appointed day for the purposes of TMA 1970 ss 59C and 103A and appointed under sub-s (7) above is 9 March 1998; Finance Act 1989, section 178(1), (Appointed Day) Order 1998, SI 1998/311.

[11] Words substituted by FA 1998 Sch 4 para 1(3) with effect for accounting periods ending on or after 1 July 1999 (the date appointed under FA 1994 s 199, by virtue of SI 1998/3173, for the purposes of corporation tax self-assessment).

[12] Sub-s (2)(*aa*) inserted by FA 1999 s 109(2), (4) with effect for instruments executed after 30 September 1999.

[13] Sub-s (2)(*p*) inserted by Tax Credits Act 1999 Sch 4 para 8(1) with effect from 7 March 2001 (by virtue of SI 2001/253).

[14] Sub-s (2)(*p*) and preceding word ", and" inserted by FA 1999 s 110(8), (9) with effect for instruments executed after 30 September 1999. It would appear that this paragraph has been incorrectly numbered.

[15] Sub-s (2)(*gh*) inserted in relation to the transfer of functions concerning the working families' tax credit and the disabled person's tax credit by Tax Credits Act 1999 s 2(3), Sch 2 para 10(2) with effect from 5 October 1999.

[16] Words in sub-s (2)(*m*) repealed by FA 2000 s 156, Sch 40 Pt II(17) with effect for relevant payments or receipts in relation to which the chargeable date for the purposes of TA 1988 Pt IV, Ch VIIA is after 31 March 2001.

[17] In sub-s (2), in para (*m*), reference "160" repealed, in para (*p*), word in italics repealed, para (*q*) numbered as such, and para (*r*) and word preceding it inserted by ITEPA 2003 ss 722, 724, Sch 6 paras 156, 162, Sch 8 with effect, for income tax purposes, from 2003–04; and for corporation tax purposes, for accounting periods ending after 5 April 2003. For transitional provisions and savings see ITEPA 2003 s 723, Sch 7.

[18] Sub-s (2)(*q*), which appears to have been numbered incorrectly, inserted by EmA 2002 ss 11, 12, Sch 1 para 8(1) with effect from 8 December 2002 (by virtue of SI 2002/2866).

[19] Sub-s (2)(*r*) inserted by FA 2003 s 123(1), Sch 18 para 4 with effect in accordance with FA 2003 s 124, Sch 19. It would appear that this provision has been incorrectly numbered.

[20] Sub-s (2)(*e*) repealed by the Land Registration Act 2002 ss 135, 136(2), Sch 13 with effect from 13 October 2003 (by virtue of SI 2003/1725).

21 Sub-s (2)(*ga*) and words in sub-s (2)(*k*) inserted, and sub-s (5) repealed, by FA 2009 s 105(5), (6)(a) with effect from 21 July 2009.

22 Sub-s (6) repealed by CTA 2010 s 1181, Sch 3 Pt 1. CTA 2010 has effect for corporation tax purposes for accounting periods ending on or after 1 April 2010, and for income and capital gains tax purposes for the tax year 2010–11 and subsequent tax years.

23 In sub-s (2)(*f*), reference "59C," repealed by the Finance Act 2009, Schedules 55 and 56 (Income Tax Self Assessment and Pension Schemes) (Appointed Days and Consequential and Savings Provisions) Order, SI 2011/702 art 12 with effect from 1 April 2011. This amendment has no effect in relation to a return or other document which is required to be made or delivered to HMRC or an amount of tax which is payable in relation to the tax year 2009–10 or any previous tax year (SI 2011/702 art 20).

24 Sub-s (2)(*u*) and preceding word "and" inserted by FA 2014 s 274, Sch 35 para 11 with effect from 17 July 2014.

25 In sub-s (2), word "and" previously preceding para (*u*) repealed, and para (*v*) and preceding word inserted, by FA 2015 s 115(4) with effect in relation to accounting periods beginning on or after 1 April 2015. For accounting periods that straddle that date, see FA 2015 s 116(2), (3).

Social Security Acts 1992: Destination Table

This Table lists the provisions of the Social Security Acts 1975–1991, so far as relevant to national insurance contributions, which are re-enacted in the Social Security Acts 1992. The 1992 Acts came into force on 1 July 1992, subject to the transitional provisions and savings in the Social Security (Consequential Provisions) Act 1992 ss 3 to 6.

The Table does not contain any entries in respect of the Social Security Pensions Act 1975 s 66(2) which provides that, with certain exceptions, that Act and the Social Security Act 1975 shall have effect as if the provisions of the Social Security Pensions Act 1975 were contained in the Social Security Act 1975. The effect is that the general provisions of the Social Security Act 1975 apply to the provisions of the Social Security Pensions Act 1975.

Note that subsequent amendments made to the 1992 provisions are not noted to this Table.

	Re-enacted in SSC&BA 1992	*Re-enacted in SSAA 1992*	*Remarks*
Social Security Act 1975			
s 1(1)	s 1(1)		Repealed in part by SSA 1986 s 86 Sch 11; SSA 1990 s 21 Sch 7 Employment Act 1990 s 16 Sch 3; amended by SSA 1990 s 16
s 1(2)	s 1(2)		Amended by SSCA 1991 s 1
s 1(3)	s 1(3)		Amended by SSA 1985 Sch 5 para 5
s 1(4)	s 1(4)		Amended by SSCA 1991 s 2
s 1(4A)	s 1(5)		Inserted by SSA 1990 s 16; amended by SSPA 1991 s 1
s 1(5)			Repealed by SSA 1989 s 31 Sch 9
s 1(5A)			Repealed by SSA 1989 s 31 Sch 9
s 1(6)	s 1(6)		Amended by SSCA 1991 s 1
s 2	s 2		
s 3(1)	s 3(1)		
s 3(1A)–(1C)	s 4(1)–(3)		Inserted by SSHBA 1982 s 37
s 3(1D)	s 4(4)		Inserted by SSA 1989 s 31 Sch 8 para 1
s 3(2)	s 3(2)		
s 3(3)	s 3(3)		
s 3(4)	s 4(5)		Inserted by SSHBA 1982 s 48 Sch 4 para 8
s 4(1)	s 5(1)		Amended by SSPA 1975 s 65 Sch 4 para 36; SSA 1985 s 7
s 4(2)	s 6(1)		Amended by Education (School-leaving Dates) Act 1976 s 2; repealed in part by SSHBA 1982 s 48 Sch 5
s 4(3)	s 6(3)		Substituted by SSA 1989 s 26 Sch 7 para 2
s 4(4), (5)	s 7		
s 4(6)–(6B)	s 8(1)–(3)		Substituted by SSA 1989 s 1
s 4(6C)	s 9(1), (4)		Inserted by SSA 1985 s 7; amended by SSA 1989 s 26 Sch 7 para 2

NIC

	Re-enacted in SSC&BA 1992	*Re-enacted in SSAA 1992*	*Remarks*
s 4(6D)	s 9(2)		Inserted by SSA 1985 s 7
s 4(6E)	s 9(3), (4)		Inserted by SSA 1985 s 7
s 4(6F)		s 146	Inserted by SSA 1985 s 7; repealed in part by SSA 1989 s 1 Sch 9
s 4(6G)		s 147	Inserted by SSA 1985 s 7
s 4(6H)		s 190(1)	Inserted by SSA 1985 s 7
s 4(6HH)		s 147(2)	Inserted by SSA 1986 ss 74 88
s 4(6J)		s 147(3)	Inserted by SSA 1985 s 7
s 4(6K)		s 147(4), (5)	Inserted by SSA 1985 s 7; amended by SSA 1990 s 21 Sch 6 para 1
s 4(7)	s 6(5)		Inserted by SSA 1979 s 14; amended by SSA 1985 s 8
s 4A	s 10		Inserted by SSCA 1991 s 1
s 7(1)	s 11(1)		Amended by Education (School-leaving Dates) Act 1976 s 2; HSSA 1984 s 17
s 7(2)–(3)			Repealed by SSPA 1975 s 3 Sch 5
s 7(4)–(6)	s 11(3)–(5)		
s 7A	s 12		Inserted by HSSA 1984 s 17; sub-s (3) amended by SI 1985/1398; SSA 1989 s 26 Sch 7 para 3, Sch 9
s 8(1)	s 13(1)		Amended by Education (School-leaving Dates) Act 1976 s 2; HSSA 1984 s 18
s 8(2)	s 13(2), (3)		Repealed in part by SSPA 1975 s 65 Sch 5
s 8(2A), (2B)	s 13(4), (5)		Inserted by HSSA 1984 s 18
s 8(2C)	s 13(6)		Inserted by HSSA 1984 s 18; amended by SI 1985/1398; SSA 1989 s 26 Sch 7 para 4
s 8(2D)	s 13(7)		Inserted by HSSA 1984 s 18
s 8(3)			Repealed by SSPA 1975 s 65 Sch 5
s 9(1)	s 15(1), (2), (5)		Amended by SSA 1989 s 26 Sch 7 para 5
s 9(2)	s 15(3)		
s 9(3)	s 16(1), (2), (6)		
s 9(4)	s 16(3)		
s 9(5)	s 16(4)		Amended by SSA 1990 s 17
s 9(6)	s 16(5)		Amended by SSA 1990 s 17
s 9(7)	s 17(1)		
s 9(8)	s 17(2)		Repealed in part by SSPA 1975 s 4 Sch 5
s 9(9)	s 17(3)–(6)		
s 10	s 18		
s 11	s 19(1)–(3)		
s 93(1)		s 17(1)	Repealed in part by Child Benefit Act 1975 s 21 Sch 4 para 30; amended by SS(MP)A 1977 s 22; SSCA 1991 s 6
s 93(2)		s 17(2)	
s 93(2A)		s 17(3)	Inserted by SSA 1989 s 21 Sch 3 para 1
s 93(3)		s 17(4)	
s 94(1)–(5)		s 18(1)–(5)	

	Re-enacted in SSC&BA 1992	Re-enacted in SSAA 1992	Remarks
s 94(6)			Repealed by Administration of Justice Act 1977 Sch 5 Pt IV; Supreme Court Act 1981 Sch 7
s 94(7), (8)		s 18(6), (7)	
s 96(1)		s 19(1)	Substituted by SSA 1986 s 52 Sch 5 para 3
s 96(2)		s 19(2), (3)	Amended by SSA 1980 ss 2, 21 Sch 1 para 9
s 114		s 58	Sub-s (2B) inserted by SSA 1986 s 52 Sch 5 para 16
s 115(1)		s 59(1)	
s 115(2)		s 59(1), Sch 3 para 1	
s 115(3), (4)		s 59(2), (3)	
s 115(4A)		s 59(4)	Inserted by SSCA 1991 ss 3, 6
s 115(6)		s 59(6)	Amended by SSA 1989 s 21 Sch 3 para 1
s 115(7)		s 59(7)	
s 117(1)		s 60(1)	Amended by Health and Social Services and Social Security Adjudications Act 1983 s 25 Sch 8 para 6
s 117(2)		s 60(2)	
s 119(1)–(2A)			Repealed by SSA 1986 s 86 Sch 11
s 119(3)		s 61(1), (3)	Repealed in part by SSA 1986 s 86 Sch 11
s 119(4)		s 61(2)	Repealed in part by SSA 1986 s 86 Sch 11
s 119(5), (6)			Repealed by SSA 1986 s 86 Sch 11
s 120(1)			Spent
s 120(2)		s 141(1)	Amended by SSPA 1975 s 65 Sch 4 para 50
s 120(3), (4)		s 141(2), (3)	
s 120(5)		s 141(4)	Repealed in part by SSPA 1975 s 65 Sch 4 para 50
s 120(6), (7)		s 141(5), (6)	
s 121(1), (2)		s 142(1), (2)	
s 121(3)		s 142(3)	Amended by SSA 1990 s 21 Sch 6 para 1
s 122(1)		s 143(1)	Amended by SSA 1985 s 29(1) Sch 5 para 9; SSA 1989 s 1(3)
s 122(2), (3)(a)		s 143(2), (3)	
s 122(3)(b), (4)			Repealed by Employment Act 1990 s 16(2) Sch 3
s 122(5)			Repealed by SSA 1989 Sch 8 para 8, Sch 9
s 122(6)		s 143(4)	Amended by SSA 1980 s 2 Sch 1 para 13; SSA 1989 s 1
s 123(1)		s 190(1)	
s 123(2)		s 144(1)	Repealed in part by Employment Act 1990 s 16 Sch 3
s 123(3)		s 144(1)	Amended by SSA 1990 s 21 Sch 6 para 1
s 123A			Inserted by SSA 1985 s 7
s 123A(1)		s 145(1)	Substituted by SSA 1989 s 1
s 123A(2)		s 145(2)	

NIC

	Re-enacted in SSC&BA 1992	*Re-enacted in SSAA 1992*	*Remarks*
s 123A(3)		s 145(3)	Amended by SSA 1989 s 1
s 123A(4)		s 145(4)	
s 123A(5)		s 147(1)	
s 123A(6)		s 190(1)	
s 123A(6A)		s 147(2)	Inserted by SSA 1986 s 74(1)
s 123A(7)		s 147(3)	
s 123A(8)		s 147(4), (5)	Amended by SSA 1990 s 21 Sch 6 para 1
s 127	s 115		
s 128(1)–(3)	s 116		
s 128(4)	s 177(3)		
s 129(1), (2)	s 117		
s 129(3)			Repealed by SS(MP)A 1977 s 1
s 130(1)	s 118		
s 130(2), (3)			Repealed by SSPA 1975 s 3 Sch 5
s 131	s 119		
s 132(1)	s 120(1)		
s 132(2)	s 120(2)		Amended by Oil and Gas (Enterprise) Act 1982 s 37 Sch 3 para 21
s 132(3)	s 120(3)		
s 142(1)		s 177(1), (5)	
s 142(2), (3)		s 177(2), (3)	
s 142(4)		s 177(4)	Amended by SSPA 1975 s 65 Sch 4 para 66; SSA 1986 s 65
s 142(5)			Repealed in part by SSA 1980 s 8 Sch 5 Pt II; re-enacted as SS (Northern Ireland) Act 1975 s 155A by SS(CP)A 1992 Sch 2 para 13
s 143(1)		s 179(1), (4)	Amended by SS(MP)A 1977 s 20; SSA 1986 s 65
s 143(1A)		s 179(2)	Inserted by SSA 1981 s 6
s 143(2)		s 179(3)	
s 146(1)		s 114(1)	Repealed in part by SSA 1986 s 86 Sch 11; amended by Criminal Justice Act 1982 ss 37, 46
s 146(2)		s 114(3)	
s 146(3)		s 114(4)	Repealed in part by SSA 1986 s 86 Sch 11
s 146(4)		s 114(5), (6)	
s 146(5)			Repealed in part by SSA 1986 s 86 Sch 11
s 148		s 117	
s 149		s 118	
s 150		s 119	
s 151(1), (2)		s 120(1), (2)	
s 151(3)		s 120(3)	Amended by SSCA 1991 s 2
s 151(3A)		s 120(4)	Inserted by SSCA 1991 s 2
s 151(4)		s 120(5)	
s 151(5)		s 120(6)	Amended by SSCA 1991 s 2
s 152(1)		s 121(1)	
s 152(2)		s 121(2)	Amended by SSPA 1975 s 65 Sch 4 para 60
s 152(3)		s 121(3)	

	Re-enacted in SSC&BA 1992	Re-enacted in SSAA 1992	Remarks
s 152(4)			Repealed by Insolvency Act 1985 Sch 10 Pt IV
s 152(5)		s 121(4)	
s 152(6)		s 121(5)	Repealed in part by SSA 1990 s 21 Sch 7
s 152(7)		s 121(6)	
s 166(1)	s 175(2)	s 189(3)	
s 166(2)	s 175(3)	s 189(4)	
s 166(3)	s 175(4)	s 189(5)	Amended by SSA 1989 s 31 Sch 8 para 10
s 166(3A)	s 175(5)	s 189(6)	Inserted by SSA 1986 s 62
s 166(4)	—	—	Unnecessary
s 166(5)	s 175(7)	s 189(9)	
s 166(5A)		s 189(10)	Inserted by SSA 1986 s 52 Sch 5 para 17
s 166(6)	s 175(8)		
s 166(7)	s 175(9)	s 189(11)	
s 167(1)	s 176(1)	s 190(1)	Amended by SSA 1986 s 62; repealed in part by SSPA 1975 s 65 Sch 5; SSA 1989 s 31 Sch 9; Employment Act 1990 s 16 Sch 3
s 167(2)	s 176(2)		Substituted by SSA 1990 s 21 Sch 6 para 8
s 167(3)	s 176(3)	s 190(3)	Substituted by SSA 1990 s 21 Sch 6 para 8
s 167(4)		s 190(4)	Substituted by SSA 1990 s 21 Sch 6 para 8
Sch 1	Sch 1		
para 1	para 1		Amended by SSA 1980 s 2 Sch 1 para 16; SSA 1985 s 29 Sch 5 para 13
para 2	para 2		
para 3	para 3		Amended by Criminal Justice Act 1982 ss 37, 46
para 4	para 4		Amended by SS(MP)A 1977 s 1
para 4A	para 5		Inserted by SSCA 1991 s 2
para 5	para 6		Amended by SSA 1990 s 17; SSCA 1991 s 2
para 5A	para 7		Inserted by SSA 1990 s 17 Sch 5; amended by SSCA 1991 s 2
para 6	para 8		Amended by SSPA 1975 s 65 Sch 4 para 61; SSA 1986 s 86 Sch 10 para 10; SSA 1989 s 2; SSA 1990 s 21 Sch 6 para 9; SSCA 1991 s 2
para 7	para 9		
para 8	para 10		
para 9	para 11		Inserted by SSHBA 1982 s 37
Sch 2	Sch 2		
para 1	para 1		Amended by TA 1988 s 844 Sch 29 para 32; CAA 1990 s 164 Sch 1 para 2
para 2	para 2		Amended by CAA 1990 s 164 Sch 1 para 2

	Re-enacted in SSC&BA 1992	*Re-enacted in SSAA 1992*	*Remarks*
para 3	para 3		Repealed in part by FA 1984 s 128 Sch 23 Pt VII; amended by FA 1985 s 42; TA 1988 s 844 Sch 29 para 32; FA 1988 Sch 3 para 31
para 4	para 9		Amended by TA 1988 s 844 Sch 29 para 32; repealed by FA 1988 Sch 14 Pt VIII
para 5	para 4		Amended by TA 1988 s 844 Sch 29 para 32
para 6	para 5		Amended by TA 1988 s 844 Sch 29 para 32
para 7	para 6		See SS(CP)A 1992 Sch 4 para 8
para 8	para 7		
para 9	para 8		
Sch 13		Sch 3	
para 1		para 2	
para 1A		para 3	Inserted by SSA 1986 Sch 5 para 19
para 2		para 4	
para 3		para 5	
para 4		para 6	
para 5		para 7	
para 11		para 12	
Sch 17		Sch 8	
Social Security Pensions Act 1975			
s 1(1)	s 5(1)		Amended by SSA 1985 s 29 Sch 5 para 15
s 1(2)	s 5(2)		Amended by SSA 1986 s 74
s 1(3)	s 5(3)		
s 3(1)	—		Spent
s 3(2), (3)	s 19(4), (5)		
s 3(4)	s 19(6)		Amended by SSA 1986 s 75 Sch 8 para 5
s 4(1)	s 6(2)		Amended and repealed in part by HSSA 1984 s 21 Sch 7 para 3
s 4(2)	s 11(2)		
s 4(3)	s 17(2)		
s 5(1)	s 14(1)		Amended by SSA 1986 s 75 Sch 8 para 6
s 5(2)	s 14(3), (4)		
s 5(3)	s 14(2)		
s 62(1)	s 176(1)(a)		Amended by SSA 1990 s 21 Sch 6 para 8; repealed by SS(CP)A 1992 Sch 1
s 62(3)			Repealed by SS(CP)A 1992 Sch 1
Social Security (Miscellaneous Provisions) Act 1977			
s 1(1)			Spent
s 1(2)		s 163(4)	
s 1(3)	Sch 1, para 1(1)		

	Re-enacted in SSC&BA 1992	*Re-enacted in SSAA 1992*	*Remarks*
s 1(4)			Spent
s 1(5)	s 14(3), (4)		
s 1(6), (7)			Spent
s 2	s 22(7)		
s 18	s 112		Repealed in part by SSA 1986 s 86 Sch 11; amended by Employment Protection (Consolidation) Act 1978 s 159 Sch 16 para 29; SSA 1986 s 86 Sch 10 para 74
Social Security Act 1980			
s 9(1)–(4)		s 170(1)–(4)	
s 9(5)			See SS(CP)A 1992 Sch 3 paras 4 6
s 9(7)		s 170(5)	Repealed in part by SSA 1986 s 86 Sch 11; SS (Northern Ireland) Order 1986 SI 1986/1888 Sch 10; amended by SSHBA 1982 s 48 Sch 4 para 30; SS (Northern Ireland) Order 1982 SI 1982/1084; Housing Benefits (Northern Ireland) Order 1983 SI 1983/1121; SSA 1989 s 31 Sch 8 para 12; SS (Northern Ireland) Order 1989 SI 1989/1342 art 31 Sch 8 para 12; SSPA 1991 s 3: Statutory Sick Pay (Northern Ireland) Order 1991 SI /765 art 5
s 10(1)		s 172(1)	Amended by SSA 1986 s 86 Sch 10 para 98; SS (Northern Ireland) Order 1986 SI 1986/1888 Sch 9 para 64
s 10(2)		s 172(3)	Repealed in part by SS (Northern Ireland) Order 1986 SI 1986/1888 Sch 10; SSA 1989 Sch 9
s 10(3)–(5)		s 174(1)–(3)	
s 10(9)		ss 172(5), 173(6), 174(4)	
s 18	s 173		
Sch 3		Sch 5	
para 1		para 1	Amended by SSHBA 1982 s 48 Sch 4 para 32
para 2		para 2	Amended by SSHBA 1982 s 48 Sch 4 para 32
paras 3–10		paras 3–10	
Sch 3		Sch 7	
para 12(2)		para 3	Amended by SSHBA 1982 s 42; SSA 1986 Sch 10 para 99
para 13(1)		para 4	Amended by SS (Northern Ireland) Order 1986 SI 1986/1888 Sch 9 para 73
para 13(1A)		para 5	Inserted by SSA 1986 Sch 10 para 106
para 15A		para 8	Inserted by SSHBA 1982 s 48 Sch 4 para 32
para 19		para 9	
para 20		para 10	

	Re-enacted in SSC&BA 1992	*Re-enacted in SSAA 1992*	*Remarks*
Social Security and Housing Benefits Act 1982			
s 1(1), (2)	s 151(1), (2)		
s 1(3)–(4)	s 151(4)–(5)		
s 1(5)	s 151(6)		Inserted by SSA 1986 s 68
s 1(6)		s 163(1)(d)	Inserted by SSA 1986 s 68
s 9(1)	s 158(1)		Amended by SSPA 1991 s 1
s 9(1A)			Repealed by SSPA 1991 Sch
s 9(1B)	s 158(2)		Inserted by SSPA 1991 s 2
s 9(1C)	s 159		Inserted by SSPA 1991 s 2
s 9(1D)	s 158(3)		Inserted by SSPA 1991 s 2
s 9(1E)		s 149	Inserted by SSPA 1991 s 2
s 9(1F)	s 176(1)(a), (c)		Inserted by SSPA 1991 s 2
s 9(2)	s 158(4)		Amended by SSPA 1991 s 2
s 9(3)	s 158(5)	s 130(4)(c)	Repealed in part by SSPA 1991 Sch; amended by SSPA 1991 s 1
s 9(4)	Sch 1 para 5(5)		
s 9(5)	Sch 1 para 5(6)		Repealed in part by SSPA 1991 Sch
s 9(6)	s 158(6)		
s 9(7)		s 163(1)	Repealed in part by SSPA 1991 Sch
s 9(8)–(10)			Repealed by SSA 1986 Sch 11
s 23	s 4(1)		
s 26(1)	s 163(1)		Amended by SSA 1985 s 21 Sch 4 para 6
s 26(7)	s 172(a)		
s 27(1), (2)	s 161(1), (2)		
s 27(3)	s 161(3)		Inserted by SSA 1989 s 26 Sch 7 para 23
s 44(1), (2)	s 172		
s 44(3), (4)			Repealed by SSA 1989 Sch 7 para 24, Sch 9
Social Security Act 1986			
s 52(4)		s 59(2)	
s 52(5)		s 117(1)	
s 56(2)(a)		s 116(2)(a)	Amended by Local Government Finance Act 1988 s 135 Sch 19 para 9
s 61(1)–(5)		s 173(1)–(5)	
s 61(8), (9)		s 176(2), (3)	
s 61(10)		s 173(7)	
s 74(5)	s 9(5), Sch 1 para 1(5)		
s 83(3)(e)	s 176(1)(c)		
Sch 5 Pt II		s 17(1)(g), (h)	

SOCIAL SECURITY CONTRIBUTIONS AND BENEFITS ACT 1992

(1992 Chapter 4)

ARRANGEMENT OF SECTIONS

PART I
CONTRIBUTIONS

PART II
CONTRIBUTORY BENEFITS
Preliminary

An Act to consolidate certain enactments relating to social security contributions and benefits with amendments to give effect to recommendations of the Law Commission and the Scottish Law Commission

[13 February 1992]

Cross references—See SSAA 1992 s 110(8)(*b*) (appointment of inspectors and inspectors' powers of search, etc in relation to offences under this Act),
SSAA 1992 s 113 (offences in consequence of breach of regulations made by virtue of this Act),
SSAA 1992 s 121(5) (unpaid contributions recovered by Secretary of State),
SSAA 1992 s 141(2)(*b*) (annual review of contributions),
SSAA 1992 s 177(5)(*a*) (co-ordination with Northern Ireland),
SSAA 1992 s 179(3), (4) (reciprocal agreements with countries outside the UK),
SSAA 1992 s 189(11) (subordinate legislation for modifications or adaptations of this Act),
SSAA 1992 s 192(2) (inter-relation of the 1992 consolidation Acts);
SS(CP)A 1992 Sch 3 para 5 (continuing powers to make transitional etc regulations).

PART I
CONTRIBUTIONS

Cross references—See SS (Employment Training: Payments) Order, SI 1988/1409 (exemption from Class 1 or Class 2 contributions in respect of payments to a person in receipt of a training premium); SS(CP)A 1992 s 2;
SSAA 1992 s 61(1)(*a*)(iii) (regulations pending determination of a person's liability for contributions under this Part of this Act),
SSAA 1992 s 110(2)(*e*)(i), (6)(*a*)(i) (appointment of inspectors and inspectors' powers of search, etc in relation to offences for contravention of provisions of this Part of this Act),
SSAA 1992 s 114(1) (offences relating to contributions under this Part of this Act),
SSAA 1992 s 141 (annual review of contributions under this Part of this Act),
SSAA 1992 s 143(1) (power to alter contributions under this Part of this Act).

Preliminary

1 Outline of contributory system

(1) The funds required—

(*a*) for paying such benefits under this Act [or any other Act][10] as are payable out of the National Insurance Fund and not out of other public money; and

(*b*) for the making of payments under section 162 of the Administration Act towards the cost of the National Health Service,

shall be provided by means of contributions payable to the [Inland Revenue][4] by earners, employers and others, together with the additions under subsection (5) below [and amounts payable under section 2 of the Social Security Act 1993][1].

(2) Contributions under this Part of this Act shall be of the following . . . [14] classes—

(*a*) Class 1, earnings-related, payable under section 6 below, being—

(i) primary Class 1 contributions from employed earners; and

(ii) secondary Class 1 contributions from employers and other persons paying earnings;

(*b*) Class 1A, payable under section 10 below . . . [6] by persons liable to pay secondary Class 1 contributions and certain other persons;

[(*bb*) Class 1B, payable under section 10A below by persons who are accountable to the Inland Revenue in respect of income tax on [general earnings][8] in accordance with a PAYE settlement agreement;][3]

(*c*) Class 2, flat-rate, payable . . . [13] under section 11 below by self-employed earners;

(*d*) Class 3, payable under section 13 [or 13A][9] below by earners and others voluntarily with a view to providing entitlement to benefit, or making up entitlement;

[(*da*) Class 3A, payable by eligible people voluntarily under section 14A with a view to obtaining units of additional pension;][14]and

(*e*) Class 4, payable under section 15 below in respect of the profits or gains of a trade, profession or vocation, or under section 18 below in respect of equivalent earnings.

(3) The amounts and rates of contributions in this Part of this Act and the other figures in it which affect the liability of contributors shall—

(*a*) be subject to regulations under sections 19(4) and 116 to 120 below; and

NIC

(*b*) to the extent provided for by Part IX of the Administration Act be subject to alteration by orders made by the [Treasury][5] from year to year under that Part,

. . .[2]

(4) Schedule 1 to this Act—

(*a*) shall have effect with respect to the computation, collection and recovery of contributions of Classes 1, 1A, [1B,][3] 2[, 3 and 3A][14], and otherwise with respect to contributions of those classes; and

(*b*) shall also, to the extent provided by regulations made under section 18 below, have effect with respect to the computation, collection and recovery of Class 4 contributions, and otherwise with respect to such contributions, . . .[4].

(5) For each financial year there shall, by way of addition to contributions, be paid out of money provided by Parliament, in such manner and at such times as the Treasury may determine, amounts the total of which for any such year is equal to the aggregate of all statutory sick pay[, statutory maternity pay, [statutory paternity pay,][12] statutory adoption pay][7] [and statutory shared parental pay][11] recovered by employers and others in that year, as estimated by the Government Actuary or the Deputy Government Actuary.

(6) No person shall—

(*a*) be liable to pay Class 1, Class 1A, [Class 1B][3] or Class 2 contributions unless he fulfils prescribed conditions as to residence or presence in Great Britain;

(*b*) be entitled to pay Class 3 contributions unless he fulfils such conditions; or

(*c*) be entitled to pay Class 1, Class 1A, [Class 1B][3] or Class 2 contributions other than those which he is liable to pay, except so far as he is permitted by regulations to pay them.

[(7) Regulations under subsection (6) above shall be made by the Treasury.][5]

Commentary—*Simon's Taxes* **E8.201, E8.281, E8.305A, E8.701.**
HMRC Manuals—National Insurance Manual NIM00002 (the structure of the NIM).
Former enactments—Sub-s (1): SSA 1975 s 1(1); SSA 1990 s 16(1), (2).
Sub-s (2): SSA 1975 s 1(2); SS (Contributions) Act 1991 s 1(2).
Sub-s (3): SSA 1975 s 1(3); SSA 1985 s 29(1), Sch 5 para 5.
Sub-s (4): SSA 1975 s 1(4); SS (Contributions) Act 1991 s 2(1)(*a*).
Sub-s (5): SSA 1975 s 1(4A); SSA 1990 s 16(2); Statutory Sick Pay Act 1991 s 1(4).
Sub-s (6): SSA 1975 s 1(6); SS (Contributions) Act 1991 s 1(3).
Regulations—Social Security (Contributions) (Amendment No. 2) Regulations, SI 2012/817.
Social Security (Contributions) (Amendment and Application of Schedule 38 to the Finance Act 2012) Regulations, SI 2013/622.
Social Security (Contributions) (Amendment) Regulations, SI 2013/718.
Social Security (Miscellaneous Amendments No 2) Regulations, SI 2015/478.
Cross references—See SS (Refunds) (Repayment of Contractual Maternity Pay) Regulations, SI 1990/536 regs 2, 3 (refund of contributions where maternity pay is repaid to employer because employee does not resume employment after child-birth); SS(CP)A 1992 s 2.
Statutory Sick Pay Act 1991 s 3(6) (effect of that Act in relation to the Crown and Crown employees).
Amendments—[1] Words in sub-s (1) added by SSA 1993 s 2.
[2] In sub-s (3), words after para (*b*) repealed by PeA 2014 s 24, Sch 13 paras 48, 49 with effect from 6 April 2016 (PeA 2014 s 56(1), (4)).
[3] Sub-s (2)(*bb*) and words in sub-ss (4)(*a*) and (6) inserted by SSA 1998 Sch 7 para 56 with effect from 8 September 1998 by virtue of the Social Security Act 1998 (Commencement No 1) Order, SI 1998/2209.
[4] Words in sub-s (1) amended and words in sub-s (4)(*b*) repealed by the Social Security Contributions (Transfer of Functions, etc) Act 1999 s 1(1) and Sch 1 para 5, and s 26(3) and Sch 10 Pt 1 with effect from 1 April 1999 by virtue of the Social Security Contributions (Transfer of Functions, etc) Act 1999 (Commencement No 1 and Transitional Provisions) Order, SI 1999/527.
[5] Words in sub-s (3)(*b*) substituted, and sub-s (7) inserted by the Social Security Contributions (Transfer of Functions, etc) Act 1999 s 2, Sch 3 para 1 with effect from 1 April 1999 by virtue of the Social Security Contributions (Transfer of Functions, etc) Act 1999 (Commencement No 1 and Transitional Provisions) Order, SI 1999/527.
[6] Words in sub-s (2)(*b*) repealed by the Child Support, Pensions and Social Security Act 2000 s 74(1), (8) with effect for the tax year beginning with 6 April 2000 and subsequent tax years.
[7] Words in sub-s (5) substituted by EmA 2002 s 6(3) with effect from 8 December 2002 (by virtue of SI 2002/2866).
[8] In sub-s (2)(*bb*), words substituted for the word "emoluments" by ITEPA 2003 s 722, Sch 6 paras 169, 170 with effect, for income tax purposes, from 2003–04; and for corporation tax purposes, for accounting periods ending after 5 April 2003. For transitional provisions and savings see ITEPA 2003 s 723, Sch 7.
[9] In sub-s (2)(*d*), words inserted by the Pensions Act 2008 s 135(1), (3) with effect from 6 April 2009.
[10] In sub-s (1)(*a*), words inserted by PeA 2014 s 23, Sch 12 paras 2, 3 with effect from 15 January 2016 (by virtue of SI 2015/2058 art 2).
[11] In sub-s (5), words inserted by the Children and Families Act 2014 s 126, Sch 7 paras 6, 7(*b*) with effect from 1 December 2014 (by virtue of SI 2014/1640 art 5).
[12] In sub-s (5), words substituted by the Children and Families Act 2014 s 126, Sch 7 paras 6, 7(*a*) with effect from 5 April 2015 (by virtue of SI 2014/1640 art 7).
[13] In sub-s (2)(*c*), word "weekly" repealed by NICA 2015 s 2, Sch 1 paras 1, 2 with effect for the tax year 2015–16 and subsequent tax years.
[14] In sub-s (2), word "six" repealed, sub-s (2)(*da*) inserted, and in sub-s (4)(*a*), words ", 3 and 3A" substituted for words "and 3" by PeA 2014 s 25, Sch 15 paras 1, 2, with effect from 12 October 2015 (by virtue of SI 2015/1475).

2 Categories of earners

(1) In this Part of this Act and Parts II to V below—

[(*a*) "employed earner" means a person who is gainfully employed in Great Britain either under a contract of service, or in an office (including elective office) with [. . . [3] earnings][2]; and

(*b*) "self-employed earner" means a person who is gainfully employed in Great Britain otherwise than in employed earner's employment (whether or not he is also employed in such employment).

(2) Regulations may provide—

(*a*) for employment of any prescribed description to be disregarded in relation to liability for contributions otherwise arising from employment of that description;

(*b*) for a person in employment of any prescribed description to be treated, for the purposes of this Act, as falling within one or other of the categories of earner defined in subsection (1) above, notwithstanding that he would not fall within that category apart from the regulations.

[(2ZA) Regulations under subsection (2)(*b*) may make provision treating a person ("P") as falling within one or other of the categories of earner in relation to an employment where arrangements have been entered into the main purpose, or one of the main purposes, of which is to secure—

(*a*) that P is not treated by other provision in regulations under subsection (2)(*b*) as falling within that category of earner in relation to the employment, or

(*b*) that a person is not treated as the secondary contributor in respect of earnings paid to or for the benefit of P in respect of the employment.

(2ZB) In subsection (2ZA) "arrangements" include any scheme, transaction or series of transactions, agreement or understanding, whether or not legally enforceable, and any associated operations.][4]

[(2A) Regulations under subsection (2) above shall be made by the Treasury and, in the case of regulations under paragraph (*b*) of that subsection, with the concurrence of the Secretary of State.][1]

(3) Where a person is to be treated by reference to any employment of his as an employed earner, then he is to be so treated for all purposes of this Act; and references throughout this Act to employed earner's employment shall be construed accordingly.

(4) Subsections (1) to (3) above are subject to the provision made by section 95 below as to the employments which are to be treated, for the purposes of industrial injuries benefit, as employed earner's employments.

(5) For the purposes of this Act, a person shall be treated as a self-employed earner as respects any week during any part of which he is such an earner (without prejudice to his being also treated as an employed earner as respects that week by reference to any other employment of his).

Commentary—*Simon's Taxes* **E8.701, E8.212**.
HMRC Manuals—National Insurance Manual NIM74100 (class 2 NIC: examiners and moderators).
Former enactments—SSA 1975 s 2.
Regulations—See the SS (Categorisation of Earners) Regulations, SI 1978/1689; SS(CP)A 1992 s 2.
The Social Security (Categorisation of Earners) (Amendment) Regulations, SI 2012/816.
The Social Security (Categorisation of Earners) (Amendment) Regulations, SI 2014/635.
Social Security (Miscellaneous Amendments No 2) Regulations, SI 2015/478.
Social Security Contributions (Limited Liability Partnership) (Amendment) Regulations, SI 2015/607.
Social Security (Miscellaneous Amendments) Regulations, SI 2017/307.
Simon's Tax Cases—2(1)(*b*), *Rashid v Garcia (Status Inspector)* [2003] STC (SCD) 36.
Amendments—[1] Sub-s (2A) substituted by the Welfare Reform and Pensions Act 1999 s 81, Sch 11 paras 1, 2 with effect from 11 November 1999.
[2] In sub-s (1)(*a*), words substituted by ITEPA 2003 s 722, Sch 6 paras 169, 171 with effect, for income tax purposes, from 2003–04; and for corporation tax purposes, for accounting periods ending after 5 April 2003. For transitional provisions and savings see ITEPA 2003 s 723, Sch 7.
[3] In sub-s (1)(*a*), word "general" repealed by NICs Act 2014 s 15(1) with effect from 14 May 2014.
[4] Sub-ss (2ZA), (2ZB) inserted by NICA 2015 s 6(3) with effect from 12 February 2015.

3 "Earnings" and "earner"

(1) In this Part of this Act and Parts II to V below—

(*a*) "earnings" includes any remuneration or profit derived from an employment; and

(*b*) "earner" shall be construed accordingly.

(2) For the purposes of this Part of this Act and of Parts II to V below other than those of Schedule 8—

(*a*) the amount of a person's earnings for any period; or

(*b*) the amount of his earnings to be treated as comprised in any payment made to him or for his benefit,

shall be calculated or estimated in such manner and on such basis as may be prescribed [by regulations made by the Treasury with the concurrence of the Secretary of State][3].

[(2A) Regulations made for the purposes of subsection (2) above may provide that, where a payment is made or a benefit provided to or for the benefit of two or more earners, a proportion (determined in such manner as may be prescribed) of the amount or value of the payment or benefit shall be attributed to each earner.][1]

(3) Regulations made for the purposes of subsection (2) above may prescribe that payments of a particular class or description made or falling to be made to or by a person shall, to such extent as may be prescribed, be disregarded or, as the case may be, be deducted from the amount of that person's earnings.

[(4) Subsection (5) below applies to regulations made for the purposes of subsection (2) above which make special provision with respect to the earnings periods of directors and former directors of companies.

(5) Regulations to which this subsection applies may make provision—

(*a*) for enabling companies, and directors and former directors of companies, to pay on account of any earnings-related contributions that may become payable by them such amounts as would be payable by way of such contributions if the special provision had not been made; and

(*b*) for requiring any payments made in accordance with the regulations to be treated, for prescribed purposes, as if they were the contributions on account of which they were made.][2]

Commentary—*Simon's Taxes* **E8.230, E8.219, E8.231, E8.250, E8.1109**.

HMRC Manuals—National Insurance Manual NIM02010 (definition of "earnings").

NIM01023 (payments of earnings after an employee's death).

NIM02030 (class 1 Nics : earnings of employees and office holders : important principles).

NIM02411 (treatment of vouchers for NIC purposes).

NIM02461 (non-cash vouchers — calculation).

NIM05020 (business expenses).

NIM05630 (car parking fines).

NIM05708 (liability for class 1 Nics).

Former enactments—Sub-s (1); SSA 1975 s 3(1).

Sub-ss (2), (3): SSA 1975 s 3(2), (3).

Press releases etc—ICAEW TAX 21/92 22-12-92 (treatment of directors' remuneration and company cars).

Contributions Agency Booklet CA 28 (detailed guidance on what is included in "earnings").

ICAEW TAX 18/95 20-6-95 para 7 (dividends which are repayable are not "earnings").

IR 19-9-95 (concessions which apply for income tax purposes are to apply for NIC purposes).

Contributions Agency 28-9-95 (mileage allowances: rates not exceeding the IR's fixed profit car scheme rates for up to 40,000 miles p.a. will not be liable to NIC).

Contributions Agency Press Release 17-11-97 (revised guidance to employers on payment into and out of FURBS).

Regulations—Social Security (Contributions) (Amendment No 2) Regulations, SI 2003/964.

Social Security (Contributions) (Amendment No 3) Regulations, SI 2003/1059.

Social Security (Contributions) (Amendment No 4) Regulations, SI 2011/1000.

Social Security (Contributions) (Amendment No 2) Regulations, SI 2012/817.

Social Security (Contributions) (Amendment and Application of Schedule 38 to the Finance Act 2012) Regulations, SI 2013/622.

Social Security (Contributions) (Amendment No 6) Regulations, SI 2014/3228.

Social Security and Tax Credits (Miscellaneous Amendments) Regulations, SI 2015/175.

Social Security (Miscellaneous Amendments No 2) Regulations, SI 2015/478.

Social Security (Contributions) (Amendment) Regulations, SI 2015/543.

Social Security Benefit (Computation of Earnings) (Amendment) Regulations, SI 2015/784.

Social Security (Contributions) (Amendment) (No 2) Regulations SI 2016/352.

Social Security (Contributions) (Amendment) (No 3) Regulations SI 2016/647.

Social Security (Contributions) (Amendment No 4) Regulations, SI 2016/1067.

Social Security (Miscellaneous Amendments) Regulations, SI 2017/307.

Cross references—See SS (Contributions) Regulations, SI 2001/1004 reg 8 (payments to directors to be treated as earnings);

SS (Contributions) Regulations, SI 2001/1004 reg 23 (sickness payments treated as remuneration);

SS (Contributions) Regulations, SI 2001/1004 regs 25–27 (payments to be disregarded).

SSC & BA 1992 s 112 (certain sums to be earnings).

Amendments—[1] Inserted by SSA 1998 s 48 with effect from 8 September 1998 by virtue of the Social Security Act 1998 (Commencement No 1) Order, SI 1998/2209.

[2] Inserted by SSA 1998 s 49 with effect from 8 September 1998 by virtue of the Social Security Act 1998 (Commencement No 1) Order, SI 1998/2209.

[3] Words in sub-s (2) inserted by the Social Security Contributions (Transfer of Functions, etc) Act 1999 s 2, Sch 3 para 3 with effect from 1 April 1999 by virtue of the Social Security Contributions (Transfer of Functions, etc) Act 1999 (Commencement No 1 and Transitional Provisions) Order, SI 1999/527.

4 Payments treated as remuneration and earnings

(1) For the purposes of section 3 above there shall be treated as remuneration derived from employed earner's employment—

(*a*) any sum paid to or for the benefit of a person in satisfaction (whether in whole or in part) of any entitlement of that person to—

(i) statutory sick pay; or

(ii) statutory maternity pay;

[(iii) . . . [10] statutory paternity pay;

(iv) . . . [9]

(v) statutory adoption pay;][8] [or

"(vi) statutory shared parental pay; and][9]

(*b*) any sickness payment made—

(i) to or for the benefit of the employed earner; and

(ii) in accordance with arrangements under which the person who is the secondary contributor in relation to the employment concerned has made, or remains liable to make, payments towards the provision of that sickness payment.

(2) Where the funds for making sickness payments under arrangements of the kind mentioned in paragraph (*b*) of subsection (1) above are attributable in part to contributions to those funds made by the employed earner, regulations may make provision for disregarding, for the purposes of that subsection, the prescribed part of any sum paid as a result of the arrangements.

(3) For the purposes of subsections (1) and (2) above "sickness payment" means any payment made in respect of absence from work due to incapacity for work . . . [1]

[(4) For the purposes of section 3 above there shall be treated as remuneration derived from an employed earner's employment—

[(*a*) the amount of any gain calculated under section 479 [of ITEPA 2003 in respect of which an amount counts as employment income of the earner under section 476 of that Act (charge on acquisition of securities pursuant to option etc), reduced by any amounts deducted under section 480(1) to (6) of that Act in arriving at the amount counting as such employment income;][7]][6]

(*b*) any sum paid (or treated as paid) to or for the benefit of the earner which is chargeable to tax by virtue of [section 225 or 226 of ITEPA 2003][6] (taxation of consideration for certain restrictive undertakings).][2]

(5) For the purposes of section 3 above regulations may make provision for treating as remuneration derived from an employed earner's employment any payment made by a body corporate to or for the benefit of any of its directors where that payment would, when made, not be earnings for the purposes of this Act.

[(6) Regulations may make provision for the purposes of this Part—

(*a*) for treating any amount on which an employed earner is chargeable to income tax under [the employment income Parts of ITEPA 2003][6] as remuneration derived from the earner's employment; and

(*b*) for treating any amount which in accordance with regulations under paragraph (*a*) above constitutes remuneration as an amount of remuneration paid, at such time as may be determined in accordance with the regulations, to or for the benefit of the earner in respect of his employment.][4]

[(7) Regulations under this section shall be made by the Treasury with the concurrence of the Secretary of State.][3]

Commentary—*Simon's Taxes* **E8.232, E8.233, E8.236, E8.521, E8.612.**

HMRC Manuals—National Insurance Manual NIM02025 (earnings of employees and office holders: payments deemed to be earnings).
NIM06810 (class 1 Nics: employment-related securities shares).
NIM06823 (securities: earnings and payments treated as earnings).
NIM09300 (statutory sick pay and statutory maternity pay: delay in paying).
NIM09310 (SSP and SMP : lump sum payments
NIM09320 (SSP and SMP : payment after employment has ended).
NIM50200 (amounts charged to income tax).

Former enactments—Sub-ss (1)–(3): SSA 1975 s 3(1A)–(1C); Social Security and Housing Benefits Act 1982 s 23.
Sub-s (4): SSA 1975 s 3(1D);
SSA 1989 s 31(1), Sch 8 para 1.
Sub-s (5): SSA 1975 s 3(4); Social Security and Housing Benefits Act 1982 s 48(5), Sch 4 para 8.

Regulations—Social Security (Contributions) (Amendment) (No 2) Regulations SI 2016/352.

Cross references—See SS (Contributions) Regulations, SI 2001/1004 reg 8 (payments to directors to be treated as earnings).
SS (Contributions) Regulations, SI 2001/1004 reg 23 (sickness payment treated as remuneration).
SS (Contributions) Regulations, SI 2001/1004 reg 25 (payments to be disregarded in computation of a person's earnings).

Simon's Tax Cases—*RCI Europe v Woods (Insp of Taxes)* [2004] STC 315.

Amendments—[1] Words omitted from sub-s (3) repealed by the Social Security (Incapacity for Work) Act 1994 Sch 1 Pt I para 1, Sch 2 with effect from 13 April 1995.

[2] Sub-s (4) substituted by SSA 1998 s 50(1) with effect in relation to any undertaking given on or after 10 July 1997 so far as relating to a sum which is chargeable to tax by virtue of TA 1988 s 313, and with effect from 8 September 1998 for all other instances by virtue of the Social Security Act 1998 (Commencement No 1) Order, SI 1998/2209.

[3] Sub-s (7) inserted by the Social Security Contributions (Transfer of Functions, etc) Act 1999 s 2, Sch 3 para 4 with effect from 1 April 1999 by virtue of the Social Security Contributions (Transfer of Functions, etc) Act 1999 (Commencement No 1 and Transitional Provisions) Order, SI 1999/527.

[4] Sub-s (6) substituted by the Child Support, Pensions and Social Security Act 2000 s 74(3), (8) with effect for the tax year beginning with 6 April 2000 and subsequent tax years (originally inserted by SSA 1998 s 50(2)).

[6] Sub-s (4)(*a*) substituted, in sub-s (4)(*b*); words substituted for the words "section 313 of the 1988 Act"; in sub-s (6)(*a*), words substituted for the words "Schedule E" by ITEPA 2003 s 722, Sch 6 paras 169, 172 with effect, for income tax purposes, from 2003–04; and for corporation tax purposes, for accounting periods ending after 5 April 2003. For transitional provisions and savings see ITEPA 2003 s 723, Sch 7.

[7] In sub-s (4)(*a*), words substituted by FA 2003 Sch 22 para 48 with effect in accordance with the provision made for the substitution of ITEPA 2003 Part 7 Chapter 5, ie with effect—

(a) after 15 April 2003 in relation to employment-related securities options which are not share options, and
(b) on and after the day appointed under FA 2003 Sch 22 para 3(2) in relation to employment-related securities options which are share options (the appointed day is 1 September 2003 (by virtue of SI 2003/1997);

and for this purpose "share options" means rights to acquire shares in a company or securities as defined in section 254(1) of the Taxes Act 1988 issued by a company: see FA 2003 Sch 22 para 10(2).

NIC

[8] Sub-s (1)(*a*)(iii)–(v) substituted for former sub-s (1)(*a*)(iii), (iv) by the Work and Families Act 2006 s 11 Sch 1 para 4 with effect from 6 April 2010 (by virtue of SI 2010/495, art 4(d)).

[9] Sub-s (1)(*a*)(iv) repealed, in sub-s (1)(*a*)(v), word substituted for word "and", and sub-s (1)(*a*)(vi) inserted, by the Children and Families Act 2014 s 126, Sch 7 paras 6, 8(b), (c) with effect from 1 December 2014 (by virtue of SI 2014/1640 art 5).

[10] In sub-s (1)(*a*)(iii), word "ordinary" repealed by the Children and Families Act 2014 s 126, Sch 7 paras 6, 8(a) with effect from 5 April 2014 (by virtue of SI 2014/1640 art 7).

[4A Earnings of workers supplied by service companies etc

(1) Regulations may make provision for securing that where—

(*a*) an individual ("the worker") personally performs, or is under an obligation personally to perform, services for the purposes of a business carried on by another person ("the client"),

(*b*) the performance of those services by the worker is (within the meaning of the regulations) referable to arrangements involving a third person (and not referable to any contract between the client and the worker), and

(*c*) the circumstances are such that, were the services to be performed by the worker under a contract between him and the client, he would be regarded for the purposes of the applicable provisions of this Act as employed in employed earner's employment by the client,

relevant payments or benefits are, to the specified extent, to be treated for those purposes as earnings paid to the worker in respect of an employed earner's employment of his.

(2) For the purposes of this section—

(*a*) "the intermediary" means—

(i) where the third person mentioned in subsection (1)(*b*) above has such a contractual or other relationship with the worker as may be specified, that third person, or

(ii) where that third person does not have such a relationship with the worker, any other person who has both such a relationship with the worker and such a direct or indirect contractual or other relationship with the third person as may be specified; and

(*b*) a person may be the intermediary despite being—

(i) a person with whom the worker holds any office or employment, or

(ii) a body corporate, unincorporated body or partnership of which the worker is a member;

and subsection (1) above applies whether or not the client is a person with whom the worker holds any office or employment.

[(2A) Regulations may also make provision for securing that, where the services of an individual ("the worker") are provided (directly or indirectly) by a managed service company ("the MSC") relevant payments or benefits are, to the specified extent, to be treated for the purposes of the applicable provisions of this Act as earnings paid to the worker in respect of an employed earner's employment of his.

(2B) In subsection (2A) "managed service company" has the same meaning as it has for the purposes of Chapter 9 of Part 2 of ITEPA 2003.][3]

(3) Regulations under this section may, in particular, make provision—

(*a*) for the worker to be treated for the purposes of the applicable provisions of this Act, in relation to the specified amount of relevant payments or benefits (the worker's "attributable earnings"), as employed in employed earner's employment by the intermediary [or the MSC (as the case requires)][3];

(*b*) for the [intermediary or the MSC (whether or not fulfilling][3] the conditions prescribed under section 1(6)(*a*) above for secondary contributors) to be treated for those purposes as the secondary contributor in respect of the worker's attributable earnings;

(*c*) for determining—

(i) any deductions to be made, and

(ii) in other respects the manner and basis in and on which the amount of the worker's attributable earnings for any specified period is to be calculated or estimated,

in connection with relevant payments or benefits;

(*d*) for aggregating any such amount, for purposes relating to contributions, with other earnings of the worker during any such period;

(*e*) for determining the date by which contributions payable in respect of the worker's attributable earnings are to be paid and accounted for;

(*f*) for apportioning payments or benefits of any specified description, in such manner or on such basis as may be specified, for the purpose of determining the part of any such payment or benefit which is to be treated as a relevant payment or benefit for the purposes of the regulations;

(*g*) for disregarding for the purposes of the applicable provisions of this Act, in relation to relevant payments or benefits, an employed earner's employment in which the worker is employed (whether by the intermediary [or the MSC][3] or otherwise) to perform the services in question;

(*h*) for otherwise securing that a double liability to pay any amount by way of a contribution of any description does not arise in relation to a particular payment or benefit or (as the case may be) a particular part of a payment or benefit;

(*i*) for securing that, to the specified extent, two or more persons, whether—

(i) connected persons (within the meaning of [section 993 of the Income Tax Act 2007][2]), or

(ii) persons of any other specified description,

are treated as a single person for any purposes of the regulations;

(*j*) (without prejudice to paragraph (*i*) above) for securing that a contract made with a person other than the client is to be treated for any such purposes as made with the client;

(*k*) for excluding or modifying the application of the regulations in relation to such cases, or payments or benefits of such description, as may be specified.

(4) Regulations made in pursuance of subsection (3)(*c*) above may, in particular, make provision—

(*a*) for the making of a deduction of a specified amount in respect of general expenses of the intermediary as well as deductions in respect of particular expenses incurred by him;

(*b*) for securing reductions in the amount of the worker's attributable earnings on account of—

(i) any secondary Class 1 contributions already paid by the intermediary [or the MSC][3] in respect of actual earnings of the worker, and

(ii) any such contributions that will be payable by [that person][3] in respect of the worker's attributable earnings.

(5) Regulations under this section may make provision for securing that, in applying any provisions of the regulations, any term of a contract or other arrangement which appears to be of a description specified in the regulations is to be disregarded.

(6) In this section—

"the applicable provisions of this Act" means this Part of this Act and Parts II to V below;

"business" includes any activity carried on—

(*a*) by a government department or public or local authority (in the United Kingdom or elsewhere), or

(*b*) by a body corporate, unincorporated body or partnership;

"relevant payments or benefits" means payments or benefits of any specified description made or provided (whether to the intermediary [or the MSC,][3] or the worker or otherwise) in connection with the performance by the worker of the services in question;

"specified" means prescribed by or determined in accordance with regulations under this section.

(7) Any reference in this section to the performance by the worker of any services includes a reference to any such obligation of his to perform them as is mentioned in subsection (1)(*a*) above.

(8) Regulations under this section shall be made by the Treasury with the concurrence of the Secretary of State.

(9) If, on any modification of the statutory provisions relating to income tax, it appears to the Treasury to be expedient to modify any of the preceding provisions of this section for the purpose of assimilating the law relating to income tax and the law relating to contributions under this Part of this Act, the Treasury may with the concurrence of the Secretary of State by order make such modifications of the preceding provisions of this section as the Treasury think appropriate for that purpose.][1]

Commentary—*Simon's Taxes* **E8.269D**.

HMRC Manuals—National Insurance Manual NIM06540 (workers supplied by service companies : employment allowance).

Regulations—Social Security Contributions (Intermediaries) Regulations, SI 2000/727.

Social Security (Miscellaneous Amendments No 2) Regulations, SI 2017/373.

Social Security (Miscellaneous Amendments No 3) Regulations, SI 2017/613.

Modifications—See the Social Security Contributions and Benefits Act 1992 (Modification of Section 4A) Order, SI 2003/1874.

Amendments—[1] This section inserted by the Welfare Reform and Pensions Act 1999 s 75, with effect from 22 December 1999.

[2] Words in sub-s (3)(*i*)(i) substituted by ITA 2007 s 1027, Sch 1 paras 288, 289, with effect for income tax purposes from 6 April 2007, and corporation tax purposes for accounting periods ending after 5 April 2007.

[3] Sub-ss (2A), (2B) inserted, and in sub-ss (3), (4), (6) words inserted and substituted, by the Social Security Contributions and Benefits Act 1992 (Modification of Section 4A) Order, SI 2007/2071 with effect from 24 July 2007..

[4AA Limited liability partnerships

(1) The Treasury may, for the purposes of this Act, by regulations—

(*a*) provide that, in prescribed circumstances—

(i) a person ("E") is to be treated as employed in employed earner's employment by a limited liability partnership (including where E is a member of the partnership), and

(ii) the limited liability partnership is to be treated as the secondary contributor in relation to any payment of earnings to or for the benefit of E as the employed earner;

(*b*) prescribe how earnings in respect of E's employed earner employment with the limited liability partnership are to be determined (including what constitutes such earnings);

(*c*) provide that such earnings are to be treated as being paid to or for the benefit of E at prescribed times.

(2) Regulations under subsection (1) may modify the definition of "employee" or "employer" in section 163, 171, 171ZJ or 171ZS below as the Treasury consider appropriate to take account of any provision falling within subsection (1)(*a*) to (*c*).

(3) If—

(*a*) a provision of the Income Tax Acts relating to limited liability partnerships or members of limited liability partnerships is passed or made, and

(*b*) in consequence, the Treasury consider it appropriate for provision to be made for the purpose of assimilating to any extent the law relating to income tax and the law relating to contributions under this Part,

the Treasury may by regulations make that provision.

(4) The provision that may be made under subsection (3) includes provision modifying any provision made by or under this Act.

(5) Regulations under this section are to be made with the concurrence of the Secretary of State.

(6) Section 4(4) of the Limited Liability Partnerships Act 2000 does not limit the provision that may be made by regulations under this section.][1]

Commentary—*Simon's Taxes* **E8.260**.

Regulations—Social Security Contributions (Limited Liability Partnership) Regulations, SI 2014/3159.

Press releases etc—Partnerships: A review of two aspects of the tax rules. HMRC Technical Note, 27 March 2014 (see *SWTI 2014, Issue 13*).

Amendments—[1] Section 4AA inserted by NICs Act 2014 s 14(1), (2) with effect from 13 March 2014.

[4B Earnings: power to make retrospective provision in consequence of retrospective tax legislation

(1) This section applies where—

(*a*) a provision of the Income Tax Acts which relates to income tax chargeable under the employment income Parts of ITEPA 2003 is passed or made so as to have retrospective effect ("the retrospective tax provision"), and

(*b*) it appears to the Treasury to be appropriate to make regulations under a relevant power for the purpose of reflecting the whole or part of the provision made by the retrospective tax provision.

(2) Those regulations may be made so as to have retrospective effect if it appears to the Treasury to be expedient, in consequence of the retrospective tax provision, for the regulations to have that effect.

(3) A "relevant power" means a power to make regulations under any of the following provisions—

(*a*) section 3 (power to prescribe the manner and basis of the calculation or estimation of earnings);

(*b*) section 4(6) (power to treat amounts chargeable to income tax under the employment income Parts of ITEPA 2003 as earnings);

(*c*) section 4A (power to treat payments or benefits to workers supplied by service companies etc as earnings).

[(*d*) section 4AA (power to make provision in relation to limited liability partnerships).][2]

(4) It does not matter whether the retrospective tax provision in question was passed or made before the day on which the National Insurance Contributions Act 2006 was passed.

(5) But nothing in subsection (2) authorises regulations to be made which have effect in relation to any time before 2nd December 2004.

(6) Regulations under a relevant power made by virtue of subsection (2) may affect, for the purposes of any contributions legislation for the purposes of which the regulations are made, the earnings in respect of an employment paid to or for the benefit of an earner at a time before the regulations are made.

(7) In such a case, subsections (8) and (9) apply and in those subsections and this subsection—

"relevant contributions legislation" means any contributions legislation for the purposes of which the regulations have the effect mentioned in subsection (6);

"the relevant time" means the time before the regulations are made mentioned in that subsection;

"the revised earnings" means the earnings, in respect of the employment, paid to or for the benefit of the earner at the relevant time as determined after applying the regulations.

(8) References in any relevant contributions legislation, or any provision made under any such legislation, which relate to—

(*a*) the earnings, in respect of the employment, paid to or for the benefit of the earner at the relevant time, or

(*b*) the amount of such earnings so paid at that time,

are to be read, in so far as they so relate, as references which relate to the revised earnings or, as the case may be, the amount of those earnings.

(9) Any matter which, at the time when the regulations are made, has been determined for the purposes of any relevant contributions legislation, or any provision made under any such legislation, wholly or partly by reference to—

(a) the earnings, in respect of the employment, paid to or for the benefit of the earner at the relevant time, or

(b) the amount of such earnings so paid at that time,

is to be redetermined as it would have been determined at the time of the original determination if it had been determined wholly or partly, as the case may be, by reference to the revised earnings or the amount of those earnings.

(10) The matters referred to in subsection (9) may include—

(a) whether Class 1 contributions are payable in respect of earnings paid to or for the benefit of the earner in a tax week, and

(b) the amount of any such contribution.

(11) Subsections (7) to (10) are subject to any express provision to the contrary (including any such provision made by regulations under section 4C(1)).

(12) The power conferred by subsection (2) is without prejudice to any powers conferred by or by virtue of any other provision of this Act or of any other enactment (including any instrument made under an Act).

(13) For the purposes of this section "contributions legislation" means any Part of this Act or provision of such a Part.][1]

Commentary—*Simon's Taxes* **E8.836, E8.1162.**

HMRC Manuals—National Insurance Manual NIM06841(employment-related securities : retrospective liability).

Regulations—Social Security Contributions (Consequential Provisions) Regulations, SI 2007/1056.

Amendments—[1] This section inserted by the National Insurance Contributions Act 2006 s 1(1) with effect from 30 March 2006.

[2] Sub-s (3)(d) inserted by NICs Act 2014 s 14(1), (3) with effect from 13 March 2014.

[4C Power to make provision in consequence of provision made by or by virtue of section 4B(2) etc

(1) The Treasury may by regulations made with the concurrence of the Secretary of State make such provision as appears to the Treasury to be expedient for any of the purposes mentioned in subsection (2) in consequence of any provision made by or by virtue of section 4B(2).

(2) Those purposes are—

(a) any purpose relating to any contributions;

(b) any purpose relating to any contributory benefit or contribution-based jobseeker's allowance;

(c) any purpose relating to any statutory payment;

(d) . . . [5]

(e) any purpose of Chapter 2 of Part 3 of that Act (reduction in state scheme contributions and benefits for members of certified schemes);

(f) such other purposes as may be prescribed by regulations made by the Treasury with the concurrence of the Secretary of State.

(3) Regulations under subsection (1) may, in particular, make provision—

(a) modifying any provision of any enactment (including this Act and any enactment passed or made on or after the commencement day);

(b) for any provision of any such enactment to apply in such cases, and with such modifications (if any), as the regulations may prescribe.

(4) Regulations under subsection (1) may be made so as to have retrospective effect but must not have effect in relation to any time before 2nd December 2004.

(5) In particular, regulations under subsection (1) made by virtue of subsection (4) may affect any of the following matters—

(a) liability to pay contributions . . . [2];

(b) the amount of any contribution . . . [2];

(c) entitlement to a contributory benefit or contribution-based jobseeker's allowance;

(d) the amount of any such benefit or allowance;

(e) entitlement to a statutory payment;

(f) the amount of any such payment;

(g) . . . [5]

(h) . . . [5]

(i) liability to make payments under section 42A(3) of the Pensions Act or to pay minimum contributions under section 43 of that Act;

(j) the amount of any such payment or contribution.

(6) In such a case, where the matter has been determined before the time when the regulations are made, the regulations may provide for the matter to be redetermined accordingly.

(7) If (ignoring this subsection) the operative provisions would directly or indirectly have effect in any case so as—

(a) to remove a person's entitlement to a contributory benefit, contribution-based jobseeker's allowance or statutory payment, or

(b) to reduce the amount of any such benefit, allowance or payment to which a person has an entitlement, those provisions are to be read with such modifications as are necessary to ensure that they do not have that effect.

(8) For the purposes of subsection (7)—

(*a*) "the operative provisions" are section 4B(7) to (10) and any provision made by virtue of section 4B(2) or under subsection (1) of this section;

(*b*) a person's "entitlement" includes any future entitlement which the person may have.

(9) The powers conferred by this section are without prejudice to any powers conferred by or by virtue of any other provision of this Act or any other enactment.

(10) In particular, any modification of any provision of an instrument by regulations made under subsection (1) is without prejudice to any other power to amend or revoke the provisions of the instrument (including the modified provision).

(11) For the purposes of this section—

"the commencement day" means the day on which the National Insurance Contributions Act 2006 was passed;

"enactment" includes an instrument made under an Act;

"statutory payment" means—

(*a*) statutory sick pay, statutory maternity pay, [statutory paternity pay,][4] statutory adoption pay [or statutory shared parental pay][3]; or

(*b*) any other payment prescribed by regulations made by the Treasury with the concurrence of the Secretary of State.][1]

Commentary—*Simon's Taxes* **E8.1162**.

HMRC Manuals—National Insurance Manual NIM50251 (when the power can be used under section 4b).

Modifications—Social Security, Occupational Pension Schemes and Statutory Payments (Consequential Provisions) Regulations, SI 2007/1154 reg 14 (modification of legislation relating to purposes in sub-s (2)(b)–(e) in relation to retrospective earnings).

Amendments—[1] This section inserted by the National Insurance Contributions Act 2006 s 1(1) with effect from 30 March 2006.

[2] In sub-s (5)(*a*), (*b*), words repealed by PeA 2014 s 24, Sch 13 paras 48, 50 with effect from 6 April 2016 (PeA 2014 s 56(1), (4)).

[3] In sub-s (11), in definition of "statutory payment", para (*a*), words inserted by the Children and Families Act 2014 s 126, Sch 7 paras 6, 9(b) with effect from 30 June 2014 (by virtue of SI 2014/1640 art 3).

[4] In sub-s (11), in definition of "statutory payment", para (*a*), words substituted by the Children and Families Act 2014 s 126, Sch 7 paras 6, 9(*a*) with effect from 5 April 2015 (by virtue of SI 2014/1640 art 7).

[5] Sub-ss (2)(*d*), (5) (*g*), (*h*) repealed by the Pensions Act 2007 s 27, Sch 4 para 42, Sch 7 Pt 7 with effect from 6 April 2015 (by virtue of SI 2011/1267 art 3(*a*)(i), (ii), (*b*)(i)).

Prospective amendments—Sub-s (5)(*I*), (*j*), to be repealed by the Pensions Act 2007 s 27, Sch 4 para 42, Sch 7 Pt 7 with effect from a date to be appointed.

In sub-ss (2)(*b*), (5)(*c*), (7)(*a*), words "contribution-based" to be repealed by the Welfare Reform Act 2012 s 147, Sch 14 Part 1 with effect from a date to be appointed.

Class 1 contributions

[5 Earnings limits and thresholds for Class 1 contributions

(1) For the purposes of this Act there shall for every tax year be—

(*a*) the following for primary Class 1 contributions—

(i) a lower earnings limit,

(ii) a primary threshold, and

(iii) an upper earnings limit; and

(*b*) a secondary threshold for secondary Class 1 contributions.

Those limits and thresholds shall be the amounts specified for that year by regulations . . . [2].

(2) . . . [4]

(3) . . . [3]

(4) Regulations may, in the case of each of the limits or thresholds mentioned in subsection (1) above, prescribe an equivalent of that limit or threshold in relation to earners paid otherwise than weekly (and references in this or any other Act to "the prescribed equivalent", in the context of any of those limits or thresholds, are accordingly references to the equivalent prescribed under this subsection in relation to such earners).

(5) The power conferred by subsection (4) above to prescribe an equivalent of any of those limits or thresholds includes power to prescribe an amount which exceeds, by not more than £1.00, the amount which is the arithmetical equivalent of that limit or threshold.

(6) Regulations under this section shall be made by the Treasury.][1]

Commentary—*Simon's Taxes* **E8.261**.

HMRC Manuals—National Insurance Manual NIM01005 (the lower earnings limit).

NIM01008 (the primary threshold ('PT') and the secondary threshold ('ST').

NIM01009 (the upper earnings limit ('UEL') and the annual maximum

Former enactments—Sub-s (1): SSA 1975 s 4(1); SS Pensions Act 1975 s 65(1), Sch 4 para 36(*a*); SSA 1985 s 7(1).

Sub-s (2): SS Pensions Act 1975 s 1(2); SSA 1986 s 74(6).

Sub-s (3): SS Pensions Act 1975 s 1(3).

Regulations—Social Security (Contributions) (Limits and Thresholds) (Amendment) Regulations, SI 2013/558.
Social Security (Contributions) (Limits and Thresholds) (Amendment) Regulations, SI 2014/569.
Social Security (Contributions) (Limits and Thresholds) (Amendment) Regulations, SI 2015/577.
Social Security (Contributions) (Limits and Thresholds Amendments and National Insurance Funds Payments) Regulations, SI 2016/343.
Social Security (Contributions) (Amendment) (No 2) Regulations SI 2016/352.
Social Security (Contributions) (Rates, Limits and Thresholds Amendments and National Insurance Funds Payments) Regulations, SI 2017/415.

Note—The appointed day for authorising the making of regulations referred to in sub-s (1) is 23 February 1999 by virtue of the Social Security Act 1998 (Commencement No 3) Order, SI 1999/418.
Words in sub-s (1) were to be substituted by the Pensions Act 2007 s 7(1), (2) with effect from the tax year 2011–12. Pensions Act 2007 s 7(2) was however repealed by the NIC Act 2008 s 4, Sch 2 with effect from 21 September 2008.

Cross references—See SS Administration Act 1992 Sch 7 para 4 (regulations under this section not requiring prior permission of Social Security Advisory Committee);
SS (Contributions) Regulations, SI 2001/1004 reg 10 (upper and lower earnings limits for the purposes of sub-s (1) above).
Employment Equality (Age) Regulations, SI 2006/1031 (minimum level of pensionable pay in relation to occupational pension schemes).
National Insurance Contributions (Rate Ceilings) Act 2015 s 3 (upper earnings limit specified in regs under sub-s (1) in relation to a tax year from 2016–17 to 2020–21 for which income tax is charged, shall not exceed the weekly equivalent of the proposed higher rate threshold for that tax year).
"Proposed higher rate threshold" for a tax year is the sum of the basic rate limit for income tax for the tax year as proposed in the pre-budget proposals for that year and the personal allowance for income tax for the tax year as so proposed (NICs (Rate Ceilings) Act 2015 s 3(3)).
The weekly equivalent of a proposed higher rate threshold for a tax year is the amount produced by dividing that threshold by 52 and rounding up or down to the nearest pound (NICs (Rate Ceilings) Act 2015 s 3(4)).

Amendments—[1] Substituted by the Welfare Reform and Pensions Act 1999, s 73 Sch 9 para 1 with effect from 22 December 1999, for the purpose of the exercise of any power to make regulations, and 6 April 2000 for all other purposes.
[2] In sub-s (1), words "which, in the case of those limits, shall be made in accordance with subsections (2) and (3) below" repealed by the NIC Act 2008 ss 1(1)(*a*), 4, Sch 2 with effect from the end of the period of two months beginning with the day on which the Act was passed. The Act was passed on 21 July 2008, therefore this amendment has effect from 21 September 2008.
[3] Sub-s (3) repealed by the NIC Act 2008 ss 1(1)(*b*), 4, Sch 2 with effect in relation to regulations specifying the upper earnings limit for 2009–10 or any subsequent tax year.
[4] Sub-s (2) repealed by the Pensions Act 2007 ss 7(1), (3), 27, Sch 7 Pt 4 with effect in relation to the tax year following "the designated tax year" and subsequent tax years. "The designated tax year" means such tax year as the Secretary of State may designate by an order made before 1 April 2011 (s 5(4)). The designated tax year, under s 5(4) is 2010–11 (SI 2010/2650 art 2), meaning that this amendment has effect for the tax year 2011–12 and subsequent tax years.

[6 Liability for Class 1 contributions

(1) Where in any tax week earnings are paid to or for the benefit of an earner over the age of 16 in respect of any one employment of his which is employed earner's employment—

(*a*) a primary Class 1 contribution shall be payable in accordance with this section and section 8 below if the amount paid exceeds the current primary threshold (or the prescribed equivalent); and

(*b*) a secondary Class 1 contribution shall be payable in accordance with this section and section 9 below if the amount paid exceeds the current secondary threshold (or the prescribed equivalent).

(2) No primary or secondary Class 1 contribution shall be payable in respect of earnings if a Class 1B contribution is payable in respect of them.

(3) Except as may be prescribed, no primary Class 1 contribution shall be payable in respect of earnings paid to or for the benefit of an employed earner after he attains pensionable age, but without prejudice to any liability to pay secondary Class 1 contributions in respect of any such earnings.

(4) The primary and secondary Class 1 contributions referred to in subsection (1) above are payable as follows—

(*a*) the primary contribution shall be the liability of the earner; and

(*b*) the secondary contribution shall be the liability of the secondary contributor;

but nothing in this subsection shall prejudice the provisions of [paragraphs 3 to 3B of Schedule 1 to this Act.][2]

(5) Except as provided by this Act, the primary and secondary Class 1 contributions in respect of earnings paid to or for the benefit of an earner in respect of any one employment of his shall be payable without regard to any other such payment of earnings in respect of any other employment of his.

(6) Regulations may provide for reducing primary or secondary Class 1 contributions which are payable in respect of persons to whom Part XI of the Employment Rights Act 1996 (redundancy payments) does not apply by virtue of section 199(2) or 209 of that Act.

(7) Regulations under this section shall be made by the Treasury.][1]

Commentary—*Simon's Taxes* **A6.952, E8.260, E8.269.**
HMRC Manuals—National Insurance Manual NIM02015 (liability for class 1 Nics).
NIM02498 (calculation of the amount of earnings).
NIM08600 (additional payments (bonuses, commissions or arrears of pay).

NIC

NIM12011 (directors: miscellaneous: consultancy fees).
NIM12012 (miscellaneous - dividends).
NIM12013 (directors: miscellaneous: concession for non-resident directors).
NIM36001 (people over state pension age).

Former enactments—Sub-s (1): SSA 1975 s 4(2); Education (School-leaving Dates) Act 1976 s 2(4).
Sub-s (2): SS Pensions Act 1975 s 4(1); Health and Social Security Act 1984 s 21, Sch 7 para 3.
Sub-s (3): SSA 1975 s 4(3); SSA 1989 s 26, Sch 7 para 2(1).
Sub-s (4): SSA 1975 s 4(2).
Sub-s (5): SSA 1975 s 4(7); SSA 1979 s 14(1); SSA 1985 s 8(1).
Sub-s (6): SSA 1986 s 74(5).

Cross references—See SS (Categorisation of Earners) Regulations, SI 1978/1689 (extending employments in respect of which an earner is to be treated as falling within the category of employed earner); SS(CP)A 1992 s 2;
Contracting-out (Recovery of Class 1 Contributions) Regulations, SI 1982/1033 reg 2 (recovery of arrears when contracting-out certificate cancelled); SS(CP)A 1992 s 2.
FA 2016 s 101(3) (application of sub-s (1)(*b*) to earnings for the purposes of the apprenticeship levy).

Simon's Tax Cases—6, *Kuehne + Nagel Drinks Logisitcs Ltd and ors v R&C Comrs* [2010] UKUT 457 (TCC), [2011] STC 576; *Forde & McHugh Ltd v R&C Comrs* [2011] UKUT 78 (TCC), [2011] STC 1428.
6(1), *Forde & McHugh Ltd v R&C Comrs* [2012] EWCA Civ 692, [2012] STC 1872.

Amendments—[1] Substituted by the Welfare Reform and Pensions Act 1999 s 73 Sch 9 para 2 with effect from 22 December 1999, for the purpose of the exercise of any power to make regulations, and 6 April 2000 for all other purposes.
[2] Words in sub-s (4) substituted by the Child Support, Pensions and Social Security Act 2000 s 77(3) with effect from 28 July 2000.

[6A Notional payment of primary Class 1 contribution where earnings not less than lower earnings limit

(1) This section applies where in any tax week earnings are paid to or for the benefit of an earner over the age of 16 in respect of any one employment of his which is employed earner's employment and the amount paid—

(*a*) is not less than the current lower earnings limit (or the prescribed equivalent), but
(*b*) does not exceed the current primary threshold (or the prescribed equivalent).

(2) Subject to any prescribed exceptions or modifications—

(*a*) the earner shall be treated as having actually paid a primary Class 1 contribution in respect of that week, and
(*b*) those earnings shall be treated as earnings upon which such a contribution has been paid,

for any of the purposes mentioned in subsection (3) below.

(3) The purposes are—

(*a*) the purposes of section 14(1)(*a*) below;
(*b*) the purposes of the provisions mentioned in section 21(5A)(*a*) to (*c*) below;
(*c*) any other purposes relating to contributory benefits; . . . [2]
(*d*) any purposes relating to jobseeker's allowance[; and
(*e*) any purposes relating to employment and support allowance.][2]

(4) Regulations may provide for any provision of this Act which, in whatever terms, refers—

(*a*) to primary Class 1 contributions being payable by a person, or
(*b*) otherwise to a person's liability to pay such contributions,

to have effect for the purposes of this section with any prescribed modifications.

(5) Except as may be prescribed, nothing in this section applies in relation to earnings paid to or for the benefit of an employed earner after he attains pensionable age.

(6) Except as provided by this Act, this section applies in relation to earnings paid to or for the benefit of an earner in respect of any one employment of his irrespective of any other such payment of earnings in respect of any other employment of his.

(7) Regulations under this section shall be made by the Treasury.][1]

Commentary—*Simon's Taxes* **E8.261, E8.1128**.

HMRC Manuals—National Insurance Manual NIM01007 (notional primary).

Modification—Sub-s (2) is modified by the Social Security (Notional Payment of Primary Class 1 Contribution) Regulations, SI 2000/747, regs 3–6, with effect from 6 April 2000.

Amendments—[1] Inserted by the Welfare Reform and Pensions Act 1999 s 73 Sch 9 para 3 with effect from 22 December 1999, for the purpose of the exercise of any power to make regulations, and 6 April 2000 for all other purposes.
[2] Words in sub-s (3) repealed and inserted by the Welfare Reform Act 2007 ss 28(1), 67, Sch 3 para 9(1), (2), Sch 8 with effect from 27 October 2008: SI 2008/787 art 2(4)(*f*).

7 "Secondary contributor"

(1) For the purposes of this Act, the "secondary contributor" in relation to any payment of earnings to or for the benefit of an employed earner, is—

(*a*) in the case of an earner employed under a contract of service, his employer;
(*b*) in the case of an earner employed in an office with [. . . [3] earnings][2], either—
(i) such person as may be prescribed in relation to that office; or
(ii) if no person is prescribed, the government department, public authority or body of persons responsible for paying the [. . . [3] earnings][2] of the office;

but this subsection is subject to subsection (2) below.

(2) In relation to employed earners who—

(*a*) are paid earnings in a tax week by more than one person in respect of different employments; or

(*b*) work under the general control or management of a person other than their immediate employer,

and in relation to any other case for which it appears to the [Treasury][1] that such provision is needed, regulations may provide that the prescribed person is to be treated as the secondary contributor in respect of earnings paid to or for the benefit of an earner.

[(2A) Regulations under subsection (2) may make provision treating a person as the secondary contributor in respect of earnings paid to or for the benefit of an earner if arrangements have been entered into the main purpose, or one of the main purposes, of which is to secure that the person is not so treated by other provision in regulations under subsection (2).

(2B) In subsection (2A) "arrangements" include any scheme, transaction or series of transactions, agreement or understanding, whether or not legally enforceable, and any associated operations.][4]

[(3) Regulations under any provision of this section shall be made by the Treasury.][1]

Commentary—*Simon's Taxes* **E8.269B, E8.901**.

HMRC Manuals—National Insurance Manual NIM20050 (self employed : residency conditions)

NIM20100 (definition of a self-employed earner).

NIM20200 (contribution week).

Former enactments—SSA 1975 s 4(4), (5).

Cross references—See the SS (Categorisation of Earners) Regulations, SI 1978/1689 (extending employments in respect of which an earner is to be treated as falling within the category of employed earner); SS(CP)A 1992 s 2;

Contracting-out (Recovery of Class 1 Contributions) Regulations, SI 1982/1033 reg 2 (recovery of arrears when contracting-out certificate cancelled); SS(CP)A 1992 s 2.

Amendments—[1] Words in sub-s (2) substituted, and sub-s (3) inserted by the Social Security Contributions (Transfer of Functions, etc) Act 1999 s 2, Sch 3 para 7 with effect from 1 April 1999 by virtue of the Social Security Contributions (Transfer of Functions, etc) Act 1999 (Commencement No 1 and Transitional Provisions) Order, SI 1999/527.

[2] In sub-s (1)(*b*), words substituted for the word "emoluments" by ITEPA 2003 s 722, Sch 6 paras 169, 173 with effect, for income tax purposes, from 2003–04; and for corporation tax purposes, for accounting periods ending after 5 April 2003. For transitional provisions and savings see ITEPA 2003 s 723, Sch 7.

[3] In sub-s (1)(*b*), word repealed in both places by NICA 2014 s 15, Sch 2 paras 1, 2 with effect from 14 May 2014.

[4] Sub-ss (2A), (2B) inserted by NICA 2015 s 6(4) with effect from 12 February 2015.

[8 Calculation of primary Class 1 contributions

(1) Where a primary Class 1 contribution is payable as mentioned in section 6(1)(*a*) above, the amount of that contribution is the aggregate of—

(*a*) the main primary percentage of so much of the earner's earnings paid in the tax week, in respect of the employment in question, as—

(i) exceeds the current primary threshold (or the prescribed equivalent); but

(ii) does not exceed the current upper earnings limit (or the prescribed equivalent); and

(*b*) the additional primary percentage of so much of those earnings as exceeds the current upper earnings limit (or the prescribed equivalent).

(2) For the purposes of this Act—

(*a*) the main primary percentage is [12][2] per cent; and

(*b*) the additional primary percentage is [2][2] per cent;

but the main primary percentage is subject to alteration under sections 143 and 145 of the Administration Act.

(3) Subsection (1) above is subject to—

(*a*) regulations under section 6(6) above;

(*b*) regulations under sections 116 to 120 below. . . . [3]

(*c*) . . .[3]][1]

Commentary—*Simon's Taxes* **T8.101**.

HMRC Manuals—National Insurance Manual NIM01208 (class 1 structural overview from April 2009: not contracted-out rate Nics.

NIM01221 —01225 (assessing primary class 1 Nics from 6 April 2009: examples).

NIM01240 (structural changes: effect on entitlement to contributory benefits).

Press releases etc—Booklet CA 28 (detailed guidance on calculation and payment of Class 1 contributions).

Cross references—See SS (Contributions) Regulations, SI 2001/1004 regs 2–6 (non-weekly and irregular earnings periods),

SS (Contributions) Regulations, SI 2001/1004 reg 12 (earnings-related contributions),

SSAA 1992 s 143(1)(*a*) (power to alter initial and main primary percentages in sub-s (2) above),

SSAA 1992 s 145(1) (power to alter initial and main primary percentages in sub-s (2) above).

National Insurance Contributions (Rate Ceilings) Act 2015 s 1 (main primary percentage shall not exceed 12% and additional primary percentage shall not exceed 2% in relation to the tax years 2016–17 to 2020–21).

Amendments—[1] This section substituted by NICA 2002 s 1(1) with effect from 2003–04.

[2] In sub-s (2)(*a*) figure substituted for previous figure "11", and in sub-s (2)(*b*) figure substituted for previous figure "1", by the National Insurance Contributions Act 2011 s 1(1) with effect from 6 April 2011.

[3] Sub-s (3)(*c*) and preceding word "and" repealed by PeA 2014 s 24, Sch 13 paras 48, 51 with effect from 6 April 2016 (PeA 2014 s 56(1), (4)).

[9 Calculation of secondary Class 1 contributions

(1) Where a secondary Class 1 contribution is payable as mentioned in section 6(1)(*b*) above, the amount of that contribution shall be [the relevant percentage][4] of so much of the earnings paid in the tax week, in respect of the employment in question, as exceeds the current secondary threshold (or the prescribed equivalent).

[(1A) For the purposes of subsection (1) "the relevant percentage" is—

(*a*) if section 9A below applies to the earnings, the age-related secondary percentage;

[(*aa*) if section 9B below (zero-rate secondary Class 1 contributions for certain apprentices) applies to the earnings, 0%;][6]

(*b*) otherwise, the secondary percentage.][4]

[(2) For the purposes of this Act the secondary percentage is [13.8][3] per cent; but that percentage is subject to alteration under sections 143 and 145 of the Administration Act.

(3) Subsection (1) above is subject to—

(*a*) regulations under section 6(6) above;

(*b*) regulations under sections 116 to 120 below; . . . [5]

(*c*) . . . [5]][2]][1]

Commentary—*Simon's Taxes* **E8.291, E8.2102.**

HMRC Manuals—National Insurance manual NIM01230 (structural changes: secondary Nics).

Cross-references—National Insurance Contributions (Rate Ceilings) Act 2015 s 2 (secondary percentage shall not exceed 13.8% in relation to the tax years 2016–17 to 2020–21).

Amendments—[1] Substituted by the Welfare Reform and Pensions Act 1999 s 73 Sch 9 para 5 with effect from 22 December 1999, for the purpose of the exercise of any power to make regulations, and 6 April 2000 for all other purposes.

[2] Sub-ss (2), (3) substituted by the National Insurance Contributions Act 2002 s 2(1) with effect from 2003–04.

[3] In sub-s (2) figure substituted for previous figure "12.8", by the National Insurance Contributions Act 2011 s 1(2) with effect from 6 April 2011.

[4] In sub-s (1), words substituted, and sub-s (1A) inserted, by NICA 2014 s 9(1), (2) with effect from 6 April 2015.

[5] Sub-s (3)(*c*) and preceding word "and" repealed by PeA 2014 s 24, Sch 13 paras 48, 52 with effect from 6 April 2016 (PeA 2014 s 56(1), (4)).

[6] Sub-s (1A)(*aa*) inserted by NICA 2015 s 1(1), (2) with effect from 6 April 2016.

[9A The age-related secondary percentage

(1) Where a secondary Class 1 contribution is payable as mentioned in section 6(1)(*b*) above, this section applies to the earnings paid in the tax week, in respect of the employment in question, if the earner falls within an age group specified in column 1 of the table in subsection (3).

[(1A) But this section does not apply to those earnings so far as section 9B below (zero-rate secondary Class 1 contributions for certain apprentices) applies to them.][2]

(2) For the purposes of section 9(1A)(*a*) above, the age-related secondary percentage is the percentage for the earner's age group specified in column 2 of the table.

(3) Here is the table—

Age group	Age-related secondary percentage
Under 21	0%

(4) The Treasury may by regulations amend the table—

(*a*) so as to add an age group in column 1 and to specify the percentage in column 2 for that age group;

(*b*) so as to reduce (or further reduce) the percentage specified in column 2 for an age group already specified in column 1 (whether for the whole of the age group or only part of it).

(5) A percentage specified under subsection (4)(*a*) must be lower than the secondary percentage.

(6) For the purposes of this Act a person is still to be regarded as being liable to pay a secondary Class 1 contribution even though the amount of the contribution is £0 because the age-related secondary percentage is 0%.

(7) The Treasury may by regulations provide that, in relation to an age group specified in the table, there is to be for every tax year an upper secondary threshold for secondary Class 1 contributions. That threshold is to be the amount specified for that year by regulations made by the Treasury.

(8) Subsections (4) and (5) of section 5 above (which confer power to prescribe an equivalent of a secondary threshold in relation to earners paid otherwise than weekly), and subsection (6) of that section as it applies for the purposes of those subsections, apply for the purposes of an upper secondary threshold in relation to an age group as they apply for the purposes of a secondary threshold.

(9) Where—

(*a*) a secondary Class 1 contribution is payable as mentioned in section 6(1)(*b*) above, (*b*) the earner falls within an age group in relation to which provision has been made under subsection (7), and

(*c*) the earnings paid in the tax week, in respect of the employment in question, exceed the current upper secondary threshold (or the prescribed equivalent) in relation to the age group,

this section is not to apply to the earnings so far as they exceed that threshold (or the prescribed equivalent); and for the purposes of section 9(1) above the relevant percentage in respect of the earnings so far as they exceed that threshold (or the prescribed equivalent) is, accordingly, to be the secondary percentage.

(10) In subsections (7) to (9) references to an age group include a part of an age group.][1]

Commentary—*Simon's Taxes* **E8.260, E8.261, E8.2102.**

HMRC Manuals—National Insurance manual NIM01296 —01299 (class 1 structural overview: abolition of secondary Nics for those employees under the age of 21).

Regulations—Social Security (Contributions) (Limits and Thresholds) (Amendment) Regulations, SI 2015/577.

Social Security (Contributions) (Limits and Thresholds Amendments and National Insurance Funds Payments) Regulations, SI 2016/343.

Social Security (Contributions) (Rates, Limits and Thresholds Amendments and National Insurance Funds Payments) Regulations, SI 2017/415.

Amendments—[1] Section 9A inserted by NICA 2014 s 9(1), (3) with effect from 6 April 2015. Note that any power conferred on the Treasury by virtue of NICA 2014 s 9 to make regulations comes into force on 14 May 2014.

[2] Sub-s (1A) inserted by NICA 2015 s 1(1), (3) with effect from 6 April 2016.

[9B Zero-rate secondary Class 1 contributions for certain apprentices

(1) Where a secondary Class 1 contribution is payable as mentioned in section 6(1)(b) above, this section applies to the earnings paid in the tax week, in respect of the employment in question, if the earner is a relevant apprentice in relation to that employment.

(2) An earner is a "relevant apprentice", in relation to an employment, if the earner—

(a) is aged under 25, and

(b) is employed, in the employment, as an apprentice.

(3) For the purposes of this Act a person is still to be regarded as being liable to pay a secondary Class 1 contribution even if the amount of the contribution is £0 because this section applies to the earnings in question.

(4) The Treasury may by regulations provide that, in relation to relevant apprentices, there is to be for every tax year an upper secondary threshold for secondary Class 1 contributions.

That threshold is to be the amount specified for that year by regulations made by the Treasury.

(5) Subsections (4) and (5) of section 5 above (which confer power to prescribe an equivalent of a secondary threshold in relation to earners paid otherwise than weekly), and subsection (6) of that section as it applies for the purposes of those subsections, apply for the purposes of an upper secondary threshold in relation to relevant apprentices as they apply for the purposes of a secondary threshold.

(6) Subsection (7) applies if—

(a) a secondary Class 1 contribution is payable as mentioned in section 6(1)(b) above,

(b) the earnings paid in the tax week, in respect of the employment in question, exceed the current upper secondary threshold (or the prescribed equivalent) in relation to relevant apprentices, and

(c) the earner is a relevant apprentice in relation to the employment.

(7) This section does not apply to those earnings so far as they exceed that threshold (or the prescribed equivalent) ("the excess earnings") and, accordingly, for the purposes of section 9(1) above the relevant percentage in respect of the excess earnings is the secondary percentage.

(8) But the Treasury may by regulations modify the effect of subsection (7) in a case in which the earner falls within an age group specified in column 1 of the table in section 9A(3) above.

(9) In subsection (2)(b) "apprentice" has such meaning as the Treasury may prescribe.

(10) The Treasury may by regulations amend subsection (2)(a) so as to alter the age that an earner must be in order to be a relevant apprentice (and regulations under this subsection may have the effect of allowing anyone who is of an age at which secondary Class 1 contributions are payable to be a relevant apprentice).][1]

Commentary—*Simon's Taxes* **E8.260, E8.261, E8.2102.**

HMRC Manuals—National Insurance manual NIM01305 —01311 (class 1 structural overview: abolition of secondary Nics for apprentices under the age of 25).

Regulations—Social Security (Contributions) (Amendment) Regulations, SI 2016/117.

Social Security (Contributions) (Limits and Thresholds Amendments and National Insurance Funds Payments) Regulations, SI 2016/343.

Social Security (Contributions) (Rates, Limits and Thresholds Amendments and National Insurance Funds Payments) Regulations, SI 2017/415.

Amendments—[1] Section 9B inserted by NICA 2015 s 1(1), (4) with effect from 6 April 2016. This section came into force for the purposes of making regulations, from 12 April 2015 (s 1(11)(*a*)).

Class 1A contributions

[10 Class 1A contributions: benefits in kind etc

(1) Where—

[(*a*) for any tax year an earner is chargeable to income tax under ITEPA 2003 on an amount of general earnings received by him from any employment ("the relevant employment"),][3]

[(*b*) the relevant employment is both—

(i) employed earner's employment, and

(ii) an employment, other than [lower-paid employment as a minister of religion][6], within the meaning of the benefits code (see Chapter 2 of Part 3 of ITEPA 2003),][3]

(*c*) the whole or a part of the [general earnings][3] falls, for the purposes of Class 1 contributions, to be left out of account in the computation of the earnings paid to or for the benefit of the earner,

a Class 1A contribution shall be payable for that tax year, in accordance with this section, in respect of that earner and so much of the [general earnings][3] as falls to be so left out of account.

(2) Subject to section 10ZA below, a Class 1A contribution for any tax year shall be payable by—

(*a*) the person who is liable to pay the secondary Class 1 contribution relating to the last (or only) relevant payment of earnings in that tax year in relation to which there is a liability to pay such a Class 1 contribution; or

(*b*) if paragraph (*a*) above does not apply, the person who, if the [general earnings][3] in respect of which the Class 1A contribution is payable were earnings in respect of which Class 1 contributions would be payable, would be liable to pay the secondary Class 1 contribution.

(3) In subsection (2) above "relevant payment of earnings" means a payment which for the purposes of Class 1 contributions is a payment of earnings made to or for the benefit of the earner in respect of the relevant employment.

(4) The amount of the Class 1A contribution in respect of any [general earnings][3] shall be the Class 1A percentage of so much of [them][3] as falls to be left out of account as mentioned in subsection (1)(*c*) above.

(5) In subsection (4) above "the Class 1A percentage" means a percentage rate equal to the [secondary percentage][2] for the tax year in question.

(6) No Class 1A contribution shall be payable for any tax year in respect of so much of any [general earnings as are taken][3] for the purposes of the making of Class 1B contributions for that year to be included in a PAYE settlement agreement.

[(7) In calculating for the purposes of this section the amount of general earnings received by an earner from an employment, a deduction under any of the excluded provisions is to be disregarded. This subsection does not apply in relation to a deduction if subsection (7A) applies in relation to it.][3]

[(7A) Where—

(*a*) a deduction in respect of a matter is allowed under an excluded provision, and

(*b*) the amount deductible is at least equal to the whole of any corresponding amount which would (but for this section) fall by reference to that matter to be included in the general earnings mentioned in subsection (7),

the whole of the corresponding amount shall be treated as not included.][3]

[(7B) For the purposes of subsections (7) and (7A) "excluded provision" means—

(*a*) any provision of Chapter 2 of Part 5 of ITEPA 2003 (deductions for employee's expenses), other than section 352 (limited deduction for agency fees paid by entertainers),

[(*aa*) any of sections 363 to 365 of ITEPA 2003 (certain deductions from benefits code earnings), or][4]

(*b*) any provision of Chapter 5 of Part 5 of ITEPA 2003 (deductions for earnings representing benefits or reimbursed expenses).][3]

(8) The Treasury may by regulations—

[(*a*) modify the effect of subsections (7) and (7A) above by amending subsection (7B) so as to include any enactment contained in the Income Tax Acts within the meaning of "excluded provision"; or][3]

(*b*) make such amendments of [subsections (7) to (7B)][3] above as appear to them to be necessary or expedient in consequence of any alteration of the provisions of the Income Tax Acts relating to the charge to tax [on employment income][3].

(9) The Treasury may by regulations provide—

(*a*) for Class 1A contributions not to be payable, in prescribed circumstances, by prescribed persons or in respect of prescribed persons or [general earnings][3];

(*b*) for reducing Class 1A contributions in prescribed circumstances.

(10) In this section "the 1988 Act" means the Income and Corporation Taxes Act 1988.[3]

[(11) The Treasury may by regulations modify the law relating to Class 1A contributions in the case of an employed earner's employment which is treated as existing by virtue of regulations under section 4AA.][5]][1]

Commentary—*Simon's Taxes* **E8.271, E8.272, E8.273, E8.275, E8.279.**

HMRC Manuals—National Insurance Manual NIM02960 (class 1A national insurance contributions).
NIM13003 (general principles).
NIM013020–13190 (class 1A NICs: the conditions necessary to be satisfied for liability to arise).
NIM014100–14510 (operation of this section: benefits exempt from Class 1A NICs).
NIM015001–15650 (revenue procedures relating to the calculation of Class 1A NICs)
NIM16001–16300 (detailed examination of particular types of benefit).
NIM16381–16389 (class 1A NICs: benefits arising from the use of a van provided by an employer).
NIM16401–16500 (class 1A NICs: Revenue procedures in respect of workers going to or coming from abroad).
NIM16600 (special class 1A NIC cases).
NIM17554 (special rules for fuel provided for private use).
Former enactments—SSA 1975 s 4A; SS (Contributions) Act 1991 s 1(5).
Press releases etc—Booklet CA 33 (detailed guidance on calculation and payment of Class 1A contributions).
Contributions Agency Press Release 19-3-98 (Class 1A national insurance contributions on cars and fuel from 6 April 1998).
Regulations—Social Security (Contributions) (Amendment No. 2) Regulations, SI 2012/817.
Social Security (Contributions) (Amendment and Application of Schedule 38 to the Finance Act 2012) Regulations, SI 2013/622.
Social Security (Contributions) (Amendment No 4) Regulations, SI 2016/1067.
Social Security (Miscellaneous Amendments) Regulations, SI 2017/307.
Cross references—See SS (Contributions) Regulations, SI 2001/1004 regs 32–38 (exceptions from liability for Class 1A contributions and their reduction); SS(CP)A 1992 s 2,
SI 2001/1004 reg 55 (repayment of Class 1A contributions); SS(CP)A 1992 s 2,
SI 2001/1004 reg 86 (contributions under this section may be paid by employees of international organisations not subject to this Act); SS(CP)A 1992 s 2,
SI 2001/1004 para 76 (interest on overdue Class 1A contributions),
SI 2001/1004 para 77 (interest on repayments of Class 1A contributions),
SI 2001/1004 para 79 (remission of interest paid by an employer on Class 1A contributions in certain circumstances).
Modification—Sub-s (7)(*a*) modified by the Social Security Contributions and Benefits Act 1992 (Modification of Section 10(7)) Regulations, SI 2001/966 reg 2.
Sub-s (7B)(*aa*) inserted by the Social Security Contributions and Benefits Act 1992 (Modification of Section 10(7B)) Regulations, SI 2007/799.
Amendments—[1] This section substituted by the Child Support, Pensions and Social Security Act 2000 s 74(2) with effect for the tax year beginning with 6 April 2000 and subsequent tax years.
[2] Words in sub-s (5) substituted by the NIC Act 2002 s 6, Sch 1 paras 1, 2 with effect from 2003–04.
[3] Sub-ss (1)(*a*), (*b*), (8)(*a*) substituted; in sub-ss (1)(*c*), (4), (6), (8)(*b*), words substituted; sub-ss (7)–(7B) substituted for sub-s (7), and sub-s (10) repealed; by ITEPA 2003 ss 722, 724, Sch 6 paras 169, 174, Sch 8 with effect, for income tax purposes, from 2003–04; and for corporation tax purposes, for accounting periods ending after 5 April 2003.
[4] Sub-s (7B)(*aa*) inserted, and preceding word "and" omitted, by the Social Security Contributions and Benefits Act 1992 (Modification of Section 10(7B)) Regulations, SI 2007/799 reg 2. These Regulations come into force on 5 April 2007 and have effect from 6 April 2006.
[5] Sub-s (11) inserted by NICA 2014 s 14(1), (4) with effect from 13 March 2014.
[6] In sub-s (1)(*b*)(ii), words substituted by FA 2015 s 13, Sch 1 para 23(1), (2) with effect for the tax year 2016–17 and subsequent tax years.

[10ZA Liability of third party provider of benefits in kind

(1) This section applies, where—

(*a*) a Class 1A contribution is payable for any tax year in respect of the whole or any part of [general earnings][2] received by an earner;

(*b*) [the general earnings, in so far as they are ones in respect of which][2] such a contribution is payable, [consist][2] in a benefit provided for the earner or a member of his family or household;

(*c*) the person providing the benefit is a person other than the person ("the relevant employer") by whom, but for this section, the Class 1A contribution would be payable in accordance with section 10(2) above; and

(*d*) the provision of the benefit by that other person has not been arranged or facilitated by the relevant employer.

(2) For the purposes of this Act if—

(*a*) the person providing the benefit pays an amount for the purpose of discharging any liability of the earner to income tax for any tax year, and

(*b*) the income tax in question is tax chargeable in respect of the provision of the benefit or of the making of the payment itself,

the amount of the payment shall be treated as if it were [general earnings][2] consisting in the provision of a benefit to the earner in that tax year and falling, for the purposes of Class 1 contributions, to be left out of account in the computation of the earnings paid to or for the benefit of the earner.

(3) Subject to subsection (4) below, the liability to pay any Class 1A contribution in respect of—

(*a*) the benefit provided to the earner, and

(*b*) any further benefit treated as so provided in accordance with subsection (2) above,

shall fall on the person providing the benefit, instead of on the relevant employer.

NIC

(4) Subsection (3) above applies in the case of a Class 1A contribution for the tax year beginning with 6th April 2000 only if the person providing the benefit in question gives notice in writing to the Inland Revenue on or before 6th July 2001 that he is a person who provides benefits in respect of which a liability to Class 1A contributions is capable of falling by virtue of this section on a person other than the relevant employer.

(5) The Treasury may by regulations make provision specifying the circumstances in which a person is or is not to be treated for the purposes of this Act as having arranged or facilitated the provision of any benefit.

(6) In this section references to a member of a person's family or household shall be construed in accordance with [section 721(5) of ITEPA 2003][2].][1]

Commentary—*Simon's Taxes* **E8.271, E8.277, E8.278.**

HMRC Manuals—National Insurance Manual NIM016351–16356 (special class 1A Nics cases: third party benefits).

Amendments—[1] This section inserted by the Child Support, Pensions and Social Security Act 2000 s 75(1), (3) with effect from the year 2000–01.

[2] In sub-ss (1), (2), (6), words substituted by ITEPA 2003 s 722, Sch 6 paras 169, 175 with effect, for income tax purposes, from 2003–04; and for corporation tax purposes, for accounting periods ending after 5 April 2003. For transitional provisions and savings see ITEPA 2003 s 723, Sch 7.

[10ZB Non-cash vouchers provided by third parties

(1) In section 10ZA above references to the provision of a benefit include references to the provision of a non-cash voucher.

(2) Where—

(*a*) a non-cash voucher is received by any person from [employment which is [lower-paid employment as a minister of religion][3], and][2]

(*b*) the case would be one in which the conditions in section 10ZA(1)(*a*) to (*d*) above would be satisfied in relation to the provision of that voucher [if that employment were not [lower-paid employment as a minister of religion][3]][2],

sections 10 and 10ZA above shall have effect in relation to the provision of that voucher, and to any such payment in respect of the provision of that voucher as is mentioned in section 10ZA(2) above, [as if that employment were not [lower-paid employment as a minister of religion][3]][2].

(3) In this section "non-cash voucher" has the same meaning as in [section 84 of ITEPA 2003][2].][1]

Commentary—*Simon's Taxes* **E8.277, E8.278.**

HMRC Manuals—National Insurance Manual NIM02438 (non-cash vouchers - exemptions - provided by third party other than employer).

NIM16357 (non-cash vouchers provided).

Amendments—[1] This section inserted by the Child Support, Pensions and Social Security Act 2000 s 75(1), (3) with effect from the year 2000–01.

[2] In sub-ss (2), (3), words substituted by ITEPA 2003 s 722, Sch 6 paras 169, 176 with effect, for income tax purposes, from 2003–04; and for corporation tax purposes, for accounting periods ending after 5 April 2003. For transitional provisions and savings see ITEPA 2003 s 723, Sch 7.

[3] In sub-s (2) words substituted by FA 2015 s 13, Sch 1 para 23(1), (3) with effect for the tax year 2016–17 and subsequent tax years.

[10ZC Class 1A contributions: power to make provision in consequence of retrospective tax legislation

(1) The Treasury may by regulations make such provision as appears to the Treasury to be expedient for any purpose of the law relating to Class 1A contributions in consequence of any relevant retrospective tax provision—

(*a*) which is passed or made at or before the time when the regulations are made, or

(*b*) which may be passed or made after that time.

(2) "Relevant retrospective tax provision" means a provision of the Income Tax Acts which—

(*a*) has retrospective effect, and

(*b*) affects the amount of general earnings received by an earner from an employment on which he is chargeable to income tax under the employment income Parts of ITEPA 2003 for a tax year.

(3) It does not matter whether the relevant retrospective tax provision was passed or made before the commencement day.

(4) Regulations under this section may, in particular, make provision—

(*a*) modifying any provision of any enactment (including this Act and any enactment passed or made on or after the commencement day);

(*b*) for any provision of any such enactment to apply in such cases, and with such modifications (if any), as the regulations may prescribe.

(5) Regulations under this section may be made so as to have retrospective effect but must not have effect in relation to any time before 2nd December 2004.

(6) In particular, regulations under this section made by virtue of subsection (5)—

(*a*) may affect matters determined before the time when the regulations are made, and

(*b*) may provide for those matters to be redetermined accordingly.

(7) Regulations under this section—

(*a*) may not impose any liability to pay a Class 1A contribution, and
(*b*) may not increase the amount of any Class 1A contribution.

(8) The powers conferred by this section are without prejudice to—
(*a*) any liability to pay a Class 1A contribution which arises by virtue of any relevant retrospective tax provision, and
(*b*) any powers conferred by or by virtue of any other provision of this Act or any other enactment.

(9) In particular, any modification of any provision of an instrument by regulations under this section is without prejudice to any other power to amend or revoke the provisions of the instrument (including the modified provision).

(10) For the purposes of this section—
"the commencement day" means the day on which the National Insurance Contributions Act 2006 was passed;
"enactment" includes an instrument made under an Act.][1]

Amendments—[1] This section inserted by the National Insurance Contributions Act 2006 s 3(1) with effect from 30 March 2006.

[Class 1B contributions

[10A Class 1B contributions

(1) Where for any tax year a person is accountable to the Inland Revenue in respect of income tax on [general earnings][5] of his employees in accordance with a PAYE settlement agreement, a Class 1B contribution shall be payable by him for that tax year in accordance with this section.

(2) The Class 1B contribution referred to in subsection (1) above is payable in respect of—
(*a*) the amount of any of [the general earnings included][5] in the PAYE settlement agreement which are chargeable emoluments; and
(*b*) the total amount of income tax in respect of which the person is accountable for the tax year in accordance with the PAYE settlement agreement.

(3) The amount of the Class 1B contribution referred to in subsection (1) above shall be the Class 1B percentage of the aggregate of the amounts mentioned in paragraphs (*a*) and (*b*) of subsection (2) above.

(4) [General earnings are chargeable emoluments][5] for the purposes of subsection (2) above if, apart from section [6(2) or 10(6)][6] above, the person accountable in accordance with the PAYE settlement agreement would be liable or entitled to pay secondary Class 1 contributions or Class 1A contributions in respect of them.

(5) Where—
(*a*) the PAYE settlement agreement was entered into after the beginning of the tax year; and
(*b*) Class 1 contributions were due in respect of any [general earnings][5] before it was entered into,

those [general earnings][5] shall not be taken to be included in the PAYE settlement agreement.

[(6) In subsection (3) above "the Class 1B percentage" means a percentage rate equal to [the secondary percentage][4] for the tax year in question.][3]

(7) [The Treasury may by regulations][2] provide for persons to be excepted in prescribed circumstances from liability to pay Class 1B contributions.][1]

Commentary—*Simon's Taxes* **E8.280, E8.281.**

HMRC Manuals—National Insurance Manual NIM18000–18050 (class 1B contributions : operations).
NIM18120–19000 (class 1B Nics: other operations).

Amendments—[1] This section inserted by SSA 1998 s 53 with effect from 8 September 1998 by virtue of the Social Security Act 1998 (Commencement No 1) Order, SI 1998/2209 for the purpose only of authorising the making of regulations or orders, and with effect from 6 April 1999 for all other purposes.

[2] Words in sub-s (7) substituted by the Social Security Contributions (Transfer of Functions, etc) Act 1999 s 2, Sch 3 para 11 with effect from 1 April 1999 by virtue of the Social Security Contributions (Transfer of Functions, etc) Act 1999 (Commencement No 1 and Transitional Provisions) Order, SI 1999/527.

[3] Sub-s (6) substituted by the Welfare Reform and Pensions Act 1999, s 77, with effect from 6 April 2000.

[4] Words in sub-s (6) substituted by NICA 2002 s 6, Sch 1 paras 1, 3 with effect from 2003–04.

[5] Words in sub-ss (1), (2), (4), (5) substituted by ITEPA 2003 s 722, Sch 6 paras 169, 177 with effect, for income tax purposes, from 2003–04; and for corporation tax purposes, for accounting periods ending after 5 April 2003. For transitional provisions and savings see ITEPA 2003 s 723, Sch 7.

[6] In sub-s (4), reference substituted by the NIC and Statutory Payments Act 2004 s 11, Schedule 1 para 1(1), (2) with effect from 1 September 2004 (by virtue of SI 2004/1943).

Class 2 contributions

[11 Class 2 contributions

(1) This section applies if an earner is in employment as a self-employed earner in a tax year (the "relevant tax year").

(2) If the earner has relevant profits of, or exceeding, the small profits threshold, the earner is liable to pay Class 2 contributions for the relevant tax year at the rate of [£2.85][2] in respect of each week in that year that the earner is in the employment.

NIC

(3) "Relevant profits" means profits, from the employment, in respect of which Class 4 contributions are payable under section 15 for the relevant tax year (or would be payable if the amount of the profits were to exceed the amount specified in subsection (3)(a) of that section in excess of which the main Class 4 percentage is payable).

(4) The "small profits threshold" is [£6,025][2].

(5) Class 2 contributions under subsection (2) are to be payable in the same manner that Class 4 contributions in respect of relevant profits are, or would be, payable (but see section 11A for the application of certain provisions in relation to such Class 2 contributions).

(6) If the earner does not have relevant profits of, or exceeding, the small profits threshold, the earner may pay a Class 2 contribution of [£2.85][2] in respect of any week in the relevant tax year that the earner is in the employment.

(7) No Class 2 contributions are to be paid under this section in respect of any week in the relevant tax year—

(a) before that in which the earner attains the age of 16, or

(b) after that in which the earner attains pensionable age.

(8) The Treasury may by regulations make provision so that, in relation to an earner, the Class 2 contribution in respect of a week is higher than that specified in subsections (2) and (6) where—

(a) in respect of any employment of the earner, the earner is treated by regulations made under section 2(2)(b) as being a self-employed earner, and

(b) in any period or periods the earner has earnings from that employment and—

(i) those earnings are such that (disregarding their amount) the earner would be liable for Class 1 contributions in respect of them if the earner were not so treated in respect of the employment, and

(ii) no Class 4 contribution is payable in respect of the earnings by virtue of regulations under section 18(1).

(9) The Treasury may by regulations—

(a) modify the meaning of "relevant profits";

(b) provide that Class 2 contributions under subsection (6) may not be paid—

(i) if the employment or the earner is of a prescribed description, or

(ii) in prescribed circumstances.

(10) Regulations under subsection (9)(a) may amend this section.

(11) Regulations under subsection (9)(b) are to be made with the concurrence of the Secretary of State.][1]

Commentary—*Simon's Taxes* **E8.303, E8.304, E8.305A, E8.308A, E8.303, E8.313, E8.314.**

HMRC Manuals—National Insurance Manual NIM70001–70300 (Class 2 contributions : general information).
NIM74001–74400 (class 2 national insurance contributions: special cases).
NIM75002 (maternity allowance : ability to pay class 2 Nics before the due date).

Note—The Government has announced its intention to abolish Class 2 NICs with effect from 6 April 2018, by repealing SSCBA 1992 ss 11, 11A and 12 (see HMRC Tax Information and Impact Note, 5 December 2016, "Abolition of Class 2 National Insurance contributions"; *see SWTI 2017, Budget Issue, 16 March 2017*).

Amendments—[1] Sections 11, 11A substituted for previous s 11 by NICA 2015 s 2, Sch 1 paras 1, 3 with effect for the tax year 2015–16 and subsequent tax years.

[2] The following amounts substituted by the Social Security (Contributions) (Rates, Limits and Thresholds Amendments and National Insurance Funds Payments) Regulations, SI 2017/415 reg 3 with effect from 6 April 2017—

– in sub-ss (2), (6) the weekly amount of Class 2 NICs is "£2.85" (previously £2.80); and
– in sub-s (4), the small profits threshold for Class 2 NICs is "£6,025" (previously £5,965).

[11A Application of certain provisions of the Income Tax Acts in relation to Class 2 contributions under section 11(2)

(1) The following provisions apply, with the necessary modifications, in relation to Class 2 contributions under section 11(2) as if those contributions were income tax chargeable under Chapter 2 of Part 2 of the Income Tax (Trading and Other Income) Act 2005 in respect of profits of a trade, profession or vocation which is not carried on wholly outside the United Kingdom—

(a) Part 2 (returns), Part 4 (assessment and claims), Part 5 (appeals), Part 5A (payment of tax), Part 6 (collection and recovery) and Part 10 (penalties) of the Taxes Management Act 1970;

(b) Schedule 24 to the Finance Act 2007 (penalties for errors);

(c) sections 101 and 102 of the Finance Act 2009 (interest);

(d) Schedules 55 and 56 to that Act (penalties for failure to make returns etc or for failure to make payments on time);

(e) Part 4 (follower notices and accelerated payments) and Part 5 (promoters of tax avoidance schemes) of the Finance Act 2014;

[(*ea*) the provisions of Schedule 18 to the Finance Act 2016 (serial tax avoidance);][2]

(f) any other provisions of the Income Tax Acts as to assessment, collection, repayment or recovery.

(2) But section 59A of the Taxes Management Act 1970 (payments on account) does not apply in relation to Class 2 contributions under section 11(2).

(3) This section and section 11(5) are subject to any contrary provision in regulations made under Schedule 1 in relation to Class 2 contributions under section 11(2).][1]

Commentary—*Simon's Taxes* **E8.305A**.

HMRC Manuals—National Insurance Manual NIM70800 (class 2 Nics: general information: enforcement).

NIM70850 (class 2 Nics: general information: appeals).

Amendments—[1] Sections 11, 11A substituted for previous s 11 by NICA 2015 s 2, Sch 1 paras 1, 3 with effect for the tax year 2015–16 and subsequent tax years.

[2] Sub-s (1)(*ea*) inserted by FA 2016 Sch 18 para 61(1), (2) with effect in relation to relevant defeats incurred after 15 September 2016, subject to FA 2016 Sch 18 para 64 (relevant defeats to be disregarded).

12 Late paid Class 2 contributions

(1) This section applies to any Class 2 contribution [under section 11(6)][2] paid in respect of a week falling within a tax year ("the contribution year") earlier than the tax year in which it is paid ("the payment year").

(2) Subject to subsections (3) [and (4)][2] below, the amount of a contribution to which this section applies shall be the amount which the earner would have had to pay if he had paid the contribution in the contribution year.

(3) Subject to subsections [(4) and (6)][2] below, in any case where—

(*a*) the earner pays an ordinary contribution to which this section applies after the end of the tax year immediately following the contribution year; and

(*b*) the weekly rate of ordinary contributions for the week in respect of which the contribution was payable in the contribution year differs from the weekly rate applicable at the time of payment in the payment year,

the amount of the contribution shall be computed by reference to the highest weekly rate of ordinary contributions in the period beginning with the week in respect of which the contribution is paid and ending with the day on which it is paid.

(4) The [Treasury][1] may by regulations direct that subsection (3) above shall have effect in relation to a higher-rate contribution to which this section applies subject to such modifications as may be prescribed.

(5) . . . [2]

(6) The [Treasury][1] may by regulations provide that the amount of any contribution which, apart from the regulations, would fall to be computed in accordance with subsection (3) . . . [2] above shall instead be computed by reference to a tax year not earlier than the contribution year but earlier—

(*a*) . . . [2] than the payment year. . . . [2]

(*b*) . . . [2]

(7) . . . [2]

(8) In this section—

"ordinary contribution" means a contribution [of the amount specified in section 11(6)][2]; and

"higher-rate contribution" means a contribution [of an amount provided for in regulations under section 11(8).][2]

Commentary—*Simon's Taxes* **E8.305**.

HMRC Manuals—National Insurance Manual NIM23002 (higher rates for contributions paid late).

NIM23600 (entitlement to pay voluntarily: higher rate provisions).

NIM70750 (class 2 Nics: general Information: higher rate provisions).

NIM72150 (class 2 Nics: payments: higher rate provisions).

NIM23005 (conditions under which higher rate provisions may be waived).

Former enactments—Sub-ss (1), (2): SSA 1975 s 7A(1), (2); Health and Social Security Act 1984 s 17(2).

Sub-s (3): SSA 1975 s 7A(3); SSA 1989 s 26, Sch 7 para 3; Health and Social Security Act 1984 s 17(2); SI 1985/1398 reg 4(2).

Sub-s (4)–(8): SSA 1975 s 7(4)–(8); Health and Social Security Act 1984 s 17(2).

Regulations—Social Security (Contributions) (Amendment and Application of Schedule 38 to the Finance Act 2012) Regulations, SI 2013/622.

Social Security (Miscellaneous Amendments No 2) Regulations, SI 2015/478.

Cross references—See SS (Contributions) Regulations, SI 2001/1004 reg 60 (treatment for purpose of contributory benefit of late paid contribution under the Act).

SS (Contributions) Regulations, SI 2001/1004 reg 60–65 (treatment of contributions paid late).

Amendments—[1] Words in sub-ss (4) and (6) substituted by the Social Security Contributions (Transfer of Functions, etc) Act 1999 s 2, Sch 3 para 13 with effect from 1 April 1999 by virtue of the Social Security Contributions (Transfer of Functions, etc) Act 1999 (Commencement No 1 and Transitional Provisions) Order, SI 1999/527.

[2] In sub-s (1) words inserted, in sub-ss (2), (3), (8) words substituted, sub-ss (5), (7) repealed, and in sub-s (6) words repealed, by NICA 2015 s 2, Sch 1 paras 1, 4 with effect in relation to a Class 2 contribution in respect of a week in the tax year 2015–16 or a subsequent tax year.

Class 3 contributions

13 Class 3 contributions

(1) [The Treasury shall by regulations][1] provide for earners and others, if over the age of 16, to be entitled if they so wish, but subject to any prescribed conditions, to pay Class 3 contributions; and, subject to the following provisions of this section, the amount of a Class 3 contribution shall be [£14.25][3].

NIC

(2) Payment of Class 3 contributions shall be allowed only with a view to enabling the contributor to satisfy . . . [2] conditions of entitlement to benefit by acquiring the requisite earnings factor for the purposes described in section 22 below.
(3) [The Secretary of State may by regulations][1] provide for Class 3 contributions, although paid in one tax year, to be appropriated in prescribed circumstances to the earnings factor of another tax year.
(4) The amount of a Class 3 contribution in respect of a tax year earlier than the tax year in which it is paid shall be the same as if it had been paid in the earlier year and in respect of that year, unless it falls to be calculated in accordance with subsection (6) below or regulations under subsection (7) below.
(5) In this section—
"the payment year" means the tax year in which a contribution is paid; and
"the contribution year" means the earlier year mentioned in subsection (4) above.
(6) Subject to subsection (7) below, in any case where—
(*a*) a Class 3 contribution is paid after the end of the next tax year but one following the contribution year; and
(*b*) the amount of a Class 3 contribution applicable had the contribution been paid in the contribution year differs from the amount of a Class 3 contribution applicable at the time of payment in the payment year,

the amount of the contribution shall be computed by reference to the highest of those two amounts and of any other amount of a Class 3 contribution in the intervening period.
(7) The [Treasury][1] may by regulations provide that the amount of a contribution which apart from the regulations would fall to be computed in accordance with subsection (6) above shall instead be computed by reference to the amount of a Class 3 contribution for a tax year earlier than the payment year but not earlier than the contribution year.

Commentary—*Simon's Taxes* **E8.402, E8.404, E8.405, E8.408.**
HMRC Manuals—National Insurance Manual NIM25101–25103 class 3 contributions — general informations).
NIM25105 (conditions of eligibility: second condition).
NIM25108 (time limit for paying).
NIM25111 (methods of payment).
NIM25029 (applying the higher rates).
Former enactments—Sub-s (1): SSA 1975 s 8(1); Education (School-leaving Dates) Act 1976 s 2(4); Health and Social Security Act 1984 s 18(1)(*a*).
Sub-s (2), (3): SSA 1975 s 8(2).
Sub-s (4): SSA 1975 s 8(2A); Health and Social Security Act 1984 s 18(1)(*b*), (3).
Sub-s (5): SSA 1975 s 8(2B); Health and Social Security Act 1984 s 18(3).
Sub-s (6): SSA 1975 s 8(2C); Health and Social Security Act 1984 s 18(3); SSA 1989 s 26, Sch 7 para 4; SI 1985/1398 reg 4(3).
Sub-s (7): SSA 1975 s 8(2D); Health and Social Security Act 1984 s 18(3).
Regulations—SS (Crediting and Treatment of Contributions, and National Insurance Numbers) Regulations, SI 2001/769.
Social Security (Contributions) (Amendment) Regulations, SI 2013/718.
Social Security (Miscellaneous Amendments No 2) Regulations, SI 2015/478.
Simon's Tax Cases—13, *Bonner and others v Revenue and Customs Comrs* [2011] STC 538.
Cross references—See the SSAA 1992 s 141(4)(*c*) (annual review of figure in sub-s (1) above),
SSAA 1992 s 143(1)(*d*) (power to alter figure in sub-s (1) above),
SSAA 1992 s 145(4) (power to alter figure in sub-s (1) above);
SS (Contributions) Regulations, SI 2001/1004 reg 48 (Class 3 contributions).
SI 2001/1004 reg 49 (precluded Class 3 contributions).
SI 2001/1004 reg 50 (contributions not paid within prescribed period).
Amendments—[1] Words in sub-ss (1), (3) and (7) substituted by the Social Security Contributions (Transfer of Functions, etc) Act 1999 s 2, Sch 3 para 14 with effect from 1 April 1999 by virtue of the Social Security Contributions (Transfer of Functions, etc) Act 1999 (Commencement No 1 and Transitional Provisions) Order, SI 1999/527.
[2] In sub-s (2), word repealed by PeA 2014 s 23, Sch 12 paras 2, 4 with effect from 6 April 2016 (PeA 2014 s 56(1), (4)).
[3] Figure in sub-s (1) substituted by the Social Security (Contributions) (Rates, Limits and Thresholds Amendments and National Insurance Funds Payments) Regulations, SI 2017/415 reg 4 with effect from 6 April 2017. Figure was previously £14.10.

[13A Right to pay additional Class 3 contributions in certain cases

(1) An eligible person is entitled, if he so wishes, but subject to any conditions prescribed by regulations made by the Treasury and to the following provisions of this section, to pay Class 3 contributions in respect of a missing year.
(2) A missing year is a tax year not earlier than 1975–76 in respect of which the person would under regulations under section 13 be entitled to pay Class 3 contributions but for a limit on the time within which contributions may be paid in respect of that year.
(3) A person is not entitled to pay contributions in respect of more than 6 tax years under this section.
(4) A person is not entitled to pay any contribution under this section after the end of 6 years beginning with the day on which he attains pensionable age.
(5) A person is an eligible person if the following conditions are satisfied.
(6) The first condition is that the person attained or will attain pensionable age in the period—
(*a*) beginning with 6th April 2008, and
(*b*) ending with 5th April 2015.

(7) The second condition is that there are at least 20 tax years each of which is a year to which subsection (8) or (10) applies.
(8) This subsection applies if—
(*a*) the year is one in respect of which the person has paid or been credited with contributions that are of a relevant class for the purposes of paragraph 5 or 5A of Schedule 3 or been credited (in the case of 1987–88 or any subsequent year) with earnings, and
(*b*) in the case of that year, the earnings factor derived as mentioned in subsection (9) is not less than the qualifying earnings factor for that year.
(9) For the purposes of subsection (8)(*b*) the earnings factor—
(*a*) in the case of 1987–88 or any subsequent year, is that which is derived from—
(i) so much of the person's earnings as did not exceed the upper earnings limit and upon which such of the contributions mentioned in subsection (8)(*a*) as are primary Class 1 contributions were paid or treated as paid or earnings credited, and
(ii) any Class 2 or Class 3 contributions for the year, or
(*b*) in the case of any earlier year, is that which is derived from the contributions mentioned in subsection (8)(*a*).
(10) This subsection applies (in the case of a person who attained or will attain pensionable age before 6th April 2010) if the year is one in which the person was precluded from regular employment by responsibilities at home within the meaning of regulations under paragraph 5(7) of Schedule 3.
(11) The third condition applies only if the person attained or will attain pensionable age before 6th April 2010.
(12) That condition is that—
(*a*) the person has, in respect of any one tax year before that in which he attains pensionable age, actually paid contributions that are of a relevant class for the purposes of paragraph 5 of Schedule 3, and
(*b*) in the case of that year, the earnings factor derived as mentioned in subsection (13) is not less than the qualifying earnings factor for that year.
(13) For the purposes of subsection (12)(*b*) the earnings factor—
(*a*) in the case of 1987–88 or any subsequent year, is that which is derived from—
(i) so much of the person's earnings as did not exceed the upper earnings limit and upon which such of the contributions mentioned in subsection (12)(*a*) as are primary Class 1 contributions were paid or treated as paid, and
(ii) any Class 2 or Class 3 contributions for the year, or
(*b*) in the case of any earlier year, is that which is derived from the contributions mentioned in subsection (12)(*a*).][1]

HMRC Manuals—National Insurance Manual NIM25101–1106 (class 3 contributions : conditions).
NIM25108 (time limit for paying).
NIM25110 (rate payable).
NIM25112 (date from which Nics are treated as paid for basic state pension and bereavement benefit purposes).
Amendments—[1] This section inserted by the Pensions Act 2008 s 135(1), (2) with effect from 6 April 2009.

14 Restriction on right to pay Class 3 contributions

(1) No person shall be entitled to pay a Class 3 contribution in respect of any tax year if his earnings factor, or the aggregate of his earnings factors, for that year derived—
(*a*) in the case of 1987–88 or any subsequent year, from earnings upon which Class 1 contributions have been paid or treated as paid or from Class 2 contributions actually paid; or
(*b*) in the case of any earlier year, from contributions actually paid,
is equal to or exceeds the qualifying earnings factor for that year; and regulations may provide for precluding the payment of Class 3 contributions in other cases.
(2) Regulations may provide for the repayment of Class 3 contributions that have been paid in cases where their payment was precluded by, or by regulations made under, subsection (1) above.
(3) Contributions repayable by virtue of regulations under subsection (2) above shall, for the purpose of determining the contributor's entitlement to any benefit, be treated as not having been paid (but nothing in this subsection shall be taken to imply that any other repayable contributions are to be treated for the purposes of benefit as having been paid).
[(4) Where primary Class 1 contributions have been paid or treated as paid on any part of a person's earnings, subsection (1)(*a*) above shall have effect as if such contributions had been paid or treated as paid on so much of those earnings as did not exceed the upper earnings limit.][1]
[(5) Regulations under subsection (1) or (2) above shall be made by the Treasury.][2]

Commentary—*Simon's Taxes* **E8.407**.
HMRC Manuals—National Insurance Manual NIM25006 (tax year is already a qualifying one for benefit purposes).
Former enactments—Sub-s (1): SS Pensions Act 1975 s 5(1); SSA 1986 s 75, Sch 8 para 6.
Sub-ss (2), (3): SS Pensions Act 1975 s 5(2); SS (Miscellaneous Provisions) Act 1977 s 1(5).
Cross reference—SS (Contributions) Regulations, SI 2001/1004 reg 48 (Class 3 contributions).
Simon's Tax Cases—13, *Bonner and others v Revenue and Customs Comrs* [2011] STC 538.

NIC

Amendments—[1] Inserted by SSA 1998 Sch 7 para 59 with effect from 6 April 1999 by virtue of the Social Security Act 1998 (Commencement No 3) Order, SI 1999/418.

[2] Sub-s (5) inserted by the Social Security Contributions (Transfer of Functions, etc) Act 1999 s 2, Sch 3 para 15 with effect from 1 April 1999 by virtue of the Social Security Contributions (Transfer of Functions, etc) Act 1999 (Commencement No 1 and Transitional Provisions) Order, SI 1999/527.

[Class 3A contributions]

[14A Class 3A contributions in return for units of additional pension

[(1) An eligible person is entitled to pay a Class 3A contribution before the cut-off date, in return for a unit of additional pension.

(1A) The cut-off date is—

(*a*) 5th April 2017, or

(*b*) if later the end of the 30-day period beginning with the day on which the person is sent information about Class 3A contributions by Her Majesty's Revenue and Customs in response to a request made before 6th April 2017.][2]

(2) A person is eligible to pay a Class 3A contribution if the person—

(*a*) is entitled to a Category A, Category B or Category D retirement pension or graduated retirement benefit, or

(*b*) has deferred entitlement to a Category A or Category B retirement pension or graduated retirement benefit.

(3) The amount of a Class 3A contribution needed to obtain a unit of additional pension is to be determined in accordance with regulations made by the Treasury.

(4) Before making those regulations the Treasury must consult the Government Actuary or the Deputy Government Actuary.

(5) A person—

(*a*) may pay Class 3A contributions on more than one occasion, but

(*b*) may not obtain more than the maximum number of units of additional pension.

(6) The maximum number of units of additional pension that a person may obtain is to be specified by the Treasury in regulations.

(7) In this section "deferred", in relation to graduated retirement benefit, has the meaning given by section 36(4A) of the National Insurance Act 1965.

(8) For the meaning of "deferred" in relation to a Category A or Category B retirement pension, see section 55(3) of this Act.][1]

Commentary—*Simon's Taxes* **E8.411**.

Regulations—Social Security Class 3A Contributions (Units of Additional Pension) Regulations, SI 2014/3240.

Amendments—[1] Sections 14A–14C and preceding crosshead inserted by PeA 2014 s 25, Sch 15 paras 1, 3 with effect from 12 October 2015 (by virtue of SI 2015/1475). Note that as PeA 2014 Sch 15 para 3 comes into force before 6 April 2016 (the day mentioned in PeA 2014 s 56(4)), this section has effect as if the reference to entitlement included the prospective entitlement of a person who has not yet reached pensionable age, but will reach pensionable age before that day (assuming that the person lives until pensionable age) (PeA 2014 Sch 15 para 4).

Note that PeA 2014 Sch 15 para 3 comes into force for the purposes only of making regulations on 1 October 2014 (by virtue of SI 2014/2377 art 2(1)(*a*)(ii), (3)(*d*)(i)).

[2] Sub-ss (1), (1A) substituted for sub-s (1) by the Social Security Class 3A Contributions (Amendment) Regulations, SI 2014/2746 reg 2 with effect from 12 October 2015. This amendment has effect in relation to Great Britain only. An identical amendment is made to the Social Security Contributions and Benefits (Northern Ireland) Act 1992 s 14A, in relation to Northern Ireland, by SI 2014/2746 reg 4. Sub-s (1) previously read as follows—

"(1) An eligible person is entitled to pay a Class 3A contribution in return for a unit of additional pension.".

[14B Class 3A contributions: repayment

(1) The Treasury may by regulations provide for a Class 3A contribution to be repaid in specified circumstances.

(2) Regulations under subsection (1) may, in particular, make provision about applications for repayments and other procedural matters.

(3) A person is to be treated as never having had a unit of additional pension if the Class 3A contribution paid in respect of it is repaid.

(4) Regulations under subsection (1) may provide for benefits paid to a person because of the unit of additional pension to be recovered by deducting them from the repayment.][1]

Regulations—Social Security Class 3A Contributions (Amendment) Regulations, SI 2014/2746.

Amendments—[1] Sections 14A–14C and preceding crosshead inserted by PeA 2014 s 25, Sch 15 paras 1, 3 with effect from 12 October 2015 (by virtue of SI 2015/1475). Note that as PeA 2014 Sch 15 para 3 comes into force before 6 April 2016 (the day mentioned in PeA 2014 s 56(4)), this section has effect as if the reference to entitlement included the prospective entitlement of a person who has not yet reached pensionable age, but will reach pensionable age before that day (assuming that the person lives until pensionable age) (PeA 2014 Sch 15 para 4).

Note that PeA 2014 Sch 15 para 3 comes into force for the purposes only of making regulations on 1 October 2014 (by virtue of SI 2014/2377 art 2(1)(*a*)(ii), (3)(*d*)(i)).

[14C Class 3A contributions: power to change eligibility or remove the option to pay

(1) The Treasury may by regulations change who is eligible to pay Class 3A contributions.

(2) The Treasury may by regulations remove the option for people to pay Class 3A contributions.

(3) Regulations under this section may, in particular, amend an Act.][1]

Regulations—Social Security Class 3A Contributions (Amendment) Regulations, SI 2014/2746.

Amendments—[1] Sections 14A–14C and preceding crosshead inserted by PeA 2014 s 25, Sch 15 paras 1, 3 with effect from 12 October 2015 (by virtue of SI 2015/1475). Note that as PeA 2014 Sch 15 para 3 comes into force before 6 April 2016 (the day mentioned in PeA 2014 s 56(4)), this section has effect as if the reference to entitlement included the prospective entitlement of a person who has not yet reached pensionable age, but will reach pensionable age before that day (assuming that the person lives until pensionable age) (PeA 2014 Sch 15 para 4).

Note that PeA 2014 Sch 15 para 3 comes into force for the purposes only of making regulations on 1 October 2014 (by virtue of SI 2014/2377 art 2(1)(*a*)(ii), (3)(*d*)(i)).

Class 4 contributions

15 Class 4 contributions recoverable under the Income Tax Acts

(1) Class 4 contributions shall be payable for any tax year in respect of all [profits][3] which—

(*a*) are immediately derived from the carrying on or exercise of one or more trades, professions or vocations, . . . [3]

(*b*) [are profits chargeable to income tax under Chapter 2 of Part 2 of the Income Tax (Trading and Other Income) Act 2005][3] for the year of assessment corresponding to that tax year [and

(*c*) are not profits of a trade, profession or vocation carried on wholly outside the United Kingdom.][3]

(2) Class 4 contributions in respect of profits . . . [3] shall be payable—

(*a*) in the same manner as any income tax which is, or would be, chargeable in respect of those profits . . . [3] (whether or not income tax in fact falls to be paid), and

(*b*) by the person on whom the income tax is (or would be) charged,

in accordance with assessments made from time to time under the Income Tax Acts.

[(3) The amount of a Class 4 contribution under this section for any tax year is equal to the aggregate of—

(*a*) the main Class 4 percentage of so much of the profits . . . [3] referred to in subsection (1) above (computed in accordance with Schedule 2 to this Act) as exceeds [£8,164][5] but does not exceed [£45,000][5]; and

(*b*) the additional Class 4 percentage of so much of those profits . . . [3] as exceeds [£45,000][5];

but the figures specified in this subsection are subject to alteration under section 141 of the Administration Act.][2]

[(3ZA) For the purposes of this Act—

(*a*) the main Class 4 percentage is [9][4] per cent; and

(*b*) the additional Class 4 percentage is [2][2] per cent;

but the main Class 4 percentage is subject to alteration under section 143 of the Administration Act.][2]

[(3A) Where income tax is (or would be) charged on a member of a limited liability partnership in respect of profits . . . [3] arising from the carrying on of a trade or profession by the limited liability partnership, Class 4 contributions shall be payable by him if they would be payable were the trade or profession carried on in partnership by the members.][1]

(4) . . . [3]

(5) For the purposes of this section the year of assessment which corresponds to a tax year is the year of assessment (within the meaning of the Tax Acts) which consists of the same period as that tax year.

Commentary—*Simon's Taxes* **E8.317, E8.318, E8.1139**.

HMRC Manuals—National Insurance Manual NIM24001 (general).

NIM24033 (changes from 6 April 2003).

NIM24040 (married women and widows with reduced rate elections).

NIM01211 (structural changes: married women and widows reduced rate Nics).

NIM70650 (class 4 is paid in addition with class 2 contributions).

NIM24522 (class 4 Nics who is liable: sleeping partners - background).

Former enactments—Sub-ss (1), (2): SSA 1975 s 9(1); SSA 1989 s 26, Sch 7 para 5(*a*), (*b*).

Sub-s (5): SSA 1975 s 9(1); SSA 1989 s 26, Sch 7 para 5(*c*).

Cross references—See SSAA 1992 s 141(4)(*d*) (annual review of figure in sub-s (3) above),

SSAA 1992 s 143(1)(*e*) (power to alter percentage rate in sub-s (3ZA) above).

Amendments—[1] Sub-s (3A) inserted by the Limited Liability Partnerships Act 2000 s 13 with effect from 6 April 2001 (by virtue of SI 2000/3316 art 2).

[2] Sub-ss (3), (3ZA) substituted for sub-s (3) by NICA 2002 s 3(1) with effect from 2003–04.

[3] In sub-s (1), words substituted, word repealed, and para (*c*) inserted; words in sub-ss (2), (3), (3A) repealed; and sub-s (4) repealed; by ITTOIA 2005 ss 882(1), 884, Sch 1 paras 419, 420, Sch 3 with effect from 6 April 2005. ITTOIA 2005 has effect—

(a) for income tax purposes, for 2005–06 and subsequent tax years, and

(b) for corporation tax purposes, for accounting periods ending after 5 April 2005: ITTOIA 2005 s 883(1).

[4] In sub-s (3ZA), in para (*a*) figure substituted for previous figure "8" and in para (*b*) figure substituted for previous figure "1", by the National Insurance Contributions Act 2011 s 2(1) with effect from 6 April 2011.

[5] In sub-s (3), the following figures substituted by the Social Security (Contributions) (Rates, Limits and Thresholds Amendments and National Insurance Funds Payments) Regulations, SI 2017/415 reg 5 with effect from 6 April 2017—

– the lower limit is "£8,164" (previously was "£8,060"); and

– the upper limit is "£45,000" (previously was "£43,000).

16 Applications of Income Tax Acts and destination of Class 4 contributions

(1) All the provisions of the Income Tax Acts, including in particular—

(*a*) provisions as to assessment, collection, repayment and recovery, and

[(*b*) the provisions of Part VA (payment of tax) and Part X (penalties) of the Taxes Management Act 1970,][1] [and

(*c*) the provisions of Schedules 55 and 56 to the Finance Act 2009 [and of Schedule 38 to the Finance Act 2012][6],][5] [and

(*d*) the provisions of Part 4 (follower notices and accelerated payments) and Part 5 (promoters of tax avoidance schemes) of the Finance Act 2014,][7]

shall, with the necessary modifications, apply in relation to Class 4 contributions under this Act and the Northern Ireland Contributions and Benefits Act as if those contributions were income tax chargeable under [Chapter 2 of Part 2 of the Income Tax (Trading and Other Income) Act 2005 in respect of the profits of a trade, profession or vocation which is not carried on wholly outside the United Kingdom[, or][4].

(*e*) the provisions of Schedule 18 to the Finance Act 2016 (serial tax avoidance),][8]

(2) Subsection (1) above is subject to any provision made by or under—

(*a*) sections 17(3) and (4) and 18 below;

(*b*) sections 17(3) and (4) and 18 of the Northern Ireland Contributions and Benefits Act; and

(*c*) Schedule 2 to this Act.

(3) Schedule 2 to this Act has effect for the application or modification, in relation to Class 4 contributions under this Act and the Northern Ireland Contributions and Benefits Act, of certain provisions of the Income Tax Acts, and the exclusion of other provisions, and generally with respect to the contributions.

(4) . . . [2]

(5) . . . [3]

Commentary—*Simon's Taxes* **E1.201A, E1.251, E8.319, E8.1013, E8.1158**.

Former enactments—Sub-ss (1)–(3): SSA 1975 s 9(3), (4).

Cross-references—See the Social Security (Contributions) (Amendment and Application of Schedule 38 to the Finance Act 2012) Regulations, SI 2013/622 reg 41 (the provisions of FA 2012 Sch 38 (tax agents: dishonest conduct) apply in relation to Class 1, Class 1A, Class 1B and Class 2 NICs as in relation to tax to the extent that they do not already apply).

Amendments—[1] Sub-s (1)(*b*) substituted by FA 1994 ss 196, 199(1), (2)(*a*), Sch 19 para 45, with effect from the year 1996–97.

[2] Sub-s (4) repealed and sub-s (5) substituted by the Social Security Contributions (Transfer of Functions, etc) Act 1999 s 2, Sch 3 para 16, and s 26(3) and Sch 10 Pt 1 with effect 1 April 1999 by virtue of the Social Security Contributions (Transfer of Functions, etc) Act 1999 (Commencement No 1 and Transitional Provisions) Order, SI 1999/527.

[3] Sub-s (5) repealed by NICA 2002 s 7, Sch 2 with effect from 2003–04.

[4] Words in sub-s (1) substituted by ITTOIA 2005 s 882(1), Sch 1 paras 419, 421 with effect from 6 April 2005. ITTOIA 2005 has effect—

(a) for income tax purposes, for 2005–06 and subsequent tax years, and

(b) for corporation tax purposes, for accounting periods ending after 5 April 2005: ITTOIA 2005 s 883(1).

[5] Sub-s (1)(*c*) and preceding word "and" inserted by the Finance Act 2009, Schedules 55 and 56 (Income Tax Self Assessment and Pension Schemes) (Appointed Days and Consequential and Savings Provisions) Order, SI 2011/702 art 13 with effect from 1 April 2011. These amendments have no effect in relation to a return or other document which is required to be made or delivered to HMRC or an amount of tax which is payable in relation to the tax year 2009–10 or any previous tax year (SI 2011/702 art 20).

[6] In sub-s (1)(*c*), words inserted by FA 2012 s 223, Sch 38 para 53 with effect from 1 April 2013 (by virtue of SI 2013/279 art 2).

[7] Sub-s (1)(*d*) inserted by NICA 2015 s 4, Sch 2 para 32 with effect from 12 April 2015.

[8] Sub-s (1)(*e*) and preceding word inserted by FA 2016 Sch 18 para 61(1), (3) with effect in relation to relevant defeats incurred after 15 September 2016, subject to FA 2016 Sch 18 para 64 (relevant defeats to be disregarded).

17 Exceptions, deferment and incidental matters relating to Class 4 contributions

(1) [The Inland Revenue may by regulations][2] provide—

(*a*) for excepting persons from liability to pay Class 4 contributions[, or any prescribed part of such contributions,][3] in accordance with sections 15 and 16(1) to (3) above; or

(*b*) for deferring any person's liability,

. . . [1]

(2) Exception from liability, or deferment, under subsection (1) above may, in particular, be by reference—

(*a*) to a person otherwise liable for contributions being under a prescribed age at the beginning of a tax year;

(*b*) to a person having attained pensionable age;

(*c*) to a person being in receipt of earnings in respect of which primary Class 1 contributions are, or may be, payable; or

(*d*) to a person not satisfying prescribed conditions as to residence or presence in the United Kingdom.

(3) [The Inland Revenue may by regulations][2] provide for any incidental matters arising out of the payment of any Class 4 contributions recovered by the Inland Revenue, including in particular the return, in whole or in part, of such contributions in cases where—

(*a*) payment has been made in error; or

(*b*) repayment ought for any other reason to be made.

(4) [The Inland Revenue may by regulations][2] provide for any matters arising out of the deferment of liability [to pay Class 4 contributions, or any part of such contributions,][3] under subsection (1) above, including in particular provision for the amount of a person's profits or gains (as computed in accordance with Schedule 2 to this Act) to be certified by the Inland Revenue to . . .[1] the person liable.

(5) . . .[4]

(6) . . .[1]

Commentary—*Simon's Taxes* **E8.324, E8.1002.**

Former enactments—SSA 1975 s 9(7)–(9).

Cross references—See the SS Administration Act 1992 s 17(2) (determination by Secretary of State of certain questions regarding Class 4 contributions under this section).

SS (Contributions) Regulations, SI 2001/1004 reg 95 (deferment in case of doubt).

SS (Contributions) Regulations, SI 2001/1004 reg 99 (calculation, and recovery of, Class 4 contributions after issue of certificate of deferment).

Amendments—[1] Words in sub-ss (1) and (4), and sub-s (6) repealed by the Social Security Contributions (Transfer of Functions, etc) Act 1999 s 26(3) and Sch 10 Pt 1 with effect from 1 April 1999 by virtue of the Social Security Contributions (Transfer of Functions, etc) Act 1999 (Commencement No 1 and Transitional Provisions) Order, SI 1999/527.

[2] Words in sub-ss (1), (3) and (4) substituted by the Social Security Contributions (Transfer of Functions, etc) Act 1999 s 2, Sch 3 para 17 with effect from 1 April 1999 by virtue of the Social Security Contributions (Transfer of Functions, etc) Act 1999 (Commencement No 1 and Transitional Provisions) Order, SI 1999/527.

[3] Words in sub-s (1) inserted, words in sub-s (4) substituted, by NICA 2002 s 6, Sch 1 paras 1, 4 with effect from 2003–04.

[4] Sub-s (5) repealed by NICA 2002 s 7, Sch 2 with effect from 2003–04.

18 Class 4 contributions recoverable under regulations

(1) [The Inland Revenue may by regulations make provision][1] so that where—

(*a*) an earner, in respect of any one or more employments of his, is treated by regulations under section 2(2)(*b*) above as being self-employed; and

(*b*) in any tax year he has earnings from any such employment (one or more) which fall within paragraph (*b*)(i) of [subsection (8)][6] of section 11 above but is not liable for a higher weekly rate of Class 2 contributions by virtue of regulations under that subsection; and

(*c*) the total of those earnings exceeds [£8,164][7],

he is to be liable, in respect of those earnings, to pay a Class 4 contribution . . .[4]

[(1A) The amount of a Class 4 contribution payable by virtue of regulations under this section is equal to the aggregate of—

(*a*) the main Class 4 percentage of so much of the total of the earnings referred to in subsection (1)(*b*) above as exceeds [£8,164][7] but does not exceed [£45,000][7]; and

(*b*) the additional Class 4 percentage of so much of that total as exceeds [£45,000][7];

but the figures specified in this subsection are subject to alteration under section 141 of the Administration Act.][3]

(2) [In relation to Class 4 contributions payable by virtue of regulations under this section][2], [regulations made by the Inland Revenue may][1]

(*a*) apply any of the provisions of Schedule 1 to this Act (except a provision conferring power to make regulations); and

(*b*) make any such provision as may be made by regulations under that Schedule, except paragraph 6 [or 7BZA][5].

Commentary—*Simon's Taxes* **E8.292, E8.318, E8.326.**

HMRC Manuals—National Insurance Manual NIM24082 (structure: special changes from 6 April 2003).

Former enactments—SSA 1975 s 10.

Cross references—See SS (Contributions) Regulations, SI 2001/1004 regs 91–110 (exceptions from Class 4 liability, deferment, calculation, etc);

SSAA 1992 s 17(2)(*b*) (determination by Secretary of State of questions arising under regulations made by virtue of this section),

SSAA 1992 s 141(5) (annual review of figure in sub-s (1) above),

SSAA 1992 s 143(2) (power to alter percentage rate in sub-s (1) above).

Amendments—[1] Words in sub-ss (1) and (2) substituted by the Social Security Contributions (Transfer of Functions, etc) Act 1999 s 2, Sch 3 para 18 with effect from 1 April 1999 by virtue of the Social Security Contributions (Transfer of Functions, etc) Act 1999 (Commencement No 1 and Transitional Provisions) Order, SI 1999/527.

[2] Words in sub-s (2) substituted by the Social Security Contributions (Transfer of Functions, etc) Act 1999 s 1(1) and Sch 1 para 7 with effect from 1 April 1999 by virtue of the Social Security Contributions (Transfer of Functions, etc) Act 1999 (Commencement No 1 and Transitional Provisions) Order, SI 1999/527.

[3] Sub-s (1A) inserted by NICA 2002 s 3(3) with effect from 2003–04.

[4] Words in sub-s (1) repealed by NICA 2002 s 7, Sch 2 with effect from 2003–04.

[5] Words in sub-s (2)(*b*) inserted by the NIC and Statutory Payments Act 2004 s 11, Schedule 1 para 1(1), (3) with effect from 1 September 2004 (by virtue of SI 2004/1943).

[6] In sub-s (1)(*b*), words substituted by NICA 2015 s 2, Sch 1 paras 1, 5 with effect for the tax year 2015–16 and subsequent tax years.

[7] In sub-ss (1), (1A) the following figures substituted by the Social Security (Contributions) (Rates, Limits and Thresholds Amendments and National Insurance Funds Payments) Regulations, SI 2017/415 reg 5 with effect from 6 April 2017—

NIC

– the lower limit is "£8,164" (previously was "£8,060"); and
– the upper limit is "£45,000" (previously was "£43,000).

[18A Class 4 contributions: partnerships

(1) The Treasury may by regulations—

(*a*) modify the way in which liabilities for Class 4 contributions of a partner in a firm are determined, or

(*b*) otherwise modify the law relating to Class 4 contributions,

as they consider appropriate to take account of the passing or making of a provision of the Income Tax Acts relating to firms or partners in firms.

(2) "Firm" has the same meaning as in the Income Tax (Trading and Other Income) Act 2005 (and includes a limited liability partnership in relation to which section 863(1) of that Act applies); and "partner" is to be read accordingly and includes a former partner.

(3) Regulations under this section may have retrospective effect; but they may not have effect before the beginning of the tax year in which they are made.][1]

Commentary—*Simon's Taxes* **E8.317**.

Regulations—Social Security (Contributions) (Amendment No 5) Regulations, SI 2014/3196.

Amendments—[1] Section 18A inserted by NICs Act 2014 s 13(1), (2) with effect from 14 May 2014.

General

19 General power to regulate liability for contributions

(1) Regulations may provide either generally or in relation to—

(*a*) any prescribed category of earners; or

(*b*) earners in any prescribed category of employments,

that their liability in a particular tax year in respect of contributions of prescribed classes[, or any prescribed part of such contributions,][2] is not to exceed such maximum amount or amounts as may be prescribed.

(2) Regulations made for the purposes of subsection (1) above may provide—

(*a*) for an earner whose liability is subject to a maximum prescribed under that subsection to be liable in the first instance for the full amount of any contributions due from him apart from the regulations, or to be relieved from liability for such contributions in prescribed circumstances and to the prescribed extent; and

(*b*) for contributions paid in excess of any such maximum to be repaid at such times, and in accordance with such conditions, as may be prescribed.

(3) Regulations may provide, in relation to earners otherwise liable for contributions of any class [or any part of such contributions][2], for excepting them from the liability for such periods, and in such circumstances, as may be prescribed.

(4) As respects any woman who was married or a widow on 6th April 1977 (the date of the coming into force of the repeal of the old provisions that primary Class 1 contributions might be paid at a reduced rate and Class 2 contributions need not be paid by a married woman or a widow) regulations shall provide—

(*a*) for enabling her to elect that [so much of her liability in respect of primary Class 1 contributions as is attributable to section 8(1)(*a*) above][2] shall be a liability to contribute at such reduced rate as may be prescribed; and

(*b*) either for enabling her to elect that her liability in respect of Class 2 contributions shall be a liability to contribute at such reduced rate as may be prescribed or for enabling her to elect that she shall be under no liability to pay such contributions; and

(*c*) for enabling her to revoke any such election.

(5) Regulations under subsection (4) above may—

(*a*) provide for the making or revocation of any election under the regulations to be subject to prescribed exceptions and conditions;

(*b*) preclude a person who has made such an election from paying Class 3 contributions while the election has effect;

(*c*) provide for treating an election made or revoked for the purpose of any provision of the regulations as made or revoked also for the purpose of any other provision of the regulations;

(*d*) provide for treating an election made in accordance with regulations under section 130(2) of the 1975 Act as made for the purpose of regulations under subsection (4) above.

[(5A) Regulations under any of subsections (1) to (5) above shall be made by the Treasury.][1]

(6) [The Secretary of State may by regulations][1] provide for earnings factors to be derived, for such purposes as may be prescribed, as follows, that is to say—

(*a*) in the case of earnings factors for 1987–88 or any subsequent tax year—

(i) from earnings upon which primary Class 1 contributions are paid at a reduced rate by virtue of regulations under subsection (4) above; or

(ii) from Class 2 contributions paid at a reduced rate by virtue of such regulations; and

(*b*) in the case of earnings factors for any earlier tax year, from contributions which are paid at a reduced rate by virtue of regulations under subsection (4) above;

and if provision is made for a person to have earnings factors so derived for the purpose of establishing entitlement to any benefit, the regulations may, in relation to that person, vary or add to the requirements for entitlement to that benefit.

Commentary—*Simon's Taxes* **A6.952, E8.266, E8.1123.**
HMRC Manuals—National Insurance Manual NIM01107 (structural changes: married women and widows reduced rate Nics).
Former enactments—Sub-ss (1)–(3): SSA 1975 s 11.
Sub-ss (4), (5): SS Pensions Act 1975 s 3(2), (3).
Sub-s (6): SS Pensions Act 1975 s 3(4); SSA 1986 s 75, Sch 8 para 5.
Cross reference—See SSAA 1992 Sch 7 para 5 (regulations under sub-s (4)(*a*) above not requiring prior submission to Social Security Advisory Committee).
Regulations—Social Security (Contributions) (Amendment No 2) Regulations, SI 2003/964.
Social Security (Contributions) (Amendment) Regulations, SI 2012/573.
The Social Security (Contributions) (Amendment No. 2) Regulations, SI 2012/817.
Social Security (Contributions) (Amendment and Application of Schedule 38 to the Finance Act 2012) Regulations, SI 2013/622.
Social Security (Miscellaneous Amendments No 2) Regulations, SI 2015/478.
Social Security (Contributions) (Amendment) (No 2) Regulations SI 2016/352.
Amendments—[1] Sub-s (5A) inserted and words in sub-s (6) substituted by the Social Security Contributions (Transfer of Functions, etc) Act 1999 s 2, Sch 3 para 19 with effect from 1 April 1999 by virtue of the Social Security Contributions (Transfer of Functions, etc) Act 1999 (Commencement No 1 and Transitional Provisions) Order, SI 1999/527.
[2] Words in sub-ss (1), (3) inserted, and words in sub-s (4)(*a*) substituted, by the NIC Act 2002 s 6, Sch 1 paras 1, 5 with effect from 2003–04.

[19A Class 1, 1A or 1B contributions paid in error.

(1) This section applies where—

(*a*) payments by way of Class 1, Class 1A or Class 1B contributions are made in respect of earnings paid to or for the benefit of an earner (or in respect of a benefit made available to an earner) in 1998–99 or a subsequent tax year ("year 1");

(*b*) the payments are made in error, in that the employment from which the earnings are derived (or by reason of which the benefit is made available) is not employed earner's employment; and

(*c*) the person making the payments has not been notified of the error by the [Inland Revenue][2] before the end of the tax year following year 1 ("year 2").

(2) After the end of year 2 the earner shall, except in such circumstances as may be prescribed, be treated for all purposes relating to—

(*a*) contributions and contributory benefits; and

(*b*) statutory sick pay and statutory maternity pay,

as if the earnings were derived from (or the benefit were made available by reason of) employed earner's employment.][1]

[(3) Regulations under subsection (2) above shall be made by the Treasury.][3]

Commentary—*Simon's Taxes* **E8.203, E8.908, E8.925.**
HMRC Manuals—National Insurance Manual NIM17100 (special refund arrangements in re-categorisation cases involving a change of employment status from employed earner to self-employed).
NIM37016–7018 (refunds: retrospective change of employment status from employed earner (class 1) to self-employed (class 2)).
Amendments—[1] Inserted by SSA 1998 s 54 with effect from 4 March 1999 for the purpose of authorising the making of regulations and 6 April 1999 for all other purposes by virtue of the Social Security Act 1998 (Commencement No 4) Order, SI 1999/526.
[2] Words in sub-s (1)(*c*) substituted by the Social Security Contributions (Transfer of Functions, etc) Act 1999 s 26(2) and Sch 9 para 4 with effect from 4 March 1999 for the purpose of authorising the making of Regulations by virtue of the Social Security Contributions (Transfer of Functions, etc) Act 1999 (Commencement No 1 and Transitional Provisions) Order, SI 1999/527.
[3] Sub-s (3) inserted by the Social Security Contributions (Transfer of Functions, etc) Act 1999 s 2, Sch 3 para 20 with effect from 1 April 1999 by virtue of the Social Security Contributions (Transfer of Functions, etc) Act 1999 (Commencement No 1 and Transitional Provisions) Order, SI 1999/527.

[19B Extended meaning of "benefit" etc in Part 1

In this Part references to "benefit" or "contributory benefit" include benefit under Part 1 of the Pensions Act 2014.]

Amendments—Section 19B inserted by PeA 2014 s 23, Sch 12 paras 2, 5 with effect from 6 April 2016 (PeA 2014 s 56(1), (4)).

PART II

CONTRIBUTORY BENEFITS

Preliminary

21 Contribution conditions

(1) Entitlement to any of the benefits specified in section 20(1) above, [other than [short-term incapacity benefit under subsection (1)(*b*) of section 30A below][6] long-term incapacity benefit under section [30A(1)(*a*)][6] below[, maternity allowance under section 35 [or 35B][13] below][4] or short-term or long-term incapacity benefit under section 40 or 41 below][1] [or a shared additional pension under section 55A [or 55AA][14] below][5], depends on contribution conditions being satisfied (either by the claimant or by some other person, according to the particular benefit).

NIC

(2) The class or classes of contribution which, for the purposes of subsection (1) above, are relevant in relation to each of those benefits are as follows—

Short-term benefit	
. . . [4]	[4]
[Short-term incapacity benefit under section [30A(1)(a)][6] below][1]	Class 1 or 2
. . . [2]	[2]
Other benefits	
[Bereavement payment][8]	Class 1, 2 or 3
Widowed mother's allowance	Class 1, 2 or 3
[Widowed parent's allowance	Class 1, 2 or 3][9]
[Bereavement allowance	Class 1, 2 or 3][9]
Widow's pension	Class 1, 2 or 3
Category A retirement pension	Class 1, 2 or 3
Category B retirement pension	Class 1, 2 or 3
Child's special allowance	Class 1, 2 or 3

(3) The relevant contribution conditions in relation to the benefits specified in subsection (2) above are those specified in Part I of Schedule 3 to this Act.

(4) Part II of Schedule 3 to this Act shall have effect as to the satisfaction of contribution conditions for benefit . . . [4] in certain cases where a claim for short-term benefit or a [bereavement payment][8] is, or has on a previous occasion been, made in the first or second year after that in which the contributor concerned first became liable for primary Class 1 or Class 2 contributions.

(5) In subsection (4) above and Schedule 3 to this Act—

(*a*) "the contributor concerned", for the purposes of any contribution condition, means the person by whom the condition is to be satisfied;

(*b*) "a relevant class", in relation to any benefit, means a class of contributions specified in relation to that benefit in subsection (2) above;

(*c*) "the earnings factor"—

(i) where the year in question is 1987–88 or any subsequent tax year, means, in relation to a person, the aggregate of his earnings factors derived from [so much of his earnings as did not exceed the upper earnings limit and][10] upon which primary Class 1 contributions have been paid or treated as paid and from his Class 2 and Class 3 contributions; and

(ii) where the year in question is any earlier tax year, means, in relation to a person's contributions of any class or classes, the aggregate of his earnings factors derived from all those contributions;

(*d*) except in the expression "benefit year", "year" means a tax year.

[(5A) Where primary Class 1 contributions have been paid or treated as paid on any part of a person's earnings, the following provisions, namely—

(*a*) subsection (5)(*c*) above;

(*b*) sections 22(1)(*a*)[, (2A)][7] and (3)(*a*), 23(3)(*a*), 24(2)(*a*), [44(6)(*za*) and (*a*)][7] . . . [11] below; and

(*c*) paragraphs 2(4)(*a*) and (5)(*a*), 4(2)(*a*), 5(2)(*b*) and (4)(*a*)[, 5A(3)(a)][12] and 7(4)(*a*) of Schedule 3 to this Act,

shall have effect as if such contributions had been paid or treated as paid on so much of the earnings as did not exceed the upper earnings limit.][3]

(6) In this Part of this Act "benefit year" means a period—

(*a*) beginning with the first Sunday in January in any calendar year, and

(*b*) ending with the Saturday immediately preceding the first Sunday in January in the following calendar year;

but for any prescribed purposes of this Part of this Act "benefit year" may by regulations be made to mean such other period (whether or not a period of 12 months) as may be specified in the regulations.

Commentary—*Simon's Taxes* **E8.919**.

HMRC Manuals—National Insurance Manual NIM25020 (class 3 Nics: benefits for which class 3 Nics count).
NIM41410 (basic state pension and bereavement benefits).

Amendments—[1] Words in sub-ss (1), (2) substituted by the Social Security (Incapacity for Work) Act 1994, s 11(1), Sch 1, para 3.

[2] Words in sub-s (2) repealed by the Jobseekers Act 1995, s 41(5), Sch 3.

[3] Sub-s (5A) inserted by the Social Security Act 1998, s 86(1), Sch 7, para 60 with effect from 6 April 1999 (by virtue of the Social Security Act 1998 (Commencement No 3) Order, SI 1999/418 art 2(2), (3)(*a*).

4 Words in sub-s (1) inserted and words in sub-ss (2), (4) repealed by the Welfare Reform and Pensions Act 1999, ss 70, 88, Sch 8, Pt VI, paras 30, 31, Sch 13, Pt V with effect from 2 April 2000 (by virtue of the Welfare Reform and Pensions Act 1999 (Commencement No 1) Order, SI 1999/3309 art 2(1)(*b*)(ii), (*c*)).

5 Words in sub-s (1) inserted by the Welfare Reform and Pensions Act 1999, s 84(1), Sch 12, Pt I, paras 14, 16 with effect from 1 December 2000 (by virtue of the Welfare Reform and Pensions Act 1999 (Commencement No 4) Order 2000, SI 2000/1047 art 2(2)(*d*), Schedule, Pt IV).

6 In sub-s (1) words inserted and substituted, and in sub-s (2) words substituted by the Welfare Reform and Pensions Act 1999, ss 70, Sch 8, Pt II, paras 20, 21 with effect from 3 Nov 2000 (by virtue of SI 2000/2958).

7 Reference in sub-s (5A)(*b*) inserted by the Child Support, Pensions and Social Security Act 2000 ss 35(2), 86 with effect from 8 January 2001 for the purposes only of making regulations and orders, from 25 January 2001 for the purposes of making reports and orders under the Pension Schemes Act 1993 ss 42, 42B, 45A and from 6 April 2002 for all other purposes.

8 Words in sub-ss (2), (4) substituted by the Welfare Reform and Pensions Act 1999, s 70, Sch 8, Pt I, paras 2, 4(1), (2)(*a*), (3) with effect from 9 April 2001 (by virtue of SI 2000/1047 art 2(2)(*a*)(ii), Schedule, Pt I).

9 In sub-s (2) entries relating to "Widowed parent's allowance" and "Bereavement allowance" inserted by the Welfare Reform and Pensions Act 1999, s 70, Sch 8, Pt I, paras 2, 4(1), (2)(*b*) with effect from 9 April 2001 (by virtue of SI 2000/1047 art 2(2)(*a*)(ii), Schedule, Pt I).

10 Words in sub-s (5)(*c*)(i) substituted by NICA 2002 s 6, Sch 1 paras 1, 6 with effect from 2003–04.

11 Words in sub-s (5A)(*b*) repealed by TCA 2002 s 60, Sch 6 with effect from 6 April 2003 (by virtue of SI 2003/962).

12 In sub-para (5A)(*c*) reference inserted by the Pensions Act 2008 s 104, Sch 4 paras 1, 2 with effect from 3 January 2012 (SI 2011/3033 art 2(*c*)(i), (ii)).

13 In sub-s (1), words inserted by the Social Security (Maternity Allowance) (Participating Wife or Civil Partner of Self-employed Earner) Regulations, SI 2014/606, reg 2(1), (2). This amendment comes into force on 1 April 2014 and has effect in relation to the payment of maternity allowance in cases where a woman's expected week of confinement (within the meaning of SSCBA 1992 s 35) begins on or after 27th July 2014.

14 In sub-s (1), words inserted by PeA 2014 s 15, Sch 11 paras 2, 3 with effect from 6 April 2016 (PeA 2014 s 56(1), (4)).

Prospective amendments—Words in sub-ss (1), (2), (4), (5A) to be repealed and inserted by the Welfare Reform Act 2007 s 67, Sch 8 with effect from a date to be appointed.

In sub-s (2), in table, entries for "bereavement payment" and "bereavement allowance" to be repealed, and sub-s (4) to be repealed by PeA 2014 s 31, Sch 16 paras 2, 4 with effect from a date to be appointed.

22 Earnings factors

(1) A person shall, for the purposes specified in subsection (2) below, be treated as having annual earnings factors derived—

(*a*) in the case of 1987–88 or any subsequent tax year, from [so much of his earnings as did not exceed the upper earnings limit and][4] upon which primary Class 1 contributions have been paid or treated as paid and from Class 2 and Class 3 contributions; and

(*b*) in the case of any earlier tax year, from his contributions of any of Classes 1, 2 and 3;

but subject to the following provisions of this section and those of section 23 below.

(2) The purposes referred to in subsection (1) above are those of—

(*a*) establishing, by reference to the satisfaction of contribution conditions, entitlement to [a contribution-based jobseeker's allowance[, to a contributory employment and support allowance][6] or to][1] any benefit specified in section 20(1) above, other than maternity allowance; . . . [8]

(*b*) calculating the additional pension in the rate of a long-term benefit[; and

(*c*) establishing entitlement to a state pension under Part 1 of the Pensions Act 2014 and, where relevant, calculating the rate of a state pension under that Part.][8]

[(2A) For the purposes specified in subsection (2)(*b*) above, in the case of the first appointed year or any subsequent tax year a person's earnings factor shall be treated as derived only from [so much of his earnings as did not exceed the [the applicable limit][5] and][4] on which primary Class 1 contributions have been paid or treated as paid.][3] [This subsection does not affect the operation of sections 44A and 44B (deemed earnings factors).][5]

[(2B) "The applicable limit" means—

(*a*) in relation to a tax year before [2009–10][7], the upper earnings limit;

(*b*) in relation to [2009–10][7] or any subsequent tax year, the upper accrual point.][5]

(3) Separate earnings factors may be derived for 1987–88 and subsequent tax years—

(*a*) from earnings [not exceeding the upper earnings limit][4] upon which primary Class 1 contributions have been paid or treated as paid;

(*b*) from earnings which have been credited;

(*c*) from contributions of different classes paid or credited in the same tax year;

(*d*) by any combination of the methods mentioned in paragraphs (*a*) to (*c*) above,

and may be derived for any earlier tax year from contributions of different classes paid or credited in the same tax year, and from contributions which have actually been paid, as opposed to those not paid but credited.

(4) Subject to regulations under section 19(4) to (6) above, no earnings factor shall be derived—

(*a*) for 1987–88 or any subsequent tax year, from earnings [in respect of which][2] primary Class 1 contributions are paid at the reduced rate, or

(*b*) for any earlier tax year, from primary Class 1 contributions paid at the reduced rate or from secondary Class 1 contributions.

(5) Regulations may provide for crediting—

(*a*) for 1987–88 or any subsequent tax year, earnings or Class 2 or Class 3 contributions, or
(*b*) for any earlier tax year, contributions of any class,

for the purpose of bringing a person's earnings factor for that tax year to a figure which will enable him to satisfy contribution conditions of entitlement to [a contribution-based jobseeker's[, to a contributory employment and support allowance][6] allowance or to][1] any prescribed description of benefit (whether his own entitlement or another person's).

[(5ZA) Regulations may provide for crediting—

(*a*) for 1987–88 or any subsequent tax year, earnings or Class 2 or Class 3 contributions, or
(*b*) for any earlier tax year, contributions of any class,

for the purpose of bringing an earnings factor for that tax year to a figure which will make that year a "qualifying year", "precommencement qualifying year" or "post-commencement qualifying year" of a person for the purposes of Part 1 of the Pensions Act 2014 (see sections 2(4) and 4(4) of that Act).

(5ZB) Regulations under subsection (5ZA) must provide for crediting a person with such contributions as may be specified in respect of periods on or after 6 April 1975 during which the person was—

(*a*) a spouse or civil partner of a member of Her Majesty's forces,
(*b*) accompanying the member on an assignment outside the United Kingdom, and
(*c*) not of a description specified in the regulations.][8]

[(5A) Section 23A makes provision for the crediting of Class 3 contributions for the purpose of determining entitlement to the benefits to which that section applies.][5]

(6) Regulations may impose limits with respect to the earnings factors which a person may have or be treated as having in respect of any one tax year.

(7) The power to amend regulations made before 30th March 1977 (the passing of the Social Security (Miscellaneous Provisions) Act 1977) under subsection (5) above may be so exercised as to restrict the circumstances in which and the purposes for which a person is entitled to credits in respect of weeks before the coming into force of the amending regulations; but not so as to affect any benefit for a period before the coming into force of the amending regulations if it was claimed before 18th March 1977.

[(8) In this section, "contributory employment and support allowance" means a contributory allowance under Part 1 of the Welfare Reform Act 2007 (employment and support allowance).][6]

[(9) References in this Act or any other Act to earnings factors derived from so much of a person's earnings as do not exceed the upper accrual point or the upper earnings limit are to be read, in relation to earners paid otherwise than weekly, as references to earnings factors derived from so much of those earnings as do not exceed the prescribed equivalent.][7]

HMRC Manuals—National Insurance Manual NIM01202 (background)
NIM01205 (class 1 structural overview from April 2009: the upper accrual point (UAP)).

Regulations—SS (Crediting and Treatment of Contributions, and National Insurance Numbers) Regulations, SI 2001/769.
Social Security (Credits) (Amendment) Regulations, SI 2010/385.
Social Security (Miscellaneous Amendments) (No 3) Regulations, SI 2013/2536.

Amendments—[1] Words in sub-ss (2)(*a*), (5) inserted by the Jobseekers Act 1995, s 41(4), Sch 2, para 22.

[2] Words in sub-s (4)(*a*) substituted by the Social Security Act 1998, s 86(1), Sch 7, para 61 with effect from 6 April 1999 (by virtue of the Social Security Act 1998 (Commencement No 3) Order, SI 1999/ 418 art 2(2), (3)(*a*)).

[3] Sub-s (2A) inserted by the Child Support, Pensions and Social Security Act 2000 ss 30(1), 86 with effect from 8 January 2001 for the purposes only of making regulations and orders, from 25 January 2001 for the purposes of making reports and orders under the Pension Schemes Act 1993 ss 42, 42B, 45A and from 6 April 2002 for all other purposes.

[4] Words in sub-ss (1)(*a*), (2A) substituted, and words in sub-s (3)(*a*) inserted, by the NIC Act 2002 s 6, Sch 1 paras 1, 7 with effect from 2003–04.

[5] Words in sub-s (2A) substituted and inserted, and sub-ss (2B), (5B) inserted, by the Pensions Act 2007 ss 3(3), 12(1), Sch 1 paras 9, 33 with effect from 26 September 2007 (s 30(3)).

[6] Words in sub-ss (2), (5),and whole of sub-s (8), inserted, by the Welfare Reform Act 2007 s 28(1), Sch 3 para 9(1), (4) with effect as follows—

- The amendment to sub-s (2) from 27 October 2008: SI 2008/787, art 2(4)(*f*).
- The amendment to sub-s (5) and the insertion of sub-s (8), for the purpose of making regulations, from 18 March 2008: SI 2008/787 art 2(1), Schedule; and for remaining purposes from 27 October 2008: SI 2008/787, art 2(4)(*f*).

[7] In sub-s (2B), words substituted for words "the flat rate introduction year" (in both places), and sub-s (9) inserted, by the NIC Act 2008 ss 3(1), (2), 4, Sch 1 para 1(1), (2) with effect from the end of the period of two months beginning with the day on which the Act was passed. The Act was passed on 21 July 2008, therefore this amendment has effect from 21 September 2008.

[8] In sub-s (2)(*a*), word "and" at the end repealed, sub-s (2)(*c*) and preceding word inserted, and sub-ss (5ZA), (5ZB) inserted, by PeA 2014 s 23, Sch 12 paras 2, 6 with effect from 6 April 2016 (PeA 2014 s 56(1), (4)).

Prospective amendments—In sub-ss (2)(*a*), (5), word "an" to be substituted for words "a contributory" by the Welfare Reform Act 2012 s 33, Sch 3 paras 1, 3 with effect from a date to be appointed.

In sub-ss (2)(*a*), (5), words "contribution-based", and whole of sub-s (8), to be repealed, by the Welfare Reform Act 2012 s 147, Sch 14 Part 13 with effect from a date to be appointed.

Sub-s (2)(*d*) and preceding word "and" to be inserted by PeA 2014 s 31, Sch 16 paras 2, 5 with effect from a date to be appointed. Sub-s (2)(*d*) as inserted to read as follows—

"(*d*) establishing entitlement to bereavement support payment under section 30 of the Pensions Act 2014.".

Unemployment benefit

[25A Determination of days for which unemployment benefit is payable]

Amendments—This section inserted by the Social Security (Incapacity for Work) Act 1994 s 11(1), Sch 1 Pt I, para 5, with effect from 13 April 1995 by virtue of SI 1994/2926 and repealed by the Jobseekers Act 1995 Sch 3, with effect from 7 October 1996 by virtue of SI 1996/2208.

Provisions relating to unemployment benefit, sickness and invalidity benefit

57 Determination of days for which benefit is payable

Amendments—This section repealed by the Social Security (Incapacity for Work) Act 1994 s 11, Sch 1 Pt I, para 14, and replaced by a new s 25A to this Act, inserted by the 1994 Act, s 11(1), Sch 1 Pt I para 5, with effect from 13 April 1995, by virtue of SI 1994/2926, and repealed by the Jobseekers Act 1995 Sch 3. with effect from 7 October 1996 by virtue of SI 1996/2208.

PART VI

MISCELLANEOUS PROVISIONS RELATING TO PARTS I TO V

Earnings

112 Certain sums to be earnings

(1) [The Treasury may by regulations made with the concurrence of the Secretary of State][2] provide—

(*a*) that any employment protection entitlement shall be deemed for the purposes of Parts I to V of this Act to be earnings payable by and to such persons as are prescribed and to be so payable in respect of such periods as are prescribed; and

(*b*) that those periods shall, so far as they are not periods of employment, be deemed for those purposes to be periods of employment.

(2) In subsection (1) above "employment protection entitlement" means—

(*a*) any sum, or a prescribed part of any sum, mentioned in subsection (3) below; and

(*b*) prescribed amounts which the regulations provide are to be treated as related to any of those sums.

[(2A) Regulations under subsection (2) above shall be made by the Treasury with the concurrence of the Secretary of State.][2]

(3) The sums referred to in subsection (2) above are the following—

(*a*) a sum payable in respect of arrears of pay in pursuance of an order for reinstatement or re-engagement under [the Employment Rights Act 1996][1];

(*b*) a sum payable by way of pay in pursuance of an order under that Act [or the Trade Union and Labour Relations (Consolidation) Act 1992][1] for the continuation of a contract of employment;

(*c*) a sum payable by way of remuneration in pursuance of a protective award under [the Trade Union and Labour Relations (Consolidation) Act 1992][1].

Commentary—*Simon's Taxes* **E8.232, E8.256.**

HMRC Manuals—National Insurance Manual NIM07021 (legislation: unfair dismissal: pay arrears under a reinstatement order: Nics treatment).

NIM07042 (unfair dismissal: pay under an order for the continuation of a contract of employment: Nics treatment).

NIM07052 (redundancy: protective awards: Nics treatment).

Former enactments—Sub-ss (1), (2); SS (Miscellaneous Provisions) Act 1977 s 18(1).

Sub-s (3): SS (Miscellaneous Provisions) Act 1977 s 18(2); Employment Protection (Consolidation) Act 1978 s 159(2), Sch 16 para 29(*d*); SSA 1986 s 86, Sch 10 para 74.

Regulations—See SS (Contributions) (Employment Protection) Regulations, SI 1977/622; SS(Contributions) Regulations, SI 2001/1004, reg 5.

Amendments—[1] Words in square brackets substituted or inserted by the Employment Rights Act 1996 s 240, Sch 1 para 51(1), (4).

[2] Words in sub-s (1) substituted and sub-s (2A) inserted by the Social Security Contributions (Transfer of Functions, etc) Act 1999 s 2, Sch 3 para 10 with effect from 1 April 1999 by virtue of the Social Security Contributions (Transfer of Functions, etc) Act 1999 (Commencement No 1 and Transitional Provisions) Order, SI 1999/527.

Special cases

115 Crown employment—Parts I to VI

(1) Subject to the provisions of this section, Parts I to V and this Part of this Act apply to persons employed by or under the Crown in like manner as if they were employed by a private person.

(2) Subsection (1) above does not apply to persons serving as members of Her Majesty's forces in their capacity as such.

(3) Employment as a member of Her Majesty's forces and any other prescribed employment under the Crown are not, and are not to be treated as, employed earner's employment for any of the purposes of Part V of this Act.

(4) The references to Parts I to V of this Act in this section and sections 116, 117, 119, 120 and 121 below do not include references to section 111 above.

Former enactments—SSA 1975 s 127.

NIC

116 Her Majesty's forces

(1) Subject to section 115(2) and (3) above and to this section, a person who is serving as a member of Her Majesty's forces shall, while he is so serving, be treated as an employed earner, in respect of his membership of those forces, for the purposes—

(*a*) of Parts I to V and this Part of this Act; and

(*b*) of any provision of the Administration Act in its application to him as an employed earner.

(2) [The Treasury may with the concurrence of the Secretary of State][4] make regulations modifying Parts I to V and this Part of this Act [and Part II of the Social Security Contributions (Transfer of Functions, etc) Act 1999][3], and any [provisions of Chapter II of Part I of the Social Security Act 1998 which correspond to][2] provisions of Part III of the 1975 Act, in such manner as [the Treasury think][4] proper, in their application to persons who are or have been members of Her Majesty's forces; and regulations under this section may in particular provide, in the case of persons who are employed earners in respect of their membership of those forces, for reducing the rate of the contributions payable in respect of their employment and for determining—

(*a*) the amounts payable on account of those contributions by the Secretary of State and the time and manner of payment, and

(*b*) the deduction (if any) to be made on account of those contributions from the pay of those persons.][1]

(3) For the purposes of Parts I to V and this Part of this Act, Her Majesty's forces shall be taken to consist of such establishments and organisations as may be prescribed [by regulations made by the Treasury with the concurrence of the Secretary of State][4], being establishments and organisations in which persons serve under the control of the Defence Council.

Commentary—*Simon's Taxes* **E8.296**.

HMRC Manuals—National Insurance Manual NIM32002–32007 (special cases- HM forces).

Former enactments—SSA 1975 s 128(1)–(3).

Cross reference—SS (Contributions) Regulations, SI 2001/1004 Sch 6 (prescribed establishments and organisations for the purposes of sub-s 116(3)).

Amendments—[1] Words in sub-s (2) substituted by the Jobseekers Act 1995 Sch 2 para 28 with effect from 7 October 1996, by virtue of SI 1996/2208.

[2] Words in sub-s (2) substituted by SSA 1998 Sch 7 para 67 with effect from 5 July 1999, for certain purposes (by virtue of the Social Security Act 1998 (Commencement No 8, and Savings and Consequential and Transitional Provisions) Order, SI 1999/1958, art 2(1)(*b*) (subject to transitional provisions contained in art 5 Sch 12 thereof)), 6 September 1999, for certain purposes (by virtue of the Social Security Act 1998 (Commencement No 9, and Savings and Consequential and Transitional Provisions) Order, SI 1999/2422, art 2(*c*) (subject to transitional provisions contained in art 4 Sch 14 thereof)), 18 October 1999, for certain purposes (by virtue of the Social Security Act 1998 (Commencement No 11, and Savings and Consequential and Transitional Provisions) Order, SI 1999/2860, art 2, Sch 1 (subject to transitional provisions contained in art 4 Schs 16–18 thereof)), 29 November 1999, for certain purposes (by virtue of the Social Security Act 1998 (Commencement No 12 and Consequential and Transitional Provisions) Order, SI 1999/3178, art 2(1), Sch 1 (subject to transitional provisions contained in art 4 Schs 21–23 thereof)),and with effect from a date to be appointed for all other purposes. Previous text read "provision of Part II of the Administration Act which replaces".

[3] Words in sub-s (2) inserted by the Social Security Contributions (Transfer of Functions, etc) Act 1999 s 18 and Sch 7 para 5 with effect from 4 March 1999 for the purpose of authorising the making of Regulations and 1 April 1999 for all other purposes by virtue of the Social Security Contributions (Transfer of Functions, etc) Act 1999 (Commencement No 1 and Transitional Provisions) Order, SI 1999/527.

[4] Words in sub-s (2) substituted, and words in sub-s (3) inserted by the Social Security Contributions (Transfer of Functions, etc) Act 1999 s 2, Sch 3 para 22 with effect from 1 April 1999 by virtue of the Social Security Contributions (Transfer of Functions, etc) Act 1999 (Commencement No 1 and Transitional Provisions) Order, SI 1999/527.

117 Mariners, airmen, etc

(1) [The Treasury may with the concurrence of the Secretary of State][2] make regulations modifying provisions of Parts I to V and this Part of this Act [and Part II of the Social Security Contributions (Transfer of Functions, etc) Act 1999][3], and any [provisions of Chapter II of Part I of the Social Security Act 1998 which correspond to][1] provisions of Part III of the 1975 Act, in such manner as [the Treasury think][2] proper, in their application to persons who are or have been, or are to be, employed on board any ship, vessel, hovercraft or aircraft.

(2) Regulations under subsection (1) above may in particular provide—

(*a*) for any such provision to apply to such persons, notwithstanding that it would not otherwise apply;

(*b*) for excepting such persons from the application of any such provision where they neither are domiciled nor have a place of residence in any part of Great Britain;

(*c*) for requiring the payment of secondary Class 1 contributions in respect of such persons, whether or not they are (within the meaning of Part I of this Act) employed earners;

(*d*) for the taking of evidence, for the purposes of any claim to benefit, in a country or territory outside Great Britain, by a British consular official or such other person as may be prescribed;

(*e*) for enabling persons who are or have been so employed to authorise the payment of the whole or any part of any benefit to which they are or may become entitled to such of their dependants as may be prescribed.

HMRC Manuals—National Insurance Manual NIM27002–27010 (application of this section to aircrew). NIM29002–29024 (application of this section to mariners).

Former enactments—SSA 1975 s 129.
Cross reference—SS (Contributions) Regulations, SI 2001/1004 regs 115–125 (treatment of mariners).
RegulationsSocial Security (Contributions) (Re-rating) Consequential Amendment Regulations, SI 2011/1001.
Social Security (Contributions) (Re-rating) Consequential Amendment Regulations, SI 2012/867.
Social Security (Contributions) (Re-rating) Consequential Amendment Regulations, SI 2013/619.
Social Security (Contributions) (Re-rating) Consequential Amendment Regulations, SI 2014/634.
Social Security (Contributions) (Re-rating) Consequential Amendment Regulations, SI 2017/416.
Amendments—[1] Words in sub-s (1) substituted by SSA 1998 Sch 7 para 68 with effect from 5 July 1999, for certain purposes (by virtue of the Social Security Act 1998 (Commencement No 8, and Savings and Consequential and Transitional Provisions) Order, SI 1999/1958, art 2(1)(*b*) (subject to transitional provisions contained in art 5 Sch 12 thereof)), 6 September 1999, for certain purposes (by virtue of the Social Security Act 1998 (Commencement No 9, and Savings and Consequential and Transitional Provisions) Order, SI 1999/2422, art 2(*c*) (subject to transitional provisions contained in art 4 Sch 14 thereof)), 18 October 1999, for certain purposes (by virtue of the Social Security Act 1998 (Commencement No 11, and Savings and Consequential and Transitional Provisions) Order, SI 1999/2860, art 2, Sch 1 (subject to transitional provisions contained in art 4 Schs 16–18 thereof)), 29 November 1999, for certain purposes (by virtue of the Social Security Act 1998 (Commencement No 12 and Consequential and Transitional Provisions) Order, SI 1999/3178, art 2(1), Sch 1 (subject to transitional provisions contained in art 4 Schs 21–23 thereof)), and with effect from a date to be appointed for all other purposes. Previous text read "provision of Part II of the Administration Act which replaces".
[2] Words in sub-s (1) substituted by the Social Security Contributions (Transfer of Functions, etc) Act 1999 s 2, Sch 3 para 23 with effect from 1 April 1999 by virtue of the Social Security Contributions (Transfer of Functions, etc) Act 1999 (Commencement No 1 and Transitional Provisions) Order, SI 1999/527.
[3] Words in sub-s (1) inserted by the Social Security Contributions (Transfer of Functions, etc) Act 1999 s 18 and Sch 7 para 6 with effect from 4 March 1999 for the purpose of authorising the making of Regulations and 1 April 1999 for all other purposes by virtue of the Social Security Contributions (Transfer of Functions, etc) Act 1999 (Commencement No 1 and Transitional Provisions) Order, SI 1999/527.

118 Married women and widows

[The Treasury may with the concurrence of the Secretary of State][1] make regulations modifying any of the following provisions of this Act, namely—

(*a*) Part I;
(*b*)–(*c*) . . . ,

in such manner as [the Treasury think][1] proper, in their application to women who are or have been married.

HMRC Manuals—National Insurance Manual NIM30002–30017 (Married women : operations of this section).
NIM31002 - 31019 (special cases and conditions: Widows: Liability of women widowed on or after 6 April 1978).
Former enactments—SSA 1975 s 130.
Note—Paras (*b*), (*c*) are outside the scope of this Publication.
Cross reference—SS (Contributions) Regulations, SI 2001/1004 regs 126–139 (treatment of married women and widows).
Regulations—Social Security (Contributions) (Amendment No 2) Regulations, SI 2003/964.
Amendments—[1] Words substituted by the Social Security Contributions (Transfer of Functions, etc) Act 1999 s 2, Sch 3 para 24 with effect from 1 April 1999 by virtue of the Social Security Contributions (Transfer of Functions, etc) Act 1999 (Commencement No 1 and Transitional Provisions) Order, SI 1999/527.

119 Persons outside Great Britain

[The Treasury may with the concurrence of the Secretary of State][3] make regulations modifying Parts I to V of this Act [and Part II of the Social Security Contributions (Transfer of Function, etc) Act 1999][2], and any [provisions of Chapter II of Part I of the Social Security Act 1998 which correspond to][1] provisions of Part III of the 1975 Act, in such manner as [the Treasury think][3] proper, in their application to persons who are or have been outside Great Britain at any prescribed time or in any prescribed circumstances.

HMRC Manuals—National Insurance Manual NIM06900 (rest of the world (ROW) countries).
NIM13021 (liability for Class 1A NICs - conditions).
NIM16475 (workers from the rest of the world: posted workers).
NIM18150 (class 1B Nics: liability: residence and presence conditions).
NIM20050 (residency conditions : calss 2 Nics).
NIM33505 -33580 (International - Row: operations under this section).
NIM34035 (specific provisions relating to the payment of the special rate of class 2 NIC: residence and presence abroad).
NIM70050 (class 2 Nics: general information: residency conditions).
Former enactments—SSA 1975 s 131.
Regulations—Social Security (Miscellaneous Amendments No 2) Regulations, SI 2015/478.
Cross reference—SS (Contributions) Regulations, SI 2001/1004 regs 145–148 (residence and persons abroad).
Amendments—[1] Words substituted by SSA 1998 Sch 7 para 69 with effect from 5 July 1999, for certain purposes (by virtue of the Social Security Act 1998 (Commencement No 8, and Savings and Consequential and Transitional Provisions) Order, SI 1999/1958, art 2(1)(*b*) (subject to transitional provisions contained in art 5 Sch 12 thereof)), 6 September 1999, for certain purposes (by virtue of the Social Security Act 1998 (Commencement No 9, and Savings and Consequential and Transitional Provisions) Order, SI 1999/2422, art 2(*c*) (subject to transitional provisions contained in art 4 Sch 14 thereof)), 18 October 1999, for certain purposes (by virtue of the Social Security Act 1998 (Commencement No 11, and Savings and Consequential and Transitional Provisions) Order, SI 1999/2860, art 2, Sch 1 (subject to transitional provisions contained in art 4 Schs 16–18 thereof)), 29 November 1999, for certain purposes (by virtue of the Social Security Act 1998 (Commencement No 12 and Consequential and Transitional Provisions) Order, SI 1999/3178, art 2(1), Sch 1 (subject to transitional provisions contained in art 4 Schs 21–23 thereof)), and with effect from a date to be appointed for all other purposes. Previous text read "provision of Part II of the Administration Act which replaces".

2 Words inserted by the Social Security Contributions (Transfer of Functions, etc) Act 1999 s 18 and Sch 7 para 7 with effect from 4 March 1999 for the purpose of authorising the making of Regulations and 1 April 1999 for all other purposes by virtue of the Social Security Contributions (Transfer of Functions, etc) Act 1999 (Commencement No 1 and Transitional Provisions) Order, SI 1999/527.

3 Words substituted by the Social Security Contributions (Transfer of Functions, etc) Act 1999 s 2, Sch 3 para 25 with effect from 1 April 1999 by virtue of the Social Security Contributions (Transfer of Functions, etc) Act 1999 (Commencement No 1 and Transitional Provisions) Order, SI 1999/527.

120 Employment at sea (continental shelf operations)

(1) [The Treasury may with the concurrence of the Secretary of State][4] make regulations modifying Parts I to V and this Part of this Act [and Part II of the Social Security Contributions (Transfer of Function, etc) Act 1999][3], and any [provisions of Chapter II of Part I of the Social Security Act 1998 which correspond to][1] provisions of Part III of the 1975 Act, in such manner as [the Treasury think][4] proper, in their application to persons [("continental shelf workers")][5] in any prescribed employment (whether under a contract of service or not) in connection with continental shelf operations.

(2) "Continental shelf operations" means any activities which, if paragraphs (*a*) and (*d*) of [subsection (8) of section 11 of the Petroleum Act 1998][2] (application of civil law to certain offshore activities) were omitted, would nevertheless fall within subsection (2) of that section.

(3) In particular (but without prejudice to the generality of subsection (1) above), [regulations under subsection (1)][5] may provide for any prescribed provision of Parts I to V and this Part of this Act to apply to any [continental shelf worker][5] notwithstanding that he does not fall within the description of an employed or self-employed earner, or does not fulfil the conditions prescribed under section 1(6) above as to residence or presence in Great Britain.

[(4) The Treasury may also, by regulations, make provision for, and in connection with, the issue by Her Majesty's Revenue and Customs of certificates to prescribed persons who are, by virtue of regulations under subsection (1), to be treated as the secondary contributor in relation to the payment of earnings to or for the benefit of one or more continental shelf workers—

(*a*) confirming that the prescribed person's liabilities to pay contributions in respect of the continental shelf workers specified or described in the certificate are being met by another person, and

(*b*) discharging the prescribed person, while the certificate is in force, from liability to make any payments in respect of the contributions, in the event that the other person fails to pay them in full.

(5) Regulations under subsection (4) may, in particular, make provision about—

(*a*) applying for a certificate;

(*b*) the circumstances in which a certificate may, or must, be issued or cancelled;

(*c*) the form and content of a certificate;

(*d*) the effect of a certificate (including provision modifying the effect mentioned in subsection (4)(b) or specifying further effects);

(*e*) the effect of cancelling a certificate.][5]

Commentary—*Simon's Taxes* **E8.718**.

HMRC Manuals—National Insurance Manual NIM28002 -28007 (continental shelf operations : class 1 Nics).

Former enactments—Sub-s (1): SSA 1975 s 132(1).

Sub-s (2): SSA 1975 s 132(2); Oil and Gas (Enterprise) Act 1982 s 37, Sch 3 para 21.

Regulations—Social Security (Contributions) (Amendment No 2) Regulations, SI 2014/572.

Social Security (Contributions) (Amendment No 4) Regulations, SI 2016/1067.

Cross reference—SS (Contributions) Regulations, SI 2001/1004 reg 114 (employment in connection with the continental shelf).

FA 2016 s 101(4) (application of sub-s (4) to the apprenticeship levy).

Amendments—1 Words in sub-s(1) substituted by SSA 1998 Sch 7 para 70 with effect from 5 July 1999, for certain purposes (by virtue of the Social Security Act 1998 (Commencement No 8, and Savings and Consequential and Transitional Provisions) Order, SI 1999/1958, art 2(1)(*b*) (subject to transitional provisions contained in art 5 Sch 12 thereof)), 6 September 1999, for certain purposes (by virtue of the Social Security Act 1998 (Commencement No 9, and Savings and Consequential and Transitional Provisions) Order, SI 1999/2422, art 2(*c*) (subject to transitional provisions contained in art 4 Sch 14 thereof)), 18 October 1999, for certain purposes (by virtue of the Social Security Act 1998 (Commencement No 11, and Savings and Consequential and Transitional Provisions) Order, SI 1999/2860, art 2, Sch 1 (subject to transitional provisions contained in art 4 Schs 16–18 thereof)), 29 November 1999, for certain purposes (by virtue of the Social Security Act 1998 (Commencement No 12 and Consequential and Transitional Provisions) Order, SI 1999/3178, art 2(1), Sch 1 (subject to transitional provisions contained in art 4 Schs 21–23 thereof)), and with effect from a date to be appointed for all other purposes. Previous text read "provision of Part II of the Administration Act which replaces".

2 Words in sub-s (2) substituted by Petroleum Act 1998 s 50, Sch 4 para 30 with effect from 15 February 1999 (by virtue of SI 1999/161).

3 Words in sub-s (1) inserted by the Social Security Contributions (Transfer of Functions, etc) Act 1999 s 18 and Sch 7 para 8 with effect from 4 March 1999 for the purpose of authorising the making of Regulations and 1 April 1999 for all other purposes by virtue of the Social Security Contributions (Transfer of Functions, etc) Act 1999 (Commencement No 1 and Transitional Provisions) Order, SI 1999/527.

4 Words in sub-s (1) substituted by the Social Security Contributions (Transfer of Functions, etc) Act 1999 s 2, Sch 3 para 26 with effect from 1 April 1999 by virtue of the Social Security Contributions (Transfer of Functions, etc) Act 1999 (Commencement No 1 and Transitional Provisions) Order, SI 1999/527.

5 In sub-s (1), words inserted, in sub-s (3) words substituted for words "the regulations" and "such person", and sub-ss (4), (5) inserted, by the NICs Act 2014 s 12 with effect from 13 March 2014.

121 Treatment of certain marriages

(1) Regulations [made by the Treasury with the concurrence of the Secretary of State][2] may provide—

(*a*) for a voidable marriage which has been annulled, whether before or after the date when the regulations come into force, to be treated for the purposes of the provisions to which this subsection applies as if it had been a valid marriage which was terminated by divorce at the date of annulment;

[(*aa*) for a voidable civil partnership which has been annulled, whether before or after the date when the regulations come into force, to be treated for the purposes of the provisions to which this subsection applies as if it had been a valid civil partnership which was dissolved at the date of annulment;][3]

(*b*) as to the circumstances in which, for the purposes of the enactments to which this section [applies, a marriage during the subsistence of which a party to it is at any time married to more than one person is to be treated as having, or as not having, the same consequences as any other marriage.][1]

(2) Subsection (1) above applies—

(*a*) to any enactment contained in Parts I . . . or this Part of this Act; and

(*b*) to regulations under any such enactment.

Commentary—*Simon's Taxes* **E8.1015**.
Former enactments—SSA 1975 s 162.
Note—Words omitted from sub-s (2)(*a*) are outside the scope of this Publication.
Regulations—The Social Security (Contributions) (Amendment No. 2) Regulations, SI 2012/817.
Amendments—[1] Words in sub-s (1)(*b*) substituted by the Private International Law (Miscellaneous Provisions) Act 1995 Schedule para 4(1) with effect from 8 January 1996.

[2] Words in sub-s (1) inserted by the Social Security Contributions (Transfer of Functions, etc) Act 1999 s 2, Sch 3 para 27 with effect from 1 April 1999 by virtue of the Social Security Contributions (Transfer of Functions, etc) Act 1999 (Commencement No 1 and Transitional Provisions) Order, SI 1999/527.

[3] Sub-s (1)(*aa*) inserted by the Civil Partnership Act 2004 s 254(1), Sch 24 para 40 with effect from 5 December 2005 (SI 2005/3175, art 2(1), Sch 1).

Interpretation

122 Interpretation of Parts I . . . and supplementary provisions

(1) In Parts I . . . above and this Part of this Act, unless the context otherwise requires—

["additional Class 4 percentage" is to be construed in accordance with section 15(3ZA)(*b*) above;][8]

["additional primary percentage" is to be construed in accordance with section 8(2)(*b*) above;][8]

["age-related secondary percentage" is to be construed in accordance with section 9A(2) above;][29]

["Bank of England base rate" means—

(*a*) the rate announced from time to time by the Monetary Policy Committee of the Bank of England as the official dealing rate, being the rate at which the Bank is willing to enter into transactions for providing short term liquidity in the money markets, or

(*b*) where an order under section 19 of the Bank of England Act 1998 is in force, any equivalent rate determined by the Treasury under that section;][12]

"beneficiary", in relation to any benefit, means the person entitled to that benefit;

"benefit" means—

(*a*) benefit under Parts II to V of this Act other than Old Cases payments;

(*b*) as respects any period before 1st July 1992 but not before 6th April 1975, benefit under Part II of the 1975 Act; or

(*c*) as respects any period before 6th April 1975, benefit under—

(i) the National Insurance Act 1946 or 1965; or

(ii) the National Insurance (Industrial Injuries) Act 1946 or 1965;

[(For the meaning of "benefit" in Part 1, see also section 19B)][13]

["the benefits code" has the meaning given by section 63(1) of ITEPA 2003;][10]

["child" has the same meaning as in Part 9 of this Act;][14]

"claim" is to be construed in accordance with "claimant";

"claimant", in relation to benefit other than industrial injuries benefit, means a person who has claimed benefit;

"claimant", in relation to industrial injuries benefit, means a person who has claimed industrial injuries benefit;

"contract of service" means any contract of service or apprenticeship whether written or oral and whether express or implied;

["contribution-based jobseeker's allowance" has the same meaning as in the Jobseekers Act 1995;][2]

"current", in relation to the lower and upper earnings limits [and primary and secondary thresholds][6] under section 5(1) above, means for the time being in force;

NIC

["day of interruption of employment" has the meaning given by section 25A(1)(*c*) above;][1]
["deferred" and "period of deferment"—

(*a*) in relation to a Category A or Category B retirement pension, have the meanings given by section 55(3), and

(*b*) in relation to a shared additional pension, have the meanings given by section 55C(3);][15]

"earner" and "earnings" are to be construed in accordance with sections 3, 4 and 112 above;
"employed earner" has the meaning assigned to it by section 2 above;
"employment" includes any trade, business, profession, office or vocation and "employed" has a corresponding meaning;
["the employment income Parts of ITEPA 2003" means Parts 2 to [7A][26] of that Act;][10]
"entitled", in relation to any benefit, is to be construed in accordance with—

(*a*) the provisions specifically relating to that benefit;

(*b*) in the case of a benefit specified in section 20(1) above, section 21 above; and

(*c*) sections 1 to 3 [of the Administration Act and section 27 of the Social Security Act 1998][16];

. . . [31]

["first appointed year" means such tax year, no earlier than 2002–03, as may be appointed by order, and "second appointed year" means such subsequent tax year as may be so appointed;][7]
["the flat rate introduction year" means such tax year as may be designated as such by order;][24]
["general earnings" has the meaning given by section 7 of ITEPA 2003 and accordingly sections 3 and 112 of this Act do not apply in relation to the word "earnings" when used in the expression "general earnings";][10]
"industrial injuries benefit" means benefit under Part V of this Act, other than under Schedule 8;
. . . [3]
"the Inland Revenue" means the Commissioners of Inland Revenue;
["ITEPA 2003" means the Income Tax (Earnings and Pensions) Act 2003;][10]
"late husband", in relation to a woman who has been more than once married, means her last husband;
"long-term benefit" has the meaning assigned to it by section 20(2) above;
"loss of physical faculty" includes disfigurement whether or not accompanied by any loss of physical faculty;
["lower earnings limit", "upper earnings limit" ["primary threshold" and secondary threshold"][6] are to be construed in accordance with subsection (1) of section 5 above, and references to the lower or upper earnings limit, or to [the primary or secondary][6] threshold, of a tax year are to whatever is (or was) for that year the limit or threshold in force under that subsection;][3]
["lower-paid employment as a minister of religion" has the meaning given by section 290D of ITEPA 2003;][31]
. . . [3]
["main Class 4 percentage" is to be construed in accordance with section 15(3ZA) above;][8]
["main primary percentage" is to be construed in accordance with section 8(2) above;][8]
"medical examination" includes bacteriological and radiographical tests and similar investigations, and "medically examined" has a corresponding meaning;
"medical treatment" means medical, surgical or rehabilitative treatment (including any course or diet or other regimen), and references to a person receiving or submitting himself to medical treatment are to be construed accordingly;
"the Northern Ireland Department" means the Department of Health and Social Services for Northern Ireland;
"Old Cases payments" means payments under Part I or II of Schedule 8 to this Act;
["PAYE settlement agreement" has the same meaning as in [Chapter 5 of Part 11 of ITEPA 2003][10];][4]
"payments by way of occupational or personal pension" means, in relation to a person, periodical payments which, in connection with the coming to an end of an employment of his, fall to be made to him—

(*a*) out of money provided wholly or partly by the employer or under arrangements made by the employer; or

(*b*) out of money provided under an enactment or instrument having the force of law in any part of the United Kingdom or elsewhere; or

(*c*) under a personal pension scheme as defined in section 84(1) of the 1986 Act; or

[(*d*) under a pension scheme registered under section 153 of the Finance Act 2004,][17]

and such other payments as are prescribed;

["pensionable age" has the meaning given by the rules in paragraph 1 of Schedule 4 to the Pensions Act 1995][18];
["PPF periodic payments" means—

(*a*) any periodic compensation payments made in relation to a person, payable under the pension compensation provisions as specified in section 162(2) of the Pensions Act 2004 or Article 146(2) of the Pensions (Northern Ireland) Order 2005 (the pension compensation provisions); or

(*b*) any periodic payments made in relation to a person, payable under section 166 of the Pensions Act 2004 or Article 150 of the Pensions (Northern Ireland) Order 2005 (duty to pay scheme benefits unpaid at assessment date etc);][19]

"pneumoconiosis" means fibrosis of the lungs due to silica dust, asbestos dust, or other dust, and includes the condition of the lungs known as dust-reticulation;

"prescribe" means prescribe by regulations;

. . . [9]

"qualifying earnings factor" means an earnings factor equal to the lower earnings limit for the tax year in question multiplied by 52;

["qualifying young person" has the same meaning as in Part 9 of this Act;][20]

["Regulation (EC) No 1408/71" means Council Regulation (EC) No 1408/71 of 14 June 1971 on the application of social security schemes to employed persons, to self-employed persons and to members of their families moving within the Community;][27]

["Regulation (EC) No 883/2004" means Regulation (EC) No 883/2004 of the European Parliament and of the Council of 29 April 2004 on the coordination of social security systems;][27]

"relative" includes a person who is a relative by marriage [or civil partnership][21];

"relevant accident" means the accident in respect of which industrial injuries benefit is claimed or payable;

"relevant injury" means the injury in respect of which industrial injuries benefit is claimed or payable;

"relevant loss of faculty" means—

(*a*) . . . [22]

(*b*) in relation to industrial injuries benefit, the loss of faculty resulting from the relevant injury;

["secondary percentage" is to be construed in accordance with section 9(2) above;][8]

"self-employed earner" has the meaning assigned to it by section 2 above;

"short-term benefit" has the meaning assigned to it by section 20(2) above;

"tax week" means one of the successive periods in a tax year beginning with the first day of that year and every seventh day thereafter, the last day of a tax year (or, in the case of a tax year ending in a leap year, the last two days) to be treated accordingly as a separate tax week;

"tax year" means the 12 months beginning with 6th April in any year, the expression "1978–79" meaning the tax year beginning with 6th April 1978, and any correspondingly framed reference to a pair of successive years being construed as a reference to the tax year beginning with 6th April in the earlier of them;

"trade or business" includes, in relation to a public or local authority, the exercise and performance of the powers and duties of that authority;

"trade union" means an association of employed earners;

["unit of additional pension" means a unit of additional pension for which a person has paid a Class 3A contribution under section 14A;][30]

["the upper accrual point" is to be construed in accordance with subsections (7) and (8) below;][24]

"week" . . . [11], means a period of 7 days beginning with Sunday.

["working life" has the meaning given by paragraph 5(8) of Schedule 3 to this Act][23].

[(1A) . . . [28]

(2) Regulations [made by the Treasury with the concurrence of the Secretary of State][5] may make provision modifying the meaning of "employment" for the purposes of any provision of Parts I . . . and this Part of this Act.

(3) Provision may be made [by the Treasury by regulations made with the concurrence of the Secretary of State][5] as to the circumstances in which a person is to be treated as residing or not residing with another person for any of the purposes of Parts I . . . and this Part of this Act and as to the circumstances in which persons are to be treated for any of those purposes as residing or not residing together.

(4)–(6) . . .

[(6A) The Treasury may by regulations prescribe an equivalent of the upper accrual point in relation to earners paid otherwise than weekly (and references in this or any other Act to "the prescribed equivalent", in the context of the upper accrual point, are to the equivalent prescribed under this subsection in relation to such earners).

(6B) The power conferred by subsection (6A) includes power to prescribe an amount which exceeds by not more than £1 the amount which is the arithmetical equivalent of the upper accrual point.][25]

(7), (8) . . . [25]

NIC

Commentary—*Simon's Taxes* **E8.249, E8.254, E8.260, E8.295, E8.318.**
HMRC Manuals—National Insurance Manual NIM08002 (general: alignment with tax weeks and months).
NIM02010 (meaning of "earnings").
Employment Income Manual EIM60066 (lower-paid employment as a minister of religion : meaning).
EIM76160 (Who qualifies for the state pension?).
Former enactments—SSA 1975 s 168(1), Sch 20; SS Pensions Act 1975 s 65(1), Sch 4 para 64; Health and Social Security Act 1984 s 13, Sch 5 para 7(*a*); SSA 1989 ss 1(9), 12(5); SSA 1990 s 21(1), Sch 6 para 11.
Note—Definitions omitted from this section are outside the scope of this Publication.
Regulations—Social Security Contributions (Intermediaries) Regulations, SI 2000/727.
SS (Crediting and Treatment of Contributions, and National Insurance Numbers) Regulations, SI 2001/769.
Social Security (Credits) (Amendment) Regulations 2010, SI 2010/385.
Social Security Benefits Up-rating Regulations, SI 2014/618.
Social Security Benefits Up-rating Regulations, SI 2015/496.
Social Security Contributions (Limited Liability Partnership) (Amendment) Regulations, SI 2015/607
Social Security (Contributions) (Amendment) (No 2) Regulations SI 2016/352.
Simon's Tax Cases—122(1), *Rashid v Garcia (Status Inspector)* [2003] STC (SCD) 36.
Amendments—[1] Definition of "day of interruption of employment" substituted by the Social Security (Incapacity for Work) Act 1994 s 11(1), Sch 1 Pt I para 30, with effect from 13 April 1995 by virtue of SI 1994/2926.
[2] Definition of "contribution-based jobseeker's allowance" inserted by the Jobseekers Act 1995 Sch 2 para 29 with effect from 7 October 1996 by virtue of SI 1996/2208.
[3] Definitions of "initial primary percentage" and "main primary percentage" repealed, definitions of "lower earnings limit", "upper earnings limit" and words in the definition of "primary percentage" substituted by SSA 1998 Sch 7 para 71 with effect from 6 April 1999 by virtue of the Social Security Act 1998 (Commencement No 3) Order, SI 1999/418.
[4] Definition of "PAYE settlement agreement" inserted by SSA 1998 Sch 7 para 71 with effect from 8 September 1998 by virtue of the Social Security Act 1998 (Commencement No 1) Order, SI 1998/2209 for the purpose only of authorising the making of regulations or orders, and with effect from 6 April 1999 in so far as it is not already in force.
[5] Words in sub-s (2) inserted and words in sub-s (3) substituted by the Social Security Contributions (Transfer of Functions, etc) Act 1999 s 2, Sch 3 para 28 with effect from 1 April 1999 by virtue of the Social Security Contributions (Transfer of Functions, etc) Act 1999 (Commencement No 1 and Transitional Provisions) Order, SI 1999/527.
[6] Words in definition "current" inserted and words in definition beginning "lower earnings limit" substituted by the Welfare Reform and Pensions Act 1999, s 84 Sch 12 paras 76, 77, with effect from 6 April 2000.
[7] Definition "first appointed year" inserted by the Child Support, Pensions and Social Security Act 2000 ss 35(1), (14), 86 with effect from 8 January 2001 for the purposes only of making regulations and orders, from 25 January 2001 for the purposes of making reports and orders under the Pension Schemes Act 1993 ss 42, 42B, 45A and from 6 April 2002 for all other purposes.
[8] Definitions "additional Class 4 percentage", "additional primary percentage", "main Class 4 percentage", "main primary percentage" and "secondary percentage" inserted by NICA 2002 s 7, Sch 1 paras 1, 12 with effect from 2003–04.
[9] Definition "primary percentage" repealed by NICA 2002 s 7, Sch 2 with effect from 2003–04.
[10] Definitions "the benefits code", "the employment income Parts of ITEPA 2003", "general earnings" and "ITEPA 2003" inserted, and in definition "PAYE settlement agreement", words substituted for the words "section 206A of the Income and Corporation Taxes Act 1988", by ITEPA 2003 s 722, Sch 6 paras 169, 178 with effect, for income tax purposes, from 2003–04; and for corporation tax purposes, for accounting periods ending after 5 April 2003. For transitional provisions and savings see ITEPA 2003 s 723, Sch 7.
[11] Words in the definition of "week" repealed by TCA 2002 s 60, Sch 6 with effect from 8 April 2003 (by virtue of SI 2003/962).
[12] In sub-s (1), definition of "Bank of England base rate" inserted by the Pensions Act 2004 s 297(4), Sch 11 paras 16, 18(*a*) with effect, for the purpose of making regulations, from 18 November 2004, and for remaining purposes, from 6 April 2005.
[13] In sub-s (1), in definition of "benefit", words inserted by PeA 2014 s 23, Sch 12 paras 2, 7 with effect from 6 April 2016 (PeA 2014 s 56(1), (4)).
[14] Definition "child" substituted by the Child Benefit Act 2005 s 1(3), Sch 1 paras 1, 8(1), (2).
[15] Definitions "'deferred' and 'period of deferment'" substituted by the Pensions Act 2004 s 297(4), Sch 11 paras 16, 18(*b*).
[16] In definition "entitled" words substituted by the Social Security Act 1998 s 86(1), Sch 7 para 71(*a*).
[17] In definition "payments by way of occupational or personal pension" para (*d*) substituted, for paras (*d*), (*e*) as originally enacted, by the Taxation of Pension Schemes (Consequential Amendments) Order, SI 2006/745 art 4(1), (3).
[18] Definition "pensionable age" substituted by the Pensions Act 1995 ss 126, 134(4), Sch 4 para 13(*a*).
[19] Definition "PPF periodic payments" inserted by the Pensions Act 2004 (PPF Payments and FAS Payments) (Consequential Provisions) Order, SI 2006/343 art 2, Schedule para 1(3).
[20] Definition "qualifying young person" inserted by the Child Benefit Act 2005 s 1(3), Sch 1 paras 1, 8(1), (3).
[21] In definition "relative" words inserted by the Civil Partnership Act 2004 s 254(1), Sch 24 para 41(1), (2).
[22] In definition "relevant loss of faculty" para (*a*) repealed by the Welfare Reform and Pensions Act 1999 s 88, Sch 13, Pt IV.
[23] Definition "working life" inserted by the Pensions Act 1995 ss 126, 134(4), Sch 4 para 13(*a*).
[24] Definition "the flat rate introduction year" inserted, by the Pensions Act 2007 ss 11(4), 12(3) with effect from 26 September 2007 (s 30(3)).
[25] In sub-s (1), definition "the upper accrual point" substituted, sub-ss (6A), (6B) inserted, and sub-ss (7), (8) repealed, by the NIC Act 2008 ss 3(1), (4), 4, Sch 2 with effect from the end of the period of two months beginning with the day on which the Act was passed. The Act was passed on 21 July 2008, therefore these amendments have effect from 21 September 2008.
[26] In sub-s (1) in the definition of "the employment income Parts of ITEPA 2003", reference substituted for reference "7", by FA 2011 s 26, Sch 2 para 50(*a*) with effect in relation to relevant steps taken on or after 6 April 2011.
[27] In sub-s (1), definitions inserted by the Social Security (Disability Living Allowance, Attendance Allowance and Carer's Allowance) (Miscellaneous Amendments) Regulations, SI 2011/2426 reg 5(1), (5) with effect from 31 October 2011.
[28] Sub-s (1A) repealed, in relation to England and Wales, by the Marriage (Same Sex Couples) Act 2013 (Consequential and Contrary Provisions and Scotland) Order, SI 2014/560 art 2, Sch 1 para 22(1), (7) with effect from 13 March 2014, and

in relation to Scotland, by the Marriage and Civil Partnership (Scotland) Act 2014 and Civil Partnership Act 2004 (Consequential Provisions and Modifications) Order, SI 2014/3229 art 5(3), Sch 4 para 2(1), (12) with effect from 16 December 2014.

29 Definition of "age-related secondary percentage" inserted by the NICs Act 2014 s 9(1), (4) with effect from 6 April 2015.

30 In sub-s (1), definition of "unit of additional pension" inserted by PeA 2014 s 25, Sch 15 paras 1, 10 with effect from 12 October 2015 (by virtue of SI 2015/1475).

31 In sub-s (1), definition of "excluded employment" repealed and the definition of "lower-paid employment as a minister of religion" inserted, by FA 2015 s 13, Sch 1 para 23 (1), (4) with effect for tax year 2016–17 and subsequent tax years.

Prospective amendments—In sub-s (1), definition of "contribution-based jobseeker's allowance" to be repealed by the Welfare Reform Act 2012 s 147, Sch 14 Part 1 with effect from a date to be appointed.

PART XI
STATUTORY SICK PAY

Cross references—See the SS Administration Act 1992 s 17(1)(*g*) (determination by Secretary of State of certain questions arising under any provision of this Part).

151 Employer's liability

(1) Where an employee has a day of incapacity for work in relation to his contract of service with an employer, that employer shall, if the conditions set out in sections 152 to 154 below are satisfied, be liable to make him, in accordance with the following provisions of this Part of this Act, a payment (to be known as "statutory sick pay") in respect of that day.

(2) Any agreement shall be void to the extent that it purports—

(*a*) to exclude, limit or otherwise modify any provision of this Part of this Act, or

(*b*) to require an employee to contribute (whether directly or indirectly) towards any costs incurred by his employer under this Part of this Act.

(3) For the avoidance of doubt, any agreement between an employer and an employee authorising any deductions from statutory sick pay which the employer is liable to pay to the employee in respect of any period shall not be void by virtue of subsection (2)(*a*) above if the employer—

(*a*) is authorised by that or another agreement to make the same deductions from any contractual remuneration which he is liable to pay in respect of the same period, or

(*b*) would be so authorised if he were liable to pay contractual remuneration in respect of that period.

(4) For the purposes of this Part of this Act [a day of incapacity for work in relation to a contract of service means a day on which][1] the employee concerned is, or is deemed in accordance with regulations to be, incapable by reason of some specific disease or bodily or mental disablement of doing work which he can reasonably be expected to do under that contract.

(5) In any case where an employee has more than one contract of service with the same employer the provisions of this Part of this Act shall, except in such cases as may be prescribed and subject to the following provisions of this Part of this Act, have effect as if the employer were a different employer in relation to each contract of service.

(6) Circumstances may be prescribed in which, notwithstanding the provisions of subsections (1) to (5) above, the liability to make payments of statutory sick pay is to be a liability of the[Commissioners of Inland Revenue][2].

[(7) Regulations under subsection (6) above must be made with the concurrence of the Commissioners of Inland Revenue.][2]

Commentary—*Simon's Taxes* **E8.601,E8.603**.

Former enactments—Sub-ss (1), (2): Social Security and Housing Benefits Act 1982 s (1), (2).

Sub-s (3): Social Security and Housing Benefits Act 1982 s 23A(1); Health and Social Security Act 1984 s 21, Sch 7 para 8.

Sub-s (4), (5): Social Security and Housing Benefits Act 1982 s 1(3), (4).

Sub-s (6): Social Security and Housing Benefits Act 1982 s 1(5); SSA 1986 s 68.

Cross references—See the Statutory Sick Pay (National Health Service Employees) Regulations, SI 1991/589 (election to treat more than one contract of employment as one contract where the employers are National Health Service Trusts).

Amendments—[1] Words in square brackets in sub-s (4) substituted by the Social Security (Incapacity for Work) Act 1994 s 11(1), Sch 1 Pt I para 34, with effect from 13 April 1995 by virtue of SI 1994/2926.

[2] Words in sub-s (6) substituted and sub-s (7) inserted by the Social Security Contributions (Transfer of Functions, etc) Act 1999 s 1(1) and Sch 1 para 9 with effect from 1 April 1999 by virtue of the Social Security Contributions (Transfer of Functions, etc) Act 1999 (Commencement No 1 and Transitional Provisions) Order, SI 1999/527.

158 Recovery by employers of amounts paid by way of statutory sick pay

Amendments—Section repealed subject to savings made by regulations under s 159A(4), by the Statutory Sick Pay Percentage Threshold Order, SI 1995/512 art 5(*a*), with effect from 6 April 1995.

159 Power to substitute provisions for s 158(2)

Amendments—Section repealed subject to savings made by regulations under s 159A(4), by the Statutory Sick Pay Percentage Threshold Order, SI 1995/512 art 5(*a*), with effect from 6 April 1995.

[159A Power to provide for recovery by employers of sums paid by way of statutory sick pay

(1) The Secretary of State may by order provide for the recovery by employers, in accordance with the order, of the amount (if any) by which their payments of, or liability incurred for, statutory sick pay in any period exceeds the specified percentage of the amount of their liability for contributions payments in respect of the corresponding period.

NIC

(2) An order under subsection (1) above may include provision—

(*a*) as to the periods by reference to which the calculation referred to above is to be made,

(*b*) for amounts which would otherwise be recoverable but which do not exceed the specified minimum for recovery not to be recoverable,

(*c*) for the rounding up or down of any fraction of a pound which would otherwise result from a calculation made in accordance with the order, and

(*d*) for any deduction from contributions payments made in accordance with the order to be disregarded for such purposes as may be specified,

and may repeal sections 158 and 159 above and make any amendments of other enactments which are consequential on the repeal of those sections.

(3) In this section—

"contributions payments" means payments which a person is required by or under any enactment to make in discharge of any liability of his as an employer in respect of primary or secondary Class 1 contributions; and

"specified" means specified in or determined in accordance with an order under subsection (1).

(4) The Secretary of State may by regulations make such transitional and consequential provision, and such savings, as he considers necessary or expedient for or in connection with the coming into force of any order under subsection (1) above.][1]

Regulations—Statutory Sick Pay Percentage Threshold Order, SI 1995/512, and Statutory Sick Pay Percentage Threshold Order 1995 (Consequential) Regulations, SI 1995/513.

Amendments—[1] Section inserted by the Statutory Sick Pay Act 1994 s 3(1), with effect from 10 February 1994.

Miscellaneous

161 Crown employment—Part XI

(1) Subject to subsection (2) below, the provisions of this Part of this Act apply in relation to persons employed by or under the Crown as they apply in relation to persons employed otherwise than by or under the Crown.

(2) The provisions of this Part of this Act do not apply in relation to persons serving as members of Her Majesty's forces, in their capacity as such.

(3) For the purposes of this section Her Majesty's forces shall be taken to consist of such establishments and organisations as may be prescribed [by regulations made by the Secretary of State with the concurrence of the Treasury][1], being establishments and organisations in which persons serve under the control of the Defence Council.

Commentary—*Simon's Taxes* **E8.603**.

Former enactments—Social Security and Housing Benefits Act 1982 s 27; SSA 1989 s 26, Sch 7 para 23.

Amendments—[1] Words in sub-s (3) inserted by the Social Security Contributions (Transfer of Functions, etc) Act 1999 s 1(1) and Sch 1 para 10 with effect from 1 April 1999 by virtue of the Social Security Contributions (Transfer of Functions, etc) Act 1999 (Commencement No 1 and Transitional Provisions) Order, SI 1999/527.

163 Interpretation of Part XI and supplementary provisions

(1) In this Part of this Act—

"contract of service" (except in paragraph (*a*) of the definition below of "employee") includes any arrangement providing for the terms of appointment of an employee;

"employee" means a person who is—

(*a*) gainfully employed in Great Britain either under a contract of service or in an office (including elective office) with [earnings (within the meaning of Parts 1 to 5 above)][2];

. . . [1]

but subject to regulations, which may provide for cases where any such person is not to be treated as an employee for the purposes of this Part of this Act and for cases where any person who would not otherwise be an employee for those purposes is to be treated as an employee for those purposes;

["employer", in relation to an employee and a contract of service of his, means a person who—

(*a*) under section 6 above is liable to pay secondary Class 1 contributions in relation to any earnings of the employee under the contract, or

(*b*) would be liable to pay such contributions but for—

(i) the condition in section 6(1)(*b*), or

(ii) the employee being under the age of 16:][1]

. . .

"period of incapacity for work" has the meaning given by section 152 above;

. . .

"prescribed" means prescribed by regulations;

. . .

"week" means any period of 7 days.

(2)–(7) . . .

Commentary—*Simon's Taxes* **E8.602**.

Modifications—The definitions of "employer" and "employee" in this section have effect for the tax year 2014–15 and subsequent tax years as if the salaried member were gainfully employed in Great Britain by the LLP under a contract of service with deemed employment income by virtue of ITTOIA 2005 s 863A or 863G(4) (see the Social Security Contributions (Limited Liability Partnership) Regulations, SI 2014/3159 reg 3(4)(*a*)).
Former enactments—Social Security and Housing Benefits Act 1982 s 26(1); SSA 1985 s 29(1), Sch 4 para 6.
Regulations—See the Statutory Sick Pay (Small Employers' Relief) Regulations, SI 1991/428; SS(CP)A 1992 s 2.
Note—Provisions omitted from this section are outside the scope of this Publication.
Amendments—[1] In sub-s (1), in definition of "employee", para (*b*) and preceding word "and" repealed, and definition of "employer" substituted, by the Employment Equality (Age) Regulations, SI 2006/1031 reg 49(1), Sch 8 para 9 with effect from 1 October 2006.
[2] In sub-s (1), in definition of "employee", in para (*a*) words substituted for words "general earnings (as defined by section 7 of the Income Tax (Earnings and Pensions) Act 2003)", by NICs Act 2014 s 15, Sch 2 paras 1, 3 with effect from 14 May 2014.

PART XII
STATUTORY MATERNITY PAY

[167 Funding of employers' liabilities in respect of statutory maternity pay

(1) Regulations shall make provision for the payment by employers of statutory maternity pay to be funded by the Commissioners of Inland Revenue to such extent as may be prescribed.
(2) Regulations under subsection (1) shall—
(*a*) make provision for a person who has made a payment of statutory maternity pay to be entitled, except in prescribed circumstances, to recover an amount equal to the sum of—
(i) the aggregate of such of those payments as qualify for small employers' relief; and
(ii) an amount equal to 92 per cent of the aggregate of such of those payments as do not so qualify; and
(*b*) include provision for a person who has made a payment of statutory maternity pay qualifying for small employers' relief to be entitled, except in prescribed circumstances, to recover an additional amount, determined in such manner as may be prescribed—
(i) by reference to secondary Class 1 contributions paid in respect of statutory maternity pay;
(ii) by reference to secondary Class 1 contributions paid in respect of statutory sick pay; or
(iii) by reference to the aggregate of secondary Class 1 contributions paid in respect of statutory maternity pay and secondary Class 1 contributions paid in respect of statutory sick pay.
(3) For the purposes of this section a payment of statutory maternity pay which a person is liable to make to a woman qualifies for small employers' relief if, in relation to that woman's maternity pay period, the person liable to make the payment is a small employer.
(4) For the purposes of this section "small employer", in relation to a woman's maternity pay period, shall have the meaning assigned to it by regulations, and, without prejudice to the generality of the foregoing, any such regulations—
(*a*) may define that expression by reference to the amount of a person's contributions payments for any prescribed period; and
(*b*) if they do so, may in that connection make provision for the amount of those payments for that prescribed period—
(i) to be determined without regard to any deductions that may be made from them under this section or under any other enactment or instrument; and
(ii) in prescribed circumstances, to be adjusted, estimated or otherwise attributed to him by reference to their amount in any other prescribed period.
(5) Regulations under subsection (1) may, in particular, make provision—
(*a*) for funding in advance as well as in arrear;
(*b*) for funding, or the recovery of amounts due under provision made by virtue of subsection (2)(*b*), by means of deductions from such amounts for which employers are accountable to the Commissioners of Inland Revenue as may be prescribed, or otherwise;
(*c*) for the recovery by the Commissioners of Inland Revenue of any sums overpaid to employers under the regulations.
(6) Where in accordance with any provision of regulations under subsection (1) an amount has been deducted from an employer's contributions payments, the amount so deducted shall (except in such cases as may be prescribed) be treated for the purposes of any provision made by or under any enactment in relation to primary or secondary Class 1 contributions—
(*a*) as having been paid (on such date as may be determined in accordance with the regulations), and
(*b*) as having been received by the Commissioners of Inland Revenue,
towards discharging the employer's liability in respect of such contributions.
(7) Regulations under this section must be made with the concurrence of the Commissioners of Inland Revenue.
(8)In this section "contributions payments", in relation to an employer, means any payments which the

employer is required, by or under any enactment, to make in discharge of any liability in respect of primary or secondary Class 1 contributions.][1]

Commentary—*Simon's Taxes* **E8.524**.

Regulations—Statutory Maternity Pay (Compensation of Employers) and Miscellaneous Amendment Regulations, SI 1994/1882.

Amendments—[1] This section substituted by EmA 2002 s 21(1) with effect from 6 April 2003 (by virtue of SI 2002/2866).

[PART 12ZA
[. . . [3] STATUTORY PATERNITY PAY[2]][1]

Modifications—SSCBA 1992 (Application of Parts 12ZA and 12ZB to Adoptions from Overseas) Regulations, SI 2003/499.

Amendments—[1] This Part inserted by EmA 2002 s 2 with effect only in relation to a person who satisfies the prescribed conditions of entitlement in respect of a child, born after 5 April 2003, or whose expected week of birth begins after that date, or, a child matched for the purposes of adoption with a person who is notified of having been matched after 5 April 2003, or placed for adoption after that date (by virtue of SI 2002/2866).

[2] Heading substituted by the Work and Families Act 2006 s 11 Sch 1 para 10 with effect from 6 April2010 (by virtue of SI 2010/495, art 4(*d*)).

[3] In heading, words repealed by the Children and Families Act 2014 s 126, Sch 7 paras 6, 10 with effect from 5 April 2015 (by virtue of SI 2014/1640 art 7).

[171ZD Liability to make payments

(1) The liability to make payments of . . . [3] statutory paternity pay under section 171ZA or 171ZB above is a liability of any person of whom the person entitled to the payments has been an employee as mentioned in subsection (2)(*b*) and (*d*) of that section.

(2) Regulations shall make provision as to a former employer's liability to pay [. . . [3] statutory paternity pay][2] to a person in any case where the former employee's contract of service with him has been brought to an end by the former employer solely, or mainly, for the purpose of avoiding [liability for . . . [3] statutory paternity pay . . . [3].][2]

(3) The Secretary of State may, with the concurrence of the Board, by regulations specify circumstances in which, notwithstanding this section, liability to make payments of statutory paternity pay is to be a liability of the Board.][1]

Commentary—*Simon's Taxes* **E8.541**.

Regulations—Statutory Paternity Pay and Statutory Adoption Pay (Parental Orders and Prospective Adopters) Regulations, SI 2014/2394.

Amendments—[1] This section inserted by EmA 2002 s 2 with effect only in relation to a person who satisfies the prescribed conditions of entitlement in respect of a child, born after 5 April 2003, or whose expected week of birth begins after that date, or, a child matched for the purposes of adoption with a person who is notified of having been matched after 5 April 2003, or placed for adoption after that date (by virtue of SI 2002/2866).

[2] In sub-s (1) word inserted, in sub-s (2) words substituted in both places by the Work and Families Act 2006 s 11 Sch 1 para 15 with effect from 6 April 2010 (by virtue of SI 2010/495, art 4(a), (d)).

[3] In sub-s (1), (2), words repealed by the Children and Families Act 2014 s 126, Sch 7 paras 6, 15 with effect from 5 April 2015 (by virtue of SI 2014/1640 art 7).

[171ZJ Part 12ZA: supplementary

(1) In this Part of this Act—

"the Board" means the Commissioners of Inland Revenue;

["employer", in relation to a person who is an employee, means a person who—

(*a*) under section 6 above is, liable to pay secondary Class 1 contributions in relation to any of the earnings of the person who is an employee; or

(*b*) would be liable to pay such contributions but for—

(i) the condition in section 6(1)(*b*), or

(ii) the employee being under the age of 16;][3]

["local authority" has the same meaning as in the Children Act 1989 (see section 105(1) of that Act);

"local authority foster parent" has the same meaning as in the Children Act 1989 (see [section 105(1)] of that Act);][7]][6]

"modifications" includes additions, omissions and amendments, and related expressions are to be read accordingly;

"prescribed" means prescribed by regulations.

(2) In this Part of this Act, "employee" means a person who is—

(*a*) gainfully employed in Great Britain either under a contract of service or in an office (including elective office) with [earnings (within the meaning of Parts 1 to 5 above)][2]; . . . [3]

(3) Regulations may provide—

(*a*) for cases where a person who falls within the definition in subsection (2) above is not to be treated as an employee for the purposes of this Part of this Act, and

(*b*) for cases where a person who would not otherwise be an employee for the purposes of this Part of this Act is to be treated as an employee for those purposes.

(4) Without prejudice to any other power to make regulations under this Part of this Act, regulations may specify cases in which, for the purposes of this Part of this Act or of such provisions of this Part of this Act as may be prescribed—

(*a*) two or more employers are to be treated as one;
(*b*) two or more contracts of service in respect of which the same person is an employee are to be treated as one.

(5) In this Part, except [section 171ZE][5], "week" means a period of 7 days beginning with Sunday or such other period as may be prescribed in relation to any particular case or class of cases.

(6) For the purposes of this Part of this Act, a person's normal weekly earnings shall, subject to subsection (8) below, be taken to be the average weekly earnings which in the relevant period have been paid to him or paid for his benefit under the contract of service with the employer in question.

(7) For the purposes of subsection (6) above, "earnings" and "relevant period" shall have the meanings given to them by regulations.

(8) In such cases as may be prescribed, a person's normal weekly earnings shall be calculated in accordance with regulations.

(9) Where—

(*a*) in consequence of the establishment of one or more National Health Service trusts under [the National Health Service Act 2006, the National Health Service (Wales) Act 2006][4] or the National Health Service (Scotland) Act 1978 (c 29), a person's contract of employment is treated by a scheme under [any of those Acts][4] as divided so as to constitute two or more contracts, or
(*b*) an order under [paragraph 26(1) of Schedule 3 to the National Health Service Act 2006][4] provides that a person's contract of employment is so divided,

regulations may make provision enabling the person to elect for all of those contracts to be treated as one contract for the purposes of this Part of this Act or such provisions of this Part of this Act as may be prescribed.

(10) Regulations under subsection (9) above may prescribe—

(*a*) the conditions that must be satisfied if a person is to be entitled to make such an election;
(*b*) the manner in which, and the time within which, such an election is to be made;
(*c*) the persons to whom, and the manner in which, notice of such an election is to be given;
(*d*) the information which a person who makes such an election is to provide, and the persons to whom, and the time within which, he is to provide it;
(*e*) the time for which such an election is to have effect;
(*f*) which one of the person's employers under two or more contracts is to be regarded for the purposes of [statutory paternity pay][5] as his employer under the contract.

(11) The powers under subsections (9) and (10) are without prejudice to any other power to make regulations under this Part of this Act.

(12) Regulations under any of subsections (4) to (10) above must be made with the concurrence of the Board.][1]

Commentary—*Simon's Taxes* **E8.541**.

Regulations—Statutory Paternity Pay and Statutory Adoption Pay (Parental Orders and Prospective Adopters) Regulations, SI 2014/2394.

Modifications—The definitions of "employer" and "employee" in this section have effect for the tax year 2014–15 and subsequent tax years as if the salaried member were gainfully employed in Great Britain by the LLP under a contract of service with deemed employment income by virtue of ITTOIA 2005 s 863A or 863G(4) (see the Social Security Contributions (Limited Liability Partnership) Regulations, SI 2014/3159 reg 3(4)(*c*)).

Amendments—[1] This section inserted by EmA 2002 s 2 with effect only in relation to a person who satisfies the prescribed conditions of entitlement in respect of a child, born after 5 April 2003, or whose expected week of birth begins after that date, or, a child matched for the purposes of adoption with a person who is notified of having been matched after 5 April 2003, or placed for adoption after that date (by virtue of SI 2002/2866).

[2] In sub-s (2)(*a*), words substituted for words "general earnings (as defined by section 7 of the Income Tax (Earnings and Pensions) Act 2003)", by NICs Act 2014 s 15, Sch 2 paras 1, 5 with effect from 14 May 2014.

[3] In sub-s (1), definition of "employer" substituted; sub-s (2)(*b*) and the word "and " preceding it omitted by the Employment Equality (Age) Regulations 2006, SI 2006/1031, reg 49(1) Sch 8 para 11 with effect in relation to an entitlement to—

(a) statutory paternity pay (birth) in respect of children whose expected week of birth begins on or after 14th January 2007;
(b) statutory paternity pay (adoption) in respect of children—
  (i) matched with a person who is notified of having been matched on or after the commencement date; or
  (ii) placed for adoption on or after the commencement date.

[4] Words in sub-s (9) substituted by the National Health Service (Consequential Provisions) Act 2006 s 2, Sch 1 paras 142, 149(*a*) with effect from 1 March 2007.

[5] In sub-ss (5), (10)(*f*), words substituted by the Children and Families Act 2014 s 126, Sch 7 paras 6, 21 with effect from 5 April 2015 (by virtue of SI 2014/1640 art 7).

[6] In sub-s (1), definitions of "local authority" and "local authority foster parent" inserted by the Children and Families Act 2014 s 121(7)(*a*) with effect from 30 June 2014 (by virtue of SI 2014/1640 art 3(1)(*e*)).

[7] In sub-s (1), in definition "local authority foster parent", words substituted by the Social Services and Well-being (Wales) Act 2014 (Consequential Amendments) Regulations, SI 2016/413 regs 130, 134 with effect from 6 April 2016.

Prospective amendments—In sub-s (9)(*a*), words "the National Health Service Act 2006," to be repealed by the Health and Social Care Act 2012 s 179, Sch 14 paras 58, 61 with effect from a date to be appointed.

PART 12ZB
STATUTORY ADOPTION PAY

Commentary—*Simon's Taxes* **E8.563, E8.564**.

Modifications—SSCBA (Application of Parts 12ZA and 12ZB to Adoptions from Overseas) Regulations, SI 2003/499.

Amendments—This Part inserted by EmA 2002 s 4. This Part came into force on 8 December 2002, with effect only in relation to a person with whom a child is, or is expected to be placed for adoption after 5 April 2003 (by virtue of SI 2002/2866).

[171ZM Liability to make payments

(1) The liability to make payments of statutory adoption pay is a liability of any person of whom the person entitled to the payments has been an employee as mentioned in section 171ZL(2)(*b*) above.

(2) Regulations shall make provision as to a former employer's liability to pay statutory adoption pay to a person in any case where the former employee's contract of service with him has been brought to an end by the former employer solely, or mainly, for the purpose of avoiding liability for statutory adoption pay.

(3) The Secretary of State may, with the concurrence of the Board, by regulations specify circumstances in which, notwithstanding this section, liability to make payments of statutory adoption pay is to be a liability of the Board.][1]

Regulations—Statutory Paternity Pay and Statutory Adoption Pay (Parental Orders and Prospective Adopters) Regulations, SI 2014/2394.

Amendments—[1] This section inserted by EmA 2002 s 4. This section came into force on 8 December 2002, with effect only in relation to a person with whom a child is, or is expected to be placed for adoption after 5 April 2003 (by virtue of SI 2002/2866).

[171ZS Part 12ZB: supplementary

(1) In this Part of this Act—

"adoption pay period" has the meaning given by section 171ZN(2) above;

"the Board" means the Commissioners of Inland Revenue;

["employer", in relation to a person who is an employee, means a person who—

(*a*) under section 6 above is liable to pay secondary Class 1 contributions in relation to any of the earnings of the person who is an employee; or

(*b*) would be liable to pay such contributions but for—

(ii) the condition in section 6(1)(*b*), or

(ii) the employee being under the age of 16;][2]

["local authority" has the same meaning as in the Children Act 1989 (see section 105(1) of that Act);][5]

["local authority foster parent" has the same meaning as in the Children Act 1989 (see [section 105(1)][6] of that Act);][5]

"modifications" includes additions, omissions and amendments, and related expressions are to be read accordingly;

"prescribed" means prescribed by regulations.

(2) In this Part of this Act, "employee" means a person who is—

(*a*) gainfully employed in Great Britain either under a contract of service or in an office (including elective office) with [earnings (within the meaning of Parts 1 to 5 above)][4];

. . . [2]

(3) Regulations may provide—

(*a*) for cases where a person who falls within the definition in subsection (2) above is not to be treated as an employee for the purposes of this Part of this Act, and

(*b*) for cases where a person who would not otherwise be an employee for the purposes of this Part of this Act is to be treated as an employee for those purposes.

(4) Without prejudice to any other power to make regulations under this Part of this Act, regulations may specify cases in which, for the purposes of this Part of this Act or of such provisions of this Part of this Act as may be prescribed—

(*a*) two or more employers are to be treated as one;

(*b*) two or more contracts of service in respect of which the same person is an employee are to be treated as one.

(5) In this Part, except sections 171ZN and 171ZP, "week" means a period of 7 days beginning with Sunday or such other period as may be prescribed in relation to any particular case or class of cases.

(6) For the purposes of this Part of this Act, a person's normal weekly earnings shall, subject to subsection (8) below, be taken to be the average weekly earnings which in the relevant period have been paid to him or paid for his benefit under the contract of service with the employer in question.

(7) For the purposes of subsection (6) above, "earnings" and "relevant period" shall have the meanings given to them by regulations.

(8) In such cases as may be prescribed, a person's normal weekly earnings shall be calculated in accordance with regulations.

(9) Where—

(*a*) in consequence of the establishment of one or more National Health Service trusts under [the National Health Service Act 2006, the National Health Service (Wales) Act 2006][3] or the National Health Service (Scotland) Act 1978 (c 29), a person's contract of employment is treated by a scheme under [any of those Acts][3] as divided so as to constitute two or more contracts, or

(*b*) an order under [paragraph 26(1) of Schedule 3 to the National Health Service Act 2006][3] provides that a person's contract of employment is so divided,

regulations may make provision enabling the person to elect for all of those contracts to be treated as one contract for the purposes of this Part of this Act or such provisions of this Part of this Act as may be prescribed.

(10) Regulations under subsection (9) above may prescribe—

(*a*) the conditions that must be satisfied if a person is to be entitled to make such an election;

(*b*) the manner in which, and the time within which, such an election is to be made;

(*c*) the persons to whom, and the manner in which, notice of such an election is to be given;

(*d*) the information which a person who makes such an election is to provide, and the persons to whom, and the time within which, he is to provide it;

(*e*) the time for which such an election is to have effect;

(*f*) which one of the person's employers under two or more contracts is to be regarded for the purposes of statutory adoption pay as his employer under the contract.

(11) The powers under subsections (9) and (10) are without prejudice to any other power to make regulations under this Part of this Act.

(12) Regulations under any of subsections (4) to (10) above must be made with the concurrence of the Board.][1]

NIC

Commentary—*Simon's Taxes* **E8.537, E8.540, E8.541**.

Regulations—Statutory Paternity Pay and Statutory Adoption Pay (Parental Orders and Prospective Adopters) Regulations, SI 2014/2394.

Modifications—The definitions of "employer" and "employee" in this section have effect for the tax year 2014–15 and subsequent tax years as if the salaried member were gainfully employed in Great Britain by the LLP under a contract of service with deemed employment income by virtue of ITTOIA 2005 s 863A or 863G(4) (see the Social Security Contributions (Limited Liability Partnership) Regulations, SI 2014/3159 reg 3(4)(*d*)).

Amendments—[1] This section inserted by EmA 2002 s 4. This section came into force on 8 December 2002, with effect only in relation to a person with whom a child is, or is expected to be placed for adoption after 5 April 2003 (by virtue of SI 2002/2866).

[2] In sub-s (1), definition of "employer" substituted; sub-s (2)(*b*) and the word "and" preceding it omitted by the Employment Equality (Age) Regulations 2006, SI 2006/1031, reg 49(1) Sch 8 para 12 with effect in relation to an entitlement to statutory adoption pay in respect of children—

(a) matched with a person who is notified of having been matched on or after the commencement date; or

(b) placed for adoption on or after that commencement.

The commencement date is 1 October 2006 (SI 2006/1031 reg 1(1)).

[3] Words in sub-s (9) substituted by the National Health Service (Consequential Provisions) Act 2006 s 2, Sch 1 paras 142, 150(*a*) with effect from 1 March 2007).

[4] In sub-s (2)(*a*), words substituted for words "general earnings (as defined by section 7 of the Income Tax (Earnings and Pensions) Act 2003)", by NICs Act 2014 s 15, Sch 2 paras 1, 6 with effect from 14 May 2014.

[5] In sub-s (1), entries inserted by the Children and Families Act 2014 s 121(7) with effect from 30 June 2014 (by virtue of SI 2014/1640 art 3).

[6] In sub-s (1), in definition "local authority foster parent", words substituted by the Social Services and Well-being (Wales) Act 2014 (Consequential Amendments) Regulations, SI 2016/413 regs 130, 137 with effect from 6 April 2016.

Prospective amendments—In sub-s (9)(*a*), words "the National Health Service Act 2006," to be repealed by the Health and Social Care Act 2012 s 179, Sch 14 paras 58, 62 with effect from a date to be appointed.

[PART 12ZC

[STATUTORY SHARED PARENTAL PAY]

Amendments—Part 12ZC inserted by the Children and Families Act 2014 s 119(1) with effect from 30 June 2014 (by virtue of SI 2014/1640 art 3).

[171ZX Liability to make payments

(1) The liability to make payments of statutory shared parental pay under section 171ZU or 171ZV is a liability of any person of whom the person entitled to the payments has been an employee as mentioned in section 171ZU(2)(*c*) or (4)(*d*) or 171ZV(2)(*c*) or (4)(*d*), as the case may be.

(2) Regulations must make provision as to a former employer's liability to pay statutory shared parental pay to a person in any case where the former employee's contract of service with the person has been brought to an end by the former employer solely, or mainly, for the purpose of avoiding liability for statutory shared parental pay.

(3) The Secretary of State may, with the concurrence of the Commissioners for Her Majesty's Revenue and Customs, by regulations specify circumstances in which, notwithstanding this section, liability to make payments of statutory shared parental pay is to be a liability of the Commissioners.][1]

Amendments—[1] Section 171ZX inserted by the Children and Families Act 2014 s 119(1) with effect from 30 June 2014 (by virtue of SI 2014/1640 art 3).

[171ZZ4 Part 12ZC: supplementary

(1) In this Part—

"adoption pay period" has the meaning given in section 171ZN(2);

"employer", in relation to a person who is an employee, means a person who—

(*a*) under section 6 is liable to pay secondary Class 1 contributions in relation to any of the earnings of the person who is an employee, or

(*b*) would be liable to pay such contributions but for—

(i) the condition in section 6(1)(*b*), or

(ii) the employee being under the age of 16;

"local authority" has the same meaning as in the Children Act 1989 (see section 105(1) of that Act);

"local authority foster parent" has the same meaning as in the Children Act 1989 (see [section 105(1)][2] of that Act);

"maternity allowance period" has the meaning given in section 35(2);

"maternity pay period" has the meaning given in section 165(1);

"modifications" includes additions, omissions and amendments, and related expressions are to be read accordingly;

"prescribed" means prescribed by regulations.

(2) In this Part "employee" means a person who is gainfully employed in Great Britain either under a contract of service or in an office (including elective office) with general earnings (as defined by section 7 of the Income Tax (Earnings and Pensions) Act 2003).

(3) Regulations may provide—

(*a*) for cases where a person who falls within the definition in subsection (2) is not to be treated as an employee for the purposes of this Part, and

(*b*) for cases where a person who would not otherwise be an employee for the purposes of this Part is to be treated as an employee for those purposes.

(4) Without prejudice to any other power to make regulations under this Part, regulations may specify cases in which, for the purposes of this Part or of such provisions of this Part as may be prescribed—

(*a*) two or more employers are to be treated as one;

(*b*) two or more contracts of service in respect of which the same person is an employee are to be treated as one.

(5) In this Part, except where otherwise provided, "week" means a period of seven days beginning with Sunday or such other period as may be prescribed in relation to any particular case or class of cases.

(6) For the purposes of this Part, a person's normal weekly earnings are, subject to subsection (8), to be taken to be the average weekly earnings which in the relevant period have been paid to the person or paid for the person's benefit under the contract of service with the employer in question.

(7) For the purposes of subsection (6) "earnings" and "relevant period" have the meanings given to them by regulations.

(8) In such cases as may be prescribed, a person's normal weekly earnings are to be calculated in accordance with regulations.

(9) Where—

(*a*) in consequence of the establishment of one or more National Health Service trusts under the National Health Service Act 2006, the National Health Service (Wales) Act 2006 or the National Health Service (Scotland) Act 1978, a person's contract of employment is treated by a scheme under any of those Acts as divided so as to constitute two or more contracts, or

(*b*) an order under paragraph 26(1) of Schedule 3 to the National Health Service Act 2006 provides that a person's contract of employment is so divided,

regulations may make provision enabling the person to elect for all of those contracts to be treated as one contract for the purposes of this Part or such provisions of this Part as may be prescribed.

(10) Regulations under subsection (9) may prescribe—

(*a*) the conditions that must be satisfied if a person is to be entitled to make such an election;

(*b*) the manner in which, and the time within which, such an election is to be made;

(*c*) the persons to whom, and the manner in which, notice of such an election is to be given;

(*d*) the information which a person who makes such an election is to provide, and the persons to whom, and the time within which, the person is to provide it;

(*e*) the time for which such an election is to have effect;

(*f*) which one of the person's employers under two or more contracts is to be regarded for the purposes of statutory shared parental pay as the person's employer under the contract.

(11) The powers under subsections (9) and (10) are without prejudice to any other power to make regulations under this Part.

(12) Regulations under any of subsections (4) to (10) must be made with the concurrence of the Commissioners for Her Majesty's Revenue and Customs.][1]

Amendments—[1] Section 171ZZ4 inserted by the Children and Families Act 2014 s 119(1) with effect from 30 June 2014 (by virtue of SI 2014/1640 art 3).

[2] In sub-s (1), in definition "local authority foster parent", words substituted by the Social Services and Well-being (Wales) Act 2014 (Consequential Amendments) Regulations, SI 2016/413 regs 130, 139 with effect from 6 April 2016.

PART XIII
GENERAL

Interpretation

172 Application of Act in relation to territorial waters

In this Act—

(*a*) any reference to Great Britain includes a reference to the territorial waters of the United Kingdom adjacent to Great Britain;

(*b*) any reference to the United Kingdom includes a reference to the territorial waters of the United Kingdom.

Commentary—*Simon's Taxes* **E8.702.**

Former enactments—Social Security and Housing Benefits Act 1982 ss 26(7), 44(2)(*a*), (*b*).

173 Age

For the purposes of this Act a person—

(*a*) is over or under a particular age if he has or, as the case may be, has not attained that age; and

(*b*) is between two particular ages if he has attained the first but not the second;

and in Scotland (as in England and Wales) the time at which a person attains a particular age expressed in years is the commencement of the relevant anniversary of the date of his birth.

Former enactments—SSA 1975 s 168(1), Sch 20.

174 References to Acts

In this Act—

"the 1975 Act" means the Social Security Act 1975;

"the 1986 Act" means the Social Security Act 1986;

"the Administration Act" means the Social Security Administration Act 1992;

"the Consequential Provisions Act" means the Social Security (Consequential Provisions) Act 1992;

"the Northern Ireland Contributions and Benefits Act" means the Social Security Contributions and Benefits (Northern Ireland) Act 1992;

. . . ; and

"the Pensions Act" means the [Pension Schemes Act 1993][1].

Note—Definition omitted is outside the scope of this Publication.

Amendments—[1] Words in definition of "the Pensions Act" substituted by the Pension Schemes Act 1993 Sch 8 para 41 with effect from 7 February 1994.

Subordinate legislation

175 Regulations, orders and schemes

(1) . . . regulations and orders under this Act shall be made by the Secretary of State.

[(1A) Subsection (1) above has effect subject to—

(*a*) any provision . . . [2] providing for regulations or an order to be made by the Treasury or by the Commissioners of Inland Revenue, . . . [2]

(*b*) . . . [2]][1]

(2) Powers under this Act to make regulations, orders or schemes shall be exercisable by statutory instrument.

(3) Except . . . in so far as this Act otherwise provides, any power under this Act to make regulations or an order may be exercised—

(*a*) either in relation to all cases to which the power extends, or in relation to those cases subject to specified exceptions, or in relation to any specified cases or classes of case;

(*b*) so as to make, as respects the cases in relation to which it is exercised—

(i) the full provision to which the power extends or any less provision (whether by way of exception or otherwise),

(ii) the same provision for all cases in relation to which the power is exercised, or different provision for different cases or different classes of case or different provision as respects the same case or class of case for different purposes of this Act,

(iii) any such provision either unconditionally or subject to any specified condition;

and where such a power is expressed to be exercisable for alternative purposes it may be exercised in relation to the same case for any or all of those purposes; and powers to make regulations or an order for the purposes of any one provision of this Act are without prejudice to powers to make regulations or an order for the purposes of any other provision.

(4) Without prejudice to any specific provision in this Act, any power conferred by this Act to make regulations or an order . . . includes power to make thereby such incidental, supplementary, consequential or transitional provision as appears to the [person making the regulations or order][1] to be expedient for the purposes of the regulations or order.

(5) Without prejudice to any specific provisions in this Act, a power conferred by any provision of this Act except—

(*a*) . . . ;

(*b*) section 122(1) above in relation to the definition of "payments by way of occupational or personal pension"; and

(*c*) Part XI,

to make regulations or an order includes power to provide for a person to exercise a discretion in dealing with any matter.

(6) . . .

(7) Any power of the Secretary of State under any provision of this Act, except the provisions mentioned in subsection (5)(*a*) *and* (*b*) above . . . , to make any regulations or order, where the power is not expressed to be exercisable with the consent of the Treasury, shall if the Treasury so direct be exercisable only in conjunction with them.

(8) . . .

(9) A power to make regulations under any of sections 116 to 120 above shall be exercisable in relation to any enactment passed after this Act which is directed to be construed as one with this Act; but this subsection applies only so far as a contrary intention is not expressed in the enactment so passed, and is without prejudice to the generality of any such direction.

(10) Any reference in this section or section 176 below to an order or regulations under this Act includes a reference to an order or regulations made under any provision of an enactment passed after this Act and directed to be construed as one with this Act; but this subsection applies only so far as a contrary intention is not expressed in the enactment so passed, and without prejudice to the generality of any such direction.

Former enactments—Sub-s (1): SSA 1975 s 168(1), Sch 20.
Sub-s (2)–(4): SSA 1975 s 166(1)–(3); SSA 1989 s 31(1), Sch 8 para 10(1).
Sub-s (5): SSA 1975 s 166(3A); SSA 1986 s 62(1).
Sub-s (7): SSA 1975 s 166(5).
Sub-s (9): SSA 1975 s 166(7).
Sub-s (10): SSA 1975 s 168(4).

Regulations—See the SS (Adjudication) Regulations, SI 1986/2218; SS(CP)A 1992 s 2.
Social Security Contributions (Intermediaries) Regulations, SI 2000/727.
SS (Crediting and Treatment of Contributions, and National Insurance Numbers) Regulations, SI 2001/769.
Social Security Contributions (Share Options) Regulations, SI 2001/1817.
Social Security (Contributions) (Amendment No. 3) Regulations, SI 2003/1059.
Social Security (Credits) (Amendment) Regulations 2010, SI 2010/385.
Social Security (Contributions) (Amendment No 4) Regulations, SI 2011/1000.
Social Security (Contributions) (Re-rating) Consequential Amendment Regulations, SI 2011/1001.
Social Security (Contributions) (Amendment) Regulations, SI 2012/573.
Social Security (Categorisation of Earners) (Amendment) Regulations, SI 2012/816.
Social Security (Contributions) (Amendment No 3) Regulations, SI 2012/821.
Social Security (Contributions) (Limits and Thresholds) (Amendment) Regulations, SI 2013/558.
Social Security (Contributions) (Re-rating) Consequential Amendment Regulations, SI 2013/619.
Social Security (Contributions) (Amendment and Application of Schedule 38 to the Finance Act 2012) Regulations, SI 2013/622.
Social Security (Contributions) (Amendment) Regulations, SI 2013/718.
Social Security (Miscellaneous Amendments) (No 3) Regulations, SI 2013/2536.
Social Security (Contributions) (Limits and Thresholds) (Amendment) Regulations, SI 2014/569.
Social Security (Contributions) (Amendment No 2) Regulations, SI 2014/572.
Social Security (Miscellaneous Amendments) Regulations, SI 2014/591.
Social Security (Contributions) (Amendment) Regulations, SI 2014/608.
Social Security Benefits Up-rating Regulations, SI 2014/618.
Social Security (Categorisation of Earners) (Amendment) Regulations, SI 2014/635.
Child Benefit (General) and Child Tax Credit (Amendment) Regulations, SI 2014/1231.
Child Benefit (General) and the Tax Credits (Residence) (Amendment) Regulations, SI 2014/1511.
Social Security (Contributions) (Amendment No 4) Regulations, SI 2014/2397.
Universal Credit and Miscellaneous Amendments (No 2) Regulations, SI 2014/2888.
Statutory Paternity Pay and Statutory Adoption Pay (Parental Orders and Prospective Adopters) Regulations, SI 2014/2394.
Social Security Contributions (Limited Liability Partnership) Regulations, SI 2014/3159.
Social Security (Contributions) (Amendment No 5) Regulations, SI 2014/3196.
Social Security (Miscellaneous Amendments) Regulations, SI 2015/67.
Social Security and Tax Credits (Miscellaneous Amendments) Regulations, SI 2015/175.
Social Security (Members of the Reserve Forces) (Amendment) Regulations, SI 2015/389.
Social Security (Miscellaneous Amendments No 2) Regulations, SI 2015/478.
Social Security Benefits Up-rating Regulations, SI 2015/496.
Social Security Contributions (Amendments in Consequence of Part 4 of the Finance Act 2014) Regulations, SI 2015/521.
Social Security (Contributions) (Amendment) Regulations, SI 2015/545.
Guardian's Allowance Up-rating Regulations, SI 2015/543.

Social Security (Contributions) (Limits and Thresholds) (Amendment) Regulations, SI 2015/577.
Social Security Contributions (Limited Liability Partnership) (Amendment) Regulations, SI 2015/607
Social Security Benefit (Computation of Earnings) (Amendment) Regulations, SI 2015/784.
Universal Credit and Miscellaneous Amendments Regulations, SI 2015/1754.
Social Security (Contributions) (Amendment) Regulations, SI 2016/117.
Social Security (Scottish Rate of Income Tax etc.) (Amendment) Regulations, SI 2016/233.
Social Security Benefit (Computation of Earnings) (Amendment) Regulations, 2016/267.
Social Security (Contributions) (Limits and Thresholds Amendments and National Insurance Funds Payments) Regulations, SI 2016/343.
Social Security (Contributions) (Amendment) (No 2) Regulations SI 2016/352.
Social Security (Miscellaneous Amendments) Regulations, SI 2017/307.
Social Security Benefits Up-rating Regulations, SI 2017/349.
Occupational Pension Schemes and Social Security (Schemes that were Contracted-out and Graduated Retirement Benefit) (Miscellaneous Amendments) Regulations, SI 2017/354.
Social Security (Miscellaneous Amendments No. 2) Regulations, SI 2017/373.
Guardian's Allowance Up-rating Regulations, SI 2017/412.
Social Security (Contributions) (Rates, Limits and Thresholds Amendments and National Insurance Funds Payments) Regulations, SI 2017/415.
Social Security (Contributions) (Re-rating) Consequential Amendment Regulations, SI 2017/416.
Social Security (Infected Blood and Thalidomide) Regulations, SI 2017/870.

Amendments—[1] Words in sub-ss (1) and (4) substituted, and sub-s (1A) inserted by the Social Security Contributions (Transfer of Functions, etc) Act 1999 s 2, Sch 3 para 29 with effect from 1 April 1999 by virtue of the Social Security Contributions (Transfer of Functions, etc) Act 1999 (Commencement No 1 and Transitional Provisions) Order, SI 1999/527.

[2] Words in sub-s (1A)(*a*) repealed, and sub-s (1A)(*b*) repealed, by TCA 2002 s 60, Sch 6 with effect from 1 April 2003 (by virtue of SI 2003/392).

Notes—Provisions omitted from this section are outside the scope of this Publication.
Section 175(7) above does not apply in relation to regulations made by the Treasury by virtue of the Tax Credits Act 1999 ss 2(1) and 25.

176 Parliamentary control

(1) Subject to the provisions of this section, a statutory instrument containing (whether alone or with other provisions)—

[(*za*) regulations under section 5 specifying the lower earnings limit for the tax year following the designated tax year (see section 5(4) of the Pensions Act 2007) or any subsequent tax year;][9]

[(*zb*) regulations under section 5 specifying the upper earnings limit;][11]

(*a*) regulations made by virtue of—

[section 4B(2);][6]
[section 4C;][6]
[section 9A(7);][13]
[section 9B(4), (8) or (10);][12]
[section 10ZC;][7]
[section 11(8) or (9)][18]
[section 14A;][16]
section 18;
section 19(4) to (6);
. . . ;
[section 45(2A);][16]
section 117;
section 118;
[section 18A;][14]
[section 130B(4);][8]
. . . ;
. . . [2];
[section 171ZE(1) [or (2)(*b*)][15];][5]
. . . [17]
. . . ;[17]
[any of sections 171ZU to 171ZY;][15]

[(*aa*) the first regulations made by virtue of section 23A(3)(*c*);][9]

[(*ab*) the first regulations made by virtue of section 130A(5) or (6);][19]

(*b*) . . . ;

(*bb*) . . . ;

(*c*) an order under—

. . . ;
. . . [2],

NIC

. . . [10]
[section 130D(2);][8]
[section 159A(1)][1]

shall not be made unless a draft of the instrument has been laid before Parliament and been approved by a resolution of each House.

(2) Subsection (1) above does not apply to a statutory instrument by reason only that it contains—

(*a*) regulations under section 117 which the instrument states are made for the purpose of making provision consequential on the making of an order under section 141, 143, 145, 146 or 162 of the Administration Act;

(*b*) regulations under powers conferred by any provision mentioned in paragraph (*a*) of that subsection . . . [2] which are to be made for the purpose of consolidating regulations to be revoked in the instrument;

(*c*) regulations which, in so far as they are made under powers conferred by any provision mentioned in paragraph (*a*) of that subsection (other than section . . . [2]), only replace provisions of previous regulations with new provisions to the same effect.

[(2A) In the case of a statutory instrument containing (whether alone or with other provisions) regulations made by virtue of section 4B(2) to which subsection (1) above applies, the draft of the instrument must be laid before Parliament before the end of the period of 12 months beginning with the appropriate date.][6]

[(2B) For the purposes of subsection (2A), the "appropriate date" means—

(*a*) where the corresponding retrospective tax provision was passed or made before the day on which the National Insurance Contributions Act 2006 was passed, the date upon which that Act was passed, and

(*b*) in any other case, the date upon which the corresponding retrospective tax provision was passed or made.][6]

[(2C) For the purposes of subsection (2B), "the corresponding retrospective tax provision" in relation to the regulations means—

(*a*) the retrospective tax provision mentioned in subsection (1) of section 4B in relation to which the regulations are to be made by virtue of subsection (2) of that section, or

(*b*) where there is more than one such tax provision, whichever of those provisions was the first to be passed or made.][6]

(3) A statutory instrument—

(*a*) which contains (whether alone or with other provisions) any order, regulations or scheme made under this Act by the Secretary of State, [the Treasury or the Commissioners of Inland Revenue,][3] . . . ; and

(*b*) which is not subject to any requirement that a draft of the instrument shall be laid before and approved by a resolution of each House of Parliament,

shall be subject to annulment in pursuance of a resolution of either House of Parliament.

[(4) Subsection (3) above does not apply to a statutory instrument by reason only that it contains an order appointing the first or second appointed year [or designating the flat rate introduction year][9] (within the meanings given by section 122(1) above).][4]

Former enactments—Sub-s (1): SSA 1975 s 167(1); SSA 1986 s 62(3).
Sub-ss (2), (3): SSA 1975 s 167(2), (3); SSA 1990 s 21(1), Sch 6 para 8(1).
Note—Provisions omitted from this section are outside the scope of this Publication.
Amendments—[1] Reference in square brackets in sub-s (1)(*c*) inserted by the Statutory Sick Pay Act 1994 s 3(2).

[2] Words omitted from sub-ss (1), (2) repealed by the Statutory Sick Pay Percentage Threshold Order, SI 1995/512 art 6(1)(*a*), with effect from 6 April 1995.

[3] Words in sub-s (3)(*a*) inserted by the Social Security Contributions (Transfer of Functions, etc) Act 1999 s 2, Sch 3 para 30 with effect from 1 April 1999 by virtue of the Social Security Contributions (Transfer of Functions, etc) Act 1999 (Commencement No 1 and Transitional Provisions) Order, SI 1999/527.

[4] Sub-s (4) inserted by the Child Support, Pensions and Social Security Act 2000 ss 35(1), (15), 86 with effect from 8 January 2001 for the purposes only of making regulations and orders, from 25 January 2001 for the purposes of making reports and orders under the Pension Schemes Act 1993 ss 42, 42B, 45A and from 6 April 2002 for all other purposes.

[5] Words in sub-s (1)(*a*) inserted by EmA 2002 s 53, Sch 7 paras 2, 7 with effect from 8 December 2002 (by virtue of SI 2002/2866).

[6] Entries in sub-s (1)(*a*) inserted, and sub-ss (2A)–(2C) inserted, by the National Insurance Contributions Act 2006 s 1(2) with effect from 30 March 2006.

[7] Entry in sub-s (1)(*a*) inserted by the National Insurance Contributions Act 2006 s 3(2) with effect from 30 March 2006.

[8] Words in sub-ss (1)(*a*), (*c*) to be inserted by the Welfare Reform Act 2007 s 31(2) with effect for the purpose of the exercise of the power to make regulations from 14 June 2007 (SI 2007/1721 art 2(1)) and for remaining purposes 1 November 2007 (SI 2007/1721 art 2(2)).

[9] Sub-s (1)(*za*), (*aa*), and words in sub-s (4), inserted by the Pensions Act 2007 ss 3(3), 7(1), (5), Sch 1 para 9(10) with effect from 26 September 2007 (s 30(3)).

[10] In sub-s (1)(*c*), entry "section 122(8);", previously inserted by the Pensions Act 2007 s 12(4), Sch 1 para 35, repealed by the National Insurance Contributions Act 2008 s 4(2), Sch 2 with effect from 21 September 2008.

[11] Sub-s (1)(*zb*) inserted by the NIC Act 2008 s 1(2) with effect in relation to regulations specifying the upper earnings limit for 2009–10 or any subsequent tax year.

12 In sub-s (1)(*a*), entry inserted by NICA 2015 s 1(5), (11) with effect from 6 April 2016. Note that, for the purposes of making regulations under SSCBA 1992 s 9B, the amendments made by NICA 2015 s 1 come into force on 12 April 2015.
13 Words in sub-s (1)(*a*) inserted by the NICs Act 2014 s 9(1), (5) with effect from 14 May 2014.
14 Words in sub-s (1)(*a*) inserted by NICs Act 2014 s 13(1), (3) with effect from 14 May 2014.
15 In sub-s (1)(*a*), entry inserted by the Children and Families Act 2014 s 119(2), with effect from 30 June 2014 (by virtue of SI 2014/1640 art 3).
16 In sub-s (1)(*a*), entries inserted by PeA 2014 s 25, Sch 15 paras 1, 11 with effect from 13 October 2014 (by virtue of SI 2014/2727 art 2).
17 In sub-s (1)(*a*), entries repealed by the Children and Families Act 2014 s 124(2) with effect from 5 April 2015 (by virtue of SI 2014/1640 arts 6, 7).
18 In sub-s (1)(*a*), words substituted by NICA 2015 s 2, Sch 1 paras 1, 8 with effect for the tax year 2015–16 and subsequent tax years.
19 In sub-s (1)(*ab*) inserted by the Welfare Reform Act 2012 s 69(4) with effect, for the purpose of making regulations only, from 27 November 2012 (by virtue of SI 2012/2946) and, for remaining purposes, with effect from 1 January 2013 (by virtue of SI 2012/2946). Note that s 69 itself is to be repealed by the Welfare Reform Act 2012 with effect from a date to be appointed.

Prospective amendments—Words in sub-s (1) to be repealed by the Welfare Reform Act 2007 s 67, Sch 8 with effect from a date to be appointed.

In sub-s (1)(*a*), words "or (2)(*b*)" to be inserted after words "section 171ZE(1)" by the Children and Families Act 2014 s 123(4) with effect from a date to be appointed.

Short title, commencement and extent

177 Short title, commencement and extent

(1) This Act may be cited as the Social Security Contributions and Benefits Act 1992.

(2) This Act is to be read, where appropriate, with the Administration Act and the Consequential Provisions Act.

(3) The enactments consolidated by this Act are repealed, in consequence of the consolidation, by the Consequential Provisions Act.

(4) Except as provided in Schedule 4 to the Consequential Provisions Act, this Act shall come into force on 1st July 1992.

(5) The following provisions extend to Northern Ireland—
section 16 and Schedule 2;
section 116(2); and
this section.

(6) Except as provided by this section, this Act does not extend to Northern Ireland.

Commentary—*Simon's Taxes* **E8.702**.

SCHEDULES

SCHEDULE 1

SUPPLEMENTARY PROVISIONS RELATING TO CONTRIBUTIONS OF CLASSES 1, 1A, [1B,][1] 2[, 3 AND 3A][2]

Section 1 (4)

Amendments—[1] Inserted by SSA 1998 Sch 7 para 77(1) with effect from 6 April 1999 by virtue of the Social Security Act 1998 (Commencement No 1) Order, SI 1998/2209.
2 In heading, words substituted for words "and 3" by PeA 2014 s 25, Sch 15 paras 1, 11 with effect from 12 October 2015 (by virtue of SI 2015/1475).

Class 1 contributions where earner employed in more than one employment

1—(1) For the purposes of determining whether Class 1 contributions are payable in respect of earnings paid to an earner in a given week and, if so, the amount of the contributions—

(*a*) all earnings paid to him or for his benefit in that week in respect of one or more employed earner's employments under the same employer shall, except as may be provided by regulations, be aggregated and treated as a single payment of earnings in respect of one such employment; and

(*b*) earnings paid to him or for his benefit in that week by different persons in respect of different employed earner's employments shall in prescribed circumstances be aggregated and treated as a single payment of earnings in respect of one such employment;

and regulations may provide that the provisions of this sub-paragraph shall have effect in cases prescribed by the regulations as if for any reference to a week there were substituted a reference to a period prescribed by the regulations.

(2), (3) . . . [3]

(4), (5) . . . [2]

[(6) . . . [3]

(7) Where any single payment of earnings is made in respect of two or more employed earner's employments under different employers, liability for Class 1 contributions shall be determined by apportioning the payment to such one or more of the employers as may be prescribed, and treating a part apportioned to any employer as a separate payment of earnings by him.
(8) Where earnings are aggregated under sub-paragraph (1)(*b*) above, liability (if any) for the secondary contribution shall be apportioned, in such manner as may be prescribed, between the secondary contributors concerned.
[(8A) Regulations under any provision of this paragraph shall be made by the Inland Revenue.][1]
(9)–(11) . . . [3]

Former enactments—Sub-para (1): SSA 1975 Sch 1 para 1(1); SS (Miscellaneous Provisions) Act 1977 s 1(3).
Sub-para (2): SSA 1975 Sch 1 para 1(1A); SSA 1980 s 2, Sch 1 para 16; SSA 1985 s 29(1), Sch 5 para 13(*a*).
Sub-paras (3), (4): SSA 1975 Sch 1 para 1(1B), (1C); SSA 1985 s 29(1), Sch 5 para 13(*b*).
Sub-para (5): SSA 1986 s 74(5).
Sub-para (6): SSA 1975 Sch 1 para 1(1D); SSA 1985 s 29(1), Sch 5 para 13(*b*).
Sub-paras (7), (8): SSA 1975 Sch 1 para 1(2), (3).
Cross reference—SS (Contributions) Regulations, SI 2001/1004 reg 13 (para 1 has effect as if references to "week" were substituted for references to "earnings period" for employees not paid weekly).
HMRC Manuals—National Insurance Manual NIM10001–10058 (operation of this para including worked examples).
Amendments—[1] Sub-para (8A) inserted by the Social Security Contributions (Transfer of Functions, etc) Act 1999 s 2, Sch 3 para 31 with effect from 1 April 1999 by virtue of the Social Security Contributions (Transfer of Functions, etc) Act 1999 (Commencement No 1 and Transitional Provisions) Order, SI 1999/527.
[2] Sub-paras (4), (5) repealed by the Welfare Reform and Pensions Act 1999 ss 84, 88, Sch 12 paras 76, 78, Sch 13, Pt VI with effect from 6 April 2000.
[3] Sub-paras (2), (3), (6), (9)–(11) repealed by PeA 2014 s 24, Sch 13 paras 48, 54 with effect from 6 April 2016 (PeA 2014 s 56(1), (4)).

Earnings not paid at normal intervals

2 Regulations [made by the Inland Revenue][1] may, for the purposes of Class 1 contributions, make provision as to the intervals at which payments of earnings are to be treated as made.
Former enactments—SSA 1975 Sch 1 para 2.
Amendments—[1] Words inserted by the Social Security Contributions (Transfer of Functions, etc) Act 1999 s 2, Sch 3 para 32 with effect from 1 April 1999 by virtue of the Social Security Contributions (Transfer of Functions, etc) Act 1999 (Commencement No 1 and Transitional Provisions) Order, SI 1999/527.

Method of paying Class 1 contributions

3—(1) Where earnings are paid to an employed earner and in respect of that payment liability arises for primary and secondary Class 1 contributions, the secondary contributor shall (except in prescribed circumstances), as well as being liable for [any secondary contribution of his own][2], be liable in the first instance to pay also the earner's primary contribution [or a prescribed part of the earner's primary contribution][5], on behalf of and to the exclusion of the earner; and for the purposes of this Act and the Administration Act contributions paid by the secondary contributor on behalf of the earner shall be taken to be contributions paid by the earner.
(2) . . . [4]
(3) A secondary contributor shall be entitled, subject to and in accordance with regulations, to recover from an earner the amount of any primary Class 1 contribution paid or to be paid by him on behalf of the earner; [and, subject to [sub-paragraphs (3A) to (5)][6] below but notwithstanding any other provision in any enactment][1] regulations under this sub-paragraph shall provide for recovery to be made by deduction from the earner's earnings, and for it not to be made in any other way.
[(3A) Sub-paragraph (3B) applies where a person ("the employee") who is employed by a particular employer ("the employer") receives earnings in a form other than money ("non-monetary earnings") from the employer in a tax year.][6]
[(3B) If and to the extent that regulations so provide, the employer may recover from the employee, in the prescribed manner, any primary Class 1 contributions paid or to be paid by him on the employee's behalf in respect of those earnings.][6]
[(4) Sub-paragraph (5) below applies in a case where—
(*a*) a person ("the employee") ceases in a particular tax year ("the cessation year") to be employed by a particular employer ("the employer"); and
(*b*) the employee receives from the employer in the cessation year, after the cessation of the employment, [or in the next tax year non-monetary earnings.][6]
(5) If and to the extent that regulations so provide, the employer may recover from the employee in such manner as may be prescribed any primary Class 1 contributions paid or to be paid by him on the employee's behalf in respect of—
(*a*) the non-monetary earnings mentioned in sub-paragraph (4) above; . . . [6]][1]
[(6) Regulations under any provision of this paragraph shall be made by the Inland Revenue.][3]
Former enactments—Sub-para (1): SSA 1975 Sch 1 para 3(1).
Sub-para (2): SSA 1975 Sch 1 para 3(2); Criminal Justice Act 1982 ss 38(2), 46(2).

Sub-para (3): SSA 1975 Sch 1 para 3(3).

Regulations—Social Security Contributions (Consequential Provisions) Regulations, SI 2007/1056 (this paragraph shall apply (to the extent that it does not otherwise) where an amount is retrospectively treated as earnings by regulations made by virtue of SSCBA 1992 s 4B(2)).

Amendments—[1] Words in sub-para (3) substituted and sub-paras (4) and (5) inserted by SSA 1998 s 55 with effect from 8 September 1998 by virtue of the Social Security Act 1998 (Commencement No 1) Order, SI 1998/2209.

[2] Words substituted by SSA 1998 Sch 7 para 77(5) with effect from 6 April 1999 by virtue of the Social Security Act 1998 (Commencement No 3) Order, SI 1999/418.

[3] Sub-para (6) inserted by the Social Security Contributions (Transfer of Functions, etc) Act 1999 s 2, Sch 3 para 33 with effect from 1 April 1999 by virtue of the Social Security Contributions (Transfer of Functions, etc) Act 1999 (Commencement No 1 and Transitional Provisions) Order, SI 1999/527.

[4] Sub-para (2) repealed by the Child Support, Pensions and Social Security Act 2000 ss 77(1), 85, Sch 9 Pt VIII with effect for the tax year beginning with 6 April 2000 and subsequent tax years.

[5] Words in sub-para (1) inserted by NICA 2002 s 6, Sch 1 paras 1, 13(1), (3) with effect from 2003–04.

[6] Words in sub-paras (3), (4) substituted; sub-paras (3A), (3B) inserted; and words in sub-para (5) repealed; by the NIC and Statutory Payments Act 2004 ss 1, 12 Sch 2 Pt 1 with effect from 1 September 2004 (by virtue of SI 2004/1943).

[Prohibition on recovery of employer's contributions

3A—(1) Subject to sub-paragraph (2) below, a person who is or has been liable to pay any secondary Class 1 or any Class 1A or Class 1B contributions shall not—

(*a*) make, from earnings paid by him, any deduction in respect of any such contributions for which he or any other person is or has been liable;

(*b*) otherwise recover any such contributions (directly or indirectly) from any person who is or has been a relevant earner; or

(*c*) enter into any agreement with any person for the making of any such deduction or otherwise for the purpose of so recovering any such contributions.

(2) Sub-paragraph (1) above does not apply to the extent that an agreement between—

(*a*) a secondary contributor, and

(*b*) any person ("the earner") in relation to whom the secondary contributor is, was or will be such a contributor in respect of the contributions to which the agreement relates,

allows the secondary contributor to recover (whether by deduction or otherwise) the whole or any part of any secondary Class 1 contribution payable in respect of [relevant employment income of that earner.][2]

[(2A) But an agreement in respect of relevant employment income is to be disregarded for the purposes of sub-paragraph (2) to the extent that it relates to[—

(*a*)] [3] relevant employment income which is employment income of the earner by virtue of Chapter 3A of Part 7 of ITEPA 2003 (employment income: securities with artificially depressed market value)[, or

(*b*) any contribution, or any part of any contribution, liability to which arises as a result of regulations being given retrospective effect by virtue of section 4B(2) (earnings: power to make retrospective provision in consequence of retrospective tax legislation)][3].][2]

[(2B) For the purposes of sub-paragraphs (2) and (2A) "relevant employment income", in relation to the earner, means—

(*a*) an amount that counts as employment income of the earner under section 426 of ITEPA 2003 (restricted securities: charge on certain post-acquisition events),

(*b*) an amount that counts as employment income of the earner under section 438 of that Act (convertible securities: charge on certain post-acquisition events), or

(*c*) a gain that is treated as remuneration derived from the earner's employment by virtue of section 4(4)(*a*) above.][2]

(3) Sub-paragraph (2) above does not authorise any recovery (whether by deduction or otherwise)—

(*a*) in pursuance of any agreement entered into before 19th May 2000; or

(*b*) in respect of any liability to a contribution arising before the day of the passing of the Child Support, Pensions and Social Security Act 2000.

(4) In this paragraph—

"agreement" includes any arrangement or understanding (whether or not legally enforceable); and

"relevant earner", in relation to a person who is or has been liable to pay any contributions, means an earner in respect of whom he is or has been so liable.][1]

Amendments—[1] Para 3A inserted by the Child Support, Pensions and Social Security Act 2000 s 77(2) with effect from 28 July 2000.

[2] Words in sub-para (2) substituted for the words "a gain that is treated as remuneration derived from that earner's employment by virtue of section 4(4)(*a*) above."; and sub-paras (2A), (2B) inserted; by the NIC and Statutory Payments Act 2004 s 3(1), (2) with effect for—

(a) agreements entered into after the date of commencement of the NIC and Statutory Payments Act 2004 s 3 which are in respect of post-commencement employment income, and

(b) elections made after that date: NIC and Statutory Payments Act 2004 s 3(4).

NIC and Statutory Payments Act 2004 s 3 came into force on 1 September 2004 (by virtue of SI 2004/1943). "Post-commencement employment income" means income which is relevant employment income within sub-para (2B) above, which, after the date of commencement of NIC and Statutory Payments Act 2004 s 3, counts as employment income for a tax year by virtue of ITEPA 2003 Pt 7: NIC and Statutory Payments Act 2004 s 3(5).

3 Words in sub-para (2A) inserted by the National Insurance Contributions Act 2006 s 5(1), (2), (4) with effect in relation to agreements and elections whether entered into or made before, or on or after, 30 March 2006 (including those entered into or made before 2 December 2004).

[Transfer of liability to be borne by earner

3B—(1) This paragraph applies where—

(*a*) an election is jointly made by—

(i) a secondary contributor, and

(ii) a person ("the earner") in relation to whom the secondary contributor is or will be such a contributor in respect of contributions on [relevant employment income of the earner][2],

for the whole or a part of any liability of the secondary contributor to contributions on any [such income][2] to be transferred to the earner; and

(*b*) the election is one in respect of which the Inland Revenue have, before it was made, given by notice to the secondary contributor their approval to both—

(i) the form of the election; and

(ii) the arrangements made in relation to the proposed election for securing that the liability transferred by the election will be met.

[(1A) In this paragraph "relevant employment income", in relation to the earner, means—

(*a*) an amount that counts as employment income of the earner under section 426 of ITEPA 2003 (restricted securities: charge on certain post-acquisition events),

(*b*) an amount that counts as employment income of the earner under section 438 of that Act (convertible securities: charge on certain post-acquisition events), or

(*c*) a gain that is treated as remuneration derived from the earner's employment by virtue of section 4(4)(*a*) above,

and references to contributions on relevant employment income are references to any secondary Class 1 contributions payable in respect of that income.][2]

(2) Any liability which—

(*a*) arises while the election is in force, and

(*b*) is a liability to pay the contributions on [relevant employment income of the earner, or the part of it][2], to which the election relates,

shall be treated for the purposes of this Act, the Administration Act and Part II of the Social Security Contributions (Transfer of Functions, etc) Act 1999 as a liability falling on the earner, instead of on the secondary contributor.

(3) Subject to [sub-paragraphs (7)(*b*) and (7B)][2] below, an election made for the purposes of sub-paragraph (1) above shall continue in force from the time when it is made until whichever of the following first occurs, namely—

(*a*) it ceases to have effect in accordance with its terms;

(*b*) it is revoked jointly by both parties to the election;

(*c*) notice is given to the earner by the secondary contributor terminating the effect of the election.

(4) An approval given to the secondary contributor for the purposes of sub-paragraph (1)(*b*) above may be given either—

(*a*) for an election to be made by the secondary contributor and a particular person; or

(*b*) for all elections to be made, or to be made in particular circumstances, by the secondary contributor and particular persons or by the secondary contributor and persons of a particular description.

(5) The grounds on which the Inland Revenue shall be entitled to refuse an approval for the purposes of sub-paragraph (1)(*b*) above shall include each of the following—

(*a*) that it appears to the Inland Revenue that adequate arrangements have not been made for securing that the liabilities transferred by the proposed election or elections will be met by the person or persons to whom they would be so transferred; and

(*b*) that it appears to the Inland Revenue that they do not have sufficient information to determine whether or not grounds falling within paragraph (*a*) above exist.

(6) If, at any time after they have given an approval for the purposes of sub-paragraph (1)(*b*) above, it appears to the Inland Revenue—

(*a*) that the arrangements that were made or are in force for securing that liabilities transferred by elections to which the approval relates are met are proving inadequate or unsatisfactory in any respect, or (*b*) that any election to which the approval relates has resulted, or is likely to result, in the avoidance or non-payment of the whole or any part of any secondary Class 1 contributions,

the Inland Revenue may withdraw the approval by notice to the secondary contributor.

(7) The withdrawal by the Inland Revenue of any approval given for the purposes of sub-paragraph (1)(*b*) above—

(*a*) may be either general or confined to a particular election or to particular elections; and

(*b*) shall have the effect that the election to which the withdrawal relates has no effect on contributions [on relevant employment income if—

(i) that income is within sub-paragraph (1A)(*a*) or (*b*) and the securities, or interest in securities, to which it relates were or was acquired after the withdrawal date, or

(ii) that income is within sub-paragraph (1A)(*c*) and the right to acquire securities to which it relates was acquired after that date.][2]

[(7A) In sub-paragraph (7)(*b*) "the withdrawal date" means—

(*a*) the date on which notice of the withdrawal of the approval is given, or

(*b*) such later date as the Inland Revenue may specify in that notice.][2]

[(7B) An election is void for the purposes of sub-paragraph (1) to the extent that it relates to[—

(*a*)] [3] relevant employment income which is employment income of the earner by virtue of Chapter 3A of Part 7 of ITEPA 2003 (employment income: securities with artificially depressed market value)[, or

(*b*) any liability, or any part of any liability, to a contribution arising as a result of regulations being given retrospective effect by virtue of section 4B(2) (earnings: power to make retrospective provision in consequence of retrospective tax legislation)][3].][2]

(8) Where the Inland Revenue have refused or withdrawn their approval for the purposes of sub-paragraph (1)(*b*) above, the person who applied for it or, as the case may be, to whom it was given may appeal . . . [4] against the Inland Revenue's decision.

(9) On an appeal under sub-paragraph (8) above [that is notified to the tribunal, the tribunal may[4]]—

(*a*) dismiss the appeal;

(*b*) remit the decision appealed against to the Inland Revenue with a direction to make such decision as the [tribunal thinks][4] fit; or

(*c*) in the case of a decision to withdraw an approval, quash that decision and direct that that decision is to be treated as never having been made.

[(10) Subject to sub-paragraph (12) below, an election under sub-paragraph (1) above shall not apply to any contributions in respect of income which, before the election was made, counted as employment income for a tax year by virtue of Part 7 of ITEPA 2003.][2]

(11) Regulations made by the Inland Revenue may make provision with respect to the making of elections for the purposes of this paragraph and the giving of approvals for the purposes of sub-paragraph (1)(*b*) above; and any such regulations may, in particular—

(*a*) prescribe the matters that must be contained in such an election;

(*b*) provide for the manner in which such an election is to be capable of being made and of being confined to particular liabilities or the part of particular liabilities; and

(*c*) provide for the making of applications for such approvals and for the manner in which those applications are to be dealt with.

(12) Where—

(*a*) an election is made under this paragraph before the end of the period of three months beginning with the date of the passing of the Child Support, Pensions and Social Security Act 2000, and

(*b*) that election is expressed to relate to liabilities for contributions arising on or after 19th May 2000 and before the making of the election,

this paragraph shall have effect in relation to those liabilities as if sub-paragraph (2) above provided for them to be deemed to have fallen on the earner (instead of on the secondary contributor); and the secondary contributor shall accordingly be entitled to reimbursement from the earner for any payment made by that contributor in or towards the discharge of any of those liabilities.

(13) . . . [2]

[(14) In this paragraph "tribunal" means the First-tier Tribunal or, where determined under Tribunal Procedure Rules, the Upper Tribunal.][4]][1]

Amendments—[1] Para 3B inserted by the Child Support, Pensions and Social Security Act 2000 s 77(2) with effect from 28 July 2000.

[2] Words in sub-paras (1), (2)(*b*), (3) and (7)(*b*) substituted; sub-paras (1A), (7A), (7B) inserted; sub-para (10) substituted, and sub-para (13) repealed; by the NIC and Statutory Payments Act 2004 ss 3(1), (3), 12, Sch 2 Pt 1 with effect for—

(a) agreements entered into after the date of commencement of the NIC and Statutory Payments Act 2004 s 3 which are in respect of post-commencement employment income, and

(b) elections made after that date: NIC and Statutory Payments Act 2004 s 3(4).

NIC and Statutory Payments Act 2004 s 3 came into force on 1 September 2004 (by virtue of SI 2004/1943).

"Post-commencement employment income" means income which is relevant employment income within SSCBA 1992 Sch 1 para 3A(2B), which, after the date of commencement of the NIC and Statutory Payments Act 2004 s 3, counts as employment income for a tax year by virtue of ITEPA 2003 Pt 7: NIC and Statutory Payments Act 2004 s 3(5).

3 Words in sub-para (7B) inserted by the National Insurance Contributions Act 2006 s 5(1), (3), (4) with effect in relation to agreements and elections whether entered into or made before, or on or after, 30 March 2006 (including those entered into or made before 2 December 2004).

4 In sub-para (8) words "to the Special Commissioners" omitted; in sub-para (9) words substituted for the words "the Special Commissioners may"; in sub-para (9)(*b*) words substituted for the words "Special Commissioners think"; sub-para (14) substituted by the Transfer of Tribunal Functions and Revenue and Customs Appeals Order, SI 2009/56 art 3, Sch 1 para 169 with effect from 1 April 2009.

General provisions as to Class 1 contributions

4 Regulations [made by the Inland Revenue][2] may, in relation to Class 1 contributions, make provision—

(*a*) for calculating the amounts payable according to a scale prepared from time to time by the [Inland Revenue][1] or otherwise adjusting them so as to avoid fractional amounts or otherwise facilitate computation;

(*b*) for requiring that the liability in respect of a payment made in a tax week, in so far as the liability depends on any conditions as to a person's age on retirement, shall be determined as at the beginning of the week or as at the end of it;

(*c*) for securing that liability is not avoided or reduced by a person following in the payment of earnings any practice which is abnormal for the employment in respect of which the earnings are paid; and

(*d*) without prejudice to sub-paragraph (*c*) above, for enabling the [Inland Revenue][1], where [they are][1] satisfied as to the existence of any practice in respect of the payment of earnings whereby the incidence of Class 1 contributions is avoided or reduced by means of irregular or unequal payments, to give directions for securing that such contributions are payable as if that practice were not followed.

Former enactments—SSA 1975 Sch 1 para 4; SS (Miscellaneous Provisions) Act 1977 s 1(4).

Amendments—[1] Words in sub-para (*a*) and (*d*) substituted by the Social Security Contributions (Transfer of Functions, etc) Act 1999 s 1(1) Sch 1 para 16 with effect from 5 Jul 1999 (by virtue of the Social Security Contributions (Transfer of Functions, etc) Act 1999 (Commencement No 2 and Consequential and Transitional Provisions) Order, SI 1999/1662).

2 Words inserted by the Social Security Contributions (Transfer of Functions, etc) Act 1999 s 2, Sch 3 para 34 with effect from 1 April 1999 (by virtue of the Social Security Contributions (Transfer of Functions, etc) Act 1999 (Commencement No 1 and Transitional Provisions) Order, SI 1999/527).

[Class 1A contributions

5 Regulations [made by the Inland Revenue][2] may—

(*a*) make provision for calculating the amount of Class 1A contributions so as to avoid fractional amounts;

(*b*) modify section 10 above in relation to cases where [something is provided or made available][3] by reason of two or more employed earner's employments under different employers.][1]

Amendments—[1] Substituted by SSA 1998 Sch 7 para 77(6) with effect from 8 September 1998 by virtue of the Social Security Act 1998 (Commencement No 1) Order, SI 1998/2209.

2 Words inserted by the Social Security Contributions (Transfer of Functions, etc) Act 1999 s 2, Sch 3 para 34 with effect from 1 April 1999 by virtue of the Social Security Contributions (Transfer of Functions, etc) Act 1999 (Commencement No 1 and Transitional Provisions) Order, SI 1999/527.

3 Words in para (*b*) substituted by the Child Support, Pensions and Social Security Act 2000 s 74(4), (8) with effect for the tax year beginning with 6 April 2000 and subsequent tax years.

[Class 1B contributions

5A Regulations [made by the Inland Revenue][2] may make provision for calculating the amount of Class 1B contributions so as to avoid fractional amounts.][1]

Amendments—[1] Inserted by SSA 1998 Sch 7 para 77(7) with effect 8 September 1998 by virtue of the Social Security Act 1998 (Commencement No 1) Order, SI 1998/2209 for the purpose only of authorising the making of regulations or orders, and with effect from 6 April 1999 in so far as it is not already in force.

2 Words inserted by the Social Security Contributions (Transfer of Functions, etc) Act 1999 s 2, Sch 3 para 34 with effect from 1 April 1999 by virtue of the Social Security Contributions (Transfer of Functions, etc) Act 1999 (Commencement No 1 and Transitional Provisions) Order, SI 1999/527.

Power to combine collection of contributions with tax

6—(1) Regulations made [by][2] the Inland Revenue may—

[(*a*) provide for Class 1, Class 1A, Class 1B or Class 2 contributions to be paid, accounted for and recovered in a similar manner to income tax in relation to which [PAYE regulations][8] have effect;][1]

(*b*) apply or extend with or without modification in relation to such contributions any of the provisions of the Income Tax Acts or of [PAYE regulations][8];

(*c*) make provision for the appropriation of the payments made by any person between his liabilities in respect of income tax and contributions.

(2) Without prejudice to the generality of sub-paragraph (1) above, the provision that may be made by virtue of paragraph (*a*) of that sub-paragraph includes in relation to Class 1[, Class 1A or Class 1B][1] contributions—

(*a*) provision for requiring the payment of interest on sums due in respect of Class 1[, Class 1A or Class 1B][1] contributions which are not paid by the due date, for determining the date (being, in the case of Class 1 contributions, not less than 14 days after the end of the tax year in respect of which the sums are due) from which such interest is to be calculated and for enabling the repayment or remission of such interest;

(*b*) provision for requiring the payment of interest on sums due in respect of Class 1[, Class 1A or Class 1B][1] contributions which fall to be repaid and for determining the date . . . [1] from which such interest is to be calculated;

(*c*) provision for, or in connection with, the imposition and recovery of penalties in relation to any returns required to be made which relate to Class 1[, Class 1A or Class 1B][1] contributions, but subject to sub-paragraph (7) and paragraph 7 below;

and any reference to contributions or income tax in paragraph (b) or (c) of sub-paragraph (1) above shall be construed as including a reference to any interest or penalty in respect of contributions or income tax, as the case may be.

(3) The rate of interest applicable for any purpose of this paragraph shall be the rate from time to time prescribed for that purpose under section 178 of the Finance Act 1989.

[(4) Where—

(*a*) a decision relating to contributions falls to be made under or by virtue of section 8, 10 or 11 of the Social Security Contributions (Transfer of Functions, etc) Act 1999; and

(*b*) the decision will affect a person's liability for, or the amount of, any interest due in respect of those contributions,

regulations under sub-paragraph (1) above shall not require any such interest to be paid until the decision has been made.][3]

[(4A) Regulations under [sub-paragraph (1) above][4] shall not require the payment of interest on a sum due in respect of a Class 1B contribution if a relevant tax appeal has been brought but not finally determined; and "a relevant tax appeal" means an appeal against a determination as to the amount of income tax in respect of which the person liable to pay the Class 1B contribution is accountable in accordance with the relevant PAYE settlement agreement.][1]

[(4B) Interest required to be paid, by virtue of sub-paragraph (2)(*a*) or (*b*) above, by regulations under sub-paragraph (1) above shall be paid without any deduction of income tax and shall not be taken into account in computing any income, profits or losses for any tax purposes.][9]

[(4C) Interest payable under section 101 of the Finance Act 2009 (late payment interest on sums due to HMRC) on sums due in respect of Class 1 contributions is not to be taken into account in computing any income, profits or losses for any tax purposes.][10]

(5) [The Secretary of State may by regulations made with the concurrence of the Inland Revenue][5] make such provision as the Secretary of State considers expedient in consequence of any provision made by or under [section 4A, 159A][7] . . . above.

(6) [Provision made in regulations under sub-paragraph (5) above may][5] in particular require the inclusion—

(*a*) in returns, certificates and other documents; or

(*b*) in any other form of record;

which the regulations require to be kept or produced or to which those regulations otherwise apply, of such particulars relating [to relevant payments or benefits within the meaning of section 4A above or (as the case may be)][7] to statutory sick pay, statutory maternity pay or deductions or payments made by virtue of section 167(1) above as may be prescribed by those regulations.

(7) Section 98 of the Taxes Management Act 1970 shall apply in relation to regulations made [under sub-paragraph (1) or (5)][5] as it applies in relation to [PAYE regulations][8].

(8) . . . [6]

Former enactments—Sub-para (1): SSA 1975 Sch 1 para 5(1); SS (Contributions) Act 1991 s 2(3).
Sub-para (2): SSA 1975 Sch 1 para 5(1A); SSA 1990 s 17(5); SS (Contributions) Act 1991 s 2(3).
Sub-paras (3), (4): SSA 1975 Sch 1 para 5(1B), (1C); SSA 1990 s 17(5).
Sub-paras (5), (6): Social Security and Housing Benefits Act 1982 s 9(4), (5).
Sub-para (7): SSA 1975 Sch 1 para 5(2).
Sub-para (8): SSA 1975 Sch 1 para 5(3); SSA 1990 s 17(6).

Regulations—Statutory Sick Pay (Additional Compensation of Employers and Consequential Amendments) Regulations, SI 1985/1411.
Statutory Maternity Pay (Compensation of Employers) Regulations, SI 1987/91.
Tax (Interest Rate) Regulations, SI 1989/1297 (reproduced in Part 1 of this work).

Contracting-out (Recovery of Class 1 Contributions) Regulations, SI 1982/1033.
Social Security Contributions (Share Options) Regulations, SI 2001/1817.
Social Security Contributions (Deferred Payments and Interest) Regulations, SI 2001/1818.
Social Security (Contributions) (Amendment No 4) Regulations 2010, SI 2010/721.
Social Security (Contributions) (Amendment No 3) Regulations, SI 2012/821.
Social Security (Contributions) (Amendment No 4) Regulations, SI 2013/2301.
Social Security (Contributions) (Amendment No 3) Regulations, SI 2014/1016.
Social Security (Contributions) (Amendment No 4) Regulations, SI 2014/2397.
Social Security and Tax Credits (Miscellaneous Amendments) Regulations, SI 2015/175.
Social Security Contributions (Amendments in Consequence of Part 4 of the Finance Act 2014) Regulations, SI 2015/521.
Social Security (Contributions) (Amendment No 4) Regulations, SI 2016/1067.

Notes—Number omitted from sub-para (5) is outside the scope of this Publication.

By virtue of Taxes (Interest Rate) Regulations, SI 1989/1297 reg 3(1)(*c*), those Regulations apply to this paragraph with effect from 6 April 1993 by virtue of FA 1989 s 178(1) (Appointed Day) Order, SI 1993/754 and Taxes (Interest Rate) (Amendment No 2) Regulations, SI 1993/758.

Cross references—See SSAA 1992 s 114(2) (penalty for failure to pay in time contributions covered by regulations under this paragraph),

SSAA 1992 s 118(1) (unpaid contributions which fall to be paid under regulations under this paragraph).

Amendments—[1] Sub-para (1)(*a*) substituted, words in sub-para (2) substituted and repealed, and sub-para (4A) inserted by SSA 1998 Sch 7 para 77. Amendments to sub-paras (1)(*a*), (2), (4A) have effect from 8 September 1998 by virtue of the Social Security Act 1998 (Commencement No 1) Order, SI 1998/2209 for the purpose only of authorising the making of regulations or orders, and with effect from 6 April 1999 in so far as they are not already in force.

[2] Words in sub-para (1) substituted by the Social Security Contributions (Transfer of Functions, etc) Act 1999 s 2 Sch 3 para 35 with effect from 1 April 1999 by virtue of the Social Security Contributions (Transfer of Functions, etc) Act 1999 (Commencement No 1 and Transitional Provisions) Order, SI 1999/527.

[3] Sub-para (4) substituted by the Social Security Contributions (Transfer of Functions, etc) Act 1999 s 18 Sch 7 para 9 with effect from 4 March 1999 for the purpose of authorising the making of Regulations and 1 April 1999 for all other purposes by virtue of the Social Security Contributions (Transfer of Functions, etc) Act 1999 (Commencement No 1 and Transitional Provisions) Order, SI 1999/527.

[4] Words in sub-para (4A) substituted by the Social Security Contributions (Transfer of Functions, etc) Act 1999 s 26(2) Sch 9 para 5 with effect from 4 March 1999 for the purpose of authorising the making of Regulations and 1 April 1999 for all other purposes by virtue of the Social Security Contributions (Transfer of Functions, etc) Act 1999 (Commencement No 1 and Transitional Provisions) Order, SI 1999/527.

[5] Words in sub-paras (5), (6) and (7) substituted by the Social Security Contributions (Transfer of Functions, etc) Act 1999 s 1(1) Sch 1 para 17 with effect from 1 April 1999 by virtue of the Social Security Contributions (Transfer of Functions, etc) Act 1999 (Commencement No 1 and Transitional Provisions) Order, SI 1999/527.

[6] Sub-para (8) repealed by the Social Security Contributions (Transfer of Functions, etc) Act 1999 s 26(3), Sch 3 para 35 and Sch 10 Pt 1 with effect from 1 April 1999 by virtue of the Social Security Contributions (Transfer of Functions, etc) Act 1999 (Commencement No 1 and Transitional Provisions) Order, SI 1999/527. The Social Security Contributions (Transfer of Functions, etc) Act 1999 Sch 1 para 17(*c*) amends words in sub-para (8), but this amendment is specifically excluded in the Commencement Order, SI 1997/527. The repeal has therefore been reflected.

[7] Words in sub-para (5) substituted and words in sub-para (6) inserted by the Welfare Reform and Pensions Act 1999, s 84, Sch 12 paras 76, 78, with effect from 6 April 2000.

[8] In sub-para (1)(*a*), words substituted for the words "regulations under section 203 of the Income and Corporation Taxes Act 1988 (PAYE)"; in sub-para (1)(*b*), words substituted for the words "regulations under that section"; and in sub-para (7), words substituted for the words "regulations made under section 203 of the Income and Corporation Taxes Act 1988 (PAYE)" by ITEPA 2003 s 722, Sch 6 paras 169, 185(*a*)–(*c*) with effect, for income tax purposes, from 2003–04; and for corporation tax purposes, for accounting periods ending after 5 April 2003. For transitional provisions and savings see ITEPA 2003 s 723, Sch 7.

[9] Sub-para (4A) inserted by FA 2003 s 147(2). In its application to the computation of income, profits or losses for an accounting period (in the case of a company) or a year of assessment (in the case of a person who is not a company), this amendment has effect for accounting periods ending after 8 April 2003, or 2003–04 and subsequent years of assessment: FA 2003 s 147(5).

[10] Sub-para (4C) inserted by the Finance Act 2009, Sections 101 and 102 (Interest on Late Payments and Repayments) (Consequential Amendments) Order, SI 2014/1293 art 2, Schedule para 1 with effect in relation to payments in respect of Class 1 National Insurance contributions and construction industry scheme payments made on or after 20 May 2014 for the tax year 2014–15 or for a subsequent tax year. "Construction industry scheme payments" means any amount deducted by a contractor from a contract payment under FA 2004 s 61 (SI 2014/1283 art 1(3).

Special penalties in the case of certain returns

7—(1) This paragraph applies where regulations under [sub-paragraph (1) of paragraph 6][4] above make provision requiring any return which is to be made in accordance with a specified provision of regulations under [that sub-paragraph][4] (the "contributions return") to be made—

(*a*) at the same time as any specified return required to be made in accordance with a provision of [PAYE regulations or regulations made under][8] [section 70(1)(*a*) or 71 (sub-contractors) of the Finance Act 2004][9] to which section 98A of the Taxes Management Act 1970 applies (the "tax return"); or

(*b*) if the circumstances are such that the return mentioned in paragraph (*a*) above does not fall to be made, at a time defined by reference to the time for making that return, had it fallen to be made;

and, in a case falling within paragraph (b) above, any reference in the following provisions of this paragraph to the tax return shall be construed as a reference to the return there mentioned.

(2) Where this paragraph applies, regulations under [paragraph 6(1)][4] above may provide that section 98A of the Taxes Management Act 1970 (penalties for late, fraudulent or negligent returns) shall apply in relation to any specified provision of regulations in accordance with which the contributions return is required to be made; and where they so provide then, subject to the following provisions of this paragraph—

(*a*) that section shall apply in relation to the contributions return as it applies in relation to the tax return; and

(*b*) sections 100 to 100D and 102 to [105][7] of that Act shall apply in relation to a penalty under section 98A of that Act to which a person is liable by virtue of this sub-paragraph as they apply in relation to any other penalty under that section.

(3) Where a person [has been required to pay][1] a penalty under paragraph (*a*) of subsection (2) of section 98A of that Act (first twelve months' default in consequence of a failure in respect of a tax return, he shall not also [be required to pay][1] a penalty under that paragraph in respect of any failure in respect of the associated contributions return.

(4) In any case where—

(*a*) a person is liable to a penalty under subsection (2)(*b*) or (4) of that section (tax-related penalties) in respect of both a tax return and its associated contributions return, and

(*b*) an officer of the Inland Revenue authorised for the purposes of section 100 of that Act has determined that a penalty is to be imposed under that provision in respect of both returns,

the penalty so imposed shall be a single penalty of an amount not exceeding the limit determined under sub-paragraph (5) below.

(5) The limit mentioned in sub-paragraph (4) above is an amount equal to the sum of—

(*a*) the maximum penalty that would have been applicable under subsection (2)(*b*) or (4) of section 98A of that Act (as the case may be) for a penalty in relation to the tax return only; and

(*b*) the maximum penalty that would have been so applicable in relation to the associated contributions return only.

(6) So much of any single penalty imposed by virtue of sub-paragraph (4) above as is recovered by the Inland Revenue shall, after the deduction of any administrative costs of the Inland Revenue attributable to its recovery, [for the purposes of making any payment into the National Insurance Fund be apportioned between income tax and contributions][5] in the ratio T:C, where—

T is the maximum penalty that could have been imposed under the provision in question in relation to the tax return only; and

C is the maximum penalty that could have been so imposed in relation to the associated contributions return only.

(7) . . . [6]

(8) [Sub-paragraph (6)][5] above shall have effect notwithstanding any provision which treats a penalty under section 98A of that Act as if it were tax charged in an assessment and due and payable.

(9) In the application of section 98A of that Act by virtue of this paragraph, any reference to a year of assessment shall be construed, in relation to a contributions return, as a reference to the tax year corresponding to that year of assessment.

(10) In the application of section 100D of that Act (court proceedings for penalties in cases of fraud) by virtue of this paragraph—

(*a*) subsection (2) shall have effect with the omission of the words "or Northern Ireland" and paragraph (*c*); and

(*b*) subsection (3) shall have effect with the omission of the words from "and any such proceedings instituted in Northern Ireland" onwards.

(11) In the application of section 103 of that Act (time limit for recovery) by virtue of this paragraph—

(*a*) any reference in subsection (1) to tax shall be taken to include a reference to Class 1 [Class 1A and Class 1B][2] contributions;

(*b*) any penalty by virtue of sub-paragraph (4) above shall be regarded as a penalty in respect of the tax return in question; and

(*c*) where, by virtue of subsection (2) (death), subsection (1)(*b*) does not apply in relation to a penalty under section 98A(2)(*b*) or (4) of that Act in respect of a tax return, it shall also not apply in relation to a penalty so imposed in respect of the associated contributions return.

[(12) A penalty under section 98A of that Act as it applies by virtue of this paragraph shall not be imposed where—

(*a*) a decision relating to contributions falls to be made under or by virtue of section 8, 10 or 11 of the Social Security Contributions (Transfer of Functions, etc) Act 1999, and has not yet been made; and

(*b*) the decision will affect a person's liability for the penalty, or the amount of it.][3]

(13) For the purposes of this paragraph—

NIC

(*a*) "contributions return" and "tax return" shall be construed in accordance with sub-paragraph (1) above; and

(*b*) a contributions return and a tax return are "associated" if the contributions return is required to be made—

(i) at the same time as the tax return, or

(ii) where sub-paragraph (1)(*b*) above applies, at a time defined by reference to the time for making the tax return.

Former enactments—Sub-paras (1)–(10): SSA 1975 Sch 1 para 5A (1)–(10); SSA 1990 s 17(7), Sch 5.
Sub-para (11): SSA 1975 Sch 1 para 5A(11); SSA 1990 s 17(7), Sch 5; SS (Contributions) Act 1991 s 2(4).
Sub-paras (12), (13): SSA 1975 Sch 1 para 5A(12), (13); SSA 1990 s 17(7), Sch 5.

Cross references—See the Social Security Contributions Regulations, SI 2001/1004 reg 86 (application of this paragraph to contributions returns);
SSAA 1992 s 119(2)(*a*).

Modification—FA 2007 s 97, Sch 24 para 30 (reference to a provision of TMA 1070 to be construed as a reference to FA 2007 Sch 24 so far as is necessary to preserve its effect).

Amendments—[1] Words in sub-para (3) substituted by SSA 1998 s 56(1) with effect from 6 April 1999 by virtue of the Social Security Act 1998 (Commencement No 4) Order, SI 1999/526.

[2] Words in sub-para (11)(a) substituted by SSA 1998 Sch 7 para 77(12) with effect from 6 April 1999 by virtue of the Social Security Act 1998 (Commencement No 1) Order, SI 1998/2209.

[3] Sub-para (12) substituted by the Social Security Contributions (Transfer of Functions, etc) Act 1999 s 18 and Sch 7 para 10 with effect from 4 March 1999 for the purpose of authorising the making of Regulations and 6 April 1999 for all other purposes by virtue of the Social Security Contributions (Transfer of Functions, etc) Act 1999 (Commencement No 1 and Transitional Provisions) Order, SI 1999/527.

[4] Words in sub-paras (1) and (2) substituted by the Social Security Contributions (Transfer of Functions, etc) Act 1999 s 1(1) and Sch 1 para 18 with effect from 1 April 1999 by virtue of the Social Security Contributions (Transfer of Functions, etc) Act 1999 (Commencement No 1 and Transitional Provisions) Order, SI 1999/527.

[5] Words in sub-paras (6) and (8) substituted by the Social Security Contributions (Transfer of Functions, etc) Act 1999 s 2, Sch 3 para 36 with effect from 1 April 1999 by virtue of the Social Security Contributions (Transfer of Functions, etc) Act 1999 (Commencement No 1 and Transitional Provisions) Order, SI 1999/527.

[6] Sub-para (7) repealed by the Social Security Contributions (Transfer of Functions, etc) Act 1999 s 26(3), Sch 3 para 36 and Sch 10 Pt 1 with effect from 1 April 1999 by virtue of the Social Security Contributions (Transfer of Functions, etc) Act 1999 (Commencement No 1 and Transitional Provisions) Order, SI 1999/527.

[7] Number in sub-para (2)(*b*) substituted by the Child Support, Pensions and Social Security Act 2000 s 76(1), (2) with effect from 28 July 2000.

[8] In sub-para (1)(*a*), words substituted for the words "regulations made by the Inland Revenue under section 203(2) or" by ITEPA 2003 s 722, Sch 6 paras 169, 185(*d*) with effect, for income tax purposes, from 2003–04; and for corporation tax purposes, for accounting periods ending after 5 April 2003. For transitional provisions and savings see ITEPA 2003 s 723, Sch 7.

[9] In para (7), words substituted by FA 2004 s 76, Sch 12, para 13 with effect for payments made on or after 6 April 2007 under contracts relating to construction operations. See SI 2006/3240, art 2.

[7A—(1) This paragraph applies where paragraph 7 above applies; and in this paragraph "contributions return" has the same meaning as in that paragraph.

(2) Without prejudice to paragraph 7(2) above or to the [other][2] powers of the Inland Revenue to penalise omissions or errors in returns, regulations [made by the Treasury][3] may provide for the [Inland Revenue][2] to impose penalties in respect of a person who, in making a contributions return, fraudulently or negligently—

(*a*) fails to provide any information or computation that he is required to provide; or

(*b*) provides any such information or computation that is incorrect.

(3) Regulations under sub-paragraph (2) above shall—

(*a*) prescribe the rates of penalty, or provide for how they are to be ascertained;

(*b*) provide for the penalty to be imposed by the [Inland Revenue][2] within six years after the date on which the penalty is incurred;

(*c*) provide for determining the date on which, for the purposes of paragraph (*b*) above, the penalty is incurred;

(*d*) prescribe the means by which the penalty is to be enforced; and

(*e*) provide for enabling the [Inland Revenue, in their][2] discretion, to mitigate or to remit the penalty, or to stay or to compound any proceedings for it.][1]

Amendments—[1] Inserted by SSA 1998 s 56(2) with effect from 4 March 1999 for the purpose of authorising the making of regulations and 6 April 1999 for all other purposes by virtue of the Social Security Act 1998 (Commencement No 4) Order, SI 1999/526.

[2] Sub-paras (2) and (3) amended by the Social Security Contributions (Transfer of Functions, etc) Act 1999 s 26(2) and Sch 9 para 6 with effect from 4 March 1999 for the purpose of authorising the making of Regulations and 1 April 1999 for all other purposes by virtue of the Social Security Contributions (Transfer of Functions, etc) Act 1999 (Commencement No 1 and Transitional Provisions) Order, SI 1999/527.

[3] Words in sub-para (2) inserted by the Social Security Contributions (Transfer of Functions, etc) Act 1999 s 2, Sch 3 para 37 with effect from 1 April 1999 by virtue of the Social Security Contributions (Transfer of Functions, etc) Act 1999 (Commencement No 1 and Transitional Provisions) Order, SI 1999/527.

Collection of contributions [otherwise than through PAYE system]

7B—(1) [The Treasury may by regulations][3] provide that, in such cases or circumstances as may be [prescribed, Class 1, Class 1A, Class 1B or Class 2 contributions shall be paid to the Inland Revenue in a manner different from that in which income tax in relation to which [PAYE regulations][5] apply is payable.][2]

(2) Regulations under this paragraph may, in particular—

(*a*) provide for returns to be made to the [Inland Revenue][2] by such date as may be prescribed;

(*b*) prescribe the form in which returns are to be made, or provide for returns to be made in such form as the [Inland Revenue][2] may approve;

(*c*) prescribe the manner in which contributions are to be paid, or provide for contributions to be paid in such manner as the [Inland Revenue][2] may approve;

(*d*) prescribe the due date for the payment of contributions;

[(*e*) require interest to be paid on contributions that are not paid by the due date, and provide for determining the date from which such interest is to be calculated;][4]

(*f*) provide for interest to be paid on contributions that fall to be repaid;

(*g*) provide for determining the date from which interest to be charged or paid pursuant to regulations under paragraph (*e*) or (*f*) above is to be calculated;

(*h*) provide for penalties to be imposed in respect of a person who—

(i) fails to submit, within the time allowed, a return required to be made in accordance with regulations under paragraph (*a*) above;

(ii) in making such a return, fraudulently or negligently fails to provide any information or computation that he is required to provide;

(iii) in making such a return, fraudulently or negligently provides any incorrect information or computation; or

(iv) fails to pay Class 2 contributions by the due date;

(*i*) provide for a penalty imposed pursuant to regulations under paragraph (*h*) above to carry interest from the date on which it becomes payable until payment.

(3) Where—

(*a*) a decision relating to contributions falls to be made under section 8, 9, 10, 12, 14 or 15 of the Social Security Act 1998; and

(*b*) the decision will affect a person's liability for, or the amount of, any interest due in respect of those contributions,

regulations under sub-paragraph (2)(e) above shall not require any such interest to be paid until the decision has been made.

(4) . . . [2]

(5) Regulations under sub-paragraph (2)(*h*) above shall—

(*a*) prescribe the rates of penalty, or provide for how they are to be ascertained;

(*b*) . . . [2] provide for the penalty to be imposed by the [Inland Revenue[2]]—

(i) within six years after the date on which the penalty is incurred; or

(ii) where the amount of the penalty is to be ascertained by reference to the amount of any contributions payable, at any later time within three years after the final determination of the amount of those contributions;

(*c*) provide for determining the date on which, for the purposes of paragraph (*b*) above, the penalty is incurred;

(*d*) prescribe the means by which the penalty is to be enforced; and

(*e*) provide for enabling the [Inland Revenue, in their][2] discretion, to mitigate or to remit the penalty, or to stay or to compound any proceedings for it.

[(5A) Regulations under this paragraph may, in relation to any penalty imposed by such regulations, make provision applying (with or without modifications) any enactment applying for the purposes of income tax that is contained in Part X of the Taxes Management Act 1970 (penalties).][4]

(6) . . . [2]

(7) . . . [6]

(8) Interest or penalties may be charged by virtue of regulations under this paragraph in respect of a period before the coming into force of section 57 of the Social Security Act 1998 but only to the extent that interest or penalties would have been chargeable if the contributions in question had been recoverable, in respect of that period, by virtue of regulations under paragraph 6 above.

(9) Any reference to contributions in sub-paragraph (1) above shall be construed as including a reference to any interest or penalty payable, in respect of contributions, by virtue of regulations under paragraph (*e*) or (*h*) of sub-paragraph (2) above.

(10) The rate of interest applicable for any purpose of this paragraph shall be the rate from time to time prescribed under section 178 of the Finance Act 1989 for the corresponding purpose of paragraph 6 above.][1]

NIC

Regulations—Social Security Contributions (Share Options) Regulations, SI 2001/1817.
Social Security (Contributions) (Amendment and Application of Schedule 38 to the Finance Act 2012) Regulations, SI 2013/622.
Social Security (Miscellaneous Amendments No 2) Regulations, SI 2015/478.
Social Security (Contributions) (Amendment) (No 2) Regulations SI 2016/352.
Cross references—See FA 2012 Sch 38 para 54 (reference in sub-para (5A) to TMA 1970 Part 10 to include a reference to FA 2012 Sch 38).
Amendments—[1] Inserted by SSA 1998 s 57 with effect from 4 March 1999 for the purpose of authorising the making of regulations and 6 April 1999 for all other purposes by virtue of the Social Security Act 1998 (Commencement No 4) Order, SI 1999/526.
[2] Words in heading and throughout para 7B amended and omitted by the Social Security Contributions (Transfer of Functions, etc) Act 1999 s 26(2) and Sch 9 para 7, and s 26(3) and Sch 10 Pt 1 with effect from 4 March 1999 for the purpose of authorising the making of Regulations and 1 April 1999 for all other purposes by virtue of the Social Security Contributions (Transfer of Functions, etc) Act 1999 (Commencement No 1 and Transitional Provisions) Order, SI 1999/527.
[3] Words in sub-para (1) substituted by the Social Security Contributions (Transfer of Functions, etc) Act 1999 s 2, Sch 3 para 38 with effect from 1 April 1999 by virtue of the Social Security Contributions (Transfer of Functions, etc) Act 1999 (Commencement No 1 and Transitional Provisions) Order, SI 1999/527.
[4] Sub-para (2)(*e*) substituted and sub-para (5A) inserted by the Child Support, Pensions and Social Security Act 2000 s 76(1), (3), (4) with effect from 28 July 2000.
[5] In sub-para (1), words substituted for the words "regulations under section 203 of the Income and Corporation Taxes Act 1988 (PAYE)" by ITEPA 2003 s 722, Sch 6 paras 169, 185(*e*) with effect, for income tax purposes, from 2003–04; and for corporation tax purposes, for accounting periods ending after 5 April 2003. For transitional provisions and savings see ITEPA 2003 s 723, Sch 7.
[6] Sub-para (7) repealed by NICA 2015 s 2, Sch 1 paras 1, 9(1), (2) with effect in relation to a Class 2 contribution in respect of a week in the tax year 2015–16 or a subsequent tax year.

[7BZA—(1) The Inland Revenue may by regulations provide for Class 1, Class 1A, Class 1B or Class 2 contributions to which regulations under paragraph 7B apply to be recovered in a similar manner to income tax.
(2) Regulations under sub-paragraph (1) may apply or extend with or without modification in relation to such contributions any of the provisions of the Income Tax Acts or of PAYE regulations.
(3) Any reference to contributions in this paragraph shall be construed as including a reference to any interest or penalty payable, in respect of contributions, by virtue of regulations under paragraph (e) or (h) of paragraph 7B(2).][1]

Amendments—[1] This paragraph inserted by the NIC and Statutory Payments Act 2004 s 5(4) with effect from 1 September 2004 (by virtue of SI 2004/1943).

[7BA The Inland Revenue may by regulations provide for amounts in respect of contributions or interest that fall to be paid or repaid in accordance with any regulations under this Schedule to be set off, or to be capable of being set off, in prescribed circumstances and to the prescribed extent, against any such liabilities under regulations under this Schedule of the person entitled to the payment or repayment as may be prescribed.][1]

Amendments—[1] This paragraph inserted by the Child Support, Pensions and Social Security Act 2000 s 76(1), (5) with effect from 28 July 2000.

[7BB (1) Regulations may provide, in connection with maternity allowance under section 35 or 35B, for a person who is, or will be, either liable or entitled to pay a Class 2 contribution in respect of a week in a tax year to be able to pay a Class 2 contribution in respect of that week at any time in the period—

(*a*) beginning with that week, and
(*b*) ending with a prescribed date.

(2) The regulations may provide that where a person pays a Class 2 contribution in respect of a week in a tax year under the regulations—

(*a*) the contribution is to be treated, before the end of the tax year, as a Class 2 contribution under section 11(6);
(*b*) the contribution is to be treated, after the end of the tax year—
  (i) if the person is liable under section 11(2) to pay a Class 2 contribution in respect of that week, as a Class 2 contribution under section 11(2);
  (ii) otherwise, as a Class 2 contribution under section 11(6).

(3) Regulations under this paragraph are to be made by the Treasury acting with the concurrence of the Secretary of State.][1]

Regulations—Social Security (Miscellaneous Amendments No 2) Regulations, SI 2015/478.
Amendments—[1] This paragraph inserted by NICA 2015 s 2, Sch 1 paras 1, 9(1), (3) with effect for the tax year 2015–16 and subsequent tax years.

Interest and penalties chargeable concurrently with Inland Revenue

[7C . . .][1]

Amendments—[1] This paragraph repealed by the Social Security Contributions (Transfer of Functions, etc) Act 1999 s 26(2) and Sch 9 para 8, and s 26(3) and Sch 10 Pt I with effect from 1 April 1999 by virtue of the Social Security Contributions (Transfer of Functions, etc) Act 1999 (Commencement No 1 and Transitional Provisions) Order, SI 1999/527. Originally inserted by SSA 1998 s 58.

General regulation-making powers

8—(1) [The appropriate authority may by regulations][4] provide—

(*a*) for requiring persons to maintain, in such form and manner as may be prescribed, records—

(i) of the earnings paid by them to and in respect of earners, and

(ii) of the contributions paid or payable in respect of earnings so paid,

for the purpose of enabling the incidence of liability for contributions of any class to be determined, and to retain the records for so long as may be prescribed;

[(*aa*) for requiring persons to maintain, in such form and manner as may be prescribed, records of such matters as may be prescribed for purposes connected with the employment allowance provisions (within the meaning of the National Insurance Contributions Act 2014), and to retain the records for so long as may be prescribed;][10]

(*b*) for requiring persons to maintain, in such form and manner as may be prescribed, records of such matters as may be prescribed for the purpose of enabling the incidence of liability for Class 1A [or Class 1B][3] contributions to be determined, and to retain the records for so long as may be prescribed;

(*c*) for treating primary Class 1 contributions, when payable on the primary contributor's behalf by the secondary contributor, but not paid, as actually paid where the failure to pay is shown not to have been with the consent or connivance of, or attributable to any negligence on the part of, the primary contributor and, in the case of contributions so treated, for treating them also as paid at a prescribed time or in respect of a prescribed period;

[(*ca*) for requiring a secondary contributor to notify a person to whom any of his liabilities are transferred by an election under paragraph 3B above of—

(i) any transferred liability that arises;

(ii) the amount of any transferred liability that arises; and

(iii) the contents of any notice of withdrawal by the Inland Revenue of any approval that relates to that election;][7]

(*d*) for treating, for the purpose of any entitlement to benefit, contributions paid at or after any prescribed time as paid at some other time (whether earlier or later) or, in the case of contributions paid after the due date for payment, or at such later date as may be prescribed, as not having been paid;

(*e*) for enabling contributions to be treated as paid in respect of a tax year earlier or later than that in respect of which they were actually paid;

(*f*) for treating (for the purposes of Class 2 contributions) a week which falls partly in one, and partly in another, tax year as falling wholly within one or the other of those tax years;

(*g*) for treating contributions of the wrong class, or at the wrong rate, or of the wrong amount, as paid on account of contributions properly payable (notwithstanding section 14 above, in the case of Class 3 contributions) or as paid (wholly or in part) in discharge of a liability for a [contributions equivalent premium][1];

(*h*) for the repayment, in prescribed cases, of the whole or a prescribed part of any contributions paid by reference to earnings which have become repayable;

(*i*) . . .[5]

[(*ia*) for the repayment, in prescribed cases, of the whole or a prescribed part [of a Class 1A or][6] of a Class 1B contribution;][3]

(*j*), (*k*) . . .[11]

(*l*) without prejudice to paragraph (*g*) above, for enabling—

(i) the whole or part of any payment of secondary Class 1 contributions to be treated as a payment of Class 1A contributions [or a Class 1B contribution][3];

(ii) the whole or part of any payment of Class 1A contributions to be treated as a payment of secondary Class 1 contributions[, or a Class 1B contribution][3] or Class 2 contributions;

[(iia) the whole or part of any payment of a Class 1B contribution to be treated as a payment of secondary Class 1 contributions, Class 1A contributions or Class 2 contributions;][3]

(iii) the whole or part of any payment of Class 2 contributions to be treated as a payment of secondary Class 1 contributions[, Class 1A contributions or a Class 1B contribution][3];

(*m*) for the return of the whole or any prescribed part of any contributions paid either in error or in such circumstances that, under any provision of Part I of this Act or of regulations, they fall to be repaid;

(*n*) for treating a person as being an employed earner, notwithstanding that his employment is outside Great Britain;

NIC

(*o*) for treating a person's employment as continuing during periods of holiday, unemployment or incapacity for work and in such other circumstances as may be prescribed;

(*p*) . . . [2];

(*q*) for any other matters incidental to the payment, collection or return of contributions.

[(1A) In sub-paragraph (1), "the appropriate authority" means the Treasury, except that, in relation to—

(*a*) provision made by virtue of paragraph (*d*) of that sub-paragraph, and

(*b*) provision made by virtue of paragraph (*q*) of that sub-paragraph in relation to the matters referred to in paragraph (*d*),

it means the Secretary of State [acting with the concurrence of the Inland Revenue][8].][4]

(2), (3) . . . [9]

Regulations—See the SS (Crediting and Treatment of Contributions, and National Insurance Numbers) Regulations, SI 2001/769.
Social Security Contributions (Share Options) Regulations, SI 2001/1817.
Social Security Class 3A Contributions (Units of Additional Pension) Regulations, SI 2014/3240.
Social Security (Miscellaneous Amendments No 2) Regulations, SI 2015/478.
Social Security (Contributions) (Amendment) (No 2) Regulations SI 2016/352.
Social Security (Miscellaneous Amendments No. 2) Regulations, SI 2017/373.

Former enactments—Sub-para (1)(*a*): SSA 1975 Sch 1 para 6(1)(*a*).
Sub-para (1)(*b*): SSA 1975 Sch 1 para 6(1)(*aa*); SS (Contributions) Act 1991 s 2(5)(*a*).
Sub-para (1)(*c*)–(*f*): SSA 1975 Sch 1 para 6(1)(*b*)–(*e*).
Sub-para (1)(*g*): SSA 1975 Sch 1 para 6(1)(*f*); SS Pensions Act 1975 s 65(1), Sch 4 para 61.
Sub-para (1)(*h*): SSA 1975 Sch 1 para 6(1)(*gg*); SSA 1989 s 2.
Sub-para (1)(*i*): SSA 1975 Sch 1 para 6(1)(*ggg*); SS (Contributions) Act 1991 s 2(5)(*c*).
Sub-para (1)(*j*), (*k*): SSA 1975 Sch 1 para 6(1)(*gh*), (*gj*); SSA 1990 s 21(1), Sch 6 para 9.
Sub-para (1)(*l*): SSA 1975 Sch 1 para 6(1)(*g*); SS (Contributions) Act 1991 s 2(5)(*b*).
Sub-para (1)(*m*): SSA 1975 Sch 1 para 6(1)(*h*); SSA 1986 s 86(1), Sch 10 para 10.
Sub-para (1)(*n*)–(*q*): SSA 1975 Sch 1 para 6(1)(*j*)–(*m*).
Sub-paras (2), (3): SSA 1975 Sch 1 para 6(2), (3).

Cross references—See the SS (Contributions) Regulations, SI 2001/1004 reg 47 (repayment of Class 2 contributions paid by low wage earners); SS(CP)A 1992 s 2.

Amendments—[1] Words in sub-para (1)(*g*) substituted for the words "state scheme premium" by the Pensions Act 1995 Sch 5 para 14 with effect from 6 April 1997, by virtue of the Pensions Act 1995 (Commencement No 10) Order, SI 1997/664 art 2, Sch Pt II.

[2] Sub-para (1)(*p*) repealed by Social Security Administration (Fraud) Act 1997 with effect from 1 July 1997 by virtue of SI 1997/1577.

[3] Words in sub-paras (1)(*b*), (*l*)(i), (ii), (iii) and sub-paras (1)(*ia*) and (1)(*l*)(iia) inserted and substituted by SSA 1998 Sch 7 para 77(14) to (16) with effect from 8 September 1998 by virtue of the Social Security Act 1998 (Commencement No 1) Order, SI 1998/2209 for the purpose only of authorising the making of regulations or orders, and with effect from 6 April 1999 in so far as it is not already in force.

[4] Words in sub-para (1) substituted, and sub-para (1A) inserted, by the Social Security Contributions (Transfer of Functions, etc) Act 1999 s 2, Sch 3 para 39 with effect from 1 April 1999 by virtue of the Social Security Contributions (Transfer of Functions, etc) Act 1999 (Commencement No 1 and Transitional Provisions) Order, SI 1999/527.

[5] Para (1)(*i*) repealed by the Child Support, Pensions and Social Security Act 2000 s 85, Sch 9 Pt VIII with effect for the tax year beginning with 6 April 2000 and subsequent tax years.

[6] Words in para (1)(*ia*) inserted by the Child Support, Pensions and Social Security Act 2000 s 74(5) with effect from 28 July 2000.

[7] Para (1)(*ca*) inserted by the Child Support, Pensions and Social Security Act 2000 s 77(4) with effect for the tax year beginning with 6 April 2000 and subsequent tax years.

[8] Words inserted by the Welfare Reform and Pensions Act 1999 s 81 Sch 11 paras 1, 3 with effect from 11 November 1999.

[9] Sub-paras (2), (3) repealed by the Welfare Reform and Pensions Act 1999, s 88, Sch 13, Pt VI with effect from 6 April 2000 (by virtue of SI 1999/3240).

[10] Sub-para (1)(*aa*) inserted by NICA 2014 s 7(1) with effect from 6 April 2014.

[11] Sub-para (1), (*j*), (*k*) repealed by NICA 2015 s 2, Sch 1 para 1, 9(1), (4) with effect for the tax year 2015–16 and subsequent tax years.

9 [The Treasury may by regulations][1] provide that—

(*a*) for the purpose of determining whether a contribution is payable in respect of any person, or

(*b*) for determining the amount or rate of any contribution,

he is to be treated as having attained at the beginning of a week, or as not having attained until the end of a week, any age which he attains during the course of that week.

Former enactments—SSA 1975 Sch 1 para 7.

Amendments—[1] Words substituted by the Social Security Contributions (Transfer of Functions, etc) Act 1999 s 2, Sch 3 para 40 with effect from 1 April 1999 by virtue of the Social Security Contributions (Transfer of Functions, etc) Act 1999 (Commencement No 1 and Transitional Provisions) Order, SI 1999/527.

Deduction of contributions from pension, etc

10—(1) Where a person is in receipt of a pension or allowance payable by the Secretary of State by virtue of any prescribed enactment or instrument, the Secretary of State may with the consent of that person pay any contributions (other than Class 1 or Class 4 contributions) payable by him and deduct the amount so paid from the pension or allowance.
(2) Sub-paragraph (1) above shall have effect notwithstanding anything in any Act, Royal Warrant, Order in Council, order or scheme.

Regulations—SS (Crediting and Treatment of Contributions, and National Insurance Numbers) Regulations, SI 2001/769.
Former enactments—SSA 1975 Sch 1 para 8.

Sickness payments counting as remuneration

11—(1) [The Treasury may by regulations][1] make provision as to the manner in which, and the person through whom, any sickness payment which, by virtue of section 4(1) above, is to be treated as remuneration derived from employed earner's employment is to be made.
(2) In any case where regulations made under sub-paragraph (1) above have the effect of requiring a registered friendly society (within the meaning of the Friendly Societies Act 1974) to make amendments to its rules, the amendments may, notwithstanding any provision of those rules, be made in accordance with the procedure prescribed by regulations made by the Chief Registrar of Friendly Societies for the purposes of this paragraph.

Former enactments—SSA 1975 Sch 1 para 9; Social Security and Housing Benefits Act 1982 s 37(2).
Amendments—[1] Words in sub-para (1) substituted by the Social Security Contributions (Transfer of Functions, etc) Act 1999 s 2, Sch 3 para 41 with effect from 1 April 1999 by virtue of the Social Security Contributions (Transfer of Functions, etc) Act 1999 (Commencement No 1 and Transitional Provisions) Order, SI 1999/527.

SCHEDULE 2

LEVY OF CLASS 4 CONTRIBUTIONS WITH INCOME TAX

Section 16 (3)

Interpretation

1 In this Schedule—
(*a*) "the Act of 1988" means the Income and Corporation Taxes Act 1988;
[(*ab*) "ITTOIA 2005" means the Income Tax (Trading and Other Income) Act 2005;][2]
[(*ac*) "ITA 2007" means the Income Tax Act 2007;][3]
(*b*) . . . [1]
(*c*) "year" means year of assessment within the meaning of [the Income Tax Acts (see section 989 of ITA 2007)][4].

Amendments—[1] Sub-para (*b*) repealed by CAA 2001 ss 578, 580, Sch 2 para 75(1), Sch 4 with effect for income tax purposes as respects allowances and charges falling to be made for chargeable periods ending after 5 April 2001.
[2] Words inserted by ITTOIA 2005 s 882(1), Sch 1 paras 419, 422(1), (2) with effect from 6 April 2005. ITTOIA 2005 has effect—
(a) for income tax purposes, for 2005–06 and subsequent tax years, and
(b) for corporation tax purposes, for accounting periods ending after 5 April 2005: ITTOIA 2005 s 883(1).
[3] Sub-para (*ac*) inserted by ITA 2007 s 1027, Sch 1 paras 288, 290(1), (2), with effect for income tax purposes from 6 April 2007, and corporation tax purposes for accounting periods ending after 5 April 2007.
[4] In sub-para (*c*) words substituted by the Income Tax Act 2007 (Amendment) Order 2010, SI 2010/588, art 2(2) with effect for the tax year 2007–08 and subsequent tax years.

Method of computing profits or gains

2 Subject to the following paragraphs, Class 4 contributions shall be payable in respect of the full amount of all [profits—
(*a*) which are the profits of any relevant trade, profession or vocation which is not carried on wholly outside the United Kingdom, and
(*b*) which are chargeable to income tax under Chapter 2 of Part 2 of ITTOIA 2005.][2] . . . [1]

Former enactments—SSA 1975 Sch 2 para 2; CAA 1990 s 164, Sch 1 para 2(*b*).
Amendments—[1] Words repealed by CAA 2001 ss 578, 580, Sch 2 para 75(2), Sch 4 with effect for income tax purposes as respects allowances and charges falling to be made for chargeable periods ending after 5 April 2001.
[2] Words substituted by ITTOIA 2005 s 882(1), Sch 1 paras 419, 422(1), (3) with effect from 6 April 2005. ITTOIA 2005 has effect—
(a) for income tax purposes, for 2005–06 and subsequent tax years, and
(b) for corporation tax purposes, for accounting periods ending after 5 April 2005: ITTOIA 2005 s 883(1).

NIC

Reliefs

3—(1) For the purposes of computing the amount of profits . . . [5] in respect of which Class 4 contributions are payable, relief shall be available under, and in the manner provided by, the following provisions of [ITA 2007[6]]—

(*a*) [sections 64 and 72][6] (set-off of trade losses against general income), but only where loss arises from activities the profits . . . [5] of which would be brought into computation for the purposes of Class 4 contributions;

(*b*) . . . [4];

(*c*) [section 83][6] (carry-forward of loss against subsequent profits); and

(*d*) [section 89][6] (carry-back of terminal losses).

(2) The following relief provisions . . . [6] shall not apply, that is to say—

(*a*) Chapter I of Part VII [of the Act of 1988 and Chapters 2 and 3 of Part 3 and sections 457, 458 and 459 of ITA 2007][6] (personal reliefs);

(*b*) [section 383 of ITA 2007][6] (relief for payment of interest);

(*c*) . . . [6]

(*d*) [sections 88 and 94 of ITA 2007][6] (treatment of interest as a loss for purposes of carry-forward or carry-back);

(*e*) . . . [3]; . . . [2]

(*f*) sections 619 and 620 (premiums or other consideration under annuity contracts and trust schemes); [and][1]

[(*g*) sections 639 (personal pension contributions).][1]

(3) . . . [8]

(4) Where in the year 1990–1991 or any subsequent year of assessment for which a person claims and is allowed relief by virtue of sub-paragraph (1) above there falls to be made in computing his [net income][6] for income tax purposes a deduction in respect of any loss in any relevant trade, profession or vocation—

(*a*) the amount of the deduction shall, as far as may be, be treated for the purpose of the charge to Class 4 contributions as reducing the person's profits . . . [5] for that year of any relevant trade, profession or vocation, and

(*b*) any excess shall be treated for that purpose as reducing such profits . . . [5] for subsequent years (being deducted as far as may be from those of the immediately following year, whether or not the person claims or is entitled to claim relief under this paragraph for that year, and, so far as it cannot be so deducted, then from those of the next year, and so on).

(5) Relief shall be allowed, in respect of—

(*a*) . . . [6]

(*b*) payments under [section 383 of ITA 2007][6] (relief for payment of interest), being payments for which relief from income tax is or can be given,

[(*c*) payments from which a sum representing income tax must be deducted under—

(i) section 900(2) of ITA 2007 (commercial payments made by individuals),

(ii) section 903(5) of that Act (patent royalties), or

(iii) section 906(5) of that Act (certain royalties etc where usual place of abode of owner is abroad),

(*d*) so much of any payment from which a sum representing income tax must be deducted under section 910(2) of ITA 2007 (proceeds of a sale of patent rights: payments to non-UK residents) as is equal to the amount referred to in that provision as "the chargeable amount", or

(*e*) a payment from which a sum representing income tax must be deducted as a result of a direction under section 944(2) of ITA 2007 (tax avoidance: certain payments to non-UK residents)][7]

[so far as the payment is incurred][7] wholly or exclusively for the purposes of any relevant trade, profession or vocation, by way of deduction from or set-off against profits . . . [5] chargeable to Class 4 contributions for the year in which the payments are made; and, in the case of any insufficiency of the profits . . . [5] of that year, the payments shall be carried forward and deducted from or set off against the profits . . . [5] of any subsequent year (being deducted or set off as far as may be from or against the profits . . . [5] of the immediately following year, whether or not relief can be claimed under this paragraph for that year, and so far as it cannot be so deducted, from or against those of the next year, and so on).

Former enactments—Sub-paras (1), (2): SSA 1975 Sch 2 para 3(1), (2): TA 1988 s 844, Sch 29 para 32 Table.
Sub-para (3): SSA 1975 Sch 2 para 3(3).
Sub-para (4): SSA 1975 Sch 2 para 3(3); FA 1988 Sch 3 para 31.
Sub-para (5): SSA 1975 Sch 2 para 3(4); TA 1988 s 844, Sch 29 para 32 Table.

Cross-reference—FA 2009 Sch 6 para 2(6) (for the purposes of the temporary carry-back of losses provisions in FA 2009 Sch 6, the reference in sub-para (1) above to ITA 2007 s 64 includes FA 2009 Sch 6 para 1).

Amendments—[1] Sub-para (2)(*g*) and the preceding word "and" inserted by the SS (Contributions) Act 1994 s 3 and deemed to have had effect from 1 July 1992.

[2] Word "and" at the end of sub-para (2)(*e*) omitted by the SS (Contributions) Act 1994 s 3 and deemed to have had effect from 1 July 1992.

[3] Sub-para (2)(*e*) repealed by FA 1996 s 147(2)(*a*), (3), Sch 41 Pt V(15) with effect from the year 1996–97.

[4] Repealed by SSA 1998 s 59(3), Sch 8 with effect from 8 September 1998 by virtue of the Social Security Act 1998 (Commencement No 1) Order, SI 1998/2209.

[5] Words in sub-paras (1), (4), (5) repealed by ITTOIA 2005 ss 882(1), 884, Sch 1 paras 419, 422(1), (4), Sch 3 with effect from 6 April 2005. ITTOIA 2005 has effect—

(a) for income tax purposes, for 2005–06 and subsequent tax years, and

(b) for corporation tax purposes, for accounting periods ending after 5 April 2005: ITTOIA 2005 s 883(1).

[6] Words in sub-paras (1), (2), (4), (5) substituted; words in sub-para (2) repealed and inserted; and words in sub-para (5) repealed, by ITA 2007 ss 1027, 1031, Sch 1 paras 288, 290(1), (3), Sch 3 Pt 1, with effect for income tax purposes from 6 April 2007, and corporation tax purposes for accounting periods ending after 5 April 2007.

[7] Sub-para (5)(*c*)–(*e*) inserted and in the para following, words substituted by the Income Tax Act 2007 (Amendment) Order 2010, SI 2010/588, art 2(3) with effect for the tax year 2007–08 and subsequent tax years.

[8] Sub-para (3) repealed by NICs Act 2014 s 17(1)(*a*) with effect for the tax year 2014–15 and subsequent tax years.

Partnerships

4—(1) Where a trade or profession is carried on by two or more persons jointly, the liability of any one of them in respect of Class 4 contributions shall arise in respect of his share of the profits . . . [2] of that trade or profession (so far as immediately derived by him from carrying it on); and for this purpose his share shall be aggregated with his share of the profits . . . [2] of any other trade, profession or vocation (so far as immediately derived by him from carrying it on or exercising it).
(2) Where sub-paragraph (1) above applies, the Class 4 contributions for which a person is liable in respect of the profits . . . [2] of the trade or profession carried on jointly (aggregated, where appropriate, as mentioned in that sub-paragraph) [shall be charged on him separately].[1]

Former enactments—SSA 1975 Sch 2 para 5; TA 1988 s 844, Sch 29 para 32 Table.

Amendments—[1] Words substituted by SSA 1998 s 59(4) with effect from 8 September 1998 by virtue of the Social Security Act 1998 (Commencement No 1) Order, SI 1998/2209.

[2] Words repealed by ITTOIA 2005 ss 882(1), 884, Sch 1 paras 419, 422(1), (4), Sch 3 with effect from 6 April 2005. ITTOIA 2005 has effect—

(a) for income tax purposes, for 2005–06 and subsequent tax years, and

(b) for corporation tax purposes, for accounting periods ending after 5 April 2005: ITTOIA 2005 s 883(1).

Trustees, etc

5 In any circumstances in which apart from this paragraph a person would—

(*a*) . . . [2]

(*b*) by virtue of [section 8 of ITTOIA 2005][1] be assessed and charged to [Class 4][2] contributions in respect of profits . . . [1] received or receivable by him in the capacity of trustee,

such contributions shall not be payable either by him or by any other person.

Former enactments—SSA 1975 Sch 2 para 6; TA 1988 s 844, Sch 29 para 32 Table.

Amendments—[1] Words repealed and words in sub-para (*b*) substituted by ITTOIA 2005 ss 882(1), 884, Sch 1 paras 419, 422(1), (5), Sch 3 with effect from 6 April 2005. ITTOIA 2005 has effect—

(a) for income tax purposes, for 2005–06 and subsequent tax years, and

(b) for corporation tax purposes, for accounting periods ending after 5 April 2005: ITTOIA 2005 s 883(1).

[2] Sub-para (*a*) repealed, and in para (*b*) words substituted, by FA 2012 s 222(4)(*c*) with effect for the tax year 2012–13 and subsequent tax years.

Other provisions

6—(1) [Section 101 of the Finance Act 2009 (late payment interest on sums due to HMRC)][3]shall apply in relation to any amount due in respect of Class 4 contributions [as it applies][1] in relation to income tax; and [section 102 of the Finance Act 2009 (repayment interest on sums to be paid by HMRC)][3] shall, with the necessary modifications, apply in relation to Class 4 contributions as it applies in relation to income tax.
(2) . . . [2]

Former enactments—SSA 1975 Sch 2 para 7(1), (2); SSA 1990 s 17(8), (9).

Cross reference—See the SS (Consequential Provisions) Act 1992 Sch 4 paras 1, 8, 9 (transitory modification of this paragraph until 19 April 1993.

Amendments—[1] Words "Section 86 of the Taxes Management Act 1970 (interest on overdue tax)" and words "as it applies" substituted SSA 1998 s 59 with effect from 8 September 1998 by virtue of the Social Security Act 1998 (Commencement No 1) Order, SI 1998/2209.

[2] Sub-para (2) repealed by the Social Security Contributions (Transfer of Functions, etc) Act 1999 s 26(3) and Sch 10 Pt 1 with effect from 1 April 1999 by virtue of the Social Security Contributions (Transfer of Functions, etc) Act 1999 (Commencement No 1 and Transitional Provisions) Order, SI 1999/527.

3 In sub-para (1), words substituted , by the Finance Act 2009, Sections 101 to 103 (Income Tax Self Assessment) (Appointed Days and Transitional and Consequential Provisions) Order, SI 2011/701 art 9 with effect from 31 October 2011. Words at the start of sub-para (1) previously substituted by SSA 1998 s 59 (see note above).

7 Where an assessment has become final and conclusive for the purposes of income tax for any year, that assessment shall also be final and conclusive for the purposes of computing liability for Class 4 contributions; and no allowance or adjustment of liability, on the ground of diminution of income or loss, shall be taken into account in computing profits . . . [1] chargeable to Class 4 contributions unless that allowance or adjustment has previously been made on an application under the special provisions of the Income Tax Acts relating to it, or falls to be allowed under paragraph 3(5) of this Schedule.

Former enactments—SSA 1975 Sch 2 para 8.

Amendments—[1] Words repealed by ITTOIA 2005 ss 882(1), 884, Sch 1 paras 419, 422(1), (6), Sch 3 with effect from 6 April 2005. ITTOIA 2005 has effect—

(a) for income tax purposes, for 2005–06 and subsequent tax years, and

(b) for corporation tax purposes, for accounting periods ending after 5 April 2005: ITTOIA 2005 s 883(1).

8 The provisions of Part V of the Taxes Management Act 1970 (appeals, etc) shall apply with the necessary modifications in relation to Class 4 contributions as they apply in relation to income tax; [but nothing in this Schedule affects the extent to which the Income Tax Acts apply with respect to any decision falling to be made—][1]

(*a*) under subsection (1) of section 17 above or subsection (1) of section 17 of the Northern Ireland Contributions and Benefits Act as to whether by regulations under that subsection a person is excepted from liability for Class 4 contributions, or his liability is deferred; or

(*b*) under regulations made by virtue of section 17(3) or (4) or 18 above or section 17(3) or (4) or 18 of the Northern Ireland Contributions and Benefits Act.

Former enactments—SSA 1975 Sch 2 para 9.

Amendments—[1] Words substituted by the Social Security Contributions (Transfer of Functions, etc) Act 1999 s 18 and Sch 7 para 11 with effect from 4 March 1999 for the purpose of authorising the making of Regulations and 1 April 1999 for all other purposes by virtue of the Social Security Contributions (Transfer of Functions, etc) Act 1999 (Commencement No 1 and Transitional Provisions) Order, SI 1999/527.

Husband and wife—1989–90 and previous years of assessment

9—

Amendments—Para 9 repealed by NICs Act 2014 s 17(1)(*b*) with effect from 13 March 2014.

SOCIAL SECURITY ADMINISTRATION ACT 1992

(1992 Chapter 5)

An Act to consolidate certain enactments relating to the administration of social security and related matters with amendments to give effect to recommendations of the Law Commission and the Scottish Law Commission.

[13 February 1992]

Cross references—See the SS Contributions and Benefits Act 1992 s 116(1) (for the purposes of this Act a member of Her Majesty's forces to be treated as an employed earner),

SSC & BA 1992 s 175(8) (subordinate legislation to modify provisions of this Act which re-enact provisions of the SSA 1975),

SSC & BA 1992 s 177(2) (inter-relation of the 1992 consolidation Acts);

SS (Consequential Provisions) Act 1992 ss 1, 2 (meaning of "the consolidating Acts" and continuity of law).

PART II
ADJUDICATION

Cross references—See the SS Contributions and Benefits Act 1992 s 116(2) (modification of any provision of this Part of this Act in its application to Her Majesty's forces and which replaces a provision of SSA 1975 Pt III),

SSC & BA 1992 s 117(1) (modification of any provision of this Part of this Act in its application to mariners, airmen, etc and which replaces a provision of SSA 1975 Pt III),

SSC & BA 1992 s 119 (modification of any provision of this Part of this Act in its application to persons who are or have been abroad and which replaces a provision of SSA 1975 Pt III),

SSC & BA 1992 s 120(1) (modification of any provision of this Part of this Act in its application to persons employed in continental shelf operations and which replaces a provision of SSA 1975 Pt III),

SSA 1998, s 4(1)(*a*) (functions of social security appeal tribunals, disability appeal tribunals and medical appeal tribunals constituted under this Part of this Act are transferred to appeal tribunals constituted under the 1998 Act, Ch 1).

Adjudication by the Secretary of State

[17 Questions for the Secretary of State

(1) Subject to this Part of this Act, any of the following questions shall be determined by the Secretary of State—

(a) a question whether a person is an earner and, if he is, as to the category of earners in which he is to be included;

(b) subject to subsection (2) below, a question whether the contribution conditions for any benefit are satisfied, or otherwise relating to a person's contributions or his earnings factor;

(c) a question whether a Class 1A contribution is payable or otherwise relating to a Class 1A contribution;

(d)–(f) . . .

(g) any question arising under any provision of Part XI of the Contributions and Benefits Act or this Act, or under any provision of regulations [or an order][1] *under that Part, as to—*

(i) whether a person is, or was, an employee or employer of another;

(ii) whether an employer is entitled to make any deduction from his contributions payments in accordance with [an order under section 159A][1] *of the Contributions and Benefits Act;*

(iii) whether a payment falls to be made to an employer in accordance with the regulations [or order][1]*;*

(iv) the amount that falls to be so deducted or paid;

(v) the amount of an employer's contributions payments for any period for the purposes of [an order under section 159A][1] *of the Contributions and Benefits Act; or*

(vi) . . .

(h), (i) . . .

(2) Subsection (1)(b) above includes any question arising—

(a) under section 17(1) of the Contributions and Benefits Act as to whether by regulations under that subsection a person is excepted from liability for Class 4 contributions, or his liability is deferred; or

(b) under regulations made by virtue of section 17(3) or (4) or 18 of that Act;

but not any other question relating to Class 4 contributions, nor any question within section 20(1)(c) below.

(3) Regulations may make provision restricting the persons who may apply to the Secretary of State for the determination of any such question as is mentioned in subsection (1) above.

(4) The Secretary of State may, if he thinks fit, before determining any such question as is mentioned in subsection (1) above, appoint a person to hold an inquiry into the question, or any matters arising in connection with it, and to report on the question, or on those matters, to the Secretary of State.][2]

Former enactments—Sub-s (1)(*a*), (*b*): SSA 1975 s 93(1)(*a*), (*b*).

Sub-s (1)(*c*): SSA 1975 s 93(1)(*bb*); SS (Contributions) Act 1991 s 3(1).

Sub-s (1)(*g*), (*h*): SSA 1986 s 52(2) and Sch 5 Pt II; Statutory Sick Pay Act 1991 s 2(3).

Sub-s (2): SSA 1975 s 93(2).

Sub-s (3): SSA 1975 s 93(2A); SSA 1989 s 21, Sch 3 para 1(1).

Sub-s (4): SSA 1975 s 93(3).

Regulations—See the SS (Adjudication) Regulations, SI 1986/2218; SS(CP)A 1992 s 2.

Note—Provisions omitted are outside the scope of this Publication.

Cross references—See SSPA 1975 s 60 (questions outside the scope of this section);

Social Security (Contributions) Regulations, SI 2001/1004 reg 106 (special Class 4 contributions: payment and notification),

Social Security (Contributions) Regulations, SI 2001/1004 reg 79 (remission of interest on Class 1A contributions);

SSA 1986 s 52(2) (questions specified in SSA 1986 Sch 5 Pt II to which this section applies);

Social Security (Adjudication) Regulations, SI 1986/2218 regs 14, 17 (application for decision, review or reference of the Secretary of State on principal questions),

Social Security (Adjudication) Regulations, SI 1986/2218 regs 15, 17 (procedure for inquiries, review or reference),

Social Security (Adjudication) Regulations, SI 1986/2218 regs 16, 17 (Secretary of State's decision and statement of grounds);

SS Contributions and Benefits Act 1992 Sch 1 para 6(4) (interest on overdue contributions regarding which questions remain to be determined under this section),

SSC & BA 1992 Sch 1 para 7(12) (penalties for late, fraudulent or negligent return of contributions regarding which questions remain to be determined under this section).

Social Security Contributions, etc (Decisions and Appeals—Transitional Modifications) Regulations, SI 1999/978.

Modifications—See Social Security Contributions, etc (Decisions and Appeals—Transitional Modifications) Regulations, SI 1999/978. Until Chapter II of Part I of the Social Security Act 1998 (social security decisions and appeals) is wholly in force, any enactment specified in column (1) of the Schedule to SI 1999/978 shall have effect subject to the modifications specified in column (2) of that Schedule.

Amendments—[1] In sub-s (1)(*g*), first and third words inserted and other words substituted by the Statutory Sick Pay Percentage Threshold Order, SI 1995/512 art 6(2)(*a*), with effect from 6 April 1995.

[2] This section is repealed by SSA 1998 s 39, Sch 8 with effect from 6 September 1999, for certain purposes (by virtue of the Social Security Act 1998 (Commencement No 9, and Savings and Consequential and Transitional Provisions) Order, SI 1999/2422 art 2(*c*) (subject to transitional provisions contained in art 4 Sch 14 thereof)), 29 November 1999, for certain purposes (by virtue of the Social Security Act 1998 (Commencement No 12 and Consequential and Transitional Provisions)

NIC

Order, SI 1999/3178, art 2(1), Sch 1 (subject to transitional provisions contained in art 4 Schs 21–23 thereof)), and with effect from a date to be appointed for all other purposes; see Modifications above.

[18 Appeal on question of law

(1) A question of law arising in connection with the determination by the Secretary of State of any such question as is mentioned in section 17(1) above may, if the Secretary of State thinks fit, be referred for decision to the High Court or, in Scotland, to the Court of Session.

(2) If the Secretary of State determines in accordance with subsection (1) above to refer any question of law to the court, he shall give notice in writing of his intention to do so—

(a) in a case where the question arises on an application made to the Secretary of State, to the applicant; and

(b) in any case to such persons as appear to him to be concerned with the question.

(3) Any person aggrieved by the decision of the Secretary of State on any question of law within subsection (1) above which is not referred in accordance with that subsection may appeal from that decision to the court.

(4) The Secretary of State shall be entitled to appear and be heard on any such reference or appeal.

(5) Rules of court shall include provision for regulating references and appeals under this section and for limiting the time within which such appeals may be brought.

(6) Notwithstanding anything in any Act, the decision of the court on a reference or appeal under this section shall be final.

(7) On any such reference or appeal the court may order the Secretary of State to pay the costs (in Scotland, the expenses) of any other person, whether or not the decision is in that other person's favour and whether or not the Secretary of State appears on the reference or appeal.][1]

Former enactments—SSA 1975 s 94.

Cross references—See the Social Security (Adjudication) Regulations, SI 1986/2218 reg 16 (obligation of Secretary of State to give reasons for his decision to enable interested person whether he may appeal under this section);

SS Contributions and Benefits Act 1992 Sch 1 para 6(4) (interest on overdue contributions regarding which an appeal under this section is pending),

SSC & BA 1992 Sch 1 para 7(12) (penalties for late, fraudulent or negligent return of contributions regarding which an appeal under this section is pending).

Amendments—[1] This section is repealed by SSA 1998 s 39, Sch 8 with effect from 6 September 1999, for certain purposes (by virtue of the Social Security Act 1998 (Commencement No 9, and Savings and Consequential and Transitional Provisions) Order, SI 1999/2422 art 2(*c*) (subject to transitional provisions contained in art 4 Sch 14 thereof)), 29 November 1999, for certain purposes (by virtue of the Social Security Act 1998 (Commencement No 12 and Consequential and Transitional Provisions) Order, SI 1999/3178, art 2(1), Sch 1 (subject to transitional provisions contained in art 4 Schs 21–23 thereof)), and with effect from a date to be appointed for all other purposes.

[19 Review of decisions

(1) Subject to subsection (2) below, the Secretary of State may review any decision given by him on any such question as is mentioned in section 17(1) above, if—

(a) new facts have been brought to his notice; or

(b) he is satisfied that the decision—

(i) was given in ignorance of some material fact;

(ii) was based on a mistake as to some material fact; or

(iii) was erroneous in point of law.

(2) A decision shall not be reviewed while an appeal under section 18 above is pending against the decision of the Secretary of State on a question of law arising in connection with it, or before the time for so appealing has expired.

(3) On a review any question of law may be referred under subsection (1) of section 18 above or, where it is not so referred, may be the subject of an appeal under subsection (3) of that section, and the other provisions of that section shall apply accordingly.][1]

Former enactments—Sub-s (1): SSA 1975 s 96(1); SSA 1986 s 52(1), Sch 5 para 3.

Sub-ss (2), (3): SSA 1975 s 96(2); SSA 1980 ss 2, 21, Sch 1 para 9.

Cross references—See the Social Security (Adjudication) Regulations, SI 1986/2218 reg 17 (procedure for review of decisions);

SS Contributions and Benefits Act 1992 Sch 1 para 6(4) (interest on overdue contributions regarding which a review under this section is pending);

SSC & BA 1992 Sch 1 para 7(12) (penalties for late, fraudulent or negligent return of contributions regarding which a review under this section is pending).

Amendments—[1] This section is repealed by SSA 1998 s 39, Sch 8 with effect from 6 September 1999, for certain purposes (by virtue of the Social Security Act 1998 (Commencement No 9, and Savings and Consequential and Transitional Provisions) Order, SI 1999/2422 art 2(*c*) (subject to transitional provisions contained in art 4 Sch 14 thereof)), 29 November 1999, for certain purposes (by virtue of the Social Security Act 1998 (Commencement No 12 and Consequential and Transitional Provisions) Order, SI 1999/3178, art 2(1), Sch 1 (subject to transitional provisions contained in art 4 Schs 21–23 thereof)), and with effect from a date to be appointed for all other purposes.

Regulations

[58 Regulations as to determination of questions and matters arising out of, or pending, reviews and appeals

(1) Subject to the provisions of this Act, provision may be made by regulations for the determination—

(a) by the Secretary of State; or

(b) by a person or tribunal appointed or constituted in accordance with the regulations,

of any question arising under or in connection with the Contributions and Benefits Act[, the Jobseekers Act 1995][1] or the former legislation, including a claim for benefit.

(2) In this section "the former legislation" means the National Insurance Acts 1965 to 1974 and the National Insurance (Industrial Injuries) Acts 1965 to 1974 and the 1975 Act and Part II of the 1986 Act.

(3) Regulations under subsection (1) above may modify, add to or exclude any provisions of this Part of this Act, so far as relating to any questions to which the regulations relate.

(4) . . .

(5) Regulations under subsection (1) above may provide for the review by the Secretary of State of decisions on questions determined by him.

(6) The Lord Chancellor may by regulations provide—

(a) for officers authorised—

(i) by the Lord Chancellor; or

(ii) in Scotland, by the Secretary of State,

to determine any question which is determinable by a Commissioner and which does not involve the determination of any appeal, application for leave to appeal or reference;

(b) for the procedure to be followed by any such officer in determining any such question;

(c) for the manner in which determinations of such questions by such officers may be called in question.

(7) A determination which would have the effect of preventing an appeal, application for leave to appeal or reference being determined by a Commissioner is not a determination of the appeal, application or reference for the purposes of subsection (6) above.

(8) Regulations under subsection (1) above may provide—

(a) for the reference to the High Court or, in Scotland, the Court of Session for decision of any question of law arising in connection with the determination of a question by the Secretary of State; and

(b) for appeals to the High Court or Court of Session from the decision of the Secretary of State on any such question of law;

and subsections (5) to (7) of section 18 above shall apply to a reference or appeal under this subsection as they apply to a reference or appeal under subsections (1) to (3) of that section.][2]

Former enactments—Sub-ss (1), (2): SSA 1975 s 114(1).
Sub-s (3): SSA 1975 s 114(2).
Sub-ss (5)–(7): SSA 1975 s 114(2B)–(2D); SSA 1986 s 52(1), Sch 5 para 16(*a*).
Sub-s (8): SSA 1975 s 114(5).

Regulations—See the SS (Adjudication) Regulations, SI 1986/2218; SS(CP)A 1992 s 2.

Note—Sub-s (4) is outside the scope of this Publication.

Amendments—[1] Words in sub-s (1) inserted by the Jobseekers Act 1995 Sch 2 para 44 with effect from 22 April 1996 by virtue of SI 1996/1126.

[2] This section is repealed by SSA 1998 s 39, Sch 8 with effect from 6 September 1999, for certain purposes (by virtue of the Social Security Act 1998 (Commencement No 9, and Savings and Consequential and Transitional Provisions) Order, SI 1999/2422 art 2(*c*) (subject to transitional provisions contained in art 4 Sch 14 thereof)), 29 November 1999, for certain purposes (by virtue of the Social Security Act 1998 (Commencement No 12 and Consequential and Transitional Provisions) Order, SI 1999/3178, art 2(1), Sch 1 (subject to transitional provisions contained in art 4 Schs 21–23 thereof)), and with effect from a date to be appointed for all other purposes.

[59 Procedure

(1) Regulations (in this section referred to as "procedure regulations") may make any such provision as is specified in Schedule 3 to this Act.

(2) . . .

(3) At any inquiry held by virtue of procedure regulations the witnesses shall, if the person holding the inquiry thinks fit, be examined on oath; and the person holding the inquiry shall have power to administer oaths for that purpose.

(4) In proceedings for the determination of a question mentioned in section 17(1)(c) above (including proceedings on an inquiry)—

(a) in England and Wales, there shall be available to a witness (other than the person who is liable, or alleged to be liable, to pay the Class 1A contribution in question) any privilege against self-incrimination or incrimination of a spouse which is available to a witness in legal proceedings; and

(b) in Scotland, section 3 of the Evidence (Scotland) Act 1853 (competence and compellability of witnesses) shall apply as it applies to civil proceedings.

(5) . . .

(6) It is hereby declared—

(a) that the power to prescribe procedure includes power to make provision as to the representation of one person, at any hearing of a case, by another person whether having professional qualifications or not; and

(b) that the power to provide for the manner in which questions arising for determination by the Secretary of State are to be raised includes power to make provision with respect to the formulation of any such questions, whether arising on a reference under section 117 below or otherwise.

(7) Except so far as it may be applied in relation to England and Wales by procedure regulations, [Part 1 of the Arbitration Act 1996][1] shall not apply to any proceedings under this Part of this Act.][2]

Former enactments—Sub-s (1): SSA 1975 s 115(1), (2).

Sub-s (3): SSA 1975 s 115(4).

Sub-s (4): SSA 1975 s 115(4A); SS (Contributions) Act 1991 s 3(2).

Sub-s (6): SSA 1975 s 115(6); SSA 1989 s 21, Sch 3 para 1(2).

Sub-s (7): SSA 1975 s 115(7).

Regulations—See the SS (Adjudication) Regulations, SI 1986/2218; SS(CP)A 1992 s 2.

Note—Sub-ss (2), (5) are outside the scope of this Publication.

Cross references—Social Security Contributions, etc (Decisions and Appeals—Transitional Modifications) Regulations, SI 1999/978.

Modifications—See Social Security Contributions, etc (Decisions and Appeals—Transitional Modifications) Regulations, SI 1999/978. Until Chapter II of Part I of the Social Security Act 1998 (social security decisions and appeals) is wholly in force, any enactment specified in column (1) of the Schedule to SI 1999/978 shall have effect subject to the modifications specified in column (2) of that Schedule.

Amendments—[1] Words substituted by the Arbitration Act 1996 s 107(1), Sch 3 para 54 with effect from 31 January 1997.

[2] This section is repealed by SSA 1998 s 39, Sch 8 with effect from 6 September 1999, for certain purposes (by virtue of the Social Security Act 1998 (Commencement No 9, and Savings and Consequential and Transitional Provisions) Order, SI 1999/2422 art 2(*c*) (subject to transitional provisions contained in art 4 Sch 14 thereof)), 29 November 1999, for certain purposes (by virtue of the Social Security Act 1998 (Commencement No 12 and Consequential and Transitional Provisions) Order, SI 1999/3178, art 2(1), Sch 1 (subject to transitional provisions contained in art 4 Schs 21–23 thereof)), and with effect from a date to be appointed for all other purposes.

[60 Finality of decisions

(1) Subject to the provisions of this Part of this Act, the decision of any claim or question in accordance with the foregoing provisions of this Part of this Act shall be final; and subject to the provisions of any regulations under section 58 above, the decision of any claim or question in accordance with those regulations shall be final.

(2) Subsection (1) above shall not make any finding of fact or other determination embodied in or necessary to a decision, or on which it is based, conclusive for the purpose of any further decision.

(3)–(5) . . .][1]

Former enactments—Sub-s (1): SSA 1975 s 117(1); Health and Social Services and Social Security Adjudications Act 1983 s 25, Sch 8 para 6.

Sub-s (2): SSA 1975 s 117(2).

Note—Sub-ss (3)–(5) are outside the scope of this Publication.

Amendments—[1] This section is repealed by SSA 1998 s 39, Sch 8 with effect from 6 September 1999, for certain purposes (by virtue of the Social Security Act 1998 (Commencement No 9, and Savings and Consequential and Transitional Provisions) Order, SI 1999/2422 art 2(*c*) (subject to transitional provisions contained in art 4 Sch 14 thereof)), 29 November 1999, for certain purposes (by virtue of the Social Security Act 1998 (Commencement No 12 and Consequential and Transitional Provisions) Order, SI 1999/3178, art 2(1), Sch 1 (subject to transitional provisions contained in art 4 Schs 21–23 thereof)), and with effect from a date to be appointed for all other purposes.

[61 Regulations about supplementary matters relating to determinations

(1) Regulations may make provision as respects matters arising—

(a) pending the determination under this Act (whether in the first instance or on an appeal or reference, and whether originally or on review)—

(i) of any claim for benefit to which this section applies; or

(ii) of any question affecting any person's right to such benefit or its receipt; or

(iii) of any person's liability for contributions . . . [1]; or

(b) out of the revision on appeal or review of any decision under this Act on any such claim or question.

(2) Without prejudice to the generality of subsection (1) above, regulations under that subsection may include provision as to the date from which any decision on a review is to have effect or to be deemed to have had effect.

(3)–(4) . . .][2]

Former enactments—SSA 1975 s 119(3), (4)(*a*).

Regulations—See the SS (Adjudication) Regulations, SI 1986/2218; SS(CP)A 1992 s 2.

Note—Sub-ss (3), (4) are outside the scope of this Publication.

Amendments—[1] Repealed by Social Security Administration (Fraud) Act 1997 with effect from 1 July 1997 by virtue of SI 1997/1577.

[2] This section is repealed by SSA 1998 s 39, Sch 8 with effect from 6 September 1999, for certain purposes (by virtue of the Social Security Act 1998 (Commencement No 9, and Savings and Consequential and Transitional Provisions) Order, SI 1999/2422 art 2(*c*) (subject to transitional provisions contained in art 4 Sch 14 thereof)), 29 November 1999, for certain purposes (by virtue of the Social Security Act 1998 (Commencement No 12 and Consequential and Transitional Provisions) Order, SI 1999/3178, art 2(1), Sch 1 (subject to transitional provisions contained in art 4 Schs 21–23 thereof)), and with effect from a date to be appointed for all other purposes.

PART VI
ENFORCEMENT

Inspection and offences

[109A Authorisations for investigators

(1) An individual who for the time being has the Secretary of State's authorisation for the purposes of this Part shall be entitled, for any one or more of the purposes mentioned in subsection (2) below, to exercise any of the powers which are conferred on an authorised officer by sections 109B and 109C below.

(2) Those purposes are—

(*a*) ascertaining in relation to any case whether a benefit is or was payable in that case in accordance with any provision of the relevant social security legislation;

(*b*) investigating the circumstances in which any accident, injury or disease which has given rise, or may give rise, to a claim for—

(i) industrial injuries benefit, or

(ii) any benefit under any provision of the relevant social security legislation,

occurred or may have occurred, or was or may have been received or contracted;

(*c*) ascertaining whether provisions of the relevant social security legislation are being, have been or are likely to be contravened (whether by particular persons or more generally);

(*d*) preventing, detecting and securing evidence of the commission (whether by particular persons or more generally) of benefit offences.

(3) An individual has the Secretary of State's authorisation for the purposes of this Part if, and only if, the Secretary of State has granted him an authorisation for those purposes and he is—

(*a*) an official of a Government department;

(*b*) an individual employed by an authority administering housing benefit or council tax benefit;

(*c*) an individual employed by an authority or joint committee that carries out functions relating to housing benefit or council tax benefit on behalf of the authority administering that benefit; or

(*d*) an individual employed by a person authorised by or on behalf of any such authority or joint committee as is mentioned in paragraph (*b*) or (*c*) above to carry out functions relating to housing benefit or council tax benefit for that authority or committee.

(4) An authorisation granted for the purposes of this Part to an individual of any of the descriptions mentioned in subsection (3) above—

(*a*) must be contained in a certificate provided to that individual as evidence of his entitlement to exercise powers conferred by this Part;

(*b*) may contain provision as to the period for which the authorisation is to have effect; and

(*c*) may restrict the powers exercisable by virtue of the authorisation so as to prohibit their exercise except for particular purposes, in particular circumstances or in relation to particular benefits or particular provisions of the relevant social security legislation.

(5) An authorisation granted under this section may be withdrawn at any time by the Secretary of State.

(6) Where the Secretary of State grants an authorisation for the purposes of this Part to an individual employed by a local authority, or to an individual employed by a person who carries out functions relating to housing benefit or council tax benefit on behalf of a local authority—

(*a*) the Secretary of State and the local authority shall enter into such arrangements (if any) as they consider appropriate with respect to the carrying out of functions conferred on that individual by or in connection with the authorisation granted to him; and

(*b*) the Secretary of State may make to the local authority such payments (if any) as he thinks fit in respect of the carrying out by that individual of any such functions.

(7) The matters on which a person may be authorised to consider and report to the Secretary of State under section 139A below shall be taken to include the carrying out by any such individual as is mentioned in subsection (3)(*b*) to (*d*) above of any functions conferred on that individual by virtue of any grant by the Secretary of State of an authorisation for the purposes of this Part.

(8) The powers conferred by sections 109B and 109C below shall be exercisable in relation to persons holding office under the Crown and persons in the service of the Crown, and in relation to premises owned or occupied by the Crown, as they are exercisable in relation to other persons and premises.

[(9) This section and sections 109B to 109C below apply as if—

(*a*) the Tax Credits Act 2002 were relevant social security legislation, and

(*b*) accordingly, child tax credit and working tax credit were relevant social security benefits for the purposes of the definition of "benefit offence".][2]][1]

Amendments—[1] This section and ss 109B, 109C substituted for s 110 by the Child Support, Pensions and Social Security Act 2000 ss 67, 86, Sch 6 paras 1, 2 with effect from 2 April 2001 (by virtue of SI 2001/1252).

[2] Sub-s (9) inserted by the Welfare Reform Act 2012 s 122 with effect from 6 June 2012 (by virtue of SI 2012/1246).

Prospective amendments—Sub-ss (3)(*b*)–(*d*), (6), (7) to be repealed by the Welfare Reform Act 2012 s 147, Sch 14 Part 1 with effect from a date to be appointed.

[109B Power to require information

(1) An authorised officer who has reasonable grounds for suspecting that a person—

(*a*) is a person falling within subsection (2) [or (2A)][2] below, and

(*b*) has or may have possession of or access to any information about any matter that is relevant for any one or more of the purposes mentioned in section 109A(2) above,

may, by written notice, require that person to provide all such information described in the notice as is information of which he has possession, or to which he has access, and which it is reasonable for the authorised officer to require for a purpose so mentioned.

(2) The persons who fall within this subsection are—

(*a*) any person who is or has been an employer or employee within the meaning of any provision made by or under the Contributions and Benefits Act;

(*b*) any person who is or has been a self-employed earner within the meaning of any such provision;

(*c*) any person who by virtue of any provision made by or under that Act falls, or has fallen, to be treated for the purposes of any such provision as a person within paragraph (*a*) or (*b*) above;

(*d*) any person who is carrying on, or has carried on, any business involving the supply of goods for sale to the ultimate consumers by individuals not carrying on retail businesses from retail premises;

(*e*) any person who is carrying on, or has carried on, any business involving the supply of goods or services by the use of work done or services performed by persons other than employees of his;

(*f*) any person who is carrying on, or has carried on, an agency or other business for the introduction or supply, to persons requiring them, of persons available to do work or to perform services;

(*g*) any local authority acting in their capacity as an authority responsible for the granting of any licence;

(*h*) any person who is or has been a trustee or manager of a personal or occupational pension scheme;

(*i*) any person who is or has been liable to make a compensation payment or a payment to the Secretary of State under section 6 of the Social Security (Recovery of Benefits) Act 1997 (payments in respect of recoverable benefits);

[(ia) a person of a prescribed description;][7] and

(*j*) the servants and agents of any such person as is specified in any of paragraphs (*a*) to [*ia*][7] above.

[(2A) The persons who fall within this subsection are—

(*a*) any bank;

[(*aa*) the Director of National Savings;][4]

(*b*) any person carrying on a business the whole or a significant part of which consists in the provision of credit (whether secured or unsecured) to members of the public;

[(*c*) any insurer;][4]

(*d*) any credit reference agency (within the meaning given by section 145(8) of the Consumer Credit Act 1974 (c 39));

(*e*) any body the principal activity of which is to facilitate the exchange of information for the purpose of preventing or detecting fraud;

(*f*) any person carrying on a business the whole or a significant part of which consists in the provision to members of the public of a service for transferring money from place to place;

(*g*) any water undertaker or sewerage undertaker, [Scottish Water or any local authority which is to collect charges by virtue of an order under section 37 of the Water Industry (Scotland) Act 2002 (asp 3)][5];

[(*h*) any person who—

(i) is the holder of a licence under section 7 of the Gas Act 1986 (c 44) to convey gas through pipes, or

(ii) is the holder of a licence under section 7A(1) of that Act to supply gas through pipes;][4]

[(*i*) any person who (within the meaning of the Electricity Act 1989 (c 29)) distributes or supplies electricity;][4]

(*j*) any person who provides a telecommunications service;

(*k*) any person conducting any educational establishment or institution;

(*l*) any body the principal activity of which is to provide services in connection with admissions to educational establishments or institutions;

(*m*) the Student Loans Company;

(*n*) any servant or agent of any person mentioned in any of the preceding paragraphs.][2]

[(2B) Subject to the following provisions of this section, the powers conferred by this section on an authorised officer to require information from any person by virtue of his falling within subsection (2A) above shall be exercisable for the purpose only of obtaining information relating to a particular person identified (by name or description) by the officer.][2]

[(2C) An authorised officer shall not, in exercise of those powers, require any information from any person by virtue of his falling within subsection (2A) above unless it appears to that officer that there are reasonable grounds for believing that the identified person to whom it relates is—

(*a*) a person who has committed, is committing or intends to commit a benefit offence; or

(*b*) a person who (within the meaning of Part 7 of the Contributions and Benefits Act) is a member of the family of a person falling within paragraph (*a*) above.][2]

[(2D) Nothing in subsection (2B) or (2C) above shall prevent an authorised officer who is an official of a Government department and whose authorisation states that his authorisation applies for the purposes of this subsection from exercising the powers conferred by this section for obtaining from—

(*a*) a water undertaker or [Scottish Water][5];

(*b*) any person who (within the meaning of the Gas Act 1986) supplies gas conveyed through pipes,

(*c*) any person who (within the meaning of the Electricity Act 1989) supplies electricity conveyed by distribution systems, or

(*d*) any servant or agent of a person mentioned in any of the preceding paragraphs,

any information which relates exclusively to whether and in what quantities water, gas or electricity are being or have been supplied to residential premises specified or described in the notice by which the information is required.][2]

[(2E) The powers conferred by this section shall not be exercisable for obtaining from any person providing a telecommunications service any information other than information which (within the meaning of section 21 of the Regulation of Investigatory Powers Act 2000 (c 23)) is communications data but not traffic data.][2]

[(2F) Nothing in subsection (2B) or (2C) above shall prevent an authorised officer from exercising the powers conferred by this section for requiring information, from a person who provides a telecommunications service, about the identity and postal address of a person identified by the authorised officer solely by reference to a telephone number or electronic address used in connection with the provision of such a service.][2]

(3) The obligation of a person to provide information in accordance with a notice under this section shall be discharged only by the provision of that information, at such reasonable time and in such form as may be specified in the notice, to the authorised officer who—

(*a*) is identified by or in accordance with the terms of the notice; or

(*b*) has been identified, since the giving of the notice, by a further written notice given by the authorised officer who imposed the original requirement or another authorised officer.

(4) The power of an authorised officer under this section to require the provision of information shall include a power to require the production and delivery up and (if necessary) creation of, or of copies of or extracts from, any such documents containing the information as may be specified or described in the notice imposing the requirement.

[(5) No one shall be required under this section to provide—

(*a*) any information that tends to incriminate either himself or, in the case of a person who is [married or is a civil partner, his spouse or civil partner][6]; or

(*b*) any information in respect of which a claim to legal professional privilege or, in Scotland, confidentiality as between client and professional legal adviser, would be successful in any proceedings;

and for the purposes of this subsection it is immaterial whether the information is in documentary form or not.][2]

[(6) Provision may be made by order—

(a) adding any person to the list of persons falling within subsection (2A) above;

(b) removing any person from the list of persons falling within that subsection;

(c) modifying that subsection for the purpose of taking account of any change to the name of any person for the time being falling within that subsection.][3]

[(7) In this section—

["bank" means—

(*a*) a person who has permission under [Part 4A][8] of the Financial Services and Markets Act 2000 (c 8) to accept deposits;

(*b*) an EEA firm of the kind mentioned in paragraph 5(b) of Schedule 3 to that Act which has permission under paragraph 15 of that Schedule (as a result of qualifying for authorisation under paragraph 12 of that Schedule) to accept deposits or other repayable funds from the public; or

(*c*) a person who does not require permission under that Act to accept deposits, in the course of his business in the United Kingdom;][4]

NIC

"credit" includes a cash loan or any form of financial accommodation, including the cashing of a cheque;

["insurer" means—

(*a*) a person who has permission under [Part 4A][8] of the Financial Services and Markets Act 2000 to effect or carry out contracts of insurance; or

(*b*) an EEA firm of the kind mentioned in paragraph 5(*d*) of Schedule 3 to that Act, which has permission under paragraph 15 of that Schedule (as a result of qualifying for authorisation under paragraph 12 of that Schedule) to effect or carry out contracts of insurance;][4]

"residential premises", in relation to a supply of water, gas or electricity, means any premises which—

(*a*) at the time of the supply were premises occupied wholly or partly for residential purposes, or

(*b*) are premises to which that supply was provided as if they were so occupied; and

"telecommunications service" has the same meaning as in the Regulation of Investigatory Powers Act 2000 (c 23).][3]

[(7A) The definitions of "bank" and "insurer" in subsection (7) must be read with—

(*a*) section 22 of the Financial Services and Markets Act 2000;

(*b*) any relevant order under that section; and

(*c*) Schedule 2 to that Act.][4]][1]

Regulations—Social Security (Persons Required to Provide Information) Regulations, SI 2013/1510.

Amendments—[1] This section and ss 109A and 109C substituted for s 110 by the Child Support, Pensions and Social Security Act 2000 ss 67, 86, Sch 6 paras 1, 2 with effect from 2 April 2001.

[2] Words in sub-s (1) inserted, sub-ss (2A)–(2F) inserted, and sub-s (5) substituted; by the Social Security Fraud Act 2001 s 1 with effect from 30 April 2002 (by virtue of SI 2002/1222).

[3] Sub-ss (6), (7) inserted by the Social Security Fraud Act 2001 s 1 with effect from 30 April 2002 (by virtue of SI 2002/1222).

[4] In sub-s (2A), para (*aa*) inserted, paras (*c*), (*h*), (*i*) substituted; in sub-s (7), definition of substituted, and that of "insurer" inserted; and sub-s (7A) inserted, by the Social Security Administration Act 1992 (Amendment) Order, SI 2002/817 arts 1–3 with effect from 1 April 2002.

[5] Words in sub-s (2A)(*g*), (2D)(*a*) substituted by the Water Industry (Scotland) Act 2002 (Consequential Modifications) Order, SI 2002/1822 art 2, Schedule para 16 with effect from 14 July 2004.

[6] Words in sub-s (5)(*a*) substituted by the Civil Partnership Act 2004 s 254(1), Sch 24 para 64 with effect from 5 December 2005 (SI 2005/3175, art 2(1), Sch 1).

[7] In sub-s (2), para (*ia*) inserted and in para (*j*) reference substituted for "(*l*)by the Welfare Reform Act 2012 s 110 with effect from 17 June 2013 for the purposes of making regulations and with effect from 1 October 2013 for all other purposes.

[8] In sub-s (7), in definitions of "bank" and "insurer" words substituted by the Financial Services Act 2012 s 114(1), Sch 18 para 74(1), 93) with effect from 1 April 2013 (by virtue of SI 2013/423 art 3, Schedule).

Prospective amendments—Sub-ss (2A)(*j*), (2F) to be repealed; in sub-s (2E), words "so as to secure the disclosure by a telecommunications operator or postal operator of communications data without the consent of the operator." to be substituted for words "for obtaining from any person providing a telecommunications service any information other than information which (within the meaning of section 21 of the Regulation of Investigatory Powers Act 2000 (c 23)) is communications data but not traffic data."; and in sub-s (7), definition of "communications data" to be inserted after definition of "bank", and definition of "postal operator" to be inserted after definition of "insurer", and definition of "telecommunications operator" to be substituted for definition of "telecommunications service" by the Investigatory Powers Act 2016 s 12(1), Sch 2, para 5 with effect from a date to be appointed. Definitions as inserted to read as follows—

""communications data" has the same meaning as in the Investigatory Powers Act 2016 (see sections 261 and 262 of that Act);".

""postal operator" has the same meaning as in the Investigatory Powers Act 2016 (see section 262 of that Act);".

Definition as substituted to read as follows—

""telecommunications operator" has the same meaning as in the Investigatory Powers Act 2016 (see section 261 of that Act).".

[109BA Power of Secretary of State to require electronic access to information

(1) Subject to subsection (2) below, where it appears to the Secretary of State—

(*a*) that a person falling within section 109B(2A) keeps any electronic records,

(*b*) that the records contain or are likely, from time to time, to contain information about any matter that is relevant for any one or more of the purposes mentioned in section 109A(2) above, and

(*c*) that facilities exist under which electronic access to those records is being provided, or is capable of being provided, by that person to other persons,

the Secretary of State may require that person to enter into arrangements under which authorised officers are allowed such access to those records.

(2) An authorised officer—

(*a*) shall be entitled to obtain information in accordance with arrangements entered into under subsection (1) above only if his authorisation states that his authorisation applies for the purposes of that subsection; and (*b*) shall not seek to obtain any information in accordance with any such arrangements other than information which relates to a particular person and could be the subject of a requirement under section 109B above.

(3) The matters that may be included in the arrangements that a person is required to enter into under subsection (1) above may include—

(*a*) requirements as to the electronic access to records that is to be made available to authorised officers;

(*b*) requirements as to the keeping of records of the use that is made of the arrangements;

(*c*) requirements restricting the disclosure of information about the use that is made of the arrangements; and

(*d*) such other incidental requirements as the Secretary of State considers appropriate in connection with allowing access to records to authorised officers.

(4) An authorised officer who is allowed access in accordance with any arrangements entered into under subsection (1) above shall be entitled to make copies of, and to take extracts from, any records containing information which he is entitled to require under section 109B.][1]

Amendments—[1] Section 109BA inserted by the Social Security Fraud Act 2001 ss 2(1), 20 with effect from 30 April 2002 (by virtue of SI 2002/1222).

[109C Powers of entry

(1) An authorised officer shall be entitled, at any reasonable time and either alone or accompanied by such other persons as he thinks fit, to enter any premises which—

(*a*) are liable to inspection under this section; and

(*b*) are premises to which it is reasonable for him to require entry in order to exercise the powers conferred by this section.

(2) An authorised officer who has entered any premises liable to inspection under this section may—

(*a*) make such an examination of those premises, and

(*b*) conduct any such inquiry there,

as appears to him appropriate for any one or more of the purposes mentioned in section 109A(2) above.

(3) An authorised officer who has entered any premises liable to inspection under this section may—

(*a*) question any person whom he finds there;

(*b*) require any person whom he finds there to do any one or more of the following—

(i) to provide him with such information,

(ii) to produce and deliver up and (if necessary) create such documents or such copies of, or extracts from, documents,

as he may reasonably require for any one or more of the purposes mentioned in section 109A(2) above; and

(*c*) take possession of and either remove or make his own copies of any such documents as appear to him to contain information that is relevant for any of those purposes.

(4) The premises liable to inspection under this section are any premises (including premises consisting in the whole or a part of a dwelling house) which an authorised officer has reasonable grounds for suspecting are—

(*a*) premises which are a person's place of employment;

(*b*) premises from which a trade or business is being carried on or where documents relating to a trade or business are kept by the person carrying it on or by another person on his behalf;

(*c*) premises from which a personal or occupational pension scheme is being administered or where documents relating to the administration of such a scheme are kept by the person administering the scheme or by another person on his behalf;

(*d*) premises where a person who is the compensator in relation to any such accident, injury or disease as is referred to in section 109A(2)(*b*) above is to be found;

(*e*) premises where a person on whose behalf any such compensator has made, may have made or may make a compensation payment is to be found.

(5) An authorised officer applying for admission to any premises in accordance with this section shall, if required to do so, produce the certificate containing his authorisation for the purposes of this Part.

(6) Subsection (5) of section 109B applies for the purposes of this section as it applies for the purposes of that section.]

Amendments—This section and ss 109A and 109B substituted for s 110 by the Child Support, Pensions and Social Security Act 2000 ss 67, 86, Sch 6 paras 1, 2 with effect from 2 April 2001 (by virtue of SI 2001/1252).

Prospective amendments—Sub-ss (6) to be substituted by the Investigatory Powers Act 2016 s 12(1), Sch 2, para 6 with effect from a date to be appointed. Sub-ss (6) as substituted to read as follows—

"(6) Subsections (2E) and (5) of section 109B apply for the purposes of this section as they apply for the purposes of that section.".

NIC

[110ZA Class 1, 1A, 1B or 2 contributions: powers to call for documents etc

[(1) Schedule 36 to the Finance Act 2008 (information and inspection powers) applies for the purpose of checking a person's position as regards relevant contributions as it applies for the purpose of checking a person's tax position, subject to the modifications in subsection (2).

(2) That Schedule applies as if—

(*a*) references to any provision of the Taxes Acts were to any provision of this Act or the Contributions and Benefits Act [or the National Insurance Contributions Act 2014][6] relating to relevant contributions,

(*b*) references to prejudice to the assessment or collection of tax were to prejudice to the assessment of liability for, and payment of, relevant contributions,

(*c*) the reference to information relating to the conduct of a pending appeal relating to tax were a reference to information relating to the conduct of a pending appeal relating to relevant contributions, and

(*d*) paragraphs 21[, 21A][4], [35(4A)(*c*), 36, 37(2) [and (2A)][4], 37A and 37B][3] of that Schedule (restrictions on giving taxpayer notice where taxpayer has made tax return) were omitted.][2]

[(2A) Part 3 of Schedule 38 to the Finance Act 2012 (power to obtain tax agent's files etc) applies in relation to relevant contributions as in relation to tax and, accordingly—

(*a*) the cases described in paragraph 7 of that Schedule (case A and case B) include cases involving conduct or an offence relating to relevant contributions,

(*b*) (whether the case involves conduct or an offence relating to tax or relevant contributions) the papers and other documents that may be sought under that Part include ones relating to relevant contributions, and

(*c*) the other Parts of that Schedule apply so far as necessary to give effect to the application of Part 3 by virtue of this subsection.][5]

(3) In this section "relevant contributions" means Class 1, Class 1A, Class 1B or Class 2 contributions.][1]

Cross-references—See the Social Security (Contributions) (Amendment and Application of Schedule 38 to the Finance Act 2012) Regulations, SI 2013/622 reg 41 (the provisions of FA 2012 Sch 38 (tax agents: dishonest conduct) apply in relation to Class 1, Class 1A, Class 1B and Class 2 NICs as in relation to tax to the extent that they do not already apply).

Amendments—[1] This section substituted by the NIC and Statutory Payments Act 2004 s 7 with effect from 6 April 2005 (by virtue of SI 2004/1943).

[2] Sub-ss (1), (2) substituted by FA 2008 s 113, Sch 36 para 84 with effect from 1 April 2009 (by virtue of SI 2009/404 art 2). In relation to a notice given on or before 31 March 2009, for the purposes of the application of TMA 1970 s 20 to this section, the amendments made by FA 2008 Sch 36 para 84 shall be disregarded (SI 2009/404 art 9).

[3] In sub-s (2)(*d*) words substituted for words "35(4)(*b*), 36 and 37(2)" by Finance Act 2009 Schedule 47 (Consequential Amendments) Order, SI 2009/2035, Art 2, Schedule para 27 with effect from 13 August 2009.

[4] In sub-s (2)(d), references inserted by the Finance Act 2009, Section 96 and Schedule 48 (Appointed Day, Savings and Consequential Amendments) Order, SI 2009/3054 art 3, Schedule para 3 with effect from 1 April 2010.

[5] Sub-s (2A) inserted by FA 2012 s 223, Sch 38 para 56 with effect from 1 April 2013 (by virtue of SI 2013/279 art 2).

[6] Words in sub-s (2)(*a*) inserted by the NICs Act 2014 s 7(6) with effect from 6 April 2014.

111 Delay, obstruction etc of inspector

(1) If a person—

(*a*) intentionally delays or obstructs an [authorised officer][3] in the exercise of any power under this Act [other than an Inland Revenue power][1];

[(*ab*) refuses or neglects to comply with any requirement under section 109BA *or 110AA*[5] or with the requirements of any arrangements entered into in accordance with subsection (1) of that section; or][3]

(*b*) refuses or neglects to answer any question or to furnish any information or to produce any document when required to do so under this Act [otherwise than in the exercise of an Inland Revenue power][1],

he shall be guilty of an offence and liable on summary conviction to a fine not exceeding level 3 on the standard scale.

(2) Where a person is convicted of an offence under [subsection (1)(*ab*) or (*b*)][3] above and the refusal or neglect is continued by him after his conviction, he shall be guilty of a further offence and liable on summary conviction to a fine not exceeding £40 for each day on which it is continued.

[(3) In subsection (1) "Inland Revenue power" means any power conferred on an officer of the Inland Revenue by [virtue of][4] section 110ZA above or by virtue of [an authorisation granted under section 109A *or 110A*[5]][2] above.][1]

[(4) . . . [4]][1]

Former enactments—SSA 1986 s 58(8), (9).

Amendments—[1] Words in sub-ss (1), and sub-ss (3) and (4) inserted by the Social Security Contributions (Transfer of Functions, etc) Act 1999 s 5 and Sch 5 para 4 with effect from 1 April 1999 by virtue of the Social Security Contributions (Transfer of Functions, etc) Act 1999 (Commencement No 1 and Transitional Provisions) Order, SI 1999/527.

[2] Words in sub-ss (3), (4) substituted by the Child Support, Pensions and Social Security Act 2000 ss 67, 86, Sch 6 paras 1, 4 with effect from 2 April 2001(by virtue of SI 2001/1252).

[3] Sub-ss (1), (2) amended, and sub-s (1)(*ab*) inserted by the Social Security Fraud Act 2001 ss 1(6), 2(3), 20 with effect from 30 April 2002 (by virtue of SI 2002/1222).

4 Words in sub-s (3) inserted, and sub-s (4) repealed, by the NIC and Statutory Payments Act 2004 ss 11, 12, Schedule 1 para 3(1), (2), Sch 2 Pt 1 with effect from 6 April 2005 (by virtue of SI 2004/1943).

5 In sub-s (1)(*ab*) words "or 110AA", and in sub-s (3) words "or 110A", repealed in so far as they relate to the abolition of council tax benefit, by the Welfare Reform Act 2012 s 147, Sch 14 Part 1 with effect from 1 April 2013 (by virtue of SI 2013/358 art 8(c)). Note that certain transitional provisions apply in relation to the abolition of council tax benefit (see SI 2013/358 art 9).

[113 Breach of regulations

(1) Regulations and schemes under any of the [legislation to which this section applies][3] may provide that any person who contravenes, or fails to comply with, any provision contained in regulations made under [that legislation[3]]—

(*a*) in the case of a provision relating to contributions, shall be liable to a penalty;

(*b*) in any other case, shall be guilty of an offence under [any enactment contained in the legislation in question][3].

[(1A) The legislation to which this section applies is—

(*a*) the relevant social security legislation; and

(*b*) the enactments specified in section 121DA(1) so far as relating to contributions . . . [4].][3]

(2) Any regulations or scheme making such provision as is mentioned in subsection (1)(*a*) above shall—

(*a*) prescribe the amount or rate of penalty, or provide for how it is to be ascertained;

(*b*) provide for the penalty to be imposed by the [Inland Revenue[2]]—

(i) within six years after the date on which the penalty is incurred; or

(ii) where the amount of the penalty is to be ascertained by reference to the amount of any contributions payable, at any later time within three years after the final determination of the amount of those contributions;

(*c*) provide for determining the date on which, for the purposes of paragraph (*b*) above, the penalty is incurred;

(*d*) prescribe the means by which the penalty is to be enforced; and

(*e*) provide for enabling the [Inland Revenue][2], in [their][2] discretion, to mitigate or to remit any such penalty, or to stay or to compound any proceedings for a penalty.

(3) A person guilty of such an offence as is mentioned in subsection (1)(*b*) above shall be liable on summary conviction—

(*a*) to a fine not exceeding level 3 on the standard scale;

(*b*) in the case of an offence of continuing a contravention or failure after conviction, to a fine not exceeding £40 for each day on which it is so continued.

(4) Any provision contained in regulations which authorises statutory sick pay or statutory maternity pay to be set off against secondary Class 1 contributions is not a provision relating to contributions for the purposes of this section.][1]

Amendments—[1] Substituted by SSA 1998 s 60 with effect from 4 March 1999 for the purpose of authorising the making of regulations and 6 April 1999 for all other purposes by virtue of the Social Security Act 1998 (Commencement No 4) Order, SI 1999/526.

2 Words in sub-s (2) substituted by the Social Security Contributions (Transfer of Functions, etc) Act 1999 s 5 and Sch 5 para 5 with effect from 6 April 1999 by virtue of the Social Security Contributions (Transfer of Functions, etc) Act 1999 (Commencement No 1 and Transitional Provisions) Order, SI 1999/527.

3 In sub-s (1) words substituted and sub-s (1A) inserted by the Child Support, Pensions and Social Security Act 2000 ss 67, 86, Sch 6 paras 1, 7 with effect from 1 November 2000 (by virtue of SI 2000/2950).

4 Words in sub-s (1A)(*b*), words repealed by the NIC and Statutory Payments Act 2004 ss 9(1), (4), 12 Sch 2 Pt 1 with effect from 6 April 2005 (by virtue of SI 2004/1943).

[113A Statutory sick pay and statutory maternity pay: breach of regulations

(1) Where a person fails to produce any document or record, or provide any information, in accordance with—

(*a*) regulations under section 5(1)(i) and (5), so far as relating to statutory sick pay or statutory maternity pay,

(*b*) regulations under section 130 or 132, or

(*c*) regulations under section 153(5)(b) of the Contributions and Benefits Act,

that person is liable to the penalties mentioned in subsection (2).

(2) The penalties are—

(*a*) a penalty not exceeding £300, and

(*b*) if the failure continues after a penalty is imposed under paragraph (a), a further penalty or penalties not exceeding £60 for each day on which the failure continues after the day on which the penalty under that paragraph was imposed (but excluding any day for which a penalty under this paragraph has already been imposed).

(3) Where a person fails to maintain a record in accordance with regulations under section 130 or 132, he is liable to a penalty not exceeding £3,000.

(4) No penalty may be imposed under subsection (1) at any time after the failure concerned has been remedied.

(5) But subsection (4) does not apply to the imposition of a penalty under subsection (2)(a) in respect of a failure to produce any document or record in accordance with regulations under section 130(5) or 132(4).

(6) Where, in the case of any employee, an employer refuses or repeatedly fails to make payments of statutory sick pay or statutory maternity pay in accordance with any regulations under section 5, the employer is liable to a penalty not exceeding £3,000.

(7) Section 118(2) of the Taxes Management Act 1970 (extra time for compliance etc) applies for the purposes of subsections (1), (3) and (6) as it applies for the purposes of that Act.

(8) Schedule 1 to the Employment Act 2002 (penalties relating to statutory paternity pay and statutory adoption pay: procedures and appeals) applies in relation to penalties imposed under this section (with the modifications set out in subsection (9)).

(9) That Schedule applies as if—

(*a*) references to a penalty under section 11 or 12 of that Act were to a penalty under this section,

(*b*) in paragraph 1(2), the reference to section 11(2)(a) of that Act were to subsection (2)(a) of this section, and

(*c*) the provisions of the Taxes Management Act 1970 having effect in relation to an appeal mentioned in paragraph 3(2) of that Schedule did not include section 50(9) of that Act.][1]

Amendments—[1] This section inserted by the NIC and Statutory Payments Act 2004 s 9(1), (5) with effect from 6 April 2005 (by virtue of SI 2004/1943).

[113B Statutory sick pay and statutory maternity pay: fraud and negligence

(1) Where a person fraudulently or negligently—

(*a*) makes any incorrect statement or declaration in connection with establishing entitlement to statutory sick pay or statutory maternity pay, or

(*b*) produces any incorrect document or record or provides any incorrect information of a kind mentioned in—

(i) regulations under section 5(1)(i) and (5), so far as relating to statutory sick pay or statutory maternity pay,

(ii) regulations under section 130 or 132, or

(iii) regulations under section 153(5)(b) of the Contributions and Benefits Act,

he is liable to a penalty not exceeding £3,000.

(2) Where an employer fraudulently or negligently makes an incorrect payment of statutory sick pay or statutory maternity pay, he is liable to a penalty not exceeding £3,000.

(3) Where an employer fraudulently or negligently receives an overpayment in pursuance of regulations under section 167 of the Contributions and Benefits Act (statutory maternity pay: advance payments to employers), he is liable to a penalty not exceeding £3,000.

(4) Schedule 1 to the Employment Act 2002 (penalties relating to statutory paternity pay and statutory adoption pay: procedures and appeals) applies in relation to penalties imposed under this section (with the modifications set out in subsection (5)).

(5) That Schedule applies as if—

(*a*) references to a penalty under section 11 or 12 of that Act were to a penalty under this section, and

(*b*) the provisions of the Taxes Management Act 1970 having effect in relation to an appeal mentioned in paragraph 3(2) of that Schedule did not include section 50(9) of that Act.][1]

Amendments—[1] This section inserted by the NIC and Statutory Payments Act 2004 s 9(1), (5) with effect from 6 April 2005 (by virtue of SI 2004/1943).

[114 Offences relating to contributions.

(1) Any person who is knowingly concerned in the fraudulent evasion of any contributions which he or any other person is liable to pay shall be guilty of an offence.

(2) A person guilty of an offence under this section shall be liable—

(*a*) on conviction on indictment, to imprisonment for a term not exceeding seven years or to a fine or to both;

(*b*) on summary conviction, to a fine not exceeding the statutory maximum.][1]

Amendments—[1] Substituted by SSA 1998 s 61 with effect from 4 March 1999 for the purpose of authorising the making of regulations and 6 April 1999 for all other purposes by virtue of the Social Security Act 1998 (Commencement No 4) Order, SI 1999/526.

[114A Penalties relating to contributions.][1]

Amendments—[1] This section substituted by SSA 1998 s 61 and subsequently repealed by the Social Security Contributions (Transfer of Functions, etc) Act 1999 s 26(3), Sch 10 Pt 1 and Sch 5 para 6 with effect from 1 April 1999 by virtue of the Social Security Contributions (Transfer of Functions, etc) Act 1999 (Commencement No 1 and Transitional Provisions) Order, SI 1999/527, without ever coming into force.

115 Offences by bodies corporate

(1) Where an offence under this Act[, or under the Jobseekers Act 1995,][1] which has been committed by a body corporate is proved to have been committed with the consent or connivance of, or to be attributable to any neglect on the part of, a director, manager, secretary or other similar officer of the body corporate, or any person who was purporting to act in any such capacity, he, as well as the body corporate, shall be guilty of that offence and be liable to be proceeded against accordingly.

(2) Where the affairs of a body corporate are managed by its members, subsection (1) above applies in relation to the acts and defaults of a member in connection with his functions of management as if he were a director of the body corporate.

Press releases etc—Contributions Agency 1-8-96 (personal assets of offenders who fail to pay NIC can be frozen—application to company directors etc).

Former enactments—SSA 1986 s 57.

Amendments—[1] Words in sub-s (1) inserted by the Jobseekers Act 1995 Sch 2 para 55 with effect from 11 June 1996 by virtue of SI 1996/1509.

[115A Penalty as alternative to prosecution

[(1) This section applies where an overpayment is recoverable from a person by, or due from a person to, the Secretary of State *or an authority*[2] under or by virtue of section 71, [71ZB,][3] 71A, 75 or 76 above and it appears to the Secretary of State *or authority*[2] that—

(a) the making of the overpayment was attributable to an act or omission on the part of that person; and

(b) there are grounds for instituting against him proceedings for an offence (under this Act or any other enactment) relating to the overpayment.

[(1A) This section also applies where—

(a) it appears to the Secretary of State *or an authority*[2] that there are grounds for instituting proceedings against a person for an offence (under this Act or any other enactment) relating to an act or omission on the part of that person in relation to any benefit, and

(b) if an overpayment attributable to the act or omission had been made, the overpayment would have been recoverable from the person by, or due from the person to, the Secretary of State *or an authority*[2] under or by virtue of section 71, 71ZB, 71A, 75 or 76 above.][4]

(2) The Secretary of State *or authority*[2] may give to the person a written notice—

(a) stating that he may be invited to agree to pay a penalty and that, if he does so in the manner specified by the Secretary of State *or authority*[2], no [proceedings referred to in subsection (1) or (1A) above][4] will be instituted against him; and

(b) containing such information relating to the operation of this section as may be prescribed.

[(3) The amount of the penalty in a case falling within subsection (1) is 50% of the amount of the overpayment (rounded down to the nearest whole penny), subject to—

(a) a minimum amount of £350, and

(b) a maximum amount of [£5000][5].

(3A) The amount of the penalty in a case falling within subsection (1A) is £350.

(3B) The Secretary of State may by order amend—

(a) the percentage for the time being specified in subsection (3);

(b) any figure for the time being specified in subsection (3)(a) or (b) or (3A).][4]

(4) If the person agrees in the specified manner to pay the penalty—

(a) the amount of the penalty shall be recoverable by the same methods as those by which the overpayment is [or would have been][4] recoverable; and

(b) no proceedings will be instituted against him for an offence (under this Act or any other enactment) relating to the overpayment [or to the act or omission referred to in subsection (1A)(a)][4].

(5) The person may withdraw his agreement to pay the penalty by notifying the Secretary of State *or authority*[2], in the manner specified by the Secretary of State *or authority*[2], at any time during the period of [14][4] days beginning with the day on which he agrees to pay it; and if he does so—

(a) so much of the penalty as has already been recovered shall be repaid; and

(b) subsection (4)(b) above shall not apply.

(6) [In a case referred to in subsection (1)][4] where, after the person has agreed to pay the penalty, it is decided on a review or appeal or in accordance with regulations that the overpayment is not recoverable or due, so much of the penalty as has already been recovered shall be repaid.

(7) [In a case referred to in subsection (1)][4] where, after the person has agreed to pay the penalty, the amount of the overpayment is revised on a review or appeal or in accordance with regulations—

(a) so much of the penalty as has already been recovered shall be repaid; and

(b) subsection (4)(b) above shall no longer apply by reason of the agreement;

but if a new agreement is made under this section in relation to the revised overpayment, the amount already recovered by way of penalty, to the extent that it does not exceed the amount of the new penalty, may be treated as recovered under the new agreement instead of being repaid.

(7A) Subject to subsection (7B) below, the Secretary of State and an authority which administers housing benefit or council tax benefit may agree that, to the extent determined by the agreement, one may carry out on the other's behalf, or may join in the carrying out of, any of the other's functions under this section.

(7B) Subsection (7A) above shall not authorise any delegation of—

(a) the function of the person by whom any overpayment is [or would have been][4] recoverable, or to whom it is [or would have been][4] due, of determining whether or not a notice should be given under subsection (2) above in respect of that overpayment; or

(b) the Secretary of State's power to make regulations for the purposes of paragraph (b) of that subsection.[2]

(8) In this section "overpayment" means—

(a) a payment which should not have been made;

(b) a sum which the Secretary of State should have received;

(c) an amount of benefit paid in excess of entitlement; or

(d) an amount equal to an excess of benefit allowed;

and the reference in subsection (1)(a) [or (1A)(b)][4] above to the making of the overpayment is to the making of the payment, the failure to receive the sum, the payment of benefit in excess of entitlement or the allowing of an excess of benefit.][1]

Orders—Social Security (Penalty as Alternative to Prosecution) (Maximum Amount) Order, SI 2015/202.

Regulations—Social Security (Miscellaneous Amendments) Regulations, SI 2014/591.

Amendments—[1] This section inserted by the Social Security Administration (Fraud) Act 1997, s 15 with effect for the purposes only of authorising the making of regulations from 21 November 1997 (SI 1997/2766, art 2(1)(a)) and for remaining purposes from 18 December 1997 (see SI 1997/2766, art 2(1)(b)).

[2] In sub-ss (1), (1A) words "or an authority", in sub-ss (2), (5) words "or authority", repealed, and sub-ss (7A), (7B) repealed, by the Welfare Reform Act 2012, s 147, Sch 14, Pt 1 with effect for certain purposes from 1 April 2013 (SI 2013/358, art 8(c)) and for remaining purposes from a date to be appointed.

[3] In sub-s (1), reference to "71ZB," inserted by the Welfare Reform Act 2012, s 105(3) with effect from 29 April 2013 (SI 2013/358, art 5(2), (3)(b)).

[4] Sub-s (1A) inserted, in sub-s (2)(a), words substituted, sub-ss (3), (3A), (3B): substituted for previous sub-s (3), in sub-ss (4), (6), (7), (7B)(a), (8) words inserted, in sub-s (5) reference substituted, by the Welfare Reform Act 2012, ss 113(1)–(5), 114(1), 115(1), (2) with effect from 8 May 2012 (SI 2012/863, art 2(3)(a), (b)).

[5] In sub-s(3)(*b*), figure substituted for previous figure "£2,000" by the Social Security (Penalty as Alternative to Prosecution) (Maximum Amount) Order, SI 2015/202 art 2 with effect from 1 April 2015.

Prospective amendments—In sub-ss (1), (1A)(b), (2) words "71A, 75 or 76", "or authority" to be repealed by the Welfare Reform Act 2012, s 147, Sch 14, Pt 1 with effect from a date to be appointed.

[115B Penalty as alternative to prosecution: colluding employers etc]

[(1) This section applies where it appears to the Secretary of State *or an authority that administers housing benefit or council tax*[5] *benefit*—

(a) that there are grounds for instituting proceedings against any person ("the responsible person") for an offence (whether or not under this Act) in respect of any conduct; and

(b) that the conduct in respect of which there are grounds for instituting the proceedings is conduct falling within subsection (2) below.

(2) Conduct in respect of which there appear to be grounds for instituting proceedings falls within this subsection if—

(a) those proceedings would be for an offence under this Act in connection with an inquiry relating to the employment of relevant employees or of any one or more particular relevant employees; or

(b) it is conduct which was such as to facilitate the commission of a benefit offence by a relevant employee (whether or not such an offence was in fact committed).

(3) The Secretary of State *or authority*[5] may give to the responsible person a written notice—

(a) specifying or describing the conduct in question;

(b) stating that he may be invited to agree to pay a penalty in respect of that conduct;

(c) stating that, if he does so in the manner specified by the Secretary of State *or authority*, no criminal proceedings will be instituted against him in respect of that conduct; and

(d) containing such information relating to the operation of this section as may be prescribed.

[(4) If the recipient of a notice under subsection (3) above agrees, in the specified manner, to pay the penalty—

(a) the amount of the penalty shall be recoverable from the recipient by the Secretary of State *or authority*[5]; and

(b) no criminal proceedings shall be instituted against the recipient in respect of the conduct to which the notice relates.

(4A) Sections 71ZC, 71ZD and 71ZE above apply in relation to amounts recoverable under subsection (4)(a) above as to amounts recoverable by the Secretary of State under section 71ZB above *(and, where the notice is given by an authority administering housing benefit or council tax benefit, those sections so apply as if references to the Secretary of State were to that authority)*[5].][4]

(5) The amount of the penalty shall be—

(a) in a case in which the conduct in question falls within paragraph (a) of subsection (2) above but not within paragraph (b) of that subsection, £1,000;
(b) in a case in which that conduct falls within paragraph (b) of that subsection and the number of relevant employees by reference to whom it falls within that subsection is five or more, £5,000; and
(c) in any other case, the amount obtained by multiplying £1,000 by the number of relevant employees by reference to whom that conduct falls within that subsection.

(6) The responsible person may withdraw his agreement to pay a penalty under this section by notifying the Secretary of State *or authority*[5], in the manner specified by the Secretary of State *or authority*[5], at any time during the period of [14][6] days beginning with the day on which he agrees to pay it.

(7) Where the responsible person withdraws his agreement in accordance with subsection (6) above—
(a) so much of the penalty as has already been recovered shall be repaid; and
(b) subsection (4)(b) above shall not apply.

(8) For the purposes of this section an individual is a relevant employee in relation to any conduct of the responsible person if—
(a) that conduct was at or in relation to a time when that individual was an employee of the responsible person;
(b) that conduct was at or in relation to a time when that individual was an employee of a body corporate of which the responsible person is or has been a director; or
(c) the responsible person, in engaging in that conduct, was acting or purporting to act on behalf of, in the interests of or otherwise by reason of his connection with, any person by whom that individual is or has been employed.

(9) In this section—
"conduct" includes acts, omissions and statements;
"director"—
(a) in relation to a company ([as defined in section 1(1) of the Companies Act 2006][3]), includes a shadow director;
(b) in relation to any such company that is a subsidiary of another, includes any director or shadow director of the other company; and
(c) in relation to a body corporate whose affairs are managed by its members, means a member of that body corporate;
"employee" means any person who—
(a) is employed under a contract of service or apprenticeship, or in an office (including an elective office), or
(b) carries out any work under any contract under which he has undertaken to provide his work,
and "employment" shall be construed accordingly;
. . .[4]
"shadow director" means a shadow director as defined in [section 251 of the Companies Act 2006][2];
"subsidiary" means a subsidiary as defined in [section 1159 of the Companies Act 2006][3].][1]

Amendments—[1] This section inserted by the Social Security Fraud Act 2001, ss 1(1), 15(1) with effect from 30 April 2002 (SI 2002/1222, art 2(f)).
[2] In sub-s (9), in definition of "shadow director", words substituted by SI 2007/2194, art 10(1), (2), Sch 4, Pt 3, para 68 with effect from 1 October 2007.
[3] In sub-s (9), in definitions of "director" and "subsidiary", words substituted by SI 2009/1941, art 2(1), Sch 1, para 129(a) with effect from 1 October 2009.
[4] Sub-ss (4), (4A) substituted for previous sub-s (4), in sub-s (9), definition of "relevant benefit" repealed, by the Welfare Reform Act 2012, s 105(4)(a), (b) with effect from 1 October 2012 (SI 2012/1246, art 2(5)(b)).
[5] In sub-s (1), words "or an authority that administers housing benefit or council tax benefit", in sub-s (3) words "or authority" in the first place they occur, in sub-ss (4)(a), (6) words "or authority", in sub-s (4A), words from "(and, where the" to the end, repealed by the Welfare Reform Act 2012, s 147, Sch 14, Pt 1 with effect for certain purposes from 1 April 2013 (SI 2013/358, art 8(c)) and for remaining purposes from a date to be appointed.
[6] In sub-s (6), reference substituted by the Welfare Reform Act 2012, s 115(1), (3) with effect from 8 May 2012 (SI 2012/863, art 2(3)(c)).

Prospective amendments—In sub-s (3)(c), words "or authority" to be repealed by the Welfare Reform Act 2012, s 147, Sch 14, Pt 1 with effect from a date to be appointed

[Civil penalties

115C Incorrect statements etc

(1) This section applies where—
(a) a person negligently makes an incorrect statement or representation, or negligently gives incorrect information or evidence—
(i) in or in connection with a claim for a relevant social security benefit, or

(ii) in connection with an award of a relevant social security benefit,

(b) the person fails to take reasonable steps to correct the error,

(c) the error results in the making of an overpayment, and

(d) the person has not been charged with an offence or cautioned, or been given a notice under section 115A, in respect of the overpayment.

(2) A penalty of a prescribed amount may be imposed by the appropriate authority—

(a) in any case, on the person;

(b) in a case where the person ("A") is making, or has made, a claim for the benefit for a period jointly with another ("B"), on B instead of A.

(3) Subsection (2)(b) does not apply if B was not, and could not reasonably be expected to have been, aware that A had negligently made the incorrect statement or representation or given the incorrect information or evidence.

(4) A penalty imposed under subsection (2) is recoverable by the appropriate authority from the person on whom it is imposed.

(5) Sections 71ZC, 71ZD and 71ZE apply in relation to amounts recoverable by the appropriate authority under subsection (4) as to amounts recoverable by the Secretary of State under section 71ZB (and, where the appropriate authority is not the Secretary of State, those sections so apply as if references to the Secretary of State were to that authority).

(6) In this section and section 115D—

"appropriate authority" means—

(a) the Secretary of State, or

(b) an authority which administers housing benefit or council tax benefit;

"overpayment" has the meaning given in section 115A(8), and the reference to the making of an overpayment is to be construed in accordance with that provision;

"relevant social security benefit" has the meaning given in section 121DA(7).][1]

Amendments—This section inserted by Welfare Reform Act 2012 s 116(1) with effect from 10 May 2012 for the purposes of prescribing amounts under sub-s (2) and from 1 October 2012 for all other purposes (SI 2013/12467, art 2(1)(*a*), (5)(*c*)).

[115D Failure to disclose information

(1) A penalty of a prescribed amount may be imposed on a person by the appropriate authority where—

(a) the person, without reasonable excuse, fails to provide information or evidence in accordance with requirements imposed on the person by the appropriate authority in connection with a claim for, or an award of, a relevant social security benefit,

(b) the failure results in the making of an overpayment, and

(c) the person has not been charged with an offence or cautioned, or been given a notice under section 115A, in respect of the overpayment.

(2) A penalty of a prescribed amount may be imposed on a person by the appropriate authority where—

(a) the person, without reasonable excuse, fails to notify the appropriate authority of a relevant change of circumstances in accordance with requirements imposed on the person under relevant social security legislation,

(b) the failure results in the making of an overpayment, and

(c) the person has not been charged with an offence or cautioned, or been given a notice under section 115A, in respect of the overpayment.

(3) Where a person is making, or has made, a claim for a benefit for a period jointly with another, and both of them fail as mentioned in subsection (1) or (2), only one penalty may be imposed in respect of the same overpayment.

(4) A penalty imposed under subsection (1) or (2) is recoverable by the appropriate authority from the person on whom it is imposed.

(5) Sections 71ZC, 71ZD and 71ZE apply in relation to amounts recoverable by the appropriate authority under subsection (4) as to amounts recoverable by the Secretary of State under section 71ZB (and, where the appropriate authority is not the Secretary of State, those sections so apply as if references to the Secretary of State were to that authority).

(6) In this section "relevant change of circumstances", in relation to a person, means a change of circumstances which affects any entitlement of the person to any benefit or other payment or advantage under any provision of the relevant social security legislation.]

Amendments—This section inserted by the Welfare Reform Act 2012 s 116(1) with effect from 10 May 2012 for the purposes of prescribing amounts under sub-ss (1), (2) and from 1 October 2012 for all other purposes (SI 2013/12467, art 2(1)(*a*), (5)(*c*)).

Legal proceedings

116 Legal proceedings

(1) Any person authorised by the Secretary of State in that behalf may conduct any proceedings [under any provision of this Act other than section 114 or under any provision of][2] [or the Jobseekers Act 1995][1] before a magistrates' court although not a barrister or solicitor.

(2) Notwithstanding anything in any Act—

(*a*) proceedings for an offence under this Act [(*other than proceedings to which paragraph (b) applies)*[5]][4][, or for an offence under the Jobseekers Act 1995,][1] may be begun at any time within the period of 3 months from the date on which evidence, sufficient in the opinion of the Secretary of State to justify a prosecution for the offence, comes to his knowledge or within a period of 12 months from the commission of the offence, whichever period last expires; and

(*b*) . . .

[(2A) . . .]

(3) For the purposes of subsection (2) above—

(*a*) a certificate purporting to be signed by or on behalf of the Secretary of State as to the date on which such evidence as is mentioned in paragraph (*a*) of that subsection came to his knowledge shall be conclusive evidence of that date; and

(*b*) . . .

(4), (5) . . .

[(5A) In relation to proceedings for an offence under section 114 above], the references in subsections (2)(a) and (3)(a) to the Secretary of State shall have effect as references to the Inland Revenue.][2]

(6) . . .

(7) In the application of this section to Scotland, the following provisions shall have effect in substitution for subsections (1) [to (5A)][2] above—

(*a*) proceedings for an offence under this Act [or the Jobseekers Act 1995][1] may, notwithstanding anything in section 331 of the Criminal Procedure (Scotland) Act 1975 be commenced at any time within the period of 3 months from the date on which evidence, sufficient in the opinion of the Lord Advocate to justify proceedings, comes to his knowledge, or within the period of 12 months from the commission of the offence, whichever period last expires;

[(*aa*) this subsection shall not be taken to impose any restriction on the time when proceedings may be commenced for an offence under section 111A above.][3]

(*b*) for the purposes of this subsection—

(i) a certificate purporting to be signed by or on behalf of the Lord Advocate as to the date on which such evidence as is mentioned above came to his knowledge shall be conclusive evidence of that date; and

(ii) subsection (3) of section 331 of the said Act of 1975 (date of commencement of proceedings) shall have effect as it has effect for the purposes of that section.

Former enactments—Sub-s (1); SSA 1986 s 56(1).
Sub-s (2): SSA 1986 s 56(2); Local Government Finance Act 1988 s 135, Sch 10 paras 1, 9(1), (2).
Sub-s (3): SSA 1986 s 56(3).
Sub-s (7): SSA 1986 s 56(5); Local Government Finance Act 1988 s 135, Sch 10 paras 1, 9(1), (5).

Note—Provisions omitted are outside the scope of this Publication.

Amendments—[1] Words in sub-ss (1), (2)(*a*), (7)(*a*) inserted by the Jobseekers Act 1995 Sch 2 para 56 with effect from 11 June 1996 by virtue of SI 1996/1509.

[2] Words in sub-ss (1) and (7) substituted and sub-s (5A) inserted by the Social Security Contributions (Transfer of Functions, etc) Act 1999 s 1(1) and Sch 1 para 21 with effect from 1 April 1999 by virtue of the Social Security Contributions (Transfer of Functions, etc) Act 1999 (Commencement No 1 and Transitional Provisions) Order, SI 1999/527.

[3] Sub-s 7(*aa*) inserted by the Social Security Fraud Act 2002 s 17 with effect from 30 April 2002 (by virtue of SI 2002/1222).

[4] In sub-s (2)(*a*), words substituted for words "other than an offence relating to housing benefit or council tax benefit" by the Welfare Reform Act 2012 s 111 with effect from 8 May 2012.

[5] In sub-s (2)(*a*) words "(other than proceedings to which paragraph (b) applies)" repealed in so far as they relate to the abolition of council tax benefit, by the Welfare Reform Act 2012 s 147, Sch 14 Part 1 with effect from 1 April 2013 (by virtue of SI 2013/358 art 8(c)). Note that certain transitional provisions apply in relation to the abolition of council tax benefit (see SI 2013/358 art 9).

[117 Issues arising in proceedings

(1) This section applies to proceedings before a court—

(*a*) for an offence under this Act or the Jobseekers Act 1995; or

(*b*) involving any question as to the payment of contributions (other than a Class 4 contribution recoverable by the Inland Revenue); or

(*c*) for the recovery of any sums due to the Secretary of State[, the Inland Revenue][2] or the National Insurance Fund.

(2) A decision of the Secretary of State which—

(*a*) falls within Part II of Schedule 3 to the Social Security Act 1998 ("the 1998 Act"); and

(*b*) relates to or affects an issue arising in the proceedings,

shall be conclusive for the purposes of the proceedings.

(3) If—

(*a*) any such decision is necessary for the determination of the proceedings; and

(*b*) the decision of the Secretary of State has not been obtained or an application with respect to the decision has been made under section 9 or 10 of the 1998 Act,

NIC

the decision shall be referred to the Secretary of State to be made in accordance (subject to any necessary modifications) with Chapter II of Part I of that Act.

(4) Subsection (2) above does not apply where, in relation to the decision—

(*a*) an appeal has been brought but not determined;

(*b*) an application for leave to appeal has been made but not determined;

(*c*) an appeal has not been brought (or, as the case may be, an application for leave to appeal has not been made) but the time for doing so has not yet expired; or

(*d*) an application has been made under section 9 or 10 of the 1998 Act.

(5) In a case falling within subsection (4) above the court shall adjourn the proceedings until such time as the final decision is known; and that decision shall be conclusive for the purposes of the proceedings.][1]

Cross references—Social Security Contributions, etc (Decisions and Appeals—Transitional Modifications) Regulations, SI 1999/978.

Modifications—See Social Security Contributions, etc (Decisions and Appeals—Transitional Modifications) Regulations, SI 1999/978. Until Chapter II of Part I of the Social Security Act 1998 (social security decisions and appeals) is wholly in force, any enactment specified in column (1) of the Schedule to SI 1999/978 shall have effect subject to the modifications specified in column (2) of that Schedule.

Amendments—[1] Substituted by SSA 1998 Sch 7 para 84 with effect from 5 July 1999 for certain purposes (by virtue of Social Security Act 1998 (Commencement No 8, and Savings and Consequential and Transitional Provisions) Order, SI 1999/1958, 29 November 1999, for certain purposes (by virtue of the Social Security Act 1998 (Commencement No 12 and Consequential and Transitional Provisions) Order, SI 1999/3178, art 2(1), Sch 1 (subject to transitional provisions contained in art 4 Schs 21–23 thereof)), and with effect from a date to be appointed for all other purposes.

[2] Words in sub-s (1)(*c*) inserted by the Social Security Contributions (Transfer of Functions, etc) Act 1999 s 18 and Sch 7 para 12 with effect from 5 July 1999.

[117A Issues arising in proceedings: contributions, etc][1]

[(1) This section applies to proceedings before a court—

(*a*) for an offence under this Act or the Jobseekers Act 1995; or

(*b*) involving any question as to the payment of contributions (other than a Class 4 contribution recoverable in accordance with section 15 of the Contributions and Benefits Act); or

(*c*) for the recovery of any sums due to the Inland Revenue or the National Insurance Fund.

(2) A decision of an officer of the Inland Revenue which—

(*a*) falls within section 8(1) of the Social Security Contributions (Transfer of Functions, etc) Act 1999; and

(*b*) relates to or affects an issue arising in the proceedings,

shall be conclusive for the purposes of the proceedings.

(3) If—

(*a*) any such decision is necessary for the determination of the proceedings, and

(*b*) the decision of an officer of the Inland Revenue has not been obtained under section 8 of the Social Security Contributions (Transfer of Functions, etc) Act 1999,

the decision shall be referred to such an officer to be made in accordance (subject to any necessary modifications) with Part II of the Social Security Contributions (Transfer of Functions, etc) Act 1999.

(4) Subsection (2) above does not apply where, in relation to the decision—

(*a*) an appeal has been brought but not determined;

(*b*) an appeal has not been brought (or, as the case may be, an application for leave to appeal has not been made) but the time for doing so has not yet expired; or

(*c*) an application for variation of the decision has been made under regulations made under section 10 of the Social Security Contributions (Transfer of Functions, etc) Act 1999.

(5) In a case falling within subsection (4) above the court shall adjourn the proceedings until such time as the final decision is known; and that decision shall be conclusive for the purposes of the proceedings.][1]

Note—NICA 2015 Sch 2 para 17 (in relation to understated NICs, s 117A does not apply to proceedings for the recovery of any amount of the accelerated payment that is unpaid at the end of the payment period).

NICA 2015 Sch 2 para 18 (in relation to proceedings before a court for recovery of relevant contributions to which an NICs appeal relates, so far as they are disputed tax specified in the notice under FA 2014 s 221(2)(b), sub-ss (4) and (5) do not apply).

NICA 2015 Sch 2 para 20 (in relation to proceedings before a court for recovery of a penalty under FA 2014 s 208 or 226 imposed under NICA 2015 Sch 2 Part 1, s 117A applies as if the assessment of the penalty were an NICs decision as to whether the person is liable for the penalty).

Simon's Tax Cases—*Goldman Sachs v R&C Comrs* [2010] STC 763.

Amendments—[1] Section 117A inserted by the Social Security Contributions (Transfer of Functions, etc) Act 1999 s 18 and Sch 7 para 13 with effect from 1 April 1999 by virtue of the Social Security Contributions (Transfer of Functions, etc) Act 1999 (Commencement No 1 and Transitional Provisions) Order, SI 1999/527.

Unpaid contributions etc

118 Evidence of non-payment

[(1) A certificate of an authorised officer that any amount by way of contributions, or by way of interest or penalty in respect of contributions, which a person is liable to pay to the [Inland Revenue][2] for any period has not been paid—

(a) to the officer; or

(b) to the best of his knowledge and belief, to any other person to whom it might lawfully be paid,

shall until the contrary is proved be sufficient evidence in any proceedings before any court that the sum mentioned in the certificate is unpaid and due.[3]

(1A), (2) . . .[2]

(3) A document purporting to be such a certificate . . .[2] *shall be deemed to be such a certificate until the contrary is proved.*[3]

(4) A statutory declaration by an officer of the [Inland Revenue][2] that the searches specified in the declaration . . .[1] for a record of the payment of a particular contribution have been made, and that . . .[1] a record of the payment of the contribution in question has not been found, is admissible in any proceedings for an offence as evidence of the facts stated in the declaration.

(5) Nothing in subsection (4) above makes a statutory declaration admissible as evidence in proceedings for an offence except in a case where, and to the extent to which, oral evidence to the like effect would have been admissible in those proceedings.

(6) Nothing in subsections (4) and (5) above makes a statutory declaration admissible as evidence in proceedings for an offence—

(*a*) unless a copy of it has, not less than 7 days before the hearing or trial, been served on the person charged with the offence in any manner in which a summons or, in Scotland, a citation in a summary prosecution may be served; or

(*b*) if that person, not later than 3 days before the hearing or trial or within such further time as the court may in special circumstances allow, gives notice to the prosecutor requiring the attendance at the trial of the person by whom the declaration was made.

[[(7) In this section "authorised officer" means any officer of the Inland Revenue authorised by them for the purposes of this section.][2]][1, 3]

Former enactments—SSA 1975 s 149.

Amendments—[1] Sub-ss (1) and (1A) substituted, words in sub-ss (3) and (4) inserted and repealed and sub-s (7) inserted by SSA 1998 s 62 with effect from 6 April 1999 by virtue of the Social Security Act 1998 (Commencement No 4) Order, SI 1999/526.

[2] Words in sub-ss (1) and (4), and sub-s (7) substituted, sub-ss (1A) and (2), and words in sub-s (3) repealed by the Social Security Contributions (Transfer of Functions, etc) Act 1999 s 5 and Sch 5 para 7, and s 26(3) and Sch 10 Pt 1 with effect from 6 April 1999 by virtue of the Social Security Contributions (Transfer of Functions, etc) Act 1999 (Commencement No 1 and Transitional Provisions) Order, SI 1999/527.

[3] Sub-ss (1), (3), (7) repealed by FA 2008 s 138, Sch 44 para 4 with effect from 21 July 2008.

119 Recovery of unpaid contributions on prosecution

(1) Where—

(*a*) a person has been convicted of an offence under section 114(1) above of failing to pay a contribution at or within the time prescribed for the purpose; and

(*b*) the contribution remains unpaid at the date of the conviction,

he shall be liable to pay to the [Inland Revenue][2] a sum equal to the amount which he failed to pay.

(2) . . .[1]

Former enactments—SSA 1975 s 150.

Amendments—[1] Repealed by SSA 1998 Sch 7 para 85 with effect from 6 April 1999 by virtue of the Social Security Act 1998 (Commencement No 4) Order, SI 1999/526.

[2] Words substituted by the Social Security Contributions (Transfer of Functions, etc) Act 1999 s 1(1) and Sch 1 para 22 with effect from 1 April 1999 by virtue of the Social Security Contributions (Transfer of Functions, etc) Act 1999 (Commencement No 1 and Transitional Provisions) Order, SI 1999/527.

120 Proof of previous offences

(1) Subject to and in accordance with subsections (2) to (5) below, where a person is convicted of an offence mentioned in section 119(1) . . .[2] above, evidence may be given of any previous failure by him to pay contributions within the time prescribed for the purpose; and in those subsections "the conviction" and "the offence" mean respectively the conviction referred to in this subsection and the offence of which the person is convicted.

(2) Such evidence may be given only if notice of intention to give it is served with the summons or warrant or, in Scotland, the complaint on which the person appeared before the court which convicted him.

(3) If the offence is one of failure to pay a Class 1 contribution, evidence may be given of failure on his part to pay (whether or not in respect of the same person) such contributions or any Class 1A [or Class 1B][3] contributions or [contributions equivalent premiums][1] on the date of the offence, or during the [6][2] years preceding that date.

(4) If the offence is one of failure to pay a Class 1A contribution, evidence may be given of failure on his part to pay (whether or not in respect of the same person or the same [amount][5]) such contributions, or any Class 1 [or Class 1B][3] contributions or [contributions equivalent premiums][1], on the date of the offence, or during the [6][2] years preceding that date.

[(4A) If the offence is one of failure to pay a Class 1B contribution, evidence may be given of failure on his part to pay such contributions, or any Class 1 or Class 1A contributions or contributions equivalent premiums, on the date of the offence, or during the 6 years preceding that date.][3]

NIC

(5) If the offence—

(*a*) is one of failure to pay Class 2 contributions; . . . [2]

(*b*) . . . [2]

evidence may be given of his failure to pay such contributions during those [6][2] years.

(6) On proof of any matter of which evidence may be given under subsection (3), (4), [(4A)][3] or (5) above, the person convicted shall be liable to pay to the [Inland Revenue][4] a sum equal to the total of all amounts which he is so proved to have failed to pay and which remain unpaid at the date of the conviction.

Former enactments—SSA 1975 s 151; SS (Contributions) Act 1991 ss 2(6), 6(5).

Amendments—[1] Words in sub-ss (3), (4) substituted for the words "state scheme premiums" by the Pensions Act 1995 Sch 5 para 15(1), (3) with effect from 6 April 1997, by virtue of the Pensions Act 1995 (Commencement No 10) Order, SI 1997/664 art 2, Sch Pt II.

[2] Words in sub-ss (1), (3), (4), (5) and (6) substituted and repealed by SSA 1998 Sch 7 para 86 with effect from 6 April 1999 by virtue of the Social Security Act 1998 (Commencement No 4) Order, SI 1999/526.

[3] Words in sub-ss (3), (4) and (6), and new sub-s (4A) inserted by SSA 1998 Sch 7 para 86 with effect from 6 April 1999 by virtue of the Social Security Act 1998 (Commencement No 1) Order, SI 1998/2209.

[4] Words in sub-s (6) to be substituted by the Social Security Contributions (Transfer of Functions, etc) Act 1999 s 1(1) and Sch 1 para 23 with effect from 1 April 1999 by virtue of the Social Security Contributions (Transfer of Functions, etc) Act 1999 (Commencement No 1 and Transitional Provisions) Order, SI 1999/527.

[5] Word in sub-s (4) substituted by the Child Support, Pensions and Social Security Act 2000 s 74(6), (8) with effect from the year 2000–01.

121 Unpaid contributions—supplementary

(1) Where in England and Wales a person charged with an offence mentioned in section 119(1) . . . [2] above is convicted of that offence in his absence under section [12(5)][1] of the Magistrates' Courts Act 1980 then if—

(*a*) it is proved to the satisfaction of the court, on oath or in the manner prescribed by [Criminal Procedure Rules][5], that notice under section 120(2) above has been duly served specifying the other contributions in respect of which the prosecutor intends to give evidence; and

(*b*) the [designated officer for][6] the court has received a statement in writing purporting to be made by the accused or by a solicitor acting on his behalf to the effect that if the accused is convicted in his absence of the offence charged he desires to admit failing to pay the other contributions so specified or any of them,

section 120 above shall have effect as if the evidence had been given and the failure so admitted had been proved, and the court shall proceed accordingly.

(2) In England and Wales, where a person is convicted of an offence mentioned in section 119(1) . . . [2] above and an order is made under [section 12 of the Powers of Criminal Courts (Sentencing) Act 2000][4] discharging him absolutely or conditionally, sections 119 and 120 above, and subsection (1) above, shall apply as if it were a conviction for all purposes.

(3) In Scotland, where a person is convicted on indictment of, or is charged before a court of summary jurisdiction with, any such offence, and an order is made under Part I of the Criminal Procedure (Scotland) Act 1975 discharging him absolutely or placing him on probation, sections 119 and 120 above shall apply as if—

(*a*) the conviction on indictment were a conviction for all purposes; or

(*b*) (as the case may be) the making of the order by the court of summary jurisdiction were a conviction.

(4) In England and Wales, any sum which a person is liable to pay under section 119 or 120 above or under subsection (1) above shall be recoverable from him as a penalty.

(5) Sums recovered by the [Inland Revenue][3] under the provisions mentioned in subsection (4) above, so far as representing contributions of any class, are to be treated for all purposes of the Contributions and Benefits Act and this Act (including in particular the application of section 162 below) as contributions of that class received by the [Inland Revenue][3].

(6) Without prejudice to subsection (5) above, in so far as such sums represent primary Class 1 or Class 2 contributions, they are to be treated as contributions paid in respect of the person in respect of whom they were originally payable; and enactments relating to earnings factors shall apply accordingly.

Former enactments—Sub-s (1): SSA 1975 s 152(1); Magistrates' Courts Act 1980 s 154, Sch 7 para 135.
Sub-s (2): SSA 1975 s 152(2); SS Pensions Act 1975 s 65(1), Sch 4 para 67.
Sub-s (3): SSA 1975 s 152(3).
Sub-ss (4)–(6): SSA 1975 s 152(5)–(7).

Amendments—[1] Words in sub-s (1) substituted by the Magistrates' Courts (Procedure) Act 1998.

[2] Words repealed by SSA 1998 Sch 7 para 87 with effect from 6 April 1999 by virtue of the Social Security Act 1998 (Commencement No 4) Order, SI 1999/526.

[3] Words in sub-s (5) substituted by the Social Security Contributions (Transfer of Functions, etc) Act 1999 s 1(1) and Sch 1 para 24 with effect from 1 April 1999 by virtue of the Social Security Contributions (Transfer of Functions, etc) Act 1999 (Commencement No 1 and Transitional Provisions) Order, SI 1999/527.

[4] Words in sub-s (2) substituted by the Powers of Criminal Courts (Sentencing) Act 2000 ss 72, 75, Sch 8 para 150 with effect from 25 August 2000.

[5] Words in sub-s (1)(*a*) substituted by the Courts Act 2003 s 109(1), Sch 8 para 355(*a*) with effect from 1 September 2004 (except in relation to the operation of this section in relation to rules of court other than Criminal Procedure Rules during the period between that date and the coming into force of the first Criminal Procedure Rules made under the Courts Act 2003 s 69) (by virtue of SI 2004/2066). To the extent that this amendment was not already in force, SI 2005/910 provided for it to come into force on 1 April 2005.

[6] In sub-s (1)(*b*), words substituted for the words "justices' chief executive for" by the Courts Act 2003 s 109(1), Sch 8 para 355(*b*) with effect from 1 April 2005 (by virtue of SI 2005/910).

[121A Recovery of contributions etc in England and Wales.

. . .

Amendments—This section repealed by FA 2008 s 129, Sch 43 para 2 with effect from 6 April 2014 (by virtue of SI 2014/906 art 2).

121B Recovery of contributions etc in Scotland.

Amendments—This section repealed by FA 2008 s 129, Sch 43 para 14 with effect from 23 November 2009 (by virtue of SI 2009/3024 art 3). Note that if, before the commencement date a warrant has been granted under this section, that warrant shall continue to have effect according to the provisions under which it was granted (SI 2009/3024 art 4(1)(b)).

[121C Liability of directors etc for company's contributions.

(1) This section applies to contributions which a body corporate is liable to pay, where—

(*a*) the body corporate has failed to pay the contributions at or within the time prescribed for the purpose; and

(*b*) the failure appears to the [Inland Revenue][2] to be attributable to fraud or neglect on the part of one or more individuals who, at the time of the fraud or neglect, were officers of the body corporate ("culpable officers").

(2) The [Inland Revenue][2] may issue and serve on any culpable officer a notice (a "personal liability notice")—

(*a*) specifying the amount of the contributions to which this section applies ("the specified amount");

(*b*) requiring the officer to pay to the Secretary of State—

(i) a specified sum in respect of that amount; and

(ii) specified interest on that sum; and

(*c*) where that sum is given by paragraph (*b*) of subsection (3) below, specifying the proportion applied by the [Inland Revenue][2] for the purposes of that paragraph.

(3) The sum specified in the personal liability notice under subsection (2)(*b*)(i) above shall be—

(*a*) in a case where there is, in the opinion of the [Inland Revenue][2], no other culpable officer, the whole of the specified amount; and

(*b*) in any other case, such proportion of the specified amount as, in the opinion of the [Inland Revenue][2], the officer's culpability for the failure to pay that amount bears to that of all the culpable officers taken together.

(4) In assessing an officer's culpability for the purposes of subsection (3)(*b*) above, the [Inland Revenue][2] may have regard both to the gravity of the officer's fraud or neglect and to the consequences of it.

(5) The interest specified in the personal liability notice under subsection (2)(*b*)(ii) above shall be [at the Class 1 rate on the Class 1 element of the specified sum, and otherwise at the prescribed rate,][4] and shall run from the date on which the notice is issued.

(6) An officer who is served with a personal liability notice shall be liable to pay to the [Inland Revenue][2] the sum and the interest specified in the notice under subsection (2)(*b*) above.

(7) Where, after the issue of one or more personal liability notices, the amount of contributions to which this section applies is reduced by a payment made by the body corporate—

(*a*) the amount that each officer who has been served with such a notice is liable to pay under this section shall be reduced accordingly;

(*b*) the [Inland Revenue][2] shall serve on each such officer a notice to that effect; and

(*c*) where the reduced liability of any such officer is less than the amount that he has already paid under this section, the difference shall be repaid to him together with interest on it [at the Class 1 rate on the Class 1 element of it and otherwise][4] at the prescribed rate.

(8) Any amount paid under a personal liability notice shall be deducted from the liability of the body corporate in respect of the specified amount.

[(8A) The amount which an officer is liable to pay under this section is to be recovered in the same manner as a Class 1 contribution to which regulations under paragraph 6 of Schedule 1 to the Contributions and Benefits Act apply and for this purpose references in those regulations to Class 1 contributions are to be construed accordingly.][3]

(9) In this section—

["the Class 1 rate"—

(*a*) in subsection (5) means the rate from time to time applicable under section 103(1) of the Finance Act 2009; and

(*b*) in subsection (7)(*c*) means the rate from time to time applicable under section 103(2) of that Act;

"the Class 1 element", in relation to any amount, means so much of that amount as is calculated by—

(*a*) multiplying that amount by so much of the specified amount as consists of Class 1 contributions; and

(*b*) dividing the product of that multiplication by the specified amount;][4]

"contributions" includes any interest or penalty in respect of contributions ["(and accordingly, in the definition of "the Class 1 element" given by this subsection, "Class 1 contributions" includes any interest or penalty in respect of Class 1 contributions)][4];

"officer", in relation to a body corporate, means—

(*a*) any director, manager, secretary or other similar officer of the body corporate, or any person purporting to act as such; and

(*b*) in a case where the affairs of the body corporate are managed by its members, any member of the body corporate exercising functions of management with respect to it or purporting to do so;

"the prescribed rate" means the rate from time to time prescribed by regulations under section 178 of the Finance Act 1989 for the purposes of the corresponding provision of Schedule 1 to the Contributions and Benefits Act, that is to say—

(*a*) in relation to subsection (5) above, paragraph 6(2)(*a*);

(*b*) in relation to subsection (7) above, paragraph 6(2)(*b*).][1]

Amendments—[1] Inserted by SSA 1998 s 64 with effect from 6 April 1999 by virtue of the Social Security Act 1998 (Commencement No 4) Order, SI 1999/526.

[2] Words "Secretary of State" substituted throughout the section by the Social Security Contributions (Transfer of Functions, etc) Act 1999 s 5 and Sch 5 para 10 with effect from 1 April 1999 by virtue of the Social Security Contributions (Transfer of Functions, etc) Act 1999 (Commencement No 1 and Transitional Provisions) Order, SI 1999/527.

[3] Sub-s (8A) inserted by the NIC and Statutory Payments Act 2004 s 5(3) with effect from 1 September 2004 (by virtue of SI 2004/1943).

[4] In sub-s (5), words substituted for words "at the prescribed rate", in sub-s (7)(*c*), words inserted, and in sub-s (9), definitions of "the Class 1 rate" and "the Class 1 element" inserted and words in definition of "contributions" inserted, by the Finance Act 2009, Sections 101 and 102 (Interest on Late Payments and Repayments) (Consequential Amendments) Order, SI 2014/1283 art 2, Schedule para 2 with effect in relation to payments in respect of Class 1 NIC and construction industry scheme payments made on or after 20 May 2014 for the tax year 2014–15 or for a subsequent tax year.

[121D Appeals in relation to personal liability notices.

(1) No appeal shall lie in relation to a personal liability notice except as provided by this section.

(2) An individual who is served with a personal liability notice may appeal to . . .[2, 5] against the [Inland Revenue's][4] decision as to the issue and content of the notice on the ground that—

(*a*) the whole or part of the amount specified under subsection (2)(*a*) of section 121C above (or the amount so specified as reduced under subsection (7) of that section) does not represent contributions to which that section applies;

(*b*) the failure to pay that amount was not attributable to any fraud or neglect on the part of the individual in question;

(*c*) the individual was not an officer of the body corporate at the time of the alleged fraud or neglect; or

(*d*) the opinion formed by the [Inland Revenue][4] under subsection (3)(*a*) or (*b*) of that section was unreasonable.

(3) The [Inland Revenue][4] shall give a copy of any notice of an appeal under this section, within 28 days of the giving of the notice, to each other individual who has been served with a personal liability notice.

(4) On an appeal under this section, the burden of proof as to any matter raised by a ground of appeal shall be on the [Inland Revenue][4].

(5) Where an appeal under this section—

(*a*) is brought on the basis of evidence not considered by the [Inland Revenue][4], or on the ground mentioned in subsection (2)(*d*) above; and

(*b*) is not allowed on some other basis or ground,

[and is notified to the tribunal, the tribunal shall][5] either dismiss the appeal or remit the case to the Inland Revenue, with any recommendations the [tribunal sees][5] fit to make, for the Inland Revenue to consider whether to vary their][2] decision as to the issue and content of the personal liability notice.

(6) In this section—

. . .[3]

"officer", in relation to a body corporate, has the same meaning as in section 121C above;

"personal liability notice" has the meaning given by subsection (2) of that section;

. . .[3]

["tribunal" means the First-tier Tribunal or, where determined under Tribunal Procedure Rules, the Upper Tribunal;][5]

"vary" means vary under regulations made under section 10 of the Social Security Contributions (Transfer of Functions, etc) Act 1999.][2]][1]

Amendments—[1] This section inserted by SSA 1998 s 64 with effect from 6 April 1999 by virtue of the Social Security Act 1998 (Commencement No 4) Order, SI 1999/526.

[2] Words in sub-ss (2) and (5) substituted, and definitions in sub-s (6) inserted by the Social Security Contributions (Transfer of Functions, etc) Act 1999 s 5 and Sch 5 para 11 with effect from 1 April 1999 by virtue of the Social Security Contributions (Transfer of Functions, etc) Act 1999 (Commencement No 1 and Transitional Provisions) Order, SI 1999/527.

[3] Definitions of "appeal tribunal" and "revise" in sub-s (6) repealed by the Social Security Contributions (Transfer of Functions, etc) Act 1999 s 5 and Sch 5 para 11, s 26(3) and Sch 10 Pt 1 with effect from 1 April 1999 by virtue of the Social Security Contributions (Transfer of Functions, etc) Act 1999 (Commencement No 1 and Transitional Provisions) Order, SI 1999/527.

[4] References to "Secretary of State" throughout this section substituted by the Social Security Contributions (Transfer of Functions, etc) Act 1999 s 5 and Sch 5 para 11 with effect from 1 April 1999 by virtue of the Social Security Contributions (Transfer of Functions, etc) Act 1999 (Commencement No 1 and Transitional Provisions) Order, SI 1999/527.

[5] The following amendments made by the Transfer of Tribunal Functions and Revenue and Customs Appeals Order, SI 2009/56 art 3, Sch 1 para 171 with effect from 1 April 2009—
– in sub-s (2) words "to the Special Commissioners" omitted;
– in sub s (5) words substituted for the words "the [Special Commissioners shall" and words substituted for the words "Special Commissioners see";
– in subsection (6) definition substituted

[121DA Interpretation of Part VI

(1) In this Part "the relevant social security legislation" means the provisions of any of the following, except so far as relating to contributions, working families' tax credit, disabled person's tax credit, statutory sick pay or statutory maternity pay, that is to say—

(*a*) the Contributions and Benefits Act;
(*b*) this Act;
(*c*) the Pensions Act, except Part III;
(*d*) section 4 of the Social Security (Incapacity for Work) Act 1994;
(*e*) the Jobseekers Act 1995;
(*f*) the Social Security (Recovery of Benefits) Act 1997;
(*g*) Parts I and IV of the Social Security Act 1998;
(*h*) Part V of the Welfare Reform and Pensions Act 1999;
[(*hh*) the State Pension Credit Act 2002;][2]
[(*hi*) Part 1 of the Welfare Reform Act 2007;][4]
[(*hj*) Part 1 of the Welfare Reform Act 2012;][6]
[(*hk*) Part 4 of that Act;][7]
[(*hl*) Part 1 of the Pensions Act 2014;][8]
(*i*) the Social Security Pensions Act 1975;
(*j*) the Social Security Act 1973;
(*k*) any subordinate legislation made, or having effect as if made, under any enactment specified in paragraphs (*a*) to (*j*) above.

(2) In this Part "authorised officer" means a person acting in accordance with any authorisation for the purposes of this Part which is for the time being in force in relation to him.

(3) For the purposes of this Part—

(*a*) references to a document include references to anything in which information is recorded in electronic or any other form;
(*b*) the requirement that a notice given by an authorised officer be in writing shall be taken to be satisfied in any case where the contents of the notice—
  (i) are transmitted to the recipient of the notice by electronic means; and
  (ii) are received by him in a form that is legible and capable of being recorded for future reference.

(4) In this Part "premises" includes—

(*a*) moveable structures and vehicles, vessels, aircraft and hovercraft;
(*b*) installations that are offshore installations for the purposes of the Mineral Workings (Offshore Installations) Act 1971; and
(*c*) places of all other descriptions whether or not occupied as land or otherwise;

and references in this Part to the occupier of any premises shall be construed, in relation to premises that are not occupied as land, as references to any person for the time being present at the place in question.

(5) In this Part—

"benefit" includes any allowance, payment, credit or loan;

["benefit offence" means—

(*a*) any criminal offence in connection with a claim for a relevant social security benefit;
(*b*) any criminal offence in connection with the receipt or payment of any amount by way of such a benefit;
(*c*) any criminal offence committed for the purpose of facilitating the commission (whether or not by the same person) of a benefit offence;
(*d*) any attempt or conspiracy to commit a benefit offence;".][3]

"compensation payment" has the same meaning as in the Social Security (Recovery of Benefits) Act 1997.

(6) In this Part—

(*a*) any reference to a person authorised to carry out any function relating to housing benefit or council tax benefit shall include a reference to a person providing services relating to the benefit directly or indirectly to an authority administering it; and

(*b*) any reference to the carrying out of a function relating to such a benefit shall include a reference to the provision of any services relating to it.[5]

(7) In this section—

["relevant social security benefit" means a benefit under any provision of the relevant social security legislation; and][3]

"subordinate legislation" has the same meaning as in the Interpretation Act 1978.][1]

Amendments—[1] Sub-ss (1), (7) inserted by the Child Support, Pensions and Social Security Act 2000 ss 67, 86, Sch 6 paras 1, 8 with effect from 1 November 2000 for the purpose of construing s 113 (by virtue of SI 2000/2950). For all other purposes this section takes effect from a day to be appointed.

[2] Sub-s (1)(*hh*) inserted by the State Pension Credit Act 2002 s 14, Sch 2 para 12 with effect from 2 July 2002 for the purpose only of exercising any power to make regulations or orders (by virtue of SI 2002/1691).

[3] In sub-s (5), the definition of "benefit offence" substituted, and in sub-s (7), definition of "relevant social security benefit" inserted by the Social Security Fraud Act 2001 ss 1(7), (8), 20 with effect from 30 April 2002 (by virtue of SI 2002/1222)

[4] Sub-s (1)(*hi*) inserted by the Welfare Reform Act 2007 s 28(1), Sch 3 para 10(1), (12) with effect as follows—

– for the purpose of making regulations, from 18 March 2008 (SI 2008/787 art 2(1), Schedule); and
– for remaining purposes, from 27 October 2008 (SI 2008/787 art 2(4)(*b*), (*f*)).

[5] Sub-s (6) repealed in so far as it relates to the abolition of council tax benefit, by the Welfare Reform Act 2012 s 147, Sch 14 Part 1 with effect from 1 April 2013 (by virtue of SI 2013/358 art 8(c)). Note that certain transitional provisions apply in relation to the abolition of council tax benefit (see SI 2013/358 art 9).

[6] In sub-s (1), para (*hj*) inserted by the Welfare Reform Act 2012 s 31, Sch 2 para 14 with effect from 29 April 2013 (by virtue of SI 2013/983 art 3(1)(*b*)(ii)).

[7] In sub-s (1), para (*hk*) inserted by the Welfare Reform Act 2012 s 91, Sch 9 paras 7, 12 with effect from 8 April 2013 in respect of persons whose only or principal residence is within a postcode listed in SI 2013/358 Sch 3 (by virtue of SI 2013/358 art 7(2)) and otherwise from 10 June 2013 (by virtue of SI 2013/1250 art 2).

[8] Sub-s (1)(*hl*) inserted by PeA 2014 s 23, Sch 12 paras 8, 13 with effect from 6 April 2016 (PeA 2014 s 56(1), (4)).

Prospective amendments—Sub-s (1)(*hm*) to be inserted by PeA 2014 s 31, Sch 16 para 26 with effect from a date to be appointed. Sub-s (1)(*hm*) as inserted to read as follows—

"(*hm*) Part 5 of the Pensions Act 2014;".

PART VII
INFORMATION

[Information relating to, or required for purposes of, contributions, statutory sick pay or statutory maternity pay

121E Supply of contributions etc information held by Inland Revenue][1]

[(1) This section applies to information which is held for the purposes of functions relating to contributions, [health in pregnancy grant,][4] statutory sick pay or statutory maternity pay [or functions under Part III of the Pensions Act[2]]—

(*a*) by the Inland Revenue, or

(*b*) by a person providing services to them, in connection with the provision of those services.

[(2) Information to which this section applies may, and . . . [6], must if an authorised officer so requires, be supplied—

(*a*) to the Secretary of State, or

(*b*) to a person providing services to the Secretary of State,

for use for the purposes of functions relating to . . . [6] war pensions . . . [6].

(2ZA) Information to which this section applies may, and . . . [6], must if an authorised officer so requires, be supplied—

(*a*) to the Northern Ireland Department, or

(*b*) to a person providing services to that Department,

for use for the purposes of functions relating to . . . [6] child support, war pensions . . . [6].][4]

(2A) . . . [6]

(3) In [this section][3] "authorised officer" means an officer of the Secretary of State or the Northern Ireland Department authorised for the purposes of this section by the Secretary of State or the Northern Ireland Department.][1]

Amendments—[1] Section 121E inserted by the Social Security Contributions (Transfer of Functions, etc) Act 1999 s 6 and Sch 6 para 1 with effect from 1 April 1999 by virtue of the Social Security Contributions (Transfer of Functions, etc) Act 1999 (Commencement No 1 and Transitional Provisions) Order, SI 1999/527.

[2] Words in sub-s (1) inserted by the Welfare Reform and Pensions Act 1999 s 81 Sch 11 paras 4, 7 with effect from 11 November 1999.

[3] Sub-s (2A) inserted, and words in sub-s (3) substituted, by EmA 2002 Sch 6 para 11 with effect from 9 September 2002 (by virtue of SI 2002/2256).

[4] In sub-s (1), words inserted by the Health and Social Care Act 2008 s 132(6) with effect in relation to England and Wales from 1 January 2009 (by virtue of SI 2008/3137 art 2), and in relation to Scotland from a date to be appointed (see the Health and Social Care Act 2008 s 170(3)).

[5] Sub-ss (2), (2ZA) substituted for previous sub-s (2), and in sub-s (2A) words inserted, by the Child Maintenance and other Payments Act 2008 s 57, Sch 7 para 2(1), (3), (4) with effect from 1 June 2009 (by virtue of SI 2009/1314 art 2(2)(*b*)(i)).

[6] In sub-ss (2), (2ZA), words repealed, and sub-s (2A) repealed, by the Welfare Reform Act 2012 s 147, Sch 14 Pt 13 with effect from 8 May 2012.

[121F Supply to Inland Revenue for purposes of contributions etc of information held by Secretary of State

[(1) This section applies to information which is held for the purposes of functions relating to . . . [7] war pensions . . . [7]

(*a*) by the Secretary of State, or

(*b*) by a person providing services to the Secretary of State, in connection with the provision of those services.

(1A) This section also applies to information which is held for the purposes of functions relating to . . . [7] child support, war pensions . . . [7]

(*a*) by the Northern Ireland Department, or

(*b*) by a person providing services to that Department, in connection with the provision of those services.][5]

(2) Information to which this section applies may, and . . . [7] must if an officer of the Inland Revenue authorised by the Inland Revenue for the purposes of this section so requires, be supplied—

(*a*) to the Inland Revenue, or

(*b*) to a person providing services to the Inland Revenue,

for use for the purposes of functions relating to contributions, [health in pregnancy grant,][4] . . . [6] statutory sick pay or statutory maternity pay [or functions under Part III of the Pensions Act][2].][1]

(2A) . . . [7]

Amendments—[1] Section 121F inserted by the Social Security Contributions (Transfer of Functions, etc) Act 1999 s 6 and Sch 6 para 1 with effect from 1 April 1999 by virtue of the Social Security Contributions (Transfer of Functions, etc) Act 1999 (Commencement No 1 and Transitional Provisions) Order, SI 1999/527.

[2] Words in sub-s (2) inserted by the Welfare Reform and Pensions Act 1999 s 81 Sch 11 paras 4, 8 with effect from 11 November 1999.

[3] Words in sub-s (2) inserted, and sub-s (2A) inserted, by EmA 2002 Sch 6 para 13 with effect from 9 September 2002 (by virtue of SI 2002/2256).

[4] In sub-s (2), words inserted by the Health and Social Care Act 2008 s 132(7) with effect in relation to England and Wales from 1 January 2009 (by virtue of SI 2008/3137 art 2), and in relation to Scotland from a date to be appointed (see the Health and Social Care Act 2008 s 170(3)).

[5] Sub-ss (1), (1A) substituted for previous sub-s (1) by the Child Maintenance and other Payments Act 2008 s 57, Sch 7 para 2(1), (5) with effect from 1 June 2009 (by virtue of SI 2009/1314 art 2(2)(*b*)(i)).

[6] In sub-s (2), words "Saving Gateway accounts," repealed by the Savings Accounts and Health in Pregnancy Grant Act 2010 s 2(2) with effect from 16 February 2011.

[7] In sub-ss (1), (1A), (2), words repealed, and sub-s (2A) repealed, by the Welfare Reform Act 2012 s 147, Sch 14 Pt 13 with effect from 8 May 2012.

Information held by tax authorities

122 Supply of information held by tax authorities for fraud prevention and verification

Amendments—Sections 122, 122ZA repealed, by the Welfare Reform Act 2012 s 147, Sch 14 Part 13 with effect from 8 May 2012.

[122ZA Supply of tax information to assess certain employment or training schemes

Amendments—Sections 122, 122ZA repealed, by the Welfare Reform Act 2012 s 147, Sch 14 Part 13 with effect from 8 May 2012.

[122AA Disclosure of contributions etc information by [Her Majesty's Revenue and Customs][3]][1]

[(1) No obligation as to secrecy imposed by statute or otherwise on [Revenue and Customs officials (within the meaning of section 18 of the Commissioners for Revenue and Customs Act 2005 (confidentiality)][3] shall prevent information held for the purposes of the functions of [Her Majesty's Revenue and Customs][3] in relation to contributions, statutory sick pay[, statutory maternity pay, [statutory paternity pay,][7] or statutory adoption pay][2] [or statutory shared parental pay][6] from being disclosed—

(*a*) to any of the authorities to which this paragraph applies, or any person authorised to exercise any function of that authority, for the purposes of the functions of that authority, or

(*b*) in a case where the disclosure is necessary for the purpose of giving effect to any agreement to which an order under section 179(1) below relates.

(2) The authorities to which subsection (1)(*a*) above applies are—

(*a*) the Health and Safety Executive,

(*b*) the Government Actuary's Department,

(*c*) the Office for National Statistics, and

(*d*) the [Pensions Regulator][4].][1]

NIC

Amendments—[1] Section 122AA inserted by the Social Security Contributions (Transfer of Functions, etc) Act 1999 s 6 and Sch 6 para 3 with effect from 1 April 1999 by virtue of the Social Security Contributions (Transfer of Functions, etc) Act 1999 (Commencement No 1 and Transitional Provisions) Order, SI 1999/527.

[2] Words in sub-s (1) amended by EA Act 2002 s 53, Sch 7 paras 8, 13 with effect from 9 September 2002 (by virtue of SI 2002/2256).

[3] Words in Heading and sub-s (1) substituted by CRCA 2005 s 50, Sch 4 paras 44, 46 with effect from 18 April 2005 (by virtue of SI 2005/1126).

[4] Words in sub-s (2)(*d*) substituted by the Pensions Act 2004 s 319(1), Sch 12 para 7 with effect from 6 April 2005 (by virtue of SI 2005/695).

[5] In sub-s (1) words substituted by the Work and Families Act 2006 s 11 Sch 1 para 25 with effect from 6 April 2010 (by virtue of SI 2010/495, art 4(a), (d)).

[6] In sub-s (1), words inserted by the Children and Families Act 2014, s 126(1), Sch 7 para 25(b) with effect from 1 December 2014 (by virtue of SI 2014/1640 art 5)

[7] In sub-s (1), words substituted by the Children and Families Act 2014, s 126(1), Sch 7 para 25(*a*) with effect from 5 April 2015 (by virtue of SI 2014/1640).

122A Supply of information by Inland Revenue for purposes of contributions

Amendments—This section repealed by the Social Security Contributions (Transfer of Functions, etc) Act 1999 s 26(3), Sch 10 Pt 1 and Sch 6 para 4 with effect from 1 April 1999 by virtue of the Social Security Contributions (Transfer of Functions, etc) Act 1999 (Commencement No 1 and Transitional Provisions) Order, SI 1999/527.

The Registration Service

124 Provisions relating to age, death and marriage

(1) Regulations made by the Registrar General under section 20 of the Registration Service Act 1953 or section 54 of the Registration of Births, Deaths and Marriages (Scotland) Act 1965 may provide for the furnishing by superintendent registrars and registrars, subject to the payment of such fee as may be prescribed by the regulations, of such information for the purposes—

(*a*) of the provisions of the Contributions and Benefits Act to which this section applies;

[(*aa*) of the provisions of Parts I and II of the Jobseekers Act 1995;][1]

[(*ab*) of the provisions of the State Pension Credit Act 2002;][3]

[(*ac*) of the provisions of Part 1 of the Welfare Reform Act 2007;][4] . . . [5]

[(*ad*) of the provisions of Part 1 of the Welfare Reform Act 2012;][5]

[(*ae*) of the provisions of Part 4 of that Act;][6]

[(*af*) of the provisions of Part 1 of the Pensions Act 2014; and][7]

(*b*) of the provisions of this Act so far as they have effect in relation to matters arising under those provisions,

including copies or extracts from the registers in their custody, as may be so prescribed.

(2) This section applies to the following provisions of the Contributions and Benefits Act—

(*a*) Parts I to VI except section 108;

(*b*)–(*f*) . . .

(3) Where the age, marriage or death of a person is required to be ascertained or proved for the purposes mentioned in subsection (1) above, any person—

(*a*) on presenting to the custodian of the register under the enactments relating to the registration of births, marriages and deaths in which particulars of the birth, marriage or death (as the case may be) of the first-mentioned person are entered, a duly completed requisition in writing in that behalf; and

(*b*) on payment of [the appropriate fee in England and Wales and a fee of][8] [£10.00][2] in Scotland,

shall be entitled to obtain a copy, certified under the hand of the custodian, of the entry of those particulars.

[(3A) Where it is required to be ascertained or proved for the purposes mentioned in subsection (1) above, that a civil partnership has been converted into a marriage, any person—

(*a*) on presenting to the superintendent registrar in whose district the conversion took place, a duly completed requisition in writing in that behalf; and

[(*b*) on payment of the appropriate fee;][8]

is entitled to obtain a copy, certified under the hand of the superintendent registrar, of the entry relating to that marriage in the register of conversions.]

(4) Requisitions for the purposes of subsection (3) above shall be in such form and contain such particulars as may from time to time be specified by the Registrar General, and suitable forms of requisition shall, on request, be supplied without charge by superintendent registrars and registrars.

(5) In this section—

(*a*) as it applies to England and Wales—

["the appropriate fee" means the fee payable to the registrar or superintendent registrar for a certified copy of an entry in the register concerned by virtue of section 38A of the Births and Deaths Registration Act 1953, section 71A of the Marriage Act 1949 or section 9 of the Marriage (Same Sex Couples) Act 2013.][8]

"Registrar General" means the Registrar General for England and Wales; and "superintendent registrar" and "registrar" mean a superintendent registrar or, as the case may be, registrar for the purposes of the enactments relating to the registration of births, deaths and marriages; and

(*b*) as it applies to Scotland—

"Registrar General" means the Registrar General of Births, Deaths and Marriages for Scotland;

"registrar" means a district registrar, senior registrar or assistant registrar for the purposes of the enactments relating to the registration of births, deaths and marriages.

Former enactments—SSA 1975 s 160.

Note—Sub-s (2)(*b*)–(*f*) are outside the scope of this Publication.

Regarding sub-s (3)(*b*) above, in relation to England and Wales, the Registration of Births, Deaths and Marriages (Fees) Order, SI 2010/441 art 2, Schedule para 21 sets out the relevant fees payable from 1 September 2014 as follows—

- certificate issued by a registrar at the time of registration: £4.00;
- certificate issued by a registrar after the time of registration: £7.00;
- certificate issued by a superintendent registrar: £10.00;
- any other custodian of the register: £10.00.

Regarding sub-s (3)(*b*) above, in relation to Scotland, the Registration of Births, Deaths and Marriages (Fees) (Scotland) Order, SSI 2010/428 art 2, Schedule, specifies the maximum amount payable to be £10.00.

Amendments—[1] Sub-s (1)(*aa*) inserted by the Jobseekers Act 1995 Sch 2 para 59 with effect from 11 June 1996 by virtue of SI 1996/1509.

[2] Figure in sub-s (3)(*b*) substituted by the Registration of Births, Deaths and Marriages (Fees) (Scotland) Order, SSI 2010/428 art 2, Schedule with effect from 1 January 2011.

[3] Sub-s (1)(*ab*) inserted by the State Pension Credit Act 2002 s 14, Sch 2 para 13 with effect from 2 July 2002 for the purpose only of exercising any power to make regulations or orders (by virtue of SI 2002/1691).

[4] Sub-s (1)(*ac*) inserted by the Welfare Reform Act 2007 s 28(1), Sch 3 para 10(1), (16). with effect from 27 October 2008 (by virtue of SI 2008/787, art 2(4)(*b*), (*f*)).

[5] In sub-s (1), in para (*ac*), the final word repealed, and para (*ad*) inserted, by the Welfare Reform Act 2012 s 31, Sch 2 para 17 with effect from 29 April 2013 (by virtue of SI 2013/983).

[6] Sub-s (1)(*ae*) inserted by the Welfare Reform Act 2012 s 91, Sch 9 paras 7, 15 with effect, in relation to personal independence payment for certain purposes, from 8 April 2013 (by virtue of SI 2013/358) and for remaining purposes, from 10 June 2013 (by virtue of SI 2013/1250).

[7] Sub-s (1)(*af*) inserted by PeA 2014 s 23, Sch 12 paras 8, 15 with effect from 6 April 2016 (PeA 2014 s 56(1), (4)).

[8] In sub-s (3)(*b*), words substituted for words "a fee of [xx.xx] in England and Wales and", sub-s (3A)(*b*) substituted, and in sub-s (5)(*a*), words inserted, by the Immigration Act 2016 s 89, Sch 15 para 36 with effect from 12 July 2016 (by virtue of SI 2016/603 art 3). Sub-s (3A)(*b*) previously read as follows–

"(*b*) on payment of a fee of £10.00;".

Prospective amendments—Sub-s (2)(*b*) to be repealed, by the Welfare Reform Act 2012 s 147, Sch 14 Part 1 with effect from a date to be appointed.

Sub-s (1)(*ag*) to be inserted by PeA 2014 s 31, Sch 16 para 28 with effect from a date to be appointed. Sub-s (1)(*ag*) as inserted to read as follows—

"(*ag*) of section 30 of the Pensions Act 2014; and".

[124A Provisions relating to civil partnership: England and Wales

(1) Regulations made by the Registrar General under section 36 of the Civil Partnership Act 2004 may provide for the furnishing by registration authorities, subject to the payment of the prescribed fee, of such information for the purposes mentioned in section 124(1) above as may be so prescribed.

(2) Where the civil partnership of a person is required to be ascertained or proved for those purposes, any person—

(*a*) on presenting to the registration authority for the area in which the civil partnership was formed a request in the prescribed manner in that behalf, and

(*b*) on payment of the prescribed fee,

shall be entitled to obtain a certified copy of such entries in the register as are prescribed by regulations made under section 36 of the 2004 Act.

(3) "The prescribed fee" means any fee prescribed under section 34(1) of the 2004 Act.

(4) "The prescribed manner" means—

(*a*) in accordance with any regulations made under section 36 of the 2004 Act, and

(*b*) in such form as is approved by the Registrar General for England and Wales,

and forms for making a request under subsection (2) shall, on request, be supplied without charge by registration authorities.][1]

Amendments—[1] This section inserted by the Civil Partnership Act 2004 (Overseas Relationships and Consequential, etc Amendments) Order 2005 SI 2005/3175 Art 4(1) Sch 1 para 4(1) with effect from 5 December 2005.

[124B Provisions relating to civil partnership: Scotland

(1) Where the civil partnership of a person is required to be ascertained or proved for the purposes mentioned in section 124(1) above, any person, on presenting to a district registrar a request in the approved manner in that behalf, shall be entitled to obtain a copy, certified by the registrar, of the entry in the civil partnership register of the particulars of the civil partnership.

(2) "The approved manner" means in such form and containing such particulars as may be approved by the Registrar General for Scotland.

(3) Forms for making a request under subsection (1) shall, on request, be supplied without charge by district registrars.

(4) "Civil partnership register" has the same meaning as in Part 3 of the Civil Partnership Act 2004.][1]

Amendments—[1] This section inserted by the Civil Partnership Act 2004 (Overseas Relationships and Consequential, etc Amendments) Order 2005 SI 2005/3175 Art 4(1) Sch 1 para 4(1) with effect from 5 December 2005.

125 Regulations as to notification of deaths

(1) Regulations [made with the concurrence of the Inland Revenue][5] may provide that it shall be the duty of any of the following persons—

(*a*) the Registrar General for England and Wales;

(*b*) the Registrar General of Births, Deaths and Marriages for Scotland;

(*c*) each registrar of births and deaths,

to furnish the Secretary of State, [or the Inland Revenue, for the purposes of their respective functions][5] under the Contributions and Benefits Act[, the Jobseekers Act 1995][1][, the Social Security (Recovery of Benefits) Act 1997][3][, the Social Security Act 1998][4] [, the State Pension Credit Act 2002][6] [, Part 1 of the Welfare Reform Act 2007][7][, Part 1 of the Welfare Reform Act 2012][8][, Part 4 of that Act][9][, Part 1 of the Pensions Act 2014][10] and this Act and the functions of the Northern Ireland Department under any Northern Ireland legislation corresponding to [any of those Acts][2], with the prescribed particulars of such deaths as may be prescribed.

(2) The regulations may make provision as to the manner in which and times at which the particulars are to be furnished.

Former enactments—SSA 1986 s 60.

Amendments—[1] Words in sub-s (1) inserted by the Jobseekers Act 1995 Sch 2 para 60 with effect from 11 June 1996 by virtue of SI 1996/1509.

[2] Words in sub-s (1) substituted for the words "either of them" by the Jobseekers Act 1995 Sch 2 para 60 with effect from 11 June 1996 by virtue of SI 1996/1509.

[3] Words in sub-s (1) inserted by Social Security (Recovery of Benefits) Act 1997 with effect from 6 October 1997 by virtue of SI 1997/2085.

[4] Inserted by SSA 1998 Sch 7 para 89 with effect from 5 July 1999, for certain purposes (by virtue of the Social Security Act 1998 (Commencement No 8, and Savings and Consequential and Transitional Provisions) Order, SI 1999/1958, art 2(1)(*b*) (subject to transitional provisions contained in art 5 Sch 12 thereof)), 6 September 1999, for certain purposes (by virtue of the Social Security Act 1998 (Commencement No 9, and Savings and Consequential and Transitional Provisions) Order, SI 1999/2422, art 2(*c*) (subject to transitional provisions contained in art 4 Sch 14 thereof)), 5 October 1999, for certain purposes (by virtue of the Social Security Act 1998 (Commencement No 10 and Transitional Provisions) Order, SI 1999/2422, art 2, Sch 1 (subject to transitional provisions contained in art 3 Sch 2 thereof)), 18 October 1999, for certain purposes (by virtue of the Social Security Act 1998 (Commencement No 11, and Savings and Consequential and Transitional Provisions) Order, SI 1999/2860, art 2, Sch 1 (subject to transitional provisions contained in art 4 Schs 16–18 thereof)), 29 November 1999, for certain purposes (by virtue of the Social Security Act 1998 (Commencement No 12 and Consequential and Transitional Provisions) Order, SI 1999/3178, art 2(1), Sch 1 (subject to transitional provisions contained in art 4 Schs 21–23 thereof)), and with effect from a date to be appointed for all other purposes.

[5] Words in sub-s (1) inserted and substituted by the Social Security Contributions (Transfer of Functions, etc) Act 1999 s 1(1) and Sch 1 para 25 with effect from 1 April 1999 by virtue of the Social Security Contributions (Transfer of Functions, etc) Act 1999 (Commencement No 1 and Transitional Provisions) Order, SI 1999/527.

[6] Words inserted by the State Pension Credit Act 2002 s 14, Sch 2 para 14 with effect from 2 July 2002 for the purpose only of exercising any power to make regulations or orders (by virtue of SI 2002/1691).

[7] Words in sub-s (1) inserted by the Welfare Reform Act 2007 s 28(1), Sch 3 para 10(1), (17) with effect from 27 October 2008 (SI 2008/787 art 2(4)(*b*), (*f*)).

[8] In sub-s (1), words inserted by the by the Welfare Reform Act 2012 s 31, Sch 2 para 18 with effect from 29 April 2013 (by virtue of SI 2013/983 art 3(1)(*b*)(ii)).

[9] In sub-s (1), words inserted by the Welfare Reform Act 2012 s 91, Sch 9 paras 7, 16 with effect from 8 April 2013 in relation to persons whose only or main residence is within a postcode listed in SI 2013/358 Sch 3 (by virtue of SI 2013/358 art 7(2)) and otherwise from 10 June 2013 (by virtue of SI 2103/1250 art 2).

[10] In sub-s (1), words inserted by PeA 2014 s 23, Sch 12 paras 8, 16 with effect from 6 April 2016 (PeA 2014 s 56(1), (4)).

Prospective amendments—In sub-s (1), words ", section 30 of that Act " to be inserted after words ", Part 1 of the Pensions Act 2014" by PeA 2014 s 31, Sch 16 para 29 with effect from a date to be appointed.

Statutory sick pay and other benefits

130 Duties of employers—statutory sick pay and claims for other benefits

(1)–(3) . . .

(4) Regulations [made with the concurrence of the Inland Revenue[1]]—

[(*za*) universal credit;][3]

(*a*)–(*b*) . . .

(*c*) may require employers who have made payments of statutory sick pay to furnish to the Secretary of State [or the Inland Revenue (as the regulations may require)][1] such documents and information, at such times, as may be prescribed.

[(5) Regulations made with the concurrence of the Inland Revenue may require employers to produce wages sheets and other documents and records to officers of the Inland Revenue, within a prescribed period, for the purpose of enabling them to satisfy themselves that statutory sick pay has been paid, and is being paid, in accordance with regulations under section 5 above, to employees or former employees who are entitled to it.][2]

Former enactments—Social Security and Housing Benefits Act 1982 s 9(3)(*a*).

Note—Provisions omitted are outside the scope of this Publication.

Amendments—[1] Words in sub-s (4) inserted by the Social Security Contributions (Transfer of Functions, etc) Act 1999 s 1(1) and Sch 1 para 26 with effect from 1 April 1999 by virtue of the Social Security Contributions (Transfer of Functions, etc) Act 1999 (Commencement No 1 and Transitional Provisions) Order, SI 1999/527.

[2] Sub-s (5) inserted by the NIC and Statutory Payments Act 2004 s 9(1), (2) with effect from 1 January 2005 (by virtue of SI 2004/1943).

[3] In sub-s (1), para (*za*) inserted by the Welfare Reform Act 2012 s 31, Sch 2 para 18 with effect from 29 April 2013 (by virtue of SI 2013/983 art 3(1)(*b*)(ii)).

[Contributions avoidance arrangements

132A Disclosure of contributions avoidance arrangements

(1) The Treasury may by regulations make provision requiring, or relating to, the disclosure of information in relation to any notifiable contribution arrangements or notifiable contribution proposal.

(2) The only provision which may be made under subsection (1) is provision applying (with or without modification), or corresponding to, any of the following provisions—

(*a*) any provision of, or made under, Part 7 of the Finance Act 2004 (disclosure of tax avoidance schemes) so far as that provision relates to income tax;

(*b*) section 98C of the Taxes Management Act 1970 (penalties for failure to comply with Part 7 of the Finance Act 2004) and any other provision of the Taxes Management Act 1970 so far as it relates to a penalty under that section;

(*c*) any provision made under section 132 of the Finance Act 1999 or section 135 of the Finance Act 2002 (electronic communications);

(*d*) any provision of any other enactment or instrument (including any enactment or instrument passed or made on or after the day on which the National Insurance Contributions Act 2006 was passed) which requires, or relates to, the disclosure of information in relation to tax avoidance arrangements which relate in whole or in part to income tax.

(3) For the purposes of subsection (1)—

"notifiable contribution arrangements" means any arrangements which—

(*a*) enable, or might be expected to enable, any person to obtain an advantage in relation to a contribution, and

(*b*) are such that the main benefit, or one of the main benefits, that might be expected to arise from the arrangements is the obtaining of that advantage;

"notifiable contribution proposal" means a proposal for arrangements which, if entered into, would be notifiable contribution arrangements (whether the proposal relates to a particular person or to any person who may seek to take advantage of it).

(4) Where, at any time after the passing of the National Insurance Contributions Act 2006, a relevant tax provision is passed or made which changes the notifiable tax matters, the Treasury may, by regulations, amend the definitions in subsection (3) so as to make an analogous change to the matters in respect of which information may be required to be disclosed by virtue of this section.

(5) In subsection (4)—

"the notifiable tax matters" means the arrangements, proposals or other matters in respect of which information is or may be required to be disclosed under a relevant tax provision;

"relevant tax provision" means a provision mentioned in subsection (2).

(6) No provision made by regulations under this section may require any person to disclose to the Commissioners for Her Majesty's Revenue and Customs, or any other person, any information with respect to which a claim to legal professional privilege, or, in Scotland, to confidentiality of communications, could be maintained in legal proceedings.

(7) In this section—

"advantage", in relation to any contribution, means—

(*a*) the avoidance or reduction of a liability for that contribution, or

(*b*) the deferral of the payment of that contribution;

"arrangements" includes any scheme, transaction or series of transactions;

"contribution" means a contribution under—

(*a*) Part 1 of the Social Security Contributions and Benefits Act 1992, or

(*b*) Part 1 of the Social Security Contributions and Benefits (Northern Ireland) Act 1992;

"tax avoidance arrangements" includes arrangements which enable, or might be expected to enable, a person to obtain an advantage in relation to any tax (within the meaning of Part 7 of the Finance Act 2004).][1]

Regulations—National Insurance Contributions (Application of Part 7 of the Finance Act 2004) Regulations, SI 2007/785.
National Insurance Contributions (Application of Part 7 of the Finance Act 2004) Regulations, SI 2012/1868.
National Insurance Contributions (Application of Part 7 of the Finance Act 2004) Regulations, SI 2015/531.
Amendments—[1] This section inserted by the National Insurance Contributions Act 2006 s 7(1), (2) with effect from 30 March 2006.

PART IX
ALTERATION OF CONTRIBUTIONS ETC

Cross references—See the SS Contributions and Benefits Act 1992 s 1(3)(*b*) (the amounts and rates of contributions are subject to alteration by subordinate legislation from year to year),
SSC & BA 1992 s 9(4)(*b*) (calculation and alteration of secondary Class 1 contributions).

141 Annual review of contributions

(1) In each tax year the [Treasury][1] shall carry out a review of the general level of earnings in Great Britain taking into account changes in that level which have taken place since [their][1] last review under this section, with a view to determining whether, in respect of Class 2, 3 or 4 contributions, an order should be made under this section, to have effect in relation to the next following tax year.

(2) For the purposes of any review under this section, the [Treasury[1]]—

(*a*) shall estimate the general level of earnings in such manner as [they think fit][1]; and

(*b*) shall take into account any other matters appearing to [them][1] to be relevant to [their][1] determination whether or not an order should be made under this section, including the current operation of the Contributions and Benefits Act.

(3) If the [Treasury determine][1], as a result of a review under this section, that having regard to changes in the general level of earnings which have taken place, and to any other matters taken into account on the review, an order under this section should be made for the amendment of Part I of the Contributions and Benefits Act, [they][1] shall prepare and lay before each House of Parliament a draft of such an order framed so as to give effect to [their][1] conclusions on the review.

(4) An order under this section may amend Part I of the Contributions and Benefits Act by altering any one or more of the following figures—

(*a*) the figure specified in [section 11(2) and (6)][3] as the weekly rate of Class 2 contributions;

(*b*) the figure specified in section 11(4) as the [small profits threshold for the purposes of Class 2 contributions][3];

(*c*) the figure specified in section 13(1) as the amount of a Class 3 contribution;

(*d*) the figures specified in [subsection (3) of section 15 as the upper limit of profits or gains to be taken into account for the purposes of Class 4 contributions under that section and as the lower limit of profits or gains to be taken into account for those purposes under paragraph (*a*) of that subsection.][2]

(5) If an order under this section contains an amendment altering either of the figures [referred to in subsection (4)(*d*) above][2], it shall make the same alteration of the corresponding figure specified in section [18 of the Contributions and Benefits Act][2].

(6) If the [Treasury determine][1] as a result of a review under this section that, having regard to [their][1] conclusions in respect of the general level of earnings and otherwise, no such amendments of Part I of the Contributions and Benefits Act are called for as can be made for the purposes of subsection (4) above, and [determine][1] accordingly not to lay a draft of an order before Parliament, [they][1] shall instead prepare and lay before each House of Parliament a report explaining [their][1] reasons for that determination.

(7) In subsection (1) above in its application to the tax year 1992–93 the reference to the last review under this section shall be construed as a reference to the last review under section 120 of the 1975 Act.

Former enactments—SSA 1975 s 120; SS Pensions Act 1975 s 65, Sch 4 para 50.
Cross reference—See SS Contributions and Benefits Act 1992 s 176(2)(*a*) (subordinate legislation not requiring parliamentary control).
Orders and Regulations—Social Security (Contributions) (Re-rating) Order, SI 2013/559.
Social Security (Contributions) (Re-rating and National Insurance Funds Payments) Order 2014, SI 2014/475.
Social Security (Contributions) (Re-rating and National Insurance Funds Payments) Order 2014, SI 2015/588.
Social Security (Contributions) (Limits and Thresholds Amendments and National Insurance Funds Payments) Regulations, SI 2016/343.
Social Security (Contributions) (Rates, Limits and Thresholds Amendments and National Insurance Funds Payments) Regulations, SI 2017/415.
Amendments—[1] Words in sub-ss (1), (2), (3) and (6) substituted by the Social Security Contributions (Transfer of Functions, etc) Act 1999 s 2 and Sch 3 para 44 with effect from 1 April 1999 by virtue of the Social Security Contributions (Transfer of Functions, etc) Act 1999 (Commencement No 1 and Transitional Provisions) Order, SI 1999/527.
[2] Words in sub-ss (4)(*d*), (5) substituted by NICA 2002 s 6, Sch 1 paras 15, 16 with effect from 2003–04.
[3] In sub-s (4)(*a*), (*b*), words substituted by NICA 2015 s 2, Sch 1 paras 19, 20 with effect for the tax year 2015–16 and subsequent tax years.

142 Orders under s 141—supplementary

(1) Where the [Treasury lay][1] before Parliament a draft of an order under section 141 above, [they shall][1] lay with it a copy of a report by the Government Actuary or the Deputy Government Actuary on the effect which, in that Actuary's opinion, the making of such an order may be expected to have on the National Insurance Fund; and, where [the Treasury determine][1] not to lay a draft order, [they shall][1] with the report laid before Parliament under section 141(6) above lay a copy of a report by the Government Actuary or the Deputy Government Actuary on the consequences for the Fund which may, in that Actuary's opinion, follow from that determination.

(2) Where the [Treasury lay][1] before Parliament a draft of an order under section 141 above, then if the draft is approved by a resolution of each House, the [Treasury][1] shall make an order in the form of the draft.

(3) An order under section 141 above shall be made so as to be in force from the beginning of the tax year following that in which it receives Parliamentary approval, and to have effect for that year and any subsequent tax year (subject to the effect of any subsequent order under this Part of this Act); and for this purpose the order is to be taken as receiving Parliamentary approval on the date on which the draft of it is approved by the second House to approve it.

Former enactments—Sub-ss (1), (2): SSA 1975 s 121(1), (2).
Sub-s (3): SSA 1975 s 121(3); SSA 1990 s 21(1), Sch 6 para 1(2).

Orders and Regulations—Social Security (Contributions) (Re-rating) Order, SI 2013/559.
Social Security (Contributions) (Re-rating and National Insurance Funds Payments) Order 2014, SI 2014/475.
Social Security (Contributions) (Re-rating and National Insurance Funds Payments) Order 2014, SI 2015/588.
Social Security (Contributions) (Limits and Thresholds Amendments and National Insurance Funds Payments) Regulations, SI 2016/343.
Social Security (Contributions) (Rates, Limits and Thresholds Amendments and National Insurance Funds Payments) Regulations, SI 2017/415.

Amendments—[1] Words in sub-ss (1) and (2) substituted by the Social Security Contributions (Transfer of Functions, etc) Act 1999 s 2 and Sch 3 para 45 with effect from 1 April 1999 by virtue of the Social Security Contributions (Transfer of Functions, etc) Act 1999 (Commencement No 1 and Transitional Provisions) Order, SI 1999/527.

143 Power to alter contributions with a view to adjusting level of National Insurance Fund

(1) Without prejudice to section 141 above, the [Treasury][2] may at any time, if [they think][2] it expedient to do so with a view to adjusting the level at which the National Insurance Fund stands for the time being and having regard to the sums which may be expected to be paid from the Fund in any future period, make an order amending Part I of the Contributions and Benefits Act by altering any one or more of the following figures—

[(*a*) the percentage rate specified as the [main primary percentage in section 8(2)(*a*)][3];

(*b*) the percentage rate specified as the secondary percentage in section 9(2);][1]

(*c*) the figure specified in [section 11(2) and (6)][6] as the weekly rate of Class 2 contributions;

(*d*) the figure specified in section 13(1) as the amount of a Class 3 contribution;

(*e*) the percentage rate [specified as the main Class 4 percentage in section 15(3ZA)(*a*)][3].

(2) . . . [4]

(3) An order under subsection (1) above may if it contains an amendment altering the figure specified in [section 11(2) and (6)][6] of the Contributions and Benefits Act as the weekly rate of Class 2 contributions and the [Treasury think][2] it expedient in consequence of that amendment, amend section 11(4) of that Act by altering the figure there specified as the [small profits threshold for the purposes of Class 2 contributions][6].

(4) No order shall be made under this section so as—

[(*a*) to increase for any tax year the [main][3] primary percentage, or the secondary percentage, to a percentage rate more than 0.25 per cent higher than that applicable at the end of the preceding tax year;][1]

(*b*) to increase the [main Class 4 percentage][3] to more than [9.25][5] per cent.

Former enactments—Sub-s (1): SSA 1975 s 122(1); SSA 1985 s 29(1), Sch 5 para 9; SSA 1989 s 1(3).
Sub-ss (2), (3): SSA 1975 s 122(2), (3)(*a*).
Sub-s (4): SSA 1975 s 122(6); SSA 1980 s 2, Sch 1 para 13; SSA 1989 s 1(5).

Cross references—See the SS Contributions and Benefits Act 1992 s 8(2)(*b*) (calculation and alteration of primary Class 1 contributions),
SSC & BA 1992 s 176(2)(*a*) (subordinate legislation not requiring parliamentary control).

Amendments—[1] Sub-ss (1)(*a*), (*b*) and (4) substituted by SSA 1998 Sch 7 para 90(1) with effect from 6 April 1999 by virtue of the Social Security Act 1998 (Commencement No 3) Order, SI 1999/418.

[2] Words in sub-ss (1) and (3) substituted by the Social Security Contributions (Transfer of Functions, etc) Act 1999 s 2 and Sch 3 para 46 with effect from 1 April 1999 by virtue of the Social Security Contributions (Transfer of Functions, etc) Act 1999 (Commencement No 1 and Transitional Provisions) Order, SI 1999/527.

[3] Words in sub-ss (1), (4)(*b*) substituted, and word in sub-s (4)(*a*) inserted, by NICA 2002 ss 6, Sch 1 paras 15, 17 with effect from 2003–04.

[4] Sub-s (2) repealed by NICA 2002 s 7, Sch 2 with effect from 2003–04.

[5] In sub-s (4)(*b*), figure substituted for previous figure "8.25" by the National Insurance Contributions Act 2011 s 2(2) with effect from 6 April 2011.

[6] In sub-ss (1)(*c*), (3), words substituted by NICA 2015 s 2, Sch 1 paras 19, 21 with effect for the tax year 2015–16 and subsequent tax years.

[143A Power to alter Class 1B contributions]

Amendments—This section repealed by the Welfare Reform and Pensions Act 1999 s 88 Sch 13, Pt VI with effect from 6 April 2000 by virtue of SI 1999/3420.

144 Orders under s 143 . . . [2]—supplementary

(1) Where (in accordance with section 190 below) the [Treasury lay][1] before Parliament a draft of an order under section 143 . . . [2] above, [they][1] shall lay with it a copy of a report by the Government Actuary or the Deputy Government Actuary on the effect which, in that Actuary's opinion, the making of such an order may be expected to have on the National Insurance Fund.

(2) An order under section 143 . . . [2] above shall be made so as to be in force from the beginning of the tax year following that in which it received Parliamentary approval, and to have effect for that year and any subsequent tax year (subject to the effect of any subsequent order under this Part of this Act); and for this purpose the order is to be taken as receiving Parliamentary approval on the date on which the draft of it is approved by the second House to approve it.

Former enactments—Sub-s (1): SSA 1975 s 123(2); Employment Act 1990 s 16(2), Sch 3.
Sub-s (2): SSA 1975 s 123(3); SSA 1990 s 21(1), Sch 6 para 1(2)(*b*).

Amendments—[1] Words in sub-s (1) substituted by the Social Security Contributions (Transfer of Functions, etc) Act 1999 s 2 and Sch 3 para 48 with effect from 1 April 1999 by virtue of the Social Security Contributions (Transfer of Functions, etc) Act 1999 (Commencement No 1 and Transitional Provisions) Order, SI 1999/527.

[2] Words in heading and sub-ss (1), (2), repealed by the Welfare Reform and Pensions Act 1999 s 88 Sch 13, Pt VI with effect from 6 April 2000 (previously inserted by SSA 1998 Sch 7 para 91) by virtue of SI 1999/3420.

145 Power to alter primary and secondary contributions

[(1) For the purpose of adjusting amounts payable by way of primary Class 1 contributions, the [Treasury][2] may at any time make an order altering the percentage rate specified as the [main primary percentage in section 8(2)(*a*)][3] of the Contributions and Benefits Act.

(2) For the purpose of adjusting amounts payable by way of secondary Class 1 contributions, the [Treasury][2] may at any time make an order altering the percentage rate specified as the secondary percentage in section 9(2) of the Contributions and Benefits Act.

(3) No order shall be made under this section so as to increase for any tax year the primary percentage, or the secondary percentage, to a percentage rate more than 0.25 per cent higher than that applicable at the end of the preceding tax year.][1]

(4) Without prejudice to section 141 or 143 above, the [Treasury][2] may make such order—

(*a*) amending [section 11(2) and (6)][4] of the Contributions and Benefits Act by altering the figure specified . . . [4] as the weekly rate of Class 2 contributions;

(*b*) amending section 13(1) of that Act by altering the figure specified in that subsection as the amount of a Class 3 contribution,

as [the Treasury think][2] fit in consequence of the coming into force of an order made or proposed to be made under subsection (1) above.

Former enactments—Sub-s (1): SSA 1975 s 123A(1); SSA 1985 s 7(5); SSA 1989 s 1(6).
Sub-s (2): SSA 1975 s 123A(2); SSA 1985 s 7(5).
Sub-s (3): SSA 1975 s 123A(3); SSA 1985 s 7(5); SSA 1989 s 1(7).
Sub-s (4): SSA 1975 s 123A(4); SSA 1985 s 7(5).

Cross references—See the SS Contributions and Benefits Act 1992 s 8(2)(*b*) (calculation and alteration of primary Class 1 contributions),
SSC & BA 1992 s 176(2)(*a*) (subordinate legislation not requiring parliamentary control).

Amendments—[1] Sub-ss (1)–(3) substituted by SSA 1998 Sch 7 para 92 with effect from 6 April 1999 by virtue of the Social Security Act 1998 (Commencement No 3) Order, SI 1999/418.

[2] Words in sub-s (4) and the words "Secretary of State" throughout substituted by the Social Security Contributions (Transfer of Functions, etc) Act 1999 s 2 and Sch 3 para 49 with effect from 1 April 1999 by virtue of the Social Security Contributions (Transfer of Functions, etc) Act 1999 (Commencement No 1 and Transitional Provisions) Order, SI 1999/527.

[3] Words in sub-s (1) substituted by NICA 2002 s 6, Sch 1 paras 15, 18 with effect from 2003–04.

[4] In sub-s (4)(*a*), words substituted and words repealed by NICA 2015 s 2, Sch 1 paras 19, 22 with effect for the tax year 2015–16 and subsequent tax years.

146 . . . [1]

Amendments—[1] Repealed by SSA 1998 Sch 7 para 93 with effect from 6 April 1999 by virtue of the Social Security Act 1998 (Commencement No 3) Order, SI 1999/418.

147 Orders under ss 145 and 146—supplementary

(1) An order under section 145 . . . [1] above may make such amendments of any enactment as appear to the [Treasury][2] to be necessary or expedient in consequence of any alteration made by it.

(2) Where (in accordance with section 190 below) the [Treasury][2] [lay][2] before Parliament a draft of an order under section 145 . . . [1] above, [they][2] shall lay with it a copy of a report by the Government Actuary or the Deputy Government Actuary on the effect which, in that Actuary's opinion, the making of such an order may be expected to have on the National Insurance Fund.

(3) An order under section 145 . . . [1] above shall be made so as to come into force—

(*a*) on a date in the tax year in which it receives Parliamentary approval; or

(*b*) on a date in the next tax year.

(4) Such an order shall have effect for the remainder of the tax year in which it comes into force and for any subsequent tax year (subject to the effect of any subsequent order under this Part of this Act).
(5) Such an order shall be taken as receiving Parliamentary approval on the date on which the draft of it is approved by the second House to approve it.

Former enactments—Sub-s (1): SSA 1975 ss 4(6G), 123A(5); SSA 1985 s 7(2).
Sub-s (2): SSA 1975 ss 4(6HH), 123A(6A); SSA 1986 ss 74(1), (2).
Sub-s (3): SSA 1975 ss 4(6J), 123A(7); SSA 1985 s 7(2).
Sub-ss (4), (5): SSA 1975 ss 4(6K), 123A(8); SSA 1985 s 7(2); SSA 1990 s 21(1), Sch 6 para 1(1), (2).
Amendments—[1] Words in sub-ss (1), (2) and (3) repealed by SSA 1998 Sch 7 para 94 with effect from 6 April 1999 by virtue of the Social Security Act 1998 (Commencement No 3) Order, SI 1999/418.
[2] Words in sub-s (2) and the words "Secretary of State" throughout substituted by the Social Security Contributions (Transfer of Functions, etc) Act 1999 s 2 and Sch 3 para 50 with effect from 1 April 1999 by virtue of the Social Security Contributions (Transfer of Functions, etc) Act 1999 (Commencement No 1 and Transitional Provisions) Order, SI 1999/527.

148 Revaluation of earnings factors

(1) This section shall have effect for the purpose of securing that earnings factors which are relevant—
(*a*) to the calculation—
(i) of the additional pension in the rate of any long-term benefit; or
(ii) of any guaranteed minimum pension; or
(*b*) to any other calculation required under Part III of the Pensions Act (including that Part as modified by or under any other enactment),
maintain their value in relation to the general level of earnings obtaining in Great Britain.
(2) The Secretary of State shall in each tax year review the general level of earnings obtaining in Great Britain and any changes in that level which have taken [place—
(*a*) since the end of the period taken into account for the last review under this section, or
(*b*) since such other date (whether earlier or later) as he may determine;
and for the purposes of any such review the Secretary of State shall estimate the general level of earnings in such manner as he thinks fit][1].
(3) If on any such review the Secretary of State concludes, having regard to earlier orders under this section, that earnings factors for any previous tax year (not being earlier than 1978-79) have not, during the period taken into account for that review, maintained their value in relation to the general level of earnings, he shall make an order under this section.
(4) An order under this section shall be an order directing that, for the purposes of any such calculation as is mentioned in subsection (1) above, the earnings factors referred to in subsection (3) above shall be increased by such percentage of their amount, apart from earlier orders under this section, as the Secretary of State thinks necessary to make up that fall in their value, during the period taken into account for the review together with other falls in their value which had been made up by such earlier orders.
(5) Subsections (3) and (4) above do not require the Secretary of State to direct any increase where it appears to him that the increase would be inconsiderable.
(6) If on any such review the Secretary of State determines that he is not required to make an order under this section, he shall instead lay before each House of Parliament a report explaining his reasons for arriving at that determination.
(7) For the purposes of this section—
(*a*) any review under [section 21 of the Social Security Pensions Act 1975] (which made provision corresponding to this section) shall be treated as a review under this section; and
(*b*) any order under that section shall be treated as an order under this section,
(but without prejudice to sections 16 and 17 of the Interpretation Act 1978).

Former enactments—Sub-s (1): SSA 1975 s 21(1); SSA 1986, s 18(1).
Sub-s (2): SSA 1975 s 21(2).
Sub-ss (3), (4): SSA 1975 ss 21(3).
Sub-s (5): SSA 1975 s 21(4).
Sub-s (6): SSA 1975 s 21(5).
Orders—Social Security Revaluation of Earnings Factors Order 1979, SI 1979/832.
Social Security Revaluation of Earnings Factors Order 1993, SI 1993/1159.
Social Security Revaluation of Earnings Factors Order 1994, SI 1994/1105.
Social Security Revaluation of Earnings Factors Order 1995, SI 1995/1070.
Social Security Revaluation of Earnings Factors Order 1996, SI 1996/1133.
Social Security Revaluation of Earnings Factors Order 1997, SI 1997/1117.
Social Security Revaluation of Earnings Factors Order 1998, SI 1998/1137.
Social Security Revaluation of Earnings Factors Order 1999, SI 1999/1235.
Social Security Revaluation of Earnings Factors Order 2000, SI 2000/1365.
Social Security Revaluation of Earnings Factors Order 2001, SI 2001/631.
Social Security Revaluation of Earnings Factors Order 2002, SI 2002/519.
Social Security Revaluation of Earnings Factors Order 2003, SI 2003/517.
Social Security Revaluation of Earnings Factors Order 2004, SI 2004/262.
Social Security Revaluation of Earnings Factors Order 2005, SI 2005/216.

Social Security Revaluation of Earnings Factors Order 2006, SI 2006/496.
Social Security Revaluation of Earnings Factors Order 2007, SI 2007/781.
Social Security Revaluation of Earnings Factors Order 2008, SI 2008/730.
Social Security Revaluation of Earnings Factors Order 2009, SI 2009/608.
Social Security Revaluation of Earnings Factors Order 2010, SI 2010/470.
Social Security Revaluation of Earnings Factors Order 2010, SI 2011/475.
Social Security Revaluation of Earnings Factors Order 2012, SI 2012/187.
Social Security Revaluation of Earnings Factors Order 2013, SI 2013/527.
Social Security Revaluation of Earnings Factors Order 2014, SI 2014/367.
Social Security Revaluation of Earnings Factors Order 2015, SI 2015/187.
Social Security Revaluation of Earnings Factors Order 2016, SI 2016/205.
Social Security Revaluation of Earnings Factors Order 2017, SI 2017/287.

Amendments—[1] Words in substituted by the Child Support, Pensions and Social Security Act 2000, s 37 with effect from 1 December 2000: see SI 2000/3166, art 2(2)(*a*).

[148A Revaluation of low earnings threshold

(1) The Secretary of State shall in the tax year preceding the first appointed year and in each subsequent tax year [up to and including the tax year 2014–15][2] review the general level of earnings obtaining in Great Britain and any changes in that level which have taken place during the review period.

(2) In this section, "the review period" means—

(*a*) in the case of the first review under this section, the period beginning with 1st October 1998 and ending on 30th September in the tax year preceding the first appointed year; and

(*b*) in the case of each subsequent review under this section, the period since—

(i) the end of the last period taken into account in a review under this section; or

(ii) such other date (whether earlier or later) as the Secretary of State may determine.

(3) If on such a review it appears to the Secretary of State that the general level of earnings has increased during the review period, he shall make an order under this section.

(4) An order under this section shall be an order directing that, for the purposes of the Contributions and Benefits Act—

(*a*) there shall be a new low earnings threshold for the tax years after the tax year in which the review takes place; and

(*b*) the amount of that threshold shall be the amount specified in subsection (5) below—

(i) increased by the percentage by which the general level of earnings increased during the review period; and

(ii) rounded to the nearest £100 (taking any amount of £50 as nearest to the next whole £100).

(5) The amount referred to in subsection (4)(*b*) above is—

(*a*) in the case of the first review under this section, £9,500; and

(*b*) in the case of each subsequent review, the low earnings threshold for the year in which the review takes place.

(6) This section does not require the Secretary of State to direct any increase where it appears to him that the increase would be inconsiderable.

(7) If on any review under subsection (1) above the Secretary of State determines that he is not required to make an order under this section, he shall instead lay before each House of Parliament a report explaining his reasons for arriving at that determination.

(8) For the purposes of any review under subsection (1) above the Secretary of State shall estimate the general level of earnings in such manner as he thinks fit.][1]

Orders—Social Security Pensions (Low Earnings Threshold) Order, SI 2013/528 (the low earnings threshold for the tax years following the tax year 2012–13 shall be £15,000).

Social Security Pensions (Low Earnings Threshold) Order, SI 2014/368 (the low earnings threshold for the tax years following the tax year 2013–14 shall be £15,100).

Social Security Pensions (Low Earnings Threshold) Order, SI 2015/186 (the low earnings threshold for the tax years following the tax year 2014–15 shall be £15,300).

Amendments—[1] This section inserted by the Child Support, Pensions and Social Security Act 2000, s 33(1).

[2] Words in sub-s (1) inserted by the Pensions Act 2014 (Consequential and Supplementary Amendments) Order, SI 2016/224 art 3(1), (2) with effect from ^ April 2016.

[148AA Revaluation of flat rate accrual amount

(1) The Secretary of State must in the tax year preceding the flat rate introduction year and in each subsequent tax year [up to and including the tax year 2014–15][2] review the general level of earnings obtaining in Great Britain and any changes in that level which have taken place during the review period.

(2) In this section "the review period" means—

(*a*) in the case of the first review under this section, the period beginning with 1st October 2004 and ending with 30th September in the tax year preceding the flat rate introduction year; and

(*b*) in the case of each subsequent review under this section, the period since—

(i) the end of the last period taken into account in a review under this section, or

(ii) such other date (whether earlier or later) as the Secretary of State may determine.

(3) If on such a review it appears to the Secretary of State that the general level of earnings has increased during the review period, he must make an order under this section.

(4) An order under this section is an order directing that for the purposes of Schedule 4B to the Contributions and Benefits Act—

(*a*) there is to be a new FRAA for the tax years after the tax year in which the review takes place, and

(*b*) the amount of that FRAA is to be the amount specified in subsection (5) below, increased by not less than the percentage by which the general level of earnings increased during the review period.

(5) The amount referred to in subsection (4)(*b*) is—

(*a*) in the case of the first review under this section, £72.80, and

(*b*) in the case of each subsequent review, the FRAA for the year in which the review takes place.

(6) The Secretary of State may, for the purposes of any provision of subsections (4) and (5), adjust any amount by rounding it up or down to such extent as he thinks appropriate.

(7) This section does not require the Secretary of State to direct any increase where it appears to him that the increase would be inconsiderable.

(8) If on any review under this section the Secretary of State determines that he is not required to make an order under this section, he must instead lay before each House of Parliament a report explaining his reasons for arriving at that determination.

(9) For the purposes of any review under this section the Secretary of State may estimate the general level of earnings in such manner as he thinks fit.

(10) In this section—

"the flat rate introduction year" has the meaning given by section 122 of the Contributions and Benefits Act (interpretation of Parts 1 to 6 etc);

"the FRAA" means the flat rate accrual amount (see paragraph 13 of Schedule 4B to the Contributions and Benefits Act (additional pension: simplified accrual rates for purposes of section 45(2)(*d*))).][1]

Orders—Social Security Pensions (Flat Rate Accrual Amount) Order, SI 2015/185 (the flat rate accrual amount for the tax year beginning 6th April 2015 and subsequent tax years shall be £93.60).

Amendments—[1] This section inserted by the Pensions Act 2007 s 11, Sch 2 para 2 with effect from 26 September 2007 (s 30(3)).

[2] Words in sub-s (1) inserted by the Pensions Act 2014 (Consequential and Supplementary Amendments) Order, SI 2016/224 art 3(1), (3) with effect from 6 April 2016.

PART XII
FINANCE

162 Destination of contributions

(1) Contributions received by the [Inland Revenue][7] . . . [2] shall be paid by [them][7] into the National Insurance Fund after deducting . . . [13] the appropriate national health service allocation . . . [13].

(2) . . . [13]

[(2A) [The reference to contributions in subsection (1) above includes][14] payments on account of contributions made in accordance with regulations under section 3(5) of the Contributions and Benefits Act (payments on account of directors' contributions).][3]

(3) The additions paid under section 1(5) of the Contributions and Benefits Act shall be paid, in accordance with any directions given by the Treasury, into the National Insurance Fund.

[(4) There shall be paid into the National Insurance Fund—

(*a*) so much of any interest recovered by the Inland Revenue by virtue of paragraph 6 of Schedule 1 to the Contributions and Benefits Act [or section 101 of the Finance Act 2009][20] [, or from persons in Great Britain by virtue of paragraph 6 of Schedule 2 to [the Contributions and Benefits Act,][20]][14] as remains after the deduction by them of any administrative costs attributable to its recovery,

(*b*) the amounts apportioned to [contributions][7] under sub-paragraph (6) of paragraph 7 of Schedule 1 to the Contributions and Benefits Act in respect of the penalties mentioned in that sub-paragraph, and

(*c*) so much of any penalty otherwise imposed by virtue of that paragraph and recovered by the Inland Revenue as remains after the deduction by them of any administrative costs attributable to its recovery.][8]

(4ZA) . . . [18]

[(4ZB) [Subsection (4)(*b*) and (*c*)][18] above shall have effect notwithstanding any provision which treats a penalty under section 98 or 98A of the Taxes Management Act 1970 as if it were tax charged in an assessment and due and payable.][9]

[(4A) The sums recovered by the [Inland Revenue][8] under regulations made under paragraph 7A[, 7B or 7BZA][18] of Schedule 1 to the Contributions and Benefits Act in respect of interest or penalties shall be paid into the National Insurance Fund.][3]

NIC

(5) In subsection (1) above "the appropriate national health service allocation" means [[50][19] per cent of the product of the additional rate together with[15]]—

(*a*) in the case of primary Class 1 contributions, [2.05][15] per cent of the amount estimated to be that of [so much of the earnings in respect of which those contributions were paid as exceeded [the primary threshold][11] but did not exceed the upper earnings limit;][1]

(*b*) in the case of secondary Class 1 contributions, [1.9][15] per cent of the amount estimated to be that of the [total][11] earnings in respect of which [primary Class 1 contributions][4] were paid;

(*c*) in the case of Class 1A contributions, [1.9][15] per cent of the amount estimated to be the aggregate of the [[general earnings][17]][12] used in calculating those contributions;

[(*ca*) in the case of Class 1B contributions, [1.9][15] per cent of the amount estimated to be the aggregate of the [general earnings][17] and the amounts of income tax in respect of which those contributions were paid;][5]

(*d*) in the case of Class 2 contributions, 15.5 per cent of the amount estimated to be the total of those contributions;

(*e*) in the case of Class 3 contributions, 15.5 per cent of the amount estimated to be the total of those contributions; and

[(*ea*) in the case of Class 3A contributions, 15.5 per cent of the amount estimated to be the total of those contributions;][21]

(*f*) in the case of Class 4 contributions, [2.15 per cent of the amount estimated to be that of so much of the profits or gains, or earnings, in respect of which those contributions were paid as exceeded the lower limit specified in paragraph (*a*) of subsection (3) of section 15, and in paragraph (*a*) of subsection (1A) of section 18, of the Contributions and Benefits Act but did not exceed the upper limit specified in those subsections][15].

[(5A) In subsection (5) above "the product of the additional rate" means the amount estimated to be the aggregate of—

(*a*) so much of the total of primary Class 1 contributions as is attributable to section 8(1)(*b*) of the Contributions and Benefits Act (additional primary percentage);

(*b*) so much of the total of Class 4 contributions under section 15 of that Act as is attributable to subsection (3)(*b*) of that section (additional Class 4 percentage); and

(*c*) so much of the total of Class 4 contributions payable by virtue of section 18 of that Act as is attributable to subsection (1A)(*b*) of that section (additional Class 4 percentage).][16]

(6) In [subsections (5) and (5A)][14] above "estimated" means estimated by the [Inland Revenue][10] in any manner which after consulting the Government Actuary or the Deputy Government Actuary [the Inland Revenue consider][10] to be appropriate and which the Treasury has approved.

[(6A) In the case of earners paid other than weekly, the reference in paragraph (*a*) of subsection (5) above to [the primary threshold or the upper earnings limit][11] shall be taken as a reference to the equivalent of [that threshold or limit prescribed under section 5(4)][11] of the Contributions and Benefits Act.][1]

(7) [The Treasury may][10] by order amend any of paragraphs (*a*) to (*f*) of subsection (5) above in relation to any tax year, by substituting for the percentage for the time being specified in that paragraph a different percentage.

(8) No order under subsection (7) above shall substitute a figure which represents an increase or decrease in the appropriate national health service allocation of more than—

(*a*) 0.1 per cent of the relevant earnings, in the case of paragraph (*a*) or (*b*);

(*b*) 0.1 per cent of the relevant aggregate, in the case of paragraph (*c*) [or (*ca*)][6];

(*c*) 4 per cent of the relevant contributions, in the case of paragraph (*d*)[, (*e*) or (*ea*)][21]; or

(*d*) 0.2 per cent of the relevant earnings, in the case of paragraph (*f*).

(9) From the national health service allocation in respect of contributions of any class there shall be deducted such amount as the [Inland Revenue][10] may estimate to be the portion of the total expenses incurred by [them][10] or any other government department in collecting contributions of that class which is fairly attributable to that allocation, and [the remainder shall be paid by the Inland Revenue to the Secretary of State towards][10] the cost—

(*a*) of the national health service in England;

(*b*) of that service in Wales; and

(*c*) of that service in Scotland,

in such shares as the Treasury may determine.

(10) The [Inland Revenue][10] shall pay any amounts deducted in accordance with subsection (9) above into the Consolidated Fund.

(11) . . . [10]

(12) The [Inland Revenue][10] may make regulations modifying this section, in such manner as [they think][10] appropriate, in relation to the contributions of persons referred to in the following sections of the Contributions and Benefits Act—

(*a*) section 116(2) (H.M. forces);

(*b*) section 117(1) (mariners, airmen, etc);

(*c*) section 120(1) (continental shelf workers),

and in relation to any contributions which are reduced under section 6(5) of that Act.

Amendments—[1] Words in square brackets in sub-s (5)(*a*) substituted, and sub-s (6A) inserted, with retrospective effect by the Social Security (Contributions) Act 1994 s 2.

[2] Words in sub-s (1) repealed by the Social Security Administration (Fraud) Act 1997 s 22, Sch 2.

[3] Sub-ss (2A), (4A) inserted by the Social Security Act 1998 s 86(1), Sch 7 para 99. Sub-s (2A) inserted with effect from 8 September 1998 (by virtue of SI 1998/2209), and sub-s (4A) inserted with effect from 6 April 1999 (by virtue of SI 1999/526).

[4] In sub-s (5)(*b*), words "primary Class 1 contributions" in square brackets substituted by the Social Security Act 1998, s 86(1), Sch 7 para 99(3) with effect from 6 April 1999 (by virtue of SI 1999/418).

[5] Sub-s (5)(*ca*) inserted by the Social Security Act 1998 s 65(2) with effect from 8 September 1998 for the purpose only of authorising the making of regulations or orders (by virtue of SI 1998/2209); and from 6 April 1999 for remaining purposes by virtue of SI 1998/2209).

[6] In sub-s (8)(*b*), words "or (*ca*)" in square brackets inserted by the Social Security Act 1998, s 86(1), Sch 7 para 99(4) with effect from 8 September 1998 for the purpose only of authorising the making of regulations or orders (by virtue of SI 1998/2209); and from 6 April 1999 for remaining purposes by virtue of SI 1998/2209).

[7] Words in sub-s (1), (2), (4)(*b*) substituted by SSC(TF)A 1999 s 2, Sch 3 para 52 with effect from 1 April 1999 (by virtue of SI 1999/527)

[8] Sub-s (4) substituted, and words in sub-s (4A) substituted, by SSC(TF)A 1999 s 1(1), Sch 1 para 28 with effect from 1 April 1999 (by virtue of SI 1999/527).

[9] Sub-ss (4ZA), (4ZB) inserted by SSC(TF) A 1999 s 5, Sch 5 para 12 with effect from 1 April 1999 (by virtue of SI 1999/527).

[10] Words in sub-ss (6), (7), (9), (10), (12), substituted; and sub-s (11) repealed; by SSC(TF)A 1999 s 2, Sch 3 para 52(1), (5)–(11), Sch 10 Pt I with effect from 1 April 1999 (by virtue of SI 1999/527).

[11] Words in sub-ss (5)(*a*), (*b*), (6A) substituted by the Welfare Reform and Pensions Act 1999 s 73, Sch 9 Pt III para 9 with effect from 6 April 2000 (by virtue of SI 1999/3420).

[12] Word in sub-s (5)(*c*) substituted by the Child Support, Pensions and Social Security Act 2000 s 74(7) with effect from 2000–01.

[13] Words in sub-s (1) repealed, and sub-s (2) repealed, by NICA 2002 s 7, Sch 2 with effect from 2003–04.

[14] In sub-ss (2A), (4)(*a*), (6) words substituted by NICA 2002 s 6, Sch 1 paras 15, 19 with effect from 2003–04.

[15] Words in sub-s (5) inserted, words in sub-s (5)(*f*) substituted, figures in sub-s (5)(*a*)–(*ca*) substituted, by NICA 2002 s 4(1), (2) with effect from 2003–04.

[16] Sub-s (5A) inserted by NICA 2002 s 4(1), (3) with effect from 2003–04.

[17] In sub-s (5)(*c*), (*ca*), words substituted for the word "emoluments" by ITEPA 2003 s 722, Sch 6 paras 186, 189 with effect, for income tax purposes, from 2003–04; and for corporation tax purposes, for accounting periods ending after 5 April 2003. For transitional provisions and savings see ITEPA 2003 s 723, Sch 7.

[18] Sub-s (4ZA) repealed, and words in sub-ss (4ZB), (4A) substituted by the NIC and Statutory Payments Act 2004 ss 11, 12, Schedule 1 para 3(1), (3), Sch 2 Pt 1 with effect from 1 September 2004 (by virtue of SI 2004/1943).

[19] In sub-s (5), figure substituted for previous figure "100" by the National Insurance Contributions Act 2011 s 3 with effect from 6 April 2011.

[20] Words in sub-s (4)(*a*) inserted and substituted by the Finance Act 2009, Sections 101 and 102 (Interest on Late Payments and Repayments), Appointed Days and Consequential Provisions Order, SI 2014/992 art 5 with effect in relation to payments due and payable in respect of the tax year 2014–15 and subsequent tax years.

[21] Sub-s (5)(*ea*) inserted, and in sub-s (8)(*c*), words substituted for words "or (*e*)" by PeA 2014 s 25, Sch 15 para 13 with effect from 12 October 2015 (by virtue of SI 2015/1475).

PART XIII
ADVISORY BODIES AND CONSULTATION

The Social Security Advisory Committee and the Industrial Injuries Advisory Council

170 The Social Security Advisory Committee

(1) The Social Security Advisory Committee (in this Act referred to as "the Committee") constituted under section 9 of the Social Security Act 1980 shall continue in being by that name—

(*a*) to give (whether in pursuance of a reference under this Act or otherwise) advice and assistance to the Secretary of State in connection with the discharge of his functions under the relevant enactments;

(*b*) to give (whether in pursuance of a reference under this Act or otherwise) advice and assistance to the Northern Ireland Department in connection with the discharge of its functions under the relevant Northern Ireland enactments; and

(*c*) to perform such other duties as may be assigned to the Committee under any enactment.

(2) Schedule 5 to this Act shall have effect with respect to the constitution of the Committee and the other matters there mentioned.

(3) The Secretary of State may from time to time refer to the Committee for consideration and advice such questions relating to the operation of any of the relevant enactments as he thinks fit (including questions as to the advisability of amending any of them).

(4) The Secretary of State shall furnish the Committee with such information as the Committee may reasonably require for the proper discharge of its functions.

(5) In this Act—

"the relevant enactments" means—

(*a*) the provisions of the Contributions and Benefits Act[, this Act and the Social Security (Incapacity for Work) Act 1994][1], except as they apply to industrial injuries benefit and Old Cases payments;

[(*aa*) the provisions of the Jobseekers Act 1995;][3]
[(*ab*) *section 10 of the Child Support Act 1995;][4] and*
[(*ac*) the provisions of the Social Security (Recovery of Benefits) Act 1997; and][5]
[(*ad*) the provisions of Chapter II of Part I of the Social Security Act 1998 and section 72 of that Act;][6]
[(*ae*) sections 60, 72 and 79 of the Welfare Reform and Pensions Act 1999;][7]
[(*af*) section 42, ...[16] and [sections 69 and 70 of the Child Support Pensions and Social Security Act 2000][17]][8],
[(*ag*) [sections 6A to 11][15] of the Social Security Fraud Act 2001;][9]
[(*ah*) the provisions of the State Pension Credit Act 2002;][10]
[(*ai*) section 7 of the Age-Related Payments Act 2004;][11]
[(*aia*) the provisions of Part 1 of the Welfare Reform Act 2007;][14]
[(*aj*) any provisions in Northern Ireland which correspond to sections 32 and 33 of the Welfare Reform Act 2007;][13]
[(*ak*) the provisions of Part 1 of the Welfare Reform Act 2012;][17]
[(*al*) Part 4 of that Act;][18]
[(*ala*) sections 96 to 97 of that Act;][21]
[(*am*) the provisions of Part 1 of the Pensions Act 2014;][19]
[(*an*) section 30 of the Pensions Act 2014;][23]
[(*ao*) sections 18, 19 and 21 of the Welfare Reform and Work Act 2016;][22]
(*b*) the provisions of Part II of Schedule 3 to the Consequential Provisions Act, except as they apply to industrial injuries benefit; and

"the relevant Northern Ireland enactments" means—
(*a*) the provisions of the Northern Ireland Contributions and Benefits Act and the Northern Ireland Administration Act, except as they apply to Northern Ireland industrial injuries benefit and payments under Part I of Schedule 8 to the Northern Ireland Contributions and Benefits Act;
[(*aa*) any provisions in Northern Ireland which correspond to provisions of the Jobseekers Act 1995; and][3]
[(*ab*) any enactment corresponding to section 10 of the Child Support Act 1995 having effect with respect to Northern Ireland; and][4] and
[(*ac*) any provisions in Northern Ireland which correspond to provisions of the Social Security (Recovery of Benefits) Act 1997; and][5]
[(*ad*) any provisions in Northern Ireland which correspond to provisions of Chapter II of Part I of the Social Security Act 1998 and section 72 of that Act;][6]
[(*ae*) any provisions in Northern Ireland which correspond to sections 60, 72 and 79 of the Welfare Reform and Pensions Act 1999;][7]
[(*af*) any provisions in Northern Ireland which correspond to section 42, any of ...[16], [sections 69 and 70 of the Child Support, Pensions and Social Security Act 2000][17]][8]
[(*ag*) any provisions in Northern Ireland which correspond to sections 7 to 11 of the Social Security Fraud Act 2001, and][9]
[(*ah*) any provisions in Northern Ireland which correspond to provisions of the State Pension Credit Act 2002; and][10]
[(*ai*) Article 9 of the Age-Related Payments (Northern Ireland) Order 2004;][12]
[(*aia*) any provisions in Northern Ireland which correspond to provisions of Part 1 of the Welfare Reform Act 2007;][14]
[(*aj*) any provisions in Northern Ireland which correspond to sections 32 and 33 of the Welfare Reform Act 2007;][13]
[(*ak*) any provisions in Northern Ireland which corresponds to the provisions of Part 1 of the Welfare Reform Act 2012.][17]
[(*al*) any provisions in Northern Ireland which correspond to Part 4 of that Act.][18]
[(*ala*) any provisions in Northern Ireland which correspond to sections 96 to 97 of that Act;][21]
[(*am*) any provisions in Northern Ireland which correspond to the provisions of Part 1 of the Pensions Act 2014;][20]
[(*an*) any provisions in Northern Ireland which correspond to section 30 of the Pensions Act 2014;][22]
[(*ao*) any provisions in Northern Ireland which correspond to sections 18, 19 and 21 of the Welfare Reform and Work Act 2016;][22]
(*b*) the provisions of Part II of Schedule 3 to the Social Security (Consequential Provisions) (Northern Ireland) Act 1992 except as they apply to Northern Ireland industrial injuries benefit; and

[(*c*) . . .][2]

and in this definition—

(i) "Northern Ireland Contributions and Benefits Act" means the Social Security Contributions and Benefits (Northern Ireland) Act 1992;

(ii) "Northern Ireland industrial injuries benefit" means benefit under Part V of the Northern Ireland Contributions and Benefits Act other than under Schedule 8 to that Act.

Former enactments—Sub-ss (1)–(4): SSA 1980 s 9(1)–(4).
Sub-s (5): SSA 1980 s 9(7); Social Security and Housing Benefits Act 1982 s 48(5), Sch 4 para 30; Statutory Sick Pay Act 1991 s 3(1)(*b*).

Amendments—[1] Para (*a*) of the definition "the relevant enactments" in sub-s (5), words in square brackets substituted by the Social Security (Incapacity for Work) Act 1994 s 11(1), Sch 1 Pt II para 51, with effect from 13 April 1995.

[2] Para (*c*) of the definition "the relevant Northern Ireland enactments" in sub-s (5) substituted by the Pension Schemes (Northern Ireland) Act 1993 s 184, Sch 7 para 26 and repealed by the Pensions (Northern Ireland) Order, SI 1995/3213 (NI 22) Sch 5, Pt III with effect from 6 April 1997.

[3] Para (*aa*) of the definitions "the relevant enactments" and "the relevant Northern Ireland enactments" in sub-s (5) inserted by the Jobseekers Act 1995 Sch 2 para 67 with effect from 22 April 1996 by virtue of SI 1996/1126.

[4] Para (*ab*) of the definitions "the relevant enactments" and "the relevant Northern Ireland enactments" in sub-s (5) inserted by the Child Support Act 1995 s 30(5) Sch 3 para 20 with effect from 14 Oct 1996 by virtue of SI 1996/2630.

[5] Para (*ac*) of the definitions "the relevant enactments" and "the relevant Northern Ireland enactments" in sub-s (5) inserted by the Social Security (Recovery of Benefits) Act 1997 with effect from 6 October 1997 by virtue of SI 1997/2085.

[6] Para (*ad*) of the definitions "the relevant enactments" and "the relevant Northern Ireland enactments" in sub-s (5) inserted by SSA 1998 Sch 7 para 104 with effect from 6 April 1999 by virtue of SI 1999/526.

[7] Para (*ae*) of the definitions "the relevant enactments" and "the relevant Northern Ireland enactments" in sub-s (5) inserted by the Welfare Reform and Pensions Act 1999, s 84 Sch 12 paras 79, 81, with effect from 11 November 1999.

[8] Para (*af*) of the definitions "the relevant enactments" and "the relevant Northern Ireland enactments" in sub-s (5) inserted by the Child Support, Pensions and Social Security Act 2000 s 73 with effect from 1 Dec 2000 in so far as each new para (*af*) refers to s 42 and as from a day to be appointed otherwise.

[9] In sub-s (5), paras (*ag*) inserted in the definitions of "the relevant enactments" and "the relevant Northern Ireland enactments", by the Social Security Fraud Act 2001 ss 12(3), 20 with effect from 1 April 2002 (by virtue of SI 2002/3689).

[10] In sub-s (5), paras (*ah*) inserted by the State Pension Credit Act 2002 s 14, Sch 2 para 12 with effect from 2 July 2002 for the purpose only of exercising any power to make regulations or orders (by virtue of SI 2002/1691).

[11] In sub-s (5), para (*ai*) in the definition of "the relevant enactments" inserted by the Age Related Payments Act 2004 s 7(5) with effect from 8 July 2004.

[12] In sub-s (5), para (*ai*) in the definition of "the relevant Northern Ireland enactments" inserted by the Age-Related Payments (Northern Ireland) Order, SI 2004/1987 art 9(6) with effect from 3 August 2004.

[13] In sub-s (5) para (*aj*) in the definition of "the relevant enactments", and para (*aj*) in the definition of "the relevant Northern Ireland enactments", inserted, by the Welfare Reform Act 2007 s 33(7) with effect as follows—

– for the purpose only of conferring power to make regulations, from 1 April 2008 (SI 2008/411 art 2(1)(*b*)); and
– for remaining purposes, from 6 October 2008 (SI 2008/411 art 2(2)).

[14] In sub-s (5) para (*aia*) in the definition of "the relevant enactments", and para (*aia*) in the definition of "the relevant Northern Ireland enactments", inserted, by the Welfare Reform Act 2007, ss 28(1), 33(7)(*b*), Sch 3, para 10(1), (28) with effect from 27 October 2008 (by virtue of SI 2008/787 art 2(4)(*b*), (*f*)).

[15] In sub-s (5), para (*ag*) of the definition of "the relevant enactments", words substituted by the Welfare Reform Act 2009, s 24(2), Sch 4, Pt 2, para 9(a) with effect from 1 April 2010 (by virtue of SI 2010/45, art 2(2)).

[16] In sub-s (5),in para (*af*) of the definition of "the relevant enactments", words repealed by the Welfare Reform Act 2009, s 58(1), Sch 7, Pt 3 with effect from 1 April 2010 (by virtue of SI 2010/293, art 2(3)(*b*)(i), (*c*), subject to art 2(4)).

[17] In sub-s (5) in definitions of "the relevant enactments" and the relevant Northern Ireland enactments", words in para (*af*) substituted and para (*ak*) inserted by the Welfare Reform Act 2012 s 31, Sch 2 para 26 with effect from 25 February 2013 (by virtue of SI 2013/358, art 3).

[18] In sub-s (5), in definitions of "the relevant enactments" and the relevant Northern Ireland enactments", para (*al*) inserted by the Welfare Reform Act 2012 s 91, Sch 9 para 26 with effect from 25 February 2013 (by virtue of SI 2013/358 art 3(*c*)).

[19] In sub-s (5), in definition of "the relevant enactments", para (*am*) inserted by PeA 2014 s 23, Sch 12 paras 8, 23(*a*) with effect from 6 April 2016 (PeA 2014 s 56(1), (4)).

[20] In sub-s (5), in definition of "the relevant Northern Ireland enactments", para (*am*) inserted by PeA 2014 s 23, Sch 12 paras 8, 23(*b*) with effect from 6 April 2016 (PeA 2014 s 56(1), (4)).

[21] In sub-s (5), in definitions of "the relevant enactments" and "the relevant Northern Ireland enactments", para (*ala*) inserted by the Welfare Reform and Work Act 2016 s 10(1) with effect from 9 June 2016 (by virtue of SI 2016/610 reg 2).

[22] In sub-s (5), in definitions of "the relevant enactments" and "the relevant Northern Ireland enactments", para (*an*) inserted by PeA 2014 s 31, Sch 16 para 32 with effect from 6 April 2017 (by virtue of SI 2017/297).

[23] In sub-s (5), in definitions of "the relevant enactments" and "the relevant Northern Ireland enactments", para (*ao*) inserted by the Welfare Reform and Work Act 2016, s 20(2)(*a*) with effect from 27 July 2017 (by virtue of SI 2017/802.

Prospective amendments—In sub-s (5), in the definition of "the relevant enactments", paragraph (*aj*) to be repealed, by the Welfare Reform Act 2012 s 147, Sch 14 Part 1 with effect from a date to be appointed.

172 Functions of Committee and Council in relation to regulations

(1) Subject—

(*a*) to subsection (3) below; and

(*b*) to section 173 below,

where the Secretary of State proposes to make regulations under any of the relevant enactments, he shall refer the proposals, in the form of draft regulations or otherwise, to the Committee.

NIC

(2) . . .
(3) Subsection (1) above does not apply to the regulations specified in Part I of Schedule 7 to this Act.
(4) . . .
(5) In relation to regulations required or authorised to be made by the Secretary of State in conjunction with the Treasury, the reference in subsection (1) above to the Secretary of State shall be construed as a reference to the Secretary of State and the Treasury.

Former enactments—Sub-s (1): SSA 1980 s 10(1); SSA 1986 s 86(1), Sch 10 para 98(*a*).
Sub-s (3): SSA 1980 s 10(2).
Sub-s (5); SSA 1980 s 10(9).
Note—Sub-ss (2), (4) are outside the scope of this Publication.

173 Cases in which consultation is not required

(1) Nothing in any enactment shall require any proposals in respect of regulations to be referred to the Committee or the Council if—
(*a*) it appears to the Secretary of State that by reason of the urgency of the matter it is inexpedient so to refer them; or
(*b*) the relevant advisory body have agreed that they shall not be referred.
(2) Where by virtue only of subsection (1)(*a*) above the Secretary of State makes regulations without proposals in respect of them having been referred, then, unless the relevant advisory body agrees that this subsection shall not apply, he shall refer the regulations to that body as soon as practicable after making them.
(3) Where the Secretary of State has referred proposals to the Committee or the Council, he may make the proposed regulations before the Committee have made their report or, as the case may be the Council have given their advice, only if after the reference it appears to him that by reason of the urgency of the matter it is expedient to do so.
(4) Where by virtue of this section regulations are made before a report of the Committee has been made, the Committee shall consider them and make a report to the Secretary of State containing such recommendations with regard to the regulations as the Committee thinks appropriate; and a copy of any report made to the Secretary of State on the regulations shall be laid by him before each House of Parliament together, if the report contains recommendations, with a statement—
(*a*) of the extent (if any) to which the Secretary of State proposes to give effect to the recommendations; and
(*b*) in so far as he does not propose to give effect to them, of his reasons why not.
(5) Except to the extent that this subsection is excluded by an enactment passed after 25th July 1986, nothing in any enactment shall require the reference to the Committee or the Council of any regulations contained in either—
(*a*) a statutory instrument made before the end of the period of 6 months beginning with the coming into force of the enactment under which those regulations are made; or
(*b*) a statutory instrument—
(i) which states that it contains only regulations made by virtue of, or consequential upon, a specified enactment; and
(ii) which is made before the end of the period of 6 months beginning with the coming into force of that specified enactment.
(6) In relation to regulations required or authorised to be made by the Secretary of State in conjunction with the Treasury, any reference in this section to the Secretary of State shall be construed as a reference to the Secretary of State and the Treasury.
(7) In this section "regulations" means regulations under any enactment, whenever passed.

Former enactments—Sub-ss (1), (2), (4): SSA 1986 s 61(1), (2), (4).
Sub-s (3): SSA 1986 s 61(3); SSA 1989 s 26, Sch 7 para 27.
Sub-s (5): SSA 1986 s 61(5); SSA 1989 s 31(1), Sch 8 para 12(3).
Sub-s (6): SSA 1980 s 10(9).
Sub-s (7): SSA 1986 s 61(10); SSA 1989 s 31(1), Sch 8 para 12(4).
Cross references—See the SS Pensions Act 1975 s 61A(1) (consultation with Social Security Advisory Committee about certain regulations).

174 Committee's report on regulations and Secretary of State's duties

(1) The Committee shall consider any proposals referred to it by the Secretary of State under section 172 above and shall make to the Secretary of State a report containing such recommendations with regard to the subject-matter of the proposals as the Committee thinks appropriate.
(2) If after receiving a report of the Committee the Secretary of State lays before Parliament any regulations or draft regulations which comprise the whole or any part of the subject-matter of the proposals referred to the Committee, he shall lay with the regulations or draft regulations a copy of the Committee's report and a statement showing—
(*a*) the extent (if any) to which he has, in framing the regulations, given effect to the Committee's recommendations; and
(*b*) in so far as effect has not been given to them, his reasons why not.

(3) In the case of any regulations laid before Parliament at a time when Parliament is not sitting, the requirements of subsection (2) above shall be satisfied as respects either House of Parliament if a copy of the report and statement there referred to are laid before that House not later than the second day on which the House sits after the laying of the regulations.
(4) In relation to regulations required or authorised to be made by the Secretary of State in conjunction with the Treasury any reference in this section to the Secretary of State shall be construed as a reference to the Secretary of State and the Treasury.

Former enactments—Sub-ss (1)–(3): SSA 1980 s 10(3)–(5).
Sub-s (4): SSA 1980 s 10(9).

PART XIV
SOCIAL SECURITY SYSTEMS OUTSIDE GREAT BRITAIN

Co-ordination

177 Co-ordination with Northern Ireland

Amendments—Section repealed by the Northern Ireland Act 1998 ss 87(8)(*a*), 100(2), Sch 15 with effect from 2 December 1999 by virtue of SI 1999/3209 art 2, Schedule.

Reciprocity

179 Reciprocal agreements with countries outside the United Kingdom

(1) For the purpose of giving effect—
(*a*) to any agreement with the government of a country outside the United Kingdom providing for reciprocity in matters relating to payments for purposes similar or comparable to the purposes of legislation to which this section applies, or
(*b*) to any such agreement as it would be if it were altered in accordance with proposals to alter it which, in consequence of any change in the law of Great Britain, the government of the United Kingdom has made to the other government in question,

Her Majesty may by Order in Council make provision for modifying or adapting such legislation in its application to cases affected by the agreement or proposed alterations.
(2) An Order made by virtue of subsection (1) above may, instead of or in addition to making specific modifications or adaptations, provide generally that legislation to which this section applies shall be modified to such extent as may be required to give effect to the provisions contained in the agreement or, as the case may be, alterations in question.
(3) The modifications which may be made by virtue of subsection (1) above include provisions—
(*a*) for securing that acts, omissions and events having any effect for the purposes of the law of the country in respect of which the agreement is made have a corresponding effect for the purposes of this Act[, the Jobseekers Act 1995][1][, Chapter II of Part I of the Social Security Act 1998][2][, Part II of the Social Security Contributions (Transfer of Functions, etc) Act 1999][3][, Part III of the Social Security Contributions (Transfer of Functions, etc) (Northern Ireland) Order 1999][4] [, the State Pension Credit Act 2002][5] [, Part 1 of the Welfare Reform Act 2007][6][, Part 1 of the Welfare Reform Act 2012][7][, Part 4 of that Act][8][, Part 1 of the Pensions Act 2014][9][, Part 5 of that Act][10] [and the Contributions and Benefits Act (but not so as to confer a right to double benefit);
(*b*) for determining, in cases where rights accrue both under such legislation and under the law of that country, which of those rights is to be available to the person concerned;
(*c*) for making any necessary financial adjustments.

(4) This section applies—
(*a*) to the Contributions and Benefits Act;
[(*aa*) to the Jobseekers Act 1995;][1] and
[(*ab*) to Chapter II of Part I of the Social Security Act 1998; and][2]
[(*ac*) to Part II of the Social Security Contributions (Transfer of Functions, etc) Act 1999; and][3]
[(*ad*) to Part III of the Social Security Contributions (Transfer of Functions, etc) (Northern Ireland) Order 1999; and][4]
[(*ae*) to the State Pension Credit Act 2002; [and
(*af*) to Part 1 of the Welfare Reform Act 2007;][6] and][5]
[*ag*) to Part 1 of the Welfare Reform Act 2012; and][8]
[(*ah*) to Part 4 of that Act;][8]
[(*ai*) to Part 1 of the Pensions Act 2014;][9]
[(*aj*) to Part 5 of the Pensions Act 2014;][10]
(*b*) to this Act,

except in relation to the following benefits—
(i) community charge benefits;
(ii) payments out of the social fund;
(iii) Christmas bonus;
(iv) statutory sick pay; and
(v) statutory maternity pay.

NIC

(5) . . .

Former enactments—Sub-s (1): SSA 1975 s 143(1); SS (Miscellaneous Provisions) Act 1977 s 20(1), (2); SSA 1986 s 65(2)(*a*).
Sub-s (2): SSA 1975 s 143(1A); SSA 1981 s 6(1), (2).
Sub-s (3): SSA 1975 s 143(2).
Sub-s (4): SSA 1975 s 143(1); SSA 1986 s 65(4); Disability Living Allowance and Disability Working Allowance Act 1991 s 7, Sch 3 para 6.
Orders—Social Security (Reciprocal Agreements) Order, SI 2012/360.
Social Security (Contributions) (Republic of Chile) Order, SI 2015/828.
Social Security (Reciprocal Agreements) Order, SI 2017/159.
Note—Sub-s (5) is outside the scope of this Publication.
Amendments—[1] Words in sub-s (3)(*a*) and sub-s (4)(*aa*) inserted by the Jobseekers Act 1995 Sch 2 para 70 with effect from 22 April 1996 by virtue of SI 1996/1126.
[2] Words in sub-s (3)(*a*) and sub-s (4)(*ab*) inserted by SSA 1998 Sch 7 para 107 with effect from 5 July 1999, for certain purposes (by virtue of the Social Security Act 1998 (Commencement No 8, and Savings and Consequential and Transitional Provisions) Order, SI 1999/1958, art 2(1)(*b*) (subject to transitional provisions contained in art 5 Sch 12 thereof)), 6 September 1999, for certain purposes (by virtue of the Social Security Act 1998 (Commencement No 9, and Savings and Consequential and Transitional Provisions) Order, SI 1999/2422, art 2(*c*) (subject to transitional provisions contained in art 4 Sch 14 thereof)), 5 October 1999, for certain purposes (by virtue of the Social Security Act 1998 (Commencement No 10 and Transitional Provisions) Order, SI 1999/2422, art 2, Sch 1 (subject to transitional provisions contained in art 3 Sch 2 thereof)), 18 October 1999, for certain purposes (by virtue of the Social Security Act 1998 (Commencement No 11, and Savings and Consequential and Transitional Provisions) Order, SI 1999/2860, art 2, Sch 1 (subject to transitional provisions contained in art 4 Schs 16–18 thereof)), 29 November 1999, for certain purposes (by virtue of the Social Security Act 1998 (Commencement No 12 and Consequential and Transitional Provisions) Order, SI 1999/3178, art 2(1), Sch 1 (subject to transitional provisions contained in art 4 Schs 21–23 thereof)), and with effect from a date to be appointed for all other purposes.
[3] Words in sub-s (3)(*a*) and sub-s (4)(*ac*) inserted by the Social Security Contributions (Transfer of Functions, etc) Act 1999 s 18 and Sch 7 para 15 with effect from 1 April 1999 by virtue of the Social Security Contributions (Transfer of Functions, etc) Act 1999 (Commencement No 1 and Transitional Provisions) Order, SI 1999/527.
[4] Words in sub-s (3)(*a*) and whole of sub-s (4)(*ad*) inserted by the Social Security Contributions (Transfer of Functions, etc) (Northern Ireland) Order, SI 1999/671 art 17 Sch 6 para 2 with effect from 1 April 1999 (by virtue of the Social Security Contributions (Transfer of Functions, etc) (1999 Order) (Commencement No 1 and Transitional Provisions) Order (Northern Ireland), SR 1999/149, art 2(*c*), Sch 2).
[5] Words on sub-s (3)(*a*) inserted, and sub-s (4)(*ae*) inserted, by the State Pension Credit Act 2002 s 14, Sch 2 para 21 with effect from 2 July 2002 for the purpose only of exercising any power to make regulations or orders (by virtue of SI 2002/1691).
[6] Words in sub-ss (3), (4) inserted by the Welfare Reform Act 2007 s 28(1), Sch 3 para 10(1), (29) with effect from 27 October 2008 (by virtue of SI 2008/787 art 2(4)(*b*), (*f*)).
[7] In sub-s (3)(*a*), words inserted and in sub-s (4), para (*ag*) inserted by the Welfare Reform Act 2012 s 31, Sch 2 para 27 with effect from 29 April 2013 (by virtue of SI 2013/983, art 3(1)(*b*)(ii)).
[8] In sub-s (3)(*a*) words inserted and in sub-s (4), para (*ah*) inserted by the Welfare Reform Act 2012 s 91, Sch 9 para 27 with effect from 8 April 2013 in relation to a person whose only or principal residence is within a postcode listed in SI 2013/358 Sch 3 (by virtue of SI 2013/358 art 7(2)) and otherwise from 10 June 2013 (by virtue of SI 2013/1250 art 2).
[9] In sub-s (3)(*a*), words inserted, sub-s (4)(*ai*) inserted, by PeA 2014 s 23, Sch 12 paras 8, 25 with effect from 7 July 2015 (by virtue of SI 2015/1475).
[10] In sub-s (3)(*a*), words inserted, and sub-s (4)(*aj*) inserted, by PeA 2014 s 31, Sch 16 para 33 with effect from 8 February 2017 (by viirtue of SI 2017/111, reg 5).
Prospective amendments—Sub-ss (4)(*b*)(i), (5)(*a*), (*d*) to be repealed, by the Welfare Reform Act 2012 s 147, Sch 14 Part 1 with effect from a date to be appointed.

PART XVI
GENERAL

Subordinate legislation

189 Regulations and orders—general

(1) Subject to . . . [1] [any provision providing for an order or regulations to be made by the Treasury or the Inland Revenue and to][2] any . . . [3] express provision of this Act, regulations and orders under this Act shall be made by the Secretary of State.

(2) . . .

(3) Powers under this Act to make regulations or orders are exercisable by statutory instrument.

(4) Except in the case of regulations under section . . . [1] ...[5] above and in so far as this Act otherwise provides, any power conferred by this Act to make an Order in Council, regulations or an order may be exercised—

(*a*) either in relation to all cases to which the power extends, or in relation to those cases subject to specified exceptions, or in relation to any specified cases or classes of case;

(*b*) so as to make, as respects the cases in relation to which it is exercised—

(i) the full provision to which the power extends or any less provision (whether by way of exception or otherwise);

(ii) the same provision for all cases in relation to which the power is exercised, or different provision for different cases or different classes of case or different provision as respects the same case or class of case for different purposes of this Act;

(iii) any such provision either unconditionally or subject to any specified condition;

and where such a power is expressed to be exercisable for alternative purposes it may be exercised in relation to the same case for any or all of those purposes; and powers to make an Order in Council, regulations or an order for the purposes of any one provision of this Act are without prejudice to powers to make regulations or an order for the purposes of any other provision.

(5) Without prejudice to any specific provision in this Act, a power conferred by this Act to make an Order in Council, regulations or an order . . . [1] includes power to make thereby such incidental, supplementary, consequential or transitional provision as appears to Her Majesty, or the authority making the regulations or order, as the case may be, to be expedient for the purposes of the Order in Council, regulations or order.

[(5A) The provision referred to in subsection (5) includes, in a case where regulations under this Act require or authorise the use of electronic communications, provision referred to in section 8(4) and (5) and 9(5) of the Electronic Communications Act 2000.

(5B) For the purposes of subsection (5A), references in section 8(4) and (5) and 9(5) of the Electronic Communications Act 2000 to an order under section 8 of that Act are to be read as references to regulations under this Act; and references to anything authorised by such an order are to be read as references to anything required or authorised by such regulations.][4]

(6) Without prejudice to any specific provisions in this Act, a power conferred by any provision of this Act, except [, . . . [1] [sections 14, 24 and 130][5], to make an Order in Council, regulations or an order includes power to provide for a person to exercise a discretion in dealing with any matter.

(7), (7A)–(8) . . .

(9) Any power of the Secretary of State under any provision of this Act, except under [sections 80 and 154][5] and 178, to make any regulations or order, where the power is not expressed to be exercisable with the consent of the Treasury, shall if the Treasury so direct be exercisable only in conjunction with them.

(10) . . . [1]

(11) A power under any of sections 177 to 179 above to make provision by regulations or Order in Council for modifications or adaptations of the Contributions and Benefits Act or this Act shall be exercisable in relation to any enactment passed after this Act which is directed to be construed as one with them, except in so far as any such enactment relates to a benefit in relation to which the power is not exercisable; but this subsection applies only so far as a contrary intention is not expressed in the enactment so passed, and is without prejudice to the generality of any such direction.

(12) Any reference in this section or section 190 below to an Order in Council, or an order or regulations, under this Act includes a reference to an Order in Council, an order or regulations made under any provision of an enactment passed after this Act and directed to be construed as one with this Act; but this subsection applies only so far as a contrary intention is not expressed in the enactment so passed, and without prejudice to the generality of any such direction.

Former enactments—Sub-ss (3), (4): SSA 1975 s 166(1), (2).
Sub-s (5): SSA 1975 ss 113(2)(*c*), 166(3).
Sub-s (6): SSA 1975 s 166(3A); SSA 1986 s 62(1), (2).
Sub-s (9): SSA 1975 s 166(5).
Sub-s (10): SSA 1975 s 166(5A); SSA 1986 s 52(1), Sch 5 para 17.
Sub-s (11): SSA 1975 s 166(7).
Sub-s (12): SSA 1975 s 166(4).

Orders and Regulations—See the SS (Adjudication) Regulations, SI 1986/2218; SS(CP)A 1992 s 2.
SS (Crediting and Treatment of Contributions, and National Insurance Numbers) Regulations, SI 2001/769.
Social Security Revaluation of Earnings Factors Order, SI 2006/496.
NIC (Application of Part 7 of the Finance Act 2004) Regulations, SI 2007/785.
Social Security Revaluation of Earnings Factors Order, SI 2007/781.
National Insurance Contributions (Application of Part 7 of the Finance Act 2004) Regulations, SI 2012/1868.
Social Security Revaluation of Earnings Factors Order, SI 2013/527.
Social Security (Overpayments and Recovery) Regulations, SI 2013/384.
Social Security Revaluation of Earnings Factors Order, SI 2014/367.
Social Security Pensions (Low Earnings Threshold) Order, SI 2014/368.
Social Security Benefits Uprating Order, SI 2014/516.
Social Security (Miscellaneous Amendments) Regulations, SI 2014/591.
Social Security Benefits Uprating Regulations, SI 2014/618.
Social Security (Miscellaneous Amendments) Regulations, SI 2015/67.
Social Security Pensions (Flat Rate Accrual Amount) Order 2015, SI 2015/185.
Social Security Pensions (Low Earnings Threshold) Order, SI 2015/186.
Social Security Revaluation of Earnings Factors Order, SI 2015/187.
Social Security (Penalty as Alternative to Prosecution) (Maximum Amount) Order, SI 2015/202.
Social Security (Fees Payable by Qualifying Lenders) (Amendment) Regulations, SI 2015/343.
Guardian's Allowance Uprating Order, SI 2015/439.
Social Security Benefits Uprating Order, SI 2015/457.
Social Security (Overpayments and Recovery) Amendment Regulations, 2015/499.
National Insurance Contributions (Application of Part 7 of the Finance Act 2004) Regulations, SI 2015/531.
Guardian's Allowance Uprating Regulations, SI 2015/543.
Social Security (Crediting and Treatment of Contributions, and National Insurance Numbers) (Amendment) Regulations, SI 2015/1828.

NIC

Social Security Revaluation of Earnings Factors Order, SI 2016/205.
Social Security Administration Act 1992 (Local Authority Investigations) Regulations, SI 2016/519.
Social Security Benefits Up-rating Order, SI 2017/260.
Social Security Revaluation of Earnings Factors Order, SI 2017/287.
Social Security Benefits Up-rating Regulations, SI 2017/349.
Guardian's Allowance Up-rating Regulations, SI 2017/412.
Social Security (Infected Blood and Thalidomide) Regulations, SI 2017/870.

Cross references—See the Scotland Act 2016 s 30 (sub-s (3) not to apply to regulations made by Scottish ministers in connection with universal credit).

Note—Sub-ss (2), (7), (7A), (8) are outside the scope of this Publication.

The functions of the Lord Advocate are hereby transferred to the Secretary of State by virtue of the Transfer of Functions (Lord Advocate and Secretary of State) Order, SI 1999/678 with effect from 19 May 1999.

Amendments—[1] Repealed by SSA 1998 Sch 7 para 109, Sch 8 with effect from 6 September 1999, for certain purposes (by virtue of the Social Security Act 1998 (Commencement No 9, and Savings and Consequential and Transitional Provisions) Order, SI 1999/2422, art 2(*c*) (subject to transitional provisions contained in art 4 Sch 14 thereof)), 5 October 1999, for certain purposes (by virtue of the Social Security Act 1998 (Commencement No 10 and Transitional Provisions) Order, SI 1999/2422, art 2, Sch 1 (subject to transitional provisions contained in art 3 Sch 2 thereof)), 18 October 1999, for certain purposes (by virtue of the Social Security Act 1998 (Commencement No 11, and Savings and Consequential and Transitional Provisions) Order, SI 1999/2860, art 2, Sch 1 (subject to transitional provisions contained in art 4 Schs 16–18 thereof)), 29 November 1999, for certain purposes (by virtue of the Social Security Act 1998 (Commencement No 12 and Consequential and Transitional Provisions) Order, SI 1999/3178, art 2(1), Sch 1 (subject to transitional provisions contained in art 4 Schs 21–23 thereof)), and with effect from a date to be appointed for all other purposes. In sub-ss (1), (4), (5), (6) previous text read as follows: "subsection (2) below and to", "24 or", "(other than the power conferred by section 24 above)" and "24," respectively. Sub-ss (2), (10) previously read as follows:

"(2) Regulations with respect to proceedings before the Commissioners (whether for the determination of any matter or for leave to appeal to or from the Commissioners) shall be made by the Lord Chancellor.".

"(10) Where the Lord Chancellor proposes to make regulations under this Act, other than under section 24 above, it shall be his duty to consult the [Secretary of State] with respect to the proposal.".

[2] Words in sub-s (1) inserted by the Social Security Contributions (Transfer of Functions, etc) Act 1999 s 2 and Sch 3 para 57 with effect from 1 April 1999 by virtue of the Social Security Contributions (Transfer of Functions, etc) Act 1999 (Commencement No 1 and Transitional Provisions) Order, SI 1999/527.

[3] Word repealed by TCA 2002 s 60, Sch 6 with effect from 26 February 2003 (by virtue of SI 2003/392).

[4] Sub-ss (5A), (5B) inserted by the Welfare Reform Act 2012 s 104(1) with effect from 25 February 2013 (by virtue of SI 2013/358).

[5] In sub-s (4), words repealed and in sub-ss (6), (9) words substituted by the Public Bodies (Abolition of Disability Living Allowance Advisory Board) Order, SI 2013/252 art 4, Sch Pt 1 with effect from 7 February 2013.

190 Parliamentary control of orders and regulations

(1) Subject to the provisions of this section, a statutory instrument containing (whether alone or with other provisions)—

[(*zzb*) regulations under section 115C(2) or 115D(1) or (2);][7]
[(*za*) regulations under section 132A(4);][6]
(*a*) an order under section 141, 143, . . . [4] 145, . . . [1], . . . above; or
[(*aza*) any order containing provision adding any person to the list of persons falling within section 109B(2A) above;][5]
(*aa*), (*ab*), (*b*) . . . ,

shall not be made unless a draft of the instrument has been laid before Parliament and been approved by a resolution of each House of Parliament.

(2) Subsection (1) above does not apply to a statutory instrument by reason only that it contains regulations under section 154 above which are to be made for the purpose of consolidating regulations to be revoked in the instrument.

(3) A statutory instrument—

(*a*) which contains (whether alone or with other provisions) orders or regulations made under this Act by the Secretary of State[, the Treasury or the Inland Revenue][3]; and
(*b*) which is not subject to any requirement that a draft of the instrument be laid before and approved by a resolution of each House of Parliament,

shall be subject to annulment in pursuance of a resolution of either House of Parliament.

(4) . . . [2]

Former enactments—Sub-s (1)(*a*): SSA 1975 ss 123A(6), 167(1)(*b*); SSA 1986 s 62(3).
Sub-ss (2)–(4): SSA 1975 s 167(2)(*b*), (3), (4); SSA 1990 s 21(1), Sch 6 para 8(1).

Regulations—Guardian's Allowance Up-rating Regulations, SI 2015/543.

Note—Sub-s (1)(*aa*), (*ab*), (*b*) and numbers omitted from sub-s (1)(*a*) are outside the scope of this Publication.

Amendments—[1] Words in sub-ss (1)(*a*) repealed by SSA 1998 Sch 7 para 110 with effect from 6 April 1999 by virtue of the Social Security Act 1998 (Commencement No 3) Order, SI 1999/418.

[2] Sub-s (4) repealed by SSA 1998 Sch 7 para 110(2) with effect from 29 November 1999, for certain purposes (by virtue of the Social Security Act 1998 (Commencement No 12 and Consequential and Transitional Provisions) Order, SI 1999/3178, art 2(1), Sch 1 (subject to transitional provisions contained in art 4 Schs 21–23 thereof)), and with effect from a date to be appointed for all other purposes..

3 Words in sub-s (3)(*a*) inserted by the Social Security Contributions (Transfer of Functions, etc) Act 1999 s 2 and Sch 3 para 58 with effect from 1 April 1999 by virtue of the Social Security Contributions (Transfer of Functions, etc) Act 1999 (Commencement No 1 and Transitional Provisions) Order, SI 1999/527.

4 Words in sub-s (1)(*a*) repealed by the Welfare Reform and Pensions Act 1999 s 88 Sch 13, Pt VI with effect from 6 April 2000 (previously inserted by SSA 1998 Sch 7 para 110) by virtue of SI 1999/3420.

5 Sub-s (1)(*aza*) inserted by the Social Security Fraud Act 2001 ss 1(9), 20 with effect from 26 February 2002 (by virtue of SI 2002 403).

6 Sub-s (1)(*za*) inserted by the National Insurance Contributions Act 2006 s 7(1), (3) with effect from 30 March 2006.

7 In sub-s (1), para (*zzb*) inserted , by the Welfare Reform Act 2012 s 116(2) with effect from 10 May 2012 (by virtue of SI 2012/1246, art 2 (1)(*b*)).

Supplementary

191 Interpretation—general

In this Act, unless the context otherwise requires—

"the 1975 Act" means the Social Security Act 1975;

"the 1986 Act" means the Social Security Act 1986;

. . .

"claim" is to be construed in accordance with "claimant";

"claimant" (in relation to contributions under Part I . . . of the Contributions and Benefits Act) means—

(*a*) a person whose right to be excepted from liability to pay, or to have his liability deferred for, or to be credited with, a contribution, is in question;

(*b*) a person who has claimed benefit;

and includes, in relation to an award or decision a beneficiary under the award or affected by the decision;

. . .

"the Consequential Provisions Act" means the Social Security (Consequential Provisions) Act 1992;

["contribution" means a contribution under Part I of the Contributions and Benefits Act;][1]

. . .

"contribution card" has the meaning assigned to it by section 114(6) above;

"the Contributions and Benefits Act" means the Social Security Contributions and Benefits Act 1992;

["contributory employment and support allowance" means a contributory allowance under Part 1 of the Welfare Reform Act 2007 (employment and support allowance);][6]

. . .

"dwelling" means any residential accommodation, whether or not consisting of the whole or part of a building and whether or not comprising separate and self-contained premises;

. . .

["income-related employment and support allowance" means an income-related allowance under Part 1 of the Welfare Reform Act 2007 (employment and support allowance);][6]

["Inland Revenue" means the Commissioners of Inland Revenue;][3]

. . .

["the Northern Ireland Department" means the Department for Social Development but—

(*a*) in section 122 and sections 122B to 122E also includes the Department of Finance and Personnel; and

(*b*) in sections 121E, 121F, 122, 122ZA, 122C and 122D also includes the Department for Employment and Learning;][4]

"the Northern Ireland Administration Act" means the Social Security (Northern Ireland) Administration Act 1992;

. . .

"prescribe" means prescribe by regulations [and "prescribed" must be construed accordingly][6];

. . .,[2]

. . .

["state pension credit" means state pension credit under the State Pension Credit Act 2002;][5]

"tax year" means the 12 months beginning with 6th April in any year;

. . .

Note—Provisions omitted are outside the scope of this Publication.

Regulations—Social Security (Overpayments and Recovery) Regulations, SI 2013/384.

Social Security (Persons Required to Provide Information) Regulations, SI 2013/1510.

Social Security (Overpayments and Recovery) Amendment Regulations, 2015/499.

Guardian's Allowance Uprating Regulations, SI 2015/543.

Guardian's Allowance Up-rating Regulations, SI 2017/412.

Amendments—1 Inserted by Social Security Administration (Fraud) Act 1997 with effect from 1 July 1997 by virtue of SI 1997/1577.

2 Definitions repealed and words in the definition of "claimant" substituted by SSA 1998 Sch 7 para 111 with effect from 29 November 1999, for certain purposes (by virtue of the Social Security Act 1998 (Commencement No 12 and Consequential

NIC

and Transitional Provisions) Order, SI 1999/3178, art 2(1), Sch 1 (subject to transitional provisions contained in art 4 Schs 21–23 thereof)), and with effect from a date to be appointed for all other purposes.

3 Definition of "Inland Revenue" inserted by the Social Security Contributions (Transfer of Functions, etc) Act 1999 s 1(1) and Sch 1 para 32 with effect from 1 April 1999 by virtue of the Social Security Contributions (Transfer of Functions, etc) Act 1999 (Commencement No 1 and Transitional Provisions) Order, SI 1999/527.

4 Definition of "the Northern Ireland Department" substituted by EmA 2002 s 53, Sch 7 paras 8, 16 with effect from 9 September 2002 (by virtue of SI 2002/2256).

5 Definition "state pension credit" inserted by the State Pension Credit Act 2002, s 14, Sch 2, Pt 2, paras 8, 24(1), (3) with effect from 2 July 2002 for the purpose only of exercising any power to make regulations or orders (by virtue of SI 2002/1691); and for remaining purposes, from a date to be appointed.

6 Definitions of "contributory employment and support allowance" and "income-related employment and support allowance", and words in definition "prescribe", inserted, by the Welfare Reform Act 2007 s 28(1), Sch 3 para 10(1), (32) with effect as follows—

- for the purpose of making regulations, from 18 March 2008 (SI 2008/787 art 2(1), Schedule); and
- for remaining purposes, from 27 July 2008 (SI 2008/787 art 2(3)(*a*)).

Prospective amendments—The following definitions to be repealed, by the Welfare Reform Act 2012 s 147, Sch 14 Part 1 with effect from a date to be appointed—

- "contributory employment and support allowance";
- "income-related employment and support allowance".

192 Short title, commencement and extent

(1) This Act may be cited as the Social Security Administration Act 1992.

(2) This Act is to be read, where appropriate, with the Contributions and Benefits Act and the Consequential Provisions Act.

(3) The enactments consolidated by this Act are repealed, in consequence of the consolidation, by the Consequential Provisions Act.

(4) Except as provided in Schedule 4 to the Consequential Provisions Act, this Act shall come into force on 1st July 1992.

(5) The following provisions extend to Northern Ireland—

. . .

. . .

[section 132A (and sections 189 and 190, but only for the purposes of regulations under section 132A);][1]

section 170 (with Schedule 5);

section 177, with Schedule 8; and

this section.

(6) Except as provided by this section, this Act does not extend to Northern Ireland.

Note—Words omitted from sub-s (5) are outside the scope of this Publication.

Amendments—[1] Entry in sub-s (5) inserted by the National Insurance Contributions Act 2006 s 7(1), (4) with effect from 30 March 2006.

SCHEDULES

SCHEDULE 3
REGULATIONS AS TO PROCEDURE

Section 59

Regulations—See the SS (Adjudication) Regulations, SI 1986/2218.

Interpretation

1 . . .

Note—This paragraph is outside the scope of this Publication.

Provision which may be made

2 Provision prescribing the procedure to be followed in connection with the consideration and determination of . . . questions by the Secretary of State, . . .

Former enactments—SSA 1975 Sch 13 para 1.

Note—Words omitted are outside the scope of this Publication.

3 Provision as to the striking out of proceedings for want of prosecution.

Former enactments—SSA 1975 Sch 13 para 1A; SSA 1986 s 52(1), Sch 5 para 19(*a*).

4 Provision as to the form which is to be used for any document, the evidence which is to be required and the circumstances in which any official record or certificate is to be sufficient or conclusive evidence.

Former enactments—SSA 1975 Sch 13 para 2.

5 Provision as to the time to be allowed—

(*a*) for producing any evidence; or

(*b*) for making an appeal.

Former enactments—SSA 1975 Sch 13 para 3.

6 Provision as to the manner in which, and the time within which, a question may be raised with a view to its decision by the Secretary of State under Part II of this Act or with a view to the review of a decision under that Part.

Former enactments—SSA 1975 Sch 13 para 4.

7 Provision for summoning persons to attend and give evidence or produce documents and for authorising the administration of oaths to witnesses.

Former enactments—SSA 1975 Sch 13 para 5.

8–11 . . .

Note—Paras 8–11 are outside the scope of this Publication.

12 Provision for requiring or authorising the Secretary of State to hold, or to appoint a person to hold, an inquiry in connection with the consideration of any question by the Secretary of State.

Former enactments—SSA 1975 Sch 13 para 11.

SCHEDULE 5

SOCIAL SECURITY ADVISORY COMMITTEE

Section 170

1 The Committee shall consist of a chairman appointed by the Secretary of State and not less than 10 nor more than 13 other members so appointed.

Former enactments—SSA 1980 Sch 3 para 1; Social Security and Housing Benefits Act 1982 s 48(5), Sch 4 para 32(2).

2—(1) Each member of the Committee shall be appointed to hold office for such period of not more than 5 years, nor less than 3 years, as the Secretary of State shall determine.

(2) The Secretary of State may, at any time before the expiration of the term of office of any member, extend or further extend that member's term of office; but no one extension shall be for a period of more than 5 years from the date when the term of office would otherwise expire.

(3) Any member—

(*a*) shall be eligible for reappointment from time to time on or after the expiration of his term of office;

(*b*) may by notice in writing to the Secretary of State resign office at any time, while remaining eligible for reappointment.

Former enactments—SSA 1980 Sch 3 para 2; Social Security and Housing Benefits Act 1982 s 48(5), Sch 4 para 32(3).

3—(1) Of the members of the Committee (other than the chairman) there shall be appointed—

(*a*) one after consultation with organisations representative of employers;

(*b*) one after consultation with organisations representative of workers; and

(*c*) one after consultation with the Head of the Northern Ireland Department;

and the Committee shall include at least one person with experience of work among, and of the needs of, the chronically sick and disabled.

(2) In selecting a person with such experience regard shall be had to the desirability of having a chronically sick or disabled person.

Former enactments—SSA 1980 Sch 3 para 3.

4 The Secretary of State may remove a member of the Committee on the ground of incapacity or misbehaviour.

Former enactments—SSA 1980 Sch 3 para 4.

5 The Secretary of State shall appoint a secretary to the Committee and may appoint such other officers and such servants to the Committee, and there shall be paid to them by the Secretary of State such salaries and allowances, as the Secretary of State may with the consent of the Treasury determine.

Former enactments—SSA 1980 Sch 3 para 5.

6 The expenses of the Committee to such an amount as may be approved by the Treasury shall be paid by the Secretary of State.

Former enactments—SSA 1980 Sch 3 para 6.

7 There may be paid as part of the expenses of the Committee—

(*a*) to all or any of the members of the Committee, such salaries or other remuneration and travelling and other allowances; and (*b*) to persons attending its meetings at the request of the Committee, such travelling and other allowances (including compensation for loss of remunerative time);

as the Secretary of State may with the consent of the Treasury determine.

Former enactments—SSA 1980 Sch 3 para 7.

8—(1) The Secretary of State may pay or make provision for paying, to or in respect of any member of the Committee, such sums by way of pensions, superannuation allowances and gratuities as the Secretary of State may determine with the consent of the Treasury.

(2) Where a person ceases to be a member of the Committee otherwise than on the expiry of his term of office and it appears to the Secretary of State that there are social circumstances which make it right for the person to receive compensation the Secretary of State may make to him a payment of such amount as the Secretary of State may determine with the consent of the Treasury.

Former enactments—SSA 1980 Sch 3 para 8.

9 The Committee may act notwithstanding any vacancy among the members.

Former enactments—SSA 1980 Sch 3 para 9.

10 The Committee may make rules for regulating its procedure (including the quorum of the Committee).

Former enactments—SSA 1980 Sch 3 para 10.

SCHEDULE 7

REGULATIONS NOT REQUIRING PRIOR SUBMISSION

Section 172

PART I

SOCIAL SECURITY ADVISORY COMMITTEE

Personal independence payment

A1 . . .

Note—This paragraph is outside the scope of this Publication.

Disability living allowance

1 . . .

Note—This paragraph is outside the scope of this Publication.

Industrial injuries

2 . . .

Note—This paragraph is outside the scope of this Publication.

Up-rating etc

3 Regulations contained in a statutory instrument which states that it contains only provisions in consequence of an order under one or more of the following provisions—

(*a*) [section 141, 143, . . . [2] or 145 above][1];

(*b*) . . .

Former enactments—SSA 1980 Sch 3 para 12(2); SSA 1986 Sch 10 para 99.

Note—Para 3(*b*) is outside the scope of this Publication.

Amendments—[1] Words substituted by SSA 1998 Sch 7 para 114(1) with effect from 8 September 1998 by virtue of the Social Security Act 1998 (Commencement No 1) Order, SI 1998/2209 for the purpose only of authorising the making of regulations or orders, and with effect from 6 April 1999 in so far as it is not already in force.

[2] Words in sub-para (*a*) repealed by the Welfare Reform and Pensions Act 1999 s 88 Sch 13, Pt VI with effect from 6 April 2000 by virtue of SI 1999/3420.

Benefit cap

3A . . .

Note—This paragraph is outside the scope of this Publication.

Earnings limits

[**4** Regulations contained in a statutory instrument which states that it contains only regulations to make provision consequential on regulations under section 5 of the Contributions and Benefits Act.][1]

Former enactments—SSA 1980 Sch 3 para 13(1).

Amendments—[1] Sub-para (4) substituted by the Social Security Contributions (Transfer of Functions, etc) Act 1999 s 2 and Sch 3 para 59 with effect from 1 April 1999 by virtue of the Social Security Contributions (Transfer of Functions, etc) Act 1999 (Commencement No 1 and Transitional Provisions) Order, SI 1999/527.

Married women and widows—reduced rate contributions

5 . . .

Former enactments—SSA 1980 Sch 3 para 13(1A); SSA 1986 Sch 10 para 106.

Amendments—This para repealed by the Social Security Contributions (Transfer of Functions, etc) Act 1999 s 26(3), Sch 3 para 59 and Sch 10 Pt 1 with effect from 1 April 1999 by virtue of the Social Security Contributions (Transfer of Functions, etc) Act 1999 (Commencement No 1 and Transitional Provisions) Order, SI 1999/527.

Child benefit

6–7 . . .

Note—Paras 6, 7 are outside the scope of this Publication.

Statutory maternity pay and statutory sick pay

8 . . .

Note—Para 8, as a consequence of amendment, is outside the scope of this Publication.

Procedural rules for tribunals

9 Regulations in so far as they consist only of procedural rules for a tribunal in respect of which consultation with the [Administrative Justice and Tribunals Council is required by paragraph 24 of Schedule 7 to the Tribunals, Courts and Enforcement Act 2007.][1].

Former enactments—SSA 1980 Sch 3 para 19.

Amendments—[1] Words substituted by the Tribunals, Courts and Enforcement Act 2007 s 48(1), Sch 8 paras 17, 19 with effect from 1 November 2007 (by virtue of SI 2007/2709 art 3(*b*)(i)).

Consolidation

10 Regulations made for the purpose only of consolidating other regulations revoked by them.

Former enactments—SSA 1980 Sch 3 para 20.

PART II
INDUSTRIAL INJURIES ADVISORY COUNCIL

11–17 . . .

Note—Paras 11–17 are outside the scope of this Publication.

SCHEDULE 8

CONSTITUTION ETC OF JOINT AUTHORITY FOR GREAT BRITAIN AND NORTHERN IRELAND

Section 177

Repeal—This Schedule repealed by the Northern Ireland Act 1998 s 100(2), Sch 15 with effect from 2 December 1999 (by virtue of SI 1999/3209 art 2, Schedule).

SOCIAL SECURITY (CONSEQUENTIAL PROVISIONS) ACT 1992

(1992 Chapter 6)

ARRANGEMENT OF SECTIONS

NIC

Schedule 4—Transitory modifications.
Part I—Provisions not yet in force.

An Act to make provision for repeals, consequential amendments, transitional and transitory matters and savings in connection with the consolidation of enactments in the Social Security Contributions and Benefits Act 1992 and the Social Security Administration Act 1992 (including provisions to give effect to recommendations of the Law Commission and the Scottish Law Commission)

[13 February 1992]

Cross references—See SSC&BA 1992 s 177(2) (inter-relation of the 1992 consolidation Acts); SSAA 1992 s 192(2) (inter-relation of the 1992 consolidation Acts).

1 Meaning of "the consolidating Acts"

In this Act—

"the consolidating Acts" means the Social Security Contributions and Benefits Act 1992 ("the Contributions and Benefits Act"), the Social Security Administration Act 1992 ("the Administration Act") and, so far as it reproduces the effect of the repealed enactments, this Act; and

"the repealed enactments" means the enactments repealed by this Act.

2 Continuity of the law

(1) The substitution of the consolidating Acts for the repealed enactments does not affect the continuity of the law.

(2) Anything done or having effect as if done under or for the purposes of a provision of the repealed enactments has effect, if it could have been done under or for the purposes of the corresponding provision of the consolidating Acts, as if done under or for the purposes of that provision.

(3) Any reference, whether express or implied, in the consolidating Acts or any other enactment, instrument or document to a provision of the consolidating Acts shall, so far as the context permits, be construed as including, in relation to the times, circumstances and purposes in relation to which the corresponding provision of the repealed enactments has effect, a reference to that corresponding provision.

(4) Any reference, whether express or implied, in any enactment, instrument or document to a provision of the repealed enactments shall be construed, so far as is required for continuing its effect, as including a reference to the corresponding provision of the consolidating Acts.

3 Repeals

(1) The enactments mentioned in Schedule 1 to this Act are repealed to the extent specified in the third column of that Schedule.

(2) . . .

(3) The repeals have effect subject to any relevant savings in Schedule 3 to this Act.

Note—Sub-s (2) is outside the scope of this Publication.

4 Consequential amendments

The enactments mentioned in Schedule 2 to this Act shall have effect with the amendments there specified (being amendments consequential on the consolidating Acts).

5 Transitional provisions and savings

(1) The transitional provisions and savings in Schedule 3 to this Act shall have effect.

(2) Nothing in that Schedule affects the general operation of section 16 of the Interpretation Act 1978 (general savings implied on repeal) or of the previous provisions of this Act.

6 Transitory modifications

The transitory modifications in Schedule 4 to this Act shall have effect.

7 Short title, commencement and extent

(1) This Act may be cited as the Social Security (Consequential Provisions) Act 1992.

(2) This Act shall come into force on 1st July 1992.

(3) Section 2 above and this section extend to Northern Ireland.

(4) Subject to subsection (5) below, where any enactment repealed or amended by this Act extends to any part of the United Kingdom, the repeal or amendment extends to that part.

(5) The repeals—

(*a*) of provisions of sections 10, . . . of the Social Security Act 1980 and Part II of Schedule 3 to that Act;

(*b*) of enactments amending those provisions;

(*c*) of paragraph 2 of Schedule 1 to the Capital Allowances Act 1990; and

(*d*) . . . ,

do not extend to Northern Ireland.

(6) Section 6 above and Schedule 4 to this Act extend to Northern Ireland in so far as they give effect to transitory modifications of provisions of the consolidating Acts which so extend.

(7) Except as provided by this section, this Act does not extend to Northern Ireland.
(8) . . .

Notes—Words omitted from sub-s (5)(*d*) are outside the scope of this Publication.
Sub-s (8) is outside the scope of this Publication.

SCHEDULES

SCHEDULE 1
REPEALS

Section 3

Note—The effect of the repeals made by this Schedule (where within the scope of this Handbook) is noted in the text of the affected legislation.

SCHEDULE 2
CONSEQUENTIAL AMENDMENTS

Section 4

Note—The effect of the amendments made by this Schedule (where within the scope of this Handbook) is noted in the text of the affected legislation.

SCHEDULE 3
TRANSITIONAL PROVISIONS AND SAVINGS (INCLUDING SOME TRANSITIONAL PROVISIONS RETAINED FROM PREVIOUS ACTS)

Section 5

PART I
GENERAL AND MISCELLANEOUS

Note—Provisions omitted or printed in italics in this Part of this Schedule are outside the scope of this Publication.

Questions relating to contributions and benefits

1—(1) A question *other than a question arising under any of sections 1 to 3 of the Administration Act*—

(*a*) *whether a person is entitled to benefit in respect of a time before 1st July 1992;*

(*b*) whether a person is liable to pay contributions in respect of such a time,

and any other question not arising under any of those sections with respect to benefit or contributions in respect of such a time is to be determined, subject to section 68 of the Administration Act, in accordance with provisions in force or deemed to be in force at that time.

(2) Subject to sub-paragraph (1) above, the consolidating Acts apply to matters arising before their commencement as to matters arising after it.

General saving for old savings

2 The repeal by this Act of an enactment previously repealed subject to savings (whether or not in the repealing enactment) does not affect the continued operation of those savings.

Documents referring to repealed enactments

3 Any document made, served or issued after this Act comes into force which contains a reference to any of the repealed enactments shall be construed, except so far as a contrary intention appears, as referring or, as the context may require, including a reference to the corresponding provision of the consolidating Acts.

Provisions relating to the coming into force of other provisions

4 The repeal by this Act of a provision providing for or relating to the coming into force of a provision reproduced in the consolidating Acts does not affect the operation of the first provision, in so far as it remains capable of having effect, in relation to the enactment reproducing the second provision.

Continuing powers to make transitional etc regulations

5 Where immediately before 1st July 1992 the Secretary of State has power under any provision of the Social Security Acts 1975 to 1991 not reproduced in the consolidating Acts by regulations to make provision or savings in preparation for or in connection with the coming into force of a provision repealed by this Act but reproduced in the consolidating Acts, the power shall be construed as having effect in relation to the provision reproducing the repealed provision.

NIC

Powers to make preparatory regulations

6 The repeal by this Act of a power by regulations to make provision or savings in preparation for or in connection with the coming into force of a provision reproduced in the consolidating Acts does not affect the power, in so far as it remains capable of having effect, in relation to the enactment reproducing the second provision.

Provisions contained in enactments by virtue of orders or regulations

7—(1) Without prejudice to any express provision in the consolidating Acts, where this Act repeals any provision contained in any enactment by virtue of any order or regulations and the provision is reproduced in the consolidating Acts, the Secretary of State shall have the like power to make orders or regulations repealing or amending the provision of the consolidating Acts which reproduces the effect of the repealed provision as he had in relation to that provision.
(2) Sub-paragraph (1) above applies to a repealed provision which was amended by Schedule 7 to the Social Security Act 1989 as it applies to a provision not so amended.

Amending orders made after passing of Act

8 An order which is made under any of the repealed enactments after the passing of this Act and which amends any of the repealed enactments shall have the effect also of making a corresponding amendment of the consolidating Acts.

PART II
SPECIFIC TRANSITIONAL PROVISIONS AND SAVINGS (INCLUDING SOME DERIVED FROM PREVIOUS ACTS)

Note—Provisions omitted from this Part of this Schedule are outside the scope of this Publication.

Interpretation

9 In this Part of this Schedule—

. . .

"the 1975 Act" means the Social Security Act 1975;

. . .

"the 1986 Act" means the Social Security Act 1986.

Social Security Pensions Act 1975

10 The repeal by this Act of any provision contained in the 1975 Act or any enactment amending such a provision does not affect the operation of that provision by virtue of section 66(2) of the Social Security Pensions Act 1975.

Additional pensions

11–23 . . .

SCHEDULE 4
TRANSITORY MODIFICATIONS

Section 6

Note—Provisions outside the scope of this Publication have been omitted from this Schedule.

PART I
PROVISIONS NOT YET IN FORCE

Introductory

1—(1) If—

(*a*) no date has been appointed as the date on which a provision mentioned in column 1 of the following Table is to come into force before 1st July 1992; or

(*b*) a date has been appointed which is later than 1st July 1992,

then the paragraph of this Schedule mentioned in column 2 of the Table opposite that provision shall have effect until the appointed day.

Table

Provision	*Paragraph of this Schedule*
Section 17(8) of the Social Security Act 1990.	Paragraph 8.

Provision	Paragraph of this Schedule
Section 17(9) of the Social Security Act 1990.	Paragraph 9.

(2) . . .

(3) In this paragraph "the appointed day" means—

(*a*) in the case mentioned in paragraph (*a*) of sub-paragraph (1) above, such day as may be appointed by the Secretary of State by order made by statutory instrument; and

(*b*) in the case mentioned in paragraph (*b*) of that sub-paragraph, the day appointed as the day on which the provision mentioned in column 1 of the Table is to come into force.

(4) An order under sub-paragraph (3) above may appoint different days for different provisions or different purposes of the same provision.

(5) . . .

Notes—SSA 1990 s 17(8), (9) mentioned in column 1 of the Table substitutes SSA 1975 Sch 2 para 7.

The appointed day for paras (*a*), (*b*) is 19 April 1993 by virtue of SS (Consequential Provisions) Act 1992 (Appointed Day) Order, SI 1993/1025.

The Contributions and Benefits Act

8 The following sub-paragraph shall be substituted for paragraph 6(1) of Schedule 2 to that Act—

"(1) Section 88(1), (4) and (5)(*a*) and (*b*) of the Taxes Management Act 1970 (interest on tax recovered to make good loss due to taxpayer's fault) shall apply in relation to any amount due in respect of Class 4 contributions as it applies in relation to income tax; but section 86 of that Act (interest on amounts overdue) shall not apply.".

9 Paragraph 6(2) of that Schedule shall be omitted.

PENSION SCHEMES ACT 1993

(1993 Chapter 48)

ARRANGEMENT OF SECTIONS

PART I

PRELIMINARY

PART III

CERTIFICATION OF PENSION SCHEMES AND EFFECTS ON MEMBERS' STATE SCHEME RIGHTS AND DUTIES

CHAPTER I

CERTIFICATION

Preliminary

General requirements for certification

Cancellation, variation, surrender and refusal of certificates

CHAPTER II

REDUCTION IN STATE SCHEME CONTRIBUTIONS AND SOCIAL SECURITY BENEFITS FOR MEMBERS OF CERTIFIED SCHEMES

Preliminary

NIC

An Act to consolidate certain enactments relating to pension schemes with amendments to give effect to recommendations of the Law Commission and the Scottish Law Commission.

[5 November 1993]

PART I
PRELIMINARY

1 Categories of pension schemes

[(1)] [2] In this Act, unless the context otherwise requires—

["occupational pension scheme" means a pension scheme—

(*a*) that—

(i) for the purpose of providing benefits to, or in respect of, people with service in employments of a description, or

(ii) for that purpose and also for the purpose of providing benefits to, or in respect of, other people,

is established by, or by persons who include, a person to whom subsection (2) applies when the scheme is established or (as the case may be) to whom that subsection would have applied when the scheme was established had that subsection then been in force, and

(*b*) that has its main administration in the United Kingdom or outside the member States,

or a pension scheme that is prescribed or is of a prescribed description;

"personal pension scheme" means a pension scheme that—

(*a*) is not an occupational pension scheme, and

(*b*) is established by a person within . . . [3] section 154(1) of the Finance Act 2004;][2]

"public service pension scheme" means an occupational pension scheme established by or under an enactment or the Royal prerogative or a Royal charter, being a scheme—

(*a*) all the particulars of which are set out in, or in a legislative instrument made under, an enactment, Royal warrant or charter, or

(*b*) which cannot come into force, or be amended, without the scheme or amendment being approved by a Minister of the Crown or government department [or by the Scottish Ministers][1],

and includes any occupational pension scheme established, with the concurrence of the Treasury, by or with the approval of any Minister of the Crown [or established by or with the approval of the Scottish Ministers][1] and any occupational pension scheme prescribed by regulations made by the Secretary of State and the Treasury jointly as being a scheme which ought in their opinion to be treated as a public service pension scheme for the purposes of this Act.

[(2) This subsection applies—

(*a*) where people in employments of the description concerned are employed by someone, to a person who employs such people,

(*b*) to a person in an employment of that description, and

(*c*) to a person representing interests of a description framed so as to include—

(i) interests of persons who employ people in employments of the description mentioned in paragraph (*a*), or

(ii) interests of people in employments of that description.

(3) For the purposes of subsection (2), if a person is in an employment of the description concerned by reason of holding an office (including an elective office) and is entitled to remuneration for holding it, the person responsible for paying the remuneration shall be taken to employ the office-holder.

(4) In the definition in subsection (1) of "occupational pension scheme", the reference to a description includes a description framed by reference to an employment being of any of two or more kinds.

(5) In subsection (1) "pension scheme" (except in the phrases "occupational pension scheme", "personal pension scheme" and "public service pension scheme") means a scheme or other arrangements, comprised in one or more instruments or agreements, having or capable of having effect so as to provide benefits to or in respect of people—

(*a*) on retirement,

(*b*) on having reached a particular age, or

(*c*) on termination of service in an employment.

(6) The power of the Treasury under section 154(4) of the Finance Act 2004 (power to amend sections 154 and 155) includes power consequentially to amend—

(*a*) paragraph (*a*) of the definition in subsection (1) of "personal pension scheme", and

(*b*) any provision in force in Northern Ireland corresponding to that paragraph.][2]

Former enactments—SSA 1973 ss 51(3), 99(1); SSPA 1975 s 66(1); SSA 1986 s 84(1).

Amendments—[1] Words in definition "public service pension scheme" inserted by the Scotland Act 1998 (Consequential Modifications) (No 2) Order, SI 1999/1820 art 4 Sch 2 Pt I para 113 with effect from 1 July 1999.

[2] Sub-s (1) numbered as such, definitions of "occupational pension scheme" and "personal pension scheme" substituted, and sub-ss (2)–(6) inserted, by the Pensions Act 2004 s 239 with effect from—

(a) for the purpose only of conferring power to make regulations, 1 July 2005; and

(b) for all other purposes—

(i) in the case of an occupational pension scheme that has its main administration in the United Kingdom, 22 September 2005; and

(ii) in all other cases, 6 April 2006.

[3] In sub-s (1), words in the definition of "personal pension scheme" repealed by FA 2007 ss 70, 114, Sch 20 paras 23(1), 24(1), Sch 27 Pt 3(2). This repeal is deemed to have come into force on 6 April 2007.

PART III

[SCHEMES THAT WERE CONTRACTED-OUT ETC] AND EFFECTS ON MEMBERS' STATE SCHEME RIGHTS . . .

Amendments—In heading, words substituted and words repealed by PeA 2014 s 24, Sch 13 paras 1, 3 with effect from 6 April 2016 (PeA 2014 s 56(1), (4)).

CHAPTER I

[SCHEMES THAT WERE CONTRACTED-OUT: GUARANTEED MINIMUM PENSIONS AND ALTERATION OF SCHEME RULES ETC]

Amendments—Heading substituted by PeA 2014 s 24, Sch 13 paras 1, 4 with effect from 6 April 2016 (PeA 2014 s 56(1), (4)).

NIC

Preliminary

7 Issue of contracting-out . . . [2] ***certificates***

[(1) Regulations shall provide for HMRC to issue certificates stating that the employment of an earner in employed earner's employment is contracted-out employment by reference to an occupational pension scheme.

(1A) In this Act such a certificate is referred to as "a contracting-out certificate".][2]

(2) The regulations shall provide for contracting-out certificates to be issued to employers and to specify—

(a) the employments which are to be treated, either generally or in relation to any specified description of earners, as contracted-out employments; and

(b) the occupational pension schemes by reference to which those employments are to be so treated.

[(2A) The regulations may provide, in the case of contracting-out certificates issued before the principal appointed day, for their cancellation by virtue of the regulations—

(a) at the end of a prescribed period beginning with that day, or

(b) if prescribed conditions are not satisfied at any time in that period,

but for them to continue to have effect until so cancelled; and the regulations may provide that a certificate having effect on and after that day by virtue of this subsection is to have effect, in relation to any earner's service on or after that day, as if issued on or after that day.][1]

[(2B) In this Part, "the principal appointed day" means the day designated by an order under section 180 of the Pensions Act 1995 as the principal appointed day for the purposes of Part III of that Act.][1]

(3) An occupational pension scheme is a contracted-out scheme in relation to an earner's employment if it is for the time being specified in a contracting-out certificate in relation to that employment; and references in this Act to the contracting-out of a scheme are references to its inclusion in such a certificate.

(4)–(6) . . . [2]

(7) Except in prescribed circumstances, no contracting-out certificate . . . [2] *shall have effect from a date earlier than that on which the certificate is issued.*

[(8) References in this Act to a contracting-out certificate, a contracted-out scheme and to contracting-out in a context relating to a money purchase contracted-out scheme are to be construed in accordance with section 181A.][2, 3]

Former enactments—Sub-s (1): SSPA 1975 ss 30(1), 31(1); SSA 1986 s 2(1)(*a*).
Sub-s (2): SSPA 1975 s 31(1).
Sub-s (3): SSPA 1975 s 32(1).
Sub-s (4): SSA 1986 s 1(8).
Sub-ss (5), (6): SSA 1986 s 2(1)(*c*), (6).
Sub-s (7): SSPA 1975 s 31(7); SSA 1986 s 2(5).

Regulations—Occupational Pension Schemes (Schemes that were Contracted-out) Regulations, SI 2015/1452.

Amendments—[1] Sub-ss (2A), (2B) inserted by the Pensions Act 1995 s 136(1) with effect from 6 April 1996, for the purpose only of authorising the making of regulations, and 6 April 1997, for all other purposes, by virtue of SI 1996/778 art 2(5)(*a*), (7).

[2] Sub-ss (1), (1A) substituted for previous sub-s (1), sub-ss (4)–(6), words "or appropriate scheme certificate" in sub-s (7) and words "and appropriate scheme" in heading, repealed, and sub-s (8) inserted, by the Pensions Act 2007 ss 11, 27, Sch 4 para 2, Sch 7 Pt 6 with effect from 26 September 2007 (s 30(3)) subject to savings in Sch 4 Pt 3.

Sub-s (1) previously read as follows—

"(1) Regulations shall provide for the Inland Revenue to issue certificates stating—

(*a*) that the employment of an earner in employed earner's employment is contracted-out employment by reference to an occupational pension scheme; or

(*b*) that a personal pension scheme is an appropriate scheme;

and in this Act a certificate under paragraph (*a*) is referred to as "a contracting-out certificate" and a certificate under paragraph (*b*) as "an appropriate scheme certificate"."

Sub-ss (4)–(6) previously read as follows—

"(4) A personal pension scheme is an appropriate scheme if there is in force an appropriate scheme certificate issued . . . in accordance with this Chapter that it is such a scheme.

(5) An appropriate scheme certificate for the time being in force in relation to a scheme shall be conclusive that the scheme is an appropriate scheme.

(6) Regulations shall provide that any question whether a personal pension scheme is or at any time was an appropriate scheme shall be determined by the Inland Revenue."

[3] Section 7 repealed by PeA 2014 s 24, Sch 13 paras 1, 5 with effect from 6 April 2016 (PeA 2014 s 56(1), (4)). Accordingly, any certificates in force under this section immediately before the repeal comes into force, cease to have effect).

Note that this section continues to have effect, despite this repeal, for the purposes of allowing or requiring the trustees or managers of a scheme that was a salary-related contracted-out scheme, and HMRC, to carry out any necessary activity relating to any period of contracted-out employment which occurred before the second abolition date (see the Pensions Act 2014 (Savings) Order, SI 2015/1502).

[7A Meaning of "the first abolition date" and "the second abolition date"

In this Act—

"the first abolition date" means 6 April 2012 (the date appointed for the commencement of section 15(1) of the Pensions Act 2007 (abolition of contracting-out for defined contribution pension schemes));

"the second abolition date" means 6 April 2016 (the date on which section 56(4) of the Pensions Act 2014 provides for the commencement of section 24(1) of that Act (abolition of contracting-out for salary related schemes)).][1]

Amendments—[1] Sections 7A, 7B inserted by PeA 2014 s 24, Sch 13 paras 1, 6 with effect from 6 April 2016 (PeA 2014 s 56(1), (4)).

[7B Meaning of "contracted-out scheme" and "appropriate scheme" etc.

(1) This section applies for the interpretation of this Act.

(2) An occupational pension scheme was "contracted-out" at a time if, at that time, there was in force a certificate under section 7 (as it then had effect) stating that the employment of an earner in employed earner's employment was contracted-out employment by reference to the scheme.

(3) "Contracting-out certificate" means a certificate of the kind mentioned in subsection (2).

(4) An occupational pension scheme was a "salary related contractedout scheme" at a time if, at that time, the scheme was contracted-out by virtue of satisfying section 9(2) (as it then had effect).

(5) An occupational pension scheme was a "money purchase contracted-out scheme" at a time if, at that time, the scheme was contracted-out by virtue of satisfying section 9(3) (as it then had effect).

(6) A personal pension scheme was an "appropriate scheme" at a time if, at that time, there was in force a certificate issued under section 7(1)(*b*) (as it then had effect) stating that the scheme was an appropriate scheme.

(7) "Appropriate scheme certificate" means a certificate of the kind mentioned in subsection (6).

(8) An appropriate scheme certificate that was in force in relation to a scheme is to be taken as conclusive that the scheme was, at that time, an appropriate scheme.][1]

Amendments—[1] Sections 7A, 7B inserted by PeA 2014 s 24, Sch 13 paras 1, 6 with effect from 6 April 2016 (PeA 2014 s 56(1), (4)).

8 Meaning of "contracted-out employment", "guaranteed minimum pension" and "minimum payment"

[(1) In relation to any period before the second abolition date, the employment of an earner in employed earner's employment was "contracted-out employment" in relation to the earner during that period if—

(*a*) the earner was under pensionable age;

(*b*) the earner's service in the employment was service which qualified the earner for a pension provided by a salary related contracted-out scheme; and

(*c*) there was in force a contracting-out certificate issued in accordance with this Chapter (as it then had effect) stating that the employment was contracted-out employment by reference to the scheme.][10]

[(1A) In addition, in relation to any period before [the first abolition date][9], the employment of an earner in employed earner's employment was "contracted-out employment" in relation to him during that period if—

(*a*) he was under pensionable age;

(*b*) his employer made minimum payments in respect of his employment to a money purchase contracted-out scheme, and

(*c*) there was in force a contracting-out certificate issued in accordance with this Chapter (as it then had effect) stating that the employment was contracted-out employment by reference to the scheme.][5]

[(1B) In the following provisions of this Act "earner", in relation to a scheme, means a person who was an earner in contracted-out employment by reference to the scheme.][10]

(2) In this Act—

"guaranteed minimum pension" means any pension which is provided[, by a scheme that was a salary related contracted-out scheme,][10] in accordance with the requirements of sections 13 and 17 to the extent to which its weekly rate is equal to the earner's or, as the case may be, the earner's [widow's, widower's[, surviving same sex spouse's][7] or surviving civil partner's][4] guaranteed minimum as determined for the purposes of those sections respectively; and

"minimum payment", in relation to an earner's employment in any tax week, means the rebate percentage of so much of the earnings paid to or for the benefit of the earner in that week as exceeds the current lower earnings limit but not [the applicable limit][6] (or the prescribed equivalents if he is paid otherwise than weekly);

[and for the purposes of this subsection "rebate percentage" means the appropriate flat rate percentage [for the tax year in which the week falls as specified in an order made under section 42B (as it had effect before [the first abolition date][9])][5]][1].

[(2A) In subsection (2) "the applicable limit" means—

NIC

(*a*) in relation to a tax year before 2009–10, the upper earnings limit;

(*b*) in relation to 2009–10 or any subsequent tax year, the upper accrual point.][6]

(3) . . .[8]

[(4) A contracting-out certificate that was in force in respect of an employed earner's employment is to be taken as conclusive that the employment was, at that time, contracted-out employment.][10]

(5) . . .[2]

Former enactments—Sub-s (1): SSPA 1975 s 30(1).
Sub-s (2): SSPA 1975 ss 26(2), 30(1A), (1B).
Sub-s (3): SSPA 1975 s 30(1C).
Sub-ss (4), (5): SSPA 1975 s 30(3), (4).

Cross references—See FA 2004 Part 4, Chapter 4 (Registered pension schemes: tax reliefs and exemptions) and FA 2004 Part 4, Chapter 5 (Registered pension schemes: tax charges).

Amendments—[1] Words in sub-s (2) substituted by the Pensions Act 1995 Sch 5 para 23(*a*) with effect from 6 April 1997, by virtue of SI 1997/664 art 2, Sch Pt II.

[2] Sub-s (5) repealed by the Pensions Act 1995 Sch 5 para 23(*b*), Sch 7 Pt III with effect from 6 April 1997, by virtue of SI 1997/664 art 2, Sch Pt II.

[3] Words in sub-s (1)(*b*) and (3)(*f*) substituted by the Social Security Contributions (Transfer of Functions, etc) Act 1999 s 1(1) and Sch 1 para 34 with effect from 1 April 1999 by virtue of the Social Security Contributions (Transfer of Functions, etc) Act 1999 (Commencement No 1 and Transitional Provisions) Order, SI 1999/527.

[4] Words in the definition of "guaranteed minimum pension" in sub-s (2) substituted by the Civil Partnership (Pensions and Benefit Payments) (Consequential, etc Provisions) Order 2005, SI 2005/2050, art 2(1) Sch 1 para 1 with effect from 5 December 2005.

[5] Words in sub-s (1) substituted, sub-s (1A) inserted, and words in sub-s (2) substituted, by the Pensions Act 2007 s 15, Sch 4 para 3 with effect from 26 September 2007 (s 30(3)) subject to savings in Sch 4 Pt 3.

[6] In sub-s (2), in definition of "minimum payment", words substituted for words "the current upper earnings limit", and sub-s (2A) inserted, by the NIC Act 2008 s 4, Sch 1 paras 7, 8 with effect from the end of the period of two months beginning with the day on which the Act was passed. The Act was passed on 21 July 2008, therefore these amendments have effect from 21 September 2008.

[7] In sub-s (2), in definition of "guaranteed minimum pension", words inserted by the Marriage (Same Sex Couples) Act 2013 s 11, Sch 4 paras 18, 19 with effect, in relation to England and Wales, from 14 March 2014 (by virtue of SI 2014/93 art 3(*j*)(iv), (v)), and in relation to Scotland from 16 December 2014 (by virtue of SI 2014/3229).

[8] Sub-s (3) repealed by the Pensions Act 2007 ss 15, 27, Sch 4 paras 46, 47, Sch 27 Pt 7 with effect from 6 April 2015 (by virtue of SI 2011/1267, art 3(*a*)(iii), (iv)).

[9] In sub-ss (1A), (2), words substituted by PeA 2014 s 24, Sch 13 paras 1, 2 with effect from 6 April 2016 (PeA 2014 s 56(1), (4)).

[10] Sub-ss (1), (4) substituted, sub-s (1B) inserted, and in sub-s (2), in definition of "guaranteed minimum pension", words substituted, by PeA 2014 s 24, Sch 13 paras 1, 7 with effect from 6 April 2016 (PeA 2014 s 56(1), (4)).

General requirements for certification

11 Elections as to employments covered by contracting-out certificates

(1) Subject to the provisions of this Part, an employment otherwise satisfying the conditions for inclusion in a contracting-out certificate shall be so included if and so long as the employer so elects and not otherwise.

(2) Subject to subsections (3) and (4), an election may be so made, and an employment so included, either generally or in relation only to a particular description of earners.

(3) Except in such cases as may be prescribed, an employer shall not, in making or abstaining from making any election under this section, discriminate between different earners on any grounds other than the nature of their employment.

(4) If the [Inland Revenue consider][1] that an employer is contravening sub-section (3) in relation to any scheme, [they][1] may—

(a) refuse to give effect to any election made by him in relation to that scheme; or

(b) cancel any contracting-out certificate held by him in respect of it.

(5) Regulations may make provision—

(a) for regulating the manner in which an employer is to make an election with a view to the issue, variation or surrender of a contracting-out certificate;

(b) for requiring an employer to give a notice of his intentions in respect of making or abstaining from making any such election in relation to any existing or proposed scheme—

(i) to employees in any employment to which the scheme applies or to which it is proposed that it should apply;

(ii) to any independent trade union recognised to any extent for the purpose of collective bargaining in relation to those employees;

(iii) to the trustees and managers of the scheme; and

(iv) to such other persons as may be prescribed;

(c) for requiring an employer, in connection with any such notice, to furnish such information as may be prescribed and to undertake such consultations as may be prescribed with any such trade union as is mentioned in paragraph (b)(ii);

(d) for empowering the [Inland Revenue][1] to refuse to give effect to an election made by an employer unless [they are][1] satisfied that he has complied with the requirements of the regulations;

(*e*) *for referring to an [employment tribunal]*[2] *any question—*

(i) *whether an organisation is such a trade union as is mentioned in paragraph* (*b*)(ii), or

(ii) *whether the requirements of the regulations as to consultation have been complied with.*[3]

Former enactments—Sub-ss (1), (2): SSPA 1975 s 31(3).
Sub-ss (3), (4): SSPA 1975 s 31(4).
Sub-s (5): SSPA 1975 s 31(5).

Regulations—Occupational Pension Schemes (Schemes that were Contracted-out) Regulations, SI 2015/1452.

Amendments—[1] Words in sub-ss (4) and (5)(*d*) substituted by the Social Security Contributions (Transfer of Functions, etc) Act 1999 s 1(1) and Sch 1 para 37 with effect from 1 April 1999 by virtue of the Social Security Contributions (Transfer of Functions, etc) Act 1999 (Commencement No 1 and Transitional Provisions) Order, SI 1999/527.

[2] Words in sub-s (5)(e) substituted by the Employment Rights (Dispute Resolution) Act 1998 s 1 with effect from 1 August 1998, by virtue of SI 1998/1658.

[3] Section 11 repealed by PeA 2014 s 24, Sch 13 paras 1, 5 with effect from 6 April 2016 (PeA 2014 s 56(1), (4)).
Note that this section continues to have effect, despite this repeal, for the purposes of allowing or requiring the trustees or managers of a scheme that was a salary-related contracted-out scheme, and HMRC, to carry out any necessary activity relating to any period of contracted-out employment which occurred before the second abolition date (see the Pensions Act 2014 (Savings) Order, SI 2015/1502).

Cancellation, variation, surrender and refusal of certificates

34 Cancellation, variation, surrender and refusal of certificates

[(1) Regulations shall provide for the cancellation, variation or surrender of a contracting-out certificate, or the issue of a new certificate—

(*a*) *on any change of circumstances affecting the treatment of an employment as contracted-out employment; or*

(*b*) *where the certificate was issued on or after the principal appointed day, if any employer of persons in the description of employment to which the scheme in question relates, or the actuary of the scheme, fails to provide HMRC, at prescribed intervals, with such documents as may be prescribed for the purpose of verifying that the conditions of section 9(2B) are satisfied.]*[4]

(2) Regulations may enable the [Inland Revenue][3] *to cancel or vary a contracting-out certificate where—*

(*a*) *[they have]*[3] *reason to suppose that any employment to which it relates ought not to be treated as contracted-out employment in accordance with the certificate; and*

(*b*) *the employer does not show that it ought to be so treated.*

(3) Where [by or by virtue of any provision of this Part the contracting-out of a scheme in relation to an employment depends on the satisfaction of a particular condition][4] *the continued contracting-out of the scheme . . .* [4] *shall be dependent on continued satisfaction of the condition; and if the condition ceases to be satisfied, that shall be a ground (without prejudice to any other) for the cancellation or variation of the contracting-out . . .* [4] *certificate.*

(4) A contracting-out certificate in respect of any employment may be withheld or cancelled by the [Inland Revenue][3] *if [they consider]*[3] *that there are circumstances which make it inexpedient that the employment should be or, as the case may be, continue to be, contracted-out employment by reference to the scheme, notwithstanding that the relevant scheme is one that [they]*[3] *would otherwise treat as proper to be contracted-out in relation to all earners in that employment.*

(5) . . . [4]

(6) . . . [1]

[(7) Without prejudice to the previous provisions of this section, failure of a scheme to comply with any requirements prescribed by virtue of section 25(2) shall be a ground on which the [Inland Revenue][3] *may, in respect of any employment to which the scheme relates, cancel a contracting-out certificate.]*[2]

(8) Except in prescribed circumstances, no cancellation, variation or surrender of a contracting-out certificate . . . [4] *shall have effect from a date earlier than that on which the cancellation, variation or surrender is made.*

[(9) A reference in this section to a contracting-out certificate does not include a reference to a contracting-out certificate issued in respect of a money purchase contracted-out scheme.][4, 5]

Former enactments—Sub-s (1): SSPA 1975 s 31(2); SSA 1986 s 2(1)(*b*).
Sub-s (2): SSPA 1975 s 31(6).
Sub-s (3): SSPA 1975 s 32(3); SSA 1986 s 2(4).
Sub-s (4): SSPA 1975 s 32(4).
Sub-s (5): SSA 1986 s 2(3).
Sub-s (6): SSA 1980 s 3(10).
Sub-s (7): SSPA 1975 s 41(2), (5).
Sub-s (8): SSPA 1975 s 31(7); SSA 1986 s 2(5).

Regulations—Occupational Pension Schemes (Schemes that were Contracted-out) Regulations, SI 2015/1452.

Amendments—[1] Sub-s (6) repealed by the Pensions Act 1995 Sch 5 para 37(*b*), Sch 7 Pt III with effect from 6 April 1996, for the purpose only of authorising the making of regulations, by virtue of SI 1996/778 art 2(5)(*a*), and otherwise from 6 April 1997, by virtue of SI 1997/664 art 2, Sch Pt II.

NIC

[2] Sub-s (7) substituted by the Pensions Act 1995 Sch 5 para 37(*c*) with effect from 6 April 1996, for the purpose only of authorising the making of regulations, by virtue of SI 1996/778 art 2(5)(*a*), and otherwise from 6 April 1997, by virtue of SI 1997/664 art 2, Sch Pt II.

[3] Words throughout the section substituted by the Social Security Contributions (Transfer of Functions, etc) Act 1999 s 1(1) and Sch 1 para 45 with effect from 1 April 1999 by virtue of the Social Security Contributions (Transfer of Functions, etc) Act 1999 (Commencement No 1 and Transitional Provisions) Order, SI 1999/527.

[4] Sub-s (1) substituted; in sub-s (3) words substituted for paras (*a*), (*b*), and words repealed; whole of sub-s (5), and words in sub-s (8), repealed; and sub-s (9) inserted; by the Pensions Act 2007 ss 15, 27, Sch 4 para 15, Sch 7 Pt 6 with effect from 26 September 2007 (s 30(3)) subject to savings in Sch 4 Pt 3.

[5] Sections 34–36 repealed by PeA 2014 s 24, Sch 13 paras 1, 22 with effect from 6 April 2016 (PeA 2014 s 56(1), (4)). Note that these sections continue to have effect, despite this repeal, for the purposes of allowing or requiring the trustees or managers of a scheme that was a salary-related contracted-out scheme, and HMRC, to carry out any necessary activity relating to any period of contracted-out employment which occurred before the second abolition date (see the Pensions Act 2014 (Savings) Order, SI 2015/1502).

35 Surrender and cancellation of contracting-out certificates: issue of further certificates

(1) This section applies in any case where—

(a) a contracting-out certificate ("the first certificate") has been surrendered by an employer or cancelled by the Board; and

(b) at any time before the end of the period of 12 months beginning with the date of the surrender or cancellation, that or any connected employer makes an election under section 11 in respect of any employment which was specified by virtue of section 7(2)(a) in the first certificate, with a view to the issue of a further contracting-out certificate.

(2) This section applies whether or not the scheme specified in the first certificate in relation to the employment concerned is the same as the scheme which would be specified in the further certificate if it were issued.

(3) The Board shall not give effect to the election referred to in subsection (1) by issuing a further certificate unless they consider that, in all the circumstances of the case, it would be reasonable to do so.

(4) Regulations may make such supplemental provision in relation to cases falling within this section as the Secretary of State considers necessary or expedient.

(5) For the purposes of subsection (1)—

(a) an employment ("the second employment") in respect of which an election of the kind referred to in subsection (1)(b) has been made; and

(b) an employment ("the first employment") which was specified by virtue of section 7(2)(a) in the first certificate,

shall be treated as one employment if, in the opinion of the Board—

(i) they are substantially the same, however described; or

(ii) the first employment falls wholly or partly within the description of the second employment or the second employment falls wholly or partly within the description of the first employment.

(6) Regulations shall prescribe the cases in which employers are to be treated as connected for the purposes of this section.[1]

Former enactments—Sub-ss (1), (3), (4), (6): SSPA 1975 s 51A(1), (4), (9), (12).
Sub-ss (2), (5): SSPA 1975 s 51A(3), (11).

Amendments—[1] Sections 34–36 repealed by PeA 2014 s 24, Sch 13 paras 1, 22 with effect from 6 April 2016 (PeA 2014 s 56(1), (4)).
Note that these sections continue to have effect, despite this repeal, for the purposes of allowing or requiring the trustees or managers of a scheme that was a salary-related contracted-out scheme, and HMRC, to carry out any necessary activity relating to any period of contracted-out employment which occurred before the second abolition date (see the Pensions Act 2014 (Savings) Order, SI 2015/1502).

36 Surrender and cancellation of contracting-out certificates: cancellation of further certificates

(1) This section applies in any case where—

(a) a contracting-out certificate ("the first certificate") has been surrendered by an employer or cancelled by the Board;

(b) a further contracting-out certificate ("the further certificate") has been issued, after the surrender or cancellation of the first certificate but before the end of the period of 12 months beginning with the date of the surrender or cancellation, in respect of any employment which was specified by virtue of section 7(2)(a) in the first certificate; and

(c) the Board have formed the opinion that had they been aware of all the circumstances of the case at the time when the further certificate was issued they would have been prevented by section 35(3) from issuing it.

(2) This section applies whether or not the scheme specified in the first certificate in relation to the employment concerned is the same as the scheme specified in the further certificate.

(3) The Board may, before the end of the period of 12 months beginning with the date on which the further certificate was issued, cancel that certificate.

(4) Where a contracting-out certificate is cancelled under subsection (3) the provisions of this Act and of any regulations and orders made under it shall have effect as if the certificate had never been issued.

(5) Regulations may make such supplemental provision in relation to cases falling within this section as the Secretary of State considers necessary or expedient.

(6) Without prejudice to subsection (5), regulations may make provision, in relation to any case in which the Board have cancelled a contracting-out certificate under subsection (3), preventing the recovery by the employer concerned (whether by deduction from emoluments or otherwise) of such arrears which he is required to pay to the Secretary of State in respect of an earner's liability under section 6(3) of the Social Security Contributions and Benefits Act 1992 as may be prescribed.

(7) For the purposes of subsection (1)—

(a) an employment ("the second employment") in respect of which a further contracting-out certificate of the kind referred to in subsection (1)(b) has been issued; and

(b) an employment ("the first employment") which was specified by virtue of section 7(2)(a) in the first certificate,

shall be treated as one employment if in the opinion of the Board—

(i) they are substantially the same, however described; or

(ii) the first employment falls wholly or partly within the description of the second employment or the second employment falls wholly or partly within the description of the first employment.[1]

Former enactments—Sub-ss (1), (3)–(5): SSPA 1975 s 51A(2), (5), (6), (9).

Sub-ss (2), (7): SSPA 1975 s 51A(3), (11).

Sub-s (6): SSPA 1975 s 51A(10).

Regulations—Occupational Pension Schemes (Schemes that were Contracted-out) Regulations, SI 2015/1452.

Amendments—[1] Sections 34–36 repealed by PeA 2014 s 24, Sch 13 paras 1, 22 with effect from 6 April 2016 (PeA 2014 s 56(1), (4)).

Note that these sections continue to have effect, despite this repeal, for the purposes of allowing or requiring the trustees or managers of a scheme that was a salary-related contracted-out scheme, and HMRC, to carry out any necessary activity relating to any period of contracted-out employment which occurred before the second abolition date (see the Pensions Act 2014 (Savings) Order, SI 2015/1502).

CHAPTER II

[REDUCTION IN SOCIAL SECURITY BENEFITS FOR MEMBERS OF SCHEMES THAT WERE CONTRACTED-OUT]

Amendments—Heading substituted by PeA 2014 s 24, Sch 13 paras 1, 26 with effect from 6 April 2016 (PeA 2014 s 56(1), (4)).

Preliminary

40 Scope of Chapter II

This Chapter has effect for the purpose—

(*a*) . . . [3]

(*b*) of providing for contributions to be paid by the [Inland Revenue][2] in respect of earners who are members of [money purchase contracted-out schemes and members of][1] appropriate personal pension schemes; and

(*c*) of making provision concerning the payment of certain social security benefits payable in respect of members and former members of [schemes that were contracted-out pension schemes][3].

Former enactments—SSPA 1975 s 26(1), (1A).

Amendments—[1] Words in para (*b*) inserted by the Pensions Act 1995 s 137(1) with effect from 13 March 1996, for the purpose only of authorising the making of orders, and 6 April 1996, for the purpose only of authorising the making of regulations, by virtue of SI 1996/778 art 2(1), (5)(*a*), and otherwise from 6 April 1997, by virtue of SI 1997/664 art 2, Sch Pt II.

[2] Words substituted by the Welfare Reform and Pensions Act 1999 s 81 Sch 11 paras 20, 21 with effect from 11 November 1999.

[3] Para (*a*) repealed, and in para (*c*), words substituted by PeA 2014 s 24, Sch 13 paras 1, 27 with effect from 6 April 2016 (PeA 2014 s 56(1), (4)).

Prospective amendments—Para (*b*) to be repealed by the Pensions Act 2007 ss 15, 27, Sch 4 paras 46, 50, Sch 27 Pt 7 with effect from a date to be appointed.

[Reduced rates of contributions for members of salary related contracted-out schemes

41 Reduced rates of Class 1 contributions

[(1) Subsections (1A) to [(1E)][2] apply where—

(*a*) the earnings paid to or for the benefit of an earner in any tax week are in respect of an employment which is contracted-out employment at the time of the payment, and

(*b*) the earner's service in the employment is service which qualifies him for a pension provided by a salary related contracted-out scheme;

and in subsections (1A) and (1B) "the relevant part", in relation to those earnings, means so much of those earnings as exceeds the current lower earnings limit but not [the upper accrual point][6] (or the prescribed equivalents if the earner is paid otherwise than weekly).

(1ZA) . . . [6]

NIC

[(1A) The amount of any primary Class 1 contribution [attributable to section 8(1)(*a*) of the Social Security Contributions and Benefits Act 1992][4] in respect of the earnings shall be reduced by an amount equal to [1.4 per cent][7] of the relevant part of the earnings ("Amount R1").

(1B) The amount of any secondary Class 1 contribution in respect of the earnings shall be reduced by an amount equal to [3.4 per cent][3, 7] of the relevant part of the earnings ("Amount R2").

(1C) The aggregate of Amounts R1 and R2 shall be set off—

(*a*) first against the aggregate amount which the secondary contributor is liable to pay in respect of the contributions mentioned in subsections (1A) and (1B); and

(*b*) then (as to any balance) against any amount which the secondary contributor is liable to pay in respect of any primary or secondary Class 1 contribution in respect of earnings—

(i) paid to or for the benefit of any other employed earner (whether in contracted-out employment or not), and

(ii) in relation to which the secondary contributor is such a contributor;

and in this subsection any reference to a liability to pay an amount in respect of a primary Class 1 contribution is a reference to such a liability under paragraph 3 of Schedule 1 to the Social Security Contributions and Benefits Act 1992.

(1D) If—

(*a*) any balance remains, and

(*b*) the secondary contributor makes an application for the purpose to the Inland Revenue,

the Inland Revenue shall, in such manner and at such time (or within such period) as may be prescribed, pay to the secondary contributor an amount equal to the remaining balance.

But regulations may make provision for the adjustment of an amount that would otherwise be payable under this subsection so as to avoid the payment of trivial or fractional amounts.

(1E) If the Inland Revenue pay any amount under subsection (1D) which they are not required to pay, they may recover that amount from the secondary contributor in such manner and at such time (or within such period) as may be prescribed.][2]]

(2) Where—

(*a*) an earner has ceased to be employed in an employment; and

(*b*) earnings are paid to him or for his benefit within the period of 6 weeks, or such other period as may be prescribed, from the day on which he so ceased,

that employment shall be treated for the purposes of subsection (1) as contracted-out employment at the time when the earnings are paid if it was contracted-out employment in relation to the earner when he was last employed in it.

(3) This section shall not affect the amount of any primary Class 1 contribution which is payable at a reduced rate by virtue of regulations under section 19(4) of the Social Security Contributions and Benefits Act 1992 (reduced rates for married women and widows).][1, 5]

Former enactments—Sub-s (1): SSPA 1975 s 27(1)–(3).
Sub-s (2): SSPA 1975 s 27(4).
Sub-s (3): SSPA 1975 s 27(5).

Amendments—[1] Substituted by SSA 1998 Sch 7 para 127 with effect from 6 April 1999 by virtue of the Social Security Act 1998 (Commencement No 3) Order, SI 1999/418.

[2] Words in sub-s (1) substituted and sub-ss (1A)–(1E) substituted for original sub-ss (1A)–(1C) by the Welfare Reform and Pensions Act 1999 s 73 Sch 9 para 6 with effect from 22 December 1999, for the purpose of the exercise of any power to make regulations, and 6 April 2000 for all other purposes.

[3] In sub-s (1B), "3.7 per cent" substituted for "3.5 per cent" by the Social Security (Reduced Rates of Class 1 Contributions, Rebates and Minimum Contributions) Order, SI 2006/1009 art 2 with effect from 6 April 2007.

[4] Words in sub-s (1A) inserted by NICA 2002 s 6, Sch 1 paras 35, 36 with effect from 2003–04.

[5] Section 41 and preceding heading repealed by PeA 2014 s 24, Sch 13 paras 1, 28, 29 with effect from 6 April 2016 (PeA 2014 s 56(1), (4)).

Note that this section continues to have effect, despite this repeal, for the purposes of allowing or requiring the trustees or managers of a scheme that was a salary-related contracted-out scheme, and HMRC, to carry out any necessary activity relating to any period of contracted-out employment which occurred before the second abolition date (see the Pensions Act 2014 (Savings) Order, SI 2015/1502).

[6] In sub-s (1) words substituted for words "the applicable limit for that week", and sub-s (1ZA) repealed, by the NIC Act 2008 s 4, Sch 1 paras 7, 10, Sch 2 with effect in relation to 2009–10 and subsequent tax years.

[7] Words substituted in sub-ss (1A), (1B) by the Social Security (Reduced Rates of Class 1 Contributions, Rebates and Minimum Contributions) Order, SI 2011/1036 art 2, in relation to England, Wales and Scotland with effect from 6 April 2012.

42 Review and alteration of rates of contributions applicable under s 41

. . .[1]

Amendments—[1] Section 42 repealed by PeA 2014 s 24, Sch 13 paras 1, 30(1) with effect from 6 April 2016 (PeA 2014 s 56(1), (4)). Before this repeal came into force, there was no duty under this section to lay any reports before Parliament (PeA 2014 Sch 13 para 30(2)).

[Reduced rates of contributions, and rebates, for members of money purchase contracted-out schemes]

[42A Reduced rates of Class I contributions, and rebates

[(1) Subsections (2) to [(2D) and (3)][4] apply where—

(*a*) the earnings paid to or for the benefit of an earner in any tax week are in respect of an employment which is contracted-out employment at the time of the payment, and

(*b*) the earner's service in the employment is service which qualifies him for a pension provided by a money purchase contracted-out scheme;

and in subsections (2) and (2A) "the relevant part", in relation to those earnings, means so much of those earnings as exceeds the current lower earnings limit but not [the upper accrual point][7] (or the prescribed equivalents if the earner is paid otherwise than weekly).

[(2) The amount of any primary Class 1 contribution [attributable to section 8(1)(*a*) of the Social Security Contributions and Benefits Act 1992][5] in respect of the earnings shall be reduced by an amount equal to the appropriate flat-rate percentage of the relevant part of the earnings ("Amount R1").

(2A) The amount of any secondary Class 1 contribution in respect of the earnings shall be reduced by an amount equal to the appropriate flat-rate percentage of the relevant part of the earnings ("Amount R2").

(2B) The aggregate of Amounts R1 and R2 shall be set off—

(*a*) first against the aggregate amount which the secondary contributor is liable to pay in respect of the contributions mentioned in subsections (2) and (2A); and

(*b*) then (as to any balance) against any amount which the secondary contributor is liable to pay in respect of a primary or secondary Class 1 contribution in respect of earnings—

(i) paid to or for the benefit of any other employed earner (whether in contracted-out employment or not), and

(ii) in relation to which the secondary contributor is such a contributor;

and in this subsection any reference to a liability to pay an amount in respect of a primary Class 1 contribution is a reference to such a liability under paragraph 3 of Schedule 1 to the Social Security Contributions and Benefits Act 1992.

(2C) If—

(*a*) any balance remains, and

(*b*) the secondary contributor makes an application for the purpose to the Inland Revenue,

the Inland Revenue shall, in such manner and at such time (or within such period) as may be prescribed, pay to the secondary contributor an amount equal to the remaining balance.

But regulations may make provision for the adjustment of an amount that would otherwise be payable under this subsection so as to avoid the payment of trivial or fractional amounts.

(2D) If the Inland Revenue pay any amount under subsection (2C) which they are not required to pay, they may recover that amount from the secondary contributor in such manner and at such time (or within such period) as may be prescribed.][4]][2]

(3) [Subject to sub-section (5A),][8] the [Inland Revenue][3] shall except in prescribed circumstances or in respect of prescribed periods pay in respect of that earner and that tax week to the [earner][9] or, in prescribed circumstances, to a prescribed person the amount by which—

(*a*) the appropriate age-related percentage of that part of those earnings,

exceeds

(*b*) the appropriate flat-rate percentage of that part of those earnings.

(4) Regulations may make provision—

(*a*) as to the manner in which and time at which or period within which payments under subsection (3) are to be made,

(*b*) for the adjustment of the amount which would otherwise be payable under that subsection so as to avoid the payment of trivial or fractional amounts,

(*c*) for earnings to be calculated or estimated in such manner and on such basis as may be prescribed for the purpose of determining whether any, and if so what, payments under subsection (3) are to be made.

(5) If the [Inland Revenue pay][3] an amount under subsection (3) which [they are][3] not required to pay or [are][3] not required to pay to the person to whom, or in respect of whom, [they pay][3] it, [they][3] may recover it from any person to whom, or in respect of whom, [they][3] paid it.

[(5A) Where a payment under subsection (3) is due in respect of an earner, HMRC are not required to make the payment if they determine that the cost to them of administering the payment would exceed the amount of the payment.][9]

(6) Where—

(*a*) an earner has ceased to be employed in an employment, and

(*b*) earnings are paid to him or for his benefit within the period of six weeks, or such other period as may be prescribed, from the day on which he so ceased,

NIC

that employment shall be treated for the purposes of this section as contracted-out employment at the time when the earnings are paid if it was contracted-out employment in relation to the earner when he was last employed in it.

(7) Subsection (3) of section 41 applies for the purposes of this section as it applies for the purposes of that.][1]

[(8) For the purposes of this section "the appropriate age-related percentage" and "the appropriate flat-rate percentage", in relation to a tax year beginning before [the first abolition date][10], are the percentages specified as such for that tax year in an order made under section 42B (as it had effect prior to that date).][6]

Cross references—SS (Reduced Rates of Class 1 Contributions and Rebates) (Money Purchase Contracted-out Schemes) Order, SI 1996/1055 (reduced rates of Class 1 contributions and rebates for the tax years 1997–98 to 2001–02).

FA 2004 Part 4, Chapter 4 (Registered pension schemes: tax reliefs and exemptions).

Regulations—SS (Reduced Rates of Class 1 Contributions, Rebates and Minimum Contributions), SI 2006/1009 art 3 (reduced rates of Class 1 contributions and rebates for the tax years 2007–08 to 2011–12).

Social Security (Reduced Rates of Class 1 Contributions, Rebates and Minimum Contributions) Order, SI 2011/1036 art 3: for the purposes of sub-s (2) the appropriate flat-rate percentage for the 2012–13 tax year is 1.4 per cent; for the purposes of sub-s (2A) the appropriate flat-rate percentage for the 2012–13 tax year is 1.0 per cent; for the purposes of sub-s (3) the appropriate age-related percentage in respect of an earner for the 2012–13 tax year is the percentage given in the table in SI 2011/1036 Schedule 1 by reference to the age of the earner on the day immediately before the start of that tax year.

Amendments—[1] Section, and preceding cross-heading, inserted by Pensions Act 1995 s 137(5) with effect from 13 March 1996, for the purpose only of authorising the making of orders, from 6 April 1996, for the purpose only of authorising the making of regulations, by virtue of SI 1996/778 art 2(1), (5)(*a*), and otherwise from 6 April 1997, by virtue of SI 1997/664 art 2, Sch Pt II.

[2] Sub-ss (1)–(2B) substituted by SSA 1998 Sch 7 para 128 with effect from 6 April 1999 by virtue of the Social Security Act 1998 (Commencement No 3) Order, SI 1999/418.

[3] Words in sub-ss (3) and (5) substituted by the Social Security Contributions (Transfer of Functions, etc) Act 1999 s 1(1) and Sch 1 para 46 with effect from 1 April 1999 by virtue of the Social Security Contributions (Transfer of Functions, etc) Act 1999 (Commencement No 1 and Transitional Provisions) Order, SI 1999/527.

[4] Words in sub-s (1) substituted and sub-ss (2)–(2D) substituted for original sub-ss (2)–(2B) by the Welfare Reform and Pensions Act 1999 s 73 Sch 9 para 7 with effect from 22 December 1999, for the purpose of the exercise of any power to make regulations, and 6 April 2000 for all other purposes.

[5] Words in sub-s (2) inserted by NICA 2002 s 6, Sch paras 35, 37 with effect from 2003–04.

[6] Sub-s (8) inserted by the Pensions Act 2007 s 15, Sch 4 para 17 with effect from 26 September 2007 (s 30(3)) subject to savings in Sch 4 Pt 3.

[7] In sub-s (1), words substituted for words "the current upper earnings limit for that week", by the NIC Act 2008 s 4, Sch 1 paras 1, 11 with effect in relation to 2009–10 and subsequent tax years.

[8] In sub-s (3), words inserted, and sub-s (5A) inserted, by the Pensions Act 2008 (Abolition of Protected Rights) (Consequential Amendments) (No. 2) Order, SI 2011/1730 art 5(1), (8) with effect from 6 April 2012.

[9] In sub-s (3), word substituted, and sub-s (5A) substituted, by the Pensions Act 2008 (Abolition of Protected Rights) (Consequential Amendments) (No 2) Order, SI 2011/1730 art 9(4) with effect from 6 April 2015.

[10] In sub-s (8), words substituted by PeA 2014 s 24, Sch 13 paras 1, 2 with effect from 6 April 2016 (PeA 2014 s 56(1), (4)).

Prospective amendments—This section to be repealed by the Pensions Act 2007 ss 15, 27, Sch 4 paras 46, 51, Sch 27 Pt 7 with effect from a date to be appointed.

[42B Determination and alteration of rates of contributions, and rebates, applicable under section 42A

(1) The Secretary of State shall at intervals of not more than five years lay before each House of Parliament—

(a) a report by the Government Actuary or the Deputy Government Actuary on the percentages which, in his opinion, are required to be specified in an order under this section so as to reflect the cost of providing benefits of an actuarial value equivalent to that of the benefits [(or parts of benefits) which, in accordance with section 48A below and Schedule 4A to the Social Security Contributions and Benefits Act 1992,][2] are foregone by or in respect of members of money purchase contracted-out schemes,

(b) a report by the Secretary of State stating what, in view of the report under paragraph (a), he considers those percentages should be, and

(c) a draft of an order under subsection (2).

(2) An order under this subsection shall have effect in relation to a period of tax years (not exceeding five) and may—

(a) specify different percentages for primary and secondary Class 1 contributions, and

(b) for each of the tax years for which it has effect—

(i) specify a percentage in respect of all earners which is "the appropriate flat-rate percentage" for the purposes of section 42A, and

(ii) specify different percentages (not being less than the percentage specified by virtue of sub-paragraph (i)) in respect of earners by reference to their ages on the last day of the preceding year (the percentage for each group of earners being "the appropriate age-related percentage" in respect of earners in that group for the purposes of section 42A).

(3) If the draft of an order under subsection (2) is approved by resolution of each House of Parliament, the Secretary of State shall make the order in the form of the draft.

(4) An order under subsection (2) shall have effect from the beginning of such tax year as may be specified in the order, not being a tax year earlier than the second after that in which the order is made.
(5) Subsection (2) is without prejudice to the generality of section 182.][1, 3]

Regulations—SS (Reduced Rates of Class 1 Contributions and Rebates) (Money Purchase Contracted-out Schemes) Order, SI 1996/1055.
SS (Reduced Rates of Class 1 Contributions, and Rebates) (Money Purchase Contracted-out Schemes) Order, SI 2001/1355.
SS (Reduced Rates of Class 1 Contributions, Rebates and Minimum Contributions), SI 2006/1009.
Social Security (Reduced Rates of Class 1 Contributions, Rebates and Minimum Contributions) Order, SI 2011/1036

Amendments—[1] Section inserted by Pensions Act 1995 s 137(5) with effect 13 March 1996, for the purpose only of authorising the making of orders, from 6 April 1996, for the purpose only of authorising the making of regulations, by virtue of SI 1996/778 art 2(1), (5)(*a*), and otherwise from 6 April 1997, by virtue of SI 1997/664 art 2, Sch Pt II.
[2] In sub-s (1)(*a*) words substituted by the Child Support, Pensions and Social Security Act 2000 ss 34, 86 with effect from 8 January 2001 for the purposes only of making regulations and orders, from 25 January 2001 for the purposes of making reports and orders under the Pension Schemes Act 1993 ss 42, 42B, 45A and from 6 April 2002 for all other purposes.
[3] This section repealed by the Pensions Act 2007 ss 15, 27, Sch 4 para 18, Sch 7 Pt 6 with effect from 26 September 2007 (s 30(3)) subject to savings in Sch 4 Pt 3.

Minimum contributions: members of appropriate personal pension schemes

43 Payment of minimum contributions to personal pension schemes

(1) Subject to the following provisions of this Part, the [Inland Revenue][1] shall, except in such circumstances [or in respect of such periods][2] as may be prescribed, pay minimum contributions in respect of an employed earner for any period during which the earner—
(*a*) is over the age of 16 but has not attained pensionable age;
(*b*) is not a married woman or widow who has made an election which is still operative that [so much of her liability in respect of primary Class 1 contributions as is attributable to section 8(1)(*a*) of the Social Security Contributions and Benefits Act 1992][3] shall be a liability to contribute at a reduced rate; and
(*c*) is a member of an appropriate personal pension scheme which is for the time being the earner's chosen scheme.

(2) Subject to subsection (3), minimum contributions in respect of an earner shall be paid to the [earner][6].
(3) In such circumstances as may be prescribed minimum contributions shall be paid to a prescribed person.
(4) Where the condition mentioned in subsection (1)(*a*) or (*c*) ceases to be satisfied in the case of an earner in respect of whom the [Inland Revenue][1] [are][1] required to pay minimum contributions, the duty of the [Inland Revenue][1] to pay them shall cease as from a date determined in accordance with regulations.
(5) If the [Inland Revenue][1] [pay][1] an amount by way of minimum contributions which [they] [are] not required to pay, [they][1] may recover it—
(*a*) from the person to whom [they][1] paid it, or
(*b*) from any person in respect of whom [they][1] paid it.
(6) If the [Inland Revenue][1] [pay][1] in respect of an earner an amount by way of minimum contributions which [they][1] [are][1] required to pay, but [do][1] not pay it to the trustees or managers of the earner's chosen scheme, [they][1] may recover it from the person to whom [they][1] paid it or from the earner.
[(6A) Where a payment under subsection (1) is due in respect of an earner, HMRC are not required to make the payment if they determine that the cost to them of administering the payment would exceed the amount of the payment.][6]
[(7) In this section "the earner's chosen scheme" means the scheme which was immediately before [the first abolition date][7] the earner's chosen scheme in accordance with section 44 (as it had effect prior to that date).][4]

Cross references—See FA 2004 Part 4, Chapter 4 (Registered pension schemes: tax reliefs and exemptions).

Amendments—[1] Words in sub-ss (1), (4)–(6) substituted by the Social Security Contributions (Transfer of Functions, etc) Act 1999 s 1(1), Sch 1 para 47(1), (2), (5) with effect from 25 February 1999, for the purpose of making regulations (SSC(TF)A 1999 s 28(2)(*b*)); and 1 April 1999 for all other purposes (SI 1999/527).
[2] Words in sub-s (1) inserted by the Pensions Act 1995, s 151, Sch 5, para 42 with effect from 6 April 1997 (by virtue of SI 1997/664 art 2(3), Schedule Pt II).
[3] Words in sub-s (1)(*b*) substituted by NICA 2002 s 6, Sch 1 paras 35, 38 with effect from 2003–04.
[4] Sub-s (7) inserted by the Pensions Act 2007 s 15, Sch 4 para 19 with effect from 26 September 2007 (s 30(3)) subject to savings in Sch 4 Pt 3.
[5] Sub-s (6A) inserted by the Pensions Act 2008 (Abolition of Protected Rights) (Consequential Amendments) (No 2) Order, SI 2011/1730 art 5(1), (9) with effect from 6 April 2012.
[6] In sub-s (2), word substituted, and sub-s (6A) substituted, by the Pensions Act 2008 (Abolition of Protected Rights) (Consequential Amendments) (No 2) Order, SI 2011/1730 art 9(5) with effect from 6 April 2015.
[7] In sub-s (7), words substituted by PeA 2014 s 24, Sch 13 paras 1, 2 with effect from 6 April 2016 (PeA 2014 s 56(1), (4)).

Prospective amendments—This section to be repealed by the Pensions Act 2007 ss 15, 27, Sch 4 paras 46, 52, Sch 27 Pt 7 with effect from a date to be appointed.

NIC

44 Earner's chosen scheme

(1) Where an earner and the trustees or managers of an appropriate personal pension scheme have jointly given notice to the [Inland Revenue][2], in such manner and form and with such supporting evidence as may be prescribed—

(a) that the earner is, or intends to become, a member of the scheme and wishes minimum contributions in respect of him to be paid to the scheme under section 43;

(b) that the trustees or managers have agreed to accept him as a member of the scheme and to receive such minimum contributions in respect of him,

[then, unless the [Inland Revenue][2] [reject][2] the notice on either or both of the grounds mentioned in subsection (1A)] that scheme is the earner's chosen scheme for the purposes of section 43 as from a date determined in accordance with regulations and specified in the notice, unless at that date some other appropriate scheme is the earner's chosen scheme for those purposes.

[(1A) The grounds referred to in subsection (1) are that the [Inland Revenue][2] [are][2] of the opinion—

(a) that section 31(5) is not being complied with in respect of any members of the scheme,

(b) that, having regard to any other provisions of sections 26 to 32 and 43 to 45, it is inexpedient to allow the scheme to be the chosen scheme of any further earners.][1]

(2) Either an earner or the trustees or managers of the scheme may cancel a notice under subsection (1) by giving notice to that effect to the [Inland Revenue][2] at such time and in such manner and form as may be prescribed.

(3) When a notice under subsection (2) is given, the scheme ceases to be the earner's chosen scheme as from a date determined in accordance with regulations and specified in the notice.[3]

Amendments—[1] Sub-s (1A) inserted by the Pensions Act 1995 s 164(*b*) with effect from 6 April 1997 (by virtue of SI 1997/664).

[2] Words in sub-ss (1), (1A) and (2) substituted by the Social Security Contributions (Transfer of Functions, etc) Act 1999 s 1(1), Sch 1 para 48(1)–(3) with effect from 25 February 1999, for certain purposes (SSC(TF)A 1999 s 28(2)(*a*)); and 1 April 1999 for all other purposes (SI 1999/527).

[3] This section repealed by the Pensions Act 2007 ss 15, 27, Sch 4 para 20, Sch 7 Pt 6 with effect from 26 September 2007 (s 30(3)) subject to savings in Sch 4 Pt 3.

45 Amount of minimum contributions

[(1) In relation to any tax week falling within a period for which the [Inland Revenue are][2] required to pay minimum contributions in respect of an earner, the amount of those contributions shall be an amount equal to the appropriate age-related percentage of so much of the earnings paid in that week (other than earnings in respect of contracted-out employment) as exceeds the current lower earnings limit but not [the upper accrual point][4] (or the prescribed equivalents if he is paid otherwise than weekly).][1]

(2) . . . [1]

(3) Regulations may make provision—

(*a*) for earnings to be calculated or estimated in such manner and on such basis as may be prescribed for the purpose of determining whether any, and if so what, minimum contributions are payable in respect of them;

(*b*) for the adjustment of the amount which would otherwise be payable by way of minimum contributions so as to avoid the payment of trivial or fractional amounts;

(*c*) for the intervals at which, for the purposes of minimum contributions, payments of earnings are to be treated as made;

(*d*) . . . [1]

(*e*) for this section to have effect in prescribed cases as if for any reference to a tax week there were substituted a reference to a prescribed period, . . .[1]

(*f*) as to the manner in which and time at which or period within which minimum contributions are to be made.

[(4) For the purposes of this section "the appropriate age-related percentage", in relation to a tax year beginning before [the first abolition date][5], is the percentage (or percentages) specified as such for that tax year in an order made under section 45A (as it had effect prior to that date).][3]

Cross references—See FA 2004 Part 4, Chapter 4 (Registered pension schemes: tax reliefs and exemptions).

SS (Reduced Rates of Class 1 Contributions, Rebates and Minimum Contributions), SI 2006/1009.

Social Security (Reduced Rates of Class 1 Contributions, Rebates and Minimum Contributions) Order, SI 2011/1036 art 4: determination of the appropriate age-related percentage in respect of earnings of an earner for the 2012–13 tax year.

Amendments—[1] Sub-s (1) substituted, sub-s (2), (3)(*d*) and words in sub-s (3)(*e*) repealed, by the Pensions Act 1995 s 138(2)–(4), 151, 177, Sch 5 para 43, Sch 7 Pt III with effect from 6 April 1997 (by virtue of SI 1997/664).

[2] Words in sub-s (1) substituted by the Social Security Contributions (Transfer of Functions, etc) Act 1999 s 1(1), Sch 1 para 49 with effect from 25 February 1999, for the purpose of making regulations (SSC(TF)A 1999 s 28(2)(*b*)), and 1 April 1999 for all other purposes (SI 1999/527).

[3] Sub-s (4) inserted by the Pensions Act 2007 s 15, Sch 4 para 21 with effect from 26 September 2007 (s 30(3)) subject to savings in Sch 4 Pt 3.

[4] In sub-s (1), words substituted for words "the current upper earnings limit for that week", by the NIC Act 2008 s 4, Sch 1 paras 1, 12 with effect in relation to 2009–10 and subsequent tax years.

[5] In sub-s (4), words substituted by PeA 2014 s 24, Sch 13 paras 1, 2 with effect from 6 April 2016 (PeA 2014 s 56(1), (4)),

Prospective amendments—This section to be repealed by the Pensions Act 2007 ss 15, 27, Sch 4 paras 46, 53, Sch 27 Pt 7 with effect from a date to be appointed.

[45A Determination and alteration of rates of minimum contributions under section 45

(1) The Secretary of State shall at intervals of not more than five years lay before each House of Parliament—

(a) a report by the Government Actuary or the Deputy Government Actuary on the percentages which, in his opinion, are required to be specified in an order under this section so as to reflect the cost of providing benefits of an actuarial value equivalent to that of the benefits [(or parts of benefits) which, in accordance with section 48A below and Schedule 4A to the Social Security Contributions and Benefits Act 1992,][2] are foregone by or in respect of members of appropriate personal pension schemes,

(b) a report by the Secretary of State stating what, in view of the report under paragraph (a), he considers those percentages should be, and

(c) a draft of an order under subsection (2).

(2) An order under this subsection—

(a) shall have effect in relation to a period of tax years (not exceeding five), and

(b) may, for each of the tax years for which it has effect, specify different percentages in respect of earners by reference to their ages on the last day of the preceding year (the percentage for each group of earners being "the appropriate age-related percentage" in respect of earners in that group for the purposes of section 45).

(3) If the draft of an order under subsection (2) is approved by resolution of each House of Parliament, the Secretary of State shall make the order in the form of the draft.

(4) An order under subsection (2) shall have effect from the beginning of such tax year as may be specified in the order, not being a tax year earlier than the second after that in which the order is made.

(5) Subsection (2) is without prejudice to the generality of section 182.][1, 3]

Regulations—See the Social Security (Minimum Contributions to Appropriate Personal Pension Schemes) Order, SI 1996/1056.
Social Security (Minimum Contributions to Appropriate Personal Pension Schemes) Order, SI 1998/944.
Social Security (Minimum Contributions to Appropriate Personal Pension Schemes) Order, SI 2001/1354.
SS (Reduced Rates of Class 1 Contributions, Rebates and Minimum Contributions), SI 2006/1009.

Amendments—[1] Inserted by the Pensions Act 1995 s 138(5) with effect from 13 March 1996 for the purpose only of authorising the making of orders (by virtue of SI 1996/778), and from 6 April 1997 for all other purposes (by virtue of SI 1997/664).

[2] Words in sub-s (1)(*a*) substituted by the Child Support, Pensions and Social Security Act 2000 s 34 with effect from 8 January 2001 for the purpose of making subordinate legislation (by virtue of SI 2000/2950), and 25 January 2001 for all other purposes (by virtue of SI 2001/153).

[3] This section repealed by the Pensions Act 2007 ss 15, 27, Sch 4 para 22, Sch 7 Pt 6 with effect from 26 September 2007 (s 30(3)) subject to savings in Sch 4 Pt 3.

45B Money purchase and personal pension schemes: verification of ages

Amendments—This section repealed by the Pensions Act 2007 ss 15, 27, Sch 4 paras 46, 54, Sch 27 Pt 7 with effect from 6 April 2015 (by virtue of SI 2011/1267 art 3(*a*)(iii), (iv)).

PART XI
GENERAL AND MISCELLANEOUS PROVISIONS

Information about schemes

158 Disclosure of information between government departments etc

(1) No obligation as to secrecy imposed by statute or otherwise on [Revenue and Customs officials][5] shall prevent information obtained or held in connection with the assessment or collection of income tax from being disclosed—

(*a*) to the Secretary of State,

(*b*) to the Department of Health and Social Services for Northern Ireland, or

(*c*) to an officer of either of them authorised to receive such information, in connection with the operation of this Act (except Chapter II of Part VII and sections 157 and 161) or of any corresponding enactment of Northern Ireland legislation.

[(1A) No obligation as to secrecy imposed by statute or otherwise on [Revenue and Customs officials][5] shall prevent information obtained or held for the purposes of Part III of this Act from being disclosed—

(*a*) to the Secretary of State,

(*b*) to the Department of Health and Social Services for Northern Ireland, or

(*c*) to an officer of either of them authorised to receive such information,

in connection with the operation of this Act or of any corresponding enactment of Northern Ireland legislation.][3]

(2)–(3) . . . [1]

(4) In relation to persons who are carrying on or have carried on [wholly or partly in the United Kingdom][4] a trade, profession or vocation income from which is chargeable to tax under [Part 2 of the Income Tax (Trading and Other Income) Act 2005 or][4] Case I or II of Schedule D, disclosure

under subsection (1) relating to that trade, profession or vocation shall be limited to information about the commencement or cessation of, and employed earners engaged in, that trade, profession or vocation, but sufficient information may also be given to identify the persons concerned.

(5) [Subsections (1) and (1A)][3] extend only to disclosure by or under the authority of the Inland Revenue.

(6) . . . [6] Information which is the subject of disclosure to any person by virtue of subsection (1) [or (1A)][3], *(2) or (3)*[1] shall not be further disclosed to any other person, except where the further disclosure is made—

(*a*) to a person to whom disclosure could by virtue of this section have been made by or under the authority of the Inland Revenue; or

(*b*) for the purposes of any civil or criminal proceedings in connection with the operation of this Act (except Chapter II of Part VII and sections 157 and 161); or

(*c*) for the purposes of [Chapter II of Part I of the Social Security Act 1998][2] or any corresponding provisions of Northern Ireland legislation; . . . [1][or

(*ca*) for the purposes of Part II of the Social Security Contributions (Transfer of Functions, etc) Act 1999 or any corresponding provisions of Northern Ireland legislation.][3]

(*d*) . . . [1]

(7) . . . [6]

(8) . . . [1]

[(9) In this section "Revenue and Customs officials" has the meaning given by section 18 of the Commissioners for Revenue and Customs Act 2005 (confidentiality).][5]

Former enactments—Sub-s (1): SSA 1973 ss 89(1), 99(1); SSA 1986 s 59(1).
Sub-s (2): SSA 1973 s 89(2).
Sub-s (3): SSA 1973 s 89(2A).
Sub-s (4): SSA 1986 s 59(2).
Sub-ss (5), (6): SSA 1973 s 89(3); SSA 1986 s 59(3).
Sub-s (7): SSPA 1975 s 59K(6).
Sub-s (8): SSPA 1975 s 57; SI 1987/1116, reg 3(9)

Amendments—[1] Sub-ss (2), (3), (6)(*d*) (and preceding word "or"), (8) repealed by the Pensions Act 1995 Sch 5 paras 18, 66, Sch 7 Pt III with effect from 6 April 1997, by virtue of SI 1997/664 art 2, Sch Pt II.

[2] Words in sub-s (6)(*c*) substituted by SSA 1998 Sch 7 para 129 with effect from 29 November 1999, for certain purposes (by virtue of the Social Security Act 1998 (Commencement No 12 and Consequential and Transitional Provisions) Order, SI 1999/3178, art 2(1), Sch 1 (subject to transitional provisions contained in art 4 Schs 21–23 thereof)), and with effect from a date to be appointed for all other purposes.

[3] Sub-s (1A), words in sub-s (6) and sub-s (6)(*ca*) inserted, and words in sub-s (5) substituted by the Social Security Contributions (Transfer of Functions, etc) Act 1999 s 6 and Sch 6 para 7 with effect from 1 April 1999 by virtue of the Social Security Contributions (Transfer of Functions, etc) Act 1999 (Commencement No 1 and Transitional Provisions) Order, SI 1999/527.

[4] Words in sub-s (4) inserted by ITTOIA 2005 s 882(1), Sch 1 paras 467, 468 with effect from 6 April 2005. ITTOIA 2005 has effect—

(a) for income tax purposes, for 2005–06 and subsequent tax years, and

(b) for corporation tax purposes, for accounting periods ending after 5 April 2005: ITTOIA 2005 s 883(1).

[5] Words substituted, and sub-s (9) inserted, by CRCA 2005 s 50, Sch 4 para 51 with effect from 18 April 2005 (by virtue of SI 2005/1126).

[6] Words in sub-s (6) repealed, and sub-s (7) repealed, by the Pensions Act 2004 s 320, Sch 13 Pt 1 with effect from 6 April 2006 (by virtue of SI 2006/560, art 2(3), Schedule, Pt 3).

[158A Other disclosures by the Secretary of State

(1) The Secretary of State may, in spite of any obligation as to secrecy or confidentiality imposed by statute or otherwise on him or on persons employed in [the Department for Work and Pensions][5], disclose [any regulated information][6] to any person specified in the first column of the following Table if he considers that the disclosure would enable or assist the person to discharge the functions specified in relation to the person in the second column of the Table.

TABLE

Persons	*Functions*
. . . [4]	. . . [4]
The Bank of England.	[Any of its functions[, apart from its functions as the Prudential Regulation Authority][8].][2]
[The Financial Conduct Authority	Any of its functions][7]
[The Prudential Regulation Authority	Any of its functions][7]

The Regulatory Authority.	Functions under this Act[, the Pensions Act 1995, the Welfare Reform and Pensions Act 1999 or the Pensions Act 2004 or any enactment in force in Northern Ireland corresponding to any of those enactments.][6].
[The Pensions Ombudsman.	Functions conferred by or by virtue of this Act or any enactment in force in Northern Ireland corresponding to it.][6]
[The Board of the Pension Protection Fund.	Functions conferred by or by virtue of Part 2 of the Pensions Act 2004 or any enactment in force in Northern Ireland corresponding to that Part.][6]
[The Ombudsman for the Board of the Pension Protection Fund.	Functions conferred by or by virtue of Part 2 of the Pensions Act 2004 or any enactment in force in Northern Ireland corresponding to that Part.][6]
[A person appointed under— (*a*) section 167 of the Financial Services and Markets Act 2000, (*b*) subsections (3) or (5) of section 168 of that Act, or (*c*) section 284 of that Act, to conduct an investigation.	Functions in relation to that investigation.][4]
[A body designated under section 326(1) of the Financial Services and Markets Act 2000	Functions in its capacity as a body designated under that section.][4]
[A recognised investment exchange or a recognised clearing house (as defined by section 285 of that Act).	Functions in its capacity as an exchange or clearing house recognised under that Act.][4]
. . .[4]	. . .[4]

[(1AA) In subsection (1), "regulated information" means information received by the Secretary of State in connection with his functions under—

(*a*) this Act,

(*b*) the Pensions Act 1995, or

(*c*) the Pensions Act 2004,

other than information supplied to him under section 235(2) of, or paragraph 2 of Schedule 10 to, the Pensions Act 2004 (supply of information for retirement planning purposes etc).][6]

[(1A) The Inland Revenue may, in spite of any obligation as to secrecy or confidentiality imposed by statute or otherwise on them or on their officers, disclose any information received by them in connection with their functions under Part III of this Act to any person specified in the first column of the Table in subsection (1) if they consider that the disclosure would enable or assist the person to discharge the functions specified in relation to the person in the second column of the Table.][3]

(2) The Secretary of State may by order—

(*a*) amend the Table in subsection (1) by—

(i) adding any person exercising regulatory functions and specifying functions in relation to that person,

(ii) removing any person for the time being specified in the Table, or

(iii) altering the functions for the time being specified in the Table in relation to any person, or

(*b*) restrict the circumstances in which, or impose conditions subject to which, disclosure may be made to any person for the time being specified in the Table.][1]

Amendments—[1] This section inserted by Pensions Act 1995 s 173, Sch 6 para 9 with effect from 6 April 1996 by virtue of SI 1996/778 art 2(4).

[2] Words amended and inserted by Bank of England Act 1998 with effect from 23 April 1998.

[3] Sub-s (1A) inserted by the Social Security Contributions (Transfer of Functions, etc) Act 1999 s 6 and Sch 6 para 8 with effect from 1 April 1999 by virtue of the Social Security Contributions (Transfer of Functions, etc) Act 1999 (Commencement No 1 and Transitional Provisions) Order, SI 1999/527.

[4] In sub-s (1), Table, words repealed, and words substituted and inserted, by the Financial Services and Markets Act 2000 (Consequential Amendments and Repeals) Order, SI 2001/3649 art 124 with effect from 1 December 2001.

[5] Words in sub-s (1) substituted by the Secretaries of State for Education and Skills and for Work and Pensions Order, SI 2002/1397 art 12, Schedule para 9(1), (3) with effect from 27 June 2002.

[6] Words in sub-s (1) substituted and sub-s (1AA) inserted by the Pensions Act 2004 s 319(1), Sch 12 paras 9, 26 with effect from 6 April 2005 (by virtue of SI 2005/275).

7 In sub-s (1), Table, entries for "The Financial Conduct Authority" and "The Prudential Regulation Authority" substituted for the former entry relating to the Financial Services Authority, by the Financial Services Act 2012 s 114(1), Sch 18 para 78(3) with effect from 1 April 2013 (by virtue of SI 2013/423 art 3, Schedule).

8 In sub-s (1), Table col 2, in entry for "Bank of England", words inserted by the Bank of England and Financial Services (Consequential Amendments) Regulations, SI 2017/80 reg 8(*a*) with effect from 1 March 2017.

170 Decisions and appeals

(1) Section 2 (use of computers) of the Social Security Act 1998 ("the 1998 Act") applies as if, for the purposes of subsection (1) of that section, this Act were a relevant enactment.

[(2) It shall be for an officer of the Inland Revenue—

(*a*) to make any decision that falls to be made under or by virtue of Part III of this Act, other than a decision which under or by virtue of that Part falls to be made by the Secretary of State;

(*b*) to decide any issue arising in connection with payments under section 7 of the Social Security Act 1986 (occupational pension schemes becoming contracted-out between 1986 and 1993); and

(*c*) to decide any issue arising by virtue of regulations made under paragraph 15 of Schedule 3 to the Social Security (Consequential Provisions) Act 1992 (continuing in force of certain enactments repealed by the Social Security Act 1973).

(3) In the following provisions of this section a "relevant decision" means any decision which under subsection (2) falls to be made by an officer of the Inland Revenue, other than a decision under section 53 . . . [5].

(4) Sections 9 and 10 of the 1998 Act (revision of decisions and decisions superseding earlier decisions) apply as if—

(*a*) any reference in those sections to a decision of the Secretary of State under section 8 of that Act included a reference to a relevant decision; and

(*b*) any other reference in those sections to the Secretary of State were, in relation to a relevant decision, a reference to an officer of the Inland Revenue.

(5) Regulations may make provision—

(*a*) generally with respect to the making of relevant decisions;

(*b*) with respect to the procedure to be adopted on any application made under section 9 or 10 of the 1998 Act by virtue of subsection (4); and

(*c*) generally with respect to such applications, revisions under section 9 and decisions under section 10;][3]

but may not prevent [a revision under section 9 or decision under section 10][3] being made without such an application.

(6) Section 12 of the 1998 Act (appeal to [First-tier Tribunal][4]) applies as if, for the purposes of subsection (1)(*b*) of that section, a relevant decision were a decision of the Secretary of State falling within Schedule 3 to the 1998 Act.

(7) The following provisions of the 1998 Act (which relate to decisions and appeals)—

sections 13 to 18,
sections 25 and 26,
section 28, and
Schedules 4 and 5,

shall apply in relation to any appeal under section 12 of the 1998 Act by virtue of subsection (6) above as if any reference to the Secretary of State were a reference to an officer of the Inland Revenue.][2][1]

Cross references—Social Security Contributions, etc (Decisions and Appeals—Transitional Modifications) Regulations, SI 1999/978.

Modifications—See Social Security Contributions, etc (Decisions and Appeals—Transitional Modifications) Regulations, SI 1999/978. Until Chapter II of Part I of the Social Security Act 1998 (social security decisions and appeals) is wholly in force, any enactment specified in column (1) of the Schedule to SI 1999/978 shall have effect subject to the modifications specified in column (2) of that Schedule.

Amendments—1 Substituted by SSA 1998 Sch 7 para 131 with effect from 4 March 1999 in so far as they authorise the making of regulations.

2 Sub-ss (2) to (4) substituted by new sub-ss (2) to (7) by the Social Security Contributions (Transfer of Functions, etc) Act 1999 s 16 with effect from 14 June 1999 for the purposes only of authorising the making of regulations, and from 5 July 1999 for all other purposes.

3 Sub-s (5)(*a*)–(*c*) substituted for sub-s (5)(*a*), (*b*) and words substituted by the Welfare Reform and Pensions Act 1999, s 81, Sch 11, paras 20, 22(*a*) with effect from 11 November 1999.

4 In sub-s (6), words substituted for words "appeal tribunal" by the Transfer of Tribunal Functions Order, SI 2008/2833 art 6, Sch 3 with effect from 3 November 2008.

5 In sub-s (3), words revoked by the Pensions Act 2008 (Abolition of Protected Rights) (Consequential Amendments) (No 2) Order, SI 2011/1730 art 5(1), (19) with effect from 6 April 2012.

173 References and appeals from the Board

Amendments—This section repealed by the Pensions Act 1995 Sch 5 paras 18, 72, Sch 7 Pt III with effect from 6 April 1997, by virtue of SI 1997/664 art 2, Sch Pt II.

PART XII
SUPPLEMENTARY PROVISIONS

Interpretation

181 General interpretation

(1) In this Act, unless the context otherwise requires—

. . . [9]

. . .

"age", in relation to any person, shall be construed so that—

(*a*) he is over or under a particular age if he has or, as the case may be, has not attained that age;

(*b*) he is between two particular ages if he has attained the first but not the second;

["appropriate scheme" and "appropriate scheme certificate" are to be construed in accordance with [section 7B][9];][12]

. . . [3]

. . .

"contracted-out employment" shall be construed in accordance with section 8;

. . .

"contracting-out certificate" and references to a contracted-out scheme and to contracting-out shall be construed in accordance with [section 7B][17];

. . .

"earner" and "earnings" shall be construed in accordance with [section 8(1B) of this Act and][9] sections 3, 4 and 112 of the Social Security Contributions and Benefits Act 1992;

. . .

["employed earner" and "self-employed earner" have the meanings given by section 2 of the Social Security Contributions and Benefits Act 1992;][8]

"employee" means a person gainfully employed in Great Britain either under a contract of service or in an office (including an elective office) with [earnings][15];

"employer" means—

(*a*) in the case of an employed earner employed under a contract of service, his employer;

(*b*) in the case of an employed earner employed in an office with emoluments—

(i) such person as may be prescribed in relation to that office; or

(ii) if no person is prescribed, the government department, public authority or body of persons responsible for paying the emoluments of the office;

"employment" includes any trade, business, profession, office or vocation and "employed" shall be construed accordingly except in the expression "employed earner";

. . . [1]

["the first abolition date" has the meaning given by section 7A;][9]

. . . [13]

"guaranteed minimum pension" has the meaning given in section 8(2);

["HMRC" means the Commissioners for Her Majesty's Revenue and Customs;][12]

"independent trade union" has the same meaning as in the Trade Union and Labour Relations (Consolidation) Act 1992;

["employment tribunal"][5] means a tribunal established or having effect as if established under [section 1(1) of the Employment Tribunals Act 1996 (previously the Industrial Tribunals Act 1996)][5];

. . .

"lower earnings limit" and "upper earnings limit" shall be construed in accordance with section 5 of the Social Security Contributions and Benefits Act 1992 and "current", in relation to those limits, means for the time being in force;

. . .

"minimum payment" has the meaning given in section 8(2);

. . .

["money purchase contracted-out scheme" is to be construed in accordance with [section 7B][9];][12]

. . .

"occupational pension scheme" has the meaning given in section 1;

. . .

["pensionable age"—

(*a*) so far as any provisions (other than sections 46 to 48) relate to guaranteed minimum pensions, means the age of 65 in the case of a man and the age of 60 in the case of a woman, and

(*b*) in any other case, has the meaning given by the rules in paragraph 1 of Schedule 4 to the Pensions Act 1995][2];

NIC

["pension debit" means a debit under section 29(1)(a) of the Welfare Reform and Pensions Act 1999;][7]

. . .

"prescribe" means prescribe by regulations and "prescribed" shall be construed accordingly;

. . . [6]

. . .

"primary Class 1 contributions" and "secondary Class 1 contributions" have the same meanings as in the Social Security Contributions and Benefits Act 1992;

. . .

["the principal appointed day" means 6 April 1997 (which is the day designated as the principal appointed day for the purposes of Part 3 of the Pensions Act 1995);][9]

"regulations" means regulations made by the Secretary of State under this Act;

. . . [8]

. . . [3]

. . .

["salary related contracted-out scheme" is to be construed in accordance with section 7B;][9]

["the second abolition date" has the meaning given by section 7A;][9]

"tax week" means one of the successive periods in a tax year beginning with the first day of that year and every seventh day thereafter, the last day of a tax year (or, in a leap year, the last two days) being treated accordingly as a separate tax week;

"tax year" means the 12 months beginning with 6th April in any year;

["the upper accrual point" has the meaning given by section 122 of the Social Security Contributions and Benefits Act 1992;][11]

. . .

(2) References to employers in the provisions of this Act (other than sections 123 to 127, 157, [and 160][4] ("the excluded provisions")) are to be treated, in relation to persons within the application of an occupational pension scheme and qualifying or prospectively qualifying for its benefits, as including references to persons who in relation to them and their employment are treated by regulations as being employers for the purposes of those provisions.

(3) Subject to any such regulations, references to an employer in any of the provisions of this Act (other than the excluded provisions or . . . [10] Chapter I of Part IV, Part VIII so far as it applies for the purposes of Chapter I of Part IV, sections . . . [3], 153(2), 158(1) to (5), 162, 163, . . . [3] and 176 . . . [3]) shall, in relation to an earner employed in an office with emoluments, be construed as references to—

(*a*) such person as may be prescribed in relation to that office; or

(*b*) if no person is prescribed, the government department, public authority or body of persons responsible for paying the emoluments of that office.

(4) Regulations may for any purpose of any provision of this Act (other than the excluded provisions or section . . . [10], . . . [14] . . . [16] . . . [14] 43 . . . [12], 111, 160, 164, 165 or 169) prescribe the persons who are to be regarded as members or prospective members of an occupational pension scheme and as to the times at which and the circumstances in which a person is to be treated as becoming, or as ceasing to be, a member or prospective member.

(5) . . .

(6) Any reference in section 185 or 186 to an order or regulations under this Act includes a reference to an order or regulations made under any provision of an enactment passed after this Act and directed to be construed as one with it; but this subsection applies only so far as a contrary intention is not expressed in the enactment so passed, and shall be without prejudice to the generality of any such direction.

(7) . . .

Regulations—Occupational and Personal Pension Schemes (Disclosure of Information) (Amendment) Regulations, SI 2015/482.

Occupational Pension Schemes (Consequential and Miscellaneous Amendments) Regulations, SI 2015/493.

Occupational and Personal Pension Schemes (Transfer Values) (Amendment and Revocation) Regulations, SI 2015/498.

Occupational Pension Schemes (Charges and Governance) Regulations, SI 2015/879

Occupational Pension Schemes (Schemes that were Contracted-out) Regulations, SI 2015/1452.

Occupational Pension Schemes and Social Security (Schemes that were Contracted-out and Graduated Retirement Benefit) (Miscellaneous Amendments) Regulations, SI 2017/354.

Note—Omitted provisions are not relevant for the purposes of this publication.

Amendments—[1] Definition "equal access requirements" in sub-s (1) repealed by Pensions Act 1995 Sch 3 para 44(*a*)(i), Sch 7 Pt I with effect from 1 January 1996 by virtue of SI 1995/3104 art 2(3).

[2] Definition "pensionable age" in sub-s (1) substituted by the Pensions Act 1995 s 126(*c*), Sch 4 Pt III para 17 with effect from 19 July 1995.

[3] Definitions "the Board" and "state scheme premium" in sub-s (1), and words in sub-s (3), repealed, by Pensions Act 1995 Sch 5 paras 18, 77(*a*)(i), (*b*), Sch 6 paras 2, 14, Sch 7 Pts III, IV with effect from 6 April 1997, by virtue of SI 1997/664 art 2, Sch Pt II.

[4] Words in sub-s (2) substituted by Pensions Act 1995 Sch 3 para 44(*b*) with effect from 6 April 1997, by virtue of SI 1997/664 art 2, Sch Pt II.

Words in definition "employment tribunal" substituted by the Employment Tribunals Act 1996 s 43, Sch 1 para 11, formerly the Industrial Tribunals Act 1996. The definition of "employment tribunal" was previously "industrial tribunal" and renamed by the Employment Rights (Dispute Resolution) Act 1998 s 1, with effect from 1 August 1998, by virtue of SI 1998/1658.
Definition of "the prescribed equivalent" repealed by the Welfare Reform and Pensions Act 1999 s 88 Sch 13, Pt VI with effect from 6 April 2000.
Definition of "pension debit" inserted by the Welfare Reform and Pensions Act 1999, s 32(5) with effect from 11 November 1999, for the purpose of the exercise of any power to make regulations (s 89(5)(*a*)) and 1 December 2000 for all other purposes (by virtue of SI 2000/1047).
Definition of "employed earner" substituted and definition of "self-employed pension arrangement" repealed by the Welfare Reform and Pensions Act 1999, s 18, Sch 2 para 3(1)(*b*), (2)(*c*), with effect from 25 April 2000 (by virtue of SI 2000/1047).
In sub-s (1), the following amendments made by PeA 2014 s 24, Sch 13 paras 1, 43 with effect from 6 April 2016 (PeA 2014 s 56(1), (4))—

- definitions inserted;
- definition of "abolition date" repealed;
- in definition of "appropriate scheme" and "appropriate scheme certificate", words substituted;
- in definition of "contracting-out certificate", words substituted;
- in definition of "earner" and "earnings", words inserted; and
- in definition of "money purchase contracted-out scheme", words substituted.

10 Words in sub-s (3), and word in sub-s (4) repealed by the Pensions Act 2004 s 320, Sch 13 Pt 1 with effect from 6 April 2005 (by virtue of SI 2005/695, art 2(7), Sch 1).
11 Definition of "the upper accrual point" inserted by the Pensions Act 2007 s 12(4), Sch 1 para 38 with effect from 26 September 2007 (s 30(3)).
12 In sub-s (1), definition of "HMRC" inserted; definition of "'appropriate scheme' and 'appropriate scheme certificate'" substituted; definition of "money purchase contracted-out scheme" substituted; and reference in sub-s (4) repealed; by the Pensions Act 2007 ss 15, 27, Sch 4 para 34, Sch 7 Pt 6 with effect from 26 September 2007 (s 30(3)) subject to savings in Sch 4 Pt 3.
13 In sub-s (1), definition of "the flat rate introduction year" repealed by the NIC Act 2008 s 4, Sch 2 with effect in relation to 2009–10 and subsequent tax years.
14 In sub-s (4), words "27, 28, 29," and "32," revoked by the Pensions Act 2008 (Abolition of Protected Rights) (Consequential Amendments) (No 2) Order, SI 2011/1730 art 5(1), (22) with effect from 6 April 2012.
15 In sub-s (1), in definition of "employee", word substituted for words "general earnings (as defined by section 7 of the Income Tax (Earnings and Pensions) Act 2003)" by NICs Act 2014 s 15, Sch 2 para 13 with effect from 14 May 2014.
16 In sub-s (4), words revoked by the Pensions Act 2008 (Abolition of Protected Rights) (Consequential Amendments) (No 2) Order, SI 2011/1730 art 9(7) with effect from 6 April 2015.

Prospective amendments—In sub-s (1) definition of "minimum contributions", and in sub-s (4) words ", 43", to be repealed by the Pensions Act 2007 ss 15, 27, Sch 4 paras 46, 58, Sch 27 Pt 7 with effect from a date to be appointed.

181A Interpretation of references to money purchase contracted-out schemes or appropriate schemes after abolition date

(1) This section applies for the interpretation of this Act on and after the abolition date.

(2) An occupational pension scheme was a money purchase contracted-out scheme at a time before the abolition date if, at that time, the scheme was contracted-out by virtue of satisfying section 9(3) (as it then had effect).

(3) A money purchase contracted-out scheme was, at a time before the abolition date, a contracted-out scheme in relation to an earner's employment if it was, at that time, specified in a contracting-out certificate in relation to that employment; and references to the contracting-out of a scheme are, in relation to a money purchase contracted-out scheme, references to its inclusion in such a certificate.

(4) Any reference to a contracting-out certificate is, in relation to a money purchase contracted-out scheme, a reference to a certificate issued by virtue of section 7, as it had effect before the abolition date, in relation to the employment of an earner in employed earner's employment which was contracted-out by reference to that scheme.

(5) Any certificate so issued that was, at a time before the abolition date, in force in respect of an employed earner's employment is to be taken as conclusive that the employment was, at that time, contracted-out employment.

(6) A personal pension scheme was an appropriate scheme at a time before the abolition date if, at that time, there was in force a certificate issued under section 7(1)(b) (as it then had effect) stating that the scheme was an appropriate scheme; and "appropriate scheme certificate" means such a certificate.

(7) Any appropriate scheme certificate in force in relation to a scheme at any time before the abolition date is to be taken as conclusive that the scheme was, at that time, an appropriate scheme.[1]

Amendments—[1] Section 181A repealed by PeA 2014 s 24, Sch 13 paras 1, 44 with effect from 6 April 2016 (PeA 2014 s 56(1), (4)).

Subordinate legislation etc

182 Orders and regulations (general provisions)

(1) Any power under this Act to make regulations or orders (except a power of . . . [1] the court to make orders) and the powers to make rules under sections 149(2) and 152(1) shall be exercisable by statutory instrument.

[(1A) Subsection (1) does not apply to the power of the Scottish Ministers to make regulations under section 97B(11).][2]

(2) Except in so far as this Act otherwise provides, any power conferred by it to make an Order in Council, regulations or an order (except an order under section 153(8)) may be exercised—

(*a*) either in relation to all cases to which the power extends, or in relation to those cases subject to specified exceptions, or in relation to any specified cases or classes of case;

(*b*) so as to make, as respects the cases in relation to which it is exercised—

(i) the full provision to which the power extends or any less provision (whether by way of exception or otherwise),

(ii) the same provision for all cases in relation to which the power is exercised, or different provision for different cases or different classes of case or different provision as respects the same case or class of case for different purposes of this Act,

(iii) any such provision either unconditionally or subject to any specified condition,

and where such a power is expressed to be exercisable for alternative purposes it may be exercised in relation to the same case for any or all of those purposes; and any power to make an Order in Council, regulations or an order for the purposes of any one provision of this Act shall be without prejudice to any power to make an Order in Council, regulations or an order for the purposes of any other provision.

(3) Any power conferred by it to make an Order in Council, regulations or an order shall include power to make such incidental, supplementary, consequential or transitional provision as appears to Her Majesty or the authority making the regulations or order to be expedient for the purposes of the Order in Council, regulations or order.

(4) Any power conferred by this Act to make an order shall include power to vary or revoke any such order by a subsequent order.

(5) Any power conferred on the Secretary of State by any provision of this Act to make any regulations or order (except an order under section 153(8)), where the power is not expressed to be exercisable with the consent of the Treasury, shall if the Treasury so direct be exercisable only in conjunction with them.

Regulations—See the Social Security (Minimum Contributions to Appropriate Personal Pension Schemes) Order, SI 2001/1354.
SS (Reduced Rates of Class 1 Contributions, Rebates and Minimum Contributions), SI 2006/1009.
Social Security (Reduced Rates of Class 1 Contributions, Rebates and Minimum Contributions) Order, SI 2011/1036
Occupational and Personal Pension Schemes (Disclosure of Information) (Amendment) Regulations, SI 2015/482.
Occupational Pension Schemes (Consequential and Miscellaneous Amendments) Regulations, SI 2015/493.
Occupational and Personal Pension Schemes (Transfer Values) (Amendment and Revocation) Regulations, SI 2015/498.
Occupational Pension Schemes (Charges and Governance) Regulations, SI 2015/879
Occupational Pension Schemes (Schemes that were Contracted-out) Regulations, SI 2015/1452.
Occupational Pension Schemes and Social Security (Schemes that were Contracted-out and Graduated Retirement Benefit) (Miscellaneous Amendments) Regulations, SI 2017/354.

Amendments—[1] Words in sub-s (1) repealed by the Pensions Act 1995 Sch 5 paras 18, 78, Sch 7 Pt III with effect from 6 April 1997, by virtue of SI 1997/664 art 2, Sch Pt II.

[2] Sub-s (1A) inserted by the Pension Schemes Act 2015 s 70(1) with effect from 6 April 2015.

183 Sub-delegation

(1) Without prejudice to any specific provisions in this Act, a power conferred by this Act to make an Order in Council, regulations or an order (other than regulations and orders made under . . . [1], Chapter I of Part IV, Part VIII so far as it applies for the purposes of Chapter I of Part IV, sections . . . [1], 153(2), 158(1) to (5), 162, 163, . . . [1] and 176 . . . [1]) includes power to provide for a person to exercise a discretion in dealing with any matter.

(2) . . . [1]

(3) . . .

Regulations—Occupational and Personal Pension Schemes (Disclosure of Information) (Amendment) Regulations, SI 2015/482.
Occupational Pension Schemes (Consequential and Miscellaneous Amendments) Regulations, SI 2015/493.
Occupational and Personal Pension Schemes (Transfer Values) (Amendment and Revocation) Regulations, SI 2015/498.
Occupational Pension Schemes (Schemes that were Contracted-out) Regulations, SI 2015/1452.
Occupational Pension Schemes and Social Security (Schemes that were Contracted-out and Graduated Retirement Benefit) (Miscellaneous Amendments) Regulations, SI 2017/354.

Note—Sub-s (3) does not relate to NIC.

Amendments—[1] Words in sub-s (1) and whole of sub-s (2) repealed by Pensions Act 1995 Sch 5 paras 18, 79, Sch 6 paras 2, 15(*a*), Sch 7 Pts III, IV with effect from 6 April 1997, by virtue of SI 1997/664 art 2, Sch Pt II.

184 Consultation with Social Security Advisory Committee about regulations under s 36(6)

(1) Subject to section 173 of the Social Security Administration Act 1992 (cases where consultation not required), where the Secretary of State proposes to make regulations under section 36(6), he shall refer the proposals, in the form of draft regulations or otherwise, to the Social Security Advisory Committee ("the Committee").

(2) The Committee shall consider any proposals referred to it by the Secretary of State under subsection (1) and shall make to the Secretary of State a report containing such recommendations with respect to the subject-matter of the proposals as the Committee thinks appropriate.

(3) If after receiving a report of the Committee the Secretary of State lays before Parliament regulations which comprise the whole or part of the subject-matter of the proposals referred to the Committee, he shall lay with the regulations a copy of the Committee's report and a statement showing—

(*a*) the extent (if any) to which he has in framing the regulations given effect to the Committee's recommendations; and

(*b*) in so far as effect has not been given to them, his reasons why not.

185 Consultations about other regulations

(1) [Subject to subsection (2), before the Secretary of State makes][1] any regulations for the purposes of Parts I to VI, Chapter . . . [2] III of Part VII, Part VIII, IX or X or section 153, 154, 155, 156, 160, 162, 163, 174 or 175 of this Act he shall [consult such persons as he may consider appropriate][1].

(2) Subsection (1) does not apply to—

(*a*) regulations prescribing actuarial tables; or

(*b*) regulations made for the purpose only of consolidating other regulations revoked by them; or

(*c*) regulations under section 36(6).

[(*d*) regulations in the case of which the Secretary of State considers consultation inexpedient because of urgency, or

(*e*) regulations which—

(i) state that they are consequential upon a specified enactment, and

(ii) are made before the end of the period of six months beginning with the coming into force of that enactment,][3]

(3), (4) . . . [2]

(5) In relation to any regulations required or authorised under this Act to be made by the Secretary of State in conjunction with the Treasury, any reference in [subsection (1)][1] to the Secretary of State shall be construed as a reference to him and the Treasury acting jointly.

[(5A Subject to subsection (5C), before the Treasury (acting alone) make any regulations under section 95, 97A or 97C they shall consult such persons as they may consider appropriate.

(5B) Subject to subsection (5C), before the Scottish Ministers make any regulations under section 97B(11) they shall consult such persons as they may consider appropriate.

(5C) Subsections (5A) and (5B) do not apply to regulations in the case of which the Treasury or (as the case may be) the Scottish Ministers consider consultation inexpedient because of urgency or to regulations of the type described in subsection (2)(*b*) or (*e*).][4]

(6) . . . [2]

(7)–(9) . . .

Note—Sub-ss (7)–(9) do not relate to NIC.

The consultation requirement in sub-s (5A) may be satisfied by things done before 3 March 2015 (the day on which the Pension Schemes Act was passed (Pension Schemes Act 2015 s 70(5)).

Amendments—[1] Words in sub-ss (1), (5) substituted by the Pensions Act 1995 Sch 5 paras 8, 80(*a*), (*d*) with effect from 6 April 1997, by virtue of SI 1997/664 art 2, Sch Pt II.

[2] Words omitted in sub-s (1) and sub-ss (3), (4), (6) repealed by the Pensions Act 1995 Sch 3 paras 22, 46, Sch 5 paras 18, 80(*c*), (*e*), Sch 7 Pts I, III with effect from 6 April 1997, by virtue of SI 1997/664 art 2, Sch Pt II.

[3] Sub-s (2)(*d*), (*e*) inserted by the Pensions Act 1995 Sch 5 paras 18, 80(*b*) with effect from 6 April 1997, by virtue of SI 1997/664 art 2, Sch Pt II.

[4] Sub-ss (5A)–(5C) inserted by the Pension Schemes Act 2015 s 70(2) with effect from 6 April 2015.

Prospective amendments—In sub-s (2)(*c*), words "or 46A(2); or" to be inserted after words "section 36(6)", by the Pensions Act 2008, s 103(1), (4) with effect from a date to be appointed.

186 Parliamentary control of orders and regulations

(1) Subject to subsections (2) and (3), a statutory instrument which contains (whether alone or with other provisions) any regulations or order made under this Act by the Secretary of State [or the Treasury][2] shall be subject to annulment in pursuance of a resolution of either House of Parliament.

(2) Subsection (1) shall not apply to any order which under any provision of this Act is required to be laid before Parliament after being made or is subject to a requirement that a draft of the instrument shall be laid before and approved by a resolution of each House of Parliament or to any order made under section 193 or paragraph 1 of Schedule 9.

(3), (4) . . .

(5) In the case of any regulations laid before Parliament at a time when Parliament is not sitting, the requirements of section 184(3) . . . [1] shall be deemed to be satisfied as respects either House of Parliament if a copy of the report and the statement in question are laid before that House not later than the second day on which the House sits after the laying of the regulations.

[(6) Regulations made by the Scottish Ministers under section 97B(11) are subject to the affirmative procedure (see Part 2 of the Interpretation and Legislative Reform (Scotland) Act 2010 (asp 10)).][2]

Note—Sub-ss (3), (4) are not relevant for the purposes of this publication.

Amendments—[1] Words in sub-s (5) repealed by the Pensions Act 1995 Sch 5 paras 18, 81, Sch 7 Pt III with effect from 6 April 1997, by virtue of SI 1997/664 art 2, Sch Pt II.

[2] Sub-s (6) inserted by the Pension Schemes Act 2015 s 70(3) with effect from 6 April 2015.

Prospective amendments—Sub-s (3)(*ba*) to be inserted by the Pension Schemes Act 2015 s 40, Sch 1 para 7 with effect from a date to be appointed. Sub-s (3)(*ba*) to read as follows—

"(*ba*) regulations under section 85A, or".

Supplemental provisions

192 Extent

(1) . . .

(2) The following provisions of this Act extend to Northern Ireland—

[section 1][1],

sections 181 to 183 (as they have effect for those purposes),

sections 185 and 186 (as they have effect for those purposes),

. . .

sections 188 to 191 (as they have effect for those purposes, but subject to subsection (1)),

this section,

section 193,

(3) Except as provided by subsection (2), this Act does not extend to Northern Ireland.

Note—Provisions omitted are not relevant for the purposes of this publication.

Amendments—[1] Words in sub-s (2) substituted by the Pensions Act 1995 Sch 5 paras 18, 82, Sch 7 Pt III with effect from 6 April 1997, by virtue of SI 1997/664 art 2, Sch Pt II.

193 Short title and commencement

(1) This Act may be cited as the Pension Schemes Act 1993.

(2) Subject to the provisions of Schedule 9, this Act shall come into force on such day as the Secretary of State may by order appoint.

(3) As respects the coming into force of—

(*a*) Part II of Schedule 5 and section 188(1) so far as it relates to it; or

(*b*) Schedule 7 and section 190 so far as it relates to it,

an order under subsection (2) may appoint different days from the day appointed for the other provisions of this Act or different days for different purposes.

Regulations—The Pension Schemes Act 1993 (Commencement No 1) Order, SI 1994/86 (bringing this Act into force on 7 February 1994 except for (i) Sch 5 Pt II and s 188(1) ante so far as it relates to Sch 5 Pt II; (ii) Sch 7 and s 190 so far as it relates to Sch 7).

SOCIAL SECURITY (CONTRIBUTIONS) ACT 1994

(1994 Chapter 1)

An Act to increase primary Class 1 contributions payable under the Social Security Contributions and Benefits Act 1992; to correct the provisions as to the appropriate national health service allocation in the case of such contributions; to clarify what reliefs are to be taken into account in assessing Class 4 contributions; and for connected purposes.

[10 February 1994]

1 Increase in primary Class 1 contributions

(1) . . .

(2) The above amendment comes into effect on 6th April 1994.

Note—Sub-s (1) amends SSC&BA 1992 s 8(2)(*b*).

2 National health service allocation

Note—This section is not relevant to this Publication.

3 Reliefs available in calculating Class 4 contributions

(1) . . .

(2) The above amendments shall be deemed to have had effect as from the commencement of those Acts; and corresponding amendments to paragraph 3(2) of Schedule 2 to the Social Security Act 1975 and the Social Security (Northern Ireland) Act 1975 shall be deemed to have had effect as from the commencement of section 31 of the Finance (No 2) Act 1987 (deduction of personal pension contributions from relevant earnings).

Note—Sub-s (1) amends SSC & BA 1992 Sch 2 para 3(2).

4 Corresponding provision for Northern Ireland

An Order in Council under paragraph 1(1)(*b*) of Schedule 1 to the Northern Ireland Act 1974 (legislation for Northern Ireland in the interim period) which states that it is made only for purposes corresponding to those of section 1 or 2 of this Act—

(*a*) shall not be subject to paragraph 1(4) and (5) of that Schedule (affirmative resolution of both Houses of Parliament), but (*b*) shall be subject to annulment in pursuance of a resolution of either House of Parliament.

5 Short title and extent

(1) This Act may be cited as the Social Security (Contributions) Act 1994.

(2) Sections 3 and 4 and this section extend to Northern Ireland, but otherwise this Act does not extend there.

FINANCE ACT 1996

(1996 Chapter 8)

[29 April 1996]

CHAPTER VI

MISCELLANEOUS PROVISIONS

Reliefs

147 Withdrawal of relief for Class 4 contributions

(1) . . . [1]

(2) (*amends* SSC&BA 1992 Sch 2 para 3(2) and SSC&B(NI)A 1992 Sch 2 para 3(2)).

(3) This section shall have effect in relation to the year 1996–97 and subsequent years of assessment.

Amendments—[1] Sub-s (1) repealed by CTA 2009 s 1326, Sch 3 Pt 1. CTA 2009 applies for accounting periods ending on or after 1 April 2009 (for corporation tax purposes) and for tax years 2009–10 onwards (for income and capital gains tax purposes).

EMPLOYMENT RIGHTS ACT 1996

(1996 Chapter 18)

[22 May 1996]

PART I

EMPLOYMENT PARTICULARS

Right to statements of employment particulars

1 Statement of initial employment particulars

(1) Where an employee begins employment with an employer, the employer shall give to the employee a written statement of particulars of employment.

(2) The statement may . . . be given in instalments and (whether or not given in instalments) shall be given not later than two months after the beginning of the employment.

(3)–(5) . . .

Note—Words omitted outside the scope of this work.

Enforcement

11 Reference to [employment tribunals][1]

(1) Where an employer does not give an employee a statement as required by section 1 . . . (either because he gives him no statement or because the statement he gives does not comply with what is required), the employee may require a reference to be made to an [employment tribunal][1] to determine what particulars ought to have been included or referred to in a statement so as to comply with the requirements of the section concerned.

(2) . . .

(3) . . .

(*a*) . . . [2]

(*b*) . . .

(4) . . .

(5) . . .

Note—Words omitted outside the scope of this work.

Amendments—[1] Words substituted by Employment Rights (Dispute Resolution) Act 1998 s 1, with effect from 1 August 1998, by virtue of SI 1998/1658.

[2] Sub-s (3)(*a*) repealed by PeA 2014 s 24, Sch 13 paras 66, 68 with effect from 6 April 2016 (PeA 2014 s 56(1), (4)).

FINANCE ACT 1997

(1997 Chapter 16)

[19 March 1997]

PART VIII
MISCELLANEOUS AND SUPPLEMENTAL

Obtaining information

110 Obtaining information from social security authorities

(1) This section applies to—

(*a*) any information held by the Secretary of State or the Department of Health and Social Services for Northern Ireland for the purposes of any of his or its functions relating to social security; and

(*b*) any information held by a person in connection with the provision by him to the Secretary of State or that Department of any services which that person is providing for purposes connected with any of those functions.

(2) Subject to the following provisions of this section, the person holding any information to which this section applies shall be entitled to supply it to—

(*a*) the Commissioners of Customs and Excise or any person by whom services are being provided to those Commissioners for purposes connected with any of their functions; or

(*b*) the Commissioners of Inland Revenue or any person by whom services are being provided to those Commissioners for purposes connected with any of their functions.

(3) Information shall not be supplied to any person under this section except for one or more of the following uses—

(*a*) use in the prevention, detection, investigation or prosecution of criminal offences which it is a function of the Commissioners of Customs and Excise, or of the Commissioners of Inland Revenue, to prevent, detect, investigate or prosecute;

(*b*) use in the prevention, detection or investigation of conduct in respect of which penalties which are not criminal penalties are provided for by or under any enactment;

(*c*) use in connection with the assessment or determination of penalties which are not criminal penalties;

(*d*) use in checking the accuracy of information relating to, or provided for purposes connected with, any matter under the care and management of the Commissioners of Customs and Excise or the Commissioners of Inland Revenue;

(*e*) use (where appropriate) for amending or supplementing any such information; and

(*f*) use in connection with any legal or other proceedings relating to anything mentioned in paragraphs (*a*) to (*e*) above.

(4) An enactment authorising the disclosure of information by a person mentioned in subsection (2)(*a*) or (*b*) above shall not authorise the disclosure by such a person of information supplied to him under this section except to the extent that the disclosure is also authorised by a general or specific permission granted by the Secretary of State or by the Department of Health and Social Services for Northern Ireland.

(5) In this section references to functions relating to social security include references to—

(*a*) functions in relation to . . . [1] social security benefits (whether contributory or not) or national insurance numbers; and

(*b*) functions under the Jobseekers Act 1995 or the Jobseekers (Northern Ireland) Order 1995.

(5AA) . . . [4]

[(5A) Nothing in this section affects any disclosure authorised by section 121F of the Social Security Administration Act 1992 (supply to Inland Revenue of information for purposes of contributions, statutory sick pay or statutory maternity pay of information held by Secretary of State) [or section 115E of the Social Security Administration (Northern Ireland) Act 1992 (supply to Inland Revenue of information for purposes of contributions, statutory sick pay or statutory maternity pay of information held by the Department of Health and Social Services for Northern Ireland)][2] [, paragraph 3 of Schedule 5 to the Tax Credits Act 1999 (supply to Inland Revenue for purposes of tax credit of information so held) or section 14 of the Employment Act 2002 (supply to Inland Revenue for purposes of [ordinary statutory paternity pay, additional statutory paternity pay][5] or statutory adoption pay of information so held)][3].][1]

(6) In this section "conduct" includes acts, omissions and statements.

(7) This section shall come into force on such day as the Treasury may by order made by statutory instrument appoint, and different days may be appointed under this subsection for different purposes.

Note—The day appointed for the purposes of this section is 2 July 1997 (Finance Act 1997, Section 110, (Appointed Day) Order, SI 1997/1603).

Amendments—[1] Words in sub-s (5)(*a*) repealed, and sub-s (5A) inserted, by the Social Security Contributions (Transfer of Functions, etc) Act 1999 s 28(3), Sch 6 para 10 with effect from 1 April 1999 by virtue of the Social Security (Transfer of Functions, etc) Act 1999 (Commencement No 1 and Transitional Provisions) Order, SI 1999/527 art 2, Sch 2.

2 Words in sub-s (5A) inserted by the Social Security Contributions (Transfer of Functions, etc) (Northern Ireland) Order, SI 1999/671, art 6, Sch 5 para 9 with effect from 1 April 1999 (by virtue of the Social Security Contributions (Transfer of Functions, etc) (1999 Order) (Commencement No 1 and Transitional Provisions) Order (Northern Ireland), SR 1999/149, art 2(*c*), Sch 2).

3 Words in sub-s (5A) substituted by EmA 2002 s 53, Sch 7 para 50 with effect from 31 July 2002 (by virtue of SI 2002/1989).

4 Sub-s (5AA) repealed by TCA 2002 s 60, Sch 6 with effect from 8 April 2003 (by virtue of SI 2003/962).

5 In sub-s (5A) words substituted by the Work and Families Act 2006 s 11 Sch 1 para 45 with effect from 6 April 2010 (by virtue of SI 2010/495 art 4(*d*)).

SOCIAL SECURITY ACT 1998

(1998 Chapter 14)

ARRANGEMENT OF SECTIONS

PART I
DECISIONS AND APPEALS

CHAPTER I
GENERAL

Decisions

Appeals

CHAPTER II
SOCIAL SECURITY DECISIONS AND APPEALS

Decisions

Appeals

Procedure etc

Supplemental

PART II
CONTRIBUTIONS

Amendments of Contributions and Benefits Act

Amendments of Administration Act

NIC

An Act to make provision as to the making of decisions and the determination of appeals under enactments relating to social security, child support, vaccine damage payments and war pensions; to make further provision with respect to social security; and for connected purposes.

[21 May 1998]

PART I
DECISIONS AND APPEALS

CHAPTER I

GENERAL

Note—Appeal tribunal under this Chapter abolished by the Transfer of Tribunal Functions Order, SI 2008/2833 art 4 with effect from 3 November 2008, except in relation to appeal tribunals constituted under this Chapter in respect of Scotland for the purposes of an appeal which is referred to such tribunal by the Scottish Ministers, or the Secretary of State on their behalf, pursuant to Health and Social Care (Community Health and Standards) Act 2003 s 158.

Decisions

1 Transfer of functions to Secretary of State

The following functions are hereby transferred to the Secretary of State, namely—

(*a*) the functions of adjudication officers appointed under section 38 of the Social Security Administration Act 1992 ("the Administration Act");

. . .

Note—Provisions omitted are outside the scope of this Publication.

2 Use of computers

(1) Any decision, determination or assessment falling to be made or certificate falling to be issued by the Secretary of State under or by virtue of a relevant enactment, or in relation to a war pension, may be made or issued not only by an officer of his acting under his authority but also—

(*a*) by a computer for whose operation such an officer is responsible; and

(*b*) in the case of a decision, determination or assessment that may be made or a certificate that may be issued by a person providing services to the Secretary of State, by a computer for whose operation such a person is responsible.

(2) In this section "relevant enactment" means any enactment contained in—

(*a*) Chapter II of this Part;

(*b*) the Social Security Contributions and Benefits Act 1992 ("the Contributions and Benefits Act");

(*c*) the Administration Act;

. . .

[(*k*) the Welfare Reform Act 2012, . . . [3]

(*l*) Part 4 of that Act][2]

[(*m*) Part 1 of the Pensions Act 2014;][3]

Note—Provisions omitted are outside the scope of this Publication.

Amendments—[1] In sub-s (2), para (*k*) inserted by the Welfare Reform Act 2012 s 31, Sch 2 para 44 with effect from 25 February 2013 for the purposes of making regulations (SI 2013/358 art 291) and otherwise from 29 April 2013 (by virtue of SI 2013/983 art 3(1)(*b*)(iii)).

[2] In sub-s (2), para (*l*) Inserted by the Welfare Reform Act 2012 s 91, Sch 9 para 38 with effect from 8 April 2013 in relation to persons whose only or principal residence is within a postcode listed in SI 2013/358 Sch 3 (by virtue of SI 2013/358 art 7(2)) and otherwise from 10 June 2013 (by virtue of SI 2013//1250 art 2).

[3] In sub-s (2)(*k*), word repealed, and sub-s (2)(*m*) inserted by PeA 2014 s 24, Sch 13 paras 31, 32 with effect from 6 April 2016 (PeA 2014 s 56(1), (4)).

Prospective amendments—Sub-s (2)(*n*) and preceding word "or" to be inserted by PeA 2014 s 31, Sch 16 paras 37, 38 with effect a date to be appointed. Sub-s (2)(*n*) as inserted to read as follows—

"(*n*) section 30 of the Pensions Act 2014;".

3 Use of information

(1) Subsection (2) below applies to information relating to [any of the matters specified in subsection (1A) below][1] which is held—

(*a*) by the Secretary of State or the Northern Ireland Department; or

(*b*) by a person providing services to the Secretary of State or the Northern Ireland Department in connection with the provision of those services.

[(1A) The matters are—

(*a*) social security, . . . [4] or war pensions;

[(*aa*) child support . . . [5]][4]

(*b*) employment or training;

(*c*) private pensions policy;

(*d*) retirement planning.

[(*e*) the investigation or prosecution of offences relating to tax credits.][6]][2]

[(*f*) the Diffuse Mesothelioma Payment Scheme.][7]

(2) Information to which this subsection applies—

(*a*) may be used for the purposes of, or for any purposes connected with, the exercise of functions in relation to [any of the matters specified in subsection (1A) above][2]; and

(*b*) may be supplied to, or to a person providing services to, the Secretary of State or the Northern Ireland Department for use for those purposes.

(3) . . . [1]

(4) In this section "the Northern Ireland Department" means the Department of Health and Social Services for Northern Ireland [or the Department for Employment and Learning in Northern Ireland][1].

[(5) In this section—

"private pensions policy" means policy relating to—

[(*a*)] [3] occupational pension schemes or personal pension schemes (within the meaning given by section 1 of the Pension Schemes Act 1993); [or

(*b*) occupational pension schemes or private pension schemes within the meaning of Part 1 of the Pensions Act 2008, if they do not fall within paragraph (*a*);][3]

"retirement planning" means promoting financial planning for retirement.][1]

Amendments—[1] Words inserted, and sub-s (3) repealed, by EmA 2002 s 54, Sch 6 paras 1, 4 Sch 8 with effect from 9 September 2002 (by virtue of SI 2002/2256).

[2] Words in sub-ss (1), (2) substituted, and sub-ss (1A), (5) inserted, by the Pensions Act 2004 s 236, Sch 10 para 1 with effect from 18 November 2004.

[3] In sub-s (5), in definition of "private pensions policy", para (*a*) numbered as such, and para (*b*) and preceding word "or" inserted, by the Pensions Act 2008 s 63(5), (6) with effect from 26 January 2009 (by virtue of SI 2009/82 art 2(1)(*a*)).

[4] In sub-s (1A)(*a*) words repealed, and sub-s (1A)(*aa*) inserted by the Child Maintenance and Other Payments Act 2008 s 57, Sch 7 para 3(1), (2) with effect from 6 April 2010 (by virtue of SI 2010/667 art 2(*b*)).

[5] In sub-s (1A)(*aa*), words "in Northern Ireland" repealed by the Public Bodies (Child Maintenance and Enforcement Commission: Abolition and Transfer of Functions) Order, SI 2012/2007 art 3(2), Schedule para 64 with effect from 1 August 2012.

[6] Sub-s (1A)(*e*) inserted by the Welfare Reform Act 2012 s 127(10) with effect from 8 May 2012.

[7] Sub-s (1A)(*f*) inserted by the Mesothelioma Act 2014 s 11, Sch 1 para 21 with effect from 31 March 2014 (by virtue of SI 2014/459 art 3(*c*)).

Appeals

4 Unified appeal tribunals

Amendments—This section repealed by the Transfer of Tribunal Functions Order, SI 2008/2833 art 6, Sch 3 paras 143, 144 with effect from 3 November 2008.

5 President of appeal tribunals

Amendments—This section repealed by the Transfer of Tribunal Functions Order, SI 2008/2833 art 6, Sch 3 paras 143, 145 with effect from 3 November 2008.

6 Panel for appointment to appeal tribunals

Amendments—This section repealed by the Transfer of Tribunal Functions Order, SI 2008/2833 art 6, Sch 3 paras 143, 146 with effect from 3 November 2008.

7 *Constitution of appeal tribunals*

Amendments—This section repealed by the Transfer of Tribunal Functions Order, SI 2008/2833 art 6, Sch 3 paras 143, 147 with effect from 3 November 2008.

CHAPTER II

SOCIAL SECURITY DECISIONS AND APPEALS

Cross references—TCA 2002 s 51, Sch 4 para 15 (references in this Chapter to a decision of the Secretary of State are, where the context so requires in consequence of TCA 2002 s 50 (functions transferred to the Board), to be construed as references to a decision of the Board, or, where the power to decide is exercised by an officer of the Board, an officer of the Board).

Decisions

8 Decisions by Secretary of State

(1) Subject to the provisions of this Chapter, it shall be for the Secretary of State—

(*a*), (*b*) . . . [and][1]

(*c*) subject to subsection (5) below, to make any decision that falls to be made under or by virtue of a relevant enactment; . . . [1]

(*d*) . . . [1]

(2), (3) . . .

(4) In this section "relevant enactment" means any enactment contained in this Chapter, the Contributions and Benefits Act, the Administration Act, the Social Security (Consequential Provisions) Act 1992[, the Jobseekers Act[, the State Pension Credit Act 2002][3]][2] [Part 1 of the Welfare Reform Act 2007 , Part 1 of the Welfare Reform Act 2012][4][, Part 4 of that Act or Part 1 of the Pensions Act 2014][5] other than one contained in—

(*a*) Part VII of the Contributions and Benefits Act so far as relating to housing benefit and council tax benefit;

(*b*) Part VIII of the Administration Act (arrangements for housing benefit and council tax benefit and related subsidies).

[(5) Subsection (1)(*c*) above does not include any decision which under section 8 of the Social Security Contributions (Transfer of Functions, etc) Act 1999 falls to be made by an officer of the Inland Revenue.][1]

Note—Provisions omitted are outside the scope of this Publication.

Cross references—TCA 2002 s 51, Sch 4 para 15 (references in this Chapter to a decision of the Secretary of State are, where the context so requires in consequence of TCA 2002 s 50 (functions transferred to the Board), to be construed as references to a decision of the Board, or, where the power to decide is exercised by an officer of the Board, an officer of the Board).

Amendments—[1] Words in sub-s (1)(*b*) inserted, sub-s (1)(*d*) repealed and sub-s (5) substituted by the Social Security Contributions (Transfer of Functions, etc) Act 1999 s 18 and Sch 7 para 22 with effect from 1 April 1999 by virtue of the Social Security Contributions (Transfer of Functions, etc) Act 1999 (Commencement No 1 and Transitional Provisions) Order, SI 1999/527.

[2] Words in sub-s (4) substituted by the State Pension Credit Act 2002 s 11, Sch 1 paras 4, 6(1), (3) with effect as follows—

- for the purpose only of exercising any power to make regulations or orders, from 2 July 2002 (SI 2002/1691 art 2(i)); and
- for remaining purposes, from 7 April 2003 (SI 2003/966 art 2(*a*)).

[3] Words in sub-s (4) substituted by the Welfare Reform Act 2007 s 28(1), Sch 3 para 17(1), (3)(*b*) with effect as follows—

- for the purpose of making regulations, from 18 March 2008 (SI 2008/787 art 2(1), Schedule); and
- for remaining purposes, from 27 July 2008 (SI 2008/787 art 2(3)(*a*)).

[4] In sub-s (4) words substituted for words "or Part 1 of the Welfare Reform Act 2007' by the Welfare Reform Act 2012 s 31, Sch 2 paras 43, 45(*b*) with effect from 29 April 2013 (by virtue of SI 2013/983 art 3(1)(*b*)(iii)).

[5] In sub-s (4), words substituted by PeA 2014 s 24, Sch 13 paras 31, 33 with effect from 6 April 2016 (PeA 2014 s 56(1), (4)).

Prospective amendments—Sub-s (3)(*ac*) to be inserted, and in sub-s (4), words "or section 30 of that Act" after words "Part 1 of the Pensions Act 2014" by PeA 2014 s 31, Sch 16 paras 37, 39 with effect a date to be appointed. Sub-s (3)(*ac*) as inserted to read as follows—

"(*ac*) bereavement support payment under section 30 of the Pensions Act 2014;".

Appeals

12 Appeal to [First-tier Tribunal][2]

(1) This section applies to any decision of the Secretary of State under section 8 or 10 above (whether as originally made or as revised under section 9 above) which—

(*a*) . . . [or][1]

(*b*) is made otherwise than on such a claim or award, and falls within Schedule 3 to this Act; . . . [1]

. . .

Notes—Provisions omitted are outside the scope of this Publication.

This section shall have effect in the case of an appeal brought against a penalty under ss 9(1), (3)(*a*) or (5)(*a*) of the Tax Credits Act 1999.

Cross references—TCA 2002 s 51, Sch 4 para 15 (references in this Chapter to a decision of the Secretary of State are, where the context so requires in consequence of TCA 2002 s 50 (functions transferred to the Board), to be construed as references to a decision of the Board, or, where the power to decide is exercised by an officer of the Board, an officer of the Board).

National Insurance Contribution Credits (Transfer of Functions) Order 2009, SI 2009/1337, arts 2, 3 (decisions to be made by HMRC Commissioners rather than the Secretary of State).

Modifications—See Tax Credits (Appeals) Regulations, SI 2002/2926 reg 4 (temporary modification of this section in respect of appeals under the Tax Credits Act 2002 s 63 for a temporary period).

Child Trust Funds (Non-tax Appeals) Regulations, SI 2005/191 reg 5 (modification of this section in relation to a child trust fund appeal to an appeal tribunal).

Amendments—[1] Words in sub-s (1)(*a*) inserted and words in sub-s (1)(*b*) omitted by the Social Security Contributions (Transfer of Functions, etc) Act 1999 s 18 and Sch 7 para 25 with effect from 1 April 1999 by virtue of the Social Security Contributions (Transfer of Functions, etc) Act 1999 (Commencement No 1 and Transitional Provisions) Order, SI 1999/527.

[2] Words in heading substituted for words "appeal tribunal" by the Transfer of Tribunal Functions Order, SI 2008/2833 art 6, Sch 3 paras 143, 149 with effect from 3 November 2008.

Procedure etc

16 Procedure

(1)–(3) . . .

(4), (5) . . . [1]

. . .

Note—Provisions omitted are outside the scope of this Publication.

Modifications—Child Trust Funds (Non-tax Appeals) Regulations, SI 2005/191 reg 11 (modification of this section in relation to a child trust fund appeal to an appeal tribunal).

Amendments—[1] Sub-ss (4) and (5) repealed by the Social Security Contributions (Transfer of Functions, etc) Act 1999 s 18 and Sch 7 para 28 with effect from 1 April 1999 by virtue of the Social Security Contributions (Transfer of Functions, etc) Act 1999 (Commencement No 1 and Transitional Provisions) Order, SI 1999/527.

18 Matters arising as respects decisions

(1) Regulations may make provision as respects matters arising—

(*a*) pending any decision under this Chapter of the Secretary of State [or the First-tier Tribunal, or any decision of the Upper Tribunal which relates to any decision under this Chapter of the First-Tier Tribunal,][2] which relates to—

(i)–(ii) . . .

(iii)–(iv) . . . [1]

. . .

Note—Provisions omitted are outside the scope of this Publication.

Cross references—TCA 2002 s 51, Sch 4 para 15 (references in this Chapter to a decision of the Secretary of State are, where the context so requires in consequence of TCA 2002 s 50 (functions transferred to the Board), to be construed as references to a decision of the Board, or, where the power to decide is exercised by an officer of the Board, an officer of the Board).

National Insurance Contribution Credits (Transfer of Functions) Order 2009, SI 2009/1337, arts 2, 3 (decisions to be made by HMRC Commissioners rather than the Secretary of State).

Amendments—[1] Sub-ss (1)(*a*)(iii) and (iv) omitted by the Social Security Contributions (Transfer of Functions, etc) Act 1999 s 18 and Sch 7 para 29 with effect from 1 April 1999 by virtue of the Social Security Contributions (Transfer of Functions, etc) Act 1999 (Commencement No 1 and Transitional Provisions) Order, SI 1999/527.

[2] Words in sub-s (1)(*a*) substituted for words ", an appeal tribunal or a Commissioner" by the Transfer of Tribunal Functions Order, SI 2008/2833 art 6, Sch 3 paras 143, 156 with effect from 3 November 2008.

Supplemental

39 Interpretation etc of Chapter II

(1) In this Chapter—

"appeal tribunal" means an appeal tribunal constituted under Chapter I of this Part;[3]

["claimant", in relation to a joint-claim couple claiming a joint-claim jobseeker's allowance (within the meaning of the Jobseekers Act 1995), means the couple or either member of the couple;][2]

"Commissioner" [(except in the expression "tax appeal Commissioners")][1] *means the Chief Social Security Commissioner or any other Social Security Commissioner, and includes a tribunal of three or more Commissioners constituted under section 16(7) above;*[3]

"relevant benefit" has the meaning given by section 8(3) above;

. . . [4]

(2) Expressions used in this Chapter to which a meaning is assigned by section 191 of the Administration Act have that meaning in this Chapter.

(3) Part II of the Administration Act, which is superseded by the foregoing provisions of this Chapter, shall cease to have effect.

Cross references—TCA 2002 s 51, Sch 4 para 15 (references in this Chapter to a decision of the Secretary of State are, where the context so requires in consequence of TCA 2002 s 50 (functions transferred to the Board), to be construed as references to a decision of the Board, or, where the power to decide is exercised by an officer of the Board, an officer of the Board).

Note—Definitions omitted are outside the scope of this publication.

Modifications—See Tax Credits (Appeals) Regulations, SI 2002/2926 reg 12 (temporary modification of this section in respect of appeals under the Tax Credits Act 2002 s 63 for a temporary period).

NIC

Amendments—[1] Words in the definition of "Commissioner", and the definition of "tax appeal Commissioners" inserted by the Social Security Contributions (Transfer of Functions, etc) Act 1999 s 18 and Sch 7 para 35 with effect from 1 April 1999 by virtue of the Social Security Contributions (Transfer of Functions, etc) Act 1999 (Commencement No 1 and Transitional Provisions) Order, SI 1999/527.

[2] Definition of "claimant" inserted by the Welfare Reform and Pensions Act 1999, s 59, Sch 7 para 17, with effect from 19 March 2001 (by virtue of SI 2000/2958).

[3] Definitions of "appeal tribunal" and "Commissioner" repealed by the Transfer of Tribunal Functions Order, SI 2008/2833 art 6, Sch 3 paras 143, 167 with effect from 3 November 2008.

[4] Definition of "tax appeal Commissioners" repealed by the Transfer of Tribunal Functions and Revenue and Customs Appeals Order, SI 2009/56 art 3, Sch 1 para 250 with effect from 1 April 2009.

PART II
CONTRIBUTIONS

Amendments of Contributions and Benefits Act

48 Apportionment of payments etc made for more than one earner

(*inserts* SSCBA 1992 s 3(2A)).

49 Payments on account of directors' contributions

(*inserts* SSCBA 1992 s 3(4)(5)).

50 Payments treated as remuneration and earnings

(1) (*substitutes* SSCBA 1992 s 4(4)).

(2) . . . [1]

(3) Subsection (1) above, so far as relating to a sum which is chargeable to tax by virtue of section 313 of the Income and Corporation Taxes Act 1988, shall have effect in relation to any undertaking given on or after 10th July 1997.

(4) Regulations under subsection (6) of section 4 of the Contributions and Benefits Act (as inserted by subsection (2) above)—

(*a*) shall not be made before the passing of the Finance Act 1998; but

(*b*) may make provision having effect in relation to acquisitions on or after 6th April 1998.

Amendments—[1] Sub-s (2) repealed by the Child Support, Pensions and Social Security Act 2000 s 85, Sch 9 Pt VIII with effect for the tax year beginning with 6 April 2000 and subsequent tax years.

51 Class 1 contributions

Substitutes SSCBA 1992 ss 5(1), 6(1), 8(1), (2), 9; *repealed* by the Welfare Reform and Pensions Act 1999 s 88 Sch 13, Pt VI with effect from 6 April 2000.)

52 Class 1A contributions

Amendments—This section repealed by the Child Support, Pensions and Social Security Act 2000 s 85, Sch 9 Pt VIII with effect for the tax year beginning with 6 April 2000 and subsequent tax years.

53 Class 1B contributions

(*inserts* SSCBA 1992 s 10A).

54 Contributions paid in error

(*inserts* SSCBA 1992 s 19A).

55 Recovery of primary Class 1 contributions by secondary contributors

In paragraph 3 of Schedule 1 to the Contributions and Benefits Act (supplementary provisions as to contributions)—

(*a*) (*amends* SSCBA 1992 Sch 1 para 3(3)).

(*b*) (*inserts* SSCBA 1992 Sch 1 para 3(4)(5)).

56 Contributions returns

(1) (*amends* SSCBA 1992 Sch 1 para 7(3)).

(2) (*inserts* SSCBA 1992 Sch 1 para 7A).

57 Collection of contributions by Secretary of State

(*inserts* SSCBA 1992 Sch 1 para 7B).

[58 Interest and penalties chargeable concurrently with Inland Revenue]

Amendments—This paragraph inserted SSCBA 1992 Sch 1 para 7C, and was repealed by the Social Security Contributions (Transfer of Functions, etc) Act 1999 s 26(2) and Sch 9 para 8, and s 26(3) and Sch 10 Pt I with effect from 1 April 1999 by virtue of the Social Security Contributions (Transfer of Functions, etc) Act 1999 (Commencement No 1 and Transitional Provisions) Order, SI 1999/527.

59 Levy of Class 4 contributions with income tax

(1) Schedule 2 to the Contributions and Benefits Act (levy of Class 4 contributions with income tax) and Schedule 2 to the Social Security Contributions and Benefits (Northern Ireland) Act 1992 (corresponding provision for Northern Ireland) shall each be amended as follows.

(2)–(5) (*amended* SSCBA 1992 Sch 2 paras 2, 4(2), 6(1) and *repealed* Sch 2 para (3)(1)(*b*), sub-s (2) *repealed by* CAA 2001 s 580, Sch 4 with effect in accordance with CAA 2001 s 579(1)).

(6) . . . [1]

Amendments—[1] Sub-s (6) repealed by the Social Security Contributions (Transfer of Functions, etc) Act 1999 s 26(3) and Sch 10 Pt 1 with effect from 1 April 1999 by virtue of the Social Security Contributions (Transfer of Functions, etc) Act 1999 (Commencement No 1 and Transitional Provisions) Order, SI 1999/527.

Amendments of Administration Act

60 Breach of regulations
(*substitutes* SSAA 1992 s 113).

61 Offences and penalties relating to contributions
(*substitutes* SSAA 1992 s 114 with SSAA 1992 s 114, 114A[1]).

Amendments—[1] This section, in so far as it relates to SSAA 1992 s 114A only, repealed by the Social Security Contributions (Transfer of Functions, etc) Act 1999 s 26(3) and Sch 10 Pt 1 with effect from 1 April 1999 by virtue of the Social Security Contributions (Transfer of Functions, etc) Act 1999 (Commencement No 1 and Transitional Provisions) Order, SI 1999/527.

62 Evidence of non-payment
(1) (substitutes SSAA 1992 s 118(1)(1A)).[2]
(2) . . .[1]
(3) (*amends* SSAA 1992 s 118(4)).
(4) . . .[1]

Amendments—[1] Sub-ss (2) and (4) repealed by the Social Security Contributions (Transfer of Functions, etc) Act 1999 s 26(3) and Sch 10 Pt 1 with effect from 6 April 1999 by virtue of the Social Security Contributions (Transfer of Functions, etc) Act 1999 (Commencement No 1 and Transitional Provisions) Order, SI 1999/527.
[2] Sub-s (1) repealed by FA 2008 s 138, Sch 44 para 11(*b*) with effect from 21 July 2008.

63 Recovery of contributions etc
(*inserts* SSAA 1992 ss 121A, 121B).

64 Liability of directors etc for company's contributions
(*inserts* SSAA 1992 ss 121C, 121D).

65 Class 1B contributions: supplemental
(1) (*inserts* SSAA 1992 s 143A; *repealed* by the Welfare Reform and Pensions Act 1999 s 88 Sch 13, Pt VI with effect from 6 April 2000).
(2) (*inserts* SSAA 1992 s 162(5)(*ca*)).

66 Payments of certain contributions out of the Consolidated Fund
(1) Subsection (4) of section 163 of the Administration Act (general financial arrangements) shall have effect, and shall be deemed always to have had effect, as if—
(*a*) for the words "a secondary contributor" there were substituted the words "any person"; and
(*b*) after the words "any secondary Class 1 contributions" there were inserted the words ", or any Class 1A contributions,".
(2) Subsection (2) of section 1 of the Social Security (Miscellaneous Provisions) Act 1977 (from which subsection (4) of section 163 is derived) shall be deemed to have had effect with the same amendments as from the commencement of the Social Security (Contributions) Act 1991.

PART IV
MISCELLANEOUS AND SUPPLEMENTAL

78 Expenditure for facilitating transfer of functions etc
(1) The Secretary of State and the Commissioners of Inland Revenue may incur expenditure in doing anything which in his or their opinion is appropriate for the purpose of facilitating either of the following things, namely—
(*a*) the transfer to the Commissioners of such of the functions of the Secretary of State as are exercisable by the Contributions Agency; and
(*b*) the exercise by the Commissioners of those functions.
(2) The powers conferred by subsection (1) above—
(*a*) shall be exercisable whether or not Parliament has given any approval on which either of the things there mentioned depends; and
(*b*) shall be without prejudice to any power conferred otherwise than by virtue of that subsection.
(3) Any expenditure incurred under this section shall be defrayed out of money provided by Parliament.
(4) In its application to Northern Ireland, this section shall have effect with the following modifications, namely—
(*a*) for the first reference to the Secretary of State there shall be substituted a reference to the Department of Health and Social Services for Northern Ireland;
(*b*) for the reference to such of the functions of the Secretary of State as are exercisable by the Contributions Agency there shall be substituted a reference to such of the functions of that Department as correspond to those functions; and
(*c*) for the reference to money provided by Parliament there shall be substituted a reference to money appropriated by Measure of the Northern Ireland Assembly.

79 Regulations and orders

(1) [Subject to subsection (2A) below,][2] regulations under this Act shall be made by the Secretary of State.

(2) . . . [2]

[(2A) Subsection (1) has effect subject to any provision providing for regulations to be made by the Treasury or the Commissioners of Inland Revenue.][1]

(3) Powers under this Act to make regulations or orders are exercisable by statutory instrument.

(4) Any power conferred by this Act to make regulations or orders may be exercised—

(*a*) either in relation to all cases to which the power extends, or in relation to those cases subject to specified exceptions, or in relation to any specified cases or classes of case;

(*b*) so as to make, as respects the cases in relation to which it is exercised—

(i) the full provision to which the power extends or any less provision (whether by way of exception or otherwise);

(ii) the same provision for all cases in relation to which the power is exercised, or different provision for different cases or different classes of case or different provision as respects the same case or class of case for different purposes of this Act;

(iii) any such provision either unconditionally or subject to any specified condition;

and where such a power is expressed to be exercisable for alternative purposes it may be exercised in relation to the same case for any or all of those purposes.

(5) Powers to make regulations for the purposes of any one provision of this Act are without prejudice to powers to make regulations for the purposes of any other provision.

(6) Without prejudice to any specific provision in this Act, a power conferred by this Act to make regulations includes power to make thereby such incidental, supplementary, consequential or transitional provision as appears to the authority making the regulations to be expedient for the purposes of those regulations.

[(6A) The provision referred to in subsection (6) includes, in a case where regulations under this Act require or authorise the use of electronic communications, provision referred to in section 8(4) and (5) and 9(5) of the Electronic Communications Act 2000.

(6B) For the purposes of subsection (6A), references in section 8(4) and (5) and 9(5) of the Electronic Communications Act 2000 to an order under section 8 of that Act are to be read as references to regulations under this Act; and references to anything authorised by such an order are to be read as references to anything required or authorised by such regulations.][4]

(7) Without prejudice to any specific provisions in this Act, a power conferred by any provision of this Act to make regulations includes power to provide for a person to exercise a discretion in dealing with any matter.

(8) Any power conferred by this Act to make regulations relating to housing benefit or council tax benefit shall include power to make different provision for different areas or different authorities.[3]

Note—The functions of the Lord Advocate are hereby transferred to the Secretary of State by virtue of the Transfer of Functions (Lord Advocate and Secretary of State) Order, SI 1999/678 with effect from 19 May 1999.

Regulations—Social Security Commissioners (Procedure) (Tax Credits Appeals) Regulations, SI 2002/3237.

Social Security (Miscellaneous Amendments) (No 3) Regulations, SI 2013/2536.

Social Security (Credits, and Crediting and Treatment of Contributions) (Consequential and Miscellaneous Amendments) Regulations, SI 2016/1145.

Modifications—Child Trust Funds (Non-tax Appeals) Regulations, SI 2005/191 reg 15 (modification of SSA 1998 ss 79, 80 and 84 in relation to a child trust fund appeal to an appeal tribunal).

Amendments—[1] Words in sub-s (1) substituted, and sub-s (2A) inserted, by TCA 2002 s 51, Sch 4 paras 12, 13 with effect from 26 February 2003 for the purpose of making subordinate legislation; 1 April 2003 for the purpose of transfer of functions etc and minor amendments; and 7 April 2003 for remaining purposes (by virtue of SI 2003/392).

[2] Words in sub-s (1) substituted, and sub-ss (2), (9) repealed, by the Transfer of Tribunal Functions Order, SI 2008/2833 art 6, Sch 3 paras 143, 168 with effect from 3 November 2008.

[3] Sub-s (8) repealed in so far as it relates to the abolition of council tax benefit, by the Welfare Reform Act 2012 s 147, Sch 14 Part 1 with effect from 1 April 2013 (by virtue of SI 2013/358 art 8(c), Sch 4). Note that certain transitional provisions apply in relation to the abolition of council tax benefit (see SI 2013/358 art 9).

[4] Sub-ss (6A), (6B) inserted by the Welfare Reform Act 2012 s 104(2) with effect from 25 February 2013 (by virtue of SI 2013/358).

80 Parliamentary control of regulations

(1) Subject to the provisions of this section, a statutory instrument containing (whether alone or with other provisions) regulations under—

(*a*) section . . . [3] . . . above; or

(*b*) . . . [3] paragraph 9 of Schedule 2 . . . [3] to this Act,

shall not be made unless a draft of the instrument has been laid before Parliament and been approved by a resolution of each House of Parliament.

(2) A statutory instrument—

(*a*) which contains (whether alone or with other provisions) regulations made under this Act by the Secretary of State[, the Treasury or the Commissioners of Inland Revenue][1]; and (*b*) which is not subject to any requirement that a draft of the instrument be laid before and approved by a resolution of each House of Parliament,

shall be subject to annulment in pursuance of a resolution of either House of Parliament.

(3), (4) . . .[3]

Note—Provisions omitted are outside the scope of this Publication.

Modifications—Child Trust Funds (Non-tax Appeals) Regulations, SI 2005/191 reg 15 (modification of SSA 1998 ss 79, 80 and 84 in relation to a child trust fund appeal to an appeal tribunal).

Amendments—[1] Words in sub-s (2) inserted by TCA 2002 s 51, Sch 4 paras 12, 14 with effect from 26 February 2003 for the purpose of making subordinate legislation; 1 April 2003 for the purpose of transfer of functions etc and minor amendments; and 7 April 2003 for remaining purposes (by virtue of SI 2003/392).

[2] Sub-s (4) inserted by the Tribunals, Courts and Enforcement Act 2007 s 50, Sch 10 para 29(1), (4) with effect from 21 July 2008 (by virtue of SI 2008/1653 art 2, subject to transitional provisions in art 3).

[3] Figure "7," in sub-s (1)(*a*), in sub-s (1)(*b*), words repealed, and sub-ss (3), (4), repealed, by the Transfer of Tribunal Functions Order, SI 2008/2833 art 6, Sch 3 paras 143, 169 with effect from 3 November 2008.

81 Reports by Secretary of State

Amendments—Section 81 repealed by the Welfare Reform Act 2012 s 143 with effect from 8 May 2012.

82 Financial provisions

(1) There shall be paid out of money provided by Parliament—

(*a*) any expenditure incurred by the Secretary of State or the Lord Chancellor under or by virtue of this Act; and

(*b*) any increase attributable to this Act in the sums which under any other Act are payable out of money so provided.

(2) There shall be paid out of or into the Consolidated Fund any increase attributable to this Act in the sums which under any other Act are payable out of or into that Fund.

83 Transitory provisions

Schedule 6 to this Act (which contains transitory provisions) shall have effect.

84 Interpretation: general

In this Act—

"the Administration Act" means the Social Security Administration Act 1992;

. . .

"the Contributions and Benefits Act" means the Social Security Contributions and Benefits Act 1992;

. . .

"prescribe" means prescribe by regulations.

Note—Provisions omitted are outside the scope of this Publication.

Regulations—Social Security Commissioners (Procedure) (Tax Credits Appeals) Regulations, SI 2002/3237.

Social Security (Credits, and Crediting and Treatment of Contributions) (Consequential and Miscellaneous Amendments) Regulations, SI 2016/1145.

Modifications—Child Trust Funds (Non-tax Appeals) Regulations, SI 2005/191 reg 15 (modification of SSA 1998 ss 79, 80 and 84 in relation to a child trust fund appeal to an appeal tribunal).

85 Provision for Northern Ireland

An Order in Council under paragraph 1(1)(*b*) of Schedule 1 to the Northern Ireland Act 1974 (legislation for Northern Ireland in the interim period) which contains a statement that it is made only for purposes corresponding to those of this Act—

(*a*) shall not be subject to paragraph 1(4) and (5) of that Schedule (affirmative resolution of both Houses of Parliament); but

(*b*) shall be subject to annulment in pursuance of a resolution of either House of Parliament.

86 Minor and consequential amendments and repeals

(1) The enactments mentioned in Schedule 7 to this Act shall have effect subject to the amendments there specified, being minor amendments and amendments consequential on the provisions of this Act.

(2) The enactments mentioned in Schedule 8 to this Act, which include some that are spent, are hereby repealed to the extent specified in the third column of that Schedule.

87 Short title, commencement and extent

(1) This Act may be cited as the Social Security Act 1998.

(2) This Act, except—

(*a*) sections 66, 69, 72 and 77 to 85, this section and Schedule 6 to this Act; and

(*b*) subsection (1) of section 50 so far as relating to a sum which is chargeable to tax by virtue of section 313 of the Income and Corporation Taxes Act 1988, and subsections (2) to (4) of that section,

shall come into force on such day as may be appointed by order made by the Secretary of State; and different days may be appointed for different provisions and for different purposes.

(3) An order under subsection (2) above may make such savings, or such transitional or consequential provision, as the Secretary of State considers necessary or expedient—

(*a*) in preparation for or in connection with the coming into force of any provision of this Act; or

(*b*) in connection with the operation of any enactment repealed or amended by a provision of this Act during any period when the repeal or amendment is not wholly in force.

. . .

Note—Provisions omitted are outside the scope of this Publication.

SCHEDULES

SCHEDULE 1

APPEAL TRIBUNALS: SUPPLEMENTARY PROVISIONS

Repeal—This Schedule repealed by the Transfer of Tribunal Functions Order, SI 2008/2833 art 6, Sch 3 paras 143, 171 with effect from 3 November 2008.

SCHEDULE 3

DECISIONS AGAINST WHICH AN APPEAL LIES

PART II

CONTRIBUTIONS DECISIONS

Categorisation of earners

10, 11. . .

Compulsory contributions

12, 13. . .

Voluntary contributions

14, 15. . .

Responsibilities at home

16 A decision whether a person was (within the meaning of regulations) precluded from regular employment by responsibilities at home.

Earnings and contributions credits

17 A decision whether a person is entitled to be credited with earnings or contributions in accordance with regulations made under section 22(5) [or (5ZA)][1] of the Contributions and Benefits Act.

Amendments—[1] Words inserted by the Pensions Act 2014 (Consequential Amendments) Order, SI 2016/931 art 3 with effect from 15 September 2016.

Statutory sick pay

18, 19. . .

Statutory maternity pay

20, 21. . .

Liability of directors etc for company's contributions

22 . . .

Preserved rights to benefit etc

23 . . .

Employment of long-term unemployed

24 . . .

Interest and penalties

25–28 . . .

Power to prescribe other decisions

29 . . .

Amendments—Paras 10–15, 18–23 and 24–29 repealed by the Social Security Contributions (Transfer of Functions, etc) Act 1999 s 18 and Sch 7 para 36 with effect from 1 April 1999 by virtue of the Social Security Contributions (Transfer of Functions, etc) Act 1999 (Commencement No 1 and Transitional Provisions) Order, SI 1999/527.

SCHEDULE 5

REGULATIONS AS TO PROCEDURE: PROVISION WHICH MAY BE MADE

Regulations—Tax Credits (Appeals) (No 2) Regulations, SI 2002/3196.

Social Security Commissioners (Procedure) (Tax Credits Appeals) Regulations, SI 2002/3237.

1 Provision prescribing the procedure to be followed in connection with—

(*a*) the making of decisions or determinations by the Secretary of State . . . [1]; and

(*b*) the withdrawal of claims, applications, appeals or references falling to be decided or determined by the Secretary of State . . . [1].

Modifications—See Tax Credits (Appeals) Regulations, SI 2002/2926 reg 9 (temporary modification of this section in respect of appeals under the Tax Credits Act 2002 s 63 for a temporary period).

Amendments—[1] Words ", an appeal tribunal or a Commissioner" repealed, in both places, by the Transfer of Tribunal Functions Order, SI 2008/2833 art 6, Sch 3 paras 143, 173 with effect from 3 November 2008.

2

Amendments—This para repealed by the Transfer of Tribunal Functions Order, SI 2008/2833 art 6, Sch 3 paras 143, 173 with effect from 3 November 2008.

3 Provision as to the form which is to be used for any document, the evidence which is to be required and the circumstances in which any official record or certificate is to be sufficient or conclusive evidence.

4 Provision as to the time within which, or the manner in which—

(*a*) any evidence is to be produced; or

(*b*) any application, reference or appeal is to be made.

5–8

Amendments—Paras 5–8 repealed by the Transfer of Tribunal Functions Order, SI 2008/2833 art 6, Sch 3 paras 143, 173 with effect from 3 November 2008.

9 Provision for the non-disclosure to a person of the particulars of any medical advice or medical evidence given or submitted for the purposes of a determination.

SCHEDULE 7

MINOR AND CONSEQUENTIAL AMENDMENTS

Income and Corporation Taxes Act 1988 (c 1)

16 (*amends* TA 1988 s 172(3); sub-para (*b*) *repealed* by the Welfare Reform and Pensions Act 1999 s 88 Sch 13, Pt VI with effect from 6 April 2000).

Social Security Contributions and Benefits Act 1992 (c 4)

56 (*amends* SSCBA 1992 s 1(2), (4)(*a*), (6)).

57 (*inserts* SSCBA 1992 s 6(2A); *repealed* by the Welfare Reform and Pensions Act 1999 s 88 Sch 13, Pt VI with effect from 6 April 2000).

58—(1) (*amends* SSCBA 1992 s 10(5)).

(2) (*inserts* SSCBA 1992 s 10(8A)).

Amendments—This paragraph repealed by the Child Support, Pensions and Social Security Act 2000 s 85, Sch 9 Pt VIII with effect for the tax year beginning with 6 April 2000 and subsequent tax years.

59 (*inserts* SSCBA 1992 s 14(4)).

. . .

67–71(*amend* SSCBA 1992 ss 116(2), 117(1), 119, 120(1), 122(1); para 71(*e*) *repealed by* NICA 2002 s 7, Sch 2).

74 (*amends* SSCBA 1992 s 163(1)).

. . .

77 (*amends* SSCBA 1992 Sch 1 heading and paras 1, 3, 5, 5A and 6; to be partly repealed by the Pensions Act 2007 s 27, Sch 7 Pt 7 with effect from a date to be appointed).

Note—Provisions omitted are outside the scope of this Publication.

(11) (*inserts* SSCBA 1992 Sch 1 para 6(4A)).

(12) (*amends* SSCBA 19m92 Sch 1 para 7(11)(*a*)).

(13) . . . [1]

(14) (*amends* SSCBA 1992 Sch 1 para 8(1)(*b*)).

(15) (*inserts* SSCBA 1992 Sch 1 para 8(1)(*ia*)).

(16) (*amends* SSCBA 1992 Sch 1 para 8(1)(*l*)).

Amendments—[1] Sub-para 13 repealed by the Social Security Contributions (Transfer of Functions, etc) Act 1999 s 26(3) and Sch 10 Pt 1 with effect from 1 April 1999 by virtue of the Social Security Contributions (Transfer of Functions, etc) Act 1999 (Commencement No 1 and Transitional Provisions) Order, SI 1999/527.

Social Security Administration Act 1992 (c 5)

83 (*repeals* SSAA 1992 s 116(6)).

84 (*substitutes* SSAA 1992 s 117).

85 (*repeals* SSAA 1992 s 119(2)).

86 (*amends* SSAA 1992 s 120).

87 (*repeals words in* SSAA 1992 s 121(1)(2)).

89 (*amends* SSAA 1992 s 125(1)).

90 (*substitutes* SSAA 1992 s 143(1)(*a*)(*b*) and 143(4)(*a*)).

91 (*amends* SSAA 1992 s 144; *repealed* by the Welfare Reform and Pensions Act 1999 s 88 Sch 13, Pt VI with effect from 6 April 2000).

92 (*substitutes* SSAA 1992 s 145(1)–(3)).

93 (*repeals* SSAA 1992 s 146).

94 (*amends* SSAA 1992 s 147).

104 (*amends* SSAA 1992 s 170(5)).

105 (*amends* SSAA 1992 s 177(5)).

107 (*amends* SSAA 1992 s 179(3)(*a*), (4)(*ab*)).

109 (*repeals words in* SSAA 1992 s 189).

110 (*amends* SSAA 1992 s 190(1)(*a*) and repeals s190(4); sub-para (*a*) *repealed* by the Welfare Reform and Pensions Act 1999 s 88 Sch 13, Pt VI with effect from 6 April 2000).

111 (*amends* SSAA 1992 s 191).

114—(1) (*amends* SSAA 1992 Sch 7 Pt I para 3(*a*)).

(2) . . .

Pension Schemes Act 1993 (c 48)

126 (*repealed* by the Pensions Act 2007 s 27, Sch 7 Pt 6 with effect from 26 September 2007).

127 (*substitutes* PSA 1993 s 41(1)(1A)(1B)(1C)).

128 (*substitutes* PSA 1993 s 42A(1)(2)(2A)(2B); to be partly repealed by the Pensions Act 2007 s 27, Sch 7 Pt 7 with effect from a date to be appointed).

129 (*amends* PSA 1993 s 158(6)(*c*)).

131 (*substitutes* PSA 1993 s 170).

SCHEDULE 8

REPEALS

Note—The effect of the repeals made by this Schedule is noted in the text of the affected legislation.

SOCIAL SECURITY CONTRIBUTIONS (TRANSFER OF FUNCTIONS, ETC) ACT 1999

(1999 Chapter 2)

ARRANGEMENT OF SECTIONS

NIC

An Act to transfer from the Secretary of State to the Commissioners of Inland Revenue or the Treasury certain functions relating to national insurance contributions, the National Insurance Fund, statutory sick pay, statutory maternity pay or pension schemes and certain associated functions relating to benefits; to enable functions relating to any of those matters in respect of Northern Ireland to be transferred to the Secretary of State, the Commissioners of Inland Revenue or the Treasury; to make further provision, in connection with the functions transferred, as to the powers of the Commissioners of Inland Revenue, the making of decisions and appeals; to provide that rebates payable in respect of members of money purchase contracted-out pension schemes are to be payable out of the National Insurance Fund; and for connected purposes.

[25 February 1999]

PART I
GENERAL

Transfer of functions

1 Transfer to Board of certain functions relating to contributions, etc

(1) Schedule 1 to this Act (which contains amendments transferring to the Board certain functions of the Secretary of State which have been exercised by the Contributions Agency and certain associated functions of the Secretary of State in relation to benefits, together with other amendments related to the transfer of those functions) shall have effect.

(2) The functions of the Secretary of State under the provisions of subordinate legislation specified in Schedule 2 to this Act are hereby transferred to the Board.

2 Transfer of other functions to Treasury or Board

Schedule 3 to this Act (which contains amendments transferring to the Treasury or the Board certain other functions of the Secretary of State, together with amendments related to the transfer of those functions) shall have effect.

Exercise by Board of functions transferred to them

3 General functions of Board

[(1) The Commissioners for Her Majesty's Revenue and Customs shall be responsible for the collection and management of contributions.][1]

(6) In Schedule 2 to the Social Security Contributions and Benefits Act 1992 (levy of Class 4 contributions with income tax) and Schedule 2 to the Social Security Contributions and Benefits (Northern Ireland) Act 1992, paragraph 6(2) (which is superseded by subsection (1) above) shall cease to have effect.

(7) In this section "contributions" includes contributions under Part I of the Social Security Contributions and Benefits (Northern Ireland) Act 1992.

Amendments—[1] Sub-s (1) substituted for sub-ss (1)–(5) by CRCA 2005 s 50, Sch 4 paras 73, 74 with effect from 18 April 2005 (by virtue of SI 2005/1126).

4 Recovery of contributions where income tax recovery provisions not applicable

The provisions of Schedule 4 shall have effect with respect to the recovery of—

(*a*) those Class 1, Class 1A [and Class 1B][3] contributions to which regulations under paragraph 6 [or 7BZA][2] of Schedule 1 to the Social Security Contributions and Benefits Act 1992 [or paragraph 6 [or 7BZA][2] of Schedule 1 to the Social Security Contributions and Benefits (Northern Ireland) Act 1992][1] (power to combine collection of contributions with income tax) do not apply,

[(*aa*) those Class 2 contributions in relation to which—

(i) the regulations mentioned in paragraph (a), and

(ii) Part 6 of the Taxes Management Act 1970 (collection and recovery),

do not apply,][3]

(*b*) . . . [2]

(*c*) interest or penalties payable under regulations made under paragraph 7A . . . [2] of Schedule 1 to [the Social Security Contributions and Benefits Act 1992 or paragraph 7A . . . [2] of Schedule 1 to the Social Security Contributions and Benefits (Northern Ireland) Act 1992][1] [and

(*d*) interest or penalties—

(i) payable under regulations made under paragraph 7B of Schedule 1 to the Social Security Contributions and Benefits Act 1992 and to which regulations under paragraph 7BZA of that Schedule do not apply, or

(ii) payable under regulations made under paragraph 7B of Schedule 1 to the Social Security Contributions and Benefits (Northern Ireland) Act 1992 and to which regulations under paragraph 7BZA of that Schedule do not apply.][2]

Amendments—[1] Words inserted and substituted by the Welfare Reform and Pensions Act 1999 s 81 Sch 11 paras 29, 31 with effect from 11 November 1999.

2 References in para (*a*) inserted; para (*b*) and the word following it repealed; words in para (*c*) repealed; and para (*d*) inserted; by the NIC and Statutory Payments Act 2004 ss 11, 12, Sch 1 para 5, Sch 2 Pt 1 with effect from 1 September 2004 (by virtue of SI 2004/1943).

3 In para (*a*) words substituted, and para (*aa*) inserted, by NICA 2015 s 2, Sch 1 paras 23, 24 with effect for the tax year 2015–16 and subsequent tax years.

5 Powers relating to enforcement

Schedule 5 to this Act (which relates to the enforcement powers of the Board in relation to functions transferred to them by this Act) shall have effect.

6 Disclosure of information

Schedule 6 to this Act (which contains amendments relating to the supply or disclosure of information) shall have effect.

7 Use of information by Board

Amendment—This section repealed by CRCA 2005 ss 50, 52, Sch 4 paras 73, 75, Sch 5 with effect from 18 April 2005 (by virtue of SI 2005/1126).

PART II
DECISIONS AND APPEALS

8 Decisions by officers of Board

(1) Subject to the provisions of this Part, it shall be for an officer of the Board—

(*a*) to decide whether for the purposes of Parts I to V of the Social Security Contributions and Benefits Act 1992 a person is or was an earner and, if so, the category of earners in which he is or was to be included,

(*b*) to decide whether a person is or was employed in employed earner's employment for the purposes of Part V of the Social Security Contributions and Benefits Act 1992 (industrial injuries),

(*c*) to decide whether a person is or was liable to pay contributions of any particular class and, if so, the amount that he is or was liable to pay,

(*d*) to decide whether a person is or was entitled to pay contributions of any particular class that he is or was not liable to pay and, if so, the amount that he is or was entitled to pay,

(*e*) to decide whether contributions of a particular class have been paid in respect of any period,

[(*ea*) to decide whether a person is or was entitled to make a deduction under section 4 of the National Insurance Contributions Act 2014 (deductions etc of employment allowance) and, if so, the amount the person is or was entitled to deduct,

(*eb*) to decide whether a person is or was entitled to a repayment under that section and, if so, the amount of the repayment,][6]

(*f*) subject to and in accordance with regulations made for the purposes of this paragraph by the Secretary of State with the concurrence of the Board, to decide any issue arising as to, or in connection with, entitlement to statutory sick pay[, statutory maternity pay, [ordinary statutory paternity pay, additional statutory paternity pay][5] or statutory adoption pay][4] [or statutory shared parental pay][7],

(*g*) to make any other decision that falls to be made [under Parts 11 [to 12ZC][7] of the Social Security Contributions and Benefits Act 1992 (statutory sick pay, statutory maternity pay, [[statutory paternity pay][8] statutory adoption pay)][4] [and statutory shared parental pay][7]

[(*ga*) to make any decision that falls to be made under regulations under section 7 of the Employment Act 2002 (funding of employers' liabilities to make payments of [[statutory paternity pay,][8] statutory adoption pay,][5] [or statutory shared parental pay][7]][4]

(*h*) to decide any question as to the issue and content of a notice under subsection (2) of section 121C of the Social Security Administration Act 1992 (liability of directors etc for company's contributions),

(*i*) to decide any issue arising under section 27 of the Jobseekers Act 1995 (employment of long-term unemployed: deductions by employers), or under any provision of regulations under that section, as to—

(i) whether a person is or was an employee or employer of another,

(ii) whether an employer is or was entitled to make any deduction from his contributions payments in accordance with regulations under section 27 of that Act,

(iii) whether a payment falls to be made to an employer in accordance with those regulations,

(iv) the amount that falls to be so deducted or paid, or

(v) whether two or more employers are, by virtue of regulations under section 27 of that Act, to be treated as one,

[(*ia*) to decide whether to give or withdraw an approval for the purposes of paragraph 3B(1)(*b*) of Schedule 1 to the Social Security Contributions and Benefits Act 1992;][3]

(*j*) . . .[2]

(*k*) to decide whether a person is liable to a penalty under—

(i) paragraph 7A(2) or 7B(2)(*h*) of Schedule 1 to the Social Security Contributions and Benefits Act 1992, or

(ii) section 113(1)(*a*) of the Social Security Administration Act 1992,

(*l*) to decide the . . . [2] penalty payable under any of the provisions mentioned in [paragraph (*k*)][2] above, and

(*m*) to decide such issues relating to contributions, other than the issues specified in paragraphs (*a*) to (*l*) above or in paragraphs 16 and 17 of Schedule 3 to the Social Security Act 1998, as may be prescribed by regulations made by the Board.

[(1A) No decision in respect of Class 2 contributions under section 11(2) of the Social Security Contributions and Benefits Act 1992 may be made under subsection (1) in relation to an issue specified in paragraph (c) or (e) of that subsection if the person to whom the decision would relate—

(*a*) has appealed under Part 5 of the Taxes Management Act 1970 in relation to that issue,

(*b*) can appeal under that Part in relation to that issue, or

(*c*) might in the future, without the agreement of Her Majesty's Revenue and Customs or permission of the tribunal, be able to appeal under that Part in relation to that issue.][9]

(2) Subsection (1)(*c*) and (*e*) above do not include any decision relating to Class 4 contributions other than a decision falling to be made—

(*a*) under subsection (1) of section 17 of the Social Security Contributions and Benefits Act 1992 as to whether by regulations under that subsection a person is or was excepted from liability for Class 4 contributions, or his liability is or was deferred, or

(*b*) under regulations made by virtue of subsection (3) or (4) of that section or section 18 of that Act.

(3) Subsection (1)(*g*) above does not include—

(*a*) any decision as to the making of subordinate legislation, or

(*b*) any decision as to whether the liability to pay statutory sick pay[, statutory maternity pay, [[statutory paternity pay,][8] statutory adoption pay][4] [or statutory shared parental pay][7] is a liability of the Board rather than the employer.

(4) . . . [1]

Regulations—See the Social Security Contributions (Intermediaries) Regulations, SI 2000/727.

Statutory Shared Parental Pay (Administration) Regulations, SI 2014/2929.

Simon's Tax Cases—*R&C Comrs v Thompson* [2007] STC 240.

Amendments—[1] Sub-s (4) repealed by the Welfare Reform and Pensions Act 1999 ss 88 Sch 13 Pt VI with effect from 6 April 2000.

[2] Sub-s (1)(*j*) repealed and words in sub-s (1)(*l*) substituted and repealed by the Child Support, Pensions and Social Security Act 2000 ss 76(6), (7), 85, Sch 9 Pt VIII with effect for interest accruing on sums becoming due in respect of the tax year beginning 6 April 2000 or any subsequent tax year.

[3] Sub-s (1)(*ia*) inserted by the Child Support, Pensions and Social Security Act 2000 s 77(5) with effect from 28 July 2000.

[4] Words in sub-ss (1)(*f*), (*g*), (3)(*b*) substituted, and sub-s (1)(*ga*) inserted, by EmA 2002 s 9 with effect from 8 December 2002 (by virtue of SI 2002/2866).

[5] In sub-ss (1)(*f*), (*g*), (*ga*), (3)(*b*) words substituted by the Work and Families Act 2006 s 11, Sch 1 para 46 with effect from 3 March 2010 (by virtue of SI 2010/495, art 3(b), (c)).

[6] Sub-s (1)(*ea*), (*eb*) inserted by the NICs Act 2014 s 6(1) with effect from 6 April 2014.

[7] In sub-s (1), in paras (*f*), (*g*), (*ga*) words inserted, in para (*g*) words substituted for words "to 12ZB", and in sub-s (3)(*b*), words inserted, by the Children and Families Act 2014 s 126, Sch 7 paras 44, 45(1), (2)(*b*), (*c*), (*e*), (*g*), (3)(*b*) with effect from 1 December 2014 (by virtue of SI 2014/1640 art 5).

[8] In sub-ss (1)(*f*), (*g*), (*ga*), (3)(*b*), words substituted by the Children and Families Act 2014 s 126, Sch 7 paras 44, 45(2)(*a*), (*d*), (*f*), (3)(*a*) with effect from 5 April 2015 (by virtue of SI 2014/1640 art 7).

[9] Sub-s (1A) inserted by NICA 2015 s 2, Sch 1 paras 23, 25 with effect for the tax year 2015–16 and subsequent tax years.

9 Regulations with respect to decisions

(1) Subject to the provisions of this Part and of the Social Security Administration Act 1992, provision may be made by the Board by regulations as to the making by their officer of any decision under or in connection with the Social Security Contributions and Benefits Act 1992, the Social Security Administration Act 1992 or the Jobseekers Act 1995 which falls to be made by such an officer.

(2) Where it appears to an officer of the Board that a matter before him involves a question of fact requiring special expertise, he may direct that in dealing with that matter he shall have the assistance of one or more experts.

(3) In subsection (2) above "expert" means a person appearing to the officer of the Board to have knowledge or experience which would be relevant in determining the question of fact requiring special expertise.

Regulations—See the Social Security Contributions (Decisions and Appeals) (Amendment) Regulations, SI 2015/174.

10 Decisions varying or superseding earlier decisions

(1) [Subject to subsection (2A) below,][1] The Board may by regulations make provision—

(*a*) for any decision of an officer of the Board under section 8 of this Act (including a decision superseding an earlier decision) to be varied either within the prescribed period or in prescribed cases or circumstances, (*b*) for any such decision to be superseded, in prescribed circumstances, by a subsequent decision made by an officer of the Board, and

(*c*) for any such decision as confirmed or varied by the [First-tier Tribunal or Upper Tribunal][2] on appeal to be superseded, in the event of a material change of circumstances since the decision was made, by a subsequent decision made by an officer of the Board.

(2) The date as from which—

(*a*) any variation of a decision, or

(*b*) any decision superseding an earlier decision,

is to take effect shall be determined in accordance with the regulations.

[(2A) The decisions in relation to which provision may be made by regulations under this section shall not include decisions falling within section 8(1)(*ia*) above.][1]

(3) In this section "prescribed" means prescribed by regulations under this section.

Amendments—[1] Words in sub-s (1) and whole of sub-s (2A) inserted by the Child Support, Pensions and Social Security Act 2000 s 77(6) with effect from 28 July 2000.

[2] In sub-s (1)(*c*) word substituted for the words "tax appeal Commissioners" by the Transfer of Tribunal Functions and Revenue and Customs Appeals Order, SI 2009/56 art 3, Sch 1 para 269 with effect from 1 April 2009.

11 Appeals against decisions of Board

(1) This section applies to any decision of an officer of the Board under section 8 of this Act or under regulations made by virtue of section 10(1)(*b*) or (*c*) of this Act (whether as originally made or as varied under regulations made by virtue of section 10(1)(*a*) of this Act).

(2) In the case of a decision to which this section applies—

(*a*) if it relates to a person's entitlement to statutory sick pay[, statutory maternity pay, [[statutory paternity pay,][5] statutory adoption pay][1] [or statutory shared parental pay][4], the employee and employer concerned shall each have a right to appeal to the [tribunal][2], and

(*b*) in any other case, the person in respect of whom the decision is made and such other person as may be prescribed shall have a right to appeal to the [tribunal][2].

(3) In subsection (2)(*b*) above "prescribed" means prescribed by the Board by regulations.

(4) This section has effect subject to section 121D of the Social Security Administration Act 1992 (appeals in relation to personal liability notices).

Regulations—See the Social Security Contributions (Decisions and Appeals) (Amendment) Regulations, SI 2015/174.

Amendments—[1] Words in sub-s (2)(*a*) substituted by the Employment Act 2002 s 9(4) with effect from 8 December 2002 (by virtue of SI 2002/2866).

[2] In sub-s (2)word substituted in both places for the words "tax appeal Commissioners" by the Transfer of Tribunal Functions and Revenue and Customs Appeals Order, SI 2009/56 art 3, Sch 1 para 270 with effect from 1 April 2009.

[3] In sub-s (2)(*a*) words substituted by the Work and Families Act 2006 s 11 Sch 1 para 47 with effect from 6 April 2010 (by virtue of SI 2010/495 art 4(*d*)).

[4] In sub-s (2)(*a*), words inserted by the Children and Families Act 2014 s 126, Sch 7 paras 44, 46(b) with effect from 1 December 2014 (by virtue of SI 2014/1640 art 5).

[5] In sub-s (2)(*a*), words "statutory paternity pay," substituted fby the Children and Families Act 2014 s 126, Sch 7 paras 44, 46(a) with effect from 5 April 2015 (by virtue of SI 2014/1640 art 7).

12 Exercise of right of appeal

(1) Any appeal against a decision must be brought by a notice of appeal in writing given within 30 days after the date on which notice of the decision was issued.

(2) The notice of appeal shall be given to the officer of the Board by whom notice of the decision was given.

[(3) The notice of appeal shall specify the grounds of appeal.][1]

(4), (5) . . . [1]

Amendments—[1] Sub-s (3) substituted, sub-ss (4), (5) repealed by the Transfer of Tribunal Functions and Revenue and Customs Appeals Order, SI 2009/56 art 3, Sch 1 para 271 with effect from 1 April 2009.

13 Regulations with respect to appeals

(1) The Board may, by regulations made with the concurrence of the Lord Chancellor and the Lord Advocate, make provision with respect to appeals to the [tribunal][1] under this Part.

(2) Regulations under subsection (1) above may, in particular—

(*a*) make provision with respect to any of the matters dealt with in the following provisions of the Taxes Management Act 1970—

(i) . . . [1]

(ii) sections 48 to 54 (appeals to the [tribunal][1] under the Taxes Acts), and

(iii) [section 56 (payment of tax where there is a further appeal)][1], or

(*b*) provide for any of those provisions of that Act to apply, with such modifications as may be specified in the regulations, in relation to an appeal to the [tribunal][1] tax appeal Commissioners under this Part.

[(2A) Regulations under subsection (1) above may provide for sections 11(2) and 13(2) of the Tribunals, Courts and Enforcement Act 2007 to apply with such modifications as may be specified in the regulations in relation to an appeal to the tribunal under this Part.][2]

(3)–(5) . . . [1]

Note—The functions of the Lord Advocate are hereby transferred to the Secretary of State by virtue of the Transfer of Functions (Lord Advocate and Secretary of State) Order, SI 1999/678 with effect from 19 May 1999.

Regulations—See the Social Security Contributions (Decisions and Appeals) (Amendment) Regulations, SI 2015/174.

Social Security Contributions (Amendments in Consequence of Part 4 of the Finance Act 2014) Regulations, SI 2015/521.

Amendments—[1] In sub-ss (1), (2)(*a*)(ii), (2)(*b*) word substituted for the words "tax appeal Commissioners"; sub-para (2)(*a*)(i) repealed; words in sub-s (2)(*a*)(iii) substituted for the words "sections 56 and 56A (appeals from their decisions)"; sub-ss (3)–(5) repealed by the Transfer of Tribunal Functions and Revenue and Customs Appeals Order, SI 2009/56 art 3, Sch 1 para 272 with effect from 1 April 2009.

[2] Sub-s (2A) inserted by the Revenue and Customs Appeals Order, SI 2009/777 art 3 with effect from 1 April 2009.

14 Matters arising as respects decisions

(1) The Board may by regulations make provision as respects matters arising—

(*a*) pending any decision of an officer of the Board under section 8 of this Act which relates to—

(i) statutory sick pay[, statutory maternity pay, [[statutory paternity pay,][5] statutory adoption pay][1] [or statutory shared parental pay][4], or

(ii) any person's liability for contributions,

(*b*) pending the determination by the [tribunal][2] of an appeal against any such decision,

(*c*) out of the variation, under regulations made under section 10 of this Act or on appeal, of any such decision, or

(*d*) out of the making of a decision which, under regulations made under that section, supersedes an earlier decision.

(2) Regulations under this section may, in particular—

(*a*) make provision making a person liable to pay contributions pending the determination by the [tribunal][2] of an appeal against a decision of an officer of the Board, and

(*b*) make provision as to the repayment in prescribed circumstances of contributions paid by virtue of the regulations.

(3) Regulations under this section must be made with the concurrence of the Secretary of State in so far as they relate to statutory sick pay[, statutory maternity pay, [[statutory paternity pay,][5] statutory adoption pay][1] [or statutory shared parental pay][4].

Amendments—[1] Words in sub-ss (1)(*a*)(i), (3) substituted by the Employment Act 2002 s 9 with effect from 8 December 2002 (by virtue of SI 2002/2866).

[2] In sub-ss (1)(*b*), (2)(*a*), word substituted for the words "tax appeal Commissioners" by the Transfer of Tribunal Functions and Revenue and Customs Appeals Order, SI 2009/56 art 3, Sch 1 para 273 with effect from 1 April 2009.

[3] In sub-ss (1)(*a*)(i), (3) words substituted by the Work and Families Act 2006 s 11 Sch 1 para 48 with effect from 6 April 2010 (by virtue of SI 2010/495 art 4(*d*)).

[4] In sub-ss (1)(*a*)(i), (3), words inserted by the Children and Families Act 2014 s 126, Sch 7 paras 44, 47(1), (2)(*b*), (3)(*b*) with effect from 30 June 2014 (by virtue of SI 2014/1640 art 3).

[5] In sub-ss (1)(*a*)(i), (3), words substituted by the Children and Families Act 2014 s 126, Sch 7 paras 44, 47(2)(*a*), (3)(*a*) with effect from 5 April 2015 (by virtue of SI 2014/1640 art 7).

15 Power to make provision for period before commencement of new social security appeal provisions

(1) The Secretary of State may by regulations modify any of the enactments to which this subsection applies during any period in which section 8 of this Act is in force but Chapter II of Part I of the Social Security Act 1998 (social security decisions and appeals) is not yet wholly in force.

(2) Subsection (1) above applies to—

(*a*) Part II of the Social Security Administration Act 1992 (adjudication), and

(*b*) the Acts amended by section 16 of, and Schedule 7 to, this Act.

16 Decisions under Pension Schemes Act 1993

(1) The function of determining the questions referred to in subsection (1) of section 170 of the Pension Schemes Act 1993, as that section has effect before the commencement of paragraph 131 of Schedule 7 to the Social Security Act 1998, is hereby transferred to an officer of the Board.

(2) (*substitutes* PSA 1993 s 170(2)–(7))

17 Arrangements for discharge of decision-making functions

(1) The Secretary of State may make arrangements with the Board for any of his functions under Chapter II of Part I of the Social Security Act 1998 in relation to—

(*a*) a decision whether a person was (within the meaning of regulations) precluded from regular employment by responsibilities at home, or

(*b*) a decision whether a person is entitled to be credited with earnings or contributions in accordance with regulations made under section 22(5) [or (5ZA)][1] of the Social Security Contributions and Benefits Act 1992,

to be discharged by the Board or by officers of the Board.

(2) No such arrangements shall affect the responsibility of the Secretary of State or the application of Chapter II of Part I of the Social Security Act 1998 in relation to any decision.

(3) Until the commencement of Chapter II of Part I of the Social Security Act 1998, the references to that Chapter in subsections (1) and (2) above shall have effect as references to Part II of the Social Security Administration Act 1992.

Amendment—[1] Words in sub-s (1)(*b*) inserted by the Pensions Act 2014 (Consequential and Supplementary Amendments) Order, SI 2016/224 art 5 with effect from 6 April 2016.

18 Amendments relating to decisions and appeals

Schedule 7 to this Act (which contains amendments relating to decisions and appeals) shall have effect.

[19 Interpretation of Part II

In this Part—

"tribunal" means the First-tier Tribunal or, where determined by or under Tribunal Procedure Rules, the Upper Tribunal.][1]

Amendment—[1] This section substituted by the Transfer of Tribunal Functions and Revenue and Customs Appeals Order, SI 2009/56 art 3, Sch 1 para 274 with effect from 1 April 2009.

[2] Words in sub-s (1) inserted by the Pensions Act 2014 (Consequential and Supplementary Amendments) Order, SI 2016/224 art 3(1), (2) with effect from 6 April 2016.

PART III

MISCELLANEOUS AND SUPPLEMENTAL

20 Payments in respect of money purchase contracted-out pension schemes to be made out of National Insurance Fund

(1) (*amends PSA 1993, s 177; para (b) repealed by the Welfare Reform and Pensions Act 1999 s 88 Sch 13, Pt VI with effect from 6 April 2000.*)

(2) (*amends the Pension Schemes (Northern Ireland) Act 1993, s 172.*)

(3) There shall be paid out of the National Insurance Fund into the Consolidated Fund such sum as the Secretary of State may estimate to be the amount of any payments made by the Secretary of State under subsection (3) of section 42A of the Pension Schemes Act 1993 during the period beginning with 1st April 1998 and ending with the passing of this Act, after deduction of the amount of any payments recovered by him under subsection (5) of that section during that period.

(4) There shall be paid out of the Northern Ireland National Insurance Fund into the Consolidated Fund of Northern Ireland such sum as the Department of Health and Social Services for Northern Ireland may estimate to be the amount of any payments made by the Department under subsection (3) of section 38A of the Pension Schemes (Northern Ireland) Act 1993 during the period beginning with 1st April 1998 and ending with the passing of this Act, after deduction of the amount of any payments recovered by it under subsection (5) of that section during that period.

(5) . . . [1]

Amendments—[1] Sub-s (5) repealed by the Welfare Reform and Pensions Act 1999, s 88 Sch 13 Pt IV, with effect from 6 April 2000.

21 Property, rights and liabilities

(1) In this section a "transfer provision" means any of the following provisions of this Act—

(*a*) section 1 and Schedules 1 and 2,

(*b*) section 2 and Schedule 3,

(*c*) section 8, and

(*d*) section 16(1).

(2) Any property, rights and liabilities to which the Secretary of State is entitled or subject immediately before the commencement of a transfer provision in connection with functions transferred to the Board or the Treasury by virtue of that provision are hereby transferred to the Board or, as the case may be, the Treasury on the commencement of that provision.

(3) A certificate issued by the Board or the Treasury that any property vested in the Secretary of State immediately before the commencement of a transfer provision has been transferred by virtue of this Act to the Board or, as the case may be, the Treasury shall be conclusive evidence of the transfer.

22 Special provision for certain contracts

(1) This section applies to—

(*a*) any contract for the supply of goods or services to the Secretary of State which relates partly to functions transferred by virtue of this Act to the Board (in this section referred to as "transferred functions") and partly to functions retained by the Secretary of State (in this section referred to as "retained functions"), and

(*b*) any contract for the supply of goods or services to the Secretary of State which relates only to transferred functions or only to retained functions, but whose terms are wholly or partly determined in accordance with a contract falling within paragraph (*a*) above.

(2) Section 21 of this Act shall not apply in relation to any contract to which this section applies.

NIC

(3) Subject to subsections (4) and (5) below, in any contract to which this section applies any term restricting the provision of goods or services under the contract to the Secretary of State or the Department of Social Security shall be treated as referring also to the Board, in connection with transferred functions.

(4) If the Secretary of State so provides by order in relation to any specified contract or class of contracts to which this section applies, the provisions of subsection (5) below shall have effect in relation to that contract, or contracts falling within that class, in place of subsection (3) above.

(5) Where this subsection applies, all rights and liabilities of the Secretary of State under the contract are by virtue of this subsection transferred to the Board on the commencement of this subsection, but any term restricting the provision of goods or services under the contract to the Secretary of State or the Department of Social Security shall be treated as referring both to the Board, in connection with transferred functions, and to the Secretary of State or that department.

23 Power to transfer functions by Order in Council

(1) Her Majesty may by Order in Council—

(*a*) provide for the transfer from the Secretary of State to the Board, or from the Board to the Secretary of State, of any transferable function,

(*b*) provide that any transferable function of the Secretary of State is to be exercisable only with the concurrence of the Board or the Treasury, or is to cease to be exercisable only with that concurrence,

(*c*) provide that any transferable function of the Board is to be exercisable only with the concurrence of the Secretary of State, or is to cease to be exercisable only with that concurrence, and

(*d*) provide that any decision to which this paragraph applies—

(i) is to be made by the Secretary of State rather than the Board, or by the Board rather than the Secretary of State, and

(ii) is to be made subject to the provisions of Chapter II of Part I of the Social Security Act 1998, or subject to the provisions of Part II of this Act rather than the provisions of that Chapter.

(2) In subsection (1) above "transferable function" means—

(*a*) any function relating to contributions or the National Insurance Fund, other than functions under section 1(1) of the Social Security Contributions and Benefits Act 1992 (receipt of contributions) or section 161(1) of the Social Security Administration Act 1992 (control and management of National Insurance Fund),

(*b*) any function relating to statutory sick pay or statutory maternity pay,

(*c*) any function under section 7 of the Social Security Act 1986 (occupational pension schemes becoming contracted-out between 1986 and 1993), so far as that section remains in force by virtue of paragraph 22 of Schedule 6 to the Pension Schemes Act 1993, or

(*d*) any function under Part III of the Pension Schemes Act 1993.

(3) The decisions to which subsection (1)(*d*) above applies are—

(*a*) any decision which is or has been specified—

(i) in section 8(1) of this Act,

(ii) in section 170(2) of the Pension Schemes Act 1993 (as amended by section 16(2) of this Act), or

(iii) in paragraph 16 or 17 of Schedule 3 to the Social Security Act 1998, and

(*b*) any other decision relating to contributions, the National Insurance Fund, statutory sick pay, statutory maternity pay or the subject-matter of Part III of the Pension Schemes Act 1993.

(4) An Order in Council under this section may contain such supplemental, consequential or transitional provision as appears to Her Majesty to be expedient, including provision—

(*a*) for the transfer of any property, rights and liabilities held, enjoyed or incurred by the Secretary of State or the Board in connection with any functions transferred,

(*b*) for the carrying on and completion by or under the authority of the person to whom any functions are transferred of anything commenced by or under the authority of the person from whom they are transferred before the date when the Order takes effect,

(*c*) as to the effect of any provision made by virtue of subsection (1)(*d*) above on decisions or proceedings made or commenced before the date when the Order takes effect,

(*d*) making such amendments of any enactment, including any enactment contained in this Act, as may be necessary for the purposes of the Order, and

(*e*) for the substitution of the person to whom any functions are transferred for the person from whom they are transferred in any instrument, contract or legal proceedings made or commenced before the date when the Order takes effect.

(5) A certificate issued by a relevant authority that any property vested in the other relevant authority immediately before an Order under this section takes effect has been transferred by virtue of the Order to the relevant authority issuing the certificate shall be conclusive evidence of the transfer; and in this subsection "relevant authority" means the Secretary of State or the Board.

(6) In the application of this section to Northern Ireland—

(*a*) references to the Secretary of State include references to the Department of Health and Social Services for Northern Ireland,

(*b*) "contributions" means contributions under Part I of the Social Security Contributions and Benefits (Northern Ireland) Act 1992,

(*c*) references to Chapter II of Part I of, and paragraphs 16 and 17 of Schedule 3 to, the Social Security Act 1998 have effect as references to Chapter II of Part II of, and paragraphs 16 and 17 of Schedule 3 to, the Social Security (Northern Ireland) Order 1998,

(*d*) the reference to the National Insurance Fund has effect as a reference to the Northern Ireland National Insurance Fund,

(*e*) references to section 1(1) of the Social Security Contributions and Benefits Act 1992 and section 161(1) of the Social Security Administration Act 1992 have effect as references to section 1(1) of the Social Security Contributions and Benefits (Northern Ireland) Act 1992 and section 141(1) of the Social Security Administration (Northern Ireland) Act 1992,

(*f*) references to section 7 of the Social Security Act 1986 and paragraph 22 of Schedule 6 to the Pension Schemes Act 1993 have effect as references to Article 9 of the Social Security (Northern Ireland) Order 1986 and paragraph 21 of Schedule 5 to the Pension Schemes (Northern Ireland) Act 1993, and

(*g*) the reference to Part III of the Pension Schemes Act 1993 has effect as a reference to Part III of the Pension Schemes (Northern Ireland) Act 1993;

and for the purposes of this section in its application to Northern Ireland any reference in section 8(1) of this Act or section 170(2) of the Pension Schemes Act 1993 to a decision is to be taken to be a reference to the corresponding decision under Northern Ireland legislation.

24 Provision for Northern Ireland

(1) Her Majesty may by Order in Council do any of the following—

(*a*) make provision for transferring from the relevant Northern Ireland authority to the Board any function in relation to Northern Ireland corresponding to a function transferred to the Board by virtue of section 1 of this Act,

(*b*) make provision for transferring from the relevant Northern Ireland authority to the Secretary of State any other function in relation to Northern Ireland which relates to any of the matters specified in paragraph 10 of Schedule 2 to the Northern Ireland Act 1998 (excepted matters),

(*c*) make provision for transferring from the relevant Northern Ireland authority to the Board or the Treasury any function in relation to Northern Ireland corresponding to a function transferred to the Board or, as the case may be, the Treasury by virtue of section 2 of this Act, and

(*d*) make other provision for Northern Ireland for purposes corresponding to any or all of the purposes of those provisions of this Act which do not extend to Northern Ireland.

(2) If an Order in Council made under this section by virtue of subsection (1)(*b*) above has transferred to the Secretary of State any function in relation to Northern Ireland which corresponds to a function transferred to the Board or the Treasury by virtue of section 2 of this Act, Her Majesty may by a further Order in Council under this section make provision for transferring that function from the Secretary of State to the Board or, as the case may be, the Treasury.

(3) An Order in Council under this section may, for the purposes of the Order—

(*a*) amend any enactment, including any enactment contained in this Act,

(*b*) confer, extend or modify any power to legislate by means of an order or regulations, and

(*c*) contain such incidental, supplemental, consequential or transitional provision as appears to Her Majesty to be expedient, including—

(i) provision modifying references in any enactment to the Northern Ireland Assembly, to statutory rules for the purposes of the Statutory Rules (Northern Ireland) Order 1979 or to the Comptroller and Auditor General for Northern Ireland,

(ii) provision for the transfer of property, rights and liabilities, and

(iii) provision for the transfer to Her Majesty's Home Civil Service of persons employed in the Northern Ireland Civil Service.

(4) A certificate issued by the Board, the Secretary of State or the Treasury that any property vested in a Northern Ireland department immediately before an Order under this section takes effect has been transferred by virtue of the Order to the Board, the Secretary of State or the Treasury, as the case may be, shall be conclusive evidence of the transfer.

(5) A certificate issued by the Board or the Treasury that any property vested in the Secretary of State immediately before an Order under this section takes effect has been transferred by virtue of the Order to the Board or the Treasury, as the case may be, shall be conclusive evidence of the transfer.

(6) Subsection (2) above does not limit the powers conferred by section 23 of this Act in relation to Northern Ireland.

(7) In this section "the relevant Northern Ireland authority", in relation to any function, means the Northern Ireland department by which the function is exercisable.

25 Orders and regulations

(1) Any power of the Secretary of State or the Board to make an order or regulations under this Act shall be exercisable by statutory instrument.

(2) Any statutory instrument containing—

(*a*) an Order in Council under section 23 or 24 of this Act, or

(*b*) regulations under any provision of this Act,

shall be subject to annulment in pursuance of a resolution of either House of Parliament.

(3) Any power conferred by this Act to make regulations may be exercised—

(*a*) either in relation to all cases to which the power extends, or in relation to those cases subject to specified exceptions, or in relation to any specified cases or classes of case;

(*b*) so as to make, as respects the cases in relation to which it is exercised—

(i) the full provision to which the power extends or any less provision (whether by way of exception or otherwise);

(ii) the same provision for all cases in relation to which the power is exercised, or different provision for different cases or different classes of case or different provision as respects the same case or class of case for different purposes of this Act;

(iii) any such provision either unconditionally or subject to any specified condition;

and where such a power is expressed to be exercisable for alternative purposes it may be exercised in relation to the same case for any or all of those purposes.

(4) Powers to make regulations for the purposes of any one provision of this Act are without prejudice to powers to make regulations for the purposes of any other provision.

(5) A power conferred by this Act to make regulations includes power to make thereby such incidental, supplementary, consequential or transitional provision as appears to the authority making the regulations to be expedient for the purposes of those regulations.

(6) A power conferred by this Act to make regulations includes power to provide for a person to exercise a discretion in dealing with any matter.

Regulations—Statutory Shared Parental Pay (Administration) Regulations, SI 2014/2929.
See the Social Security Contributions (Decisions and Appeals) (Amendment) Regulations, SI 2015/174.
Social Security Contributions (Amendments in Consequence of Part 4 of the Finance Act 2014) Regulations, SI 2015/521.

26 Savings, transitional provisions, consequential amendments, repeals and revocations

(1) The provisions of this Act shall have effect subject to the savings and transitional provisions in Schedule 8 to this Act.

(2) Schedule 9 to this Act (further consequential amendments) shall have effect

(3) Schedule 10 to this Act (repeals and revocations) shall have effect.

27 Interpretation

In this Act, unless a contrary intention appears—

"the Board" means the Commissioners of Inland Revenue;

"contributions" means contributions under Part I of the Social Security Contributions and Benefits Act 1992.

28 Short title, commencement and extent

(1) This Act may be cited as the Social Security Contributions (Transfer of Functions, etc) Act 1999.

(2) The following provisions of this Act—

(*a*) section 1(1) (with Schedule 1), so far as enabling the Secretary of State to make subordinate legislation conferring functions on the Board,

(*b*) sections 8 to 15, so far as conferring any power to make subordinate legislation,

(*c*) section 17,

(*d*) section 20,

(*e*) section 22(4), so far as conferring the power to make an order,

(*f*) sections 24 and 25,

(*g*) section 26(1) (with Schedule 8), and

(*h*) section 27 and this section,

shall come into force on the passing of this Act.

(3) Except as provided by subsection (2) above, the provisions of this Act shall come into force on such day as the Secretary of State may by order appoint; and different days may be appointed for different purposes.

(4) An order under subsection (3) above may make such savings, or such transitional or consequential provision, as the Secretary of State considers necessary or expedient—

(*a*) in preparation for or in connection with the coming into force of any provision of this Act, or

(*b*) in connection with the operation of any enactment repealed or amended by a provision of this Act during any period when the repeal or amendment is not wholly in force.

(5) The following provisions of this Act extend to Northern Ireland—

(*a*) section 1 and Schedule 1, so far as they amend the Income and Corporation Taxes Act 1988,

(*b*) section 2 and Schedule 3, so far as they amend section 177 of the Social Security Administration Act 1992 or section 88 of the Northern Ireland Act 1998,
(*c*) section 3,
(*d*) section 4 and Schedule 4,
(*e*) section 5 and Schedule 5, so far as they amend the Taxes Management Act 1970,
(*f*) section 18 and Schedule 7, so far as they amend the Taxes Management Act 1970, Schedule 2 to the Social Security Contributions and Benefits Act 1992 or Schedule 2 to the Social Security Contributions and Benefits (Northern Ireland) Act 1992,
(*g*) section 6 and Schedule 6, so far as they amend the Finance Act 1989 or the Finance Act 1997,
(*h*) section 7,
(*i*) sections 23 to 25,
(*j*) section 26(3) and Schedule 10, so far as they relate to any enactment which extends to Northern Ireland, and
(*k*) section 27 and this section.

(6) Section 20(2) and (4) of this Act extends to Northern Ireland only.

(7) Except as provided by subsections (5) and (6) above, this Act does not extend to Northern Ireland.

SCHEDULE 1

TRANSFER OF CONTRIBUTIONS AGENCY FUNCTIONS AND ASSOCIATED FUNCTIONS

Section 1(1)

The amendments made by this Schedule to the Income and Corporation Taxes Act 1988, the Social Security Contributions and Benefits Act 1992, the Social Security Administration Act 1992, and the Pension Schemes Act 1993 are already in effect and are not reproduced here.

SCHEDULE 2

TRANSFER OF FUNCTIONS UNDER SUBORDINATE LEGISLATION

Section 1(2)

Number	Title	Provisions conferring functions transferred
SI 1979/591	The Social Security (Contributions) Regulations 1979.	All the regulations except regulations 36 to 39, 41 to 42 and 44.
. . .	. . .	
SI 1990/536	The Social Security (Refunds) (Repayment of Contractual Maternity Pay) Regulations 1990.	Regulations 2 and 3.
. . .	. . .	. . .
SI 1994/1882	The Statutory Maternity Pay (Compensation of Employers) and Miscellaneous Amendment Regulations 1994.	Regulations 3 and 6.
SI 1995/512	The Statutory Sick Pay Percentage Threshold Order 1995.	Article 4.
. . .	. . .	. . .

Note—Provisions omitted are outside the scope of this Publication.

SCHEDULE 3

TRANSFER OF OTHER FUNCTIONS TO TREASURY OR BOARD

Section 2

Amendments made to the Social Security Contributions and Benefits Act 1992, and Social Security Administration Act 1992 are already in effect and are not reproduced here.

SCHEDULE 4

RECOVERY OF CONTRIBUTIONS WHERE INCOME TAX RECOVERY PROVISIONS NOT APPLICABLE

Section 4

Interpretation

1 In any provision of this Schedule "authorised officer" means an officer of the Board authorised by them for the purposes of that provision.

Magistrates' courts

2—(1) Any amount which—

(*a*) is due by way of contributions or by way of interest or penalty in respect of contributions, and

(*b*) does not exceed the prescribed sum,

shall, without prejudice to any other remedy, be recoverable summarily as a civil debt in proceedings commenced in the name of an authorised officer.

(2) All or any of the sums due from any one person in respect of contributions, or interest or penalties in respect of contributions, (being sums which are by law recoverable summarily) may be included in the same complaint, summons, order, warrant or other document required by law to be laid before justices or to be issued by justices, and every such document shall, as respects each such sum, be construed as a separate document and its invalidity as respects any one such sum shall not affect its validity as respects any other such sum.

(3) Proceedings under this paragraph in England and Wales may be brought—

(*a*) in the case of Class 2 contributions or interest or penalties in respect of such contributions, at any time before the end of the year following the tax year in which the contributor becomes liable to pay the contributions, and

(*b*) in any other case, not later than the first anniversary of the day on which the contributions became due.

(4) In sub-paragraph (1) above, the expression "recoverable summarily as a civil debt" in respect of proceedings in Northern Ireland means recoverable in proceedings under Article 62 of the Magistrates' Courts (Northern Ireland) Order 1981.

(5) In this paragraph—

"the prescribed sum" means the sum for the time being specified in section 65(1) of the Taxes Management Act 1970 (recovery of income tax, etc in magistrates' courts);

"tax year" means the twelve months beginning with 6th April in any year.

County courts

3—(1) Without prejudice to any other remedy, any sum which is due by way of contributions or by way of interest or penalty in respect of contributions may—

(*a*) in England and Wales, and

(*b*) in Northern Ireland, where the amount does not exceed the limit specified in Article 10(1) of the County Courts (Northern Ireland) Order 1980,

be sued for and recovered from the person liable as a debt due to the Crown by proceedings [in England and Wales in the county court or in Northern Ireland][2] in a county court commenced in the name of an authorised officer[1].

(2) An authorised officer may conduct any proceedings under this paragraph before a county court in England and Wales, although not a barrister or solicitor.[1]

(3) In this paragraph as it applies in Northern Ireland, "county court" means a county court held for a division under the County Courts (Northern Ireland) Order 1980.

(4) Sections 21 and 42(2) of the Interpretation Act (Northern Ireland) 1954 shall apply as if any reference in those provisions to any enactment included a reference to this paragraph, and Part III of the County Courts (Northern Ireland) Order 1980 (general civil jurisdiction) shall apply for the purposes of this paragraph in Northern Ireland.

Amendments—[1] Words in sub-para (1), and whole of sub-para (2), repealed by FA 2008 s 137(5) with effect from 21 July 2008. This amendment does not affect proceedings commenced or brought in the name of a collector or authorised officer before 21 July 2008 (FA 2008 s 137(7).

[2] In para 3(1), words inserted by the Crime and Courts Act 2013 s 17, Sch 19 para 129 with effect from 22 April 2014 (by virtue of SI 2014/954 art 2(*a*)).

Prospective amendment—Sub-para (3) to be repealed by the Justice Act (Northern Ireland) 2015 ss 6, 105, Sch 1 para 118, Sch 9 Pt 1 with effect from a date to be appointed.

Sheriff courts in Scotland

4—(1) In Scotland, any sum which is due by way of contributions or by way of interest or penalty in respect of contributions may, without prejudice to any other remedy, be sued for and recovered from the person liable as a debt due to the Crown by proceedings commenced in the sheriff court in the name of an authorised officer.

(2) An authorised officer may conduct any proceedings under this paragraph, although not an advocate or solicitor.

(3) Paragraphs 2 and 3 above shall not apply in Scotland.

General

5—(1) Proceedings may be brought for the recovery of the total amount of Class 1 or Class 1A contributions which an employer has become liable to pay on a particular date and any sum due by way of interest or penalty in respect of those contributions without distinguishing the amounts which the employer is liable to pay in respect of each employee and without specifying the employees in question; and for the purposes of proceedings under any of paragraphs 2 to 4 above that total amount shall be one cause of action or one matter of complaint.
(2) Nothing in sub-paragraph (1) above shall prevent the bringing of separate proceedings for the recovery of each of the several amounts of Class 1 or Class 1A contributions which the employer is liable to pay.

SCHEDULE 5
ENFORCEMENT

Section 5

The amendments made by this Schedule to the Taxes Management Act 1970, the Social Security Administration Act 1992 are already in effect and have not been reproduced here.

SCHEDULE 6
INFORMATION

Section 6

The amendments made by this Schedule to the Social Security Administration Act 1992, the Pension Schemes Act 1993, the Finance Act 1989, and the Finance Act 1997 are already in effect and have not been reproduced here.

SCHEDULE 7
DECISIONS AND APPEALS

Section 18

The amendments made by this Schedule to the Taxes Management Act 1970, the Social Security Contributions and Benefits Act 1992, the Social Security Administration Act 1992, the Social Security Act 1998 are already in effect and have not been reproduced here.

SCHEDULE 8
SAVINGS AND TRANSITIONAL PROVISIONS

Section 26(1)

General savings

1—(1) In this paragraph—

"transfer provision" has the meaning given by section 21(1) of this Act;

"instrument" includes in particular Royal Charters, Orders in Council, Letters Patent, judgments, decrees, orders, rules, regulations, schemes, bye-laws, awards, contracts and other agreements, memoranda and articles of association, warrants, certificates and other documents.

(2) A transfer provision shall not affect the validity of anything done by or in relation to the Secretary of State before the commencement of the transfer provision; and anything which at that date is in the process of being done by or in relation to the Secretary of State may—

(*a*) if it relates to functions transferred by virtue of the transfer provision to the Board, be continued by or in relation to the Board, and

(*b*) if it relates to functions transferred by virtue of the transfer provision to the Treasury, be continued by or in relation to the Treasury.

(3) Any authority, appointment, determination, approval, consent or direction given or made or other thing done, or having effect as if given, made or done, by the Secretary of State in connection with functions transferred by virtue of a transfer provision shall have effect as if given, made or done by the Board or, as the case requires, the Treasury in so far as that is required for continuing its effect after the commencement of the transfer provision.

(4) Any instrument made before the commencement of a transfer provision shall have effect, so far as may be necessary for the purposes of or in consequence of that provision or section 21 or 22 of this Act, as if—

(*a*) any reference to the Secretary of State were or included a reference to the Board or the Treasury, as the case requires; and

(*b*) any reference to the Department of Social Security or any officer of that Department were or included a reference to the Board or any officer of theirs.

Documents and forms

2 Documents or forms produced for use in connection with any function transferred by virtue of this Act to the Board may be used even though they contain references to the Secretary of State or to the Department of Social Security or to any officer of that Department; and those references shall be construed as far as necessary as references to the Board or to any officer of the Board.

3, 4(*Repealed* by the Welfare Reform and Pensions Act 1999 s 88 Sch 13, Pt VI with effect from 6 April 2000).

SCHEDULE 9

FURTHER CONSEQUENTIAL AMENDMENTS

Section 26(2)

Debtors (Scotland) Act 1987 (c 18)

1 In section 1(5)(*f*)(iv) (competence of time to pay direction) and section 5(4)(*f*)(iv) (competence of time to pay order) of the Debtors (Scotland) Act 1987, as amended by paragraph 12 of Schedule 7 to the Social Security Act 1998, for "Secretary of State" there is substituted "Commissioners of Inland Revenue".

2 In paragraph 35(*dd*) of Schedule 5 to the Debtors (Scotland) Act 1987 (interpretation), as inserted by paragraph 14 of Schedule 7 to the Social Security Act 1998, for "Secretary of State" there is substituted "Commissioners of Inland Revenue".

Social Security Contributions and Benefits Act 1992 (c 4)

3 (*inserted* SSCBA 1992 s 12(7)(*aa*);*repealed* by NICA 2015 s 2, Sch 1 paras 23, 27)

4 (*amends* SSCBA 1992 s (1)(*c*))

5 (*amends* SSCBA 1992 Sch 1 para 6(4A))

6 (*amends* SSCBA 1992 Sch 1 para 7A(2), (3))

7 (*amends* SSCBA 1992 Sch 1 para 7B(1), (2), (5), *omits* paras (4), (6))

8 (*repeals* SSCBA 1992 Sch 1 para 7C)

SCHEDULE 10

REPEALS AND REVOCATIONS

Section 26(3)

PART I
REPEALS

Note—The repeals made under this heading are already in effect and have therefore been omitted.

PART II
REVOCATIONS

Note—The table of revocations has been omitted as it is outside the scope of this Publication.

SOCIAL SECURITY CONTRIBUTIONS (SHARE OPTIONS) ACT 2001

(2001 Chapter 20)

ARRANGEMENT OF SECTIONS

An Act to make provision about the payment of National Insurance Contributions in respect of share options and similar rights obtained by persons as directors or employees during the period beginning with 6th April 1999 and ending with 19th May 2000.

[11 May 2001]

1 Notices relating to share options acquired before 19th May 2000

(1) Where—

(*a*) a right to acquire shares in a body corporate was obtained by any person in the period beginning with 6th April 1999 and ending with 19th May 2000,

(*b*) that right is one to which subsection (2) applies,

(*c*) a notice in respect of that right is given in accordance with the following provisions of this section to the Inland Revenue before the end of the period of ninety-two days beginning with the day on which this Act is passed,

liability to contributions in respect of gains realised after 7th November 2000 on the exercise, assignment or release of that right shall be determined in accordance with section 2.

(2) This subsection applies to a right obtained by any person in the period mentioned in subsection (1)(*a*) if—

(*a*) were a gain to be realised after the passing of this Act on the exercise, assignment or release of that right, the gain would or (if circumstances changed) might be one falling, by virtue of section 4(4)(*a*) of the Contributions and Benefits Act, to be treated for the purposes of that Act as remuneration derived from that person's employment; or

(*b*) a gain that has been realised after 7th November 2000 and before the passing of this Act on any exercise, assignment or release of that right has fallen, by virtue of section 4(4)(*a*) of that Act, to be so treated.

(3) The person who may give a notice under this section in respect of any right to which subsection (2) applies by virtue of paragraph (*a*) of that subsection is—

(*a*) where neither of the following paragraphs apply, the person who would be the secondary contributor in relation to any liability to pay secondary Class 1 contributions in respect of a gain realised on an exercise, assignment or release, of that right on the day of the notice;

(*b*) where an election for the purposes of paragraph 3B(1) of Schedule 1 to the Contributions and Benefits Act which is in force on the day of the notice would relate to the whole of any such gain—

(i) the person on whom (apart from this Act) any such liability would fall by virtue of the election; or

(ii) the secondary contributor on whom (apart from this Act) any such liability would fall were no election in force;

(*c*) where an election for the purposes of paragraph 3B(1) of that Schedule which is in force on the day of the notice would relate to only a part of any such gain, the persons mentioned in paragraph (*b*)(i) and (ii), acting jointly.

(4) The person who may give a notice under this section in respect of any right to which subsection (2) applies by virtue of paragraph (*b*) of that subsection is—

(*a*) the person on whom (apart from this Act) the liability for secondary Class 1 contributions payable in respect of the gain mentioned in that paragraph did fall; and

(*b*) if different parts of that liability fell (apart from this Act) on different persons, those persons acting jointly.

(5) A notice under this section in respect of any right—

(*a*) must be given in writing or by such electronic means as may be authorised by regulations made by the Inland Revenue;

(*b*) must contain such matters and be in such form as may be required by any such regulations; and

(*c*) once given, shall be irrevocable.

(6) For the purposes of this Act where, in the case of any right to acquire shares, the person entitled or (if there is more than one) each of the persons entitled to give a notice under this section in respect of that right is a person whose liability by virtue of the giving of such a notice to pay a special contribution under section 2 in respect of that right would be nil, that person or, as the case may be, each of those persons acting jointly shall be deemed—

(*a*) to have given such a notice in respect of that right in accordance with this section and immediately before the end of the period specified in subsection (1)(*c*);

(*b*) to have accompanied that notice with a notification to the Inland Revenue that the liability arising by virtue of that notice was nil; and

(*c*) to have given that notification in the belief that the facts reasonably ascertainable by him at the time at which he is deemed to have given it were grounds for giving it.

Regulations—See the Social Security Contributions (Share Options) Regulations, SI 2001/1817.

NIC

2 Effect of notice under s 1

(1) Subject to subsections (3) and (4) and section 3, where liability to contributions in respect of gains realised after 7th November 2000 on the exercise, assignment or release of any right falls under section 1 to be determined in accordance with this section—

(*a*) no liability to pay any Class 1 contributions in respect of any gain realised after the passing of this Act shall arise on the exercise, assignment or release of that right;

(*b*) any liability to pay Class 1 contributions in respect of any gain realised after 7th November 2000 and before the passing of this Act on any exercise, assignment or release of that right shall be deemed never to have arisen; and

(*c*) the person who gave the notice under that section in respect of that right shall become liable to pay a special contribution in respect of that right under this section.

(2) The amount of the special contribution in respect of any right shall be—

(*a*) 12.2 per cent of the amount (if any) in respect of which Class 1 contributions would have been payable by virtue of section 4(4)(*a*) of the Contributions and Benefits Act if the right had been exercised in full on 7th November 2000 without the giving of any further consideration for the shares acquired by the exercise of that right; or

(*b*) where there is no such amount, nil.

(3) Neither paragraph (*a*) nor paragraph (*b*) of subsection (1) shall apply in relation to any liability to pay Class 1 contributions in respect of so much of any gain realised on the assignment or release of a right as is equal to the amount (if any) by which the first of the following amounts exceeds the second, that is to say—

(*a*) the amount of any valuable consideration given for the assignment or release; and

(*b*) the amount which (in accordance with the provisions of [section 479 of the Income Tax (Earnings and Pensions) Act 2003][1]) would have been taken to be the amount of the gain realised by an exercise in full of that right immediately before the time of its assignment or release [(less any deductible amounts under section 480(1) to (6) of that Act)][2].

(4) Subject to subsection (5), where—

(*a*) a person becomes liable to pay to the Inland Revenue a special contribution under this section in respect of any right, but

(*b*) that liability is not discharged before the end of the period of ninety-two days beginning with the day on which this Act is passed,

the Contributions and Benefits Act and this Act shall have effect as if no notice had been given under section 1 of this Act in respect of that right.

(5) If it appears to the Inland Revenue that a person who has given a notice under section 1 in respect of any right and who would (but for subsection (4) of this section), be liable by virtue of that notice to pay a special contribution under this section—

(*a*) did, within the period of ninety-two days mentioned in that subsection, make a payment in respect of that liability to the Inland Revenue of an amount which he had reasonable grounds for believing was the correct amount of his liability,

(*b*) did, within that period, give notification to the Inland Revenue, in the belief on reasonable grounds that it was correct, that the liability arising by virtue of that notice was nil, or

(*c*) has a reasonable excuse for having failed to do either of those things within that period,

the Inland Revenue may, if they think fit, direct that, in relation to that notice, subsection (1) of section 1 and subsection (4) of this section are to be treated as having had effect with the period of ninety-two days mentioned in those subsections extended by such further period as they may determine.

(6) A decision as to the giving or refusal of a direction under subsection (5) shall be made by an officer of the same description and be subject to the same rights of appeal as any decision, to which the giving of the direction is or would be relevant, as to whether a person is or has been liable to pay contributions of any particular class.

(7) Where paragraph (*b*) of subsection (1) applies in relation to any liability to pay Class 1 contributions and amounts have already been paid to the Inland Revenue in respect of that liability before the passing of this Act—

(*a*) all such repayments shall be made as may be necessary by virtue of that paragraph; but

(*b*) any amount which it would otherwise be necessary to repay in respect of a secondary Class 1 contribution paid by a person who has become liable to pay a special contribution under this section may be retained and set against any undischarged liability of his to pay that special contribution.

Amendments—[1] In sub-s (3)(*b*), words substituted for the words "section 135(3)(*a*) of the Income and Corporation Taxes Act 1988" by ITEPA 2003 s 722, Sch 6 paras 259, 260 with effect, for income tax purposes, from 2003–04; and for corporation tax purposes, for accounting periods ending after 5 April 2003. For transitional provisions and savings see ITEPA 2003 s 723, Sch 7.

[2] In sub-s (3)(*b*), words inserted by FA 2003 s 140, Sch 22 paras 55, 56 with effect on or after the day appointed under FA 2003 Sch 22 para 3(2).

3 Special provision for roll-overs

(1) This section applies where—

(*a*) a right to acquire shares in a body corporate was obtained by any person in the period beginning with 6th April 1999 and ending with 19th May 2000 ("the original right"); and

(*b*) the original right is or has been assigned or released (whether before or after the passing of this Act) for a consideration that consists of or includes another right ("the replacement right") to acquire shares in that or any other body corporate.

(2) If the replacement right or any subsequent replacement right was obtained on or before 7th November 2000, that right shall be treated for the purposes of sections 1 and 2 and this section, but subject to subsection (5), as a right obtained in the period beginning with 6th April 1999 and ending with 19th May 2000.

(3) Where the replacement right is or has been obtained after 7th November 2000 a notice may be given under section 1 in respect of the original right, notwithstanding that the assignment or release of that right was before the giving of the notice.

(4) The liability by virtue of section 2(3) to pay Class 1 contributions in respect of a gain realised on the assignment or release of the original right shall be determined—

(*a*) as if (notwithstanding anything in [[section 483(1) to (4)][2] of the Income Tax (Earnings and Pensions) Act 2003][1]) the replacement right were or, as the case may be, were part of the valuable consideration given for the assignment or release; and

(*b*) as if the value of so much of that consideration as is represented by the replacement right were equal to whichever is the smaller of the following amounts—

(i) the amount which (in accordance with the provisions of [section 479][1] of that Act) would have been taken to be the gain realised by an exercise in full of the original right immediately before the time of its assignment or release [(less any deductible amounts under section 480(1) to (6) of that Act)][2]; and

(ii) the amount which (in accordance with those provisions) would have been taken to be the amount of the gain realised by an exercise in full of the replacement right at that time which falls immediately after it is given in consideration of the assignment or release.

(5) Paragraphs (*a*) and (*b*) of section 2(1) shall not, where this section applies—

(*a*) prevent a liability to pay Class 1 contributions from arising after the passing of this Act in respect of any gain realised on the exercise, assignment or release of the replacement right or of any subsequent replacement right, or

(*b*) have the effect of deeming any such liability not to have arisen on any such gain,

but those paragraphs shall have effect (instead) as if they provided for the amount of any such liability to be determined, or to be deemed to have been determined in accordance with the following provisions of this section.

[(6) Subject to subsection (7), in relation to the replacement right or any subsequent right, [section 483(1) to (3)][2] of the Income Tax (Earnings and Pensions) Act 2003 (application of Chapter 5 of Part 7 where share option exchanged for another) shall be deemed to have effect (or, as the case may be, to have had effect) for the purposes of the determination mentioned in subsection (5) of this section—

(*a*) as if that section had effect (or, as the case may be, had had effect) in relation to that right to the extent only that it is a right to acquire additional shares; and

(*b*) as if the value of the consideration for the grant of the original right had been nil.][1]

(7) Where—

(*a*) the whole or any part of any consideration given for the assignment or release of the replacement right or of any subsequent replacement right does not (or did not) comprise a subsequent replacement right, and

(*b*) as a consequence, a gain would (but for this Act) be taken for the purposes of [Chapter 5 of Part 7 of the Income Tax (Earnings and Pensions) Act 2003][1] to be realised (or to have been realised) on that assignment or release,

that gain shall be taken for the purposes of the determination mentioned in subsection (5) to be (or, as the case may be, to have been) equal to the amount in respect of which liability to pay Class 1 contributions would have been preserved, on the assumptions mentioned in subsection (8), by virtue of section 2(3) (read with subsection (4) of this section) or, if no such liability would have been so preserved, to nil.

(8) Those assumptions are—

(*a*) that (subject to paragraph (*c*)) the right assigned or released is a right the liability to pay Class 1 contributions in respect of which is a liability to which section 2(1)(*a*) or (*b*) applied;

(*b*) that references in subsection (4) of this section to the original right and to the replacement right are references, respectively, to the right that is assigned or released and to the right comprised in the consideration for the assignment or release; and

(*c*) that so much of the right assigned or released as is a right to acquire additional shares is to be disregarded for the purposes of both section 2(3) and subsection (4) of this section.

NIC

(9) Nothing in the preceding provisions of this section shall limit or remove, or be deemed to have limited or removed, any liability to pay Class 1 contributions in respect of a gain arising on the exercise, assignment or release of the replacement right, or of any subsequent replacement right, in any case in which the right in question or that gain derives (directly or indirectly) from a transaction the purpose, or one of the main purposes, of which was to make use of the provisions of this Act to avoid the payment of such contributions in respect of a benefit conferred after 19th May 2000.

(10) For the purposes of this section shares are additional shares, in relation to any right ("the new right") constituting or comprised in the consideration for the assignment or release of another right ("the old right"), to the extent that they are shares obtainable in exercise of the new right in addition to shares obtainable in exercise of the new right with a value that matches the value of the shares (other than any that were themselves additional shares) which were obtainable by the exercise of the old right.

(11) For the purposes of subsection (10) shares obtainable by the exercise of the new right shall be taken to have a value that matches the value of the shares obtainable in exercise of the old right to the extent, and to the extent only, that the following amounts are the same—

(*a*) the amount which (in accordance with the provisions of [section 479 of the Income Tax (Earnings and Pensions) Act 2003][1]) would be taken to be the amount of the gain realised by an exercise of the new right at the relevant time (assuming it to be exercisable at that time) for obtaining the shares [(less any deductible amounts under section 480(1) to (6)][2]; and

(*b*) the amount which would have been taken (in accordance with those provisions) to be the gain realised by a full exercise of the old right immediately before the time of its assignment or release;

and in this subsection "the relevant time", in relation to the new right, means the time which falls immediately after it is given in consideration of the assignment or release of the old right.

(12) Where any question arises for the purposes of this Act, in relation to any partial exercise, assignment or release of any right, whether the shares obtainable under so much of the right as has been exercised, assigned or released were additional shares, it shall be assumed that the right in so far as it is a right to acquire additional shares must be exercised, assigned or released before the exercise, assignment or release of any part of that right that is a right to acquire shares that are not additional shares.

(13) All such apportionments as may be necessary shall be made in determining for the purposes of this section, in a case in which the number of additional shares cannot be a whole number, to what extent a liability to pay Class 1 contributions arises in relation to the exercise, assignment or release of a right to acquire any such shares.

(14) Nothing in this section shall apply (where the replacement right was granted on or before 7th November 2000) for determining the amount of any special contribution payable under section 2.

(15) Where subsection (5) applies in relation to any liability to pay Class 1 contributions and amounts have already been paid to the Inland Revenue in respect of that liability before the passing of this Act—

(*a*) all such repayments shall be made as may be necessary by virtue of that subsection; but

(*b*) any amount which it would otherwise be necessary to repay in respect of a secondary Class 1 contribution paid by a person who has become liable to pay a special contribution under section 2 may be retained and set against any undischarged liability of his to pay that special contribution.

(16) In this section references to a subsequent replacement right are references to any right to acquire shares in a body corporate which are or have been obtained by any person as, or as part of, the consideration for the assignment or release by him of the replacement right or of a subsequent replacement right.

Amendments—[1] In sub-s (4)(*a*), words substituted for the words "section 136(1) of the Income and Corporation Taxes Act 1988"; in sub-s (4)(*b*)(i), words substituted for the words "section 135(3)(*a*)"; sub-s (6) substituted; in sub-s (7)(*b*), words substituted for the words "section 135 of the Income and Corporation Taxes Act 1988"; and in sub-s (11)(*a*), words substituted for the words "section 135(3)(*a*) of the Income and Corporation Taxes Act 1988"; by ITEPA 2003 s 722, Sch 6 paras 259, 261 with effect, for income tax purposes, from 2003–04; and for corporation tax purposes, for accounting periods ending after 5 April 2003. For transitional provisions and savings see ITEPA 2003 s 723, Sch 7.

[2] In sub-s (4), words "section 483(1) to (4)" substituted for the words "section 485(1) to (4)"; at the end of sub-s (4)(*b*)(i) words." to be inserted; in sub-s (6), words "483(1) to (3)" substituted for the words "485(1) to (3)"; and words inserted at the end of sub-s (11)(*a*) by FA 2003 s 140, Sch 22 paras 55, 57 with effect on or after the day appointed under FA 2003 Sch 22 para 3(2).

4 Consequential changes to tax relief provisions

Amendment—This section repealed by ITEPA 2003 s 724, Sch 8 with effect, for income tax purposes, from 2003–04; and for corporation tax purposes, for accounting periods ending after 5 April 2003. For transitional provisions and savings see ITEPA 2003 s 723, Sch 7.

5 Interpretation

(1) In this Act—

"the Administration Act" means—

(*a*) in the application of this Act to Great Britain, the Social Security Administration Act 1992 (c 5); and

(*b*) in the application of this Act to Northern Ireland, the Social Security Administration (Northern Ireland) Act 1992 (c 8);

"the Contributions and Benefits Act" means—

(*a*) in the application of this Act to Great Britain, the Social Security Contributions and Benefits Act 1992 (c 4); and

(*b*) in the application of this Act to Northern Ireland, the Social Security Contributions and Benefits (Northern Ireland) Act 1992 (c 7).

(2) In this Act—

(*a*) a reference to shares in a body corporate includes a reference to stock in that body corporate and to securities issued by that body corporate;

(*b*) a reference to the release of a right includes a reference to agreeing to a restriction of the exercise of the right; and

(*c*) references to the assignment or release of a right to acquire shares, and to gains realised on such an assignment or release, shall be construed as if [section [477(6)][2] of the Income Tax (Earnings and Pensions) Act 2003][1] applied for the purposes of this Act as it applies for the purposes of [Chapter 5 of Part 7 of that Act][1].

(3) Where any assumption that a right has been exercised at any time is made for the purposes of any provision of this Act, that assumption shall be taken to include the assumption that that right was capable of being exercised at that time.

(4) A special contribution under section 2 shall be treated for the purposes of any provision made by or under any enactment—

(*a*) as a contribution of a class provided for by the Contributions and Benefits Act; and

(*b*) as due at the end of the period of ninety-two days beginning with the day on which this Act is passed;

and any reference in Schedule 1 to that Act or in any of the provisions of the Administration Act to a Class 1A contribution shall have effect as if it included a reference to a special contribution under section 2 of this Act.

(5) This Act shall be construed, and the provisions of the Contributions and Benefits Act shall have effect, as if the provisions of this Act were contained in Part 1 of that Act.

Amendments—[1] In sub-s (2)(*c*), words substituted for the words "subsection (8) of section 135 of the Income and Corporation Taxes Act 1988 (c 1)" and "that section " by ITEPA 2003 s 722, Sch 6 paras 259, 262 with effect, for income tax purposes, from 2003–04; and for corporation tax purposes, for accounting periods ending after 5 April 2003. For transitional provisions and savings see ITEPA 2003 s 723, Sch 7.

[2] In sub-s (2)(*c*), " 483(1) to (4)" substituted for "477(6)" by FA 2003 s 140, Sch 22 paras 55, 58 with effect on or after the day appointed under FA 2003 Sch 22 para 3(2).

6 Short title and extent

(1) This Act may be cited as the Social Security Contributions (Share Options) Act 2001.

(2) This Act extends to Northern Ireland.

NATIONAL INSURANCE CONTRIBUTIONS ACT 2002

(2002 Chapter 19)

An Act to make provision for, and in connection with, increasing national insurance contributions and for applying the increases towards the cost of the national health service.

[8 July 2002]

Increases in contributions

1 Primary Class 1 contributions

(1) (*substitutes* SSCBA 1992 s 8).

(2) (*substitutes* SSCBA(NI)A s 8).

2 Secondary Class 1 contributions

(1) (*substitutes* SSCBA 1992 s 9(2), (3)).

(2) (*substitutes* SSCBA 1992 s 9(2), (3))

3 Class 4 contributions

(1) (*substitutes* SSCBA 1992 s 15(3)).

(2) (*substitutes* SSCB(NI)A 1992 s 15(3)).

(3) (*inserts* SSCBA 1992 s 18(1A)).

(4) (*inserts* SSCBA 1992 s 18(1A)).

Application towards cost of national health service

4 Appropriate national health service allocation: Great Britain
(*amends* SSAA 1992 s 162).

5 Appropriate health service allocation: Northern Ireland
(*amends* SSA(NI)A 1992 s 142).

Supplementary

6 Consequential amendments
Schedule 1 (consequential amendments) has effect.

7 Repeals and revocations
Schedule 2 (repeals and revocations) has effect.

8 Short title, commencement and extent
(1) This Act may be cited as the National Insurance Contributions Act 2002.
(2) This Act has effect in relation to the tax year 2003–04 and subsequent tax years; and for this purpose "tax year" has the meaning given by section 122(1) of the Social Security Contributions and Benefits Act 1992 (c 4).
(3) The amendments, repeals and revocations made by this Act have the same extent as the provisions to which they relate.
(4) Subject to that, this Act extends to Northern Ireland (as well as to England and Wales and Scotland).

SCHEDULES

SCHEDULE 1

CONSEQUENTIAL AMENDMENTS

Note—The amendments made by this Schedule are already in force and have therefore been omitted.

SCHEDULE 2

REPEALS AND REVOCATIONS

Note—The repeals and revocations made by this Schedule are already in force and have therefore been omitted.

EMPLOYMENT ACT 2002

(2002 Chapter 22)

ARRANGEMENT OF SECTIONS

PART 1
STATUTORY LEAVE AND PAY

CHAPTER 1
PATERNITY AND ADOPTION

Rights to leave and pay

PART 4
MISCELLANEOUS AND GENERAL
General

An Act to make provision for statutory rights to paternity and adoption leave and pay; to amend the law relating to statutory maternity leave and pay; to amend the Employment Tribunals Act 1996; to make provision for the use of statutory procedures in relation to employment disputes; to amend the law relating to particulars of employment; . . . to amend the law relating to maternity allowance; . . . to make provision about the use of information for, or relating to, employment and training; and for connected purposes.

[8 July 2002]

PART 1
STATUTORY LEAVE AND PAY

CHAPTER 1
PATERNITY AND ADOPTION
Rights to leave and pay

2 Statutory paternity pay
(*inserts* SSCBA 1992 Pt 12ZA).

4 Statutory adoption pay
(*inserts* SSCBA 1992 Pt 12ZB).

Administration and enforcement: pay

5 General functions of the Board

Amendment—This section repealed by CRCA 2005 ss 50, 52, Sch 4 para 93, Sch 5 with effect from 18 April 2005 (by virtue of SI 2005/1126).

6 Financial arrangements
(3) (*amends* SSCBA 1992 s 1(5))

7 Funding of employers' liabilities
(1) The Secretary of State shall by regulations make provision for the payment by employers of [statutory paternity pay,][3] statutory adoption pay [and statutory shared parental pay][2] to be funded by the Board to such extent as the regulations may specify.
(2) Regulations under subsection (1) shall—
(*a*) make provision for a person who has made a payment of [statutory paternity pay,][3] statutory adoption pay [or statutory shared parental pay][2] to be entitled, except in such circumstances as the regulations may provide, to recover an amount equal to the sum of—
(i) the aggregate of such of those payments as qualify for small employers' relief; and
(ii) an amount equal to 92 per cent of the aggregate of such of those payments as do not so qualify; and
(*b*) include provision for a person who has made a payment of [statutory paternity pay,][3] statutory adoption pay [or statutory shared parental pay][2] qualifying for small employers' relief to be entitled, except in such circumstances as the regulations may provide, to recover an additional amount equal to the amount to which the person would have been entitled under section 167(2)(*b*) of the Social Security Contributions and Benefits Act 1992 (corresponding provision for statutory maternity pay) had the payment been a payment of statutory maternity pay.
(3) For the purposes of subsection (2), [a payment of][1] [statutory paternity pay,][3] or statutory adoption pay [or statutory shared parental pay][2] qualifies for small employers' relief if it would have so qualified were it a payment of statutory maternity pay, [treating—
(*a*) the period for which the payment of statutory paternity pay is made,
(*a*) the payee's adoption pay period, or
(*a*) the period for which the payment of statutory shared parental pay is made,

as the maternity pay period.][2]

(4) Regulations under subsection (1) may, in particular—

(*a*) make provision for funding in advance as well as in arrear;

(*b*) make provision for funding, or the recovery of amounts due under provision made by virtue of subsection (2)(*b*), by means of deductions from such amounts for which employers are accountable to the Board as the regulations may provide, or otherwise;

(*c*) make provision for the recovery by the Board of any sums overpaid to employers under the regulations.

(5) Where in accordance with any provision of regulations under subsection (1) an amount has been deducted from an employer's contributions payments, the amount so deducted shall (except in such cases as the Secretary of State may by regulations provide) be treated for the purposes of any provision made by or under any enactment in relation to primary or secondary Class 1 contributions—

(*a*) as having been paid (on such date as may be determined in accordance with the regulations), and

(*b*) as having been received by the Board,

towards discharging the employer's liability in respect of such contributions.

(6) Regulations under this section must be made with the concurrence of the Board.

(7) In this section, "contributions payments", in relation to an employer, means any payments which the employer is required, by or under any enactment, to make in discharge of any liability in respect of primary or secondary Class 1 contributions.

Amendments—[1] In sub-ss (1)–(3) words substituted by the Work and Families Act 2006 s 11(1), Sch 1 para 50 with effect from 3 March 2010 (by virtue of SI 2010/495, art 3(*b*), (*c*)).

[2] In sub-ss (1), (2)(*a*), (*b*), (3), words inserted, and in sub-s (3), words substituted for words "treating the period for which the payment is made, in the case of ordinary statutory paternity pay, additional statutory paternity pay, or the payee's adoption pay period, in the case of statutory adoption pay, as the maternity pay period." by the Children and Families Act 2014 s 126, Sch 7 paras 50, 51(1), (2)(*b*), (3)(*a*)(ii), (*b*)(ii), (4)(*b*), (*c*) with effect from 30 June 2014 (by virtue of SI 2014/1640 art 3). Note that the substitution of text in sub-s (3) does not have effect in relation to children whose expected week of birth ends on or before 4 April 2015 or children placed for adoption on or before 4 April 2015 (SI 2014/1640 art 9).

[3] In sub-ss (1), (2)(*a*), (*b*), (3), words substituted by the Children and Families Act 2014 s 126, Sch 7 paras 50, 51(2)(*a*), (3)(*a*)(i), (*b*)(i), (4)(*a*) with effect from 5 April 2015 (by virtue of SI 2014/1640 art 7).

8 Regulations about payment

(1) The Secretary of State may make regulations with respect to the payment by employers of [statutory paternity pay,][2] statutory adoption pay [and statutory shared parental pay][1].

(2) Regulations under subsection (1) may, in particular, include provision—

(*a*) about the records to be kept by employers in relation to payments of [statutory paternity pay,][2] statutory adoption pay [and statutory shared parental pay][1], including the length of time for which they are to be retained;

(*b*) for the production of wages sheets and other documents and records to officers of the Board for the purpose of enabling them to satisfy themselves that [statutory paternity pay,][2] statutory adoption pay [and statutory shared parental pay][1] have been paid and are being paid, in accordance with the regulations, to employees who are entitled to them;

(*c*) for requiring employers to provide information to employees (in their itemised pay statements or otherwise);

(*d*) for requiring employers to make returns to the Board containing such particulars with respect to payments of [statutory paternity pay,][2] statutory adoption pay [and statutory shared parental pay][1] as the regulations may provide.

(3) Regulations under subsection (1) must be made with the concurrence of the Board.

Amendments—[1] In sub-ss (1), (2), words inserted by the Children and Families Act 2014 s 126, Sch 7 paras 50, 52(1), (2)(*b*), (3)(*a*)(ii), (*b*)(ii), (*c*)(ii) with effect from 30 June 2014 (by virtue of SI 2014/1640 art 3).

[2] In sub-ss (1), (2), words substituted by the Children and Families Act 2014 s 126, Sch 7 paras 50, 52(2)(*a*), (3)(*a*)(i), (*b*)(i), (*c*)(i) with effect from 5 April 2015 (by virtue of SI 2014/1640 art 7).

9 Decisions and appeals

(*amends* SSC(TF)A 1999 ss 8, 11, 14).

10 Powers to require information

(1) The Secretary of State may by regulations make provision enabling an officer of the Board authorised by the Board for the purposes of this section to require persons of a description specified in the regulations to provide, or produce for inspection, within such period as the regulations may require, such information or documents as the officer may reasonably require for the purpose of ascertaining whether [statutory paternity pay,][2] statutory adoption pay [or statutory shared parental pay][1] is or was payable to or in respect of any person.

(2) The descriptions of person which may be specified by regulations under subsection (1) include, in particular—

(*a*) any person claiming to be entitled to [statutory paternity pay,][2] statutory adoption pay [or statutory shared parental pay][1], (*b*) any person who is, or has been, the spouse or partner of such a person as is mentioned in paragraph (*a*),

(*c*) any person who is, or has been, an employer of such a person as is mentioned in paragraph (*a*),

(*d*) any person carrying on an agency or other business for the introduction or supply to persons requiring them of persons available to do work or to perform services, and

(*e*) any person who is a servant or agent of any such person as is specified in paragraphs (*a*) to (*d*).

(3) Regulations under subsection (1) must be made with the concurrence of the Board.

Amendments—[1] In sub-ss (1), (2), words inserted by the Children and Families Act 2014 s 126, Sch 7 paras 50, 53(1), (2)(*b*), (3)(*b*) with effect from 30 June 2014 (by virtue of SI 2014/1640 art 3).

[2] In sub-ss (1), (2), words substituted by the Children and Families Act 2014 s 126, Sch 7 paras 50, 53(2)(*a*), (3)(*a*) with effect from 5 April 2015 (by virtue of SI 2014/1640 art 7).

11 Penalties: failures to comply

(1) Where a person—

(*a*) fails to produce any document or record, provide any information or make any return, in accordance with regulations under section 8, or

(*b*) fails to provide any information or document in accordance with regulations under section 10,

he shall be liable to the penalties mentioned in subsection (2) below (subject to subsection (4)).

(2) The penalties are—

(*a*) a penalty not exceeding £300, and

(*b*) if the failure continues after a penalty is imposed under paragraph (*a*), a further penalty or penalties not exceeding £60 for each day on which the failure continues after the day on which the penalty under that paragraph was imposed (but excluding any day for which a penalty under this paragraph has already been imposed).

(3) Where a person fails to keep records in accordance with regulations under section 8I, he shall be liable to a penalty not exceeding £3,000.

(4) Subject to subsection (5), no penalty shall be imposed under subsection (2) or (3) at any time after the failure concerned has been remedied.

(5) Subsection (4) does not apply to the imposition of a penalty under subsection (2)(*a*) in respect of a failure within subsection (1)(*a*).

(6) Where, in the case of any employee, an employer refuses or repeatedly fails to make payments of [statutory paternity pay,][2] statutory adoption pay [or statutory shared parental pay][1] in accordance with any regulations under section 8, the employer shall be liable to a penalty not exceeding £3,000.

(7) Section 118(2) of the Taxes Management Act 1970 (c 9) (extra time for compliance etc) shall apply for the purposes of subsections (1), (3) and (6) as it applies for the purposes of that Act.

(8) Schedule 1 to this Act (penalties: procedure and appeals) has effect in relation to penalties under this section.

Amendments—[1] In sub-s (6), words inserted by the Children and Families Act 2014 s 126, Sch 7 paras 50, 54(*b*) with effect from 1 December 2014 (by virtue of SI 2014/1640 art 5).

[2] In sub-s (6), words substituted by the Children and Families Act 2014 s 126, Sch 7 paras 50, 54(*a*) with effect from 5 April 2015 (by virtue of SI 2014/1640 art 7).

12 Penalties: fraud etc

(1) Where a person fraudulently or negligently—

(*a*) makes any incorrect statement or declaration in connection with establishing entitlement to [. . . [3] statutory paternity pay][1], or

(*b*) provides any incorrect information or document of a kind mentioned in regulations under section 10(1) so far as relating to [. . . [3]statutory paternity pay][1],

he shall be liable to a penalty not exceeding £300.

(2) Where a person fraudulently or negligently—

(*a*) makes any incorrect statement or declaration in connection with establishing entitlement to statutory adoption pay [or [statutory shared parental pay][2]][1], or

(*b*) provides any incorrect information or document of a kind mentioned in regulations under section 10(1) so far as relating to statutory adoption pay [or [statutory shared parental pay][2]][1],

he shall be liable to a penalty not exceeding £3,000.

(3) Where an employer fraudulently or negligently makes incorrect payments of [. . . [3] statutory paternity pay][1], he shall be liable to a penalty not exceeding £300.

(4) Where an employer fraudulently or negligently makes incorrect payments of statutory adoption pay [or [statutory shared parental pay][2]][1], he shall be liable to a penalty not exceeding £3,000.

(5) Where an employer fraudulently or negligently—

(*a*) produces any incorrect document or record, provides any incorrect information or makes any incorrect return, of a kind mentioned in regulations under section 8E, or

(*b*) receives incorrect payments in pursuance of regulations under section 7,

he shall be liable to a penalty not exceeding £3,000 or, if the offence relates only to [. . . [3] statutory paternity pay][1], £300.

NIC

(6) Schedule 1 (penalties: procedure and appeals) has effect in relation to penalties under this section.

Amendments—[1] In sub-ss (1), (3), (5) words substituted; in sub-ss (2), (4), words inserted by the Work and Families Act 2006 s 11 Sch 1 para 54 with effect from 6 April 2010 (by virtue of SI 2010/495, art 4(*c*), (*d*)).

[2] In sub-ss (2)(*a*), (*b*), (4), words substituted for words "additional statutory paternity pay" by the Children and Families Act 2014 s 126, Sch 7 paras 50, 55(1), (3), (5) with effect from 1 December 2014 (by virtue of SI 2014/1640 art 5).

[3] In sub-ss (1)(*a*), (*b*), (3), (5) word repealed by the Children and Families Act 2014 s 126, Sch 7 paras 50, 55(2), (4), (6) with effect from 5 April 2015 (by virtue of SI 2014/1640 art 7).

13 Supply of information held by the Board

(1) This section applies to information which is held for the purposes of functions relating to [statutory paternity pay,][5] statutory adoption pay [or statutory shared parental pay[4]]—

(*a*) by the Board, or

(*b*) by a person providing services to the Board, in connection with the provision of those services.

(2) Information to which this section applies may be supplied—

(*a*) to the Secretary of State[, . . . [3]][1] or the Department, or

(*b*) to a person providing services to the Secretary of State[, . . . [3]][1] or the Department,

for use for the purposes of functions relating to social security, child support or war pensions . . . [3].

Amendments—[1] In sub-s (2) words inserted by the Child Support (Consequential Provisions) (No 2) Regulations, SI 2008/2656 reg 2 with effect from 1 November 2008.

[3] In sub-s (2)(*a*), (*b*), words "the Child Maintenance and Enforcement Commission" repealed, and in the final words, words "and in relation to the Child Maintenance and Enforcement Commission, any function of that Commission" repealed, by the Public Bodies (Child Maintenance and Enforcement Commission: Abolition and Transfer of Functions) Order, SI 2012/2007 art 3(2), Schedule para 66 with effect from 1 August 2012.

[4] In sub-s (1), words inserted by the Children and Families Act 2014 s 126, Sch 7 paras 50, 56(*b*) with effect from 1 December 2014 (by virtue of SI 2014/1640 art 5).

[5] In sub-s (1), words "statutory paternity pay," substituted for words "ordinary statutory paternity pay, additional statutory paternity pay or" by the Children and Families Act 2014 s 126, Sch 7 paras 50, 56(*a*) with effect from 5 April 2015 (by virtue of SI 2014/1640 art 7). This amendment has effect subject to transitional provisions in SI 2014/1640 art 19(3) (SI 2014/1640 art 19(1)).

14 Supply of information held by the Secretary of State

(1) This section applies to information which is held for the purposes of functions relating to [statutory paternity pay,][2] statutory adoption pay [or statutory shared parental pay[1]]—

(*a*) by the Secretary of State or the Department, or

(*b*) by a person providing services to the Secretary of State or the Department, in connection with the provision of those services.

(2) Information to which this section applies may be supplied—

(*a*) to the Board, or

(*b*) to a person providing services to the Board,

for use for the purposes of functions relating to [statutory paternity pay,][2] statutory adoption pay [or statutory shared parental pay][1].

Amendments—[1] In sub-ss (1), (2), words inserted by the Children and Families Act 2014 s 126, Sch 7 paras 50, 57(1), (2)(*b*), (3)(*b*) with effect from 1 December 2014 (by virtue of SI 2014/1640 art 5).

[2] In sub-ss (1), (2), words "statutory paternity pay," substituted for words "ordinary statutory paternity pay, additional statutory paternity pay or" by the Children and Families Act 2014 s 126, Sch 7 paras 50, 57(2)(*a*), (3)(*a*) with effect from 5 April 2015 (by virtue of SI 2014/1640 art 7). This amendment has effect subject to transitional provisions in SI 2014/1640 art 19(3) (SI 2014/1640 art 19(1)).

15 Use of information by the Board

(1) Information which is held—

(*a*) by the Board, or

(*b*) by a person providing services to the Board, in connection with the provision of those services,

for the purposes of any functions specified in any paragraph of subsection (2) below may be used for the purposes of, or for any purposes connected with, the exercise of any functions specified in any other paragraph of that subsection, and may be supplied to any person providing services to the Board for those purposes.

(2) The functions referred to in subsection (1) above are—

(*a*) the functions of the Board in relation to . . . [2] statutory paternity pay;

(*aa*) . . . [2]

(*b*) their functions in relation to statutory adoption pay; . . . [1]

[(*ba*) their functions in relation to statutory shared parental pay; and][1]

(*c*) their functions in relation to tax, contributions, statutory sick pay, statutory maternity pay or tax credits, or functions under Part 3 of the Pension Schemes Act 1993 (c 48) [(schemes that were contracted-out etc)][3] or Part 3 of the Pension Schemes (Northern Ireland) Act 1993 (c 49) (corresponding provisions for Northern Ireland).

(3) In subsection (2)(*c*) above, "contributions" means contributions under Part 1 of the Social Security Contributions and Benefits Act 1992 (c 4) or Part 1 of the Social Security Contributions and Benefits (Northern Ireland) Act 1992 (c 7).

Amendments—[1] In sub-s (2)(*b*), word "and" at the end repealed, and sub-s (2)(*ba*) inserted, by the Children and Families Act 2014 s 126, Sch 7 paras 50, 58(*b*), (*c*) with effect from 1 December 2014 (by virtue of SI 2014/1640 art 5).
[2] In sub-s (2)(*a*), word "ordinary" repealed, and sub-s (2)(*aa*) repealed by the Children and Families Act 2014 s 126, Sch 7 paras 50, 58(*a*), (*b*) with effect from 5 April 2015 (by virtue of SI 2014/1640 art 7). This amendment has effect subject to transitional provisions in SI 2014/1640 art 19(3) (SI 2014/1640 art 19(1)).
[3] In sub-s (2)(*c*) words substituted by PeA 2014 s 24, Sch 13 para 72 with effect from 6 April 2016.

16 Interpretation

In sections 5 to 15—

"the Board" means the Commissioners of Inland Revenue;

"the Department" means the Department for Social Development or the Department for Employment and Learning;

"employer" and "employee" have the same meanings as in Parts 12ZA and 12ZB of the Social Security Contributions and Benefits Act 1992.

CHAPTER 2

MATERNITY

21 Funding of employers' liabilities: statutory maternity pay

(*substitutes* SSCBA 1992 s 167 and SSCB(NI)A 1992 s 163).

PART 4

MISCELLANEOUS AND GENERAL

General

51 Orders and regulations

(1) Any power of the Secretary of State to make orders or regulations under this Act includes power—

(*a*) to make different provision for different cases or circumstances;

(*b*) to make such incidental, supplementary, consequential or transitional provision as the Secretary of State thinks fit.

(2) Any power of the Secretary of State to make orders or regulations under this Act is exercisable by statutory instrument.

(3) No order may be made under this Act unless a draft of the order has been laid before and approved by resolution of each House of Parliament.

(4) No regulations may be made under section . . . 45 unless a draft of the regulations has been laid before and approved by resolution of each House of Parliament.

(5) A statutory instrument containing regulations under any other provision of this Act shall be subject to annulment in pursuance of a resolution of either House of Parliament.

(6) This section does not apply to orders under section 55(2).

Amendments—In sub-s (4), words repealed by the Employment Act 2008 s 20, Schedule Pt 1 with effect from 6 April 2009 (by virtue of SI 2008/3232 art 2).

52 Financial provisions

(1) There shall be paid out of money provided by Parliament—

(*a*) any expenses incurred by a Minister of the Crown or government department in consequence of this Act, and

(*b*) any increase attributable to this Act in the sums so provided under any other Act.

(2) There shall be paid into the Consolidated Fund any increase attributable to this Act in the sums payable into that Fund under any other Act.

53 Minor and consequential amendments

Schedule 7 (which makes minor and consequential amendments) has effect.

54 Repeals and revocations

The enactments and instruments specified in Schedule 8 are hereby repealed or revoked to the extent specified there.

55 Short title etc

(1) This Act may be cited as the Employment Act 2002.

(2) This Act, except sections 45, 46, 51 and 52 and this section, shall come into force on such day as the Secretary of State may by order made by statutory instrument appoint, and different days may be so appointed for different purposes.

(3) An order under subsection (2) may contain such transitional provisions and savings as the Secretary of State considers necessary or expedient in connection with the coming into force of any of the provisions of this Act.

(4) The Secretary of State may by regulations make such transitional provisions and savings as he considers necessary or expedient for the purposes of or in connection with—

(*a*) the coming into force of section 19 or 48, or Schedule 7 so far as relating to any amendment made in consequence of either of those sections; or

(*b*) the operation of any enactment amended by any of those provisions during any period when the amendment is not wholly in force.

(5) Subject to subsections (6) and (7), this Act extends to England and Wales and Scotland only.

(6) The following provisions also extend to Northern Ireland—

(*a*) section 5;

(*b*) sections 13 to 15, and section 16 so far as relating thereto;

(*c*) paragraphs 1, 4, 9 and 10 of Schedule 6, and section 50 so far as relating thereto;

(*d*) sections 51 and 52;

(*e*) paragraphs 1, 50, 52 and 53 of Schedule 7, and section 53 so far as relating thereto;

(*f*) Schedule 8, so far as relating to the repeal of section 3(3) of the Social Security Act 1998 (c 14), and section 54 so far as relating thereto;

(*g*) this section.

(7) The following provisions extend to Northern Ireland only—

(*a*) sections 21(2) and 46;

(*b*) paragraphs 7, 8, 12 and 14 of Schedule 6, and section 50 so far as relating thereto;

(*c*) paragraph 17 of Schedule 7, and section 53 so far as relating thereto;

(*d*) Schedule 8, so far as relating to—

(i) the repeal in the Social Security Administration (Northern Ireland) Act 1992 (c 8), and

(ii) the revocations in the Social Security Administration (Fraud) (Northern Ireland) Order 1997 (SI 1997/1182 (NI 11)) and the Social Security Contributions (Transfer of Functions, etc) (Northern Ireland) Order 1999 (SI 1999/671),

and section 54 so far as relating thereto.

(8) In sections 5 and 13 to 15 and paragraph 53 of Schedule 7, references to [statutory paternity pay,][1] statutory adoption pay [or statutory shared parental pay][2] include statutory pay under Northern Ireland legislation corresponding to Part 12ZA[, Part 12ZB or Part 12ZC][2] of the Social Security Contributions and Benefits Act 1992 (c 4).

Amendments—[1] In sub-s (8), words substituted by the Children and Families Act 2014 s 126, Sch 7 paras 50, 59(*a*) with effect from 5 April 2015 (by virtue of SI 2014/1640 art 7).

[2] In sub-s (8), words inserted and substituted by the Children and Families Act 2014 s 126, Sch 7 paras 50, 59(*b*), (*c*) with effect from 15 March 2015, being the day on which Northern Ireland legislation containing provision corresponding to SSCBA 1992 Part 12ZC comes into force (by virtue of SI 2014/1640 art 8).

SCHEDULES

SCHEDULE 1

PENALTIES: PROCEDURE AND APPEALS

Section 11

Determination of penalties by officer of Board

1—(1) Subject to sub-paragraph (2) and except where proceedings have been instituted under paragraph 5, an officer of the Board authorised by the Board for the purposes of this paragraph may make a determination—

(*a*) imposing a penalty under section 11 or 12, and

(*b*) setting it at such amount as, in his opinion, is correct or appropriate.

(2) Sub-paragraph (1) does not apply to the imposition of such a penalty as is mentioned in section 11(2)(*a*).

(3) Notice of a determination of a penalty under this paragraph shall be served on the person liable to the penalty and shall state the date on which it is issued and the time within which an appeal against the determination may be made.

(4) After the notice of a determination under this paragraph has been served the determination shall not be altered except in accordance with this paragraph or on appeal.

(5) If it is discovered by an officer of the Board authorised by the Board for the purposes of this paragraph that the amount of a penalty determined under this paragraph is or has become insufficient, the officer may make a determination in a further amount so that the penalty is set at the amount which, in his opinion, is correct or appropriate.

Provisions supplementary to paragraph 1

2—(1) A penalty determined under paragraph 1 above shall be due and payable at the end of the period of thirty days beginning with the date of the issue of the notice of determination.

(2) Part 6 of the Taxes Management Act 1970 (c 9) shall apply in relation to a penalty determined under paragraph 1 as if it were tax charged in an assessment and due and payable.

Appeals against penalty determinations

3—(1) An appeal may be brought against the determination of a penalty under paragraph 1.

(2) The provisions of the Taxes Management Act 1970 relating to appeals, except section 50(6) to (8), shall have effect in relation to an appeal against such a determination as they have effect in relation to an appeal against an assessment to tax [except that references to the tribunal shall be taken to be references to the First-tier Tribunal][1].

(3) On an appeal by virtue of sub-paragraph (2) against the determination of a penalty under paragraph 1, the [First-tier Tribunal][1] may—

(a) if it appears . . . [1] that no penalty has been incurred, set the determination aside;

(*b*) if the amount determined appears . . . [1] to be appropriate, confirm the determination;

(*c*) if the amount determined appears . . . [1] to be excessive, reduce it to such other amount (including nil) as [the tribunal considers][1] appropriate;

(d) if the amount determined appears . . . [1] to be insufficient, increase it to such amount not exceeding the permitted maximum as [the tribunal considers][1] appropriate.

[(4) In addition to any right of appeal on a point of law under section 11(2) of the Tribunals, Courts and Enforcement Act 2007, the person liable to the penalty may appeal to the Upper Tribunal against the amount of the penalty which had been determined under sub-paragraph (3), but not against any decision which falls under section 11(5)(*d*) or (*e*) of that Act and was made in connection with the determination of the amount of the penalty.

(4A) Section 11(3) and (4) of the Tribunals, Courts and Enforcement Act 2007 applies to the right of appeal under sub-paragraph (4) as it applies to the right of appeal under section 11(2) of that Act.

(4B) On an appeal under this paragraph the Upper Tribunal has the like jurisdiction as is conferred on the First-tier Tribunal by virtue of this paragraph.][1]

Amendments—[1] In sub-para (2) words inserted, in sub-para (3), words substituted and repealed, and sub-paras (4)–(4B) substituted for previous sub-para (4), by the Transfer of Tribunal Functions and Revenue and Customs Appeals Order, SI 2009/56, art 3(1), Sch 1, paras 321, 322 with effect from 1 April 2009.

Penalty proceedings before [First-tier Tribunal]

4—(1) An officer of the Board authorised by the Board for the purposes of this paragraph may commence proceedings for any penalty to which sub-paragraph (1) of paragraph 1 does not apply by virtue of sub-paragraph (2) of that paragraph.

[(2) The person liable to the penalty shall be a party to the proceedings.][1]

(3) Part 6 of the Taxes Management Act 1970 (c 9) shall apply in relation to a penalty determined in proceedings under this paragraph as if it were tax charged in an assessment and due and payable.

[(4) In addition to any right of appeal on a point of law under section 11(2) of the Tribunals, Courts and Enforcement Act 2007, the person liable to the penalty may appeal to the Upper Tribunal against the determination of a penalty in proceedings under sub-paragraph (1), but not against any decision which falls under section 11(5)(*d*) or (*e*) of that Act and was made in connection with the determination of the amount of the penalty.

(4A) Section 11(3) and (4) of the Tribunals, Courts and Enforcement Act 2007 applies to the right of appeal under sub-paragraph (4) as it applies to the right of appeal under section 11(2) of that Act.][1]

(5) On any such appeal the [Upper Tribunal][1] may—

(*a*) if it appears that no penalty has been incurred, set the determination aside;

(*b*) if the amount determined appears to be appropriate, confirm the determination;

(*c*) if the amount determined appears to be excessive, reduce it to such other amount (including nil) as the [Upper Tribunal][1] considers appropriate;

(*d*) if the amount determined appears to be insufficient, increase it to such amount not exceeding the permitted maximum as the [Upper Tribunal][1] considers appropriate.

Amendments—[1] In heading, words substituted for words "Commissioners", sub-paras (2), (4), (4A) substituted, and in sub-para (5), words substituted for word "court", by the Transfer of Tribunal Functions and Revenue and Customs Appeals Order, SI 2009/56, art 3(1), Sch 1, paras 321, 323 with effect from 1 April 2009.

Penalty proceedings before court

5—(1) Where in the opinion of the Board the liability of any person for a penalty under section 11 or 12 arises by reason of the fraud of that or any other person, proceedings for the penalty may be instituted before the High Court or, in Scotland, the Court of Session as the Court of Exchequer in Scotland.

(2) Subject to sub-paragraph (3), proceedings under this paragraph shall be instituted—

(*a*) in England and Wales, in the name of the Attorney General, and

(*b*) in Scotland, in the name of the Advocate General for Scotland.

(3) Sub-paragraph (2) shall not prevent proceedings under this paragraph being instituted in England and Wales under the Crown Proceedings Act 1947 (c 44) by and in the name of the Board as an authorised department for the purposes of that Act.
(4) Any proceedings under this paragraph instituted in England and Wales shall be deemed to be civil proceedings by the Crown within the meaning of Part 2 of the Crown Proceedings Act 1947.
(5) If in proceedings under this paragraph the court does not find that fraud is proved but considers that the person concerned is nevertheless liable to a penalty, the court may determine a penalty notwithstanding that, but for the opinion of the Board as to fraud, the penalty would not have been a matter for the court.

Mitigation of penalties

6 The Board may in their discretion mitigate any penalty under section 11 or 12, or stay or compound any proceedings for a penalty, and may also, after judgment, further mitigate or entirely remit the penalty.

Time limits for penalties

7 A penalty under section 11 or 12 may be determined by an officer of the Board, or proceedings for the penalty may be commenced before the [tribunal][1] or the court, at any time within six years after the date on which the penalty was incurred or began to be incurred.

Amendments—[1] Word substituted for word "Commissioners", by the Transfer of Tribunal Functions and Revenue and Customs Appeals Order, SI 2009/56, art 3(1), Sch 1, paras 321, 324 with effect from 1 April 2009.

Interest on penalties

8—(1) (*inserts* FA 1989 s 178(2)(*q*)).
(2) A penalty under section 11 or 12 shall carry interest at the rate applicable under section 178 of the Finance Act 1989 from the date on which it becomes due and payable until payment.

Interpretation

9 In this Schedule—
"the Board" means the Commissioners of Inland Revenue;
. . . [1]

Amendments—[1] Definition of "General Commissioners" and "Special Commissioners" repealed by the Transfer of Tribunal Functions and Revenue and Customs Appeals Order, SI 2009/56, art 3(1), Sch 1, paras 321, 325 with effect from 1 April 2009.

SCHEDULE 6

USE OF INFORMATION FOR, OR RELATING TO, EMPLOYMENT AND TRAINING

Note—Provisions omitted are outside the scope of this work.

Supply and use of employment or training information by Secretary of State etc

4 (*repeals* SSA 1998 s 3(3)).

Supply of tax information for employment or training purposes

5 (*amended* SSAA 1992 s 122; *repealed by* the Welfare Reform Act 2012 s 147, Sch 14 Pt 1)

6 (*inserted* SSAA 1992 s 122ZA; *repealed by* the Welfare Reform Act 2012 s 147, Sch 14 Pt 1)

7 (*amended* SSA(NI)A 1992 s 116; *repealed by* the Welfare Reform (Northern Ireland) Order, SI 2015/2006 art 140, Sch 12 Pt 12)

8 (*inserted* SSAA 1992 s 116ZA; *repealed by* the Welfare Reform (Northern Ireland) Order, SI 2015/2006 art 140, Sch 12 Pt 12)

Supply of Inland Revenue tax credits information for employment or training purposes

9 . . .

Amendment—This paragraph repealed by TCA 2002 s 60, Sch 6 with effect from 8 April 2003 (by virtue of SI 2003/962).

Supply to Inland Revenue of employment or training information for purposes of tax credits

10 . . .

Amendment—This paragraph repealed by TCA 2002 s 60, Sch 6 with effect from 8 April 2003 (by virtue of SI 2003/962).

Supply of other Inland Revenue information for employment or training purposes

11 (*amended* SSAA 1992 s 121E); *repealed in part by* the Welfare Reform Act 2012 s 147, Sch 14 Pt 13)

Prospective amendment—Para 11(*a*) to be repealed by the Child Maintenance and Other Payments Act 2008 s 58, Sch 8 with effect from a date to be appointed.

Supply to Inland Revenue of employment or training information for other purposes

13 (*amended* SSAA 1992 s 121F; *repealed in part by* the Welfare Reform Act 2012 s 147, Sch 14 Pt 13)

Prospective amendment—Para 13(*a*) to be repealed by the Child Maintenance and Other Payments Act 2008 s 58, Sch 8 with effect from a date to be appointed.

SCHEDULE 7

MINOR AND CONSEQUENTIAL AMENDMENTS

Section 53

Social Security Contributions and Benefits Act 1992 (c 4)

2 The Social Security Contributions and Benefits Act 1992 is amended as follows.

3 (*amended* SSCBA 1992 s 4; *repealed* by the Work and Families Act 2006 s 15 Sch 2).

4–6 (outside the scope of this work).

7 (*amends* SSCBA 1992 s 176).

Social Security Administration Act 1992 (c 5)

8 The Social Security Administration Act 1992 is amended as follows.

9–12(outside the scope of this work).

13 (*amends* SSAA 1992 s 122AA).

14, 15 (outside the scope of this work).

16 (*amends* SSAA 1992 s 191).

Finance Act 1997 (c 16)

50 (*amended* FA 1997 s 110; *repealed by* the Welfare Reform Act 2012 s 147, Sch 14 Pt 13)

Tax Credits Act 1999 (c 10)

52 (*amended* TCA 1999 s 18; *repealed by* TCA 2002 s 60, Sch 6 with effect from 8 April 2003 (by virtue of SI 2003/962))

Finance Act 1999 (c 16)

53 Sections 132 and 133 of the Finance Act 1999 shall have effect as if statutory maternity pay, statutory paternity pay and statutory adoption pay were matters which are under the care and management of the Commissioners of Inland Revenue.

SCHEDULE 8

REPEALS AND REVOCATIONS

Section 54

Note—The repeals and revocations made by this Schedule are already in force and have therefore been omitted.

NATIONAL INSURANCE CONTRIBUTIONS AND STATUTORY PAYMENTS ACT 2004

(2004 Chapter 3)

An Act to make provision relating to the payment and administration of national insurance contributions and the provision of information in connection with the payment of statutory sick pay and statutory maternity pay, and for connected purposes.

[13 May 2004]

Payment of Class 1 contributions

1 Payment of Class 1 contributions: Great Britain

(*amends* SSCBA 1992 Sch 1 para 3)

NIC

2 Payment of Class 1 contributions: Northern Ireland
(*amends* SSCB(NI)A 1992 Sch 1 para 3)

3 Agreements and joint elections: Great Britain
(1)–(3) (*amend* SSCBA 1992 Sch 1 paras 3A, 3B)
(4) The amendments made by this section have effect in relation to—
(*a*) agreements entered into after the date of commencement of this section which are in respect of post-commencement employment income, and
(*b*) elections made after that date.
(5) For the purposes of subsection (4), "post-commencement employment income" means income which is relevant employment income within paragraph 3A(2B) of Schedule 1 to the Social Security Contributions and Benefits Act 1992 (c 4) which, after the date of commencement of this section, counts as employment income for a tax year by virtue of Part 7 of the Income Tax (Earnings and Pensions) Act 2003 (c 1).

4 Agreements and joint elections: Northern Ireland
(1)–(3) (*amend* SSCB(NI)A 1992 Sch 1 paras 3A, 3B)
(4) The amendments made by this section have effect in relation to—
(*a*) agreements entered into after the date of commencement of this section which are in respect of post-commencement employment income, and
(*b*) elections made after that date.
(5) For the purposes of subsection (4), "post-commencement employment income" means income which is relevant employment income within paragraph 3A(2B) of Schedule 1 to the Social Security Contributions and Benefits (Northern Ireland) Act 1992 (c 7) which, after the date of commencement of this section, counts as employment income for a tax year by virtue of Part 7 of the Income Tax (Earnings and Pensions) Act 2003 (c 1).

Method of recovery of contributions etc

5 Recovery of contributions, etc: Great Britain
(1) (*amended* SSAA 1992 ss 121A(1)(*b*); *revoked* by FA 2008 s 129 Sch 43 para 11(*c*) with effect from 6 April 2014)
(2), (3) (*amend* SSAA 1992 ss . 121B(1), 121C)
(4) (*inserts* SSCBA 1992 Sch 1 para 7BZA)

6 Recovery of contributions, etc: Northern Ireland
(1), (2) (*substitute* SSA(NI)A 1992 s 115A, *insert* SSA(NI)A 1992 s 1158(8A))
(3) (*inserts* SSCB(NI)A 1992 Sch 1 para 7BZA)

Provision of information

7 Class 1, 1A, 1B or 2 contributions: powers to call for documents etc: Great Britain
(*substitutes* SSAA 1992 s 110ZA)

8 Class 1, 1A, 1B or 2 contributions: powers to call for documents etc: Northern Ireland
(*substitutes* SSA(NI)A 1992 s 104ZA)

Statutory sick pay and statutory maternity pay

9 Compliance regime for statutory sick pay and statutory maternity pay: Great Britain
(*amends* SSAA 1992 ss 113,130, 132, *inserts* ss 113A, 113B)

10 Compliance regime for statutory sick pay and statutory maternity pay: Northern Ireland
(*amends* SSA(NI)A 1992 ss 107, 122, 124; *inserts* ss 107A, 107B)

Miscellaneous and general

11 Minor and consequential amendments
Schedule 1 (which makes minor and consequential amendments) has effect.

12 Repeals and revocations
The enactments and instruments mentioned in Schedule 2 are repealed or revoked to the extent specified.

13 Commencement
(1) The preceding provisions of this Act come into force in accordance with provision made by the Treasury by order.
(2) The power to make an order under subsection (1) is exercisable by statutory instrument.
(3) An order under this section—
(*a*) may include incidental, supplementary, consequential or transitional provision or savings;
(*b*) may make different provision for different purposes.

14 Extent
(1) Sections 1, 3, 5, 7 and 9 extend to England and Wales and Scotland only.
(2) Sections 2, 4, 6, 8 and 10 extend to Northern Ireland only.

(3) An amendment, repeal or revocation contained in Schedule 1 or 2 has the same extent as the enactment or instrument to which it relates.

(4) Subject to subsections (1) to (3) this Act extends to England and Wales, Scotland and Northern Ireland.

15 Short title

This Act may be cited as the National Insurance Contributions and Statutory Payments Act 2004.

SCHEDULE 1

MINOR AND CONSEQUENTIAL AMENDMENTS

Section 11

1 (*amends* SSCBA 1992 ss 10A, 18)

2 (*amends* SSCB(NI)A 1992 ss 10A, 18)

3 (*amends* SSAA 1992 ss 111, 162)

4 (*amends* SSA(NI)A 1992 ss 105, 142)

5 (*amends* SSC(TF)A 1999 s 4)

SCHEDULE 2

REPEALS AND REVOCATIONS

Section 12

Note—The repeals and revocations provided for in this Schedule are already in effect, and where relevant to this publication, have been noted under the affected provisions.

PENSIONS ACT 2004

(2004 Chapter 35)

An Act to make provision relating to pensions and financial planning for retirement and provision relating to entitlement to bereavement payments, and for connected purposes.

[18 November 2004]

Note—Please see Part 1 of this work for the text of the relevant provisions of this Act.

COMMISSIONERS FOR REVENUE AND CUSTOMS ACT 2005

(2005 Chapter 11)

An Act to make provision for the appointment of Commissioners to exercise functions presently vested in the Commissioners of Inland Revenue and the Commissioners of Customs and Excise; for the establishment of a Revenue and Customs Prosecutions Office; and for connected purposes.

[7 April 2005]

Note—Please see Part 1 of this publication for the text of this Act.

PENSIONS ACT 2007

(2007 Chapter 22)

An Act to make provision about pensions and other benefits payable to persons in connection with bereavement or by reference to pensionable age; to make provision about the establishment and functions of the Personal Accounts Delivery Authority; and for connected purposes.

[26 July 2007]

PART 1

STATE PENSION

Entitlement to Category A and B retirement pensions

1 Category A and B retirement pensions: single contribution condition

(4) Part 1 of Schedule 1 contains consequential amendments.

2 Category B retirement pension: removal of restriction on entitlement

(4) Part 2 of Schedule 1 contains consequential amendments.

(5) The amendments made by this section and that Part of that Schedule have effect as from 6th April 2010.

7 Removal of link between lower earnings limit and basic pension

(1) Section 5 of the SSCBA (earnings limits and thresholds for Class 1 contributions) is amended as follows.

(2) . . . [1]

(3) Omit subsection (2) (link between lower earnings limit and weekly rate of basic pension).

(4) Subsections (2) and (3) have effect in relation to the tax year following the designated tax year (see section 5(4)) and subsequent tax years.

(5) (inserts SSCBA 1992 s 176(1)(*za*)).

Amendments—[1] Sub-s (2) repealed by the NIC Act 2008 s 4, Sch 2 with effect from the end of the period of two months beginning with the day on which the Act was passed. The Act was passed on 21 July 2008, therefore this amendment has effect from 21 September 2008.

8 Removal of link between lower earnings limit and basic pension: Northern Ireland

(1) Section 5 of the Social Security Contributions and Benefits (Northern Ireland) Act 1992 (c 7) (earnings limits and thresholds for Class 1 contributions) is amended as follows.

(2) . . . [1]

(3) Omit subsection (2) (link between lower earnings limit and weekly rate of basic pension).

(4) Subsections (2) and (3) have effect in relation to the tax year following the designated tax year (see section 5(4)) and subsequent tax years.

(5) (*amends* SSCB(NI)A 1992 s 172)

Amendments—[1] Sub-s (2) repealed by the NIC Act 2008 s 4, Sch 2 with effect from the end of the period of two months beginning with the day on which the Act was passed. The Act was passed on 21 July 2008, therefore this amendment has effect from 21 September 2008.

12 Additional pension: upper accrual point

(1) (*amends* SSCBA 1992 s 22)

(2) (*amends* SSCBA 1992 s 44)

(3) (*amends* SSCBA 1992 s 112)

(4) Part 7 of Schedule 1 contains consequential amendments.

(5) Subsection (6) applies if it appears to the Secretary of State that (apart from that subsection) he would be required to make an order under section 148A of the Administration Act (revaluation of low earnings threshold) by virtue of which the low earnings threshold for the following tax year would be an amount not less than the upper accrual point.

(6) In that event the Secretary of State—

(*a*) is not required to make such an order under section 148A of the Administration Act, and

(*b*) instead must make an order abolishing the low earnings threshold and the upper accrual point as from the beginning of the following tax year.

(7) An order under subsection (6) may make—

(*a*) such consequential, incidental or supplemental provision, and

(*b*) such transitional, transitory or saving provision,

as the Secretary of State thinks necessary or expedient in connection with, or in consequence of, the abolition of the low earnings threshold and the upper accrual point.

(8) An order under subsection (6) may in particular amend, repeal or revoke any provision of any Act or subordinate legislation (whenever passed or made).

(9) No order may be made under subsection (6) unless a draft of the order has been laid before and approved by a resolution of each House of Parliament.

(10) In this section—

"the low earnings threshold" has the meaning given by section 44A(5) of the SSCBA;

"the upper accrual point" has the meaning given by section 122(7) and (8) of that Act.

PART 2

OCCUPATIONAL AND PERSONAL PENSION SCHEMES

15 Abolition of contracting-out for defined contribution pension schemes

(1) Any certificate which is either—

(*a*) a contracting-out certificate in relation to a money purchase contracted-out scheme, or

(*b*) an appropriate scheme certificate,

and is in force immediately before [6 April 2012][1], ceases to have effect on that date.

(2) In this section—

. . . [1]

"contracting-out certificate", "money purchase contracted-out scheme" and "appropriate scheme certificate" have the meanings given by section 181(1) of the Pension Schemes Act 1993 (c 48) (as in force immediately before that day).

(3) In Schedule 4—

(*a*) Parts 1 and 2 contain amendments which are consequential on, or related to, the provision made by subsection (1), and

(*b*) Part 3 contains savings relating to amendments made by Part 1.

(4) The amendments made by Part 1 of that Schedule have effect as from [6 April 2012][1] (but any power to make regulations conferred by those amendments may be exercised at any time so as to make regulations having effect as from [6 April 2012][1]).

(5) The Secretary of State may by regulations make—

(*a*) such consequential, incidental or supplemental provision, and

(*b*) such transitional, transitory or saving provision,

as he thinks necessary or expedient in connection with, or in consequence of, the provisions of subsection (1) and Schedule 4.

(6) Regulations under subsection (5) may in particular amend, repeal or revoke any provision of any Act or subordinate legislation (whenever passed or made).

(7) No regulations which amend or repeal any provision of an Act may be made under this section unless a draft of the regulations has been laid before and approved by a resolution of each House of Parliament.

(8) A statutory instrument containing regulations under this section that do not fall within subsection (7) is subject to annulment in pursuance of a resolution of either House of Parliament.

Commencement—Pensions Act 2007 (Commencement No 4) Order, SI 2011/1267 art 2(a) (sub-s (1) comes into force on 6 April 2012).

Amendments—[1] In sub-ss (1), (4) words substituted, and in sub-s (2) definition of "the abolition date" repealed, by PeA 2014 s 24, Sch 13 paras 77, 78 with effect from 6 April 2016 (PeA 2014 s 56(1), (4)).

PART 3
PERSONAL ACCOUNTS DELIVERY AUTHORITY

20 Personal Accounts Delivery Authority

Amendments—This section repealed by the Personal Accounts Delivery Authority Winding Up Order 2010, SI 2010/911 art 8(1)(*a*) with effect from 5 July 2010.

21 Initial function of the Authority

Amendments—Section 21 repealed by the Pensions Act 2008 s 79(1) with effect from 26 November 2008.

22 Management of the Authority

Amendments—Section 22 repealed by the Personal Accounts Delivery Authority Winding Up Order 2010, SI 2010/911 art 8(1)(*a*) with effect from 5 July 2010.

23 Winding up of the Authority

[(1) The Secretary of State may by order provide for the winding up and dissolution of the Authority.][1]

(2)–(4) . . . [1]

(5) An order under this section may, in particular—

(*a*) provide for the transfer of property, rights or liabilities of the Authority to the Secretary of State [or any other person][1];

(*b*) provide, in connection with provision made under paragraph (*a*)—

(i) for the creation of interests in property transferred;

(ii) for the creation of rights and liabilities in relation to such property;

(iii) for interests, rights and liabilities to be extinguished;

(*c*) provide for the payment by the Secretary of State or the Authority of compensation to any person who suffers loss or damage as a result of the provision made for the winding up of the Authority.

(6) An order under this section may make—

(*a*) such consequential, incidental or supplemental provision, and

(*b*) such transitional, transitory or saving provision,

as the Secretary of State thinks necessary or expedient in connection with, or in consequence of, the winding up and dissolution of the Authority.

(7) An order under this section may also contain provision repealing any provision of—

[(*a*)] [1]sections 20 to 22 or Schedule 6[;

(*b*) sections 79 to 85 of the Pensions Act 2008.][1]

(8) No order may be made under this section unless a draft of the order has been laid before and approved by a resolution of each House of Parliament.

Orders—Personal Accounts Delivery Authority Winding Up Order 2010, SI 2010/911.

Amendments—[1] Sub-s (1) substituted, sub-ss (2)–(4) repealed, in sub-s (5)(*a*) words inserted, and in sub-s (7), para (*a*) numbered as such and para (*b*) inserted, by the Pensions Act 2008 ss 86, 148, Sch 11 Pt 1, with effect from 26 November 2008.

PART 4
GENERAL

24 Review of operation of Act

(1) The Secretary of State must, before the end of 2014, prepare a report on the operation of the provisions of this Act.

NIC

(2) The Secretary of State may prepare subsequent reports on the operation of the provisions of this Act.

(3) The Secretary of State must lay a copy of any report prepared under this section before Parliament.

25 Orders and regulations

(1) Any order or regulations under this Act must be made by statutory instrument.

(2) Any power of the Secretary of State to make an order or regulations under this Act includes power to make different provision for different purposes or cases.

(3) Before the Secretary of State makes any regulations by virtue of—

(*a*) section 15(5), or

(*b*) section 18(9),

he must consult such persons as he considers appropriate.

(4) Subsection (3) does not apply—

(*a*) to regulations made for the purpose only of consolidating other regulations revoked by them,

(*b*) in a case where it appears to the Secretary of State that by reason of urgency consultation is inexpedient,

(*c*) to regulations made before the end of the period of 6 months beginning with the coming into force of the provision mentioned in subsection (3) by virtue of which the regulations are made, or

(*d*) to regulations which—

(i) state that they are consequential upon a specified enactment, and

(ii) are made before the end of the period of 6 months beginning with the coming into force of that enactment.

(5) In subsection (4) "enactment" includes an enactment comprised in subordinate legislation.

Orders—Personal Accounts Delivery Authority Winding Up Order 2010, SI 2010/911.

26 Interpretation

In this Act—

"the Administration Act" means the Social Security Administration Act 1992 (c 5);

"the SSCBA" means the Social Security Contributions and Benefits Act 1992 (c 4);

"subordinate legislation" has the same meaning as in the Interpretation Act 1978 (c 30);

"tax year" has the same meaning as in Parts 1 to 6 of the SSCBA (see section 122(1) of that Act).

27 Consequential etc provision, repeals and revocations

(1) The Secretary of State may by order make—

(*a*) such supplementary, incidental or consequential provision, or

(*b*) such transitory, transitional or saving provision,

as he considers appropriate for the general purposes, or any particular purposes, of this Act, or in consequence of, or for giving full effect to, any provision made by this Act.

(2) Schedule 7 contains repeals and revocations.

(3) The following repeals have effect at the end of the period of 2 months beginning with the day on which this Act is passed—

(*a*) the repeals in Part 2 of Schedule 7 of the provisions of the Pensions Act 1995 (c 26) other than paragraphs 19 and 20 of Schedule 4 to that Act;

(*b*) the repeal in Part 2 of Schedule 7 of paragraph 36 of Schedule 24 to the Civil Partnership Act 2004 (c 33);

(*c*) the repeals in Parts 3 and 5 of Schedule 7.

(4) The following repeals and revocations have effect on 6th April 2010—

(*a*) the repeals and revocations in Part 1 of Schedule 7;

(*b*) the repeals in Part 2 of that Schedule other than those falling within subsection (3).

(5) The repeals in Part 4 of that Schedule have effect on 6th April in the tax year following the designated tax year (see section 5(4)).

(6) The repeals and revocations in Part 6 of that Schedule have effect on [6 April 2012][1].

(7) The other repeals contained in that Schedule have effect on the date on which they come into force by virtue of an order made under section 30.

(8) A statutory instrument containing an order under subsection (1) is subject to annulment in pursuance of a resolution of either House of Parliament.

Amendments—[1] In sub-s (6), words substituted by PeA 2014 s 24, Sch 13 paras 77, 79 with effect from 6 April 2016 (PeA 2014 s 56(1), (4)).

28 Financial provisions

(1) There is to be paid out of money provided by Parliament—

(*a*) any expenditure incurred by the Secretary of State by virtue of this Act; and (*b*) any increase attributable to this Act in the sums payable under any other Act out of money so provided.

(2) There is to be paid into the Consolidated Fund any increase in the sums payable into that Fund under any other Act.

29 Extent

(1) The following provisions of this Act extend to England and Wales, Scotland and Northern Ireland—

(*a*) sections 18 and 19,

(*b*) Part 3, and

(*c*) this Part.

(2) But section 24 extends to Northern Ireland in accordance with subsection (1) only as respects the provisions of this Act extending there.

(3) Section 8 and the repeal in the Social Security Contributions and Benefits (Northern Ireland) Act 1992 (c 7) in Part 4 of Schedule 7 extend to Northern Ireland only.

(4) The amendments made by Schedule 5 have the same extent as the enactments amended.

(5) The other provisions of this Act extend to England and Wales and Scotland.

30 Commencement

(1) The following provisions of this Act come into force on the day on which it is passed—

(*a*) sections 5 and 6, and Part 5 of Schedule 1, so far as relating to the amounts mentioned in subsection (1)(*d*) of the new section 150A inserted into the Administration Act by section 5(1);

(*b*) sections 18(4) to (11) and 19;

(*c*) Part 3;

(*d*) this Part.

(2) The following provisions of this Act come into force on such day as the Secretary of State may by order appoint—

(*a*) section 14;

(*b*) section 15(1), Part 2 of Schedule 4 and Part 7 of Schedule 7;

(*c*) section 17, Schedule 5 and Part 8 of Schedule 7;

(*d*) section 18(1) to (3).

(3) The other provisions of this Act come into force at the end of the period of 2 months beginning with the day on which it is passed.

(4) An order under subsection (2) may—

(*a*) appoint different days for different purposes;

(*b*) make such provision as the Secretary of State considers necessary or expedient for transitory, transitional or saving purposes in connection with the coming into force of any provision falling within subsection (2).

31 Short title

This Act may be cited as the Pensions Act 2007.

SCHEDULE 1

STATE PENSION: CONSEQUENTIAL AND RELATED AMENDMENTS

Sections 1 to 5, 9, 12 and 13

PART 3

CONTRIBUTIONS CREDITS FOR RELEVANT PARENTS AND CARERS

Social Security Contributions and Benefits Act 1992 (c 4)

9 (*inserts* SSCBA 1992 s 22(5A)).

10 (*inserts* SSCBA 1992 s 176(1)(*aa*)).

PART 6

DEEMED EARNINGS FACTORS FOR PURPOSES OF ADDITIONAL PENSION

33 (*amends* SSCBA 1992 s 22).

PART 7

ADDITIONAL PENSION: SIMPLIFIED ACCRUAL RATES

Social Security Contributions and Benefits Act 1992 (c 4)

35 In section 176 of the SSCBA (parliamentary control)—

(*a*) . . . [1]

NIC

(*b*) (*amends* SSCBA 1992 s 176(4)).

Amendments—[1] Sub-para (*a*) repealed by the NIC Act 2008 s 4, Sch 2 with effect from the end of the period of two months beginning with the day on which the Act was passed. The Act was passed on 21 July 2008, therefore this amendment has effect from 21 September 2008.

Pension Schemes Act 1993 (c 48)

37

Amendments—This para repealed by the NIC Act 2008 s 4, Sch 2 with effect in relation to 2009–10 and subsequent tax years.

38 (*amends* Pension Schemes Act 1993 s 181(1)).

SCHEDULE 2

ADDITIONAL PENSION: SIMPLIFIED ACCRUAL RATES

Section 11

PART 2

REVALUATION OF FLAT RATE ACCRUAL AMOUNT

2 (*inserts* SSAA 1992 s 148AA)

PART 3

CONSEQUENTIAL AND RELATED AMENDMENTS

Pension Schemes Act 1993 (c 48)

12 (*amends* PSA 1993 s 42(1)(*a*)(ii)).

SCHEDULE 4

ABOLITION OF CONTRACTING-OUT FOR DEFINED CONTRIBUTION PENSION SCHEMES

PART 1

AMENDMENTS HAVING EFFECT AS FROM ABOLITION DATE

Pension Schemes Act 1993 (c 48)

1 The Pension Schemes Act 1993 has effect subject to the following amendments.

2—(1) Section 7 (issue of contracting-out and appropriate scheme certificates) is amended as follows.
(2) (*substitutes* PSA 1993 s 7(1), (1A)).
(3) (*repeals* PSA 1993 s 7(4)–(6)).
(4) (*amends* PSA 1993 s 7(7)).
(5) (*inserts* PSA 1993 s 7(8)).
(6) (*amends* sidenote to PSA 1993 s 7).

3—(1) Section 8 (definitions of certain terms) is amended as follows.
(2) (*substitutes* PSA 1993 s 8(1)(*a*), (*aa*)).
(3) (*inserts* PSA 1993 s 8(1A)).
(4) (*amends* PSA 1993 s 8(2)).

15—(1) Section 34 (cancellation, variation, surrender and refusal of certificates) is amended as follows.
(2) (*substitutes* PSA 1993 s 34(1)).
(3) (*amends* PSA 1993 s 34(3)).
(4) (*repeals* PSA 1993 s 34(5)).
(5) (*amends* PSA 1993 s 34(8)).
(6) (*inserts* PSA 1993 s 34(9)).

17 (*inserts* PSA 1993 s 42A(8)).

18 (*repeals* PSA 1993 s 42B).

19 (*inserts* PSA 1993 s 43(7)).

20 (*repeals* PSA 1993 s 44).

21 (*inserts* PSA 1993 s 45(4)).

22 (*repeals* PSA 1993 s 45A).

23—(1) Section 48A (additional pension and other benefits) is amended as follows.
(2) (*amends* PSA 1993 s 48A(1)(*a*)).
(3) (*amends* PSA 1993 s 48A(1)(*b*)).

34—(1) Section 181 (general interpretation) is amended as follows.
(2) (*amends* PSA 1993 s 181(1)(*a*)).
(3) (*amends* PSA 1993 s 181(4)).

35 (*inserts* PSA 1993 s 181A).

PART 2
FURTHER AMENDMENTS

Social Security Contributions and Benefits Act 1992 (c 4)

42—(1) Section 4C of the SSCBA (power to make provision in consequence of provision made by or by virtue of section 4B(2) etc) is amended as follows.
(2) In subsection (2) (purposes for which regulations may be made) omit paragraph (*d*) (purposes relating to minimum payments).
(3) In subsection (5) (matters in respect of which regulations may have retrospective effect)—
- (*a*) in paragraph (*b*) (amount of rebate under section 41(1D) or 42A(2C) of the Pension Schemes Act 1993 (c 48)) omit "or 42A(2C)";
- (*b*) omit paragraphs (*g*) and (*h*) (liability to make, and amount of, minimum payments);
- (*c*) omit paragraphs (i) and (j) (liability to make, and amount of, payments under section 42A(3) of that Act or minimum contributions).

Commencement—Pensions Act 2007 (Commencement No 4) Order, SI 2011/1267 art 3(*a*)(i), (ii) (para 42(1), in so far as it relates to para 42(2), (3)(*b*), and para 42(2), (3)(*b*), come into force on 6 April 2015).

43 In section 8 of the SSCBA (calculation of primary Class 1 contributions) in subsection (3) (provisions to which calculation is subject) in paragraph (*c*), for "sections 41 and 42A" substitute "section 41".

44 In section 9 of the SSCBA (calculation of secondary Class 1 contributions) in subsection (3) (provisions to which calculation is subject) in paragraph (*c*), for "sections 41 and 42A" substitute "section 41".

45—(1) In Schedule 1 to the SSCBA (supplementary provisions relating to contributions of Classes 1, 1A, 1B, 2 and 3) paragraph 1 (Class 1 contributions where earner is in more than one employment) is amended as follows.
(2) In sub-paragraph (3) (determination of amount of primary Class 1 contributions where aggregate earnings include earnings from contracted-out employment)—
- (*a*) omit paragraphs (*a*) and (*b*);
- (*b*) in paragraph (*c*), for sub-paragraphs (i) and (ii) substitute "to such part of the aggregated earnings attributable to COSRS service as exceeds the current primary threshold and does not exceed the current upper earnings limit";
- (*c*) in paragraph (*d*), for "part or parts attributable to COMPS or COSRS service" substitute "part attributable to COSRS service".

(3) In sub-paragraph (6) (determination of amount of secondary Class 1 contributions where aggregate earnings include earnings from contracted-out employment) omit paragraphs (*a*) and (*b*).
(4) In sub-paragraph (9) (interpretation) omit the definition of "COMPS service".

Pension Schemes Act 1993 (c 48)

46 The Pension Schemes Act 1993 has effect subject to the following amendments.

Commencement—Pensions Act 2007 (Commencement No 4) Order, SI 2011/1267 art 2(*b*)(i) (para 46, in so far as it relates to paras 59(1), (2), (4), 60 comes into force on 6 April 2012).
Pensions Act 2007 (Commencement No 4) Order, SI 2011/1267 art 3(*a*)(iii) (para 46, in so far as it relates to paras 47, 49, 54, 59(1), (3) comes into force on 6 April 2015).

47 In section 8 (meaning of, among other things, "minimum payment") omit subsection (3) (regulations may make provision about manner in which minimum payments to be made etc).

Commencement—Pensions Act 2007 (Commencement No 4) Order, SI 2011/1267 art 3(*a*)(iv) (para 47 comes into force on 6 April 2015).

50 In section 40 (scope of Chapter 2 of Part 3) omit paragraph (*b*) (which relates to contributions to be paid by HMRC in respect of members of money purchase contracted-out schemes or of appropriate personal pension schemes).

51 Omit section 42A (reduced rates of contributions, and rebates, for members of money purchase contracted-out schemes etc).

NIC

52 Omit section 43 (payment of minimum contributions to personal pension schemes).

53 Omit section 45 (amount of minimum contributions).

54 Omit section 45B (money purchase and personal pension schemes: verification of ages).

Commencement—Pensions Act 2007 (Commencement No 4) Order, SI 2011/1267 art 3(*a*)(iv) (para 54 comes into force on 6 April 2015).

58—(1) Section 181 (interpretation) is amended as follows.
(2) In subsection (1), omit the definition of "minimum contributions".
(3) In subsection (4) (regulations may prescribe the persons who are to be regarded as members or prospective members of an occupational scheme etc) omit ", 43".

PART 3
SAVINGS

Issue and cancellation etc of certificates for periods before the abolition date

61 Nothing in the relevant amendments and repeals affects the continued operation of any regulations in force under section 7(1) and (7) of the PSA 1993 (issue of certificates) immediately before [6 April 2012][1] in relation to the issue of a certificate having effect for a period before [6 April 2012][1].

Amendments—[1] Words substituted by PeA 2014 s 24, Sch 13 paras 77, 80(1), (2) with effect from 6 April 2016 (PeA 2014 s 56(1), (4)).

62—(1) Nothing in the relevant amendments and repeals affects the continued operation of section 34 of the PSA 1993 (cancellation, variation, surrender and refusal of certificates), or any regulations in force under it immediately before [6 April 2012][1], for the purposes of a retrospective act.
(2) In sub-paragraph (1) "a retrospective act" means the cancellation, variation, surrender or refusal of a certificate, or the issue of an amended certificate, where—
(*a*) the certificate was in force for a period beginning before [6 April 2012][1] (or, in the case of a refusal of a certificate, would have related to such a period if it had been issued), and
(*b*) the cancellation, variation, surrender, refusal or issue—
(i) is made after [6 April 2012][1], but
(ii) has effect from a date before that date.
(3) An amended certificate issued by virtue of this paragraph must provide for it to cease to have effect as from [6 April 2012][1].
(4) In this paragraph and paragraph 61 "a certificate" means an appropriate scheme certificate or a contracting-out certificate in respect of a money purchase contracted-out scheme, and each of those terms has the meaning given by section 181(1) of the PSA 1993.

Amendments—[1] In sub-paras (1), (2)(*a*), (*b*)(i), (3), words substituted by PeA 2014 s 24, Sch 13 paras 77, 80(1), (2) with effect from 6 April 2016 (PeA 2014 s 56(1), (4)).

63 Nothing in the relevant amendments and repeals affects the continued operation of section 164(2) of the PSA 1993 (persons employed by or under the Crown to be treated as employed earners for the purposes of certain provisions) in relation to the provisions of that Act saved by paragraphs 61 and 62.

64 Nothing in the relevant amendments and repeals affects the continued operation of section 177(3)(*b*)(ii) of the PSA 1993 (administrative expenses of the Secretary of State, other than those arising out of certain provisions, to be paid out of the National Insurance Fund into the Consolidated Fund) in relation to the estimated administrative expenses of the Secretary of State in carrying into effect the provisions of that Act saved by paragraphs 61 and 62.

Determination of question whether scheme was appropriate scheme

65 Nothing in the relevant amendments and repeals affects the continued operation of any regulations in force under section 7(6) of the PSA 1993 (issue of certificates) immediately before [6 April 2012][1].

Amendments—[1] Words substituted by PeA 2014 s 24, Sch 13 paras 77, 80(1), (2) with effect from 6 April 2016 (PeA 2014 s 56(1), (4)).

Preservation of earner's chosen scheme

66—(1) Nothing in the relevant amendments and repeals—
(*a*) prevents the giving of a preceding tax year notice, or
(*b*) otherwise affects the operation of section 44 of the PSA 1993 in relation to such a notice.

(2) In sub-paragraph (1) a "preceding tax year notice" means a notice within section 44(1) of the PSA 1993 which is given on or after [6 April 2012][1] but in which the date specified in accordance with that provision falls before [6 April 2012][1].

Amendments—[1] In sub-para (2), words substituted by PeA 2014 s 24, Sch 13 paras 77, 80(1), (2) with effect from 6 April 2016 (PeA 2014 s 56(1), (4)).

Interpretation etc

67—(1) In this Part of this Schedule—

. . . [1]

"the PSA 1993" means the Pension Schemes Act 1993 (c 48);

"the relevant amendments and repeals" means—

(*a*) the amendments and repeals made by Part 1 of this Schedule, and

(*b*) the consequential repeals and revocations in Part 6 of Schedule 7.

(2) Nothing in this Part of this Schedule is to be read as affecting the generality of section 16 of the Interpretation Act 1978 (c 30) (general savings).

Amendments—[1] In sub-para (1), definition of "the abolition date" repealed by PeA 2014 s 24, Sch 13 paras 77, 80(1), (3) with effect from 6 April 2016 (PeA 2014 s 56(1), (4)).

SCHEDULE 6

THE PERSONAL ACCOUNTS DELIVERY AUTHORITY

Amendments—This Schedule repealed by the Personal Accounts Delivery Authority Winding Up Order 2010, SI 2010/911 art 8(1)(*b*) subject to savings (see arts 8(2), (3)) with effect from 5 July 2010.

Section 20

SCHEDULE 7

REPEALS AND REVOCATIONS

Section 27

Note—This Schedule repealed by the Personal Accounts Delivery Authority Winding Up Order 2010, SI 2010/911 art 8(1)(*b*) subject to savings (see arts 8(2), (3)) with effect from 5 July 2010.

PART 4

REMOVAL OF LINK BETWEEN LOWER EARNINGS LIMIT AND BASIC PENSION

Citation	*Extent of repeal*
Social Security Contributions and Benefits Act 1992	Section 5(2).
Social Security Contributions and Benefits (Northern Ireland) Act 1992 (c 7)	Section 5(2).

PART 6

ABOLITION OF CONTRACTING-OUT FOR DEFINED CONTRIBUTION PENSION SCHEMES: REPEALS AND REVOCATIONS HAVING EFFECT ON ABOLITION DATE

Citation or reference	*Extent of repeal or revocation*
Pension Schemes Act 1993 (c 48)	In section 7—
	(a) subsections (4) to (6); (b) in subsection (7), the words "or appropriate scheme certificate";
	(c) in the sidenote, the words "and appropriate scheme".
	In section 34—
	(a) in subsection (3), the words "or, as the case may be, the scheme's continuing to be an appropriate scheme" and "or appropriate scheme";
	(b) subsection (5);
	(c) in subsection (8), the words "or appropriate scheme certificate".
	Section 42B.
	Section 44.
	Section 45A.

	In section 181(4) ", 44".
Social Security Act 1998 (c 14)	In Schedule 7, paragraph 126.
Social Security Contributions (Transfer of Functions, etc) Act 1999 (c 2)	In Schedule 1, paragraphs 33, 35(3), 41 and 48.

PART 7
ABOLITION OF CONTRACTING-OUT FOR DEFINED CONTRIBUTION PENSION SCHEMES: FURTHER REPEALS

Citation	*Extent of repeal*
Social Security Contributions and Benefits Act 1992 (c 4)	In section 4C—
	(a) subsection (2)(d);
	(b) in subsection (5)(b), "or 42A(2C)";
	(c) subsection (5)(g) to (j).
	In paragraph 1 of Schedule 1—
	(a) sub-paragraph (3)(a) and (b);
	(b) sub-paragraph (6)(a) and (b);
	(c) in sub-paragraph (9), the definition of "COMPS service".
Pension Schemes Act 1993 (c 48)	Section 8(3).
	Section 42A.
	Section 43.
	Section 45.
	Section 45B.
	In section 181—
	(a) in subsection (1), the definition of "minimum contributions";
	(b) in subsection (4), ", 43".
	In paragraph 2 of Schedule 4—
	(a) sub-paragraphs (2) and (3);
	(b) in the opening words of sub-paragraph (3A), "or (3)";
	(c) in sub-paragraph (3A)(a), the words "or (2) (as the case may be)";
	(d) in sub-paragraph (5), the definition of "appropriate flat-rate percentage."
Social Security Act 1998 (c 14)	In Schedule 7, paragraphs 77(4)(a) and 128.
	Social Security Contributions (Transfer of Functions, etc) Act 1999 (c 2)
	In Schedule 1, paragraphs 34(b), 43, 46, 47, 49, 50 and 61(3)(a).
National Insurance Contributions Act 2002 (c 19)	In Schedule 1, paragraphs 37 and 38.

Commencement—Pensions Act 2007 (Commencement No 4) Order, SI 2011/1267 art 3(a)(iv) (Pt 7 in so far as it relates to the repeals of SSCBA 1992 4C(2)*d*), (5)(*g*), (h) and PSA 1993 s 8(3) comes into force on 6 April 2015).

FINANCE ACT 2009

(2009 Chapter 10)

CONTENTS

PART 7
ADMINISTRATION

Interest

An Act to Grant certain duties, to alter other duties, and to amend the law relating to the National Debt and the Public Revenue, and to make further provision in connection with finance.

[21 July 2009]

PART 7
ADMINISTRATION

Interest

101 Late payment interest on sums due to HMRC

(1) This section applies to any amount that is payable by a person to HMRC under or by virtue of an enactment.

(2) But this section does not apply to—

(*a*) an amount of corporation tax,

(*b*) an amount of petroleum revenue tax, or

(*c*) an amount of any description specified in an order made by the Treasury.

(3) An amount to which this section applies carries interest at the late payment interest rate from the late payment interest start date until the date of payment.

(4) The late payment interest start date in respect of any amount is the date on which that amount becomes due and payable.

(5) In Schedule 53—

(*a*) Part 1 makes special provision as to the amount on which late payment interest is calculated,

(*b*) Part 2 makes special provision as to the late payment interest start date,

(*c*) Part 3 makes special provision as to the date to which late payment interest runs, and

(*d*) Part 4 makes provision about the effect that the giving of a relief has on late payment interest.

(6) Subsection (3) applies even if the late payment interest start date is a non-business day within the meaning of section 92 of the Bills of Exchange Act 1882.

(7) Late payment interest is to be paid without any deduction of income tax.

(8) Late payment interest is not payable on late payment interest.

(9) For the purposes of this section any reference to the payment of an amount to HMRC includes a reference to its being set off against an amount payable by HMRC (and, accordingly, the reference to the date on which an amount is paid includes a reference to the date from which the set-off takes effect).

[(10) The reference in subsection (1) to amounts payable to HMRC includes—

(*a*) amounts of UK VAT payable under a non-UK special scheme;

(*b*) amounts of UK VAT payable under a special scheme;

and references in Schedule 53 to amounts due or payable to HMRC are to be read accordingly.

(11) In subsection (10)—

(*a*) expressions used in paragraph (a) have the meaning given by paragraph 23(1) of Schedule 3B to VATA 1994 (non- Union scheme);

(*b*) expressions used in paragraph (b) have the meaning given by paragraph 38(1) of Schedule 3BA to VATA 1994 (Union scheme).][1]

Commentary—*Simon's Taxes* **A4.620.**

Commencement—Finance Act 2009, Sections 101 to 103 (Appointed Day and Supplemental Provision) Order, SI 2010/1878 (day appointed as the day on which FA 2009 ss 101–103 come into force for the purposes of bank payroll tax (including any penalties assessed in relation to that tax) is 31 August 2010).

Finance Act 2009, Sections 101 to 103 (Income Tax Self Assessment) (Appointed Days and Transitional and Consequential Provisions) Order, SI 2011/701 (for the purposes of any self–assessment amount payable by a person to HMRC, ss 101 and 103 come into force on 31 October 2011; for the purposes of any self-assessment amount payable or repayable by HMRC to any person, ss 102 and 103 come into force on 31 October 2011).

Finance (No 3) Act 2010, Schedule 10 and the Finance Act 2009, Schedule 55 and Sections 101 to 103 (Appointed Day, etc) (Construction Industry Scheme) Order, SI 2011/2391 (the day appointed for the coming into force of ss 101–103 is 6 October 2011, but only in relation to a penalty under Sch 55 paras 7–13 (Construction Industry Scheme).

NIC

Finance Act 2009, Sections 101 and 102 (Machine Games Duty) (Appointed Day) Order, SI 2013/67 (the day appointed for the coming into force of ss 101 and 102 is 1 February 2013 for the purposes of machine games duty, including any penalties assessed in relation to that duty).

Finance Act 2009, Section 101 (Tax Agents: Dishonest Conduct) (Appointed Day) Order, SI 2013/280 (the day appointed for the coming into force of s 101 is 1 April 2013 for the purposes of penalties assessed under FA 2012 Sch 38 Parts 3–5 (penalties for dishonest conduct or for failure to comply with a file access notice).

Finance Act 2009, Sections 101 and 102 (Annual Tax on Enveloped Dwellings) (Appointed Day) Order, SI 2013/2472 (the day appointed for the coming into force of ss 101 and 102 for the purposes of the annual tax on enveloped dwellings and penalties assessed in relation to that tax is 1 October 2013).

Finance Act 2009, Sections 101 and 102 (Interest on Late Payments and Repayments), Appointed Days and Consequential Provisions Order, SI 2014/992 (the day appointed for the coming into force of ss 101 and 102 is 6 May 2014 for the purposes of PAYE and Class 1 contributions payable by, or repayable by HMRC to, an employer, and any CIS amount either payable by, or repayable by HMRC to, a contractor).

Finance Act 2009, Schedules 55 and 56 and Sections 101 and 102 (Stamp Duty Reserve Tax) (Appointed Days, Consequential and Transitional Provision) Order, SI 2014/3269 art 4 (the day appointed as the day on which ss 101 and 102 come into force for the purposes of stamp duty reserve tax (including any penalties assessed in relation to that tax) is 1 January 2015. This only applies to a charge with a due and payable date falling after 31 December 2014.).

Finance Act 2009, Sections 101 and 102 (Remote Gambling Taxes) (Appointed Day) Order, SI 2014/3324 art 3 (the day appointed as the day on which ss 101 and 102 come into force for the purposes of remote gambling taxes is 1 January 2015).

Finance Act 2009, Sections 101 and 102 (Diverted Profits Tax) (Appointed Day) Order, SI 2015/974 (the day appointed for the coming into force of ss 101, 102 for the purposes of diverted profits tax and penalties assessed in relation to that tax is 1 April 2015).

Regulations—Taxes and Duties, etc (Interest Rate) Regulations, SI 2011/2446 (formula for calculating late payment interest rate for the purposes of this section).

Cross-references—See FA 2014 s 176 in relation to interest charged under s 101 in relation to general betting duty, pool betting duty and remote gaming duty (outside the scope of this work).

SSCBA 1992 s 11A (this section applies with the necessary modifications, in relation to Class 2 contributions under SSCBA 1992 s 11(2) as if those contributions were income tax chargeable under ITTOIA 2005 Pt 2 Ch 2 in respect of profits of a trade, profession or vocation which is not carried on wholly outside the United Kingdom).

Education (Postgraduate Master's Degree Loans) Regulations, SI 2016/606 regs 49, 68, 80 (application of this section to loans for postgraduate master's degree courses which begin on or after 1 August 2016).

Amendments—[1] Sub-ss (10), (11) inserted by FA 2014 s 103, Sch 22 para 20(1), (2) with effect from 17 July 2014.

Prospective amendment—Sub-s (2)(*a*), (*b*) to be repealed by F(No 3)A 2010 s 25, Sch 9 Pt 1 paras 1, 2, Pt 2 paras 13, 14 with effect from a day to be appointed by Treasury order (F(No 3)A 2010 s 25).

102 Repayment interest on sums to be paid by HMRC

(1) This section applies to—

(*a*) any amount that is payable by HMRC to any person under or by virtue of an enactment, and

(*b*) a relevant amount paid by a person to HMRC that is repaid by HMRC to that person or to another person.

(2) But this section does not apply to—

(*a*) an amount constituting a repayment of corporation tax,

(*b*) an amount constituting a repayment of petroleum revenue tax, or

(*c*) an amount of any description specified in an order made by the Treasury.

(3) An amount to which this section applies carries interest at the repayment interest rate from the repayment interest start date until the date on which the payment or repayment is made.

(4) In Schedule 54—

(*a*) Parts 1 and 2 define the repayment interest start date, and

(*b*) Part 3 makes supplementary provision.

(5) Subsection (3) applies even if the repayment interest start date is a non-business day within the meaning of section 92 of the Bills of Exchange Act 1882.

(6) Repayment interest is not payable on an amount payable in consequence of an order or judgment of a court having power to allow interest on the amount.

(7) Repayment interest is not payable on repayment interest.

(8) For the purposes of this section—

(*a*) "relevant amount" means any sum that was paid in connection with any liability (including any purported or anticipated liability) to make a payment to HMRC under or by virtue of an enactment, and

(*b*) any reference to the payment or repayment of an amount by HMRC includes a reference to its being set off against an amount owed to HMRC (and, accordingly, the reference to the date on which an amount is paid or repaid by HMRC includes a reference to the date from which the set-off takes effect).

Commentary—*Simon's Taxes* **A4.629.**

Commencement—Finance Act 2009, Sections 101 to 103 (Appointed Day and Supplemental Provision) Order, SI 2010/1878 (day appointed as the day on which FA 2009 ss 101–103 come into force for the purposes of bank payroll tax (including any penalties assessed in relation to that tax) is 31 August 2010).

Finance Act 2009, Sections 101 to 103 (Income Tax Self Assessment) (Appointed Days and Transitional and Consequential Provisions) Order, SI 2011/701 (for the purposes of any self-assessment amount payable by a person to HMRC, ss 101 and 103 come into force on 31 October 2011; for the purposes of any self-assessment amount payable or repayable by HMRC to any person, ss 102 and 103 come into force on 31 October 2011).

Finance (No 3) Act 2010, Schedule 10 and the Finance Act 2009, Schedule 55 and Sections 101 to 103 (Appointed Day, etc) (Construction Industry Scheme) Order, SI 2011/2391 (the day appointed for the coming into force of ss 101–103 is 6 October 2011, but only in relation to a penalty under Sch 55 paras 7–13 (Construction Industry Scheme).

Finance Act 2009, Sections 101 and 102 (Machine Games Duty) (Appointed Day) Order, SI 2013/67 (the day appointed for the coming into force of ss 101 and 102 is 1 February 2013 for the purposes of machine games duty, including any penalties assessed in relation to that duty).

Finance Act 2009, Sections 101 and 102 (Annual Tax on Enveloped Dwellings) (Appointed Day) Order, SI 2013/2472 (the day appointed for the coming into force of ss 101 and 102 for the purposes of the annual tax on enveloped dwellings and penalties assessed in relation to that tax is 1 October 2013).

Finance Act 2009, Sections 101 and 102 (Interest on Late Payments and Repayments), Appointed Days and Consequential Provisions Order, SI 2014/992 (the day appointed for the coming into force of ss 101 and 102 is 6 May 2014 for the purposes of PAYE and Class 1 contributions payable by, or repayable by HMRC to, an employer, and any CIS amount either payable by, or repayable by HMRC to, a contractor).

Finance Act 2009, Schedules 55 and 56 and Sections 101 and 102 (Stamp Duty Reserve Tax) (Appointed Days, Consequential and Transitional Provision) Order, SI 2014/3269 art 4 (the day appointed as the day on which ss 101 and 102 come into force for the purposes of stamp duty reserve tax (including any penalties assessed in relation to that tax) is 1 January 2015. This only applies to a charge with a due and payable date falling after 31 December 2014.).

Finance Act 2009, Sections 101 and 102 (Remote Gambling Taxes) (Appointed Day) Order, SI 2014/3324 art 3 (the day appointed as the day on which ss 101 and 102 come into force for the purposes of remote gambling taxes is 1 January 2015).

Finance Act 2009, Sections 101 and 102 (Diverted Profits Tax) (Appointed Day) Order, SI 2015/974 art 2 (the day appointed for the coming into force of ss 101, 102 for the purposes of diverted profits tax and penalties assessed in relation to that tax is 1 April 2015).

Cross-references—See SSCBA 1992 s 11A (this section applies with the necessary modifications, in relation to Class 2 contributions under SSCBA 1992 s 11(2) as if those contributions were income tax chargeable under ITTOIA 2005 Pt 2 Ch 2 in respect of profits of a trade, profession or vocation which is not carried on wholly outside the United Kingdom).

Regulations—Taxes and Duties, etc (Interest Rate) Regulations, SI 2011/2446 (formula for calculating repayment payment interest rate for the purposes of this section).

Prospective amendment—Sub-s (2)(*a*), (*b*) to be repealed, and sub-s (4)(*za*) to be inserted before sub-s (4)(*a*), by F(No 3)A 2010 s 25, Sch 9 Pt 1 paras 1, 3, Pt 2 paras 13, 15 with effect from a day to be appointed by Treasury order (F(No 3)A 2010 s 25). Sub-s (4)(*za*) as inserted to read—

"(*za*) Part A1 makes special provision as to the amount of corporation tax on which repayment interest is calculated,".

103 Rates of interest

(1) The late payment interest rate is the rate provided for in regulations made by the Treasury under this subsection.

(2) The repayment interest rate is the rate provided for in regulations made by the Treasury under this subsection.

(3) Regulations under subsection (1) or (2)—

(*a*) may make different provision for different purposes,

(*b*) may either themselves specify a rate of interest or make provision for such a rate to be determined (and to change from time to time) by reference to such rate, or the average of such rates, as may be referred to in the regulations,

(*c*) may provide for rates to be reduced below, or increased above, what they otherwise would be by specified amounts or by reference to specified formulae,

(*d*) may provide for rates arrived at by reference to averages to be rounded up or down,

(*e*) may provide for circumstances in which alteration of a rate of interest is or is not to be take place, and

(*f*) may provide that alterations of rates are to have effect for periods beginning on or after a day determined in accordance with the regulations in relation to interest running from before that day as well as from or from after that day.

Commencement—Finance Act 2009, Sections 101 to 103 (Appointed Day and Supplemental Provision) Order, SI 2010/1878 (day appointed as the day on which FA 2009 ss 101–103 come into force for the purposes of bank payroll tax (including any penalties assessed in relation to that tax) is 31 August 2010).

Finance Act 2009, Sections 101 to 103 (Income Tax Self Assessment) (Appointed Days and Transitional and Consequential Provisions) Order, SI 2011/701 (for the purposes of any self–assessment amount payable by a person to HMRC, ss 101 and 103 come into force on 31 October 2011; for the purposes of any self-assessment amount payable or repayable by HMRC to any person, ss 102 and 103 come into force on 31 October 2011).

Finance (No 3) Act 2010, Schedule 10 and the Finance Act 2009, Schedule 55 and Sections 101 to 103 (Appointed Day, etc) (Construction Industry Scheme) Order, SI 2011/2391 (the day appointed for the coming into force of ss 101–103 is 6 October 2011, but only in relation to a penalty under Sch 55 paras 7–13 (Construction Industry Scheme).

Finance Act 2009, Section 103 (Appointed Day) Order, SI 2011/2401 (the day appointed as the day on which s 103 comes into force generally is 6 October 2011).

Regulations—Taxes and Duties, etc (Interest Rate) Regulations, SI 2011/2446.

SCHEDULES

SCHEDULE 55

PENALTY FOR FAILURE TO MAKE RETURNS ETC

Section 106

Commencement—Finance Act 2009, Schedules 55 and 56 (Income Tax Self Assessment and Pension Schemes) (Appointed Days and Consequential and Savings Provisions) Order, SI 2011/702 art 2 (appointed day for the coming into force of Sch 55 is 6 April 2011 in relation to a return or other document which is required to be made or delivered to HMRC in relation to the tax year 2010–11 or any subsequent tax year and falls within item 1, 2 or 3 of the Table in para 1).

Finance (No 3) Act 2010, Schedule 10 and the Finance Act 2009, Schedule 55 and Sections 101 to 103 (Appointed Day, etc) (Construction Industry Scheme) Order, SI 2011/2391 (the day appointed for the coming into force of the following paras of Sch 55 is 6 October 2011, with effect only in relation to a return within item 6 of Sch 55 para 1(5), and for which the filing date for the purposes of Sch 55 is after 19 October 2011—

– para 1 (but only in relation to item 6 in the Table in para 1(5);
– paras 7–13; and
– 14–24, 26, and 27(1)–(4) but only as relevant to paras 7–13).

FA 2013 Sch 34 para 7(2) (Sch 55, as amended by FA 2013 Sch 34 para 7(1), is taken to have come into force for the purposes of annual tax on enveloped dwellings on 17 July 2013).

Finance Act 2009, Schedule 55 (Penalties for failure to make returns) (Appointed Days and Consequential Provision) Order, SI 2014/2395 (appoints various days for the coming into force of Sch 55 in relation to a return falling within item 4 of the Table in para 1). The effect of SI 2014/2395, along with SI 2014/2396, is to bring into force the penalties for late returns of in-year PAYE information under the real time information regime with effect from 6 October 2014 for existing large RTI employers (50 or more employees), and 6 March 2015 for remaining employers.

Finance Act 2009, Schedules 55 and 56 and Sections 101 and 102 (Stamp Duty Reserve Tax) (Appointed Days, Consequential and Transitional Provision) Order, SI 2014/3269 art 2 (the day appointed for the coming into force of Sch 55 is 1 January 2015 in relation to a charge to tax which is specified in item 11 of the Table in para 1 (SDRT)).

FA 2015 Sch 7 para 59 (Sch 55, as amended by FA 2015 Sch 7 para 59(2), is taken to have come into force for the purposes of NRCGT returns on 26 March 2015).

Cross-references—See FA 2014 ss 208–214, Sch 30 (follower notices: penalties).

SSCBA 1992 s 11A (this Schedule applies with the necessary modifications, in relation to Class 2 contributions under SSCBA 1992 s 11(2) as if those contributions were income tax chargeable under ITTOIA 2005 Pt 2 Ch 2 in respect of profits of a trade, profession or vocation which is not carried on wholly outside the United Kingdom).

Education (Postgraduate Master's Degree Loans) Regulations, SI 2016/606 reg 50 (this schedule applies to failure to disclose required information about loans for postgraduate master's degree courses which begin on or after 1 August 2016).

Penalty for failure to make returns etc'

1—(1) A penalty is payable by a person ("P") where P fails to make or deliver a return, or to deliver any other document, specified in the Table below on or before the filing date.
(2) Paragraphs 2 to 13 set out—
(*a*) the circumstances in which a penalty is payable, and
(*b*) subject to paragraphs 14 to 17, the amount of the penalty.
(3) If P's failure falls within more than one paragraph of this Schedule, P is liable to a penalty under each of those paragraphs (but this is subject to paragraph 17(3)).
(4) In this Schedule—
"filing date", in relation to a return or other document, means the date by which it is required to be made or delivered to HMRC;
"penalty date", in relation to a return or other document [falling within any of items 1 to 3 and 5 to 13 in the Table][3], means the date on which a penalty is first payable for failing to make or deliver it (that is to say, the day after the filing date).
[(4A) The Treasury may by order make such amendments to item 4 in the Table as they think fit in consequence of any amendment, revocation or re-enactment of the regulations mentioned in that item.][3]
(5) In the provisions of this Schedule which follow the Table—
(*a*) any reference to a return includes a reference to any other document specified in the Table, and

(*b*) any reference to making a return includes a reference to delivering a return or to delivering any such document.

	Tax to which return etc relates	*Return or other document*
1	Income tax or capital gains tax	(a) Return under section 8(1)(a) of TMA 1970 (b) Accounts, statement or document required under section 8(1)(b) of TMA 1970
2	Income tax or capital gains tax	(a) Return under section 8A(1)(a) of TMA 1970 (b) Accounts, statement or document required under section 8A(1)(b) of TMA 1970
[2A	Capital gains tax	NRCGT return under section 12ZB of TMA 1970][4]
3	Income tax or corporation tax	(a) Return under section 12AA(2)(a) or (3)(a) of TMA 1970 (b) Accounts, statement or document required under section 12AA(2)(b) or (3)(b) of TMA 1970
4	Income tax	[Return under any of the following provisions of the Income Tax (PAYE) Regulations 2003 (SI 2003/2682)— (a) regulation 67B (real time returns) (b) regulation 67D (exceptions to regulation 67B)][3]
[4A	Apprenticeship levy	Return under regulations under section 105 of FA 2016][6]
5	Income tax	Return under section 254 of FA 2004 (pension schemes)
6	Deductions on account of tax under Chapter 3 of Part 3 of FA 2004 (construction industry scheme)	Return under regulations under section 70 of FA 2004
7	Corporation tax	Company tax return under paragraph 3 of Schedule 18 to FA 1998
8	Inheritance tax	Account under section 216 or 217 of IHTA 1984
9	Stamp duty land tax	Land transaction return under section 76 of FA 2003 or further return under section 81 of that Act
10	Stamp duty land tax	Return under paragraph 3, 4 or 8 of Schedule 17A to FA 2003
11	Stamp duty reserve tax	Notice of charge to tax under regulations under section 98 of FA 1986
[11A	Annual tax on enveloped dwellings	Annual tax on enveloped dwellings return under section 157 of FA 2013
11B	Annual tax on enveloped dwellings	Return of adjusted chargeable amount under section 158 of FA 2013][2]
12	Petroleum revenue tax	Return under paragraph 2 of Schedule 2 to OTA 1975
13	Petroleum revenue tax	Statement under section 1(1)(a) of PRTA 1980
[20A	Excise duties	Return under regulations under section 60A of the Customs and Excise Management Act 1979][5]
[29	Machine games duty	Return under regulations under paragraph 18 of Schedule 24 to FA 2012][1]

Commencement—Finance Act 2009, Schedules 55 and 56 (Income Tax Self Assessment and Pension Schemes) (Appointed Days and Consequential and Savings Provisions) Order, SI 2011/702 art 2 (appointed day for the coming into force of Sch 55 is 6 April 2011 in relation to a return or other document which is required to be made or delivered to HMRC in relation to the tax year 2010–11 or any subsequent tax year and falls within item 1, 2 or 3 of the Table in para 1).

Finance (No 3) Act 2010, Schedule 10 and the Finance Act 2009, Schedule 55 and Sections 101 to 103 (Appointed Day, etc) (Construction Industry Scheme) Order, SI 2011/2391 (the day appointed for the coming into force of the following paras of Sch 55 is 6 October 2011, with effect only in relation to a return within item 6 of Sch 55 para 1(5), and for which the filing date for the purposes of Sch 55 is after 19 October 2011—

- para 1 (but only in relation to item 6 in the Table in para 1(5);
- paras 7–13; and
- 14–24, 26, and 27(1)–(4) but only as relevant to paras 7–13).

NIC

Finance Act 2009, Schedule 55 (Penalties for failure to make returns) (Appointed Days and Consequential Provision) Order, SI 2014/2395 provides dates for the coming into force of Sch 55 in relation to returns falling within item 4 of the table (PAYE returns), as follows—

- **11 September 2014:** powers to make regulations in relation to quanta of RTI late-filing penalties in para 6C(5), (7), (8), (9), (11) (see also SI 2014/2396).
- **6 October 2014:** provisions of Sch 55 relating to failures to make returns under the PAYE Regulations (SI 2003/2682) regs 67B and 67D where the employer is a large existing employer (an employer which as at 6 October 2014 employs at least 50 employees). Affected returns are those required to be made or delivered to HMRC on or after 6 October 2014.
- **6 March 2015:** provisions of Sch 55 relating to failures to make returns under regs 67B and 67D where the employer is a small existing employer (an employer which as at 6 October 2014 employs no more than 49 employees) or is a new employer. Affected returns are those required to be made or delivered to HMRC on or after 6 March 2015.

Cross references See FA 2016 s 91 (this para does not apply to a NRCGT return made under TMA 1970 s 12ZBA).

Modifications—FA 2009 Sch 55 has effect as if a bank payroll tax return were specified in the Table in this para (and bank payroll tax were specified in relation to it) (FA 2010 s 22, Sch 1 para 38(1)(*a*)).

Amendments—[1] Item 29 inserted by FA 2012 s 191, Sch 24 para 31 with effect in relation to the playing of machine games on or after 1 February 2013 (and Schs 55, 56, as amended by FA 2012 Sch 24 Part 1, are taken to have come into force for the purposes of machine games duty on that date).

[2] In table, entries inserted by FA 2013 s 164, Sch 34 para 7 with effect from 17 July 2013. Note that Sch 55 is taken to have come into force for the purposes of annual tax on enveloped dwellings on 17 July 2013 (FA 2013 Sch 34 para 7(2)).

[3] In sub-para (4), in definition of "penalty date" words inserted, sub-para (4A) inserted, and in Table, in item 4, words in the third column substituted, by FA 2013 s 230, Sch 50 paras 2–4, with effect for the tax year 2014–15 and subsequent tax years in relation to failures to make returns with a filing date (as defined in FA 2009 Sch 55 para 1(4)) on or after 6 April 2014.

[4] In table, entry inserted by FA 2015 s 37, Sch 7 para 59 with effect for the purposes of NRCGT returns from 26 March 2015.

[5] In Table, item 20A inserted by FA 2014 s 101, Sch 21 para 7 with effect from 1 April 2015 (by virtue of SI 2015/812 art 2).

[6] In Table, item 4A inserted by FA 2016 s 113(5), (6) with effect from 15 September 2016.

Prospective amendments—In sub-para (2), figure"13J" to be substituted for figure "13", in sub-para (4), in the definition of "filing date" at the end, words "(or, in the case of a return mentioned in item 7AA or 7AB of the Table, to the tax authorities to whom the return is required to be delivered)" to be inserted, and in the table, entries to be inserted after item 7, by F(No 3)A 2010 s 26, Sch 10 paras 1, 2 (as amended by FA 2014 s 103, Sch 22 para 21) with effect from a day to be appointed by Treasury order. Note that entries 23, 24 and 28 are amended by FA 2014 s 196, Sch 28 paras 28, 29 with effect from a date to be appointed). Entries as inserted to read as follows—

"7A	Value added tax	Return under regulations under paragraph 2 of Schedule 11 to VATA 1994
7AA	Value added tax	Relevant non-UK return (as defined in paragraph 20(3) of Schedule 3BA to VATA 1994)
7AB	Value added tax	Relevant special scheme return (as defined in paragraph 16(3) of Schedule 3B to VATA 1994)
7B	Insurance premium tax	Return under regulations under section 54 of FA 1994".

and

"14	Aggregates levy	Return under regulations under section 25 of FA 2001
15	Climate change levy	Return under regulations under paragraph 41 of Schedule 6 to FA 2000
16	Landfill tax	Return under regulations under section 49 of FA 1996
17	Air passenger duty	Return under regulations under section 38 of FA 1994
18	Alcoholic liquor duties	Return under regulations under section 13, 49, 56 or 62 of ALDA 1979
19	Tobacco products duty	Return under regulations under section 7 of TPDA 1979
20	Hydrocarbon oil duties	Return under regulations under section 21 of HODA 1979
21	Excise duties	Return under regulations under section 93 of the Customs and Excise Management Act 1979
22	Excise duties	Return under regulations under section 100G or 100H of the Customs and Excise Management Act 1979
23	General betting duty	Return under regulations under [section 166 of FA 2014]

24	Pool betting duty	Return under regulations under [section 166 of FA 2014]
25	Bingo duty	Return under regulations under paragraph 9 of Schedule 3 to BGDA 1981
26	Lottery duty	Return under regulations under section 28(2) of FA 1993
27	Gaming duty	Return under directions under paragraph 10 of Schedule 1 to FA 1997
28	Remote gaming duty	Return under regulations under [166 of FA 2014]".

In sub-para (4), in definition of "penalty date", "13A" to be substituted for "13", and in table, entry 13A to be inserted, by FA 2017 s 56, Sch 11 para 4(1)–(3) with effect from a date to be appointed. Once appointed, the charge to soft drinks industry levy will arise on chargeable events which occur on or after 6 April 2018 (FA 2017 s 31(1)). Entry 13A to read as follows—

"13A	Soft drinks industry levy	Return under regulations under section 52 of FA 2017".

Amount of penalty: occasional returns and annual returns

2 Paragraphs 3 to 6 apply in the case of a return falling within any of items [1 to 3, 5][1] and 7 to 13 in the Table.

Commencement—Finance Act 2009, Schedules 55 and 56 (Income Tax Self Assessment and Pension Schemes) (Appointed Days and Consequential and Savings Provisions) Order, SI 2011/702 art 2 (appointed day for the coming into force of Sch 55 is 6 April 2011 in relation to a return or other document which is required to be made or delivered to HMRC in relation to the tax year 2010–11 or any subsequent tax year and falls within item 1, 2 or 3 of the Table in para 1).

Modifications—FA 2009 Sch 55 has effect as if the reference in this para to a return falling within certain items in the Table included a reference to a bank payroll tax return (FA 2010 s 22, Sch 1 para 38(1)(*b*)).

Amendments—[1] Words substituted by FA 2013 s 230, Sch 50 paras 2, 5, with effect for the tax year 2014–15 and subsequent tax years in relation to failures to make returns with a filing date (as defined in FA 2009 Sch 55 para 1(4)) on or after 6 April 2014.

Prospective amendments—This para and preceding cross-head to be substituted by F(No 3)A 2010 s 26, Sch 10 paras 1, 3 with effect from a day to be appointed by Treasury order. This para as substituted to read—

"*Amount of penalty: occasional returns and returns for periods of 6 months or more*

(1) Paragraphs 3 to 6 apply in the case of—

(a) a return falling within any of items 1 to 5, 7 and 8 to 13 in the Table,

(b) a return falling within any of items 7A, 7B and 14 to 28 which relates to a period of 6 months or more, and

(c) a return falling within item 7A which relates to a transitional period for the purposes of the annual accounting scheme.

(2) In sub-paragraph (1)(*c*), a transitional period for the purposes of the annual accounting scheme is a prescribed accounting period (within the meaning of section 25(1) of VATA 1994) which—

(a) ends on the day immediately preceding the date indicated by the Commissioners for Her Majesty's Revenue and Customs in a notification of authorisation under regulation 50 of the Value Added Tax Regulations 1995 (SI 1995/2518) (admission to annual accounting scheme), or

(b) begins on the day immediately following the end of the last period of 12 months for which such an authorisation has effect.".

In sub-para (1)(*b*) (as substituted), "29" to be substituted for "28", by FA 2012 s 191, Sch 24 para 32(*a*), with effect in relation to the playing of machine games on or after 1 February 2013 (and Schs 55, 56, as amended by FA 2012 Sch 24 Part 1, are taken to have come into force for the purposes of machine games duty on that date).

3 P is liable to a penalty under this paragraph of £100.

Commencement—Finance Act 2009, Schedules 55 and 56 (Income Tax Self Assessment and Pension Schemes) (Appointed Days and Consequential and Savings Provisions) Order, SI 2011/702 art 2 (appointed day for the coming into force of Sch 55 is 6 April 2011 in relation to a return or other document which is required to be made or delivered to HMRC in relation to the tax year 2010–11 or any subsequent tax year and falls within item 1, 2 or 3 of the Table in para 1).

4— (1) P is liable to a penalty under this paragraph if (and only if)—

(*a*) P's failure continues after the end of the period of 3 months beginning with the penalty date,

(*b*) HMRC decide that such a penalty should be payable, and

(*c*) HMRC give notice to P specifying the date from which the penalty is payable.

(2) The penalty under this paragraph is £10 for each day that the failure continues during the period of 90 days beginning with the date specified in the notice given under sub-paragraph (1)(*c*).

(3) The date specified in the notice under sub-paragraph (1)(*c*)—

(*a*) may be earlier than the date on which the notice is given, but

(*b*) may not be earlier than the end of the period mentioned in sub-paragraph (1)(*a*).

NIC

Commencement—Finance Act 2009, Schedules 55 and 56 (Income Tax Self Assessment and Pension Schemes) (Appointed Days and Consequential and Savings Provisions) Order, SI 2011/702 art 2 (appointed day for the coming into force of Sch 55 is 6 April 2011 in relation to a return or other document which is required to be made or delivered to HMRC in relation to the tax year 2010–11 or any subsequent tax year and falls within item 1, 2 or 3 of the Table in para 1).

Simon's Tax Cases—*R&C Comrs v Donaldson* [2014] UKUT 536 (TCC), [2015] STC 689; *R&C Comrs v Donaldson* [2016] EWCA Civ 761, [2016] STC 2511.

5—(1) P is liable to a penalty under this paragraph if (and only if) P's failure continues after the end of the period of 6 months beginning with the penalty date.

(2) The penalty under this paragraph is the greater of—

(*a*) 5% of any liability to tax which would have been shown in the return in question, and

(*b*) £300.

Commencement—Finance Act 2009, Schedules 55 and 56 (Income Tax Self Assessment and Pension Schemes) (Appointed Days and Consequential and Savings Provisions) Order, SI 2011/702 art 2 (appointed day for the coming into force of Sch 55 is 6 April 2011 in relation to a return or other document which is required to be made or delivered to HMRC in relation to the tax year 2010–11 or any subsequent tax year and falls within item 1, 2 or 3 of the Table in para 1).

Cross references—FA 2014 s 212 (application of this paragraph in calculation of aggregate penalties for failure to take corrective action in response to a follower notice).

6—(1) P is liable to a penalty under this paragraph if (and only if) P's failure continues after the end of the period of 12 months beginning with the penalty date.

(2) Where, by failing to make the return, P [deliberately][1] withholds information which would enable or assist HMRC to assess P's liability to tax, the penalty under this paragraph is determined in accordance with sub-paragraphs (3) and (4).

(3) If the withholding of the information is deliberate and concealed, the penalty is the greater of—

(*a*) [the relevant percentage][2] of any liability to tax which would have been shown in the return in question, and

(*b*) £300.

[(3A) For the purposes of sub-paragraph (3)(*a*), the relevant percentage is—

(*a*) for the withholding of category 1 information, 100%,

(*b*) for the withholding of category 2 information, 150%, and

(*c*) for the withholding of category 3 information, 200%.][2]

(4) If the withholding of the information is deliberate but not concealed, the penalty is the greater of—

(*a*) [the relevant percentage][2] of any liability to tax which would have been shown in the return in question, and

(*b*) £300.

[(4A) For the purposes of sub-paragraph (4)(*a*), the relevant percentage is—

(*a*) for the withholding of category 1 information, 70%,

(*b*) for the withholding of category 2 information, 105%, and

(*c*) for the withholding of category 3 information, 140%.][2]

(5) In [any case not falling within sub-paragraph (2)][1], the penalty under this paragraph is the greater of—

(*a*) 5% of any liability to tax which would have been shown in the return in question, and

(*b*) £300.

[(6) Paragraph 6A explains the 3 categories of information.][2]

Commencement—Finance Act 2009, Schedules 55 and 56 (Income Tax Self Assessment and Pension Schemes) (Appointed Days and Consequential and Savings Provisions) Order, SI 2011/702 art 2 (appointed day for the coming into force of Sch 55 is 6 April 2011 in relation to a return or other document which is required to be made or delivered to HMRC in relation to the tax year 2010–11 or any subsequent tax year and falls within item 1, 2 or 3 of the Table in para 1).

Cross references—FA 2014 s 212 (application of this paragraph in calculation of aggregate penalties for failure to take corrective action in response to a follower notice).

FA 2015 Sch 21 (penalties in connection with offshore asset moves).

FA 2016 Sch 20 (penalties for enablers of offshore tax evasion or non-compliance).

FA 2016 Sch 22 (asset-based penalty for offshore inaccuracies and failures).

Amendments—[1] In sub-para (2) word inserted, and in sub-para (5) words substituted, by F(No 3)A 2010 s 26, Sch 10 paras 1, 4 with effect as follows (by virtue of SI 2011/703)—

– from 6 April 2011 in relation to a return or other document which is required to be made or delivered to HMRC in relation to the tax year 2010–11 or any subsequent tax year, and falls within item 1, 2 or 3 of the Table in Sch 55 para 1; and

– from 1 April 2011 in relation to a return under FA 2004 s 254 to be made in respect of a return period ending on or after 31 March 2011.

[2] In sub-parsa (3)(*a*), (4)(*a*), words substituted, and sub-paras (3A), (4A), (6) inserted, by FA 2010 s 35, Sch 10 paras 10, 11 with effect from 6 April 2011 in relation to a return or other document which is required to be made or delivered to HMRC in relation to the tax year 2011–12 or any subsequent tax year, and falls within item 1, 2 or 3 of the Table in FA 2009 Sch 55 para 1. Note that these changes do not have effect in relation to Sch 55 in relation to a return or other document which is required to be made or delivered to HMRC in relation to the tax year 2010–11 or any previous tax year (SI 2011/975 art 5).

Prospective amendments—Sub-paras (3A)(*za*), (4A)(*za*) to be inserted before sub-paras (3A)(*a*), (4A)(*a*), in sub-para (3A)(*a*), figure "125%" to be substituted for "100%", in sub-para (4A)(*a*), figure "87.5%" to be substituted for "70%", and in sub-para (6), figure "4" to be substituted for figure "3" by FA 2015 s 120, Sch 20 paras 14, 15 with effect from a day to be appointed. Sub-para (3A)(*za*) as inserted to read as follows—

"(za) for the withholding of category 0 information, 100%,".

Sub-para (4A)(*za*) as inserted to read as follows—

"(za) for the withholding of category 0 information, 70%,".

[6A (1) Information is category 1 information if—

(*a*) it involves a domestic matter, or

(*b*) it involves an offshore matter and—

(i) the territory in question is a category 1 territory, or

(ii) it is information which would enable or assist HMRC to assess P's liability to a tax other than income tax or capital gains tax.

(2) Information is category 2 information if—

(*a*) it involves an offshore matter [or an offshore transfer][2],

(*b*) the territory in question is a category 2 territory, and

(*c*) it is information which would enable or assist HMRC to assess P's liability to income tax[, capital gains tax or inheritance tax][2].

(3) Information is category 3 information if—

(*a*) it involves an offshore matter [or an offshore transfer][2],

(*b*) the territory in question is a category 3 territory, and

(*c*) it is information which would enable or assist HMRC to assess P's liability to income tax[, capital gains tax or inheritance tax][2].

(4) Information "involves an offshore matter" if the liability to tax which would have been shown in the return includes a liability to tax charged on or by reference to—

(*a*) income arising from a source in a territory outside the UK,

(*b*) assets situated or held in a territory outside the UK,

(*c*) activities carried on wholly or mainly in a territory outside the UK, or

(*d*) anything having effect as if it were income, assets or activities of a kind described above.

[(4A) If the liability to tax which would have been shown in the return is a liability to inheritance tax, assets are treated for the purposes of sub-paragraph (4) as situated or held in a territory outside the UK if they are so situated or held immediately after the transfer of value by reason of which inheritance tax becomes chargeable.

(4B) Information "involves an offshore transfer" if—

(*a*) it does not involve an offshore matter,

(*b*) it is information which would enable or assist HMRC to assess P's liability to income tax, capital gains tax or inheritance tax,

(*c*) by failing to make the return, P deliberately withholds the information (whether or not the withholding of the information is also concealed), and

(*d*) the applicable condition in paragraph 6AA is satisfied.][2]

(5) Information "involves a domestic matter" if [it does not involve an offshore matter or an offshore transfer][2].

(6) If the information which P withholds falls into more than one category—

(*a*) P's failure to make the return is to be treated for the purposes of this Schedule as if it were separate failures, one for each category of information according to the matters [or transfers][2] which the information involves, and

(*b*) for each separate failure, the liability to tax which would have been shown in the return in question is taken to be such share of the liability to tax which would have been shown in the return mentioned in paragraph (*a*) as is just and reasonable.

(7) For the purposes of this Schedule—

(*a*) paragraph 21A of Schedule 24 to FA 2007 (classification of territories) has effect, but

(*b*) an order under that paragraph does not apply to a failure if the filing date is before the date on which the order comes into force.

(8) . . . [2]

(9) In this paragraph [and paragraph 6AA[2]]—

"assets" has the meaning given in section 21(1) of TCGA 1992, but also includes sterling;

"UK" means the United Kingdom, including the territorial sea of the United Kingdom.][1]

Commencement—Finance Act 2009, Schedules 55 and 56 (Income Tax Self Assessment and Pension Schemes) (Appointed Days and Consequential and Savings Provisions) Order, SI 2011/702 art 2 (appointed day for the coming into force of Sch 55 is 6 April 2011 in relation to a return or other document which is required to be made or delivered to HMRC in relation to the tax year 2010–11 or any subsequent tax year and falls within item 1, 2 or 3 of the Table in para 1).

NIC

Amendments—[1] Para 6A inserted by FA 2010 s 35, Sch 10 paras 10, 12 with effect from 6 April 2011 in relation to a return or other document which is required to be made or delivered to HMRC in relation to the tax year 2011–12 or any subsequent tax year, and falls within item 1, 2 or 3 of the Table in FA 2009 Sch 55 para 1. Note that these changes do not have effect in relation to Sch 55 in relation to a return or other document which is required to be made or delivered to HMRC in relation to the tax year 2010–11 or any previous tax year (SI 2011/975 art 5).

[2] In sub-paras (2)(*a*), (3)(*a*), (6)(*a*), (9), words inserted, in sub-paras (2)(*c*). (3)(*c*), (5), words substituted, sub-paras (4A), (4B) inserted, and sub-para (8) repealed by FA 2015 s 120, Sch 20 paras 14, 16(3)–(9) with effect from 6 April 2016 (by virtue of SI 2016/456 art 5) in relation to a return or other document which—

- is required to be made or delivered to HMRC in relation to a tax year commencing on or after that date; and
- falls within item 1, 2 or 3 of the Table in FA 2009 Sch 55 para 1(5)).

Prospective amendments—Sub-paras (A1), (1) to be substituted for sub-para (1) by FA 2015 s 120, Sch 20 paras 14, 16 with effect from a day to be appointed. Sub-paragraphs (A1), (1) as substituted to read as follows—

"(A1) Information is category 0 information if—

(a) it involves a domestic matter,

(b) it involves an offshore matter or an offshore transfer, the territory in question is a category 0 territory and it is information which would enable or assist HMRC to assess P's liability to income tax, capital gains tax or inheritance tax, or

(c) it involves an offshore matter and it is information which would enable or assist HMRC to assess P's liability to a tax other than income tax, capital gains tax or inheritance tax.

(1) Information is category 1 information if—

(a) it involves an offshore matter or an offshore transfer,

(b) the territory in question is a category 1 territory, and

(c) it is information which would enable or assist HMRC to assess P's liability to income tax, capital gains tax or inheritance tax.".

[6AA (1) This paragraph makes provision in relation to offshore transfers.

(2) Where the liability to tax which would have been shown in the return is a liability to income tax, the applicable condition is satisfied if the income on or by reference to which the tax is charged, or any part of the income—

(*a*) is received in a territory outside the UK, or

(*b*) is transferred before the relevant date to a territory outside the UK.

(3) Where the liability to tax which would have been shown in the return is a liability to capital gains tax, the applicable condition is satisfied if the proceeds of the disposal on or by reference to which the tax is charged, or any part of the proceeds—

(*a*) are received in a territory outside the UK, or

(*b*) are transferred before the relevant date to a territory outside the UK.

(4) Where the liability to tax which would have been shown in the return is a liability to inheritance tax, the applicable condition is satisfied if—

(*a*) the disposition that gives rise to the transfer of value by reason of which the tax becomes chargeable involves a transfer of assets, and

(*b*) after that disposition but before the relevant date the assets, or any part of the assets, are transferred to a territory outside the UK.

(5) In the case of a transfer falling within sub-paragraph (2)(*b*), (3)(*b*) or (4)(*b*), references to the income, proceeds or assets transferred are to be read as including references to any assets derived from or representing the income, proceeds or assets.

(6) In relation to an offshore transfer, the territory in question for the purposes of paragraph 6A is the highest category of territory by virtue of which the information involves an offshore transfer.

(7) "Relevant date" means the date on which P becomes liable to a penalty under paragraph 6.][1]

Amendments—[1] Paragraphs 6AA, 6AB inserted by FA 2015 s 120, Sch 20 paras 14, 17 with effect from 6 April 2016 (by virtue of SI 2016/456 art 5) in relation to a return or other document which—

- is required to be made or delivered to HMRC in relation to a tax year commencing on or after that date; and
- falls within item 1, 2 or 3 of the Table in FA 2009 Sch 55 para 1(5)).

[6AB Regulations under paragraph 21B of Schedule 24 to FA 2007 (location of assets etc) apply for the purposes of paragraphs 6A and 6AA of this Schedule as they apply for the purposes of paragraphs 4A and 4AA of that Schedule.][1]

Amendments—[1] Paragraphs 6AA, 6AB inserted by FA 2015 s 120, Sch 20 paras 14, 17 with effect from 6 April 2016 (by virtue of SI 2016/456 art 5) in relation to a return or other document which—

- is required to be made or delivered to HMRC in relation to a tax year commencing on or after that date; and
- falls within item 1, 2 or 3 of the Table in FA 2009 Sch 55 para 1(5)).

[Amount of penalty: real time information for PAYE [and apprenticeship levy]

6B Paragraphs 6C and 6D apply in the case of a return falling within item 4 [or 4A][2] in the Table.][1]

Commencement—Finance Act 2009, Schedule 55 (Penalties for failure to make returns) (Appointed Days and Consequential Provision) Order, SI 2014/2395 provides dates for the coming into force of Sch 55 in relation to returns falling within item 4 of the table in para 1 above (PAYE returns), as follows—

– **11 September 2014:** powers to make regulations in relation to quanta of RTI late-filing penalties in para 6C(5), (7), (8), (9), (11) (see also SI 2014/2396).
– for paras 1, 6B, 6C(1)–(4), (6), (10), 6D, 16–24, 26, 27 (relating to failures to make returns under the PAYE Regulations (SI 2003/2682) regs 67B and 67D):
  (a) **6 October 2014:** where the employer is a large existing employer (an employer which as at 6 October 2014 employs at least 50 employees). Affected returns are those required to be made or delivered to HMRC on or after 6 October 2014.
  (b) **6 March 2015:** where the employer is a small existing employer (an employer which as at 6 October 2014 employs no more than 49 employees) or is a new employer. Affected returns are those required to be made or delivered to HMRC on or after 6 March 2015.

Amendments—[1] Paragraphs 6B–6D and preceding cross-head inserted by FA 2013 s 230, Sch 50 paras 2, 6 with effect for the tax year 2014–15 and subsequent tax years in relation to failures to make returns with a filing date (as defined in FA 2009 Sch 55 para 1(4)) on or after 6 April 2014.

[2] Words inserted by FA 2016 s 113(5), (7), (8) with effect from 15 September 2016 in relation to the apprenticeship levy which applies for 2017–18 and subsequent tax years.

[**6C**—(1) If P fails during a tax month to make a return on or before the filing date, P is liable to a penalty under this paragraph in respect of that month.

(2) But this is subject to sub-paragraphs (3) and (4).

(3) P is not liable to a penalty under this paragraph in respect of a tax month as a result of any failure to make a return on or before the filing date which occurs during the initial period.

(4) P is not liable to a penalty under this paragraph in respect of a tax month falling in a tax year if the month is the first tax month in that tax year during which P fails to make a return on or before the filing date (disregarding for this purpose any failure which occurs during the initial period).

(5) In sub-paragraphs (3) and (4) "the initial period" means the period which—

(*a*) begins with the day in the first tax year on which P is first required to make a return, and

(*b*) is of such duration as is specified in regulations made by the Commissioners,

and for this purpose "the first tax year" means the first tax year in which P is required to make returns.

(6) P may be liable under this paragraph to no more than one penalty in respect of each tax month.

(7) The penalty under this paragraph is to be calculated in accordance with regulations made by the Commissioners.

(8) Regulations under sub-paragraph (7) may provide for a penalty under this paragraph in respect of a tax month to be calculated by reference to either or both of the following matters—

(*a*) the number of persons employed by P, or treated as employed by P for the purposes of PAYE regulations;

(*b*) the number of previous penalties incurred by P under this paragraph in the same tax year.

(9) The Commissioners may by regulations disapply sub-paragraph (3) or (4) in such circumstances as are specified in the regulations.

(10) If P has elected under PAYE regulations to be treated as different employers in relation to different groups of employees, this paragraph applies to P as if—

(*a*) in respect of each group P were a different person, and

(*b*) each group constituted all of P's employees.

(11) Regulations made by the Commissioners under this paragraph may—

(*a*) make different provision for different cases, and

(*b*) include incidental, consequential and supplementary provision.][1]

Commencement—Finance Act 2009, Schedule 55 (Penalties for failure to make returns) (Appointed Days and Consequential Provision) Order, SI 2014/2395 provides dates for the coming into force of Sch 55 in relation to returns falling within item 4 of the table in para 1 above (PAYE returns), as follows—

– **11 September 2014:** powers to make regulations in relation to quanta of RTI late-filing penalties in para 6C(5), (7), (8), (9), (11) (see also SI 2014/2396).
– for paras 1, 6B, 6C(1)–(4), (6), (10), 6D, 16–24, 26, 27 (relating to failures to make returns under the PAYE Regulations (SI 2003/2682) regs 67B and 67D):
  (a) **6 October 2014:** where the employer is a large existing employer (an employer which as at 6 October 2014 employs at least 50 employees). Affected returns are those required to be made or delivered to HMRC on or after 6 October 2014.
  (b) **6 March 2015:** where the employer is a small existing employer (an employer which as at 6 October 2014 employs no more than 49 employees) or is a new employer. Affected returns are those required to be made or delivered to HMRC on or after 6 March 2015.

Regulations—Income Tax (Pay As You Earn) (Amendment No 3) Regulations, SI 2014/2396 (inserting regs 67I–67K into the PAYE Regulations (SI 2003/2682)).

Cross-references—See Income Tax (Pay As You Earn) Regulations, SI 2003/2682 regs 67I–67K (amount of penalties for employers who fail to file a return by the relevant filing date).

Amendments—[1] Paragraphs 6B–6D and preceding cross-head inserted by FA 2013 s 230, Sch 50 paras 2, 6 with effect for the tax year 2014–15 and subsequent tax years in relation to failures to make returns with a filing date (as defined in FA 2009 Sch 55 para 1(4)) on or after 6 April 2014.

[**6D**—(1) P may be liable to one or more penalties under this paragraph in respect of extended failures.

NIC

(2) In this paragraph an "extended failure" means a failure to make a return on or before the filing date which continues after the end of the period of 3 months beginning with the day after the filing date.

(3) P is liable to a penalty or penalties under this paragraph if (and only if)—

(*a*) HMRC decide at any time that such a penalty or penalties should be payable in accordance with sub-paragraph (4) or (6), and

(*b*) HMRC give notice to P specifying the date from which the penalty, or each penalty, is payable.

(4) HMRC may decide under sub-paragraph (3)(*a*) that a separate penalty should be payable in respect of each unpenalised extended failure in the tax year to date.

(5) In that case the amount of the penalty in respect of each failure is 5% of any liability to make payments which would have been shown in the return in question.

(6) HMRC may decide under sub-paragraph (3)(*a*) that a single penalty should be payable in respect of all the unpenalised extended failures in the tax year to date.

(7) In that case the amount of the penalty in respect of those failures is 5% of the sum of the liabilities to make payments which would have been shown in each of the returns in question.

(8) For the purposes of this paragraph, an extended failure is unpenalised if a penalty has not already been imposed in respect of it under this paragraph (whether in accordance with subparagraph (4) or (6)).

(9) The date specified in the notice under sub-paragraph (3)(*b*) in relation to a penalty—

(*a*) may be earlier than the date on which the notice is given, but

(*b*) may not be earlier than the end of the period mentioned in sub-paragraph (2) in relation to the relevant extended failure.

(10) In sub-paragraph (9)(*b*) "the relevant extended failure" means—

(*a*) the extended failure in respect of which the penalty is payable, or

(*b*) if the penalty is payable in respect of more than one extended failure (in accordance with sub-paragraph (6)), the extended failure with the latest filing date.][1]

Commencement—Finance Act 2009, Schedule 55 (Penalties for failure to make returns) (Appointed Days and Consequential Provision) Order, SI 2014/2395 provides dates for the coming into force of Sch 55 in relation to returns falling within item 4 of the table in para 1 above (PAYE returns), as follows—

– **11 September 2014:** powers to make regulations in relation to quanta of RTI late-filing penalties in para 6C(5), (7), (8), (9), (11) (see also SI 2014/2396).

– for paras 1, 6B, 6C(1)–(4), (6), (10), 6D, 16–24, 26, 27 (relating to failures to make returns under the PAYE Regulations (SI 2003/2682) regs 67B and 67D):

(a) **6 October 2014:** where the employer is a large existing employer (an employer which as at 6 October 2014 employs at least 50 employees). Affected returns are those required to be made or delivered to HMRC on or after 6 October 2014.

(b) **6 March 2015:** where the employer is a small existing employer (an employer which as at 6 October 2014 employs no more than 49 employees) or is a new employer. Affected returns are those required to be made or delivered to HMRC on or after 6 March 2015.

Amendments—[1] Paragraphs 6B–6D and preceding cross-head inserted by FA 2013 s 230, Sch 50 paras 2, 6 with effect for the tax year 2014–15 and subsequent tax years in relation to failures to make returns with a filing date (as defined in FA 2009 Sch 55 para 1(4)) on or after 6 April 2014.

Amount of penalty: CIS returns

7 Paragraphs 8 to 13 apply in the case of a return falling within item 6 in the Table.

Commencement—Finance Act 2009, Schedules 55 and 56 (Income Tax Self Assessment and Pension Schemes) (Appointed Days and Consequential and Savings Provisions) Order, SI 2011/702 art 2 (appointed day for the coming into force of Sch 55 is 6 April 2011 in relation to a return or other document which is required to be made or delivered to HMRC in relation to the tax year 2010–11 or any subsequent tax year and falls within item 1, 2 or 3 of the Table in para 1).

Finance (No 3) Act 2010, Schedule 10 and the Finance Act 2009, Schedule 55 and Sections 101 to 103 (Appointed Day, etc) (Construction Industry Scheme) Order, SI 2011/2391 (the day appointed for the coming into force of the following paras of Sch 55 is 6 October 2011, with effect only in relation to a return within item 6 of Sch 55 para 1(5), and for which the filing date for the purposes of Sch 55 is after 19 October 2011—

– para 1 (but only in relation to item 6 in the Table in para 1(5);
– paras 7–13; and
– 14–24, 26, and 27(1)–(4) but only as relevant to paras 7–13).

8 P is liable to a penalty under this paragraph of £100.

Commencement—Finance Act 2009, Schedules 55 and 56 (Income Tax Self Assessment and Pension Schemes) (Appointed Days and Consequential and Savings Provisions) Order, SI 2011/702 art 2 (appointed day for the coming into force of Sch 55 is 6 April 2011 in relation to a return or other document which is required to be made or delivered to HMRC in relation to the tax year 2010–11 or any subsequent tax year and falls within item 1, 2 or 3 of the Table in para 1).

Finance (No 3) Act 2010, Schedule 10 and the Finance Act 2009, Schedule 55 and Sections 101 to 103 (Appointed Day, etc) (Construction Industry Scheme) Order, SI 2011/2391 (the day appointed for the coming into force of the following paras of Sch 55 is 6 October 2011, with effect only in relation to a return within item 6 of Sch 55 para 1(5), and for which the filing date for the purposes of Sch 55 is after 19 October 2011—

- para 1 (but only in relation to item 6 in the Table in para 1(5);
- paras 7–13; and
- 14–24, 26, and 27(1)–(4) but only as relevant to paras 7–13).

9—(1) P is liable to a penalty under this paragraph if (and only if) P's failure continues after the end of the period of 2 months beginning with the penalty date.

(2) The penalty under this paragraph is £200.

Commencement—Finance Act 2009, Schedules 55 and 56 (Income Tax Self Assessment and Pension Schemes) (Appointed Days and Consequential and Savings Provisions) Order, SI 2011/702 art 2 (appointed day for the coming into force of Sch 55 is 6 April 2011 in relation to a return or other document which is required to be made or delivered to HMRC in relation to the tax year 2010–11 or any subsequent tax year and falls within item 1, 2 or 3 of the Table in para 1).

Finance (No 3) Act 2010, Schedule 10 and the Finance Act 2009, Schedule 55 and Sections 101 to 103 (Appointed Day, etc) (Construction Industry Scheme) Order, SI 2011/2391 (the day appointed for the coming into force of the following paras of Sch 55 is 6 October 2011, with effect only in relation to a return within item 6 of Sch 55 para 1(5), and for which the filing date for the purposes of Sch 55 is after 19 October 2011—

- para 1 (but only in relation to item 6 in the Table in para 1(5);
- paras 7–13; and
- 14–24, 26, and 27(1)–(4) but only as relevant to paras 7–13).

10—(1) P is liable to a penalty under this paragraph if (and only if) P's failure continues after the end of the period of 6 months beginning with the penalty date.

(2) The penalty under this paragraph is the greater of—

(*a*) 5% of any liability to make payments which would have been shown in the return in question, and

(*b*) £300.

Commencement—Finance Act 2009, Schedules 55 and 56 (Income Tax Self Assessment and Pension Schemes) (Appointed Days and Consequential and Savings Provisions) Order, SI 2011/702 art 2 (appointed day for the coming into force of Sch 55 is 6 April 2011 in relation to a return or other document which is required to be made or delivered to HMRC in relation to the tax year 2010–11 or any subsequent tax year and falls within item 1, 2 or 3 of the Table in para 1).

Finance (No 3) Act 2010, Schedule 10 and the Finance Act 2009, Schedule 55 and Sections 101 to 103 (Appointed Day, etc) (Construction Industry Scheme) Order, SI 2011/2391 (the day appointed for the coming into force of the following paras of Sch 55 is 6 October 2011, with effect only in relation to a return within item 6 of Sch 55 para 1(5), and for which the filing date for the purposes of Sch 55 is after 19 October 2011—

- para 1 (but only in relation to item 6 in the Table in para 1(5);
- paras 7–13; and
- 14–24, 26, and 27(1)–(4) but only as relevant to paras 7–13).

11—(1) P is liable to a penalty under this paragraph if (and only if) P's failure continues after the end of the period of 12 months beginning with the penalty date.

(2) Where, by failing to make the return, P [deliberately][1] withholds information which would enable or assist HMRC to assess the amount that P is liable to pay to HMRC in accordance with Chapter 3 of Part 3 of FA 2004, the penalty under this paragraph is determined in accordance with sub-paragraphs (3) and (4).

(3) If the withholding of the information is deliberate and concealed, the penalty is the greater of—

(*a*) 100% of any liability to make payments which would have been shown in the return in question, and

(*b*) £3,000.

(4) If the withholding of the information is deliberate but not concealed, the penalty is the greater of—

(*a*) 70% of any liability to make payments which would have been shown in the return in question, and

(*b*) £1,500.

(5) In [any case not falling within sub-paragraph (2)][1], the penalty under this paragraph is the greater of—

(*a*) 5% of any liability to make payments which would have been shown in the return in question, and

(*b*) £300.

Commencement—Finance Act 2009, Schedules 55 and 56 (Income Tax Self Assessment and Pension Schemes) (Appointed Days and Consequential and Savings Provisions) Order, SI 2011/702 art 2 (appointed day for the coming into force of Sch 55 is 6 April 2011 in relation to a return or other document which is required to be made or delivered to HMRC in relation to the tax year 2010–11 or any subsequent tax year and falls within item 1, 2 or 3 of the Table in para 1).

Finance (No 3) Act 2010, Schedule 10 and the Finance Act 2009, Schedule 55 and Sections 101 to 103 (Appointed Day, etc) (Construction Industry Scheme) Order, SI 2011/2391 (the day appointed for the coming into force of the following paras of Sch 55 is 6 October 2011, with effect only in relation to a return within item 6 of Sch 55 para 1(5), and for which the filing date for the purposes of Sch 55 is after 19 October 2011—

- para 1 (but only in relation to item 6 in the Table in para 1(5);
- paras 7–13; and
- 14–24, 26, and 27(1)–(4) but only as relevant to paras 7–13).

Amendments—[1] In sub-para (2) word inserted, and in sub-para (5) words substituted for words "any other case", by F(No 3)A 2010 s 26, Sch 10 paras 1, 5 with effect from 6 October 2011 (by virtue of SI 2011/2391). These amendments have effect in relation to a return within item 6 of Sch 55 para 1(5), and for which the filing date for the purposes of Sch 55 is after 19 October 2011 (SI 2011/2391 art 3(1)).

12—(1) P is liable to a penalty under this paragraph if (and only if)—

(*a*) P's failure continues after the end of the period of 12 months beginning with the penalty date, and

(*b*) the information required in the return relates only to persons registered for gross payment (within the meaning of Chapter 3 of Part 3 of FA 2004).

(2) Where, by failing to make the return, P [deliberately][1] withholds information which relates to such persons, the penalty under this paragraph is—

(*a*) if the withholding of the information is deliberate and concealed, £3,000, and

(*b*) if the withholding of the information is deliberate but not concealed, £1,500.

Commencement—Finance Act 2009, Schedules 55 and 56 (Income Tax Self Assessment and Pension Schemes) (Appointed Days and Consequential and Savings Provisions) Order, SI 2011/702 art 2 (appointed day for the coming into force of Sch 55 is 6 April 2011 in relation to a return or other document which is required to be made or delivered to HMRC in relation to the tax year 2010–11 or any subsequent tax year and falls within item 1, 2 or 3 of the Table in para 1).

Finance (No 3) Act 2010, Schedule 10 and the Finance Act 2009, Schedule 55 and Sections 101 to 103 (Appointed Day, etc) (Construction Industry Scheme) Order, SI 2011/2391 (the day appointed for the coming into force of the following paras of Sch 55 is 6 October 2011, with effect only in relation to a return within item 6 of Sch 55 para 1(5), and for which the filing date for the purposes of Sch 55 is after 19 October 2011—

– para 1 (but only in relation to item 6 in the Table in para 1(5);
– paras 7–13; and
– 14–24, 26, and 27(1)–(4) but only as relevant to paras 7–13).

Amendments—[1] In sub-para (2) word inserted by F(No 3)A 2010 s 26, Sch 10 paras 1, 6 with effect from 6 October 2011 (by virtue of SI 2011/2391). This amendment has effect in relation to a return within item 6 of Sch 55 para 1(5), and for which the filing date for the purposes of Sch 55 is after 19 October 2011 (SI 2011/2391 art 3(1)).

13—(1) This paragraph applies—

(*a*) at any time before P first makes a return falling within item 6 in the Table, to any return falling within that item, and

(*b*) at any time after P first makes a return falling within that item, to that return and any earlier return.

(2) In respect of any return or returns to which this paragraph applies—

(*a*) paragraphs 10(2)(*b*) and 11(5)(*b*) do not apply, and

(*b*) P is not liable to penalties under paragraphs 8 and 9 which exceed, in total, £3,000.

(3) In sub-paragraph (1)(*b*) "earlier return" means any return falling within item 6 which has a filing date earlier than the date on which P first made a return.

Commencement—Finance Act 2009, Schedules 55 and 56 (Income Tax Self Assessment and Pension Schemes) (Appointed Days and Consequential and Savings Provisions) Order, SI 2011/702 art 2 (appointed day for the coming into force of Sch 55 is 6 April 2011 in relation to a return or other document which is required to be made or delivered to HMRC in relation to the tax year 2010–11 or any subsequent tax year and falls within item 1, 2 or 3 of the Table in para 1).

Finance (No 3) Act 2010, Schedule 10 and the Finance Act 2009, Schedule 55 and Sections 101 to 103 (Appointed Day, etc) (Construction Industry Scheme) Order, SI 2011/2391 (the day appointed for the coming into force of the following paras of Sch 55 is 6 October 2011, with effect only in relation to a return within item 6 of Sch 55 para 1(5), and for which the filing date for the purposes of Sch 55 is after 19 October 2011—

– para 1 (but only in relation to item 6 in the Table in para 1(5);
– paras 7–13; and
– 14–24, 26, and 27(1)-(4) but only as relevant to paras 7–13).

[Amount of penalty: returns for periods of between 2 and 6 months

13A—*(1) Paragraphs 13B to 13E apply in the case of a return falling within any of items 7A to 7B and 14 to [29]*[1] *in the Table which relates to a period of less than 6 months but more than 2 months.*

(2) But those paragraphs do not apply in the case of a return mentioned in paragraph 2(1)(c).]

Commencement—Finance Act 2009, Schedules 55 and 56 (Income Tax Self Assessment and Pension Schemes) (Appointed Days and Consequential and Savings Provisions) Order, SI 2011/702 art 2 (appointed day for the coming into force of Sch 55 is 6 April 2011 in relation to a return or other document which is required to be made or delivered to HMRC in relation to the tax year 2010–11 or any subsequent tax year and falls within item 1, 2 or 3 of the Table in para 1).

Amendments—[1] In sub-para (1) figure substituted by FA 2012 s 191, Sch 24 para 32(*b*), with effect in relation to the playing of machine games on or after 1 February 2013 (and Schs 55, 56, as amended by FA 2012 Sch 24 Part 1, are taken to have come into force for the purposes of machine games duty on that date).

Prospective amendments—Paras 13A–13J and preceding cross-heads to be inserted by F(No 3)A 2010 s 26, Sch 10 paras 1, 7 (as amended by FA 2014 s 103, Sch 22 para 21) with effect from a day to be appointed by Treasury order.

[13B—*(1) P is liable to a penalty under this paragraph of £100.*

(2) In addition, a penalty period begins to run on the penalty date for the return.

(3) The penalty period ends with the day 12 months after the filing date for the return, unless it is extended under paragraph 13C(2)(c) or 13H(2)(*c*).]

Commencement—Finance Act 2009, Schedules 55 and 56 (Income Tax Self Assessment and Pension Schemes) (Appointed Days and Consequential and Savings Provisions) Order, SI 2011/702 art 2 (appointed day for the coming into force of Sch 55 is 6 April 2011 in relation to a return or other document which is required to be made or delivered to HMRC in relation to the tax year 2010–11 or any subsequent tax year and falls within item 1, 2 or 3 of the Table in para 1).

Prospective amendment—Paras 13A–13J and preceding cross-heads to be inserted by F(No 3)A 2010 s 26, Sch 10 paras 1, 7 with effect from a day to be appointed by Treasury order.

[**13C**—(1) This paragraph applies if—

(*a*) a penalty period has begun under paragraph 13B or 13G because P has failed to make a return ("return A"), and

(*b*) before the end of the period, P fails to make another return ("return B") falling within the same item in the Table as return A.

(2) In such a case—

(*a*) paragraph 13B(1) and (2) do not apply to the failure to make return B, but

(*b*) P is liable to a penalty under this paragraph for that failure, and

(*c*) the penalty period that has begun is extended so that it ends with the day 12 months after the filing date for return B.

(3) The amount of the penalty under this paragraph is determined by reference to the number of returns that P has failed to make during the penalty period.

(4) If the failure to make return B is P's first failure to make a return during the penalty period, P is liable, at the time of the failure, to a penalty of £200.

(5) If the failure to make return B is P's second failure to make a return during the penalty period, P is liable, at the time of the failure, to a penalty of £300.

(6) If the failure to make return B is P's third or a subsequent failure to make a return during the penalty period, P is liable, at the time of the failure, to a penalty of £400.

(7) For the purposes of this paragraph—

(*a*) in accordance with sub-paragraph (1)(*b*), the references in sub-paragraphs (3) to (6) to a return are references to a return falling within the same item in the Table as returns A and B, and

(*b*) a failure to make a return counts for the purposes of those sub-paragraphs if (but only if) the return relates to a period of less than 6 months.

(8) A penalty period may be extended more than once under sub-paragraph (2)(*c*).

Commencement—Finance Act 2009, Schedules 55 and 56 (Income Tax Self Assessment and Pension Schemes) (Appointed Days and Consequential and Savings Provisions) Order, SI 2011/702 art 2 (appointed day for the coming into force of Sch 55 is 6 April 2011 in relation to a return or other document which is required to be made or delivered to HMRC in relation to the tax year 2010–11 or any subsequent tax year and falls within item 1, 2 or 3 of the Table in para 1).

Prospective amendment—Paras 13A–13J and preceding cross-heads to be inserted by F(No 3)A 2010 s 26, Sch 10 paras 1, 7 with effect from a day to be appointed by Treasury order.

[**13D**—(1) P is liable to a penalty under this paragraph if (and only if) P's failure continues after the end of the period of 6 months beginning with the penalty date.

(2) The penalty under this paragraph is the greater of—

(*a*) 5% of any liability to tax which would have been shown in the return in question, and

(*b*) £300.]

Commencement—Finance Act 2009, Schedules 55 and 56 (Income Tax Self Assessment and Pension Schemes) (Appointed Days and Consequential and Savings Provisions) Order, SI 2011/702 art 2 (appointed day for the coming into force of Sch 55 is 6 April 2011 in relation to a return or other document which is required to be made or delivered to HMRC in relation to the tax year 2010–11 or any subsequent tax year and falls within item 1, 2 or 3 of the Table in para 1).

Prospective amendment—Paras 13A–13J and preceding cross-heads to be inserted by F(No 3)A 2010 s 26, Sch 10 paras 1, 7 with effect from a day to be appointed by Treasury order.

[**13E**—(1) P is liable to a penalty under this paragraph if (and only if) P's failure continues after the end of the period of 12 months beginning with the penalty date.

(2) Where, by failing to make the return, P deliberately withholds information which would enable or assist HMRC to assess P's liability to tax, the penalty under this paragraph is determined in accordance with sub-paragraphs (3) and (4).

(3) If the withholding of the information is deliberate and concealed, the penalty is the greater of—

(*a*) 100% of any liability to tax which would have been shown in the return in question, and

(*b*) £300.

(4) If the withholding of the information is deliberate but not concealed, the penalty is the greater of—

(*a*) 70% of any liability to tax which would have been shown in the return in question, and

(*b*) £300.

(5) In any case not falling within sub-paragraph (2), the penalty under this paragraph is the greater of—

(*a*) 5% of any liability to tax which would have been shown in the return in question, and

(*b*) £300.]

Commencement—Finance Act 2009, Schedules 55 and 56 (Income Tax Self Assessment and Pension Schemes) (Appointed Days and Consequential and Savings Provisions) Order, SI 2011/702 art 2 (appointed day for the coming into force of Sch 55 is 6 April 2011 in relation to a return or other document which is required to be made or delivered to HMRC in relation to the tax year 2010–11 or any subsequent tax year and falls within item 1, 2 or 3 of the Table in para 1).

Prospective amendment—Paras 13A–13J and preceding cross-heads to be inserted by F(No 3)A 2010 s 26, Sch 10 paras 1, 7 with effect from a day to be appointed by Treasury order.

[Amount of penalty: returns for periods of 2 months or less

13F (1) Paragraphs 13G to 13J apply in the case of a return falling within any of items 7A, 7B and 14 to [29][1] in the Table which relates to a period of 2 months or less.

(2) But those paragraphs do not apply in the case of a return mentioned in paragraph 2(1)(*c*).]

Commencement—Finance Act 2009, Schedules 55 and 56 (Income Tax Self Assessment and Pension Schemes) (Appointed Days and Consequential and Savings Provisions) Order, SI 2011/702 art 2 (appointed day for the coming into force of Sch 55 is 6 April 2011 in relation to a return or other document which is required to be made or delivered to HMRC in relation to the tax year 2010–11 or any subsequent tax year and falls within item 1, 2 or 3 of the Table in para 1).

Amendments—[1] In sub-para (1), "29" substituted for "28", by FA 2012 s 191, Sch 24 para 32(*a*), with effect in relation to the playing of machine games on or after 1 February 2013 (and Schs 55, 56, as amended by FA 2012 Sch 24 Part 1, are taken to have come into force for the purposes of machine games duty on that date).

Prospective amendments—Paras 13A–13J and preceding cross-heads to be inserted by F(No 3)A 2010 s 26, Sch 10 paras 1, 7 with effect from a day to be appointed by Treasury order.

[13G—(1) P is liable to a penalty under this paragraph of £100.

(2) In addition, a penalty period begins to run on the penalty date for the return.

(3) The penalty period ends with the day 12 months after the filing date for the return, unless it is extended under paragraph 13C(2)(*c*) or 13H(2)(*c*).]

Commencement—Finance Act 2009, Schedules 55 and 56 (Income Tax Self Assessment and Pension Schemes) (Appointed Days and Consequential and Savings Provisions) Order, SI 2011/702 art 2 (appointed day for the coming into force of Sch 55 is 6 April 2011 in relation to a return or other document which is required to be made or delivered to HMRC in relation to the tax year 2010–11 or any subsequent tax year and falls within item 1, 2 or 3 of the Table in para 1).

Prospective amendment—Paras 13A–13J and preceding cross-heads to be inserted by F(No 3)A 2010 s 26, Sch 10 paras 1, 7 with effect from a day to be appointed by Treasury order.

[13H—(1) This paragraph applies if—

(*a*) a penalty period has begun under paragraph 13B or 13G because P has failed to make a return ("return A"), and

(*b*) before the end of the period, P fails to make another return ("return B") falling within the same item in the Table as return A.

(2) In such a case—

(*a*) paragraph 13G(1) and (2) do not apply to the failure to make return B, but

(*b*) P is liable to a penalty under this paragraph for that failure, and

(*c*) the penalty period that has begun is extended so that it ends with the day 12 months after the filing date for return B.

(3) The amount of the penalty under this paragraph is determined by reference to the number of returns that P has failed to make during the penalty period.

(4) If the failure to make return B is P's first, second, third, fourth or fifth failure to make a return during the penalty period, P is liable, at the time of the failure, to a penalty of £100.

(5) If the failure to make return B is P's sixth or a subsequent failure to make a return during the penalty period, P is liable, at the time of the failure, to a penalty of £200.

(6) For the purposes of this paragraph—

(*a*) in accordance with sub-paragraph (1)(*b*), the references in sub-paragraphs (3) to (5) to a return are references to a return falling within the same item in the Table as returns A and B, and

(*b*) a failure to make a return counts for the purposes of those sub-paragraphs if (but only if) the return relates to a period of less than 6 months.

(7) A penalty period may be extended more than once under sub-paragraph (2)(*c*).]

Commencement—Finance Act 2009, Schedules 55 and 56 (Income Tax Self Assessment and Pension Schemes) (Appointed Days and Consequential and Savings Provisions) Order, SI 2011/702 art 2 (appointed day for the coming into force of Sch 55 is 6 April 2011 in relation to a return or other document which is required to be made or delivered to HMRC in relation to the tax year 2010–11 or any subsequent tax year and falls within item 1, 2 or 3 of the Table in para 1).

Prospective amendment—Paras 13A–13J and preceding cross-heads to be inserted by F(No 3)A 2010 s 26, Sch 10 paras 1, 7 with effect from a day to be appointed by Treasury order.

[13I—(1) P is liable to a penalty under this paragraph if (and only if) P's failure continues after the end of the period of 6 months beginning with the penalty date.

(2) The penalty under this paragraph is the greater of—

(*a*) 5% of any liability to tax which would have been shown in the return in question, and

(*b*) £300.]

Commencement—Finance Act 2009, Schedules 55 and 56 (Income Tax Self Assessment and Pension Schemes) (Appointed Days and Consequential and Savings Provisions) Order, SI 2011/702 art 2 (appointed day for the coming into force of Sch 55 is 6 April 2011 in relation to a return or other document which is required to be made or delivered to HMRC in relation to the tax year 2010–11 or any subsequent tax year and falls within item 1, 2 or 3 of the Table in para 1).

Prospective amendment—Paras 13A–13J and preceding cross-heads to be inserted by F(No 3)A 2010 s 26, Sch 10 paras 1, 7 with effect from a day to be appointed by Treasury order.

[13J—(1) P is liable to a penalty under this paragraph if (and only if) P's failure continues after the end of the period of 12 months beginning with the penalty date.

(2) Where, by failing to make the return, P deliberately withholds information which would enable or assist HMRC to assess P's liability to tax, the penalty under this paragraph is determined in accordance with sub-paragraphs (3) and (4).

(3) If the withholding of the information is deliberate and concealed, the penalty is the greater of—

(*a*) 100% of any liability to tax which would have been shown in the return in question, and

(*b*) £300.

(4) If the withholding of the information is deliberate but not concealed, the penalty is the greater of—

(*a*) 70% of any liability to tax which would have been shown in the return in question, and

(*b*) £300.

(5) In any case not falling within sub-paragraph (2), the penalty under this paragraph is the greater of—

(*a*) 5% of any liability to tax which would have been shown in the return in question, and

(*b*) £300.]

Commencement—Finance Act 2009, Schedules 55 and 56 (Income Tax Self Assessment and Pension Schemes) (Appointed Days and Consequential and Savings Provisions) Order, SI 2011/702 art 2 (appointed day for the coming into force of Sch 55 is 6 April 2011 in relation to a return or other document which is required to be made or delivered to HMRC in relation to the tax year 2010–11 or any subsequent tax year and falls within item 1, 2 or 3 of the Table in para 1).

Prospective amendment—Paras 13A–13J and preceding cross-heads to be inserted by F(No 3)A 2010 s 26, Sch 10 paras 1, 7 with effect from a day to be appointed by Treasury order.

Reductions for disclosure

14—[(A1) In this paragraph, "relevant information" means information which has been withheld by a failure to make a return.][1]

(1) Paragraph 15 provides for reductions in the penalty under paragraph 6(3) or (4) [where P discloses relevant information that involves a domestic matter][1] or 11(3) or (4) where P discloses [relevant information][1].

[(1A) Paragraph 15A provides for reductions in the penalty under paragraph 6(3) or (4) where P discloses relevant information that involves an offshore matter or an offshore transfer.

(1B) Sub-paragraph (2) applies where—

(*a*) P is liable to a penalty under paragraph 6(3) or (4) and P discloses relevant information that involves a domestic matter, or

(*b*) P is liable to a penalty under any of the other provisions mentioned in sub-paragraph (1) and P discloses relevant information.][1]

(2) P discloses relevant information by—

(*a*) telling HMRC about it,

(*b*) giving HMRC reasonable help in quantifying any tax unpaid by reason of its having been withheld, and

(*c*) allowing HMRC access to records for the purpose of checking how much tax is so unpaid.

[(2A) Sub-paragraph (2B) applies where P is liable to a penalty under paragraph 6(3) or (4) and P discloses relevant information that involves an offshore matter or an offshore transfer.

(2B) P discloses relevant information by—

(*a*) telling HMRC about it,

(*b*) giving HMRC reasonable help in quantifying any tax unpaid by reason of its having been withheld,

(*c*) allowing HMRC access to records for the purpose of checking how much tax is so unpaid, and

(*d*) providing HMRC with additional information.][1]

(2C) The Treasury must make regulations setting out what is meant by "additional information" for the purposes of sub-paragraph (2B)(*d*).

(2D) Regulations under sub-paragraph (2C) are to be made by statutory instrument.

(2E) An instrument containing regulations under sub-paragraph (2C) is subject to annulment in pursuance of a resolution of the House of Commons.][1]

(3) Disclosure of relevant information—

(*a*) is "unprompted" if made at a time when P has no reason to believe that HMRC have discovered or are about to discover the relevant information, and (*b*) otherwise, is "prompted".

(4) In relation to disclosure "quality" includes timing, nature and extent.

[(5) Paragraph 6A(4) to (5) applies to determine whether relevant information involves an offshore matter, an offshore transfer or a domestic matter for the purposes of this paragraph.][1]

Commencement—Finance Act 2009, Schedules 55 and 56 (Income Tax Self Assessment and Pension Schemes) (Appointed Days and Consequential and Savings Provisions) Order, SI 2011/702 art 2 (appointed day for the coming into force of Sch 55 is 6 April 2011 in relation to a return or other document which is required to be made or delivered to HMRC in relation to the tax year 2010–11 or any subsequent tax year and falls within item 1, 2 or 3 of the Table in para 1).

Finance (No 3) Act 2010, Schedule 10 and the Finance Act 2009, Schedule 55 and Sections 101 to 103 (Appointed Day, etc) (Construction Industry Scheme) Order, SI 2011/2391 (the day appointed for the coming into force of the following paras of Sch 55 is 6 October 2011, with effect only in relation to a return within item 6 of Sch 55 para 1(5), and for which the filing date for the purposes of Sch 55 is after 19 October 2011—

- para 1 (but only in relation to item 6 in the Table in para 1(5);
- paras 7–13; and
- 14–24, 26, and 27(1)-(4) but only as relevant to paras 7–13).

Regulations—

Penalties Relating to Offshore Matters and Offshore Transfers (Additional Information) Regulations, SI 2017/345.

Amendments—[1] Sub-paras (A1), (1A), (1B) (2A)–(2E), (5) inserted, and in sub-para (1), words inserted and words substituted, by FA 2016 s 163, Sch 21 paras 9, 10 with effect, by virtue of SI 2017/259 regs 2, 3—

- for inheritance tax purposes, in relation to transfers of value made on or after 1 April 2017;
- for income tax and capital gains tax purposes, in relation to any tax year commencing on or after 6 April 2016; and
- for the purpose of making regulations, from 8 March 2017.

Prospective amendments—In sub-para (1), words ", 11(3) or (4), 13E(3) or (4) or 13J(3) or (4)" to be substituted for words "or 11(3) or (4)" by F(No 3)A 2010 s 26, Sch 10 paras 1, 8 with effect from a day to be appointed by Treasury order.

15—[(1) If a person who would otherwise be liable to a penalty of a percentage shown in column 1 of the Table (a "standard percentage") has made a disclosure, HMRC must reduce the standard percentage to one that reflects the quality of the disclosure.

(2) But the standard percentage may not be reduced to a percentage that is below the minimum shown for it—

(*a*) in the case of a prompted disclosure, in column 2 of the Table, and

(*b*) in the case of an unprompted disclosure, in column 3 of the Table.

[Standard %	*Minimum % for prompted disclosure*	*Minimum % for unprompted disclosure*
70%	35%	20%
100%	50%	30%][2]

(3) . . . [1]

(4) . . . [1]

(5) But HMRC must not under this paragraph—

(*a*) reduce a penalty under paragraph 6(3) or (4) below £300, or

(*b*) reduce a penalty under paragraph 11(3) or (4) below the amount set by paragraph 11(3)(*b*) or (4)(*b*) (as the case may be).

Commencement—Finance Act 2009, Schedules 55 and 56 (Income Tax Self Assessment and Pension Schemes) (Appointed Days and Consequential and Savings Provisions) Order, SI 2011/702 art 2 (appointed day for the coming into force of Sch 55 is 6 April 2011 in relation to a return or other document which is required to be made or delivered to HMRC in relation to the tax year 2010–11 or any subsequent tax year and falls within item 1, 2 or 3 of the Table in para 1).

Finance (No 3) Act 2010, Schedule 10 and the Finance Act 2009, Schedule 55 and Sections 101 to 103 (Appointed Day, etc) (Construction Industry Scheme) Order, SI 2011/2391 (the day appointed for the coming into force of the following paras of Sch 55 is 6 October 2011, with effect only in relation to a return within item 6 of Sch 55 para 1(5), and for which the filing date for the purposes of Sch 55 is after 19 October 2011—

- para 1 (but only in relation to item 6 in the Table in para 1(5);
- paras 7–13; and
- 14–24, 26, and 27(1)-(4) but only as relevant to paras 7–13).

Amendments—[1] Sub-paras (1), (2) substituted, and sub-paras (3), (4) repealed, by FA 2010 s 35, Sch 10 paras 10, 13 with effect from 6 April 2011 in relation to a return or other document which is required to be made or delivered to HMRC in relation to the tax year 2011–12 or any subsequent tax year, and falls within item 1, 2 or 3 of the Table in FA 2009 Sch 55 para 1. Note that these changes do not have effect in relation to Sch 55 in relation to a return or other document which is required to be made or delivered to HMRC in relation to the tax year 2010–11 or any previous tax year (SI 2011/975 art 5).

[2] In sub-para (2), Table substituted by FA 2016 s 163, Sch 21 paras 9, 11 with effect, by virtue of SI 2017/259 regs 2, 3—

- for inheritance tax purposes, in relation to transfers of value made on or after 1 April 2017; and
- for income tax and capital gains tax purposes, in relation to any tax year commencing on or after 6 April 2016.

Prospective amendments—In sub-para (5), words "sub-paragraph (3) or (4) of any of paragraphs 11, 13E and 13J" to be substituted for words "paragraph 11(3) or (4)", and words "paragraph (*b*) of that sub-paragraph" to be substituted for words "paragraph 11(3)(*b*) or (4)(*b*) (as the case may be)", by F(No 3)A 2010 s 26, Sch 10 paras 1, 9 with effect from a day to be appointed by Treasury order.

In sub-para (2), the following Table entries to be inserted at the appropriate places by FA 2015 s 120, Sch 20 paras 14, 18 with effect from a day to be appointed—

"87.5%	43.75%	25%"
"125%	62.5%	40%".

[15A—(1) If a person who would otherwise be liable to a penalty of a percentage shown in column 1 of the Table (a "standard percentage") has made a disclosure, HMRC must reduce the standard percentage to one that reflects the quality of the disclosure.

(2) But the standard percentage may not be reduced to a percentage that is below the minimum shown for it—

(*a*) in the case of a prompted disclosure, in column 2 of the Table, and

(*b*) in the case of an unprompted disclosure, in column 3 of the Table.

Standard %	*Minimum % for prompted disclosure*	*Minimum % for unprompted disclosure*
70%	45%	30%
87.5%	53.75%	35%
100%	60%	40%
105%	62.5%	40%
125%	72.5%	50%
140%	80%	50%
150%	85%	55%
200%	110%	70%

(3) But HMRC must not under this paragraph reduce a penalty below £300.][1]

Amendments—[1] Paragraph 15A inserted by FA 2016 s 163, Sch 21 paras 9, 12 with effect, by virtue of SI 2017/259 regs 2, 3—

- for inheritance tax purposes, in relation to transfers of value made on or after 1 April 2017; and
- for income tax and capital gains tax purposes, in relation to any tax year commencing on or after 6 April 2016.

Special reduction

16—(1) If HMRC think it right because of special circumstances, they may reduce a penalty under any paragraph of this Schedule.

(2) In sub-paragraph (1) "special circumstances" does not include—

(*a*) ability to pay, or

(*b*) the fact that a potential loss of revenue from one taxpayer is balanced by a potential overpayment by another.

(3) In sub-paragraph (1) the reference to reducing a penalty includes a reference to—

(*a*) staying a penalty, and

(*b*) agreeing a compromise in relation to proceedings for a penalty.

Commencement—Finance Act 2009, Schedules 55 and 56 (Income Tax Self Assessment and Pension Schemes) (Appointed Days and Consequential and Savings Provisions) Order, SI 2011/702 art 2 (appointed day for the coming into force of Sch 55 is 6 April 2011 in relation to a return or other document which is required to be made or delivered to HMRC in relation to the tax year 2010–11 or any subsequent tax year and falls within item 1, 2 or 3 of the Table in para 1).

Finance (No 3) Act 2010, Schedule 10 and the Finance Act 2009, Schedule 55 and Sections 101 to 103 (Appointed Day, etc) (Construction Industry Scheme) Order, SI 2011/2391 (the day appointed for the coming into force of the following paras of Sch 55 is 6 October 2011, with effect only in relation to a return within item 6 of Sch 55 para 1(5), and for which the filing date for the purposes of Sch 55 is after 19 October 2011—

- para 1 (but only in relation to item 6 in the Table in para 1(5);
- paras 7–13; and
- 14–24, 26, and 27(1)–(4) but only as relevant to paras 7–13).

Finance Act 2009, Schedule 55 (Penalties for failure to make returns) (Appointed Days and Consequential Provision) Order, SI 2014/2395 provides dates for the coming into force of Sch 55 in relation to returns falling within item 4 of the table in para 1 above (PAYE returns), as follows—

- **11 September 2014:** powers to make regulations in relation to quanta of RTI late-filing penalties in para 6C(5), (7), (8), (9), (11) (see also SI 2014/2396).
- for paras 1, 6B, 6C(1)–(4), (6), (10), 6D, 16–24, 26, 27 (relating to failures to make returns under the PAYE Regulations (SI 2003/2682) regs 67B and 67D):

NIC

(a) **6 October 2014:** where the employer is a large existing employer (an employer which as at 6 October 2014 employs at least 50 employees). Affected returns are those required to be made or delivered to HMRC on or after 6 October 2014.

(b) **6 March 2015:** where the employer is a small existing employer (an employer which as at 6 October 2014 employs no more than 49 employees) or is a new employer. Affected returns are those required to be made or delivered to HMRC on or after 6 March 2015.

Interaction with other penalties and late payment surcharges

17—(1) Where P is liable for a penalty under any paragraph of this Schedule which is determined by reference to a liability to tax, the amount of that penalty is to be reduced by the amount of any other penalty incurred by P, if the amount of the penalty is determined by reference to the same liability to tax.

(2) In sub-paragraph (1) the reference to "any other penalty" does not include—

(*a*) a penalty under any other paragraph of this Schedule, or

(*b*) a penalty under Schedule 56 (penalty for late payment of tax)[, or

(*c*) a penalty under Part 4 of FA 2014 (penalty where corrective action not taken after follower notice etc)[, or][2]

(*d*) a penalty under Schedule 22 to FA 2016 (asset-based penalty).][3]

(3) Where P is liable for a penalty under more than one paragraph of this Schedule which is determined by reference to a liability to tax, the aggregate of the amounts of those penalties must not exceed [the relevant percentage][1] of the liability to tax.

[(4) The relevant percentage is—

(*a*) if one of the penalties is a penalty under paragraph 6(3) or (4) and the information withheld is category 3 information, 200%,

(*b*) if one of the penalties is a penalty under paragraph 6(3) or (4) and the information withheld is category 2 information, 150%, and

(*c*) in all other cases, 100%.][1]

Commencement—Finance Act 2009, Schedules 55 and 56 (Income Tax Self Assessment and Pension Schemes) (Appointed Days and Consequential and Savings Provisions) Order, SI 2011/702 art 2 (appointed day for the coming into force of Sch 55 is 6 April 2011 in relation to a return or other document which is required to be made or delivered to HMRC in relation to the tax year 2010–11 or any subsequent tax year and falls within item 1, 2 or 3 of the Table in para 1).

Finance (No 3) Act 2010, Schedule 10 and the Finance Act 2009, Schedule 55 and Sections 101 to 103 (Appointed Day, etc) (Construction Industry Scheme) Order, SI 2011/2391 (the day appointed for the coming into force of the following paras of Sch 55 is 6 October 2011, with effect only in relation to a return within item 6 of Sch 55 para 1(5), and for which the filing date for the purposes of Sch 55 is after 19 October 2011—

– para 1 (but only in relation to item 6 in the Table in para 1(5);
– paras 7–13; and
– 14–24, 26, and 27(1)–(4) but only as relevant to paras 7–13).

Finance Act 2009, Schedule 55 (Penalties for failure to make returns) (Appointed Days and Consequential Provision) Order, SI 2014/2395 provides dates for the coming into force of Sch 55 in relation to returns falling within item 4 of the table in para 1 above (PAYE returns), as follows—

– **11 September 2014:** powers to make regulations in relation to quanta of RTI late-filing penalties in para 6C(5), (7), (8), (9), (11) (see also SI 2014/2396).
– for paras 1, 6B, 6C(1)–(4), (6), (10), 6D, 16–24, 26, 27 (relating to failures to make returns under the PAYE Regulations (SI 2003/2682) regs 67B and 67D):

(a) **6 October 2014:** where the employer is a large existing employer (an employer which as at 6 October 2014 employs at least 50 employees). Affected returns are those required to be made or delivered to HMRC on or after 6 October 2014.

(b) **6 March 2015:** where the employer is a small existing employer (an employer which as at 6 October 2014 employs no more than 49 employees) or is a new employer. Affected returns are those required to be made or delivered to HMRC on or after 6 March 2015.

Amendments—[1] In sub-para (3) words substituted for figure "100%", and sub-s (4) inserted, by FA 2010 s 35, Sch 10 paras 10, 14 with effect from 6 April 2011 in relation to a return or other document which is required to be made or delivered to HMRC in relation to the tax year 2011–12 or any subsequent tax year, and falls within item 1, 2 or 3 of the Table in FA 2009 Sch 55 para 1. Note that these changes do not have effect in relation to Sch 55 in relation to a return or other document which is required to be made or delivered to HMRC in relation to the tax year 2010–11 or any previous tax year (SI 2011/975 art 5).

[2] Sub-para (2)(*c*) and preceding word "or" inserted by FA 2014 s 233, Sch 33 para 5 with effect from 17 July 2014.

[3] Sub-para (2)(*d*) and preceding word "or" inserted by FA 2016 Sch 22 para 20(5) with effect—

– for inheritance tax purposes, in relation to transfers of value (within the meaning of IHTA 1984 s 3) made on or after that day; and
– for income tax and capital gains tax purposes, in relation to any tax year commencing on or after 6 April 2016.

Prospective amendments—Para 17(4)(*ba*) to be inserted by FA 2015 s 120, Sch 20 paras 14, 19 with effect from a day to be appointed. Para 17(4)(*ba*) as inserted to read as follows—

"(*ba*) if one of the penalties is a penalty under paragraph 6(3) or (4) and the information withheld is category 1 information, 125%, and".

[Cancellation of penalty

17A—(1) This paragraph applies where—

(*a*) P is liable for a penalty under any paragraph of this Schedule in relation to a failure to make a return falling within item 1 or 2 in the Table, and

(*b*) [HMRC decide to give P a notice under section 8B withdrawing][2] a notice under section 8 or 8A of that Act.

(2) The notice under section 8B of TMA 1970 may include provision under this paragraph cancelling liability to the penalty from the date specified in the notice.][1]

Commencement—Finance Act 2009, Schedule 55 (Penalties for failure to make returns) (Appointed Days and Consequential Provision) Order, SI 2014/2395 provides dates for the coming into force of Sch 55 in relation to returns falling within item 4 of the table in para 1 above (PAYE returns), as follows—

– **11 September 2014:** powers to make regulations in relation to quanta of RTI late-filing penalties in para 6C(5), (7), (8), (9), (11) (see also SI 2014/2396).

– for paras 1, 6B, 6C(1)–(4), (6), (10), 6D, 16–24, 26, 27 (relating to failures to make returns under the PAYE Regulations (SI 2003/2682) regs 67B and 67D):

(a) **6 October 2014:** where the employer is a large existing employer (an employer which as at 6 October 2014 employs at least 50 employees). Affected returns are those required to be made or delivered to HMRC on or after 6 October 2014.

(b) **6 March 2015:** where the employer is a small existing employer (an employer which as at 6 October 2014 employs no more than 49 employees) or is a new employer. Affected returns are those required to be made or delivered to HMRC on or after 6 March 2015.

Amendments—[1] Paragraphs 17A, 17B and preceding cross-head inserted by FA 2013 s 233, Sch 51 para 8 with effect in relation to a return—

(a) under TMA 1970 s 12AA for a partnership which includes one or more companies, for a relevant period beginning on or after 6 April 2012; and

(b) under TMA 1970 s 12AA for any other partnership, or a return under TMA 1970 s 8 or s 8A, for a year of assessment beginning on or after 6 April 2012.

A "relevant period" means a period in respect of which a return is required: FA 2013 Sch 51 para 9(2).

[2] In sub-para (1)(*b*), words substituted by FA 2016 s 169(1), (6) with effect in relation to any notice under TMA 1970 s 8 or s 8A given in relation to the tax year 2014–15 or any subsequent year. It is immaterial whether the notice was given before or after 15 September 2016.

[**17B**—(1) This paragraph applies where—

(*a*) P is liable for a penalty under any paragraph of this Schedule in relation to a failure to make a return falling within item 3 in the Table, and

(*b*) a request is made under section 12AAA of TMA 1970 for HMRC to withdraw a notice under section 12AA of that Act.

(2) The notice under section 12AAA of TMA 1970 may include provision under this paragraph cancelling liability to the penalty from the date specified in the notice.][1]

Commencement—Finance Act 2009, Schedule 55 (Penalties for failure to make returns) (Appointed Days and Consequential Provision) Order, SI 2014/2395 provides dates for the coming into force of Sch 55 in relation to returns falling within item 4 of the table in para 1 above (PAYE returns), as follows—

– **11 September 2014:** powers to make regulations in relation to quanta of RTI late-filing penalties in para 6C(5), (7), (8), (9), (11) (see also SI 2014/2396).

– for paras 1, 6B, 6C(1)–(4), (6), (10), 6D, 16–24, 26, 27 (relating to failures to make returns under the PAYE Regulations (SI 2003/2682) regs 67B and 67D):

(a) **6 October 2014:** where the employer is a large existing employer (an employer which as at 6 October 2014 employs at least 50 employees). Affected returns are those required to be made or delivered to HMRC on or after 6 October 2014.

(b) **6 March 2015:** where the employer is a small existing employer (an employer which as at 6 October 2014 employs no more than 49 employees) or is a new employer. Affected returns are those required to be made or delivered to HMRC on or after 6 March 2015.

Amendments—[1] Paragraphs 17A, 17B and preceding cross-head inserted by FA 2013 s 233, Sch 51 para 8 with effect in relation to a return—

(a) under TMA 1970 s 12AA for a partnership which includes one or more companies, for a relevant period beginning on or after 6 April 2012; and

(b) under TMA 1970 s 12AA for any other partnership, or a return under TMA 1970 s 8 or s 8A, for a year of assessment beginning on or after 6 April 2012.

A "relevant period" means a period in respect of which a return is required: FA 2013 Sch 51 para 9(2).

Assessment

18—(1) Where P is liable for a penalty under any paragraph of this Schedule HMRC must—

(*a*) assess the penalty,

(*b*) notify P, and

(*c*) state in the notice the period in respect of which the penalty is assessed.

(2) A penalty under any paragraph of this Schedule must be paid before the end of the period of 30 days beginning with the day on which notification of the penalty is issued.

(3) An assessment of a penalty under any paragraph of this Schedule—

(*a*) is to be treated for procedural purposes in the same way as an assessment to tax (except in respect of a matter expressly provided for by this Schedule),

(*b*) may be enforced as if it were an assessment to tax, and

(*c*) may be combined with an assessment to tax.

(4) A supplementary assessment may be made in respect of a penalty if an earlier assessment operated by reference to an underestimate of the liability to tax which would have been shown in a return.

[(5) Sub-paragraph (6) applies if—

(*a*) an assessment in respect of a penalty is based on a liability to tax that would have been shown in a return, and

(*b*) that liability is found by HMRC to be excessive.

(6) HMRC may by notice to P amend the assessment so that it is based upon the correct amount.

(7) An amendment under sub-paragraph (6)—

(*a*) does not affect when the penalty must be paid;

(*b*) may be made after the last day on which the assessment in question could have been made under paragraph 19.][1]

Commencement—Finance Act 2009, Schedules 55 and 56 (Income Tax Self Assessment and Pension Schemes) (Appointed Days and Consequential and Savings Provisions) Order, SI 2011/702 art 2 (appointed day for the coming into force of Sch 55 is 6 April 2011 in relation to a return or other document which is required to be made or delivered to HMRC in relation to the tax year 2010–11 or any subsequent tax year and falls within item 1, 2 or 3 of the Table in para 1).

Finance (No 3) Act 2010, Schedule 10 and the Finance Act 2009, Schedule 55 and Sections 101 to 103 (Appointed Day, etc) (Construction Industry Scheme) Order, SI 2011/2391 (the day appointed for the coming into force of the following paras of Sch 55 is 6 October 2011, with effect only in relation to a return within item 6 of Sch 55 para 1(5), and for which the filing date for the purposes of Sch 55 is after 19 October 2011—

– para 1 (but only in relation to item 6 in the Table in para 1(5);
– paras 7–13; and
– 14–24, 26, and 27(1)–(4) but only as relevant to paras 7–13).

Finance Act 2009, Schedule 55 (Penalties for failure to make returns) (Appointed Days and Consequential Provision) Order, SI 2014/2395 provides dates for the coming into force of Sch 55 in relation to returns falling within item 4 of the table in para 1 above (PAYE returns), as follows—

– **11 September 2014:** powers to make regulations in relation to quanta of RTI late-filing penalties in para 6C(5), (7), (8), (9), (11) (see also SI 2014/2396).
– for paras 1, 6B, 6C(1)–(4), (6), (10), 6D, 16–24, 26, 27 (relating to failures to make returns under the PAYE Regulations (SI 2003/2682) regs 67B and 67D):
  (a) **6 October 2014:** where the employer is a large existing employer (an employer which as at 6 October 2014 employs at least 50 employees). Affected returns are those required to be made or delivered to HMRC on or after 6 October 2014.
  (b) **6 March 2015:** where the employer is a small existing employer (an employer which as at 6 October 2014 employs no more than 49 employees) or is a new employer. Affected returns are those required to be made or delivered to HMRC on or after 6 March 2015.

Amendments—[1] Sub-paras (5)–(7) substituted for sub-para (5) by FA 2013 s 230, Sch 50 paras 2, 7 with effect for the tax year 2014–15 and subsequent tax years in relation to failures to make returns with a filing date (as defined in FA 2009 Sch 55 para 1(4)) on or after 6 April 2014.

19—(1) An assessment of a penalty under any paragraph of this Schedule in respect of any amount must be made on or before the later of date A and (where it applies) date B.

(2) Date A is[—

(*a*) in the case of an assessment of a penalty under paragraph 6C, the last day of the period of 2 years beginning with the end of the tax month in respect of which the penalty is payable,

(*b*) in the case of an assessment of a penalty under paragraph 6D, the last day of the period of 2 years beginning with the filing date for the relevant extended failure (as defined in paragraph 6D(10)), and

(*c*) in any other case,][1] the last day of the period of 2 years beginning with the filing date.

(3) Date B is the last day of the period of 12 months beginning with—

(*a*) the end of the appeal period for the assessment of the liability to tax which would have been shown in the return, [or returns (as the case may be in relation to penalties under section 6C or 6D)][1] or

(*b*) if there is no such assessment, the date on which that liability is ascertained or it is ascertained that the liability is nil.

(4) In sub-paragraph (3)(*a*) "appeal period" means the period during which—

(*a*) an appeal could be brought, or

(*b*) an appeal that has been brought has not been determined or withdrawn.

(5) Sub-paragraph (1) does not apply to a re-assessment under paragraph 24(2)(*b*).

Commencement—Finance Act 2009, Schedules 55 and 56 (Income Tax Self Assessment and Pension Schemes) (Appointed Days and Consequential and Savings Provisions) Order, SI 2011/702 art 2 (appointed day for the coming into force of Sch 55 is

6 April 2011 in relation to a return or other document which is required to be made or delivered to HMRC in relation to the tax year 2010–11 or any subsequent tax year and falls within item 1, 2 or 3 of the Table in para 1).

Finance (No 3) Act 2010, Schedule 10 and the Finance Act 2009, Schedule 55 and Sections 101 to 103 (Appointed Day, etc) (Construction Industry Scheme) Order, SI 2011/2391 (the day appointed for the coming into force of the following paras of Sch 55 is 6 October 2011, with effect only in relation to a return within item 6 of Sch 55 para 1(5), and for which the filing date for the purposes of Sch 55 is after 19 October 2011—

– para 1 (but only in relation to item 6 in the Table in para 1(5);
– paras 7–13; and
– 14–24, 26, and 27(1)–(4) but only as relevant to paras 7–13).

Finance Act 2009, Schedule 55 (Penalties for failure to make returns) (Appointed Days and Consequential Provision) Order, SI 2014/2395 provides dates for the coming into force of Sch 55 in relation to returns falling within item 4 of the table in para 1 above (PAYE returns), as follows—

– **11 September 2014:** powers to make regulations in relation to quanta of RTI late-filing penalties in para 6C(5), (7), (8), (9), (11) (see also SI 2014/2396).
– for paras 1, 6B, 6C(1)–(4), (6), (10), 6D, 16–24, 26, 27 (relating to failures to make returns under the PAYE Regulations (SI 2003/2682) regs 67B and 67D):
  (a) **6 October 2014:** where the employer is a large existing employer (an employer which as at 6 October 2014 employs at least 50 employees). Affected returns are those required to be made or delivered to HMRC on or after 6 October 2014.
  (b) **6 March 2015:** where the employer is a small existing employer (an employer which as at 6 October 2014 employs no more than 49 employees) or is a new employer. Affected returns are those required to be made or delivered to HMRC on or after 6 March 2015.

Amendments—[1] In sub-paras (2), (3)(*a*) words inserted by FA 2013 s 230, Sch 50 paras 2, 8 with effect for the tax year 2014–15 and subsequent tax years in relation to failures to make returns with a filing date (as defined in FA 2009 Sch 55 para 1(4)) on or after 6 April 2014.

Appeal

20—(1) P may appeal against a decision of HMRC that a penalty is payable by P.

(2) P may appeal against a decision of HMRC as to the amount of a penalty payable by P.

Commencement—Finance Act 2009, Schedules 55 and 56 (Income Tax Self Assessment and Pension Schemes) (Appointed Days and Consequential and Savings Provisions) Order, SI 2011/702 art 2 (appointed day for the coming into force of Sch 55 is 6 April 2011 in relation to a return or other document which is required to be made or delivered to HMRC in relation to the tax year 2010–11 or any subsequent tax year and falls within item 1, 2 or 3 of the Table in para 1).

Finance (No 3) Act 2010, Schedule 10 and the Finance Act 2009, Schedule 55 and Sections 101 to 103 (Appointed Day, etc) (Construction Industry Scheme) Order, SI 2011/2391 (the day appointed for the coming into force of the following paras of Sch 55 is 6 October 2011, with effect only in relation to a return within item 6 of Sch 55 para 1(5), and for which the filing date for the purposes of Sch 55 is after 19 October 2011—

– para 1 (but only in relation to item 6 in the Table in para 1(5);
– paras 7–13; and
– 14–24, 26, and 27(1)–(4) but only as relevant to paras 7–13).

Finance Act 2009, Schedule 55 (Penalties for failure to make returns) (Appointed Days and Consequential Provision) Order, SI 2014/2395 provides dates for the coming into force of Sch 55 in relation to returns falling within item 4 of the table in para 1 above (PAYE returns), as follows—

– **11 September 2014:** powers to make regulations in relation to quanta of RTI late-filing penalties in para 6C(5), (7), (8), (9), (11) (see also SI 2014/2396).
– for paras 1, 6B, 6C(1)–(4), (6), (10), 6D, 16–24, 26, 27 (relating to failures to make returns under the PAYE Regulations (SI 2003/2682) regs 67B and 67D):
  (a) **6 October 2014:** where the employer is a large existing employer (an employer which as at 6 October 2014 employs at least 50 employees). Affected returns are those required to be made or delivered to HMRC on or after 6 October 2014.
  (b) **6 March 2015:** where the employer is a small existing employer (an employer which as at 6 October 2014 employs no more than 49 employees) or is a new employer. Affected returns are those required to be made or delivered to HMRC on or after 6 March 2015.

21—(1) An appeal under paragraph 20 is to be treated in the same way as an appeal against an assessment to the tax concerned (including by the application of any provision about bringing the appeal by notice to HMRC, about HMRC review of the decision or about determination of the appeal by the First-tier Tribunal or Upper Tribunal).

(2) Sub-paragraph (1) does not apply—

(*a*) so as to require P to pay a penalty before an appeal against the assessment of the penalty is determined, or

(*b*) in respect of any other matter expressly provided for by this Act.

Commencement—Finance Act 2009, Schedules 55 and 56 (Income Tax Self Assessment and Pension Schemes) (Appointed Days and Consequential and Savings Provisions) Order, SI 2011/702 art 2 (appointed day for the coming into force of Sch 55 is 6 April 2011 in relation to a return or other document which is required to be made or delivered to HMRC in relation to the tax year 2010–11 or any subsequent tax year and falls within item 1, 2 or 3 of the Table in para 1).

Finance (No 3) Act 2010, Schedule 10 and the Finance Act 2009, Schedule 55 and Sections 101 to 103 (Appointed Day, etc) (Construction Industry Scheme) Order, SI 2011/2391 (the day appointed for the coming into force of the following paras of Sch 55 is 6 October 2011, with effect only in relation to a return within item 6 of Sch 55 para 1(5), and for which the filing date for the purposes of Sch 55 is after 19 October 2011—

– para 1 (but only in relation to item 6 in the Table in para 1(5);
– paras 7–13; and
– 14–24, 26, and 27(1)–(4) but only as relevant to paras 7–13).

Finance Act 2009, Schedule 55 (Penalties for failure to make returns) (Appointed Days and Consequential Provision) Order, SI 2014/2395 provides dates for the coming into force of Sch 55 in relation to returns falling within item 4 of the table in para 1 above (PAYE returns), as follows—

– **11 September 2014:** powers to make regulations in relation to quanta of RTI late-filing penalties in para 6C(5), (7), (8), (9), (11) (see also SI 2014/2396).
– for paras 1, 6B, 6C(1)–(4), (6), (10), 6D, 16–24, 26, 27 (relating to failures to make returns under the PAYE Regulations (SI 2003/2682) regs 67B and 67D):
  (a) **6 October 2014:** where the employer is a large existing employer (an employer which as at 6 October 2014 employs at least 50 employees). Affected returns are those required to be made or delivered to HMRC on or after 6 October 2014.
  (b) **6 March 2015:** where the employer is a small existing employer (an employer which as at 6 October 2014 employs no more than 49 employees) or is a new employer. Affected returns are those required to be made or delivered to HMRC on or after 6 March 2015.

22—(1) On an appeal under paragraph 20(1) that is notified to the tribunal, the tribunal may affirm or cancel HMRC's decision.

(2) On an appeal under paragraph 20(2) that is notified to the tribunal, the tribunal may—

(*a*) affirm HMRC's decision, or

(*b*) substitute for HMRC's decision another decision that HMRC had power to make.

(3) If the tribunal substitutes its decision for HMRC's, the tribunal may rely on paragraph 16—

(*a*) to the same extent as HMRC (which may mean applying the same percentage reduction as HMRC to a different starting point), or

(*b*) to a different extent, but only if the tribunal thinks that HMRC's decision in respect of the application of paragraph 16 was flawed.

(4) In sub-paragraph (3)(*b*) "flawed" means flawed when considered in the light of the principles applicable in proceedings for judicial review.

(5) In this paragraph "tribunal" means the First-tier Tribunal or Upper Tribunal (as appropriate by virtue of paragraph 21(1)).

Commencement—Finance Act 2009, Schedules 55 and 56 (Income Tax Self Assessment and Pension Schemes) (Appointed Days and Consequential and Savings Provisions) Order, SI 2011/702 art 2 (appointed day for the coming into force of Sch 55 is 6 April 2011 in relation to a return or other document which is required to be made or delivered to HMRC in relation to the tax year 2010–11 or any subsequent tax year and falls within item 1, 2 or 3 of the Table in para 1).

Finance (No 3) Act 2010, Schedule 10 and the Finance Act 2009, Schedule 55 and Sections 101 to 103 (Appointed Day, etc) (Construction Industry Scheme) Order, SI 2011/2391 (the day appointed for the coming into force of the following paras of Sch 55 is 6 October 2011, with effect only in relation to a return within item 6 of Sch 55 para 1(5), and for which the filing date for the purposes of Sch 55 is after 19 October 2011—

– para 1 (but only in relation to item 6 in the Table in para 1(5);
– paras 7–13; and
– 14–24, 26, and 27(1)–(4) but only as relevant to paras 7–13).

Finance Act 2009, Schedule 55 (Penalties for failure to make returns) (Appointed Days and Consequential Provision) Order, SI 2014/2395 provides dates for the coming into force of Sch 55 in relation to returns falling within item 4 of the table in para 1 above (PAYE returns), as follows—

– **11 September 2014:** powers to make regulations in relation to quanta of RTI late-filing penalties in para 6C(5), (7), (8), (9), (11) (see also SI 2014/2396).
– for paras 1, 6B, 6C(1)–(4), (6), (10), 6D, 16–24, 26, 27 (relating to failures to make returns under the PAYE Regulations (SI 2003/2682) regs 67B and 67D):
  (a) **6 October 2014:** where the employer is a large existing employer (an employer which as at 6 October 2014 employs at least 50 employees). Affected returns are those required to be made or delivered to HMRC on or after 6 October 2014.
  (b) **6 March 2015:** where the employer is a small existing employer (an employer which as at 6 October 2014 employs no more than 49 employees) or is a new employer. Affected returns are those required to be made or delivered to HMRC on or after 6 March 2015.

Reasonable excuse

23—(1) Liability to a penalty under any paragraph of this Schedule does not arise in relation to a failure to make a return if P satisfies HMRC or (on appeal) the First-tier Tribunal or Upper Tribunal that there is a reasonable excuse for the failure.

(2) For the purposes of sub-paragraph (1)—

(*a*) an insufficiency of funds is not a reasonable excuse, unless attributable to events outside P's control,

(*b*) where P relies on any other person to do anything, that is not a reasonable excuse unless P took reasonable care to avoid the failure, and

(*c*) where P had a reasonable excuse for the failure but the excuse has ceased, P is to be treated as having continued to have the excuse if the failure is remedied without unreasonable delay after the excuse ceased.

Commencement—Finance Act 2009, Schedules 55 and 56 (Income Tax Self Assessment and Pension Schemes) (Appointed Days and Consequential and Savings Provisions) Order, SI 2011/702 art 2 (appointed day for the coming into force of Sch 55 is 6 April 2011 in relation to a return or other document which is required to be made or delivered to HMRC in relation to the tax year 2010–11 or any subsequent tax year and falls within item 1, 2 or 3 of the Table in para 1).

Finance (No 3) Act 2010, Schedule 10 and the Finance Act 2009, Schedule 55 and Sections 101 to 103 (Appointed Day, etc) (Construction Industry Scheme) Order, SI 2011/2391 (the day appointed for the coming into force of the following paras of Sch 55 is 6 October 2011, with effect only in relation to a return within item 6 of Sch 55 para 1(5), and for which the filing date for the purposes of Sch 55 is after 19 October 2011—

- para 1 (but only in relation to item 6 in the Table in para 1(5);
- paras 7–13; and
- 14–24, 26, and 27(1)–(4) but only as relevant to paras 7–13).

Finance Act 2009, Schedule 55 (Penalties for failure to make returns) (Appointed Days and Consequential Provision) Order, SI 2014/2395 provides dates for the coming into force of Sch 55 in relation to returns falling within item 4 of the table in para 1 above (PAYE returns), as follows—

- **11 September 2014:** powers to make regulations in relation to quanta of RTI late-filing penalties in para 6C(5), (7), (8), (9), (11) (see also SI 2014/2396).
- for paras 1, 6B, 6C(1)–(4), (6), (10), 6D, 16–24, 26, 27 (relating to failures to make returns under the PAYE Regulations (SI 2003/2682) regs 67B and 67D):
  - (a) **6 October 2014:** where the employer is a large existing employer (an employer which as at 6 October 2014 employs at least 50 employees). Affected returns are those required to be made or delivered to HMRC on or after 6 October 2014.
  - (b) **6 March 2015:** where the employer is a small existing employer (an employer which as at 6 October 2014 employs no more than 49 employees) or is a new employer. Affected returns are those required to be made or delivered to HMRC on or after 6 March 2015.

Prospective amendment—Sub-para (1) to be substituted by F(No 3)A 2010 s 26, Sch 10 paras 1, 11 with effect from a day to be appointed by Treasury order. Sub-para (1) as substituted to read as follows—

"(1) If P satisfies HMRC or (on appeal) the First-tier Tribunal or Upper Tribunal that there is a reasonable excuse for a failure to make a return—

(a) liability to a penalty under any paragraph of this Schedule does not arise in relation to that failure, and

(b) the failure does not count for the purposes of paragraphs 13B(2), 13C, 13G(2) and 13H.".

Determination of penalty geared to tax liability where no return made

24—(1) References to a liability to tax which would have been shown in a return are references to the amount which, if a complete and accurate return had been delivered on the filing date, would have been shown to be due or payable by the taxpayer in respect of the tax concerned for the period to which the return relates.

(2) In the case of a penalty which is assessed at a time before P makes the return to which the penalty relates—

(*a*) HMRC is to determine the amount mentioned in sub-paragraph (1) to the best of HMRC's information and belief, and

(*b*) if P subsequently makes a return, the penalty must be re-assessed by reference to the amount of tax shown to be due and payable in that return (but subject to any amendments or corrections to the return).

(3) In calculating a liability to tax which would have been shown in a return, no account is to be taken of any relief under [section 458 of CTA 2010][1] (relief in respect of repayment etc of loan) which is deferred under [subsection (5)][1] of that section.

Commencement—Finance Act 2009, Schedules 55 and 56 (Income Tax Self Assessment and Pension Schemes) (Appointed Days and Consequential and Savings Provisions) Order, SI 2011/702 art 2 (appointed day for the coming into force of Sch 55 is 6 April 2011 in relation to a return or other document which is required to be made or delivered to HMRC in relation to the tax year 2010–11 or any subsequent tax year and falls within item 1, 2 or 3 of the Table in para 1).

Finance (No 3) Act 2010, Schedule 10 and the Finance Act 2009, Schedule 55 and Sections 101 to 103 (Appointed Day, etc) (Construction Industry Scheme) Order, SI 2011/2391 (the day appointed for the coming into force of the following paras of Sch 55 is 6 October 2011, with effect only in relation to a return within item 6 of Sch 55 para 1(5), and for which the filing date for the purposes of Sch 55 is after 19 October 2011—

- para 1 (but only in relation to item 6 in the Table in para 1(5);
- paras 7–13; and
- 14–24, 26, and 27(1)–(4) but only as relevant to paras 7–13).

Finance Act 2009, Schedule 55 (Penalties for failure to make returns) (Appointed Days and Consequential Provision) Order, SI 2014/2395 provides dates for the coming into force of Sch 55 in relation to returns falling within item 4 of the table in para 1 above (PAYE returns), as follows—

- **11 September 2014:** powers to make regulations in relation to quanta of RTI late-filing penalties in para 6C(5), (7), (8), (9), (11) (see also SI 2014/2396).
- for paras 1, 6B, 6C(1)–(4), (6), (10), 6D, 16–24, 26, 27 (relating to failures to make returns under the PAYE Regulations (SI 2003/2682) regs 67B and 67D):
  - (a) **6 October 2014:** where the employer is a large existing employer (an employer which as at 6 October 2014 employs at least 50 employees). Affected returns are those required to be made or delivered to HMRC on or after 6 October 2014.

(b) **6 March 2015:** where the employer is a small existing employer (an employer which as at 6 October 2014 employs no more than 49 employees) or is a new employer. Affected returns are those required to be made or delivered to HMRC on or after 6 March 2015.

Amendments—[1] In sub-para (3) words substituted for words "subsection (4) of section 419 of ICTA" and "subsection (4A)" by CTA 2010 s 1177, Sch 1 paras 706, 723. CTA 2010 has effect for corporation tax purposes for accounting periods ending on or after 1 April 2010, and for income and capital gains tax purposes for the tax year 2010–11 and subsequent tax years.

Partnerships

25—(1) This paragraph applies where—

(*a*) the representative partner, or

(*b*) a successor of the representative partner,

fails to make a return falling within item 3 in the Table (partnership returns).

(2) A penalty in respect of the failure is payable by every relevant partner.

(3) In accordance with sub-paragraph (2), any reference in this Schedule to P is to be read as including a reference to a relevant partner.

(4) An appeal under paragraph 20 in connection with a penalty payable by virtue of this paragraph may be brought only by—

(*a*) the representative partner, or

(*b*) a successor of the representative partner.

(5) Where such an appeal is brought in connection with a penalty payable in respect of a failure, the appeal is to treated as if it were an appeal in connection with every penalty payable in respect of that failure.

(6) In this paragraph—

"relevant partner" means a person who was a partner in the partnership to which the return relates at any time during the period in respect of which the return was required;

"representative partner" means a person who has been required by a notice served under or for the purposes of section 12AA(2) or (3) of TMA 1970 to deliver any return;

"successor" has the meaning given by section 12AA(11) of TMA 1970.

Commencement—Finance Act 2009, Schedules 55 and 56 (Income Tax Self Assessment and Pension Schemes) (Appointed Days and Consequential and Savings Provisions) Order, SI 2011/702 art 2 (appointed day for the coming into force of Sch 55 is 6 April 2011 in relation to a return or other document which is required to be made or delivered to HMRC in relation to the tax year 2010–11 or any subsequent tax year and falls within item 1, 2 or 3 of the Table in para 1).

Double jeopardy

26 P is not liable to a penalty under any paragraph of this Schedule in respect of a failure or action in respect of which P has been convicted of an offence.

Commencement—Finance Act 2009, Schedules 55 and 56 (Income Tax Self Assessment and Pension Schemes) (Appointed Days and Consequential and Savings Provisions) Order, SI 2011/702 art 2 (appointed day for the coming into force of Sch 55 is 6 April 2011 in relation to a return or other document which is required to be made or delivered to HMRC in relation to the tax year 2010–11 or any subsequent tax year and falls within item 1, 2 or 3 of the Table in para 1).

Finance (No 3) Act 2010, Schedule 10 and the Finance Act 2009, Schedule 55 and Sections 101 to 103 (Appointed Day, etc) (Construction Industry Scheme) Order, SI 2011/2391 (the day appointed for the coming into force of the following paras of Sch 55 is 6 October 2011, with effect only in relation to a return within item 6 of Sch 55 para 1(5), and for which the filing date for the purposes of Sch 55 is after 19 October 2011—

– para 1 (but only in relation to item 6 in the Table in para 1(5);
– paras 7–13; and
– 14–24, 26, and 27(1)–(4) but only as relevant to paras 7–13).

Finance Act 2009, Schedule 55 (Penalties for failure to make returns) (Appointed Days and Consequential Provision) Order, SI 2014/2395 provides dates for the coming into force of Sch 55 in relation to returns falling within item 4 of the table in para 1 above (PAYE returns), as follows—

– **11 September 2014:** powers to make regulations in relation to quanta of RTI late-filing penalties in para 6C(5), (7), (8), (9), (11) (see also SI 2014/2396).
– for paras 1, 6B, 6C(1)–(4), (6), (10), 6D, 16–24, 26, 27 (relating to failures to make returns under the PAYE Regulations (SI 2003/2682) regs 67B and 67D):

(a) **6 October 2014:** where the employer is a large existing employer (an employer which as at 6 October 2014 employs at least 50 employees). Affected returns are those required to be made or delivered to HMRC on or after 6 October 2014.

(b) **6 March 2015:** where the employer is a small existing employer (an employer which as at 6 October 2014 employs no more than 49 employees) or is a new employer. Affected returns are those required to be made or delivered to HMRC on or after 6 March 2015.

Interpretation

27—(1) This paragraph applies for the construction of this Schedule.

(2) The withholding of information by P is—

(*a*) "deliberate and concealed" if P deliberately withholds the information and makes arrangements to conceal the fact that the information has been withheld, and (*b*) "deliberate but not concealed" if P deliberately withholds the information but does not make arrangements to conceal the fact that the information has been withheld.

[(2A) "The Commissioners" means the Commissioners for Her Majesty's Revenue and Customs.][1]

(3) "HMRC" means Her Majesty's Revenue and Customs.

[(3A) "Tax month" means the period beginning with the 6th day of a month and ending with the 5th day of the following month.][1]

(4) References to a liability to tax, in relation to a return falling within item 6 in the Table (construction industry scheme), are to a liability to make payments in accordance with Chapter 3 of Part 3 of FA 2004.

(5) References to an assessment to tax, in relation to inheritance tax and stamp duty reserve tax, are to a determination.

Commencement—Finance Act 2009, Schedules 55 and 56 (Income Tax Self Assessment and Pension Schemes) (Appointed Days and Consequential and Savings Provisions) Order, SI 2011/702 art 2 (appointed day for the coming into force of Sch 55 is 6 April 2011 in relation to a return or other document which is required to be made or delivered to HMRC in relation to the tax year 2010–11 or any subsequent tax year and falls within item 1, 2 or 3 of the Table in para 1).

Finance (No 3) Act 2010, Schedule 10 and the Finance Act 2009, Schedule 55 and Sections 101 to 103 (Appointed Day, etc) (Construction Industry Scheme) Order, SI 2011/2391 (the day appointed for the coming into force of the following paras of Sch 55 is 6 October 2011, with effect only in relation to a return within item 6 of Sch 55 para 1(5), and for which the filing date for the purposes of Sch 55 is after 19 October 2011—

- para 1 (but only in relation to item 6 in the Table in para 1(5);
- paras 7–13; and
- 14–24, 26, and 27(1)–(4) but only as relevant to paras 7–13).

Finance Act 2009, Schedule 55 (Penalties for failure to make returns) (Appointed Days and Consequential Provision) Order, SI 2014/2395 provides dates for the coming into force of Sch 55 in relation to returns falling within item 4 of the table in para 1 above (PAYE returns), as follows—

- **11 September 2014:** powers to make regulations in relation to quanta of RTI late-filing penalties in para 6C(5), (7), (8), (9), (11) (see also SI 2014/2396).
- for paras 1, 6B, 6C(1)–(4), (6), (10), 6D, 16–24, 26, 27 (relating to failures to make returns under the PAYE Regulations (SI 2003/2682) regs 67B and 67D):
  - (a) **6 October 2014:** where the employer is a large existing employer (an employer which as at 6 October 2014 employs at least 50 employees). Affected returns are those required to be made or delivered to HMRC on or after 6 October 2014.
  - (b) **6 March 2015:** where the employer is a small existing employer (an employer which as at 6 October 2014 employs no more than 49 employees) or is a new employer. Affected returns are those required to be made or delivered to HMRC on or after 6 March 2015.

Amendments—[1] Sub-paras (2A), (3A) inserted by FA 2013 s 230, Sch 50 paras 2, 9 with effect for the tax year 2014–15 and subsequent tax years in relation to failures to make returns with a filing date (as defined in FA 2009 Sch 55 para 1(4)) on or after 6 April 2014.

SCHEDULE 56

PENALTY FOR FAILURE TO MAKE PAYMENTS ON TIME

Section 107

Commencement—Finance Act 2009, Schedule 56 (Appointed Day and Consequential Provisions) Order, SI 2010/466 (6 April 2010 appointed as day on which Sch 56 comes into force for certain purposes).

Finance Act 2009, Schedules 55 and 56 (Income Tax Self Assessment and Pension Schemes) (Appointed Days and Consequential and Savings Provisions) Order, SI 2011/702 art 2 (appointed day for the coming into force of Sch 56 is 6 April 2011 in relation to an amount of tax which is payable in relation to the tax year 2010–11 or any subsequent tax year and falls within item 1, 12, 18 or 19 of the Table in para 1, or in so far as the tax falls within item 1 of that Table, item 17, 23 or 24 of that Table).

FA 2013 Sch 34 para 12 (Sch 56, as amended by FA 2013 Sch 34 para 9, is taken to have come into force for the purposes of the annual tax on enveloped dwellings on 17 July 2013).

Finance Act 2009, Schedules 55 and 56 and Sections 101 and 102 (Stamp Duty Reserve Tax) (Appointed Days, Consequential and Transitional Provision) Order, SI 2014/3269 art 3 (the day appointed for the coming into force of Sch 56 is 1 January 2015 in relation to an amount of SDRT which is in item 10, 17, 23 or 24 of the Table in para 1).

Finance Act 2016 s 113(18) (for the purposes of apprenticeship levy, Sch 56 as amended by FA 2016 s 113 is taken to come into force on 15 September 2016).

Cross-references—See SSCBA 1992 s 11A (this Schedule applies with the necessary modifications, in relation to Class 2 contributions under SSCBA 1992 s 11(2) as if those contributions were income tax chargeable under ITTOIA 2005 Pt 2 Ch 2 in respect of profits of a trade, profession or vocation which is not carried on wholly outside the United Kingdom).

Education (Postgraduate Master's Degree Loans) Regulations, SI 2016/606 regs 46, 85 (this schedule applies to loans for postgraduate master's degree courses which begin on or after 1 August 2016).

Penalty for failure to pay tax

1—(1) A penalty is payable by a person ("P") where P fails to pay an amount of tax specified in column 3 of the Table below on or before the date specified in column 4.

(2) Paragraphs 3 to 8 set out—

(*a*) the circumstances in which a penalty is payable, and

(*b*) subject to paragraph 9, the amount of the penalty.

(3) If P's failure falls within more than one provision of this Schedule, P is liable to a penalty under each of those provisions.

(4) In the following provisions of this Schedule, the "penalty date", in relation to an amount of tax, means [the day after the date specified in or for the purposes of column 4 of the Table in relation to that amount.][5]

	Tax to which payment relates	*Amount of tax payable*	*Date after which penalty is incurred*
PRINCIPAL AMOUNTS			
1	Income tax or capital gains tax	Amount payable under section 59B(3) or (4) of TMA 1970	The date falling 30 days after the date specified in section 59B(3) or (4) of TMA 1970 as the date by which the amount must be paid
2	Income tax	Amount payable under PAYE regulations . . . [1]	The date determined by or under PAYE regulations as the date by which the amount must be paid
3	Income tax	Amount shown in return under section 254(1) of FA 2004	The date falling 30 days after the date specified in section 254(5) of FA 2004 as the date by which the amount must be paid
[3A	Income tax	Amount payable under regulations under section 244L(2)(*a*) of FA 2004	The date falling 30 days after the due date determined by or under the regulations][10]
[4A	Apprenticeship levy	Amount payable under regulations under section 105 of FA 2016	The date determined by or under regulations under section 105 of FA 2016][9]
4	Deductions on account of tax under Chapter 3 of Part 3 of FA 2004 (construction industry scheme)	Amount payable under section 62 of FA 2004 (except an amount falling within item 17, 23 or 24)	The date determined by or under regulations under [section 71][1] of FA 2004 as the date by which the amount must be paid
5	Corporation tax	Amount shown in company tax return under paragraph 3 of Schedule 18 to FA 1998	The filing date for the company tax return for the accounting period for which the tax is due (see paragraph 14 of Schedule 18 to FA 1998)
6	Corporation tax	Amount payable under regulations under section 59E of TMA 1970 (except an amount falling within item 17, 23 or 24)	The filing date for the company tax return for the accounting period for which the tax is due (see paragraph 14 of Schedule 18 to FA 1998)
[6ZZA	Corporation tax	Amount payable under section 357YQ of CTA 2010	The end of the period within which, in accordance with section 357YQ(5), the amount must be paid.][8]

	Tax to which payment relates	*Amount of tax payable*	*Date after which penalty is incurred*
[6ZA	Corporation tax	Amount payable under an exit charge payment plan entered into in accordance with Schedule 3ZB to TMA 1970	The later of— (*a*) the first day after the period of 12 months beginning immediately after the migration accounting period (as defined in Part 1 or 2 of Schedule 3ZB to TMA 1970, as the case may be), and (*b*) the date on which the amount is payable under the plan.][3]
[6ZB	Diverted profits tax	Amount of diverted profits tax payable under Part 3 of FA 2015	The date when, in accordance with section 98(2) of FA 2015, the amount must be paid][7]
7	Inheritance tax	Amount payable under section 226 of IHTA 1984 (except an amount falling within item 14 or 21)	The filing date (determined under section 216 of IHTA 1984) for the account in respect of the liability for that amount
8	Inheritance tax	Amount payable under section 227 or 229 of IHTA 1984 (except an amount falling within item 14 or 21)	For the first instalment, the filing date (determined under section 216 of IHTA 1984) for the account in respect of the liability for that amount For any later instalment, the date falling 30 days after the date determined under section 227 or 229 of IHTA 1984 as the date by which the instalment must be paid
9	Stamp duty land tax	Amount payable under section 86(1) or (2) of FA 2003	The date falling 30 days after the date specified in section 86(1) or (2) of FA 2003 as the date by which the amount must be paid
10	Stamp duty reserve tax	Amount payable under section 87, 93 or 96 of FA 1986 or Schedule 19 to FA 1999 (except an amount falling within item 17, 23 or 24)	The date falling 30 days after the date determined by or under regulations under section 98 of FA 1986 as the date by which the amount must be paid
[10A	Annual tax on enveloped dwellings	Amount payable under section 161(1) or (2) of FA 2013 (except an amount falling within item 23).	The date falling 30 days after the date specified in section 161(1) or (2) of FA 2013 as the date by which the amount must be paid][4]
11	Petroleum revenue tax	Amount charged in an assessment under paragraph 11(1) of Schedule 2 to OTA 1975	The date falling 30 days after the date determined in accordance with paragraph 13 of Schedule 2 to OTA 1975 as the date by which the amount must be paid
[11GA	Excise duties	Amount payable under regulations under section 60A of the Customs and Excise Management Act 1979 (except an amount falling within item 17A, 23 or 24).	The date determined by or under regulations under section 60A of the Customs and Excise Management Act 1979 as the date by which the amount must be paid][6]
[11N	Machine games duty	Amount payable under paragraph 6 of Schedule 24 to FA 2012 (except an amount falling within item 17A, 23 or 24)	The date determined by or under regulations under paragraph 19 of Schedule 24 to FA 2012 as the date by which the amount must be paid][2]

	Tax to which payment relates	*Amount of tax payable*	*Date after which penalty is incurred*
AMOUNTS PAYABLE IN DEFAULT OF A RETURN BEING MADE			
12	Income tax or capital gains tax	Amount payable under section 59B(5A) of TMA 1970	The date falling 30 days after the date specified in section 59B(5A) of TMA 1970 as the date by which the amount must be paid
13	Corporation tax	Amount shown in determination under paragraph 36 or 37 of Schedule 18 to FA 1998	The filing date for the company tax return for the accounting period for which the tax is due (see paragraph 14 of Schedule 18 to FA 1998)
14	Inheritance tax	Amount shown in a determination made by HMRC in the circumstances set out in paragraph 2	The filing date (determined under section 216 of IHTA 1984) for the account in respect of the liability for that amount
15	Stamp duty land tax	Amount shown in determination under paragraph 25 of Schedule 10 to FA 2003 (including that paragraph as applied by section 81(3) of that Act)	The date falling 30 days after the filing date for the return in question
[15A	Annual tax on enveloped dwellings	Amount shown in determination under paragraph 18 of Schedule 31 to FA 2013	The date falling 30 days after the filing date for the return in question][4]
16	Petroleum revenue tax	Amount charged in an assessment made where participator fails to deliver return for a chargeable period	The date falling 6 months and 30 days after the end of the chargeable period
17	Tax falling within any of items 1 to 6, 9[, 10 or 10A][3]	Amount (not falling within any of items 12 to [15A][3]) which is shown in an assessment or determination made by HMRC in the circumstances set out in paragraph 2	The date falling 30 days after the date by which the amount would have been required to be paid if it had been shown in the return in question
AMOUNT SHOWN TO BE DUE IN OTHER ASSESSMENTS, DETERMINATIONS, ETC			
18	Income tax or capital gains tax	Amount payable under section 55 of TMA 1970	The date falling 30 days after the date determined in accordance with section 55(3), (4), (6) or (9) of TMA 1970 as the date by which the amount must be paid
19	Income tax or capital gains tax	Amount payable under section 59B(5) or (6) of TMA 1970	The date falling 30 days after the date specified in section 59B(5) or (6) of TMA 1970 as the date by which the amount must be paid
20	. . .[1]		
21	Inheritance tax	Amount shown in— (*a*) an amendment or correction of a return showing an amount falling within item 7 or 8, or (*b*) a determination made by HMRC in circumstances other than those set out in paragraph 2	The later of— (*a*) the filing date (determined under section 216 of IHTA 1984) for the account in respect of the liability for that amount, and (*b*) the date falling 30 days after the date on which the amendment, correction, assessment or determination is made

	Tax to which payment relates	*Amount of tax payable*	*Date after which penalty is incurred*
22	Petroleum revenue tax	Amount charged in an assessment, or an amendment of an assessment, made in circumstances other than those set out in items 11 and 16	The date falling 30 days after— (*a*) the date by which the amount must be paid, or (*b*) the date on which the assessment or amendment is made, whichever is later
23	Tax falling within any of items 1 to 6, 9 or 10	Amount (not falling within any of items 18 to 20) shown in an amendment or correction of a return showing an amount falling within any of items 1 to 6, 9 or 10	The date falling 30 days after— (*a*) the date by which the amount must be paid, or (*b*) the date on which the amendment or correction is made, whichever is later
24	Tax falling within any of items 1 to 6, 9 or 10	Amount (not falling within any of items 18 to 20) shown in an assessment or determination made by HMRC in circumstances other than those set out in paragraph 2	The date falling 30 days after— (*a*) the date by which the amount must be paid, or (*b*) the date on which the assessment or determination is made, whichever is later

[(5) Sub-paragraph (4) is subject to paragraph 2A.][1]

Commentary—*Simon's Taxes* **A4.560.**

Modifications—FA 2009 Sch 56 has effect as if the Table in this para included references to bank payroll tax (FA 2010 s 22, Sch 1 para 39 (1)–(4)).

FA 2013 Sch 34 para 10(1) (until F(No 3)A 2010 Sch 11 para 2(13)(*a*), (14)(*a*) come into force, this para has effect as if—

- in item 23 the references in the second and third columns to items 1 to 6, 9 or 10 included item 10A, and
- in item 24 the reference in the second column to items 1 to 6, 9 or 10 included item 10A.

Commencement—Finance Act 2009, Schedule 56 (Appointed Day and Consequential Provisions) Order, SI 2010/466: 6 April 2010 appointed as day on which Sch 56 comes into force for the following amounts specified in column 3 of the Table—items 2–4, and items 17, 23 and 24 but only in so far as the tax falls within any of items 2, 3 or 4 (see SI 2010/466 art 3).

Finance Act 2009, Schedules 55 and 56 (Income Tax Self Assessment and Pension Schemes) (Appointed Days and Consequential and Savings Provisions) Order, SI 2011/702 art 2 (appointed day for the coming into force of Sch 56 is 6 April 2011 in relation to an amount of tax which is payable in relation to the tax year 2010–11 or any subsequent tax year and falls within item 1, 12, 18 or 19 of the Table in para 1, or in so far as the tax falls within item 1 of that Table, item 17, 23 or 24 of that Table).

FA 2009 Sch 56, as amended by FA 2013 Sch 34 para 9, is taken to have come into force for the purposes of the annual tax on enveloped dwellings on 17 July 2013 (FA 2013 Sch 34 para 12).

Amendments—[1] Sub-para (5) inserted; in Table, in item 2 column 3, words "(except an amount falling within item 20)" repealed, in item 4 column 4, words substituted for words "section 62", and item 20 repealed, by F(No 3)A 2010 s 27, Sch 11 paras 1, 2(1), (3), (5), (6), (12) with effect from 25 January 2011 (by virtue of SI 2011/132 art 2(*a*)).

[2] Item 11N inserted, and in items 17A, 23, 24 (as to be inserted by F(No 3)A 2010: see prospective amendment note below) reference "11N" to be substituted for reference "11M" by FA 2012 s 191, Sch 24 paras 33, 34 with effect in relation to the playing of machine games on or after 1 February 2013 (and Schs 55, 56, as amended by FA 2012 Sch 24 Part 1, are taken to have come into force for the purposes of machine games duty on that date).

[3] In sub-para (4), in Table, item 6ZA inserted by FA 2013 s 229, Sch 49 paras 1, 7. This amendment is treated as having come into force on 11 December 2012 in relation to an accounting period if the relevant day in relation to that period falls on or after 11 December 2012, subject to transitional provisions where the relevant day falls between 11 December 2012 and 31 March 2013 (inclusive): FA 2013 Sch 49 para 8(3).

NIC

The relevant day, in relation to an accounting period, means the first day after the period of 9 months beginning immediately after the accounting period: FA 2013 Sch 49 para 8(2).

4 In Table, items 10A, 15A inserted, and in item 17, in second column words substituted for words "or 10", and in third column reference substituted for reference "15", by FA 2013 s 164, Sch 34 paras 8, 9 with effect from 17 July 2013.

5 In sub-para (4), words substituted by FA 2013 s 230, Sch 50 paras 10, 11 with effect for defaults made in relation to the tax year 2014–15 and subsequent tax years (see FA 2009 Sch 56 para 6(2), as amended by FA 2013 Sch 50 para 12(3), as to when a default is made in relation to a tax year).

6 In Table, item 11GA inserted by FA 2014 s 101, Sch 21 para 8 with effect from 1 April 2015 (by virtue of SI 2015/812).

7 In Table, item 6ZB inserted by FA 2015 s 104(1), (2) with effect in relation to accounting periods beginning on or after 1 April 2015. For accounting periods that straddle that date, see FA 2015 s 116(2).

8 In Table, item 6ZZA inserted by F(No 2)A 2015 s 38(6), (7) with effect in relation to payments of restitution interest in respect of awards that are finally determined on or after 21 October 2015, whether the interest arose before, on or after that date. HMRC must deduct tax from a payment of restitution interest made on or after 26 October 2015 (see F(No 2)A 2015 s 38(10)). Note however that this Schedule is not yet in force except to the extent specified: see Commencement note above.

9 In Table, item 4A inserted by FA 2016 s 113(9), (10) with effect from 15 September 2016. Note that Sch 56, as amended by FA 2016 s 113, is taken to come into force for the purposes of apprenticeship levy on 15 September 2016 (FA 2016 s 113(18)).

10 In Table, item 3A inserted by FA 2017 s 10, Sch 4 para 20 with effect in relation to transfers made on or after 9 March 2017.

11 In Table, entry inserted by FA 2017 s 56, Sch 11 para 5(1), (2) with effect from 27 April 2017.

Prospective amendments—The following amendments are to be made by F(No 3)A 2010 s 27, Sch 11 paras 1, 2 (as amended by FA 2014 s 103, Sch 22 para 22(1)–(5)) with effect from a date to be appointed by Treasury order.

Note that the inserted text is amended by FA 2012 Sch 24 para 34 with effect in relation to the playing of machine games on or after 1 February 2013, as per the above footnote. See also the modification note above in relation to the application of this para until the coming into force of F(No 3)A 2010 Sch 11 para 2(13)(*a*), (14)(*a*)

Note that the inserted text is also amended by FA 2014 s 196, Sch 28 paras 28, 30 with effect from a date to be appointed. The FA 2014 amendments substitute items 11H, 11I and 11M; these changes are accounted for in the text below—

- in sub-para (2) figure "8J" to be substituted for figure "8";
- in Table—
  - entries to be inserted after items 6, 11, 13, 16 and 17;
  - item 20 to be repealed;
  - in item 23 columns 2, 3, item 24 column 2, words "items 1 to 6A, 6BA, 6BB, 6C, 9, 10 or 11A to 11M" to be substituted for words "items 1 to 6, 9 or 10";
  - in items 23, 24 column 3, words "item 18 or 19" to be substituted for words "any of items 18 to 20".

Table entries as inserted to read as follows—

"6A	Value added tax	Amount payable under section 25(1) of VATA 1994 (except an amount falling within item 6B, 13A, 23 or 24)	The date determined— (*a*) by or under regulations under section 25 of VATA 1994, or (*b*) in accordance with an order under section 28 of that Act, as the date by which the amount must be paid
6B	Value added tax	Amount payable under section 25(1) of VATA 1994 which is an instalment of an amount due in respect of a period of 9 months or more ("amount A")	The date on or before which P must pay any balancing payment or other outstanding payment due in respect of amount A
6BA	Value added tax	Amount payable under relevant special scheme return (as defined in paragraph 16(3) of Schedule 3B to VATA 1994) (except an amount falling within item 13A, 13AA, 13AB, 23 or 24)	The date by which the amount must be paid under the law of the member State which has established the special scheme
6BB	Value added tax	Amount payable under relevant non-UK return (as defined in paragraph 20(3) of Schedule 3BA to VATA 1994) (except an amount falling within item 13A, 13AA, 13AB, 23 or 24)	The date by which the amount must be paid under the law of the member State which has established the non-UK special scheme

6C	Insurance premium tax	Amount payable under regulations under section 54 of FA 1994 (except an amount falling within item 13B, 23 or 24)	The date determined by or under regulations under section 54 of FA 1994 as the date by which the amount must be paid".

"11A	Aggregates levy	Amount payable under regulations under section 25 of FA 2001 (except an amount falling within item 16A, 23 or 24)	The date determined by or under regulations under section 25 of FA 2001 as the date by which the amount must be paid
11B	Climate change levy	Amount payable under regulations under paragraph 41 of Schedule 6 to FA 2000 (except an amount falling within item 16B, 23 or 24)	The date determined by or under regulations under paragraph 41 of Schedule 6 to FA 2000 as the date by which the amount must be paid
11C	Landfill tax	Amount payable under regulations under section 49 of FA 1996 (except an amount falling within item 16C, 23 or 24)	The date determined by or under regulations under section 49 of FA 1996 as the date by which the amount must be paid
11D	Air passenger duty	Amount payable under regulations under section 38 of FA 1994 (except an amount falling within item 17A, 23 or 24)	The date determined by or under regulations under section 38 of FA 1994 as the date by which the amount must be paid
11E	Alcoholic liquor duties	Amount payable under regulations under section 13, 49, 56 or 62 of ALDA 1979 (except an amount falling within item 17A, 23 or 24)	The date determined by or under regulations under section 13, 49, 56 or 62 of ALDA 1979 as the date by which the amount must be paid
11F	Tobacco products duty	Amount payable under regulations under section 7 of TPDA 1979 (except an amount falling within item 17A, 23 or 24)	The date determined by or under regulations under section 7 of TPDA 1979 as the date by which the amount must be paid
11G	Hydrocarbon oil duties	Amount payable under regulations under section 21 or 24 of HODA 1979 (except an amount falling within item 17A, 23 or 24)	The date determined by or under regulations under section 21 or 24 of HODA 1979 as the date by which the amount must be paid
[11H	General betting duty	Amount payable under section 142 of FA 2014	The date determined— (*a*) under section 142 of FA 2014, or (*b*) by or under regulations under section 163 or 167 of that Act, as the date by which the amount must be paid
11I	Pool betting duty	Amount payable under section 151 of FA 2014	The date determined— (*a*) under section 151 of FA 2014, or (*b*) by or under regulations under section 163 or 167 of that Act, as the date by which the amount must be paid]

NIC

11J	Bingo duty	Amount payable under regulations under paragraph 9 of Schedule 3 to BGDA 1981 (except an amount falling within item 17A, 23 or 24)	The date determined by or under regulations under paragraph 9 of Schedule 3 to BGDA 1981 as the date by which the amount must be paid
11K	Lottery duty	Amount payable under section 26 of FA 1993 (except an amount falling within item 17A, 23 or 24)	The date determined — (*a*) by section 26 of FA 1993, or (*b*) by or under regulations under that section, as the date by which the amount must be paid
11L	Gaming duty	Amount payable under section 12 of FA 1997 (except an amount falling within item 17A, 23 or 24)	The date determined by or under regulations under — (*a*) section 12 of FA 1997, or (*b*) paragraph 11 of Schedule 1 to that Act, as the date by which the amount must be paid
[11M	Remote gaming duty	Amount payable under section 162 of FA 2014	The date determined by or under regulations under section 163 or 167 of FA 2014 as the date by which the amount must be paid]".

"13A	Value added tax	Amount assessed under section 73(1) of VATA 1994 in the absence of a return	The date by which the amount would have been required to be paid if it had been shown in the return
13AA	Value added tax	Amount assessed under section 73(1) of VATA 1994, by virtue of paragraph 16 of Schedule 3B to that Act, in the absence of a value added tax return (as defined in paragraph 23(1) of that Schedule)	The date by which the amount would have been required to be paid under the law of the member State under whose law the return was required
13AB	Value added tax	Amount assessed under section 73(1) of VATA 1994, by virtue of paragraph 20 of Schedule 3BA to that Act, in the absence of a relevant non-UK return (as defined in paragraph 38(1) of that Schedule)	The date by which the amount would have been required to be paid under the law of the member State under whose law the return was required
13B	Insurance premium tax	Amount assessed under section 56(1) of FA 1994 in the absence of a return	The date by which the amount would have been required to be paid if it had been shown in the return".

"16A	Aggregates levy	Amount assessed under paragraph 2 or 3 of Schedule 5 to FA 2001 in the absence of a return	The date by which the amount would have been required to be paid if it had been shown in the return
16B	Climate change levy	Amount assessed under paragraph 78 or 79 of Schedule 6 to FA 2000 in the absence of a return	The date by which the amount would have been required to be paid if it had been shown in the return
16C	Landfill tax	Amount assessed under section 50(1) of FA 1996 in the absence of a return	The date by which the amount would have been required to be paid if it had been shown in the return".

"17A	Tax falling within any of items 11D to 11M	Amount assessed under section 12(1) of FA 1994 in the absence of a return	The date by which the amount would have been required to be paid if it had been shown in the return".

In items 17A, 23 and 24 (as inserted), "11N" to be substituted for "11M" by FA 2012 s 191, Sch 24 para 34(*a*) with effect in relation to the playing of machine games on or after 1 February 2013 (and Schs 55, 56, as amended by FA 2012 Sch 24 Part 1, are taken to have come into force for the purposes of machine games duty on that date).

The following amendments to be made by FA 2013 Sch 34 para 10(2) with effect from the coming into force of F(No 3)A 2010 Sch 11 para 2(13)(*a*), (14)(*a*)—

– in item 23, in the second and third columns, for "9, 10" substitute "9 to 10A"; and
– in item 24, in the second column, for "9, 10" substitute "9 to 10A".

In para 1, Table entry to be inserted by FA 2016 s 167, Sch 23 para 9(1), (2) with effect from a day to be appointed. Table entry as inserted to read as follows—

"1A	Income tax or capital gains tax	Amount payable under section 59BA(4) or (5) of TMA 1970	The date falling 30 days after the date specified in section 59BA(4) or (5) of TMA 1970 as the date by which the amount must be paid.".

In para 1, Table entry to be inserted by FA 2017 s 56, Sch 11 para 5(1), (2) with effect from a date to be appointed. Once appointed, the charge to soft drinks industry levy will arise on chargeable events which occur on or after 6 April 2018 (FA 2017 s 31(1)). Table entry as inserted to read as follows—

"11ZA	Soft drinks industry levy	Amount payable under regulations under section 52 of FA 2017 or paragraphs 6 or 14 of Schedule 8 to that Act	The date determined by or under regulations under section 52 of FA 2017".

Assessments and determinations in default of return

2 The circumstances referred to in items 14, 17, 21 and 24 are where—

(*a*) P or another person is required to make or deliver a return falling within any item in the Table in Schedule 55,

(*b*) that person fails to make or deliver the return on or before the date by which it is required to be made or delivered, and

(*c*) if the return had been made or delivered as required, the return would have shown that an amount falling within any of items 1 to 10 was due and payable.

Modifications—FA 2009 Sch 56 has effect as if the reference to a return in this para included a reference to a bank payroll tax return (FA 2010 s 22, Sch 1 para 39(1), (5)).

Until F(No 3)A 2010 Sch 11 para 3 comes into force, para 2(*c*) has effect as if the reference in that para to items 1 to 10 were to items 1 to 10A (FA 2013 Sch 34 para 11).

Commencement—Finance Act 2009, Schedule 56 (Appointed Day and Consequential Provisions) Order, SI 2010/466: 6 April 2010 appointed as day on which Sch 56 comes into force for the following amounts specified in column 3 of the Table—items 2–4, and items 17, 23 and 24 but only in so far as the tax falls within any of items 2, 3 or 4 (see SI 2010/466 art 3).

Finance Act 2009, Schedules 55 and 56 (Income Tax Self Assessment and Pension Schemes) (Appointed Days and Consequential and Savings Provisions) Order, SI 2011/702 art 2 (appointed day for the coming into force of Sch 56 is 6 April 2011 in relation to an amount of tax which is payable in relation to the tax year 2010–11 or any subsequent tax year and falls within item 1, 12, 18 or 19 of the Table in para 1, or in so far as the tax falls within item 1 of that Table, item 17, 23 or 24 of that Table).

Prospective amendments—In sub-para (*c*) figure "11M" to be substituted for figure "10" by F(No 3)A 2010 s 27, Sch 11 paras 1, 3 with effect from a date to be appointed by Treasury order. Also see Modification note above.

In sub-para (*c*) "11N" substituted for "11M" (as prospectively substituted by F(No 3)A 2010) by FA 2012 s 191, Sch 24 para 34(*b*) with effect in relation to the playing of machine games on or after 1 February 2013 (and Schs 55, 56, as amended by FA 2012 Sch 24 Part 1, are taken to have come into force for the purposes of machine games duty on that date).

[Different penalty date for certain PAYE payments

2A—(1) PAYE regulations may provide that, in relation to specified payments of tax falling within item 2, the penalty date is a specified date later than that determined in accordance with column 4 of the Table.

(2) In sub-paragraph (1) "specified" means specified in the regulations.][1]

Commencement—Finance Act 2009, Schedules 55 and 56 (Income Tax Self Assessment and Pension Schemes) (Appointed Days and Consequential and Savings Provisions) Order, SI 2011/702 art 2 (appointed day for the coming into force of Sch 56 is 6 April 2011 in relation to an amount of tax which is payable in relation to the tax year 2010–11 or any subsequent tax year and falls within item 1, 12, 18 or 19 of the Table in para 1, or in so far as the tax falls within item 1 of that Table, item 17, 23 or 24 of that Table).

Amendments—[1] This para and preceding cross-head inserted by F(No 3)A 2010 s 27, Sch 11 paras 1, 4 with effect from 25 January 2011 (by virtue of SI 2011/132 art 2(*b*)).

Amount of penalty: occasional amounts and amounts in respect of periods of 6 months or more

3—(1) This paragraph applies in the case of—

(*a*) a payment of tax falling within any of items 1, 3 and 7 to 24 in the Table,

[(*aa*) a payment of tax falling within [item 4A or][2] item 6ZB in the Table,][1]

(*b*) a payment of tax falling within item 2 or 4 which relates to a period of 6 months or more, and

(*c*) a payment of tax falling within item 2 which is payable under regulations under section 688A of ITEPA 2003 (recovery from other persons of amounts due from managed service companies).

[(*ca*) an amount in respect of apprenticeship levy falling within item 4A which is payable by virtue of regulations under section 106 of FA 2016 (recovery from third parties).][2]

(2) P is liable to a penalty of 5% of the unpaid tax.

(3) If any amount of the tax is unpaid after the end of the period of 5 months beginning with the penalty date, P is liable to a penalty of 5% of that amount.

(4) If any amount of the tax is unpaid after the end of the period of 11 months beginning with the penalty date, P is liable to a penalty of 5% of that amount.

Modifications—FA 2009 Sch 56 has effect as if sub-para (1)(*a*) included a reference to a payment of bank payroll tax (FA 2010 s 22, Sch 1 para 39(1), (6)).

Commencement—Finance Act 2009, Schedule 56 (Appointed Day and Consequential Provisions) Order, SI 2010/466: 6 April 2010 appointed as day on which Sch 56 comes into force for the following amounts specified in column 3 of the Table—items 2–4, and items 17, 23 and 24 but only in so far as the tax falls within any of items 2, 3 or 4 (see SI 2010/466 art 3).

Finance Act 2009, Schedules 55 and 56 (Income Tax Self Assessment and Pension Schemes) (Appointed Days and Consequential and Savings Provisions) Order, SI 2011/702 art 2 (appointed day for the coming into force of Sch 56 is 6 April 2011 in relation to an amount of tax which is payable in relation to the tax year 2010–11 or any subsequent tax year and falls within item 1, 12, 18 or 19 of the Table in para 1, or in so far as the tax falls within item 1 of that Table, item 17, 23 or 24 of that Table).

Amendments—[1] Sub-para (1)(*aa*) inserted by FA 2015 s 104(1), (3) with effect in relation to accounting periods beginning on or after 1 April 2015. For accounting periods that straddle that date, see FA 2015 s 116(2).

[2] Words in sub-para (1)(*b*) inserted, and sub-para (1)(*ca*) inserted by FA 2016 s 113(9), (11) with effect from 15 September 2016.

Prospective amendments—In sub-para (1)(*a*) words "items 1, 3, 6B, 7 to 11 and 12 to 24" to be substituted for words "items 1, 3 and 7 to 24", in sub-para (1)(*b*) words "any of items 2, 4, 6A, 6C and 11A to 11M" to be substituted for words "item 2 or 4" and word "and" at the end to be repealed, and sub-paras (1)(*d*) and preceding word "and", and (1A) to be inserted, by F(No 3)A 2010 s 27, Sch 11 paras 1, 5 with effect from a date to be appointed by Treasury order. Sub-paras (1)(*d*), (1A) as inserted to read—

"(*d*) a payment of tax falling within item 6A which relates to a transitional period for the purposes of the annual accounting scheme.".

"(1A) In sub-paragraph (1)(*d*), a transitional period for the purposes of the annual accounting scheme is a prescribed accounting period (within the meaning of section 25(1) of VATA 1994) which—

(a) ends on the day immediately preceding the date indicated by the Commissioners for Her Majesty's Revenue and Customs in a notification of authorisation under regulation 50 of the Value Added Tax Regulations 1995 (SI 1995/2518) (admission to annual accounting scheme), or

(b) begins on the day immediately following the end of the last period of 12 months for which such an authorisation has effect.".

In sub-para (1)(*b*) "11N" to be substituted for "11M" by FA 2012 s 191, Sch 24 para 34(*c*) with effect in relation to the playing of machine games on or after 1 February 2013 (and Schs 55, 56, as amended by FA 2012 Sch 24 Part 1, are taken to have come into force for the purposes of machine games duty on that date).

In sub-para (1)(*a*), words "1A," to be inserted after words "items 1," by FA 2016 s 167, Sch 23 para 9(1), (3) with effect from a day to be appointed.

4—(1) This paragraph applies in the case of a payment of tax falling within item 5[, 6 or 6ZZA][1] in the Table.

(2) P is liable to a penalty of 5% of the unpaid tax.

(3) If any amount of the tax is unpaid after the end of the period of 3 months beginning with the penalty date, P is liable to a penalty of 5% of that amount.

(4) If any amount of the tax is unpaid after the end of the period of 9 months beginning with the penalty date, P is liable to a penalty of 5% of that amount.

Commencement—Finance Act 2009, Schedules 55 and 56 (Income Tax Self Assessment and Pension Schemes) (Appointed Days and Consequential and Savings Provisions) Order, SI 2011/702 art 2 (appointed day for the coming into force of Sch 56 is 6 April 2011 in relation to an amount of tax which is payable in relation to the tax year 2010–11 or any subsequent tax year and falls within item 1, 12, 18 or 19 of the Table in para 1, or in so far as the tax falls within item 1 of that Table, item 17, 23 or 24 of that Table).

Amendments—[1] In sub-para (1), words substituted for words "or 6" by F(No 2)A 2015 s 38(6), (8) with effect in relation to payments of restitution interest in respect of awards that are finally determined on or after 21 October 2015, whether the interest arose before, on or after that date. HMRC must deduct tax from a payment of restitution interest made on or after 26 October 2015 (see F(No 2)A 2015 s 38(10)). Note however that this Schedule is not yet in force except to the extent specified: see Commencement note above.

Amount of penalty: PAYE and CIS amounts [etc.]

5—(1) Paragraphs 6 to 8 apply in the case of a payment of tax falling within item 2[, 4 or 4A][1] in the Table.

(2) But those paragraphs do not apply in the case of a payment mentioned in paragraph 3(1)(*b*) [, (*c*) or (*ca*).][1]

Commencement—Finance Act 2009, Schedule 56 (Appointed Day and Consequential Provisions) Order, SI 2010/466: 6 April 2010 appointed as day on which Sch 56 comes into force for the following amounts specified in column 3 of the Table—items 2–4, and items 17, 23 and 24 but only in so far as the tax falls within any of items 2, 3 or 4 (see SI 2010/466 art 3).

Finance Act 2009, Schedules 55 and 56 (Income Tax Self Assessment and Pension Schemes) (Appointed Days and Consequential and Savings Provisions) Order, SI 2011/702 art 2 (appointed day for the coming into force of Sch 56 is 6 April 2011 in relation to an amount of tax which is payable in relation to the tax year 2010–11 or any subsequent tax year and falls within item 1, 12, 18 or 19 of the Table in para 1, or in so far as the tax falls within item 1 of that Table, item 17, 23 or 24 of that Table).

Amendments—[1] Word in heading inserted, words in sub-para (1) substituted for words "or 4", and words in sub-para (2) substituted for words "or (*c*)", by FA 2016 s 113(9), (12), (13), (15) with effect from 15 September 2016.

[6—[(1) P is liable to a penalty under this paragraph, in relation to each tax, each time that P makes a default in relation to a tax year.][2]

(2) For the purposes of this paragraph, P makes a default [in relation to a tax year][2] when P fails to make one of the following payments (or to pay an amount comprising two or more of those payments) in full on or before the date on which it becomes due and payable—

(*a*) a payment under PAYE regulations [of tax payable in relation to the tax year][2];

(*b*) a payment of earnings-related contributions within the meaning of the Social Security (Contributions) Regulations 2001 (SI 2001/1004) [payable in relation to the tax year][2];

[(*ba*) a payment under regulations under section 105 of FA 2016 of an amount in respect of apprenticeship levy payable in relation to the tax year;][2]

(*c*) a payment due under the Income Tax (Construction Industry Scheme) Regulations 2005 (SI 2005/2045) [payable in relation to the tax year][2];

(*d*) a repayment in respect of a student loan due under the Education (Student Loans) (Repayments) Regulations 2009 (SI 2009/470) or the Education (Student Loans) (Repayments) Regulations (Northern Ireland) 2000 (S.R. 2000 No 121) [and due for the tax year][2].

[(3) But where a failure to make one of those payments (or to pay an amount comprising two or more of those payments) would, apart from this sub-paragraph, constitute the first default in relation to a tax year, that failure does not count as a default in relation to that year for the purposes of a penalty under this paragraph.

(4) The amount of the penalty for a default made in relation to a tax year is determined by reference to—

(*a*) the amount of the tax comprised in the default, and

(*b*) the number of previous defaults that P has made in relation to the same tax year.

(5) If the default is P's 1st, 2nd or 3rd default in relation to the tax year, P is liable, at the time of the default, to a penalty of 1% of the amount of tax comprised in the default.

(6) If the default is P's 4th, 5th or 6th default in relation to the tax year, P is liable, at the time of the default, to a penalty of 2% of the amount of tax comprised in the default.

(7) If the default is P's 7th, 8th or 9th default in relation to the tax year, P is liable, at the time of the default, to a penalty of 3% of the amount of tax comprised in the default.

(7A) If the default is P's 10th or subsequent default in relation to the tax year, P is liable, at the time of the default, to a penalty of 4% of the amount of tax comprised in the default.][2]

(8) For the purposes of this paragraph—

(*a*) the amount of a tax comprised in a default is the amount of that tax comprised in the payment which P fails to make;

[(*b*) a previous default counts for the purposes of subparagraphs (5) to (7A) even if it is remedied before the time of the default giving rise to the penalty.][2]

[(8A) Regulations made by the Commissioners for Her Majesty's Revenue and Customs may specify—

(*a*) circumstances in which, for the purposes of sub-paragraph (2), a payment of less than the full amount may be treated as a payment in full;

(*b*) circumstances in which sub-paragraph (3) is not to apply.

(8B) Regulations under sub-paragraph (8A) may—

(*a*) make different provision for different cases, and

(*b*) include incidental, consequential and supplementary provision.][2]

(9) The Treasury may by order made by statutory instrument make such amendments to sub-paragraph (2) as they think fit in consequence of any amendment, revocation or re-enactment of the regulations mentioned in that sub-paragraph.][1]

Commencement—Finance Act 2009, Schedule 56 (Appointed Day and Consequential Provisions) Order, SI 2010/466: 6 April 2010 appointed as day on which Sch 56 comes into force for the following amounts specified in column 3 of the Table—items 2–4, and items 17, 23 and 24 but only in so far as the tax falls within any of items 2, 3 or 4 (see SI 2010/466 art 3).

Finance Act 2009, Schedules 55 and 56 (Income Tax Self Assessment and Pension Schemes) (Appointed Days and Consequential and Savings Provisions) Order, SI 2011/702 art 2 (appointed day for the coming into force of Sch 56 is 6 April 2011 in relation to an amount of tax which is payable in relation to the tax year 2010–11 or any subsequent tax year and falls within item 1, 12, 18 or 19 of the Table in para 1, or in so far as the tax falls within item 1 of that Table, item 17, 23 or 24 of that Table).

Regulations—Income Tax (Pay As You Earn) and the Income Tax (Construction Industry Scheme) (Amendment) Regulations, SI 2014/472.

Amendments—[1] This para substituted by F(No 3)A 2010 s 27, Sch 11 paras 1, 6 with effect from 25 January 2011 (by virtue of SI 2011/132 art 2(*b*)).

[2] Sub-paras (1), (8)(*b*) substituted, sub-paras (3)–(7A) substituted for sub-paras (3)–(7), in sub-para (2), (2)(*a*)–(*d*), words inserted, and sub-paras (8A), (8B) inserted, by FA 2013 s 230, Sch 50 paras 10, 12 with effect for defaults made in relation to the tax year 2014–15 and subsequent tax years (see FA 2009 Sch 56 para 6(2), as amended by FA 2013 Sch 50 para 12(3), as to when a default is made in relation to a tax year)—

7 If any amount of the tax is unpaid after the end of the period of 6 months beginning with the penalty date, P is liable to a penalty of 5% of that amount.

Commencement—Finance Act 2009, Schedule 56 (Appointed Day and Consequential Provisions) Order, SI 2010/466: 6 April 2010 appointed as day on which Sch 56 comes into force for the following amounts specified in column 3 of the Table—items 2–4, and items 17, 23 and 24 but only in so far as the tax falls within any of items 2, 3 or 4 (see SI 2010/466 art 3).

Finance Act 2009, Schedules 55 and 56 (Income Tax Self Assessment and Pension Schemes) (Appointed Days and Consequential and Savings Provisions) Order, SI 2011/702 art 2 (appointed day for the coming into force of Sch 56 is 6 April 2011 in relation to an amount of tax which is payable in relation to the tax year 2010–11 or any subsequent tax year and falls within item 1, 12, 18 or 19 of the Table in para 1, or in so far as the tax falls within item 1 of that Table, item 17, 23 or 24 of that Table).

8 If any amount of the tax is unpaid after the end of the period of 12 months beginning with the penalty date, P is liable to a penalty of 5% of that amount.

Commencement—Finance Act 2009, Schedule 56 (Appointed Day and Consequential Provisions) Order, SI 2010/466: 6 April 2010 appointed as day on which Sch 56 comes into force for the following amounts specified in column 3 of the Table—items 2–4, and items 17, 23 and 24 but only in so far as the tax falls within any of items 2, 3 or 4 (see SI 2010/466 art 3).

Finance Act 2009, Schedules 55 and 56 (Income Tax Self Assessment and Pension Schemes) (Appointed Days and Consequential and Savings Provisions) Order, SI 2011/702 art 2 (appointed day for the coming into force of Sch 56 is 6 April 2011 in relation to an amount of tax which is payable in relation to the tax year 2010–11 or any subsequent tax year and falls within item 1, 12, 18 or 19 of the Table in para 1, or in so far as the tax falls within item 1 of that Table, item 17, 23 or 24 of that Table).

[Amount of penalty: amounts in respect of periods of between 2 and 6 months

8A—(1) Paragraphs 8B to 8E apply in the case of a payment of tax falling within any of items 6A, 6BA, 6BB, 6C and 11A to [11N] in the Table which relates to a period of less than 6 months but more than 2 months.

(2) But those paragraphs do not apply in the case of a payment mentioned in paragraph 3(1)(*d*).

(3) Paragraph 8K sets out how payments on account of VAT (item 6A) are to be treated for the purposes of paragraphs 8B to 8E.]

Commencement—Finance Act 2009, Schedules 55 and 56 (Income Tax Self Assessment and Pension Schemes) (Appointed Days and Consequential and Savings Provisions) Order, SI 2011/702 art 2 (appointed day for the coming into force of Sch 56 is 6 April 2011 in relation to an amount of tax which is payable in relation to the tax year 2010–11 or any subsequent tax year and falls within item 1, 12, 18 or 19 of the Table in para 1, or in so far as the tax falls within item 1 of that Table, item 17, 23 or 24 of that Table).

Prospective amendments—Paras 8A–8J and preceding cross-heads to be inserted by F(No 3)A 2010 s 27, Sch 11 paras 1, 7 (as amended by FA 2014 s 103, Sch 22 para 22(6)) with effect from a date to be appointed by Treasury order.

In sub-para (1) "11N" substituted for "11M" by FA 2012 s 191, Sch 24 para 34(*d*) with effect in relation to the playing of machine games on or after 1 February 2013 (and Schs 55, 56, as amended by FA 2012 Sch 24 Part 1, are taken to have come into force for the purposes of machine games duty on that date).

[8B—(1) A penalty period begins to run on the penalty date for the payment of tax.
(2) The penalty period ends with the day 12 months after the date specified in or for the purposes of column 4 for the payment, unless it is extended under paragraph 8C(2)(*c*) or 8H(2)(*c*).]

Commencement—Finance Act 2009, Schedules 55 and 56 (Income Tax Self Assessment and Pension Schemes) (Appointed Days and Consequential and Savings Provisions) Order, SI 2011/702 art 2 (appointed day for the coming into force of Sch 56 is 6 April 2011 in relation to an amount of tax which is payable in relation to the tax year 2010–11 or any subsequent tax year and falls within item 1, 12, 18 or 19 of the Table in para 1, or in so far as the tax falls within item 1 of that Table, item 17, 23 or 24 of that Table).

Prospective amendments—Paras 8A–8J and preceding cross-heads to be inserted by F(No 3)A 2010 s 27, Sch 11 paras 1, 7 with effect from a date to be appointed by Treasury order.

[8C—(1) This paragraph applies if—

(*a*) a penalty period has begun under paragraph 8B or 8G because P has failed to make a payment ("payment A"), and

(*b*) before the end of the period, P fails to make another payment ("payment B") falling within the same item in the Table as payment A.

(2) In such a case—

(*a*) paragraph 8B(1) does not apply to the failure to make payment B,

(*b*) P is liable to a penalty under this paragraph for that failure, And

(*c*) the penalty period that has begun is extended so that it ends with the day 12 months after the date specified in or for the purposes of column 4 for payment B.

(3) The amount of the penalty under this paragraph is determined by reference to the number of defaults that P has made during the penalty period.

(4) If the default is P's first default during the penalty period, P is liable, at the time of the default, to a penalty of 2% of the amount of the default.

(5) If the default is P's second default during the penalty period, P is liable, at the time of the default, to a penalty of 3% of the amount of the default.

(6) If the default is P's third or a subsequent default during the penalty period, P is liable, at the time of the default, to a penalty of 4% of the amount of the default.

(7) For the purposes of this paragraph—

(*a*) P makes a default when P fails to pay an amount of tax in full on or before the date on which it becomes due and payable;

(*b*) in accordance with sub-paragraph (1)(*b*), the references in sub-paragraphs (3) to (6) to a default are references to a default in relation to the tax to which payments A and B relate;

(*c*) a default counts for the purposes of those sub-paragraphs if (but only if) the period to which the payment relates is less than 6 months;

(*d*) the amount of a default is the amount which P fails to pay.

(8) A penalty period may be extended more than once under subparagraph (2)(*c*).]

Commencement—Finance Act 2009, Schedules 55 and 56 (Income Tax Self Assessment and Pension Schemes) (Appointed Days and Consequential and Savings Provisions) Order, SI 2011/702 art 2 (appointed day for the coming into force of Sch 56 is 6 April 2011 in relation to an amount of tax which is payable in relation to the tax year 2010–11 or any subsequent tax year and falls within item 1, 12, 18 or 19 of the Table in para 1, or in so far as the tax falls within item 1 of that Table, item 17, 23 or 24 of that Table).

Prospective amendments—Paras 8A–8J and preceding cross-heads to be inserted by F(No 3)A 2010 s 27, Sch 11 paras 1, 7 with effect from a date to be appointed by Treasury order.

[8D If any amount of the tax is unpaid after the end of the period of 6 months beginning with the penalty date, P is liable to a penalty of 5% of that amount.]

Commencement—Finance Act 2009, Schedules 55 and 56 (Income Tax Self Assessment and Pension Schemes) (Appointed Days and Consequential and Savings Provisions) Order, SI 2011/702 art 2 (appointed day for the coming into force of Sch 56 is 6 April 2011 in relation to an amount of tax which is payable in relation to the tax year 2010–11 or any subsequent tax year and falls within item 1, 12, 18 or 19 of the Table in para 1, or in so far as the tax falls within item 1 of that Table, item 17, 23 or 24 of that Table).

Prospective amendments—Paras 8A–8J and preceding cross-heads to be inserted by F(No 3)A 2010 s 27, Sch 11 paras 1, 7 with effect from a date to be appointed by Treasury order.

[8E If any amount of the tax is unpaid after the end of the period of 12 months beginning with the penalty date, P is liable to a penalty of 5% of that amount.]

Commencement—Finance Act 2009, Schedules 55 and 56 (Income Tax Self Assessment and Pension Schemes) (Appointed Days and Consequential and Savings Provisions) Order, SI 2011/702 art 2 (appointed day for the coming into force of Sch 56 is 6 April 2011 in relation to an amount of tax which is payable in relation to the tax year 2010–11 or any subsequent tax year and falls within item 1, 12, 18 or 19 of the Table in para 1, or in so far as the tax falls within item 1 of that Table, item 17, 23 or 24 of that Table).

Prospective amendments—Paras 8A–8J and preceding cross-heads to be inserted by F(No 3)A 2010 s 27, Sch 11 paras 1, 7 with effect from a date to be appointed by Treasury order.

NIC

[Amount of penalty: amounts in respect of periods of 2 months or less

8F—(1) Paragraphs 8G to 8J apply in the case of a payment of tax falling within any of items 6A, 6C and 11A to [11N] in the Table which relates to a period of 2 months or less.

(2) But those paragraphs do not apply in the case of a payment mentioned in paragraph 3(1)(*d*).]

Commencement—Finance Act 2009, Schedules 55 and 56 (Income Tax Self Assessment and Pension Schemes) (Appointed Days and Consequential and Savings Provisions) Order, SI 2011/702 art 2 (appointed day for the coming into force of Sch 56 is 6 April 2011 in relation to an amount of tax which is payable in relation to the tax year 2010–11 or any subsequent tax year and falls within item 1, 12, 18 or 19 of the Table in para 1, or in so far as the tax falls within item 1 of that Table, item 17, 23 or 24 of that Table).

Prospective amendments—Paras 8A–8J and preceding cross-heads to be inserted by F(No 3)A 2010 s 27, Sch 11 paras 1, 7 with effect from a date to be appointed by Treasury order.

In sub-para (1) "11N" substituted for "11M" by FA 2012 s 191, Sch 24 para 34(*e*) with effect in relation to the playing of machine games on or after 1 February 2013 (and Schs 55, 56, as amended by FA 2012 Sch 24 Part 1, are taken to have come into force for the purposes of machine games duty on that date).

[8G—(1) A penalty period begins to run on the penalty date for the payment of tax.

(2) The penalty period ends with the day 12 months after the date specified in or for the purposes of column 4 for the payment, unless it is extended under paragraph 8C(2)(*c*) or 8H(2)(*c*).]

Commencement—Finance Act 2009, Schedules 55 and 56 (Income Tax Self Assessment and Pension Schemes) (Appointed Days and Consequential and Savings Provisions) Order, SI 2011/702 art 2 (appointed day for the coming into force of Sch 56 is 6 April 2011 in relation to an amount of tax which is payable in relation to the tax year 2010–11 or any subsequent tax year and falls within item 1, 12, 18 or 19 of the Table in para 1, or in so far as the tax falls within item 1 of that Table, item 17, 23 or 24 of that Table).

Prospective amendments—Paras 8A–8J and preceding cross-heads to be inserted by F(No 3)A 2010 s 27, Sch 11 paras 1, 7 with effect from a date to be appointed by Treasury order.

[8H—(1) This paragraph applies if—

(*a*) a penalty period has begun under paragraph 8B or 8G because P has failed to make a payment ("payment A"), and

(*b*) before the end of the period, P fails to make another payment ("payment B") falling within the same item in the Table as payment A.

(2) In such a case—

(*a*) paragraph 8G(1) does not apply to the failure to make payment B,

(*b*) P is liable to a penalty under this paragraph for that failure, and

(*c*) the penalty period that has begun is extended so that it ends with the day 12 months after the date specified in or for the purposes of column 4 for payment B.

(3) The amount of the penalty under this paragraph is determined by reference to the number of defaults that P has made during the penalty period.

(4) If the default is P's first, second or third default during the penalty period, P is liable, at the time of the default, to a penalty of 1% of the amount of the default.

(5) If the default is P's fourth, fifth or sixth default during the penalty period, P is liable, at the time of the default, to a penalty of 2% of the amount of the default.

(6) If the default is P's seventh, eighth or ninth default during the penalty period, P is liable, at the time of the default, to a penalty of 3% of the amount of the default.

(7) If the default is P's tenth or a subsequent default during the penalty period, P is liable, at the time of the default, to a penalty of 4% of the amount of the default.

(8) For the purposes of this paragraph—

(*a*) P makes a default when P fails to pay an amount of tax in full on or before the date on which it becomes due and payable;

(*b*) in accordance with sub-paragraph (1)(*b*), the references in sub-paragraphs (3) to (7) to a default are references to a default in relation to the tax to which payments A and B relate;

(*c*) a default counts for the purposes of those sub-paragraphs if (but only if) the period to which the payment relates is less than 6 months;

(*d*) the amount of a default is the amount which P fails to pay.

(9) A penalty period may be extended more than once under subparagraph (2)(*c*).]

Commencement—Finance Act 2009, Schedules 55 and 56 (Income Tax Self Assessment and Pension Schemes) (Appointed Days and Consequential and Savings Provisions) Order, SI 2011/702 art 2 (appointed day for the coming into force of Sch 56 is 6 April 2011 in relation to an amount of tax which is payable in relation to the tax year 2010–11 or any subsequent tax year and falls within item 1, 12, 18 or 19 of the Table in para 1, or in so far as the tax falls within item 1 of that Table, item 17, 23 or 24 of that Table).

Prospective amendments—Paras 8A–8J and preceding cross-heads to be inserted by F(No 3)A 2010 s 27, Sch 11 paras 1, 7 with effect from a date to be appointed by Treasury order.

[8I If any amount of the tax is unpaid after the end of the period of 6 months beginning with the penalty date, P is liable to a penalty of 5% of that amount.]

Commencement—Finance Act 2009, Schedules 55 and 56 (Income Tax Self Assessment and Pension Schemes) (Appointed Days and Consequential and Savings Provisions) Order, SI 2011/702 art 2 (appointed day for the coming into force of Sch 56 is

6 April 2011 in relation to an amount of tax which is payable in relation to the tax year 2010–11 or any subsequent tax year and falls within item 1, 12, 18 or 19 of the Table in para 1, or in so far as the tax falls within item 1 of that Table, item 17, 23 or 24 of that Table).

Prospective amendments—Paras 8A–8J and preceding cross-heads to be inserted by F(No 3)A 2010 s 27, Sch 11 paras 1, 7 with effect from a date to be appointed by Treasury order.

[8J If any amount of the tax is unpaid after the end of the period of 12 months beginning with the penalty date, P is liable to a penalty of 5% of that amount.]

Commencement—Finance Act 2009, Schedules 55 and 56 (Income Tax Self Assessment and Pension Schemes) (Appointed Days and Consequential and Savings Provisions) Order, SI 2011/702 art 2 (appointed day for the coming into force of Sch 56 is 6 April 2011 in relation to an amount of tax which is payable in relation to the tax year 2010–11 or any subsequent tax year and falls within item 1, 12, 18 or 19 of the Table in para 1, or in so far as the tax falls within item 1 of that Table, item 17, 23 or 24 of that Table).

Prospective amendments—Paras 8A–8J and preceding cross-heads to be inserted by F(No 3)A 2010 s 27, Sch 11 paras 1, 7 with effect from a date to be appointed by Treasury order.

[Calculation of unpaid VAT: treatment of payments on account

8K—(1) Where P is required, by virtue of an order under section 28 of VATA 1994, to make any payment on account of VAT—

(*a*) each payment is to be treated for the purposes of this Schedule as relating to the prescribed accounting period in respect of which it is to be paid (and not as relating to the interval between the dates on which payments on account are required to be made), and

(*b*) the amount of tax unpaid in respect of the prescribed accounting period is the total of the amounts produced by paragraphs (*a*) and (*b*) of sub-paragraph (3).

(2) In determining that total—

(*a*) if there is more than one amount of POAD or POAT, those amounts are to be added together, and

(*b*) if the amount produced by sub-paragraph (3)(*b*) is less than zero, that amount is to be disregarded.

(3) The amounts are—

(*a*) POAD – POAT, and

(*b*) BPD – BPT.

(4) In this paragraph—

POAD is the amount of any payment on account due in respect of the prescribed accounting period,

POAT is the amount of any payment on account paid on time (that is, on or before the date on which it was required to be made),

BPD (which is the balancing payment due in respect of the prescribed accounting period) is equal to PAPD – POAD, and

BPT (which is the amount paid on time in satisfaction of any liability to pay BPD) is equal to PAPP – POAP.

(5) In sub-paragraph (4)—

PAPD is the amount of VAT due in respect of the prescribed accounting period,

PAPP is the total amount paid, on or before the last day on which P is required to make payments in respect of that period, in satisfaction of any liability to pay PAPD, and

POAP is the total amount paid, on or before that day (but whether or not paid on time), in satisfaction of any liability to pay POAD.]

Commencement—Finance Act 2009, Schedules 55 and 56 (Income Tax Self Assessment and Pension Schemes) (Appointed Days and Consequential and Savings Provisions) Order, SI 2011/702 art 2 (appointed day for the coming into force of Sch 56 is 6 April 2011 in relation to an amount of tax which is payable in relation to the tax year 2010–11 or any subsequent tax year and falls within item 1, 12, 18 or 19 of the Table in para 1, or in so far as the tax falls within item 1 of that Table, item 17, 23 or 24 of that Table).

Prospective amendments—Para 8K and preceding cross-head to be inserted by F(No 3)A 2010 s 27, Sch 11 paras 1, 8 with effect from a date to be appointed by Treasury order.

Special reduction

9—(1) If HMRC think it right because of special circumstances, they may reduce a penalty under any paragraph of this Schedule.

(2) In sub-paragraph (1) "special circumstances" does not include—

(*a*) ability to pay, or

(*b*) the fact that a potential loss of revenue from one taxpayer is balanced by a potential over-payment by another.

(3) In sub-paragraph (1) the reference to reducing a penalty includes a reference to—

(*a*) staying a penalty, and

(*b*) agreeing a compromise in relation to proceedings for a penalty.

Commencement—Finance Act 2009, Schedule 56 (Appointed Day and Consequential Provisions) Order, SI 2010/466: 6 April 2010 appointed as day on which Sch 56 comes into force for the following amounts specified in column 3 of the Table—items 2–4, and items 17, 23 and 24 but only in so far as the tax falls within any of items 2, 3 or 4 (see SI 2010/466 art 3).
Finance Act 2009, Schedules 55 and 56 (Income Tax Self Assessment and Pension Schemes) (Appointed Days and Consequential and Savings Provisions) Order, SI 2011/702 art 2 (appointed day for the coming into force of Sch 56 is 6 April 2011 in relation to an amount of tax which is payable in relation to the tax year 2010–11 or any subsequent tax year and falls within item 1, 12, 18 or 19 of the Table in para 1, or in so far as the tax falls within item 1 of that Table, item 17, 23 or 24 of that Table).
Cross-references—See FA 2014 s 226(7) (application of paras 9–18 of this Schedule, with any necessary modifications, to penalties for failure to pay accelerated payment).

[Interaction with other penalties and late payment surcharges

9A In the application of the following provisions, no account shall be taken of a penalty under this Schedule—

(*a*) section 97A of TMA 1970 (multiple penalties),

(*b*) paragraph 12(2) of Schedule 24 to FA 2007 (interaction with other penalties), and

(*c*) paragraph 15(1) of Schedule 41 to FA 2008 (interaction with other penalties).][1]

Cross-references—See FA 2014 s 226(7) (application of paras 9–18 of this Schedule, with any necessary modifications, to penalties for failure to pay accelerated payment).
Amendments—[1] Paragraph 9A and preceding cross-head inserted by FA 2013 s 230, Sch 50 paras 10, 13 with effect for defaults made in relation to the tax year 2014–15 and subsequent tax years (see FA 2009 Sch 56 para 6(2), as amended by FA 2013 Sch 50 para 12(3), as to when a default is made in relation to a tax year).

Suspension of penalty during currency of agreement for deferred payment

10—(1) This paragraph applies if—

(*a*) P fails to pay an amount of tax when it becomes due and payable,

(*b*) P makes a request to HMRC that payment of the amount of tax be deferred, and

(*c*) HMRC agrees that payment of that amount may be deferred for a period ("the deferral period").

(2) If P would (apart from this sub-paragraph) become liable, between the date on which P makes the request and the end of the deferral period, to a penalty under any paragraph of this Schedule for failing to pay that amount, P is not liable to that penalty.

(3) But if—

(*a*) P breaks the agreement (see sub-paragraph (4)), and

(*b*) HMRC serves on P a notice specifying any penalty to which P would become liable apart from sub-paragraph (2),

P becomes liable, at the date of the notice, to that penalty.

(4) P breaks an agreement if—

(*a*) P fails to pay the amount of tax in question when the deferral period ends, or

(*b*) the deferral is subject to P complying with a condition (including a condition that part of the amount be paid during the deferral period) and P fails to comply with it.

(5) If the agreement mentioned in sub-paragraph (1)(*c*) is varied at any time by a further agreement between P and HMRC, this paragraph applies from that time to the agreement as varied.

Commencement—Finance Act 2009, Schedule 56 (Appointed Day and Consequential Provisions) Order, SI 2010/466: 6 April 2010 appointed as day on which Sch 56 comes into force for the following amounts specified in column 3 of the Table—items 2–4, and items 17, 23 and 24 but only in so far as the tax falls within any of items 2, 3 or 4 (see SI 2010/466 art 3).
Finance Act 2009, Schedules 55 and 56 (Income Tax Self Assessment and Pension Schemes) (Appointed Days and Consequential and Savings Provisions) Order, SI 2011/702 art 2 (appointed day for the coming into force of Sch 56 is 6 April 2011 in relation to an amount of tax which is payable in relation to the tax year 2010–11 or any subsequent tax year and falls within item 1, 12, 18 or 19 of the Table in para 1, or in so far as the tax falls within item 1 of that Table, item 17, 23 or 24 of that Table).
Cross-references—See FA 2014 s 226(7) (application of paras 9–18 of this Schedule, with any necessary modifications, to penalties for failure to pay accelerated payment).

Assessment

11—(1) Where P is liable for a penalty under any paragraph of this Schedule HMRC must—

(*a*) assess the penalty,

(*b*) notify P, and

(*c*) state in the notice the period in respect of which the penalty is assessed.

(2) A penalty under any paragraph of this Schedule must be paid before the end of the period of 30 days beginning with the day on which notice of the assessment of the penalty is issued.

(3) An assessment of a penalty under any paragraph of this Schedule—

(*a*) is to be treated for procedural purposes in the same way as an assessment to tax (except in respect of a matter expressly provided for by this Schedule),

(*b*) may be enforced as if it were an assessment to tax, and

(*c*) may be combined with an assessment to tax.

(4) A supplementary assessment may be made in respect of a penalty if an earlier assessment operated by reference to an underestimate of an amount of [tax which was due or payable][1].

[(4A) If an assessment in respect of a penalty is based on an amount of tax due or payable that is found by HMRC to be excessive, HMRC may by notice to P amend the assessment so that it is based upon the correct amount.

(4B) An amendment made under sub-paragraph (4A)—

(*a*) does not affect when the penalty must be paid;

(*b*) may be made after the last day on which the assessment in question could have been made under paragraph 12.][2]

(5) . . . [2]

Commencement—Finance Act 2009, Schedule 56 (Appointed Day and Consequential Provisions) Order, SI 2010/466: 6 April 2010 appointed as day on which Sch 56 comes into force for the following amounts specified in column 3 of the Table—items 2–4, and items 17, 23 and 24 but only in so far as the tax falls within any of items 2, 3 or 4 (see SI 2010/466 art 3).

Finance Act 2009, Schedules 55 and 56 (Income Tax Self Assessment and Pension Schemes) (Appointed Days and Consequential and Savings Provisions) Order, SI 2011/702 art 2 (appointed day for the coming into force of Sch 56 is 6 April 2011 in relation to an amount of tax which is payable in relation to the tax year 2010–11 or any subsequent tax year and falls within item 1, 12, 18 or 19 of the Table in para 1, or in so far as the tax falls within item 1 of that Table, item 17, 23 or 24 of that Table).

Cross-references—See FA 2014 s 226(7) (application of paras 9–18 of this Schedule, with any necessary modifications, to penalties for failure to pay accelerated payment).

Amendments—[1] In sub-para (4) words substituted for words "unpaid tax", and sub-para (4A) inserted, by (F(No 3)A 2010 s 27, Sch 11 paras 1, 9 with effect from 6 April 2011 in relation to an amount of tax which is payable in relation to the tax year 2010–11 or any subsequent tax year, and falls within item 1, 12, 18 or 19 of the Table in FA 2009 Sch 56 para 1, or insofar as the tax falls within item 1 of that Table, item 17, 23 or 24 of that Table (by virtue of SI 2011/703 art 3).

[2] Sub-paras (4A), (4B) substituted for sub-para (4A), and sub-para (5) repealed, by FA 2013 s 230, Sch 50 paras 10, 14 with effect for defaults made in relation to the tax year 2014–15 and subsequent tax years (see FA 2009 Sch 56 para 6(2), as amended by FA 2013 Sch 50 para 12(3), as to when a default is made in relation to a tax year).

12—(1) An assessment of a penalty under any paragraph of this Schedule in respect of any amount must be made on or before the later of date A and (where it applies) date B.

(2) Date A is the last day of the period of 2 years beginning with the date specified in or for the purposes of column 4 of the Table (that is to say, the last date on which payment may be made without incurring a penalty).

(3) Date B is the last day of the period of 12 months beginning with—

(*a*) the end of the appeal period for the assessment of the amount of tax in respect of which the penalty is assessed, or

(*b*) if there is no such assessment, the date on which that amount of tax is ascertained.

(4) In sub-paragraph (3)(*a*) "appeal period" means the period during which—

(*a*) an appeal could be brought, or

(*b*) an appeal that has been brought has not been determined or withdrawn.

Commencement—Finance Act 2009, Schedule 56 (Appointed Day and Consequential Provisions) Order, SI 2010/466: 6 April 2010 appointed as day on which Sch 56 comes into force for the following amounts specified in column 3 of the Table—items 2–4, and items 17, 23 and 24 but only in so far as the tax falls within any of items 2, 3 or 4 (see SI 2010/466 art 3).

Finance Act 2009, Schedules 55 and 56 (Income Tax Self Assessment and Pension Schemes) (Appointed Days and Consequential and Savings Provisions) Order, SI 2011/702 art 2 (appointed day for the coming into force of Sch 56 is 6 April 2011 in relation to an amount of tax which is payable in relation to the tax year 2010–11 or any subsequent tax year and falls within item 1, 12, 18 or 19 of the Table in para 1, or in so far as the tax falls within item 1 of that Table, item 17, 23 or 24 of that Table).

Cross-references—See FA 2014 s 226(7) (application of paras 9–18 of this Schedule, with any necessary modifications, to penalties for failure to pay accelerated payment).

Appeal

13—(1) P may appeal against a decision of HMRC that a penalty is payable by P.

(2) P may appeal against a decision of HMRC as to the amount of a penalty payable by P.

Commencement—Finance Act 2009, Schedule 56 (Appointed Day and Consequential Provisions) Order, SI 2010/466: 6 April 2010 appointed as day on which Sch 56 comes into force for the following amounts specified in column 3 of the Table—items 2–4, and items 17, 23 and 24 but only in so far as the tax falls within any of items 2, 3 or 4 (see SI 2010/466 art 3).

Finance Act 2009, Schedules 55 and 56 (Income Tax Self Assessment and Pension Schemes) (Appointed Days and Consequential and Savings Provisions) Order, SI 2011/702 art 2 (appointed day for the coming into force of Sch 56 is 6 April 2011 in relation to an amount of tax which is payable in relation to the tax year 2010–11 or any subsequent tax year and falls within item 1, 12, 18 or 19 of the Table in para 1, or in so far as the tax falls within item 1 of that Table, item 17, 23 or 24 of that Table).

Cross-references—See FA 2014 s 226(7) (application of paras 9–18 of this Schedule, with any necessary modifications, to penalties for failure to pay accelerated payment).

14—(1) An appeal under paragraph 13 is to be treated in the same way as an appeal against an assessment to the tax concerned (including by the application of any provision about bringing the appeal by notice to HMRC, about HMRC review of the decision or about determination of the appeal by the First-tier Tribunal or Upper Tribunal).

(2) Sub-paragraph (1) does not apply—

NIC

(*a*) so as to require P to pay a penalty before an appeal against the assessment of the penalty is determined, or

(*b*) in respect of any other matter expressly provided for by this Act.

Commencement—Finance Act 2009, Schedule 56 (Appointed Day and Consequential Provisions) Order, SI 2010/466: 6 April 2010 appointed as day on which Sch 56 comes into force for the following amounts specified in column 3 of the Table—items 2–4, and items 17, 23 and 24 but only in so far as the tax falls within any of items 2, 3 or 4 (see SI 2010/466 art 3).

Finance Act 2009, Schedules 55 and 56 (Income Tax Self Assessment and Pension Schemes) (Appointed Days and Consequential and Savings Provisions) Order, SI 2011/702 art 2 (appointed day for the coming into force of Sch 56 is 6 April 2011 in relation to an amount of tax which is payable in relation to the tax year 2010–11 or any subsequent tax year and falls within item 1, 12, 18 or 19 of the Table in para 1, or in so far as the tax falls within item 1 of that Table, item 17, 23 or 24 of that Table).

Cross-references—See FA 2014 s 226(7) (application of paras 9–18 of this Schedule, with any necessary modifications, to penalties for failure to pay accelerated payment).

15—(1) On an appeal under paragraph 13(1) that is notified to the tribunal, the tribunal may affirm or cancel HMRC's decision.

(2) On an appeal under paragraph 13(2) that is notified to the tribunal, the tribunal may—

(*a*) affirm HMRC's decision, or

(*b*) substitute for HMRC's decision another decision that HMRC had power to make.

(3) If the tribunal substitutes its decision for HMRC's, the tribunal may rely on paragraph 9—

(*a*) to the same extent as HMRC (which may mean applying the same percentage reduction as HMRC to a different starting point), or

(*b*) to a different extent, but only if the tribunal thinks that HMRC's decision in respect of the application of paragraph 9 was flawed.

(4) In sub-paragraph (3)(*b*) "flawed" means flawed when considered in the light of the principles applicable in proceedings for judicial review.

(5) In this paragraph "tribunal" means the First-tier Tribunal or Upper Tribunal (as appropriate by virtue of paragraph 14(1)).

Commencement—Finance Act 2009, Schedule 56 (Appointed Day and Consequential Provisions) Order, SI 2010/466: 6 April 2010 appointed as day on which Sch 56 comes into force for the following amounts specified in column 3 of the Table—items 2–4, and items 17, 23 and 24 but only in so far as the tax falls within any of items 2, 3 or 4 (see SI 2010/466 art 3).

Finance Act 2009, Schedules 55 and 56 (Income Tax Self Assessment and Pension Schemes) (Appointed Days and Consequential and Savings Provisions) Order, SI 2011/702 art 2 (appointed day for the coming into force of Sch 56 is 6 April 2011 in relation to an amount of tax which is payable in relation to the tax year 2010–11 or any subsequent tax year and falls within item 1, 12, 18 or 19 of the Table in para 1, or in so far as the tax falls within item 1 of that Table, item 17, 23 or 24 of that Table).

Cross-references—See FA 2014 s 226(7) (application of paras 9–18 of this Schedule, with any necessary modifications, to penalties for failure to pay accelerated payment).

Reasonable excuse

16—(1) Liability to a penalty under any paragraph of this Schedule does not arise in relation to a failure to make a payment if P satisfies HMRC or (on appeal) the First-tier Tribunal or Upper Tribunal that there is a reasonable excuse for the failure.

(2) For the purposes of sub-paragraph (1)—

(*a*) an insufficiency of funds is not a reasonable excuse unless attributable to events outside P's control,

(*b*) where P relies on any other person to do anything, that is not a reasonable excuse unless P took reasonable care to avoid the failure, and

(*c*) where P had a reasonable excuse for the failure but the excuse has ceased, P is to be treated as having continued to have the excuse if the failure is remedied without unreasonable delay after the excuse ceased.

Commencement—Finance Act 2009, Schedule 56 (Appointed Day and Consequential Provisions) Order, SI 2010/466: 6 April 2010 appointed as day on which Sch 56 comes into force for the following amounts specified in column 3 of the Table—items 2–4, and items 17, 23 and 24 but only in so far as the tax falls within any of items 2, 3 or 4 (see SI 2010/466 art 3).

Finance Act 2009, Schedules 55 and 56 (Income Tax Self Assessment and Pension Schemes) (Appointed Days and Consequential and Savings Provisions) Order, SI 2011/702 art 2 (appointed day for the coming into force of Sch 56 is 6 April 2011 in relation to an amount of tax which is payable in relation to the tax year 2010–11 or any subsequent tax year and falls within item 1, 12, 18 or 19 of the Table in para 1, or in so far as the tax falls within item 1 of that Table, item 17, 23 or 24 of that Table).

Cross-references—See FA 2014 s 226(7) (application of paras 9–18 of this Schedule, with any necessary modifications, to penalties for failure to pay accelerated payment).

Amendments—Sub-para (1) substituted by F(No 3)A 2010 s 27, Sch 11 paras 1, 10 with effect as follows—

– from 25 January 2011 in respect of the following amounts of tax specified in column 3 of the Table in Sch 56 para 1—
  – item 2 (PAYE regulations);
  – item 3 (returns under FA 2004 s 254(1));
  – item 4 (FA 2004 s 62); and
  – items 17, 23 and 24 but only insofar as the tax falls within any of items 2, 3 or 4.

for remaining purposes from a date to be appointed by Treasury order.

Sub-para (1) as substituted reads as follows—

"(1) If P satisfies HMRC or (on appeal) the First-tier Tribunal or Upper Tribunal that there is a reasonable excuse for a failure to make a payment—

(a) liability to a penalty under any paragraph of this Schedule does not arise in relation to that failure, and

(b) the failure does not count as a default for the purposes of paragraphs 6, 8B, 8C, 8G and 8H.".

Double jeopardy

17 P is not liable to a penalty under any paragraph of this Schedule in respect of a failure or action in respect of which P has been convicted of an offence.

Commencement—Finance Act 2009, Schedule 56 (Appointed Day and Consequential Provisions) Order, SI 2010/466: 6 April 2010 appointed as day on which Sch 56 comes into force for the following amounts specified in column 3 of the Table—items 2–4, and items 17, 23 and 24 but only in so far as the tax falls within any of items 2, 3 or 4 (see SI 2010/466 art 3).

Finance Act 2009, Schedules 55 and 56 (Income Tax Self Assessment and Pension Schemes) (Appointed Days and Consequential and Savings Provisions) Order, SI 2011/702 art 2 (appointed day for the coming into force of Sch 56 is 6 April 2011 in relation to an amount of tax which is payable in relation to the tax year 2010–11 or any subsequent tax year and falls within item 1, 12, 18 or 19 of the Table in para 1, or in so far as the tax falls within item 1 of that Table, item 17, 23 or 24 of that Table).

Cross-references—See FA 2014 s 226(7) (application of paras 9–18 of this Schedule, with any necessary modifications, to penalties for failure to pay accelerated payment).

Interpretation

18—(1) This paragraph applies for the construction of this Schedule.

(2) "HMRC" means Her Majesty's Revenue and Customs.

(3) References to tax include construction industry deductions under Chapter 3 of Part 3 of FA 2004.

(4) References to a determination, in relation to an amount payable under PAYE regulations or under Chapter 3 of Part 3 of FA 2004, include a certificate.

(5) References to an assessment to tax, in relation to inheritance tax and stamp duty reserve tax, are to a determination.

Commencement—Finance Act 2009, Schedule 56 (Appointed Day and Consequential Provisions) Order, SI 2010/466: 6 April 2010 appointed as day on which Sch 56 comes into force for the following amounts specified in column 3 of the Table—items 2–4, and items 17, 23 and 24 but only in so far as the tax falls within any of items 2, 3 or 4 (see SI 2010/466 art 3).

Finance Act 2009, Schedules 55 and 56 (Income Tax Self Assessment and Pension Schemes) (Appointed Days and Consequential and Savings Provisions) Order, SI 2011/702 art 2 (appointed day for the coming into force of Sch 56 is 6 April 2011 in relation to an amount of tax which is payable in relation to the tax year 2010–11 or any subsequent tax year and falls within item 1, 12, 18 or 19 of the Table in para 1, or in so far as the tax falls within item 1 of that Table, item 17, 23 or 24 of that Table).

Cross-references—See FA 2014 s 226(7) (application of paras 9–18 of this Schedule, with any necessary modifications, to penalties for failure to pay accelerated payment).

NATIONAL INSURANCE CONTRIBUTIONS ACT 2011

(2011 Chapter 3)

An Act to make provision for and in connection with increasing rates of national insurance contributions and a regional secondary Class 1 contributions holiday for new businesses.

[22 March 2011]

PART 1
INCREASES IN RATES

1 Class 1 contributions

(1) In section 8(2) of SSCBA 1992 and SSCB(NI)A 1992 (calculation of primary Class 1 percentages)—

(a) in paragraph (a) (main primary percentage), for "11" substitute "12", and

(b) in paragraph (b) (additional primary percentage), for "1" substitute "2".

(2) In section 9(2) of SSCBA 1992 and SSCB(NI)A 1992 (calculation of secondary Class 1 percentage), for "12.8" substitute "13.8".

2 Class 4 contributions

(1) In section 15(3ZA) of SSCBA 1992 and SSCB(NI)A 1992 (Class 4 percentages)—

(a) in paragraph (a) (main Class 4 percentage), for "8" substitute "9", and

(b) in paragraph (b) (additional Class 4 percentage), for "1" substitute "2".

(2) In section 143(4)(b) of SSAA 1992 (power to alter contributions with a view to adjusting level of National Insurance Fund: main Class 4 percentage not to be increased to more than 8.25 per cent), for "8.25" substitute "9.25".

3 Increased product of additional rates to be paid into National Insurance Fund

In section 162(5) of SSAA 1992 and section 142(5) of SSA(NI)A 1992 (destination of contributions: 100 per cent of product of additional primary percentage rate and additional Class 4 percentage rate to form part of health service allocation), for "100" substitute "50".

PART 2
REGIONAL SECONDARY CONTRIBUTIONS HOLIDAY FOR NEW BUSINESSES

4 Holiday for new businesses

(1) This section applies where—

(a) a person, or a number of persons in partnership, ("P") starts a new business during the relevant period,

(b) the principal place at which the new business is carried on when it is started is not in any of the excluded regions, and

(c) one or more persons are qualifying employees in relation to the new business.

(2) The appropriate amount in respect of each qualifying employee may be—

(a) deducted from Class 1 contributions payments which P is liable to make, or

(b) refunded to P.

(3) Section 5 defines what is meant by "starting a new business".

(4) "The relevant period" is the period—

(a) beginning with 22 June 2010, and

(b) ending with 5 September 2013.

(5) "The excluded regions" are Greater London, the South East Region and the Eastern Region.

(6) Section 6 specifies when a person is a qualifying employee in relation to a new business.

(7) Section 7 specifies what is the appropriate amount in respect of a qualifying employee.

(8) Section 8 explains how a deduction or refund is made.

(9) Section 9 makes provision requiring the retention of records.

(10) Section 10 contains an anti-avoidance rule.

(11) Section 11 makes provision for the interpretation of this Part.

5 Starting a new business

(1) P "starts" a new business when P begins to carry on a new business.

(2) A business is not a "new" business if—

(a) P has, at any time during the period of 6 months ending with the time when P begins to carry it on, carried on another business consisting of the activities of which the business consists (or most of them), or

(b) P carries it on as a result of a transfer (within the meaning of subsection (3)).

(3) P carries on a business as a result of a transfer if P begins to carry on the business on another person ceasing to carry on the activities of which it consists (or most of them) in consequence of arrangements involving P and the other person.

(4) For the purposes of subsection (3) P is to be taken to begin to carry on a business on another person ceasing to carry on such activities if—

(a) the business begins to be carried on by P otherwise than in partnership on such activities ceasing to be carried on by persons in partnership, or

(b) P is a number of persons in partnership who begin to carry on the business on such activities ceasing to be carried on—

(i) by a person, or a number of persons, otherwise than in partnership,

(ii) by persons in a partnership not consisting only of all the persons constituting P, or

(iii) partly as mentioned in sub-paragraph (i) and partly as mentioned in sub-paragraph (ii).

(5) P is not to be regarded as starting a new business by beginning to carry on a business if—

(a) before P begins to carry on the business, P is a party to arrangements under which P may (at any time during the relevant period) carry on as part of the business activities carried on by any other person, and

(b) the business would have been prevented by subsection (2)(b) from being a new business had—

(i) P begun to carry on the activities when beginning to carry on the business, and

(ii) the other person at that time ceased to carry them on.

(6) In this section "business" means something which is—

(a) a trade, profession or vocation for the purposes of the Income Tax Acts or the Corporation Tax Acts,

(b) a property business (within the meaning of section 263(6) of the Income Tax (Trading and Other Income) Act 2005), or

(c) an investment business (that is, a business consisting wholly or partly of making investments).

6 Qualifying employees

(1) A person is a "qualifying employee" in relation to a new business if—

(a) the person first becomes employed as an employed earner for the purposes of the new business before the end of the initial period, and

(b) P is the secondary contributor in relation to any payment of earnings to or for the benefit of the person in respect of the employment at any time during the period that is the holiday period in relation to the person.

(2) Where (apart from this subsection) there would be more than 10 qualifying employees, only the first 10 persons who become qualifying employees are qualifying employees.

(3) The "initial period" means the period of one year beginning with—

(a) the date on which P starts the new business, or

(b) if earlier, the first date on which a person first becomes employed as an employed earner for the purposes of the new business,

but if the first date on which a person first becomes employed as an employed earner for the purposes of the new business is before 22 June 2010, the person is to be taken for the purposes of paragraph (b) as first so employed on that date.

(4) The "holiday period", in relation to a person, is the period—

(a) beginning with the day on which the person first becomes employed as an employed earner for the purposes of the new business or, if the person first becomes so employed before 6 September 2010, with that date, and

(b) ending with the earlier of—

(i) the end of the period of one year beginning with the day on which it begins, and

(ii) the end of the relevant period.

(5) None of the following has effect for the purposes of this Part—

(a) the Social Security Contributions (Intermediaries) Regulations 2000 (SI 2000/727) and the Social Security Contributions (Intermediaries) (Northern Ireland) Regulations 2000 (SI 2000/728) (which provide in certain cases for an intermediary to be treated as the secondary contributor in relation to the payment of earnings), and

(b) the Social Security Contributions (Managed Service Companies) Regulations 2007 (SI 2007/2070) (which provide in certain cases for a managed service company to be treated as the secondary contributor in relation to the payment of earnings).

7 The appropriate amount

(1) The appropriate amount in respect of a qualifying employee is the relevant amount of secondary Class 1 contributions.

(2) "The relevant amount of secondary Class 1 contributions" is the amount of secondary Class 1 contributions which P is liable to pay in respect of relevant earnings.

(3) "Relevant earnings" are earnings paid to or for the benefit of the qualifying employee, in respect of employment as an employed earner for the purposes of the new business, at any time during the holiday period when the principal place at which the business is carried on is not in any of the excluded regions.

(4) But if (apart from this subsection) the relevant amount of secondary Class 1 contributions would exceed £5,000, it is the first £5,000 which P becomes liable to pay.

(5) In the case of a qualifying employee who is a mariner, the reference in subsection (3) to earnings paid at any time during the holiday period includes, in relation to earnings paid for a voyage beginning in the holiday period but ending after it, earnings earned in the part of the voyage period falling within the holiday period.

"Mariner" and "voyage period" have the meaning given by regulation 115 of the 2001 Regulations.

(6) If P is liable to pay secondary Class 1 contributions at the contracted-out rate, P is to be treated for the purposes of subsection (2) as liable to pay them at the non-contracted-out rate; and for this purpose "contracted-out rate" and "non-contracted-out rate" have the same meaning as in the 2001 Regulations.

8 Making of deductions or refunds

(1) To the extent that the appropriate amount is attributable to secondary Class 1 contributions payable in respect of earnings paid in a tax year it may be deducted from any one or more Class 1 contributions payments made by P in respect of that tax year.

(2) If the amount which P would be entitled to deduct under this section exceeds the amount of the payments from which it can be deducted, HMRC must instead refund the excess to P if P requests them to do so.

(3) No deduction or refund may be made under this section until an application has been submitted to, and granted by, HMRC.

(4) An application must contain such information, and must be made in such form and manner, as is specified by HMRC.

(5) No application may be made for a refund in respect of a qualifying employee after the end of the period of 4 years beginning with the day on which the last deduction could be made in respect of the qualifying employee.

(6) For the purposes of—

(a) Part 2 of the Social Security Contributions (Transfer of Functions, etc) Act 1999, and

(b) Part 3 of the Social Security Contributions (Transfer of Functions, etc) (Northern Ireland) Order 1999 (SI 1999/671),

(decisions and appeals), the decisions to which this subsection applies are decisions of an officer of Revenue and Customs under section 8 of that Act or Article 7 of that Order.

(7) Subsection (6) applies to—

(a) a decision whether P is or was entitled to make a deduction under this section and, if so, the amount that P is or was entitled to deduct, and

(b) a decision whether P is entitled to a refund under this section and, if so, the amount of the refund.

9 Retention of records

(1) This section applies where P is or was entitled to make a deduction under section 8 in respect of a qualifying employee.

(2) P must keep and preserve any documents or records relating to—

(a) P's entitlement to make a deduction in respect of the employee, and

(b) the calculation of any amount that has been, or could have been, deducted,

for not less than 3 years beginning with the date on which the last deduction under section 8 is, or could be, made in respect of the employee.

(3) Accordingly, the duty imposed by paragraph 26(1) of Schedule 4 to the 2001 Regulations (retention by employer of contribution and election records) does not apply to any such documents or records.

(4) The duty imposed by this section may be discharged by preserving the documents or records in any form or by any means.

(5) For the purposes of Schedule 36 to the Finance Act 2008 (information and inspection powers), as applied by section 110ZA of SSAA 1992 and section 104ZA of SSA(NI)A 1992, the duty imposed by this section is to be treated as if it were a duty imposed under or by virtue of SSCBA 1992 or SSCB(NI)A 1992.

10 Anti-avoidance

(1) This Part does not apply if P starts the new business pursuant to avoidance arrangements.

(2) Arrangements are "avoidance arrangements" if the main purpose, or one of the main purposes, of P in being a party to them is to secure that activities which might otherwise have been carried on as part of another business (whether by Por any other person) are carried on by P as part of the new business in order to obtain deductions or refunds (or increased deductions or refunds) under this Part.

11 Interpretation of Part 2

(1) In this Part—

"the 2001 Regulations" means the Social Security (Contributions) Regulations 2001 (SI 2001/1004);

"the appropriate amount" is to be read in accordance with section 7;

"arrangements" includes any agreement, understanding, scheme, transaction or series of transactions (whether or not legally enforceable);

"Class 1 contributions payments" means payments under—

(a) paragraph 10 of Schedule 4 to the 2001 Regulations (monthly payments), or

(b) paragraph 11 of that Schedule (quarterly payments);

"the Eastern Region" means—

(a) the counties of Bedford, Cambridgeshire, Central Bedfordshire, Essex, Hertfordshire, Norfolk and Suffolk, and

(b) the non-metropolitan districts of Luton, Peterborough, Southend-on-Sea and Thurrock;

"the excluded regions" has the meaning given by section 4(5);

"HMRC" means the Commissioners for Her Majesty's Revenue and Customs;

"holiday period" has the meaning given by section 6(4);

"qualifying employee" has the meaning given by section 6;

"the relevant period" has the meaning given by section 4(4);

"the South East Region" means—

(a) the counties of Buckinghamshire, East Sussex, Hampshire, the Isle of Wight, Kent, Oxfordshire, Surrey and West Sussex, and

(b) the non-metropolitan districts of Bracknell Forest, Brighton and Hove, Medway, Milton Keynes, Portsmouth, Reading, Slough, Southampton, West Berkshire, Windsor and Maidenhead and Wokingham.

(2) Expressions used in this Part and in Part 1 of SSCBA 1992 or SSCB(NI)A 1992 have the same meaning for the purposes of this Part as they have for the purposes of that Part.

PART 3
GENERAL

12 Abbreviations of Acts

In this Act—

"SSAA 1992" means the Social Security Administration Act 1992;

"SSA(NI)A 1992" means the Social Security Administration (Northern Ireland) Act 1992;

"SSCBA 1992" means the Social Security Contributions and Benefits Act 1992;

"SSCB(NI)A 1992" means the Social Security Contributions and Benefits (Northern Ireland) Act 1992.

13 Commencement

(1) Part 1 comes into force on 6 April 2011.

(2) Part 2 and this Part come into force on the day on which this Act is passed.

14 Extent

(1) The amendments made by Part 1 have the same extent as the provisions to which they relate.

(2) Part 2 and this Part extend to England and Wales, Scotland and Northern Ireland.

15 Short title

This Act may be cited as the National Insurance Contributions Act 2011.

WELFARE REFORM ACT 2012

(2012 Chapter 5)

An Act to make provision for universal credit and personal independence payment; to make other provision about social security and tax credits; to make provision about the functions of the registration service, child support maintenance and the use of jobcentres; to establish the Social Mobility and Child Poverty Commission and otherwise amend the Child Poverty Act 2010; and for connected purposes.

[8 March 2012]

PART 1
UNIVERSAL CREDIT

CHAPTER 3

SUPPLEMENTARY AND GENERAL

Supplementary and consequential

31 Supplementary and consequential amendments

Schedule 2 contains supplementary and consequential amendments.

Commencement—Welfare Reform Act 2012 (Commencement No 8 and Savings and Transitional Provisions) Order, SI 2013/358, art 3(*b*) (appoints 25 February 2013 as the day for the coming into force of s 31 in so far as it relates to Sch 2 para 26).

Welfare Reform Act 2012 (Commencement No 8 and Savings and Transitional Provisions) Order, SI 2013/358, art 5(5) (appoints 29 April 2013 as the day for the coming into force of s 31 in so far as it relates to Sch 2 para 9 and Sch 2 para 3 in so far as it relates to para 9).

Welfare Reform Act 2012 (Commencement No 8 and Savings and Transitional Provisions Order), SI 2013/358 art 6(4)(*d*) (appoints 1 April 2013 as the day for the coming into force of s 31 in so far as it relates to Sch 2 para 51, and Sch 2 para 43 in so far as it relates to para 51, Sch 2 paras 57, 58(2) (and para 58(1) in so far as it relates to para 58(2)), para 59(2) (and para 59(1) insofar as it relates to para 59(2), para 62, and para 56 in so far as it relates to paras 57, 58(2), 59(2), 62).

Welfare Reform Act 2012 (Commencement No 9 and Transitional and Transitory Provisions and Commencement No 8 and Savings and Transitional Provisions (Amendment)) Order, SI 2013/983 art 3(1)(b) (appoints 29 April 2013 as the day for the coming into force of s 31 in so far as it relates to the following paras of Sch 2: paras 1, 2, 32–35, 37–42, 52–55, 65; paras 4, 8, 10–23, 25, 27–31 and para 3 in so far as it relates to those paragraphs; and paras 44, 45, 47, 49, 50(2) and 50(1) in so far as it relates to 50(2), and para 43 in so far as it relates to those paragraphs and sub-paragraphs).

Universal credit and other benefits

33 Abolition of benefits

(1) The following benefits are abolished—

(a) income-based jobseeker's allowance under the Jobseekers Act 1995;

(b) income-related employment and support allowance under Part 1 of the Welfare Reform Act 2007;

(c) income support under section 124 of the Social Security Contributions and Benefits Act 1992;

(d) housing benefit under section 130 of that Act;

(e) council tax benefit under section 131 of that Act;

(f) child tax credit and working tax credit under the Tax Credits Act 2002.

NIC

(2) In subsection (1)—
(a) "income-based jobseeker's allowance" has the same meaning as in the Jobseekers Act 1995;
(b) "income-related employment and support allowance" means an employment and support allowance entitlement to which is based on section 1(2)(b) of the Welfare Reform Act 2007.
(3) Schedule 3 contains consequential amendments.

PART 4
PERSONAL INDEPENDENCE PAYMENT

General

91 Amendments

Schedule 9 contains amendments relating to this Part.

Commencement—Welfare Reform Act 2012 (Commencement No. 8 and Savings and Transitional Provisions) Order, SI 2013/358, art 3(*d*) (appoints 25 February 2013 as the day for the coming into force of s 91 (amendments) in so far as they relate to Sch 9 para 26.

Welfare Reform Act 2012 (Commencement No. 8 and Savings and Transitional Provisions) Order, SI 2013/358, art 7(*k*) (appoints 8 April 2013 as the day for the coming into force of s 91 (amendments) in so far as they relate to Sch 9 paras 1–3, 5–25, 27–50 (to the extent that they are not already in force) in relation to a person whose only or principal residence is listed in SI 2013/358 Sch 3.

Welfare Reform Act 2012 (Commencement No 10) Order, SI 2013/1250 art 2 (appoints 10 June 2013 as the day for the coming into force of s 91 (amendments) in so far as they relate to Sch 9 paras 1–3, 5–25, 27–50 (to the extent that they are not already in force) other than in relation to a person whose only or principal residence is listed in SI 2013/358 Sch 3.

PART 5
SOCIAL SECURITY: GENERAL

Investigation and prosecution of offences

110 Powers to require information relating to investigations

(*amends* SSAA 1992 s 109B(2))

Commencement—Welfare Reform Act 2012 (Commencement No 10) Order, SI 2013/1250, art 3 (appoints 17 June 2013 as the day for the coming into force of s 110 for the purposes of making regulations and 1 October 2013 for all other purposes).

111 Time limits for legal proceedings

(*amends* SSAA 1992 s 116(2))

Commencement—This section came into force on 8 May 2012 (two months after the Act was passed in accordance with s 150(2)(*e*).

Prospective amendment—This section to be repealed by WRA 2012 s 147, Sch 14 Pt 1 with effect from a date to be appointed.

112 Prosecution powers of local authorities

(1) The Social Security Administration Act 1992 is amended as follows.
(2) (*inserts* SSAA 1992 s 116ZA)
(3)–(6) (*amend* SSAA 1992 s116A(2), (4)(b) and heading)

Commencement—Welfare Reform Act 2012 (Commencement No 28) Order, SI 2016/511, arts 3, 4 (appoints 20 April 2016 as the day for the coming into force of s 112(2), and s 112(1) of the Act in so far as it relates to section 112(2) for the purpose of making regulations, and 24 May 2016 for all other purposes, and appoints 24 May 2016 for the coming into force of s 112 (3)–(6)).

Civil penalties

116 Civil penalties for incorrect statements and failures to disclose information

(1) (*inserts* SSAA 1992 ss 115C, 115D)
(2) (*inserts* SSAA 1992 s 190(1)(zzb))

Commencement—Welfare Reform Act 2012 (Commencement No 2) Order, SI 2012/1246, art 2 (appoints 10 May 2012 as the day for the coming into force of s 116(1) for the purpose of prescribing amounts under SSAA 1992 ss 115C(2), 115D(1), (2) and 1 October 2012 as the day for the coming into force of s 116(1) for all other purposes; and appoints 10 May 2012 as the day for the coming into force of s 116(2)).

Information-sharing: Secretary of State and HMRC

127 Information-sharing between Secretary of State and HMRC

(1) This subsection applies to information which is held for the purposes of any HMRC functions—
(a) by the Commissioners for Her Majesty's Revenue and Customs, or
(b) by a person providing services to them.
(2) Information to which subsection (1) applies may be supplied—
(a) to the Secretary of State, or to a person providing services to the Secretary of State, or
(b) to a Northern Ireland Department, or to a person providing services to a Northern Ireland Department,
for use for the purposes of departmental functions.
(3) This subsection applies to information which is held for the purposes of any departmental functions—
(a) by the Secretary of State, or by a person providing services to the Secretary of State, or

(b) by a Northern Ireland Department, or by a person providing services to a Northern Ireland Department.

(4) Information to which subsection (3) applies may be supplied—

(a) to the Commissioners for Her Majesty's Revenue and Customs, or

(b) to a person providing services to them,

for use for the purposes of HMRC functions.

(5) Information supplied under this section must not be supplied by the recipient of the information to any other person or body without—

(a) the authority of the Commissioners for Her Majesty's Revenue and Customs, in the case of information supplied under subsection (2);

(b) the authority of the Secretary of State, in the case of information held as mentioned in subsection (3)(a) and supplied under subsection (4);

(c) the authority of the relevant Northern Ireland Department, in the case of information held as mentioned in subsection (3)(b) and supplied under subsection (4).

(6) Where information supplied under this section has been used for the purposes for which it was supplied, it is lawful for it to be used for any purposes for which information held for those purposes could be used.

(7) In this section—

"departmental functions" means functions relating to—

(*a*) social security,

(*b*) employment or training, . . . [1]

(*c*) the investigation or prosecution of offences relating to tax credits; [or

(*d*) child support;][1]

"HMRC function" means any function—

(a) for which the Commissioners for Her Majesty's Revenue and Customs are responsible by virtue of section 5 of the Commissioners for Revenue and Customs Act 2005, . . . [3]

(b) which relates to a matter listed in Schedule 1 to that Act, . . . [4]

[(c) which is conferred by or under the Childcare Payments Act 2014][3] [, or

(d) which is conferred by or under section 2 of, or Schedule 2 to, the Savings (Government Contributions) Act 2017 (bonuses in respect of savings in Help-to-Save accounts);][4]

"Northern Ireland Department" means any of the following—

(a) the Department for Social Development;

(b) the Department of Finance and Personnel;

(c) the Department for Employment and Learning.

(8) For the purposes of this section any reference to functions relating to social security includes a reference to functions relating to—

(a) statutory payments as defined in section 4C(11) of the Social Security Contributions and Benefits Act 1992;

(b) maternity allowance under section 35 of that Act;

(c) statutory payments as defined in section 4C(11) of the Social Security Contributions and Benefits (Northern Ireland) Act 1992;

(d) maternity allowance under section 35 [or 35B][2] of that Act.

(9) This section does not limit the circumstances in which information may be supplied apart from this section.

(10) (*inserts* SSA 1998 s 3(1A)(*d*))

Commencement—This section came into effect on 8 May 2012 (two months after the Act was passed by virtue of s 150(2)(*f*).

Amendments—[1] In sub-s (7), in definition "departmental functions", word "or" in para (*b*) repealed, and para (*d*) and preceding word "or" inserted, by the Public Bodies (Child Maintenance and Enforcement Commission: Abolition and Transfer of Functions) Order, SI 2012/2007 art 3(2), Schedule paras 101, 102 with effect from 1 August 2012.

[2] Words inserted in sub-s (8)(d) by the Social Security (Maternity Allowance) (Participating Wife or Civil Partner of Self-employed Earner) Regulations, SI 2014/606 reg 4 with effect in relation to the payment of maternity allowance in cases where a woman's expected week of confinement (within the meaning of SSCBA 1992 s 35) begins on or after 27 July 2014.

[3] In sub-s (7), in definition of "HMRC function", word ", or" at the end of para (a) repealed, and para (c) and preceding word "or" inserted, by the Childcare Payments Act 2014 s 27(6)(a) with effect for the powers to make regulations only, from 17 December 2014, and for remaining purposes, from a date to be appointed (the Childcare Payments Act 2014 s 75(1)(c), (2)).

[4] In sub-s (7), in definition of "HMRC function", words ", or" at the end of para (b) repealed, and para (d) and preceding word "or" inserted, by the Savings (Government Contributions) Act 2017 s 2, Sch 2 para 17(8) with effect from 17 January 2017.

PART 7
FINAL

147 Repeals

Schedule 14 contains consequential repeals.

Commencement—This section came into effect on 8 March 2012 (date of Royal Assent: s 150(1(*f*).

NIC

148 Financial provision

There shall be paid out of money provided by Parliament—

(a) sums paid by the Secretary of State by way of universal credit or personal independence payment;

(b) any other expenditure incurred in consequence of this Act by a Minister of the Crown or the Commissioners for Her Majesty's Revenue and Customs;

(c) any increase attributable to this Act in the sums payable under any other Act out of money so provided.

Commencement—This section came into effect on 8 March 2012 (date of Royal Assent: s 150(1(*f*).

149 Extent

(1) This Act extends to England and Wales and Scotland only, subject as follows.

(2) The following provisions extend to England and Wales, Scotland and Northern Ireland—

(a) section 32 (power to make consequential and supplementary provision: universal credit);

(b) section 33 (abolition of benefits);

(c) section 76 (calculation of working tax credit);

(d) section 92 (power to make consequential and supplementary provision: personal independence payment);

(e) section 126(1) to (13) (tax credits: transfer of functions etc);

(f) section 127(1) to (9) (information-sharing between Secretary of State and HMRC);

(g) this Part, excluding Schedule 14 (repeals).

(3) Sections 128 and 129 extend to England and Wales only.

(4) Any amendment or repeal made by this Act has the same extent as the enactment to which it relates.

Commencement—This section came into effect on 8 March 2012 (date of Royal Assent: s 150(1(*f*).

150 Commencement

(1) The following provisions of this Act come into force on the day on which it is passed—

(a) section 76 (calculation of working tax credit);

(b) section 103 and Schedule 12 (supersession of decisions of former appellate bodies) (but see section 103(2));

(c) section 108 (application of Limitation Act 1980) (but see section 108(4));

(d) section 109 (recovery of fines etc by deductions from employment and support allowance) (but see section 109(3));

(e) section 126 (tax credits: transfer of functions etc);

(f) this Part, excluding Schedule 14 (repeals).

(2) The following provisions of this Act come into force at the end of the period of two months beginning with the day on which it is passed—

(a) section 50 (dual entitlement to employment and support allowance and jobseeker's allowance);

(b) section 60 and Part 6 of Schedule 14 (claimants dependent on drugs etc);

(c) sections 71 and 72 (social fund: purposes of discretionary payments and determination of amount or value of budgeting loan);

(d) section 107 (recovery of child benefit and guardian's allowance);

(e) section 111 (time limit for legal proceedings);

(f) section 127 and Part 13 of Schedule 14 (information-sharing between Secretary of State and HMRC);

(g) section 134 (information-sharing for social security or employment purposes etc);

(h) section 135 (functions of registration service);

(i) section 142 (exclusion of child support maintenance from individual voluntary arrangements);

(j) section 145 and Schedule 13 (Social Mobility and Child Poverty Commission);

(k) Part 2 of Schedule 14 (entitlement to jobseeker's allowance without seeking employment).

(3) The remaining provisions of this Act come into force on such day as the Secretary of State may by order made by statutory instrument appoint.

(4) An order under subsection (3) may—

(a) appoint different days for different purposes;

(b) appoint different days for different areas in relation to—

(i) any provision of Part 1 (universal credit) or of Part 1 of Schedule 14;

(ii) section 61 or 62 (entitlement to work: jobseeker's allowance and employment and support allowance);

(iii) any provision of Part 4 (personal independence payment) or of Part 9 of Schedule 14;

(iv) section 102 (consideration of revision before appeal);

(c) make such transitory or transitional provision, or savings, as the Secretary of State considers necessary or expedient.

Orders—Welfare Reform Act 2012 (Commencement No 1) Order, SI 2012/863.
Welfare Reform Act 2012 (Commencement No 2) Order, SI 2012/1246.
Welfare Reform Act 2012 (Commencement No 2) (Amendment) Order, SI 2012/1440.
Welfare Reform Act 2012 (Commencement No 3, Savings Provision) Order, SI 2012/1651.
Welfare Reform Act 2012 (Commencement No 4) Order, SI 2012/2530.
Welfare Reform Act 2012 (Commencement No 5) Order, SI 2012/2946.
Welfare Reform Act 2012 (Commencement No 6 and Savings Provisions) Order, SI 2012/3090.
Welfare Reform Act 2012 (Commencement No 7) Order, SI 2013/178.
Welfare Reform Act 2012 (Commencement No 8 and Savings and Transitional Provisions) Order, SI 2013/358.
Welfare Reform Act 2012 (Commencement No 9 and Transitional and Transitory Provisions and Commencement No 8 and Savings and Transitional Provisions (Amendment)) Order 2013, SI 2013/983.
Welfare Reform Act 2012 (Commencement No 10) Order 2013, SI 2013/1250.
Welfare Reform Act 2012 (Commencement No 11 and Transitional and Transitory Provisions and Commencement No 9 and Transitional and Transitory Provisions (Amendment)) Order 2013, SI 2013/1511.
Welfare Reform Act 2012 (Commencement No 12) Order 2013, SI 2013/2534.
Welfare Reform Act 2012 (Commencement No 13 and Transitional and Transitory Provisions) Order, SI 2013/2657.
Welfare Reform Act 2012 (Commencement No 14 and Transitional and Transitory Provisions) Order 2013, SI 2013/2846.
Child Maintenance and Other Payments Act 2008 (Commencement No 12 and Savings Provisions) and the Welfare Reform Act 2012 (Commencement No 15) Order 2013, SI 2013/2947.
Welfare Reform Act 2012 (Commencement No 16 and Transitional and Transitory Provisions) Order 2014, SI 2014/209.
Welfare Reform Act 2012 (Commencement No 9, 11, 13, 14 and 16 and Transitional and Transitory Provisions (Amendment)) Order 2014, SI 2014/1452
Welfare Reform Act 2012 (Commencement No 17 and Transitional and Transitory Provisions) Order 2014, SI 2014/1583
Child Maintenance and Other Payments Act 2008 (Commencement No 14 and Transitional Provisions) and the Welfare Reform Act 2012 (Commencement No 18 and Transitional and Savings Provisions) Order, SI 2014/1635.
Welfare Reform Act 2012 (Commencement No 9, 11, 13 14, 16 and 17 and Transitional and Transitory Provisions (Amendment)) Order 2014, SI 2014/1661.
Welfare Reform Act 2012 (Commencement No 9, 11, 13, 14, 16 and 17 and Transitional and Transitory Provisions (Amendment) (No 2)) Order 2014, SI 2014/1923.
Welfare Reform Act 2012 (Commencement No 19 and Transitional and Transitory Provisions and Commencement No 9 and Transitional and Transitory Provisions (Amendment)) Order 2014, SI 2014/2321.
Welfare Reform Act 2012 (Commencement No 9, 11, 13 14, 16, 17 and 19 and Transitional and Transitory Provisions (Amendment)) Order 2014, SI 2014/3067.
Welfare Reform Act 2012 (Commencement No 9, 11, 13, 14, 16, 17 and 19 and Transitional and Transitory Provisions (Amendment)) Order 2015, SI 2015/32.
Welfare Reform Act 2012 (Commencement No 21 and Transitional and Transitory Provisions) Order 2015, SI 2015/33.
Welfare Reform Act 2012 (Commencement No 22 and Transitional and Transitory Provisions) Order 2015, SI 2015/101.
Welfare Reform Act 2012 (Commencement No 23 and Transitional and Transitory Provisions) Order 2015, SI 2015/634.
Welfare Reform Act 2012 (Commencement No 23 and Transitional and Transitory Provisions) (Amendment) Order 2015, SI 2015/740.
Welfare Reform Act 2012 (Commencement No 24 and Transitional and Transitory Provisions and Commencement No 9 and Transitional and Transitory Provisions (Amendment)) Order 2015, SI 2015/1537.
Welfare Reform Act 2012 (Commencement No 25 and Transitional and Transitory Provisions) Order, SI 2015/1930.
Welfare Reform Act 2012 (Commencement No 26 and Transitional and Transitory Provisions and Commencement No 22, 23 and 24 and Transitional and Transitory Provisions (Modification)) Order, SI 2016/33.
Welfare Reform Act 2012 (Commencement No 27 and Transitional and Transitory Provisions and Commencement No 22, 23 and 24 and Transitional and Transitory Provisions (Modification)) Order, SI 2016/407.
Welfare Reform Act 2012 (Commencement No 28) Order 2016, SI 2016/511.

151 Short title

This Act may be cited as the Welfare Reform Act 2012.

SCHEDULES

SCHEDULE 2

UNIVERSAL CREDIT: AMENDMENTS

Section 31

Social Security Administration Act 1992 (c 5)

3–31(*amend* the Social Security Administration Act 1992)

Social Security Act 1998 (c 14)

43–51(*amend* the Social Security Act 1998)

SCHEDULE 3

ABOLITION OF BENEFITS: CONSEQUENTIAL AMENDMENTS

Section 33

Social Security Contributions and Benefits Act 1992 (c 4)

1–3(*amend* the Social Security Contributions and Benefits Act 1992)

Social Security Administration Act 1992 (c 5)

4–8(*amend* the Social Security Administration Act 1992)

SCHEDULE 4

HOUSING CREDIT ELEMENT OF STATE PENSION CREDIT

Section 34

PART 2

AMENDMENTS TO OTHER ACTS

Social Security Administration Act 1992 (c 5)

9–12(*amend* the Social Security Administration Act 1992)

SCHEDULE 9

PERSONAL INDEPENDENCE PAYMENT: AMENDMENTS

Section 91

Social Security Contributions and Benefits Act 1992 (c 4)

3–6(*amend* the Social Security Contributions and Benefits Act 1992)

Social Security Administration Act 1992 (c 5)

7–33(*amend* the Social Security Administration Act 1992)

Social Security Act 1998 (c 14)

37–43(*amend* the Social Security Act 1998)

SCHEDULE 14

REPEALS

Note—The effect of the repeals made by this Schedule (where within the scope of this Handbook) is noted in the text of the affected legislation.

Section 147

FINANCE ACT 2012

(2012 Chapter 14)

An Act to grant certain duties, to alter other duties, and to amend the law relating to the National Debt and the Public Revenue, and to make further provision in connection with finance.

[17 July 2012]

PART 9

MISCELLANEOUS MATTERS

Incapacitated persons and minors

222 Removal of special provision for incapacitated persons and minors

(1) (*repeals* TMA 1970 ss 42(8), 72, 73)

(2) (*repeals* FA 2003 s 106(1), (2))

(3) Accordingly, incapacitated persons are (and minors remain) assessable and chargeable to the taxes in question.

(4) In consequence of the amendments made by subsections (1) and (2)—

(a) (*amends* TMA 1970 s 118(1))

(b) (*repeals* the Age of Legal Capacity (Scotland) Act 1991 Sch 1 paras 33, 34)

(c) (*amends* SSCBA 1992 Sch 2 para 5)

(d) (*amends* SSCB(NI)A 1992 Sch 2 para 5)
(e) (*repeals* FA 2003 s 81B(4)(*b*))

(5) The amendments made by subsections (1) and (4)(a) to (d) have effect for the tax year 2012–13 and subsequent tax years.

(6) The amendments made by subsections (2) and (4)(e) have effect in relation to land transactions of which the effective date is on or after the day on which this Act is passed.

Commentary—*Simon's Taxes* **A1.153, A1.411, A1.421, A1.441**.

Administration

223 Tax agents: dishonest conduct

(1) Schedule 38 contains provision about tax agents who engage in dishonest conduct.

(2) That Schedule comes into force on such day as the Treasury may by order appoint.

(3) An order under subsection (2)—
(a) may make different provision for different purposes, and
(b) may include transitional provision and savings.

(4) The Treasury may by order make any incidental, supplemental, consequential, transitional or saving provision in consequence of Schedule 38.

(5) An order under subsection (4) may—
(a) make different provision for different purposes, and
(b) make provision amending, repealing or revoking any provision made by or under an Act (whenever passed or made).

(6) An order under this section is to be made by statutory instrument.

(7) A statutory instrument containing an order under subsection (4) is subject to annulment in pursuance of a resolution of the House of Commons.

Orders—Finance Act 2012, Schedule 38 (Tax Agents: Dishonest Conduct) (Appointed Day and Savings) Order, SI 2013/279.
Commentary—*Simon's Taxes* **I11.703**.

SCHEDULES

SCHEDULE 38

TAX AGENTS: DISHONEST CONDUCT

Section 223

Commentary—*Simon's Taxes* **A6.321**.

Commencement—Finance Act 2012, Schedule 38 (Tax Agents: Dishonest Conduct) (Appointed Day and Savings) Order, SI 2013/279 art 2(appointed day for the coming into force of Sch 38 is 1 April 2013).

Cross-references—See the Social Security (Contributions) (Amendment and Application of Schedule 38 to the Finance Act 2012) Regulations, SI 2013/622 reg 41 (the provisions of FA 2012 Sch 38 (tax agents: dishonest conduct) apply in relation to Class 1, Class 1A, Class 1B and Class 2 NICs as in relation to tax to the extent that they do not already apply).

Note—*Please see the IHT section for the full text of Sch 38.*

PART 7

CONSEQUENTIAL PROVISIONS

Social Security Contributions and Benefits Act 1992

53 (*amends* SSCBA 1992 s 16)

54 (*amends* SSCBA 1992 Sch 1 para 7B)

Social Security Contributions and Benefits (Northern Ireland) Act 1992

55 (*amends* SSCB(NI)A 1992 Sch 1 para 7B)

Social Security Administration Act 1992

56 (*amends* SSAA 1992 s 110ZA)

Social Security Administration (Northern Ireland) Act 1992

57 (*amends* SSA(NI)A 1992 s 104ZA)

FINANCE ACT 2013

(2013 Chapter 29)

AN ACT TO Grant certain duties, to alter other duties, and to amend the law relating to the National Debt and the Public Revenue, and to make further provision in connection with finance.

[17 July 2013]

CONTENTS

PART 5
GENERAL ANTI-ABUSE RULE

206–215 General anti-abuse rule

Note—Please see *IHT* section above for the text of these sections.

SCHEDULES

SCHEDULE 43

GENERAL ANTI-ABUSE RULE: PROCEDURAL REQUIREMENTS

Section 209

Note—Please see *IHT* section above for the text of this Schedule.

[SCHEDULE 43A

PROCEDURAL REQUIREMENTS: POOLING NOTICES AND NOTICES OF BINDING]

Note—Please see *IHT* section above for the text of this Schedule.

[SCHEDULE 43B

PROCEDURAL REQUIREMENTS: GENERIC REFERRAL OF TAX ARRANGEMENTS]

Note—Please see *IHT* section above for the text of this Schedule.

[SCHEDULE 43C

PENALTY UNDER SECTION 212A: SUPPLEMENTARY PROVISION]

Note—Please see *IHT* section above for the text of this Schedule.

NATIONAL INSURANCE CONTRIBUTIONS ACT 2014

(2014 Chapter 7)

An Act to make provision in relation to national insurance contributions; and for connected purposes.

[13 March 2014]

BE IT ENACTED by the Queen's most Excellent Majesty, by and with the advice and consent of the Lords Spiritual and Temporal, and Commons, in this present Parliament assembled, and by the authority of the same, as follows:—

Press releases etc—National Insurance Contributions Act 2014 receives Royal Assent: HM Treasury press release 13 March 2014 (see *SWTI 2014, Issue 11*).

Employment allowance

1 Employment allowance for national insurance contributions

(1) A person qualifies for an employment allowance for a tax year if, in the tax year—

(a) the person is the secondary contributor in relation to payments of earnings to, or for the benefit of, one or more employed earners, and

(b) in consequence, the person incurs liabilities to pay secondary Class 1 contributions, under SSCBA 1992 or SSCB(NI)A 1992 (or both).

(2) The person's employment allowance for the tax year is—

(a) [£3,000][1], or

(b) if less, an amount equal to the total amount of the liabilities mentioned in subsection (1)(b) which are not excluded liabilities.

(3) Subsection (1) is subject to sections 2 and 3 (and Schedule 1).

(4) Sections 2 and 3 (and Schedule 1) set out cases in which a person cannot qualify for an employment allowance for a tax year.

(5) Section 2 also sets out the cases in which liabilities to pay secondary Class 1 contributions are "excluded liabilities".

(6) Section 4 provides for a person who qualifies for an employment allowance for a tax year to receive it by way of deductions or a repayment under that section.

(7) In this Act references to "the employment allowance provisions" are to this section, sections 2 to 4 and Schedule 1.

(8) In the employment allowance provisions and section 5 terms used which are also used in Part 1 of SSCBA 1992 or SSCB(NI)A 1992 have the same meaning as they have in that Part.

Press releases etc—Employment Allowance—guidance on eligibility, claiming, record keeping and penalties: HMRC Notice 6 February 2014 (see *SWTI 2014, Issue 6*).

Amendments—[1] In sub-s (2)(a), "£3,000" substituted for "£2,000" by the Employment Allowance (Increase of Maximum Amount) Regulations, SI 2016/63 reg 2 with effect from 6 April 2016.

2 Exceptions

Public authorities

(1) A person cannot qualify for an employment allowance for a tax year if, at any time in the tax year, the person is a public authority which is not a charity.

(2) In subsection (1)—

"charity" has the same meaning as in the Small Charitable Donations Act 2012 (see section 18(1) of that Act), and

"public authority" includes any person whose activities involve, wholly or mainly, the performance of functions (whether or not in the United Kingdom) which are of a public nature.

Personal, family or household affairs

(3) Liabilities to pay secondary Class 1 contributions incurred by a person ("P") are "excluded liabilities" if they are incurred in respect of an employed earner who is employed (wholly or partly) for purposes connected with P's personal, family or household affairs.

[(3A) But the liabilities mentioned in subsection (3) are not "excluded liabilities" by virtue of that subsection if all the duties of the employed earner's employment which relate to P's personal, family or household affairs are performed for an individual who needs those duties to be performed because of the individual's—

(a) old age,

(b) mental or physical disability,

(c) past or present dependence on alcohol or drugs,

(d) past or present illness, or

(e) past or present mental disorder.][1]

Workers supplied by service companies etc

(4) Liabilities to pay secondary Class 1 contributions are "excluded liabilities" if they are incurred by virtue of regulations made under section 4A of SSCBA 1992 or SSCB(NI)A 1992 (earnings of workers supplied by service companies etc).

[Excluded companies

(4A) A body corporate ("C") cannot qualify for an employment allowance for a tax year if—

(a) all the payments of earnings in relation to which C is the secondary contributor in that year are paid to, or for the benefit of, the same employed earner, and

(b) when each of those payments is made, that employed earner is a director of C.][2]

Transfers of businesses

(5) Subsection (6) applies if a business, or a part of a business, is transferred to a person ("P") in a tax year.

(6) Liabilities to pay secondary Class 1 contributions incurred by P in the tax year are "excluded liabilities" if they are incurred in respect of an employed earner who is employed (wholly or partly) for purposes connected with the transferred business or part.

(7) For the purposes of subsection (5) a business, or a part of a business, is transferred to P in a tax year if, in the tax year—

(a) another person ("Q") is carrying on the business or part, and

(b) in consequence of arrangements involving P and Q, P begins to carry on the business or part on or following Q ceasing to do so.

(8) In subsection (7)(b) "arrangements" includes any agreement, understanding, scheme, transaction or series of transactions (whether or not legally enforceable).

(9) In subsections (5) to (7) "business" includes—

(a) anything which is a trade, profession or vocation for the purposes of the Income Tax Acts or the Corporation Tax Acts;

(b) a property business (as defined in section 263(6) of the Income Tax (Trading and Other Income) Act 2005);

(c) any charitable or not-for-profit undertaking or any similar undertaking;

(d) functions of a public nature.

Anti-avoidance

(10) A person cannot qualify for an employment allowance for a tax year if, apart from this subsection, the person would qualify in consequence of avoidance arrangements.

(11) In a case not covered by subsection (10), liabilities to pay secondary Class 1 contributions incurred by a person ("P") in a tax year are "excluded liabilities" if they are incurred by P, or are incurred by P in that tax year (as opposed to another tax year), in consequence of avoidance arrangements.

(12) In subsections (10) and (11) "avoidance arrangements" means arrangements the main purpose, or one of the main purposes, of which is to secure that a person benefits, or benefits further, from the application of the employment allowance provisions.

(13) In subsection (12) "arrangements" includes any agreement, understanding, scheme, transaction or series of transactions (whether or not legally enforceable).

Amendments—[1] Sub-s (3A) inserted by the Employment Allowance (Care and Support Workers) Regulations, SI 2015/578 reg 2 with effect from 6 April 2015.

[2] Sub-s (4A) and preceding heading inserted by the Employment Allowance (Excluded Companies) Regulations, SI 2016/344 reg 2 with effect from 6 April 2016.

3 Connected persons

(1) This section applies if—

(a) at the beginning of a tax year, two or more companies which are not charities are connected with one another, and

(b) apart from this section, two or more of those companies would qualify for an employment allowance for the tax year.

(2) This section also applies if—

(a) at the beginning of a tax year, two or more charities are connected with one another, and

(b) apart from this section, two or more of those charities would qualify for an employment allowance for the tax year.

(3) Only one of the companies or charities mentioned in subsection (1)(b) or (2)(b) (as the case may be) can qualify for an employment allowance for the tax year.

(4) It is up to the companies or charities so mentioned to decide which of them that will be.

(5) Part 1 of Schedule 1 sets out the rules for determining if two or more companies are "connected" with one another for the purposes of subsection (1).

(6) Part 2 of Schedule 1 sets out the rules for determining if two or more charities are "connected" with one another for the purposes of subsection (2).

(7) In this section and Schedule 1—

"charity" has the same meaning as in the Small Charitable Donations Act 2012 (see section 18(1) of that Act), subject to paragraph 8(5) of Schedule 1, and

"company" has the meaning given by section 1121(1) of the Corporation Tax Act 2010 (meaning of "company") and includes a limited liability partnership.

4 How does a person who qualifies for an employment allowance receive it?

(1) Her Majesty's Revenue and Customs ("HMRC") must (from time to time) make such arrangements as HMRC consider appropriate for persons who qualify for an employment allowance for a tax year to receive it by making deductions from qualifying payments which they are required to make under regulations made under paragraph 6 of Schedule 1 to SSCBA 1992 or SSCB(NI)A 1992 (regulations combining collection of contributions with tax).

(2) In this section "qualifying payment", in relation to a person who qualifies for an employment allowance for a tax year, means a payment in respect of any of the person's liabilities mentioned in section 1(1)(b) which are not excluded liabilities (see section 2).

(3) If under HMRC's arrangements a person is permitted to make a deduction from a qualifying payment, the person must make the deduction and must make it before any other deductions which the person is permitted to make from the payment under any other legislation.

(4) HMRC's arrangements may (in particular)—

(a) require deductions to be made at the earliest opportunity in a tax year;

(b) provide that deductions may not be made in specified cases;

(c) place limits on the amounts of deductions;

(d) provide that a person is not permitted to make deductions unless the person has first given notice to HMRC in such form and manner, and containing such information, as HMRC may require.

(5) Subsections (6) to (8) apply in relation to a person who qualifies for an employment allowance for a tax year if the person has not deducted under this section the full amount of the employment allowance by the end of the month of April in which the tax year ends.

(6) The person may apply to HMRC for a repayment, up to the outstanding amount of the employment allowance, of qualifying payments made by the person; and HMRC must make the repayment.

(7) The person's application must be made in such form and manner, and contain such information, as HMRC may require.

(8) The person's application must be made before the end of the 4th tax year after the tax year mentioned in subsection (5).

(9) In the application of section 102 of the Finance Act 2009 (repayment interest on sums to be paid by HMRC) in relation to a repayment under this section, the repayment interest start date is the date on which HMRC receive the person's application.

(10) A repayment under this section, and any interest in respect of it under section 102 of the Finance Act 2009, are to be paid out of the National Insurance Fund or the Northern Ireland National Insurance Fund.

(11) A person who qualifies for an employment allowance for a tax year may not receive it otherwise than by way of deductions or a repayment under this section.

5 Power to amend the employment allowance provisions

(1) The Treasury may by regulations amend the employment allowance provisions—

(a) so as to increase or decrease a person's employment allowance for a tax year, or

(b) so as to add to, reduce or modify the cases in which a person cannot qualify for an employment allowance for a tax year or in which liabilities to pay secondary Class 1 contributions are "excluded liabilities".

(2) Section 175(3) to (5) of SSCBA 1992 (various supplementary powers) applies to the power to make regulations conferred by this section.

(3) The power conferred by section 175(4) of SSCBA 1992, as applied by subsection (2), includes (in particular) power to make the provision mentioned in section 175(4) by way of amendments to the employment allowance provisions.

(4) Regulations under this section must be made by statutory instrument.

(5) A statutory instrument containing (with or without other provision)—

(a) regulations falling within subsection (1)(a) which decrease a person's employment allowance for a tax year, or

(b) regulations falling within subsection (1)(b),

may not be made unless a draft has been laid before, and approved by a resolution of, each House of Parliament.

(6) A statutory instrument—

(a) which contains regulations falling within subsection (1)(a) which increase a person's employment allowance for a tax year, and

(b) which does not have to be approved in draft under subsection (5),

must be laid before Parliament after being made.

(7) Regulations contained in a statutory instrument which is required to be laid before Parliament under subsection (6) cease to have effect at the end of the period of 40 days after the day on which the instrument is made unless, before the end of that period, the instrument is approved by a resolution of each House of Parliament.

(8) If regulations cease to have effect as a result of subsection (7), that does not—

(a) affect anything previously done by virtue of the regulations, or

(b) prevent the making of new regulations to the same or a similar effect.

(9) In calculating the period of 40 days for the purposes of subsection (7), no account is to be taken of any time during which Parliament is dissolved or prorogued or during which either House is adjourned for more than 4 days.

Regulations—Employment Allowance (Increase of Maximum Amount) Regulations, SI 2016/63.

6 Decisions and appeals about entitlements to make deductions etc

(1) In Part 2 of the Social Security Contributions (Transfer of Functions, etc) Act 1999 (decisions and appeals), in section 8(1) (decisions of officers of Revenue and Customs), after paragraph (e) insert—

"(ea) to decide whether a person is or was entitled to make a deduction under section 4 of the National Insurance Contributions Act 2014 (deductions etc of employment allowance) and, if so, the amount the person is or was entitled to deduct,

(eb) to decide whether a person is or was entitled to a repayment under that section and, if so, the amount of the repayment,".

NIC

(2) In Part 3 of the Social Security Contributions (Transfer of Functions, etc) (Northern Ireland) Order 1999 (SI 1999/671) (decisions and appeals), in Article 7(1) (decisions of officers of Revenue and Customs), after paragraph (e) insert—

"(ea) to decide whether a person is or was entitled to make a deduction under section 4 of the National Insurance Contributions Act 2014 (deductions etc of employment allowance) and, if so, the amount the person is or was entitled to deduct,

(eb) to decide whether a person is or was entitled to a repayment under that section and, if so, the amount of the repayment,".

7 Retention of records etc

(1) In Schedule 1 to SSCBA 1992 (supplementary provisions relating to national insurance contributions), in paragraph 8(1) (general regulation-making powers), after paragraph (a) insert—

"(aa) for requiring persons to maintain, in such form and manner as may be prescribed, records of such matters as may be prescribed for purposes connected with the employment allowance provisions (within the meaning of the National Insurance Contributions Act 2014), and to retain the records for so long as may be prescribed;".

(2) In Schedule 1 to SSCB(NI)A 1992 (supplementary provisions relating to national insurance contributions), in paragraph 8(1) (general regulation-making powers), after paragraph (a) insert—

"(aa) for requiring persons to maintain, in such form and manner as may be prescribed, records of such matters as may be prescribed for purposes connected with the employment allowance provisions (within the meaning of the National Insurance Contributions Act 2014), and to retain the records for so long as may be prescribed;".

(3) In paragraph 26 of Schedule 4 to the Social Security (Contributions) Regulations 2001 (SI 2001/1004) (retention of records), after sub-paragraph (4) insert—

"(4A) Sub-paragraph (4B) applies in relation to an employer who makes deductions, or applies for a repayment, under section 4 of the National Insurance Contributions Act 2014 on account of an employment allowance for which the employer qualifies for a tax year (or who intends to do so).

(4B) So far as they are not otherwise covered by sub-paragraph (4), "contribution records" includes any documents or records relating to—

(a) the employer's qualification for the employment allowance, or

(b) the calculation of any amount that has been, or could be, deducted or repaid under section 4 of the National Insurance Contributions Act 2014 on account of the employment allowance."

(4) The amendment made by subsection (3) is to be treated as having been made by the Treasury using the powers conferred by paragraph 8(1)(aa) of Schedule 1 to SSCBA 1992 (as inserted by subsection (1)) and paragraph 8(1)(aa) of Schedule 1 to SSCB(NI)A 1992 (as inserted by subsection (2)).

(5) In section 110ZA of the Social Security Administration Act 1992 (powers to call for documents etc), in subsection (2)(a), after "Benefits Act" insert "or the National Insurance Contributions Act 2014".

(6) In section 104ZA of the Social Security Administration (Northern Ireland) Act 1992 (powers to call for documents etc), in subsection (2)(a), after "Benefits Act" insert "or the National Insurance Contributions Act 2014".

Press releases etc—Employment Allowance—guidance on eligibility, claiming, record keeping and penalties: HMRC Notice 6 February 2014 (see *SWTI 2014, Issue 6*).

8 Commencement of the employment allowance provisions etc

Sections 1 to 7 and Schedule 1 come into force on 6 April 2014.

Introduction of age-related secondary percentage

9 Reduction of secondary Class 1 contributions for certain age groups

(1) SSCBA 1992 is amended as follows.

(2) In section 9 (calculation of secondary Class 1 contributions)—

(a) in subsection (1) for "the secondary percentage" substitute "the relevant percentage", and

(b) after subsection (1) insert—

"(1A) For the purposes of subsection (1) "the relevant percentage" is—

(a) if section 9A below applies to the earnings, the age-related secondary percentage;

(b) otherwise, the secondary percentage."

(3) After section 9 insert—

"9A The age-related secondary percentage

(1) Where a secondary Class 1 contribution is payable as mentioned in section 6(1)(b) above, this section applies to the earnings paid in the tax week, in respect of the employment in question, if the earner falls within an age group specified in column 1 of the table in subsection (3).

(2) For the purposes of section 9(1A)(a) above, the age-related secondary percentage is the percentage for the earner's age group specified in column 2 of the table.

(3) Here is the table—

Age group	Age-related secondary percentage
Under 21	0%

(4) The Treasury may by regulations amend the table—

(a) so as to add an age group in column 1 and to specify the percentage in column 2 for that age group;

(b) so as to reduce (or further reduce) the percentage specified in column 2 for an age group already specified in column 1 (whether for the whole of the age group or only part of it).

(5) A percentage specified under subsection (4)(a) must be lower than the secondary percentage.

(6) For the purposes of this Act a person is still to be regarded as being liable to pay a secondary Class 1 contribution even though the amount of the contribution is £0 because the age-related secondary percentage is 0%.

(7) The Treasury may by regulations provide that, in relation to an age group specified in the table, there is to be for every tax year an upper secondary threshold for secondary Class 1 contributions.

That threshold is to be the amount specified for that year by regulations made by the Treasury.

(8) Subsections (4) and (5) of section 5 above (which confer power to prescribe an equivalent of a secondary threshold in relation to earners paid otherwise than weekly), and subsection (6) of that section as it applies for the purposes of those subsections, apply for the purposes of an upper secondary threshold in relation to an age group as they apply for the purposes of a secondary threshold.

(9) Where—

(a) a secondary Class 1 contribution is payable as mentioned in section 6(1)(b) above,

(b) the earner falls within an age group in relation to which provision has been made under subsection (7), and

(c) the earnings paid in the tax week, in respect of the employment in question, exceed the current upper secondary threshold (or the prescribed equivalent) in relation to the age group,

this section is not to apply to the earnings so far as they exceed that threshold (or the prescribed equivalent); and for the purposes of section 9(1) above the relevant percentage in respect of the earnings so far as they exceed that threshold (or the prescribed equivalent) is, accordingly, to be the secondary percentage.

(10) In subsections (7) to (9) references to an age group include a part of an age group."

(4) In section 122(1) (interpretation of Parts 1 to 6), at the appropriate place insert—

""age-related secondary percentage" is to be construed in accordance with section 9A(2) above;".

(5) In section 176(1)(a) (parliamentary control: instruments subject to affirmative procedure) after "section 4C;" insert—

"section 9A(7);".

(6) SSCB(NI)A 1992 is amended as follows.

(7) In section 9 (calculation of secondary Class 1 contributions)—

(a) in subsection (1) for "the secondary percentage" substitute "the relevant percentage", and

(b) after subsection (1) insert—

"(1A) For the purposes of subsection (1) "the relevant percentage" is—

(a) if section 9A below applies to the earnings, the age-related secondary percentage;

(b) otherwise, the secondary percentage."

(8) After section 9 insert—

"9A The age-related secondary percentage

(1) Where a secondary Class 1 contribution is payable as mentioned in section 6(1)(b) above, this section applies to the earnings paid in the tax week, in respect of the employment in question, if the earner falls within an age group specified in column 1 of the table in subsection (3).

NIC

(2) For the purposes of section 9(1A)(a) above, the age-related secondary percentage is the percentage for the earner's age group specified in column 2 of the table.

(3) Here is the table—

Age group	Age-related secondary percentage
Under 21	0%

(4) The Treasury may by regulations amend the table—

(a) so as to add an age group in column 1 and to specify the percentage in column 2 for that age group;

(b) so as to reduce (or further reduce) the percentage specified in column 2 for an age group already specified in column 1 (whether for the whole of the age group or only part of it).

(5) A percentage specified under subsection (4)(a) must be lower than the secondary percentage.

(6) For the purposes of this Act a person is still to be regarded as being liable to pay a secondary Class 1 contribution even though the amount of the contribution is £0 because the age-related secondary percentage is 0%.

(7) The Treasury may by regulations provide that, in relation to an age group specified in the table, there is to be for every tax year an upper secondary threshold for secondary Class 1 contributions.

That threshold is to be the amount specified for that year by regulations made by the Treasury.

(8) Subsections (4) and (5) of section 5 above (which confer power to prescribe an equivalent of a secondary threshold in relation to earners paid otherwise than weekly), and subsection (6) of that section as it applies for the purposes of those subsections, apply for the purposes of an upper secondary threshold in relation to an age group as they apply for the purposes of a secondary threshold.

(9) Where—

(a) a secondary Class 1 contribution is payable as mentioned in section 6(1)(b) above,

(b) the earner falls within an age group in relation to which provision has been made under subsection (7), and

(c) the earnings paid in the tax week, in respect of the employment in question, exceed the current upper secondary threshold (or the prescribed equivalent) in relation to the age group,

this section is not to apply to the earnings so far as they exceed that threshold (or the prescribed equivalent); and for the purposes of section 9(1) above the relevant percentage in respect of the earnings so far as they exceed that threshold (or the prescribed equivalent) is, accordingly, to be the secondary percentage.

(10) In subsections (7) to (9) references to an age group include a part of an age group."

(9) In section 121(1) (interpretation of Parts 1 to 6), at the appropriate place insert—

""age-related secondary percentage" is to be construed in accordance with section 9A(2) above;"

(10) In section 172(11A) (parliamentary control: instruments subject to affirmative procedure) after "4C," insert "9A(7),".

(11) The following come into force at the end of the period of 2 months beginning with the day on which this Act is passed—

(a) any power conferred on the Treasury by virtue of this section to make regulations, and

(b) the amendments made by subsections (5) and (10).

(12) So far as not already brought into force by subsection (11), the amendments made by this section come into force on 6 April 2015.

Application of general anti-abuse rule to national insurance contributions

10 GAAR to apply to national insurance contributions

(1) In Part 5 of the Finance Act 2013 (general anti-abuse rule)—

(a) references to tax, other than in references to particular taxes, include national insurance contributions, and

(b) references to a charge to tax include a liability to pay national insurance contributions.

(2) Section 206(3) of that Act (list of taxes to which the general anti-abuse rule applies) has effect as if it included a reference to national insurance contributions.

(3) Section 207 of that Act (meaning of "tax arrangements" and "abusive") has effect as if, in subsection (4)(a), after "income," there were inserted "earnings (within the meaning of Part 1 of the Social Security Contributions and Benefits Act 1992 or Part 1 of the Social Security Contributions and Benefits (Northern Ireland) Act 1992),".

(4) Adjustments to be made in respect of national insurance contributions under section 209 of the Finance Act 2013 (counteracting the tax advantages) may be made by a notice given under paragraph 12 of Schedule 43 to that Act (notice of final decision)[, paragraph 8 or 9 of Schedule 43A to that Act (pooling of tax arrangements: notice of final decision) or paragraph 8 of Schedule 43B to that Act (generic referral of arrangements: notice of final decision)][1].

(5) For the purposes of section 210 of that Act (consequential relieving adjustments)—

(a) if a claim under that section relates to Class 4 national insurance contributions, Schedule 1A to the Taxes Management Act 1970 (as that Schedule applies in relation to such contributions) applies to it, and

(b) if a claim under that section relates to any other class of national insurance contributions, it must be made in such form and manner, and contain such information, as HMRC may require.

(6) Adjustments to be made in respect of national insurance contributions under that section may be made by a notice given under subsection (7) of that section.

[(6A) Where, by virtue of this section, a case falls within paragraph 4A of Schedule 43 to the Finance Act 2013 (referrals of single schemes: relevant corrective action) or paragraph 4 of Schedule 43A to that Act (pooled schemes: relevant corrective action)—

(*a*) the person ("P") mentioned in sub-paragraph (1) of that paragraph takes the "relevant corrective action" for the purposes of that paragraph if (and only if)—

(i) in a case in which the tax advantage in question can be counteracted by making a payment to HMRC, P makes that payment and notifies HMRC that P has done so, or

(ii) in any case, P takes all necessary action to enter into an agreement in writing with HMRC for the purpose of relinquishing the tax advantage, and

(*b*) accordingly, sub-paragraphs (2) to (8) of that paragraph do not apply.][1]

(7) This section has effect in relation to tax arrangements (within the meaning of Part 5 of the Finance Act 2013 as modified by this section) entered into on or after the day on which this Act is passed.

(8) Subsections (9) and (10) apply where the tax arrangements—

(a) would not have been tax arrangements but for the modifications made by this section, and

(b) form part of other arrangements entered into before the day on which this Act is passed.

(9) The other arrangements are to be ignored for the purposes of section 207(3) of the Finance Act 2013, subject to subsection (10).

(10) Account is to be taken of the other arrangements for the purposes of that section if, as a result, the tax arrangements would not be abusive.

(11) In this section—

"abusive", "arrangements"[, "HMRC" and "tax advantage"][1] have the same meaning as in Part 5 of the Finance Act 2013 [(as modified by this section)][1];

"national insurance contributions" means contributions under either Part 1 of SSCBA 1992 or Part 1 of SSCB(NI)A 1992.

[(12) See section 10A for further modifications of Part 5 of the Finance Act 2013.][1]

Amendments—[1] In sub-s (4), words inserted, sub-ss (6A), (12) inserted, in sub-s (11)(*a*), words inserted, and in sub-s (11)(*b*), words substituted for words "and "HMRC", by FA 2016 s 157(12)–(16) with effect in relation to tax arrangements (within the meaning of FA 2013 Pt 5) entered into at any time (whether before on or after 15 September 2016).

[10A Application of GAAR in relation to penalties

(1) For the purposes of this section a penalty under section 212A of the Finance Act 2013 is a "relevant NICs-related penalty" so far as the penalty relates to a tax advantage in respect of relevant contributions.

(2) A relevant NICs-related penalty may be recovered as if it were an amount of relevant contributions which is due and payable.

(3) Section 117A of the Social Security Administration Act 1992 or (as the case may be) section 111A of the Social Security Administration (Northern Ireland) Act 1992 (issues arising in proceedings: contributions etc) has effect in relation to proceedings before a court for recovery of a relevant NICs-related penalty as if the assessment of the penalty were a NICs decision as to whether the person is liable for the penalty.

(4) Accordingly, paragraph 5(4)(*b*) of Schedule 43C to the Finance Act 2013 (assessment of penalty to be enforced as if it were an assessment to tax) does not apply in relation to a relevant NICs-related penalty.

(5) In the application of Schedule 43C to the Finance Act 2013 in relation to a relevant NICs-related penalty, paragraph 9(5) has effect as if the reference to an appeal against an assessment to the tax concerned were to an appeal against a NICs decision.

(6) In paragraph 8 of that Schedule (aggregate penalties), references to a "relevant penalty provision" include—

(*a*) any provision mentioned in sub-paragraph (5) of that paragraph, as applied in relation to any class of national insurance contributions by regulations (whenever made);

(*b*) section 98A of the Taxes Management Act 1970, as applied in relation to any class of national insurance contributions by regulations (whenever made);
(*c*) any provision in regulations made by the Treasury under which a penalty can be imposed in respect of any class of national insurance contributions.

(7) The Treasury may by regulations—
(*a*) disapply, or modify the effect of, subsection (6)(*a*) or (*b*);
(*b*) modify paragraph 8 of Schedule 43C to the Finance Act 2013 as it has effect in relation to a relevant penalty provision by virtue of subsection (6)(*b*) or (*c*).

(8) Section 175(3) to (5) of SSCBA 1992 (various supplementary powers) applies to a power to make regulations conferred by subsection (7).

(9) Regulations under subsection (7) must be made by statutory instrument.

(10) A statutory instrument containing regulations under subsection (7) is subject to annulment in pursuance of a resolution of either House of Parliament.

(11) In this section "NICs decision" means a decision under section 8 of the Social Security Contributions (Transfer of Functions, etc) Act 1999 or Article 7 of the Social Security Contributions (Transfer of Functions, etc) (Northern Ireland) Order 1999 (SI 1999/671).

(12) In this section "relevant contributions" means the following contributions under Part 1 of SSCBA 1992 or Part 1 of SSCB(NI)A 1992—
(*a*) Class 1 contributions;
(*b*) Class 1A contributions;
(*c*) Class 1B contributions;
(*d*) Class 2 contributions which must be paid but in relation to which section 11A of the Act in question (application of certain provisions of the Income Tax Acts in relation to Class 2 contributions under section 11(2) of that Act) does not apply.][1]

Amendments—[1] Section 10A inserted by FA 2016 s 157(12), (17) with effect in relation to tax arrangements (within the meaning of FA 2013 Pt 5) entered into at any time (whether before on or after 15 September 2016).

11 Power to modify application of GAAR to national insurance contributions

(1) Where a modification is made to Part 5 of the Finance Act 2013 (general anti-abuse rule) that does not apply in relation to national insurance contributions ("the tax only modification"), the Treasury may by regulations—
(a) make provision for the purpose of applying the tax only modification in relation to national insurance contributions (with or without modifications),
(b) make provision in relation to national insurance contributions corresponding to the tax only modification, or
(c) otherwise modify the general anti-abuse rule, as it has effect in relation to national insurance contributions, in consequence of, or for the purpose of making provision supplementary or incidental to, the tax only modification.

(2) Regulations under this section—
(a) may amend, repeal or revoke any provision of an Act or instrument made under an Act (whenever passed or made),
(b) may make consequential, incidental, supplementary, transitional, transitory or saving provision, and
(c) may make different provision for different cases, classes of national insurance contributions or purposes.

(3) Regulations under this section must be made by statutory instrument.

(4) A statutory instrument containing (with or without other provision) regulations under this section that amend or repeal a provision of an Act may not be made unless a draft has been laid before, and approved by a resolution of, each House of Parliament.

(5) A statutory instrument containing regulations under this section that does not have to be approved in draft under subsection (4) is subject to annulment in pursuance of a resolution of either House of Parliament.

(6) In this section—
"general anti-abuse rule" has the same meaning as in Part 5 of the Finance Act 2013;
"national insurance contributions" means contributions under either Part 1 of SSCBA 1992 or Part 1 of SSCB(NI)A 1992.

Oil and gas workers on the continental shelf

12 Oil and gas workers on the continental shelf: secondary contributors etc

(1) Section 120 of SSCBA 1992 (employment at sea: continental shelf operations) is amended as follows.

(2) In subsection (1), after "persons" insert "("continental shelf workers")".

(3) In subsection (3)—
(a) for "the regulations" substitute "regulations under subsection (1)", and
(b) for "such person" substitute "continental shelf worker".

(4) After that subsection insert—

"(4) The Treasury may also, by regulations, make provision for, and in connection with, the issue by Her Majesty's Revenue and Customs of certificates to prescribed persons who are, by virtue of regulations under subsection (1), to be treated as the secondary contributor in relation to the payment of earnings to or for the benefit of one or more continental shelf workers—

(a) confirming that the prescribed person's liabilities to pay contributions in respect of the continental shelf workers specified or described in the certificate are being met by another person, and

(b) discharging the prescribed person, while the certificate is in force, from liability to make any payments in respect of the contributions, in the event that the other person fails to pay them in full.

(5) Regulations under subsection (4) may, in particular, make provision about—

(a) applying for a certificate;

(b) the circumstances in which a certificate may, or must, be issued or cancelled;

(c) the form and content of a certificate;

(d) the effect of a certificate (including provision modifying the effect mentioned in subsection (4)(b) or specifying further effects);

(e) the effect of cancelling a certificate."

Press releases etc—Offshore employment intermediaries—technical note and draft guidance: HMRC Technical Note 19 December 2013 (see *SWTI 2014, Issue 1*).

Partnerships

13 Class 4 contributions: partnerships

(1) SSCBA 1992 is amended as follows.

(2) After section 18 insert—

"18A Class 4 contributions: partnerships

(1) The Treasury may by regulations—

(a) modify the way in which liabilities for Class 4 contributions of a partner in a firm are determined, or

(b) otherwise modify the law relating to Class 4 contributions,

as they consider appropriate to take account of the passing or making of a provision of the Income Tax Acts relating to firms or partners in firms.

(2) "Firm" has the same meaning as in the Income Tax (Trading and Other Income) Act 2005 (and includes a limited liability partnership in relation to which section 863(1) of that Act applies); and "partner" is to be read accordingly and includes a former partner.

(3) Regulations under this section may have retrospective effect; but they may not have effect before the beginning of the tax year in which they are made."

(3) In section 176(1)(a) (parliamentary control: instruments subject to affirmative procedure), after "section 18;" insert—

"section 18A;".

(4) SSCB(NI)A 1992 is amended as follows.

(5) After section 18 insert—

"18A Class 4 contributions: partnerships

(1) The Treasury may by regulations—

(a) modify the way in which liabilities for Class 4 contributions of a partner in a firm are determined, or

(b) otherwise modify the law relating to Class 4 contributions,

as they consider appropriate to take account of the passing or making of a provision of the Income Tax Acts relating to firms or partners in firms.

(2) "Firm" has the same meaning as in the Income Tax (Trading and Other Income) Act 2005 (and includes a limited liability partnership in relation to which section 863(1) of that Act applies); and "partner" is to be read accordingly and includes a former partner.

(3) Regulations under this section may have retrospective effect; but they may not have effect before the beginning of the tax year in which they are made."

(6) In section 172(11A) (parliamentary control: instruments subject to affirmative procedure), after "18," insert "18A,".

(7) The amendments made by this section come into force at the end of the period of 2 months beginning with the day on which this Act is passed.

Press releases etc—Partnerships—A review of two aspects of the tax rules—technical note and guidance: HMRC Technical Note 10 December 2013 (see *SWTI 2014, Issue 1*).

14 Limited liability partnerships

(1) SSCBA 1992 is amended as follows.

(2) After section 4A insert—

"4AA Limited liability partnerships

(1) The Treasury may, for the purposes of this Act, by regulations—

(a) provide that, in prescribed circumstances—

(i) a person ("E") is to be treated as employed in employed earner's employment by a limited liability partnership (including where E is a member of the partnership), and

(ii) the limited liability partnership is to be treated as the secondary contributor in relation to any payment of earnings to or for the benefit of E as the employed earner;

(b) prescribe how earnings in respect of E's employed earner employment with the limited liability partnership are to be determined (including what constitutes such earnings);

(c) provide that such earnings are to be treated as being paid to or for the benefit of E at prescribed times.

(2) Regulations under subsection (1) may modify the definition of "employee" or "employer" in section 163, 171, 171ZJ or 171ZS below as the Treasury consider appropriate to take account of any provision falling within subsection (1)(a) to (c).

(3) If—

(a) a provision of the Income Tax Acts relating to limited liability partnerships or members of limited liability partnerships is passed or made, and

(b) in consequence, the Treasury consider it appropriate for provision to be made for the purpose of assimilating to any extent the law relating to income tax and the law relating to contributions under this Part,

the Treasury may by regulations make that provision.

(4) The provision that may be made under subsection (3) includes provision modifying any provision made by or under this Act.

(5) Regulations under this section are to be made with the concurrence of the Secretary of State.

(6) Section 4(4) of the Limited Liability Partnerships Act 2000 does not limit the provision that may be made by regulations under this section."

(3) In section 4B (power to make retrospective provision in consequence of retrospective tax legislation), in subsection (3), after paragraph (c) insert—

"(d) section 4AA (power to make provision in relation to limited liability partnerships)".

(4) In section 10 (Class 1A contributions: benefits in kind etc), at the end, insert—

"(11) The Treasury may by regulations modify the law relating to Class 1A contributions in the case of an employed earner's employment which is treated as existing by virtue of regulations under section 4AA."

(5) SSCB(NI)A 1992 is amended as follows.

(6) After section 4A insert—

"4AA Limited liability partnerships

(1) The Treasury may, for the purposes of this Act, by regulations—

(a) provide that, in prescribed circumstances—

(i) a person ("E") is to be treated as employed in employed earner's employment by a limited liability partnership (including where E is a member of the partnership), and

(ii) the limited liability partnership is to be treated as the secondary contributor in relation to any payment of earnings to or for the benefit of E as the employed earner;

(b) prescribe how earnings in respect of E's employed earner employment with the limited liability partnership are to be determined (including what constitutes such earnings);

(c) provide that such earnings are to be treated as being paid to or for the benefit of E at prescribed times.

(2) Regulations under subsection (1) may modify the definition of "employee" or "employer" in section 159, 167, 167ZJ or 167ZS below as the Treasury consider appropriate to take account of any provision falling within subsection (1)(a) to (c).

(3) If—

(a) a provision of the Income Tax Acts relating to limited liability partnerships or members of limited liability partnerships is passed or made, and

(b) in consequence, the Treasury consider it appropriate for provision to be made for the purpose of assimilating to any extent the law relating to income tax and the law relating to contributions under this Part, the Treasury may by regulations make that provision.

(4) The provision that may be made under subsection (3) includes provision modifying any provision made by or under this Act.

(5) Regulations under this section are to be made with the concurrence of the Department.

(6) Section 4(4) of the Limited Liability Partnerships Act 2000 does not limit the provision that may be made by regulations under this section."

(7) In section 4B (power to make retrospective provision in consequence of retrospective tax legislation), in subsection (3), after paragraph (c) insert—

"(d) section 4AA (power to make provision in relation to limited liability partnerships)".

(8) In section 10 (Class 1A contributions: benefits in kind etc), at the end, insert—

"(11) The Treasury may by regulations modify the law relating to Class 1A contributions in the case of an employed earner's employment which is treated as existing by virtue of regulations under section 4AA."

Regulations—Social Security Contributions (Limited Liability Partnership) Regulations, SI 2014/3159.

Press releases etc—Partnerships: A review of two aspects of the tax rules. HMRC Technical Note, 27 March 2014 (see *SWTI 2014, Issue 13*).

Other provision

15 Office holders who receive "earnings" to be employed earners

(1) In section 2(1)(a) of SSCBA 1992 (definition of "employed earner"), omit "general".

(2) In section 2(1)(a) of SSCB(NI)A 1992 (definition of "employed earner"), omit "general".

(3) Schedule 2 makes provision that is consequential upon office holders in receipt of "earnings" (as opposed to "general earnings") being employed earners.

(4) The amendments made by this section and Schedule 2 come into force at the end of the period of 2 months beginning with the day on which this Act is passed.

16 Armed Forces early departure payments retrospectively disregarded

Paragraph 10A of Part 6 of Schedule 3 to the Social Security (Contributions) Regulations 2001 (SI 2001/1004) (payments under the Armed Forces Early Departure Payments Scheme Order 2005 (SI 2005/437) to be disregarded) also has effect for the tax years 2005–06 to 2012–13 inclusive.

17 Repeal of certain redundant reliefs relating to Class 4 contributions

(1) In Schedule 2 to SSCBA 1992 (levy of Class 4 contributions with income tax)—

(a) omit paragraph 3(3), and

(b) omit paragraph 9 (and the heading immediately before it).

(2) In Schedule 2 to SSCB(NI)A 1992 (levy of Class 4 contributions with income tax)—

(a) omit paragraph 3(3), and

(b) omit paragraph 9 (and the heading immediately before it).

(3) The amendments made by subsections (1)(a) and (2)(a) have effect for the tax year after the one during which this Act is passed and for subsequent tax years.

18 Certain orders and regulations in respect of Northern Ireland

(1) Section 172 of SSCB(NI)A 1992 (Assembly etc control of regulations and orders) is amended as follows.

(2) In subsection (11), for "(9)" substitute "(10)".

(3) In subsection (11B)—

(a) after "contains" insert

"—

(a)

(b) after "129" insert "or 142(7)", and

(c) after "Act" insert

",

(b) regulations under powers conferred by any provision mentioned in that subsection which are to be made for the purpose of consolidating regulations to be revoked in the instrument, or

(c) regulations which, in so far as they are made under powers conferred by any provision mentioned in that subsection, only replace provisions of previous regulations with new provisions to the same effect."

(4) Section 165 of the Social Security Administration (Northern Ireland) Act 1992 (regulations and orders—general) is amended as follows.

(5) In subsection (1), after "to be made by" insert "the Secretary of State,".

(6) In subsection (3), after "the Department" insert ", the Secretary of State".

(7) The amendments made by this section come into force at the end of the period of 2 months beginning with the day on which this Act is passed.

General

19 HMRC administrative expenses: financial provision

(1) In section 165 of the Social Security Administration Act 1992 (adjustments between the National Insurance Fund and Consolidated Fund), in subsection (5)(a), after "adoption pay" insert "or the National Insurance Contributions Act 2014".

(2) In section 145 of the Social Security Administration (Northern Ireland) Act 1992 (adjustments between the National Insurance Fund and Consolidated Fund), in subsection (5)(a), after "adoption pay" insert "or the National Insurance Contributions Act 2014".

20 Abbreviations of Acts

In this Act—

"SSCBA 1992" means the Social Security Contributions and Benefits Act 1992;

"SSCB(NI)A 1992" means the Social Security Contributions and Benefits (Northern Ireland) Act 1992.

21 Short title and extent

(1) This Act may be cited as the National Insurance Contributions Act 2014.

(2) Subject to subsection (3), this Act extends to England and Wales, Scotland and Northern Ireland.

(3) An amendment or repeal made by this Act has the same extent as the provision amended or repealed.

SCHEDULES

SCHEDULE 1

EMPLOYMENT ALLOWANCE: RULES FOR DETERMINING IF PERSONS ARE "CONNECTED"

Section 3

PART 1

COMPANIES

Application

1 This Part applies for the purposes of section 3(1).

The basic rule

2 (1) Two companies are "connected" with one another if—

(a) one of the two has control of the other, or

(b) both are under the control of the same person or persons.

(2) In sub-paragraph (1) "control" has the same meaning as in Part 10 of CTA 2010 (see sections 450 and 451 of that Act) (and a limited liability partnership is to be treated as a company for the purposes of that Part as applied by this sub-paragraph).

(3) For this purpose, where under section 450 of that Act "C" is a limited liability partnership, subsection (3) of that section has effect as if before paragraph (a) there were inserted—

"(za) rights to a share of more than half the assets, or of more than half the income, of C,".

(4) Sub-paragraphs (1) to (3) are subject to paragraphs 3 to 6.

(5) Paragraph 7 provides for further connections.

(6) In this Part "CTA 2010" means the Corporation Tax Act 2010.

Companies whose relationship is not one of substantial commercial interdependence

3 (1) This paragraph applies for the purpose of determining under paragraph 2(1) if two companies are connected with one another if the relationship between the companies is not one of substantial commercial interdependence.

(2) In the application of section 451 of CTA 2010 for the purposes of the determination, any person to whom rights and duties fall to be attributed under subsections (4) and (5) of that section is to be treated, for the purposes of those subsections, as having no associates.

(3) In determining for the purposes of sub-paragraph (1) if two companies have a relationship of "substantial commercial interdependence", the following factors are to be taken into account—

(a) the degree to which the companies are financially interdependent (see sub-paragraph (4)),

(b) the degree to which the companies are economically interdependent (see sub-paragraph (5)), and

(c) the degree to which the companies are organisationally interdependent (see sub-paragraph (6)).

(4) Two companies are "financially interdependent" if (in particular)—
(a) one gives financial support (directly or indirectly) to the other, or
(b) each has (directly or indirectly) a financial interest in the other's activities.
(5) Two companies are "economically interdependent" if (in particular)—
(a) they seek to realise the same economic objective,
(b) the activities of one benefit the other, or
(c) their activities involve common customers.
(6) Two companies are "organisationally interdependent" if (in particular) they have—
(a) common management,
(b) common employees,
(c) common premises, or
(d) common equipment.

Fixed-rate preference shares

4 (1) In determining for the purposes of paragraph 2(1) if a company is under the control of another, fixed-rate preference shares held by a company are ignored if the company holding them—
(a) is not a close company,
(b) takes no part in the management or conduct of the company which issued the shares, or in the management or conduct of its business, and
(c) subscribed for the shares in the ordinary course of a business which includes the provision of finance.
(2) In sub-paragraph (1) "fixed-rate preference shares" means shares which—
(a) were issued wholly for new consideration,
(b) do not carry any right either to conversion into shares or securities of any other description or to the acquisition of any additional shares or securities, and
(c) do not carry any right to dividends other than dividends which—
(i) are of a fixed amount or at a fixed rate per cent of the nominal value of the shares, and
(ii) together with any sum paid on redemption, represent no more than a reasonable commercial return on the consideration for which the shares were issued.
(3) In sub-paragraph (2)(a) "new consideration" has the meaning given by section 1115 of CTA 2010.
(4) In sub-paragraph (1)(a) "close company" is to be read in accordance with Chapter 2 of Part 10 of CTA 2010 (see, in particular, section 439 of that Act).

Connection through a loan creditor

5 (1) A company ("A") is not under the control of another company ("B") for the purposes of paragraph 2(1) if—
(a) B is a loan creditor of A,
(b) there is no other connection between A and B, and
(c) either—
(i) B is not a close company, or
(ii) B's relationship to A as a loan creditor arose in the ordinary course of a business which B carries on.
(2) Sub-paragraph (3) applies if—
(a) two companies ("A" and "B") are under the control of the same person who is a loan creditor of each of them,
(b) there is no other connection between A and B, and
(c) either—
(i) the loan creditor is a company which is not a close company, or
(ii) the loan creditor's relationship to each of A and B as a loan creditor arose in the ordinary course of a business which the loan creditor carries on.
(3) In determining under paragraph 2(1) if A and B are connected with one another, rights which the loan creditor has as a loan creditor of A, or as a loan creditor of B, are ignored.
(4) In sub-paragraph (2)(a) "control" has the same meaning as in paragraph 2(1).
(5) In this paragraph—
(a) "close company" is to be read in accordance with Chapter 2 of Part 10 of CTA 2010 (see, in particular, section 439 of that Act),
(b) "connection" includes a connection in the past as well as a connection in the present and references to a connection between two companies include any dealings between them, and
(c) references to a loan creditor of a company are to be read in accordance with section 453 of CTA 2010.

Connection through a trustee

6 (1) Sub-paragraph (2) applies if—

(a) two companies ("A" and "B") are under the control of the same person by virtue of rights or powers (or both) held in trust by that person, and

(b) there is no other connection between A and B.

(2) In determining under paragraph 2(1) if A and B are connected with one another, the rights and powers mentioned in sub-paragraph (1)(a) are ignored.

(3) In sub-paragraph (1)—

(a) "control" has the same meaning as in paragraph 2(1), and

(b) "connection" includes a connection in the past as well as a connection in the present and the reference to a connection between A and B includes any dealings between them.

Further connections

7 (1) This paragraph applies if—

(a) a company ("A") is connected with another company ("B"), and

(b) B is connected with another company ("C").

(2) A and C are also connected with one another (if that would not otherwise be the case).

(3) In sub-paragraph (1)(a) the reference to a company being connected with another company is to that company being so connected by virtue of paragraphs 2 to 6 or this paragraph, and in sub-paragraph (1)(b) the reference to a company being connected with another company is to that company being so connected by virtue of paragraphs 2 to 6.

PART 2
CHARITIES

8 (1) Two charities are connected with one another for the purposes of section 3(2) if—

(a) they are connected with one another in accordance with section 993 of the Income Tax Act 2007 (meaning of "connected" persons), and

(b) their purposes and activities are the same or substantially similar.

(2) In the application of section 993 of the Income Tax Act 2007 for the purposes of sub-paragraph (1)(a)—

(a) a charity which is a trust is to be treated as if it were a company (and accordingly a person), including in this sub-paragraph;

(b) a charity which is a trust has "control" of another person if the trustees (in their capacity as trustees of the charity) have, or any of them has, control of the person;

(c) a person (other than a charity regulator) has "control" of a charity which is a trust if—

(i) the person is a trustee of the charity and some or all of the powers of the trustees of the charity could be exercised by the person acting alone or by the person acting together with any other persons who are trustees of the charity and who are connected with the person,

(ii) the person, alone or together with other persons, has power to appoint or remove a trustee of the charity, or

(iii) the person, alone or together with other persons, has any power of approval or direction in relation to the carrying out by the trustees of any of their functions.

(3) A charity which is a trust is also connected with another charity which is a trust for the purposes of section 3(2) if at least half of the trustees of one of the charities are—

(a) trustees of the other charity,

(b) persons who are connected with persons who are trustees of the other charity, or

(c) a combination of both,

and the charities' purposes and activities are the same or substantially similar.

(4) In determining if a person is connected with another person for the purposes of sub-paragraph (2)(c)(i) or (3)(b), apply section 993 of the Income Tax Act 2007 with the omission of subsection (3) of that section (and without the modifications in sub-paragraph (2)).

(5) If a charity ("A") controls a company ("B") which, apart from this sub-paragraph, would not be a charity—

(a) B is to be treated as if it were a charity for the purposes of section 3 and this Part (including this sub-paragraph), and

(b) A and B are connected with one another for the purposes of section 3(2).

(6) In sub-paragraph (5) "control" is to be read in accordance with—

(a) paragraph 2(2) and (3) (but ignoring paragraphs 3 to 6), and

(b) sub-paragraph (2)(b) of this paragraph.

9 (1) This paragraph applies if—

(a) a charity ("A") is connected with another charity ("B") for the purposes of section 3(2), and

(b) B is connected with another charity ("C") for the purposes of section 3(2).

(2) A and C are also connected with one another for the purposes of section 3(2) (if that would not otherwise be the case).

(3) In sub-paragraph (1)(a) the reference to a charity being connected with another charity for the purposes of section 3(2) is to that charity being so connected by virtue of paragraph 8 or this paragraph, and in sub-paragraph (1)(b) the reference to a charity being connected with another charity for the purposes of section 3(2) is to that charity being so connected by virtue of paragraph 8.

SCHEDULE 2

OFFICE HOLDERS IN RECEIPT OF "EARNINGS" TO BE EMPLOYED EARNERS: CONSEQUENTIAL PROVISION

Section 15

SSCBA 1992

1 SSCBA 1992 is amended as follows.

2 In section 7(1)(b) (definition of "secondary contributor" in relation to office holders), omit "general" in both places it appears.

3 In section 163(1) (interpretation of Part 11 of that Act: statutory sick pay), in paragraph (a) of the definition of "employee", for "general earnings (as defined by section 7 of the Income Tax (Earnings and Pensions) Act 2003)" substitute "earnings (within the meaning of Parts 1 to 5 above)".

4 In section 171(1) (interpretation of Part 12 of that Act: statutory maternity pay), in paragraph (a) of the definition of "employee", for "general earnings (as defined by section 7 of the Income Tax (Earnings and Pensions) Act 2003)" substitute "earnings (within the meaning of Parts 1 to 5 above)".

5 In section 171ZJ(2)(a) (definition of "employee" for Part 12ZA of that Act: ordinary and additional statutory paternity pay), for "general earnings (as defined by section 7 of the Income Tax (Earnings and Pensions) Act 2003)" substitute "earnings (within the meaning of Parts 1 to 5 above)".

6 In section 171ZS(2)(a) (definition of "employee" for Part 12ZB of that Act: statutory adoption pay), for "general earnings (as defined by section 7 of the Income Tax (Earnings and Pensions) Act 2003)" substitute "earnings (within the meaning of Parts 1 to 5 above)".

SSCB(NI)A 1992

7 SSCB(NI)A 1992 is amended as follows.

8 In section 7(1)(b) (definition of "secondary contributor" in relation to office holders), omit "general" in both places it appears.

9 In section 159(1) (interpretation of Part 11 of that Act: statutory sick pay), in paragraph (a) of the definition of "employee", for "general earnings (as defined by section 7 of the Income Tax (Earnings and Pensions) Act 2003)" substitute "earnings (within the meaning of Parts 1 to 5 above)".

10 In section 167(1) (interpretation of Part 12 of that Act: statutory maternity pay), in paragraph (a) of the definition of "employee", for "general earnings (as defined by section 7 of the Income Tax (Earnings and Pensions) Act 2003)" substitute "earnings (within the meaning of Parts 1 to 5 above)".

11 In section 167ZJ(2)(a) (definition of "employee" for Part 12ZA of that Act: ordinary and additional statutory paternity pay), for "emoluments chargeable to income tax under Schedule E" substitute "earnings (within the meaning of Parts 1 to 5 above)".

12 In section 167ZS(2)(a) (definition of "employee" for Part 12ZB of that Act: statutory adoption pay), for "emoluments chargeable to income tax under Schedule E" substitute "earnings (within the meaning of Parts 1 to 5 above)".

Pension Schemes Act 1993 (c 48)

13 In section 181(1) of the Pension Schemes Act 1993 (general interpretation), in the definition of "employee", for "general earnings (as defined by section 7 of the Income Tax (Earnings and Pensions) Act 2003)" substitute "earnings".

Pension Schemes (Northern Ireland) Act 1993 (c 49)

14 In section 176(1) of the Pension Schemes (Northern Ireland) Act 1993 (general interpretation), in the definition of "employee", for "general earnings (as defined by section 7 of the Income Tax (Earnings and Pensions) Act 2003)" substitute "earnings".

FINANCE ACT 2014

(2014 Chapter 26)

AN ACT TO Grant certain duties, to alter other duties, and to amend the law relating to the National Debt and the Public Revenue, and to make further provision in connection with finance.

[17 July 2014]

CONTENTS

PART 4
FOLLOWER NOTICES AND ACCELERATED PAYMENTS
CHAPTER 1
INTRODUCTION

Note—FA 2014 Part 4 has effect for NICs purposes with the modifications set out in NICA 2015 Sch 2 Part 1, with effect from 12 April 2015. These modifications include the following—

– references to tax or a relevant tax, other than references to particular taxes, include relevant contributions;
– references to a charge to tax include a liability to pay relevant contributions and references to a person being chargeable to tax, or to tax being charged, are to be construed accordingly;
– references to an assessment to tax include an NICs decision relating to a person's liability for relevant contributions;
– references to a tax enquiry include a relevant contributions dispute;
– references to a return into which a tax enquiry is in progress include a notification of dispute in relation to which a relevant contributions dispute is in progress;
– references to a tax appeal include a NICs appeal;
– references to a provision of FA 2004 Part 7 (DOTAS) includes a reference to that DOTAS provision as applied by regulations under SSAA 1992 s 132A, and any provision of regulations under that section that corresponds to that DOTAS provision, whenever the regulations are made;

See also NICA 2015 generally for application of the follower notices and accelerated payments legislation in relation to NICs.

Press releases etc—Tackling marketed tax avoidance—summary of responses to the consultation on extension of "accelerated payments": HMRC Notice 28 March 2014 (see *SWTI 2014, Issue 13*).

HMRC publishes list of avoidance schemes facing accelerated payments: HMRC Notice 15 July 2014 (see *SWTI 2014, Issue 29*).

Cross-references—See SSCBA 1992 s 11A (Parts 4 and 5 of FA 2014 apply with the necessary modifications, in relation to Class 2 contributions under SSCBA 1992 s 11(2) as if those contributions were income tax chargeable under ITTOIA 2005 Pt 2 Ch 2 in respect of profits of a trade, profession or vocation which is not carried on wholly outside the United Kingdom).

Overview

199 Overview of Part 4

In this Part—

(a) sections 200 to 203 set out the main defined terms used in the Part,
(b) Chapter 2 makes provision for follower notices and for penalties if account is not taken of judicial rulings which lay down principles or give reasoning relevant to tax cases,
(c) Chapter 3 makes—
 (i) provision for accelerated payments to be made on account of tax,
 (ii) provision restricting the circumstances in which payments of tax can be postponed pending an appeal, . . . [1]
 (iii) provision to enable a court to prevent repayment of tax, for the purpose of protecting the public revenue[, and
 (iv) provision restricting the surrender of losses and other amounts for the purposes of group relief.][1]
(d) Chapter 4—
 (i) makes special provision about the application of this Part in relation to stamp duty land tax and annual tax for enveloped dwellings,
 (ii) confers a power to extend the provisions of this Part to other taxes, and
 (iii) makes amendments consequential on this Part.

Amendments—[1] Word "and" at the end of para (*c*)(ii) repealed, and para (*c*)(iv) and preceding word inserted, by FA 2015 s 118, Sch 18 paras 1, 2 with effect from 26 March 2015.

Main definitions

200 "Relevant tax"

In this Part, "relevant tax" means—

(a) income tax,
(b) capital gains tax,
(c) corporation tax, including any amount chargeable as if it were corporation tax or treated as if it were corporation tax,
[(ca) apprenticeship levy,][1]
(d) inheritance tax,
(e) stamp duty land tax, and
(f) annual tax on enveloped dwellings.

Note—For NICs purposes, the definition of "relevant tax" has effect as if it includes relevant contributions (NICA 2015 Sch 2 para 12).

Cross-references—FA 2014 s 232 (Treasury power to amend s 200 to extend follower notices and accelerated payments provisions to any other tax).

Amendments[1] Para (*ca*) inserted by FA 2016 s 104(3), (4) with effect from 15 September 2016.

201 "Tax advantage" and "tax arrangements"

(1) This section applies for the purposes of this Part.
(2) "Tax advantage" includes—

NIC

(a) relief or increased relief from tax,
(b) repayment or increased repayment of tax,
(c) avoidance or reduction of a charge to tax or an assessment to tax,
(d) avoidance of a possible assessment to tax,
(e) deferral of a payment of tax or advancement of a repayment of tax, and
(f) avoidance of an obligation to deduct or account for tax.

(3) Arrangements are "tax arrangements" if, having regard to all the circumstances, it would be reasonable to conclude that the obtaining of a tax advantage was the main purpose, or one of the main purposes, of the arrangements.

(4) "Arrangements" includes any agreement, understanding, scheme, transaction or series of transactions (whether or not legally enforceable).

202 "Tax enquiry" and "return"

(1) This section applies for the purposes of this Part.

(2) "Tax enquiry" means—
(a) an enquiry under section 9A or 12AC of TMA 1970 (enquiries into self-assessment returns for income tax and capital gains tax), including an enquiry by virtue of notice being deemed to be given under section 9A of that Act by virtue of section 12AC(6) of that Act,
(b) an enquiry under paragraph 5 of Schedule 1A to that Act (enquiry into claims made otherwise than by being included in a return),
(c) an enquiry under paragraph 24 of Schedule 18 to FA 1998 (enquiry into company tax return for corporation tax etc), including an enquiry by virtue of notice being deemed to be given under that paragraph by virtue of section 12AC(6) of TMA 1970,
(d) an enquiry under paragraph 12 of Schedule 10 to FA 2003 (enquiries into SDLT returns),
(e) an enquiry under paragraph 8 of Schedule 33 to FA 2013 (enquiries into annual tax for enveloped dwellings returns), or
(f) a deemed enquiry under subsection (6).

(3) The period during which an enquiry is in progress—
(a) begins with the day on which notice of enquiry is given, and
(b) ends with the day on which the enquiry is completed.

(4) Subsection (3) is subject to subsection (6).

(5) In the case of inheritance tax, each of the following is to be treated as a return—
(a) an account delivered by a person under section 216 or 217 of IHTA 1984 (including an account delivered in accordance with regulations under section 256 of that Act);
(b) a statement or declaration which amends or is otherwise connected with such an account produced by the person who delivered the account;
(c) information or a document provided by a person in accordance with regulations under section 256 of that Act;

and such a return is to be treated as made by the person in question.

(6) An enquiry is deemed to be in progress, in relation to a return to which subsection (5) applies, during the period which—
(a) begins with the time the account is delivered or (as the case may be) the statement, declaration, information or document is produced, and
(b) ends when the person is issued with a certificate of discharge under section 239 of that Act, or is discharged by virtue of section 256(1)(b) of that Act, in respect of the return (at which point the enquiry is to be treated as completed).

203 "Tax appeal"

In this Part "tax appeal" means—
(a) an appeal under section 31 of TMA 1970 (income tax: appeals against amendments of self-assessment, amendments made by closure notices under section 28A or 28B of that Act, etc), including an appeal under that section by virtue of regulations under Part 11 of ITEPA 2003 (PAYE),
(b) an appeal under paragraph 9 of Schedule 1A to TMA 1970 (income tax: appeals against amendments made by closure notices under paragraph 7(2) of that Schedule, etc),
(c) an appeal under section 705 of ITA 2007 (income tax: appeals against counteraction notices),
(d) an appeal under paragraph 34(3) or 48 of Schedule 18 to FA 1998 (corporation tax: appeals against amendment of a company's return made by closure notice, assessments other than self-assessments, etc),
(e) an appeal under section 750 of CTA 2010 (corporation tax: appeals against counteraction notices),
[(ea) an appeal under section 114 of FA 2016 (apprenticeship levy: appeal against an assessment),][1]

(f) an appeal under section 222 of IHTA 1984 (appeals against HMRC determinations) other than an appeal made by a person against a determination in respect of a transfer of value at a time when a tax enquiry is in progress in respect of a return made by that person in respect of that transfer,
(g) an appeal under paragraph 35 of Schedule 10 to FA 2003 (stamp duty land tax: appeals against amendment of self-assessment, discovery assessments, etc),
(h) an appeal under paragraph 35 of Schedule 33 to FA 2013 (annual tax on enveloped dwellings: appeals against amendment of self-assessment, discovery assessments, etc), or
(i) an appeal against any determination of—
  (i) an appeal within paragraphs (a) to (h), or
  (ii) an appeal within this paragraph.

Commentary—*Simon's Taxes* **A7.247**.
Amendments[1] Para (*ea*) inserted by FA 2016 s 104(3), (5) with effect from 15 September 2016.

CHAPTER 2

FOLLOWER NOTICES

Giving of follower notices

204 Circumstances in which a follower notice may be given

(1) HMRC may give a notice (a "follower notice") to a person ("P") if Conditions A to D are met.
(2) Condition A is that—
(a) a tax enquiry is in progress into a return or claim made by P in relation to a relevant tax, or
(b) P has made a tax appeal (by notifying HMRC or otherwise) in relation to a relevant tax, but that appeal has not yet been—
  (i) determined by the tribunal or court to which it is addressed, or
  (ii) abandoned or otherwise disposed of.
(3) Condition B is that the return or claim or, as the case may be, appeal is made on the basis that a particular tax advantage ("the asserted advantage") results from particular tax arrangements ("the chosen arrangements").
(4) Condition C is that HMRC is of the opinion that there is a judicial ruling which is relevant to the chosen arrangements.
(5) Condition D is that no previous follower notice has been given to the same person (and not withdrawn) by reference to the same tax advantage, tax arrangements, judicial ruling and tax period.
(6) A follower notice may not be given after the end of the period of 12 months beginning with the later of—
(a) the day on which the judicial ruling mentioned in Condition C is made, and
(b) the day the return or claim to which subsection (2)(a) refers was received by HMRC or (as the case may be) the day the tax appeal to which subsection (2)(b) refers was made.

Note—For the purposes of s 204, Condition B is also met if, in a relevant contributions dispute, a person disputes liability for relevant contributions on the basis mentioned in sub-s (3) (regardless of whether the notification of dispute was given on that basis). (NICA 2015 Sch 2 para 13).
Cross-references—FA 2014 s 217 (transitional provision in relation to judicial rulings made before Royal Assent).
FA 2014 Sch 31 para 3 (follower notices in relation to partnership returns).
NICA 2015 Sch 2 para 14 (application of this section in a case in which, by virtue of NICA 2015 Sch 2 Part 1, a follower notice is given by virtue of sub-s (2)(a)).

205 "Judicial ruling" and circumstances in which a ruling is "relevant"

(1) This section applies for the purposes of this Chapter.
(2) "Judicial ruling" means a ruling of a court or tribunal on one or more issues.
(3) A judicial ruling is "relevant" to the chosen arrangements if—
(a) it relates to tax arrangements,
(b) the principles laid down, or reasoning given, in the ruling would, if applied to the chosen arrangements, deny the asserted advantage or a part of that advantage, and
(c) it is a final ruling.
(4) A judicial ruling is a "final ruling" if it is—
(a) a ruling of the Supreme Court, or
(b) a ruling of any other court or tribunal in circumstances where—
  (i) no appeal may be made against the ruling,
  (ii) if an appeal may be made against the ruling with permission, the time limit for applications has expired and either no application has been made or permission has been refused,
  (iii) if such permission to appeal against the ruling has been granted or is not required, no appeal has been made within the time limit for appeals, or
  (iv) if an appeal was made, it was abandoned or otherwise disposed of before it was determined by the court or tribunal to which it was addressed.

(5) Where a judicial ruling is final by virtue of sub-paragraph (ii), (iii) or (iv) of subsection (4)(b), the ruling is treated as made at the time when the sub-paragraph in question is first satisfied.

206 Content of a follower notice

A follower notice must—

(a) identify the judicial ruling in respect of which Condition C in section 204 is met,

(b) explain why HMRC considers that the ruling meets the requirements of section 205(3), and

(c) explain the effects of sections 207 to 210.

Representations

207 Representations about a follower notice

(1) Where a follower notice is given under section 204, P has 90 days beginning with the day that notice is given to send written representations to HMRC objecting to the notice on the grounds that—

(a) Condition A, B or D in section 204 was not met,

(b) the judicial ruling specified in the notice is not one which is relevant to the chosen arrangements, or

(c) the notice was not given within the period specified in subsection (6) of that section.

(2) HMRC must consider any representations made in accordance with subsection (1).

(3) Having considered the representations, HMRC must determine whether to—

(a) confirm the follower notice (with or without amendment), or

(b) withdraw the follower notice, and notify P accordingly.

Cross-references—FA 2014 s 231(6) (annual tax on enveloped dwellings: where follower notice or accelerated payment notice is given to more than one person, power conferred on P by this section is exercisable by each of those persons separately or by two or more jointly).

Penalties

208 Penalty if corrective action not taken in response to follower notice

(1) This section applies where a follower notice is given to P (and not withdrawn).

(2) P is liable to pay a penalty if the necessary corrective action is not taken in respect of the denied advantage (if any) before the specified time.

(3) In this Chapter "the denied advantage" means so much of the asserted advantage (see section 204(3)) as is denied by the application of the principles laid down, or reasoning given, in the judicial ruling identified in the follower notice under section 206(a).

(4) The necessary corrective action is taken in respect of the denied advantage if (and only if) P takes the steps set out in subsections (5) and (6).

(5) The first step is that—

(a) in the case of a follower notice given by virtue of section 204(2)(a), P amends a return or claim to counteract the denied advantage;

(b) in the case of a follower notice given by virtue of section 204(2)(b), P takes all necessary action to enter into an agreement with HMRC (in writing) for the purpose of relinquishing the denied advantage.

(6) The second step is that P notifies HMRC—

(a) that P has taken the first step, and

(b) of the denied advantage and (where different) the additional amount which has or will become due and payable in respect of tax by reason of the first step being taken.

(7) In determining the additional amount which has or will become due and payable in respect of tax for the purposes of subsection (6)(b), it is to be assumed that, where P takes the necessary action as mentioned in subsection (5)(b), the agreement is then entered into.

(8) In this Chapter—

"the specified time" means—

(a) if no representations objecting to the follower notice were made by P in accordance with subsection (1) of section 207, the end of the 90 day post-notice period;

(b) if such representations were made and the notice is confirmed under that section (with or without amendment), the later of—

(i) the end of the 90 day post-notice period, and

(ii) the end of the 30 day post-representations period;

"the 90 day post-notice period" means the period of 90 days beginning with the day on which the follower notice is given;

"the 30 day post-representations period" means the period of 30 days beginning with the day on which P is notified of HMRC's determination under section 207.

(9) No enactment limiting the time during which amendments may be made to returns or claims operates to prevent P taking the first step mentioned in subsection (5)(a) before the tax enquiry is closed (whether or not before the specified time).

(10) No appeal may be brought, by virtue of a provision mentioned in subsection (11), against an amendment made by a closure notice in respect of a tax enquiry to the extent that the amendment takes into account an amendment made by P to a return or claim in taking the first step mentioned in subsection (5)(a) (whether or not that amendment was made before the specified time).

(11) The provisions are—

(a) section 31(1)(b) or (c) of TMA 1970,

(b) paragraph 9 of Schedule 1A to TMA 1970,

(c) paragraph 34(3) of Schedule 18 to FA 1998,

(d) paragraph 35(1)(b) of Schedule 10 to FA 2003, and

(e) paragraph 35(1)(b) of Schedule 33 to FA 2013.

Definitions—"denied advantage" in relation to partnerships, FA 2014 Sch 31 para 4(3).

Modifications—NICA 2015 Sch 2 para 14: in a case where a follower notice has been issued whilst a NICs dispute is in progress, NICA 2015 Sch 2 para 14(2) specifies what necessary corrective action is to be taken by a person receiving a follower notice for the purposes of s 208. Schedule 2 para 14 also disapplies sub-ss (4)–(7) and (9)–(11) in relation to NICs, and the reference in s 209(3)(*a*) to P amending a return or claim is to be treated as a reference to P making a corrective payment.

NICA 2015 Sch 2 para 20: a penalty under s 208 or 226 imposed by virtue of NICA 2015 Sch 2 Part 1 may be recovered as if it were an amount of relevant contributions which is due and payable.

FA 2014 Sch 31 para 4(2), (4): in relation to a partnership follower notice, sub-s (2) applies as if reference to P were to each relevant partner; in sub-s (6)(*b*), words from "and (where different)" to the end to be ignored and sub-s (7) not to apply.

Cross-references—See FA 2014 Sch 31 para 4 (penalty for failure to take corrective action in response to partnership follower notice).

209 Amount of a section 208 penalty

(1) The penalty under section 208 is 50% of the value of the denied advantage.

(2) Schedule 30 contains provision about how the denied advantage is valued for the purposes of calculating penalties under this section.

(3) Where P before the specified time—

(a) amends a return or claim to counteract part of the denied advantage only, or

(b) takes all necessary action to enter into an agreement with HMRC (in writing) for the purposes of relinquishing part of the denied advantage only,

in subsections (1) and (2) the references to the denied advantage are to be read as references to the remainder of the denied advantage.

Modifications—NICA 2015 Sch 2 para 14 (in a case where a follower notice has been issued whilst a NICs dispute is in progress, NICA 2015 Sch 2 para 14(2) specifies what necessary corrective action is to be taken by a person receiving a follower notice for the purposes of s 208. Schedule 2 para 14 also disapplies sub-ss (4)–(7) and (9)–(11) in relation to NICs, and the reference in s 209(3)(*a*) to P amending a return or claim is to be treated as a reference to P making a corrective payment.).

FA 2014 Sch 31 para 5(2): in relation to a partnership follower notice, this section applies with the following modifications—

– the total amount of the penalties under s 208(2) for which the relevant partners are liable is 20% of the value of the denied advantage;

– the amount of the penalty for which each relevant partner is liable is that partner's appropriate share of that total amount; and

– the value of the denied advantage for the purposes of calculating the total amount of the penalties is: (i) in the case of a notice given under s 204(2)(*a*), the net amount of the amendments required to be made to the partnership return to counteract the denied advantage, and (ii) in the case of a notice given under s 204(2)(*b*), the net amount of the amendments that have been made to the partnership return to counteract the denied advantage, (and Sch 30 does not apply).

The Treasury has the power to vary the percentage rate (FA 2014 Sch 31 para 5(11)).

210 Reduction of a section 208 penalty for co-operation

(1) Where—

(a) P is liable to pay a penalty under section 208 of the amount specified in section 209(1),

(b) the penalty has not yet been assessed, and

(c) P has co-operated with HMRC,

HMRC may reduce the amount of that penalty to reflect the quality of that cooperation.

(2) In relation to co-operation, "quality" includes timing, nature and extent.

(3) P has co-operated with HMRC only if P has done one or more of the following—

(a) provided reasonable assistance to HMRC in quantifying the tax advantage;

(b) counteracted the denied advantage;

(c) provided HMRC with information enabling corrective action to be taken by HMRC;

(d) provided HMRC with information enabling HMRC to enter an agreement with P for the purpose of counteracting the denied advantage;

(e) allowed HMRC to access tax records for the purpose of ensuring that the denied advantage is fully counteracted.

(4) But nothing in this section permits HMRC to reduce a penalty to less than 10% of the value of the denied advantage.

Modifications—FA 2014 Sch 31 para 5(4), (5): in relation to a partnership follower notice, where—

– the relevant partners are liable to pay a penalty under s 208(2) as modified (see modification note following s 208),

– the penalties have not yet been assessed, and

NIC

– P has co-operated with HMRC,

sub-s (1) does not apply, but HMRC may reduce the total amount of the penalties determined in accordance with Sch 31 para 5(2)(*a*) to reflect the quality of that co-operation.

For these purposes—

– sub-ss (2), (3) apply in relation to the quality of co-operation, and

– HMRC may not reduce the total amount of the penalties to less than 4% of the value of the denied advantage.

The Treasury has the power to vary the minimum percentage (FA 2014 Sch 31 para 5(11)).

211 Assessment of a section 208 penalty

(1) Where a person is liable for a penalty under section 208, HMRC may assess the penalty.

(2) Where HMRC assess the penalty, HMRC must—

(a) notify the person who is liable for the penalty, and

(b) state in the notice a tax period in respect of which the penalty is assessed.

(3) A penalty under section 208 must be paid before the end of the period of 30 days beginning with the day on which the person is notified of the penalty under subsection (2).

(4) An assessment—

(a) is to be treated for procedural purposes in the same way as an assessment to tax (except in respect of a matter expressly provided for by this Chapter),

(b) may be enforced as if it were an assessment to tax, and

(c) may be combined with an assessment to tax.

(5) No penalty under section 208 may be notified under subsection (2) later than—

(a) in the case of a follower notice given by virtue of section 204(2)(a) (tax enquiry in progress), the end of the period of 90 days beginning with the day the tax enquiry is completed, and

(b) in the case of a follower notice given by virtue of section 204(2)(b) (tax appeal pending), the end of the period of 90 days beginning with the earliest of—

(i) the day on which P takes the necessary corrective action (within the meaning of section 208(4)),

(ii) the day on which a ruling is made on the tax appeal by P, or any further appeal in that case, which is a final ruling (see section 205(4)), and

(iii) the day on which that appeal, or any further appeal, is abandoned or otherwise disposed of before it is determined by the court or tribunal to which it is addressed.

(6) In this section a reference to an assessment to tax, in relation to inheritance tax, is to a determination.

Modifications—NICA 2015 Sch 2 para 20 (sub-s (4)(*b*) does not apply in relation to a penalty under s 208 imposed by virtue of NICA 2015 Sch 2 Part 1).

212 Aggregate penalties

(1) Subsection (2) applies where—

(a) two or more penalties are incurred by the same person and fall to be determined by reference to an amount of tax to which that person is chargeable,

(b) one of those penalties is incurred under section 208, and

(c) one or more of the other penalties are incurred under a relevant penalty provision.

(2) The aggregate of the amounts of the penalties mentioned in subsection (1)(b) and (c), so far as determined by reference to that amount of tax, must not exceed—

(a) the relevant percentage of that amount, or

(b) in a case where at least one of the penalties is under paragraph 5(2)(b) or 6(3)(b), (4)(b) or (5)(b) of Schedule 55 to FA 2009, £300 (if greater).

(3) In the application of section 97A of TMA 1970 (multiple penalties), no account is to be taken of a penalty under section 208.

(4) "Relevant penalty provision" means—

(a) Schedule 24 to FA 2007 (penalties for errors),

(b) Schedule 41 to FA 2008 (penalties: failure to notify etc), [1]

(c) Schedule 55 to FA 2009 (penalties for failure to make returns etc)[, ...[2]

(*d*) Part 5 of Schedule 18 to FA 2016 (serial tax avoidance)[,or][1]

(*e*) section 212A of FA 2013 (general anti-abuse rule).][2]

(5) "The relevant percentage" means—

(a) 200% in a case where at least one of the penalties is determined by reference to the percentage in—

(i) paragraph 4(4)(c) of Schedule 24 to FA 2007,

(ii) paragraph 6(4)(a) of Schedule 41 to FA 2008, or

(iii) paragraph 6(3A)(c) of Schedule 55 to FA 2009,

(b) 150% in a case where paragraph (a) does not apply and at least one of the penalties is determined by reference to the percentage in—

(i) paragraph 4(3)(c) of Schedule 24 to FA 2007,

(ii) paragraph 6(3)(a) of Schedule 41 to FA 2008, or

(iii) paragraph 6(3A)(b) of Schedule 55 to FA 2009,

(c) 140% in a case where neither paragraph (a) nor paragraph (b) applies and at least one the penalties is determined by reference to the percentage in—
   (i) paragraph 4(4)(b) of Schedule 24 to FA 2007,
   (ii) paragraph 6(4)(b) of Schedule 41 to FA 2008,
   (iii) paragraph 6(4A)(c) of Schedule 55 to FA 2009,

(d) 105% in a case where none of paragraphs (a), (b) and (c) applies and at least one of the penalties is determined by reference to the percentage in—
   (i) paragraph 4(3)(b) of Schedule 24 to FA 2007,
   (ii) paragraph 6(3)(b) of Schedule 41 to FA 2008,
   (iii) paragraph 6(4A)(b) of Schedule 55 to FA 2009, and

(e) in any other case, 100%.

Modifications—NICA 2015 Sch 2 para 15 (in s 212, references to a "relevant penalty provision" include any provision mentioned in sub-s (4), as applied in relation to relevant contributions by regulations (whenever made), TMA 1970 s 98A, as applied in relation to relevant contributions by regulations (whenever made) and any provision specified in regulations made by the Treasury under which a penalty can be imposed in respect of relevant contributions).

Cross-references—See FA 2014 Sch 31 para 5(6): for the purposes of this section, a penalty imposed on a relevant partner by virtue of FA 2014 Sch 31 para 4(2) is to be treated as if it were determined by reference to such additional amount of tax as is due and payable by the relevant partner as a result of the counteraction of the denied advantage.

Amendments—[1] In sub-s (4)(*b*) word "or" at the end repealed, and para (*d*) and preceding word inserted, by FA 2016 Sch 18 para 60 with effect in relation to relevant defeats incurred after 15 September 2016 subject to FA 2016 Sch 18 para 64 (relevant defeats to be disregarded).

[2] In sub-s (4)(*c*), word "or" at the end repealed, and para (*e*) and preceding word inserted, by FA 2016 s 158(11) with effect in relation to tax arrangements (within the meaning of FA 2013 Pt 5) entered into on or after 15 September 2016.

213 Alteration of assessment of a section 208 penalty

(1) After notification of an assessment has been given to a person under section 211(2), the assessment may not be altered except in accordance with this section or on appeal.

(2) A supplementary assessment may be made in respect of a penalty if an earlier assessment operated by reference to an underestimate of the value of the denied advantage.

(3) An assessment or supplementary assessment may be revised as necessary if it operated by reference to an overestimate of the denied advantage; and, where more than the resulting assessed penalty has already been paid by the person to HMRC, the excess must be repaid.

214 Appeal against a section 208 penalty

(1) P may appeal against a decision of HMRC that a penalty is payable by P under section 208.

(2) P may appeal against a decision of HMRC as to the amount of a penalty payable by P under section 208.

(3) The grounds on which an appeal under subsection (1) may be made include in particular—
   (a) that Condition A, B or D in section 204 was not met in relation to the follower notice,
   (b) that the judicial ruling specified in the notice is not one which is relevant to the chosen arrangements,
   (c) that the notice was not given within the period specified in subsection (6) of that section, or
   (d) that it was reasonable in all the circumstances for P not to have taken the necessary corrective action (see section 208(4)) in respect of the denied advantage.

(4) An appeal under this section must be made within the period of 30 days beginning with the day on which notification of the penalty is given under section 211.

(5) An appeal under this section is to be treated in the same way as an appeal against an assessment to the tax concerned (including by the application of any provision about bringing the appeal by notice to HMRC, about HMRC's review of the decision or about determination of the appeal by the First-tier Tribunal or Upper Tribunal).

(6) Subsection (5) does not apply—
   (a) so as to require a person to pay a penalty before an appeal against the assessment of the penalty is determined, or
   (b) in respect of any other matter expressly provided for by this Part.

(7) In this section a reference to an assessment to tax, in relation to inheritance tax, is to a determination.

(8) On an appeal under subsection (1), the tribunal may affirm or cancel HMRC's decision.

(9) On an appeal under subsection (2), the tribunal may—
   (a) affirm HMRC's decision, or
   (b) substitute for HMRC's decision another decision that HMRC had power to make.

(10) The cancellation under subsection (8) of HMRC's decision on the ground specified in subsection (3)(d) does not affect the validity of the follower notice, or of any accelerated payment notice or partner payment notice under Chapter 3 related to the follower notice.

(11) In this section "tribunal" means the First-tier Tribunal or Upper Tribunal (as appropriate by virtue of subsection (5)).

Cross-references—See FA 2014 Sch 31 para 5(7)–(9): the right of appeal under this section extends to—

– a decision that penalties are payable by the relevant partners by virtue of Sch 31 para 5, and

NIC

– a decision as to the total amount of those penalties payable by those partners, but not to a decision as to the appropriate share of, or the amount of a penalty payable by, a relevant partner.

Such an appeal may be brought only by the representative partner or, if that partner is no longer available, the person who is for the time being the successor of that partner.

Partners and partnerships

215 Follower notices: treatment of partners and partnerships

Schedule 31 makes provision about the application of this Chapter in relation to partners and partnerships.

Appeals out of time

216 Late appeal against final judicial ruling

(1) This section applies where a final judicial ruling ("the original ruling") is the subject of an appeal by reason of a court or tribunal granting leave to appeal out of time.

(2) If a follower notice has been given identifying the original ruling under section 206(a), the notice is suspended until such time as HMRC notify P that—

(a) the appeal has resulted in a judicial ruling which is a final ruling, or

(b) the appeal has been abandoned or otherwise disposed of (before it was determined).

(3) Accordingly the period during which the notice is suspended does not count towards the periods mentioned in section 208(8).

(4) When a follower notice is suspended under subsection (2), HMRC must notify P as soon as reasonably practicable.

(5) If the new final ruling resulting from the appeal is not a judicial ruling which is relevant to the chosen arrangements (see section 205), the follower notice ceases to have effect at the end of the period of suspension.

(6) In any other case, the follower notice continues to have effect after the end of the period of suspension and, in a case within subsection (2)(a), is treated as if it were in respect of the new final ruling resulting from the appeal.

(7) The notice given under subsection (2) must—

(a) state whether subsection (5) or (6) applies, and

(b) where subsection (6) applies in a case within subsection (2)(a), make any amendments to the follower notice required to reflect the new final ruling.

(8) No new follower notice may be given in respect of the original ruling unless the appeal has been abandoned or otherwise disposed of before it is determined by the court or tribunal to which it is addressed.

(9) Nothing in this section prevents a follower notice being given in respect of a new final ruling resulting from the appeal.

(10) Where the appeal is abandoned or otherwise disposed of before it is determined by the court or tribunal to which it is addressed, for the purposes of the original ruling the period beginning when leave to appeal out of time was granted, and ending when the appeal is disposed of, does not count towards the period of 12 months mentioned in section 204(6).

Cross-references—FA 2014 s 217 (transitional provision in relation to judicial rulings made before Royal Assent).

Transitional provision

217 Transitional provision

(1) In the case of judicial rulings made before the day on which this Act is passed, this Chapter has effect as if for section 204(6) there were substituted—

"(6) A follower notice may not be given after—

(a) the end of the period of 24 months beginning with the day on which this Act is passed, or

(b) the end of the period of 12 months beginning with the day the return or claim to which subsection (2)(a) refers was received by HMRC or (as the case may be) with the day the tax appeal to which subsection (2)(b) refers was made,

whichever is later."

(2) Accordingly, the reference in section 216(10) to the period of 12 months includes a reference to the period of 24 months mentioned in the version of section 204(6) set out in subsection (1) above.

Defined terms

218 Defined terms used in Chapter 2

For the purposes of this Chapter—

"arrangements" has the meaning given by section 201(4);

"the asserted advantage" has the meaning given by section 204(3);

"the chosen arrangements" has the meaning given by section 204(3);

"the denied advantage" has the meaning given by section 208(3);

"follower notice" has the meaning given by section 204(1);

"HMRC" means Her Majesty's Revenue and Customs;

"judicial ruling", and "relevant" in relation to a judicial ruling and the chosen arrangements, have the meaning given by section 205;
"relevant tax" has the meaning given by section 200;
"the specified time" has the meaning given by section 208(8);
"tax advantage" has the meaning given by section 201(2);
"tax appeal" has the meaning given by section 203;
"tax arrangements" has the meaning given by section 201(3);
"tax enquiry" has the meaning given by section 202(2);
"tax period" means a tax year, accounting period or other period in respect of which tax is charged;
"P" has the meaning given by section 204(1);
"the 30 day post-representations period" has the meaning given by section 208(8);
"the 90 day post-notice period" has the meaning given by section 208(8).

CHAPTER 3
ACCELERATED PAYMENT

Press releases etc—Tackling marketed tax avoidance—summary of responses to the consultation on extension of "accelerated payments": HMRC Notice 28 March 2014 (see *SWTI 2014, Issue 13*).
HMRC publishes list of avoidance schemes facing accelerated payments: HMRC Notice 15 July 2014 (see *SWTI 2014, Issue 29*).
Commentary—*Simon's Taxes* **A4.230**.

Accelerated payment notices

219 Circumstances in which an accelerated payment notice may be given

(1) HMRC may give a notice (an "accelerated payment notice") to a person ("P") if Conditions A to C are met.
(2) Condition A is that—
(a) a tax enquiry is in progress into a return or claim made by P in relation to a relevant tax, or
(b) P has made a tax appeal (by notifying HMRC or otherwise) in relation to a relevant tax but that appeal has not yet been—
(i) determined by the tribunal or court to which it is addressed, or
(ii) abandoned or otherwise disposed of.
(3) Condition B is that the return or claim or, as the case may be, appeal is made on the basis that a particular tax advantage ("the asserted advantage") results from particular arrangements ("the chosen arrangements").
(4) Condition C is that one or more of the following requirements are met—
(a) HMRC has given (or, at the same time as giving the accelerated payment notice, gives) P a follower notice under Chapter 2—
(i) in relation to the same return or claim or, as the case may be, appeal, and
(ii) by reason of the same tax advantage and the chosen arrangements;
(b) the chosen arrangements are DOTAS arrangements;
(c) a GAAR counteraction notice has been given in relation to the asserted advantage or part of it and the chosen arrangements (or is so given at the same time as the accelerated payment notice) in a case where the stated opinion of at least two of the members of the sub-panel of the GAAR Advisory Panel which considered the matter under paragraph 10 of Schedule 43 to FA 2013 was as set out in paragraph 11(3)(b) of that Schedule (entering into tax arrangements not reasonable course of action etc).
[(*d*) a notice has been given under paragraph 8(2) or 9(2) of Schedule 43A to FA 2013 (notice of final decision after considering Panel's opinion about referred or counteracted arrangements) in relation to the asserted advantage or part of it and the chosen arrangements (or is so given at the same time as the accelerated payment notice) in a case where the stated opinion of at least two of the members of the sub-panel of the GAAR Advisory Panel about the other arrangements (see subsection (8)) was as set out in paragraph 11(3)(*b*) of Schedule 43 to FA 2013;
(*e*) a notice under paragraph 8(2) of Schedule 43B to FA 2013 (GAAR: generic referral of tax arrangements) has been given in relation to the asserted advantage or part of it and the chosen arrangements (or is so given at the same time as the accelerated payment notice) in a case where the stated opinion of at least two of the members of the sub-panel of the GAAR Advisory Panel which considered the generic referral in respect of those arrangements under paragraph 6 of Schedule 43B to FA 2013 was as set out in paragraph 6(4)(*b*) of that Schedule.][1]
(5) "DOTAS arrangements" means—
(a) notifiable arrangements to which HMRC has allocated a reference number under section 311 of FA 2004,
(b) notifiable arrangements implementing a notifiable proposal where HMRC has allocated a reference number under that section to the proposed notifiable arrangements, or

(c) arrangements in respect of which the promoter must provide prescribed information under section 312(2) of that Act by reason of the arrangements being substantially the same as notifiable arrangements within paragraph (a) or (b).

(6) But the notifiable arrangements within subsection (5) do not include arrangements in relation to which HMRC has given notice under section 312(6) of FA 2004 (notice that promoters not under duty imposed to notify client of reference number).

(7) "GAAR counteraction notice" means a notice under paragraph 12 of Schedule 43 to FA 2013 (notice of final decision to counteract under the general anti-abuse rule).

[(8) In subsection (4)(*d*) "other arrangements" means—

(*a*) in relation to a notice under paragraph 8(2) of Schedule 43A to FA 2013, the referred arrangements (as defined in that paragraph);

(*b*) in relation to a notice under paragraph 9(2) of that Schedule, the counteracted arrangements (as defined in paragraph 2 of that Schedule).][1]

Modifications—NICA 2015 Sch 2 para 16 (for the purposes of s 219, Condition B is also met if, in a relevant contributions dispute, a person disputes liability for relevant contributions on the basis mentioned in sub-s (3) (regardless of whether the notification of dispute was given on that basis)).

Cross-references—See NICA 2015 Sch 2 para 18 (effect of accelerated payment notice in respect of an NICs appeal).

Amendments—[1] Sub-ss (4)(*d*), (*e*), (8) inserted by FA 2016 s 157(18)–(20) with effect in relation to tax arrangements (within the meaning of FA 2013 Pt 5) entered into at any time (whether before on or after 15 September 2016).

220 Content of notice given while a tax enquiry is in progress

(1) This section applies where an accelerated payment notice is given by virtue of section 219(2)(a) (notice given while a tax enquiry is in progress).

(2) The notice must—

(a) specify the paragraph or paragraphs of section 219(4) by virtue of which the notice is given,

(b) specify the payment [(if any)][1] required to be made under section 223 and the requirements of that section, . . . [1]

(c) explain the effect of sections 222 and 226, and of the amendments made by sections 224 and 225 (so far as relating to the relevant tax in relation to which the accelerated payment notice is given)[, and

(*d*) if the denied advantage consists of or includes an asserted surrenderable amount, specify that amount and any action which is required to be taken in respect of it under section 225A.][1]

(3) The payment required to be made under section 223 is an amount equal to the amount which a designated HMRC officer determines, to the best of that officer's information and belief, as the understated tax.

(4) "The understated tax" means the additional amount that would be due and payable in respect of tax if—

(a) in the case of a notice given by virtue of section 219(4)(a) (cases where a follower notice is given)—

(i) it were assumed that the explanation given in the follower notice in question under section 206(b) is correct, and

(ii) the necessary corrective action were taken under section 208 in respect of what the designated HMRC officer determines, to the best of that officer's information and belief, as the denied advantage;

(b) in the case of a notice given by virtue of section 219(4)(b) (cases where the DOTAS requirements are met), such adjustments were made as are required to counteract what the designated HMRC officer determines, to the best of that officer's information and belief, as the denied advantage;

(c) in the case of a notice given by virtue of section 219(4)(c)[, (*d*) or (*e*)][2] (cases involving counteraction under the general anti-abuse rule), such of the adjustments set out in the GAAR counteraction notice as have effect to counteract the denied advantage were made.

[(4A) "Asserted surrenderable amount" means so much of a surrenderable loss as a designated HMRC officer determines, to the best of that officer's information and belief, to be an amount—

(*a*) which would not be a surrenderable loss of P if the position were as stated in paragraphs (*a*), (*b*) or (*c*) of subsection (4), and

(*b*) which is not the subject of a claim by P for relief from corporation tax reflected in the understated tax amount (and hence in the payment required to be made under section 223).

(4B) "Surrenderable loss" means a loss or other amount within section 99(1) of CTA 2010 (or part of such a loss or other amount).][1]

(5) "The denied advantage"—

(a) in the case of a notice given by virtue of section 219(4)(a), has the meaning given by section 208(3),

(b) in the case of a notice given by virtue of section 219(4)(b), means so much of the asserted advantage as is not a tax advantage which results from the chosen arrangements or otherwise, and

(c) in the case of a notice given by virtue of section 219(4)(c)[, (*d*) or (*e*)][2], means so much of the asserted advantage as would be counteracted by making the adjustments set out in the GAAR counteraction notice.

(6) If a notice is given by reason of two or all of the requirements in section 219(4) being met, [any payment specified under subsection (2)(*b*) or amount specified under subsection (2)(*d*)][1] is to be determined as if the notice were given by virtue of such one of them as is stated in the notice as being used for this purpose.

(7) "The GAAR counteraction notice" means the notice [under—

(*a*) paragraph 12 of Schedule 43 to FA 2013,

(*b*) paragraph 8 or 9 of Schedule 43A to that Act, or

(*c*) paragraph 8 of Schedule 43B to that Act,

as the case may be.][2]

Amendments—[1] In sub-s (2)(*b*), words inserted and word "and" repealed, sub-s (2)(*d*) and preceding word inserted, sub-ss (4A), (4B) inserted, and in sub-s (6), words substituted, by FA 2015 s 118, Sch 18 paras 1, 3 with effect from 26 March 2015.

[2] In sub-ss (4)(*c*), (5)(*c*), words inserted, and in sub-s (7), words substituted for words "under paragraph 12 of Schedule 43 to FA 2013 (notice of final decision to counteract under the general anti-abuse rule)." by FA 2016 s 157(21) with effect in relation to tax arrangements (within the meaning of FA 2013 Pt 5) entered into at any time (whether before on or after 15 September 2016).

221 Content of notice given pending an appeal

(1) This section applies where an accelerated payment notice is given by virtue of section 219(2)(b) (notice given pending an appeal).

(2) The notice must—

(a) specify the paragraph or paragraphs of section 219(4) by virtue of which the notice is given,

(b) specify the disputed tax [(if any)][1], . . . [1]

(c) explain the effect of section 222 and of the amendments made by sections 224 and 225 so far as relating to the relevant tax in relation to which the accelerated payment notice is given[, and

(*d*) if the denied advantage consists of or includes an asserted surrenderable amount (within the meaning of section 220(4A)), specify that amount and any action which is required to be taken in respect of it under section 225A.][1]

(3) "The disputed tax" means so much of the amount of the charge to tax arising in consequence of—

(a) the amendment or assessment to tax appealed against, or

(b) where the appeal is against a conclusion stated by a closure notice, that conclusion,

as a designated HMRC officer determines, to the best of the officer's information and belief, as the amount required to ensure the counteraction of what that officer so determines as the denied advantage.

(4) "The denied advantage" has the same meaning as in section 220(5).

(5) If a notice is given by reason of two or all of the requirements in section 219(4) being met, the denied advantage is to be determined as if the notice were given by virtue of such one of them as is stated in the notice as being used for this purpose.

(6) In this section a reference to an assessment to tax, in relation to inheritance tax, is to a determination.

Amendments—[1] In sub-s (2)(*b*), words inserted and word "and" repealed, and sub-s (2)(*d*) and preceding word inserted, by FA 2015 s 118, Sch 18 paras 1, 4 with effect from 26 March 2015.

222 Representations about a notice

(1) This section applies where an accelerated payment notice has been given under section 219 (and not withdrawn).

(2) P has 90 days beginning with the day that notice is given to send written representations to HMRC—

(a) objecting to the notice on the grounds that Condition A, B or C in section 219 was not met, . . . [1]

(b) objecting to the amount specified in the notice under section 220(2)(b) or section 221(2)(b)[, or

(*c*) objecting to the amount specified in the notice under section 220(2)(*d*) or section 221(2)(*d*).][1]

(3) HMRC must consider any representations made in accordance with subsection (2).

(4) Having considered the representations, HMRC must—

(a) if representations were made under subsection (2)(a), determine whether—

(i) to confirm the accelerated payment notice (with or without amendment), or

(ii) to withdraw the accelerated payment notice, . . . [1]

(b) if representations were made under subsection (2)(b) (and the notice is not withdrawn under paragraph (a)), determine whether a different amount [(or no amount)][1] ought to have been specified under section 220(2)(b) or section 221(2)(b), and then—

(i) confirm the amount specified in the notice, . . . [1]

(ii) amend the notice to specify a different amount[, or

(iii) remove from the notice the provision made under section 220(2)(*b*) or section 221(2)(*b*), and

(*c*) if representations were made under subsection (2)(*c*) (and the notice is not withdrawn under paragraph (*a*)), determine whether a different amount (or no amount) ought to have been specified under section 220(2)(*d*) or 221(2)(*d*), and then—

(i) confirm the amount specified in the notice,

(ii) amend the notice to specify a different amount, or

(iii) remove from the notice the provision made under section 220(2)(*d*) or section 221(2)(*d*),][1]

and notify P accordingly.

Cross-references—FA 2014 s 231(6) (annual tax on enveloped dwellings: where follower notice or accelerated payment notice is given to more than one person, power conferred on P by this section is exercisable by each of those persons separately or by two or more jointly).

Amendments—[1] In sub-ss (2)(*a*), (4)(*a*)(ii), (*b*)(i), word repealed, sub-s (2)(*c*) and preceding word inserted, in sub-s (4)(*b*), words inserted, and sub-s (4)(*b*)(iii), (*c*) inserted, by FA 2015 s 118, Sch 18 paras 1, 5 with effect from 26 March 2015.

Forms of accelerated payment

223 Effect of notice given while tax enquiry is in progress[: accelerated payment]

[(1) This section applies where—

(*a*) an accelerated payment notice is given by virtue of section 219(2)(*a*) (notice given while a tax enquiry is in progress) (and not withdrawn), and

(*b*) an amount is stated in the notice in accordance with section 220(2)(*b*).][1]

(2) P must make a payment ("the accelerated payment") to HMRC of [that amount][1].

(3) The accelerated payment is to be treated as a payment on account of the understated tax (see section 220).

(4) The accelerated payment must be made before the end of the payment period.

(5) "The payment period" means—

(a) if P made no representations under section 222, the period of 90 days beginning with the day on which the accelerated payment notice is given, and

(b) if P made such representations, whichever of the following periods ends later—

(i) the 90 day period mentioned in paragraph (a);

(ii) the period of 30 days beginning with the day on which P is notified under section 222 of HMRC's determination.

(6) But where the understated tax would be payable by instalments by virtue of an election made under section 227 of IHTA 1984, to the extent that the accelerated payment relates to tax payable by an instalment which falls to be paid at a time after the payment period, the accelerated payment must be made no later than that time.

(7) If P pays any part of the understated tax before the accelerated payment in respect of it, the accelerated payment is treated to that extent as having been paid at the same time.

(8) Any tax enactment which relates to the recovery of a relevant tax applies to an amount to be paid on account of the relevant tax under this section in the same manner as it applies to an amount of the relevant tax.

(9) "Tax enactment" means provisions of or made under—

(a) the Tax Acts,

(b) any enactment relating to capital gains tax,

(c) IHTA 1984 or any other enactment relating to inheritance tax,

(d) Part 4 of FA 2003 or any other enactment relating to stamp duty land tax, or

(e) Part 3 of FA 2013 or any other enactment relating to annual tax on enveloped dwellings.

Modifications—NICA 2015 Sch 2 para 17 (sub-ss (3) and (7)–(9) do not apply in relation to an accelerated payment of understated NICs).

Cross-references—See NICA 2015 Sch 2 para 17 for recovery of accelerated payments in relation to understated NICs.

FA 2014 s 226 (where sub-s (6) applies to require an amount of the accelerated payment to be paid before a later time than the end of the payment period, references in sub-ss (2) and (5) to the end of that period are to be read, in relation to that amount, as references to that later time).

Amendments—[1] In heading, words inserted, sub-s (1) substituted, and words in sub-s (2) substituted, by FA 2015 s 118, Sch 18 paras 1, 6 with effect from 26 March 2015.

224 Restriction on powers to postpone tax payments pending initial appeal

(1) In section 55 of TMA 1970 (recovery of tax not postponed), after subsection (8A) insert—

"(8B) Subsections (8C) and (8D) apply where a person has been given an accelerated payment notice or partner payment notice under Chapter 3 of Part 4 of the Finance Act 2014 and that notice has not been withdrawn.

(8C) Nothing in this section enables the postponement of the payment of (as the case may be)—

(a) the understated tax to which the payment specified in the notice under section 220(2)(b) of that Act relates,

(b) the disputed tax specified in the notice under section 221(2)(b) of that Act, or
(c) the understated partner tax to which the payment specified in the notice under paragraph 4(1)(b) of Schedule 32 to that Act relates.

(8D) Accordingly, if the payment of an amount of tax within subsection (8C)(b) is postponed by virtue of this section immediately before the accelerated payment notice is given, it ceases to be so postponed with effect from the time that notice is given, and the tax is due and payable—
(a) if no representations were made under section 222 of that Act in respect of the notice, on or before the last day of the period of 90 days beginning with the day the notice or partner payment notice is given, and
(b) if representations were so made, on or before whichever is later of—
(i) the last day of the 90 day period mentioned in paragraph (a), and
(ii) the last day of the period of 30 days beginning with the day on which HMRC's determination in respect of those representations is notified under section 222 of that Act."

(2) In section 242 of IHTA 1984 (recovery of tax), after subsection (3) insert—

"(4) Where a person has been given an accelerated payment notice under Chapter 3 of Part 4 of the Finance Act 2014 and that notice has not been withdrawn, nothing in this section prevents legal proceedings being taken for the recovery of (as the case may be)—
(a) the understated tax to which the payment specified in the notice under section 220(2)(b) of that Act relates, or
(b) the disputed tax specified in the notice under section 221(2)(b) of that Act."

(3) In Schedule 10 to FA 2003 (SDLT: returns, enquiries, assessments and appeals), in paragraph 39 (direction by the tribunal to postpone payment), after sub-paragraph (8) insert—

"(9) Sub-paragraphs (10) and (11) apply where a person has been given an accelerated payment notice under Chapter 3 of Part 4 of the Finance Act 2014 and that notice has not been withdrawn.

(10) Nothing in this paragraph enables the postponement of the payment of (as the case may be)—
(a) the understated tax to which the payment specified in the notice under section 220(2)(b) of that Act relates, or
(b) the disputed tax specified in the notice under section 221(2)(b) of that Act.

(11) Accordingly, if the payment of an amount of tax within sub-paragraph (10)(b) is postponed by virtue of this paragraph immediately before the accelerated payment notice is given, it ceases to be so postponed with effect from the time that notice is given, and the tax is due and payable—
(a) if no representations were made under section 222 of that Act in respect of the notice, on or before the last day of the period of 90 days beginning with the day the notice is given, and
(b) if representations were so made, on or before whichever is later of—
(i) the last day of the 90 day period mentioned in paragraph (a), and
(ii) the last day of the period of 30 days beginning with the day on which HMRC's determination in respect of those representations is notified under section 222 of that Act."

(4) In paragraph 40 of that Schedule (agreement to postpone payment of tax), after sub-paragraph (3) insert—

"(4) Sub-paragraphs (9) to (11) of paragraph 39 apply for the purposes of this paragraph as they apply for the purposes of paragraph 39."

(5) In Schedule 33 to FA 2013 (annual tax on enveloped dwellings: returns, enquiries, assessments and appeals), in paragraph 48 (application for payment of tax to be postponed), after sub-paragraph (8) insert—

"(8A) Sub-paragraphs (8B) and (8C) apply where a person has been given an accelerated payment notice under Chapter 3 of Part 4 of FA 2014 and that notice has not been withdrawn.

(8B) Nothing in this paragraph enables the postponement of the payment of (as the case may be)—
(a) the understated tax to which the payment specified in the notice under section 220(2)(b) of that Act relates, or
(b) the disputed tax specified in the notice under section 221(2)(b) of that Act.

(8C) Accordingly, if the payment of an amount of tax within sub-paragraph (8B)(b) is postponed by virtue of this paragraph immediately before the accelerated payment notice is given, it ceases to be so postponed with effect from the time that notice is given, and the tax is due and payable—

(a) if no representations were made under section 222 of that Act in respect of the notice, on or before the last day of the period of 90 days beginning with the day the notice is given, and

(b) if representations were so made, on or before whichever is later of—

(i) the last day of the 90 day period mentioned in paragraph (a), and

(ii) the last day of the period of 30 days beginning with the day on which HMRC's determination in respect of those representations is notified under section 222 of that Act."

(6) In paragraph 49 of that Schedule (agreement to postpone payment of tax), after sub-paragraph (3) insert—

"(4) Sub-paragraphs (8A) to (8C) of paragraph 48 apply for the purposes of this paragraph as they apply for the purposes of paragraph 48."

225 Protection of the revenue pending further appeals

(1) In section 56 of TMA 1970 (payment of tax where there is a further appeal), after subsection (3) insert—

"(4) Subsection (5) applies where—

(a) an accelerated payment notice or partner payment notice has been given to a party to the appeal under Chapter 3 of Part 4 of the Finance Act 2014 (and not withdrawn), and

(b) the assessment has effect, or partly has effect, to counteract the whole or part of the asserted advantage (within the meaning of section 219(3) of that Act) by reason of which the notice was given.

(5) If, on the application of HMRC, the relevant court or tribunal considers it necessary for the protection of the revenue, it may direct that subsection (2) does not apply so far as the tax relates to the counteraction of the whole or part of the asserted advantage, and—

(a) give permission to withhold all or part of any repayment, or

(b) require the provision of adequate security before repayment is made.

(6) "Relevant court or tribunal" means the tribunal or court from which permission or leave to appeal is sought."

(2) In Schedule 10 to FA 2003 (SDLT: returns, enquiries, assessments and appeals), in paragraph 43 (payment of stamp duty land tax where there is a further appeal), after sub-paragraph (2) insert—

"(3) Sub-paragraph (4) applies where—

(a) an accelerated payment notice has been given to a party to the appeal under Chapter 3 of Part 4 of the Finance Act 2014 (and not withdrawn), and

(b) the assessment to which the appeal relates has effect, or partly has effect, to counteract the whole or part of the asserted advantage (within the meaning of section 219(3) of that Act) by reason of which the notice was given.

(4) If, on the application of HMRC, the relevant court or tribunal considers it necessary for the protection of the revenue, it may direct that sub-paragraph (1) does not apply so far as the stamp duty land tax relates to the counteraction of the whole or part of the asserted advantage, and—

(a) give permission to withhold all or part of any repayment, or

(b) require the provision of adequate security before repayment is made.

(5) "Relevant court or tribunal" means the tribunal or court from which permission or leave to appeal is sought."

(3) In Schedule 33 to FA 2013 (annual tax on enveloped dwellings: returns, enquiries, assessments and appeals), in paragraph 53 (payment of tax where there is a further appeal), after sub-paragraph (2) insert—

"(3) Sub-paragraph (4) applies where—

(a) an accelerated payment notice has been given to a party to the appeal under Chapter 3 of Part 4 of FA 2014 (and not withdrawn), and

(b) the assessment to which the appeal relates has effect, or partly has effect, to counteract the whole or part of the asserted advantage (within the meaning of section 219(3) of that Act) by reason of which the notice was given.

(4) If, on the application of HMRC, the relevant court or tribunal considers it necessary for the protection of the revenue, it may direct that sub-paragraph (1) does not apply so far as the tax relates to the counteraction of the whole or part of the asserted advantage, and—

(a) give permission to withhold all or part of any repayment, or

(b) require the provision of adequate security before repayment is made.

(5) "Relevant court or tribunal" means the tribunal or court from which permission or leave to appeal is sought."

[Prevention of surrender of losses

225A Effect of notice: surrender of losses ineffective, etc

(1) This section applies where—

(*a*) an accelerated payment notice is given (and not withdrawn), and

(*b*) an amount is specified in the notice in accordance with section 220(2)(*d*) or 221(2)(*d*).

(2) P may not consent to any claim for group relief in respect of the amount so specified.

(3) Subject to subsection (2), paragraph 75 (other than sub-paragraphs (7) and (8)) of Schedule 18 to FA 1998 (reduction in amount available for surrender) has effect as if the amount so specified ceased to be an amount available for surrender at the time the notice was given to P.

(4) For the purposes of subsection (3), paragraph 75 of that Schedule has effect as if, in sub-paragraph (2) of that paragraph for "within 30 days" there were substituted "before the end of the payment period (within the meaning of section 223(5) of the Finance Act 2014)".

(5) The time limits otherwise applicable to amendment of a company tax return do not prevent an amendment being made in accordance with paragraph 75(6) of Schedule 18 to FA 1998 where, pursuant to subsection (3), a claimant company receives—

(*a*) notice of the withdrawal of consent under paragraph 75(3) of that Schedule, or

(*b*) a copy of a notice containing directions under paragraph 75(4) of that Schedule.

(6) Subsection (7) applies where—

(*a*) a company makes such an amendment to its company tax return at a time when an enquiry is in progress into the return, and

(*b*) paragraph 31(3) of that Schedule prevents the amendment from taking effect until the enquiry is completed.

(7) Section 219 (circumstances in which an accelerated payment notice may be given) has effect, in its application to that company in a case where section 219(2)(*a*) applies (tax enquiry in progress), as if—

(*a*) for the purposes of section 219(3), that amendment to the return had not been made,

(*b*) in section 219(4), after paragraph (*c*) there were inserted—

"(*d*) P has amended its company tax return, in accordance with paragraph 75(6) of Schedule 18 to FA 1998, in circumstances where pursuant to section 225A(3), P has received—

(i) notice of the withdrawal of consent under paragraph 75(3) of that Schedule, or

(ii) a copy of a notice containing directions under paragraph 75(4) of that Schedule,

but paragraph 31(3) of that Schedule prevents that amendment having effect.",

(*c*) in section 220(4), after paragraph (*c*) there were inserted—

"(*d*) in the case of a notice given by virtue of section 219(4)(*d*) (cases involving withdrawal of consent for losses claimed), it were assumed that P had never made the claim to group relief to which the amendment to its company tax return relates.", and

(*d*) in section 227(10), for "or (*c*)" there were substituted ", (*c*) or (*d*)".

(8) Subsections (2) and (3) are subject to—

(*a*) section 227(14) to (16) (provision about claims for group relief, and consents to claims, following amendment or withdrawal of an accelerated payment notice), and

(*b*) section 227A (provision about claims for group relief, and consents to claims, once tax position finally determined).][1]

Amendments—[1] Section 225A and preceding crosshead inserted by FA 2015 s 118, Sch 18 paras 1, 7 with effect from 26 March 2015. Subsection (3) has effect in relation to an amount specified in a notice in accordance with FA 2014 s 220(2)(*d*) or s 221(2)(*d*), whether the consent to a claim for group relief was given, or the claim itself was made, before or on or after 26 March 2015.

Penalties

226 Penalty for failure to pay accelerated payment

(1) This section applies where an accelerated payment notice is given by virtue of section 219(2)(a) (notice given while tax enquiry is in progress) (and not withdrawn).

(2) If any amount of the accelerated payment is unpaid at the end of the payment period, P is liable to a penalty of 5% of that amount.

(3) If any amount of the accelerated payment is unpaid after the end of the period of 5 months beginning with the penalty day, P is liable to a penalty of 5% of that amount.

(4) If any amount of the accelerated payment is unpaid after the end of the period of 11 months beginning with the penalty day, P is liable to a penalty of 5% of that amount.

(5) "The penalty day" means the day immediately following the end of the payment period.

NIC

(6) Where section 223(6) (accelerated payment payable by instalments when it relates to inheritance tax payable by instalments) applies to require an amount of the accelerated payment to be paid before a later time than the end of the payment period, references in subsections (2) and (5) to the end of that period are to be read, in relation to that amount, as references to that later time.

(7) Paragraphs 9 to 18 (other than paragraph 11(5)) of Schedule 56 to FA 2009 (provisions which apply to penalties for failures to make payments of tax on time) apply, with any necessary modifications, to a penalty under this section in relation to a failure by P to pay an amount of the accelerated payment as they apply to a penalty under that Schedule in relation to a failure by a person to pay an amount of tax.

Modifications—NICA 2015 Sch 2 para 19: sub-s (7) applies in relation to a penalty under this section imposed by virtue of NICA 2015 Sch 2 Part 1, but the reference in sub-s (7) to tax does not include relevant contributions.

But, in their application in relation to NICs, the provisions of FA 2009 Sch 56 mentioned in sub-s (7) have effect as follows—

- as if references to an assessment to tax were to an NICs decision relating to a person's liability for relevant contributions;
- as if a reference to an appeal against an assessment to the tax concerned were a reference to an appeal against an NICs decision;
- as if para 11(3)(*b*) were omitted (but this is subject to NICA 2015 Sch 2 para 20); and
- with any other necessary modifications.

NICA 2015 Sch 2 para 20: a penalty under s 208 or 226 imposed by virtue of NICA 2015 Sch 2 Part 1 may be recovered as if it were an amount of relevant contributions which is due and payable.

Cross-references—See FA 2014 Sch 32 para 7 (application of this section in relation to accelerated partner payments).

FA 2014 s 231 (annual tax on enveloped dwellings: joint and several liability in respect of accelerated payment or penalty under this section).

Withdrawal etc of accelerated payment notice

227 Withdrawal, modification or suspension of accelerated payment notice

(1) In this section a "Condition C requirement" means one of the requirements set out in Condition C in section 219.

(2) Where an accelerated payment notice has been given, HMRC may, at any time, by notice given to P—

(a) withdraw the notice,

(b) where the notice is given by virtue of more than one Condition C requirement being met, withdraw it to the extent it is given by virtue of one of those requirements (leaving the notice effective to the extent that it was also given by virtue of any other Condition C requirement and has not been withdrawn), . . . [1]

(c) reduce the amount specified in the accelerated payment notice under section 220(2)(b) or 221(2)(b)[, or

(*d*) reduce the amount specified in the accelerated payment notice under section 220(2)(*d*) or 221(2)(*d*).][1]

(3) Where—

(a) an accelerated payment notice is given by virtue of the Condition C requirement in section 219(4)(a), and

(b) the follower notice to which it relates is withdrawn,

HMRC must withdraw the accelerated payment notice to the extent it was given by virtue of that requirement.

(4) Where—

(a) an accelerated payment notice is given by virtue of the Condition C requirement in section 219(4)(a), and

(b) the follower notice to which it relates is amended under section 216(7)(b) (cases where there is a new relevant final judicial ruling following a late appeal),

HMRC may by notice given to P make consequential amendments (whether under subsection (2)(c) [or (d)][1] or otherwise) to the accelerated payment notice.

(5) Where—

(a) an accelerated payment notice is given by virtue of the Condition C requirement in section 219(4)(b), and

(b) HMRC give notice under section 312(6) of FA 2004 with the result that promoters are no longer under the duty in section 312(2) of that Act in relation to the chosen arrangements,

HMRC must withdraw the notice to the extent it was given by virtue of that requirement.

(6) Subsection (7) applies where—

(a) an accelerated payment notice is withdrawn to the extent that it was given by virtue of a Condition C requirement,

(b) that requirement is the one stated in the notice for the purposes of section 220(6) or 221(5) (calculation of amount of the accelerated payment or of the denied advantage [etc][1]), and

(c) the notice remains effective to the extent that it was also given by virtue of any other Condition C requirement.

(7) HMRC must, by notice given to P—

(*a*) modify the accelerated payment notice so as to state the remaining, or one of the remaining, Condition C requirements for the purposes of section 220(6) or 221(5), . . .[1]

(*b*) if the amount of the accelerated payment or (as the case may be) the amount of the disputed tax determined on the basis of the substituted Condition C requirement is less than the amount specified in the notice, amend that notice under subsection (2)(c) to substitute the lower amount[, and

(*c*) if the amount of the asserted surrenderable amount is less than the amount specified in the notice, amend the notice under subsection (2)(*d*) to substitute the lower amount.][1]

(8) If a follower notice is suspended under section 216 (appeals against final rulings made out of time) for any period, an accelerated payment notice in respect of the follower notice is also suspended for that period.

(9) Accordingly, the period during which the accelerated payment notice is suspended does not count towards the periods mentioned in the following provisions—

(a) section 223;

(b) section 55(8D) of TMA 1970;

(c) paragraph 39(11) of Schedule 10 to FA 2003;

(d) paragraph 48(8C) of Schedule 33 to FA 2013.

(10) But the accelerated payment notice is not suspended under subsection (8) if it was also given by virtue of section 219(4)(b) or (c) and has not, to that extent, been withdrawn.

(11) In a case within subsection (10), subsections (6) and (7) apply as they would apply were the notice withdrawn to the extent that it was given by virtue of section 219(4)(a), except that any change made to the notice under subsection (7) has effect during the period of suspension only.

(12) Where an accelerated payment notice is withdrawn, it is to be treated as never having had effect (and any accelerated payment made in accordance with, or penalties paid by virtue of, the notice are to be repaid).

[(12A) Where, as a result of an accelerated payment notice specifying an amount under section 220(2)(*d*) or 221(2)(*d*), a notice of consent by P to a claim for group relief in respect of the amount specified (or part of it) became ineffective by virtue of section 225A(3), nothing in subsection (12) operates to revive that notice.][1]

(13) If, as a result of a modification made under subsection (2)(c), more than the resulting amount of the accelerated payment has already been paid by P, the excess must be repaid.

[(14) If the accelerated payment notice is amended under subsection (2)(*d*) or withdrawn—

(*a*) section 225A(2) and (3) (which prevents consent being given to group relief claims) cease to apply in relation to the released amount, and

(*b*) a claim for group relief may be made in respect of any part of the released amount within the period of 30 days after the day on which the notice is amended or withdrawn.

(15) The time limits otherwise applicable to amendment of a company tax return do not apply to the extent that it makes a claim for group relief within the time allowed by subsection (14).

(16) "The released amount" means—

(*a*) in a case where the accelerated payment notice is amended under subsection (2)(*d*), the amount represented by the reduction, and

(*b*) in a case where the accelerated payment notice is withdrawn, the amount specified under section 220(2)(*d*) or 221(2)(*d*).][1]

Modifications—NICA 2015 Sch 20 para 21 (subsection (9) has effect as if the provisions mentioned therein included NICA 2015 Sch 2 para 18(2) (payment of disputed contributions where accelerated payment notice issued when NICs appeal pending).

Cross-references—See FA 2014 Sch 32 para 8 (application of this section in relation to accelerated partner payment notices).

Amendments—[1] The following amendments made by FA 2015 s 118, Sch 18 paras 1, 8 with effect from 26 March 2015—

– in sub-ss (2)(*b*), (7)(*a*), words repealed;
– sub-ss (2)(*d*), (7)(*c*) and preceding words inserted;
– in sub-ss (4), (6)(*b*), word inserted; and
– sub-ss (12A), (14)–(16) inserted.

[Group relief claims after accelerated payment notices

227A Group relief claims after accelerated payment notices

(1) This section applies where as a result of an accelerated payment notice given to P—

(*a*) P was prevented from consenting to a claim for group relief in respect of an amount under section 225A(2), or

(*b*) pursuant to section 225A(3), a consent given by P to a claim for group relief in respect of an amount was ineffective.

(2) If a final determination establishes that the amount P has available to surrender consists of or includes the amount referred to in subsection (1)(*a*) or (*b*) or a part of it ("the allowed amount")—

(*a*) section 225A(2) and (3) (which prevents consent being given to group relief claims) ceases to apply in relation to the allowed amount, and

(*b*) a claim for group relief in respect of any part of the allowed amount may be made within the period of 30 days after the relevant time.

(3) The time limits otherwise applicable to amendment of a company tax return do not apply to an amendment to the extent that it makes a claim for group relief in respect of any part of the allowed amount within the time limit allowed by subsection (2)(*b*).

(4) In this section—

"final determination" means—

(*a*) a conclusion stated in a closure notice under paragraph 34 of Schedule 18 to FA 1998 against which no appeal is made;

(*b*) the final determination of a tax appeal within paragraph (*d*) or (*e*) of section 203;

"relevant time" means—

(*a*) in a case within paragraph (*a*) above, the end of the period during which the appeal could have been made;

(*b*) in the case within paragraph (*b*) above, the end of the day on which the final determination occurs.][1]

Amendments—[1] Section 227A and preceding crosshead inserted by FA 2015 s 118, Sch 18 paras 1, 9 with effect from 26 March 2015.

Partners and partnerships

228 Accelerated partner payments

Schedule 32 makes provision for accelerated partner payments and modifies this Chapter in relation to partnerships.

Defined terms

229 Defined terms used in Chapter 3

In this Chapter—

"the accelerated payment" has the meaning given by section 223(2);

"accelerated payment notice" has the meaning given by section 219(1);

"arrangements" has the meaning given by section 201(4);

"the asserted advantage" has the meaning given by section 219(3);

"the chosen arrangements" has the meaning given by section 219(3), except in Schedule 32 where it has the meaning given by paragraph 3(3) of that Schedule;

"the denied advantage" has the meaning given by section 220(5), except in paragraph 4 of Schedule 32 where it has the meaning given by paragraph 4(4) of that Schedule;

"designated HMRC officer" means an officer of Revenue and Customs who has been designated by the Commissioners for the purposes of this Part;

"follower notice" has the meaning given by section 204(1);

"HMRC" means Her Majesty's Revenue and Customs;

"P" has the meaning given by section 219(1);

"partner payment notice" has the meaning given by paragraph 3 of Schedule 32;

"relevant tax" has the meaning given by section 200;

"tax advantage" has the meaning given by section 201(2);

"tax appeal" has the meaning given by section 203;

"tax enquiry" has the meaning given by section 202(2).

CHAPTER 4
MISCELLANEOUS AND GENERAL PROVISION

Stamp duty land tax and annual tax on enveloped dwellings

230 Special case: stamp duty land tax

(1) This section applies to modify the application of this Part in the case of—

(a) a return or claim in respect of stamp duty land tax, or

(b) a tax appeal within section 203(g), or any appeal within section 203(i) which derives from such an appeal.

(2) If two or more persons acting jointly are the purchasers in respect of the land transaction—

(a) anything required or authorised by this Part to be done in relation to P must be done in relation to all of those persons, and

(b) any liability of P in respect of an accelerated payment, or a penalty under this Part, is a joint and several liability of all of those persons.

(3) Subsection (2) is subject to subsections (4) to (8).

(4) If the land transaction was entered into by or on behalf of the members of a partnership—

(a) anything required or authorised to be done under this Part in relation to P is required or authorised to be done in relation to all the responsible partners, and

(b) any liability of P in respect of an accelerated payment, or a penalty under this Part, is a joint and several liability of the responsible partners.

(5) But nothing in subsection (4) enables—

(a) an accelerated payment to be recovered from a person who did not become a responsible partner until after the effective date of the transaction in respect of which the tax to which the accelerated payment relates is payable, or

(b) a penalty under this Part to be recovered from a person who did not become a responsible partner until after the time when the omission occurred that caused the penalty to become payable.

(6) Where the trustees of a settlement are liable to pay an accelerated payment or a penalty under this Part, the payment or penalty may be recovered (but only once) from any one or more of the responsible trustees.

(7) But nothing in subsection (6) enables a penalty to be recovered from a person who did not become a responsible trustee until after the time when the omission occurred that caused the penalty to become payable.

(8) Where a follower notice or accelerated payment notice is given to more than one person, the power conferred on P by section 207 or 222 is exercisable by each of those persons separately or by two or more of them jointly.

(9) In this section—

"the accelerated payment" has the meaning given by section 223(2);

"accelerated payment notice" has the meaning given by section 219(1);

"effective date", in relation to a land transaction, has the meaning given by section 119 of FA 2003;

"follower notice" has the meaning given by section 204(1);

"the responsible partners", in relation to a land transaction, has the meaning given by paragraph 6(2) of Schedule 15 to that Act;

"the responsible trustees" has the meaning given by paragraph 5(3) of Schedule 16 to that Act;

"P"—

(a) in relation to Chapter 2, has the meaning given by section 204(1);

(b) in relation to Chapter 3, has the meaning given by section 219.

231 Special case: annual tax on enveloped dwellings

(1) This section applies to modify the application of this Part in the case of—

(a) a return or claim in respect of annual tax on enveloped dwellings, or

(b) a tax appeal within section 203(h), or any appeal within section 203(i) which derives from such an appeal.

(2) If the responsible partners of a partnership are the chargeable person in relation to the tax to which the return or claim or appeal relates—

(a) anything required or authorised by this Part to be done in relation to P must be done in relation to all of those partners, and

(b) any liability of P in respect of an accelerated payment, or a penalty under this Part, is a joint and several liability of all of those persons.

(3) Where—

(a) a follower notice is given by virtue of a tax enquiry into the return or claim or the appeal, and

(b) by virtue of section 97 or 98 of FA 2013, two or more persons would have been jointly and severally liable for an additional amount of tax had the necessary corrective action been taken before the specified time for the purposes of section 208,

any liability of P in respect of a penalty under that section is a joint and several liability of all of them.

(4) Where—

(a) an accelerated payment notice is given by virtue of a tax enquiry into the return or claim or the appeal, and

(b) two or more persons would, by virtue of section 97 or 98 of FA 2013, be jointly and severally liable for the understated tax relating to the accelerated payment specified in the notice or (as the case may be) the disputed tax specified in the notice,

any liability of P in respect of the accelerated payment or a penalty under section 226 is a joint and several liability of all of them.

(5) Accordingly—

(a) where a follower notice is given in a case where subsection (3) applies, or

(b) an accelerated payment notice is given in a case to which subsection (4) applies,

HMRC must also give a copy of the notice to any other person who would be jointly and severally liable for a penalty or payment, in relation to the notice, by virtue of this section.

(6) Where a follower notice or accelerated payment notice is given to more than one person, the power conferred on P by section 207 or 222 is exercisable by each of those persons separately or by two or more of them jointly.

(7) In this section—

"the accelerated payment" has the meaning given by section 223(2);

"accelerated payment notice" has the meaning given by section 219(1);

NIC

"the chargeable person" has the same meaning as in Part 3 of FA 2013 (annual tax on enveloped dwellings);
"follower notice" has the same meaning as in Chapter 2;
"P"—
(a) in relation to Chapter 2, has the meaning given by section 204(1);
(b) in relation to Chapter 3, has the meaning given by section 219;
"the responsible partners" has the same meaning as in Part 3 of FA 2013 (annual tax on enveloped dwellings).

Extension of Part by order

232 Extension of this Part by order

(1) The Treasury may by order amend section 200 (definition of "relevant tax") so as to extend this Part to any other tax.
(2) An order under this section may include—
(a) provision in respect of that other tax corresponding to the provision made by sections 224 and 225,
(b) consequential and supplemental provision, and
(c) transitional and transitory provision and savings.
(3) For the purposes of subsection (1) or (2) an order under this section may amend this Part (other than this section) or any other enactment whenever passed or made.
(4) The power to make orders under this section is exercisable by statutory instrument.
(5) An order under this section may only be made if a draft of the instrument containing the order has been laid before and approved by a resolution of the House of Commons.
(6) In this section "tax" includes duty.

Consequential amendments

233 Consequential amendments

Schedule 33 contains consequential amendments.

PART 5
PROMOTERS OF TAX AVOIDANCE SCHEMES

Note—FA 2014 Part 5 has effect for NICs purposes with the modifications set out in NICA 2015 Sch 2 Part 2 with effect from 12 April 2015. These modifications include the following—
– references to tax, other than in references to particular taxes, include relevant contributions;
– references to a tax advantage include the avoidance or reduction of a liability to pay relevant contributions; and
– references to a provision of FA 2004 Part 7 (DOTAS) include references to that DOTAS provision as applied by regulations under SSAA 1992 s 132A, and any provision of regulations under that section that corresponds to that DOTAS provision, whenever the regulations are made;

NICA 2015 Sch 2 Part 2 comes into force for the purposes of making regulations under FA 2014 Part 5 with effect from 12 February 2015.
See also NICA 2015 generally for application of the POTAS legislation in relation to NICs.
Commentary—*Simon's Taxes* **A7.250**.
Cross-references—See SSCBA 1992 s 11A (Parts 4 and 5 of FA 2014 apply with the necessary modifications, in relation to Class 2 contributions under SSCBA 1992 s 11(2) as if those contributions were income tax chargeable under ITTOIA 2005 Pt 2 Ch 2 in respect of profits of a trade, profession or vocation which is not carried on wholly outside the United Kingdom).

Introduction

234 Meaning of "relevant proposal" and "relevant arrangements"

(1) "Relevant proposal" means a proposal for arrangements which (if entered into) would be relevant arrangements (whether the proposal relates to a particular person or to any person who may seek to take advantage of it).
(2) Arrangements are "relevant arrangements" if—
(a) they enable, or might be expected to enable, any person to obtain a tax advantage, and
(b) the main benefit, or one of the main benefits, that might be expected to arise from the arrangements is the obtaining of that advantage.
(3) "Tax advantage" includes—
(a) relief or increased relief from tax,
(b) repayment or increased repayment of tax,
(c) avoidance or reduction of a charge to tax or an assessment to tax,
(d) avoidance of a possible assessment to tax,
(e) deferral of a payment of tax or advancement of a repayment of tax, and
(f) avoidance of an obligation to deduct or account for tax.
(4) "Arrangements" includes any agreement, scheme, arrangement or understanding of any kind, whether or not legally enforceable, involving a single transaction or two or more transactions.

235 Carrying on a business "as a promoter"

(1) A person carrying on a business in the course of which the person is, or has been, a promoter in relation to a relevant proposal or relevant arrangements carries on that business "as a promoter".

(2) A person is a "promoter" in relation to a relevant proposal if the person—
(a) is to any extent responsible for the design of the proposed arrangements,
(b) makes a firm approach to another person in relation to the relevant proposal with a view to making the proposal available for implementation by that person or any other person, or
(c) makes the relevant proposal available for implementation by other persons.
(3) A person is a "promoter" in relation to relevant arrangements if the person—
(a) is by virtue of subsection (2)(b) or (c), a promoter in relation to a relevant proposal which is implemented by the arrangements, or
(b) is responsible to any extent for the design, organisation or management of the arrangements.
(4) For the purposes of this Part a person makes a firm approach to another person in relation to a relevant proposal if—
(a) the person communicates information about the relevant proposal to the other person at a time when the proposed arrangements have been substantially designed,
(b) the communication is made with a view to that other person or any other person entering into transactions forming part of the proposed arrangements, and
(c) the information communicated includes an explanation of the tax advantage that might be expected to be obtained from the proposed arrangements.
(5) For the purposes of subsection (4) proposed arrangements have been substantially designed at any time if by that time the nature of the transactions to form them (or part of them) has been sufficiently developed for it to be reasonable to believe that a person who wished to obtain the tax advantage mentioned in subsection (4)(c) might enter into—
(a) transactions of the nature developed, or
(b) transactions not substantially different from transactions of that nature.
(6) A person is not a promoter in relation to a relevant proposal or relevant arrangements by reason of anything done in prescribed circumstances.
(7) Regulations under subsection (6) may contain provision having retrospective effect.

Regulations—Promoters of Tax Avoidance Schemes (Prescribed Circumstances under Section 235) Regulations, SI 2015/130.

236 Meaning of "intermediary"

For the purposes of this Part a person ("A") is an intermediary in relation to a relevant proposal if—
(a) A communicates information about the relevant proposal to another person in the course of a business,
(b) the communication is made with a view to that other person, or any other person, entering into transactions forming part of the proposed arrangements, and
(c) A is not a promoter in relation to the relevant proposal.

Conduct notices

237 Duty to give conduct notice

(1) Subsections (5) to (9) apply if an authorised officer becomes aware at any time that a person ("P") who is carrying on a business as a promoter—
(a) has, in the period of 3 years ending with that time, met one or more threshold conditions, and
(b) was carrying on a business as a promoter when P met that condition.
[(1A) Subsections (5) to (9) also apply if an authorised officer becomes aware at any time ("the relevant time") that—
(*a*) a person has, in the period of 3 years ending with the relevant time, met one or more threshold conditions,
(*b*) at the relevant time another person ("P") meets one or more of those conditions by virtue of Part 2 of Schedule 34 (meeting the threshold conditions: bodies corporate and partnerships), and
(*c*) P is, at the relevant time, carrying on a business as a promoter.][1]
(2) Part 1 of Schedule 34 sets out the threshold conditions and describes how they are met.
(3) Part 2 of that Schedule contains provision about [when a person is treated as meeting a threshold condition][1].
(4) See also Schedule 36 (which contains provision about the meeting of threshold conditions and other conditions by partnerships).
[(5) The authorised officer must determine—
(*a*) in a case within subsection (1), whether or not P's meeting of the condition mentioned in subsection (1)(*a*) (or, if more than one condition is met, the meeting of all of those conditions, taken together) should be regarded as significant in view of the purposes of this Part, or
(*b*) in a case within subsection (1A), whether or not—
(i) the meeting of the condition by the person as mentioned in subsection (1A)(*a*) (or, if more than one condition is met, the meeting of all of those conditions, taken together), and
(ii) P's meeting of the condition (or conditions) as mentioned in subsection (1A)(*b*),

should be regarded as significant in view of those purposes.][1]

(6) Subsection (5) does not apply if a conduct notice or a monitoring notice already has effect in relation to P.

(7) If the authorised officer determines under [subsection (5)(*a*)][1] that P's meeting of the condition or conditions in question should be regarded as significant, the officer must give P a conduct notice, unless subsection (8) applies.

[(7A) If the authorised officer determines under subsection (5)(*b*) that both—

(*a*) the meeting of the condition or conditions by the person as mentioned in subsection (1A)(*a*), and

(*b*) P's meeting of the condition or conditions as mentioned in subsection (1A)(*b*),

should be regarded as significant, the officer must give P a conduct notice, unless subsection (8) applies.][1]

(8) This subsection applies if the authorised officer determines that, having regard to the extent of the impact that P's activities as a promoter are likely to have on the collection of tax, it is inappropriate to give P a conduct notice.

(9) The authorised officer must determine under subsection (5) that the meeting of the condition (or all the conditions) . . . [1] should be regarded as significant if the condition (or any of the conditions) is in any of the following paragraphs of Schedule 34—

(a) paragraph 2 (deliberate tax defaulters);

(b) paragraph 3 (breach of Banking Code of Practice);

(c) paragraph 4 (dishonest tax agents);

(d) paragraph 6 (persons charged with certain offences);

(e) paragraph 7 (opinion notice of GAAR Advisory Panel).

[(10) If, as a result of subsection (1A), subsections (5) to (9) apply to a person, this does not prevent the giving of a conduct notice to the person mentioned in subsection (1A)(*a*).][1]

Press releases etc—Queen's Speech 2014—Bills with tax implications (including NICs Bill proposals which would mirror the Finance Act 2014 conduct notices and monitoring provisions for NICs purposes) (see *SWTI 2014, Issue 23*)

Definitions—"authorised officer" (for the purposes of Part 5), s 283(2); "threshold condition", Sch 34 paras 2–12.

Cross-references—See FA 2014 Sch 32 paras 5, 6 (conduct notices and monitoring notices given to partnerships).

Amendments—[1] Sub-ss (1A), (7A), (10) inserted, sub-s (5) substituted, words in sub-ss (3), (7) substituted, and in sub-s (9), words repealed, by FA 2015 s 119, Sch 19 paras 1, 2 with effect for the purposes of determining whether a person meets a threshold condition in a period of three years ending on or after 26 March 2015.

[237A Duty to give conduct notice: defeat of promoted arrangements

(1) If an authorised officer becomes aware at any time ("the relevant time") that a person ("P") who is carrying on a business as a promoter meets any of the conditions in subsections (11) to (13), the officer must determine whether or not P's meeting of that condition should be regarded as significant in view of the purposes of this Part.

But see also subsection (14).

(2) An authorised officer must make the determination set out in subsection (3) if the officer becomes aware at any time ("the section 237A(2) relevant time") that—

(*a*) a person meets a condition in subsection (11), (12) or (13), and

(*b*) at the section 237A(2) relevant time another person ("P"), who is carrying on a business as a promoter, meets that condition by virtue of Part 4 of Schedule 34A (meeting the section 237A conditions: bodies corporate and partnerships).

(3) The authorised officer must determine whether or not—

(*a*) the meeting of the condition by the person as mentioned in subsection (2)(*a*), and

(*b*) P's meeting of the condition as mentioned in subsection (2)(*b*),

should be regarded as significant in view of the purposes of this Part.

(4) Subsections (1) and (2) do not apply if a conduct notice or monitoring notice already has effect in relation to P.

(5) Subsection (1) does not apply if, at the relevant time, an authorised officer is under a duty to make a determination under section 237(5) in relation to P.

(6) Subsection (2) does not apply if, at the section 237A(2) relevant time, an authorised officer is under a duty to make a determination under section 237(5) in relation to P.

(7) But in a case where subsection (1) does not apply because of subsection (5), or subsection (2) does not apply because of subsection (6), subsection (5) of section 237 has effect as if—

(*a*) the references in paragraph (*a*) of that subsection to "subsection (1)", and "subsection (1)(*a*)" included subsection (1) of this section, and

(*b*) in paragraph (*b*) of that subsection the reference to "subsection (1A)(*a*)" included a reference to subsection (2)(*a*) of this section and the reference to subsection (1A)(*b*) included a reference to subsection (2)(*b*) of this section.

(8) If the authorised officer determines under subsection (1) that P's meeting of the condition in question should be regarded as significant, the officer must give P a conduct notice, unless subsection (10) applies.

(9) If the authorised officer determines under subsection (3) that—

(*a*) the meeting of the condition by the person as mentioned in subsection (2)(*a*), and (*b*) P's meeting of the condition as mentioned in subsection (2)(*b*), should be regarded as significant in view of the purposes of this Part, the officer must give P a conduct notice, unless subsection (10) applies.

(10) This subsection applies if the authorised officer determines that, having regard to the extent of the impact that P's activities as a promoter are likely to have on the collection of tax, it is inappropriate to give P a conduct notice.

(11) The condition in this subsection is that in the period of 3 years ending with the relevant time at least 3 relevant defeats have occurred in relation to P.

(12) The condition in this subsection is that at least two relevant defeats have occurred in relation to P at times when a single defeat notice under section 241A(2) or (6) had effect in relation to P.

(13) The condition in this subsection is that at least one relevant defeat has occurred in relation to P at a time when a double defeat notice under section 241A(3) had effect in relation to P.

(14) A determination that the condition in subsection (12) or (13) is met cannot be made unless—

(*a*) the defeat notice in question still has effect when the determination is made, or

(*b*) the determination is made on or before the 90th day after the day on which the defeat notice in question ceased to have effect.

(15) Schedule 34A sets out the circumstances in which a "relevant defeat" occurs in relation to a person and includes provision limiting what can amount to a further relevant defeat in relation to a person (see paragraph 6).][1]

Cross-references—See FA 2016 s 160(20)–(25) (circumstances in which defeats are treated for the purposes of this section as not having occurred).

Amendments—[1] Sections 237A–237D inserted by FA 2016 s 160(1), (2) with effect from 15 September 2016.

[237B Duty to give further conduct notice where provisional notice not complied with

(1) An authorised officer must give a conduct notice to a person ("P") who is carrying on a business as a promoter if—

(*a*) a conduct notice given to P under section 237A(8)—

(i) has ceased to have effect otherwise than as a result of section 237D(2) or 241(3) or (4), and

(ii) was provisional immediately before it ceased to have effect,

(*b*) the officer determines that P had failed to comply with one or more conditions in the conduct notice,

(*c*) the conduct notice relied on a Case 3 relevant defeat,

(*d*) since the time when the conduct notice ceased to have effect, one or more relevant defeats falling within subsection (2) have occurred in relation to—

(i) P, and

(ii) any arrangements to which the Case 3 relevant defeat also relates, and

(*e*) had that relevant defeat or (as the case may be) those relevant defeats, occurred before the conduct notice ceased to have effect, an authorised officer would have been required to notify the person under section 237C(3) that the notice was no longer provisional.

(2) A relevant defeat falls within this subsection if it occurs by virtue of Case 1 or Case 2 in Schedule 34A.

(3) Subsection (1) does not apply if the authorised officer determines that, having regard to the extent of the impact that the person's activities as a promoter are likely to have on the collection of tax, it is inappropriate to give the person a conduct notice.

(4) Subsection (1) does not apply if a conduct notice or monitoring notice already has effect in relation to the person.

(5) For the purposes of this Part a conduct notice "relies on a Case 3 relevant defeat" if it could not have been given under the following condition.

The condition is that paragraph 9 of Schedule 34A had effect with the substitution of "100% of the tested arrangements" for "75% of the tested arrangements".][1]

Amendments—[1] Sections 237A–237D inserted by FA 2016 s 160(1), (2) with effect from 15 September 2016.

[237C When a conduct notice given under section 237A(8) is "provisional"

(1) This section applies to a conduct notice which—

(*a*) is given to a person under section 237A(8), and

(*b*) relies on a Case 3 relevant defeat.

(2) The notice is "provisional" at all times when it has effect, unless an authorised officer notifies the person that the notice is no longer provisional.

(3) An authorised officer must notify the person that the notice is no longer provisional if subsection (4) or (5) applies.

(4) This subsection applies if—

(*a*) the condition in subsection (5)(*a*) is not met, and

(*b*) a full relevant defeat occurs in relation to P.

(5) This subsection applies if—

(a) two, or all three, of the relevant defeats by reference to which the conduct notice is given would not have been relevant defeats if paragraph 9 of Schedule 34A had effect with the substitution of "100% of the tested arrangements" for "75% of the tested arrangements", and

(b) the same number of full relevant defeats occur in relation to P.

(6) A "full relevant defeat" occurs in relation to P if—

(a) a relevant defeat occurs in relation to P otherwise than by virtue of Case 3 in paragraph 9 of Schedule 34A, or

(b) circumstances arise which would be a relevant defeat in relation to P by virtue of paragraph 9 of Schedule 34A if that paragraph had effect with the substitution of "100% of the tested arrangements" for "75% of the tested arrangements".

(7) In determining under subsection (6) whether a full relevant defeat has occurred in relation to P, assume that in paragraph 6 of Schedule 34A (provision limiting what can amount to a further relevant defeat in relation to a person) the first reference to a "relevant defeat" does not include a relevant defeat by virtue of Case 3 in paragraph 9 of Schedule 34A.][1]

Amendments—[1] Sections 237A–237D inserted by FA 2016 s 160(1), (2) with effect from 15 September 2016.

[237D Judicial ruling upholding asserted tax advantage: effect on conduct notice which is provisional

(1) Subsection (2) applies if at any time—

(a) a conduct notice which relies on a Case 3 relevant defeat (see section 237B(5)) is provisional, and

(b) a court or tribunal upholds a corresponding tax advantage which has been asserted in connection with any of the related arrangements to which that relevant defeat relates (see paragraph 5(2) of Schedule 34A).

(2) The conduct notice ceases to have effect when that judicial ruling becomes final.

(3) An authorised officer must give the person to whom the conduct notice was given a written notice stating that the conduct notice has ceased to have effect.

(4) For the purposes of this section, a tax advantage is "asserted" in connection with any arrangements if a person makes a return, claim or election on the basis that the tax advantage arises from those arrangements.

In relation to the arrangements mentioned in paragraph (b) of subsection (1) "corresponding tax advantage" means a tax advantage corresponding to any tax advantage the counteraction of which contributed to the relevant defeat mentioned in that paragraph.

(5) For the purposes of this section a court or tribunal "upholds" a tax advantage if—

(a) the court or tribunal makes a ruling to the effect that no part of the tax advantage is to be counteracted, and

(b) that judicial ruling is final.

(6) For the purposes of this Part a judicial ruling is "final" if it is—

(a) a ruling of the Supreme Court, or

(b) a ruling of any other court or tribunal in circumstances where—

(i) no appeal may be made against the ruling,

(ii) if an appeal may be made against the ruling with permission, the time limit for applications has expired and either no application has been made or permission has been refused,

(iii) if such permission to appeal against the ruling has been granted or is not required, no appeal has been made within the time limit for appeals, or

(iv) if an appeal was made, it was abandoned or otherwise disposed of before it was determined by the court or tribunal to which it was addressed.

(7) In this section references to "counteraction" include anything referred to as a counteraction in any of Conditions A to F in paragraphs 11 to 16 of Schedule 34A.][1]

Note—In this section, "tax" includes VAT, and "tax advantage" has the meaning given by s 234(3) and also includes a tax advantage as defined in VATA 1994 Sch 11A para 1.

Amendments—[1] Sections 237A–237D inserted by FA 2016 s 160(1), (2) with effect from 15 September 2016.

238 Contents of a conduct notice

(1) A conduct notice is a notice requiring the person to whom it has been given ("the recipient") to comply with conditions specified in the notice.

(2) Before deciding on the terms of a conduct notice, the authorised officer must give the person to whom the notice is to be given an opportunity to comment on the proposed terms of the notice.

(3) A notice may include only conditions that it is reasonable to impose for any of the following purposes—

(a) to ensure that the recipient provides adequate information to its clients about relevant proposals, and relevant arrangements, in relation to which the recipient is a promoter;

(b) to ensure that the recipient provides adequate information about relevant proposals in relation to which it is a promoter to persons who are intermediaries in relation to those proposals;

(c) to ensure that the recipient does not fail to comply with any duty under a specified disclosure provision;
(d) to ensure that the recipient does not discourage others from complying with any obligation to disclose to HMRC information of a description specified in the notice;
(e) to ensure that the recipient does not enter into an agreement with another person ("C") which relates to a relevant proposal or relevant arrangements in relation to which the recipient is a promoter, on terms which—
(i) impose a contractual obligation on C which falls within paragraph 11(2) or (3) of Schedule 34 (contractual terms restricting disclosure), or
(ii) impose on C obligations within both paragraph 11(4) and (5) of that Schedule (contractual terms requiring contribution to fighting funds and restricting settlement of proceedings);
(f) to ensure that the recipient does not promote relevant proposals or relevant arrangements which rely on, or involve a proposal to rely on, one or more contrived or abnormal steps to produce a tax advantage;
(g) to ensure that the recipient does not fail to comply with any stop notice which has effect under paragraph 12 of Schedule 34.

(4) References in subsection (3) to ensuring that adequate information is provided about proposals or arrangements include—
(a) ensuring the adequacy of the description of the arrangements or proposed arrangements;
(b) ensuring that the information includes an adequate assessment of the risk that the arrangements or proposed arrangements will fail;
(c) ensuring that the information does not falsely state, and is not likely to create a false impression, that HMRC have (formally or informally) considered, approved or expressed a particular opinion in relation to the proposal or arrangements.

(5) In subsection (3)(c) "specified disclosure provision" means a disclosure provision that is specified in the notice; and for this purpose "disclosure provision" means any of the following—
(a) section 308 of FA 2004 (disclosure of tax avoidance schemes: duties of promoter);
(b) section 312 of FA 2004 (duty of promoter to notify client of number);
(c) sections 313ZA and 313ZB of FA 2004 (duties to provide details of clients and certain others);
(d) Part 1 of Schedule 36 to FA 2008 (duties to provide information and produce documents).

(6) In subsection (4)(b) "fail", in relation to arrangements or proposed arrangements, means not result in a tax advantage which the arrangements or (as the case may be) proposed arrangements might be expected to result in.

(7) The Treasury may by regulations amend the definition of "disclosure provision" in subsection (5).

Definitions—"authorised officer" (for the purposes of Part 5), s 283(2).
Cross-references—See FA 2014 Sch 32 paras 5, 6 (conduct notices and monitoring notices given to partnerships).

239 Section 238: supplementary

(1) In section 238 the following expressions are to be interpreted as follows.

(2) "Adequate" means adequate having regard to what it might be reasonable for a client or (as the case may be) an intermediary to expect; and "adequacy" is to be interpreted accordingly.

(3) A person ("C") is a "client" of a promoter, if at any time when a conduct notice has effect, the promoter—
(a) makes a firm approach to C in relation to a relevant proposal with a view to the promoter making the proposal available for implementation by C or another person;
(b) makes a relevant proposal available for implementation by C;
(c) takes part in the organisation or management of relevant arrangements entered into by C.

(4) The recipient of a conduct notice "promotes" a relevant proposal if it—
(a) takes part in designing the proposal,
(b) makes a firm approach to a person in relation to the proposal with a view to making the proposal available for implementation by that person or another person, or
(c) makes the proposal available for implementation by persons (other than the recipient).

(5) The recipient of a conduct notice "promotes" relevant arrangements if it takes part in designing, organising or managing the arrangements.

240 Amendment or withdrawal of conduct notice

(1) This section applies where a conduct notice has been given to a person.

(2) An authorised officer may at any time amend the notice.

(3) An authorised officer—
(a) may withdraw the notice if the officer thinks it is not necessary for it to continue to have effect, and
(b) in considering whether or not that is necessary must take into account the person's record of compliance, or failure to comply, with the conditions in the notice.

NIC

Definitions—"authorised officer" (for the purposes of Part 5), s 283(2).

241 Duration of conduct notice

(1) A conduct notice has effect from the date specified in it as its commencement date.

(2) A conduct notice ceases to have effect—

(a) at the end of the period of two years beginning with its commencement date, or

(b) if an earlier date is specified in it as its termination date, at the end of that day.

(3) A conduct notice ceases to have effect if withdrawn by an authorised officer under section 240.

(4) A conduct notice ceases to have effect in relation to a person when a monitoring notice takes effect in relation to that person.

[(5) See also section 237D(2) (provisional conduct notice affected by judicial ruling).][1]

Definitions—"authorised officer" (for the purposes of Part 5), s 283(2).

Amendments—[1] Sub-s (5) inserted by FA 2016 s 160(6) with effect from 15 September 2016.

[Defeat notices

241A Defeat notices

(1) This section applies in relation to a person ("P") only if P is carrying on a business as a promoter.

(2) An authorised officer, or an officer of Revenue and Customs with the approval of an authorised officer, may give P a notice if the officer concerned has become aware of one (and only one) relevant defeat which has occurred in relation to P in the period of 3 years ending with the day on which the notice is given.

(3) An authorised officer, or an officer of Revenue and Customs with the approval of an authorised officer, may give P a notice if the officer concerned has become aware of two (but not more than two) relevant defeats which have occurred in relation to P in the period of 3 years ending with the day on which the notice is given.

(4) A notice under this section must be given by the end of the 90 days beginning with the day on which the matters mentioned in subsection (2) or (as the case may be) (3) come to the attention of HMRC.

(5) Subsection (6) applies if—

(*a*) a single defeat notice which had been given to P (under subsection (2) or (6)) ceases to have effect as a result of section 241B(1), and

(*b*) in the period when the defeat notice had effect a relevant defeat ("the further relevant defeat") occurred in relation to P.

(6) An authorised officer or an officer of Revenue and Customs with the approval of an authorised officer may give P a notice in respect of the further relevant defeat (regardless of whether or not it occurred in the period of 3 years ending with the day on which the notice is given).

(7) In this Part—

(*a*) "single defeat notice" means a notice under subsection (2) or (6);

(*b*) "double defeat notice" means a notice under subsection (3);

(*c*) "defeat notice" means a single defeat notice or a double defeat notice.

(8) A defeat notice must—

(*a*) set out the dates on which the look-forward period for the notice begins and ends;

(*b*) in the case of a single defeat notice, explain the effect of section 237A(12);

(*c*) in the case of a double defeat notice, explain the effect of section 237A(13).

(9) HMRC may specify what further information must be included in a defeat notice.

(10) "Look-forward period"—

(*a*) in relation to a defeat notice under subsection (2) or (3), means the period of 5 years beginning with the day after the day on which the notice is given;

(*b*) in relation to a defeat notice under subsection (6), means the period beginning with the day after the day on which the notice is given and ending at the end of the period of 5 years beginning with the day on which the further relevant defeat mentioned in subsection (6) occurred in relation to P.

(11) A defeat notice has effect throughout its look-forward period unless it ceases to have effect earlier in accordance with section 241B(1) or (4).][1]

Cross-references—See FA 2016 s 160(20)–(25) (circumstances in which defeats are treated for the purposes of this section as not having occurred).

Amendments—[1] Sections 241A, 241B and preceding crosshead inserted by FA 2016 s 160(1), (3) with effect from 15 September 2016.

[241B Judicial ruling upholding asserted tax advantage: effect on defeat notice

(1) If the relevant defeat to which a single defeat notice relates is overturned (see subsection (5)), the notice has no further effect on and after the day on which it is overturned.

(2) Subsection (3) applies if one (and only one) of the relevant defeats in respect of which a double defeat notice was given is overturned.

(3) The notice is to be treated for the purposes of this Part (including this section) as if it had always been a single defeat notice given (in respect of the other of the two relevant defeats) on the date on which the notice was in fact given.

The look-forward period for the notice is accordingly unchanged.

(4) If both the relevant defeats to which a double defeat notice relates are overturned (on the same date), that notice has no further effect on and after that date.

(5) A relevant defeat specified in a defeat notice is "overturned" if—

(*a*) the notice could not have specified that relevant defeat if paragraph 9 of Schedule 34A had effect with the substitution of "100% of the tested arrangements" for "75% of the tested arrangements", and

(*b*) at a time when the notice has effect a court or tribunal upholds a corresponding tax advantage which has been asserted in connection with any of the related arrangements to which the relevant defeat relates (see paragraph 5(2) of Schedule 34A).

Accordingly the relevant defeat is overturned on the day on which the judicial ruling mentioned in paragraph (*b*) becomes final.

(6) If a defeat notice ceases to have effect as a result of subsection (1) or (4) an authorised officer, or an officer of Revenue and Customs with the approval of an authorised officer, must notify the person to whom the notice was given that it has ceased to have effect.

(7) If subsection (3) has effect in relation to a defeat notice, an authorised officer, or an officer of Revenue and Customs with the approval of an authorised officer, must notify the person of the effect of that subsection.

(8) For the purposes of this section, a tax advantage is "asserted" in connection with any arrangements if a person makes a return, claim or election on the basis that the tax advantage arises from those arrangements.

(9) In relation to the arrangements mentioned in paragraph (*b*) of subsection (5) "corresponding tax advantage" means a tax advantage corresponding to any tax advantage the counteraction of which contributed to the relevant defeat mentioned in that paragraph.

(10) For the purposes of this section a court or tribunal "upholds" a tax advantage if—

(*a*) the court or tribunal makes a ruling to the effect that no part of the tax advantage is to be counteracted, and

(*b*) that judicial ruling is final.

(11) In this section references to "counteraction" include anything referred to as a counteraction in any of Conditions A to F in paragraphs 11 to 16 of Schedule 34A.][1]

Note—In this section, "tax" includes VAT, and "tax advantage" has the meaning given by s 234(3) and also includes a tax advantage as defined in VATA 1994 Sch 11A para 1.

Amendments—[1] Sections 241A, 241B and preceding crosshead inserted by FA 2016 s 160(1), (3) with effect from 15 September 2016.

Monitoring notices: procedure and publication

242 Monitoring notices: duty to apply to tribunal

(1) If—

(a) a conduct notice has effect in relation to a person who is carrying on a business as a promoter, and

(b) an authorised officer determines that the person has failed to comply with one or more conditions in the notice,

the authorised officer must apply to the tribunal for approval to give the person a monitoring notice.

(2) An application under subsection (1) must include a draft of the monitoring notice.

(3) Subsection (1) does not apply if—

(a) the condition (or all the conditions) mentioned in subsection (1)(b) were imposed under subsection (3)(a), (b) or (c) of section 238, and

(b) the authorised officer considers that the failure to comply with the condition (or all the conditions, taken together) is such a minor matter that it should be disregarded for the purposes of this section.

(4) Where an authorised officer makes an application to the tribunal under subsection (1), the officer must at the same time give notice to the person to whom the application relates.

(5) The notice under subsection (4) must state which condition (or conditions) the authorised officer has determined under subsection (1)(b) that the person has failed to comply with and the reasons for that determination.

[(6) At a time when a notice given under section 237A is provisional, no determination is to be made under subsection (1) in respect of the notice.

(7) If a promoter fails to comply with conditions in a conduct notice at a time when the conduct notice is provisional, nothing in subsection (6) prevents those failures from being taken into account under subsection (1) at any subsequent time when the conduct notice is not provisional.][1]

Definitions—"authorised officer" (for the purposes of Part 5), s 283(2).

Cross-references—See FA 2014 Sch 32 paras 5, 6 (conduct notices and monitoring notices given to partnerships).

Amendments—[1] Sub-ss (6), (7) inserted by FA 2016 s 160(1), (4) with effect from 15 September 2016.

243 Monitoring notices: tribunal approval

(1) On an application under section 242, the tribunal may approve the giving of a monitoring notice only if—

(a) the tribunal is satisfied that, in the circumstances, the authorised officer would be justified in giving the monitoring notice, and

(b) the person to whom the monitoring notice is to be given ("the affected person") has been given a reasonable opportunity to make representations to the tribunal.

(2) The tribunal may amend the draft notice included with the application under section 242.

(3) If the representations that the affected person makes to the tribunal include a statement that in the affected person's view it was not reasonable to include the condition mentioned in section 242(1)(b) in the conduct notice, the tribunal must refuse to approve the giving of the monitoring notice if it is satisfied that it was not reasonable to include that condition (but see subsection (4)).

(4) If the representations made to the tribunal include the statement described in subsection (3) and the determination under section 242(1)(b) is a determination that there has been a failure to comply with more than one condition in the conduct notice—

(a) subsection (3) does not apply, but

(b) in deciding whether or not to approve the giving of the monitoring notice, the tribunal is to assume, in the case of any condition that the tribunal considers it was not reasonable to include in the conduct notice, that there has been no failure to comply with that condition.

Definitions—"authorised officer" (for the purposes of Part 5), s 283(2).

244 Monitoring notices: content and issuing

(1) Where the tribunal has approved the giving of a monitoring notice, the authorised officer must give the notice to the person to whom it relates.

(2) A monitoring notice given under subsection (1) or paragraph 9 or 10 of Schedule 36 must—

(a) explain the effect of the monitoring notice and specify the date from which it takes effect;

(b) inform the recipient of the right to request the withdrawal of the monitoring notice under section 245.

(3) In addition, a monitoring notice must—

(a) if given under subsection (1), state which condition (or conditions) it has been determined the person has failed to comply with and the reasons for that determination;

(b) if given under paragraph 9 or 10 of Schedule 36, state the date of the original monitoring notice and name the partnership to which that notice was given.

(4) The date specified under subsection (2)(a) must not be earlier than the date on which the monitoring notice is given.

(5) In this Part, a person in relation to whom a monitoring notice has effect is called a "monitored promoter".

Definitions—"authorised officer" (for the purposes of Part 5), s 283(2).

245 Withdrawal of monitoring notice

(1) A person in relation to whom a monitoring notice has effect may, at any time after the end of the period of 12 months beginning with the end of the appeal period, request that the notice should cease to have effect.

(2) The "appeal period" means—

(a) the period during which an appeal could be brought against the approval by the tribunal of the giving of the monitoring notice, or

(b) where an appeal mentioned in paragraph (a) has been brought, the period during which that appeal has not been finally determined, withdrawn or otherwise disposed of.

(3) A request under this section is to be made in writing to an authorised officer.

(4) Where a request is made under this section, an authorised officer must within 30 days beginning with the day on which the request is received determine either—

(a) that the monitoring notice is to cease to have effect, or

(b) that the request is to be refused.

(5) The matters to be taken into account by an authorised officer in making a determination under subsection (4) include—

(a) whether or not the person subject to the monitoring notice has, since the time when the notice took effect, engaged in behaviour of a sort that conditions included in a conduct notice in accordance with section 238(3) could be used to regulate;

(b) whether or not it appears likely that the person will in the future engage in such behaviour;

(c) the person's record of compliance, or failure to comply, with obligations imposed on it under this Part, since the time when the monitoring notice took effect.

(6) An authorised officer—

(a) may withdraw a monitoring notice if the officer thinks it is not necessary for it to continue to have effect, and

(b) in considering whether or not that is necessary, the officer must take into account the matters in paragraphs (a) to (c) of subsection (5).

(7) If the authorised officer makes a determination under subsection (4)(a), or decides to withdraw a monitoring notice under subsection (6), the officer must also determine that the person is, or is not, to be given a follow-on conduct notice.

(8) "Follow-on conduct notice" means a conduct notice taking effect immediately after the monitoring notice ceases to have effect.

(9) Where the monitoring notice mentioned in subsection (1) is a replacement monitoring notice—

(a) in subsection (1) the reference to the end of the appeal period is to be read as a reference to whichever is the later of the end of the appeal period for the original monitoring notice and the date the replacement monitoring notice takes effect, and

(b) in subsection (5)(a) and (c) the time referred to is to be read as the time when the original monitoring notice (see paragraph 11(2) of Schedule 36) took effect.

Definitions—"authorised officer" (for the purposes of Part 5), s 283(2).

246 Notification of determination under section 245

(1) Where an authorised officer makes a determination under section 245(4), that officer, or an officer of Revenue and Customs with that officer's approval, must notify the person who made the request of the determination.

(2) If the determination is that the monitoring notice is to cease to have effect, the notice must—

(a) specify the date from which the monitoring notice is to cease to have effect, and

(b) inform the person of the determination made under section 245(7).

(3) If the determination is that the request is to be refused, the notice must inform the person who made the request—

(a) of the reasons for the refusal, and

(b) of the right to appeal under section 247.

Definitions—"authorised officer" (for the purposes of Part 5), s 283(2).

247 Appeal against refusal to withdraw monitoring notice

(1) A person may appeal against a refusal by an authorised officer of a request that a monitoring notice should cease to have effect.

(2) Notice of appeal must be given—

(a) in writing to the officer who gave the notice of the refusal under section 245, and

(b) within the period of 30 days beginning with the day on which notice of the refusal was given.

(3) The notice of appeal must state the grounds of appeal.

(4) On an appeal that is notified to the tribunal, the tribunal may—

(a) confirm the refusal, or

(b) direct that the monitoring notice is to cease to have effect.

(5) Subject to this section, the provisions of Part 5 of TMA 1970 relating to appeals have effect in relation to an appeal under this section.

Definitions—"authorised officer" (for the purposes of Part 5), s 283(2).

248 Publication by HMRC

(1) An authorised officer may publish the fact that a person is a monitored promoter.

(2) Publication under subsection (1) may also include the following information about the monitored promoter—

(a) its name;

(b) its business address or registered office;

(c) the nature of the business mentioned in section 242(1)(a);

(d) any other information that the authorised officer considers it appropriate to publish in order to make clear the monitored promoter's identity.

(3) The reference in subsection (2)(a) to the monitored promoter's name includes any name under which it carries on a business as a promoter and any previous name or pseudonym.

(4) Publication under subsection (1) may also include a statement of which of the conditions in a conduct notice it has been determined that the person (or, in the case of a replacement monitoring notice, the person to whom the original monitoring notice was given) has failed to comply with.

(5) Publication may not take place before the end of the appeal period (or, in the case of a replacement monitoring notice, the appeal period for the original monitoring notice).

(6) The "appeal period", in relation to a monitoring notice, means—

(a) the period during which an appeal could be brought against the approval by the tribunal of the giving of the notice, or

(b) where an appeal mentioned in paragraph (a) has been brought, the period during which that appeal has not been finally determined, withdrawn or otherwise disposed of.

(7) Publication under this section is to be in such manner as the authorised officer thinks fit; but see subsection (8).

(8) If an authorised officer publishes the fact that a person is a monitored promoter and the monitoring notice is withdrawn, the officer must publish the fact of the withdrawal in the same way as the officer published the fact that the person was a monitored promoter.

Definitions—"authorised officer" (for the purposes of Part 5), s 283(2).

Cross-references—See FA 2014 Sch 36 para 14 (where the monitored promoter referred to in sub-s (2) above is a partnership, paras (*a*), (*b*) and (*d*) of that subsection are to be read as referring to details of the partnership, not to details of particular partners).

NIC

249 Publication by monitored promoter

(1) A person who is given a monitoring notice ("the monitored promoter") must give the persons mentioned in subsection (6) a notice stating—

(a) that it is a monitored promoter, and

(b) which of the conditions in a conduct notice it has been determined that it (or, if the monitoring notice is a replacement monitoring notice, the person to whom that notice was given) has failed to comply with.

(2) If the monitoring notice is a replacement monitoring notice, the notice under subsection (1) must also identify the original monitoring notice.

(3) If regulations made by the Commissioners so require, the monitored promoter must publish on the internet—

(a) the information mentioned in paragraph (a) and (b) of subsection (1), and

(b) its promoter reference number (see section 250).

(4) Subsection (1) and any duty imposed under subsection (3) or (10) do not apply until the end of the period of 10 days beginning with the end of the appeal period (and also see subsection (9)).

(5) The "appeal period" means—

(a) the period during which an appeal could be brought against the approval by the tribunal of the giving of the monitoring notice, or

(b) where an appeal mentioned in paragraph (a) has been brought, the period during which that appeal has not been finally determined, withdrawn or otherwise disposed of.

(6) The notice under subsection (1) must be given—

(a) to any person who becomes a client of the monitored promoter while the monitoring notice has effect, and

(b) (except in a case where the monitoring notice is a replacement monitoring notice) any person who is a client of the monitored promoter at the time the monitoring notice takes effect.

(7) A person ("C") is a client of a monitored promoter at the time a monitoring notice takes effect if during the period beginning with the date the conduct notice mentioned in subsection (1)(b) takes effect and ending with that time the promoter—

(a) made a firm approach to C in relation to a relevant proposal with a view to the promoter making the proposal available for implementation by C or another person;

(b) made a relevant proposal available for implementation by C;

(c) took part in the organisation or management of relevant arrangements entered into by C.

(8) A person becomes a client of a monitored promoter if the promoter does any of the things mentioned in paragraph (a) to (c) of subsection (7) in relation to that person.

(9) In the case of a person falling within subsection (6)(a), notice under subsection (1) may be given within the period of 10 days beginning with the day on which the person first became a client of the monitored promoter if that period would expire at a later date than the date on which notification would otherwise be required by virtue of subsection (4).

(10) A monitored promoter must also include in any prescribed publication or prescribed correspondence—

(a) the information mentioned in paragraph (a) and (b) of subsection (1), and

(b) its promoter reference number (see section 250).

(11) Notification under subsection (1), publication under subsection (3) or inclusion of the information required by subsection (10) is to be in such form and manner as is prescribed.

(12) Where the monitoring notice mentioned in subsection (1) is a replacement monitoring notice, the reference in subsection (4) to the end of the appeal period is to be read as a reference to whichever is the later of the end of the appeal period for the original monitoring notice and the date the replacement monitoring notice takes effect.

Definitions—"authorised officer" (for the purposes of Part 5), s 283(2).

Cross-references—See FA 2014 Sch 35 (penalties for failure to comply with duties under this section)

Allocation and distribution of promoter reference number

250 Allocation of promoter reference number

(1) Where a monitoring notice is given to a person ("the monitored promoter") HMRC must as soon as practicable after the end of the appeal period—

(a) allocate the monitored promoter a reference number, and

(b) notify the relevant persons of that number.

(2) "Relevant persons" means—

(a) the monitored promoter, and

(b) if the monitored promoter is resident outside the United Kingdom, any person who HMRC know is an intermediary in relation to a relevant proposal of the monitored promoter.

(3) The "appeal period" means—

(a) the period during which an appeal could be brought against the approval by the tribunal of the giving of the monitoring notice, or

(b) where an appeal mentioned in paragraph (a) has been brought, the period during which that appeal has not been finally determined, withdrawn or otherwise disposed of.

(4) The duty in subsection (1) does not apply if the monitoring notice is set aside following an appeal.

(5) A number allocated to a person under this section is referred to in this Part as a "promoter reference number".

(6) Where the monitoring notice mentioned in subsection (1) is a replacement monitoring notice—

(a) in subsection (1) the reference to the end of the appeal period is to be read as a reference to whichever is the later of the end of the appeal period for the original monitoring notice and the date the replacement monitoring notice takes effect, and

(b) in subsection (4) the reference to the monitoring notice is to be read as a reference to the original monitoring notice.

251 Duty of monitored promoter to notify clients and intermediaries of number

(1) This section applies where a person who is a monitored promoter ("the monitored promoter") is notified under section 250 of a promoter reference number.

(2) The monitored promoter must, within the relevant period, notify the promoter reference number to—

(a) any person who has become its client at any time in the period beginning with the day on which the monitoring notice in relation to the monitored promoter took effect and ending with the day on which the monitored promoter was notified of that number,

(b) any person who becomes its client after the end of the period mentioned in paragraph (a) but while the monitoring notice has effect,

(c) any person who the monitored promoter could reasonably be expected to know falls within subsection (4), and

(d) any person who the monitored promoter could reasonably be expected to know is a relevant intermediary in relation to a relevant proposal of the monitored promoter.

(3) A person ("C") becomes a client of a monitored promoter if the promoter does any of the following in relation to C—

(a) makes a firm approach to C in relation to a relevant proposal with a view to the promoter making the proposal available for implementation by C or another person;

(b) makes a relevant proposal available for implementation by C;

(c) takes part in the organisation or management of relevant arrangements entered into by C.

(4) A person falls within this subsection if during the period beginning with the date the conduct notice took effect and ending with the date on which the monitoring notice took effect the person has entered into transactions forming part of relevant arrangements and those arrangements—

(a) enable, or are likely to enable, the person to obtain a tax advantage during the time a monitoring notice has effect, and

(b) are either relevant arrangements in relation to which the monitored promoter is or was a promoter or implement a relevant proposal in relation to which the monitored promoter was a promoter.

(5) A person is a relevant intermediary in relation to a relevant proposal of a monitored promoter if the person meets the conditions in section 236(a) to (c) (meaning of "intermediary") at any time while the monitoring notice in relation to the monitored promoter has effect.

(6) The "relevant period" means—

(a) in the case of a person falling within subsection (2)(a), the period of 30 days beginning with the day of the notification mentioned in subsection (1),

(b) in the case of a person falling within subsection (2)(b), the period of 30 days beginning with the day on which the person first became a client in relation to the monitored promoter,

(c) in the case of a person falling within subsection (2)(c), the period of 30 days beginning with the later of the day of the notification mentioned in subsection (1) and the first day on which the monitored promoter could reasonably be expected to know that the person fell within subsection (4), and

(d) in the case of a person falling within subsection (2)(d), the period of 30 days beginning with the later of the day of the notification mentioned in subsection (1) and the first day on which the monitored promoter could reasonably be expected to know that the person was a relevant intermediary in relation to a relevant proposal of the monitored promoter.

(7) In this section "the conduct notice" means the conduct notice that the monitored promoter failed to comply with which resulted in the monitoring notice being given to the monitored promoter.

(8) Subsection (2)(c) is to be ignored in a case where the monitoring notice is a replacement monitoring notice.

Cross-references—See FA 2014 Sch 35 (penalties for failure to comply with duties under this section)

252 Duty of those notified to notify others of promoter's number

(1) In this section "notified client" means—

(a) a person who is notified of a promoter reference number under section 250 by reason of being a person falling within subsection (2)(b) of that section, and

(b) a person who is notified of a promoter reference number under section 251.

NIC

(2) A notified client must, within 30 days of being notified as described in subsection (1), provide the promoter reference number to any other person who the notified client might reasonably be expected to know has become, or is likely to have become, a client in relation to the monitored promoter concerned at a time when the monitoring notice in relation to that monitored promoter had effect.

(3) A person ("C") becomes a client of a monitored promoter if the promoter does any of the following in relation to C—

(a) makes a firm approach to C in relation to a relevant proposal with a view to the promoter making the proposal available for implementation by C or another person;

(b) makes a relevant proposal available for implementation by C;

(c) takes part in the organisation or management of relevant arrangements entered into by C.

(4) Where the notified client is an intermediary in relation to a relevant proposal of the monitored promoter concerned, the notified client must also, within 30 days, provide the promoter reference number to—

(a) any person to whom the notified client has, since the monitoring notice in relation to the monitored promoter concerned took effect, communicated in the course of a business information about a relevant proposal of the monitored promoter, and

(b) any person who the notified client might reasonably be expected to know has, since that monitoring notice took effect, entered into, or is likely to enter into, transactions forming part of relevant arrangements in relation to which that monitored promoter is a promoter.

(5) Subsection (2) or (4) does not impose a duty on a notified client to notify a person of a promoter reference number if the notified client reasonably believes that the person has already been notified of the promoter reference number (whether as a result of a duty under this section or as a result of any of the other provision of this Part).

Cross-references—See FA 2014 Sch 35 (penalties for failure to comply with duties under this section)

253 Duty of persons to notify the Commissioners

(1) If a person ("N") is notified of a promoter reference number under section 250, 251 or 252, N must report the number to the Commissioners if N expects to obtain a tax advantage from relevant arrangements in relation to which the monitored promoter to whom the reference number relates (whether that is N or another person) is the promoter.

(2) A report under this section—

(a) must be made in (or, if prescribed circumstances exist, submitted with) each tax return made by N for a period that is or includes a period for which the arrangements enable N to obtain a tax advantage (whether in relation to the tax to which the return relates or another tax);

(b) if no tax return falls within paragraph (a), or in the case mentioned in subsection (3), must contain such information, and be made in such form and manner and within such time, as is prescribed.

(3) The case is that the tax return in which the report would (apart from this subsection) have been made is not submitted—

(a) by the filing date, or

(b) if there is no filing date in relation to the tax return concerned, by such other time that the tax return is required to be submitted by or under any enactment.

(4) Where N expects to obtain the tax advantage referred to in subsection (1) in respect of inheritance tax, stamp duty land tax, stamp duty reserve tax or petroleum revenue tax—

(a) subsection (2) does not apply in relation to that tax advantage, and

(b) a report under this section in respect of that tax must be in such form and manner and contain such information and be made within such time as is prescribed.

(5) Where the relevant arrangements referred to in subsection (1) give rise to N making a claim under section 261B of TCGA 1992 (treating trade loss as CGT loss) or for loss relief under Part 4 of ITA 2007 and that claim is not contained in a tax return, a report under this section must also be made in that claim.

(6) In this section "tax return" means any of the following—

(a) a return under section 8 of TMA 1970 (income tax and capital gains tax: personal return);

(b) a return under section 8A of TMA 1970 (income tax and capital gains tax: trustee's return);

(c) a return under section 12AA of TMA 1970 (income tax and corporation tax: partnership return);

(d) a company tax return under paragraph 3 of Schedule 18 to the FA 1998 (company tax return);

[(da) a return under regulations made under section 105 of FA 2016 (apprenticeship levy)][1]

(e) a return under section 159 or 160 of FA 2013 (returns and further returns for annual tax on enveloped dwellings).

Modifications—NICA 2015 Sch 2 para 27 (in this section, references to a tax return include a return relating to relevant contributions that is required to be made by or under an enactment).

Cross-references—See FA 2014 Sch 35 (penalties for failure to comply with duties under this section)

Amendments[1] Sub-s (6)(*da*) inserted by FA 2016 s 104(6), (7) with effect from 15 September 2016.

Prospective amendments—In sub-s (6)(*c*), words ", or regulations under paragraph 10 of Schedule A1 to," to be inserted after words "section 12AA of" by F(No 2)A 2017 s 61(1), Sch 14 paras 43, 44 with effect from a day to be appointed.

Obtaining information and documents

254 Meaning of "monitored proposal" and "monitored arrangements"

(1) For the purposes of this Part a relevant proposal in relation to which a person ("P") is a promoter is a "monitored proposal" in relation to P if any of the following dates fell on or after the date on which a monitoring notice took effect—

(a) the date on which P first made a firm approach to another person in relation to the relevant proposal;

(b) the date on which P first made the relevant proposal available for implementation by any other person;

(c) the date on which P first became aware of any transaction forming part of the proposed arrangements being entered into by any person.

(2) For the purposes of this Part relevant arrangements in relation to which a person ("P") is a promoter are "monitored arrangements" in relation to P if—

(a) P was by virtue of section 235(2)(b) or (c) a promoter in relation to a relevant proposal which was implemented by the arrangements and any of the following fell on or after the date on which the monitoring notice took effect—

(i) the date on which P first made a firm approach to another person in relation to the relevant proposal;

(ii) the date on which P first made the relevant proposal available for implementation by any other person;

(iii) the date on which P first became aware of any transaction forming part of the proposed arrangements being entered into by any person,

(b) the date on which P first took part in designing, organising or managing the arrangements fell on or after the date on which a monitoring notice took effect, or

(c) the arrangements enable, or are likely to enable, the person who has entered into transactions forming them to obtain the tax advantage by reason of which they are relevant arrangements, at any time on or after the date on which a monitoring notice took effect.

255 Power to obtain information and documents

(1) An authorised officer, or an officer of Revenue and Customs with the approval of an authorised officer, may by notice in writing require any person ("P") to whom this section applies—

(a) to provide information, or

(b) to produce a document,

if the information or document is reasonably required by the officer for any of the purposes in subsection (3).

(2) This section applies to—

(a) any person who is a monitored promoter, and

(b) any person who is a relevant intermediary in relation to a monitored proposal of a monitored promoter,

and in either case that monitored promoter is referred to below as "the relevant monitored promoter".

(3) The purposes mentioned in subsection (1) are—

(a) considering the possible consequences of implementing a monitored proposal of the relevant monitored promoter for the tax position of persons implementing the proposal,

(b) checking the tax position of any person who the officer reasonably believes has implemented a monitored proposal of the relevant monitored promoter, or

(c) checking the tax position of any person who the officer reasonably believes has entered into transactions forming monitored arrangements of the relevant monitored promoter.

(4) A person is a "relevant intermediary" in relation to a monitored proposal if the person meets the conditions in section 236(a) to (c) (meaning of "intermediary") in relation to the proposal at any time after the person has been notified of a promoter reference number of a person who is a promoter in relation to the proposal.

(5) In this section "checking" includes carrying out an investigation or enquiry of any kind.

(6) In this section "tax position", in relation to a person, means the person's position as regards any tax, including the person's position as regards—

(a) past, present and future liability to pay any tax,

(b) penalties and other amounts that have been paid, or are or may be payable, by or to the person in connection with any tax,

(c) claims, elections, applications and notices that have been or may be made or given in connection with the person's liability to pay any tax,

(d) deductions or repayments of tax, or of sums representing tax, that the person is required to make—

(i) under PAYE regulations, or

(ii) by or under any other provision of the Taxes Acts, and

(e) the withholding by the person of another person's PAYE income (as defined in section 683 of ITEPA 2003).

(7) In this section the reference to the tax position of a person—

(a) includes the tax position of a company that has ceased to exist and an individual who has died, and

(b) is to the person's tax position at any time or in relation to any period.

(8) A notice under subsection (1) which is given for the purpose of checking the tax position of a person mentioned in subsection (3)(b) or (c) may not be given more than 4 years after the person's death.

(9) A notice under subsection (1) may specify or describe the information or documents to be provided or produced.

(10) Information or a document required as a result of a notice under subsection (1) must be provided or produced within—

(a) the period of 10 days beginning with the day on which the notice was given, or

(b) such longer period as the officer who gives the notice may direct.

Modifications—NICA 2015 Sch 2 para 28 (in this section, references to a person's tax position include the person's position as regards deductions or repayments of relevant contributions, or of sums representing relevant contributions, that the person is required to make by or under an enactment).

Definitions—"authorised officer" (for the purposes of Part 5), s 283(2).

Cross-references—See FA 2014 s 264 (power to apply to tribunal to require promoter to provide information or documents where reasonable grounds to suspect not all information or documents have been provided by promoter).

FA 2014 s 266 (right of appeal against notice imposing information etc requirements).

FA 2014 s 267 (form and manner of providing information).

FA 2014 s 268 (compliance with requirement to produce documents by producing copies).

FA 2014 ss 278, 279 (offence of concealing documents).

FA 2014 Sch 35 (penalties for failure to comply with duties under this section)

256 Tribunal approval for certain uses of power under section 255

(1) An officer of Revenue and Customs may not, without the approval of the tribunal, give a notice under section 255 requiring a person ("A") to provide information or produce a document which relates (in whole or in part) to a person who is neither A nor an undertaking in relation to which A is a parent undertaking.

(2) An officer of Revenue and Customs may apply to the tribunal for the approval required by subsection (1); and an application for approval may be made without notice.

(3) The tribunal may approve the giving of the notice only if—

(a) the application for approval is made by, or with the agreement of, an authorised officer,

(b) the tribunal is satisfied that, in the circumstances, the officer giving the notice is justified in doing so,

(c) the person to whom the notice is to be given has been informed that the information or documents referred to in the notice are required and given a reasonable opportunity to make representations to an officer of Revenue and Customs, and

(d) the tribunal has been given a summary of any representations made by that person.

(4) Where a notice is given under section 255 with the approval of the tribunal, it must state that it is given with that approval.

(5) Paragraphs (c) and (d) of subsection (3) do not apply to the extent that the tribunal is satisfied that taking the action specified in those paragraphs might prejudice the assessment or collection of tax.

(6) In subsection (1) "parent undertaking" and "undertaking" have the same meaning as in the Companies Acts (see section 1161 and 1162 of, and Schedule 7 to, the Companies Act 2006).

(7) A decision of the tribunal under this section is final (despite the provisions of sections 11 and 13 of the Tribunals, Courts and Enforcement Act 2007).

Definitions—"authorised officer" (for the purposes of Part 5), s 283(2).

Cross-references—See FA 2014 s 278 (offence of concealing documents).

257 Ongoing duty to provide information following HMRC notice

(1) An authorised officer, or an officer of Revenue and Customs with the approval of an authorised officer, may give a notice to a person ("P") in relation to whom a monitoring notice has effect.

(2) A person to whom a notice is given under subsection (1) must provide prescribed information and produce prescribed documents relating to—

(a) all the monitored proposals and all the monitored arrangements in relation to which the person is a promoter at the time of the notice, and

(b) all the monitored proposals and all the monitored arrangements in relation to which the person becomes a promoter after that time.

(3) The duty under subsection (2)(b) does not apply in relation to any proposals or arrangements in relation to which the person first becomes a promoter after the monitoring notice ceases to have effect.

(4) A notice under subsection (1) must specify the time within which information must be provided or a document produced and different times may be specified for different cases.

Definitions—"authorised officer" (for the purposes of Part 5), s 283(2).

Cross-references—See FA 2014 s 264 (power to apply to tribunal to require promoter to provide information or documents where reasonable grounds to suspect not all information or documents have been provided by promoter).
FA 2014 s 266 (right of appeal against notice imposing information etc requirements).
FA 2014 s 268 (compliance with requirement to produce documents by producing copies).
FA 2014 Sch 35 (penalties for failure to comply with duties under this section)

258 Duty of person dealing with non-resident monitored promoter

(1) This section applies where a monitored promoter who is resident outside the United Kingdom has failed to comply with a duty under section 255 or 257 to provide information about a monitored proposal or monitored arrangements.

(2) An authorised officer, or an officer of Revenue and Customs with the approval of an authorised officer, may give a notice to a relevant person which—

(a) specifies or describes the information which the monitored promoter has failed to provide, and

(b) requires the person to provide the information.

(3) A "relevant person" means—

(a) any person who is an intermediary in relation to the monitored proposal concerned, and

(b) any person ("A") to whom the monitored promoter has made a firm approach in relation to the monitored proposal concerned with a view to making the proposal available for implementation by a person other than A.

(4) If an authorised officer is not aware of any person to whom a notice could be given under subsection (2) the authorised officer, or an officer of Revenue and Customs with the approval of the authorised officer, may give a notice to any person who has implemented the proposal which—

(a) specifies or describes the information which the monitored promoter has failed to provide, and

(b) requires the person to provide the information.

(5) If the duty mentioned in subsection (1) relates to monitored arrangements an authorised officer, or an officer of Revenue and Customs with the approval of an authorised officer, may give a notice to any person who has entered into any transaction forming part of the monitored arrangements concerned which—

(a) specifies or describes the information which the monitored promoter has failed to provide, and

(b) requires the person to provide the information.

(6) A notice under this section may be given only if the officer giving the notice reasonably believes that the person to whom the notice is given is able to provide the information requested.

(7) Information required as a result of a notice under this section must be provided within—

(a) the period of 10 days beginning with the day on which the notice was given, or

(b) such longer period as the officer who gives the notice may direct.

Definitions—"authorised officer" (for the purposes of Part 5), s 283(2).

Cross-references—See FA 2014 s 264 (power to apply to tribunal to require promoter to provide information or documents where reasonable grounds to suspect not all information or documents have been provided by promoter).
FA 2014 s 266 (right of appeal against notice imposing information etc requirements).
FA 2014 s 272 (notice given under sub-s (4) or (5) to tax adviser).
FA 2014 Sch 35 (penalties for failure to comply with duties under this section)

259 Monitored promoters: duty to provide information about clients

(1) An authorised officer, or an officer of Revenue and Customs with the approval of an authorised officer, may give notice to a person in relation to whom a monitoring notice has effect ("the monitored promoter").

(2) A person to whom a notice is given under subsection (1) must, for each relevant period, give the officer who gave the notice the information set out in subsection (9) in respect of each person who was its client with reference to that relevant period (see subsections (5) to (8)).

(3) Each of the following is a "relevant period"—

(a) the calendar quarter in which the notice under subsection (1) was given but not including any time before the monitoring notice takes effect,

(b) the period (if any) beginning with the date the monitoring notice takes effect and ending immediately before the beginning of the period described in paragraph (a), and

(c) each calendar quarter after the period described in paragraph (a) but not including any time after the monitoring notice ceases to have effect.

(4) Information required as a result of a notice under subsection (1) must be given—

(a) within the period of 30 days beginning with the end of the relevant period concerned, or

(b) in the case of a relevant period within subsection (3)(b), within the period of 30 days beginning with the day on which the notice under subsection (1) was given if that period would expire at a later time than the period given by paragraph (a).

(5) A person ("C") is a client of the monitored promoter with reference to a relevant period if—

(a) the promoter did any of the things mentioned in subsection (6) in relation to C at any time during that period, or

(b) the person falls within subsection (7).

NIC

(6) Those things are that the monitored promoter—
(a) made a firm approach to C in relation to a relevant proposal with a view to the promoter making the proposal available for implementation by C or another person;
(b) made a relevant proposal available for implementation by C;
(c) took part in the organisation or management of relevant arrangements entered into by C.
(7) A person falls within this subsection if the person has entered into transactions forming part of relevant arrangements and those arrangements—
(a) enable the person to obtain a tax advantage either in that relevant period or a later relevant period, and
(b) are either relevant arrangements in relation to which the monitored promoter is or was a promoter, or implement a relevant proposal in relation to which the monitored promoter was a promoter.
(8) But a person is not a client of the monitored promoter with reference to a relevant period if—
(a) the person has previously been a client of the monitored promoter with reference to a different relevant period,
(b) the promoter complied with the duty in subsection (2) in respect of the person for that relevant period, and
(c) the information provided as a result of complying with that duty remains accurate.
(9) The information mentioned in subsection (2) is—
(a) the person's name and address, and
(b) such other information about the person as may be prescribed.
(10) Where the monitoring notice mentioned in subsection (1) is a replacement monitoring notice, subsection (5)(b) does not impose a duty on the monitored promoter concerned to provide information about a person who has entered into transactions forming part of relevant arrangements (as described in subsection (7)) if the monitored promoter reasonably believes that information about that person has, in relation to those arrangements, already been provided under the original monitoring notice.

Definitions—"authorised officer" (for the purposes of Part 5), s 283(2).

Cross-references—See FA 2014 s 264 (power to apply to tribunal to require promoter to provide information or documents where reasonable grounds to suspect not all information or documents have been provided by promoter).
FA 2014 s 266 (right of appeal against notice imposing information etc requirements).
FA 2014 Sch 35 (penalties for failure to comply with duties under this section)

260 Intermediaries: duty to provide information about clients

(1) An authorised officer, or an officer of Revenue and Customs with the approval of an authorised officer, may give notice to a person ("the intermediary") who is an intermediary in relation to a relevant proposal which is a monitored proposal of a person in relation to whom a monitoring notice has effect ("the monitored promoter").
(2) A person to whom a notice is given under subsection (1) must, for each relevant period, give the officer who gave the notice the information set out in subsection (7) in respect of each person who was its client with reference to that relevant period (see subsections (5) to (6)).
(3) Each of the following is a "relevant period"—
(a) the calendar quarter in which the notice under subsection (1) was given but not including any time before the intermediary was first notified under section 250, 251 or 252 of the promoter reference number of the monitored promoter,
(b) the period (if any) beginning with the date of the notification under section 250, 251 or 252 and ending immediately before the beginning of the period described in paragraph (a), and
(c) each calendar quarter after the period described in paragraph (a) but not including any time after the monitoring notice mentioned in subsection (1) ceases to have effect.
(4) Information required as a result of a notice under subsection (1) must be given—
(a) within the period of 30 days beginning with the end of the relevant period concerned, or
(b) in the case of a relevant period within subsection (3)(b), within the period of 30 days beginning with the day on which the notice under subsection (1) was given if that period would expire at a later time than the period given by paragraph (a).
(5) A person ("C") is a client of the intermediary with reference to a relevant period if during that period—
(a) the intermediary communicated information to C about a monitored proposal in the course of a business, and
(b) the communication was made with a view to C, or any other person, entering into transactions forming part of the proposed arrangements.
(6) But a person is not a client of the intermediary with reference to a relevant period if—
(a) the person has previously been a client of the intermediary with reference to a different relevant period,
(b) the intermediary complied with the duty in subsection (2) in respect of the person for that relevant period, and
(c) the information provided as a result of complying with that duty remains accurate.
(7) The information mentioned in subsection (2) is—

(a) the person's name and address, and
(b) such other information about the person as may be prescribed.

Definitions—"authorised officer" (for the purposes of Part 5), s 283(2).
Cross-references—See FA 2014 s 264 (power to apply to tribunal to require promoter to provide information or documents where reasonable grounds to suspect not all information or documents have been provided by promoter).
FA 2014 s 266 (right of appeal against notice imposing information etc requirements).
FA 2014 Sch 35 (penalties for failure to comply with duties under this section)

261 Enquiry following provision of client information

(1) This section applies where—
(a) a person ("the notifying person") has provided information under section 259 or 260 about a person who was a client of the notifying person with reference to a relevant period (within the meaning of the section concerned) in connection with a particular relevant proposal or particular relevant arrangements, and
(b) an authorised officer suspects that a person in respect of whom information has not been provided under section 259 or 260—
(i) has at any time been, or is likely to be, a party to transactions implementing the proposal, or
(ii) is a party to a transaction forming (in whole or in part) particular relevant arrangements.
(2) The authorised officer may by notice in writing require the notifying person to provide prescribed information in relation to any person whom the notifying person might reasonably be expected to know—
(a) has been, or is likely to be, a party to transactions implementing the proposal, or
(b) is a party to a transaction forming (in whole or in part) the relevant arrangements.
(3) But a notice under subsection (2) does not impose a requirement on the notifying person to provide information which the notifying person has already provided to an authorised officer under section 259 or 260.
(4) The notifying person must comply with a requirement under subsection (2) within—
(a) 10 days of the notice, or
(b) such longer period as the authorised officer may direct.

Definitions—"authorised officer" (for the purposes of Part 5), s 283(2).
Cross-references—See FA 2014 s 264 (power to apply to tribunal to require promoter to provide information or documents where reasonable grounds to suspect not all information or documents have been provided by promoter).
FA 2014 s 266 (right of appeal against notice imposing information etc requirements).
FA 2014 Sch 35 (penalties for failure to comply with duties under this section)

262 Information required for monitoring compliance with conduct notice

(1) This section applies where a conduct notice has effect in relation to a person.
(2) An authorised officer, or an officer of Revenue and Customs with the approval of an authorised officer, may (as often as is necessary for the purpose mentioned below) by notice in writing require the person—
(a) to provide information, or
(b) to produce a document,
if the information or document is reasonably required for the purpose of monitoring whether and to what extent the person is complying with the conditions in the conduct notice.

Definitions—"authorised officer" (for the purposes of Part 5), s 283(2).
Cross-references—See FA 2014 s 264 (power to apply to tribunal to require promoter to provide information or documents where reasonable grounds to suspect not all information or documents have been provided by promoter).
FA 2014 s 266 (right of appeal against notice imposing information etc requirements).
FA 2014 s 268 (compliance with requirement to produce documents by producing copies).
FA 2014 Sch 35 (penalties for failure to comply with duties under this section)

263 Duty to notify HMRC of address

If, on the last day of a calendar quarter, a monitoring notice has effect in relation to a person ("the monitored promoter") the monitored promoter must within 30 days of the end of the calendar quarter inform an authorised officer of its current address.

Definitions—"authorised officer" (for the purposes of Part 5), s 283(2).
Cross-references—See FA 2014 Sch 35 (penalties for failure to comply with duties under this section)

264 Failure to provide information: application to tribunal

(1) This section applies where—
(a) a person ("P") has provided information or produced a document in purported compliance with section 255, 257, 258, 259, 260, 261 or 262, but
(b) an authorised officer suspects that P has not provided all the information or produced all the documents required under the section concerned.
(2) The authorised officer, or an officer of Revenue and Customs with the approval of the authorised officer, may apply to the tribunal for an order requiring P to—
(a) provide specified information about persons who are its clients for the purposes of the section to which the application relates,

NIC

(b) provide specified information, or information of a specified description, about a monitored proposal or monitored arrangements,

(c) produce specified documents relating to a monitored proposal or monitored arrangements.

(3) The tribunal may make an order under subsection (2) in respect of information or documents only if satisfied that the officer has reasonable grounds for suspecting that the information or documents—

(a) are required under section 255, 257, 258, 259, 260, 261 or 262 (as the case may be), or

(b) will support or explain information required under the section concerned.

(4) A requirement by virtue of an order under subsection (2) is to be treated as part of P's duty under section 255, 257, 258, 259, 260, 261 or 262 (as the case may be).

(5) Information or a document required as a result of subsection (2) must be provided, or the document produced, within the period of 10 days beginning with the day on which the order under subsection (2) was made.

(6) An authorised officer may, by direction, extend the 10 day period mentioned in subsection (5).

Definitions—"authorised officer" (for the purposes of Part 5), s 283(2).
Cross-references—FA 2014 s 267 (form and manner of providing information).

265 Duty to provide information to monitored promoter

(1) This section applies where a person has been notified of a promoter reference number—

(a) under section 250 by reason of being a person falling within subsection (2)(b) of that section, or

(b) under section 251 or 252.

(2) The person notified ("C") must within 10 days notify the person whose promoter reference number it is of—

(a) C's national insurance number (if C has one), and

(b) C's unique tax reference number (if C has one).

(3) If C has neither a national insurance number nor a unique tax reference number, C must within 10 days inform the person whose promoter reference number it is of that fact.

(4) A unique tax reference number is an identification number allocated to a person by HMRC.

(5) Subsection (2) or (3) does not impose a duty on C to provide information which C has already provided to the person whose promoter reference number it is.

Cross-references—See FA 2014 Sch 35 (penalties for failure to comply with duties under this section)

Obtaining information and documents: appeals

266 Appeals against notices imposing information etc requirements

(1) This section applies where a person is given a notice under section 255, 257, 258, 259, 260, 261 or 262.

(2) The person to whom the notice is given may appeal against the notice or any requirement under the notice.

(3) Subsection (2) does not apply—

(a) to a requirement to provide any information or produce any document that forms part of the person's statutory records, or

(b) if the tribunal has approved the giving of the notice under section 256.

(4) For the purposes of this section, information or a document forms part of a person's statutory records if it is information or a document which the person is required to keep and preserve under or by virtue of—

(a) the Taxes Acts, or

(b) any other enactment relating to a tax.

(5) Information and documents cease to form part of a person's statutory records when the period for which they are required to be preserved by the enactments mentioned in subsection (4) has expired.

(6) Notice of appeal must be given—

(a) in writing to the officer who gave the notice, and

(b) within the period of 30 days beginning with the day on which the notice was given.

(7) The notice of appeal must state the grounds of the appeal.

(8) On an appeal that is notified to the tribunal, the tribunal may—

(a) confirm the notice or a requirement under the notice,

(b) vary the notice or such a requirement, or

(c) set aside the notice or such a requirement.

(9) Where the tribunal confirms or varies the notice or a requirement, the person to whom the notice was given must comply with the notice or requirement—

(a) within such period as is specified by the tribunal, or

(b) if the tribunal does not specify a period, within such period as is reasonably specified in writing by an officer of Revenue and Customs following the tribunal's decision.

(10) A decision of the tribunal on an appeal under this section is final (despite the provisions of sections 11 and 13 of the Tribunals, Courts and Enforcement Act 2007).

(11) Subject to this section, the provisions of Part 5 of TMA 1970 relating to appeals have effect in relation to an appeal under this section.

Obtaining information and documents: supplementary

267 Form and manner of providing information

(1) The Commissioners may specify the form and manner in which information required to be provided or documents required to be produced by sections 255 to 264 must be provided or produced if the provision is to be complied with.

(2) The Commissioners may specify that a document must be produced for inspection—

- (a) at a place agreed between the person and an officer of Revenue and Customs, or
- (b) at such place (which must not be a place used solely as a dwelling) as an officer of Revenue and Customs may reasonably specify.

(3) The production of a document in compliance with a notice under this Part is not to be regarded as breaking any lien claimed on the document.

268 Production of documents: compliance

(1) Where the effect of a notice under section 255, 257 or 262 is to require a person to produce a document, the person may comply with the requirement by producing a copy of the document, subject to any conditions or exceptions that may be prescribed.

(2) Subsection (1) does not apply where—

- (a) the effect of the notice is to require the person to produce the original document, or
- (b) an authorised officer, or an officer of Revenue and Customs with the approval of an authorised officer, subsequently makes a request in writing to the person for the original document.

(3) Where an officer requests a document under subsection (2)(b), the person to whom the request is made must produce the document—

- (a) within such period, and
- (b) at such time and by such means,

as is reasonably requested by the officer.

Definitions—"authorised officer" (for the purposes of Part 5), s 283(2).
Cross-references—See FA 2014 s 278 (offence of concealing documents: exception in cases where sub-s (1) above applies).

269 Exception for certain documents or information

(1) Nothing in this Part requires a person to provide or produce—

- (a) information that relates to the conduct of a pending appeal relating to tax or any part of a document containing such information,
- (b) journalistic material (as defined in section 13 of the Police and Criminal Evidence Act 1984) or information contained in such material, or
- (c) personal records (as defined in section 12 of the Police and Criminal Evidence Act 1984) or information contained in such records (but see subsection (2)).

(2) A notice under this Part may require a person—

- (a) to produce documents, or copies of documents, that are personal records, omitting any information whose inclusion (whether alone or with other information) makes the original documents personal records ("personal information"), and
- (b) to provide any information contained in such records that is not personal information.

270 Limitation on duty to produce documents

Nothing in this Part requires a person to produce a document—

- (a) which is not in the possession or power of that person, or
- (b) if the whole of the document originates more than 6 years before the requirement to produce it would, if it were not for this section, arise.

271 Legal professional privilege

(1) Nothing in this Part requires any person to disclose to HMRC any privileged information.

(2) "Privileged information" means information with respect to which a claim to legal professional privilege by the person who would (ignoring the effect of this section) be required to disclose it, could be maintained in legal proceedings.

(3) In the case of legal proceedings in Scotland, the reference in subsection (2) to legal professional privilege is to be read as a reference to confidentiality of communications.

272 Tax advisers

(1) This section applies where a notice is given under section 258(4) or (5) and the person to whom the notice is given is a tax adviser.

(2) The notice does not require a tax adviser—

- (a) to provide information about relevant communications, or
- (b) to produce documents which are the tax adviser's property and consist of relevant communications.

NIC

(3) Subsection (2) does not have effect in relation to—

(a) information explaining any information or document which the person to whom the notice is given has, as tax accountant, assisted any person in preparing for, or delivering to, HMRC, or

(b) a document which contains such information.

(4) But subsection (2) is not disapplied by subsection (3) if the information in question has already been provided, or a document containing the information has already been produced, to an officer of Revenue and Customs.

(5) In this section—

"relevant communications" means communications between the tax adviser and—

(a) a person in relation to whose tax affairs the tax adviser has been appointed, or

(b) any other tax adviser of such a person,

the purpose of which is the giving or obtaining of advice about any of those tax affairs, and

"tax adviser" means a person appointed to give advice about the tax affairs of another person (whether appointed directly by that person or by another tax adviser of that person).

273 Confidentiality

(1) No duty of confidentiality or other restriction on disclosure (however imposed) prevents the voluntary disclosure by a relevant client or a relevant intermediary to HMRC of information or documents about—

(a) a monitored promoter, or

(b) relevant proposals or relevant arrangements in relation to which a monitored promoter is a promoter.

(2) "Relevant client" means a person in relation to whom the monitored promoter mentioned in subsection (1)(a) or (b)—

(a) has made a firm approach in relation to a relevant proposal with a view to making the proposal available for implementation by that person or another person;

(b) has made a relevant proposal available for implementation by that person;

(c) took part in the organisation or management of relevant arrangements entered into by that person.

(3) "Relevant intermediary" means a person who is an intermediary in relation to a relevant proposal in relation to which the monitored promoter mentioned in subsection (1)(a) or (b) is a promoter.

(4) The relevant proposal or relevant arrangements mentioned in subsection (2) or (3) need not be the relevant proposals or relevant arrangements to which the disclosure relates.

Penalties

274 Penalties

Schedule 35 contains provision about penalties for failure to comply with provisions of this Part.

275 Failure to comply with Part 7 of the Finance Act 2004

In section 98C of TMA 1970 (notification under Part 7 of FA 2004), after subsection (2E) insert—

"(2EA) Where a person fails to comply with—

(a) section 309 of that Act and the promoter for the purposes of that section is a monitored promoter for the purposes of Part 5 of the Finance Act 2014, or

(b) section 310 of that Act and the arrangements for the purposes of that section are arrangements of such a monitored promoter,

then for the purposes of section 118(2) of this Act legal advice which the person took into account is to be disregarded in determining whether the person had a reasonable excuse, if the advice was given or procured by that monitored promoter.

(2EB) In determining for the purpose of section 118(2) of this Act whether or not a person who is a monitored promoter within the meaning of Part 5 of the Finance Act 2014 had a reasonable excuse for a failure to do anything required to be done under a provision mentioned in subsection (2), reliance on legal advice is to be taken automatically not to constitute a reasonable excuse if either—

(a) the advice was not based on a full and accurate description of the facts, or

(b) the conclusions in the advice that the person relied on were unreasonable."

276 Limitation of defence of reasonable care

(1) Subsection (2) applies where—

(a) *a person gives HMRC a document of a kind listed in the Table in paragraph 1 of Schedule 24 to FA 2007 (penalties for providing inaccurate documents to HMRC), and*

(b) *the document contains an inaccuracy.*

(2) In determining whether or not the inaccuracy was careless for the purposes of paragraph 3(1)(a) of Schedule 24 to FA 2007, reliance by the person on legal advice relating to relevant arrangements in relation to which a monitored promoter is a promoter is to be disregarded if the advice was given or procured by a person who was a monitored promoter in relation to the arrangements.

Modifications—NICA 2015 Sch 2 para 29 (in this section, the reference in sub-s (1) to a document of a kind listed in the Table FA 2007 Sch 24 para 1 includes a document, relating to relevant contributions, in relation to which Sch 24 applies (and, accordingly, the reference to Sch 24 in sub-s (2) includes Sch 24 as it so applies)).

Amendments—This section repealed by F(No 2)A 2017 s 64(1), (4) with effect in relation to any document of a kind listed in the Table in FA 2007 Sch 24 para 1 which is given to HMRC on or after 16 November 2017 and which relates to a tax period beginning on or after 6 April 2017 and ending on or after 16 November 2017. "Tax period", and the reference to giving a document to HMRC have the same meaning as in FA 2007 Sch 24 para 28 (F(No 2)A 2017 s 64(6)).

277 Extended time limit for assessment

(1) In section 36 of TMA 1970 (loss of tax brought about carelessly or deliberately), in subsection (1A)—

(a) omit the "or" following paragraph (b), and

(b) at the end of paragraph (c) insert " or

(d) attributable to arrangements which were expected to give rise to a tax advantage in respect of which the person was under an obligation to notify the Commissioners for Her Majesty's Revenue and Customs under section 253 of the Finance Act 2014 (duty to notify Commissioners of promoter reference number) but failed to do so,".

(2) In paragraph 12B of Schedule 2 to OTA 1975 (extended time limits for assessment of petroleum revenue tax)—

(a) in sub-paragraph (1), after "sub-paragraph (2)" insert "and (2A)",

(b) after sub-paragraph (2) insert—

"(2A) In a case involving a relevant situation brought about by arrangements which were expected to give rise to a tax advantage in respect of which a participator (or a person acting on behalf of a participator) was under an obligation to notify the Board under section 253 of the Finance Act 2014 (duty to notify Commissioners of promoter reference number) but failed to do so, an assessment (or an amendment of an assessment) on the participator may be made at any time not more than 20 years after the end of the relevant chargeable period.",

(c) in sub-paragraph (5), for "or (2)" substitute ", (2) or (2A)", and

(d) in sub-paragraph (6), for "or (2)" substitute ", (2) or (2A)".

(3) In section 240 of IHTA 1984 (underpayments)—

(a) in subsection (3) for "and (5)" substitute "to (5A)",

(b) in subsection (5), for "those dates" substitute "the dates in subsection (2)(a) and (b)",

(c) after subsection (5) insert—

"(5A) Proceedings in a case involving a loss of tax attributable to arrangements which were expected to give rise to a tax advantage in respect of which a person liable for the tax was under an obligation to make a report under section 253 of the Finance Act 2014 (duty to notify Commissioners of promoter reference number) but failed to do so, may be brought at any time not more than 20 years after the later of the dates in subsection (2)(a) and (b).", and

(d) in subsection (8), for ", (5) and (6)" substitute "to (6)".

(4) In paragraph 46 of Schedule 18 to FA 1998 (general time limits for assessments to corporation tax), in sub-paragraph (2A)—

(a) omit the "or" following paragraph (b), and

(b) at the end of paragraph (c) insert " or

(d) attributable to arrangements which were expected to give rise to a tax advantage in respect of which the company was under an obligation to notify the Commissioners for Her Majesty's Revenue and Customs under section 253 of the Finance Act 2014 (duty to notify Commissioners of promoter reference number) but failed to do so,".

(5) In paragraph 31 of Schedule 10 to FA 2003 (time limit for assessment of stamp duty land tax), in sub-paragraph (2A)—

(a) omit the "or" following paragraph (b), and

(b) at the end of paragraph (c) insert " or

(d) attributable to arrangements which were expected to give rise to a tax advantage in respect of which the person was under an obligation to notify the Commissioners for Her Majesty's Revenue and Customs under section 253 of the Finance Act 2014 (duty to notify Commissioners of promoter reference number) but failed to do so,".

(6) In paragraph 25 of Schedule 33 to FA 2013 (time limit for assessment: annual tax on enveloped dwellings), in sub-paragraph (4)—

(a) omit the "or" following paragraph (b), and

(b) at the end of paragraph (c) insert ", or

(d) attributable to arrangements which were expected to give rise to a tax advantage in respect of which the person was under an obligation to notify the Commissioners for Her Majesty's Revenue and Customs under section 253 of FA 2014 (duty to notify Commissioners of promoter reference number) but failed to do so."

Offences

278 Offence of concealing etc documents

(1) A person is guilty of an offence if—

(a) the person is required to produce a document by a notice given under section 255,

(b) the tribunal approved the giving of the notice under section 256, and

(c) the person conceals, destroys or otherwise disposes of, or arranges for the concealment, destruction or disposal of, that document.

(2) Subsection (1) does not apply if the person acts after the document has been produced to an officer of Revenue and Customs in accordance with section 255, unless the officer has notified the person in writing that the document must continue to be available for inspection (and has not withdrawn the notification).

(3) Subsection (1) does not apply, in a case to which section 268(1) applies, if the person acts after the end of the expiry of 6 months beginning with the day on which a copy of the document was produced in accordance with that section unless, before the expiry of that period, an officer of Revenue and Customs makes a request for the original document under section 268(2)(b).

Cross-references—See FA 2014 s 280 (penalties for offences under ss 278 or 279).

279 Offence of concealing etc documents following informal notification

(1) A person is guilty of an offence if the person conceals, destroys or otherwise disposes of, or arranges for the concealment, destruction or disposal of, a document after an officer of Revenue and Customs has informed the person in writing that—

(a) the document is, or is likely, to be the subject of a notice under section 255, and

(b) the officer of Revenue and Customs intends to seek the approval of the tribunal to the giving of the notice.

(2) A person is not guilty of an offence under this section if the person acts after—

(a) at least 6 months has expired since the person was, or was last, informed as described in subsection (1), or

(b) a notice has been given to the person under section 255, requiring the document to be produced.

Cross-references—See FA 2014 s 280 (penalties for offences under ss 278 or 279).

280 Penalties for offences

(1) A person who is guilty of an offence under section 278 or 279 is liable—

(a) on summary conviction, to—

(i) in England and Wales, a fine, or

(ii) in Scotland or Northern Ireland, a fine not exceeding the statutory maximum, or

(b) on conviction on indictment, to imprisonment for a term not exceeding 2 years or to a fine or both.

(2) In relation to an offence committed before section 85(1) of the Legal Aid, Sentencing and Punishment of Offenders Act 2012 comes into force, subsection (1)(a)(i) has effect as if the reference to "a fine" were a reference to "a fine not exceeding the statutory maximum".

Supplemental

281 Partnerships

Schedule 36 contains provision about the application of this Part to partnerships.

[281A VAT [and other indirect taxes]

(1) In the provisions mentioned in subsection (2)—

(*a*) "tax" includes value added tax [and other indirect taxes]², and

(*b*) "tax advantage" has the meaning given by section 234(3) and also includes a tax advantage as defined [for VAT in paragraph 6, and for other indirect taxes in paragraph 7, of Schedule 17 to FA 2017 (disclosure of tax avoidance schemes: VAT and other indirect taxes)."]²

(2) Those provisions are—

(*a*) section 237D;

(*b*) section 241B;

(*c*) Schedule 34A.

(3) Other references in this Part to "tax" are to be read as including value added tax [or other indirect taxes]² so far as that is necessary for the purposes of sections 237A to 237D, 241A and 241B and Schedule 34A; but "tax" does not include value added tax [or other indirect taxes]² in section 237A(10) or 237B(3).

[(4) In this section "indirect tax" has the same meaning as in Schedule 17 to FA 2017.]²]¹

Amendments—[1] Section 281A inserted by FA 2016 s 160(7) with effect from 15 September 2016.
[2] The following amendments made by F(No 2)A 2017 s 66, Sch 17 paras 52, 53 with effect from 1 January 2018—
- in heading, sub-ss (1)(*a*), (3) (in both places), words inserted;
- in sub-s (1)(*b*), words substituted for words "in paragraph 1 of Schedule 11A to VATA 1994."; and
- sub-s (4) inserted.

282 Regulations under this Part

(1) Regulations under this Part are to be made by statutory instrument.

(2) Apart from an instrument to which subsection (3) applies, a statutory instrument containing regulations made under this Part is subject to annulment in pursuance of a resolution of the House of Commons.

(3) A statutory instrument containing (whether alone or with other provision) regulations made under—

(a) section 238(7),
(b) paragraph 14 of Schedule 34,
[(*ba*) paragraph 31 of Schedule 34A,][1]
(c) paragraph 5(1) of Schedule 35, or
(d) paragraph 21 of Schedule 36,

may not be made unless a draft of the instrument has been laid before and approved by a resolution of the House of Commons.

(4) Regulations under this Part—

(a) may make different provision for different purposes;
(b) may include transitional provision and savings.

Amendments—[1] Sub-s (3)(*ba*) inserted by FA 2016 s 160(8) with effect from 15 September 2016.

283 Interpretation of this Part

(1) In this Part—

"arrangements" has the meaning given by section 234(4);
"the Commissioners" means the Commissioners for Her Majesty's Revenue and Customs;
"calendar quarter" means a period of 3 months beginning with 1 January, 1 April, 1 July or 1 October;
"conduct notice" means a notice of the description in section 238 that is given under—

(a) section 237(7) [or (7A)][1],
[(*aa*) section 237A(8),
(*ab*) section 237B(1),][2]
(b) section 245(7), or
(c) paragraph 8(2) or (3) or 10(3)(a) or (4)(a) of Schedule 36;

["contract settlement" means an agreement in connection with a person's liability to make a payment to the Commissioners under or by virtue of an enactment;][2]
["defeat", in relation to arrangements, has the meaning given by paragraph 10 of Schedule 34A;][2]
["defeat notice" has the meaning given by section 241A(7);][2]
["double defeat notice" has the meaning given by section 241A(7);][2]
["final", in relation to a judicial ruling, is to be interpreted in accordance with section 237D(6);][1]

"firm approach" has the meaning given by section 235(4);
"HMRC" means Her Majesty's Revenue and Customs;

["judicial ruling" means a ruling of a court or tribunal on one or more issues;][2]
["look-forward period", in relation to a defeat notice, has the meaning given by section 241A(10);][2]

"monitored promoter" has the meaning given by section 244(5);
"monitored proposal" and "monitored arrangements" have the meaning given by section 254;
"monitoring notice" means a notice given under section 244(1) or paragraph 9(2) or (3) or 10(3)(b) or (4)(b) of Schedule 36;
"the original monitoring notice" has the meaning given by paragraph 11(2) of Schedule 36;
"prescribed" means prescribed, or of a description prescribed, in regulations made by the Commissioners;
"promoter reference number" has the meaning given by section 250(5);

["provisional", in relation to a conduct notice given under section 237A(8), is to be interpreted in accordance with section 237C;][2]
["related", in relation to arrangements, is to be interpreted in accordance with paragraph 2 of Schedule 34A;][2]

"relevant arrangements" has the meaning given by section 234(2);

["relevant defeat", in relation to a person, is to be interpreted in accordance with Schedule 34A;][2]

"relevant proposal" has the meaning given by section 234(1);

["relies on a Case 3 relevant defeat" is to be interpreted in accordance section 237B(5);][2]

"replacement conduct notice" has the meaning given by paragraph 11(1) of Schedule 36;

"replacement monitoring notice" has the meaning given by paragraph 11(1) of Schedule 36;

["single defeat notice" has the meaning given by section 241A(7).][2]

"tax" [(except in provisions to which section 281A applies)][2] means—

(a) income tax,

(b) capital gains tax,

(c) corporation tax,

(d) petroleum revenue tax,

[(da) apprenticeship levy,][3]

(e) inheritance tax,

(f) stamp duty land tax,

(g) stamp duty reserve tax, or

(h) annual tax on enveloped dwellings;

"tax advantage" has the meaning given by section 234(3) [(but see also section 281A)][2];

"Taxes Acts" has the same meaning as in TMA 1970 (see section 118(1) of that Act);

"the tribunal" means the First-tier Tribunal or, where determined by or under Tribunal Procedure Rules, the Upper Tribunal.

(2) A reference in a provision of this Part to an authorised officer is to an officer of Revenue and Customs who is, or is a member of a class of officers who are, authorised by the Commissioners for the purposes of that provision.

(3) A reference in a provision of this Part to meeting a threshold condition is to meeting one of the conditions described in paragraphs 2 to 12 of Schedule 34.

Modifications—NICA 2015 Sch 2 para 30 (definition of "tax" in sub-s (1) has effect as if it included relevant contributions).

Regulations—Promoters of Tax Avoidance Schemes (Prescribed Circumstances under Section 235) Regulations, SI 2015/130.

Definitions—"threshold condition", Sch 34 paras 2–12.

Amendments—[1] In definition of "conduct notice", words inserted by FA 2015 s 119, Sch 19 paras 1, 3 with effect for the purposes of determining whether a person meets a threshold condition in a period of three years ending on or after 26 March 2015.

[2] In sub-s (1), in definition of "conduct notice", sub-paras (*aa*), (*ab*) inserted, in definitions of "tax" and "tax advantage", words inserted, and definitions inserted, by FA 2016 s 160(9) with effect from 15 September 2016.

[3] In sub-s (1), in definition of "tax", para (*da* inserted by FA 2016 s 104(6), (8) with effect from 15 September 2016.

SCHEDULES

SCHEDULE 30

SECTION 208 PENALTY: VALUE OF THE DENIED ADVANTAGE

Section 209

Commentary—*Simon's Taxes* **A7.247**.

Introduction

1 This Schedule applies for the purposes of calculating penalties under section 209.

Value of denied advantage: normal rule

2 (1) The value of the denied advantage is the additional amount due or payable in respect of tax as a result of counteracting the denied advantage.

(2) The reference in sub-paragraph (1) to the additional amount due or payable includes a reference to—

(a) an amount payable to HMRC having erroneously been paid by way of repayment of tax, and

(b) an amount which would be repayable by HMRC if the denied advantage were not counteracted.

(3) The following are ignored in calculating the value of the denied advantage—

(a) group relief, and

(b) any relief under section 458 of CTA 2010 (relief in respect of repayment etc of loan) which is deferred under subsection (5) of that section.

(4) This paragraph is subject to paragraphs 3 and 4.

Value of denied advantage: losses

3 (1) To the extent that the denied advantage has the result that a loss is wrongly recorded for purposes of direct tax and the loss has been wholly used to reduce the amount due or payable in respect of tax, the value of the denied advantage is determined in accordance with paragraph 2.

(2) To the extent that the denied advantage has the result that a loss is wrongly recorded for purposes of direct tax and the loss has not been wholly used to reduce the amount due or payable in respect of tax, the value of the denied advantage is—

(a) the value under paragraph 2 of so much of the denied advantage as results from the part (if any) of the loss which is used to reduce the amount due or payable in respect of tax, plus

(b) 10% of the part of the loss not so used.

(3) Sub-paragraphs (1) and (2) apply both—

(a) to a case where no loss would have been recorded but for the denied advantage, and

(b) to a case where a loss of a different amount would have been recorded (but in that case sub-paragraphs (1) and (2) apply only to the difference between the amount recorded and the true amount).

(4) To the extent that a denied advantage creates or increases an aggregate loss recorded for a group of companies—

(a) the value of the denied advantage is calculated in accordance with this paragraph, and

(b) in applying paragraph 2 in accordance with sub-paragraphs (1) and (2), group relief may be taken into account (despite paragraph 2(3)).

(5) To the extent that the denied advantage results in a loss, the value of it is nil where, because of the nature of the loss or P's circumstances, there is no reasonable prospect of the loss being used to support a claim to reduce a tax liability (of any person).

Value of denied advantage: deferred tax

4 (1) To the extent that the denied advantage is a deferral of tax, the value of that advantage is—

(a) 25% of the amount of the deferred tax for each year of the deferral, or

(b) a percentage of the amount of the deferred tax, for each separate period of deferral of less than a year, equating to 25% per year,

or, if less, 100% of the amount of the deferred tax.

(2) This paragraph does not apply to a case to the extent that paragraph 3 applies.

SCHEDULE 31

FOLLOWER NOTICES AND PARTNERSHIPS

Section 215

Commentary—*Simon's Taxes* **A7.247**.

Introduction

1 This Schedule makes special provision about the application of Chapter 2 to partners and partnerships.

Interpretation

2 (1) This paragraph applies for the purposes of this Schedule.

(2) "Partnership follower notice" means a follower notice given by reason of—

(a) a tax enquiry being in progress into a partnership return, or

(b) an appeal having been made in relation to an amendment of a partnership return or against a conclusion stated by a closure notice in relation to a tax enquiry into a partnership return.

(3) "Partnership return" means a return in pursuance of a notice under section 12AA(2) or (3) of TMA 1970.

(4) "The representative partner", in relation to a partnership return, means the person who was required by a notice served under or for the purposes of section 12AA(2) or (3) of TMA 1970 to deliver the return.

(5) "Relevant partner", in relation to a partnership return, means a person who was a partner in the partnership to which the return relates at any time during the period in respect of which the return was required.

(6) References to a "successor", in relation to the representative partner are to be construed in accordance with section 12AA(11) of TMA 1970.

Prospective amendments—The following amendments to be made by F(No 2)A 2017 s 61(1), Sch 14 paras 43, 45(1), (2) with effect from a day to be appointed—

– in sub-para (3), words from "in pursuance" to the end to be numbered as para (*a*), in that para, words "(a "section 12AA partnership return"), or" to be inserted at the end, and sub-para (3)(*b*) to be inserted;

– in sub-para (4), words "section 12AA" to be inserted after words "in relation to a"; and

– sub-para (4A) to be inserted.

Sub-para (3)(*b*) as inserted to read as follows—

"(*b*) required by regulations under paragraph 10 of Schedule A1 to TMA 1970 (a "Schedule A1 partnership return").".

Sub-para (4A) as inserted to read as follows—

"(4A) "The nominated partner", in relation to a Schedule A1 partnership return, has the meaning given by paragraph 5 of Schedule A1 to TMA 1970.".

Giving of follower notices in relation to partnership returns

3 (1) If the representative partner in relation to a partnership return is no longer available, then, for the purposes of section 204 the return, or an appeal in respect of the return, is to be regarded as made by the person who is for the time being the successor of that partner (if that would not otherwise be the case).

(2) Where, at any time after a partnership follower notice is given to P, P is no longer available, any reference in this Chapter (other than section 204 and this sub-paragraph) to P is to be read as a reference to the person who is, for the time being, the successor of the representative partner.

(3) For the purposes of Condition B in section 204 a partnership return, or appeal in respect of a partnership return, is made on the basis that a particular tax advantage results from particular tax arrangements if—

(a) it is made on the basis that an increase or reduction in one or more of the amounts mentioned in section 12AB(1) of TMA 1970 (amounts in the partnership statement in a partnership return) results from those tax arrangements, and

(b) that increase or reduction results in that tax advantage for one or more of the relevant partners.

(4) For the purposes of Condition D in section 204—

(a) a notice given to a person in the person's capacity as the representative partner of a partnership, or a successor of that partner, and a notice given to that person otherwise than in that capacity are not to be treated as given to the same person, and

(b) all notices given to the representative partner and successors of that partner, in that capacity, are to be treated as given to the same person.

(5) In this paragraph references to a person being "no longer available" have the same meaning as in section 12AA(11) of TMA 1970.

Prospective amendments—The following amendments to be made by F(No 2)A 2017 s 61(1), Sch 14 paras 43, 45(1), (3) with effect from a day to be appointed—

- in sub-para (1), words "section 12AA" to be inserted after words "in relation to a";
- sub-para (1A) to be inserted.
- in sub-para (2), words ", or the nominated partner (as the case may be)." to be inserted at the end;
- in sub-para (4)(*a*), words "or as the nominated partner of a partnership," to be inserted after words "or a successor of that partner,"; and
- in sub-para (4)(*b*), words "or to a nominated partner" to be inserted after words "successors of that partner".

Sub-para (1A) as inserted to read as follows—

"(1A) For the purposes of section 204 a Schedule A1 partnership return, or an appeal in respect of the return, is to be regarded as made by the person who is for the time being the nominated partner (if that would not otherwise be the case).".

Penalty if corrective action not taken in response to partnership follower notice

4 (1) Section 208 applies, in relation to a partnership follower notice, in accordance with this paragraph.

(2) Subsection (2) applies as if the reference to P were to each relevant partner.

(3) References to the denied advantage are to be read as references to the increase or reduction in an amount in the partnership statement mentioned in paragraph 3(3) which is denied by the application of the principles laid down or the reasoning given in the judicial ruling identified in the partnership follower notice under section 206(a) or, if only part of any increase or reduction is so denied, that part.

(4) In subsection (6)(b) the words from "and (where different)" to the end are to be ignored, and accordingly subsection (7) does not apply.

Calculation of penalty etc

5 (1) This paragraph applies in relation to a partnership follower notice.

(2) Section 209 applies subject to the following modifications—

(a) the total amount of the penalties under section 208(2) for which the relevant partners are liable is 20% of the value of the denied advantage,

(b) the amount of the penalty for which each relevant partner is liable is that partner's appropriate share of that total amount, and

(c) the value of the denied advantage for the purposes of calculating the total amount of the penalties is—

(i) in the case of a notice given under section 204(2)(a), the net amount of the amendments required to be made to the partnership return to counteract the denied advantage, and

(ii) in the case of a notice given under section 204(2)(b), the net amount of the amendments that have been made to the partnership return to counteract the denied advantage,

(and, accordingly, Schedule 30 does not apply).

(3) For the purposes of sub-paragraph (2), a relevant partner's appropriate share is—

(a) the same share as the share in which any profits or loss for the period to which the return relates would be apportioned to that partner in accordance with the firm's profit-sharing arrangements, or

(b) if HMRC do not have sufficient information from P to establish that share, such share as is determined for the purposes of this paragraph by an officer of HMRC.

(4) Where—

(a) the relevant partners are liable to pay a penalty under section 208(2) (as modified by this paragraph),

(b) the penalties have not yet been assessed, and

(c) P has co-operated with HMRC,

section 210(1) does not apply, but HMRC may reduce the total amount of the penalties determined in accordance with sub-paragraph (2)(a) to reflect the quality of that co-operation.

Section 210(2) and (3) apply for the purposes of this sub-paragraph.

(5) Nothing in sub-paragraph (4) permits HMRC to reduce the total amount of the penalties to less than 4% of the value of the denied advantage (as determined in accordance with sub-paragraph (2)(c)).

(6) For the purposes of section 212, a penalty imposed on a relevant partner by virtue of paragraph 4(2) is to be treated as if it were determined by reference to such additional amount of tax as is due and payable by the relevant partner as a result of the counteraction of the denied advantage.

(7) The right of appeal under section 214 extends to—

(a) a decision that penalties are payable by the relevant partners by virtue of this paragraph, and

(b) a decision as to the total amount of those penalties payable by those partners,

but not to a decision as to the appropriate share of, or the amount of a penalty payable by, a relevant partner.

(8) Section 214(3) applies to an appeal by virtue of sub-paragraph (7)(a) as it applies to an appeal under section 214(1).

(9) Section 214(8) applies to an appeal by virtue of sub-paragraph (7)(a), and section 214(9) to an appeal by virtue of sub-paragraph (7)(b).

(10) An appeal by virtue of sub-paragraph (7) may be brought only by the representative partner or, if that partner is no longer available, the person who is for the time being the successor of that partner.

(11) The Treasury may by order made by statutory instrument vary the rates for the time being specified in sub-paragraphs (2)(a) and (5).

(12) Any statutory instrument containing an order under sub-paragraph (11) is subject to annulment in pursuance of a resolution of the House of Commons.

Prospective amendments—In sub-para (10), words from "the representative partner" to the end to be numbered as para (*a*), in that para, words "(in relation to a section 12AA partnership return), or" to be inserted at the end, and sub-para (10)(*b*) to be inserted, by F(No 2)A 2017 s 61(1), Sch 14 paras 43, 45(1), (4) with effect from a day to be appointed. Sub-para (10)(*b*) as inserted to read as follows—

"(*b*) the nominated partner (in relation to a Schedule A1 partnership return).".

SCHEDULE 32

ACCELERATED PAYMENTS AND PARTNERSHIPS

Section 228

Commentary—*Simon's Taxes* **A4.233**.

Simon's Tax Cases—*R (on the appn of Sword Services Ltd and ors) v R&C Comrs* [2016] EWHC 1473 (Admin), [2017] STC 596.

Interpretation

1 (1) This paragraph applies for the purposes of this Schedule.

(2) "Partnership return" means a return in pursuance of a notice under section 12AA(2) or (3) of TMA 1970.

(3) "The representative partner", in relation to a partnership return, means the person who was required by a notice served under or for the purposes of section 12AA(2) or (3) of TMA 1970 to deliver the return.

(4) "Relevant partner", in relation to a partnership return, means a person who was a partner in the partnership to which the return relates at any time during the period in respect of which the return was required.

NIC

(5) References to a "successor", in relation to the representative partner, are to be construed in accordance with section 12AA(11) of TMA 1970.

Prospective amendments—The following amendments to be made by F(No 2)A 2017 s 61(1), Sch 14 paras 43, 46(1), (2) with effect from a day to be appointed—

- in sub-para (2), words from "in pursuance" to the end to be numbered as para (*a*), in that para, words "(a "section 12AA partnership return"), or" to be inserted at the end, and sub-para (2)(*b*) to be inserted;
- in sub-para (3), words "section 12AA" to be inserted after words "in relation to a"; and
- sub-para (3A) to be inserted.

Sub-para (2)(*b*) as inserted to read as follows—

"(*b*) required by regulations under paragraph 10 of Schedule A1 to TMA 1970 (a "Schedule A1 partnership return")".

Sub-para (4A) as inserted to read as follows—

"(4A) "The nominated partner", in relation to a Schedule A1 partnership return, has the meaning given by paragraph 5 of Schedule A1 to TMA 1970.".

Restriction on circumstances when accelerated payment notices can be given

2 (1) This paragraph applies where—

(a) a tax enquiry is in progress in relation to a partnership return, or

(b) an appeal has been made in relation to an amendment of such a return or against a conclusion stated by a closure notice in relation to a tax enquiry into such a return.

(2) No accelerated payment notice may be given to the representative partner of the partnership, or a successor of that partner, by reason of that enquiry or appeal.

(3) But this Schedule makes provision for partner payment notices and accelerated partner payments in such cases.

Prospective amendments—In sub-para (2), words "(in relation to a section 12AA partnership return), or to the nominated partner of the partnership (in relation to a Schedule A1 partnership return)" to be inserted after words "a successor of that partner" by F(No 2)A 2017 s 61(1), Sch 14 paras 43, 46(1), (3) with effect from a day to be appointed.

Circumstances in which partner payment notices may be given

3 (1) Where a partnership return has been made in respect of a partnership, HMRC may give a notice (a "partner payment notice") to each relevant partner of the partnership if Conditions A to C are met.

(2) Condition A is that—

(a) a tax enquiry is in progress in relation to the partnership return, or

(b) an appeal has been made in relation to an amendment of the return or against a conclusion stated by a closure notice in relation to a tax enquiry into the return.

(3) Condition B is that the return or, as the case may be, appeal is made on the basis that a particular tax advantage ("the asserted advantage") results from particular arrangements ("the chosen arrangements").

(4) Paragraph 3(3) of Schedule 31 applies for the purposes of sub-paragraph (3) as it applies for the purposes of Condition B in section 204(3).

(5) Condition C is that one or more of the following requirements are met—

(a) HMRC has given (or, at the same time as giving the partner payment notice, gives) the representative partner, or a successor of that partner, a follower notice under Chapter 2—

(i) in relation to the same return or, as the case may be, appeal, and

(ii) by reason of the same tax advantage and the chosen arrangements;

(b) the chosen arrangements are DOTAS arrangements (within the meaning of section 219(5) and (6));

(c) the relevant partner in question has been given a GAAR counteraction notice in respect of any tax advantage resulting from the asserted advantage or part of it and the chosen arrangements (or is given such a notice at the same time as the partner payment notice) in a case where the stated opinion of at least two of the members of the sub-panel of the GAAR Advisory Panel which considered the matter under paragraph 10 of Schedule 43 to FA 2013 was as set out in paragraph 11(3)(b) of that Schedule (entering into tax arrangements not reasonable course of action etc).

[(d) the relevant partner in question has been given a notice under paragraph 8(2) or 9(2) of Schedule 43A to FA 2013 (notice of final decision after considering Panel's opinion about referred or counteracted arrangements) in respect of any tax advantage resulting from the asserted advantage or part of it and the chosen arrangements (or is given such a notice at the same time as the partner payment notice) in a case where the stated opinion of at least two of the members of the sub-panel of the GAAR Advisory Panel about the other arrangements (see sub-paragraph (7)) was as set out in paragraph 11(3)(*b*) of Schedule 43 to FA 2013;

(e) the relevant partner in question has been given a notice under paragraph 8(2) of Schedule 43B to FA 2013 (GAAR: generic referral of arrangements) in respect of any tax advantage resulting from the asserted advantage or part of it and the chosen arrangements (or is given such a notice at the same time as the partner payment notice) in a case where the stated opinion of at least two of the members of the sub-panel of the GAAR Advisory Panel which considered the generic referral in respect of those arrangements was as set out in paragraph 6(4)(*b*) of that Schedule.][1]

(6) "GAAR counteraction notice" has the meaning given by section 219(7).

[(7) "Other arrangements" means—

(a) in relation to a notice under paragraph 8(2) of Schedule 43A to FA 2013, the referred arrangements (as defined in that paragraph);

(b) in relation to a notice under paragraph 9(2) of that Schedule, the counteracted arrangements (as defined in paragraph 2 of that Schedule).][1]

Amendments—[1] Sub-paras (5)(*d*), (*e*), (7) inserted by FA 2016 s 157(26)–(28) with effect in relation to tax arrangements (within the meaning of FA 2013 Pt 5) entered into at any time (whether before on or after 15 September 2016.

Prospective amendments—In sub-para (5)(*a*), words "(in relation to a section 12AA partnership return), or to the nominated partner (in relation to a Schedule A1 partnership return)" to be inserted after words "or a successor of that partner" by F(No 2)A 2017 s 61(1), Sch 14 paras 43, 46(1), (4) with effect from a day to be appointed.

Content of partner payment notices

4 (1) The partner payment notice given to a relevant partner must—

(a) specify the paragraph or paragraphs of paragraph 3(5) by virtue of which the notice is given,

(b) specify the payment [(if any)][1] required to be made under paragraph 6, . . . [1]

(c) explain the effect of paragraphs 5 and 6, and of the amendments made by sections 224 and 225 (so far as relating to the relevant tax in relation to which the partner payment notice is given)[, and

(*d*) if the denied advantage consists of or includes an asserted surrenderable amount, specify that amount and any action which is required to be taken in respect of it under paragraph 6A.][1]

(2) The payment required to be made under paragraph 6 is an amount equal to the amount which a designated HMRC officer determines, to the best of the officer's information and belief, as the understated partner tax.

(3) "The understated partner tax" means the additional amount that would become due and payable by the relevant partner in respect of tax if—

(a) in the case of a notice given by virtue of paragraph 3(5)(a) (case where a partnership follower notice is given)—

(i) it were assumed that the explanation given in the follower notice in question under section 206(b) is correct, and

(ii) what the officer may determine to the best of the officer's information and belief as the denied advantage is counteracted to the extent that it is reflected in a return or claim of the relevant partner;

(b) in the case of a notice given by virtue of paragraph 3(5)(b) (cases where the DOTAS arrangements are met), such adjustments were made as are required to counteract so much of what the designated HMRC officer so determines as the denied advantage as is reflected in a return or claim of the relevant partner;

(c) in the case of a notice given by virtue of paragraph 3(5)(c) (cases involving counteraction under the general anti-abuse rule), such of the adjustments set out in the GAAR counteraction notice are made as have effect to counteract so much of the denied advantage as is reflected in a return or claim of the relevant partner.

(4) "The denied advantage"—

(a) in the case of the notice given by virtue of paragraph 3(5)(a), has the meaning given by paragraph 4(3) of Schedule 31,

(b) in the case of a notice given by virtue of paragraph 3(5)(b), means so much of the asserted advantage as is not a tax advantage which results from the chosen arrangements or otherwise, and

(c) in the case of a notice given by virtue of paragraph 3(5)(c), means so much of the asserted advantage as would be counteracted by making the adjustments set out in the GAAR counteraction notice.

[(4A) "Asserted surrenderable amount" means so much of a surrenderable loss which the relevant partner asserts to have as a designated HMRC officer determines, to the best of that officer's information and belief, to be an amount—

(*a*) which would not be a surrenderable loss of that partner if the position were as stated in paragraphs (*a*), (*b*) or (*c*) of sub-paragraph (3), and

NIC

(*b*) which is not the subject of a claim by the relevant partner to relief from corporation tax which is reflected in the amount of the understated partner tax of that partner (and hence in the payment required to be made under paragraph 6).

(4B) "Surrenderable loss" means a loss or other amount within section 99(1) of CTA 2010 (or part of such a loss or other amount).][1]

(5) If a notice is given by reason of two or all of the requirements of paragraph 3(5) being met, [any payment specified under sub-paragraph (1)(*b*) or amount specified under sub-paragraph (1)(*d*)][1] is to be determined as if the notice were given by virtue of such one of them as is stated in the notice as being used for this purpose.

Amendments—[1] In sub-para (1)(*b*), words inserted and word repealed, sub-para (4)(*d*) and preceding word inserted, sub-paras (4A), (4B) inserted, and in sub-para (5), words substituted, by FA 2015 s 118, Sch 18 paras 1, 10(1), (2) with effect from 26 March 2015.

Representations about a partner payment notice

5 (1) This paragraph applies where a partner payment notice has been given to a relevant partner under paragraph 3 (and not withdrawn).

(2) The relevant partner has 90 days beginning with the day that notice is given to send written representations to HMRC—

(a) objecting to the notice on the grounds that Condition A, B or C in that paragraph was not met, . . . [1]

(b) objecting to the amount specified in the notice under paragraph 4(1)(b)[, or

(*c*) objecting to the amount specified in the notice under paragraph 4(1)(*d*).][1]

(3) HMRC must consider any representations made in accordance with sub-paragraph (2).

(4) Having considered the representations, HMRC must—

(a) if representations were made under sub-paragraph (2)(a), determine whether—

(i) to confirm the partner payment notice (with or without amendment), or

(ii) to withdraw the partner payment notice, . . . [1]

(b) if representations were made under sub-paragraph (2)(b) (and the notice is not withdrawn under paragraph (a)), determine whether a different amount [(or no amount)][1] ought to have been specified as the understated partner tax, and then—

(i) confirm the amount specified in the notice, . . . [1]

(ii) amend the notice to specify a different amount[, or

(iii) remove from the notice the provision made under paragraph 4(1)(*b*),][1] [and

(*c*) if representations were made under sub-paragraph (2)(*c*) (and the notice is not withdrawn under paragraph (*a*)), determine whether a different amount (or no amount) ought to have been specified under paragraph 4(1)(*d*), and then—

(i) confirm the amount specified in the notice,

(ii) amend the notice to specify a different amount, or

(iii) remove from the notice the provision made under paragraph 4(1)(*d*),][1]

and notify P accordingly.

Amendments—[1] In sub-paras (2)(*a*), (4)(*a*), (*b*)(i), word repealed, sub-paras (2)(*c*), (4)(*b*) (iii), (*c*) and preceding words inserted, and in sub-para (4)(*b*), words inserted, by FA 2015 s 118, Sch 18 paras 1, 10(1), (3) with effect from 26 March 2015.

Effect of partner payment notice

6 [(1) This paragraph applies where—

(*a*) a partner payment notice has been given to a relevant partner (and not withdrawn), and

(*b*) an amount is stated in the notice in accordance with paragraph 4(1)(*b*).][1]

(2) The relevant partner must make a payment ("the accelerated partner payment") to HMRC of [that amount][1].

(3) The accelerated partner payment is to be treated as a payment on account of the understated partner tax (see paragraph 4).

(4) The accelerated partner payment must be made before the end of the payment period.

(5) "The payment period" means—

(a) if the relevant partner made no representations under paragraph 5, the period of 90 days beginning with the day on which the partner payment notice is given;

(b) if the relevant partner made such representations, whichever of the following ends later—

(i) the 90 day period mentioned in paragraph (a);

(ii) the period of 30 days beginning with the day on which the relevant partner is notified under paragraph 5 of HMRC's determination.

(6) If the relevant partner pays any part of the understated partner tax before the accelerated partner payment in respect of it, the accelerated partner payment is treated to that extent as having been paid at the same time.

(7) Subsections (8) and (9) of section 223 apply in relation to a payment under this paragraph as they apply to a payment under that section.

Cross-references—F(No 2)A 2015 Sch 8 para 2(3)(*b*) (sums due under this para are relevant sums for the purposes of scheme for enforcement by deduction from accounts (direct recovery of debts)).

Amendments—[1] Sub-para (1) substituted, and words in sub-para (2) substituted, by FA 2015 s 118, Sch 18 paras 1, 10(1), (4) with effect from 26 March 2015.

[6A (1) This paragraph applies where—

(*a*) an accelerated payment notice is given (and not withdrawn), and

(*b*) an amount is specified in the notice in accordance with paragraph 4(1)(*d*).

(2) The relevant partner may not at any time when the notice has effect consent to any claim for group relief in respect of the amount so specified.

(3) Subject to sub-paragraph (2), paragraph 75 (other than sub-paragraphs (7) and (8)) of Schedule 18 to FA 1998 (reduction in amount available for surrender) has effect at any time when the notice has effect as if that specified amount ceased to be an amount available for surrender at the time the notice was given to the relevant partner.

(4) For the purposes of sub-paragraph (3), paragraph 75 of that Schedule has effect as if, in sub-paragraph (2) of that paragraph for "within 30 days" there were substituted "before the end of the payment period (within the meaning of paragraph 6(5) of Schedule 32 to the Finance Act 2014)".

(5) The time limits otherwise applicable to amendment of a company tax return do not prevent an amendment being made in accordance with paragraph 75(6) of Schedule 18 to FA 1998 where the relevant partner withdraws consent by virtue of sub-paragraph (3).][1]

Amendments—[1] Paragraph 6A inserted by FA 2015 s 118, Sch 18 paras 1, 10(1), (5) with effect from 26 March 2015. Sub-para (3) has effect in relation to an amount specified in a notice in accordance with FA 2014 Sch 32 para 4(1)(*d*) whether the consent to a claim for group relief was given, or the claim itself was made, before or on or after 26 March 2015 (FA 2015 Sch 18 para 12(2)).

Penalty for failure to comply with partner payment notice

7 Section 226 (penalty for failure to make accelerated payment on time) applies to accelerated partner payments as if—

(a) references in that section to the accelerated payment were to the accelerated partner payment,

(b) references to P were to the relevant partner, and

(c) "the payment period" had the meaning given by paragraph 6(5).

Withdrawal, suspension or modification of partner payment notices

8 (1) Section 227 (withdrawal, modification or suspension of accelerated payment notice) applies in relation to a relevant partner, a partner payment notice, Condition C in paragraph 3 and an accelerated partner payment as it applies in relation to P, an accelerated payment notice, Condition C in section 219 and an accelerated payment.

(2) Accordingly, for this purpose—

[(*za*) section 227(2)(*d*), (12A) and (16) has effect as if the references to section 220(2)(*d*) or 221(2)(*d*) were to paragraph 4(1)(*d*) of this Schedule,][1]

(a) section 227(6)(b) and (7)(a) has effect as if the references to section 220(6) were to paragraph 4(5) of this Schedule, . . . [1]

(b) the provisions listed in section 227(9) are to be read as including paragraph 6(5) of this Schedule[, or

(*c*) section 227(12A) has effect as if the reference to section 225A(3) were to paragraph 6A(3) of this Schedule.][1]

Amendments—[1] Sub-para (2)(*za*) inserted, in sub-para (2)(*a*), word repealed, and sub-para (2)(*c*) and preceding word inserted, by FA 2015 s 118, Sch 18 paras 1, 10(1), (6) with effect from 26 March 2015.

SCHEDULE 33

PART 4: CONSEQUENTIAL AMENDMENTS

Section 233

Taxes Management Act 1970

1 (*amends* TMA 1970 s 9B(1))

2 (*inserts* TMA 1970 s 103ZA(h))

Finance Act 2007

3 (*inserts* FA 2007 Sch 24 para 12(2A))

Finance Act 2008

4 (*inserts* FA 2008 Sch 41 para 15(1A))

Finance Act 2009

5 (*inserts* FA 2009 Sch 55 para 17(2)(c))

SCHEDULE 34
PROMOTERS OF TAX AVOIDANCE SCHEMES: THRESHOLD CONDITIONS

Section 237

Commentary—*Simon's Taxes* **A7.252.**

PART 1
MEETING THE THRESHOLD CONDITIONS: GENERAL

Meaning of "threshold condition"

1 Each of the conditions described in paragraphs 2 to 12 is a "threshold condition".

Deliberate tax defaulters

2 A person meets this condition if the Commissioners publish information about the person in reliance on section 94 of FA 2009 (publishing details of deliberate tax defaulters).

Breach of the Banking Code of Practice

3 A person meets this condition if the person is named in a report under section 285 as a result of the Commissioners determining that the person breached the Code of Practice on Taxation for Banks by reason of promoting arrangements which the person cannot have reasonably believed achieved a tax result which was intended by Parliament.

Dishonest tax agents

4 A person meets this condition if the person is given a conduct notice under paragraph 4 of Schedule 38 to FA 2012 (tax agents: dishonest conduct) and either—

(a) the time period during which a notice of appeal may be given in relation to the notice has expired, or

(b) an appeal against the notice has been made and the tribunal has confirmed the determination referred to in sub-paragraph (1) of paragraph 4 of that Schedule.

Non-compliance with Part 7 of FA 2004

5 (1) A person meets this condition if the person fails to comply with any of the following provisions of Part 7 of FA 2004 (disclosure of tax avoidance schemes)—

(a) section 308(1) and (3) (duty of promoter in relation to notifiable proposals and notifiable arrangements);

(b) section 309(1) (duty of person dealing with promoter outside the United Kingdom);

(c) section 310 (duty of parties to notifiable arrangements not involving promoter);

(d) section 313ZA (duty of promoter to provide details of clients).

[(2) For the purposes of sub-paragraph (1), a person ("P") fails to comply with a provision mentioned in that sub-paragraph if and only if any of conditions A to C are met.

(3) Condition A is met if—

(*a*) the tribunal has determined that P has failed to comply with the provision concerned,

(*b*) the appeal period has ended, and

(*c*) the determination has not been overturned on appeal.

(4) Condition B is met if—

(*a*) the tribunal has determined for the purposes of section 118(2) of TMA 1970 that P is to be deemed not to have failed to comply with the provision concerned as P had a reasonable excuse for not doing the thing required to be done,

(*b*) the appeal period has ended, and

(*c*) the determination has not been overturned on appeal.

(5) Condition C is met if P has admitted in writing to HMRC that P has failed to comply with the provision concerned.

(6) The "appeal period" means—

(*a*) the period during which an appeal could be brought against the determination of the tribunal, or (*b*) where an appeal mentioned in paragraph (*a*) has been brought, the period during which that appeal has not been finally determined, withdrawn or otherwise disposed of.][1]

Amendments—[1] Sub-paras (2)–(6) substituted for previous sub-para (2) by FA 2015 s 119, Sch 19 para 6 with effect for the purposes of determining whether a person meets a threshold condition in a period of three years ending on or after 26 March 2015.

Criminal offences

6 (1) A person meets this condition if the person is charged with a relevant offence.

(2) The fact that a person has been charged with an offence is disregarded for the purposes of this paragraph if—

(a) the person has been acquitted of the offence, or

(b) the charge has been dismissed or the proceedings have been discontinued.

(3) An acquittal is not taken into account for the purposes of sub-paragraph (2) if an appeal has been brought against the acquittal and has not yet been disposed of.

(4) "Relevant offence" means any of the following—

(a) an offence at common law of cheating in relation to the public revenue;

(b) in Scotland, an offence at common law of—

(i) fraud;

(ii) uttering;

(c) an offence under section 17(1) of the Theft Act 1968 or section 17 of the Theft Act (Northern Ireland) 1969 (c. 16 (NI)) (false accounting);

(d) an offence under section 106A of TMA 1970 (fraudulent evasion of income tax);

(e) an offence under section 107 of TMA 1970 (false statements: Scotland);

(f) an offence under any of the following provisions of CEMA 1979—

(i) section 50(2) (improper importation of goods with intent to defraud or evade duty);

(ii) section 167 (untrue declarations etc);

(iii) section 168 (counterfeiting documents etc);

(iv) section 170 (fraudulent evasion of duty);

(v) section 170B (taking steps for the fraudulent evasion of duty);

(g) an offence under any of the following provisions of VATA 1994—

(i) section 72(1) (being knowingly concerned in the evasion of VAT);

(ii) section 72(3) (false statement etc);

(iii) section 72(8) (conduct involving commission of other offence under section 72);

(h) an offence under section 1 of the Fraud Act 2006 (fraud);

(i) an offence under any of the following provisions of CRCA 2005—

(i) section 30 (impersonating a Commissioner or officer of Revenue and Customs);

(ii) section 31 (obstruction of officer of Revenue and Customs etc);

(iii) section 32 (assault of officer of Revenue and Customs);

(j) an offence under [regulation 86(1) of the Money Laundering, Terrorist Financing and Transfer of Funds (Information on the Payer) Regulations 2017][1];

(k) an offence under section 49(1) of the Criminal Justice and Licensing (Scotland) Act 2010 (asp 13) (possession of articles for use in fraud).

Amendments—[1] In sub-para (4)(j), words substituted for words "regulation 45(1) of the Money Laundering Regulations 2007 (SI 2007/2157)" by the Money Laundering, Terrorist Financing and Transfer of Funds (Information on the Payer) Regulations, SI 2017/692 reg 109, Sch 7 para 10 with effect from 26 June 2017.

Opinion notice of GAAR Advisory Panel

7 A person meets this condition if—

(a) arrangements in relation to which the person is a promoter[—

(i) have been referred to the GAAR Advisory Panel under Schedule 43 to FA 2013 (referrals of single schemes),

(ii) are in a pool in respect of which a referral has been made to that Panel under Schedule 43B to that Act (generic referrals), or

(iii) have been referred to that Panel under paragraph 26 of Schedule 16 to F(No. 2)A 2017 (referrals in relation to penalties for enablers of defeated tax avoidance),][2]

(b) one or more opinion notices are given [in respect of the referral][1] [under (as the case may be)—

(i) paragraph 11(3)(*b*) of Schedule 43 to FA 2013,

(ii) paragraph 6(4)(*b*) of Schedule 43B to that Act, or

(iii) paragraph 34(3)(*b*) of Schedule 16 to F(No. 2)A 2017,

(opinion of sub-panel of GAAR Advisory Panel that arrangements are not reasonable), and][2]

(c) the notice, or the notices taken together, either—

(i) state the joint opinion of all the members of the sub-panel arranged under ...[1] that Schedule, or

(ii) state the opinion of two or more members of that sub-panel.

Amendments—[1] In paras (*a*), (*b*), words inserted, in para (*b*), words substituted for words "in relation to the arrangements", and in para (*c*), words "paragraph 10 of" repealed, by FA 2016 s 157(29) with effect in relation to tax arrangements (within the meaning of FA 2013 Pt 5) entered into at any time (whether before on or after 15 September 2016).

[2] In para (*a*), words substituted for words "have been referred to the GAAR Advisory Panel under Schedule 43 to FA 2013, (referrals of single schemes) or are in a pool in respect of which a referral has been made to that Panel under Schedule 43B to that Act (generic referrals),", and in para (b), words substituted for words "under paragraph 11(3)(b) or (as the case may be) 6(4)(*b*) of that Schedule (opinion of sub-panel of GAAR Advisory Panel that arrangements are not reasonable), and", by F(No 2)A 2017 s 65, Sch 16 para 61 with effect in relation to arrangements entered into on or after 16 November 2017. In determining in relation to any particular arrangements whether a person is a person who enabled the arrangements, any action of the person carried out before 16 November 2017 is to be disregarded, and these amendments do not apply in relation to a person who is a promoter in relation to arrangements if that person is not a person who enabled the arrangements (F(No 2)A 2017 Sch 16 para 62(2), (3)).

Disciplinary action [against a member of a trade or profession]

8 [(1) A person who carries on a trade or profession that is regulated by a professional body meets this condition if all of the following conditions are met—

(*a*) the person is found guilty of misconduct of a prescribed kind,

(*b*) action of a prescribed kind is taken against the person in relation to that misconduct, and

(*c*) a penalty of a prescribed kind is imposed on the person as a result of that misconduct.][1]

(2) Misconduct may only be prescribed for the purposes of sub-paragraph (1)(a) if it is misconduct other than misconduct in matters (such as the payment of fees) that relate solely or mainly to the person's relationship with the professional body.

(3) A "professional body" means—

(a) the Institute of Chartered Accountants in England and Wales;

(b) the Institute of Chartered Accountants of Scotland;

(c) the General Council of the Bar;

(d) the Faculty of Advocates;

(e) the General Council of the Bar of Northern Ireland;

(f) the Law Society;

(g) the Law Society of Scotland;

(h) the Law Society [of][1] Northern Ireland;

(i) the Association of Accounting Technicians;

(j) the Association of Chartered Certified Accountants;

(k) the Association of Taxation Technicians;

(l) any other prescribed body with functions relating to the regulation of a trade or profession.

Amendments—[1] Sub-para (1) substituted, and words in heading and word in sub-para (3)(*h*) substituted, by FA 2015 s 119, Sch 19 para 7 with effect for the purposes of determining whether a person meets a threshold condition in a period of three years ending on or after 26 March 2015.

Disciplinary action by a regulatory authority

9 (1) A person meets this condition if a regulatory authority imposes a relevant sanction on the person.

(2) A "relevant sanction" is a sanction which is—

(a) imposed in relation to misconduct other than misconduct in matters (such as the payment of fees) that relate solely or mainly to the person's relationship with the regulatory authority, and

(b) prescribed.

(3) The following are regulatory authorities for the purposes of this paragraph—

(a) the Financial Conduct Authority;

(b) the Financial Services Authority;

(c) any other authority that may be prescribed.

(4) Only authorities that have functions relating to the regulation of financial institutions may be prescribed under sub-paragraph (3)(c).

Exercise of information powers

10 (1) A person meets this condition if the person fails to comply with an information notice given under any of paragraphs 1, 2, 5 and 5A of Schedule 36 to FA 2008.

(2) For the purposes of section 237, the failure to comply is taken to occur when the period within which the person is required to comply with the notice expires (without the person having complied with it).

Restrictive contractual terms

11 (1) A person ("P") meets this condition if P enters into an agreement with another person ("C") which relates to a relevant proposal or relevant arrangements in relation to which P is a promoter, on terms which—

(a) impose a contractual obligation on C which falls within sub-paragraph (2) or (3), or

(b) impose on C both obligations within sub-paragraph (4) and obligations within sub-paragraph (5).

(2) A contractual obligation falls within this sub-paragraph if it prevents or restricts the disclosure by C to HMRC of information relating to the proposals or arrangements, whether or not by referring to a wider class of persons.

(3) A contractual obligation falls within this sub-paragraph if it requires C to impose on any tax adviser to whom C discloses information relating to the proposals or arrangements a contractual obligation which prevents or restricts the disclosure of that information to HMRC by the adviser.

(4) A contractual obligation falls within this sub-paragraph if it requires C to—

(a) meet (in whole or in part) the costs of, or contribute to a fund to be used to meet the costs of, any proceedings relating to arrangements in relation to which P is a promoter (whether or not implemented by C), or

(b) take out an insurance policy which insures against the risk of having to meet the costs connected with proceedings relating to arrangements which C has implemented and in relation to which P is a promoter.

(5) A contractual obligation falls within this paragraph if it requires C to obtain the consent of P before—

(a) entering into any agreement with HMRC regarding arrangements which C has implemented and in relation to which P is a promoter, or

(b) withdrawing or discontinuing any appeal against any decision regarding such arrangements.

(6) In sub-paragraph (5)(b), the reference to withdrawing or discontinuing an appeal includes any action or inaction which results in an appeal being discontinued.

(7) In this paragraph—

"proceedings" includes any sort of proceedings for resolving disputes (and not just proceedings in court), whether commenced or contemplated;

"tax adviser" means a person appointed to give advice about the tax affairs of another person (whether appointed directly by that person or by another tax adviser of that person).

Continuing to promote certain arrangements

12 (1) A person ("P") meets this condition if P has been given a stop notice and after the end of the notice period P—

(a) makes a firm approach to another person ("C") in relation to an affected proposal with a view to making the affected proposal available for implementation by C or another person, or

(b) makes an affected proposal available for implementation by other persons.

(2) "Affected proposal" means a relevant proposal that is in substance the same as the relevant proposal specified in the stop notice in accordance with sub-paragraph (4)(c).

(3) An authorised officer may give a person ("P") a notice (a "stop notice") if each of these conditions is met—

(a) a person has been given a follower notice under section 204 (circumstances in which a follower notice may be given) in relation to particular relevant arrangements;

(b) P is a promoter in relation to a relevant proposal that is implemented by those arrangements;

(c) 90 days have elapsed since the follower notice was given and—

(i) the follower notice has not been withdrawn, and

(ii) if representations objecting to the follower notice were made under section 207 (representations about a follower notice), HMRC have confirmed the follower notice.

(4) A stop notice must—

(a) specify the arrangements which are the subject of the follower notice mentioned in sub-paragraph (3)(a),

(b) specify the judicial ruling identified in that follower notice,

(c) specify a relevant proposal in relation to which the condition in sub-paragraph (3)(b) is met, and

(d) explain the effect of the stop notice.

(5) An authorised officer may determine that a stop notice given to a person is to cease to have effect.

(6) If an authorised officer makes a determination under sub-paragraph (5) the officer must give the person written notice of the determination.

(7) The notice must specify the date from which it takes effect, which may be earlier than the date on which the notice is given.

NIC

(8) In this paragraph—

"the notice period" means the period of 30 days beginning with the day on which a stop notice is given;

"judicial ruling" means a ruling of a court or tribunal.

PART 2
MEETING THE THRESHOLD CONDITIONS: BODIES CORPORATE [AND PARTNERSHIPS]

Amendments—In heading, words inserted by FA 2015 s 119, Sch 19 para 4(1), (2) with effect for the purposes of determining whether a person meets a threshold condition in a period of three years ending on or after 26 March 2015.

[Interpretation

13A (1) This paragraph contains definitions for the purposes of this Part of this Schedule.

(2) Each of the following is a "relevant body"—

(*a*) a body corporate, and

(*b*) a partnership.

(3) "Relevant time" means the time referred to in section 237(1A) (duty to give conduct notice to person treated as meeting threshold condition).

(4) "Relevant threshold condition" means a threshold condition specified in any of the following paragraphs of this Schedule—

(*a*) paragraph 2 (deliberate tax defaulters);

(*b*) paragraph 4 (dishonest tax agents);

(*c*) paragraph 6 (criminal offences);

(*d*) paragraph 7 (opinion notice of GAAR advisory panel);

(*e*) paragraph 8 (disciplinary action against a member of a trade or profession);

(*f*) paragraph 9 (disciplinary action by regulatory authority);

(*g*) paragraph 10 (failure to comply with information notice).

(5) A person controls a body corporate if the person has power to secure that the affairs of the body corporate are conducted in accordance with the person's wishes—

(*a*) by means of the holding of shares or the possession of voting power in relation to the body corporate or any other relevant body,

(*b*) as a result of any powers conferred by the articles of association or other document regulating the body corporate or any other relevant body, or

(*c*) by means of controlling a partnership.

[(6) Two or more persons together control a body corporate if together they have the power to secure that the affairs of the body corporate are conducted in accordance with their wishes in any way specified in sub-paragraph (5)(*a*) to (*c*).

(7) A person controls a partnership if the person is a member of the partnership and—

(*a*) has the right to a share of more than half the assets, or more than half the income, of the partnership, or

(*b*) directs, or is on a day-to-day level in control of, the management of the business of the partnership.

(8) Two or more persons together control a partnership if they are members of the partnership and together they—

(*a*) have the right to a share of more than half the assets, or of more than half the income, of the partnership, or

(*b*) direct, or are on a day-to-day level in control of, the management of the business of the partnership.

(9) Paragraph 19(2) to (5) of Schedule 36 (connected persons etc) applies to a person referred to in sub-paragraph (7) or (8) as if references to "P" were to that person.

(10) A person has significant influence over a body corporate or partnership if the person—

(*a*) does not control the body corporate or partnership, but

(*b*) is able to, or actually does, exercise significant influence over it (whether or not as the result of a legal entitlement).

(11) Two or more persons together have significant influence over a body corporate or partnership if together those persons—

(*a*) do not control the body corporate or partnership, but

(*b*) are able to, or actually do, exercise significant influence over it (whether or not as the result of a legal entitlement).

(12) References to a person being a promoter are to the person carrying on business as a promoter.][2]][1]

Commentary—*Simon's Taxes* **A7.251, A7.252A, A7.259** .

Press releases etc—HMRC TIIN (Budget 2017), "Promoters of Tax Avoidance Schemes—associated and successor entities rules", 8 March 2017 (see *SWTI 2017, Budget Edition*).

Amendments—[1] Paragraphs 13A–13D substituted for previous para 13 by FA 2015 s 119, Sch 19 para 4(1), (3) with effect for the purposes of determining whether a person meets a threshold condition in a period of three years ending on or after 26 March 2015.

[2] Sub-paras (6)–(12) substituted for previous sub-paras (6)–(8) by FA 2017 s 24(1) with effect for the purposes of determining whether a person meets a threshold condition in a period of three years ending on or after 8 March 2017.

[Relevant bodies controlled etc by other persons treated as meeting a threshold condition

13B (1) A relevant body is treated as meeting a threshold condition at the relevant time if any of Conditions A to C is met.

(2) Condition A is that—

(*a*) a person met the threshold condition at a time when the person was a promoter, and

(*b*) the person controls or has significant influence over the relevant body at the relevant time.

(3) Condition B is that—

(*a*) a person met the threshold condition at a time when the person controlled or had significant influence over the relevant body,

(*b*) the relevant body was a promoter at that time, and

(*c*) the person controls or has significant influence over the relevant body at the relevant time.

(4) Condition C is that—

(*a*) two or more persons together controlled or had significant influence over the relevant body at a time when one of those persons met the threshold condition,

(*b*) the relevant body was a promoter at that time, and

(*c*) those persons together control or have significant influence over the relevant body at the relevant time.

(5) Where the person referred to in sub-paragraph (2)(*a*) or (3)(*a*) or (4)(*a*) as meeting a threshold condition is an individual, sub-paragraph (1) only applies if the threshold condition is a relevant threshold condition.

(6) For the purposes of sub-paragraph (2) it does not matter whether the relevant body existed at the time referred to in sub-paragraph (2)(*a*).][1]

Commentary—*Simon's Taxes* **A7.259** .

Press releases etc—HMRC TIIN (Budget 2017), "Promoters of Tax Avoidance Schemes—associated and successor entities rules", 8 March 2017 (see *SWTI 2017, Budget Edition*).

Amendments—[1] Paragraphs 13B–13D substituted by FA 2017 s 24(2) with effect for the purposes of determining whether a person meets a threshold condition in a period of three years ending on or after 8 March 2017.

[Persons who control etc a relevant body treated as meeting a threshold condition

13C (1) If at a time when a person controlled or had significant influence over a relevant body—

(*a*) the relevant body met a threshold condition, and

(*b*) the relevant body, or another relevant body which the person controlled or had significant influence over, was a promoter,

the person is treated as meeting the threshold condition at the relevant time.

(2) It does not matter whether any relevant body referred to sub-paragraph (1) exists at the relevant time.][1]

Commentary—*Simon's Taxes* **A7.259** .

Press releases etc—HMRC TIIN (Budget 2017), "Promoters of Tax Avoidance Schemes—associated and successor entities rules", 8 March 2017 (see *SWTI 2017, Budget Edition*).

Amendments—[1] Paragraphs 13B–13D substituted by FA 2017 s 24(2) with effect for the purposes of determining whether a person meets a threshold condition in a period of three years ending on or after 8 March 2017.

[Relevant bodies controlled etc by the same person treated as meeting a threshold condition

13D (1) If—

(*a*) a person controlled or had significant influence over a relevant body at a time when it met a threshold condition, and

(*b*) at that time that body, or another relevant body which the person controlled or had significant influence over, was a promoter,

any relevant body which the person controls or has significant influence over at the relevant time is treated as meeting the threshold condition at the relevant time.

(2) If—

(*a*) two or more persons together controlled or had significant influence over a relevant body at a time when it met a threshold condition, and

(*b*) at that time that body, or another relevant body which those persons together controlled or had significant influence over, was a promoter,

any relevant body which those persons together control or have significant influence over at the relevant time is treated as meeting the threshold condition at the relevant time.

NIC

(3) It does not matter whether—

(*a*) a relevant body referred to in sub-paragraph (1)(*a*) or (*b*) or (2)(*a*) or (*b*) exists at the relevant time, or

(*b*) a relevant body existing at the relevant time existed at the time referred to in sub-paragraph (1)(*a*) or (2)(*a*).][1]

Commentary—*Simon's Taxes* **A7.259** .

Press releases etc—HMRC TIIN (Budget 2017), "Promoters of Tax Avoidance Schemes—associated and successor entities rules", 8 March 2017 (see *SWTI 2017, Budget Edition*).

Amendments—[1] Paragraphs 13B–13D substituted by FA 2017 s 24(2) with effect for the purposes of determining whether a person meets a threshold condition in a period of three years ending on or after 8 March 2017.

PART 3
POWER TO AMEND

14 (1) The Treasury may by regulations amend this Schedule.

(2) An amendment made by virtue of sub-paragraph (1) may, in particular—

(a) vary or remove any of the conditions set out in paragraphs 2 to 12;

(b) add new conditions;

[(*c*) vary any of the circumstances described in paragraphs 13B to 13D in which a person is treated as meeting a threshold condition (including by amending paragraph 13A);

(*d*) add new circumstances in which a person will be so treated.][1]

(3) Regulations under sub-paragraph (1) may include any amendment of this Part of this Act that is appropriate in consequence of an amendment made by virtue of sub-paragraph (1).

Amendments—[1] Sub-para (2)(*c*), (*d*) inserted by FA 2015 s 119, Sch 19 para 8 with effect from 26 March 2015.

[SCHEDULE 34A
PROMOTERS OF TAX AVOIDANCE SCHEMES: DEFEATED ARRANGEMENTS

Note—In this Schedule, "tax" includes VAT, and "tax advantage" has the meaning given by s 234(3) and also includes a tax advantage as defined in VATA 1994 Sch 11A para 1.

Amendments—Schedule 34A inserted by FA 2016 s 160(1), (5) with effect from 15 September 2016.

PART 1
INTRODUCTION]

Amendments—Schedule 34A inserted by FA 2016 s 160(1), (5) with effect from 15 September 2016.

[1 In this Schedule—

(*a*) Part 2 is about the meaning of "relevant defeat";

(*b*) Part 3 contains provision about when a relevant defeat is treated as occurring in relation to a person;

(*c*) Part 4 contains provision about when a person is treated as meeting a condition in subsection (11), (12) or (13) of section 237A;

(*d*) Part 5 contains definitions and other supplementary provisions.][1]

Amendments—[1] Schedule 34A inserted by FA 2016 s 160(1), (5) with effect from 15 September 2016.

[PART 2
MEANING OF "RELEVANT DEFEAT"

"Related" arrangements

2 (1) For the purposes of this Part of this Act, separate arrangements which persons have entered into are "related" to one another if (and only if) they are substantially the same.

(2) Sub-paragraphs (3) to (6) set out cases in which arrangements are to be treated as being "substantially the same" (if they would not otherwise be so treated under sub-paragraph (1)).

(3) Arrangements to which the same reference number has been allocated under Part 7 of FA 2004 (disclosure of tax avoidance schemes) are treated as being substantially the same. For this purpose arrangements in relation to which information relating to a reference number has been provided in compliance with section 312 of FA 2004 are treated as arrangements to which that reference number has been allocated under Part 7 of that Act.

(4) Arrangements to which the same reference number has been allocated under paragraph 9 of Schedule 11A to VATA 1994 (disclosure of avoidance schemes) [or paragraph 22 of Schedule 17 to FA 2017 (disclosure of avoidance schemes: VAT and other indirect taxes)][2] are treated as being substantially the same.

(5) Any two or more sets of arrangements which are the subject of follower notices given by reference to the same judicial ruling are treated as being substantially the same.

(6) Where a notice of binding has been given in relation to any arrangements ("the bound arrangements") on the basis that they are, for the purposes of Schedule 43A to FA 2013, equivalent arrangements in relation to another set of arrangements (the "lead arrangements")—

(*a*) the bound arrangements and the lead arrangements are treated as being substantially the same, and

(*b*) the bound arrangements are treated as being substantially the same as any other arrangements which, as a result of this sub-paragraph, are treated as substantially the same as the lead arrangements.][1]

Amendments—[1] Schedule 34A inserted by FA 2016 s 160(1), (5) with effect from 15 September 2016.

[2] In sub-para (4), words inserted by F(No 2)A 2017 s 66, Sch 17 paras 52, 54(1), (2) with effect from 1 January 2018.

["Promoted arrangements"

3 (1) For the purposes of this Schedule arrangements are "promoted arrangements" in relation to a person if—

(*a*) they are relevant arrangements or would be relevant arrangements under the condition stated in sub-paragraph (2), and

(*b*) the person is carrying on a business as a promoter and—

(i) the person is or has been a promoter in relation to the arrangements, or

(ii) that would be the case if the condition in subparagraph (2) were met.

(2) That condition is that the definition of "tax" in section 283 includes, and has always included, value added tax.][1]

Amendments—[1] Schedule 34A inserted by FA 2016 s 160(1), (5) with effect from 15 September 2016.

[Relevant defeat of single arrangements

4 (1) A defeat of arrangements (entered into by any person) which are promoted arrangements in relation to a person ("the promoter") is a "relevant defeat" in relation to the promoter if the condition in subparagraph (2) is met.

(2) The condition is that the arrangements are not related to any other arrangements which are promoted arrangements in relation to the promoter.

(3) For the meaning of "defeat" see paragraphs 10 to 16.][1]

Amendments—[1] Schedule 34A inserted by FA 2016 s 160(1), (5) with effect from 15 September 2016.

[Relevant defeat of related arrangements

5 (1) This paragraph applies if arrangements (entered into by any person) ("Set A")—

(*a*) are promoted arrangements in relation to a person ("P"), and

(*b*) are related to other arrangements which are promoted arrangements in relation to P.

(2) If Case 1, 2 or 3 applies (see paragraphs 7 to 9) a relevant defeat occurs in relation to P and each of the related arrangements.

(3) "The related arrangements" means Set A and the arrangements mentioned in sub-paragraph (1)(*b*).][1]

Amendments—[1] Schedule 34A inserted by FA 2016 s 160(1), (5) with effect from 15 September 2016.

[Limit on number of separate relevant defeats in relation to the same, or related, arrangements

6 In relation to a person, if there has been a relevant defeat of arrangements (whether under paragraph 4 or 5) there cannot be a further relevant defeat of—

(*a*) those particular arrangements, or

(*b*) arrangements which are related to those arrangements.][1]

Amendments—[1] Schedule 34A inserted by FA 2016 s 160(1), (5) with effect from 15 September 2016.

[Case 1: counteraction upheld by judicial ruling

7 (1) Case 1 applies if—

(*a*) any of Conditions A to E is met in relation to any of the related arrangements, and

(*b*) in the case of those arrangements the decision to make the relevant counteraction has been upheld by a judicial ruling (which is final).

(2) In sub-paragraph (1) "the relevant counteraction" means the counteraction mentioned in paragraph 11(*d*), 12(1)(*b*), 13(1)(*d*), 14(1)(*d*) or 15(1)(*d*) (as the case requires).][1]

Amendments—[1] Schedule 34A inserted by FA 2016 s 160(1), (5) with effect from 15 September 2016.

[Case 2: judicial ruling that avoidance-related rule applies

8 Case 2 applies if Condition F is met in relation to any of the related arrangements.][1]

Amendments—[1] Schedule 34A inserted by FA 2016 s 160(1), (5) with effect from 15 September 2016.

[Case 3: proportion-based relevant defeat

9 (1) Case 3 applies if—

(*a*) at least 75% of the tested arrangements have been defeated, and

(*b*) no final judicial ruling in relation to any of the related arrangements has upheld a corresponding tax advantage which has been asserted in connection with any of the related arrangements.

(2) In this paragraph "the tested arrangements" means so many of the related arrangements (as defined in paragraph 5(3)) as meet the condition in sub-paragraph (3) or (4).

(3) Particular arrangements meet this condition if a person has made a return, claim or election on the basis that a tax advantage results from those arrangements and—

(*a*) there has been an enquiry or investigation by HMRC into the return, claim or election, or

(*b*) HMRC assesses the person to tax on the basis that the tax advantage (or any part of it) does not arise, or

(*c*) a GAAR counteraction notice has been given in relation to the tax advantage or part of it and the arrangements.

(4) Particular arrangements meet this condition if HMRC takes other action on the basis that a tax advantage which might be expected to arise from those arrangements, or is asserted in connection with them, does not arise.

(5) For the purposes of this paragraph a tax advantage has been "asserted" in connection with particular arrangements if a person has made a return, claim or election on the basis that the tax advantage arises from those arrangements.

(6) In sub-paragraph (1)(*b*) "corresponding tax advantage" means a tax advantage corresponding to any tax advantage the counteraction of which is taken into account by HMRC for the purposes of subparagraph (1)(*a*).

(7) For the purposes of this paragraph a court or tribunal "upholds" a tax advantage if—

(*a*) the court or tribunal makes a ruling to the effect that no part of the tax advantage is to be counteracted, and

(*b*) that judicial ruling is final.

(8) In this paragraph references to "counteraction" include anything referred to as a counteraction in any of Conditions A to F in paragraphs 11 to 16.

(9) In this paragraph "GAAR counteraction notice" means—

(*a*) a notice such as is mentioned in sub-paragraph (2) of paragraph 12 of Schedule 43 to FA 2013 (notice of final decision to counteract),

(*b*) a notice under paragraph 8(2) or 9(2) of Schedule 43A to that Act (pooling or binding of arrangements) stating that the tax advantage is to be counteracted under the general anti-abuse rule, or

(*c*) a notice under paragraph 8(2) of Schedule 43B to that Act (generic referrals) stating that the tax advantage is to be counteracted under the general anti-abuse rule.][1]

Amendments—[1] Schedule 34A inserted by FA 2016 s 160(1), (5) with effect from 15 September 2016.

["Defeat" of arrangements

10 For the purposes of this Part of this Act a "defeat" of arrangements occurs if any of Conditions A to F (in paragraphs 11 to 16) is met in relation to the arrangements.][1]

Amendments—[1] Schedule 34A inserted by FA 2016 s 160(1), (5) with effect from 15 September 2016.

[11 Condition A is that—

(*a*) a person has made a return, claim or election on the basis that a tax advantage arises from the arrangements,

(*b*) a notice given to the person under paragraph 12 of Schedule 43 to, paragraph 8(2) or 9(2) of Schedule 43A to or paragraph 8(2) of Schedule 43B to FA 2013 stated that the tax advantage was to be counteracted under the general anti-abuse rule,

(*c*) the tax advantage has been counteracted (in whole or in part) under the general anti-abuse rule, and

(*d*) the counteraction is final.][1]

Amendments—[1] Schedule 34A inserted by FA 2016 s 160(1), (5) with effect from 15 September 2016.

[12 (1) Condition B is that a follower notice has been given to a person by reference to the arrangements (and not withdrawn) and—

(*a*) the person has complied with subsection (2) of section 208 of FA 2014 by taking the action specified in subsections (4) to (6) of that section in respect of the denied tax advantage (or part of it), or

(*b*) the denied tax advantage has been counteracted (in whole or in part) otherwise than as mentioned in paragraph (*a*) and the counteraction is final.

(2) In this paragraph "the denied tax advantage" is to be interpreted in accordance with section 208(3) of FA 2014.

(3) In this Schedule "follower notice" means a follower notice under Chapter 2 of Part 4 of FA 2014.][1]

Amendments—[1] Schedule 34A inserted by FA 2016 s 160(1), (5) with effect from 15 September 2016.

[13 (1) Condition C is that—

(*a*) the arrangements are DOTAS arrangements,

(*b*) a person ("the taxpayer") has made a return, claim or election on the basis that a relevant tax advantage arises,

(*c*) the relevant tax advantage has been counteracted, and

(*d*) the counteraction is final.

(2) For the purposes of sub-paragraph (1) "relevant tax advantage" means a tax advantage which the arrangements might be expected to enable the taxpayer to obtain.

(3) For the purposes of this paragraph the relevant tax advantage is "counteracted" if adjustments are made in respect of the taxpayer's tax position on the basis that the whole or part of that tax advantage does not arise.][1]

Amendments—[1] Schedule 34A inserted by FA 2016 s 160(1), (5) with effect from 15 September 2016.

[14 (1) Condition D is that—

(*a*) the arrangements are disclosable VAT [or other indirect tax][2] arrangements to which a . . . [2] person is a party,

(*b*) the . . . [2] person has made a return or claim on the basis that a relevant tax advantage arises,

(*c*) the relevant tax advantage has been counteracted, and

(*d*) the counteraction is final.

(2) For the purposes of sub-paragraph (1) "relevant tax advantage" means a tax advantage which the arrangements might be expected to enable the . . . [2] person to obtain.

(3) For the purposes of this paragraph the relevant tax advantage is "counteracted" if adjustments are made in respect of the . . . [2] person's tax position on the basis that the whole or part of that tax advantage does not arise.][1]

Amendments—[1] Schedule 34A inserted by FA 2016 s 160(1), (5) with effect from 15 September 2016.

[2] In sub-para (1)(*a*), words inserted, and in sub-paras (1)(*a*), (*b*), (2), (3), word "taxable" repealed, by F(No 2)A 2017 s 66, Sch 17 paras 52, 54(1), (3) with effect from 1 January 2018.

[15 (1) Condition E is that the arrangements are disclosable VAT arrangements to which a taxable person ("T") is a party and—

(*a*) the arrangements relate to the position with respect to VAT of a person other than T ("S") who has made supplies of goods or services to T,

(*b*) the arrangements might be expected to enable T to obtain a tax advantage in connection with those supplies of goods or services,

(*c*) the arrangements have been counteracted, and

(*d*) the counteraction is final.

(2) For the purposes of this paragraph the arrangements are "counteracted" if—

(*a*) HMRC assess S to tax or take any other action on a basis which prevents T from obtaining (or obtaining the whole of) the tax advantage in question, or

(*b*) adjustments are made on a basis such as is mentioned in paragraph (*a*).][1]

Amendments—[1] Schedule 34A inserted by FA 2016 s 160(1), (5) with effect from 15 September 2016.

[16 (1) Condition F is that—

(*a*) a person has made a return, claim or election on the basis that a relevant tax advantage arises,

(*b*) the tax advantage, or part of the tax advantage would not arise if a particular avoidance-related rule (see paragraph 25) applies in relation to the person's tax affairs,

(*c*) it is held in a judicial ruling that the relevant avoidance-related rule applies in relation to the person's tax affairs, and

(*d*) the judicial ruling is final.

(2) For the purposes of sub-paragraph (1) "relevant tax advantage" means a tax advantage which the arrangements might be expected to enable the person to obtain.][1]

Amendments—[1] Schedule 34A inserted by FA 2016 s 160(1), (5) with effect from 15 September 2016.

[PART 3

RELEVANT DEFEATS: ASSOCIATED PERSONS

Attribution of relevant defeats

17 (1) Sub-paragraph (2) applies if—

NIC

(*a*) there is (or has been) a person ("Q"),
(*b*) arrangements ("the defeated arrangements") have been entered into,
(*c*) an event occurs such that either—
(i) there is a relevant defeat in relation to Q and the defeated arrangements, or
(ii) the condition in sub-paragraph (i) would be met if Q had not ceased to exist,
(*d*) at the time of that event a person ("P") is carrying on a business as a promoter (or is carrying on what would be such a business under the condition in paragraph 3(2)), and
(*e*) Condition 1 or 2 is met in relation to Q and P.

(2) The event is treated for all purposes of this Part of this Act as a relevant defeat in relation to P and the defeated arrangements (whether or not it is also a relevant defeat in relation to Q, and regardless of whether or not P existed at any time when those arrangements were promoted arrangements in relation to Q).

(3) Condition 1 is that—
(*a*) P is not an individual,
(*b*) at a time when the defeated arrangements were promoted arrangements in relation to Q—
(i) P was a relevant body controlled by Q, or
(ii) Q was a relevant body controlled by P, and
(*c*) at the time of the event mentioned in sub-paragraph (1)(*c*)—
(i) Q is a relevant body controlled by P,
(ii) P is a relevant body controlled by Q, or
(iii) P and Q are relevant bodies controlled by a third person.

(4) Condition 2 is that—
(*a*) P and Q are relevant bodies,
(*b*) at a time when the defeated arrangements were promoted arrangements in relation to Q, a third person ("C") controlled Q, and
(*c*) C controls P at the time of the event mentioned in subparagraph (1)(*c*).

(5) For the purposes of sub-paragraphs (3)(*b*) and (4)(*b*), the question whether arrangements are promoted arrangements in relation to Q at any time is to be determined on the assumption that the reference to "design" in paragraph (*b*) of section 235(3) (definition of "promoter" in relation to relevant arrangements) is omitted.][1]

Amendments—[1] Schedule 34A inserted by FA 2016 s 160(1), (5) with effect from 15 September 2016.

[Deemed defeat notices

18 (1) This paragraph applies if—
(*a*) an authorised officer becomes aware at any time ("the relevant time") that a relevant defeat has occurred in relation to a person ("P") who is carrying on a business as a promoter,
(*b*) there have occurred, more than 3 years before the relevant time—
(i) one third party defeat, or
(ii) two third party defeats, and
(*c*) conditions A1 and B1 (in a case within paragraph (*b*)(i)), or conditions A2 and B2 (in a case within paragraph (*b*)(ii)), are met.

(2) Where this paragraph applies by virtue of sub-paragraph (1)(*b*)(i), this Part of this Act has effect as if an authorised officer had (with due authority), at the time of the time of the third party defeat, given P a single defeat notice under section 241A(2) in respect of it.

(3) Where this paragraph applies by virtue of sub-paragraph (1)(*b*)(ii), this Part of this Act has effect as if an authorised officer had (with due authority), at the time of the second of the two third party defeats, given P a double defeat notice under section 241A(3) in respect of the two third party defeats.

(4) Section 241A(8) has no effect in relation to a notice treated as given as mentioned in sub-paragraph (2) or (3).

(5) Condition A1 is that—
(*a*) a conduct notice or a single or double defeat notice has been given to the other person (see sub-paragraph (9)) in respect of the third party defeat,
(*b*) at the time of the third party defeat an authorised officer would have had power by virtue of paragraph 17 to give P a defeat notice in respect of the third party defeat, had the officer been aware that it was a relevant defeat in relation to P, and
(*c*) so far as the authorised officer mentioned in sub-paragraph (1)(*a*) is aware, the conditions for giving P a defeat notice in respect of the third party defeat have never been met (ignoring this paragraph).

(6) Condition A2 is that—
(*a*) a conduct notice or a single or double defeat notice has been given to the other person (see sub-paragraph (9)) in respect of each, or both, of the third party defeats,

(*b*) at the time of the second third party defeat an authorised officer would have had power by virtue of paragraph 17 to give P a double defeat notice in respect of the third party defeats, had the officer been aware that either of the third party defeats was a relevant defeat in relation to P, and

(*c*) so far as the authorised officer mentioned in sub-paragraph(1)(*a*) is aware, the conditions for giving P a defeat notice in respect of those third party defeats (or either of them) have never been met (ignoring this paragraph).

(7) Condition B1 is that, had an authorised officer given P a defeat notice in respect of the third party defeat at the time of that relevant defeat, that defeat notice would still have effect at the relevant time (see subparagraph (1)).

(8) Condition B2 is that, had an authorised officer given P a defeat notice in respect of the two third party defeats at the time of the second of those relevant defeats, that defeat notice would still have effect at the relevant time.

(9) In this paragraph "third party defeat" means a relevant defeat which has occurred in relation to a person other than P.][1]

Amendments—[1] Schedule 34A inserted by FA 2016 s 160(1), (5) with effect from 15 September 2016.

[Meaning of "relevant body" and "control"

19 (1) In this Part of this Schedule "relevant body" means—

(*a*) a body corporate, or

(*b*) a partnership.

(2) For the purposes of this Part of this Schedule a person controls a body corporate if the person has power to secure that the affairs of the body corporate are conducted in accordance with the person's wishes—

(*a*) by means of the holding of shares or the possession of voting power in relation to the body corporate or any other relevant body,

(*b*) as a result of any powers conferred by the articles of association or other document regulating the body corporate or any other relevant body, or

(*c*) by means of controlling a partnership.

(3) For the purposes of this Part of this Schedule a person controls a partnership if the person is a controlling member or the managing partner of the partnership.

(4) In this paragraph "controlling member" has the same meaning as in Schedule 36 (partnerships).

(5) In this paragraph "managing partner", in relation to a partnership, means the member of the partnership who directs, or is on a day-today level in control of, the management of the business of the partnership.][1]

Amendments—[1] Schedule 34A inserted by FA 2016 s 160(1), (5) with effect from 15 September 2016.

[PART 4

MEETING SECTION 237A CONDITIONS: BODIES CORPORATE AND PARTNERSHIPS

[Relevant bodies controlled etc by other persons treated as meeting section 237A condition

20 (1) A relevant body is treated as meeting a section 237A condition at the section 237A(2) relevant time if any of Conditions A to C is met.

(2) Condition A is that—

(*a*) a person met the section 237A condition at a time when the person was a promoter, and

(*b*) the person controls or has significant influence over the relevant body at the section 237A(2) relevant time.

(3) Condition B is that—

(*a*) a person met the section 237A condition at a time when the person controlled or had significant influence over the relevant body,

(*b*) the relevant body was a promoter at that time, and

(*c*) the person controls or has significant influence over the relevant body at the section 237A(2) relevant time.

(4) Condition C is that—

(*a*) two or more persons together controlled or had significant influence over the relevant body at a time when one of those persons met the section 237A condition,

(*b*) the relevant body was a promoter at that time, and

(*c*) those persons together control or have significant influence over the relevant body at the section 237A(2) relevant time.

(5) Sub-paragraph (1) does not apply where the person referred to in sub-paragraph (2)(*a*), (3)(*a*), or (4)(*a*) as meeting a section 237A condition is an individual.

(6) For the purposes of sub-paragraph (2) it does not matter whether the relevant body existed at the time referred to in sub-paragraph (2)(*a*).][2]][1]

Commentary—*Simon's Taxes* **A7.252A**.

Press releases etc—HMRC TIIN (Budget 2017), "Promoters of Tax Avoidance Schemes—associated and successor entities rules", 8 March 2017 (see *SWTI 2017, Budget Edition*).

Amendments—[1] Schedule 34A inserted by FA 2016 s 160(1), (5) with effect from 15 September 2016.

[2] Paras 20–22 substituted by FA 2017 s 24(2) with effect for the purposes of determining whether a person meets a section 237A condition in a period of three years ending on or after 8 March 2017.

[Persons who control etc a relevant body treated as meeting a section 237A condition

21 (1) If at a time when a person controlled or had significant influence over a relevant body—

(*a*) the relevant body met a section 237A condition, and

(*b*) the relevant body, or another relevant body which the person controlled or had significant influence over, was a promoter,

the person is treated as meeting the section 237A condition at the section 237A(2) relevant time.

(2) It does not matter whether any relevant body referred to sub-paragraph (1) exists at the section 237A(2) relevant time.][1]

Commentary—*Simon's Taxes* **A7.252A**.

Press releases etc—HMRC TIIN (Budget 2017), "Promoters of Tax Avoidance Schemes—associated and successor entities rules", 8 March 2017 (see *SWTI 2017, Budget Edition*).

Amendments—[1] Paras 20–22 substituted by FA 2017 s 24(2) with effect for the purposes of determining whether a person meets a section 237A condition in a period of three years ending on or after 8 March 2017.

[Relevant bodies controlled etc by the same person treated as meeting a section 237A condition

22 (1) If—

(*a*) a person controlled or had significant influence over a relevant body at a time when it met a section 237A condition, and

(*b*) at that time that body, or another relevant body which the person controlled or had significant influence over, was a promoter,

any relevant body which the person controls or has significant influence over at the section 237A(2) relevant time is treated as meeting the section 237A condition at the section 237A(2) relevant time.

(2) If—

(*a*) two or more persons together controlled or had significant influence over a relevant body at a time when it met a section 237A condition, and

(*b*) at that time that body, or another relevant body which those persons together controlled or had significant influence over, was a promoter,

any relevant body which those persons together control or have significant influence over at the section 237A(2) relevant time is treated as meeting the section 237A condition at the section 237A(2) relevant time.

(3) It does not matter whether—

(*a*) a relevant body referred to in sub-paragraph (1)(*a*) or (*b*) or (2)(*a*) or (*b*) exists at the section 237A(2) relevant time, or

(*b*) a relevant body existing at the section 237A(2) relevant time existed at the time referred to in sub-paragraph (1)(*a*) or (2)(*a*).][1]

Commentary—*Simon's Taxes* **A7.252A**.

Press releases etc—HMRC TIIN (Budget 2017), "Promoters of Tax Avoidance Schemes—associated and successor entities rules", 8 March 2017 (see *SWTI 2017, Budget Edition*).

Amendments—[1] Paras 20–22 substituted by FA 2017 s 24(2) with effect for the purposes of determining whether a person meets a section 237A condition in a period of three years ending on or after 8 March 2017.

[Interpretation

23 (1) In this Part of this Schedule—

["control" and "significant influence" have the same meanings as in Part 4 of Schedule 34 (see paragraph 13A(5) to (11));

references to a person being a promoter are to the person carrying on business as a promoter;][2]

"relevant body" has the same meaning as in Part 3 of this Schedule;

"section 237A(2) relevant time" means the time referred to in section 237A(2);

"section 237A condition" means any of the conditions in section 237A(11), (12) and (13).

(2) For the purposes of paragraphs [20 to 22][2], the condition in section 237A(11) (occurrence of 3 relevant defeats in the 3 years ending with the relevant time) is taken to have been met by a person at any time if at least 3 relevant defeats have occurred in relation to the person in the period of 3 years ending with that time.][1]

Commentary—*Simon's Taxes* **A7.252A**.

Press releases etc—HMRC TIIN (Budget 2017), "Promoters of Tax Avoidance Schemes—associated and successor entities rules", 8 March 2017 (see *SWTI 2017, Budget Edition*).

Amendments—[1] Schedule 34A inserted by FA 2016 s 160(1), (5) with effect from 15 September 2016.
[2] In sub-para (1), definition of "control" substituted, and in sub-para (2), words substituted, by FA 2017 s 24(4) with effect for the purposes of determining whether a person meets a section 237A condition in a period of three years ending on or after 8 March 2017.

[PART 5
SUPPLEMENTARY

"Adjustments"

24 In this Schedule "adjustments" means any adjustments, whether by way of an assessment, the modification of an assessment or return, the amendment or disallowance of a claim, the entering into of a contract settlement or otherwise (and references to "making" adjustments accordingly include securing that adjustments are made by entering into a contract settlement).][1]

Amendments—[1] Schedule 34A inserted by FA 2016 s 160(1), (5) with effect from 15 September 2016.

[Meaning of "avoidance-related rule"

25 (1) In this Schedule "avoidance-related rule" means a rule in Category 1 or 2.

(2) A rule is in Category 1 if—

(*a*) it refers (in whatever terms) to the purpose or main purpose or purposes of a transaction, arrangements or any other action or matter, and

(*b*) to whether or not the purpose in question is or involves the avoidance of tax or the obtaining of any advantage in relation to tax (however described).

(3) A rule is also in Category 1 if it refers (in whatever terms) to—

(*a*) expectations as to what are, or may be, the expected benefits of a transaction, arrangements or any other action or matter, and

(*b*) whether or not the avoidance of tax or the obtaining of any advantage in relation to tax (however described) is such a benefit.

For the purposes of paragraph (*b*) it does not matter whether the reference is (for instance) to the "sole or main benefit" or "one of the main benefits" or any other reference to a benefit.

(4) A rule falls within Category 2 if as a result of the rule a person may be treated differently for tax purposes depending on whether or not purposes referred to in the rule (for instance the purposes of an actual or contemplated action or enterprise) are (or are shown to be) commercial purposes.

(5) For example, a rule in the following form would fall within Category 1 and within Category 2—

"Example rule

Section X does not apply to a company in respect of a transaction if the company shows that the transaction meets Condition A or B.

Condition A is that the transaction is effected—

(*a*) for genuine commercial reasons, or

(*b*) in the ordinary course of managing investments.

Condition B is that the avoidance of tax is not the main object or one of the main objects of the transaction."][1]

Amendments—[1] Schedule 34A inserted by FA 2016 s 160(1), (5) with effect from 15 September 2016.

["DOTAS arrangements"

26 (1) For the purposes of this Schedule arrangements are "DOTAS arrangements" at any time if at that time a person—

(*a*) has provided, information in relation to the arrangements under section 308(3), 309 or 310 of FA 2004, or

(*b*) has failed to comply with any of those provisions in relation to the arrangements.

(2) But for the purposes of this Schedule "DOTAS arrangements" does not include arrangements in respect of which HMRC has given notice under section 312(6) of FA 2004 (notice that promoters not under duty to notify client of reference number).

(3) For the purposes of sub-paragraph (1) a person who would be required to provide information under subsection (3) of section 308 of FA 2004—

(*a*) but for the fact that the arrangements implement a proposal in respect of which notice has been given under subsection (1) of that section, or

(*b*) but for subsection (4A), (4C) or (5) of that section,

is treated as providing the information at the end of the period referred to in subsection (3) of that section.][1]

Amendments—[1] Schedule 34A inserted by FA 2016 s 160(1), (5) with effect from 15 September 2016.

NIC

[Disclosable VAT or other indirect tax arrangements"

26A (1) For the purposes of this Schedule arrangements are "disclosable VAT or other indirect tax arrangements" at any time if at that time—

(*a*) the arrangements are disclosable Schedule 11A arrangements, or

(*b*) sub-paragraph (2) applies.

(2) This sub-paragraph applies if a person—

(*a*) has provided information in relation to the arrangements under paragraph 12(1), 17(2) or 18(2) of Schedule 17 to FA 2017, or

(*b*) has failed to comply with any of those provisions in relation to the arrangements.

(3) But for the purposes of this Schedule arrangements in respect of which HMRC have given notice under paragraph 23(6) of that Schedule (notice that promoters not under duty to notify client of reference number) are not to be regarded as disclosable VAT or other indirect tax arrangements.

(4) For the purposes of sub-paragraph (2) a person who would be required to provide information under paragraph 12(1) of that Schedule—

(*a*) but for the fact that the arrangements implement a proposal in respect of which notice has been given under paragraph 11(1) of that Schedule, or

(*b*) but for paragraph 13, 14 or 15 of that Schedule,

is treated as providing the information at the end of the period referred to in paragraph 12(1).][1]

Amendments—[1] Paragraph 26A inserted by F(No 2)A 2017 s 66, Sch 17 paras 52, 54(1), (4) with effect from 1 January 2018.

[“Disclosable [Schedule 11A] VAT arrangements”

27 For the purposes of [paragraph 26A][2] arrangements are "disclosable [Schedule 11A][2] VAT arrangements" at any time if at that time—

(*a*) a person has complied with paragraph 6 of Schedule 11A to VATA 1994 in relation to the arrangements (duty to notify Commissioners),

(*b*) a person under a duty to comply with that paragraph in relation to the arrangements has failed to do so, or

(*c*) a reference number has been allocated to the scheme under paragraph 9 of that Schedule (voluntary notification of avoidance scheme which is not a designated scheme).][1]

Amendments—[1] Schedule 34A inserted by FA 2016 s 160(1), (5) with effect from 15 September 2016.

[2] In heading, words inserted, and in opening words, words inserted and words substituted for words "this Schedule", by F(No 2)A 2017 s 66, Sch 17 paras 52, 54(1), (5), (6) with effect from 1 January 2018.

[Paragraphs 26 [to 27]: supplementary

28 (1) A person "fails to comply" with any provision mentioned in paragraph 26(1)(*a*) [26A(2)(*a*)][2] or 27(*b*) if and only if any of the conditions in subparagraphs (2) to (4) is met.

(2) The condition in this sub-paragraph is that—

(*a*) the tribunal has determined that the person has failed to comply with the provision concerned,

(*b*) the appeal period has ended, and

(*c*) the determination has not been overturned on appeal.

(3) The condition in this sub-paragraph is that—

(*a*) the tribunal has determined for the purposes of section 118(2) of TMA 1970 that the person is to be deemed not to have failed to comply with the provision concerned as the person had a reasonable excuse for not doing the thing required to be done,

(*b*) the appeal period has ended, and

(*c*) the determination has not been overturned on appeal.

(4) The condition in this sub-paragraph is that the person admitted in writing to HMRC that the person has failed to comply with the provision concerned.

(5) In this paragraph "the appeal period" means—

(*a*) the period during which an appeal could be brought against the determination of the tribunal, or

(*b*) where an appeal mentioned in paragraph (*a*) has been brought, the period during which that appeal has not been finally determined, withdrawn or otherwise disposed of.][1]

Amendments—[1] Schedule 34A inserted by FA 2016 s 160(1), (5) with effect from 15 September 2016.

[2] In heading, words substituted for words "and 27", and in sub-para (1), words inserted, by F(No 2)A 2017 s 66, Sch 17 paras 52, 54(1), (7), (8) with effect from 1 January 2018.

["Final" counteraction

29 For the purposes of this Schedule the counteraction of a tax advantage or of arrangements is "final" when the assessment or adjustments made to effect the counteraction, and any amounts arising as a result of the assessment or adjustments, can no longer be varied, on appeal or otherwise.][1]

Amendments—[1] Schedule 34A inserted by FA 2016 s 160(1), (5) with effect from 15 September 2016.

[Inheritance tax, stamp duty reserve tax, VAT and petroleum revenue tax

30 (1) In this Schedule, in relation to inheritance tax, each of the following is treated as a return—

(*a*) an account delivered by a person under section 216 or 217 of IHTA 1984 (including an account delivered in accordance with regulations under section 256 of that Act);

(*b*) a statement or declaration which amends or is otherwise connected with such an account produced by the person who delivered the account;

(*c*) information or a document provided by a person in accordance with regulations under section 256 of that Act;

and such a return is treated as made by the person in question.

(2) In this Schedule references to an assessment to tax, in relation to inheritance tax, stamp duty reserve tax and petroleum revenue tax, include a determination.

(3) In this Schedule an expression used in relation to VAT has the same meaning as in VATA 1994.][1]

Amendments—[1] Schedule 34A inserted by FA 2016 s 160(1), (5) with effect from 15 September 2016.

[Power to amend

31 (1) The Treasury may by regulations amend this Schedule (apart from this paragraph).

(2) An amendment by virtue of sub-paragraph (1) may, in particular, add, vary or remove conditions or categories (or otherwise vary the meaning of "avoidance-related rule").

(3) Regulations under sub-paragraph (1) may include any amendment of this Part of this Act that is appropriate in consequence of an amendment made by virtue of sub-paragraph (1).][1]

Amendments—[1] Schedule 34A inserted by FA 2016 s 160(1), (5) with effect from 15 September 2016.

NIC

SCHEDULE 35

PROMOTERS OF TAX AVOIDANCE SCHEMES: PENALTIES

Section 274

Commentary—*Simon's Taxes* **A7.264**.

Introduction

1 In this Schedule a reference to an "information duty" is to a duty arising under any of the following provisions to provide information or produce a document—

(a) section 255 (duty to provide information or produce document);

(b) section 257 (ongoing duty to provide information);

(c) section 258 (duty of person dealing with non-resident promoter);

(d) section 259 (monitored promoter: duty to provide information about clients);

(e) section 260 (intermediaries: duty to provide information about clients);

(f) section 261 (duty to provide information about clients following enquiry);

(g) section 262 (information required for monitoring compliance with conduct notice);

(h) section 263 (information about monitored promoter's address).

Penalties for failure to comply

2 (1) A person who fails to comply with a duty imposed by or under this Part mentioned in column 1 of the Table is liable to a penalty not exceeding the amount shown in relation to that provision in column 2 of the Table.

Table

Column 1 *Provision*	*Column 2* *Maximum penalty (£)*
Section 249(1) (duty to notify clients of monitoring notice)	5,000
Section 249(3) (duty to publicise monitoring notice)	1,000,000
Section 249(10) (duty to include information on correspondence etc)	1,000,000
Section 251 (duty of promoter to notify clients and intermediaries of reference number)	5,000
Section 252 (duty of those notified to notify others of promoter's number)	5,000

Section 253 (duty to notify HMRC of reference number)	the relevant amount (see sub-paragraph (3))
Section 255 (duty to provide information or produce document)	1,000,000
Section 257 (ongoing duty to provide information or produce document)	1,000,000
Section 258 (duty of person dealing with non-resident promoter)	1,000,000
Section 259 (monitored promoter: duty to provide information about clients)	5,000
Section 260 (intermediaries: duty to provide information about clients)	5,000
Section 261 (duty to provide information about clients following an enquiry)	10,000
Section 262 (duty to provide information required to monitor compliance with conduct notice)	5,000
Section 263 (duty to provide information about address)	5,000
Section 265 (duty to provide information to promoter)	5,000

(2) In relation to a failure to comply with section 249(1), 251, 252, 259 or 260 the maximum penalty specified in column 2 of the Table is a maximum penalty which may be imposed in respect of each person to whom the failure relates.

(3) In relation to a failure to comply with section 253, the "relevant amount" is—

(a) £5,000, unless paragraph (b) or (c) applies;

(b) £7,500, where a person has previously failed to comply with section 253 on one (and only one) occasion during the period of 36 months ending with the date on which the current failure occurred;

(c) £10,000, where a person has previously failed to comply with section 253 on two or more occasions during the period mentioned in paragraph (b).

(4) The amount of a penalty imposed under sub-paragraph (1) is to be arrived at after taking account of all relevant considerations, including the desirability of setting it at a level which appears appropriate for deterring the person, or other persons, from similar failures to comply on future occasions having regard (in particular)—

(a) in the case of a penalty imposed for a failure to comply with section 255 or 257, to the amount of fees received, or likely to have been received, by the person in connection with the monitored proposal, arrangements implementing the monitored proposal or monitored arrangements to which the information or document required as a result of section 255 or 257 relates,

(b) in the case of a penalty imposed in relation to a failure to comply with section 258(4) or (5), to the amount of any tax advantage gained, or sought to be gained, by the person in relation to the monitored arrangements or the arrangements implementing the monitored proposal.

Daily default penalties for failure to comply

3 (1) If the failure to comply with an information duty continues after a penalty is imposed under paragraph 2(1), the person is liable to a further penalty or penalties not exceeding the relevant sum for each day on which the failure continues after the day on which the penalty under paragraph 2(1) was imposed.

(2) In sub-paragraph (1) "the relevant sum" means—

(a) £10,000, in a case where the maximum penalty which could have been imposed for the failure was £1,000,000;

(b) £600, in cases not falling within paragraph (a).

Penalties for inaccurate information and documents

4 (1) If—

(a) in complying with an information duty, a person provides inaccurate information or produces a document that contains an inaccuracy, and

(b) condition A, B or C is met,

the person is liable to a penalty not exceeding the relevant sum.

(2) Condition A is that the inaccuracy is careless or deliberate.

(3) An inaccuracy is careless if it is due to a failure by the person to take reasonable care.

(4) For the purpose of determining whether or not a person who is a monitored promoter took reasonable care, reliance on legal advice is to be disregarded if either—

- (a) the advice was not based on a full and accurate description of the facts, or
- (b) the conclusions in the advice that the person relied on were unreasonable.

(5) For the purpose of determining whether or not a person who complies with a duty under section 258 took reasonable care, reliance on legal advice is to be disregarded if the advice was given or procured by the monitored promoter mentioned in subsection (1) of that section.

(6) Condition B is that the person knows of the inaccuracy at the time the information is provided or the document produced but does not inform HMRC at that time.

(7) Condition C is that the person—

- (a) discovers the inaccuracy some time later, and
- (b) fails to take reasonable steps to inform HMRC.

(8) The "relevant sum" means—

- (a) £1,000,000, where the information is provided or document produced in compliance with a duty under section 255, 257 or 258;
- (b) £10,000, where the information is provided in compliance with a duty under section 261;
- (c) £5,000, where the information is provided or document produced in compliance with a duty under section 259, 260, 262 or 263.

(9) If the information or document contains more than one inaccuracy, one penalty is payable under this paragraph whatever the number of inaccuracies.

Power to change amount of penalties

5 (1) If it appears to the Treasury that there has been a change in the value of money since the last relevant date, they may by regulations substitute for the sums for the time being specified in paragraph 2, 3 or 4 such other sums as appear to them to be justified by the change.

(2) Regulations under sub-paragraph (1) may include any amendment of paragraph 10(b) that is appropriate in consequence of an amendment made by virtue of sub-paragraph (1).

(3) The "relevant date", in relation to a specified sum, means—

- (a) the date on which this Act is passed, and
- (b) each date on which the power conferred by sub-paragraph (1) has been exercised in relation to that sum.

Concealing, destroying etc documents following imposition of a duty to provide information

6 (1) A person must not conceal, destroy or otherwise dispose of, or arrange for the concealment, destruction or disposal of, a document which is subject to a duty under section 255, 257 or 262.

(2) Sub-paragraph (1) does not apply if the person acts after the document has been produced to an officer of Revenue and Customs in accordance with the duty, unless the officer has notified the person in writing that the document must continue to be available for inspection (and has not withdrawn the notification).

(3) Sub-paragraph (1) does not apply, in a case to which section 268(1) applies, if the person acts after the expiry of the period of 6 months beginning with the day on which a copy of the document was produced in accordance with that section unless, before the expiry of that period, an officer of Revenue and Customs makes a request for the original document under section 268(2)(b).

(4) A person who conceals, destroys or otherwise disposes of, or arranges for the concealment, destruction or disposal of, a document in breach of sub-paragraph (1), is taken to have failed to comply with the duty to produce the document under the provision concerned (but see sub-paragraph (5)).

(5) If a person conceals, destroys or otherwise disposes of, or arranges for the concealment, destruction or disposal of, a document which is subject to a duty under more than one of the provisions mentioned in sub-paragraph (1) then—

- (a) in a case where a duty under section 255 applies, the person will be taken to have failed to comply only with that provision, or
- (b) in a case where a duty under section 255 does not apply, the person will be taken to have failed to comply only with section 257.

Concealing, destroying etc documents following informal notification

7 (1) A person must not conceal, destroy or otherwise dispose of, or arrange for the concealment, destruction or disposal of, a document if an officer of Revenue and Customs has informed the person in writing that the person is, or is likely, to be given a notice under 255, 257 or 262 the effect of which will, or is likely to, require the production of the document.

(2) Sub-paragraph (1) does not apply if the person acts—

- (a) at least 6 months after the person was, or was last, informed as described in sub-paragraph (1), or

NIC

(b) after the person becomes subject to a duty under 255, 257 or 262 which requires the document to be produced.

(3) A person who conceals, destroys or otherwise disposes of, or arranges for the concealment, destruction or disposal of, a document in breach of sub-paragraph (1), is taken to have failed to comply with the duty to produce the document under the provision concerned (but see sub-paragraph (4)).

(4) If a person conceals, destroys or otherwise disposes of, or arranges for the concealment, destruction or disposal of, a document which is subject to a duty under more than one of the provisions mentioned in sub-paragraph (1) then—

(a) in a case where a duty under section 255 applies, the person will be taken to have failed to comply only with that provision, or

(b) in a case where a duty under section 255 does not apply, the person will be taken to have failed to comply only with section 257.

Failure to comply with time limit

8 A failure to do anything required to be done within a limited period of time does not give rise to liability to a penalty under this Schedule if the person did it within such further time, if any, as an officer of Revenue and Customs or the tribunal may have allowed.

Reasonable excuse

9 (1) Liability to a penalty under this Schedule does not arise if there is a reasonable excuse for the failure.

(2) For the purposes of this paragraph—

(a) an insufficiency of funds is not a reasonable excuse unless attributable to events outside the person's control,

(b) if the person relies on any other person to do anything, that is not a reasonable excuse unless the first person took reasonable care to avoid the failure,

(c) if the person had a reasonable excuse for the failure but the excuse has ceased, the person is to be treated as having continued to have the excuse if the failure is remedied without unreasonable delay after the excuse ceased,

(d) reliance on legal advice is to be taken automatically not to constitute a reasonable excuse where the person is a monitored promoter if either—

(i) the advice was not based on a full and accurate description of the facts, or

(ii) the conclusions in the advice that the person relied on were unreasonable, and

(e) reliance on legal advice is to be taken automatically not to constitute a reasonable excuse in the case of a penalty for failure to comply with section 258, if the advice was given or procured by the monitored promoter mentioned in subsection (1) of that section.

Assessment of penalty and appeals

10 Part 10 of TMA 1970 (penalties, etc) has effect as if—

(a) the reference in section 100(1) to the Taxes Acts were read as a reference to the Taxes Acts and this Schedule,

(b) in subsection (2) of section 100, there were inserted a reference to a penalty under this Schedule, other than a penalty under paragraph 3 of this Schedule in respect of which the relevant sum is £600.

Interest on penalties

11 (1) A penalty under this Schedule is to carry interest at the rate applicable under section 178 of FA 1989 from the date it is determined until payment.

(2) (*inserts* FA 1989 s 178(2)(u))

Double jeopardy

12 A person is not liable to a penalty under this Schedule in respect of anything in respect of which the person has been convicted of an offence.

Overlapping penalties

13 A person is not liable to a penalty under—

(a) Schedule 24 to the FA 2007 (penalties for errors),

(b) Part 7 of FA 2004, or

(c) any other provision which is prescribed,

by reason of any failure to include in any return or account a reference number required by section 253.

SCHEDULE 36

PROMOTERS OF TAX AVOIDANCE SCHEMES: PARTNERSHIPS

Section 281

Commentary—*Simon's Taxes* **A7.259**.

PART 1

PARTNERSHIPS AS PERSONS

"Person" includes a partnership

1 (1) Persons carrying on a business in partnership—

(a) are regarded as a person for the purposes of this Part of this Act;

(b) are referred to in this Part as a "partnership".

(2) But in this Part of this Act "partnership" does not include a body of persons forming a legal person that is distinct from themselves (and paragraphs 2 to 21 may accordingly be disregarded in applying this Part of this Act to such a body of persons).

(3) In the references in this Part to carrying on a business in partnership, "partnership" has the same meaning as in the Partnership Act 1890.

Continuity of partnerships

2 A partnership is regarded for the purposes of this Part of this Act as continuing to be the same partnership (and the same person) regardless of a change in membership, provided that a person who was a member before the change remains a member after the change.

Meeting of conditions

3 (1) Accordingly, for the purposes of this Part of this Act a partnership is taken—

(a) to have done any act that bound the members, and

(b) to have failed to comply with any obligation of the firm which the members failed to comply with;

but see sub-paragraph (3).

(2) In sub-paragraph (1), "the members" means those who were the members of the partnership or (in the case of a limited partnership) the general partners of the partnership at the time when the act was done or the failure to comply occurred.

(3) Where a member of a partnership ("M") has done, or failed to do, an act at any time ("the earlier time"), the partnership is not treated at any later time as having done, or failed to do, that act unless—

(a) M, or

(b) another person who was a member of the partnership at the earlier time,

is a member of the partnership at the later time.

(4) In this paragraph "firm" has the same meaning as in the Partnership Act 1890.

4 . . .

Commentary—*Simon's Taxes* **A7.259** .

Amendments—Paragraph 4 and preceding crosshead repealed by FA 2015 s 119, Sch 19 para 5(*a*) with effect for the purposes of determining whether a person meets a threshold condition in a period of three years ending on or after 26 March 2015.

PART 2

CONDUCT NOTICES AND MONITORING NOTICES

[Defeat notices

4A A defeat notice that is given to a partnership must state that it is a partnership defeat notice.][1]

Amendments—[1] Paragraph 4A inserted by FA 2016 s 160(10), (11) with effect from 15 September 2016.

Conduct notices

5 (1) A conduct notice that is given to a partnership must state that it is a partnership conduct notice.

(2) In accordance with paragraphs 1 and 2, where the person to whom a conduct notice is given is a partnership, section 238 authorises the imposition of conditions relating to—

(a) the persons who are members of the partnership when the conduct notice is given, and

(b) any person who becomes a member of the partnership after the conduct notice is given.

Monitoring notices

6 A monitoring notice that is given to a partnership must state that it is a partnership monitoring notice.

Person continuing to carry on partnership business as a sole trader

7 (1) This paragraph applies where—

(a) a person or persons have ceased to be members of a partnership,

(b) immediately before the cessation, a [defeat notice,][1] conduct notice or monitoring notice had effect in relation to the partnership, and

(c) immediately after the cessation, a person who was a member of the partnership immediately before the cessation is carrying on the business of the partnership, but not in partnership.

(2) Where this paragraph applies, the [defeat notice,][1] conduct notice or monitoring notice continues (despite paragraphs 1 and 2) to have effect in relation to the person mentioned in sub-paragraph (1)(c) (but, in relation to times when the business is not being carried on in partnership, the notice is not regarded for the purposes of this Part of this Act as a notice that has been given to a partnership.)

Amendments—[1] In sub-paras (1)(*b*), (2), words inserted by FA 2016 s 160(10), (12), (13) with effect from 15 September 2016.

[Persons leaving partnership: defeat notices

7A (1) Sub-paragraphs (2) and (3) apply where—

(*a*) a person ("P") who was a controlling member of a partnership at the time when a defeat notice ("the original notice") was given to the partnership has ceased to be a member of the partnership,

(*b*) the defeat notice had effect in relation to the partnership at the time of that cessation, and

(*c*) P is carrying on a business as a promoter.

(2) An authorised officer may give P a defeat notice.

(3) If P is carrying on a business as a promoter in partnership with one or more other persons and is a controlling member of that partnership ("the new partnership"), an authorised officer may give a defeat notice to the new partnership.

(4) A defeat notice given under sub-paragraph (3) ceases to have effect if P ceases to be a member of the new partnership.

(5) A notice under sub-paragraph (2) or (3) may not be given after the original notice has ceased to have effect.

(6) A defeat notice given under sub-paragraph (2) or (3) is given in respect of the relevant defeat or relevant defeats to which the original notice relates.][1]

Amendments—[1] Paragraph 7A inserted by FA 2016 s 160(10), (14) with effect from 15 September 2016.

Persons leaving a partnership: conduct notices

8 (1) Sub-paragraphs (2) and (3) apply where—

(a) a person ("P") who was a controlling member of a partnership at the time when a conduct notice ("the original notice") was given to the partnership has ceased to be a member of the partnership,

(b) the conduct notice had effect in relation to the partnership at the time of that cessation, and

(c) P is carrying on a business as a promoter.

(2) An authorised officer may give P a conduct notice.

(3) If P is carrying on a business as a promoter in partnership with one or more other persons and is a controlling member of that partnership ("the new partnership"), an authorised officer may give a conduct notice to the new partnership.

(4) A conduct notice given under sub-paragraph (3) ceases to have effect if P ceases to be a member of the new partnership.

(5) A notice under sub-paragraph (2) or (3) may not be given after the termination date of the original notice (under section 241(2)(a) or (b)).

Persons leaving a partnership: monitoring notices

9 (1) Sub-paragraphs (2) and (3) apply where—

(a) a person ("P") who was a controlling member of a partnership at the time when a monitoring notice was given to the partnership has ceased to be a member of the partnership,

(b) the monitoring notice had effect in relation to the partnership at the time of that cessation, and

(c) P is carrying on a business as a promoter.

(2) An authorised officer may give P a monitoring notice.

(3) If P is carrying on a business as a promoter in partnership with one or more other persons, and is a controlling member of that partnership ("the new partnership"), an authorised officer may give a monitoring notice to the new partnership.

(4) A monitoring notice given under sub-paragraph (3) ceases to have effect if P ceases to be a member of the new partnership.

Cross-references—See FA 2014 s 244(2), (3) (monitoring notice given under Sch 36 para 9 or 10 must explain the effect of the notice, the date of the notice, the date from which it takes effect, the name of the partnership to which it was given, and inform the recipient of the right to request withdrawal under s 245).

Division of partnership business

10 (1) This paragraph applies if—

(a) a person ("a departing partner") who has been carrying on a business in partnership ceases to carry on the business in partnership,

(b) a [defeat notice, conduct notice or][1] monitoring notice had effect in relation to the partnership immediately before the departing partner ceased to carry on the business in partnership, and

(c) the departing partner is continuing to carry on part (but not the whole) of the business ("the transferred part").

(2) The notice mentioned in sub-paragraph (1)(b) is referred to in this paragraph as "the original notice".

(3) An authorised officer may give the departing partner—

[(za) a defeat notice (if the original notice is a defeat notice);][1]

(a) a conduct notice (if the original notice is a conduct notice);

(b) a monitoring notice (if the original notice is a monitoring notice).

(4) If the departing partner is itself carrying on the transferred part of the business in partnership, the authorised officer may give that partnership ("the new partnership")—

[(za) a defeat notice (if the original notice is a defeat notice);][1]

(a) a conduct notice (if the original notice is a conduct notice);

(b) a monitoring notice (if the original notice is a monitoring notice).

(5) A notice given under sub-paragraph (4) ceases to have effect if the departing partner ceases to be a member of the new partnership.

[(5A) A notice under sub-paragraph (3)(za) or (4)(za) may not be given after the end of the look-forward period of the original notice.][1]

(6) A notice given under sub-paragraph (3)(a) or (4)(a) may not be given after the termination date of the original notice (under section 241(2)(a) or (b)).

(7) It does not matter whether one, some or all of the persons who were carrying on the business in partnership are departing partners by virtue of sub-paragraph (1).

Cross-references—See FA 2014 s 244(2), (3) (monitoring notice given under Sch 36 para 9 or 10 must explain the effect of the notice, the date of the notice, the date from which it takes effect, the name of the partnership to which it was given, and inform the recipient of the right to request withdrawal under s 245).

Amendments—[1] In sub-para (1)(*b*), words substituted for words "conduct notice or a", and sub-paras (3)(*za*), (4)(*za*), (5A) inserted, by FA 2016 s 160(10), (15) with effect from 15 September 2016.

Notices under paragraphs 8 to 10: general

11 (1) In this Part of this Act—

"replacement conduct notice" means a notice under paragraph 8(2) or (3) or 10(3)(a) or (4)(a);

"replacement monitoring notice" means a notice given under paragraph 9(2) or (3) or 10(3)(b) or (4)(b).

(2) In this Part of this Act, "the original monitoring notice" means—

(a) in relation to a replacement monitoring notice given under paragraph 9(2), the monitoring notice mentioned in paragraph 9(1), and

(b) in relation to a replacement monitoring notice given under paragraph 10(3)(b) or (4)(b), the monitoring notice mentioned in paragraph 10(2),

and that original monitoring notice is also the "original monitoring notice" in relation to any monitoring notice that (under paragraph 9(2) or (3) or 10(3)(b) or (4)(b)) replaces a replacement monitoring notice.

[11A The look-forward period for a notice under paragraph 7A(2) or (3) or 10(3)(za) or (4)(za)—

(a) begins on the day after the day on which the notice is given, and

(b) continues to the end of the look-forward period for the original notice (as defined in paragraph 7A(1)(a) or 10(2), as the case may be).][1]

Amendments—[1] Paragraph 11A inserted by FA 2016 s 160(10), (16) with effect from 15 September 2016.

12 A notice under paragraph 8(2) or (3) or 10(3)(a) or (4)(a)—

(a) has no effect after the termination date of the original notice;

(b) must state that that date is its termination date.

13 An authorised officer may not give a replacement conduct notice or replacement monitoring notice to a person if a conduct notice or monitoring notice previously given to the person still has effect in relation to the person.

Publication under section 248

14 Where the monitored promoter referred to in section 248(2) is a partnership, paragraphs (a), (b) and (d) of that subsection are to be read as referring to details of the partnership (for instance, the name under which the business of the partnership is carried on), not to details of particular partners.

PART 3
RESPONSIBILITY OF PARTNERS

Responsibility of partners

15 (1) A notice given to a partnership under this Part of this Act has effect, at any time, in relation to the persons who are members of the partnership at that time ("the responsible partners").

(2) Sub-paragraph (1) does not affect any liability of a person who has ceased to be a member of a partnership in respect of things that the responsible partners did or failed to do before that person ceased to be a member of the partnership.

(3) Anything required to be done by the responsible partners under or by virtue of a provision of this Part of this Act is required to be done by all the responsible partners (but see paragraph 18).

(4) In relation to any right (such as a right of appeal) conferred by this Part of this Act references to a person have the meaning that is appropriate in consequence of sub-paragraphs (1) to (3).

Joint and several liability of responsible partners

16 (1) Where the responsible partners are liable to a penalty under this Part of this Act, or to interest on such a penalty, their liability is joint and several.

(2) No amount may be recovered under sub-paragraph (1) from a person who did not become a responsible partner until after the relevant time.

(3) "The relevant time" means—

(a) in relation to so much of the penalty as is payable in respect of any day, or to interest on so much of a penalty as is so payable, the beginning of that day;

(b) in relation to any other penalty, or interest on such a penalty, the time when the act or omission occurred that caused the penalty to become payable.

Service of notices

17 (1) Any notice given to a partnership by an officer of Revenue and Customs under this Part of this Act must be served either—

(a) on all the persons who are members of the partnership when the notice is given, or

(b) on a representative partner.

(2) "Representative partner" means—

(a) a nominated partner, or

(b) if no partner has been nominated under paragraph 18(2), a partner designated by an authorised officer as a representative partner.

(3) A designation under sub-paragraph (2), or the revocation of such a designation, has effect only when notice of the designation, or revocation, has been given to the partnership by an authorised officer.

Nominated partners

18 (1) Anything required to be done by the responsible partners under this Part of this Act may instead be done by any nominated partner.

(2) "Nominated partner" means a partner nominated by a majority of the partners to act as the representative of the partnership for the purposes of this Part of this Act.

(3) A nomination under sub-paragraph (2), or the revocation of such a nomination, has effect only after notice of the nomination, or revocation, has been given to an authorised officer.

PART 4
INTERPRETATION

Meaning of "controlling member"

19 (1) For the purposes of this Schedule a person ("P") is a "controlling member" of a partnership at any time when the person has a right to a share of more than half the assets, or of more than half the income, of the partnership.
(2) For that purpose there are to be attributed to P any interests or rights of—
(a) any individual who is connected with P (if P is an individual), and
(b) any body corporate that P controls.
(3) An individual is "connected" with P if the individual is—
(a) P's spouse or civil partner;
(b) a relative of P;
(c) the spouse or civil partner of a relative of P;
(d) a relative of P's spouse or civil partner, or
(e) the spouse or civil partner of a relative of P's spouse or civil partner.
(4) In sub-paragraph (3) "relative" means brother, sister, ancestor or lineal descendant.
(5) P controls a body corporate ("B") if P has power to secure—
(a) by means of the holding of shares or the possession of voting power in relation to B or any other body corporate, or
(b) as a result of any powers conferred by the articles of association or other document regulating that or any other body corporate,
that the affairs of B are conducted in accordance with P's wishes.

. . .

20 . . .

Amendments—Paragraph 20 and preceding crosshead repealed by FA 2015 s 119, Sch 19 para 5(*b*) with effect for the purposes of determining whether a person meets a threshold condition in a period of three years ending on or after 26 March 2015.

Power to amend definitions

21 (1) The Treasury may by regulations amend paragraph 19 . . . [1].
(2) Regulations under sub-paragraph (1) may include any amendment of this Schedule that is necessary in consequence of any amendment made by virtue of sub-paragraph (1).

Amendments—[1] Words in sub-para (1) repealed by FA 2015 s 119, Sch 19 para 5(*c*) with effect for the purposes of determining whether a person meets a threshold condition in a period of three years ending on or after 26 March 2015.

NATIONAL INSURANCE CONTRIBUTIONS ACT 2015

(2015 Chapter 5)

An Act to make provision in relation to national insurance contributions; and for connected purposes.

[12 February 2015]

CONTENTS

Secondary Class 1 contributions: apprentices under 25

1 Zero-rate secondary Class 1 contributions for apprentices under 25

(1) SSCBA 1992 is amended as follows.

(2) In section 9 (calculation of secondary Class 1 contributions), in subsection (1A), after paragraph (a) insert—

"(aa) if section 9B below (zero-rate secondary Class 1 contributions for certain apprentices) applies to the earnings, 0%;".

(3) In section 9A (the age-related secondary percentage), after subsection (1) insert—

"(1A) But this section does not apply to those earnings so far as section 9B below (zero-rate secondary Class 1 contributions for certain apprentices) applies to them."

(4) After section 9A insert—

"9B Zero-rate secondary Class 1 contributions for certain apprentices

(1) Where a secondary Class 1 contribution is payable as mentioned in section 6(1)(b) above, this section applies to the earnings paid in the tax week, in respect of the employment in question, if the earner is a relevant apprentice in relation to that employment.

(2) An earner is a "relevant apprentice", in relation to an employment, if the earner—

(a) is aged under 25, and

(b) is employed, in the employment, as an apprentice.

(3) For the purposes of this Act a person is still to be regarded as being liable to pay a secondary Class 1 contribution even if the amount of the contribution is £0 because this section applies to the earnings in question.

(4) The Treasury may by regulations provide that, in relation to relevant apprentices, there is to be for every tax year an upper secondary threshold for secondary Class 1 contributions.

That threshold is to be the amount specified for that year by regulations made by the Treasury.

(5) Subsections (4) and (5) of section 5 above (which confer power to prescribe an equivalent of a secondary threshold in relation to earners paid otherwise than weekly), and subsection (6) of that section as it applies for the purposes of those subsections, apply for the purposes of an upper secondary threshold in relation to relevant apprentices as they apply for the purposes of a secondary threshold.

(6) Subsection (7) applies if—

(a) a secondary Class 1 contribution is payable as mentioned in section 6(1)(b) above,

(b) the earnings paid in the tax week, in respect of the employment in question, exceed the current upper secondary threshold (or the prescribed equivalent) in relation to relevant apprentices, and

(c) the earner is a relevant apprentice in relation to the employment.

(7) This section does not apply to those earnings so far as they exceed that threshold (or the prescribed equivalent) ("the excess earnings") and, accordingly, for the purposes of section 9(1) above the relevant percentage in respect of the excess earnings is the secondary percentage.

(8) But the Treasury may by regulations modify the effect of subsection (7) in a case in which the earner falls within an age group specified in column 1 of the table in section 9A(3) above.

(9) In subsection (2)(b) "apprentice" has such meaning as the Treasury may prescribe.

(10) The Treasury may by regulations amend subsection (2)(a) so as to alter the age that an earner must be in order to be a relevant apprentice (and regulations under this subsection may have the effect of allowing anyone who is of an age at which secondary Class 1 contributions are payable to be a relevant apprentice)."

(5) In section 176(1)(a) (regulations subject to affirmative procedure), after "section 9A(7);" insert—
"section 9B(4), (8) or (10);".

(6) SSCB(NI)A 1992 is amended as follows.

(7) In section 9 (calculation of secondary Class 1 contributions), in subsection (1A), after paragraph (a) insert—

"(aa) if section 9B below (zero-rate secondary Class 1 contributions for certain apprentices) applies to the earnings, 0%;".

(8) In section 9A (the age-related secondary percentage), after subsection (1) insert—

"(1A) But this section does not apply to those earnings so far as section 9B below (zero-rate secondary Class 1 contributions for certain apprentices) applies to them."

(9) After section 9A insert—

"9B Zero-rate secondary Class 1 contributions for certain apprentices

(1) Where a secondary Class 1 contribution is payable as mentioned in section 6(1)(b) above, this section applies to the earnings paid in the tax week, in respect of the employment in question, if the earner is a relevant apprentice in relation to that employment.

(2) An earner is a "relevant apprentice", in relation to an employment, if the earner—

(a) is aged under 25, and

(b) is employed, in the employment, as an apprentice.

(3) For the purposes of this Act a person is still to be regarded as being liable to pay a secondary Class 1 contribution even if the amount of the contribution is £0 because this section applies to the earnings in question.

(4) The Treasury may by regulations provide that, in relation to relevant apprentices, there is to be for every tax year an upper secondary threshold for secondary Class 1 contributions.

That threshold is to be the amount specified for that year by regulations made by the Treasury.

(5) Subsections (4) and (5) of section 5 above (which confer power to prescribe an equivalent of a secondary threshold in relation to earners paid otherwise than weekly), and subsection (6) of that section as it applies for the purposes of those subsections, apply for the purposes of an upper secondary threshold in relation to relevant apprentices as they apply for the purposes of a secondary threshold.

(6) Subsection (7) applies if—

(a) a secondary Class 1 contribution is payable as mentioned in section 6(1)(b) above,

(b) the earnings paid in the tax week, in respect of the employment in question, exceed the current upper secondary threshold (or the prescribed equivalent) in relation to relevant apprentices, and

(c) the earner is a relevant apprentice in relation to the employment.

(7) This section does not apply to those earnings so far as they exceed that threshold (or the prescribed equivalent) ("the excess earnings") and, accordingly, for the purposes of section 9(1) above the relevant percentage in respect of the excess earnings is the secondary percentage.

(8) But the Treasury may by regulations modify the effect of subsection (7) in a case in which the earner falls within an age group specified in column 1 of the table in section 9A(3) above.

(9) In subsection (2)(b) "apprentice" has such meaning as the Treasury may prescribe.

(10) The Treasury may by regulations amend subsection (2)(a) so as to alter the age that an earner must be in order to be a relevant apprentice (and regulations under this subsection may have the effect of allowing anyone who is of an age at which secondary Class 1 contributions are payable to be a relevant apprentice)."

(10) In section 172(11A) (regulations subject to affirmative procedure), after "9A(7)," insert "section 9B(4), (8) or (10),".

(11) The amendments made by this section come into force—

(a) for the purposes of making regulations under section 9B of SSCBA 1992 or section 9B of SSCB(NI)A 1992, at the end of the period of 2 months beginning with the day on which this Act is passed, and

(b) for remaining purposes, on 6 April 2016.

Class 2 contributions

2 Reform of Class 2 contributions

Schedule 1 contains provision relating to Class 2 national insurance contributions.

3 Consequential etc power

(1) The Treasury may by regulations make consequential, incidental or supplementary provision in connection with the provision made in Schedule 1.

(2) Regulations under this section may modify any provision of an Act or an instrument made under an Act.

(3) In subsection (2) "modify" includes amend, repeal or revoke.

(4) Section 175(3) to (5) of SSCBA 1992 (various supplementary powers) applies to the power to make regulations conferred by this section.

(5) Regulations under this section must be made by statutory instrument.

(6) A statutory instrument containing (with or without other provision) regulations under this section that amend or repeal a provision of an Act may not be made unless a draft of the instrument has been laid before, and approved by a resolution of, each House of Parliament.

NIC

(7) A statutory instrument containing regulations under this section that does not have to be approved in draft under subsection (6) is subject to annulment in pursuance of a resolution of either House of Parliament.

Regulations—Social Security (Miscellaneous Amendments No 2) Regulations, SI 2015/478.

Follower notices, accelerated payments and promoters of avoidance

4 Application of Parts 4 and 5 of FA 2014 to national insurance contributions

(1) Part 1 of Schedule 2 applies Part 4 of FA 2014 (follower notices and accelerated payments) to Class 1, 1A, 1B and certain Class 2 contributions.

(2) Part 2 of that Schedule applies Part 5 of that Act (promoters of tax avoidance schemes) to Class 1, 1A, 1B and certain Class 2 contributions.

(3) Part 3 of that Schedule applies Parts 4 and 5 of that Act to Class 4 contributions.

(4) Part 4 of that Schedule contains commencement and transitory provision.

5 Provision in consequence etc of tax-only changes to Part 4 or 5 of FA 2014

(1) Where a modification is made to Part 4 of FA 2014 (follower notices and accelerated payments) or Part 5 of that Act (promoters of tax avoidance schemes) that does not apply in relation to national insurance contributions ("the tax-only modification"), the Treasury may by regulations—

(a) make provision for the purpose of applying the tax-only modification in relation to national insurance contributions (with or without modifications),

(b) make provision in relation to national insurance contributions corresponding to the tax-only modification, or

(c) otherwise modify the Part concerned, as it has effect in relation to national insurance contributions, in consequence of, or for the purpose of making provision supplementary or incidental to, the tax-only modification.

(2) Regulations under this section—

(a) may amend, repeal or revoke any provision of an Act or instrument made under an Act (whenever passed or made),

(b) may make consequential, incidental, supplementary, transitional, transitory or saving provision, and

(c) may make different provision for different cases, classes of national insurance contributions or purposes.

(3) Regulations under this section must be made by statutory instrument.

(4) A statutory instrument containing (with or without other provision) regulations under this section that amend or repeal a provision of an Act may not be made unless a draft of the instrument has been laid before, and approved by a resolution of, each House of Parliament.

(5) A statutory instrument containing regulations under this section that does not have to be approved in draft under subsection (4) is subject to annulment in pursuance of a resolution of either House of Parliament.

(6) In this section "national insurance contributions" means contributions under Part 1 of SSCBA 1992 or Part 1 of SSCB(NI)A 1992.

(7) This section comes into force at the end of the period of 2 months beginning with the day on which this Act is passed.

Anti-avoidance

6 Categorisation of earners etc: anti-avoidance

(1) In the Social Security (Categorisation of Earners) Regulations 1978 (SI 1978/1689) ("the 1978 GB regulations"), after regulation 5 insert—

"5A Anti-avoidance

(1) Paragraph (2) applies if—

(a) an earner has an employment in which the earner personally provides services to a person who is resident or present or has a place of business in Great Britain,

(b) a third person enters into relevant avoidance arrangements, and

(c) but for paragraph (2), the earner would not be, and would not be treated as falling within the category of, an employed earner in relation to the employment.

(2) The earner is to be treated as falling within the category of an employed earner in relation to the employment.

(3) In paragraph (1)(b) "relevant avoidance arrangements" means arrangements the main purpose, or one of the main purposes, of which is to secure—

(a) that the earner is not treated under paragraph 2 of Schedule 1 as falling within the category of employed earner in relation to the employment, or

(b) that a person is not treated under paragraph 2 or 9(b) or (d) of Schedule 3 as the secondary Class 1 contributor in respect of payments of earnings to or for the benefit of the earner in respect of the employment.

(4) Paragraph (5) applies if—

(a) a person ("P") enters into arrangements the main purpose, or one of the main purposes, of which is to secure that P is not treated under a relevant provision as the secondary Class 1 contributor in respect of payments of earnings to or for the benefit of an employed earner in respect of an employment, and

(b) but for paragraph (5), no person who is resident or present or has a place of business in Great Britain would—

(i) be the secondary Class 1 contributor in respect of such payments, or

(ii) be treated, under a provision other than paragraph 2(a) or (b) or 9(g) or (h) in column (B) of Schedule 3, as the secondary Class 1 contributor in respect of such payments.

(5) If P is resident or present or has a place of business in Great Britain, P is to be treated as the secondary Class 1 contributor in respect of such payments.

(6) In paragraph (4)(a) a "relevant provision" means any provision of—

(a) paragraph 2 of Schedule 3, other than sub-paragraphs (a) and (b) of that paragraph in column (B), or

(b) paragraph 9(a) to (d) of that Schedule.

(7) In this regulation "arrangements" include any scheme, transaction or series of transactions, agreement or understanding, whether or not legally enforceable, and any associated operations."

(2) In the Social Security (Categorisation of Earners) Regulations (Northern Ireland) 1978 (S.R. (NI) 1978 No 401) ("the 1978 NI regulations"), after regulation 5 insert—

"5A Anti-avoidance

(1) Paragraph (2) applies if—

(a) an earner has an employment in which the earner personally provides services to a person who is resident or present or has a place of business in Northern Ireland,

(b) a third person enters into relevant avoidance arrangements, and

(c) but for paragraph (2), the earner would not be, and would not be treated as falling within the category of, an employed earner in relation to the employment.

(2) The earner is to be treated as falling within the category of an employed earner in relation to the employment.

(3) In paragraph (1)(b) "relevant avoidance arrangements" means arrangements the main purpose, or one of the main purposes, of which is to secure—

(a) that the earner is not treated under paragraph 2 of Schedule 1 as falling within the category of employed earner in relation to the employment, or

(b) that a person is not treated under paragraph 2 or 7(b) or (d) of Schedule 3 as the secondary Class 1 contributor in respect of payments of earnings to or for the benefit of the earner in respect of the employment.

(4) Paragraph (5) applies if—

(a) a person ("P") enters into arrangements the main purpose, or one of the main purposes, of which is to secure that P is not treated under a relevant provision as the secondary Class 1 contributor in respect of payments of earnings to or for the benefit of an employed earner in respect of an employment, and

(b) but for paragraph (5), no person who is resident or present or has a place of business in Northern Ireland would—

(i) be the secondary Class 1 contributor in respect of such payments, or

(ii) be treated, under a provision other than paragraph 2(a) or (b) or 7(g) or (h) in column (B) of Schedule 3, as the secondary Class 1 contributor in respect of such payments.

(5) If P is resident or present or has a place of business in Northern Ireland, P is to be treated as the secondary Class 1 contributor in respect of such payments.

(6) In paragraph (4)(a) a "relevant provision" means any provision of—

(a) paragraph 2 of Schedule 3, other than sub-paragraphs (a) and (b) of that paragraph in column (B), or

(b) paragraph 7(a) to (d) of that Schedule.

(7) In this regulation "arrangements" include any scheme, transaction or series of transactions, agreement or understanding, whether or not legally enforceable, and any associated operations."

(3) In section 2 of SSCBA 1992 (categories of earner), after subsection (2) insert—

"(2ZA) Regulations under subsection (2)(b) may make provision treating a person ("P") as falling within one or other of the categories of earner in relation to an employment where arrangements have been entered into the main purpose, or one of the main purposes, of which is to secure—

(a) that P is not treated by other provision in regulations under subsection (2)(b) as falling within that category of earner in relation to the employment, or

(b) that a person is not treated as the secondary contributor in respect of earnings paid to or for the benefit of P in respect of the employment.

(2ZB) In subsection (2ZA) "arrangements" include any scheme, transaction or series of transactions, agreement or understanding, whether or not legally enforceable, and any associated operations."

(4) In section 7 of SSCBA 1992 ("secondary contributor"), after subsection (2) insert—

"(2A) Regulations under subsection (2) may make provision treating a person as the secondary contributor in respect of earnings paid to or for the benefit of an earner if arrangements have been entered into the main purpose, or one of the main purposes, of which is to secure that the person is not so treated by other provision in regulations under subsection (2).

(2B) In subsection (2A) "arrangements" include any scheme, transaction or series of transactions, agreement or understanding, whether or not legally enforceable, and any associated operations."

(5) In section 2 of SSCB(NI)A 1992 (categories of earner), after subsection (2) insert—

"(2ZA) Regulations under subsection (2)(b) may make provision treating a person ("P") as falling within one or other of the categories of earner in relation to an employment where arrangements have been entered into the main purpose, or one of the main purposes, of which is to secure—

(a) that P is not treated by other provision in regulations under subsection (2)(b) as falling within that category of earner in relation to the employment, or

(b) that a person is not treated as the secondary contributor in respect of earnings paid to or for the benefit of P in respect of the employment.

(2ZB) In subsection (2ZA) "arrangements" include any scheme, transaction or series of transactions, agreement or understanding, whether or not legally enforceable, and any associated operations."

(6) In section 7 of SSCB(NI)A 1992 ("secondary contributor"), after subsection (2) insert—

"(2A) Regulations under subsection (2) may make provision treating a person as the secondary contributor in respect of earnings paid to or for the benefit of an earner if arrangements have been entered into the main purpose, or one of the main purposes, of which is to secure that the person is not so treated by other provision in regulations under subsection (2).

(2B) In subsection (2A) "arrangements" include any scheme, transaction or series of transactions, agreement or understanding, whether or not legally enforceable, and any associated operations."

(7) Subsections (1) and (2)—

(a) are to be treated as having come into force on 6 April 2014 for the purposes of inserting regulation 5A(1) to (5), (6)(a) and (7), and

(b) come into force for the purposes of inserting regulation 5A(6)(b) on the day on which this Act is passed.

(8) Paragraphs (4) and (5) of regulation 5A have effect in relation to arrangements entered into on or after 6 April 2014 the main purpose, or one of the main purposes of which, is to secure that a person is not treated, under a provision mentioned in paragraph (6)(b) of that regulation, as the secondary Class 1 contributor in respect of payments of earnings to or for the benefit of an employed earner in respect of an employment.

(9) But regulation 5A(5) only applies as a result of arrangements mentioned in subsection (8) in relation to payments of earnings that are made on or after the day on which this Act is passed.

(10) In subsections (7) to (9) references to regulation 5A are to regulation 5A—

(a) inserted by subsection (1) into the 1978 GB regulations;

(b) inserted by subsection (2) into the 1978 NI regulations.

(11) The amendments made by subsections (1) and (2) are without prejudice to any power to make regulations amending or revoking the provision inserted.

General

7 HMRC administrative expenses: financial provision

(1) In section 165 of SSAA 1992 (adjustments between the National Insurance Fund and Consolidated Fund)—

(a) in subsection (5)(a), for the words from "other" to "Act 2014" substitute "relevant legislation";

(b) after subsection (5A) insert—

"(5B) In subsection (5)(a) "relevant legislation" means—

(a) legislation relating to ordinary statutory paternity pay, additional statutory paternity pay or statutory adoption pay,

(b) the National Insurance Contributions Act 2014, or
(c) the National Insurance Contributions Act 2015."

(2) In section 145 of SSA(NI)A 1992 (adjustments between the National Insurance Fund and Consolidated Fund)—

(a) in subsection (5)(a), for the words from "other" to "Act 2014" substitute "relevant legislation";

(b) after subsection (5A) insert—

"(5B) In subsection (5)(a) "relevant legislation" means—

(a) legislation relating to ordinary statutory paternity pay, additional statutory paternity pay or statutory adoption pay,
(b) the National Insurance Contributions Act 2014, or
(c) the National Insurance Contributions Act 2015."

8 Abbreviations of Acts

In this Act—

"CRCA 2005" means the Commissioners for Revenue and Customs Act 2005;
"FA", followed by a year, means the Finance Act of that year;
"JA 1995" means the Jobseekers Act 1995;
"PA 2014" means the Pensions Act 2014;
"SSAA 1992" means the Social Security Administration Act 1992;
"SSA(NI)A 1992" means the Social Security Administration (Northern Ireland) Act 1992;
"SSCBA 1992" means the Social Security Contributions and Benefits Act 1992;
"SSCB(NI)A 1992" means the Social Security Contributions and Benefits (Northern Ireland) Act 1992;
"SSC(TF)A 1999 means the Social Security Contributions (Transfer of Functions, etc) Act 1999;
"TMA 1970" means the Taxes Management Act 1970;
"WRA 2007" means the Welfare Reform Act 2007;
"Welfare Reform Act 2012 c 5>WRA 2012 means the Welfare Reform Act 2012.

9 Short title and extent

(1) This Act may be cited as the National Insurance Contributions Act 2015.
(2) Subject to subsection (3), this Act extends to England and Wales, Scotland and Northern Ireland.
(3) An amendment, repeal or revocation made by this Act has the same extent as the provision amended, repealed or revoked.

SCHEDULES

SCHEDULE 1

REFORM OF CLASS 2 CONTRIBUTIONS

Section 2

SSCBA 1992

1 SSCBA 1992 is amended as follows.

2 In section 1 (outline of contributory system), in subsection (2)(c), omit "weekly".

3 For section 11 (liability for Class 2 contributions) substitute—

"Class 2 contributions

11

(1) This section applies if an earner is in employment as a self-employed earner in a tax year (the "relevant tax year").

(2) If the earner has relevant profits of, or exceeding, the small profits threshold, the earner is liable to pay Class 2 contributions for the relevant tax year at the rate of £2.80 in respect of each week in that year that the earner is in the employment.

(3) "Relevant profits" means profits, from the employment, in respect of which Class 4 contributions are payable under section 15 for the relevant tax year (or would be payable if the amount of the profits were to exceed the amount specified in subsection (3)(a) of that section in excess of which the main Class 4 percentage is payable).

(4) The "small profits threshold" is £5,965.

(5) Class 2 contributions under subsection (2) are to be payable in the same manner that Class 4 contributions in respect of relevant profits are, or would be, payable (but see section 11A for the application of certain provisions in relation to such Class 2 contributions).

NIC

(6) If the earner does not have relevant profits of, or exceeding, the small profits threshold, the earner may pay a Class 2 contribution of £2.80 in respect of any week in the relevant tax year that the earner is in the employment.

(7) No Class 2 contributions are to be paid under this section in respect of any week in the relevant tax year—

(a) before that in which the earner attains the age of 16, or

(b) after that in which the earner attains pensionable age.

(8) The Treasury may by regulations make provision so that, in relation to an earner, the Class 2 contribution in respect of a week is higher than that specified in subsections (2) and (6) where—

(a) in respect of any employment of the earner, the earner is treated by regulations made under section 2(2)(b) as being a self-employed earner, and

(b) in any period or periods the earner has earnings from that employment and—

(i) those earnings are such that (disregarding their amount) the earner would be liable for Class 1 contributions in respect of them if the earner were not so treated in respect of the employment, and

(ii) no Class 4 contribution is payable in respect of the earnings by virtue of regulations under section 18(1).

(9) The Treasury may by regulations—

(a) modify the meaning of "relevant profits";

(b) provide that Class 2 contributions under subsection (6) may not be paid—

(i) if the employment or the earner is of a prescribed description, or

(ii) in prescribed circumstances.

(10) Regulations under subsection (9)(a) may amend this section.

(11) Regulations under subsection (9)(b) are to be made with the concurrence of the Secretary of State.

Application of certain provisions of the Income Tax Acts in relation to Class 2 contributions under section 11(2)

11A

(1) The following provisions apply, with the necessary modifications, in relation to Class 2 contributions under section 11(2) as if those contributions were income tax chargeable under Chapter 2 of Part 2 of the Income Tax (Trading and Other Income) Act 2005 in respect of profits of a trade, profession or vocation which is not carried on wholly outside the United Kingdom—

(a) Part 2 (returns), Part 4 (assessment and claims), Part 5 (appeals), Part 5A (payment of tax), Part 6 (collection and recovery) and Part 10 (penalties) of the Taxes Management Act 1970;

(b) Schedule 24 to the Finance Act 2007 (penalties for errors);

(c) sections 101 and 102 of the Finance Act 2009 (interest);

(d) Schedules 55 and 56 to that Act (penalties for failure to make returns etc or for failure to make payments on time);

(e) Part 4 (follower notices and accelerated payments) and Part 5 (promoters of tax avoidance schemes) of the Finance Act 2014;

(f) any other provisions of the Income Tax Acts as to assessment, collection, repayment or recovery.

(2) But section 59A of the Taxes Management Act 1970 (payments on account) does not apply in relation to Class 2 contributions under section 11(2).

(3) This section and section 11(5) are subject to any contrary provision in regulations made under Schedule 1 in relation to Class 2 contributions under section 11(2)."

4 (1) Section 12 (late paid Class 2 contributions) is amended as follows.

(2) In subsection (1), after "Class 2 contribution" insert "under section 11(6)".

(3) In subsection (2), for "to (5)" substitute "and (4)".

(4) In subsection (3), for "(4) to (6)" substitute "(4) and (6)".

(5) Omit subsection (5).

(6) In subsection (6)—

(a) omit "or (5)";

(b) in paragraph (a), omit "in a case falling within subsection (3) above,";

(c) omit paragraph (b) and the word "and" preceding it.

(7) Omit subsection (7).

(8) In subsection (8)—

(a) in the definition of "ordinary contribution", for "under section 11(1) above" substitute "of the amount specified in section 11(6)";

(b) in the definition of "higher-rate contribution", for the words from "under regulations" to the end substitute "of an amount provided for in regulations under section 11(8)".

5 In section 18 (Class 4 contributions recoverable under regulations), in subsection (1)(b), for "subsection (3)" substitute "subsection (8)".

6 In section 35A (appropriate weekly rate of maternity allowance under section 35), in subsection (5)(c)—

(a) in sub-paragraph (i), after "she" insert "has";

(b) in sub-paragraph (ii), for "was excepted (under section 11(4) above) from liability for" substitute "could have paid, but has not paid,".

7 In section 35B (state maternity allowance for participating wife or civil partner of self-employed earner), in subsection (1)(c), for "is liable to pay" substitute "has paid".

8 In section 176(1)(a) (parliamentary control: instruments subject to affirmative procedure), for "section 11(3)" substitute "section 11(8) or (9)".

9 (1) Schedule 1 (supplementary provisions) is amended as follows.

(2) In paragraph 7B, omit sub-paragraph (7).

(3) After paragraph 7BA insert—

"7BB

(1) Regulations may provide, in connection with maternity allowance under section 35 or 35B, for a person who is, or will be, either liable or entitled to pay a Class 2 contribution in respect of a week in a tax year to be able to pay a Class 2 contribution in respect of that week at any time in the period—

(a) beginning with that week, and

(b) ending with a prescribed date.

(2) The regulations may provide that where a person pays a Class 2 contribution in respect of a week in a tax year under the regulations—

(a) the contribution is to be treated, before the end of the tax year, as a Class 2 contribution under section 11(6);

(b) the contribution is to be treated, after the end of the tax year—

(i) if the person is liable under section 11(2) to pay a Class 2 contribution in respect of that week, as a Class 2 contribution under section 11(2);

(ii) otherwise, as a Class 2 contribution under section 11(6).

(3) Regulations under this paragraph are to be made by the Treasury acting with the concurrence of the Secretary of State."

(4) In paragraph 8(1), omit paragraphs (j) and (k).

SSCB(NI)A 1992

10 SSCB(NI)A 1992 is amended as follows.

11 In section 1 (outline of contributory system), in subsection (2)(c), omit "weekly".

12 For section 11 (liability for Class 2 contributions) substitute—

"Class 2 contributions

11

(1) This section applies if an earner is in employment as a self-employed earner in a tax year (the "relevant tax year").

(2) If the earner has relevant profits of, or exceeding, the small profits threshold, the earner is liable to pay Class 2 contributions for the relevant tax year at the rate of £2.80 in respect of each week in that year that the earner is in the employment.

(3) "Relevant profits" means profits, from the employment, in respect of which Class 4 contributions are payable under section 15 for the relevant tax year (or would be payable if the amount of the profits were to exceed the amount specified in subsection (3)(a) of that section in excess of which the main Class 4 percentage is payable).

(4) The "small profits threshold" is £5,965.

(5) Class 2 contributions under subsection (2) are to be payable in the same manner that Class 4 contributions in respect of relevant profits are, or would be, payable (but see section 11A for the application of certain provisions in relation to such Class 2 contributions).

(6) If the earner does not have relevant profits of, or exceeding, the small profits threshold, the earner may pay a Class 2 contribution of £2.80 in respect of any week in the relevant tax year that the earner is in the employment.

(7) No Class 2 contributions are to be paid under this section in respect of any week in the relevant tax year—

(a) before that in which the earner attains the age of 16, or

(b) after that in which the earner attains pensionable age.

(8) The Treasury may by regulations make provision so that, in relation to an earner, the Class 2 contribution in respect of a week is higher than that specified in subsections (2) and (6) where—

(a) in respect of any employment of the earner, the earner is treated by regulations made under section 2(2)(b) as being a self-employed earner, and

(b) in any period or periods the earner has earnings from that employment and—

(i) those earnings are such that (disregarding their amount) the earner would be liable for Class 1 contributions in respect of them if the earner were not so treated in respect of the employment, and

(ii) no Class 4 contribution is payable in respect of the earnings by virtue of regulations under section 18(1).

(9) The Treasury may by regulations—

(a) modify the meaning of "relevant profits";

(b) provide that Class 2 contributions under subsection (6) may not be paid—

(i) if the employment or the earner is of a prescribed description, or

(ii) in prescribed circumstances.

(10) Regulations under subsection (9)(a) may amend this section.

(11) Regulations under subsection (9)(b) are to be made with the concurrence of the Department.

Application of certain provisions of the Income Tax Acts in relation to Class 2 contributions under section 11(2)

11A

(1) The following provisions apply, with the necessary modifications, in relation to Class 2 contributions under section 11(2) as if those contributions were income tax chargeable under Chapter 2 of Part 2 of the Income Tax (Trading and Other Income) Act 2005 in respect of profits of a trade, profession or vocation which is not carried on wholly outside the United Kingdom—

(a) Part 2 (returns), Part 4 (assessment and claims), Part 5 (appeals), Part 5A (payment of tax), Part 6 (collection and recovery) and Part 10 (penalties) of the Taxes Management Act 1970;

(b) Schedule 24 to the Finance Act 2007 (penalties for errors);

(c) sections 101 and 102 of the Finance Act 2009 (interest);

(d) Schedules 55 and 56 to that Act (penalties for failure to make returns etc or for failure to make payments on time);

(e) Part 4 (follower notices and accelerated payments) and Part 5 (promoters of tax avoidance schemes) of the Finance Act 2014;

(f) any other provisions of the Income Tax Acts as to assessment, collection, repayment or recovery.

(2) But section 59A of the Taxes Management Act 1970 (payments on account) does not apply in relation to Class 2 contributions under section 11(2).

(3) This section and section 11(5) are subject to any contrary provision in regulations made under Schedule 1 in relation to Class 2 contributions under section 11(2)."

13 (1) Section 12 (late paid Class 2 contributions) is amended as follows.

(2) In subsection (1), after "Class 2 contribution" insert "under section 11(6)".

(3) In subsection (2), for "to (5)" substitute "and (4)".

(4) In subsection (3), for "(4) to (6)" substitute "(4) and (6)".

(5) Omit subsection (5).

(6) In subsection (6)—

(a) omit "or (5)";

(b) in paragraph (a), omit "in a case falling within subsection (3) above,";

(c) omit paragraph (b) and the word "and" preceding it.

(7) Omit subsection (7).

(8) In subsection (8)—

(a) in the definition of "ordinary contribution", for "under section 11(1) above" substitute "of the amount specified in section 11(6)";

(b) in the definition of "higher-rate contribution", for the words from "under regulations" to the end substitute "of an amount provided for in regulations under section 11(8)".

14 In section 18 (Class 4 contributions recoverable under regulations), in subsection (1)(b), for "subsection (3)" substitute "subsection (8)".

15 In section 35A (appropriate weekly rate of maternity allowance under section 35), in subsection (5)(c)—

(a) in sub-paragraph (i), after "she" insert "has";

(b) in sub-paragraph (ii), for "was excepted (under section 11(4) above) from liability for" substitute "could have paid, but has not paid,".

16 In section 35B (state maternity allowance for participating wife or civil partner of self-employed earner), in subsection (1)(c), for "is liable to pay" substitute "has paid".

17 In section 172(11A) (instruments subject to Parliamentary affirmative procedure), for "11(3)" substitute "11(8) or (9)".

18 (1) Schedule 1 (supplementary provisions) is amended as follows.

(2) In paragraph 7B, omit sub-paragraph (7).

(3) After paragraph 7BA insert—

"7BB

(1) Regulations may provide, in connection with maternity allowance under section 35 or 35B, for a person who is, or will be, either liable or entitled to pay a Class 2 contribution in respect of a week in a tax year to be able to pay a Class 2 contribution in respect of that week at any time in the period—

(a) beginning with that week, and

(b) ending with a prescribed date.

(2) The regulations may provide that where a person pays a Class 2 contribution in respect of a week in a tax year under the regulations—

(a) the contribution is to be treated, before the end of the tax year, as a Class 2 contribution under section 11(6);

(b) the contribution is to be treated, after the end of the tax year—

(i) if the person is liable under section 11(2) to pay a Class 2 contribution in respect of that week, as a Class 2 contribution under section 11(2);

(ii) otherwise, as a Class 2 contribution under section 11(6).

(3) Regulations under this paragraph are to be made by the Treasury acting with the concurrence of the Department."

(4) In paragraph 8(1), omit paragraphs (j) and (k).

SSAA 1992

19 SSAA 1992 is amended as follows.

20 In section 141 (annual review of contributions), in subsection (4)—

(a) in paragraph (a), for "section 11(1)" substitute "section 11(2) and (6)";

(b) in paragraph (b), for the words from "amount" to the end substitute "small profits threshold for the purposes of Class 2 contributions".

21 (1) Section 143 (power to alter contributions with a view to adjusting the level of the National Insurance Fund) is amended as follows.

(2) In subsection (1)(c), for "section 11(1)" substitute "section 11(2) and (6)".

(3) In subsection (3)—

(a) for "section 11(1)" substitute "section 11(2) and (6)";

(b) for the words from "amount" to the end substitute "small profits threshold for the purposes of Class 2 contributions".

22 In section 145 (power to alter primary and secondary contributions), in subsection (4)(a)—

(a) for "section 11(1)" substitute "section 11(2) and (6)";

(b) omit "in that subsection".

SSC(TF)A 1999

23 SSC(TF)A 1999 is amended as follows.

24 In section 4 (recovery of contributions where income tax recovery provisions not applicable)—

(a) in paragraph (a), for ", Class 1B and Class 2" substitute "and Class 1B";

(b) after paragraph (a) insert—

"(aa) those Class 2 contributions in relation to which—

(i) the regulations mentioned in paragraph (a), and

NIC

(ii) Part 6 of the Taxes Management Act 1970 (collection and recovery),

do not apply,".

25 In section 8 (decisions by officers of HMRC), after subsection (1) insert—

"(1A) No decision in respect of Class 2 contributions under section 11(2) of the Social Security Contributions and Benefits Act 1992 may be made under subsection (1) in relation to an issue specified in paragraph (c) or (e) of that subsection if the person to whom the decision would relate—

(a) has appealed under Part 5 of the Taxes Management Act 1970 in relation to that issue,

(b) can appeal under that Part in relation to that issue, or

(c) might in the future, without the agreement of Her Majesty's Revenue and Customs or permission of the tribunal, be able to appeal under that Part in relation to that issue."

26 In Schedule 3 (transfer of other functions to the Treasury or Board), omit paragraph 12.

27 In Schedule 9 (further consequential amendments), omit paragraphs 3 and 7(7).

Social Security Contributions (Transfer of Functions, etc) (Northern Ireland) Order 1999 (SI 1999/671)

28 The Social Security Contributions (Transfer of Functions, etc) (Northern Ireland) Order 1999 is amended as follows.

29 In Article 7 (decisions by officers of HMRC), after paragraph (1) insert—

"(1A) No decision in respect of Class 2 contributions under section 11(2) of the Contributions and Benefits Act may be made under paragraph (1) in relation to an issue specified in sub-paragraph (c) or (e) of that paragraph if the person to whom the decision would relate—

(a) has appealed under Part 5 of the Taxes Management Act 1970 in relation to that issue,

(b) can appeal under that Part in relation to that issue, or

(c) might in the future, without the agreement of Her Majesty's Revenue and Customs or permission of the tribunal, be able to appeal under that Part in relation to that issue."

30 In Schedule 3 (transfer of other functions to the Treasury or Board), omit paragraph 13.

31 In Schedule 8 (further consequential amendments), omit paragraphs 1 and 5(7).

Social Security (Contributions) Regulations 2001 (SI 2001/1004)

32 The Social Security (Contributions) Regulations 2001 are amended as follows.

33 (1) In regulation 125 (share fishermen), in paragraph (c), for "section 11(1) of the Act (Class 2 contributions), be £3.40" substitute "section 11(2) and (6) of the Act (Class 2 contributions), be £3.45".

(2) The amendment made by sub-paragraph (1) is without prejudice to any power to make regulations amending or revoking the provision amended.

34 (1) In regulation 127 (elections by married women and widows), in paragraph (3)(b), after "Class 2 contribution" insert ", nor shall she be entitled to pay any such contribution,".

(2) The amendment made by sub-paragraph (1) is without prejudice to any power to make regulations amending or revoking the provision inserted.

Commencement

35 The amendments made by this Schedule, other than those mentioned in paragraph 36, have effect for the tax year 2015-16 and subsequent tax years.

36 The amendments made by paragraphs 4, 9(2), 13, 18(2), 27 and 31 have effect in relation to a Class 2 contribution in respect of a week in the tax year 2015-16 or a subsequent tax year.

37 The Treasury may by regulations made by statutory instrument make transitional or transitory provision or savings in connection with the coming into force of any of the amendments made by this Schedule.

SCHEDULE 2

APPLICATION OF PARTS 4 AND 5 OF FA 2014 TO NATIONAL INSURANCE CONTRIBUTIONS

Section 4

PART 1

FOLLOWER NOTICES & ACCELERATED PAYMENTS: CLASS 1, 1A, 1B AND CERTAIN CLASS 2

Introduction

1 Part 4 of FA 2014 (follower notices and accelerated payments) has effect with the following modifications.

General

2 References to tax or a relevant tax, other than references to particular taxes, include relevant contributions.

3 References to a charge to tax include a liability to pay relevant contributions and references to a person being chargeable to tax, or to tax being charged, are to be construed accordingly.

4 References to an assessment to tax include a NICs decision relating to a person's liability for relevant contributions.

5 References to a tax enquiry include a relevant contributions dispute.

6 A "relevant contributions dispute" arises if—

(a) without making a NICs decision, HMRC notifies a person in writing that HMRC considers the person to be liable to pay an amount of relevant contributions, and

(b) the person notifies HMRC in writing (a "notification of dispute") that the person disputes liability for some or all of the contributions ("the disputed contributions").

7 The relevant contributions dispute is in progress, in relation to the notification of dispute, during the period which—

(a) begins with the day on which the person gives the notification of dispute, and

(b) ends (at which point it is to be treated as completed) with the day on which—

(i) the disputed contributions are paid in full,

(ii) HMRC and the person enter into an agreement in writing as to the person's liability for the disputed contributions and any amount of those contributions that the person is to pay under that agreement is paid,

(iii) an officer of Revenue and Customs makes a NICs decision in relation to the person's liability for the disputed contributions, or

(iv) without making a NICs decision, HMRC notifies the person in writing that HMRC no longer considers the person to be liable to pay the disputed contributions.

8 References to a return into which a tax enquiry is in progress include a notification of dispute in relation to which a relevant contributions dispute is in progress.

9 References to a tax appeal include a NICs appeal.

10 A "NICs appeal" means—

(a) an appeal, under section 11 of SSC(TF)A 1999 or Article 10 of the Social Security Contributions (Transfer of Functions, etc) (Northern Ireland) Order 1999 (SI 1999/671), against a NICs decision relating to relevant contributions, or

(b) an appeal against any determination of—

(i) an appeal within paragraph (a), or

(ii) an appeal within this paragraph.

11 (1) A reference to a provision of Part 7 of FA 2004 (disclosure of tax avoidance schemes) (a "DOTAS provision") includes a reference to—

(a) that DOTAS provision as applied by regulations under section 132A of SSAA 1992 (disclosure of contributions avoidance arrangements);

(b) any provision of regulations under that section that corresponds to that DOTAS provision, whenever the regulations are made.

(2) Regulations under section 132A of SSAA 1992 may disapply, or modify the effect of, sub-paragraph (1).

List of relevant taxes

12 The definition of "relevant tax" in section 200 ("relevant tax") has effect as if relevant contributions were listed in it.

Circumstances in which follower notice may be given

13 For the purposes of section 204 (circumstances in which a follower notice may be given), Condition B is also met if, in a relevant contributions dispute, a person disputes liability for relevant contributions on the basis mentioned in subsection (3) of that section (regardless of whether the notification of dispute was given on that basis).

Follower notices: corrective action and penalties

14 (1) This paragraph applies in a case in which, by virtue of this Part of this Schedule, a follower notice is given by virtue of section 204(2)(a).
(2) For the purposes of section 208 (penalty if corrective action not taken in response to follower notice), the necessary corrective action is taken in respect of the denied advantage if (and only if)—
- (a) in a case in which the denied advantaged can be counteracted by making a payment to HMRC, P makes that payment and notifies HMRC that P has done so, or
- (b) in any case, P takes all necessary action to enter into an agreement in writing with HMRC for the purpose of relinquishing the denied advantage.

(3) Accordingly—
- (a) subsections (4) to (7) and (9) to (11) of section 208 do not apply, and
- (b) the reference in section 209(3)(a) to P amending a return or claim is to be treated as a reference to P making a payment mentioned in sub-paragraph (2)(a).

(4) Terms used in this paragraph that are defined for the purposes of section 208 have the same meaning as in that section.

Follower notices: aggregate penalties

15 (1) In section 212 (aggregate penalties), references to a "relevant penalty provision" include—
- (a) any provision mentioned in subsection (4) of that section, as applied in relation to relevant contributions by regulations (whenever made);
- (b) section 98A of TMA 1970, as applied in relation to relevant contributions by regulations (whenever made);
- (c) any provision specified in regulations made by the Treasury under which a penalty can be imposed in respect of relevant contributions.

(2) The Treasury may by regulations disapply, or modify the effect of, sub-paragraph (1)(a) or (b).
(3) The Treasury may by regulations modify section 212 as it has effect in relation to a relevant penalty provision by virtue of sub-paragraph (1)(b) or (c).
(4) Section 175(3) to (5) of SSCBA 1992 (various supplementary powers) applies to a power to make regulations conferred by this paragraph.
(5) Regulations under this paragraph must be made by statutory instrument.
(6) A statutory instrument containing regulations under this paragraph is subject to annulment in pursuance of a resolution of either House of Parliament.

Circumstances in which accelerated payment notice may be given

16 For the purposes of section 219 (circumstances in which an accelerated payment notice may be given), Condition B is also met if, in a relevant contributions dispute, a person disputes liability for relevant contributions on the basis mentioned in subsection (3) of that section (regardless of whether the notification of dispute was given on that basis).

Nature and recovery of accelerated payment

17 (1) This paragraph applies in relation to an accelerated payment (see section 223(2)) so far as (but only so far as) it represents understated tax (see section 220) that consists of an additional amount that would be due and payable in respect of relevant contributions ("the understated contributions").
(2) The accelerated payment is a payment of the understated contributions (and not a payment on account of them).
(3) Accordingly, subsections (3) and (7) to (9) of section 223 do not apply in relation to the accelerated payment.
(4) The accelerated payment must be paid before the end of the payment period regardless of whether P brings a NICs appeal that relates to the understated contributions.

(5) Section 117A of SSAA 1992 and section 111A of SSA(NI)A 1992 (issues arising in proceedings: contributions etc) do not apply to proceedings for the recovery of any amount of the accelerated payment that is unpaid at the end of the payment period.

(6) A certificate of an officer of Revenue and Customs under section 25A of CRCA 2005 (certificates of debt) that the accelerated payment has not been paid is to be treated as conclusive evidence that the amount is unpaid.

(7) If some or all of the understated contributions are subsequently repaid to P—

(a) the contributions repaid are to be treated, for the purposes of determining a person's entitlement to benefit, or the amount of a person's benefit, as not having been paid, but

(b) that does not affect any payments of benefit made to a person before the repayment.

(8) In sub-paragraph (7) "benefit" means a contributory benefit or a statutory payment.

(9) Terms used in this paragraph that are defined for the purposes of section 223 have the same meaning as in that section.

Effect of accelerated payment notice in respect of appeal

18 (1) This paragraph applies where—

(a) a person ("P") has been given an accelerated payment notice by virtue of section 219(2)(b) (notice given when appeal pending), which has not been withdrawn, and

(b) the appeal by virtue of which the notice could be given was a NICs appeal in relation to relevant contributions.

(2) P must pay the disputed contributions (see sub-paragraph (8))—

(a) if no representations were made under section 222 in respect of the notice, on or before the last day of the period of 90 days beginning with the day the notice is given, and

(b) if representations were so made, on or before whichever is later of—

(i) the last day of the 90 day period mentioned in paragraph (a), and

(ii) the last day of the period of 30 days beginning with the day on which HMRC's determination in respect of those representations is notified under section 222.

(3) Subsections (4) and (5) of section 117A of SSAA 1992 or (as the case may be) of section 111A of SSA(NI)A 1992 (decision of officer of HMRC not conclusive if subject to appeal and proceedings for recovery to be adjourned pending appeal) do not apply to proceedings before a court for recovery of the disputed contributions.

(4) Accordingly, if proceedings have been adjourned under subsection (5) of either of those sections, they cease to be adjourned, so far as they relate to the recovery of the disputed contributions, from the end of the applicable period under sub-paragraph (2).

(5) A certificate of an officer of Revenue and Customs under section 25A of CRCA 2005 (certificates of debt) that the disputed contributions have not been paid is to be treated as conclusive evidence that the disputed contributions are unpaid.

(6) If some or all of the disputed contributions are subsequently repaid to P—

(a) the contributions repaid are to be treated, for the purposes of determining a person's entitlement to benefit, or the amount of a person's benefit, as not having been paid, but

(b) that does not affect any payments of benefit made to a person before the repayment.

(7) In sub-paragraph (6) "benefit" means a contributory benefit or a statutory payment.

(8) In this paragraph "the disputed contributions" means the relevant contributions to which the NICs appeal relates so far as they are disputed tax specified in the notice under section 221(2)(b).

Penalty for failure to pay accelerated payment

19 (1) Subsection (7) of section 226 (penalty for failure to pay accelerated payment) applies in relation to a penalty under that section imposed by virtue of this Part of this Schedule, but the reference in that subsection to tax does not include relevant contributions.

(2) But in their application by virtue of sub-paragraph (1), the provisions of Schedule 56 to FA 2009 mentioned in that subsection have effect—

(a) as if references to an assessment to tax were to a NICs decision relating to a person's liability for relevant contributions,

(b) as if a reference to an appeal against an assessment to the tax concerned were a reference to an appeal against a NICs decision,

(c) as if sub-paragraph (3)(b) of paragraph 11 were omitted (but see paragraph 20 of this Schedule), and

(d) with any other necessary modifications.

Recovery of penalties under Part 4 of FA 2014

20 (1) A penalty under section 208 or 226 imposed by virtue of this Part of this Schedule may be recovered as if it were an amount of relevant contributions which is due and payable.

NIC

(2) Section 117A of SSAA 1992 or (as the case may be) section 111A of SSA(NI)A 1992 (issues arising in proceedings: contributions etc) has effect in relation to proceedings before a court for recovery of the penalty as if the assessment of the penalty were a NICs decision as to whether the person is liable for the penalty.
(3) Accordingly, section 211(4)(b) (assessment of penalty to be enforced as if it were an assessment to tax) does not apply in relation to a penalty under section 208 imposed by virtue of this Part of this Schedule.

Withdrawal, modification or suspension of accelerated payment notice

21 In section 227 (withdrawal, modification or suspension of accelerated payment notice), subsection (9) has effect as if the provisions mentioned there included paragraph 18(2) of this Schedule.

Interpretation

22 In this Part of this Schedule—

"accelerated payment notice" means an accelerated payment notice under Chapter 3 of Part 4 of FA 2014;

"contributory benefit" means—

(a) a contributory benefit under Part 2 of SSCBA 1992,
(b) a jobseeker's allowance under JA 1995,
(c) an employment and support allowance under Part 1 of WRA 2007,
(d) state pension or a lump sum under Part 1 of PA 2014,
(e) bereavement support payment under section 30 of that Act, or
(f) any corresponding benefit in Northern Ireland;

"the disputed contributions", other than in paragraph 18, has the meaning given by paragraph 6(b);

"HMRC" means Her Majesty's Revenue and Customs;

"NICs appeal" has the meaning given by paragraph 10;

"NICs decision" means a decision under section 8 of SSC(TF)A 1999 or Article 7 of the Social Security Contributions (Transfer of Functions, etc) (Northern Ireland) Order 1999 (SI 1999/671);

"notification of dispute" has the meaning given by paragraph 6(b);

"relevant contributions" means the following contributions under Part 1 of SSCBA 1992 or Part 1 of SSCB(NI)A 1992—

(a) Class 1 contributions;
(b) Class 1A contributions;
(c) Class 1B contributions;
(d) Class 2 contributions which a person is, or is alleged to be, liable to pay but in relation to which section 11A of the Act in question (application of certain provisions of the Income Tax Acts in relation to Class 2 contributions under section 11(2) of that Act) does not, or would not, apply;

"relevant contributions dispute" has the meaning given by paragraphs 6 and 7;

"statutory payment" means a statutory payment for the purposes of section 4C of SSCBA 1992 or section 4C of SSCB(NI)A 1992;

and references to sections are to sections of FA 2014, unless otherwise indicated.

PART 2

PROMOTERS OF AVOIDANCE SCHEMES: CLASS 1, 1A, 1B AND CERTAIN CLASS 2

Introduction

23 Part 5 of FA 2014 (promoters of tax avoidance schemes) has effect with the following modifications.

General

24 References to tax, other than in references to particular taxes, include relevant contributions.

25 References to a tax advantage include the avoidance or reduction of a liability to pay relevant contributions.

26 (1) A reference to a provision of Part 7 of FA 2004 (disclosure of tax avoidance schemes) (a "DOTAS provision") includes a reference to—

(a) that DOTAS provision as applied by regulations under section 132A of SSAA 1992 (disclosure of contributions avoidance arrangements);

(b) any provision of regulations under that section that corresponds to that DOTAS provision,

whenever the regulations are made.

(2) Regulations under section 132A of SSAA 1992 may disapply, or modify the effect of, sub-paragraph (1).

Duty to notify Commissioners

27 In section 253 (duty of persons to notify the Commissioners), references to a tax return include a return relating to relevant contributions that is required to be made by or under an enactment.

Power to obtain information and documents

28 In section 255 (power to obtain information and documents), references to a person's tax position include the person's position as regards deductions or repayments of relevant contributions, or of sums representing relevant contributions, that the person is required to make by or under an enactment.

Limitation of defence of reasonable care

29 In section 276 (limitation of defence of reasonable care), the reference in subsection (1) to a document of a kind listed in the Table in paragraph 1 of Schedule 24 to FA 2007 includes a document, relating to relevant contributions, in relation to which that Schedule applies (and, accordingly, the reference to that Schedule in subsection (2) of that section includes that Schedule as it so applies).

List of taxes

30 The definition of "tax" in section 283(1) (interpretation) has effect as if relevant contributions were listed in it.

[Threshold conditions

30A (1) In paragraph 5 of Schedule 34 (non-compliance with Part 7 of FA 2004), in sub-paragraph (4)—

(a) paragraph (a) includes a reference to a decision having been made for corresponding NICs purposes that P is to be deemed not to have failed to comply with the provision concerned as P had a reasonable excuse for not doing the thing required to be done, and

(b) the reference in paragraph (c) to a determination is to be read accordingly.

(2) In this paragraph "corresponding NICs purposes" means the purposes of any provision of regulations under section 132A of SSAA 1992.][1]

Amendments—[1] Paragraphs 30A, 30B inserted by FA 2016 s 160(17), (18) with effect from 15 September 2016.

[Relevant defeats

30B (1) Schedule 34A (promoters of tax avoidance schemes: defeated arrangements) has effect with the following modifications.

(2) References to an assessment (or an assessment to tax) include a NICs decision relating to a person's liability for relevant contributions.

(3) References to adjustments include a payment in respect of a liability to pay relevant contributions (and the definition of "adjustments" in paragraph 24 accordingly has effect as if such payments were included in it).

(4) In paragraph 9(3) the reference to an enquiry into a return includes a relevant contributions dispute (as defined in paragraph 6 of this Schedule).

(5) In paragraph 28(3)—

(a) paragraph (a) includes a reference to a decision having been made for corresponding NICs purposes that the person is to be deemed not to have failed to comply with the provision concerned as the person had a reasonable excuse for not doing the thing required to be done, and

(b) the reference in paragraph (c) to a determination is to be read accordingly.

"Corresponding NICs purposes" means the purposes of any provision of regulations under section 132A of SSAA 1992.][1]

Amendments—[1] Paragraphs 30A, 30B inserted by FA 2016 s 160(17), (18) with effect from 15 September 2016.

Interpretation

31 In this Part of this Schedule—

[(za) "NICs decision" means a decision under section 8 of SSC(TF)A 1999 or Article 7 of the Social Security Contributions (Transfer of Functions, etc) (Northern Ireland) Order 1999 (SI 1999/671);][1]

(a) "relevant contributions" means the following contributions under Part 1 of SSCBA 1992 or Part 1 of SSCB(NI)A 1992—
   (i) Class 1 contributions;
   (ii) Class 1A contributions;
   (iii) Class 1B contributions;
   (iv) Class 2 contributions which must be paid but in relation to which section 11A of the Act in question (application of certain provisions of the Income Tax Acts in relation to Class 2 contributions under section 11(2) of that Act) does not apply;

(b) references to sections [or Schedules are to sections of, or Schedules to][1] FA 2014, unless otherwise indicated.

Amendments—[1] Sub-para (*za*) inserted, and in sub-para (*b*), words substituted for words "are to sections of", by FA 2016 s 160(17), (19) with effect from 15 September 2016.

PART 3

APPLICATION OF PARTS 4 AND 5 OF FA 2014: CLASS 4

32 In section 16 of SSCBA 1992 (application of Income Tax Acts and destination of Class 4 contributions), in subsection (1), at the end of paragraph (c) insert
"and

(d) the provisions of Part 4 (follower notices and accelerated payments) and Part 5 (promoters of tax avoidance schemes) of the Finance Act 2014,".

PART 4

COMMENCEMENT AND TRANSITORY PROVISION

33 (1) Parts 1 and 3 of this Schedule come into force at the end of the period of 2 months beginning with the day on which this Act is passed.

(2) Part 2 of this Schedule comes into force—

(a) for the purposes of making regulations under Part 5 of FA 2014, on the day on which this Act is passed, and

(b) for remaining purposes, at the end of the period of 2 months beginning with the day on which this Act is passed.

34 Before the coming into force of the repeals in section 4C of SSCBA 1992 made by Part 1 of Schedule 14 to Welfare Reform Act 2012 c 5 (WRA 2012) (abolition of benefits superseded by universal credit), the reference in paragraph 22 to a jobseeker's allowance is to be treated as a reference to a contribution-based jobseeker's allowance (within the meaning of JA 1995).

35 Before the coming into force of the repeal of section 22(8) of SSCBA 1992 made by Part 1 of Schedule 14 to Welfare Reform Act 2012 c 5 (WRA 2012) (abolition of benefits superseded by universal credit), the reference in paragraph 22 to an employment and support allowance is to be treated as a reference to a contributory allowance (within the meaning of Part 1 of WRA 2007).

FINANCE (NO 2) ACT 2015

2015 Chapter 33

An Act to grant certain duties, to alter other duties, and to amend the law relating to the National Debt and the Public Revenue, and to make further provision in connection with finance.

18 November 2015

PART 6

ADMINISTRATION AND ENFORCEMENT

51 Enforcement by deduction from accounts

Please see IHT section.

52 Rate of interest applicable to judgment debts etc in taxation matters

(1) This section applies if a sum payable to or by the Commissioners under a judgment or order given or made in any court proceedings relating to a taxation matter (a "tax-related judgment debt") carries interest as a result of a relevant enactment.

(2) The "relevant enactments" are—

(*a*) section 17 of the Judgments Act 1838 (judgment debts to carry interest), and

(*b*) any order under section 74 of the County Courts Act 1984 (interest on judgment debts etc).

(3) The relevant enactment is to have effect in relation to the tax-related judgment debt as if for the rate specified in section 17(1) of the Judgments Act 1838 and any other rate specified in an order under section 74 of the County Courts Act 1984 there were substituted—

(*a*) in the case of a sum payable to the Commissioners, the late payment interest rate provided for in regulations made by the Treasury under section 103(1) of FA 2009, and

(*b*) in the case of a sum payable by the Commissioners, the special repayment rate.

(4) Subsection (3) does not affect any power of the court under the relevant enactment to prevent any sum from carrying interest or to provide for a rate of interest which is lower than (and incapable of exceeding) that for which the subsection provides.

(5) If section 44A of the Administration of Justice Act 1970 (interest on judgment debts expressed otherwise than in sterling), or any corresponding provision made under section 74 of the County Courts Act 1984 in relation to the county court, applies to a tax-related judgment debt—

(*a*) subsection (3) does not apply, but

(*b*) the court may not specify in an order under section 44A of the Administration of Justice Act 1970, or under any provision corresponding to that section which has effect under section 74 of the County Courts Act 1984, an interest rate which exceeds (or is capable of exceeding)—

(i) in the case of a sum payable to the Commissioners, the rate mentioned in subsection (3)(*a*), or

(ii) in the case of a sum payable by the Commissioners, the special repayment rate.

(6) The "special repayment rate" is the percentage per annum given by the formula—

BR + 2

where BR is the official Bank rate determined by the Bank of England Monetary Policy Committee at the operative meeting.

(7) "The operative meeting", in relation to the special repayment rate applicable in respect of any day, means the most recent meeting of the Bank of England Monetary Policy Committee apart from any meeting later than the 13th working day before that day.

(8) The Treasury may by regulations made by statutory instrument—

(*a*) repeal subsections (6) and (7), and

(*b*) provide that the "special repayment rate" for the purposes of this section is the rate provided for in the regulations.

(9) Regulations under subsection (8)—

(*a*) may make different provision for different purposes,

(*b*) may either themselves specify a rate of interest or make provision for such a rate to be determined (and to change from time to time) by reference to such rate, or the average of such rates, as may be referred to in the regulations,

(*c*) may provide for rates to be reduced below, or increased above, what they would otherwise be by specified amounts or by reference to specified formulae,

(*d*) may provide for rates arrived at by reference to averages to be rounded up or down,

(*e*) may provide for circumstances in which the alteration of a rate of interest is or is not to take place, and

(*f*) may provide that alterations of rates are to have effect for periods beginning on or after a day determined in accordance with the regulations ("the effective date") regardless of—

(i) the date of the judgment or order in question, and

(ii) whether interest begins to run on or after the effective date, or began to run before that date.

(10) A statutory instrument containing regulations under subsection (8) is subject to annulment in pursuance of a resolution of the House of Commons.

(11) To the extent that a tax-related judgment debt consists of an award of costs to or against the Commissioners, the reference in section 24(2) of the Crown Proceedings Act 1947 (which relates to interest on costs awarded to or against the Crown) to the rate at which interest is payable upon judgment debts due from or to the Crown is to be read as a reference to the rate at which interest is payable upon tax-related judgment debts.

(12) This section has effect in relation to interest for periods beginning on or after 8 July 2015, regardless of—

(*a*) the date of the judgment or order in question, and

(*b*) whether interest begins to run on or after 8 July 2015, or began to run before that date.

(13) Subsection (14) applies where, at any time during the period beginning with 8 July 2015 and ending immediately before the day on which this Act is passed ("the relevant period")—

(*a*) a payment is made in satisfaction of a tax-related judgment debt, and

(*b*) the payment includes interest under a relevant enactment in respect of any part of the relevant period.

(14) The court by which the judgment or order in question was given or made must, on an application made to it under this subsection by the person who made the payment, order the repayment of the amount by which the interest paid under the relevant enactment in respect of days falling within the relevant period exceeds the interest payable under the relevant enactment in respect of those days in accordance with the provisions of this section.

(15) In this section—

"the Commissioners" means the Commissioners for Her Majesty's Revenue and Customs;

"taxation matter" means anything . . . [1] the collection and management of which is the responsibility of the Commissioners (or was the responsibility of the Commissioners of Inland Revenue or Commissioners of Customs and Excise);

"working day" means any day other than a non-business day as defined in section 92 of the Bills of Exchange Act 1882.

(16) This section extends to England and Wales only.

Amendments—[1] In sub-s (15), in definition of "taxation matter", words ", other than national insurance contributions," repealed by FA 2016 s 172 with effect in relation to interest for periods beginning on or after 15 September 2016, regardless of—

- the date of the judgment or order in question; and
- whether interest begins to run on or after 15 September 2016, or began to run before that date.

This amendment extends to England and Wales only.

SCHEDULES

SCHEDULE 8

ENFORCEMENT BY DEDUCTION FROM ACCOUNTS

Section 51

Please see IHT section.

NATIONAL INSURANCE CONTRIBUTIONS (RATE CEILINGS) ACT 2015

(2015 Chapter 35)

An Act to set a ceiling on the main and additional primary percentages, the secondary percentage and the upper earnings limit in relation to Class 1 national insurance contributions.

[17 December 2015]

Be it enacted by the Queen's most Excellent Majesty, by and with the advice and consent of the Lords Spiritual and Temporal, and Commons, in this present Parliament assembled, and by the authority of the same, as follows:—

CONTENTS

Rate Ceilings

1 Main and additional primary percentages

(1) In relation to primary Class 1 contributions payable in respect of any period in a tax year to which this section applies—

(a) the main primary percentage shall not exceed 12%, and

(b) the additional primary percentage shall not exceed 2%.

(2) This section applies to a tax year which begins after the day on which this Act comes into force but before the date of the first parliamentary general election after that day.

(3) In this section, "main primary percentage" and "additional primary percentage" are to be construed in accordance with section 8(2)(a) and (b) of SSCBA 1992 and SSCB(NI)A 1992.

2 Secondary percentage

(1) In relation to secondary Class 1 contributions payable in respect of any period in a tax year to which this section applies, the secondary percentage shall not exceed 13.8%.

(2) This section applies to a tax year which begins after the day on which this Act comes into force but before the date of the first parliamentary general election after that day.

(3) In this section, "secondary percentage" is to be construed in accordance with section 9(2) of SSCBA 1992 and SSCB(NI)A 1992.

3 Upper earnings limit

(1) The upper earnings limit specified in regulations under section 5(1) of SSCBA 1992 and SSCB(NI)A 1992 for any tax year to which this section applies shall not exceed the weekly equivalent of the proposed higher rate threshold for that tax year.

(2) This section applies to a tax year—

(a) which begins after the day on which this Act comes into force but before the date of the first parliamentary general election after that day, and

(b) for which income tax is charged.

(3) For the purposes of this section, the "proposed higher rate threshold" for a tax year is the sum of—

(a) the basic rate limit for income tax for the tax year as proposed in the pre-budget proposals for that year, and

(b) the personal allowance for income tax for the tax year as so proposed.

(4) For the purposes of this section, the weekly equivalent of a proposed higher rate threshold for a tax year is the amount produced by dividing that threshold by 52 and rounding up or down to the nearest pound.

(5) In this section "pre-budget proposals" means the government's pre-budget fiscal proposals for a tax year which are contained in a document presented to Parliament by the Chancellor of the Exchequer by Command of Her Majesty.

Final

4 Interpretation

In this Act—

"SSCBA 1992" means the Social Security Contributions and Benefits Act 1992;

"SSCB(NI)A 1992" means the Social Security Contributions and Benefits (Northern Ireland) Act 1992.

5 Extent, commencement and short title

(1) This Act extends to England and Wales, Scotland and Northern Ireland.

(2) This Act comes into force on the day on which it is passed.

(3) This Act may be cited as the National Insurance Contributions (Rate Ceilings) Act 2015.

FINANCE ACT 2016

2016 Chapter 24

An Act to grant certain duties, to alter other duties, and to amend the law relating to the National Debt and the Public Revenue, and to make further provision in connection with finance.

15 September 2016

PART 10
TAX AVOIDANCE AND EVASION

General anti-abuse rule

157 General anti-abuse rule: binding of tax arrangements to lead arrangements

(1) Part 5 of FA 2013 (general anti-abuse rule) is amended in accordance with subsections (2) to (11).

(2) (*inserts* FA 2013 Sch 43A)

(3) (*inserts* FA 2013 Sch 43B)

(4) In section 209 (counteracting tax advantages), in subsection (6)(*a*), after "Schedule 43" insert ", 43A or 43B".

(5) In section 210 (consequential relieving adjustments), in subsection (1)(*b*), after "Schedule 43," insert "paragraph 8 or 9 of Schedule 43A or paragraph 8 of Schedule 43B,".

(6) In section 211 (proceedings before a court or tribunal), in subsection (2)(*b*), for the words from "Panel" to the end substitute "Panel given—

(i) under paragraph 11 of Schedule 43 about the arrangements or any tax arrangements which are, as a result of a notice under paragraph 1 or 2 of Schedule 43A, the referred or (as the case may be) counteracted arrangements in relation to the arrangements, or

(ii) under paragraph 6 of Schedule 43B in respect of a generic referral of the arrangements."

(7) Section 214 (interpretation of Part 5) is amended in accordance with subsections (8) to (10).

(8) Renumber section 214 as subsection (1) of section 214.

NIC

(9) In subsection (1) (as renumbered), at the appropriate places insert—

""designated HMRC officer" has the meaning given by paragraph 2 of Schedule 43;".

""notice of binding" has the meaning given by paragraph 2(2) of Schedule 43A;

""pooling notice" has the meaning given by paragraph 1(4) of Schedule 43A;"

""tax appeal" has the meaning given by paragraph 1A of Schedule 43;"

""tax enquiry" has the meaning given by section 202(2) of FA 2014."

(10) After subsection (1) insert—

"(2) In this Part references to any "opinion of the GAAR Advisory Panel" about any tax arrangements are to be interpreted in accordance with paragraph 11(5) of Schedule 43.

(3) In this Part references to tax arrangements which are "equivalent" to one another are to be interpreted in accordance with paragraph 11 of Schedule 43A."

(11) In Schedule 43 (general anti-abuse rule: procedural requirements), in paragraph 6, after sub-paragraph (2) insert—

"(3) The officer must, as soon as reasonably practicable after deciding whether or not the matter is to be referred to the GAAR Advisory Panel, give the taxpayer written notice of the decision."

(12) Section 10 of the National Insurance Contributions Act 2014 (GAAR to apply to national insurance contributions) is amended in accordance with subsections (13) to (16).

(13) In subsection (4), at the end insert ", paragraph 8 or 9 of Schedule 43A to that Act (pooling of tax arrangements: notice of final decision) or paragraph 8 of Schedule 43B to that Act (generic referral of arrangements: notice of final decision)".

(14) After subsection (6) insert—

"(6A) Where, by virtue of this section, a case falls within paragraph 4A of Schedule 43 to the Finance Act 2013 (referrals of single schemes: relevant corrective action) or paragraph 4 of Schedule 43A to that Act (pooled schemes: relevant corrective action)—

(*a*) the person ("P") mentioned in sub-paragraph (1) of that paragraph takes the "relevant corrective action" for the purposes of that paragraph if (and only if)—

(i) in a case in which the tax advantage in question can be counteracted by making a payment to HMRC, P makes that payment and notifies HMRC that P has done so, or

(ii) in any case, P takes all necessary action to enter into an agreement in writing with HMRC for the purpose of relinquishing the tax advantage, and

(*b*) accordingly, sub-paragraphs (2) to (8) of that paragraph do not apply."

(15) In subsection (11)—

(*a*) for "and HMRC" substitute ", "HMRC" and "tax advantage"";

(*b*) after "2013" insert "(as modified by this section)".

(16) After subsection (11) insert—

"(12) See section 10A for further modifications of Part 5 of the Finance Act 2013."

(17) (*inserts* NICA 2014 s 10A)

(18) Section 219 of FA 2014 (circumstances in which an accelerated payment notice may be given) is amended in accordance with subsections (19) and (20).

(19) In subsection (4), after paragraph (*c*) insert—

"(*d*) a notice has been given under paragraph 8(2) or 9(2) of Schedule 43A to FA 2013 (notice of final decision after considering Panel's opinion about referred or counteracted arrangements) in relation to the asserted advantage or part of it and the chosen arrangements (or is so given at the same time as the accelerated payment notice) in a case where the stated opinion of at least two of the members of the sub-panel of the GAAR Advisory Panel about the other arrangements (see subsection (8)) was as set out in paragraph 11(3)(*b*) of Schedule 43 to FA 2013;

(*e*) a notice under paragraph 8(2) of Schedule 43B to FA 2013 (GAAR: generic referral of tax arrangements) has been given in relation to the asserted advantage or part of it and the chosen arrangements (or is so given at the same time as the accelerated payment notice) in a case where the stated opinion of at least two of the members of the sub-panel of the GAAR Advisory Panel which considered the generic referral in respect of those arrangements under paragraph 6 of Schedule 43B to FA 2013 was as set out in paragraph 6(4)(*b*) of that Schedule."

(20) After subsection (7) insert—

"(8) In subsection (4)(*d*) "other arrangements" means—

(*a*) in relation to a notice under paragraph 8(2) of Schedule 43A to FA 2013, the referred arrangements (as defined in that paragraph);

(*b*) in relation to a notice under paragraph 9(2) of that Schedule, the counteracted arrangements (as defined in paragraph 2 of that Schedule).

(21) In section 220 of FA 2014 (content of notice given while a tax enquiry is in progress)—

(*a*) in subsection (4)(*c*), after "219(4)(*c*)" insert ", (*d*) or (*e*)";

(*b*) in subsection (5)(*c*), after "219(4)(*c*)" insert ", (*d*) or (*e*)";

(*c*) in subsection (7), for the words from "under" to the end substitute "under—

(*a*) paragraph 12 of Schedule 43 to FA 2013,

(*b*) paragraph 8 or 9 of Schedule 43A to that Act, or

(*c*) paragraph 8 of Schedule 43B to that Act,

as the case may be."

(22) Section 287 of FA 2014 (Code of Practice on Taxation for Banks) is amended in accordance with subsections (23) to (25).

(23) In subsection (4), after "(5)" insert "or (5A)".

(24) In subsection (5)(*b*), after "Schedule" insert "or paragraph 8 or 9 of Schedule 43A to that Act".

(25) After subsection (5) insert—

"(5A) This subsection applies to any conduct—

(*a*) in relation to which there has been given—

(i) an opinion notice under paragraph 6(4)(*b*) of Schedule 43B to FA 2013 (GAAR advisory panel: opinion that such conduct unreasonable) stating the joint opinion of all the members of a sub-panel arranged under that paragraph, or

(ii) one or more such notices stating the opinions of at least two members of such a sub-panel, and

(*b*) in relation to which there has been given a notice under paragraph 8 of that Schedule (HMRC final decision on tax advantage) stating that a tax advantage is to be counteracted.

(5B) For the purposes of subsection (5), any opinions of members of the GAAR advisory panel which must be considered before a notice is given under paragraph 8 or 9 of Schedule 43A to FA 2013 (opinions about the lead arrangements) are taken to relate to the conduct to which the notice relates."

(26) In Schedule 32 to FA 2014 (accelerated payments and partnerships), paragraph 3 is amended in accordance with subsections (27) and (28).

(27) In sub-paragraph (5), after paragraph (*c*) insert—

"(*d*) the relevant partner in question has been given a notice under paragraph 8(2) or 9(2) of Schedule 43A to FA 2013 (notice of final decision after considering Panel's opinion about referred or counteracted arrangements) in respect of any tax advantage resulting from the asserted advantage or part of it and the chosen arrangements (or is given such a notice at the same time as the partner payment notice) in a case where the stated opinion of at least two of the members of the sub-panel of the GAAR Advisory Panel about the other arrangements (see sub-paragraph (7)) was as set out in paragraph 11(3)(*b*) of Schedule 43 to FA 2013;

(*e*) the relevant partner in question has been given a notice under paragraph 8(2) of Schedule 43B to FA 2013 (GAAR: generic referral of arrangements) in respect of any tax advantage resulting from the asserted advantage or part of it and the chosen arrangements (or is given such a notice at the same time as the partner payment notice) in a case where the stated opinion of at least two of the members of the sub-panel of the GAAR Advisory Panel which considered the generic referral in respect of those arrangements was as set out in paragraph 6(4)(*b*) of that Schedule."

(28) After sub-paragraph (6) insert—

"(7) "Other arrangements" means—

(*a*) in relation to a notice under paragraph 8(2) of Schedule 43A to FA 2013, the referred arrangements (as defined in that paragraph);

(*b*) in relation to a notice under paragraph 9(2) of that Schedule, the counteracted arrangements (as defined in paragraph 2 of that Schedule)."

(29) In Schedule 34 to FA 2014 (promoters of tax avoidance schemes: threshold conditions), in paragraph 7—

(*a*) in paragraph (*a*), at the end insert "(referrals of single schemes) or are in a pool in respect of which a referral has been made to that Panel under Schedule 43B to that Act (generic referrals),";

(*b*) in paragraph (*b*)—

(i) for "in relation to the arrangements" substitute "in respect of the referral";

(ii) after "11(3)(*b*)" insert "or (as the case may be) 6(4)(*b*)";

(*c*) in paragraph (*c*)(i) omit "paragraph 10 of".

(30) The amendments made by this section have effect in relation to tax arrangements (within the meaning of Part 5 of FA 2013) entered into at any time (whether before or on or after the day on which this Act is passed).

NIC

158 General anti-abuse rule: penalty

(1) Part 5 of FA 2013 (general anti-abuse rule) is amended as follows.

(2) (*inserts* FA 2013 s 212A)

(3) (*inserts* FA 2013 Sch 43C)

(4) In section 209 (counteracting the tax advantages), after subsection (7) insert—

"(8) Where a matter is referred to the GAAR Advisory Panel under paragraph 5 or 6 of Schedule 43, the taxpayer (as defined in paragraph 3 of that Schedule) must not make any GAAR-related adjustments in relation to the taxpayer's tax affairs in the period (the "closed period") which—

(*a*) begins with the 31st day after the end of the 45 day period mentioned in paragraph 4(1) of that Schedule, and

(*b*) ends immediately before the day on which the taxpayer is given the notice under paragraph 12 of Schedule 43 (notice of final decision after considering opinion of GAAR Advisory Panel).

(9) Where a person has been given a pooling notice or a notice of binding under Schedule 43A in relation to any tax arrangements, the person must not make any GAAR-related adjustments in the period ("the closed period") that—

(*a*) begins with the 31st day after that on which that notice is given, and

(*b*) ends—

(i) in the case of a pooling notice, immediately before the day on which the person is given a notice under paragraph 8(2) or 9(2) of Schedule 43A, or a notice under paragraph 8(2) of Schedule 43B, in relation to the tax arrangements (notice of final decision after considering opinion of GAAR Advisory Panel), or

(ii) in the case of a notice of binding, with the 30th day after the day on which the notice is given.

(10) In this section "GAAR-related adjustments" means—

(*a*) for the purposes of subsection (8), adjustments which give effect (wholly or in part) to the proposed counteraction set out in the notice under paragraph 3 of Schedule 43;

(*b*) for the purposes of subsection (9), adjustments which give effect (wholly or partly) to the proposed counteraction set out in the notice of pooling or binding (as the case may be)."

(5) Schedule 43 (general anti-abuse rule: procedural requirements) is amended in accordance with subsections (6) to (9).

(6) (*inserts* FA 2013 Sch 43 para 1A)

(7) In paragraph 3(2)(*e*), for "of paragraphs 5 and 6" substitute "of—

(i) paragraphs 5 and 6, and

(ii) sections 209(8) and (9) and 212A."

(8) (*inserts* FA 2013 Sch 43 para 4A)

(9) Before paragraph 5 (but after the heading "Referral to GAAR Advisory Panel") insert—

"4B Paragraphs 5 and 6 apply if the taxpayer does not take the relevant corrective action (see paragraph 4A) by the beginning of the closed period mentioned in section 209(8)."

(10) In section 103ZA of TMA 1970 (disapplication of sections 100 to 103 in the case of certain penalties)—

(*a*) omit "or" at the end of paragraph (*g*), and

(*b*) after paragraph (*g*) insert

"(*ga*) section 212A of the Finance Act 2013 (general anti-abuse rule), or"

(11) In section 212 of FA 2014 (follower notices: aggregate penalties) (as amended by Schedule 18), in subsection (4)—

(*a*) omit "or" at the end of paragraph (*c*), and

(*b*) after paragraph (*d*) insert ", or

(*e*) section 212A of FA 2013 (general anti-abuse rule)."

(12) FA 2015 is amended in accordance with subsections (13) and (14).

(13) In section 120 (penalties in connection with offshore matters and offshore transfers), in subsection (1), omit "and" before paragraph (*c*) and after paragraph (*c*) insert— ", and

(*d*) Schedule 43C to FA 2013 (as amended by FA 2016)."

(14) (*inserts* FA 2013 Sch 20 para 20)

(15) The amendments made by this section have effect in relation to tax arrangements (within the meaning of Part 5 of FA 2013) entered into on or after the day on which this Act is passed.

Tackling frequent avoidance

160 Promoters of tax avoidance schemes

(1) Part 5 of FA 2014 (promoters of tax avoidance schemes) is amended as follows.

(2) (*inserts* FA 2014 ss 237A–237D)

(3) (*inserts* FA 2014 ss 241A, 241B)

(4) In section 242 (monitoring notices: duty to apply to tribunal), after subsection (5) insert—

"(6) At a time when a notice given under section 237A is provisional, no determination is to be made under subsection (1) in respect of the notice.

(7) If a promoter fails to comply with conditions in a conduct notice at a time when the conduct notice is provisional, nothing in subsection (6) prevents those failures from being taken into account under subsection (1) at any subsequent time when the conduct notice is not provisional."

(5) (*inserts* FA 2014 Sch 34A)

(6) In section 241 (duration of conduct notice), after subsection (4) insert—

"(5) See also section 237D(2) (provisional conduct notice affected by judicial ruling)."

(7) (*inserts* FA 2014 s 281A)

(8) In section 282 (regulations), in subsection (3), after paragraph (*b*) insert—

"(*ba*) paragraph 31 of Schedule 34A,".

(9) In section 283(1) (interpretation of Part 5)—

(*a*) in the definition of "conduct notice", after paragraph (*a*) insert—

"(*aa*) section 237A(8),

(*ab*) section 237B(1),";

(*b*) in the definition of "tax", after ""tax"" insert "(except in provisions to which section 281A applies)";

(*c*) in the definition of ""tax advantage"", after "234(3)" insert "(but see also section 281A)";

(*d*) at the appropriate places insert—

""contract settlement" means an agreement in connection with a person's liability to make a payment to the Commissioners under or by virtue of an enactment;"

""defeat", in relation to arrangements, has the meaning given by paragraph 10 of Schedule 34A;"

""defeat notice" has the meaning given by section 241A(7);"

""double defeat notice" has the meaning given by section 241A(7);"

""final", in relation to a judicial ruling, is to be interpreted in accordance with section 237D(6);"

""judicial ruling" means a ruling of a court or tribunal on one or more issues;"

""look-forward period, in relation to a defeat notice, has the meaning given by section 241A(10);"

""provisional", in relation to a conduct notice given under section 237A(8), is to be interpreted in accordance with section 237C;"

""relevant defeat", in relation to a person, is to be interpreted in accordance with Schedule 34A;"

""related", in relation to arrangements, is to be interpreted in accordance with paragraph 2 of Schedule 34A;"

""relies on a Case 3 relevant defeat" is to be interpreted in accordance section 237B(5);"

""single defeat notice" has the meaning given by section 241A(7)."

(10) Schedule 36 (promoters of tax avoidance schemes: partnerships) is amended in accordance with subsections (11) to (16).

(11) (*inserts* FA 2014 Sch 36 para 4A)

(12) In paragraph 7(1)(*b*) after "a" insert "defeat notice,".

(13) In paragraph 7(2) after "the" insert "defeat notice,".

(14) (*inserts* FA 2014 Sch 36 para 7A)

(15) In paragraph 10—

(*a*) in sub-paragraph (1)(*b*) for "conduct notice or a" substitute ", defeat notice, conduct notice or";

(*b*) in sub-paragraph (3), after "partner—" insert—

"(*za*) a defeat notice (if the original notice is a defeat notice);".

(*c*) in sub-paragraph (4), after "("the new partnership")—" insert—

"(*za*) a defeat notice (if the original notice is a defeat notice);".

(*d*) after sub-paragraph (5) insert—

"(5A) A notice under sub-paragraph (3)(*za*) or (4)(*za*) may not be given after the end of the look-forward period of the original notice."

(16) (*inserts* FA 2014 Sch 36 para 11A)
(17) Part 2 of Schedule 2 to the National Insurance Contributions Act 2015 (application of Part 5 of FA 2014 to national insurance contributions) is amended in accordance with subsections (18) and (19).
(18) After paragraph 30 insert—

"Threshold conditions

30A

(1) In paragraph 5 of Schedule 34 (non-compliance with Part 7 of FA 2004), in sub-paragraph (4)—

(*a*) paragraph (*a*) includes a reference to a decision having been made for corresponding NICs purposes that P is to be deemed not to have failed to comply with the provision concerned as P had a reasonable excuse for not doing the thing required to be done, and

(*b*) the reference in paragraph (*c*) to a determination is to be read accordingly.

(2) In this paragraph "corresponding NICs purposes" means the purposes of any provision of regulations under section 132A of SSAA 1992.

Relevant defeats

30B

(1) Schedule 34A (promoters of tax avoidance schemes: defeated arrangements) has effect with the following modifications.
(2) References to an assessment (or an assessment to tax) include a NICs decision relating to a person's liability for relevant contributions.
(3) References to adjustments include a payment in respect of a liability to pay relevant contributions (and the definition of "adjustments" in paragraph 24 accordingly has effect as if such payments were included in it).
(4) In paragraph 9(3) the reference to an enquiry into a return includes a relevant contributions dispute (as defined in paragraph 6 of this Schedule).
(5) In paragraph 28(3)—

(*a*) paragraph (*a*) includes a reference to a decision having been made for corresponding NICs purposes that the person is to be deemed not to have failed to comply with the provision concerned as the person had a reasonable excuse for not doing the thing required to be done, and

(*b*) the reference in paragraph (*c*) to a determination is to be read accordingly.

"Corresponding NICs purposes" means the purposes of any provision of regulations under section 132A of SSAA 1992."
(19) In paragraph 31 (interpretation)—

(*a*) before paragraph (*a*) insert—

"(*za*) "NICs decision" means a decision under section 8 of SSC(TF)A 1999 or Article 7 of the Social Security Contributions (Transfer of Functions, etc) (Northern Ireland) Order 1999 (SI 1999/671);"

(*b*) in paragraph (*b*), for "are to sections of" substitute "or Schedules are to sections of, or Schedules to".

(20) For the purposes of sections 237A and 241A of FA 2014, a defeat (by virtue of any of Conditions A to F in Schedule 34A to that Act) of arrangements is treated as not having occurred if—

(*a*) there has been a final judicial ruling on or before the day on which this Act is passed as a result of which the counteraction referred to in paragraph 11(*d*), 12(1)(*b*), 13(1)(*d*), 14(1)(*d*) or 15(1)(*d*) (as the case may be) is final for the purposes of Schedule 34A of that Act, or

(*b*) (in the case of a defeat by virtue of Condition F in Schedule 34A) the judicial ruling mentioned in paragraph 16(1)(*d*) of that Schedule becomes final on or before the day on which this Act is passed.

(21) Subsection (20) does not apply in relation to a person (who is carrying on a business as a promoter) if at any time after 17 July 2014 that person or an associated person takes action as a result of which the person taking the action—

(*a*) becomes a promoter in relation to the arrangements, or arrangements related to those arrangements, or

(*b*) would have become a promoter in relation to arrangements mentioned in paragraph (*a*) had the person not already been a promoter in relation to those arrangements.

(22) For the purposes of sections 237A and 241A of FA 2014, a defeat of arrangements is treated as not having occurred if it would (ignoring this subparagraph) have occurred—

(*a*) on or before the first anniversary of the day on which this Act is passed, and

(*b*) by virtue of any of Conditions A to E in Schedule 34A to FA 2014, but otherwise than as a result of a final judicial ruling.

(23) For the purposes of subsection (21) a person ("Q") is an "associated person" in relation to another person ("P") at any time when any of the following conditions is met—

(*a*) P is a relevant body which is controlled by Q;

(*b*) Q is a relevant body, P is not an individual and Q is controlled by P;

(*c*) P and Q are relevant bodies and a third person controls P and Q.

(24) In subsection (23) "relevant body" and "control" are to be interpreted in accordance with paragraph 19 of Schedule 34A to FA 2014.

(25) In subsections (20) to (22) expressions used in Part 5 of FA 2014 (as amended by this section) have the same meaning as in that Part.

PART 11

ADMINISTRATION, ENFORCEMENT AND SUPPLEMENTARY POWERS

Judgment debts

172 Rate of interest applicable to judgment debts etc: England and Wales

(1) In section 52 of F(No 2)A 2015 (rates of interest applicable to judgment debts etc in taxation matters: England and Wales), in subsection (15), in the definition of "taxation matter" omit ", other than national insurance contributions,".

(2) This section has effect in relation to interest for periods beginning on or after the day on which this Act is passed, regardless of—

(*a*) the date of the judgment or order in question, and

(*b*) whether interest begins to run on or after the day on which this Act is passed, or began to run before that date.

(3) This section extends to England and Wales only.

SCHEDULES

SCHEDULE 18

SERIAL TAX AVOIDANCE

Section 159

Please see IHT section.

SCHEDULE 20

PENALTIES FOR ENABLERS OF OFFSHORE TAX EVASION OR NON-COMPLIANCE

Section 162

Please see IHT section.

SCHEDULE 22

ASSET-BASED PENALTY FOR OFFSHORE INACCURACIES AND FAILURES

Section 165

Please see IHT section.

FINANCE ACT 2017

2017 Chapter 10

An Act to grant certain duties, to alter other duties, and to amend the law relating to the national debt and the public revenue, and to make further provision in connection with finance.

27 April 2017

PART 1

DIRECT AND INDIRECT TAXES

Avoidance

24 Promoters of tax avoidance schemes: threshold conditions etc

(1) In Part 2 of Schedule 34 to FA 2014 (meeting the threshold conditions: bodies corporate and partnerships), in paragraph 13A (interpretation), for sub-paragraphs (6) to (8) substitute—

NIC

"(6) Two or more persons together control a body corporate if together they have the power to secure that the affairs of the body corporate are conducted in accordance with their wishes in any way specified in sub-paragraph (5)(a) to (c).

(7) A person controls a partnership if the person is a member of the partnership and—

(a) has the right to a share of more than half the assets, or more than half the income, of the partnership, or

(b) directs, or is on a day-to-day level in control of, the management of the business of the partnership.

(8) Two or more persons together control a partnership if they are members of the partnership and together they—

(a) have the right to a share of more than half the assets, or of more than half the income, of the partnership, or

(b) direct, or are on a day-to-day level in control of, the management of the business of the partnership.

(9) Paragraph 19(2) to (5) of Schedule 36 (connected persons etc) applies to a person referred to in sub-paragraph (7) or (8) as if references to "P" were to that person.

(10) A person has significant influence over a body corporate or partnership if the person—

(a) does not control the body corporate or partnership, but

(b) is able to, or actually does, exercise significant influence over it (whether or not as the result of a legal entitlement).

(11) Two or more persons together have significant influence over a body corporate or partnership if together those persons—

(a) do not control the body corporate or partnership, but

(b) are able to, or actually do, exercise significant influence over it (whether or not as the result of a legal entitlement).

(12) References to a person being a promoter are to the person carrying on business as a promoter."

(2) In Part 2 of Schedule 34 to FA 2014, for paragraphs 13B to 13D substitute—

"Relevant bodies controlled etc by other persons treated as meeting a threshold condition

13B

(1) A relevant body is treated as meeting a threshold condition at the relevant time if any of Conditions A to C is met.

(2) Condition A is that—

(a) a person met the threshold condition at a time when the person was a promoter, and

(b) the person controls or has significant influence over the relevant body at the relevant time.

(3) Condition B is that—

(a) a person met the threshold condition at a time when the person controlled or had significant influence over the relevant body,

(b) the relevant body was a promoter at that time, and

(c) the person controls or has significant influence over the relevant body at the relevant time.

(4) Condition C is that—

(a) two or more persons together controlled or had significant influence over the relevant body at a time when one of those persons met the threshold condition,

(b) the relevant body was a promoter at that time, and

(c) those persons together control or have significant influence over the relevant body at the relevant time.

(5) Where the person referred to in sub-paragraph (2)(a) or (3)(a) or (4)(a) as meeting a threshold condition is an individual, sub-paragraph (1) only applies if the threshold condition is a relevant threshold condition.

(6) For the purposes of sub-paragraph (2) it does not matter whether the relevant body existed at the time referred to in sub-paragraph (2)(a).

Persons who control etc a relevant body treated as meeting a threshold condition

13C

(1) If at a time when a person controlled or had significant influence over a relevant body—

(a) the relevant body met a threshold condition, and

(b) the relevant body, or another relevant body which the person controlled or had significant influence over, was a promoter,

the person is treated as meeting the threshold condition at the relevant time.

(2) It does not matter whether any relevant body referred to sub-paragraph (1) exists at the relevant time.

Relevant bodies controlled etc by the same person treated as meeting a threshold condition

13D

(1) If—

(a) a person controlled or had significant influence over a relevant body at a time when it met a threshold condition, and

(b) at that time that body, or another relevant body which the person controlled or had significant influence over, was a promoter,

any relevant body which the person controls or has significant influence over at the relevant time is treated as meeting the threshold condition at the relevant time.

(2) If—

(a) two or more persons together controlled or had significant influence over a relevant body at a time when it met a threshold condition, and

(b) at that time that body, or another relevant body which those persons together controlled or had significant influence over, was a promoter,

any relevant body which those persons together control or have significant influence over at the relevant time is treated as meeting the threshold condition at the relevant time.

(3) It does not matter whether—

(a) a relevant body referred to in sub-paragraph (1)(a) or (b) or (2)(a) or (b) exists at the relevant time, or

(b) a relevant body existing at the relevant time existed at the time referred to in sub-paragraph (1)(a) or (2)(a)."

(3) In Part 4 of Schedule 34A to FA 2014 (meeting section 237A conditions: bodies corporate and partnerships), for paragraphs 20 to 22 substitute—

"Relevant bodies controlled etc by other persons treated as meeting section 237A condition

20

(1) A relevant body is treated as meeting a section 237A condition at the section 237A(2) relevant time if any of Conditions A to C is met.

(2) Condition A is that—

(a) a person met the section 237A condition at a time when the person was a promoter, and

(b) the person controls or has significant influence over the relevant body at the section 237A(2) relevant time.

(3) Condition B is that—

(a) a person met the section 237A condition at a time when the person controlled or had significant influence over the relevant body,

(b) the relevant body was a promoter at that time, and

(c) the person controls or has significant influence over the relevant body at the section 237A(2) relevant time.

(4) Condition C is that—

(a) two or more persons together controlled or had significant influence over the relevant body at a time when one of those persons met the section 237A condition,

(b) the relevant body was a promoter at that time, and

(c) those persons together control or have significant influence over the relevant body at the section 237A(2) relevant time.

(5) Sub-paragraph (1) does not apply where the person referred to in sub-paragraph (2)(a), (3)(a), or (4)(a) as meeting a section 237A condition is an individual.

(6) For the purposes of sub-paragraph (2) it does not matter whether the relevant body existed at the time referred to in sub-paragraph (2)(a).

Persons who control etc a relevant body treated as meeting a section 237A condition

21

(1) If at a time when a person controlled or had significant influence over a relevant body—

(a) the relevant body met a section 237A condition, and

(b) the relevant body, or another relevant body which the person controlled or had significant influence over, was a promoter,

the person is treated as meeting the section 237A condition at the section 237A(2) relevant time.

(2) It does not matter whether any relevant body referred to sub-paragraph (1) exists at the section 237A(2) relevant time.

Relevant bodies controlled etc by the same person treated as meeting a section 237A condition

22

(1) If—

(a) a person controlled or had significant influence over a relevant body at a time when it met a section 237A condition, and

(b) at that time that body, or another relevant body which the person controlled or had significant influence over, was a promoter,

any relevant body which the person controls or has significant influence over at the section 237A(2) relevant time is treated as meeting the section 237A condition at the section 237A(2) relevant time.

(2) If—

(a) two or more persons together controlled or had significant influence over a relevant body at a time when it met a section 237A condition, and

(b) at that time that body, or another relevant body which those persons together controlled or had significant influence over, was a promoter,

any relevant body which those persons together control or have significant influence over at the section 237A(2) relevant time is treated as meeting the section 237A condition at the section 237A(2) relevant time.

(3) It does not matter whether—

(a) a relevant body referred to in sub-paragraph (1)(a) or (b) or (2)(a) or (b) exists at the section 237A(2) relevant time, or

(b) a relevant body existing at the section 237A(2) relevant time existed at the time referred to in sub-paragraph (1)(a) or (2)(a)."

(4) In Part 4 of Schedule 34A to FA 2014, in paragraph 23 (interpretation)—

(a) in sub-paragraph (1), for the definition of "control" substitute—

""control" and "significant influence" have the same meanings as in Part 4 of Schedule 34 (see paragraph 13A(5) to (11));

references to a person being a promoter are to the person carrying on business as a promoter;";

(b) in sub-paragraph (2), for "20(1)(a), 21(1)(a) and 22(1)(a)" substitute "20 to 22".

(5) The amendments made by subsections (1) and (2) have effect for the purposes of determining whether a person meets a threshold condition in a period of three years ending on or after 8 March 2017.

(6) The amendments made by subsections (3) and (4) have effect for the purposes of determining whether a person meets a section 237A condition in a period of three years ending on or after 8 March 2017.

Commentary—*Simon's Taxes* **A7.251, A7.252A, A7.259**.

Press releases etc—HMRC TIIN (Budget 2017), "Promoters of Tax Avoidance Schemes—associated and successor entities rules", 8 March 2017 (see *SWTI 2017, Budget Edition*).

FINANCE (NO 2) ACT 2017

16 November 2017

An Act To Grant certain duties, to alter other duties, and to amend the law relating to the national debt and the public revenue, and to make further provision in connection with finance.

PART 4

ADMINISTRATION, AVOIDANCE AND ENFORCEMENT

Avoidance etc

65 Penalties for enablers of defeated tax avoidance

Please see IHT section.

SCHEDULE 16

PENALTIES FOR ENABLERS OF DEFEATED TAX AVOIDANCE

Section 65

Please see IHT section.

Statutory Instruments

Contents

Chronological list of printed Statutory Instruments

Note—

For a chronological list of current and amending statutory instruments, *see below*.

SI 1975/556 Social Security (Credits) Regulations 1975

SI 1977/622 Social Security (Contributions) (Employment Protection) Regulations 1977

SI 1978/1689 Social Security (Categorisation of Earners) Regulations 1978

SI 1979/591 Social Security (Contributions) Regulations 1979 (revoked)

SI 1979/676 Social Security (Earnings Factor) Regulations 1979

SI 1982/1033 Contracting-out (Recovery of Class 1 Contributions) Regulations 1982 (revoked)

SI 1988/1409 Social Security (Employment Training: Payments) Order 1988

SI 1989/1297 Taxes (Interest Rate) Regulations 1989 (see Part 2 of this work)

SI 1990/536 Social Security (Refunds) (Repayment of Contractual Maternity Pay) Regulations 1990

SI 1991/589 Statutory Sick Pay (National Health Service Employees) Regulations 1991

SI 1994/1882 Statutory Maternity Pay (Compensation of Employers) and Miscellaneous Amendment Regulations 1994

SI 1995/512 Statutory Sick Pay Percentage Threshold Order 1995 (revoked by SI 2014/897)

SI 1995/1801 Social Security (Adjudication) Regulations 1995 (revoked)

SI 1996/1055 Social Security (Reduced Rates of Class 1 Contributions and Rebates) (Money Purchase Contracted-out Schemes) Order 1996

SI 1996/1056 Social Security (Minimum Contributions to Appropriate Personal Pension Schemes) Order 1996

SI 1998/944 Social Security (Minimum Contributions to Appropriate Personal Pension Schemes) Order 1998

SI 1998/945 Social Security (Reduced Rates of Class 1 Contributions, and Rebates) (Money Purchase Contracted-out Schemes) Order 1998

SI 1998/2209 Social Security Act 1998 (Commencement No 1) Order 1998

SI 1998/2211 Social Security (Contributions) Amendments (No 3) Regulations 1998 (revoked)

SI 1999/3 Social Security (Categorisation of Earners) Regulations 1999 (revoked)

SI 1999/418 Social Security Act 1998 (Commencement No 3) Order 1999

SI 1999/527 Social Security Contributions (Transfer of Functions, etc) Act 1999 (Commencement No 1 and Transitional Provisions) Order 1999

SI 1999/978 Social Security Contributions, etc (Decisions and Appeals—Transitional Modifications) Regulations 1999

SI 1999/1027 Social Security Contributions (Decisions and Appeals) Regulations 1999

SI 1999/1662 Social Security Contributions (Transfer of Functions, etc) Act 1999 (Commencement No 2 and Consequential and Transitional Provisions) Order 1999

SI 1999/1958 Social Security Act 1998 (Commencement No 8, and Savings and Consequential and Transitional Provisions) Order 1999

SI 1999/2422 Social Security Act 1998 (Commencement No 9, and Savings and Consequential and Transitional Provisions) Order 1999

SI 1999/2739 Social Security Act 1998 (Commencement No 10 and Transitional Provisions) Order 1999

SI 1999/2860 Social Security Act 1998 (Commencement No 11, and Savings and Consequential and Transitional Provisions) Order 1999

SI 1999/3178 Social Security Act 1998 (Commencement No 12 and Consequential and Transitional Provisions) Order 1999

SI 2000/727 Social Security Contributions (Intermediaries) Regulations 2000

SI 2000/747 Social Security Contributions (Notional Payment of Primary Class 1 Contribution) Regulations 2000

SI 2000/750 Occupational Pension Schemes (Contracting-out) (Payment and Recovery of Remaining Balances) Regulations 2000

SI 2001/769 Social Security (Crediting and Treatment of Contributions, and National Insurance Numbers) Regulations 2001

SI 2001/1004 Social Security (Contributions) Regulations 2001

SI 2001/1354 Social Security (Minimum Contributions to Appropriate Personal Pension Schemes) Order 2001

SI 2001/1355 Social Security (Reduced Rates of Class 1 Contributions, and Rebates) (Money Purchase Contracted-out Schemes) Order 2001

Chronological list of Statutory Instruments

Note—

The following is the list of current and amending instruments.

For the list of current instruments which are printed on the following pages, *see above*.

SI 1976/1736 Social Security (Miscellaneous Amendments) Regulations 1976 (amend SI 1975/556)
SI 1977/622 Social Security (Contributions) (Employment Protection) Regulations 1977
SI 1977/788 Social Security (Credits) Amendment Regulations 1977 (amend SI 1975/556)
SI 1978/409 Social Security (Credits) Amendment and (Earnings Factor) Transitional Regulations 1978 (amend SI 1975/556)
SI 1978/1689 Social Security (Categorisation of Earners) Regulations 1978
SI 1979/591 Social Security (Contributions) Regulations 1979 (revoked)
SI 1979/676 Social Security (Earnings Factor) Regulations 1979
SI 1980/1713 Social Security (Categorisation of Earners) Amendment Regulations 1980 (amend SI 1978/1689)
SI 1981/1501 Social Security (Unemployment, Sickness and Invalidity Benefit and Credits) Amendment Regulations 1981 (amend SI 1975/556)
SI 1982/96 Social Security (Unemployment, Sickness and Invalidity Benefit and Credits) Amendment Regulations 1982 (amend SI 1975/556)
SI 1982/1033 Contracting-out (Recovery of Class 1 Contributions) Regulations 1982 (revoked)
SI 1983/197 Social Security (Credits) Amendment Regulations 1983 (amend SI 1975/556)
SI 1983/463 Social Security and Supplementary Benefit (Miscellaneous Provisions) Amendment Regulations 1983 (amend SI 1975/556)
SI 1984/350 Social Security (Categorisation of Earners) Amendment Regulations 1984 (amend SI 1978/1689)
SI 1987/414 Social Security (Credits) Amendment Regulations 1987 (amend SI 1975/556)
SI 1987/687 Social Security (Credits) Amendment (No 2) Regulations 1987 (amend SI 1975/556)
SI 1988/516 Social Security (Credits) Amendment Regulations 1988 (amend SI 1975/556)
SI 1988/1230 Social Security (Credits) Amendment (No 2) Regulations 1988 (amend SI 1975/556)
SI 1988/1409 Social Security (Employment Training: Payments) Order 1988
SI 1988/1439 Social Security (Credits) Amendment (No 3) Regulations 1988 (amend SI 1975/565)
SI 1988/1545 Social Security (Credits) Amendment (No 4) Regulations 1988 (amend SI 1975/556)
SI 1989/345 Social Security (Contributions) Amendment Regulations 1989 (amend SI 1979/591)
SI 1989/572 Social Security (Contributions) Amendment (No 3) Regulations 1989 (amend SI 1979/591)
SI 1989/1297 Taxes (Interest Rate) Regulations 1989 (see Part 2 of this work)
SI 1989/1627 Social Security (Credits) Amendment Regulations 1989 (amend SI 1975/556)
SI 1990/536 Social Security (Refunds) (Repayment of Contractual Maternity Pay) Regulations 1990
SI 1990/1894 Social Security (Categorisation of Earners) Amendment Regulations 1990 (amend SI 1978/1689)
SI 1990/2208 Social Security (Miscellaneous Provisions) Amendment Regulations 1990 (amend SI 1990/536)
SI 1991/387 Enterprise (Scotland) Consequential Amendments Order 1991 (amend SI 1975/556)
SI 1991/589 Statutory Sick Pay (National Health Service Employees) Regulations 1991
SI 1991/2772 Social Security (Credits) Amendment Regulations 1991 (amend SI 1975/556)
SI 1992/726 Social Security (Credits) Amendment Regulations 1992 (amend SI 1975/556)
SI 1994/544 Social Security (Contributions) (Re-rating and National Insurance Fund Payments) Order 1994 (amend SSCBA 1992 ss 9, 11, 13, 15, 18)
SI 1994/726 Social Security (Categorisation of Earners) Amendment Regulations 1994 (amend SI 1978/1689)
SI 1994/1230 Maternity Allowance and Statutory Maternity Pay Regulations 1994 (amend SSCBA 1992 ss 35, 166, 167)
SI 1994/1837 Social Security (Credits) Amendment Regulations 1994 (amend SI 1975/556)
SI 1994/1882 Statutory Maternity Pay (Compensation of Employers) and Miscellaneous Amendment Regulations 1994
SI 1995/512 Statutory Sick Pay Percentage Threshold Order 1995 (revoked by SI 2014/897)
SI 1995/561 Social Security (Contributions) (Re-rating and National Insurance Fund Payments) Order 1995 (amend SSCBA 1992 ss 9, 11, 13, 15, 18)

SI 1995/566 Statutory Maternity Pay (Compensation of Employers) Amendment Regulations 1995 (amend SI 1994/1230)
SI 1995/829 Social Security (Incapacity Benefit) (Consequential and Transitional Amendments and Savings) Regulations 1995 (amend SI 1975/556)
SI 1995/1801 Social Security (Adjudication) Regulations 1995 (revoked)
SI 1995/2558 Social Security (Credits) Amendment Regulations 1995 (amend SI 1975/556)
SI 1996/597 Social Security (Contributions) (Re-rating and National Insurance Fund Payments) Order 1996 (amend SSCBA 1992 ss 9, 11, 13, 15, 18)
SI 1996/668 Statutory Maternity Pay (Compensation of Employers) Amendment Regulations 1996 (amend SI 1994/1230)
SI 1996/1055 Social Security (Reduced Rates of Class 1 Contributions and Rebates) (Money Purchase Contracted-out Schemes) Order 1996
SI 1996/1056 Social Security (Minimum Contributions to Appropriate Personal Pension Schemes) Order 1996
SI 1996/1133 Social Security Revaluation of Earnings Factors Order 1996
SI 1996/2367 Social Security (Credits and Contributions) (Jobseeker's Allowance Consequential and Miscellaneous Amendments) Regulations 1996 (amend SI 1975/556)
SI 1997/574 Statutory Maternity Pay (Compensation of Employers) Amendment Regulations 1997 (amend SI 1994/1882)
SI 1997/1117 Social Security Revaluation of Earnings Factors Order 1997
SI 1997/2939 Registration of Births, Deaths and Marriages (Fees) Order 1997 (revoked)
SI 1998/522 Statutory Maternity Pay (Compensation of Employers) Amendment Regulations 1998 (amend SI 1994/1882)
SI 1998/944 Social Security (Minimum Contributions to Appropriate Personal Pension Schemes) Order 1998
SI 1998/945 Social Security (Reduced Rates of Class 1 Contributions, and Rebates) (Money Purchase Contracted-out Schemes) Order 1998
SI 1998/1728 Social Security (Categorisation of Earners) Amendment Regulations 1998 (amending)
SI 1998/2209 Social Security Act 1998 (Commencement No 1) Order 1998
SI 1998/2211 Social Security (Contributions)Amendments (No 3) Regulations 1998 (revoked)
SI 1998/3171 Registration of Births, Deaths and Marriages (Fees) Order 1998 (amending (revoked SI 1997/2939))
SI 1999/3 Social Security (Categorisation of Earners) Amendment Regulations 1999 (revoked)
SI 1999/263 Social Security (Contributions) (Re-rating and National Insurance Fund Payments) Order 1999 (amend SSCBA 1992 ss 9, 11, 13, 15, 18)
SI 1999/363 Statutory Maternity Pay (Compensation of Employers) Amendment Regulations 1999 (amend SI 1994/1882)
SI 1999/418 Social Security Act 1998 (Commencement No 3) Order 1999
SI 1999/527 Social Security Contributions (Transfer of Functions, etc) Act 1999 (Commencement No 1 and Transitional Provisions) Order 1999
SI 1999/671 Social Security Contributions (Transfer of Functions, etc) (Northern Ireland) Order 1999 (amend SI 1988/1012 and other SIs)
SI 1999/678 Transfer of Functions (Lord Advocate and Secretary of State) Order 1999 (amend SI 1989/469)
SI 1999/978 Social Security Contributions, etc (Decisions and Appeals—Transitional Modifications) Regulations 1999
SI 1999/1027 Social Security Contributions (Decisions and Appeals) Regulations 1999
SI 1999/1042 Scotland Act 1998 (Consequential Modifications) (No 1) Order 1999 (amends various Acts)
SI 1999/1958 Social Security Act 1998 (Commencement No 8, and Savings and Consequential and Transitional Provisions) Order 1999
SI 1999/1662 Social Security Contributions (Transfer of Functions, etc) Act 1999 (Commencement No 2 and Consequential and Transitional Provisions) Order 1999
SI 1999/2422 Social Security Act 1998 (Commencement No 9, and Savings and Consequential and Transitional Provisions) Order 1999
SI 1999/2739 Social Security Act 1998 (Commencement No 10 and Transitional Provisions) Order 1999
SI 1999/2860 Social Security Act 1998 (Commencement No 11, and Savings and Consequential and Transitional Provisions) Order 1999
SI 1999/3178 Social Security Act 1998 (Commencement No 12 and Consequential and Transitional Provisions) Order 1999

SI 2000/694 Health Act 1999 (Supplementary, Consequential etc Provisions) (No 2) Order 2000
SI 2000/727 Social Security Contributions (Intermediaries) Regulations 2000
SI 2000/747 Social Security Contributions (Notional Payment of Primary Class 1 Contribution) Regulations 2000
SI 2000/750 Occupational Pension Schemes (Contracting-out) (Payment and Recovery of Remaining Balances) Regulations 2000
SI 2000/755 Social Security (Contributions) (Re-rating and National Insurance Funds Payments) Order 2000 (amend SSCBA 1992 ss 9, 11, 13, 15, 18)
SI 2000/1483 Social Security (Benefits for Widows and Widowers) (Consequential Amendments) Regulations 2000 (amend SI 1975/556)
SI 2000/2666 Child Support, Pensions and Social Security Act 2000 (Commencement No 1) Order 2000
SI 2000/2950 Child Support, Pensions and Social Security Act 2000 (Commencement No 2) Order 2000
SI 2000/2994 Child Support, Pensions and Social Security Act 2000 (Commencement No 3) Order 2000
SI 2000/3120 Social Security (Incapacity Benefit) Miscellaneous Amendments Regulations 2000 (amend SI 1975/556)
SI 2001/477 Social Security (Contributions) (Re-rating and National Insurance Funds Payments) Order 2001 (amends SSCBA ss 9, 11, 13, 15)
SI 2001/518 Social Security Amendment (Joint Claims) Regulations 2001 (amend SI 1975/556)
SI 2001/573 Social Security (Credits and Incapacity Benefit) Amendment Regulations 2001
SI 2001/769 Social Security (Crediting and Treatment of Contributions, and National Insurance Numbers) Regulations 2001
SI 2001/1004 Social Security (Contributions) Regulations 2001
SI 2001/1354 Social Security (Minimum Contributions to Appropriate Personal Pension Schemes) Order 2001
SI 2001/1355 Social Security (Reduced Rates of Class 1 Contributions, and Rebates) (Money Purchase Contracted-out Schemes) Order 2001
SI 2001/1356 Social Security (Reduced Rates of Class 1 Contributions) (Salary Related Contracted-out Schemes) Order 2001 (amends PSA 1993 s 41)
SI 2001/1817 Social Security Contributions (Share Options) Regulations 2001
SI 2001/1818 Social Security Contributions (Deferred Payments and Interest) Regulations 2001
SI 2001/2187 Social Security (Contributions) (Amendment No 4) Regulations 2001 (amend SI 2001/1004)
SI 2001/2412 Social Security (Contributions) (Amendment No 5) Regulations 2001 (amend SI 2001/1004).
SI 2001/3728 Social Security (Contributions) (Amendment No 6) Regulations 2001 (amend SI 2001/1004)
SI 2001/1711 Social Security (Breach of Community Order) (Consequential Amendments) Regulations 2001 (amend SI 1975/556)
SI 2001/3629 Financial Services and Markets Act 2000 (Consequential Amendments) (Taxes) Order 2002 (amends SI 2001/1004)
SI 2001/4023 Social Security Contributions (Decisions and Appeals) (Amendment) Regulations 2001 (amend SI 1999/1027)
SI 2002/225 Statutory Maternity Pay (Compensation of Employers) Amendment Regulations (amend SI 1994/1882)
SI 2002/238 Social Security (Contributions) (Amendment) Regulations 2002 (amend SI 2001/1004)
SI 2002/307 Social Security (Contributions) (Amendment No 2) Regulations 2002 (amend SI 2001/1004)
SI 2002/490 Social Security (Loss of Benefit) (Consequential Amendments) Regulations 2002 (amend SI 1975/556)
SI 2002/2256 Employment Act 2002 (Commencement No 2) Order 2002
SI 2002/2366 Social Security (Contributions) (Amendment No 3) Regulations 2002 (amend SI 2001/769 and SI 2001/1004)
SI 2002/2469 National Health Service Reform and Health Care Professions Act 2002 (Supplementary, Consequential etc Provisions) Regulations 2002 (amend SI 1991/589)

SI 2006/127 Social Security (Contributions) (Amendment) Regulations 2006 (amend SI 2001/1004)
SI 2006/576 Social Security (Contributions) (Amendment No 2) Regulations 2006 (amend SI 2001/1004)
SI 2006/624 Social Security (Contributions) (Re-rating and National Insurance Funds Payments) Order 2006 (amends SSCBA 1992)
SI 2006/883 Social Security (Contributions) (Amendment No 3) Regulations 2006 (amend SI 2001/1004)
SI 2006/2003 Social Security (Contributions) (Amendment No 4) Regulations 2006 (amend SI 2001/1004)
SI 2006/2829 Social Security (Contributions) (Amendment No 5) Regulations 2006 (amend SI 2001/1004)
SI 2006/2924 Social Security (Contributions) (Amendment No 6) Regulations 2006
SI 2007/118 Social Security (Contributions) (Amendment) Regulations 2007
SI 2007/770 Social Security (Contributions, Categorisation of Earners and Intermediaries) (Amendment) Regulations 2007
SI 2007/781 Social Security Revaluation of Earnings Factors Order 2007
SI 2007/785 National Insurance Contributions (Application of Part 7 of the Finance Act 2004) Regulations 2007 (revoked)
SI 2007/795 Social Security Contributions and Benefits (Northern Ireland) Act 1992 (Modification of Section 10(7B)) Regulations 2007
SI 2007/799 Social Security Contributions and Benefits Act 1992 (Modification of Section 10(7B)) Regulations 2007
SI 2007/824 Tax Credits (Miscellaneous Amendments) Regulations 2007
SI 2007/1052 Social Security (Contributions) (Re-rating and National Insurance Funds Payments) Order 2007
SI 2007/1056 Social Security Contributions (Consequential Provisions) Regulations 2007
SI 2007/1057 Social Security (Contributions) (Amendment No 2) Regulations 2007
SI 2007/1094 Social Security (Contributions) (Re-rating) Consequential Amendment Regulations 2007
SI 2007/1154 Social Security, Occupational Pension Schemes and Statutory Payments (Consequential Provisions) Regulations 2007
SI 2007/1838 Social Security (Contributions) (Amendment No 4) Regulations 2007
SI 2007/2070 Social Security Contributions (Managed Service Companies) Regulations 2007
SI 2007/2071 Social Security Contributions and Benefits Act 1992 (Modification of Section 4A) Order 2007
SI 2007/2091 Social Security (Contributions) (Amendment No 6) Regulations 2007
SI 2007/2401 Social Security (Contributions) (Amendment No 7) Regulations 2007
SI 2007/2520 Social Security (Contributions) (Amendment No 8) Regulations 2007
SI 2007/2582 Social Security (National Insurance Credits) Amendment Regulations 2007 (revoked)
SI 2007/2905 Social Security (Contributions) (Amendment No 9) Regulations 2007
SI 2008/223 Social Security (National Insurance Numbers) Amendment Regulations 2008
SI 2008/607 Social Security (Contributions) (Amendment No 2) Regulations 2008
SI 2008/636 Social Security (Contributions) (Amendment No 3) Regulations 2008
SI 2008/579 Social Security (Contributions) (Re-rating) Order 2008
SI 2008/703 Social Security (Contributions) (Re-rating) Consequential Amendment Regulations 2008
SI 2008/954 Companies Act 2006 (Consequential Amendments) (Taxes and National Insurance) Order 2008
SI 2008/1431 Social Security (Contributions) (Amendment No 4) Regulations 2008
SI 2008/1432 Financial Assistance Scheme (Miscellaneous Provisions) Regulations 2008
SI 2008/1554Employment and Support Allowance (Consequential Provisions) (No 2) Regulations 2009
SI 2008/2624Social Security (Contributions) (Amendment No 5) Regulations 2008
SI 2008/2678 National Insurance Contributions (Application of Part 7 of the Finance Act 2004) (Amendment) Regulations 2008 (revoked)
SI 2008/2683 Tribunals, Courts and Enforcement Act 2007 (Transitional and Consequential Provisions) Order 2009
SI 2008/2685 Tribunal Procedure (First-tier Tribunal) (Social Entitlement Chamber) Rules 2008
SI 2008/2833 Transfer of Tribunal Functions Order 2008

SI 2013/559 Social Security (Contributions) (Re-rating) Order 2013
SI 2013/591 Armed Forces and Reserve Forces Compensation Scheme (Consequential Provisions: Subordinate Legislation) Order 2013
SI 2013/619 Social Security (Contributions) (Re-rating) Consequential Amendment Regulations 2013
SI 2013/622 Social Security (Contributions) (Amendment and Application of Schedule 38 to the Finance Act 2012) Regulations 2013
SI 2013/718 Social Security (Contributions) (Amendment) Regulations 2013
SI 2013/1510 Social Security (Persons Required to Provide Information) Regulations 2013
SI 2013/1907 Social Security (Contributions) (Amendment No 3) Regulations 2013
SI 2013/2067 Tribunal Procedure (Amendment No 4) Rules 2013
SI 2013/2301 Social Security (Contributions) (Amendment No 4) Regulations 2013
SI 2013/2536 Social Security (Miscellaneous Amendments) (No 3) Regulations 2013
SI 2013/2600 National Insurance Contributions (Application of Part 7 of the Finance Act 2004) (Amendment) Regulations 2013
SI 2013/3165 Social Security (Crediting and Treatment of Contributions, and National Insurance Numbers) (Amendment) Regulations 2013
SI 2014/367 Social Security Revaluation of Earnings Factors Order 2014
SI 2014/368 Social Security Pensions (Low Earnings Threshold) Order 2014.
SI 2014/475 Social Security (Contributions) (Re-rating and National Insurance Funds Payments) Order 2014
SI 2014/514 Tribunal Procedure (Amendment) Rules 2014
SI 2014/516 Social Security Benefits Up-rating Order 2014
SI 2014/569 Social Security (Contributions) (Limits and Thresholds) (Amendment) Regulations 2014
SI 2014/572 Social Security (Miscellaneous Amendments) Regulations 2014
SI 2014/591 Social Security (Miscellaneous Amendments) Regulations 2014
SI 2014/608 Social Security (Contributions) (Amendment) Regulations 2014
SI 2014/618 Social Security Benefits Up-rating Regulations 2014 (revoked)
SI 2014/634 Social Security (Contributions) (Re-rating) Consequential Amendment Regulations 2014
SI 2014/635 Social Security (Categorisation of Earners) (Amendment) Regulations 2014
SI 2014/897 Statutory Sick Pay Percentage Threshold (Revocations, Transitional and Saving Provisions) (Great Britain and Northern Ireland) Order 2014
SI 2014/992 Finance Act 2009, Sections 101 and 102 (Interest on Late Payments and Repayments), Appointed Days and Consequential Provisions Order 2014
SI 2014/1016 Social Security (Contributions) (Amendment No 3) Regulations 2014
SI 2014/1231 Child Benefit (General) and Child Tax Credit (Amendment) Regulations 2014
SI 2014/1283 Finance Act 2009, Sections 101 and 102 (Interest on Late Payments and Repayments) (Consequential Amendments) Order 2014
SI 2014/1511 Child Benefit (General) and Tax Credits (Residence) (Amendment) Regulations 2014
SI 2014/2727 Pensions Act 2014 (Commencement No. 3) Order 2014
SI 2014/3061 Marriage (Same Sex Couples) Act 2013 and Marriage and Civil Partnership (Scotland) Act 2014 (Consequential Provisions) Order 2014
SI 2014/3159 Social Security Contributions (Limited Liability Partnership) Regulations 2014
SI 2014/3240 Social Security Class 3A Contributions (Units of Additional Pension) Regulations 2014
SI 2015/118 Occupational Pension Schemes (Power to Amend Schemes to Reflect Abolition of Contracting-out) Regulations 2015
SI 2015/174 Social Security Contributions (Decisions and Appeals) (Amendment) Regulations 2015
SI 2015/175 Social Security and Tax Credits (Miscellaneous Amendments) Regulations 2015
SI 2015/185 Social Security Pensions (Flat Rate Accrual Amount) Order 2015
SI 2015/186 Social Security Pensions (Low Earnings Threshold) Order 2015
SI 2015/187 Social Security Revaluation of Earnings Factors Order 2015
SI 2015/202 Social Security (Penalty as Alternative to Prosecution) (Maximum Amount) Order 2015
SI 2015/343 Social Security (Fees Payable by Qualifying Lenders) (Amendment) Regulations 2015
SI 2015/389 Social Security (Members of the Reserve Forces) (Amendment) Regulations 2015

Statutory Instruments

1975/556

SOCIAL SECURITY (CREDITS) REGULATIONS 1975

Made by the Secretary of State for Social Services under SSA 1975 s 13(4) and SS(CP)A 1975 s 2(1) and Sch 3 para 3

Note—Social Security Acts 1992 which consolidate provisions under which this statutory instrument is made come into effect on 1 July 1992. Social Security (Consequential Provisions) Act 1992 s 2 provides for the continuity of this instrument after 30 June 1992.

Made .... 3 April 1975
Laid before Parliament .... 4 April 1975
Coming into Operation .... 6 April 1975

1 Citation and commencement

These regulations may be cited as the Social Security (Credits) Regulations 1975 and shall come into operation on 6th April 1975.

2 Interpretation

(1) In these regulations, unless the context otherwise require,—

"the Act" means the Social Security Act 1975;

["the 2012 Act" means the Welfare Reform Act 2012;][17]

["benefit"—

(*a*) includes—

(i) a contribution-based jobseeker's allowance;

(ii) a contributory employment and support allowance;

(*b*) does not include—

(i) an income-based jobseeker's allowance;

(ii) an income-related employment and support allowance;

(iii) state pension under Part 1 of the Pensions Act 2014;][18]

. . . [19]

. . . [19]

[. . . [9]][1]

["contribution-based jobseeker's allowance" means an allowance under the Jobseekers Act 1995 as amended by the provisions of Part 1 of Schedule 14 to the 2012 Act that remove references to an income-based allowance, and a contribution-based allowance under the Jobseekers Act 1995 as that Act has effect apart from those provisions;][17]

["contributory employment and support allowance" means an allowance under Part 1 of the Welfare Reform Act as amended by the provisions of Schedule 3, and Part 1 of Schedule 14, to the 2012 Act that remove references to an income-related allowance, and a contributory allowance under Part 1 of the Welfare Reform Act as that Part has effect apart from those provisions;][17]

["the Contributions and Benefits Act" means the Social Security Contributions and Benefits Act 1992;][5]

"credits" and "a credit" shall be construed in accordance with regulation 3;

[. . . [14]][11]

[. . . [9]][1]

[. . . [9]][1]

["income-based jobseeker's allowance" has the same meaning as in the Jobseekers Act 1995;][6]

["income-related employment and support allowance" means an income-related allowance under Part 1 of the Welfare Reform Act (employment and support allowance);][16]

["jobseeker's allowance" means an allowance payable under Part I of the Jobseekers Act 1995;][6]

[. . . [9]][1]

[. . . [9]][1]

["reckonable year" means a year for which the relevant earnings factor of the contributor concerned was sufficient to satisfy—

(*a*) in relation to short-term incapacity benefit, widowed mother's allowance, [widowed parent's allowance, . . . [19],][15] widow's pension or Category A or Category B retirement pension, paragraph (*b*) of the second contribution condition specified in relation to that benefit in Schedule 3 to the Contributions and Benefits Act; . . . [16]

(*b*) in relation to contribution-based jobseeker's allowance, the additional condition specified in section 2(3) of the Jobseekers Act 1995; [or

(*c*) in relation to a contributory employment and support allowance, the condition specified in paragraph 2(1) of Schedule 1 to the Welfare Reform Act (conditions relating to national insurance).][16]][7]

["relevant benefit year" has the same meaning as it has—

(*a*) in relation to short-term incapacity benefit, in paragraph 2(6)(*b*) of Schedule 3 to the Contributions and Benefits Act; . . . [16]

(*b*) in relation to contribution-based jobseeker's allowance, in section 2(4)(*b*) of the Jobseekers Act 1995; [and

(*c*) in relation to a contributory employment and support allowance, in paragraph 3(1)(*f*) of Schedule 1 to the Welfare Reform Act (conditions relating to national insurance);][16]][7]

"relevant earnings factor", [in relation to any benefit—

(*a*) [if the benefit is a contribution-based jobseeker's allowance or if the contributions relevant to the benefit under section 21 of the Contributions and Benefits Act][8] are Class 1 contributions, the earnings factor derived from earnings [in respect of which][10] primary Class 1 contributions have been paid or treated as paid, or credited earnings;

(*b*) if the contributions relevant to that benefit under [that section][8] are Class 1 and Class 2 contributions, the earnings factor or the aggregate of the earnings factors derived from—

(i) earnings [in respect of which][10] primary Class 1 contributions have been paid or treated as paid, or credited earnings, and

(ii) Class 2 contributions;

(*c*) if the contributions relevant to that benefit under [that section][8] are Class 1, Class 2 and Class 3 contributions, the earnings factor or the aggregate of the earnings factors derived from—

(i) earnings [in respect of which][10] primary contributions have been paid or treated as paid, or credited earnings,

(ii) Class 2 contributions, and

(iii) Class 3 contributions paid or credited][2];

["relevant past year" means the last complete year before the beginning of the relevant benefit year;][4]

["universal credit" means universal credit under Part 1 of the 2012 Act;][17]

["the Welfare Reform Act" means the Welfare Reform Act 2007;][16]

["widowed parent's allowance" means an allowance referred to in section 39A of the Contributions and Benefits Act;][13]

[["working tax credit" means a working tax credit under section 10 of the Tax Credits Act 2002][14]][12]

["year" means tax year;][3]

and other expressions have the same meanings as in the Act.

(2) The rules for the construction of Acts of Parliament contained in the Interpretation Act 1889[a] shall apply for the purposes of the interpretation of these regulations as they apply for the purposes of the interpretation of a Act of Parliament.

(3) Unless the context otherwise requires, any reference in these regulations—

(*a*) to a numbered section is a reference to the section of the Act bearing that number;

(*b*) to a numbered regulation is a reference to the regulation bearing that number in these regulations, and any reference in a regulation to a numbered paragraph is a reference to the paragraph of that regulation bearing that number;

(*c*) to any provision made by or contained in any enactment or instrument shall be construed as a reference to that provision as amended or extended by any enactment or instrument and as including a reference to any provision which it re-enacts or replaces or which may re-enact or replace it with or without modification.

(4) Nothing in these regulations shall be construed as entitling any person to be credited with contributions for the purposes of any benefit for a day, period or event occurring before 6th April 1975.

Note—[a] Interpretation Act 1978.

Amendments—[1] Definitions inserted by the Social Security (Unemployment, Sickness and Invalidity Benefit and Credits) Amendment Regulations, SI 1982/96 reg 5.

[2] In definition of "relevant earnings factor" words substituted by the Social Security (Credits) Amendment Regulations, SI 1987/414, regs 2, 11, with effect in respect of periods after 5 April 1987.

[3] Definition of "year" inserted by the Social Security (Credits) Amendment (No 2) Regulations, SI 1988/1230.

4 Definition of "relevant past year" substituted by the Social Security (Credits) Amendment (No 4) Regulations, SI 1988/1545 reg 2(2).

5 Definition of "the Contributions and Benefits Act" inserted by the Social Security (Incapacity Benefit) (Consequential and Transitional Amendments and Savings) Regulations, SI 1995/829 reg 6(2), with effect from 13 April 1995.

6 Definitions of "contribution-based jobseeker's allowance", "income-based jobseeker's allowance" and "jobseeker's allowance" inserted by the Social Security (Credits and Contributions) (Jobseeker's Allowance Consequential and Miscellaneous Amendments) Regulations, SI 1996/2367 reg 2(1), (2)(*a*) with effect from 7 October 1996.

7 Definitions "reckonable year" and "relevant benefit year" substituted by SI 1996/2367 reg 2(1), (2)(*b*), (*c*) with effect from 7 October 1996.

8 In definition of "relevant earnings factor" words in sub-paras (*a*)–(*c*) substituted by SI 1996/2367 reg 2(1), (2)(*d*) with effect from 7 October 1996.

9 Definitions "charity", "health authority", "health board", "local authority" and "preserved board" omitted by SI 1996/2367 reg 2(1), (2)(*e*) with effect from 7 October 1996.

10 In definition of "relevant earnings factor" words substituted by the Social Security (Contributions and Credits) (Miscellaneous Amendments) Regulations, SI 1999/568 reg 20 with effect from 6 April 1999.

11 Definition of "disabled person's tax credit" substituted for definition "disability working allowance" by the Social Security and Child Support (Tax Credits) Consequential Amendments Regulations, SI 1999/2566 reg 2(3)(*a*), Sch 2 Pt III with effect from 5 October 1999.

12 Definition of "working families' tax credit" inserted by SI 1999/2566 reg 2(3)(*b*), Sch 2 Pt III with effect from 5 October 1999.

13 Definition of "widowed parent's allowance" inserted by the Social Security (Benefits for Widows and Widowers) (Consequential Amendments) Regulations, SI 2000/1483 reg 3(1), (2) with effect from 9 April 2001.

14 Definition of "disabled persons' tax credit" revoked, and definition of "working tax credit" substituted for the definition of "working families' tax credit", by the Social Security (Working Tax Credit and Child Tax Credit) (Consequential Amendments) Regulations, SI 2003/455 reg 6, Sch 4 para 1(*a*) with effect from 7 April 2003.

15 Words in definition of "reckonable year" inserted by the Social Security (Miscellaneous Amendments) (No 3) Regulations, SI 2007/1749 reg 8(1), (2) with effect from 16 July 2007.

16 In para (1), definitions of "contributory employment and support allowance", "income-related employment and support allowance" and "the Welfare Reform Act" inserted, in the definition of "reckonable year", word "or " in sub-para (*a*) repealed and sub-para (*c*) and preceding word "or" inserted, in the definition of "relevant benefit year", word "and " in sub-para (*a*) repealed and sub-para (*c*) and preceding word "and" inserted, by the Employment and Support Allowance (Consequential Provisions) (No 2) Regulations, SI 2008/1554 reg 48(1), (2) with effect from 27 October 2008.

17 In para (1), definitions of "the 2012 Act" and "universal credit' inserted, and definitions of "contribution-based jobseeker's allowance" and "contributory employment and support allowance" substituted, by the Universal Credit (Consequential, Supplementary, Incidental and Miscellaneous Provisions) Regulations, SI 2013/630 reg 70(1), (2) with effect from 29 April 2013.

18 In para (1), definition of "benefit" substituted by the Pensions Act 2014 (Consequential, Supplementary and Incidental Amendments) Order, SI 2015/1985 art 2 with effect from 6 April 2016.

19 In para (1), definitions of "bereavement allowance" and "bereavement benefit" revoked, and in definition of "reckonable year", words revoked, by the Pensions Act 2014 (Consequential, Supplementary and Incidental Amendments) Order, SI 2017/422 art 4(1), (2) with effect from 6 April 2017 (the day on which Pensions Act 2014 s 30 comes into effect for all purposes).

3 General provisions relating to the crediting of contributions [and earnings]

[(1) Any contributions or earnings credited in accordance with these Regulations shall be only for the purpose of enabling the person concerned to satisfy—

([*aa*) in relation to short-term incapacity benefit, the second contribution condition specified in paragraph 2(3) of Schedule 3 (contribution conditions for entitlement to benefit) to the Contributions and Benefits Act;

(*ab*) in relation to—

(*i*) widowed mother's allowance;

(*ii*) widowed parent's allowance;

(*iii*) . . .[7] and

(*iv*) widow's pension,

the second contribution condition specified in paragraph 5(3) of Schedule 3 to the Contributions and Benefits Act;

(*ac*) in relation to a Category A or Category B retirement pension—

(*i*) in the case of a retirement pension to which paragraph 5 of Schedule 3 to the Contributions and Benefits Act applies, the second contribution condition specified in paragraph 5(3); and

(*ii*) otherwise, the contribution condition specified in paragraph 5A(2) of Schedule 3 to that Act;otherwise, the contribution condition specified in paragraph 5A(2) of Schedule 3 to that Act;][6]

(*b*) in relation to contribution-based jobseeker's allowance, the condition specified in section 2(1)(*b*) of the Jobseekers Act 1995, [or

(*c*) in relation to a contributory employment and support allowance, the condition specified in paragraph 2(1) of Schedule 1 to the Welfare Reform Act,][5]

and accordingly, where under any of the provisions of these Regulations a person would, but for this paragraph, be entitled to be credited with any contributions or earnings for a year, or in respect of any

NIC

week in a year, he shall be so entitled for the purposes of any benefit only if and to no greater extent than that by which his relevant earnings factor for that year falls short of the level required to make that year a reckonable year.][4]

(2) Where under these regulations a person is entitled for the purposes of any benefit to—

(*a*) [be credited with earnings][1] for a year, he is to be credited with such amount of [earnings][1] as may be required to bring his relevant earnings factor to the level required to make that year a reckonable year;

(*b*) . . . [2]

(3) Where under these regulations a person is entitled to [be credited with earnings or a contribution][3] in respect of a week which is partly in one tax year and partly in another, he shall be entitled to [be credited with those earnings or that contribution][3] for the tax year in which that week began and not for the following year.

Amendments—Words in heading added by the Social Security (Credits) Amendment Regulations, SI 1987/414, regs 3(*a*), 11, with effect in respect of periods after 5 April 1987.

1 Words in para (2)(*a*) substituted by SI 1987/414, regs 3(*c*)(i), (ii), 11, with effect in respect of periods after 5 April 1987.

2 Para 2(*b*) revoked by SI 1987/414, regs 3(*c*)(iii), 11, with effect in respect of periods after 5 April 1987.

3 Words in para (3) substituted by SI 1987/414, regs 3(*d*), 11, with effect in respect of periods after 5 April 1987.

4 Para (1) substituted by the Social Security (Credits and Contributions) (Jobseeker's Allowance Consequential and Miscellaneous Amendments) Regulations, SI 1996/2367 reg 2(1), (3) with effect from 7 October 1996.

5 In para (1)(*a*), word "or" repealed, and para (1)(*c*) and preceding word "or" inserted, by the Employment and Support Allowance (Consequential Provisions) (No 2) Regulations, SI 2008/1554 reg 48(1), (3) with effect from 27 October 2008.

6 Para (1)(*aa*)–(*ac*) substituted for former para (1)(*a*) by the Social Security (State Pension and National Insurance Credits) Regulations 2009, SI 2009/2206 regs 28, 29 with effect from 6 April 2010.

7 Para (1)(*ab*)(iii) revoked by the Pensions Act 2014 (Consequential, Supplementary and Incidental Amendments) Order, SI 2017/422 art 4(1), (3) with effect from 6 April 2017 (the day on which Pensions Act 2014 s 30 comes into effect for all purposes).

4 Starting credits for the purposes of a retirement pension, a widowed mother's allowance[, a widowed parent's allowance . . .] and a widow's pension

(1) [Subject to paragraph (1A),][3]For the purposes of entitlement to a Category A or a Category B retirement pension, a widowed mother's allowance[, a widowed parent's allowance . . .[4]][2] or a widow's pension [by virtue of a person's earnings or contributions][1], he shall be credited with such number of Class 3 contributions as may be required to bring his relevant earnings factor in respect of the tax year in which he attained the age of 16 and for each of the 2 following tax years to the level required to make those years reckonable years; so however that, subject to paragraph (2), no contribution shall be credited under this regulation in respect of any tax year commencing before 6th April 1975.

[(1A) For the purposes of entitlement to a Category A or a Category B retirement pension, no contribution shall be credited under this regulation—

(*a*) in respect of any tax year commencing on or after 6th April 2010;

(*b*) in respect of any other tax year, where an application under regulation 9 (application for allocation of national insurance number) of the Social Security (Crediting and Treatment of Contributions, and National Insurance Numbers) Regulations 2001 is made on or after 6th April 2010.][3]

(2) Where a person was in Great Britain on 6th April 1975 and had attained the age of 16 but was not an insured person under the National Insurance Act 1965 he shall be credited with contributions under paragraph(1) in respect of the tax year commencing on 6th April 1974.

Amendments—1 Words in para (1) substituted by the Social Security (Credits) Amendment (No 4) Regulations, SI 1988/1545 reg 2(5).

2 Words in cross-heading and para (1) inserted by the Social Security (Benefits for Widows and Widowers) (Consequential Amendments) Regulations, SI 2000/1483 reg 3(1), (4) with effect as from 9 April 2001.

3 Words in para (1) inserted, and para (1A) inserted, by the National Insurance Contributions Credits (Miscellaneous Amendments) Regulations, SI 2011/709 reg 2(1), (2) with effect from 5 April 2011.

4 In heading and para (1), words revoked by the Pensions Act 2014 (Consequential, Supplementary and Incidental Amendments) Order, SI 2017/422 art 4(1), (4) with effect from 6 April 2017 (the day on which Pensions Act 2014 s 30 comes into effect for all purposes).

7 Credits for approved training

(1) For the purposes of entitlement to any benefit [by virtue of a person's earnings or contributions][1] he shall, subject to paragraphs [(2) to (4)][6], be entitled to [be credited with earnings equal to the lower earnings limit then in force][2] in respect of each week in any part of which he was undergoing (otherwise than in pursuance of his employment as an employed earner) a course of . . .[3] training approved by the Secretary of State for the purposes of this regulation.

[(2) Paragraph (1) shall apply to a person only if—

(*a*) the course is—

(i) a course of full-time training; or

(ii) a course of training which he attends for not less than 15 hours in the week in question and he is a disabled person within the meaning of the Disabled Persons (Employment) Act 1944; or

(iii) a course of training introductory to a course to which paragraph (i) or (ii) above applies; and

(*b*) when the course began it was not intended to continue for more than 12 months or, if he was a disabled person within the meaning of the Disabled Persons (Employment) Act 1944 and the training was provided under the Employment and Training Act 1973 [or the Enterprise and New Towns (Scotland) Act 1990][4], for such longer period as is reasonable in the circumstances of his case; and

(*c*) he had attained the age of 18 before the beginning of the tax year in which the week in question began.][3]

(3) Paragraph (1) shall not apply to a woman in respect of any week in any part of which she was a married woman in respect of whom an election made by her under regulations made [under section 3(2) of the Social Security Pensions Act 1975[a]][5] had effect.

[(4) Paragraph (1) shall not apply to a person in respect of any week in any part of which that person was entitled to universal credit.][6]

Notes—[a] SSCBA 1992 s 19(4).

Amendments—[1] Words in para (1) substituted by the Social Security (Credits) Amendment (No 4) Regulations, SI 1988/1545 reg 2(5).

[2] Words in para (1) substituted by the Social Security (Credits) Amendment Regulations, SI 1987/414, regs 5(*a*), 11, with effect in respect of periods after 5 April 1987.

[3] Words omitted in para (1), and para (2), substituted by the Social Security (Credits) Amendment (No 3) Regulations, SI 1988/1439, with effect in respect of periods after 3 September 1988.

[4] Words in para (2)(*b*) inserted by the Enterprise (Scotland) Consequential Amendments Order, SI 1991/387 art 3(*a*), with effect from 1 April 1991.

[5] Words in para (3) substituted by the Social Security (Credits) Amendment and (Earnings Factor) Transitional Regulations, SI 1978/409 reg 2(2).

[6] In para (1), words substituted, and para (4) inserted, by the Universal Credit (Consequential, Supplementary, Incidental and Miscellaneous Provisions) Regulations, SI 2013/630 reg 70(1), (3) with effect from 29 April 2013.

7A [Credits for invalid care allowance

(1) For the purposes of entitlement to any benefit [by virtue of a person's contributions][2] he shall, subject to paragraph (2), be entitled to [be credited with earnings equal to the lower earnings limit then in force][3] in respect of each week for any part of which an invalid care allowance is paid to him [or would be paid to him but for a restriction under section 7 of the Social Security Fraud Act 2001 (loss of benefit provisions)][7], or in the case of a [widow, widower or surviving civil partner][8], would have been so payable but for the provisions of the Social Security (Overlapping Benefits) Regulations 1975, as amended by the Social Security (Invalid Care Allowance) Regulations 1976, requiring adjustment of an invalid care allowance against widow's benefit[, [widowed parent's allowance][9]][6] or benefit by virtue of section 39(4) corresponding to a widowed mother's allowance or a widow's pension.

(2) Paragraph (1) shall not apply—

(*a*) to a person in respect of any week where he is entitled to [be credited with earnings][3] under [regulation 8A or 8B][5] in respect of the same week; or

(*b*) to a woman in respect of any week in any part of which she was a married woman in respect of whom an election made by her under regulations made [under section 3(2) of the Social Security Pensions Act 1975][4] had effect.][1]

Notes—[a] SSCBA 1992 s 19(4).

Amendments—[1] Reg 7A inserted by the Social Security (Invalid Care Allowance) Regulations, SI 1976/409 reg 19.

[2] Words in para (1) substituted by the Social Security (Credits) Amendment (No 4) Regulations, SI 1988/1545 reg 2 (5).

[3] Words in para (1), (2)(*a*) substituted by the Social Security (Credits) Amendment Regulations, SI 1987/414, regs 6, 11, with effect in respect of periods after 5 April 1987.

[4] Words in para (2)(*b*) substituted by the Social Security (Credits) Amendment and (Earnings Factor) Transitional Regulations, SI 1978/409 reg 2(2).

[5] Words in para (2)(*a*) substituted by the Social Security (Credits and Contributions) (Jobseeker's Allowance Consequential and Miscellaneous Amendments) Regulations, SI 1996/2367 reg 2(1), (4) with effect from 7 October 1996.

[6] Words in para (1) inserted by the Social Security (Benefits for Widows and Widowers) (Consequential Amendments) Regulations, SI 2000/1483 reg 3(1), (5) with effect from 9 April 2001.

[7] Words in para (1) inserted by the Social Security (Loss of Benefit) (Consequential Amendments) Regulations, SI 2002/490 reg 3(*a*) with effect from 1 April 2002.

[8] Words in para (1) substituted by the Civil Partnership (Pensions, Social Security and Child Support) (Consequential, etc Provisions) Order 2005, SI 2005/2877 Art 2(3), Sch 3 para 4(2) with effect from 5 December 2005.

[9] In para (1), words substituted by the Pensions Act 2014 (Consequential, Supplementary and Incidental Amendments) Order, SI 2017/422 art 4(1), (5) with effect from 6 April 2017 (the day on which Pensions Act 2014 s 30 comes into effect for all purposes).

7B [Credits for [disability element of working tax credit]]

(1) For the purposes of entitlement to any benefit by virtue of a person's earnings or contributions he shall, subject to paragraphs (2) and (3), be credited with earnings equal to the lower earnings limit then in force in respect of each week for any part of which [the disability element or the severe disability element of working tax credit as specified in regulation 20(1)(*b*) and (*f*) of the Working Tax Credit (Entitlement and Maximum Rate) Regulations 2002 is included in an award of working tax credit which][3] is paid to him.

(2) Paragraph (1) shall apply to a person only if he is—

(*a*) an employed earner; . . .[4]

(*b*) a self-employed earner who is excepted from liability to pay Class 2 contributions by virtue of his earnings being less than or being treated by regulations as less than the amount specified in section 7(5) of the Act (exception from liability for Class 2 contributions on account of small earnings).

(3) Paragraph (1) shall not apply—

(*a*) to a person in respect of any week where he is entitled to be credited with earnings under [regulation 8A or 8B][2] in respect of the same week; or

[(*b*) self-employed earner whose profits for the year are below the small profits threshold specified in section 11(4) of the Contributions and Benefits Act, who would otherwise be liable to pay a Class 2 contribution; or

(*c*) excepted from liability to pay a Class 2 contribution by virtue of regulation 43 of the Social Security (Contributions) Regulations 2001(d).][4]][1]

Amendments—[1] Reg. 7B inserted by the Social Security (Credits) Amendment Regulations, SI 1991/2772 reg 3, with effect from 6 April 1992.

[2] Words in para (3)(*a*) substituted by the Social Security (Credits and Contributions) (Jobseeker's Allowance Consequential and Miscellaneous Amendments) Regulations, SI 1996/2367 reg 2(1), (4) with effect from 7 October 1996.

[3] Words in Heading and para (1) substituted by the Social Security (Working Tax Credit and Child Tax Credit) (Consequential Amendments) Regulations, SI 2003/455 reg 6, Sch 4 para 1(*b*), (*c*) with effect from 7 April 2003.

[4] In para (2)(*a*), word "or" revoked, and para (2)(*b*), (*c*) substituted for previous para (2)(*b*), by the Social Security (Credits, and Crediting and Treatment of Contributions) (Consequential and Miscellaneous Amendments) Regulations, SI 2016/1145 reg 3(1), (2) with effect from 1 January 2017.

7C [Credits for [working tax credit]

(1) [Subject to regulation 7B,][4] for the purposes of entitlement to a Category A or a Category B retirement pension, a widowed mother's allowance[, a widowed parent's allowance . . .[7]][3] or a widow's pension by virtue of a person's earnings or contributions, where [working tax credit][4] is paid for any week in respect of—

(*a*) an employed earner; . . .[6]

[(*b*) a self-employed earner—

(i) whose profits for the year are below the small profits threshold specified in section 11(4) of the Contributions and Benefits Act, who would otherwise be liable to pay a Class 2 contribution; or

(ii) who is excepted from liability to pay a Class 2 contribution by virtue of regulation 43 of the Social Security (Contributions) Regulations 2001,][6]

(2) The reference in paragraph (1) to the person in respect of whom [working tax credit][4] is paid—

(*a*) where it is paid to one of [a couple][5], is a reference to the member of that couple specified in paragraph (3); and

(*b*) in any other case, is a reference to the person to whom it is paid.

(3) The member of [a couple][5] specified for the purposes of paragraph (2)(*a*) is—

(*a*) where only one member is assessed for the purposes of the award of [working tax credit][4] as having income consisting of earnings, that member;

(*b*) . . .[4] or

(*c*) where the earnings of each member are assessed . . .[4], the member to whom [working tax credit][4] is paid.

(4) Paragraph (1) shall not apply—

(*a*) to a person in respect of any week where he is entitled to be credited with earnings under [regulation 8A or 8B][2] in respect of the same week; or

(*b*) to a woman in respect of any week in any part of which she is a married woman in respect of whom an election made by her under regulations made under section 19(4) of the Contributions and Benefits Act has effect.

(5) . . .[4]

(6) In this regulation ["couple" has][5] the same meaning as in Part VII of the Contributions and Benefits Act.][1]

Amendments—[1] Reg 7C inserted by the Social Security (Credits) Amendment Regulations, SI 1995/2558, reg 2, with effect from 1 November 1995.

[2] Words in para (4)(*a*) substituted by the Social Security (Credits and Contributions) (Jobseeker's Allowance Consequential and Miscellaneous Amendments) Regulations, SI 1996/2367 reg 2(1), (4) with effect from 7 October 1996.

3 Words in para (1) inserted by the Social Security (Benefits for Widows and Widowers) (Consequential Amendments) Regulations, SI 2000/1483 reg 3(1), (6) with effect from 9 April 2001.
4 Words in para (1) inserted, words in paras (1)–(3) substituted, and sub-para (3)(*b*), para (5), and words in sub-para (3)(*c*) revoked, by the Social Security (Working Tax Credit and Child Tax Credit) (Consequential Amendments) Regulations, SI 2003/455 reg 6, Sch 4 para 1(*d*), (*e*) with effect from 7 April 2003.
5 Words in paras (2)(*a*), (3), (6) substituted by the Civil Partnership (Pensions, Social Security and Child Support) (Consequential, etc Provisions) Order 2005, SI 2005/2877 Art 2(3), Sch 3 para 4(3) with effect from 5 December 2005.
6 In para (1)(*a*), word "or" revoked, and para (1)(*b*) substituted, by the Social Security (Credits, and Crediting and Treatment of Contributions) (Consequential and Miscellaneous Amendments) Regulations, SI 2016/1145 reg 3(1), (3) with effect from 1 January 2017.
7 In para (1), words revoked by the Pensions Act 2014 (Consequential, Supplementary and Incidental Amendments) Order, SI 2017/422 art 4(1), (6) with effect from 6 April 2017 (the day on which Pensions Act 2014 s 30 comes into effect for all purposes).

8 Credits on termination of full-time education, training or apprenticeship

[(1) For the purposes of his entitlement to [a contribution-based jobseeker's allowance][5] [, short-term incapacity benefit or a contributory employment and support allowance][6] a person shall be entitled to be credited with earnings equal to the lower earnings limit then in force for either one of the last two complete years before the beginning of the relevant benefit year if—

(*a*) during any part of that year he was—

(i) undergoing a course of full-time education; or

(ii) undergoing—

(*a*) a course of training which was full-time and which was arranged under section 2(1) of the Employment and Training Act 1973 [or section 2(3) of the Enterprise and New Towns (Scotland) Act 1990][2]; or

(*b*) any other full-time course the sole or main purpose of which was the acquisition of occupational or vocational skills; or

(*c*) if he is a disabled person within the meaning of the Disabled Persons (Employment) Act 1944 a part-time course attended for at least 15 hours a week which, if it was full-time, would fall within either of heads (*a*) or (*b*) above; or

(iii) an apprentice; and

(*b*) the other year is, in his case, a reckonable year; and

(*c*) that course or, as the case may be, his apprenticeship has terminated.][1]

(2) Paragraph (1) shall not apply—

(*a*) where the course of education or training or the apprenticeship commenced after the person had attained the age of 21;

(*b*) to a woman in respect of any tax year immediately before the end of which she was a married woman and an election made by her under regulations made [under section 3(2) of the Social Security Pensions Act 1975[7]][3] had effect[;]

[(*c*) to a person in respect of any tax year before that in which he attains the age of 18.][4]

Amendments—1 Para (1) substituted by the Social Security (Credits) Amendment Regulations, SI 1989/1627 reg 3, with effect from 1 October 1989.
2 Words in para (1)(*a*)(ii) inserted by the Enterprise (Scotland) Consequential Amendments Order, SI 1991/387 art 3(*b*), with effect from 1 April 1991.
3 Words in para (2)(*b*) substituted by the Social Security (Credits) Amendment and (Earnings Factor) Transitional Regulations, SI 1978/409 reg 2(2).
4 Para (2)(*c*) inserted, and punctuation in para (2)(*b*) substituted, by SI 1988/1230, reg 2(1), (3)(*b*), (*c*).
5 Words in para (1) substituted by the Social Security (Credits and Contributions) (Jobseeker's Allowance Consequential and Miscellaneous Amendments) Regulations, SI 1996/2367 reg 2(1), (5) with effect from 7 October 1996.
6 In para (1), words substituted for words "or short-term incapacity benefit", by the Employment and Support Allowance (Consequential Provisions) (No 2) Regulations, SI 2008/1554 reg 48(1), (4) with effect from 27 October 2008.
7 SSCBA 1992 s 19(4).

8A [Credits for unemployment

(1) . . . [2] for the purposes of entitlement to any benefit by virtue of a person's earnings or contributions, he shall be entitled to be credited with earnings equal to the lower earnings limit then in force, in respect of each week to which this regulation applies.

(2) Subject to paragraph (5) this regulation applies to a week which, in relation to the person concerned, is—

(*a*) a week for the whole of which he was paid a jobseeker's allowance; or

[(*b*) a week for the whole of which the person in relation to old style JSA—

(i) satisfied or was treated as having satisfied the conditions set out in paragraphs (a), (c) and (e) to (h) of section 1(2) of the Jobseekers Act 1995 (conditions for entitlement to a jobseeker's allowance); and

(ii) satisfied the further condition specified in paragraph (3) below; or

(*ba*) a week for the whole of which the person in relation to new style JSA—

NIC

(i) satisfied or was treated as having satisfied the conditions set out in paragraphs (*e*) to (*h*) of section 1(2) of the Jobseekers Act 1995 (conditions for entitlement to a jobseeker's allowance);

(ii) satisfied or was treated as having satisfied the work-related requirements under section 6D and 6E of the Jobseekers Act 1995 (work search and work availability requirements); and

(iii) satisfied the further condition specified in paragraph (3) below; or][8]

(*c*) a week which would have been a week described in sub-paragraph (*b*) [or (*ba*)][8] but for the fact that he was incapable of work [or had limited capability for work][6] for part of it [or

(*d*) a week in respect of which he would have been paid a jobseeker's allowance but for a restriction imposed pursuant to . . .[7] [section 7, 8 or 9 of the Social Security Fraud Act 2001] (loss of benefit provisions).][5]][4]

(3) The further condition referred to in paragraph (2)(*b*) [and (*ba*)][8] is that the person concerned—

(*a*) furnished to the Secretary of State notice in writing of the grounds on which he claims to be entitled to be credited with earnings—

(i) on the first day of the period for which he claims to be so entitled in which the week in question fell; or

(ii) within such further time as may be reasonable in the circumstances of the case; and

(*b*) has provided any evidence required by the Secretary of State that the conditions referred to in paragraph (2)(*b*) [or the conditions and requirements in paragraph (2)(*ba*)][8] are satisfied.

(4) . . .[9]

(5) This regulation shall not apply to—

(*a*) a week in respect of which the person concerned was not entitled to a jobseeker's allowance (or would not have been if he had claimed it) because of section 14 of the Jobseekers Act 1995 (trade disputes); or

(*b*) a week in respect of which, in relation to the person concerned, there was in force a direction under section 16 of that Act (which relates to persons who have reached the age of 16 but not the age of 18 and who are in severe hardship); or

[(*c*) a week in respect of which, in relation to the person concerned—

(i) an old style JSA was reduced in accordance with section 19 or 19A, or regulations made under section 19B, of the Jobseekers Act 1995; or

(ii) a new style JSA was reduced in accordance with section 6J or 6K of the Jobseekers Act 1995; or][8]

[(*cc*) a week in respect of which a joint-claim jobseeker's allowance was not payable or was reduced pursuant to section 20A of that Act because the person was subject to sanctions for the purposes of that section, even though the couple of which he was a member satisfied the conditions for entitlement to that allowance;][3]

(*d*) a week in respect of which a jobseeker's allowance was payable to the person concerned only by virtue of regulation 141 of the Jobseeker's Allowance Regulations 1996 (circumstances in which an income-based jobseeker's allowance is payable to a person in hardship); or

[(*dd*) a week in respect of which a joint-claim jobseeker's allowance was payable in respect of a joint-claim couple of which the person is a member only by virtue of regulation 146C of the Jobseeker's Allowance Regulations 1996 (circumstances in which a joint-claim jobseeker's allowance is payable where a joint-claim couple is a couple in hardship);][3]

[(*de*) a week where paragraph (2)(*b*), (*ba*) or (*c*) apply and the person concerned was entitled to universal credit for any part of that week; or][8]

(*e*) where the person concerned is a married woman, a week in respect of any part of which an election made by her under regulations made under section 19(4) of the Contributions and Benefits Act had effect.

[(6) In this regulation—

"new style JSA" means a jobseeker's allowance under the Jobseekers Act 1995 as amended by the provisions of Part 1 of Schedule 14 to the 2012 Act that remove references to an income-based allowance;

"old style JSA" means a jobseeker's allowance under the Jobseekers Act 1995 as it has effect apart from the amendments made by Part 1 of Schedule 14 to the 2012 Act that remove references to an income-based allowance.][8]][1]

Amendments—[1] This regulation inserted by the Social Security (Credits and Contributions) (Jobseeker's Allowance Consequential and Miscellaneous Amendments) Regulations, SI 1996/2367 reg 2(1), (6) with effect from 7 October 1996.

[2] In para (1) words "Subject to regulation 9," revoked by the Social Security (Incapacity Benefit) Miscellaneous Amendments Regulations, SI 2000/3120 reg 4(a) with effect from 6 April 2001.

[3] Paras (5)(*cc*), (*dd*) inserted by the Social Security Amendment (Joint Claims) Regulations, SI 2001/518 reg 3 with effect from 19 March 2001.

[4] Para (2)(*d*) and word preceding it inserted by the Social Security (Breach of Community Order) (Consequential Amendments) Regulations, SI 2001/1711 art 2(3) with effect from 15 October 2001.

5 Words in para (2)(*d*) added by the Social Security (Loss of Benefit) (Consequential Amendments) Regulations, SI 2002/490 reg 3(*b*) with effect from 1 April 2002.

6 In para (2)(*c*) words inserted by the Employment and Support Allowance (Consequential Provisions) (No 2) Regulations, SI 2008/1554 reg 48(1), (5) with effect from 27 October 2008.

7 In para (2)(*d*) words repealed by the Welfare Reform Act 2009 (Section 26) (Consequential Amendments) Regulations 2010, SI 2010/424 reg 2 with effect from 2 April 2010.

8 In para (2), sub-paras (*b*), (*ba*) substituted for previous sub-para (*b*), and words in sub-para (*c*) inserted; in para (3) words inserted; para (5)(c) substituted and paras (5)(*de*), (6) inserted; by the Universal Credit (Consequential, Supplementary, Incidental and Miscellaneous Provisions) Regulations, SI 2013/630 reg 70(1), (4) with effect from 29 April 2013.

9 Para (4) revoked by the Social Security (Miscellaneous Amendments) (No 3) Regulations, SI 2013/2536 reg 3 with effect from 29 October 2013.

8B [Credits for incapacity for work [or limited capability for work]

(1) . . .[2] for the purposes of entitlement to any benefit by virtue of a person's earnings or contributions, he shall be entitled to be credited with earnings equal to the lower earnings limit then in force, in respect of each week to which this regulation applies.

(2) Subject to paragraphs [(2A),][7] (3) and (4) this regulation applies to—

[(*a*) a week in which, in relation to the person concerned, each of the days—

(i) was a day of incapacity for work under section 30C of the Contributions and Benefits Act (incapacity benefit: days and periods of incapacity for work); or

(ii) would have been such a day had the person concerned claimed short-term incapacity benefit or maternity allowance within the prescribed time; or

(iii) was a day of incapacity for work for the purposes of statutory sick pay under section 151 of the Contributions and Benefits Act and fell within a period of entitlement under section 153 of that Act; or

(iv) was a day of limited capability for work for the purposes of Part 1 of the Welfare Reform Act (limited capability for work) or would have been such a day had the person concerned been entitled to an employment and support allowance by virtue of section 1(2)(*a*) of the Welfare Reform Act; or

[(iva) would have been a day of limited capability for work for the purposes of Part 1 of the Welfare Reform Act (limited capability for work) where the person concerned would have been entitled to an employment and support allowance but for the application of section 1A of that Act; or][6]

(v) would have been a day of limited capability for work for the purposes of Part 1 of the Welfare Reform Act (limited capability for work) had that person claimed an employment and support allowance or maternity allowance within the prescribed time;][4]

[(aa) a week in which, in relation to the person concerned, each of the days—

(i) was a day of limited capability for work for the purposes of Part 1 of the Welfare Reform Act (limited capability for work) or would have been such a day had that person been entitled to an employment and support allowance by virtue of section 1 of the Welfare Reform Act; or

(ii) would have been such a day had the person concerned claimed an employment and support allowance or maternity allowance within the prescribed time; or][5]

[(*b*) a week for any part of which an unemployability supplement or allowance was payable by virtue of—

(i) Schedule 7 to the Contributions and Benefits Act;

[(ii) Article 12 of the Naval, Military and Air Forces Etc (Disablement and Death) Service Pensions Order 2006;][4]

(iii) Article 18 of the Personal Injuries (Civilians) Scheme 1983.][3]

[(2A) This regulation shall not apply to a week where—

(*a*) under paragraph (2)(a)(i) the person concerned was not entitled to incapacity benefit, severe disablement allowance or maternity allowance;

(*b*) paragraph (2)(*a*)(ii), (iva) or (v) apply; or

(*c*) under paragraph (2)(*a*)(iv) the person concerned was not entitled to an employment and support allowance by virtue of section 1(2)(*a*) of the Welfare Reform Act,

and the person concerned was entitled to universal credit for any part of that week.][7]

(3) Where the person concerned is a married woman, this regulation shall not apply to a week in respect of any part of which an election made by her under regulations made under section 19(4) of the Contributions and Benefits Act had effect.

(4) A day shall not be a day to which paragraph (2)(*a*) applies unless the person concerned has—

(*a*) before the end of the benefit year immediately following the year in which that day fell; or

(*b*) within such further time as may be reasonable in the circumstances of the case,

furnished to the Secretary of State notice in writing of the grounds on which he claims to be entitled to be credited with earnings.][1]

Amendments—[1] This regulation inserted by the Social Security (Credits and Contributions) (Jobseeker's Allowance Consequential and Miscellaneous Amendments) Regulations, SI 1996/2367 reg 2(1), (6) with effect from 7 October 1996.

[2] In para (1), the words "Subject to regulation 9," revoked by the Social Security (Incapacity Benefit) Miscellaneous Amendments Regulations 2000 reg 4(*b*) with effect from 6 April 2001.

[3] In para (2), words in sub-para (*a*)(i) inserted, and sub-para (*b*) substituted, by the Social Security (Credits) Amendment Regulations, SI 2003/521 reg 2(1), (2) with effect from 6 April 2003.

[4] Paras (2)(*a*) and (2)(*b*)(ii) substituted by the Social Security (Credits) (Amendment) Regulations 2010, SI 2010/385 reg 2 with effect from 6 April 2010.

[5] In heading, words inserted, and para (2)(*aa*) inserted, by the Employment and Support Allowance (Consequential Provisions) (No 2) Regulations, SI 2008/1554 reg 48(1), (6) with effect from 27 October 2008. Para (2)(*aa*) subsequently repealed by the Social Security (Credits) (Amendment) Regulations 2010, SI 2010/385 reg 2(b) with effect from 6 April 2010.

[6] Para (2)(*a*)(iva) inserted by the Employment and Support Allowance (Duration of Contributory Allowance) (Consequential Amendments) Regulations, SI 2012/913 reg 2 with effect from 1 May 2012.

[7] Words in para (2), and whole of para (2A), inserted, by the Universal Credit (Consequential, Supplementary, Incidental and Miscellaneous Provisions) Regulations, SI 2013/630 reg 70(1), (5) with effect from 29 April 2013.

8C [Credits on termination of bereavement benefits

(1) This regulation applies for the purpose only of enabling a person who previously received a bereavement benefit ("the recipient") to satisfy, as the case may be, the condition referred to in—

(*a*) paragraph 2(3)(*b*) of Schedule 3 to the Contributions and Benefits Act in relation to short-term incapacity benefit; . . .[3]

(*b*) section 2(1)(*b*) of the Jobseekers Act 1995 in relation to contribution-based jobseeker's allowance [or

(*c*) paragraph 2(1) of Schedule 1 to the Welfare Reform Act in relation to a contributory employment and support allowance.][3]

(2) For every year up to and including that in which the recipient ceased to be entitled to a bereavement benefit otherwise than by reason of remarriage[, forming a civil partnership,][2] or living together with [another person as a married couple][4], the recipient shall be credited with such earnings as may be required to enable the condition referred to above to be satisfied.]

[(3) In this regulation, "bereavement benefit" means—

(*a*) a bereavement payment referred to in section 36 of the Contributions and Benefits Act as in force immediately before it was repealed by paragraph 8 of Schedule 16 to the Pensions Act 2014;

(*b*) a bereavement allowance referred to in section 39B of the Contributions and Benefits Act as in force immediately before it was repealed by paragraph 13 of Schedule 16 to the Pensions Act 2014; and

(*c*) widowed parent's allowance.][5]][1]

Amendments—[1] This regulation inserted by the Social Security (Benefits for Widows and Widowers) (Consequential Amendments) Regulations, SI 2000/1483 reg 3(1), (7) with effect from 9 April 2001.

[2] Words in para (2) inserted by the Civil Partnership (Pensions, Social Security and Child Support) (Consequential, etc Provisions) Order 2005, SI 2005/2877 Art 2(3), Sch 3 para 4(4) with effect from 5 December 2005.

[3] In para (1), words "or" in sub-para (*a*) repealed, and sub-para (*c*) and preceding word "or" inserted, by the Employment and Support Allowance (Consequential Provisions) (No 2) Regulations, SI 2008/1554 reg 48(1), (7) with effect from 27 October 2008.

[4] Words in para (2) substituted by the Marriage (Same Sex Couples) Act 2013 and Marriage and Civil Partnership (Scotland) Act 2014 (Consequential Provisions) Order, SI 2014/3061 art 2, Schedule para 4(1), (2) with effect, in relation to England and Wales, from 10 December 2014, and in relation to Scotland, from 16 December 2014.

[5] Para (3) inserted by the Pensions Act 2014 (Consequential, Supplementary and Incidental Amendments) Order, SI 2017/422 art 4(1), (7) with effect from 6 April 2017 (the day on which Pensions Act 2014 s 30 comes into effect for all purposes).

8D [Credits for the purposes of entitlement to incapacity benefit following official error

(1) This regulation applies for the purpose only of enabling a person who was previously entitled to incapacity benefit to satisfy the condition referred to in paragraph 2(3)(*b*) of Schedule 3 to the Contributions and Benefits Act in respect of a subsequent claim for incapacity benefit where his period of incapacity for work is, together with a previous period of incapacity for work, to be treated as one period of incapacity for work under section 30C of that Act.

(2) Where—

(*a*) a person was previously entitled to incapacity benefit;

(*b*) the award of incapacity benefit was as a result of satisfying the condition referred to in paragraph (1) by virtue of being credited with earnings for incapacity for work or approved training in the tax years from 1993–94 to 2007–08;

(*c*) some or all of those credits were credited by virtue of official error derived from the failure to transpose correctly information relating to those credits from the Department for Work and Pensions' Pension Strategy Computer System to Her Majesty's Revenue and Customs' computer system (NIRS2) or from related clerical procedures;

(*d*) that person makes a further claim for incapacity benefit; and

(*e*) his period of incapacity for work is, together with the period of incapacity for work to which his previous entitlement referred to in sub-paragraph (*a*) related, to be treated as one period of incapacity for work under section 30C of the Contributions and Benefits Act,

that person shall be credited with such earnings as may be required to enable the condition referred to in paragraph (1) to be satisfied.

(3) In this regulation and in regulations 8E and 8F, "official error" means an error made by—

(*a*) an officer of the Department for Work and Pensions or an officer of Revenue and Customs acting as such which no person outside the Department or Her Majesty's Revenue and Customs caused or to which no person outside the Department for Work and Pensions or Her Majesty's Revenue and Customs materially contributed; or

(*b*) a person employed by a service provider and to which no person who was not so employed materially contributed,

but excludes any error of law which is shown to have been an error by virtue of a subsequent decision of a Commissioner or the court.

(4) In paragraph (3)—

"Commissioner" means the Chief Social Security Commissioner or any other Social Security Commissioner and includes a tribunal of three or more Commissioners constituted under section 16(7) of the Social Security Act 1998;

"service provider" means a person providing services to the Secretary of State for Work and Pensions or to Her Majesty's Revenue and Customs.][1]

Amendments—[1] This regulation inserted by the Social Security (National Insurance Credits) Amendment Regulations, SI 2007/2582 reg 2 with effect from 1 October 2007: SI 2007/2582 reg 1.

8E [Credits for the purposes of entitlement to retirement pension following official error

(1) This regulation applies for the purpose only of enabling the condition referred to in paragraph 5(3)(*a*) of Schedule 3 to the Contributions and Benefits Act to be satisfied in respect of a claim for retirement pension made by a person ("the claimant")—

(*a*) who would attain pensionable age no later than 31st May 2008;

(*b*) not falling within sub-paragraph (*a*) but based on the satisfaction of that condition by another person—

(i) who would attain, or would have attained, pensionable age no later than 31st May 2008; or

(ii) in respect of whose death the claimant received a bereavement benefit.

(2) Where—

(*a*) a person claims retirement pension;

(*b*) the satisfaction of the condition referred to in paragraph (1) would be based on earnings credited for incapacity for work or approved training in the tax years from 1993–94 to 2007–08; and

(*c*) some or all of those credits were credited by virtue of official error derived from the failure to transpose correctly information relating to those credits from the Department for Work and Pensions' Pension Strategy Computer System to Her Majesty's Revenue and Customs' computer system (NIRS2) or from related clerical procedures,

those earnings shall be credited.

(3) In this regulation, "bereavement benefit" means a bereavement allowance [referred to in section 39B of the Contributions and Benefits Act as in force immediately before it was repealed by paragraph 13 of Schedule 16 to the Pensions Act 2014][2], a widowed mother's allowance, a widowed parent's allowance or a widow's pension.][1]

Amendments—[1] This regulation inserted by the Social Security (National Insurance Credits) Amendment Regulations, SI 2007/2582 reg 2 with effect from 1 October 2007: SI 2007/2582 reg 1.

[2] In para (3), words inserted by the Pensions Act 2014 (Consequential, Supplementary and Incidental Amendments) Order, SI 2017/422 art 4(1), (8) with effect from 6 April 2017 (the day on which Pensions Act 2014 s 30 comes into effect for all purposes).

8F [Credits for the purposes of entitlement to contribution-based jobseeker's allowance following official error]

(1) This regulation applies for the purpose only of enabling a person to satisfy the condition referred to in section 2(1)(*b*) of the Jobseekers Act 1995.

(2) Where—

(*a*) a person claims a jobseeker's allowance;

(*b*) the satisfaction of the condition referred to in paragraph (1) would be based on earnings credited for incapacity for work or approved training in the tax years from 1993–94 to 2007–08; and

(*c*) some or all of those credits were credited by virtue of official error derived from the failure to transpose correctly information relating to those credits from the Department for Work and Pensions' Pension Strategy Computer System to Her Majesty's Revenue and Customs' computer system (NIRS2) or from related clerical procedures,

that person shall be credited with those earnings.][1]

Amendments—[1] This regulation inserted by the Social Security (National Insurance Credits) Amendment Regulations, SI 2007/2582 reg 2 with effect from 1 October 2007: SI 2007/2582 reg 1.

NIC

[8G Credits for persons entitled to universal credit

(1) For the purposes of entitlement to a benefit to which this regulation applies, a person shall be credited with a Class 3 contribution in respect of a week if that person is entitled to universal credit under Part 1 of the Welfare Reform Act 2012 for any part of that week

(2) This regulation applies to—

(*a*) a Category A retirement pension;

(*b*) a Category B retirement pension;

(*c*) a widowed parent's allowance;

(*d*) . . . [2]][1]

Amendments—[1] Reg 8G inserted by the Universal Credit (Consequential, Supplementary, Incidental and Miscellaneous Provisions) Regulations, SI 2013/630 reg 70(1), (6) with effect from 29 April 2013.

[2] Para (2)(*d*) revoked by the Pensions Act 2014 (Consequential, Supplementary and Incidental Amendments) Order, SI 2017/422 art 4(1), (9) with effect from 6 April 2017 (the day on which Pensions Act 2014 s 30 comes into effect for all purposes).

9 [Crediting of earnings for the purposes of entitlement to short-term incapacity benefit—further conditions

. . .

Amendments—Regulation revoked by the Social Security (Incapacity Benefit) Miscellaneous Amendments Regulations, SI 2000/3120 reg 4(*c*) with effect from 6 April 2001.

[9A [Credits for persons approaching pensionable age]

(1) For the purposes of entitlement to any benefit by virtue of a person's earnings or contributions [a person to whom this regulation applies][3] shall, subject to the following paragraphs, be credited with such earnings as may be required to bring his relevant earnings factor in respect of a tax year to which this regulation applies to the level required to make that year a reckonable year.

[(1A) This regulation applies to a man born before 6th October 1954 but who has not attained the age of 65.][3]

[(2) This regulation shall apply to—

(*a*) the tax year in which a man attains the age which is pensionable age in the case of a woman born on the same day as that man; and

(*b*) to any succeeding tax year,

but not including the tax year in which he attains the age of 65 or any subsequent tax year.][3]

(3) Paragraph (1) shall apply, in the case of a self-employed earner, only if he is—

(*a*) liable to pay a Class 2 contribution in respect of any week in a tax year to which this regulation applies; or

(*b*) excepted from liability to pay Class 2 contributions in respect of any week in a tax year to which this regulation applies by virtue of his earnings being less than, or being treated by regulations as less than, the amount specified in section 11(4) of the Social Security Contributions and Benefits Act 1992 (exception from liability for Class 2 contributions on account of small earnings),

so that he shall be credited with earnings equal to the lower earnings limit then in force in respect of each week for which he is not so liable.

(4) . . . [2]

(5) Where in any tax year to which this regulation applies a person is absent from Great Britain for more than 182 days, he shall not by virtue of this regulation be credited with any earnings or contributions in that tax year.][1]

Amendments—[1] Reg 9A (as inserted by SI 1983/463 reg 2(2)) substituted by the Social Security (Credits) Amendment Regulations, SI 1994/1837 reg 3, with effect from 8 August 1994.

[2] Para (4) omitted by the Social Security (Credits and Contributions) (Jobseeker's Allowance Consequential and Miscellaneous Amendments) Regulations, SI 1996/2367 reg 2(1), (8) with effect from 7 October 1996.

[3] In para (1) words substituted, para (1A) inserted, para (2) substituted by the Social Security (State Pension and National Insurance Credits) Regulations 2009, SI 2009/2206, regs 28, 30 with effect from 6 April 2010.

9B [Credits for jury service

(1) Subject to paragraphs (2) and (3), for the purposes of entitlement to any benefit [by virtue of a person's earnings or contributions][2] he shall be entitled to be credited with earnings equal to the lower earnings limit then in force, in respect of each week for any part of which he attended at Court for jury service.

(2) A person shall be entitled to be credited with earnings in respect of a week by virtue of the provisions of this regulation only if—

(*a*) his earnings in respect of that week from any employment of his as an employed earner are below the lower earnings limit then in force; and

(*b*) he furnished to the Secretary of State notice in writing of his claim to be entitled to be credited with earnings and did so before the end of the benefit year immediately following the tax year in which that week or part of that week fell or within such further time as may be reasonable in the circumstances of his case.

(3) Paragraph (1) shall not apply—

(*a*) to a woman in respect of any week in any part of which she was a married woman in respect of whom an election made by her under Regulations made under section 3(2) of the Social Security Pensions Act 1975 had effect; or

(*b*) in respect of any week falling wholly or partly within a year commencing before 6th April 1988.][1] [or][3]

[(*c*) to a person in respect of any week in any part of which he is a self-employed earner.][3]

Amendments—[1] Regulation 9B inserted by the Social Security (Credits) Amendment Regulations, SI 1988/516 regs 2(3), 3(2), with effect in respect of periods after 5 April 1988.

2 Words in para (1) substituted by the Social Security (Credits) Amendment (No 4) Regulations, SI 1988/1545 reg 2(5).

3 Para (3)(*c*) and the word "or" immediately preceding it added by the Social Security (Credits) Amendment Regulations, SI 1994/1837 reg 4, with effect from 8 August 1994.

9C [[Credits for adoption pay period, [shared parental pay period,][3] additional paternity pay period and maternity pay period]

(1) For the purposes of entitlement to any benefit by virtue of—

(*a*) in the case of a person referred to in paragraph (2)(*a*) [or (*aa*)][2], that person's earnings or contributions;

(*b*) in the case of a woman referred to in paragraph (2)(*b*), her earnings or contributions,

that person or that woman, as the case may be, shall be entitled to be credited with earnings equal to the lower earnings limit then in force in respect of each week to which this regulation applies.

(2) Subject to paragraphs (3) and (4), this regulation applies to each week during—

(*a*) the adoption pay period in respect of which statutory adoption pay was paid to a person; or

[(*aa*) the additional paternity pay period in respect of which additional statutory paternity pay was paid to a person; or][2]

(*b*) the maternity pay period in respect of which statutory maternity pay was paid to a woman[; or

(*c*) the shared parental pay period in respect of which statutory shared parental pay is paid to a person.][3]

(3) A person or woman referred to above shall be entitled to be credited with earnings in respect of a week by virtue of this regulation only if he or she—

(*a*) furnished to the Secretary of State notice in writing of his or her claim to be entitled to be credited with earnings; and

(*b*) did so—

(i) before the end of the benefit year immediately following the tax year in which that week began, or

(ii) within such further time as may be reasonable in the circumstances of his or her case.

(4) This regulation shall not apply to a woman in respect of any week in any part of which she was a married woman in respect of whom an election made by her under regulations made under section 19(4) of the Contributions and Benefits Act had effect.

(5) In this regulation[—

(*a*) "adoption pay period", ["additional paternity pay period",] "maternity pay period", "statutory adoption pay" ["additional statutory paternity pay"][2] and "statutory maternity pay" have the same meaning as in the Contributions and Benefits Act.

(*b*) "statutory shared parental pay" means statutory shared parental pay payable in accordance with Part 12ZC of that Act and "shared parental pay period" means the weeks in respect of which statutory shared parental pay is payable to a person under section 171ZY(2) of that Act.][3]][1].

Amendments—[1] This regulation substituted by the Social Security (Credits) Amendment Regulations, SI 2003/521 reg 2(1), (3) with effect from 6 April 2003.

2 Heading substituted, words in para (1)(*a*) inserted, para (2)(*aa*) inserted, and words in para (5) inserted, by the Social Security (Credits) (Amendment) Regulations, SI 2012/766 reg 2 with effect from 5 April 2012.

3 In heading, words inserted, para (2)(*c*) and preceding word inserted, and in para (5), sub-para (*a*) numbered as such and sub-para (*b*) inserted, by the Shared Parental Leave and Statutory Shared Parental Pay (Consequential Amendments to Subordinate Legislation) Order, SI 2014/3255 art 2 with effect from 5 April 2015.

9D [Credits for certain periods of imprisonment or detention in legal custody

(1) Subject to paragraphs (2) and (4), for the purposes of entitlement to any benefit by virtue of a person's earnings or contributions, where—

(*a*) a person is imprisoned or otherwise detained in legal custody by reason of his conviction of an offence or convictions in respect of 2 or more offences;

(*b*) that conviction or, as the case may be, each of those convictions is subsequently quashed by the Crown Court, the Court of Appeal or the High Court of Justiciary; and

(*c*) he is released from that imprisonment or detention, whether prior, or pursuant, to the quashing of that conviction or, as the case may be, each of those convictions,

that person shall, if he has made an application in writing to the Secretary of State for the purpose, be entitled to be credited with earnings or, in the case of any year earlier than 1987–88, contributions, in accordance with paragraph (3).

(2) Paragraph (1) shall not apply in respect of any period during which the person was also imprisoned or otherwise detained in legal custody for reasons unconnected with the conviction or convictions referred to in that paragraph.

(3) The earnings or, as the case may be, the contributions referred to in paragraph (1) are, in respect of any week in any part of which the person was—

(*a*) detained in legal custody—

(i) prior to the conviction or convictions referred to in that paragraph, but,

(ii) for the purposes of any proceedings in relation to any offence referred to in sub-paragraph (*a*) of that paragraph; or

(*b*) imprisoned or otherwise detained in legal custody by reason of that conviction or those convictions,

those necessary for the purpose of bringing his earnings factor, for the year in which such a week falls, to the level required to make that year a reckonable year.

(4) Subject to paragraph (5), paragraph (1) shall not apply to a woman in respect of any week referred to in paragraph (3) in any part of which she was a married woman in respect of whom an election made by her under regulations made under section 19(4) of the Contributions and Benefits Act had effect.

(5) Paragraph (4) shall not apply to any woman—

(*a*) who was imprisoned or otherwise detained in legal custody as referred to in paragraph (3) for a continuous period which included 2 complete years; and

(*b*) whose election ceased to have effect in accordance with regulation 101(1)(c) of the Social Security (Contributions) Regulations 1979 (which provides for an election to cease to have effect at the end of 2 consecutive years which began on or after 6th April 1978 during which the woman is not liable for primary Class 1 or Class 2 contributions).

(6) An application referred to in paragraph (1) may be transmitted by electronic means.][1]

Amendments—[1] Regulation 9D inserted by the Social Security (Credits and Incapacity Benefit) Amendment Regulations 2001, SI 2001/573 reg 2 with effect from 26 March 2001.

9E [Credits for certain spouses and civil partners of members of Her Majesty's forces

(1) For the purposes of entitlement to any benefit by virtue of a person's earnings or contributions, that person shall, subject to the following paragraphs, be entitled to be credited with earnings equal to the lower earnings limit then in force, in respect of each week to which paragraph (2) applies.

(2) This paragraph applies to each week for any part of which the person is—

(*a*) the spouse or civil partner of a member of Her Majesty's forces or treated as such by the Secretary of State for the purposes of occupying accommodation, and

(*b*) accompanying the member of Her Majesty's forces on an assignment outside the United Kingdom or treated as such by the Secretary of State.

(3) A person referred to in paragraph (2) shall be entitled to be credited with earnings in respect of a week by virtue of this regulation only if that person has made an application to the Secretary of State for the purpose.

(4) An application under paragraph (3) must—

(*a*) be properly completed and on a form approved by the Secretary of State, or in such manner as the Secretary of State accepts as sufficient in the particular circumstances, and

(*b*) include—

(i) a statement confirming that the conditions referred to in paragraph (2) are met and signed by or on behalf of the Defence Council or a person authorised by them, and

(ii) such other information as the Secretary of State may require.

(5) An application under paragraph (3) is to be made—

(*a*) once the end date of the assignment referred to in paragraph (2) has been confirmed, or

(*b*) at such earlier time as the Secretary of State is prepared to accept in the particular circumstances of the case.

(6) An application made in accordance with paragraph (5)(*a*) must be made before the end of the tax year immediately following the tax year in which the assignment referred to in paragraph (2) ended, or within such further time as may be reasonable in the circumstances of the case.

(7) Where the Secretary of State accepts an application in accordance with paragraph (5)(*b*), this regulation entitles the person referred to in paragraph (2) to be credited with earnings in respect of any week subsequent to that application only if that person has made a further application to the Secretary of State in accordance with paragraphs (3) to (6).

(8) This regulation shall not apply—

(*a*) to a person in respect of any week where the person is entitled to be credited with earnings under regulation 7A, 8A or 8B in respect of the same week;

(*b*) to a woman in respect of any week in any part of which she was a married woman in respect of whom an election made by her under regulations made under section 19(4) of the Contributions and Benefits Act had effect; or

(*c*) in respect of any week commencing before 6th April 2010.][1]

Amendments—[1] Regulation 9E inserted by the Social Security (Credits) Amendment Regulations, SI 2010/385 reg 2(1), (3) with effect from 6 April 2010.

9F [Credits for persons providing care for a child under the age of 12

(1) Subject to paragraphs (2), (5) and (6), the contributor concerned in the case of a benefit listed in paragraph (3) shall be credited with a Class 3 contribution for each week ("the relevant week") falling after 6th April 2011 during which that contributor satisfied the conditions in paragraph (4).

(2) Contributions shall only be credited in so far as is necessary to enable the contributor concerned to satisfy—

(*a*) in relation to a Category A or Category B retirement pension, the contribution condition specified in paragraph 5A(2) of Schedule 3 to the Contributions and Benefits Act;

(*b*) in relation to a widowed parent's allowance . . . [2], the second contribution condition specified in paragraph 5(3) of Schedule 3 to the Contributions and Benefits Act.

(3) This regulation applies to the following benefits—

(*a*) a Category A retirement pension in a case where the contributor concerned attains pensionable age on or after 6thApril 2012;

(*b*) a Category B retirement pension payable by virtue of section 48A of the Contributions and Benefits Act in a case where the contributor concerned attains pensionable age on or after that date;

(*c*) a Category B retirement pension payable by virtue of section 48B of that Act in a case where the contributor concerned dies on or after that date without having attained pensionable age before that date;

(*d*) a widowed parent's allowance payable in a case where the contributor concerned dies on or after that date;

(*e*) . . . [2]

(4) The conditions are that in the relevant week the contributor concerned—

(*a*) provided care in respect of a child under the age of 12;

(*b*) is, in relation to that child, a person specified in the Schedule (other than a person who is a relevant carer for the purposes of section 23A of the Contributions and Benefits Act); and

(*c*) was ordinarily resident in Great Britain.

(5) Only one contributor may be credited with Class 3 contributions under this Regulation in respect of any relevant week.

(6) The contributor concerned shall not be credited with Class 3 contributions by virtue of paragraph (1) unless—

(*a*) a person other than that contributor satisfies the conditions in paragraph (7); and

(*b*) an application to the Secretary of State to be so credited is made in accordance with paragraph (8).

(7) The conditions are that—

(*a*) child benefit was awarded to that other person in relation to the child for whom, and in respect of the week in which, child care was provided by the contributor concerned; and

(*b*) the aggregate of that other person's earnings factors, where those earnings factors are derived from so much of that person's earnings as do not exceed the upper earnings limit and upon which Class 1 contributions have been paid or treated as paid, exceed the qualifying earnings factor for the year in which the relevant week falls.

(8) An application under paragraph (6)(b) must—

(*a*) include the name and date of birth of the child cared for;

(*b*) where requested by the Secretary of State or the Commissioners for Her Majesty's Revenue and Customs, include a declaration by the person awarded child benefit in respect of that child that the conditions in paragraph (4) are satisfied;

(*c*) specify the relevant week or weeks in which the child was cared for; and

(*d*) be received after the end of the tax year in which a week, which is the subject of the application, falls.

(9) In this regulation, "the contributor concerned" has the meaning given in section 21(5)(*a*) of the Contributions and Benefits Act.][1]

Amendments—[1] Reg 9F inserted by the National Insurance Contributions Credits (Miscellaneous Amendments) Regulations, SI 2011/709 reg 2(1), (3) with effect from 5 April 2011.

[2] In para (2)(*b*), words revoked, and para (3)(*e*) revoked, by the Pensions Act 2014 (Consequential, Supplementary and Incidental Amendments) Order, SI 2017/422 art 4(1), (10) with effect from 6 April 2017 (the day on which Pensions Act 2014 s 30 comes into effect for all purposes).

[SCHEDULE

PERSONS WHO MAY QUALIFY AS CARERS FOR A CHILD UNDER THE AGE OF 12

Regulation 9F(4)(*b*)

1—(1) Parent.

(2) Grandparent.

(3) Great-grandparent.

(4) Great-great-grandparent.
(5) Sibling.
(6) Parent's sibling.
(7) Spouse or former spouse of any of the persons listed in sub-paragraphs (1) to (6).
(8) (8) Civil partner or former civil partner of any of the persons listed in sub-paragraphs (1) to (6).
(9) Partner or former partner of any of the persons listed in sub-paragraphs (1) to (8).
(10) (10) Son or daughter of persons listed in sub-paragraphs (5) to (9).
(11) In respect of the son or daughter of a person listed in sub-paragraph (6), that person's—
(*a*) spouse or former spouse;
(*b*) civil partner or former civil partner; or
(*c*) partner or former partner.

2 For the purposes of paragraph 1(5) and (6), a sibling includes a sibling of the half blood, a step sibling and an adopted sibling.

3 For the purposes of paragraph 1(9) and (11)(*c*), a partner is the other member of a couple consisting of [two people who are not married to or civil partners of each other but are living together as a married couple.][2]
(*a*) . . . [2]
(*b*) . . . [2]][1]

Amendments—[1] Schedule inserted by the National Insurance Contributions Credits (Miscellaneous Amendments) Regulations, SI 2011/709 reg 2(1), (4) with effect from 5 April 2011.
[2] Words inserted and sub-paras (*a*), (*b*) repealed, by the Marriage (Same Sex Couples) Act 2013 and Marriage and Civil Partnership (Scotland) Act 2014 (Consequential Provisions) Order, SI 2014/3061 art 2, Schedule para 4(1), (3) with effect, in relation to England and Wales, from 10 December 2014, and in relation to Scotland, from 16 December 2014.

1977/622

SOCIAL SECURITY (CONTRIBUTIONS) (EMPLOYMENT PROTECTION) REGULATIONS 1977

Made by the Secretary of State for Social Services under s 18 of the Social Security (Miscellaneous Provisions) Act 1977, now Social Security Contributions and Benefits Act 1992 s 112

Made . . . . . *31 March 1977*
Laid before Parliament . . . . . *1 April 1977*
Coming into Operation . . . . . *6 April 1977*

Note—Social Security Acts 1992 which consolidate provisions under which this statutory instrument is made come into effect on 1 July 1992. Social Security (Consequential Provisions) Act 1992 s 2 provides for the continuity of this instrument after 30 June 1992.

1 Citation, interpretation and commencement

(1) These regulations may be cited as the Social Security (Contributions) (Employment Protection) Regulations 1977 and shall come into operation on 6th April 1977.
(2) In these regulations, unless the context otherwise requires—
"the Act" means the Social Security Act 1975[1];
"maternity pay" has the meaning assigned to it by section 126(1) of the Employment Protection Act 1975;
and other expressions have the same meanings as in the Act.
(3) The rules for the construction of Acts of Parliament contained in the Interpretation Act 1889[2] shall apply for the purposes of the interpretation of these regulations as they apply for the purposes of the interpretation of any Act of Parliament.

Notes—[1] SSCBA 1992, SSAA 1992.
[2] Interpretation Act 1978.

2 Certain sums to be earnings

For the purposes of the Act—
(*a*) any such sum as is referred to in section 18(2)(*a*) or (*b*) of the Social Security (Miscellaneous Provisions) Act 1977[1] (certain sums to be earnings for social security purposes) shall be deemed to be earnings payable by the person liable to pay the maternity pay, to the person entitled to receive such sum and to be so payable in respect of the period for which it is paid;
(*b*) any such sum as is referred to in section 18(2)(*c*) to (*e*) of the said Act[2] shall be deemed to be earnings payable by the person liable to make such payment to the person entitled to receive it and to be so payable in respect of the period to which the order or as the case may be award relates;
(*c*) any amount (save where such amount is a payment of earnings from another employment) taken into account for the purpose of calculating the amount payable by way of any such sum

as is referred to in sub-paragraph (*b*) above so as to reduce the amount payable shall be treated as related to such sum and shall be deemed to be earnings payable by and to the persons referred to in the said sub-paragraph (*b*) and to be so payable in respect of the period referred to in that sub-paragraph;

(*d*) any period referred to in this regulation shall, so far as it is not a period of employment, be deemed to be a period of employment.

Notes—[1] Social Security (Miscellaneous Provisions) Act 1977 s 18(2)(*a*), (*b*) repealed by Social Security Act 1986 s 86, Sch 11 with effect from 6 April 1987. SSMPA 1977 s 18 re-enacted in SSCBA 1992 s 112.

[2] SSCBA 1992 s 112(3).

3 Modification of sections 42 and 44 of the Employment Protection Act 1975

(Spent).

1978/1689

SOCIAL SECURITY (CATEGORISATION OF EARNERS) REGULATIONS 1978

Made by the Secretary of State for Social Services, in exercise of powers conferred on him by SSSA 1975 ss 2(2), 4(4) and (5), and Sch 1 para 6(1)(k) [now SSCBA 1992 s 2(2), 7(1), (2) and Sch 1 para 8(1)(o)] and of all other powers enabling him

Made . . . . *24 November 1978*

Laid before Parliament . . . . *6 December 1978*

Coming into Operation . . . . *27 December 1978*

Note—Social Security Acts 1992 which consolidate provisions under which this statutory instrument is made come into effect on 1 July 1992. Social Security (Consequential Provisions) Act 1992 s 2 provides for the continuity of this instrument after 30 June 1992.

1 Citation, commencement and interpretation

(1) These regulations may be cited as the Social Security (Categorisation of Earners) Regulations 1978, and shall come into operation on 27th December 1978.

(2) In these regulations, unless the context otherwise requires—

"the Act" means the Social Security Act 1975;[6]

["an agency" in paragraph 2 of Schedule 1 and paragraphs 2 and 9 of Schedule 3 to these regulations means either a UK agency or a foreign agency;][5]

["category A, B, C or D waters" has the meaning given in the Merchant Shipping (Categorisation of Waters) Regulations 1992;][3]

["end client" in paragraph 2 of Schedule 1 and paragraphs 2 and 9 of Schedule 3 to these regulations means a person (including any connected person within the meaning given by section 993 of the Income Tax Act 2007) who has a place of business, residence or presence in Great Britain and to whom the worker personally provides services;

"foreign agency" in paragraph 2 of Schedule 1 and paragraphs 2 and 9 of Schedule 3 to these regulations means a person (including a body of persons unincorporate of which the employed person is a member) who does not have a place of business, residence or presence in Great Britain;][5]

. . .[4]

. . .[5]

["foreign employer" in paragraph 9 of Schedule 3 to these regulations means a person—

(*a*) who does not fulfil the conditions as to residence or presence in Great Britain prescribed under section 1(6)(*a*) of the Social Security Contributions and Benefits Act 1992; and

(*b*) who, if he did fulfil those conditions as to residence or presence in Great Britain referred to in (*a*) above, would be the secondary contributor in relation to any payment of earnings to or for the benefit of the person employed;][1]

["host employer" in paragraph 9 of Schedule 3 to these regulations means a person having a place of business[, residence or presence][5] in Great Britain;][1]

["mariner" has the meaning given in regulation 115 of the Social Security (Contributions) Regulations 2001;][3]

]"remuneration"—

(*a*) in paragraph 2 of Schedule 1 and paragraphs 2 and 9 of Schedule 3 to these regulations means—

(i) every form of payment, profit, gratuity or benefit, but

(ii) does not include anything that would not have constituted employed earner's earnings if it had been receivable in connection with an employment but for those paragraphs; and

(*b*) in paragraph 8 of Schedule 3 to these regulations includes any payment in respect of stipend or salary and excludes—

NIC

(i) any payment disregarded or, as the case may be, deducted from the amount of a person's earnings by virtue of regulations made under section 3(3) of the Act[7]; or

(ii) any specific and distinct payment made towards the maintenance or education of a dependent of the person receiving the payment;][5]

["UK agency" in paragraph 2 of Schedule 1 and paragraphs 2 and 9 of Schedule 3 to these regulations means a person (including a body of persons unincorporate of which the employed person is a member) who has a place of business, residence or presence in Great Britain;

"worker" in paragraph 2 of Schedule 1 and paragraphs 2 and 9 of Schedule 3 to these regulations means the person providing services under or in consequence of the contract;][5]

and other expressions have the same meaning as in the Act.

(3) Any reference in these regulations to any provision made by or contained in any enactment or instrument shall, except in so far as the context otherwise requires, be construed as including a reference to that provision as amended or extended by any enactment or instrument, and as including a reference to any provision which it re-enacts or replaces with or without modification.

(4) The rules for the construction of Acts of Parliament contained in the *Interpretation Act 1889*[8] shall apply for the purposes of the interpretation of these regulations as they apply for the purposes of the interpretation of an Act of Parliament.

Amendments—[1] Definitions of "foreign employer" and "host employer" in para (2) inserted by the SS (Categorisation of Earners) Amendment Regulations, SI 1994/726 regs 1, 2 with effect from 6 April 1994.

[2] Definition of "entertainer" in para (2) inserted by the SS (Categorisation of Earners) Amendment Regulations, SI 1998/1728 reg 2 with effect from 17 July 1998.

[3] Definitions of "category A, B, C or D waters" and "mariner" inserted by the Social Security (Categorisation of Earners) (Amendment No 2) Regulations, SI 2003/2420 regs 2, 3 with effect from 13 October 2003.

[4] Definition of "educational establishment" in para (2) revoked by the Social Security (Categorisation of Earners) (Amendment) Regulations, SI 2012/816 regs 2, 3 with effect from 6 April 2012.

[5] In para (2), definitions of "an agency", "end client", "foreign agency", "UK agency", and "worker" inserted, definition of "entertainer" revoked, in definition of "host emploeyer", words inserted, and definition of "remuneration" substituted, by the Social Security (Categorisation of Earners) (Amendment) Regulations, SI 2014/635 reg 2(1), (2) with effect from 6 April 2014.

[6] SSCBA 1992, SSAA 1992.

[7] SSA 1975 s 3(3) is re-enacted in SSCBA 1992 s 3(3).

[8] The Interpretation Act 1889 was repealed and replaced by the Interpretation Act 1978.

2 Treatment of earners in one category of earners as falling within another category and disregard of employments

(1) For the purposes of the Act an earner in one category of earners shall be treated as falling within another category in accordance with the following provisions of this regulation.

(2) Subject to the provisions of paragraph (4) of this regulation, every earner shall, in respect of any employment described in any paragraph in column (A) of Part I of Schedule 1 to these regulations, be treated as falling within the category of an employed earner in so far as he is gainfully employed in such employment and is not a person specified in the corresponding paragraph in column (B) of that Part, notwithstanding that the employment is not under a contract of service, or in an office (including elective office) with [. . . [2] earnings][1].

(3) Subject to the provisions of paragraph (4) of this regulation, every earner shall, in respect of any employment described in any paragraph in column (A) of Part II of the said Schedule 1, be treated as falling within the category of a self-employed earner in so far as he is gainfully employed in such employment and is not a person specified in the corresponding paragraph in column (B) of that Part, notwithstanding that the employment is under a contract of service, or in an office (including elective office) with [. . . [2] earnings][1].

(4) Every employment described in any paragraph in column (A) of Part III of the said Schedule 1 shall, in relation to liability for contributions otherwise arising from employment of that description, be disregarded, except in so far as it is employment of a person specified in the corresponding paragraph in column (B) of that Part.

Simon's Tax Cases—reg 2(2), *ITV Services Ltd v R&C Comrs* [2012] UKUT 47 (TCC), [2012] STC 1213.

Amendments—[1] Words in paras (2), (3) substituted by the Social Security (Contributions, Categorisation of Earners and Intermediaries) (Amendment) Regulations, SI 2004/770 reg 34(1), (2) with effect from 6 April 2004.

[2] Word revoked in each place by the Social Security (Miscellaneous Amendments No 2) Regulations, SI 2015/478 reg 25(1), (2) with effect from 6 April 2015.

3 Employments treated as continuing

For the purposes of the Act with respect to the computation, collection and recovery of, and otherwise with respect to, contributions (other than Class 4 contributions which under section 9 of the Act[1] are to be recovered by the Inland Revenue), the employment of a person shall be treated as continuing in the circumstances specified in Schedule 2 to these regulations.

Notes—[1] SSA 1975 s 9 is re-enacted in SSCBA 1992 ss 15,16.

4 Special provisions with respect to persons declared by the High Court to be persons falling within a particular category of earners

(1) Where, under the provisions of the Act relating to references and appeals to the High Court, the High Court decides any question whether in respect of any employment a person is an earner and, if so, as to the category of earners in which he is to be included, and that decision is inconsistent with some previous determination of a question by the Secretary of State, then, if the Secretary of State is satisfied that contributions appropriate to another category of earners have been paid by or in respect of any person by reason of that determination or in the reasonable belief that that determination was applicable, the Secretary of State may, if it appears to him that it would be in the interests of the person by or in respect of whom such contributions have been paid, or of any claimant or beneficiary by virtue of that person's contributions, so to do, direct that that person shall be treated as though he had been included in the category of earners corresponding to the contributions paid during the period for which contributions appropriate to that other category were so paid before the date on which the decision of the High Court was given, and, if such a direction is given, that person shall be deemed to have been included in that category accordingly for such period.

(2) Where the Secretary of State, on review under section 96(1) of the Act[1], has revised a determination of a question previously given by him, the provisions of this regulation shall apply with the necessary modifications in the same manner as they apply where the High Court has given a decision inconsistent with a determination previously given by the Secretary of State.

(3) In the application of this regulation to Scotland, for any reference to the High Court, there shall be substituted a reference to the Court of Session.

Note—[1] SSA 1975 s 96(1) is re-enacted in SSAA 1992 s 19.

5 Persons to be treated as secondary contributors

[(1)] For the purposes of section 4 of the Act[1] (Class 1 contributions), in relation to any payment of earnings to or for the benefit of an employed earner in any employment described in any paragraph in column (A) of Schedule 3 to these regulations, the person specified in the corresponding paragraph in column (B) of that Schedule shall be treated as the secondary Class 1 contributor in relation to that employed earner.

[(2) Paragraph 9 of Schedule 3 applies to mariners notwithstanding anything in regulations 122 and 124(1) of the Social Security (Contributions) Regulations 2001.]

Note—[1] SSA 1975 s 4 is re-enacted in SSCBA ss 7, 9.

Cross reference—Social Security Contributions and Benefits Act 1992 s 7 (meaning of "secondary contributor").

Amendments—Para (1) numbered as such, and para (2) inserted, by the Social Security (Categorisation of Earners) (Amendment No 2) Regulations, SI 2003/2420 regs 2, 4 with effect from 13 October 2003.

5A Anti-avoidance

(1) Paragraph (2) applies if—

(a) an earner has an employment in which the earner personally provides services to a person who is resident or present or has a place of business in Great Britain,

(b) a third person enters into relevant avoidance arrangements, and

(c) but for paragraph (2), the earner would not be, and would not be treated as falling within the category of, an employed earner in relation to the employment.

(2) The earner is to be treated as falling within the category of an employed earner in relation to the employment.

(3) In paragraph (1)(b) "relevant avoidance arrangements" means arrangements the main purpose, or one of the main purposes, of which is to secure—

(a) that the earner is not treated under paragraph 2 of Schedule 1 as falling within the category of employed earner in relation to the employment, or

(b) that a person is not treated under paragraph 2 or 9(b) or (d) of Schedule 3 as the secondary Class 1 contributor in respect of payments of earnings to or for the benefit of the earner in respect of the employment.

(4) Paragraph (5) applies if—

(a) a person ("P") enters into arrangements the main purpose, or one of the main purposes, of which is to secure that P is not treated under a relevant provision as the secondary Class 1 contributor in respect of payments of earnings to or for the benefit of an employed earner in respect of an employment, and

(b) but for paragraph (5), no person who is resident or present or has a place of business in Great Britain would—

(i) be the secondary Class 1 contributor in respect of such payments, or

(ii) be treated, under a provision other than paragraph 2(a) or (b) or 9(g) or (h) in column (B) of Schedule 3, as the secondary Class 1 contributor in respect of such payments.

(5) If P is resident or present or has a place of business in Great Britain, P is to be treated as the secondary Class 1 contributor in respect of such payments.

(6) In paragraph (4)(a) a "relevant provision" means any provision of—

(a) paragraph 2 of Schedule 3, other than sub-paragraphs (a) and (b) of that paragraph in column (B), or

(b) paragraph 9(a) to (d) of that Schedule.

(7) In this regulation "arrangements" include any scheme, transaction or series of transactions, agreement or understanding, whether or not legally enforceable, and any associated operations.][1]

Amendments—[1] Reg 5A inserted by NICA 2015 s 6(1).

Paras (1)–(5), (6)(a), (7) are to be treated as having come into force on 6 April 2014.

Para (6)(b) came into force on 12 February 2015 (NICA 2015 s 6(7)).

Paras (4), (5) have effect in relation to arrangements entered into on or after 6 April 2014 the main purpose, or one of the main purposes of which, is to secure that a person is not treated, under a provision mentioned in para (6)(b), as the secondary Class 1 contributor in respect of payments of earnings to or for the benefit of an employed earner in respect of an employment. But para (5) only applies as a result of such arrangements in relation to payments of earnings that are made on or after 12 February 2015 (NICA 2015 s 6(8), (9)).

6 Revocation and general savings

(1) The regulations specified in column (1) of Schedule 4 to these regulations are hereby revoked to the extent mentioned in column (3) of that Schedule.

(2) Anything whatsoever done under or by virtue of any regulation revoked by these regulations shall be deemed to have been done under or by virtue of the corresponding provision of these regulations and anything whatsoever begun under any such regulation may be continued under these regulations as if begun thereunder.

SCHEDULE 1

Regulation 2

PART I

Column (A)	Column (B)
Employments in respect of which, subject to the provisions of regulation 2 and to the exceptions in column (B) of this Part, earners are treated as falling within the category of employed earner	Persons excepted from the operation of column (A)
[1. Employment— (*a*) as an office cleaner or as an operative in any similar capacity in any premises other than those used as a private dwelling-house; or (*b*) as a cleaner of any telephone apparatus and associated fixtures, other than of apparatus and fixtures in premises used as a private dwelling-house.][6]	1. None.
[2. Employment (not being an employment in which the employed earner is treated as an employed earner under the provisions of paragraph 1, 3 or 5 of this Schedule) where—	[2. Any person in employment described in paragraph 2 in column (A)—
(*a*) the worker personally provides services to the end client;	(*a*) where the worker carries out the employment wholly in their own home or on other premises not under the control or management of the end client (except where the other premises are premises at which the employed person is required, by reason of working for the client, to work); or
(*b*) there is a contract between the end client and an agency under or in consequence of which— (i) the services are provided, or (ii) the end client pays, or otherwise provides consideration for the services,	(*b*) who works for the end client as an actor, singer, musician or other entertainer, or as a fashion, photographic or artist's model; or
(*c*) remuneration is receivable by the worker (from any person) in consequence of providing the services.][8]	(*c*) where it is shown that the manner in which the worker provides the services is not subject to (or to the right of) supervision, direction or control by any person.][8]

3. Employment of a person by his or her spouse [or civil partner][4] for the purposes of the [employment of the spouse or civil partner][4].	3. None.
...[5, 7]	...[7]
5. Employment as a minister of religion, not being employment under a contract of service or in an office with [. . . [9] earnings][3].	5. Any person in employment described in paragraph 5 of column (A) whose remuneration in respect of that employment (disregarding any payment in kind) does not consist wholly or mainly of stipend or salary.
5A. . . . [8]	5A . . . [8]

Simon's Tax Cases—Column A, para 5A, Column B, para 5A, *ITV Services Ltd v R&C Comrs* [2012] UKUT 47 (TCC), [2012] STC 1213.

Amendments—[1] Words in Column B para 2(*b*) omitted and para 5A in columns (A) and (B) inserted by the Social Security (Categorisation of Earners) Amendment Regulations, SI 1998/1728 reg 3(*a*), (*b*) with effect from 17 July 1998 and continuing in effect after 1 February 1999 by virtue of the Social Security (Categorisation of Earners) Amendment Regulations, SI 1999/3 reg 2.

[2] Para 5A in column (B) substituted by the Social Security (Categorisation of Earners) Amendment Regulations, SI 2003/736 reg 3 with effect from 6 April 2003.

[3] Words in paras 5, 5A substituted by the Social Security (Contributions, Categorisation of Earners and Intermediaries) (Amendment) Regulations, SI 2004/770 reg 34(1), (3) with effect from 6 April 2004.

[4] Words in para 3 inserted and substituted by the Social Security (Categorisation of Earners) (Amendment) Regulations, SI 2005/3133 regs 2, 3(1), (2) with effect from 5 December 2005.

[5] Para 4(a) in column (A) revoked, and former para 4 in column (B) substituted, by the Social Security (Categorisation of Earners) Amendment Regulations, SI 1984/350 reg 2 with effect from 6 April 1984.

[6] Para 1 in column (A) substituted by the Social Security (Categorisation of Earners) Amendment Regulations, SI 1990/1894 reg 2 with effect from 16 October 1990.

[7] Para 4 in column (A) and para 4 in column (B) revoked by the Social Security (Categorisation of Earners) (Amendment) Regulations, SI 2012/816 regs 2, 4 with effect from 6 April 2012.

[8] Para 2 in columns (A) and (B) substituted, and para 5A in columns (A) and (B) revoked by the Social Security (Categorisation of Earners) (Amendment) Regulations, SI 2014/635 reg 2(1), (3) with effect from 6 April 2014.

[9] In para 5 in column A, word revoked by the Social Security (Miscellaneous Amendments No 2) Regulations, SI 2015/478 reg 25(1), (3) with effect from 6 April 2015.

PART II

Column (A)	Column (B)
Employments in respect of which, subject to the provisions of regulation 2 and to the exceptions in column (B) of this Part, earners are treated as falling within the category of self-employed earner	Persons excepted from the operation of column (A)
6. Employment (not being employment described in paragraph 2 in column (A) of this Schedule) by any person responsible for the conduct or administration of any examination leading to any certificate, diploma, degree or professional qualification— (*a*) as an examiner, moderator or invigilator or in any similar capacity; or (*b*) in which the person employed is engaged to set questions or tests for any such examination, Under a contract where the whole of the work to be performed is to be performed in less than twelve months.	6. None.

PART III

Column (A)	Column (B)
Employments which, subject to the exceptions in column (B) of this Part are to be disregarded	Employments excepted from the operation of column (A)

NIC

7. Employment by the father, mother, grandfather, grandmother, stepfather, stepmother, son, daughter, grandson, granddaughter, stepson, stepdaughter, brother, sister, half-brother or half-sister of the person employed, in so far as the employment— (*a*) is employment in a private dwelling-house in which both the person employed and the employer reside; and (*b*) is not employment for the purposes of any trade or business carried on there by the employer.	7. None.
8. Employment (whether or not under a contract of service) of a person by his or her spouse [or civil partner][3] otherwise than for the purposes of the [employment of the spouse or civil partner][3].	8. None.
9. Any employment or employments as a self-employed earner (including any employment in respect of which a person is, under these regulations, treated as falling within the category of a self-employed earner) where the earner is not ordinarily employed in such employment or employments.	9. None.
10. Employment for the purpose of any election or referendum authorised by Act of Parliament— (*a*) as a returning officer or acting returning officer; or (*b*) as a Chief Counting Officer or counting officer; or (*c*) of any person by any officer referred to in (*a*) or (*b*) above.	10. None.
[11. Employment: (*a*) as a member of the naval, military or air forces of a country to which a provision of the Visiting Forces Act 1952 applies by virtue of section 1 thereof; (*b*) as a civilian by any such force.][1]	[11. Any employment described in paragraph 11(*b*) in column (A) of a person who is ordinarily resident in the United Kingdom.][1]
12. Employment as a member of any international headquarters or defence organisation designated under section 1 of the International Headquarters and Defence Organisations Act 1964.][1]	12. Any employment described in paragraph 12 in column (A) of a person who is— (*a*) a serving member of the regular naval, military or air forces of the Crown [— (i) raised in the United Kingdom; or (ii) having its depot or headquarters in the United Kingdom][4] (*b*) a civilian ordinarily resident in the United Kingdom who is not a member of a [scheme providing a pension, lump sum, gratuity or like benefit on cessation of the employment which is][2] established under arrangements made by the international headquarters or, as the case may be, defence organisation of which he is a member.][1]
13. . . .[4]	13. . . .[4]

[14. Employment by the International Finance Corporation ("IFC") of a person who is— (*a*) exempt from tax by virtue of article 3 of, and section 9 of article 6 of the Agreement establishing the IFC as set out in the Schedule to, the International Finance Corporation Order 1955, and (*a*) a member of a scheme established by or on behalf of the IFC which provides for a pension or any other benefit on cessation of the employment.	[14. None.][5]
15. Employment by the Asian Infrastructure Investment Bank ("AIIB") of a person who is— (*a*) exempt from tax by virtue of regulation 18(2) of the Asian Infrastructure Investment Bank (Immunities and Privileges) Order 2015, and (*b*) a member of a scheme established by or on behalf of the AIIB which provides for a pension or any other benefit on cessation of the employment.][5]	[15. None.][5]

Amendments—[1] Paras 11 and 12 in columns (A) and (B) inserted by the Social Security (Categorisation of Earners) Amendment Regulations, SI 1980/1713 reg 2 with effect from 1 December 1980.

[2] Words in para 12(*b*) in column (B) substituted by the Social Security (Categorisation of Earners) Amendment Regulations, SI 1984/350 reg 3 with effect from 6 April 1984.

[3] Words in para 8 inserted and substituted by the Social Security (Categorisation of Earners) (Amendment) Regulations, SI 2005/3133 regs 2, 3(2), (3) with effect from 5 December 2005.

[4] Words in para 12(*a*) substituted for the words "raised in the United Kingdom, and any officer of the Brigade of Gurkhas holding Her Majesty's commission who is not a Queen's Gurkha officer; or "; and in entries in para 13 revoked, by the Social Security (Categorisation of Earners) (Amendment) Regulations, SI 2006/1530 with effect from 5 July 2006.

[5] Paras 14 and 15 inserted by the Social Security (Miscellaneous Amendments) Regulations, SI 2017/307 reg 5 with effect from 6 April 2017.

SCHEDULE 2

CIRCUMSTANCES IN WHICH EMPLOYMENT IS TREATED AS CONTINUING

Regulation 3

Where a person is employed as a self-employed earner or in an employment in respect of which he is, under these regulations, treated as falling within the category of a self-employed earner, the employment shall in either case be treated as continuing unless and until he is no longer ordinarily employed in that employment.

SCHEDULE 3

EMPLOYMENTS IN RESPECT OF WHICH PERSONS ARE TREATED AS SECONDARY CLASS 1 CONTRIBUTORS

Regulation 5

Column (A) Employments	Column (B) Persons treated as secondary Class 1 contributors
[1. Employment— (*a*) as an office cleaner or as an operative in any similar capacity in any premises other than those used as a private dwelling-house; or	1. (*a*) Where the person employed is supplied by, or through the agency of, some third person and receives his remuneration from, or through the agency of, that third person, that third person;p[
(*b*) as a cleaner of any telephone apparatus and associated fixtures, other than of apparatus and fixtures in premises used as a private dwelling-house.][2]	(*b*) in any other case, except where the employment is also one described in paragraph 4 in column (A) of this Schedule, the person with whom the person employed contracted to do the work.

NIC

[2. Employment (not being an employment described in paragraph 2 of column (B) of Schedule 1 to these regulations or an employment to which paragraph 1, 4, 5, 7 or 8 of this Schedule applies) where—	[2. The UK agency who is party to the contract with the end client; or—
(*a*) the worker personally provides services to the end client;	(*a*) where, at any time, the end client provides to the UK agency fraudulent documents in connection with the control, direction or supervision which is to be exercised over the employed person, the end client; or
(*b*) there is a contract between the end client and a UK agency under or in consequence of which—	(*b*) where, at any time, a person (other the end client) who is resident in Great Britain and who has a contractual relationship with the UK agency provides to the UK agency fraudulent documents in connection with the purported deduction or payment of contributions in connection with the employed person, the person who provides the fraudulent documents.][11]
(i) the services are provided, or	
(ii) the end client pays, or otherwise provides consideration for the services, and	
(*c*) remuneration is receivable by the worker (from any person) in consequence of providing the services.][11]	
3. Employment of a person by his or her spouse [or civil partner][9] for the purposes of [the employment of the spouse or civil partner][9].	3. The spouse [or civil partner][9].
4. Employment (not being employment in respect of which a secondary contributor, in any particular case, is prescribed in paragraph (1)(a) in column (B) of this Schedule, and not being employment described in paragraph 2 in column (A) of that Schedule) by a company, being a company within the meaning of the Companies Act 1948 and in voluntary liquidation but carrying on business under a liquidator.	4. The person who at the time of the employment holds the office of liquidator.
5. Employment in chambers as a barrister's clerk.	5. The head of chambers.
...[1 10]	...[10]
7. Employment as a minister of the Church of England, not being employment under a contract of service.	7. The Church Commissioners for England.
8. Employment as a minister of religion not being employment— (*a*) as a minister of the Church of England; or	8. (*a*) Where the remuneration in respect of the employment is paid from one fund, the person responsible for the administration of that fund;
(*b*) under a contract of service; or	(*b*) where the remuneration in respect of the employment is paid from more than one fund and—
(*c*) described in paragraph 5 in column (B) of Schedule 1 to these regulations.	(i) remuneration is also paid from one of those funds to other ministers of religion, the person responsible for the administration of that fund;
	(ii) remuneration is also paid from two or more of those funds to other ministers of religion, the person responsible for the administration of the fund from which remuneration is paid to the greatest number of ministers of religion who carry out their duties in Great Britain;

	(iii) no person falls to be treated as secondary contributor by virtue of sub-paragraph (*b*)(i) or (ii) of this paragraph, the person responsible for the administration of the fund from which the minister of religion first receives a payment of remuneration in the tax year.
[9. Employment—	[9. Where the employment is—
(*a*) (not being an employment described in sub-paragraphs (b) to (f)) by a foreign employer where the employed person, under an arrangement involving the foreign employer and the host employer, provides, or is personally involved in the provision of services, to a host employer;	(*a*) employment within paragraph 9(*a*) of column (A), the host employer;
(*b*) under or in consequence of a contract between a foreign agency and an end client where the worker provides services to that end client;	(*b*) employment within paragraph 9(*b*) of column (A), the end client;
(*c*) by a foreign employer where the worker provides services to an end client under or in consequence of a contract between that end client and a UK agency;	(*c*) employment within paragraph 9(*c*) of column (A), the UK agency who has the contractual relationship with the end client;
(*d*) by a foreign agency where the worker provides services to an end client under or in consequence of a contract between that end client and a UK agency;	(*d*) employment within paragraph 9(*d*) of column (A), the UK agency who has the contractual relationship with the end client;
(*e*) by a UK employer where the worker provides services to a person outside the United Kingdom under or in consequence of a contract between that person and a UK agency and the worker is eligible to pay contributions in the United Kingdom in relation to that employment; or	(*e*) employment within paragraph 9(*e*) of column (A), the UK employer or UK agency who has the contractual relationship with the person outside the United Kingdom; or
(*f*) by a foreign employer where the worker provides services to a person outside the United Kingdom under or in consequence of a contract between that person and a UK agency and the worker is eligible to pay contributions in the United Kingdom in relation to that employment.][11]	(*f*) employment within paragraph 9(*f*) of column (A), the UK agency who has the contractual relationship with the person outside the United Kingdom;
	(*g*) employment within paragraphs 9(*c*) or (*d*) of column (A) and the end client provides at any time to the UK agency fraudulent documents in connection with the control, direction or supervision which is to be exercised over the employed person, the end client; or
	(*h*) employment within paragraphs 9(*c*) or (*d*) of column (A) and a person who is resident in Great Britain (who is not the end client) with a contractual relationship with the UK agency provides at any time to the UK agency fraudulent documents in connection with the purported deduction or payment of contributions in connection with the employed person, the person who provides the fraudulent documents.][11]
[Where the employment is as a mariner, this paragraph only applies where the duties of the employment are performed wholly or mainly in category A, B, C or D waters.][7]	
10. . . .[11]	[10. . . .[11]

Amendments—[1] Words omitted in para 6 in column (A) revoked by the Social Security (Categorisation of Earners) Amendment Regulations, SI 1984/350 reg 4 with effect from 6 April 1984.

[2] Para 1 in column (A) substituted by the Social Security (Categorisation of Earners) Amendment Regulations, SI 1990/1894 reg 3(1) with effect from 16 October 1990.

3 Words substituted in para 2(*c*) in column (B) by the Social Security (Categorisation of Earners) Amendment Regulations, SI 1990/1894 reg 3(2) with effect from 16 October 1990.

4 Para 9 in columns (A) and (B) inserted by the Social Security (Categorisation of Earners) Amendment Regulations, SI 1994/726 regs 1, 4 with effect from 6 April 1994.

5 Para 10 in columns (A) and (B) inserted by the Social Security (Categorisation of Earners) Amendment Regulations, SI 1998/1728 reg 4 with effect from 17 July 1998.

6 Para 10 in column (B) substituted by the Social Security (Categorisation of Earners) Amendment Regulations, SI 2003/736 reg 4 with effect from 6 April 2003.

7 Words inserted in column (A) of para 9 by the Social Security (Categorisation of Earners) (Amendment No 2) Regulations, SI 2003/2420 regs 2, 5 with effect from 13 October 2003.

8 Words in para 10 of Column (A) substituted by the Social Security (Contributions, Categorisation of Earners and Intermediaries) (Amendment) Regulations, SI 2004/770 reg 34(1), (4) with effect from 6 April 2004.

9 Words in para 3 inserted and substituted by the Social Security (Categorisation of Earners) (Amendment) Regulations, SI 2005/3133 regs 2, 4 with effect from 5 December 2005.

10 Para 6 in column (A) and para 6 in column (B) revoked by the Social Security (Categorisation of Earners) Regulations, SI 2012/816 regs 2, 5 with effect from 6 April 2012.

11 Para 2, in columns (A) and (B) substituted, in para 9, words in column (A) and the whole of column (B) substituted, and para 10 in columns (A) and (B) revoked, by the Social Security (Categorisation of Earners) (Amendment) Regulations, SI 2014/635 reg 2(1), (4) with effect from 6 April 2014.

1979/591

SOCIAL SECURITY (CONTRIBUTIONS) REGULATIONS 1979

Note—These Regulations have been revoked by the Social Security (Contributions) Regulations, SI 2001/1004 reg 157, Sch 8 Pt I with effect from 6 April 2001. SI 2001/1004 consolidates the regulations relating to social security contributions.

1979/676

SOCIAL SECURITY (EARNINGS FACTOR) REGULATIONS 1979

Made by the Secretary of State for Social Services under SSA 1975 ss 13(5), 115(1) and Sch 13 para 2 [see now SSCBA 1992 s 23(1), SSAA 1992 s 59(1) Sch 3, para 4], SSPA 1975 s 35(3) and SS(MP)A 1977 s 1(5)

Made . . . . *18 June 1979*
Laid before Parliament . . . . *25 June 1979*
Coming into Operation . . . . *16 July 1979*

Notes—These Regulations are made for the purpose only of consolidating the Regulations hereby revoked and, accordingly, by virtue of section 139(2) of, and paragraph 20 of Schedule 15 to, the Social Security Act 1975 and by virtue of section 61(2) of the Social Security Pensions Act 1975 as amended by section 21(4) of, and paragraph 21 of Schedule 3 to, the Social Security Act 1979 no reference of them has been made either to the National Insurance Advisory Committee or to the Occupational Pensions Board.

The Regulations prescribe rules for deriving from contributions paid, or paid and credited, under the Social Security Act 1975 the earnings factors by reference to which the contribution conditions for contributory benefits are expressed in Schedule 3 to that Act, the rate of earnings-related supplement or addition to certain benefits is calculated under Schedule 6 to that Act, the additional component in the rate of long-term benefits is calculated by virtue of section 6 of the Social Security Pensions Act 1975 and an earner's guaranteed minimum is calculated under section 35 of the latter Act. Provision is also made for treating as paid or as not repaid contributions by reference to which an earner's guaranteed minimum is calculated under the said section 35.

Social Security Acts 1992 which consolidate provisions under which this statutory instrument is made come into effect on 1 July 1992. Social Security (Consequential Provisions) Act 1992 s 2 provides for the continuity of this instrument after 30 June 1992.

1 Citation, commencement and interpretation

(1) These regulations may be cited as the Social Security (Earnings Factor) Regulations 1979 and shall come into operation on 16th July 1979.

(2) In these regulations—

"the Act" means the Social Security Act 1975[3];

. . .[1]

"the Contributions Regulations" means the Social Security (Contributions) Regulations 1979;

"year" means tax year;

and other expressions have the same meanings as in the Act.

[(3) In these regulations references to contributions of any class are to contributions actually of that class notwithstanding that for the purposes of any benefit they may be treated as or be deemed to be contributions of another class.][2]

Amendments—[1] Words in para (2) revoked by the Social Security (Earnings Factor) Amendment (No 2) Regulations, SI 1987/411 regs 2(2)(*a*), 3, with effect for the ascertainment of earnings factors in respect of the tax year 1987–88 and subsequent years.

[2] Para (3) inserted by the Social Security (Earnings Factor) Amendment (No 2) Regulations, SI 1987/411 regs 2(2)(*b*), 3, with effect for the ascertainment of earnings factors in respect of the tax year 1987–88 and subsequent years.

[3] SSCBA 1992; SSAA 1992.

2 [Ascertainment of earnings factors

(1) The earnings factors derived from a person's earnings paid in, or from earnings credited or Class 2 or Class 3 contributions in respect of, any year shall, subject to paragraph (2) of this regulation, be ascertained in accordance with the rules contained in Schedule 1 to these Regulations.

(2) A person's earnings factors in respect of the year commencing on 6th April 1988, or any subsequent year, shall not in respect of any such year together exceed an amount equal to 58 times the upper earnings limit of that year.][1]

Amendments—[1] Regulation 2 was substituted by the Social Security (Earnings Factor) Amendment Regulations, SI 1988/429 regs 2(2), 3 with effect from 4 April 1988.

3 Evidence of official records

For the purposes of Part III of the Act (determination of claims and questions) a certificate signed by a duly authorised officer of the Department of Health and Social Security, as to the manner in which any contributions paid or treated as having been paid or as not repaid have been or are to be recorded in the records of that Department, shall be sufficient evidence of the facts so certified; and any document purporting to be so signed shall be deemed to be so signed unless the contrary is proved.

4 Contributions to be treated as having been paid or as not repaid

For the purposes of [paragraph 5][1] of Schedule 1 to these regulations—

(*a*) any contributions which would have been payable by the person in question but for the fact that they are not payable by virtue of regulation 49 of the Contributions Regulations, or

(*b*) any contributions repayable or repaid to him under regulation 32 of those regulations as having been paid in excess of the amount prescribed in regulation 17 of those regulations (annual maximum)

shall be treated as having been paid and in the case of repaid contributions as not repaid.

Amendments—[1] Words substituted by the Social Security (Earnings Factor) Amendment Regulations, SI 1991/1165 reg 2 with effect from 6 June 1991.

5 Revocations

The regulations specified in Schedule 2 to these regulations are hereby revoked.

SCHEDULE 1

RULES FOR THE ASCERTAINMENT OF EARNINGS FACTORS

(Regulation 2)

[PART I][1]

CLASS 1 CONTRIBUTIONS

Amendments—[1] This Part substituted by the Social Security (Earnings Factor) Amendment Regulations, SI 1991/1165 with effect from 6 June 1991.

1—(1) In this Part of this Schedule—

["Class 1 contributions" means primary Class 1 contributions paid or treated as paid on so much of a person's earnings as do not exceed the current upper earnings limit or the prescribed equivalent if he is paid otherwise than weekly;][1]

["contracted-out contributions" means primary Class 1 contributions paid or treated as paid on so much of a person's earnings in respect of any contracted-out employment as exceed the current lower earnings limit but do not exceed the current upper earnings limit or the prescribed equivalents if he is paid otherwise than weekly;][1]

"the standard level" in relation to any year means that year's lower earnings limit for [primary][1] Class 1 contributions multiplied by 50; and

each paragraph has effect subject to the provisions of all later paragraphs.

(2) Paragraphs 2, 3 and 4 below shall apply for the purposes specified in section 13(2) of the Act[2] [or section 2(4) of the Pensions Act 2014][3], and paragraph 5 below for the purposes of section 35 of the Social Security Pensions Act 1975 (earner's guaranteed minimum).

Amendments—[1] Definitions of "Class 1 contributions" and "contracted-out contributions" substituted, and word in the definition of "the standard level" inserted, by the Social Security (Earnings Factor) Amendment Regulations, SI 2003/608 with effect from 6 April 2003. However, for the purpose of ascertaining a person's earnings factors in respect of the year commencing on 6 April 2002 and any preceding year, these regulations (ie SI 1979/676) shall have effect as if the above amendments had not been made: SI 2003/608 reg 3.

[2] SSCBA 1992 s 22(2).

3 In sub-para (2), words inserted by the Pensions Act 2014 (Consequential, Supplementary and Incidental Amendments) Order, SI 2015/1985 art 6(*a*) with effect from 6 April 2016.

2—(1) Subject to sub-paragraph (2) below, a person's earnings factor derived in respect of the year commencing on 6th April 1987, or any subsequent year, from—

(*a*) those of his earnings paid in that year upon which Class 1 contributions have been paid or treated as paid in respect of that year, and

(*b*) earnings with which he has been credited in respect of that year,

shall be equal to the amount of those actual and credited earnings.

(2) Any earnings factor ascertained under sub-paragraph (1) above shall be rounded down to the nearest whole pound.

3 Where a person's earnings paid in the year commencing on 6th April 1987, or in any subsequent year, are earnings upon which Class 1 contributions have been paid or treated as paid in respect of that year and are, or are to be, recorded as separate sums in the records of the Department of Social Security, the earnings factor derived from those earnings shall be equal to the aggregate of the amounts ascertained by rounding down each sum separately to the nearest whole pound.

4 Where Class 1 contributions have been paid or treated as paid in respect of the year commencing on 6th April 1987, or any subsequent year, upon a person's earnings paid in that year and, but for this paragraph, the ascertainment of any earnings factor of his in respect of such year by the application of paragraphs 2 or 3 above would have the effect that—

(*a*) his earnings factor derived from those earnings, or

(*b*) the aggregate of his earnings factors derived from those earnings, and any earnings credited in respect of the same year, together with any derived from Class 2 or Class 3 contributions paid or credited in that year

would fall short of—

(i) the qualifying earnings factor, by an amount not exceeding £50, or

(ii) the standard level, by an amount not exceeding £50, or

(iii) one-half of the standard level, by an amount not exceeding £25,

the amount of that earnings factor as so ascertained shall, for the purpose of section 13(2)(*a*) of the Act [or section 2(4) of the Pensions Act 2014][1], be increased by the amount of the shortfall, and the amount resulting shall be rounded up to the nearest whole pound.

Amendments—[1] Words inserted by the Pensions Act 2014 (Consequential, Supplementary and Incidental Amendments) Order, SI 2015/1985 art 6(*b*) with effect from 6 April 2016.

5—(1) Subject to sub-paragraphs (2) and (3) below, a person's earnings factor derived in respect of the year commencing on 6th April 1987, or any subsequent year, from those of his earnings in contracted-out employment upon which contracted-out contributions have been paid, or treated as paid, in respect of such year, shall be equal to the amount of those earnings.

(2) Any earnings factor ascertained under sub-paragraph (1) above shall be rounded down to the nearest whole pound.

(3) Where a person's earnings paid in the year commencing on 6th April 1987, or in any subsequent year, are earnings upon which contracted-out contributions have been paid or treated as paid in respect of that year and are, or are to be, recorded as separate sums in the records of the Department of Social Security, the earnings factor derived from those earnings shall be equal to the aggregate of the amounts ascertained by rounding down each sum separately to the nearest whole pound.

PART II
CLASS 2 AND CLASS 3 CONTRIBUTIONS

8 Subject to the provisions of paragraph 9, the earnings factor derived from a person's Class 2 or Class 3 contributions, being in each case contributions actually paid or contributions paid or credited, in respect of any year shall be that year's lower earnings limit for Class 1 contributions multiplied by the number of the contributions from which the earnings factor is to be derived.

9 Where any earnings factor ascertained by applying the rule contained in paragraph 8 above would not, but for this paragraph, be expressed as a whole number of pounds, it shall be so expressed by the rounding down of any fraction of a pound less than one-half and the rounding up of any other fraction of a pound.

1982/1033

CONTRACTING-OUT (RECOVERY OF CLASS 1 CONTRIBUTIONS) REGULATIONS 1982

Note—These Regulations are revoked by the Social Security (Contributions) Regulations, SI 2001/1004 reg 157, Sch 8 Pt I with effect from 6 April 2001.

1988/1409

SOCIAL SECURITY (EMPLOYMENT TRAINING: PAYMENTS) ORDER 1988

Made by the Secretary of State for Social Security under EA 1988 s 26(1)(d), (2), (4)

Made ....*8 August 1988*
Laid before Parliament ....*12 August 1988*
Coming into force ....*4 September 1988*

Note—This Order modifies SSA 1975 Pt I so as to provide that payments made to persons undergoing Employment Training who are in receipt of a training premium shall not attract liability to pay Class 1 or Class 2 NICs.

1 Citation, commencement and interpretation

(1) This Order may be cited as the Social Security (Employment Training: Payments) Order 1988 and shall come into force on 4th September 1988.

(2) In this Order, "Class 1 contributions", "primary Class 1 contributions", "secondary Class 1 contributions" and "Class 2 contributions" shall have the same meanings as in the Social Security Act 1975.

2 Treatment of payments for purposes of the Social Security Act 1975

No primary or secondary Class 1 contributions shall be payable, and no person shall be liable to pay Class 1 or Class 2 contributions, in respect of payments to any person in receipt of a training premium under provision made under section 2 of the Employment and Training Act 1973 being payments under provision made under that section in connection with his use of facilities provided in pursuance of arrangements, known by the name of Employment Training, under that section; and Part I (Contributions) of the Social Security Act 1975 shall be modified accordingly.

1989/1297

TAXES (INTEREST RATE) REGULATIONS 1989

Note—These regulations are reproduced in Part 2 of this work; reference should be made to regs 3(1)(*c*) and 3AB(*b*) in relation to interest rates on unpaid contributions.

1990/536

SOCIAL SECURITY (REFUNDS) (REPAYMENT OF CONTRACTUAL MATERNITY PAY) REGULATIONS 1990

Made by the Secretary of State for Social Security under SSA 1975 s 166(2) and Sch 1 para 6(1)(*gg*), (*m*) and Sch 20, see now SSCBA 1992 s 175(3), SSAA 1992 s 189(4), SSCBA 1992 Sch 1, para 8(1)(*i*), (*q*).

Made ....*8 March 1990*
Laid before Parliament ....*9 March 1990*
Coming into force ....*31 March 1990*

Note—Social Security Acts 1992 which consolidate provisions under which this statutory instrument is made come into effect on 1 July 1992. SS (Consequential Provisions) Act 1992 s 2 provides for the continuity of this instrument after 30 June 1992.

Functions of the Secretary of State are hereby transferred to the Board of Inland Revenue by the Social Security Contributions (Transfer of Functions, etc.) Act 1999 s 1(2) and Sch 2 with effect from 1 April 1999 for regs 2 and 3, by virtue of the Social Security Contributions (Transfer of Functions, etc) Act 1999 (Commencement No 1 and Transitional Provisions) Order, SI 1999/527.

1 Citation, commencement and interpretation

(1) These Regulations may be cited as the Social Security (Refunds) (Repayment of Contractual Maternity Pay) Regulations 1990 and shall come into force on 31st March 1990.

(2) In these Regulations "the Act" means the Social Security Act 1975[1] and "the Contributions Regulations" means the Social Security (Contributions) Regulations 1979.

Notes—[1] SSCBA 1992; SSAA 1992.

NIC

2 Refunds of contributions

(1) Where contractual maternity pay becomes repayable after 31st March 1990 and—

(*a*) subject to paragraph (2) below, an application for refund of contributions paid in respect of that pay is made in accordance with paragraph (3) below; and

(*b*) the net amount of the refund which would, but for this sub-paragraph, be payable exceeds the amount of one fifteenth of a standard rate primary Class 1 contribution payable on earnings at the upper earnings limit in respect of primary Class 1 contributions prescribed in regulation 7 of the Contributions Regulations (lower and upper earnings limits) for the last or only year in respect of which the contributions were paid,

the Secretary of State shall refund the whole of any primary or secondary Class 1 contributions paid in respect of that pay or, as the case may be, such part of those contributions as is prescribed in regulation 3 below.

(2) No application under this regulation may be made unless—

(*a*) where the application is by the employee, the contractual maternity pay has been repaid; or

(*b*) where the application is by the employer, he has been repaid the contractual maternity pay or can satisfy the Secretary of State that he has taken all reasonable steps to recover it.

(3) A person desiring to apply for the refund of any contribution under this regulation shall make the application in writing and within the period of 6 years from the end of the year in which that contribution was paid or, if the Secretary of State is satisfied that the person making the application had good cause for not making it within the said period, within such longer period as the Secretary of State may allow.

(4) In this regulation—

(*a*) "contractual maternity pay" means earnings payable under a contract of service by reason of pregnancy or confinement and repayable to the employer in the event of the employee failing to resume that employment after the birth or confinement; and

(*b*) "standard rate" means the appropriate percentage rate specified in section 4(6A) of the Act[1] for primary Class 1 contributions.

Notes—[1] SSCBA 1992 s 8(2).

Functions of the Secretary of State are transferred to the Board of Inland Revenue by SSC(TF)A 1999 s 1(2) and Sch 2 with effect from 1 April 1999 (SI 1999/527).

3 Refund of part of contributions

Where there has been paid an amount by way of any of the contributory benefits (as described in section 12(1) of the Act[2]) which would not have been paid had any of the contributions (in respect of which an application for their refund is duly made in accordance with regulation 2 above) not been paid in the first instance, the Secretary of State shall refund that part of the contributions remaining after the deduction of [that amount][1] paid by way of such benefits.

Amendments—[1] Words substituted by the Social Security (Miscellaneous Provisions) Amendment Regulations, SI 1990/2208 reg 19, with effect from 5 December 1990.

[2] SSCBA 1992 s 20(1).

Functions of the Secretary of State are transferred to the Board of Inland Revenue by SSC(TF)A 1999 s 1(2) and Sch 2 with effect from 1 April 1999 (SI 1999/527).

4 (Revoked by SI 2001/1004 reg 157, Sch 8 Pt I.)

1991/589

STATUTORY SICK PAY (NATIONAL HEALTH SERVICE EMPLOYEES) REGULATIONS 1991

Note—Social Security Acts 1992 which consolidate provisions under which this statutory instrument is made come into effect on 1 July 1992. SS (Consequential Provisions) Act 1992 s 2 provides for the continuity of this instrument after 30 June 1992.

Made .... *11 March 1991*
Laid before Parliament .... *11 March 1991*
Coming into force .... *1 April 1991*

The Secretary of State for Social Security in exercise of the powers conferred by sections 26(1) and (5A), 45(1) and 47 of the Social Security and Housing Benefits Act 1982 and of all other powers enabling him in that behalf, by this instrument, which contains only regulations consequential upon paragraph 16 of Schedule 6 to the Social Security Act 1990 hereby makes the following Regulations:

1 Citation, commencement and interpretation

(1) These Regulations may be cited as the Statutory Sick Pay (National Health Service Employees) Regulations 1991 and shall come into force on 1st April 1991.

(2) In these Regulations, a "health authority" [shall in relation to Wales have the same meaning it has in section 8][2] of the National Health Service Act 1977 and in relation to Scotland mean the health board within the meaning of section 2 of the National Health Service (Scotland) Act 1978.

(3) . . .[1]

[(4) . . .[1]

[(5) In these Regulations, a reference to "NHS trust" shall be construed to include a reference to an NHS foundation trust within the meaning of section 1(1) of the Health and Social Care (Community Health and Standards) Act 2003 where the application for authorisation to become an NHS foundation trust was made by an NHS trust.][3]

Amendments—[1] Paras 3, 4 revoked by the National Treatment Agency (Abolition) and the Health and Social Care Act 2012 (Consequential, Transitional and Saving Provisions) Order, SI 2013/235 art 11, Sch 2 para 15(1), (2) with effect from 1 April 2013.

[2] Words in para (2) substituted, and para (4) inserted, by the National Health Service Reform and Health Care Professions Act 2002 (Supplementary, Consequential etc Provisions) Regulations, SI 2002/2469 reg 4, Sch 1 para 50 with effect from 1 October 2002.

[3] Para (5) inserted by the Health and Social Care (Community Health and Standards) Act 2003 (Supplementary and Consequential Provision) (NHS Foundation Trusts) Order, SI 2004/696 art 3(17), Sch 17 with effect for certain specified purposes (see SI 2004/696 arts 1(2), 3(16), Sch 16) from 5 July 2004, and otherwise from 1 April 2004: SI 2004/696 art 1(1).

2 Treatment of more than one contract of employment as one contract

Where, in consequence of the establishment of one or more National Health Service Trusts under Part I of the National Health Service and Community Care Act 1990 or the National Health Service (Scotland) Act 1978 a person's contract of employment is treated by a scheme under that Part or Act as divided so as to constitute two or more contracts . . .[1] he may elect for all those contracts to be treated as one contract for the purposes of Part I of the Social Security and Housing Benefits Act 1982.

Amendments—[1] Words revoked by the National Treatment Agency (Abolition) and the Health and Social Care Act 2012 (Consequential, Transitional and Saving Provisions) Order, SI 2013/235 art 11, Sch 2 para 15(1), (3) with effect from 1 April 2013.

3 Notification of election

A person who makes an election under regulation 2 above shall give written notification of that election to each of his employers under the two or more contracts of service mentioned in that regulation, before the end of the fourth day of incapacity for work in the period of incapacity for work in relation to a contract of service with the employer with whom this day first occurs.

4 Provision of information by employees

A person who makes an election under regulation 2 above shall, as soon as is reasonably practicable after giving notice of that election, provide each of his employers under the two or more contracts of service mentioned in that regulation with the following information—

(*a*) the name and address of each of his employers; and

(*b*) the date his employment with each of those employers commenced; and

(*c*) details of his earnings during the relevant period and for this purpose "earnings" and "relevant period" have the same meanings as they have for the purposes of section 26(2) of the Social Security and Housing Benefits Act 1982.

5 Treatment of two or more employers as one

The employer to be regarded for the purposes of statutory sick pay as the employee's employer under the one contract where 2 or more contracts of service are treated as one in accordance with regulation 2 above, shall be—

[(*a*) in the case of a person whose contract of employment is treated by a scheme under Part I of the National Health Service and Community Care Act 1990 or the National Health Service (Scotland) Act 1978 as divided—

(i) the Health Authority . . .[3] from which the employee was transferred, in a case where any one of the employee's contracts of service is with that Health Authority . . .[3]; or

(ii) the first NHS trust to which a contract of service was transferred in a case where none of the employee's contracts of service are with the Health Authority or Primary Care Trust from which he was transferred;

. . .[3]

(b) in the case of a person whose contract of employment is divided as provided by an order under paragraph 23(1) of Schedule 5A to the National Health Service Act 1977—

(i) the [Strategic Health Authority][2], NHS trust or Primary Care Trust from which the employee was transferred, in a case where any one of the employee's contracts of service is with that body; or

(ii) the first Primary Care Trust to which a contract of service was transferred in a case where none of the employee's contracts of service are with the body from which he was transferred.][1], [3]

NIC

Amendments—[1] Paras (*a*), (*b*) substituted by the Health Act 1999 (Supplementary, Consequential etc Provisions) (No 2) Order, SI 2000/694 art 3 Schedule, para 2(1), (4), with effect from 1 April 2000.

[2] Words substituted by the National Health Service Reform and Health Care Professions Act 2002 (Supplementary, Consequential etc Provisions) Regulations, SI 2002/2469 reg 6, Sch 3 with effect from 1 October 2002.

[3] In para (*a*), words "or Primary Trust revoked in both places, and para (*b*) and preceding word "or" revoked by the National Treatment Agency (Abolition) and the Health and Social Care Act 2012 (Consequential, Transitional and Saving Provisions) Order, SI 2013/235 art 11, Sch 2 para 15(1), (4) with effect from 1 April 2013. These amendments extend to England and Wales only (SI 2013/235 art 1(3)) and do not affect the continuing validity or effect of any election made before 1st April 2013 under reg 2 above, and do not prevent a person employed immediately before that date ("the employee") from making an election under that regulation on or after that date (SI 2013/235 art 12, Sch 3 para 1(1)).

6 Time for which an election is to have effect

An election made under regulation 2 shall lapse at the end of the period of incapacity for work in relation to the contract of service with the employer mentioned in regulation 5.

1994/1882

STATUTORY MATERNITY PAY (COMPENSATION OF EMPLOYERS) AND MISCELLANEOUS AMENDMENTS REGULATIONS 1994

Made by the Secretary of State for Social Security under the Social Security Contributions and Benefits Act 1992 ss 35(3), 167(1), (1A), (1B), (4), 171(1), 175(1)–(4)

Made .... *14 July 1994*
Laid before Parliament .... *15 July 1994*
Coming into force in accordance with regulation 1(2) and (3)
regulations 1 and 9 .... *31 July 1994*
regulations 2 to 8 .... *4 September 1994*

Note—Functions of the Secretary of State are hereby transferred to the Board of Inland Revenue by the Social Security Contributions (Transfer of Functions, etc.) Act 1999 s 1(2) and Sch 2 with effect from 1 April 1999 for regs 3 and 6, by virtue of the Social Security Contributions (Transfer of Functions, etc) Act 1999 (Commencement No 1 and Transitional Provisions) Order, SI 1999/527.

1 Citation, commencement and interpretation

(1) These Regulations may be cited as the Statutory Maternity Pay (Compensation of Employers) and Miscellaneous Amendment Regulations 1994 and regulations 2 to 7 shall have effect in relation to payments of statutory maternity pay due on or after 4th September 1994.

(2) This regulation and regulation 9 shall come into force on 31st July 1994.

(3) Regulations 2 to 8 shall come into force on 4th September 1994.

(4) In these Regulations—

["the Board" means the Commissioners of Inland Revenue;][1]

"the Contributions and Benefits Act" means the Social Security Contributions and Benefits Act 1992;

["contributions payments" has the same meaning as in section 167(8) of the Contributions and Benefits Act;][1]

["the Contributions Regulations" means the Social Security (Contributions) Regulations 2001;][1]

"the Maternity Allowance Regulations" means the Social Security (Maternity Allowance) Regulations 1987;

. . .[1]

"employer" shall include a person who was previously an employer of a woman to whom a payment of statutory maternity pay was made, whether or not that person remains her employer at the date any deduction from contributions payments is made by him in accordance with regulation 5 or, as the case may be, any payment is received by him in accordance with regulation 6;

["the Employment Act" means the Employment Act 2002;][1]

"income tax month" means the period beginning on the 6th day of any calendar month and ending on the 5th day of the following calendar month;

["income tax quarter" means, in any tax year, the period beginning on 6th April and ending on 5th July, the period beginning on 6th July and ending on 5th October, the period beginning on 6th October and ending on 5th January, or the period beginning on 6th January and ending on 5th April;][1]

. . .[1]

"qualifying day" means the first day in the week immediately preceding the 14th week before the expected week of confinement in which a woman who is or has been an employee first satisfies the conditions of entitlement to statutory maternity pay for which a deduction from a contributions payment is made by her employer in respect of a payment of statutory maternity pay made by him;

"qualifying tax year" means the tax year preceding the tax year in which the qualifying day in question falls;

["statutory adoption pay" means any payment under section 171ZL of the Contributions and Benefits Act;][1]

["statutory paternity pay" means any payment under section 171ZA or 171ZB of the Contributions and Benefits Act;][1]

["tax year" means the period of 12 months beginning on 6th April in any year;][1]

["writing" includes writing delivered by means of electronic communications approved by directions issued by the Board pursuant to regulations made under section 132 of the Finance Act 1999.][1]

[(5) Any reference in these Regulations to the employees of any employer includes, where the context permits, a reference to his former employees.][1]

(6) . . .[1]

Amendments—[1] Definitions of "contributions payments" and "payment of statutory maternity pay" revoked; other definitions inserted; para (5) substituted; and para (6) revoked; by the SMP (Compensation of Employers) Amendment Regulations, SI 2003/672 reg 2 with effect from 6 April 2003.

2 Meaning of "small employer"

(1) Subject to the following provisions of this regulation, a small employer is an employer whose contributions payments for the qualifying tax year do not exceed [£45,000][1].

(2) For the purposes of this regulation, the amount of an employer's contributions payments shall be determined without regard to any deductions that may be made from them under any enactment or instrument.

(3) Where in the qualifying tax year an employer has made contributions payments in one or more, but less than 12, of the income tax months, the amount of his contributions payments for that tax year shall be estimated by adding together all of those payments, dividing the total amount by the number of those months in which he has made those payments and multiplying the resulting figure by 12.

(4) Where in the qualifying tax year an employer has made no contributions payments, but does have such payments in one or more income tax months which fall both—

(*a*) in the tax year in which the qualifying day falls, and

(*b*) before the qualifying day or, where there is more than one such day in that tax year, before the first of those days,

then the amount of his contributions payments for the qualifying tax year shall be estimated in accordance with paragraph (3) but as if the amount of the contributions payments falling in those months had fallen instead in the corresponding tax months in the qualifying tax year.

Amendments—[1] Figure in para (1) substituted by the Statutory Maternity Pay (Compensation of Employers) Amendment Regulations, SI 2004/698 reg 2 with effect for payments of statutory maternity pay made after 5 April 2004.

3 Determination of the amount of additional payment to which a small employer shall be entitled

In respect of any payment of statutory maternity pay [made in the tax year commencing [6th April 2011][3], or in any subsequent tax year,][1] a small employer shall be [entitled to recover an additional amount][2] being an amount equal to [3.0%][3] of such payment, that percentage being the total amount of secondary Class 1 contributions estimated by the Secretary of State as to be paid in respect of statutory maternity pay by all employers in that year, expressed as a percentage of the total amount of statutory maternity pay estimated by him to be paid by all employers in that year.

Note—Functions of the Secretary of State are hereby transferred to the Board of Inland Revenue by the Social Security Contributions (Transfer of Functions, etc.) Act 1999 s 1(2) and Sch 2 with effect from 1 April 1999 by virtue of the Social Security Contributions (Transfer of Functions, etc) Act 1999 (Commencement No 1 and Transitional Provisions) Order, SI 1999/527.

Amendments—[1] Words inserted and substituted respectively by the Statutory Maternity Pay (Compensation of Employers) Amendment Regulations, SI 1995/566 reg 2 with effect from 6 April 1995.

[2] Words substituted by the SMP (Compensation of Employers) Amendment Regulations, SI 2003/672 reg 3 with effect from 6 April 2003.

[3] Words substituted by the Statutory Maternity Pay (Compensation of Employers) Amendment Regulations, SI 2011/725 reg 2 with effect in relation to payments of statutory maternity pay made on or after 6 April 2011.

4 [Right of employers to prescribed amount

An employer who has made, or is liable to make, any payment of statutory maternity pay shall be entitled to recover—

(*a*) an amount equal to 92 per cent of such payment; or

(*b*) if he is a small employer—

(i) an amount equal to such payment, and

(ii) an additional amount under regulation 3,

in accordance with the provisions of these Regulations.][1]

Amendments—[1] Regulations 4–6A substituted by the SMP (Compensation of Employers) Amendment Regulations, SI 2003/672 reg 4 with effect from 6 April 2003.

NIC

5 [Application for advance funding from the Board

(1) If an employer is entitled to recover an amount determined in accordance with regulation 4 in respect of statutory maternity pay which he is required to pay to an employee or employees in any income tax month or income tax quarter and the amount exceeds the aggregate of—

(*a*) the total amount of tax which the employer is required to pay to the collector of taxes in respect of deductions from the emoluments of his employees in accordance with the Income Tax (Employments) Regulations 1993 for that income tax month or income tax quarter;

(*b*) the total amount of deductions made by the employer from the emoluments of his employees for that income tax month or income tax quarter in accordance with regulations made under section 22(5) of the Teaching and Higher Education Act 1998 or section 73B of the Education (Scotland) Act 1980 or in accordance with Article 3(5) of the Education (Student Support) (Northern Ireland) Order 1988;

(*c*) the total amount of contributions payments which the employer is required to pay to the collector of taxes in respect of the emoluments of his employees (whether by means of deduction or otherwise) in accordance with the Contributions Regulations for that income tax month or income tax quarter;

(*d*) the total amount of payments which the employer is required to pay to the collector of taxes in respect of deductions made on account of tax from payments to sub-contractors in accordance with section 559 of the Income and Corporation Taxes Act 1988 for that income tax month or income tax quarter; and

(*e*) the statutory paternity pay, statutory adoption pay and statutory maternity pay which the employer is required to pay to his employees in that income tax month or income tax quarter,

the employer may apply to the Board in accordance with paragraph (2) for funds ("advance funding") to pay that excess (or so much of it as remains outstanding) to the employee or employees.

(2) Where—

(*a*) the conditions in paragraph (1) are satisfied; or

(*b*) the employer considers that the conditions in paragraph (1) will be satisfied on the date of any subsequent payment of emoluments to one or more employees who are entitled to a payment of statutory maternity pay,

the employer may apply to the Board for advance funding on a form approved for that purpose by the Board.

(3) An application by an employer under paragraph (2) shall be for an amount not exceeding the amount of statutory maternity pay which the employer is entitled to recover in accordance with regulation 4 and which he is required to pay to an employee or employees for the income tax month or income tax quarter to which the payment of emoluments relates.][1]

Amendments—[1] Regulations 4–6A substituted by the SMP (Compensation of Employers) Amendment Regulations, SI 2003/672 reg 4 with effect from 6 April 2003.

6 [Deductions from payments to the Board

An employer who is entitled to recover an amount under regulation 4 may do so by making one or more deductions from the aggregate of the amounts specified in sub-paragraphs (*a*) to (*e*) of regulation 5(1), except where and insofar as—

(*a*) those amounts relate to earnings paid before the beginning of the income tax month or income tax quarter in which the payment of statutory maternity pay was made;

(*b*) those amounts are paid by him later than six years after the tax year in which the payment of statutory maternity pay was made;

(*c*) the employer has received advance funding from the Board in accordance with an application under regulation 5; or

(*d*) the employer has made a request in writing under regulation 5 that the amount which he is entitled to recover under regulation 4 be paid to him and he has not received notification by the Board that such request is refused.][1]

Amendments—[1] Regulations 4–6A substituted by the SMP (Compensation of Employers) Amendment Regulations, SI 2003/672 reg 4 with effect from 6 April 2003.

6A [Payments to employers by the Board

If, in an income tax month or an income tax quarter—

(*a*) the total amount that the employer is entitled to deduct under regulation 6 is less than the amount which the employer is entitled to recover under regulation 4;

(*b*) the Board is satisfied that this is so; and

(*c*) the employer has so requested in writing,

the Board shall pay to the employer the sum that the employer is unable to deduct under regulation 6.][1]

Amendments—[1] Regulations 4–6A substituted by the SMP (Compensation of Employers) Amendment Regulations, SI 2003/672 reg 4 with effect from 6 April 2003.

7 Date when certain contributions are to be treated as paid

Where an employer has made a deduction from a contributions payment under [regulation 6][1], the date on which it is to be treated as having been paid for the purposes of [section 167(6)][1] of the Contributions and Benefits Act (amount deducted to be treated as paid and received towards discharging liability in respect of Class 1 contributions) is—

(*a*) in a case where the deduction did not extinguish the contributions payment, the date on which the remainder of the contributions payment or, as the case may be, the first date on which any part of the remainder of the contributions payment was paid; and

(*b*) in a case where the deduction extinguished the contributions payment, the 14th day after the end of the income tax month during which there were paid the earnings in respect of which the contributions payment was payable.

Amendments—[1] Words substituted by the SMP (Compensation of Employers) Amendment Regulations, SI 2003/672 reg 5 with effect from 6 April 2003.

7A [Overpayments

(1) Where advance funding has been provided to an employer in accordance with an application under regulation 5, the Board may recover any part of it not used to pay statutory maternity pay ("the overpayment").

(2) An officer of the Board shall decide to the best of his judgement the amount of the overpayment and shall give notice in writing of his decision to the employer.

(3) A decision under paragraph (2) may be in respect of funding provided in accordance with regulation 5 for one or more income tax months or income tax quarters in a tax year—

(*a*) in respect of one or more classes of employees specified in a decision notice (where a notice does not name any individual employee); or

(*b*) in respect of one or more individual employees named in a decision notice.

(4) Subject to paragraphs (5), (6) or (7), Part 6 of the Taxes Management Act 1970 (collection and recovery) shall apply with any necessary modifications to a decision under this regulation as if the amount specified were an assessment and as if the amount set out in the notice were income tax charged on the employer.

(5) Where a decision under paragraph (2) relates to more than one employee, proceedings may be brought to recover the amount overpaid without distinguishing the sum to be repaid in respect of each employee and without specifying the employee in question.

(6) A decision to recover an amount made in accordance with this regulation shall give rise to one cause of action or matter of complaint for the purpose of proceedings under section 65, 66 or 67 of the Taxes Management Act 1970.

(7) Nothing in paragraph (5) shall prevent separate proceedings being brought for the recovery of any amount which the employer is liable to repay in respect of each employee to whom the decision relates.][1]

Amendments—[1] Regulation 7A inserted by the SMP (Compensation of Employers) Amendment Regulations, SI 2003/672 reg 6 with effect from 6 April 2003.

8 Revocation

The Statutory Maternity Pay (Compensation of Employers) Regulations 1987 are hereby revoked.

9 (Amends SI 1987/416.)

NIC

1995/512

STATUTORY SICK PAY PERCENTAGE THRESHOLD ORDER 1995

Revocation—This Order revoked by the Statutory Sick Pay Percentage Threshold (Revocations, Transitional and Saving Provisions) (Great Britain and Northern Ireland) Order, SI 2014/589, art 2(*a*) with effect from 6 April 2014. Notwithstanding the revocation, this Order continues to have effect for the period of two years beginning with 6 April 2014 for the purposes of entitling an employer to recover an amount of statutory sick pay (whether paid before, on or after 6 April 2014) in respect of any day of incapacity for work falling before 6th April 2014.

Note—Functions of the Secretary of State are hereby transferred to the Board of Inland Revenue by the Social Security Contributions (Transfer of Functions, etc.) Act 1999 s 1(2) and Sch 2 with effect from 1 April 1999 for art 4, by virtue of the Social Security Contributions (Transfer of Functions, etc) Act 1999 (Commencement No 1 and Transitional Provisions) Order, SI 1999/527.

Made by the Secretary of State for Social Security under the Social Security Contributions and Benefits Act 1992 ss 159A, 175(3), (4)

Made . . . . *1 March 1995*

Coming into force . . . . *6 April 1995*

1 Citation, commencement and interpretation

(1) This Order may be cited as the Statutory Sick Pay Percentage Threshold Order 1995 and shall come into force on 6th April 1995.

(2) In this Order, unless the context otherwise requires, "income tax month" means the period beginning on the 6th day of any calendar month and ending on the 5th day of the following calendar month.
(3) A reference in this Order to a payment of statutory sick pay shall not include any such payment made in respect of a day of incapacity for work before the coming into force of this Order.
(4) Unless the context otherwise requires, any reference in this Order to a numbered article is a reference to the article bearing that number in this Order and any reference in an article to a numbered paragraph is a reference to the paragraph of that article bearing that number.

2 Right of employer to recover statutory sick pay

(1) Subject to paragraph (2) an employer is entitled to recover in accordance with articles 3 and 4 the amount, if any, by which the payments of statutory sick pay made by him in any income tax month exceed 13 per cent of the amount of his liability for contributions payments in respect of that income tax month.
(2) For the purposes of calculating the amount an employer is entitled to recover under paragraph (1), there shall be excluded any payment of statutory sick pay which was not made—
- (*a*) in the income tax month in which he received notice, in accordance with regulation 7 of the Statutory Sick Pay (General) Regulations 1982, of the day or days of incapacity for work to which the payment related;
- (*b*) in a case where it would have been impracticable to make the payment in that income tax month in view of the employer's methods of accounting for and paying remuneration, in the following income tax month; or
- (*c*) in a case where a decision had been made by an adjudication officer, social security appeal tribunal or Commissioner that the employee was entitled to that payment, within the time limits set out in regulation 9 of those Regulations.

3 Recovery by deduction from contributions payments

(1) An employer may recover an amount determined in accordance with article 2 in respect of any income tax month by making one or more deductions from his contributions payments for that or any following income tax month within 6 years from the end of the tax year in which he became entitled to recover that amount, except where and insofar as—
- (*a*) that amount has been repaid to him by or on behalf of the Secretary of State under article 4; or
- (*b*) he has made a request in writing under article 4 that that amount be repaid to him, and he has not received notification by or on behalf of the Secretary of State that the request is refused.

(2) A deduction from contributions payments made in accordance with paragraph (1) shall be disregarded for the purposes of determining whether an employer has discharged any liability of his in respect of Class 1 contributions.

4 Recovery from the Secretary of State

(1) If the amount which an employer is or would otherwise be entitled to deduct under article 3 exceeds the amount of his contributions payments in respect of earnings paid in an income tax month, and the Secretary of State is satisfied that that is so, then provided that the employer has requested him in writing to do so, there shall be repaid to the employer by or on behalf of the Secretary of State such amount as the employer was unable to deduct.
(2) If an employer is not liable for any contributions payments in an income tax month but would otherwise be entitled to deduct an amount under article 3, and the Secretary of State is satisfied that that is so, then provided the employer has in writing requested him to do so, that amount shall be repaid to the employer by or on behalf of the Secretary of State.

Note—Functions of the Secretary of State are hereby transferred to the Board of Inland Revenue by the Social Security Contributions (Transfer of Functions, etc.) Act 1999 s 1(2) and Sch 2 with effect from 1 April 1999 by virtue of the Social Security Contributions (Transfer of Functions, etc) Act 1999 (Commencement No 1 and Transitional Provisions) Order, SI 1999/527.

5 Repeals and revocations

Subject to the savings made by regulations under section 159A(4) of the Social Security Contributions and Benefits Act 1992—
- (*a*) sections 158 and 159 of the Social Security Contributions and Benefits Act 1992 shall be repealed; and
- (*b*) the Statutory Sick Pay (Compensation of Employers) and Miscellaneous Provisions Regulations 1983 and the Statutory Sick Pay (Small Employers' Relief) Regulations 1991 shall be revoked.

6 Consequential amendments

. . .

Note—Amends Social Security Contributions and Benefits Act 1992 s 176, Sch 1; and Social Security Administration Act 1992 ss 17, 149, Sch 7.

1995/1801

SOCIAL SECURITY (ADJUDICATION) REGULATIONS 1995

Made .... *13 July 1995*
Laid before Parliament .... *20 July 1995*
Coming into Operation .... *10 August 1995*

Revoked by SI 1999/991 reg 59, Sch 4 with effect from 1 June 1999 in so far as these Regulations relate to child support; 5 July 1999 in so far as they relate to industrial injuries benefit, guardian's allowance, child benefit and a decision made by virtue of the Pension Schemes Act 1993, s 170(2); 6 September 1999 in so far as they relate to retirement pension, widow's benefit, incapacity benefit, severe disablement allowance and maternity allowance; 5 October 1999 in so far as they relate to family credit and disability working allowance; 18 October 1999 in so far as they relate to attendance allowance, disability living allowance, invalid care allowance, jobseeker's allowance, credits of contributions or earnings, home responsibilities protection and vaccine damage payments; 29 November 1999 for all remaining purposes: see SI 1999/991 reg 1(2), and for provision as to the continued effect of these Regulations up to and including 28 November 1999 see reg 59(2) thereof.

1996/1055

SOCIAL SECURITY (REDUCED RATES OF CLASS 1 CONTRIBUTIONS AND REBATES) (MONEY PURCHASE CONTRACTED-OUT SCHEMES) ORDER 1996

Made by the Secretary of State for Social Security under PSA 1993 s 42B

Made .... *3 April 1996*
Coming into Operation .... *6 April 1997*

NIC

1 Citation and commencement

This Order may be cited as the Social Security (Reduced Rates of Class 1 Contributions and Rebates) (Money Purchase Contracted-out Schemes) Order 1996 and shall come into force on 6th April 1997.

2 Reduced rates of Class 1 contributions and rebates

For the purposes of section 42A of the Pension Schemes Act 1993—

(*a*) the appropriate flat-rate percentage in respect of earners for the tax years 1997–98 [and 1998–99][1], in the case of a primary Class 1 contribution is 1·6 per cent and, in the case of a secondary Class 1 contribution is 1·5 per cent;

(*b*) the appropriate age-related percentages in respect of earners in the tax years 1997–98 to [and 1998–99][1] are those specified in the Table in the Schedule to this Order by reference to their ages on the last day of the preceding tax year.

Note—Social Security (Reduced Rates of Class 1 Contributions, and Rebates) (Money Purchase Contracted-out Schemes) Order, SI 1998/945 gives percentage details for 1999–00 to 2001–02.

Amendments—[1] Article 2 amended by the Social Security (Reduced Rates of Class 1 Contributions, and Rebates) (Money Purchase Contracted-out Schemes) Order, SI 1998/945 with effect from 6 April 1999.

SCHEDULE

TABLE

Appropriate age-related percentages of earnings exceeding the lower earnings limit but not the upper earnings limit.

	Appropriate age-related percentages for the tax year	
Age on last day of preceding tax year	*1997–98*	*1998–99*
15	3.1	3.1
16	3.2	3.2
17	3.2	3.2
18	3.3	3.3
19	3.3	3.3
20	3.4	3.4
21	3.4	3.4
22	3.5	3.5
23	3.5	3.5

24	3.6	3.6
25	3.6	3.7
26	3.7	3.7
27	3.8	3.8
28	3.8	3.8
29	3.9	3.9
30	3.9	3.9
31	4.0	4.0
32	4.0	4.0
33	4.1	4.1
34	4.2	4.2
35	4.3	4.2
36	4.5	4.4
37	4.6	4.5
38	4.8	4.7
39	5.0	4.9
40	5.2	5.1
41	5.4	5.3
42	5.8	5.5
43	6.4	5.9
44	7.2	6.5
45	8.0	7.3
46	8.9	8.1
47	9.0	9.0
48	9.0	9.0
49	9.0	9.0
50	9.0	9.0
51	9.0	9.0
52	9.0	9.0
53	9.0	9.0
54	9.0	9.0
55	9.0	9.0
56	9.0	9.0
57	9.0	9.0
58	9.0	9.0
59	9.0	9.0
60	9.0	9.0
61	9.0	9.0
62	9.0	9.0
63	9.0	9.0

Note—See Social Security (Reduced Rates of Class 1 Contributions, and Rebates) (Money Purchase Contracted-out Schemes) Order, SI 1998/945 for age-related percentages for 1999–00 to 2001–02.

Amendments—Columns relating to the tax years 1999–00, 2000–01 and 2001–02 omitted by the Social Security (Reduced Rates of Class 1 Contributions, and Rebates) (Money Purchase Contracted-out Schemes) Order, SI 1998/945 with effect from 6 April 1999.

1996/1056

SOCIAL SECURITY (MINIMUM CONTRIBUTIONS TO APPROPRIATE PERSONAL PENSION SCHEMES) ORDER 1996

Made by the Secretary of State under PSA 1993 s 45A

Made . . . . *3 April 1996*

1 Citation and commencement

This Order may be cited as the Social Security (Minimum Contributions to Appropriate Personal Pension Schemes) Order 1996, and shall come into force on 6th April 1997.

2 Appropriate age-related percentage

For the purposes of section 45 of the Pension Schemes Act 1993 (amount of minimum contributions) the appropriate age-related percentages in respect of earners in the tax years 1997–98 [and 1998–99][1] are those specified in the Table in the Schedule to this Order by reference to their ages on the last day of the preceding tax year.

Amendments—[1] Words substituted by the Social Security (Minimum Contributions to Appropriate Personal Pension Schemes) Order, SI 1998/944 art 3(*a*) with effect from 6 April 1999.

SCHEDULE

Article 2

TABLE

Appropriate age-related percentages of earnings exceeding the lower earnings limit but not the upper earnings limit.

Age on last day of preceding tax year	*Appropriate age-related percentages for the tax year*				
	1997–98	*1998–99*	. . .	. . .	. . .
15	3.4	3.4	. . .	. . .	. . .
16	3.4	3.4	. . .	. . .	. . .
17	3.5	3.5	. . .	. . .	. . .
18	3.5	3.5	. . .	. . .	. . .
19	3.6	3.6	. . .	. . .	. . .
20	3.6	3.6	. . .	. . .	. . .
21	3.7	3.7	. . .	. . .	. . .
22	3.7	3.7	. . .	. . .	. . .
23	3.8	3.8	. . .	. . .	. . .
24	3.8	3.8	. . .	. . .	. . .
25	3.9	3.9	. . .	. . .	. . .
26	3.9	3.9	. . .	. . .	. . .
27	4.0	4.0	. . .	. . .	. . .
28	4.0	4.0	. . .	. . .	. . .
29	4.1	4.1	. . .	. . .	. . .
30	4.2	4.2	. . .	. . .	. . .
31	4.2	4.2	. . .	. . .	. . .
32	4.3	4.3	. . .	. . .	. . .
33	4.3	4.3	. . .	. . .	. . .
34	4.4	4.4	. . .	. . .	. . .
35	4.5	4.4	. . .	. . .	. . .
36	4.7	4.6	. . .	. . .	. . .
37	4.9	4.8	. . .	. . .	. . .
38	5.0	4.9	. . .	. . .	. . .
39	5.2	5.1	. . .	. . .	. . .
40	5.4	5.3	. . .	. . .	. . .
41	5.6	5.5	. . .	. . .	. . .
42	6.0	5.7	. . .	. . .	. . .
43	6.7	6.1	. . .	. . .	. . .
44	7.4	6.8	. . .	. . .	. . .
45	8.2	7.5	. . .	. . .	. . .
46	9.0	8.3	. . .	. . .	. . .
47	9.0	9.0	. . .	. . .	. . .
48	9.0	9.0	. . .	. . .	. . .

49	9.0	9.0	. . .	. . .	. . .
50	9.0	9.0	. . .	. . .	. . .
51	9.0	9.0	. . .	. . .	. . .
52	9.0	9.0	. . .	. . .	. . .
53	9.0	9.0	. . .	. . .	. . .
54	9.0	9.0	. . .	. . .	. . .
55	9.0	9.0	. . .	. . .	. . .
56	9.0	9.0	. . .	. . .	. . .
57	9.0	9.0	. . .	. . .	. . .
58	9.0	9.0	. . .	. . .	. . .
59	9.0	9.0	. . .	. . .	. . .
60	9.0	9.0	. . .	. . .	. . .
61	9.0	9.0	. . .	. . .	. . .
62	9.0	9.0	. . .	. . .	. . .
63	9.0	9.0	. . .	. . .	. . .

Amendments—Columns 4, 5, 6 relating to the tax years 1999–00, 2000–01 and 2001–02 revoked by the Social Security (Minimum Contributions to Appropriate Personal Pension Schemes) Order, SI 1998/944 art 3(*b*) with effect from 6 April 1999.

1998/944

SOCIAL SECURITY (MINIMUM CONTRIBUTIONS TO APPROPRIATE PERSONAL PENSION SCHEMES) ORDER 1998

Made by the Secretary of State for Social Security under PSA 1993

Made . . . . *1 April 1998*
Coming into force . . . . *6 April 1999*

1 Citation and commencement
This Order may be cited as the Social Security (Minimum Contributions to Appropriate Personal Pension Schemes) Order 1998 and shall come into force on 6th April 1999.

2 Appropriate age-related percentages
For the purposes of section 45 of the Pension Schemes Act 1993 (amount of minimum contributions) the appropriate age-related percentages in respect of earners in the tax years 1999–2000 to 2001–2002 are those specified in the Table in the Schedule to this Order by reference to their ages on the last day of the preceding tax year.

3 Amendment of previous Order
(amends SI 1996/1056 arts 2, Schedule)

SCHEDULE

Article 2

TABLE

Appropriate age-related percentages of earnings exceeding the lower earnings limit but not the upper earnings limit.

Age on last day of preceding tax year	*Appropriate age-related percentages for the tax year*		
	1999–2000	*2000–2001*	*2001–2002*
15	3.8	3.8	3.8
16	3.8	3.8	3.8
17	3.9	3.9	3.9
18	3.9	3.9	3.9
19	4.0	4.0	4.0
20	4.0	4.0	4.0
21	4.1	4.1	4.1
22	4.1	4.1	4.1
23	4.2	4.2	4.2

24	4.2	4.2	4.2
25	4.3	4.3	4.3
26	4.3	4.3	4.3
27	4.4	4.4	4.4
28	4.4	4.4	4.4
29	4.5	4.5	4.5
30	4.5	4.5	4.5
31	4.6	4.6	4.6
32	4.6	4.6	4.6
33	4.7	4.7	4.7
34	4.7	4.7	4.7
35	4.8	4.8	4.8
36	4.8	4.8	4.8
37	5.0	4.9	4.9
38	5.1	5.0	4.9
39	5.3	5.2	5.1
40	5.5	5.4	5.3
41	5.7	5.5	5.4
42	5.9	5.7	5.6
43	6.1	5.9	5.8
44	6.5	6.1	6.0
45	7.1	6.6	6.2
46	7.9	7.2	6.6
47	8.7	8.0	7.3
48	9.0	8.8	8.1
49	9.0	9.0	8.9
50	9.0	9.0	9.0
51	9.0	9.0	9.0
52	9.0	9.0	9.0
53	9.0	9.0	9.0
54	9.0	9.0	9.0
55	9.0	9.0	9.0
56	9.0	9.0	9.0
57	9.0	9.0	9.0
58	9.0	9.0	9.0
59	9.0	9.0	9.0
60	9.0	9.0	9.0
61	9.0	9.0	9.0
62	9.0	9.0	9.0
63	9.0	9.0	9.0

NIC

1998/945

SOCIAL SECURITY (REDUCED RATES OF CLASS 1 CONTRIBUTIONS, AND REBATES) (MONEY PURCHASE CONTRACTED-OUT SCHEMES) ORDER 1998

Made by the Secretary of State for Social Security under PSA 1993 s 42B

Made . . . . *1 April 1998*
Coming into force . . . . *6 April 1999*

1 Citation and commencement

This Order may be cited as the Social Security (Reduced Rates of Class 1 Contributions, and Rebates) (Money Purchase Contracted-out Schemes) Order 1998 and shall come into force on 6th April 1999.

2 Reduced rates of Class 1 contributions, and rebates

For the purposes of section 42A of the Pension Schemes Act 1993 (reduced rates of Class 1 contributions, and rebates)—

(*a*) the appropriate flat-rate percentage in respect of earners for the tax years 1999–2000 to 2001–2002, in the case of a primary Class 1 contribution is 1.6 per cent, and in the case of a secondary Class 1 contribution is 0.6 per cent;

(*b*) the appropriate age-related percentages in respect of earners for the tax years 1999–2000 to 2001–2002 are the percentages specified in the Table set out in the Schedule to this Order, by reference to the earners' ages on the last day of the preceding tax year.

3 Amendment of previous Order

[amends SI 1996/1055 reg 2 and Schedule.]

SCHEDULE

TABLE

Appropriate age-related percentages of earnings exceeding the lower earnings limit but not the upper earnings limit.

	Appropriate age-related percentages for the tax year		
Age on last day of preceding tax year	*1999–2000*	2000–2001	2001–2002
15	2.2	2.2	2.2
16	2.2	2.2	2.2
17	2.3	2.3	2.3
18	2.3	2.3	2.3
19	2.3	2.4	2.4
20	2.4	2.4	2.4
21	2.5	2.5	2.5
22	2.5	2.5	2.5
23	2.6	2.6	2.6
24	2.6	2.6	2.6
25	2.7	2.7	2.7
26	2.7	2.7	2.7
27	2.8	2.8	2.8
28	2.9	2.9	2.9
29	2.9	2.9	2.9
30	3.0	3.0	3.0
31	3.0	3.0	3.0
32	3.1	3.1	3.1
33	3.2	3.2	3.2
34	3.2	3.2	3.3
35	3.3	3.3	3.3
36	3.4	3.4	3.4
37	3.5	3.5	3.5
38	3.7	3.6	3.5
39	3.8	3.8	3.7
40	4.0	3.9	3.8
41	4.2	4.1	4.0
42	4.4	4.3	4.2
43	4.6	4.5	4.4
44	5.0	4.7	4.6

45	5.6	5.1	4.8
46	6.3	5.7	5.2
47	7.1	6.4	5.8
48	8.0	7.2	6.6
49	8.8	8.2	7.4
50	9.0	9.0	8.4
51	9.0	9.0	9.0
52	9.0	9.0	9.0
53	9.0	9.0	9.0
54	9.0	9.0	9.0
55	9.0	9.0	9.0
56	9.0	9.0	9.0
57	9.0	9.0	9.0
58	9.0	9.0	9.0
59	9.0	9.0	9.0
60	9.0	9.0	9.0
61	9.0	9.0	9.0
62	9.0	9.0	9.0
63	9.0	9.0	9.0

NIC

1998/2209

SOCIAL SECURITY ACT 1998 (COMMENCEMENT NO 1) ORDER 1998

Made by the Secretary of State for Social Security under SSA 1998 ss 79(3), 87(2), (3)

Made . . . . *7 September 1998*

1 Citation and interpretation

(1) This Order may be cited as the Social Security Act 1998 (Commencement No 1) Order 1998.

(2) In this Order, except where the context otherwise requires, references to sections and Schedules are references to sections of and Schedules to the Social Security Act 1998.

2 Appointed days

Subject to article 3 below, the day appointed for the coming into force of—

(*a*) the provisions of the Social Security Act 1998 which are specified in Part I of the Schedule to this Order is 8th September 1998;

(*b*) the provisions of that Act which are specified in Part II of the Schedule to this Order, in so far as they authorise the making of Regulations or Orders, is 8th September 1998;

(*c*) the provisions of that Act which are specified in Part III of the Schedule to this Order, in so far as they are not already in force, is 6th April 1999;

(*d*) section 73 (statutory sick pay not precluded by maternity allowance), Schedule 8 in respect of the repeal in the Social Security Contributions and Benefits Act 1992, Schedule 11, paragraph 2(*d*), of the words "(ii) she was entitled to a maternity allowance, or" and section 86(2) in so far as it refers to that repeal, is 6th April 1999;

(*e*) section 75 (overpayments out of social fund) is 5th October 1998.

3 Saving

Notwithstanding the appointment of 8th September 1998 for the coming into force of section 59(5) and (6), section 88 of the Taxes Management Act 1970 shall continue to have effect with respect to the levy of Class 4 national insurance contributions with income tax, where—

(*a*) an assessment has been made for the purpose of making good to the Crown a loss of tax wholly or partly attributable to—

(i) a failure to give a notice, make a return or produce or furnish a document or other information required by or under the Taxes Acts, or

(ii) an error in any information, return, accounts or other document delivered to an inspector or other officer of the Board of Inland Revenue; and

(*b*) that assessment is in respect of the tax year 1996–1997 in respect of a partnership whose trade, profession or business was set up and commenced before 6th April 1994.

SCHEDULE

Article 2(a) to (c)

PART I

PROVISIONS COMING INTO FORCE ON 8TH SEPTEMBER 1998

Provisions of the Social Security Act 1998	*Subject Matter*
Section 2 (except section 2(2)(*a*))	Use of computers.
Section 3	Use of information.
Section 16(4) and (5) (except section 16(4)(*b*))	Procedure.
Section 48	Apportionment of payments etc made for more than one earner.
Section 49	Payments on account of directors' contributions.
Section 50(1) in so far as not already in force	Payments treated as remuneration and earnings.
Section 52	Class 1A contributions.
Section 55	Recovery of primary Class 1 contributions by secondary contributors.
Section 59	Levy of Class 4 contributions with income tax.
Section 68	Rates of short-term incapacity benefit.
Schedule 7 in the respects specified below and section 86(1) so far as it relates to them—	Minor and consequential amendments.
Paragraph 27(*a*)	Information required by Secretary of State.
Paragraph 49	Local authority records.
Paragraphs 77(6) and 99(1)	National Insurance contributions.
Schedule 8 in respect of the repeals specified below and section 86(2) in so far as it relates to them—	Repeals.
in the Child Support Act 1991—	
in section 14, subsections (2) and (2A);	Information.
in Schedule 2 to that Act, paragraph 2;	
in Schedule 2 to the Social Security Contributions and Benefits Act 1992, paragraph 3(1)(*b*) and, in paragraph 6(2), the words "or 88";	National Insurance contributions.
in Schedule 2 to the Social Security Contributions and Benefits (Northern Ireland) Act 1992, paragraph 3(1)(*b*) and in paragraph 6(2), the words "or 88";	National Insurance contributions.
in Schedule 2 to the Jobseekers Act 1995, paragraph 20(3);	Information.
in Schedule 3 to the Child Support Act 1995, paragraph 3(2).	Information.

PART II

PROVISIONS COMING INTO FORCE ON 8TH SEPTEMBER 1998 FOR THE PURPOSE ONLY OF AUTHORISING THE MAKING OF REGULATIONS OR ORDERS

Provisions of the Social Security Act 1998	*Subject Matter*
Section 53	Class 1B contributions.
Section 65	Class 1B contributions: Supplemental.
Schedule 7 in the respects specified below and section 86(1) so far as it relates to them—	Minor and consequential amendments.

Paragraphs 56, 71(*d*), 77(7) to (9), (11) and (14) to (16), 91, 99(4) and 110(1)(*a*)	National Insurance contributions.
Paragraph 114	Regulations not requiring prior submission to Social Security Advisory Committee.

PART III

PROVISIONS COMING INTO FORCE ON 6TH APRIL 1999

Provisions of the Social Security Act 1998	*Subject Matter*
Section 16(4)(*b*)	Procedure.
Section 53 so far as not already in force	Class 1B contributions.
Section 65 so far as not already in force	Class 1B contributions: Supplemental.
Schedule 7 in the respects specified below (so far as not already in force) and section 86(1) so far as it relates to them—	
paragraphs 56, 57, 58(2), 71(*d*), 77(1), (7) to (9), (11), (12) and (14) to (16), 86(2)(*a*), (3)(*a*), (4) and (6), 91, 99(4), 100(1) and 110(1)(*a*);	National Insurance contributions.
paragraph 114	
Schedule 8 in respect of the repeal specified below and section 86(2) in so far as it relates to it—	
in Schedule 1 to the Social Security Contributions and Benefits Act 1992, in paragraph 6(2)(*b*), the words "(being not less than one year after the end of the tax year in respect of which the sums are due)".	

1998/2211

SOCIAL SECURITY (CONTRIBUTIONS) AMENDMENTS (NO 3) REGULATIONS 1998

Note—These Regulations revoked by the Social Security (Contributions) Regulations, SI 2001/1004 reg 157, Sch 8 Pt I with effect from 6 April 2001.

1999/3SOCIAL SECURITY

SOCIAL SECURITY (CATEGORISATION OF EARNERS) AMENDMENT REGULATIONS 1999

Made . . . . *6 January 1999*
Laid before Parliament . . . . *8 January 1999*
Coming into force . . . . *31 January 1999*

Revocation—These Regs revoked by the Social Security (Categorisation of Earners) (Amendment) Regulations, SI 2014/635 reg 4, Schedule with effect from 6 April 2014.

1999/418

SOCIAL SECURITY ACT 1998 (COMMENCEMENT NO 3) ORDER 1999

Made by the Secretary of State for Social Security under SSA 1998 ss 79(3) and 87(2)

Made . . . . *22 February 1999*

1 Citation and interpretation

(1) This Order may be cited as the Social Security Act 1998 (Commencement No 3) Order 1999.

(2) In this Order references to sections and Schedules are references to sections of and Schedules to the Social Security Act 1998.

2 Appointed days

(1) The day appointed for the coming into force of section 51 (Class 1 contributions)—

(*a*) for the purpose only of authorising the making of Regulations is 23rd February 1999; and

(*b*) for all other purposes is 6th April 1999.

(2) The day appointed for the coming into force of the provisions specified in paragraph (3) below is 6th April 1999.

(3) The provisions specified in this paragraph are—

(*a*) paragraphs 16, 58(1), 59 to 61, 71(*b*), (*c*) and (*e*), 74, 75, 77(2) to (5), 90, 92 to 94, 99(3), 110(1)(*b*), 126 to 128 and 133 of Schedule 7 and section 86(1) in so far as it relates to those paragraphs;

(*b*) in Schedule 8 the repeals of the provisions of the Social Security Administration Act 1992 specified below and section 86(2) in so far as it relates to them—

(i) section 146;

(ii) in section 147(1), (2) and (3) the words "or 146"; and

(iii) in section 190, in subsection (1)(*a*) the word "146,"; and

(*c*) in Schedule 8 the repeals of the provisions specified below and section 86(2) in so far as it relates to them—

(i) the definitions of "initial primary percentage" and "main primary percentage" in section 122(1) of the Social Security Contributions and Benefits Act 1992; and

(ii) section 137(2) of the Pensions Act 1995.

1999/527

SOCIAL SECURITY CONTRIBUTIONS (TRANSFER OF FUNCTIONS, ETC) ACT 1999 (COMMENCEMENT NO 1 AND TRANSITIONAL PROVISIONS) ORDER 1999

Made by the Secretary of State for Social Security under the Social Security Contributions (Transfer of Functions, etc) Act 1999 s 28(3), (4)

Made . . . . *3 March 1999*

1 Citation and interpretation

(1) This Order may be cited as the Social Security Contributions (Transfer of Functions, etc) Act 1999 (Commencement No 1 and Transitional Provisions) Order 1999.

(2) In this Order, unless the context otherwise requires—

"The Act" means the Social Security Contributions (Transfer of Functions, etc) Act 1999;

"the Administration Act" means the Social Security Administration Act 1992;

"the Contributions and Benefits Act" means the Social Security Contributions and Benefits Act 1992; and

"transfer provision" has the meaning given by section 21(1) of the Act,

and references to sections and Schedules are references to sections of, and Schedules to, the Act.

2 Appointed day

Subject to articles 3 to 6 below, the day appointed for the coming into force of—

(*a*) the provisions of the Act which are specified in Schedule 1 to this Order, for purposes connected with the making of Regulations under or in consequence of provisions of the Act, is 4th March 1999;

(*b*) the provisions of the Act which are specified in Schedule 2 to this Order, in so far as they are not already in force, is 1st April 1999; and

(*c*) the provisions of the Act which are specified in Schedule 3 to this Order, in so far as they are not already in force, is 6th April 1999.

3 Regulations under Schedule 1 to the Contributions and Benefits Act

(1) Any regulations made under paragraph 6 of Schedule 1 to the Contributions and Benefits Act before 1st April 1999 shall—

(*a*) to the extent that they are made by virtue of sub-paragraph (5) of that paragraph, be treated on and after that date as made under that sub-paragraph with the concurrence of the Board, and

(*b*) to the extent that they are not made by virtue of that sub-paragraph, shall be treated on and after that date as made under paragraph 6(1).

(2) Any regulations made under paragraph 8(1) of Schedule 1 to the Contributions and Benefits Act before 1st April 1999 shall—

(*a*) to the extent that they are made by virtue of paragraph 8(1)(*d*), or are made by virtue of paragraph 8(1)(*q*) and relate to the matter referred to in paragraph 8(1)(*d*), shall be treated on and after that date as made by the Secretary of State, and

(*b*) to the extent that they are not so made, shall be treated on and after that date as made by the Treasury.

4 Decisions and appeals

(1) Subject to paragraph (2) below, where—

(*a*) a person has before 1st April applied—

(i) in accordance with regulations made under section 58 of the Administration Act for the determination by the Secretary of State of any such question as is mentioned in section 17(1) of that Act, or

(ii) in accordance with regulations made under paragraph (*b*) of subsection (3) of section 20 of that Act for the determination by an adjudication officer of any question mentioned in that subsection; and

(*b*) that question has not been determined before that date,

the question shall on or after that date be treated in accordance with paragraph (3) below as being for the decision of an officer of the Board under section 8(1) of the Act.

(2) Paragraph (1) above—

(*a*) shall apply in relation to any such question as is mentioned in paragraph (*b*) of section 17(1) of the Administration Act only in so far as that question raises an issue of a kind specified in paragraph (*c*), (*d*) or (*e*) of section 8(1) of the Act; and

(*b*) shall not apply in relation to any such question as is mentioned in paragraph (*e*) or (*f*) of that section 17(1).

(3) A question to which paragraph (1) above applies—

(*a*) by virtue only of paragraph (2)(*a*) above, shall be treated as falling to be decided under paragraph (*c*), (*d*) or, as the case may be, (*e*) of section 8(1) of the Act;

(*b*) in any other case, shall be treated as falling to be decided under such provision of the Act as is specified in column (2) of the Table below in relation to the provision of the Administration Act (specified in column (1) of that Table) in which that question is mentioned.

(1) *Provision of Administration Act*	(2) *Provision of the Act*
Section 17(1)(*a*)	Section 8(1)(*a*)
Section 17(1)(*c*)	Section 8(1)(*c*)
Section 17(1)(*d*)	Section 8(1)(*b*)
Section 17(1)(*g*)(i) or (vi)	Section 8(1)(*f*)
Section 17(1)(*g*)(ii) to (v)	Section 8(1)(*g*)
Section 17(1)(*h*)(i) or (v)	Section 8(1)(*f*)
Section 17(1)(*h*)(ii) to (iv)	Section 8(1)(*g*)
Section 17(1)(*i*)	Section 8(1)(*i*)
Section 20(3)	Section 8(1)(*f*)

(4) Where, by virtue of paragraph (1)(*a*)(i) above, a question falls to be decided by an officer of the Board, that question shall until the relevant date be treated for the purposes of paragraphs (2)(*b*) and (3)(*c*)(ii) of regulation 28D of Schedule 1 to the Social Security (Contributions) Regulations 1979 (remission of interest pending determination of questions) as if it were a question for determination under section 17(1) of the Administration Act.

(5) In paragraph (4) above, "the relevant date" means the date on which—

(*a*) the question is determined by the officer of the Board; or

(*b*) those provisions of that regulation 28D cease to be in force,

whichever first occurs.

(6) Notwithstanding paragraph 1(2) of Schedule 8 (which provides for certain determinations made by the Secretary of State to have effect as if made by the Board), Part II of the Act shall not apply with respect to any decision given before 1st April 1999—

(*a*) by the Secretary of State on any such question as is mentioned in section 17(1) of the Administration Act;

(*b*) by the Secretary of State of any such question as is mentioned in section 170(1) of the Pensions Schemes Act 1993 (which includes such a question among the questions to which section 17(1) of the Administration Act applies); or

(*c*) by an adjudication officer of the question mentioned in section 20(3) of that Act.

(7) Where, before 1st April 1999, the Secretary of State has determined a question to which section 170(7) of the Pension Schemes Act 1993 applies (certain questions arising under Part III of that Act), that determination shall, on and after that date, be treated for the purposes of the Occupational and Personal Pension Schemes (Contracting-out etc: Review of Determinations) Regulations 1997 as if it had been made by the Board.

NIC

5 Accounts of the National Insurance Fund

Notwithstanding the coming into force of paragraph 51 of Schedule 3 (which provides for the National Insurance Fund to be maintained under the control and management of the Board, and for its accounts to be prepared by them), the accounts of the National Insurance Fund in relation to the year ending on 31st March 1999 shall be prepared by the Secretary of State in accordance with section 161(2) of the Administration Act as in force prior to its amendment by that paragraph.

6 Complaints to the Parliamentary Commissioner for Administration

A complaint made under the Parliamentary Commissioner Act 1967 to the Parliamentary Commissioner for Administration in relation to the Department of Social Security, whether made before, on or after 1st April 1999, shall, in so far as it relates to any function transferred by virtue of a transfer provision to the Board, be treated on and after that date as if it were a complaint made in relation to the Board.

SCHEDULE 1

PROVISIONS COMING INTO FORCE ON 4TH MARCH 1999 FOR PURPOSES CONNECTED WITH THE MAKING OF REGULATIONS

Article 2(a)

Provisions of the Act	*Subject matter*
Section 18 and Schedule 7, in so far as they relate to paragraphs 1 to 3, 5 to 11 and 17 of that Schedule	Amendments relating to decisions and appeals
Section 19	Interpretation of Part II of the Act
Section 26(2) and Schedule 9 in so far as they relate to paragraphs 4 to 7 of that Schedule	Further consequential amendments of provisions concerned with Class 1B contributions and certain penalties and interest payable in connection with contributions

SCHEDULE 2

PROVISIONS COMING INTO FORCE ON 1ST APRIL 1999

Article 2(b)

Provisions of the Act	*Subject matter*
Section 1(1) and Schedule 1, except in relation to paragraph 17(c), in so far as it amends paragraph 6(8) of Schedule 1 to the Contributions and Benefits Act, and paragraph 66(3) of that Schedule	Transfer to Board of certain functions relating to contributions etc
Section 1(2) and Schedule 2, except in relation to functions which are, by virtue of article 4 of the Pensions Act 1995 (Commencement No 10) Order 1997, exercisable under regulation 20(2)(*b*) of the Occupational Pension Schemes (Contracting-out) Regulations 1984	Transfer to Board of certain functions under subordinate legislation
Section 2 and Schedule 3	Transfer of other functions to Treasury or Board
Section 3, except for subsection (3)(c)	General functions of Board
Section 4(*a*), except in so far as it relates to Class 1B contributions, and (*b*) and Schedule 4 to that extent	Recovery of contributions where income tax recovery provisions not applicable
Section 5 and Schedule 5, except in relation to paragraphs 5 and 7 of that Schedule	Powers relating to enforcement
Section 6 and Schedule 6	Disclosure of information
Section 7	Use of information
Section 8, except for subsection (1)(*h*) and (*j*) to (1)	Decisions by officers of Board
Sections 9 and 10	Regulations with respect to decisions, and decisions varying or superseding earlier decisions

Section 11(1) to (3)	Appeals against decisions of Board
Section 12, except for the words from "section 121D" to "and to" in subsection (4)	Exercise of right of appeal
Sections 13 to 15	Regulations about appeals, matters arising as respects decisions, and provision for period before commencement of provisions about social security decisions and appeals
Section 18 and Schedule 7, in so far as they relate to paragraphs 1 to 3, 5–8, 11, 13, 15–17, 18 (except in relation to sub-paragraph (3) thereof), 21–23, 25–27, 29–32 and 35 of that Schedule, and paragraph 36 of that Schedule in so far as it relates to paragraph 23 of Schedule 3 to the Social Security Act 1998	Amendments relating to decisions and appeals
Section 19	Interpretation of Part II
Sections 21 and 22	Property, rights and liabilities, and special provision for certain contracts
Section 23	Power to Transfer functions by Order in Council
Section 26(2) and Schedule 9, except in relation to paragraphs 1 and 2 of that Schedule	Further consequential amendments
Section 26(3) and Schedule 10, except in respect of the repeals in section 118 of the Administration Act, of section 167(3) of the Pension Schemes Act 1993, and in sections 16 and 62 of, and of paragraph 23 of Schedule 3 and paragraphs 130 and 132 of Schedule 7 to, the Social Security Act 1998.	Repeals and revocations

SCHEDULE 3
PROVISIONS COMING INTO FORCE ON 6TH APRIL 1999
Article 2(c)

Provisions of the Act	*Subject matter*
Section 4(*a*), as it relates to Class 1B contributions, and (*c*) and Schedule 4 to that extent	Recovery of Class 1B contributions, interest and penalties where income tax recovery provisions not applicable
Section 5 and Schedule 5 in so far as they relate to paragraphs 5 and 7 of that Schedule	Powers relating to enforcement—breach of regulations, and evidence of non-payment of contributions
Sections 8(1)(*h*) and (*j*) to (*l*)	Decisions by officers of Board in relation to liability of company directors for contributions, and to certain penalties and interest
Section 11(4)	Appeals against decisions of Board—liability of company directors for contributions
Section 12(4) as it relates to section 121D of the Administration Act	Exercise of right of appeal in connection with liability of company directors for contributions
Section 18 and Schedule 7 in so far as they relate to paragraphs 9 and 10 of that Schedule	Decisions and appeals
Section 26(2) and Schedule 9 in so far as they relate to paragraphs 1 and 2 of that Schedule	Consequential amendment of the Debtors (Scotland) Act 1987
Section 26(3) and Schedule 10 in so far as they relate to repeals in section 118 of the Administration Act, and section 62 of the Social Security Act 1998	Repeals

NIC

1999/978

SOCIAL SECURITY CONTRIBUTIONS, ETC (DECISIONS AND APPEALS—TRANSITIONAL MODIFICATIONS) REGULATIONS 1999

Made by the Secretary of State for Social Security under the Social Security Contributions (Transfer of Functions, etc) Act 1999 ss 15(1) and 25(3)

Made .... *25 March 1999*
Laid before Parliament .... *29 March 1999*
Coming into force .... *1 April 1999*

1 Citation, commencement and interpretation

(1) These Regulations may be cited as the Social Security Contributions, etc (Decisions and Appeals—Transitional Modifications) Regulations 1999 and shall come into force on 1st April 1999.

(2) In these Regulations "the Act" means the Social Security Contributions (Transfer of Functions, etc) Act 1999.

2 Modification of enactments

(1) Subject to paragraph (2) below, until Chapter II of Part I of the Social Security Act 1998 (social security decisions and appeals) is wholly in force, any enactment specified in column (1) of the Schedule to these Regulations shall have effect subject to the modifications specified in column (2) of that Schedule.

(2) Paragraph (1) above shall not apply with respect to—

(*a*) any such question as is mentioned in—

(i) paragraph (*b*) of section 17(1) of the Social Security Administration Act 1992 (questions for the Secretary of State) in so far as that question does not raise an issue of a kind specified in paragraph (*c*), (*d*) or (*e*) of section 8(1) of the Act (decisions by officers of Board of Inland Revenue), or

(ii) paragraph (*e*) or (*f*) of that section 17(1);

(*b*) any question which is, by virtue of section 170(1) of the Pension Schemes Act 1993 (determination of questions by the Secretary of State), included in the questions to which that section 17(1) applies; or

(*c*) any decision to which article 4(6) of the Social Security Contributions (Transfer of Functions, etc) Act 1999 (Commencement No 1 and Transitional Provisions) Order 1999 (decisions to which Part II of the Act is not to apply) applies.

SCHEDULE

Regulation 2(1)

MODIFICATION OF ENACTMENTS

(1) Enactment	*(2) Modification*
Social Security Contributions and Benefits Act 1992—	
Section 95 (meaning of "employed earner's employment" in industrial injuries and diseases provisions)	As if, in subsection (5)(*c*), after the words "Administration Act" there were inserted the words "or Part II of the Social Security Contributions (Transfer of Functions, etc.) Act 1999".
Social Security Administration Act 1992—	
Section 17 (questions for the Secretary of State)	As if—
	(*a*) in subsection (1)
	(i) paragraphs (*a*), (*c*), (*d*) and (*g*) to (*l*) were omitted, and
	(ii) in paragraph (*b*), the words "contributions or his" were omitted; and
	(*b*) subsection (2) were omitted.
Section 20 (claims and questions to be submitted to adjudication officer)	As if—
	(*a*) subsection (3) were omitted; and
	(*b*) in subsection (6), paragraphs (*g*) and (*h*) were omitted.
Section 21 (decision of adjudication officer)	As if—

	(*a*) subsection (4) were omitted; (*b*) in subsection (5), for the words "In any other case notice" there were substituted the word "Notice"; and (*c*) in subsection (6), the words "(4) or" were omitted.
Section 22 (appeal to social security appeal tribunal)	As if— (*a*) in subsection (1), for the words from "allowance", in the third place where it occurs, to the end of that subsection there were substituted the words "allowance, the claimant shall have the right to appeal to a social security appeal tribunal."; (*b*) in subsection (3)(*a*), after the words "this Act" there were inserted the words "or Part II of the Social Security Contributions (Transfer of Functions, etc.) Act 1999"; and (*c*) in subsection (5), paragraphs (*d*) and (*e*) were omitted.
Section 23 (appeal from social security appeal tribunal to Commissioner)	As if— (*a*) subsection (2) were omitted; (*b*) in subsection (3), for the words "In any other case an appeal" there were substituted the words "An appeal"; and (*c*) in subsection (6), the word "(2)," were omitted.
Section 37 (reference of special questions)	As if, in subsection (1)(*a*), after the words "this Act" there were inserted the words "or Part II of the Social Security Contributions (Transfer of Functions, etc.) Act 1999".
Section 59 (procedure)	As if subsection (4) were omitted.
Section 117 (questions arising in proceedings)	As if, in subsection (1), paragraph (*b*) were omitted.
Section 166 (financial review and report)	As if— (*a*) in subsection (1)(*d*), for the words "so far as it relates" there were substituted the words "and Part II of the Social Security Contributions (Transfer of Functions, etc.) Act 1999 so far as they relate"; and (*b*) in subsection (2)(*c*), for the words "so far as it relates" there were substituted the words "and Part II of the Social Security Contributions (Transfer of Functions, etc) Act 1999 so far as they relate".
Pension Schemes Act 1993—	
Section 170 (determination of questions by the Secretary of State)	As if, in subsection (7)(*b*), for the words "Secretary of State" there were substituted the words "Inland Revenue".

1999/1027

SOCIAL SECURITY CONTRIBUTIONS (DECISIONS AND APPEALS) REGULATIONS 1999

Made by the Commissioners of Inland Revenue under the Social Security Contributions (Transfer of Functions, etc) Act 1999 ss 9, 10, 11, 13, 24 and 25 and the Social Security Contributions (Transfer of Functions, etc) (Northern Ireland) Order 1999 Arts 8, 9, 10, 12 and 23 and, in relation to Part III of this instrument, with the concurrence of the Lord Chancellor and the Lord Advocate, hereby make the following Regulations:

NIC

Made . . . . *30 March 1999*
Laid before Parliament . . . . *30 March 1999*
Coming into force . . . . *1 April 1999*

PART I
INTRODUCTORY

1 Citation and commencement

These Regulations may be cited as the Social Security Contributions (Decisions and Appeals) Regulations 1999 and shall come into force on 1st April 1999.

2 Interpretation

In these Regulations unless the context otherwise requires—

"the Board" means the Commissioners of Inland Revenue;

"the Management Act" means the Taxes Management Act 1970;

"notice" means notice in writing and "notify" and "notification" shall be construed accordingly;

"the Transfer Act" means the Social Security Contributions (Transfer of Functions, etc.) Act 1999;

"the Transfer Order" means the Social Security Contributions (Transfer of Functions, etc.) (Northern Ireland) Order 1999.

PART II
DECISIONS

3 Decisions—general

(1) A decision which, by virtue of section 8 of the Transfer Act or Article 7 of the Transfer Order, falls to be made by an officer of the Board under or in connection with the Social Security Contributions and Benefits Act 1992, the Social Security Administration Act 1992, the Social Security Contributions and Benefits (Northern Ireland) Act 1992, the Social Security Administration (Northern Ireland) Act 1992, the Jobseekers Act 1995 or the Jobseekers (Northern Ireland) Order 1995—

(*a*) must be made to the best of his information and belief, and

(*b*) must state the name of every person in respect of whom it is made and—

(i) the date from which it has effect, or

(ii) the period for which it has effect.

(2) Where an officer of the Board has resolved to make a decision of a kind referred to in paragraph (1), he may entrust to some other officer of the Board responsibility for completing the procedure for making the decision, whether by means involving the use of a computer or otherwise, including responsibility for serving notice of the decision on any person named in it.

(3) In the case of a decision to which section 11 of the Transfer Act or Article 10 of the Transfer Order applies, other than one which relates to a person's entitlement to [statutory sick pay, statutory maternity pay, [statutory paternity pay][3], [4][,statutory shared parental pay][5] [or statutory adoption pay][1], each person who is named in the decision has a right to appeal . . . [2].

Amendments—[1] Words in para (3) substituted by the Social Security Contributions (Decisions and Appeals) Regulations, SI 2002/3120 reg 3(1), (2)(*a*) with effect from 7 January 2003.

[2] In para (3), words "to the tax appeal Commissioners" revoked, by the Transfer of Tribunal Functions and Revenue and Customs Appeals Order, SI 2009/56 art 3, Sch 2 paras 59, 60 with effect from 1 April 2009.

[3] Words in para (3) substituted for words "statutory paternity pay" by the Social Security Contributions (Decisions and Appeals) (Amendment) Regulations, SI 2010/2451 reg 2 with effect from 14 November 2010.

[4] Words in para (3) substituted for words "ordinary statutory paternity pay, additional statutory paternity pay" by the Social Security Contributions (Decisions and Appeals) (Amendment) Regulations, SI 2015/174 reg 2(*a*) with effect from 5 April 2015. This amendment does not have effect where an appeal under this regulation relates to a person's entitlement to ordinary statutory paternity pay or additional statutory paternity pay (SI 2014/174 reg 3).

[5] Words in para (3) inserted by the Social Security Contributions (Decisions and Appeals) (Amendment) Regulations, SI 2015/174 reg 2(*b*) with effect from 5 March 2015.

4 Notice of decision

(1)— Notice of a decision by an officer of the Board referred to in regulation 3(1) must be given—

(*a*) in the case of a decision relating to a person's entitlement to [statutory sick pay, statutory maternity pay, [statutory paternity pay][2], [3][,statutory shared parental pay][4] or statutory adoption pay][1], to the employee and employer concerned, and

(*b*) in any other case, to every person named in the decision.

(2) A notice under this regulation must state the date on which it is issued and may be served by post addressed to any person to whom it is to be given at his usual or last known place of residence, or his place of business or employment.

(3) Where notice is to be given to a company, it may be served by post addressed to its registered office or its principal place of business.

Amendments—[1] Words in para (1)(*a*) substituted by the Social Security Contributions (Decisions and Appeals) Regulations, SI 2002/3120 reg 3(1), (2)(*b*) with effect from 7 January 2003.

[2] Words in para (1)(*a*) substituted for words "statutory paternity pay" by the Social Security Contributions (Decisions and Appeals) (Amendment) Regulations, SI 2010/2451 reg 2 with effect from 14 November 2010.

[3] Words in para (1)(*a*) substituted for words "ordinary statutory paternity pay, additional statutory paternity pay" by the Social Security Contributions (Decisions and Appeals) (Amendment) Regulations, SI 2015/174 reg 2(*a*) with effect from 5 April 2015.

[4] Words in para (1)(*a*) inserted by the Social Security Contributions (Decisions and Appeals) (Amendment) Regulations, SI 2015/174 reg 2(*b*) with effect from 5 March 2015.

5 Variation of decision

(1) An officer of the Board may vary a decision under section 8 of the Transfer Act or Article 7 of the Transfer Order if he has reason to believe that it was incorrect at the time that it was made.

(2) Notice of a variation of a decision must be given to the same persons and in the same manner as notice of the decision was given.

(3) A variation of a decision may state that it has effect for any period in respect of which the decision could have had effect, if the reason for the variation had been known to the person making the decision at the time that it was made.

(4) A decision which is under appeal may be varied at any time before the [tribunal determines][1] the appeal.

Amendments—[1] In para (4), words substituted for words "tax appeal Commissioners determine", by the Transfer of Tribunal Functions and Revenue and Customs Appeals Order, SI 2009/56 art 3, Sch 2 paras 59, 61 with effect from 1 April 2009.

6 Decision superseding earlier decision

(1) An officer of the Board may make a decision superseding an earlier decision, whether as originally made or as varied in accordance with regulation 5, which has become inappropriate for any reason.

(2) A decision superseding an earlier decision which is made in these circumstances has effect from the date of the change in circumstances which rendered the earlier decision inappropriate and the earlier decision ceases to have effect as soon as the superseding decision has effect.

PART III
APPEALS

7 [Application of the Taxes Management Act 1970 in relation to reviews and appeals with modifications

(1) In this regulation reference to a section alone is reference to the section so numbered in the Management Act.

(2) For the purposes of these regulations, sections 49A to 49I of the Management Act shall apply to appeals with the following modifications—

(*a*) in section 49A(4) for "in accordance with section 54" substitute "in accordance with regulation 11 of the Social Security Contributions (Decisions and Appeals) Regulations 1999",

(*b*) in section 49C(4) for "agreement in writing under section 54(1)" substitute "agreement under regulation 11 of the Social Security Contributions (Decisions and Appeals) Regulations 1999",

(*c*) omit section 49C(5),

(*d*) in section 49F(2) for "agreement in writing under section 54(1)" substitute "agreement under regulation 11 of the Social Security Contributions (Decisions and Appeals) Regulations 1999",

(*e*) omit section 49F(3)][1]

Amendments—[1] Reg 7 substituted by the Transfer of Tribunal Functions and Revenue and Customs Appeals Order, SI 2009/56 art 3, Sch 2 paras 59, 62 with effect from 1 April 2009.

8 Multiple appeals

Amendments—Regs 8, 8A revoked by the Transfer of Tribunal Functions and Revenue and Customs Appeals Order, SI 2009/56 art 3, Sch 2 paras 59, 63 with effect from 1 April 2009.

8A [Transfer of proceedings to the Special Commissioners etc

Amendments—Regs 8, 8A revoked by the Transfer of Tribunal Functions and Revenue and Customs Appeals Order, SI 2009/56 art 3, Sch 2 paras 59, 63 with effect from 1 April 2009.

9 Proceedings brought out of time

(1) Section 49 of the Management Act applies to appeals to the [tribunal][1] under Part II of the Transfer Act and Part III of the Transfer Order which are brought out of time with the modifications specified in this regulation.

(2) In that section "the Taxes Acts" includes Part II of the Transfer Act and Part III of the Transfer Order and "inspector of the Board" includes an officer of the Board.

Amendments—[1] Words substituted for words "tax appeal Commissioners", by the Transfer of Tribunal Functions and Revenue and Customs Appeals Order, SI 2009/56 art 3, Sch 2 paras 59, 64 with effect from 1 April 2009.

10 Determination of appeals by [the tribunal]

If, on an appeal . . . [1] under Part II of the Transfer Act or Part III of the Transfer Order [that is notified to the tribunal][1], it appears to the [tribunal][1] that the decision should be varied in a particular manner, the decision shall be varied in that manner, but otherwise shall stand good.

Amendments—[1] In heading, words substituted for words "tax appeal Commissioners", words "to the tax appeal Commissioners" revoked, words inserted, and words substituted for words "majority of the Commissioners present at the hearing, by examination of the appellant on oath or affirmation or by other evidence,", by the Transfer of Tribunal Functions and Revenue and Customs Appeals Order, SI 2009/56 art 3, Sch 2 paras 59, 65 with effect from 1 April 2009.

11 Settling of appeals by agreement

(1) Subject to the provisions of this regulation, where before an appeal is determined by the [tribunal][2], an officer of the Board and every person who has appealed against the decision come to an agreement, whether in writing or otherwise, that the decision under appeal should be treated as upheld without variation, as varied in a particular manner or as superseded by a further decision, the like consequences ensue for all purposes as would have ensued if, at the time when the agreement was come to, the officer of the Board had made a decision in the same terms as the decision under appeal, had varied the decision in that manner or had made a decision superseding the decision under appeal in the same terms as that further decision, as the case may be.

(2) Where an agreement is come to in the manner described in paragraph (1) the appeals of all persons who have appealed against the decision lapse.

(3) Notice of the agreement must be given by the officer of the Board to the persons named in the decision who have not appealed against it.

(4) Where an agreement is not in writing—

(*a*) the preceding provisions of this regulation do not apply unless the fact that an agreement was come to, and the terms agreed, are confirmed by notice given by the officer of the Board to the appellant and any other person who has appealed against the decision or by the appellant or any other person who has appealed against the decision to the officer of the Board; and

(*b*) the references in those provisions to the time when the agreement was come to shall be construed as references to the time of the giving of the notice of confirmation.

(5) Where before an appeal is determined by the [tribunal[2]]—

(*a*) a person who has appealed against a decision notifies the officer of the Board and every other person named in the decision, whether orally or in writing, that he does not wish to proceed with the appeal, and

(*b*) thirty days have elapsed since the giving of the notification without the officer of the Board or any other person named in the decision giving notice to the appellant and any other person named in the decision or the officer of the Board, as the case may be, indicating that he is unwilling that the appeal should be treated as withdrawn,

the preceding provisions of this regulation have effect as if, at the date of the appellant's notification, the appellant and the officer of the Board and every other person named in the decision had come to an agreement, orally or in writing, as the case may be, that the decision under appeal should be upheld without variation.

(6) The references in this regulation to an agreement being come to with an appellant and other persons named in the decision and the giving of notice or notification to or by an appellant or any other person named in the decision include references to an agreement being come to with, and the giving of notice or notification to or by, a person acting on behalf of the appellant or any of the other persons named in the decision in relation to the appeal.

(7) In this regulation "any other person named in the decision" includes, in the case of a decision relating to a person's entitlement to [statutory sick pay, statutory maternity pay, [statutory paternity pay][3], [4][,statutory shared parental pay][5] or statutory adoption pay][1], the employee and the employer concerned.

Amendments—[1] Words in para (7) substituted by the Social Security Contributions (Decisions and Appeals) Regulations, SI 2002/3120 reg 3(1), (2)(*d*) with effect from 7 January 2003.

[2] In paras (1), (5) words substituted for words "tax appeal Commissioners", by the Transfer of Tribunal Functions and Revenue and Customs Appeals Order, SI 2009/56 art 3, Sch 2 paras 59, 66 with effect from 1 April 2009.

[3] Words in para (7) substituted for words "statutory paternity pay" by the Social Security Contributions (Decisions and Appeals) (Amendment) Regulations, SI 2010/2451 reg 2 with effect from 14 November 2010.

[4] Words in para (7) substituted for words "ordinary statutory paternity pay, additional statutory paternity pay" by the Social Security Contributions (Decisions and Appeals) (Amendment) Regulations, SI 2015/174 reg 2(*a*) with effect from 5 April 2015. This amendment does not have effect where a settlement under this regulation relates to a person's entitlement to ordinary statutory paternity pay or additional statutory paternity pay (SI 2014/174 reg 3).

[5] Words in para (7) inserted by the Social Security Contributions (Decisions and Appeals) (Amendment) Regulations, SI 2015/174 reg 2(*b*) with effect from 5 March 2015.

12 [Appeals from the tribunal

(1) Section 56 of the Management Act (payment of tax where there is a further appeal) shall apply to appeals from the tribunal under Part II of the Transfer Act and Part III of the Transfer Order.

(2) For the purposes of sections 11(2) and 13(2) of the Tribunals, Courts and Enforcement Act 2007 a party to the case includes—

(*a*) the appellant and HMRC;
(*b*) in the case of an appeal against a decision relating to a person's entitlement to statutory sick pay, statutory maternity pay, [statutory paternity pay][2], [3][,statutory shared parental pay][4] or statutory adoption pay, the employee or employer concerned; and
(*c*) in any other case, any other person named in the decision.][1]

[(3) The reference to section 56 of the Taxes Management Act 1970 in this regulation includes a reference to that section as amended by section 225(1) of the Finance Act 2014 (protection of the revenue pending further appeals).][2]

Amendments—[1] Reg 12 substituted by the Revenue and Customs Appeals Order, SI 2009/777 art 6 with effect from 1 April 2009. Note that this reg was previously substituted by the Transfer of Tribunal Functions and Revenue and Customs Appeals Order, SI 2009/56 art 3, Sch 2 paras 59, 67 with effect from 1 April 2009.

2 Words in para (2)(*b*) substituted for words "statutory paternity pay" by the Social Security Contributions (Decisions and Appeals) (Amendment) Regulations, SI 2010/2451 reg 2 with effect from 14 November 2010.

3 Words in para (2)(*b*) substituted for words "ordinary statutory paternity pay, additional statutory paternity pay" by the Social Security Contributions (Decisions and Appeals) (Amendment) Regulations, SI 2015/174 reg 2(*a*) with effect from 5 April 2015.

4 Words in para (2)(*b*) inserted by the Social Security Contributions (Decisions and Appeals) (Amendment) Regulations, SI 2015/174 reg 2(*b*) with effect from 5 March 2015.

5 Paragraph (3) inserted by the Social Security Contributions (Amendments in Consequence of Part 4 of the Finance Act 2014) Regulations, SI 2015/521 reg 2 with effect from 12 April 2015.

1999/1958

SOCIAL SECURITY ACT 1998 (COMMENCEMENT NO 8, AND SAVINGS AND CONSEQUENTIAL AND TRANSITIONAL PROVISIONS) ORDER 1999

Made by the Secretary of State for Social Security under SSA 1998 ss 79(3), (4), 87(2), (3)
Made . . . .*4 July 1999*

1 Citation and interpretation

(1) This Order may be cited as the Social Security Act 1998 (Commencement No 8, and Savings and Consequential and Transitional Provisions) Order 1999.

(2) In this Order, unless the context otherwise requires—

"the Act" means the Social Security Act 1998;

"the Administration Act" means the Social Security Administration Act 1992;

and references to sections and Schedules are references to sections of, and Schedules to, the Act.

2 Appointed day

(1) Subject to paragraph (2) below and to articles 3 and 5 of this Order, 5th July 1999 is the day appointed for the coming into force of—

(*a*) . . .
(*b*) the provisions of the Act specified in Schedule 1 to this Order, in so far as those provisions are not already in force, for the purposes of—
(i) guardian's allowance under Part III of the Social Security Contributions and Benefits Act 1992,
(ii) benefits under Part V of that Act (benefits for industrial injuries),
(iii) child benefit, and
(iv) any matter to which, by virtue of section 170 of the Pension Schemes Act 1993, provisions of Chapter II of Part I of the Act are to apply.

(2) . . .

5 Transitional provisions

Schedule 12 to this Order shall have effect.

SCHEDULE 1

PROVISIONS BROUGHT INTO FORCE ON 5TH JULY 1999 FOR PURPOSES SPECIFIED IN ARTICLE 2(1)(*B*)

Article 2

Provision of the Act	*Subject matter*
Section 39	Interpretation etc of Chapter II of Part I of the Act
Schedule 7 in the respects specified below, and section 86(1) in so far as it relates to them—	Minor and consequential amendments—
paragraphs 88 and 89	Disclosure of information, and notification of deaths

NIC

paragraphs 106 to 108	reciprocal agreements, and travelling expenses
paragraph 111(b)	definition of "claimant"

SCHEDULE 12

TRANSITIONAL PROVISIONS

Article 5

1—(1) In this Schedule, unless the context otherwise requires—

"adjudicating authority" means an adjudication officer, an adjudicating medical practitioner, a specially qualified adjudicating medical practitioner, a medical board or a special medical board;

"appellate authority" means a medical appeal tribunal or a social security appeal tribunal;

"the Adjudication Regulations" means the Social Security (Adjudication) Regulations 1995;

"decision" in relation to any period before 5th July 1999, includes a determination, and "decided" is to be construed accordingly;

"legally qualified panel member" has the same meaning as in the Regulations;

"the Regulations" means the Social Security and Child Support (Decisions and Appeals) Regulations 1999; and

"relevant benefit" means any of the benefits mentioned in article 2(1)(*b*)(i) to (iii) of this Order.

(2) Any reference in paragraphs 6 to 12 of this Schedule to—

(*a*) an appeal to an appellate authority is to be construed as a reference to an appeal in relation to the decision of an adjudicating authority as respects a relevant benefit; and

(*b*) a decision of an appellate authority is to be construed as a reference to a decision of such an appeal.

2 Any matter which before 5th July 1999 fell to be decided in relation to a relevant benefit by an adjudicating authority but which has not been decided immediately before that date shall be decided on or after that date by the Secretary of State under paragraph (a) or, as the case may be, paragraph (c) of section 8(1).

3—(1) Any application duly made before 5th July 1999 for a review of a decision of an adjudicating authority in relation to a relevant benefit which was not decided before that date shall on or after that date be treated as an application to the Secretary of State—

(*a*) where the application was made within one month of the date on which the applicant was notified of the decision, or within such longer period as may be allowed under sub-paragraph (2) below, for a revision of that decision under section 9; or

(*b*) in any other case, for a decision under section 10 to supersede that decision.

(2) Subject to sub-paragraphs (3) and (4) below, the period of one month specified in sub-paragraph (1)(*a*) above may be extended where an application for such an extension is made before 5th August 2000 by a claimant or a person acting on his behalf containing—

(*a*) the grounds on which an extension of time is sought; and

(*b*) sufficient details of the decision to enable it to be identified.

(3) An application for an extension of time shall not be granted under sub-paragraph (2) above unless the Secretary of State is satisfied that—

(*a*) it is reasonable to grant that application;

(*b*) the application for review has merit; and

(*c*) special circumstances are relevant to the application for extension of time as a result of which it was not practicable for the application for review to be made within one month of the date of the adjudicating authority's decision being notified to the claimant.

(4) In deciding whether to grant an extension of time no account shall be taken of the following factors—

(*a*) that the claimant or any person acting for him misunderstood or was unaware of the law applicable to his case (including misunderstanding or being unaware of the period specified in sub-paragraph (1)(*a*) above); or

(*b*) that a Social Security Commissioner or a court has taken a different view of the law from that previously understood and applied by the adjudicating authority.

(5) Where, by virtue of sub-paragraph (1)(*b*) above—

(*a*) a decision is made under section 10 which is advantageous to the applicant; and

(*b*) the same decision could have been made by the adjudicating authority prior to 5th July 1999 on the application for review,

that decision shall take effect from the date from which it would have taken effect had the decision been so made.

4—(1) Where, before 5th July 1999, a decision has been made by an adjudicating authority in relation to a relevant benefit, that decision shall be treated on or after that date as a decision of the Secretary of State under paragraph (*a*) or, as the case may be, paragraph (*c*) of section 8(1).
(2) Where, before that date, any person was required to give notice to the claimant of that decision of the adjudicating authority, and such notice has not been given to the claimant before that date, the Secretary of State shall on or after that date give notice to the claimant of that decision.

5—(1) Where—

(*a*) a decision of an adjudicating authority in relation to a relevant benefit has been made before 5th July 1999; and

(*b*) the period within which an appeal may be made in relation to that decision has not expired before that date,

regulation 3 of the Adjudication Regulations as it relates to the period within which an appeal may be made, or any extension of that period, shall, notwithstanding regulation 59 of the Regulations, continue to have effect, subject to the modifications in sub-paragraph (2) below, with respect to any appeal to an appeal tribunal on or after that date in relation to that decision.
(2) The modifications referred to in sub-paragraph (1) above are—

(*a*) as if references to a chairman or to a person considering the application were references to a legally qualified panel member;

(*b*) as if references to a tribunal were references to an appeal tribunal constituted under section 7; and

(*c*) as if in paragraph (3E) for the words from "6 years" to the end of the paragraph there were substituted the words "5th August 2000".

6 An appeal to an appellate authority which was duly made before 5th July 1999 and which has not been determined before that date shall, without prejudice to Chapter III of Part V of the Regulations, be treated on or after that date as an appeal duly made to an appeal tribunal in relation to a decision of the Secretary of State under section 8.

7—(1) This paragraph applies where a clerk to an appellate authority has before 5th July 1999 given a direction under regulation 22(1) of the Adjudication Regulations in connection with an appeal to that authority, and the notification mentioned in paragraph (1A) of that regulation 22 has not been received by the clerk before that date.
(2) A notification in response to such a direction given under that regulation 22(1) shall be in writing and shall be made within 14 days of receipt of the direction or within such other period as the clerk to an appeal tribunal may direct.
(3) An appeal may be struck out by the clerk to an appeal tribunal where the notification referred to in sub-paragraph (2) above is not received within the period specified in that sub-paragraph.
(4) An appeal which has been struck out in accordance with sub-paragraph (3) above shall be treated for the purpose of reinstatement as if it had been struck out under regulation 46 of the Regulations.
(5) An oral hearing of the appeal shall be held where—

(*a*) a notification is received by the clerk to the appeal tribunal under sub-paragraph (2) above; or

(*b*) the chairman or, in the case of an appeal tribunal which has only one member, that member of the appeal tribunal is satisfied that such a hearing is necessary to enable the appeal tribunal to reach a decision.

8 Where an appeal to an appellate authority has been struck out under regulation 7 of the Adjudication Regulations, a legally qualified panel member may on or after 5th July 1999, on an application made by any party to the proceedings not later than three months from the date of the order under paragraph (1) of that regulation, reinstate the appeal if he is satisfied that—

(*a*) the applicant did not receive a notice under paragraph (2) of that regulation; and

(*b*) the conditions in paragraph (2A) of that regulation were not satisfied,

and the appeal shall then be treated as an appeal to an appeal tribunal in relation to a decision of the Secretary of State under section 8.

9 An appeal tribunal shall completely rehear any appeal to an appellate authority which stands adjourned immediately before 5th July 1999.

10 A copy of a statement of—

(*a*) the reasons for a decision of an appellate authority; and

(*b*) its findings on questions of fact material thereto,

shall be supplied by the Secretary of State to each party to the proceedings before that authority, if requested by any such party within 21 days of the date on which notification of that decision was given or sent.

11—(1) Subject to sub-paragraph (2) below, any decision of an appellate authority shall, for the purposes of sections 13 and 14, be treated as a decision of an appeal tribunal.
(2) Where sub-paragraph (1) above applies, any application for leave to appeal which is made for the purposes of section 14(10)(*a*) shall be made no later than 3 months after the date on which a copy of the statement of the decision of the appellate authority was given or sent to the applicant.

12—(1) Subject to sub-paragraph (3) below, regulation 10 of the Adjudication Regulations, and regulation 3 of those Regulations in so far as it relates to that regulation 10, shall, notwithstanding regulation 59 of the Regulations, continue to have effect on and after 5th July 1999, subject to the modifications specified in sub-paragraph (2) below, in relation to any application to set aside a decision of an appellate authority.
(2) The modifications referred to in sub-paragraph (1) above are—
(*a*) as if, in that regulation 3, or in paragraph (1) of that regulation 10 any reference to the adjudicating authority which gave the decision or to an authority of like status were a reference to an appeal tribunal constituted under section 7; and
(*b*) as if, in that regulation 3, for the reference to a chairman there were substituted a reference to a legally qualified panel member.
(3) Paragraph (1) above shall not apply in any case where an application to set aside a decision of an appellate authority is made after 5th August 2000.

13 Where, immediately before 5th July 1999, payment of a relevant benefit was suspended or withheld by virtue of any provision of Part V of the Social Security (Claims and Payments) Regulations 1987 (suspension and extinguishment), the provisions of Chapter I of Part III of the Regulations (suspension and termination) shall, on or after that date, apply with respect to that suspension or withholding as if it were a suspension imposed by virtue of those provisions.

1999/1662

SOCIAL SECURITY CONTRIBUTIONS (TRANSFER OF FUNCTIONS, ETC) ACT 1999 (COMMENCEMENT NO 2 AND CONSEQUENTIAL AND TRANSITIONAL PROVISIONS) ORDER 1999

Made by the Secretary of State for Social Security under the Social Security Contributions (Transfer of Functions, etc) Act 1999 s 28(3), (4)

Made . . . . *13 June 1999*

1 Citation and interpretation

(1) This Order may be cited as the Social Security Contributions (Transfer of Functions, etc) Act 1999 (Commencement No 2 and Consequential and Transitional Provisions) Order 1999.
(2) In this Order, unless the context otherwise requires—
"the Act" means the Social Security Contributions (Transfer of Functions, etc) Act 1999; and references to sections and Schedules are references to sections of, and Schedules to, the Act.

2 Appointed days

Subject to article 4 below, the day appointed for the coming into force of—
(*a*) the provisions of the Act which are specified in Part I of the Schedule to this Order, in so far as they authorise the making of Regulations, is 14th June 1999;
(*b*) the provisions of the Act which are specified in Part II of that Schedule, in so far as they are not already in force, is 5th July 1999.

3 Consequential amendments

(1) Subject to article 4 below, the Social Security and Child Support (Decisions and Appeals) Regulations 1999 shall on 5th July 1999 be amended in accordance with the following paragraphs of this article.
(2) In regulation 1 (interpretation)—
(*a*) in paragraph (3)—
(i) after the definition of "appeal" there shall be inserted the following definition—
" "the Board" means the Commissioners of Inland Revenue;",
(ii) in paragraph (*b*) of the definition of "claimant", for "the Secretary of State" there shall be substituted "an officer of the Board", and
(iii) in the definition of "official error", after "Social Security" there shall be inserted ",the Board", and for "either Department" (in both places where those words occur) there shall be substituted "any of those Departments";
(*b*) after paragraph (3) there shall be inserted the following paragraph—

"(3A) In these Regulations as they relate to any decision made under the Pension Schemes Act 1993 by virtue of section 170(2) of that Act, any reference to the Secretary of State is to be construed as if It were a reference to an officer of the Board.".

(3) In regulation 3 (revision of decisions)—

(*a*) in paragraph (4), for "the Secretary of State" there shall be substituted "an officer of the Board"; and

(*b*) in paragraph (11), after sub-paragraph (*b*) there shall be inserted "; or

(*c*) in the case of a contributions decision which falls within Part II of Schedule 3 to the Act, any National Insurance Contributions office of the Board or any office of the Department of Social Security; or

(*d*) in the case of a decision made under the Pension Schemes Act 1993 by virtue of section 170(2) of that Act, any National Insurance Contributions office of the Board.".

(4) In regulation 33(2) (making of appeals and applications—meaning of "appropriate office")—

(*a*) in sub-paragraph (*c*) after "office" there shall be inserted "of the Board, or any office of the Department of Social Security"; and

(*b*) after sub-paragraph (*c*) there shall be inserted the following sub-paragraph—

"(*cc*) in the case of a decision made under the Pension Schemes Act 1993 by virtue of section 170(2) of that Act, any National Insurance Contributions office of the Board;".

4 Transitional provision

Notwithstanding paragraph 1(2) of Schedule 8 (which provides for certain determinations made by the Secretary of State to have effect as if made by the Board) section 16(2) shall not apply with respect to any decision given before 5th July 1999 by the Secretary of State of any such question as is mentioned in section 170(1) of the Pension Schemes Act 1993 (which includes such a question among the questions to which section 17(1) of the Social Security Administration Act 1992 applies).

SCHEDULE

PART I

PROVISIONS OF THE ACT COMING INTO FORCE ON 14TH JUNE 1999 FOR THE PURPOSE ONLY OF AUTHORISING THE MAKING OF REGULATIONS

Provisions of the Act	*Subject matter*
Section 16(2)	Decisions under the Pension Schemes Act 1993
Schedule 7 in the respects specified below, and section 18 in so far as it relates to them—	Amendments relating to decisions and appeals—
paragraph 24	reference of issues by Secretary of State to Inland Revenue
paragraph 33	appeals dependent on issues falling to be decided by Inland Revenue

PART II

PROVISIONS OF THE ACT COMING INTO FORCE ON 5TH JULY 1999

Provisions of the Act	*Subject matter*
Section 16	Decisions under the Pension Schemes Act 1993
Schedule 7 in the respects specified below, and section 18 in so far as it relates to them—	Amendments relating to decisions and appeals—
paragraph 4	provisions concerned with industrial injuries and diseases
paragraph 12	issues for Inland Revenue arising in legal proceedings
paragraph 14	financial review and report as to operation of social security legislation
paragraph 18(3)	application to pension schemes of social security provision for determination of questions

NIC

paragraph 19	questions under the Pension Schemes Act 1993 arising in legal proceedings
paragraph 20	reports by Inland Revenue about decision-making
paragraph 24	reference of issues by Secretary of State to Inland Revenue
paragraph 33	appeals dependent on issues falling to be decided by Inland Revenue
paragraph 34	correction of errors and setting aside of decisions
paragraph 36, in so far as it relates to paragraph 23 of Schedule 3 to the Social Security Act 1998	decisions against which an appeal lies
Schedule 10, in respect of the repeals specified below, and section 26(3) in so far as it relates to them—	Repeals and revocations—
in the Pension Schemes Act 1993, section 167(3)	application to pension schemes of social security provision for determination of questions
in the Social Security Act 1998—	decisions against which an appeal lies
in Schedule 3 to that Act, paragraph 23	
in Schedule 7 to that Act, paragraphs 130(1) and 132	

1999/2422

SOCIAL SECURITY ACT 1998 (COMMENCEMENT NO 9, AND SAVINGS AND CONSEQUENTIAL AND TRANSITIONAL PROVISIONS) ORDER 1999

Made by the Secretary of State for Social Security under SSA 1998 ss 79(3), (4), 87(2), (3) of the Social Security Act 1998

Made . . . . *2 September 1999*

1 Citation and interpretation

(1) This Order may be cited as the Social Security Act 1998 (Commencement No 9, and Savings and Consequential and Transitional Provisions) Order 1999.

(2) In this Order, unless the context otherwise requires—

(*a*) "the Act" means the Social Security Act 1998;

(*b*) "the Regulations" means the Social Security and Child Support (Decisions and Appeals) Regulations 1999;

(*c*) "relevant benefit" means any of the benefits to which article 2(*c*) of this Order refers,

[(*d*) "relevant benefit" also means the following benefits under the Social Security Act 1975—

(i) sickness benefit under section 14;

(ii) unemployment benefit under section 14;

(iii) invalidity pension under section 15; and

(iv) invalidity allowance under section 16;][1]

and references to sections and Schedules are references to sections of, and Schedules to, the Act.

Amendments—[1] Sub-para (2)(*d*) inserted by the Social Security Act 1998 (Commencement Nos 9 and 11) (Amendment) Order, SI 2006/2540 art 2(1), (2) with effect from 16 October 2006.

2 Appointed day

6th September 1999 is the day appointed for the coming into force of—

(*a*) section 31;

(*b*) section 39(3) in so far as it provides that section 61A of the Administration Act shall cease to have effect, and section 86(2) and Schedule 8 in so far as they repeal that section 61A; and

(*c*) the provisions specified in Schedule 1 to this Order, in so far as those provisions are not already in force, for the purposes of—

(i) benefits under Part II of the Contributions and Benefits Act except child's special allowance;

(ii) severe disablement allowance under sections 68 and 69 of that Act;

(iii) benefits for the aged under sections 78 and 79 of that Act;

(iv) increases for dependants under Part IV of that Act; and

(v) graduated retirement benefit under sections 36 and 37 of the National Insurance Act 1965.

3 Consequential amendments and modifications

. . .

Note—This Regulation is not relevant to this publication.

4 Transitional provisions

Schedule 14 to this Order shall have effect as from 6th September 1999.

5 Savings

Notwithstanding the coming into force of section 39(3) (Part II of the Administration Act to cease to have effect) or regulation 59 (revocations) of the Regulations—

(*a*) sections 18 and 19 of the Administration Act (appeals on questions of law, and review of decisions);

(*b*) sections 59 to 61 of, and Schedule 3 to, that Act (regulations about procedural and supplementary matters) as they relate to regulations made in relation to those sections; and

(*c*) any regulations made under or in connection with the operation of any of those sections or that Schedule,

shall continue to have effect with respect to any decision given before 6th September 1999 by the Secretary of State under section 17 of that Act (questions for the Secretary of State).

SCHEDULE 1

PROVISIONS BROUGHT INTO FORCE ON 6TH SEPTEMBER 1999 FOR THE PURPOSES SPECIFIED IN ARTICLE 2(C)

Article 2(c)

Provision of the Act	*Subject matter*
Section 39	Interpretation etc of Chapter II of Part I of the Act
Schedule 7 in the respects specified below, and section 86(1) in so far as it relates to them—	Minor and consequential amendments—
. . .	. . .
paragraph 62	Category A and Category B retirement pensions—supplemental provisions
paragraphs 66 to 71(*a*)	miscellaneous provisions relating to benefits
paragraphs 88 and 89	disclosure of information, and notification of deaths
paragraphs 107 and 108	reciprocal agreements and travelling expenses
paragraph 109	regulations and orders under the Administration Act
. . .	. . .

Note—Words omitted not relevant to this publication.

SCHEDULE 14

TRANSITIONAL PROVISIONS

Article 4

1 In this Schedule—

"the Adjudication Regulations" means the Social Security (Adjudication) Regulations 1995;

"all work test" has the meaning it bears in regulation 2(1) of the Social Security (Incapacity for Work) (General) Regulations 1995;

"relevant enactment" has the meaning it bears in section 8(4); and

"medically qualified panel member" and "legally qualified panel member" have the meanings they bear in regulation 1(3) of the Regulations.

2—(1) Subject to sub-paragraph (4) below, a decision which fell to be made before 6th September 1999 (but which was not made before that date)—

(*a*) on a claim for; or

(*b*) under or by virtue of Part II of the Administration Act in relation to,

a relevant benefit (other than a decision which fell to be made on appeal) shall be made by the Secretary of State under paragraph (*a*) or, as the case may be, paragraph (*c*) of section 8(1).

NIC

(2) Subject to sub-paragraph (4) below, any reference of a disablement question made in relation to a relevant benefit which fell to be determined before 6th September 1999 but which was not determined before that date shall be determined by the Secretary of State.

(3) In sub-paragraph (2) above "disablement question" shall be construed in accordance with section 45 of the Administration Act.

(4) An appeal tribunal shall determine any case referred to a medical appeal tribunal under section 46(3)(*b*) of the Administration Act for a decision in relation to a relevant benefit which was not determined before 6th September 1999.

3—(1) Any application duly made before 6th September 1999 under Part II of the Administration Act for a review of a decision (other than a decision given on appeal) in relation to a relevant benefit which was not decided before that date shall on or after that date be treated as an application to the Secretary of State—

(*a*) where the application is made—

(i) within three months of the date on which the applicant was notified of the decision, or within such longer period as may be allowed under sub-paragraph (3) below; and

(ii) other than on the ground of a relevant change of circumstances,

for a revision of that decision under section 9; or

(*b*) in any other case, for a decision under section 10 to supersede that decision.

(2) Any application duly made before 6th September 1999 under Part II of the Administration Act for a review of a decision given on appeal in relation to a relevant benefit shall on or after that date be treated as an application to the Secretary of State for a decision under section 10 to supersede that decision.

(3) Subject to sub-paragraphs (4) and (5) below, the period of three months specified in sub-paragraph (1)(*a*) above may be extended where an application for such an extension is made before 6th October 2000 by a claimant or a person acting on his behalf containing—

(*a*) the grounds on which an extension of time is sought; and

(*b*) sufficient details of the decision to enable it to be identified.

(4) An application for an extension of time shall not be granted under sub-paragraph (3) above unless the Secretary of State is satisfied that—

(*a*) it is reasonable to grant that application;

(*b*) the application for review has merit; and

(*c*) special circumstances are relevant to the application for extension of time as a result of which it was not practicable for the application for review to be made within three months of the date of the adjudication officer's decision being notified to the claimant.

(5) In deciding whether to grant an extension of time no account shall be taken of the following factors—

(*a*) that the claimant or any person acting for him misunderstood or was unaware of the law applicable to his case (including misunderstanding or being unaware of the period specified in sub-paragraph (1)(*a*) above); or

(*b*) that a Commissioner or a court has taken a different view of the law from that previously understood and applied by the adjudication officer.

(6) Where, by virtue of sub-paragraph (1)(*b*) or (2) above—

(*a*) a decision is made under section 10 which is advantageous to the applicant; and

(*b*) the same decision could have been made on a review prior to 6th September 1999,

that decision shall take effect from the date on which it would have taken effect had the decision been so made.

4—(1) A decision (other than a decision of a social security appeal tribunal, a medical appeal tribunal or a Commissioner), made before 6th September 1999—

(*a*) on a claim for . . . [1]

[(*aa*) under or by virtue of Part III of the Social Security Act 1975; or][1]

(*b*) under or by virtue of Part II of the Administration Act in relation to,

a relevant benefit, shall be treated on or after that date as a decision of the Secretary of State under paragraph (*a*) or, as the case may be, paragraph (*c*) of section 8(1).

(2) Where, before 6th September 1999, any person was required to give notice to the claimant of a decision referred to in paragraph (1) above, and such notice has not been given to the claimant before that date, the Secretary of State shall on or after that date give notice to the claimant of that decision.

Amendments—[1] Word "or" in sub-para (1)(*a*) repealed, and sub-para (1)(*aa*) inserted, by the Social Security Act 1998 (Commencement Nos 9 and 11) (Amendment) Order, SI 2006/2540 art 2(1), 4 with effect from 16 October 2006.

5—(1) This paragraph applies where the time limit for making an appeal to a social security appeal tribunal or a medical appeal tribunal in respect of a decision in relation to a relevant benefit made before 6th September 1999 has not expired before that date.

(2) Where sub-paragraph (1) applies, regulation 3 of the Adjudication Regulations as it relates to the period within which an appeal may be made, or an extension of that period, shall, notwithstanding regulation 59 of the Regulations, continue to have effect, subject to the modifications in sub-paragraph (3) below, with respect to any appeal to an appeal tribunal made on or after 6th September 1999 in relation to that decision.

(3) The modifications referred to in sub-paragraph (2) above are as if—

(*a*) references to—

(i) a chairman or a person considering the application were references to a legally qualified panel member;

(ii) a tribunal were references to an appeal tribunal constituted under Chapter I of Part I of the Act;

(*b*) in paragraph (3E) for the words from "6 years" to the end of the paragraph there were substituted the words "6th October 2000".

(4) Notwithstanding regulation 3 of the Regulations, the Secretary of State may revise under section 9 a decision given before 6th September 1999 on a claim for or award of a relevant benefit (other than a decision given on appeal)—

(*a*) pursuant to an application for a review of a decision made within three months of the notification of that decision; or

(*b*) where an appeal has been duly made against that decision but not determined.

(5) Where a decision is revised pursuant to sub-paragraph (4) above the appeal shall lapse unless the decision as revised is not more advantageous to the appellant than the decision before it was revised.

6 An appeal to a social security appeal tribunal or a medical appeal tribunal in relation to a relevant benefit which was duly made before 6th September 1999 and which has not been determined before that date shall, without prejudice to Chapter III of Part V of the Regulations, be treated on or after that date as an appeal duly made to an appeal tribunal in relation to a decision of the Secretary of State under section 8.

7—(1) This paragraph applies where a clerk to—

(*a*) a social security appeal tribunal; or

(*b*) a medical appeal tribunal,

has before 6th September 1999 given a direction under regulation 22(1) or, as the case may be, 38(1) of the Adjudication Regulations in connection with an appeal in relation to a relevant benefit to that tribunal, and the notification mentioned in paragraph (1A) of that regulation 22 or paragraph (1A) of that regulation 38 has not been received by the clerk before that date.

(2) A notification in response to such a direction given under that regulation 22(1) or regulation 38(1) shall be—

(*a*) in writing; and

(*b*) made within 14 days of receipt of the direction or within such other period as the clerk to an appeal tribunal may direct.

(3) An appeal may be struck out by the clerk to an appeal tribunal where the notification referred to in sub-paragraph (2) above is not received within the period specified in that sub-paragraph.

(4) An appeal which has been struck out in accordance with sub-paragraph (3) above shall be treated for the purpose of reinstatement as if it had been struck out under regulation 46 of the Regulations.

(5) An oral hearing of the appeal shall be held where—

(*a*) a notification is received by the clerk to the appeal tribunal under sub-paragraph (2) above; or

(*b*) the chairman of the appeal tribunal or, in the case of an appeal tribunal which has only one member, that member is satisfied that such a hearing is necessary to enable the appeal tribunal to reach a decision.

8 Where an appeal to a social security appeal tribunal or a medical appeal tribunal in relation to a relevant benefit has been struck out under regulation 7 of the Adjudication Regulations, a legally qualified panel member may on or after 6th September 1999, on an application made by any party to the proceedings not later than three months from the date of the order under paragraph (1) of that regulation, reinstate the appeal if he is satisfied that—

(*a*) the applicant did not receive a notice under paragraph (2) of that regulation; and

(*b*) the conditions in paragraph (2A) of that regulation were not satisfied,

and the appeal shall then be treated as an appeal to an appeal tribunal in relation to a decision of the Secretary of State under section 8.

9 An appeal tribunal shall completely rehear any appeal to a social security appeal tribunal or a medical appeal tribunal in relation to a relevant benefit which stands adjourned immediately before 6th September 1999.

10 A copy of a statement of—

(*a*) the reasons for a decision of a social security appeal tribunal or, as the case may be, a medical appeal tribunal in relation to a relevant benefit; and

(*b*) its findings on questions of fact material thereto,

shall be supplied to each party to the proceedings before that tribunal, if requested by any such party within 21 days of the date on which notification of that decision was given or sent.

11—(1) Subject to sub-paragraph (2) below, any decision of a social security appeal tribunal or a medical appeal tribunal in relation to a relevant benefit shall be treated as a decision of an appeal tribunal made under section 12.

(2) Where sub-paragraph (1) above applies, any application for leave to appeal which is made for the purposes of section 14(10)(*a*) shall be made no later than three months after the date on which a copy of the statement of the decision of the social security appeal tribunal or, as the case may be, the medical appeal tribunal was given or sent to the applicant.

12—(1) Subject to sub-paragraph (3) below, regulation 10 of the Adjudication Regulations, and regulation 3 of those Regulations in so far as it relates to that regulation 10, shall, notwithstanding regulation 59 of the Regulations, continue to have effect, subject to the modifications specified in sub-paragraph (2) below, in relation to any application to set aside a decision of a social security appeal tribunal or a medical appeal tribunal in relation to a relevant benefit.

(2) The modifications referred to in sub-paragraph (1) above are as if in—

(*a*) regulation 3 for the reference to a chairman there were substituted a reference to a legally qualified panel member; and

(*b*) regulation 10(1) the first reference to the adjudicating authority which gave the decision or to an authority of like status were a reference to an appeal tribunal constituted under Chapter I of Part I of the Act.

(3) Paragraph (1) above shall not apply in any case where an application to set aside a decision of a social security appeal tribunal or a medical appeal tribunal is made after 6th October 2000.

13 Where, immediately before 6th September 1999, payment of a relevant benefit was suspended or withheld by virtue of any provision of Part V of the Social Security (Claims and Payments) Regulations 1987 (suspension and extinguishment), the provisions of Chapter I of Part III of the Regulations (suspension and termination) shall apply with respect to that suspension or withholding as if it were a suspension imposed by virtue of those provisions.

14 For the purpose of section 10(1)(b), a decision of a Commissioner made before 6th September 1999 as respects a relevant benefit shall be treated as a decision of a Commissioner made under section 14.

15 A determination of the Secretary of State (including a determination made following a change of circumstances) whether a person is, or is to be treated as, capable or incapable of work shall be conclusive for the purposes of any decision which falls to be made—

(*a*) under a relevant enactment; or

(*b*) on a claim for or award of—

(i) housing benefit; or

(ii) council tax benefit.

16—(1) Where before 29th November 1999, in relation to a determination for any purpose to which Part XIIA of the Contributions and Benefits Act applies, a determination falls to be made as to—

(*a*) whether a person is, or is to be treated as, capable or incapable of work in respect of any period; or

(*b*) whether a person is terminally ill,

that determination shall be made by the Secretary of State, notwithstanding—

(i) regulation 1(2)(*e*) and (*f*) of the Regulations; and

(ii) that other matters fall to be determined by another authority.

(2) An appeal shall lapse where the Secretary of State makes a determination pursuant to sub-paragraph (1) above in relation to a case where an appeal against a decision of an adjudication officer has been made but not determined provided that the decision as revised is more advantageous to the appellant than the decision before it was revised.

(3) Where—

(*a*) the Secretary of State reverses a determination under section 171C of the Contributions and Benefits Act that a person satisfies or is treated as satisfying the all work test; and

(*b*) that determination which is reversed is necessary to or embodied in a decision in relation to which Part II of the Administration Act continues to have effect,

an adjudication officer shall revise that decision upon review in consequence of that reversal.

17—(1) An appeal made by or on behalf of a person against a decision of an adjudication officer (other than a decision in relation to a relevant benefit) which incorporates a determination as to whether the all work test is satisfied or treated as satisfied—

(*a*) shall be heard by a social security appeal tribunal which consists of two persons, one being a medically qualified panel member and the other being a legally qualified panel member; and

(*b*) may be heard with an appeal made by or on behalf of the same person against a decision of the Secretary of State which incorporates such a determination.

(2) Where an appeal to which sub-paragraph (1) above applies is heard with an appeal to an appeal tribunal—

(*a*) section 13 shall not apply in relation to the appeal to the appeal tribunal; and

(*b*) notwithstanding regulation 59 of the Regulations, regulation 24 of the Adjudication Regulations and regulation 3 of, and Schedule 2 to, those Regulations in so far as they relate to regulation 24 shall have effect on and after 6th September 1999 in relation to the appeal to the appeal tribunal subject to the modifications specified in sub-paragraph (3) below.

(3) The modifications referred to in sub-paragraph (2) above are as if references in the provisions described in that sub-paragraph to—

(*a*) an adjudication officer were to the Secretary of State;

(*b*) an appeal tribunal were to an appeal tribunal constituted under Chapter I of Part I of the Act;

(*c*) the clerk to the tribunal were to a clerk to an appeal tribunal constituted under Chapter I of Part I of the Act;

(*d*) the chairman of an appeal tribunal and a chairman of appeal tribunals were to a chairman of an appeal tribunal constituted under Chapter I of Part I of the Act or, in the case of a tribunal which has only one member, that member; and

(*e*) the words "under section 41(4) of the Administration Act" were omitted.

1999/2739

SOCIAL SECURITY ACT 1998 (COMMENCEMENT NO 10 AND TRANSITIONAL PROVISIONS) ORDER 1999

Made by the Secretary of State for Social Security under the Social Security Act 1998 ss 79(3), (4), 87(2) and (3) and all other enabling powers

Made . . . .*4 October 1999*

1 Citation and interpretation

(1) This Order may be cited as the Social Security Act 1998 (Commencement No 10 and Transitional Provisions) Order 1999.

(2) In this Order, unless the context otherwise requires "the Act" means the Social Security Act 1998; and references to sections and Schedules are references to sections of, and Schedules to, the Act.

2 Appointed day

5th October 1999 is the day appointed for the coming into force of the provisions specified in Schedule 1 to this Order, in so far as those provisions are not already in force, for the purposes of family credit and disability working allowance under Part VII of the Contributions and Benefits Act.

3 Transitional provisions

Schedule 2 to this Order shall have effect as from 5th October 1999.

SCHEDULE 1

PROVISIONS BROUGHT INTO FORCE ON 5TH OCTOBER 1999 FOR THE PURPOSES SPECIFIED IN ARTICLE 2

Article 2

Provision of the Act	*Subject matter*
Section 39	Interpretation etc of Chapter II of Part I of the Act
. . .	. . .
Schedule 7 in the respects specified below, and section 86(1) in so far as it relates to them—	Minor and consequential amendments—
. . .	. . .
paragraphs 88 and 89	Disclosure of information, and notification of deaths
paragraphs 106 to 108	Reciprocal agreements and travelling expenses

paragraph 109	Regulations and orders under the Administration Act
. . .	. . .

Note—Words omitted are not relevant to this publication.

SCHEDULE 2

TRANSITIONAL PROVISIONS

Article 3

1 In this Schedule—

"the Adjudication Regulations" means the Social Security (Adjudication) Regulations 1995;

"the Regulations" means the Social Security and Child Support (Decisions and Appeals) Regulations 1999; and

"legally qualified panel member" has the meaning it bears in regulation 1(3) of the Regulations.

2 A decision which fell to be made before 5th October 1999 (but which was not made before that date)—

(*a*) on a claim for; or

(*b*) under or by virtue of Part II of the Administration Act in relation to,

family credit or disability working allowance (other than a decision which fell to be made on appeal) shall be made by the Secretary of State under paragraph (*a*) or, as the case may be, paragraph (*c*) of section 8(1).

3—(1) Any application duly made before 5th October 1999 under Part II of the Administration Act for a review of a decision (other than a decision made on appeal) in relation to family credit or disability working allowance which was not decided before that date shall on or after that date be treated as an application to the Secretary of State—

(*a*) where the application is made—

(i) within three months of the date on which the applicant was notified of the decision, or within such longer period as may be allowed under sub-paragraph (3) below; and

(ii) other than on the ground of a relevant change of circumstances,

for a revision of that decision under section 9; or

(*b*) in any other case, for a decision under section 10 to supersede that decision.

(2) Any application duly made before 5th October 1999 under Part II of the Administration Act for a review of a decision in relation to family credit or disability working allowance made on appeal shall on or after that date be treated as an application to the Secretary of State for a decision under section 10 to supersede that decision.

(3) Subject to sub-paragraphs (4) and (5) below, the period of three months specified in sub-paragraph (1)(*a*) above may be extended where an application for such an extension is made before 5th November 2000 by a claimant or a person acting on his behalf containing—

(*a*) the grounds on which an extension of time is sought; and

(*b*) sufficient details of the decision to enable it to be identified.

(4) An application for an extension of time shall not be granted under sub-paragraph (3) above unless the Secretary of State is satisfied that—

(*a*) it is reasonable to grant that application;

(*b*) the application for review has merit; and

(*c*) special circumstances are relevant to the application for extension of time as a result of which it was not practicable for the application for review to be made within three months of the date of the adjudication officer's decision being notified to the claimant.

(5) In deciding whether to grant an extension of time no account shall be taken of the following factors—

(*a*) that the claimant or any person acting for him misunderstood or was unaware of the law applicable to his case (including misunderstanding or being unaware of the period specified in sub-paragraph (1)(*a*) above); or

(*b*) that a Commissioner or a court has taken a different view of the law from that previously understood and applied by the adjudication officer.

(6) Where, by virtue of sub-paragraph (1)(*b*) or (2) above—

(*a*) a decision is made under section 10 which is advantageous to the applicant; and

(*b*) the same decision could have been made on a review prior to 5th October 1999,

that decision shall have effect as from the date on which it would have taken effect had the decision been so made.

4—(1) A decision (other than a decision of a social security appeal tribunal, a disability appeal tribunal or a Commissioner), made before 5th October 1999—

(*a*) on a claim for; or

(*b*) under or by virtue of Part II of the Administration Act in relation to,

family credit or disability working allowance, shall be treated on or after that date as a decision of the Secretary of State under paragraph (*a*) or, as the case may be, paragraph (*c*) of section 8(1).

(2) Where, before 5th October 1999, any person was required to give notice to the claimant of the decision referred to in sub-paragraph (1) above, and such notice has not been given to the claimant before that date, the Secretary of State shall on or after that date give notice to the claimant of that decision.

5—(1) This paragraph applies where the time limit for making an appeal to a social security appeal tribunal or a disability appeal tribunal in respect of a decision relating to family credit or disability working allowance made before 5th October 1999 has not expired before that date.

(2) Where sub-paragraph (1) above applies, regulation 3 of the Adjudication Regulations as it relates to the period within which an appeal may be made, or an extension of that period, shall, notwithstanding regulation 59 of the Regulations, continue to have effect, subject to the modifications in sub-paragraph (3) below, with respect to any appeal to an appeal tribunal made on or after 5th October 1999 in relation to that decision.

(3) The modifications referred to in sub-paragraph (2) above are as if—

(*a*) references to—

(i) a chairman or to a person considering the application were references to a legally qualified panel member; and

(ii) a tribunal were references to an appeal tribunal constituted under Chapter I of Part I of the Act; and

(*b*) in paragraph (3E) for the words from "6 years" to the end of the paragraph there were substituted the words "5th November 2000".

(4) Notwithstanding regulation 3 of the Regulations, the Secretary of State may revise under section 9 a decision made before 5th October 1999 on a claim for or award of family credit or disability working allowance (other than a decision made on appeal)—

(*a*) pursuant to an application for a review of a decision made within three months of the notification of that decision; or

(*b*) where an appeal has been duly made against that decision but not determined.

(5) Where a decision is revised pursuant to sub-paragraph (4) above the appeal shall lapse unless the decision as revised is not more advantageous to the appellant than the decision before it was revised.

6 An appeal to a social security appeal tribunal or a disability appeal tribunal in relation to family credit or disability working allowance which was duly made before 5th October 1999 and which has not been determined before that date shall, without prejudice to Chapter III of Part V of the Regulations, be treated on or after that date as an appeal duly made to an appeal tribunal in relation to a decision of the Secretary of State under section 8.

7—(1) This paragraph applies where a clerk to a social security appeal tribunal or a disability appeal tribunal has before 5th October 1999 given a direction under regulation 22(1) or, as the case may be, regulation 29(1) of the Adjudication Regulations in connection with an appeal in relation to family credit or disability working allowance to that tribunal, and the notification mentioned in paragraph (1A) of that regulation 22 or paragraph (1A) of that regulation 29 has not been received by the clerk before that date.

(2) A notification in response to such direction given under that regulation 22(1) or regulation 29(1) shall be—

(*a*) in writing; and

(*b*) made within 14 days of receipt of the direction or within such other period as the clerk to an appeal tribunal may direct.

(3) An appeal may be struck out by the clerk to an appeal tribunal where the notification referred to in sub-paragraph (2) above is not received within the period specified in that sub-paragraph.

(4) An appeal which has been struck out in accordance with sub-paragraph (3) above shall be treated for the purpose of reinstatement as if it had been struck out under regulation 46 of the Regulations.

(5) An oral hearing of the appeal shall be held where—

(*a*) a notification is received by the clerk to the appeal tribunal under sub-paragraph (2) above; or

(*b*) the chairman or, in the case of an appeal tribunal which has only one member, that member is satisfied that such a hearing is necessary to enable the appeal tribunal to reach a decision.

8 Where an appeal to a social security appeal tribunal or a disability appeal tribunal in relation to family credit or disability working allowance has been struck out under regulation 7 of the Adjudication Regulations, a legally qualified panel member may on or after 5th October 1999, on an application made by any party to the proceedings not later than three months from the date of the order under paragraph (1) of that regulation, reinstate the appeal if he is satisfied that—

(*a*) the applicant did not receive a notice under paragraph (2) of that regulation; and

(*b*) the conditions in paragraph (2A) of that regulation were not satisfied,

and the appeal shall then be treated as an appeal to an appeal tribunal in relation to a decision of the Secretary of State under section 8.

9 An appeal tribunal shall completely rehear any appeal to a social security appeal tribunal or a disability appeal tribunal in relation to family credit or disability working allowance which stands adjourned immediately before 5th October 1999.

10 A copy of a statement of—

(*a*) the reasons for a decision of a social security appeal tribunal or, as the case may be, a disability appeal tribunal in relation to family credit or disability working allowance; and

(*b*) its findings on questions of fact material thereto,

shall be supplied to each party to the proceedings before that tribunal, if requested by any such party within 21 days of the date on which notification of that decision was given or sent.

11—(1) Subject to sub-paragraph (2) below, any decision of a social security appeal tribunal or a disability appeal tribunal in relation to family credit or disability working allowance shall be treated as a decision of an appeal tribunal made under section 12.

(2) Where sub-paragraph (1) above applies, any application for leave to appeal which is made for the purposes of section 14(10)(*a*) shall be made no later than three months after the date on which a copy of the statement of the reasons for the decision of the social security appeal tribunal or, as the case may be, the disability appeal tribunal was given or sent to the applicant.

12—(1) Subject to sub-paragraph (3) below, regulation 10 of the Adjudication Regulations, and regulation 3 of those Regulations in so far as it relates to that regulation 10, shall, notwithstanding regulation 59 of the Regulations, continue to have effect, subject to the modifications specified in sub-paragraph (2) below, in relation to any application to set aside a decision of a social security appeal tribunal or a disability appeal tribunal in relation to family credit or disability working allowance.

(2) The modifications referred to in sub-paragraph (1) above are as if in—

(*a*) regulation 3 for the reference to a chairman there were substituted a reference to a legally qualified panel member; and

(*b*) regulation 10(1) the first reference to the adjudicating authority who gave the decision and the reference to an authority of like status were a reference to an appeal tribunal which consists of a legally qualified panel member.

(3) Paragraph (1) above shall not apply in any case where an application to set aside a decision of a social security appeal tribunal or a disability appeal tribunal is made after 5th November 2000.

13 Where, immediately before 5th October 1999, payment of family credit or disability working allowance was suspended or withheld by virtue of any provision of Part V of the Social Security (Claims and Payments) Regulations 1987 (suspension and extinguishment), the provisions of Chapter I of Part III of the Regulations (suspension and termination) shall apply with respect to that suspension or withholding as if it were a suspension imposed by virtue of those provisions.

14 For the purpose of section 10(1)(b), a decision of a Commissioner as respects family credit or disability working allowance made before 5th October 1999 shall be treated as a decision of a Commissioner made under section 14.

1999/2860

SOCIAL SECURITY ACT 1998 (COMMENCEMENT NO 11, AND SAVINGS AND CONSEQUENTIAL AND TRANSITIONAL PROVISIONS) ORDER 1999

Made by the Secretary of State for Social Security under the Social Security Act 1998, ss 79(3), (4), 87(2), (3)

Made . . . . *16 October 1999*

1 Citation and interpretation

(1) This Order may be cited as the Social Security Act 1998 (Commencement No 11, and Savings and Consequential and Transitional Provisions) Order 1999.

(2) In this Order, unless the context otherwise requires—

(*a*) "the Act" means the Social Security Act 1998;
(*b*) "the Regulations" means the Social Security and Child Support (Decisions and Appeals) Regulations 1999;
(*c*) "relevant benefit" means any of the benefits to which article 2(*c*)(i) and (ii) of this Order refers,
[(*d*) "relevant benefit" also means—
(i) an attendance allowance under section 35 of the Social Security Act 1975;
(ii) a mobility allowance under section 37A of that Act;
(iii) supplementary benefit under section 1 of the Supplementary Benefit Act 1976][1]

and references to sections and Schedules are references to sections of, and Schedules to, the Act.

Amendments—[1] Sub-para (1)(*d*) inserted by the Social Security Act 1998 (Commencement Nos 9 and 11) (Amendment) Order, SI 2006/2540 art 3(1), (2) with effect from 16 October 2006.

2 Appointed Day

18th October 1999 is the day appointed for the coming into force of—
(*a*) sections 18(2), 32 and 34;
(*b*) section 39(3) in so far as it provides that section 63 of the Administration Act shall cease to have effect, and section 86(2) and Schedule 8 in so far as they repeal that section 63; and
(*c*) the provisions specified in Schedule 1 to this Order, in so far as those provisions are not already in force, for the purposes of—
(i) attendance allowance, disability living allowance and invalid care allowance under Part III of the Contributions and Benefits Act;
(ii) jobseeker's allowance under Part I of the Jobseekers Act and any sum payable under section 26 of that Act;
(iii) vaccine damage payments under the Vaccine Damage Payments Act;
(iv) decisions whether a person is entitled to be credited with earnings or contributions in accordance with regulations made under section 22(5) of the Contributions and Benefits Act; and
(v) decisions whether a person was, within the meaning of regulations, precluded from regular employment by responsibilities at home.

3 Consequential amendments and modifications

. . .

Note—This Regulation is not relevant to this publication.

4 Transitional provisions

Schedules 16 to 18 to this Order shall have effect as from 18th October 1999 in relation to relevant benefit, vaccine damage payments, and credits of contributions or earnings and home responsibilities protection respectively.

5 Savings

. . .

Note—This Regulation is not relevant to this publication.

SCHEDULE 1

PROVISIONS BROUGHT INTO FORCE ON 18TH OCTOBER 1999 FOR THE PURPOSES SPECIFIED IN ARTICLE 2(C)

Article 2(*c*)

Provision of the Act	*Subject matter*
. . .	. . .
Section 39	Interpretation etc of Chapter II of Part I of the Act
. . .	
Schedule 7 in the respects specified below, and section 86(1) in so far as it relates to them—	Minor and consequential amendments—
. . .	. . .
Paragraphs 66 to 71(a)	miscellaneous provisions relating to benefits
. . .	. . .
Paragraphs 88 and 89	disclosure of information, and notification of deaths
. . .	. . .

Paragraph 109	regulations and orders under the Administration Act
.....	.....

Note—Words omitted not relevant to this publication.

SCHEDULE 16

TRANSITIONAL PROVISIONS IN RELATION TO RELEVANT BENEFIT

Article 4

1 In this Schedule—

"the Adjudication Regulations" means the Social Security (Adjudication) Regulations 1995;

"the Claims and Payments Regulations" means the Social Security (Claims and Payments) Regulations 1987;

"claimant" and "legally qualified panel member" have the meanings they bear in regulation 1(3) of the Regulations; and

any reference to a decision includes a reference to a decision which fell to be made under the Social Security (Introduction of Disability Living Allowance) Regulations 1991 or the Jobseeker's Allowance (Transitional Provisions) Regulations 1996.

2 A decision which fell to be made before 18th October 1999, but which was not made before that date—

(*a*) on a claim for; or

(*b*) under or by virtue of Part II of the Administration Act in relation to,

a relevant benefit (other than a decision which fell to be made on appeal) shall be made by the Secretary of State under paragraph (a) or, as the case may be, paragraph (c) of section 8(1).

3—(1) Any application duly made before 18th October 1999 under Part II of the Administration Act for a review of a decision (other than a decision made on appeal) in relation to a relevant benefit which was not decided before that date shall on or after that date be treated as an application to the Secretary of State—

(*a*) where the application is made—

(i) within three months of the date on which the applicant was notified of the decision, or within such longer period as may be allowed under sub-paragraph (3) below; and

(ii) other than on the ground of a relevant change of circumstances,

for a revision of that decision under section 9; or

(*b*) in any other case, for a decision under section 10 to supersede that decision.

(2) Any application duly made before 18th October 1999 under Part II of the Administration Act for a review of a decision made on appeal in relation to a relevant benefit shall on or after that date be treated as an application to the Secretary of State for a decision under section 10 to supersede that decision.

(3) Subject to sub-paragraphs (4) and (5) below, the period of three months specified in sub-paragraph (1)(*a*) above may be extended where an application for such an extension is made before 18th November 2000 by a claimant or a person acting on his behalf containing—

(*a*) the grounds on which an extension of time is sought; and

(*b*) sufficient details of the decision to enable it to be identified.

(4) An application for an extension of time shall not be granted under sub-paragraph (3) above unless the Secretary of State is satisfied that—

(*a*) it is reasonable to grant that application;

(*b*) the application for review has merit; and

(*c*) special circumstances are relevant to the application for extension of time as a result of which it was not practicable for the application for review to be made within three months of the date of the adjudication officer's decision being notified to the claimant.

(5) In deciding whether to grant an extension of time no account shall be taken of the following factors—

(*a*) that the claimant or any person acting for him misunderstood or was unaware of the law applicable to his case (including misunderstanding or being unaware of the period specified in sub-paragraph (1)(*a*) above); or

(*b*) that a Commissioner or a court has taken a different view of the law from that previously understood and applied by the adjudication officer.

(6) Where, by virtue of sub-paragraph (1)(*b*) or (2) above—

(*a*) a decision is made under section 10 which is advantageous to the applicant; and

(*b*) the same decision could have been made on a review prior to 18th October 1999, that decision shall take effect from the date on which it would have taken effect had the decision been so made.

(7) Notwithstanding regulation 7(9) of the Regulations, but subject to sub-paragraph (6) above, where in any case relating to attendance allowance or disability living allowance a decision is made under section 10, on the basis of a relevant change of circumstances which occurred before 18th October 1999 and the decision is advantageous to the claimant, the decision shall take effect from—

(*a*) where the decision is made on the Secretary of State's own initiative, the date of that decision;

(*b*) in a case where the change is relevant to the question of entitlement to a particular rate of benefit and the claimant notifies the change before a date one month after he satisfies the conditions of entitlement to that rate or within such longer period as may be allowed under regulation 8 of the Regulations, the first pay day (as specified in Schedule 6 to the Claims and Payments Regulations) after he satisfied those conditions;

(*c*) in a case where the change is relevant to the question of whether benefit is payable and the claimant notifies the change before a date one month after the change or within such longer period as may be allowed under regulation 8 of the Regulations, the first pay day (as specified in Schedule 6 to the Claims and Payments Regulations) after the change occurred; or

(*d*) in any other case, the date of the application for the superseding decision.

4—(1) A decision (other than a decision of a social security appeal tribunal, a disability appeal tribunal, a medical appeal tribunal or a Commissioner) made before 18th October 1999—

(*a*) on a claim for; . . . [1]

[(*aa*) under or by virtue of Part III of the Social Security Act 1975; or][1]

(*b*) under or by virtue of Part II of the Administration Act in relation to,

a relevant benefit, shall be treated on or after that date as a decision of the Secretary of State under paragraph (*a*) or, as the case may be, paragraph (*c*) of section 8(1).

(2) Where, before 18th October 1999, any person was required to give notice to the claimant of a decision referred to in sub-paragraph (1) above, and such notice has not been given to the claimant before that date, the Secretary of State shall on or after that date give notice to the claimant of that decision.

Amendments—[1] Word "or" in sub-para (1)(*a*) revoked, and sub-para (1)(*aa*) inserted, by the Social Security Act 1998 (Commencement Nos 9 and 11) (Amendment) Order, SI 2006/2540 art 3(1), (4) with effect from 16 October 2006.

5—(1) This paragraph applies where the time limit for making an appeal to a social security appeal tribunal, a disability appeal tribunal or a medical appeal tribunal in respect of a decision in relation to a relevant benefit made before 18th October 1999 has not expired before that date.

(2) Where sub-paragraph (1) applies, regulation 3 of the Adjudication Regulations as it relates to the period within which an appeal may be made, or an extension of that period, shall, notwithstanding regulation 59 of the Regulations, continue to have effect, subject to the modifications in sub-paragraph (3) below, with respect to an appeal tribunal made on or after 18th October 1999 in relation to that decision.

(3) The modifications referred to in sub-paragraph (2) above are as if—

(*a*) references to—

(i) a chairman or a person considering the application were references to a legally qualified panel member;

(ii) a tribunal where references to an appeal tribunal constituted under Chapter I of Part I of the Act;

(*b*) in paragraph (3E) for the words from "6 years" to the end of the paragraph there were substituted the words "18th November 2000".

(4) Notwithstanding regulation 3 of the Regulations, the Secretary of State may revise under section 9 of the Act a decision made before 18th October 1999 on a claim for or award of a relevant benefit (other than a decision made on appeal)—

(*a*) pursuant to an application for a review of a decision made within three months of the notification of that decision; or

(*b*) where an appeal has been duly made against that decision but not determined.

(5) Where a decision is revised pursuant to sub-paragraph (4) the appeal shall lapse unless the decision as revised is not more advantageous to the appellant than the decision before it was revised.

6 An appeal to a social security appeal tribunal, a disability appeal tribunal or a medical appeal tribunal in relation to a relevant benefit which was duly made before 18th October 1999 and which has not been determined before that date shall, without prejudice to Chapter III of Part V of the Regulations, be treated on or after that date as an appeal duly made to an appeal tribunal in relation to a decision of the Secretary of State under section 8.

NIC

7—(1) This paragraph applies where a clerk to a social security appeal tribunal, a disability appeal tribunal or a medical appeal tribunal has before 18th October 1999 given a direction under regulation 22(1), regulation 29(1) or regulation 38(1), as the case may be, of the Adjudication Regulations in connection with an appeal in relation to a relevant benefit to the tribunal, and the notification mentioned in paragraph (1A) of that regulation 22, paragraph (1A) of that regulation 29 or paragraph (1A) of that regulation 38 has not been received by the clerk before that date.

(2) A notification in response to such a direction given under that regulation 22(1), regulation 29(1) or regulation 38(1) shall be—

(*a*) in writing; and

(*b*) made within 14 days of receipt of the direction or within such other period as the clerk to an appeal tribunal may direct.

(3) An appeal may be struck out by the clerk to an appeal tribunal where the notification referred to in sub-paragraph (2) above is not received within the period specified in that sub-paragraph.

(4) An appeal which has been struck out in accordance with sub-paragraph (3) above shall be treated for the purpose of reinstatement as if it had been struck out under regulation 46 of the Regulations.

(5) An oral hearing of the appeal shall be held where—

(*a*) a notification is received by the clerk to the appeal tribunal under sub-paragraph (2) above; or

(*b*) the chairman of the appeal tribunal or, in the case of an appeal tribunal which has only one member, that member of the appeal tribunal is satisfied that such a hearing is necessary to enable the appeal tribunal to reach a decision.

8 Where an appeal to a social security appeal tribunal, a disability appeal tribunal or a medical appeal tribunal in relation to a relevant benefit has been struck out under regulation 7 of the Adjudication Regulations, a legally qualified panel member may on or after 18th October 1999, on an application made by any party to the proceedings not later than three months from the date of the order under paragraph (1) of that regulation, reinstate the appeal if he is satisfied that—

(*a*) the applicant did not receive a notice under paragraph (2) of that regulation; and

(*b*) the conditions in paragraph (2A) of that regulation were not satisfied,

and the appeal shall then be treated as an appeal to an appeal tribunal in relation to a decision of the Secretary of State under section 8.

9 An appeal tribunal shall completely rehear any appeal to a social security appeal tribunal, a disability appeal tribunal or a medical appeal tribunal in relation to a relevant benefit which stands adjourned immediately before 18th October 1999.

10 Where, before 18th October 1999, a case fell to be referred by a medical appeal tribunal to an adjudication officer under any provision of the Social Security (Introduction of Disability Living Allowance) Regulations 1991, the appeal tribunal hearing the appeal on or after that date shall refer the case to the Secretary of State to be decided under section 8.

11 A copy of a statement of—

(*a*) the reasons for a decision of a social security appeal tribunal, a disability appeal tribunal or, as the case may be, a medical appeal tribunal in relation to a relevant benefit; and

(*b*) its findings on questions of fact material thereto,

shall be supplied to each party to the proceedings before that tribunal, if requested by any such party within 21 days of the date on which notification of that decision was given or sent.

12—(1) Subject to sub-paragraph (2) below, any decision of a social security appeal tribunal, a disability appeal tribunal or a medical appeal tribunal in relation to a relevant benefit shall be treated as a decision of an appeal tribunal made under section 12.

(2) Where sub-paragraph (1) above applies, any application for leave to appeal which is made for the purposes of section 14(10)(*a*) shall be made no later than three months after the date on which a copy of the statement of the reasons for the decision of the social security appeal tribunal, disability appeal tribunal or, as the case may be, medical appeal tribunal was given or sent to the applicant.

13—(1) Subject to sub-paragraph (3) below, regulation 10 of the Adjudication Regulations, and regulation 3 of those Regulations in so far as it relates to that regulation 10, shall, notwithstanding regulation 59 of the Regulations, continue to have effect, subject to the modifications specified in sub-paragraph (2) below, in relation to any application to set aside a decision of a social security appeal tribunal, disability appeal tribunal or medical appeal tribunal in relation to a relevant benefit.

(2) The modifications referred to in sub-paragraph (1) above are as if in regulation 3 for the reference to a chairman and in regulation 10(1) the first reference to the adjudicating authority which gave the decision and to an authority of like status, there were substituted references to a legally qualified panel member.

(3) Paragraph (1) above shall not apply in any case where an application to set aside a decision of a social security appeal tribunal, disability appeal tribunal or medical appeal tribunal is made after 18th November 2000.

14 Where, immediately before 18th October 1999, payment of a relevant benefit was suspended or withheld by virtue of any provision of Part V of the Claims and Payments Regulations (suspension and extinguishment), the provisions of Chapter I of Part III of the Regulations (suspension and termination) shall apply with respect to that suspension or withholding as if it were a suspension imposed by virtue of those provisions.

15 For the purpose of section 10(1)(b), a decision of a Commissioner made before 18th October 1999 as respects a relevant benefit shall be treated as a decision of a Commissioner made under section 14.

SCHEDULE 18

TRANSITIONAL PROVISION IN RELATION TO CREDITS OF CONTRIBUTIONS OR EARNINGS AND HOME RESPONSIBILITIES PROTECTION

Article 4

A decision which fell to be made, but which was now made, before 18th October 1999 under or by virtue of Part II of the Administration Act as to whether—

(*a*) a person is entitled to be credited with earnings or contributions in accordance with regulations made under section 22(5) of the Contributions and Benefits Act; or

(*b*) a person was (within the meaning of regulations) precluded from regular employment by responsibilities at home,

shall be made by the Secretary of State under paragraph (*c*) of section 8(1).

1999/3178

SOCIAL SECURITY ACT 1998 (COMMENCEMENT NO 12 AND CONSEQUENTIAL AND TRANSITIONAL PROVISIONS) ORDER 1999

Made by the Secretary of State for Social Security under the Social Security Act 1998, ss 79(3), (4), 87(2), (3)

Made . . . . *25 November 1999*

1 Citation and interpretation

(1) This Order may be cited as the Social Security Act 1998 (Commencement No 12 and Consequential and Transitional Provisions) Order 1999.

(2) In this Order, unless the context otherwise requires—

(*a*) "the Act" means the Social Security Act 1998;

(*b*) "the 1997 Regulations" means the Social Security (Recovery of Benefits) (Appeals) Regulations 1997;

(*c*) "the Adjudication Regulations" means the Social Security (Adjudication) Regulations 1995;

(*d*) "legally qualified panel member" has the meaning it bears in regulation 1(3) of the Regulations;

(*e*) "the No 8 Order" means the Social Security Act 1998 (Commencement No 8, and Savings and Consequential and Transitional Provisions) Order 1999;

(*f*) "the No 9 Order" means the Social Security Act 1998 (Commencement No 9, and Savings and Consequential and Transitional Provisions) Order 1999;

(*g*) "the No 11 Order" means the Social Security Act 1998 (Commencement No 11, and Savings and Consequential and Transitional Provisions) Order 1999;

(*h*) "the Regulations" means the Social Security and Child Support (Decisions and Appeals) Regulations 1999; and

(*i*) "relevant benefit" means income support, child's special allowance under section 56 of the Contributions and Benefits Act or, as the case may be, a social fund payment mentioned in section 138(1)(*a*) or (2) of that Act,

and references to sections and Schedules are references to sections of, and Schedules to, the Act.

2 Appointed day

(1) Subject to paragraph (2) below, 29th November 1999 is the day appointed for the coming into force of—

(*a*) the provisions specified in Schedule 1 to this Order; and

(*b*) sections 1 and 4 to 7 in relation to—

(i) statutory sick pay under Part XI of the Contributions and Benefits Act; and

(ii) statutory maternity pay under Part XII of that Act,

in so far as those provisions are not already in force.

NIC

(2) Paragraph (1)(*a*) above shall not apply in relation to—

(*a*) housing benefit;

(*b*) council tax benefit; nor

(*c*) decisions to which article 4(6) of the Social Security Contributions (Transfer of Functions, etc) Act 1999 (Commencement No 1 and Transitional Provisions) Order 1999 applies.

(3) 31st March 2000 is the day appointed for the coming into force of paragraph 10 of Schedule 1 (appeal tribunals: supplementary provisions) and sections 5(3) and 7(7) in so far as they relate to it.

3 Consequential amendments

. . .

Note—This Regulation is not relevant to this publication.

4 Transitional provisions

Schedules 21 to 23 to this Order shall take effect as from 29th November 1999.

SCHEDULE 1

PROVISIONS BROUGHT INTO FORCE ON 29TH NOVEMBER 1999

Article 2(1)

Provision of the Act	*Subject matter*
. . .	. . .
Section 39	Interpretation etc of Chapter II of Part I of the Act
. . .	. . .
Schedule 7 in the respects specified below, and section 86(1) in so far as it relates to them—	Minor and consequential amendments
. . .	. . .
Paragraphs 66 to 73	Miscellaneous provisions relating to benefits, and social fund
. . .	. . .
Paragraph 84	Issues arising in proceedings
. . .	. . .
Paragraph 89	Regulations as to notification of deaths
. . .	
Paragraph 101	Destination of payments
. . .	. . .
Paragraphs 106 to 108	Reciprocal agreements, and travelling expenses
Paragraph 109	Regulations and orders under the Administration Act
. . .	. . .
Paragraph 111	Interpretation of the Administration Act
. . .	. . .
Paragraph 129	Pension Schemes—disclosure of information between government departments etc
. . .	. . .
Schedule 8 in respect of the legislation specified below, and section 86(2) in so far as it relates to it—	Repeals
. . .	. . .
In the Administration Act—	
Part II	
. . .	. . .

Note—Words omitted not relevant to this publication.

SCHEDULE 21

TRANSITIONAL PROVISIONS IN RELATION TO THE RECOVERY OF BENEFITS

Article 4

1—(1) Regulation 2 of the 1997 Regulations shall, notwithstanding regulation 59 of the Regulations continue to have effect until 29th December 2000 in relation to any certificate of recoverable benefits in respect of which a right of appeal arose before 29th November 1999 subject to the modifications specified in sub-paragraph (2) below.

(2) The modifications referred to in sub-paragraph (1) above are as if—

(*a*) for the word "chairman" in each place in which it occurs there were substituted the words "legally qualified panel member";

(*b*) in paragraph (2) the words "of a medical appeal tribunal" were omitted;

(*c*) for paragraph (7) there were substituted the following paragraph—

"(7) Notwithstanding paragraph (2), no appeal may be brought after 29th December 2000.";

(*d*) in paragraph (18) the words from ", notwithstanding that a condition" to the end were omitted; and

(*e*) after paragraph (18) there were added the following paragraph—

"(19) In this regulation "legally qualified panel member" has the meaning it bears in regulation 1(3) of the Social Security and Child Support (Decisions and Appeals) Regulations 1999.".

2 An appeal duly made (but not determined) before 29th November 1999 against a certificate of recoverable benefits shall be referred to and determined by an appeal tribunal under section 12 of the Social Security (Recovery of Benefits) Act 1997.

3—(1) Notwithstanding regulation 39 and Chapter III of Part V of the Regulations, this paragraph applies where a direction ("the direction") was given under regulation 4(1) of the 1997 Regulations.

(2) An appeal tribunal shall hold an oral hearing of an appeal if—

(*a*) sub-paragraph (3) below applies; or

(*b*) the chairman or, in the case of an appeal tribunal which has only one member, that member, is satisfied that such a hearing is necessary to enable the tribunal to reach a decision.

(3) This sub-paragraph applies where a notification that a party to the proceedings wishes an oral hearing to be held is received by a clerk to a medical appeal tribunal before 29th November 1999 or by a clerk to an appeal tribunal (notwithstanding that it was sent to a clerk to a medical appeal tribunal) after that date within—

(*a*) 10 days of receipt by that party of the direction; or

(*b*) such other period as—

(i) the clerk to, or the chairman of, the medical appeal tribunal may have directed; or

(ii) where head (i) above does not apply, a clerk to an appeal tribunal may direct.

(4) An appeal tribunal shall determine an appeal without an oral hearing where sub-paragraph (2) does not apply.

4 An appeal tribunal shall completely rehear any appeal to a medical appeal tribunal in relation to a certificate of recoverable benefits which stands adjourned immediately before 29th November 1999.

5 A copy of a statement of—

(*a*) the reasons for a decision of a medical appeal tribunal in relation to a certificate of recoverable benefits; and

(*b*) its findings on questions of fact material thereto,

shall be supplied to each party to the proceedings before that tribunal, if requested by any such party within 21 days of the date on which notification of that decision was given or sent.

6—(1) Subject to paragraph 1(2) above and sub-paragraph (3) below—

(*a*) regulation 11; and

(*b*) regulations 2(16) and (17) and 12 in so far as they relate to regulation 11,

of the 1997 Regulations shall, notwithstanding regulation 59 of the Regulations, continue to have effect, subject to the modifications specified in sub-paragraph (2) below, in relation to any application to set aside a decision of a medical appeal tribunal in relation to a certificate of recoverable benefits.

(2) The modifications referred to in sub-paragraph (1) above are as if in—

(*a*) regulation 2(16), for the words "the chairman" there were substituted the words "the legally qualified panel member";

NIC

(*b*) regulation 11(1), for the words "the tribunal which gave the decision or by another medical appeal tribunal" there were substituted the words "a legally qualified panel member within the meaning of regulation 1(3) of the Social Security and Child Support (Decisions and Appeals) Regulations 1999";

(*c*) regulation 11(2)—

(i) for the words "the tribunal shall" in both places in which they occur there were substituted the words "the legally qualified panel member shall"; and

(ii) for the words "it is satisfied" there were substituted the words "he is satisfied";

(*d*) regulation 11(3)(*b*), after the words "the office of the clerk to the tribunal which made the relevant decision" there were inserted the words "or to a clerk to an appeal tribunal"; and

(*e*) regulation 11(4)—

(i) for the words "the chairman of the tribunal" there were substituted the words "a legally qualified panel member"; and

(ii) for the words "a chairman" there were substituted the words "a legally qualified panel member".

(3) Sub-paragraph (1) above shall not apply in any case where an application to set aside a decision of a medical appeal tribunal is made after 29th December 2000.

7—(1) Subject to sub-paragraph (2) below, any decision of a medical appeal tribunal under section 12 of the Social Security (Recovery of Benefits) Act 1997 shall be treated as a decision of an appeal tribunal under that section.

(2) Where sub-paragraph (1) above applies, any application for leave to appeal which is made for the purposes of section 14(10)(*a*) shall be—

(*a*) made no later than three months after the date on which a copy of the statement of the reasons for the decision of the medical appeal tribunal was given or sent to the applicant; and

(*b*) determined by a legally qualified panel member.

SCHEDULE 22

TRANSITIONAL PROVISIONS IN RELATION TO RELEVANT BENEFITS

Article 4

1 A decision which fell to be made before 29th November 1999, but which was not made before that date—

(*a*) on a claim for; or

(*b*) under or by virtue of Part II of the Administration Act in relation to,

a relevant benefit (other than a decision which fell to be made on review or on appeal) shall be made by the Secretary of State under paragraph (*a*) or, as the case may be, paragraph (*c*) of section 8(1).

2—(1) Any application duly made before 29th November 1999 under Part II of the Administration Act for a review of a decision in relation to a relevant benefit which was not decided before that date shall on and after that date be treated as an application to the Secretary of State—

(*a*) where the application is not in respect of a decision given on appeal and is made—

(i) within three months of the date on which the applicant was notified of the decision, or within such longer period as may be allowed under sub-paragraph (2) below; and

(ii) other than on the ground of a relevant change of circumstances,

for a revision of that decision under section 9; or

(*b*) in any other case, for a decision under section 10 to supersede that decision.

(2) Subject to sub-paragraphs (3) and (4) below, the period of three months specified in sub-paragraph (1)(*a*) above may be extended where an application for such an extension is made before 29th December 2000 by a claimant or a person acting on his behalf containing—

(*a*) the grounds on which an extension of time is sought; and

(*b*) sufficient details of the decision to enable it to be identified.

(3) An application for an extension of time shall not be granted under sub-paragraph (2) above unless the Secretary of State is satisfied that—

(*a*) it is reasonable to grant that application;

(*b*) the application for review has merit; and

(*c*) special circumstances are relevant to the application for an extension of time as a result of which it was not practicable for the application for review to be made within three months of the date of the adjudication officer's decision being notified to the claimant.

(4) In deciding whether to grant an extension of time no account shall be taken of the following factors—

(*a*) that the claimant or any person acting for him misunderstood or was unaware of the law applicable to his case (including misunderstanding or being unaware of the period specified in sub-paragraph (1)(*a*) above); or (*b*) that a Commissioner or a court has taken a different view of the law from that previously understood and applied by the adjudication officer.

(5) Where, by virtue of sub-paragraph (1)(*b*) above—

(*a*) a decision is made under section 10 which is advantageous to the applicant; and

(*b*) the same decision could have been made on a review prior to 29th November 1999,

that decision shall take effect from the date on which it would have taken effect had the decision been so made.

3—(1) A decision (other than a decision of a social security appeal tribunal or a Commissioner) made before 29th November 1999—

(*a*) on a claim for; or

(*b*) under or by virtue of Part II of the Administration Act in relation to,

a relevant benefit shall be treated as a decision of the Secretary of State under paragraph (*a*) or, as the case may be, paragraph (*c*) of section 8(1).

(2) Where, before 29th November 1999, any person was required to give notice to the claimant of a decision referred to in sub-paragraph (1) above, and such notice was not given before that date, the Secretary of State shall give notice to the claimant of that decision.

4—(1) This paragraph applies where the time limit for making an appeal to a social security appeal tribunal in respect of a decision in relation to a relevant benefit made before 29th November 1999 has not expired before that date.

(2) Where sub-paragraph (1) above applies, regulation 3 of the Adjudication Regulations as it relates to the period within which an appeal may be made, or an extension of that period, shall, notwithstanding regulation 59 of the Regulations, continue to have effect, subject to the modifications in sub-paragraph (3) below, with respect to any appeal to an appeal tribunal made on or after 29th November 1999 in relation to that decision.

(3) The modifications referred to in sub-paragraph (2) above are as if—

(*a*) references to a tribunal, a chairman or a person considering the application were references to a legally qualified panel member; and

(*b*) in paragraph (3E), for the words from "6 years" to the end of the paragraph there were substituted the words "29th December 2000".

(4) Notwithstanding regulation 3 of the Regulations, the Secretary of State may revise under section 9 a decision made before 29th November 1999 on a claim for or award of a relevant benefit (other than a decision made on appeal)—

(*a*) pursuant to an application for a review of a decision made within three months of the notification of that decision; or

(*b*) where an appeal has been duly made against that decision but not determined.

(5) Where a decision is revised pursuant to sub-paragraph (4) above the appeal shall lapse unless the decision as revised is not more advantageous to the appellant than the decision before it was revised.

5 An appeal to a social security appeal tribunal in relation to a relevant benefit which was duly made before 29th November 1999 and which was not determined before that date shall, without prejudice to Chapter III of Part V of the Regulations, be treated as an appeal duly made to an appeal tribunal in relation to a decision of the Secretary of State under section 8.

6—(1) This paragraph applies where a clerk to a social security appeal tribunal has before 29th November 1999 given a direction under regulation 22(1) of the Adjudication Regulations in connection with an appeal in relation to a relevant benefit to that tribunal, and the notification mentioned in paragraph (1A) of that regulation 22 has not been received by the clerk before that date.

(2) A notification in response to such a direction given under that regulation 22(1) shall be—

(*a*) in writing; and

(*b*) made within 14 days of receipt of the direction or within such other period as the clerk to an appeal tribunal may direct.

(3) An appeal may be struck out by the clerk to an appeal tribunal where the notification referred to in sub-paragraph (2) above is not received within the period specified in that sub-paragraph.

(4) An appeal which has been struck out in accordance with sub-paragraph (3) above shall be treated for the purpose of reinstatement as if it had been struck out under regulation 46 of the Regulations.

(5) An oral hearing of the appeal shall be held where—

(*a*) a notification is received by the clerk to the appeal tribunal under sub-paragraph (2) above; or

(*b*) the chairman of the appeal tribunal or, in the case of an appeal tribunal which has only one member, that member, is satisfied that such a hearing is necessary to enable the tribunal to reach a decision.

NIC

7 Where an appeal to a social security appeal tribunal in relation to a relevant benefit has been struck out under regulation 7 of the Adjudication Regulations, a legally qualified panel member may reinstate the appeal on an application by any party to the proceedings made not later than three months from the date of the order under paragraph (1) of that regulation if he is satisfied that—

(*a*) the applicant did not receive a notice under paragraph (2) of that regulation; and

(*b*) the conditions in paragraph (2A) of that regulation were not satisfied,

and the appeal shall be treated as an appeal to an appeal tribunal in relation to a decision of the Secretary of State under section 8.

8 An appeal tribunal shall completely rehear any appeal to a social security appeal tribunal in relation to a relevant benefit which stands adjourned immediately before 29th November 1999.

9 A copy of a statement of—

(*a*) the reasons for a decision of a social security appeal tribunal in relation to a relevant benefit; and

(*b*) its findings on questions of fact material thereto,

shall be supplied to each party to the proceedings before that tribunal, if requested by any such party within 21 days of the date on which notification of that decision was given or sent.

10—(1) Subject to sub-paragraph (2) below, any decision of a social security appeal tribunal in relation to a relevant benefit shall be treated as a decision of an appeal tribunal made under section 12.

(2) Where sub-paragraph (1) above applies, any application for leave to appeal which is made for the purposes of section 14(10)(*a*) shall be—

(*a*) made no later than three months after the date on which a copy of the statement of the reasons for the decision of the social security appeal tribunal was given or sent to the applicant; and

(*b*) determined by a legally qualified panel member.

11—(1) Subject to sub-paragraph (3) below, regulation 10 of the Adjudication Regulations and regulation 3 of those Regulations in so far as it relates to that regulation 10, shall, notwithstanding regulation 59 of the Regulations, continue to have effect, subject to the modifications specified in sub-paragraph (2) below, in relation to any application to set aside a decision of a social security appeal tribunal in relation to a relevant benefit.

(2) The modifications referred to in sub-paragraph (1) above are as if in regulation 3 for the reference to a chairman and in regulation 10(1) the first reference to the adjudicating authority which gave the decision and to an authority of like status, there were substituted references to a legally qualified panel member.

(3) Paragraph (1) above shall not apply in any case where an application to set aside a decision of a social security appeal tribunal is made after 29th December 2000.

12 Where, immediately before 29th November 1999, a payment of relevant benefit was suspended or withheld by virtue of any provision of Part V of the Social Security (Claims and Payments) Regulations 1987 (suspension and extinguishment), the provisions of Chapter I of Part III of the Regulations (suspension and termination) shall apply with respect to that suspension or withholding as if it were a suspension imposed by virtue of those provisions.

13 For the purpose of section 10(1)(b), a decision of a Commissioner made before 29th November 1999 in relation to a relevant benefit shall be treated as a decision of a Commissioner made under section 14.

SCHEDULE 23

TRANSITIONAL PROVISIONS IN RELATION TO THE SOCIAL FUND

Article 4

1 An application to—

(*a*) the social fund shall, from 29th November 1999, be determined by an appropriate officer;

(*b*) to a social fund officer for a review shall, from 29th November 1999, be treated as an application for a review by an appropriate officer.

2 A determination of a social fund officer shall be treated as a determination of an appropriate officer from 29th November 1999.

3 In this Schedule "appropriate officer" has the meaning it bears in section 36(1).

2000/727

SOCIAL SECURITY CONTRIBUTIONS (INTERMEDIARIES) REGULATIONS 2000

Made by the Treasury under SSCBA 1992 ss 4A, 122(1), 175(1A), (2)–(4) and the Inland Revenue under SSC(TF)A 1999 s 8(1)(*m*)

Made . . . .*13 March 2000*
Laid before Parliament . . . .*13 March 2000*
Coming into force . . . .*6 April 2000*

Commentary—*Simon's Taxes* **E4.205**.
Press releases etc—IR Tax Bulletin October 2001 p 819 (Providing services through an intermediary—IR35–what happens next?).

1 Citation, commencement and effect

(1) These Regulations may be cited as the Social Security Contributions (Intermediaries) Regulations 2000 and shall come into force on 6th April 2000.
(2) These Regulations have effect for the tax year 2000–01 and subsequent years and apply in relation to services performed, or to be performed, on or after 6th April 2000.
(3) Payments or other benefits in respect of such services received before that date shall be treated as if received in the tax year 2000–01.

[PART 1:
INTERMEDIARIES – GENERAL PROVISIONS]

2 Interpretation

(1) In these Regulations unless the context otherwise requires—
. . . [5]
"associate" has the meaning given by regulation 3;
"attributable earnings" in relation to a worker shall be construed in accordance with regulation 6(3)(*a*);
["the Board" means the Commissioners for Her Majesty's Revenue and Customs;][4]
. . . [2]
"Class 1A contributions" has the meaning given by section 10 of the Contributions and Benefits Act;
. . . [5]
"company" means any body corporate or unincorporated association, but does not include a partnership;
"the Contributions and Benefits Act" means the Social Security Contributions and Benefits Act 1992;
["the Contributions Regulations" means the Social Security (Contributions) Regulations 2001;][1]
["CTA 2010" means the Corporation Taxes Act 2010(b);][5]
. . . [5]
["public authority" has the meaning given by regulation 3A;][5]
"relevant benefit" means any benefit falling within regulation 4 that is provided to the intermediary or to or on behalf of the worker under the arrangements;
"relevant payment" means any payment made to an intermediary or to or on behalf of the worker under the arrangements;
"secondary Class 1 contributions" has the meaning given by section 6 of the Contributions and Benefits Act;
"secondary contributor" has the meaning given by section 7 of the Contributions and Benefits Act;
["statutory auditor" has the meaning given by Part 42 of the Companies Act 2006;][5]
"the Taxes Act" means the Income and Corporation Taxes Act 1988;
"tax year" means year of assessment;
. . . . [5]

(2) References in these Regulations to payments or benefits received or receivable from a partnership or unincorporated association include payments or benefits to which a person is or may be entitled in his capacity as a member of the partnership or association.
(3) For the purposes of these Regulations—
(*a*) anything done by or in relation to an associate of an intermediary is treated as done by or in relation to the intermediary, and
(*b*) a payment or other benefit provided to a member of an individual's family or household is treated as provided to the individual.
(4) The reference in paragraph (3)(*b*) to an individual's family or household shall be construed in accordance with [sections 721(4) and (5) of ITEPA 2003][3].

NIC

(5) For the purposes of these Regulations a man and a woman living together as husband and wife are treated as if they were married to each other.

[(6) For the purposes of these Regulations two people of the same sex living together as if they were civil partners of each other are treated as if they were civil partners of each other; and, for the purposes of these Regulations, two people of the same sex are to be regarded as living together as if they were civil partners if, but only if, they would be regarded as living together as husband and wife were they instead two people of the opposite sex.][4]

[(7) For the purposes of these Regulations "connected" shall be construed in accordance with section 993 of the Income Tax Act 2007.

(8) For the purposes of these Regulations "controlled" shall be construed in accordance with section 995 of the Income Tax Act 2007.][5]

Amendments—[1] Definition of "the Contributions Regulations" substituted by the Social Security Contributions (Intermediaries) (Amendment) Regulations, SI 2002/703 reg 3 with effect from 6 April 2002.

[2] Definition of "business" revoked by the Social Security Contributions (Intermediaries) (Amendment) Regulations, SI 2003/2079 regs 3, 4 with effect from 2003–04. This amendment applies to services performed or due to be performed after 31 August 2003.

[3] Words in para (4) substituted by the Social Security (Contributions, Categorisation of Earners and Intermediaries) (Amendment) Regulations, SI 2004/770 reg 35(1), (2) with effect from 6 April 2004.

[4] In para (1), definition of "the Board" substituted, and para (6) inserted, by the Social Security Contributions (Intermediaries) (Amendment) Regulations, SI 2005/3131 regs 3, 4 with effect from 2005–06. The amendments apply in relation to services performed, or to be performed, on or after 5 December 2005.

[5] In para (1), definitions of "arrangements", "client", "intermediary" and "worker" revoked (and moved to reg 2A below), definitions of "CTA 2010", "public authority" and "statutory auditor" inserted, and paras (7), (8) inserted, by the Social Security (Miscellaneous Amendments No 2) Regulations, SI 2017/373 reg 2(1)–(4) with effect from 6 April 2017. Revoked definitions previously read as follows—

' "arrangements" means the arrangements referred to in regulation 6(1)(*b*);

"client" shall be construed in accordance with regulation 6(1)(*a*);

"intermediary" has the meaning given by regulation 5;

"worker" means the individual referred to in regulation 6(1)(*a*)'.

[2A Definitions for the purposes of Part 1

In this Part—

"arrangements" means the arrangements referred to in regulation 6(1)(b);
"client" shall be construed in accordance with regulation 6(1)(b);
"intermediary" has the meaning given by regulation 5; and
"worker" means the individual referred to in regulation 6(1)(a).][1]

Amendments—[1] Para 2A inserted by the Social Security (Miscellaneous Amendments No 2) Regulations, SI 2017/373 reg 2(1), (5) with effect from 6 April 2017.

3 Meaning of associate

(1) In these Regulations "associate"—

(*a*) in relation to an individual, has the meaning given by section 417(3) and (4) of the Taxes Act, subject to the following provisions of this regulation;

(*b*) in relation to a company, means a person connected with the company within the meaning of section 839 of the Taxes Act; and

(*c*) in relation to a partnership, means any associate of a member of the partnership.

(2) Where an individual has an interest in shares or obligations of the company as a beneficiary of an employee benefit trust, the trustees are not regarded as associates of his by reason only of that interest except in the following circumstances.

(3) The exception is where—

(*a*) the individual, either on his own or with one or more of his associates, or

(*b*) any associate of his, with or without other such associates,

has been the beneficial owner of, or able (directly or through the medium of other companies or by any other indirect means) to control, more than 5 per cent of the ordinary share capital of the company.

(4) In paragraph (2) "employee benefit trust" has the same meaning as in [sections 550 and 551 of ITEPA 2003][1].

Amendments—[1] Words in para (4) substituted by the Social Security (Contributions, Categorisation of Earners and Intermediaries) (Amendment) Regulations, SI 2004/770 reg 35(1), (3) with effect from 6 April 2004.

[3A Meaning of public authority

(1) In these Regulations "public authority" means—

(*a*) a public authority as defined by the Freedom of Information Act 2000,

(*b*) a Scottish public authority as defined by the Freedom of Information (Scotland) Act 2002,

(*c*) the Corporate Officer of the House of Commons,

(*d*) the Corporate Officer of the House of Lords,

(*e*) the National Assembly for Wales Commission, or

(*f*) the Northern Ireland Assembly Commission.

(2) An authority within paragraph (1)(*a*) or (*b*) is a public authority for the purposes of these Regulations in relation to all its activities even if provisions of the Act mentioned in that paragraph do not apply to all information held by the authority.

(3) Paragraph (1) is subject to paragraph (4).

(4) A primary-healthcare provider is a public authority for the purposes of these Regulations only if the primary-healthcare provider—

(*a*) has a registered patient list for the purposes of relevant medical-services regulations,

(*b*) is within paragraph 43A in Part 3 of Schedule 1 to the Freedom of Information Act 2000 (providers of primary healthcare services in England and Wales) by reason of being a person providing primary dental services,

(*c*) is within paragraph 51 in that Part of that Schedule (providers of healthcare services in Northern Ireland) by reason of being a person providing general dental services, or

(*d*) is within paragraph 33 in Part 4 of Schedule 1 to the Freedom of Information (Scotland) Act 2002 (providers of healthcare services in Scotland) by reason of being a person providing general dental services.

(5) In paragraph (4)—

"primary-healthcare provider" means an authority that is within paragraph (1)(*a*) or (*b*) only because it is within a relevant paragraph,

"relevant paragraph" means—

(*a*) any of paragraphs 43A to 45A and 51 in Part 3 of Schedule 1 to the Freedom of Information Act 2000, or

(*b*) any of paragraphs 33 to 35 in Part 4 of Schedule 1 to the Freedom of Information (Scotland) Act 2002, and

"relevant medical-services regulations" means any of the following—

(*a*) the Primary Medical Services (Sale of Goodwill and Restrictions on Sub-contracting) Regulations 2004,

(*b*) the Primary Medical Services (Sale of Goodwill and Restrictions on Sub-contracting) (Wales) Regulations 2004,

(*c*) the Primary Medical Services (Sale of Goodwill and Restrictions on Sub-contracting) (Scotland) Regulations 2004, and

(*d*) the Primary Medical Services (Sale of Goodwill and Restrictions on Sub-contracting) Regulations (Northern Ireland) 2004.][1]

Amendments—[1] Regulation 3A substituted by the Social Security (Miscellaneous Amendments No 3) Regulations, SI 2017/613 reg 2 with effect from 18 May 2017. Regulation 3A previously read as follows—

"3A **Meaning of public authority**In these Regulations "public authority" means—

(*a*) a public authority as defined by the Freedom of Information Act 2000,

(*b*) a Scottish public authority as defined by the Freedom of Information (Scotland) Act 2002,

(*c*) the Corporate Officer of the House of Commons,

(*d*) the Corporate Officer of the House of Lords,

(*e*) the National Assembly for Wales Commission, or

(*f*) the Northern Ireland Assembly Commission.

An authority within paragraph (*a*) or (*b*) is a public authority for the purposes of these Regulations in relation to all its activities even if provisions of the Act mentioned in that paragraph do not apply to all information held by the authority.".

4 Meaning of benefit

[(1) For the purposes of these Regulations a "benefit" means anything that, if received by an employee for performing the duties of an employment, would be general earnings of the employment.][1]

(2) The amount of a benefit is taken to be—

(*a*) in the case of a cash benefit, the amount received, and

(*b*) in the case of a non-cash benefit, the cash equivalent of the benefit.

(3) The cash equivalent of a non-cash benefit is taken to be whichever is the greater of—

[(*a*) the amount that would, for income tax purposes, be general earnings if the benefit were general earnings from an employment, and][1]

[(*b*) the cash equivalent determined in accordance with section 398(2)(*b*) of ITEPA 2003.][1]

(4) For the purposes of these Regulations a benefit is treated as received—

(*a*) in the case of a cash benefit, when payment is made of or on account of the benefit; and

(*b*) in the case of a non-cash benefit, when it is used or enjoyed.

Amendments—[1] Paras (1), (3)(*a*), (*b*) substituted by the Social Security (Contributions, Categorisation of Earners and Intermediaries) (Amendment) Regulations, SI 2004/770 reg 35(1), (4) with effect from 6 April 2004.

5 Meaning of intermediary

(1) [In this Part][3] "intermediary" means any person, including a partnership or unincorporated association of which the worker is a member—

(*a*) whose relationship with the worker in any tax year satisfies the conditions specified in paragraph (2), (6), (7) or (8), and

(*b*) from whom the worker, or an associate of the worker—

(i) receives, directly or indirectly, in that year a payment or benefit that is not chargeable to tax [as employment income under ITEPA 2003][1], or

(ii) is entitled to receive, or in any circumstances would be entitled to receive, directly or indirectly, in that year any such payment or benefit.

(2) Where the intermediary is a company the conditions are that—

(*a*) the intermediary is not an associated company of the client, within the meaning of section 416 of the Taxes Act by reason of the intermediary and the client both being under the control of the worker, or under the control of the worker and another person; and

(*b*) either—

(i) the worker has a material interest in the intermediary, or

(ii) the payment or benefit is received or receivable by the worker directly from the intermediary, and can reasonably be taken to represent remuneration for services provided by the worker to the client.

(3) A worker is treated as having a material interest in a company for the purposes of paragraph (2)(*a*) if—

(*a*) the worker, alone or with one or more associates of his, or

(*b*) an associate of the worker, with or without other such associates,

has a material interest in the company.

(4) For this purpose a material interest means—

(*a*) beneficial ownership of, or the ability to control, directly or through the medium of other companies or by any other indirect means, more than 5 per cent of the ordinary share capital of the company; or

(*b*) possession of, or entitlement to acquire, rights entitling the holder to receive more than 5 per cent of any distributions that may be made by the company; or

(*c*) where the company is a close company, possession of, or entitlement to acquire, rights that would in the event of the winding up of the company, or in any other circumstances, entitle the holder to receive more than 5 per cent of the assets that would then be available for distribution among the participators.

In sub-paragraph (*c*) "close company" has the meaning given by sections 414 and 415 of the Taxes Act, and "participator" has the meaning given by section 417(1) of that Act.

(5) Where the intermediary is a partnership the conditions are as follows.

(6) In relation to payments or benefits received or receivable by the worker as a member of the partnership, the conditions are—

(*a*) that the worker, alone or with one or more relatives, is entitled to 60 per cent or more of the profits of the partnership; or

(*b*) that most of the profits of the partnership derive from the provision of services under the arrangements—

(i) to a single client, or

(ii) to a single client together with an associate or associates of that client; or

(*c*) that under the profit sharing arrangements the income of any of the partners is based on the amount of income generated by that partner by the provision of services under the arrangements.

In sub-paragraph (*a*) "relative" means [spouse or civil partner][2], parent [or child or remoter relation in the direct line, or brother or sister.][3]

(7) In relation to payments or benefits received or receivable by the worker otherwise than as a member of the partnership, the conditions are that the payment or benefit—

(*a*) is received or receivable by the worker directly from the intermediary, and

(*b*) can reasonably be taken to represent remuneration for services provided by the worker to the client.

(8) Where the intermediary is an individual the conditions are that the payment or benefit—

(*a*) is received or receivable by the worker directly from the intermediary, and

(*b*) can reasonably be taken to represent remuneration for services provided by the worker to the client.

Amendments—[1] Words in para (1)(*b*)(i) substituted by the Social Security (Contributions, Categorisation of Earners and Intermediaries) (Amendment) Regulations, SI 2004/770 reg 35(1), (5) with effect from 6 April 2004.

[2] Words in para (6) substituted by the Social Security Contributions (Intermediaries) (Amendment) Regulations, SI 2005/3131 regs 3, 5 with effect from 2005–06. The amendments apply in relation to services performed, or to be performed, on or after 5 December 2005. See SI 2005/3131 reg 7 for transitional provisions.

[3] In para (1), words substituted for words "In these Regulations", and in para (6), words substituted for words "or remoter forebear, child or remoter issue, or brother or sister", by the Social Security (Miscellaneous Amendments No 2) Regulations, SI 2017/373 reg 2(1), (7), (8) with effect from 6 April 2017.

6 Provision of services through intermediary

(1) [This Part applies][2] where—

(*a*) an individual ("the worker") personally performs, or is under an obligation personally to perform, services [for another person][1] ("the client"),

[(*aa*) the client is not a public authority,][2]

(*b*) the performance of those services by the worker is carried out, not under a contract directly between the client and the worker, but under arrangements involving an intermediary, and

(*c*) the circumstances are such that, had the arrangements taken the form of a contract between the worker and the client, the worker would be regarded for the purposes of Parts I to V of the Contributions and Benefits Act as employed in employed earner's employment by the client.

(2) Paragraph (1)(*b*) has effect irrespective of whether or not—

(*a*) there exists a contract between the client and the worker, or

(*b*) the worker is the holder of an office with the client.

[(2A) Holding office as a statutory auditor of the client does not count as the worker being the holder of an office with the client for the purposes of paragraph 6(2)(*b*).][2]

(3) Where these Regulations apply—

(*a*) the worker is treated, for the purposes of Parts I to V of the Contributions and Benefits Act, and in relation to the amount deriving from relevant payments and relevant benefits that is calculated in accordance with regulation 7 ("the worker's attributable earnings"), as employed in employed earner's employment by the intermediary, and

(*b*) the intermediary, whether or not he fulfils the conditions prescribed under section 1(6)(*a*) of the Contributions and Benefits Act for secondary contributors, is treated for those purposes as the secondary contributor in respect of the worker's attributable earnings,

and Parts I to V of that Act have effect accordingly.

(4) Any issue whether the circumstances are such as are mentioned in paragraph (1)(*c*) is an issue relating to contributions that is prescribed for the purposes of section 8(1)(*m*) of the Social Security Contributions (Transfer of Functions, etc) Act 1999 (decision by officer of the Board).

Simon's Tax Cases—reg 6(1), *Battersby v Campbell (Insp of Taxes)* [2001] STC (SCD) 189; *Lime-IT Ltd v Justin (Officer of the Board of Inland Revenue)* [2003] STC (SCD) 15; *Synaptek Ltd v Young (Insp of Taxes)* [2003] STC 543; *Future Online Ltd (a firm) v Foulds (Insp of Taxes)* [2005] STC 198; *Dragonfly Consultancy Ltd v R&C Comrs* [2008] STC 3030; *R&C Comrs v Larkstar Data Ltd* [2009] STC 1161.

Amendments—[1] Words in para (1)(*a*) substituted by the Social Security Contributions (Intermediaries) (Amendment) Regulations, SI 2003/2079 regs 3, 5 with effect from 2003–04. This amendment applies to services performed or due to be performed after 31 August 2003. However see SI 2003/2079 art 7 for transitional provisions.

[2] In para (1), words substituted for words "These Regulations apply", and paras (1)(*aa*), (2A) inserted, by the Social Security (Miscellaneous Amendments No 2) Regulations, SI 2017/373 reg 2(1), (9)–(11) with effect from 6 April 2017.

7 Worker's attributable earnings—calculation

(1) For the purposes of regulation 6(3)(*a*) the amount of the worker's attributable earnings for a tax year is calculated as follows—

Step one

Find the total amount of all payments and benefits received by the intermediary in that year under the arrangements [but excluding amounts on which Class 1 or Class 1A contributions are payable by virtue of regulation 3 or 4 of the Social Security Contributions (Limited Liability Partnership) Regulations 2014][6], and reduce that amount by 5 per cent.

Step two

Add the amount of any payments and benefits received by the worker in that year under the arrangements, otherwise than from the intermediary, that—

(*a*) are not chargeable to income tax [as employment income under ITEPA 2003][2], and

(*b*) would be so chargeable if the worker were employed by the client.

Step three

Deduct the amount of any expenses met in that year by the intermediary that under [ITEPA 2003][2] would have been deductible from the [taxable earnings of the employment, within the meaning of section 10 of ITEPA 2003, in accordance with section 327(3) to (5) of that Act][2] if the worker had been employed by the client and the expenses had been met by the worker out of [those earnings][2].

Step four

Deduct the amount of any capital allowances in respect of expenditure incurred by the intermediary in that year that could have been claimed by the worker [under Part 2 of the Capital Allowances Act 2001 (plant and machinery allowances) by virtue of section 15(1)(i) of that Act (which provides that employment is a qualifying activity for the purposes of that Part)][2] if the worker had been employed by the client and had incurred the expenditure.

Step five

NIC

Deduct any contributions made in that year for the benefit of the worker by the intermediary to [a registered pension scheme for the purposes of Part 4 of the Finance Act 2004][5] that if made by an employer for the benefit of an employee would not be chargeable to income tax as income of the employee[, and any payments made in that year in respect of the worker by the intermediary in respect of any of the Pensions Act levies][4].

This does not apply to excess contributions made and later repaid.

Step six

Deduct the amount of secondary Class 1 contributions and Class 1A contributions paid by the intermediary for that year in respect of earnings of the worker.

Step seven

Deduct—

(*a*) the amount of any payments made by the intermediary to the worker in that year that constitute remuneration derived from the worker's employment by that intermediary including, where the intermediary is a body corporate and the worker is a director of that body corporate, payments treated as remuneration derived from that employment by virtue of regulation [22(2)][1] of the Contributions Regulations (payments to directors to be treated as earnings), but excluding payments which represent items in respect of which a deduction was made under Step three [and payments within paragraph 25 of Part 10 of Schedule 3 to the Contributions Regulations][6], and

(*b*) the amount of any benefits provided by the intermediary to the worker in that year, being benefits that constitute amounts of [general earnings][3] in respect of which Class 1A contributions are payable, but excluding any benefits which represent items in respect of which a deduction was made under Step three.

If the result at this point is nil or a negative amount, there are no worker's attributable earnings for that year.

Step eight

Find the amount that, together with the amount of secondary Class 1 contributions payable in respect of it, is equal to the amount resulting from Step seven (if that amount is a positive amount).

Step nine

The result is the amount of the worker's attributable earnings for that year.

(2) Where section 559 of the Taxes Act applies (sub-contractors in the construction industry—payments to be made under deduction) the intermediary is treated for the purposes of Step one of the calculation in paragraph (1) as receiving the amount that would have been received had no deduction been made under that section.

(3) For the purpose of calculating the amount of deductible expenses referred to in Step three of the calculation in paragraph (1) it shall be assumed that all engagements of the worker under the arrangements involving the intermediary are undertaken in the course of the same employment.

(4) For the purposes of this regulation any necessary apportionment shall be made on a just and reasonable basis of amounts received by the intermediary that are referable—

(*a*) to the services of more than one worker, or

(*b*) partly to the services of the worker and partly to other matters.

(5) For the purposes of this regulation the time when payments are received by the intermediary or the worker under the arrangements shall be found in accordance with the rules contained in [sections 18 and 19 of ITEPA 2003, subject to the qualification that the worker shall not be treated, by virtue of Rule 2 in section 18, as receiving a payment prior to the time of its actual receipt.][2]

[(6) The reference in Step Three of the calculation in paragraph (1) to expenses met by the intermediary includes expenses met by the worker and reimbursed by the intermediary.][1]

[(7) Where the intermediary is a partnership and the worker is a member of the partnership, expenses met by the worker for and on behalf of the intermediary shall be treated for the purposes of paragraph (6) as expenses met by the worker and reimbursed by the intermediary.][1]

[(8) Where—

(*a*) the intermediary provides a vehicle for the worker, and

(*b*) the worker would have been entitled to an amount of mileage allowance relief under [section 231 of ITEPA 2003][2] for a tax year in respect of the use of the vehicle if the worker had been employed by the client, or would have been so entitled if the worker had been employed by the client and the vehicle had not been a company vehicle,

Step Three of the calculation in paragraph (1) shall have effect as if that amount were an amount of expenses deductible under that Step.][1]

[(9) Where—

(*a*) the intermediary is a partnership,

(*b*) the worker is a member of the partnership, and

(*c*) the worker provides a vehicle for the purposes of the business of the partnership, then for the purposes of paragraph (8) the vehicle shall be regarded as provided by the intermediary for the worker.][1]

[(10) Where the intermediary makes payments to the worker that are exempt from income tax [as employment income under ITEPA 2003][2] by virtue of [section 229 or 233 of ITEPA 2003][2] (mileage allowance payments and passenger payments), paragraph (*a*) of Step Seven of the calculation in paragraph (1) shall have effect as if the intermediary had made payments to the worker that constituted remuneration derived from the worker's employment by the intermediary.][1]

[(11) In this regulation "the Pensions Act levies" means—

(*a*) the administration levy referred to in section 117(1) of the Pensions Act 2004;

(*b*) the initial levy referred to in section 174(1) of that Act;

(*c*) the risk-based pension protection levy referred to in section 175(1)(*a*) of that Act;

(*d*) the scheme-based pension protection levy referred to in section 175(1)(*b*) of that Act;

(*e*) the fraud compensation levy referred to in section 189(1) of that Act;

(*f*) a levy in respect of eligible schemes imposed by regulations made under section 209(7) of that Act (the Ombudsman for the Board of the Pension Protection Fund).][4]

Modifications—See the Social Security Contributions (Intermediaries) (Amendment) Regulations, SI 2003/2079 reg 7 (modification of this regulation for the purposes of the relevant year).

See the Social Security Contributions (Intermediaries) (Amendment) Regulations, SI 2005/3131 reg 7 (modification of this regulation for the purposes of 2005–06).

Amendments—[1] Reference in para (*a*) of step seven substituted, and paras (6)–(10) added, by the Social Security (Contributions) (Intermediaries) (Amendment) Regulations, SI 2002/703 regs 4, 5 with effect from 6 April 2002.

[2] Words in sub-paras (1), (5), (8)(*b*) and (10) substituted by the Social Security Contributions (Intermediaries) (Amendment) Regulations, SI 2003/2079 regs 3, 6 with effect from 2003–04. This amendment applies to services performed or due to be performed after 31 August 2003.

[3] Words in para (1) substituted by the Social Security (Contributions, Categorisation of Earners and Intermediaries) (Amendment) Regulations, SI 2004/770 reg 35(1), (6) with effect from 6 April 2004.

[4] Words in para (1) inserted, and para (11) inserted, by the Social Security Contributions (Intermediaries) (Amendment) Regulations, SI 2005/3131 regs 3, 6 with effect from 2005–06. The amendments apply in relation to services performed, or to be performed, on or after 5 December 2005.

[5] Words substituted by the Social Security Contributions (Intermediaries) (Amendment) Regulations, SI 2005/3131 regs 3, 8, coming into force on 6 April 2006, with effect from 2006–07. The amendments apply in relation to services performed, or to be performed, on or after 6 April 2006.

[6] In para (1), words in steps one and seven inserted by the Social Security Contributions (Limited Liability Partnership) Regulations, SI 2014/3159 reg 6 with effect in relation only to England, Wales and Scotland for the tax year 2014–15 and subsequent tax years.

8 Worker's attributable earnings—deemed payment

(1) The amount referred to in Step nine of the calculation in regulation 7(1) is treated, for the purposes of Parts I to V of the Contributions and Benefits Act, as a single payment of the worker's attributable earnings made by the intermediary on the 5th April in the tax year concerned or, as the case may be, on the date found in accordance with paragraphs (4) to (7), and those Parts of that Act shall have effect accordingly.

(2) The worker's attributable earnings shall be aggregated with any other earnings paid to the worker by the intermediary in the year concerned to or for the benefit of the worker in respect of employed earner's employment, and the amount of earnings related contributions payable in respect of that aggregate amount shall be assessed in accordance with the appropriate earnings period specified in regulation [8][1] of the Contributions Regulations (earnings period for directors), whether or not the worker is a director of a company during that year.

(3) Where the intermediary is a partnership or unincorporated association, the amount referred to in Step nine of the calculation in regulation 7(1) is treated, for the purposes of Parts I to V of the Contributions and Benefits Act, as received by the worker in his personal capacity and not as income of the partnership or association.

(4) If in a tax year—

(*a*) an amount of the worker's attributable earnings is treated as made under paragraph (1), and

(*b*) before the date on which the payment would be treated as made under that paragraph any relevant event (as defined below) occurs in relation to the intermediary,

that amount is treated, for the purposes of Parts I to V of the Contributions and Benefits Act, as having been made immediately before that event or, if there is more than one, immediately before the first of them.

(5) Where the intermediary is a company the following are relevant events—

(*a*) where the worker is a member of the company, his ceasing to be such a member;

(*b*) where the worker holds an office with the company, his ceasing to hold such an office;

(*c*) where the worker is employed by the company, his ceasing to be so employed;

[(*d*) the company ceasing to trade.][1]

(6) Where the intermediary is a partnership the following are relevant events—

(*a*) the dissolution of the partnership or the partnership ceasing to trade or a partner ceasing to act as such;

(*b*) where the worker is employed by the partnership, his ceasing to be so employed.

(7) Where the intermediary is an individual and the worker is employed by him, it is a relevant event if the worker ceases to be so employed.

NIC

(8) The fact that an amount of the worker's attributable earnings is treated as made under paragraph (1) before the end of the tax year concerned does not affect what payments and benefits are taken into account in calculating that amount.

Modifications—See the Social Security Contributions (Intermediaries) (Amendment) Regulations, SI 2003/2079 reg 7 (modification of this regulation for the purposes of the relevant year).

Amendments—[1] Figure in para (2) substituted, and para (5)(*d*) added, by the Social Security (Contributions) (Intermediaries) (Amendment) Regulations, SI 2002/703 reg 6 with effect from 6 April 2002.

9 Multiple intermediaries—general

(1) Regulations 10 and 11 apply where in any tax year the arrangements involve more than one intermediary.

(2) Except as provided by regulations 10 and 11, the provisions of [this Part apply][1] separately in relation to each intermediary.

Amendments—[1] In para (2), words substituted for words "these regulations apply" by the Social Security (Miscellaneous Amendments No 2) Regulations, SI 2017/373 reg 2(1), (12) with effect from 6 April 2017. Publisher's Note: the official version of SI 2017/373 reg 2(12) provides the substituted words "this Part applies", which appears to be a typographical error.

10 Multiple intermediaries—avoidance of double-counting

(1) This regulation applies where a payment or benefit has been made or provided, directly or indirectly, from one intermediary to another intermediary under the arrangements.

(2) In that case, the amount taken into account in relation to any intermediary in Step one or Step two of the calculation in regulation 7(1) shall be reduced to such extent as is necessary to avoid double-counting having regard to the amount so taken into account in relation to any other intermediary.

11 Multiple intermediaries—joint and several liability

(1) Where the arrangements involve more than one intermediary, all the intermediaries are jointly and severally liable, subject to paragraph (3), to pay contributions in respect of the amount of the worker's attributable earnings treated in accordance with regulation 8(1) as paid by any of them—

(*a*) under those arrangements, or

(*b*) under those arrangements together with other arrangements.

(2) For the purposes of paragraph (1), each amount of the worker's attributable earnings shall be aggregated, and the aggregate amount shall be treated for the purposes of regulation 8(1) as a single payment of the worker's attributable earnings, but so that the total liability of the intermediaries to pay contributions in respect of that aggregate amount is not less than it would have been if the arrangements had involved a single intermediary and that aggregate amount had been an amount treated as paid in accordance with regulation 8(1) by a single intermediary.

(3) An intermediary is not jointly and severally liable as mentioned in paragraph (1) if the intermediary has not received any payment or benefit under the arrangements concerned or under any such other arrangements as are mentioned in sub-paragraph (*b*) of that paragraph.

12 Social Security (Categorisation of Earners) Regulations 1978—Saving

Nothing in these Regulations affects the operation of regulation 2 of the Social Security (Categorisation of Earners) Regulations 1978 (treatment of earners in one category of earners as falling within another category and disregard of employments) as that regulation applies to employment listed in paragraph 2 in column (A) of Part I of Schedule 1 to those Regulations (earner supplied through a third person treated as employed earner).

[PART 2—
INTERMEDIARIES – WORKER'S SERVICES PROVIDED TO PUBLIC AUTHORITIES

13 Engagements to which this Part applies

(1) Regulations 14 to 18 apply where—

(*a*) an individual ("the worker") personally performs, or is under an obligation personally to perform, services for another person ("the client"),

(*b*) the client is a public authority,

(*c*) the services are provided not under a contract directly between the client and the worker but under arrangements involving a third party ("the intermediary"), and

(*d*) the circumstances are such that—

(i) if the services were provided under a contract directly between the client and the worker, the worker would be regarded for the purposes of Parts I to V of the Contributions and Benefits Act as employed in employed earner's employment by the client, or

(ii) the worker is an office-holder who holds that office under the client and the services relate to that office.

(2) The references in sub-paragraph (1)(c) to "third party" includes a partnership or unincorporated association of which the worker is a member.

(3) The circumstances referred to in sub-paragraph (1)(*d*) includes the terms on which the services are provided, having regard to the terms of the contracts forming part of the arrangements under which the services are provided.

(4) Holding office as a statutory auditor of the client does not count as holding office under the client for the purposes of sub-paragraph (1)(*d*).

Commentary—*Simon's Taxes* **E4.1001**.

Press releases etc—HMRC Notice, 5 December 2016, "Responses to consultation on intermediaries legislation for public sector off-payroll work" (*SWTI 2016, Issue 49*).

HMRC Guidance Note, 3 February 2017, "Off-payroll working in the public sector—guidance on intermediaries legislation" (*SWTI 2017, Issue 6*).

HMRC Guidance Note, 3 February 2017, "Off-payroll working in the public sector—guidance for fee-payers" (*SWTI 2017, Issue 6*).

HMRC Guidance Note, 3 February 2017, "Off-payroll working in the public sector—guidance for individuals using PSCs" (*SWTI 2017, Issue 6*).

HMRC Guidance Note, 3 February 2017, "Off-payroll working in the public sector—guidance for engagers" (*SWTI 2017, Issue 6*).

HMRC Technical Note, 1 March 2017, "Off-payroll working in the public sector—information for agents" (*SWTI 2017, Issue 9*).

HMRC Guidance Note, 1 March 2017, "Off-payroll working in the public sector—scope of the reform and preparing for 6 April 2017" (*SWTI 2017, Issue 9*).

Amendments—[1] Part 2 (regs 13–23) inserted by the Social Security (Miscellaneous Amendments No 2) Regulations, SI 2017/373 reg 2(1), (13) with effect from 6 April 2017.

[14 Worker treated as receiving earnings from employment

(1) If one of conditions A to C in paragraphs (9) to (11) is met, identify the chain of two or more persons where—

(*a*) the highest person in the chain is the client,

(*b*) the lowest person in the chain is the intermediary, and

(*c*) each person in the chain above the lowest makes a chain payment to the person immediately below them in the chain.

(See regulation 21 for cases where one of conditions A to C is treated as being met).

(2) In this Part—

(*a*) "chain payment" means a payment, or money's worth that can reasonably be taken to be for the worker's services to the client,

(*b*) "make" in relation to a chain payment that is money's worth, means transfer, and

(*c*) "the fee-payer" means the person in the chain immediately above the lowest.

(3) The fee-payer is treated as making to the worker, and the worker is treated as receiving, a payment ("the deemed direct earnings") which is to be treated for the purposes of Parts 1 to 5 of the Contributions and Benefits Act as earnings from an employed earner's employment, but this is subject to paragraphs (5) to (7) and regulations 20 and 22.

(4) The deemed direct earnings are treated as paid at the same time as the chain payment made by the fee-payer.

(5) Paragraphs (6) and (7) apply, subject to regulations 20 and 22, if the fee-payer—

(*a*) is not the client, and

(*b*) is not a qualifying person.

(6) If there is no person in the chain below the highest and above the lowest who is a qualifying person, paragraphs (3) and (4) have effect as if for any reference to the fee-payer there were substituted a reference to the client.

(7) Otherwise, paragraphs (3) and (4) have effect as if for any reference to the fee-payer there were substituted a reference to the person in the chain who—

(*a*) is above the lowest,

(*b*) is a qualifying person, and

(*c*) is lower in the chain than any other person in the chain who—

(i) is above the lowest, and

(ii) is a qualifying person.

(8) In paragraphs (5) to (7) a "qualifying person" is a person who—

(*a*) is resident in the United Kingdom or has a place of business in the United Kingdom,

(*b*) is not a person who is controlled by—

(i) the worker, alone or with one or more associates of the worker, or

(ii) an associate of the worker, with or without other associates of the worker, and

(*c*) if a company, is not one in which—

(i) the worker, alone or with one or more associates of the worker, or

(ii) an associate of the worker, with or without other associates of the worker,

has a material interest (within the meaning given by section 51(4) and (5) of ITEPA 2003(meaning of material interest)).

(9) Condition A is that—

(*a*) the intermediary is a company, and

(*b*) the conditions in regulation 15 are met in relation to the intermediary.

(10) Condition B is that—

(*a*) the intermediary is a partnership,

(*b*) the worker is a member of the partnership,

NIC

(*c*) the provision of the services is by the worker as a member of the partnership, and

(*d*) the condition in regulation 16 is met in relation to the intermediary.

(11) Condition C is that the intermediary is an individual.

(12) Where a payment or money's worth can reasonably be taken to be for both—

(*a*) the worker's services to the client, and

(*b*) anything else,

then, for the purposes of this Part, so much of it as can, on a just and reasonable apportionment, be taken to be for the worker's services is to be treated as (and the rest is to be treated as not being) a payment or money's worth, that can reasonably be taken to be for the worker's services.][1]

Amendments—[1] Part 2 (regs 13–23) inserted by the Social Security (Miscellaneous Amendments No 2) Regulations, SI 2017/373 reg 2(1), (13) with effect from 6 April 2017.

[15 Conditions where intermediary is a company

(1) The conditions mentioned in regulation 14(9)(b) are that—

(*a*) the intermediary is not an associated company of the client that falls within sub-paragraph (2), and

(*b*) the worker has a material interest in the intermediary.

(2) An associated company of the client falls within this paragraph if it is such a company by reason of the intermediary and the client being under the control—

(*a*) of the worker, or

(*b*) of the worker and other persons.

(3) The worker is treated as having a material interest in the intermediary if—

(*a*) the worker, alone or with one or more associates of the worker, or

(*b*) an associate of the worker, with or without other associates of the worker,

has a material interest in the intermediary.

(4) For this purpose "material interest" has the meaning given by section 51(4) and (5) of ITEPA 2003.

(5) In this regulation "associated company" has the meaning given by section 449 of CTA 2010.][1]

Amendments—[1] Part 2 (regs 13–23) inserted by the Social Security (Miscellaneous Amendments No 2) Regulations, SI 2017/373 reg 2(1), (13) with effect from 6 April 2017.

[16 Conditions where intermediary is a partnership

(1) The condition mentioned in regulation 14(10)(*d*) is—

(*a*) that the worker, alone or with one or more relatives, is entitled to 60 per cent or more of the profits of the partnership, or

(*b*) that most of the profits of the partnership derive from the provision of services under engagements to which one or other of this Part and Part 1 applies—

(i) to a single client, or

(ii) to a single client together with associates of that client, or

(*c*) that under the profit sharing arrangements the income of any of the partners is based on the amount of income generated by that partner by the provision of services under engagements to which one or other of this Part and Part 1 applies.

(2) In sub-paragraph (1)(*a*) "relative" means spouse or civil partner, parent or child or remoter relation in the direct line, or brother or sister.

(3) For the purposes of this regulation section 61(4) and (5) of ITEPA 2003 apply as they apply for the purposes of Chapter 8 of that Act.][1]

Amendments—[1] Part 2 (regs 13–23) inserted by the Social Security (Miscellaneous Amendments No 2) Regulations, SI 2017/373 reg 2(1), (13) with effect from 6 April 2017.

[17 Calculation of deemed direct earnings

(1) The amount of the deemed direct earnings is the amount resulting from the following steps—

Step 1

Identify the amount or value of the chain payment made by the person who is treated as making the deemed direct earnings, and deduct from that amount so much of it (if any) as is in respect of value added tax.

Step 2

Deduct, from the amount resulting from Step 1, so much of that amount as represents the direct cost to the intermediary of materials used, or to be used, in the performance of the services.

Step 3

Deduct, at the option of the person treated as making the deemed direct earnings, from the amount resulting from Step 2, so much of that amount as represents expenses met by the intermediary that under ITEPA 2003 would have been deductible from the taxable earnings of the employment under section 10 ITEPA 2003, in accordance with section 327(3) to (5) of that Act, if—

(*a*) the worker had been employed by the client, and

(*b*) the expenses had been met by the worker out of those earnings.

Step 4

If the amount resulting from the preceding Steps is nil or negative, there are no deemed direct earnings. Otherwise, that amount is the amount of the deemed direct earnings.
(2) For the purposes of Step 1 of paragraph (1), exclude amounts on which Class 1 or Class 1A contributions are payable by virtue of regulation 3 or 4 of the Social Security Contributions (Limited Liability Partnership) Regulations 2014.
(3) In paragraph (1), the reference to the amount or value of the chain payment means the amount or value of that payment before the deduction (if any) permitted under regulation 19.
(4) If the actual amount or value of the chain payment mentioned in Step 1 of paragraph (1) is such that its recipient bears the cost of amounts due under the Income Tax (Pay As You Earn) Regulations 2003 or the Contributions Regulations in respect of the deemed direct earnings, that Step applies as if the amount or value of the chain payment were what it would be if the burden of that cost were not being passed on through the setting of the level of the payment.
(5) In Step 3 of paragraph (1), the reference to "expenses met by the intermediary" includes—
(*a*) expenses met by the worker and reimbursed by the intermediary, and
(*b*) where the intermediary is a partnership and the worker is a member of the partnership, expenses met by the worker for and on behalf of the partnership.
(6) The deemed direct earnings are to be assessed on the amount of such earnings paid, or treated as paid, in the earnings period specified in regulations 3 to 6 or 8 of the Contributions Regulations.
(7) For the purposes of paragraph (6), the definition of "regular interval" in regulation 1(2) of the Contributions Regulations is to be read as if "employed earner" were replaced with "intermediary" and the words "of earnings" were deleted.][1]

Amendments—[1] Part 2 (regs 13–23) inserted by the Social Security (Miscellaneous Amendments No 2) Regulations, SI 2017/373 reg 2(1), (13) with effect from 6 April 2017.

[18 Application of Social Security Contributions and Benefits Act 1992 to deemed employment

(1) This regulation applies where deemed direct earnings are treated as having been paid in any tax year under regulation 14.
(2) For the purposes of Parts 1 to 5 of the Contributions and Benefits Act—
(*a*) the amount of any deemed direct earnings calculated under regulation 17 shall be treated as remuneration derived from an employed earner's employment,
(*b*) the worker shall be treated, in relation to the deemed direct earnings as employed in employed earner's employment by the person treated as making the payment of deemed direct earnings,
(*c*) the services were performed, or are to be performed, by the worker in the course of performing the duties of that employment, and
(*d*) the person treated as making the payment of deemed direct earnings shall be treated as the secondary contributor in relation to the deemed direct earnings.][1]

Amendments—[1] Part 2 (regs 13–23) inserted by the Social Security (Miscellaneous Amendments No 2) Regulations, SI 2017/373 reg 2(1), (13) with effect from 6 April 2017.

[19 Deductions from chain payments

(1) This regulation applies if, as a result of regulation 18, a person who is treated as making a payment of deemed direct earnings is required under the Contributions Regulations to pay primary Class 1 contributions to the Commissioners for Her Majesty's Revenue and Customs (the Commissioners) in respect of the payment.
(But see paragraph (4)).
(2) The person may deduct from the underlying chain payment an amount which is equal to the amount payable to the Commissioners in respect of primary Class 1 contributions, but where the amount or value of the underlying chain payment is treated by regulation 17(4) as increased by the cost of any amount due under the Contributions Regulations, the amount that may be deducted is limited to the difference (if any) between the amount of primary Class 1 contributions payable to the Commissioners and the amount of that increase.
(3) Where a person in the chain other than the intermediary receives a chain payment from which an amount has been deducted in reliance on paragraph (2) or this paragraph, that person may deduct the same amount from the chain payment made by them.
(4) This regulation does not apply in a case to which regulation 22(2) applies.
(5) In paragraph (2) "the underlying chain payment" means the chain payment whose amount is used at Step 1 of regulation 17(1) as the starting point for calculating the amount of the deemed direct earnings.][1]

Amendments—[1] Part 2 (regs 13–23) inserted by the Social Security (Miscellaneous Amendments No 2) Regulations, SI 2017/373 reg 2(1), (13) with effect from 6 April 2017.

[20 Information to be provided by clients and consequences of failure

(1) If the conditions in regulation 13(1)(*a*) to (*c*) are met in any case, and a person as part of the arrangements mentioned in regulation 13(1)(*c*) enters into a contract with the client, the client must inform that person (in the contract or otherwise) of which one of the following is applicable—

(*a*) the client has concluded that the condition in regulation 13(1)(*d*) is met in the case;

(*b*) the client has concluded that the condition in regulation 13(1)(*d*) is not met in the case.

(2) If the contract is entered into on or after 6th April 2017, the duty under paragraph (1) must be complied with—

(*a*) on or before the time of entry into the contract, or

(*b*) if the services begin to be performed at a later time, before that later time.

(3) If the contract is entered into before 6th April 2017, the duty under paragraph (1) must be complied with on or before the date the first payment is made under the contract on or after 6th April 2017.

(4) If the information which paragraph (1) requires the client to give to a person has been given (whether in the contract, as required by paragraph (2) or (3) or otherwise), the client must, on a written request by the person, provide the person with a written response to any questions raised by the person about the client's reasons for reaching the conclusion identified in the information.

(5) A response required by paragraph (4) must be provided before the end of 31 days beginning with the day the request for it is received by the client.

(6) If—

(*a*) the client fails to comply with the duty under paragraph (1) within the time allowed by paragraph (2) or (3), or

(*b*) the client fails to provide a response required by paragraph (4) within the time allowed by paragraph (5), or

(*c*) the client complies with the duty under paragraph (1) but fails to take reasonable care in coming to its conclusion as to whether the condition in regulation 13(1)(*d*) is met in the case,

regulations 14(3) and (4) have effect in the case as if for any reference to the fee-payer there were substituted a reference to the client, but this is subject to regulation 22.][1]

Amendments—[1] Part 2 (regs 13–23) inserted by the Social Security (Miscellaneous Amendments No 2) Regulations, SI 2017/373 reg 2(1), (13) with effect from 6 April 2017.

[21 Information to be provided by worker and consequences of failure

(1) In the case of an engagement to which this Part applies, the worker must inform the potential deemed employer of which one of the following is applicable—

(*a*) that one of conditions A to C in regulation 14 is met in the case,

(*b*) that none of conditions A to C in regulation 14 is met in the case.

(2) If the worker has not complied with paragraph (1), then for the purposes of regulation 14(1), one of conditions A to C in regulation 14 is to be treated as met.

(3) In this regulation, "the potential deemed employer" is the person who, if one of conditions A to C in regulation 14 were met, would be treated as making a payment of deemed direct earnings to the worker under regulation 14(3).][1]

Amendments—[1] Part 2 (regs 13–23) inserted by the Social Security (Miscellaneous Amendments No 2) Regulations, SI 2017/373 reg 2(1), (13) with effect from 6 April 2017.

[22 Consequences of providing fraudulent information

(1) Paragraph (2) applies if in any case—

(*a*) a person ("the deemed employer") would, but for this paragraph, be treated by regulation 14(3) as making a payment to another person ("the services-provider"), and

(*b*) the fraudulent documentation condition is met.

(2) Regulation 14(3) has effect in the case as if the reference to the fee-payer were a reference to the services-provider, but

(*a*) regulation 14(4) continues to have effect as if the reference to the fee-payer were a reference to the deemed employer, and

(*b*) Step 1 of regulation 17(1) continues to have effect as referring to the chain payment to be made by the deemed employer.

(3) Paragraph (2) has effect even though that involves the services-provider being treated as both employer and employee in relation to the deemed employment under regulation 14(3).

(4) "The fraudulent documentation condition" is that a relevant person provided any person with a fraudulent document intended to constitute evidence—

(*a*) that the case is not an engagement to which this Part applies, or

(*b*) that none of the conditions A to C in regulation 14 is met in the case.

(5) For the purposes of this regulation a "relevant person" is—

(*a*) the services-provider,

(*b*) a person connected with the services-provider,

(*c*) if the intermediary in the case is a company, an office-holder in that company.][1]

Amendments—[1] Part 2 (regs 13–23) inserted by the Social Security (Miscellaneous Amendments No 2) Regulations, SI 2017/373 reg 2(1), (13) with effect from 6 April 2017.

[23 Prevention of double liability to national insurance contributions and allowance of certain deductions

(1) Paragraph (2) applies where—

(*a*) a person ("the payee") receives a payment ("the end-of-line remuneration") from another person ("the paying intermediary"),

(*b*) the end-of-line remuneration can reasonably be taken to represent remuneration for services of the payee to a public authority,

(*c*) a payment ("the deemed payment") has been treated by regulation 14(3) as paid to the payee,

(*d*) the underlying chain payment can reasonably be taken to be for the same services of the payee to that public authority, and

(*e*) the recipient of the underlying chain payment has (whether by deduction from that payment or otherwise) borne the cost of any amounts due, under Income Tax (Pay As You Earn) Regulations 2003 and Contributions Regulations in respect of the deemed payment from the person treated by regulation 14(3) as making the deemed payment.

(2) For national insurance contributions purposes, the paying intermediary may treat the amount of the end-of-line remuneration as reduced (but not below nil) by the amount (see regulation 17) of the deemed payment less the amount of income tax and primary Class 1 national insurance contributions deducted from that amount.

(3) Nothing in paragraph (2) shall be read as removing a worker's entitlement to Statutory Maternity Pay which would have existed but for the operation of that paragraph.

(4) In sub-paragraph (1)(*d*) "the underlying chain payment" means the chain payment whose amount is used at Step 1 of regulation 17(1) as the starting point for calculating the amount of the deemed direct earnings.][1]

Amendments—[1] Part 2 (regs 13–23) inserted by the Social Security (Miscellaneous Amendments No 2) Regulations, SI 2017/373 reg 2(1), (13) with effect from 6 April 2017.

2000/747

SOCIAL SECURITY CONTRIBUTIONS (NOTIONAL PAYMENT OF PRIMARY CLASS 1 CONTRIBUTION) REGULATIONS 2000

Made by the Treasury under SSCBA 1992 ss 3(2), 6A(2) and (7), 119, 122(1) and 175(3) and (4) and the Commissioners of Inland Revenue, SSCBA 1992, Sch 1, paras 1(1), (8A), 6(1).

Made .... *13 March 2000*

Laid before Parliament .... *14 March 2000*

Coming into force .... *6 April 2000*

1 Citation and commencement

These Regulations may be cited as the Social Security Contributions (Notional Payment of Primary Class 1 Contribution) Regulations 2000 and shall come into force on 6th April 2000.

2 Interpretation

In these Regulations unless the context otherwise requires—

"the Contributions and Benefits Act" means the Social Security Contributions and Benefits Act 1992;

"the principal Regulations" means the Social Security (Contributions) Regulations 1979;

"section 6A(2)" means section 6A(2) of the Contributions and Benefits Act.

3 Introductory

Section 6A(2) (notional payment of primary Class 1 contribution where in any tax week payment of earnings is not less than the current lower earnings limit but does not exceed the current primary threshold) has effect subject to the modifications and exceptions prescribed by regulations 4 to 6 of these Regulations.

4 Prescribed modifications and exceptions

The modification prescribed by this regulation is that section 6A(2) has effect to the extent only that, if the amount of earnings paid in the tax week concerned had exceeded the current primary threshold, the earner would have been liable or entitled under the Contributions and Benefits Act and the principal Regulations to pay a primary Class 1 contribution in respect of those earnings.

5 The exception prescribed by this regulation is that section 6A(2) does not have effect for the purposes of regulation 32 of the principal Regulations (return of contributions).

6 The modification prescribed by this regulation is that, where the earner is a woman who has made an election under regulation 100 of the principal Regulations (elections by married women and widows for liability to pay primary Class 1 contributions at the reduced rate) and that election has not ceased to have effect, section 6A(2) has effect as if the primary Class 1 contribution there referred to had been paid at the reduced rate.

7–9 Consequential amendments to the principal Regulations
(*Revoked by the Social Security (Contributions) Regulations, SI 2001/1004 reg 157, Sch 8 Pt I*).

2000/750

OCCUPATIONAL PENSION SCHEMES (CONTRACTING-OUT) (PAYMENT AND RECOVERY OF REMAINING BALANCES) REGULATIONS 2000

Made by the Secretary of State for Social Security under PSA 1993, ss 41(1D), (1E), 42A(2C), (2D) and 183(1) and the PS(NI)A 1993 ss 37(1D), (1E), 38A(2C), (2D) and 178(1).

Made . . . . *14 March 2000*
Laid before Parliament . . . . *16 March 2000*
Coming into force . . . . *6 April 2000*

1 Citation, commencement and interpretation
(1) These Regulations may be cited as the Occupational Pension Schemes (Contracting-out) (Payment and Recovery of Remaining Balances) Regulations 2000 and shall come into force on 6th April 2000.
(2) In these Regulations—
"the Act" means the Pension Schemes Act 1993;
"the Inland Revenue" means the Commissioners of Inland Revenue;
"the Northern Ireland Act" means the Pension Schemes (Northern Ireland) Act 1993.

2 Payments of amounts to Inland Revenue
(1) A payment by the Inland Revenue of an amount referred to in—
(*a*) subsection (1D) of section 41 of the Act or subsection (1D) of section 37 of the Northern Ireland Act (reduced rates for members of salary related contracted-out schemes—payment of remaining balance);
(*b*) subsection (2C) of section 42A of the Act or subsection (2C) of section 38A of the Northern Ireland Act (reduced rates for members of money purchase contracted-out schemes—payment of remaining balance);
shall be made in accordance with paragraph (2) below.
(2) The payments shall be made—
(*a*) by automated credit transfer into a bank or building society account which relates to the secondary contributor and which accepts payments by automated credit transfer; or
(*b*) in such other manner as the Inland Revenue may in their discretion approve.
(3) Where an amount to which paragraph (1) above applies would otherwise not be a whole number of pence, it shall be adjusted to the nearest whole number of pence, and any amount of a half penny or less shall be disregarded.

3 Recovery of amounts by Inland Revenue
Where the Inland Revenue are, by virtue of section 41(1E) or 42A(2D) of the Act or section 37(1E) or [section 38A(2D) of the Northern Ireland Act][1], entitled to recover an amount from a secondary contributor, that amount—
(*a*) may, where the amount was originally paid by automated credit transfer under regulation 2(2)(*a*) above, be recovered in the same manner; or
(*b*) may be recovered as a debt owed by the secondary contributor to the Inland Revenue.

Amendments—[1] Words substituted by the Occupational and Personal Pension Schemes (Contracting-out) (Miscellaneous Amendments) Regulations, SI 2002/681 reg 10 with effect from 6 April 2002.

2001/769

SOCIAL SECURITY (CREDITING AND TREATMENT OF CONTRIBUTIONS, AND NATIONAL INSURANCE NUMBERS) REGULATIONS 2001

The Secretary of State for Social Security, with the concurrence of the Inland Revenue in so far as required, in exercise of powers conferred by sections 13(3), 22(5), 122(1) and 175(1) to (4) of, and paragraphs 8(1)(*d*) and (1A) and 10 of Schedule 1 to, the Social Security Contributions and Benefits Act 1992 and sections 182C and 189(1) and (3) to (6) of the Social Security Administration Act 1992 and of all other powers enabling him in that behalf and for the purpose only of consolidating other regulations hereby revoked, hereby makes the following Regulations:

Made . . . . *7 March 2001*
Laid before Parliament . . . . *13 March 2001*

Coming into force ....6 April 2001

1 Citation, commencement and interpretation

(1) These Regulations may be cited as the Social Security (Crediting and Treatment of Contributions, and National Insurance Numbers) Regulations 2001 and shall come into force on 6th April 2001.

(2) In these Regulations, including this regulation—

"the Act" means the Social Security Contributions and Benefits Act 1992;

"the Contributions Regulations" means the Social Security (Contributions) Regulations [2001][6];

["contribution-based jobseeker's allowance" means an allowance under the Jobseekers Act 1995 as amended by the provisions of Part 1 of Schedule 14 to the Welfare Reform Act 2012 that remove references to an income-based allowance, and a contribution-based allowance under the Jobseekers Act 1995 as that Act has effect apart from those provisions;][5]

"contribution week" means a period of seven days beginning with midnight between Saturday and Sunday;

"contributory benefit" includes a contribution-based jobseeker's allowance but not an income-based jobseeker's allowance [and includes a contributory employment and support allowance but not an income-related employment and support allowance][3];

["contributory employment and support allowance" means an allowance under Part 1 of the Welfare Reform Act as amended by the provisions of Schedule 3, and Part 1 of Schedule 14, to the Welfare Reform Act 2012 that remove references to an income-related allowance, and a contributory allowance under Part 1 of the Welfare Reform Act as that Part has effect apart from those provisions;][5]

[""due date" (subject to regulation 4(11)) means, in relation to—

(*a*) any Class 1 contribution, the date by which payment falls to be made;

(*b*) any Class 2 contribution which a person is liable or entitled to pay, the 31st January following the end of the year in respect of which it is payable;

(*c*) any Class 3 contribution, the date 42 days after the end of the year in respect of which it is paid;][6]

"earnings factor" has the meaning assigned to it in section 21(5)(*c*) of the Act;

["income-based jobseeker's allowance" has the same meaning as in the Jobseekers Act 1995;][5]

["income-related employment and support allowance" means an income-related allowance under Part 1 of the Welfare Reform Act (employment and support allowance);][3]

"relevant benefit year" has the meaning assigned to it in—

(*a*) section 2(4)(*b*) of the Jobseekers Act 1995, in relation to a contribution-based jobseeker's allowance;

(*b*) paragraph 2(6)(*b*) of Schedule 3 to the Act (contribution conditions for entitlement to short-term incapacity benefit), in relation to short-term incapacity benefit;

[(*c*) paragraph 3(1)(*f*) of Schedule 1 to the Welfare Reform Act (conditions relating to national insurance), in relation to a contributory employment and support allowance.][3]

"relevant time", in relation to short-term incapacity benefit, has the meaning assigned to it in paragraph 2(6)(*a*) of Schedule 3 to the Act;

["the Welfare Reform Act" means the Welfare Reform Act 2007;][3]

"year" means tax year.

[(3) In these Regulations, "official error" means an error made by—

(*a*) an officer of the Department for Work and Pensions or an officer of Revenue and Customs acting as such which no person outside the Department or Her Majesty's Revenue and Customs caused or to which no person outside the Department or Her Majesty's Revenue and Customs materially contributed; or

(*b*) a person employed by a service provider and to which no person who was not so employed materially contributed,

but excludes any error of law which is shown to have been an error by virtue of a subsequent decision of [the Upper Tribunal][4] or the court.

(4) In paragraph (3)—

. . . [4]

"service provider" means a person providing services to the Secretary of State for Work and Pensions or to Her Majesty's Revenue and Customs.][2]

Amendments—[2] Paras (3), (4) inserted by the Social Security (National Insurance Credits) Amendment Regulations, SI 2007/2582 reg 4(1), (2) with effect from 1 October 2007: SI 2007/2582 reg 1.

[3] In para (1), in definition of "contributory benefit", words inserted, definitions of "income-related employment and support allowance" and "the Welfare Reform Act" inserted, and in definition of "relevant benefit year" sub-para (*c*) inserted, by the Employment and Support Allowance (Consequential Provisions) (No 2) Regulations, SI 2008/1554 reg 49(1), (2) with effect from 27 October 2008.

[4] In para (3), words substituted, and in para (4), definition of "Commissioner" repealed, by the Tribunals, Courts and Enforcement Act 2007 (Transitional and Consequential Provisions) Order, SI 2008/2683 art 6(1), Sch 1 para 147 with effect from 3 November 2008.

5 In para (2), definitions substituted for previous definitions " 'contribution-based jobseeker's allowance' and 'income-based jobseeker's allowance' " and ' "contributory employment and support allowance' ", and definition "income-based jobseeker's allowance" inserted, by the Universal Credit (Consequential, Supplementary, Incidental and Miscellaneous Provisions) Regulations, SI 2013/630 reg 71 with effect from 29 April 2013.

6 In para 1, in definition "the Contribution Regulations", year substituted for year "1979", and definition "due date substituted, by the Social Security (Credits, and Crediting and Treatment of Contributions) (Consequential and Miscellaneous Amendments) Regulations, SI 2016/1145 reg 5(1), (2) with effect from 1 January 2017. Definition "due date" previously read as follows—

""due date" (subject to regulation 4(11)) means, in relation to any contribution which a person is—

(*a*) liable to pay, the date by which payment falls to be made in accordance with Part IV of the Contributions Regulations;

(*b*) entitled, but not liable, to pay, the date 42 days after the end of the year in respect of which it is paid;".

2 Appropriation of Class 3 contributions

Any person paying Class 3 contributions in one year may appropriate such contributions to the earnings factor of another year if such contributions are payable in respect of that other year or, in the absence of any such appropriation, the Inland Revenue may, with the consent of the contributor, make such appropriation.

3 Crediting of Class 3 contributions

Where, for any year, a contributor's earnings factor derived from—

(*a*) earnings upon which primary Class 1 contributions have been paid or treated as paid;

(*b*) credited earnings;

(*c*) Class 2 or Class 3 contributions paid by or credited to him; or

(*d*) any or all of such earnings and contributions,

falls short of a figure which is 52 times that year's lower earnings limit for Class 1 contributions by an amount which is equal to, or less than, half that year's lower earnings limit, that contributor shall be credited with a Class 3 contribution for that year.

4 Treatment for the purpose of any contributory benefit of late paid contributions

(1) Subject to the provisions of regulations 5 [to 6C][4] below and regulation [61][6] of the Contributions Regulations (voluntary Class 2 contributions not paid within permitted period), for the purpose of entitlement to any contributory benefit, [paragraphs (1B)][5] to (9) below shall apply to contributions ("relevant contributions")—

(*a*) paid after the due date; or

(*b*) treated as paid after the due date under regulation 7(2) below.

[(1A) Any relevant contribution which is paid—

(*a*) by virtue of an official error; and

(*b*) more than six years after the end of the year in which the contributor was first advised of that error,

shall be treated as not paid.][2]

[(1B) Where contributions are paid in accordance with regulation 63A of the Social Security (Contributions) Regulations 2001 (collection of unpaid Class 2 contributions through PAYE code), any relevant contributions are to be treated as paid on 5th April of the tax year in which they are paid.][5]

(2) Subject to the provisions of paragraph (4) below, any relevant contribution other than one referred to in paragraph (3) below—

(*a*) if paid [after the end of the second year][6]—

(i) . . . [6] following the year in which liability for that contribution arises, [or][6]

[(ii) following the year in respect of which a person is entitled, but not liable, to pay the contribution,][6]

shall be treated as not paid;

(*b*) if paid before the end of the said second year, shall, subject to paragraphs (7) and (8) below, be treated as paid on the date on which payment of the contribution is made.

(3) Subject to the provisions of paragraph (4) below, any relevant Class 2 contribution payable in respect of a contribution week after 5th April 1983 or any relevant Class 3 contribution payable in respect of a year after 5th April 1982—

(*a*) if paid [after the end of the sixth year][6]—

(i) . . . [6] following the year in which liability for that contribution arises, [or][6]

[(ii) following the year in respect of which a person is entitled, but not liable, to pay the contribution,][6]

shall be treated as not paid;

(*b*) if paid before the end of the said sixth year, shall, subject to paragraphs (7) [or][6] (8) below, be treated as paid on the date on which payment of the contribution is made.

(4) A Class 3 contribution payable by a person to whom regulation [48(3)(*b*)(ii) or (iii)][6] of the Contributions Regulations (which specify the conditions to be complied with before a person may pay a Class 3 contribution) applies in respect of a year which includes a period of education, apprenticeship, training, imprisonment or detention in legal custody such as is specified in that regulation—

(*a*) if paid after the end of the sixth year specified in that regulation, shall be treated as not paid;

(*b*) if paid before the end of the said sixth year shall, subject to the provisions of paragraphs (7) and (8) below, be treated as paid on the date on which payment of the contribution is made.

(5) Notwithstanding the provisions of paragraph (4) above, for the purpose of entitlement to any contributory benefit, where—

(*a*) a Class 3 contribution other than one referred to in sub-paragraph (*b*) below which is payable in respect of a year specified in that sub-paragraph, is paid after—

(i) the due date, and

(ii) the end of the second year following the year preceding that in which occurred the relevant time or, as the case may be, the relevant event,

that contribution shall be treated as not paid;

(*b*) in respect of a year after 5th April 1982, a Class 3 contribution which is payable in respect of a year specified in paragraph (4) above, is paid after—

(i) the due date, and

(ii) the end of the sixth year following the year preceding that in which occurred the relevant time or, as the case may be, the relevant event,

that contribution shall be treated as not paid.

(6) For the purposes of paragraph (5) above, "relevant event" means the date on which the person concerned attained pensionable age or, as the case may be, died under that age.

(7) Notwithstanding the provisions of paragraphs (2), (3) and (4) above, in determining whether the relevant contribution conditions are satisfied in whole or in part for the purpose of entitlement to any contributory benefit, any relevant contribution which is paid within the time specified in paragraph (2)(*b*), (3)(*b*) or, as the case may be, (4)(*b*) above shall be treated—

(*a*) for the purpose of entitlement in respect of any period before the date on which the payment of the contribution is made, as not paid; and

(*b*) subject to the provisions of paragraph (8) below, for the purpose of entitlement in respect of any other period, as paid on the date on which the payment of the contribution is made.

[(7A) In determining whether the relevant contribution conditions are satisfied in whole or in part for the purpose of entitlement to any contributory benefit, any relevant contribution which is treated as paid on the date specified in paragraph (1B) shall be treated—

(*a*) for the purpose of entitlement in respect of any period before the date on which payment of the contribution is treated as paid, as not paid; and

(*b*) subject to the provisions of paragraph (8) below, for the purpose of entitlement in respect of any other period, as paid on the date specified in paragraph (1B).][5]

[(8) For the purpose of determining whether the second contribution condition for entitlement to a contribution-based jobseeker's allowance or a contributory employment and support allowance is satisfied in whole or in part a relevant contribution is to be treated—

(*a*) if a Class 1 contribution paid before the beginning of the relevant benefit year, as paid on the due date;

(*b*) if, subject to paragraph (2)(*a*), a Class 1 contribution paid after the end of the benefit year immediately preceding the relevant benefit year or, subject to paragraph (3)(*a*), a Class 2 contribution—

(i) as not paid in relation to the benefit claimed in respect of any day before the expiry of a period of 42 days (including Sundays) commencing with the date on which the payment of that contribution is made; and

(ii) as paid at the expiry of that period in relation to entitlement to such benefit in respect of any other period.][6]

(9) For the purposes of paragraph (8) above, "second contribution condition" in relation to—

(*a*) a contribution-based jobseeker's allowance is a reference to the condition specified in section 2(1)(*b*) of the Jobseekers Act 1995;

(*b*) short-term incapacity benefit is a reference to the condition specified in paragraph 2(3) of Schedule 3 to the Act;

[(*c*) a contributory employment and support allowance is a reference to the condition specified in paragraph 2(1) of Schedule 1 to the Welfare Reform Act][3].

(10) This regulation shall not apply to Class 4 contributions.

NIC

[(11) Where an amount is retrospectively treated as earnings ("retrospective earnings") by regulations made by virtue of section 4B(2) of the Act, the "due date" for earnings-related contributions in respect of those earnings is the date given by paragraph 11A of Schedule 4 to the Social Security (Contributions) Regulations 2001, for the purposes of this regulation and regulations 5 and 5A.][1]

Amendments—[1] Paragraph (11) inserted by the Social Security, Occupational Pension Schemes and Statutory Payments (Consequential Provisions) Regulations, SI 2007/1154 reg 2(1), (3). These Regulations come into force on 6 April 2007 and have effect from 2 December 2004.

[2] Para (1A) inserted, by the Social Security (National Insurance Credits) Amendment Regulations, SI 2007/2582 reg 4(3) with effect from 1 October 2007: SI 2007/2582 reg 1.

[3] In para (8), words substituted, and para (9)(*c*) inserted, by the Employment and Support Allowance (Consequential Provisions) (No 2) Regulations, SI 2008/1554 reg 49(1), (3) with effect from 27 October 2008.

[4] In para (1), reference substituted by the Social Security (Additional Class 3 National Insurance Contributions) Amendment Regulations, SI 2009/659 reg 3(1), (2) with effect from 6 April 2009.

[5] In para (1), words substituted, and paras (1B), (7A) inserted by the Social Security (Crediting and Treatment of Contributions, and National Insurance Numbers) (Amendment) Regulations, SI 2013/3154 reg 2 with effect from 6 April 2014.

[6] The following amendments made by the Social Security (Credits, and Crediting and Treatment of Contributions) (Consequential and Miscellaneous Amendments) Regulations, SI 2016/1145 reg 5(1), (3) with effect from 1 January 2017—

- in para (1), reference substituted for reference "40", and in para (4) reference substituted for reference "27(3)(*b*)(ii) or (iii)";
- in paras (2)(*a*), (3)(*a*), words inserted;
- in para (2)(*a*)(i), words "after the end of the second year" revoked, and in para (3)(*a*)(i), words "after the end of the sixth year" revoked;
- paras (2)(*a*)(ii), (3)(*a*)(ii), (8) revoked; and
- in para (3)(*b*), word substituted for word "and".

Para (2)(*a*)(ii) previously read as follows—

"(ii) following the due date for that contribution in the case of a contribution which a person is entitled, but not liable, to pay,".

Para (3)(*a*)(ii) previously read as follows—

"(ii) following the due date for that contribution in the case of a contribution which a person is entitled, but not liable, to pay,".

Para (8) previously read as follows—

"(8) For the purpose of determining whether the second contribution condition for entitlement to a contribution-based jobseeker's allowance[, short-term incapacity benefit or a contributory employment and support allowance][3] is satisfied in whole or in part, any relevant contribution shall be treated—

(*a*) if paid before the beginning of the relevant benefit year, as paid on the due date;

(*b*) if paid after the end of the benefit year immediately preceding the relevant benefit year, as not paid in relation to the benefit claimed in respect of any day before the expiry of a period of 42 days (including Sundays) commencing with the date on which the payment of that contribution is made, and, subject to the provisions of paragraphs (2)(*a*) and (3)(*a*) above, as paid at the expiry of that period in relation to entitlement to such benefit in respect of any other period.".

5 Treatment for the purpose of any contributory benefit of late paid primary Class 1 contributions where there was no consent, connivance or negligence by the primary contributor

(1) This regulation applies where a primary Class 1 contribution which is payable on a primary contributor's behalf by a secondary contributor—

(*a*) is paid after the due date; or

(*b*) in relation to any claim for—

(i) a contribution-based jobseeker's allowance, is not paid before the beginning of the relevant benefit year, . . . [2]

(ii) short-term incapacity benefit, is not paid before the relevant time, [or

(iii) a contributory employment and support allowance, is not paid before the beginning of the relevant benefit year,][2]

and the delay in making payment is shown to the satisfaction of [an officer of][1] the Inland Revenue not to have been with the consent or connivance of, or attributable to any negligence on the part of, the primary contributor.

(2) Where paragraph (1) above applies, the primary Class 1 contribution shall be treated—

(*a*) for the purpose of the first contribution condition of entitlement to a contribution-based jobseeker's allowance or short-term incapacity benefit, as paid on the day on which payment is made of the earnings in respect of which the contribution is payable; and

(*b*) for any other purpose relating to entitlement to any contributory benefit, as paid on the due date.

(3) For the purposes of this regulation—

(*a*) "first contribution condition" in relation to—

(i) a contribution-based jobseeker's allowance is a reference to the condition specified in section 2(1)(*a*) of the Jobseekers Act 1995,

(ii) short-term incapacity benefit is a reference to the condition specified in paragraph 2(2) of Schedule 3 to the Act;

[(iii) a contributory employment and support allowance is a reference to the condition specified in paragraph 1(1) of Schedule 1 to the Welfare Reform Act;][2]

(*b*) "primary contributor" means the person liable to pay a primary Class 1 contribution in accordance with section 6(4)(*a*) of the Act (liability for Class 1 contributions);

(*c*) "secondary contributor" means the person who, in respect of earnings from employed earner's employment, is liable to pay a secondary Class 1 contribution in accordance with section 6(4)(*b*) of the Act.

Amendments—[1] Words in para (1) inserted by the Social Security (Contributions) (Amendment No 3) Regulations, SI 2002/2366 reg 19(1), (2) with effect from 8 October 2002.

[2] In para (1)(*b*), word in sub-para (i) repealed and sub-para (iii) and preceding word inserted, and para (3)(*a*)(iii) inserted, by the Employment and Support Allowance (Consequential Provisions) (No 2) Regulations, SI 2008/1554 reg 49(1), (4) with effect from 27 October 2008.

5A [Treatment for the purpose of any contributory benefit of duly paid primary Class 1 contributions in respect of retrospective earnings

Where a primary Class 1 contribution payable in respect of retrospective earnings is paid by the due date, it shall be treated—

(*a*) for the purposes of the first contribution condition of entitlement to a contribution-based jobseeker's allowance[, short-term incapacity benefit or a contributory employment and support allowance][2], as paid on the day on which payment is made of the retrospective earnings in respect of which the contribution is payable; and

(*b*) for any other purpose relating to entitlement to any contributory benefit, as paid on the due date.[1]

[1] Regulation inserted by the Social Security, Occupational Pension Schemes and Statutory Payments (Consequential Provisions) Regulations, SI 2007/1154 reg 2(1), (4). These Regulations come into force on 6 April 2007 and have effect from 2 December 2004.

[2] In para (a), words substituted by the Employment and Support Allowance (Consequential Provisions) (No 2) Regulations, SI 2008/1554 reg 49(1), (5) with effect from 27 October 2008.

6 Treatment for the purpose of any contributory benefit of contributions under the Act paid late through ignorance or error

(1) In the case of a contribution paid by or in respect of a person after the due date, where—

(*a*) the contribution is paid after the time when it would, under regulation 4 or 5 above, have been treated as paid for the purpose of entitlement to contributory benefit; and

(*b*) it is shown to the satisfaction of [an officer of][1] the Inland Revenue that the failure to pay the contribution before that time is attributable to ignorance or error on the part of that person or the person making the payment and that that ignorance or error was not due to any failure on the part of such person to exercise due care and diligence,

[an officer of the Inland Revenue may direct][1] that, for the purposes of those regulations, the contribution shall be treated as paid on such earlier day as [the officer considers][1] appropriate in the circumstances, and those regulations shall have effect subject to any such direction.

(2) This regulation shall not apply to a Class 4 contribution.

Simon's Tax Cases—*R&C Comrs v Thompson* [2007] STC 240.

Amendments—[1] Words in para (1) substituted by the Social Security (Contributions) (Amendment No 3) Regulations, SI 2002/2366 reg 19(1), (3) with effect from 8 October 2002.

6A [Treatment for the purposes of any contributory benefit of certain Class 3 contributions

(1) For the purposes of entitlement to any contributory benefit, this regulation applies in the case of a Class 3 contribution paid after the due date—

(*a*) which would otherwise under regulation 4—

(i) have been treated as paid on a day other than on the day on which it was actually paid; or

(ii) have been treated as not paid; and

(*b*) which is paid in respect of a year after 5th April 1996 but before 6th April 2002.

(2) A contribution referred to in paragraph (1), where it is paid on or before 5th April 2009 by or in respect of a person who attains pensionable age on or after 6th April 2008, shall be treated as paid on the day on which it is paid.

(3) A contribution referred to in paragraph (1), where it is paid on or before 5th April 2009 by or in respect of a person who attains pensionable age on or after 24th October 2004 but before 6th April 2008, shall be treated as paid on—

(*a*) the day on which it is paid; or

(*b*) the date on which the person attained pensionable age,

whichever is the earlier.

NIC

(4) A contribution referred to in paragraph (1), where it is paid on or before 5th April 2010 by or in respect of a person who attains pensionable age on or after 6th April 1998 but before 24th October 2004, shall be treated as paid on—

(*a*) 1st October 1998; or

(*b*) the date on which the person attained pensionable age,

whichever is the later.][1]

Amendments—[1] Regulation 6A inserted by the Social Security (Crediting and Treatment of Contributions, and National Insurance Numbers) Amendment Regulations, SI 2004/1361 reg 2(*b*) with effect from 17 May 2004.

6B [Treatment for the purpose of any contributory benefit of certain Class 2 or Class 3 contributions

For the purpose of entitlement to any contributory benefit, a Class 2 or a Class 3 contribution paid after the due date—

(*a*) which would otherwise under regulation 4 (apart from paragraph (1A) of that regulation)—

(i) have been treated as paid on a day other than the day on which it was actually paid; or

(ii) have been treated as not paid; and

(*b*) which was paid after the due date by virtue of an official error,

shall be treated as paid on the day on which it is paid.][1]

Amendments—[1] Regulation 6B inserted, by the Social Security (National Insurance Credits) Amendment Regulations, SI 2007/2582 reg 4(4) with effect from 1 October 2007: SI 2007/2582 reg 1.

6C [Treatment of Class 3 contributions paid under section 13A of the Act

(1) This regulation applies to a Class 3 contribution paid by an eligible person under section 13A (right to pay additional Class 3 contributions in certain cases) of the Act.

(2) A contribution paid after 5th April 2009 but before 6th April 2011 shall be treated as paid on—

(*a*) the day on which it is paid; or

(*b*) the date on which the person attained pensionable age,

whichever is the earlier.

(3) A contribution paid after 5th April 2011 shall be treated as paid on the day on which it is paid.][1]

Amendments—[1] Regulation 6C inserted by the Social Security (Additional Class 3 National Insurance Contributions) Amendment Regulations, SI 2009/659 reg 3(1), (3) with effect from 6 April 2009.

7 [Treatment for the purpose of any contributory benefit of contributions paid under certain provisions relating to the payment and collection of contributions][1]

[(1) Subject to the provisions of paragraph (2), for the purpose of entitlement to any contributory benefit except a contribution-based jobseeker's allowance or a contributory employment and support allowance, where—

(*a*) person pays a Class 2 contribution under section 11(2) or (6) of the Act, or a Class 3 contribution in accordance with regulation 89, 89A, 90 or 148C of the Contributions Regulations (provisions relating to the method of, and time for, payment of Class 2 and Class 3 contributions etc.); and

(*b*) the due date for payment of that contribution is a date after the relevant day,

that contribution is treated as paid by the relevant day.][1]

(2) Where, in respect of any part of a late notification period, a person pays a Class 2 contribution which he is liable [or entitled][1] to pay, that contribution shall be treated as paid after the due date, whether or not it was paid by the due date.

(3) For the purposes of this regulation—

(*a*) "late notification period" means the period beginning with the day a person liable [or entitled][1] to pay a Class 2 contribution was first required to notify the Inland Revenue in accordance with the provisions of regulation [87, 87A or 87AA][1] of the Contributions Regulations (notification of commencement or cessation of payment of Class 2 or Class 3 contributions) and ending on the [day on][1] which he gives that notification;

(*b*) "relevant day" means the first day in respect of which a person would have been entitled to receive the contributory benefit in question if any contribution condition relevant to that benefit had already been satisfied;

(c) "contribution quarter" means one of the four periods of not less than 13 contribution weeks commencing on the first day of the first, fourteenth, twenty-seventh or fortieth contribution week, in any year.[1]

Amendments—[1] The following amendments made by the Social Security (Credits, and Crediting and Treatment of Contributions) (Consequential and Miscellaneous Amendments) Regulations, SI 2016/1145 reg 5(1), (4) with effect from 1 January 2017—

– heading and para (1) substituted;
– in paras (2), (3)(*a*), words inserted;
– in para (3)(*a*), reference substituted for reference "53A", and words substituted for words "last day of the contribution quarter immediately before the contribution quarter in"; and
– para (3)(*c*) revoked.

Heading previously read as follows—

"Treatment for the purpose of any contributory benefit of contributions paid under regulation 54 of the Contributions Regulations".

Para (1) previously read as follows—

"(1) Subject to the provisions of paragraph (2) below, for the purpose of entitlement to any contributory benefit, where—

(*a*) a person pays a Class 2 or Class 3 contribution in accordance with regulation 54 of the Contributions Regulations (method of, and time for, payment of Class 2 and Class 3 contributions etc.); and

(*b*) the due date for payment of that contribution is a date after the relevant day,

that contribution shall be treated as paid by the relevant day.".

[7A Treatment for the purpose of a contribution-based jobseeker's allowance or a contributory employment and support allowance of Class 2 contributions paid in accordance with the Act

(1) For the purpose of entitlement to a contribution-based jobseeker's allowance or a contributory employment and support allowance, a Class 2 contribution is to be treated as paid as set out in paragraph (2) if the contribution is paid—

(*a*) in relation to—

(i) a contribution-based jobseeker's allowance, on or after the first day of the week for which the jobseeker's allowance is claimed; or

(ii) contributory employment and support allowance, on or after the first day of the relevant benefit week; and

(*b*) by the due date.

(2) The contribution is treated as paid—

(*a*) in relation to a contribution-based jobseeker's allowance, before the week for which the jobseeker's allowance is claimed; or

(*b*) in relation to a contributory employment and support allowance, before the relevant benefit week.

(3) "Relevant benefit week" has the meaning given in paragraph 5 of Schedule 1 to the Welfare Reform Act.][1]

Amendments—[1] Regulation 7A inserted by the Social Security (Credits, and Crediting and Treatment of Contributions) (Consequential and Miscellaneous Amendments) Regulations, SI 2016/1145 reg 5(1), (5) with effect from 1 January 2017.

8 Treatment for the purpose of any contributory benefit of contributions paid under an arrangement

For the purposes of regulations 4 to [7A][1] above and regulation [61][1] of the Contributions Regulations (voluntary Class 2 contributions not paid within permitted period)—

(*a*) where a contribution is paid under an arrangement to which regulations [68 and 84][1] or, as the case may be, regulation [90][1] of the Contributions Regulations (other methods of collection and recovery of earnings-related contributions; special provisions relating to primary Class 1 contributions and arrangements approved by the Inland Revenue for method of, and time for, payment of Class 2 and Class 3 contributions respectively) apply, the date by which, but for the said regulations 4 to [7A][1] and [61][1], the contribution would have fallen due to be paid shall, in relation to that contribution, be the due date;

(*b*) any payment made of, or as on account of, a contribution in accordance with any such arrangement shall, on and after the due date, be treated as a contribution paid on the due date.

Amendments—[1] References substituted for references "7", "40", "46 and 48" and "54A", by the Social Security (Credits, and Crediting and Treatment of Contributions) (Consequential and Miscellaneous Amendments) Regulations, SI 2016/1145 reg 5(1), (6) with effect from 1 January 2017.

9 Application for allocation of national insurance number

(1) Subject to the provisions of [paragraphs (2) and (2A)][3] below, every person, who is over the age of 16 and satisfies the conditions specified in regulation 87 or 119 of the Contributions Regulations (conditions of domicile or residence and conditions as to residence or presence in Great Britain respectively), shall, unless he has already been allocated a national insurance number under the Act, the Social Security Act 1975 or the National Insurance Act 1965, apply either to the Secretary of State or to the Inland Revenue for the allocation of a national insurance number and shall make such application at such time and in such manner as the Secretary of State shall direct.

[(1A) An application under paragraph (1) shall be accompanied by a document of a description specified [in Schedule 1][2]][1]

(2) As respects any person who is neither an employed earner nor a self-employed earner the provisions of paragraph (1) above shall not apply unless and until that person wishes to pay a Class 3 contribution.

[(2A) The provisions of paragraph (1) shall not apply to a person in respect of whom the Secretary of State or the Commissioners for Her Majesty's Revenue and Customs are notified that a biometric immigration document is to be issued pursuant to regulation 13 [or 13A][4] of the Immigration (Biometric Registration) Regulations 2008.][3]

NIC

(3) The Secretary of State may authorise arrangements for the allocation of a national insurance number to any person during the 12 months before that person reaches the age of 16, and in particular may direct that a person who will attain the age of 16 within 12 months after such direction shall apply for the allocation of a national insurance number before attaining the age of 16, and any such person shall accordingly comply with such direction.

[(4) Where a person—

(*a*) qualifies for a loan made in accordance with regulations made under section 22 of the Teaching and Higher Education Act 1998 (new arrangements for giving financial support to students) or sections 73 to 74(1) of the Education (Scotland) Act 1980 in connection with an academic year beginning on or after 1st September 2007; and

(*b*) has been required as a condition of entitlement to payment of the loan to provide his national insurance number,

he shall, unless he has already been allocated a national insurance number, apply to the Secretary of State or the Commissioners for Her Majesty's Revenue and Customs for one to be allocated to him, and the Secretary of State or, as the case may be, the Commissioners may direct how the application is to be made.][1]

Amendments—[1] Paras (1A), (4) inserted by the Social Security (National Insurance Numbers) Amendment Regulations, SI 2006/2897 reg 2 with effect from 1 March 2007.

[2] Words in para (1A) substituted by the Social Security (National Insurance Numbers) Amendment Regulations, SI 2008/223 reg 2(1), (2) with effect from 29 February 2008.

[3] In para (1), words substituted for words "paragraph (2)", and para (2A) inserted, by the Social Security (Miscellaneous Amendments) Regulations, SI 2015/67 reg 5 with effect from 23 February 2015.

[4] In para (2A), words inserted by the Social Security (Crediting and Treatment of Contributions, and National Insurance Numbers) (Amendment) Regulations, SI 2015/1828 reg 2 with effect from 30 Novemebr 2015.

10 Deduction of contribution from pensions etc—prescribed enactments and instruments under which payable

For the purposes of paragraph 10 of Schedule 1 to the Act (power to deduct contributions from a pension or allowance payable by the Secretary of State by virtue of any prescribed enactment or instrument), the enactments and instruments are—

(*a*) Order in Council 19th December 1881;
(*b*) The Royal Warrant 27th October 1884;
(*c*) The Naval and Military War Pensions Act 1915;
(*d*) The War Pensions Act 1920;
(*e*) The War Pensions Act 1921;
(*f*) Order by His Majesty 14th January 1922;
(*g*) The War Pensions (Coastguards) Scheme 1944;
(*h*) The Royal Warrant 1964;
(*i*) The Order by Her Majesty 1964;
(*j*) The War Pensions (Naval Auxiliary Personnel) Scheme 1964;
(*k*) The Pensions (Polish Forces) Scheme 1964;
(*l*) The War Pensions (Mercantile Marine) Scheme 1964;
(*m*) The Order by Her Majesty (Ulster Defence Regiment) 1971;
(*n*) The Personal Injuries (Civilians) Scheme 1983;
(*o*) The Naval, Military and Air Forces etc (Disablement and Death) Service Pensions Order 1983.

11 Consequential amendments to the Contributions Regulations

(1) The Contributions Regulations shall be amended in accordance with the following provisions of this regulation.

(2) In regulation 1(2) (definitions), in the definition of "week" omit the words "for the purposes of regulation 38(7) it has the meaning assigned to it in regulation 38(8), and".

(3) In regulation 39 (treatment for the purpose of any contributory benefit of late paid or unpaid primary Class 1 contributions where there was no consent, connivance or negligence by the primary contributor)—

(*a*) in the heading, omit the words "late paid or";
(*b*) in paragraph (1), omit the words "is paid after the due date or" and "delay or".

12 Revocations

The regulations set out in column (1) of [Schedule 2][1] to these Regulations are hereby revoked to the extent mentioned in column (3) of that Schedule.

Amendments—[1] Words substituted by the Social Security (National Insurance Numbers) Amendment Regulations, SI 2008/223 reg 2(1), (4) with effect from 29 February 2008.

[SCHEDULE 1
DOCUMENTS TO ACCOMPANY AN APPLICATION FOR A NATIONAL INSURANCE NUMBER

Regulation 9(1A)

1 Any document specified for the time being in paragraphs 1 to 6 of List A of the Schedule to the Immigration (Restrictions on Employment) Order 2007.

2 Any document specified for the time being in paragraphs 1 to 6 of List B of the Schedule to the Immigration (Restrictions on Employment) Order 2007.

3 Any of the following documents—

(*a*) a full birth certificate issued in the United Kingdom which includes the name(s) of at least one of the holder's parents;

(*b*) a full adoption certificate issued in the United Kingdom which includes the name(s) of at least one of the holder's adoptive parents;

(*c*) a birth certificate issued in the Channel Islands, the Isle of Man or Ireland;

(*d*) an adoption certificate issued in the Channel Islands, the Isle of Man or Ireland;

(*e*) a certificate of registration or naturalisation as a British Citizen;

(*f*) an Immigration Status Document issued by the Home Office or the Border and Immigration Agency to the holder with an endorsement indicating that the person named in it is allowed to stay indefinitely in the United Kingdom or has no time limit on their stay in the United Kingdom;

(*g*) a letter issued by the Home Office or the Border and Immigration Agency to the holder which indicates that the person named in it is allowed to stay indefinitely in the United Kingdom;

(*h*) an Immigration Status Document issued by the Home Office or the Border and Immigration Agency to the holder with an endorsement indicating that the person named in it can stay in the United Kingdom, and is allowed to do the type of work in question;

(*i*) a letter issued by the Home Office or the Border and Immigration Agency to the holder or the employer or prospective employer, which indicates that the person named in it can stay in the United Kingdom and is allowed to do the work in question.][1]

Amendments—[1] Schedule 1 inserted by the Social Security (National Insurance Numbers) Amendment Regulations, SI 2008/223 reg 2(1), (5) with effect from 29 February 2008.

[SCHEDULE 2][1]
REGULATIONS REVOKED

Regulation 12

Column (1) *Citation*	*Column (2)* *Statutory Instrument*	*Column (3)* *Extent of Revocation*
The Social Security (Contributions) Regulations 1979	SI 1979/591	Regulations 30, 36, 38, 38A, 41, 41A, 42, 44 and 55
The Social Security (Contributions) Amendment Regulations 1980	SI 1980/1975	Regulation 4
The Social Security (Contributions) Amendment Regulations 1984	SI 1984/77	Regulation 13
The Social Security (Contributions) Amendment (No 2) Regulations 1987	SI 1987/413	Regulations 8 and 9
The Social Security (Contributions) Amendment (No 5) Regulations 1992	SI 1992/669	Regulations 2 and 4
The Social Security (Contributions) Amendment (No 6) Regulations 1993	SI 1993/2094	Regulations 3, 4 and 5
The Social Security (Contributions) Amendment (No 2) Regulations 1994	SI 1994/1553	Regulation 3
The Social Security (Incapacity Benefit) (Consequential and Transitional Amendments and Savings) Regulations 1995	SI 1995/829	Regulation 13(4)

The Social Security (Credits and Contributions) (Jobseeker's Allowance Consequential and Miscellaneous Amendments) Regulations 1996	SI 1996/2367	Regulation 3(4)
The Social Security Contributions, Statutory Maternity Pay and Statutory Sick Pay (Miscellaneous Amendments) Regulations 1999	SI 1999/567	Regulation 7
The Social Security (Contributions and Credits) (Miscellaneous Amendments) Regulations 1999	SI 1999/568	Regulation 13
The Social Security (Contributions) (Amendment No 8) Regulations 2000	SI 2000/2207	Regulation 6

Amendments—[1] Schedule 2 numbered as such, by the Social Security (National Insurance Numbers) Amendment Regulations, SI 2008/223 reg 2(1), (3) with effect from 29 February 2008.

SOCIAL SECURITY (CONTRIBUTIONS) REGULATIONS 2001

Made . . . .*5 March 2001*

Laid before Parliament . . . .*5 March 2001*

Coming into force in accordance with . . . .*regulation 1*

ARRANGEMENT OF REGULATIONS

NIC

NIC

The Treasury, with the concurrence of the Secretary of State for Social Security and the Department for Social Development in so far as required, in exercise of the powers set out in column (1) of Part I of Schedule 1 to these Regulations and the Commissioners of Inland Revenue, in exercise of the powers set out in column (1) of Part II of that Schedule 1 (in both cases as amended in particular by the provisions set out in column (2) of that Schedule), and of all other powers enabling them in that behalf, for the purpose only of consolidating the Regulations revoked by this instrument, hereby make the following Regulations—

PART 1
GENERAL

1 Citation, commencement and interpretation

(1) These Regulations may be cited as the Social Security (Contributions) Regulations 2001 and shall come into force on 6th April 2001 immediately after—

(*a*) the Social Security (Contributions) (Amendment No 2) Regulations 2001;
(*b*) the Social Security (Contributions) (Amendment No 2) (Northern Ireland) Regulations 2001;
(*c*) the Social Security (Contributions) (Amendment No 3) Regulations 2001;
(*d*) the Social Security (Contributions) (Amendment No 3) (Northern Ireland) Regulations 2001;
(*e*) the Social Security (Crediting and Treatment of Contributions, and National Insurance Numbers) Regulations 2001); and
(*f*) the Social Security (Crediting and Treatment of Contributions, and National Insurance Numbers) Regulations (Northern Ireland) 2001.

(2) In these Regulations, unless the context otherwise requires—

["the acquired gender" has the same meaning as it has in the Gender Recognition Act 2004;][6]

"the Act" means the Social Security Contributions and Benefits Act 1992;

"the Administration Act" means the Social Security Administration Act 1992;

"aggregation" means the aggregating and treating as a single payment under paragraph 1(1) of Schedule 1 to the Act (Class 1 contributions; more than one employment) of two or more payments or earnings and "aggregated" shall be construed accordingly;

"apportionment" means the apportioning under paragraph 1(7) of Schedule 1 to the Act to one or more employers of a single payment of earnings made to or for the benefit of an employed earner in respect of two or more employments, or, as the case may be, the apportioning under paragraph 1(8) of that Schedule of contribution liability between two or more employers in respect of earnings which have been aggregated under paragraph 1(1)(*b*) of that Schedule, and in either case "apportioning" and "apportioned" shall be construed accordingly;

["approved method of electronic communications" in relation to the delivery of information or the making of a payment in accordance with a provision of these Regulations, means a method of electronic communications which has been approved, by specific or general directions issued by the Board, for the delivery of information of that kind or the making of a payment of that kind under that provision;][4]

"the Board" means the Commissioners of Inland Revenue, and subject to section 4A of the Inland Revenue Regulation Act 1890, includes any officer or servant of theirs;

["business travel" has the meaning given in section 236(1) of ITEPA 2003 [and includes journeys which are treated as business travel by section 235A of ITEPA 2003 (journeys made by members of local authorities etc)][19];][4]

["cash voucher" has the meaning given to it in section 75 of ITEPA 2003;][4]

. . .[13]

"company" means a company within the meaning of section [1][14] of the Companies Act [2006][14] or a body corporate to which, by virtue of [regulations made under section 1043 of [that Act][14], any provision of [that Act][14]][11] applies;

. . .[15]

"conditional interest in shares" means an interest which is conditional for the purposes of [Chapter 2 of Part 7 of ITEPA 2003 as originally enacted][4];

. . .[20]

. . .[20]

"contribution week" means a period of seven days beginning with midnight between Saturday and Sunday;

"contribution year" shall be construed in accordance with section 12(1) or (as the case requires) section 13(5) of the Act (late paid Class 2 or Class 3 contributions);

["contribution-based jobseeker's allowance" means an allowance under the Jobseekers Act 1995 as amended by the provisions of Part 1 of Schedule 14 to the Welfare Reform Act 2012 that remove references to an income-based allowance, and a contribution-based allowance under the Jobseekers Act 1995 as that Act has effect apart from those provisions;][16]

"contributory benefit" includes a contribution-based jobseeker's allowance but not an income-based jobseeker's allowance;

. . .[2]

NIC

. . .[20]

"director" means—

(*a*) in relation to a company whose affairs are managed by a board of directors or similar body, a member of that board or similar body;

(*b*) in relation to a company whose affairs are managed by a single director or similar person, that director or person; and

(*c*) any person in accordance with whose directions or instructions the company's directors as defined in paragraphs (*a*) and (*b*) above are accustomed to act; and for this purpose a person is not to be treated as such a person by reason only that the directors act on advice given by him in his professional capacity;

["due date" in Part 6 means, in relation to—

(*a*) any Class 1 contribution, the date by which payment falls to be made;

(*b*) any Class 2 contribution which a person is liable or entitled to pay, the 31st January following the end of the tax year in respect of which it is paid or payable; and

(*c*) any Class 3 contribution, the date 42 days after the end of the year in respect of which it is paid.][17]

"earnings period" means the period referred to in regulation 2;

"earnings-related contributions" means contributions payable under the Act in respect of earnings paid to or for the benefit of an earner in respect of employed earner's employment;

["employment and support allowance" has the same meaning as in the Welfare Reform Act 2007;][17]

["electronic communications" includes any communications conveyed by means of an electronic communications network;][3]

["full gender recognition certificate" means a certificate issued under section 4 of the Gender Recognition Act 2004;][6]

["HMRC" means Her Majesty's Revenue and Customs;][10]

"an income-based jobseeker's allowance" has the same meaning as in the Jobseekers Act 1995;

. . .[4]

"national insurance number" means the national insurance number allocated within the meaning of regulation 9 of the Social Security (Crediting and Treatment of Contributions, and National Insurance Numbers) Regulations 2001;

["non-cash voucher" has the meaning given to it in section 84 of ITEPA 2003;][4]

. . .[20]

. . .[20]

. . .[20]

["official computer system" means a computer system maintained by or on behalf of the Board;][4]

[. . .[17]

["the PAYE Regulations" means the Income Tax (Pay As You Earn) Regulations 2003;][4]

. . .[8]

. . .[20]

"profits or gains" for the purposes of Part 8 means profits or gains which, subject to the provisions of Schedule 2 to the Act, are chargeable to income tax under Case I or Case II of Schedule D;

"readily convertible asset" has the meaning given in [section 702 of ITEPA 2003 as amended by the Finance Act 2003;][2]

["registered pension scheme" has the meaning given in section 150(2) of the Finance Act 2004;][7]

["relevant employment income" has the meaning given in paragraph 3B(1A) of Schedule 1 to the Act;][5]

"regular interval" for the purposes of regulations 3, 4 and 7 includes only such interval as is in accordance with an express or implied agreement between the employed earner and the secondary contributor as to the intervals at which payments of earnings normally fall to be made, being intervals of substantially equal length;

["restricted securities" and "restricted interest in securities" have the meanings given in sections 423 and 424 of ITEPA 2003 as substituted by the Finance Act 2003;][2]

"retirement benefits scheme" has the meaning given in section 611 of the Taxes Act;

["retrospective contributions", in relation to an amount of retrospective earnings, means the amount of earnings-related contributions based on those earnings which the employee is liable to pay under section 6(4)(*a*) of the Act (primary contributions);][8]

["retrospective contributions regulations" means regulations made by virtue of section 4B(2) of the Act and, in relation to an amount of retrospective earnings, "the relevant retrospective contributions regulations" means the regulations which treat that amount as earnings;][8]

["retrospective earnings" means an amount retrospectively treated as earnings by retrospective contributions regulations;][8]

. . .[4]

"secondary contributor" means the person who, in respect of earnings from employed earner's employment, is liable to pay a [a secondary Class 1 contribution][9] under section 6(4)(*b*) of the Act (liability for Class 1 contributions);

["securities" and "securities option" have the meaning given by section 420 of ITEPA 2003 as substituted by the Finance Act 2003;][2]

[. . .[17]

"serving member of the forces" means a person, other than one mentioned in Part 2 of Schedule 6, who, being over the age of 16, is a member of any establishment or organisation specified in Part I of that Schedule (being a member who gives full pay service) but does not include any such person while absent on desertion;

"the Taxes Act" means the Income and Corporation Taxes Act 1988;

["tax month" has the meaning given in paragraph 1(2) of Schedule 4;][4]

"training" means full-time training at a course approved by the Board;

"the Transfer Act" means the Social Security Contributions (Transfer of Functions, etc) Act 1999;

["tribunal" means the First-tier tribunal or, where determined by or under Tribunal Procedure Rules, the Upper Tribunal;][12]

"week" means tax week, except in relation to Case C of Part 9, where "week" and "weekly" have the meanings given in regulation 115;

"the Welfare Reform Act" means the Welfare Reform and Pensions Act 1999;

"year" means tax year;

"year of assessment" has the meaning given to it in section 832(1) of the Taxes Act;

(3) For the purposes of regulations 52, 57, 67 and 116, references to "contributions", "Class 1 contributions" and "earnings-related contributions" shall, unless the context otherwise requires, include any amount paid on account of earnings-related contributions in accordance with regulation 8(6).

[(3A In these Regulations, references to—

(*a*) Schedule 24 to the Finance Act 2007 (penalties for errors); and

(*b*) Schedule 55 to the Finance Act 2009 (penalties for failure to make a return)

include references to these Schedules as amended by paragraphs 3 and 5 of Schedule 33 to the Finance Act 2014 (Part 4: Consequential Amendments).][18]

(4) Where, by any provision of these Regulations—

(*a*) any notice or other document is required to be given or sent to the Board, that notice or document shall be treated as having been given or sent on the day that it is received by the Board; and

(*b*) any notice or other document is required to be given or sent by the Board to any person, that notice or document shall, if sent by post to that person's last known address, be treated as having been given or sent on the day that is was posted.

(5) Unless the context otherwise requires—

(*a*) any reference in these Regulations to a numbered regulation is a reference to the regulation bearing that number in these Regulations;

(*b*) any reference in these Regulations to a numbered Part or Schedule is to the Part of, or Schedule to, these Regulations bearing that number;

(*c*) any reference in a regulation or a Schedule to a numbered paragraph is a reference to the paragraph bearing that number in that regulation or Schedule;

(*d*) any reference in a paragraph of a regulation or a Schedule to a numbered or lettered sub-paragraph is a reference to the sub-paragraph bearing that number or letter in that paragraph; and

(*e*) any reference in a sub-paragraph to a numbered head is a reference to the head in that sub-paragraph bearing that number.

Commentary—*Simon's Taxes* **E8.233, E8.249, E8.260, E8.290, E8.1123, E8.1156.**

HMRC Manuals—National Insurance Manual NIM02715 (registered pension schemes: definition).

NIM02413 (non-cash vouchers - definition).

NIM02497 (cash vouchers - definition).

NIM06822 (securities: meaning of securities).

NIM06835 (securities: readily convertible assets).

NIM20200 (contribution week).

NIM12002 (directors: definition of director: class 1 Nics).

NIM08002 (general: alignment with tax weeks and months).

HMRC Directions—The following directions (dated 13 March 2012) were published on the HMRC website on 19 March 2012—

HMRC directions for approved methods of electronic communications from April 2012

NIC

Directions under regulations 189 and 205(2) of the Income Tax (Pay As You Earn) Regulations 2003 (SI 2003/2682) and regulation 1(2) of the Social Security (Contributions) Regulations 2001 (SI 2001/1004) and Approval under regulation 211(5) of the Income Tax (Pay As You Earn) Regulations 2003 (SI 2003/2682) and 80(3A) of the Social Security (Contributions) Regulations 2001 (SI 2001/1004)

Interpretation

In these directions and this approval—

'EDI' means the Electronic Data Interchange;

'PAYE Regulations' means the Income Tax (Pay As You Earn) Regulations 2003 (S.I. 2003/2682);

'Contributions Regulations' means the Social Security (Contributions) Regulations 2001 (S.I. 2001/1004).

Directions

The Commissioners for Her Majesty's Revenue and Customs (HMRC) give the following directions about approved methods of electronic communications for the delivery of information and the making of payments and approve the specified manner of authentication of employers' annual returns delivered electronically.

The directions and approval have effect from 6 April 2012.

Approved methods of electronic communications for delivery of information by employers or persons acting on behalf of employers to HMRC

1. The methods of electronic communications approved for the delivery of the information listed in column 1 of the table by an employer or a person acting on behalf of an employer are:

(a) the internet services provided through PAYE Online for Employers and PAYE Online for Agents, where indicated in column 2, and

(b) the EDI services provided through PAYE Online for Employers and PAYE Online for Agents, where indicated in column 3.

1.	2.	3.
Description of the kind of information to be delivered	Internet	EDI
PAYE Regulations[1]		
Simplified deductions scheme: deductions working sheet. Form P12 (regulation 35).	Yes	No
Simplified deductions scheme: annual return of deductions working sheets. Form P37 (regulation 35).	Yes	No
Cessation of employment. Form P45, Part 1 (regulation 36).	Yes	Yes
Death of employee. Form P45, Part 1 (regulation 38).	Yes	Yes
Death of pensioner. Form P45, Part 1 (regulation 39).	Yes	Yes
Procedure if new employer receives Form P45. Form P45, Part 3 (regulation 42).	Yes	Yes
Information to be provided if code not known. Form P46 (regulations 47, 48 and 49).	Yes	Yes
Late presentation of Form P45. Form P45, Part 3 (regulation 52).	Yes	Yes
Information on retirement. Form P46 (Pen) (regulation 55).	Yes	Yes
Procedure if new pension payer receives Form P45. Form P45, Part 3 (regulation 56).	Yes	Yes
Information to be provided if code not known (non-UK resident pensioners). Form P46 (Pen) (regulation 57).	Yes	Yes
Information to be provided if code not known (UK resident pensioners). Form P46 (Pen) (regulation 58).	Yes	Yes
Late presentation of Form P45. Form P45, Part 3 (regulation 60).	Yes	Yes
Annual return of relevant payments liable to deduction of tax. Forms P35 and P14 (regulation 73).	Yes	Yes
Annual return of relevant payments not liable to deduction of tax. Form P38A (regulation 74).	Yes	Yes
Employers: annual return of other PAYE income: benefits code employee. Form P11D (regulation 85).	Yes	Yes
Quarterly return of cars becoming available or unavailable. Form P46 (Car) (regulation 90).	Yes	Yes
Contributions Regulations		

1.	2.	3.
Description of the kind of information to be delivered	Internet	EDI
Return by employer of Class 1A National Insurance contributions. Form P11D(b) (regulation 80(1)).	Yes	Yes
Return by employer at end of year. Forms P35 and P14 (paragraph 22 of Schedule 4)	Yes	Yes

[1]Regulation 211 permits electronic delivery of certain information. This direction approves the methods of electronic communications for delivery of that information.

Approved methods of electronic communications for mandatory electronic filing of specified information

2. The methods of electronic communications approved for the delivery of specified information, by an employer or a person acting on behalf of an employer, in accordance with regulation 205 of the PAYE Regulations (and, in accordance with paragraph 22 of Schedule 4 and regulation 90N(1) of the Contributions Regulations) are the internet services and the EDI services provided through PAYE Online for Employers and PAYE Online for Agents.

Approved methods of electronic communications for delivery of information by HMRC to employers or persons acting on behalf of employers

3. The methods of electronic communications approved for delivery of the information listed in column 1 of the table by HMRC to an employer or a person acting on behalf of an employer are:

(a) the internet services provided through PAYE Online for Employers and PAYE Online for Agents, where indicated in column 2, and

(b) the EDI services provided through PAYE Online for Employers and PAYE Online for Agents, where indicated in column 3.

1.	2.	3.
Description of the kind of information to be delivered	Internet	EDI
PAYE Regulations[2]		
Issue of code to employer or agent. Form P6 or P9 (regulations 8 and 20).	Yes	Yes
Notice to employer to amend codes. Form P7X or P9X (regulation 20).	Yes	Yes
Notice to employer of payments and total net tax deducted. Form P6 (regulation 53).	Yes	Yes
Notice to pension payer of payments and total net tax deducted. Form P6 (regulation 61).	Yes	Yes

[2] Regulation 213 permits electronic delivery of certain information. This direction approves the methods of electronic communications for delivery of that information.

Approved method of authentication of the return required by regulation 73 (annual return of relevant payments liable to deduction of tax, Forms P35 and P14) of the PAYE Regulations and regulation 80 (Return by employer) of the Contributions Regulations where the return is delivered electronically

4. The method approved for authenticating a return required by regulation 73 of the PAYE Regulations or regulation 80 of the Contributions Regulations and delivered by a method of electronic communications is the completion of any certificate or declaration contained in the electronic return or form and, where the sender is acting on behalf of an employer, completion of the following procedure before the information is sent:

(a) the sender must make a copy of the information before it is sent, and

(b) the employer must confirm to the sender that the information is complete and accurate to the best of his knowledge and belief.

Approved methods of electronic communications for the making of a payment

5. The methods of electronic communications approved for the making of payments required by the PAYE Regulations and the Contributions Regulations are the services known as Direct Debit, BACS Direct Credit (including telephone and internet banking), CHAPS, debit and credit card over the internet ('BillPay'), Government Banking Service (formerly known as Paymaster), Bank Giro and payments made through the Post Office.

The following Direction (dated 24 September 2012) was published on the HMRC website on 4 October 2012—

Direction under regulations 2A(1)(b) and (2) and 2B(1)(b) and (2)of the Income Tax (Pay As You Earn) Regulations 2003 and paragraph 1(4) and (5) of Schedule 4 to the Social Security (Contributions) Regulations 2001

Real Time Information employers and Real Time Information pension payers: migration during tax year 2013-14

NIC

The Commissioners for Her Majesty's Revenue and Customs give the following direction under regulation 2A(1)(b) and (2) and regulation 2B(1)(b) and (2) of the Income Tax (Pay As You Earn) Regulations 2003 (SI 2003/2682) and paragraph 1(4) and (5) of Schedule 4 to the Social Security (Contributions) Regulations 2001 (SI 2001/1004):

Real Time Information employers

1. Any employer who, apart from this direction, is not a Real Time Information employer for the purposes of the PAYE Regulations and the Contributions Regulations is required to deliver to HMRC returns under regulation 67B of the PAYE Regulations and paragraph 21A of Schedule 4 to the Contributions Regulations with effect from the date mentioned in paragraph 2.

2. The date is 6th April 2013 unless HMRC specifies a later date.

Real Time Information pension payers

3. Any pension payer who, apart from this direction, is not a Real Time Information pension payer for the purposes of the PAYE Regulations is required to deliver to HMRC returns under regulation 67B of the PAYE Regulations with effect from the date mentioned in paragraph 4.

4. The date is 6th April 2013 unless HMRC specifies a later date.

Interpretation

5. In this direction:

"the Contributions Regulations" means the Social Security (Contributions) Regulations 2001 (SI 2001/1004);

"the PAYE Regulations" means the Income Tax (Pay As You Earn) Regulations 2003 (SI 2003/2682);

"employer":

(a) so far as this direction relates to the PAYE Regulations, has the meaning given in regulation 2(1) of those Regulations, and

(b) so far as this direction relates to the Contributions Regulations, has the meaning given in paragraph 1(2) of Schedule 4 to those Regulations;

"HMRC" means Her Majesty's Revenue and Customs; and

"pension payer" has the meaning given in regulation 2(1) of the PAYE Regulations.

Amendments—[2] Definition of "convertible shares" revoked, words substituted in the definition of "readily convertible asset"; and definitions of "restricted securities" and "restricted interest in securities", and "securities" and "securities option" inserted, by the Social Security Contributions (Amendment) (No 5) Regulations, SI 2003/2085 regs 3, 4 with effect from 1 September 2003.

[3] In para (2), definition of "electronic communications" substituted by the Communications Act (Consequential Amendments) Order, SI 2003/2155 art 3(1), Sch 1 para 23(1)(*d*), (2) with effect from 17 September 2003.

[4] In para (2), definitions of "approved method of electronic communications", "official computer system", "the PAYE regulations" and "tax month" inserted; definitions of "business travel", "cash voucher", and "non-cash voucher" substituted; words in definition of "conditional interest in shares" substituted; and definitions of "income tax month" and "month", and "Schedule E" revoked; by the Social Security (Contributions, Categorisation of Earners and Intermediaries) (Amendment) Regulations, SI 2004/770 regs 2, 3, 36, Schedule with effect from 6 April 2004.

[5] Definition of "relevant employment income" inserted by the Social Security (Contributions) (Amendment No 4) Regulations, SI 2004/2096 regs 2, 3 with effect from 1 September 2004. SI 2004/2096 has effect in relation to—

(a) agreements entered into after 1 September 2004 which are in respect of post-commencement employment income, and

(b) elections made after that date.

[6] Definition of "the acquired gender" and "full gender recognition certificate" inserted by the Social Security (Contributions) (Amendment No 3) Regulations, SI 2005/778 regs 2, 3 with effect from 6 April 2005.

[7] Definition of "registered pension scheme" inserted by the Social Security (Contributions) (Amendment No 2) Regulations, SI 2006/576 regs 2, 3 with effect from 6 April 2006.

[8] Definitions of "retrospective contributions", "retrospective earnings" and "retrospective contributions regulations" inserted, by the Social Security Contributions (Consequential Provisions) Regulations, SI 2007/1056 regs 3, 4 with effect from 6 April 2007.

[9] Words in definition of "secondary contributor" substituted by the Social Security Contributions (Managed Service Companies) Regulations, SI 2007/2070 reg 5 with effect from 6 August 2007.

[10] Definition of "the Commissioner", "official error" and "service provider" inserted by the Social Security (Contributions) (Amendment No 8) Regulations, SI 2007/2520 regs 2, 3 with effect from 1 October 2007: SI 2007/2520 reg 1.

[11] In para (2), words in definition of "company" substituted by the Companies Act 2006 (Consequential Amendments) (Taxes and National Insurance) Order, SI 2008/954 art 50 with effect from 6 April 2008.

[12] Definitions of "HMRC" and "tribunal" inserted by the Social Security (Contributions) (Amendment No 3) Regulations, SI 2009/600 regs 2, 3 with effect from 1 April 2009.

[13] Definition of "the Commissioner" revoked and, in definition of "official error", words substituted, by the Tribunals, Courts and Enforcement Act 2007 (Transitional and Consequential Provisions) Order, SI 2008/2683 art 6(1), Sch 1 para 164 with effect from 3 November 2008.

[14] In para (2), figures and words substituted by the Companies Act 2006 (Consequential Amendments) (Taxes and National Insurance) Order, SI 2009/1890 art 3(9) with effect from 1 October 2009.

[15] In para (2), definition of "COMPS employment" revoked by the Social Security (Contributions) (Amendment No 2) Regulations, SI 2012/817 regs 2, 3 with effect from 6 April 2012. These amendments do not affect the operation of the Social

Security (Contributions) Regulations, SI 2001/1004 in relation to obligations arising in connection with tax years beginning prior to 6 April 2012 (SI 2012/817 reg 11(1)).

16 In para (2), definition substituted for previous definition "a contribution-based jobseeker's allowance", by the Universal Credit (Consequential, Supplementary, Incidental and Miscellaneous Provisions) Regulations, SI 2013/630 reg 72 with effect from 29 April 2013.

17 In para (2), definition of "due date" substituted, definition of "employment and support allowance" inserted and definitions of "official error" and "service provider" revoked by the Social Security (Miscellaneous Amendments No 2) Regulations, SI 2015/478 regs 2, 3, 24(1)(*a*) with effect from 6 April 2015.

18 Paragraph (3A) inserted by the Social Security Contributions (Amendments in Consequence of Part 4 of the Finance Act 2014) Regulations, SI 2015/521 reg 3 with effect from 12 April 2015.

19 Words in definition of "business travel" inserted by the Social Security (Contributions) (Amendment) (No 2) Regulations SI 2016/352, regs 2, 3 with effect from 6 April 2016.

20 Definitions of "contracted-out employment", "contracted-out rate", "COSRS employment", "non-contracted-out employment", "non-contracted out rate", "normal rate" and "the Pensions Act" revoked by the Social Security (Contributions) (Amendment) (No 2) Regulations, SI 2016/352 reg 8 with effect from 6 April 2016 and subject to savings in relation to rights or obligations arising in connection with tax years beginning before 6 April 2016.

PART 2
ASSESSMENT OF EARNINGS-RELATED CONTRIBUTIONS

2 Earnings periods

Except where regulation 8 applies, the amount, if any, of earnings-related contributions payable or, where section 6A of the Act applies, treated as having been paid, in respect of earnings paid to or for the benefit of an earner in respect of an employed earner's employment shall, subject to regulations 7 and 12 to 19, be assessed on the amount of such earnings paid, or treated as paid, in the earnings period specified in regulation 3, 4, 5, 6, or 9.

Commentary—*Simon's Taxes* **A2.248.**
HMRC Manuals—National Insurance Manual NIM08001 (general).

[3 Earnings period for earnings normally paid or treated as paid at regular intervals

(1) If any part of earnings paid to or for the benefit of an earner is normally paid, or is treated under regulation 7 as paid, at regular intervals, the earnings period in respect of those earnings shall be the period found in accordance with the following Table, subject to paragraphs (2) to (6).

Earnings Periods

Case	*Applicable earnings period*
Earnings paid at an interval of 7 days or more	The length of the interval
Earnings paid at intervals of different lengths, each of which is 7 days or more	The length of the shorter or shortest of those intervals
Earnings paid at one or more intervals of less than 7 days	A week.
Earnings paid at one or more intervals of less than 7 days and at one or more intervals of more than 7 days.	A week.][1]

[(2) In any year, the earnings period for the earnings mentioned in paragraph (1) shall only be that found by the Table in that paragraph if the period in which the earnings are paid is one of a succession of periods and—

(*a*) the periods are the same length;
(*b*) the first period begins on the first day of the year; and
(*c*) the subsequent periods begin immediately after the end of the preceding period.

For the purpose of this paragraph, if all the periods in the succession mentioned above, apart from the last in the year in question, are the same length, the last period in the year shall be treated as if it were the same length as the others.
This paragraph is subject to the following qualification.][1]

[(2A) Paragraph (2B) applies if it appears to an officer of the Board that—

(*a*) it is the employer's practice to pay the greater part of the earnings referred to in paragraph (2) at intervals of greater length than the shorter or shortest of the earnings periods produced by the application of that paragraph; and
(*b*) that practice is likely to continue.][1]

[(2B) If this paragraph applies the officer may, and if requested to do so by the earner or the secondary contributor shall, decide whether to give a notice to the earner and the secondary contributor specifying the longer or longest of the earnings periods produced by the application of paragraph (2) to be the earnings period applicable to those earnings.][1]

[(2C) A notice under paragraph (2B) shall—

(*a*) be given to both the earner and the secondary contributor; and
(*b*) specify the date from which the change of earnings period is to take effect.

NIC

The date specified shall not be earlier than that on which the notice is given.][1]

[(2D) A notice given under paragraph (2B) shall have effect until an officer of the Board decides (either of his own motion or on an application by the earner or the secondary contributor) that the practice to which it relates has ceased.

If an officer of the Board decides that a notice is to cease to have effect, he shall notify the earner and the secondary contributor accordingly.][1]

(3) If the length of the earnings period determined in accordance with [paragraph (2B)][1] is a year, then notwithstanding [paragraph (2)][1], where the change in the length of the earnings period takes effect during the course of a year, the length of the earnings period in respect of any earnings in that year which are paid or treated as paid on or after the change shall be the number of weeks remaining in that year commencing with the week in which the change takes effect.

(4) . . . [1]

(5) Where—

(*a*) the employment in respect of which the earnings are paid has ended;

(*b*) the employment in respect of which the earnings are paid was one in which, during its continuance, earnings were paid or treated under regulation 7 as paid at a regular interval; and

(*c*) after the end of the employment, a payment of earnings is made which satisfies either or both of the conditions specified in paragraph (6),

the earnings period in respect of such payment of earnings shall, notwithstanding regulation 7, be the week in which the payment is made.

(6) The conditions referred to in paragraph (5) are that the payment is—

(*a*) by way of addition to a payment made before the end of the employment; and

(*b*) not in respect of a regular interval.

Commentary—*Simon's Taxes* **E8.249, E8.249A, E8.249B, E8.249C , E8.1002.**

HMRC Manuals—National Insurance Manual NIM08010 - 08030 (earnings paid at regular intervals: fitting them into tax years).
NIM08300 (employee starts work).
NIM08312 (employee starts work part-way through an earnings period but is not paid until the end of the next earnings period).
NIM08400 - NIM08410 (payments after the employment has ended: regular pattern of payments).
NIM08610 (additional payments at regular intervals).
NIM09110 (holiday pay: payment on normal payday).
NIM09510 - NIM09560 (earnings periods: Notification issued in accordance with this regulation).

Amendments—[1] Paras (1)–(2D) substituted for paras (1), (2), figures in para (3) substituted, and para (4) revoked, by the Social Security (Contributions) (Amendment No 3) Regulations, SI 2002/2366 regs 3, 4 with effect from 8 October 2002.

4 Earnings period for earnings normally paid otherwise than at regular intervals and not treated as paid at regular intervals

Subject to regulation 3(5) or regulation 5, where earnings are paid to or for the benefit of an earner in respect of an employed earner's employment, but no part of those earnings is normally paid or treated under regulation 7 as paid at regular intervals, the earnings period in respect of those earnings shall be a period of one of the following lengths—

(*a*) the length of the period of that part of the employment for which the earnings are paid or a week, whichever is the longer; or

(*b*) where it is not reasonably practicable to determine that period under paragraph (*a*)—

(i) the length of the period from the date on which the last payment of earnings, before the payment in question, was paid during the employment in respect of the employment (or, if there has been no such payment, from the date on which the employment began) to the date of the payment in question, unless the period so calculated would be of a length less than that of a week, in which case the earnings period shall be a week, or

(ii) where the payment is made before the employment begins or after it ends, a week.

Commentary—*Simon's Taxes* **E8.249D, E8.249E.**

HMRC Manuals—National Insurance Manual NIM08100 (employee has no regular earnings period).
NIM09910 (special cases: irregular harvest casuals).

5 Earnings period for sums deemed to be earnings by virtue of regulations made under section 112 of the Act

Where any sum or amount is deemed to be earnings by virtue of any regulations made under section 112 of the Act (sums to be earnings for the purposes of Part I to V of the Act)—

(*a*) the earnings period in respect of any payment of those earnings shall be the length of the protected period (as referred to in section 189 of the Trade Union and Labour Relations (Consolidation) Act 1992) or, as the case may be, that part of it in respect of which the sum is paid, or a week whichever is the longer;

(*b*) contributions paid in respect of such earnings shall, if the employed earner so requests—

(i) if the period to which the payment of earnings relates falls wholly in a year other than the year in which they are paid, be treated as paid in respect of the year in which the period to which the payment of earnings relates falls, or

(ii) if the period to which the payment of earnings relates falls partly in the year in which they are paid and partly in one or more other years, be treated as paid proportionately in respect of each of the years in which the period to which the payment of earnings relates falls, or

(iii) if the period to which the payment of earnings relates falls wholly in two or more years other than the year in which they are paid, be treated as paid proportionately in respect of each of the years in which the period to which the payment of earnings relates falls.

Commentary—*Simon's Taxes* **E8.256, E8.265, E8.1146.**

HMRC Manuals—National Insurance Manual NIM07062 (payments made under a protective award).

NIM07066 (re-allocating primary Nics paid on a payment made under a reinstatement order).

6 Earnings period for earnings to be aggregated where the earnings periods for those earnings otherwise would be of different lengths

(1) Paragraphs (2) and (3) apply where—

(*a*) earnings paid in respect of two or more employed earner's employments fall to be aggregated; and

(*b*) the earnings periods in respect of those earnings are, by virtue of regulation 3, 4 or 5, of different lengths.

(2) In a case to which this regulation applies, where (but for its provisions) the earnings period in respect of earnings derived from any of the employments is of a different length from the designated earnings period, the earnings period in respect of any payment of those earnings shall be the designated earnings period.

[(3) In this regulation "the designated earnings period" means the shorter, or as the case may be the shortest, of the earnings periods in respect of earnings derived from such employments.][1]

Commentary—*Simon's Taxes* **E8.289C.**

HMRC Manuals—National Insurance Manual NIM10012–NIM10017 (calculating Nics: earnings periods: all jobs).

Amendments—[1] Sub-para (3) substituted by the Social Security (Contributions) (Amendment) (No 2) Regulations, SI 2016/352 reg 9 with effect from 6 April 2016 and subject to savings in relation to rights or obligations arising in connection with tax years beginning before 6 April 2016.

7 Treatment of earnings paid otherwise than at regular intervals

(1) Subject to regulation 3(5) and paragraphs (2) and (3), for the purposes of assessing earnings-related contributions—

(*a*) if on any occasion a payment of earnings which would normally fall to be made at regular interval is made otherwise than at the regular interval, it shall be treated as if it were a payment made at that regular interval;

(*b*) if payments of earnings are made at irregular intervals which secure that one and only one payment is made in each of a succession of periods consisting of the same number of days, weeks or calendar months, those payments shall be treated as if they were payments made at the regular interval of one of those periods of days, weeks or, as the case may be, calendar months;

(*c*) if payments of earnings, other than those specified in sub-paragraph (*b*), are made in respect of regular intervals, but otherwise than at regular intervals, each such payment shall be treated as made at the regular interval in respect of which it is due.

(2) Where under paragraph (1) a payment of earnings is treated as made at a regular interval, it shall for the purposes of assessment under these regulations of earnings-related contributions also be treated as paid—

(*a*) in a case falling within paragraph (1)(*a*), on the date on which it would normally have fallen to be made;

(*b*) in any other case, on the last day of the regular interval at which it is treated as paid.

(3) Paragraphs (1) and (2) shall not apply to a payment of earnings made in one year where by virtue of those paragraphs that payment would be treated as made in another year.

(4) Notwithstanding regulation 15, a payment to which paragraph (3) applies ("the relevant payment") shall not be aggregated with any other earnings unless—

(*a*) other earnings to which paragraphs (1) to (2) do not apply by virtue only of paragraph (3) are paid in the earnings period in which the relevant payment falls; and

(*b*) those other earnings would have been aggregated with the relevant payment had paragraph (3) not applied.

(5) A relevant payment shall be aggregated only with the other earnings specified in paragraph (4).

Commentary—*Simon's Taxes* **E8.246, E8.249C.**

HMRC Manuals—National Insurance Manual NIM07085 (insolvency of employer: payments made out of the national insurance fund).

NIM08040–08070 (earnings paid at regular intervals: occasional changes in pay interval).

NIM08620 (regular additional payment made later).

NIM08700–08710 (payments not paid on their usual payday: general).

NIC

8 Earnings periods for directors

(1) Where a person is, or is appointed, or ceases to be a director of a company during any year the amount, if any, of earnings-related contributions payable in respect of earnings paid to or for the benefit of that person in respect of any employed earner's employment with that company shall, subject to regulations 12 and 14 to 17, be assessed on the amount of all such earnings paid (whether or not paid weekly) in the earnings periods specified in paragraphs (2) to (5).

(2) Where on one or more than one occasion a person is appointed a director of a company during the course of a year the earnings period in respect of such earnings as are paid in so much of the year as remains in the period commencing with the week in which he is appointed or, as the case may be, first appointed shall be the number of weeks in that period.

(3) Where a person is a director of a company at the beginning of a year the earnings period in respect of such earnings shall be that year, whether or not he remains such a director throughout that year.

(4) Where the earnings paid in respect of two or more employed earner's employments fall to be aggregated and the earnings periods in respect of those earnings would be of different lengths, then—

(*a*) if those periods are determined only by paragraphs (1) to (3); or

(*b*) if the length of one or more of those periods is determined by those paragraphs and the length of one or more of the others is determined by any other provision of these Regulations,

the earnings period in respect of all those earnings shall be the period determined by those paragraphs or, where there is more than one such period, the longer or longest period so determined.

(5) Where a person is no longer a director of a company and, in any year after that in which he ceased to be a director of that company, he is paid earnings in respect of any period during which he was such a director, then—

(*a*) notwithstanding regulation 15, those earnings shall not be aggregated with any other earnings with which they would otherwise fall to be aggregated; and

(*b*) the earnings period in respect of those earnings shall be the year in which they are paid.

(6) Without prejudice to the paragraphs (1) to (5), a director and any company employing him may pay on account of any earnings-related contributions that may become payable by them such amounts as would be payable by way of such contributions if those paragraphs did not apply.

[(7) If a full gender recognition certificate is issued under the Gender Recognition Act 2004 to a person aged at least 60 but not more than 64—

(*a*) whose gender before its issue was female; and

(*b*) whose acquired gender is male;

the periods in the year of issue respectively falling before and after its issue shall be treated, for the purpose of computing liability for primary Class 1 contributions, as separate earnings periods.][1]

Commentary—*Simon's Taxes* **E8.246, E8.250, E8.902.**

HMRC Manuals—National Insurance Manual NIM12003 (definition of director: annual earnings period). NIM12021–12026 (annual earnings periods : directors).

Amendments—[1] Para (7) inserted by the Social Security (Contributions) (Amendment No 3) Regulations, SI 2005/778 regs 2, 4 with effect from 6 April 2005.

9 Earnings period for statutory maternity pay[, [statutory paternity pay], statutory adoption pay][, statutory shared parental pay] and statutory sick pay paid by the Board

(1) In this regulation the expression "week"—

(*a*) in paragraph (2)(*a*); and

(*b*) in paragraph (2)(*b*) where it first occurs,

has the same meaning as in section 171(1) of the Act.

[(2) If the Board make a payment of statutory maternity pay, [statutory paternity pay][2], [3][, statutory shared parental pay][4] or statutory adoption pay under regulations made under the relevant provision—

(*a*) that payment of statutory maternity pay, [statutory paternity pay][2], [3][, statutory shared parental pay][4] or statutory adoption pay (as the case may be) shall not be aggregated with any other earnings; and

(*b*) the earnings period in respect of that payment for any week shall be a week.][1]

[(2A) In paragraph (2) "the relevant provision" means—

(*a*) in relation to statutory maternity pay, section 164(9)(*b*),

[(*b*) in relation to . . . [3]statutory paternity pay, section 171ZD(3),

(*ba*) . . . [3][,][4]][2]

(*c*) in relation to statutory adoption pay, section 171ZM(3), [and

(*d*) in relation to statutory shared parental pay, section 171ZX(3),][4]

of the Act (liability to make payments of the relevant statutory pay to be that of the Board).][1]

(3) If the Board make a payment of statutory sick pay under regulations made under section 151(6) of the Act (circumstances in which the Board are liable to pay statutory sick pay), the earnings period for that payment shall be—

(*a*) a period of the same length as the period in respect of which the payment is made, or

(*b*) a week,

whichever is the longer.

Commentary—*Simon's Taxes* **E8.24, E8.255**.

Amendments—[1] Words in heading inserted, and paras (2), (2A) substituted for para (2) as originally enacted, by the Social Security (Contributions) (Amendment) Regulations, SI 2003/193 regs 2, 4 with effect from 2003–04.

[2] Words in heading and in para (2) substituted for words "statutory paternity pay", and para (2A)(*b*), (*ba*) substituted for previous para (2A)(*b*), by the Social Security (Contributions) (Amendment) (No 5) Regulations, SI 2010/2450, regs 2, 3 with effect from 14 November 2010.

[3] In heading, para (2) in both places, words substituted, in para (2A)(*b*), word revoked, and para (2A)(*ba*) revoked by the Social Security and Tax Credits (Miscellaneous Amendments) Regulations, SI 2015/175 regs 2, 3(1), (2)(*a*), (3)(*a*), (4)(*a*), (*b*) with effect from 5 April 2015. These amendments do not have effect where they relate to ordinary statutory paternity pay or additional statutory paternity pay, or ordinary statutory paternity pay or additional statutory paternity pay paid on or after 5 April 2015: SI 2015/175 reg 9.

[4] In heading and para (2) in both places, words inserted, in para (2A)(*ba*), comma substituted for word "and", and para (2A)(*d*) and preceding word inserted by the Social Security and Tax Credits (Miscellaneous Amendments) Regulations, SI 2015/175 regs 2, 3(1), (2)(*b*), (3)(*b*), (4)(*c*), (*d*) with effect from 5 March 2015.

10 Earnings limits and thresholds

For the purposes of [sections 5(1)[, 9A and 9B][2]][1] of the Act (earnings limits and thresholds to be specified for each tax year in respect of Class 1 contributions), for the tax year which begins on 6th April [2016][2]—

(*a*) the lower earnings limit (for primary Class 1 contributions) shall be [£113][3];

(*b*) the upper earnings limit (for primary Class 1 contributions) shall be [£866][3];

(*c*) the primary threshold (for primary Class 1 contributions) shall be [£157][3]; . . . [1]

(*d*) the secondary threshold (for secondary Class 1 contributions) shall be [£157][3][; . . . [2]

(*e*) the upper secondary threshold for secondary Class 1 contributions in relation to the Under 21 group (for the upper limit of the age-related secondary percentage) shall be [£866][3, 1][; and

[(*f*) the upper secondary threshold for secondary Class 1 contributions in relation to relevant apprentices (for the upper limit of zero-rate secondary Class 1 contributions) shall be £866][3].

Commentary—*Simon's Taxes* **E8.261**.

HMRC Manuals—National Insurance Manual NIM01005 (the lower earnings limit).

NIM01009(the upper earnings limit & the annual maximum).

NIM01203 (class 1 structural overview from April 2009: the lower earnings limit).

NIM01204 (class 1 structural overview from April 2009: the PT & the ST).

Amendments—[1] Words and figures substituted, word at the end of para (*c*) revoked and para (*e*) and preceding word inserted, by the Social Security (Contributions) (Limits and Thresholds) (Amendment) Regulations, SI 2015/577 regs 2, 3 with effect from 6 April 2015.

[2] Words and figures substituted, and para (*f*) and preceding word inserted, by the Social Security (Contributions) (Limits and Thresholds Amendments and National Insurance Funds Payments) Regulations, SI 2016/343 regs 3, 4 with effect from 6 April 2016.

[3] The following figures substituted by the Social Security (Contributions) (Rates, Limits and Thresholds Amendments and National Insurance Funds Payments) Regulations, SI 2017/415 regs 6, 7 with effect from 6 April 2017—

- the Class 1 weekly primary lower earnings limit is "£113" (previously "£112");
- the Class 1 weekly primary upper earnings limit is "£866" (previously "£827");
- the Class 1 weekly primary threshold is "£157" (previously "£155");
- the Class 1 weekly secondary threshold is "£157" (previously "£156");
- the Class 1 weekly upper secondary threshold for under 21s is "£866" (previously "£827"); and
- the Class 1 weekly upper secondary threshold for apprentices under 25 is "£866" (previously "£827").

11 Prescribed equivalents

(1) The prescribed equivalents of the lower and upper earnings limits[, the primary and secondary thresholds and the upper secondary thresholds][5], for the purposes of—

(*a*) sections 6(1), 6A(1), 8(1), [9(1), 9A(9), and 9B(6)][5] of the Act (which provide liability for Class 1 contributions, notional payment of primary Class 1 contribution where earnings are not less than the lower earnings limit, the calculation of primary Class 1 contributions[, the calculation of secondary Class 1 contributions, the calculation of secondary Class 1 contributions in relation to the Under 21 age group and the calculation of secondary Class 1 contributions in relation to relevant apprentices][5] respectively); [and][6]

[(*aa*) section 22 of the Act (earnings factors);][1]

(*b*) . . . [6]

shall be determined in accordance with paragraphs (2) to (5).

(1A) . . . [6]

[(2) Subject to paragraphs (4) and (5), the prescribed equivalents of the lower earnings limit . . . [6] shall be—

(*a*) where the earnings period is a multiple of a week, the [amount][6] calculated by multiplying the lower earnings limit . . . [6] by the corresponding multiple;][1]

(*b*) where the earnings period is a month, the [amount][6] calculated by multiplying [the lower earnings limit][6] by 4¹/₃;

(*c*) where the earnings period is a multiple of a month, the [amount][6] calculated by multiplying [the lower earnings limit][6] by 4¹/₃ and multiplying [the result][6] by the corresponding multiple;

NIC

(*d*) in any other case, the [amount][6] calculated by dividing [the lower earnings limit][6] by 7 and multiplying [the result][6] by the number of days in the earnings period concerned.

[(2A) Subject to paragraphs (4) and (5), the prescribed equivalents of the upper earnings limit shall be—

(*a*) where the earnings period is a month, [£3,750][7];

(*b*) where the earnings period is a year, [£45,000][7];

(*c*) where the earnings period is a multiple of a week, the amount calculated by dividing the figure in sub-paragraph (*b*) by 52 and multiplying the result by the corresponding multiple;

(*d*) where the earnings period is a multiple of a month, the amount calculated by dividing the figure in sub-paragraph (*b*) by 12 and multiplying the result by the corresponding multiple;

(*e*) in any other case, the amount calculated by dividing the figure in sub-paragraph (*b*) by 365 and multiplying the result by the number of days in the earnings period concerned.][1]

(3) Subject to paragraphs (4) and (5), [the prescribed equivalents of the primary threshold][2] shall be—

(*a*) where the earnings period is a month, [£680][7];

(*b*) where the earnings period is a year, [£8,164][7];

(*c*) where the earnings period is a multiple of a week, the amount calculated by dividing the figure in sub-paragraph (*b*) by 52 and multiplying the result by the corresponding multiple;

(*d*) where the earnings period is a multiple of a month, the amount calculated by dividing the figure in sub-paragraph (*b*) by 12 and multiplying the result by the corresponding multiple;

(*e*) in any other case, the amount calculated by dividing the figure in sub-paragraph (*b*) by 365 and multiplying the result by the number of days in the earnings period concerned.

[(3A) Subject to paragraphs (4) and (5), the prescribed equivalents of the secondary threshold shall be—

(*a*) where the earnings period is a month, [£680][7];

(*b*) where the earnings period is a year, [£8,164][7];

(*c*) where the earnings period is a multiple of a week, the amount calculated by dividing the figure in sub-paragraph (*b*) by 52 and multiplying the result by the corresponding multiple;

(*d*) where the earnings period is a multiple of a month, the amount calculated by dividing the figure in sub-paragraph (*b*) by 12 and multiplying the result by the corresponding multiple;

(*e*) in any other case, the amount calculated by dividing the figure in sub-paragraph (*b*) by 365 and multiplying the result by the number of days in the earnings period concerned.][2]

[(3B) Subject to paragraphs (4) and (5), the prescribed equivalents of the upper secondary threshold for secondary Class 1 contributions in relation to the Under 21 age group shall be—

(*a*) where the earnings period is a month, [£3,750][7];

(*b*) where the earnings period is a year, [£45,000][7];

(*c*) where the earnings period is a multiple of a week, the amount calculated by dividing the figure in sub-paragraph (*b*) by 52 and multiplying the result by the corresponding multiple;

(*d*) where the earnings period is a multiple of a month, the amount calculated by dividing the figure in sub-paragraph (*b*) by 12 and multiplying the result by the corresponding multiple;

(*e*) in any other case, the amount calculated by dividing the figure in sub-paragraph (*b*) by 365 and multiplying the result by the number of days in the earnings period concerned.][3]

[(3C) Subject to paragraphs (4) and (5), the prescribed equivalents of the upper secondary threshold for secondary Class 1 contributions in relation to relevant apprentices shall be—

(*a*) where the earnings period is a month, [£3,750][7];

(*b*) where the earnings period is a year, [£45,000][7];

(*c*) where the earnings period is a multiple of a week, the amount calculated by dividing the figure in sub-paragraph (*b*) by 52 and multiplying the result by the corresponding multiple;

(*d*) where the earnings period is a multiple of a month, the amount calculated by dividing the figure in sub-paragraph (*b*) by 12 and multiplying the result by the corresponding multiple;

(*e*) in any other case, the amount calculated by dividing the figure in sub-paragraph (*b*) by 365 and multiplying the result by the number of days in the earnings period concerned.][5]

[(4) The amounts determined in accordance with paragraphs (2)(*b*) and (*c*), paragraph (2A)(*c*) and (*d*)[, paragraph (3)(*c*) and (*d*)[, paragraph (3A)(*c*) and (*d*)[, paragraph (3B)(*c*) and (*d*) and paragraph (3C)(*c*) and (*d*)][5]][4]][2] if not whole pounds, shall be rounded up to the next whole pound.][1]

(5) The amounts determined in accordance with [paragraph (2)(*d*), paragraph (2A)(*e*)[, paragraph (3)(*e*), [paragraph (3A)(*e*)[, paragraph (3B)(*e*) and paragraph (3C)(*e*)][5]][4]][2]][1] shall be calculated to the nearest penny, and any amount of a halfpenny or less shall be disregarded.

(6) . . .[6]

Commentary—*Simon's Taxes* **E8.261**.

HMRC Manuals—National Insurance Manual NIM01010 (earnings limits & thresholds for pay intervals other than a week).
NIM01206 (calculating earnings limits & thresholds for pay intervals of other than a week).
NIM02472 (how to calculate the exempt amount - the simplified method).

Amendments—[1] In para (1), sub-para (*aa*) inserted, paras (2A) inserted, in paras (2), (5), words substituted, and para (4) substituted, by the Social Security (Contributions) (Amendment) Regulations, SI 2009/111 regs 2, 3 with effect from 6 April 2009.

2 Words in para (3) substituted, para (3A) inserted, and in paras (4), (5), words substituted, by the Social Security (Contributions) (Amendment No 2) Regulations, SI 2011/940 regs 2, 4 with effect from 6 April 2011.

3 Para (3B) inserted by the (Social Security (Contributions) (Limits and Thresholds) (Amendment) Regulations, SI 2015/577 regs 2, 4 with effect from 6 April 2015.

4 In paras (4), (5), words substituted by the Social Security (Contributions) (Limits and Thresholds) (Amendment) Regulations 2015, SI 2015/577 regs 4(e) and (f) with effect from 6 April 2015.

5 In paras (1), (4), (5), words substituted, and para (3C) inserted, by the Social Security (Contributions) (Limits and Thresholds Amendments and National Insurance Funds Payments) Regulations, SI 2016/343 regs 3, 5 with effect from 6 April 2016.

6 In para (1) word at end of sub-para (*a*) inserted and sub-para (*b*) revoked, paras (1A), (6) revoked, and in para (2) words revoked and substituted, by the Social Security (Contributions) (Amendment) (No 2) Regulations, SI 2016/352 reg 10 with effect from 6 April 2016 and subject to savings in relation to rights or obligations arising in connection with tax years beginning before 6 April 2016.

7 The following prescribed equivalent figures for monthly and yearly earnings periods are substituted by the Social Security (Contributions) (Rates, Limits and Thresholds Amendments and National Insurance Funds Payments) Regulations, SI 2017/415 regs 6, 8 with effect from 6 April 2017—

- the upper earnings limit in para (2A) is: monthly "£3,750" (previously "£3,583"); and yearly "£45,000" (previously "£43,000");
- the primary threshold in para (3) is: monthly "£680" (previously "£672"); and yearly "£8,164" (previously "£8,060");
- the secondary threshold in para (3A) is: monthly "£680" (previously "£676"); and yearly "£8,164" (previously "£8,112");
- the upper secondary threshold for under 21s in para (3B) is: monthly "£3,750" (previously "£3,583"); and yearly "£45,000" (previously "£43,000"); and
- the upper secondary threshold for apprentices under 25 in para (3C) is: monthly "£3,750" (previously "£3,583"); and yearly "£45,000" (previously "£43,000").

12 Calculation of earnings-related contributions

[(1) Subject to paragraphs (3) and (4), primary and secondary Class 1 contributions under section 6 of the Act (liability for Class 1 contributions) shall be calculated to the nearest penny and any amount of a halfpenny or less shall be disregarded.][1]

(2) In the alternative, but subject to the provisions of paragraphs (3) to (5), the contributions specified in paragraph (1) may be calculated in accordance with the appropriate scale or, for contributions payable on earnings above the upper earnings limit or the prescribed equivalent of that limit, a contributions calculator prepared by the Board.

(3) Where the amount of earnings to which—

(*a*) the appropriate scale is to be applied does not appear in the scale, the amount of contributions payable shall be calculated by reference to the next smaller amount of earnings in the appropriate column in the scale;

(*b*) the appropriate contributions calculator is to be applied does not appear in the calculator, the amount of contributions payable shall be calculated—

(i) by obtaining from the calculator the amounts of contributions payable on the largest components of the earnings provided for in the calculator, and

(ii) by adding together the amounts so obtained.

(4) Where a scale or a contributions calculator would, but for the period to which it relates, be appropriate and the earnings period in question is a multiple of the period in the scale or, as the case may be, calculator, the scale or calculator shall be applied by dividing the earnings in question so as to obtain the equivalent earnings for the period to which the scale or calculator relates and—

(*a*) in the case of the scale, by multiplying the amount of contributions shown in the scale as appropriate to those equivalent earnings by the same factor as the earnings were divided;

(*b*) in the case of the calculator, by multiplying the amount of contributions shown in the calculator as appropriate to those equivalent earnings or, where no equivalent earnings are shown, the amount of contributions calculated in accordance with paragraph (3)(*b*), by the same factor as the earnings were divided.

(5) Unless the Board agree to the contrary, all the contributions payable in a year in respect of the earnings paid to or for the benefit of an earner in respect of his employed earner's employment or, where he has more than one such employment and the earnings from those employments are aggregated under paragraph 1(1) of Schedule 1 to the Act (Class 1 contributions where more than one employment), in respect of those employments, shall be calculated either in accordance with paragraph (1) or paragraph (2) but not partly in accordance with one and partly in accordance with the other of those paragraphs, save that the contributions calculator may also be used where the contributions have been calculated in accordance with paragraph (1).

Commentary—*Simon's Taxes* **E8.249D.**

HMRC Manuals—NIM11001 (Class 1: calculating & recording earnings : general).
NIM11002 (exact percentage method).

Amendments—[1] Para (1) substituted by the Social Security (Contributions) (Amendment) (No 2) Regulations, SI 2016/352 reg 11 with effect from 6 April 2016 and subject to savings in relation to rights or obligations arising in connection with tax years beginning before 6 April 2016.

NIC

13 General provisions as to aggregation

Where on one or more occasions the whole or any part of a person's earnings in respect of employed earner's employment is not paid weekly (whether or not it is treated for the purpose of earnings-related contributions as paid weekly), paragraph 1 of Schedule 1 to the Act (Class 1 contributions where more than one employment) shall have effect as if for the references to "week" there were substituted references to "earnings period".

Commentary—*Simon's Taxes* **E8.243**.

14 Aggregation of earnings paid in respect of separate employed earner's employments under the same employer

For the purpose of earnings-related contributions, where an earner is concurrently employed in more than one employed earner's employment under the same employer, the earnings paid to or for the benefit of the earner in respect of those employments shall not be aggregated if such aggregation is not reasonably practicable because the earnings in the respective employment are separately calculated.

Commentary—*Simon's Taxes* **E8.241**.

HMRC Manuals—National Insurance Manual NIM10002 (one or more employments with the same employer).

15 Aggregation of earnings paid in respect of different employed earner's employments by different persons and apportionment of contribution liability

(1) Subject to regulation 7, for the purposes of determining whether earnings-related contributions are payable in respect of earnings paid to or for the benefit of an earner in a given earnings period, and, if so, the amount of contributions, where in that period earnings in respect of different employed earner's employments are paid to or for the benefit of the earner—

(*a*) by different secondary contributors who in respect of those employments carry on business in association with each other;

(*b*) by different employers, one of whom is, by virtue of Schedule 3 to the Social Security (Categorisation of Earners) Regulations 1978, treated as the secondary contributor in respect of each of those employments; or

(*c*) by different persons, in respect of work performed for those persons by the earner in those employments and in respect of those earnings, some other person is, by virtue of that Schedule, treated as the secondary contributor,

the earnings paid in respect of each of the employments referred to in this paragraph shall, unless in a case falling under sub-paragraph (*a*) it is not reasonably practicable to do so, be aggregated and treated as a single payment of earnings in respect of one such employment.

(2) Where, under paragraph (1), earnings are aggregated, liability for the secondary contributions payable in respect of those earnings shall, in a case falling within paragraph (1)(*a*), be apportioned between the secondary contributors in such proportions as they shall agree amongst themselves, or, in default of agreement, in the proportions which the earnings paid by each bearer to the total amount of the aggregated earnings.

Commentary—*Simon's Taxes* **E8.242 , E8.244, E8.613**.

HMRC Manuals—National Insurance Manual NIM 10003-10006 (more than one employment with different employers). NIM10010 (definition of 'business in association').

16 Aggregation of earnings paid after pensionable age

Notwithstanding the provisions of regulation 15, a payment of earnings to which regulation 28 applies shall not be aggregated with any other earnings.

Commentary—*Simon's Taxes* **E8.247**.

HMRC Manuals—National Insurance Manual NIM10007 (earnings paid after state pension age).

17 Apportionment of single payment of earnings in respect of different employed earner's employments by different secondary contributors

Where any single payment of earnings is made in respect of two or more employed earner's employments under different secondary contributions, liability for earnings-related contributions shall be determined by apportioning the payment as follows—

(*a*) where the secondary contributors are, in respect of those employments, carrying on business in association with each other, to the secondary contributor who makes the payment;

(*b*) where the secondary contributors are not so carrying on business in association with each other, to each of those secondary contributors in the proportion which the earnings due in respect of that secondary contributor's employment bears to the total of the single payment.

Commentary—*Simon's Taxes* **E8.245**.

HMRC Manuals—National Insurance Manual NIM10008 (single payments of earnings to cover employments with different secondary contributors).

18 Change of earnings period

(1) Paragraphs (2) and (3) apply where, by reason of a change in the regular interval at which any part of an earner's earnings is paid or treated as paid in respect of employed earner's employment ("the regular interval of payment"), that person's earnings period in any employment or employments under the same secondary contributor is, or is in the process of being, changed.

(2) Subject to paragraph (3), in relation to any payments made on or after the date of change the earnings period shall be determined in accordance with the new interval.

(3) Where the new period is longer than the old period and during the first new period any payment has also been made at the old interval, the earnings-related contributions payable on any payment made on or after the date of change shall not exceed in amount the total which would have been payable if all the payments during the new period had been made at the new interval.

(4) In this regulation—

(*a*) the regular interval of payment which has been discontinued is referred to as "the old interval" and the interval which has, or is to, become the regular interval of payment is referred to as "the new interval";

(*b*) the earnings period determined according to the old interval is referred to as "the old period" and that determined according to the new interval is referred to as "the new period";

(*c*) reference to payment means payment of earnings actually made or, as the case may be, treated under regulation 7 as made, at an interval or date; and

(*d*) "date of change" means the date on which the first payment of earnings at the new interval is made.

Commentary—*Simon's Taxes* **E8.249C**.

HMRC Manuals—Nation Insurance Manual NIM08500 (change of earnings period with the same employer : change to shorter interval).

NIM08510 (change of earnings period with the same employer: change to longer interval).

19 Holiday payments

Where as respects an employed earner's employment in which the earner is paid or would, but for paragraph (*b*), be treated under regulation 7 as paid at a regular interval of a week or a fixed number of weeks, a payment of earnings includes or comprises a payment in respect of a period of holiday entitlement other than such a payment made to an earner in respect of a period of holiday entitlement outstanding on termination of that employment, for the purposes of calculating the earnings-related contributions payable in respect of that payment of earnings—

(*a*) the earnings period may be the length of the period in respect of which the payment is made, but where the length of that earnings period includes a fraction of a week that fraction shall be treated as a whole week; and

(*b*) where the earnings period is so determined, regulation 7 shall not apply.

Commentary—*Simon's Taxes* **E8.257**.

HMRC Manuals—NIM09100 - NIM09160 (holiday pay and its calculations).

20 [Joint employment of spouses or civil partners]

For the purposes of earnings-related contributions, where [spouses or civil partners][1] are jointly employed in employed earner's employment and earnings in respect of the employment are paid to them jointly, the amount of the earnings of each shall be calculated upon the same basis as that upon which those earnings are calculated for the purposes of income tax and, in the absence of such calculation, upon such basis as may be approved by the Board.

Commentary—*Simon's Taxes* **E8.236**.

Amendments—[1] Words substituted by the Social Security (Contributions) (Amendment No 6) Regulations, SI 2005/3130 regs 2, 3 with effect from 5 December 2005.

21 [Annual maxima for those with more than one employment

(1) For the purposes of section 19(1) and (2) of the Act (power to prescribe maximum amounts of contributions and repayments of excess) if an earner is employed in more than one employment his liability in any year—

(*a*) for primary Class 1 contributions; or

(*b*) where both primary Class 1 contributions and Class 2 contributions are payable by him, for both primary Class 1 contributions and Class 2 contributions,

shall not exceed an amount which equals the amount found in accordance with paragraph (2).

(2) The amount is found as follows.

Step One

Calculate—

$$53 \times (\text{UEL} - \text{PT})$$

Here *UEL* is the upper earnings limit, and *PT* the primary threshold, specified for the year.

Step Two

Multiply the result of Step One by [12 per cent][2].

Step Three

Add together, in respect of all of the employed earner's employments, so much of the earnings in each of those employments as exceeds the primary threshold and does not exceed the upper earnings limit.

Step Four

From the sum produced by Step Three subtract the amount found by the formula in Step One.

Step Five

If the result produced by Step Four is a positive value, multiply it by [2 per cent][2].

If that result is nil or a negative value, it is treated for the purposes of Step Eight as nil.

Step Six

Add together, in respect of all of the employed earner's employments, so much of the earnings in each of those employments as exceeds the upper earnings limit.

Step Seven

Multiply the sum produced by Step Six by [2 per cent][2]

Step Eight

Add together the amounts produced by Steps Two, Five and Seven.

The result of Step Eight is the annual maximum, subject to the further qualifications in paragraphs (3) and (4).

[(3) For the purpose only of determining the extent of the earner's liability for contributions under paragraph (2), the amount of a primary Class 1 contribution which is paid at a rate less than 12 per cent because the earner is a married woman who has made an election to pay contributions at the reduced rate as mentioned in regulation 127, shall be treated as equal to the amount of the primary Class 1 contribution which would be payable if the election had not been made.][3]

(4) Paragraph (2) is subject to—

(*a*) section 12 of the Act (late paid Class 2 contributions); and

(*b*) regulations 63 to 65 (special provisions about Class 2 and Class 3 contributions paid late).

(5) Notwithstanding paragraphs (1) to (4), an earner shall be liable, in the first instance, for the full amount of the contributions which would have been payable but for this regulation.][1]

Commentary—*Simon's Taxes* **E8.266, E8.267.**

HMRC Manuals—National Insurance Manual NIM01009 (the upper earnings limit ('UEL') & the annual maximum).
NIM01251 - 01253 (the class 1 and 2 annual maximum).
NIM20725 (deferment and the annual maximum).

Amendments—[1] Regulation 21 substituted by the Social Security (Contributions) (Amendment) Regulations, SI 2003/193 regs 2, 6 with effect from 2003–04.

[2] Percentages substituted by the Social Security (Contributions) (Amendment) Regulations, SI 2012/573 reg 2(1), (2) with effect in relation to contributions paid in respect of the tax year 2011–12 and subsequent tax years.

[3] Para (3) substituted by the Social Security (Contributions) (Amendment) (No 2) Regulations, SI 2016/352 reg 12 with effect from 6 April 2016 and subject to savings in relation to rights or obligations arising in connection with tax years beginning before 6 April 2016.

22 [Amounts] to be treated as earnings

(1) For the purposes of section 3 of the Act (earnings), the amounts specified in paragraphs [(2) to (13)][4] shall be treated as remuneration derived from an employed earner's employment.

(2) The amount specified in this paragraph is the amount of any payment by a company to or for the benefit of any of its directors if—

(*a*) apart from this regulation the payment would, when made, not be earnings for the purposes of the Act; and

(*b*) the payment is made on account of or by way of an advance on a sum which would be earnings for those purposes.

[(3) The amount specified in this paragraph is the amount equal to the cash equivalent in respect of car fuel which is treated as earnings from the employment of the earner for income tax purposes by virtue of section 149 of ITEPA 2003.][1]

[(4) The amount specified in this paragraph is the amount which is treated as earnings from the employment of the employed earner by virtue of section 222(2) of ITEPA 2003.][1]

[(5) The amount specified in this paragraph is the amount which counts as employment income of the employed earner under Chapter 2 of Part 7 of ITEPA 2003 computed in accordance with section 428 of ITEPA 2003 in respect of conditional shares or interests in conditional shares acquired before 16th April 2003.

References in this paragraph and paragraph (6) to ITEPA 2003 are to that Act as originally enacted.][1]

[(6) The amount specified in this paragraph is the amount which counts as employment income of the employed earner by virtue of Chapter 4 of Part 7 of ITEPA 2003 (shares: post-acquisition charges) in respect of shares or interests in shares acquired before 16th April 2003.][1]

[(7) The amounts specified in this paragraph are those—

(*a*) which count as employment income of the employed earner in relation to employment-related securities (within the meaning given by section 421B(8) of ITEPA 2003); and

(*b*) to which section 698 of ITEPA 2003 (PAYE: special charges on employment-related securities) applies.

References in this paragraph [and paragraphs (9) and (10)][2] to ITEPA 2003 are to that Act as amended . . . [2].][1]

[(8) The amount specified in this paragraph is the amount—

(*a*) which counts as employment income of the employed earner by virtue of sections 500 to 508 of ITEPA 2003; and

(*b*) in respect of which income tax is recoverable in accordance with PAYE regulations.][1]

[(9) The amount specified in this paragraph is any amount—

(*a*) which, by reason of the operation of Schedule 2 to the Finance (No 2) Act 2005, counts as employment income of the employed earner under any of Chapters 2 to 4 of Part 7 of ITEPA 2003; and

(*b*) where the relevant date for that income determined under section 698(6) of ITEPA 2003 (whether or not the PAYE Regulations apply to that income) is on or after 2nd December 2004 and before 20th July 2005.

(10) The amount specified in this paragraph is any amount—

(*a*) which by virtue of the operation of section 92 of the Finance Act 2006 counts as employment income of the employed earner under any of Chapters 2 to 4 of Part 7 of ITEPA 2003; and

(*b*) where the relevant date for that income determined under section 698(6) of ITEPA 2003 (whether or not the PAYE Regulations apply to that income) is on or after 2nd December 2004 and before 19th July 2006.][2]

[(11) The amount specified in this paragraph is the amount treated as earnings from the employment by virtue of section 226A of ITEPA 2003 (amount treated as earnings).][3]

[(12) The amount specified in this paragraph is any amount—

(*a*) paid or reimbursed to an employed earner in respect of expenses;

(*b*) provided pursuant to relevant salary sacrifice arrangements within the meaning of section 289A(5) of ITEPA 2003; and

(*c*) which is not a payment or reimbursement of relevant motoring expenditure within the meaning of paragraph (3) of regulation 22A.

(13) The amount specified in this paragraph is any amount paid or reimbursed to an employed earner in respect of expenses which is calculated according to a set rate rather than by reference to the actual amount incurred in respect of the expenses where such a rate is not—

(*a*) contained in regulations made by the Commissioners for Her Majesty's Revenue and Customs under section 289A(6)(*a*); or

(*b*) approved under section 289B of ITEPA 2003.][4]

Commentary—*Simon's Taxes* **E8.233, E8.234, E8.236, E8.269D, E8.1113, E8.1123**.

HMRC Manuals—NIM06807 (employment - related securities: shares - early acquisition of shares from a share incentive plan).

NIM06814 (class 1 Nics: employment-related securities shares: employee shareholder status).

NIM06826 -NIM06834 (securities: amount treated as earnings).

NIM06842-06843 (class 1 Nics: employment-related securities -retrospective liability - rights under contracts of insurance).

NIM12014 (directors loan accounts and payments on account of earnings: introduction).

NIM12016-12020 (directors loan accounts: related issues).

Amendments—[1] Word in cross-heading substituted, and paras (3)–(8) substituted for previous paras (3)–(5), by the Social Security (Contributions) (Amendment No 5) Regulations, SI 2003/2085 regs 3, 5 with effect from 1 September 2003.

[2] Words in para (7) inserted and revoked, and paras (9), (10) inserted, by the Social Security (Contributions) (Amendment No 2) Regulations, SI 2007/1057 reg 2. These changes come into force on 6 April 2007 and have effect generally from 2 December 2004. The revocation of words in para (7) has effect from 20 July 2005.

[3] Para (11) inserted, by the Social Security (Contributions) (Amendment No 3) Regulations, SI 2013/1907 regs 2, 3 with effect from 1 September 2013.

[4] In para (1), references substituted, and paras (12), (13) inserted, by the Social Security (Contributions) (Amendment) (No 2) Regulations SI 2016/352, regs 2, 4 with effect from 6 April 2016.

22A [Amounts to be treated as earnings in connection with the use of qualifying vehicles other than cycles

(1) To the extent that it would not otherwise be earnings, the amount specified in paragraph (2) shall be so treated.

(2) The amount is that produced by the formula—

$$RME - QA$$

Here—

RME is the aggregate of relevant motoring expenditure within the meaning of paragraph (3) in the earnings period; and

QA is the qualifying amount calculated in accordance with paragraph (4).

(3) A payment is relevant motoring expenditure if—

(*a*) it is a mileage allowance payment within the meaning of [section 229(2) of ITEPA 2003][2];

(*b*) it would be such a payment but for the fact that it is paid to another for the benefit of the employee; or

NIC

(*c*) it is any other form of payment, except a payment in kind, made by or on behalf of the employer, and made to, or for the benefit of, the employee in respect of the use by the employee of a qualifying vehicle.

[Here "qualifying vehicle" means a vehicle to which section 235 of ITEPA 2003 applies,][2] but does not include a cycle within the meaning of section 192(1) of the Road Traffic Act 1988.

(4) The qualifying amount is the product of the formula—

$$M \times R$$

Here—

M is the sum of—

(*a*) the number of miles of business travel undertaken, at or before the time when the payment is made—

(i) in respect of which the payment is made, and

(ii) in respect of which no other payment has been made; and

(*b*) the number of miles of business travel undertaken—

(i) since the last payment of relevant motoring expenditure was made, or, if there has been no such payment, since the employment began, and

(ii) for which no payment has been, or is to be, made; and

R is the rate applicable to the vehicle in question, at the time when the payment is made, in accordance with [section 230(2) of ITEPA 2003][2] and, if more than one rate is applicable to the class of vehicle in question, is the higher or highest of those rates.][1]

Commentary—*Simon's Taxes* **E8.235**.

HMRC Manuals—National Insurance Manual NIM05802 (main features of the Nics motoring expenses scheme).

NIM05815 -05816 (relevant motoring expenditure).

NIM05830-05831 (the qualifying amount: business travel).

NIM05840-05842 (calculating class 1 Nics : mileage allowance).

NIM05860 (determining whether payments are for an employee's use of a qualifying vehicle: motor cycles).

Simon's Tax Cases—*Cheshire Employer and Skills Development Ltd v R&C Comrs* [2011] UKUT 329 (TCC), [2012] STC 69.

Amendments—[1] Regulation 22A inserted by the Social Security (Contributions) (Amendment No 2) Regulations, SI 2002/307 regs 2, 4 with effect from 6 April 2002.

[2] Words in paras (3), (4) substituted by the Social Security (Contributions, Categorisation of Earners and Intermediaries) (Amendment) Regulations, SI 2004/770 regs 2, 4 with effect from 6 April 2004.

22B [Amounts to be treated as earnings: Part 7A of ITEPA 2003

(1) For the purposes of section 3 of the Act (earnings), the amount specified in paragraph (2) shall be treated as remuneration derived from an employed earner's employment.

(2) The amount is the amount which counts as employment income of the employed earner by virtue of Chapter 2 of Part 7A of ITEPA 2003.

(3) Paragraph (2) does not apply if the relevant step which gives rise to the amount which counts as employment income by virtue of Chapter 2 of Part 7A of ITEPA 2003 would otherwise give rise to earnings for the purposes of the Act.

(4) In paragraph (3) "relevant step" means a relevant step for the purposes of Part 7A of ITEPA 2003.][1]

Commentary—*Simon's Taxes* **E4.801, E8.1110, E8.1113**.

HMRC Manuals—National Insurance Manual NIM52100 (treating employment income as earnings).

NIM52150 (class 1 Nics liability arises).

NIM52650 (prevention of Nics on same amounts twice).

NIM52900 (employer financed retirement benefit schemes – payments disregarded from earnings).

Press releases etc—HMRC Notice, 5 January 2012: National Insurance Contributions on disguised remuneration—Frequently Asked Questions.

HMRC Notice, 5 September 2012: Employee Benefit Trusts—update on "settlement opportunity" and FAQs (see *SWTI 2012, Issue 36*).

Amendments—[1] Regulation 22B inserted by the Social Security (Contributions) (Amendment No 5) Regulations, SI 2011/2700 regs 2, 3 with effect from 6 December 2011. This amendment does not apply in relation to an amount which counts as employment income by virtue of ITEPA 2003 Part 7A Chapter 2 if that Chapter applies because of FA 2011 Sch 2 para 53 or para 54 (SI 2011/2700 reg 1(2)).

23 Manner of making sickness payments treated as remuneration

Where by virtue of section 4(1) of the Act (payments treated as remuneration and earnings) a sickness payment is treated as remuneration derived from an employed earner's employment, that payment shall be made through the person who is the secondary contributor in relation to the employment concerned except where—

(*a*) the payment is payable by another person;

(*b*) that person has agreed with the secondary contributor to make the payment; and (*c*) arrangements have been made between them for the person who has agreed to make the payment to furnish the secondary contributor with the information specified in paragraph 3(5)(*a*) of Schedule 4 (intermediate employers).

Commentary—*Simon's Taxes* **E8.260, E8.908**.

24 Calculation of earnings for the purposes of earnings-related contributions

For the purpose of determining the amount of earnings-related contributions, the amount of a person's earnings from employed earner's employment shall be calculated on the basis of his gross earnings from the employment or employments in question.

This is subject to the provisions of Schedule 2 (calculation of earnings for the purposes of earnings-related contributions in particular cases) and Schedule 3 (payments to be disregarded in the calculation of earnings for the purposes of earnings-related contributions).

Commentary—*Simon's Taxes* **E8.231**.
HMRC Manuals—National Insurance Manual NIM02411 (class 1: vouchers - introduction).
NIM02464 (non-cash vouchers - calculation of the amount of earnings).
NIM02499 (calculation of the amount of earnings - voucher provided to two or more employees).

25 Payments to be disregarded in the calculation of earnings for the purposes of earnings-related contributions

Schedule 3 specifies payments which are to be disregarded in the calculation of earnings from employed earner's employment for the purpose of earnings-related contributions.

HMRC Manuals—National Insurance Manual NIM02020 (payments excluded from class 1 liability).
NIM02162 (NIC liability where schemes are granted interim approval for tax purposes).
NIM02102-02104 (Class 1 Nics : employer pays all or part expenses for an employee in provided accommodation).
NIM02108 (credit card reward payments).
NIM05610 (call-out expenses).
NIM02218 (long service awards).
NIM05625 (parking fees incurred at the permanent workplace).

26 Certain payments by trustees to be disregarded

(1) For the purposes of earnings-related contributions, there shall be excluded from the calculation of a person's earnings in respect of any employed earner's employment any payment, or any part of a payment—

(*a*) which is made by trustees before 6th April 1990;
(*b*) the amount of which is or may be dependent upon the exercise by the trustees of a discretion or the performance by them of a duty arising under the trust;
(*c*) not being a sickness payment which by virtue of section 4(1) of the Act (payments treated as remuneration and earnings) is treated as remuneration derived from an employed earner's employment,

and in respect of which either paragraph (2) or (3) is satisfied.

(2) This paragraph is satisfied if the trust, under which the payment is made, was created before 6th April 1985.

(3) This paragraph is satisfied if—

(*a*) the trust, under which the payment is made, was created on or after 6th April 1985;
(*b*) that trust took effect immediately on the termination of a trust created before 6th April 1985;
(*c*) the person to whom the payment is made either—
  (i) was a beneficiary under the earlier trust, or
  (ii) would have been such a beneficiary if, while the earlier trust was subsisting, he had held the employment in respect of which the payment is made; and
(*d*) there were or are payments under the earlier trust which in the case of payments made on or after 6th October 1987, are payments made in circumstances to which sub-paragraphs (*a*), (*b*) and (*c*) apply.

27 Payments to directors which are to be disregarded

(1) For the purposes of earnings-related contributions, there shall be excluded from the calculation of a person's earnings any payment in so far as it is a payment—

(*a*) by a company;
(*b*) to or for the benefit of a director of that company;
(*c*) in respect of any employed earner's employment of that director with that company; and
(*d*) in respect of which paragraph (2), (3) or (4) is satisfied.

(2) This paragraph is satisfied if—

(*a*) the director is a partner in a firm carrying on a profession;
(*b*) being a director of a company is a normal incident of membership of that profession and of membership of the firm of the director;
(*c*) the director is required by the terms of his partnership to account to his firm for the payment; and
(*d*) the payment forms an insubstantial part of that firm's gross returns.

NIC

(3) This paragraph is satisfied if—

(*a*) the director was appointed to that office by a company having the right to do so by virtue of its shareholding in, or an agreement with, the company making the payment;

(*b*) by virtue of an agreement with the company that appointed him, the director is required to account for the payment to that company; and

(*c*) the payment forms part of the profits brought into charge to corporation tax or income tax of the company that appointed the director.

(4) This paragraph is satisfied if—

(*a*) the director was appointed to that office by a company other than the company making the payment;

(*b*) by virtue of an agreement with the company that appointed him, the director is required to account for the payment to that company;

(*c*) the payment forms part of the profits brought into charge to corporation tax of the company that appointed the director; and

(*d*) the company that appointed the director is not one over which—

(i) the director has, or

(ii) any person connected with the director has, or

(iii) the director and any persons connected with him together have,

control.

(5) In this regulation—

(*a*) "company" has the meaning given by section 832(1) . . . [1] of the Taxes Act (interpretation of the Tax Acts) [and Part 2 of Schedule 1 to ITEPA 2003][1];

(*b*) "the director" means the director to or for the benefit of whom the payment referred to in paragraph (1) is made; and

(*c*) in paragraph (4)(*d*)—

(i) "control" has the same meaning as in section 840 of the Taxes Act,

(ii) "any person connected with the director" means any of the following, namely the spouse, [civil partner,][2] parent, child, son-in-law or daughter-in-law of the director.

Commentary—*Simon's Taxes* **E8.290, E8.609, E8.1136**.

HMRC Manuals—National Insurance Manual NIM12004–12010 (directors: fees received by professional partnerships and other companies).

Amendments—[1] In para (5)(*a*), words revoked and inserted by the Social Security (Contributions, Categorisation of Earners and Intermediaries) (Amendment) Regulations, SI 2004/770 regs 2, 5 with effect from 6 April 2004.

[2] Words in para (5) inserted by the Social Security (Contributions) (Amendment No 6) Regulations, SI 2005/3130 regs 2, 4 with effect from 5 December 2005.

28 Liability for Class 1 contributions in respect of earnings normally paid after pensionable age

Where in the year in which an earner attains pensionable age a payment of earnings is made to or for his benefit before the date he reaches pensionable age, and those earnings would normally fall to be paid in a year following that year, he shall be excepted from liability for primary Class 1 contributions payable in respect of those earnings.

Commentary—*Simon's Taxes* **E8.269**.

HMRC Manuals—National Insurance Manual NIM36001 (people over state pension age).

NIM41270 (non-benefit credits: post-1975 credited earnings: credits for spouses and civil partners of HM forces).

29 Liability for Class 1 contributions of persons over pensionable age

If—

(*a*) earnings are paid to or for the benefit of an earner after he attains pensionable age; and

(*b*) those earnings would normally fall to be paid before the date on which he reaches pensionable age,

section 6(3) of the Act (liability for Class 1 contributions) shall not operate to except him from liability for primary Class 1 contributions in respect of those earnings.

Commentary—*Simon's Taxes* **E8.269**.

30 [Abnormal pay practices

(1) If an officer of the Board is satisfied that—

(*a*) a secondary contributor has followed or is following a practice in the payment of earnings which is abnormal for the employment in question ("an abnormal pay practice"); and

(*b*) by reason of that practice the liability for earnings-related contributions is or has been avoided or reduced,

paragraph (2) applies.

(2) If this paragraph applies the officer may, and if requested to do so by the earner or the secondary contributor shall, decide any question relating to a person's earnings-related contributions as if the secondary contributor had not followed an abnormal pay practice, but had followed a practice normal for the employment in question.

(3) A decision under this regulation shall not apply to contributions based on payments made more than one year before the beginning of the year in which that decision is given.][1]

Commentary—*Simon's Taxes* **E8.1008, E8.1009**.

HMRC Manuals—National Insurance Manual NIM09500 (notifications & directions: their purpose).
NIM09600 (directions issued in accordance with regulation).

Amendments—[1] This paragraph substituted by the Social Security (Contributions) (Amendment No 3) Regulations, SI 2002/2366 regs 3, 5 with effect from 8 October 2002.

31 [Practices avoiding or reducing liability for contributions

(1) If an officer of the Board is satisfied that—

(*a*) a practice exists as to the making of irregular or unequal payments of earnings; and

(*b*) by reason of the practice the liability for earnings-related contributions is avoided or reduced,

he may, and if requested to do so by either the earner or the secondary contributor shall, decide whether to issue a direction to secure that the same contributions are payable as would be payable if the practice were not followed.

(2) A direction under paragraph (1)—

(*a*) shall specify the date from which it is to have effect, which shall not be earlier than that on which it is given;

(*b*) shall have effect until—

(i) the direction is superseded by the giving of a further direction, or

(ii) an officer of the Board is satisfied that the practice has ceased, or has ceased to have the effect mentioned in paragraph (1)(*b*); and

(*c*) shall be given to the earner and the secondary contributor concerned.

This is subject to the qualification in paragraph (3).

(3) A direction under paragraph (1) need not be given to an earner if the officer of the Board is for any reason unable to ascertain his identity or whereabouts.

(4) This regulation does not limit the operation of regulation 30.][1]

Commentary—*Simon's Taxes* **E8.1002, E8.1009**.

HMRC Manuals—NIM09650–09680 (directions issued in accordance with regulation 31).

Amendments—[1] This paragraph substituted by the Social Security (Contributions) (Amendment No 3) Regulations, SI 2002/2366 regs 3, 6 with effect from 8 October 2002.

PART 3

CLASS 1A CONTRIBUTIONS

32 Interpretation for the purposes of this Part

Amendment—Regulations 32–35 revoked by the Social Security (Contributions, Categorisation of Earners and Intermediaries) (Amendment) Regulations, SI 2004/770 regs 2, 6, 36, Schedule with effect from 6 April 2004.

33 Exception from liability to pay Class 1A contributions in respect of cars made available to members of an employed earner's family or household in certain circumstances

Amendment—Regulations 32–35 revoked by the Social Security (Contributions, Categorisation of Earners and Intermediaries) (Amendment) Regulations, SI 2004/770 regs 2, 6, 36, Schedule with effect from 6 April 2004.

34 Class 1A contributions payable where two or more cars are made available concurrently

Amendment—Regulations 32–35 revoked by the Social Security (Contributions, Categorisation of Earners and Intermediaries) (Amendment) Regulations, SI 2004/770 regs 2, 6, 36, Schedule with effect from 6 April 2004.

35 Reduction of certain Class 1A contributions in the case of a car provided or made available by reason of two or more employments or to two or more employed earners

Amendment—Regulations 32–35 revoked by the Social Security (Contributions, Categorisation of Earners and Intermediaries) (Amendment) Regulations, SI 2004/770 regs 2, 6, 36, Schedule with effect from 6 April 2004.

36 Reduction of certain Class 1A contributions on account of the number of employments in the cases of something provided or made available by reason of two or more employments and of something provided or made available to two or more employed earners

(1) This regulation applies if something is provided or made available—

(*a*) an employed earner by reason of two or more employed earner's employments, whether under the same employer or different employers; or

(*b*) two or more employed earners concurrently by reason of their respective employed earner's employments under the same employer,

and all of those employed earner's employments are employments [other than excluded employments within the meaning of the benefits code (see Chapter 2 of Part 3 of ITEPA 2003)][1].

(2) If this regulation applies the amount of any Class 1A contribution payable for the year by the person liable to pay such contribution shall be reduced . . . [1] by deducting from that amount an amount equal to the fraction—

NIC

$$\frac{(X-1)}{X}$$

of the amount which would be payable but for this regulation.

Here X is the total number of employments in respect of which the thing is provided or made available.

Commentary—*Simon's Taxes* **E8.272, E8.275.**

HMRC Manuals—National Insurance Manual NIM16022 (cars provided for home to work travel only). NIM16024 (fuel provided).

Amendments—[1] Words in para (1) substituted, and words in para (2) revoked, by the Social Security (Contributions, Categorisation of Earners and Intermediaries) (Amendment) Regulations, SI 2004/770 regs 2, 7 with effect from 6 April 2004.

37 Reduction of certain Class 1A contributions in respect of cars made available to disabled employed earners

Amendments—This regulation revoked by the Social Security (Contributions, Categorisation of Earners and Intermediaries) (Amendment) Regulations, SI 2004/770 regs 2, 8, 36, Schedule with effect from 6 April 2004.

38 Exception from liability to pay Class 1 contributions in respect of cars made available to disabled employed earners only for business and home to work travel

(1) If the conditions mentioned in paragraphs (2) to (5) are satisfied, the person who would otherwise be liable to pay the Class 1A contribution for that year in respect of the employer earner and the car mentioned in those paragraphs shall be excepted from that liability.

(2) The first condition is that the car is made available to an earner who is disabled.

(3) The second condition is that the car is made available to the earner by reason of his employment.

(4) The third condition is that the car is made available account of the earner's disability for the purposes of, or for purposes which include assisting, the earner's travelling between the earner's home and place of employment.

(5) The fourth condition is that the terms on which the car is made available to the earner prohibit private use other than—

(*a*) by the earner to whom it is made available; and

(*b*) in travelling between the earner's home and place of employment.

(6) The fifth condition is that no prohibited private use of the car has been made in the year.

39 Calculation of Class 1A contributions

Where a person is liable to pay a Class 1A contribution in accordance with section 10 of the Act (Class 1A contributions: benefits in kind, etc) the amount of that contribution shall be calculated to the nearest penny, and any amount of a halfpenny or less shall be disregarded.

Commentary—*Simon's Taxes* **E8.279E.**

40 Prescribed [general earnings] in respect of which Class 1A contributions not payable

(1) Class 1A contributions shall not be payable in respect of the [general earnings][2] prescribed by paragraphs (2) to (7).

(2) The [general earnings][2] prescribed by this paragraph are [those][2] which are excluded from the calculation of a person's earnings in respect of any employed earner's employment by virtue of the following provisions of Schedule 3—

(*za*) . . . [8]

(*a*) in Part VI, [paragraphs 2(*b*), 3 to 5, 7, 10 and 11;][6]

[(*ab*) in Part 7, paragraph 12;][4]

(*b*) in Part VIII, paragraphs [4 to 5][9] and 13;

(*c*) in Part IX, paragraphs [3 to 7A][3]; and

(*d*) in Part X, paragraphs 5, [9, 11 to 13 and 15][1].

(3) The [general earnings][2] prescribed by this paragraph are [those][2] which are payments which are not excluded from the calculation of a person's earnings in respect of any employed earner's employment by virtue of paragraph 1 of Part II of Schedule 3 (payments in kind), but which are so excluded by virtue of paragraph 3 of Part VIII of Schedule 3 (qualifying travelling expenses) or paragraph 9 of that Part (specific and distinct expenses).

(4) . . . [7]

(5) . . . [5]

(6), (6A) . . . [6]

(7) [The general earnings prescribed by this paragraph are so much of any general earnings as are not charged to income tax as employment income by virtue of][2] any of the following extra-statutory concessions published by the Board as at 1st September 2000—

(*a*) . . . [1]

(*b*) . . . [2]

(*c*) A11 (residence in the United Kingdom: year of commencement or cessation of residence);

(*d*) . . . [2]

(*e*) A37 (tax treatment of directors' fees received by partnerships and other companies);

(*f*) A56 (benefits in kind: tax treatment of accommodation in Scotland provided for employees);
(*g*)–(*o*) . . . [2]
(*p*) A91 (living accommodation provided by reason of employment);
(*q*) A97 (Jobmatch programme).
[Sub-paragraph (*f*) applies only to Scotland and sub-paragraph (q) does not apply to Northern Ireland.][2]
(8), (9) . . . [5]

HMRC Manuals—National Insurance Manual NIM02960 (class 1A national insurance contributions).
NIM14301 (exemptions from class 1A Nics: benefits covered by extra statutory concessions).
NIM14320–14322 (extra statutory concession).
NIM14501(general).

Note—Extra-statutory Concession A11 is obsolete for tax years 2013–14 onwards. For income tax split-year treatment from 6 April 2013 onwards, see FA 2013 Sch 45 Part 3.

Amendments—[1] Words in para (2)(*d*) substituted, and para (7)(*a*) repealed, by the Social Security (Contributions) (Amendment No 5) Regulations, SI 2001/2412 regs 2, 3 with effect from 26 July 2001.
[2] Words in cross-heading and in paras (1)–(7) substituted, former para (4)(*b*) substituted, paras (6)(*a*), (7)(*b*), (*d*), (*g*)–(*o*), and in para (8), definition of "emolument" revoked, and para (6A) inserted, by the Social Security (Contributions) (Amendment No 5) Regulations, SI 2003/2085 regs 3, 6 with effect from 1 September 2003.
[3] References in para (2)(*c*) substituted, words in para (6)(*c*) inserted, and words in para (8) substituted, by the Social Security (Contributions, Categorisation of Earners and Intermediaries) (Amendment) Regulations, SI 2004/770 regs 2, 9 with effect from 6 April 2004.
[4] Para (2)(*ab*) inserted by the Social Security (Contributions) (Amendment No 2) Regulations, SI 2005/728 regs 2, 3 with effect from 6 April 2005. This insertion has effect in relation to payments of earnings made in respect of the academic year beginning on 1 September 2005 and subsequent academic years: SI 2005/728 reg 1.
[5] Paras (5), (8), (9) revoked by the Social Security (Contributions) (Amendment No 3) Regulations, SI 2005/778 regs 2, 5 with effect from 6 April 2005.
[6] Words in para (2)(*a*) substituted, and paras (6), (6A) revoked, by the Social Security (Contributions) (Amendment No 2) Regulations, SI 2006/576 regs 2, 4 with effect from 6 April 2006.
[7] Para (4) revoked by the Social Security (Contributions) (Amendment No 2) Regulations, SI 2012/817 regs 2, 7(1) with effect from 6 April 2012.
[8] Para (2)(*za*) revoked by the Security (Contributions) (Amendment and Application of Schedule 38 to the Finance Act 2012) Regulations, SI 2013/622 reg 33 with effect in relation to the tax year 2013–14 and subsequent tax years.
[9] In para (2)(*b*), words substituted for words "4, 5" by the Social Security (Contributions) (Amendment No 4) Regulations, SI 2016/1067 regs 2, 3 with effect from 28 November 2016.

[40A Exception from liability to pay Class 1A contributions in respect of an amount representing an amount on which Class 1 or Class 1A contributions have already been paid pursuant to the Social Security Contributions (Limited Liability Partnership) Regulations 2014

Class 1A contributions shall not be payable in respect of a benefit in kind provided by an employer to an employed earner which represents an amount on which Class 1 or Class 1A contributions are payable by a limited liability partnership in respect of that earner by virtue of regulation 3 or 4 of the Social Security Contributions (Limited Liability Partnership) Regulations 2014.][1]

Amendments—[1] Regulation 40A inserted by the Social Security Contributions (Limited Liability Partnership) Regulations, SI 2014/3159 reg 5(1), (2) with effect for the tax year 2014–15 and subsequent tax years.

[40B Exception from liability to pay Class 1A contributions for tax year 2017–18 in respect of sporting testimonial payments

(1) Paragraph (2) applies to Class 1A contributions payable for the tax year 2017–18 where—
(*a*) the whole or part of the general earnings in respect of which the Class 1A contribution is payable consists of a sporting testimonial payment, and
(*b*) the person making the sporting testimonial payment is the controller of the independent sporting testimonial committee.

(2) Class 1A contributions shall not be payable by the secondary contributor in respect of the sporting testimonial payment for the tax year 2017–18.

(3) In this regulation—
(*a*) "controller" means the person who controls the disbursement of any money raised by the independent sporting testimonial committee for or for the benefit of an individual who is or has been employed as a professional sports person,
(*b*) "independent sporting testimonial committee" means a committee which acts independently of the secondary contributor in organising a sporting testimonial and making the sporting testimonial payment, and
(*c*) "sporting testimonial" and "sporting testimonial payment" have the meaning given in section 226E of ITEPA 2003 (sporting testimonial payments).][1]

Amendments—[1] Regulation 40B inserted by the Social Security (Miscellaneous Amendments) Regulations, SI 2017/307 regs 2, 3 with effect from 6 April 2017.

PART 4
CLASS 1B CONTRIBUTIONS

41 Calculation of Class 1B contributions

Where a person is liable to pay a Class 1B contribution in accordance with section 10A of the Act (Class 1B contributions), the amount of that contribution shall be calculated to the nearest penny, and any amount of a half penny or less shall be disregarded.

Commentary—*Simon's Taxes* **E8.282.**

42 Exception from liability to pay Class 1B contributions

(1) A person shall be excepted from liability to pay a Class 1B contribution for any year in respect of—

(*a*) the amount of any [general earnings which are chargeable emoluments][1] under section 10A(4) of the Act of an employee included in a PAYE settlement agreement; and

(*b*) the total amount of income tax in respect of which that person is accountable to the Board in relation to [general earnings][1] of such an employee in accordance with a PAYE settlement agreement,

where the employee is a person falling within paragraph (2) or (3).

(2) The employee falls within this paragraph if he is subject to the legislation of a contracting party, other than the United Kingdom, to the Agreement on the European Economic Area signed at Oporto on 2nd May 1992 as adjusted by the Protocol signed at Brussels on 17th March 1993.

(3) The employee falls within this paragraph if he is subject to the legislation of a country outside the United Kingdom in respect of which there is an Order in Council under section 179 of the Administration Act (reciprocal agreements with countries outside the United Kingdom) giving effect to a reciprocal agreement.

(4) If a person is excepted from liability to pay a Class 1B contribution for any year under paragraphs (1) to (3), he shall be entitled, if he so wishes, to pay that contribution for that year.

Commentary—*Simon's Taxes* **E8.281.**

Amendments—[1] Words in para (1) substituted by the Social Security (Contributions, Categorisation of Earners and Intermediaries) (Amendment) Regulations, SI 2004/770 regs 2, 10 with effect from 6 April 2004.

PART 5
EXCEPTION FROM LIABILITY FOR CLASS 2 CONTRIBUTIONS, PROVISIONS ABOUT CLASS 3 CONTRIBUTIONS, AND REALLOCATION AND REFUND OF CONTRIBUTIONS (OTHER THAN CLASS 4)

43 Exception from . . . [2] for Class 2 contributions

(1) Subject to paragraphs (2) and (3), a self-employed earner shall be excepted from [paying][2] a Class 2 contribution for any contribution week—

(*a*) in respect of the whole of which the earner is in receipt of incapacity benefit;

[(*ab*) in respect of the whole of which the earner is in receipt of employment and support allowance;][2]

(*b*) throughout the whole of which the earner is incapable of work;

(*c*) in respect of which the earner is in receipt of maternity allowance;

(*d*) throughout the whole of which he is undergoing imprisonment or detention in legal custody; or

(*e*) in respect of any part of which the earner is in receipt of [carer's allowance][1] or an unemployability supplement.

(2) For the purposes of paragraph (1), in computing the period of a contribution week—

(*a*) subject to sub-paragraph (*b*), Sunday shall be disregarded;

(*b*) in the case of a self-employed earner who objects on religious grounds to working on a specific day in each contribution week other than Sunday, and does not object to working on Sunday, that specific day shall be disregarded instead of Sunday.

(3) If a self-employed earner is excepted from [paying][2] a Class 2 contribution for any contribution week by virtue of paragraph (1), he shall be entitled, subject to Part 6, to pay a contribution for that week if he so wishes.

Commentary—*Simon's Taxes* **E8.311, E8.312.**

Amendments—[1] In para (1)(*e*), words substituted by the Social Security (Contributions) (Amendment No 4) Regulations, SI 2002/2924 regs 2, 3 with effect from 1 April 2003.

[2] In heading, words revoked, in paras (1), (3), word substituted, and para (1)(*ab*) inserted by the Social Security (Miscellaneous Amendments No 2) Regulations, SI 2015/478 regs 2, 4 with effect from 6 April 2015.

44 Application for, and duration and cancellation of, certificates of exception

. . .

Amendments—Regulations 44–47 revoked by the Social Security (Miscellaneous Amendments No 2) Regulations, SI 2015/478 regs 2, 24(1)(*b*) with effect from 6 April 2015.

45 Earnings for the purposes of certificates of exception

. . .

Amendments—Regulations 44–47 revoked by the Social Security (Miscellaneous Amendments No 2) Regulations, SI 2015/478 regs 2, 24(1)(*b*) with effect from 6 April 2015.

46 Certificates of exception: exception from liability for, and entitlement to pay, Class 2 contributions

. . .

Amendments—Regulations 44–47 revoked by the Social Security (Miscellaneous Amendments No 2) Regulations, SI 2015/478 regs 2, 24(1)(*b*) with effect from 6 April 2015.

47 Return of Class 2 contributions paid by low earners

. . .

Amendments—Regulations 44–47 revoked by the Social Security (Miscellaneous Amendments No 2) Regulations, SI 2015/478 regs 2, 24(1)(*b*) with effect from 6 April 2015.

48 Class 3 contributions

(1) Subject to sections 13(2) and 14(1) of the Act (Class 3 contributions only payable for purposes of satisfying certain . . . [4] conditions and circumstances in which persons shall not be entitled to pay Class 3 contributions) and these Regulations, any person who is over the age of 16 and fulfils the conditions as to residence or presence in Great Britain or in Northern Ireland prescribed in regulation 145, may, if he so wishes, pay Class 3 contributions.

(2) It shall be a condition of a person's right to pay a Class 3 contribution that he—

(*a*) complies with Part 7 in so far as it applies to persons paying such a contribution, and

(*b*) complies with either of the two conditions specified in paragraph (3).

(3) The conditions are that the person specified in paragraph (1) shall either—

(*a*) pay the contribution not later than 42 days after the end of the year in respect of which it is paid; or

(*b*) subject to [regulations 50, 50A[. . . [3] and 50C][2]][1] and Part 6, pay the contribution—

(i) where the contribution is payable in respect of any year before 6th April 1982, before the end of the second year following the year in respect of which it is paid; and where the contribution is payable in respect of any year after 5th April 1982, before the end of the sixth year following the year in respect of which it is paid; or

(ii) where the year in respect of which it is paid includes a period of at least 6 months throughout which the contributor has been undergoing full-time education, or full-time apprenticeship or training for which, in either case, any earnings are less than the lower earnings limit, or has been undergoing imprisonment or detention in legal custody, before the end of the sixth year following the year in which the education, or apprenticeship or training, or imprisonment or detention terminated; and

(iii) where the year first mentioned in head (ii) is immediately preceded or followed by a year in which the conditions specified in that head are not satisfied in respect only of the length of the period specified in that head, in respect of that preceding or following year, before the end of the sixth year following the year in which the education, apprenticeship, training, imprisonment or detention described in that head terminated.

Commentary—*Simon's Taxes* **E8.405**.

Amendments—[1] Reference in para (3)(*b*) substituted by the Social Security (Contributions) (Amendment No 8) Regulations, SI 2007/2520 regs 2, 4 with effect from 1 October 2007: SI 2007/2520 reg 1.

[2] In para (3)(*b*), words substitutedby the Security (Contributions) (Amendment and Application of Schedule 38 to the Finance Act 2012) Regulations, SI 2013/622 reg 34 with effect in relation to the tax year 2013–14 and subsequent tax years.

[3] In para (3)(*b*), words revoked by the Social Security (Miscellaneous Amendments No 2) Regulations, SI 2015/478 regs 2, 24(2) with effect from 6 April 2015.

[4] In para (1), word revoked by the Pensions Act 2014 (Consequential, Supplementary and Incidental Amendments) Order, SI 2015/1985 art 21(1), (2) with effect from 6 April 2016.

49 Precluded Class 3 contributions

(1) Subject to paragraph (2), no person shall be entitled to pay a Class 3 contribution—

(*a*) in respect of any year if he would, but for the payment of such a contribution, be entitled to be credited with a contribution;

(*b*) in respect of any year in which the aggregate of his earnings factors derived from earnings in respect of which [primary Class 1 contributions, payable at the main primary percentage,][2] have been paid, credited earnings, or Class 2 or Class 3 contributions paid or credited is less than 25 times the lower earnings limit and either the period has passed within which any Class 3 contributions may be treated as paid for that year under regulation 4 of the Social Security (Crediting and Treatment of Contributions, and National Insurance Numbers) Regulations 2001 or he has sooner, in accordance with regulation 56, applied for the return of any Class 3 contributions paid in respect of that year;

(*c*) in respect of any year if the aggregate of his earnings factors derived from earnings in respect of which [primary Class 1 contributions, payable at the main primary percentage,][2] have been paid, credited earnings, or Class 2 or Class 3 contributions paid or credited is more than 25 times the lower earnings limit but less than the qualifying earnings factor and either—

(i) the period referred to in sub-paragraph (*b*) has passed, or

(ii) he has sooner applied under regulation 56 for the return of any Class 3 contributions paid in respect of that year;

(*d*) in respect of any year if it causes the aggregate of his earnings factors derived from earnings in respect of which [primary Class 1 contributions, payable at the main primary percentage,][2] have been paid, credited earnings, or Class 2 or Class 3 contributions paid or credited to exceed the qualifying earnings factor by an amount which is half or more than half that year's lower earnings limit;

(*e*) . . .[3]

(*f*) in respect of the year in which he attains 17 or 18 years of age if in an earlier year he has satisfied the first contribution condition for retirement pension or widow's pension or widowed mother's allowance.

[Sub-paragraphs (*a*), (*b*) and (*c*) are subject to the following qualification.][1]

(2) . . .[1] a person shall be entitled to pay a Class 3 contribution in respect of any year if it would enable him to satisfy—

(*a*) the first contribution condition for retirement pension [widowed mother's allowance, widowed parent's allowance . . .[5] or widow's pension][1] and he has not satisfied that condition at the beginning of that year; or

(*b*) the contribution condition for . . .[5] widow's payment and he has not satisfied that condition at the beginning of that year.

[(2A) No person shall be entitled to pay a Class 3 contribution in respect of the year in which he attains pensionable age or any subsequent year.

This is subject to the following qualification.][3]

[(2B) A person—

(*a*) who has attained the age of 60;

(*b*) to whom a full gender recognition certificate is issued; and

(*c*) whose acquired gender is male;

is not precluded from paying Class 3 contributions for the relevant years.][3]

[(2C) For the purposes of paragraph (2B) the relevant years are—

(*a*) the year in which the person attains the age of 60;

(*b*) any subsequent year before that in which the full gender recognition certificate is issued; and

(*c*) the year in which the full gender recognition certificate is issued.][3]

(3) In this regulation "credited" means credited for the purposes of retirement pension, [a state pension under section 2 or 4 of the Pensions Act 2014,][4] widowed mother's allowance[, widowed parent's allowance . . .[5]][1] and widow's pension.

Commentary—*Simon's Taxes* **E8.408**.

Amendments—[1] Words in para (1) inserted; words in para (2) revoked, words in para (2)(*a*) substituted, and words in paras (2)(*b*), (3) inserted, by the Social Security (Contributions) (Amendment No 6) Regulations, SI 2001/3728 art 2 with effect from 12 December 2001.

[2] Words in para (1) substituted by the Social Security (Contributions) (Amendment) Regulations, SI 2003/193 regs 2, 7 with effect from 2003–04.

[3] Para (1)(*e*) revoked, and paras (2A)–(2C) inserted, by the Social Security (Contributions) (Amendment No 3) Regulations, SI 2005/778 regs 2, 6 with effect from 6 April 2005.

[4] In para (3), words inserted by the Pensions Act 2014 (Consequential, Supplementary and Incidental Amendments) Order, SI 2015/1985 art 21(1), (3) with effect from 6 April 2016.

[5] In paras (2), (3), words revoked by the Pensions Act 2014 (Consequential, Supplementary and Incidental Amendments) Order, SI 2017/422 art 18 with effect from 6 April 2017 (the day on which Pensions Act 2014 s 30 comes into effect for all purposes).

49A [Conditions relating to Class 3 contributions: transfers to the Communities' pension scheme

(1) The entitlement of a person to pay a Class 3 contribution is subject to the condition set out in paragraph (2).

(2) The condition is that a person may not pay a Class 3 contribution for any part of the period to which that person's Communities transfer relates.

(3) For the purposes of this regulation, paragraph (3) of regulation 148A applies to determine the meaning of a Communities transfer in the same way as it applies to determine the meaning of that expression for the purposes of that regulation.][1]

Amendments—[1] This regulation inserted by the Social Security (Contributions) (Amendment No 4) Regulations, SI 2007/1838 regs 2, 3 with effect from 18 July 2007: SI 2007/1838 reg 1.

[50 Class 3 contributions not paid within prescribed periods

(1) If—

(*a*) a person ("the contributor")—

(i) was entitled to pay a Class 3 contribution under regulation 48, 146(2)(*b*) or 147; and

(ii) failed to pay that contribution in the appropriate period specified for its payment; and

(*b*) the condition in paragraph (2) is satisfied,

the contributor may pay the contribution within such further period as an officer of the Board may direct.

(2) The condition is that an officer of the Board is satisfied that—

(*a*) the failure to pay is attributable to the contributor's ignorance or error; and

(*b*) that ignorance or error was not the result of the contributor's failure to exercise due care and diligence.][1]

Simon's Tax Cases—*R&C Comrs v Kearney* [2008] STC 1506.

Amendments—[1] This paragraph substituted by the Social Security (Contributions) (Amendment No 3) Regulations, SI 2002/2366 regs 3, 7 with effect from 8 October 2002.

50A [Class 3 contributions: tax years 1996–97 to 2001–02

(1) This regulation applies to Class 3 contributions payable in respect of the tax years 1996–97 to 2001–02 ("the relevant years").

(2) If a person ("the contributor")—

(*a*) was entitled to pay a Class 3 contribution in respect of any of the relevant years under regulation 48, 146(2)(*b*) or 147;

(*b*) had not, before the coming into force of these Regulations, paid that contribution; and

(*c*) had not, before 1st November 2003, received notice—

(i) in the case of a contributor in Great Britain, from the Department for Work and Pensions, the former Department of Social Security or the Board, or

(ii) in the case of a contributor in Northern Ireland, from the Department for Social Development, the former Department for Health and Social Services for Northern Ireland or the Board,

that he was entitled to pay a Class 3 contribution for that relevant year;

he may pay the contribution within the period specified in paragraph (3).

(3) The period within which the contribution may be paid is the period beginning with the coming into force of these Regulations and ending—

(*a*) in the case of a contributor who has reached or will reach pensionable age before 24th October 2004, on 5th April 2010; and

(*b*) in the case of a contributor who will reach pensionable age on or after 24th October 2004, on 5th April 2009.

(4) Nothing in this regulation limits the application of [regulation 50 or 50B][2].][1]

Amendments—[1] This regulation inserted by the Social Security (Contributions) (Amendment No 3) Regulations, SI 2004/1362 regs 2, 4 with effect from 17 May 2004.

[2] Reference in para (4) substituted for reference "regulation 50" by the Social Security (Contributions) (Amendment No 8) Regulations, SI 2007/2520 regs 2, 5 with effect from 1 October 2007: SI 2007/2520 reg 1.

50B [Class 3 contributions: tax years 1993–94 to 2007–08

. . .

Amendments—Regulation 50B revoked by the Social Security (Miscellaneous Amendments No 2) Regulations, SI 2015/478 regs 2, 24(1)(*c*) with effect from 6 April 2015.

[50C Class 3 contributions: tax years 2006-07 to 2015-16: unavailability of pension statements 2013-14 to 2016-17

(1) This regulation applies to Class 3 contributions payable in respect of one or more of the tax years 2006-07 to 2015-16 ("the relevant contribution years").

(2) Paragraph (3) applies if a person ("the contributor")—

(*a*) was entitled under regulation 48, 146(2)(*b*) or 147(1)(*b*) to pay a Class 3 contribution in respect of one or more of the relevant contribution years;

(*b*) had not, before the coming into force of this regulation, paid that contribution; and

(*c*) will reach pensionable age on or after 6th April [2016][2].

(3) The contributor may pay a Class 3 contribution under this regulation, in respect of any of the relevant contribution years, within the period specified in paragraph (4).

(4) The period within which the contribution may be paid is the period beginning on 6th April 2013 and ending on 5th April 2023.

(5) Notwithstanding section 13(6) of the Act, the amount of a Class 3 contribution payable under this regulation shall be—

(*a*) in respect of contribution years 2006-07 to 2009-10, the amount payable in relation to tax year 2012-13; or

(*b*) in respect of contribution years 2010-11 to 2015-16, the amount payable in the contribution year to which the payment relates.

(6) Paragraph (5) does not apply to a Class 3 contribution paid on or after 6th April 2019.

(7) Nothing in this regulation limits the application of regulations 50, 50A and 50B.][1]

NIC

Amendments—[1] Reg 50C inserted by the Security (Contributions) (Amendment and Application of Schedule 38 to the Finance Act 2012) Regulations, SI 2013/622 reg 35 with effect in relation to the tax year 2013–14 and subsequent tax years.
[2] In para (2)(*c*) "2016" substituted for "2017" by Social Security (Contributions) (Amendment) Regulations, SI 2013/718 reg 2 with effect from 18 April 2013. Note that, where the contributor reaches pensionable age on or after 6 April 2016 but before 6 April 2017, the reference to 6 April 2013 in para (4) is to be read as a reference to 18 April 2013 (SI 2013/718 reg 3).

51 Disposal of contributions not properly paid

(1) Where contributions (other than Class 1A, Class 1B or Class 4 contributions) are paid which are of the wrong class, or at the wrong rate, or of the wrong amount, [HMRC][2] may treat them as paid on account of contributions properly payable under the Act.

(2) Where the whole or any part of a Class 1A contribution or a Class 1B contribution falls to be returned by [HMRC][2] to any person under [regulation 52 or 52A][1] or any part of a Class 1A contribution falls to be repaid by [HMRC][2] [to any person under regulation 55(1), or regulation 55A,][2], [HMRC][2] may treat—

(*a*) the amount of the Class 1A contribution or, as the case may be, any part of such a contribution, as a payment on account of any secondary Class 1 contributions, Class 1B contributions or Class 2 contributions;

(*b*) the amount of that Class 1B contribution or, as the case may be, any part of such a contribution, as a payment on account of any secondary Class 1 contributions, Class 1A contribution or Class 2 contributions,

properly payable by that person.

Commentary—*Simon's Taxes* **E8.279E.**

Amendments—[1] Words in para (2) substituted by the Social Security (Contributions, Categorisation of Earners and Intermediaries) (Amendment) Regulations, SI 2004/770 regs 2, 11 with effect only in respect of contributions payable in respect of 2003–04 and subsequent years.
[2] In each place, "HMRC" substituted for words "the Board", and in para (2), words substituted for words "to any person under regulation 55(1)", by the Social Security (Contributions) (Amendment No 3) Regulations, SI 2011/797 regs 2, 4 with effect from 6 April 2011.

52 [Return of contributions paid in error

(1) This regulation applies if a contribution other than a Class 4 contribution has been paid in error. This regulation is subject to regulations 51 and 57.

(2) If this regulation applies, an application may be made to the Board for the return of the contribution paid in error.

(3) An application under paragraph (2) shall be made to the Board—

(*a*) in writing, or in such form and by such means of electronic communications as are approved; and

(*b*) within the time permitted by paragraph (8).

(4) On the making of an application under paragraph (2) the Board shall return the contribution paid in error.

This is subject to paragraphs (5) and (6).

(5) Paragraph (4) does not require the return of contributions unless the amount to be returned exceeds—

(*a*) in the case of Class 1 contributions, 1/15 of a contribution at the main primary percentage payable on earnings at the upper earnings limit in respect of primary Class 1 contributions prescribed in regulation 10 for the last or only year in respect of which the contributions were paid; or

(*b*) in the case of a Class 1A or Class 1B contribution, 50 pence.

(6) Paragraph (4) does not require the return of a primary Class 1 contribution which is treated as properly paid by regulation 3 of the Social Security (Additional Pension) (Contributions Paid in Error) Regulations 1996.

(7) Contributions paid by a secondary contributor on behalf of any person in error—

(*a*) if they are not recovered from that person by the secondary contributor, may be returned to the secondary contributor; and

(*b*) if they are recovered by the secondary contributor from that person may be returned—

(i) to that person; or

(ii) with that person's consent given in writing or in such form and by such means of electronic communications as may be approved, to the secondary contributor.

(8) An application for the return of any contribution paid in error shall be made within the period of six years from the end of the year in which the contribution was due to be paid.

This is subject to the following qualification.

If the application is made after the end of that period, an officer of the Board shall admit it if satisfied that—

(*a*) the person making the application had reasonable excuse for not making the application within that period; and

(*b*) the application was made without unreasonable delay after the excuse had ceased.

(9) In this regulation "error" means, and means only, an error which—

(*a*) is made at the time of the payment; and

(*b*) relates to some past or present matter.][1]

Commentary—*Simon's Taxes* **E8.284, E8.308**.

Simon's Tax Cases—52, *Bonner and others v Revenue and Customs Comrs* [2011] STC 538.

Amendments—[1] Regulations 52, 52A substituted regulation 52 by the Social Security (Contributions, Categorisation of Earners and Intermediaries) (Amendment) Regulations, SI 2004/770 regs 2, 12 with effect only in respect of contributions payable in respect of 2003–04 and subsequent years.

52A [Return of contributions paid in excess of maxima prescribed in regulation 21

(1) This regulation applies if there has been a payment of contributions in excess of the maximum determined in accordance with regulation 21 (annual maxima for those with more than one employment) in the particular case.

This regulation is subject to regulations 51, 52 and 57.

(2) If this regulation applies, an application may be made to the Board, in writing or in such form and by such means of electronic communications as may be approved for the return of so much of the payment of contributions as exceeds the maximum determined in accordance with regulation 21 in the particular case.

(3) On the making of an application under paragraph (2) the Board shall, subject to the following provisions of this regulation, return so much of the [contributions actually paid by the earner][5] as exceeds the maximum determined in accordance with regulation 21 in the particular case.

(4) Paragraph (3) does not require the return of—

(*a*) a payment of Class 1 or Class 2 contributions unless the amount to be returned exceeds 1/15 of a contribution at the primary percentage payable on earnings at the upper-earnings limit in respect of main primary Class 1 contributions prescribed in regulation 10 for the last or only year in respect of which the contributions were paid;

(*b*) a primary Class 1 contribution to which regulation 3 of the Social Security (Additional Pension) (Contributions Paid in Error) Regulations 1996 (purposes for which primary Class 1 contributions paid in error are to be treated as properly paid) applies.

(5) Contributions to which this regulation applies shall be returned in the following order—

(*a*) primary Class 1 contributions at the reduced rate;

(*b*) Class 2 contributions;

(*c*) primary Class 1 contributions at the main primary percentage[.][5]

(*d*) . . . [5]

(*e*) . . . [5]

(6)–(8) . . . [5]

(9) Contributions paid by a secondary contributor on behalf of any person in excess of the amount specified in regulation 21—

(*a*) if they are not recovered from that person by the secondary contributor, may be returned to the secondary contributor; and

(*b*) if they are recovered by the secondary contributor from that person may be returned—

(i) to that person; or

(ii) with that person's consent given in writing or in such form and by such means of electronic communications as may be approved, to the secondary contributor.][1]

Commentary—*Simon's Taxes* **E8.267**.

Amendments—[1] Regulations 52, 52A substituted by the Social Security (Contributions, Categorisation of Earners and Intermediaries) (Amendment) Regulations, SI 2004/770 regs 2, 12 with effect only in respect of contributions payable in respect of 2003–04 and subsequent years.

[2] In paras (3), (5)(*c*), words substituted, and paras (5)(*d*), (*e*), (6)–(8) revoked, by the Social Security (Contributions) (Amendment) (No 2) Regulations, SI 2016/352 reg 13 with effect from 6 April 2016 and subject to savings in relation to rights or obligations arising in connection with tax years beginning before 6 April 2016.

53 Return of contributions: further provisions

Amendment—This regulation revoked by the Social Security (Contributions) (Amendment No 2) Regulations, SI 2006/576 regs 2, 5 with effect from 6 April 2006.

54 Return of Class 1 contributions paid at the non-contracted out rate instead of at the contracted-out rate

Amendment—This regulation revoked by the Social Security (Contributions) (Amendment) (No 2) Regulations, SI 2016/352 reg 14 with effect from 6 April 2016, subject to savings in relation to rights or obligations arising in connection with tax years beginning before 6 April 2016.

55 Repayment of Class 1A contributions

(1) Subject to regulations 51 and 57 and paragraphs (2) and (3), where, in a case specified in paragraph (2), in the light of information provided to the Board, it appears that too much has been paid in respect of a Class 1A contribution, they shall repay to the person paying that contribution the amount which has been overpaid, unless that amount does not exceed 50 pence.

(2) The cases to which paragraph (1) applies are those in which a person has paid a Class 1A contribution and—

(*a*) in calculating the amount of that contribution the person used information which later proves to have been inaccurate or incomplete; or

(*b*) the employee who received the [general earnings][2] in respect of which the contribution was payable is later found to have been a person not residing in the United Kingdom for the purposes of income tax at the time of receipt.

(3) The repayment of part of a Class 1A contribution under paragraph (1) is subject to the condition that the person referred to in that paragraph [("the applicant")][1] shall make an application to that effect in writing to the Board and within the period of 6 years from the end of the year in which the Class 1A contribution was due to be paid.

This is subject to the following qualification.

If the application is made after the end of that period, an officer of the Board shall admit it if satisfied that—

(*a*) the applicant had reasonable excuse for not making the application within that period; and

(*b*) the application was made without unreasonable delay after the excuse had ceased.][1]

Commentary—*Simon's Taxes* **E8.279E.**

Amendments—[1] Words in para (3) inserted and substituted by the Social Security (Contributions) (Amendment No 3) Regulations, SI 2002/2366 regs 3, 10 with effect from 8 October 2002.

[2] Words in para (2) substituted by the Social Security (Contributions, Categorisation of Earners and Intermediaries) (Amendment) Regulations, SI 2004/770 regs 2, 13 with effect from 6 April 2004.

[55A [Repayment of Class 1A contributions: certain earnings no longer treated as earnings for income tax purposes

(1) Subject to regulations 51 and 57 and to paragraph (2), where an officer of Revenue and Customs is satisfied that an amount treated as earnings in respect of which a Class 1A contribution was paid is no longer treated as earnings in accordance with the provisions of sections 100A and 100B of the Income Tax (Earnings and Pensions) Act 2003 (homes outside UK owned through company etc), the amount paid shall be repaid to the person who paid that contribution.

(2) The repayment of all or part of a Class 1A contribution under paragraph (1) is subject to the condition that an application shall be made in writing to HMRC on or before 6th April 2015.][1]

Amendments—[1] Reg 55A inserted by the Social Security (Contributions) (Amendment No 3) Regulations, SI 2011/797 regs 2, 3 with effect from 6 April 2011.

56 Return of precluded Class 3 contributions

(1) Subject to regulations 51 and 57 and to paragraph (2), where a contributor has paid a Class 3 contribution which by virtue of section 14(1) of the Act (restriction on the right to pay Class 3 contributions) or regulation 49 he was not entitled to pay, the Board shall, on application of the contributor, return that contribution to the contributor.

(2) A contributor wishing to apply for the return of a contribution falling within paragraph (1) shall make an application to the Board either—

(*a*) in writing; or

(*b*) in such form, and by such means of electronic communications, as are approved.

[56A Repayment of Class 3A contributions

(1) Where a Class 3A contribution has been paid, the contribution shall be repaid if one or more of the following conditions are satisfied—

(*a*) the person who paid the contribution ("the contributor") dies within the period of 90 days beginning with the date of payment of the contribution, or

(*b*) the contributor makes an application to HMRC for repayment within the period of 90 days beginning with the date of payment of the contribution.

(2) Where a Class 3A contribution is repaid, any amounts received under section 45(1)(*b*) or (2)(*e*) of the Act in return for that contribution shall be deducted from the repayment.][1]

Amendments—[1] Reg 56A inserted by the Social Security Class 3A Contributions (Amendment) Regulations, SI 2014/2746 reg 4 with effect from 12 October 2015.

57 Calculation of return of contributions

(1) In calculating the amount of any return of contributions to be made under [regulation 52, 52A[, 55, 55A][2] or 56][1], there shall be deducted—

(*a*) the amount of any contribution which has under regulation 51 been treated as paid on account of other contributions;

(*b*) in the case of such contributions paid in error in respect of any person, the amount, if any, paid to that person (and to any other person on the basis of that error) by way of contributory benefit which would not have been paid had any of the contributions (in respect of which an application for their return is duly made in accordance with [regulation 52(8)][1]) not been paid in the first instance;

(*c*) the amount of any contributions equivalent premium payable under Chapter III of Part III of the Pensions Act;

(*d*) the amount of any minimum contributions paid by the Board under section 43 of the Pensions Act (minimum contributions to personal pension schemes);

(*e*) the amount of any payment made by the Board under section 7 of the Social Security Act 1986 (schemes becoming contracted-out between 1986 and 1993); and

(*f*) in the case of such contributions paid in error in respect of any person, the amount of any payment made by the Board under section 42A(3) of the Pensions Act (age-related rebates).

(2) Paragraph (1)(*b*) is subject to the qualification that, if the Secretary of State certifies that a deduction of an additional amount of income support or income-based jobseeker's allowance has been made under regulation 13 of the Social Security (Payments on account, Overpayments and Recovery) Regulations 1988 ("the 1988 Regulations") (sums to be deducted in calculating the recoverable amount), paragraph (3) applies.

(3) If this paragraph applies, the amount to be returned shall be reduced by applying the formula—

$$CB - IS$$

Here—

CB is the amount of contributory benefit specified in paragraph (1)(*b*) and

IS is the amount of income support or income-based jobseeker's allowance specified in regulation 13(*b*) of the 1988 Regulations.

(4) In this regulation the expression "contributions equivalent premium" has the same meaning as in section 55(2) of the Pensions Act.

Amendments—[1] Words in para (1) substituted by the Social Security (Contributions, Categorisation of Earners and Intermediaries) (Amendment) Regulations, SI 2004/770 regs 2, 14 with effect only in respect of contributions payable in respect of 2003–04 and subsequent years.

[2] Words in para (1) inserted by the Social Security (Contributions) (Amendment No 3) Regulations, SI 2011/797 regs 2, 5 with effect from 6 April 2011.

58 Reallocation of contributions for benefit purposes

(1) Where any payment of earnings is made in one year which, but for regulation 7(3), would by virtue of that regulation have been treated as paid at an interval falling within another year, the contributions paid in respect of those earnings shall, on the application of the employed earner or the direction of the Secretary of State, be treated, for the purposes of entitlement to benefit, as paid in respect of that other year.

(2) Where—

(*a*) an employed earner's employment commences in one year;

(*b*) the first payment of earnings in respect of that employment is made in the following year; and

(*c*) earnings in respect of that employment which fall to be paid in that later year are paid at regular intervals,

the contributions paid in respect of the first payment of earnings shall, on the application of the employed earner to the Secretary of State, be treated, for the purposes of entitlement to benefit, as paid in respect of the year in which the employment commenced.

Commentary—*Simon's Taxes* **E8.249C**.

59 Circumstances in which two-year limit for refunds of Class 1, 1A or 1B contributions not to apply

(1) Section 19A(1) of the Act (repayment of Class 1, 1A or 1B contributions paid in error) does not apply where the three circumstances prescribed in paragraphs (2), (3) and (4) exist.

(2) The first circumstance is that, in respect of the earnings derived in year 1 from an employment of the earner, Class 1, 1A or 1B contributions have been paid.

(3) The second circumstance is that in respect of that employment and before the end of year 2—

(*a*) an application for the determination of a question as to the category of earners in which the earner is or was to be included ("the categorisation question") has been made under section 17(1)(*a*) of the Administration Act in accordance with regulation 13(1) of the Social Security (Adjudication) Regulations 1995;

(*b*) the question of law arising in connection with the categorisation question has been referred by the Secretary of State to a court under section 18 of the Administration Act;

(*c*) a request in writing has been made that an officer of the Board—

(i) decide the categorisation question under section 8(1)(*a*) of the Transfer Act, or

(ii) vary a decision made under that section; or

(*d*) the amount of income tax, which is liable to be paid in respect of year 1 and in respect of which the person liable to pay a Class 1B contribution is accountable, has been the subject of a relevant tax appeal.

(4) The third circumstance is that the question, reference, request or appeal referred to in paragraph (3) has not been determined or finally disposed of, as the case may be, at the end of year 2.

(5) For the purposes of this regulation—

"relevant tax appeal" has the meaning given by paragraph 6(4A) of Schedule 1 to the Act;

NIC

"year 1" and "year 2" have the meanings given by section 19A(1) of the Act,
and a question, reference, request or appeal shall only be taken to be determined or finally disposed of when the time for appealing against it has expired or no further appeal is possible.

PART 6
LATE PAID AND UNPAID CONTRIBUTIONS (OTHER THAN CLASS 4 CONTRIBUTIONS)

60 Treatment for the purpose of contributory benefit of unpaid primary Class 1 contributions where no consent, connivance or negligence on the part of the primary contributor

(1) If a primary Class 1 contribution payable on a primary contributor's behalf by a secondary contributor is not paid, and the failure to pay that contribution is shown to the satisfaction [of an officer of the Board][1] not to have been with the consent or connivance of, or attributable to any negligence on the part of the primary contributor, that contribution shall be treated—

(*a*) for the purpose of the first contribution condition of entitlement to a contribution-based jobseeker's allowance or short term incapacity benefit as paid on the date on which payment is made of the earnings in respect of which the contribution is payable; and

(*b*) for any other purpose of entitlement to contributory benefit, as paid on the due date.

(2) In paragraph (1)(*a*) "the first contribution condition", in relation to a contribution-based jobseeker's allowance means the condition specified in section 2(1)(*a*) of the Jobseeker's Act 1995.

[(3) Where—

(*a*) an amount is retrospectively treated as earnings by retrospective contributions regulations, and

(*b*) the primary Class 1 contribution payable in respect of those earnings is not paid, and the failure to pay that contribution is shown to the satisfaction of an officer of the Board not to have been with the consent or connivance of, or attributable to any negligence on the part of the primary contributor,

that contribution shall be treated in accordance with paragraph (1)(*a*) and (*b*).][2]

Commentary—*Simon's Taxes* **E8.1117**.

Amendments—[1] Words in para (1) substituted by the Social Security (Contributions) (Amendment No 3) Regulations, SI 2002/2366 regs 3, 11 with effect from 8 October 2002.

[2] Para (3) inserted by the Social Security Contributions (Consequential Provisions) Regulations, SI 2007/1056 regs 3, 5 with effect from 6 April 2007.

[61 Voluntary Class 2 contributions not paid within permitted period

(1) If a person who was entitled, but not liable, to pay a Class 2 contribution ("the contributor") fails to pay that contribution within the period within which it may be paid, and the condition in paragraph (2) is satisfied, the contribution may be paid within such further period as an officer of the Board may direct.

(2) The condition is that an officer of the Board is satisfied that—

(*a*) the failure was attributable to the contributor's ignorance or error; and

(*b*) that ignorance or error was not the result of the contributor's failure to exercise due care and diligence.][1]

Commentary—*Simon's Taxes* **E8.314**.

Amendments—[1] This paragraph substituted by the Social Security (Contributions) (Amendment No 3) Regulations, SI 2002/2366 regs 3, 12 with effect from 8 October 2002.

61A Voluntary Class 2 contributions: tax years 1993–94 to 2007–08

. . .

Amendments—Regulations 44–47 revoked by the Social Security (Miscellaneous Amendments No 2) Regulations, SI 2015/478 regs 2, 24(1)(*d*) with effect from 6 April 2015.

[61B Voluntary Class 2 contributions: tax years 2006-07 to 2015-16: unavailability of pension statements 2013-14 to 2016-17

(1) This regulation applies to Class 2 contributions which a person ("the contributor") was entitled, but not liable, to pay in respect of one or more of the tax years 2006-07 to 2015-16 ("the relevant contribution years").

(2) Paragraph (3) applies if the contributor—

(*a*) was entitled . . . [3] to pay a Class 2 contribution in respect of one or more of the relevant contribution years;

(*b*) had not, before the coming into force of this regulation, paid that contribution; and

(*c*) will reach pensionable age on or after 6th April [2016][2].

(3) The contributor may pay a Class 2 contribution under this regulation, in respect of any of the relevant contribution years, within the period specified in paragraph (4).

(4) The period within which the contribution may be paid is the period beginning on 6th April 2013 and ending on 5th April 2023.

(5) Notwithstanding section 12(3) of the Act, the amount of a Class 2 contribution payable under this regulation shall be—

(a) in respect of contribution years 2006-07 to 2010-11, the amount payable in relation to tax year 2012-13; or

(b) in respect of contribution years 2011-12 to 2015-16, the amount payable in the contribution year to which the payment relates.

(6) Paragraph (5) does not apply to a Class 2 contribution paid on or after 6th April 2019.

(7) Nothing in this regulation limits the application of [[regulation][3] 61 . . . [3].][1]

Amendments—[1] Regulation 61B inserted by the Social Security (Contributions) (Amendment and Application of Schedule 38 to the Finance Act 2012) Regulations, SI 2013/622 reg 37 with effect in relation to the tax year 2013–14 and subsequent tax years.

[2] In para (2)(c) "2016" substituted for "2017" by Social Security (Contributions) (Amendment) Regulations, SI 2013/718 reg 2 with effect from 18 April 2013. Note that, where the contributor reaches pensionable age on or after 6 April 2016 but before 6 April 2017, the reference to 6 April 2013 in para (4) is to be read as a reference to 18 April 2013 (SI 2013/718 reg 3).

[3] In para (2)(a), words revoked, and in para (7), words revoked and words substituted by the Social Security (Miscellaneous Amendments No 2) Regulations, SI 2015/478 regs 2, 5, 24(3)with effect from 6 April 2015.

62 Payment of contributions after death of contributor

If a person dies, any contributions which, immediately before his death he was entitled, but not liable, to pay, may be paid, notwithstanding his death, subject to the same provisions with respect to the time for payment as were applicable to that person.

Commentary—*Simon's Taxes* **E8.303**.

63 Class 2 contributions paid late in accordance with a payment undertaking

(1) This regulation applies to any Class 2 contributions which—

(a) the earner has failed to pay on or by the due date and which, after that date, is payable in accordance with the provisions of an undertaking to pay such a contribution entered into after that date; and

(b) would when paid fall to be computed in accordance with section 12(3) of the Act.

(2) In the case of a contribution to which this regulation applies—

(a) which is paid in accordance with the provisions of an undertaking entered into in the contribution year or the year immediately following that year, the amount of such a contribution shall be computed by reference to the weekly rate applicable in the contribution year;

(b) which is paid in accordance with the provisions of an undertaking entered into in any year other than a year specified in sub-paragraph (a), the amount of such a contribution shall be computed by reference to the highest weekly rate of such a contribution in the period beginning with the contribution week in respect of which the contribution is paid and ending with the day on which the undertaking was entered into;

(c) which is not paid in accordance with the provisions of the undertaking, the amount of such a contribution shall be computed by reference to the highest weekly rate of such a contribution—

(i) where the contribution is paid in accordance with a further undertaking, in the period beginning with the contribution week in respect of which the contribution is paid and ending with the day on which the further undertaking was entered into, or

(ii) where the contribution is paid otherwise than in accordance with a further undertaking, in the period beginning with the contribution week in respect of which the contribution is paid and ending with the day on which it is paid.

(3) In this regulation "undertaking" means an arrangement between the Board and an earner under which the Board have agreed to accept payment of arrears of Class 2 contributions by instalments.

Commentary—*Simon's Taxes* **E8.305**.

[63A Collection of unpaid Class 2 contributions through PAYE code

(1) Where—

(a) the amount of any Class 2 contributions ("relevant debt") would fall to be computed in accordance with section 12(3) of the Act (late paid Class 2 contributions), and

(b) paragraph (2) applies,

the amount of the relevant debt must be computed in accordance with paragraph (4).

(2) This paragraph applies where—

(a) the code ("the PAYE code") required by regulation 13 of the PAYE Regulations (determination of code by Inland Revenue) for use by an employer for a year in respect of the person liable to pay the relevant debt is determined in accordance with regulation 14A of the PAYE Regulations (determination of code in respect of recovery of relevant debts) so as to effect recovery of the relevant debt;

(b) the determination of the PAYE code is made assuming the amount of the relevant debt is the amount computed in accordance with paragraph (4); and

(c) the relevant debt is paid in the year in respect of which the PAYE code is determined for use by an employer of the person liable to pay the relevant debt.

NIC

(3) For the purpose of determining whether a relevant debt is paid in accordance with paragraph (2)(*c*), the amount of the relevant debt must be assumed to be the amount computed in accordance with paragraph (4).

(4) The amount referred to in paragraphs (1), (2)(*b*) and (3) is the highest weekly rate of a Class 2 contribution in the period beginning with the . . . [2] week to which the relevant debt relates and ending with the day the PAYE code mentioned in paragraph (2)(a) is determined.][1]

Amendments—[1] Regulation 63A inserted by the Social Security (Contributions) (Amendment and Application of Schedule 38 to the Finance Act 2012) Regulations, SI 2013/622 reg 38 with effect in relation to the tax year 2013–14 and subsequent tax years.

[2] In para (4), word revoked by the Social Security (Miscellaneous Amendments No 2) Regulations, SI 2015/478 regs 2, 6 with effect from 6 April 2015.

64 Class 2 and Class 3 contributions paid within a month from notification of amount of arrears

(1) This regulation applies to any Class 2 or Class 3 contribution—

(*a*) which would when paid fall to be computed in accordance with section 12(3) or 13(6) of the Act; and

(*b*) the amount of that contribution has been notified to the contributor by the Board in the last month of a year.

(2) Where a contribution to which this regulation applies is paid—

(*a*) within one calendar month from the date of such notification; and

(*b*) in the year following that in which the amount was so notified;

the amount of that contribution shall be computed by reference to the weekly rate or, as the case may be, amount of such a contribution calculated in accordance with section 12 or 13 of the Act as if the contribution had been paid on the last day of the year in which the notification was given.

65 Class 2 and Class 3 contributions paid late through ignorance or error

(1) This regulation applies to any Class 2 or Class 3 contribution which would when paid fall to be computed at a rate or, as the case may be, an amount other than that applicable in the contribution year in accordance with section 12(3) or 13(6) of the Act.

(2) Where—

(*a*) it is shown [to the satisfaction of an officer of the Board][1] that, by reason of ignorance or error on the part of the earner, not being ignorance or error due to any failure on his part to exercise due care and diligence, he has failed to pay a Class 2 contribution to which this regulation applies for any period on or by the due date; and

(*b*) payment of that contribution is made in a year later than that in which the period commenced;

the amount of that contribution shall be calculated by reference to the weekly rate at which a contribution paid under section 12 of the Act would have been payable if it had been paid at the time when the period began.

(3) Where a Class 3 contribution would otherwise fall to be calculated in accordance with section 13(6) of the Act, but it is shown [to the satisfaction of an officer of the Board][1] that the contributor has not paid that contribution before the end of the second year following the contribution year by reason of ignorance or error on the part of the earner, not being ignorance or error due to any failure on his part to exercise due care and diligence, the amount of that contribution shall be computed by reference to the amount of such a contribution applicable to the period for which the contribution is paid.

(4) Where—

(*a*) a Class 3 contribution would when paid fall to be computed in accordance with section 13(6) of the Act,

(*b*) such a contribution remains unpaid for a period commencing at any time after the end of the second year following the contribution year ("the relevant period"), and

(*c*) it is shown [to the satisfaction of an officer of the Board][1] that the contributor has not, during the relevant period only, paid such a contribution by reason of ignorance or error not being ignorance or error due to any failure on the contributor's part to exercise due care and diligence,

paragraph (5) applies.

(5) If this paragraph applies to a contribution, the amount of that contribution shall be calculated in accordance with section 13(6) of the Act as if the contribution had been paid at the time when the relevant period commenced.

Commentary—*Simon's Taxes* **E8.305**.

Amendments—[1] Words in paras (2)(*a*), (3) and (4)(*c*) substituted by the Social Security (Contributions) (Amendment No 3) Regulations, SI 2002/2366 regs 3, 13 with effect from 8 October 2002.

65ZA Amounts of Class 2 and Class 3 contributions in certain cases where earnings removed

. . .

Amendments—Regulations 44–47 revoked by the Social Security (Miscellaneous Amendments No 2) Regulations, SI 2015/478 regs 2, 24(1)(*e*) with effect from 6 April 2015.

65A [Amount of Class 3 contributions payable by virtue of regulation 50A

The amount of a contribution payable by virtue of regulation 50A during the period mentioned in paragraph (3) of that regulation shall, notwithstanding section 13(6) of the Act, be calculated by reference to the weekly rate which would have been applicable if it had been paid during the contribution year to which it relates.][1]

Amendments—[1] Regulation 65A inserted by the Social Security (Contributions) (Amendment No 3) Regulations, SI 2004/1362 regs 2, 5 with effect from 17 May 2004.

65B [Amount of Class 3 contributions payable after issue of a full gender recognition certificate

The amount of a contribution payable by virtue of regulation 49(2B) (Class 3 contributions not precluded where gender recognition certificate issued) which is paid in the year in which the full gender recognition certificate is issued or the following year shall, notwithstanding section 13(6) of the Act, be calculated by reference to the weekly rate which would have been applicable if it had been paid during the contribution year to which it relates.][1]

Amendments—[1] Regulation 65B inserted by the Social Security (Contributions) (Amendment No 3) Regulations, SI 2005/778 regs 2, 7 with effect from 6 April 2005.

65C Late payment of voluntary Class 2 and 3 contributions for tax year 2005–06

. . .

Amendments—Regulations 44–47 revoked by the Social Security (Miscellaneous Amendments No 2) Regulations, SI 2015/478 regs 2, 24(1)(*f*) with effect from 6 April 2015.

65D Late payment of voluntary Class 2 and 3 contributions for tax year 2006–07

. . .

Amendments—Regulations 44–47 revoked by the Social Security (Miscellaneous Amendments No 2) Regulations, SI 2015/478 regs 2, 24(1)(*g*) with effect from 6 April 2015.

PART 7

COLLECTION OF CONTRIBUTIONS (OTHER THAN CLASS 4 CONTRIBUTIONS) AND RELATED MATTERS

66 Notification of national insurance numbers to secondary contributors

Every employed earner, in respect of whom any person is liable to pay an earnings-related contribution, shall, on request, supply his national insurance number to that person.

Commentary—*Simon's Taxes* **E8.812**.

67 Collection and recovery of earnings-related contributions, and Class 1B contributions

(1) Subject to the provisions of regulations 68 and 70, earnings-related contributions and Class 1B contributions shall be paid, accounted for and recovered in like manner as income tax deducted from the [[PAYE income][4] by virtue of regulations under section 684 of ITEPA 2003 (PAYE Regulations)][1].

[(1A) PAYE income has the meaning given in section 683 of ITEPA 2003.][4]

(2) . . . [2] the provisions contained in Schedule 4, (which contains provisions derived from the Income Tax Acts and [the PAYE Regulations][1] with extensions and modifications) shall apply to and for the purposes of earnings-related contributions and Class 1B contributions.

[(3) Schedules 4A (real time returns) and 4B (additional information about payments) apply to and for the purposes of earnings related contributions.][3]

Amendments—[1] Words substituted by the Social Security (Contributions, Categorisation of Earners and Intermediaries) (Amendment) Regulations, SI 2004/770 regs 2, 15 with effect from 6 April 2004.

[2] Words in para (2) revoked by the Social Security (Contributions) (Amendment No 3) Regulations, SI 2008/636 regs 2, 3 with effect from 1 April 2008.

[3] Para (3) inserted by the Social Security (Contributions) (Amendment No 3) Regulations, SI 2012/821 regs 2, 3 with effect from 6 April 2012.

[4] Words in para (1) substituted, and para (1A) inserted by the Social Security (Miscellaneous Amendments No 2) Regulations, SI 2015/478 regs 2, 7 with effect from 6 April 2015.

67A [Penalty for failure to make payments on time: Class 1 contributions

[(1)] [2]Schedule 56 to the Finance Act 2009 ("Schedule 56 FA 2009") (penalty for failure to make payments on time) shall apply in relation to the late payment of Class 1 contributions, as if—

(*a*) the Class 1 contributions were an amount of tax falling within item 2 of the Table in paragraph 1 of Schedule 56 FA 2009 ("the Table"),

(*b*) references to the PAYE Regulations were references to these Regulations, and

(*c*) references to "an assessment or determination" in item 24 of the Table were references to a decision made under section 8(1)(*c*) of the Social Security Contributions (Transfer of Functions, etc) Act 1999.][1]

[(2) Regulation 69A of the PAYE Regulations (circumstances in which payment of a lesser amount is to be treated as payment in full for the purposes of paragraph 6(2) of Schedule 56 to the Finance Act 2009) applies in relation to the late payment of Class 1 contributions as if—

NIC

(*a*) the Class 1 contributions were an amount of tax falling within item 2 of the Table in paragraph 1 of that Schedule,

(*b*) references to regulations 67G and 67H(2) were references to paragraphs 10 and 11 of Schedule 4 to these Regulations, and

(*c*) references to earnings-related contributions were references to tax deducted under the PAYE Regulations][2],

Amendments—[1] Regs 67A, 67B inserted by the Social Security (Contributions) (Amendment No 4) Regulations, SI 2010/721, regs 2, 3 with effect in relation to the tax year 2010–11 and subsequent tax years.

[2] Sub-para (1) numbered as such, and sub-para (2) inserted by the Social Security (Contributions) (Amendment) Regulations, SI 2014/608 regs 2, 3. These amendments come into force on 6 April 2014 and have effect in relation to a payment made in relation to the tax year 2014–15 and subsequent tax years.

67B [Penalty for failure to make payments on time: Class 1A and Class 1B contributions

Schedule 56 to the Finance Act 2009 ("Schedule 56 FA 2009") shall apply in relation to the late payment of Class 1A and Class 1B contributions, as if—

(*a*) the Class 1A and Class 1B contributions were an amount of tax falling within item 3 of the table in paragraph 1 of Schedule 56 FA 2009,

(*b*) in the case of Class 1B contributions, the reference to "amount shown in return under section 254(1) of FA 2004" was a reference to the amount payable under section 10A of the Act, and

(*c*) the reference to section 254(5) of the Finance Act 2004 was a reference to these Regulations."][1]

Amendments—[1] Regs 67A, 67B inserted by the Social Security (Contributions) (Amendment No 4) Regulations, SI 2010/721, regs 2, 3 with effect in relation to the tax year 2010–11 and subsequent tax years.

68 Other methods of collection and recovery of earnings-related contributions

(1) The Board may authorise arrangements under which earnings-related contributions are to be paid in a different manner from that prescribed by regulation 67.

(2) The provisions of regulation 67 shall be in addition to any remedy otherwise available for the recovery of earnings-related contributions.

69 Transfer of liability from secondary contributor to employed earner: [relevant employment income]

Schedule 5 contains provisions which have effect with respect to elections made jointly by a secondary contributor and an employed earner that the liability of the secondary contributor in respect of [relevant employment income][1] shall be transferred to the employed earner.

Commentary—*Simon's Taxes* **E8.233**.

Amendments—[1] Words substituted by the Social Security (Contributions) (Amendment No 4) Regulations, SI 2004/2096 regs 2, 4 with effect from 1 September 2004. SI 2004/2096 has effect in relation to—

(a) agreements entered into after 1 September 2004 which are in respect of post-commencement employment income, and

(b) elections made after that date.

70 Payment of Class 1A contributions

(1) In the cases prescribed by paragraph (2), contributions shall be paid to the Board in accordance with regulations 71 to 83.

(2) The cases prescribed by this paragraph are cases where an employer is liable to pay a Class 1A contribution to the Board.

(3) For the purposes of this regulation and regulations 71 to 83 where—

(*a*) any payment to the Board is made by cheque; and

(*b*) the cheque is paid on its first presentation to the banker on whom it is drawn,

the payment shall be treated as made on the day on which the cheque was received by the Board, and related expressions shall be construed accordingly.

(4) In this regulation, and in regulations 71 to 83, "employer" [means the person liable, in accordance with section 10(2) or 10ZA of the Act, to pay a Class 1A contribution.][1].

Commentary—*Simon's Taxes* **E8.278**.

Amendments—[1] Words in para (4) substituted by the Social Security (Contributions) (Amendment No 5) Regulations, SI 2002/2929 reg 3 with effect from 28 November 2002.

71 Due date for payment of a Class 1A contribution

(1) Subject to regulation 72(2) or 73(2), as the case may be, an employer who is liable to pay a Class 1A contribution to the Board shall pay that contribution to them not later than 19th July [or, where payment is made by an approved method of electronic communications in respect of earnings paid after 5th April 2004, not later than 22nd July][1] in the year immediately following the end of the year in respect of which it is payable.

(2) A Class 1A contribution paid to the Board in accordance with paragraph (1) shall be shown in a return made to them in accordance with regulation 80(1).

Commentary—*Simon's Taxes* **A6.913, E8.279E**.

Amendments—[1] Words in para (1) inserted by the Social Security (Contributions, Categorisation of Earners and Intermediaries) (Amendment) Regulations, SI 2004/770 regs 2, 16 with effect from 6 April 2004.

72 Provisions relating to a Class 1A contribution due on succession to business

(1) Paragraphs (2) and (3) apply in relation to the payment of a Class 1A contribution if—

(*a*) there is a change in the employer who is liable to pay [. . . [2] earnings][1] to or for the benefit of all the persons who are employed in a business in respect of their employment in that business; and

(*b*) the employees in question are those who ceased to be employed in that business before the change of employer occurred.

(2) Not later than 14 days [or, where payment is made by an approved method of electronic communications in respect of earnings paid after 5th April 2004, 17 days][1] after the end of the relevant final [tax month][1], the employer shall pay to the Board—

(*a*) any Class 1A contribution referred to in paragraph (1) in respect of the relevant final year; and

(*b*) where the relevant final [tax month][1] is the month beginning on 6th April, 6th May or 6th June, any Class 1A contribution referred to in paragraph (1) in respect of the year immediately preceding the relevant final year.

(3) The employer shall include the amount of any Class 1A contribution which is payable in accordance with paragraph (2)(*a*) in the return required by regulation 80(1) for the relevant final year.

(4) In this regulation—

"business" includes any trade, concern or undertaking;

"employer" means the employer before the change referred to in paragraph (1)(*a*);

. . . [2]

"relevant final [tax month[1]]" means the [tax month][1] in which the employer has made any payments of emoluments which were, by reason of the change of employer referred to in paragraph (1)(*a*) in respect of the employment of all those persons who were employed by him in that [tax month][1], the [final payment of . . . [2] earnings][1] to be made by him in the year in which those payments were made; . . . [1]; and

"relevant final year" means the year in which the relevant final [tax month][1] occurs.

Commentary—*Simon's Taxes* **E8.831**.

Amendments—[1] Words in paras (1), (2), (4) substituted, words in para (2) inserted, in para (4), definition of "general earnings" inserted, and words in definition of "relevant final tax month" revoked, by the Social Security (Contributions, Categorisation of Earners and Intermediaries) (Amendment) Regulations, SI 2004/770 regs 2, 17, 36, Schedule with effect from 6 April 2004.

[2] In para (1)(*a*), word revoked, and para (4), definition of "general earnings" revoked and in definition of "relevant final tax month", word revoked by the Social Security (Miscellaneous Amendments No 2) Regulations, SI 2015/478 regs 2, 8 with effect from 6 April 2015.

73 Provisions relating to Class 1A contribution due on cessation of business

(1) Paragraphs (2) and (3) apply in relation to the payment of a Class 1A contribution if—

(*a*) an employer ceases to carry on business and upon that cessation no other person becomes liable to pay [. . . [2] earnings][1] to or for the benefit of any employee in respect of his employment in that business; and

(*b*) the employees are all those who were employed in that business at any time in the relevant final year or the year immediately preceding the relevant final year.

(2) Not later than 14 days [or where payment is made by an approved method of electronic communications in respect of earnings paid after 5th April 2004, 17 days][1] after the end of the relevant final [tax month][1], the employer shall pay to the Board—

(*a*) any Class 1A contribution referred to in paragraph (1) in respect of the relevant final year; and

(*b*) where the relevant final [tax month][1] is the month beginning on 6th April, 6th May or 6th June any Class 1A contribution referred to in paragraph (1) in respect of the year immediately preceding the relevant final year.

(3) The employer shall include the amount of any Class 1A contribution which is payable in accordance with paragraph (2)(*a*) in the return required by regulation 80 for the relevant final year.

(4) In this regulation—

"business" includes any trade, concern or undertaking;

"employer" means the employer before the cessation of business referred to in paragraph (1)(*a*);

. . . [2]

"relevant final [tax month[1]]" means the [tax month][1] in which the employer has made any payments of emoluments which were, by reason of the cessation of business referred to in paragraph (1)(*a*) in respect of the employment of all those persons who were employed by him in that [tax month][1], the [final payment of . . . [2] earnings][1] to be made by him in the year in which those payments were made; . . . [1]

"relevant final year" means the year in which the relevant final [tax month][1] occurs.

Commentary—*Simon's Taxes* **E8.831**.

NIC

Amendments—[1] Words in paras (1), (2), (4) substituted, words in para (2) inserted, in para (4), definition of "general earnings" inserted, and words in definition of "relevant final tax month" revoked, by the Social Security (Contributions, Categorisation of Earners and Intermediaries) (Amendment) Regulations, SI 2004/770 regs 2, 18, 36, Schedule with effect from 6 April 2004.
[2] In para (1)(*a*), word revoked, and para (4), definition of "general earnings" revoked and in definition of "relevant final tax month", word revoked by the Social Security (Miscellaneous Amendments No 2) Regulations, SI 2015/478 regs 2, 9 with effect from 6 April 2015.

74 Employer failing to pay a Class 1A contribution

(1) If—

(*a*) the employer has paid no amount of a Class 1A contribution to the Board by the date which applies to him under regulation 71(1), 72(2) or 73(2) (as the case may be); and

(*b*) the Board are unaware of the amount, if any, which the employer is liable so to pay, they may give notice to the employer requiring him to render, within 14 days, a return in the prescribed form showing the amount of a Class 1A contribution which the employer is liable to pay to them under that regulation in respect of the year in question.

(2) A notice may be given by the Board under paragraph (1) notwithstanding that an amount of a Class 1A contribution has been paid to them by the employer under regulation 71(1), 72(2) or 73(2), in respect of the year in question, if they are not satisfied that the amount so paid is the full amount which the employer is liable to pay to them for that year and the provisions of this regulation shall have effect accordingly.

(3) Upon receipt of a return made by an employer under paragraph (1) the Board may prepare a certificate showing the amount of a Class 1A contribution which the employer is liable to pay to them for the year in question.

(4) The production of the return made by the employer under paragraph (1) and of the certificate of the Board under paragraph (3) shall be sufficient evidence that the amount shown in the certificate is the amount of a Class 1A contribution which the employer is liable to pay to the Board in respect of the year in question.

(5) Any document purporting to be a certificate under paragraph (3) shall be presumed to be such a certificate until the contrary is proved.

Commentary—*Simon's Taxes* **E8.815**.

75 Specified amount of a Class 1A contribution

(1) If, following the date which applies to him under regulation 71(1), 72(2) or 73(2) (as the case may be), the employer has paid no amount of a Class 1A contribution to the Board in respect of the year in question and there is reason to believe that the employer is liable so to pay, the Board—

(*a*) in the case of the first year in which the employer is liable to pay such a contribution, upon consideration of any information which has been provided to them by the employer relating to his liability to pay such contributions; or

(*b*) in the case of any later year, upon consideration of the employer's record of past payments;

may to the best of their judgment specify the amount of a Class 1A contribution which they consider the employer is liable to pay and give notice to him of that amount.

(2) If, on the expiration of the period of 7 days allowed in the notice, the specified amount of a Class 1A contribution or any part of that amount is unpaid, the amount so unpaid—

(*a*) shall be treated for the purposes of these Regulations to be an amount of a Class 1A contribution which the employer was liable to pay in respect of the year in question in accordance with regulation 71(1), 72(2) or 73(2); and

(*b*) may be certified by the Board.

(3) Paragraph (2) does not apply if, during the period allowed in the notice—

(*a*) the employer pays to the Board the full amount of a Class 1A contribution which he is liable to pay under regulation 71(1), 72(2) or 73(2), in respect of the year in question; or

(*b*) the employer satisfies the Board that no amount of such a contribution is due.

(4) The production of a certificate such as is mentioned in paragraph (2)(*b*) shall, until the contrary is established, be sufficient evidence that the employer is liable to pay to the Board the amount shown in the certificate, and any document purporting to be such a certificate shall be deemed to be such a certificate until the contrary is proved.

(5) A notice may be given by the Board under paragraph (1) notwithstanding that an amount of a Class 1A contribution has been paid to them by the employer under regulation 71(1), 72(2) or 73(2) in respect of the year in question, if, after seeking the employer's explanation as to the amount of a Class 1A contribution paid, they are not satisfied that the amount so paid is the full amount which the employer is liable to pay to them in respect of that year, and this regulation shall have effect accordingly, but paragraph (2) shall not apply if, during the period allowed in the notice, the employer satisfies the Board that no further amount of a Class 1A contribution is due in respect of that year.

(6) Where, during the period allowed in a notice given by the Board under paragraph (1), the employer claims, but does not satisfy the Board, that the payment of a Class 1A contribution made in respect of the year specified in the notice is the full amount of a Class 1A contribution which he is

liable to pay to the Board in respect of that year, the employer may require the Board to inspect his documents and records as if they had called upon him to produce those documents and records in accordance with [Schedule 36 to the Finance Act 2008 (information and inspection powers)][1].

(7) If the employer does require the Board to inspect his documents and records in accordance with paragraph (6), the provisions of [paragraph 26A][1] of Schedule 4 shall apply in relation to that inspection and the notice given by the Board under paragraph (1) shall be disregarded.

Amendments—[1] Words in paras (6), (7) substituted, by the Social Security (Contributions) (Amendment No 3) Regulations, SI 2009/600 regs 2, 4 with effect from 1 April 2009.

76 Interest on an overdue Class 1A contribution

(1) Where an employer has not paid a Class 1A contribution, which he is liable to pay, by the date which applies to him under regulation 71(1), 72(2) or 73(2) (as the case may be), any contribution not so paid shall carry interest at the rate applicable under paragraph 6(3) of Schedule 1 to the Act from the reckonable date until payment.

(2) Interest payable under this regulation shall be recoverable as if it were a Class 1A contribution which an employer is liable to pay to the Board under regulation 71(1), 72(2) or 73(2), as the case may be).

(3) A contribution to which paragraph (1) applies shall carry interest from the reckonable date even if that date is a non-business day within the meaning of section 92 of the Bills of Exchange Act 1882.

(4) A certificate of the Board that any amount of interest payable under this regulation has not been paid to the Board or, to the best of the Board's knowledge and belief, to any person acting on their behalf, shall be sufficient evidence that the employer is liable to pay to the Board the amount of interest shown on the certificate and that the sum is unpaid and due to be paid, and any document purporting to be such a certificate shall be deemed to be a certificate until the contrary is proved.

(5) For the purposes of this regulation, "the reckonable date" means the 19th July [or where payment is made by an approved method of electronic communications in respect of earnings paid after 5th April 2004, the 22nd July][1] in the year immediately following the end of the year in respect of which the Class 1A contribution is payable to the Board.

Commentary—*Simon's Taxes* **A6.922**.

Amendments—[1] Words inserted by the Social Security (Contributions, Categorisation of Earners and Intermediaries) (Amendment) Regulations, SI 2004/770 regs 2, 19 with effect from 6 April 2004.

77 Payment of interest on a repaid Class 1A contribution

(1) Where—

(*a*) a Class 1A contribution paid by an employer to the Board in respect of the year ended 5th April 1999 or any subsequent year is repaid to him; and

(*b*) that repayment is made after the relevant date,

any such repaid contribution shall carry interest at the rate applicable under paragraph 6(3) of Schedule 1 to the Act from the relevant date until the order for the repayment is issued.

(2) For the purposes of this regulation, "the relevant date" means—

(*a*) the 14th day after the end of the year in respect of which the Class 1A contribution was paid; or

(*b*) if later than that day, the date on which the contribution was paid.

78 Repayment of interest paid on a Class 1A contribution

If an employer has paid interest on a Class 1A contribution, that interest shall be repaid to him where—

(*a*) the interest paid is found not to have been due to be paid, although the contribution in respect of which it was paid was due to be paid;

(*b*) the Class 1A contribution in respect of which interest was paid is returned or repaid to the employer in accordance with the provisions of regulation 52 or 55.

79 Remission of interest on a Class 1A contribution

(1) Where interest is payable in accordance with regulation 76 it shall be remitted for the period commencing on the first relevant date and ending on the second relevant date in the circumstances specified in paragraph (2).

(2) For the purposes of paragraph (1), the circumstances are that the liability, or a greater liability, to pay interest in respect of a Class 1A contribution arises as the result of an official error being made.

(3) For the purposes of this regulation—

"official error" means a mistake made, or something omitted to be done, by an officer of, or person employed in relation to, the Board acting as such, where the employer or any person acting on his behalf has not caused, or materially contributed to, that mistake or omission;

"the first relevant date" means the date defined in regulation 76(5) or, if later, the date on which the official error occurs; and

NIC

"the second relevant date" means the date 14 days after the date on which the official error is rectified and the employer is advised of its rectification.

80 Return by employer

(1) Where a Class 1A contribution is payable to the Board in accordance with regulation 71(1), 72(2) or 73(2), the employer shall render to them a return, not later than 6th July following the end of the year, showing—

(*a*) such particulars as they may require for the identification of the employer;

(*b*) the year to which the return relates;

(*c*) the amounts which are [general earnings][2] in respect of which a Class 1A contribution is payable; and

(*d*) the amount of any Class 1A contribution payable in respect of that year.

[(1A) The employer must render the return required by paragraph (1)—

(*a*) by sending it to the Board; or

(*b*) arranging for the information which it would contain to be delivered to an official computer system by an approved method of electronic communications.][2]

(1B)–(1F) . . .[1, 2]

(2) The return shall include a declaration by the person making the return to the effect that the return is, to the best of his knowledge, correct and complete.

[(3) The declaration must be —

(*a*) signed by the employer; or,

(*b*) where the employer is a body corporate, signed either by the secretary or by a director.][3]

[(3A) Where the return referred to in this regulation is rendered as mentioned in paragraph (1A)(*b*) the declaration must, instead of being signed, be authenticated by or on behalf of the employer in such a manner as may be approved by HMRC.][3]

(4) If, by the date which applies to him under regulation 71(1), 72(2) or 73(2) (as the case may be), an employer has failed to pay a Class 1A contribution which he is liable to pay, the Board may prepare a certificate showing the total amount of a Class 1A contribution remaining unpaid in respect of the year in question and regulation 76(1) and (2) shall, with any necessary modifications, apply to the amount shown in that certificate.

Commentary—*Simon's Taxes* **E8.815**.

Amendments—[1] Paras (1A)–(1F) inserted by the Social Security (Contributions) (Amendment No 4) Regulations, SI 2001/2187 reg 3 with effect from 6 July 2001.

[2] Words in para (1)(*c*) inserted, para (1A) substituted, and paras (1B)–(1F) revoked, by the Social Security (Contributions, Categorisation of Earners and Intermediaries) (Amendment) Regulations, SI 2004/770 regs 2, 20, 36, Schedule with effect from 6 April 2004.

[3] Para (3) substituted and para (3A) inserted, by the Social Security (Contributions) (Amendment No 3) Regulations, SI 2012/821 regs 2, 19 with effect from 6 April 2012.

80A [Returns rendered electronically on another's behalf . . .

Amendment—This regulation revoked by the Social Security (Contributions, Categorisation of Earners and Intermediaries) (Amendment) Regulations, SI 2004/770 regs 2, 21 with effect from 6 April 2004.

81 Penalties for failure to make a return and incorrect returns

[(1) Schedule 24 to the Finance Act 2007 (penalties for errors) applies to the return of contributions referred to in regulation 80(1) (return by employer) as if—

(*a*) Class 1A contributions were a tax; and

(*b*) that tax and the return of contributions in relation to it were listed in the table in paragraph 1 of that Schedule.

(1A) That Schedule also applies to decisions made under section 8(1)(*c*) of the Social Security Contributions (Transfer of Functions, etc) Act 1999 regarding Class 1A contributions and for that purpose a reference in the Schedule to an assessment is to be treated as if it included a reference to a decision and "under-assessment" shall be construed accordingly.

(1B) Paragraphs (6) to (9) do not apply in relation to penalties under paragraphs (1) and (1A).[1]

(2) Any person who fails to make a return referred to in paragraph (1) by the date which applies to him under regulation 71(1), 72(2) or 73(2), may be liable—

(*a*) within 6 years after the date of that failure, to a penalty of the relevant monthly amount for each month (or part of a month) during which the failure continues but excluding any month after the twelfth, or for which a penalty under this paragraph has already been imposed; and

(*b*) if the failure continues beyond 12 months, to a penalty not exceeding so much of the amount payable by him in accordance with the regulations for the year to which the return relates as remains unpaid at the end of 19th July after the end of that year.

(3) The penalty referred to in paragraph (2)(*b*) is without prejudice to any penalty which may be imposed under paragraph (2)(*a*) and may be imposed within six years after the date of the failure referred to in paragraph (2) or at any later time within three years of the final determination of the amount of a Class 1A contribution by reference to which the amount of that penalty is to be ascertained.

(4) For the purposes of paragraph (2), "the relevant monthly amount" in the case of a failure to make a return is—

(*a*) where the number of earners in respect of whom particulars of the amount of any Class 1A contribution payable should be included in the return is 50 or less, £100; or

(*b*) where that number is greater than 50, £100 for each 50 such earners and an additional £100 where that number is not a multiple of 50.

(5) The total penalty payable under paragraph (2)(*a*) shall not exceed the total amount of Class 1A contributions payable in respect of the year to which the return in question relates.

(6) Any penalty imposed in accordance with this regulation shall be recoverable as if it were a Class 1A contribution which the employer is liable to pay to the Board under regulation 71.

(7) A penalty imposed in accordance with this regulation shall be due and payable at the end of 30 days beginning with the date on which notice of the decision to impose it was issued.

(8) The Board may, in their discretion, mitigate any penalty, or stay or compound any proceedings for any penalty, imposed in accordance with the provisions of this regulation, and may also, after judgment, further mitigate or entirely remit such a penalty.

(9) For the purposes of this regulation a person shall be deemed not to have failed to have done anything required to be done within a limited time if he—

(*a*) did it within such further time as the Board allowed; or

(*b*) had a reasonable excuse for the failure and if that excuse ceased, did it without unreasonable delay after that excuse ceased.

Commentary—*Simon's Taxes* **E8.815**.

Amendments—[1] Paras (1)–(1B) substituted for former para (1) by the Social Security (Contributions) (Amendment No 4) Regulations, SI 2010/721, regs 2, 4 with effect in relation to the tax year 2010–11 and subsequent tax years.

82 Application of the Management Act to penalties for failure to make a return and incorrect returns

(1) Section 100 of the Management Act (determination of penalties by an officer of the Board) shall apply with any necessary modifications in relation to the determination of any penalty under regulation 81 as it applies to the determination of a penalty under the Taxes Acts.

(2) Section 100D of the Management Act (penalty proceedings before court) shall apply with any necessary modifications in relation to any proceedings for a penalty under regulation 81 as it applies to proceedings for a penalty under the Taxes Acts.

(3) Section 104 of the Management Act (saving for criminal proceedings) shall apply with any necessary modifications in relation to the provisions of regulation 81 as it applies to the provisions of the Taxes Acts.

(4) Section 105 of the Management Act (evidence in cases of fraudulent conduct) shall apply with any necessary modifications in respect of any proceedings for a penalty under regulation 81, or on appeal against the determination of such a penalty, as it applies in relation to any proceedings for a penalty, or on appeal against the determination of a penalty, under the Management Act.

(5) In this regulation—

"the Management Act" means the Taxes Management Act 1970; and

"the Taxes Acts" has the same meaning as in section 118(1) of the Management Act (interpretation).

Commentary—*Simon's Taxes* **E8.815**.

83 Set-off of Class 1A contributions falling to be repaid against earnings-related contributions

(1) In the circumstance prescribed by paragraph (2), an amount in respect of a Class 1A contribution that falls to be repaid in accordance with these Regulations may be set off against liabilities under them to the extent prescribed in paragraph (3).

(2) The circumstance is that an employer has paid to the Board in accordance with regulations 70 to 82 an amount, in respect of Class 1A contributions, which he was not liable to pay.

(3) The extent of the set-off is that the employer shall be entitled to deduct the amount which he was not liable to pay in respect of Class 1A contributions from any payment in respect of secondary earnings-related contributions which he is subsequently liable to pay to a Collector under paragraph 10 or 11 of Schedule 4 for any income tax period in the same year.

(4) In this regulation "Collector", "income tax period" and "year" have the meanings given in paragraph 1(2) of Schedule 4.

Commentary—*Simon's Taxes* **E8.279E**.

83A [Requirement to give security or further security for amounts of Class 1A contributions

Paragraphs 29M to 29X of Schedule 4 (security for payment of Class 1 contributions) apply in relation to Class 1A contributions as they apply in relation to Class 1 contributions but as if—

(*a*) in paragraph 29N—

(i) the reference to "Class 1 contributions" were a reference to "Class 1A contributions"; and

(ii) the reference to "paragraph 10, 11 or 11A" were a reference to "section 10 or 10ZA of the Social Security Contributions and Benefits Act 1992, or section 10 or 10ZA of the Social Security Contributions and Benefits (Northern Ireland) Act 1992, as the case may be"; and

(*b*) in paragraph 29O(1) for "within the meaning given in paragraph 1(2)" there were substituted "within the meaning given in regulation 70(4).][1]

Amendments—[1] Reg 83A and preceding heading inserted by the Social Security (Contributions) (Amendment No 3) Regulations, SI 2012/821 regs 2, 17 with effect from 6 April 2012.

[84 Special provisions relating to primary Class 1 contributions

(1) If in accordance with an arrangement authorised under regulation 68, notwithstanding paragraph 3(1) of Schedule 1 to the Act (method of paying Class 1 contributions), an earner is required to make direct payments in respect of primary Class 1 contributions in respect of earnings paid to him or for his benefit, the following provisions of this regulation apply.

(2) In a case to which this regulation applies—

(*a*) the earner shall be liable for such of the primary Class 1 contributions as are specified in the arrangements authorised under regulation 68, and

(*b*) the secondary contributor shall be liable for any other Class 1 contributions,

in respect of earnings paid to the earner or for the earner's benefit from the employment in question.

(3) The Board shall notify the secondary contributor in writing of—

(*a*) the arrangement,

(*b*) the contributions for which, notwithstanding the arrangement, he will remain accountable to the Board, and

(*c*) the period to which the arrangement relates ("the relevant period").

(4) During the relevant period, paragraph 3(1) of Schedule 1 to the Act (method of paying Class 1 contributions) shall not apply to the secondary contributor in respect of those contributions—

(*a*) to which the arrangement relates, and

(*b*) for which he would otherwise have been accountable to the Board,

unless and until the arrangement has been cancelled before the end of the period and the secondary contributor has been notified in writing of its cancellation.][1]

Amendments—[1] Regulation 84 substituted by the Social Security (Contributions) (Amendment) Regulations, SI 2003/193 regs 2, 8 with effect from 2003–04.

85 Exception in relation to earnings to which regulation 84 applies

Amendment—Regulation 85 revoked by the Social Security (Contributions) (Amendment) Regulations, SI 2003/193 regs 2, 9 with effect from 2003–04.

86 Special provisions relating to culpable employed earners and to secondary contributors or employers exempted by treaty etc, from enforcement of the Act or liability under it

(1) As respects any employed earner's employment—

(*a*) where there has been a failure to pay any primary contribution which a secondary contributor is, or but for the provisions of this regulation would be, liable to pay on behalf of the earner and

[(i)] [1]the failure was due to an act or default of the earner and not to any negligence on the part of the secondary contributor[, or

(ii) it is shown to the satisfaction of an officer of the Board that the earner knows that the secondary contributor has wilfully failed to pay the primary contribution which the secondary contributor was liable to pay on behalf of the earner and has not recovered that primary contribution from the earner][1]; or

(*b*) where the secondary contributor is a person against whom, by reason of any international treaty or convention as mentioned in paragraph 30 of Schedule 4, the provisions of the Act are not enforceable and who is not willing to pay on behalf of the earner any contribution due in respect of earnings paid to or for the benefit of the earner in respect of that employment,

the provisions of paragraph 3(1) of Schedule 1 to the Act (method of paying Class 1 contributions) shall not apply in relation to that contribution.

(2) Where, as respects any employed earner's employment the employer is a person who by reason of any such international treaty or convention is exempt from the provisions of the Act, he may, if he so wishes, pay contributions in respect of any earnings paid to or for the benefit of the earner in respect of the employment, or contributions under section 10 of the Act . . . [1], in either case to the same extent to which he could have paid such contributions if he had not been so exempt.

(3) In this regulation "employer" has the same meaning as it has in paragraph 30 of Schedule 4.

Commentary—*Simon's Taxes* **A6.944**.

Amendments—[1] Words in para (1) inserted, and words in para (2) revoked, by the Social Security (Contributions, Categorisation of Earners and Intermediaries) (Amendment) Regulations, SI 2004/770 regs 2, 22, 36, Schedule with effect from 6 April 2004.

87 Notification of commencement or cessation of payment of Class 2 or Class 3 contributions [on or before 5th April 2009]

(1) Every person to whom paragraph (2) applies shall immediately notify the relevant date to the Board in writing or by such means of electronic communications as may be approved.

(2) This paragraph applies to a person who [on or before 5th April 2009[1]]—

(*a*) becomes, or ceases to be, liable to pay a Class 2 contribution;

(*b*) becomes, or ceases to be, entitled to pay a Class 2 contribution although not liable to do so; or

(*c*) is entitled to pay a Class 3 contribution and wishes either to do so or to cease doing so.

(3)–(8) . . . [2]

Commentary—*Simon's Taxes* **E8.305, E8.1106.**

Amendments—[1] Words in heading and para (2) inserted, by the Social Security (Contributions) (Amendment No 3) Regulations, SI 2009/600 regs 2, 5 with effect from 6 April 2009.

[2] Paragraphs (3)–(8) revoked by the Social Security (Miscellaneous Amendments No 2) Regulations, SI 2015/478 regs 2, 24(1)(*h*) with effect from 6 April 2015.

87A [Notification of commencement or cessation of payment of Class 2 or Class 3 contributions on or after 6th April 2009 [but before 6th April 2015][2]

(1) A person (P) to whom paragraph (2) applies shall immediately notify the relevant date to HMRC in writing or by such means of electronic communications as may be approved.

(2) This paragraph applies where P on or after 6th April 2009 [but before 6th April 2015][2]

(*a*) becomes, or ceases to be, liable to pay a Class 2 contribution;

(*b*) becomes, or ceases to be, entitled to pay a Class 2 contribution although not liable to do so; or

(*c*) is entitled to pay a Class 3 contribution and wishes either to do so or to cease doing so.

(3) In paragraph (1) "the relevant date" means—

(*a*) in relation to a person to whom paragraph (2)(*a*) applies, the date on which P commences or ceases to be a self-employed earner;

(*b*) in relation to a person to whom paragraph (2)(*b*) or (*c*) applies, the date on which P wishes to commence or cease paying either Class 2 or Class 3 contributions, as the case may be.

(4) P is to be treated as having immediately notified HMRC in accordance with paragraph (1) if P has notified HMRC within such further time, if any, as HMRC may allow.][1]

Commentary—*Simon's Taxes* **E8.305.**

Amendments—[1] Regulations 87A–87G inserted by the Social Security (Contributions) (Amendment No 3) Regulations, SI 2009/600 regs 2, 6 with effect from 6 April 2009.

[2] Words in heading and para (2) inserted by the Social Security (Miscellaneous Amendments No 2) Regulations, SI 2015/478 regs 2, 10 with effect from 6 April 2015.

[87AA Notification of commencement or cessation of self-employment or Class 3 contributions on or after 6th April 2015

(1) A person (P) to whom paragraph (2) applies shall immediately notify the relevant date to HMRC in writing or by such means of electronic communication as may be approved.

(2) This paragraph applies where P on or after 6th April 2015—

(*a*) commences or ceases to be a self-employed earner; or

(*b*) is entitled to pay a Class 3 contribution and either wishes to do so or cease doing so.

(3) In paragraph (1) "the relevant date" means—

(*a*) in relation to a person to whom paragraph (2)(*a*) applies, the date on which P commences or ceases to be a self-employed earner;

(*b*) in relation to a person to whom paragraph (2)(*b*) applies, the date on which P wishes to commence or cease paying Class 3 contributions.

(4) P is to be treated as having immediately notified HMRC in accordance with paragraph (1) if P has notified HMRC within such further time, if any, as HMRC may allow.][1]

Commentary—*Simon's Taxes* **E8.305.**

Amendments—[1] This regulation inserted by the Social Security (Miscellaneous Amendments No 2) Regulations, SI 2015/478 regs 2, 11 with effect from 6 April 2015.

87B Penalty for failure to notify

. . .

Amendments—Regulations 87B–87G revoked by the Social Security (Miscellaneous Amendments No 2) Regulations, SI 2015/478 regs 2, 24(1)(*l*) with effect from 6 April 2015.

87C Disclosure

. . .

Amendments—Regulations 87B–87G revoked by the Social Security (Miscellaneous Amendments No 2) Regulations, SI 2015/478 regs 2, 24(1)(*l*) with effect from 6 April 2015.

87D Reduction of penalty for disclosure

. . .

NIC

Amendments—Regulations 87B–87G revoked by the Social Security (Miscellaneous Amendments No 2) Regulations, SI 2015/478 regs 2, 24(1)(*l*) with effect from 6 April 2015.

87E Special reduction

. . .

Amendments—Regulations 87B–87G revoked by the Social Security (Miscellaneous Amendments No 2) Regulations, SI 2015/478 regs 2, 24(1)(*l*) with effect from 6 April 2015.

87F Notice of decision etc

. . .

Amendments—Regulations 87B–87G revoked by the Social Security (Miscellaneous Amendments No 2) Regulations, SI 2015/478 regs 2, 24(1)(*l*) with effect from 6 April 2015.

87G Double jeopardy

. . .

Amendments—Regulations 87B–87G revoked by the Social Security (Miscellaneous Amendments No 2) Regulations, SI 2015/478 regs 2, 24(1)(*l*) with effect from 6 April 2015.

88 Notification of change of address

A person liable to pay Class 2 contributions; or paying Class 2 contributions (although not liable to do so) or Class 3 contributions, shall immediately notify the Board of any change of his address in writing or by such means of electronic communications as may be approved.

Commentary—*Simon's Taxes* **E8.305**.

89 Method of, and time for, payment of Class 2 and Class 3 contributions etc

(1) Where Class 2 or Class 3 contributions are payable by a person other than in accordance with [the Taxes Management Act 1970 (as modified by section 11A of the Act) or in accordance with,][2] arrangements approved under regulation 90 [or in accordance with regulation 90ZA or 148C][2], such contributions shall be paid in accordance with paragraph (2), . . . [2] (3) or (4), as the case may be.

(1A) . . . [2]

(2) . . . [2]

[(2A) Where—

(*a*) a person who is entitled, although not liable, to pay a Class 2 contribution in any year has notified HMRC of his entitlement in accordance with the provisions of regulation 87[,][2] 87A [or 87AA][2]; and

(*b*) HMRC has, no later than the notification date, issued him with written notice of the amount he may pay in respect of his entitlement in that period;

that person may, if the person so wishes, pay to HMRC a sum not exceeding that amount.][1]

(3) Where—

(*a*) a person . . . [1] who is entitled to pay a Class 3 contribution, in any year, has notified [HMRC][1] of his entitlement in accordance with the provisions of regulation 87[, 87A or 87AA][2]; and

(*b*) [HMRC][1], within 14 days after the end of a contribution quarter which commences in that year, have issued him with written notice of the amount he may pay in respect of his entitlement in that quarter;

that person may, if he so wishes, pay to [HMRC][1] a sum not exceeding that amount.

(4) Where—

(*a*) paragraph (5) . . . [2] applies to a person; and

(*b*) [HMRC][1] have then, in respect of that . . . [2] entitlement to pay Class 2 or Class 3 contributions, issued or re-issued him, as the case may be, with written notice of . . . [2] the amount of his entitlement;

that person . . . [2] may pay a sum not exceeding the amount of his entitlement, to [HMRC][1].

[(5) This paragraph applies to a person who—

(*a*) has notified HMRC in accordance with the provisions of regulation 87[, 87A or 87AA][2] that—

(*i*) . . . [2]

(ii) he is entitled although not liable to pay a Class 2 contribution in a [tax year][2], or is entitled to pay a Class 3 contribution in a contribution quarter; and

(*b*) has—

(i) not, by the notification date, had written notice issued to him in respect of that week or weeks of the kind referred to in paragraph (2A);

(ii) not had written notice issued to him in respect of that week or weeks of a kind mentioned in paragraph (3) and more than 14 days have elapsed since the end of the contribution quarter in question; or

(iii) notified HMRC in accordance with regulation 87[[, 87A or 87AA][2] that he has . . . [2] ceased to be entitled to pay Class 2 or Class 3 contributions . . . [2].

(6) . . . [2]

(7) In this regulation—

(*a*) . . . [2]
(*b*) . . . [2]
(*c*) . . . [2]
(*d*) "contribution quarter" means one of the four periods of not less than 13 contribution weeks commencing on the first, fourteenth, twenty-seventh or fortieth contribution week, as the case may be, in any year;
[(*e*) "notification date" means 31st October following the end of the tax year.][2]

Commentary—*Simon's Taxes* **E8.305**.

Amendments—[1] In para (1), words inserted, paras (1A), (2A) inserted, paras (2), (5)–(7) substituted, in para (3)(*a*), words revoked, words inserted and word substituted in each place, and in para (4) words substituted in each place, by the Social Security (Contributions) (Amendment No 3) Regulations, SI 2011/797 regs 2, 6 with effect in relation to Class 2 contributions in respect of contribution weeks beginning on or after 10 April 2011.

[2] The following amendments made by the Social Security (Miscellaneous Amendments No 2) Regulations, SI 2015/478 regs 2, 12 with effect from 6 April 2015—

- in para (1), words inserted and revoked;
- paras (1A), (2), (6), (7)(*a*)–(*a*) revoked;
- in para (2A), words inserted and substituted;
- in paras (4), (7), words revoked;
- in para (5), words inserted, revoked and substituted; and
- in para (7)(*e*) substituted

[89A Class 2 contributions for tax years up to 2014–15

(1) This regulation applies where a person (P) is liable to pay a Class 2 contribution in respect of any contribution week in a tax year up to and including the 2014–15 tax year.

(2) An officer of HMRC may issue P with written notice of the amount of Class 2 contributions for which P is liable in respect of any tax year up to and including the 2014–15 tax year.

(3) P shall pay the amount of contributions for which he is liable no later than the date specified in the notice. This paragraph is subject to paragraphs (4) and (5).

(4) Where P—

(*a*) is liable to pay a Class 2 contribution in respect of any contribution week falling within the period defined in paragraph (5) ("the specified contribution period"); and

(*b*) has notified HMRC of such liability in accordance with the provisions of regulation 87 or 87A,

HMRC shall issue P with written notice of the amount of Class 2 contributions for which P is liable to pay in respect of the specified contribution period no later than 1st June 2015 and P shall pay the amount set out in that notice to HMRC no later than 31st July 2015.

(5) For the purposes of paragraph (4), the specified contribution period is the period of not less than 26 contribution weeks falling within the 2014–15 tax year commencing with the first day of the twenty seventh contribution week in that year.][1]

Amendments—[1] This regulation inserted by the Social Security (Miscellaneous Amendments No 2) Regulations, SI 2015/478 regs 2, 13 with effect from 6 April 2015.

90 Arrangements approved by the Board for method of, and time for, payment of Class 2 and Class 3 contributions

(1) The Board may from time to time approve arrangements under which contributions are paid at times or in a manner different from those prescribed by regulation 89.

This is subject to paragraphs (2) to (4).

(2) When granting approval under paragraph (1), the Board may impose such conditions as they see fit.

(3) The Board may, in particular, grant approval under paragraph (1) if, as respects any year in which a person is both an employed earner and a self-employed earner, the condition in paragraph (4) is satisfied.

(4) The condition is that the Board are satisfied that the [total amounts of primary Class 1 contributions and Class 2 contributions][1] likely to be paid by or in respect of that person in respect of that year will exceed [the amount equal to 53 primary Class 1 contributions payable on earnings at the upper earnings limit for that year at the main primary percentage][1].

(5) The provisions of these Regulations shall, subject to the provisions of the arrangements, apply to the person affected by the arrangements.

(6) Where in respect of an earner arrangements are approved under paragraph (1) for payment of contributions by way of direct debit of a bank, those arrangements shall be subject to the condition that any payment by way of direct debit on account of such contributions after the authority of the bank to make such payment has for any reason ceased to be effective, shall not be a payment of contributions for the purposes of the Act.

Commentary—*Simon's Taxes* **E8.305, E8.306**.

Amendments—[1] Words in para (4) substituted by the Social Security (Contributions) (Amendment) Regulations, SI 2003/193 regs 2, 10 with effect from 2003–04.

[90ZA Class 2 contributions - maternity allowance

(1) This regulation applies in connection with maternity allowance under section 35 or 35B of the Act.

(2) A person who is, or will be, either liable or entitled to pay a Class 2 contribution in respect of a week in a tax year may pay a Class 2 contribution in respect of that week at any time in the period—

(*a*) beginning with that week; and

(*b*) ending with 31st January next following the end of the relevant tax year.

(3) Where a person pays a Class 2 contribution in accordance with paragraph (2)—

(*a*) the contribution is to be treated, before the end of the tax year, as a Class 2 contribution under section 11(6) of the Act, and

(*b*) the contribution is to be treated after the end of the tax year—

(i) if the person is liable under section 11(2) of the Act to pay a Class 2 contribution in respect of that week, as a Class 2 contribution under section 11(2) of the Act; or

(ii) otherwise, as a Class 2 contribution under section 11(6) of the Act.][1]

Amendments—[1] This regulation inserted by the Social Security (Miscellaneous Amendments No 2) Regulations, SI 2015/478 regs 2, 14 with effect from 6 April 2015.

[PART 7A
ELECTRONIC COMMUNICATIONS][1]

Amendments—[1] Part 7A inserted by the Social Security (Contributions, Categorisation of Earners and Intermediaries) (Amendment) Regulations, SI 2004/770 regs 2, 23 with effect from 6 April 2004.

90A [Whether information has been delivered electronically

(1) For the purposes of these Regulations, information is taken to have been delivered to an official computer system by an approved method of electronic communications only if it is accepted by that official computer system.

(2) References in these Regulations to information and to the delivery of information must be construed in accordance with section 135(8) of the Finance Act 2002 (mandatory e-filing).][1]

Amendments—[1] Part 7A inserted by the Social Security (Contributions, Categorisation of Earners and Intermediaries) (Amendment) Regulations, SI 2004/770 regs 2, 23 with effect from 6 April 2004.

90B [Proof of content of electronic delivery

(1) A document certified by the Board to be a printed-out version of any information delivered by an approved method of electronic communications is evidence, unless the contrary is proved, that the information—

(*a*) was delivered by an approved method of electronic communications on that occasion, and

(*b*) constitutes everything which was delivered on that occasion.

(2) A document which purports to be a certificate given in accordance with paragraph (1) is presumed to be such a certificate unless the contrary is proved.][1]

Commentary—*Simon's Taxes* **E8.835**.

Amendments—[1] Part 7A inserted by the Social Security (Contributions, Categorisation of Earners and Intermediaries) (Amendment) Regulations, SI 2004/770 regs 2, 23 with effect from 6 April 2004.

90C [Proof of identity of person sending or receiving electronic delivery

The identity of—

(*a*) the person sending any information delivered by an approved method of electronic communications to the Board,

(*b*) the person receiving any information delivered by an approved method of electronic communications by the Board,

is presumed, unless the contrary is proved, to be the person recorded as such on an official computer system.][1]

Commentary—*Simon's Taxes* **E8.835**.

Amendments—[1] Part 7A inserted by the Social Security (Contributions, Categorisation of Earners and Intermediaries) (Amendment) Regulations, SI 2004/770 regs 2, 23 with effect from 6 April 2004.

90D [Information sent electronically on behalf of a person

(1) Any information delivered by an approved method of electronic communications—

(*a*) to the Board, or

(*b*) to an official computer system,

on behalf of a person is taken to have been delivered by that person.

(2) But this does not apply if the person proves that the information was delivered without the person's knowledge or connivance.][1]

Commentary—*Simon's Taxes* **E8.835**.

Amendments—[1] Part 7A inserted by the Social Security (Contributions, Categorisation of Earners and Intermediaries) (Amendment) Regulations, SI 2004/770 regs 2, 23 with effect from 6 April 2004.

90E [Proof of delivery of information sent electronically

(1) The use of an approved method of electronic communications is presumed, unless the contrary is proved, to have resulted in the delivery of information—

(*a*) to the Board, if the delivery of the information has been recorded on an official computer system;

(*b*) by the Board, if the despatch of the information has been recorded on an official computer system.

(2) The use of an approved method of electronic communications is presumed, unless the contrary is proved, not to have resulted in the delivery of information—

(*a*) to the Board, if the delivery of the information has not been recorded on an official computer system;

(*b*) by the Board, if the despatch of the information has not been recorded on an official computer system.

(3) The time of receipt or despatch of any information delivered by an approved method of electronic communications is presumed, unless the contrary is proved, to be the time recorded on an official computer system.][1]

Commentary—*Simon's Taxes* **E8.835.**

Amendments—[1] Part 7A inserted by the Social Security (Contributions, Categorisation of Earners and Intermediaries) (Amendment) Regulations, SI 2004/770 regs 2, 23 with effect from 6 April 2004.

90F [Proof of payment sent electronically

(1) The use of a method of electronic communications is presumed, unless the contrary is proved, to have resulted in the making of a payment—

(*a*) to the Board, if the making of the payment has been recorded on an official computer system;

(*b*) by the Board, if the despatch of the payment has been recorded on an official computer system.

(2) The use of a method of electronic communications is presumed, unless the contrary is proved, not to have resulted in the making of a payment—

(*a*) to the Board, if the making of the payment has not been recorded on an official computer system;

(*b*) by the Board, if the despatch of the payment has not been recorded on an official computer system.

(3) The time of receipt or despatch of any payment sent by a method of electronic communications is presumed, unless the contrary is proved, to be the time recorded on an official computer system.][1]

Commentary—*Simon's Taxes* **E8.835.**

Amendments—[1] Part 7A inserted by the Social Security (Contributions, Categorisation of Earners and Intermediaries) (Amendment) Regulations, SI 2004/770 regs 2, 23 with effect from 6 April 2004.

90G [Use of unauthorised method of electronic communications

(1) This regulation applies to information which is required to be delivered to the Board or to an official computer system under a provision of these Regulations.

(2) The use of a method of electronic communications for the purpose of delivering such information is conclusively presumed not to have resulted in the delivery of that information, unless that method of electronic communications is for the time being approved for delivery of that kind under that provision.][1]

Commentary—*Simon's Taxes* **E8.835.**

Amendments—[1] Part 7A inserted by the Social Security (Contributions, Categorisation of Earners and Intermediaries) (Amendment) Regulations, SI 2004/770 regs 2, 23 with effect from 6 April 2004.

90H [Mandatory electronic payment

[(1) An employer who is a large employer within the meaning of regulation [198A (large employers)][4] of the PAYE Regulations must pay the specified payment using an approved method of electronic communications.][3]

(2) Paragraph (1) applies regardless of whether a payment of tax is due under regulation [67G or][5] 68 of the PAYE Regulations (payment and recovery of tax by employer).

(3) If the Board have given a direction under regulation 199(3) of the PAYE Regulations requiring a particular method of electronic communications to be used in the case of an employer, he must use that method.][1]

[(4) This regulation does not apply to a payment of contributions, whether primary or secondary, in respect of retrospective earnings where those earnings relate to a tax year which is closed (see paragraph 1(2) of Schedule 4) at the time the relevant retrospective contributions regulations come into force.][2]

[(5) A specified payment is not treated as received in full by HMRC on or before the date by which that specified payment is required in accordance with paragraph 10 or paragraph 11 of Schedule 4 unless it is made in a manner which secures (in a case where the specified payment is made otherwise than in cash) that, on or before that date, all transactions can be completed which need to be completed before the whole amount of the specified payment becomes available to the Commissioners for Her Majesty's Revenue and Customs.][3]

Amendments—[1] Part 7A inserted by the Social Security (Contributions, Categorisation of Earners and Intermediaries) (Amendment) Regulations, SI 2004/770 regs 2, 23 with effect from 6 April 2004.
[2] Para (4) inserted by the Social Security Contributions (Consequential Provisions) Regulations, SI 2007/1056 regs 3, 6 with effect from 6 April 2007.
[3] Para (1) substituted, and para (5) inserted, by the Social Security (Contributions) (Amendment No 4) Regulations, SI 2010/721 regs 2, 5(*a*), (*c*)with effect in relation to the tax year 2010–11 and subsequent tax years.
[4] In para (1) words substitued by the Social Security (Contributions) (Amendment No 4) Regulations, SI 2010/721 regs 2, 5(*b*) with effect in relation to the tax year 2011–12 and subsequent tax years.
[5] In para (2), reference inserted by the Social Security (Contributions) (Amendment No 3) Regulations, SI 2012/821 regs 2, 4 with effect from 6 April 2012.

90I Employer in default if specified payment not received by applicable due date

Amendments—Regs 90I–90L repealed by the Social Security (Contributions) (Amendment No 4) Regulations, SI 2010/721, regs 2, 6 with effect in relation to the tax year 2010–11 and subsequent tax years.

90J Default notice and appeal

Amendments—Regs 90I–90L repealed by the Social Security (Contributions) (Amendment No 4) Regulations, SI 2010/721, regs 2, 6 with effect in relation to the tax year 2010–11 and subsequent tax years.

90K Default surcharge

Amendments—Regs 90I–90L repealed by the Social Security (Contributions) (Amendment No 4) Regulations, SI 2010/721, regs 2, 6 with effect in relation to the tax year 2010–11 and subsequent tax years.

90L Surcharge notice and appeal

Amendments—Regs 90I–90L repealed by the Social Security (Contributions) (Amendment No 4) Regulations, SI 2010/721, regs 2, 6 with effect in relation to the tax year 2010–11 and subsequent tax years.

90M [Paragraph 22 return and specified payments]

In this Part—

["paragraph 22 return" means the return and accompanying information required by paragraph 22 of Schedule 4 (return by employer at the end of the year);][2] and

["specified payments" means payments of earnings-related contributions under paragraph 10 (payments made monthly by employer) or paragraph 11 (payments made quarterly by employer) of Schedule 4.][3]][1]

Amendments—[1] Part 7A inserted by the Social Security (Contributions, Categorisation of Earners and Intermediaries) (Amendment) Regulations, SI 2004/770 regs 2, 23 with effect from 6 April 2004.
[2] Heading substituted, and definition of "paragraph 22 return" substituted, by the Social Security (Contributions) (Amendment No 4) Regulations, SI 2009/2028 regs 2, 5 with effect in relation to the tax year 2009–10 and subsequent tax years.
[3] Definition of "specified payments" substituted by the Social Security (Contributions) (Amendment No 4) Regulations, SI 2010/721, regs 2, 7 with effect in relation to the tax year 2010–11 and subsequent tax years.

90N [Mandatory use of electronic communications

(1) An employer (as to which see regulation 90NA) must deliver a paragraph 22 return to an official computer system using an approved method of electronic communications.

(2) If the Commissioners for Her Majesty's Revenue and Customs have made a direction under regulation [205(2)][2] of the PAYE Regulations requiring a particular method of electronic communication to be used in the case of an employer, the employer must use that method.

(3) This regulation does not apply to a return in respect of retrospective earnings where those earnings relate to a tax year which is closed (see paragraph 1(2) of Schedule 4) at the time the relevant retrospective contributions regulations come into force.[1]

Commentary—*Simon's Taxes* **E8.835**.

Amendments—[1] Regs 90N, 90NA substituted for former reg 90N by the Social Security (Contributions) (Amendment No 4) Regulations, SI 2010/721, regs 2, 8(1) with effect in relation to the tax year 2010–11 and subsequent tax years.
[2] In para (2), reference substituted by the Social Security (Contributions) (Amendment No 4) Regulations, SI 2010/721, regs 2, 8(2) with effect in relation to the tax year 2011–12 and subsequent tax years.

90NA [Employers

(1) For the purposes of regulation 90N, the following shall not be regarded as employers—

(*a*) an individual who is a practising member of a religious society or order whose beliefs are incompatible with the use of electronic communications,

(*b*) a partnership, if all the partners fall within sub-paragraph (*a*),

(*c*) a company, if all the directors and company secretary fall within sub-paragraph (*a*),

(*d*) . . .[2]and

(*e*) a care and support employer.

(2) In paragraph (1)(*c*), "company" means a body corporate or unincorporated association but does not include a partnership.

(3) In paragraph (1)(*e*), a "care and support employer" means an individual ("the employer") who employs a person to provide domestic or personal services at or from the employer's home where—

(*a*) the services are provided to the employer or a member of the employer's family,

(*b*) the recipient of the services has a physical or mental disability, or is elderly or infirm,

(*c*) the employer has not received an incentive payment in respect of the last 3 tax years, and (*d*) it is the employer who delivers the paragraph 22 return (and not some other person on the employer's behalf).

(4) In this regulation "incentive payment" means an incentive payment received under the Income Tax (Incentive Payments for Voluntary Electronic Communication of PAYE Returns) Regulations 2003.][1]

Amendments—[1] Regs 90N, 90NA substituted for 90N by the Social Security (Contributions) (Amendment No 4) Regulations, SI 2010/721, regs 2, 8 with effect in relation to the tax year 2010–11 and subsequent tax years.

[2] Para (1)(*d*) (but not the word "and" after it) revoked by the Social Security (Contributions) (Amendment and Application of Schedule 38 to the Finance Act 2012) Regulations, SI 2013/622 regs 2, 3 with effect in relation to the tax year 2014–15.

90O [Standards of accuracy and completeness

(1) [Any paragraph 22 return][2] delivered by a method of electronic communications must meet the standards of accuracy or completeness set by specific or general directions given by the Board.

(2) [Any paragraph 22 return][2] which fails to meet those standards must be treated as not having been delivered.][1]

Commentary—*Simon's Taxes* **E8.835**.

Amendments—[1] Part 7A inserted by the Social Security (Contributions, Categorisation of Earners and Intermediaries) (Amendment) Regulations, SI 2004/770 regs 2, 23 with effect from 6 April 2004.

[2] Words substituted by the Social Security (Contributions) (Amendment No 4) Regulations, SI 2009/2028 regs 2, 7 with effect in relation to the tax year 2009–10 and subsequent tax years.

90P [Penalties and appeals

(1) An employer who fails to deliver [a paragraph 22 return][2] or any part of it in accordance with regulation 90N is liable to a penalty.

[(2) Table 2 sets out the penalties for employers for the tax year ending 5th April 2010, depending on the number of employees for whom particulars should have been included with the paragraph 22 return.

Table 2
Penalties: tax year ending 5th April 2010

1 Number of employees for whom particulars should have been included with the return	*2 Penalty*
1–5	0
6-49	£100
50–249	£600
250-399	£900
400–499	£1200
500–599	£1500
600-699	£1800
700–799	£2100
800-899	£2400
900–999	£2700
1000 or more	£3000

(2A) Table 3 sets out the penalties for employers for the tax years ending 5th April 2011 and subsequent years, depending on the number of employees for whom particulars should have been included with the paragraph 22 return.

Table 3
Penalties: tax year ending 5th April 2011 and subsequent tax years

1 Number of employees for whom particulars should have been included with the return	*2 Penalty*
1–5	£100
6–49	£300
50-249	£600
250–399	£900
400-499	£1200
500–599	£1500
600-699	£1800
700–799	£2100
800–899	£2400

NIC

900–999	£2700
1000 or more	£3000][2]

(3) An employer is not liable to a penalty if the employer had—

(*a*) a reasonable excuse for failing to comply with regulation 90N which had not ceased at the time the [paragraph 22 return][2] was delivered, or

[(*b*) been subject to a penalty for failing to deliver the return and accompanying information required by regulation 73 of the PAYE Regulations (annual return of relevant payments liable to deduction of tax (Forms P35 and P14)) in accordance with regulation 205 (mandatory use of electronic communication) of those Regulations.][4]

(4) A notice of appeal against a determination under section 100 of the Management Act of a penalty under this paragraph can only be on the grounds that—

(*a*) the employer did comply with regulation 90N,

[(*aa*) the employer is not regarded as an employer for the purposes of regulation 90N,][3]

(*b*) the amount of the penalty is incorrect, or

(*c*) paragraph (3) applies.

(5) Section 103A of the Management Act (interest on penalties) applies to penalties payable under this paragraph.][1]

Commentary—*Simon's Taxes* **E8.835.**

Amendments—[1] Part 7A inserted by the Social Security (Contributions, Categorisation of Earners and Intermediaries) (Amendment) Regulations, SI 2004/770 regs 2, 23 with effect from 6 April 2004.

[2] In paras (1), (3)(*a*), words substituted, paras (2), (2A) substituted, and para (3)(*b*) substituted, by the Social Security (Contributions) (Amendment No 4) Regulations, SI 2009/2028 regs 2, 7 with effect in relation to the tax year 2009–10 and subsequent tax years.

[3] Para 4(*aa*) inserted by the Social Security (Contributions) (Amendment No 4) Regulations, SI 2010/721, regs 2, 9(*b*) with effect in relation to the tax year 2010–11 and subsequent tax years.

[4] Para (3)(*b*) substituted by the Social Security (Contributions) (Amendment No 4) Regulations, SI 2010/721, regs 2, 9(*a*) with effect in relation to the tax year 2011–12 and subsequent tax years. Para (*b*) previously by the Social Security (Contributions) (Amendment No 4) Regulations, SI 2009/2028 regs 2, 7 with effect in relation to the tax year 2009–10 and subsequent tax years.

90Q [Appeals: supplementary provisions

[(1) Section 31A(5) of the Management Act applies to appeals under regulation 90J as it applies to an appeal under section 31 of that Act.][2]

(2), (3) . . . [2]][1]

Amendments—[1] Part 7A inserted by the Social Security (Contributions, Categorisation of Earners and Intermediaries) (Amendment) Regulations, SI 2004/770 regs 2, 23 with effect from 6 April 2004.

[2] Para (1) substituted, and paras (2), (3) revoked, by the Transfer of Tribunal Functions and Revenue and Customs Appeals Order, SI 2009/56 art 3, Sch 2 para 75 with effect from 1 April 2009.

90R [Interpretation

In this Part "the Management Act" means the Taxes Management Act 1970.][1]

Amendments—[1] Part 7A inserted by the Social Security (Contributions, Categorisation of Earners and Intermediaries) (Amendment) Regulations, SI 2004/770 regs 2, 23 with effect from 6 April 2004.

PART 8

CLASS 4 CONTRIBUTIONS

91 Exception from Class 4 liability of persons over pensionable age and persons not resident in the United Kingdom

Any earner who—

(*a*) at the beginning of a year of assessment is over pensionable age; or

(*b*) for the purposes of income tax is not resident in the United Kingdom in the year of assessment;

shall be excepted from liability for contributions under section 15 of the Act (Class 4 contributions).

Commentary—*Simon's Taxes* **E8.324.**

92 Exception of divers and diving supervisors from liability for Class 4 contributions

A person who performs the duties of an employment to which section 314 of the Taxes Act applies (divers and diving supervisors) shall be excepted from liability for contributions under section 15 of the Act on so much of his profits or gains as are derived from that employment.

Commentary—*Simon's Taxes* **E8.324.**

93 Exception of persons under the age of 16 from liability for Class 4 contributions

(1) Where, as respects any year of assessment, a person to whom this regulation applies wishes to be excepted from liability to pay contributions under section 15 of the Act for that year, the following provisions of this regulation shall apply, subject to the provisions of regulations 97 and 98.

(2) Any such person shall make application to the Board for a certificate of exception for that year.

(3) If it is shown to the satisfaction of the Board that the applicant is a person to whom this regulation applies and the application is made before the beginning of the year of assessment to which it relates, the Board shall issue in respect of the applicant such a certificate of exception for that year.
(4) If the application is not made until the beginning of the year of assessment to which it relates, but is made before contributions under that section 15 of the Act for that year become due and payable and it is shown to the satisfaction of the Board that the applicant is a person to whom this regulation applies, the Board may issue in respect of the applicant a certificate of exception for that year.
(5) Where under paragraphs (1) to (4) a certificate of exception has been issued in respect of an applicant for any year of assessment, the Board shall not collect any contributions under section 15 of the Act from the applicant for that year.
(6) This regulation applies to any person who at the beginning of the year of assessment is under the age of 16.

Commentary—*Simon's Taxes* **E8.324.**

94 [Exception from Class 4 liability in respect of earnings from employed earner's employment chargeable to income tax under Schedule D]

[(1) If, for any year of assessment—
(*a*) an earner has earnings from employment which is employed earner's employment; and
(*b*) those earnings are chargeable to income tax under Schedule D;
the earner shall be excepted from liability to pay contributions under section 15 of the Act on those earnings.
This is subject to the following qualification.][1]
(2) It shall be a condition of exception from liability that the earner makes an application for such an exception to the Board before the beginning of the year of assessment to which the application relates, or before such later date as the Board may allow.
(3) An application under paragraph (2) shall be made in such manner as the Board may direct and, for the purpose of enabling the Board to determine whether the earner is entitled to the exception, the earner shall furnish the Board with such information and evidence as the Board may require, whether the requirement is made at the time of the application or later.
(4) Without prejudice to the earner's right to any such exception, nothing in paragraphs (1) to (3) shall affect the Board's powers under regulation 95 to defer, pending the determination of the application, the earner's liability under section 15 of the Act.

Amendments—[1] Heading and para (1) substituted by the Social Security (Contributions) (Amendment) Regulations, SI 2003/193 regs 2, 11 with effect from 2003–04.

94A [Exception from Class 4 liability in respect of certain amounts chargeable to income tax under Schedule D

Where—
(*a*) an earner has earnings from employment which is employed earner's employment; and
(*b*) an amount representing those earnings is included in the calculation of the profits chargeable to income tax under Schedule D,
the earner shall be excepted from liability to pay contributions under section 15 of the Act (Class 4 contributions) on that amount.][1]

Commentary—*Simon's Taxes* **E8.326.**

Amendments—[1] Regulation 94A inserted by the Social Security (Contributions) (Amendment No 7) Regulations, SI 2003/2958 regs 2, 4 with effect from 2003–04.

[94B Liability of a partner in an AIFM firm for Class 4 contributions

(1) This regulation applies if an AIFM firm makes an election under section 863H of ITTOIA 2005 (election for special provision for alternative investment fund managers to apply).
(2) Where a partner ("P") in an AIFM firm allocates a profit ("the allocated profit") to that firm as provided for in section 863I(2) of ITTOIA 2005 (allocation of profit to the AIFM firm), no Class 4 contributions are payable in respect of that allocated profit by virtue of the allocation.
(3) Paragraph (4) applies if all or part of the allocated profit vests in P at a time when P is carrying on the AIFM trade (whether as a partner in the AIFM firm or otherwise).
(4) The amount treated as a profit under section 863J(2) and (5) of ITTOIA 2005 (vesting of remuneration represented by the allocated profit) is to be treated for the purposes of the Act as if it were profits—
(*a*) to which section 15(1) of the Act (class 4 contributions recoverable under the Income Tax Acts) applies; and
(*b*) made by P in the tax year in which that profit is chargeable to income tax under Chapter 2 of Part 2 of ITTOIA 2005.
(5) In this regulation—
"AIFM firm" and "AIFM trade" have the meanings given in section 863H(3) and (4) of ITTOIA 2005; and
"ITTOIA 2005" means the Income Tax (Trading and Other Income) Act 2005.][1]

NIC

Amendments—[1] Regulation 94B inserted by the Social Security (Contributions) (Amendment No 5) Regulations, SI 2014/3196 reg 2 with effect for the tax year 2014–15 and subsequent tax years.

95 Deferment of Class 4 liability where such liability is in doubt

Where, as respects any year of assessment [before the tax year 2015–16][2], it appears to the Board that, by virtue of the provisions of this Part, there is doubt as to the extent, if any, of an earner's liability to pay contributions under section 15 of the Act (Class 4 contributions) for that year, or that at the date on which any application under regulation 96 is made, it is not possible to determine whether, having regard to the provisions of these Regulations, the earner is or will be liable to pay such contributions for that year, the Board may issue in respect of the earner a certificate of deferment deferring that earner's liability for such contributions [and for such period][1] as the Board may direct.

Commentary—*Simon's Taxes* **E8.323**.

Amendments—[1] Words substituted by the Social Security (Contributions) (Amendment) Regulations, SI 2003/193 regs 2, 12 with effect from 2003–04.

[2] Words inserted by the Social Security (Miscellaneous Amendments No 2) Regulations, SI 2015/478 regs 2, 15 with effect from 6 April 2015.

96 Application for deferment of Class 4 liability

(1) If a person wishes his liability to pay contributions under section 15 of the Act for any year of assessment to be deferred, he shall make an application for that purpose to the Board.

(2) Any such application—

(*a*) shall be made before the beginning of that year or before such later date as the Board may allow; and

(*b*) is subject to regulations 97 and 98.

97 General conditions for application for, and issue of, certificates of exception and deferment

(1) Any application made under any of regulations 91 to 96, for a certificate of exception from, or deferment of, liability to pay contributions under section 15 of the Act for any particular year of assessment shall be made in such form and in such manner as the Board may approve.

(2) Any person making such application shall furnish, or cause to be furnished, to the Board such information or evidence as they may require for the purpose of enabling them to determine whether such a certificate should be issued in respect of that person.

(3) On the issue of such a certificate the person in respect of whom the certificate is issued shall be excepted from liability to pay the contributions to which the certificate relates or his liability for such payment shall be deferred.

This is subject to paragraph (4).

(4) If, for the purpose of obtaining a certificate of exception or deferment, the person making the application furnishes or causes to be furnished to the Board information which is erroneous, or fails to furnish or cause to be furnished to them information which is relevant, and but for such furnishing or failure the certificate would not have been issued for any particular year of assessment—

(*a*) the Board may revoke the certificate in so far as it relates to that year; and

(*b*) the person who made the application shall be liable to pay contributions under section 15 of the Act for that year to the extent to which he would have been so liable if the certificate had not been issued.

98 Revocation of certificates of exception and deferment

Where under regulation 97(4)(*a*) the Board revoke a certificate of exception or deferment—

(*a*) they shall be responsible for calculating the contributions due under section 15 of the Act for the year specified in paragraph 97(4)(*b*) (being the current or a past year) and for the collection of those contributions;

(*b*) the applicant shall—

(i) furnish, or cause to be furnished, to the Board all such information or evidence as they may require for the purpose of calculating those contributions, and

(ii) within such period as the Board may direct, pay to them the contributions so calculated.

99 Calculation of liability for, and recovery of, Class 4 contributions after issue of certificate of deferment

(1) Where a certificate of deferment has been issued in respect of any earner under regulations 91 to 98—

(*a*) the profits or gains of that earner, in respect of which contributions would be payable under section 15 of the Act (Class 4 contributions), but for the issue of the certificate of deferment, shall be assessed under the Income Tax Acts for each year to which the certificate relates, in all respects as if no such certificate had been issued, provided that (without prejudice to the validity of the assessment of the amount of the earner's profits or gains and his right of appeal against that assessment) no figure representing [contributions, the payment of which has been deferred][1] shall be shown in any such assessment or on any notice of such assessment nor shall any of the provisions of the Income Tax Acts (as applied or modified by section 16 of, and Schedule 2 to, the Act) as to collection, repayment or recovery apply to any such assessment; and

(*b*) the Board shall be responsible for the calculation, administration and recovery of Class 4 contributions ultimately payable in respect of the profits or gains so assessed for any year of assessment to which the certificate of deferment relates.

(2) Any such calculation shall be subject to the provisions of regulations 94 and 100 and for the purpose of the calculation where the total amount of the profits or gains for any year of assessment to which the certificate relates includes a fraction of £1, that fraction shall be disregarded.

(3) For the purpose of enabling the Board to make the calculation, they shall certify the amount of the earner's profits or gains, computed under Schedule 2 to the Act for each year of assessment. [This is subject to the following qualification.][1]

(4) Notwithstanding paragraph (3), the Board shall not be required to certify the amount referred to in that paragraph unless the assessment made under this regulation has become [final and conclusive.][1]

(5) The Board, on making the calculation referred to in paragraph (3), shall give notice to the earner of the amount of the contributions due from him under section 15 of the Act for each year to which the certificate of deferment relates.

(6) The earner shall pay to the Board those contributions within the period of 28 days from the receipt of the notice from them, unless before the expiry of that period the earner—

(*a*) has appealed out of time or made a claim or appealed against the decision on a claim made under the Income Tax Acts on any matter concerning the amount of the profits or gains certified as mentioned in paragraph (3), and has notified the Board accordingly; or

(*b*) has appealed against a decision made under section 8 of the Transfer Act relating to those contributions.

(7) If the amount of any assessment made under this regulation for any year is altered for any reason, or if a further assessment is made in respect of that year, subsequently to the certification by the Board of the amount of an earner's profits or gains computed in accordance with the provisions of this regulation and that alteration or further assessment affects the amount of the earner's profits or gains so computed they shall immediately, or in the case of a further assessment when that further assessment has become final and conclusive, certify to the earner the altered amount of the earner's profits or gains.

Commentary—*Simon's Taxes* **E8.319, E8.323.**

Amendments—[1] Words in paras (1)(*a*), (3), (4) substituted by the Social Security (Contributions) (Amendment) Regulations, SI 2003/193 regs 2, 13 with effect from 2003–04.

100 [Annual maximum of Class 4 contributions due under section 15 of the Act

(1) If, in respect of any year, there are payable by or in respect of an earner Class 4 contributions under section 15 of the Act and also—

(*a*) primary Class 1 contributions or Class 2 contributions; or

(*b*) primary Class 1 contributions and Class 2 contributions,

paragraph (2) applies.

(2) If this paragraph applies, the earner's liability for Class 4 contributions shall not exceed the maximum found in accordance with paragraph (3).

(3) The maximum is found as follows.

Step One

Subtract the lower profits limit from the upper profits limit for the year.

Step Two

Multiply the result of Step One by [9 per cent][2].

Step Three

Add to the result of Step Two 53 times the weekly amount of the appropriate Class 2 contribution.

Step Four

Subtract from the result of Step Three the aggregate amount of any Class 2 contributions and primary Class 1 contributions paid at the main primary percentage.

The application of the following steps is determined by reference to the following three Cases.

Case 1

If the result of this step is a positive value, and exceeds the aggregate of—

(*a*) primary Class 1 contributions payable at the main primary percentage,

(*b*) Class 2 contributions; and

(*c*) Class 4 contributions payable at the main Class 4 percentage,

in respect of the earner's earnings, profits and gains for the year, the result of this step is the maximum amount of Class 4 contributions payable.

Case 2

If the result of this step is a positive value, but does not exceed the aggregate mentioned in Case 1, the result of this step is the maximum amount of Class 4 contributions payable at the main Class 4 percentage.

Case 3

If the result of this step is a negative value, the maximum amount of a Class 4 contribution payable at the main Class 4 percentage is nil and the result of this step is treated as nil.

If Case 1 applies, Steps Five to Nine do not, but if Case 2 or Case 3 applies those Steps do apply.

Step Five

Multiply the result of Step Four by [100/9][2]

Step Six

Subtract the lower profits limit from the lesser of the upper profits limit and the amount of profits for the year.

Step Seven

Subtract the result of Step Five from the result of Step Six.

If the result of this step is a negative value, it is treated as nil.

Step Eight

Multiply the result of Step Seven by [2 per cent][2].

Step Nine

Multiply the amount by which the profits and gains for the year exceed the upper profits limit for the year by [2 per cent][2].

The maximum amount of Class 4 contributions payable is—

(*a*) where Case 1 of Step Four applies, the result of that step, and

(*b*) where Case 2 or Case 3 of Step Four applies, the amount produced by adding together the results of Steps Four, Eight and Nine.

This is subject to the qualifications in paragraphs (4) to (6).

In this paragraph—

"lower profits limit" means the lesser of the two monetary sums specified in section 15(3)(*a*) of the Act; and

"upper profits limit" means the greater of those sums.

[(4) For the purpose only of determining the extent of the earner's liability for contributions under paragraph (3), the amount of a primary Class 1 contribution which would otherwise be payable at the main primary percentage but which is paid at a rate less than 12 per cent because the earner is a married woman who has made an election to pay contributions at the reduced rate as mentioned in regulation 127, shall be treated as equal to the amount of the primary Class 1 contribution payable at the main primary percentage, which would be so payable if the election had not been made.][3]

(5) Paragraph (2) is subject to the provisions of section 12 of the Act and to regulations 63 to 65.

(6) Notwithstanding paragraphs (1) to (5), an earner shall be liable, in the first instance, for the full amount of the contributions which would have been payable but for this regulation.][1]

Commentary—*Simon's Taxes* **E8.321**.

Amendments—[1] Regulation 100 substituted by the Social Security (Contributions) (Amendment) Regulations, SI 2003/193 regs 2, 14 with effect from 2003–04.

[2] In para (3), in steps two, eight and nine, percentages substituted, and in para (3), in step five, fraction substituted, by the Social Security (Contributions) (Amendment) Regulations, SI 2012/573 reg 2(1), (3) with effect in relation to contributions paid in respect of the tax year 2011–12 and subsequent tax years.

[3] Para (4) substituted by the Social Security (Contributions) (Amendment) (No 2) Regulations, SI 2016/352 reg 15 with effect from 6 April 2016, subject to savings in relation to rights or obligations arising in connection with tax years beginning before 6 April 2016.

101 Disposal of Class 4 contributions under section 15 of the Act which are not due

Where for any year of assessment any payment is made by an earner as on account of contributions under section 15 of the Act (Class 4 contributions) and—

(*a*) a certificate of exception is issued for that year, or would have been so issued if application had been made for its issue before the beginning of that year;

(*b*) that payment is made in error . . . [1];

(*c*) the payment is in excess of the amount which, subject to an exception under regulation 94, is due from that earner for that year or would have been so due if application for exception had been made under that regulation before the beginning of that year; or

(*d*) the payment is in excess of the amount calculated in accordance with regulation 100,

the Board may treat that payment as made on account of other contributions properly payable by that person under the Act.

Amendments—[1] Words in para (*b*) revoked by the Social Security (Contributions) (Amendment No 3) Regulations, SI 2002/2366 regs 3, 14 with effect from 8 October 2002.

102 Repayment of Class 4 contributions under section 15 of the Act which are not due

(1) Subject to paragraph (2), any payment such as is specified in regulation 101 shall, except in so far as it is, under that regulation, treated by the Board as made on account of contributions under the Act, be repaid [to the earner][1], unless the net amount of such repayment would not exceed in value 50 pence.

[(2) It is a condition of repayment under this regulation that the earner makes an application for the repayment—

(*a*) in such form and manner as the Board may determine; and

(*b*) in the case of contributions falling within paragraph (*b*) of regulation 101, within the time prescribed in paragraph (3).][1]

(3) The period referred to in paragraph (2) is one of—

(*a*) six years beginning with 6th April in the year of assessment next following that in respect of which the payment was made where the application is in respect of any year of assessment ending before 6th April 1996,

(*b*) five years beginning with 1st February in the year of assessment next following that in respect of which the payment was made where the application is in respect of any year of assessment beginning on or after 6th April 1996, or

(*c*) if later than sub-paragraph (*a*) or (*b*), two years beginning with 6th April in the year of assessment next following that in which the payment was made.

Amendments—[1] Words in para (1) substituted, and para (2) substituted, by the Social Security (Contributions) (Amendment No 3) Regulations, SI 2002/2366 regs 3, 15 with effect from 8 October 2002.

103 Class 4 liability of earners treated as self-employed earners who would otherwise be employed earners

(1) Subject to regulation 108, where—

(*a*) an earner, in respect of any one or more employments of his, is treated by regulations under section 2(2)(*b*) of the Act (treatment of a person in employment of any prescribed description as falling in one or other of the categories of earner) as being self-employed;

(*b*) in any year he has earnings from any such employment (one or more) which fall within section 11(3) of the Act (higher weekly rate of Class 2 contributions), but is not liable for a higher weekly rate of Class 2 contributions by virtue of regulations under that section;

(*c*) those earnings are chargeable to income tax [as general earnings][2]; and

(*d*) the total of those earnings exceeds the sum specified in section 18(1)(*c*) of the Act,

paragraph (2) applies.

(2) If this paragraph applies, the earner shall be liable, in respect of the earnings mentioned in paragraph (1), to pay a Class 4 contribution (referred to in this Part as a "special Class 4 contribution") [of an amount equal to the aggregate of—

(*a*) the main Class 4 percentage of so much of the total of those earnings as exceeds the lower, but does not exceed the higher, of the money sums, and

(*b*) the additional Class 4 percentage of so much of the total of those earnings as exceeds the higher of the money sums,

for the time being specified in section 18(1A).][1]

Commentary—*Simon's Taxes* **E8.326.**

Amendments—[1] Words in para (2) substituted by the Social Security (Contributions) (Amendment) Regulations, SI 2003/193 regs 2, 15 with effect from 2003–04.

[2] Words in para (1)(*c*) substituted by the Social Security (Contributions, Categorisation of Earners and Intermediaries) (Amendment) Regulations, SI 2004/770 regs 2, 24 with effect from 6 April 2004.

104 Notification of national insurance number and recording of category letter on deductions working sheet

(1) Any earner to whom regulation 103 applies shall, on request, notify his national insurance number to the person who pays him the earnings referred to in that regulation.

(2) The person who pays those earnings shall record on the earner's deductions working sheet the earner's national insurance number, and the appropriate category letter as indicated by the Board.

(3) In this regulation "deductions working sheet" has the same meaning as in Schedule 4.

Commentary—*Simon's Taxes* **E8.326.**

105 Calculation of earnings for the purposes of special Class 4 contributions

For the purpose of the calculation of an earner's liability for a special Class 4 contribution for any year—

(*a*) the earnings of that earner for that year shall, subject to paragraph (*b*), be calculated by the Board on the basis that they are earnings to which regulations 24 and 25 and Schedules 2 and 3 apply;

(*b*) in the calculation of these earnings, if the total amount of the earnings for the year includes a fraction of a pound, that fraction shall be disregarded.

NIC

106 Notification and payment of special Class 4 contributions due

The Board shall, subject to any other arrangements notified by them to the earner specified in regulation 105, give notice to the earner of the special Class 4 contribution due from him for any year, and the earner shall pay that contribution to the Board within the period of 28 days from the receipt of the notice unless, before the expiry of that period, the earner has appealed against a decision made under section 8 of the Transfer Act relating to that contribution.

107 Recovery of deferred Class 4 and special Class 4 contributions after appeal, claim or further assessment under the Income Tax Acts or appeal under section 8 of the Transfer Act

(1) Where—

(*a*) the Board have been notified that there has been such a claim or appeal as is specified in regulation 99(6) or regulation 106; or

(*b*) the Board have certified in accordance with regulation 99(7) an altered amount of earner's profits or gains,

paragraph (2) applies.

(2) If this paragraph applies, the Board shall, as soon as may be after the prescribed time, give to the earner notice or, as the case may be, revised notice of such contributions as might, having regard to the final decision on the claim or appeal or, the altered amount of profits or gains, be due from the earner—

(*a*) under section 15 of the Act (Class 4 contributions) for the year or years to which the certificate referred to in regulation 99(7) relates; or

(*b*) by way of a special Class 4 contribution for the year to which the notice specified in regulation 106 relates,

and the earner shall within 28 days of receipt of that notice pay to the Board the contribution or contributions specified in that notice.

(3) In this regulation "prescribed time" means—

(*a*) except where sub-paragraph (*c*) applies—

(i) in the case of an appeal out of time, the date of the determination of the appeal, and

(ii) in the case of a claim or appeal against a decision on a claim made under the Income Tax Acts, the date on which the time for appealing against the decision on the claim expires, or the date of the determination of the appeal, whichever is the later;

(*b*) in the case of an appeal under section 8 of the Transfer Act, the date on which the time for appealing against that decision expires or the date of the determination of the appeal, whichever is the later;

(*c*) in the case of an altered amount of profits or gains being certified by the Board, the date on which they are so certified.

Commentary—*Simon's Taxes* **E8.319**.

108 Annual maximum of special Class 4 contribution

(1) Where for any year there are payable (or, but for this regulation, there would be payable) by or in respect of an earner a special Class 4 contribution and also any contribution under section 15 of the Act (in this regulation referred to as "an ordinary Class 4 contribution") or any primary Class 1 contribution or any Class 2 contribution, or any combination of such contributions, the maximum amount of the special Class 4 contribution payable for that year shall not exceed the maximum specified in paragraph (2).

(2) The maximum is—

(*a*) in the case of a special Class 4 contribution and an ordinary Class 4 contribution, the amount (if any) equal to the difference between the maximum amount of a special Class 4 contribution for which provision is made in section 18(1) of the Act and the amount of the ordinary Class 4 contributions ultimately payable for that year; or

(*b*) in any other case (whether or not a Class 4 contribution is also payable), the amount (if any) equal to the difference between the maximum amount prescribed in regulation 100 and the amount of such Class 4, primary Class 1 and Class 2 contributions as are ultimately payable for that year.

(3) Paragraphs (1) and (2) are without prejudice to the earner's liability in the first instance for the full amount payable apart from those paragraphs.

Commentary—*Simon's Taxes* **E8.326**.

109 Disposal of special Class 4 contributions paid in excess or error

Where any payment has been made by a person on account of a special Class 4 contribution and that payment has been made in excess of the amount prescribed under regulation 108 or has been made in error, the Board may treat that payment as made on account of other contributions properly payable by that person under the Act.

Commentary—*Simon's Taxes* **E8.326**.

110 Return of special Class 4 contributions paid in excess or error

(1) Subject to regulation 109 and paragraphs (2) and (3), where any payment has been made by a person as on account of a special Class 4 contribution and that payment has been made in excess of the amount prescribed in regulation 108 or has been made in error, that payment shall be returned by the Board to that person, unless the net amount to be returned does not exceed 50 pence, if application is made to the Board, in writing or in such other form and manner as the Board may allow, within the time specified in paragraph (3).

(2) In calculating the amount of any return of a special Class 4 contribution to be made under paragraph (1) there shall be deducted the amount (if any) treated under regulation 109 as paid on account of other contributions.

(3) Any person desiring to apply for the return of a special Class 4 contribution ["the applicant"][1] shall make the application within the period of six years from the end of the year in which the contribution [was due to be paid.

This is subject to the following qualification.

If the application is made after the end of that period, an officer of the Board shall admit it if satisfied that—

(*a*) the applicant had reasonable excuse for not making the application within that period; and

(*b*) the application was made without unreasonable delay after the excuse had ceased.][1]

Commentary—*Simon's Taxes* **E8.326**.

Amendments—[1] Words in para (3) inserted and substituted, by the Social Security (Contributions) (Amendment No 3) Regulations, SI 2002/2366 regs 3, 16 with effect from 8 October 2002.

PART 9

SPECIAL CLASSES OF EARNERS

CASE A

AIRMEN

111 Interpretation

In this Case, unless the context otherwise requires—

"airman" means a person who is, or has been, employed under a contract of service either as a pilot, commander, navigator or other member of the crew of any aircraft, or in any other capacity on board any aircraft where—

(*a*) the employment in that other capacity is for the purposes of the aircraft or its crew or of any passengers or cargo or mails carried on that aircraft; and

(*b*) the contract is entered into in the United Kingdom with a view to its performance (in whole or in part) while the aircraft is in flight,

but does not include a person in so far as his employment is as a serving member of the forces;

"British aircraft" means any aircraft belonging to Her Majesty and any aircraft registered in the United Kingdom of which the owner (or managing owner if there is more than one owner) resides or has his principal place of business in the United Kingdom, and references to the owner of an aircraft shall, in relation to an aircraft which has been hired, be taken as referring to the person for the time being entitled as hirer to possession and control of the aircraft by virtue of the hiring or any subordinate hiring.

112 Modification of employed earner's employment

(1) Subject to paragraphs (2) and (3), where an airman is employed as such on board any aircraft, and the employer of that airman or the person paying the airman his earnings in respect of the employment (whether or not the person making the payment is acting as agent for the employer) or the person under whose directions the terms of the airman's employment and the amount of the earnings to be paid in respect of that employment are determined has—

(*a*) in the case of the aircraft being a British aircraft, a place of business in Great Britain or Northern Ireland; or

(*b*) in any other case, his principal place of business in Great Britain or Northern Ireland,

then, notwithstanding that the airman does not fulfil the conditions of section 2(1)(*a*) of the Act (definition of employed earner), he shall be treated as employed in employed earner's employment and, for the purposes of regulation 145(1)(*a*), in respect of that employment, as present in Great Britain or Northern Ireland (as the case requires).

(2) Subject to paragraph (3), notwithstanding that an airman is employed in an employment to which the provisions of paragraph (1) applies, if that airman is neither domiciled nor has a place of residence in Great Britain or Northern Ireland (as the case requires) no contributions shall be payable by or in respect of him as an employed earner.

(3) Paragraph (2) is subject to any Order in Council giving effect to any reciprocal agreement made under section 179 of the Administration Act (reciprocal agreements with countries outside the United Kingdom).

113 Application of the Act and regulations

Part I of the Act and so much of Part VI of the Act as relates to contributions and the regulations made under those provisions, so far as they are not inconsistent with this Case, apply to an airman with the modification that, where an airman is, on account of his being outside the United Kingdom by reason of his employment as an airman, unable to perform an act required to be done either immediately or upon the happening of a certain event or within a specified time, he shall be deemed to have complied with such requirement if he performs the act as soon as is reasonably practicable, although after the happening of the event or the expiration of the specified time.

CASE B

CONTINENTAL SHELF

114 Application to employment in connection with continental shelf of Part I of the Act and so much of Part VI of the Act as relates to contributions

(1) For the purposes of section 120 of the Act (employment at sea (continental shelf operations)), prescribed employment shall be any employment (whether under a contract of service or not) in any area which may from time to time be designated by Order in Council under section 1(7) of the Continental Shelf Act 1964, where the employment is in connection with any activity mentioned in section 11(2) of the Petroleum Act 1998 in the designated area.

(2) Where a person is employed in any employment specified in paragraph (1), the provisions of Part I of the Act and so much of Part VI of the Act as relates to contributions shall, subject to the provisions of paragraph (3), apply as though the area so designated were in Great Britain, and notwithstanding that he does not satisfy the conditions as of residence or presence in Great Britain prescribed in regulation 145(1)(*a*).

(3) Where a person employed in any employment specified in paragraph (1) is, on account of his being outside Great Britain by reason of that employment, unable to perform any act required to be done either immediately or on the happening of a certain event or within a specified time, he shall be deemed to have complied with the requirement if he performs the act as soon as reasonably practicable, although after the happening of the event or the expiration of the specified time.

[(4) Where a continental shelf worker is employed in any employment specified in paragraph (1) and that employment is on or in connection with an offshore installation the secondary contributor is—

(*a*) where the employer is present in Great Britain, the employer; or,

(*b*) where the employer is not present in Great Britain but has an associated company present in Great Britain, the associated company; or,

(*c*) where the employer is not present and does not have an associated company present in Great Britain, the oil field licensee.

Where the employer has more than one associated company present in Great Britain the associated company to which sub-paragraph (*b*) applies is the company which has the greatest taxable total profit within the meaning of section 4 of the Corporation Tax Act 2010 for the accounting period which precedes the tax year in which the contributions are due.

(5) The modifications in paragraph (4) do not apply to a continental shelf worker—

(*a*) who is employed in a capacity described in Column (A) of Table 1,

(*b*) who holds a certificate of a description in Column (B) of that table, and

(*c*) whose presence on the ship is required in order to meet the requirement of [regulation 46(1)(*c*) of the Merchant Shipping (Standards of Training, Certification and Watchkeeping) Regulations 2015][2].

[Table 1

Column (A): capacity in which the continental shelf worker is employed	*Column (B): description of the certificate*
Master or chief mate on a ship of 3000 gross tonnage or more.	A certificate which complies with regulation 6 of the Merchant Shipping Regulations.
Master on a ship of between 500 gross tonnage and 2999 gross tonnage not engaged on near-coastal voyages.	A certificate which complies with regulation 6 of the Merchant Shipping Regulations.
Chief mate on a ship of between 500 gross tonnage and 2999 gross tonnage.	A certificate which complies with regulation 6 of the Merchant Shipping Regulations.

Officer in charge of an engineering watch in a manned engine-room, or designated duty engineer officer in a periodically unmanned engine-room, on a ship powered by main propulsion machinery of 750 kilowatts propulsion power or more.	A certificate which complies with regulation 6 of the Merchant Shipping Regulations.
Chief engineer officer and second engineer officer on a ship powered by main propulsion machinery of between 750 and 3000 kilowatts propulsion power.	A certificate which complies with regulation 6 of the Merchant Shipping Regulations.
Rating forming part of a navigational watch on a ship of 500 gross tonnage or more (who is not under training and whose duties are skilled in nature).	A certificate which complies with regulation 14 of the Merchant Shipping Regulations.
Rating forming part of an engine-room watch or designated to perform duties in a periodically unmanned engine-room on a ship powered by main propulsion machinery of 750 kilowatts propulsion power or more (who is not under training and whose duties are skilled in nature).	A certificate which complies with regulation 15 of the Merchant Shipping Regulations.][2]

(6) In Table 1 "Merchant Shipping Regulations" means [the Merchant Shipping (Standards of Training, Certification and Watchkeeping) Regulations 2015][2];

(7) To the extent that where this regulation and regulations 115 to 125 (case C Mariners) apply, this regulation takes precedence.][1]

Amendments—[1] Paragraphs (4)–(7) inserted by the Social Security (Contributions) (Amendment No 2) Regulations, SI 2014/572 reg 2(1), (2) with effect from 6 April 2014.

[2] In para (5), words in sub-para (*c*), substituted for words "regulation 5(1)(*c*) of the Merchant Shipping (Safe manning, Hours of Work and Watchkeeping) Regulations 1997", and Table 1 substituted, and in para (6), words substituted for words "the Merchant Shipping (Training and Certification) Regulations 1997", by the Social Security (Contributions) (Amendment No 4) Regulations, SI 2016/1067 regs 2, 4 with effect from 28 November 2016. Table 1 previously read as follows—

"Table 1

Column (A): capacity in which the continental shelf worker is employed	*Column (B): description of the certificate*
Master or chief mate on a ship of 3000 gross tons or more.	A certificate which complies with regulation 7 of the Merchant Shipping Regulations.
Master or chief mate on a ship of less than 3000 gross tons.	A certificate which complies with regulation 7 of the Merchant Shipping Regulations.
Officer in charge of an engineering watch in a manned engine-room, or a designated duty engineer officer in a periodically unmanned engine-room, on a ship powered by main propulsion machinery of 750kW propulsion power or more.	A certificate which complies with regulation 7 of the Merchant Shipping Regulations.
Chief engineer officer or second engineer officer on a ship powered by main propulsion machinery of between 750kW and 3000kW propulsion power.	A certificate which complies with regulation 7 of the Merchant Shipping Regulations.
Rating forming part of a navigational watch on a ship of 500 gross tons or more and whose duties are skilled in nature.	A certificate issued under regulation 8 of the Merchant Shipping Regulations.
Rating forming part of an engine-room watch or designated to perform duties in a periodically unmanned engine-room on a ship powered by main propulsion machinery of 750kW propulsion power or more.	A certificate issued under regulation 8 of the Merchant Shipping Regulations.".

[Continental shelf workers: provisions relating to certificates

114A Application for certificate

(1) An employer who meets the conditions in paragraph (2) may apply to HMRC for the issue of a UKCS continental shelf workers certificate.

(2) The conditions are that—

(*a*) the employer supplies or intends to supply a continental shelf worker for whom the secondary contributor, under regulation 114(4) (application of Part 1 and Part 6 of the Act to employment in connection with the continental shelf), is the oil field licensee;

(*b*) the employer has or intends to have a contractual relationship under which the employer acts, directly or indirectly, as an agent of the oil field licensee for the purposes of National Insurance; and

(*c*) the employer or an associated company has not had a certificate cancelled previously for a failure to comply with their obligations and responsibilities under regulation 114B.

(3) An application under this regulation must be made in writing and must include—

(*a*) the name and address of the employer and employer's PAYE reference;

(*b*) the name and address of a person in Great Britain who is authorised to accept service on behalf of the employer;

(*c*) confirmation that the employer understands and intends to discharge the obligations contained in regulation 114B; and

(*d*) the name, address, and employer's PAYE reference of any associated company which is a current or former holder of a UKCS continental shelf workers certificate.

(4) When the employer makes the first application under this regulation, the employer may also comply with the obligation under regulation 114B(*e*) by including those details (if known) in the application.

(5) An application made under this regulation may be combined with an application made under an equivalent PAYE provision.

(6) Upon receipt of an application under this regulation, an officer of Revenue and Customs may, if they are satisfied the conditions in paragraph (2) are met, issue a UKCS continental shelf workers certificate.

(7) A UKCS continental shelf workers certificate must include—

(*a*) the name of the UKCS continental shelf workers certificate holder;

(*b*) the employer's PAYE reference of the UKCS continental shelf workers certificate holder; and

(*c*) the date on which the certificate is issued.

(8) A UKCS continental shelf workers certificate may be issued to—

(*a*) the person authorised to accept service on behalf of the employer;

(*b*) the employer; or

(*c*) both the person authorised to accept service on behalf of the employer and the employer.

(9) A certificate may be combined with a certificate issued under an equivalent PAYE provision.

(10) Where an employer ceases to meet the conditions in paragraph (2) or to comply with its obligations under regulation 114B, or an equivalent PAYE provision, an officer of Revenue and Customs may, by notice in writing to the person authorised to accept service on behalf of the employer, cancel the UKCS continental shelf workers certificate from the date specified in the notice of cancellation.

(11) The date specified in paragraph (10) may not be earlier than 10 working days after the date of the notice.

(12)]A notice under paragraph (10) may be combined with a notice under an equivalent PAYE provision.[1]

Amendments—[1] Regulations 114A–114D and preceding crosshead inserted by the Social Security (Contributions) (Amendment No 2) Regulations, SI 2014/572 reg 2(1), (3) with effect from 6 April 2014.

[114B UKCS continental shelf workers certificate holder: obligations and responsibilities

A UKCS continental shelf workers certificate holder must—

(*a*) make such deductions, returns and repayments as are required of a secondary contributor;

(*b*) keep written records of—

(i) the name, date of birth, and national insurance number of the continental shelf workers supplied;

(ii) the name, registered office and oil field licence number of the oil field licensee to whom each of the workers were supplied;

(iii) the offshore installation to which each of the workers were supplied; and

(iv) the dates between which the workers worked on the offshore installation;

(*c*) keep the records required by sub-paragraph (*b*) for a period of 6 years from the end of the tax year to which they relate;

(*d*) where an officer of Revenue and Customs requires them in writing to do so, provide copies of the records required by sub-paragraph (*b*) to HMRC within 30 days of the date of the request; and (*e*) before supplying the oil field licensee with continental shelf workers for the first time, inform HMRC in writing of the details of the oil field licensee including name, business address, and oil field licence number of the oil field licensee.][1]

Amendments—[1] Regulations 114A–114D and preceding crosshead inserted by the Social Security (Contributions) (Amendment No 2) Regulations, SI 2014/572 reg 2(1), (3) with effect from 6 April 2014.

[114C UKCS oil field licensee certificate

(1) Where a UKCS continental shelf workers certificate holder has notified HMRC that the employer intends to supply continental shelf workers to an oil field licensee an officer of Revenue and Customs must issue a UKCS oil field licensee certificate to the oil field licensee.

(2) The UKCS oil field licensee certificate must include—

(*a*) the name of the oil field licensee;

(*b*) the registered office of that oil field licensee;

(*c*) the oil field licence number;

(*d*) the name of the UKCS continental shelf workers certificate holder;

(*e*) the date on which it is issued; and

(*f*) a description of the continental shelf workers to whom it applies.

(3) Where a UKCS oil field licensee certificate is in force the holder of that certificate is not liable to pay any contributions in respect of any continental shelf worker of a description set out in the certificate.

(4) If a UKCS continental shelf workers certificate is cancelled by an officer of Revenue and Customs that officer must also, by notice in writing, cancel the UKCS oil field licensee certificate.

(5) A notice under paragraph (4) must—

(*a*) be sent on the same day as the notice cancelling the UKCS continental shelf workers certificate;

(*b*) specify the date of cancellation of the UKCS oil field licensee certificate; and

(*c*) notify the oil field licensee that it is liable to meet its obligations as a secondary contributor.

(6) The date of cancellation of the UKCS oil field licensee certificate must be the same date as that specified in the UKCS continental shelf workers certificate cancellation notice.][1]

Amendments—[1] Regulations 114A–114D and preceding crosshead inserted by the Social Security (Contributions) (Amendment No 2) Regulations, SI 2014/572 reg 2(1), (3) with effect from 6 April 2014.

[114D Interpretation of regulations 114 to 114C

In regulations 114 to 114C—

"associated company" means any company within the meaning of section 449 of the Corporation Tax Act 2010;

"an equivalent PAYE provision" means any provision in the PAYE Regulations which has an equivalent effect to the provisions in regulations 114A to 114C;

"employer's PAYE reference" has the meaning given in regulation 2(1) of the PAYE Regulations;

"offshore installation" means—

(*a*) a structure which is, is to be, or has been, put to a relevant use while in water;

(*b*) but a structure is not an offshore installation if—

(i) it has permanently ceased to be put to a relevant use,

(ii) it is not, and is not to be, put to any other relevant use, and

(iii) since permanently ceasing to be put to a relevant use, it has been put to a use which is not a relevant use;

(*c*) a use is a relevant use if it is—

(i) for the purposes of exploiting mineral resources,

(ii) for the purposes of exploration with a view to exploiting mineral resources,

(iii) for the storage of gas in or under the shore or the bed of any waters,

(iv) for the recovery of gas so stored,

(v) for the conveyance of things by means of a pipe,

(vi) mainly for the provision of accommodation for individuals who work on or from a structure which is, is to be, or has been put to any of the above uses while in the water,

(vii) for the purposes of decommissioning any structure which has been used for or in connection with any of the relevant uses above;

(*d*) a structure is put to use while in water if it is put to use while—

(i) standing in any waters,

(ii) stationed (by whatever means) in any waters, or

(iii) standing on the foreshore or other land intermittently covered with water;

(*e*) a "structure" includes a ship or other vessel except where it is used wholly or mainly—

(i) for the transport of supplies;

(ii) as a safety vessel;

(iii) for a combination of (i) and (ii); or

(iv) for the laying of cables; and

"oil field licensee" means the holder of a licence under Part 1 of the Petroleum Act 1998 in respect of the area in which the duties of the continental shelf worker's employment are performed;

"UKCS continental shelf workers certificate" means a certificate issued under regulation 114A;

"UKCS oil field licensee certificate" means a certificate issued under regulation 114C(1).][1]

Amendments—[1] Regulations 114A–114D and preceding crosshead inserted by the Social Security (Contributions) (Amendment No 2) Regulations, SI 2014/572 reg 2(1), (3) with effect from 6 April 2014.

CASE C

MARINERS

115 Interpretation

In this Case—

"British ship" means—

(*a*) any ship or vessel belonging to Her Majesty; or

(*b*) any ship or vessel whose port of registry is a port in the United Kingdom; or

(*c*) a hovercraft which is registered in the United Kingdom;

"foreign-going ship" means any ship or vessel which is not a home-trade ship;

"home-trade ship" includes—

(*a*) every ship or vessel employed in trading or going within the following limits, that is to say, the United Kingdom (including for this purpose the Republic of Ireland), the Channel Islands, the Isle of Man, and the continent of Europe between the river Elbe and Brest inclusive;

(*b*) every fishing vessel not proceeding beyond the following limits—

on the South, Latitude 48°30'N,

on the West, Longitude 12°W, and

on the North, Latitude 61°N;

"managing owner" means the owner of any ship or vessel who, where there is more than one such owner, is responsible for the control and management of that ship or vessel;

"mariner" means a person who is or has been in employment under a contract of service either as a master or member of the crew of any ship or vessel, or in any other capacity on board any ship or vessel where—

(*a*) the employment in that other capacity is for the purposes of that ship or vessel or her crew or any passengers or cargo or mails carried by the ship or vessel; and

(*b*) the contract is entered into in the United Kingdom with a view to its performance (in whole or in part) while the ship or vessel is on her voyage;

but does not include a person in so far as his employment is as a serving member of the forces;

"owner" in relation to any ship or vessel, means the person to whom the ship or vessel belongs and who, subject to the right of control of the captain or master of the ship or vessel ("the master's rights"), is entitled to control of that ship or vessel, and references to the owner of a ship or vessel shall, in relation to a ship or vessel which has been demised, be construed as referring to the person who for the time being is entitled as charterer to possession and, subject to the master's rights, to control of the ship or vessel by virtue of the demise or any sub-demise;

"passenger" means any person carried on a ship except—

(*a*) a person employed or engaged in any capacity on board the ship on the business of the ship; or

(*b*) a person on board the ship either in pursuance of the obligation to carry shipwrecked, distressed or other persons, or by reason of any circumstance that neither the master nor the owner nor the charterer (if any) could have prevented or forestalled;

"pay period" in relation to any payment of a mariner's earnings means the period in respect of which the payment is made;

"radio officer" means a mariner employed in connection with the radio apparatus of any ship or vessel and holding a certificate of competence in radio telephony granted by the Secretary of State or by an authority empowered in that behalf by the legislature of some part of the Commonwealth or of the Republic of Ireland and recognised by the Secretary of State as equivalent to the like certificate granted by him;

"share fisherman" means any person who—

(*a*) is ordinarily employed in the fishing industry, otherwise than under a contract of service as the master or a member of the crew of any United Kingdom fishing vessel within the meaning of section 1(3) of the Merchant Shipping Act 1995, manned by more than one person, and who is remunerated in respect of that employment in whole or in part by a share of the profits or gross earnings of the fishing vessel, or

(*b*) has ordinarily been so employed, but who by reason of age or infirmity permanently ceases to be so employed and becomes ordinarily engaged in employment ashore in the United Kingdom, otherwise than under a contract of service, making or mending any gear appurtenant to a United Kingdom fishing vessel or performing other services ancillary to or in connection with that vessel and is remunerated in respect of that employment in whole or in part by a share of the profits or gross earnings of that vessel and has not ceased to be ordinarily engaged in such employment;

"ship or vessel" for the purposes of this Case other than those of regulations 116 to 120 includes hovercraft;

"voyage period" means a pay period comprising an entire voyage or series of voyages (including any period of leave on pay which immediately follows the day on which the termination of that voyage or series of voyages occurs);

"week" means a period of 7 consecutive days and "weekly" shall be construed accordingly.

Commentary—*Simon's Taxes* **E8.291, E8.292**.

116 Modification of section 162(5) of the Administration Act

In section 162 of the Administration Act (destination of contributions), subsection (5) (which specifies the amount of the national health service allocation to be deducted from each class of contribution prior to their payment into the National Insurance Fund) shall be modified, in the case of contributions paid at the rate reduced in accordance with regulation 119(1), as if, instead of the percentage figure specified in paragraph (*b*) of that subsection, there were specified the percentage figure "0.6".

117 Conditions of domicile or residence

(1) As respects any employment of a person as a mariner and liability for payment of any contribution under the Act as an employed earner by or on behalf, or in respect, of that mariner in respect of that employment—

(*a*) the provisions of Case F of these Regulations relating to conditions as to residence or presence in Great Britain or Northern Ireland (as the case requires) shall not apply; but

(*b*) it shall be a condition of liability to pay a contribution under the Act that the mariner is domiciled or resident in Great Britain or Northern Ireland (as the case requires); and

(*c*) it shall be a condition of liability to pay a secondary contribution under the Act that the secondary contributor is resident or has a place of business in Great Britain or Northern Ireland (as the case requires).

This is subject to the following qualification.

(2) This regulation has effect subject to any Order in Council giving effect to any reciprocal agreement made under section 179 of the Administration Act (reciprocal agreements with countries outside the United Kingdom).

Commentary—*Simon's Taxes* **E8.291, E8.292**.

118 Modification of employed earner's employment

Where a mariner—

(*a*) is employed as such and—

(i) the employment is on board a British ship, or

(ii) the employment is on board a ship and the contract in respect of the employment is entered into in the United Kingdom with a view to its performance (in whole or in part) while the ship or vessel is on her voyage, and

(iii) in a case to which sub-paragraph (ii) applies, the person by whom the mariner's earnings are paid, or, in the case of employment as a master or member of the crew of a ship or vessel, either that person or the owner of the ship or vessel (or the managing owner if there is more than one owner) has a place of business in Great Britain or Northern Ireland (as the case requires); or

(*b*) is employed as a master, member of the crew or as a radio officer on board any ship or vessel, not being a mariner to whom paragraph (*a*) applies, and—

(i) in the case of employment as a radio officer, if the contract under which the employment is performed is entered into in the United Kingdom, the employer or the person paying the radio officer his earnings for that employment has a place of business in Great Britain or Northern Ireland (as the case requires), or

(ii) in the case of the employment being a master, member of the crew or as a radio officer, if the contract is not entered into in the United Kingdom, the employer or the person paying the earnings has his principal place of business in Great Britain or Northern Ireland (as the case requires), then, notwithstanding that he does not fulfil the conditions of section 2(1)(*a*) of the Act (definition of employed earner), the employment of the mariner as mentioned above shall be treated as employed earner's employment.

Commentary—*Simon's Taxes* **E8.291**.

119 Modification of section 9(2) of the Act

(1) As respects earnings paid to or for the benefit of a mariner for employment as such in any employment specified in paragraph (2), being employment which by virtue of regulation 118 is treated as employed earner's employment, from the figure specified as the secondary percentage in section 9(2) of the Act there shall be subtracted 0.5 per cent and section 9 of the Act shall be modified accordingly.

(2) The employment referred to in paragraph (1) is employment as a master or member of the crew of a ship where—

(*a*) the employment is on a foreign-going ship and the payment of earnings is exclusively in respect of that employment; or

(*b*) the employment is partly on a foreign-going ship and partly otherwise than on such a ship and the payment of earnings in respect of that employment is made during the employment on the foreign-going ship.

(3) In this regulation the word "employment" includes any period of leave, other than leave for the purpose of study, accruing from the employment.

120 Earnings periods for mariners and apportionment of earnings

(1) For the purposes of liability for and calculation of earnings-related contributions, paragraphs (2) to (9) apply where earnings are paid to or for the benefit of a mariner in respect of his employment as such for a voyage period.

(2) In this regulation "a relevant change" means a change affecting the calculation of earnings-related contributions under the Act not being—

(*a*) a change in the amount of the mariner's earnings; or

(*b*) a change in one or more of the following figures applicable in respect of the mariner's employment—

(i) [the main primary percentage or the additional primary percentage][1] for a primary Class 1 contribution specified in section 8(2) of the Act or the percentage rate for a secondary Class 1 contribution specified in section 9(2) of the Act,

(ii) . . . [2]

(iii) the amount by which the percentage rate of a secondary Class 1 contribution is reduced in accordance with regulation 119(1),

(iv) the lower or upper earnings limit for primary Class 1 contributions specified in section 5(1) of the Act.

(3) Where a voyage period falls wholly in one year, then—

(*a*) if no relevant change occurs during the voyage period, the earnings period shall be the voyage period;

(*b*) if one or more than one relevant change occurs during the voyage period the earnings shall be apportioned to such periods as comprise—

(i) the day on which the voyage period began and the day immediately before which the change occurred, and for any subsequent change, the day on which the immediately preceding change occurred and the day before which the next succeeding change occurred, and

(ii) so much of the voyage period as remains,

according to the amounts earned in each period, and the earnings period in respect of each amount so apportioned shall be the length of the period to which it is apportioned.

(4) Where a voyage period falls partly in one or more other years, then if no relevant change occurs during the voyage period—

(*a*) the earnings shall be apportioned to those years according to the amounts earned in each year; and

(*b*) the earnings period in respect of each amount shall be the length of the period to which that amount is apportioned.

(5) Where a voyage period falls partly in one and partly in one or more other years and one or more than one relevant change occurs during the voyage period, then—

(*a*) in respect of a year during which a relevant change or more than one relevant change occurs the earnings shall be apportioned to such periods as comprise—

(i) the day on which the voyage period began, or where it began in another year, the beginning of the year in which the change occurred, and the day immediately before which the change occurred, and for any subsequent change, the day on which the immediately preceding change occurred and the day before which the next succeeding change occurred, and

(ii) so much of the voyage period as remains in the year,

according to the amounts earned in each period, and the earnings period in respect of each amount so apportioned shall be the length of the period to which it is apportioned; and

(*b*) in respect of other years, the earnings shall be apportioned to those years according to the amounts earned in each year and the earnings period in respect of each amount so apportioned shall be the length of the period to which it is apportioned.

(6) Where under paragraphs (3) to (5) an earnings period—

(*a*) is less than a week, that period shall for the purposes of those paragraphs be treated as a week;

(*b*) exceeds a week or a whole multiple of a week by a part of a week,

(i) if that part of a week is a period in excess of 3 days, that part of a week shall be treated as a week for the purposes of paragraphs (3) to (5), and

(ii) if that part of a week is a period of 3 days or less, it shall be disregarded for those purposes.

(7) For the purposes of paragraphs (3) to (5)—

(*a*) where a period of leave on pay immediately follows the day on which the termination of an entire voyage or series of voyages occurs—

(i) the earnings for that period of leave shall be treated as if they were earned during that period and shall be excluded from the earnings for any other period or periods, and

(ii) for the purpose of apportionment, the earnings for the period of leave shall be deemed to accrue from day to day by equal daily amounts; and

(*b*) "earned" includes treated as earned under this paragraph.

(8) Where under paragraphs (1) to (7) earnings are apportioned to a period—

(*a*) each amount so apportioned shall be treated as paid at the end of the period to which it is apportioned; and

(*b*) contributions paid in respect of the amount so apportioned shall be treated as paid in respect of the year in which the end of that period falls.

(9) Notwithstanding paragraphs (3) to (5) and (8), where a voyage period extends beyond the date on which the earnings are paid, any amount of earnings which, by virtue of paragraphs (1) to (8), would be apportioned to a period in the year following that in which the earnings are paid—

(*a*) shall be treated as paid at the end of the year in which the earnings are paid but shall not be aggregated with any other amount of earnings paid or treated as paid at the end of that year; and

(*b*) the earnings period in respect of that amount shall be a period of the same length as that to which it is apportioned.

Commentary—*Simon's Taxes* **E8.291**.

Amendment—[1] Words in sub-para (2)(*b*)(i) substituted by the Social Security (Contributions) (Amendment No 2) Regulations, SI 2003/964 regs 3, 4 with effect from 6 April 2003.

[2] Para (2)(*b*)(ii) revoked by the Social Security (Contributions) (Amendment) (No 2) Regulations, SI 2016/352 reg 16 with effect from 6 April 2016, subject to savings in relation to rights or obligations arising in connection with tax years beginning before 6 April 2016.

121 Calculation of earnings-related contributions for mariners

(1) For the purpose of the calculation of earnings-related contributions payable in respect of earnings paid to or for the benefit of a person in respect of that person's employment as a mariner—

(*a*) regulation 12(1) shall apply, save that in the case of a contribution payable on earnings above the upper earnings limit or the prescribed equivalent of that limit, the appropriate contributions calculator prepared by the Board may be applied;

(*b*) in the alternative, paragraphs (2), (3) or (4) and (5) of that regulation shall, except in relation to secondary Class 1 contributions payable at a rate reduced in accordance with regulation 119, apply in respect of those earnings.

(2) Subject to paragraphs (3), (4) and (5) of regulation 12 where the secondary Class 1 contribution is payable at a rate reduced in accordance with regulation 119, that contribution may be calculated in accordance with the scale prepared by the Board appropriate to that rate or, in the case of such a contribution payable on earnings above the upper limit or the prescribed equivalent of that limit, a contributions calculator appropriate to that rate, prepared by the Board.

Commentary—*Simon's Taxes* **E8.291**.

122 Prescribed secondary contributors

In relation to any payment of earnings to or for the benefit of a mariner in respect of employment to which the provisions of regulation 118 apply, where the person employing the mariner does not satisfy the conditions specified in regulation 117(1)(*c*), but the person who pays the mariner those earnings does satisfy either of those conditions, that person shall be treated as the secondary contributor, whether or not he makes the payment as agent for the employer.

123 Payments to be disregarded

Commentary—*Simon's Taxes* **E8.291, E8.540**.

Amendments—This regulation revoked by the Social Security (Contributions) (Amendment No 2) Regulations, SI 2012/817 regs 2, 7(2) with effect from 6 April 2012.

124 Application of the Act and regulations

(1) Part I of the Act and so much of Part VI of the Act as relates to contributions and the regulations made under those provisions shall, insofar as they are not inconsistent with the provisions of this Case, apply to mariners with the modification set out in paragraph (2).

(2) The modification is that, where a mariner is, on account of his being at sea or outside Great Britain or Northern Ireland (as the case requires) by reason of his employment as a mariner, unable to perform an act required to be done either immediately or on the happening of a certain event or within a specified time, he shall be deemed to have complied with that requirement if he performs the act as soon as is reasonably practicable, although after the happening of the event or the expiration of the specified time.

Commentary—*Simon's Taxes* **E8.291**.

125 Modification in relation to share fishermen of Part I of the Act and so much of Part VI of the Act as relates to contributions

Part I of the Act and so much of Part VI of the Act as relates to contributions shall apply to share fishermen with the modification that—

(*a*) employment as a share fisherman shall be employment as a self-employed earner notwithstanding that it is not employment in the United Kingdom;

(*b*) as respects liability of a share fishermen to pay Class 2 contributions in respect of his employment as a share fisherman, regulation 117(1)(*a*) and (*b*) and (2) shall apply as if the share fisherman were a mariner and as if the reference in regulation 117(1) to an employed earner were a reference to a self-employed earner and as if the words "or on behalf, or in respect, of" were omitted;

(*c*) for the purposes of entitlement to a contribution-based job seeker's allowance, the weekly rate of any Class 2 contribution payable by a share fisherman for any contribution week while he is ordinarily employed as a share fisherman shall, notwithstanding the provisions of [section 11(2) and (6) of the Act (Class 2 contributions), be [£3.50][3]][2];

(*d*) regulations 21, 100 and 108 shall apply to contributions payable at the weekly rate specified in paragraph (*c*) of this regulation as if references in those regulations to Class 2 contributions included, as may be appropriate, references to Class 2 contributions at that rate;

(*e*) regulation 43 shall apply to a share fisherman as if there were included at the end of paragraph (1)(*a*) of that regulation the words "or is entitled to a contribution-based jobseeker's allowance or, but for a failure to satisfy the contribution conditions for that benefit, would be so entitled";

(*f*) insofar as Class 4 contributions in respect of the profits or gains of a share fisherman in respect of his employment as such are not collected by the Board under section 16 of the Act (assessment and collection, etc of Class 4 contributions) regulations 103 to 110 shall apply as if the share fisherman were a person to whom section 18(1)(*a*) and (*b*) of the Act applied (Class 4 contributions for persons treated under section 2(2)(*b*) of the Act as self-employed earners); and

(*g*) for the purposes of section 12 of the Act and for the purposes of that section as modified by regulations 63 to 65, where an earner was a share fisherman when [the earner became entitled to pay Class 2 contributions][1], any reference in section 12 to an ordinary contribution, and any reference in those regulations to the weekly applicable rate of a contribution, shall be a reference to the rate of Class 2 contributions prescribed for a share fisherman.

Commentary—*Simon's Taxes* **E8.292**.

Amendment—[1] Words in para (*a*) substituted by NICA 2015 s 2, Sch 1 paras 32, 33 with effect for the tax year 2015–16 and subsequent tax years.

[2] Words in para (*g*) substituted by the Social Security (Miscellaneous Amendments No 2) Regulations, SI 2015/478 regs 2, 16 with effect from 6 April 2015.

[3] Figure in para (*c*) substituted by the Social Security (Contributions) (Re-rating) Consequential Amendment Regulations, SI 2017/416 reg 2 with effect from 6 April 2017.

CASE D

MARRIED WOMEN AND WIDOWS

126 Interpretation

(1) In this Case, unless the context otherwise requires—

"personal death benefit" means any death benefit which, apart from any regulations made under section 73 of the Administration Act (overlapping benefits—general), is payable to a person otherwise than in respect of another person who is a child or an adult dependant;

"Personal Injuries Scheme" means any scheme made under the Personal Injuries (Emergency Provisions) Act 1939 or under the Pensions (Navy, Army, Air Force and Mercantile Marine) Act 1939;

"qualifying widow" has the meaning assigned to it in regulation 127(1);

"reduced rate" means the rate specified in regulation 131;

"regulation 91 of the 1975 Regulations" and "regulation 94 of the 1975 Regulations" mean respectively regulation 91 and regulation 94 of the Social Security (Contributions) Regulations 1975 before section 3(1) of the Social Security Pensions Act 1975 (married women and widows) came into force and sections 5(3) and 130(2) of the Social Security Act 1975 (Class 1 reduced rate and married women and widows) were repealed;

"Service Pensions Instrument" means those provisions and only those provisions of any Royal Warrant, Order in Council or other instrument (not being a 1914–1918 War Injuries Scheme) under which a death or disablement pension (not including a pension calculated by reference to length of service) and allowances for dependants payable with either such pension may be paid out of public funds in respect of any death or disablement, wound, injury or disease due to service in the naval, military or air forces of the Crown or in any nursing service or other auxiliary service of any of those forces or in the Home Guard or in any other organisation established under the control of the Defence Council or formerly established under the control of the Admiralty, the Army Council or the Air Council;

"1914–1918 War Injuries Scheme" means any scheme made under the Injuries in War (Compensation) Act 1914 or under the Injuries in War Compensation Act 1914 (Session 2) or under any Government scheme for compensation in respect of persons injured in any merchant ship or fishing vessel as a result of hostilities during the 1914–1918 War.

(2) Where by any provision of this Case notice is required to be or may be given in writing it shall be given on a form approved by the Board or in such other manner, being in writing, as they may accept as sufficient in any case.

127 Elections by married women and widows

(1) A woman who on 6th April 1977 (the date on which section 3(1) of the [Social Security Pensions Act 1975][1] (married women and widows) came into force) was married or was a widow who satisfied the conditions prescribed in paragraph (8) ("a qualifying widow") may—

(*a*) elect that her liability in respect of primary Class 1 contributions shall be a liability to contribute at the reduced rate; and

(*b*) elect that she shall be under no liability to pay Class 2 contributions.

(2) Any election made for the purpose of paragraph (1)(*a*) shall be treated as also made for the purpose of paragraph (1)(*b*) and any election made for the purpose of paragraph (1)(*b*) shall be treated as also made for the purpose of paragraph (1)(*a*) and any revocation of an election for the one purpose shall be treated also as a revocation of an election for the other purpose.

[(3) Where a woman has made an election to which this regulation applies—

(*a*) any primary Class 1 contributions which are—

(i) attributable to section 8(1)(*a*) of the Act, and

(ii) payable in respect of earnings paid to her or for her benefit in the period during which the election has effect under the following provisions of this Case,

shall be payable at the reduced rate; and

(*b*) she shall be under no liability to pay any Class 2 contribution[, nor shall she be entitled to pay any such contribution,][2] for any contribution week in that period.][1]

(4) Subject to regulation 134, no woman shall be entitled to make an election specified in paragraph (1) after 11th May 1977.

(5) Every election shall be made by notice in writing to the Board and by notice in writing to the Board may be revoked by the woman who made the election.

(6) Any revocation may be cancelled by notice in writing to the Board before the date upon which the notice of revocation is to have effect, and upon cancellation the revocation shall cease to have effect.

(7) Every woman who makes an election under this regulation shall furnish such certificates, documents, information and other evidence for the purpose of enabling the Board to consider the validity of the election as the Board may require.

(8) The conditions referred to in paragraph (1) are that the widow—

(*a*) was entitled to—

(i) widow's benefit under the Social Security Act 1975,

(ii) any personal death benefit which was payable to her as a widow under the provisions of Chapter IV of Part II of that Act at a weekly rate which was not less than the basic pension specified for the time being in section 6(1)(*a*) of the Social Security Pensions Act 1975 (rate of Category A retirement pension),

NIC

(iii) any personal death benefit by way of pension or allowance payable to her as a widow under any Personal Injuries Scheme or Service Pensions Instrument or any 1914–1918 War Injuries Scheme (not being a pension or allowance calculated by reference to the needs of the beneficiary), the rate of which is as set out in head (ii) above, or

(iv) benefit under section 39(4) of the Social Security Act 1975 (retirement benefits for the aged), other than a Category C retirement pension; and

(*b*) was not disentitled to payment of any such benefit by reason of her living with a man, to whom she was not married, as his wife.

Commentary—*Simon's Taxes* **E8.304, E8.313**.

Amendment—[1] Words in paras (1), (3) substituted by the Social Security (Contributions) (Amendment No 2) Regulations, SI 2003/964 regs 3, 5 with effect from 6 April 2003.

[2] Words in para (3)*b*) inserted by NICA 2015 s 2, Sch 1 paras 32, 34 with effect for the tax year 2015–16 and subsequent tax years.

128 Duration of effect of election

(1) Subject to paragraph (2), any election made under regulation 127 shall have effect from and including 6th April 1977 (the date on which section 3(1) of the Social Security Pensions Act 1975 (married women and widows) came into force) until whichever of the following events first occurs after the date of the election, namely—

(*a*) the date on which the woman ceases to be married otherwise than by reason of the death of her husband;

(*b*) the end of the year in which she ceases to be a qualifying widow;

(*c*) the end of any two consecutive years which begin on or after 6th April 1978 and in which the woman who made the election has no earnings in respect of which any primary Class 1 contributions are payable in those years and in which that woman is not at any time a self-employed earner;

(*d*) in the case of a revocation which has not been cancelled in accordance with regulation 127(6), the end of the week in which the notice of revocation is given or, if the woman so wishes, the end of any subsequent week in the same year specified in the notice;

(*e*) where in any year after 5th April 1982 a payment ("an erroneous payment") is made by or on behalf of a woman on account of primary Class 1 contributions at the contracted-out rate and the woman wishes to pay contributions at the [main primary percentage][1] from the beginning of the year next following that year, the end of the year in respect of which the erroneous payment is made; or

(*f*) where—

(i) in any year after 5th April 1982 a payment is made by or on behalf of a woman on account of primary Class 1 contributions at the non-contracted-out rate, ("an erroneous payment"), or more than one such payment is made,

(ii) from the time of making that payment or, if there is more than one such payment, the first, to the time at which she notifies the Board in accordance with head (v), no contributions have been paid by her or on her behalf at the reduced rate and no contributions have been payable by her or on her behalf in respect of any contracted-out employment,

(iii) she has not procured a refund in respect of any erroneous payment,

(iv) she wishes to pay contributions at the [main primary percentage][1] from the date on which the only or first erroneous payment was made, and

(v) after 5th April 1983 and on or before the 31st December in the next complete calendar year following the end of the year in which any erroneous payment was made, she notifies the Board of her wish to pay contributions at the [main primary percentage][1] in accordance with head (iv),

the date on which the only or first erroneous payment was made.

(2) Where a woman, to whom paragraph (1)(*b*) applies, remarries or again becomes a qualifying widow before the end of the year in which she ceases to be a qualifying widow, that woman's election shall, notwithstanding that sub-paragraph, but without prejudice to the application of paragraph (1)(*c*), (*d*), (*e*) or (*f*), continue to have effect from the end of that year.

Commentary—*Simon's Taxes* **E8.293**.

Amendment—[1] Words in sub-paras (1)(*e*), (*f*)(iv)–(v) substituted by the Social Security (Contributions) (Amendment No 2) Regulations, SI 2003/964 regs 3, 9(1), (2)(*a*) with effect from 6 April 2003.

129 Continuation of elections under regulation 91 of the 1975 Regulations

Where, but for regulation 91 of the 1975 Regulations ceasing to have effect on 6th April 1977 (the date on which section 130(2) of the Social Security Act 1975 was repealed) an election made under that regulation before that date would have continued to have effect on that date, that election shall be treated as made under regulation 127 and this Case shall apply accordingly.

130 Continuation of elections on widowhood

(1) If on 6th April 1977 (the date on which section 3(1) of the Social Security Pensions Act 1975 came into force) a woman—

(*a*) was married and subsequently becomes a widow; or

(*b*) was a widow and subsequently remarries and again becomes a widow,

paragraph (2) applies to her.

(2) Where this paragraph applies to a woman any election—

(*a*) which she had made under regulation 127 before the death of the husband which renders a widow; or

(*b*) which she is, by virtue of regulation 129, treated as having made under regulation 127 before that death;

and which is still effective at the time of the husband's death, shall, subject to paragraphs (4) and (5) and notwithstanding regulation 128, continue to have effect until the end of the appropriate period.

(3) For the purposes of this regulation the end of the appropriate period is—

(*a*) the earliest of—

(i) the end of the second year specified in regulation 128(1)(*c*),

(ii) the end of the period specified in regulation 128(1)(*d*) or (*e*), or

(iii) the date specified in regulation 128(1)(*f*); or

(*b*) subject to sub-paragraph (*a*) and paragraphs (4) and (5)—

(i) where the husband's death occurs before 1st October in any year, the end of that year,

(ii) where the husband's death occurs after 30th September in any year, the end of the year next following that in which the death occurs.

(4) Subject to regulation 128(1)(*c*), (*d*), (*e*) and (*f*) and to paragraph (5), if at the end of the year specified in head (i) or head (ii) of paragraph (3)(*b*) there is pending a claim or application made by or on behalf of the woman as a widow within 182 days (including Sundays) of her husband's death for any benefit specified in head (i) or (iv) or, irrespective of its rate, in head (ii) or (iii) of regulation 127(8)(*a*), the end of the appropriate period shall be the end of the year in which the claim or application is determined.

(5) If at the end of the year specified in head (i) or (ii) of paragraph (3)(*b*) or, as the case may be, in paragraph (4) the woman is a qualifying widow or married, the election shall continue to have effect, unless she is then a person to whom regulation 128(1)(*c*), (*d*), (*e*) or (*f*) applies.

131 [Reduced rate of primary Class 1 contributions otherwise payable at the main primary percentage

On and after [6th April 2011][2], the reduced rate of contribution for the purposes of section 19(4) of the Act (power to regulate liability in respect of certain married women and widows) in respect of so much of a married woman's liability for primary Class 1 contributions as is attributable to section 8(1)(*a*) of the Act shall be [5.85][2] per cent.][1]

Commentary—*Simon's Taxes* **E8.293.**

Amendments—[1] Regulation 131 substituted by the Social Security (Contributions) (Amendment No 2) Regulations, SI 2003/964 regs 3, 6 with effect from 6 April 2003.

[2] Date and sum substituted by the Social Security (Contributions) (Amendment No 2) Regulations, SI 2011/940 regs 2, 5 with effect from 6 April 2011.

132 Class 3 contributions

A woman who has made, or is under the regulations 126 to 131 treated as having made, an election under regulation 127 shall be precluded from paying Class 3 contributions for any year in respect of the whole of which that election has effect.

Commentary—*Simon's Taxes* **E8.408.**

133 Certificates of election

(1) As represents any election made, or by virtue of regulation 129 as treated as made, under regulation 127—

(*a*) where a woman makes an election under regulation 127, the Board shall issue without charge, a certificate of election ("a certificate") to her;

(*b*) where a woman is treated as making such an election, the Board shall, on application without charge, issue a certificate to her; and

(*c*) the certificate shall remain the property of the Board.

(2) A woman to whom a certificate has been issued shall be responsible for its custody unless and until it is delivered to a secondary contributor or returned to the Board.

(3) A woman in respect of whom an election has effect in accordance with regulations 126 to 132 shall, if any primary Class 1 contribution is payable by her or on her behalf, immediately deliver to the secondary contributor a certificate which is currently in force in respect of her and upon the delivery of the certificate, the secondary contributor shall become responsible for its custody unless and until it is delivered again to the woman or to the Board.

(4) Where a certificate has ceased to be in force, the woman in respect of whom the certificate was issued shall immediately return it to the Board and for that purpose, if at the time when the certificate ceases to be in force it is in the custody of a secondary contributor, that contributor shall immediately return it to the woman.
(5) The Board may at any time require the person for the time being responsible for the custody of a certificate to return it to the Board, and if at that time the election to which that certificate relates continues to have effect, the Board shall issue to that person a replacement certificate.
(6) Where a woman in respect of whom an election has effect has more than one employed earner's employment the Board shall issue to her without charge, on her application, such number of certificates as will enable her to comply with the requirements of paragraph (3) in relation to each secondary contributor.
(7) Where a certificate has been lost or destroyed the person responsible for its custody shall inform the Board of that loss or destruction.
(8) When a woman gives notice in writing to the Board that she revokes an election she shall—
(*a*) if the certificate is with a secondary contributor, recover it from him; and
(*b*) deliver the certificate to the Board.
(9) Where a secondary contributor holds a certificate and—
(*a*) is informed by the woman to whom it was issued that she intends to revoke her election and is requested to return the certificate to her so that she may return it to the Board; or
(*b*) the employment by him of the woman to whom the certificate was issued has terminated,
he shall immediately return the certificate to her.
(10) Where under the foregoing provisions of this Case an election has been made by a woman [to pay at the reduced rate in respect of so much of her liability for primary Class 1 contributions as is attributable to section 8(1)(*a*) of the Act][1] and that election ceases to have effect, it shall be the duty of that woman to inform the secondary contributor accordingly.
(11) Any certificate issued for the purpose of an election made or deemed to have been made under the regulation 91 of the 1975 Regulations shall, if by virtue of regulation 124 the election is treated as made under regulation 127, continue in force for the purposes of that regulation.

Commentary—*Simon's Taxes* **E8.293**.
Amendments—[1] Words in para (10) substituted by the Social Security (Contributions) (Amendment No 2) Regulations, SI 2003/964 regs 3, 7 with effect from 6 April 2003.

134 Special transitional provisions consequent upon passing of the Social Security Pensions Act 1975

(1) Any woman to whom this regulation applies—
(*a*) shall, in respect of [so much of her liability for primary Class 1 contributions as is attributable to section 8(1)(*a*) of the Act][1], be liable to pay [those contributions][1] at the reduced rate; and
(*b*) shall not be liable to pay any Class 2 contribution which, apart from the provisions of this paragraph, she would be liable to pay.
(2) Subject to paragraphs (3) to (7), this regulation applies to any woman—
(*a*) to whom, before 6th April 1977 (the date on which section 3(1) of the Social Security Pensions Act 1975 came into force and sections 5(3) and 130(2) of the Social Security Act 1975 were repealed), the provisions of section 5(3) of the Social Security Act 1975 or of regulation 94 of the 1975 Regulations (newly widowed woman) applied and to whom those provisions would have continued to apply but for those provisions having been repealed or, as the case may be, having ceased to have effect on that date;
(*b*) who, not being a person to whom regulation 130 applies—
(i) on 6th April 1977 was a married woman and became a widow during the period from and including that date to 6th April 1978, or
(ii) on 6th April 1977 was a qualifying widow, remarried after that date and again became a widow during that period; or
(*c*) who on 6th April 1977 was married or a qualifying widow and had attained the age of 59.
(3) In the case of a woman specified in paragraph (2)(*a*) or (*b*), the provisions of paragraph (1) shall, subject to the provisions of paragraphs (4) and (5), apply only during the period which—
(*a*) in the case of a woman specified in paragraph (2)(*a*)—
(i) began at the beginning of the year in which section 3(1) came into force; and
(ii) ended at the end of that year;
(*b*) in the case of a woman specified in paragraph (2)(*b*)—
(i) began on the date on which that woman became or, as the case may be, again became a widow, and
(ii) ends at the end of whichever of the two periods specified in regulation 130(2)(*b*) is appropriate in her case in so far as that regulation relates to the date of the death of the husband.
(4) In the case of a woman to whom paragraph (3)(*a*) or (*b*) applies, those sub-paragraphs shall be subject to regulation 130(4) and paragraph (5) below with the modification that—

(*a*) in regulation 130(4), the reference to sub-paragraphs (*d*) and (*e*) of regulation 128(1) shall be omitted;

(*b*) in so far as the provisions of regulation 128(1)(*c*) are incorporated in regulation 130(4) as modified for the purposes of this regulation, references in regulation 128(1)(*c*) to any election made under regulation 127 and to a woman who made the election shall respectively be construed as references to the application of paragraph (1) and to the woman to whom that paragraph applies.

(5) Any woman—

(*a*) who by virtue of paragraph (1)—

(i) was, in respect of [so much of her liability for primary Class 1 contributions as is attributable to section 8(1)(*a*) of the Act][1], liable to pay that contribution at the reduced rate, or

(ii) was not liable to pay any Class 2 contribution which apart from the provisions of that paragraph she would have been liable to pay; but

(*b*) to whom by virtue of paragraphs (2) to (4), paragraph (1) ceases so to apply; and

(*c*) who has not, in relation to the application of paragraph (1), given the notice prescribed in paragraph (7),

may, subject to the conditions prescribed in paragraph (6), make an election under and in accordance with regulation 127, notwithstanding that she has not done so before the date prescribed in that regulation, and regulations 126 to 133 shall apply accordingly from the end of the year in which paragraph (1) ceases to apply to her.

(6) The conditions referred to in paragraph (5) are that the woman—

(*a*) shall make the election not later than 11th May next following the end of the year in which paragraph (1) ceases to apply to her; and

(*b*) is, at the beginning of the year next following the year in which paragraph (1) so ceases to apply, married or a qualifying widow.

(7) Any woman to whom, by virtue of paragraph (2)(*a*) or (*b*), paragraph (1) applies may give notice in writing to the Board that she does not wish paragraph (1) to apply to her and upon the giving of such notice it shall accordingly cease to apply.

Amendment—[1] Words in sub-paras (1)(*a*), (5)(*a*)(i) substituted by the Social Security (Contributions) (Amendment No 2) Regulations, SI 2003/964 regs 3, 8 with effect from 6 April 2003.

135 Deemed election of married women and widows excepted from contribution liability under the National Insurance Act 1965

Where immediately before 6th April 1975 there was, or is deemed to have been, in issue a current certificate of exception under regulation 9(3) or (4A) of the National Insurance (Contributions) Regulations 1969 (exception for certain widows), or there was current an election under regulation 2(1)(*a*) of the National Insurance (Married Women) Regulations 1973 (married women who are employed persons), or a women then was, or but for any exception under or by virtue of another provision of the National Insurance Act 1965 would have been, excepted under regulation 3(1)(*a*) of the 1973 Regulations (married women who are self-employed persons) from liability for contributions as a self-employed person under that Act and in any of these cases on that day the woman is a widow or, as the case may be, a married woman, that woman shall be deemed to have made an election under regulation 91 of the 1975 Regulations.

136 Special transitional provisions regarding deemed elections

(1) If, under regulation 135 a woman is deemed to have made an election under regulation 91 of the 1975 Regulations, this regulation applies.

(2) Before the woman first becomes liable to pay a primary Class 1 contribution she may revoke any such election by notice in writing given to the Board and, if she so specified in that notice, the revocation shall have effect from and including the beginning of the year in which the notice is given.

(3) If no notice of revocation is given and—

(*a*) in the first year (not being more than 2 years after 6th April 1978) in which the woman becomes liable to pay primary Class 1 contributions—

(i) she shall be entitled to choose whether with effect from the beginning of that year, to pay such contributions at the [main primary percentage][1] or at the reduced rate,

(ii) she shall notify any secondary contributor whether he is to pay such contributions on her behalf at the [main primary percentage][1] or the reduced rate, and

(iii) such secondary contributor shall pay those contributions in accordance with that notification until the woman notifies him to the contrary in accordance with the provisions of regulation 133(10);

(*b*) in that first year (not being more than 2 years after 6th April 1978) any primary Class 1 contribution at the standard rate is paid by or on behalf of the woman, unless it is shown to the satisfaction of the Board that the woman did not intend, by the making of that payment, to revoke the election she shall be deemed to have revoked the election.

Amendment—[1] Words in sub-paras (3)(*a*)(i)–(ii) substituted by the Social Security (Contributions) (Amendment No 2) Regulations, SI 2003/964 regs 3, 9(1), (2)(*b*) with effect from 6 April 2003.

137 Application of regulations 126 to 134 to elections and revocation of elections deemed made under regulations 135 and 136

(1) Subject to paragraph (2), regulations 126 to 134, save only in so far as inconsistent with regulations 135 and 136, shall apply to any election deemed to have been made under regulation 91 of the 1975 Regulations by virtue of regulation 135 as if it had been made under, and in accordance with, regulation 127 except that the Board shall not be obliged to issue a certificate, and as if any revocation which is deemed to be made under regulation 136 were made under, and in accordance with, regulation 127(5).

(2) Where a woman who under regulation 135 is not liable for a primary Class 1 contribution otherwise than at the reduced rate and to whom no certificate of election under the Act has been issued becomes employed in employed earner's employment, she shall make application in writing to the Board for such a certificate and, notwithstanding paragraph (1), the Board shall issue such a certificate to her.

138 Savings

For the purpose of facilitating the introduction of the scheme of social security contributions within the meaning of paragraph 9(1)(*a*)(i) of Schedule 3 to the Social Security (Consequential Provisions) Act 1975 regulations 2(2) (married women who are employed persons), 3(2) (married women who are self-employed persons), 4(2) (married women who are non-employed persons) and 16 (notice of marriage) of the National Insurance (Married Woman) Regulations 1973 shall be saved.

139 Modification of the Act

[Part 1, Part 2 (except section 60), and Parts 3 and 4 of the Act][1] shall have effect as respects married woman and widows subject to the modifications contained in this Case.

CASE E

MEMBERS OF THE FORCES

140 Establishments and organisations of which Her Majesty's forces are taken to consist

Except in relation to the employment in any of the establishments or organisations specified in Part I of Schedule 6 of any person specified in Part II of that Schedule, Her Majesty's forces shall, for the purpose of the Act, be taken to consist of the establishments and organisations specified in Part I of that Schedule, and this Case shall be construed accordingly.

141 Treatment of serving members of the forces as present in Great Britain

For the purposes of regulation 145(1)(*a*) a serving member of the forces shall, in respect of his employment as such, be treated as present in Great Britain.

Commentary—*Simon's Taxes* **E8.219D**.

142 Treatment of contributions paid after that date

For the purpose of any entitlement to benefit, any earnings-related contributions paid after the due date in respect of earnings paid to or for the benefit of a person in respect of his employment as a member of the forces shall be treated as paid on that date.

143 Special provisions concerning earnings-related contributions

(1) For the purposes of earnings-related contributions, there shall be excluded from the computation of a person's earnings as a serving member of the forces any payment in so far as it is—

(*a*) a payment of or in respect of an Emergence Service grant;

(*b*) a payment of any sum referred to in [sections 297 and 298 of ITEPA 2003 (armed forces' food, drink and mess allowances and reserve and auxiliary forces' training allowances)][1]; or

(*c*) a payment of liability bounty in recognition of liability for immediate call-up in times of emergency.

(2) The earnings period for a person who is a serving member of the forces shall be as follows—

(*a*) in the case of a person serving in the regular naval, military or air forces of the Crown, whatever is the accounting period from time to time applying in his case under the Naval Pay Regulations or, as the case may be, the Army Pay Warrant, Queen's Regulations for the Army or for the Royal Air Force or the Air Council Instructions; or

(*b*) in the case of a person undergoing training in any of the establishments or organisations specified in paragraphs 2 to 9 of Part I of Schedule 6, a month.

Commentary—*Simon's Taxes* **E8.238, E8.251**.

Amendments—[1] Words in para (1)(*b*) substituted by the Social Security (Contributions, Categorisation of Earners and Intermediaries) (Amendment) Regulations, SI 2004/770 regs 2, 25 with effect from 6 April 2004.

144 Application of the Act and regulations

(1) The provisions of Part I of the Act and so much of Part VI of the Act as relates to contributions and the regulations made under those provisions shall, in so far as they are not inconsistent and the provisions of this Case, apply in relation to persons who are serving members of the forces with the modification prescribed in paragraph (2).

(2) The modification is that where any such person is, on account of his being at sea or outside the United Kingdom by reason of his employment as a serving member of the forces, unable to perform an act required to be done either immediately or on the happening of a certain event or within a specified time, he shall be deemed to have complied with that requirement if he performs the act as soon as is reasonably practicable, although after the happening of the event or the expiration of the specified time,

Commentary—*Simon's Taxes* **E8.833**.

CASE F

RESIDENCE AND PERSONS ABROAD

145 Condition as to residence or presence in Great Britain or Northern Ireland

(1) Subject to [paragraph (2)][1], for the purposes of section 1(6) of the Act (conditions as to residence or presence in Great Britain for liability or entitlement to pay Class 1 or Class 2 contributions, liability to pay Class 1A or Class 1B contributions or entitlement to pay Class 3 Contributions) the conditions as to residence or presence in Great Britain or Northern Ireland (as the case requires) shall be—

(*a*) as respects liability of an employed earner to pay primary Class 1 contributions in respect of earnings for an employed earner's employment, that the employed earner is resident or present in Great Britain or Northern Ireland(or but for any temporary absence would be present in Great Britain or Northern Ireland) at the time of that employment or is then ordinarily resident in Great Britain or Northern Ireland (as the case may be);

(*b*) as respect liability to pay secondary Class 1 contributions, Class 1A contributions or Class 1B contributions that the person who, but for any conditions as to residence or presence in Great Britain or Northern Ireland (as the case may be and including the having of a place of business in Great Britain or Northern Ireland), would be the secondary contributor or the person liable for the payment of Class 1B contributions (in this Case referred to as "the employer") is resident or present in Great Britain or Northern Ireland when such contributions become payable or then has a place of business in Great Britain or Northern Ireland (as the case may be), so however that nothing in this paragraph shall prevent the employer paying the said contributions if he so wishes;

(*c*) as respects entitlement of a self-employed earner to pay Class 2 contributions, that that earner is present in Great Britain or Northern Ireland (as the case may be) in the contribution week for which the contribution is to be paid;

(*d*) as respects liability of a self-employed earner to pay Class 2 contributions, that the self-employed earner is ordinarily resident in Great Britain or Northern Ireland (as the case may be), or, if he is not so ordinarily resident, that before the period in respect of which any such contributions are to be paid he has been resident in Great Britain (as the case may be) for a period of at least 26 out of the immediately preceding 52 contribution weeks under the Act, the Social Security Act 1975 or the National Insurance Act 1965 or under some or all of those Acts.

(*e*) as respects entitlement of a person to pay Class 3 contributions in respect of any year, either that—

(i) that person is resident in Great Britain or Northern Ireland (as the case may be) throughout the year,

(ii) that person has arrived in Great Britain or Northern Ireland (as the case may be) during that year and has been or is liable to pay Class 1 or Class 2 contributions in respect of an earlier period during that year,

(iii) that person has arrived in Great Britain or Northern Ireland (as the case may be) during that year and was either ordinarily resident in Great Britain or Northern Ireland (as the case may be) throughout the whole of that year or became ordinarily resident during the course of it, or

(iv) that person not being ordinarily resident in Great Britain or Northern Ireland (as the case may be), has arrived in that year or the previous year and has been continuously present in Great Britain or Northern Ireland (as the case may be) for 26 complete contribution weeks, entitlement where the arrival has been in the previous year arising in respect only of the next year.

(2) Where a person is ordinarily neither resident nor employed in the United Kingdom and, in pursuance of employment which is mainly employment outside the United Kingdom by an employer whose place of business is outside the United Kingdom (whether or not he also has a place of

business in the United Kingdom) that person is employed for a time in Great Britain or Northern Ireland (as the case may be) as an employed earner and, but for the provisions of this paragraph, the provisions of sub-paragraph (*a*) of paragraph (1) would apply, the conditions prescribed in that sub-paragraph and in sub-paragraph (*b*) of that paragraph shall apply subject to the proviso that—

(*a*) no primary or secondary Class 1 contribution shall be payable in respect of the earnings of the employed earner for such employment;

(*b*) no Class 1A contribution shall be payable in respect of something which is made available to the employed earner or to a member of his family or household by reason of such employment; and

(*c*) no Class 1B contribution shall be payable in respect of any PAYE settlement agreement in connection with such employment, after the date of the earner's last entry into Great Britain or Northern Ireland (as the case may be) and before he has been resident in Great Britain or Northern Ireland (as the case may be) for a continuous period of 52 contribution weeks from the beginning of the contribution week following that in which that date falls.

(3) . . . [1]

Commentary—*Simon's Taxes* **E8.1109**.

Amendments—[1] In para (1), words substituted, and para (3) revoked, by the Social Security (Contributions) (Amendment No 2) Regulations, SI 2012/817 regs 2, 7(3) with effect from 6 April 2012.

146 Payment of contributions for periods abroad

(1) Where an earner is gainfully employed outside the United Kingdom, and that employment, if it had been in Great Britain or Northern Ireland, would have been employed earner's employment, that employment outside the United Kingdom shall be treated as employed earner's employment for the period for which under paragraph (2)(*a*) contributions are payable in respect of the earnings paid to the earner in respect of that employment provided that—

(*a*) the employer has a place of business in Great Britain or Northern Ireland (as the case may be);

(*b*) the earner is ordinarily resident in Great Britain or Northern Ireland (as the case may be); and

(*c*) immediately before the commencement of the employment the earner was resident in Great Britain or Northern Ireland (as the case may be).

(2) Where, under paragraph (1), the employment outside the United Kingdom is treated as an employed earner's employment, the following provisions shall apply in respect of the payment of contributions—

(*a*) primary and secondary Class 1 contributions shall be payable in respect of any payment of earnings for the employment outside the United Kingdom during the period of 52 contribution weeks from the beginning of the contribution week in which that employment begins to the same extent as that to which such contributions would have been payable if the employment had been in Great Britain or Northern Ireland (as the case may be);

(*b*) subject to [regulations 148 and 148A][1], any earner by or in respect of whom contributions are or have been payable under sub-paragraph (*a*) shall be entitled to pay Class 3 contributions in respect of any year during which the earner is outside the United Kingdom from and including that in which the employment outside the United Kingdom begins until that in which he next returns to Great Britain or Northern Ireland (as the case may be);

(*c*) Class 1A contributions and Class 1B contributions shall be payable in respect of the period specified in sub-paragraph (*a*).

Amendments—[1] Words in para (2)(*b*) substituted by the Social Security (Contributions) (Amendment No 4) Regulations, SI 2007/1838 regs 2, 4 with effect from 18 July 2007: SI 2007/1838 reg 1.

147 Class 2 and Class 3 contributions for periods abroad

(1) Subject to [regulations 148 and 148A][1], a person (other than a person to whom regulation 146(2)(*a*) applies) may, notwithstanding the provisions of regulation 145(1)(*c*) and (*e*), if he so wishes and if he satisfies the conditions specified in paragraph (3) below pay contributions in respect of periods during which he is outside the United Kingdom as follows—

(*a*) in respect of any contribution week throughout which he is gainfully employed outside the United Kingdom in employment which is not employment in respect of earnings from which Class 1 contributions are payable, he may, if immediately before he last left Great Britain or Northern Ireland (as the case may be), he was ordinarily an employed earner or a self-employed earner, pay a contribution as a self-employed earner;

(*b*) in respect of any year which includes a period during which he is outside the United Kingdom he may pay Class 3 contributions.

(2) A person who is gainfully employed outside Great Britain and falls within the provisions of paragraph (1)(*a*) shall for the purposes of that paragraph be treated as being outside the United Kingdom for any period during which he is temporarily in the United Kingdom.

(3) Subject to paragraph (4), the conditions referred to in paragraph (1) are that—

(*a*) the person has been resident in Great Britain or Northern Ireland (as the case may be) for a continuous period of not less than three years at any time before the period for which the contributions are to be paid;

(*b*) there have been paid by or on behalf of that person contributions of the appropriate amount—
(i) for each of 3 years ending at any time before the relevant period,
(ii) for each of 2 years ending at any time before the relevant period and, in addition, 52 contributions under either or both the Social Security Act 1975 or the National Insurance Act 1965, or
(iii) for any one year ending at any time before the relevant period and, in addition, 104 contributions under either or both the Social Security Act 1975 or the National Insurance Act 1965, or
(*c*) there have been paid by or on behalf of that person 156 contributions under either or both the Social Security Act 1975 or the National Insurance Act 1965.

(4) In paragraph (3)—
"contributions of the appropriate amount" means contributions under the Act the earnings factor derived from which is not less than 52 times the lower earnings limit for the time being for primary Class 1 contributions;
"contributions under either or both the Social Security Act 1975 or the National Insurance Act 1965" means contributions of any class under section 4, 7 or 8 of the Social Security Act 1975 or section 3 of the National Insurance Act 1965 in respect of any period; and
"the relevant period" means the period for which it is desired to pay the Class 2 or Class 3 contributions specified in paragraph (1).

Amendments—[1] Words in para (1) substituted by the Social Security (Contributions) (Amendment No 4) Regulations, SI 2007/1838 regs 2, 5 with effect from 18 July 2007: SI 2007/1838 reg 1.

148 Conditions of payment of Class 2 or Class 3 contributions for periods abroad

Entitlement to pay Class 2 or Class 3 contributions under regulations 146 and 147 shall be subject to the following conditions—
(*a*) that the payment is made within the period specified in regulation 48(3)(*b*)(i); and
(*b*) that the payment is made only to the extent to which it could have been made if the contributor had been present in Great Britain or Northern Ireland (as the case may by) and otherwise entitled to make it.

148A Conditions of payment of Class 3 contributions: transfers to the Communities' pension scheme

(1) Entitlement to pay Class 3 contributions under regulations 146 and 147 is subject to the condition set out in paragraph (2).
(2) The condition is that a person may not pay a Class 3 contribution for any part of the period to which that person's Communities transfer relates.
(3) For the purposes of this regulation—
a "Communities transfer" means a transfer to the Communities pension scheme of rights to relevant benefits;
"the Communities' pension scheme" means the pension scheme provided for officials and other servants of Community institutions and bodies in accordance with regulations adopted by the Council of the European Communities;
"relevant benefits" means benefits under—
(*a*) Parts 2 to 5 and 10 of the Act,
(*b*) sections 36 and 37 of the National Insurance Act 1965 (graduated retirement benefit), and
(*c*) sections 1(2) and 2 of the Jobseekers Act 1995 (contribution-based jobseeker's allowance).][1]

Amendments—[1] This regulation inserted by the Social Security (Contributions) (Amendment No 4) Regulations, SI 2007/1838 regs 2, 6 with effect from 18 July 2007: SI 2007/1838 reg 1.

[148B (1) This regulation applies, in relation to a tax year, in respect of a person who is in that tax year—
(*a*) in employment as a self-employed earner; and
(*b*) a person to whom the Act applies by virtue of Regulation (EC) No 1408/71 or Regulation (EC) No 883/2004.

(2) Section 11 of the Act has effect in relation to the employment as if for subsection (3) there were substituted—
"(3) "Relevant profits" means profits from the employment in respect of which Class 4 contributions would be payable under section 15 for the relevant tax year if—
(*a*) for the purposes of income tax, the earner were resident in the United Kingdom in that year;
(*b*) the employment were carried on by the earner in Great Britain;
(*c*) the amount of the profits were to exceed the amount specified in subsection (3)(*a*) of that section in excess of which the main Class 4 percentage is payable; and

NIC

(*d*) any applicable arrangements having effect under section 2 of the Taxation (International and Other Provisions) Act 2010 (double taxation arrangements) were to be disregarded.".][1]

Amendments—[1] This regulation inserted by the Social Security (Miscellaneous Amendments No 2) Regulations, SI 2015/478 regs 2, 17 with effect from 6 April 2015.

[148C (1) This regulation applies in relation to a person (P)—

(*a*) who is liable under section 11(2) of the Act, or entitled under section 11(6) of the Act, to pay one or more Class 2 contributions in respect of a contribution week in a relevant tax year;

(*b*) who does not carry on a trade, profession or vocation the profits of which (if any) would be chargeable to income tax under Chapter 2 of Part 2 of the Income Tax (Trading and Other Income) Act 2005 for the relevant tax year; and

(*c*) in respect of whom regulation 148B applies in relation to the relevant tax year.

(2) Section 11(5) of the Act (Class 2 contributions payable in the same manner as Class 4 contributions) does not apply in relation to the Class 2 contributions (if it would otherwise do so).

(3) Section 12 of the Act (late paid Class 2 contributions) is to apply to the Class 2 contributions that P is liable to pay under section 11(2) of the Act as it applies to contributions paid under section 11(6) of the Act.

(4) If P is liable to pay the Class 2 contributions, P must, no later than 31st January next following the end of the relevant tax year—

(*a*) pay the Class 2 contributions for which P is liable in respect of any contribution weeks in that tax year; and

(*b*) make a return in such form as may be approved by HMRC.

(5) If P is entitled to pay a Class 2 contribution under section 11(6) of the Act, P may—

(*a*) make a return in such form as may be approved by HMRC; and

(*b*) pay the contribution.

(6) P must keep such records as may be necessary for the purposes of calculating P's—

(*a*) relevant profits from the employment for the purposes of section 11(2) of the Act; and

(*b*) liability or, as the case may be, entitlement to pay a Class 2 contribution,

for the relevant tax year and preserve such records until the sixth anniversary of the 31st January next following the end of the relevant tax year.]

Amendments—[1] This regulation inserted by the Social Security (Miscellaneous Amendments No 2) Regulations, SI 2015/478 regs 2, 18 with effect from 6 April 2015.

CASE G

VOLUNTEER DEVELOPMENT WORKERS

149 Interpretation

(1) In this Case "volunteer development worker" means a person in respect of whom the Board has certified that it is consistent with the proper administration of the Act that, subject to the satisfaction of the conditions in paragraph (2), that person should be entitled to pay Class 2 contributions under regulation 151.

(2) The conditions are—

(*a*) that that person is ordinarily resident in Great Britain or Northern Ireland (as the case may be); and

(*b*) that he is employed [outside the United Kingdom][1].

Amendments—[1] Words in para (2)(*b*) substituted by the Social Security (Contributions) (Amendment No 3) Regulations, SI 2002/2366 regs 3, 17 with effect from 8 October 2002.

150 Certain volunteer development workers to be self-employed earners

Any employment as a volunteer development worker, which is not employment in respect of earnings from which Class 1 contributions are payable, or, where section 6A of the Act applies, are treated as having been paid, shall be employment as a self-employed earner notwithstanding that it is not employment in Great Britain or Northern Ireland.

151 Option to pay Class 2 contributions

Notwithstanding section 11(1) of the Act and regulation 150, a volunteer development worker who by virtue of that regulation is a self-employer earner—

(*a*) . . . [1]

(*b*) shall be entitled to pay [a Class 2][1] contribution if he so wishes at the rate prescribed in regulation 152(*b*).

Amendments—[1] Para (*a*) revoked, and words in para (*b*) substituted by the Social Security (Miscellaneous Amendments No 2) Regulations, SI 2015/478 regs 2, 19 with effect from 6 April 2015.

152 Special provision as to residence, rate, annual maximum and method of payment

In relation to the Class 2 contributions a volunteer development worker is entitled to pay by virtue of regulation 151—

(*a*) the provision of Case F of these Regulations shall not apply;

(*b*) the weekly rate of any Class 2 contributions payable by a volunteer development worker for any contribution week while he is ordinarily employed as a volunteer development worker shall, notwithstanding the provisions of section [11(2)][1] of the Act (Class 2 contributions) be 5 per cent of the lower earnings limit for the year in which falls the week in respect of which the contribution is paid;

(*c*) for the purpose of determining the extent of an earner's liability for contributions under regulation 21 the amount prescribed in that regulation shall be reduced by the amount of any contributions paid in respect of the year in question by virtue of regulation 151; and

(*d*) regulation 89 shall not apply.

Commentary—*Simon's Taxes* **E8.315**.

Amendments—[1] Reference in para (*b*) substituted by the Social Security (Miscellaneous Amendments No 2) Regulations, SI 2015/478 regs 2, 20 with effect from 6 April 2015.

153 Late paid contributions

(1) This regulation applies to any Class 2 contribution a volunteer development worker is entitled to pay by virtue of regulation 151, which is paid in respect of a week falling within a tax year ("the contribution year") earlier than the tax year in which it is paid.

(2) Section 12 of the Act (late paid Class 2 contributions) shall not apply.

(3) Subject to paragraph (4), the amount of a contribution to which this regulation applies shall be the amount which the volunteer development worker would have had to pay if he had paid the contribution in the contribution year.

(4) In any case where—

(*a*) the volunteer development worker pays a contribution to which this regulation applies after the end of the tax year immediately following the contribution year; and

(*b*) the weekly rate of contributions applicable under regulation 152(*b*), for the week in respect of which the contribution is paid, differs from the weekly rate so applicable at the time of payment,

the amount of the contributions shall be computed by reference to the highest weekly rate of contributions applicable in the period from the week in respect of which the contribution is paid to the day on which it is paid.

154 Modification of the Act and these Regulations

Part 1 of the Act and these Regulations shall have effect as respects volunteer development workers subject to the modification contained in this Case.

[CASE H

154A Apprentices: zero-rate secondary Class 1 contributions

(1) For the purposes of section 9B (zero-rate secondary Class 1 contributions for certain apprentices) of the Act, an apprentice is a person who falls within paragraphs (2) and (3).

(2) The person is employed under—

(*a*) an approved English apprenticeship agreement within the meaning of section A1 of the Apprenticeships, Skills, Children and Learning Act 2009 ("the 2009 Act"),

(*b*) an English apprenticeship agreement within the meaning of section 32 of the 2009 Act as saved by paragraph 2 of Part 2 of the Schedule to the Deregulation Act 2015 (Commencement No 1 and Transitional and Saving Provisions) Order 2015,

(*c*) a Welsh apprenticeship agreement within the meaning of section 32 of the 2009 Act,

(*d*) arrangements made by the Secretary of State or the Scottish Ministers under section 2 of the Employment and Training Act 1973,

(*e*) arrangements made by the Secretary of State or the Scottish Ministers under section 2 of the Enterprise and New Towns (Scotland) Act 1990, or

(*f*) arrangements made by the Secretary of State or Northern Ireland Ministers under section 1 of the Employment and Training Act (Northern Ireland) 1950.

(3) The person is being trained pursuant to arrangements—

(*a*) in relation to which the Secretary of State has secured the provision of financial resources under section 100 of the 2009 Act, or

(*b*) which are set out in a written agreement made between that person, the employer and the training provider containing the following information—

(i) the type of apprenticeship framework or standard being followed,

(ii) the start date of the apprenticeship, and

(iii) the expected completion date of the apprenticeship.][1]

Amendments—[1] Regulation 154A and preceding heading inserted by the Social Security (Contributions) (Amendment) Regulations, SI 2016/117 reg 2 with effect from 6 April 2016.

NIC

PART 10
MISCELLANEOUS PROVISIONS

155 Treatment of contribution week falling in two years

For the purposes of Class 2 contributions, where a contribution week falls partly in one year and partly in another, it shall be treated as falling wholly within the year in which it begins.

Commentary—*Simon's Taxes* **E8.311**.

155A [Decisions taken by officers of the Inland Revenue in respect of contributions which are prescribed for the purposes of section 8(1)(m) of the Transfer Act

(1) For the purposes of section 8(1)(*m*) of the Transfer Act the decisions specified in paragraphs (2) to (5) are prescribed.

(2) The decisions specified in this paragraph are—

(*a*) whether a notice should be given under regulation 3(2B) and, if so, the terms of such a notice;

(*b*) whether a notice given under regulation 3(2B) should cease to have effect;

(*c*) whether a direction should be given under regulation 31 and, if so, the terms of the direction;

(*d*) whether the condition in regulation 50(2) is satisfied;

(*e*) whether a late application under [regulation 52(8)][2] for the refund of a contribution should be admitted;

(*f*) . . . [3]

(*g*) whether a late application under regulation 55(3) for the repayment of a Class 1A contribution should be admitted;

(*h*) whether, in a case where the secondary contributor has failed to pay a primary Class 1 contribution on behalf of the primary contributor, that failure was with the consent or connivance of the primary contributor or attributable to any negligence on the part of the primary contributor, as mentioned in regulation 60;

(*i*) whether the condition in regulation 61(2) is satisfied;

(*j*) whether, in the case of a Class 2 contribution remaining unpaid by the due date, the reason for the non-payment is the contributor's ignorance or error, and, if so, whether that ignorance or error was due to his failure to exercise due care and diligence, as mentioned in regulation 65(2);

(*k*) whether the reason for a contributor's failure to pay a Class 3 contribution within the period prescribed for its payment is his ignorance or error, and, if so, whether that ignorance or error was due to his failure to exercise due care and diligence, as mentioned in regulation 65(3);

(*l*) whether the reason for a contributor's failure to pay a Class 3 contribution falling to be computed under section 13(6) of the Act and which remains unpaid after the end of the second year following the contribution year, is his ignorance or error and if so whether that ignorance or error was due to his failure to exercise due care and diligence, as mentioned in regulation 65(4); and

(*m*) whether a late application under regulation 110(3) for the return of a special Class 4 contribution should be admitted.

(3) The decisions specified in this paragraph are—

(*a*) whether a contribution (other than a Class 4 contribution) has been paid in error as mentioned in [regulation 52(1)][2]; and

(*b*) whether there has been a payment of contributions in excess of the amount specified in regulation 21, as mentioned in [regulation 52A(1)][2],

to the extent that they are not decisions falling within section 8(1)(*c*) or (*d*) (decisions as to liability and entitlement to pay contributions) of the Transfer Act.

(4) The decisions specified in this paragraph are—

(*a*) whether the delay in making payment of a contribution, payable by an employer on behalf of an insured person, was neither with the consent or connivance of the insured person nor attributable to any negligence on the part of the insured person, as mentioned in regulation 23 of the National Insurance (Contributions) Regulations 1969;

(*b*) whether, in the case of a contribution paid after the due date, the failure to pay the contribution before that time was attributable to ignorance or error on the part of the insured person, and, if so, whether that ignorance or error was due to the failure on the part of the insured person to exercise due care and diligence, as mentioned in regulation 24 of those Regulations; and

(*c*) whether the failure to pay a contribution to which regulation 32 of those Regulations applies within the prescribed period was attributable to ignorance or error on the part of the person entitled to pay it and, if so, whether that ignorance or error was due to the failure of the person entitled to pay the contribution to exercise due care and diligence.

(5) The decisions specified in this paragraph are—

(*a*) whether the delay in making payment of a primary Class 1 contribution which is payable on a primary contributor's behalf by a secondary contributor was neither with the consent or connivance of the primary contributor nor attributable to any negligence on the part of the primary contributor, as mentioned in regulation 5 of the Social Security (Crediting and Treatment of Contributions, and National Insurance Numbers) Regulations 2001 (treatment for the purpose of any contributory benefit of late paid primary Class 1 contributions where there was no consent, connivance or negligence by the primary contributor); and

(*b*) whether, in the case of a contribution paid by or in respect of a person after the due date, the failure to pay the contribution before that time was attributable to ignorance or error on the part of that person or the person making the payment and if so whether that ignorance or error was due to the failure on the part of such person to exercise due care and diligence, as mentioned in regulation 6 of the Social Security (Crediting and Treatment of Contributions, and National Insurance Numbers) Regulations 2001 (treatment for the purpose of any contributory benefit of contributions under the Act paid late through ignorance or error).][1]

Commentary—*Simon's Taxes* **E8.1002**.

Amendments—[1] This reg inserted by the Social Security (Contributions) (Amendment No 3) Regulations, SI 2002/2366 regs 3, 18 with effect from 8 October 2002.

[2] Words in paras (1)(*e*), (3) substituted by the Social Security (Contributions, Categorisation of Earners and Intermediaries) (Amendment) Regulations, SI 2004/770 regs 2, 26 with effect only in respect of contributions payable in respect of 2003–04 and subsequent years.

[3] Para (2)(*f*) revoked by the Social Security (Contributions) (Amendment) (No 2) Regulations, SI 2016/352 reg 17 with effect from 6 April 2016, subject to savings in relation to rights or obligations arising in connection with tax years beginning before 6 April 2016.

156 Northern Ireland

(1) Except where otherwise provided, the provisions of these Regulations shall apply to Northern Ireland as they apply to Great Britain.

(2) Paragraph (1) does not apply to the provisions of Case B . . . [1] of Part 9 of these Regulations.

(3) In the application of these Regulations to Northern Ireland other than this regulation, a reference to a provision of an enactment, which applies only to Great Britain shall be construed so far as necessary as including a reference to the corresponding enactment applying in Northern Ireland.

(4) Schedule 7 contains a Table showing, in column (1) details of enactments applying in Great Britain for which the enactment shown in column (2) is the corresponding enactment in Northern Ireland.

Neither this paragraph nor Schedule 7 limits the operation of paragraph (3).

(5) The reference—

(*a*) to an Order in Council under section 179 of the Administration Act shall be taken to include a reference to an order under section 155 of the Social Security Administration (Northern Ireland) Act 1992; and

(*b*) to the Secretary of State in regulation 59(3)(*b*) shall be taken to include a reference to the Department of Health and Social Services for Northern Ireland, but any other reference to the Secretary of State shall be taken to include a reference to the Department for Social Development.

(6) The rate of interest prescribed for the purposes of regulations 75 and 76(1) and paragraphs 17(1) and 18(1) and (3) of Schedule 4, in their application to Northern Ireland, is the rate applicable under paragraph 6(3)(*a*) of Schedule 1 to the Social Security Contributions and Benefits (Northern Ireland) Act 1992 for the purpose of paragraph 6(3) of Schedule 1 to the Social Security Contributions and Benefits Act 1992.

Amendments—[1] Words in para (2) revoked by the Social Security (Contributions) (Amendment No 2) Regulations, SI 2003/964 regs 3, 11 with effect from 6 April 2003.

157 Revocations

(1) The Regulations specified in column (1) of Parts I and II of Schedule 8 are revoked to the extent mentioned in column (3) of that Schedule.

Part I of Schedule 8 contains revocations of provisions which extend either to Great Britain or to the whole of the United Kingdom, whilst Part II contains revocations of provisions which extend only to Northern Ireland.

(2) Anything done, permitted to be done or required to be done, under any provision of the instruments revoked by these Regulations shall be treated as though it had been done or were permitted or required to be done (as the case may be) under the corresponding provision of these Regulations.

(3) Without prejudice to the generality of paragraph (2), a person who would have been liable, immediately before the revocation of regulation 53A(4) of the Social Security (Contributions) Regulations 1979 by paragraph (1) to a penalty in respect of a failure which commenced before these Regulations come into force shall continue to be liable to that penalty.

(4) The revocation by these Regulations of an instrument which itself revoked an earlier instrument subject to savings does not prevent the continued operation of those savings, insofar as they are capable of continuing to have effect.

(5) In this regulation "instrument" includes a Statutory Rule of Northern Ireland.

SCHEDULE 1

PROVISIONS CONFERRING POWERS EXERCISED IN MAKING THESE REGULATIONS

Preamble

In this Schedule—

"the 1998 Act" means the Social Security Act 1998;

"the 1988 Order" means the Social Security (Northern Ireland Order 1998;

"the 2000 Act" means the Child Support, Pensions and Social Security Act 2000;

"the Transfer Act" means the Social Security Contributions (Transfer of Functions, etc) Act 1999

"the Transfer Order" means the Social Security Contributions (Transfer of Functions, etc) (Northern Ireland) Order 1999; and

"the Welfare Reform Act" means the Welfare Reform and Pensions Act 1999.

PART I
POWERS EXERCISED BY THE TREASURY

Column (1) *Enabling power*	*Column (2)* *Relevant amendment*
Social Security Contributions and Benefits Act 1992	
Section 1(6) and (7)	Paragraph 56(3) of Schedule 7 to the 1998 Act and paragraph 1(3) of Schedule 3 to the Transfer Act.
Section 3(2), (2A), (3) and (5)	Section 48 and 49 of the 1998 Act and paragraph 3 of Schedule 3 to the Transfer Act.
Section 4(5), (6) and (7)	Section 50 of the 1998 Act, paragraph 4 of Schedule 3 to the Transfer Act and section 74(3) of the 2000 Act.
Section 5(1), (4) and (6)	Paragraph 1 of Schedule 9 to the Welfare Reform Act.
Section 6(3), (6) and (7)	Paragraph 2 of Schedule 9 to the Welfare Reform Act.
Section 6A(2) and (7)	Paragraph 3 of Schedule 9 to the Welfare Reform Act.
Section 10(9)	
Section 10A(7)	Paragraph 11 of Schedule 3 to the Transfer Act.
Section 11(3), (4) and (5)	Paragraph 12 of Schedule 3 to the Transfer Act and article 3 of SI 2001/477.
Section 12(6)	Paragraph 13 of Schedule 3 to the Transfer Act.
Section 13(1) and (7)	Paragraph 14(2) and (4) of Schedule 3 to the Transfer Act, and article 4 of SI 2001/477.
Section 14(1), (2) and (5)	Paragraph 15 of Schedule 3 to the Transfer Act.
Section 19(1) to (5A)	Paragraph 19(2) of Schedule 3 to the Transfer Act.
Section 19A(2) and (3)	Paragraph 20 of Schedule 3, and paragraph 4 of Schedule 9, to the Transfer Act.
Section 116(2) and (3)	Paragraph 28 of Schedule 2 to the Jobseekers Act 1995, paragraph 67 of Schedule 7 to the 1998 Act and paragraph 22 of Schedule 3, and paragraph 5 of Schedule 7 to the Transfer Act.
Section 117	Paragraph 68 of Schedule 7 to the 1998 Act and paragraph 23 of Schedule 3 to, and paragraph 6 of Schedule 7 to, the Transfer Act.
Section 118	Paragraph 24 of Schedule 3 to the Transfer Act.
Section 119	Paragraph 69 of Schedule 7 to the 1998 Act and paragraph 25 of Schedule 3, and paragraph 7 of Schedule 7 to, the Transfer Act.
Section 120	Paragraph 70 of Schedule 7 to the 1998 Act and paragraph 26 of Schedule 3, and paragraph 8 of Schedule 7 to the Transfer Act.
Section 122(1)	
Section 175(3), (4) and (5)	Paragraph 29(4) of Schedule 3 to the Transfer Act.
Schedule 1	

Column (1) *Enabling power*	*Column (2)* *Relevant amendment*
Paragraph 7A	Paragraph 37 of Schedule 3 to, and paragraph 6 of Schedule 9 to, the Transfer Act.
Paragraph 7B	Paragraph 38 of Schedule 3, and paragraph 7 of Schedule 9, and the relevant entry in Part I of Schedule 10, to the Transfer Act, and section 76(3) and (4) of the 2000 Act.
Paragraph 8(1)(a), (c), (ca), (e), (f), (g), (h), (ia), (j), (k), (l), (m) and (q) and (1A)	Paragraph 14 of Schedule 5 to the Pensions Act 1995, paragraph 77(15) and (16) of Schedule 7 to the 1998 Act, paragraph 39 of Schedule 3 to the Transfer Act and section 74(5) and 77(4) and (5) of the 2000 Act.
Paragraph 11	Paragraph 41 of Schedule 3 to the Transfer Act.
Social Security Contributions and Benefits (Northern Ireland) Act 1992	
Section 1(6) and (7)	Paragraph 38(3) of Schedule 6 to the 1998 Order and paragraph 2 of Schedule 3 to the Transfer Order.
Section 3(2), (2A), (3) and (5)	Articles 45 and 46 of the 1998 Order and paragraph 4 of Schedule 3 to the Transfer Order.
Section 4(5), (6) and (7)	Paragraph 5 of Schedule 3 to the Transfer Order and section 78(3) of the 2000 Act.
Section 5(1), (4) and (6)	Paragraph 1 of Schedule 10 to the Welfare Reform Act.
Section 6(3), (6) and (7)	Paragraph 2 of Schedule 10 to the Welfare Reform Act.
Section 6(a)(2) and (7)	
Section 10(9)	
Section 10A(7)	Paragraph 12 of Schedule 3 to the Transfer Order.
Section 11(3), (4) and (5)	Paragraph 13 of Schedule 3 to the Transfer Order and article 3 of SI 2001/477.
Section 12(6)	Paragraph 14 of Schedule 3 to the Transfer Order.
Section 13(1) and (7)	Paragraph 15(2) and (4) of Schedule 3 to the Transfer Order and article 4 of SI 2001/477.
Section 14(1), (2) and (5)	Paragraph 16 of Schedule 3 to the Transfer Order.
Section 19(1) to (5A)	Paragraph 19(2) of Schedule 3 to the Transfer Order.
Section 116(2) and (3)	Paragraph 11 of Schedule 2 to the Jobseekers (Northern Ireland) Order 1995, paragraph 49 of Schedule 6 to the 1998 Order and paragraph 22 of Schedule 3, and paragraph 4 of Schedule 6 to the Transfer Order.
Section 117	Paragraph 50 of Schedule 6 to the 1998 Order and paragraph 23 of Schedule 3, and paragraph 5 of Schedule 6 to, the Transfer Order.
Section 118	Paragraph 24 of Schedule 3 to the Transfer Order.
Section 119	Paragraph 51 of Schedule 6 to the 1998 Order and paragraph 25 of Schedule 3, and paragraph 6 of Schedule 6 to the Transfer Order.
Section 121(1)	
Section 171(3), (4), (5) and (10)	Paragraph 36 of Schedule 1 to the Social Security (Incapacity for Work) (Northern Ireland) Order 1994
Schedule 1	
Paragraph 7A	Paragraph 36 of Schedule 3, and paragraph 4 of Schedule 8, to the Transfer Order.
Paragraph 7B	Paragraph 37 of Schedule 3, and paragraph 5 of Schedule 8, and the relevant entry in Part 1 of Schedule 9 to the Transfer Order and section 80(3) and (4) of the 2000 Act.
Paragraph 8(1)(a), (c), (ca), (e), (f), (g), (h), (ia), (j), (k), (l), (m) and (q) and (1A)	Paragraph 11 of Schedule 3 to the Pensions (Northern Ireland) Order 1995, paragraph 58(15) and (16) of Schedule 6 to the 1998 Order, paragraph 38 of Schedule 3 to the Transfer Order and sections 78(5) and 81(4) and (5) of the 2000 Act.

Column (1) *Enabling power*	*Column (2)* *Relevant amendment*
Paragraph 10	Paragraph 19 of Schedule 21 to the Friendly Societies Act 1992 and paragraph 40 of Schedule 3 to the Transfer Order.

PART II

POWERS EXERCISED BY THE COMMISSIONERS OF THE INLAND REVENUE

Column (1) *Enabling power*	*Column (2)* *Relevant amendment*
Social Security Contributions and Benefits Act 1992	
Section 17(1), (2), (3) and (4)	Paragraph 6 of Schedule 1, paragraph 17 of Schedule 3, and the relevant entry in Part I of Schedule 10 to, the Transfer Act.
Section 18	Paragraph 7 of Schedule 1, and paragraph 18 of Schedule 3, to the Transfer Act and article 5 of SI 2001/477.
Section 122(1)	
Schedule 1	
Paragraph 1	Section 148(2), (3) and (4) of the Pensions Act 1995, paragraph 77(2), (3) and (4) of Schedule 7 to the 1998 Act, paragraph 31 of Schedule 3 to the Transfer Act and paragraph 78(2) to (5) of Schedule 12 to, and Part VI of Schedule 13, to the Welfare Reform Act.
Paragraph 2	Paragraph 32 of Schedule 3 to the Transfer Act.
Paragraph 3	Section 55 of, and paragraph 77(5) of Schedule 7 to the 1998 Act, paragraph 33 of Schedule 3 to the Transfer Act, section 77(1) of and Part VIII of Schedule 9 to the 2000 Act.
Paragraph 3B(11)	
Paragraph 4	Paragraph 16 of Schedule 1 and paragraph 34 of Schedule 3 to the Transfer Act.
Paragraph 5	Paragraph 77(6) of Schedule 7 to the 1998 Act, paragraph 34 of Schedule 3 to the Transfer Act and section 74(4) of the 2000 Act.
Paragraph 5A	Paragraph 34 of Schedule 3 to the Transfer Act.
Paragraph 6	Paragraph 77(8), (9), and (11) of Schedule 7 to, and the relevant entry in Schedule 8 to the 1998 Act and paragraph 17 of Schedule 1, paragraph 35 of Schedule 3, paragraph 9 of Schedule 7, paragraph 5 of Schedule 9, and the relevant entry in Part 1 of Schedule 10, to the Transfer Act
Paragraph 7BA	
The Social Security Administration Act 1992	
Section 113	Section 60 of the 1998 Act, paragraph 5 of Schedule 5 to the Transfer Act and paragraph 7 of Schedule 6 to the 2000 Act.
Section 162(12)	Paragraph 52(11) of Schedule 3 to the Transfer Act.
Section 191	
Social Security Contributions and Benefit (Northern Ireland) Act 1992	
Section 17	Paragraph 7 of Schedule 1, paragraph 17 of Schedule 3, and the relevant entry in Part I of Schedule 9 to, the Transfer Order.

Column (1) *Enabling power*	*Column (2)* *Relevant amendment*
Section 18	Paragraph 8 of Schedule 1 to, and paragraph 18 of Schedule 3 to the Transfer Order and article 5 of SI 2001/477.
Section 121(1)	
Schedule 1	
Paragraph 1	Article 145(2), (3) and (4) of the Pensions (Northern Ireland) Order 1995, paragraph 58(1) to (4) of Schedule 6 to the 1998 Order, paragraph 30 of Schedule 3 to the Transfer Order and paragraph 86(2) to (5) of Schedule 12, and the relevant entry in Part VI of Schedule 13 to, the Welfare Reform Act.
Paragraph 2	Paragraph 31 of Schedule 3 to the Transfer Order.
Paragraph 3	Article 52 of, and paragraph 58(5) of Schedule 6 to, the 1998 Order, paragraph 32 of Schedule 3 to the Transfer Order, section 81(1) of, and the relevant entry in Part VIII of Schedule 9 to, the 2000 Act.
Paragraph 3B(11)	
Paragraph 4	Paragraph 16 of Schedule 1, and paragraph 33 of Schedule 3 to the Transfer Order.
Paragraph 5	Paragraph 58(6) of Schedule 7 to the 1998 Order, paragraph 34 of Schedule 3 to the Transfer Order and section 78(4) of the 2000 Act.
Paragraph 5A	Paragraph 33 of Schedule 3 to the Transfer Order.
Paragraph 6	Paragraph 58(8), (9) and (11) of Schedule 6, and the relevant entry in Schedule 7, to the 1998 Order, paragraph 20 of Schedule 1, paragraph 34 of Schedule 3, paragraph 7 of Schedule 6, paragraph 3 of Schedule 8, and the relevant entry in Part I of Schedule 9 to the Transfer Order.
Paragraph 7BA	
Social Security Administration (Northern Ireland) Act 1992	
Section 107	Article 56 of the 1998 Order, paragraph 5 of Schedule 4 to the Transfer Order and paragraph 7 of Schedule 6 to the Child Support, Pensions and Social Security Act (Northern Ireland) 2000.
Section 142(12)	Paragraph 45(12) of Schedule 3 to the Transfer Order.
Section 167(1)	
Finance Act 1999	
Section 133(1)	

SCHEDULE 2

CALCULATION OF EARNINGS FOR THE PURPOSES OF EARNINGS-RELATED CONTRIBUTIONS IN PARTICULAR CASES

Regulation 24

Calculation of earnings

1 This Schedule contains rules for the calculation of earnings in the assessment of earnings-related contributions in particular cases.

Calculation of earnings in respect of beneficial interest in assets within Part IV of Schedule 3

2—(1) Except where paragraph 3, 4, 5 or 6 applies, the amount of earnings comprised in any payment by way of the conferment of any beneficial interest in any asset specified in Part IV of Schedule 3, which falls to be taken into account in the computation of a person's earnings shall be calculated or estimated at a price which that beneficial interest might reasonably be expected to fetch if sold in the open market on the day on which it is conferred.

NIC

(2) For the purposes of sub-paragraph (1), where any asset is not quoted on a recognised stock exchange within the meaning of section 841 of the Taxes Act, it shall be assumed that, in the open market which is postulated, there is available to any prospective purchaser of the beneficial interest in the asset in question all the information which a prudent prospective purchaser might reasonably require if he were proposing to purchase if from a willing vendor by private treaty and at arm's length.

Valuation of beneficial interest in units in a unit trust scheme

3 The amount of earnings which is comprised in any payment by way of the conferment of a beneficial interest in any units in a unit trust scheme (within the meaning of section [237 of the Financial Services and Markets Act 2000][1] having a published selling price and which falls to be taken into account in the calculation of a person's earnings shall be calculated or estimated by reference to the published selling price on the day in question.
Here "published selling price" means the lowest selling price published on the date on which the payment in question is made, and where no such price is published on that date, it means the lowest selling price published on the last previous date on which such a price was published.

Amendments—[1] Words substituted by the Financial Services and Markets Act 2000 (Consequential Amendments) (Taxes) Order, SI 2001/3629 arts 1(2)(*b*), 190, 191 with effect from 1 December 2001, immediately after the coming into force of the Financial Services and Markets Act 2000 ss 411, 432(1), Sch 20 (and SI 2001/3629 Pts 1 and 2).

Conferment of a beneficial interest in an option to acquire asset falling within Part IV of Schedule 3

4 The amount of earnings which is comprised in a payment by way of the conferment of a beneficial interest in an option to acquire any asset falling within Part IV of Schedule 3 shall be calculated or estimated by reference to the amount which would be comprised in accordance with paragraph 2, or, if paragraph 3, 5 or 6 would apply in accordance with that paragraph, in a payment by way of the conferment of a beneficial interest—

(*a*) in the asset which may be acquired by the exercise of the option; or

(*b*) where that asset (the first asset) may be exchanged for another asset (the second asset) and the value of the beneficial interest in the second asset is greater than that in the first, in that second asset,

on the day on which the beneficial interest in the option is conferred.
The amount shall be reduced by the amount or value, or, if variable, the least amount or value, of the consideration for which the asset may be so acquired.

Readily convertible assets

5—(1) The amount of earnings which is comprised in—

(*a*) any payment by way of the conferment of a beneficial interest in any asset falling within Part III of Schedule 3;

(*b*) any payment by way of the conferment of a beneficial interest in any asset falling within Part IV of Schedule 3 which is a readily convertible asset;

(*c*) any payment by way of—

(i) a voucher, stamp or similar document falling within paragraph 12 of Part IV of that Schedule where the asset for which it is capable of being converted is a readily convertible asset;

(ii) a non-cash voucher not falling within Part V (whether or not also falling within paragraph 12 of Part IV of that Schedule) which is capable of being exchanged for a readily convertible asset;

and which is to be taken into account in computing a person's earnings, shall be calculated in accordance with sub-paragraph (2) to (5).

(2) In the case of an asset falling within paragraph 1 of Part III of Schedule 3 the amount is the best estimate which can reasonably be made of [the amount of general earnings][1] in respect of the provision of the asset.

(3) In the case of an asset falling within paragraph 2 of Part III of Schedule 3, the amount is the best estimate that can reasonably be made of [the amount of general earnings][1] in respect of the enhancement of its value.

(4) In the case of a voucher, stamp or similar document falling within—

(*a*) sub-paragraph(1)(*c*); or

(*b*) paragraph 3 of Part III of Schedule 3,

the amount is the best estimate that can reasonably be made of [the amount of general earnings][1] in respect of the provision of any asset for which the voucher is capable of being exchanged.

(5) In the case of an asset falling within sub-paragraph(1)(*b*), the amount is the best estimate that can reasonably be made of [the amount of general earnings][1] in respect of the provision of the asset.

Amendments—[1] Words in sub-paras (2)–(5) substituted by the Social Security (Contributions) (Amendment No 5) Regulations, SI 2003/2085 regs 3, 7(1), (2) with effect from 1 September 2003.

Assets not readily convertible: beneficial interests in alcoholic liquor on which duty has not been paid, gemstones and certain vouchers and non-cash vouchers

6 The amount of earnings comprised in any payment by way of the conferment of a beneficial interest in—

(*a*) an asset which—

(i) falls within paragraph 9 or 10 of Part IV of Schedule 3 (payments by way of alcoholic liquor on which duty has not been paid or by way of gemstones not to be disregarded as payments in kind), and

(ii) is not a readily convertible asset;

(*b*) a voucher, stamp or similar document which falls within paragraph 12 of Part IV of that Schedule and which is not capable of being exchanged for a readily convertible asset; or

(*c*) a non-cash voucher not excluded by virtue of Part 5 of that Schedule and which falls within paragraph 12 of Part IV of that Schedule (assets not to be disregarded as payments in kind) which is not capable of being exchanged for a readily convertible asset;

shall be calculated or estimated on the basis of the cost of the asset in question.

Here "the cost of the asset" in relation to any voucher, stamp or similar document includes the cost of any asset for which that voucher, stamp or similar document is capable of being exchanged.

Convertible and restricted interests in securities and convertible and restricted securities

[7—(1) The amount of earnings comprised in any payment by way of the conferment of—

(*a*) a convertible interest in securities;

(*b*) a restricted interest in securities; or

(*c*) an interest in convertible or restricted securities,

falling to be taken into account in computing a person's earnings from employed earner's employment shall be computed in the same manner, and shall be taken into account at the same time, as applies under Chapters 1 to 5 of Part 7 of ITEPA 2003, for the purpose of computing his employment income.

This is subject to the following qualification.

(2) For the purpose of sub-paragraph (1) no account shall be taken of any relief obtained under sections 428A or 442A of ITEPA 2003 (relief for secondary Class 1 contributions met by employee).][1]

Amendments—[1] This paragraph substituted by the Social Security (Contributions) (Amendment No 4) Regulations, SI 2004/2096 regs 2, 5 with effect from 1 September 2004. SI 2004/2096 has effect in relation to—

(a) agreements entered into after 1 September 2004 which are in respect of post-commencement employment income, and

(b) elections made after that date.

Convertible interest in shares

8 . . .

Amendment—This paragraph revoked by the Social Security (Contributions) (Amendment No 5) Regulations, SI 2003/2085 regs 3, 7(1), (4) with effect from 1 September 2003.

Assignment or release of right to acquire shares where neither right nor shares readily convertible

9 . . .

Amendment—This paragraph revoked by the Social Security (Contributions) (Amendment No 5) Regulations, SI 2003/2085 regs 3, 7(1), (4) with effect from 1 September 2003.

Assignment or release of a right, acquired as director or employee before 6th April 1999, to acquire shares where neither right nor shares readily convertible

10 . . .

Amendment—This paragraph revoked by the Social Security (Contributions) (Amendment No 5) Regulations, SI 2003/2085 regs 3, 7(1), (4) with effect from 1 September 2003.

[Exercise of a replacement right to acquire shares, obtained as an earner before 6th April 1999

11—(1) This paragraph applies if—

(*a*) an earner obtained, before 6th April 1999, a right to acquire shares in a body corporate;

(*b*) the earner subsequently obtained a replacement right (within the meaning given in paragraph 16A(3) of Part 9 of Schedule 3);

(*c*) the replacement right is exercised;
(*d*) paragraph 11A of this Schedule does not apply; and
(*e*) paragraph 16A of Part 9 of Schedule 3 does not apply because sub-paragraph (4) of that paragraph is not satisfied.

(2) If this paragraph applies, the amount of earnings comprised in any payment realised by the exercise of the replacement right shall be calculated or estimated in accordance with sub-paragraph (3).

(3) The basis for calculating the amount of a gain realised by the exercise of the replacement right shall be the best estimate that can reasonably be made of the amount found as follows.

Step One

Find the amount (if any) by which the sum of—

(*a*) the market value of the shares acquired by the exercise of the replacement right; and
(*b*) the market value of any other benefit in money or money's worth obtained by the exercise of the replacement right;

exceeds the amount required to be paid for the exercise of that right.

Step Two

Find the amount (if any) by which the market value of the shares, which were the subject of the right assigned or released on the first occasion in respect of which the condition in paragraph 16A(4) of Part 9 of Schedule 3 is not satisfied, exceeds the amount required to be paid for the exercise of that right immediately before that time.

Step Three

Subtract the amount found by Step Two from the amount found by Step One.

Step Four

Subtract from the result of Step Three—

(*a*) any amount taken into account in computing the earner's earnings for the purposes of Class 1 contributions at the time of the grant of the first right; and
(*b*) any amount given by or on behalf of the earner as consideration for the acquisition of the first right or any replacement right, but "consideration" does not include the value of any right assigned or released in exchange for the acquisition of a replacement right.

Subject to the following qualification, the result of this step is the amount of earnings referred to in sub-paragraph (2) above.

If the result of this step is a negative value, it is treated as nil for the purposes of computing the earner's earnings.

(4) In this paragraph—

(*a*) "market value" means the price which the shares which are the subject of the right in question might reasonably be expected to fetch on a sale in the open market;
(*b*) neither the consideration given for the grant of any right to acquire shares, nor any entire consideration, shall be taken to include the performance of the duties in connection with the office or employment by reason of which the right was granted;
(*c*) no amount or value of the consideration given for the grant of a right to acquire shares shall be taken into account more than once;
(*d*) "shares" includes stock;
(*e*) "body corporate" includes—
 (i) a body corporate constituted under the law of a country or territory outside the United Kingdom; and
 (ii) an unincorporated association wherever constituted; and
(*f*) references to the release of a share option include agreeing to the restriction of the exercise of the option.][1]

Amendment—[1] This paragraph substituted by the Social Security (Contributions) (Amendment No 5) Regulations, SI 2003/2085 regs 3, 7(1), (5) with effect from 1 September 2003.

[Exercise, assignment or release of share option — market value of option or resulting shares increased by things done otherwise than for genuine commercial purposes

11A—(1) This paragraph applies for calculating or estimating the amount of earnings which is comprised in a payment which—

(*a*) would be disregarded in the computation of earnings for the purposes of earnings-related contributions by virtue of paragraph 16 of Part 9 of Schedule 3; but
(*b*) is not disregarded because paragraph 17 of that Part applies to it.

(2) If this paragraph applies, the amount of earnings to be taken into account for the purpose of earnings related contributions is the amount which would, but for paragraph 16 [or 16A][2] of Part 9 of Schedule 3, have been taken into account by virtue of section 4(4)(*a*) of the Act.

This is subject to the following qualification.

(3) If—

(*a*) the right to acquire shares in a body corporate is not capable of being exercised more than ten years after the date on which it was obtained,

(*b*) an amount of earnings was taken into account for the purpose of earnings-related contributions in respect of the earner's obtaining that right, at the time he obtained it ("the deductible amount"), and

(*c*) no exercise, assignment or release of the whole or any part of—

(i) that right,

(ii) any right replacing that right ("a replacement right"), or

(iii) any subsequent replacement right, has occurred on or after 10th April 2003, the deductible amount may be deducted from the amount otherwise to be taken into account by virtue of this paragraph.][1]

Amendments—[1] Para 11A inserted by the Social Security (Contributions) (Amendment No 3) Regulations, SI 2003/1059 regs 2, 3(1), (3) with effect from 10 April 2003.

[2] Words in sub-para (2) inserted by the Social Security (Contributions) (Amendment No 5) Regulations, SI 2003/2085 regs 3, 7(1), (6) with effect from 1 September 2003.

Interpretation of paragraphs 9, 10 and 11

12 . . .

Amendment—This paragraph revoked by the Social Security (Contributions) (Amendment No 5) Regulations, SI 2003/2085 regs 3, 7(1), (7) with effect from 1 September 2003.

Apportionment of a payment [to] a retirement benefits scheme for the benefit of two or more people

13 . . .

Amendment—Paragraph 13 revoked by the Social Security (Contributions) (Amendment No 2) Regulations, SI 2006/576 regs 2, 7 with effect from 6 April 2006.

Valuation of non-cash vouchers

14—(1) The amount of earnings comprised in any payment by way of a non-cash voucher which is not otherwise disregarded by these Regulations and which falls to be taken into account in calculating an employed earner's earnings shall be calculated on the basis set out in sub-paragraph (2).

(2) The basis referred to in sub-paragraph (1) is that of an amount equal to the expense incurred ("the chargeable expense")—

(*a*) by the person at whose cost the voucher and the money, goods or services, for which it is capable or being exchanged, are provided;

(*b*) in, or in connection with that provision,

and any money, goods or services obtained by the employed earner or any other person in exchange for the voucher shall be disregarded.

This is subject to the following [qualifications][1].

[(3) For the purposes of sub-paragraph (2) the chargeable expense shall be reduced by any part of that which the employed earner makes good to the person incurring it.][2]

[(4) The valuation of qualifying childcare vouchers is determined in accordance with paragraph 7 of Part 5 of Schedule 3.][1]

Amendments—[1] Word in sub-para (2) substituted, and sub-para (4) inserted, by the Social Security (Contributions) (Amendment No 3) Regulations, SI 2005/778 regs 2, 8 with effect from 6 April 2005.

[2] Sub-para (3) substituted by the Social Security (Contributions) (Amendment and Application of Schedule 38 to the Finance Act 2012) Regulations, SI 2013/622 reg 39 with effect in relation to the tax year 2013–14 and subsequent tax years.

Apportionment of earnings comprised in a cash or non-cash voucher provided for benefit of two or more employed earners

15—(1) The amount of earnings comprised in any payment by way of a cash voucher or a non-cash voucher provided for the benefit of two or more employed earners and which falls to be taken into account in computing the earnings of each of those earners shall be calculated or estimated on the basis set out in whichever of sub-paragraphs (2) or (3) applies.

(2) If the respective proportion of the benefit of the voucher to which each of those earners is entitled is know at the time of the payment, the basis is that of a separate payment equal to that proportion.

(3) In any case where the respective proportions are not know at the time of the payment, the basis is equal apportionment between all those earners.

(4) In this paragraph—

(*a*) "chargeable expense" has the same meaning, and is calculated in the same way, as in paragraph 14; and

(*b*) if an employed earner makes good any part of the chargeable expense to the person incurring it, that chargeable expense in relation to that employed earner shall be reduced by that part.

SCHEDULE 3

PAYMENTS TO BE DISREGARDED IN THE CALCULATION OF EARNINGS FOR THE PURPOSES OF EARNINGS-RELATED CONTRIBUTIONS

Regulation 25

PART I

INTRODUCTORY

Introduction

1—(1) This Schedule contains provisions about payments which are to be disregarded in the calculation of earnings for the purposes of earnings-related contributions.

(2) Part II contains provisions about the treatment of payments in kind.

(3) Part III and IV specifies payments by way of assets which are not to be disregarded by virtue of paragraph 1 of Part II.

(4) Part V specifies non-cash vouchers which are to be disregarded by virtue of paragraph 1 of Part II.

(5) In computing earnings there are also to be disregarded—

(*a*) the pensions and pension contributions specified in Part VI;

(*b*) the payments in respect of training and similar courses specified in Part VII;

(*c*) the travelling, relocation and overseas expenses specified in Part VIII;

(*d*) the [incentives by way of securities][1] specified in Part IX; and

(*e*) the miscellaneous payments specified in Part X.

Amendments—[1] Words in sub-para (5)(*d*) substituted by the Social Security (Contributions) (Amendment No 5) Regulations, SI 2003/2085 regs 3, 8, 9 with effect from 1 September 2003.

Interpretation

2—(1) In this Schedule, unless the context otherwise requires—

(*a*) a reference to a numbered Part is a reference to the Part of this Schedule which bears that number;

(*b*) a reference in a Part, to a numbered paragraph is a reference to the paragraph of that Part which bears that number; and.

(*c*) a reference in a paragraph to a lettered or numbered sub-paragraph is a reference to the sub-paragraph of that paragraph which bears that letter or number.

PART II

PAYMENTS IN KIND

Certain payments in kind to be disregarded

1 A payment in kind, or by way of the provision of services, board and lodging or other facilities is to be disregarded in the calculation of earnings.

This is subject to the paragraph 2 and also to any provision about a payment in kind of a particular description or in particular circumstances in any other Part of this Schedule.

Payments by way of assets not to be disregarded

2 Payments falling within paragraph 1 do not include any payment by way of—

(*a*) the conferment of any beneficial interest in—

(i) any asset mentioned in Part III or Part IV,

[(ii) any contract of long-term insurance which falls within paragraph I, III or VI of Part II of Schedule 1 to the Financial Services and Markets Act 2000 (Regulated Activities) Order 2001;][1]

(*b*) a non-cash voucher not of a description mentioned in Part V or to which paragraph 4 of Part X applies.

(2) Sub-paragraph (1)(*a*)(i) is subject to the qualification that an asset, which falls within either Part III or Part IV, shall nevertheless be disregarded under paragraph 1 [if no liability to income tax arises by virtue of section 323 of ITEPA 2003 (long service awards)][2].

(3) For the purposes of sub-paragraph (1)(*a*)(ii), if the [contract—

(*a*) falls within Part II of Schedule 1 to the Financial Services and Markets Act 2000 (Regulated Activities) Order 2001 and Part I of that Schedule; or

(*b*) is treated for the purposes of that Order as falling within Part II of that Schedule by Article 3(3) of that Order,

that contract shall be treated as a contract of long-term insurance.][1]

Amendments—[1] Sub-para (1)(*a*)(ii) and words in sub-para (3) substituted by the Financial Services and Markets Act 2000 (Consequential Amendments) (Taxes) Order, SI 2001/3629 arts 1(2)(*b*), 190, 192(1), (2) with effect from 1 December 2001, immediately after the coming into force of the Financial Services and Markets Act 2000 ss 411, 432(1), Sch 20 (and SI 2001/3629 Pts 1 and 2).

[2] Words in sub-para (2) substituted by the Social Security (Contributions, Categorisation of Earners and Intermediaries) (Amendment) Regulations, SI 2004/770 regs 2, 28(1), (2) with effect from 6 April 2004.

PART III

PAYMENTS BY WAY OF READILY CONVERTIBLE ASSETS NOT DISREGARDED AS PAYMENTS IN KIND

[1 A readily convertible asset within the meaning of section 702 of ITEPA 2003.][1]

Amendments—[1] Substituted by the Social Security (Contributions) (Amendment No 5) Regulations, SI 2003/2085 regs 3, 8, 10 with effect from 1 September 2003.

[2 An asset which, in accordance with section 697 of ITEPA 2003 (PAYE: enhancing the value of an asset), would be treated, for the purposes of section 696 of that Act, as a readily convertible asset.][1]

Amendments—[1] Substituted by the Social Security (Contributions) (Amendment No 5) Regulations, SI 2003/2085 regs 3, 8, 10 with effect from 1 September 2003.

3 Any voucher, stamp or similar document—

(*a*) whether used singularly or together with other such vouchers, stamps or documents; and

(*b*) which is capable of being exchanged for an asset falling within paragraph 1 or 2.

PART IV

PAYMENTS BY WAY OF SPECIFIC ASSETS NOT DISREGARDED AS PAYMENTS IN KIND

[Securities

1 Securities.]

Amendments—Substituted by the Social Security (Contributions) (Amendment No 5) Regulations, SI 2003/2085 regs 3, 8, 11(*a*) with effect from 1 September 2003.

Certain debentures and other securities for loans

2 . . .

Amendment—Revoked by the Social Security (Contributions) (Amendment No 5) Regulations, SI 2003/2085 regs 3, 8, 11(*b*) with effect from 1 September 2003.

Loans stocks of public and local authorities

3 . . .

Amendment—Revoked by the Social Security (Contributions) (Amendment No 5) Regulations, SI 2003/2085 regs 3, 8, 11(*b*) with effect from 1 September 2003.

Warrants etc for loan stock and debentures

4 . . .

Amendment—Revoked by the Social Security (Contributions) (Amendment No 5) Regulations, SI 2003/2085 regs 3, 8, 11(*b*) with effect from 1 September 2003.

Units in collective investment schemes

5 . . .

Amendment—Revoked by the Social Security (Contributions) (Amendment No 5) Regulations, SI 2003/2085 regs 3, 8, 11(*b*) with effect from 1 September 2003.

Options to acquire assets, currency, precious metals or other options

6 Options to acquire, or dispose of—

(*a*) currency of the United Kingdom or any other country or territory;

(*b*) gold, silver, palladium or platinum;

(*c*) an asset falling within any other paragraph of this Part of this Schedule;

(*d*) an option to acquire, or dispose of, an asset falling within sub-paragraph (*a*), (*b*) or (*c*).

Contracts for futures

7 . . .

Amendment—Revoked by the Social Security (Contributions) (Amendment No 5) Regulations, SI 2003/2085 regs 3, 8, 11(*c*) with effect from 1 September 2003.

Contracts for differences or to secure profit by reference to movements of indices

8 . . .

Amendment—Revoked by the Social Security (Contributions) (Amendment No 5) Regulations, SI 2003/2085 regs 3, 8, 11(*c*) with effect from 1 September 2003.

Alcoholic liquor on which duty has not been paid

9 Any alcoholic liquor, within the meaning of section 1 of the Alcoholic Liquor Duties Act 1979 in respect of which no duty has been paid under that Act.

Gemstones

10 Any gemstone, including stones such as diamond, emerald, ruby, sapphire, amethyst, jade, opal or topaz and organic gemstones such as amber or pearl, whether cut or uncut and whether or not having an industrial use.

Certificates etc conferring rights in respect of assets

11 Certificates or other instruments which confer—

(*a*) property rights in respect of any asset falling within paragraphs [1][1], 9 or 10;

(*b*) any right to acquire, dispose of, underwrite or convert an asset, being a right to which the holder would be entitled if he held any such asset to which the certificate or instrument relates; or

(*c*) a contractual right, other than an option, to acquire any such asset otherwise than by subscription.

Amendments—[1] Reference substituted by the Social Security (Contributions) (Amendment No 5) Regulations, SI 2003/2085 regs 3, 8, 11(*d*) with effect from 1 September 2003.

Vouchers

12 Any voucher, stamp or similar document—

(*a*) whether used singularly or together with other such vouchers, stamps or documents; and

(*b*) which is capable of being exchanged for an asset falling within any other paragraph of this Part.

PART V
CERTAIN NON-CASH VOUCHERS TO BE DISREGARDED AS PAYMENTS IN KIND

1—(1) Subject to sub-paragraph (2), a non-cash voucher provided, to or for the benefit of the employed earner, by the employer or any other person on his behalf is to be disregarded in the calculation of an employed earner's earnings by virtue of paragraph 1 of Part II only if it falls within any of paragraphs 2 to [9][3].

[(2) A non-cash voucher may also be disregarded—

(*a*) by virtue of paragraph 7D of Part VIII (car fuel); . . .

[(*aa*) by virtue of paragraph 7E of Part 8 (van fuel); or][4]

(*b*) in the circumstances specified in paragraph 4 of Part X (payments by way of [incidental overnight expenses][2]).][1]

Amendments—[1] Sub-para (2) substituted by the Social Security (Contributions) (Amendment No 2) Regulations, SI 2002/307 regs 2, 6 with effect from 6 April 2002.

[2] Words in sub-para (2)(*b*) substituted by the Social Security (Contributions, Categorisation of Earners and Intermediaries) (Amendment) Regulations, SI 2004/770 regs 2, 28(1), (3)(*a*) with effect from 6 April 2004.

[3] Reference in sub-para (1) substituted by the Social Security (Contributions) (Amendment No 6) Regulations, SI 2007/2091 reg 2(1), (2) with effect from 14 August 2007: SI 2007/2091 reg 1.

[4] Word in sub-para (2)(*a*) revoked, and sub-para (2)(*aa*) inserted, by the Social Security (Contributions) (Amendment No 2) Regulations, SI 2008/607 regs 2, 4(1), (2) with effect from 6 April 2008.

2 A non-cash voucher which is not treated as [general earnings][1] from employment for the purposes of [section 86 of ITEPA 2003 (transport vouchers under pre-26th March arrangements).][1] [This paragraph only applies in the case of an employee who is in lower paid employment, within the meaning of section 217 of ITEPA 2003][1].

Amendments—[1] Words substituted by the Social Security (Contributions, Categorisation of Earners and Intermediaries) (Amendment) Regulations, SI 2004/770 regs 2, 28(1), (3)(*b*) with effect from 6 April 2004.

3 A non-cash voucher exempted from liability to income tax under Chapter 4 of Part 3 by virtue of sections 266(1)(*a*) or 269 of ITEPA 2003 (exemptions: non-cash vouchers and credit-tokens).][1]

Amendments—[1] Para 3 substituted for paras 3, 4 by the Social Security (Contributions, Categorisation of Earners and Intermediaries) (Amendment) Regulations, SI 2004/770 regs 2, 28(1), (3)(*c*) with effect from 6 April 2004.

[5 A non-cash voucher in respect of which no liability to income tax arises by virtue of section 266(1) of ITEPA 2003 to the extent that the voucher is used to obtain anything the direct provision of which would fall within any of the following provisions of that Act—

(*a*) section 246 (transport between work and home for disabled employees: general);

(*b*) section 247 (provision of cars for disabled employees);

(*c*) section 248 (transport home: late night working and failure of car-sharing arrangements)[;][2]

[(*d*) section 320C (recommended medical treatment).][2]][1]

Amendments—[1] Paras 5–6 substituted for paras 5, 6 by the Social Security (Contributions) (Amendment No 7) Regulations, SI 2003/2958 regs 2, 5(1), (2) with effect from 10 December 2003.

[2] Sub-para (*d*) inserted by the Social Security (Contributions) (Amendment No 6) Regulations, SI 2014/3228 regs 2, 3 with effect from 1 January 2015.

[5A A non-cash voucher in respect of which no liability to income tax arises by virtue of section 266(2) of ITEPA 2003 if the voucher evidences entitlement to use anything the direct provision of which would fall within any of the following provisions of that Act—

(*a*) section 242 (works transport services);

(*b*) section 243 (support for public bus services);

(*c*) section 244 (cycles and cyclist's safety equipment);][1]

[(*d*) section 319 (mobile telephones).][2]

Amendments—[1] Paras 5–6 substituted for paras 5, 6 by the Social Security (Contributions) (Amendment No 7) Regulations, SI 2003/2958 regs 2, 5(1), (2) with effect from 10 December 2003.

[2] Para (5)(*d*) inserted by the Social Security (Contributions) (Amendment No 4) Regulations, SI 2006/2003 reg 2(2) with effect from 14 August 2006.

[5B A non-cash voucher in respect of which no liability to income tax arises by virtue of section 266(3) of ITEPA 2003 if the voucher can be used only to obtain anything the direct provision of which would fall within any of the following provisions of that Act—

(*a*) section 245 (travelling and subsistence during public transport strikes);

(*b*) section 261 (recreational benefits);

(*c*) section 264 (annual parties and functions);

(*d*) section 296 (armed forces' leave travel facilities);

(*e*) section 317 (subsidised meals);][1]

[(*f*) section 320A (eye tests and special corrective appliances).][2]

Amendments—[1] Paras 5–6 substituted for paras 5, 6 by the Social Security (Contributions) (Amendment No 7) Regulations, SI 2003/2958 regs 2, 5(1), (2) with effect from 10 December 2003.

[2] Para (5)(*f*) inserted by the Social Security (Contributions) (Amendment No 4) Regulations, SI 2006/2003 reg 2(2) with effect from 14 August 2006.

[6 A non-cash voucher to the extent that no liability to income tax arises by virtue of any of the following sections of ITEPA 2003—

(*a*) section 270 (exemption for small gifts of vouchers and tokens from third parties);

(*b*) section 305 (offshore oil and gas workers: mainland transfers);

(*c*) section 321 (suggestion awards);

(*d*) section 323 (long service awards);

[(*da*) section 323A(a) (trivial benefits provided by employers);][2]

(*e*) section 324 (small gifts from third parties).][1]

Amendments—[1] Paras 5–6 substituted for paras 5, 6 by the Social Security (Contributions) (Amendment No 7) Regulations, SI 2003/2958 regs 2, 5(1), (2) with effect from 10 December 2003.

[2] Sub-para (*da*) inserted by the Social Security (Contributions) (Amendment No 4) Regulations, SI 2016/1067 regs 2, 5 with effect from 28 November 2016.

[Meal vouchers

6A 15 pence per working day up to a maximum of £1.05 per week of the value of one or more non-cash vouchers which can only be exchanged for meals.][1], [2]

Amendments—[1] Para 6A inserted by the Social Security (Contributions) (Amendment No 5) Regulations, SI 2001/2412 regs 2, 5(1), (2)(*b*) with effect from 26 July 2001 (note that reg 5(2)(*b*) is revoked by SI 2013/622 reg 42(c) with effect in relation to the tax year 2013–14 and subsequent tax years).

[2] Para 6A revoked by the Social Security (Contributions) (Amendment and Application of Schedule 38 to the Finance Act 2012) Regulations, SI 2013/622 reg 40(*a*)(i) with effect in relation to the tax year 2013–14 and subsequent tax years.

NIC

[Interpretation—qualifying childcare vouchers

6B In paragraphs 7 and 7A—

(*a*) "care", "child" and "parental responsibility" have the same meaning as in section 318B of ITEPA 2003;

(*b*) "chargeable expense" has the meaning given in paragraph 14 of Schedule 2;

(*c*) "qualifying child care" has the same meaning as in section 318C of ITEPA 2003;

(*d*) "qualifying week" means a tax week in respect of which a qualifying childcare voucher is received;

(*e*) "relevant salary sacrifice arrangements" means arrangements (whenever made) under which the employees for whom the vouchers are provided give up the right to receive an amount of general earnings or specific employment income in return for the provision of the vouchers;

(*f*) "relevant flexible remuneration arrangements" means arrangements (whenever made) under which the employees for whom the vouchers are provided agree with the employer that they are to be provided with the vouchers rather than receive some other description of employment income;

(*g*) "relevant low-paid employees" means any of the employer's employees who are remunerated by the employer at a rate such that, if the relevant salary sacrifice arrangements or relevant flexible remuneration arrangements applied to them, the rate at which they would then be so remunerated would be likely to be lower than the national minimum wage;

(*h*) "scheme" means the manner by which an employer provides qualifying childcare vouchers and an employee is taken to join a scheme or have joined a scheme when the employer has agreed that vouchers will be provided to the employee under the scheme and there is a child falling within Condition A of paragraph 7(7); and

(*i*) the administration costs for a voucher means the difference between the cost of provision of a voucher and its face value and the face value is the amount stated on or recorded in the voucher as the value of the provision of care for a child that may be obtained by using it.][1]

Amendments—[1] Para 6B inserted by the Social Security (Contributions) (Amendment No 4) Regulations, SI 2011/1000 regs 2, 3 with ffect from 6 April 2011.

[[Qualifying childcare vouchers for employees who joined a scheme before 6th April 2011

7—[(1) A qualifying childcare voucher, where an employee joined a scheme—

(*a*) before 6th April 2011;

(*a*) before 6th April 2011 but ceased to be employed by the employer and was subsequently re-employed by the employer and re-joined the scheme before 6th April 2011; or

(*a*) before 6th April 2011 and there was a continuous period of 52 weeks ending before 6th April 2011 throughout which vouchers were not being provided for the employee under the scheme,

subject to the qualifications in sub-paragraphs (2) and (5).][4]

(1A) . . . [4]

(2) Where the chargeable expense of the voucher exceeds the exempt amount, only that amount shall be disregarded by virtue of sub-paragraph (1).

(3) The exempt amount is the amount found by the formula—

$$E \times QW$$

Here—

E is the sum of—

(*a*) [£55][2]; and

(*b*) the administration costs for the qualifying childcare voucher;

QW is the number of qualifying weeks—

(*a*) for which the earner has been employed by the secondary contributor during the tax year in which the qualifying childcare voucher is provided; and

(*b*) for which no other qualifying childcare voucher has been provided by the secondary contributor.

(4) Where an earner has two or more employed earner's employments, the earnings from which fall to be aggregated in accordance with regulation 14 or 15, the reference to the secondary contributor in paragraph (*b*) of the definition of QW is a reference to the secondary contributor in respect any of those employments.

(5) An earner is only entitled to one exempt amount even if childcare vouchers are provided in respect of more than one child.

[(6) In this paragraph "qualifying childcare voucher" means a non-cash voucher in relation to which Conditions A to C are met.][3]

[(7) Condition A is that the voucher is provided to enable an employee to obtain care for a child who—

(*a*) is a child or stepchild of the employee and is maintained (wholly or partly) at the employee's expense; or

(*b*) is resident with the employee and is a person in respect of whom the employee has parental responsibility.

(8) Condition B is that the voucher can only be used to obtain qualifying child care.

(9) Condition C is that the vouchers are provided under a scheme that is open—

(*a*) to the employer's employees generally; or

(*b*) generally to those at a particular location,

subject to sub-paragraph (10).

(10) Where the scheme under which the vouchers are provided involves—

(*a*) relevant salary sacrifice arrangements; or

(*b*) relevant flexible remuneration arrangements,

Condition C is not prevented from being met by reason only that the scheme is not open to relevant low-paid employees.][3]][1]

Amendments—[1] Paragraph 7 substituted by the Social Security (Contributions) (Amendment No 3) Regulations, SI 2005/778 regs 2, 9(1), (2) with effect from 6 April 2005. However—

(a) in relation to qualifying childcare vouchers provided during the period beginning on 6 April 2005 and ending on 5 October 2005 ("the transitional period"), sub-para (3) above shall have effect as if, for the purposes of paragraph (*a*) of QW, the number of qualifying weeks were 26. This is subject to the following qualification.

(b) The sum of the exempt amounts which may be disregarded, in computing earnings during the transitional period, by virtue of sub-para (3) above, as modified in (*a*) above, shall not exceed £1,300: SI 2005/778 reg 10 (as amended by SI 2005/1086).

[2] Figure in sub-para (3) substituted by the Social Security (Contributions) (Amendment No 3) Regulations, SI 2006/883 with effect from 6 April 2006.

[3] Heading, and sub-para (1) substituted, and sub-paras (1A), (7)–(1) inserted, by the Social Security (Contributions) (Amendment No 4) Regulations, SI 2011/1000 regs 2, 4 with effect for employees who joined a scheme before 6 April 2011.

[4] Sub-para (1) substituted and sub-para (1A) revoked, by the Social Security (Contributions) (Amendment No 5) Regulations, SI 2011/2700 regs 2, 5 with effect from 6 December 2011.

[[Qualifying childcare vouchers for employees who joined a scheme on or after 6th April 2011, or before 6th April 2011 where there has been a break in employment or a 52 week break in receiving vouchers recommencing on or after 6th April 2011]

7A—[(1) A qualifying childcare voucher, where an employee joined a scheme—

(*a*) on or after 6th April 2011;

(*a*) before 6th April 2011 but ceased to be employed by the employer and was subsequently re-employed by the employer and re-joined the scheme on or after 6th April 2011; or

(*a*) before 6th April 2011 and there was a continuous period of 52 weeks ending on or after 6th April 2011 throughout which vouchers were not being provided for the employee under the scheme

subject to the qualifications in sub-paragraphs (3) and (6).][2]

(2) In this paragraph a "qualifying childcare voucher" means a non-cash voucher in relation to which conditions A to D (see sub-paragraphs (7) to (11)) are met.

(3) Where the chargeable expense of the voucher exceeds the exempt amount, only that amount shall be disregarded by virtue of sub-paragraph (1).

(4) The exempt amount is the amount found by the formula—

$$E \times QW$$

Here—

E is, in the case of an employee the sum of—

(*a*) [£25][3], if the relevant earnings amount for the tax year, as estimated in accordance with Condition D, exceeds the higher rate limit for the tax year;

(*b*) £28, if the relevant earnings amount for the tax year, as estimated in accordance with Condition D, exceeds the basic rate limit but does not exceed the higher rate limit for the tax year; or

(*c*) £55, in any other case; and

(*d*) the administration costs for the qualifying childcare voucher;

QW is the number of qualifying weeks—

(*a*) for which the earner has been employed by the secondary contributor during the tax year in which the qualifying childcare voucher is provided; and

(*b*) for which no other qualifying childcare voucher has been provided by the secondary contributor.

NIC

(5) Where an earner has two or more employed earner's employments, the earnings from which fall to be aggregated in accordance with regulation 14 or 15, the reference to the secondary contributor in paragraph (*b*) of the definition of QW is a reference to the secondary contributor in respect of any of those employments.

(6) An earner is only entitled to one exempt amount even if childcare vouchers are provided in respect of more than one child.

(7) Condition A is that the voucher is provided to enable an employee to obtain care for a child who—

(*a*) is a child or stepchild of the employee and is maintained (wholly or partly) at the employee's expense; or

(*b*) is resident with the employee and is a person in respect of whom the employee has parental responsibility.

(8) Condition B is that the voucher can only be used to obtain qualifying child care.

(9) Condition C is that the vouchers are provided under a scheme that is open—

(*a*) to the employer's employees generally; or

(*b*) generally to those at a particular location,

subject to sub-paragraph (10).

(10) Where the scheme under which the vouchers are provided involves—

(*a*) relevant salary sacrifice arrangements; or

(b) relevant flexible remuneration arrangements,

Condition C is not prevented from being met by reason only that the scheme is not open to relevant low-paid employees.

(11) Condition D is that the employer has, at the required time, made an estimate of the employee's relevant earnings amount for the tax year in respect of which the voucher is provided.

(12) In sub-paragraph (11) "the required time", in the case of an employee, means—

(*a*) if the employee joins the scheme under which the vouchers are provided at a time during the tax year, that time, and

(*b*) otherwise, the beginning of the tax year.

(13) In sub-paragraph (11) the "relevant earnings amount", in the case of an employee provided with vouchers by an employer for any qualifying week in a tax year, and subject to sub-paragraph (14), means—

(*a*) the aggregate of—

(i) the amount of any relevant earnings (see sub-paragraph (15)) for the tax year from employment by the employer; and

(ii) any amounts to be treated under Chapters 2 to 12 of Part 3 of ITEPA 2003 as earnings from such employment; less

(*b*) the aggregate of any excluded amounts (see sub-paragraph (16)).

(14) But if the employee becomes employed by the employer during the tax year, what would otherwise be the amount of the aggregate mentioned in sub-paragraph (13)(*a*) is the relevant multiple of that amount; and the relevant multiple is—

365 / *RD*

where—

RD is the number of days in the period beginning with the day on which the employee becomes employed by the employer and ending with the tax year.

(15) In sub-paragraph (13)(*a*) "relevant earnings" means—

(*a*) salary, wages or fees, . . . [2]

[(*b*) guaranteed contractual bonuses;

(*c*) contractual commission;

(*d*) guaranteed overtime payments;

(*e*) location or cost of living allowances;

(*f*) shift allowances;

(*g*) skills allowances;

(*h*) retention and recruitment allowances; and

(*i*) market rate supplements.][2]

(16) For the purposes of sub-paragraph (13)(*b*) the following are "excluded amounts"—

[(*za*) contributions under a pension scheme if the employee has authorised the employer to make the deductions from relevant payments (as defined by regulation 4 of the PAYE Regulations) for which relief at source is given under section 192(1) of the Finance Act 2004 (relief at source);][2]

(*a*) contributions under a . . . [2] pension scheme allowed under section 193(2) of Finance Act 2004 (relief under net pay arrangements) to be deducted by the employer from the employee's employment income for the tax year [in accordance with the PAYE Regulations][2];

(*b*) donations for which a deduction is made under section 713 of ITEPA 2003 (payroll giving) in calculating the employee's net taxable earnings from employment by the employer for the tax year [in accordance with the PAYE Regulations][2];

(*c*) expenses within Chapter 3 of Part 3 of ITEPA 2003 (expenses payments) which the employer is authorised to exclude from the employee's taxable earnings for the tax year in accordance with [the][2] PAYE Regulations;

(*d*) payments in respect of removal expenses to which section 271 of ITEPA 2003 applies (as defined in section 272) and which are taxable earnings of the employee from employment by the employer for the tax year;

[(*e*) amounts equivalent to the amount of the personal allowance under section 35(1) of the Income Tax Act 2007, and in addition if applicable, the amount of the blind person's allowance under section 38 of that Act.][2]][1]

Amendments—[1] Para 7A inserted by the Social Security (Contributions) (Amendment No 4) Regulations, SI 2011/1000 regs 2, 5 with effect for employees who join a scheme on or after 6 April 2011.

[2] Heading and sub-para (1) substituted; in sub-para (15), in para (*a*) word "and" revoked, and paras (*b*)–(*i*) substituted for previous para (*b*); in sub-para (16), para (*za*) inserted, in para (*a*) word "registered" revoked and words inserted, in paras (*b*), (*c*) words inserted, and para (*e*) substituted; by the Social Security (Contributions) (Amendment No 5) Regulations, SI 2011/2700 regs 2, 5 with effect from 6 December 2011.

[3] In sub-para (4), in para (*a*) of definition of E, figure substituted by the Social Security (Contributions) (Amendment and Application of Schedule 38 to the Finance Act 2012) Regulations, SI 2013/622 reg 40(*a*)(ii) with effect in relation to the tax year 2013–14 and subsequent tax years.

8 A non-cash voucher provided to or for the benefit of an employed earner in respect of employed earner's employment by a person who is not the secondary contributor in respect of the provision of that voucher.

[**9** A non-cash voucher providing for health screening or medical check-ups to the extent that no liability to income tax arises in the provision of such health screening or medical check-ups [by virtue of any provision of or under the Income Tax (Earnings and Pensions) Act 2003 which exempts from liability to income tax the provision by employers to employees of health screening and medical check-ups.][2]][1]

Amendments—[1] This paragraph inserted by the Social Security (Contributions) (Amendment No 6) Regulations, SI 2007/2091 reg 2(1), (3) with effect from 14 August 2007: SI 2007/2091 reg 1.

[2] Words substituted by the Social Security (Contributions) (Amendment No 3) Regulations, SI 2009/600 regs 2, 7(1) with effect from 6 April 2009. For the purposes of this amendment, any limitation of provision under ITEPA 2003 by virtue of which an exemption is conditional on the benefit being made available to the employer's employees generally on similar terms, is disregarded (SI 2009/600 reg 7(2)).

PART VI

PENSIONS AND PENSION CONTRIBUTIONS

[Pension payments and pension contributions disregarded

1 The payments mentioned in [this Part][2] are disregarded in the calculation of earnings for the purposes of earnings-related contributions.][1]

Amendments—[1] Paragraph 1 substituted by the Social Security (Contributions) (Amendment No 2) Regulations, SI 2006/576 regs 2, 8(1), (2) with effect from 6 April 2006.

[2] Words substituted by the Social Security (Contributions) (Amendment) Regulations, SI 2015/543 regs 2, 3 with effect from 6 April 2015.

[Contributions to, and benefits from, registered pension schemes

2 A payment—

(*a*) by way of employer's contribution towards a registered pension scheme to which section 308 . . . [2] of ITEPA 2003 (exemption of contributions to registered pension scheme) applies;

(*b*) by way of any benefit pursuant to a registered pension scheme to which—

(i) section 204(1) (authorised pensions and lump sums) of, and Schedule 31 (taxation of benefits under registered pension schemes) to, the Finance Act 2004 applies; or

(ii) section 208 or 209 of that Act (unauthorised payments) applies.][1]

Amendments—[1] Paragraphs 2, 3 substituted by the Social Security (Contributions) (Amendment No 2) Regulations, SI 2006/576 regs 2, 8(1), (3) with effect from 6 April 2006.

NIC

[2] In sub-para (*a*), subsection reference revoked by the Social Security (Contributions) (Amendment No 2) Regulations, SI 2012/817 regs 2, 6(*a*) with effect from 6 April 2012. This amendment does not affect the operation of the Social Security (Contributions) Regulations, SI 2001/1004 in relation to obligations arising in connection with tax years beginning prior to 6 April 2012 (SI 2012/817 reg 11(1)).

[Migrant member relief and corresponding relief [etc]

3—[(1)] [2] A payment by way of—

(*a*) an employer's contribution to which paragraph 2 of Schedule 33 of the Finance Act 2004 (relief for employers' contributions) applies [and any benefit referable to that contribution][2];

(*b*) an employer's contribution to which article 15(2) of the Taxation of Pension Schemes (Transitional Provisions) Order 2006 (employers with pre-commencement entitlement to corresponding relief) applies [and any benefit referable to that contribution][2]; . . . [2]

[(*ba*) an employer's contribution to a pension scheme established by a government outside the United Kingdom for the benefit of its employees or primarily for their benefit, and any benefit referable to such a contribution (whenever made);][2]

(*c*) . . . [2]

[(*d*) benefits from a pension scheme which are referable to contributions made before 6th April 2006, provided that section 386 of ITEPA 2003 did not apply to those contributions by virtue of section 390 of that Act; or

(*e*) benefits subject to the unauthorised payment charge imposed by section 208 of the Finance Act 2004 as applied to a relevant non-UK scheme by virtue of paragraph 1 of Schedule 34 to that Act.][2]

[(2) Expressions defined in Schedule 34 to the Finance Act 2004 have the same meaning in this paragraph as they have there.][2]][1]

Amendments—[1] Paragraphs 2, 3 substituted by the Social Security (Contributions) (Amendment No 2) Regulations, SI 2006/576 regs 2, 8(1), (3) with effect from 6 April 2006.

[2] Sub-para (1) numbered as such; words in heading and paras (*a*), (*b*) inserted; paras (*ba*), (*d*), (*e*) and sub-para (2) inserted; word "or" in para (*b*) and whole of para (*c*) revoked, by the Social Security (Contributions) (Amendment No 5) Regulations, SI 2006/2829 regs 2, 3 with effect from 16 November 2006.

Funded unapproved retirement benefit schemes

4 A payment by way of relevant benefits pursuant to a retirement benefits scheme which has not been approved by the Board for the purposes of Chapter I of Part XIV of the Taxes Act and attributable to payments prior to 6th April 1998.

Here "relevant benefits" has the meaning given in section 612 of the Taxes Act.

Payments to pension previously taken into account in calculating earnings

5 A payment by way of any benefit pursuant to a retirement benefits scheme which has not been approved by the Board for the purposes of Chapter I of Part XIV of the Taxes Act and attributable to payments on or after 6th April 1998 [and before 6th April 2006][1] which have previously been included in a person's earnings for the purpose of the assessment of his liability for earnings-related contributions.

Amendments—[1] Words inserted by the Social Security (Contributions) (Amendment No 2) Regulations, SI 2006/576 regs 2, 8(1), (4) with effect from 6 April 2006.

Payments in good faith to scheme solely for providing approved benefits

6

Amendment—Paragraph 6 revoked by the Social Security (Contributions) (Amendment No 2) Regulations, SI 2006/576 regs 2, 8(1), (5) with effect from 6 April 2006.

[Payments to [and benefits from] pension schemes] exempt from UK taxation under double taxation agreements

7—(1) A payment to a pension scheme which is afforded relief from taxation by virtue of [any of the following provisions, and any benefit referable to that payment[3]]—

(*a*) Article 25(8) of the Convention set out in the Schedule to the Double Taxation Relief (Taxes on Income) (France) Order 1968;

(*b*) Article 17A of the Convention set out in the Schedule to the Double Taxation Relief (Taxes on Income) (Republic of Ireland) Order 1976;

[(*bb*) Article 27(2) of the Convention set out in the Schedule to the Double Taxation Relief (Taxes on Income) (Canada) Order 1980;][2]

(*c*) Article 28(3) of the Convention set out in the Schedule to the Double Taxation Relief (Taxes on Income) (Denmark) Order 1980;

[(*d*) Article 18 of the Convention set out in the Schedule to the Double Taxation Relief (Taxes on Income) (The United States of America) Order 2002.][1]

[(*e*) Article 17(3) of the Convention set out in the Schedule to the Double Taxation Relief (Taxes on Income) (South Africa) Order 2002;][1]

[(*f*) Article 17(3) of the Convention set out in the Schedule to the Double Taxation Relief (Taxes on Income) (Chile) Order 2003.][1]

(2) . . . [2]

Amendments—[1] Words in heading substituted, and sub-para (1)(*d*) inserted, by the Social Security (Contributions) (Amendment No 3) Regulations, SI 2005/778 regs 2, 9(1), (3) with effect from 6 April 2005.

[2] Sub-para (1)(*bb*), (*e*), (*f*) inserted, and sub-para (2) revoked, by the Social Security (Contributions) (Amendment No 2) Regulations, SI 2006/576 regs 2, 8(1), (6) with effect from 6 April 2006.

[3] Words in heading and in sub-para (1) inserted, by the Social Security (Contributions) (Amendment No 5) Regulations, SI 2011/2700 regs 2, 6 with effect from 6 December 2011.

[Contributions to, and benefits from, employer-financed retirement benefits schemes

8 A payment by way of—

(*a*) an employer's contribution towards an employer-financed retirement benefits scheme; and

(*b*) benefits, pursuant to an employer-financed retirement benefits scheme, to which paragraph 10 applies.

Here and in paragraph 10 "employer-financed retirement benefits scheme" has the meaning given in section 393A of ITEPA 2003.][1]

Amendments—[1] Paragraphs 8–10, 11 inserted by the Social Security (Contributions) (Amendment No 2) Regulations, SI 2006/576 regs 2, 8(1), (7) with effect from 6 April 2006.

[Contributions to, and pension payments from, employer-financed pension only schemes

9—(1) A payment by way of—

(*a*) an employer's contribution towards an employer-financed pension only scheme; and

(*b*) a pension, pursuant to an employer-financed pension only scheme, which is income charged to tax pursuant to Part 9 of ITEPA 2003 to which paragraph 10 applies.

(2) In this paragraph "employer-financed pension only scheme" means a scheme—

(*a*) financed by payments made by or on behalf of the secondary contributor, and

(*b*) providing only a pension (and which is accordingly not an employer-financed retirement benefits scheme because it does not provide relevant benefits).

Here "relevant benefits" has the meaning given in section 393B of ITEPA 2003.][1]

Amendments—[1] Paragraphs 8–10, 11 inserted by the Social Security (Contributions) (Amendment No 2) Regulations, SI 2006/576 regs 2, 8(1), (7) with effect from 6 April 2006.

[Payments from employer-financed retirement benefits schemes and employer-financed pension only schemes

10—(1) This paragraph applies to payments in paragraphs 8(*b*) and 9(1)(*b*) which—

(*a*) if the scheme had been a registered pension scheme—

(i) would have been authorised member payments under any of the provisions of section 164 of the Finance Act 2004 (authorised member payments) listed in sub-paragraph (4); and

(ii) would satisfy any of the conditions in sub-paragraph (5); and

(*b*) are made after the employment of the employed earner by—

(i) the secondary contributor,

(ii) a subsidiary of the secondary contributor, or

(iii) a person connected with the secondary contributor or a subsidiary of the secondary contributor,

has ceased.

For the purposes of this sub-paragraph—

"subsidiary" has the meaning given in section 838 of the Taxes Act 1988; and

an employer is connected with any of the persons with respect to whom he would be a connected person by virtue of section 839 of that Act.

(2) In the following provisions of this paragraph—

(*a*) "the Act" means the Finance Act 2004;

(*b*) a reference to a numbered section or Schedule (without more) is a reference to the section or Schedule bearing that number in the Act; and

(*b*) any reference to a numbered pension rule is to the pension rule contained in section 165 bearing that number.

NIC

(3) In applying any provision of the Act for the purposes of this paragraph, a reference to the scheme administrator is to be read as a reference to—

(*a*) the responsible person, within the meaning of section 399A of ITEPA 2003, in relation to the employer-financed retirement benefits scheme, or

(*b*) the person who would be the responsible person if the scheme were an employer-financed retirement benefits scheme.

(4) The provisions referred to in sub-paragraph (1)(*a*)(i) are—

(*a*) [section 164(1)(*a*)][2] (pensions permitted by the pension rules (see section 165)),

(*b*) [section 164(1)(*b*)][2] (lump sums permitted by the lump sum rule (see section 166)),

(*c*) [section 164(1)(*e*)][2] (payments pursuant to a pension sharing order or provision), and

(*d*) [section 164(1)(*f*)][2] (payments of a description prescribed by regulations made by the Commissioners for Revenue and Customs).

(5) The conditions referred to in sub-paragraph (1)(*a*)(ii) are that, if the scheme had been a registered pension scheme—

[(*a*) any pension payable under its rules would have satisfied pension rules 1, 3 and 4;][3]

(*b*) in relation to any lump sum payable under its rules, section 166(1)(*a*) (pension commencement lump sum) and paragraphs 1 to 3 of Schedule 29, as modified by sub-paragraph (6) below, would have been satisfied;

(*c*) in relation to any lump sum payable under its rules, section 166(1)(*b*) (serious ill-health lump sum) and paragraph 4 of Schedule 29, as modified by sub-paragraph (6) below, would have been satisfied; and

(*d*) any pension is payable until the member's death in instalments at least annually.

(6) The amount to be disregarded shall be computed in accordance with Part 1 of Schedule 29 (lump sum rule) as if that Part were modified as follows—

(*a*) in paragraph 1 (pension commencement lump sum)—

(i) paragraphs (*b*) and (*f*) of sub-paragraph (1) were omitted,

(ii) for sub-paragraph (2) there were substituted—

"(2) But if a lump sum falling within sub-paragraph (1) exceeds the permitted lump sum, no part of it shall be disregarded.";

(iii) sub-paragraph (4) were omitted; and

(iv) for sub-paragraph (5) there were substituted—

"(5) Paragraph 2 defines the permitted lump sum.";

(*b*) for paragraph 2 there were substituted—

"2

The permitted lump sum is the higher of—

$$\frac{MVF}{4} \text{ and } \frac{LS + (MAP \times 20)}{4}$$

where—

MVF is the market value of the employee's employer-financed retirement benefits scheme fund at the time the benefit is paid to the individual,

LS is the amount of the lump sum, and

MAP is the maximum annual pension which could be paid to the member under the arrangement.";

(*c*) paragraph 3 were omitted;

(*d*) in paragraph 4, paragraphs (*b*) and (*c*) of sub-paragraph (1) and [sub-paragraphs (2) and (3)][2] were omitted.

(7) No payment by way of benefits shall be disregarded by virtue of this paragraph if they are payable in respect of a period during which an earner is—

(*a*) engaged as a self-employed earner under a contract for services with, or

(*b*) re-employed as an employed earner by,

the secondary contributor from employment with whom the benefits were derived.][1]

Amendments—[1] Paragraphs 8–10, 11 inserted by the Social Security (Contributions) (Amendment No 2) Regulations, SI 2006/576 regs 2, 8(1), (7) with effect from 6 April 2006.

[2] In sub-paras (4)(*a*)–(*d*), (6)(*d*), words substituted, and sub-para (5)(*a*)(iii) revoked, by the Social Security (Contributions) (Amendment No 5) Regulations, SI 2011/2700 regs 2, 6(*c*) with effect from 6 December 2011.

[3] Sub-para (5)(*a*) substituted by the Social Security (Contributions) (Amendment No 2) Regulations, SI 2012/817 regs 2, 6(*b*) with effect from 6 April 2012. This amendment does not affect the operation of the Social Security (Contributions) Regulations, SI 2001/1004 in relation to obligations arising in connection with tax years beginning prior to 6 April 2012 (SI 2012/817 reg 11(1)).

[Armed forces early departure scheme payments

10A A payment under a scheme established by the Armed Forces Early Departure Payments Scheme Order 2005 (SI 2005/437) [or by the Armed Forces Early Departure Payments Scheme Regulations 2014 (S.I. 2014/2328)][2].][1]

Note—Para 10A also has effect for the tax years 2005–06 to 2012–13 inclusive (NICs Act 2014 s 16).

Amendments—[1] Paragraph 10A inserted by the Social Security (Contributions) (Amendment and Application of Schedule 38 to the Finance Act 2012) Regulations, SI 2013/622 reg 40(*b*) with effect in relation to the tax year 2013–14 and subsequent tax years. By virtue of the NICs Act 2014 s 16, para 10A also has effect for the tax years 2005–06 to 2012–13 inclusive.

[2] Words inserted by the Social Security (Miscellaneous Amendments No 2) Regulations, SI 2015/478 regs 2, 21(1), (2) with effect from 1 April 2015.

[Superannuation funds to which section 615(3) of the Taxes Act applies

11 A payment by way of employer's contribution to a superannuation fund to which section 615(3) of the Taxes Act applies, and a payment by way of [a pension or][2] an annuity paid by such a fund . . .[2].][1]

Amendments—[1] Paragraphs 8–10, 11 inserted by the Social Security (Contributions) (Amendment No 2) Regulations, SI 2006/576 regs 2, 8(1), (7) with effect from 6 April 2006.

[2] Words inserted and words revoked by the Social Security (Contributions) (Amendment No 5) Regulations, SI 2006/2829 arts 2, 4 with effect from 16 November 2006.

[Independent advice in respect of conversions and transfers of pension scheme benefits

12 A payment or reimbursement to which no liability to income tax arises by virtue of section 308B of ITEPA 2003 (independent advice in respect of conversions and transfers of pension scheme benefits).][1]

Amendments—[1] Para 12 inserted by the Social Security (Contributions) (Amendment) Regulations, SI 2015/543 regs 2, 4 with effect from 6 April 2015.

[Payments and reimbursements of the cost of pensions advice

13 (1) A payment or reimbursement of costs incurred, by or in respect of an employee or former or prospective employee, in obtaining relevant pensions advice, if Condition A or B is met.

(2) This paragraph does not apply in relation to a person in a tax year so far as the total amount of any payments and reimbursements under sub-paragraph (1) in the person's case in that year exceeds £500.

(3) If in a tax year there is in relation to an individual more than one person who is an employer or former employer, sub-paragraphs (1) and (2) apply in relation to the individual as employee or former or prospective employee of any one of those persons separately from their application in relation to the individual as employee or former or prospective employee of any other of those persons.

(4) "Relevant pensions advice", in relation to a person, means information or advice in connection with—

(*a*) the person's pension arrangements; or

(*b*) the use of the person's pension funds.

(5) Condition A is that the payment or reimbursement is provided under a scheme that is open—

(*a*) to the employer's employees generally; or

(*b*) generally to the employer's employees at a particular location.

(6) Condition B is that the payment or reimbursement is provided under a scheme that is open generally to the employer's employees, or generally to those of the employer's employees at a particular location, who—

(*a*) have reached the minimum qualifying age; or

(*b*) meet the ill-health condition.

(7) The "minimum qualifying age", in relation to an employee, means the employee's relevant pension age less 5 years.

(8) "Relevant pension age", in relation to an employee, means—

(*a*) where paragraph 22 or 23 of Schedule 36 to the Finance Act 2004 applies in relation to the employee and a registered pension scheme of which the employee is a member, the employee's protected pension age (see paragraphs 22(8) and 23(8) of Schedule 36 to the Finance Act 2004); or

(*b*) in any other case, the employee's normal minimum pension age, as defined by section 279(1) of the Finance Act 2004.

(9) The "ill-health condition" is met by an employee if the employer is satisfied, on the basis of evidence provided by a registered medical practitioner, that the employee is (and will continue to be) incapable of carrying on his or her occupation because of physical or mental impairment.][1]

Amendments—[1] Para 13 inserted by the Social Security (Miscellaneous Amendments) Regulations, SI 2017/307 regs 2, 4 with effect from 6 April 2017.

PART VII
PAYMENTS IN RESPECT OF TRAINING AND SIMILAR COURSES

Payments in respect of training and similar payment disregarded

1 The training payments and vouchers mentioned in this Part are disregarded in the calculation of an employed earner's earnings.
[Paragraphs 5 to 8][1] do not apply to Northern Ireland.

Amendments—[1] Words substituted for the words "Paragraphs 5 to 9" by the Social Security (Contributions) (Amendment No 5) Regulations, SI 2005/2422 with effect from 3 October 2005. The amendment extends only to Northern Ireland.

Work-related training

2 A payment of, or contribution towards, expenditure incurred on providing work-related training which, by virtue of [sections 250 to 254 of ITEPA 2003 (exemption for work-related training)][1], is not to be taken as [general earnings][1] of the office or employment in connection with which it is provided.

Amendments—[1] Words substituted by the Social Security (Contributions, Categorisation of Earners and Intermediaries) (Amendment) Regulations, SI 2004/770 regs 2, 28(1), (5)(*a*) with effect from 6 April 2004.

Education and training funded by employers

3 A payment in respect of expenditure which, by virtue of [section 255 of ITEPA 2003 (exemption for contributions to individual learning account training)][1], is not to be taken as [general earnings][1] of the office or employment in connection with which it is provided.

Amendments—[1] Words substituted by the Social Security (Contributions, Categorisation of Earners and Intermediaries) (Amendment) Regulations, SI 2004/770 regs 2, 28(1), (5)(*b*) with effect from 6 April 2004.

New Deal 50plus: employment grant and training credit

4 A payment to a person, as a participant in the scheme arranged under section 2(2) of the Employment and Training Act 1973 and known as New Deal 50plus, of an employment credit or a training grant under that scheme.

Retraining courses for recipients of jobseeker's allowance

5 A payment to a person as a participant in a scheme of the kind mentioned in section 60(1) of the Welfare Reform and Pensions Act 1999 (special schemes for claimants for jobseeker's allowances).

Payments to Jobmatch participants

6 A payment made to a participant in a Jobmatch Scheme (including a pilot) arranged under section 2(1) of the Employment and Training Act 1973 in his capacity as such.

Vouchers provided to Jobmatch participants

7 A payment by way of the discharge of any liability by the use of a voucher given to a participant in a Jobmatch Scheme (including a pilot), arranged under section 2(1) of the Employment and Training Act 1973, in his capacity as such.

[Employment Retention and Advancement payments

8 A payment made to a participant in an Employment Retention and Advancement Scheme, arranged under section 2(1) of the Employment and Training Act 1973, in his capacity as such.][1]

Amendments—[1] Inserted by the Social Security (Contributions) (Amendment No 6) Regulations, SI 2003/2340 regs 1, 2(1), (3) with effect from 1 October 2003.

[Return to Work Credit

9 A payment made to a participant in a Return to Work Credit Scheme, arranged under section 2(1) of the Employment and Training Act 1973 in his capacity as such.][1]

Amendments—[1] Inserted by the Social Security (Contributions) (Amendment No 6) Regulations, SI 2003/2340 regs 1, 2(1), (3) with effect from 1 October 2003, and substituted by the Social Security (Contributions) (Amendment No 7) Regulations, SI 2003/2958 regs 2, 5(1), (3) with effect from 10 December 2003.

[Working Neighbourhoods Pilot

10 A payment made to a participant in a Working Neighbourhoods Pilot, arranged under section 2(1) of the Employment and Training Act 1973, in his capacity as such.][1]

Amendments—[1] Paragraphs 10, 11 inserted by the Social Security (Contributions, Categorisation of Earners and Intermediaries) (Amendment) Regulations, SI 2004/770 regs 2, 28(1), (5)(*c*) with effect from 6 April 2004.

[In-Work Credit

11 A payment made to a participant in an In-Work Credit scheme, arranged under section 2(1) of the Employment and Training Act 1973, in his capacity as such.][1]

Amendments—[1] Paragraphs 10, 11 inserted by the Social Security (Contributions, Categorisation of Earners and Intermediaries) (Amendment) Regulations, SI 2004/770 regs 2, 28(1), (5)(*c*) with effect from 6 April 2004.

[Payments made by employers to earners in full-time attendance at universities &c

12—(1) A payment to an employed earner receiving full-time instruction at a university, technical college or similar educational establishment (within the meaning of section 331 of the Taxes Act) if the conditions in sub-paragraphs (2) to (6) are satisfied, but subject to the exclusion in sub-paragraph (7).

(2) The employed earner must have enrolled at the educational establishment for a course lasting at least one academic year at the time when payment is made.

(3) The secondary contributor must require the employed earner to attend the course for an average of at least twenty weeks in an academic year.

(4) The educational establishment—

(*a*) must be open to members of the public generally,

(*b*) must offer more than one course of practical or academic instruction.

(5) The educational establishment must not be run by—

(*a*) the secondary contributor, or a person who would be treated by section 839 of the Taxes Act as connected with him; or

(*b*) a trade organisation of which the secondary contributor is a member.

(6) The total amount of earnings payable to the earner in respect of his attendance, including lodging, travelling and subsistence allowances, but excluding any tuition fees, must not exceed [£15,480][2] in respect of an academic year.

(7) This paragraph does not apply to any payment made by the secondary contributor to the employed earner for, or in respect of, work done for the secondary contributor by the earner (whether during vacations or otherwise).

(8) This paragraph has effect in respect of payments made in relation to the academic year beginning on 1st September 2005 and subsequent academic years.

(9) In this paragraph—

"academic year" means the period beginning on 1st September of one calendar year and ending on 31st August of the following calendar year.

"trade organisation" means an organisation of secondary contributors (in their capacity as employers) the members of which carry on a particular profession or trade for the purposes of which the organisation exists.][1]

Amendments—[1] Paragraph 12 inserted by the Social Security (Contributions) (Amendment No 2) Regulations, SI 2005/728 regs 2, 4 with effect from 6 April 2005. This insertion has effect in relation to payments of earnings made in respect of the academic year beginning on 1 September 2005 and subsequent academic years: SI 2005/728 reg 1.

[2] Reference in sub-para (6) substituted by the Social Security (Contributions) (Amendment No 7) Regulations, SI 2007/2401 reg 2 with effect in relation to payments of earnings on or after 5 September 2007 in respect of the academic year beginning on 1 September 2007 and subsequent academic years: SI 2007/2401 reg 1(*b*).

PART VIII
TRAVELLING, RELOCATION AND OTHER EXPENSES AND ALLOWANCES OF THE EMPLOYMENT

Travelling, relocation and incidental expenses disregarded

1 The travelling, relocation and other expenses and allowances mentioned in this Part are disregarded in the calculation of an employed earner's earnings.

[1A For the purposes of this paragraph none of the following amounts are to be disregarded in the calculation of an employed earner's earnings—

(*a*) any amount paid or reimbursed pursuant to relevant salary sacrifice arrangements as provided for in section 289A(5);

(*b*) any amount paid or reimbursed to an employed earner which falls within regulation 22(13); and

(*c*) any amount paid to an employed earner in respect of anticipated expenses that have yet to be incurred (whether or not such expenses are actually incurred after the payment is made).][1]

Amendments—[1] Para 1A inserted by the Social Security (Contributions) (Amendment) (No 2) Regulations, SI 2016/352 regs 2, 5(1), (2) with effect from 6 April 2016.

NIC

Relocation expenses

2—(1) A payment of, or contribution towards, expenses reasonably incurred by a person in relation to a change of residence in connection with the commencement of, or an alteration in the duties of the person's employment or the place where those duties are normally to be performed is disregarded if the conditions in sub-paragraphs (2) to (6) are met.

(2) The first condition is that—

(*a*) the payment or contribution—

[(i) is not, by virtue of section 271 of ITEPA 2003 (limited exemption of removal benefits and expenses) liable to income tax as general earnings under that Act; or][1]

(ii) would not have been so regarded, but is in fact disregarded [by virtue of another provision of ITEPA 2003; . . . [2]][1]

(*b*) . . . [2]

(3) The second condition is that the change of residence must result from—

(*a*) the employee becoming employed by an employer;

(*b*) an alteration of the duties of the employee's employment (where his employer remains the same); or

(*c*) an alteration of the place where the employee is normally to perform the duties of his employment (where both the employer and the duties which the employee is to perform remains the same).

(4) The third condition is that the change of residence must be made wholly or mainly to allow the employee to have his residence within a reasonable daily travelling distance of—

(*a*) the place where he performs, or is to perform, the duties of his employment (in a case falling within paragraph (3)(*a*);

(*b*) the place where he performs, or is to perform, the duties of his employment (in a case falling within paragraph (3)(*b*); or

(*c*) the new place where he performs, or is to perform, the duties of his employment (in a case falling within paragraph (3)(*c*).

References in this sub-paragraph and sub-paragraph (5) to the place where the employee performs, or is to perform, the duties of his employment are references to the place where he normally performs, or is normally to perform, the duties of the employment.

(5) The fourth condition is that the employee's former residence must not be within a reasonable daily travelling distance of the place where the employee performs or is to perform the duties of the employment.

(6) . . . [2]

[(7) For the purposes of this paragraph, Chapter 7 of Part 4 of ITEPA 2003 shall be read as if sections 272 (1)(*b*), 272 (3)(*b*), 274 and 287 were omitted.][1]

Amendments—[1] Sub-paras (2)(*a*)(i), (7) substituted, and words in sub-para (2)(*a*)(ii) substituted, by the Social Security (Contributions, Categorisation of Earners and Intermediaries) (Amendment) Regulations, SI 2004/770 regs 2, 28(1), (6)(*a*) with effect from 6 April 2004.

[2] Sub-para (2)(*b*) and preceding word "and", and sub-para (6), revoked, by the Social Security (Contributions) (Amendment No 2) Regulations, SI 2012/817 regs 2, 7(4) with effect from 6 April 2012.

Travelling expenses—general

3 A payment of, or a contribution towards, [travelling expenses][1] which the holder of an office or employment is obliged to incur and [pay as the holder of that office or employment][1] [but this paragraph is subject to paragraph 1A][2].

For the purposes of this paragraph—

(*za*) "ordinary commuting" means travel between—

(i) the employee's home and a permanent workplace; or

(ii) a place that is not a workplace and a permanent workplace;

(*zb*) "private travel" means travel between—

(i) the employee's home and a place that is not a workplace; or

(ii) two places neither of which is a workplace;][2]

[(*a*) "travel expenses" means amounts necessarily expended on travelling in the performance of the duties of the office or employment or other expenses of travelling which are attributable to the necessary attendance at any place of the holder of the office or employment in the performance of the duties of the office or employment and are not expenses of—

(i) ordinary commuting;

(ii) travel between any two places that is for practical purposes substantially ordinary commuting;

(iii) travel between any two places that is for practical purposes substantially private travel; or

(iv) private travel.][2]

[(*b*) . . . [2]

(*c*) expenses of travel by the holder of an office or employment between two places at which he performs the duties of different offices or employments under or with companies in the same group are treated as necessarily expended in the performance of the duties which he is to perform at his destination; and

(*d*) for purpose of sub-paragraph (*c*) companies are to be taken to be members of the same group if and only if—

(i) one is a 51 per cent subsidiary of the other; or

(ii) both are 51 per cent subsidiaries of a third company

within the meaning of section 838(1)(a) of the Taxes Act (subsidiaries).

Amendments—[1] Words substituted by the Social Security (Contributions, Categorisation of Earners and Intermediaries) (Amendment) Regulations, SI 2004/770 regs 2, 28(1), (6)(*b*) with effect from 6 April 2004.

[2] Words inserted, sub-paras (*za*), (*zb*) inserted, sub-para (*a*) substituted and sub-para (*b*) revoked, by the Social Security (Contributions) (Amendment) (No 2) Regulations, SI 2016/352 regs 2, 5(1), (3) with effect from 6 April 2016.

[Meaning of "workplace" and "permanent workplace"

3ZA—(1) For the purposes of paragraph 3—

(*a*) "workplace", in relation to an employment, means a place at which the employee's attendance is necessary in the performance of the duties of the employment,

(*b*) "permanent workplace", in relation to an employment, means a place which—

(i) the employee regularly attends in the performance of the duties of the employment, and

(ii) is not a temporary workplace.

This is subject to sub-paragraphs (3) to (7).

(2) In sub-paragraph (1)(*b*) "temporary workplace", in relation to an employment, means a place which the employee attends in the performance of the duties of the employment—

(*a*) for the purpose of performing a task of limited duration, or

(*b*) for some other temporary purpose.

This is subject to sub-paragraphs (3) and (4).

(3) A place which the employee regularly attends in the performance of the duties of the employment is treated as a permanent workplace and not a temporary workplace if—

(*a*) it forms the base from which those duties are performed, or

(*b*) the tasks to be carried out in the performance of those duties are allocated there.

(4) A place is not regarded as a temporary workplace if the employee's attendance is—

(*a*) in the course of a period of continuous work at that place—

(i) lasting more than 24 months, or

(ii) comprising all or almost all of the period for which the employee is likely to hold the employment, or

(*b*) at a time when it is reasonable to assume that it will be in the course of such a period.

(5) For the purposes of sub-paragraph (4), a period is a period of continuous work at a place if over the period the duties of the employment are performed to a significant extent at the place.

(6) An actual or contemplated modification of the place at which duties are performed is to be disregarded for the purpose of sub-paragraphs (4) and (5) if it does not, or would not, have any substantial effect on the employee's journey, or expenses of travelling, to and from the place where they are performed.

(7) An employee is treated as having a permanent workplace consisting of an area if—

(*a*) the duties of the employment are defined by reference to an area (whether or not they also require attendance at places outside it),

(*b*) in the performance of those duties the employee attends different places within the area,

(*c*) none of the places the employee attends in the performance of those duties is a permanent workplace, and

(*d*) the area would be a permanent workplace if sub-paragraphs (1)(*b*), (2), (4), (5) and (6) referred to the area where they refer to a place.][1]

Amendments—[1] Paras 3ZA, 3ZB inserted by the Social Security (Contributions) (Amendment) (No 2) Regulations, SI 2016/352 regs 2, 5(1), (4) with effect from 6 April 2016.

[Travel for necessary attendance: employment intermediaries

3ZB—(1) This paragraph applies where an individual ("the worker")—

(*a*) personally provides services (which are not excluded services) to another person ("the client"), and (*b*) the services are provided not under a contract directly between the client or a person connected with the client and the worker but under arrangements involving an employment intermediary.

This is subject to the following provisions of this paragraph.

(2) Where this paragraph applies, each engagement is for the purposes of paragraphs 3 and 3ZA to be regarded as a separate employment.

(3) This paragraph does not apply if it is shown that the manner in which the worker provides the services is not subject to (or to the right of) supervision, direction or control by any person.

(4) Sub-paragraph (3) does not apply in relation to an engagement if—

(*a*) Chapter 8 of Part 2 of ITEPA 2003 applies in relation to the engagement,

(*b*) the conditions in section 51, 52 or 53 of that Act are met in relation to the employment intermediary, and

(*c*) the employment intermediary is not a managed service company.

(5) This paragraph does not apply in relation to an engagement if—

(*a*) Chapter 8 of Part 2 of ITEPA 2003 does not apply in relation to the engagement merely because the circumstances in section 49(1)(*c*) of ITEPA 2003 are not met,

(*b*) assuming those circumstances were met, the conditions in section 51, 52 or 53 of that Act would be met in relation to the employment intermediary, and

(*c*) the employment intermediary is not a managed service company.

(6) In determining for the purposes of sub-paragraphs (4) to (5) whether the conditions in section 51, 52 or 53 of ITEPA 2003 are or would be met in relation to the employment intermediary—

[(*a*) in section 51(1) of that Act—

(i) disregard "either" in the opening words, and

(ii) disregard paragraph (b) (and the preceding "or"), and][2]

(*b*) read references to the intermediary as references to the employment intermediary.

[(6A) Sub-paragraph (6B) applies if—

(*a*) the client or a relevant person provides the employment intermediary (whether before or after the worker begins to provide the services) with a fraudulent document which is intended to constitute evidence that, by virtue of sub-paragraph (3), this paragraph does not or will not apply in relation to the services,

(*b*) that paragraph is taken not to apply in relation to the services, and

(*c*) in consequence, the employment intermediary does not under these Regulations deduct and account for an amount that would have been deducted and accounted for if this paragraph had been taken to apply in relation to the services.

(6B) For the purpose of recovering the amount referred to in sub-paragraph (6A)(*c*) ("the unpaid contributions")—

(*a*) the worker is to be treated as having an employment with the client or relevant person who provided the document, the duties of which consist of the services, and

(*b*) the client or relevant person is under these Regulations to account for the unpaid contributions as if they arose in respect of earnings from that employment.

(6C) In sub-paragraphs (6A) and (6B) "relevant person" means a person, other than the client, the worker or a person connected with the employment intermediary, who—

(*a*) is resident, or has a place of business, in the United Kingdom, and

(*b*) is party to a contract with the employment intermediary or a person connected with the employment intermediary under or in consequence of which—

(i) the services are provided, or

(ii) the employment intermediary, or a person connected with the employment intermediary makes payments in respect of the services.][3]

[(6D) Sub-paragraph (3) does not apply in relation to an engagement if—

(*a*) regulations 14 to 18 of the Social Security Contributions (Intermediaries) Regulations 2000 apply in relation to the engagement,

(*b*) one of conditions A to C in regulation 14 of those Regulations is met in relation to the employment intermediary, and

(*c*) the employment intermediary is not a managed service company.

(6E) This paragraph does not apply in relation to an engagement if—

(*a*) regulations 14 to 18 of the Social Security Contributions (Intermediaries) Regulations 2000 do not apply in relation to the engagement because the circumstances in regulation 13(1)(*d*) of those Regulations are not met,

(*b*) assuming those circumstances were met, one of conditions A to C in regulation 14 of those regulations would be met in relation to the employment intermediary, and

(*c*) the employment intermediary is not a managed service company.

(6F) In determining for the purposes of sub-paragraph (6D) or (6E) whether one of conditions A to C in regulation 14 is or would be met in relation to the employment intermediary, read references to the intermediary as references to the employment intermediary.][4]

(7) In determining whether this paragraph applies, no regard is to be had to any arrangements the main purpose, or one of the main purposes, of which is to secure that this paragraph does not to any extent apply.

(8) In this paragraph—

"arrangements" includes any such scheme, transaction or series of transactions, agreement or understanding, whether or not enforceable, and any associated operations;

"employment intermediary" means a person, other than the worker or the client, who carries on a business (whether or not with a view to profit and whether or not in conjunction with any other business) of supplying labour;

"engagement" means any such provision of services as is mentioned in sub-paragraph (1)(*a*);

"excluded services" means services provided wholly in the client's home;

"managed service company" means a company which—

(*a*) is a managed service company within the meaning given by section 61B of ITEPA 2003, or

(*b*) would be such a company disregarding subsection (1)(*c*) of that section.][1]

Commentary—*Simon's Taxes* **E4.1001**.

Cross-references—See the Social Security Contributions (Intermediaries) Regulations, SI 2000/727 Part 2 (intermediaries: special rules where workers' services are provided to public authorities).

Amendments—[1] Paras 3ZA, 3ZB inserted by the Social Security (Contributions) (Amendment) (No 2) Regulations, SI 2016/352 regs 2, 5(1), (4) with effect from 6 April 2016.

[2] Sub-para (6)(*a*) substituted by the Social Security (Contributions) (Amendment No 3) Regulations, SI 2016/647 reg 2 with effect from 6 July 2016. Sub-para (6)(*a*) previously read as follows—

"(a) in section 50(1)(*b*) of that Act, disregard the words "that is not employment income", and,".

[3] Sub-paras (6A)–(6C) inserted by the Social Security (Contributions) (Amendment No 4) Regulations, SI 2016/1067 regs 2, 6 with effect from 28 November 2016.

[4] Sub-paras (6D)–(6F) inserted by the Social Security (Miscellaneous Amendments No 2) Regulations, SI 2017/373 reg 4(1), (2) with effect from 6 April 2017.

[Travel by unpaid directors of not-for-profit companies

3A—(1) A payment of, or contribution towards, the expenses of the earner's employment if or to the extent that payment or contribution is paid wholly and exclusively for the purposes of paying or reimbursing travel expenses in respect of which conditions A to C are met.

(2) Condition A is that—

(*a*) the earner is obliged to incur the expenses as holder of the employment, and

(*b*) the expenses are attributable to the earner's necessary attendance at any place in the performance of the duties of the employment.

(3) Condition B is that the employment is employment as a director of a not-for-profit company.

(4) Condition C is that the employment is one from which the earner receives no earnings other than sums—

(*a*) paid to the earner in respect of expenses, and

(*b*) which are so paid by reason of the employment.

(5) In this paragraph—

(*a*) "director" has the same meaning as in the benefits code (see section 67 of ITEPA 2003), and

(*b*) "not-for-profit company" means a company that does not carry on activities for the purpose of making profits for distribution to its members or others.][1]

Amendments—[1] Paras 3A–3C inserted by the Social Security (Contributions) (Amendment) Regulations, SI 2014/608 regs 2, 4. These amendments come into force on 6 April 2014 and have effect in relation to expenses incurred on or after 6th April 2014.

[Travel where directorship held as part of a trade or profession

3B A payment of, or contribution towards, the expenses of the earner's employment to the extent that those expenses are travel expenses which are exempt from income tax in accordance with section 241B of ITEPA 2003 (travel where directorship held as part of a trade or profession).][1]

Amendments—[1] Paras 3A–3C inserted by the Social Security (Contributions) (Amendment) Regulations, SI 2014/608 regs 2, 4. These amendments come into force on 6 April 2014 and have effect in relation to expenses incurred on or after 6th April 2014.

[Travel between linked employments

3C A payment of, or contribution towards, the expenses of the earner's employment to the extent that those expenses are travel expenses deductible for income tax purposes in accordance with section 340A of ITEPA 2003 (travel between linked employments).

[This paragraph is subject to paragraph 1A.][2]][1]

Amendments—[1] Paras 3A–3C inserted by the Social Security (Contributions) (Amendment) Regulations, SI 2014/608 regs 2, 4. These amendments come into force on 6 April 2014 and have effect in relation to expenses incurred on or after 6th April 2014.

[2] Words inserted by the Social Security (Contributions) (Amendment) (No 2) Regulations, SI 2016/352 regs 2, 5(1), (5) with effect from 6 April 2016.

[Travel at start or finish of overseas employment

4 A payment of, or a contribution towards, the expenses of the earner's employment to the extent that those expenses—

(*a*) are deductible for income tax purposes in accordance with section 341 of ITEPA 2003 (travel at start or finish of overseas employment); or

(*b*) would be so deductible if—

(i) Conditions B and C were omitted from that section; and

(ii) the earnings of the employment were subject to income tax as employment income under that Act.

[This paragraph is subject to paragraph 1A.][2]][1]

Amendments—[1] Paras 4–5 substituted for paras 4, 5 by the Social Security (Contributions, Categorisation of Earners and Intermediaries) (Amendment) Regulations, SI 2004/770 regs 2, 28(1), (6)(*c*) with effect from 6 April 2004.

[2] Words inserted by the Social Security (Contributions) (Amendment) (No 2) Regulations, SI 2016/352 regs 2, 5(1), (5) with effect from 6 April 2016.

[Travel between employments where duties performed abroad

4A A payment of, or a contribution towards, the expenses of the earner's employment to the extent that those expenses—

(*a*) are deductible for income tax purposes in accordance with section 342 of ITEPA 2003 (travel between employments where duties performed abroad), or

(*b*) would be so deductible if—

(i) Conditions E and F were omitted from that section; and

(ii) the earnings of the employment were subject to income tax as employment income under that Act.

[This paragraph is subject to paragraph 1A.][2]][1]

Amendments—[1] Paras 4–5 substituted for paras 4, 5 by the Social Security (Contributions, Categorisation of Earners and Intermediaries) (Amendment) Regulations, SI 2004/770 regs 2, 28(1), (6)(*c*) with effect from 6 April 2004.

[2] Words inserted by the Social Security (Contributions) (Amendment) (No 2) Regulations, SI 2016/352 regs 2, 5(1), (5) with effect from 6 April 2016.

[Travel costs and expenses where duties performed abroad: earner's travel

4B—(1) So much of an employed earner's earnings as equals the amount in sub-paragraph (2).

(2) The amount in this sub-paragraph is—

(*a*) the included amount within the meaning of section 370 of ITEPA 2003 (travel costs and expenses where duties performed abroad: employee's travel); or

(*b*) the amount which would be the included amount within the meaning of that section if the earner were resident and ordinarily resident in the United Kingdom.

[This paragraph is subject to paragraph 1A.][2]][1]

Amendments—[1] Paras 4–5 substituted for paras 4, 5 by the Social Security (Contributions, Categorisation of Earners and Intermediaries) (Amendment) Regulations, SI 2004/770 regs 2, 28(1), (6)(*c*) with effect from 6 April 2004.

[2] Words inserted by the Social Security (Contributions) (Amendment) (No 2) Regulations, SI 2016/352 regs 2, 5(1), (5) with effect from 6 April 2016.

[Travel costs and expenses where duties performed abroad: visiting spouse's[, civil partner's] or child's travel

4C—(1) So much of an employed earner's earnings as equals the amount in sub-paragraph (2).

(2) The amount in this sub-paragraph is—

(*a*) the included amount within the meaning of section 371 of ITEPA 2003 (travel costs and expenses where duties performed abroad: visiting spouse's[, civil partner's][2] or child's travel); or

(*b*) the amount which would be the included amount within the meaning of that section if the earner were resident and ordinarily resident in the United Kingdom.

[This paragraph is subject to paragraph 1A.][3]][1]

Amendments—[1] Paras 4–5 substituted for paras 4, 5 by the Social Security (Contributions, Categorisation of Earners and Intermediaries) (Amendment) Regulations, SI 2004/770 regs 2, 28(1), (6)(*c*) with effect from 6 April 2004.

[2] Words in cross-heading and para (2) inserted by the Social Security (Contributions) (Amendment No 6) Regulations, SI 2005/3130 regs 2, 5(1), (2) with effect from 5 December 2005.

[3] Words inserted by the Social Security (Contributions) (Amendment) (No 2) Regulations, SI 2016/352 regs 2, 5(1), (5) with effect from 6 April 2016.

[Foreign accommodation and subsistence costs and expenses (overseas employments)

4D So much of an employed earner's earnings as equals the amount of the deduction—

(*a*) permitted for income tax purposes under section 376 of ITEPA 2003 (foreign accommodation and subsistence costs and expenses (overseas employments)); or

(*b*) which would be so permitted if the earnings of the employment were subject to tax as employment income under ITEPA 2003.

[This paragraph is subject to paragraph 1A.][2]][1]

Amendments—[1] Paras 4–5 substituted for paras 4, 5 by the Social Security (Contributions, Categorisation of Earners and Intermediaries) (Amendment) Regulations, SI 2004/770 regs 2, 28(1), (6)(*c*) with effect from 6 April 2004.

[2] Words inserted by the Social Security (Contributions) (Amendment) (No 2) Regulations, SI 2016/352 regs 2, 5(1), (5) with effect from 6 April 2016.

[[Travel costs and expenses of non-domiciled employee or the employee's spouse, civil partner or child where duties performed in the United Kingdom]

5 So much of an employed earner's earnings as equals the aggregate amount of the deductions—

(*a*) permitted for income tax purposes under sections 373 and 374 of ITEPA 2003 (travel costs and expenses of a non-domiciled employee or the employee's spouse[, civil partner][2] or child where duties are performed in the United Kingdom); or

(*b*) which would be so permitted if the earnings of the employment were subject to tax as employment income under ITEPA 2003.

[This paragraph is subject to paragraph 1A.][3]][1]

Amendments—[1] Paras 4–5 substituted for paras 4, 5 by the Social Security (Contributions, Categorisation of Earners and Intermediaries) (Amendment) Regulations, SI 2004/770 regs 2, 28(1), (6)(*c*) with effect from 6 April 2004.

[2] Heading substituted, and words in para (*a*) inserted, by the Social Security (Contributions) (Amendment No 6) Regulations, SI 2005/3130 regs 2, 5(1), (3), (4) with effect from 5 December 2005.

[3] Words inserted by the Social Security (Contributions) (Amendment) (No 2) Regulations, SI 2016/352 regs 2, 5(1), (5) with effect from 6 April 2016.

Travelling expenses of workers on offshore gas and oil rigs

6 A payment of, or a contribution towards, expenses where that payment or contribution is disregarded for the purposes of calculating [general earnings under section 305 of ITEPA 2003 (offshore oil and gas workers: mainland transfers).][1]

Amendments—[1] Words substituted by the Social Security (Contributions, Categorisation of Earners and Intermediaries) (Amendment) Regulations, SI 2004/770 regs 2, 28(1), (6)(*d*) with effect from 6 April 2004.

[Payments connected with cars and vans and exempt heavy goods vehicles provided for private use]

7 A payment—

(*a*) by way of the discharge of any liability which by virtue of [section 239(1) of ITEPA 2003 (payments and benefits connected with taxable cars and vans and exempt heavy goods vehicles)][1]; or

(*b*) of expenses, which by virtue of [section 239(2)][1] of that Act;

is not treated as [general earnings][1] of the employment chargeable to income tax . . . [1].

Amendments—[1] Heading and words substituted, and words revoked, by the Social Security (Contributions, Categorisation of Earners and Intermediaries) (Amendment) Regulations, SI 2004/770 regs 2, 28(1), (6)(*e*) with effect from 6 April 2004.

[Qualifying amounts of relevant motoring expenditure

7A To the extent that it would otherwise be earnings, the qualifying amount calculated in accordance with regulation 22A(4).][1]

Amendments—[1] Paragraphs 7A–7D inserted by the Social Security (Contributions) (Amendment No 2) Regulations, SI 2002/307 regs 2, 7 with effect from 6 April 2002.

[Qualifying amounts of mileage allowance payment in respect of cycles

7B—(1) To the extent that it would otherwise be earnings, the qualifying amount of a mileage allowance payment in respect of a cycle.

(2) The qualifying amount is that which would be produced by the formula in regulation 22A(4) if the value for R were the rate for the time being approved under [section 230(2) of ITEPA 2003][2] in respect of a cycle.

(3) In this paragraph—

"cycle" has the meaning given in section 192(1) of the Road Traffic Act 1988; and

NIC

"mileage allowance payment" has the meaning given in [section 229(2) of ITEPA 2003][2]][1]

Amendments—[1] Paragraphs 7A–7D inserted by the Social Security (Contributions) (Amendment No 2) Regulations, SI 2002/307 regs 2, 7 with effect from 6 April 2002.

[2] Words in paras (2), (3) substituted by the Social Security (Contributions, Categorisation of Earners and Intermediaries) (Amendment) Regulations, SI 2004/770 regs 2, 28(1), (6)(*f*) with effect from 6 April 2004.

[Qualifying amounts of passenger payment

7C—(1) To the extent that it would otherwise be earnings, the qualifying amount of a passenger payment.

(2) The qualifying amount is that which would be produced by the formula in regulation 22A(4) if—

(*a*) references to business travel were to business travel for which the employee [receives passenger payments within the meaning of section 233(3) of ITEPA 2003; and][2]

(*b*) the value for R were the rate for the time being approved for a passenger payment under [section 234 of ITEPA 2003][2].

(3) In this paragraph—

"passenger payment" has the meaning given in [section 233(3) of ITEPA 2003][2]; and

. . . [2]][1]

Amendments—[1] Paragraphs 7A–7D inserted by the Social Security (Contributions) (Amendment No 2) Regulations, SI 2002/307 regs 2, 7 with effect from 6 April 2002.

[2] Words in sub-para (2) substituted, in sub-para (3), words in definition of "passenger payment" substituted, and definition of "qualifying passenger" revoked, by the Social Security (Contributions, Categorisation of Earners and Intermediaries) (Amendment) Regulations, SI 2004/770 regs 2, 28(1), (6)(*g*) with effect from 6 April 2004.

[Car fuel

7D A payment by way of the provision of car fuel which is chargeable to income tax under section 149 of ITEPA 2003.][1]

Amendments—[1] This paragraph (which was inserted by SI 2002/307 regs 2, 7) substituted by the Social Security (Contributions, Categorisation of Earners and Intermediaries) (Amendment) Regulations, SI 2004/770 regs 2, 28(1), (6)(*h*) with effect from 6 April 2004.

[Van fuel

7E A payment by way of the provision of van fuel which is chargeable to income tax under section 160 of ITEPA 2003.][1]

Amendments—[1] Para 7E inserted, by the Social Security (Contributions) (Amendment No 2) Regulations, SI 2008/607 regs 2, 4(1), (3)(*a*) with effect from 6 April 2008.

Car parking facilities

8 A payment of, or a contribution towards, the provision of car parking facilities at or near the earner's place of employment which, by virtue of [section 237 of ITEPA 2003][1], is not regarded as [general earnings][1] of the earner's employment.

Amendments—[1] Words substituted by the Social Security (Contributions, Categorisation of Earners and Intermediaries) (Amendment) Regulations, SI 2004/770 regs 2, 28(1), (6)(*i*) with effect from 6 April 2004.

[Amounts exempted from income tax under section 289A of ITEPA 2003

8A Any amount which is exempted from income tax under section 289A of ITEPA 2003.][1]

Amendments—[1] Para 8A inserted by the Social Security (Contributions) (Amendment) (No 2) Regulations, SI 2016/352 regs 2, 5(1), (6) with effect from 6 April 2016.

Specific and distinct payments of, or towards, expenses actually incurred

9[—(1)] [1] For the avoidance of doubt, [there][2] shall be disregarded any specific and distinct payment of, or contribution towards, expenses which an employed earner actually incurs in carrying out his employment.

[This is subject to the following [qualifications][2].][1]

[(2) Sub-paragraph (1) does not authorise the disregard of any amount by way of relevant motoring expenditure, within the meaning of paragraph (3) of regulation 22A, in excess of that permitted by the formula in paragraph (4) of that regulation.][1]

[(3) Sub-paragraph (1) does not authorise the disregard of any amount which—

(*a*) falls within paragraphs (12) or (13) of regulation 22; or

(*b*) is paid to an employed earner in respect of anticipated expenses that have yet to be incurred (whether or not such expenses are actually incurred after the payment is made).][2]

Amendments—[1] Sub-para (1) numbered as such, and para (2) added, by the Social Security (Contributions) (Amendment No 2) Regulations, SI 2002/307 regs 2, 7 with effect from 6 April 2002.

[2] Words in sub-para (1) substituted, and sub-para (3) inserted, by the Social Security (Contributions) (Amendment) (No 2) Regulations, SI 2016/352 regs 2, 5(1), (7) with effect from 6 April 2016.

[Council tax or water or sewerage charges] on accommodation provided for employee's use

10 A payment of, or a contribution towards meeting a person's liability for [council tax or water or sewerage charges][1] in respect of accommodation occupied by him and provided for him by reason of his employment if by virtue of [sections 99 or 100 of ITEPA 2003 (accommodation provided for performance of duties or as a result of a security threat)][1], [he is not liable to income tax[1]] . . . [1] in respect of the provision of that accommodation.

This paragraph does not extend to Northern Ireland.

Amendments—[1] Words substituted by the Social Security (Contributions, Categorisation of Earners and Intermediaries) (Amendment) Regulations, SI 2004/770 regs 2, 28(1), (6)(*j*), (*k*) with effect from 6 April 2004.

[Rates or water or sewerage charges] on accommodation provided for employee's use

11 A payment of, or a contribution towards meeting, a person's liability for [rates or water or sewerage charges][1] in respect of accommodation occupied by him and provided for him by reason of his employment if by virtue of [sections 99 or 100 of ITEPA 2003 (accommodation provided for performance of duties or as a result of a security threat)][1], he is not liable to income tax . . . [1] in respect of the provision of that accommodation.

This paragraph extends only to Northern Ireland.

Amendments—[1] Words substituted by the Social Security (Contributions, Categorisation of Earners and Intermediaries) (Amendment) Regulations, SI 2004/770 regs 2, 28(1), (6)(*k*), (*l*) with effect from 6 April 2004.

Foreign service allowance

12 A payment by way of an allowance which is not regarded as income for any income tax purpose by virtue of [section 299 of ITEPA 2003 (Crown employees' foreign service allowance)][1].

Amendments—[1] Words substituted by the Social Security (Contributions, Categorisation of Earners and Intermediaries) (Amendment) Regulations, SI 2004/770 regs 2, 28(1), (6)(*m*) with effect from 6 April 2004.

[HM Forces' Operational Allowance

12A—(1) A payment of the Operational Allowance to members of the armed forces of the Crown.

(2) The Operational Allowance is an allowance designated as such under a Royal Warrant made under section 333 of the Armed Forces Act 2006]

][1]

Amendments—[1] Para 12A substituted by the Social Security (Contributions) (Amendment No 2) Regulations, SI 2012/817 regs 2, 9(*a*) with effect from 6 April 2012.

[HM Forces' Council Tax Relief

12B—(1) A payment of Council Tax Relief to members of the armed forces of the Crown.

(2) Council Tax Relief is a payment designated as such under a Royal Warrant made under section 333 of the Armed Forces Act 2006.][1]

Amendments—[1] Para 12B substituted by the Social Security (Contributions) (Amendment No 2) Regulations, SI 2012/817 regs 2, 9(*b*) with effect from 6 April 2012.

[HM Forces' Continuity of Education Allowance

12C—(1) A payment of the Continuity of Education Allowance to or in respect of members of the armed forces of the Crown.

(2) The Continuity of Education Allowance is an allowance designated as such under a Royal Warrant made under section 333 of the Armed Forces Act 2006.][1]

Amendments—[1] Para 12C inserted by the Social Security (Contributions) (Amendment No 2) Regulations, SI 2012/817 regs 2, 9(*c*) with effect from 6 April 2012.

Commonwealth War Graves Commission and British Council: extra cost of living allowance

13 A payment by way of an allowance to a person in the service of the Commonwealth War Graves Commission or the British Council paid with a view to compensating him for the extra cost of living outside the United Kingdom in order to perform the duties of his employment.

Overseas medical treatment

14 A payment of, or a contribution towards, expenses incurred in—

(*a*) providing an employee with medical treatment outside the United Kingdom (including providing for him to be an in-patient) in a case where the need for the treatment arises while the employee is outside the United Kingdom for the purposes of performing the duties of his employment; or

(*b*) providing insurance for the employee against the cost of such treatment in a case falling within sub-paragraph (*a*).

Here "medical treatment" includes all forms of treatment for, and all procedures for diagnosing, any physical or mental ailment, infirmity or defect.

[Recommended medical treatment

14A A payment or reimbursement to which no liability to income tax arises by virtue of section 320C of ITEPA 2003 (recommended medical treatment).][1]

Amendments—[1] Paragraph 14A inserted by the Social Security (Contributions) (Amendment No 6) Regulations, SI 2014/3228 regs 2, 4 with effect from 1 January 2015.

[Experts Seconded to European Commission

15 A payment in respect of daily subsistence allowances paid by the European Commission to persons whose services are made available to the Commission by their employers under the detached national experts scheme which is exempt from income tax by virtue of section 304 of ITEPA 2003 (experts seconded to European Commission).][1]

Amendments—[1] This paragraph inserted by the Social Security (Contributions, Categorisation of Earners and Intermediaries) (Amendment) Regulations, SI 2004/770 regs 2, 28(1), (6)(*n*) with effect from 6 April 2004.

[Experts seconded to a body of the European Union

15A A payment in respect of subsistence allowances paid—

(*a*) by a body of the European Union that is located in the United Kingdom and listed in the table below;

(*b*) to persons who, because of their expertise in matters relating to the subject matter of the functions of the body, are seconded to the body by their employers.

Bodies of the European Union located in the United Kingdom
The European Medicines Agency
The European Police College
The European Banking Authority][1]

Amendments—[1] Para 15A inserted by the Social Security (Contributions) (Amendment No 3) Regulations, SI 2011/797 regs 2, 7 with effect from 6 April 2011.

[Expenses of MPs and other representatives

16 A payment to which no liability to income tax arises by virtue of any of the following provisions of ITEPA 2003—

(*a*) section 292 (accommodation expenses of MPs);

(*b*) section 293 (overnight expenses of other elected representatives);

(*c*) section 293A (UK travel and subsistence expenses of MPs);

(*ca*) section 293B (UK travel expenses of other elected representatives);][2]

(*d*) section 294 (European travel expenses of MPs and other representatives).][1]

Amendments—[1] This para inserted by the Social Security (Contributions) (Amendment) Regulations, SI 2011/225 regs 2, 3 with effect from 28 February 2011.

[2] Para (*ca*) inserted by the Social Security (Contributions) (Amendment No 3) Regulations, SI 2013/1907 regs 2, 4(*a*) with effect from 1 September 2013.

[Travel expenses of members of local authorities etc

17 A payment to which no liability to income tax arises by virtue of section 295A of ITEPA 2003 (travel expenses of members of local authorities etc).][1]

Amendments—[1] Para 17 inserted by the Social Security (Contributions) (Amendment) (No 2) Regulations, SI 2016/352 regs 2, 5(1), (8) with effect from 6 April 2016.

PART IX
[INCENTIVES BY WAY OF SECURITIES][1]

Amendments—[1] Heading substituted by the Social Security (Contributions) (Amendment No 5) Regulations, SI 2003/2085 regs 3, 8, 12(1), (2) with effect from 1 September 2003.

[Certain payments by way of securities, restricted securities and restricted interests in securities, and gains arising from them, disregarded

1 Payments by way of securities, restricted securities and restricted interests in securities, and gains arising from them, are disregarded in the calculation of an employed earner's earnings to the extent mentioned in this Part.][1]

Amendments—[1] Substituted by the Social Security (Contributions) (Amendment No 5) Regulations, SI 2003/2085 regs 3, 8, 12(1), (3) with effect from 1 September 2003.

Shares in secondary contributor or associated body

2 . . .

Amendment—Revoked by the Social Security (Contributions) (Amendment No 5) Regulations, SI 2003/2085 regs 3, 8, 12(1), (4) with effect from 1 September 2003.

[Rights to acquire securities

3 A payment by way of a right to acquire securities.][1]

Amendments—[1] Substituted by the Social Security (Contributions) (Amendment No 5) Regulations, SI 2003/2085 regs 3, 8, 12(1), (5) with effect from 1 September 2003.

"Short" share options granted on or after 6th April 1999

3A . . .

Amendment—Revoked by the Social Security (Contributions) (Amendment No 5) Regulations, SI 2003/2085 regs 3, 8, 12(1), (6) with effect from 1 September 2003.

Enterprise management incentives

4 . . .

Amendment—Revoked by the Social Security (Contributions) (Amendment No 5) Regulations, SI 2003/2085 regs 3, 8, 12(1), (6) with effect from 1 September 2003.

[Priority share allocations

5 A payment by way of an allocation of shares in priority to members of the public in respect of which no liability to income tax arises by virtue of section 542 of ITEPA 2003.][1]

Amendments—[1] Substituted by the Social Security (Contributions) (Amendment No 5) Regulations, SI 2003/2085 regs 3, 8, 12(1), (7) with effect from 1 September 2003.

Partnership share agreements

6 A payment that is deducted from the earnings of the employment under a partnership share agreement.

Here "partnership share agreement" has the meaning given in [paragraph 44 of Schedule 2 to ITEPA 2003.][1]

Amendments—[1] Words substituted by the Social Security (Contributions) (Amendment No 5) Regulations, SI 2003/2085 regs 3, 8, 12(1), (8) with effect from 1 September 2003.

[Shares under share incentive plans

7 A payment by way of an award of shares under a share incentive plan within the meaning of Schedule 2 to ITEPA 2003.][1]

Amendments—[1] Substituted, together with paragraph 7A below, for the original paragraph 7, by the Social Security (Contributions) (Amendment No 5) Regulations, SI 2003/2085 regs 3, 8, 12(1), (9) with effect from 1 September 2003.

[Securities and interests in securities which are not readily convertible assets

7A A payment by way of the acquisition of securities, interests in securities or securities options in connection with employed earner's employment if, or to the extent that, what is acquired is not a readily convertible asset.

Here "acquisition" includes acquisition pursuant to an employment-related securities option within the meaning of section 471(5) of ITEPA 2003 as substituted by the Finance Act 2003.][1]

Amendments—[1] Substituted, together with paragraph 7 above, for the original paragraph 7 by the Social Security (Contributions) (Amendment No 5) Regulations, SI 2003/2085 regs 3, 8, 12(1), (9) with effect from 1 September 2003.

Shares under approved profit sharing schemes

8 . . .

Amendment—Revoked by the Social Security (Contributions) (Amendment No 5) Regulations, SI 2003/2085 regs 3, 8, 12(1), (10) with effect from 1 September 2003.

[Restricted securities and restricted interests in securities

9—(1) A payment by way of the acquisition of restricted securities, or a restricted interest in securities, where those securities are, or that interest is, employment-related, if no charge to income tax arises under section 425 of ITEPA 2003 other than by virtue of subsection (2) of that section.

This is subject to the following qualification.

(2) This paragraph does not apply if an election has been made as mentioned in subsection (3) of section 425 of ITEPA 2003.

(3) References in this paragraph to section 425 of ITEPA 2003 are to that section as substituted by paragraph 3(1) of Schedule 22 to the Finance Act 2003.][1]

Amendments—[1] Substituted by the Social Security (Contributions) (Amendment No 5) Regulations, SI 2003/2085 regs 3, 8, 12(1), (11) with effect from 1 September 2003.

Conditional interest in shares: gains from exercise etc of share options

10 . . .

Amendment—Revoked by the Social Security (Contributions) (Amendment No 5) Regulations, SI 2003/2085 regs 3, 8, 12(1), (12) with effect from 1 September 2003.

Convertible shares

11 . . .

Amendment—Revoked by the Social Security (Contributions) (Amendment No 5) Regulations, SI 2003/2085 regs 3, 8, 12(1), (12) with effect from 1 September 2003.

Convertible shares: gains from the exercise etc of share options

12 . . .

Amendment—Revoked by the Social Security (Contributions) (Amendment No 5) Regulations, SI 2003/2085 regs 3, 8, 12(1), (12) with effect from 1 September 2003.

Share option gains by directors and employees

13 . . .

Amendment—Revoked by the Social Security (Contributions) (Amendment No 5) Regulations, SI 2003/2085 regs 3, 8, 12(1), (12) with effect from 1 September 2003.

Shares acquired under options granted before 9th April 1998

14 . . .

Amendment—Revoked by the Social Security (Contributions) (Amendment No 5) Regulations, SI 2003/2085 regs 3, 8, 12(1), (12) with effect from 1 September 2003.

Assignment or release of option

15 . . .

Amendment—Revoked by the Social Security (Contributions) (Amendment No 5) Regulations, SI 2003/2085 regs 3, 8, 12(1), (12) with effect from 1 September 2003.

[Exercise of options acquired before 6th April 1999

16—(1) A gain realised by the exercise (in whole or in part) of a right, obtained before 6th April 1999, to acquire shares in a body corporate unless paragraph 17 applies, but only to the extent that the gain realised consists of the shares acquired.

(2) In this paragraph and paragraphs 16A and 17—

"shares" includes stock; and

"body corporate" includes—

(*a*) a body corporate constituted under the law of a country or territory outside the United Kingdom; and

(*b*) an unincorporated association wherever constituted.][1]

Amendments—[1] Substituted, together with paragraph 16A for paragraph 16, by the Social Security (Contributions) (Amendment No 5) Regulations, SI 2003/2085 regs 3, 8, 12(1), (13) with effect from 1 September 2003.

[Exercise of replacement share options where original option acquired before 6th April 1999

16A—(1) A gain realised by the exercise of a replacement right to acquire shares in a body corporate where the original right was obtained before 6th April 1999 provided that—

(*a*) sub-paragraph (4) is satisfied, and

(*b*) paragraph 17 does not apply,

The disregard conferred by this paragraph is subject to the following limitation.

(2) Only the value of the shares acquired by the exercise of the replacement right shall be disregarded.

(3) In this paragraph and paragraph 17—

"the original right" means the right, acquired before 6th April 1999, to acquire shares in a body corporate; and

"replacement right" means a right to acquire shares, obtained, whether as the result of one transaction or a series of transactions, and whether directly or indirectly, in consequence of—

(*a*) the assignment or release of the original right; or

(*b*) the assignment or release of a right which was itself obtained in consequence of the assignment or release of that right.

(4) This sub-paragraph is satisfied in respect of a transaction through which the replacement right was obtained if **A** is not substantially greater than **R**.

Here—

A is the market value of the shares which may be obtained by the exercise of the right acquired on that occasion, less any consideration which would have to be given on that occasion by or on behalf of the earner if that right were to be exercised immediately after its acquisition (disregarding any restriction on its exercise); and

R is the market value of the shares subject to the right assigned or released on that occasion, immediately before that occasion, less any consideration which would have been required to be given by or on behalf of the earner for the exercise of that right, disregarding any restriction on its exercise, subject to the following qualification.

If a transaction involves only a partial replacement of an earlier right, the amount of the earlier consideration to be deducted in computing R shall be proportionately reduced.][1]

Amendments—[1] Substituted, together with paragraph 16 for paragraph 16, by the Social Security (Contributions) (Amendment No 5) Regulations, SI 2003/2085 regs 3, 8, 12(1), (13) with effect from 1 September 2003.

[Payments resulting from exercise, assignment or release of options which are not disregarded by virtue of paragraph 16

17—(1) This paragraph applies to a payment—

(*a*) made on or after 10th April 2003, and

(*b*) which would otherwise fall to be disregarded by virtue of paragraph 16 [or 16A][2] of this Part, where the market value of the shares has been increased by more than 10% by things done, on or after 6th April 1999, otherwise than for genuine commercial purposes.

(2) For the purposes of sub-paragraph (1) "the shares" includes—

(*a*) the shares subject to the right currently being exercised; and

(*b*) where the right to acquire shares held on 6th April 1999 has been replaced by a [replacement right][2], includes the shares subject to [a replacement right.][2]

(3) The following are among the things that are, for the purposes of this paragraph, done otherwise than for genuine commercial purposes—

(*a*) anything done as part of a scheme or arrangement the main purpose, or one of the main purposes, of which is the avoidance of tax or of contributions under the Act; and

(*b*) any transaction between companies which, at the time of the transaction, are members of the same group on terms which are not such as might be expected to be agreed between persons acting at arm's length.

(4) But sub-paragraph (3)(*b*) does not apply to a payment for group relief within the meaning given in section 402(6) of the Taxes Act.

(5) In sub-paragraph (3)(*b*) "group" means a body corporate and its 51% subsidiaries (within the meaning of section 838 of the Taxes Act), and other expressions used in this paragraph which are defined in, or for the purposes of, paragraph 16 have the same meaning here as they have in that paragraph.][1]

Amendments—[1] Para 17 inserted by the Social Security (Contributions) (Amendment No 3) Regulations, SI 2003/1059 regs 2, 4(1), (3) with effect from 10 April 2003.

[2] Reference in sub-para (1)(*b*) inserted, and words in sub-para (2)(*b*) substituted, by the Social Security (Contributions) (Amendment No 5) Regulations, SI 2003/2085 regs 3, 8, 12(1), (14) with effect from 1 September 2003.

[Payments made to internationally mobile employees

18—(1) So much of any payment as equals the amount in sub-paragraph (3).

(2) For the purposes of calculating the amount in sub-paragraph (3) treat amounts which count as employment income under Chapters 2 to 5 of Part 7 of ITEPA 2003 as having been paid in equal instalments on each day of the "relevant period" as determined in accordance with section 41G of ITEPA 2003.

(3) The amount in this sub-paragraph is calculated by adding together every instalment which would satisfy the condition in sub-paragraph (4), (5) or (6) on the day on which the instalment is treated as having been paid.

(4) The condition in this sub-paragraph is that the instalment does not give rise to a liability to pay earnings-related contributions because the employed earner does not fulfil the prescribed conditions as to residence or presence in Great Britain or Northern Ireland (as the case requires) set out in paragraph (1) of regulation 145 or because the proviso in paragraph (2) of that regulation applies.

(5) The condition in this sub-paragraph is that the instalment does not give rise to a liability to pay earnings-related contributions because the employed earner is determined in accordance with Title II of Regulation No (EC) 883/2004 and Title II of Regulation No (EC) 987/2009 to be subject only to the legislation of another EEA State or Switzerland.

(6) The condition in this sub-paragraph is that the instalment does not give rise to a liability to pay earnings-related contributions because the employed earner is determined to be subject only to the legislation of a country outside the United Kingdom pursuant to an Order in Council having effect under section 179 of the Administration Act.][1]

Amendments—[1] Para 18 inserted by the Social Security (Miscellaneous Amendments No 2) Regulations, SI 2015/478 regs 2, 21(1), (3) with effect from 6 April 2015.

PART X
MISCELLANEOUS AND SUPPLEMENTAL

Press releases etc—HMRC Notice, 5 January 2012: National Insurance Contributions on disguised remuneration—Frequently Asked Questions (*SWTI 2012, Issue 2*).

Other miscellaneous payments to be disregarded

1—(1) The payments listed in [this Part][1] are disregarded in the calculation of earnings.

(2) Paragraph 4 contains additional rules about the way in which the components of a payment by way of expenses incidental to a qualifying absence from home are to be treated for the purpose of earnings-related contributions if the permitted maximum is exceeded.

Amendments—[1] In sub-para (1), words substituted by the Social Security (Contributions) (Amendment) Regulations, SI 2011/225 regs 2, 4(*a*) with effect from 28 February 2011.

Payments on account of sums already included in the computation of earnings

2 A payment on account of a person's earnings in respect of his employment as an employed earner which comprises, or represents and does not exceed sums which have previously been included in his earnings for the purpose of his assessment of earnings-related contributions.

[Payments connected to amounts within regulation 22B

2A—(1) A payment ("A") the subject of which represents, or arises or derives (whether wholly or partly or directly or indirectly) from, an amount ("B") treated as remuneration under regulation 22B which has previously been included in an employed earner's earnings for the purposes of assessing earnings-related contributions.

(2) Paragraph (1) does not apply to the extent that A exceeds B.

(3) For the purposes of determining whether paragraph (1) applies, A is to be treated as including the value of any payment made before A which represents, or arises or derives (whether wholly or partly or directly or indirectly) from, B.][1]

Press releases etc—HMRC Notice, 5 January 2012: National Insurance Contributions on disguised remuneration—Frequently Asked Questions.

HMRC Notice, 5 September 2012: Employee Benefit Trusts—update on "settlement opportunity" and FAQs (see *SWTI 2012, Issue 36*).

Amendments—[1] Para 2A inserted by the Social Security (Contributions) (Amendment No 5) Regulations, SI 2011/2700 regs 2, 7 with effect from 6 December 2011.

Payments discharging liability for secondary Class 1 contributions following election under paragraph 3B of Schedule 1 to the Contributions and Benefits Act

3 A payment by way of the discharge of any liability for secondary Class 1 contributions which has been transferred from the secondary contributor to the employed earner by election made jointly by them for the purposes of paragraph 3B(1) of Schedule 1 to the Contributions and Benefits Act (elections about contribution liability in respect of [relevant employment income][1]).

Amendments—[1] Words substitutedby the Social Security (Contributions) (Amendment No 4) Regulations, SI 2004/2096 regs 2, 6 with effect from 1 September 2004. SI 2004/2096 has effect in relation to—

(a) agreements entered into after 1 September 2004 which are in respect of post-commencement employment income, and

(b) elections made after that date.

Payments by way of incidental [overnight] expenses

4—[(1) A payment by way of incidental overnight expenses, in whatever form, which by virtue of section 240 of ITEPA 2003 are not general earnings liable to income tax under that Act.][1]

[(2) If a payment is made by way of incidental overnight expenses in connection with a qualifying period, but the amount of that payment (calculated in accordance with section 241 of ITEPA 2003) exceeds the permitted amount, sub-paragraphs (3) to (6) apply.][1]

(3) So much of the payment as is made by way of cash shall be included in the calculation of earnings.

(4) The amount of cash for which a cash voucher can be exchanged shall be included in the calculation of earnings.

(5) The cost of provision of any non-cash voucher shall be included in the calculation of earnings and anything for which the voucher can be exchanged shall be disregarded in that calculation.

(6) Any payment by way of a benefit in kind shall be disregarded in the calculation of earnings.

(7) In this paragraph—

"the cost of provision" in relation to a non-cash voucher is the cost incurred by the person at whose expense the voucher is provided;

"the permitted amount" has the meaning given in section 241(3) of ITEPA 2003; and

"qualifying period" has the meaning given in section 240(1)(*b*) and (4) of ITEPA 2003.][1]

Amendments—[1] Words in heading inserted, and sub-paras (1), (2), (7) substituted by the Social Security (Contributions, Categorisation of Earners and Intermediaries) (Amendment) Regulations, SI 2004/770 regs 2, 28(1), (7)(*a*) with effect from 6 April 2004.

Gratuities and offerings

5—(1) A payment of, or in respect of, a gratuity or offering [which—

(*a*) satisfies the condition in either sub-paragraph (2) or (3); and

(*b*) is not within sub-paragraph (4) or (5).][1]

(2) [The condition in this sub-paragraph][1] is that the payment—

(*a*) is not made, directly or indirectly, by the secondary contributor; and

(*b*) does not comprise or represent sums previously paid to the secondary contributor.

(3) [The condition in this sub-paragraph][1] is that the secondary contributor does not allocate the payment, directly or indirectly, to the earner.

[(4) A payment made to the earner by a person who is connected with the secondary contributor is within this sub-paragraph unless—

(*a*) it is—

(i) made in recognition for personal services rendered to the connected person by the earner or by another earner employed by the same secondary contributor; and

(ii) similar in amount to that which might reasonably be expected to be paid by a person who is not so connected; or

(*b*) the person making the payment does so in his capacity as a tronc-master.][1]

[(5) A payment made to the earner is within this sub-paragraph if it is made by a trustee holding property for any persons who include, or any class of persons which includes, the earner.

In this sub-paragraph "trustee" does not include a tronc-master.][1]

[(6) A person is connected with the secondary contributor for the purposes of this paragraph if his relationship with the secondary contributor, or where the employer and secondary contributor are different, with either of them, is as described in subsection (2), (3), (4), (5), (6) or (7) of section 839 of the Taxes Act (connected persons).][1]

Press releases etc—Tips, gratuities, service charges & troncs – the NICs position (April 2006, Tax Bulletin article). See also Booklet E24 on the HMRC website.

Amendments—[1] Words in sub-paras (1)–(3) substituted, and sub-paras (4)–(6) inserted, by the Social Security (Contributions) (Amendment) Regulations, SI 2004/173 with effect from 23 February 2004.

Redundancy payments

6 For the avoidance of doubt, in calculating the earnings paid to or for the benefit of an earner in respect of an employed earner's employment, any payment by way of a redundancy payment shall be disregarded.

NIC

Sickness payments attributable to contributions made by employed earner

7 If the funds for making a sickness payment under arrangements of the kind mentioned in section 4(1)(b) of the Contributions and Benefits Act are attributable in part to contributions to those funds made by the employed earner, for the purposes of section 4(1) of that Act the part of that payment which is attributable to those contributions shall be disregarded.

[Expenses and other payments not charged to income tax under miscellaneous exemptions

8 A payment which is not charged to tax under any of the following provisions of ITEPA 2003—

(*a*) section 245 (travelling and subsistence during public transport strikes);

(*b*) section 246 (transport between work and home for disabled employees: general);

(*c*) section 248 (transport home: late night working and failure of car-sharing arrangements);

(*d*) section 290A (accommodation outgoings of ministers of religion);

(*e*) section 290B (allowances paid to ministers of religion in respect of accommodation outgoings);

(*f*) section 321 (suggestion awards).][1]

Amendments—[1] This paragraph substituted by the Social Security (Contributions) (Amendment No 2) Regulations, SI 2010/188 reg 2 with effect from 6 April 2010.

VAT on the supply of goods and services by employed earner

9 If—

(*a*) goods or services are supplied by an earner in employed earner's employment;

(*b*) earnings paid to or for the benefit of the earner in respect of that employment include the remuneration for the supply of those goods or services; and

(*c*) value added tax is chargeable on that supply;

an amount equal to the value added tax chargeable on that supply shall be excluded from the calculation of those earnings.

[Employee's liabilities and indemnity insurance

10 A payment which by virtue of section 346 of ITEPA 2003 (deduction for employee liabilities) is deductible from the general earnings of the employment chargeable to tax under that Act. [This paragraph is subject to paragraph 1A of Part 8 of this Schedule.][2]][1]

Amendments—[1] This paragraph substituted by the Social Security (Contributions, Categorisation of Earners and Intermediaries) (Amendment) Regulations, SI 2004/770 regs 2, 28(1), (7)(*c*) with effect from 6 April 2004.

[2] Words inserted by the Social Security (Contributions) (Amendment) (No 2) Regulations, SI 2016/352 regs 2, 6(1), (2) with effect from 6 April 2016.

Fees and subscriptions to professional bodies, learned societies etc

11 A payment of, or a contribution towards any fee, contribution or annual subscription which, under [section 343 or 344 of ITEPA 2003 (deduction for professional membership fees or annual subscriptions) is deductible from the general earnings of any office or employment. [This paragraph is subject to paragraph 1A of Part 8 of this Schedule.][2]][1]

Amendments—[1] Words substituted by the Social Security (Contributions, Categorisation of Earners and Intermediaries) (Amendment) Regulations, SI 2004/770 regs 2, 28(1), (7)(*d*) with effect from 6 April 2004.

[2] Words inserted by the Social Security (Contributions) (Amendment) (No 2) Regulations, SI 2016/352 regs 2, 6(1), (3) with effect from 6 April 2016.

Holiday pay

12

Amendments—This para revoked by the Social Security (Contributions) (Amendment No 9) Regulations, SI 2007/2905 reg 2(1), (2) with effect from 30 October 2007: SI 2007/2905 reg 1(1).

This para continued to have effect until the fifth anniversary of 30 October 2007 in the case of holiday pay derived from an employed earner's employment if—

Payments to ministers of religion

13 A payment of a fee in respect of employment as a minister of religion which does not form part of the stipend or salary paid in respect of that employment.

[Payments to miners and former miners, etc in lieu of coal

14—(1) A payment in lieu of the provision of coal or smokeless fuel, if the employee is—

(*a*) a colliery worker;

(*b*) a former colliery worker;

and the condition in sub-paragraph (2) is met.

(2) The condition is that the amount of coal or fuel in respect of which the payment is made does not substantially exceed the amount reasonably required for personal use.

(3) That condition is assumed to be met unless the contrary is shown.

(4) In this paragraph, "colliery worker" means a coal miner or any other person employed at or about a colliery otherwise than in clerical, administrative or technical work; and "former colliery worker" shall be construed accordingly.

(5) This paragraph does not apply to Northern Ireland.][1]

Amendments—[1] This paragraph substituted by the Social Security (Contributions, Categorisation of Earners and Intermediaries) (Amendment) Regulations, SI 2004/770 regs 2, 28(1), (7)(*e*) with effect from 6 April 2004.

[Rewards for assistance with lost or stolen cards

15—(1) A payment made by an issuer of charge cards, cheque guarantee cards, credit cards or debit cards, as a reward to an individual who assists in identifying or recovering lost or stolen cards in the course of his or her employment as an employed earner (other than employment by the issuer), together with any income tax paid by the issuer for the purpose of discharging any liability of the individual to income tax on the payment.

(2) In this paragraph—

"charge card" means a credit card, the terms of which include the obligation to settle the account in full at the end of a specified period;

"cheque guarantee card" means a card issued by a bank or building society for the purpose of guaranteeing a payment or supporting the encashment of a cheque up to a specified value;

"credit card" means a card which—

(*a*) may be used on its own to pay for goods or services or to withdraw cash, and

(*b*) enables the holder to make purchases and to draw cash up to a prearranged limit; and

"debit card" means a card linked to a bank or building society current account, used to pay for goods or services by debiting the holder's account.][1]

Amendments—[1] Para 15 inserted by the Social Security (Contributions) (Amendment No 5) Regulations, SI 2001/2412 regs 2, 5(1), (4)(*b*) with effect from 26 July 2001.

[Student loans

16—(1) A payment made in accordance with Regulations made under section 186 of the Education Act 2002 in respect of the repayment, reduction or extinguishing of the amounts payable in respect of a loan.

(2) A payment for the purpose of discharging any liability of the earner to income tax for any tax year where the income tax in question is tax chargeable in respect of —

(*a*) the payment referred to in paragraph (1), or

(*b*) the payment made for the purpose of discharging the income tax liability itself.][1]

Amendments—[1] This paragraph inserted by the Social Security (Contributions) (Amendment No 4) Regulations, SI 2002/2924 regs 2, 4(*b*) with effect from 17 December 2002.

[Payment of PAYE tax in respect of notional payment

17 A payment by way of income tax for which the employer is required to account to the Board under section 710(1) of ITEPA 2003 (notional payments: accounting for tax).][1]

Amendments—[1] This paragraph inserted by the Social Security (Contributions) (Amendment No 5) Regulations, SI 2003/2085 regs 3, 8, 13(*b*) with effect from 1 September 2003.

[Payments made from the In-Work Emergency Discretion Fund

18 Any In-Work Emergency Discretion Fund payment made to a person pursuant to arrangements made by the Secretary of State under section 2 of the Employment and Training Act 1973.

This paragraph does not apply in Northern Ireland.][1]

Amendments—[1] Paras 18, 19 inserted by the Social Security (Contributions) (Amendment No 2) Regulations, SI 2008/607 regs 2, 4(1), (4)(*b*) with effect from 6 April 2008.

[Payments made from the In-Work Emergency Fund

19 Any In-Work Emergency Fund payment made to a person pursuant to arrangements made by the Department of Economic Development under section 1 of the Employment and Training Act (Northern Ireland) 1950.

This paragraph applies only in Northern Ireland.][1]

NIC

Amendments—[1] Paras 18, 19 inserted by the Social Security (Contributions) (Amendment No 2) Regulations, SI 2008/607 regs 2, 4(1), (4)(*b*) with effect from 6 April 2008.

[Up-Front Childcare Fund payments

20 Any Up-Front Childcare Fund payment made pursuant to arrangements made by the Secretary of State under section 2 of the Employment and Training Act 1973.

This paragraph does not apply to Northern Ireland.][1]

Amendments—[1] Regulation inserted by the Social Security (Contributions) (Amendment No 4) Regulations, SI 2008/1431 reg 2(1), (2)(*b*) with effect from 1 July 2008.

[Better off in Work Credit payments

21 Any Better off in Work Credit payment made pursuant to arrangements made by the Secretary of State under section 2 of the Employment and Training Act 1973.

This paragraph does not apply to Northern Ireland.][1]

Amendments—[1] Para 21 inserted by the Social Security (Contributions) (Amendment No 5) Regulations, SI 2008/2624 reg 2(1), (2)(*b*) with effect from 27 October 2008.

[Fees relating to the Protection of Vulnerable Groups (Scotland) Scheme

22 A payment of a fee in respect of an application to join the scheme administered under section 44 of the Protection of Vulnerable Groups (Scotland) Act 2007 (scheme to collate and disclose information about individuals working with vulnerable persons).][1]

Amendments—[1] This para inserted by the Social Security (Contributions) (Amendment) Regulations, SI 2011/225 regs 2, 4(*b*)with effect from 28 February 2011.

[Fees relating to the Disclosure and Barring Service

23—(1) A fee paid by virtue of section 116A(4)(b) or (5)(b) of the Police Act 1997 ("the Police Act") (fee for up-dating certificates).

(2) A fee paid under—

(*a*) section 113A(1)(b) of the Police Act (fee for criminal record certificates);

(*b*) section 113B(1)(b) of the Police Act (fee for enhanced criminal record certificates);

(*c*) section 114(1)(b) of the Police Act (fee for criminal record certificates: Crown employment); or

(*d*) section 116(1)(b) of the Police Act (fee for enhanced criminal record certificates: judicial appointments and Crown employment);

where the application is made at the same time as an application under section 116A(4) or (5) of the Police Act for the certificate to be subject to up-date arrangements.][1]

Amendments—[1] This para inserted by the Social Security (Contributions) (Amendment No 2) Regulations, SI 2013/1142 reg 2 with effect from 10 June 2013.

[Advice relating to proposed employee shareholder agreements

24—(1) A payment, or reimbursement, in accordance with section 205A(7) of the Employment Rights Act 1996 (employee shareholder status), of any reasonable costs in obtaining relevant advice.

(2) "Relevant advice" has the same meaning as section 326B(2) of ITEPA 2003 (advice relating to proposed employee shareholder agreements).][1]

Amendments—[1] This para inserted by the Social Security (Contributions) (Amendment No 3) Regulations, SI 2013/1907 regs 2, 4(*b*) with effect from 1 September 2013.

[25 Payments on which Class 1 or Class 1A contributions have been paid pursuant to the Social Security Contributions (Limited Liability Partnership) Regulations 2014

A payment made by an employer to an employed earner which represents an amount on which Class 1 or Class 1A contributions are payable by a limited liability partnership in respect of that earner by virtue of regulation 3 or 4 of the Social Security Contributions (Limited Liability Partnership) Regulations 2014.][1]

Amendments—[1] Para 25 inserted by the Social Security Contributions (Limited Liability Partnership) Regulations, SI 2014/3159 reg 5(1), (3) with effect for the tax year 2014–15 and subsequent tax years.

SCHEDULE 4

[PROVISIONS DERIVED FROM THE INCOME TAX ACTS AND THE INCOME TAX (PAY AS YOU EARN) REGULATIONS 2003][1]

Regulation 67(2)

Amendments—[1] Heading substituted by the Social Security (Contributions, Categorisation of Earners and Intermediaries) (Amendment) Regulations, SI 2004/770 regs 2, 29 with effect from 6 April 2004.

PART I
GENERAL

Interpretation

1—[(1) In this Schedule the "PAYE Regulations" means the Income Tax (Pay As You Earn) Regulations 2003.][1]

[(2) In this Schedule, except where the context otherwise requires—

"aggregated" means aggregated and treated as a single payment under paragraph 1(1) of Schedule 1 to the Act;

"allowable pension contributions" means any sum paid by an employee by way of contribution towards a pension fund or scheme which is withheld from the payment of PAYE income and for which a deduction must be allowed from employment income under section 592(7) or 594(1) of the Taxes Act (exempt approved schemes and exempt statutory schemes);

["closed tax year" means any year preceding the current year and cognate expressions shall be construed accordingly;][2]

"Compensation of Employers Regulations" means the Statutory Maternity Pay (Compensation of Employers) and Miscellaneous Amendments Regulations 1994 . . . [9]

"deductions working sheet" means any form of record on or in which are to be kept the matters required by this Schedule in connection with an employee's general earnings and earnings-related contributions . . . [8] . . . [7];

"earnings-related contributions" means contributions payable under the Act by or in respect of an employed earner in respect of employed earner's employment;

"employed earner" and "employed earner's employment" have the same meaning as in the Act;

"employee" means any person in receipt of . . . [10] earnings;

"employer" means the secondary contributor determined—

(*a*) by section 7 of the Act;

(*b*) under regulation 5 of, and Schedule 3 to, the Social Security (Categorisation of Earners) Regulations 1978; or

(*c*) under regulation 122;

. . . [10]

. . . [3]

"Inland Revenue" means any officer of the Board of Inland Revenue;

"mariner" has the same meaning as in regulation 115;

["non-Real Time Information employer" means an employer other than one within sub-paragraph (4);][4]

["Real Time Information employer" has the meaning given in sub-paragraph (4);][4]

. . . [5]

"tax month" means the period beginning on the 6th day of any calendar month and ending on the 5th day of the following calendar month;

"tax period" means a tax quarter where paragraph 11 has effect, but otherwise means a tax month;

"tax quarter" means the period beginning on 6th April and ending on 5th July, or beginning on 6th July and ending on 5th October, or beginning on 6th October and ending on 5th January, or beginning on 6th January and ending on 5th April;

"voyage period" has the same meaning as in regulation 115;

"year" means tax year;

and other expressions have the same meaning as in the Income Tax Acts.][1]

(3) For the purposes of paragraphs 7(13), 9, 10, 11 and 22, "primary Class 1 contributions" and "earnings-related contributions" shall, unless the context otherwise requires, include any amount paid on account of earnings-related contributions in accordance with the provisions of regulation 8(6).

[(4) The following are Real Time Information employers for the purposes of this Schedule—

(*a*) an employer who has entered into an agreement with HMRC to comply with the provisions of this Schedule which are expressed as relating to Real Time Information employers;

(*b*) an employer within sub-paragraph (5);

(*c*) . . . [6] and

(*d*) on and after 6th October 2013, all employers.

(5) An employer is within this paragraph if the employer has been given a general or specific direction by the Commissioners for Her Majesty's Revenue and Customs before 6th October 2013 to deliver to HMRC returns under paragraph 21A of this Schedule (real time returns of information about payments of . . . [10] earnings).][4]

NIC

Amendments—[1] Paras(1), (2) substituted by the Social Security (Contributions, Categorisation of Earners and Intermediaries) (Amendment) Regulations, SI 2004/770 regs 2, 30(1), (2) with effect from 6 April 2004.
[2] Definition of "closed tax year" inserted by the Social Security Contributions (Consequential Provisions) Regulations, SI 2007/1056 regs 3, 8 with effect from 6 April 2007.
[3] Definition of "HMRC" revoked, by the Social Security (Contributions) (Amendment No 3) Regulations, SI 2009/600 regs 2, 8(1), (2) with effect from 1 April 2009.
[4] In sub-para (2), definitions of "non-Real Time Information employer" and "Real Time Information employer" and paras (4), (5) inserted, by the Social Security (Contributions) (Amendment No 3) Regulations, SI 2012/821 regs 2, 5 with effect from 6 April 2012.
[5] In sub-para (2), definition of "general earnings" substituted and definition of "the Reimbursement Regulations" revoked by the Social Security (Contributions) (Amendment No 3) Regulations, SI 2012/821 regs 2, 20 with effect from 6 April 2012.
[6] Sub-para (4)(*c*) revoked by the Security (Contributions) (Amendment and Application of Schedule 38 to the Finance Act 2012) Regulations, SI 2013/622 regs 5, 6 with effect in relation to the tax year 2013–14 and subsequent tax years.
[7] In sub-para (2), in the definition of "deductions working sheet", words revoked by the Social Security (Contributions) (Amendment and Application of Schedule 38 to the Finance Act 2012) Regulations, SI 2013/622 regs 2, 4(1), (2) with effect in relation to the tax year 2014–15.
[8] In sub-para (2), in definition of "deductions working sheet", words revoked by the Social Security (Contributions) (Amendment) Regulations, SI 2014/608 regs 2, 5, 6. This amendment comes into force on 6 April 2014.
[9] In sub-para (2), in definition of "Compensation of Employers Regulations", words revoked by the Social Security (Contributions) (Amendment No 4) Regulations, SI 2014/2397 regs 2, 3(1), (2) with effect from 6 October 2014.
[10] In sub-para (2), word in definition of "employee" revoked and definition of "general earnings" revoked, and in sub-para (5), word revoked by the Social Security (Miscellaneous Amendments No 2) Regulations, SI 2015/478 regs 2, 22(1), (2)(*a*), (*b*) with effect from 6 April 2015.

[Multiple employers

2—(1) If—

(*a*) an employer has made an election under regulation 98 of the PAYE Regulations to be treated as a different employer in respect of each group of employees specified in the election, and

(*b*) no improper purpose notice has been given, or if one has been given it has been withdrawn,

he shall be treated as having made an identical election for the purposes of this Schedule.

(2) In this paragraph an "improper purpose notice" is a notice issued to the employer stating that it appears to the Inland Revenue that the election is made wholly or mainly for an improper purpose within the meaning of regulation 99(2) of the PAYE Regulations.][1]

Amendments—[1] This paragraph substituted by the Social Security (Contributions, Categorisation of Earners and Intermediaries) (Amendment) Regulations, SI 2004/770 regs 2, 30(1), (3) with effect from 6 April 2004.

Intermediate employers

3—(1) Where an employee works for a person who is not his immediate employer, that person shall be treated as the employer for the purpose of this Schedule, and the immediate employer shall furnish the principal employer with such particulars of the employee's [. . . [2] earnings][1] as may be necessary to enable the principal employer to comply with the provisions of this Schedule. This is subject to the qualification in sub-paragraph (4).

(2) In this paragraph—

"the principal employer" means the person specified as the relevant person in the direction referred to in sub-paragraph (4), and

"the immediate employer" means the person specified as the contractor in that direction.

(3) If the [employee's . . . [2] earnings][1] are actually paid to him by the immediate employer—

(*a*) the immediate employer shall be notified by the principal employer of the amount of earnings-related contributions which may be deducted when [those earnings][1] are paid to the employee, and may deduct the amount so notified to him accordingly; and

(*b*) the principal employer may make a corresponding deduction on making to the immediate employer the payment out of which [those earnings][1] will be paid.

(4) This paragraph only applies if a direction has been given by the Board under [section 691 of ITEPA 2003][1] (PAYE: mobile UK workforce).

(5) Where an employee is paid a sickness payment which by virtue of regulation 23 is not made through the secondary contributor in relation to the employment—

(*a*) the person making that payment shall furnish the secondary contributor with such particulars of that payment as may be necessary to enable the secondary contributor to comply with this Schedule; and

(*b*) for the purposes only of this Schedule the secondary contributor shall be deemed to have made the sickness payment.

Amendments—[1] Words in paras (1), (3), (4) substituted by the Social Security (Contributions, Categorisation of Earners and Intermediaries) (Amendment) Regulations, SI 2004/770 regs 2, 30(1), (4) with effect from 6 April 2004.
[2] Word revoked in each place by the Social Security (Miscellaneous Amendments No 2) Regulations, SI 2015/478 regs 2, 22(1), (2)(*c*) with effect from 6 April 2015.

Employer's earnings-related contributions

4 If, under this Schedule, a person [pays][1] any earnings-related contributions which, under section 6(4) of the Act, another person is liable to pay, his payment of those contributions shall be made as agent for that other person.

Amendments—[1] Word substituted by the Social Security (Contributions) (Amendment No 5) Regulations, SI 2002/2929 reg 5 with effect from 28 November 2002.

[Intermediaries

4A—(1) Where any payment of [. . . [2] earnings][2] of an employee is made by an intermediary of the employer, the employer shall be treated, for the purposes of this Schedule other than—

(*a*) paragraph 7(1),

(*b*) paragraph 7(3)(*a*),

(*c*) the references to a subsequent payment of [. . . [2] earnings][2] or of monetary earnings in paragraph 7(3) and (8), and

(*d*) paragraph 7(11), as making the payment of those [. . . [2] earnings][2] to the employee.

(2) For the purposes of this paragraph, a payment of [. . . [2] earnings][2] of an employee is made by an intermediary of the employer if it is made—

(*a*) either—

(i) by a person acting on behalf of the employer and at the expense of the employer, or

(ii) by a person connected with him, or

(*b*) by trustees holding property for any persons who include, or class of persons which includes, the employee.

(3) Section 839 of the Taxes Act (connected persons) applies for the purposes of this paragraph.][1]

Amendments—[1] Regulation 4A inserted by the Social Security (Contributions) (Amendment No 5) Regulations, SI 2002/2929 reg 6 with effect from 28 November 2002.

[2] Words substituted by the Social Security (Contributions, Categorisation of Earners and Intermediaries) (Amendment) Regulations, SI 2004/770 regs 2, 30(1), (5) with effect from 6 April 2004.

[Continuation of proceedings etc

5 Any legal proceedings or administrative act authorised by or done for the purposes of this Schedule and begun by one Inland Revenue officer may be continued by another officer, and any officer may act for any division or other area.][1]

Amendments—[1] This paragraph substituted by the Social Security (Contributions, Categorisation of Earners and Intermediaries) (Amendment) Regulations, SI 2004/770 regs 2, 30(1), (6) with effect from 6 April 2004.

PART II
DEDUCTION OF EARNINGS-RELATED CONTRIBUTIONS

Deduction of earnings-related contributions

6—(1) Every employer, on making during any year to any employee any payment of [. . . [5] earnings][1] in respect of which earnings-related contributions are payable, or are treated as payable . . . [5]

(*a*) shall, if he has not already done so, prepare . . . [4] a deductions working sheet for that employee, and

(*b*) may deduct earnings-related contributions in accordance with this Schedule.

[(1A) Where a liability to pay retrospective contributions has arisen in respect of an employee, an employer shall amend the relevant deductions working sheet or where necessary prepare one in respect of that employee.][3]

(2) Subject to sub-paragraph (3), an employer shall not be entitled to recover any earnings-related contributions paid or to be paid by him on behalf of any employee otherwise than by deduction in accordance with this Schedule.

(3) Sub-paragraph (2) does not apply to secondary Class 1 contributions in respect of which an election has been made jointly by the secondary contributor and the employed earner for the purposes of paragraph 3B(1) of Schedule 1 to the Act (election in respect of transfer of secondary contribution liability on [relevant employment income][2]) if the election provides for the collection of the amount in respect of which liability is transferred.

Amendments—[1] Words in sub-para (1) substituted by the Social Security (Contributions, Categorisation of Earners and Intermediaries) (Amendment) Regulations, SI 2004/770 regs 2, 31(1), (2) with effect from 6 April 2004.

[2] In sub-para (3), words substituted by the Social Security (Contributions) (Amendment No 4) Regulations, SI 2004/2096 regs 2, 7(*a*) with effect from 1 September 2004. SI 2004/2096 has effect in relation to—

(a) agreements entered into after 1 September 2004 which are in respect of post-commencement employment income, and

(b) elections made after that date.

3 Para (1A) inserted by the Social Security Contributions (Consequential Provisions) Regulations, SI 2007/1056 regs 3, 8(1), (3) with effect from 6 April 2007.
4 In sub-para (1)(*a*), words revoked by the Social Security (Contributions) (Amendment and Application of Schedule 38 to the Finance Act 2012) Regulations, SI 2013/622 regs 2, 4(1), (3) with effect in relation to the tax year 2014–15.
5 Words in sub-para (1) revoked by the Social Security (Miscellaneous Amendments No 2) Regulations, SI 2015/478 regs 2, 22(1), (3)(*a*) with effect from 6 April 2015.

Calculation of deduction

7—(1) Subject to sub-paragraph (2), on making any payment of [. . . [14] earnings][5] to the employee, the employer may deduct from those [. . . [14] earnings][5] the amount of the earnings-related contributions based on those [. . . [14] earnings][5] . . . [1] which the employee is liable to pay under section 6(4) of the Act [(the "section 6(4)(*a*) amount")][1].

[(1A) On making any chain payment the fee-payer may deduct the amount of earnings related contributions calculated by reference to the deemed direct earnings which the fee-payer is liable to pay.][15]

(2) Where two or more payments of [. . . [14] earnings][5] fall to be aggregated, the employer may deduct the amount of the earnings-related contributions based on those [. . . [14] earnings][5], which are payable by the employee, either wholly from one such payment or partly from one and partly from the other or any one or more of the others.

[(3) If the employer—

(*a*) on making any payment of [. . . [14] earnings][5] to an employee does not deduct from those [. . . [14] earnings][5] the full section 6(4)(*a*) amount, or

(*b*) is treated as making a payment of [. . . [14] earnings][5] by paragraph 4A, he may recover, in a case falling within paragraph (*a*) the amount not so deducted or, in a case falling within paragraph (*b*) the section 6(4)(*a*) amount, by deduction from any subsequent payment of [. . . [14] earnings][5] made by the employer to that employee during [the same year and, where the case falls within paragraph (*b*) [or sub-paragraph 4(*a*) or (*f*)][5], during the following year][3].

This sub-paragraph is subject to sub-paragraphs (4) and (5).][1]

[(3A) Where an amount has been treated as retrospective earnings paid to or for the benefit of an employee, the employer may deduct the retrospective contributions based on those earnings from any payment of . . . [14] earnings made by him to that employee—

(*a*) after the relevant retrospective contributions regulations come into force, and

(*b*) during the same and the following year.

This sub-paragraph is subject to sub-paragraph (5).][8]

(4) Sub-paragraph (3) applies only where—

(*a*) the under-deduction occurred by reason of an error made by the employer in good faith;

(*b*) the [. . . [14] earnings][5] in respect of which the under-deduction occurred are treated as earnings by virtue of regulations made under section 112 of the Act (certain sums to be earnings);

(*c*) . . . [10]

(*d*) the [. . . [14] earnings][5] in respect of which the under-deduction occurred are, by virtue of regulation 23, not paid through the secondary contributor in relation to the employment[; . . . [5]

(*e*) the employer is treated as making a payment of [. . . [14] earnings][5] by paragraph 4A][1][; or

(*f*) the payment in question is made to a person whose place of employment is outside the United Kingdom and on whose . . . [14] earnings Class 1 contributions are, but income tax is not, payable.][5]

(5) For the purposes of sub-paragraphs (3), [(3A),][7] (4), (8) and (11)—

(*a*) the amount which by virtue of those sub-paragraphs may be deducted from any payment, or from any payments which fall to be aggregated, shall be an amount in addition to, but not in excess of, the amount deductible from those payments under the other provisions of this Schedule; and

(*b*) for the purposes of Part III of this Schedule an additional amount which may be deducted by virtue of those sub-paragraphs [in a case falling within paragraph (*a*) of any of those sub-paragraphs][1] [except sub-paragraph (3A)][7] shall be treated as an amount deductible under this Schedule only in so far as the amount of the corresponding under-deduction has not been so treated.

[This is subject to the following qualification.][3]

(5A) Where a payment—

(*a*) falls within sub-paragraph (4)(*e*) [or (*f*)][5],

(*b*) comprises a beneficial interest in [securities][4], or

(*c*) is treated as earnings within the meaning of Part 7 of the Income Tax (Earnings and Pensions) Act 2003, sub-paragraph (5B) applies.][3]

[(5B) If this sub-paragraph applies—

(*a*) sub-paragraph (5)(*a*) shall have effect as if ", but not in excess of," were omitted; and

(*b*) sub-paragraph (8) shall have effect as if at the end there were added "or the following year".][3]

(6) Sub-paragraph (8) applies where an employer makes a payment consisting either solely of non-monetary earnings, or a combination of monetary and non-monetary earnings, to—

(*a*) an employee;

(*b*) an ex-employee,

and at the time of the payment of those earnings there are no, or insufficient, monetary earnings from which the employer could deduct the [section 6(4)(*a*) amount][1].

(7) In sub-paragraph (6)(*b*) "ex-employee" means a person who—

(*a*) ceases to be employed by the employer in a particular year ("the cessation year"); and

(*b*) receives such earnings from the employer after the cessation of employment but in the cessation year.

[(8) Where, in the circumstances specified in sub-paragraph (6), the employer—

(*a*) does not deduct from the earnings referred to in that sub-paragraph the full section 6(4)(*a*) amount, or

(*b*) is treated as making a payment of [. . . [14] earnings][5] by paragraph 4A, he may recover, in a case falling within paragraph (*a*) the amount not so deducted or, in a case falling within paragraph (*b*) the section 6(4)(*a*) amount, by deduction from any subsequent payment of monetary earnings to that employee, or ex-employee (as the case may be) during the same year.

This sub-paragraph is subject to sub-paragraph (5).][1]

[(9) Sub-paragraph (11) applies where—

(*a*) an employee receives non-monetary earnings comprising, or derived from, relevant securities; or

(*b*) during the post-cessation period a former employee receives non-monetary earnings—

(i) comprising, or derived from, relevant securities; and

(ii) in connection with the former employment.

Here "the post-cessation period" means the period beginning with the day on which the employment ceased and ending with the last day of the next tax year.][6]

(10) . . . [5]

[(11) Where this sub-paragraph applies, the employer or former employer may—

(*a*) retain such of the relevant securities as is necessary to enable him to recover the whole or any part of the primary Class 1 contributions in respect of those securities; and

(*b*) sell those securities.

This sub-paragraph is subject to sub-paragraphs (12) and (12A).][6]

[(11A) In sub-paragraphs (9), (11), (12) and (12A) "relevant securities" means securities in respect of which an amount is chargeable to income tax as employment income.][6]

[(12) The employer or former employer shall not retain or sell relevant securities without the prior written consent of the employee or former employee.][6]

[(12A) An employer or former employer who has retained relevant securities in accordance with sub-paragraph (11) shall account to the employee or former employee in respect of so much of the proceeds of sale as is not required to enable the employer or former employer to recover the primary Class 1 contributions in respect of those securities.][6]

(13) Subject to sub-paragraph (14), the employer shall record on the deductions working sheet for that employee the name and national insurance number of the employee, the year to which the working sheet relates, the appropriate category letter in relation to the employee (being the appropriate category letter indicated by the Board) and, in so far as relevant to that category letter, the following particulars regarding every payment of [general earnings][5] which he makes to the employee namely—

(*a*) the date of payment;

(*b*) the amount of—

(i) earnings up to and including the current lower earnings limit where earnings equal or exceed that figure,

(ii) [earnings which exceed the current lower earnings limit but do not exceed the current primary threshold,][11]

(iii) [earnings which exceed the current primary threshold but do not exceed the [current upper earnings limit][10],][11]

(iii*a*) . . . [15]

[(iv) the sum of the primary Class 1 contributions and secondary Class 1 contributions payable on all the employee's earnings, other than contributions recovered under sub-paragraph (3); and][2]

NIC

[(v) the primary Class 1 contributions payable on the employee's earnings;][2]
(vi) any statutory maternity pay;
[(vii) any . . . [12] statutory paternity pay;
(viia) . . . [12] . . . [13]][9]
[(viii) any statutory adoption pay][2][; and
(ix) any statutory shared parental pay.][13]
. . . [10]

(*c*) . . . [2]

(14) Where 2 or more payments of [. . . [14] earnings][5] fall to be aggregated, the employer, instead of recording under heads (iv) and (v) of sub-paragraph (13)(*b*) separate amounts in respect of each such payment, shall under each head record a single amount, being the total of the contributions appropriate to the description specified in that head, in respect of the aggregated payments.

(15) When an employer pays [. . . [14] earnings][1] he shall record under the name of the employee to whom he pays the [general earnings[1]]—

(*a*) the date of payment;
(*b*) the amount of the [. . . [14] earnings][5], excluding any allowable [pension][5] contributions; and
(*c*) any allowable [pension][5] contributions;

and retain the record for a period of three years after the end of the tax year in which the [. . . [14] earnings][5] were paid.

Cross-references—See the Social Security Contributions (Intermediaries) Regulations, SI 2000/727 Part 2 (intermediaries: special rules where workers' services are provided to public authorities).

Amendments—[1] Words in sub-para (1) revoked, words in sub-paras (1), (5) inserted, sub-paras (3), (8) substituted, words in sub-paras (6) substituted, and sub-para (4)(*e*) inserted, by the Social Security (Contributions) (Amendment No 5) Regulations, SI 2002/2929 reg 7 with effect from 28 November 2002.

[2] Sub-paras (13)(*b*)(iv), (v) substituted; sub-paras (13)(*b*)(vii), (viii); and sub-para (13)(*c*) revoked; by the Social Security (Contributions) (Amendment) Regulations, SI 2003/193 regs 2, 16(1), (2) with effect from 2003–04.

[3] Words in sub-para (3) substituted, words in sub-para (5) inserted, and sub-paras (5A), (5B) inserted, by the Social Security (Contributions) (Amendment No 4) Regulations, SI 2003/1337 reg 2 with effect from 10 June 2003.

[4] Word in sub-para (5A)(*b*) substituted by the Social Security (Contributions) (Amendment No 5) Regulations, SI 2003/2085 regs 3, 14(1), (2) with effect from 1 September 2003.

[5] Words substituted; words in sub-para (4) revoked, and inserted; words in sub-para (5A) inserted; and para (10) revoked; by the Social Security (Contributions, Categorisation of Earners and Intermediaries) (Amendment) Regulations, SI 2004/770 regs 2, 31(1), (3), 36, Schedule with effect from 6 April 2004.

[6] Sub-para 9 substituted, and sub-paras (11)–(12A) substituted for sub-paras (11), (12), by the Social Security (Contributions) (Amendment No 5) Regulations, SI 2004/2246 with effect from 22 September 2004.

[7] Sub-para (3A) and words in sub-para (5) inserted, by the Social Security Contributions (Consequential Provisions) Regulations, SI 2007/1056 regs 3, 8(4) with effect from 6 April 2007.

[8] In sub-para (13)(*b*), words substituted and inserted by the Social Security (Contributions) (Amendment) Regulations, SI 2009/111 regs 2, 4 with effect from 6 April 2009.

[9] Sub-para (13)(*b*)(vii), (vii*a*) substituted for previous sub-para (13)(*b*)(vii), by the Social Security (Contributions) (Amendment) (No 5) Regulations, SI 2010/2450 regs 2, 4 with effect from 14 November 2010.

[10] Para (4)(*c*) revoked, and in para (13)(*b*) words substituted and revoked, by the Social Security (Contributions) (Amendment) (No 2) Regulations, SI 2016/352 reg 18(*a*) with effect from 6 April 2016, subject to savings in relation to rights or obligations arising in connection with tax years beginning before 6 April 2016.

[11] In sub-para (13)(*b*), paras (ii), (iii) substituted by the Social Security (Contributions) (Amendment No 3) Regulations, SI 2012/821 regs 2, 21 with effect from 6 April 2012.

[12] In sub-para (13)(*b*), word "ordinary" in para (vii) revoked and para (viia) revoked by the Social Security and Tax Credits (Miscellaneous Amendments) Regulations, SI 2015/175 regs 2, 4(1), (2)(*a*), (*b*) with effect from 5 April 2015. These amendments do not have effect where they relate to ordinary statutory paternity pay or additional statutory paternity pay, or ordinary statutory paternity pay or additional statutory paternity pay paid on or after 5 April 2015: SI 2015/175 reg 9.

[13] In sub-para (13)(*b*), word "and" and the end of para (viia) revoked, and para (ix) and preceding word inserted by the Social Security and Tax Credits (Miscellaneous Amendments) Regulations, SI 2015/175 regs 2, 4(1), (2)(*c*), (*d*) with effect from 5 March 2015.

[14] Word revoked in each place by the Social Security (Miscellaneous Amendments No 2) Regulations, SI 2015/478 regs 2, 22(1), (3)(*b*) with effect from 6 April 2015.

[15] Sub-para (1A) inserted by the Social Security (Miscellaneous Amendments No 2) Regulations, SI 2017/373 reg 4(1), (3) with effect from 6 April 2017.

[Records where liability transferred from secondary contributor to employed earner: relevant employment income

8 Where an election has been made for the purposes of paragraph 3B(1) of Schedule 1 to the Act (elections about transfer of liability for secondary contributions in respect of relevant employment income), the secondary contributor shall maintain records containing—

(*a*) a copy of any such election;
(*b*) a copy of the notice of approval issued by the Inland Revenue under paragraph 3B(1)(*b*) of that Schedule;

(*c*) the name and address of the secondary contributor who has entered into the election;
(*d*) the name of the employed earner; and
(*e*) the national insurance number allocated to the employed earner.][1]

Amendments—[1] This paragraph substituted by the Social Security (Contributions) (Amendment No 4) Regulations, SI 2004/2096 regs 2, 7(*b*) with effect from 1 September 2004. SI 2004/2096 has effect in relation to—
(a) agreements entered into after 1 September 2004 which are in respect of post-commencement employment income, and
(b) elections made after that date.

Certificate of contributions paid

9—(1) Where the employer is required to give the employee a certificate in accordance with [regulation 67 of the PAYE Regulations (information to employees about payments and tax deducted (Form P 60))][3], the employer shall enter on the certificate, in respect of the year to which the certificate relates—

(*a*) the amount of any earnings up to and including the current lower earnings limit where earnings equal or exceed that figure;
(*b*) the amount of any earnings in respect of which primary Class 1 contributions were, by virtue of section 6A of the Act, treated as having been paid, which exceed the current lower earnings limit but do not exceed the current primary threshold . . .[4]
(*c*) the amount of any earnings in respect of which primary Class 1 contributions were payable which exceed the current primary threshold but do not exceed the [current upper earnings limit][4] . . . [4]
(*ca*) . . .[4]
(*d*) the amount of the earnings, if any, recorded under paragraphs (*b*) and (*c*), above the current lower earnings limit, in respect of which primary Class 1 contributions were payable or, where section 6A of the Act and regulation 127 applies, were treated as having been paid, at the reduced rate;
(*e*) the amount of primary Class 1 contributions paid by the employee;
[(*f*) the amount of statutory maternity pay paid to the employee;][1]
[(*g*) the amount of . . . [8] statutory paternity pay paid to the employee;
(*ga*) . . . [8] . . . [9]][6]
[(*h*) the amount of statutory adoption pay paid to the employee][1][; and
(*i*) the amount of statutory shared parental pay paid to the employee;][9]

and shall enter the amounts under [paragraph (e)][1] under the appropriate category letter indicated by the [Inland Revenue][5] [and

(2) Where the employer is not required to give the employee a certificate in accordance with [regulation 67 of the PAYE Regulations][3], because no tax has been deducted from the employee's [relevant payments][7] during the year concerned, . . . [5], [but the employee—

(*a*) has paid, or
(*b*) is treated, by virtue of section 6A of the Act, as having paid,

primary Class 1 contributions in that year, the employer shall nevertheless give the employee such a certificate showing the information referred to in sub-paragraph (1).][2]

[(3) In sub-paragraph (2), "relevant payments" has the meaning given in the PAYE Regulations.][7]

Amendments—[1] Sub-paras (1)(*f*)–(*h*) inserted; and words substituted; by the Social Security (Contributions) (Amendment) Regulations, SI 2003/193 regs 2, 16(1), (3) with effect from 2003–04.

[2] Words in sub-para (2) substituted by the Social Security (Contributions) (Amendment No 4) Regulations, SI 2003/1337 reg 3 with effect from 10 June 2003.

[3] Words in sub-paras (1), (2) substituted by the Social Security (Contributions, Categorisation of Earners and Intermediaries) (Amendment) Regulations, SI 2004/770 regs 2, 31(1), (4) with effect from 6 April 2004.

[4] In sub-para (1)(*b*), words revoked, in sub-para (1)(*c*), words substituted and revoked, and sub-para (1)(*ca*) revoked, by the Social Security (Contributions) (Amendment) (No 2) Regulations, SI 2016/352 reg 18(*b*) with effect from 6 April 2016, subject to savings in relation to rights or obligations arising in connection with tax years beginning before 6 April 2016.

[5] Words "or the employee was not in the employer's employment on the last day of the tax year" in para (2) repealed by the Social Security (Contributions) (Amendment No 4) Regulations, SI 2010/721 regs 2, 10 with effect only in relation to the tax year 2010–11 and subsequent tax years.

[6] sub-paras (1)(*g*), (*ga*) substituted for previous sub-para (*g*), by the Social Security (Contributions) (Amendment) (No 5) Regulations, SI 2010/2450, regs 2, 4 with effect from 14 November 2010.

[7] In sub-para (2) words substituted, and sub-para (3) inserted, by the Social Security (Contributions) (Amendment No 3) Regulations, SI 2012/821 regs 2, 22 with effect from 6 April 2012.

[8] In sub-para (1)(*g*), word revoked, and sub-para (1)(*ga*) revoked, by the Social Security and Tax Credits (Miscellaneous Amendments) Regulations, SI 2015/175 regs 2, 4(1), (3)(*a*), (*b*) with effect from 5 April 2015. These amendments do not have effect where they relate to ordinary statutory paternity pay or additional statutory paternity pay, or ordinary statutory paternity pay or additional statutory paternity pay paid on or after 5 April 2015: SI 2015/175 reg 9.

[9] In sub-para (1)(*ga*), word "and" at the end revoked, and sub-para (1)(*i*) and preceding word inserted by the Social Security and Tax Credits (Miscellaneous Amendments) Regulations, SI 2015/175 regs 2, 4(1), (3)(*c*), (*d*) with effect from 5 March 2015.

PART III
PAYMENT AND RECOVERY OF EARNINGS-RELATED CONTRIBUTIONS, CLASS 1A CONTRIBUTIONS AND CLASS 1B CONTRIBUTIONS, ETC

Payment of earnings-related contributions monthly by employer

10—(1) Subject to [sub-paragraph (1A) and][2] paragraph 11 and 15(8), the employer shall pay the amount specified in sub-paragraph (2) to the [Inland Revenue][1] within 14 days [or, if payment is made by an approved method of electronic communications in respect of earnings paid after 5th April 2004, within 17 days][1] of the end of every . . . [1] tax month.

[(1A) This paragraph does not apply in respect of amounts of retrospective earnings.][2]

(2) The amount specified in this sub-paragraph is the total amount of earnings-related contributions due in respect of [. . . [7] earnings][1] paid by the employer in that . . . [1] tax month [(and, where required, reported under paragraph 21A or 21D)][3], other than amounts deductible under paragraph 7(2) which he did not deduct and amounts which he deducted under the Compensation of Employers Regulations . . . [4].

(3) For the purposes of sub-paragraph (2), if two or more payments of [. . . [7] earnings][1] fall to be aggregated, the employer shall be treated as having deducted from the last of those payments the amount of any earnings-related contributions deductible from those payments which he did not deduct from the earlier payments.

[(3A) The amount specified in sub-paragraph (2) must be adjusted to take account of errors corrected under paragraph 21E(5), other than in cases where paragraph 21E(4) applies[, or failures rectified under paragraph 21EA(2)][5].][3]

[(4) Where the amount specified in sub-paragraph (2) has been adjusted to take account of an error as provided for in sub-paragraph (3A) and the value of the adjustment is a negative amount, that amount is treated as having been paid to HMRC—

(*a*) 17 days after the end of the tax month in which the correction is made if payment is made using an approved method of electronic communications, and

(*b*) 14 days after the end of the tax month in which the correction is made, in any other case.][6]

Amendments—[1] Words substituted, words inserted in sub-para (1), and words revoked in sub-paras (1), (2), by the Social Security (Contributions, Categorisation of Earners and Intermediaries) (Amendment) Regulations, SI 2004/770 regs 2, 32(1), (2) with effect from 6 April 2004.

[2] Words in sub-para (1) and whole of sub-para (1A) inserted, by the Social Security Contributions (Consequential Provisions) Regulations, SI 2007/1056 regs 3, 8(5) with effect from 6 April 2007.

[3] Words in sub-para (2), and para (3A), inserted, by the Social Security (Contributions) (Amendment No 3) Regulations, SI 2012/821 regs 2, 6 with effect from 6 April 2012.

[4] In sub-para (2), words revoked by the Social Security (Contributions) (Amendment No 3) Regulations, SI 2012/821 regs 2, 23 with effect from 6 April 2012.

[5] Words in sub-para (3A)inserted by the Security (Contributions) (Amendment and Application of Schedule 38 to the Finance Act 2012) Regulations, SI 2013/622 regs 5, 7 with effect in relation to the tax year 2013–14 and subsequent tax years.

[6] Sub-para (4) inserted by the Social Security (Contributions) (Amendment No 3) Regulations, SI 2014/1016 reg 2(*a*) with effect in relation to amounts due and payable for the tax year 2014–15 and subsequent tax years.

[7] Word revoked in each place by the Social Security (Miscellaneous Amendments No 2) Regulations, SI 2015/478 regs 2, 22(1), (4)(*a*) with effect from 6 April 2015.

Payments of earnings-related contributions quarterly by employer

11—(1) Subject to [sub-paragraph (1A) and][4] paragraph 15(8), the employer shall pay the amount specified in sub-paragraph (2) to the [Inland Revenue][2] within 14 days of the end of every . . . [2] tax quarter [or, if payment is made by an approved method of electronic communications in respect of earnings paid after 5th April 2004, within 17 days of the end of every tax quarter][2] where—

(*a*) the employer has reasonable grounds for believing that the condition specified in sub-paragraph (4) applies and chooses to pay the amount specified in sub-paragraph (2) quarterly; or

(*b*) . . . [5]

[(1A) This paragraph does not apply in respect of amounts of retrospective earnings.][4]

(2) The amount specified in this sub-paragraph is the total amount of earnings-related contributions due in respect of [. . . [5] earnings][2] paid by the employer in that . . . [2] tax quarter [(and, where required, reported under paragraph 21A or 21D)][6], other than amounts deductible under paragraph 7(2) which he did not deduct and amounts which he deducted under the Compensation of Employers Regulations . . . [7].

(3) For the purposes of sub-paragraph (2), where two or more payments [of . . . [5] earnings][2] fall to be aggregated, the employer shall be deemed to have deducted from the last of those payments the amount of any earnings-related contributions deductible from those payments which he did not deduct from the earlier payments.

[(3A) The amount specified in sub-paragraph (2) must be adjusted to take account of errors corrected under paragraph 21E(5), other than in cases where paragraph 21E(4) applies[, or failures rectified under paragraph 21EA(2)][8].][6]

[(3B) Where the amount specified in sub-paragraph (2) has been adjusted to take account of an error as provided for in sub-paragraph (3A) and the value of the adjustment is a negative amount, that amount is treated as having been paid to HMRC—

(*a*) 17 days after the end of the tax quarter in which the correction is made if payment is made using an approved method of electronic communications, and

(*b*) 14 days after the end of the tax quarter in which the correction is made, in any other case.][9]

[(4) The condition specified in this sub-paragraph is that for [tax months][2] falling within the current year, the average monthly amount found by the formula below will be less than £1500.

The formula is—

$$[(N+P+L+S)-(SP+CD)]^3$$

The expressions used in the formula have the following values.

N is the amount which would be payable to the [Inland Revenue][2] under the Social Security Contributions and Benefits Act 1992 and these Regulations but disregarding—

(*a*) any amount of secondary Class 1 contributions in respect of which liability has been transferred to the employed earner by an election made jointly by the employed earner and the secondary contributor for the purpose of paragraph 3B(1) of Schedule 1 to the Act (transfer of liability to be borne by the earner); and

[(*aa*) any amount payable in respect of retrospective earnings;][4]

(*b*) . . . [3]

["P" is the amount which would be payable to HMRC under regulation [67G or][6] 68 of the PAYE Regulations but disregarding any amount payable in respect of retrospective employment income (within the meaning of regulation 2 of those Regulations);][4]

L is the amount which would be payable to the [Inland Revenue][2] under [regulation 54(1) of the Education (Student Loans) (Repayment) Regulations 2009 (payment of repayments deducted to HMRC)][7] if the reduction referred to in paragraph (3) of that regulation . . . [3] were disregarded.

S is the sum of the amounts which the employer would be liable to deduct, under section 559 of the Taxes Act and the Income Tax (Sub-contractors in the Construction Industry) Regulations 1993, from payments made by him.

T . . . .[3]

SP is the amount—

(*a*) recoverable by the employer from the Board, or

(*b*) deductible from amounts for which the employer would otherwise be accountable to the [Inland Revenue][2],

in respect of payments to his employees by way of . . . [10] statutory maternity pay, [statutory paternity pay][11] [, statutory shared parental pay][12] and statutory adoption pay.

CD is the amount which would be deducted by others from sums due to the employer, in his position as a sub-contractor, under section 559 of the Taxes Act.][1]

Amendments—[1] Sub-para (4) substituted; by the Social Security (Contributions) (Amendment) Regulations, SI 2003/193 regs 2, 16(1), (4) with effect from 2003–04.

[2] Words substituted, words in sub-paras (1), (3) revoked, and sub-para (1)(*b*) also revoked, by the Social Security (Contributions, Categorisation of Earners and Intermediaries) (Amendment) Regulations, SI 2004/770 regs 2, 32(1), (3) with effect from 6 April 2004.

[3] In sub-para (4), formula substituted, and words revoked, by the Social Security (Contributions) (Amendment No 2) Regulations, SI 2006/576 regs 2, 9 with effect from 6 April 2006.

[4] Words in sub-para (1) and whole of sub-para (1A) inserted, and words in sub-para (4) inserted and substituted, by the Social Security Contributions (Consequential Provisions) Regulations, SI 2007/1056 regs 3, 8(6) with effect from 6 April 2007.

[5] Word revoked in each place by the Social Security (Miscellaneous Amendments No 2) Regulations, SI 2015/478 regs 2, 22(1), (4)(*a*) with effect from 6 April 2015.

[6] In sub-paras (2), (4), words inserted, and sub-para (3A) inserted, by the Social Security (Contributions) (Amendment No 3) Regulations, SI 2012/821 regs 2, 7 with effect from 6 April 2012.

[7] In sub-para (2), words revoked, and in sub-para (4) words substituted, by the Social Security (Contributions) (Amendment No 3) Regulations, SI 2012/821 regs 2, 24, 25 with effect from 6 April 2012.

[8] Words in sub-para (3A) inserted by the Security (Contributions) (Amendment and Application of Schedule 38 to the Finance Act 2012) Regulations, SI 2013/622 regs 5, 8 with effect in relation to the tax year 2013–14 and subsequent tax years.

[9] Sub-para (3B) inserted by the Social Security (Contributions) (Amendment No 3) Regulations, SI 2014/1016 reg 2(*b*) with effect in relation to amounts due and payable for the tax year 2014–15 and subsequent tax years.

[10] In sub-para (4), in definition of "SP", words revoked by the Social Security (Contributions) (Amendment No 4) Regulations, SI 2014/2397 regs 2, 3(1), (3) with effect from 6 October 2014.

[11] In sub-para (4), words substituted by the Social Security and Tax Credits (Miscellaneous Amendments) Regulations, SI 2015/175 regs 2, 4(1), (4)(*a*) with effect from 5 April 2015. These amendments do not have effect where they relate to ordinary statutory paternity pay or additional statutory paternity pay, or ordinary statutory paternity pay or additional statutory paternity pay paid on or after 5 April 2015: SI 2015/175 reg 9.

[12] In sub-para (4), words inserted by the Social Security and Tax Credits (Miscellaneous Amendments) Regulations, SI 2015/175 regs 2, 4(1), (4)(*b*) with effect from 5 March 2015.

[Payments to and recoveries from HMRC for each tax period by Real Time Information employers: returns under paragraph 21E(6) [or 21EA(3)]

11ZA—(1) This paragraph applies if, during any tax period, an employer makes a return under paragraph 21E(6) (returns under paragraph 21A and 21D: amendments) other than by virtue of paragraph 21E(4)[, or paragraph 21EA(3) (failure to make a return under paragraph 21A or 21D of Schedule 4)][2].

(2) The amount specified in paragraph 10(2) or, as the case may be, 11(2) for the final tax period in the year covered by the return is to be adjusted to take account of the information in the return.

(3) If the value of the adjustment required by paragraph (2) is a negative amount, the employer may recover that amount—

(*a*) by setting it off against the amount the employer is liable to pay under paragraph 10(2) or, as the case may be, 11(2) for the tax period the return is made in; or

(*b*) from the Commissioners for Her Majesty's Revenue and Customs.

[(3A) Where sub-paragraph (3) applies the negative amount is treated as having been paid to HMRC—

(*a*) 17 days after the end of the final tax period in the year covered by the return where payment is made using an approved method of electronic communication, and

(*b*) 14 days after the end of the final tax period in the year covered by the return in any other case.][3]

(4) But paragraph (3) does not apply in relation to primary Class 1 contributions in a case where those contributions were deducted in error and the excess deduction has not been refunded to the employee.][1]

Amendments—[1] Para 11ZA and preceding heading inserted by the Social Security (Contributions) (Amendment No 3) Regulations, SI 2012/821 regs 2, 8 with effect from 6 April 2012.

[2] Words in heading and words in sub-para (1) inserted by the Security (Contributions) (Amendment and Application of Schedule 38 to the Finance Act 2012) Regulations, SI 2013/622 regs 5, 9 with effect in relation to the tax year 2013–14 and subsequent tax years.

[3] Sub-para (3A) inserted by the Social Security (Contributions) (Amendment No. 3) Regulations, SI 2014/1016 reg 2(*c*) with effect in relation to amounts due and payable for the tax year 2014–15 and subsequent tax years.

[Payments of earnings-related contributions in respect of retrospective earnings

11A—(1) This paragraph applies where there are retrospective earnings in respect of which contributions (whether primary or secondary contributions) are payable.

(2) The employer shall pay the contributions referred to in sub-paragraph (1) to HMRC within 14 days or, if payment is made in respect of the current year by an approved method of electronic communications, 17 days of the end of the tax month immediately following the tax month in which the relevant retrospective contributions regulations came into force.][1]

Amendments—[1] Paragraph inserted by the Social Security Contributions (Consequential Provisions) Regulations, SI 2007/1056 regs 3, 8(7) with effect from 6 April 2007.

Payment of earnings-related contributions by employer (further provisions)

12—[(1) The Inland Revenue shall give a receipt to the employer for the total amount paid under paragraph [10, 11 or 11A][2] if so requested, but if a receipt is given for the total amount of earnings-related contributions and any tax paid at the same time, a separate receipt need not be given for earnings-related contributions.][1]

(2) Subject to sub-paragraph (3), if the employer has paid to the [Inland Revenue][1] on account of earnings-related contributions under paragraph [10, 11 or 11A][2] an amount which he was not liable to pay, or which has been refunded in accordance with regulation 2 of the Social Security (Refunds) (Repayment of Contractual Maternity Pay) Regulations 1990 (refunds of contributions), the amounts which he is liable to pay subsequently in respect of other payments of [. . . [3] earnings][1] made by him during the same year shall be reduced by the amount overpaid, so however that if there was a corresponding over-deduction from any payment of [general earnings][1] to an employee, this paragraph shall apply only in so far as the employer has reimbursed the employee for that over-deduction.

(3) Sub-paragraph (2) applies only if—

(*a*) the over-deduction occurred by reason of an error by the employer in good faith;

(*b*) . . . [4]; or

(*c*) a refund has been made under regulation 2 of the Social Security (Refunds) (Repayment of Contractual Maternity Pay) Regulations 1990.

Amendments—[1] Sub-para (1) substituted, and words in sub-para (2) substituted, by the Social Security (Contributions, Categorisation of Earners and Intermediaries) (Amendment) Regulations, SI 2004/770 regs 2, 32(1), (4) with effect from 6 April 2004.

2 References substituted by the Social Security Contributions (Consequential Provisions) Regulations, SI 2007/1056 regs 3, 8(8) with effect from 6 April 2007.

3 In sub-para (2), word revoked by the Social Security (Miscellaneous Amendments No 2) Regulations, SI 2015/478 regs 2, 22(1), (4)(*a*) with effect from 6 April 2015.

4 Sub-para (3)(*b*) revoked by the Social Security (Contributions) (Amendment) (No 2) Regulations, SI 2016/352 reg 18(*c*) with effect from 6 April 2016, subject to savings in relation to rights or obligations arising in connection with tax years beginning before 6 April 2016.

Payment of Class 1B contributions

13—(1) A person who is liable to pay a Class 1B contribution ("the employer"), shall pay that Class 1B contribution to the [Inland Revenue][1] not later than 19th October [or, if payment is made by an approved method of electronic communications in respect of earnings paid after 5th April 2004, not later than 22nd October][1] in the year immediately following the end of the year in respect of which that contribution is payable.

(2) If the employer has paid to the [Inland Revenue][1] under this paragraph an amount in respect of Class 1B contributions which he was not liable to pay, he shall be entitled to deduct the amount overpaid from any payment in respect of secondary earnings-related contributions which he is liable to pay subsequently to the [Inland Revenue][1] under paragraph 10 or 11 for any . . . [1] tax period in the same year.

Amendments—[1] Words substituted, words inserted in sub-para (1), and word revoked in sub-para (2), by the Social Security (Contributions, Categorisation of Earners and Intermediaries) (Amendment) Regulations, SI 2004/770 regs 2, 32(1), (5) with effect from 6 April 2004.

Employer failing to pay earnings-related contributions

14—(1) If within [17 days][1] of the end of any . . . [1] tax period [a non-Real Time Information employer][2] has paid no amount of earnings-related contributions to the [Inland Revenue][1] under paragraph 10 or 11 for that . . . [1] tax period and the [Inland Revenue][1] is unaware of the amount, if any, which the employer is liable so to pay, the [Inland Revenue][1] may give notice to the employer requiring him to render, within 14 days, a return in the prescribed form showing the amount of earnings-related contributions which the employer is liable to pay to the [Inland Revenue][1] under that paragraph in respect of the . . . [1] tax period in question.

(2) Where a notice given by the [Inland Revenue][1] under sub-paragraph (1) extends to two or more consequent . . . [1] tax periods, the provisions of this Schedule shall have effect as if those . . . [1] tax periods were one . . . [1] tax period.

(3) If the [Inland Revenue][1] is not satisfied that an amount of earnings-related contributions paid . . . [1] under paragraph 10 or 11 for any . . . [1] tax period is the full amount which the employer is liable to pay . . . [1], the [Inland Revenue][1] may give a notice under sub-paragraph (1) despite the payment of that amount.

Amendments—[1] Words substituted and revoked, and words inserted in sub-para (1), by the Social Security (Contributions, Categorisation of Earners and Intermediaries) (Amendment) Regulations, SI 2004/770 regs 2, 32(1), (6) with effect from 6 April 2004.

2 Words substituted by the Social Security (Contributions) (Amendment No 3) Regulations, SI 2012/821 regs 2, 9 with effect from 6 April 2012.

Specified amount of earnings-related contributions payable by the employer

15—(1) If after [17 days][1] following the end of any . . . [1] tax period the employer has paid no amount of earnings-related contributions to [HMRC][2] under paragraph 10 or 11 for that . . . [1] tax period and there is reason to believe that the employer is liable to pay such contributions, [HMRC][2], upon consideration of the employer's record of past payments [whether of earnings-related contributions or of combined amounts,][2] may to the best of [their judgment][1] specify the amount of earnings-related contributions [or of a combined amount][2] which [they consider][1] the employer is liable to pay and give notice to him of that amount.

[(1A) For the purposes of this paragraph "combined amount" is an amount which includes earnings-related contributions due under these regulations and one or more of the following—

(*a*) tax due under the PAYE Regulations;

(*b*) amounts due under the Income Tax (Construction Industry Scheme) Regulations 2005;

(*c*) payments of repayments of student loans due under the [Education (Student Loans) (Repayment) Regulations 2009][5].][2]

[(1B) In arriving at an amount under paragraph (1), HMRC may also take into account any returns made by the employer under this Schedule in the tax period in question or earlier tax periods.][4]

(2) If, on the expiration of the period of 7 days allowed in the notice, the specified amount . . . [2] or any part thereof is unpaid, the amount so unpaid—

(*a*) shall be treated for the purposes of this Schedule as an amount of earnings-related contributions [or as including an amount of earnings-related contributions][2] which the employer was liable to pay for that . . . [1] tax period in accordance with paragraph 10 or 11; and

NIC

(*b*) may be certified by [HMRC][2].

(3) The provisions of sub-paragraph (2) shall not apply if, during the period allowed in the notice, the employer pays to [HMRC][2] the full amount of earnings-related contributions which the employer is liable to pay under paragraph 10 or 11 for that . . . [1] tax period, or the employer satisfies [HMRC][2] that no amount of such contributions is due.

(4) The production of a certificate such as is mentioned in sub-paragraph (2) shall, until the contrary is established, be sufficient evidence that the employer is liable to pay to the [HMRC][2] the amount shown in it; and any document purporting to be such a certificate as aforesaid shall be deemed to be such a certificate until the contrary is proved.

Paragraph 16 shall apply, with any necessary modifications, to the amount shown in the certificate.

(5) Where the employer has paid no amount of earnings-related contributions under paragraph 10 or 11 for any . . . [1] tax periods, a notice may be given by [HMRC][2] under sub-paragraph (1) which extends to two or more consecutive . . . [1] tax periods, and this Schedule shall have effect as if those . . . [1] tax periods were the latest . . . [1] tax period specified in the notice.

(6) A notice may be given by [HMRC][2] under sub-paragraph (1) notwithstanding that an amount of earnings-related contributions has been paid . . . [1] by the employer under paragraph 10 or 11 for any . . . [1] tax period, if, after seeking the employer's explanation as to the amount of earnings-related contributions paid, [HMRC][2] is not satisfied that the amount so paid is the full amount which the employer is liable to pay . . . [1] for that period, and this paragraph shall have effect accordingly, save that sub-paragraph (2) shall not apply if, during the period allowed in the notice, the employer satisfies [HMRC][2] that no further amount of earnings-related contributions is due for the relevant . . . [1] tax period.

(7) Where, during the period allowed in a notice given by [HMRC][2] under sub-paragraph (1), the employer claims, but does not satisfy [HMRC][2], that the payment . . . [2] made in respect of any . . . [1] tax period specified in the notice is [or includes][2] the full amount of earnings-related contributions he is liable to pay to [HMRC][2] for that period, the employer may require [HMRC][2] to inspect the employer's documents and records as if [HMRC][2] had called upon the employer to produce those documents and records in accordance with [Schedule 36 to the Finance Act 2008 (information and inspection powers) and the provisions of paragraph 26A][3] shall apply in relation to that inspection, and the notice given by [HMRC][2] under sub-paragraph (1) shall be disregarded in relation to any subsequent time.

(8) Notwithstanding anything in this paragraph, if the employer pays any amount of earnings-related contributions certified by [HMRC][2] under it [whether separately or as part of a combined amount][2] and that amount exceeds the amount which he would have been liable to pay in respect of that . . . [1] tax period apart from this paragraph, he shall be entitled to set off such excess against any amount which he is liable to pay to [HMRC][2] under paragraph 10 or 11 for any subsequent . . . [1] tax period.

(9) If, after the end of the year, the employer renders the return required by paragraph 22(1) and the total earnings-related contributions he has paid in respect of that year in accordance with this Schedule exceeds the total amount of such contributions due for that year, any excess not otherwise recovered by set-off shall be repaid.

Amendments—[1] Words substituted and revoked by the Social Security (Contributions, Categorisation of Earners and Intermediaries) (Amendment) Regulations, SI 2004/770 regs 2, 32(1), (7) with effect from 6 April 2004.

[2] References to "the Inland Revenue" substituted throughout, words in sub-paras (1), (8) and whole of sub-para (1A) inserted, words in sub-paras (2), (7) revoked and inserted, by the Social Security (Contributions) (Amendment No 3) Regulations, SI 2008/636 regs 2, 4 with effect from 6 April 2008.

[3] Words in sub-para (7) substituted, by the Social Security (Contributions) (Amendment No 3) Regulations, SI 2009/600 regs 2, 8(1), (3) with effect from 1 April 2009.

[4] Sub-para (1B) inserted by the Social Security (Contributions) (Amendment No 3) Regulations, SI 2012/821 regs 2, 10 with effect from 6 April 2012.

[5] In sub-para (1A) words substituted by the Social Security (Contributions) (Amendment No 3) Regulations, SI 2012/821 regs 2, 26(*a*) with effect from 6 April 2012.

Recovery of earnings-related contributions or Class 1B contributions

16—(1) The Income Tax Acts and any regulations under [section 684 of ITEPA 2003 (PAYE regulations)][1] relating to the recovery of tax shall apply to the recovery of—

(*a*) any amount of earnings-related contributions which an employer is liable to pay [HMRC][2] for any . . . [1] tax period in accordance with paragraph 10 or 11 or which he is treated as liable to [HMRC][2] [whether separately or as part of a combined amount][2] for any . . . [1] tax period under paragraph 15; or

(*b*) any amount of Class 1B contributions which an employer is liable to pay to [HMRC][2] in respect of any year in accordance with paragraph 13(1),

as if each of those amounts had been charged to tax by way of an assessment on the employer [as employment income under ITEPA 2003][1].

(2) Sub-paragraph (1) is subject to the qualification that, in the application to any proceedings taken, by virtue of this paragraph, of any of the relevant provisions limiting the amount which is recoverable in those proceedings, there shall be disregarded any [other component of a combined amount][2] which may, by virtue of sub-paragraphs (3) to (5), be included as part of the cause of action or matter of complaint in those proceedings.

(3) Proceedings may be brought for the recovery of the total amount of—

(*a*) earnings-related contributions which the employer is liable to pay to [HMRC][2] for any . . . [1] tax period;

(*b*) Class 1B contributions which the employer is liable to pay to [HMRC][2] in respect of any year;

(*c*) a combination of those classes of contributions as specified in heads (*a*) and (*b*); or

(*d*) any of the contributions as specified in heads (*a*), (*b*), or (*c*) in addition to any [other component of a combined amount][2] which the employer is liable to pay to [HMRC][2] for any . . . [1] tax period,

without specifying the respective amount of those contributions and of [other component of a combined amount][2], or distinguishing the amounts which the employer is liable to pay in respect of each employee and without specifying the employees in question.

(4) For the purposes of—

(*a*) proceedings under section 66 of the Taxes Management Act 1970 (including proceedings under that section as applied by the provisions of this paragraph);

(*b*) summary proceedings (including in Scotland proceedings in the sheriff court or in the sheriff's small debt court),

the total amount of contributions, in addition to any [other component of the combined amount][2] which the employer is liable to pay to [HMRC][2] for any . . . [1] tax period, referred to in sub-paragraph (3) shall, subject to sub-paragraph (2), be one cause of action or one matter of complaint.

(5) Nothing in sub-paragraph (3) or (4) shall prevent the bringing of separate proceedings for the recovery of each of the several amounts of—

(*a*) earnings-related contributions which the employer is liable to pay for any . . . [1] tax period in respect of each of his several employees;

(*b*) Class 1B contributions which the employer is liable to pay in respect of any year in respect of each of his several employees; . . .

(*c*) tax which the employer is liable to pay for any . . . [1] tax period in respect of each of his several employees.

[(*d*) amounts due under the Income Tax (Construction Industry Scheme) Regulations 2005; or

(*e*) payments of repayments of student loans due under the [Education (Student Loans) (Repayment) Regulations 2009][3].][2]

[(6) For the purposes of this paragraph "combined amount" has the meaning given in paragraph 15(1A).][2]

Amendments—[1] Words substituted and revoked by the Social Security (Contributions, Categorisation of Earners and Intermediaries) (Amendment) Regulations, SI 2004/770 regs 2, 32(1), (8) with effect from 6 April 2004.

[2] References to "the Inland Revenue" substituted throughout, words in sub-para (1) inserted, words in sub-paras (2)–(4) substituted, in sub-para (5) word revoked and paras (*d*), (*e*) inserted, and sub-para (6) inserted, by the Social Security (Contributions) (Amendment No 3) Regulations, SI 2008/636 regs 2, 5 with effect from 6 April 2008.

[3] In sub-para (5)(*e*), words substituted by the Social Security (Contributions) (Amendment No 3) Regulations, SI 2012/821 regs 2, 26(*b*) with effect from 6 April 2012.

Interest on overdue earnings-related contributions or Class 1B contributions

17—(1) [Subject to [sub-paragraph (4A) and][2] paragraph 21][1], where, in relation to the year ended 5th April 1993 or any subsequent year, an employer has not—

(*a*) . . . [4]

(*b*) paid a Class 1B contribution by 19th October [or, if payment is made by an approved method of electronic communications in respect of earnings paid after 5th April 2004, not later than 22nd October][1] next following the year in respect of which it was due,

any contribution not so paid shall carry interest at the rate applicable under paragraph 6(3) of Schedule 1 to the Act from the reckonable date until payment.

(2) Interest payable under this paragraph shall be recoverable as if it were an earnings-related contribution or a Class 1B contribution, as the case may be, in respect of which an employer is liable under paragraph 10, 11, or 13 to pay to [HMRC][3].

(3) For the purposes of this paragraph—

(*a*) "employer" means, in relation to a Class 1B contribution, the person liable to pay such a contribution in accordance with section 10A of the Act;

(*b*) "the reckonable date" means, in relation to—

(*i*) . . . [4]

NIC

(ii) a Class 1B contribution, the 19th October [or, if payment was made by an approved method of electronic communications in respect of earnings paid after 5th April 2004, the 22nd October][1] next following the year in respect of which it was due.

[(iii) a contribution payable in respect of retrospective earnings relating to a tax year which is closed at the time that the relevant retrospective contributions regulations come into force, the 14th day after the end of the tax month immediately following the tax month in which those regulations came into force.][2]

(4) A contribution to which sub-paragraph (1) applies shall carry interest from the reckonable date even if the date is a non-business day within the meaning of section 92 of the Bills of Exchange Act 1882.

[(4A) Where an employer has not paid contributions in respect of retrospective earnings relating to a closed tax year by the date set out in paragraph 11A, any contribution not so paid shall carry interest at the rate applicable under paragraph 6(3) of Schedule 1 to the Act from the reckonable date until payment.][2]

[(5) A certificate of [HMRC][3] that, to the best of their knowledge and belief, any amount of interest payable under this paragraph has not been paid by an employer or employee is sufficient evidence that the amount mentioned in the certificate is unpaid and due to be paid, and any document purporting to be such a certificate shall be presumed to be a certificate until the contrary is proved.][1]

[(6) HMRC may prepare a certificate certifying the total amount of interest payable in respect of the whole or any component of a combined amount without specifying what component of the combined amount the interest relates to.

Sub-paragraph (5) shall apply, with any necessary modifications, to the certificate.][3]

[(7) For the purposes of this paragraph "combined amount" has the meaning given in paragraph 15(1A).][3]

Amendments—[1] Words in sub-para (1), (2) substituted, words inserted in sub-paras (1), (3), and sub-para (5) substituted, by the Social Security (Contributions, Categorisation of Earners and Intermediaries) (Amendment) Regulations, SI 2004/770 regs 2, 32(1), (9) with effect from 6 April 2004.

[2] Words in sub-para (1), and whole of sub-paras (3)(*b*)(iii), (4A) inserted, by the Social Security Contributions (Consequential Provisions) Regulations, SI 2007/1056 regs 3, 8(9) with effect from 6 April 2007.

[3] Reference to "the Inland Revenue" substituted throughout, and sub-paras (6), (7) inserted, by the Social Security (Contributions) (Amendment No 3) Regulations, SI 2008/636 regs 2, 6 with effect from 6 April 2008.

[4] Sub-paras (1)(*a*), (3)(*b*)(i) revoked by the Finance Act 2009, Sections 101 and 102 (Interest on Late Payments and Repayments), Appointed Days and Consequential Provisions Order, SI 2014/992 art 10(1), (2) with effect in relation to payments due and payable in respect of the tax year 2014–15 and subsequent tax years.

[Application of paragraphs 16 and 17 in cases of wilful failure to pay

17A—(1) If regulation 86(1)(*a*) applies paragraphs 16 and 17[", and section 101 of the Finance Act 2009, in respect of an earnings-related contribution,][2] shall apply to the employed earner to the extent of the primary contribution which the secondary contributor wilfully failed to pay.

(2) For the purpose of sub-paragraph (1) any reference in paragraph 16 and 17 to an employer shall be construed as a reference to the employed earner.][1]

Amendments—[1] Paragraph 17A inserted by the Social Security (Contributions, Categorisation of Earners and Intermediaries) (Amendment) Regulations, SI 2004/770 regs 2, 32(1), (10) with effect from 6 April 2004.

[2] Words in sub-para (1) inserted by the Finance Act 2009, Sections 101 and 102 (Interest on Late Payments and Repayments), Appointed Days and Consequential Provisions Order, SI 2014/992 art 10(1), (3) with effect in relation to payments due and payable in respect of the tax year 2014–15 and subsequent tax years.

Payment of interest on repaid earnings-related contributions or Class 1B contributions

18—(1) Where an earnings-related contribution paid by an employer in respect of the year ended 5th April 1993 or any subsequent year not later than the year ended 5th April 1999 is repaid to him and that repayment is made after the relevant date, any such repaid contribution shall carry interest at the rate applicable under paragraph 6(3) of Schedule 1 to the Act from the relevant date until the order for the repayment is issued.

(2) For the purposes of sub-paragraph (1) "the relevant date" is—

(*a*) in the case of an earnings-related contribution overpaid more than 12 months after the end of the year in respect of which the payment was made, the last day of the year in which it was paid; and

(*b*) in any other case, the last day of the year after the year in respect of which the contribution in question was paid.

(3) Where . . . [1] a Class 1B contribution paid by an employer in respect of the year ended 5th April 2000 or any subsequent year is repaid to him and that repayment is made after the relevant date, any such repaid contribution shall carry interest at the rate applicable under paragraph 6(3) of Schedule 1 to the Act from the relevant date until the order for the repayment is issued.

(4) For the purpose of sub-paragraph (3) "the relevant date" is—

(*a*) in the case of—

(*i*) . . . [1]

(ii) a Class 1B contribution, the 19th October next following the year in respect of which that contribution was paid; or

(*b*) the date on which the . . . [1] or Class 1B contribution was paid if that date is later than the date referred to in paragraph (*a*).

Amendments—[1] Words in sub-paras (3), (4)(*b*) revoked, and sub-para (4)(*a*)(i) revoked, by the Finance Act 2009, Sections 101 and 102 (Interest on Late Payments and Repayments), Appointed Days and Consequential Provisions Order, SI 2014/992 art 10(1), (4) with effect in relation to payments due and payable in respect of the tax year 2014–15 and subsequent tax years.

Repayment of interest

19 Where a secondary contributor or a person liable to pay a Class 1B contribution has paid interest on an earnings-related contribution or a Class 1B contribution, that interest shall be repaid to him [if[2]]—

(*a*) the interest paid is found not to have been due to be paid, although the contribution in respect of which it was paid was due to be paid;

(*b*) the earnings-related contribution or Class 1B contribution in respect of which interest was paid is returned or repaid to him in accordance with the provisions of regulation [52, 52A or 55][1].

Amendments—[1] References in sub-para (*b*) substituted by the Social Security (Contributions, Categorisation of Earners and Intermediaries) (Amendment) Regulations, SI 2004/770 regs 2, 32(1), (11) with effect only in respect of contributions payable in respect of 2003–04 and subsequent years: SI 2004/770 reg 1(2).

[2] Word inserted by the Social Security Contributions (Consequential Provisions) Regulations, SI 2007/1056 regs 3, 8(10) with effect from 6 April 2007.

Remission of interest for official error

20—(1) Where interest is payable in accordance with paragraph 17[, or section 101 of the Finance Act 2009 in relation to any earnings-related contribution,][1] it shall be remitted for the period commencing on the first relevant date and ending on the second relevant date in the circumstances specified in sub-paragraph (2).

(2) For the purposes of sub-paragraph (1), the circumstances are that the liability, or a greater liability, to pay interest in respect of an earnings-related contribution or a Class 1B contribution arises as the result of an official error being made.

(3) In this paragraph—

(*a*) "an official error" means a mistake made, or something omitted to be done, by an officer of the Board, where the employer or any person acting on his behalf has not caused, or materially contributed to, that mistake or omission;

(*b*) "the first relevant date" means the reckonable date as defined in paragraph 17(3) or, if later, the date on which the official error occurs;

(*c*) "the second relevant date" means the date 14 days after the date on which the official error has been rectified and the employer is advised of its rectification.

Amendments—[1] Words in sub-para(1) inserted by the Finance Act 2009, Sections 101 and 102 (Interest on Late Payments and Repayments), Appointed Days and Consequential Provisions Order, SI 2014/992 art 10(1), (5) with effect in relation to payments due and payable in respect of the tax year 2014–15 and subsequent tax years.

Application of paragraphs 10, 12, 16, 17, 18, 19 and 20

21—(1) This paragraph applies where—

(*a*) secondary Class 1 contributions are payable in respect of [relevant employment income; and][1];

(*b*) an amount or proportion (as the case may be) of the liability of the secondary contributor to those contributions is transferred to the employed earner by an election made jointly by them for the purposes of paragraph 3B(1) of Schedule 1 to the Act.

(2) Paragraphs 10, 12, 16, 17, 18, 19 and 20 shall apply to the employed earner to the extent of the liability transferred by the election and, to that extent, those paragraphs shall not apply to the employer.

(3) For the purposes of sub-paragraph (2)—

(*a*) any reference in paragraphs 10, 12, 16, 17, 18 and 20 to an employer; and

(*b*) the reference in paragraph 19 to a secondary contributor,

shall be construed as a reference to the employed earner to whom the liability is transferred by the election.

Amendments—[1] In sub-para (1)(*a*), words substituted by the Social Security (Contributions) (Amendment No 4) Regulations, SI 2004/2096 regs 2, 7(*c*) with effect from 1 September 2004. SI 2004/2096 has effect in relation to—

(a) agreements entered into after 1 September 2004 which are in respect of post-commencement employment income, and

(b) elections made after that date.

NIC

[Real time returns of information about payments of . . . [5] earnings

21A—(1) [Subject to [sub-paragraph (1A)][4],][3] on or before making any payment of . . . [5] earnings to an employee a Real Time Information employer must deliver to HMRC the information specified in Schedule 4A (real time returns) in accordance with this paragraph [unless—

(*a*) the employer is not required to maintain a deductions working sheet for any employees, or

(*b*) an employee's earnings are below the lower earnings limit and the employer is required to make a return under regulation 67B(1), regulation 67D(3), regulation 67E(6) or regulation 67EA(3) of the PAYE Regulations.][2]

[(1A) But a Real Time Information employer—

(*a*) which for the tax year 2014–15 meets Conditions A and B, or

(*b*) which for the tax year 2015–16 meets Conditions A and C,

may instead for that tax year deliver to HMRC the information specified in Schedule 4A (real time returns) in respect of every payment of . . . [5] earnings made to an employee in a tax month on or before making the last payment of . . . [5] earnings in that month.

(1B) Condition A is that at 5th April 2014 the employer is one to whom HMRC has issued an employer's PAYE reference.

(1C) Condition B is that at 6th April 2014 the Real Time Information employer employs no more than 9 employees.

(1D) Condition C is that at 6th April 2015 the Real Time Information employer employs no more than 9 employees.

(1E) In this paragraph "employer's PAYE reference" means—

(*a*) the combination of letters, numbers, or both, used by HMRC to identify an employer for the purposes of the PAYE Regulations, and

(*b*) the number which identifies the employer's HMRC office.][4]

(2) The information must be included in a return.

(3) Subject to paragraph (4), if payments of . . . [5] earnings are made to more than one employee at the same time, the return under sub-paragraph (2) must include the information required by Schedule 4A in respect of each employee to whom a payment of . . . [5] earnings is made at that time.

(4) If payments of . . . [5] earnings are made to more than one employee at the same time but the employer operates more than one payroll, the employer must make a return in respect of each payroll.

(5) The return is to be made using an approved method of electronic communications and regulation 90N(2) (mandatory use of electronic communications) applies as if the return was a paragraph 22 return within the meaning given by regulation 90M (paragraph 22 return and specified payments).

(6), (7) . . . [2]

(8) Schedule 24 to the Finance Act 2007 (penalties for errors), as that Schedule applies to income tax returns, shall apply in relation to the requirement to make a return contained in sub-paragraph (2).][1]

Cross-references—See Social Security (Contributions) (Amendment No 3) Regulations, SI 2012/821 reg 16 (real time information transitional provisions: postponement of first return).

Social Security (Contributions) (Amendment and Application of Schedule 38 to the Finance Act 2012) Regulations, SI 2013/622 regs 29–32 (transitional arrangements in relation to information requirements under real time information).

Amendments—[1] Para 21A and preceding heading inserted by the Social Security (Contributions) (Amendment No 3) Regulations, SI 2012/821 regs 2, 11 with effect from 6 April 2012.

[2] In sub-para (1), words substituted, and sub-paras 6), (7) revoked, by the Security (Contributions) (Amendment and Application of Schedule 38 to the Finance Act 2012) Regulations, SI 2013/622 regs 5, 10 with effect in relation to the tax year 2013–14 and subsequent tax years.

[3] Words in sub-para (1), and whole of sub-paras (1A), (1B), inserted, by the Social Security (Contributions) (Amendment No 4) Regulations, SI 2013/2301 regs 2, 3 with effect in relation to any payment of general earnings made in the period beginning on 6 October 2013 and ending on 5 April 2014 (SI 2013/2301 reg 1(2)).

[4] In sub-para (1), words substituted, and sub-paras (1A)–(1E) substituted for previous sub-paras (1A), (1B) by the Social Security (Contributions) (Amendment) Regulations, SI 2014/608 regs 2, 5, 7. These amendments come into force on 6 April 2014.

[5] Word revoked in heading and in each place by the Social Security (Miscellaneous Amendments No 2) Regulations, SI 2015/478 regs 2, 22(1), (4)(*b*) with effect from 6 April 2015.

[Employees in respect of whom employer is not required to maintain a deductions worksheet

21AA—(1) This paragraph applies if an employer makes a payment of . . . [2] earnings to an employee in respect of whom the employer is not required to maintain a deductions working sheet.

(2) The employer need not deliver the information required by paragraph 21A in respect of that employee on or before making the payment.

(3) The employer must deliver that information no later than the end of the period of 7 days starting with the day following the day on which the payment is made.][1]

Amendments—[1] Paras 21AA–21AD inserted by the Security (Contributions) (Amendment and Application of Schedule 38 to the Finance Act 2012) Regulations, SI 2013/622 regs 5, 11 with effect in relation to the tax year 2013–14 and subsequent tax years
[2] In sub-para (1), word revoked by the Social Security (Miscellaneous Amendments No 2) Regulations, SI 2015/478 regs 2, 22(1), (4)(*c*) with effect from 6 April 2015.

[Employees paid in specified circumstances

21AB—(1) This paragraph applies if—

(*a*) an employer makes a payment of . . . [2] earnings to an employee, and

(*b*) all of the circumstances in sub-paragraph (2) apply.

(2) The circumstances are that—

(*a*) the payment includes an amount of . . . [2] earnings which is for work undertaken by the employee on—

(i) the day the payment is made, or

(ii) provided that the payment is made before the employee leaves the place of work at the end of the employee's period of work, the day before the payment is made,

(*b*) in respect of the work mentioned in paragraph (a), it was not reasonably practicable for the employer to calculate the payment due before the completion of the work, and

(*c*) it is not reasonably practicable for the employer to deliver the information required by paragraph 21A on or before making the payment.

(3) The employer need not deliver the information required by paragraph 21A on or before making the payment.

(4) The employer must deliver that information no later than the end of the period of 7 days starting with the day following the day on which the payment is made.][1]

Amendments—[1] Paras 21AA–21AD inserted by the Security (Contributions) (Amendment and Application of Schedule 38 to the Finance Act 2012) Regulations, SI 2013/622 regs 5, 11 with effect in relation to the tax year 2013–14 and subsequent tax years.
[2] In sub-paras (1), (2), word revoked by the Social Security (Miscellaneous Amendments No 2) Regulations, SI 2015/478 regs 2, 22(1), (4)(*c*) with effect from 6 April 2015.

[Paragraphs 21AA and 21AB: supplementary

21AC Where paragraph 21AA or 21AB applies, the information required by paragraph 21A in respect of the payment of . . . [2] earnings may be included in a return with the information for any other payment of general earnings.][1]

Amendments—[1] Paras 21AA–21AD inserted by the Security (Contributions) (Amendment and Application of Schedule 38 to the Finance Act 2012) Regulations, SI 2013/622 regs 5, 11 with effect in relation to the tax year 2013–14 and subsequent tax years.
[2] Word revoked by the Social Security (Miscellaneous Amendments No 2) Regulations, SI 2015/478 regs 2, 22(1), (4)(*c*) with effect from 6 April 2015.

[Benefits and expenses—returns under regulations 85 to 87 of the PAYE Regulations

21AD—(1) This paragraph applies if an employer makes a payment of . . . [2] earnings to an employee which, for the purposes of tax, falls to be included in a return under—

(*a*) regulations 85 and 86 of the PAYE Regulations (employers: annual return of other earnings (Forms P11D and P9D)—information which must be provided for each employee), or

(*b*) regulations 85 and 87 of the PAYE Regulations (employers: annual return of other earnings (Forms P11D and P9D)—information which must also be provided for benefits code employees) or would fall to be so included if the employee's employment was subject to the benefits code for the purposes of regulation 85 of the PAYE Regulations.

(2) If the employer is unable to comply with the requirement in paragraph 21A(1) to deliver the information required by that paragraph on or before making the payment, the employer must instead deliver the information as soon as reasonably practicable after the payment is made and in any event no later than 14 days after the end of the tax month in which the payment is made.][1]

Amendments—[1] Paras 21AA–21AD inserted by the Security (Contributions) (Amendment and Application of Schedule 38 to the Finance Act 2012) Regulations, SI 2013/622 regs 5, 11 with effect in relation to the tax year 2013–14 and subsequent tax years.
[2] In sub-para (1), word revoked by the Social Security (Miscellaneous Amendments No 2) Regulations, SI 2015/478 regs 2, 22(1), (4)(*c*) with effect from 6 April 2015.

[Modification of the requirements of paragraph 21A: notional payments

21B—(1) This [paragraph][2] applies if an employer makes a payment of . . . [3] earnings to an employee which, for the purposes of tax, is a notional payment within the meaning given by section 710(2) of ITEPA 2003 (including a notional payment arising by virtue of a retrospective tax provision).

(2) If the employer is unable to comply with the requirement in paragraph 21A(1) to deliver the information required by that paragraph on or before making the payment, the employer must instead deliver the information as soon as reasonably practicable after the payment is made and in any event no later than—

(*a*) the time at which the employer delivers the information required by regulation 67B of the PAYE Regulations (real time returns of information about relevant payments) in respect of the payment;

(*b*) . . . [2] or

(*c*) 14 days after the end of the tax month the payment is made in,

whichever is earliest.][1]

Amendments—[1] Para 21B and preceding heading inserted by the Social Security (Contributions) (Amendment No 3) Regulations, SI 2012/821 regs 2, 11 with effect from 6 April 2012.

[2] In sub-para (1) word substituted for word "regulation", and sub-para (2)(*b*) revoked by the Security (Contributions) (Amendment and Application of Schedule 38 to the Finance Act 2012) Regulations, SI 2013/622 regs 5, 12 with effect in relation to the tax year 2013–14 and subsequent tax years.

[3] In sub-para (1), word revoked by the Social Security (Miscellaneous Amendments No 2) Regulations, SI 2015/478 regs 2, 22(1), (4)(*c*) with effect from 6 April 2015.

[Relationship between paragraph 21A and aggregation of earnings

21C—(1) Where an employee's earnings are aggregated, a Real Time Information employer or, as the case may be, Real Time Information employers must make such arrangements as are necessary to ensure that the information specified in paragraph (2) in respect of all the aggregated earnings is included in the information given in respect of one of the employee's employments only.

(2) The information specified in this paragraph is the information specified in paragraphs 7 and 10(b) and (d) of Schedule 4A (real time returns).][1]

Amendments—[1] Para 21C and preceding heading inserted by the Social Security (Contributions) (Amendment No 3) Regulations, SI 2012/821 regs 2, 11 with effect from 6 April 2012.

[Notifications of payments of general earnings to and by providers of certain electronic payment methods

21CA—(1) A Real Time Information employer who makes a payment of . . . [2] earnings using an approved method of electronic communications which falls to be included in a return under paragraph 21A must—

(*a*) generate a reference and include it in that return,

(*b*) notify the service provider that the payment is a payment of . . . [2] earnings, and

(*c*) generate a sub-reference in respect of the payment of . . . [2] earnings and notify the service provider of that sub-reference.

(2) A service provider who receives a notification under paragraph (1)(*b*) must notify HMRC of the information it holds that is required for generating a reference in relation to the payment of . . . [2] earnings.

(3) In sub-paragraphs (1) and (2), "service provider" means the provider of the approved method of electronic communications by which the payment is made.

(4) For the purposes of sub-paragraphs (1) and (3), an "approved method of electronic communications" is any method of electronic communications which has been approved for the purposes of regulation 90H (mandatory electronic payment).

(5) Any direction given under regulation 67CA of the PAYE Regulations (notification of relevant payments to and by providers of certain electronic payment methods) applies for the purposes of the obligations in this paragraph as if it referred to payments of . . . [2] earnings.][1]

Amendments—[1] Para 21CA inserted by the Security (Contributions) (Amendment and Application of Schedule 38 to the Finance Act 2012) Regulations, SI 2013/622 regs 5, 13 with effect in relation to the tax year 2013–14 and subsequent tax years.

[2] Word revoked in each place by the Social Security (Miscellaneous Amendments No 2) Regulations, SI 2015/478 regs 2, 22(1), (4)(*c*) with effect from 6 April 2015.

[Exceptions to paragraph 21A

21D—(1) This paragraph applies to—

(*a*) an individual who is a practising member of a religious society or order whose beliefs are incompatible with the use of electronic communications;

(*b*) a partnership, if all the partners fall within sub-paragraph (*a*);

(*c*) a company, if all the directors and the company secretary fall within sub-paragraph (*a*);

(*d*) a care and support employer;

[(*e*) an employer to whom a direction has been given under sub-paragraph (12).][2]

[But this is subject to sub-paragraph (2B).][3]

(2) A Real Time Information employer to whom this paragraph applies may proceed in accordance with this paragraph instead of paragraph 21A.

[(2A) Before 6th April 2014, a Real Time Information employer to whom this paragraph applies may proceed as if the employer were a non-Real Time Information employer and accordingly the provisions of this Schedule apply to such an employer.][2]

[(2B) This paragraph does not apply if a Real Time Information employer within sub-paragraph (1) makes a return using an approved method of electronic communications.][3]

(3) [On and after 6th April 2014, the][2] Real Time Information employer must deliver to HMRC the information specified in Schedule 4A in respect of each employee to whom a payment of . . . [4] earnings is made in a tax [quarter][3] unless the employer is not required to maintain a deductions working sheet for any employees and, for the purposes of this paragraph, references in Schedule 4A to a payment of general earnings shall be read as if they were references to all the payments made to the employee in the tax [quarter][3].

(4) The information must be included in a return in such a form as HMRC may approve or prescribe.

(5) The return required under sub-paragraph (4) must be delivered within 14 days after the end of the tax [quarter][3] the return relates to.

(6) If payments of . . . [4] earnings have been made to more than one employee in the tax [quarter][3], the return under sub-paragraph (4) must include the information required by Schedule 4A in respect of each employee to whom a payment of . . . [4] earnings has been made.

(7), (8) . . . [2]

(9) Schedule 24 to the Finance Act 2007, as that Schedule applies to income tax returns, shall apply in relation to the requirement to make a return contained in sub-paragraph (4).

(10) In sub-paragraph (1)(*c*), "company" means a body corporate or unincorporated association but does not include a partnership.

(11) In sub-paragraph (1)(*d*), "care and support employer" means an individual ("the employer") who employs a person to provide domestic or personal services at or from the employer's home where—

(*a*) the services are provided to the employer or a member of the employer's family;

(*b*) the recipient of the services has a physical or mental disability, or is elderly or infirm; and

(*c*) it is the employer who delivers the return (and not some other person on the employer's behalf).

[(12) Where the Commissioners for Her Majesty's Revenue and Customs are satisfied that—

(*a*) it is not reasonably practicable for an employer to make a return using an approved method of electronic communications, and

(*b*) it is the employer who delivers the return (and not some other person on the employer's behalf),

they may make a direction specifying that the employer is not required to make a return using an approved method of electronic communications.][2]][1]

Cross-references—See Social Security (Contributions) (Amendment No 3) Regulations, SI 2012/821 reg 16 (real time information transitional provisions: postponement of first return).

Social Security (Contributions) (Amendment and Application of Schedule 38 to the Finance Act 2012) Regulations, SI 2013/622 regs 29–32 (transitional arrangements in relation to information requirements under real time information).

Amendments—[1] Para 21D and preceding heading inserted by the Social Security (Contributions) (Amendment No 3) Regulations, SI 2012/821 regs 2, 11 with effect from 6 April 2012.

[2] Sub-paras (1)(*e*), (2A), (12) inserted, in sub-para (3) words substituted for word "A", and sub-paras (7), (8) revoked, by the Security (Contributions) (Amendment and Application of Schedule 38 to the Finance Act 2012) Regulations, SI 2013/622 regs 5, 14 with effect in relation to the tax year 2013–14 and subsequent tax years.

[3] In sub-para (1), words inserted, sub-para (2B) inserted, and word in sub-paras (3), (5), (6) substituted, by the Social Security (Contributions) (Amendment) Regulations, SI 2014/608 regs 2, 5, 8. These amendments come into force on 6 April 2014.

[4] In sub-paras (3), (6), word revoked by the Social Security (Miscellaneous Amendments No 2) Regulations, SI 2015/478 regs 2, 22(1), (4)(*c*) with effect from 6 April 2015.

[Returns under paragraphs 21A and 21D: amendments

21E—(1) This paragraph applies where [there is an inaccuracy in a return, whether careless or deliberate,][3] made under paragraph 21A (real time returns of information about payments of . . . [4] earnings) or 21D (exceptions to paragraph 21A) and sub-paragraph (2), (3) or (4) applies.

(2) This sub-paragraph applies where the [inaccuracy][3] relates to the information given in the return in respect of an employee under [one or more of paragraphs 3A, 7][2], 10(*b*), 10(*d*), 13, 14, 15, 16 or 18 of Schedule 4A (real time returns).

(3) This sub-paragraph applies where the [inaccuracy][3] was the omission of details of a payment of . . . [4] earnings to an employee.

(4) This sub-paragraph applies where retrospective earnings increase the total amount of the . . . [4] earnings paid to the employee for any tax year in which the employer was a Real Time Information employer.

[(5) When the employer becomes aware of an inaccuracy in a return under paragraph 21A or 21D, the employer must provide the correct information in the next return for the tax year in question.][3]

NIC

(6) But if the information given has not been corrected before 20th April following the end of the tax year in question, the employer must make a return under this sub-paragraph.

(7) A return under sub-paragraph (6)—

(*a*) must include the following—

(i) the information specified in paragraphs [2 to 7 and 10 to 12][2] of Schedule 4A,

(ii) . . . [2]

(iii) the value of the adjustment, if any, to the information given under each of the paragraphs of Schedule 4A referred to in sub-paragraph (2) in the final return under paragraph 21A or 21D containing information in respect of the employee in the tax year in question,

(iv) if an adjustment is made to the information given under paragraph 7 or 10(*b*) or (*d*) of Schedule 4A, the information specified in paragraph 6 of that Schedule,

(v) if an adjustment is made to the information given under paragraph 10(*d*) of Schedule 4A that decreases the amount reported under that paragraph, an indication of whether the employer has refunded the primary Class 1 contributions paid in error to the employee, and

(vi) if an adjustment is made to the information given under paragraph 16 of Schedule 4A, the information specified in paragraph 17 of that Schedule if it has not already been provided;

(*b*) must be made as soon as reasonably practicable after the [employer becomes aware of the inaccuracy][3]; and

(*c*) must be made using an approved method of electronic communications [and regulation 90N(2) (mandatory use of electronic communications) applies as if the return was a paragraph 22 return within the meaning given by regulation 90M (paragraph 22 return and specified payments)][2].

(8) In the application of sub-paragraphs (6) and (7) to cases within sub-paragraph (3), if no information was given in any returns under paragraph 21A or 21D in respect of the employee in the tax year, the value of any adjustments required must be calculated as if there was a final return containing information for the employee in the year and the figure requiring adjustment was zero.

(9) Sub-paragraph (7)(*c*) does not apply if the employer is one to whom paragraph 21D applies but in those circumstances the return must be in such a form as HMRC may approve or prescribe.][1]

Amendments—[1] Para 21E and preceding heading inserted by the Social Security (Contributions) (Amendment No 3) Regulations, SI 2012/821 regs 2, 11 with effect from 6 April 2012.

[2] In sub-paras (2), (7)(*a*)(i), words substituted, para (*a*)(ii) revoked, and words in para (*c*) inserted, by the Security (Contributions) (Amendment and Application of Schedule 38 to the Finance Act 2012) Regulations, SI 2013/622 regs 5, 15 with effect in relation to the tax year 2013–14 and subsequent tax years.

[3] In sub-paras (1), (7)(*b*), words substituted, in sub-paras (2), (3), word substituted, and sub-para (5) substituted, by the Social Security (Contributions) (Amendment) Regulations, SI 2014/608 regs 2, 5, 9. These amendments come into force on 6 April 2014.

[4] In sub-paras (1), (3), (4), word revoked by the Social Security (Miscellaneous Amendments No 2) Regulations, SI 2015/478 regs 2, 22(1), (4)(*c*) with effect from 6 April 2015.

[Failure to make a return under paragraph 21A or 21D

21EA—(1) This paragraph applies where an employer does not make a return required by paragraph 21A (real time returns of information about payments of . . . [4] earnings) or 21D (exceptions to paragraph 21A).

(2) The employer must provide the information in the next return made under paragraph 21A or 21D for the tax year in question.

(3) But if the information has not been provided before 20th April following the end of the tax year in question, the employer must submit a return under this sub-paragraph . . . [2].

(4) A return under sub-paragraph (3) must—

(*a*) include the information specified in Schedule 4A,

(*b*) be made as soon as reasonably practicable after the discovery of the failure to make the return, and

(*c*) be made using an approved method of electronic communications and regulation 90N(2) (mandatory use of electronic communications) applies as if the return were a paragraph 22 return within the meaning given by regulation 90M (paragraph 22 return and specified payments).

(5) Sub-paragraph (4)(*c*) does not apply if the employer is one to whom paragraph 21D applies but in those circumstances the return must be in such a form as HMRC may approve or prescribe.

(6) [If a return under sub-paragraph (3) is not made before 20th May following the tax year in question][2] section 98A of TMA 1970 (special penalties in the case of certain returns) applies to [that return][2][, but this sub-paragraph does not apply to a return in respect of the tax year 2014–15 or a subsequent tax year][3].][1]

Amendments—[1] Para 21EA inserted by the Security (Contributions) (Amendment and Application of Schedule 38 to the Finance Act 2012) Regulations, SI 2013/622 regs 5, 16 with effect in relation to the tax year 2013–14 and subsequent tax years.

[2] In sub-para (3), words revoked, and in sub-para (6), words at beginning inserted and words substituted, by the Social Security (Contributions) (Amendment No 4) Regulations, SI 2013/2301 regs 2, 4 with effect from 6 October 2013.

[3] In sub-para (6), words inserted by the Social Security (Contributions) (Amendment No 4) Regulations, SI 2014/2397 regs 2, 3(1), (4) with effect in relation to a failure to deliver a return to HMRC in respect of any payment of general earnings made on or after 6 October 2014.

[4] In sub-para (1), word revoked by the Social Security (Miscellaneous Amendments No 2) Regulations, SI 2015/478 regs 2, 22(1), (4)(*c*) with effect from 6 April 2015.

[Additional information about payments

21F—(1) A Real Time Information employer must inform HMRC of each of the amounts specified in Schedule 4B (additional information about payments) for each tax period unless sub-paragraph (4) or (5) applies.

(2) The information must be given in a return.

(3) The return must be delivered within 14 days after the end of the tax period.

(4) This sub-paragraph applies if—

(*a*) all of the amounts are zero; and

(*b*) the employer has not made a return under sub-paragraph (2) in the tax year.

(5) This paragraph applies if none of the amounts has changed in the tax period.

(6) If an employer makes an error in a return under this paragraph, the employer must provide the correct information in the first return made under sub-paragraph (2) after the discovery of the error.

(7) But if the information given has not been corrected before 20th April following the end of the year in question, the employer must provide the correct information for the year in question in a return under this sub-paragraph.

[(7A) A Real Time Information employer may send to HMRC a notification (included within a return under this paragraph or otherwise) if—

(*a*) for a tax period, the employer was not required to make any returns in accordance with paragraph 21A or 21D because no payments of . . . [3] earnings were made during the tax periods, or

(*b*) the employer has sent the final return under paragraph 21A or 21D that the employer expects to make—

(i) in the circumstances described in paragraph 5 of Schedule A1 to the PAYE Regulations (real time returns); or

(ii) for the year.][2]

(8) A return under sub-paragraph (2) or (7) [and a notification under paragraph (7A)][2]—

(*a*) must state—

(i) the year to which the return relates,

(ii) the employer's HMRC office number,

(iii) the employer's PAYE reference, . . . [2]

(iv) the employer's accounts office reference[; and

(v) if the notification is under sub-paragraph (7A)(*b*)(i), include the date of cessation;][2]

(*b*) is to be made using an approved method of electronic communications.

(9) . . . [2]

(10) For the purposes of sub-paragraph (8)(b), regulation 90N(2) (mandatory use of electronic communications) applies as if the return was a paragraph 22 return within the meaning given by regulation 90M (paragraph 22 return and specified payments).

(11) The requirement to use an approved method of electronic communications does not apply if the employer is one to whom paragraph 21D (exceptions to paragraph 21A) applies but in those circumstances the return must be in such a form as HMRC may approve or prescribe.

(12) Schedule 24 to the Finance Act 2007 (penalties for errors), as that Schedule applies to income tax returns, shall apply in relation to the requirement to make a return contained in sub-paragraph (2) or (7).][1]

Amendments—[1] Para 21F and preceding heading inserted by the Social Security (Contributions) (Amendment No 3) Regulations, SI 2012/821 regs 2, 11 with effect from 6 April 2012.

[2] Sub-para (7A) inserted, in sub-para (8) words inserted and word "and" revoked, and sub-para (9) revoked, by the Security (Contributions) (Amendment and Application of Schedule 38 to the Finance Act 2012) Regulations, SI 2013/622 regs 5, 17 with effect in relation to the tax year 2013–14 and subsequent tax years.

[3] In sub-para (7A), word revoked by the Social Security (Miscellaneous Amendments No 2) Regulations, SI 2015/478 regs 2, 22(1), (4)(*c*) with effect from 6 April 2015.

[Penalty: failure to comply with paragraph 21A or 21D

21G—(1) Where a Real Time Information employer fails to deliver a return in accordance with paragraph 21A (real time returns of information about payments of . . . [2] earnings) to paragraph 21AB (employees paid in specific circumstances), paragraph 21AD (benefits and expenses – returns under the PAYE Regulations), paragraph 21B (modification of the requirements of paragraph 21A: notional payments) or paragraph 21D (exceptions to paragraph 21A), Schedule 55 to the Finance Act 2009 (amount of penalty: real time information for PAYE) and regulations 67I to 67K of the PAYE Regulations (penalties) apply in relation that failure as if—

(*a*) the return under paragraph 21A (real time returns of information about payments of . . . [2] earnings) or paragraph 21D (exceptions to paragraph 21A), as the case may be, were a return falling within item 4 of the Table in paragraph 1 of Schedule 55, and

(*b*) references to the PAYE Regulations were references to these Regulations, but this is subject to [sub-paragraphs (2) and (2A)][3].

(2) Where a Real Time Information employer (P) is liable to a penalty in consequence of a failure to deliver a return ("the tax return") under regulation 67B (real time returns of information about relevant payments) or regulation 67D (exceptions to regulation 67B) of the PAYE Regulations, P shall not also be liable to a penalty in respect of any failure in relation to an associated return under paragraph 21A (real time returns of information about payments of . . . [2] earnings) or 21D (exceptions to paragraph 21A).

[(2A) Sub-paragraph (2) does not apply to a penalty imposed under paragraph 6D of Schedule 55 to the Finance Act 2009 (amount of penalty: real time information for PAYE).][3]

(3) A tax return and a return under paragraph 21A or 21D are "associated" if the return under paragraph 21A or 21D is required to be delivered at the same time as the tax return.][1]

Amendments—[1] Para 21G inserted by the Social Security (Contributions) (Amendment No 4) Regulations, SI 2014/2397 regs 2, 3(1), (5) with effect in relation to a failure to deliver a return to HMRC in respect of any payment of general earnings made—

– on or after 6 October 2014 where the employer is a large existing Real Time Information employer; and

– on or after 6 March 2015 where the employer is a small existing Real Time Information employer or a person becomes a new Real Time Information employer after 6 October 2014.

[2] Word in each place revoked by the Social Security (Miscellaneous Amendments No 2) Regulations, SI 2015/478 regs 2, 22(1), (4)(*c*) with effect from 6 April 2015.

[3] Words substituted, and sub-para (2A) inserted, by the Social Security (Contributions) (Amendment) (No 2) Regulations, SI 2016/352 regs 2, 7 with effect from 6 April 2016.

Return by employer at end of year

22—[(A1) This regulation applies to—

(*a*) non-Real Time Information employers;

(*b*) Real Time Information employers in relation to years in which they were, for the whole of the year, non-Real Time information employers; and

(*c*) Real Time Information employers to whom HMRC has given a notice requiring a return under regulation 73 of the PAYE Regulations (annual return of relevant payments liable to deduction of tax (Forms P35 and P14) in respect of a tax year.][7]

(1) [Before 20th May following the end of the year the employer shall render to [HMRC][3] in such form as they may approve or prescribe][2], a return showing in respect of each employee, in respect of whom he was required at any time during the year to prepare or maintain a deductions working sheet in accordance with this Schedule—

(*a*) such particulars as [HMRC][3] may require for the identification of the employee,

(*b*) the year to which the return relates,

(*c*) in respect of each and under each of the category letters, the total amounts for the year shown under—

(i) each of [sub-paragraphs (i) to (v)][1] severally of paragraph 7(13)(*b*) (such amounts being rounded down to the next whole pound if not already whole pounds) in the case of paragraphs (i) [to (iii)][13]),

(ii), (iii) . . . [1]

(*d*) the total amount of any statutory maternity pay paid during the year; . . . [1]

[(*da*) the total amount of [. . . [11] statutory paternity pay][6] paid during the year;][1]

(*daa*) [11] . . . . . . [12]

[(*db*) the total amount of statutory adoption pay paid during the year][1][; and

(*dc*) the total amount of statutory shared parental pay paid during the year.][12]

(*e*) . . . [8]

(2) The return required by sub-paragraph (1) shall include a statement and declaration in the form approved or prescribed by [HMRC][3] containing a list of all deductions working sheets on which the employer was obliged to keep records in accordance with this Schedule in respect of that year, and shall also include a certificate showing—

(*a*) the total amount of earnings-related contributions payable by him in respect of each employee during that year;

(*b*) the total amount of earnings-related contributions payable in respect of all his employees during that year;

(*c*) . . . [13]

(*d*) in respect of statutory maternity pay paid during that year to all his employees, the total of amounts determined under regulation 3 of the Compensation of Employers Regulations and deducted by virtue of regulation 4 of those Regulations; . . . [1]

[(*da*) in respect of [. . . [11] statutory paternity pay][6] paid during that year to all his employees the total of the amounts determined under regulation 5 of the Statutory Paternity Pay and Statutory Adoption Pay (Administration) Regulations 2002;][1]

(*daa*) . . . [11] . . . [12]

[(*db*) in respect of statutory adoption pay paid during that year to all his employees the total of the amounts determined under regulation 5 of the Statutory Paternity Pay and Statutory Adoption Pay (Administration) Regulations 2002][1][; and

(*dc*) in respect of statutory shared parental pay paid during the year to all his employees the total of the amounts determined under regulation 5 (deductions from payments to the Commissioners) of the Statutory Shared Parental Pay (Administration) Regulations 2014.][12]

(*e*) . . . [8]

[(2A) Where a liability arises to pay contributions in respect of retrospective earnings relating to a closed tax year, the employer shall render a replacement return, or where necessary prepare one, in respect of the employee for that closed tax year before 20th May following the end of the year in which the relevant retrospective contributions regulations came into force, in accordance with paragraphs (*a*) to (*c*) of sub-paragraph (1), setting out the revised earnings and earnings-related contributions.

(2B) The return required by sub-paragraph (2A) shall include a statement and declaration in a form prescribed by HMRC containing a list of all deductions working sheets in accordance with paragraph 6(1A) of this Schedule in respect of that year, and shall also include a certificate showing—

(*a*) the total amount of earnings-related contributions originally payable (in accordance with sub-paragraph (2)(*a*)) in respect of each employee to whom sub-paragraph (2A) applies;

(*b*) the total amount of earnings-related contributions originally payable (in accordance with sub-paragraph (2)(*b*)) in respect of all employees to whom sub-paragraph (2A) applies;

(*c*) the total amount of revised earnings-related contributions payable in respect of each of those employees;

(*d*) the total amount of revised earnings-related contributions payable in respect of all those employees,

(*e*) the difference between the amount certified in paragraph (*b*) and paragraph (*d*) of this sub-paragraph in respect of all of those employees[.][13]

(*f*) . . . [13]][3]

(3) . . . [10]

(4) If the employer is a body corporate, [the declarations][3] and [the certificates][3] referred to in [sub-paragraphs (2) and (2B)][3] shall be signed by the secretary or by a director of the body corporate.

(5) If, within 14 days of the end of any year, an employer has failed to pay to [HMRC][3] the total amount of earnings-related contributions which he is liable so to pay, [HMRC][3] may prepare a certificate showing the amount of such contributions remaining unpaid for the year in question, excluding any amount deducted by the employer by virtue of the Compensation of Employers Regulations.

The provisions of paragraph 17 shall apply with any necessary modifications to the amount shown in that certificate.

(6) Notwithstanding sub-paragraphs (2) to (5), [the returns referred to in sub-paragraphs (1) and (2A)][3] may be made in such other form as [HMRC][3] and the employer approve, and in that case—

(*a*) sub-paragraphs (2) to (5) shall not apply; and

(*b*) the making of [the returns][3] shall be subject to such conditions as [HMRC][3] may direct as to the method of making it.

(7) [Section 98A of the Taxes Management Act 1970 (special penalties in the case of certain returns) and Schedule 24 to the Finance Act 2007 (penalties for errors) as that Schedule applies to income tax returns][4] as modified by the provisions of paragraph 7 of Schedule 1 to the Act shall apply in relation to the requirement to make a return contained in sub-paragraph (1) [and (2A)][3].

Amendments—[1] Words in sub-para (1)(*c*) substituted; sub-paras (1)(*c*)(ii), (iii), and word in sub-paras (1)(*d*), (2)(*d*) revoked; and sub-paras (1)(*da*), (*db*), and (2)(*da*), (*db*) inserted; by the Social Security (Contributions) (Amendment) Regulations, SI 2003/193 regs 2, 16(1), (5) with effect from 2003–04.

[2] Words substituted by the Social Security (Contributions, Categorisation of Earners and Intermediaries) (Amendment) Regulations, SI 2004/770 regs 2, 32(1), (12) with effect from 6 April 2004.

[3] Words in sub-paras (1), (2), (4)–(6) substituted; sub-paras (2A), (2B), and words in sub-para (7), inserted; by the Social Security Contributions (Consequential Provisions) Regulations, SI 2007/1056 regs 3, 8(11)–(15) with effect from 6 April 2007.

[4] Words in sub-para (7) substituted by the Social Security (Contributions) (Amendment No 3) Regulations, SI 2008/636 regs 2, 7(*a*) with effect from 1 April 2008.

[6] Words in sub-paras (1)(*da*), (2)(*da*) substituted for words "statutory paternity pay", and sub-paras (1)(*daa*) and (2)(*daa*) inserted, by the Social Security (Contributions) (Amendment No 5) Regulations, SI 2010/2450, regs 2, 4 with effect from 14 November 2010.

[7] Sub-para (A1) inserted by the Social Security (Contributions) (Amendment No 3) Regulations, SI 2012/821 regs 2, 12 with effect from 6 April 2012.

[8] In sub-paras (1)(*daa*), (2)(*daa*) words inserted, in sub-paras (1)(*db*), (2)(*db*) full stop substituted, and sub-paras (1)(*e*), (2)(*e*) revoked, by the Social Security (Contributions) (Amendment No 3) Regulations, SI 2012/821 regs 2, 27, 28 with effect from 6 April 2012.

[9] In sub-para (A1) word substituted by the Security (Contributions) (Amendment and Application of Schedule 38 to the Finance Act 2012) Regulations, SI 2013/622 regs 5, 18 with effect in relation to the tax year 2013–14 and subsequent tax years.

[10] Sub-para (3) revoked by the Social Security (Contributions) (Amendment No 4) Regulations, SI 2014/2397 regs 2, 3(1), (6) with effect from 6 October 2014.

[11] In sub-paras (1)(*da*), (2)(*da*), word revoked, and sub-paras (1)(*daa*), (2)(*daa*) revoked by the Social Security and Tax Credits (Miscellaneous Amendments) Regulations, SI 2015/175 regs 2, 4(1), (5)(*a*)(i), (ii), (*b*)(i), (ii) with effect from 5 April 2015. These amendments do not have effect where they relate to ordinary statutory paternity pay or additional statutory paternity pay, or ordinary statutory paternity pay or additional statutory paternity pay paid on or after 5 April 2015: SI 2015/175 reg 9.

[12] In sub-paras (1)(*daa*), (2)(*daa*), word "and" at the end revoked, and sub-paras (1)(*dc*), (2)(*dc*) and preceding word inserted by the Social Security and Tax Credits (Miscellaneous Amendments) Regulations, SI 2015/175 regs 2, 4(1), (5)(*a*)(iii), (iv), (*b*)(iii), (iv) with effect from 5 March 2015.

[13] In sub-para (1)(*c*)(i), words substituted, and sub-paras (2)(*c*), (2B)(*f*) revoked, by the Social Security (Contributions) (Amendment) (No 2) Regulations, SI 2016/352 reg 18(*d*) with effect from 6 April 2016, subject to savings in relation to rights or obligations arising in connection with tax years beginning before 6 April 2016.

[Notification by employer at end of year that an agreement described in paragraph 3A(2) or an election under paragraph 3B(1) of Schedule 1 to the Act has been operated in relation to a Secondary Class 1 contribution

23—(1) An employer must notify HMRC on or before 6th July if a relevant agreement or relevant election has been operated in relation to a Secondary Class 1 contribution payable in respect of the relevant employment income of a person ("the earner") in the year immediately preceding the year in which that day falls.

(2) A relevant agreement has been operated in relation to the contribution described in sub-paragraph (1) if the employer has recovered the whole or any part of it pursuant to an agreement described in paragraph 3A(2) of Schedule 1 to the Act.

(3) A relevant election has been operated in relation to the contribution described in subparagraph (1) if the liability for the whole or any part of it has been transferred to the earner pursuant to an election under paragraph 3B of that Schedule.][1]

Amendments—[1] Paragraph 23 substituted by the Social Security (Miscellaneous Amendments No 2) Regulations, SI 2015/478 regs 2, 22(1), (5) with effect in relation to returns made by employers for the tax year 2014–15 and subsequent tax years.

Special return by employer at end of voyage period

24—(1) This paragraph applies where earnings-related contributions are assessed in accordance with regulation 120(4) or (5) (earnings periods for mariners and apportionment of earnings).

(2) Not later than 14 days after the end of the voyage period the employer shall render to the [Inland Revenue][1] in such form as the [Inland Revenue][1] may authorise a return in respect of each mariner showing—

(*a*) his name, discharge book number and national insurance number;

(*b*) the earnings periods and the amounts of [. . . [3] earnings][1] apportioned to each such period in the voyage period;

(*c*) the appropriate category letter for each apportionment of [. . . [3] earnings][1];

(*d*) the amounts of all the earnings-related contributions payable on each apportionment of [. . . [3] earnings][1] otherwise than under paragraph 7(3);

(*e*) the amounts of primary Class 1 contributions included in the amounts shown under paragraph (*d*) for each apportionment of [. . . [3] earnings][1]; [and][4]

[(*f*) the total amount of any earnings in respect of which primary Class 1 contributions were payable.][4]

(*g*) . . . [4]

(*h*) . . . [2], [1].

Amendments—[1] Words substituted by the Social Security (Contributions, Categorisation of Earners and Intermediaries) (Amendment) Regulations, SI 2004/770 regs 2, 32(1), (14) with effect from 6 April 2004.

[2] Sub-para 2(*h*) revoked, by the Social Security (Contributions (Amendment No 3) Regulations, SI 2012/821 regs 2, 29 with effect from 6 April 2012.

[3] In sub-para (2), word revoked in each place by the Social Security (Miscellaneous Amendments No 2) Regulations, SI 2015/478 regs 2, 22(1), (4)(*d*) with effect from 6 April 2015.

[4] In sub-para (2), word at end of para (*e*) inserted, para (*f*) substituted, and para (*g*) revoked, by the Social Security (Contributions) (Amendment) (No 2) Regulations, SI 2016/352 reg 18(*e*) with effect from 6 April 2016, subject to savings in relation to rights or obligations arising in connection with tax years beginning before 6 April 2016.

Return by employer of recovery under the Statutory Sick Pay Percentage Threshold Order

25—

Amendments—Para 25 revoked by the Social Security (Contributions) (Amendment No 4) Regulations, SI 2014/2397 regs 2, 3(1), (7) with effect from 6 October 2014.

[Retention by employer of contribution and election records

26—(1) An employer must keep and preserve all contribution records which are not required to be sent to HMRC by other provisions in these Regulations for not less than—

(*a*) three years after the end of the tax year to which they relate; or

(*b*) for documents or records relating to information about the amounts of Class 1A and Class 1B contributions, three years after the end of the year in which a contribution became payable.

(2) The duty under paragraph (1) may be discharged by preserving the contribution records in any form or by any means.

(3) Where an election has been made jointly by the secondary contributor and the employed earner for the purposes of paragraph 3B(1) of Schedule 1 to the Act, the records which the secondary contributor is obliged by paragraph 8 to maintain shall be retained by the secondary contributor throughout the period for which the election is in force and for six years after the end of that period.

(4) In this paragraph "contribution records" means wages sheets, deductions working sheets . . . [2] and other documents or records relating to—

(*a*) the calculation of payment of earnings to the employer's employees or the amount of the earnings-related contributions payable for those earnings;

(*b*) the amount of any Class 1A contributions or Class 1B contributions payable by the employer; and

(*c*) any information about the amounts of Class 1A and Class 1B contributions.

[(4A) Sub-paragraph (4B) applies in relation to an employer who makes deductions, or applies for a repayment, under section 4 of the National Insurance Contributions Act 2014 on account of an employment allowance for which the employer qualifies for a tax year (or who intends to do so).

(4B) So far as they are not otherwise covered by sub-paragraph (4), "contribution records" includes any documents or records relating to—

(*a*) the employer's qualification for the employment allowance, or

(*b*) the calculation of any amount that has been, or could be, deducted or repaid under section 4 of the National Insurance Contributions Act 2014 on account of the employment allowance.][3]

(5) For the purposes of this paragraph "employer"—

(*a*) includes, in relation to a Class 1A contribution, the person liable to pay such a contribution in accordance with section 10ZA of the Act (liability of third party provider of benefits in kind); and

(*b*) means, in relation to a Class 1B contribution, the person liable to pay such a contribution in accordance with section 10A of the Act.][1]

Amendments—[1] Paras 26, 26A substituted for previous para 26, by the Social Security (Contributions) (Amendment No 3) Regulations, SI 2009/600 regs 2, 8(1), (4) with effect from 1 April 2009.

[2] In sub-para (4), words "(other than deductions working sheets issued under regulation 35 of the PAYE Regulations (simplified deduction schemes: records))" revoked by the Social Security (Contributions) (Amendment and Application of Schedule 38 to the Finance Act 2012) Regulations, SI 2013/622 regs 2, 4(1), (4) with effect in relation to the tax year 2014–15.

[3] Sub-paras (4A), (4B) inserted by the NICs Act 2014 s 7(3) with effect from 6 April 2014.

[Certificate of employer's liability to pay contributions after inspection of documents

26A—(1) An officer of Revenue and Customs may, by reference to the information obtained from an inspection of the documents and records produced under Schedule 36 to the Finance Act 2008 (information and inspection powers), and on the occasion of each inspection, prepare a certificate showing—

(*a*) the amount of earnings-related contributions which it appears that the employer is liable to pay to HMRC, excluding any amount deducted by the employer by virtue of the Compensation of Employers Regulations for the years or tax periods covered by the inspection; or (*b*) the amount of any Class 1B contributions which it appears that the employer is liable to pay to HMRC for the years covered by the inspection, or such an amount in addition to an amount referred to in paragraph (*a*);

together with any amount of earnings-related contributions or Class 1B contributions or a combination of those classes of contributions, which has not been paid to HMRC or, to the best of the officer's knowledge and belief, to any other person to whom it might lawfully be paid.

(2) The production of a certificate mentioned in sub-paragraph (1) shall, unless the contrary is proved, be sufficient evidence that the employer is liable to pay to HMRC in respect of the years or, as the case may be, tax periods mentioned in the certificate, the amount shown in the certificate as unpaid; and any document purporting to be such a certificate shall be treated as such a certificate until the contrary is proved.

(3) The provisions of paragraph 16 shall apply with any necessary modifications to the amount shown in such a certificate.

(4) For the purposes of this paragraph "employer" has the meaning given by paragraph 26(5).][1]

Amendments—[1] Paras 26, 26A substituted for previous para 26, by the Social Security (Contributions) (Amendment No 3) Regulations, SI 2009/600 regs 2, 8(1), (4) with effect from 1 April 2009.

Death of an employer

27 If an employer dies, anything which he would have been liable to do under this Schedule shall be done by his personal representatives, or, in the case of an employer who paid [. . . [2] earnings][1] on behalf of another person, by the person succeeding him or, if no person succeeds him, the person on whose behalf he paid [. . . [2] earnings][1].

Amendments—[1] Words substituted by the Social Security (Contributions, Categorisation of Earners and Intermediaries) (Amendment) Regulations, SI 2004/770 regs 2, 32(1), (17) with effect from 6 April 2004.

[2] Word revoked in both places by the Social Security (Miscellaneous Amendments No 2) Regulations, SI 2015/478 regs 2, 22(1), (4)(*d*) with effect from 6 April 2015.

Succession to a business, etc

28—(1) This paragraph applies where there has been a change in the employer from whom an employee receives [. . . [3] earnings][1] in respect of his employment in any trade, business, concern or undertaking, or in connection with any property, or from whom an employee receives any annuity other than a pension.

(2) Where this paragraph applies, in relation to any matter arising after the change, the employer after the change shall be liable to do anything which the employer before the change would have been liable to do under this Schedule if the change had not taken place.

(3) Sub-paragraph (2) is subject to the qualification that the employer after the change shall not be liable for the payment of any earnings-related contributions which were deductible from [general earnings][1] paid to the employee before, unless they are also deductible from [general earnings][1] paid to [the employee after][2], the change took place, or of any corresponding employer's earnings-related contributions.

Amendments—[1] Words substituted by the Social Security (Contributions, Categorisation of Earners and Intermediaries) (Amendment) Regulations, SI 2004/770 regs 2, 32(1), (17) with effect from 6 April 2004.

[2] Words in sub-para (3) substituted by SI 2004/770 regs 2, 32(1), (18) with effect from 6 April 2004. Note, SI 2004/770 reg 32(18) provides as follows—

"(18) In paragraph 28(3) for "the employer after" substitute "the employee after".".

It is the publisher's view that the legislator's intention was to substitute the second occurrence only.

[3] In sub-paras (1), (3), word revoked by the Social Security (Miscellaneous Amendments No 2) Regulations, SI 2015/478 regs 2, 22(1), (4)(*d*) with effect from 6 April 2015.

Payments by cheque

29—(1) Sub-paragraph (2) applies for the purposes of paragraphs 10, 11, 13, 15, 17 and 18.

(2) If any payment to the [Inland Revenue][1] is made by cheque, and the cheque is paid on its first presentation to the banker on whom it is drawn, the payment shall be treated as made on the day on which the cheque was received by the [Inland Revenue][1], and "pay", "paid", "unpaid" and "overpaid" shall be construed accordingly.

Amendments—[1] Words in sub-para (2) substituted by the Social Security (Contributions, Categorisation of Earners and Intermediaries) (Amendment) Regulations, SI 2004/770 regs 2, 32(1), (19) with effect from 6 April 2004.

[PART IIIA
DEBTS OF MANAGED SERVICE COMPANIES]

Amendments—Part 3A (paras 29A–29L) inserted by the Social Security (Contributions) (Amendment No 5) Regulations, SI 2007/2068 reg 2 with effect from 6 August 2007.

[Interpretation of this Part

29A—(1) In this Part of this Schedule—

"HM Revenue and Customs" means Her Majesty's Revenue and Customs;

"lower amount" means the amount mentioned in paragraph 29C(5);

"managed service company" has the meaning given by section 61B of ITEPA;

"paragraph (*b*) associate" means a person who—

(*a*) is within section 688A(2)(*d*), and

(*b*) is within that provision by virtue of a connection with a person who is within section 688A(2)(*b*);

"paragraph (*c*) associate" means a person who—

(*a*) is within section 688A(2)(*d*), and

(*b*) is within that provision by virtue of a connection with a person who is within section 688A(2)(*c*);

"qualifying period" means a tax period beginning on or after [the date on which these amending Regulations come into force];

"relevant contributions debt" means a debt specified in paragraph 29B;

"specified amount" means the amount mentioned in paragraph 29C(1)(*b*);

"transfer notice" means the notice mentioned in paragraph 29C(4);

"transferee" means the person mentioned in paragraph 29C(4).

(2) In this Part of this Schedule references to section 688A, however expressed, are references to section 688A of ITEPA.][1]

Amendments—[1] Part 3A (paras 29A–29L) inserted by the Social Security (Contributions) (Amendment No 5) Regulations, SI 2007/2068 reg 2 with effect from 6 August 2007.

[Relevant contributions debts of managed service companies

29B—(1) A managed service company has a relevant contributions debt if—

(*a*) a managed service company must pay an amount of contributions for a qualifying period, and

(*b*) one of conditions A to E is met.

(2) Condition A is met if—

(*a*) a decision has been made in accordance with section 8 of the Social Security Contributions (Transfer of Functions, etc.) Act 1999 that an amount of Class 1 National Insurance contributions is due in respect of a qualifying period, and

(*b*) any part of the amount has not been paid within 14 days from the date on which the decision became final and conclusive.

(3) Condition B is met if—

(*a*) an employer delivers a return under paragraph 22(1) (return by employer at end of year) for the tax year 2007-08, or any later tax year, showing an amount of total contributions deducted by the employer for that tax year,

(*b*) HM Revenue and Customs prepare a certificate under paragraph 22(5) (certificate that contributions specified in return under paragraph 22(1) remain unpaid) showing how much of that amount remains unpaid, and

(*c*) any part of that amount remains unpaid at the end of a period of 14 days beginning with the date on which the certificate is prepared.

(4) Condition C is met if—

(*a*) HM Revenue and Customs prepare a certificate under paragraph 14(1) (employer failing to pay earnings-related contributions) showing an amount of contributions which the employer is liable to pay for a qualifying period, and

(*b*) any part of that amount remains unpaid at the end of a period of 14 days beginning with the date on which the certificate is prepared.

(5) Condition D is met if—

(*a*) HM Revenue and Customs serve notice on an employer under paragraph 15(1) (specified amount of earnings-related contributions payable by the employer) requiring payment of the amount of Class 1 contributions which they consider the employer is liable to pay, and

(*b*) any part of that amount remains unpaid at the end of a period of 14 days beginning with the date on which the notice is prepared.

(6) Condition E is met if—

(*a*) HM Revenue and Customs prepare a certificate under [paragraph 26A (certificate of employer's liability to pay contributions after inspection of documents)][2] showing an amount of contributions which it appears that the employer is liable to pay for a qualifying period,

(*b*) HM Revenue and Customs make a written demand for payment of that amount of contributions, and (*c*) any part of that amount remains unpaid at the end of a period of 14 days beginning with the date on which the written demand for payment is made.][1]

Amendments—[1] Part 3A (paras 29A–29L) inserted by the Social Security (Contributions) (Amendment No 5) Regulations, SI 2007/2068 reg 2 with effect from 6 August 2007.

[2] In sub-para (6)(*a*), words substituted, by the Social Security (Contributions) (Amendment No 3) Regulations, SI 2009/600 regs 2, 8(1), (5) with effect from 1 April 2009.

[Transfer of debt of managed service company

29C—(1) This paragraph applies if—

(*a*) a managed service company has a relevant contributions debt, and

(*b*) an officer of Revenue and Customs is of the opinion that the relevant contributions debt or a part of the relevant contributions debt (the "specified amount") is irrecoverable from the managed service company within a reasonable period.

(2) HM Revenue and Customs may make a direction authorising the recovery of the specified amount from the persons specified in section 688A(2) (managed service companies: recovery from other persons).

(3) Upon the making of a direction under sub-paragraph (2), the persons specified in section 688A(2) become jointly and severally liable for the relevant contributions debt, but subject to what follows.

(4) HM Revenue and Customs may not recover the specified amount from any person in accordance with a direction made under sub-paragraph (2) until they have served a notice (a "transfer notice") on the person in question (the "transferee").

(5) If an officer of Revenue and Customs is of the opinion that it is appropriate to do so, HM Revenue and Customs may accept an amount less than the specified amount (the "lower amount") from a transferee; but this acceptance shall not prejudice the recovery of the specified amount from any other transferee.

(6) HM Revenue and Customs may not serve a transfer notice on a person mentioned in section 688A(2)(*c*), or on a paragraph (*c*) associate, if the relevant contributions debt is incurred before 6th January 2008.

(7) HM Revenue and Customs may not serve a transfer notice on a person mentioned in section 688A(2)(*c*), or on a paragraph (*c*) associate, unless an officer of Revenue and Customs certifies that, in his opinion, it is impracticable to recover the specified amount from persons mentioned in paragraphs (*a*) and (*b*) of section 688A(2) and from paragraph (*b*) associates.

(8) In determining, for the purposes of sub-paragraph (7), whether it is impracticable to recover from the persons mentioned in paragraphs (*a*) and (*b*) of section 688A(2) and from paragraph (*b*) associates the officer of Revenue and Customs may have regard to all managed service companies in relation to which a person is a person mentioned in paragraph (*a*) or (*b*) of section 688A(2) or a paragraph (*b*) associate.

(9) In determining which of the persons mentioned in section 688A(2)(*c*) and which of the paragraph (*c*) associates are to be served with transfer notices and the amount of those notices, HM Revenue and Customs must have regard to the degree and extent to which those persons are persons who (directly or indirectly) have encouraged or been actively involved in the provision by the managed service company of the services of the individual mentioned in that provision.][1]

Amendments—[1] Part 3A (paras 29A–29L) inserted by the Social Security (Contributions) (Amendment No 5) Regulations, SI 2007/2068 reg 2 with effect from 6 August 2007.

[Time limits for issue of transfer notices

29D—(1) A transfer notice must be served before the end of the period specified in this paragraph.

(2) Sub-paragraphs (3) to (7) apply if the transfer notice is served on a person mentioned in paragraph (*a*) or (*b*) or section 688A(2) or on a paragraph (*b*) associate.

(3) In a case in which condition A in paragraph 29B is met, the transfer notice must be served before the end of a period of 12 months beginning with the date on which the decision became final and conclusive.

(4) In a case in which condition B in paragraph 29B is met, the transfer notice must be served before the end of a period of 12 months beginning with the date on which HM Revenue and Customs received the return delivered under paragraph 22.

(5) In a case in which condition C in paragraph 29B is met, the transfer notice must be served before the end of a period of 12 months beginning with the date on which HM Revenue and Customs prepare the certificate under paragraph 14(1).

(6) In a case in which condition D in paragraph 29B is met, the transfer notice must be served before the end of a period of 12 months beginning with the date on which HM Revenue and Customs serve notice to the employer under paragraph 15(1).

(7) In a case in which condition E in paragraph 29B is met, the transfer notice must be served before the end of a period of 12 months beginning with the date on which HM Revenue and Customs carry out the inspection of the employer's contribution records under [Schedule 36 to the Finance Act 2008][2].

(8) If the transfer notice is served on a person mentioned in paragraph (*c*) of section 688A(2), or on a paragraph (*c*) associate, the transfer notice must be served before the end of a period of there months beginning with the date on which the officer of Revenue and Customs certifies the matters specified in paragraph 29C(7).][1]

Amendments—[1] Part 3A (paras 29A–29L) inserted by the Social Security (Contributions) (Amendment No 5) Regulations, SI 2007/2068 reg 2 with effect from 6 August 2007.

[2] In sub-para (7), words substituted, by the Social Security (Contributions) (Amendment No 3) Regulations, SI 2009/600 regs 2, 8(1), (6) with effect from 1 April 2009.

[Contents of transfer notice

29E—(1) A transfer notice must contain the following information—

(*a*) the name of the managed service company to which the relevant contributions debt relates;

(*b*) the address of the managed service company to which the relevant contributions debt relates;

(*c*) the amount of the relevant contributions debt;

(*d*) the tax periods to which the relevant contributions debt relates;

(*e*) if the tax periods to which the relevant contributions debt relates are comprised in more than one tax year, the apportionment of the relevant contributions debt among those tax years;

(*f*) which of the conditions A to E specified in paragraph 29B is met;

(*g*) the transferee's name;

(*h*) the transferee's address;

(*j*) whether the transferee is a person mentioned in paragraph (*a*), (*b*) or (*c*) of section 688A, a paragraph (*b*) associate or a paragraph (*c*) associate;

(*k*) if the transferee is a person mentioned in paragraph (*c*) of section 688A or a paragraph (*c*) associate—

(i) the date on which the officer of Revenue and Customs certified the matters specified in paragraph 29C(7), and

(ii) the names of the persons from whom it has been impracticable to recover the specified amount;

(*l*) the specified amount;

(*m*) the tax periods to which the specified amount relates;

(*n*) if the tax periods to which the specified amount relates are comprised in more than one tax year, the apportionment of the specified amount among those tax years;

(*o*) the address to which payment must be sent;

(*p*) the address to which an appeal must be sent.

(2) The transfer notice may specify the lower amount if HM Revenue and Customs are prepared to accept the lower amount from the transferee.

(3) The transfer notice must also contain a statement, made by the officer of Revenue and Customs serving the notice, that in his opinion the specified amount is irrecoverable from the managed service company within a reasonable period.][1]

Amendments—[1] Part 3A (paras 29A–29L) inserted by the Social Security (Contributions) (Amendment No 5) Regulations, SI 2007/2068 reg 2 with effect from 6 August 2007.

[Payment of the specified amount

29F—(1) If a transfer notice is served, the transferee must pay the specified amount to HM Revenue and Customs at the address specified in the transfer notice.

(2) The transferee must pay the specified amount within 30 days beginning with the date on which the transfer notice is served (the "specified period").

(3) If a transfer notice is served on a person mentioned in paragraph (*a*) or (*b*) of section 688A(2), or on a paragraph (*b*) associate, the specified amount carries interest from the reckonable date until the date on which payment is made.

(4) If a transfer notice is served on a person mentioned in paragraph (*c*) of section 688A(2), or on a paragraph (*c*) associate, the specified amount carries interest from the day following the expiry of the specified period until the date on which payment is made.

[(5) For the purposes of sub-paragraph (3) "the reckonable date" has the meaning given by paragraph 17(3)(*b*)(i).][2]][1]

Amendments—[1] Part 3A (paras 29A–29L) inserted by the Social Security (Contributions) (Amendment No 5) Regulations, SI 2007/2068 reg 2 with effect from 6 August 2007.

[2] Sub-para (5) inserted by the Social Security (Contributions) (Amendment No 3) Regulations, SI 2009/600 regs 2, 8(1), (7) with effect from 1 April 2009.

[Appeals

29G—(1) A transferee may appeal against the transfer notice.

(2) A notice of appeal must—

NIC

(*a*) be given to HM Revenue and Customs at the address specified in the transfer notice within 30 days beginning with the date on which the transfer notice was served, and

(*b*) specify the grounds of the appeal.

(3) The grounds of appeal are any of the following—

(*a*) that the relevant contributions debt (or part of the relevant contributions debt) is not due from the managed service company to HM Revenue and Customs;

(*b*) that the specified amount does not relate to a company which is a managed service company;

(*c*) that the specified amount is not irrecoverable from the managed service company within a reasonable period;

(*d*) that the transferee is not a person mentioned in section 688A(2);

(*e*) that the transferee was not a person mentioned in section 688A(2) during the tax periods to which the specified amount relates;

(*f*) that the transferee was not a person mentioned in section 688A(2) during some part of the tax periods to which the specified amount relates;

(*g*) that the transfer notice was not served before the end of the period specified in paragraph 29D;

(*h*) that the transfer notice does not satisfy the requirements specified in paragraph 29E;

(*j*) in the case of a transferee mentioned in section 688A(2)(*c*) or of a paragraph (*c*) associate, that it is not impracticable to recover the specified amount from persons mentioned in paragraphs (*a*) and (*b*) of section 688A(2) or from paragraph (*b*) associates;

(*k*) in the case of a transferee mentioned in section 688A(2)(*c*) or of a paragraph (*c*) associate, that the amount specified in the transfer notice does not have regard to the degree and extent to which the transferee is a person who (directly or indirectly) has encouraged or been actively involved in the provision by the managed service company of the services of the individual mentioned in that provision.

(4) Sub-paragraph (3)(*a*) is subject to paragraph 29H(4).

(5) The appeal is to the Special Commissioners.[2]][1]

Amendments—[1] Part 3A (paras 29A–29L) inserted by the Social Security (Contributions) (Amendment No 5) Regulations, SI 2007/2068 reg 2 with effect from 6 August 2007.

[2] Sub-para (5) revoked by the Transfer of Tribunal Functions and Revenue and Customs Appeals Order, SI 2009/56 art 3, Sch 2 para 76(1), (2) with effect from 1 April 2009.

[Procedure on appeals

29H—(1) On an appeal [that is notified to the tribunal, the tribunal][2] shall uphold or quash the transfer notice.

(2) The general rule in sub-paragraph (1) is subject to the following qualifications.

(3) In the case of the ground of appeal specified in paragraph 29G(3)(*a*), the [tribunal][2] shall investigate the matter and shall—

(*a*) uphold the amount of the relevant contributions debt specified in the transfer notice, or

(*b*) reduce or increase the amount of the relevant contributions debt specified in the transfer notice to such amount as in [the tribunal's][2] opinion is just and reasonable.

(4) If the [tribunal determines][2] the amount of the relevant contributions debt of a managed service company under sub-paragraph (3), that amount is conclusive as to the amount of that relevant contributions debt in any later appeal relating to that debt.

(5) In the case of the ground of appeal specified in paragraph 29G(3)(*f*), the [tribunal][2] may reduce the amount specified in the transfer notice to an amount determined in accordance with the equation—

$$RA = \frac{P}{TP} \times AS$$

(6) In paragraph (5)—

RA means the reduced amount;

P means the number of days in the tax periods specified in the transfer notice during which the transferee was a person mentioned in section 688A(2);

TP means the number of days in the tax periods specified in the transfer notice;

AS means the amount specified in the transfer notice.

(7) In the case of the ground of appeal specified in paragraph 29G(3)(*l*), the [tribunal][2] may reduce the amount specified in the transfer notice to such amount as in [the tribunal's][2] opinion is just and reasonable.][1]

Amendments—[1] Part 3A (paras 29A–29L) inserted by the Social Security (Contributions) (Amendment No 5) Regulations, SI 2007/2068 reg 2 with effect from 6 August 2007.

2 In sub-paras (1), (3)–(5), (7), words substituted by the Transfer of Tribunal Functions and Revenue and Customs Appeals Order, SI 2009/56 art 3, Sch 2 para 76(1), (3) with effect from 1 April 2009.

[Withdrawal of transfer notices

29J—(1) A transfer notice shall be withdrawn if the [tribunal quashes][2] it.

(2) A transfer notice may be withdrawn if, in the opinion of an officer of Revenue and Customs, it is appropriate to do so.

(3) If a transfer notice is withdrawn, HM Revenue and Customs must give written notice of that fact to the transferee.][1]

Amendments—[1] Part 3A inserted by the Social Security (Contributions) (Amendment No 5) Regulations, SI 2007/2068 reg 2 with effect from 6 August 2007.

2 In sub-para (1), words substituted by the Transfer of Tribunal Functions and Revenue and Customs Appeals Order, SI 2009/56 art 3, Sch 2 para 76(1), (4) with effect from 1 April 2009.

[Application of Part 6 of the Taxes Management Act 1970

29K—(1) For the purposes of this Chapter, Part 6 of the Taxes Management Act 1970 (collection and recovery) applies as if—

(*a*) the transfer notice were an assessment of tax on employment income, and

(*b*) the amount of earnings-related contributions specified in the transfer notice, and any interest payable on that amount under sub-paragraph (3) or (4) of paragraph 29F were income tax charged on the transferee;

and that Part of that Act applies with the modification specified in sub-paragraph (2) and any other necessary modifications.

(2) Summary proceedings for the recovery of the specified amount may be brought in England and Wales or Northern Ireland at any time before the end of a period of 12 months beginning immediately after the expiry of the period mentioned in paragraph 29F(2).

(3) The specified amount is one cause of action or one matter of complaint for the purposes of proceedings under sections 65, 66 and 67 of the Taxes Management Act 1970 (magistrates' courts, county courts and inferior courts in Scotland).

(4) But sub-paragraph (3) does not prevent the bringing of separate proceedings for the recovery of each of the amounts which the transferee is liable to pay for any tax period.][1]

Amendments—[1] Part 3A (paras 29A–29L) inserted by the Social Security (Contributions) (Amendment No 5) Regulations, SI 2007/2068 reg 2 with effect from 6 August 2007.

[Repayment of surplus amounts

29L—(1) This paragraph applies if the amounts paid to HM Revenue and Customs in respect of a relevant contributions debt exceed the specified amount.

(2) HM Revenue and Customs shall repay the difference on a just and equitable basis and without unreasonable delay.

(3) Interest on any sum repaid shall be paid in accordance with paragraph 18 (payment of interest on repaid earnings-related contributions).][1]

Amendments—[1] Part 3A (paras 29A–29L) inserted by the Social Security (Contributions) (Amendment No 5) Regulations, SI 2007/2068 reg 2 with effect from 6 August 2007.

[PART 3B

SECURITY FOR THE PAYMENT OF CLASS 1 CONTRIBUTIONS]

Amendments—Part 3B (paras 29M–29X) inserted by the Social Security (Contributions) (Amendment No 3) Regulations, SI 2012/821 regs 2, 18 with effect from 6 April 2012.

[Interpretation

29M In this Part—

"employer" has the meaning given in paragraph 29O(1);

"a further notice" has the meaning given in paragraph 29U(3);

"PGS" has the meaning given in paragraph 29S(1).][1]

Amendments—[1] Part 3B (paras 29M–29X) inserted by the Social Security (Contributions) (Amendment No 3) Regulations, SI 2012/821 regs 2, 18 with effect from 6 April 2012.

[Requirement for security

29N In circumstances where an officer of Revenue and Customs considers it necessary for the protection of Class 1 contributions, the officer may require a person described in paragraph 29P(1) to give security or further security for the payment of amounts which an employer is or may be liable to pay to HMRC under paragraph 10, 11[, 11ZA][2] or 11A.][1]

Amendments—[1] Part 3B (paras 29M–29X) inserted by the Social Security (Contributions) (Amendment No 3) Regulations, SI 2012/821 regs 2, 18 with effect from 6 April 2012.

[2] Reference inserted by the Security (Contributions) (Amendment and Application of Schedule 38 to the Finance Act 2012) Regulations, SI 2013/622 regs 5, 19 with effect in relation to the tax year 2013–14 and subsequent tax years.

[Employers

29O (1) An "employer" is any employer within the meaning given in paragraph 1(2) other than—

(*a*) the Crown;

(*b*) a person to whom sub-paragraph (2) applies;

(*c*) . . . [2] and

(*d*) a care and support employer within the meaning given in regulation 90NA(3) of these Regulations.

(2) This sub-paragraph applies to persons who at the relevant time could not be liable to a penalty under Schedule 56 to the Finance Act 2009 by virtue of paragraph 10 of that Schedule (suspension of penalty for failure to make payments on time during currency of agreement for deferred payment).

(3) In sub-paragraph (2), the relevant time is a time at which, but for sub-paragraph (1)(*b*), the officer would require security.][1]

Amendments—[1] Part 3B (paras 29M–29X) inserted by the Social Security (Contributions) (Amendment No 3) Regulations, SI 2012/821 regs 2, 18 with effect from 6 April 2012.

[2] Sub-para (1)(*c*) (but not the word "and" after it) revoked by the Social Security (Contributions) (Amendment and Application of Schedule 38 to the Finance Act 2012) Regulations, SI 2013/622 regs 2, 4(1), (5) with effect in relation to the tax year 2014–15.

[Persons from whom security can be required

29P—(1) The persons are—

(*a*) the employer;

(*b*) any of the following in relation to the employer—

(i) a director;

(ii) a company secretary;

(iii) any other similar officer; or

(iv) any person purporting to act in such a capacity; and

(*c*) in a case where the employer is a limited liability partnership, a member of the limited liability partnership.

(2) An officer of Revenue and Customs may require—

(*a*) a person to give security or further security of a specified value in respect of the employer; or

(*b*) more than one person to give security or further security of a specified value in respect of the employer, and where the officer does so those persons shall be jointly and severally liable to give that security or further security.][1]

Amendments—[1] Part 3B (paras 29M–29X) inserted by the Social Security (Contributions) (Amendment No 3) Regulations, SI 2012/821 regs 2, 18 with effect from 6 April 2012.

[Notice of requirement

29Q—(1) An officer of Revenue and Customs must give notice of a requirement for security to each person from whom security is required and the notice must specify—

(*a*) the value of security to be given;

(*b*) the manner in which security is to be given;

(*c*) the date on or before which security is to be given; and

(*d*) the period of time for which security is required.

(2) The notice must include, or be accompanied by, an explanation of—

(*a*) the employer's right to make a request under paragraph 10(1) of Schedule 56 to the Finance Act 2009; and

(*b*) the effect of paragraph 29R(2) and (3).

(3) In a case which falls within paragraph 29P(2)(*b*), the notice must include, or be accompanied by, the names of each other person from whom security is required.

(4) The notice may contain such other information as the officer considers necessary.

(5) A person shall not be treated as having been required to provide security unless HMRC comply with this paragraph and paragraph 29R(1).

(6) Notwithstanding anything in regulation 1(4)(*b*), where the notice, or a further notice, ("contributions notice") is to be given with a notice or further notice mentioned in regulations 97Q(1) and 97U(3) of the PAYE Regulations ("PAYE notice") the contributions notice shall be taken to be given at the same time that the PAYE notice is given.][1]

Amendments—[1] Part 3B (paras 29M–29X) inserted by the Social Security (Contributions) (Amendment No 3) Regulations, SI 2012/821 regs 2, 18 with effect from 6 April 2012.

[Date on which security is due

29R—(1) The date specified under paragraph 29Q(1)(*c*) may not be earlier than the 30th day after the day on which the notice is given.

(2) If, before the date specified under paragraph 29Q(1)(*c*), the employer makes a request under paragraph 10(1) of Schedule 56 to the Finance Act 2009, the requirement to give security on or before that date does not apply.

(3) In a case which falls within sub-paragraph (2), if HMRC does not agree to the employer's request, security is to be given on or before the 30th day after the day on which HMRC notifies the employer of that decision.][1]

Amendments—[1] Part 3B (paras 29M–29X) inserted by the Social Security (Contributions) (Amendment No 3) Regulations, SI 2012/821 regs 2, 18 with effect from 6 April 2012.

[Application for reduction in the value of security held

29S—(1) A person who has given security ("PGS") may apply to an officer of Revenue and Customs for a reduction in the value of security held by HMRC if—

(*a*) PGS' circumstances have changed since the day the security was given because—

(i) of hardship; or

(ii) PGS has ceased to be a person mentioned in paragraph 29P(1); or

(*b*) since the day the security was given there has been a significant reduction in the number of employed earners of the employer to whom the security relates or that employer has ceased to be an employer.

(2) Where paragraph 29P(2)(*b*) applies, a person who has not contributed to the value of the security given may not make an application under sub-paragraph (1).][1]

Amendments—[1] Part 3B (paras 29M–29X) inserted by the Social Security (Contributions) (Amendment No 3) Regulations, SI 2012/821 regs 2, 18 with effect from 6 April 2012.

[Outcome of application under paragraph 29S

29T—(1) If an application under paragraph 29S(1) is successful, the officer must inform PGS of the reduced value of security that is still required or, where that value is nil, that the requirement for security has been cancelled.

(2) HMRC may make such arrangements as they think fit to ensure the necessary reduction in the value of security held.][1]

Amendments—[1] Part 3B (paras 29M–29X) inserted by the Social Security (Contributions) (Amendment No 3) Regulations, SI 2012/821 regs 2, 18 with effect from 6 April 2012.

[Outcome of application under paragraph 29S: further provision

29U (1) This paragraph applies—

(*a*) in cases which fall within paragraph 29P(2)(*b*); and

(*b*) where PGS' application is made under paragraph 29S(1)(*a*).

(2) As a consequence of arrangements made under paragraph 29T(2), an officer of Revenue and Customs may require any other person who was given notice under paragraph 29Q in relation to the security ("the original security"), or any other person mentioned in paragraph 29P(1), to provide security in substitution for the original security.

(3) Where an officer of Revenue and Customs acts in reliance on sub-paragraph (2), the officer must give notice ("a further notice").

(4) Paragraph 29Q(1) to (5) and paragraph 29R apply in relation to a further notice.

(5) Subject to sub-paragraph (6), paragraph 29V(1) applies in relation to a further notice.

(6) A person who is given a further notice and who was also given notice under paragraph 29Q in relation to the original security may only appeal on the grounds that the person is not a person mentioned in paragraph 29P(1).][1]

Amendments—[1] Part 3B (paras 29M–29X) inserted by the Social Security (Contributions) (Amendment No 3) Regulations, SI 2012/821 regs 2, 18 with effect from 6 April 2012.

[Appeals

29V—(1) A person who is given notice under paragraph 29Q may appeal against the notice or any requirement in it.

(2) PGS may appeal against—

(*a*) the rejection by an officer of Revenue and Customs of an application under paragraph 29S(1); and

(*b*) a smaller reduction in the value of security held than PGS applied for.

(3) Notice of an appeal under this paragraph must be given—

(*a*) before the end of the period of 30 days beginning with—

(i) in the case of an appeal under sub-paragraph (1), the day after the day on which the notice was given; and

(ii) in the case of an appeal under sub-paragraph (2), the day after the day on which PGS was notified of the outcome of the application; and

(*b*) to the officer of Revenue and Customs by whom the notice was given or the decision on the application was made, as the case may be.

(4) Notice of an appeal under this paragraph must state the grounds of appeal.

(5) On an appeal under sub-paragraph (1) that is notified to the tribunal, the tribunal may—

(*a*) confirm the requirements in the notice;

(*b*) vary the requirements in the notice; or

(*c*) set aside the notice.

(6) On an appeal under sub-paragraph (2) that is notified to the tribunal, the tribunal may—

(*a*) confirm the decision on the application; or

(*b*) vary the decision on the application.

(7) On the final determination of an appeal under this paragraph—

(*a*) subject to any alternative determination by a tribunal or court, any security to be given is due on the 30th day after the day on which the determination is made; or

(*b*) HMRC may make such arrangements as they think fit to ensure the necessary reduction in the value of the security held.

(8) Part 5 of the Taxes Management Act 1970 (appeals and other proceedings) applies in relation to an appeal under this paragraph as it applies in relation to an appeal under the Taxes Acts but as if—

(*a*) sections 46D, 47B, 50(6) to (9) and (11)(*c*) and 54A to 57 were omitted; and

(*b*) in section 48(1)—

(i) in paragraph (*a*) the reference to "the Taxes Acts" were a reference to "paragraph 29V of Schedule 4 to the Social Security (Contributions) Regulations 2001"; and

(ii) in paragraph (*b*) the reference to "any provision of the Taxes Acts" were a reference to "paragraph 29V of Schedule 4 to the Social Security (Contributions) Regulations 2001".][1]

Amendments—[1] Part 3B (paras 29M–29X) inserted by the Social Security (Contributions) (Amendment No 3) Regulations, SI 2012/821 regs 2, 18 with effect from 6 April 2012.

[Appeals: further provision for cases which fall within paragraph 29R

29W In a case which falls within paragraph 29R(2), if the request mentioned in that provision is made before an appeal under paragraph 29V(1), paragraph 29V(3)(*a*)(i) applies as if the words "the day after the day on which the notice was given" were "the day after the day on which HMRC notifies the employer of its decision".][1]

Amendments—[1] Part 3B (paras 29M–29X) inserted by the Social Security (Contributions) (Amendment No 3) Regulations, SI 2012/821 regs 2, 18 with effect from 6 April 2012.

[Offence

29X—(1) Section 684(4A) of the Income Tax (Earnings and Pensions) Act 2003 (PAYE regulations – security for payment of PAYE: offence) applies in relation to a requirement imposed under these Regulations as it applies in relation to a requirement imposed under the PAYE Regulations.

(2) For the purposes of section 684(4A) as it applies by virtue of sub-paragraph (1)—

(*a*) in relation to a requirement for security under a notice under paragraph 29Q the period specified is the period which starts with the day the notice is given and ends with—

(i) the first day after the date specified under paragraph 29Q(1)(*c*); or

(ii) in a case which falls within paragraph 29R(2), the first day after the date determined under paragraph 29R(3);

(*b*) in relation to a requirement for security under a further notice the period specified is the period which starts with the day the further notice is given and ends with—

(i) the first day after the date specified under paragraph 29Q(1)(*c*) as it applies in relation to the further notice; or

(ii) in a case which falls within paragraph 29R(2), the first day after the date determined under paragraph 29R(3) as it applies in relation to the further notice; and

(*c*) in relation to a requirement for security to which paragraph 29V(7)(*a*) applies the period specified is the period which starts with the day the determination is made and ends with the first day after—

(i) the day the tribunal or court determines to be the day that the security is to be given; or

(ii) the day determined in accordance with that paragraph,

as the case may be.][1]

Amendments—[1] Part 3B (paras 29M–29X) inserted by the Social Security (Contributions) (Amendment No 3) Regulations, SI 2012/821 regs 2, 18 with effect from 6 April 2012.

[PART 3C
CERTAIN DEBTS OF COMPANIES UNDER PARAGRAPH 3ZB OF PART 8 OF SCHEDULE 3 (TRAVEL EXPENSES OF WORKERS PROVIDING SERVICES THROUGH EMPLOYMENT INTERMEDIARIES)]

Amendments—Part 3C (paras 29Y–29Z5) inserted by the Social Security (Contributions) (Amendment No 4) Regulations, SI 2016/1076 regs 2, 7 with effect from 28 November 2016.

[Interpretation of Part 3C: "relevant contributions debt" and "relevant date"

29Y (1) In this Part "relevant contributions debt", in relation to a company means an amount within any of sub-paragraphs (2) to (5).

(2) An amount within this sub-paragraph is an amount that the company is to account for in accordance with paragraph 3ZB(6A) to (6C) (persons providing fraudulent documents).

(3) An amount within this sub-paragraph is an amount which a company is to deduct and pay by virtue of paragraph 3ZB in circumstances where—

(*a*) a company is an employment intermediary,

(*b*) on the basis that paragraph 3ZB does not apply by virtue of sub-paragraph (3) of that paragraph the company has not deducted and paid the amount, but

(*c*) the company has not been provided by any other person with evidence from which it would be reasonable in all the circumstances to conclude that sub-paragraph (3) of that paragraph applied (and the mere assertion by a person that the manner in which the worker provided the services was not subject to (or to the right of) supervision, direction or control by any person is not such evidence).

(4) An amount within this sub-paragraph is an amount that the company is to deduct and pay in accordance with paragraph 3ZB in circumstances where sub-paragraph (4) of that paragraph applies (services provided under arrangements made by intermediaries).

(5) An amount within this sub-paragraph is any interest or penalty in respect of an amount within any of sub-paragraphs (2) to (4) for which the company is liable.

(6) In this paragraph "paragraph 3ZB" means paragraph 3ZB of Part 8 of Schedule 3 to these Regulations.

(7) In this Part "the relevant date" in relation to a relevant contributions debt means the date on which the first payment is due on which contributions are not accounted for.][1]

Amendments—[1] Part 3C (paras 29Y–29Z5) inserted by the Social Security (Contributions) (Amendment No 4) Regulations, SI 2016/1076 regs 2, 7 with effect from 28 November 2016.

[Interpretation of Part 3C: general

29Z In this Part—

"company" includes a limited liability partnership;

"director" has the meaning given by section 67 of ITEPA 2003;

"personal liability notice" has the meaning given by paragraph 29Z1(2);

"the specified amount" has the meaning given by paragraph 29Z1(2)(*a*).][1]

Amendments—[1] Part 3C (paras 29Y–29Z5) inserted by the Social Security (Contributions) (Amendment No 4) Regulations, SI 2016/1076 regs 2, 7 with effect from 28 November 2016.

[Liability of directors for relevant contributions debts

29Z1 (1) This paragraph applies in relation to an amount of relevant contributions debt of a company if the company does not deduct that amount by the time by which the company is required to do so.

(2) HMRC may serve a notice ("personal liability notice") on any person who was, on the relevant date, a director of the company—

(*a*) specifying the amount of relevant contributions debt in relation to which this paragraph applies ("the specified amount"), and

(*b*) requiring the director to pay HMRC—

(i) the specified amount, and

(ii) specified interest on that amount.

(3) The interest specified in the personal liability notice—

(*a*) is to be at the rate applicable under section 178 of the Finance Act 1989 for the purposes of section 86 of the Taxes Management Act 1970, and

(*b*) is to run from the date the notice is served.

NIC

(4) A director who is served with a personal liability notice is liable to pay to HMRC the specified amount and the interest specified in the notice within 30 days beginning with the day the notice is served.

(5) If HMRC serve personal liability notices on more than one director of the company in respect of the same amount of relevant contributions debt, the directors are jointly and severally liable to pay to HMRC the specified amount and the interest specified in the notices.][1]

Amendments—[1] Part 3C (paras 29Y–29Z5) inserted by the Social Security (Contributions) (Amendment No 4) Regulations, SI 2016/1076 regs 2, 7 with effect from 28 November 2016.

[Appeals in relation to personal liability notices

29Z2 (1) A person who is served with a personal liability notice in relation to an amount of relevant contributions debt of a company may appeal against the notice.

(2) A notice of appeal must—

(*a*) be given to HMRC within 30 days beginning with the day the personal liability notice is served, and

(*b*) specify the grounds of the appeal.

(3) The grounds of appeal are—

(*a*) that all or part of the specified amount does not represent an amount of relevant contributions debt, of the company, to which paragraph 29Z1 applies, or

(*b*) that the person was not a director of the company on the relevant date.

(4) But a person may not appeal on the ground mentioned in sub-paragraph (3)(*a*) if it has already been determined, on an appeal by the company, that—

(*a*) the specified amount is a relevant contributions debt of the company, and

(*b*) the company did not deduct, account for, or (as the case may be) pay the debt by the time by which the company was required to do so.

(5) Subject to sub-paragraph (6), on an appeal that is notified to the tribunal, the tribunal is to uphold or quash the personal liability notice.

(6) In a case in which the ground of appeal mentioned in sub-paragraph (3)(*a*) is raised, the tribunal may also reduce or increase the specified amount so that it does represent an amount of relevant contributions debt, of the company, to which paragraph 29Z1 applies.][1]

Amendments—[1] Part 3C (paras 29Y–29Z5) inserted by the Social Security (Contributions) (Amendment No 4) Regulations, SI 2016/1076 regs 2, 7 with effect from 28 November 2016.

[Withdrawal of personal liability notices

29Z3 (1) A personal liability notice is withdrawn if the tribunal quashes it.

(2) An officer of Revenue and Customs may withdraw a personal liability notice if the officer considers it appropriate to do so.

(3) If a personal liability notice is withdrawn, HMRC must give notice of that fact to the person upon whom the notice was served.][1]

Amendments—[1] Part 3C (paras 29Y–29Z5) inserted by the Social Security (Contributions) (Amendment No 4) Regulations, SI 2016/1076 regs 2, 7 with effect from 28 November 2016.

[Recovery of sums due under personal liability notice: application of Part 6 of Taxes Management Act 1970

29Z4 (1) For the purposes of this Part, Part 6 of the Taxes Management Act 1970 (collection and recovery) applies as if—

(*a*) the personal liability notice were an assessment, and

(*b*) the specified amount and any interest on that amount under paragraph 29Z1(2)(*b*)(ii) were income tax charged on the director upon whom the notice is served, and that Part of that Act applies with the modification in paragraph (2) and any other necessary modifications.

(2) Summary proceedings for the recovery of the specified amount, and any interest on that amount under paragraph 29Z1(2)(*b*)(ii), may be brought in England and Wales or Northern Ireland at any time before the end of the period of 12 months beginning with the day after the day on which personal liability notice is served.][1]

Amendments—[1] Part 3C (paras 29Y–29Z5) inserted by the Social Security (Contributions) (Amendment No 4) Regulations, SI 2016/1076 regs 2, 7 with effect from 28 November 2016.

[Repayment of surplus amounts

29Z5 (1) This paragraph applies if—

(*a*) one or more personal liability notices are served in respect of an amount of relevant contributions debt of a company, and (*b*) the amounts paid to HMRC (whether by directors upon whom notices are served or the company) exceed the aggregate of the specified amount and any interest on it under paragraph 29Z1(2)(*b*)(ii).

(2) HMRC is to repay the difference on a just and equitable basis and without unreasonable delay.

(3) HMRC is to pay interest on any sum repaid.

(4) The interest—

(*a*) is to be at the rate applicable under section 178 of the Finance Act 1989 for the purposes of section 824 of the Taxes Act, and

(*b*) is to run from the date the amounts paid to HMRC come to exceed the aggregate mentioned in sub-paragraph (1)(*b*).][1]

Amendments—[1] Part 3C (paras 29Y–29Z5) inserted by the Social Security (Contributions) (Amendment No 4) Regulations, SI 2016/1076 regs 2, 7 with effect from 28 November 2016.

PART IV
ASSESSMENT AND DIRECT COLLECTION

Provisions for direct payment

30 In cases of employed earner's employment, where the employer does not fulfil the conditions prescribed in regulation 145(1)(b) as to residence or presence in Great Britain or Northern Ireland or is a person who, by reason of any international treaty to which the United Kingdom is a party or of any international convention binding on the United Kingdom, is exempt from the provisions of the Act or is a person against whom, for a similar reason, the provisions of the Act are not enforceable, the provisions of paragraph 31 shall apply to the employee, unless the employer, being a person entitled to pay the primary contributions due in respect of the earnings from the said employment, is willing to pay those contributions.

[Application of paragraphs 31 and 31A

30A—(1) Paragraph 31(4) to (7) does not apply on or after 6th April 2014.

(2) Paragraph 31(7A) and (7B) applies only in relation to closed tax years ending on or before 5th April 2014.

(3) Paragraph 31A applies on and after 6th April 2014.][1]

Amendments—[1] Para 30A inserted by the Security (Contributions) (Amendment and Application of Schedule 38 to the Finance Act 2012) Regulations, SI 2013/622 regs 5, 20 with effect in relation to the tax year 2013–14 and subsequent tax years.

Direct collection involving deductions working sheets

31—(1) In any case falling within paragraph 30, . . .[5] sub-paragraphs (2) to (8) shall apply.

(2) The employee . . .[5] shall record on [a working sheet][5] his name, national insurance number and category letter indicated by [HMRC][2], and whenever, in respect of an employment such as is specified in paragraph 30, the employee receives any [. . .[6] earnings][1] during [the relevant tax year][5], he shall also record on that working sheet the amount of the [earnings][1], the date on which he received them, and the earnings-related contributions payable by him in respect of those [earnings][1].

(3) Not later than the time for the payment of income tax, if any, the employee shall pay to [HMRC][2] the amount of the earnings-related contributions payable by the employee in respect of the [. . .[6] earnings][1] which have been received by him and for which the income tax is or would have been payable.

[(3A) Before 20 May 2014 the employee must deliver to HMRC a return in the prescribed form for the tax year 2013–14 showing the following information:

(*a*) the total amount of the . . .[6] earnings and earnings-related contributions payable during the tax year 2013–14,

(*b*) the appropriate category letter,

(*c*) the employee's name and address, and

(*d*) the employee's national insurance number, and

the provisions of paragraph 22(5) regarding the certification and recovery of earnings-related contributions remaining unpaid by an employer for any year shall apply in the case of any earnings-related contributions remaining unpaid by the employee.][5]

(4) If, by the time specified in sub-paragraph (3), the employee has paid no amount of earnings-related contributions to [HMRC][2] in respect of the [. . .[6] earnings][1] mentioned in that sub-paragraph, and [HMRC][2] is unaware of the amount, if any, which the employee is liable so to pay, or if an amount has been paid but [HMRC][2] is not satisfied that it is the full amount which the employee is liable to pay *to him* in respect of those [earnings][1], sub-paragraph (5) applies.

(5) If this sub-paragraph applies, [HMRC][2] may give notice to the employee requiring him to render within the time limited in the notice, a return in the prescribed form containing particulars of all [. . . [6] earnings][1] received by him during the period specified in the notice and such other particulars affecting the calculations of the earnings-related contributions payable in respect of the [earnings][1] in question as may be specified in the notice, and in such a case the provisions of—

(*a*) paragraph 14 regarding the ascertaining and certifying by [HMRC][2] of earnings-related contributions payable by an employer, and

(*b*) paragraph 16 regarding the recovery of those contributions

shall apply with the necessary modifications for the purposes of ascertaining, certifying and recovering the earnings-related contributions payable by the employee.

(6) If the employee ceases to receive [. . . [6] earnings][1] falling within sub-paragraph (2), he shall immediately render to [[HMRC][2], in such form as they may prescribe][1], a return showing such particulars as they may require for the identification of the employee, the year to which the return relates, the appropriate category letter, the last date on which he received any such [earnings][1], the total of those [earnings][1] and the earnings-related contributions payable from the beginning of the year to that date.

(7) [Before 20th May following][1] the end of the year, the employee shall (unless sub-paragraph (6) has applied) render to [[HMRC][2], in such form as they may prescribe][1], a return showing such particulars as they may require for the identification of the employee, the year to which the return relates, the total of the [. . . [6] earnings][1] and earnings-related contributions payable during the year, together with the appropriate category letter, and the provisions of paragraph 22(5) regarding the certification and recovery of earnings-related contributions remaining unpaid by an employer for any year shall apply in the case of any earnings-related contributions remaining unpaid by the employee.

[(7A) Where a liability arises to pay contributions in respect of retrospective earnings relating to a closed tax year, the [employee][4] shall render a replacement return for the closed tax year before 20th May following the end of the year in which the relevant retrospective contributions regulations came into force in accordance with sub-paragraph (7), setting out the revised earnings and earnings-related contributions.

(7B) Where sub-paragraph (7A) applies, the [employee][4] shall amend the relevant deductions working sheet or where necessary prepare one in accordance with sub-paragraph (2)][2]

(8) The employee shall retain deductions working sheets . . . [5] for not less than three years after the end of the year to which they relate.

[Section 98A of the Taxes Management Act 1970 (special penalties in the case of certain returns) and Schedule 24 to the Finance Act 2007 (penalties for errors) as that Schedule applies to income tax returns][3] as modified by the provisions of paragraph 7 to Schedule 1 to the Act, shall apply in relation to the requirement to make a return contained in sub-paragraphs [[(3A)][5] and (7A)][2].

Note—As a result of the substitution of the words "HMRC" (formerly "Inland Revenue") for "Collector" in sub-para (4), the words "to him" in that sub-paragraph would appear to be superfluous.

Amendments—[1] Words substituted by the Social Security (Contributions, Categorisation of Earners and Intermediaries) (Amendment) Regulations, SI 2004/770 regs 2, 33 with effect from 6 April 2004.

[2] Words substituted, and sub-paras (7A), (7B) inserted, by the Social Security Contributions (Consequential Provisions) Regulations, SI 2007/1056 regs 3, 8(16) with effect from 6 April 2007.

[3] Words in sub-para (8) substituted by the Social Security (Contributions) (Amendment No 3) Regulations, SI 2008/636 regs 2, 7(*b*) with effect from 1 April 2008.

[4] Words in sub-para (1) inserted, and in sub-paras (7A), (7B) word substituted for word "employer", by the Security (Contributions) (Amendment and Application of Schedule 38 to the Finance Act 2012) Regulations, SI 2013/622 regs 5, 21 with effect in relation to the tax year 2013–14 and subsequent tax years.

[5] In sub-paras (1), (8), words revoked, in sub-para (2), words substituted and revoked, sub-para (3A) inserted, and in sub-para (9) reference substituted, by the Social Security (Contributions) (Amendment) Regulations, SI 2014/608 regs 2, 5, 10. These amendments come into force on 6 April 2014.

[6] Word revoked in each place by the Social Security (Miscellaneous Amendments No 2) Regulations, SI 2015/478 regs 2, 22(1), (6)(with effect from 6 April 2015.

[Direct collection involving deductions working sheets on and after 6th April 2014

31A—(1) On receiving any . . . [1] earnings which fall to be recorded on a deductions working sheet under paragraph 31(2), subject to sub-paragraph (2), an employee must proceed in accordance with paragraph 21A(1), (2) and (5).

(2) If the employee falls within paragraph 21D(1)(a), the employee may instead proceed in accordance with paragraph 21D(3), (4) and (5).

(3) For the purposes of sub-paragraph (1), paragraph 21A(8) and paragraphs 21AB, 21AC, 21AD, 21B and 21C apply as if the employee were a Real Time Information employer.

(4) For the purposes of sub-paragraph (2), paragraph 21D(9) applies as if the employee were a Real Time Information employer.

(5) For the purposes of sub-paragraphs (1) and (2), paragraphs 15, 16, 21E, 21EA and 21F(7A) and (8) and Schedule 4A apply as if the employee were a Real Time Information employer, but the information required by paragraph 10(a) and (b) of that Schedule need not be provided.][1]

Amendments—[1] Para 31A inserted by the Security (Contributions) (Amendment and Application of Schedule 38 to the Finance Act 2012) Regulations, SI 2013/622 regs 5, 22 with effect in relation to the tax year 2013–14 and subsequent tax years.
[2] In sub-para (1), word revoked by the Social Security (Miscellaneous Amendments No 2) Regulations, SI 2015/478 regs 2, 22(1), (6) with effect from 6 April 2015.

[SCHEDULE 4A

REAL TIME RETURNS

Regulation 67(3)]

Cross-references—See the Income Tax (Pay As You Earn) (Amendment) Regulations, SI 2012/822 reg 54 (real time information: transitional provisions in relation to information about payments made to employees)
Amendments—Schedule 4A inserted by the Social Security (Contributions) (Amendment No 3) Regulations, SI 2012/821 regs 2, 14, Schedule with effect from 6 April 2012.

[1 The information specified in this Schedule is as follows and terms used in this Schedule which are defined for the purposes of Schedule 4 bear the same meaning as in that Schedule.][1]

Amendments—[1] Schedule 4A inserted by the Social Security (Contributions) (Amendment No 3) Regulations, SI 2012/821 regs 2, 14, Schedule with effect from 6 April 2012.

[Information about the employer and employee

2 The information specified in paragraphs 2 to [6, 8 to 15 and 18 to 20][2] of Schedule A1 (real time returns) to the PAYE Regulations.][1]

Amendments—[1] Schedule 4A inserted by the Social Security (Contributions) (Amendment No 3) Regulations, SI 2012/821 regs 2, 14, Schedule with effect from 6 April 2012.
[2] Words substituted for words "4 and 8 to 14" by the Security (Contributions) (Amendment and Application of Schedule 38 to the Finance Act 2012) Regulations, SI 2013/622 regs 23, 24 with effect in relation to the tax year 2013–14 and subsequent tax years.

[2A For the purposes of paragraph 2, the references in paragraphs 5 and 6 of Schedule A1 to the PAYE Regulations to regulation 67F of those Regulations shall be taken as references to paragraph 21F of Schedule 4 to these Regulations.][1]

Amendments—[1] Para 2A by the Security (Contributions) (Amendment and Application of Schedule 38 to the Finance Act 2012) Regulations, SI 2013/622 regs 23, 25 with effect in relation to the tax year 2013–14 and subsequent tax years.

[Information about payments to the employee, etc

3 The amount of the payment made that is included in the amount of the employee's earnings from the employment for the purposes of determining the amount of earnings-related contributions payable.][1]

Amendments—[1] Schedule 4A inserted by the Social Security (Contributions) (Amendment No 3) Regulations, SI 2012/821 regs 2, 14, Schedule with effect from 6 April 2012.

[3A The total of the amounts referred to in paragraph 3 in the year to date.][1]

Amendments—[1] Para 3A by the Security (Contributions) (Amendment and Application of Schedule 38 to the Finance Act 2012) Regulations, SI 2013/622 regs 23, 26 with effect in relation to the tax year 2013–14 and subsequent tax years.

[4 For the purposes of assessing earnings-related contributions based on the payment, the number of earnings periods the payment relates to.][1]

Amendments—[1] Schedule 4A inserted by the Social Security (Contributions) (Amendment No 3) Regulations, SI 2012/821 regs 2, 14, Schedule with effect from 6 April 2012.

[5 Where—

(*a*) the earner is concurrently employed in more than one employed earner's employment under the same employer but regulation 14 (aggregation of earnings paid in respect of separate employed earner's employments under the same employer) does not apply; or

(*b*) regulation 15 (aggregation of earnings paid in respect of different employed earner's employments by different persons and apportionment of contribution liability) applies in relation to the earner,

an indication of whether the return relates to earnings which have been or will be aggregated.][1]

Cross-references—See the Income Tax (Pay As You Earn) (Amendment) Regulations, SI 2012/822 reg 54 (real time information: transitional provisions in relation to information about payments made to employees)
Amendments—[1] Schedule 4A inserted by the Social Security (Contributions) (Amendment No 3) Regulations, SI 2012/821 regs 2, 14, Schedule with effect from 6 April 2012.

[6 The appropriate category letter or, as the case may be, letters in relation to the employee (being the appropriate letter or letters indicated by HMRC).][1]

NIC

Cross-references—See the Income Tax (Pay As You Earn) (Amendment) Regulations, SI 2012/822 reg 54 (real time information: transitional provisions in relation to information about payments made to employees)

Amendments—[1] Schedule 4A inserted by the Social Security (Contributions) (Amendment No 3) Regulations, SI 2012/821 regs 2, 14, Schedule with effect from 6 April 2012.

[7 For the category letter or, as the case may be, each category letter in relation to the employee (being the appropriate letter or letters indicated by HMRC), the total of the amounts required to be recorded by paragraph 7(13)(*b*)(i) [to (iii)][2] of Schedule 4 (calculation of deduction) for the year to date.][1]

Cross-references—See the Income Tax (Pay As You Earn) (Amendment) Regulations, SI 2012/822 reg 54 (real time information: transitional provisions in relation to information about payments made to employees)

Amendments—[1] Schedule 4A inserted by the Social Security (Contributions) (Amendment No 3) Regulations, SI 2012/821 regs 2, 14, Schedule with effect from 6 April 2012.

[2] Words substituted by the Social Security (Contributions) (Amendment) (No 2) Regulations, SI 2016/352 reg 19(i) with effect from 6 April 2016, subject to savings in relation to rights or obligations arising in connection with tax years beginning before 6 April 2016.

[8 If the employee is a director, in so far as relevant to the relevant category letter (being the appropriate category letter indicated by HMRC) in relation to the employee—

(*a*) an indication of whether, for the purposes of assessing earnings-related contributions based on the payment, the employer has relied on regulation 8(2) or (3) (earnings periods for directors), or

(*b*) an indication of whether, for the purposes of assessing earnings-related contributions based on the payment, the employer has relied or, if the earnings fall to be aggregated, will rely on regulation 8(6).][1]

Cross-references—See the Income Tax (Pay As You Earn) (Amendment) Regulations, SI 2012/822 reg 54 (real time information: transitional provisions in relation to information about payments made to employees)

Amendments—[1] Schedule 4A inserted by the Social Security (Contributions) (Amendment No 3) Regulations, SI 2012/821 regs 2, 14, Schedule with effect from 6 April 2012.

[9 Where regulation 8(2) applies and the appointment was in the current tax year, the week in which the appointment was made.][1]

Cross-references—See the Income Tax (Pay As You Earn) (Amendment) Regulations, SI 2012/822 reg 54 (real time information: transitional provisions in relation to information about payments made to employees)

Amendments—[1] Schedule 4A inserted by the Social Security (Contributions) (Amendment No 3) Regulations, SI 2012/821 regs 2, 14, Schedule with effect from 6 April 2012.

[10 In so far as relevant to the relevant category letter or, as the case may be, letters (being the appropriate category letter or letters indicated by HMRC) in relation to the employee—

(*a*) the total amount of secondary Class 1 contributions payable on the employee's earnings in the earnings period in which the return is made,

(*b*) the total amount of secondary Class 1 contributions payable on the employee's earnings in the year to date,

(*c*) the total amount of primary Class 1 contributions payable on the employee's earnings in the earnings period in which the return is made, and

(*d*) the total amount of primary Class 1 contributions payable on the employee's earnings in the year to date.][1]

Cross-references—See the Income Tax (Pay As You Earn) (Amendment) Regulations, SI 2012/822 reg 54 (real time information: transitional provisions in relation to information about payments made to employees)

Amendments—[1] Schedule 4A inserted by the Social Security (Contributions) (Amendment No 3) Regulations, SI 2012/821 regs 2, 14, Schedule with effect from 6 April 2012.

[11 In a case where the earnings the return relates to will fall to be aggregated with other earnings in the same earnings period, the information required by paragraphs 6, 7 and 10 need only be provided when the final payment of . . . [2] earnings in the earnings period is made.][1]

Amendments—[1] Schedule 4A inserted by the Social Security (Contributions) (Amendment No 3) Regulations, SI 2012/821 regs 2, 14, Schedule with effect from 6 April 2012.

[2] Word revoked by the Social Security (Miscellaneous Amendments No 2) Regulations, SI 2015/478 regs 2, 23 with effect from 6 April 2015.

12 . . . [1]

Amendments—[1] Para 12 revoked by the Social Security (Contributions) (Amendment) (No 2) Regulations, SI 2016/352 reg 19(ii) with effect from 6 April 2016, subject to savings in relation to rights or obligations arising in connection with tax years beginning before 6 April 2016.

[12A Whether, during the period since the employer last made a return under paragraph 21A or 21D of Schedule 4 containing information about the employee—

(*a*) the employee has been absent from the employment because of a trade dispute at the employer's place of work, or (*b*) the employee has been absent from the employment without pay for any other reason.][1]

Amendments—[1] Paras 12A–12D inserted by the Security (Contributions) (Amendment and Application of Schedule 38 to the Finance Act 2012) Regulations, SI 2013/622 regs 23, 28 with effect in relation to the tax year 2013–14 and subsequent tax years.

[12B In cases—

(*a*) falling within paragraph 30 of Schedule 4, or

(*b*) where the employer has no obligation to deduct or repay tax in accordance with regulation 21 of the PAYE Regulations

the amount of the payment after statutory deductions, being the amount of the payment referred to in paragraph 3 minus the total amount of primary Class 1 contributions for the period (see paragraph 10(c)) minus the value of the deduction due under the Education (Student Loans) (Repayment) Regulations 2009 or the Education (Student Loans) (Repayment) Regulations (Northern Ireland) 2009.][1]

Amendments—[1] Paras 12A–12D inserted by the Security (Contributions) (Amendment and Application of Schedule 38 to the Finance Act 2012) Regulations, SI 2013/622 regs 23, 28 with effect in relation to the tax year 2013–14 and subsequent tax years.

[12C The value of any amount which is not subject to tax or national insurance contributions paid to the employee at the same time as the payment.][1]

Amendments—[1] Paras 12A–12D inserted by the Security (Contributions) (Amendment and Application of Schedule 38 to the Finance Act 2012) Regulations, SI 2013/622 regs 23, 28 with effect in relation to the tax year 2013–14 and subsequent tax years.

[12D The value of any deductions made from the payment which do not otherwise fall to be reported under Schedule 4.][1]

Amendments—[1] Paras 12A–12D inserted by the Security (Contributions) (Amendment and Application of Schedule 38 to the Finance Act 2012) Regulations, SI 2013/622 regs 23, 28 with effect in relation to the tax year 2013–14 and subsequent tax years.

[information about statutory sick pay

13 *In a case where the employer is entitled to recover an amount in accordance with article 2 (right of employer to recover statutory sick pay) of the Statutory Sick Pay Percentage Threshold Order 1995 in respect of a payment of statutory sick pay, the total amount of statutory sick pay paid during the year to date in this employment.]*[1, 2]

Amendments—[1] Sch 4A inserted by the Social Security (Contributions) (Amendment No. 3) Regulations, SI 2012/821 reg 14 and Schedule with effect from 6 April 2012.

[2] Para 13 revoked by the Social Security (Contributions) (Amendment No 4) Regulations, SI 2014/2397 regs 2, 3(1), (8) with effect from 6 October 2014.

[Information about statutory maternity pay

14 If any, the total amount of statutory maternity pay paid during the year to date in this employment.][1]

Amendments—[1] Schedule 4A inserted by the Social Security (Contributions) (Amendment No 3) Regulations, SI 2012/821 regs 2, 14, Schedule with effect from 6 April 2012.

[Information about ordinary statutory paternity pay

15 If any, the total amount of . . . [2] statutory paternity pay paid during the year to date in this employment.][1]

Amendments—[1] Schedule 4A inserted by the Social Security (Contributions) (Amendment No 3) Regulations, SI 2012/821 regs 2, 14, Schedule with effect from 6 April 2012.

[2] Word "ordinary" revoked by the Social Security and Tax Credits (Miscellaneous Amendments) Regulations, SI 2015/175 regs 2, 5(1), (2) with effect from 5 April 2015. These amendments do not have effect where they relate to ordinary statutory paternity pay or additional statutory paternity pay, or ordinary statutory paternity pay or additional statutory paternity pay paid on or after 5 April 2015: SI 2015/175 reg 9.

[Information about additional statutory paternity pay

16 *If any, the total amount of additional statutory paternity pay paid during the year to date in this employment.]*[1, 2]

Amendments—[1] Schedule 4A inserted by the Social Security (Contributions) (Amendment No 3) Regulations, SI 2012/821 regs 2, 14, Schedule with effect from 6 April 2012.

[2] Paragraphs 16, 17 revoked by the Social Security and Tax Credits (Miscellaneous Amendments) Regulations, SI 2015/175 regs 2, 5(1), (3) with effect from 5 April 2015. These amendments do not have effect where they relate to additional statutory paternity pay and additional statutory paternity pay that has been paid on or after 5 April 2015, or ordinary statutory paternity pay and ordinary statutory paternity pay that has been paid on or after 5 April 2015: SI 2015/175 reg 9.

[17 Where additional statutory paternity pay has been paid during the year to date, the following information from the employee's application for the payment under, as the case may be, regulation 8, 10, 15 or 17 (applications) of the Additional Statutory Paternity Pay (General) Regulations 2010—

a) the name of the mother or, as the case may be, the adopter of the child the application relates to, and

(b) the national insurance number of the mother or, as the case may be, the adopter of the child the application relates to.][1], [2]

Amendments—[1] Schedule 4A inserted by the Social Security (Contributions) (Amendment No 3) Regulations, SI 2012/821 regs 2, 14, Schedule with effect from 6 April 2012.

[2] Paragraphs 16, 17 revoked by the Social Security and Tax Credits (Miscellaneous Amendments) Regulations, SI 2015/175 regs 2, 5(1), (3) with effect from 5 April 2015. These amendments do not have effect where they relate to additional statutory paternity pay and additional statutory paternity pay that has been paid on or after 5 April 2015, or ordinary statutory paternity pay and ordinary statutory paternity pay that has been paid on or after 5 April 2015: SI 2015/175 reg 9.

[Information about statutory shared parental pay

17A If any, the total amount of statutory shared parental pay paid during the year to date in this employment.][1]

Amendments—[1] Paragraphs 17A, 17B and preceding cross-head inserted by the Social Security and Tax Credits (Miscellaneous Amendments) Regulations, SI 2015/175 regs 2, 5(1), (4) with effect from 5 March 2015.

[17B Where statutory shared parental pay has been paid during the year to date, the following information from the employee's application for the payment under, as the case may be, regulation 6, 7, 19, or 20 (notification and evidential requirements) of the Statutory Shared Parental Pay (General) Regulations 2014—

(*a*) the name of the employee's spouse or partner who has the main responsibility (apart from the employee) for the care of the child to which the application relates, and

(*b*) where there is such a number, the national insurance number of the employee's spouse or partner who has the main responsibility (apart from the employee) for the care of the child to whom the application relates.

For the purposes of this regulation "partner" has the meaning given in regulation 2(1) of the Statutory Shared Parental Pay (General) Regulations 2014.][1]

Amendments—[1] Paragraphs 17A, 17B and preceding cross-head inserted by the Social Security and Tax Credits (Miscellaneous Amendments) Regulations, SI 2015/175 regs 2, 5(1), (4) with effect from 5 March 2015.

[Information about statutory adoption pay

18 If any, the total amount of statutory adoption pay paid in the year to date in this employment.][1]

Amendments—[1] Schedule 4A inserted by the Social Security (Contributions) (Amendment No 3) Regulations, SI 2012/821 regs 2, 14, Schedule with effect from 6 April 2012.

[SCHEDULE 4B

ADDITIONAL INFORMATION ABOUT PAYMENTS

Regulation 67(3)]

Amendments—Schedule 4B inserted by the Social Security (Contributions) (Amendment No 3) Regulations, SI 2012/821 regs 2, 14, Schedule with effect from 6 April 2012.

[**1** The amounts specified in this Schedule are as follows and terms used in this Schedule which are defined for the purposes of Schedule 4 bear the same meaning as in that Schedule.][1]

Amendments—[1] Schedule 4B inserted by the Social Security (Contributions) (Amendment No 3) Regulations, SI 2012/821 regs 2, 14, Schedule with effect from 6 April 2012.

[Deductions in respect of statutory payments

2 In respect of statutory maternity pay paid during the year to date to all employees the total of the amounts determined under regulation 3 (determination of the amount of additional payment to which a small employer shall be entitled) of the Statutory Maternity Pay (Compensation of Employers) and Miscellaneous Amendments Regulations 1994 and deducted by virtue of regulation 4 (right of employer to prescribed amount) of those Regulations.][1]

Amendments—[1] Schedule 4B inserted by the Social Security (Contributions) (Amendment No 3) Regulations, SI 2012/821 regs 2, 14, Schedule with effect from 6 April 2012.

[**3** In respect of . . . [2] statutory paternity pay paid during the year to date to all employees, the total of the amounts determined under regulation 5 (deductions from payments to HMRC) of the Statutory Paternity Pay and Statutory Adoption Pay (Administration) Regulations 2002.][1]

Amendments—[1] Schedule 4B inserted by the Social Security (Contributions) (Amendment No 3) Regulations, SI 2012/821 regs 2, 14, Schedule with effect from 6 April 2012.

2 Word "ordinary" revoked by the Social Security and Tax Credits (Miscellaneous Amendments) Regulations, SI 2015/175 regs 2, 6(1), (2) with effect from 5 April 2015. These amendments do not have effect where they relate to ordinary statutory paternity pay or additional statutory paternity pay, or ordinary statutory paternity pay or additional statutory paternity pay paid on or after 5 April 2015: SI 2015/175 reg 9.

4

Amendments—This paragraph revoked by the Social Security and Tax Credits (Miscellaneous Amendments) Regulations, SI 2015/175 regs 2, 6(1), (3) with effect from 5 April 2015. These amendments do not have effect where they relate to ordinary statutory paternity pay or additional statutory paternity pay, or ordinary statutory paternity pay or additional statutory paternity pay paid on or after 5 April 2015: SI 2015/175 reg 9.

[**4A** In respect of statutory shared parental pay paid during the year to all employees, the total amounts determined under regulation 5 (deductions from payments to the Commissioners) of the Statutory Shared Parental Pay (Administration) Regulations 2014.][1]

Amendments—[1] This paragraph inserted by the Social Security and Tax Credits (Miscellaneous Amendments) Regulations, SI 2015/175 regs 2, 6(1), (4) with effect from 5 March 2015.

[**5** In respect of statutory adoption pay paid during the year to date to all employees, the total of the amounts determined under regulation 5 of the Statutory Paternity Pay and Statutory Adoption Pay (Administration) Regulations 2002.]

Amendments—[1] Schedule 4B inserted by the Social Security (Contributions) (Amendment No 3) Regulations, SI 2012/821 regs 2, 14, Schedule with effect from 6 April 2012.

6

Amendments—Para 6 revoked by the Social Security (Contributions) (Amendment No 4) Regulations, SI 2014/2397 regs 2, 3(1), (9) with effect from 6 October 2014.

[Regional secondary contributions holiday for new businesses

7 The total of the appropriate amounts within the meaning given by section 7 of the National Insurance Contributions Act 2011 (regional secondary contributions holiday for new businesses) deducted by or refunded to the employer under section 4 of that Act in the year to date.][1]

Amendments—[1] Schedule 4B inserted by the Social Security (Contributions) (Amendment No 3) Regulations, SI 2012/821 regs 2, 14, Schedule with effect from 6 April 2012.

SCHEDULE 5

ELECTIONS ABOUT [SECURITIES OPTIONS, RESTRICTED SECURITIES AND CONVERTIBLE SECURITIES][1]

Regulation 69

Amendments—[1] Words substituted by the Social Security (Contributions) (Amendment No 4) Regulations, SI 2004/2096 regs 2, 8(*a*) with effect from 1 September 2004. SI 2004/2096 has effect in relation to—

(a) agreements entered into after 1 September 2004 which are in respect of post-commencement employment income, and

(b) elections made after that date.

1—(1) An election for the purposes of paragraph 3B(1) of Schedule 1 to the Act shall contain—

[(*a*) details of the securities options, restricted securities and convertible securities to which it relates, or of the period to which it relates, within which these are intended to be awarded or acquired;][1]

[(*b*) a statement that the election relates to relevant employment income arising from the securities or securities options referred to in sub-paragraph (1)(*a*) on which the employed earner is liable to pay secondary Class 1 contributions under—

(i) in the case of securities options, section 476 of ITEPA 2003 and section 4(4)(*a*) of the Act;

(ii) in the case of restricted securities, section 426 of ITEPA 2003 and regulation 22(7);

(iii) in the case of convertible securities, section 438 of ITEPA 2003 and regulation 22(7), and

an explanation of the effect of the relevant provision;][1]

(*c*) the amount or proportion (as the case may be) of the liability for secondary Class 1 contributions to be transferred;

(*d*) a statement that its purpose is to transfer the liability for the secondary Class 1 contributions referred to in paragraph (*c*) from the secondary contributor to the employed earner;

[(*dd*) a statement that it does not apply in relation to any liability, or any part of any liability, arising as a result of regulations being given retrospective effect by virtue of section 4B(2) of either the Social Security Contributions and Benefits Act 1992 or the Social Security Contributions and Benefits (Northern Ireland) Act 1992;][2]

(*e*) a statement as to the method by which the secondary contributor will secure that the liability for amounts of contributions, transferred under the election, is met;

NIC

(*f*) a statement as to the circumstances in which it shall cease to have effect;

(*g*) a declaration by the employed earner that he agrees to be bound by its terms; and

(*h*) evidence sufficient to show that the secondary contributor agrees to be bound by its terms.

(2) The declaration referred to in sub-paragraph (1)(*g*) must either be signed by the employed earner or, if it is made by electronic communications, made by him in such electronic form and by such means of electronic communications as may be authorised by the Board.

Amendments—[1] Sub-para (1)(*a*), (*b*) substituted by the Social Security (Contributions) (Amendment No 4) Regulations, SI 2004/2096 regs 2, 8(*b*) with effect from 1 September 2004. SI 2004/2096 has effect in relation to—

(a) agreements entered into after 1 September 2004 which are in respect of post-commencement employment income, and

(b) elections made after that date.

[2] Sub-para (1)(*dd*) inserted by the Social Security (Contributions) (Amendment No 3) Regulations, SI 2007/1175 reg 2 with effect from 6 April 2007. This amendment does not affect the continuing validity of any election made prior to the coming into force of SI 2007/1175, but subject to the National Insurance Contributions Act 2006 s 5(4).

2—(1) An election to which this Schedule applies shall be made either in writing or in such electronic form and by such means of electronic communications as may be authorised by the Board.

(2) An election to which this Schedule applies may be contained in two documents, one made by the employed earner and the other by the secondary contributor, in which case—

(*a*) the document made by the employed earner shall contain the matters listed in paragraph 1(1)(*a*) to (*g*); and

(*b*) the document made by the secondary contributor shall contain the matters listed in paragraph 1(1)(*a*) to (*f*) and (*h*).

3—(1) Where an election to which this Schedule applies has been made, the secondary contributor shall notify the employed earner to whom any of his liabilities are transferred by the election of—

(*a*) any transferred liability that arises;

(*b*) the amount of any transferred liability that arises; and

(*c*) the contents of any notice of withdrawal by the Board of any approval that relates to the election.

(2) The secondary contributor shall notify the employed earner of the matters set out in sub-paragraph (1)(*a*) and (*b*) as soon as reasonably practicable.

(3) The secondary contributor shall notify the employed earner of the matters set out in sub-paragraph (1)(*c*) within 14 days of receipt of the notice of withdrawal in question.

SCHEDULE 6

Regulation 140

PART I

PRESCRIBED ESTABLISHMENTS AND ORGANISATIONS FOR THE PURPOSES OF SECTION 116(3) OF THE ACT

1 Any of the regular naval, military or air forces of the Crown.

2 Royal Fleet Reserve.

3 Royal Naval Reserve.

4 Royal Marines Reserve.

5 Army Reserve.

6 Territorial Army.

7 Royal Air Force Reserve.

8 Royal Auxiliary Air Force.

9 The Royal Irish Regiment, to the extent that its members are not members of any force falling within paragraph 1.

PART II

ESTABLISHMENTS AND ORGANISATIONS OF WHICH HER MAJESTY'S FORCES SHALL NOT CONSIST

10 By virtue of regulation 140, Her Majesty's forces shall not be taken to consist of any of the establishments or organisations specified in Part I of this Schedule by virtue only of the employment in such establishment or organisation of the following persons—

(*a*) any person who is serving as a member of any naval force of Her Majesty's forces and who (not having been an insured person under the National Insurance Act 1965 and not being a contributor under the Social Security Act 1975 or the Act) locally entered that force at an overseas base;

(*b*) any person who is serving as a member of any military force of Her Majesty's forces and who entered that force, or was recruited for that force outside the United Kingdom, and the depot of whose unit is situated outside the United Kingdom;

(*c*) any person who is serving as a member of any air force of Her Majesty's forces and who entered that force, or was recruited for that force, outside the United Kingdom, and is liable under the terms of his engagement to serve only in a specified part of the world outside the United Kingdom.

SCHEDULE 7

CORRESPONDING NORTHERN IRELAND ENACTMENTS

Regulation 156(4)

1 In this Schedule—

"the 1998 Order" means the Social Security (Northern Ireland) Order 1998;

"the 2000 Act" means the Child Support, Pensions and Social Security Act 2000;

"the Transfer Order" means the Social Security Contributions (Transfer of Functions, etc) (Northern Ireland) Order 1999;

"the Welfare Reform Act" means the Welfare Reform and Pensions Act 1999; and

"the Welfare Reform Order" means the Welfare Reform and Pensions (Northern Ireland) Order 1999.

PART I

ENACTMENTS CORRESPONDING TO PRIMARY LEGISLATION APPLICABLE TO GREAT BRITAIN

Enactment applying in Great Britain	*Corresponding enactment applying in Northern Ireland*	*Relevant Northern Ireland amendment*
National Insurance Act 1965	National Insurance Act (Northern Ireland) 1996	
Section 3	Section 3	
Employment and Training Act 1973	Employment and Training Act (Northern Ireland) 1950	
Section 2(2)	Section 1	Article 3 of the Employment and Training (Amendment) (Northern Ireland) Order 1988 and Article 5 of the Industrial Training (Northern Ireland) Order 1990.
Social Security Act 1975	Social Security (Northern Ireland) Act 1975	
Section 4	Section 4	
Section 5(3)	Section 5(3)	
Section 7	Section 7	
Section 8	Section 8	
Section 39(4)	Section 39(4)	
Section 130(2)	Section 125(2)	
Social Security Pensions Act 1975	Social Security Pensions (Northern Ireland) Order 1975	
Section 3(1)	Article 5(1)	
Section 6(1)(*a*)	Article 8(1)(*a*)	
Companies Act 1985	Companies (Northern Ireland) Order 1986	
Section 718	Article 667	Amended by paragraph 8 of Schedule 8 to SR 1997 No 251.
Section 735 (definition of "company")	Article 3(1)	
Social Security Act 1986	Social Security (Northern Ireland) Order 1986	

NIC

Section 7	Article 9	
Children Act 1999	Children (Northern Ireland) Order 1995	
Part X	Part XI	
Section 71(13) (definition of "nanny")	Article 119(6)	
Section 105(1) (definition of "relative")	Article 2(2)	
Social Security Contributions and Benefits Act 1992	Social Security Contributions and Benefits (Northern Ireland) Act 1992	
Section 1(6)	Section 1(6)	Paragraph 38(3) of Schedule 6 to the 1998 Order and paragraph 2 of Schedule 3 to the Transfer Order.
Section 2(1) and (2)	Section 2(1) and (2)	
Section 3	Section 3	Articles 45 and 46 of the 1998 Order and paragraph 4 of Schedule 3 to the Transfer Order.
Section 4(1) and (4)	Section 4(1) and (4)	Subsection (4) was substituted by Article 47(1) of the 1998 Order.
Section 5(1)	Section 5(1)	Substituted by paragraph 1 of Part I of Schedule 10 to the Welfare Reform Act.
Section 6	Section 6	Substituted by paragraph 2 of Part I of Schedule 10 to the Welfare Reform Act and amended by section 81(3) of the 2000 Act.
Section 6A	Section 6A	
Section 8(1) and (2)	Section 8(1) and (2)	Section 8 was substituted by paragraph 4 of Part I of Schedule 10 to the Welfare Reform Act.
Section 9	Section 9	Substituted by paragraph 5 of Part I of Schedule 10 to the Welfare Reform Act.
Section 10	Section 10	Substituted by section 78(2) of the 2000 Act.
Section 10ZA	Section 10ZA	
Section 10A	Section 10A	Paragraph 12 of Schedule 3 to the Transfer Order and section 78 of the Welfare Reform Act.
Section 11	Section 11	Paragraph 13 of Schedule 3 to Transfer Order and article 3 of SI 2001/477.
Section 12	Section 12	Paragraph 14 of Schedule 3, and paragraph 1 of Schedule 8 to the Transfer Order.
Section 13	Section 13	Paragraph 15 of Schedule 3 to the Transfer Order and article 4 of SI 2001/477.
Section 14(1)	Section 14(1)	
Section 15	Section 15	Article 4 of SI 2000/755 and article 5 of SI 2001/477.
Section 16	Section 16	Paragraph 6 of Schedule 1 to the Transfer Order.

Section 17	Section 17	Paragraph 7 of Schedule 1, paragraph 17 of Schedule 3 and Schedule 9 to the Transfer Order.
Section 18	Section 18	Paragraph 8 of Schedule 1, paragraph 18 of Schedule 3 to the Transfer Order, article 4 of SI 2000/755 and article 5 of SI 2001/477.
Section 19(1), (2) and (4)	Section 19(1), (2) and (4) respectively	
Section 19A	Section 19A	Paragraph 20 of Schedule 3 and paragraph 2 of Schedule 8 to the Transfer Order.
Section 20(1)	Section 20(1)	Paragraph 2(2) of Schedule 1 to the Social Security (Incapacity for Work) (Northern Ireland) Order 1994, Schedule 3 to the Jobseekers (Northern Ireland) Order 1995, paragraph 18(1) of Schedule 2 to the Pensions (Northern Ireland) Order 1995 and paragraph 2(2) of Schedule 8, paragraph 5(2) of Schedule 9 and Part V of Schedule 10 to the Welfare Reform Order.
Section 112	Section 112	Schedule 1 to the Employment Rights (Northern Ireland) Order 1996 and paragraph 21 of Schedule 3 to the Transfer Order.
Section 122(1) (definition of "pensionable age")	Section 121(1) (definition of "pensionable age")	Paragraph 9 of Schedule 2 to the Pensions (Northern Ireland) Order 1995.
Section 151(6)	Section 147 (6)	Paragraph 10 of Schedule 1 to the Transfer Order.
Section 164(9)(*b*)	Section 160(9)(*b*)	Paragraph 14(2) of Schedule 1 to the Transfer Order.
Schedule 1	Schedule 1	
Paragraph 1(1)	Paragraph 1(1)	
Paragraph 1(7)	Paragraph 1(7)	
Paragraph 1(8)	Paragraph 1(8)	
Paragraph 3(1)	Paragraph 3(1)	Paragraph 58(5) of Schedule 6 to the 1998 Order.
Paragraph 3B	Paragraph 3B	
Paragraph 6(3) and (4A)	Paragraph 6(3) and (4A)	Amended by paragraph 3 of Schedule 8 to the Transfer Order.
Schedule 2	Schedule 2	
Social Security Administration Act 1992	Social Security Administration (Northern Ireland) Act 1992	
Section 17	Section 15	
Section 18	Section 16	
Section 73	Section 71	Paragraph 32 of Schedule 2 to the Jobseekers (Northern Ireland) Order 1995.

NIC

Section 162(5)	Section 142(5)	Article 4(1) of the Social Security (Contributions) (Northern Ireland) Order 1994, Article 61(2) of the 1998 Order, paragraph 9(2) of Part III of Schedule 10 to the Welfare Reform Act and section 78(7) of the 2000 Act.
Section 179	Section 155	Paragraph 48 of Schedule 2 to the Jobseekers (Northern Ireland) Order 1995, paragraph 84 of Schedule 6 to the 1998 Order and paragraph 5 of Schedule 1 to the Tax Credits Act 1999.
Trade Union and Labour Relations (Consolidation) Act 1992	Employment Rights (Northern Ireland) Order 1996	
Section 189	Article 217	Regulation 10 of SR 1999 No 432.
Pension Schemes Act 1993	Pension Schemes (Northern Ireland) Act 1993	
Section 8(1)	Section 4(1)	Article 133(2) of, and paragraph 14 of Schedule 3 to the Pensions (Northern Ireland) Order 1995 and paragraph 37(a) of Schedule 1 to the Transfer Order.
Section 9(2)	Section 5(2)	Article 133(3) of the Pensions (Northern Ireland) Order 1995.
Section 9(3)	Section 5(3)	Article 133(4) of, and paragraph 17 of Schedule 3 to the Pensions (Northern Ireland) Order 1995, and paragraph 38(3) of Schedule 3 to the Transfer Order.
Section 41(1) to (1B)	Section 37(1) to (1B)	Subsection (1) was amended by paragraph 95 of Schedule 6 to the 1998 Order and further amended by paragraph 6(2), and subsections (1A) and (1B) were substituted by paragraph 6(3), of Part II of Schedule 10 to the Welfare Reform Act.
Section 42A(1) to (2A)	Section 38A(1) to (2A)	Section 38A was inserted by Article 134(4) of the Pensions (Northern Ireland) Order 1995, subsections (1) to (2A) were substituted by paragraph 96 of Schedule 6 to the 1998 Order and subsections (2) and (2A) were further substituted by paragraph 7(3) of Part I of Schedule 10 to the Welfare Reform Act.
Section 43	Section 39	Paragraph 34 of Schedule 3 to the Pensions (Northern Ireland) Order 1995 and paragraph 54 of Schedule 1 to the Transfer Order.

Section 44(1)	Section 40(1)	Article 160(a) of the Pensions (Northern Ireland) Order 1995 and paragraph 55(2) and (3) of Schedule 1 to the Transfer Order.
Section 55(2)	Section 51(2)	Substituted by Article 138 of the Pensions (Northern Ireland) Order 1995 and amended by paragraph 7(2) of Schedule 2 to the Welfare Reform Act.
Jobseekers Act 1995	Jobseekers (Northern Ireland) Order 1995	
Section 2(1)(*a*)	Article 4(1)(*a*)	
Social Security Contributions (Transfer of Functions, etc) Act 1999	The Transfer Order	
Section 8(1)(*a*) and (*k*)(ii)	Article 7(1)(*a*) and (*k*)(ii)	

PART II

ENACTMENTS CORRESPONDING TO SUBORDINATE LEGISLATION APPLICABLE TO GREAT BRITAIN

Subordinate legislation applying in Great Britain	*Subordinate legislation applying in Northern Ireland*	*Relevant amendment to the Northern Ireland provision*
National Insurance (Contributions) Regulations 1969	National Insurance (Contributions) Regulations (Northern Ireland) 1962	SR & O (NI) 1963 No 59 and 1970 No 295.
Regulation 9(3) and (4A)	Regulation 10(3) and (4A) respectively	
National Insurance (Married Women) Regulations 1973—	National Insurance (Married Women) Regulations (Northern Ireland) 1973	
Regulation 2(1)(*a*)	Regulation 2(1)(*a*)	
Regulation 2(2)	Regulation 2(2)	
Regulation 3(1)(*a*)	Regulation 3(1)(*a*)	
Regulation 3(2)	Regulation 3(2)	
Regulation 4(2)	Regulation 4(2)	
Regulation 16	Regulation 16	
Social Security (Contributions) Regulations 1975	Social Security (Contributions) Regulations (Northern Ireland) 1975	
Regulation 91	Regulation 89	
Regulation 94	Regulation 92	
Social Security (Categorisation of Earners) Regulations 1978	Social Security (Categorisation of Earners) Regulations (Northern Ireland) 1978	
Schedule 3	Schedule 3	Regulation 4 of SR 1984 No 81, regulation 3 of SR 1990 No 339, regulation 4 of SR 1994 No 92 and regulation 4 of SR 1998 No 250. See also SR 1999 No 2.
Social Security (Payments on account, Overpayments and Recovery) Regulations 1988	Social Security (Payments on account, Overpayments and Recovery) Regulations (Northern Ireland) 1988	

Regulation 13	Regulation 13	Regulation 15(3) of SR 1996 No 289 and regulation 11 of SI 1999/2573.
Social Security (Refunds) (Repayment of Contractual Maternity Pay) Regulations 1990	Social Security (Refunds) (Repayment of Contractual Maternity Pay) Regulations (Northern Ireland) 1990	
Regulation 2	Regulation 2	
Statutory Maternity Pay (Compensation of Employers) and Miscellaneous Amendments Regulations 1994	Statutory Maternity Pay (Compensation of Employers) and Miscellaneous Amendments Regulations (Northern Ireland) 1994	
Regulation 3	Regulation 3	
Regulation 4	Regulation 4	
. . . [2]	. . . [2]	
Social Security (Adjudication) Regulations 1995	Social Security (Adjudication) Regulations (Northern Ireland) 1995	
Regulation 13	Regulation 13	
Social Security (Additional Pension) (Contributions Paid in Error) Regulations 1996	Social Security (Additional Pension) (Contributions Paid in Error) Regulations (Northern Ireland) 1996	
Regulation 3	Regulation 3	
Employer's Contributions Reimbursement Regulations 1996	Employer's Contributions Reimbursement Regulations (Northern Ireland) 1996	
Regulations 5, 6 and 8	Regulations 5, 6 and 8 respectively	
[Education (Student Loans) (Repayment) Regulations 2009][1]	[Education (Student Loans) (Repayment) Regulations (Northern Ireland) 2009][1]	
Regulation 39(1)	Regulation 39(1)	
Social Security (Crediting and Treatment of Contributions, and National Insurance Numbers) Regulations 2001	Social Security (Crediting and Treatment of Contributions, and National Insurance Numbers) Regulations (Northern Ireland) 2001	
Regulation 4	Regulation 4	
Regulation 9	Regulation 9	

Amendments—[1] Entries substituted by the Social Security (Contributions) (Amendment No 3) Regulations, SI 2012/821 regs 2, 26(*c*), 31 with effect from 6 April 2012.

[2] In first column, entry for "Statutory Sick Pay Percentage Threshold Order 1995" revoked, and in second column, entry for "Statutory Sick Pay Percentage Threshold Order (Northern Ireland) 1995" revoked, by the Social Security (Contributions) (Amendment No 4) Regulations, SI 2014/2397 regs 2, 3(1), (10) with effect from 6 October 2014.

SCHEDULE 8

REVOCATIONS

Regulation 157

PART I

REVOCATIONS APPLICABLE TO GREAT BRITAIN OR TO THE UNITED KINGDOM

Column (1)	*Column (2)*	*Column (3)*
Regulations revoked	*References*	*Extent of revocation*
The Social Security (Contributions) Regulation 1979	SI 1979/591	The whole of the Regulations

The Social Security (Contributions) Amendment Regulations 1980	SI 1980/1975	The whole of the Regulations
The Social Security (Contributions) Amendment Regulations 1981	SI 1981/82	The whole of the Regulations
The Social Security (Contributions) (Mariners) Amendment Regulations 1982	SI 1982/206	The whole of the Regulations
The Contracting-out (Recovery of Class 1 Contributions) Regulations 1982	SI 1982/1033	The whole of the Regulations
The Social Security (Contributions) Amendment Regulations 1982	SI 1982/1573	The whole of the Regulations
The Social Security and Statutory Sick Pay (Oil and Gas (Enterprise) Act 1982) (Consequential) Regulations 1982	SI 1982/1738	Regulation 4
The Social Security (Contributions) Amendment (No 2) Regulations 1982	SI 1982/1739	The whole of the Regulations
The Social Security (Contributions) Amendment Regulations 1983	SI 1983/10	The whole of the Regulations
The Social Security (Contributions) Amendment (No 2) Regulations 1983	SI 1983/53	The whole of the Regulations
The Social Security (Contributions, Re-rating) Consequential Amendment Regulations 1983	SI 1983/73	The whole of the Regulations
The Social Security (Contributions) Amendment (No 4) Regulations 1983	SI 1983/395	The whole of the Regulations
The Social Security (Contributions) Amendment (No 3) Regulations 1983	SI 1983/496	The whole of the Regulations
The Social Security (Contributions) Amendment (No 5) Regulations 1983	SI 1983/1689	The whole of the Regulations
The Social Security (Contributions) Amendment Regulations 1984	SI 1984/77	The whole of the Regulations
The Social Security (Contributions, Re-rating) Consequential Amendment Regulations 1984	SI 1984/146	The whole of the Regulations
The Social Security (Contributions) Amendment (No 2) Regulations 1984	SI 1984/1756	The whole of the Regulations
The Social Security (Contributions, Re-rating) Consequential Amendment Regulations 1985	SI 1985/143	The whole of the Regulations
The Social Security (Contributions) Amendment Regulations 1985	SI 1985/396	The whole of the Regulations
The Social Security (Contributions) Amendment (No 2) Regulations 1985	SI 1985/397	The whole of the Regulations
The Social Security (Contributions) Amendment (No 3) Regulations 1985	SI 1985/398	The whole of the Regulations
The Social Security (Contributions) Amendment (No 4) Regulations 1985	SI 1985/399	The whole of the Regulations
The Social Security (Contributions) Amendment (No 5) Regulations 1985	SI 1985/400	The whole of the Regulations
The Social Security (Contributions and Credits) (Transitional and Consequential Provisions) Regulations 1985	SI 1985/1398	Regulations 2, 4, 5 and 6
The Social Security (Contributions) Amendment (No 6) Regulations 1985	SI 1985/1726	The whole of the Regulations
The Social Security (Contributions, Re-rating) Consequential Amendment Regulations 1986	SI 1986/198	The whole of the Regulations
The Social Security (Contributions) Amendment Regulations 1986	SI 1986/485	The whole of the Regulations
The Social Security (Contributions) Amendment (No 2) Regulations 1987	SI 1987/413	The whole of the Regulations

The Social Security (Contributions) Amendment (No 3) Regulations 1987	SI 1987/1590	The whole of the Regulations
The Social Security (Contributions) Amendment (No 4) Regulations 1987	SI 1987/2111	The whole of the Regulations
The Social Security (Contributions) Amendment Regulations 1988	SI 1988/299	The whole of the Regulations
The Social Security (Contributions) Amendment (No 2) Regulations 1988	SI 1988/674	The whole of the Regulations
The Social Security (Contributions) Amendment (No 3) Regulations 1988	SI 1988/860	The whole of the Regulations
The Social Security (Contributions) Amendment (No 4) Regulations 1988	SI 1988/992	The whole of the Regulations
The Social Security (Contributions) Amendment Regulations 1989	SI 1989/345	The whole of the Regulations
The Social Security (Contributions) Amendment (No 2) Regulations 1989	SI 1989/571	The whole of the Regulations
The Social Security (Contributions) Amendment (No 3) Regulations 1989	SI 1989/572	The whole of the Regulations
The Social Security (Contributions) (Transitional and Consequential Provisions) Regulations 1989	SI 1989/1677	The whole of the Regulations
The Social Security (Refunds) (Repayment of Contractual Maternity Pay) Regulations 1990	SI 1990/536	Regulation 4
The Social Security (Contributions) Amendment Regulations 1990	SI 1990/604	The whole of the Regulations
The Social Security (Contributions) Amendment (No 2) Regulations 1990	SI 1990/605	The whole of the Regulations
The Social Security (Contributions) (Re-rating) Consequential Amendment Regulations 1990	SI 1990/906	The whole of the Regulations
The Social Security (Contributions) Amendment (No 3) Regulations 1990	SI 1990/1779	The whole of the Regulations
The Social Security (Contributions) Amendment (No 4) Regulations 1990	SI 1990/1935	The whole of the Regulations
The Social Security (Contributions) Amendment Regulations 1991	SI 1991/504	The whole of the Regulations
The Social Security (Contributions) Amendment (No 2) Regulations 1991	SI 1991/639	The whole of the Regulations
The Social Security (Contributions) Amendment (No 3) Regulations 1991	SI 1991/640	The whole of the Regulations
The Social Security (Contributions) Amendment (No 4) Regulations 1991	SI 1991/1632	The whole of the Regulations
The Social Security (Contributions) Amendment (No 5) Regulations 1991	SI 1991/1935	The whole of the Regulations
The Social Security (Contributions) Amendment (No 6) Regulations 1991	SI 1991/2505	The whole of the Regulations
The Social Security (Contributions) Amendment Regulations 1992	SI 1992/97	The whole of the Regulations
The Social Security (Contributions) Amendment (No 2) Regulations 1992	SI 1992/318	The whole of the Regulations
The Social Security (Contributions) Amendment (No 3) Regulations 1992	SI 1992/667	The whole of the Regulations
The Social Security (Contributions) Amendment (No 4) Regulations 1992	SI 1992/668	The whole of the Regulations
The Social Security (Contributions) Amendment (No 5) Regulations 1992	SI 1992/669	The whole of the Regulations
The Social Security (Contributions) Amendment (No 6) Regulations 1992	SI 1992/1440	The whole of the Regulations

The Social Security (Contributions) Amendment Regulations 1993	SI 1993/260	The whole of the Regulations
The Social Security (Contributions) Amendment (No 2) Regulations 1993	SI 1993/281	The whole of the Regulations
The Social Security (Contributions) Amendment (No 3) Regulations 1993	SI 1993/282	The whole of the Regulations
The Social Security (Contributions) Amendment (No 4) Regulations 1993	SI 1993/583	The whole of the Regulations
The Social Security (Contributions) Amendment (No 5) Regulations 1993	SI 1993/821	The whole of the Regulations
The Social Security (Contributions) Amendment (No 6) Regulations 1993	SI 1993/2094	The whole of the Regulations
The Social Security (Miscellaneous Amendments) Regulations 1993	SI 1993/2736	The whole of the Regulations
The Social Security (Contributions) Amendment (No 7) Regulations 1993	SI 1993/2925	The whole of the Regulations
The Social Security (Contributions) Amendment Regulations 1994	SI 1994/563	The whole of the Regulations
The Social Security (Contributions) (Miscellaneous Amendments) Regulations 1994	SI 1994/667	The whole of the Regulations
The Social Security (Contributions) Amendment (No 2) Regulations 1994	SI 1994/1553	The whole of the Regulations
The Social Security (Contributions) Amendment (No 3) Regulations 1994	SI 1994/2194	The whole of the Regulations
The Social Security (Contributions) Amendment (No 4) Regulations 1994	SI 1994/2299	The whole of the Regulations
The Statutory Sick Pay Percentage Threshold Order 1995	SI 1995/512	Article 6(3)
The Social Security (Contributions) Amendment Regulations 1995	SI 1995/514	The whole of the Regulations
The Social Security (Contributions) Amendment (No 2) Regulations 1995	SI 1995/714	The whole of the Regulations
The Social Security (Contributions) Amendment (No 3) Regulations 1995	SI 1995/730	The whole of the Regulations
The Social Security (Incapacity Benefit) (Consequential and Transitional Amendments and Savings) Regulations 1995	SI 1995/829	Regulation 13
The Social Security (Contributions) Amendment (No 4) Regulations 1995	SI 1995/1003	The whole of the Regulations
The Social Security (Contributions) Amendment (No 5) Regulations 1995	SI 1995/1570	The whole of the Regulations
The Employer's Contributions Reimbursement Regulations 1996	SI 1996/195	Regulation 13
The Social Security (Contributions) Amendment Regulations 1996	SI 1996/486	The whole of the Regulations
The Social Security (Contributions) Amendment (No 2) Regulations 1996	SI 1996/663	The whole of the Regulations
The Social Security (Contributions) Amendment (No 3) Regulations 1996	SI 1996/700	The whole of the Regulations
The Social Security Contributions, Statutory Maternity Pay and Statutory Sick Pay (Miscellaneous Amendments) Regulations 1996	SI 1996/777	Regulation 5
The Social Security (Contributions) Amendment (No 4) Regulations 1996	SI 1996/1047	The whole of the Regulations
The Social Security (Additional Pension) (Contributions Paid in Error) Regulations 1996	SI 1996/1245	Regulation 4
The Social Security (Credits and Contributions) (Jobseeker's Allowance Consequential and Miscellaneous Amendments) Regulations 1996	SI 1996/2367	Regulation 3

The Social Security (Contributions) Amendment (No 5) Regulations 1996	SI 1996/2407	The whole of the Regulations
The Social Security (Contributions) Amendment (No 6) Regulations 1996	SI 1996/3031	The whole of the Regulations
The Social Security (Contributions) Amendments Regulations 1997	SI 1997/545	The whole of the Regulations
The Social Security (Contributions) Amendment (No 2) Regulations 1997	SI 1997/575	The whole of the Regulations
The Social Security (Contributions) Amendment (No 3) Regulations 1997	SI 1997/820	The whole of the Regulations
The Social Security (Contributions) Amendment (No 4) Regulations 1997	SI 1997/1045	The whole of the Regulations
The Social Security (Contributions) Amendment Regulations 1998	SI 1998/523	The whole of the Regulations
The Social Security (Contributions) (Re-rating) Consequential Amendment Regulations 1998	SI 1998/524	The whole of the Regulations
The Social Security (Contributions) Amendment (No 2) Regulations 1998	SI 1998/680	The whole of the Regulations
The Social Security (Contributions) Amendment (No 3) Regulations 1998	SI 1998/2211	The whole of the Regulations
The Social Security (Contributions) Amendment (No 4) Regulations 1998	SI 1998/2320	The whole of the Regulations
The Social Security (Contributions) Amendment (No 5) Regulations 1998	SI 1998/2894	The whole of the Regulations
The Social Security (Contributions) (Re-rating) Consequential Amendment Regulations 1999	SI 1999/361	The whole of the Regulations
The Social Security (Contributions) Amendment Regulations 1999	SI 1999/561	The whole of the Regulations
The Social Security Contributions, Statutory Maternity Pay and Statutory Sick Pay (Miscellaneous Amendments) Regulations 1999	SI 1999/567	Regulations 2 to 6 and 8 to 11
The Social Security (Contributions and Credits) (Miscellaneous Amendments) Regulations 1999	SI 1999/568	Regulations 2 to 12 and 14 to 19
The Social Security (Contributions) Amendment (No 2) Regulations 1999	SI 1999/827	The whole of the Regulations
The Social Security (Contributions) Amendment (No 3) Regulations 1999	SI 1999/975	The whole of the Regulations
The Social Security (Contributions) (Amendment No 4) Regulations 1999	SI 1999/1965	The whole of the Regulations
The Social Security (Contributions) (Amendment No 5) Regulations 1999	SI 1999/2736	The whole of the Regulations
The Social Security (Contributions) (Amendment) Regulations 2000	SI 2000/175	The whole of the Regulations
The Social Security (Contributions) (Amendment No 2) Regulations 2000	SI 2000/723	The whole of the Regulations
The Social Security (Contributions) (Amendment No 3) Regulations 2000	SI 2000/736	The whole of the Regulations
The Social Security Contributions (Notional Payment of Primary Class 1 Contribution) Regulations 2000	SI 2000/747	Regulations 7 to 9
The Social Security (Contributions) (Re-rating) Consequential Amendment Regulations 2000	SI 2000/760	The whole of the Regulations
The Social Security (Contributions) (Amendment No 4) Regulations 2000	SI 2000/761	The whole of the Regulations
The Social Security (Contributions) (Amendment No 5) Regulations 2000	SI 2000/1149	The whole of the Regulations

The Social Security (Contributions) (Amendment No 6) Regulations 2000	SI 2000/2084	The whole of the Regulations
The Social Security (Contributions) (Amendment No 7) Regulations 2000	SI 2000/2077	The whole of the Regulations
The Social Security (Contributions) (Amendment No 8) Regulations 2000	SI 2000/2207	The whole of the Regulations
The Social Security (Contributions) (Amendment No 9) Regulations 2000	SI 2000/2343	The whole of the Regulations
The Social Security (Contributions) (Amendment No 10) Regulations 2000	SI 2000/2744	The whole of the Regulations
The Social Security (Contributions) (Amendment) Regulations 2001	SI 2001/45	The whole of the Regulations
The Social Security (Contributions) (Amendment No 2) Regulations 2001	SI 2001/313	The whole of the Regulations
The Social Security (Contributions) (Amendment No 3) Regulations 2001	SI 2001/596	The whole of the Regulations
The Social Security (Crediting and Treatment of National Insurance Contributions) Regulations 2001	SI 2001/769	Regulation 11

PART II

REVOCATIONS APPLICABLE TO NORTHERN IRELAND

Note—This revocation table is not reproduced.

2001/1354

SOCIAL SECURITY (MINIMUM CONTRIBUTIONS TO APPROPRIATE PERSONAL PENSION SCHEMES) ORDER 2001

Made by the Secretary of State for Social Security under PSA 1993 ss 45A, 182(2), and PS(NI)A 1993 ss 41A, 181(9A)

Made . . . . *3 April 2001*
Coming into force . . . . *6 April 2002*

1 Citation and commencement

(1) This Order may be cited as the Social Security (Minimum Contributions to Appropriate Personal Pension Schemes) Order 2001 and shall come into force on 6th April 2002.

(2) In this Order—

(*a*) "LET" means the low earnings threshold for the tax year in question as specified in—

(i) section 44A of the Social Security Contributions and Benefits Act 1992 or,

(ii) in relation to Northern Ireland, section 44A of the Social Security Contributions and Benefits (Northern Ireland) Act 1992;

(*b*) "qualifying earnings factor" means the same as in—

(i) section 122(1) of the Social Security Contributions and Benefits Act 1992 or,

(ii) in relation to Northern Ireland, section 121(1) of the Social Security Contributions and Benefits (Northern Ireland) Act 1992;

(*c*) "QEF" means the qualifying earnings factor for that tax year;

(*d*) "2QEF" means the amount produced by doubling QEF, rounded to the nearest £100 (taking any amount of £50 as nearest to the previous whole £100).

2 Appropriate age-related percentages

(1) For the purposes of section 45 of the Pension Schemes Act 1993 and section 41 of the Pension Schemes (Northern Ireland) Act 1993 (amount of minimum contributions) the appropriate age-related percentages in respect of earners—

(*a*) for the tax year 2002–03 are those specified in the Table set out in Schedule 1 to this Order;

(*b*) for the tax year 2003–04 are those specified in the Table set out in Schedule 2 to this Order;

(*c*) for the tax year 2004–05 are those specified in the Table set out in Schedule 3 to this Order;

(*d*) for the tax year 2005–06 are those specified in the Table set out in Schedule 4 to this Order;

(*e*) for the tax year 2006–07 are those specified in the Table set out in Schedule 5 to this Order,

by reference to their ages on the last day of the preceding tax year.

(2) The appropriate age-related percentage in respect of an earner whose age on that day is specified in Column A of any such Table—

NIC

(*a*) in the case of an earner whose earnings do not exceed LET, shall be the percentage specified in Column B;

(*b*) in the case of an earner whose earnings which exceed LET but do not exceed 3LET – 2QEF, shall—

(i) in so far as those earnings do not exceed LET, be the percentage specified in Column B,

(ii) in so far as those earnings exceed LET, be the percentage specified in Column C;

(*c*) in the case of an earner whose earnings exceed 3LET – 2QEF, shall—

(i) in so far as those earnings do not exceed LET, be the percentage specified in Column B,

(ii) in so far as those earnings exceed LET but do not exceed 3LET – 2QEF, be the percentage specified in Column C,

(iii) in so far as those earnings exceed 3LET – 2QEF, be the percentage specified in Column D.

SCHEDULE 1

APPROPRIATE AGE-RELATED PERCENTAGES FOR THE TAX YEAR 2002–03

Article 2(1)(a)

Column A	*Column B*	*Column C*	*Column D*
Age on last day of preceding tax year	*Earnings not exceeding LET*	*Earnings exceeding LET but not 3LET – 2QEF*	*Earnings exceeding 3LET – 2QEF*
15	8.4	2.10	4.2
16	8.4	2.10	4.2
17	8.4	2.10	4.2
18	8.6	2.15	4.3
19	8.6	2.15	4.3
20	8.8	2.20	4.4
21	8.8	2.20	4.4
22	9.0	2.25	4.5
23	9.0	2.25	4.5
24	9.0	2.25	4.5
25	9.2	2.30	4.6
26	9.2	2.30	4.6
27	9.4	2.35	4.7
28	9.4	2.35	4.7
29	9.6	2.40	4.8
30	9.6	2.40	4.8
31	9.8	2.45	4.9
32	9.8	2.45	4.9
33	10.0	2.50	5.0
34	10.0	2.50	5.0
35	10.0	2.50	5.0
36	10.2	2.55	5.1
37	10.2	2.55	5.1
38	10.4	2.60	5.2
39	10.4	2.60	5.2
40	10.8	2.70	5.4
41	11.2	2.80	5.6
42	11.4	2.85	5.7
43	11.8	2.95	5.9
44	12.2	3.05	6.1
45	12.6	3.15	6.3
46	13.0	3.25	6.5
47	14.0	3.50	7.0
48	15.6	3.90	7.8

Column A	*Column B*	*Column C*	*Column D*
Age on last day of preceding tax year	*Earnings not exceeding LET*	*Earnings exceeding LET but not 3LET – 2QEF*	*Earnings exceeding 3LET – 2QEF*
49	17.6	4.40	8.8
50	19.8	4.95	9.9
51	21.0	5.25	10.5
52	21.0	5.25	10.5
53	21.0	5.25	10.5
54	21.0	5.25	10.5
55	21.0	5.25	10.5
56	21.0	5.25	10.5
57	21.0	5.25	10.5
58	21.0	5.25	10.5
59	21.0	5.25	10.5
60	21.0	5.25	10.5
61	21.0	5.25	10.5
62	21.0	5.25	10.5
63	21.0	5.25	10.5

SCHEDULE 2

APPROPRIATE AGE-RELATED PERCENTAGES FOR THE TAX YEAR 2003–04

Article 2(1)(*b*)

Column A	*Column B*	*Column C*	*Column D*
Age on last day of preceding tax year	*Earnings not exceeding LET*	*Earnings exceeding LET but not 3LET – 2QEF*	*Earnings exceeding 3LET – 2QEF*
15	8.4	2.10	4.2
16	8.4	2.10	4.2
17	8.4	2.10	4.2
18	8.6	2.15	4.3
19	8.6	2.15	4.3
20	8.8	2.20	4.4
21	8.8	2.20	4.4
22	9.0	2.25	4.5
23	9.0	2.25	4.5
24	9.0	2.25	4.5
25	9.2	2.30	4.6
26	9.2	2.30	4.6
27	9.4	2.35	4.7
28	9.4	2.35	4.7
29	9.6	2.40	4.8
30	9.6	2.40	4.8
31	9.8	2.45	4.9
32	9.8	2.45	4.9
33	10.0	2.50	5.0
34	10.0	2.50	5.0
35	10.0	2.50	5.0
36	10.2	2.55	5.1
37	10.2	2.55	5.1
38	10.4	2.60	5.2
39	10.4	2.60	5.2

Column A	*Column B*	*Column C*	*Column D*
Age on last day of preceding tax year	*Earnings not exceeding LET*	*Earnings exceeding LET but not 3LET – 2QEF*	*Earnings exceeding 3LET – 2QEF*
40	10.6	2.65	5.3
41	11.0	2.75	5.5
42	11.2	2.80	5.6
43	11.6	2.90	5.8
44	12.0	3.00	6.0
45	12.4	3.10	6.2
46	12.8	3.20	6.4
47	13.2	3.30	6.6
48	14.2	3.55	7.1
49	15.8	3.95	7.9
50	17.8	4.45	8.9
51	20.0	5.00	10.0
52	21.0	5.25	10.5
53	21.0	5.25	10.5
54	21.0	5.25	10.5
55	21.0	5.25	10.5
56	21.0	5.25	10.5
57	21.0	5.25	10.5
58	21.0	5.25	10.5
59	21.0	5.25	10.5
60	21.0	5.25	10.5
61	21.0	5.25	10.5
62	21.0	5.25	10.5
63	21.0	5.25	10.5

SCHEDULE 3

APPROPRIATE AGE-RELATED PERCENTAGES FOR THE TAX YEAR 2004–05

Article 2(1)(*c*)

Column A	*Column B*	*Column C*	*Column D*
Age on last day of preceding tax year	*Earnings not exceeding LET*	*Earnings exceeding LET but not 3LET – 2QEF*	*Earnings exceeding 3LET – 2QEF*
15	8.4	2.10	4.2
16	8.4	2.10	4.2
17	8.4	2.10	4.2
18	8.6	2.15	4.3
19	8.6	2.15	4.3
20	8.8	2.20	4.4
21	8.8	2.20	4.4
22	9.0	2.25	4.5
23	9.0	2.25	4.5
24	9.0	2.25	4.5
25	9.2	2.30	4.6
26	9.2	2.30	4.6
27	9.4	2.35	4.7
28	9.4	2.35	4.7
29	9.6	2.40	4.8
30	9.6	2.40	4.8

Column A	*Column B*	*Column C*	*Column D*
Age on last day of preceding tax year	*Earnings not exceeding LET*	*Earnings exceeding LET but not 3LET – 2QEF*	*Earnings exceeding 3LET – 2QEF*
31	9.8	2.45	4.9
32	9.8	2.45	4.9
33	10.0	2.50	5.0
34	10.0	2.50	5.0
35	10.2	2.55	5.1
36	10.2	2.55	5.1
37	10.2	2.55	5.1
38	10.4	2.60	5.2
39	10.4	2.60	5.2
40	10.6	2.65	5.3
41	10.6	2.65	5.3
42	11.0	2.75	5.5
43	11.4	2.85	5.7
44	11.8	2.95	5.9
45	12.0	3.00	6.0
46	12.4	3.10	6.2
47	12.8	3.20	6.4
48	13.2	3.30	6.6
49	14.4	3.60	7.2
50	16.0	4.00	8.0
51	18.0	4.50	9.0
52	20.2	5.05	10.1
53	21.0	5.25	10.5
54	21.0	5.25	10.5
55	21.0	5.25	10.5
56	21.0	5.25	10.5
57	21.0	5.25	10.5
58	21.0	5.25	10.5
59	21.0	5.25	10.5
60	21.0	5.25	10.5
61	21.0	5.25	10.5
62	21.0	5.25	10.5
63	21.0	5.25	10.5

SCHEDULE 4

APPROPRIATE AGE-RELATED PERCENTAGES FOR THE TAX YEAR 2005–06

Article 2(1)(*d*)

Column A	*Column B*	*Column C*	*Column D*
Age on last day of preceding tax year	*Earnings not exceeding LET*	*Earnings exceeding LET but not 3LET – 2QEF*	*Earnings exceeding 3LET – 2QEF*
15	8.4	2.10	4.2
16	8.4	2.10	4.2
17	8.4	2.10	4.2
18	8.6	2.15	4.3
19	8.6	2.15	4.3
20	8.8	2.20	4.4
21	8.8	2.20	4.4

NIC

Column A	*Column B*	*Column C*	*Column D*
Age on last day of preceding tax year	*Earnings not exceeding LET*	*Earnings exceeding LET but not 3LET – 2QEF*	*Earnings exceeding 3LET – 2QEF*
22	9.0	2.25	4.5
23	9.0	2.25	4.5
24	9.0	2.25	4.5
25	9.2	2.30	4.6
26	9.2	2.30	4.6
27	9.4	2.35	4.7
28	9.4	2.35	4.7
29	9.6	2.40	4.8
30	9.6	2.40	4.8
31	9.8	2.45	4.9
32	9.8	2.45	4.9
33	10.0	2.50	5.0
34	10.0	2.50	5.0
35	10.2	2.55	5.1
36	10.2	2.55	5.1
37	10.4	2.60	5.2
38	10.4	2.60	5.2
39	10.4	2.60	5.2
40	10.6	2.65	5.3
41	10.6	2.65	5.3
42	10.8	2.70	5.4
43	11.2	2.80	5.6
44	11.4	2.85	5.7
45	11.8	2.95	5.9
46	12.2	3.05	6.1
47	12.6	3.15	6.3
48	13.0	3.25	6.5
49	13.4	3.35	6.7
50	14.6	3.65	7.3
51	16.0	4.00	8.0
52	18.0	4.50	9.0
53	20.4	5.10	10.2
54	21.0	5.25	10.5
55	21.0	5.25	10.5
56	21.0	5.25	10.5
57	21.0	5.25	10.5
58	21.0	5.25	10.5
59	20.4	5.10	10.2
60	21.0	5.25	10.5
61	21.0	5.25	10.5
62	21.0	5.25	10.5
63	21.0	5.25	10.5

SCHEDULE 5

APPROPRIATE AGE-RELATED PERCENTAGES FOR THE TAX YEAR 2006–07

Article 2(1)(*e*)

Column A	*Column B*	*Column C*	*Column D*
Age on last day of preceding tax year	*Earnings not exceeding LET*	*Earnings exceeding LET but not 3LET – 2QEF*	*Earnings exceeding 3LET – 2QEF*
15	8.4	2.10	4.2
16	8.4	2.10	4.2
17	8.4	2.10	4.2
18	8.6	2.15	4.3
19	8.6	2.15	4.3
20	8.8	2.20	4.4
21	8.8	2.20	4.4
22	9.0	2.25	4.5
23	9.0	2.25	4.5
24	9.0	2.25	4.5
25	9.2	2.30	4.6
26	9.2	2.30	4.6
27	9.4	2.35	4.7
28	9.4	2.35	4.7
29	9.6	2.40	4.8
30	9.6	2.40	4.8
31	9.8	2.45	4.9
32	9.8	2.45	4.9
33	10.0	2.50	5.0
34	10.0	2.50	5.0
35	10.2	2.55	5.1
36	10.2	2.55	5.1
37	10.4	2.60	5.2
38	10.4	2.60	5.2
39	10.6	2.65	5.3
40	10.6	2.65	5.3
41	10.8	2.70	5.4
42	10.8	2.70	5.4
43	11.0	2.75	5.5
44	11.2	2.80	5.6
45	11.6	2.90	5.8
46	12.0	3.00	6.0
47	12.4	3.10	6.2
48	12.8	3.20	6.4
49	13.2	3.30	6.6
50	13.6	3.40	6.8
51	14.6	3.65	7.3
52	16.2	4.05	8.1
53	18.2	4.55	9.1
54	20.6	5.15	10.3
55	21.0	5.25	10.5
56	21.0	5.25	10.5
57	21.0	5.25	10.5
58	21.0	5.25	10.5
59	19.6	4.90	9.8

Column A	*Column B*	*Column C*	*Column D*
Age on last day of preceding tax year	*Earnings not exceeding LET*	*Earnings exceeding LET but not 3LET – 2QEF*	*Earnings exceeding 3LET – 2QEF*
60	20.6	5.15	10.3
61	21.0	5.25	10.5
62	21.0	5.25	10.5
63	21.0	5.25	10.5

2001/1355

SOCIAL SECURITY (REDUCED RATES OF CLASS 1 CONTRIBUTIONS, AND REBATES) (MONEY PURCHASE CONTRACTED-OUT SCHEMES) ORDER 2001

Made by the Secretary of State for Social Security under PSA 1993 s 42B, and PS(NI)A 1993 ss 38B, 181(9A)

Made . . . .*3 April 2001*
Coming into force . . . .*6 April 2002*

1 Citation and commencement

This Order may be cited as the Social Security (Reduced Rates of Class 1 Contributions, and Rebates) (Money Purchase Contracted-out Schemes) Order 2001 and shall come into force on 6th April 2002.

2 Reduced rates of Class 1 contributions, and rebates

For the purposes of section 42A of the Pension Schemes Act 1993 and section 38A of the Pension Schemes (Northern Ireland) Act 1993 (reduced rates of Class 1 contributions, and rebates)—

(*a*) the appropriate flat-rate percentage in respect of earners for the tax years 2002–2003 to 2006–2007—

(i) in the case of a primary Class 1 contribution is 1.6 per cent, and

(ii) in the case of a secondary Class 1 contribution is 1 per cent;

(*b*) the appropriate age-related percentages in respect of earners for each of the tax years 2002–2003 to 2006–2007 are the percentages specified in relation to that year in the Table set out in the Schedule to this Order, by reference to the earners' ages on the last day of the preceding tax year.

SCHEDULE

Article 2

TABLE

APPROPRIATE AGE-RELATED PERCENTAGES OF EARNINGS EXCEEDING THE LOWER EARNINGS LIMIT BUT NOT THE UPPER EARNINGS LIMIT

Age on last day of preceding tax year	*Appropriate age-related percentages for the tax year*				
	2002–03	2003–04	2004–05	2005–06	2006–07
15	2.6	2.6	2.6	2.6	2.6
16	2.6	2.6	2.6	2.6	2.6
17	2.7	2.7	2.7	2.7	2.7
18	2.7	2.7	2.7	2.7	2.7
19	2.8	2.8	2.8	2.8	2.8
20	2.8	2.8	2.8	2.8	2.8
21	2.9	2.9	2.9	2.9	2.9
22	2.9	2.9	2.9	2.9	3.0
23	3.0	3.0	3.0	3.0	3.0
24	3.1	3.1	3.1	3.1	3.1
25	3.1	3.1	3.1	3.1	3.1
26	3.2	3.2	3.2	3.2	3.2

27	3.2	3.2	3.2	3.2	3.2
28	3.3	3.3	3.3	3.3	3.3
29	3.4	3.4	3.4	3.4	3.4
30	3.4	3.4	3.4	3.4	3.4
31	3.6	3.6	3.6	3.6	3.6
32	3.6	3.6	3.6	3.6	3.6
33	3.7	3.7	3.7	3.7	3.7
34	3.8	3.8	3.8	3.8	3.8
35	3.8	3.8	3.8	3.8	3.8
36	3.9	3.9	3.9	3.9	3.9
37	4.0	4.0	4.0	4.0	4.0
38	4.1	4.1	4.1	4.1	4.1
39	4.1	4.1	4.1	4.1	4.1
40	4.3	4.2	4.2	4.2	4.2
41	4.4	4.4	4.3	4.3	4.3
42	4.6	4.5	4.4	4.4	4.4
43	4.8	4.7	4.6	4.5	4.4
44	5.0	4.9	4.8	4.7	4.6
45	5.3	5.1	5.0	4.9	4.8
46	5.5	5.4	5.3	5.1	5.0
47	6.0	5.6	5.5	5.4	5.3
48	6.8	6.1	5.7	5.6	5.5
49	7.8	6.9	6.2	5.8	5.7
50	9.0	7.9	7.1	6.4	5.9
51	10.3	9.1	8.1	7.2	6.5
52	10.5	10.5	9.3	8.2	7.4
53	10.5	10.5	10.5	9.5	8.4
54	10.5	10.5	10.5	10.5	9.7
55	10.5	10.5	10.5	10.5	10.5
56	10.5	10.5	10.5	10.5	10.5
57	10.5	10.5	10.5	10.5	10.5
58	10.5	10.5	10.5	10.5	10.5
59	10.5	10.5	10.1	9.7	9.3
60	10.5	10.5	10.5	10.3	9.9
61	10.5	10.5	10.5	10.5	10.5
62	10.5	10.5	10.5	10.5	10.5
63	10.5	10.5	10.5	10.5	10.5

2001/1817

SOCIAL SECURITY CONTRIBUTIONS (SHARE OPTIONS) REGULATIONS 2001

The Treasury, in exercise of the powers conferred upon them by section 175(3) and (4) of, and paragraphs 7B(1) and (2)(*e*), (*f*) and (*g*) and 8(1)(*b*) and (*q*) and (1A) of Schedule 1 to, the Social Security Contributions and Benefits Act 1992, section 171(3) and (4) of, and paragraphs 7B(1), (2)(*e*), (*f*) and (*g*) and (10) and 8(1)(*b*) and (*q*) and (1A) of Schedule 1 to, the Social Security Contributions and Benefits (Northern Ireland) Act 1992 and section 5(3) of the Social Security Contributions (Share Options) Act 2001, and the Commissioners of Inland Revenue, in exercise of the powers conferred upon them by section 175(3) and (4) of, and paragraph 6(1)(*b*) of Schedule 1 to, the Social Security Contributions and Benefits Act 1992, section 171(3) and (4) of, and paragraph 6(1)(*b*) of Schedule 1 to, the Social Security Contributions and Benefits (Northern Ireland) Act 1992 and section 1(5)(*a*) and (*b*) of the Social Security Contributions (Share Options)

NIC

Act 2001, hereby make, immediately after the passing of the Social Security Contributions (Share Options) Act 2001, the following Regulations:

Made . . . . *11 May 2001*
Laid before Parliament . . . . *11 May 2001*
Coming into force . . . . *12 May 2001*

1 Citation and commencement

These Regulations may be cited as the Social Security Contributions (Share Options) Regulations 2001 and shall come into force on 12th May 2001.

2 Interpretation

In these Regulations—

"the Act" means the Social Security Contributions (Share Options) Act 2001 and references to a numbered section, without more, are references to the section bearing that number in the Act;

"the Contributions and Benefits Act" means—

(*a*) in the application of these Regulations to Great Britain, the Social Security Contributions and Benefits Act 1992; and

(*b*) in the application of these Regulations to Northern Ireland, the Social Security Contributions and Benefits (Northern Ireland) Act 1992;

"the day on which the Act is passed" means 11th May 2001;

"special contribution" means the contribution payable to the Inland Revenue under section 2.

3 Matters to be contained in notices under section 1

(1) A notice under section 1 must contain the following—

(*a*) the name and address of the person giving the notice;

(*b*) the name and national insurance number of the person who has obtained a right to acquire shares in respect of which the notice is given;

(*c*) the date on which the right was granted;

(*d*) the amount that a person might reasonably have expected to have obtained from a sale in the open market on 7th November 2000 of each share to which the right relates together with a statement as to whether or not that amount has been agreed with Inland Revenue Shares Valuation;

(*e*) the price at which each share may be acquired by exercise of the right;

(*f*) any amount paid in consideration of the grant of the right, or, in cases where section 3 applies, the grant of the original right, by the person who has obtained it;

(*g*) the amount in respect of which Class 1 contributions would have been payable by virtue of section 4(4)(*a*) of the Contributions and Benefits Act if the right had been exercised in full on 7th November 2000 without the giving of any further consideration for the shares acquired by exercise of that right;

(*h*) the amounts of any Class 1 contributions that have already been paid to the Inland Revenue in respect of any liability to pay Class 1 contributions in respect of any gain realised on an exercise, assignment or release of the right after 7th November 2000 and before the day on which the Act is passed; and

(*i*) confirmation that the person giving the notice understands that the notice is irrevocable.

(2) In cases where an election for the purposes of paragraph 3B(1) of Schedule 1 to the Contributions and Benefits Act which is in force on the day of the notice would relate to any gain realised on an exercise, assignment or release of the right on the day of the notice, the notice must also contain the following—

(*a*) a statement as to whether the person paying the special contribution is the person on whom (apart from the Act) any liability to pay secondary Class 1 contributions in respect of that gain would fall by virtue of the election;

(*b*) if different parts of that liability would fall (apart from the Act) on different persons by virtue of the election, a statement as to how much of the special contribution is being paid by the secondary contributor on whom (apart from the Act) that liability would fall if no election were in force; and

(*c*) if the notice is given—

(i) by the secondary contributor on whom (apart from the Act) any liability to pay secondary Class 1 contributions in respect of that gain would fall if no election were in force,

(ii) on behalf of the person on whom (apart from the Act) that liability would fall by virtue of the election,

a declaration that that person has consented to the notice being given by the secondary contributor.

(3) In cases where section 3 applies, the notice must also contain confirmation that the person on whom any liability to pay Class 1 contributions in respect of any gain realised on the exercise, assignment or release of the replacement right referred to in that section or any subsequent replacement right would fall understands that section 2(1)(*a*) and (*b*) does not—

(*a*) prevent any such liability in respect of any such gain; or

(*b*) have the effect of deeming any such liability not to have arisen on any such gain.

4 Form of, and manner of giving, notices under section 1

(1) A notice under section 1 given in writing must be signed by the person giving it.

(2) A notice under section 1 may also be given by electronic communication containing an electronic signature of the person giving the notice.

(3) Where a notice under section 1 is to be given by a company, section 108(1) of the Taxes Management Act 1970 shall apply to that notice as it applies to a notice to be given by a company under the Taxes Acts.

(4) In this regulation—

["electronic communication" includes any communication conveyed by means of an electronic communications network;][1]

"electronic signature" has the meaning given by section 7(2) of the Electronic Communications Act 2000;

"the Taxes Acts" has the same meaning as is given by section 118(1) of the Taxes Management Act 1970.

Amendments—[1] In para (4), definition of "electronic communication" substituted by the Social Security Contributions (Share Options) Regulations, SI 2003/2155, art 3(1), Sch 1 para 24(1)(*d*), (2) with effect from 17 September 2003.

5 Payment of special contributions

(1) Any special contribution must be paid to the Inland Revenue before the end of the period of ninety-two days beginning with the day on which the Act is passed or before the end of that period as extended by any such further period determined by the Inland Revenue under section 2(5).

(2) For the purpose of this regulation and regulations 6 to 9 where—

(*a*) any payment to the Inland Revenue is made by cheque; and

(*b*) the cheque is paid on its first presentation to the banker on whom it is drawn,

the payment shall be treated as made on the day on which the cheque was received by the Inland Revenue and cognate expressions shall be construed accordingly.

6 Interest on overdue special contributions

(1) A special contribution which is not paid to the Inland Revenue before the end of the period of ninety-two days beginning with the day on which the Act is passed shall carry interest at the rate applicable under paragraph 6(3) of Schedule 1 to the Social Security Contributions and Benefits Act 1992 from the end of that period until payment.

(2) Interest payable under this regulation shall be recoverable as if it were a Class 1A contribution.

(3) A certificate of the Inland Revenue that any amount of interest payable under this regulation has not been paid to them, or, to the best of their knowledge and belief, to any person acting on their behalf, shall be sufficient evidence that a person is liable to pay to them the amount of interest shown on the certificate and that the sum is unpaid and due to be paid, and any document purporting to be such a certificate shall be deemed to be such a certificate until the contrary is proved.

7 Payment of interest on repaid special contributions

Where a special contribution is repaid to a person by the Inland Revenue, the repayment shall carry interest at the rate applicable under paragraph 6(3) of Schedule 1 to the Social Security Contributions and Benefits Act 1992 from the end of the period of ninety-two days beginning with the day on which the Act is passed, or, if later, from the date on which the special contribution was paid to the Inland Revenue, until the order for repayment is issued.

8 Repayment of interest paid on special contributions

Where a person has paid interest in respect of a special contribution, the Inland Revenue shall repay the interest to that person if—

(*a*) the interest is found not to have been due to be paid; or

(*b*) the special contribution is returned, or repaid, to that person.

9 Remission of interest on special contributions

(1) Interest payable in respect of a special contribution shall be remitted for the period commencing on the first relevant date and ending on the second relevant date in the circumstances specified in paragraph (2).

(2) The circumstances specified in this paragraph are that the liability, or a part of the liability, to pay the interest arises as the result of an official error being made.

(3) In this regulation—

"official error" means a mistake made, or something omitted to be done, by an officer of, or person employed in relation to, the Inland Revenue acting as such, where the person by whom the interest was payable, or any person acting on his behalf, does not cause, or materially contribute to, that error or omission;

"the first relevant date" means the date after the end of the period of ninety-two days beginning with the day on which the Act is passed or, if later, the date on which the official error occurs;

"the second relevant date" means the date which is fourteen days after the date on which the official error is rectified and the person by whom the interest was payable is advised of its rectification.

10 Records to be maintained

(1) A person who has given a notice under section 1 must maintain the following records—

(*a*) a copy of the notice;

(*b*) evidence of the price at which each share may be acquired by exercise of the right in respect of which the notice is given;

(*c*) evidence of the amount that a person might reasonably have expected to have obtained from a sale in the open market on 7th November 2000 of each share to which the right relates;

(*d*) evidence that the special contribution was paid to the Inland Revenue before the end of the period of ninety-two days beginning with the day on which the Act is passed; and

(*e*) in cases where sub-paragraph (*c*) of regulation 3(2) applies, evidence of the consent referred to in that sub-paragraph.

(2) Subject to paragraph (3), the records referred to in paragraph (1) must be retained by the person required to maintain them for a period of not less than three years beginning with 6th April following the date on which a gain is realised on the exercise, assignment or release of the right in respect of which the notice under section 1 is given.

(3) In cases where—

(*a*) section 3 applies; and

(*b*) the notice under section 1 is given in respect of the original right,

the records referred to in paragraph (1) must be retained by the person required to maintain them for a period of not less than three years beginning with 6th April following the date on which a gain is realised on the exercise, assignment or release of the replacement right or any subsequent replacement right.

11 Inspection of records

(1) The following provisions of this regulation, which are a modified version of paragraphs (1) and (3) to (7) of regulation 55 of the Income Tax (Employments) Regulations 1993, shall apply in relation to every person required to maintain records under regulation 10 of these Regulations.

(2) Every person required to maintain records under regulation 10, whenever called upon to do so by any authorised officer of the Inland Revenue, must produce those records to that officer for inspection, at such time as that officer may reasonably require, at the prescribed place.

(3) "The prescribed place" mentioned in paragraph (2) means—

(*a*) such place in the United Kingdom as the person and the officer may agree upon;

(*b*) in default of such agreement, the place in the United Kingdom at which the records referred to in paragraph (2) are normally kept; or

(*c*) in default of such agreement and if there is no such place as is referred to in sub-paragraph (*b*), the person's principal place of business in the United Kingdom.

(4) The authorised officer may—

(*a*) take copies of, or make extracts from, any document produced to him for inspection in accordance with paragraph (2); and

(*b*) remove any document so produced if it appears to him to be necessary to do so, at a reasonable time and for a reasonable period.

(5) Where any document is removed in accordance with paragraph (4)(*b*), the authorised officer must provide—

(*a*) a receipt for any documents so removed; and

(*b*) a copy of the document, free of charge, within seven days, to the person by whom it was produced or caused to be produced where the document is reasonably required for the proper conduct of a business.

(6) Where a lien is claimed on a document produced in accordance with paragraph (2), the removal of the document under paragraph (4)(*b*) shall not be regarded as breaking the lien.

(7) Where records are maintained by computer, the person required to make them available for inspection shall provide the authorised officer with all facilities necessary for obtaining information from them.

2001/1818

SOCIAL SECURITY CONTRIBUTIONS (DEFERRED PAYMENTS AND INTEREST) REGULATIONS 2001

The Commissioners of Inland Revenue, in exercise of the powers conferred upon them by paragraph 6(1)(b) of Schedule 1 to the Social Security Contributions and Benefits Act 1992 and paragraph 6(1)(*b*) of Schedule 1 to the Social Security Contributions and Benefits (Northern Ireland) Act 1992, after the signifying of Royal Assent to the Finance Act 2001 [11 May 2001], hereby make the following Regulations:

Made . . . . *11 May 2001*
Laid before Parliament . . . . *11 May 2001*
Coming into force . . . . *12 May 2001*

1 Citation and commencement

These Regulations may be cited as the Social Security Contributions (Deferred Payments and Interest) Regulations 2001 and shall come into force on 12th May 2001.

2 Application of section 107 of the Finance Act 2001 for the purposes of Class 1 contributions, Class 1A contributions and Class 1B contributions

(1) For the purposes of Class 1 contributions, Class 1A contributions and Class 1B contributions, section 107 of the Finance Act 2001 (interest on unpaid tax, etc: foot-and-mouth disease) shall apply with the following modifications.

(2) In subsection (1)—

(*a*) after "of tax", where it first occurs, add "or a relevant contribution"; and

(*b*) for the second paragraph substitute—

"For this purpose—

"relevant contribution" means a Class 1 contribution, a Class 1A contribution or a Class 1B contribution, within the meaning of section 1(2) of the Social Security Contributions and Benefits Act 1992, or, in the case of a contribution payable in Northern Ireland, section 1(2) of the Social Security Contributions and Benefits (Northern Ireland) Act 1992, in respect of which interest would apart from this section be chargeable; and

"tax" includes any amount chargeable by way of tax, or as a result of the non-payment of tax, in respect of which interest would apart from this section be chargeable.".

(3) In subsection (2) for "31st January 2001" substitute "12th May 2001".

(4) In subsection (6)(*a*) for "the passing of this Act" substitute "the coming into force of the Social Security Contributions (Deferred Payments and Interest) Regulations 2001".

2003/499

SOCIAL SECURITY CONTRIBUTIONS AND BENEFITS ACT 1992 (APPLICATION OF PARTS 12ZA[, 12ZB AND 12ZC] TO ADOPTIONS FROM OVERSEAS) REGULATIONS 2003

Made by the Secretary of State under the Social Security Contributions and Benefits Act 1992 ss 171ZK and 171ZT

Made . . . . *5 March 2003*
Laid before Parliament . . . . *6 March 2003*
So far as applying enabling powers . . . . *10 March 2003*

Amendments—In heading to these regs, words substituted for words "and 12ZB" by the Social Security Contributions and Benefits Act 1992 (Application of Parts 12ZA and 12ZB to Adoptions from Overseas) (Amendment) Regulations, SI 2014/2857 regs 2, 3 with effect from 19 November 2014.

1 Citation, commencement and interpretation

(1) These Regulations may be cited as the Social Security Contributions and Benefits Act 1992 (Application of Parts 12ZA[, 12ZB and 12ZC][1] to Adoptions from Overseas) Regulations 2003 and shall come into force, in so far as they apply powers to make regulations, on 10th March 2003, and for all other purposes on 6th April 2003.

(2) In these Regulations—

"adoption from overseas" means the adoption of a child who enters Great Britain from outside the United Kingdom in connection with or for the purposes of adoption which does not involve the placement of the child for adoption under the law of any part of the United Kingdom;

"the Act" means the Social Security Contributions and Benefits Act 1992.

Amendments—[1] In para (1), words substituted by the Social Security Contributions and Benefits Act 1992 (Application of Parts 12ZA and 12ZB to Adoptions from Overseas) (Amendment) Regulations, SI 2014/2857 regs 2, 4 with effect from 19 November 2014.

2 Application of Part 12ZA of the Act to adoptions from overseas

Part 12ZA of the Act . . .[2] shall apply in relation to adoptions from overseas, with the modifications of sections 171ZB, 171ZE [171ZEB, 171ZEE][1] and 171ZJ of the Act specified in the second column of Schedule 1.

Amendments—[1] Words inserted in both places by the Social Security Contributions and Benefits Act 1992 (Application of Parts 12ZA and 12ZB to Adoptions from Overseas) Regulations 2003 (Amendment) Regulations 2010, SI 2010/153, reg 2 with effect from 6 April 2010.

[2] Words revoked by the Shared Parental Leave and Statutory Shared Parental Pay (Consequential Amendments to Subordinate Legislation) Order, SI 2014/3255 art 14(1), (2) with effect from 5 April 2015.

3 Application of Part 12ZB of the Act to adoptions from overseas

Part 12ZB of the Act shall apply in relation to adoptions from overseas, with the modifications of sections 171ZL and 171ZS of the Act specified in the second column of Schedule 2.

[4 Application of Part 12ZC of the Act to adoptions from overseas

Part 12ZC of the Act shall apply in relation to adoptions from overseas, with the modifications of section 171ZV of the Act(a) specified in the second column of Schedule 3.][1]

Amendments—[1] Para 4 inserted by the Social Security Contributions and Benefits Act 1992 (Application of Parts 12ZA and 12ZB to Adoptions from Overseas) (Amendment) Regulations, SI 2014/2857 regs 2, 5 with effect from 19 November 2014.

SCHEDULE 1

APPLICATION OF PART 12ZA OF THE ACT TO ADOPTIONS FROM OVERSEAS

Regulation 2

Provision	*Modification*
Section 171ZB(2)	. . .[1] In paragraph (*a*)(i), for "who is placed for adoption under the law of any part of the United Kingdom" substitute "who is adopted from overseas". In paragraph (*a*)(ii), for "a person with whom the child is so placed for adoption" substitute "an adopter of the child". [In paragraph (*b*), omit "ending with the relevant week"][1] In paragraph (*d*), for "the day on which the child is placed for adoption" substitute "the day on which the child enters Great Britain". In paragraph (*e*), for "a person with whom the child is placed for adoption" substitute "an adopter of the child".
Section 171ZB(3)	[For subsection (3) substitute— "(3) The references in subsection (2)(*c*) and (*d*) to the relevant week are to— (*a*)the week in which official notification is sent to the adopter, or (*b*)the week at the end of which the person satisfies the condition in subsection (2)(*b*), whichever is the later.[1]]" . . .[1]
Section 171ZB(6)	For "the placement for adoption of more than one child as part of the same arrangement" substitute "the adoption from overseas of more than one child as part of the same arrangement".
Section 171ZB(7)	Omit subsection (7).
Section 171ZE(3)	In paragraph (*b*), for "with the date of the child's placement for adoption" substitute "with the date of the child's entry into Great Britain".
Section 171ZE(10)	For subsection (10) substitute— "(10) Where more than one child is the subject of adoption from overseas as part of the same arrangement, and the date of entry of each child is different, the reference in subsection (3)(*b*) to the date of the child's entry into Great Britain shall be interpreted as a reference to the date of the entry of the first child to enter Great Britain.".
. . .[2]	. . .[2]
. . .[2]	. . .[2]

Provision	*Modification*
. . . [2]	. . . [2]
. . . [2]	. . . [2]
. . . [2]	. . . [2]
Section 171ZJ(1)	In the appropriate places in the alphabetical order, insert— " "adopter", in relation to a child, means a person by whom the child has been or is to be adopted;" " "adoption from overseas" means the adoption of a child who enters Great Britain from outside the United Kingdom in connection with or for the purposes of adoption which does not involve the placement of the child for adoption under the law of any part of the United Kingdom, and the references to a child adopted from overseas shall be construed accordingly;" " "official notification" means written notification, issued by or on behalf of the relevant domestic authority, that it is prepared to issue a certificate to the overseas authority concerned with the adoption of the child, or has issued a certificate and sent it to that authority, confirming, in either case, that the adopter is eligible to adopt and has been assessed and approved as being a suitable adoptive parent;" " "relevant domestic authority" means— (*a*) in the case of an adopter to whom the Intercountry Adoption (Hague Convention) Regulations 2003 apply and who is habitually resident in Wales, the National Assembly of Wales;(*b*) in the case of an adopter to whom the [Adoptions with a Foreign Element (Scotland) Regulations 2009][3] apply and who is habitually resident in Scotland, the Scottish Ministers; (*c*) in any other case, the Secretary of State.".

Amendments—[1] In entry relating to Section 171ZB(2), words revoked, and words inserted; and in entry relating to Section 171ZB(3), words substituted, and words revoked; by the Statutory Paternity Pay and Statutory Adoption Pay (Amendment) Regulations, SI 2004/488 reg 3(1), (2) with effect from 6 April 2004.

[2] Entries revoked by the Shared Parental Leave and Statutory Shared Parental Pay (Consequential Amendments to Subordinate Legislation) Order, SI 2014/3255 art 14(1), (3) with effect from 5 April 2015.

[3] In the entry relating to the modification of s 171ZJ(1), words substituted by the Adoptions with a Foreign Element (Scotland) Regulations SI 2011/159 reg 9(2) m 21 March 2011. Change also made by the Adoption and Children (Scotland) Act 2007 (Consequential Modifications) Order, Si 2011/1740 art 3 and Sch 2 para 7(1), 92) with effect from 15 July 2011.

SCHEDULE 2

APPLICATION OF PART 12ZB OF THE ACT TO ADOPTIONS FROM OVERSEAS

Regulation 3

Provision	*Modification*
Section 171ZL(2)	[1] In paragraph (*a*), for "with whom a child is, or is expected to be, placed for adoption under the law of any part of the United Kingdom" substitute "who is, or is expected to be, an adopter of a child from overseas". [In paragraph (*b*), omit "ending with the relevant week"][1]
Section 171ZL(3)	[For subsection (3) substitute— "(3) The reference in subsection (2)(*d*) to the relevant week is to— (*a*) the week in which official notification is sent to the adopter, or (*b*) the week at the end of which the person satisfies the condition in subsection (2)(*b*), whichever is the later."][1]
	. . . [1]
Section 171ZL(4)	In paragraph (*b*), for "placed for adoption with him" substitute "adopted by him".

Provision	*Modification*
Section 171ZL(5)	For "the placement, or expected placement, for adoption of more than one child" substitute "the adoption, or expected adoption, from overseas of more than one child".
Section 171ZS(1)	In the appropriate places in the alphabetical order, insert— " "adopter", in relation to a child, means a person by whom a child has been or is to be adopted;" " "adoption from overseas" means the adoption of a child who enters Great Britain from outside the United Kingdom in connection with or for the purposes of adoption which does not involve the placement of the child for adoption under the law of any part of the United Kingdom, and the reference to an adopter from overseas shall be construed accordingly;" " "official notification" means written notification, issued by or on behalf of the relevant domestic authority, that it is prepared to issue a certificate to the overseas authority concerned with the adoption of the child, or has issued a certificate and sent it to that authority, confirming, in either case, that the adopter is eligible to adopt and has been assessed and approved as being a suitable adoptive parent;" " "relevant domestic authority" means— (*a*) in the case of an adopter to whom the Intercountry Adoption (Hague Convention) Regulations 2003 apply and who is habitually resident in Wales, the National Assembly of Wales; (*b*) in the case of an adopter to whom the [Adoptions with a Foreign Element (Scotland) Regulations 2009][2] apply and who is habitually resident in Scotland, the Scottish Ministers; (*c*) in any other case, the Secretary of State.".

Amendments—[1] In entry relating to Section 171ZL(2), words revoked, and words inserted; and in entry relating to Section 171ZL(3), words substituted; by the Statutory Paternity Pay and Statutory Adoption Pay (Amendment) Regulations, SI 2004/488 reg 3(1), (3) with effect from 6 April 2004.

[2] In the entry modifying s 171ZS, words substituted by the Adoptions with a Foreign Element (Scotland) Regulations SI 2011/159 reg 9(3) with effect from 21 March 2011. Change also made by the Adoption and Children (Scotland) Act 2007 (Consequential Modifications) Order, Si 2011/1740 art 3 and Sch 2 para 7(1), 92) with effect from 15 July 2011.

[SCHEDULE 3

APPLICATION OF PART 12ZC OF THE ACT TO ADOPTIONS FROM OVERSEAS

Regulation 4

Provision	*Modification*
Section 171ZV	In subsection (1), for "with whom a child is, or is expected to be, placed for adoption under the law of any part of the United Kingdom" substitute "by whom a child is, or is expected to be, adopted from overseas". In paragraph (*g*) of subsection (2), for "placement for adoption of the child" substitute "adoption of the child from overseas". In paragraph (*a*) of subsection (4), for "with whom a child is, or is expected to be, placed for adoption under the law of any part of the United Kingdom" substitute "by whom a child is, or is expected to be, adopted from overseas". In paragraph (*h*) of subsection (4), for "placement for adoption of the child" substitute "adoption of the child from overseas". In subsection (16), for "placement for adoption" substitute "adoption from overseas".

Provision	*Modification*
	After subsection (16) insert— "(16A) For the purposes of this section, a person adopts a child from overseas if the person adopts a child who enters Great Britain from outside the United Kingdom in connection with or for the purposes of adoption which does not involve the placement of the child for adoption under the law of any part of the United Kingdom.". Omit subsection (17). Omit subsection (18).][1]

Amendments—[1] Schedule 3 inserted by the Social Security Contributions and Benefits Act 1992 (Application of Parts 12ZA and 12ZB to Adoptions from Overseas) (Amendment) Regulations, SI 2014/2857 regs 2, 6, Schedule with effect from 19 November 2014.

2003/736

SOCIAL SECURITY (CATEGORISATION OF EARNERS) AMENDMENT REGULATIONS 2003

Made . . . . *14 March 2003*
Laid before Parliament . . . . *14 March 2003*
Coming into force . . . . *6 April 2003*

Revocation—These Regs revoked by the Social Security (Categorisation of Earners) (Amendment) Regulations, SI 2014/635 reg 4, Schedule with effect from 6 April 2014.

2003/1874

SOCIAL SECURITY CONTRIBUTIONS AND BENEFITS ACT 1992 (MODIFICATION OF SECTION 4A) ORDER 2003

Made by the Treasury, with the concurrence of the Secretary of State, under SSCBA 1992 s 4A(9)

Made . . . . *17 July 2003*
Laid . . . . *18 July 2003*
Coming into force . . . . *8 August 2003*

1 Citation and commencement

This Order may be cited as the Social Security Contributions and Benefits Act 1992 (Modification of Section 4A) Order 2003 and shall come into force on 8th August 2003.

2 Modification of the Social Security Contributions and Benefits Act 1992

Section 4A of Part 1 of the Social Security Contributions and Benefits Act 1992 is modified as follows.

3 In subsection (1)(*a*) for "for the purposes of a business carried on by another person" substitute "for another person".

4 In consequence of the above modification omit the definition of "business" in subsection (6).

2003/2079

SOCIAL SECURITY CONTRIBUTIONS (INTERMEDIARIES) (AMENDMENT) REGULATIONS 2003

Made by the Treasury under SSCBA 1992 ss 4A, 175(3), (4)

Made . . . . *11 August 2003*
Laid before Parliament . . . . *11 August 2003*
Coming into force . . . . *1 September 2003*

1 Citation, commencement and effect

(1) These Regulations may be cited as the Social Security Contributions (Intermediaries) (Amendment) Regulations 2003 and shall come into force on 1st September 2003.

(2) These Regulations have effect for the tax year 2003–04 and subsequent years and apply in relation to services performed or due to be performed on or after 1st September 2003.

NIC

2 Interpretation

In these Regulations—

"the principal Regulations" means the Social Security Contributions (Intermediaries) Regulations 2000;

"intermediary" has the meaning given in regulation 5 of the principal Regulations;

"worker" has the meaning given in regulation 6(1)(*a*) of the principal Regulations.

3–6 Amendment of the principal Regulations

(*amend SI 2000/727 regs 2, 6, and 7*).

7 Transitional provision

(1) This regulation applies for the purposes of the tax year 2003–04 ("the relevant year") in the case of a worker to whom the principal Regulations apply only by virtue of the amendment made by regulation 5 of these Regulations.

(2) For the purposes of the relevant year regulation 7(1) of the principal Regulations shall have effect as if—

(*a*) for "a tax year" there were substituted "the relevant period";

(*b*) for each of the references to "in that year" there were substituted "in that period";

(*c*) in Step Six for "for that year" there were substituted "for the relevant period"; and

(*d*) at the end there were added—

"In this paragraph "the relevant period" means the period beginning with 1st September 2003 and ending with 5th April 2004.".

(3) Paragraph (4) applies for the purpose of the relevant year in the case of a worker who is not a director of the intermediary through which services are provided under the arrangements.

(4) Where this paragraph applies, regulation 8(2) of the principal Regulations shall have effect as if—

(*a*) for "the year concerned" there were substituted "the relevant period";

(*b*) for "during that year" there were substituted "during that period"; and

(*c*) at the end there were added—

"In this paragraph "the relevant period" has the same meaning as in regulation 7(1).".

2005/3131

SOCIAL SECURITY CONTRIBUTIONS (INTERMEDIARIES) (AMENDMENT) REGULATIONS 2005

Made by the Treasury, with the concurrence of the Secretary of State, in exercise of the powers conferred on them by SSCBA 1992 ss 4A, 122(1) and 175(3) and (4)

Made . . . . 10 November 2005

Laid before Parliament . . . . 11 November 2005

Coming into force in accordance with . . . . regulation 1(2) and (3)

1 Citation, commencement and effect

(1) These Regulations may be cited as the Social Security Contributions (Intermediaries) (Amendment) Regulations 2005.

(2) Except for regulation 8, these Regulations shall come into force on 5th December 2005, have effect for the tax year 2005–06 and subsequent tax years, and apply in relation to services performed, or to be performed, on or after 5th December 2005.

(3) Regulation 8 shall come into force on 6th April 2006, have effect for the tax year 2006–07 and subsequent tax years, and apply in relation to services performed, or to be performed, on or after 6th April 2006.

2 Interpretation

In these Regulations—

"the principal Regulations" means the Social Security Contributions (Intermediaries) Regulations 2000;

"intermediary" has the meaning given in regulation 5 of the principal Regulations;

"tax year" means the 12 months beginning with 6th April in any year;

"worker" has the meaning given in regulation 6(1)(*a*) of the principal Regulations.

3 Amendment of the principal Regulations

The principal Regulations are amended as follows.

4 (*amends SI 2000/727 reg 2*)

5 (*amends SI 2000/727 reg 5*)

6 (*amends SI 2000/727 reg 7*)

7 Transitional provision

(1) This regulation applies for the purposes of the tax year 2005–06 ("the relevant year") in the case of a worker to whom the principal Regulations apply only by virtue of the amendment made by regulation 5 of these Regulations.

(2) For the purposes of the relevant year regulation 7(1) of the principal Regulations shall have effect as if—

(*a*) for "a tax year" there were substituted "the relevant period";

(*b*) for each of the references to "in that year" there were substituted "in that period";

(*c*) in Step Six for "for that year" there were substituted "for the relevant period"; and

(*d*) at the end there were added—

"In this paragraph "the relevant period" means the period beginning with 5th December 2005 and ending with 5th April 2006.".

8 Further amendment of the principal Regulations

(*amends SI 2000/727 reg 7(1)*).

2007/781

SOCIAL SECURITY REVALUATION OF EARNINGS FACTORS ORDER 2007

Made . . . . *8 March 2007*
Laid before Parliament . . . . *15 March 2007*
Coming into force . . . . *6 April 2007*

The Secretary of State for Work and Pensions has reviewed the general level of prices obtaining in Great Britain as required by section 148 of the Social Security Administration Act 1992.

In accordance with that section, he has considered earlier orders made under it and concluded that the earnings factors for the relevant previous tax years have not maintained their value in relation to those earnings during the review period.

Accordingly, the Secretary of State, in exercise of the powers conferred upon him by sections 148(3) and (4) and 189(1), (4) and (5) of the Social Security Administration Act 1992 makes the following Order.

1 Citation and commencement

This Order may be cited as the Social Security Revaluation of Earnings Factors Order 2007 and shall come into force on 6th April 2007.

2 Revaluation of earnings factors

The earnings factors for tax years specified in the Schedule to this Order in so far as they are relevant—

(*a*) to the calculation—

(i) of the additional pension in the rate of any long-term benefit; or

(ii) of any guaranteed minimum pension; or

(*b*) to any other calculation required under Part III of the Pension Schemes Act 1993 (including that Part as modified by or under any other enactment),

are directed to be increased for those tax years by the percentage of their amount shown opposite those tax years in that Schedule.

3 Rounding of fractional amounts

Where any earnings factor relevant to the calculation specified in article 2(*a*)(i) of this Order, as increased in accordance with this Order, would not but for this article be expressed as a whole number of pounds, it shall be so expressed by the rounding down of any fraction of a pound less than one half and the rounding up of any other fraction of a pound.

SCHEDULE

Article 2

Tax Year	*Percentage*
1978–79	623.0
1979–80	538.8
1980–81	433.7
1981–82	347.0
1982–83	306.0
1983–84	276.9

NIC

1984–85	249.0
1985–86	227.4
1986–87	200.7
1987–88	179.9
1988–89	157.5
1989–90	132.4
1990–91	116.6
1991–92	96.7
1992–93	84.7
1993–94	75.9
1994–95	70.7
1995–96	63.5
1996–97	59.0
1997–98	51.4
1998–99	44.8
1999–2000	38.9
2000–2001	30.7
2001–2002	25.7
2002–2003	20.5
2003–2004	16.3
2004–2005	12.1
2005–2006	7.6
2006–2007	4.1

2007/785

NATIONAL INSURANCE CONTRIBUTIONS (APPLICATION OF PART 7 OF THE FINANCE ACT 2004) REGULATIONS 2007

Made by the Treasury under SSAA 1992 ss 132A(1) and 189(4) and (5)

Made . . . . *12 March 2007*
Laid before Parliament . . . . *12 March 2007*
Coming into force . . . . *1 May 2007*

Revocation—These Regs revoked by the National Insurance Contributions (Application of Part 7 of the Finance Act 2004) Regulations, SI 2012/1868 reg 29 with effect from 1 September 2012.

2007/795

SOCIAL SECURITY CONTRIBUTIONS AND BENEFITS (NORTHERN IRELAND) ACT 1992 (MODIFICATION OF SECTION 10(7B)) REGULATIONS 2007

Made by the Treasury under SSCB(NI)A 1992 s 10(8)

Made . . . . *12 March 2007*
Laid before Parliament . . . . *13 March 2007*
Coming into force in accordance with . . . . *regulation 1*

1 Citation, commencement and effect

These Regulations may be cited as the Social Security Contributions and Benefits (Northern Ireland) Act 1992 (Modification of Section 10(7B)) Regulations 2007, shall come into force on 5th April 2007 and shall have effect in relation to the tax year beginning with 6th April 2006 and subsequent tax years.

2 Modification of Section 10(7B) of the Social Security Contributions and Benefits (Northern Ireland) Act 1992

In section 10(7B) of the Social Security Contributions and Benefits (Northern Ireland) Act 1992—

(*a*) at the end of paragraph (*a*) omit "and"; and
(*b*) after paragraph (*a*) insert—
"(*aa*) any of sections 363 to 365 of ITEPA 2003 (certain deductions from benefits code earnings), or".

2007/799

SOCIAL SECURITY CONTRIBUTIONS AND BENEFITS ACT 1992 (MODIFICATION OF SECTION 10(7B)) REGULATIONS 2007

Made by the Treasury under SSCBA 1992 s 10(8)

Made . . . . *12 March 2007*
Laid before Parliament . . . . *13 March 2007*
Coming into force in accordance . . . . *with regulation 1*

1 Citation, commencement and effect

These Regulations may be cited as the Social Security Contributions and Benefits Act 1992 (Modification of Section 10(7B)) Regulations 2007, shall come into force on 5th April 2007 and shall have effect in relation to the tax year beginning on 6th April 2006 and subsequent tax years.

2 Modification of Section 10(7B) of the Social Security Contributions and Benefits Act 1992

In section 10(7B) of the Social Security Contributions and Benefits Act 1992—
(*a*) at the end of paragraph (*a*) omit "and"; and
(*b*) after paragraph (*a*) insert—
"(*aa*) any of sections 363 to 365 of ITEPA 2003 (certain deductions from benefits code earnings), or".

2007/1154

SOCIAL SECURITY, OCCUPATIONAL PENSION SCHEMES AND STATUTORY PAYMENTS (CONSEQUENTIAL PROVISIONS) REGULATIONS 2007

Made by the Treasury under SSCBA 1992 ss 4C(1)–(6), 175(3), (4) and SSCB(NI)A 1992 ss 4C(1)–(6), 171(3), (4).

Made . . . . *31 March 2007*
Coming into force . . . . *6 April 2007*

1 Citation, commencement and effect

(1) These Regulations may be cited as the Social Security, Occupational Pension Schemes and Statutory Payments (Consequential Provisions) Regulations 2007 and shall come into force on 6th April 2007.
(2) These Regulations have effect from 2nd December 2004.

2 (*amends the Social Security (Crediting and Treatment of Contributions, and National Insurance Numbers) Regulations, SI 2001/769 regs 1, 4, 5A*).

3–13 . . .

14 Modifications to other contributions legislation (contributory benefits, statutory payments etc)

(1) In this regulation—
"relevant legislation" means legislation relating to purposes mentioned in section 4C(2)(*b*) to (*e*) of the Social Security Contributions and Benefits Act 1992 ("the Act") or section 4C(2)(*b*) to (*e*) of the Social Security Contributions and Benefits (Northern Ireland) Act 1992 ("the Northern Ireland Act");
"retrospective contributions regulations" means regulations made by virtue of section 4B(2) of the Act or of the Northern Ireland Act, as the case may be and, in relation to an amount retrospectively treated as earnings, "the relevant retrospective contributions regulations" means the regulations which treated that amount as earnings;
"the relevant time" means the time before the relevant retrospective contributions regulations are made; and
"the revised earnings" means the earnings, in respect of the employment, paid to or for the benefit of the earner at the relevant time as determined after applying the relevant retrospective contributions regulations.

(2) References in any relevant legislation, or any provision made under any such legislation, which relate to—

(*a*) the earnings in respect of the employment, paid to or for the benefit of the earner at the relevant time, or

(*b*) the amount of such earnings so paid at that time,

are to be read, to the extent they would not otherwise be and in so far as they so relate, as references which relate to the revised earnings or, as the case may be, the amount of those earnings.

(3) Any matter which, at the time when the relevant retrospective contributions regulations are made, has been determined for the purposes of any relevant legislation, or any provision made under any such legislation, wholly or partly by reference to—

(*a*) the earnings, in respect of the employment, paid to or for the benefit of the earner at the relevant time, or

(*b*) the amount of such earnings so paid at that time,

is to be re-determined (to the extent it would not otherwise be) as it would have been determined at the time of the original determination if it had been determined wholly or partly, as the case may be, by reference to the revised earnings or the amount of those earnings.

Note—Regulations 3–13 beyond the scope of this work.

2007/2070

SOCIAL SECURITY CONTRIBUTIONS (MANAGED SERVICE COMPANIES) REGULATIONS 2007

Made . . . .*25 July 2007*
Laid before Parliament . . . .*26 July 2007*
Coming into force . . . .*6 August 2007*

The Treasury and the Commissioners for Her Majesty's Revenue and Customs make these Regulations.

The powers exercised by the Treasury are those conferred by section 4A, 122(1) and 175(1A) of the Social Security Contributions and Benefits Act 1992 and sections 4A, 121 and 171(1) of the Social Security Contributions and Benefits (Northern Ireland) Act 1992.

The powers exercised by the Commissioners for Her Majesty's Revenue and Customs are those contained in section 8(1)(*m*) of the Social Security Contributions (Transfer of Functions, etc) Act 1999 and Article 7(1)(*m*) of the Social Security Contributions (Transfer of Functions, etc) (Northern Ireland) Order 1999 and now exercisable by them.

The Secretary of State and the Department for Social Development concur in the making of these Regulations.

1 Citation and commencement

These Regulations may be cited as the Social Security Contributions (Managed Service Companies) Regulations 2007 and shall come into force on 6th August 2007.

2 Interpretation

(1) In these Regulations "ITEPA" means the Income Tax (Earnings and Pensions) Act 2003, and the following expressions have the same meaning as they have for the purposes of Chapter 9 of Part 2 of that Act—

"associate";
"managed service company";
"payment or benefit";
"worker".

(2) In these Regulations—

"attributable earnings" has the meaning given by regulation 3(2);
"secondary Class 1 contributions" has the meaning given by section 6 of SSCBA;
"secondary contributor" has the meaning given by section 7 of SSCBA;
"SSCBA" means the Social Security Contributions and Benefits Act 1992;
"SSCR" means the Social Security (Contributions) Regulations 2001.

(3) In the application of these Regulations to Northern Ireland a reference to an enactment applying to Great Britain is to be read as a reference to the corresponding enactment applying in Northern Ireland.

3 Payments and benefits received by workers treated as earnings

(1) This regulation applies if—

(*a*) the services of an individual ("the worker") are provided (directly or indirectly) by a managed service company ("the MSC"),

(*b*) the worker, or an associate of the worker, receives (from any person) a payment or benefit which can reasonably be taken to be in respect of the services, and (*c*) the payment or benefit is not earnings derived from an employed earner's employment of the worker with the MSC.

(2) Where this regulation applies, the MSC is treated as making to the worker, and the worker is treated as receiving, a payment or benefit which is to be treated as earnings from an employed earner's employment ("the worker's attributable earnings").

(3) The amount of the worker's attributable earnings comprised in any payment or benefit is computed in accordance with section 61E of ITEPA.

(4) The time at which a worker is treated as receiving that payment or benefit is determined in accordance with section 61F of ITEPA.

(5) The worker's attributable earnings shall be aggregated with any other earnings paid to or for the benefit of the worker by the MSC in respect of the earnings period in which the payment or benefit mentioned in paragraph (1)(*b*) is received by the worker, and the amount of contributions shall be assessed in accordance with the appropriate earnings period determined in accordance with regulations 3 to 6 of SSCR.

(6) Any issue whether the circumstances are such as are mentioned in paragraph (1) is an issue relating to contributions that is prescribed for the purposes of section 8(1)(*m*) of the Social Security Contributions (Transfer of Functions, etc) Act 1999 (decision by officer of Revenue and Customs).

4 Deemed employed earner's employment

Where regulation 3 applies—

(*a*) the worker is treated, for the purposes of Parts 1 to 5 of SSCBA, and in relation to the worker's attributable earnings, as employed in employed earner's employment by the MSC, and

(*b*) the MSC, whether or not it fulfils the conditions prescribed under section 1(6)(*a*) of SSCBA for secondary contributors, is treated for those purposes as the secondary contributor in respect of the worker's attributable earnings

and Parts 1 to 5 of SSCBA have effect accordingly.

5 Amendment of SSCR

In regulation 1(2) of SSCR (interpretation) in the definition of "secondary contributor" for "a second Class 1 contribution" substitute "a secondary Class 1 contribution".

2007/2071

SOCIAL SECURITY CONTRIBUTIONS AND BENEFITS ACT 1992 (MODIFICATION OF SECTION 4A) ORDER 2007

Made . . . .*23 July 2007*
Laid before Parliament . . . .*23 July 2007*
Coming into force . . . .*24 July 2007*

The provisions of Part 2 of the Income Tax (Earnings and Pensions) Act 2003 are modified by paragraphs 3 and 4 of Schedule 3 to the Finance Act 2007.

It appears to the Treasury to be expedient, in consequence of those modifications, to modify the provisions of section 4A of the Social Security Contributions and Benefits Act 1992 which precede subsection (9) for the purpose of assimilating the law relating to income tax and the law relating to contributions under Part 1 of that Act.

This Order contains modifications which the Treasury think appropriate in consequence of the first recital above.

Accordingly, the Treasury make the following Order in exercise of the power conferred upon them by section 4A(9) of the Social Security Contributions and Benefits Act 1992.

The Secretary of State concurs in the making of this Order.

1 Citation and commencement

This Order may be cited as the Social Security Contributions and Benefits Act 1992 (Modification of Section 4A) Order 2007 and shall come into force on 24th July 2007.

2 Modification of section 4A of the Social Security Contributions and Benefits Act 1992

(1) Section 4A of the Social Security Contributions and Benefits Act 1992 is modified as follows.

(2) After subsection (2) insert—

"(2A) Regulations may also make provision for securing that, where the services of an individual ("the worker") are provided (directly or indirectly) by a managed service company ("the MSC") relevant payments or benefits are, to the specified extent, to be treated for the purposes of the applicable provisions of this Act as earnings paid to the worker in respect of an employed earner's employment of his.

(2B) In subsection (2A) "managed service company" has the same meaning as it has for the purposes of Chapter 9 of Part 2 of ITEPA 2003.".

(3) In subsection (3)—

(*a*) in paragraph (*a*) after "by the intermediary" insert "or the MSC (as the case requires)";

(*b*) in paragraph (*b*) for "intermediary (whether or not he fulfils" substitute "intermediary or the MSC (whether or not fulfilling";

(*c*) in paragraph (*g*) after "the intermediary" insert "or the MSC".

(4) In subsection (4)(*b*)—

(*a*) in sub-paragraph (i) after "intermediary" insert "or the MSC"; and

(*b*) in sub-paragraph (ii) for "him" substitute "that person".

(5) In subsection (6) in the definition of "relevant payments or benefit" after "the intermediary" insert "or the MSC,".

2008/2685

TRIBUNAL PROCEDURE (FIRST-TIER TRIBUNAL) (SOCIAL ENTITLEMENT CHAMBER) RULES 2008

Made .... *9 October 2008*

Laid before Parliament .... *15 October 2008*

Coming into force .... *3 November 2008*

After consulting in accordance with paragraph 28(1) of Schedule 5 to, the Tribunals, Courts and Enforcement Act 2007, the Tribunal Procedure Committee has made the following Rules in exercise of the powers conferred by sections 20(2) and (3) of the Social Security Act 1998 and sections 9(3), 22 and 29(3) of, and Schedule 5 to, the Tribunals, Courts and Enforcement Act 2007.

The Lord Chancellor has allowed the Rules in accordance with paragraph 28(3) of Schedule 5 to the Tribunals, Courts and Enforcement Act 2007.

PART 1
INTRODUCTION

1 Citation, commencement, application and interpretation

(1) These Rules may be cited as the Tribunal Procedure (First-tier Tribunal) (Social Entitlement Chamber) Rules 2008 and come into force on 3rd November 2008.

(2) [These rules apply to proceedings before Social Entitlement Chapter of the First Tier Tribunal.][3]

(3) In these Rules—

"the 2007 Act" means the Tribunals, Courts and Enforcement Act 2007;

"appeal" includes an application under section 19(9) of the Tax Credits Act 2002;

"appellant" means a person who makes an appeal to the Tribunal, or a person substituted as an appellant under rule 9(1) (substitution of parties);

"asylum support case" means proceedings concerning the provision of support for an asylum seeker[, a failed asylum seeker or a person designated under section 130 of the Criminal Justice and Immigration Act 2008 (designation), or the dependants of any such person][1];

"criminal injuries compensation case" means proceedings concerning the payment of compensation under a scheme made under the Criminal Injuries Compensation Act 1995 [or section 47 of the Crime and Security Act 2010][5];

"decision maker" means the maker of a decision against which an appeal has been brought;

"dispose of proceedings" includes, unless indicated otherwise, disposing of a part of the proceedings;

"document" means anything in which information is recorded in any form, and an obligation under these Rules to provide or allow access to a document or a copy of a document for any purpose means, unless the Tribunal directs otherwise, an obligation to provide or allow access to such document or copy in a legible form or in a form which can be readily made into a legible form;

"hearing" means an oral hearing and includes a hearing conducted in whole or in part by video link, telephone or other means of instantaneous two-way electronic communication;

"legal representative" means [a person who, for the purposes of the Legal Services Act 2007, is an authorised person in relation to an activity which constitutes the exercise of a right of audience or the conduct of litigation within the meaning of that Act][2], an advocate or solicitor in Scotland or a barrister or solicitor in Northern Ireland;

"party" means—

(*a*) a person who is an appellant or respondent in proceedings before the Tribunal;

(*b*) a person who makes a reference to the Tribunal under section 28D of the Child Support Act 1991;

(*c*) a person who starts proceedings before the Tribunal under paragraph 3 of Schedule 2 to the Tax Credits Act 2002; or

(*d*) if the proceedings have been concluded, a person who was a party under paragraph (*a*), (*b*) or (*c*) when the Tribunal finally disposed of all issues in the proceedings;

"practice direction" means a direction given under section 23 of the 2007 Act;

"respondent" means—

(*a*) in an appeal against a decision, the decision maker and any person other than the appellant who had a right of appeal against the decision;

(*b*) in a reference under section 28D of the Child Support Act 1991—

(i) the absent parent or non-resident parent;

(ii) the person with care; and

(iii) in Scotland, the child if the child made the application for a departure direction or a variation;

(*c*) in proceedings under paragraph 3 of Schedule 2 to the Tax Credits Act 2002, a person on whom it is proposed that a penalty be imposed; . . .[6]

[(*cc*) an affected party within the meaning of section 61(5) of the Childcare Payments Act 2014, other than an appellant; or][6]

(*d*) a person substituted or added as a respondent under rule 9 (substitution and addition of parties);

. . .[4]

"social security and child support case" means any case allocated to the Social Entitlement Chamber [of the First-tier Tribunal][4] except an asylum support case or a criminal injuries compensation case;

"Tribunal" means the First-tier Tribunal.

Amendments—[1] In para (3), in definition of "asylum support case", words substituted by the Tribunal Procedure (Amendment) Rules, SI 2009/274 rule 2 with effect from 1 April 2009.

[2] In para (3), in definition of "legal representative", words substituted by the Tribunal Procedure (Amendment) Rules, SI 2010/43 rule 3 with effect from 18 January 2010.

[3] Para (2) substituted by the Tribunal Procedure (Amendment No 3) Rules SI 2010/2553 rule 5(2) with effect from 29 November 2010.

[4] In para (3), definition of "Social entitlement Chamber" revoked, and in definition of "social security and child support case" words inserted by the Tribunal Procedure (Amendment Rules), SI 2011/651 rule 4(1), (2) with effect from 1 April 2011.

[5] In para (3), in definition of "criminal injuries compensation case", words inserted by the Tribunal Procedure (Amendment) Rules, SI 2013/477 rules 22, 23 with effect from 8 April 2013.

[6] In para (3), word "or" in sub-para (*c*) revoked, and sub-para (*cc*) inserted by the Tribunal Procedure (Amendment) Rules, SI 2015/1510 arts 11, 12 with effect from 21 August 2015.

2 Overriding objective and parties' obligation to co-operate with the Tribunal

(1) The overriding objective of these Rules is to enable the Tribunal to deal with cases fairly and justly.

(2) Dealing with a case fairly and justly includes—

(*a*) dealing with the case in ways which are proportionate to the importance of the case, the complexity of the issues, the anticipated costs and the resources of the parties;

(*b*) avoiding unnecessary formality and seeking flexibility in the proceedings;

(*c*) ensuring, so far as practicable, that the parties are able to participate fully in the proceedings;

(*d*) using any special expertise of the Tribunal effectively; and

(*e*) avoiding delay, so far as compatible with proper consideration of the issues.

(3) The Tribunal must seek to give effect to the overriding objective when it—

(*a*) exercises any power under these Rules; or

(*b*) interprets any rule or practice direction.

(4) Parties must—

(*a*) help the Tribunal to further the overriding objective; and

(*b*) co-operate with the Tribunal generally.

3 Alternative dispute resolution and arbitration

(1) The Tribunal should seek, where appropriate—

(*a*) to bring to the attention of the parties the availability of any appropriate alternative procedure for the resolution of the dispute; and

(*b*) if the parties wish and provided that it is compatible with the overriding objective, to facilitate the use of the procedure.

(2) Part 1 of the Arbitration Act 1996 does not apply to proceedings before the Tribunal.

PART 2
GENERAL POWERS AND PROVISIONS

4 Delegation to staff

(1) Staff appointed under section 40(1) of the 2007 Act (tribunal staff and services) may, with the approval of the Senior President of Tribunals, carry out functions of a judicial nature permitted or required to be done by the Tribunal.

(2) The approval referred to at paragraph (1) may apply generally to the carrying out of specified functions by members of staff of a specified description in specified circumstances.

(3) Within 14 days after the date on which the Tribunal sends notice of a decision made by a member of staff under paragraph (1) to a party, that party may apply in writing to the Tribunal for that decision to be considered afresh by a judge.

5 Case management powers

(1) Subject to the provisions of the 2007 Act and any other enactment, the Tribunal may regulate its own procedure.

(2) The Tribunal may give a direction in relation to the conduct or disposal of proceedings at any time, including a direction amending, suspending or setting aside an earlier direction.

(3) In particular, and without restricting the general powers in paragraphs (1) and (2), the Tribunal may—

- (*a*) extend or shorten the time for complying with any rule, practice direction or direction;
- (*aa*) . . . [2,1]
- (*b*) consolidate or hear together two or more sets of proceedings or parts of proceedings raising common issues, or treat a case as a lead case (whether in accordance with rule 18 (lead cases) or otherwise);
- (*c*) permit or require a party to amend a document;
- (*d*) permit or require a party or another person to provide documents, information, evidence or submissions to the Tribunal or a party;
- (*e*) deal with an issue in the proceedings as a preliminary issue;
- (*f*) hold a hearing to consider any matter, including a case management issue;
- (*g*) decide the form of any hearing;
- (*h*) adjourn or postpone a hearing;
- (*i*) require a party to produce a bundle for a hearing;
- (*j*) stay (or, in Scotland, sist) proceedings;
- (*k*) transfer proceedings to another court or tribunal if that other court or tribunal has jurisdiction in relation to the proceedings and—
  - (i) because of a change of circumstances since the proceedings were started, the Tribunal no longer has jurisdiction in relation to the proceedings; or
  - (ii) the Tribunal considers that the other court or tribunal is a more appropriate forum for the determination of the case; or
- (*l*) suspend the effect of its own decision pending the determination by the Tribunal or the Upper Tribunal of an application for permission to appeal against, and any appeal or review of, that decision.

Amendments—[1] Para (3)(*aa*) inserted by the Tribunal Procedure (Amendment No 4) Rules, SI 2013/2067 rules 22, 23 with effect from 1 November 2013.

[2] Para (3)(*aa*) revoked by the Tribunal Procedure (Amendment) Rules, SI 2015/1510 arts 11, 13 with effect from 21 August 2015.

6 Procedure for applying for and giving directions

(1) The Tribunal may give a direction on the application of one or more of the parties or on its own initiative.

(2) An application for a direction may be made—

- (*a*) by sending or delivering a written application to the Tribunal; or
- (*b*) orally during the course of a hearing.

(3) An application for a direction must include the reason for making that application.

(4) Unless the Tribunal considers that there is good reason not to do so, the Tribunal must send written notice of any direction to every party and to any other person affected by the direction.

(5) If a party or any other person sent notice of the direction under paragraph (4) wishes to challenge a direction which the Tribunal has given, they may do so by applying for another direction which amends, suspends or sets aside the first direction.

7 Failure to comply with rules etc

(1) An irregularity resulting from a failure to comply with any requirement in these Rules, a practice direction or a direction, does not of itself render void the proceedings or any step taken in the proceedings.

(2) If a party has failed to comply with a requirement in these Rules, a practice direction or a direction, the Tribunal may take such action as it considers just, which may include—

- (*a*) waiving the requirement;

(*b*) requiring the failure to be remedied;
(*c*) exercising its power under rule 8 (striking out a party's case); or
(*d*) exercising its power under paragraph (3).

(3) The Tribunal may refer to the Upper Tribunal, and ask the Upper Tribunal to exercise its power under section 25 of the 2007 Act in relation to, any failure by a person to comply with a requirement imposed by the Tribunal—

(*a*) to attend at any place for the purpose of giving evidence;
(*b*) otherwise to make themselves available to give evidence;
(*c*) to swear an oath in connection with the giving of evidence;
(*d*) to give evidence as a witness;
(*e*) to produce a document; or
(*f*) to facilitate the inspection of a document or any other thing (including any premises).

8 Striking out a party's case

(1) The proceedings, or the appropriate part of them, will automatically be struck out if the appellant has failed to comply with a direction that stated that failure by a party to comply with the direction would lead to the striking out of the proceedings or that part of them.

(2) The Tribunal must strike out the whole or a part of the proceedings if the Tribunal—

(*a*) does not have jurisdiction in relation to the proceedings or that part of them; and
(*b*) does not exercise its power under rule 5(3)(k)(i) (transfer to another court or tribunal) in relation to the proceedings or that part of them.

(3) The Tribunal may strike out the whole or a part of the proceedings if—

(*a*) the appellant has failed to comply with a direction which stated that failure by the appellant to comply with the direction could lead to the striking out of the proceedings or part of them;
(*b*) the appellant has failed to co-operate with the Tribunal to such an extent that the Tribunal cannot deal with the proceedings fairly and justly; or
(*c*) the Tribunal considers there is no reasonable prospect of the appellant's case, or part of it, succeeding.

(4) The Tribunal may not strike out the whole or a part of the proceedings under paragraph (2) or (3)(*b*) or (*c*) without first giving the appellant an opportunity to make representations in relation to the proposed striking out.

(5) If the proceedings, or part of them, have been struck out under paragraph (1) or (3)(*a*), the appellant may apply for the proceedings, or part of them, to be reinstated.

(6) An application under paragraph (5) must be made in writing and received by the Tribunal within 1 month after the date on which the Tribunal sent notification of the striking out to the appellant.

(7) This rule applies to a respondent as it applies to an appellant except that—

(*a*) a reference to the striking out of the proceedings is to be read as a reference to the barring of the respondent from taking further part in the proceedings; and
(*b*) a reference to an application for the reinstatement of proceedings which have been struck out is to be read as a reference to an application for the lifting of the bar on the respondent from taking further part in the proceedings.

(8) If a respondent has been barred from taking further part in proceedings under this rule and that bar has not been lifted, the Tribunal need not consider any response or other submission made by that respondent [and may summarily determine any or all issues against that respondent][1].

Amendments—[1] In para (8) words inserted by the Tribunal Procedure (Amedment No. 3) Rules SI 201/2653 rule 5(3) with effect from 29 November 2010.

9 Substitution and addition of parties

(1) The Tribunal may give a direction substituting a party if—

(*a*) the wrong person has been named as a party; or
(*b*) the substitution has become necessary because of a change in circumstances since the start of proceedings.

(2) The Tribunal may give a direction adding a person to the proceedings as a respondent.

(3) If the Tribunal gives a direction under paragraph (1) or (2) it may give such consequential directions as it considers appropriate.

10 No power to award costs

The Tribunal may not make any order in respect of costs (or, in Scotland, expenses).

11 Representatives

(1) A party may appoint a representative (whether a legal representative or not) to represent that party in the proceedings.

(2) Subject to paragraph (3), if a party appoints a representative, that party (or the representative if the representative is a legal representative) must send or deliver to the Tribunal written notice of the representative's name and address.

(3) In a case to which rule 23 (cases in which the notice of appeal is to be sent to the decision maker) applies, if the appellant (or the appellant's representative if the representative is a legal representative) provides written notification of the appellant's representative's name and address to the decision maker before the decision maker provides its response to the Tribunal, the appellant need not take any further steps in order to comply with paragraph (2).

(4) If the Tribunal receives notice that a party has appointed a representative under paragraph (2), it must send a copy of that notice to each other party.

(5) Anything permitted or required to be done by a party under these Rules, a practice direction or a direction may be done by the representative of that party, except signing a witness statement.

(6) A person who receives due notice of the appointment of a representative—

- (*a*) must provide to the representative any document which is required to be provided to the represented party, and need not provide that document to the represented party; and
- (*b*) may assume that the representative is and remains authorised as such until they receive written notification that this is not so from the representative or the represented party.

(7) At a hearing a party may be accompanied by another person whose name and address has not been notified under paragraph (2) or (3) but who, with the permission of the Tribunal, may act as a representative or otherwise assist in presenting the party's case at the hearing.

(8) Paragraphs (2) to (6) do not apply to a person who accompanies a party under paragraph (7).

12 Calculating time

(1) Except in asylum support cases, an act required by these Rules, a practice direction or a direction to be done on or by a particular day must be done by 5pm on that day.

(2) If the time specified by these Rules, a practice direction or a direction for doing any act ends on a day other than a working day, the act is done in time if it is done on the next working day.

(3) In this rule "working day" means any day except a Saturday or Sunday, Christmas Day, Good Friday or a bank holiday under section 1 of the Banking and Financial Dealings Act 1971.

13 Sending and delivery of documents

(1) Any document to be provided to the Tribunal under these Rules, a practice direction or a direction must be—

- (*a*) sent by pre-paid post or delivered by hand to the address specified for the proceedings;
- (*b*) sent by fax to the number specified for the proceedings; or
- (*c*) sent or delivered by such other method as the Tribunal may permit or direct.

(2) Subject to paragraph (3), if a party provides a fax number, email address or other details for the electronic transmission of documents to them, that party must accept delivery of documents by that method.

(3) If a party informs the Tribunal and all other parties that a particular form of communication (other than pre-paid post or delivery by hand) should not be used to provide documents to that party, that form of communication must not be so used.

(4) If the Tribunal or a party sends a document to a party or the Tribunal by email or any other electronic means of communication, the recipient may request that the sender provide a hard copy of the document to the recipient. The recipient must make such a request as soon as reasonably practicable after receiving the document electronically.

(5) The Tribunal and each party may assume that the address provided by a party or its representative is and remains the address to which documents should be sent or delivered until receiving written notification to the contrary.

14 Use of documents and information

(1) The Tribunal may make an order prohibiting the disclosure or publication of—

- (*a*) specified documents or information relating to the proceedings; or
- (*b*) any matter likely to lead members of the public to identify any person whom the Tribunal considers should not be identified.

(2) The Tribunal may give a direction prohibiting the disclosure of a document or information to a person if—

- (*a*) the Tribunal is satisfied that such disclosure would be likely to cause that person or some other person serious harm; and
- (*b*) the Tribunal is satisfied, having regard to the interests of justice, that it is proportionate to give such a direction.

(3) If a party ("the first party") considers that the Tribunal should give a direction under paragraph (2) prohibiting the disclosure of a document or information to another party ("the second party"), the first party must—

- (*a*) exclude the relevant document or information from any documents that will be provided to the second party; and
- (*b*) provide to the Tribunal the excluded document or information, and the reason for its exclusion, so that the Tribunal may decide whether the document or information should be disclosed to the second party or should be the subject of a direction under paragraph (2).

(4) The Tribunal must conduct proceedings as appropriate in order to give effect to a direction given under paragraph (2).
(5) If the Tribunal gives a direction under paragraph (2) which prevents disclosure to a party who has appointed a representative, the Tribunal may give a direction that the documents or information be disclosed to that representative if the Tribunal is satisfied that—
(*a*) disclosure to the representative would be in the interests of the party; and
(*b*) the representative will act in accordance with paragraph (6).
(6) Documents or information disclosed to a representative in accordance with a direction under paragraph (5) must not be disclosed either directly or indirectly to any other person without the Tribunal's consent.

15 Evidence and submissions

(1) Without restriction on the general powers in rule 5(1) and (2) (case management powers), the Tribunal may give directions as to—
(*a*) issues on which it requires evidence or submissions;
(*b*) the nature of the evidence or submissions it requires;
(*c*) whether the parties are permitted or required to provide expert evidence;
(*d*) any limit on the number of witnesses whose evidence a party may put forward, whether in relation to a particular issue or generally;
(*e*) the manner in which any evidence or submissions are to be provided, which may include a direction for them to be given—
(i) orally at a hearing; or
(ii) by written submissions or witness statement; and
(*f*) the time at which any evidence or submissions are to be provided.
(2) The Tribunal may—
(*a*) admit evidence whether or not—
(i) the evidence would be admissible in a civil trial in the United Kingdom; or
(ii) the evidence was available to a previous decision maker; or
(*b*) exclude evidence that would otherwise be admissible where—
(i) the evidence was not provided within the time allowed by a direction or a practice direction;
(ii) the evidence was otherwise provided in a manner that did not comply with a direction or a practice direction; or
(iii) it would otherwise be unfair to admit the evidence.
(3) The Tribunal may consent to a witness giving, or require any witness to give, evidence on oath, and may administer an oath for that purpose.

16 Summoning or citation of witnesses and orders to answer questions or produce documents

(1) On the application of a party or on its own initiative, the Tribunal may—
(*a*) by summons (or, in Scotland, citation) require any person to attend as a witness at a hearing at the time and place specified in the summons or citation; or
(*b*) order any person to answer any questions or produce any documents in that person's possession or control which relate to any issue in the proceedings.
(2) A summons or citation under paragraph (1)(*a*) must—
(*a*) give the person required to attend 14 days' notice of the hearing or such shorter period as the Tribunal may direct; and
(*b*) where the person is not a party, make provision for the person's necessary expenses of attendance to be paid, and state who is to pay them.
(3) No person may be compelled to give any evidence or produce any document that the person could not be compelled to give or produce on a trial of an action in a court of law in the part of the United Kingdom where the proceedings are due to be determined.
(4) A summons, citation or order under this rule must—
(*a*) state that the person on whom the requirement is imposed may apply to the Tribunal to vary or set aside the summons, citation or order, if they have not had an opportunity to object to it; and
(*b*) state the consequences of failure to comply with the summons, citation or order.

17 Withdrawal

(1) Subject to paragraph (2), a party may give notice of the withdrawal of its case, or any part of it—
(*a*) . . . [1] by sending or delivering to the Tribunal a written notice of withdrawal; or
(*b*) orally at a hearing.
(2) In the circumstances described in paragraph (3), a notice of withdrawal will not take effect unless the Tribunal consents to the withdrawal.
(3) The circumstances referred to in paragraph (2) are where a party gives notice of withdrawal—
(*a*) . . . [1] in a criminal injuries compensation case; . . .

(*b*) in a social security and child support case where the Tribunal has directed that notice of withdrawal shall take effect only with the Tribunal's consent; or

(*c*) at a hearing.][1]

[(4) An application for a withdrawn case to be reinstated may be made by—

(*a*) the party who withdrew the case;

(*b*) where an appeal in a social security and child support case has been withdrawn, a respondent.

(5) An application under paragraph (4) must be made in writing and be received by the Tribunal within 1 month after the earlier of—

(*a*) the date on which the applicant was sent notice under paragraph (6) that the withdrawal had taken effect; or

(*b*) if the applicant was present at the hearing when the case was withdrawn orally under paragraph (1)(*b*), the date of that hearing.][2]

(6) The Tribunal must notify each party in writing [that a withdrawal has taken effect][1] under this rule.

Amendments—[1] In paras (1)(*a*), (3)(*a*), words revoked; in para (3), sub-paras (*b*), (*c*) substituted for previous sub-para (*b*) and preceding word "or"; and in para (6), words substituted, by the Tribunal Procedure (Amendment) Rules, SI 2013/477 rules 22, 24 with effect from 8 April 2013.

[2] Paras (4), (5) substituted by the Tribunal Procedure (Amendment) Rules, SI 2015/1510 arts 11, 14 with effect from 21 August 2015.

18 Lead cases

(1) This rule applies if—

(*a*) two or more cases have been started before the Tribunal;

(*b*) in each such case the Tribunal has not made a decision disposing of the proceedings; and

(*c*) the cases give rise to common or related issues of fact or law.

(2) The Tribunal may give a direction—

(*a*) specifying one or more cases falling under paragraph (1) as a lead case or lead cases; and

(*b*) staying (or, in Scotland, sisting) the other cases falling under paragraph (1) ("the related cases").

(3) When the Tribunal makes a decision in respect of the common or related issues—

(*a*) the Tribunal must send a copy of that decision to each party in each of the related cases; and

(*b*) subject to paragraph (4), that decision shall be binding on each of those parties.

(4) Within 1 month after the date on which the Tribunal sent a copy of the decision to a party under paragraph (3)(*a*), that party may apply in writing for a direction that the decision does not apply to, and is not binding on the parties to, a particular related case.

(5) The Tribunal must give directions in respect of cases which are stayed or sisted under paragraph (2)(*b*), providing for the disposal of or further directions in those cases.

(6) If the lead case or cases lapse or are withdrawn before the Tribunal makes a decision in respect of the common or related issues, the Tribunal must give directions as to—

(*a*) whether another case or other cases are to be specified as a lead case or lead cases; and

(*b*) whether any direction affecting the related cases should be set aside or amended.

[19 Confidentiality in social security and child support cases

(1) Paragraph (4) applies to—

(*a*) proceedings under the Child Support Act 1991 in the circumstances described in paragraph (2), other than an appeal against a reduced benefit decision (as defined in section 46(10)(*b*) of the Child Support Act 1991, as that section had effect prior to the commencement of section 15(*b*) of the Child Maintenance and Other Payments Act 2008);

(*b*) proceedings where the parties to the appeal include former joint claimants who are no longer living together in the circumstances described in paragraph (3).

(2) The circumstances referred to in paragraph (1)(*a*) are that the absent parent, non-resident parent or person with care would like their address or the address of the child to be kept confidential and has given notice to that effect—

(*a*) in the notice of appeal or when notifying the Secretary of State or the Tribunal of any subsequent change of address; or

(*b*) within 14 days after an enquiry is made by the recipient of the notice of appeal or the notification referred to in sub-paragraph (*a*).

(3) The circumstances referred to in paragraph (1)(*b*) are that one of the former joint claimants would like their address to be kept confidential and has given notice to that effect—

(*a*) in the notice of appeal or when notifying the decision maker or the tribunal of any subsequent change of address; or

(*b*) within 14 days after an enquiry is made by the recipient of the notice of appeal or the notification referred to in sub-paragraph (*a*).

(4) Where this paragraph applies, the Secretary of State or other decision maker and the Tribunal must take appropriate steps to secure the confidentiality of the address and of any information which could reasonably be expected to enable a person to identify the address, to the extent that the address or that information is not already known to each other party.
(5) In this rule—
"absent parent", "non-resident parent" and "person with care" have the meanings set out in section 3 of the Child Support Act 1991;
"joint claimants" means the persons who made a joint claim for a jobseeker's allowance under the Jobseekers Act 1995, a tax credit under the Tax Credits Act 2002 or in relation to whom an award of universal credit is made under Part 1 of the Welfare Reform Act 2012.][1]

Amendments—[1] Rule 19 substituted by the Tribunal Procedure (Amendment No 3) Rules, SI 2014/2128 rr 33, 35 with effect from 20 October 2014.

20 Expenses in criminal injuries compensation cases
(1) This rule applies only to criminal injuries compensation cases.
(2) The Tribunal may meet reasonable expenses—
(*a*) incurred by the appellant, or any person who attends a hearing to give evidence, in attending the hearing; or
(*b*) incurred by the appellant in connection with any arrangements made by the Tribunal for the inspection of the appellant's injury.

21 Expenses in social security and child support cases
(1) This rule applies only to social security and child support cases.
(2) The Secretary of State may pay such travelling and other allowances (including compensation for loss of remunerative time) as the Secretary of State may determine to any person required to attend a hearing in proceedings under section 20 of the Child Support Act 1991, section 12 of the Social Security Act 1998 or paragraph 6 of Schedule 7 to the Child Support, Pensions and Social Security Act 2000.

PART 3

PROCEEDINGS BEFORE THE TRIBUNAL

CHAPTER 1

BEFORE THE HEARING

22 Cases in which the notice of appeal is to be sent to the Tribunal
[(1) This rule applies to all cases except those to which—
(*a*) rule 23 (cases in which the notice of appeal is to be sent to the decision maker), or
(*b*) rule 26 (social security and child support cases started by reference or information in writing),
applies.][1]
(2) An appellant must start proceedings by sending or delivering a notice of appeal to the Tribunal so that it is received—
(*a*) in asylum support cases, within 3 days after the date on which the appellant received written notice of the decision being challenged;
(*b*) in criminal injuries compensation cases, within 90 days after the date of the decision being challenged[;
(*c*) in appeals under the Vaccine Damage Payments Act 1979, at any time;
(*d*) in other cases—
(i) if mandatory reconsideration applies, within 1 month after the date on which the appellant was sent notice of the result of mandatory reconsideration;
(ii) if mandatory reconsideration does not apply, within the time specified in Schedule 1 to these Rules [(time limits for providing notices of appeal in social security and child support cases where mandatory reconsideration does not apply)][3].
(3) The notice of appeal must be in English or Welsh, must be signed by the appellant and must state—
(*a*) the name and address of the appellant;
(*b*) the name and address of the appellant's representative (if any);
(*c*) an address where documents for the appellant may be sent or delivered;
(*d*) the name and address of any respondent [other than the decision maker][1];
(*e*) . . .[1]; and
(*f*) the grounds on which the appellant relies.
(4) The appellant must provide with the notice of appeal—
[(*a*) a copy of—

(i) the notice of the result of mandatory reconsideration, in any social security and child support case to which mandatory reconsideration applies;

(ii) the decision being challenged, in any other case;][1]

(*b*) any statement of reasons for that decision that the appellant has[; and][1]

(*c*) any documents in support of the appellant's case which have not been supplied to the respondent. . . . [1]

(*d*) . . . [1]

(5) In asylum support cases the notice of appeal must also—

(*a*) state whether the appellant will require an interpreter at any hearing, and if so for which language or dialect; and

(*b*) state whether the appellant intends to attend or be represented at any hearing.

(6) If the appellant provides the notice of appeal to the Tribunal later than the time required by paragraph (2) or by an extension of time allowed under rule 5(3)(*a*) . . . [2] (power to extend time)—

(*a*) the notice of appeal must include a request for an extension of time and the reason why the notice of appeal was not provided in time; and

(*b*) [subject to paragraph (8)][1] unless the Tribunal extends time for the notice of appeal under rule 5(3)(*a*) . . . [2] (power to extend time) the Tribunal must not admit the notice of appeal.

(7) The Tribunal must send a copy of the notice of appeal and any accompanying documents to each other party—

(*a*) in asylum support cases, on the day that the Tribunal receives the notice of appeal, or (if that is not reasonably practicable) as soon as reasonably practicable on the following day;

(*b*) in [all other][1] cases, as soon as reasonably practicable after the Tribunal receives the notice of appeal.

[(7A) Her Majesty's Revenue and Customs must, upon receipt of the notice of appeal from the Tribunal under the Childcare Payments Act 2014, inform the Tribunal whether there are any affected parties within the meaning of section 61(5) of that Act other than the appellant and, if so, provide their names and addresses.][3]

[(8) Where an appeal in a social security and child support case is not made within the time specified in paragraph (2)—

(*a*) it will be treated as having been made in time, unless the Tribunal directs otherwise, if it is made within not more than 12 months of the time specified and neither the decision maker nor any other respondent objects;

(*b*) the time for bringing the appeal may not be extended under rule 5(3)(*a*) by more than 12 months.

[(9) For the purposes of this rule, mandatory reconsideration applies where—

(*a*) the notice of the decision being challenged includes a statement to the effect that there is a right of appeal in relation to the decision only if the decision-maker has considered an application for the revision, reversal, review or reconsideration (as the case may be) of the decision being challenged; or

(*b*) the appeal is brought against a decision made by Her Majesty's Revenue and Customs.][3]

Amendments—[1] The following amendments made by the Tribunal Procedure (Amendment) Rules, SI 2013/477 rules 22, 25 with effect from 8 April 2013—

- para (1) substituted;
- para (2)(*c*), (*d*) inserted;
- in para (3), words in sub-para (*d*) inserted, and sub-para (e) revoked (except for the word ": and";
- in para (4), sub-para (*a*) substituted, in sub-para (*b*), word substituted, and sub-para (*d*) and preceding word "and" revoked;
- in para (6)(*b*) words inserted;
- in para (7)(*b*), words substituted for words "criminal injuries compensation cases" (Publisher's Note: it is assumed that the intention was to retain the word "cases"); and
- paras (8), (9) inserted.

[2] In para (6), words revoked in both places by the Tribunal Procedure (Amendment) Rules, SI 2014/514 rr 21, 22 with effect from 6 April 2014.

[3] In para (2)(*d*)(ii), words substituted, para (7A) inserted and para (9) substituted by the Tribunal Procedure (Amendment) Rules, SI 2015/1510 arts 11, 15 with effect from 21 August 2015.

23 Cases in which the notice of appeal is to be sent to the decision maker

[(1) This rule applies to [appeals under paragraph 6 of Schedule 7 to the Child Support, Pensions and Social Security Act 2000 (housing benefit and council tax benefit: revisions and appeals) or under section 22 of the Child Trust Funds Act 2004][5].

(2) An appellant must start proceedings by sending or delivering a notice of appeal to the decision maker so that it is received [no later than the latest of—

(*a*) in a housing benefit or council tax benefit case—

(i) one month after the date on which notice of the decision being challenged was sent to the appellant;

(ii) if a written statement of reasons for the decision was requested within that month, 14 days after the later of—

(aa) the end of that month; or

(ab) the date on which the written statement of reasons was provided; or

(iii) if the appellant made an application for revision of the decision under regulation 4(1)(*a*) of the Housing Benefit and Council Tax Benefit (Decisions and Appeals) Regulations 2001 and that application was unsuccessful, one month after the date on which notice that the decision would not be revised was sent to the appellant;

(*b*) in an appeal under section 22 of the Child Trust Funds Act 2004, the period of 30 days specified in section 23(1) of that Act.][5]

(3) If the appellant provides the notice of appeal to the decision maker later than the time required by [paragraph (2)(*a*)][5] the notice of appeal must include the reason why the notice of appeal was not provided in time.

(4) Subject to paragraph (5), where an appeal is not made within the time specified in [paragraph (2)][5], it will be treated as having been made in time [if neither the decision maker nor any other respondent objects][2].

(5) No appeal may be made more than 12 months after the time specified in [paragraph (2)][5].

(6) The notice of appeal must be in English or Welsh, must be signed by the appellant and must state—

(*a*) the name and address of the appellant;

(*b*) the name and address of the appellant's representative (if any);

(*c*) an address where documents for the appellant may be sent or delivered;

(*d*) details of the decision being appealed; and

(*e*) the grounds on which the appellant relies.

(7) The decision maker must refer the case to the Tribunal immediately if—

(*a*) the appeal has been made after the time specified in [paragraph (2)][5] and the decision maker [or any other respondent][2] objects to it being treated as having been made in time; or

(*b*) the decision maker considers that the appeal has been made more than 12 months after the time specified in [paragraph (2)][5].

[(8) Notwithstanding rule 5(3)(*a*) . . . [5] (case management powers) and rule 7(2) (failure to comply with rules etc.), the Tribunal must not extend the time limit in paragraph (5).][1]

Amendments—[1] Para (8) inserted by the Tribunal Procedure (Amendment No. 2) Rules 2009, SI 2009/1975 rs 2, 3 with effect from 1 September 2009.

[2] In para (4), words substituted for words "if the decision maker does not object", and in para (7)(*a*) words inserted, by the Tribunal Procedure (Amendment) Rules, SI 2012/500 rule 4 with effect from 6 April 2012.

[3] Para (1) substituted by the Tribunal Procedure (Amendment) Rules, SI 2013/477 rules 22, 26 with effect from 8 April 2013.

[4] In para (8), words inserted by the Tribunal Procedure (Amendment No 4) Rules, SI 2013/2067 rules 22, 26 with effect from 1 November 2013.

[5] In para (1)–(5), (7)(*a*), (*b*), words substituted, and in para (8), words revoked by the Tribunal Procedure (Amendment) Rules, SI 2015/1510 arts 11, 16 with effect from 21 August 2015.

24 Responses and replies

[(1) When a decision maker receives a copy of a notice of appeal from the Tribunal under rule 22(7), the decision maker must send or deliver a response to the Tribunal—

(*a*) in asylum support cases, so that it is received within 3 days after the date on which the Tribunal received the notice of appeal;

(*b*) in—

(i) criminal injuries compensation cases, or

(ii) appeals under the Child Support Act 1991,

within 42 days after the date on which the decision maker received the copy of the notice of appeal; and

(*c*) in other cases, within 28 days after the date on which the decision maker received the copy of the notice of appeal.

(1A) Where a decision maker receives a notice of appeal from an appellant under rule 23(2), the decision maker must send or deliver a response to the Tribunal so that it is received as soon as reasonably practicable after the decision maker received the notice of appeal.][2]

(2) The response must state—

(*a*) the name and address of the decision maker;

(*b*) the name and address of the decision maker's representative (if any);

(*c*) an address where documents for the decision maker may be sent or delivered;

(*d*) the names and addresses of any other respondents and their representatives (if any);

(*e*) whether the decision maker opposes the appellant's case and, if so, any grounds for such opposition which are not set out in any documents which are before the Tribunal; and

(*f*) any further information . . . [2] required by a practice direction or direction.

(3) The response may include a submission as to whether it would be appropriate for the case to be disposed of without a hearing.

NIC

(4) The decision maker must provide with the response—

(*a*) a copy of any written record of the decision under challenge, and any statement of reasons for that decision, if they were not sent with the notice of appeal;

(*b*) copies of all documents relevant to the case in the decision maker's possession, unless a practice direction or direction states otherwise; and

(*c*) in cases to which rule 23 (cases in which the notice of appeal is to be sent to the decision maker) applies, a copy of the notice of appeal, any documents provided by the appellant with the notice of appeal and (if they have not otherwise been provided to the Tribunal) the name and address of the appellant's representative (if any).

(5) The decision maker must provide a copy of the response and any accompanying documents to each other party at the same time as it provides the response to the Tribunal.

(6) The appellant and any other respondent may make a written submission and supply further documents in reply to the decision maker's response.

(7) Any submission or further documents under paragraph (6) must be provided to the Tribunal within 1 month after the date on which the decision maker sent the response to the party providing the reply, and the Tribunal must send a copy to each other party.

Amendments—[1] In para (1), word "and" at end of sub-para (*a*) revoked, and sub-para (*aa*) inserted, by the Tribunal Procedure (Amendment) Rules, SI 2011/651 rule 4(1), (3) with effect from 1 April 2011.

[2] Paras (1), (1A) substituted for previous para (1), and in para (2)(*f*), words "or documents" revoked, by the Tribunal Procedure (Amendment) Rules, SI 2013/477 rules 22, 27 with effect from 1 October 2014.

Note that SI 2013/477 r 27(*a*), which substitutes para (1) above, was itself amended by the Tribunal Procedure (Amendment No 3) Rules, SI 2014/2128 rr 36, 37 with effect from 1 September 2014, ie before it had come into effect. This amendment replaced sub-para (**b**) in the substituted para (1). This amendment has been incorporated into the text.

25 Medical and physical examination in appeals under section 12 of the Social Security Act 1998

(1) This rule applies only to appeals under section 12 of the Social Security Act 1998.

(2) At a hearing an appropriate member of the Tribunal may carry out a physical examination of a person if the case relates to—

(*a*) the extent of that person's disablement and its assessment in accordance with section 68(6) of and Schedule 6 to, or section 103 of, the Social Security Contributions and Benefits Act 1992; or

(*b*) diseases or injuries prescribed for the purpose of section 108 of that Act.

(3) If an issue which falls within Schedule 2 to these Rules (issues in relation to which the Tribunal may refer a person for medical examination) is raised in an appeal, the Tribunal may exercise its power under section 20 of the Social Security Act 1998 to refer a person to a health care professional approved by the Secretary of State for—

(*a*) the examination of that person; and

(*b*) the production of a report on the condition of that person.

(4) Neither paragraph (2) nor paragraph (3) entitles the Tribunal to require a person to undergo a physical test for the purpose of determining whether that person is unable to walk or virtually unable to do so.

26 Social security and child support cases started by reference or information in writing

(1) This rule applies to proceedings under section 28D of the Child Support Act 1991 and paragraph 3 of Schedule 2 to the Tax Credits Act 2002.

(2) A person starting proceedings under section 28D of the Child Support Act 1991 must send or deliver a written reference to the Tribunal.

(3) A person starting proceedings under paragraph 3 of Schedule 2 to the Tax Credits Act 2002 must send or deliver an information in writing to the Tribunal.

(4) The reference or the information in writing must include—

(*a*) an address where documents for the person starting proceedings may be sent or delivered;

(*b*) the names and addresses of the respondents and their representatives (if any); and

(*c*) a submission on the issues that arise for determination by the Tribunal.

(5) Unless a practice direction or direction states otherwise, the person starting proceedings must also provide a copy of each document in their possession which is relevant to the proceedings.

(6) Subject to any obligation under rule 19(3) (confidentiality in child support cases), the person starting proceedings must provide a copy of the written reference or the information in writing and any accompanying documents to each respondent at the same time as they provide the written reference or the information in writing to the Tribunal.

(7) Each respondent may send or deliver to the Tribunal a written submission and any further relevant documents within one month of the date on which the person starting proceedings sent a copy of the written reference or the information in writing to that respondent.

CHAPTER 2

HEARINGS

27 Decision with or without a hearing

(1) Subject to the following paragraphs, the Tribunal must hold a hearing before making a decision which disposes of proceedings unless—

(*a*) each party has consented to, or has not objected to, the matter being decided without a hearing; and

(*b*) the Tribunal considers that it is able to decide the matter without a hearing.

(2) This rule does not apply to decisions under Part 4.

(3) The Tribunal may in any event dispose of proceedings without a hearing under rule 8 (striking out a party's case).

(4) In a criminal injuries compensation case—

(*a*) the Tribunal may make a decision which disposes of proceedings without a hearing; and

(*b*) subject to paragraph (5), if the Tribunal makes a decision which disposes of proceedings without a hearing, any party may make a written application to the Tribunal for the decision to be reconsidered at a hearing.

(5) An application under paragraph (4)(*b*) may not be made in relation to a decision—

(*a*) not to extend a time limit;

(*b*) not to set aside a previous decision;

(*c*) not to allow an appeal against a decision not to extend a time limit; or

(*d*) not to allow an appeal against a decision not to reopen a case.

(6) An application under paragraph (4)(*b*) must be received within 1 month after the date on which the Tribunal sent notice of the decision to the party making the application.

28 Entitlement to attend a hearing

Subject to rule 30(5) (exclusion of a person from a hearing), each party to proceedings is entitled to attend a hearing.

29 Notice of hearings

(1) The Tribunal must give each party entitled to attend a hearing reasonable notice of the time and place of the hearing (including any adjourned or postponed hearing) and any changes to the time and place of the hearing.

(2) The period of notice under paragraph (1) must be at least 14 days except that—

(*a*) in an asylum support case the Tribunal must give at least 1 day's and not more than 5 days' notice; and

(*b*) the Tribunal may give shorter notice—

(i) with the parties' consent; or

(ii) in urgent or exceptional circumstances.

30 Public and private hearings

(1) Subject to the following paragraphs, all hearings must be held in public.

(2) A hearing in a criminal injuries compensation case must be held in private unless—

(*a*) the appellant has consented to the hearing being held in public; and

(*b*) the Tribunal considers that it is in the interests of justice for the hearing to be held in public.

(3) The Tribunal may give a direction that a hearing, or part of it, is to be held in private.

(4) Where a hearing, or part of it, is to be held in private, the Tribunal may determine who is permitted to attend the hearing or part of it.

(5) The Tribunal may give a direction excluding from any hearing, or part of it—

(*a*) any person whose conduct the Tribunal considers is disrupting or is likely to disrupt the hearing;

(*b*) any person whose presence the Tribunal considers is likely to prevent another person from giving evidence or making submissions freely;

(*c*) any person who the Tribunal considers should be excluded in order to give effect to a direction under rule 14(2) (withholding information likely to cause harm); or

(*d*) any person where the purpose of the hearing would be defeated by the attendance of that person.

(6) The Tribunal may give a direction excluding a witness from a hearing until that witness gives evidence.

31 Hearings in a party's absence

If a party fails to attend a hearing the Tribunal may proceed with the hearing if the Tribunal—

(*a*) is satisfied that the party has been notified of the hearing or that reasonable steps have been taken to notify the party of the hearing; and

(*b*) considers that it is in the interests of justice to proceed with the hearing.

CHAPTER 3

DECISIONS

32 Consent orders

(1) The Tribunal may, at the request of the parties but only if it considers it appropriate, make a consent order disposing of the proceedings and making such other appropriate provision as the parties have agreed.

(2) Notwithstanding any other provision of these Rules, the Tribunal need not hold a hearing before making an order under paragraph (1), or provide reasons for the order.

33 Notice of decisions

(1) The Tribunal may give a decision orally at a hearing.

(2) Subject to rule 14(2) (withholding information likely to cause harm), the Tribunal must provide to each party as soon as reasonably practicable after making [a decision (other than a decision under Part 4) which finally disposes of all issues in the proceedings or of a preliminary issue dealt with following a direction under rule 5(3)(*e*)][1]

(*a*) a decision notice stating the Tribunal's decision;

(*b*) where appropriate, notification of the right to apply for a written statement of reasons under rule 34(3); and

(*c*) notification of any right of appeal against the decision and the time within which, and the manner in which, such right of appeal may be exercised.

(3) In asylum support cases the notice and notifications required by paragraph (2) must be provided at the hearing or sent on the day that the decision is made.

Amendments—[1] In para (2), words substituted by the Tribunal Procedure (Amendment) Rules, SI 2013/477 rules 22, 28 with effect from 8 April 2013.

34 Reasons for decisions

(1) In asylum support cases the Tribunal must send a written statement of reasons for a decision which disposes of proceedings (except a decision under Part 4) to each party—

(*a*) if the case is decided at a hearing, within 3 days after the hearing; or

(*b*) if the case is decided without a hearing, on the day that the decision is made.

(2) In all other cases the Tribunal may give reasons for a decision which disposes of proceedings (except a decision under Part 4)—

(*a*) orally at a hearing; or

(*b*) in a written statement of reasons to each party.

(3) Unless the Tribunal has already provided a written statement of reasons under paragraph (2)(*b*), a party may make a written application to the Tribunal for such statement following a decision [which finally disposes of—[1]

(*a*) all issues in the proceedings; or

(*b*) a preliminary issue dealt with following a direction under rule 5(3)(*e*).][1]

(4) An application under paragraph (3) must be received within 1 month of the date on which the Tribunal sent or otherwise provided to the party a decision notice relating to the decision . . . [1].

(5) If a party makes an application in accordance with paragraphs (3) and (4) the Tribunal must, subject to rule 14(2) (withholding information likely to cause harm), send a written statement of reasons to each party within 1 month of the date on which it received the application or as soon as reasonably practicable after the end of that period.

Amendments—[1] In para (3), words substituted, and in para (4), words revoked, by the Tribunal Procedure (Amendment) Rules, SI 2013/477 rules 22, 29 with effect from 8 April 2013.

PART 4

CORRECTING, SETTING ASIDE, REVIEWING AND APPEALING TRIBUNAL DECISIONS

35 Interpretation

In this Part—

"appeal" means the exercise of a right of appeal—

(*a*) under paragraph 2(2) or 4(1) of Schedule 2 to the Tax Credits Act 2002;

(*b*) under section 21(10) of the Child Trust Funds Act 2004; or

(*c*) on a point of law under section 11 of the 2007 Act; and

"review" means the review of a decision by the Tribunal under section 9 of the 2007 Act.

36 Clerical mistakes and accidental slips or omissions

The Tribunal may at any time correct any clerical mistake or other accidental slip or omission in a decision, direction or any document produced by it, by—

(*a*) sending notification of the amended decision or direction, or a copy of the amended document, to all parties; and (*b*) making any necessary amendment to any information published in relation to the decision, direction or document.

37 Setting aside a decision which disposes of proceedings

(1) The Tribunal may set aside a decision which disposes of proceedings, or part of such a decision, and re-make the decision, or the relevant part of it, if—

(*a*) the Tribunal considers that it is in the interests of justice to do so; and

(*b*) one or more of the conditions in paragraph (2) are satisfied.

(2) The conditions are—

(*a*) a document relating to the proceedings was not sent to, or was not received at an appropriate time by, a party or a party's representative;

(*b*) a document relating to the proceedings was not sent to the Tribunal at an appropriate time;

(*c*) a party, or a party's representative, was not present at a hearing related to the proceedings; or

(*d*) there has been some other procedural irregularity in the proceedings.

(3) A party applying for a decision, or part of a decision, to be set aside under paragraph (1) must make a written application to the Tribunal so that it is received no later than 1 month after the date on which the Tribunal sent notice of the decision to the party.

38 Application for permission to appeal

(1) This rule does not apply to asylum support cases or criminal injuries compensation cases.

(2) A person seeking permission to appeal must make a written application to the Tribunal for permission to appeal.

(3) An application under paragraph (2) must be sent or delivered to the Tribunal so that it is received no later than 1 month after the latest of the dates that the Tribunal sends to the person making the application—

[(*za*) the relevant decision notice;][1]

(*a*) written reasons for the decision[, if the decision disposes of—

(i) all issues in the proceedings; or

(ii) subject to paragraph (3A), a preliminary issue dealt with following a direction under rule 5(3)(*e*);][1]

(*b*) notification of amended reasons for, or correction of, the decision following a review; or

(*c*) notification that an application for the decision to be set aside has been unsuccessful.

[(3A) The Tribunal may direct that the 1 month within which a party may send or deliver an application for permission to appeal against a decision that disposes of a preliminary issue shall run from the date of the decision that disposes of all issues in the proceedings.][1]

(4) The date in paragraph (3)(*c*) applies only if the application for the decision to be set aside was made within the time stipulated in rule 37 (setting aside a decision which disposes of proceedings) or any extension of that time granted by the Tribunal.

(5) If the person seeking permission to appeal sends or delivers the application to the Tribunal later than the time required by paragraph (3) or by any extension of time under rule 5(3)(*a*) (power to extend time)—

(*a*) the application must include a request for an extension of time and the reason why the application was not provided in time; and

(*b*) unless the Tribunal extends time for the application under rule 5(3)(*a*) (power to extend time) the Tribunal must not admit the application.

(6) An application under paragraph (2) must—

(*a*) identify the decision of the Tribunal to which it relates;

(*b*) identify the alleged error or errors of law in the decision; and

(*c*) state the result the party making the application is seeking.

(7) If a person makes an application under paragraph (2) [in respect of a decision that disposes of proceedings or of a preliminary issue dealt with following a direction under rule 5(3)(*e*)][1] when the Tribunal has not given a written statement of reasons for its decision—

(*a*) if no application for a written statement of reasons has been made to the Tribunal, the application for permission must be treated as such an application;

(*b*) unless the Tribunal decides to give permission and directs that this sub-paragraph does not apply, the application is not to be treated as an application for permission to appeal; and

(*c*) if an application for a written statement of reasons has been, or is, refused because of a delay in making the application, the Tribunal must only admit the application for permission if the Tribunal considers that it is in the interests of justice to do so.

Amendments—[1] Paras (3)(*za*), (3A) inserted, and words in paras (3)(*a*), (7) inserted, by the Tribunal Procedure (Amendment) Rules, SI 2013/477 rules 22, 30 with effect from 8 April 2013.

39 Tribunal's consideration of application for permission to appeal

(1) On receiving an application for permission to appeal the Tribunal must first consider, taking into account the overriding objective in rule 2, whether to review the decision in accordance with rule 40 (review of a decision).

(2) If the Tribunal decides not to review the decision, or reviews the decision and decides to take no action in relation to the decision, or part of it, the Tribunal must consider whether to give permission to appeal in relation to the decision or that part of it.

(3) The Tribunal must send a record of its decision to the parties as soon as practicable.

(4) If the Tribunal refuses permission to appeal it must send with the record of its decision—

(*a*) a statement of its reasons for such refusal; and

(*b*) notification of the right to make an application to the Upper Tribunal for permission to appeal and the time within which, and the method by which, such application must be made.

(5) The Tribunal may give permission to appeal on limited grounds, but must comply with paragraph (4) in relation to any grounds on which it has refused permission.

40 Review of a decision

(1) This rule does not apply to asylum support cases or criminal injuries compensation cases.

(2) The Tribunal may only undertake a review of a decision—

(*a*) pursuant to rule 39(1) (review on an application for permission to appeal); and

(*b*) if it is satisfied that there was an error of law in the decision.

(3) The Tribunal must notify the parties in writing of the outcome of any review, and of any right of appeal in relation to the outcome.

(4) If the Tribunal takes any action in relation to a decision following a review without first giving every party an opportunity to make representations, the notice under paragraph (3) must state that any party that did not have an opportunity to make representations may apply for such action to be set aside and for the decision to be reviewed again.

41 Power to treat an application as a different type of application

The Tribunal may treat an application for a decision to be corrected, set aside or reviewed, or for permission to appeal against a decision, as an application for any other one of those things.

SCHEDULES

[SCHEDULE 1

TIME LIMITS FOR PROVIDING NOTICES OF APPEAL IN SOCIAL SECURITY AND CHILD SUPPORT CASES WHERE MANDATORY RECONSIDERATION DOES NOT APPLY

Rule 22

	Type of proceedings	*Time for providing notice of appeal*
1	Appeal against a certification of NHS charges under section 157(1) of the Health and Social Care (Community Health and Standards) Act 2003	(*a*) 3 months after the latest of— (i) the date on the certificate; (ii) the date on which the compensation payment was made; (iii) if the certificate has been reviewed, the date the certificate was confirmed or a fresh certificate was issued; or (iv) the date of any agreement to treat an earlier compensation payment as having been made in final discharge of a claim made by or in respect of an injured person and arising out of the injury or death; or (*b*) if the person to whom the certificate has been issued makes an application under section 157(4) of the Health and Social Care (Community Health and Standards) Act 2003, one month after— (i) the date of the decision on that application; or (ii) if the person appeals against that decision under section 157(6) of that Act, the date on which the appeal is decided or withdrawn.
2	Appeal against a waiver decision under section 157(6) of the Health and Social Care (Community Health and Standards) Act 2003	One month after the date of the decision.

3	Appeal against a certificate of NHS charges under section 7 of the Road Traffic (NHS Charges) Act 1999	3 months after the latest of— (*a*) the date on which the liability under section 1(2) of the Road Traffic (NHS Charges) Act 1999 was discharged; (*b*) if the certificate has been reviewed, the date the certificate was confirmed or a fresh certificate was issued; or (*c*) the date of any agreement to treat an earlier compensation payment as having been made in final discharge of a claim made by or in respect of a traffic casualty and arising out of the injury or death.
4	Appeal against a certificate of recoverable benefits under section 11 of the Social Security (Recovery of Benefits) Act 1997	One month after the latest of— (*a*) the date on which any payment to the Secretary of State required under section 6 of the Social Security (Recovery of Benefits) Act 1997 was made; (*b*) if the certificate has been reviewed, the date the certificate was confirmed or a fresh certificate was issued; (*c*) the date of any agreement to treat an earlier compensation payment as having been made in final discharge of a claim made by or in respect of an injured person and arising out of the accident, injury or disease.
5	Cases other than those listed above	The latest of— (*a*) one month after the date on which notice of the decision being challenged was sent to the appellant; (*b*) if a written statement of reasons for the decision was requested within that month, 14 days after the later of— (i) the end of that month; or (ii) the date on which the written statement of reasons was provided; (*c*) if the appellant made an application for the revision of the decision under— (i) regulation 17(1)(*a*) of the Child Support (Maintenance Assessment Procedure) Regulations 1992; (ii) regulation 3(1) or (3) or 3A(1)(*a*) of the Social Security and Child Support (Decisions and Appeals) Regulations 1999; (iii) regulation 14(1)(*a*) of the Child Support Maintenance Calculation Regulations 2012; or (iv) regulation 5 of the Universal Credit, Personal Independence Payment, Jobseeker's Allowance and Employment and Support Allowance (Decisions and Appeals) Regulations 2013, and the application was unsuccessful, one month after the date on which notice that the decision would not be revised was sent to the appellant.][1]

Amendments—[1] Schedule 1 substituted by the Tribunal Procedure (Amendment) Rules, SI 2015/1510 arts 11, 17, Schedule with effect from 21 August 2015.

SCHEDULE 2

ISSUES IN RELATION TO WHICH THE TRIBUNAL MAY REFER A PERSON FOR MEDICAL EXAMINATION UNDER SECTION 20(2) OF THE SOCIAL SECURITY ACT 1998

Rule 25(3)

An issue falls within this Schedule if the issue—

(*a*) is whether the claimant satisfies the conditions for entitlement to—

(i) an attendance allowance specified in section 64 and 65(1) of the Social Security Contributions and Benefits Act 1992;

(ii) severe disablement allowance under section 68 of that Act;

(iii) the care component of a disability living allowance specified in section 72(1) and (2) of that Act;

(iv) the mobility component of a disability living allowance specified in section 73(1), (8) and (9) of that Act; . . . [1]

(v) a disabled person's tax credit specified in section 129(1)(*b*) of that Act.

[(vi) the daily living component of personal independence payment specified in section 78 of the Welfare Reform Act 2012; or

(vii) the mobility component of personal independence payment specified in section 79 of the Welfare Reform Act 2012.][1]

(*b*) relates to the period throughout which the claimant is likely to satisfy the conditions for entitlement to an attendance allowance or a disability living allowance;
(*c*) is the rate at which an attendance allowance is payable;
(*d*) is the rate at which the care component or the mobility component of a disability living allowance is payable;
(*e*) is whether a person is incapable of work for the purposes of the Social Security Contributions and Benefits Act 1992;
(*f*) relates to the extent of a person's disablement and its assessment in accordance with Schedule 6 to the Social Security Contributions and Benefits Act 1992;
(*g*) is whether the claimant suffers a loss of physical or mental faculty as a result of the relevant accident for the purposes of section 103 of the Social Security Contributions and Benefits Act 1992;
(*h*) relates to any payment arising under, or by virtue of a scheme having effect under, section 111 of, and Schedule 8 to, the Social Security Contributions and Benefits Act 1992 (workmen's compensation);
(*i*) is whether a person has limited capability for work or work-related activity for the purposes of the Welfare Reform Act 2007[;
(*j*) is the rate at which the daily living component or mobility component of personal independence payment is payable.][1]

Amendments—[1] In para (*a*)(iv), word "or" revoked, para (*a*)(vi), (vii) inserted, and para (*j*) inserted, by the Tribunal Procedure (Amendment) Rules, SI 2013/477 rules 22, 32 with effect from 8 April 2013

2008/2833

TRANSFER OF TRIBUNAL FUNCTIONS ORDER 2008

Made . . . . *29 October 2008*
Coming into force . . . . *3 November 2008*

The Lord Chancellor makes the following Order in exercise of the powers conferred by sections 30(1) and (4), 31(1), (2) and (9), 32(3) and (5), 33(2) and (3), 34(2) and (3), 37(1), 38 and 145 of, and paragraph 30 of Schedule 5 to, the Tribunals, Courts and Enforcement Act 2007. The Scottish Ministers have consented to the making of this order in so far as their consent is required by section 30(7) of that Act.

A draft of this Order was laid before Parliament and approved by a resolution of each House of Parliament in accordance with section 49(5) of that Act.

1 Citation, commencement, interpretation and extent

(1) This Order may be cited as the Transfer of Tribunal Functions Order 2008 and comes into force on 3rd November 2008.

(2) A reference in this Order to a Schedule by a number alone is a reference to the Schedule so numbered in this Order.

(3) Subject as follows, this Order extends to England and Wales, Scotland and Northern Ireland.

(4) Except as provided by paragraph (5) or (6), an amendment, repeal or revocation of any enactment by any provision of Schedule 3 extends to the part or parts of the United Kingdom to which the enactment extends.

(5) For the purposes of article 3(3)(*a*) and (*b*) the following amendments, repeals and revocations made by the provisions of that Schedule do not extend to Scotland—
(*a*) paragraphs 145 to 147;
(*b*) paragraph 150;
(*c*) paragraph 151(*d*);
(*d*) paragraph 152;
(*e*) paragraph 154;
(*f*) paragraphs 167 to 173; and
(*g*) paragraph 228(*h*), (*l*), (*n*) and (*r*).

(6) The amendments and repeals made by paragraphs 198 to 201 of Schedule 3 do not extend to Scotland.

2 Additions to the list of tribunals in Schedule 6

(*amends* TCEA 2007 Sch 6 Part 4).

3 Transfer of functions of certain tribunals

(1) Subject to paragraph (3), the functions of the tribunals listed in Table 1 of Schedule 1 are transferred to the First-tier Tribunal.

(2) Subject to paragraph (3), the functions of the tribunals listed in Table 2 of Schedule 1 are transferred to the Upper Tribunal.

(3) The following functions are not transferred—

(*a*) the determination by an appeal tribunal constituted under Chapter 1 of Part 1 of the Social Security Act 1998 of an appeal which is referred to such tribunal by the Scottish Ministers, or the Secretary of State on their behalf, pursuant to section 158 (appeal tribunals) of the Health and Social Care (Community Health and Standards) Act 2003 ("the 2003 Act"); and

(*b*) the determination by a Social Security Commissioner of an appeal made under section 159 (appeal to social security commissioner) of the 2003 Act against a decision falling within sub-paragraph (*a*).

4 Abolition of tribunals transferred under section 30(1)

The tribunals listed in Table 1 and Table 2 of Schedule 1 are abolished except for—

(*a*) appeal tribunals constituted under Chapter 1 of Part 1 of the Social Security Act 1998 in respect of Scotland for the purposes of the function described in article 3(3)(*a*); and

(*b*) the Social Security Commissioners in respect of Scotland for the purposes of the function described in article 3(3)(*b*).

5 Transfer of persons into the First-tier Tribunal and the Upper Tribunal

(1) A person holding an office listed in a table in Schedule 2 who was, was a member of, or was an authorised decision-maker for, a tribunal listed in the corresponding table in Schedule 1 immediately before the functions of that tribunal were transferred under article 3 shall hold the corresponding office or offices.

(2) In paragraph (1) "corresponding" means appearing in the corresponding entry in the table below.

Table in Schedule 1	Table in Schedule 2	Office or offices
Table 1	Table 1	Transferred-in judge of the First-tier Tribunal
Table 1	Table 2	Transferred-in other member of the First-tier Tribunal
Table 1	Table 3	Transferred in judge of the First-tier Tribunal and deputy judge of the Upper Tribunal
Table 2	Table 4	Transferred-in judge of the Upper Tribunal
Table 1 or 2	Table 5	Transferred-in other member of the Upper Tribunal

6 Appeal to Upper Tribunal from tribunals in Wales

(1) An appeal against a decision of a tribunal listed in paragraph (2) lies to the Upper Tribunal.

(2) The tribunals referred to in paragraph (1) are—

(*a*) the Mental Health Review Tribunal for Wales established under section 65 of the Mental Health Act 1983; and

(*b*) the Special Educational Needs Tribunal for Wales established under section 336ZA of the Education Act 1996.

7 Appeal to Upper Tribunal from tribunals in Scotland

An appeal against a decision of the Pensions Appeal Tribunal in Scotland under section 5 of the Pensions Appeal Tribunals Act 1943 (assessment decision) lies to the Upper Tribunal.

8 Appeal to Upper Tribunal from tribunals in Northern Ireland

An appeal against a decision of the Pensions Appeal Tribunal in Northern Ireland under section 5 of the Pensions Appeal Tribunals Act 1943 (assessment decision) lies to the Upper Tribunal.

9 Minor, consequential and transitional provisions

(1) Schedule 3 contains minor, consequential and supplemental amendments, and repeals and revocations as a consequence of those amendments.

(2) Schedule 4 contains transitional provisions.

SCHEDULE 1

FUNCTIONS TRANSFERRED TO THE FIRST-TIER TRIBUNAL AND UPPER TRIBUNAL

Articles 3, 4 and 5

Table 1: Functions transferred to the First-tier Tribunal

Tribunal	*Enactment*
Adjudicator	Section 5 of the Criminal Injuries Compensation Act 1995 (c 53)
Appeal tribunal	Chapter 1 of Part 1 of the Social Security Act 1998 (c 14)

Tribunal	*Enactment*
Asylum Support Adjudicators	Section 102 of the Immigration and Asylum Act 1999 (c 33)
Mental Health Review Tribunal for a region of England	Section 65(1) and (1A)(*a*) of the Mental Health Act 1983 (c 20)
Pensions Appeal Tribunal in England and Wales	Section 8(2) of the War Pensions (Administrative Provisions) Act 1919 (c 53) and paragraph 1(1) of the Schedule to the Pensions Appeal Tribunals Act 1943 (c 39)
Special Educational Needs and Disability Tribunal	Section 28H of the Disability Discrimination Act 1995 (c 50) and section 333 of the Education Act 1996 (c 56) and
Tribunal, except in respect of its functions under section 4 of the Safeguarding Vulnerable Groups Act 2006 (c 47)	Section 9 of the Protection of Children Act 1999 (c 14)

Table 2: Functions transferred to the Upper Tribunal

Tribunal	*Enactment*
Child Support Commissioner	Section 22 of the Child Support Act 1991 (c 48)
Social Security Commissioner	Schedule 4 to the Social Security Act 1998 (c 14)
Tribunal, in respect of its functions under section 4 of the Safeguarding Vulnerable Groups Act 2006 (c 47)	Section 9 of the Protection of Children Act 1999 (c 14)

SCHEDULE 2

PERSONS TRANSFERRED AS JUDGES AND MEMBERS OF THE FIRST-TIER TRIBUNAL AND UPPER TRIBUNAL

Article 5

Table 1: Members becoming transferred-in judges of the First-tier Tribunal

Tribunal Member	*Enactment*
A legal member of the Criminal Injuries Compensation Appeals Panel	Section 5 of the Criminal Injuries Compensation Act 1995 (c 53) and the Criminal Injuries Compensation Schemes
A legally qualified panel member	Section 6 of the Social Security Act 1998 (c 14)
The Deputy Chief Asylum Support Adjudicator or an adjudicator	Section 102 of and paragraph 1(*a*) and (*c*) of Schedule 10 to the Immigration and Asylum Act 1999 (c 33)
A legal member	Paragraph 1(*a*) of Schedule 2 to the Mental Health Act 1983 (c 20)
The Deputy President of Pensions Appeal Tribunals or a legally qualified member	Paragraphs 2A(1)(*a*) and 2B(1) of the Schedule to the Pensions Appeal Tribunals Act 1943 (c 39)
A member of the chairmen's panel	Section 333(2)(*b*) of the Education Act 1996 (c 56)
A member of the chairmen's panel	Paragraph 1(1)(*a*) of the Schedule to the Protection of Children Act 1999 (c 14)

Table 2: Members becoming transferred-in other members of the First-tier Tribunal

Tribunal Member	*Enactment*
A member of the Criminal Injuries Compensation Appeals Panel other than the Chairman or a legal member	Section 5 of the Criminal Injuries Compensation Act 1995 (c 53) and the Criminal Injuries Compensation Schemes

Tribunal Member	*Enactment*
A financially qualified panel member, a medically qualified panel member or a panel member with a disability qualification	Section 6 of the Social Security Act 1998 (c 14)
A medical member or other member	Paragraph 1(*b*) or (*c*) of Schedule 2 to the Mental Health Act 1983 (c 20)
A medically qualified member, a member with knowledge or experience of service, or other member	Paragraph 2A(1)(*b*), (*c*) or (*d*) of the Schedule to the Pensions Appeal Tribunals Act 1943 (c 39)
A member of the lay panel	Section 333(2)(*c*) of the Education Act 1996 (c 56)
A member of the lay panel, other than a member in Table 5	Paragraph 1(1)(*c*) of the Schedule to the Protection of Children Act 1999 (c 14)

Table 3: Members becoming transferred-in judges of the First-tier Tribunal and deputy judges of the Upper Tribunal

Tribunal Member	*Enactment*
The Chairman	Section 5(3)(*b*) of the Criminal Injuries Compensation Act 1995 (c 53) and the Criminal Injuries Compensation Schemes
The President	Section 5 of the Social Security Act 1998 (c 14)
The Chief Asylum Support Adjudicator	Section 102 of and paragraph 1(*b*) of Schedule 10 to the Immigration and Asylum Act 1999 (c 33)
A chairman of a Mental Health Review Tribunal	Paragraph 3 of Schedule 2 to the Mental Health Act 1983 (c 20)
A President of Pensions Appeal Tribunals	Paragraph 2B(1) of the Schedule to the Pensions Appeal Tribunals Act 1943 (c 39)
A President	Section 333(2)(*a*) of the Education Act 1996 (c 56)
The President	Paragraph 1(1)(*a*) of the Schedule to the Protection of Children Act 1999 (c 14)
The Deputy President	Appointed as a member of the chairmen's panel under paragraph 1(1)(*b*) of the Schedule to the Protection of Children Act 1999 (c 14) and also appointed as deputy president of the Tribunal
A deputy Child Support Commissioner	Paragraph 4 of Schedule 4 to the Child Support Act 1991 (c 48)
A deputy Commissioner	Paragraph 1(2) of Schedule 4 to the Social Security Act 1998 (c 14)

Table 4: Members becoming transferred-in judges of the Upper Tribunal

Tribunal Member	*Enactment*
The Chief Child Support Commissioner or a Child Support Commissioner	Section 22 of the Child Support Act 1991 (c 48)
The Chief Social Security Commissioner or a Social Security Commissioner	Paragraph 1 of Schedule 4 to the Social Security Act 1998 (c 14)

Table 5: Members becoming transferred-in other members of the Upper Tribunal

Tribunal Member	*Enactment*
A member of the lay panel who was appointed on the ground that the member satisfied the requirements referred to in regulation 41(1) of the Protection of Children Act Tribunal Regulations 2000 (SI 2000/2619) or regulation 3(1)(*a*) or (*b*) of the Protection of Children and Vulnerable Adults and Care Standards Tribunal Regulations 2002 (SI 2002/816)	Paragraph 1(1)(*c*) of the Schedule to the Protection of Children Act 1999 (c 14)

SCHEDULE 3

MINOR, CONSEQUENTIAL AND SUPPLEMENTAL PROVISIONS

Article 6

Note—The amendments made by this Schedule are already in force and are therefore not reproduced.

SCHEDULE 4

TRANSITIONAL PROVISIONS

Article 6

TRANSITIONAL PROVISIONS

1 Subject to article 3(3)(*a*) any proceedings before a tribunal listed in Table 1 of Schedule 1 which are pending immediately before 3rd November 2008 shall continue on and after 3rd November 2008 as proceedings before the First-tier Tribunal.

2 Subject to article 3(3)(*b*) any proceedings before a tribunal listed in Table 2 of Schedule 1 which are pending immediately before 3rd November 2008 shall continue on and after 3rd November 2008 as proceedings before the Upper Tribunal.

3—(1) The following sub-paragraphs apply where proceedings are continued in the First-tier Tribunal or Upper Tribunal by virtue of paragraph 1 or 2.

(2) Where a hearing began before 3rd November 2008 but was not completed by that date, the First-tier Tribunal or the Upper Tribunal, as the case may be, must be comprised for the continuation of that hearing of the person or persons who began it.

(3) The First-tier Tribunal or Upper Tribunal, as the case may be, may give any direction to ensure that proceedings are dealt with fairly and, in particular, may—

(*a*) apply any provision in procedural rules which applied to the proceedings before 3rd November 2008; or

(*b*) disapply provisions of Tribunal Procedure Rules.

(4) In sub-paragraph (3) "procedural rules" means provision (whether called rules or not) regulating practice or procedure before a tribunal.

(5) Any direction or order given or made in proceedings which is in force immediately before 3rd November 2008 remains in force on and after that date as if it were a direction or order of the First-tier Tribunal or Upper Tribunal, as the case may be.

(6) A time period which has started to run before 3rd November 2008 and which has not expired shall continue to apply.

(7) An order for costs may only be made if, and to the extent that, an order could have been made before 3rd November 2008.

4 Subject to article 3(3)(*a*) and (*b*) where an appeal lies to a Child Support or Social Security Commissioner from any decision made before 3rd November 2008 by a tribunal listed in Table 1 of Schedule 1, section 11 of the 2007 Act (right to appeal to Upper Tribunal) shall apply as if the decision were a decision made on or after 3rd November 2008 by the First-tier Tribunal.

5 Subject to article 3(3)(*b*) where an appeal lies to a court from any decision made before 3rd November 2008 by a Child Support or Social Security Commissioner, section 13 of the 2007 Act (right to appeal to Court of Appeal etc) shall apply as if the decision were a decision made on or after 3rd November 2008 by the Upper Tribunal.

6 Subject to article 3(3)(*a*) and (*b*) any case to be remitted by a court on or after 3rd November 2008 in relation to a tribunal listed in Schedule 1 shall be remitted to the First-tier Tribunal or Upper Tribunal as the case may be.

SAVINGS PROVISIONS

7—(1) Section 78(8) of the Mental Health Act 1983 shall continue to apply to any decision given by a Mental Health Review Tribunal before 3rd November 2008 as if the amendments to it in Schedule 3 had not been made.

(2) Section 11(1) of the Tribunals and Inquiries Act 1992 shall continue to apply to any decision given by the Special Educational Needs and Disability Tribunal or the Special Educational Needs Tribunal for Wales before 3rd November 2008 as if the amendments to it in Schedule 3 had not been made.

(3) Section 9(6) of the Protection of Children Act 1999 shall continue to apply to any decision given by the tribunal under section 9(1) of that Act before 3rd November 2008 as if the amendments to it in Schedule 3 had not been made.

2009/1377

NATIONAL INSURANCE CONTRIBUTION CREDITS (TRANSFER OF FUNCTIONS) ORDER 2009

Made by Her Majesty, in pursuance of the powers conferred on Her by SSCTFA 1999 s 23(1)(*d*), (3)(*b*) and (4)(*d*)

Made . . . . *10 June 2009*
Laid before Parliament . . . . *17 June 2009*
Coming into force . . . . *6 April 2010*

1 Citation, commencement and extent

(1) This Order may be cited as the National Insurance Contribution Credits (Transfer of Functions) Order 2009 and shall come into force on 6th April 2010.

(2) This Order extends to England and Wales and to Scotland.

2 Transfer of functions

(1) The decisions to which this article applies are to be made by the Commissioners for Her Majesty's Revenue and Customs (rather than the Secretary of State).

(2) This article applies to any decision which relates to the crediting of Class 3 contributions for a week falling after 6th April 2010 under section 23A(2) of the Social Security Contributions and Benefits Act 1992 (contributions credits for relevant carers) by virtue of the contributor concerned being a relevant carer in respect of that week under—

(*a*) section 23A(3)(*a*) (persons awarded child benefit in respect of a child under the age of 12);
(*b*) section 23A(3)(*b*) (foster parents, within the meaning of regulations); or
(*c*) regulations providing, for the purposes of section 23A(3)(*c*) (other persons engaged in caring, within the meaning given by regulations), that a person is engaged in caring in any week if that person is the partner of a person to whom section 23A(3)(*a*) applies.

3 Decisions and appeals

(1) The following provisions of Chapter 2 (social security decisions and appeals) of Part 1 (decisions and appeals) of the Social Security Act 1998 apply to a decision to which article 2 applies as they apply in relation to a decision of the Secretary of State mentioned in section 8(1) (decisions by the Secretary of State) of that Act.

(2) The provisions are—

(*a*) section 9 (revision of decisions);
(*b*) section 10 (decisions superseding earlier decisions);
(*c*) section 11 (regulations with respect to decisions);
(*d*) section 12 (appeal to First-tier Tribunal), except for subsections (4) and (5);
(*e*) section 13 (redetermination etc of appeals by tribunal);
(*f*) section 14 (appeal from First-tier Tribunal to Upper Tribunal), except for subsections (3)(*c*) and (4) to (6);
(*g*) section 15 (applications for permission to appeal against a decision of the Upper Tribunal);
(*h*) section 15A (functions of Senior President of Tribunals);
(*i*) section 16 (procedure), except for subsections (4) and (5);
(*j*) section 17 (finality of decisions);
(*k*) section 18 (matters arising as respects decisions), except for subsection (2);
(*l*) section 21 (suspension in prescribed circumstances);
(*m*) section 22 (suspension for failure to furnish information etc), except for subsection (4);
(*n*) section 23 (termination in cases of failure to furnish information);

NIC

(*o*) section 25 (decisions involving issues that arise on appeal in other cases);
(*p*) section 26 (appeals involving issues that arise on appeal in other cases);
(*q*) section 27 (restrictions on entitlement to benefit in certain cases of error);
(*r*) section 28 (correction of errors and setting aside of decisions), except for subsection (1A); and
(*s*) section 39ZA (certificates).

4—(1) In the application of the provisions listed in article 3(2) to a decision to which article 2 applies, any reference to the Secretary of State (other than in a reference to a decision of the Secretary of State under section 8(1)) is to have effect as a reference to the Commissioners for Her Majesty's Revenue and Customs.
(2) Paragraph (1) does not apply to references contained in sections 21 to 23.

5 Amendment of the Social Security Contributions and Benefits Act 1992

In section 23A(4)(*b*) of the Social Security Contributions and Benefits Act 1992, after "the Secretary of State" insert "or to the Commissioners for Her Majesty's Revenue and Customs".

2010/19

SOCIAL SECURITY (CONTRIBUTIONS CREDITS FOR PARENTS AND CARERS) REGULATIONS 2010

Made ....*5 January 2010*
Coming into force ....*6 April 2010*

The Secretary of State makes the following Regulations in exercise of the powers conferred by section 23A(3)(*c*), (4) and (9) and section 175(1), (4) and (5) of the Social Security Contributions and Benefits Act 1992.
A draft of this instrument was laid before and approved by a resolution of each House of Parliament in accordance with section 176(1)(*aa*) of that Act.
The Social Security Advisory Committee has agreed that proposals in respect of these Regulations should not be referred to it.

PART 1
GENERAL PROVISIONS

1 Citation and commencement

These Regulations may be cited as the Social Security (Contributions Credits for Parents and Carers) Regulations 2010 and shall come into force on 6th April 2010.

2 Interpretation

(1) In these Regulations—
"partner" means the person with whom another person—
(*a*) resides; and
(*b*) shares responsibility for a child under the age of 12;
"relevant benefit" means—
(*a*) attendance allowance in accordance with section 64 (entitlement);
(*b*) the care component of disability living allowance in accordance with section 72 (the care component), at the middle or highest rate prescribed in accordance with subsection (3) of that section;
(*c*) an increase in the rate of disablement pension in accordance with section 104 (increase where constant attendance needed);
(*d*) any benefit by virtue of—
(i) the Pneumoconiosis, Byssinosis and Miscellaneous Diseases Benefit Scheme 1983; or
(ii) regulations made under paragraph 7(2) in Part 2 (regulations providing for benefit) of Schedule 8 (industrial injuries and diseases (old cases)),
which is payable as if the injury or disease were one in respect of which a disablement pension were for the time being payable in respect of an assessment of 100 per cent.;
(*e*) a constant attendance allowance payable by virtue of—
(i) article 8 (constant attendance allowance) of the Naval, Military and Air Forces etc (Disablement and Death) Service Pensions Order 2006; or
(ii) article 14 (constant attendance allowance) of the Personal Injuries (Civilians) Scheme 1983.

[(*f*) the daily living component of personal independence payment in accordance with section 78 of the Welfare Reform Act 2012.][1]

[(*g*) armed forces independence payment in accordance with the Armed Forces and Reserve Forces (Compensation Scheme) Order 2011.][2]

(2) In these Regulations, a reference to a section or Schedule by number alone is a reference to the section or Schedule so numbered in the Social Security Contributions and Benefits Act 1992.

Amendments—[1] In para (1), in definition of "relevant benefit", sub-para (*f*) inserted by the Personal Independence Payment (Supplementary Provisions and Consequential Amendments) Regulations, SI 2013/388 reg 8, Sch para 46 with effect from 8 April 2013.

In para (1), in definition of "relevant benefit", sub-para (*g*) inserted by the Armed Forces and Reserve Forces Compensation Scheme (Consequential Provisions: Subordinate Legislation) Order, SI 2013/591 art 7, Schedule para 44 with effect from 8 April 2013.

3 Transitional provision

For the period of 12 weeks from the date on which these Regulations come into force, regulation 7(1)(*a*) has effect as if the reference in regulation 7(1) to 12 weeks were a reference to the number of complete weeks since these Regulations came into force.

PART 2
MEANING OF "FOSTER PARENT" AND "ENGAGED IN CARING"

4 Meaning of "foster parent"

(1) For the purposes of subsection (3)(*b*) of section 23A (contributions credits for relevant parents and carers), a foster parent is a person approved as—

(*a*) a foster parent in accordance with Part 4 (approval of foster parents) of the Fostering Services Regulations 2002; . . . [1]

[(*aa*) a kinship carer in accordance with Part 5 (kinship care) of the Looked After Children (Scotland) Regulations 2009;][1]

(*b*) a foster carer in accordance with Part 7 (fostering) of the Looked After Children (Scotland) Regulations 2009[; or

(*c*) a foster parent in accordance with Part 2 (approvals and placements) of the Foster Placement (Children) Regulations (Northern Ireland) 1996][1].

(2) Paragraph (1) is subject to regulation 8.

Amendments—[1] In para (1), word "or" at end of sub-para (*a*) revoked, and sub-paras (*aa*), (*c*) (and preceding word "or") inserted, by the National Insurance Contributions Credits (Miscellaneous Amendments) Regulations, SI 2011/709 reg 3 with effect from 5 April 2011.

5 Meaning of "engaged in caring"

(1) For the purposes of subsection (3)(*c*) of section 23A, a person is engaged in caring in a week—

(*a*) if that person is the partner of a person who is awarded child benefit for any part of that week in respect of a child under the age of 12;

(*b*) if that person is caring for another person or persons for a total of 20 or more hours in that week and—

(i) that other person is, or each of the persons cared for are, entitled to a relevant benefit for that week; or

(ii) the Secretary of State considers that level of care to be appropriate;

(*c*) if that person is one to whom any of paragraphs 4 to 6 (persons caring for another person) of Schedule 1B (prescribed categories of person) to the Income Support (General) Regulations 1987 applies.

(2) Paragraph (1) is subject to regulations 6 to 8.

6 Limit on the period in respect of partners of persons awarded child benefit

(1) Regulation 5(1)(*a*) does not apply to any week which falls within a tax year in respect of which the person awarded child benefit satisfies the following condition.

(2) The condition is that that person's earnings factor for the purposes of section 45 (additional pension in a Category A retirement pension) does not exceed the qualifying earnings factor for that year.

(3) In calculating a person's earnings factor for the purposes of paragraph (2), no account is to be taken of any earnings factor derived from contributions credited by virtue of that person being a relevant carer due to an award of child benefit.

7 Additional period in respect of entitlement to carer's allowance and relevant benefits

(1) A person is engaged in caring for a period of 12 weeks—

(*a*) prior to the date on which that person becomes entitled to carer's allowance by virtue of subsection (1) of section 70 (carer's allowance);

(*b*) subject to paragraph (2), following the end of the week in which that person ceases to be entitled to carer's allowance by virtue of that subsection;

(*c*) following the end of a week in which regulation 5(1)(*b*) ceases to be satisfied.

NIC

(2) For the purposes of paragraph (1)(*b*), a person is not engaged in caring in a week in respect of which that person is entitled, under regulations made under subsection (5) of section 22 (earnings factors), to be credited with contributions by virtue of being entitled to an allowance under section 70.

8 Disqualification due to residence or imprisonment

A person is not a foster parent or engaged in caring for the purposes of section 23A during any period in respect of which that person is—

(*a*) not ordinarily resident in Great Britain; or

(*b*) undergoing imprisonment or detention in legal custody.

PART 3

APPLICATIONS

9 Applications: foster parents and partners of persons awarded child benefit

A person shall not be entitled to be credited with Class 3 contributions under—

(*a*) subsection (3)(*b*) (foster parent) of section 23A; or

(*b*) subsection (3)(*c*) (person engaged in caring) of section 23A by virtue of regulation 5(1)(*a*)

unless an application to be so credited is received by the Commissioners for Her Majesty's Revenue and Customs.

10 Applications: carers for 20 or more hours per week

(1) A person shall not be entitled to be credited with Class 3 contributions under subsection (3)(*c*) of section 23A by virtue of regulation 5(1)(*b*) unless an application to be so credited is received by the Secretary of State.

(2) Paragraph (1) does not apply where that person—

(*a*) . . . [1]

(*b*) is a married woman who is not entitled to be credited with contributions under paragraph (1) of regulation 7A (credits for carer's allowance) of the Social Security (Credits) Regulations 1975 by virtue of paragraph (2)(*b*) (reduced contribution rate election under regulations under section 19(4)) of that regulation.

Amendments—[1] Para (2)(*a*) repealed by Social Security (Credits) (Amendment) Regulations 2010, SI 2010/385 reg 3 with effect from 6 April 2010.

11 Provision of information: carers for 20 or more hours per week

(1) With respect to an application to which regulation 10(1) applies, the application must include—

(*a*) a declaration by the applicant that the applicant cares for a person or persons for 20 or more hours per week;

(*b*) the name and, where known, the national insurance number of each person cared for;

(*c*) where applicable, which relevant benefit each person cared for is entitled to; and

(*d*) where requested by the Secretary of State, a declaration signed by an appropriate person as to the level of care which is required for each person cared for.

(2) For the purposes of paragraph (1)(*d*), an appropriate person is a person who is—

(*a*) involved in the health care or social care of the person cared for; and

(*b*) considered by the Secretary of State as appropriate to make a declaration as to the level of care required.

12 Time limit for applications

An application under regulation 9 or 10 must be received—

(*a*) before the end of the tax year following the tax year in which a week, which is the subject of the application, falls; or

(*b*) within such further time as the Secretary of State or the Commissioners for Her Majesty's Revenue and Customs, as the case may be, consider reasonable in the circumstances.

2010/154

ADDITIONAL STATUTORY PATERNITY PAY (BIRTH, ADOPTION AND ADOPTIONS FROM OVERSEAS) (ADMINISTRATION) REGULATIONS 2010

Made . . . . *28 January 2010*

Laid before Parliament . . . . *1 February 2010*

Coming into force . . . . *6 April 2010*

The Secretary of State makes these Regulations in the exercise of powers conferred by sections 7, 8, 10 and 51(1) of the Employment Act 2002 and sections 8(1)(f) and (ga) and 25 of the Social

Security Contributions (Transfer of Functions, etc) Act 1999 and with the concurrence of the Commissioners for Her Majesty's Revenue and Customs.

1 Citation and commencement

These Regulations may be cited as the Additional Statutory Paternity Pay (Birth, Adoption and Adoptions from Overseas) (Administration) Regulations 2010 and shall come into force on 6th April 2010.

2 Interpretation

(1) In these Regulations—

"the 1992 Act" means the Social Security Contributions and Benefits Act 1992;

"the 1996 Act" means the Employment Rights Act 1996;

"the 2002 Act" means the Employment Act 2002;

"additional statutory paternity pay period" means the period determined in accordance with section 171ZEE(2) of the 1992 Act, or section 171ZEE(2) of the 1992 Act as it applies to adoptions from overseas, as the period in respect of which additional statutory paternity pay is payable to a person;

"additional statutory paternity pay" means any payment under section 171ZEA or section 171ZEB of the 1992 Act, or under section 171ZEB of the 1992 Act as it applies to adoptions from overseas;

"adoption from overseas" means the adoption of a child who enters Great Britain from outside the United Kingdom in connection with or for the purposes of adoption which does not involve placement of the child for adoption under the law of any part of the United Kingdom;

"the Commissioners" means the Commissioners for Her Majesty's Revenue and Customs;

"contributions payments" has the same meaning as in section 7 of the 2002 Act;

"the Contributions Regulations" means the Social Security (Contributions) Regulations 2001;

"income tax month" means the period beginning on the 6th day of any calendar month and ending on the 5th day of the following calendar month;

"income tax quarter" means the period beginning on the 6th day of April and ending on the 5th day of July, the period beginning on the 6th day of July and ending on the 5th day of October, the period beginning on the 6th day of October and ending on the 5th day of January or the period beginning on the 6th day of January and ending on the 5th day of April;

"tax year" means the 12 months beginning with 6th April in any year;

"writing" includes writing delivered by means of electronic communications approved by directions issued by the Commissioners pursuant to regulations under section 132 of the Finance Act 1999.

(2) Any reference in these Regulations to the employees of an employer includes the employer's former employees.

3 Funding of employers' liabilities to make payments of additional statutory paternity pay

(1) An employer who has made any payment of additional statutory paternity pay shall be entitled—

(*a*) to an amount equal to 92% of such payment; or

(*b*) if the payment qualifies for small employer's relief by virtue of section 7(3) of the 2002 Act—

(i) to an amount equal to such payment; and

(ii) to an additional payment equal to the amount to which the employer would have been entitled under section 167(2)(b) of the 1992 Act had the payment been a payment of statutory maternity pay.

(2) The employer shall be entitled in either case (*a*) or case (*b*) to apply for advance funding in respect of such payment in accordance with regulation 4, or to deduct it in accordance with regulation 5 from amounts otherwise payable by the employer.

4 Application for funding from the Commissioners

(1) If an employer is entitled to a payment determined in accordance with regulation 3 in respect of additional statutory paternity pay which the employer is required to pay to an employee or employees for an income tax month or income tax quarter, and the payment exceeds the aggregate of—

(*a*) the total amount of tax which the employer is required to pay to the collector of taxes in respect of the deductions from the emoluments of employees in accordance with the Income Tax (Pay as You Earn) Regulations 2003 for the same income tax month or income tax quarter,

(*b*) the total amount of the deductions made by the employer from the emoluments of employees for the same income tax month or income tax quarter in accordance with regulations under section 22(5) of the Teaching and Higher Education Act 1998 or section 73B of the Education (Scotland) Act 1980 or in accordance with article 3(5) of the Education (Student Support) (Northern Ireland) Order 1998,

NIC

(*c*) the total amount of contributions payments which the employer is required to pay to the collector of taxes in respect of the emoluments of employees (whether by means of deduction or otherwise) in accordance with the Contributions Regulations for the same income tax month or income tax quarter, and

(*d*) the total amount of payments which the employer is required to pay to the collector of taxes in respect of the deductions made on account of tax from payments to sub-contractors in accordance with section 61 of the Finance Act 2004 for the same income tax month or income tax quarter,

the employer may apply to the Commissioners in accordance with paragraph (2) for funds to pay the additional statutory paternity pay (or so much of it as remains outstanding) to the employee or employees.

(2) Where—

(*a*) the condition in paragraph (1) is satisfied, or

(*b*) the employer considers that the condition in paragraph (1) will be satisfied on the date of any subsequent payment of emoluments to one or more employees who are entitled to payment of additional statutory paternity pay,

the employer may apply to the Commissioners for funding in a form approved for that purpose by the Commissioners.

(3) An application by an employer under paragraph (2) shall be for an amount up to, but not exceeding, the amount of the payment to which the employer is entitled in accordance with regulation 3 in respect of additional statutory paternity pay which the employer is required to pay to an employee or employees for the income tax month or income tax quarter to which the payment of emoluments relates.

5 Deductions from payments to the Commissioners

An employer who is entitled to a payment determined in accordance with regulation 3 may recover such payment by making one or more deductions from the aggregate of the amounts specified in sub-paragraphs (*a*) to (*d*) of regulation 4(1) except where and in so far as—

(*a*) those amounts relate to earnings paid before the beginning of the income tax month or income tax quarter in which the payment of additional statutory paternity pay was made;

(*b*) those amounts are paid by the employer later than six years after the end of the tax year in which the payment of additional statutory paternity pay was made;

(*c*) the employer has received payment from the Commissioners under regulation 4; or

(*d*) the employer has made a request in writing under regulation 4 that the payment to which the employer is entitled in accordance with regulation 3 be paid and the employer has not received notification by the Commissioners that the request is refused.

6 Payments to employers by the Commissioners

If the total amount which an employer is or would otherwise be entitled to deduct under regulation 5 is less than the payment to which the employer is entitled in accordance with regulation 3 in an income tax month or income tax quarter, and the Commissioners are satisfied that this is so, then provided that the employer has in writing requested them to do so, the Commissioners shall pay the employer such amount as the employer was unable to deduct.

7 Date when certain contributions are to be treated as paid

Where an employer has made a deduction from a contributions payment under regulation 5, the date on which it is to be treated as having been paid for the purposes of section 7(5) of the 2002 Act (when amount deducted from contributions payment to be treated as paid and received by the Commissioners) is—

(*a*) in a case where the deduction did not extinguish the contributions payment, the date on which the remainder of the contributions payment or, as the case may be, the first date on which any part of the remainder of the contributions payment was paid; and

(*b*) in a case where the deduction extinguished the contributions payment, the 14th day after the end of the income tax month or income tax quarter during which there were paid the earnings in respect of which the contributions payment was payable.

8 Overpayments

(1) This regulation applies where funds have been provided to the employer pursuant to regulation 4 in respect of one or more employees and it appears to an officer of Revenue and Customs that the employer has not used the whole or part of those funds to pay additional statutory paternity pay.

(2) An officer of Revenue and Customs shall decide to the best of the officer's judgement the amount of funds provided pursuant to regulation 4 and not used to pay additional statutory paternity pay and shall serve notice in writing of this decision on the employer.

(3) A decision under this regulation may cover funds provided pursuant to regulation 4—

(*a*) for any one income tax month or income tax quarter, or more than one income tax month or income tax quarter, in a tax year, and

(*b*) in respect of a class or classes of employees specified in the decision notice (without naming the individual employees), or in respect of one or more employees named in the decision notice.

(4) Subject to the following provisions of this regulation, Part 6 of the Taxes Management Act 1970 (collection and recovery) shall apply with any necessary modifications to a decision under this regulation as if it were an assessment and as if the amount of funds determined were income tax charged on the employer.

(5) Where an amount of funds determined under this regulation relates to more than one employee, proceedings may be brought for the recovery of that amount without distinguishing the amounts making up that sum which the employer is liable to repay in respect of each employee and without specifying the employee in question, and the amount determined under this regulation shall be one cause of action or one matter of complaint for the purposes of proceedings under section 65, 66 or 67 of the Taxes Management Act 1970.

(6) Nothing in paragraph (5) prevents the bringing of separate proceedings for the recovery of any amount which the employer is liable to repay in respect of each employee.

9 Records to be maintained by employers

Every employer shall maintain for three years after the end of a tax year in which the employer made payments of additional statutory paternity pay to any employee a record of—

(*a*) if the employee's additional statutory paternity pay period began in that year—

(i) the date on which that period began, and

(ii) the evidence of entitlement to additional statutory paternity pay provided by the employee pursuant to regulations made under section 171ZEC(3)(*c*) of the 1992 Act or under section 171ZEC(3)(*c*) of the 1992 Act as it applies to adoptions from overseas;

(*b*) the weeks in that tax year in which additional statutory paternity pay was paid to the employee and the amount paid in each week; and

(*c*) any week in that tax year which was within the employee's additional statutory paternity pay period but for which no payment of additional statutory paternity pay was made to the employee and the reason no payment was made.

10 Inspection of employers' records

(1) Every employer, whenever called upon to do so by any authorised officer of Revenue and Customs, shall produce the documents and records specified in paragraph (2) to that officer for inspection, at such time as that officer may reasonably require, at the prescribed place.

(2) The documents and records specified in this paragraph are—

(*a*) all wages sheets, deductions working sheets, records kept in accordance with regulation 9 and other documents and records whatsoever relating to the calculation or payment of additional statutory paternity pay to employees in respect of the years specified by such officer; or

(*b*) such of those wages sheets, deductions working sheets, or other documents and records as may be specified by the authorised officer.

(3) The "prescribed place" mentioned in paragraph (1) means—

(*a*) such place in Great Britain as the employer and the authorised officer may agree upon; or

(*b*) in default of such agreement, the place in Great Britain at which the documents and records referred to in paragraph (2)(*a*) are normally kept; or

(*c*) in default of such agreement and if there is no such place as is referred to in sub-paragraph (*b*), the employer's principal place of business in Great Britain.

(4) The authorised officer may—

(*a*) take copies of, or make extracts from, any document or record produced to the authorised officer for inspection in accordance with paragraph (1);

(*b*) remove any document or record so produced if it appears to the authorised officer to be necessary to do so, at a reasonable time and for a reasonable period.

(5) Where any document or record is removed in accordance with paragraph (4)(*b*), the authorised officer shall provide—

(*a*) a receipt for the document or record so removed; and

(*b*) a copy of the document or record, free of charge, within seven days, to the person by whom it was produced or caused to be produced where the document or record is reasonably required for the proper conduct of a business.

(6) Where a lien is claimed on a document produced in accordance with paragraph (1), the removal of the document under paragraph (4)(*b*) shall not be regarded as breaking the lien.

(7) Where records are maintained by computer, the person required to make them available for inspection shall provide the authorised officer with all facilities necessary for obtaining information from them.

11 Provision of information relating to entitlement to additional statutory paternity pay

(1) Where an employer, who has been given evidence of entitlement to additional statutory paternity pay pursuant to regulations made under section 171ZEC(3)(*c*) of the 1992 Act or under section 171ZEC(3)(*c*) of the 1992 Act as it applies to adoptions from overseas by a person who is or has been an employee, decides that they have no liability to make payments of additional statutory paternity pay to the employee, the employer shall furnish the employee with details of the decision and the reasons for it.

(2) Where an employer who has been given such evidence of an entitlement to additional statutory paternity pay has made one or more payments of additional statutory paternity pay to the employee but decides, before the end of the additional statutory paternity pay period, that they have no liability to make further payments to the employee because the employee has been detained in legal custody or sentenced to a term of imprisonment which was not suspended, the employer shall furnish the employee with—

(*a*) details of the employer's decision and the reasons for it; and

(*b*) details of the last week in respect of which a liability to pay additional statutory paternity pay arose and the total number of weeks within the additional statutory paternity pay period in which such a liability arose.

(3) The employer shall—

(*a*) return to the employee any evidence provided by the employee as referred to in paragraph (1) or (2); and

(*b*) comply with the requirements imposed by paragraph (1) within 28 days of the day the employee gave notice of intended absence; and

(*c*) comply with the requirements imposed by paragraph (2) within seven days of being notified of the employee's detention or sentence.

12 Application for the determination of any issue arising as to, or in connection with, entitlement to additional statutory paternity pay

(1) An application for the determination of any issue arising as to, or in connection with, entitlement to additional statutory paternity pay may be submitted to an officer of Revenue and Customs by the employee concerned.

(2) Such an issue shall be decided by an officer of Revenue and Customs only on the basis of such an application or on their own initiative.

13 Applications in connection with additional statutory paternity pay

(1) An application for the determination of any issue referred to in regulation 12 shall be made in a form approved for the purpose by the Commissioners.

(2) Where such an application is made by an employee, it shall—

(*a*) be made to an officer of Revenue and Customs within six months of the earliest day in respect of which entitlement to additional statutory paternity pay is in issue;

(*b*) state the period in respect of which entitlement to additional statutory paternity pay is in issue; and

(*c*) state the grounds (if any) on which the applicant's employer had denied liability for additional statutory paternity pay in respect of the period specified in the application.

14 Provision of information

(1) Any person specified in paragraph (2) shall, where information or documents are reasonably required from the person to ascertain whether additional statutory paternity pay is or was payable, furnish that information or those documents within 30 days of receiving a notification from an officer of Revenue and Customs requesting such information or documents.

(2) The requirement to provide such information or documents applies to—

(*a*) any person claiming to be entitled to additional statutory paternity pay;

(*b*) any person who is, or has been, the spouse, civil partner or partner of such a person as is specified in paragraph (*a*);

(*c*) any person who is, or has been, an employer of such a person as is specified in paragraph (*a*);

(*d*) any person carrying on an agency or other business for the introduction or supply to persons requiring them of persons available to do work or to perform services; and

(*e*) any person who is a servant or agent of any such person as is specified in paragraphs (*a*) to (*d*).

2010/426

SOCIAL SECURITY (MAXIMUM ADDITIONAL PENSION) REGULATIONS 2010

Made . . . . *18 February 2010*

Laid before Parliament . . . . .25 February 2010
Coming into force . . . . .6 April 2010

The Secretary of State for Work and Pensions makes the following Regulations in exercise of the powers conferred by sections 52(3), 122(1), 175(1) of the Social Security Contributions and Benefits Act 1992.

The Social Security Advisory Committee has agreed that proposals in respect of these Regulations should not be referred to it.

1 Citation and commencement

These Regulations may be cited as the Social Security (Maximum Additional Pension) Regulations 2010 and shall come into force on 6th April 2010.

2 Interpretation

(1) In these Regulations—

"applicable limit" has the meaning given by section 44(7)(*c*);

["relevant day" means the day on which the survivor would, but for section 43 (persons entitled to more than one retirement pension), have become entitled to both—

(*a*) a Category A retirement pension; and

(*b*) a Category B retirement pension by virtue of the contributions of a spouse or civil partner who has died,

or would have become so entitled if the survivor's entitlement to a Category A or Category B retirement pension had not been deferred;][1]

"relevant year" has the meaning given by section 44(7)(*a*);

"survivor" means surviving spouse or surviving civil partner.

(2) In these Regulations a reference to a section by number alone is a reference to the section so numbered in the Social Security Contributions and Benefits Act 1992.

Amendments—[1] In para (1), definition of "relevant day" inserted by the Pensions Act 2014 (Consequential, Supplementary and Incidental Amendments) Order, SI 2015/1985 art 33(1), (2) with effect from 6 April 2016.

3 Prescribed maximum additional pension

[(A1) This regulation applies to a survivor whose relevant day is before 6th April 2016.][1]

(1) For the purposes of section 52(3) (increase of additional pension in the Category A retirement pension for surviving spouses) the maximum additional pension shall be the amount of additional pension to which a person is entitled where that person—

(*a*) has reached pensionable age on [the survivor's relevant day][1]; and

(*b*) in respect of each relevant year has an earnings factor specified in paragraph (3).

(2) . . . [1]

(3) For the purposes of paragraph (1)(*b*), the specified earnings factor is an earnings factor which—

(*a*) is equal to 53 times that year's applicable limit, before any increase under section 148 of the Social Security Administration Act 1992 (revaluation of earnings factors); and

(*b*) is derived from earnings on which primary Class 1 contributions were paid.

Amendments—[1] Para (A1) inserted, in para (1)(*a*), words substituted, and para (2) revoked, by the Pensions Act 2014 (Consequential, Supplementary and Incidental Amendments) Order, SI 2015/1985 art 33(1), (3) with effect from 6 April 2016.

[3A Prescribed maximum additional pension for survivors who become entitled on or after 6th April 2016

(1) This regulation applies to a survivor whose relevant day is on or after 6th April 2016.

(2) For the purposes of section 52(3), the maximum additional pension shall be £165.60.][1]

Amendments—[1] Regulation 3A inserted by the Pensions Act 2014 (Consequential, Supplementary and Incidental Amendments) Order, SI 2015/1985 art 33(1), (4) with effect from 6 April 2016.

4 Revocations

The following instruments are revoked—

(*a*) the Social Security (Maximum Additional Pension) Regulations 1978;

(*b*) the Social Security (Maximum Additional Pension) Amendment Regulations 1979.

2010/926

RECOVERY OF SOCIAL SECURITY CONTRIBUTIONS DUE IN OTHER MEMBER STATES REGULATIONS 2010

Made . . . . .23 March 2010
Laid before Parliament . . . . .24 March 2010
Coming into force . . . . .1 May 2010

The Treasury are a government department designated for the purposes of section 2(2) of the European Communities Act 1972 in relation to mutual assistance between states for the recovery of claims relating to social security contributions and interest, fines, costs and penalties related to such claims.

The Treasury make the following Regulations in exercise of the powers conferred by section 2(2) of the European Communities Act 1972.

1 Citation and commencement

These Regulations may be cited as the Recovery of Social Security Contributions Due in Other Member States Regulations 2010 and come into force on 1st May 2010.

2 Interpretation

In these Regulations—

"applicant party" has the meaning assigned to it by Article 75 of Council Regulation (EC) No 987/2009;

"claim" has the meaning assigned to it by Article 75 of Council Regulation (EC) No 987/2009, except for the second and third times it occurs in regulation 4(1) of these Regulations;

"Commissioners" means the Commissioners for Her Majesty's Revenue and Customs;

"instrument permitting enforcement" means—

(i) any instrument issued by an applicant party in relation to a claim; or

(ii) a decision relating to a claim given in favour of an applicant party in any member State by a court or tribunal or other competent body in that State which permits recovery of that claim, or part thereof, in that State;

"officer" means an officer of Revenue and Customs.

3 Enforcement of claims

(1) An instrument permitting enforcement of a claim, recognised by the Commissioners as an instrument authorising enforcement of the claim in the United Kingdom, together with a certificate of an officer that payment of the claim has not been made to that officer, or, to the best of that officer's knowledge and belief, to any other person acting on behalf of the Commissioners, or to the applicant party, is sufficient evidence that the sum mentioned in the instrument is unpaid and is due to the applicant party.

(2) A certificate of an officer that interest is payable under regulation 4(1) and that payment of the interest has not been made to that officer, or, to the best of that officer's knowledge and belief, to any other person acting on behalf of the Commissioners, or to the applicant party, is sufficient evidence that the sum mentioned in the instrument is unpaid and is due to the applicant party.

(3) For the purposes of this regulation, any document purporting to be such a certificate as is mentioned in paragraph (1) or (2) is deemed to be such a certificate unless the contrary is proved.

4 Interest for late payment of claims

(1) A claim corresponding to a claim for outstanding Class 1, 1A, 1B or 4 national insurance contributions carries interest in respect of the principal amount and any penalty claimed at the rate applicable to the corresponding claim [under—

(*a*) section 178 of the Finance Act 1989 for the purposes of Class 1, 1A and 1B national insurance contributions, or

(*b*) sections 101 and 103 of the Finance Act 2009 for the purposes of Class 4 national insurance contributions,

from the date of recognition until the date of payment inclusive.][1].

(2) In this Regulation "the date of recognition" means the earlier of—

(i) the date following the expiry of three months from the date of receipt by the Commissioners of the request for recovery of the claim; and

(ii) the date the instrument permitting enforcement of the claim is recognised by the Commissioners as an instrument authorising enforcement of the claim in the United Kingdom.

(3) Interest is payable under this regulation without any deduction of income tax.

(4) For the purposes of this regulation, where—

(*a*) any payment is made by cheque to—

(i) the Commissioners, or

(ii) the applicant party, and

(*b*) the cheque is paid on its first presentation to the banker on whom it is drawn;

the payment shall be treated as made on the date on which the cheque was received by the Commissioners or the applicant party.

(5) Interest payable under this regulation shall be recoverable as if it were interest charged under a provision of the Taxes Management Act 1970.

Amendments—

In para (1), words substituted by the Finance Act 2009, Sections 101 to 103 (Income Tax Self Assessment) (Appointed Days and Transitional and Consequential Provisions) Order, SI 2011/701 art 111 with effect from 31 October 2011.

2011/475

SOCIAL SECURITY REVALUATION OF EARNINGS FACTORS ORDER 2011

Made . . . .*22nd February 2011*

Laid before Parliament . . . .*28th February 2011*

Coming into force . . . . *6th April 2011*

In accordance with section 148(2) (revaluation of earnings factors) of the Social Security Administration Act 1992, the Secretary of State has reviewed the general level of earnings obtaining in Great Britain.

The Secretary of State has concluded, having regard to earlier orders made under section 148, that earnings factors for the relevant tax years have not, during the period taken into account for that review, maintained their value in relation to the general level of earnings.

The Secretary of State makes the following Order in exercise of the powers conferred upon him by section 148(3) and (4) and section 189(1), (4) and (5) of the Social Security Administration Act 1992.

1 Citation and commencement

This Order may be cited as the Social Security Revaluation of Earnings Factors Order 2011 and shall come into force on 6th April 2011.

2 Revaluation of earnings factors

The earnings factors for tax years specified in the Schedule to this Order in so far as they are relevant—

(*a*) to the calculation—

(i) of the additional pension in the rate of any long-term benefit, or

(ii) of any guaranteed minimum pension; or

(*b*) to any other calculation required under Part 3 of the Pension Schemes Act 1993 (including that Part as modified by or under any other enactment),

are directed to be increased for those tax years by the percentage of their amount shown opposite those tax years in that Schedule.

3 Rounding of fractional amounts

Where any earnings factor relevant to the calculation specified in article 2(a)(i) of this Order, as increased in accordance with this Order, would not but for this article be expressed as a whole number of pounds, it shall be so expressed by rounding down any fraction of a pound less than one half and rounding up any other fraction of a pound.

SCHEDULE

PERCENTAGE INCREASE OF EARNINGS FACTOR FOR SPECIFIED TAX YEARS

Article 2

Tax year	*Percentage increase*
1978—1979	705.0
1979—1980	610.5
1980—1981	493.6
1981—1982	397.1
1982—1983	351.5
1983—1984	319.2
1984—1985	288.2
1985—1986	264.2
1986—1987	234.4
1987—1988	211.3
1988—1989	186.4
1989—1990	158.5

NIC

1990—1991	140.9
1991—1992	118.8
1992—1993	105.5
1993—1994	95.7
1994—1995	89.8
1995—1996	81.8
1996—1997	76.8
1997—1998	68.4
1998—1999	61.0
1999—2000	54.5
2000—2001	45.4
2001—2002	39.8
2002—2003	34.0
2003—2004	29.4
2004—2005	24.6
2005—2006	19.7
2006—2007	15.8
2007—2008	11.2
2008—2009	6.7
2009—2010	3.5
2010—2011	2.3

2011/1036

SOCIAL SECURITY (REDUCED RATES OF CLASS 1 CONTRIBUTIONS, REBATES AND MINIMUM CONTRIBUTIONS) ORDER 2011

Made . . . . *31 March 2011*
Coming into force. . . . . *6 April 2012*

This Order is made in exercise of the powers conferred by sections 42, 42B, 45A and 182(2) of the Pension Schemes Act 1993 and sections 38, 38B, 41A and 177(2) of the Pension Schemes (Northern Ireland) Act 1993.

The Secretary of State for Work and Pensions has, under section 42(1) of the Pension Schemes Act 1993, laid before each House of Parliament a report by the Government Actuary, and the Secretary of State's report stating whether the Secretary of State considers that, in view of the report of the Government Actuary under section 42(1) of that Act, there should be an alteration in the percentages applying under section 41(1A) and (1B) of that Act and if so, what alteration is in the Secretary of State's opinion required.

The Secretary of State for Work and Pensions has, under section 42B(1) of that Act, laid before each House of Parliament a report by the Government Actuary, and the Secretary of State's report stating what, in view of the report of the Government Actuary under section 42B(1) of that Act, the Secretary of State considers the percentages applying under section 42A(2), (2A) and (3) of that Act should be.

The Secretary of State for Work and Pensions has, under section 45A(1) of that Act, laid before each House of Parliament a report by the Government Actuary, and the Secretary of State's report stating what, in view of the report of the Government Actuary under section 45A(1) of that Act, the Secretary of State considers the percentages applying under section 45(1) of that Act should be.

A draft of this instrument has been laid before Parliament in accordance with sections 42(3), 42B(1) and 45A(1) of the Pension Schemes Act 1993 and section 181(9A) of the Pension Schemes (Northern Ireland) Act 1993 and approved by a resolution of each House of Parliament.

The Secretary of State for Work and Pensions makes the following Order:—

1 Citation, commencement, interpretation and extent

(1) This Order may be cited as the Social Security (Reduced Rates of Class 1 Contributions, Rebates and Minimum Contributions) Order 2011 and shall come into force on 6th April 2012.

(2) In this Order—

"the 1993 Act" means the Pension Schemes Act 1993;

"the low earnings threshold", in relation to a tax year, means the low earnings threshold for that tax year as specified in—

(*a*) section 44A of the Social Security Contributions and Benefits Act 1992 (deemed earnings factors); or

(*b*) in relation to Northern Ireland, section 44A of the Social Security Contributions and Benefits (Northern Ireland) Act 1992 (deemed earnings factors);

"the Northern Ireland Act" means the Pension Schemes (Northern Ireland) Act 1993.

(3) These provisions of this Order extend to England and Wales and Scotland—

(*a*) articles 2 to 4;

(*b*) this article, and the Schedules, so far as they relate to articles 2 to 4.

(4) These provisions of this Order extend to Northern Ireland—

(*a*) articles 5 to 7;

(*b*) this article, and the Schedules, so far as they relate to articles 5 to 7.

2 Alteration of reduced rates of Class 1 contributions for salary related contracted-out schemes

(1) This article applies for the purposes of section 41 of the 1993 Act (reduced rates of Class 1 contributions).

(2) In section 41(1A) of the 1993 Act (reduced rates of primary Class 1 contributions in contracted-out employment) for "1.6 per cent" substitute "1.4 per cent".

(3) In section 41(1B) of the 1993 Act (reduced rates of secondary Class 1 contributions in contracted-out employment) for "3.7 per cent" substitute "3.4 per cent".

3 Reduced rates of Class 1 contributions and rebates for money purchase contracted-out schemes

(1) This article applies for the purposes of section 42A of the 1993 Act (reduced rates of Class 1 contributions, and rebates).

(2) For the purposes of section 42A(2) of the 1993 Act (reduction of primary Class 1 contributions), the appropriate flat-rate percentage for the 2012–2013 tax year is 1.4 per cent.

(3) For the purposes of section 42A(2A) of the 1993 Act (reduction of secondary Class 1 contributions), the appropriate flat-rate percentage for the 2012–2013 tax year is 1.0 per cent.

(4) For the purposes of section 42A(3) of the 1993 Act (appropriate age-related percentage), the appropriate age-related percentage in respect of an earner for the 2012–2013 tax year is the percentage given in the table in Schedule 1 by reference to the age of the earner on the day immediately before the start of that tax year.

4 Appropriate age-related percentages for appropriate personal pension schemes

(1) This article applies for the purposes of section 45(1) of the 1993 Act (amount of minimum contributions).

(2) For the 2012–2013 tax year, the appropriate age-related percentage in respect of earnings of an earner is determined in accordance with paragraph (3) or (4).

(3) If the earnings do not exceed the low earnings threshold, the appropriate age-related percentage is the column B percentage.

(4) If the earnings exceed the low earnings threshold, then—

(*a*) in respect of the part of the earnings that does not exceed the low earnings threshold, the appropriate age-related percentage is the column B percentage; and

(*b*) in respect of the part of the earnings that exceeds the low earnings threshold, the appropriate age-related percentage is the column C percentage.

(5) In respect of earnings of an earner—

(*a*) the column B percentage is the percentage given in column B of the table in Schedule 2 by reference to the age of the earner on the day immediately before the start of the 2012–2013 tax year; and

(*b*) the column C percentage is the percentage given in column C of the table in Schedule 2 by reference to the age of the earner on the day immediately before the start of the 2012–2013 tax year.

5 Alteration of reduced rates of Class 1 contributions for salary related contracted-out schemes—Northern Ireland

(1) This article applies for the purposes of section 37 of the Northern Ireland Act (reduced rates of Class 1 contributions).

(2) In section 37(1A) of the Northern Ireland Act (reduced rates of primary Class 1 contributions) for "1.6 per cent" substitute "1.4 per cent".

(3) In section 37(1B) of the Northern Ireland Act (reduced rates of secondary Class 1 contributions) for "3.7 per cent" substitute "3.4 per cent".

6 Reduced rates of Class 1 contributions and rebates for money purchase contracted-out schemes—Northern Ireland

(1) This article applies for the purposes of section 38A of the Northern Ireland Act (reduced rates of Class 1 contributions, and rebates).

(2) For the purposes of section 38A(2) of the Northern Ireland Act (reduction of primary Class 1 contributions), the appropriate flat-rate percentage for the 2012–2013 tax year is 1.4 per cent.

(3) For the purposes of section 38A(2A) of the Northern Ireland Act (reduction of secondary Class 1 contributions), the appropriate flat-rate percentage for the 2012–2013 tax year is 1.0 per cent.

(4) For the purposes of section 38A(3) of the Northern Ireland Act (appropriate age-related percentage), the appropriate age-related percentage in respect of an earner for the 2012–2013 tax year is the percentage given in the table in Schedule 1 by reference to the age of the earner on the day immediately before the start of that tax year.

7 Appropriate age-related percentages for appropriate personal pension schemes—Northern Ireland

(1) This article applies for the purposes of section 41(1) of the Northern Ireland Act (amount of minimum contributions).

(2) For the 2012–2013 tax year, the appropriate age-related percentage in respect of earnings of an earner is determined in accordance with paragraph (3) or (4).

(3) If the earnings do not exceed the low earnings threshold, the appropriate age-related percentage is the column B percentage.

(4) If the earnings exceed the low earnings threshold, then—

(*a*) in respect of the part of the earnings that does not exceed the low earnings threshold, the appropriate age-related percentage is the column B percentage; and

(*b*) in respect of the part of the earnings that exceeds the low earnings threshold, the appropriate age-related percentage is the column C percentage.

(5) In respect of earnings of an earner—

(*a*) the column B percentage is the percentage given in column B of the table in Schedule 2 by reference to the age of the earner on the day immediately before the start of the 2012–2013 tax year; and

(*b*) the column C percentage is the percentage given in column C of the table in Schedule 2 by reference to the age of the earner on the day immediately before the start of the 2012–2013 tax year.

SCHEDULE 1

APPROPRIATE AGE-RELATED PERCENTAGES FOR MONEY PURCHASE CONTRACTED-OUT SCHEMES FOR THE 2012–2013 TAX YEAR

Articles 3(4) and 6(4)

Age on last day of preceding tax year	*Appropriate age-related percentage*
15	2.4%
16	2.5%
17	2.5%
18	2.6%
19	2.7%
20	2.7%
21	2.8%
22	2.9%
23	2.9%
24	3.0%
25	3.1%
26	3.1%
27	3.2%
28	3.3%
29	3.4%
30	3.4%
31	3.5%
32	3.6%
33	3.7%

34	4.1%
35	4.2%
36	4.3%
37	4.4%
38	4.5%
39	4.7%
40	4.8%
41	5.0%
42	5.1%
43	5.7%
44	5.9%
45	6.0%
46	6.2%
47	6.3%
48	6.5%
49	6.6%
50	6.9%
51	7.3%
52	7.4%
53	7.4%
55	7.4%
56	7.4%
57	7.4%
58	7.4%
59	7.4%
60	7.4%
61	7.4%
62	7.4%
63	7.4%

SCHEDULE 2

APPROPRIATE AGE-RELATED PERCENTAGES FOR APPROPRIATE PERSONAL PENSION SCHEMES FOR THE 2012–2013 TAX YEAR

Articles 4 and 7

Column A	*Column B*	*Column C*
Age on last day of preceding tax year	*Earnings not exceeding low earnings threshold*	*Earnings exceeding low earnings threshold*
15	7.6%	1.9%
16	7.8%	1.95%
17	8.0%	2.0%
18	8.0%	2.0%
19	8.2%	2.05%
20	8.2%	2.05%
21	8.4%	2.1%
22	8.6%	2.15%
23	8.6%	2.15%
24	8.8%	2.2%
25	9.0%	2.25%
26	9.0%	2.25%
27	9.2%	2.3%
28	9.2%	2.3%

29	9.4%	2.35%
30	9.6%	2.4%
31	9.6%	2.4%
32	9.8%	2.45%
33	10.0%	2.5%
34	10.8%	2.7%
35	11.0%	2.75%
36	11.2%	2.8%
37	11.4%	2.85%
38	11.6%	2.9%
39	11.8%	2.95%
40	12.2%	3.05%
41	12.4%	3.1%
42	12.6%	3.15%
43	13.8%	3.45%
44	14.0%	3.5%
45	14.2%	3.55%
46	14.6%	3.65%
47	14.8%	3.7%
48	14.8%	3.7%
49	14.8%	3.7%
50	14.8%	3.7%
51	14.8%	3.7%
52	14.8%	3.7%
53	14.8%	3.7%
55	14.8%	3.7%
56	14.8%	3.7%
57	14.8%	3.7%
58	14.8%	3.7%
59	14.8%	3.7%
60	14.8%	3.7%
61	14.8%	3.7%
62	14.8%	3.7%
63	14.8%	3.7%

2012/187

SOCIAL SECURITY REVALUATION OF EARNINGS FACTORS ORDER 2012

Made. . . . .*26 January 2012*

Laid before Parliament. . . . .*31 January 2012*

Coming into force. . . . .*6 April 2012*

In accordance with section 148(2) (revaluation of earnings factors) of the Social Security Administration Act 1992, the Secretary of State has reviewed the general level of earnings obtaining in Great Britain.

The Secretary of State has concluded, having regard to earlier orders made under section 148, that earnings factors for the relevant tax years have not, during the period taken into account for that review, maintained their value in relation to the general level of earnings.

The Secretary of State makes the following Order in exercise of the powers conferred upon him by section 148(3) and (4) and section 189(1), (4) and (5) of the Social Security Administration Act 1992.

1 Citation and commencement

This Order may be cited as the Social Security Revaluation of Earnings Factors Order 2012 and shall come into force on 6th April 2012.

2 Revaluation of earnings factors

The earnings factors for tax years specified in the Schedule to this Order in so far as they are relevant—

(*a*) to the calculation—

(i) of the additional pension in the rate of any long-term benefit, or

(ii) of any guaranteed minimum pension; or

(*b*) to any other calculation required under Part 3 of the Pension Schemes Act 1993 (including that Part as modified by or under any other enactment),

are directed to be increased for those tax years by the percentage of their amount shown opposite those tax years in that Schedule.

3 Rounding of fractional amounts

Where any earnings factor relevant to the calculation specified in article 2(a)(i) of this Order, as increased in accordance with this Order, would not but for this article be expressed as a whole number of pounds, it shall be so expressed by rounding down any fraction of a pound less than one half and rounding up any other fraction of a pound.

SCHEDULE

PERCENTAGE INCREASE OF EARNINGS FACTOR FOR SPECIFIED TAX YEARS

Article 2

Tax year	*Percentage increase*
1978–1979	719.5
1979–1980	623.3
1980–1981	504.3
1981–1982	406.1
1982–1983	359.6
1983–1984	326.8
1984–1985	295.2
1985–1986	270.7
1986–1987	240.4
1987–1988	217.0
1988–1989	191.6
1989–1990	163.2
1990–1991	145.3
1991–1992	122.8
1992–1993	109.2
1993–1994	99.2
1994–1995	93.2
1995–1996	85.1
1996–1997	80.0
1997–1998	71.5
1998–1999	63.9
1999–2000	57.3
2000–2001	48.0
2001–2002	42.3
2002–2003	36.4
2003–2004	31.7
2004–2005	26.9
2005–2006	21.9
2006–2007	17.9
2007–2008	13.2
2008–2009	8.7
2009–2010	5.4
2010–2011	4.1

2011–2012	1.8

2012/1868

NATIONAL INSURANCE CONTRIBUTIONS (APPLICATION OF PART 7 OF THE FINANCE ACT 2004) REGULATIONS 2012

Made . . . . *16 July 2012*
Laid before Parliament . . . . *17 July 2012*
Coming into force . . . . *1st September 2012*

The Treasury make the following Regulations in exercise of the powers conferred upon them by sections 132A(1) and 189(4) and (5) of the Social Security Administration Act 1992.

PART 1
INTRODUCTION

1 Citation and commencement

These Regulations may be cited as the National Insurance Contributions (Application of Part 7 of the Finance Act 2004) Regulations 2012 and shall come into force on 1st September 2012.

2 Interpretation

In these Regulations—

"the Descriptions Regulations" means the Tax Avoidance Schemes (Prescribed Descriptions of Arrangements) Regulations 2006 as modified by these Regulations.

"the Information Regulations" means the Tax Avoidance (Information) Regulations 2012 as modified by these Regulations.

"introducer", in relation to a notifiable contribution proposal, has the meaning given by regulation 7(2);

"HMRC" means the Commissioners for Her Majesty's Revenue and Customs;

"notifiable arrangements" and "notifiable proposal" have the meaning given to them in section 306 of the Finance Act 2004;

"Part 7" means Part 7 of the Finance Act 2004 (disclosure of tax avoidance schemes) and a reference to a numbered section (without more) is a reference to a section of Part 7;

"prescribed" means prescribed by the Information Regulations, unless the context otherwise requires;

"promoter", in relation to notifiable contribution arrangements or a notifiable contribution proposal, has the meaning given by regulation 7;

"reference number" means the reference number allocated under regulation 12 or section 311 as the case may be;

"tribunal" means the First-tier Tribunal or, where determined by or under Tribunal Procedure Rules, the Upper Tribunal.

["working day" means a day which is not a Saturday or a Sunday, Christmas Day, Good Friday or a bank holiday under the Banking and Financial Dealings Act 1971 in any part of the United Kingdom.][1]

Amendments—[1] Definition of "working day" inserted by the National Insurance Contributions (Application of Part 7 of the Finance Act 2004) (Amendment) Regulations, SI 2015/531 regs 2, 3 with effect in relation to prescribed information about notifiable contribution proposals or notifiable contribution arrangements provided by a person in compliance, or purported compliance, with regs 8, 10, 11 of these regulations, on or after 12th April 2015. "Prescribed" has the meaning given in this regulation: SI 2015/531 reg 1(3).

3 Structure of the Regulations

(1) Regulations 5 to 21 make provision corresponding to Part 7 (other than section 314 (legal professional privilege)) in so far as that Part applies to income tax.

(2) Regulations 22 to 24 make provision corresponding to section 98C and section 118(2) of the Taxes Management Act 1970 (penalties for failure to comply with Part 7 of the Finance Act 2004) and other provisions of the Taxes Management Act 1970 in so far as they relate to a penalty under section 98C.

(3) Regulations 25 to 28 modify regulations made under Part 7 in so far as they apply to income tax.

4 Revocations

(1) The regulations described in Regulation 29 are revoked.

(2) Anything begun under or for the purpose of any regulations revoked by these Regulations shall be continued under or, as the case may be, for the purpose of the corresponding provision of these Regulations.

(3) Where any document refers to a provision of a regulation revoked by these Regulations, such reference shall, unless the context otherwise requires, be construed as a reference to the corresponding provision of these Regulations.

PART 2
PROVISIONS CORRESPONDING TO PART 7 OF THE FINANCE ACT 2004

5 Application of Part 2

(1) This Part applies to—

(*a*) notifiable contribution arrangements; and

(*b*) notifiable contribution proposals

which fall within any description prescribed by the Descriptions Regulations.

(2) The Table below shows which of the following regulations corresponds to which provision of Part 7.

Section within Part 7	*Corresponding provision of these Regulations*
Section 306 (meaning of "notifiable arrangements" and "notifiable proposal")	Regulation 5
Section 306A (doubt as to notifiability)	Regulation 6
Section 307 (meaning of promoter)	Regulation 7
Section 308 (duties of promoter)	Regulation 8
Section 308A (supplemental information)	Regulation 9
Section 309 (duty of person dealing with promoter outside the United Kingdom)	Regulation 10
Section 310 (duty of parties to notifiable arrangements not involving promoter)	Regulation 11
[Section 310A (duty to provide further information requested by HMRC)	Regulation 11A
Section 310B (failure to provide information under section 310A: application to the Tribunal)	Regulation 11B][2]
Section 311 (arrangements to be given reference number)	Regulation 12
Section 312 (duty of promoter to notify client of number)	Regulation 13
Section 312A (duty of client to notify parties of number)	Regulation 14
[Section 312B (duty of client to provide information to promoter)	Regulation 14A][1]
Section 313 (duty of parties to notifiable arrangements to notify Board of number etc)	Regulation 15
Section 313ZA (duty of promoter to provide details of clients)	Regulation 16
[Section 313ZB (enquiry following disclosure of client details)	Regulation 16A][1]
Section 313A (pre-disclosure enquiry)	Regulation 17
Section 313B (reasons for non-disclosure: supporting information)	Regulation 18
Section 313C (information provided to introducers)	Regulation 19
Section 314A (order to disclose)	Regulation 20
Section 316 (information to be provided in form and manner specified by Board)	Regulation 21

Amendments—[1] In sub-para (2), entries in table inserted by the National Insurance Contributions (Application of Part 7 of the Finance Act 2004) (Amendment) Regulations, SI 2013/2600 regs 2, 3 with effect from 4 November 2013. Note that SI 2013/2600 does not have effect for the purposes of reg 8(1), (3) if the relevant date falls before 4 November 2013, or if the date on which the promoter first becomes aware of any transaction forming part of notifiable contribution arrangements falls before 4 November 2013. "Relevant date" has the meaning given by reg 8(2) (SI 2013/2600 art 1(2), (3)).

[2] Table entries inserted by the National Insurance Contributions (Application of Part 7 of the Finance Act 2004) (Amendment) Regulations, SI 2015/531 regs 2, 4 with effect in relation to prescribed information about notifiable contribution proposals or notifiable contribution arrangements provided by a person in compliance, or purported compliance, with regs 8, 10, 11 of these regulations, on or after 12th April 2015. "Prescribed" has the meaning given in reg 2 of these regulations: SI 2015/531 reg 1(3).

6 Doubt as to notifiabilty

(1) HMRC may apply to the tribunal for an order that—

(*a*) a proposal is to be treated as a notifiable contribution proposal; or

(*b*) arrangements are to be treated as notifiable contribution arrangements.

(2) An application must specify—

(*a*) the proposal or arrangements in respect of which the order is sought; and

(*b*) the promoter.

(3) On an application the tribunal may make the order only if satisfied that HMRC—

(*a*) have taken all reasonable steps to establish whether the proposal is a notifiable contribution proposal or the arrangements are notifiable contribution arrangements; and

(*b*) have reasonable grounds for suspecting that the proposal may be a notifiable contribution proposal or the arrangements may be notifiable contribution arrangements.

(4) Reasonable steps under paragraph (3)(*a*) may (but need not) include taking action under regulation 17 or 18.

(5) Grounds for suspicion under paragraph (3)(*b*) may include—

(*a*) the fact that the relevant arrangements fall within a description prescribed by the Descriptions Regulations;

(*b*) an attempt by the promoter to avoid or delay providing information or documents about the proposal or arrangements under or by virtue of regulation 17 or 18;

(*c*) the promoter's failure to comply with a requirement under or by virtue of regulation 17 or 18 or section 313A or 313B in relation to another proposal or other arrangements.

(6) Where an order is made under this regulation in respect of a proposal or arrangements, the period for the purposes of paragraphs (1) and (3) of regulation 8 is that prescribed.

(7) An order under this regulation in relation to a proposal or arrangements is without prejudice to the possible application of regulation 8, other than by virtue of this regulation, to the proposal or arrangements.

7 Meaning of promoter

(1) For the purposes of this Part a person is a promoter—

(*a*) in relation to a notifiable contribution proposal if, in the course of a relevant business, the person ("P")—

(i) is to any extent responsible for the design of the proposed arrangements;

(ii) makes a firm approach to another person ("C") in relation to the proposal with a view to P making the proposal available for implementation by C or any other person; or

(iii) makes the notifiable contribution proposal available for implementation by other persons; and

(*b*) in relation to notifiable contribution arrangements, if the person ("P") is by virtue of sub-paragraph (*a*)(ii) or (iii) a promoter in relation to a notifiable contribution proposal which is implemented by those arrangements or if, in the course of a relevant business, P is to any extent responsible for—

(i) the design of the arrangements, or

(ii) the organisation or management of the arrangements.

(2) For the purposes of this Part a person is an introducer in relation to a notifiable contribution proposal if the person makes a marketing contact with another person in relation to the proposal.

(3) In this regulation "relevant business" means any trade, profession or business which—

(*a*) involves the provision to other persons of services relating to national insurance contributions, or

(*b*) is carried on by a bank, as defined by section 1120 of the Corporation Tax Act 2010, or by a securities house, as defined by section 1009(3) of that Act.

(4) For the purposes of this regulation anything done by a company is to be taken to be done in the course of a relevant business if it is done for the purposes of a relevant business falling within paragraph (3)(*b*) carried on by another company which is a member of the same group.

(5) Section 170 of the Taxation of Chargeable Gains Act 1992 has effect for determining for the purposes of paragraph (4) whether two companies are members of the same group, but as if in that section—

(*a*) for each of the references to a 75% subsidiary there were substituted a reference to a 51% subsidiary, and

(*b*) subsection (3)(*b*) and subsections (6) to (8) were omitted.

(6) For the purposes of this Part a person makes a firm approach to another person in relation to a notifiable contribution proposal if the person makes a marketing contact with the other person in relation to the proposal at a time when the proposed arrangements have been substantially designed.

(7) For the purposes of this Part a person makes a marketing contact with another person in relation to a notifiable contribution proposal if—

(*a*) the person communicates information about the proposal to the other person;

(*b*) the communication is made with a view to that other person, or any other person, entering into transactions forming part of the proposed arrangements; and (*c*) the information communicated includes an explanation of the advantage in relation to any contribution that might be expected to be obtained from the proposed arrangements.

(8) For the purposes of paragraph (6) proposed contribution arrangements have been substantially designed at any time if by that time the nature of the transactions to form part of them has been sufficiently developed for it to be reasonable to believe that a person who wished to obtain the advantage mentioned in paragraph (7)(*c*) might enter into—

(*a*) transactions of the nature developed; or

(*b*) transactions not substantially different from transactions of that nature.

(9) A person is not to be treated as a promoter or introducer for the purposes of this Part by reason of anything done in circumstances prescribed by the Tax Avoidance Schemes (Promoters and Prescribed Circumstances) Regulations 2004 as modified by these Regulations.

(10) In the application of this Part to a proposal which is not a notifiable contribution proposal or arrangements which are not notifiable contribution arrangements, a reference to a promoter or introducer is a reference to a person who would be a promoter or introducer under paragraphs (1) to (9) if the proposal were a notifiable contribution proposal or arrangements were notifiable contribution arrangements.

8 Duties of promoter

(1) A person who is a promoter in relation to a notifiable contribution proposal must, within the prescribed period after the relevant date, provide HMRC with the prescribed information relating to the notifiable contribution proposal.

(2) In paragraph (1) "the relevant date" means the earliest of the following—

(*a*) the date on which the promoter first makes a firm approach to another person in relation to a notifiable contribution proposal;

(*b*) the date on which the promoter makes the notifiable contribution proposal available for implementation by any other person; or

(*c*) the date on which the promoter first becomes aware of any transaction forming part of notifiable contribution arrangements implementing the notifiable contribution proposal.

(3) A person who is a promoter in relation to notifiable contribution arrangements must, within the prescribed period after the date on which the person first becomes aware of any transaction forming part of the notifiable contribution arrangements, provide HMRC with the prescribed information relating to those arrangements, unless those arrangements implement a proposal in respect of which notice has been given under paragraph (1).

(4) Paragraph (5) applies where a person complies with paragraph (1) in relation to a notifiable contribution proposal for arrangements and another person is—

(*a*) also a promoter in relation to the notifiable contribution proposal or is a promoter in relation to a notifiable contribution proposal for arrangements which are substantially the same as the proposed arrangements (whether they relate to the same or different parties); or

(*b*) a promoter in relation to notifiable contribution arrangements implementing the notifiable contribution proposal or notifiable contribution arrangements which are substantially the same as notifiable contribution arrangements implementing the notifiable contribution proposal (whether they relate to the same or different parties).

(5) Any duty of the other person under paragraph (1) or (3) in relation to the notifiable contribution proposal or notifiable contribution arrangements is discharged if—

(*a*) the person who complied with paragraph (1) has notified the identity and address of the other person to HMRC or the other person holds the reference number allocated to the proposed notifiable contribution arrangements under regulation 12; and

(*b*) the other person holds the information provided to HMRC in compliance with paragraph (1).

(6) Paragraph (7) applies where a person complies with section 308(1) in relation to a notifiable proposal and another person is—

(*a*) a promoter in relation to a notifiable contribution proposal for arrangements which are substantially the same as the notifiable proposal (whether they relate to the same or different parties); or

(*b*) a promoter in relation to notifiable contribution arrangements which are substantially the same as notifiable arrangements implementing the notifiable proposal (whether they relate to the same or different parties).

(7) Any duty of the other person under paragraph (1) or (3) in relation to the notifiable contribution proposal or notifiable contribution arrangements is discharged if—

(*a*) the person who complied with section 308(1) in relation to the notifiable proposal has notified the identity and address of the other person to HMRC or the other person holds the reference number allocated to the proposed notifiable arrangements under section 311; and

(*b*) the other person holds the information provided to HMRC in compliance with section 308(1).

(8) Paragraph (9) applies where a person complies with paragraph (3) in relation to notifiable contribution arrangements and another person is—

NIC

(*a*) a promoter in relation to a notifiable contribution proposal for arrangements which are substantially the same as the notifiable contribution arrangements (whether they relate to the same or different parties); or

(*b*) also a promoter in relation to the notifiable contribution arrangements or notifiable contribution arrangements which are substantially the same (whether they relate to the same or different parties).

(9) Any duty of the other person under paragraph (1) or (3) in relation to the notifiable contribution proposal or notifiable contribution arrangements is discharged if—

(*a*) the person who complied with paragraph (3) has notified the identity and address of the other person to HMRC or the other person holds the reference number allocated to the notifiable contribution arrangements under regulation 12; and

(*b*) the other person holds the information provided to HMRC in compliance with paragraph (3).

(10) Paragraph (11) applies where a person complies with section 308(3) in relation to notifiable arrangements and another person is a promoter in relation to a notifiable contribution proposal for arrangements or notifiable contribution arrangements which are substantially the same as the notifiable arrangements (whether they relate to the same or different parties).

(11) Any duty of the other person under paragraph (1) or (3) in relation to the notifiable contribution proposal or notifiable contribution arrangements is discharged if—

(*a*) the person who complied with section 308(3) in relation to the notifiable contribution arrangements has notified the identity and address of the other person to HMRC or the other person holds the reference number allocated to the notifiable contribution arrangements under section 311;and

(*b*) the other person holds the information provided to HMRC in compliance with section 308(3).

(12) Where a person is a promoter in relation to two or more notifiable contribution proposals or sets of notifiable contribution arrangements which are substantially the same (whether they relate to the same parties or different parties), that person need not provide information under paragraph (1) or (3) if that person has already provided information under either of those paragraphs in relation to any of the other contribution proposals or contribution arrangements.

Cross-reference See the National Insurance Contributions (Application of Part 7 of the Finance Act 2004) (Amendment) Regulations, SI 2013/2600 reg 1(2), (3) (those regulations not to have effect for the purposes of reg 8(1), (3) above if the relevant date falls before 4 November 2013, or if the date on which the promoter first becomes aware of any transaction forming part of notifiable contribution arrangements falls before 4 November 2013. "Relevant date" has the meaning given by reg 8(2) above.

9 Supplemental information

(1) This regulation applies where—

(*a*) a promoter ("P") has provided information in purported compliance with paragraph (1) or (3) of regulation 8; but

(*b*) HMRC believe that P has not provided all the prescribed information.

(2) HMRC may apply to the tribunal for an order requiring P to provide specified information about, or documents relating to, the notifiable contribution proposal or notifiable contribution arrangements.

(3) The tribunal may make an order under paragraph (2) in respect of information or documents only if satisfied that HMRC have reasonable grounds for suspecting that the information or documents—

(*a*) form part of the prescribed information; or

(*b*) will support or explain the prescribed information.

(4) A requirement by virtue of paragraph (2) shall be treated as part of P's duty under paragraph (1) or (3) of regulation 8.

(5) In so far as P's duty under paragraph (1) or (3) of regulation 8 arises out of a requirement by virtue of paragraph (2) above, the period for the purposes of those paragraphs of regulation 8 and the date after which it begins are those prescribed.

(6) In so far as P's duty under paragraph (1) or (3) of regulation 8 arises out of a requirement by virtue of paragraph (2) above, the prescribed period may be extended by HMRC by direction.

10 Duty of person dealing with promoter outside United Kingdom

(1) Any person ("the client") who enters into any transaction forming part of any notifiable contribution arrangements in relation to which—

(*a*) a promoter is resident outside the United Kingdom, and

(*b*) no promoter is resident in the United Kingdom,

must provide HMRC with the prescribed information relating to the notifiable contribution arrangements within the prescribed period.

(2) Compliance with regulation 8(1) by any promoter in relation to the notifiable contribution arrangements discharges the duty of the client under paragraph (1).

11 Duty of parties to notifiable contribution arrangements not involving promoter

Any person who enters into any transaction forming part of notifiable contribution arrangements as respects which neither that person nor any other person in the United Kingdom is liable to comply with regulation 8 or regulation 10 must at the prescribed time provide HMRC with the prescribed information relating to the notifiable contribution arrangements.

[11A Duty to provide further information requested by HMRC

(1) This regulation applies where—

(*a*) a person has provided the prescribed information about notifiable contribution proposals or notifiable contribution arrangements in compliance with regulation 8, 10 or 11, or

(*b*) a person has provided information in purported compliance with regulation 10 or 11 but HMRC believe that the person has not provided all the prescribed information.

(2) HMRC may require the person to provide—

(*a*) further specified information about the notifiable contribution proposals or notifiable contribution arrangements (in addition to the prescribed information under regulation 8, 10 or 11);

(*b*) documents relating to the notifiable contribution proposals or notifiable contribution arrangements.

(3) Where HMRC impose a requirement on a person under this regulation, the person must comply with the requirement within—

(*a*) the period of 10 working days beginning with the day on which HMRC imposed the requirement, or

(*b*) such longer period as HMRC may direct.][1]

Amendments—[1] Regulations 11A, 11B inserted by the National Insurance Contributions (Application of Part 7 of the Finance Act 2004) (Amendment) Regulations, SI 2015/531 regs 2, 5 with effect in relation to prescribed information about notifiable contribution proposals or notifiable contribution arrangements provided by a person in compliance, or purported compliance, with regs 8, 10, 11 of these regulations, on or after 12th April 2015. "Prescribed" has the meaning given in reg 2 of these regulations: SI 2015/531 reg 1(3).

[11B Failure to provide information under regulation 11A: application to the Tribunal

(1) This regulation applies where HMRC—

(*a*) have required a person to provide information or documents under regulation 11A, but

(*b*) believe that the person has failed to provide the information or documents required.

(2) HMRC may apply to the tribunal for an order requiring the person to provide the information or documents required.

(3) The tribunal may make an order under paragraph (2) only if satisfied that HMRC have reasonable grounds for suspecting that the information or documents will assist HMRC in considering the notifiable contribution proposals or notifiable contribution arrangements.

(4) Where the tribunal makes an order under paragraph (2), the person must comply with it within—

(*a*) the period of 10 working days beginning with the day on which the tribunal made the order, or

(*b*) such longer period as HMRC may direct.][1]

Amendments—[1] Regulations 11A, 11B inserted by the National Insurance Contributions (Application of Part 7 of the Finance Act 2004) (Amendment) Regulations, SI 2015/531 regs 2, 5 with effect in relation to prescribed information about notifiable contribution proposals or notifiable contribution arrangements provided by a person in compliance, or purported compliance, with regs 8, 10, 11 of these regulations, on or after 12th April 2015. "Prescribed" has the meaning given in reg 2 of these regulations: SI 2015/531 reg 1(3).

12 Arrangements to be given reference number

(1) Where a person complies or purports to comply with regulation 8(1) or (3), regulation 10(1) or regulation 11 in relation to any notifiable contribution proposal or notifiable contribution arrangements, HMRC—

(*a*) may within 30 days allocate a reference number in relation to the notifiable contribution arrangements, or in the case of a notifiable contribution proposal, to the proposed notifiable contribution arrangements; and

(*b*) if they do so, must notify that number to the person and (where the person is one who has complied or purported to comply with paragraph (1) or (3) of regulation 8) to any other person—

(i) who is a promoter in relation to the notifiable contribution proposal (or arrangements implementing the notifiable contribution proposal) or the notifiable contribution arrangements (or proposal implemented by the notifiable contribution arrangements), and

(ii) whose identity and address has been notified to HMRC by the person,

except that where the arrangements or proposal concern both national insurance contributions and tax, HMRC shall allocate a single reference number in respect of both matters.

(2) The allocation of a reference number to any notifiable contribution arrangements (or proposed notifiable contribution arrangements) is not to be regarded as constituting any indication by HMRC that the arrangements could as a matter of law result in the obtaining by any person of an advantage in relation to a contribution.

13 Duty of promoter to notify client of number

(1) This regulation applies where a person who is a promoter in relation to notifiable contribution arrangements is providing (or has provided) services to any person ("the client") in connection with the notifiable contribution arrangements.

(2) The promoter must, within 30 days after the relevant date, provide the client with the prescribed information relating to any reference number (or, if more than one, any one reference number) that has been notified to the promoter (whether by HMRC or any other person) in relation to—

(*a*) the notifiable contribution arrangements; or

(*b*) any arrangements, including notifiable arrangements, which are substantially the same as the notifiable contribution arrangements (whether involving the same or different parties).

(3) In paragraph (2) "the relevant date" means the later of—

(*a*) the date on which the promoter becomes aware of any transaction which forms part of the notifiable contribution arrangements; and

(*b*) the date on which the reference number is notified to the promoter.

(4) But where the conditions in paragraph (5) are met the duty imposed on the promoter under paragraph (2) to provide the client with information in relation to notifiable contribution arrangements is discharged.

(5) Those conditions are that—

(*a*) the promoter is also a promoter in relation to a notifiable contribution proposal and provides services to the client in connection with them both;

(*b*) the notifiable contribution proposal and the notifiable contribution arrangements are substantially the same; and

(*c*) the promoter has provided to the client, in a form and manner specified by HMRC, prescribed information relating to the reference number that has been notified to the promoter in relation to the proposed notifiable contribution arrangements.

(6) HMRC may give notice that, in relation to notifiable contribution arrangements specified in the notice, promoters are not under the duty under paragraph (2) after the date specified in the notice.

14 Duty of client to notify parties of number

(1) This regulation applies where a person (the "client") to whom a person who is a promoter in relation to notifiable contribution arrangements or a notifiable contribution proposal is providing (or has provided) services in connection with the notifiable contribution arrangements or notifiable contribution proposal receives prescribed information relating to the reference number allocated to—

(*a*) the notifiable contribution arrangements,

(*b*) the notifiable contribution proposal, or

(*c*) proposed notifiable arrangements, or notifiable arrangements, which are substantially the same as the notifiable contribution proposal or notifiable contribution arrangements.

(2) The client must, within the prescribed period, provide the prescribed information relating to the reference number to any other person—

(*a*) who the client might reasonably be expected to know is or is likely to be a party to the arrangements or proposed arrangements, and

(*b*) who might reasonably be expected to gain an advantage by reason of the arrangements or proposed arrangements.

(3) HMRC may give notice that, in relation to notifiable contribution arrangements or a notifiable contribution proposal specified in the notice, persons are not under the duty under paragraph (2) after the date specified in the notice.

(4) The duty under paragraph (2) does not apply in the prescribed circumstances.

[14A Duty of client to provide information to promoter

(1) This regulation applies where a person who is a promoter in relation to notifiable contribution arrangements has provided a person ("the client") with information under regulation 13(2) (duty of promoter to notify client of reference number).

(2) The client must, within the prescribed period, provide the promoter with the prescribed information relating to the client.][1]

Amendments—[1] Regulation 14A inserted by the National Insurance Contributions (Application of Part 7 of the Finance Act 2004) (Amendment) Regulations, SI 2013/2600 regs 2, 4 with effect from 4 November 2013. Note that SI 2013/2600 does not have effect for the purposes of reg 8(1), (3) if the relevant date falls before 4 November 2013, or if the date on which the promoter first becomes aware of any transaction forming part of notifiable contribution arrangements falls before 4 November 2013. "Relevant date" has the meaning given by reg 8(2) (SI 2013/2600 art 1(2), (3)).

15 Duty of parties to notifiable contribution arrangements to notify HMRC of number etc

(1) Any person who is a party to any notifiable contribution arrangements must, at the prescribed time or times, provide HMRC with the prescribed information relating to—

(*a*) any reference number notified to him, whether the reference number was allocated under regulation 12 or section 311, and
(*b*) the time when he obtains or expects to obtain by virtue of the arrangements an advantage in relation to any contribution.

(2) HMRC may give notice that, in relation to notifiable contribution arrangements specified in the notice, persons are not under the duty under paragraph (1) after the date specified in the notice.

16 Duty to provide details of clients

(1) This regulation applies where a person who is a promoter in relation to notifiable contribution arrangements is providing (or has provided) services to any person ("the client") in connection with the notifiable contribution arrangements and either—
(*a*) the promoter is subject to the reference number information requirement; or
(*b*) the promoter has failed to comply with regulation 8(1) or (3) in relation to the notifiable contributions arrangements (or the notifiable contribution proposal for them) but would be subject to the reference number information requirement if a reference number had been allocated to the notifiable contribution arrangements.

(2) For the purposes of this regulation "the reference number information requirement" is the requirement under regulation 13(2) to provide to the client prescribed information relating to the reference number allocated to the notifiable contribution arrangements.

(3) The promoter must, within the prescribed period after the end of the relevant period, provide HMRC with the prescribed information in relation to the client.

(4) In paragraph (3) "the relevant period" means the prescribed period during which the promoter is or would be subject to the reference number information requirement.

(5) The promoter need not comply with paragraph (3) in relation to any notifiable contribution arrangements at any time after HMRC have given notice under regulation 13(6) in relation to the arrangements.

[16A Enquiry following disclosure of client details

(1) This regulation applies where—
(*a*) a person who is a promoter in relation to notifiable contribution arrangements has provided HMRC with information in relation to a person ("the client") under regulation 16(3) (duty to provide details of clients); and
(*b*) HMRC suspect that a person other than the client is or is likely to be a party to the arrangements.

(2) HMRC may by written notice require the promoter to provide the prescribed information in relation to any person other than the client who the promoter might reasonably be expected to know is or is likely to be a party to the arrangements.

(3) The promoter must comply with a requirement under or by virtue of paragraph (2) within—
(*a*) the prescribed period; or
(*b*) such longer period as HMRC may direct.][1]

Amendments—[1] Regulation 16A inserted by the National Insurance Contributions (Application of Part 7 of the Finance Act 2004) (Amendment) Regulations, SI 2013/2600 regs 2, 5 with effect from 4 November 2013. Note that SI 2013/2600 does not have effect for the purposes of reg 8(1), (3) if the relevant date falls before 4 November 2013, or if the date on which the promoter first becomes aware of any transaction forming part of notifiable contribution arrangements falls before 4 November 2013. "Relevant date" has the meaning given by reg 8(2) (SI 2013/2600 art 1(2), (3)).

17 Pre-disclosure enquiry

(1) Where HMRC suspect that a person ("P") is the promoter or introducer of a proposal or arrangements which may be a notifiable contribution proposal or notifiable contribution arrangements, HMRC may by written notice require P to state—
(*a*) whether in P's opinion the proposal or arrangements are notifiable by P, and
(*b*) if not, the reasons for P's opinion.

(2) A notice must specify the proposal or arrangements to which it relates.

(3) For the purpose of paragraph (1)(b)—
(*a*) it is not sufficient to refer to the fact that a lawyer or other professional has given an opinion,
(*b*) the reasons must show, by reference to this Part and the Descriptions Regulations why P thinks the proposal or arrangements are not notifiable by P, and
(*c*) in particular, if P asserts that the arrangements do not fall within any description prescribed by the Descriptions Regulations the reasons must provide sufficient information to enable HMRC to confirm the assertion.

(4) P must comply with a requirement under or by virtue of paragraph (1) within—
(*a*) the prescribed period, or
(*b*) such longer period as HMRC may direct.

NIC

18 Reasons for non-disclosure: supporting information

(1) Where HMRC receive from a person ("P") a statement of reasons why a proposal or arrangements are not notifiable by P, HMRC may apply to the tribunal for an order requiring P to provide specified information or documents in support of the reasons.

(2) P must comply with a requirement under or by virtue of paragraph (1) within—

(*a*) the prescribed period, or

(*b*) such longer period as HMRC may direct.

(3) The power under paragraph (1)—

(*a*) may be exercised more than once, and

(*b*) applies whether or not the statement of reasons was received under regulation 17(1)(*b*).

19 Information provided to introducers

(1) Where HMRC suspect—

(*a*) that a person ("P") is an introducer in relation to a proposal; and

(*b*) that the proposal may be a notifiable contribution proposal,

HMRC may by written notice require P to provide HMRC with the prescribed information in relation to each person who has provided P with any information relating to the proposal.

(2) A notice must specify the proposal to which it relates.

(3) P must comply with a requirement under paragraph (1) within—

(*a*) the prescribed period; or

(*b*) such longer period as HMRC may direct.

20 Order to disclose

(1) HMRC may apply to the tribunal for an order that—

(*a*) a proposal is a notifiable contribution proposal, or

(*b*) arrangements are notifiable contribution arrangements.

(2) An application must specify—

(*a*) the proposal or arrangements in respect of which the order is sought, and

(*b*) the promoter.

(3) On an application the tribunal may make the order only if satisfied that section 132A(3) of the Social Security Administration Act 1992 applies to the relevant arrangements and that they are within a description prescribed by the Descriptions Regulations.

21 Information to be provided in form and manner specified by HMRC

(1) HMRC may specify the form and manner in which information required to be provided by any of the information provisions must be provided if the provision is to be complied with.

(2) The "information provisions" are regulations 8(1) and (3), 10(1), 11, [11A,][1] 13(2), 14(2), 15(1) and 16(3) and the Information Regulations.

Amendments—[1] In para (2), reference inserted by the National Insurance Contributions (Application of Part 7 of the Finance Act 2004) (Amendment) Regulations, SI 2015/531 regs 2, 6 with effect in relation to prescribed information about notifiable contribution proposals or notifiable contribution arrangements provided by a person in compliance, or purported compliance, with regs 8, 10, 11 of these regulations, on or after 12th April 2015. "Prescribed" has the meaning given in reg 2 of these regulations: SI 2015/531 reg 1(3).

PART 3
PROVISIONS CORRESPONDING TO SECTION 98C AND SECTION 118(2) OF THE TAXES MANAGEMENT ACT 1970 AND MODIFICATIONS OF RELATED PROVISIONS

22 Notification under Part 2

(1) A person who fails to comply with any of the provisions of Part 2 mentioned in paragraph (2) below shall be liable—

(*a*) to a penalty not exceeding—

(i) in the case of a provision mentioned in sub-paragraph (*a*), (*b*)[, (*c*) or (*ca*)][1] of that paragraph, £600 for each day during the initial period (but see also paragraphs (5), (7) and (8) below); and

(ii) in any other case, £5,000; and

(*b*) if the failure continues after a penalty is imposed under sub-paragraph (*a*) above, to a further penalty or penalties not exceeding £600 for each day on which the failure continues after the day on which the penalty under sub-paragraph (*a*) was imposed (but excluding any day for which a penalty under this paragraph has already been imposed).

This is subject to paragraph (14).

(2) Those provisions are—

(*a*) regulation 8(1) and (3) (duty of promoter in relation to notifiable contribution proposals and notifiable contribution arrangements),

(*b*) regulation 10(1) (duty of person dealing with promoter outside United Kingdom),

(*c*) regulation 11 (duty of parties to notifiable contribution arrangements not involving promoter),

[(*ca*) regulation 11A (duty to provide further information requested by HMRC),][2]
(*d*) regulation 13(2) (duty of promoter to notify client of reference number),
(*e*) regulation 14(2) (duty of client to notify parties of reference number),
[(*ea*) regulation 14A(2) (duty of client to provide information to promoter),][1]
(*f*) regulation 16 (duty of promoter to provide details of clients),
[(*fa*) regulation 16A (duty of promoter to provide further information),][1]
(*g*) regulations 17 and 18 (duty of promoter to respond to inquiry), and
(*h*) regulation 19 (duty of introducer to give details of persons who have provided information).

(3) In this regulation "the initial period" means the period—
(*a*) beginning with the relevant day; and
(*b*) ending with the earlier of the day on which the penalty under paragraph (1)(*a*)(i) is determined and the last day before the failure ceases;

and for this purpose "the relevant day" is the day specified in relation to the failure in the following table.

TABLE

Failure	*Relevant day*
A failure to comply with paragraph (1) or (3) of regulation 8 in so far as the paragraph applies by virtue of an order under regulation 6	The first day of the prescribed period
A failure to comply with paragraph (1) or (3) of regulation 8 in so far as the paragraph applies by virtue of an order under regulation 9(2)	The first day after the end of the prescribed period (as it may have been extended by a direction under regulation 9(6))
Any other failure to comply with paragraph (1) of regulation 8	The first day after the end of the prescribed period
Any other failure to comply with paragraph (3) of regulation 8	The first day after the end of the prescribed period
A failure to comply with paragraph (1) of regulation 10	The first day after the end of the prescribed period
A failure to comply with regulation 11	The first day after the latest time by which regulation 11 must be complied with in the case concerned
[A failure to comply with regulation 11A	The first day after the end of the period within which the person must comply with regulation 11A][1]

(4) The amount of a penalty under paragraph (1)(*a*)(i) is to be arrived at after taking account of all relevant considerations, including the desirability of its being set at a level which appears appropriate for deterring the person, or other persons, from similar failures to comply on future occasions having regard (in particular)-
(*a*) in the case of a penalty for a [promoter's][1] failure to comply with regulation 8(1) or (3) [or regulation 11A][1], to the amount of any fees received, or likely to have been received, by the [promoter][1] in connection with the notifiable contribution proposal (or arrangements implementing the notifiable contribution proposal), or with the notifiable contribution arrangements;
(*b*) in the case of a penalty for the [relevant][1] person's failure to comply with regulation 10(1)[, 11 or 11A][1], to the amount of any advantage gained, or sought to be gained, by the [relevant][1] person in relation to any contribution.

[(4A) In paragraph 4—
(*a*) "promoter" has the same meaning as in regulation 7, and
(*b*) "relevant person" means a person who enters into any transaction forming part of notifiable contribution arrangements within the meaning of regulation 5.][1]

(5) If the maximum penalty under paragraph (1)(*a*)(i) above appears inappropriately low after taking account of those considerations, the penalty is to be of such amount not exceeding £1 million as appears appropriate having regard to those considerations.

(6) Where it appears to an officer of Revenue and Customs that a penalty under paragraph (1)(*a*)(i) above has been determined on the basis that the initial period begins with a day later than that which the officer considers to be the relevant day, an officer of Revenue and Customs may commence proceedings for a re-determination of the penalty.

NIC

(7) Where a failure to comply with a provision mentioned in paragraph (2) concerns a proposal or arrangements in respect of which an order has been made under regulation 6 (doubt as to notifiability), the amounts specified in paragraph (1)(*a*)(i) and (*b*) shall be increased to the sum prescribed by the Tax Avoidance Schemes (Penalty) Regulations 2007 (as modified by these Regulations).

(8) Where a failure to comply with a provision mentioned in paragraph (2) concerns a proposal or arrangements in respect of which an order has been made under regulation 20 (order to disclose), the amounts specified in paragraph (1)(*a*)(i) and (*b*) shall be increased to the sum prescribed by the Tax Avoidance Schemes (Penalty) Regulations 2007 (as modified by these Regulations) in relation to the days falling after the prescribed period.

(9) The making of an order under regulation 6 or 20 does not of itself mean that, for the purposes of regulation 23, a person either did or did not have a reasonable excuse for non-compliance before the order was made.

(10) Where an order is made under regulation 6 or 20 then for the purposes of regulation 23—

(*a*) the person identified in the order as the promoter of the proposal or arrangements cannot, in respect of any time after the end of the period mentioned in paragraph (8), rely on doubt as to notifiability as an excuse for failure to comply with regulation 8, and

(*b*) any delay in compliance with that regulation after the end of that period is unreasonable unless attributable to something other than doubt as to notifiability.

[(10A) Where a person fails to comply with—

(*a*) regulation 10 and the promoter for the purposes of that regulation is a monitored promoter for the purposes of Part 5 of the Finance Act 2014, or

(*b*) regulation 11 and the notifiable contribution arrangements for the purposes of that regulation are arrangements of such a monitored promoter,

then for the purposes of regulation 23 (interpretation) legal advice which the person took into account is to be disregarded in determining whether the person had a reasonable excuse, if the advice was given or procured by that monitored promoter.

(10B) In determining for the purpose of regulation 23 whether or not a person who is a monitored promoter within the meaning of Part 5 of the Finance Act 2014 had a reasonable excuse for a failure to do anything required to be done under a provision mentioned in paragraph (2), reliance on legal advice is to be taken automatically not to constitute a reasonable excuse if either—

(*a*) the advice was not based on a full and accurate description of the facts, or

(*b*) the conclusions in the advice that the person relied on were unreasonable.][1]

(11) A person who fails to comply with regulation 15(1) (duty of parties to notifiable contribution arrangements to notify HMRC of number, etc) or regulation 10 of the Information Regulations shall be liable to a penalty of the relevant sum.

This is subject to paragraph (14).

(12) In paragraph (11) "the relevant sum" means—

(*a*) in relation to a person not falling within sub-paragraph (*b*) or (*c*) below, £100 in respect of each scheme to which the failure relates,

(*b*) in relation to a person who has previously failed to comply with regulation 15(1) or regulation 10 of the Information Regulations on one (and only one) occasion during the period of 36 months ending with the date on which the current failure to comply with that provision began, £500 in respect of each scheme to which the current failure relates (whether or not the same as the scheme to which the previous failure relates), or

(*c*) in relation to a person who has previously failed to comply with regulation 15(1) or regulation 10 of the Information Regulations on two or more occasions during the period of 36 months ending with the date on which the current failure to comply with that provision began, £1,000 in respect of each scheme to which the current failure relates (whether or not the same as the schemes to which any of the previous failures relates).

(13) In paragraph (12) above "scheme" means any notifiable contribution arrangements which fall within any description prescribed by the Descriptions Regulations.

(14) Where the notifiable contribution arrangements or proposed notifiable contribution arrangements are, or are substantially the same as, a notifiable arrangements or proposed notifiable arrangements under Part 7 in relation to which a penalty has been imposed under section 98C of the Taxes Management Act 1970 in respect of a failure to comply with the provisions of Part 7, this regulation shall not apply to impose a penalty in respect of the failure to comply with the corresponding provision of these Regulations.

Amendments—[1] Sub-para (2)(*ea*), (*fa*) inserted by the National Insurance Contributions (Application of Part 7 of the Finance Act 2004) (Amendment) Regulations, SI 2013/2600 regs 2, 6 with effect from 4 November 2013. Note that SI 2013/2600 does not have effect for the purposes of reg 8(1), (3) if the relevant date falls before 4 November 2013, or if the date on which the promoter first becomes aware of any transaction forming part of notifiable contribution arrangements falls before 4 November 2013. "Relevant date" has the meaning given by reg 8(2) (SI 2013/2600 art 1(2), (3)).

[2] The following amendments made by the National Insurance Contributions (Application of Part 7 of the Finance Act 2004) (Amendment) Regulations, SI 2015/531 regs 2, 7 with effect in relation to prescribed information about notifiable contribution

proposals or notifiable contribution arrangements provided by a person in compliance, or purported compliance, with regs 8, 10, 11 of these regulations, on or after 12th April 2015. "Prescribed" has the meaning given in reg 2 of these regulations: SI 2015/531 reg 1(3)—

- in paras(1)(*a*)(i), (4)(*a*), (*b*), words substituted;
- paras (2)(*ca*), (4A), (10A), (10B) and table entry in para (3) inserted; and
- in paras (4)(*a*), (4)(*b*), words inserted.

23 Interpretation

For the purposes of this Part—

(*a*) a person shall be deemed not to have failed to do anything required to be done within a limited time if it was done within such further time, if any, as HMRC may have allowed; and

(*b*) where a person had a reasonable excuse for not doing anything required to be done—

(i) that person shall be deemed not to have failed to do it unless the excuse ceased; and

(ii) after the excuse ceased, that person shall be deemed not to have failed to do it if it was done without unreasonable delay after the excuse had ceased.

24 Modification of Part 10 of the Taxes Management Act 1970

(1) Part 10 of the Taxes Management Act 1970 so far as it relates to a penalty under section 98C of that Act shall apply in relation to a penalty under regulation 22 with the following modifications.

(2) In section 100 (determination of penalties by officer of Board) for subsection (2)(*f*) (penalties to which subsection (1) of the section does not apply) substitute—

"(*f*) regulation 22(1)(*a*) of the National Insurance Contributions (Application of Part 7 of the Finance Act 2004) Regulations 2012.".

PART 4

MODIFICATION OF REGULATIONS UNDER PART 7

25 Modification of the Descriptions Regulations

(1) The Descriptions Regulations apply to notifiable contribution arrangements and notifiable contribution proposals with the following modifications and any reference in those Regulations to sections 306 to 313C and section 314A shall be construed as a reference to the corresponding provision of these Regulations (see regulation 5(2)).

(2) In regulation 1 (citation, commencement and effect) omit paragraphs (2) and (3).

(3) In regulation 5 (prescribed descriptions of arrangements)—

(*a*) in paragraph (1) for "income tax, corporation tax and capital gains tax" substitute "national insurance contributions", and

(*b*) in paragraph (2) omit [sub-paragraphs (*f*) to (*g*)][1].

(4) In Part 3—

(*a*) for "tax advantage" wherever it occurs substitute "advantage within the meaning given by section 132A(7) of the Social Security Administration Act 1992"; and

(*b*) for "a tax advantage" wherever it occurs substitute "an advantage within the meaning given by section 132A(7) of the Social Security Administration Act 1992".

(5) In regulation 10 (Description 5: standardised tax products), in the heading and paragraphs (1) and (3) for "tax product" substitute "national insurance contributions product".

(6) Omit regulations [12 to 17][1].

Amendments—[1] In sub-paras (3)(*b*), (6), words substituted by the National Insurance Contributions (Application of Part 7 of the Finance Act 2004) (Amendment) Regulations, SI 2013/2600 regs 2, 7 with effect from 4 November 2013. Note that SI 2013/2600 does not have effect for the purposes of reg 8(1), (3) if the relevant date falls before 4 November 2013, or if the date on which the promoter first becomes aware of any transaction forming part of notifiable contribution arrangements falls before 4 November 2013. "Relevant date" has the meaning given by reg 8(2) (SI 2013/2600 art 1(2), (3)).

26 The Information Regulations

(1) The Information Regulations apply to notifiable contribution arrangements and notifiable contribution proposals with the following modifications and—

(*a*) any reference in those Regulations to sections 306 to 313C and section 314A shall be construed as a reference to the corresponding provision of these Regulations (see regulation 5(2)); and

(*b*) any reference in those Regulations to section 98C of the Taxes Management Act 1970 shall be construed as a reference to regulation 22 of these Regulations.

(2) In regulation 2 (interpretation)—

(*a*) insert the following definition immediately before the definition of "employment"—

""contributions" means national insurance contributions;";

[(*aa*) in sub-paragraph (*a*) of the definition of "the filing date" omit "or in the case of inheritance tax the last day of the period mentioned in regulation 9(5)(*b*);][1]

(*b*) after the definition of "filing date" insert—

""notifiable contribution arrangements" has the meaning given by section 132A(3) of the Social Security Administration Act 1992;

"notifiable contribution proposal" has the meaning given by section 132A(3) of the Social Security Administration Act 1992;";

(*c*) omit the definition of "the prescribed taxes".

(3) In regulation 4 (prescribed information in respect of notifiable proposals and arrangements)—

(*a*) wherever the words appear—

(i) for "any of the prescribed taxes" substitute "the contributions";

(ii) for "notifiable arrangements" substitute "notifiable contribution arrangements";

(iii) for "notifiable proposal" substitute "notifiable contribution proposal"; and

(iv) for "tax advantage" substitute "advantage";

(*b*) in paragraphs (1)(*b*), (2)(*c*) and (3)(*b*) omit "[, the ATED Arrangements Regulations, the IHT Arrangements Regulations or the SDLT Arrangements Regulations"][1]; and

(*c*) in paragraph (5) omit the definitions of [""the ATED Arrangements Regulations",][1] "the IHT Arrangements Regulations" and "the SDLT Arrangements Regulations".

(4) In regulation 5 (time for providing information under section 308, 308A, 309 or 310)—

(*a*) in paragraph (2) for "proposal or arrangements" substitute "contribution proposal or contribution arrangements";

(*b*) in paragraph (3) for "notifiable proposal or arrangements" substitute "notifiable contribution proposal or notifiable contribution arrangements"; and

(*c*) in paragraphs (6), (7) and (8) for "notifiable arrangements" substitute "notifiable contribution arrangements".

(5) In regulation 7 (time for providing information under section 312A) for "notifiable arrangements" substitute "notifiable contribution arrangements".

(6) In regulation 8 (exemption from duty under section 312A)—

(*a*) for "a tax advantage in respect of income tax or capital gains tax" substitute "an advantage"; and

(*b*) for "notifiable arrangements" substitute "notifiable contribution arrangements".

[(6A) In regulation 8A (prescribed information under section 312B: information and timing) for "notifiable arrangements" wherever it occurs substitute "notifiable contribution arrangements".][1]

(7) Omit regulation 9.

(8) For regulation 10 (prescribed cases under section 313(3)(b)) substitute—

"10 Prescribed information under regulation 15 of the National Insurance Contributions (Application of Part 7 of the Finance Act 2004) Regulations 2012: timing and manner of delivery

(1) For the purposes of regulation 15 of the National Insurance Contributions (Application of Part 7 of the Finance Act 2004) Regulations 2012 (duty of parties to notifiable contribution arrangements to notify HMRC of number, etc) the prescribed information is—

(*a*) the reference number allocated by HMRC under regulation 12 to the notifiable contribution arrangements or notifiable contribution proposal;

(*b*) the earnings period in which the person making the notification expects an advantage to be obtained; and

(*c*) the employer's name, address and Unique Taxpayer Reference (UTR).

(2) The prescribed information shall be provided by the employer to HMRC in such form and manner as they may specify.

(3) Unless paragraph (4) applies, the prescribed time at which a person who is a party to notifiable contribution arrangements must provide HMRC with information under regulation 15 is whichever of (a) or (b) below applies in respect of the tax year in which the employer first enters into a transaction forming part of the notifiable contribution arrangements and whichever applies in respect of each subsequent year until an advantage ceases to apply to any person—

(*a*) in the case of a non-Real Time Information employer any time before the date on which the return under paragraph 22(1) of Schedule 4 to the Social Security (Contributions) Regulations 2001 (return by employer at end of year) is or would be due; or

(*b*) in the case of a Real Time Information employer, 14 days after the end of the final tax period of the tax year.

In this paragraph, "non-Real Time Information employer" and "Real Time Information employer" have the meanings given in paragraph 1 of Schedule 4 to the Social Security Contributions Regulations 2001 (interpretation; provisions derived from the Income Tax Acts and the Income Tax (Pay As You Earn) Regulations 2003).

(4) Where the advantage which is expected to arise from the notifiable contribution arrangements relates to Class 1A contributions only, and the transactions which comprise the notifiable contribution arrangements do not give rise to an advantage in relation to tax, the prescribed time is any time before the date on which the return under regulation 80(1) of the Social Security (Contributions) Regulations 2001 (return by employer) is or would be due—

(*a*) for the year in which the employer first enters into a transaction forming part of the notifiable contribution arrangements; and

(*b*) for each subsequent year until the advantage ceases to apply to any person.

In this paragraph the term "an advantage in relation to tax" shall be construed in accordance with section 318(1).".

(9) Omit regulations 11 and 12.

(10) In regulation 13(1)(*b*)(i) (prescribed information under section 313ZA: information and timing) before "arrangements" insert "contribution".

[(10A) In regulation 13A(1)(*b*)(i) (prescribed information under section 313ZB: information and timing) for "a tax advantage" substitute "an advantage".][1]

(11) In regulation 15(1)(*b*) (prescribed information under section 313C: information and timing) before "proposal" insert "contribution".

(12) In regulation 17 (electronic delivery of information)—

(*a*) in paragraph (2)—

(i) for sub-paragraph (*a*) substitute—

"(*a*) it is authorised by virtue of Part 7A of the Social Security (Contributions) Regulations 2001 (electronic communications); and";

(ii) in paragraph (*b*) for "section" substitute "Part".

(*b*) in paragraph (3)(*a*) for "regulations under section 132 of the Finance Act 1999" substitute "Part 7A of the Social Security (Contributions) Regulations 2001 (electronic communications)".

(13) Omit regulation 18.

Amendments—[1] Sub-paras (2)(*aa*), (6), (10A) inserted, in sub-para (3)(*b*), words substituted, and in sub-para (3)(*b*), words inserted by the National Insurance Contributions (Application of Part 7 of the Finance Act 2004) (Amendment) Regulations, SI 2013/2600 regs 2, 8–12 with effect from 4 November 2013. Note that SI 2013/2600 does not have effect for the purposes of reg 8(1), (3) if the relevant date falls before 4 November 2013, or if the date on which the promoter first becomes aware of any transaction forming part of notifiable contribution arrangements falls before 4 November 2013. "Relevant date" has the meaning given by reg 8(2) (SI 2013/2600 art 1(2), (3)).

27 The Tax Avoidance Schemes (Promoters and Prescribed Circumstances) Regulations 2004

(1) The Tax Avoidance Schemes (Promoters and Prescribed Circumstances) Regulations 2004 apply to notifiable contribution arrangements and notifiable contribution proposals as they apply to income tax with the following modifications and any reference in those Regulations to sections 306 to 313C and section 314A shall be construed as a reference to the corresponding provision of these Regulations (see regulation 5(2)).

(2) In regulation 1 (citation, commencement and interpretation) for paragraph (2) substitute—

"(2) In these Regulations—

"notifiable contribution arrangements" and "notifiable contribution proposal" have the meanings given by section 132A(3) of the Social Security Administration Act 1992.".

(3) In regulation 4 (persons not to be treated as promoters under section 307(1)(*a*)(i) or (*b*)(i))—

(*a*) for "tax advice" wherever it occurs substitute "advice about national insurance contributions"; and

(*b*) for "tax advantage" wherever it occurs substitute "advantage".

(4) In regulation 6 (legal professional privilege) for "section 314" substitute "section 132A(6) of the Social Security Administration Act 1992".

28 The Tax Avoidance Schemes (Penalty) Regulations 2007

The Tax Avoidance Schemes (Penalty) Regulations 2007 apply to notifiable contribution arrangements and notifiable contribution proposals as they apply to income tax and—

(*a*) any reference in those Regulations to sections 306 to 313C and section 314A shall be construed as a reference to the corresponding provision of these Regulations (see regulation 5(2)); and

(*b*) any reference in those Regulations to section 98C of the Taxes Management Act 1970 shall be construed as a reference to regulation 22 of these Regulations.

PART 5
REVOCATIONS

29 The following instruments are revoked.

(*a*) the National Insurance Contributions (Application of Part 7 of the Finance Act 2004) Regulations 2007;

(*b*) the National Insurance Contributions (Application of Part 7 of the Finance Act 2004) (Amendment) Regulations 2008;

(*c*) the National Insurance Contributions (Application of Part 7 of the Finance Act 2004) (Amendment) Regulations 2009;

NIC

(*d*) the National Insurance Contributions (Application of Part 7 of the Finance Act 2004) (Amendment) (No 2) Regulations 2009; and

(*e*) the National Insurance Contributions (Application of Part 7 of the Finance Act 2004) (Amendment) Regulations 2010.

2013/527

SOCIAL SECURITY REVALUATION OF EARNINGS FACTORS ORDER 2013

Made..*6 March 2013*

Laid before Parliament..........................*11 March 2013*

Coming into force...............................*6 April 2013*

In accordance with section 148(2) (revaluation of earnings factors) of the Social Security Administration Act 1992, the Secretary of State has reviewed the general level of earnings obtaining in Great Britain.

The Secretary of State has concluded, having regard to earlier orders made under section 148, that earnings factors for the relevant tax years have not, during the period taken into account for that review, maintained their value in relation to the general level of earnings.

The Secretary of State makes the following Order in exercise of the powers conferred by sections 148(3) and (4) and 189(1), (4) and (5) of the Social Security Administration Act 1992.

1 Citation and commencement

This Order may be cited as the Social Security Revaluation of Earnings Factors Order 2013 and shall come into force on 6th April 2013.

2 Revaluation of earnings factors

The earnings factors for tax years specified in the Schedule to this Order in so far as they are relevant—

(*a*) to the calculation—

(i) of the additional pension in the rate of any long-term benefit, or

(ii) of any guaranteed minimum pension; or

(*b*) to any other calculation required under Part 3 of the Pension Schemes Act 1993 (including that Part as modified by or under any other enactment),

are directed to be increased for those tax years by the percentage of their amount shown opposite those tax years in that Schedule.

3 Rounding of fractional amounts

Where any earnings factor relevant to the calculation specified in article 2(*a*)(i) of this Order, as increased in accordance with this Order, would not but for this article be expressed as a whole number of pounds, it shall be so expressed by rounding down any fraction of a pound less than one half and rounding up any other fraction of a pound.

SCHEDULE

PERCENTAGE INCREASE OF EARNINGS FACTOR FOR SPECIFIED TAX YEARS

Article 2

Tax year	Percentage increase
1978–1979	734.2
1979–1980	636.3
1980–1981	515.1
1981–1982	415.2
1982–1983	367.9
1983–1984	334.5
1984–1985	302.3
1985–1986	277.4
1986–1987	246.5
1987–1988	222.7
1988–1989	196.8
1989–1990	167.9
1990–1991	149.7

1991–1992	126.8
1992–1993	112.9
1993–1994	102.8
1994–1995	96.7
1995–1996	88.4
1996–1997	83.3
1997–1998	74.5
1998–1999	66.9
1999–2000	60.1
2000–2001	50.7
2001–2002	44.9
2002–2003	38.9
2003–2004	34.1
2004–2005	29.2
2005–2006	24.1
2006–2007	20.0
2007–2008	15.3
2008–2009	10.6
2009–2010	7.3
2010–2011	6.0
2011–2012	3.6
2012–2013	1.8

2013/622

SOCIAL SECURITY (CONTRIBUTIONS) (AMENDMENT AND APPLICATION OF SCHEDULE 38 TO THE FINANCE ACT 2012) REGULATIONS 2013

Made . . . . 14 March 2013

Laid before Parliament . . . . 15 March 2013

Coming into force in accordance with Regulation 1

These Regulations are made by the Treasury and the Commissioners for Her Majesty's Revenue and Customs with the concurrence of the Secretary of State and the Department for Social Development in relation to regulations 33, 39, 40 and 42 and to regulation 2 in so far as it relates to regulations 33, 39, 40 and 42.

The powers exercised by the Treasury are those conferred by sections 1(6), 3(2) and (3), 10(9), 12(6), 13(1) and (7), 19(1) and (5A), and 175(3) and (4) of, and paragraph 7B(5A) of Schedule 1 to, the Social Security Contributions and Benefits Act 1992 and sections 1(6), 3(2) and (3), 10(9), 12(6), 13(1) and (7), 19(1) and (5A) and 171(3), (4) and (10) of, and paragraph 7B(5A) of Schedule 1 to, the Social Security Contributions and Benefits (Northern Ireland) Act 1992 and now exercisable by them.

The powers exercised by the Commissioners for Her Majesty's Revenue and Customs are those conferred by section 175(4) of, and paragraph 6(1) and (2) of Schedule 1 to, the Social Security Contributions and Benefits Act 1992 and section 171(4) and (10) of, and paragraph 6(1) and (2) of Schedule 1 to, the Social Security Contributions and Benefits (Northern Ireland) Act 1992 and now exercisable by them.

PART 1
GENERAL

1 Citation, commencement, effect and interpretation

(1) These Regulations may be cited as the Social Security (Contributions) (Amendment and Application of Schedule 38 to the Finance Act 2012) Regulations 2013.

(2) Regulations 1, 2 and 5 to 42 come into force on 6th April 2013 and apply in relation to the tax year 2013–14 and subsequent tax years.

(3) Regulations 3 and 4 come into force on 6th April 2014 and apply in relation to the tax year 2014–15.

(4) The amendments made by regulation 36 have effect in relation to contributions paid in respect of the tax year 2012–2013 and subsequent tax years.

(5) In these Regulations "the 2001 Regulations" mean the Social Security (Contributions) Regulations 2001.

2 Amendment of the 2001 Regulations

The 2001 Regulations are amended as provided for in regulations 3 to 28 and 33 to 40.

PART 3

REAL TIME INFORMATION

CHAPTER 2

REAL TIME INFORMATION: TRANSITIONAL PROVISIONS

29 Information about employees

On becoming a Real Time Information employer, an employer must provide to HMRC—

(*a*) the information specified in paragraphs 2 to 4 of Schedule A1 to the PAYE Regulations,

(*b*) the income tax year in which the employer became a Real Time Information employer,

(*c*) the following information about each of the employer's employees during the tax year in which the employer became a Real Time Information employer—

(i) the employee's name,

(ii) the employee's date of birth,

(iii) the employee's current gender,

(iv) if known, the employee's national insurance number,

(v) the employee's address, and

(vi) the number used by the employer to identify the employee, if any.

30 Information about payments to employees

(1) Within one month of making the first return under paragraph 21A or 21D of Schedule 4 to the 2001 Regulations, a Real Time Information employer must provide to HMRC the information specified in paragraph (2) in respect of—

(*a*) each employee who has been employed in the tax year the return was made in but whose employment had ceased before the date on which the return was made, and

(*b*) each employee to whom the relevant payments are made on an irregular basis and—

(i) in respect of whom information was not included on that return, and

(ii) to whom the employer does not expect to make a relevant payment within one month of making the return.

(2) The information specified in this paragraph is that specified in—

(*a*) paragraphs 3A, 6 to 9, 10(*b*), 10(*d*) and 12 of Schedule 4A to the 2001 Regulations, and

(*b*) paragraphs 2 to 4 of Schedule A1 to the PAYE Regulations.

31 Provision of information under regulations 29 and 30

(1) If an employer is one to whom paragraph (3) applies, the information required by regulation 27 must be provided before the employer makes any returns under paragraph 21A or 21D of Schedule 4 to the 2001 Regulations.

(2) Any other employer may provide the information required by regulation 27 as part of the first return the employer makes under paragraph 21A or 21D of Schedule 4 to the 2001 Regulations.

(3) This paragraph applies to an employer who, on the day the employer becomes a Real Time Information employer, employs 250 or more employees.

(4) The information required by regulations 29 and 30 must be provided using an approved method of electronic communications unless the employer is one to whom paragraph 21D of Schedule 4 to the 2001 Regulations applies in which case the information must be provided in the form specified by HMRC.

32 Regulations 29 to 31 interpretation

Terms used in regulations 29 to 31 have the same meaning as they have in the 2001 Regulations.

PART 5

TAX AGENTS: DISHONEST CONDUCT

41 Application of Schedule 38 to the Finance Act 2012

The provisions of Schedule 38 to the Finance Act 2012 (tax agents: dishonest conduct) apply in relation to Class 1, Class 1A, Class 1B and Class 2 National Insurance contributions as in relation to tax to the extent that they do not already apply.

PART 6
REPEALS

42 Amendment of the Social Security (Contributions) (Amendment No 5) Regulations 2001

In the Social Security (Contributions) (Amendment No 5) Regulations 2001 omit—

(*a*) regulation 3(2)(*a*);
(*b*) regulation 4; and
(*c*) regulation 5(2)(*b*).

2013/1510

SOCIAL SECURITY (PERSONS REQUIRED TO PROVIDE INFORMATION) REGULATIONS 2013

Made . . . . *20 June 2013*
Laid before Parliament . . . . *27 June 2013*
Coming into force . . . . *1 October 2013*

The Secretary of State for Work and Pensions makes the following Regulations in exercise of the powers conferred by sections 109B(2)(*ia*), 189(1) and (5) and 191 of the Social Security Administration Act 1992.

In accordance with section 176(1) of that Act, the Secretary of State has consulted with organisations appearing to him to be representative of the authorities concerned.

This instrument has not been referred to the Social Security Advisory Committee because it contains only regulations made by virtue of section 110 of the Welfare Reform Act 2012 and is made before the end of the period of 6 months beginning with the coming into force of that section.

1 Citation and commencement

(1) These Regulations may be cited as the Social Security (Persons Required to Provide Information) Regulations 2013.

(2) They come into force on 1st October 2013.

2 Persons required to provide information

(1) The following are prescribed as descriptions of persons for the purpose of section 109B(2)(ia) of the Social Security Administration Act 1992 (power of authorised officers to require information)—

(*a*) a person who provides relevant childcare;
(*b*) a person to whom a person in receipt of universal credit ("C") is liable to make rent payments in respect of accommodation which C occupies, or purports to occupy, as their home where C's award of universal credit includes an amount in respect of such payments;
(*c*) a rent officer to the extent that the information required relates to the rent officer's functions under section 122 of the Housing Act 1996;
(*d*) a local authority which administers a council tax reduction scheme to the extent that the information required relates to such a scheme.

(2) In this regulation—

(*a*) "UC Regulations" means the Universal Credit Regulations 2013;
(*b*) "council tax reduction scheme"—
 (i) in England and Wales, has the meaning given in section 13A(9) of the Local Government Finance Act 1992 and includes a default scheme within the meaning of paragraph 4 of Schedule 1A (or in Wales paragraph 6(1)(*e*) of Schedule 1B) to that Act; and
 (ii) in Scotland, means a means-tested reduction to an individual's council tax liability in accordance with the Council Tax Reduction (Scotland) Regulations 2012 or the Council Tax Reduction (State Pension Credit) (Scotland) Regulations 2012;
(*c*) "relevant childcare" has the meaning given in regulation 35 of the UC Regulations;
(*d*) "rent payments" has the meaning given in paragraph 2 of Schedule 1 to the UC Regulations;
(*e*) "universal credit" means universal credit under Part 1 of the Welfare Reform Act 2012.

2014/367

SOCIAL SECURITY REVALUATION OF EARNINGS FACTORS ORDER 2014

Made . . . . *19 February 2014*
Laid before Parliament . . . . *26 February 2014*
Coming into force . . . . *6 April 2014*

NIC

In accordance with section 148(2) (revaluation of earnings factors) of the Social Security Administration Act 1992, the Secretary of State has reviewed the general level of earnings obtaining in Great Britain.

The Secretary of State has concluded, having regard to earlier orders made under section 148, that earnings factors for the relevant tax years have not, during the period taken into account for that review, maintained their value in relation to the general level of earnings.

The Secretary of State makes the following Order in exercise of the powers conferred by sections 148(3) and (4) and 189(1), (4) and (5) of the Social Security Administration Act 1992.

1 Citation and commencement

This Order may be cited as the Social Security Revaluation of Earnings Factors Order 2014 and shall come into force on 6th April 2014.

2 Revaluation of earnings factors

The earnings factors for tax years specified in the Schedule to this Order in so far as they are relevant—

(*a*) to the calculation—

(i) of the additional pension in the rate of any long-term benefit, or

(ii) of any guaranteed minimum pension; or

(*b*) to any other calculation required under Part 3 of the Pension Schemes Act 1993 (including that Part as modified by or under any other enactment),

are directed to be increased for those tax years by the percentage of their amount shown opposite those tax years in that Schedule.

3 Rounding of fractional amounts

Where any earnings factor relevant to the calculation specified in article 2(*a*)(i) of this Order, as increased in accordance with this Order, would not but for this article be expressed as a whole number of pounds, it shall be so expressed by rounding down any fraction of a pound less than one half and rounding up any other fraction of a pound.

SCHEDULE

PERCENTAGE INCREASE OF EARNINGS FACTOR FOR SPECIFIED TAX YEARS

Article 2

Tax year	*Percentage increase*
1978–1979	741.7
1979–1980	642.9
1980–1981	520.7
1981–1982	419.8
1982–1983	372.1
1983–1984	338.4
1984–1985	305.9
1985–1986	280.8
1986–1987	249.7
1987–1988	225.6
1988–1989	199.5
1989–1990	170.3
1990–1991	151.9
1991–1992	128.8
1992–1993	114.8
1993–1994	104.6
1994–1995	98.5
1995–1996	90.1
1996–1997	84.9
1997–1998	76.1
1998–1999	68.4
1999–2000	61.6
2000–2001	52.0

2001–2002	46.2
2002–2003	40.1
2003–2004	35.3
2004–2005	30.3
2005–2006	25.2
2006–2007	21.1
2007–2008	16.3
2008–2009	11.6
2009–2010	8.3
2010–2011	7.0
2011–2012	4.6
2012–2013	2.7
2013–2014	0.9

2014/368

SOCIAL SECURITY PENSIONS (LOW EARNINGS THRESHOLD) ORDER 2014

Made . . . . *19 February 2014*
Laid before Parliament . . . . *25 February 2014*
Coming into force . . . . *6 April 2014*

In accordance with section 148A(1) (revaluation of low earnings threshold) of the Social Security Administration Act 1992, the Secretary of State has reviewed the general level of earnings obtaining in Great Britain.

It appears to the Secretary of State that the general level of earnings has increased during the review period.

The Secretary of State makes the following Order in exercise of the powers conferred by sections 148A(3) to (5) and 189(1), (4) and (5) of the Social Security Administration Act 1992.

1 Citation and commencement

This Order may be cited as the Social Security Pensions (Low Earnings Threshold) Order 2014 and shall come into force on 6th April 2014.

2 Low earnings threshold

For the purposes of the Social Security Contributions and Benefits Act 1992, it is directed that the low earnings threshold for the tax years following the tax year 2013–2014 shall be £15,100.

2014/3159

SOCIAL SECURITY CONTRIBUTIONS (LIMITED LIABILITY PARTNERSHIP) REGULATIONS 2014

Made . . . . *4 December 2014*
Coming into force . . . . *5 December 2014*

The Treasury make the following Regulations in exercise of the powers conferred by sections 4AA and 175(3) and (4) of the Social Security Contributions and Benefits Act 1992, 4AA and 171(3) and (4) of the Social Security Contributions and Benefits (Northern Ireland) Act 1992 and, as it appears to the Treasury to be expedient for these Regulations to have retrospective effect in consequence of retrospective tax provisions, namely sections 863A to 863G of the Income Tax (Trading and Other Income) Act 2005, by section 4B of those Acts.

Accordingly, the Treasury, with the concurrence of the Secretary of State and the Department for Social Development in so far as required, make the following Regulations:

A draft of this instrument has been laid before each House of Parliament in accordance with section 176(1) of the Social Security Contributions and Benefits Act 1992 and section 172(11A) of the Social Security Contributions and Benefits (Northern Ireland) Act 1992 and approved by resolution of each House.

1 Citation, commencement, effect and extent

(1) These Regulations may be cited as the Social Security Contributions (Limited Liability Partnership) Regulations 2014.

NIC

(2) These Regulations come into force on the day after the day on which they are made, and have effect for the tax year 2014–15 and subsequent tax years.

[(2A) Regulations 2A, 2B and 2C have effect for the tax year 2015-16 and subsequent tax years.][1]

(3) Regulations [2B,][1] 3 and 6 extend only to England and Wales and to Scotland and regulations [2B,][1] 4 and 7 extend only to Northern Ireland.

Amendments—[1] Para (2A) inserted and words in para (3) inserted by the Social Security Contributions (Limited Liability Partnership) (Amendment) Regulations, SI 2015/607 regs 2, 3 with effect from 6 April 2015.

2 Interpretation

In these Regulations—

"employment income" has the meaning given by section 7 of ITEPA 2003;

"ITTOIA 2005" means the Income Tax (Trading and Other Income) Act 2005;

"LLP" means limited liability partnership;

"SSCBA 1992" means the Social Security Contributions and Benefits Act 1992; and

"SSCB(NI)A 1992" means the Social Security Contributions and Benefits (Northern Ireland) Act 1992.

[2A Members of LLPs: employment

(1) The modification in paragraph (2) applies to—

(*a*) Part 1 and so much of Part 6 of SSCBA 1992 as relates to contributions, and

(*b*) Part 1 and so much of Part 6 of SSCB(NI)A 1992 as relates to contributions.

(2) The modification is that "employment" includes membership of an LLP which carries on a trade, profession or business with a view to profit.][1]

Amendments—[1] Regulations 2A–2C inserted by the Social Security Contributions (Limited Liability Partnership) (Amendment) Regulations, SI 2015/607 regs 2, 4 with effect from 6 April 2015.

[2B Members of LLPs: Great Britain

A person in employment in Great Britain as a member of an LLP which carries on a trade, profession or business with a view to profit is, unless regulation 3 applies, to be treated as a self-employed earner for the purposes of SSCBA 1992.

Amendments—Regulations 2A–2C inserted by the Social Security Contributions (Limited Liability Partnership) (Amendment) Regulations, SI 2015/607 regs 2, 4 with effect from 6 April 2015.

[2C Members of LLPs: Northern Ireland

A person in employment in Northern Ireland as a member of an LLP which carries on a trade, profession or business with a view to profit is, unless regulation 4 applies, to be treated as a self-employed earner for the purposes of SSCB(NI)A 1992.

Amendments—Regulations 2A–2C inserted by the Social Security Contributions (Limited Liability Partnership) (Amendment) Regulations, SI 2015/607 regs 2, 4 with effect from 6 April 2015.

3 Salaried Members of LLPs: Great Britain

(1) This regulation applies where—

(*a*) for the purposes of the Income Tax Acts an individual is treated by section 863A of ITTOIA 2005 (limited liability partnerships: salaried members) as being employed by an LLP under a contract of service, including where that is the case by virtue of section 863G of ITTOIA 2005 (anti-avoidance), ("the deemed tax employment"); and

(*b*) if the services performed, or to be performed, by the individual as a member of the LLP in the relevant period (as defined in section 863B(3) of ITTOIA 2005) were actually performed (or to be performed) under a contract of service with the LLP, the employment under that contract of service would be employment in Great Britain.

(2) For the purposes of SSCBA 1992—

(*a*) the individual ("the Salaried Member") is to be treated as employed in employed earner's employment by the LLP (being the deemed tax employment);

(*b*) any amount treated by virtue of section 863A or 863G(4) of ITTOIA 2005 as employment income from the deemed tax employment, other than employment income under Chapters 2 to 11 of Part 3 of ITEPA 2003 (the benefits code), is to be treated as an amount of earnings paid to or for the benefit of the Salaried Member in respect of the Salaried Member's employed earner's employment with the LLP;

(*c*) the secondary contributor in relation to those earnings is the LLP; and

(*d*) in the case of an amount of earnings which is an amount of employment income by virtue of section 863G(4) of ITTOIA 2005, the earnings are to be treated as being paid by the LLP to the Salaried Member when the amount mentioned in section 863G(2)(*d*) of that Act arises.

(3) The reference in paragraph (1)(*b*) to services performed (or to be performed) by the individual as a member of the LLP includes services personally performed by the individual for the LLP under arrangements by virtue of which section 863G(4) of ITTOIA 2005 applies.

(4) The definitions of "employer" and "employee" in—

(*a*) section 163 (interpretation of Part 11 and supplementary provisions);

(*b*) section 171 (interpretation of Part 12 and supplementary provisions);
(*c*) section 171ZJ (Part 12ZA: supplementary); and
(*d*) section 171ZS (Part 12ZB: supplementary)

of the SSCBA 1992 have effect as if the Salaried Member were gainfully employed in Great Britain by the LLP under a contract of service with the earnings mentioned in paragraph (2)(b).

4 Salaried Members of LLPs: Northern Ireland

(1) This regulation applies where—

(*a*) for the purposes of the Income Tax Acts an individual is treated by section 863A of ITTOIA 2005 (limited liability partnerships: salaried members) as being employed by an LLP under a contract of service, including where that is the case by virtue of section 863G of ITTOIA 2005 (anti-avoidance), ("the deemed tax employment"); and

(*b*) if the services performed, or to be performed, by the individual as a member of the LLP in the relevant period (as defined in section 863B(3) of ITTOIA 2005) were actually performed (or to be performed) under a contract of service, the employment under that contract of service would be employment in Northern Ireland.

(2) For the purposes of SSCB(NI)A 1992—

(*a*) the individual ("the Salaried Member") is to be treated as employed in employed earner's employment by the LLP (being the deemed tax employment);

(*b*) any amount treated as employment income by virtue of section 863A or section 863G(4) of ITTOIA 2005 as employment income from the deemed tax employment, other than employment income under Chapters 2 to 11 of Part 3 of ITEPA 2003 (the benefits code), is to be treated as an amount of earnings paid to or for the benefit of the Salaried Member in respect of the Salaried Member's employed earner's employment with the LLP;

(*c*) the secondary contributor in relation to those earnings is the LLP; and

(*d*) in the case of an amount of earnings which is an amount of employment income by virtue of section 863G(4) of ITTOIA 2005, the earnings are to be treated as being paid by the LLP to the Salaried Member when the amount mentioned in section 863G(2)(*d*) of that Act arises.

(3) The reference in paragraph (1)(*b*) to services performed by the individual as a member of the LLP includes services personally performed by the individual for the LLP under arrangements by virtue of which section 863G(4) of ITTOIA 2005 applies.

(4) The definitions of "employer" and "employee" in—

(*a*) section 159 (interpretation of Part 11 and supplementary provisions);
(*b*) section 167 (interpretation of Part 12, etc);
(*c*) section 167ZJ (Part 12ZA: supplementary); and
(*d*) section 167ZS (Part 12ZB: supplementary)

of SSCB(NI)A 1992 have effect as if the Salaried Member were gainfully employed in Northern Ireland by the LLP under a contract of service with the earnings mentioned in sub- paragraph (2)(b).

5 Consequential amendment to the Social Security (Contributions) Regulations 2001

(1) The Social Security (Contributions) Regulations 2001 are amended as follows.
(2) (*inserts* SI 2001/1004 reg 40A)
(3) (*inserts* SI 2001/1004 Sch 3 para 25)

6 Consequential amendments to the Social Security Contributions (Intermediaries) Regulations 2000

(1) The Social Security Contributions (Intermediaries) Regulations 2000 are amended as follows.
(2) (*amends* SI 2000/727 reg 7(1))

7 Consequential amendments to the Social Security Contributions (Intermediaries) (Northern Ireland) Regulations 2000

(1) The Social Security Contributions (Intermediaries) (Northern Ireland) Regulations 2000 are amended as follows.
(2) (*amends* SI 2000/728 reg 7(1))

2014/3240

SOCIAL SECURITY CLASS 3A CONTRIBUTIONS (UNITS OF ADDITIONAL PENSION) REGULATIONS 2014

Made . . . . .8 December 2014

Coming into force in accordance with regulation 1(2) and (3)

These Regulations are made by the Treasury and the Secretary of State.

The powers exercised by the Treasury are those conferred by section 14A(3) (the Treasury having consulted the Government Actuary) and 14A(6) of, and paragraph 8(1)(*q*) of Schedule 1 to, the Social Security Contributions and Benefits Act 1992 and section 14A(3) (the Treasury having

NIC

consulted the Government Actuary) and 14A(6) of, and paragraph 8(1)(*q*) of Schedule 1 to, the Social Security Contributions and Benefits (Northern Ireland) Act 1992 and now exercisable by them. The powers exercised by the Secretary of State are those conferred by section 45(2A) of the Social Security Contributions and Benefits Act 1992. Regulation 4 of this instrument is made before the end of the period of six months beginning with the coming into force of the relevant amendments made to the Social Security Contributions and Benefits Act 1992.

1 Citation and commencement

(1) These Regulations may be cited as the Social Security Class 3A Contributions (Units of Additional Pension) Regulations 2014.

(2) These Regulations come into force in Great Britain on 12th October 2015.

(3) Regulations 1, 2 and 3 come into force in Northern Ireland on the same day as the coming into force for all purposes of paragraph 17 of Schedule 15 to the Pensions Act 2014.

2 Determination of amount of a Class 3A contribution needed to obtain a unit of additional pension

(1) The amount of a Class 3A contribution needed by an eligible person to obtain a unit of additional pension is determined by the Table, subject to paragraph (2).

Age of person on the date of payment	*Amount of Class 3A contribution needed to obtain a unit of additional pension*
62 (women only)	£956
63 (women only)	£934
64 (women only)	£913
65	£890
66	£871
67	£847
68	£827
69	£801
70	£779
71	£761
72	£738
73	£719
74	£694
75	£674
76	£646
77	£625
78	£596
79	£574
80	£544
81	£514
82	£484
83	£454
84	£424
85	£394
86	£366
87	£339
88	£314
89	£291
90	£270
91	£251
92	£232
93	£216
94	£200
95	£185
96	£172

97	£159
98	£148
99	£137
100 and over	£127

(2) If an eligible person pays a Class 3A contribution before reaching pensionable age the amount of contribution needed to obtain a unit of additional pension is the amount that that person would have needed to pay if on the date of payment the person had reached pensionable age.

(3) The date of payment for a Class 3A contribution is the date the contribution is received by Her Majesty's Revenue and Customs.

3 Maximum number of units of additional pension

The maximum number of units of additional pension that a person may obtain is 25.

4 Specified amount for each unit of additional pension

The specified amount for the purposes of section 45(1)(*b*) and (2)(*e*) of the Social Security Contributions and Benefits Act 1992 (the additional pension in a category A retirement pension) is £1.

2015/118

OCCUPATIONAL PENSION SCHEMES (POWER TO AMEND SCHEMES TO REFLECT ABOLITION OF CONTRACTING-OUT) REGULATIONS 2015

Made..*25 February 2015*

Laid before Parliament..............................*4 March 2015*

Coming into force...................................*6 April 2015*

The Secretary of State for Work and Pensions, in exercise of the powers conferred by sections 24(5) and 54(5) and (6), of and paragraphs 2(3) and (4), 4, 6, 10(1), 12, 13, and 14(1) and (2) of Schedule 14 to, the Pensions Act 2014, makes the following Regulations:

1 Citation and commencement

(1) These Regulations may be cited as the Occupational Pension Schemes (Power to Amend Schemes to Reflect Abolition of Contracting-out) Regulations 2015.

(2) These Regulations come into force on 6th April 2015.

2 Interpretation

In these Regulations—

"the Act" means the Pensions Act 2014;

"the 2004 Act" means the Pensions Act 2004;

"actuarial valuation" has the meaning given by section 224(2)(a) of the 2004 Act (actuarial valuations and reports);

"the actuary" means the actuary appointed in accordance with regulation 10(2);

"the amendment date" means the date amendments made using the power take effect;

"the calculation date" means the date chosen in accordance with regulation 8(7);

"effective date" means the date referred to in section 224(2)(b) of the 2004 Act;

"the power" means the power under section 24(2) of the Act to amend an occupational pension scheme;

"principal employer" means, in relation to a multi-employer scheme—

(*a*) a person nominated by the employers, or by rules of the scheme, to act on behalf of the employers for the purposes of section 229 of the 2004 Act (matters requiring agreement of the employer), or

(*b*) where there is no such nominee, a person nominated by the employers to act on their behalf for the purposes of the use of the power;

"proposed amendments" means the amendments to be certified under paragraph 6(1) of Schedule 14 to the Act;

"segregated scheme" means a multi-employer scheme which is divided into two or more sections where—

(*a*) any contributions payable to the scheme by an employer in relation to the scheme, or by a member employed by that employer, are allocated to that employer's section, and if more than one section applies to an employer, to the section to which the employment relates, and

(*b*) a specified proportion of the assets of the scheme is attributable to each section of the scheme and cannot be used for the purposes of any other section; and "technical provisions" has the meaning given by section 222(2) of the 2004 Act (the statutory funding objective).

3 Protected persons to whom the power does not apply

(1) For the purposes of section 24(4)(*a*) of the Act (when the power may not be used) a person listed in this regulation is a "protected person in relation to a scheme".

(2) A person who is a "protected employee" as defined by regulation 2(1) of the Electricity (Protected Persons) (England and Wales) Pension Regulations 1990 (interpretation) on or after the amendment date.

(3) A person who is a "protected employee" as defined by regulation 2(1) of the Electricity (Protected Persons) (Scotland) Pension Regulations 1990 (interpretation) on or after the amendment date.

(4) A person who is a "protected employee" as defined by article 1(2) of the Railway Pensions (Protection and Designation of Schemes) Order 1994 (citation, commencement and interpretation) to whom Part II of that Order has effect in relation to relevant pension rights, within the meaning of paragraph 6(3) of Schedule 11 to the Railways Act 1993 (the powers of protection), accruing on or after the amendment date.

(5) A person who is a "protected employee" as defined by regulation 2(1) of the Coal Industry (Protected Persons) Pensions Regulations 1994 (interpretation) on or after the amendment date.

(6) A person who is a "protected person" as defined by article 1(3) of the London Transport Pension Arrangements Order 2000 (citation, commencement and interpretation) to whom that Order has effect on or after the amendment date.

(7) A person who falls within paragraph 9(5) of Schedule 8 to the Energy Act 2004 (persons entitled to pension protection under paragraphs 10 and 11) and to whom paragraph 9(2) of that Schedule applies.

4 Total annual employee contributions of the relevant members

(1) For the purposes of paragraph 2(3)(*a*) of Schedule 14 to the Act (what can the power be used to do?), the "total annual employee contributions of the relevant members" means the total annual amount of employee contributions for the relevant members calculated using the employee contribution rates shown in the schedule of contributions adopted in relation to the scheme for the purposes of Part 3 of the 2004 Act (scheme funding) as at the calculation date.

(2) The actuary is to calculate the increase, due to the proposed amendments, in the total annual employee contributions of the relevant members—

(*a*) estimated to be payable over the period of one year beginning with the calculation date;
(*b*) using the earnings data specified in regulation 7; and
(*c*) in accordance with the requirements in regulation 8.

5 Annual increase in an employer's national insurance contributions in respect of the relevant members

(1) For the purposes of paragraph 2(3)(*b*) of Schedule 14 to the Act, the "annual increase in an employer's national insurance contributions in respect of the relevant members" means the increase of 3.4% in the annual amount of national insurance contributions payable by the employer in respect of so much of the earnings of relevant members as exceeds the applicable lower earnings limit but not the upper accrual point (or the prescribed equivalents if the earner is paid otherwise than weekly).

(2) The actuary is to calculate the annual increase in the employer's national insurance contributions in respect of the relevant members—

(*a*) estimated to be payable over the period of one year beginning with the calculation date;
(*b*) using the earnings data specified in regulation 7; and
(*c*) in accordance with the requirements in regulation 8.

(3) In this regulation—

"the 1992 Act" means the Social Security Contributions and Benefits Act 1992;

"applicable" in relation to the lower earnings limit, means the limit or limits in force during the one year after the calculation date;

"lower earnings limit" is to be construed in accordance with section 5 of the 1992 Act (earnings limits and thresholds for class 1 contributions);

"the prescribed equivalents"—

(*a*) in the context of the lower earnings limit, means the equivalent prescribed under section 5(4) of the 1992 Act, and
(*b*) in the context of the upper accrual point, means the equivalent prescribed under section 122(6A) of that Act (interpretation); and

"the upper accrual point" has the meaning given by section 122(1) of the 1992 Act.

6 Scheme liabilities in respect of the benefits that accrue annually for or in respect of the relevant members

(1) For the purposes of paragraph 2(3)(*c*) of Schedule 14 to the Act, a "scheme's liabilities in respect of the benefits that accrue annually for or in respect of the relevant members" means any liabilities which arise by virtue of any rights accruing to future benefits under the scheme rules for or in respect of the relevant members.

(2) Where those rights include discretionary benefits, the discretionary benefits are to be taken into account in the same way as in the scheme's technical provisions—

(*a*) where the calculation date is the same date as the effective date of an actuarial valuation, calculated by reference to that date, or

(*b*) where the calculation date is not the same date as that date, calculated by reference to the date of the most recent actuarial valuation before the calculation date.

(3) Where those rights include money purchase benefits, the money purchase benefits are not to be taken into account.

(4) The actuary is to calculate the reduction, due to the proposed amendments, in the scheme's liabilities in respect of the benefits that accrue annually for or in respect of the relevant members—

(*a*) estimated for the period of one year beginning with the calculation date;

(*b*) using the earnings data specified in regulation 7; and

(*c*) in accordance with the requirements of regulation 8.

(5) In this regulation, "money purchase benefits" have the meaning given by section 181 of the Pension Schemes Act 1993 (general interpretation) .

7 Earnings data

(1) The actuary must use earnings data which, except where paragraph (3) applies, is for the period of one year ending with the calculation date.

(2) Where paragraph (3) applies, calculations may be made using earnings data which refers to the period of three years ending with the calculation date.

(3) This paragraph applies where—

(*a*) the actuary is satisfied that the earnings data for some or all of the relevant members for the period of one year ending with the calculation date is significantly abnormal; and

(*b*) the—

(i) principal employer in a case falling within regulation 14 or 15, or

(ii) employer in any other case;

writes to the actuary stating that it is also so satisfied.

8 General calculation requirements

(1) The actuary must comply with the following requirements in carrying out the calculations under regulations 4(2), 5(2) and 6(4).

(2) The calculations are to be carried out—

(*a*) as if the proposed amendments took effect on the calculation date;

(*b*) taking account only of the effect of the proposed amendments;

(*c*) at the present value at the calculation date; and

(*d*) where an assumption is used in more than one calculation, using the same assumption for each calculation in which it is used.

(3) Any data used in the calculations, other than earnings data, must be data—

(*a*) the actuary considers is relevant; and

(*b*) which—

(i) is as at the calculation date, or

(ii) refers to the period of one year ending with the calculation date,

as the actuary considers appropriate.

(4) Calculations must be made using—

(*a*) the methods and assumptions used to calculate the scheme's technical provisions—

(i) where the calculation date is the same date as the effective date of an actuarial valuation, calculated by reference to that date, or

(ii) where the calculation date is not the same date as that date, calculated by reference to the date of the most recent actuarial valuation before the calculation date, updated if necessary to reflect market conditions at the calculation date; and

(*b*) any other assumptions which the actuary considers necessary and which are consistent with the assumptions used to calculate the scheme's technical provisions, updated if necessary to reflect market conditions at the calculation date.

(5) Where paragraph (6) applies, the actuary must adjust the requested assumptions to a best estimate basis by removing any margin for prudence provided the actuary is satisfied such adjustments are consistent with the principles that would be used by the trustees or managers of the scheme in

calculating an initial cash equivalent under regulation 7B of the Occupational Pension Schemes (Transfer Values) Regulations 1996 (initial cash equivalents for salary related benefits other than cash balance benefits not calculated by reference to final salary) at the calculation date.

(6) This paragraph applies where the—

(*a*) principal employer in a case falling within regulation 14 or 15; or

(*b*) employer in any other case,

writes to the actuary instructing the actuary to adjust any assumptions ("the requested assumptions") to remove any margin for prudence.

(7) Subject to regulation 8(8), the—

(*a*) principal employer in a case falling within regulation 14 or 15; or

(*b*) employer in any other case,

must choose a calculation date which may be any date after 31st December 2011.

(8) Where the power is used in relation to the same members in the same scheme on a second or subsequent occasion the calculation date must be the same date as on the first occasion the power was used.

(9) In this regulation, "any margin for prudence" means any margin for adverse deviation allowed for in accordance with regulation 5(4)(*a*) of the Occupational Pension Schemes (Scheme Funding) Regulations 2005 (calculation of technical provisions).

9 Further restrictions on the use of the power

(1) The power may not be used to make amendments which would remove a power to determine any matter from the trustees or managers of a scheme.

10 Actuary

(1) For the purposes of paragraph 6(2)(*a*) of Schedule 14 to the Act (requirement for actuary's certificate), "actuary" means a Fellow of the Institute and Faculty of Actuaries.

(2) The—

(*a*) principal employer in a case falling within regulation 14 or 15; or

(*b*) employer in any other case,

must appoint an actuary.

11 Requirement for actuary's certificate

(1) Except in a case where regulation 8(8) applies, the actuary must certify whether, in the actuary's opinion—

(*a*) the proposed amendments comply with paragraph 2(2) of Schedule 14 to the Act; and

(*b*) the calculations have been made in accordance with the requirements of regulations 4(2), 5(2), 6(2) to (4), 7 and 8(2) to (6).

(2) In a case where regulation 8(8) applies, the actuary must certify whether, in the actuary's opinion—

(*a*) all the amendments comply with the requirement in paragraph (1)(*a*) as if all the amendments are being made on this second or subsequent (as appropriate) occasion; and

(*b*) the calculations have been made in accordance with the requirements in paragraph (1)(*b*) and regulation 8(8).

(3) For the purposes of this regulation, "all the amendments" means the proposed amendments and the amendments made by the previous use, or uses, of the power in relation to the same members in the same scheme as covered by the proposed amendments.

(4) The actuary must provide a certificate under this regulation that includes the information specified in the Schedule.

(5) The actuary must issue a certificate under this regulation to the trustees or managers of the scheme and—

(*a*) the principal employer in a case falling within regulation 14 or 15; or

(*b*) in any other case, the employer,

before any amendments are made.

12 Information

(1) The trustees or managers of an occupational pension scheme must provide any information reasonably requested by—

(*a*) the principal employer in a case falling within regulation 14 or 15; or

(*b*) in any other case, the employer,

in connection with the use of the power.

(2) The information must be provided in writing within such reasonable period as agreed with the principal employer or employer as applicable.

(3) Where the trustees or managers of a scheme have failed to take all reasonable steps to comply with any requirement imposed on them by this regulation, section 10 of the Pensions Act 1995 (civil penalties) applies.

13 Segregated schemes with single employer sections

(1) This regulation applies to a section of a segregated scheme where there is one employer in relation to that section of the scheme.

(2) Section 24 of the Act (abolition of contracting-out for salary related schemes etc) and Schedule 14 to the Act (power to amend schemes to reflect abolition of contracting-out) apply with the following modifications.

(3) In section 24(2) the reference to—

(*a*) "an employer" is to be read as a reference to "an employer in relation to a section of an occupational pension scheme"; and

(*b*) "an occupational pension scheme" is to be read as a reference to "that section of an occupational pension scheme".

(4) In Schedule 14 in paragraphs 2(2), 3(1), 9 and 15, references to a "scheme" are to be read as references to a "section of a scheme".

(5) Where these Regulations (apart from this regulation) apply to a section of a segregated scheme where there is one employer in relation to that section of the scheme, they shall apply to that section as if the section were a separate scheme.

14 Non-segregated multi-employer schemes

(1) This regulation applies to multi-employer schemes which are not segregated schemes.

(2) Section 24 of the Act and Schedule 14 to the Act apply with the following modifications.

(3) In section 24(2) the reference to—

(*a*) "an employer" is to be read as a reference to "the principal employer"; and

(*b*) "the employer's national insurance contributions" is to be read as a reference to "the employers' national insurance contributions".

(4) In Schedule 14—

(*a*) in paragraph 2(2), references to "the employer's national insurance contributions" are to be read as references to "the employers' national insurance contributions"; and

(*b*) in paragraph 2(5), the reference to "the employer is" is to be read as a reference to "the employers are".

NIC

15 Segregated schemes with multi-employer sections

(1) This regulation applies to a section of a segregated scheme where there is more than one employer in relation to that section of the scheme.

(2) Section 24 of the Act and Schedule 14 to the Act apply with the following modifications.

(3) In section 24(2) the reference to—

(*a*) "an employer" is to be read as a reference to "the principal employer in relation to a section of an occupational pension scheme";

(*b*) "an occupational pension scheme" is to be read as a reference to "that section of an occupational pension scheme"; and

(*c*) "the employer's national insurance contributions" is to be read as a reference to "the employers' national insurance contributions".

(4) In Schedule 14—

(*a*) in paragraph 2(2), references to "the employer's national insurance contributions" are to be read as references to "the employers' national insurance contributions"; and

(*b*) in paragraphs 2(2), 3(1), 9 and 15, references to a "scheme" are to be read as references to a "section of a scheme".

(5) Where these Regulations (apart from this regulation) apply to a section of a segregated scheme where there is more than one employer in relation to that section of the scheme, they shall apply to that section as if the section were a separate scheme.

16 Notification of amendment date

(1) Following the issue of a certificate by the actuary in accordance with regulation 11(5), the—

(*a*) principal employer in a case falling within regulation 14 or 15; or

(*b*) employer in any other case,

must consult the trustees or managers of the scheme about an appropriate amendment date.

(2) The principal employer or employer as applicable, must, as soon as reasonably practicable after consultation, notify the trustees or managers of the scheme of the amendment date.

(3) The notification required by paragraph (2) must be in writing.

(4) Amendments may not have effect before 6th April 2016.

SCHEDULE

INFORMATION TO BE INCLUDED IN ACTUARY'S CERTIFICATE

Regulation 11

Name and address of employer/principal employer

Name and Scheme Contracted-out Number (SCON(s)) of scheme/section

The amendments proposed to be made.

Data and assumptions used

Calculation date

Date of scheme actuarial valuation

Any additional assumptions used

Any assumptions which the employer requested were adjusted to remove the margin for prudence

What earnings data used:1 year to calculation date or 3 years to calculation date

Other data sources used

Estimates of values of scheme amendments

A statement that the Actuary's estimate of the following values is for the proposed amendments as set out in the certificate and on the basis of the data referred to, the methods and assumptions used to calculate the scheme's technical provisions and the additional assumptions set out in the certificate.

The values for—

the annual increase in the employer's national insurance contributions in respect of the earnings of relevant members as exceeds the lower earnings limit but not the upper accrual point

the increase in the total annual employee contributions of the relevant members (if applicable)

the reduction in the scheme's liabilities in respect of the benefits that accrue annually for or in respect of the relevant members (if applicable)

the sum of the increase in the total annual employee contributions and the reduction in the scheme's liabilities in respect of the benefits that accrue annually for or in respect of the relevant members (if applicable).

Note: In a case where the power is being used on a second or subsequent occasion, estimates should be for the changes due to all the amendments, those proposed and the amendments made by the previous use or uses of the power.

Certification

A statement that, in the actuary's opinion—

The proposed amendments to the scheme/section set out in this certificate comply with paragraph 2(2) of Schedule 14 to the Pensions Act 2014.

The calculations have been made in accordance with the requirements of regulations 4(2), 5(2), 6(2) to (4), 7 and 8(2) to (6) of the Occupational Pension Schemes (Power to Amend Schemes to Reflect Abolition of Contracting-out) Regulations 2015.

Alternative certification where the power is being used on a second or subsequent occasion

A statement that, in the actuary's opinion—

All the amendments to the scheme/section, those proposed and set out in this certificate and those made by the previous use or uses of the power and set out in resolutions (give dates) comply with paragraph 2(2) of Schedule 14 to the Pensions Act 2014.

The calculations have been made in accordance with the requirements of regulations 4(2), 5(2), 6(2) to (4), 7, 8(2) to (6) and 8(8) of the Occupational Pension Schemes (Power to Amend Schemes to Reflect Abolition of Contracting-out) Regulations 2015.

Signature:

Date:

Name:

Qualification:

Address:

2015/186

SOCIAL SECURITY PENSIONS (LOW EARNINGS THRESHOLD) ORDER 2015

Made . . . . *9 February 2015*

Laid before Parliament . . . . *16 February 2015*

Coming into force . . . . *6 April 2015*

In accordance with section 148A(1) (revaluation of low earnings threshold) of the Social Security Administration Act 1992, the Secretary of State has reviewed the general level of earnings obtaining in Great Britain.

It appears to the Secretary of State that the general level of earnings has increased during the review period.

The Secretary of State makes the following Order in exercise of the powers conferred by sections 148A(3) to (5) and 189(1), (4) and (5) of the Social Security Administration Act 1992.

1 Citation and commencement

This Order may be cited as the Social Security Pensions (Low Earnings Threshold) Order 2015 and shall come into force on 6th April 2015.

2 Low earnings threshold

For the purposes of the Social Security Contributions and Benefits Act 1992, it is directed that the low earnings threshold for the tax years following the tax year 2014–2015 shall be £15,300.

2015/187

SOCIAL SECURITY REVALUATION OF EARNINGS FACTORS ORDER 2015

Made . . . .*9 February 2015*
Laid before Parliament . . . .*16 February 2015*
Coming into force . . . .*6 April 2015*

In accordance with section 148(2) (revaluation of earnings factors) of the Social Security Administration Act 1992, the Secretary of State has reviewed the general level of earnings obtaining in Great Britain.

The Secretary of State has concluded, having regard to earlier orders made under section 148, that earnings factors for the relevant tax years have not, during the period taken into account for that review, maintained their value in relation to the general level of earnings.

The Secretary of State makes the following Order in exercise of the powers conferred by sections 148(3) and (4) and 189(1), (4) and (5) of the Social Security Administration Act 1992.

1 Citation and commencement

This Order may be cited as the Social Security Revaluation of Earnings Factors Order 2015 and shall come into force on 6th April 2015.

2 Revaluation of earnings factors

The earnings factors for tax years specified in the Schedule to this Order in so far as they are relevant—

(*a*) to the calculation—

(i) of the additional pension in the rate of any long-term benefit, or

(ii) of any guaranteed minimum pension; or

(*b*) to any other calculation required under Part 3 of the Pension Schemes Act 1993 (including that Part as modified by or under any other enactment),

are directed to be increased for those tax years by the percentage of their amount shown opposite those tax years in that Schedule.

3 Rounding of fractional amounts

Where any earnings factor relevant to the calculation specified in article 2(*a*)(i) of this Order, as increased in accordance with this Order, would not but for this article be expressed as a whole number of pounds, it shall be so expressed by rounding down any fraction of a pound less than one half and rounding up any other fraction of a pound.

SCHEDULE

PERCENTAGE INCREASE OF EARNINGS FACTOR FOR SPECIFIED TAX YEARS

Article 2

Tax year	*Percentage increase*
1978–1979	754.4
1979–1980	654.1
1980–1981	530.0
1981–1982	427.6
1982–1983	379.2
1983–1984	345.0
1984–1985	312.0
1985–1986	286.5
1986–1987	254.9
1987–1988	230.4
1988–1989	204.0
1989–1990	174.4

NIC

1990–1991	155.7
1991–1992	132.2
1992–1993	118.1
1993–1994	107.7
1994–1995	101.4
1995–1996	93.0
1996–1997	87.7
1997–1998	78.8
1998–1999	70.9
1999–2000	64.0
2000–2001	54.3
2001–2002	48.4
2002–2003	42.2
2003–2004	37.3
2004–2005	32.3
2005–2006	27.1
2006–2007	22.9
2007–2008	18.0
2008–2009	13.3
2009–2010	9.9
2010–2011	8.6
2011–2012	6.1
2012–2013	4.3
2013–2014	2.4
2014–2015	1.5

2015/1502

PENSIONS ACT 2014 (SAVINGS) ORDER 2015

Made . . . . 14 July 2015

The Secretary of State for Work and Pensions makes the following Order in exercise of the powers conferred by section 56(8) of the Pensions Act 2014:

1 Citation, commencement and interpretation

(1) This Order may be cited as the Pensions Act 2014 (Savings) Order 2015.
(2) This Order comes into force on 6th April 2016.
(3) Articles 2(1) and (2) cease to have effect on 6th April 2019.
(4) In this Order—

"the Act" means the Pensions Act 2014;

"the 1993 Act" means the Pension Schemes Act 1993;

"contracted-out employment" and "contributions equivalent premium" have the meanings given in section 181(1) of the 1993 Act;

"earner" has the meaning given in section 181(1) of the 1993 Act;

"HMRC" means the Commissioners for Her Majesty's Revenue and Customs;

"PPF assessment period" means an assessment period in relation to the Board of the Pension Protection Fund within the meaning of section 132 of the Pensions Act 2004;

"salary related contracted-out scheme" and "the second abolition date" have the meanings given in section 181(1) of the 1993 Act.

2 Savings

(1) The provisions of the 1993 Act specified in paragraph (2) and repealed by paragraphs 5, 8, 9 to 11, 22, 28, 29, 33, 36, 37 and 46(1), (2) and (4) of Schedule 13 to the Act (abolition of contracting-out for salary related schemes) continue to have effect, despite those repeals, for the purposes of allowing or requiring the trustees or managers of a scheme that was a salary related contracted-out scheme, and HMRC, to carry out any necessary activity relating to any period of contracted-out employment which occurred before the second abolition date.
(2) The provisions are—

(*a*) section 7 (issue of contracting-out certificates);
(*b*) section 9 (requirements for certification of schemes: general);
(*c*) section 11 (elections as to employment covered by contracting-out certificates);
(*d*) sections 12A to 12D (requirements for certification of occupational pension schemes applying from 6th April 1997);
(*e*) sections 34 to 36 (cancellation, variation, surrender and refusal of certificates);
(*f*) section 41 (reduced rates of Class 1 contributions);
(*g*) section 50 (powers of HMRC to approve arrangements for scheme ceasing to be certified);
(*h*) section 53(3) (supervision: former contracted-out schemes);
(*i*) sections 55 to 68 (state scheme premiums);
(*j*) Schedule 2, paragraphs 1 to 4 and 6 to 8 (certification regulations).

(3) Section 16(2) of the 1993 Act (revaluation of earnings factors for the purposes of section 14: early leavers etc) continues to have effect, as if that subsection had not been substituted by paragraph 16 of Schedule 13 to the Act, in relation to earners whose service in contracted-out employment ended before the second abolition date.

(4) Sections 55 to 68 of the 1993 Act continue to have effect as if they had not been repealed by paragraph 37 of Schedule 13 to the Act, for the purposes of allowing or requiring the trustees or managers of a scheme described in paragraph (5) to elect to pay, and pay, a contributions equivalent premium in relation to members of the scheme whose contracted-out employment ended on or before the second abolition date.

(5) A scheme referred to in paragraph (4) is—
(*a*) one which started to wind up before the second abolition date; or
(*b*) one—
(i) which had not started to wind up before the second abolition date;
(ii) which entered a PPF assessment period before 6th April 2016, and where the assessment period continues after 6th April 2019; and
(iii) where the trustees or managers of the scheme elected to pay a contributions equivalent premium after the start of the PPF assessment period but cannot make that payment during the assessment period due to the restriction in section 135(4)(b) of the Pensions Act 2004 (restrictions on winding up, discharge of liabilities etc).

NIC

2016/205

SOCIAL SECURITY REVALUATION OF EARNINGS FACTORS ORDER 2016

Made . . . . *22 February 2016*
Laid before Parliament . . . . *29 February 2016*
Coming into force . . . . *6 April 2016*

In accordance with section 148(2) of the Social Security Administration Act 1992, the Secretary of State has reviewed the general level of earnings obtaining in Great Britain.

The Secretary of State has concluded, having regard to earlier orders made under section 148 of that Act, that earnings factors for the relevant tax years have not, during the period taken into account for that review, maintained their value in relation to the general level of earnings.

The Secretary of State makes the following Order in exercise of the powers conferred by sections 148(3) and (4) and 189(1), (4) and (5) of the Social Security Administration Act 1992.

1 Citation and commencement

This Order may be cited as the Social Security Revaluation of Earnings Factors Order 2016 and shall come into force on 6th April 2016.

2 Revaluation of earnings factors

The earnings factors for tax years specified in the Schedule to this Order in so far as they are relevant—
(*a*) to the calculation—
(i) of the additional pension in the rate of any long-term benefit, or
(ii) of any guaranteed minimum pension; or
(*b*) to any other calculation required under Part 3 of the Pension Schemes Act 1993 (including that Part as modified by or under any other enactment),

are directed to be increased for those tax years by the percentage of their amount shown opposite those tax years in that Schedule.

3 Rounding of fractional amounts

Where any earnings factor relevant to the calculation specified in article 2(a)(i) of this Order, as increased in accordance with this Order, would not but for this article be expressed as a whole number of pounds, it shall be so expressed by rounding down any fraction of a pound less than one half and rounding up any other fraction of a pound.

SCHEDULE

PERCENTAGE INCREASE OF EARNINGS FACTOR FOR SPECIFIED TAX YEARS

Article 2

Tax year	*Percentage increase*
1978–1979	771.5
1979–1980	669.2
1980–1981	542.6
1981–1982	438.2
1982–1983	388.8
1983–1984	353.9
1984–1985	320.2
1985–1986	294.2
1986–1987	262.0
1987–1988	237.1
1988–1989	210.1
1989–1990	179.9
1990–1991	160.8
1991–1992	136.9
1992–1993	122.4
1993–1994	111.8
1994–1995	105.5
1995–1996	96.8
1996–1997	91.4
1997–1998	82.3
1998–1999	74.3
1999–2000	67.3
2000–2001	57.4
2001–2002	51.3
2002–2003	45.1
2003–2004	40.0
2004–2005	34.9
2005–2006	29.6
2006–2007	25.3
2007–2008	20.4
2008–2009	15.5
2009–2010	12.1
2010–2011	10.7
2011–2012	8.3
2012–2013	6.3
2013–2014	4.5
2014–2015	3.5
2015–2016	2.0

2017/287

SOCIAL SECURITY REVALUATION OF EARNINGS FACTORS ORDER 2017

Made . . . . *7 March 2017*
Laid before Parliament . . . . *13 March 2017*
Coming into force . . . . *6 April 2017*

In accordance with section 148(2) of the Social Security Administration Act 1992, the Secretary of State for Work and Pensions has reviewed the general level of earnings obtaining in Great Britain.

The Secretary of State has concluded, having regard to earlier orders made under section 148 of that Act, that earnings factors for the relevant tax years have not, during the period taken into account for that review, maintained their value in relation to the general level of earnings.

The Secretary of State makes the following Order in exercise of the powers conferred by sections 148(3) and (4) and 189(1), (4) and (5) of the Social Security Administration Act 1992.

1 Citation and commencement

This Order may be cited as the Social Security Revaluation of Earnings Factors Order 2017 and shall come into force on 6th April 2017.

2 Revaluation of earnings factors

The earnings factors for tax years specified in the Schedule to this Order in so far as they are relevant—

(*a*) to the calculation—

(i) of the additional pension in the rate of any long-term benefit, or

(ii) of any guaranteed minimum pension; or

(*b*) to any other calculation required under Part 3 of the Pension Schemes Act 1993 (including that Part as modified by or under any other enactment),

are directed to be increased for those tax years by the percentage of their amount shown opposite those tax years in that Schedule.

3 Rounding of fractional amounts

Where any earnings factor relevant to the calculation specified in article 2(*a*)(i), as increased in accordance with this Order, would not but for this article be expressed as a whole number of pounds, it shall be so expressed by rounding down any fraction of a pound less than one half and rounding up any other fraction of a pound.

SCHEDULE

PERCENTAGE INCREASE OF EARNINGS FACTOR FOR SPECIFIED TAX YEARS

Article 2

Tax year	*Percentage increase*
1978–1979	794.1
1979–1980	689.2
1980–1981	559.3
1981–1982	452.2
1982–1983	401.5
1983–1984	365.7
1984–1985	331.2
1985–1986	304.5
1986–1987	271.4
1987–1988	245.8
1988–1989	218.1
1989–1990	187.1
1990–1991	167.6
1991–1992	143.0
1992–1993	128.2
1993–1994	117.3
1994–1995	110.8
1995–1996	101.9
1996–1997	96.4
1997–1998	87.1
1998–1999	78.8
1999–2000	71.6
2000–2001	61.5
2001–2002	55.3
2002–2003	48.9
2003–2004	43.7

2004–2005	38.4
2005–2006	33.0
2006–2007	28.6
2007–2008	23.5
2008–2009	18.6
2009–2010	15.0
2010–2011	13.6
2011–2012	11.1
2012–2013	9.1
2013–2014	7.2
2014–2015	6.2
2015–2016	4.7
2016–2017	2.6

EU Legislation

Contents

COUNCIL REGULATION OF 14 JUNE 1971 ON THE APPLICATION OF SOCIAL SECURITY SCHEMES TO EMPLOYED PERSONS, TO SELF-EMPLOYED PERSONS AND TO MEMBERS OF THEIR FAMILIES MOVING WITHIN THE COMMUNITY.

(1408/71/EEC)

Note—See OJ L149 05.07.71 p 2.

Prospective repeal—This Regulation repealed from 1 May 2010, the date of implementation of Regulation (EC) No 883/2004 of the European Parliament and of the Council of 29 April 2004 on the coordination of social security systems: Council Regulation (EC) 883/2004, art 90 (see OJ L166, 30.04.04, p 1). However, Council Regulation (EEC) 1408/71 shall remain in force and shall continue to have legal effect for the purposes of—

(a) Council Regulation (EC) 859/2003 of 14 May 2003 extending the provisions of Regulation (EEC) 1408/71 and Regulation (EEC) 574/72 to nationals of third countries who are not already covered by those provisions solely on the ground of their nationality, for as long as that Regulation has not been repealed or modified;

(b) Council Regulation (EEC) 1661/85 of 13 June 1985 laying down the technical adaptations to the Community rules on social security for migrant workers with regard to Greenland, for as long as that Regulation has not been repealed or modified;

(c) the Agreement on the European Economic Area and the Agreement between the European Community and its Member States, of the one part, and the Swiss Confederation, of the other part, on the free movement of persons and other agreements which contain a reference to Regulation (EEC) 1408/71, for as long as those agreements have not been modified in the light of this Regulation.

TITLE I
GENERAL PROVISIONS

Article 1 Definitions

For the purpose of this Regulation:

(*a*) "employed person" and "self-employed person" mean respectively:

[(i) any person who is insured, compulsorily or on an optional continued basis, for one or more of the contingencies covered by the branches of a social security scheme for employed or self-employed persons or by a special scheme for civil servants;][1]

(ii) any person who is compulsorily insured for one or more of the contingencies covered by the branches of social security dealt with in this Regulation, under a social security scheme for all residents or for the whole working population, if such person:

— can be identified as an employed or self-employed person by virtue of the manner in which such scheme is administered or financed, or,

— failing such criteria, is insured for some other contingency specified in Annex I under a scheme for employed or self-employed persons, or under a scheme referred to in (iii), either compulsorily or on an optional continued basis, or, where no such scheme exists in the Member State concerned, complies with the definition given in Annex I;

(iii) any person who is compulsorily insured for several of the contingencies covered by the branches dealt with in this Regulation, under a standard social security scheme for the whole rural population in accordance with the criteria laid down in Annex I;

(iv) any person who is voluntarily insured for one or more of the contingencies covered by the branches dealt with in this Regulation, under a social security scheme of a Member State for employed or self-employed persons or for all residents or for certain categories of residents:

— if such person carries out an activity as an employed or self-employed person, or

— if such person has previously been compulsorily insured for the same contingency under a scheme for employed or self-employed persons of the same Member State;

(*b*) "frontier worker" means any employed or self-employed person who pursues his occupation in the territory of a Member State and resides in the territory of another Member State to which he returns as a rule daily or at least once a week; however, a frontier worker who is posted elsewhere in the territory of the same or another Member State by the undertaking to which he is normally attached, or who engages in the provision of services elsewhere in the territory of the same or another Member State, shall retain the status of frontier worker for a period not exceeding four months, even if he is prevented, during that period, from returning daily or at least once a week to the place where he resides;

(*c*) "seasonal worker" means any employed person who goes to the territory of a Member State other than the one in which he is resident to do work there of a seasonal nature for an undertaking or an employer of that State for a period which may on no account exceed eight

NIC

months, and who stays in the territory of the said State for the duration of his work; work of a seasonal nature shall be taken to mean work which, being dependent on the succession of the seasons, automatically recurs each year;

[(*ca*) "student" means any person other than an employed or self-employed person or a member of his family or survivor within the meaning of this Regulation who studies or receives vocational training leading to a qualification officially recognised by the authorities of a Member State, and is insured under a general social security scheme or a special social security scheme applicable to students;][2]

(*d*) "refugee" shall have the meaning assigned to it in Article 1 of the Convention on the Status of Refugees, signed at Geneva on 28th July 1951;

(*e*) "stateless person" shall have the meaning assigned to it in Article 1 of the Convention on the Status of Stateless Persons, signed in New York on 28th September 1954;

(*f*), (*g*) . . .

(*h*) "residence" means habitual residence;

(*i*) "stay" means temporary residence;

(*j*) "legislation" means in respect of each Member State, statutes, regulations, and other provisions and all other implementing measures, present or future, relating to the branches and schemes of social security covered by Article 4(1) and (2);

This term excludes provisions of existing or future industrial agreements, whether or not they have been the subject of a decision by the authorities rendering them compulsory or extending their scope. However, in so far as such provisions:

(*i*) serve to put into effect compulsory insurance imposed by the laws and regulations referred to in the preceding sub-paragraph; or

(ii) set up a scheme administered by the same institution as that which administers the schemes set up by the laws and regulations referred to in the preceding sub-paragraph,

the limitation on the term may at any time be lifted by a declaration by the Member State concerned, specifying the schemes of such a kind to which this Regulation applies. Such a declaration shall be notified and published in accordance with the provisions of Article 97.

The provisions of the preceding sub-paragraph shall not have the effect of exempting from application of this Regulation the schemes to which Regulation No 3 applied;

The term "legislation" also excludes provisions governing special schemes for self-employed persons the creation of which is left to the initiatives of those concerned or which apply only to a part of the territory of the Member State concerned, irrespective of whether or not the authorities decided to make them compulsory or extend their scope. The special schemes in question are specified in Annex II;

[(*ja*) "special scheme for civil servants" means any social security scheme which is different from the general social security scheme applicable to employed persons in the Member States concerned and to which all, or certain categories of, civil servants or persons treated as such are directly subject;][1]

(*k*) "social security convention" means any bilateral or multilateral instrument which binds or will bind two or more Member States exclusively, and any other multilateral instrument which binds or will bind at least two Member States and one or more other States in the field of social security, for all or part of the branches and schemes set out in Article 4(1) and (2), together with agreements, of whatever kind, concluded pursuant to the said instruments;

(*l*) "competent authority" means, in respect of each Member State, the Minister, Ministers or other equivalent authority responsible for social security schemes throughout or in any part of the territory of the State in question;

(*m*) "Administrative Commission" means the Commission referred to in Article 80;

(*n*) "institution" means, in respect of each Member State, the body or authority responsible for administering all or part of the legislation;

(*o*) "competent institution" means:

(*i*) the institution with which the person concerned is insured at the time of the application for benefit, or

(ii) the institution from which the person concerned is entitled or would be entitled to benefits if he or a member or members of his family were resident in the territory of the Member State in which the institution is situated, or

(iii) the institution designated by the competent authority of the Member State concerned, or

(iv) in the case of a scheme relating to an employer's liability in respect of the benefits set out in Article 4(1), either the employer or the insurer involved or, in default thereof, a body or authority designated by the competent authority of the Member State concerned;

(*p*) "institution of the place of residence" and "institution of the place of stay" mean respectively the institution which is competent to provide benefits in the place where the person concerned resides and the institution which is competent to provide benefits in the place where the person concerned is staying, under the legislation administered by that institution or, where no such institution exists, the institution designated by the competent authority of the Member State in question;

(*q*) "competent State" means the Member State in whose territory the competent institution is situated;

(*r*) "periods of insurance" means periods of contribution or periods of employment or self-employment as defined or recognised as periods of insurance by the legislation under which they were completed or considered as completed, and all periods treated as such, where they are regarded by the said legislation as equivalent to periods of insurance; [periods completed under a special scheme for civil servants are also considered as periods of insurance;][1]

(*s*) "periods of employment" and "periods of self-employment" mean periods so defined or recognised by the legislation under which they were completed, and all periods treated as such, where they are regarded by the said legislation as equivalent to periods of employment or of self-employment; [periods completed under a special scheme for civil servants are also considered as periods of employment;][1]

(*sa*)–(*v*) . . .

Note—Words omitted are not relevant to this work.

Amendments—[1] Para (*a*)(i) substituted and para (*ja*) and words at the end of paras (*r*), (*s*) inserted by EC Council Regulation 1606/98 of 29 June 1998, OJ L209, 25.7.98 p 1.

[2] Para (*ca*) inserted by EC Council Regulation 307/99 of 8 February 1999, OJ L38, 12.02.1999, p 1–5.

Article 2 Persons covered

[1. This Regulation shall apply to employed or self-employed persons and to students who are or have been subject to the legislation of one or more Member States and who are nationals of one of the Member States or who are stateless persons or refugees residing within the territory of one of the Member States, as well as to the members of their families and their survivors.

2. This Regulation shall apply to the survivors of employed or self-employed persons and of students who have been subject to the legislation of one or more Member States, irrespective of the nationality of such persons, where their survivors are nationals of one of the Member States, or stateless persons or refugees residing within the territory of one of the Member States.][1]

Note—Words omitted are not relevant to this work.

Amendment—[1] Article 2 substituted by EC Council Regulation 307/99 of 8 February 1999, OJ L38, 12.02.1999, pp 1–5.

Article 3 Equality of treatment

(1) Subject to the special provisions of this Regulation, persons . . . [1] to whom this Regulation applies shall be subject to the same obligations . . . under the legislation of any Member State as the nationals of that State.

(2) . . .

(3) Save as provided in Annex III, the provisions of social security conventions which remain in force pursuant to . . . . . . [1], shall apply to all persons to whom this Regulation applies.

Note—Words omitted are not relevant to this work.

Amendment—[1] Words in paras (1), (3) repealed by Parliament and Council Regulation (EC) 647/2005 art 1(1) (OJ L 117; 4.5.2005 p 1).

Article 4 Matters covered

(1) This Regulation shall apply to all legislation concerning the following branches of social security:

(*a*) sickness and maternity benefits;
(*b*) invalidity benefits, including those intended for the maintenance or improvement of earning capacity;
(*c*) old-age benefits;
(*d*) survivors' benefits;
(*e*) benefits in respect of accidents at work and occupational diseases;
(*f*) death grants;
(*g*) unemployment benefits;
(*h*) family benefits.

(2) This Regulation shall apply to all general and special social security schemes, whether contributory or non-contributory, and to schemes concerning the liability of an employer or ship owner in respect of the benefits referred to in paragraph (1).

(4) This Regulation shall not apply to social and medical assistance, to benefit schemes for victims of war or its consequences, . . . [1]

Note—Words omitted are not relevant to this work.

Amendments—[1] In para (4) words repealed by EC Council Regulation 1606/98 of 29 June 1998, OJ L209, 25.7.98 p 1.

Article 5 Declarations of Member States on the scope of this Regulation

The Member States shall specify the legislation and schemes referred to in Article 4(1) and (2) . . . in declarations to be notified and published in accordance with Article 97.

Note—This article has been amended by EEC Council Regulation 1247/92, OJ L136, 19.5.92, p 2, but the amendment (ie words omitted) is not relevant to this work.

Article 6 Social security conventions replaced by this Regulation

Subject to the provisions of Articles . . . 8 . . . this Regulation shall, as regards persons and matters which it covers, replace the provisions of any social security convention binding either:

(*a*) two or more Member States exclusively, or

(*b*) at least two Member States and one or more other States, where settlement of the cases concerned does not involve any institution of one of the latter States.

Note—Words omitted are not relevant to this work.

Article 8 Conclusion of conventions between Member States

(1) Two or more Member States may, as need arises, conclude conventions with each other based on the principles and in the spirit of this Regulation.

(2) Each Member State shall notify, in accordance with the provisions of Article 97(1), any convention concluded with another Member State under the provisions of paragraph (1).

Article 9 Admission to voluntary or optional continued insurance

(1) The provisions of the legislation of any Member State which make admission to voluntary or optional continued insurance conditional upon residence in the territory of that State shall not apply to persons resident in the territory of another Member State, provided that at some time in their past working life they were subject to the legislation of the first State as employed or as self-employed persons.

(2) Where, under the legislation of a Member State, admission to voluntary or optional continued insurance is conditional upon completion of periods of insurance, the periods of insurance or residence completed under the legislation of another Member State shall be taken into account, to the extent required, as if they were completed under the legislation of the first State.

Cross reference—See EEC Council Regulation 574/72, Art 6 (implementation of this Article).

TITLE II

DETERMINATION OF THE LEGISLATION APPLICABLE

Article 13 General rules

[(1) Subject to Articles 14c and 14f, persons to whom this Regulation applies shall be subject to the legislation of a single Member State only. That legislation shall be determined in accordance with the provisions of this Title;][2]

(2) Subject to Articles 14 to 17:

(*a*) a person employed in the territory of one Member State shall be subject to the legislation of that State even if he resides in the territory of another Member State or if the registered office or place of business of the undertaking or individual employing him is situated in the territory of another Member State;

(*b*) a person who is self-employed in the territory of one Member State shall be subject to the legislation of that State even if he resides in the territory of another Member State.

(*c*) a person employed on board a vessel flying the flag of a Member State shall be subject to the legislation of that State;

(*d*) civil servants and persons treated as such shall be subject to the legislation of the Member State to which the administration employing them is subject;

(*e*) a person called up or recalled for service in the armed forces, or for civilian service, of a Member State shall be subject to the legislation of that State. If entitlement under that legislation is subject to the completion of periods of insurance before entry into or after release from such military or civilian service, periods of insurance completed under the legislation of any other Member State shall be taken into account, to the extent necessary, as if they were periods of insurance completed under the legislation of the first State. The employed or self-employed person called up or recalled for service in the armed forces or for civilian service shall retain the status of employed or self-employed person.

[(*f*) a person to whom the legislation of a Member State ceases to be applicable, without the legislation of another Member State becoming applicable to him in accordance with one of the rules laid down in the aforegoing subparagraphs or in accordance with one of the exceptions or special provisions laid down in Articles 14 to 17 shall be subject to the legislation of the Member State in whose territory he resides in accordance with the provisions of that legislation alone.][1]

Cross reference—See EEC Council Regulation 574/72, Art 11 (implementation of this Article).

Amendments—[1] Para (2)(*f*) added by EEC Council Regulation 2195/91, art 1(2); OJ L206, 29.7.1991, p 2.

[2] Para (1) substituted by EC Council Regulation 1606/98 of 29 June 1998, OJ L209, 25.7.98 p 1.

Article 14 Special rules applicable to persons, other than mariners, engaged in paid employment

Article 13(2)(*a*) shall apply subject to the following exceptions and circumstances:

(1)

(*a*) A person employed in the territory of a Member State by an undertaking to which he is normally attached who is posted by that undertaking to the territory of another Member State to perform work there for that undertaking shall continue to be subject to the legislation of the first Member State, provided that the anticipated duration of that work does not exceed 12 months and that he is not sent to replace another person who has completed his term of posting;

(*b*) if the duration of the work to be done extends beyond the duration originally anticipated, owing to unforeseeable circumstances, and exceeds 12 months, the legislation of the first Member State shall continue to apply until the completion of such work, provided that the competent authority of the Member State in whose territory the person concerned is posted or the body designated by that authority gives its consent; such consent must be requested before the end of the initial 12-month period. Such consent cannot, however, be given for a period exceeding 12 months.

(2) A person normally employed in the territory of two or more Member States shall be subjected to the legislation determined as follows:

(*a*) a person who is a member of the travelling or flying personnel of an undertaking which, for hire or reward or on its own account, operates international transport services for passengers or goods by rail, road, air or inland waterway and has its registered office or place of business in the territory of a Member State, shall be subject to the legislation of the latter State, with the following restrictions:

(*i*) where the said undertaking has a branch or permanent representation in the territory of a Member State other than that in which it has its registered office or place of business, a person employed by such branch or permanent representation shall be subject to the legislation of the Member State in whose territory such branch or permanent representation is situated;

(ii) where a person is employed principally in the territory of the Member State in which he resides, he shall be subject to the legislation of that State, even if the undertaking which employs him has no registered office or place of business or branch or permanent representation in that territory;

(*b*) a person other than that referred to in (*a*) shall be subject:

(*i*) to the legislation of the Member State in whose territory he resides, if he pursues his activity partly in that territory or if he is attached to several undertakings or several employers who have their registered offices or places of business in the territory of different Member States;

(ii) to the legislation of the Member State in whose territory is situated the registered office or place of business of the undertaking or individual employing him, if he does not reside in the territory of any of the Member States where he is pursuing his activity.

(3) A person who is employed in the territory of one Member State by an undertaking which has its registered office or place of business in the territory of another Member State and which straddles the common frontier of these States shall be subject to the legislation of the Member State in whose territory the undertaking has its registered office or place of business.

Cross reference—See EEC Council Regulation 574/72, Arts 11, 12 and 12a (implementation of this Article).

Article 14a Special rules applicable to persons, other than mariners, who are self-employed

Article 13(2)(*b*) shall apply subject to the following exceptions and circumstances:

(1)

(*a*) A person normally self-employed in the territory of a Member State and who performs work in the territory of another Member State shall continue to be subject to the legislation of the first Member State, provided that the anticipated duration of that work does not exceed 12 months;

(*b*) if the duration of the work to be done extends beyond the duration originally anticipated, owing to unforeseeable circumstances, and exceeds 12 months, the legislation of the first Member State shall continue to apply until the completion of such work, provided that the competent authority of the Member State in whose territory the person concerned has entered to perform the work in question or the body appointed by that authority gives its consent; such consent must be requested before the end of the initial 12-month period. Such consent cannot, however, be given for a period exceeding 12 months.

(2) A person normally self-employed in the territory of two or more the Member States shall be subject to the legislation of the Member State in whose territory he resides if he pursues any part of his activity in the territory of the Member State. If he does not pursue any activity in the territory of the Member State in which he resides, he shall be subject to the legislation of the Member State in whose territory he pursues his main activity. The criteria used to determine the principal activity are laid down in the Regulation referred to in Article 98.

NIC

(3) A person who is self-employed in an undertaking which has its registered office or place of business in the territory of one Member State and which straddles the common frontier of two Member States shall be subject to the legislation of the Member State in whose territory the undertaking has its registered office or place of business.

(4) If the legislation to which a person should be subject in accordance with paragraphs (2) or (3) does not enable that person, even on a voluntary basis, to join a pension scheme, the person concerned shall be subject to the legislation of the other Member State which would apply apart from these particular provisions or, should the legislations of two or more Member States apply in this way, he shall be subject to the legislation decided on by common agreement amongst the Member States concerned or their competent authorities.

Cross reference—See EEC Council Regulation 574/72, Arts 11a and 12a (implementation of this Article).

Article 14b Special rules applicable to mariners

Article 13(2)(*c*) shall apply subject to the following exceptions and circumstances:

(1) A person employed by an undertaking to which he is normally attached, either in the territory of a Member State or on board a vessel flying the flag of a Member State, who is posted by that undertaking on board a vessel flying the flag of another Member State to perform work there for that undertaking shall, subject to the conditions provided in Article 14(1), continue to be subject to the legislation of the first Member State.

(2) A person normally self-employed, either in the territory of a Member State or on board a vessel flying the flag of a Member State and who performs work on his own account on board a vessel flying the flag of another Member State shall, subject to the conditions provided in Article 14a(1), continue to be subject to the legislation of the first Member State.

(3) A person who, while not being normally employed at sea, performs work in the territorial waters or in a port of a Member State on a vessel flying the flag of another Member State within those territorial waters or in that port, but is not a member of the crew of the vessel, shall be subject to the legislation of the first Member State.

(4) A person employed on board a vessel flying the flag of a Member State and remunerated for such employment by an undertaking or a person whose registered office or place of business is in the territory of another Member State shall be subject to the legislation of the latter State if he is resident in the territory of that State; the undertaking or person paying the remuneration shall be considered as the employer for the purposes of the said legislation.

Cross reference—See EEC Council Regulation 574/72, Arts 11, 11a and 12 (implementation of this Article).

Article 14c Special rules applicable to persons who are simultaneously employed in the territory of one Member State and self-employed in the territory of another Member State

A person who is simultaneously employed in the territory of one Member State and self-employed in the territory of another Member State shall be subject:

(*a*) save as otherwise provided in subparagraph (*b*) to the legislation of the Member State in the territory of which he is engaged in paid employment or, where he pursues such an activity in the territory of two or more Member States, to the legislation determined in accordance with Article 14(2) or (3);

(*b*) in the cases mentioned in Annex VII:

— to the legislation of the Member State in the territory of which he is engaged in paid employment, that legislation having been determined in accordance with the provisions of Article 14(2) or (3), where he pursues such an activity in the territory of two or more Member States, and

— to the legislation of the Member State in the territory of which he is self-employed, that legislation having been determined in accordance with Article 14a(2), (3) or (4), where he pursues such an activity in the territory of two or more Member States.

Cross reference—See EEC Council Regulation 574/72, Art 12a (implementation of this Article).
Amendment—Article 14c substituted by Council Regulation 3811/86/EEC; OJ L355, 16.12.1986, p 5; art 1(1).

Article 14d Miscellaneous provisions

[(1) The person referred to in Article 14(2) and (3), Article 14a(2), (3) and (4), Article 14c(a) and Article 14e shall be treated, for the purposes of application of the legislation laid down in accordance with these provisions, as if he pursued all his professional activity or activities in the territory of the Member State concerned.][1]

[(2) The person referred to in Article 14c(*b*) shall be treated, for the purposes of determining the rates of contributions to be charged to self-employed workers under the legislation of the Member State in whose territory he is self-employed, as if he pursued his paid employment in the territory of the Member State concerned.]

(3) . . .

Note—Words omitted are not relevant to this work.
Amendments—Para (2) substituted by Council Regulation 3811/86/EEC; OJ L355, 16.12.1986, p 5; art 1(1).
[1] Para (1) substituted by EC Council Regulation 1606/98 of 29 June 1998, OJ L209, 25.7.98 p 1.

[Article 14e Special rules applicable to persons insured in a special scheme for civil servants who are simultaneously employed and/or self-employed in the territory of one or more other Member States

A person who is simultaneously employed as a civil servant or a person treated as such and insured in a special scheme for civil servants in one Member State and who is employed and/or self-employed in the territory of one or more other Member States shall be subject to the legislation of the Member State in which he is insured in a special scheme for civil servants.]

Amendments—This article inserted by EC Council Regulation 1606/98 of 29 June 1998, OJ L209, 25.7.98 p 1.

[Article 14f Special rules applicable to civil servants simultaneously employed in more than one Member State and insured in one of these States in a special scheme

A person who is simultaneously employed in two or more Member States as a civil servant or person treated as such and insured in at least one of those Member States in a special scheme for civil servants shall be subject to the legislation of each of these Member States.]

Amendments—This article inserted by EC Council Regulation 1606/98 of 29 June 1998, OJ L209, 25.7.98 p 1.

Article 15 Rules concerning voluntary insurance or optional continued insurance

(1) Articles 13 to 14d shall not apply to voluntary insurance or to optional continued insurance unless, in respect of one of the branches referred to in Article 4, there exists in any Member State only a voluntary scheme of insurance.

(2) Where application of the legislations of two or more Member States entails overlapping of insurance:

- under a compulsory insurance scheme and one or more voluntary or optional continued insurance schemes, the person concerned shall be subject exclusively to the compulsory insurance scheme;
- under two or more voluntary or optional continued insurance schemes, the person concerned may join only the voluntary or optional continued insurance scheme for which he has opted.

(3) However, in respect of invalidity, old age and death (pensions), the person concerned may join the voluntary or optional continued insurance scheme of a Member State, even if he is compulsorily subject to the legislation of another Member State, to the extent that such overlapping is explicitly or implicitly admitted in the first Member State.

Article 16 Special rules regarding persons employed by diplomatic missions and consular posts, and auxiliary staff of the European Communities

(1) The provision of Article 13(2)(*a*) shall apply to persons employed by diplomatic missions and consular posts and to the private domestic staff of agents of such missions or posts.

(2) However, employed persons covered by paragraph (1) who are nationals of the Member State which is the accrediting or sending State may opt to be subject to the legislation of that State. Such right of option may be renewed at the end of each calendar year and shall not have retrospective effect.

(3) Auxiliary staff of the European Communities may opt to be subject to the legislation of the Member State in whose territory they are employed, to the legislation of the Member State to which they were last subject or to the legislation of the Member State whose nationals they are, in respect of provisions other than those relating to family allowances, the granting of which is governed by the conditions of employment applicable to such staff. This right of option, which may be exercised once only, shall take effect from the date of entry into employment.

Cross reference—See EEC Council Regulation 574/72, Arts 13 and 14 (implementation of this Article).

[Article 17 Exceptions to Articles 13 to 16

Two or more Member States, the competent authorities of those States or the bodies designated by these authorities may by common agreement provide for exceptions to the provisions of Articles 13 to 16 in the interests of certain categories of persons or of certain persons.]

Amendment—Article 17 substituted by EEC Council Regulation 2195/91; OJ L206, 29.7.1991, p 2.

[Article 17a Special rules concerning recipients of pensions due under the legislation of one or more Member State

The recipient of a pension due under the legislation of a Member State or of pensions due under the legislation of several Member States who resides in the territory of another Member State may at his request be exempted from the legislation of the latter State provided that he is not subject to that legislation because of the pursuit of an occupation.]

Amendment—Article 17a inserted by EEC Council Regulation 2195/91; OJ L206, 29.7.1991, p 2.

TITLE VI
MISCELLANEOUS PROVISIONS

Article 84 Co-operation between competent authorities

(1) The competent authorities of Member States shall communicate to each other all information regarding:

(*a*) measures taken to implement this Regulation;

NIC

(*b*) changes in their legislation which are likely to affect the implementation of this Regulation.

(2) For the purposes of implementing this Regulation, the authorities and institutions of Member States shall lend their good offices and act as though implementing their own legislation. The administrative assistance furnished by the said authorities and institutions shall, as a rule, be free of charge. However, the competent authorities of the Member States may agree to certain expenses being reimbursed.

(3) The authorities and institutions of Member States may, for the purpose of implementing this Regulation, communicate directly with one another and with the persons concerned or their representatives.

(4), (5) . . .

Note—Words omitted are not relevant to this work.

[Article 84a Relations between the institutions and the persons covered by this Regulation

(1) The institutions and persons covered by this Regulation shall have a duty of mutual information and cooperation to ensure the correct implementation of this Regulation.

The institutions, in accordance with the principle of good administration, shall respond to all queries within a reasonable period of time and shall in this connection provide the persons concerned with any information required for exercising the rights conferred on them by this Regulation.

The persons concerned shall inform the institutions of the competent State and of the State of residence as soon as possible of any changes in their personal or family situation which affect their right to benefits under this Regulation.

(2) Failure to respect the obligation of information referred to in paragraph 1, third subparagraph, may result in the application of proportionate measures in accordance with national law. Nevertheless, these measures shall be equivalent to those applicable to similar situations under domestic law and shall not make it impossible or excessively difficult in practice for claimants to exercise the rights conferred on them by this Regulation.

(3) In the event of difficulties in the interpretation or application of this Regulation which could jeopardise the rights of a person covered by it, the institution of the competent State or of the State of residence of the person involved shall contact the institution(s) of the Member State(s) concerned. If a solution cannot be found within a reasonable period, the authorities concerned may call on the Administrative Commission to intervene.][1]

Amendment—[1] Article 84a inserted by European Parliament and Council Regulation 631/2004 art 1(8) (OJ L 100; 6.4.2004 p 1).

Article 91 Contributions chargeable to employers or undertakings not established in the competent State

An employer shall not be bound to pay increased contributions by reason of the fact that his place of business or the registered office or place of business of his undertaking is in the territory of a Member State other than the competent State.

92 Collection of contributions

(1) Contributions payable to an institution of one Member State may be collected in the territory of another Member State in accordance with the administrative procedure and with the guarantees and privileges applicable to the collection of contributions payable to the corresponding institution of the latter State.

(2) The procedure for the implementation of paragraph (1) shall be governed, in so far as is necessary, by the implementing Regulation referred to in Article 98 or by means of agreements between Member States. Such implementing procedure may also cover procedure for enforcing payment.

TITLE VII

TRANSITIONAL AND FINAL PROVISIONS

Article 97 Notifications pursuant to certain provisions

(1) The notifications referred to in Articles 1(*j*), 5 and 8(2) shall be addressed to the President of the Council of the European Communities. They shall indicate the date of entry into force of the laws and schemes in question or, in the case of the notifications referred to in Article 1(*j*), the date from which this Regulation shall apply to the schemes mentioned in the declarations of the Member States.

(2) Notifications received in accordance with the provisions of paragraph (1) shall be published in the *Official Journal of the European Communities*.

Article 98 Implementing Regulation

A further Regulation shall lay down the procedure for implementing this Regulation.

Cross reference—See EEC Council Regulation 574/72.

ANNEX I

PERSONS COVERED BY THE REGULATION

Note—Annex I and heading substituted by Council Regulation 3095/95 (OJ L335, 30.12.95, p 1). The categories in this Annex have been re-ordered, and new categories inserted, by the Act of Accession of the Czech Republic, Estonia, Cyprus, Latvia, Lithuania, Hungary, Malta, Poland, Slovenia and the Slovak Republic. See art 20, Annex II thereof.

I.

EMPLOYED PERSONS AND/OR SELF-EMPLOYED PERSONS (ARTICLE 1(A)(II) AND (III) OF THE REGULATION)

A.

Belgium

Does not apply.

[B.

Bulgaria

Any person working without an employment contract within the meaning of points 5 and 6 of Article 4(3) of the Social Security Code shall be considered a self-employed person within the meaning of Article 1(a)(ii) of the Regulation.][1]

Amendment—[1] Entry inserted by Council Regulation (EC) No 1791/2006 art 1, Annex para 2 (OJ L 363, 20.12.2006, p 1).

C.

Czech Republic.

Does not apply.

D.

Denmark

1 Any person who, from the fact of pursuing an activity as an employed person, is subject:

(*a*) to the legislation on accidents at work and occupational diseases for the period prior to 1 September 1977;

(*b*) to the legislation on supplementary pensions for employed persons (arbejdsmarkedets tillaegspension, ATP) for a period commencing on or after 1 September 1977,

shall be considered as an employed person within the meaning of Article 1(a)(ii) of the Regulation.

2 Any person who, pursuant to the law on daily cash benefits in the event of sickness or maternity, is entitled to such benefits on the basis of an earned income other than a wage or salary shall be considered a self-employed person within the meaning of Article 1(*a*)(ii) of the Regulation.

E.

Germany

If the competent institution for granting family benefits in accordance with Chapter 7 of Title III of the Regulation is a German institution, then within the meaning of Article 1(*a*)(ii) of the Regulation:

(*a*) "employed person" means any person compulsorily insured against unemployment or any person who, as a result of such insurance, obtains cash benefits under sickness insurance or comparable benefits [or any established civil servant in receipt of a salary in respect of his/her civil servant status which is at least equal to that which, in the case of an employed person, would result in compulsory insurance against unemployment][1];

(*b*) "self-employed person" means any person pursuing self-employment which is bound:

— to join, or pay contributions in respect of, an old-age insurance within a scheme for self-employed persons, or

— to join a scheme within the framework of compulsory pension insurance.

Amendment—[1] Words in sub-s (*a*) inserted by Council Regulation 1399/99/EEC, OJ L 164, 30.6.1999, p 4 with effect from 1 September 1999.

F.

Estonia

Does not apply.

G.

Greece

1 Persons insured under the OGA scheme who pursue exclusively activities as employed persons or who are or have been subject to the legislation of another Member State and who consequently are or have been "employed persons" within the meaning of Article 1(*a*) of the Regulation are considered as employed persons within the meaning of Article 1(*a*)(iii) of the Regulation.

2 For the purposes of granting the national family allowances, persons referred to in Article 1(*a*)(i) and (iii) of the Regulation are considered as employed persons within the meaning of Article 1(*a*)(ii) of the Regulation.

H.

Spain

Does not apply.

[I.

France

If a French Institution is the competent institution for the grant of family benefits in accordance with Title III, Chapter 7 of the Regulation:

1 "employed person" within the meaning of Article 1(*a*)(ii) of the Regulation shall be deemed to mean any person who is compulsorily insured under the social security scheme in accordance with Article L 311-2 of the Social Security Code and who fulfils the minimum conditions regarding work or remuneration provided for in Article L 313-1 of the Social Security Code in order to benefit from cash benefits under sickness insurance, maternity and invalidity cover or the person who benefits from these cash benefits;
"self-employed person" within the meaning of Article 1(*a*)(ii) of the Regulation shall be deemed to mean any person who performs a self-employed activity and who is required to take out insurance and to pay old-age benefit contributions to a self-employed persons' scheme.][1]

Amendment—[1] Substituted by Council Regulation 3427/89/EEC, OJ L 331, 16.11.1989, p 3.

J.

Ireland

[1 1. Any person who is compulsorily or voluntarily insured pursuant to the provisions of Sections 12, 24 and 70 of the Social Welfare Consolidation Act 2005 shall be considered an employed person within the meaning of Article 1(*a*)(ii) of the Regulation.
2. Any person who is compulsorily or voluntarily insured pursuant to the provisions of Sections 20 and 24 of the Social Welfare Consolidation Act 2005 shall be considered a self-employed person within the meaning of Article 1(*a*)(ii) of the Regulation.][1]

Amendments—[1] Para 1 substituted by Regulation (EC) 592/2008 of the European Parliament and of the Council art 1, Annex 1 (OJ L 177, 4.7.2008 p 1).

[2 Any person who is compulsorily or voluntarily insured pursuant to the provisions of [Sections 17 and 21 of the Social Welfare (Consolidation) Act 1993][2] shall be considered a self-employed person within the meaning of Article 1 (*a*) (ii) of the Regulation.][1]

Amendments—[1] Para 2 substituted by Council Regulation (EEC) 1945/93 art 1 para 1 (OJ L 181, 23.7.1993 p 1).
[2] Words substituted by Council Regulation (EC) 1223/98 art 1 para 3 (OJ L 168, 13.6.1998 p 1).

K.

Italy

Does not apply.

L.

Cyprus

Does not apply.

M.

Latvia

Does not apply.

N.

Lithuania

Does not apply.

O.

Luxembourg

Does not apply.

P.

Hungary.

Does not apply.

Q.

Malta.

Does not apply.

R.

Netherlands

Any person pursuing an activity or occupation without a contract of employment shall be considered a self-employed person within the meaning of Article 1(*a*)(ii) of the Regulation.

[S.

Austria

Does not apply.][1]

Amendments—[1] Annex I, Part I amended by Act of Accession 1994; OJ L1, 1.1.1995, p 23.

T.

Poland

Does not apply.

U.

Portugal

Does not apply.

[V.

Romania

Does not apply.][1]

Amendments—[1] Entry for Romania inserted by Council Regulation (EC) No 1791/2006 art 1, Annex para 2 (OJ L 363, 20.12.2006, p 1).

W.

Slovenia

Does not apply.

[X.

Slovakia

For the purpose of determining entitlement to benefits in kind pursuant to the provisions of Chapter 1 of title III of the Regulation, "member of the family" means a spouse and/or a dependent child as defined by the Act on Child Allowance][1]

Amendments—[1] Entry for Slovakia substituted by European Parliament Regulation (EC) 629/2006 art 1, Annex para 1 (OJ L 114, 27.4.2006, p 1).

[Y.

Finland

Any person who is an employed or self-employed person within the meaning of the legislation on the Employment Pensions Scheme shall be considered respectively as employed or self-employed within the meaning of Article 1(*a*)(ii) of the Regulation.

NIC

[Z.

Sweden

Persons who are engaged in gainful activity and who pay their own contributions on this income pursuant to Chapter 3, paragraph 3, of the Social Insurance Contributions Act (2000:980) shall be considered as self-employed.][2]][1]

Amendments—[1] Annex I, Part I amended by Act of Accession 1994; OJ L1, 1.1.1995, p 23.

[2] Entry for Sweden substituted by European Parliament and Council Regulation (EC) No 1992/2006 art 1, Annex para 1 (OJ L 392, 30.12.2006, p 1). Note, this entry, as substituted, is preceded by a letter "X". This appears to be a drafting error which ignores previous re-ordering of entries by Council Regulation (EC) No 1791/2006. The publisher has therefore retained the preceding letter "Z".

AA.

United Kingdom

Any person who is an "employed earner" or a "self-employed earner" within the meaning of the legislation of Great Britain or of the legislation of Northern Ireland shall be regarded respectively as an employed person or a self-employed person within the meaning of Article 1(*a*)(ii) of the Regulation. Any person in respect of whom contributions are payable as an "employed person" or a "self-employed person" in accordance with the legislation of Gibraltar shall be regarded respectively as an employed person or a self-employed person within the meaning of Article 1(*a*)(ii) of the Regulation.

Note—Entries re-ordered as a result of insertion of entries for Bulgaria and Romania, by Council Regulation (EC) No 1791/2006 art 1, Annex para 2 (OJ L 363, 20.12.2006, p 1).

II.

MEMBERS OF THE FAMILY
(SECOND SENTENCE OF ARTICLE 1(F) OF THE REGULATION)

. . .

ANNEX II

Note—The categories in this Annex have been re-ordered, and new categories inserted, by the Act of Accession of the Czech Republic, Estonia, Cyprus, Latvia, Lithuania, Hungary, Malta, Poland, Slovenia and the Slovak Republic. See art 20, Annex II thereof.

I.

SPECIAL SCHEMES FOR SELF-EMPLOYED PERSONS EXCLUDED FROM THE SCOPE OF THE REGULATION PURSUANT TO THE FOURTH SUB-PARAGRAPH OF ARTICLE 1(J) (ARTICLE 1(J) AND (U) OF THE REGULATION)

A.

Belgium

Does not apply.

[B.

Bulgaria

Does not apply.][1]

Amendments—[1] Entry for Bulgaria inserted by Council Regulation (EC) No 1791/2006 art 1, Annex para 2 (OJ L 363, 20.12.2006, p 1).

C.

Czech Republic

Does not apply.

D.

Denmark

Does not apply.

E.

Germany

[Does not apply][1]

Amendments—[1] Substituted by Parliament and Council Regulation (EC) 647/2005 art 10, Annex I para 1 (OJ L 117; 4.5.2005 p 1).

F.

Estonia

Does not apply.

G.

Greece

Does not apply.

H.

Spain

[1 Self-employed persons as referred to in Article 10 (2) (c) of the Consolidated Text of the General Law on Social Security (Royal Legislative Decree No 1/1994 of 20 June 1994) and in Article 3 of Decree No 2530/1970 of 20 August 1970 regulating the special scheme for self-employed persons who join a professional association and decide to become members of the mutual insurance society set up by the said association instead of joining the special social security scheme for self-employed persons.][1]

Amendments—[1] Substituted by EEC Council Regulation 1290/97; OJ L176, 4.7.1997, p 1.

2 Welfare system and/or with the character of social assistance or a charity, managed by institutions not subject to the General Law on Social Security or to the Law of 6 December 1941.

[I.

France

[1 Supplementary benefit schemes for self-employed persons in craft trades, industrial or commercial occupations or the liberal professions, supplementary old-age insurance schemes for self-employed persons in the liberal professions, supplementary insurance schemes for self-employed persons in the liberal professions covering invalidity or death, and supplementary old-age benefit schemes for contracted medical practitioners and auxiliaries, as referred to respectively in Articles L.615-20, L.644-1, L.644-2, L.645-1 and L.723-14 of the Social Security Code.][1]

Amendments—[1] Para 1 substituted by Regulation (EC) 592/2008 of the European Parliament and of the Council art 1, Annex 1(2) (OJ L 177, 4.7.2008 p 1).

2 Supplementary sickness and maternity insurance schemes for self-employed workers in agriculture, as referred to in Article L.727–1 of the Rural Code.][1]

Amendments—[1] Substituted by Parliament Regulation (EC) 629/2006 art 1, Annex para 2 (OJ L 114; 27.4.2006).

J.

Ireland

Does not apply.

K.

Italy

Does not apply.

L.

Cyprus

1 Pension scheme for doctors in private practice set up under the Medical (Pensions and Allowances) Regulations of 1999 (PI 295/99) issued under the Medical (Associations, Discipline and Pension Fund) Law of 1967 (Law 16/67), as amended.

2 Advocates' pension scheme set up under the Advocates (Pensions and Allowances) Regulations of 1966 (PI 642/66), as amended, issued under the Advocates Law, Cap. 2, as amended.

M.

Latvia

Does not apply.

N.

Lithuania

Does not apply.

O.

Luxembourg

Does not apply.

P.

Hungary

Does not apply.

Q.

Malta

Does not apply

[R.

Netherlands

For the purpose of determining entitlement to benefits pursuant to Chapters 1 and 4 of Title III of this Regulation, "member of the family" means a spouse, registered partner or child under the age of 18.][1]

Amendments—[1] Entry for the Netherlands substituted by European Parliament and Council Regulation (EC) No 1992/2006 art 1, Annex para 1 (OJ L 392, 30.12.2006, p 1). Note, this entry, as substituted, is preceded by a letter "Q". This appears to be a drafting error which ignores previous re-ordering of entries by Council Regulation (EC) No 1791/2006. The publisher has therefore retained the preceding letter "R".

S.

Austria

[Does not apply]

T.

Poland

Does not apply.

U.

Portugal

Does not apply.

[V.

Romania

For the purposes of determining entitlement to benefits in kind pursuant to the provisions of Chapter 1 of Title III of the Regulation, "member of the family" means a spouse, a dependent parent, a child under the age of 18 (or under the age of 26 and dependent).][1]

Amendments—[1] Entry for Romania inserted by Council Regulation (EC) No 1791/2006 art 1, Annex para 2 (OJ L 363, 20.12.2006, p 1).

W.

Slovenia

Does not apply.

X.

Slovakia

Does not apply.

Y.

Finland

Does not apply.

Z.

Sweden

Does not apply.

AA.

United Kingdom

Does not apply.

Note—Entries re-ordered as a result of insertion of entries for Bulgaria and Romania, by Council Regulation (EC) No 1791/2006 art 1, Annex para 2 (OJ L 363, 20.12.2006, p 1).

ANNEX III

Note—This Annex substituted by Act of Accession 1985 (OJ L 302, 15.11.1985, p 170). The categories in this Annex have been re-ordered, and new categories inserted, by the Act of Accession of the Czech Republic, Estonia, Cyprus, Latvia, Lithuania, Hungary, Malta, Poland, Slovenia and the Slovak Republic. See art 20, Annex II thereof.

(Articles 7(2)(*c*) and 3(3) of the Regulation)

Provisions of social security conventions remaining applicable notwithstanding Article 6 of the Regulation—Provisions of social security conventions which do not apply to all persons to whom the Regulation applies

GENERAL COMMENTS

1 In so far as the provisions contained in this Annex provide for references to the provisions of other conventions, those references shall be replaced by references to the corresponding provisions of this Regulation, unless the provisions of the conventions in question are themselves contained in this Annex.

2 The termination clause provided for in a social security convention, some of whose provisions are contained in this Annex, shall continue to apply as regards those provisions.

[3 Account being taken of the provisions of Article 6 of this Regulation, it is to be noted that the provisions of bilateral Conventions which do not fall within the scope of this Regulation and which remain in force between Member States are not listed in this Annex, inter alia, provisions providing for aggregation of insurance periods fulfilled in a third country.][1]

Amendments—[1] Paragraph 3 inserted by Parliament and Council Regulation (EC) 647/2005 art 10, Annex I para 3 (OJ L 117; 4.5.2005 p 1).

A.
PROVISIONS OF SOCIAL SECURITY CONVENTIONS REMAINING APPLICABLE NOTWITHSTANDING ARTICLE 6 OF THE REGULATION

(Article 7(2)(*c*) of the Regulation)

[23][2].

Germany—United Kingdom

[(*a*) Article 7(5) and (6) of the Convention on social security of 20 April 1960 (legislation applicable to civilians serving the military forces);][1]

[(*b*) Article 5(5) and (6) of the Convention on unemployment insurance of 20 April 1960 (legislation applicable to civilians serving the military forces)][1]

. . .

Amendments[1] Words substituted by Parliament and Council Regulation (EC) 647/2005 art 10, Annex I para 3 (OJ L 117; 4.5.2005 p 1).

[2] Renumbered, by Council Regulation (EC) No 1791/2006 art 1, Annex para 2 (OJ L 363, 20.12.2006, p 1).

[25][2].

Ireland—United Kingdom

[Article 8 of the Agreement of 14 September 1971 on social security (concerning the transfer and reckoning of certain disability credits)][1]

. . .

Amendments[1] Words substituted by Parliament and Council Regulation (EC) 647/2005 art 10, Annex I para 3 (OJ L 117; 4.5.2005 p 1).

[2] Renumbered, by Council Regulation (EC) No 1791/2006 art 1, Annex para 2 (OJ L 363, 20.12.2006, p 1).

24.

Belgium—United Kingdom

Amendments—Repealed by Parliament and Council Regulation (EC) 647/2005 art 10, Annex I para 3 (OJ L 117; 4.5.2005 p 1).

[[30][2].

Portugal—United Kingdom

(*a*) Article 2(1) of the Protocol on medical treatment of 15 November 1978.

(*b*) As regards Portuguese employed persons, and for the period from 22 October 1987 to the end of the transitional period provided for in Article 220(1) of the Act relating to the conditions of accession of Spain and Portugal: Article 26 of the Social Security Convention of 15 November 1978, as amended by the Exchange of Letters of 28 September 1987.][1]

Amendments—[1] Substituted by Council Regulation 2332/89/EEC, OJ L 224, 2.8.1989, p 1.
[2] Renumbered by Parliament and Council Regulation (EC) 629/2006 art 1, Annex para 5 (OJ L 114; 27.4.2006).

47.

Czech Republic—United Kingdom

Amendment—Repealed by Parliament and Council Regulation (EC) 629/2006 art 1, Annex para 5 (OJ L 114; 27.4.2006).

69.

Denmark—United Kingdom

Amendments—Repealed by Parliament and Council Regulation (EC) 647/2005 art 10, Annex I para 3 (OJ L 117; 4.5.2005 p 1).

110.

Estonia—United Kingdom

Amendment—Repealed by Parliament and Council Regulation (EC) 629/2006 art 1, Annex para 5 (OJ L 114; 27.4.2006).

129.

Greece—United Kingdom

Amendments—Repealed by Parliament and Council Regulation (EC) 647/2005 art 10, Annex I para 3 (OJ L 117; 4.5.2005 p 1).

147.

Spain—United Kingdom

Amendments—Repealed by Parliament and Council Regulation (EC) 647/2005 art 10, Annex I para 3 (OJ L 117; 4.5.2005 p 1).

164.

France—United Kingdom

Amendments—Repealed by Parliament and Council Regulation (EC) 647/2005 art 10, Annex I para 3 (OJ L 117; 4.5.2005 p 1).

195.

Italy—United Kingdom

Amendments—Repealed by Parliament and Council Regulation (EC) 647/2005 art 10, Annex I para 3 (OJ L 117; 4.5.2005 p 1).

209.

Cyprus—United Kingdom

Amendment—Repealed by Parliament and Council Regulation (EC) 629/2006 art 1, Annex para 5 (OJ L 114; 27.4.2006).

222.

Latvia—United Kingdom

Amendment—Repealed by Parliament and Council Regulation (EC) 629/2006 art 1, Annex para 5 (OJ L 114; 27.4.2006).

234.

Lithuania—United Kingdom.

Amendment—Repealed by Parliament and Council Regulation (EC) 629/2006 art 1, Annex para 5 (OJ L 114; 27.4.2006).

245.

Luxembourg—United Kingdom

Amendments—Repealed by Parliament and Council Regulation (EC) 647/2005 art 10, Annex I para 3 (OJ L 117; 4.5.2005 p 1).

255.

Hungary—United Kingdom

Amendment—Repealed by Parliament and Council Regulation (EC) 629/2006 art 1, Annex para 5 (OJ L 114; 27.4.2006).

264.

Malta—United Kingdom

Amendment—Repealed by Parliament and Council Regulation (EC) 629/2006 art 1, Annex para 5 (OJ L 114; 27.4.2006).

272.

Netherlands—United Kingdom

Amendments—Repealed by Parliament and Council Regulation (EC) 647/2005 art 10, Annex I para 3 (OJ L 117; 4.5.2005 p 1).

279.

Austria—United Kingdom

Amendments—Repealed by Parliament and Council Regulation (EC) 647/2005 art 10, Annex I para 3 (OJ L 117; 4.5.2005 p 1).

285.

Poland—United Kingdom

Amendment—Repealed by Parliament and Council Regulation (EC) 629/2006 art 1, Annex para 5 (OJ L 114; 27.4.2006).

294.

Slovenia—United Kingdom

Amendment—Repealed by Parliament and Council Regulation (EC) 629/2006 art 1, Annex para 5 (OJ L 114; 27.4.2006).

297.

Slovakia—United Kingdom

Amendment—Repealed by Parliament and Council Regulation (EC) 629/2006 art 1, Annex para 5 (OJ L 114; 27.4.2006).

299.

Finland—United Kingdom

Amendments—Repealed by Parliament and Council Regulation (EC) 647/2005 art 10, Annex I para 3 (OJ L 117; 4.5.2005 p 1).

300.

Sweden—United Kingdom

Amendments—Repealed by Parliament and Council Regulation (EC) 647/2005 art 10, Annex I para 3 (OJ L 117; 4.5.2005 p 1).

B.

PROVISIONS OF CONVENTIONS WHICH DO NOT APPLY TO ALL PERSONS TO WHOM THE REGULATION APPLIES

(Article 3(3) of the Regulation)

. . .

24.

Belgium—United Kingdom

Amendment—Repealed by Parliament and Council Regulation (EC) 647/2005 art 10, Annex I para 3 (OJ L 117; 4.5.2005 p 1).

47.

Czech Republic—United Kingdom

Amendment—Repealed by Parliament and Council Regulation (EC) 629/2006 art 1, Annex para 5 (OJ L 114; 27.4.2006).

69.

Denmark—United Kingdom

Amendment—Repealed by Parliament and Council Regulation (EC) 647/2005 art 10, Annex I para 3 (OJ L 117; 4.5.2005 p 1).

90.

Germany—United Kingdom

Amendment—Repealed by Parliament and Council Regulation (EC) 647/2005 art 10, Annex I para 3 (OJ L 117; 4.5.2005 p 1).

110.

Estonia—United Kingdom

Amendment—Repealed by Parliament and Council Regulation (EC) 629/2006 art 1, Annex para 5 (OJ L 114; 27.4.2006).

129.

Greece—United Kingdom

Amendment—Repealed by Parliament and Council Regulation (EC) 647/2005 art 10, Annex I para 3 (OJ L 117; 4.5.2005 p 1).

147.

Spain—United Kingdom

Amendment—Repealed by Parliament and Council Regulation (EC) 647/2005 art 10, Annex I para 3 (OJ L 117; 4.5.2005 p 1).

164.

France—United Kingdom

Amendment—Repealed by Parliament and Council Regulation (EC) 647/2005 art 10, Annex I para 3 (OJ L 117; 4.5.2005 p 1).

180.

Ireland—United Kingdom

Amendment—Repealed by Parliament and Council Regulation (EC) 647/2005 art 10, Annex I para 3 (OJ L 117; 4.5.2005 p 1).

195.

Italy—United Kingdom

Amendment—Repealed by Parliament and Council Regulation (EC) 647/2005 art 10, Annex I para 3 (OJ L 117; 4.5.2005 p 1).

209.

Cyprus—United Kingdom

Amendment—Repealed by Parliament and Council Regulation (EC) 629/2006 art 1, Annex para 5 (OJ L 114; 27.4.2006).

222.

Latvia—United Kingdom

Amendment—Repealed by Parliament and Council Regulation (EC) 629/2006 art 1, Annex para 5 (OJ L 114; 27.4.2006).

234.

Lithuania—United Kingdom

Amendment—Repealed by Parliament and Council Regulation (EC) 629/2006 art 1, Annex para 5 (OJ L 114; 27.4.2006).

245.

Luxembourg—United Kingdom

Amendment—Repealed by Parliament and Council Regulation (EC) 647/2005 art 10, Annex I para 3 (OJ L 117; 4.5.2005 p 1).

255.

Hungary—United Kingdom

Amendment—Repealed by Parliament and Council Regulation (EC) 629/2006 art 1, Annex para 5 (OJ L 114; 27.4.2006).

264.

Malta—United Kingdom

Amendment—Repealed by Parliament and Council Regulation (EC) 629/2006 art 1, Annex para 5 (OJ L 114; 27.4.2006).

272.

Netherlands—United Kingdom

Amendment—Repealed by Parliament and Council Regulation (EC) 647/2005 art 10, Annex I para 3 (OJ L 117; 4.5.2005 p 1).

279.

Austria—United Kingdom

Amendment—Repealed by Parliament and Council Regulation (EC) 647/2005 art 10, Annex I para 3 (OJ L 117; 4.5.2005 p 1).

285.

Poland—United Kingdom

Amendment—Repealed by Parliament and Council Regulation (EC) 629/2006 art 1, Annex para 5 (OJ L 114; 27.4.2006).

290.

Portugal—United Kingdom

Amendment—Repealed by Parliament and Council Regulation (EC) 647/2005 art 10, Annex I para 3 (OJ L 117; 4.5.2005 p 1).

294.

Slovenia—United Kingdom

Amendment—Repealed by Parliament and Council Regulation (EC) 629/2006 art 1, Annex para 5 (OJ L 114; 27.4.2006).

297.

Slovakia—United Kingdom

Amendment—Repealed by Parliament and Council Regulation (EC) 629/2006 art 1, Annex para 5 (OJ L 114; 27.4.2006).

299.

Finland—United Kingdom

Amendment—Repealed by Parliament and Council Regulation (EC) 647/2005 art 10, Annex I para 3 (OJ L 117; 4.5.2005 p 1).

300.

Sweden—United Kingdom

Amendment—Repealed by Parliament and Council Regulation (EC) 647/2005 art 10, Annex I para 3 (OJ L 117; 4.5.2005 p 1).

[ANNEX VII

INSTANCES IN WHICH A PERSON SHALL BE SIMULTANEOUSLY SUBJECT TO THE LEGISLATION OF TWO MEMBER STATES

(Article 14c(1)(b) of the Regulation)

1. Where he is self-employed in Belgium and gainfully employed in any other Member State.
2. Where a person is self-employed in Bulgaria and gainfully employed in any other Member State.
3. Where a person is self-employed in the Czech Republic and gainfully employed in any other Member State.
4. Where a person resident in Denmark is self-employed in Denmark and gainfully employed in any other Member State.
5. For the agricultural accident insurance scheme and the old-age insurance scheme for farmers: where he is self-employed in farming in Germany and gainfully employed in any other Member State.
6. Where a person resident in Estonia is self-employed in Estonia and gainfully employed in any other Member State.
7. For the pension insurance scheme for self-employed persons: where he is self-employed in Greece and gainfully employed in any other Member State.
8. Where a person resident in Spain is self-employed in Spain and gainfully employed in any other Member State.
9. Where he is self-employed in France and gainfully employed in any other Member State, except Luxembourg.
10. Where he is self-employed in farming in France and gainfully employed in Luxembourg.
11. Where he is self-employed in Italy and gainfully employed in any other Member State.
12. Where a person resident in Cyprus is self-employed in Cyprus and gainfully employed in any other Member State.
13. Where a person is self-employed in Malta and gainfully employed in any other Member State.
14. Where he is self-employed in Portugal and gainfully employed in any other Member State.
15. Where a person is self-employed in Romania and gainfully employed in any other Member State.
16. Where a person resident in Finland is self-employed in Finland and gainfully employed in any other Member State.
17. Where a person is self-employed in Slovakia and gainfully employed in any other Member State.
18. Where a person resident in Sweden is self-employed in Sweden and gainfully employed in any other Member State.[1]

Amendments—[1] Annex substituted by Council Regulation (EC) No 1791/2006 art 1, Annex para 2 (OJ L 363, 20.12.2006, p 1).

COUNCIL REGULATION (EC) OF 14 MAY 2003

EXTENDING THE PROVISIONS OF REGULATION (EEC) NO 1408/71 AND REGULATION (EEC) NO 574/72 TO NATIONALS OF THIRD COUNTRIES WHO ARE NOT ALREADY COVERED BY THOSE PROVISIONS SOLELY ON THE GROUND OF THEIR NATIONALITY

(859/03/EC)

Note—This Regulation is repealed between the member states that are bound by this Regulation, by Regulation 1231/2010/EU (OJ 344, 29.12.2010 p 1)

THE COUNCIL OF THE EUROPEAN UNION,

Having regard to the Treaty establishing the European Community and in particular Article 63, point 4 thereof,

Having regard to the proposal from the Commission[1],

Having regard to the opinion of the European Parliament[2],

Whereas:

(1) As its special meeting in Tampere on 15 and 16 October 1999, the European Council proclaimed that the European Union should ensure fair treatment of third-country nationals who reside legally in the territory of its Member States, grant them rights and obligations comparable to those of EU citizens, enhance non-discrimination in economic, social and cultural life and approximate their legal status to that of Member States' nationals.

(2) In its resolution of 27 October 1999[3], the European Parliament called for prompt action on promises of fair treatment for third-country nationals legally resident in the Member States and on the definition of their legal status, including uniform rights as close as possible to those enjoyed by the citizens of the European Union.

(3) The European Economic and Social Committee has also appealed for equal treatment of Community nationals and third-country nationals in the social field, notably in its opinion of 26 September 1991 on the status of migrant workers from third countries[4].

(4) Article 6(2) of the Treaty on European Union provides that the Union shall respect fundamental rights, as guaranteed by the European Convention on the Protection of Human Rights and Fundamental Freedoms signed in Rome on 4 November 1950 and as they result from the constitutional traditions common to the Member States, as general principles of Community law.

(5) This Regulation respects the fundamental rights and observes the principles recognised in particular by the Charter of Fundamental Rights of the European Union, in particular the spirit of its Article 34(2).

(6) The promotion of a high level of social protection and the raising of the standard of living and quality of life in the Member States are objectives of the Community.

(7) As regards the conditions of social protection of third-country nationals, and in particular the social security scheme applicable to them, the Employment and Social Policy Council argued in its conclusions of 3 December 2001 that the coordination applicable to third-country nationals should grant them a set of uniform rights as near as possible to those enjoyed by EU citizens.

(8) Currently, Council Regulation (EEC) No 1408/71 of 14 June 1971 on the application of social security schemes to employed persons and their families moving within the Community[5], which is the basis for the coordination of the social security schemes of the different Member States, and Council Regulation (EEC) No 574/72 of 21 March 1972, laying down the procedure for implementing Regulation (EEC) No 1408/71[6], apply only to certain third-country nationals. The number and diversity of legal instruments used in an effort to resolve problems in connection with the coordination of the Member States' social security schemes encountered by nationals of third countries who are in the same situation as Community nationals give rise to legal and administrative complexities. They create major difficulties for the individuals concerned, their employers, and the competent national social security bodies.

(9) Hence, it is necessary to provide for the application of the coordination rules of Regulation (EEC) No 1408/71 and Regulation (EEC) No 574/72 to third-country nationals legally resident in the Community who are not currently covered by the provisions of these Regulations on grounds of their nationality and who satisfy the other conditions provided for in this Regulation; such an extension is in particular important with a view to the forthcoming enlargement of the European Union.

(10) The application of Regulation (EEC) No 1408/71 and Regulation (EEC) No 574/72 to these persons does not give them any entitlement to enter, to stay or to reside in a Member State or to have access to its labour market.

(11) The provisions of Regulation (EEC) No 1408/71 and Regulation (EEC) No 574/72 are, by virtue of this Regulation, applicable only in so far as the person concerned is already legally resident in the territory of a Member State. Being legally resident is therefore a prerequisite for the application of these provisions.

(12) The provisions of Regulation (EEC) No 1408/71 and Regulation (EEC) No 574/72 are not applicable in a situation which is confined in all respects within a single Member State. This concerns, inter alia, the situation of a third country national who has links only with a third country and a single Member State.

(13) The continued right to unemployment benefit, as laid down in Article 69 of Regulation (EEC) No 1408/71, is subject to the condition of registering as a job-seeker with the employment services of each Member State entered. Those provisions may therefore apply to a third-country national only provided he/she has the right, where appropriate pursuant to his/her residence permit, to register as a job-seeker with the employment services of the Member State entered and the right to work there legally.

(14) Transitional provisions should be adopted to protect the persons covered by this Regulation and to ensure that they do not lose rights as a result of its entry into force.

(15) To achieve these objectives it is necessary and appropriate to extend the scope of the rules coordinating the national social security schemes by adopting a Community legal instrument which is binding and directly applicable in every Member State which takes part in the adoption of this Regulation.

(16) This Regulation is without prejudice to rights and obligations arising from international agreements with third countries to which the Community is a party and which afford advantages in terms of social security.

(17) Since the objectives of the proposed action cannot be sufficiently achieved by the Member States and can therefore, by reason of the scale or effects of the proposed action, be better achieved at Community level, the Community may take measures in accordance with the principle of subsidiarity enshrined in Article 5 of the Treaty. In compliance with the principle of proportionality as set out in that Article, this Regulation does not go beyond what is necessary to achieve these objectives.

(18) In accordance with Article 3 of the Protocol on the position of the United Kingdom and Ireland annexed to the Treaty on the European Union and to the Treaty establishing the European Community, Ireland and the United Kingdom gave notice, by letters of 19 and 23 April 2002, of their wish to take part in the adoption and application of this Regulation.

(19) In accordance with Articles 1 and 2 of the Protocol on the position of Denmark annexed to the Treaty on the European Union and to the Treaty establishing the European Community, Denmark is not taking part in the adoption of this Regulation and is not therefore bound by or subject to it,

Notes—[1] OJ C 126 E, 28.5.2002, p. 388.
[2] Opinion of 21 November 2002 (not yet published in the Official Journal).
[3] OJ C 154, 5.6.2000, p. 63.
[4] OJ C 339, 31.12.1991, p. 82.
[5] OJ L 149, 5.7.1971, p. 2; Regulation last amended by Regulation (EC) No 1386/2001 of the European Parliament and of the Council (OJ L 187, 10.7.2001, p. 1).
[6] OJ L 74, 27.3.1972, p. 1; Regulation last amended by Commission Regulation (EC) No 410/2002 (OJ L 62, 5.3.2002, p. 17).

NIC

HAS ADOPTED THIS REGULATION:

Article 1

Subject to the provisions of the Annex to this Regulation, the provisions of Regulation (EEC) No 1408/71 and Regulation (EEC) No 574/72 shall apply to nationals of third countries who are not already covered by those provisions solely on the ground of their nationality, as well as to members of their families and to their survivors, provided they are legally resident in the territory of a Member State and are in a situation which is not confined in all respects within a single Member State.

Article 2

(1) This Regulation shall not create any rights in respect of the period before 1 June 2003.

(2) Any period of insurance and, where appropriate, any period of employment, self-employment or residence completed under the legislation of a Member State before 1 June 2003 shall be taken into account for the determination of rights acquired in accordance with the provisions of this Regulation.

(3) Subject to the provisions of paragraph 1, a right shall be acquired under this Regulation even if it relates to a contingency arising prior to 1 June 2003.

(4) Any benefit that has not been awarded or that has been suspended on account of the nationality or the residence of the person concerned shall, at the latter's request, be awarded or resumed from 1 June 2003, provided that the rights for which benefits were previously awarded did not give rise to a lump-sum payment.

(5) The rights of persons who prior to 1 June 2003, obtained the award of a pension may be reviewed at their request, account being taken of the provisions of this Regulation.

(6) If the request referred to in paragraph 4 or paragraph 5 is lodged within two years from 1 June 2003, rights deriving from this Regulation shall be acquired from that date and the provisions of the legislation of any Member State on the forfeiture or lapse of rights may not be applied to the persons concerned.

(7) If the request referred to in paragraph 4 or paragraph 5 is lodged after expiry of the deadline referred to in paragraph 6, rights not forfeited or lapsed shall be acquired from the date of such request, subject to any more favourable provisions of the legislation of any Member State.

Article 3

This Regulation shall enter into force on the first day of the month following its publication in the Official Journal of the European Union.

This Regulation shall be binding in its entirety and directly applicable in the Member States in accordance with the Treaty establishing the European Community.

Done at Brussels, 14 May 2003.

ANNEX

SPECIAL PROVISIONS REFERRED TO IN ARTICLE 1

I.
GERMANY

In the case of family benefits, this Regulation shall apply only to third-country nationals who are in possession of a residence permit meeting the definition in German law of the "Aufenthaltserlaubnis" or "Aufenthaltsberechtigung".

II.
AUSTRIA

In the case of family benefits, this Regulation shall apply only to third-country nationals who fulfil the conditions laid down by Austrian legislation for permanent entitlement to family allowances.

REGULATION (EC) NO 883/2004
OF THE EUROPEAN PARLIAMENT AND OF THE COUNCIL
OF 29 APRIL 2004
ON THE COORDINATION OF SOCIAL SECURITY SYSTEMS

(883/2004/EC)

Notes—The text of this Regulation includes the amendments made by the following—

- Regulation 988/2009/EC with effect from 1 May 2010;
- Commission Regulation 1244/2010/EU with effect from 11 January 2011;
- Commission Regulation 465/2012/EU with effect from 28 June 2012;
- Commission Regulation 1224/2012/EU with effect from 8 January 2013
- Council Regulation 517/2013/EU with effect from 1 July 2013
- Commission Regulation 1372/2013/EU with effect from 1 January 2014; and
- Commission Regulation (EU) 2017/492 with effect from 11 April 2017.

This Regulation shall apply to nationals of third countries who are not already covered by these Regulations solely on the ground of their nationality, as well as to members of their families and to their survivors, provided that they are legally resident in the territory of a Member State and are in a situation which is not confined in all respects within a single Member State (Regulation 1231/2010/EU Art 1, OJ L 344, 29.12.2010, p 1).

THE EUROPEAN PARLIAMENT AND THE COUNCIL OF THE EUROPEAN UNION,

Having regard to the Treaty establishing the European Community, and in particular Articles 42 and 308 thereof,

Having regard to the proposal from the Commission presented after consultation with the social partners and the Administrative Commission on Social Security for Migrant Workers [1],

Having regard to the opinion of the European Economic and Social Committee [2],

Acting in accordance with the procedure laid down in Article 251 of the Treaty [3],

Whereas:

(1) The rules for coordination of national social security systems fall within the framework of free movement of persons and should contribute towards improving their standard of living and conditions of employment.

(2) The Treaty does not provide powers other than those of Article 308 to take appropriate measures within the field of social security for persons other than employed persons.

(3) Council Regulation (EEC) No 1408/71 of 14 June 1971 on the application of social security schemes to employed persons, to self-employed persons and to members of their families moving within the Community [4] has been amended and updated on numerous occasions in order to take into account not only developments at Community level, including judgments of the Court of Justice, but also changes in legislation at national level. Such factors have played their part in making the Community coordination rules complex and lengthy. Replacing, while modernising and simplifying, these rules is therefore essential to achieve the aim of the free movement of persons.

(4) It is necessary to respect the special characteristics of national social security legislation and to draw up only a system of coordination.

(5) It is necessary, within the framework of such coordination, to guarantee within the Community equality of treatment under the different national legislation for the persons concerned.

(6) The close link between social security legislation and those contractual provisions which complement or replace such legislation and which have been the subject of a decision by the

public authorities rendering them compulsory or extending their scope may call for similar protection with regard to the application of those provisions to that afforded by this Regulation. As a first step, the experience of Member States who have notified such schemes might be evaluated.

(7) Due to the major differences existing between national legislation in terms of the persons covered, it is preferable to lay down the principle that this Regulation is to apply to nationals of a Member State, stateless persons and refugees resident in the territory of a Member State who are or have been subject to the social security legislation of one or more Member States, as well as to the members of their families and to their survivors.

(8) The general principle of equal treatment is of particular importance for workers who do not reside in the Member State of their employment, including frontier workers.

(9) The Court of Justice has on several occasions given an opinion on the possibility of equal treatment of benefits, income and facts; this principle should be adopted explicitly and developed, while observing the substance and spirit of legal rulings.

(10) However, the principle of treating certain facts or events occurring in the territory of another Member State as if they had taken place in the territory of the Member State whose legislation is applicable should not interfere with the principle of aggregating periods of insurance, employment, self-employment or residence completed under the legislation of another Member State with those completed under the legislation of the competent Member State. Periods completed under the legislation of another Member State should therefore be taken into account solely by applying the principle of aggregation of periods.

(11) The assimilation of facts or events occurring in a Member State can in no way render another Member State competent or its legislation applicable.

(12) In the light of proportionality, care should be taken to ensure that the principle of assimilation of facts or events does not lead to objectively unjustified results or to the overlapping of benefits of the same kind for the same period.

(13) The coordination rules must guarantee that persons moving within the Community and their dependants and survivors retain the rights and the advantages acquired and in the course of being acquired.

(14) These objectives must be attained in particular by aggregating all the periods taken into account under the various national legislation for the purpose of acquiring and retaining the right to benefits and of calculating the amount of benefits, and by providing benefits for the various categories of persons covered by this Regulation.

(15) It is necessary to subject persons moving within the Community to the social security scheme of only one single Member State in order to avoid overlapping of the applicable provisions of national legislation and the complications which could result therefrom.

(16) Within the Community there is in principle no justification for making social security rights dependent on the place of residence of the person concerned; nevertheless, in specific cases, in particular as regards special benefits linked to the economic and social context of the person involved, the place of residence could be taken into account.

(17) With a view to guaranteeing the equality of treatment of all persons occupied in the territory of a Member State as effectively as possible, it is appropriate to determine as the legislation applicable, as a general rule, that of the Member State in which the person concerned pursues his/her activity as an employed or self-employed person.

(17a) Once the legislation of a Member State becomes applicable to a person under Title II of this Regulation, the conditions for affiliation and entitlement to benefits should be defined by the legislation of the competent Member State while respecting Community law.

(18) In specific situations which justify other criteria of applicability, it is necessary to derogate from that general rule.

(18a) The principle of single applicable legislation is of great importance and should be enhanced. This should not mean, however, that the grant of a benefit alone, in accordance with this Regulation and comprising the payment of insurance contributions or insurance coverage for the beneficiary, renders the legislation of the Member State, whose institution has granted that benefit, the applicable legislation for that person.

(18b) In Annex III to Council Regulation (EEC) No 3922/91 of 16 December 1991 on the harmonization of technical requirements and administrative procedures in the field of civil aviation (*), the concept of "home base" for flight crew and cabin crew members is defined as the location nominated by the operator to the crew member from where the crew member normally starts and ends a duty period, or a series of duty periods, and where, under normal conditions, the operator is not responsible for the accommodation of the crew member concerned. In order to facilitate the application of Title II of this Regulation for flight crew and cabin crew members, it is justified to use the concept of "home base" as the criterion for determining the applicable legislation for flight crew and cabin crew members. However, the applicable legislation for flight crew and cabin crew members should remain stable and the

NIC

home base principle should not result in frequent changes of applicable legislation due to the industry's work patterns or seasonal demands.

(19) In some cases, maternity and equivalent paternity benefits may be enjoyed by the mother or the father and since, for the latter, these benefits are different from parental benefits and can be assimilated to maternity benefits *strictu sensu* in that they are provided during the first months of a new-born child's life, it is appropriate that maternity and equivalent paternity benefits be regulated jointly.

(20) In the field of sickness, maternity and equivalent paternity benefits, insured persons, as well as the members of their families, living or staying in a Member State other than the competent Member State, should be afforded protection.

(21) Provisions on sickness, maternity and equivalent paternity benefits were drawn up in the light of Court of Justice caselaw. Provisions on prior authorisation have been improved, taking into account the relevant decisions of the Court of Justice.

(22) The specific position of pension claimants and pensioners and the members of their families makes it necessary to have provisions governing sickness insurance adapted to this situation.

(23) In view of the differences between the various national systems, it is appropriate that Member States make provision, where possible, for medical treatment for family members of frontier workers in the Member State where the latter pursue their activity.

(24) It is necessary to establish specific provisions regulating the non-overlapping of sickness benefits in kind and sickness benefits in cash which are of the same nature as those which were the subject of the judgments of the Court of Justice in Case C-215/99 *Jauch* and C-160/96 *Molenaar*, provided that those benefits cover the same risk.

(25) In respect of benefits for accidents at work and occupational diseases, rules should be laid down, for the purpose of affording protection, covering the situation of persons residing or staying in a Member State other than the competent Member State.

(26) For invalidity benefits, a system of coordination should be drawn up which respects the specific characteristics of national legislation, in particular as regards recognition of invalidity and aggravation thereof.

(27) It is necessary to devise a system for the award of old-age benefits and survivors' benefits where the person concerned has been subject to the legislation of one or more Member States.

(28) There is a need to determine the amount of a pension calculated in accordance with the method used for aggregation and pro rata calculation and guaranteed by Community law where the application of national legislation, including rules concerning reduction, suspension or withdrawal, is less favourable than the aforementioned method.

(29) To protect migrant workers and their survivors against excessively stringent application of the national rules concerning reduction, suspension or withdrawal, it is necessary to include provisions strictly governing the application of such rules.

(30) As has constantly been reaffirmed by the Court of Justice, the Council is not deemed competent to enact rules imposing a restriction on the overlapping of two or more pensions acquired in different Member States by a reduction of the amount of a pension acquired solely under national legislation.

(31) According to the Court of Justice, it is for the national legislature to enact such rules, bearing in mind that it is for the Community legislature to fix the limits within which the national provisions concerning reduction, suspension or withdrawal are to be applied.

(32) In order to foster mobility of workers, it is particularly appropriate to facilitate the search for employment in the various Member States; it is therefore necessary to ensure closer and more effective coordination between the unemployment insurance schemes and the employment services of all the Member States.

(33) It is necessary to include statutory pre-retirement schemes within the scope of this Regulation, thus guaranteeing both equal treatment and the possibility of exporting pre-retirement benefits as well as the award of family and health-care benefits to the person concerned, in accordance with the provisions of this Regulation; however, the rule on the aggregation of periods should not be included, as only a very limited number of Member States have statutory pre-retirement schemes.

(34) Since family benefits have a very broad scope, affording protection in situations which could be described as classic as well as in others which are specific in nature, with the latter type of benefit having been the subject of the judgments of the Court of Justice in Joined Cases C-245/94 and C-312/94 *Hoever and Zachow* and in Case C-275/96 *Kuusijärvi*, it is necessary to regulate all such benefits.

(35) In order to avoid unwarranted overlapping of benefits, there is a need to lay down rules of priority in the case of overlapping of rights to family benefits under the legislation of

the competent Member State and under the legislation of the Member State of residence of the members of the family.

(36) Advances of maintenance allowances are recoverable advances intended to compensate for a parent's failure to fulfil his/her legal obligation of maintenance to his/her own child, which is an obligation derived from family law. Therefore, these advances should not be considered as a direct benefit from collective support in favour of families. Given these particularities, the coordinating rules should not be applied to such maintenance allowances.

(37) As the Court of Justice has repeatedly stated, provisions which derogate from the principle of the exportability of social security benefits must be interpreted strictly. This means that they can apply only to benefits which satisfy the specified conditions. It follows that Chapter 9 of Title III of this Regulation can apply only to benefits which are both special and non-contributory and listed in Annex X to this Regulation.

(38) It is necessary to establish an Administrative Commission consisting of a government representative from each Member State, charged in particular with dealing with all administrative questions or questions of interpretation arising from the provisions of this Regulation, and with promoting further cooperation between the Member States.

(39) The development and use of data-processing services for the exchange of information has been found to require the creation of a Technical Commission, under the aegis of the Administrative Commission, with specific responsibilities in the field of data-processing.

(40) The use of data-processing services for exchanging data between institutions requires provisions guaranteeing that the documents exchanged or issued by electronic means are accepted as equivalent to paper documents. Such exchanges are to be carried out in accordance with the Community provisions on the protection of natural persons with regard to the processing and free movement of personal data.

(41) It is necessary to lay down special provisions which correspond to the special characteristics of national legislation in order to facilitate the application of the rules of coordination.

(42) In line with the principle of proportionality, in accordance with the premise for the extension of this Regulation to all European Union citizens and in order to find a solution that takes account of any constraints which may be connected with the special characteristics of systems based on residence, a special derogation by means of an Annex XI — 'DENMARK' entry, limited to social pension entitlement exclusively in respect of the new category of non-active persons, to whom this Regulation has been extended, was deemed appropriate due to the specific features of the Danish system and in the light of the fact that those pensions are exportable after a 10-year period of residence under the Danish legislation in force (Pension Act).

(43) In line with the principle of equality of treatment, a special derogation by means of an Annex XI — 'FINLAND' entry, limited to residence-based national pensions, is deemed appropriate due to the specific characteristics of Finnish social security legislation, the objective of which is to ensure that the amount of the national pension cannot be less than the amount of the national pension calculated as if all insurance periods completed in any Member State were completed in Finland.

(44) It is necessary to introduce a new Regulation to repeal Regulation (EEC) No 1408/71. However, it is necessary that Regulation (EEC) No 1408/71 remain in force and continue to have legal effect for the purposes of certain Community acts and agreements to which the Community is a party, in order to secure legal certainty.

(45) Since the objective of the proposed action, namely the coordination measures to guarantee that the right to free movement of persons can be exercised effectively, cannot be sufficiently achieved by the Member States and can therefore, by reason of the scale and effects of that action, be better achieved at Community level, the Community may adopt measures in accordance with the principle of subsidiarity as set out in Article 5 of the Treaty. In accordance with the principle of proportionality as set out in that article, this Regulation does not go beyond what is necessary, in order to achieve that objective,

HAVE ADOPTED THIS REGULATION:

[1] OJ C 38, 12.2.1999, p. 10.

[2] OJ C 75, 15.3.2000, p. 29.

[3] Opinion of the European Parliament of 3 September 2003 (not yet published in the Official Journal). Council Common Position of 26 January 2004 (OJ C 79 E, 30.3.2004, p. 15) and Position of the European Parliament of 20 April 2004 (not yet published in the Official Journal). Decision of the Council of 26 April 2004.

[4] OJ L 149, 5.7.1971, p. 2. Regulation as last amended by Regulation (EC) No 1386/2001 of the European Parliament and of the Council (OJ L 187, 10.7.2001, p. 1).

TITLE I
GENERAL PROVISIONS

Article 1 Definitions

For the purposes of this Regulation:

(*a*) 'activity as an employed person' means any activity or equivalent situation treated as such for the purposes of the social security legislation of the Member State in which such activity or equivalent situation exists;

(*b*) 'activity as a self-employed person' means any activity or equivalent situation treated as such for the purposes of the social security legislation of the Member State in which such activity or equivalent situation exists;

(*c*) 'insured person', in relation to the social security branches covered by Title III, Chapters 1 and 3, means any person satisfying the conditions required under the legislation of the Member State competent under Title II to have the right to benefits, taking into account the provisions of this Regulation;

(*d*) 'civil servant' means a person considered to be such or treated as such by the Member State to which the administration employing him/her is subject;

(*e*) 'special scheme for civil servants' means any social security scheme which is different from the general social security scheme applicable to employed persons in the Member State concerned and to which all, or certain categories of, civil servants are directly subject;

(*f*) 'frontier worker' means any person pursuing an activity as an employed or self-employed person in a Member State and who resides in another Member State to which he/she returns as a rule daily or at least once a week;

(*g*) 'refugee' shall have the meaning assigned to it in Article 1 of the Convention relating to the Status of Refugees, signed in Geneva on 28 July 1951;

(*h*) 'stateless person' shall have the meaning assigned to it in Article 1 of the Convention relating to the Status of Stateless Persons, signed in New York on 28 September 1954;

(*i*) 'member of the family' means:

1.

(i) any person defined or recognised as a member of the family or designated as a member of the household by the legislation under which benefits are provided;

(ii) with regard to benefits in kind pursuant to Title III, Chapter 1 on sickness, maternity and equivalent paternity benefits, any person defined or recognised as a member of the family or designated as a member of the household by the legislation of the Member State in which he/she resides;

2. if the legislation of a Member State which is applicable under subparagraph 1 does not make a distinction between the members of the family and other persons to whom it is applicable, the spouse, minor children, and dependent children who have reached the age of majority shall be considered members of the family;

3. if, under the legislation which is applicable under subparagraphs 1 and 2, a person is considered a member of the family or member of the household only if he/she lives in the same household as the insured person or pensioner, this condition shall be considered satisfied if the person in question is mainly dependent on the insured person or pensioner;

(*j*) 'residence' means the place where a person habitually resides;

(*k*) 'stay' means temporary residence;

(*l*) 'legislation' means, in respect of each Member State, laws, regulations and other statutory provisions and all other implementing measures relating to the social security branches covered by Article 3(1);

This term excludes contractual provisions other than those which serve to implement an insurance obligation arising from the laws and regulations referred to in the preceding subparagraph or which have been the subject of a decision by the public authorities which makes them obligatory or extends their scope, provided that the Member State concerned makes a declaration to that effect, notified to the President of the European Parliament and the President of the Council of the European Union. Such declaration shall be published in the *Official Journal of the European Union*;

(*m*) 'competent authority' means, in respect of each Member State, the Minister, Ministers or other equivalent authority responsible for social security schemes throughout or in any part of the Member State in question;

(*n*) 'Administrative Commission' means the commission referred to in Article 71;

(*o*) 'Implementing Regulation' means the Regulation referred to in Article 89;

(*p*) 'institution' means, in respect of each Member State, the body or authority responsible for applying all or part of the legislation;

(*q*) 'competent institution' means:

(i) the institution with which the person concerned is insured at the time of the application for benefit;

or

(ii) the institution from which the person concerned is or would be entitled to benefits if he/she or a member or members of his/her family resided in the Member State in which the institution is situated;

or

(iii) the institution designated by the competent authority of the Member State concerned;

or

(iv) in the case of a scheme relating to an employer's obligations in respect of the benefits set out in Article 3(1), either the employer or the insurer involved or, in default thereof, the body or authority designated by the competent authority of the Member State concerned;

(*r*) 'institution of the place of residence' and 'institution of the place of stay' mean respectively the institution which is competent to provide benefits in the place where the person concerned resides and the institution which is competent to provide benefits in the place where the person concerned is staying, in accordance with the legislation administered by that institution or, where no such institution exists, the institution designated by the competent authority of the Member State concerned;

(*s*) 'competent Member State' means the Member State in which the competent institution is situated;

(*t*) 'period of insurance' means periods of contribution, employment or self-employment as defined or recognised as periods of insurance by the legislation under which they were completed or considered as completed, and all periods treated as such, where they are regarded by the said legislation as equivalent to periods of insurance;

(*u*) 'period of employment' or 'period of self-employment' mean periods so defined or recognised by the legislation under which they were completed, and all periods treated as such, where they are regarded by the said legislation as equivalent to periods of employment or to periods of self-employment;

(*v*) 'period of residence' means periods so defined or recognised by the legislation under which they were completed or considered as completed;

(*va*) 'Benefits in kind' means:

(i) for the purposes of Title III, Chapter 1 (sickness, maternity and equivalent paternity benefits), benefits in kind provided for under the legislation of a Member State which are intended to supply, make available, pay directly or reimburse the cost of medical care and products and services ancillary to that care. This includes long-term care benefits in kind;

(ii) for the purposes of Title III, Chapter 2 (accidents at work and occupational diseases), all benefits in kind relating to accidents at work and occupational diseases as defined in point (i) above and provided for under the Member States' accidents at work and occupational diseases schemes;

(*w*) 'pension' covers not only pensions but also lump-sum benefits which can be substituted for them and payments in the form of reimbursement of contributions and, subject to the provisions of Title III, revaluation increases or supplementary allowances;

(*x*) 'pre-retirement benefit' means: all cash benefits, other than an unemployment benefit or an early old-age benefit, provided from a specified age to workers who have reduced, ceased or suspended their remunerative activities until the age at which they qualify for an old-age pension or an early retirement pension, the receipt of which is not conditional upon the person concerned being available to the employment services of the competent State; 'early old-age benefit' means a benefit provided before the normal pension entitlement age is reached and which either continues to be provided once the said age is reached or is replaced by another old-age benefit;

(*y*) 'death grant' means any one-off payment in the event of death excluding the lump-sum benefits referred to in subparagraph w;

(*z*) 'family benefit' means all benefits in kind or in cash intended to meet family expenses, excluding advances of maintenance payments and special childbirth and adoption allowances mentioned in Annex I.

Article 2 Persons covered

1. This Regulation shall apply to nationals of a Member State, stateless persons and refugees residing in a Member State who are or have been subject to the legislation of one or more Member States, as well as to the members of their families and to their survivors.
2. It shall also apply to the survivors of persons who have been subject to the legislation of one or more Member States, irrespective of the nationality of such persons, where their survivors are nationals of a Member State or stateless persons or refugees residing in one of the Member States.

Article 3 Matters covered

1. This Regulation shall apply to all legislation concerning the following branches of social security:

NIC

(*a*) sickness benefits;
(*b*) maternity and equivalent paternity benefits;
(*c*) invalidity benefits;
(*d*) old-age benefits;
(*e*) survivors' benefits;
(*f*) benefits in respect of accidents at work and occupational diseases;
(*g*) death grants;
(*h*) unemployment benefits;
(*i*) pre-retirement benefits;
(*j*) family benefits.

2. Unless otherwise provided for in Annex XI, this Regulation shall apply to general and special social security schemes, whether contributory or non-contributory, and to schemes relating to the obligations of an employer or shipowner.

3. This Regulation shall also apply to the special non-contributory cash benefits covered by Article 70.

4. The provisions of Title III of this Regulation shall not, however, affect the legislative provisions of any Member State concerning a shipowner's obligations.

5. This Regulation shall not apply to:
(*a*) social and medical assistance or
(*b*) benefits in relation to which a Member State assumes the liability for damages to persons and provides for compensation, such as those for victims of war and military action or their consequences; victims of crime, assassination or terrorist acts; victims of damage occasioned by agents of the Member State in the course of their duties; or victims who have suffered a disadvantage for political or religious reasons or for reasons of descent.

Article 4 Equality of treatment

Unless otherwise provided for by this Regulation, persons to whom this Regulation applies shall enjoy the same benefits and be subject to the same obligations under the legislation of any Member State as the nationals thereof.

Article 5 Equal treatment of benefits, income, facts or events

Unless otherwise provided for by this Regulation and in the light of the special implementing provisions laid down, the following shall apply:
(*a*) where, under the legislation of the competent Member State, the receipt of social security benefits and other income has certain legal effects, the relevant provisions of that legislation shall also apply to the receipt of equivalent benefits acquired under the legislation of another Member State or to income acquired in another Member State;
(*b*) where, under the legislation of the competent Member State, legal effects are attributed to the occurrence of certain facts or events, that Member State shall take account of like facts or events occurring in any Member State as though they had taken place in its own territory.

Article 6 Aggregation of periods

Unless otherwise provided for by this Regulation, the competent institution of a Member State whose legislation makes:
— the acquisition, retention, duration or recovery of the right to benefits,
— the coverage by legislation,
or
— the access to or the exemption from compulsory, optional continued or voluntary insurance,

conditional upon the completion of periods of insurance, employment, self-employment or residence shall, to the extent necessary, take into account periods of insurance, employment, self-employment or residence completed under the legislation of any other Member State as though they were periods completed under the legislation which it applies.

Article 7 Waiving of residence rules

Unless otherwise provided for by this Regulation, cash benefits payable under the legislation of one or more Member States or under this Regulation shall not be subject to any reduction, amendment, suspension, withdrawal or confiscation on account of the fact that the beneficiary or the members of his/her family reside in a Member State other than that in which the institution responsible for providing benefits is situated.

Article 8 Relations between this Regulation and other coordination instruments

1. This Regulation shall replace any social security convention applicable between Member States falling under its scope. Certain provisions of social security conventions entered into by the Member States before the date of application of this Regulation shall, however, continue to apply provided that they are more favourable to the beneficiaries or if they arise from specific historical

circumstances and their effect is limited in time. For these provisions to remain applicable, they shall be included in Annex II. If, on objective grounds, it is not possible to extend some of these provisions to all persons to whom the Regulation applies this shall be specified.

2. Two or more Member States may, as the need arises, conclude conventions with each other based on the principles of this Regulation and in keeping with the spirit thereof.

Article 9 Declarations by the Member States on the scope of this Regulation

1. The Member States shall notify the European Commission in writing of the declarations made in accordance with point (l) of Article 1, the legislation and schemes referred to in Article 3, the conventions entered into as referred to in Article 8(2), the minimum benefits referred to in Article 58, and the lack of an insurance system as referred to in Article 65a(1), as well as substantive amendments. Such notifications shall indicate the date from which this Regulation will apply to the schemes specified by the Member States therein.

2. These notifications shall be submitted to the European Commission every year and shall be given the necessary publicity.

Article 10 Prevention of overlapping of benefits

Unless otherwise specified, this Regulation shall neither confer nor maintain the right to several benefits of the same kind for one and the same period of compulsory insurance.

TITLE II
DETERMINATION OF THE LEGISLATION APPLICABLE

Article 11 General rules

1. Persons to whom this Regulation applies shall be subject to the legislation of a single Member State only. Such legislation shall be determined in accordance with this Title.

2. For the purposes of this Title, persons receiving cash benefits because or as a consequence of their activity as an employed or self-employed person shall be considered to be pursuing the said activity. This shall not apply to invalidity, old-age or survivors' pensions or to pensions in respect of accidents at work or occupational diseases or to sickness benefits in cash covering treatment for an unlimited period.

3. Subject to Articles 12 to 16:

(*a*) a person pursuing an activity as an employed or self-employed person in a Member State shall be subject to the legislation of that Member State;

(*b*) a civil servant shall be subject to the legislation of the Member State to which the administration employing him/her is subject;

(*c*) a person receiving unemployment benefits in accordance with Article 65 under the legislation of the Member State of residence shall be subject to the legislation of that Member State;

(*d*) a person called up or recalled for service in the armed forces or for civilian service in a Member State shall be subject to the legislation of that Member State;

(*e*) any other person to whom subparagraphs (*a*) to (*d*) do not apply shall be subject to the legislation of the Member State of residence, without prejudice to other provisions of this Regulation guaranteeing him/her benefits under the legislation of one or more other Member States.

4. For the purposes of this Title, an activity as an employed or selfemployed person normally pursued on board a vessel at sea flying the flag of a Member State shall be deemed to be an activity pursued in the said Member State. However, a person employed on board a vessel flying the flag of a Member State and remunerated for such activity by an undertaking or a person whose registered office or place of business is in another Member State shall be subject to the legislation of the latter Member State if he/she resides in that State. The undertaking or person paying the remuneration shall be considered as the employer for the purposes of the said legislation.

5. An activity as a flight crew or cabin crew member performing air passenger or freight services shall be deemed to be an activity pursued in the Member State where the home base, as defined in Annex III to Regulation (EEC) No 3922/91, is located.

Article 12 Special rules

1. A person who pursues an activity as an employed person in a Member State on behalf of an employer which normally carries out its activities there and who is posted by that employer to another Member State to perform work on that employer's behalf shall continue to be subject to the legislation of the first Member State, provided that the anticipated duration of such work does not exceed 24 months and that he/she is not sent to replace another posted person.

2. A person who normally pursues an activity as a self-employed person in a Member State who goes to pursue a similar activity in another Member State shall continue to be subject to the legislation of the first Member State, provided that the anticipated duration of such activity does not exceed 24 months.

Article 13 Pursuit of activities in two or more Member States

1. A person who normally pursues an activity as an employed person in two or more Member States shall be subject:

NIC

(*a*) to the legislation of the Member State of residence if he/she pursues a substantial part of his/her activity in that Member State; or

(*b*) if he/she does not pursue a substantial part of his/her activity in the Member State of residence:

(i) to the legislation of the Member State in which the registered office or place of business of the undertaking or employer is situated if he/she is employed by one undertaking or employer; or

(ii) to the legislation of the Member State in which the registered office or place of business of the undertakings or employers is situated if he/she is employed by two or more undertakings or employers which have their registered office or place of business in only one Member State; or

(iii) to the legislation of the Member State in which the registered office or place of business of the undertaking or employer is situated other than the Member State of residence if he/she is employed by two or more undertakings or employers, which have their registered office or place of business in two Member States, one of which is the Member State of residence; or

(iv) to the legislation of the Member State of residence if he/she is employed by two or more undertakings or employers, at least two of which have their registered office or place of business in different Member States other than the Member State of residence.

2. A person who normally pursues an activity as a self-employed person in two or more Member States shall be subject to:

(*a*) the legislation of the Member State of residence if he/she pursues a substantial part of his/her activity in that Member State;

or

(*b*) the legislation of the Member State in which the centre of interest of his/her activities is situated, if he/she does not reside in one of the Member States in which he/she pursues a substantial part of his/her activity.

3. A person who normally pursues an activity as an employed person and an activity as a self-employed person in different Member States shall be subject to the legislation of the Member State in which he/she pursues an activity as an employed person or, if he/she pursues such an activity in two or more Member States, to the legislation determined in accordance with paragraph 1.

4. A person who is employed as a civil servant by one Member State and who pursues an activity as an employed person and/or as a self-employed person in one or more other Member States shall be subject to the legislation of the Member State to which the administration employing him/her is subject.

5. Persons referred to in paragraphs 1 to 4 shall be treated, for the purposes of the legislation determined in accordance with these provisions, as though they were pursuing all their activities as employed or self-employed persons and were receiving all their income in the Member State concerned.

Article 14 Voluntary insurance or optional continued insurance

1. Articles 11 to 13 shall not apply to voluntary insurance or to optional continued insurance unless, in respect of one of the branches referred to in Article 3(1), only a voluntary scheme of insurance exists in a Member State.

2. Where, by virtue of the legislation of a Member State, the person concerned is subject to compulsory insurance in that Member State, he/she may not be subject to a voluntary insurance scheme or an optional continued insurance scheme in another Member State. In all other cases in which, for a given branch, there is a choice between several voluntary insurance schemes or optional continued insurance schemes, the person concerned shall join only the scheme of his/her choice.

3. However, in respect of invalidity, old age and survivors' benefits, the person concerned may join the voluntary or optional continued insurance scheme of a Member State, even if he/she is compulsorily subject to the legislation of another Member State, provided that he/she has been subject, at some stage in his/her career, to the legislation of the first Member State because or as a consequence of an activity as an employed or self-employed person and if such overlapping is explicitly or implicitly allowed under the legislation of the first Member State.

4. Where the legislation of a Member State makes admission to voluntary insurance or optional continued insurance conditional upon residence in that Member State or upon previous activity as an employed or self-employed person, Article 5(*b*) shall apply only to persons who have been subject, at some earlier stage, to the legislation of that Member State on the basis of an activity as an employed or self-employed person.

Article 15 Contract staff of the European Communities

Contract staff of the European Communities may opt to be subject to the legislation of the Member State in which they are employed, to the legislation of the Member State to which they were last subject or to the legislation of the Member State whose nationals they are, in respect of provisions other than those relating to family allowances, provided under the scheme applicable to such staff. This right of option, which may be exercised once only, shall take effect from the date of entry into employment.

Article 16 Exceptions to Articles 11 to 15

1. Two or more Member States, the competent authorities of these Member States or the bodies designated by these authorities may by common agreement provide for exceptions to Articles 11 to 15 in the interest of certain persons or categories of persons.

2. A person who receives a pension or pensions under the legislation of one or more Member States and who resides in another Member State may at his/her request be exempted from application of the legislation of the latter State provided that he/she is not subject to that legislation on account of pursuing an activity as an employed or self-employed person.

TITLE III

SPECIAL PROVISIONS CONCERNING THE VARIOUS CATEGORIES OF BENEFITS

CHAPTER 1

SICKNESS, MATERNITY AND EQUIVALENT PATERNITY BENEFITS

SECTION 1

INSURED PERSONS AND MEMBERS OF THEIR FAMILIES, EXCEPT PENSIONERS AND MEMBERS OF THEIR FAMILIES

Article 17 Residence in a Member State other than the competent Member State

An insured person or members of his/her family who reside in a Member State other than the competent Member State shall receive in the Member State of residence benefits in kind provided, on behalf of the competent institution, by the institution of the place of residence, in accordance with the provisions of the legislation it applies, as though they were insured under the said legislation.

Article 18 Stay in the competent Member State when residence is in another Member State – Special rules for the members of the families of frontier workers

1. Unless otherwise provided for by paragraph 2, the insured person and the members of his/her family referred to in Article 17 shall also be entitled to benefits in kind while staying in the competent Member State. The benefits in kind shall be provided by the competent institution and at its own expense, in accordance with the provisions of the legislation it applies, as though the persons concerned resided in that Member State.

2. The members of the family of a frontier worker shall be entitled to benefits in kind during their stay in the competent Member State.

Where the competent Member State is listed in Annex III however, the members of the family of a frontier worker who reside in the same Member State as the frontier worker shall be entitled to benefits in kind in the competent Member State only under the conditions laid down in Article 19(1).

Article 19 Stay outside the competent Member State

1. Unless otherwise provided for by paragraph 2, an insured person and the members of his/her family staying in a Member State other than the competent Member State shall be entitled to the benefits in kind which become necessary on medical grounds during their stay, taking into account the nature of the benefits and the expected length of the stay. These benefits shall be provided on behalf of the competent institution by the institution of the place of stay, in accordance with the provisions of the legislation it applies, as though the persons concerned were insured under the said legislation.

2. The Administrative Commission shall establish a list of benefits in kind which, in order to be provided during a stay in another Member State, require for practical reasons a prior agreement between the person concerned and the institution providing the care.

Article 20 Travel with the purpose of receiving benefits in kind — authorisation to receive appropriate treatment outside the Member State of residence

1. Unless otherwise provided for by this Regulation, an insured person travelling to another Member State with the purpose of receiving benefits in kind during the stay shall seek authorisation from the competent institution.

2. An insured person who is authorised by the competent institution to go to another Member State with the purpose of receiving the treatment appropriate to his/her condition shall receive the benefits in kind provided, on behalf of the competent institution, by the institution of the place of stay, in accordance with the provisions of the legislation it applies, as though he/she were insured under the said legislation. The authorisation shall be accorded where the treatment in question is among the benefits provided for by the legislation in the Member State where the person concerned resides and where he/she cannot be given such treatment within a time limit which is medically justifiable, taking into account his/her current state of health and the probable course of his/her illness.

3. Paragraphs 1 and 2 shall apply *mutatis mutandis* to the members of the family of an insured person.
4. If the members of the family of an insured person reside in a Member State other than the Member State in which the insured person resides, and this Member State has opted for reimbursement on the basis of fixed amounts, the cost of the benefits in kind referred to in paragraph 2 shall be borne by the institution of the place of residence of the members of the family. In this case, for the purposes of paragraph 1, the institution of the place of residence of the members of the family shall be considered to be the competent institution.

Article 21 Cash benefits

1. An insured person and members of his/her family residing or staying in a Member State other than the competent Member State shall be entitled to cash benefits provided by the competent institution in accordance with the legislation it applies. By agreement between the competent institution and the institution of the place of residence or stay, such benefits may, however, be provided by the institution of the place of residence or stay at the expense of the competent institution in accordance with the legislation of the competent Member State.
2. The competent institution of a Member State whose legislation stipulates that the calculation of cash benefits shall be based on average income or on an average contribution basis shall determine such average income or average contribution basis exclusively by reference to the incomes confirmed as having been paid, or contribution bases applied, during the periods completed under the said legislation.
3. The competent institution of a Member State whose legislation provides that the calculation of cash benefits shall be based on standard income shall take into account exclusively the standard income or, where appropriate, the average of standard incomes for the periods completed under the said legislation.
4. Paragraphs 2 and 3 shall apply *mutatis mutandis* to cases where the legislation applied by the competent institution lays down a specific reference period which corresponds in the case in question either wholly or partly to the periods which the person concerned has completed under the legislation of one or more other Member States.

Article 22 Pension claimants

1. An insured person who, on making a claim for a pension, or during the investigation thereof, ceases to be entitled to benefits in kind under the legislation of the Member State last competent, shall remain entitled to benefits in kind under the legislation of the Member State in which he/she resides, provided that the pension claimant satisfies the insurance conditions of the legislation of the Member State referred to in paragraph 2. The right to benefits in kind in the Member State of residence shall also apply to the members of the family of the pension claimant.
2. The benefits in kind shall be chargeable to the institution of the Member State which, in the event of a pension being awarded, would become competent under Articles 23 to 25.

SECTION 2

PENSIONERS AND MEMBERS OF THEIR FAMILIES

Article 23 Right to benefits in kind under the legislation of the Member State of residence

A person who receives a pension or pensions under the legislation of two or more Member States, of which one is the Member State of residence, and who is entitled to benefits in kind under the legislation of that Member State, shall, with the members of his/her family, receive such benefits in kind from and at the expense of the institution of the place of residence, as though he/she were a pensioner whose pension was payable solely under the legislation of that Member State.

Article 24 No right to benefits in kind under the legislation of the Member State of residence

1. A person who receives a pension or pensions under the legislation of one or more Member States and who is not entitled to benefits in kind under the legislation of the Member State of residence shall nevertheless receive such benefits for himself/herself and the members of his/her family, in so far as he/she would be entitled thereto under the legislation of the Member State or of at least one of the Member States competent in respect of his/her pensions, if he/she resided in that Member State. The benefits in kind shall be provided at the expense of the institution referred to in paragraph 2 by the institution of the place of residence, as though the person concerned were entitled to a pension and benefits in kind under the legislation of that Member State.
2. In the cases covered by paragraph 1, the cost of benefits in kind shall be borne by the institution as determined in accordance with the following rules:

(*a*) where the pensioner is entitled to benefits in kind under the legislation of a single Member State, the cost shall be borne by the competent institution of that Member State;

(*b*) where the pensioner is entitled to benefits in kind under the legislation of two or more Member States, the cost thereof shall be borne by the competent institution of the Member State to whose legislation the person has been subject for the longest period of time;

should the application of this rule result in several institutions being responsible for the cost of benefits, the cost shall be borne by the institution applying the legislation to which the pensioner was last subject.

Article 25 Pensions under the legislation of one or more Member States other than the Member State of residence, where there is a right to benefits in kind in the latter Member State

Where the person receiving a pension or pensions under the legislation of one or more Member States resides in a Member State under whose legislation the right to receive benefits in kind is not subject to conditions of insurance, or of activity as an employed or selfemployed person, and no pension is received from that Member State, the cost of benefits in kind provided to him/her and to members of his/her family shall be borne by the institution of one of the Member States competent in respect of his/her pensions determined in accordance with Article 24(2), to the extent that the pensioner and the members of his/her family would be entitled to such benefits if they resided in that Member State.

Article 26 Residence of members of the family in a Member State other than the one in which the pensioner resides

Members of the family of a person receiving a pension or pensions under the legislation of one or more Member States who reside in a Member State other than the one in which the pensioner resides shall be entitled to receive benefits in kind from the institution of the place of their residence in accordance with the provisions of the legislation it applies, in so far as the pensioner is entitled to benefits in kind under the legislation of a Member State. The costs shall be borne by the competent institution responsible for the costs of the benefits in kind provided to the pensioner in his/her Member State of residence.

Article 27 Stay of the pensioner or the members of his/her family in a Member State other than the Member State in which they reside — stay in the competent Member State — authorisation for appropriate treatment outside the Member State of residence

1. Article 19 shall apply *mutatis mutandis* to a person receiving a pension or pensions under the legislation of one or more Member States and entitled to benefits in kind under the legislation of one of the Member States which provide his/her pension(s) or to the members of his/her family who are staying in a Member State other than the one in which they reside.

2. Article 18(1) shall apply *mutatis mutandis* to the persons described in paragraph 1 when they stay in the Member State in which is situated the competent institution responsible for the cost of the benefits in kind provided to the pensioner in his/her Member State of residence and the said Member State has opted for this and is listed in Annex IV.

3. Article 20 shall apply *mutatis mutandis* to a pensioner and/or the members of his/her family who are staying in a Member State other than the one in which they reside with the purpose of receiving there the treatment appropriate to their condition.

4. Unless otherwise provided for by paragraph 5, the cost of the benefits in kind referred to in paragraphs 1 to 3 shall be borne by the competent institution responsible for the cost of benefits in kind provided to the pensioner in his/her Member State of residence.

5. The cost of the benefits in kind referred to in paragraph 3 shall be borne by the institution of the place of residence of the pensioner or of the members of his/her family, if these persons reside in a Member State which has opted for reimbursement on the basis of fixed amounts. In these cases, for the purposes of paragraph 3, the institution of the place of residence of the pensioner or of the members of his/her family shall be considered to be the competent institution.

Article 28 Special rules for retired frontier workers

1. A frontier worker who has retired because of old-age or invalidity is entitled in the event of sickness to continue to receive benefits in kind in the Member State where he/she last pursued his/her activity as an employed or self-employed person, in so far as this is a continuation of treatment which began in that Member State. 'Continuation of treatment' means the continued investigation, diagnosis and treatment of an illness for its entire duration.

The first sub-paragraph shall apply *mutatis mutandis* to the members of the family of the former frontier worker unless the Member State where the frontier worker last pursued his/her activity is listed in Annex III.

2. A pensioner who, in the five years preceding the effective date of an old-age or invalidity pension has been pursuing an activity as an employed or self-employed person for at least two years as a frontier worker shall be entitled to benefits in kind in the Member State in which he/she pursued such an activity as a frontier worker, if this Member State and the Member State in which the competent institution responsible for the costs of the benefits in kind provided to the pensioner in his/her Member State of residence is situated have opted for this and are both listed in Annex V.

NIC

3. Paragraph 2 shall apply *mutatis mutandis* to the members of the family of a former frontier worker or his/her survivors if, during the periods referred to in paragraph 2, they were entitled to benefits in kind under Article 18(2), even if the frontier worker died before his/her pension commenced, provided he/she had been pursuing an activity as an employed or self-employed person as a frontier worker for at least two years in the five years preceding his/her death.
4. Paragraphs 2 and 3 shall be applicable until the person concerned becomes subject to the legislation of a Member State on the basis of an activity as an employed or self-employed person.
5. The cost of the benefits in kind referred to in paragraphs 1 to 3 shall be borne by the competent institution responsible for the cost of benefits in kind provided to the pensioner or to his/her survivors in their respective Member States of residence.

Article 29 Cash benefits for pensioners

1. Cash benefits shall be paid to a person receiving a pension or pensions under the legislation of one or more Member States by the competent institution of the Member State in which is situated the competent institution responsible for the cost of benefits in kind provided to the pensioner in his/her Member State of residence. Article 21 shall apply *mutatis mutandis*.
2. Paragraph 1 shall also apply to the members of a pensioner's family.

Article 30 Contributions by pensioners

1. The institution of a Member State which is responsible under the legislation it applies for making deductions in respect of contributions for sickness, maternity and equivalent paternity benefits, may request and recover such deductions, calculated in accordance with the legislation it applies, only to the extent that the cost of the benefits pursuant to Articles 23 to 26 is to be borne by an institution of the said Member State.
2. Where, in the cases referred to in Article 25, the acquisition of sickness, maternity and equivalent paternity benefits is subject to the payment of contributions or similar payments under the legislation of a Member State in which the pensioner concerned resides, these contributions shall not be payable by virtue of such residence.

SECTION 3

COMMON PROVISIONS

Article 31 General provision

Articles 23 to 30 shall not apply to a pensioner or the members of his/her family who are entitled to benefits under the legislation of a Member State on the basis of an activity as an employed or self-employed person. In such a case, the person concerned shall be subject, for the purposes of this Chapter, to Articles 17 to 21.

Article 32 Prioritising of the right to benefits in kind — special rule for the right of members of the family to benefits in the Member State of residence

1. An independent right to benefits in kind based on the legislation of a Member State or on this Chapter shall take priority over a derivative right to benefits for members of a family. A derivative right to benefits in kind shall, however, take priority over independent rights, where the independent right in the Member State of residence exists directly and solely on the basis of the residence of the person concerned in that Member State.
2. Where the members of the family of an insured person reside in a Member State under whose legislation the right to benefits in kind is not subject to conditions of insurance or activity as an employed or self-employed person, benefits in kind shall be provided at the expense of the competent institution in the Member State in which they reside, if the spouse or the person caring for the children of the insured person pursues an activity as an employed or self-employed person in the said Member State or receives a pension from that Member State on the basis of an activity as an employed or self-employed person.

Article 33 Substantial benefits in kind

1. An insured person or a member of his/her family who has had a right to a prosthesis, a major appliance or other substantial benefits in kind recognised by the institution of a Member State, before he/she became insured under the legislation applied by the institution of another Member State, shall receive such benefits at the expense of the first institution, even if they are awarded after the said person has already become insured under the legislation applied by the second institution.
2. The Administrative Commission shall draw up the list of benefits covered by paragraph 1.

Article 34 Overlapping of long-term care benefits

1. If a recipient of long-term care benefits in cash, which have to be treated as sickness benefits and are therefore provided by the Member State competent for cash benefits under Articles 21 or 29, is, at the same time and under this Chapter, entitled to claim benefits in kind intended for the same purpose from the institution of the place of residence or stay in another Member State, and an institution in the first Member State is also required to reimburse the cost of these benefits in kind under Article 35, the general provision on prevention of overlapping of benefits laid down in Article

10 shall be applicable, with the following restriction only: if the person concerned claims and receives the benefit in kind, the amount of the benefit in cash shall be reduced by the amount of the benefit in kind which is or could be claimed from the institution of the first Member State required to reimburse the cost.

2. The Administrative Commission shall draw up the list of the cash benefits and benefits in kind covered by paragraph 1.

3. Two or more Member States, or their competent authorities, may agree on other or supplementary measures which shall not be less advantageous for the persons concerned than the principles laid down in paragraph 1.

Article 35 Reimbursements between institutions

1. The benefits in kind provided by the institution of a Member State on behalf of the institution of another Member State under this Chapter shall give rise to full reimbursement.

2. The reimbursements referred to in paragraph 1 shall be determined and effected in accordance with the arrangements set out in the Implementing Regulation, either on production of proof of actual expenditure, or on the basis of fixed amounts for Member States the legal or administrative structures of which are such that the use of reimbursement on the basis of actual expenditure is not appropriate.

3. Two or more Member States, and their competent authorities, may provide for other methods of reimbursement or waive all reimbursement between the institutions coming under their jurisdiction.

CHAPTER 2

BENEFITS IN RESPECT OF ACCIDENTS AT WORK AND OCCUPATIONAL DISEASES

Article 36 Right to benefits in kind and in cash

1. Without prejudice to any more favourable provisions in paragraphs 2 and 2a of this Article, Articles 17, 18(1), 19(1) and 20(1) shall also apply to benefits relating to accidents at work or occupational diseases.

2. A person who has sustained an accident at work or has contracted an occupational disease and who resides or stays in a Member State other than the competent Member State shall be entitled to the special benefits in kind of the scheme covering accidents at work and occupational diseases provided, on behalf of the competent institution, by the institution of the place of residence or stay in accordance with the legislation which it applies, as though he/she were insured under the said legislation.

2a. The competent institution may not refuse to grant the authorisation provided for in Article 20(1) to a person who has sustained an accident at work or who has contracted an occupational disease and who is entitled to benefits chargeable to that institution, where the treatment appropriate to his/her condition cannot be given in the Member State in which he/she resides within a time-limit which is medically justifiable, taking into account his/her current state of health and the probable course of the illness.

3. Article 21 shall also apply to benefits falling within this Chapter.

Article 37 Costs of transport

1. The competent institution of a Member State whose legislation provides for meeting the costs of transporting a person who has sustained an accident at work or is suffering from an occupational disease, either to his/her place of residence or to a hospital, shall meet such costs to the corresponding place in another Member State where the person resides, provided that that institution gives prior authorisation for such transport, duly taking into account the reasons justifying it. Such authorisation shall not be required in the case of a frontier worker.

2. The competent institution of a Member State whose legislation provides for meeting the costs of transporting the body of a person killed in an accident at work to the place of burial shall, in accordance with the legislation it applies, meet such costs to the corresponding place in another Member State where the person was residing at the time of the accident.

Article 38 Benefits for an occupational disease where the person suffering from such a disease has been exposed to the same risk in several Member States

When a person who has contracted an occupational disease has, under the legislation of two or more Member States, pursued an activity which by its nature is likely to cause the said disease, the benefits that he/she or his/her survivors may claim shall be provided exclusively under the legislation of the last of those States whose conditions are satisfied.

Article 39 Aggravation of an occupational disease

In the event of aggravation of an occupational disease for which a person suffering from such a disease has received or is receiving benefits under the legislation of a Member State, the following rules shall apply:

(*a*) if the person concerned, while in receipt of benefits, has not pursued, under the legislation of another Member State, an activity as an employed or self-employed person likely to cause or aggravate the disease in question, the competent institution of the first Member State shall bear the cost of the benefits under the provisions of the legislation which it applies, taking into account the aggravation;

(*b*) if the person concerned, while in receipt of benefits, has pursued such an activity under the legislation of another Member State, the competent institution of the first Member State shall bear the cost of the benefits under the legislation it applies without taking the aggravation into account. The competent institution of the second Member State shall grant a supplement to the person concerned, the amount of which shall be equal to the difference between the amount of benefits due after the aggravation and the amount which would have been due prior to the aggravation under the legislation it applies, if the disease in question had occurred under the legislation of that Member State;

(*c*) the rules concerning reduction, suspension or withdrawal laid down by the legislation of a Member State shall not be invoked against persons receiving benefits provided by institutions of two Member States in accordance with sub-paragraph (*b*).

Article 40 Rules for taking into account the special features of certain legislation

1. If there is no insurance against accidents at work or occupational diseases in the Member State in which the person concerned resides or stays, or if such insurance exists but there is no institution responsible for providing benefits in kind, those benefits shall be provided by the institution of the place of residence or stay responsible for providing benefits in kind in the event of sickness.

2. If there is no insurance against accidents at work or occupational diseases in the competent Member State, the provisions of this Chapter concerning benefits in kind shall nevertheless be applied to a person who is entitled to those benefits in the event of sickness, maternity or equivalent paternity under the legislation of that Member State if that person sustains an accident at work or suffers from an occupational disease during a residence or stay in another Member State. Costs shall be borne by the institution which is competent for the benefits in kind under the legislation of the competent Member State.

3. Article 5 shall apply to the competent institution in a Member State as regards the equivalence of accidents at work and occupational diseases which either have occurred or have been confirmed subsequently under the legislation of another Member State when assessing the degree of incapacity, the right to benefits or the amount thereof, on condition that:

(*a*) no compensation is due in respect of an accident at work or an occupational disease which had occurred or had been confirmed previously under the legislation it applies;

and

(*b*) no compensation is due in respect of an accident at work or an occupational disease which had occurred or had been confirmed subsequently, under the legislation of the other Member State under which the accident at work or the occupational disease had occurred or been confirmed.

Article 41 Reimbursements between institutions

1. Article 35 shall also apply to benefits falling within this Chapter, and reimbursement shall be made on the basis of actual costs.

2. Two or more Member States, or their competent authorities, may provide for other methods of reimbursement or waive all reimbursement between the institutions under their jurisdiction.

CHAPTER 3

DEATH GRANTS

Article 42 Right to grants where death occurs in, or where the person entitled resides in, a Member State other than the competent Member State

1. When an insured person or a member of his/her family dies in a Member State other than the competent Member State, the death shall be deemed to have occurred in the competent Member State.

2. The competent institution shall be obliged to provide death grants payable under the legislation it applies, even if the person entitled resides in a Member State other than the competent Member State.

3. Paragraphs 1 and 2 shall also apply when the death is the result of an accident at work or an occupational disease.

Article 43 Provision of benefits in the event of the death of a pensioner

1. In the event of the death of a pensioner who was entitled to a pension under the legislation of one Member State, or to pensions under the legislations of two or more Member States, when that pensioner was residing in a Member State other than that of the institution responsible for the cost of benefits in kind provided under Articles 24 and 25, the death grants payable under the legislation administered by that institution shall be provided at its own expense as though the pensioner had been residing at the time of his/her death in the Member State in which that institution is situated.

2. Paragraph 1 shall apply *mutatis mutandis* to the members of the family of a pensioner.

CHAPTER 4

INVALIDITY BENEFITS

Article 44 Persons subject only to type A legislation

1. For the purposes of this Chapter, 'type A legislation' means any legislation under which the amount of invalidity benefits is independent of the duration of the periods of insurance or residence and which is expressly included by the competent Member State in Annex VI, and 'type B legislation' means any other legislation.

2. A person who has been successively or alternately subject to the legislation of two or more Member States and who has completed periods of insurance or residence exclusively under type A legislations shall be entitled to benefits only from the institution of the Member State whose legislation was applicable at the time when the incapacity for work followed by invalidity occurred, taking into account, where appropriate, Article 45, and shall receive such benefits in accordance with that legislation.

3. A person who is not entitled to benefits under paragraph 2 shall receive the benefits to which he/she is still entitled under the legislation of another Member State, taking into account, where appropriate, Article 45.

4. If the legislation referred to in paragraph 2 or 3 contains rules for the reduction, suspension or withdrawal of invalidity benefits in the case of overlapping with other income or with benefits of a different kind within the meaning of Article 53(2), Articles 53(3) and 55(3) shall apply *mutatis mutandis*.

Article 45 Special provisions on aggregation of periods

The competent institution of a Member State whose legislation makes the acquisition, retention or recovery of the right to benefits conditional upon the completion of periods of insurance or residence shall, where necessary, apply Article 51(1) *mutatis mutandis*.

Article 46 Persons subject either only to type B legislation or to type A and B legislation

1. A person who has been successively or alternately subject to the legislation of two or more Member States, of which at least one is not a type A legislation, shall be entitled to benefits under Chapter 5, which shall apply *mutatis mutandis* taking into account paragraph 3.

2. However, if the person concerned has been previously subject to a type B legislation and suffers incapacity for work leading to invalidity while subject to a type A legislation, he/she shall receive benefits in accordance with Article 44, provided that:

— he satisfies the conditions of that legislation exclusively or of others of the same type, taking into account, where appropriate, Article 45, but without having recourse to periods of insurance or residence completed under a type B legislation,

and

— he does not assert any claims to old-age benefits, taking into account Article 50(1).

3. A decision taken by an institution of a Member State concerning the degree of invalidity of a claimant shall be binding on the institution of any other Member State concerned, provided that the concordance between the legislation of these Member States on conditions relating to the degree of invalidity is acknowledged in Annex VII.

Article 47 Aggravation of invalidity

1. In the case of aggravation of an invalidity for which a person is receiving benefits under the legislation of one or more Member States, the following provisions shall apply, taking the aggravation into account:

(*a*) the benefits shall be provided in accordance with Chapter 5, applied *mutatis mutandis*;

(*b*) however, where the person concerned has been subject to two or more type A legislations and since receiving benefit has not been subject to the legislation of another Member State, the benefit shall be provided in accordance with Article 44(2).

2. If the total amount of the benefit or benefits payable under paragraph 1 is lower than the amount of the benefit which the person concerned was receiving at the expense of the institution previously competent for payment, that institution shall pay him/her a supplement equal to the difference between the two amounts.

3. If the person concerned is not entitled to benefits at the expense of an institution of another Member State, the competent institution of the Member State previously competent shall provide the benefits in accordance with the legislation it applies, taking into account the aggravation and, where appropriate, Article 45.

Article 48 Conversion of invalidity benefits into old-age benefits

1. Invalidity benefits shall be converted into old-age benefits, where appropriate, under the conditions laid down by the legislation or legislations under which they are provided and in accordance with Chapter 5.

2. Where a person receiving invalidity benefits can establish a claim to old-age benefits under the legislation of one or more other Member States, in accordance with Article 50, any institution which is responsible for providing invalidity benefits under the legislation of a Member State shall continue to provide such a person with the invalidity benefits to which he/she is entitled under the legislation it applies until paragraph 1 becomes applicable in respect of that institution, or otherwise for as long as the person concerned satisfies the conditions for such benefits.

3. Where invalidity benefits provided under the legislation of a Member State, in accordance with Article 44, are converted into old age benefits and where the person concerned does not yet satisfy the conditions laid down by the legislation of one or more of the other Member States for receiving those benefits, the person concerned shall receive, from that or those Member States, invalidity benefits from the date of the conversion.

Those invalidity benefits shall be provided in accordance with Chapter 5 as if that Chapter had been applicable at the time when the incapacity for work leading to invalidity occurred, until the person concerned satisfies the qualifying conditions for old-age benefit laid down by the national legislations concerned or, where such conversion is not provided for, for as long as he/she is entitled to invalidity benefits under the latter legislation or legislations.

4. The invalidity benefits provided under Article 44 shall be recalculated in accordance with Chapter 5 as soon as the beneficiary satisfies the qualifying conditions for invalidity benefits laid down by a type B legislation, or as soon as he/she receives old-age benefits under the legislation of another Member State.

Article 49 Special provisions for civil servants

Articles 6, 44, 46, 47 and 48 and Article 60(2) and (3) shall apply *mutatis mutandis* to persons covered by a special scheme for civil servants.

CHAPTER 5

OLD-AGE AND SURVIVORS' PENSIONS

Article 50 General provisions

1. All the competent institutions shall determine entitlement to benefit, under all the legislations of the Member States to which the person concerned has been subject, when a request for award has been submitted, unless the person concerned expressly requests deferment of the award of old-age benefits under the legislation of one or more Member States.

2. If at a given moment the person concerned does not satisfy, or no longer satisfies, the conditions laid down by all the legislations of the Member States to which he/she has been subject, the institutions applying legislation the conditions of which have been satisfied shall not take into account, when performing the calculation in accordance with Article 52(1)(*a*) or (*b*), the periods completed under the legislations the conditions of which have not been satisfied, or are no longer satisfied, where this gives rise to a lower amount of benefit.

3. Paragraph 2 shall apply *mutatis mutandis* when the person concerned has expressly requested deferment of the award of old-age benefits.

4. A new calculation shall be performed automatically as and when the conditions to be fulfilled under the other legislations are satisfied or when a person requests the award of an old-age benefit deferred in accordance with paragraph 1, unless the periods completed under the other legislations have already been taken into account by virtue of paragraph 2 or 3.

Article 51 Special provisions on aggregation of periods

1. Where the legislation of a Member State makes the granting of certain benefits conditional upon the periods of insurance having been completed only in a specific activity as an employed or self-employed person or in an occupation which is subject to a special scheme for employed or self-employed persons, the competent institution of that Member State shall take into account periods completed under the legislation of other Member States only if completed under a corresponding scheme or, failing that, in the same occupation, or where appropriate, in the same activity as an employed or self-employed person.

If, account having been taken of the periods thus completed, the person concerned does not satisfy the conditions for receipt of the benefits of a special scheme, these periods shall be taken into account for the purposes of providing the benefits of the general scheme or, failing that, of the scheme applicable to manual or clerical workers, as the case may be, provided that the person concerned had been affiliated to one or other of those schemes.

2. The periods of insurance completed under a special scheme of a Member State shall be taken into account for the purposes of providing the benefits of the general scheme or, failing that, of the scheme applicable to manual or clerical workers, as the case may be, of another Member State, provided that the person concerned had been affiliated to one or other of those schemes, even if those periods have already been taken into account in the latter Member State under a special scheme.

3. Where the legislation or specific scheme of a Member State makes the acquisition, retention or recovery of the right to benefits conditional upon the person concerned being insured at the time of the materialisation of the risk, this condition shall be regarded as having been satisfied if that person

has been previously insured under the legislation or specific scheme of that Member State and is, at the time of the materialisation of the risk, insured under the legislation of another Member State for the same risk or, failing that, if a benefit is due under the legislation of another Member State for the same risk. The latter condition shall, however, be deemed to be fulfilled in the cases referred to in Article 57.

Article 52 Award of benefits

1. The competent institution shall calculate the amount of the benefit that would be due:
 (*a*) under the legislation it applies, only where the conditions for entitlement to benefits have been satisfied exclusively under national law (independent benefit);
 (*b*) by calculating a theoretical amount and subsequently an actual amount (pro rata benefit), as follows:
  (i) the theoretical amount of the benefit is equal to the benefit which the person concerned could claim if all the periods of insurance and/or of residence which have been completed under the legislations of the other Member States had been completed under the legislation it applies on the date of the award of the benefit. If, under this legislation, the amount does not depend on the duration of the periods completed, that amount shall be regarded as being the theoretical amount;
  (ii) the competent institution shall then establish the actual amount of the pro rata benefit by applying to the theoretical amount the ratio between the duration of the periods completed before materialisation of the risk under the legislation it applies and the total duration of the periods completed before materialisation of the risk under the legislations of all the Member States concerned.

2. Where appropriate, the competent institution shall apply, to the amount calculated in accordance with sub-paragraphs 1(*a*) and (*b*), all the rules relating to reduction, suspension or withdrawal, under the legislation it applies, within the limits provided for by Articles 53 to 55.

3. The person concerned shall be entitled to receive from the competent institution of each Member State the higher of the amounts calculated in accordance with sub-paragraphs 1(*a*) and (*b*).

4. Where the calculation pursuant to paragraph 1(a) in one Member State invariably results in the independent benefit being equal to or higher than the pro rata benefit, calculated in accordance with paragraph 1(*b*), the competent institution shall waive the pro rata calculation, provided that:
 (i) such a situation is set out in Part 1 of Annex VIII;
 (ii) no legislation containing rules against overlapping, as referred to in Articles 54 and 55, is applicable unless the conditions laid down in Article 55(2) are fulfilled; and
 (iii) Article 57 is not applicable in relation to periods completed under the legislation of another Member State in the specific circumstances of the case.

5. Notwithstanding the provisions of paragraphs 1, 2 and 3, the pro rata calculation shall not apply to schemes providing benefits in respect of which periods of time are of no relevance to the calculation, subject to such schemes being listed in part 2 of Annex VIII. In such cases, the person concerned shall be entitled to the benefit calculated in accordance with the legislation of the Member State concerned.

Article 53 Rules to prevent overlapping

1. Any overlapping of invalidity, old age and survivors' benefits calculated or provided on the basis of periods of insurance and/or residence completed by the same person shall be considered to be overlapping of benefits of the same kind.

2. Overlapping of benefits which cannot be considered to be of the same kind within the meaning of paragraph 1 shall be considered to be overlapping of benefits of a different kind.

3. The following provisions shall be applicable for the purposes of rules to prevent overlapping laid down by the legislation of a Member State in the case of overlapping of a benefit in respect of invalidity, old age or survivors with a benefit of the same kind or a benefit of a different kind or with other income:
 (*a*) the competent institution shall take into account the benefits or incomes acquired in another Member State only where the legislation it applies provides for benefits or income acquired abroad to be taken into account;
 (*b*) the competent institution shall take into account the amount of benefits to be paid by another Member State before deduction of tax, social security contributions and other individual levies or deductions, unless the legislation it applies provides for the application of rules to prevent overlapping after such deductions, under the conditions and the procedures laid down in the Implementing Regulation;
 (*c*) the competent institution shall not take into account the amount of benefits acquired under the legislation of another Member State on the basis of voluntary insurance or continued optional insurance;

(*d*) if a single Member State applies rules to prevent overlapping because the person concerned receives benefits of the same or of a different kind under the legislation of other Member States or income acquired in other Member States, the benefit due may be reduced solely by the amount of such benefits or such income.

Article 54 Overlapping of benefits of the same kind

1. Where benefits of the same kind due under the legislation of two or more Member States overlap, the rules to prevent overlapping laid down by the legislation of a Member State shall not be applicable to a pro rata benefit.

2. The rules to prevent overlapping shall apply to an independent benefit only if the benefit concerned is:

(*a*) a benefit the amount of which does not depend on the duration of periods of insurance or residence,

or

(*b*) a benefit the amount of which is determined on the basis of a credited period deemed to have been completed between the date on which the risk materialised and a later date, overlapping with:

(i) a benefit of the same type, except where an agreement has been concluded between two or more Member States to avoid the same credited period being taken into account more than once,

or

(ii) a benefit referred to in sub-paragraph (*a*).

The benefits and agreements referred to in sub-paragraphs (*a*) and (*b*) are listed in Annex IX.

Article 55 Overlapping of benefits of a different kind

1. If the receipt of benefits of a different kind or other income requires the application of the rules to prevent overlapping provided for by the legislation of the Member States concerned regarding:

(*a*) two or more independent benefits, the competent institutions shall divide the amounts of the benefit or benefits or other income, as they have been taken into account, by the number of benefits subject to the said rules;

however, the application of this sub-paragraph cannot deprive the person concerned of his/her status as a pensioner for the purposes of the other chapters of this Title under the conditions and the procedures laid down in the Implementing Regulation;

(*b*) one or more pro rata benefits, the competent institutions shall take into account the benefit or benefits or other income and all the elements stipulated for applying the rules to prevent overlapping as a function of the ratio between the periods of insurance and/or residence established for the calculation referred to in Article 52(1)(*b*)(ii);

(*c*) one or more independent benefits and one or more pro-rata benefits, the competent institutions shall apply *mutatis mutandis* sub-paragraph (*a*) as regards independent benefits and sub-paragraph (*b*) as regards pro rata benefits.

2. The competent institution shall not apply the division stipulated in respect of independent benefits, if the legislation it applies provides for account to be taken of benefits of a different kind and/or other income and all other elements for calculating part of their amount determined as a function of the ratio between periods of insurance and/or residence referred to in Article 52(1)(*b*)(ii).

3. Paragraphs 1 and 2 shall apply *mutatis mutandis* where the legislation of one or more Member States provides that a right to a benefit cannot be acquired in the case where the person concerned is in receipt of a benefit of a different kind, payable under the legislation of another Member State, or of other income.

Article 56 Additional provisions for the calculation of benefits

1. For the calculation of the theoretical and pro rata amounts referred to in Article 52(1)(b), the following rules shall apply:

(*a*) where the total length of the periods of insurance and/or residence completed before the risk materialised under the legislations of all the Member States concerned is longer than the maximum period required by the legislation of one of these Member States for receipt of full benefit, the competent institution of that Member State shall take into account this maximum period instead of the total length of the periods completed; this method of calculation shall not result in the imposition on that institution of the cost of a benefit greater than the full benefit provided for by the legislation it applies. This provision shall not apply to benefits the amount of which does not depend on the length of insurance;

(*b*) the procedure for taking into account overlapping periods is laid down in the Implementing Regulation;

(*c*) if the legislation of a Member State provides that the benefits are to be calculated on the basis of incomes, contributions, bases of contributions, increases, earnings, other amounts or a combination of more than one of them (average, proportional, fixed or credited), the competent institution shall:

(i) determine the basis for calculation of the benefits in accordance only with periods of insurance completed under the legislation it applies;

(ii) use, in order to determine the amount to be calculated in accordance with the periods of insurance and/or residence completed under the legislation of the other Member States, the same elements determined or recorded for the periods of insurance completed under the legislation it applies;

where necessary in accordance with the procedures laid down in Annex XI for the Member State concerned;

(*d*) In the event that point (c) is not applicable because the legislation of a Member State provides for the benefit to be calculated on the basis of elements other than periods of insurance or residence which are not linked to time, the competent institution shall take into account, in respect of each period of insurance or residence completed under the legislation of any other Member State, the amount of the capital accrued, the capital which is considered as having been accrued or any other element for the calculation under the legislation it administers divided by the corresponding units of periods in the pension scheme concerned.

2. The provisions of the legislation of a Member State concerning the revalorisation of the elements taken into account for the calculation of benefits shall apply, as appropriate, to the elements to be taken into account by the competent institution of that Member State, in accordance with paragraph 1, in respect of the periods of insurance or residence completed under the legislation of other Member States.

Article 57 Periods of insurance or residence of less than one year

1. Notwithstanding Article 52(1)(*b*), the institution of a Member State shall not be required to provide benefits in respect of periods completed under the legislation it applies which are taken into account when the risk materialises, if:

— the duration of the said periods is less than one year,

and

— taking only these periods into account no right to benefit is acquired under that legislation.

For the purposes of this Article, 'periods' shall mean all periods of insurance, employment, self-employment or residence which either qualify for, or directly increase, the benefit concerned.

2. The competent institution of each of the Member States concerned shall take into account the periods referred to in paragraph 1, for the purposes of Article 52(1)(*b*)(i).

3. If the effect of applying paragraph 1 would be to relieve all the institutions of the Member States concerned of their obligations, benefits shall be provided exclusively under the legislation of the last of those Member States whose conditions are satisfied, as if all the periods of insurance and residence completed and taken into account in accordance with Articles 6 and 51(1) and (2) had been completed under the legislation of that Member State.

4. This Article shall not apply to schemes listed in Part 2 of Annex VIII.

Article 58 Award of a supplement

1. A recipient of benefits to whom this chapter applies may not, in the Member State of residence and under whose legislation a benefit is payable to him/her, be provided with a benefit which is less than the minimum benefit fixed by that legislation for a period of insurance or residence equal to all the periods taken into account for the payment in accordance with this chapter.

2. The competent institution of that Member State shall pay him/her throughout the period of his/her residence in its territory a supplement equal to the difference between the total of the benefits due under this chapter and the amount of the minimum benefit.

Article 59 Recalculation and revaluation of benefits

1. If the method for determining benefits or the rules for calculating benefits are altered under the legislation of a Member State, or if the personal situation of the person concerned undergoes a relevant change which, under that legislation, would lead to an adjustment of the amount of the benefit, a recalculation shall be carried out in accordance with Article 52.

2. On the other hand, if, by reason of an increase in the cost of living or changes in the level of income or other grounds for adjustment, the benefits of the Member State concerned are altered by a percentage or fixed amount, such percentage or fixed amount shall be applied directly to the benefits determined in accordance with Article 52, without the need for a recalculation.

Article 60 Special provisions for civil servants

1. Articles 6, 50, 51(3) and 52 to 59 shall apply *mutatis mutandis* to persons covered by a special scheme for civil servants.

2. However, if the legislation of a competent Member State makes the acquisition, liquidation, retention or recovery of the right to benefits under a special scheme for civil servants subject to the condition that all periods of insurance be completed under one or more special schemes for civil servants in that Member State, or be regarded by the legislation of that Member State as equivalent to such periods, the competent institution of that State shall take into account only the periods which can be recognised under the legislation it applies.

If, account having been taken of the periods thus completed, the person concerned does not satisfy the conditions for the receipt of these benefits, these periods shall be taken into account for the award of benefits under the general scheme or, failing that, the scheme applicable to manual or clerical workers, as the case may be.

3. Where, under the legislation of a Member State, benefits under a special scheme for civil servants are calculated on the basis of the last salary or salaries received during a reference period, the competent institution of that State shall take into account, for the purposes of the calculation, only those salaries, duly revalued, which were received during the period or periods for which the person concerned was subject to that legislation.

CHAPTER 6

UNEMPLOYMENT BENEFITS

Article 61 Special rules on aggregation of periods of insurance, employment or self-employment

1. The competent institution of a Member State whose legislation makes the acquisition, retention, recovery or duration of the right to benefits conditional upon the completion of either periods of insurance, employment or self-employment shall, to the extent necessary, take into account periods of insurance, employment or self-employment completed under the legislation of any other Member State as though they were completed under the legislation it applies.

However, when the applicable legislation makes the right to benefits conditional on the completion of periods of insurance, the periods of employment or self-employment completed under the legislation of another Member State shall not be taken into account unless such periods would have been considered to be periods of insurance had they been completed in accordance with the applicable legislation.

2. Except in the cases referred to in Article 65(5)(*a*), the application of paragraph 1 of this Article shall be conditional on the person concerned having the most recently completed, in accordance with the legislation under which the benefits are claimed:

— periods of insurance, if that legislation requires periods of insurance,

— periods of employment, if that legislation requires periods of employment,

or

— periods of self-employment, if that legislation requires periods of self-employment.

Article 62 Calculation of benefits

1. The competent institution of a Member State whose legislation provides for the calculation of benefits on the basis of the amount of the previous salary or professional income shall take into account exclusively the salary or professional income received by the person concerned in respect of his/her last activity as an employed or self-employed person under the said legislation.

2. Paragraph 1 shall also apply where the legislation administered by the competent institution provides for a specific reference period for the determination of the salary which serves as a basis for the calculation of benefits and where, for all or part of that period, the person concerned was subject to the legislation of another Member State.

3. By way of derogation from paragraphs 1 and 2, as far as the unemployed persons covered by Article 65(5)(*a*) are concerned, the institution of the place of residence shall take into account the salary or professional income received by the person concerned in the Member State to whose legislation he/she was subject during his/her last activity as an employed or self-employed person, in accordance with the Implementing Regulation.

Article 63 Special provisions for the waiving of residence rules

For the purpose of this Chapter, Article 7 shall apply only in the cases provided for by Articles 64, 65 and 65a and within the limits prescribed therein.

Article 64 Unemployed persons going to another Member State

1. A wholly unemployed person who satisfies the conditions of the legislation of the competent Member State for entitlement to benefits, and who goes to another Member State in order to seek work there, shall retain his/her entitlement to unemployment benefits in cash under the following conditions and within the following limits:

(*a*) before his/her departure, the unemployed person must have been registered as a person seeking work and have remained available to the employment services of the competent Member State for at least four weeks after becoming unemployed. However, the competent services or institutions may authorise his/her departure before such time has expired;

(*b*) the unemployed person must register as a person seeking work with the employment services of the Member State to which he/she has gone, be subject to the control procedure organised there and adhere to the conditions laid down under the legislation of that Member State. This condition shall be considered satisfied for the period before registration if the person concerned registers within seven days of the date on which he/she ceased to be available to the employment services of the Member State which he/she left. In exceptional cases, the competent services or institutions may extend this period;

(*c*) entitlement to benefits shall be retained for a period of three months from the date when the unemployed person ceased to be available to the employment services of the Member State which he/she left, provided that the total duration for which the benefits are provided does not exceed the total duration of the period of his/her entitlement to benefits under the legislation of that Member State; the competent services or institutions may extend the period of three months up to a maximum of six months;

(*d*) the benefits shall be provided by the competent institution in accordance with the legislation it applies and at its own expense.

2. If the person concerned returns to the competent Member State on or before the expiry of the period during which he/she is entitled to benefits under paragraph 1(*c*), he/she shall continue to be entitled to benefits under the legislation of that Member State. He/she shall lose all entitlement to benefits under the legislation of the competent Member State if he/she does not return there on or before the expiry of the said period, unless the provisions of that legislation are more favourable. In exceptional cases the competent services or institutions may allow the person concerned to return at a later date without loss of his/her entitlement.

3. Unless the legislation of the competent Member State is more favourable, between two periods of employment the maximum total period for which entitlement to benefits shall be retained under paragraph 1 shall be three months; the competent services or institutions may extend that period up to a maximum of six months.

4. The arrangements for exchanges of information, cooperation and mutual assistance between the institutions and services of the competent Member State and the Member State to which the person goes in order to seek work shall be laid down in the Implementing Regulation.

Article 65 Unemployed persons who resided in a Member State other than the competent State

1. A person who is partially or intermittently unemployed and who, during his/her last activity as an employed or self-employed person, resided in a Member State other than the competent Member State shall make himself/herself available to his/her employer or to the employment services in the competent Member State. He/she shall receive benefits in accordance with the legislation of the competent Member State as if he/she were residing in that Member State. These benefits shall be provided by the institution of the competent Member State.

2. A wholly unemployed person who, during his/her last activity as an employed or self-employed person, resided in a Member State other than the competent Member State and who continues to reside in that Member State or returns to that Member State shall make himself/herself available to the employment services in the Member State of residence. Without prejudice to Article 64, a wholly unemployed person may, as a supplementary step, make himself/herself available to the employment services of the Member State in which he/she pursued his/her last activity as an employed or self-employed person. An unemployed person, other than a frontier worker, who does not return to his/her Member State of residence, shall make himself/herself available to the employment services in the Member State to whose legislation he/she was last subject.

3. The unemployed person referred to in the first sentence of paragraph 2 shall register as a person seeking work with the competent employment services of the Member State in which he/she resides, shall be subject to the control procedure organised there and shall adhere to the conditions laid down under the legislation of that Member State. If he/she chooses also to register as a person seeking work in the Member State in which he/she pursued his/her last activity as an employed or self-employed person, he/she shall comply with the obligations applicable in that State.

4. The implementation of the second sentence of paragraph 2 and of the second sentence of paragraph 3, as well as the arrangements for exchanges of information, cooperation and mutual assistance between the institutions and services of the Member State of residence and the Member State in which he/she pursued his/her last occupation, shall be laid down in the Implementing Regulation.

5.

(*a*) The unemployed person referred to in the first and second sentences of paragraph 2 shall receive benefits in accordance with the legislation of the Member State of residence as if he/she had been subject to that legislation during his/her last activity as an employed or self-employed person. Those benefits shall be provided by the institution of the place of residence.

(*b*) However, a worker other than a frontier worker who has been provided benefits at the expense of the competent institution of the Member State to whose legislation he/she was last subject shall firstly receive, on his/her return to the Member State of residence, benefits in accordance with Article 64, receipt of the benefits in accordance with (*a*) being suspended for the period during which he/she receives benefits under the legislation to which he/she was last subject.

6. The benefits provided by the institution of the place of residence under paragraph 5 shall continue to be at its own expense. However, subject to paragraph 7, the competent institution of the Member State to whose legislation he/she was last subject shall reimburse to the institution of the place of residence the full amount of the benefits provided by the latter institution during the first three months. The amount of the reimbursement during this period may not be higher than the amount payable, in the case of unemployment, under the legislation of the competent Member State. In the case referred to in paragraph 5(b), the period during which benefits are provided under Article 64 shall be deducted from the period referred to in the second sentence of this paragraph. The arrangements for reimbursement shall be laid down in the Implementing Regulation.
7. However, the period of reimbursement referred to in paragraph 6 shall be extended to five months when the person concerned has, during the preceding 24 months, completed periods of employment or self-employment of at least 12 months in the Member State to whose legislation he/she was last subject, where such periods would qualify for the purposes of establishing entitlement to unemployment benefits.
8. For the purposes of paragraphs 6 and 7, two or more Member States, or their competent authorities, may provide for other methods of reimbursement or waive all reimbursement between the institutions falling under their jurisdiction.

Article 65a Special provisions for wholly unemployed self- employed frontier workers where no unemployment benefits system covering self-employed persons exists in the Member State of residence

1. By way of derogation from Article 65, a wholly unemployed person who, as a frontier worker, has most recently completed periods of insurance as a self-employed person or periods of self-employment recognised for the purposes of granting unemployment benefits in a Member State other than his/her Member State of residence and whose Member State of residence has submitted notification that there is no possibility for any category of self-employed persons to be covered by an unemployment benefits system of that Member State, shall register with and make himself/herself available to the employment services in the Member State in which he/she pursued his/her last activity as a self-employed person and, when he/she applies for benefits, shall continuously adhere to the conditions laid down under the legislation of the latter Member State. The wholly unemployed person may, as a supplementary step, make himself/herself available to the employment services of the Member State of residence.
2. Benefits shall be provided to the wholly unemployed person referred to in paragraph 1 by the Member State to whose legislation he/she was last subject in accordance with the legislation which that Member State applies.
3. If the wholly unemployed person referred to in paragraph 1 does not wish to become or remain available to the employment services of the Member State of last activity after having been registered there, and wishes to seek work in the Member State of residence, Article 64 shall apply mutatis mutandis, except Article 64(1)(a). The competent institution may extend the period referred to in the first sentence of Article 64(1)(c) up to the end of the period of entitlement to benefits.'.

CHAPTER 7

PRE-RETIREMENT BENEFITS

Article 66 Benefits

When the applicable legislation makes the right to pre-retirement benefits conditional on the completion of periods of insurance, of employment or of self-employment, Article 6 shall not apply.

CHAPTER 8

FAMILY BENEFITS

Article 67 Members of the family residing in another Member State

A person shall be entitled to family benefits in accordance with the legislation of the competent Member State, including for his/her family members residing in another Member State, as if they were residing in the former Member State. However, a pensioner shall be entitled to family benefits in accordance with the legislation of the Member State competent for his/her pension.

Article 68 Priority rules in the event of overlapping

1. Where, during the same period and for the same family members, benefits are provided for under the legislation of more than one Member State the following priority rules shall apply:
   (*a*) in the case of benefits payable by more than one Member State on different bases, the order of priority shall be as follows: firstly, rights available on the basis of an activity as an employed or self-employed person, secondly, rights available on the basis of receipt of a pension and finally, rights obtained on the basis of residence;
   (*b*) in the case of benefits payable by more than one Member State on the same basis, the order of priority shall be established by referring to the following subsidiary criteria:

(i) in the case of rights available on the basis of an activity as an employed or self-employed person: the place of residence of the children, provided that there is such activity, and additionally, where appropriate, the highest amount of the benefits provided for by the conflicting legislations. In the latter case, the cost of benefits shall be shared in accordance with criteria laid down in the Implementing Regulation;

(ii) in the case of rights available on the basis of receipt of pensions: the place of residence of the children, provided that a pension is payable under its legislation, and additionally, where appropriate, the longest period of insurance or residence under the conflicting legislations;

(iii) in the case of rights available on the basis of residence: the place of residence of the children.

2. In the case of overlapping entitlements, family benefits shall be provided in accordance with the legislation designated as having priority in accordance with paragraph 1. Entitlements to family benefits by virtue of other conflicting legislation or legislations shall be suspended up to the amount provided for by the first legislation and a differential supplement shall be provided, if necessary, for the sum which exceeds this amount. However, such a differential supplement does not need to be provided for children residing in another Member State when entitlement to the benefit in question is based on residence only.

3. If, under Article 67, an application for family benefits is submitted to the competent institution of a Member State whose legislation is applicable, but not by priority right in accordance with paragraphs 1 and 2 of this Article:

(*a*) that institution shall forward the application without delay to the competent institution of the Member State whose legislation is applicable by priority, inform the person concerned and, without prejudice to the provisions of the Implementing Regulation concerning the provisional award of benefits, provide, if necessary, the differential supplement mentioned in paragraph 2;

(*b*) the competent institution of the Member State whose legislation is applicable by priority shall deal with this application as though it were submitted directly to itself, and the date on which such an application was submitted to the first institution shall be considered as the date of its claim to the institution with priority.

Article 68a Provision of benefits

In the event that family benefits are not used by the person to whom they should be provided for the maintenance of the members of the family, the competent institution shall discharge its legal obligations by providing those benefits to the natural or legal person in fact maintaining the members of the family, at the request and through the agency of the institution in their Member State of residence or of the designated institution or body appointed for that purpose by the competent authority of their Member State of residence.

Article 69 Additional provisions

1. If, under the legislation designated by virtue of Articles 67 and 68, no right is acquired to the payment of additional or special family benefits for orphans, such benefits shall be paid by default, and in addition to the other family benefits acquired in accordance with the abovementioned legislation, under the legislation of the Member State to which the deceased worker was subject for the longest period of time, in so far as the right was acquired under that legislation. If no right was acquired under that legislation, the conditions for the acquisition of such right under the legislations of the other Member States shall be examined and benefits provided in decreasing order of the length of periods of insurance or residence completed under the legislation of those Member States.

2. Benefits paid in the form of pensions or supplements to pensions shall be provided and calculated in accordance with Chapter 5.

CHAPTER 9

SPECIAL NON-CONTRIBUTORY CASH BENEFITS

Article 70 General provision

1. This Article shall apply to special non-contributory cash benefits which are provided under legislation which, because of its personal scope, objectives and/or conditions for entitlement, has characteristics both of the social security legislation referred to in Article 3(1) and of social assistance.

2. For the purposes of this Chapter, 'special non-contributory cash benefits' means those which:

(*a*) are intended to provide either:

(i) supplementary, substitute or ancillary cover against the risks covered by the branches of social security referred to in Article 3(1), and which guarantee the persons concerned a minimum subsistence income having regard to the economic and social situation in the Member State concerned;

NIC

or

(ii) solely specific protection for the disabled, closely linked to the said person's social environment in the Member State concerned,

and

(*b*) where the financing exclusively derives from compulsory taxation intended to cover general public expenditure and the conditions for providing and for calculating the benefits are not dependent on any contribution in respect of the beneficiary. However, benefits provided to supplement a contributory benefit shall not be considered to be contributory benefits for this reason alone,

and

(*c*) are listed in Annex X.

3. Article 7 and the other chapters of this Title shall not apply to the benefits referred to in paragraph 2 of this Article.

4. The benefits referred to in paragraph 2 shall be provided exclusively in the Member State in which the persons concerned reside, in accordance with its legislation. Such benefits shall be provided by and at the expense of the institution of the place of residence.

TITLE IV

ADMINISTRATIVE COMMISSION AND ADVISORY COMMITTEE

Article 71 Composition and working methods of the Administrative Commission

1. The Administrative Commission for the Coordination of Social Security Systems (hereinafter called the Administrative Commission) attached to the European Commission shall be made up of a government representative from each of the Member States, assisted, where necessary, by expert advisers. A representative of the European Commission shall attend the meetings of the Administrative Commission in an advisory capacity.

2. The Administrative Commission shall act by a qualified majority as defined by the Treaties, except when adopting its rules which shall be drawn up by mutual agreement among its members.

Decisions on questions of interpretation referred to in Article 72(a) shall be given the necessary publicity.

3. Secretarial services for the Administrative Commission shall be provided by the European Commission.

Article 72 Tasks of the Administrative Commission

The Administrative Commission shall:

(*a*) deal with all administrative questions and questions of interpretation arising from the provisions of this Regulation or those of the Implementing Regulation, or from any agreement concluded or arrangement made thereunder, without prejudice to the right of the authorities, institutions and persons concerned to have recourse to the procedures and tribunals provided for by the legislation of the Member States, by this Regulation or by the Treaty;

(*b*) facilitate the uniform application of Community law, especially by promoting exchange of experience and best administrative practices;

(*c*) foster and develop cooperation between Member States and their institutions in social security matters in order, *inter alia*, to take into account particular questions regarding certain categories of persons; facilitate realisation of actions of crossborder cooperation activities in the area of the coordination of social security systems;

(*d*) encourage as far as possible the use of new technologies in order to facilitate the free movement of persons, in particular by modernising procedures for exchanging information and adapting the information flow between institutions for the purposes of exchange by electronic means, taking account of the development of data processing in each Member State; the Administrative Commission shall adopt the common structural rules for data processing services, in particular on security and the use of standards, and shall lay down provisions for the operation of the common part of those services;

(*e*) undertake any other function falling within its competence under this Regulation and the Implementing Regulation or any agreement or arrangement concluded thereunder;

(*f*) make any relevant proposals to the European Commission concerning the coordination of social security schemes, with a view to improving and modernising the Community *acquis* by drafting subsequent Regulations or by means of other instruments provided for by the Treaty;

(*g*) establish the factors to be taken into account for drawing up accounts relating to the costs to be borne by the institutions of the Member States under this Regulation and to adopt the annual accounts between those institutions, based on the report of the Audit Board referred to in Article 74.

Article 73 Technical Commission for Data Processing

1. A Technical Commission for Data Processing (hereinafter called the Technical Commission) shall be attached to the Administrative Commission. The Technical Commission shall propose to the Administrative Commission common architecture rules for the operation of data-processing services, in particular on security and the use of standards; it shall deliver reports and a reasoned opinion before decisions are taken by the Administrative Commission pursuant to Article 72(*d*). The composition and working methods of the Technical Commission shall be determined by the Administrative Commission.

2. To this end, the Technical Commission shall:

(*a*) gather together the relevant technical documents and undertake the studies and other work required to accomplish its tasks;

(*b*) submit to the Administrative Commission the reports and reasoned opinions referred to in paragraph 1;

(*c*) carry out all other tasks and studies on matters referred to it by the Administrative Commission;

(*d*) ensure the management of Community pilot projects using data-processing services and, for the Community part, operational systems using data-processing services.

Article 74 Audit Board

1. An Audit Board shall be attached to the Administrative Commission. The composition and working methods of the Audit Board shall be determined by the Administrative Commission.

The Audit Board shall:

(*a*) verify the method of determining and calculating the annual average costs presented by Member States;

(*b*) collect the necessary data and carry out the calculations required for establishing the annual statement of claims of each Member State;

(*c*) give the Administrative Commission periodic accounts of the results of the implementation of this Regulation and of the Implementing Regulation, in particular as regards the financial aspect;

(*d*) provide the data and reports necessary for decisions to be taken by the Administrative Commission pursuant to Article 72(*g*);

(*e*) make any relevant suggestions it may have to the Administrative Commission, including those concerning this Regulation, in connection with sub-paragraphs (*a*), (*b*) and (*c*);

(*f*) carry out all work, studies or assignments on matters referred to it by the Administrative Commission.

Article 75 Advisory Committee for the Coordination of Social Security Systems

1. An Advisory Committee for the Coordination of Social Security Systems (hereinafter referred to as Advisory Committee) is hereby established, comprising, from each Member State:

(*a*) one government representative;

(*b*) one representative from the trade unions;

(*c*) one representative from the employers' organisations.

For each of the categories referred to above, an alternate member shall be appointed for each Member State.

The members and alternate members of the Advisory Committee shall be appointed by the Council. The Advisory Committee shall be chaired by a representative of the European Commission. The Advisory Committee shall draw up its Rules of Procedure.

2. The Advisory Committee shall be empowered, at the request of the European Commission, the Administrative Commission or on its own initiative:

(*a*) to examine general questions or questions of principle and problems arising from the implementation of the Community provisions on the coordination of social security systems, especially regarding certain categories of persons;

(*b*) to formulate opinions on such matters for the Administrative Commission and proposals for any revisions of the said provisions.

TITLE V

MISCELLANEOUS PROVISIONS

Article 76 Cooperation

1. The competent authorities of the Member States shall communicate to each other all information regarding:

(*a*) measures taken to implement this Regulation;

(*b*) changes in their legislation which may affect the implementation of this Regulation.

2. For the purposes of this Regulation, the authorities and institutions of the Member States shall lend one another their good offices and act as though implementing their own legislation. The administrative assistance given by the said authorities and institutions shall, as a rule, be free of charge. However, the Administrative Commission shall establish the nature of reimbursable expenses and the limits above which their reimbursement is due.

3. The authorities and institutions of the Member States may, for the purposes of this Regulation, communicate directly with one another and with the persons involved or their representatives.

4. The institutions and persons covered by this Regulation shall have a duty of mutual information and cooperation to ensure the correct implementation of this Regulation.

The institutions, in accordance with the principle of good administration, shall respond to all queries within a reasonable period of time and shall in this connection provide the persons concerned with any information required for exercising the rights conferred on them by this Regulation.

The persons concerned must inform the institutions of the competent Member State and of the Member State of residence as soon as possible of any change in their personal or family situation which affects their right to benefits under this Regulation.

5. Failure to respect the obligation of information referred to in the third subparagraph of paragraph 4 may result in the application of proportionate measures in accordance with national law. Nevertheless, these measures shall be equivalent to those applicable to similar situations under domestic law and shall not make it impossible or excessively difficult in practice for claimants to exercise the rights conferred on them by this Regulation.

6. In the event of difficulties in the interpretation or application of this Regulation which could jeopardise the rights of a person covered by it, the institution of the competent Member State or of the Member State of residence of the person concerned shall contact the institution(s) of the Member State(s) concerned. If a solution cannot be found within a reasonable period, the authorities concerned may call on the Administrative Commission to intervene.

7. The authorities, institutions and tribunals of one Member State may not reject applications or other documents submitted to them on the grounds that they are written in an official language of another Member State, recognised as an official language of the Community institutions in accordance with Article 290 of the Treaty.

Article 77 Protection of personal data

1. Where, according to this Regulation or to the Implementing Regulation, the authorities or institutions of a Member State communicate personal data to the authorities or institutions of another Member State, such communication shall be subject to the data protection legislation of the Member State transmitting them. Any communication from the authority or institution of the receiving Member State as well as the storage, alteration and destruction of the data provided by that Member State shall be subject to the data protection legislation of the receiving Member State.

2. Data required for the application of this Regulation and the Implementing Regulation shall be transmitted by one Member State to another Member State in accordance with Community provisions on the protection of natural persons with regard to the processing and free movement of personal data.

Article 78 Data processing

1. Member States shall progressively use new technologies for the exchange, access and processing of the data required to apply this Regulation and the Implementing Regulation. the European Commission shall lend its support to activities of common interest as soon as the Member States have established such data-processing services.

2. Each Member State shall be responsible for managing its own part of the data-processing services in accordance with the Community provisions on the protection of natural persons with regard to the processing and the free movement of personal data.

3. An electronic document sent or issued by an institution in conformity with this Regulation and the Implementing Regulation may not be rejected by any authority or institution of another Member State on the grounds that it was received by electronic means, once the receiving institution has declared that it can receive electronic documents. Reproduction and recording of such documents shall be presumed to be a correct and accurate reproduction of the original document or representation of the information it relates to, unless there is proof to the contrary.

4. An electronic document shall be considered valid if the computer system on which the document is recorded contains the safeguards necessary in order to prevent any alteration, disclosure or unauthorised access to the recording. It shall at any time be possible to reproduce the recorded information in an immediately readable form. When an electronic document is transferred from one social security institution to another, appropriate security measures shall be taken in accordance with the Community provisions on the protection of natural persons with regard to the processing and the free movement of personal data.

Article 79 Funding of activities in the social security field

In connection with this Regulation and the Implementing Regulation, the European Commission may fund in full or in part:

(*a*) activities aimed at improving exchanges of information between the social security authorities and institutions of the Member States, particularly the electronic exchange of data;

(*b*) any other activity aimed at providing information to the persons covered by this Regulation and their representatives about the rights and obligations deriving from this Regulation, using the most appropriate means.

Article 80 Exemptions

1. Any exemption from or reduction of taxes, stamp duty, notarial or registration fees provided for under the legislation of one Member State in respect of certificates or documents required to be produced in application of the legislation of that Member State shall be extended to similar certificates or documents required to be produced in application of the legislation of another Member State or of this Regulation.

2. All statements, documents and certificates of any kind whatsoever required to be produced in application of this Regulation shall be exempt from authentication by diplomatic or consular authorities.

Article 81 Claims, declarations or appeals

Any claim, declaration or appeal which should have been submitted, in application of the legislation of one Member State, within a specified period to an authority, institution or tribunal of that Member State shall be admissible if it is submitted within the same period to a corresponding authority, institution or tribunal of another Member State. In such a case the authority, institution or tribunal receiving the claim, declaration or appeal shall forward it without delay to the competent authority, institution or tribunal of the former Member State either directly or through the competent authorities of the Member States concerned. The date on which such claims, declarations or appeals were submitted to the authority, institution or tribunal of the second Member State shall be considered as the date of their submission to the competent authority, institution or tribunal.

Article 82 Medical examinations

Medical examinations provided for by the legislation of one Member State may be carried out at the request of the competent institution, in another Member State, by the institution of the place of residence or stay of the claimant or the person entitled to benefits, under the conditions laid down in the Implementing Regulation or agreed between the competent authorities of the Member States concerned.

Article 83 Implementation of legislation

Special provisions for implementing the legislation of certain Member States are referred to in Annex XI.

Article 84 Collection of contributions and recovery of benefits

1. Collection of contributions due to an institution of one Member State and recovery of benefits provided by the institution of one Member State but not due may be effected in another Member State in accordance with the procedures and with the guarantees and privileges applicable to the collection of contributions due to the corresponding institution of the latter Member State and the recovery of benefits provided by it but not due.

2. Enforceable decisions of the judicial and administrative authorities relating to the collection of contributions, interest and any other charges or to the recovery of benefits provided but not due under the legislation of one Member State shall be recognised and enforced at the request of the competent institution in another Member State within the limits and in accordance with the procedures laid down by the legislation and any other procedures applicable to similar decisions of the latter Member State. Such decisions shall be declared enforceable in that Member State in so far as the legislation and any other procedures of that Member State so require.

3. Claims of an institution of one Member State shall in enforcement, bankruptcy or settlement proceedings in another Member State enjoy the same privileges as the legislation of the latter Member State accords to claims of the same kind.

4. The procedure for implementing this Article, including costs reimbursement, shall be governed by the Implementing Regulation or, where necessary and as a complementary measure, by means of agreements between Member States.

Article 85 Rights of institutions

1. If a person receives benefits under the legislation of one Member State in respect of an injury resulting from events occurring in another Member State, any rights of the institution responsible for providing benefits against a third party liable to provide compensation for the injury shall be governed by the following rules:

(*a*) where the institution responsible for providing benefits is, under the legislation it applies, subrogated to the rights which the beneficiary has against the third party, such subrogation shall be recognised by each Member State;

(*b*) where the institution responsible for providing benefits has a direct right against the third party, each Member State shall recognise such rights.

2. If a person receives benefits under the legislation of one Member State in respect of an injury resulting from events occurring in another Member State, the provisions of the said legislation which determine the cases in which the civil liability of employers or of their employees is to be excluded shall apply with regard to the said person or to the competent institution.
Paragraph 1 shall also apply to any rights of the institution responsible for providing benefits against employers or their employees in cases where their liability is not excluded.
3. Where, in accordance with Article 35(3) and/or Article 41(2), two or more Member States or their competent authorities have concluded an agreement to waive reimbursement between institutions under their jurisdiction, or, where reimbursement does not depend on the amount of benefits actually provided, any rights arising against a liable third party shall be governed by the following rules:

(*a*) where the institution of the Member State of residence or stay accords benefits to a person in respect of an injury sustained in its territory, that institution, in accordance with the provisions of the legislation it applies, shall exercise the right to subrogation or direct action against the third party liable to provide compensation for the injury;

(*b*) for the application of (*a*):

(i) the person receiving benefits shall be deemed to be insured with the institution of the place of residence or stay,

and

(ii) that institution shall be deemed to be the institution responsible for providing benefits;

(*c*) paragraphs 1 and 2 shall remain applicable in respect of any benefits not covered by the waiver agreement or a reimbursement which does not depend on the amount of benefits actually provided.

Article 86 Bilateral agreements

As far as relations between, on the one hand, Luxembourg and, on the other hand, France, Germany and Belgium are concerned, the application and the duration of the period referred to in Article 65(7) shall be subject to the conclusion of bilateral agreements.

TITLE VI
TRANSITIONAL AND FINAL PROVISIONS

Article 87 Transitional provisions

1. No rights shall be acquired pursuant to this Regulation for the period before its date of application.
2. Any period of insurance and, where appropriate, any period of employment, self-employment or residence completed under the legislation of a Member State prior to the date of application of this Regulation in the Member State concerned shall be taken into consideration for the determination of rights acquired under this Regulation.
3. Subject to paragraph 1, a right shall be acquired under this Regulation even if it relates to a contingency arising before its date of application in the Member State concerned.
4. Any benefit which has not been awarded or which has been suspended by reason of the nationality or place of residence of the person concerned shall, at the request of that person, be provided or resumed with effect from the date of application of this Regulation in the Member State concerned, provided that the rights for which benefits were previously provided have not given rise to a lump-sum payment.
5. The rights of a person to whom a pension was provided prior to the date of application of this Regulation in a Member State may, at the request of the person concerned, be reviewed, taking into account this Regulation.
6. If a request referred to in paragraph 4 or 5 is submitted within two years from the date of application of this Regulation in a Member State, the rights acquired in accordance with this Regulation shall have effect from that date, and the legislation of any Member State concerning the forfeiture or limitation of rights may not be invoked against the persons concerned.
7. If a request referred to in paragraph 4 or 5 is submitted after the expiry of the two-year period following the date of application of this Regulation in the Member State concerned, rights not forfeited or not time-barred shall have effect from the date on which the request was submitted, subject to any more favourable provisions under the legislation of any Member State.
8. If, as a result of this Regulation, a person is subject to the legislation of a Member State other than that determined in accordance with Title II of Regulation (EEC) No 1408/71, that legislation shall continue to apply while the relevant situation remains unchanged and in any case for no longer than 10 years from the date of application of this Regulation unless the person concerned requests that he/she be subject to the legislation applicable under this Regulation. The request shall be submitted within 3 months after the date of application of this Regulation to the competent institution of the Member State whose legislation is applicable under this Regulation if the person concerned is to be subject to the legislation of that Member State as of the date of application of this Regulation. If the request is made after the time limit indicated, the change of applicable legislation shall take place on the first day of the following month.

9. Article 55 of this Regulation shall apply only to pensions not subject to Article 46c of Regulation (EEC) No 1408/71 on the date of application of this Regulation.
10. The provisions of the second sentences of Article 65(2) and (3) shall be applicable to Luxembourg at the latest two years after the date of application of this Regulation.
10a. The entries in Annex III corresponding to Estonia, Spain, Italy, Lithuania, Hungary and the Netherlands shall cease to have effect 4 years after the date of application of this Regulation.
10b. The list contained in Annex III shall be reviewed no later than 31 October 2014 on the basis of a report by the Administrative Commission. That report shall include an impact assessment of the significance, frequency, scale and costs, both in absolute and in relative terms, of the application of the provisions of Annex III. That report shall also include the possible effects of repealing those provisions for those Member States which continue to be listed in that Annex after the date referred to in paragraph 10a. In the light of that report, the Commission shall decide whether to submit a proposal concerning a review of the list, with the aim in principle of repealing the list unless the report of the Administrative Commission provides compelling reasons not to do so.
11. Member States shall ensure that appropriate information is provided regarding the changes in rights and obligations introduced by this Regulation and the Implementing Regulation.

Article 87a Transitional provision for application of Regulation (EU) No 465/2012

1. If as a result of the entry into force of Regulation (EU) No 465/2012, a person is subject, in accordance with Title II of this Regulation, to the legislation of a different Member State than that to which he/she was subject before that entry into force, the legislation of the Member State applicable before that date shall continue to apply to him/her for a transitional period lasting for as long as the relevant situation remains unchanged and, in any case, for no longer than 10 years from the date of entry into force of Regulation (EU) No 465/2012. Such a person may request that the transitional period no longer applies to him/her. Such request shall be submitted to the institution designated by the competent authority of the Member State of residence. Requests submitted by 29 September 2012 shall be deemed to take effect on 28 June 2012. Requests submitted after 29 September 2012 shall take effect on the first day of the month following that of their submission.
2. No later than 29 June 2014, the Administrative Commission shall evaluate the implementation of the provisions laid down in Article 65a of this Regulation and present a report on their application. On the basis of this report, the European Commission may, as appropriate, submit proposals to amend those provisions.

Article 88 Updating of the Annexes

The Annexes of this Regulation shall be revised periodically.

Article 89 Implementing Regulation

A further Regulation shall lay down the procedure for implementing this Regulation.

Article 90 Repeal

1. Council Regulation (EEC) No 1408/71 shall be repealed from the date of application of this Regulation.
However, Regulation (EEC) No 1408/71 shall remain in force and shall continue to have legal effect for the purposes of:

(*a*) Council Regulation (EC) No 859/2003 of 14 May 2003 extending the provisions of Regulation (EEC) No 1408/71 and Regulation (EEC) No 574/72 to nationals of third countries who are not already covered by those provisions solely on the ground of their nationality[1], for as long as that Regulation has not been repealed or modified;

(*b*) Council Regulation (EEC) No 1661/85 of 13 June 1985 laying down the technical adaptations to the Community rules on social security for migrant workers with regard to Greenland[2], for as long as that Regulation has not been repealed or modified;

(*c*) the Agreement on the European Economic Area[3] and the Agreement between the European Community and its Member States, of the one part, and the Swiss Confederation, of the other part, on the free movement of persons[4] and other agreements which contain a reference to Regulation (EEC) No 1408/71, for as long as those agreements have not been modified in the light of this Regulation.

2 References to Regulation (EEC) No 1408/71 in Council Directive 98/49/EC of 29 June 1998 on safeguarding the supplementary pension rights of employed and self-employed persons moving within the Community[5] are to be read as referring to this Regulation.

[1] OJ L 124, 20.5.2003, p. 1.
[2] OJ L 160, 20.6.1985, p. 7.
[3] OJ L 1, 3.1.1994, p. 1.
[4] OJ L 114, 30.4.2002, p. 6. Agreement as last amended by Decision No 2/2003 of the EU-Swiss Committee (OJ L 187, 26.7.2003, p. 55).
[5] OJ L 209, 25.7.1998, p. 46.

Article 91 Entry into force

This Regulation shall enter into force on the 20th day after its publication in the *Official Journal of the European Union.*

NIC

It shall apply from the date of entry into force of the Implementing Regulation.
This Regulation shall be binding in its entirety and directly applicable in all Member States.

ANNEX I

ADVANCES OF MAINTENANCE PAYMENTS AND SPECIAL CHILDBIRTH AND ADOPTION ALLOWANCES

(Article 1(z))

I.

ADVANCES OF MAINTENANCE PAYMENTS

BELGIUM

Advances of maintenance allowances under the law of 21 February 2003 creating a maintenance payments agency within the federal public service, Finance Department

BULGARIA

Maintenance payments made by the State under Article 92 of the Family Code

DENMARK

Advance payment of child support laid down in the Act on Child Benefits Advance payment of child support consolidated by Law No 765 of 11 September 2002

GERMANY

Advances of maintenance payments under the German law on advances of maintenance payments (Unterhaltsvorschussgesetz) of 23 July 1979

ESTONIA

Maintenance allowances under the Maintenance Allowance Act of 21 February 2007

SPAIN

Advances of maintenance payments under the Royal Decree 1618/2007 of 7 December 2007

FRANCE

Family support allowance paid to a child one of whose parents or both of whose parents are in default or are unable to meet their maintenance obligations or the payment of a maintenance allowance laid down by a court decision

[CROATIA

Temporary advances paid by Centres for Social Welfare on the basis of the obligation to provide temporary maintenance pursuant to the Family Act (OG 116/03, as amended)]

LITHUANIA

Payments from the Children's Maintenance Fund under the Law on the Children's Maintenance Fund.

LUXEMBOURG

Advances and recovery of maintenance payments within the meaning of the Act of 26 July 1980

AUSTRIA

Advances of maintenance payments under the Federal Law on the grant of advances of child maintenance (Unterhaltsvorschussgesetz 1985 – UVG)

POLAND

Benefits from the Alimony Fund under the Act of Assistance to the Persons Entitled to Alimony

PORTUGAL

Advances of maintenance payments (Act No 75/98, 19 November, on the guarantee of maintenance for minors)

SLOVENIA

Maintenance replacement in accordance with the Act of Public Guarantee and Maintenance Fund of the Republic of Slovenia of 25 July 2006

SLOVAKIA

Substitute alimony benefit (substitute maintenance payment) pursuant to the Act No 452/2004 Coll. on substitute alimony benefit as amended by later regulations

FINLAND

Maintenance allowance under the Security of Child Maintenance Act (671/1998)

SWEDEN

Maintenance allowance under the Maintenance Support Act (1996:1030)

II.
SPECIAL CHILDBIRTH AND ADOPTION ALLOWANCES

BELGIUM

Childbirth allowance and adoption grant

BULGARIA

Maternity lump sum allowance (Law on Family Allowances for Children)

CZECH REPUBLIC

Childbirth allowance

ESTONIA

(*a*) Childbirth allowance

(*b*) Adoption allowance

SPAIN

Single payment birth and adoption grants

FRANCE

Birth or adoption grants as part of the 'early childhood benefit', except when they are paid to a person who remains subject to French legislation pursuant to Article 12 or Article 16

[CROATIA

One-off cash benefit for a newborn child under the Maternity and Parental Benefits Act (OG 85/08, as amended)

One-off cash benefit for an adopted child under the Maternity and Parental Benefits Act (OG 85/08, as amended)

One-off cash benefits for a newborn child or an adopted child provided by regulations on local and regional self- government pursuant to Article 59 of the Maternity and Parental Benefits Act (OG 85/08, as amended)]

LATVIA

(*a*) Childbirth grant

(*b*) Adoption allowance

LITHUANIA

Child lump sum grant

LUXEMBOURG

Antenatal allowances

Childbirth allowances

HUNGARY

Maternity grant

POLAND

Single payment birth grant (Act on Family Benefits)

ROMANIA

(*a*) Childbirth allowance

(*b*) Layette for newborn children

SLOVENIA

Childbirth grant

SLOVAKIA

(*a*) Childbirth allowance

(*b*) Supplement to childbirth allowance

FINLAND

Maternity package, maternity lump-sum grant and assistance in the form of a lump sum intended to offset the cost of international adoption pursuant to the Maternity Grant Act.

ANNEX II
PROVISIONS OF CONVENTIONS WHICH REMAIN IN FORCE AND WHICH, WHERE APPLICABLE, ARE RESTRICTED TO THE PERSONS COVERED THEREBY

(Article 8(1))

General comments—It is to be noted that the provisions of bilateral conventions which do not fall within the scope of this Regulation and which remain in force between Member States are not listed in this Annex. This includes obligations between Member States arising from conventions providing, for example, for provisions regarding aggregation of insurance periods fulfilled in a third country.

Provisions of social security conventions remaining applicable:

BELGIUM-GERMANY

Articles 3 and 4 of the Final Protocol of 7 December 1957 to the General Convention of that date, as set out in the Complementary Protocol of 10 November 1960 (reckoning of insurance periods completed in some border regions before, during and after the Second World War).

BELGIUM-LUXEMBOURG

Convention of 24 March 1994 on social security for frontier workers (relating to the complementary flat rate reimbursement).

BULGARIA-GERMANY

Article 28(1)(b) of the Convention on social security of 17 December 1997 (maintenance of conventions concluded between Bulgaria and the former German Democratic Republic for persons who already received a pension before 1996).

[BULGARIA-CROATIA

Article 35(3) of the Convention on Social Security of 14 July 2003 (recognition of periods of insurance completed until 31 December 1957 at the expense of the contracting state in which the insured person resided on 31 December 1957).]

BULGARIA-AUSTRIA

Article 38(3) of the Convention on social security of 14 April 2005 (reckoning of periods of insurance completed before 27 November 1961); the application of that provision remains restricted to the persons covered by that Convention.

BULGARIA-SLOVENIA

Article 32(2) of the Convention on Social Security of 18 December 1957 (reckoning of periods of insurance completed until 31 December 1957).

CZECH REPUBLIC-GERMANY

Article 39(1)(b) and (c) of the Convention on Social Security of 27 July 2001 (maintenance of the convention concluded between the former Czechoslovak Republic and the former German Democratic Republic for persons who already received a pension before 1996; reckoning of periods of insurance completed in one of the contracting States for persons who already received a pension for these periods on 1 September 2002 from the other contracting State, while residing in its territory).

CZECH REPUBLIC-CYPRUS

Article 32(4) of the Convention on Social Security of 19 January 1999 (determining competence for the calculation of periods of employment completed under the relevant Convention of 1976); the application of that provision remains restricted to the persons covered by it.

CZECH REPUBLIC-LUXEMBOURG

Article 52(8) of the Convention on Social Security of 17 November 2000 (reckoning of pension insurance periods for political refugees).

CZECH REPUBLIC-AUSTRIA

Article 32(3) of the Convention on social security of 20 July 1999 (reckoning of periods of insurance completed before 27 November 1961); the application of that provision remains restricted to the persons covered by it.

CZECH REPUBLIC-SLOVAKIA

Articles 12, 20 and 33 of the Convention on Social Security of 29 October 1992 (Article 12 determines competence for a grant of survivor's benefits; Article 20 determines competence for calculation of insurance periods completed until the day of dissolution of the Czech and Slovak Federal Republic; Article 33 determines competence for payment of pensions awarded before the day of the dissolution of the Czech and Slovak Federal Republic).

DENMARK-FINLAND

Article 7 of the Nordic Convention on social security of 18 August 2003 (concerning coverage of extra travel expenses in case of sickness during stay in another Nordic country increasing the cost of return travel to the country of residence).

DENMARK-SWEDEN

Article 7 of the Nordic Convention on social security of 18 August 2003 (concerning coverage of extra travel expenses in case of sickness during stay in another Nordic country increasing the cost of return travel to the country of residence).

GERMANY-SPAIN

Article 45(2) of the Social Security Convention of 4 December 1973 (representation by diplomatic and consular authorities).

GERMANY-FRANCE

(*a*) Complementary Agreement No 4 of 10 July 1950 to the General Convention of the same date, as set out in Supplementary Agreement No 2 of 18 June 1955 (reckoning of periods of insurance completed between 1 July 1940 and 30 June 1950);

(*b*) Title I of that Supplementary Agreement No 2 (reckoning of periods of insurance completed before 8 May 1945);
(*c*) points 6, 7 and 8 of the General Protocol of 10 July 1950 to the General Convention of the same date (administrative arrangements);
(*d*) Titles II, III and IV of the Agreement of 20 December 1963 (social security in the Saar).
[GERMANY-CROATIA
Article 41 of the Convention on Social Security of 24 November 1997 (settlement of rights acquired before 1 January 1956 under the social security scheme of the other contracting state); the application of that provision remains restricted to the persons covered by it.]
GERMANY-LUXEMBOURG
Articles 4, 5, 6 and 7 of the Convention of 11 July 1959 (reckoning of insurance periods completed between September 1940 and June 1946).
GERMANY-HUNGARY
Article 40(1)(b) of the Convention on social security of 2 May 1998 (maintenance of the convention concluded between the former German Democratic Republic and Hungary for persons who already received a pension before 1996).
GERMANY-NETHERLANDS
Articles 2 and 3 of Complementary Agreement No 4 of 21 December 1956 to the Convention of 29 March 1951 (settlement of rights acquired under the German social insurance scheme by Dutch workers between 13 May 1940 and 1 September 1945).
GERMANY-AUSTRIA
(*a*) Article 1(5) and Article 8 of the Convention on Unemployment Insurance of 19 July 1978 and Article 10 of the Final Protocol to this Convention (granting of unemployment allowances to frontier workers by the previous State of employment) shall continue to apply to persons who have exercised an activity as a frontier worker on or before 1 January 2005 and become unemployed before 1 January 2011;
(*b*) Article 14(2)(g), (h), (i) and (j) of the Convention on social security of 4 October 1995 (determination of competencies between both countries with regard to former insurance cases and acquired insurance periods); the application of that provision remains restricted to the persons covered by it.
GERMANY-POLAND
(*a*) Convention of 9 October 1975 on old-age and work injury provisions, under the conditions and the scope defined by Article 27(2) to (4) of the Convention on social security of 8 December 1990 (maintenance of legal status, on the basis of the Convention of 1975, of the persons who had established their residence in the territory of Germany or Poland before 1 January 1991 and who continue to reside there);
(*b*) Articles 27(5) and 28(2) of the Convention on social security of 8 December 1990 (maintenance of entitlement to a pension paid on the basis of the Convention of 1957 concluded between the former German Democratic Republic and Poland; reckoning of periods of insurance completed by Polish employees under the Convention of 1988 concluded between the former German Democratic Republic and Poland).
GERMANY-ROMANIA
Article 28(1)(b) of the Convention on social security of 8 April 2005 (maintenance of the Convention concluded between the former German Democratic Republic and Romania for persons who already received a pension before 1996).
GERMANY-SLOVENIA
Article 42 of the Convention on social security of 24 September 1997 (settlement of rights acquired before 1 January 1956 under the social security scheme of the other contracting state); the application of that provision remains restricted to the persons covered by it.
GERMANY-SLOVAKIA
Article 29(1), second and third sub-paragraphs of the Agreement of 12 September 2002 (maintenance of the Convention concluded between the former Czechoslovak Republic and the former German Democratic Republic for persons who already received a pension before 1996; reckoning of periods of insurance completed in one of the contracting States for persons who already received a pension for these periods on 1 December 2003 from the other contracting State, while residing in its territory).
GERMANY-UNITED KINGDOM
(*a*) Article 7(5) and (6) of the Convention on social security of 20 April 1960 (legislation applicable to civilians serving in the military forces);
(*b*) Article 5(5) and (6) of the Convention on unemployment insurance of 20 April 1960 (legislation applicable to civilians serving in the military forces).

IRELAND-UNITED KINGDOM

Article 19(2) of the Agreement of 14 December, 2004 on social security (concerning the transfer and reckoning of certain disability credits).

SPAIN-PORTUGAL

Article 22 of the General Convention of 11 June 1969 (export of unemployment benefits). This entry will remain valid for 2 years from the date of application of this Regulation.

[CROATIA-ITALY

(*a*) The Agreement between Yugoslavia and Italy on Regulation of Mutual Obligations in Social Insurance with Reference to Paragraph 7 of Annex XIV to the Peace Treaty, concluded by exchange of notes on 5 February 1959 (reckoning of periods of insurance completed before 18 December 1954); the application remains restricted to the persons covered by that Agreement;

(*b*) Article 44(3) of the Convention on Social Security between the Republic of Croatia and the Italian Republic of 27 June 1997, concerning ex Zone B of the Free Territory of Trieste (reckoning of periods of insurance completed before 5 October 1956); the application of that provision remains restricted to persons covered by that Convention.

CROATIA-HUNGARY

Article 43(6) of the Convention on Social Security of 8 February 2005 (recognition of periods of insurance completed until 29 May 1956 at the expense of the contracting state in which the insured person resided on 29 May 1956).

CROATIA-AUSTRIA

Article 35 of the Convention on Social Security of 16 January 1997 (reckoning of periods of insurance completed before 1 January 1956); the application of that provision remains restricted to the persons covered by it.

CROATIA-SLOVENIA

(*a*) Article 35(3) of the Agreement on Social Security of 28 April 1997 (recognition of periods with bonus under the legislation of the former common State);

(*b*) Articles 36 and 37 of the Agreement on Social Security of 28 April 1997 (benefits acquired before 8 October 1991 remain the obligation of the contracting state that granted them; pensions granted between 8 October 1991 and 1 February 1998, the date of entry into force of the said Agreement, in respect of the periods of insurance completed in the other contracting state until 31 January 1998, are subject to recalculation).]

ITALY-SLOVENIA

(*a*) Agreement on regulation of mutual obligations in social insurance with reference to paragraph 7 of Annex XIV to the Peace Treaty, concluded by exchange of notes on 5 February 1959 (reckoning of periods of insurance completed before 18 December 1954); the application of that provision remains restricted to the persons covered by that Agreement;

(*b*) Article 45(3) of the Convention on social security of 7 July 1997 concerning ex-Zone B of the Free Territory of Trieste (reckoning of periods of insurance completed before 5 October 1956); the application of that provision remains restricted to the persons covered by that Convention.

LUXEMBOURG-PORTUGAL

Agreement of 10 March 1997 (on the recognition of decisions by institutions in one contracting party concerning the state of invalidity of applicants for pensions from institutions in the other contracting party).

LUXEMBOURG-SLOVAKIA

Article 50(5) of the Convention on Social Security of 23 May 2002 (reckoning of pension insurance periods for political refugees).

HUNGARY-AUSTRIA

Article 36(3) of the Convention on social security of 31 March 1999 (reckoning of periods of insurance completed before 27 November 1961); the application of that provision remains restricted to the persons covered by it.

HUNGARY-SLOVENIA

Article 31 of the Convention on social security of 7 October 1957 (reckoning of periods of insurance completed before 29 May 1956); the application of that provision remains restricted to the persons covered by it.

HUNGARY-SLOVAKIA

Article 34(1) of the Convention on social security of 30 January 1959 (Article 34(1) of that Convention provides that the insurance periods awarded before the day of signing that Convention are the insurance periods of the contracting State on which territory the entitled person had a residence); the application of that provision remains restricted to the persons covered by it.

AUSTRIA-POLAND

Article 33(3) of the Convention on social security of 7 September 1998 (reckoning of periods of insurance completed before 27 November 1961); the application of that provision remains restricted to the persons covered by it.

AUSTRIA-ROMANIA

Article 37(3) of the Agreement on social security of 28 October 2005 (reckoning of periods of insurance completed before 27 November 1961); the application of that provision remains restricted to the persons covered by it.

AUSTRIA-SLOVENIA

Article 37 of the Convention on social security of 10 March 1997 (reckoning of periods of insurance completed before 1 January 1956); the application of that provision remains restricted to the persons covered by it.

AUSTRIA-SLOVAKIA

Article 34(3) of the Convention of 21 December 2001 on Social Security (reckoning of periods of insurance completed before 27 November 1961); the application of that provision remains restricted to the persons covered by it.

FINLAND-SWEDEN

Article 7 of the Nordic Convention on social security of 18 August 2003 (concerning coverage of extra travel expenses in case of sickness during stay in another Nordic country increasing the cost of return travel to the country of residence).

ANNEX III

RESTRICTION OF RIGHTS TO BENEFITS IN KIND FOR MEMBERS OF THE FAMILY OF A FRONTIER WORKER

(referred to in Article 18(2))

DENMARK

ESTONIA (this entry will be valid during the period referred to in Article 87(10a))

IRELAND

SPAIN (this entry will be valid during the period referred to in Article 87(10a))

[CROATIA]

ITALY (this entry will be valid during the period referred to in Article 87(10a))

LITHUANIA (this entry will be valid during the period referred to in Article 87(10a))

HUNGARY (this entry will be valid during the period referred to in Article 87(10a))

NETHERLANDS (this entry will be valid during the period referred to in Article 87(10a))

FINLAND

SWEDEN

UNITED KINGDOM

ANNEX IV

MORE RIGHTS FOR PENSIONERS RETURNING TO THE COMPETENT MEMBER STATE

(Article 27(2))

BELGIUM

BULGARIA

CZECH REPUBLIC

GERMANY

GREECE

SPAIN

FRANCE

CYPRUS

LUXEMBOURG

HUNGARY

THE NETHERLANDS

AUSTRIA

POLAND

SLOVENIA

SWEDEN

ANNEX V

MORE RIGHTS FOR FORMER FRONTIER WORKERS WHO RETURN TO THEIR PREVIOUS MEMBER STATE OF ACTIVITY AS AN EMPLOYED OR SELF-EMPLOYED PERSON (APPLICABLE ONLY IF THE MEMBER STATE IN WHICH THE COMPETENT INSTITUTION RESPONSIBLE FOR THE COSTS OF THE BENEFITS IN KIND PROVIDED TO THE PENSIONER IN HIS/HER MEMBER STATE OF RESIDENCE IS SITUATED ALSO APPEARS ON THE LIST)

(Article 28(2))

BELGIUM

GERMANY

SPAIN

FRANCE

LUXEMBOURG

AUSTRIA

PORTUGAL

ANNEX VI

IDENTIFICATION OF TYPE A LEGISLATION WHICH SHOULD BE SUBJECT TO SPECIAL COORDINATION

(Article 44(1))

CZECH REPUBLIC

Full disability pension for persons whose total disability arose before reaching 18 years of age and who were not insured for the required period (Section 42 of the Pension Insurance Act No 155/1995 Coll.)

ESTONIA

(*a*) Invalidity pensions granted before 1 April 2000 under the State Allowances Act and which are retained under the State Pension Insurance Act

(*b*) National pensions granted on the basis of invalidity according to the State Pension Insurance Act

(*c*) Invalidity pensions granted according to the Defence Forces Service Act, Police Service Act, Prosecutor's Office Act, Status of Judges Act, Members of the Riigikogu Salaries, Pensions and Other Social Guarantees Act and President of the Republic Official Benefits Act

[(*d*) Work ability allowance granted under the Work Ability Allowance Act']

IRELAND

Part 2, Chapter 17 of the Social Welfare Consolidation Act 2005

GREECE

Legislation relating to the agricultural insurance scheme (OGA), under Law No 4169/1961

[CROATIA

(*a*) Invalidity pension due to occupational injury or disease according to Article 52(5) of the Pension Insurance Act (OG 102/98, as amended).

(*b*) Physical damage allowance according to Article 56 of the Pension Insurance Act (OG 102/98, as amended).]

LATVIA

Invalidity pensions (third group) under Article 16(1)(2) of the Law on State Pensions of 1 January 1996

[HUNGARY

As from 1 January 2012 pursuant to the Act CXCI of 2011 on the benefits for persons with changed working capacity and amendments of certain other acts:

(*a*) the rehabilitation benefit;

(*b*) the invalidity benefit.

SLOVAKIA

Invalidity pension for a person who became invalid as a dependent child or during full-time doctoral studies while under the age of 26 years and who is always deemed to have fulfilled the required period of insurance (Article 70(2), Article 72(3) and Article 73(3) and (4) of Act No 461/2003 on social insurance, as amended).]

FINLAND

National Pensions to persons who are born disabled or become disabled at an early age (the National Pension Act, 568/2007);

Invalidity pensions determined according to transitional rules and awarded prior to 1 January 1994 (Act on Enforcement of the National Pensions Act, 569/2007).

[SWEDEN

Income-related sickness compensation and income-related activity compensation (Chapter 34 of the Social Insurance Code).]

[UNITED KINGDOM

Employment and Support Allowance (ESA)

(*a*) For awards granted before 1 April 2016 ESA is a cash sickness benefit for the initial 91 days (Assessment Phase). From the 92nd day ESA (Main Phase) becomes an invalidity benefit.

(*b*) For awards granted on or after 1 April 2016 ESA is a cash sickness benefit for the initial 365 days (Assessment Phase). From the 366th day ESA (Support Group) becomes an invalidity benefit.

Great Britain legislation: Part 1 of the Welfare Reform Act 2007.

Northern Ireland legislation: Part 1 of the Welfare Reform Act (Northern Ireland) 2007.]

ANNEX VII

CONCORDANCE BETWEEN THE LEGISLATIONS OF MEMBER STATES ON CONDITIONS RELATING TO THE DEGREE OF INVALIDITY

(Article 46(3) of the Regulation)

BELGIUM

Member State	Schemes administered by institutions of Member States which have taken a decision recognising the degree of invalidity	Schemes administered by Belgian institutions on which the decision is binding in cases of concordance				
		General scheme	Miners' scheme		Mariners' scheme	Ossom
			General invalidity	Occupational invalidity		
FRANCE	1. General scheme:					
	– Group III (constant attendance)	Concordance	Concordance	Concordance	Concordance	No concordance
	– Group II	Concordance	Concordance	Concordance	Concordance	No concordance
	– Group I	Concordance	Concordance	Concordance	Concordance	No concordance
	2. Agricultural scheme					
	– Total, general invalidity	Concordance	Concordance	Concordance	Concordance	No concordance
	– Two-thirds general invalidity	Concordance	Concordance	Concordance	Concordance	No concordance
	– Constant attendance	Concordance	Concordance	Concordance	Concordance	No concordance
	3. Miners' scheme:					
	– Partial, general invalidity	Concordance	Concordance	Concordance	Concordance	No concordance
	– Constant attendance	Concordance	Concordance	Concordance	Concordance	No concordance
	– Occupational invalidity	No concordance	No concordance	Concordance	No concordance	No concordance
	4. Mariners' scheme:					
	– General invalidity	Concordance	Concordance	Concordance	Concordance	No concordance

ITALY	– Constant attendance	Concordance	Concordance	Concordance	Concordance	No concordance
	– Occupational invalidity	No concordance	No concordance	No concordance	No concordance	No concordance
	1. General scheme:					
	– Invalidity — manual workers	No concordance	Concordance	Concordance	Concordance	No concordance
	– Invalidity — clerical staff	No concordance	Concordance	Concordance	Concordance	No concordance
	2. Mariners' scheme:					
	– Unfitness for seafaring	No concordance	No concordance	No concordance	No concordance	No concordance

FRANCE

Member State	Schemes administered by institutions of Member States which have taken a decision recognising the degree of invalidity	Schemes administered by French institutions on which the decision is binding in cases of concordances											
		General scheme			Agricultural scheme			Miners' scheme			Mariners' scheme		
		Group I	Group II	Group III Constant attendance	2/3 Invalidity	Total invalidity	Constant attendance	2/3 General invalidity	Constant attendance	Occupational invalidity	2/3 General invalidity	Total occupational invalidity	Constant attendance
BELGIUM	1. General scheme	Concordance	No concordance	No concordance	Concordance	No concordance	No concordance	Concordance	No concordance	No concordance	No concordance	No concordance	No concordance
	2. Miners' scheme												

NIC

	– partial general invalidity	Concordance	No concordance	No concordance	Concordance	No concordance	No concordance	Concordance	No concordance	No concordance	No concordance	No concordance	No concordance
	– occupational invalidity	No concordance	No concordance	No concordance	No concordance	No concordance	No concordance	No concordance	No concordance	Concordance [2]			
	3. Mariners' scheme	Concordance [1]	No concordance	No concordance	Concordance [1]	No concordance	No concordance	Concordance [1]	No concordance	No concordance	No concordance	No concordance	No concordance
ITALY	1. General scheme												
	– invalidity — manual workers	Concordance	No concordance	No concordance	Concordance	No concordance	No concordance	Concordance	No concordance	No concordance	No concordance	No concordance	No concordance
	– invalidity — clerical staff	Concordance	No concordance	No concordance	Concordance	No concordance	No concordance	Concordance	No concordance	No Concordance	No concordance	No concordance	No concordance
	2. Mariners' scheme												
	– unfitness for seafaring	No concordance	No concordance	No concordance	No Concordance	No Concordance	No concordance	No concordance	No concordance	No concordance	No concordance	No concordance	No concordance

[1] In so far as the invalidity recognised by the Belgian institutions is general invalidity.
[2] Only if the Belgian institution has recognised that the worker is unfit for work underground or at ground level.

ITALY

Member State	Schemes administered by institutions of Member States which have taken a decision recognising the degree of invalidity	Schemes administered by Italian institutions on which the decision is binding in cases of concordance		
		General scheme		Mariners unfit for navigation
		Manual workers	Clerical staff	
BELGIUM	1. General scheme	No concordance	No concordance	No concordance
	2. Miners' scheme			
	– partial general invalidity	Concordance	Concordance	No concordance
	– occupational invalidity	No concordance	No concordance	No concordance
	3. Mariners' scheme	No concordance	No concordance	No concordance
FRANCE	1. General scheme			
	– Group III (constant attendance)	Concordance	Concordance	No concordance
	– Group II	Concordance	Concordance	No concordance
	– Group I	Concordance	Concordance	No concordance
	2. Agricultural scheme			
	– total general invalidity	Concordance	Concordance	No concordance
	– partial general invalidity	Concordance	Concordance	No concordance
	– constant attendance	Concordance	Concordance	No concordance
	3. Miners' scheme			
	– partial general invalidity	Concordance	Concordance	No concordance
	– constant attendance	Concordance	Concordance	No concordance
	– occupational invalidity	No concordance	No concordance	No concordance
	4. Mariners' scheme			
	– partial general invalidity	No concordance	No concordance	No concordance
	– constant attendance	No concordance	No concordance	No concordance
	– occupational invalidity			

NIC

ANNEX VIII

CASES IN WHICH THE PRO RATA CALCULATION SHALL BE WAIVED OR SHALL NOT APPLY

(Article 52(4) and 52(5))

Part 1: Cases in which the pro rata calculation shall be waived pursuant to Article 52(4)

DENMARK

All applications for pensions referred to in the law on social pensions, except for pensions mentioned in Annex IX.

IRELAND

All applications for state pension (transition), state pension (contributory), widow's (contributory) pension and widower's (contributory) pension.

CYPRUS

All applications for old age, invalidity, widow's and widower's pensions.

LATVIA

(*a*) All applications for invalidity pensions (Law on State Pensions of 1 January 1996);

(*b*) All applications for survivor's pensions (Law on State pensions of 1 January 1996; Law on State funded pensions of 1 July 2001).

LITHUANIA

All applications for State social insurance survivor's pensions calculated on the basis of the basic amount of survivor's pension (Law on State Social Insurance Pensions).

NETHERLANDS

All applications for old-age pensions under the law on general old-age insurance (AOW).

AUSTRIA

(*a*) All applications for benefits under the Federal Act of 9 September 1955 on General Social Insurance – ASVG, the Federal Act of 11 October 1978 on social insurance for self-employed persons engaged in trade and commerce – GSVG, the Federal Act of 11 October 1978 on social insurance for self-employed farmers – BSVG and the Federal Act of 30 November 1978 on social insurance for the self-employed in the liberal professions (FSVG);

(*b*) All applications for invalidity pensions based on a pension account pursuant to the General Pensions Act (APG) of 18 November 2004;

[(*c*) All applications for survivors' pensions based on a pension account pursuant to the General Pensions Act (APG) of 18 November 2004, with the exception of cases under Part 2.]

(*d*) All applications for invalidity and survivors' pensions of the Austrian Provincial Chambers of Physicians (Landesärztekammer) based on basic provision (basic and any supplementary benefit, or basic pension);

(*e*) All applications for permanent occupational invalidity support and survivors' support from the pension fund of the Austrian Chamber of Veterinary Surgeons;

(*f*) All applications for benefits from occupational invalidity, widows and orphans pensions according to the statutes of the welfare institutions of the Austrian bar associations, Part A.

[(*g*) All applications for benefits under the Notary Insurance Act of 3 February 1972 – NVG 1972.]

[POLAND

All applications for disability pensions, old-age under the defined benefits scheme and survivors' pensions, except for the cases where the totalised periods of insurance completed under the legislation of more than one Member State are equal to or longer than 20 years for women and 25 years for men but the national periods of insurance are inferior to these limits (and not less than 15 years for women and 20 years for men), and the calculation is made under Articles 27 and 28 of the Act of 17 December 1998 (O.J. 2015, item 748).]

PORTUGAL

All applications for invalidity, old-age and survivors' pension claims, except for the cases where the totalised periods of insurance completed under the legislation of more than one Member State are equal to or longer than 21 calendar years but the national periods of insurance are equal or inferior to 20 years, and the calculation is made under Articles 32 and 33 of Decree-Law No 187/2007 of 10 May 2007.

SLOVAKIA

(*a*) All applications for survivors' pension (widow's pension, widower's and orphan's pension) calculated according to the legislation in force before 1 January 2004, the amount of which is derived from a pension formerly paid to the deceased;

(*b*) All applications for pensions calculated pursuant to Act No 461/2003 Coll. on social security as amended.

[SWEDEN

(*a*) Applications for an old-age pension in the form of a guaranteed pension (Chapters 66 and 67 of the Social Insurance Code).

(*b*) Applications for an old-age pension in the form of a supplementary pension (Chapter 63 of the Social Insurance Code).]

UNITED KINGDOM

[All applications for retirement pension, state pension pursuant to Part 1 of the Pensions Act 2014, widows' and bereavement benefits, with the exception of those for which during a tax year beginning on or after 6 April 1975:]

(*i*) the party concerned had completed periods of insurance, employment or residence under the legislation of the United Kingdom and another Member State; and one (or more) of the tax years was not considered a qualifying year within the meaning of the legislation of the United Kingdom;

(ii) the periods of insurance completed under the legislation in force in the United Kingdom for the periods prior to 5 July 1948 would be taken into account for the purposes of Article 52(1)(b) of the Regulation by application of the periods of insurance, employment or residence under the legislation of another Member State.

All applications for additional pension pursuant to the Social Security Contributions and Benefits Act 1992, section 44, and the Social Security Contributions and Benefits (Northern Ireland) Act 1992, section 44.

Part 2: Cases in which Article 52(5) applies

BULGARIA

Old age pensions from the Supplementary Compulsory Pension Insurance, under Part II, Title II, of the Social Insurance Code.

[CZECH REPUBLIC

Pensions paid from the Second Pillar scheme established by Act No 426/2011 Coll., on pension savings.][1]

[DENMARK

(*a*) Personal pensions;

(*b*) Benefits in the event of death (accrued based on contributions to Arbejdsmarkedets Tillægspension related to the time before 1 January 2002);

(*c*) Benefits in the event of death (accrued based on contributions to Arbejdsmarkedets Tillægspension related to the time after 1 January 2002) referred to in the Consolidated Act on Labour Market Supplementary Pension (Arbejdsmarkedets Tillægspension) 942:2009.]

ESTONIA

Mandatory funded old-age pension scheme.

FRANCE

Basic or supplementary schemes in which old-age benefits are calculated on the basis of retirement points.

[CROATIA

Pensions from the compulsory insurance scheme based on the individual capitalised savings according to the Compulsory and Voluntary Pension Funds Act (OG 49/99, as amended) and the Act on Pension Insurance Companies and Payment of Pensions Based on Individual Capitalised Savings (OG 106/99, as amended), except in the cases provided by Articles 47 and 48 of the Compulsory and Voluntary Pension Funds Act (invalidity pension based on general incapacity to work and survivor's pension).]

LATVIA

Old-age pensions (Law on State pensions of 1 January 1996; Law on State funded pensions of 1 July 2001).

HUNGARY

Pension benefits based on membership of private pension funds.

AUSTRIA

[(*a*) Old-age pensions and survivor's pensions derived thereof based on a pension account pursuant to the General Pensions Act (APG) of 18 November 2004;][1]

(*b*) Compulsory allowances under Article 41 of the Federal Law of 28 December 2001, BGBl I Nr. 154 on the general salary fund of Austrian pharmacists (Pharmazeutische Gehaltskasse für Österreich);

(*c*) Retirement and early retirement pensions of the Austrian Provincial Chambers of Physicians based on basic provision (basic and any supplementary benefit, or basic pension), and all pension benefits of the Austrian Provincial Chambers of Physicians based on additional provision (additional or individual pension);

(*d*) Old-age support from the pension fund of the Austrian Chamber of Veterinary Surgeons;

(*e*) Benefits according to the statutes of the welfare institutions of the Austrian bar associations, Parts A and B, with the exception of applications for benefits from disability, widows' and orphans' pensions according to the statutes of the welfare institutions of the Austrian bar associations, Part A;
(*f*) Benefits by the welfare institutions of the Federal Chamber of Architects and Consulting Engineers under the Austrian Civil Engineers' Chamber Act (Ziviltechnikerkammergesetz) 1993 and the statutes of the welfare institutions, with the exception of benefits on grounds of occupational invalidity and survivors' benefits deriving from the last-named benefits;
(*g*) Benefits according to the statute of the welfare institution of the Federal Chamber of Professional Accountants and Tax Advisors under the Austrian Professional Accountants and Tax Advisors' Act (Wirtschaftstreuhandberufsgesetz).

POLAND

Old-age pensions under the defined contribution scheme.

PORTUGAL

Supplementary pensions granted pursuant to Decree-Law No 26/2008 of 22 February 2008 (public capitalisation scheme).

SLOVENIA

Pension from compulsory supplementary pension insurance.

SLOVAKIA

Mandatory old-age pension saving.

[SWEDEN

Old-age pension in the form of an income pension and a premium pension (Chapters 62 and 64 of the Social Insurance Code).]

UNITED KINGDOM

Graduated retirement benefits paid pursuant to the National Insurance Act 1965, sections 36 and 37, and the National Insurance Act (Northern Ireland) 1966, sections 35 and 36.

Amendments—[1] In entry for Austria, point (a) substituted, and entry for Croatia inserted, by Commission Regulation 1372/2013/EU art 1(1) with effect from 1 January 2014 (OJ L 346, 20.12.2013, p 27).

ANNEX IX

BENEFITS AND AGREEMENTS WHICH ALLOW THE APPLICATION OF ARTICLE 54

I.

BENEFITS REFERRED TO IN ARTICLE 54(2)(A) OF THE REGULATION, THE AMOUNT OF WHICH IS INDEPENDENT OF THE LENGTH OF PERIODS OF INSURANCE OR RESIDENCE COMPLETED

BELGIUM

Benefits relating to the general invalidity scheme, the special invalidity scheme for miners and the special scheme for merchant navy mariners

Benefits on insurance for self-employed persons against incapacity to work

Benefits relating to invalidity in the overseas social insurance scheme and the invalidity scheme for former employees of the Belgian Congo and Rwanda-Urundi

DENMARK

The full Danish national old-age pension acquired after 10 years' residence by persons who will have been awarded a pension by 1 October 1989

IRELAND

Type A Invalidity pension

GREECE

Benefits under Law No 4169/1961 relating to the agricultural insurance scheme (OGA)

SPAIN

Survivors' pensions granted under the general and special schemes, with the exception of the Special Scheme for Civil Servants

FRANCE

Invalidity pension under the general social security system or under the agricultural workers scheme

Widower's or widow's invalidity pension under the general social security system or under the agricultural workers scheme where it is calculated on the basis of the deceased spouse's invalidity pension settled in accordance with Article 52(1)(*a*)

LATVIA

Invalidity pensions (third group) under Article 16(1)(2) of the Law on State Pensions of 1 January 1996

NETHERLANDS

Disability Insurance Act of 18 February 1966, as amended (WAO)

Self-employed Persons Disablement Benefits Act of 24 April 1997, as amended (WAZ)

General Surviving Relatives Act of 21 December 1995 (ANW)

The Work and Income according to Labour Capacity Act of 10 November 2005 (WIA)

FINLAND

National pensions to persons who are born disabled or become disabled at an early age (the National Pensions Act, 568/2007)

National pensions and spouse's pensions determined according to the transitional rules and awarded prior to the 1 of January 1994 (Act on Enforcement of the National Pensions Act, 569/2007)

The additional amount of child's pension when calculating independent benefit according to the National Pension Act (the National Pension Act, 568/2007)

[SWEDEN

Income-related sickness compensation and income-related activity compensation (Chapter 34 of the Social Insurance Code)

Guaranteed pension and guaranteed compensation which replaced the full state pensions provided under the legislation on the state pension which applied before 1 January 1993, and the full state pension awarded under the transitional rules of the legislation applying from that date';

II.

BENEFITS REFERRED TO IN ARTICLE 54(2)(B) OF THE REGULATION, THE AMOUNT OF WHICH IS DETERMINED BY REFERENCE TO A CREDITED PERIOD DEEMED TO HAVE BEEN COMPLETED BETWEEN THE DATE ON WHICH THE RISK MATERIALISED AND A LATER DATE

GERMANY

Invalidity and survivors' pensions, for which account is taken of a supplementary period

Old-age pensions, for which account is taken of a supplementary period already acquired

SPAIN

The pensions for retirement or retirement for permanent disability (invalidity) under the Special Scheme for Civil Servants due under Title I of the consolidated text of the Law on State Pensioners if at the time of materialisation of the risk the beneficiary was an active civil servant or treated as such; death and survivors' (widows'/widowers', orphans' and parents') pensions due under Title I of the consolidated text of the Law on State Pensioners if at the time of death the civil servant was active or treated as such

ITALY

Italian pensions for total incapacity for work (inabilità)

LATVIA

Survivors' pension calculated on the basis of assumed insurance periods (Article 23(8) of the Law on State Pensions of 1 January 1996)

LITHUANIA

(*a*) State social insurance work incapacity pensions, paid under the Law on State Social Insurance Pensions

(*b*) State social insurance survivors' and orphans' pensions, calculated on the basis of the work incapacity pension of the deceased under the Law on State Social Insurance Pensions

LUXEMBOURG

Invalidity and survivors' pensions

SLOVAKIA

(*a*) Slovak invalidity pension and survivors' pension derived therefrom

(*b*) . . .

FINLAND

Employment pensions for which account is taken of future periods according to the national legislation

[SWEDEN

Sickness compensation and activity compensation in the form of guarantee compensation (Chapter 35 of the Social Insurance Code)

Survivors' pension calculated on the basis of credited insurance periods (Chapters 76-85 of the Social Insurance Code).]

III.

AGREEMENTS REFERRED TO IN ARTICLE 54(2)(B)(I) OF THE REGULATION INTENDED TO PREVENT THE SAME CREDITED PERIOD BEING TAKEN INTO ACCOUNT TWO OR MORE TIMES:

The Social Security Agreement of 28 April 1997 between the Republic of Finland and the Federal Republic of Germany

The Social Security Agreement of 10 November 2000 between the Republic of Finland and the Grand Duchy of Luxembourg

Nordic Convention on social security of 18 August 2003

ANNEX X

SPECIAL NON-CONTRIBUTORY CASH BENEFITS

(Article 70(2)(*c*))

BELGIUM

(*a*) Income replacement allowance (Law of 27 February 1987);

(*b*) Guaranteed income for elderly persons (Law of 22 March 2001).

BULGARIA

Social Pension for old age (Article 89 of the Social Insurance Code).

CZECH REPUBLIC

Social allowance (State Social Support Act No 117/1995 Sb.).

DENMARK

Accommodation expenses for pensioners (Law on individual accommodation assistance, consolidated by Law No 204 of 29 March 1995).

GERMANY

(*a*) Basic subsistence income for the elderly and for persons with reduced earning capacity under Chapter 4 of Book XII of the Social Code;

(*b*) Benefits to cover subsistence costs under the basic provision for jobseekers unless, with respect to these benefits, the eligibility requirements for a temporary supplement following receipt of unemployment benefit (Article 24(1) of Book II of the Social Code) are fulfilled.

ESTONIA

(*a*) Disabled adult allowance (Social Benefits for Disabled Persons Act of 27 January 1999);

(*b*) State unemployment allowance (Labour Market Services and Support Act of 29 September 2005).

IRELAND

(*a*) Jobseekers' allowance (Social Welfare Consolidation Act 2005, Part 3, Chapter 2);

(*b*) State pension (non-contributory) (Social Welfare Consolidation Act 2005, Part 3, Chapter 4);

(*c*) Widow's (non-contributory) pension and widower's (non-contributory) pension (Social Welfare Consolidation Act 2005, Part 3, Chapter 6);

(*d*) Disability allowance (Social Welfare Consolidation Act 2005, Part 3, Chapter 10);

(*e*) Mobility allowance (Health Act 1970, Section 61);

(*f*) Blind pension (Social Welfare Consolidation Act 2005, Part 3, Chapter 5).

GREECE

Special benefits for the elderly (Law 1296/82).

SPAIN

(*a*) Minimum income guarantee (Law No 13/82 of 7 April 1982);

(*b*) Cash benefits to assist the elderly and invalids unable to work (Royal Decree No 2620/81 of 24 July 1981);

(*c*)

(*i*) Non-contributory invalidity and retirement pensions as provided for in Article 38(1) of the Consolidated Text of the General Law on Social Security, approved by Royal Legislative Decree No 1/1994 of 20 June 1994; and

(ii) the benefits which supplement the above pensions, as provided for in the legislation of the Comunidades Autonómas, where such supplements guarantee a minimum subsistence income having regard to the economic and social situation in the Comunidades Autonómas concerned;

(*d*) Allowances to promote mobility and to compensate for transport costs (Law No 13/1982 of 7 April 1982).

FRANCE

(*a*) Supplementary allowances of:

(*i*) the Special Invalidity Fund; and

(ii) the Old Age Solidarity Fund in respect of acquired rights (Law of 30 June 1956, codified in Book VIII of the Social Security Code);

(*b*) Disabled adults' allowance (Law of 30 June 1975, codified in Book VIII of the Social Security Code);

(*c*) Special allowance (Law of 10 July 1952, codified in Book VIII of the Social Security Code) in respect of acquired rights;

(*d*) Old-age solidarity allowance (ordinance of 24 June 2004, codified in Book VIII of the Social Security Code) as of 1 January 2006.

ITALY

(*a*) Social pensions for persons without means (Law No 153 of 30 April 1969);

(*b*) Pensions and allowances for the civilian disabled or invalids (Laws No 118 of 30 March 1971, No 18 of 11 February 1980 and No 508 of 23 November 1988);

(*c*) Pensions and allowances for the deaf and dumb (Laws No 381 of 26 May 1970 and No 508 of 23 November 1988);

(*d*) Pensions and allowances for the civilian blind (Laws No 382 of 27 May 1970 and No 508 of 23 November 1988);

(*e*) Benefits supplementing the minimum pensions (Laws No 218 of 4 April 1952, No 638 of 11 November 1983 and No 407 of 29 December 1990);

(*f*) Benefits supplementing disability allowances (Law No 222 of 12 June 1984);

(*g*) Social allowance (Law No 335 of 8 August 1995);

(*h*) Social increase (Article 1(1) and (12) of Law No 544 of 29 December 1988 and successive amendments).

CYPRUS

(*a*) Social Pension (Social Pension Law of 1995 (Law 25(I)/95), as amended);

(*b*) Severe motor disability allowance (Council of Ministers' Decisions Nos 38210 of 16 October 1992, 41370 of 1 August 1994, 46183 of 11 June 1997 and 53675 of 16 May 2001);

(*c*) Special grant to blind persons (Special Grants Law of 1996 (Law 77(I)/96), as amended).

LATVIA

(*a*) State Social Security Benefit (Law on State Social Benefits of 1 January 2003);

(*b*) Allowance for the compensation of transportation expenses for disabled persons with restricted mobility (Law on State Social Benefits of 1 January 2003).

LITHUANIA

(*a*) Social assistance pension (Law of 2005 on State Social Assistance Benefits, Article 5);

(*b*) Relief compensation (Law of 2005 on State Social Assistance Benefits, Article 15);

(*c*) Transport compensation for the disabled who have mobility problems (Law of 2000 on Transport Compensation, Article 7).

LUXEMBOURG

Income for the seriously disabled (Article 1(2), Law of 12 September 2003), with the exception of persons recognised as being disabled workers and employed on the mainstream labour market or in a sheltered environment.

HUNGARY

(*a*) Invalidity annuity (Decree No 83/1987 (XII 27) of the Council of Ministers on Invalidity Annuity);

(*b*) Non-contributory old age allowance (Act III of 1993 on Social Administration and Social Benefits);

(*c*) Transport allowance (Government Decree No 164/1995 (XII 27) on Transport Allowances for Persons with Severe Physical Handicap).

MALTA

(*a*) Supplementary allowance (Section 73 of the Social Security Act (Cap. 318) 1987);

(*b*) Age pension (Social Security Act (Cap. 318) 1987).

NETHERLANDS

(*a*) Work and Employment Support for Disabled Young Persons Act of 24 April 1997 (Wet Wajong).

(*b*) Supplementary Benefits Act of 6 November 1986 (TW).

AUSTRIA

Compensatory supplement (Federal Act of 9 September 1955 on General Social Insurance — ASVG, Federal Act of 11 October 1978 on Social insurance for persons engaged in trade and commerce — GSVG and Federal Act of 11 October 1978 on Social insurance for farmers — BSVG).

POLAND

Social pension (Act of 27 June 2003 on social pensions).

PORTUGAL

NIC

(*a*) Non-contributory State old-age and invalidity pension (Decree-Law No 464/80 of 13 October 1980);

(*b*) Non-contributory widowhood pension (Regulatory Decree No 52/81 of 11 November 1981);

(*c*) Solidarity supplement for the elderly (Decree – Law No 232/2005 of 29 December 2005, amended by Decree – Law No 236/2006 of 11 December 2006).

SLOVENIA

(*a*) State pension (Pension and Disability Insurance Act of 23 December 1999);

(*b*) Income support for pensioners (Pension and Disability Insurance Act of 23 December 1999);

(*c*) Maintenance allowance (Pension and Disability Insurance Act of 23 December 1999).

SLOVAKIA

(*a*) Adjustment awarded before 1 January 2004 to pensions constituting the sole source of income;

(*b*) Social pension which has been awarded before 1 January 2004.

FINLAND

(*a*) Housing allowance for pensioners (Act concerning the Housing Allowance for pensioners, 571/2007);

(*b*) Labour market support (Act on Unemployment Benefits 1290/2002);

(*c*) Special assistance for immigrants (Act on Special Assistance for Immigrants, 1192/2002).

SWEDEN

(*a*) Housing supplements for persons receiving a pension (Law 2001:761);

(*b*) Financial support for the elderly (Law 2001:853).

UNITED KINGDOM

(*a*) State Pension Credit (State Pension Credit Act 2002 and State Pension Credit Act (Northern Ireland) 2002);

(*b*) Income-based allowances for jobseekers (Jobseekers Act 1995 and Jobseekers (Northern Ireland) Order 1995);

(*c*) . . .

(*d*) Disability Living Allowance mobility component (Social Security Contributions and Benefits Act 1992 and Social Security Contributions and Benefits (Northern Ireland) Act 1992);

(*e*) Employment and Support Allowance Income-related (Welfare Reform Act 2007 and Welfare Reform Act (Northern Ireland) 2007).

ANNEX XI

SPECIAL PROVISIONS FOR THE APPLICATION OF THE LEGISLATION OF THE MEMBER STATES

(Articles 51(3), 56(1) and 83)

BULGARIA

Article 33(1) of the Bulgarian Health Insurance Act shall apply to all persons for whom Bulgaria is the competent Member State under Chapter 1 of Title III of this Regulation.

CZECH REPUBLIC

For the purposes of defining members of the family according to Article 1(i), 'spouse' also includes registered partners as defined in the Czech act no. 115/2006 Coll., on registered partnership.

DENMARK

1.

(*a*) For the purpose of calculating the pension under the 'lov om social pension' (Social Pension Act), periods of activity as an employed or self-employed person completed under Danish legislation by a frontier worker or a worker who has gone to Denmark to do work of a seasonal nature are regarded as periods of residence completed in Denmark by the surviving spouse in so far as, during those periods, the surviving spouse was linked to the abovementioned worker by marriage without separation from bed and board or de facto separation on grounds of incompatibility, and provided that, during those periods, the spouse resided in the territory of another Member State. For the purposes of this point, 'work of a seasonal nature' means work which, being dependent on the succession of the seasons, automatically recurs each year.

(*b*) For the purpose of calculating the pension under the 'lov om social pension' (Social Pension Act), periods of activity as an employed or self-employed person completed under Danish legislation before 1 January 1984 by a person to whom point 1(a) does not apply shall be regarded as periods of residence completed in Denmark by the surviving spouse, in so far as, during those periods, the surviving spouse was linked to the person by marriage without separation from bed and board or de facto separation on grounds of incompatibility, and provided that, during those periods, the spouse resided in the territory of another Member State.

(*c*) Periods to be taken into account under points (a) and (b) shall not be taken into consideration if they coincide with the periods taken into account for the calculation of the pension due to the person concerned under the legislation on compulsory insurance of another Member State or with the periods during which the person concerned received a pension under such legislation. These periods shall, however, be taken into consideration if the annual amount of the said pension is less than half the basic amount of the social pension.

2.

(*a*) Notwithstanding the provisions of Article 6 of this Regulation, persons who have not been gainfully employed in one or more Member States are entitled to a Danish social pension only if they have been, or have previously been, permanent residents of Denmark for at least 3 years, subject to the age limits prescribed by Danish legislation. Subject to Article 4 of this Regulation, Article 7 does not apply to a Danish social pension to which entitlement has been acquired by such persons.

(*b*) The abovementioned provisions do not apply to Danish social pension entitlement for the members of the family of persons who are or have been gainfully employed in Denmark, or for students or the members of their families.

3. The temporary benefit for unemployed persons who have been admitted to the ledighedsydelse (flexible job' scheme) (Law No 455 of 10 June 1997) is covered by Title III, Chapter 6 of this Regulation. As regards unemployed persons going to another Member State, Articles 64 and 65 will be applicable when this Member State has similar employment schemes for the same category of persons.

4. Where the beneficiary of a Danish social pension is also entitled to a survivor's pension from another Member State, these pensions for the implementation of Danish legislation shall be regarded as benefits of the same kind within the meaning of Article 53(1) of this Regulation, subject to the condition, however, that the person whose periods of insurance or of residence serve as the basis for the calculation of the survivor's pension had also acquired a right to a Danish social pension.

GERMANY

1. Notwithstanding Article 5(*a*) of this Regulation and Article 5(4) point 1 of the Sozialgesetzbuch VI (Volume VI of the Social Code), a person who receives a full old-age pension under the legislation of another Member State may request to be compulsorily insured under the German pension insurance scheme.

2. Notwithstanding Article 5(a) of this Regulation and Article 7 of the Sozialgesetzbuch VI (Volume VI of the Social Code), a person who is compulsorily insured in another Member State or receives an old-age pension under the legislation of another Member State may join the voluntary insurance scheme in Germany.

3. For the purpose of granting cash benefits under §47(1) of SGB V, §47(1) of SGB VII and §200(2) of the Reichsversicherungsordnung to insured persons who live in another Member State, German insurance schemes calculate net pay, which is used to assess benefits, as if the insured person lived in Germany, unless the insured person requests an assessment on the basis of the net pay which he actually receives.

4. Nationals of other Member States whose place of residence or usual abode is outside Germany and who fulfil the general conditions of the German pension insurance scheme may pay voluntary contributions only if they had been voluntarily or compulsorily insured in the German pension insurance scheme at some time previously; this also applies to stateless persons and refugees whose place of residence or usual abode is in another Member State.

5. The pauschale Anrechnungszeit (fixed credit period) pursuant to Article 253 of the Sozialgesetzbuch VI (Volume VI of the Social Code) shall be determined exclusively with reference to German periods.

6. In cases where the German pension legislation, in force on 31 December 1991, is applicable for the recalculation of a pension, only the German legislation applies for the purposes of crediting German Ersatzzeiten (substitute periods).

7. The German legislation on accidents at work and occupational diseases to be compensated for under the law governing foreign pensions and on benefits for insurance periods which can be credited under the law governing foreign pensions in the territories named in paragraph 1(2)(3) of the Act on affairs of displaced persons and refugees (Bundesvertriebenengesetz) continues to apply within the scope of application of this Regulation, notwithstanding the provisions of paragraph 2 of the Act on foreign pensions (Fremdrentengesetz).

8. For the calculation of the theoretical amount referred to in Article 52(1)(*b*)(i) of this Regulation, in pension schemes for liberal professions, the competent institution shall take as a basis, in respect of each of the years of insurance completed under the legislation of any other Member State, the average annual pension entitlement acquired during the period of membership of the competent institution through the payment of contributions.

ESTONIA

For the purpose of calculating parental benefits, periods of employment in Member States other than Estonia shall be considered to be based on the same average amount of Social Tax as paid during the periods of employment in Estonia with which they are aggregated. If during the reference year the person has been employed only in other Member States, the calculation of the benefit shall be considered to be based on the average Social Tax paid in Estonia between the reference year and the maternity leave.

IRELAND

1. Notwithstanding Articles 21(2) and 62 of this Regulation, for the purposes of calculating the prescribed reckonable weekly earnings of an insured person for the grant of sickness or unemployment benefit under Irish legislation, an amount equal to the average weekly wage of employed persons in the relevant prescribed year shall be credited to that insured person in respect of each week of activity as an employed person under the legislation of another Member State during that prescribed year.

2. Where Article 46 of this Regulation applies, if the person concerned suffers incapacity for work leading to invalidity while subject to the legislation of another Member State, Ireland shall, for the purposes of Section 118(1)(a) of the Social Welfare Consolidation Act 2005, take account of any periods during which, in respect of the invalidity that followed that incapacity for work, he/she would have been regarded as being incapable of work under Irish legislation.

GREECE

1. Law No 1469/84 concerning voluntary affiliation to the pension insurance scheme for Greek nationals and foreign nationals of Greek origin is applicable to nationals of other Member States, stateless persons and refugees, where the persons concerned, regardless of their place of residence or stay, have at some time in the past been compulsorily or voluntarily affiliated to the Greek pension insurance scheme.

2. Notwithstanding Article 5(*a*) of this Regulation and Article 34 of Law 1140/1981, a person who receives a pension in respect of accidents at work or occupational diseases under the legislation of another Member State may request to be compulsorily insured under the legislation applied by OGA, to the extent that he/she pursues an activity falling within the scope of that legislation.

SPAIN

1. For the purposes of implementing Article 52(1)(*b*)(i) of this Regulation, the years which the worker lacks to reach the pensionable or compulsory retirement age as stipulated under Article 31(4) of the consolidated version of the Ley de Clases Pasivas del Estado (Law on State Pensioners) shall be taken into account as actual years of service to the State only if at the time of the event in respect of which invalidity or death pensions are due, the beneficiary was covered by Spain's special scheme for civil servants or was performing an activity assimilated under the scheme, or if, at the time of the event in respect of which the pensions are due, the beneficiary was performing an activity that would have required the person concerned to be included under the State's special scheme for civil servants, the armed forces or the judiciary, had the activity been performed in Spain.

2.

(*a*) Under Article 56(1)(c) of this Regulation, the calculation of the theoretical Spanish benefit shall be carried out on the basis of the actual contributions of the person during the years immediately preceding payment of the last contribution to Spanish social security. Where, in the calculation of the basic amount for the pension, periods of insurance and/or residence under the legislation of other Member States have to be taken into account, the contribution basis in Spain which is closest in time to the reference periods shall be used for the aforementioned periods, taking into account the development of the retail price index.

(*b*) The amount of the pension obtained shall be increased by the amount of the increases and revaluations calculated for each subsequent year for pensions of the same nature.

3. Periods completed in other Member States which must be calculated in the special scheme for civil servants, the armed forces and the judicial administration, will be treated in the same way, for the purposes of Article 56 of this Regulation, as the periods closest in time covered as a civil servant in Spain.

4. The additional amounts based on age referred to in the Second Transitional Provision of the General Law on Social Security shall be applicable to all beneficiaries of the Regulation who have contributions to their name under the Spanish legislation prior to 1 January 1967; it shall not be possible, by application of Article 5 of this Regulation, to treat periods of insurance credited in another Member State prior to the aforementioned date as being the same as contributions paid in Spain, solely for the present purposes. The date corresponding to 1 January 1967 shall be 1 August 1970 for the Special Scheme for Seafarers and 1 April 1969 for the Special Social Security Scheme for Coal Mining.

FRANCE

1. . . .

2. For persons receiving benefits in kind in France pursuant to Articles 17, 24 or 26 of this Regulation who are resident in the French departments of Haut-Rhin, Bas-Rhin or Moselle, benefits in kind provided on behalf of the institution of another Member State which is responsible for bearing their cost include benefits provided by both the general sickness insurance scheme and the obligatory supplementary local sickness insurance scheme of Alsace- Moselle.

3. French legislation applicable to a person engaged, or formerly engaged, in an activity as an employed or self-employed person for the application of Chapter 5 of Title III of this Regulation includes both the basic old-age insurance scheme(s) and the supplementary retirement scheme(s) to which the person concerned was subject.

CYPRUS

For the purpose of applying the provisions of Articles 6, 51 and 61 of this Regulation, for any period commencing on or after 6 October 1980, a week of insurance under the legislation of the Republic of Cyprus is determined by dividing the total insurable earnings for the relevant period by the weekly amount of the basic insurable earnings applicable in the relevant contribution year, provided that the number of weeks so determined shall not exceed the number of calendar weeks in the relevant period.

MALTA

Special provisions for civil servants

(*a*) Solely for the purposes of the application of Articles 49 and 60 of this Regulation, persons employed under the Malta Armed Forces Act (Chapter 220 of the Laws of Malta), the Police Act (Chapter 164 of the Laws of Malta) and the Prisons Act (Chapter 260 of the Laws of Malta) shall be treated as civil servants.

(*b*) Pensions payable under the above Acts and under the Pensions Ordinance (Chapter 93 of the Laws of Malta) shall, solely for the purposes of Article 1(*e*) of the Regulation, be considered as 'special schemes for civil servants'.

NETHERLANDS

1. Health care insurance

(*a*) As regards entitlement to benefits in kind under Dutch legislation, persons entitled to benefits in kind for the purpose of the implementation of Chapters 1 and 2 of Title III of this Regulation shall mean:

(i) persons who, under Article 2 of the Zorgverzekeringswet (Health Care Insurance Act), are obliged to take out insurance under a health care insurer; and

(ii) in so far as they are not already included under point (i), members of the family of active military personnel who are living in another Member State and persons who are resident in another Member State and who, under this Regulation are entitled to health care in their state of residence, the costs being borne by the Netherlands.

(*b*) The persons referred to in point 1(*a*)(i) must, in accordance with the provisions of the Zorgverzekeringswet (Health Care Insurance Act) take out insurance with a health care insurer, and the persons referred to in point 1(*a*)(ii) must register with the College voor zorgverzekeringen (Health Care Insurance Board).

(*c*) The provisions of the Zorgverzekeringswet (Health Care Insurance Act) and the Algemene Wet Bijzondere Ziektekosten (General Act on Exceptional Medical Expenses) concerning liability for the payment of contributions shall apply to the persons referred to in point (a) and the members of their families. In respect of members of the family, the contributions shall be levied on the person from whom the right to health care is derived with the exception of the members of the family of military personnel living in another Member State, who shall be levied directly.

(*d*) The provisions of the Zorgverzekeringswet (Health Care Insurance Act) concerning late insurance shall apply *mutatis mutandis* in the event of late registration with the College voor zorgverzekeringen (Health Care Insurance Board) in respect of the persons referred to in point 1(a)(ii).

(*e*) Persons entitled to benefits in kind by virtue of the legislation of a Member State other than the Netherlands who reside in the Netherlands or stay temporarily in the Netherlands shall be entitled to benefits in kind in accordance with the policy offered to insured persons in the Netherlands by the institution of the place of residence or the place of stay, taking into account Article 11(1), (2) and (3) and Article 19(1) of the Zorgverzekeringswet (Health Care Insurance Act), as well as to benefits in kind provided for by the Algemene Wet Bijzondere Ziektekosten (General Act on Exceptional Medical Expenses).

(*f*) For the purposes of Articles 23 to 30 of this Regulation, the following benefits (in addition to pensions covered by Title III, Chapters 4 and 5 of this Regulation) shall be treated as pensions due under Dutch legislation:

— pensions awarded under the Law of 6 January 1966 on pensions for civil servants and their survivors (Algemene burgerlijke pensioenwet) (Netherlands Civil Service Pensions Act),

NIC

- — pensions awarded under the Law of 6 October 1966 on pensions for military personnel and their survivors (Algemene militaire pensioenwet) (Military Pensions Act),
- — benefits for incapacity for work awarded under the Law of 7 June 1972 on benefits for incapacity for work for military personnel (Wetarbeidsongeschiktheidsvoorziening militairen) (Military Personnel Incapacity for Work Act),
- — pensions awarded under the Law of 15 February 1967 on pensions for employees of the NV Nederlandse Spoorwegen (Dutch Railway Company) and their survivors (Spoorwegpensioenwet) (Railway Pensions Act),
- — pensions awarded under the Reglement Dienstvoorwaarden Nederlandse Spoorwegen (Regulation governing conditions of employment of the Netherlands Railway Company),
- — benefits awarded to retired persons before reaching the pensionable age of 65 years under a pension designed to provide income for former employed persons in their old age, or benefits provided in the event of premature exit from the labour market under a scheme set up by the state or by an industrial agreement for persons aged 55 or over,
- — benefits awarded to military personnel and civil servants under a scheme applicable in the event of redundancy, superannuation and early retirement.

[(*fa*) Any person as referred to in Article 69(1) of the Zorgverzekeringswet (Health Care Insurance Act) who, on the last day of the month preceding that in which he or she reaches the age of 65, is receiving a pension or benefit which, on the basis of paragraph 1(f) of this Section is treated as a pension payable under Dutch legislation, shall be regarded as a pension claimant as referred to in Article 22 of this Regulation until he or she reaches the pension age as referred to in Article 7a of the Algemene Ouderdomswet (General Old Age Pensions Act).][1]

(*g*) . . .

(*h*) For the purposes of Article 18(1) of this Regulation, the persons referred to in point 1(a)(ii) of this Annex who stay temporarily in the Netherlands shall be entitled to benefits in kind in accordance with the policy offered to insured persons in the Netherlands by the institution of the place of stay, taking into account Article 11(1), (2) and (3) and Article 19(1) of the Zorgverzekeringswet (Health Care Insurance Act), as well as to benefits in kind provided for by the Algemene Wet Bijzondere Ziektekosten (General Act on Exceptional Medical Expenses).

2. Application of the Algemene Ouderdomswet (AOW) (General Old Age Pensions Act)

(*a*) The reduction referred to in Article 13(1) of the Algemene Ouderdomswet (AOW) (General Old Age Pensions Act) shall not be applied for calendar years before 1 January 1957 during which a recipient not satisfying the conditions for having such years treated as periods of insurance:

- — resided in the Netherlands between the ages of 15 and 65, or
- — while residing in another Member State, worked in the Netherlands for an employer established in the Netherlands, or
- — worked in another Member State during periods regarded as periods of insurance under the Dutch social security system.

By way of derogation from Article 7 of the AOW, anyone who resided or worked in the Netherlands in accordance with the above conditions only prior to 1 January 1957 shall also be regarded as being entitled to a pension.

(*b*) The reduction referred to in Article 13(1) of the AOW shall not apply to calendar years prior to 2 August 1989 during which, between the ages of 15 and 65, a person who is or was married was not insured under the above legislation, while being resident in the territory of a Member State other than the Netherlands, if these calendar years coincide with periods of insurance completed by the person's spouse under the above legislation or with calendar years to be taken into account under point 2(*a*), provided that the couple's marriage subsisted during that time.

By way of derogation from Article 7 of the AOW, such a person shall be regarded as entitled to a pension.

(*c*) The reduction referred to in Article 13(2) of the AOW shall not apply to calendar years before 1 January 1957 during which a pensioner's spouse who fails to satisfy the conditions for having such years treated as periods of insurance:

- — resided in the Netherlands between the ages of 15 and 65, or
- — while residing in another Member State, worked in the Netherlands for an employer established in the Netherlands, or
- — worked in another Member State during periods regarded as periods of insurance under the Netherlands social security system.

(*d*) The reduction referred to in Article 13(2) of the AOW shall not apply to calendar years prior to 2 August 1989 during which, between the ages of 15 and 65, a pensioner's spouse resident in a Member State other than the Netherlands was not insured under the above legislation, if those calendar years coincide with periods of insurance completed by the pensioner under that legislation or with calendar years to be taken into account under point 2(*a*), provided that the couple's marriage subsisted during that time.

(*e*) Points 2(*a*), 2(*b*), 2(*c*) and 2(*d*) shall not apply to periods which coincide with:

— periods which may be taken into account for calculating pension rights under the old-age insurance legislation of a Member State other than the Netherlands, or

— periods for which the person concerned has drawn an old-age pension under such legislation.

Periods of voluntary insurance under the system of another Member State shall not be taken into account for the purposes of this provision.

(*f*) Points 2(*a*), 2(*b*), 2(*c*) and 2(*d*) shall apply only if the person concerned has resided in one or more Member States for 6 years after the age of 59 and only for such time as that person is resident in one of those Member States.

(*g*) By way of derogation from Chapter IV of the AOW, anyone resident in a Member State other than the Netherlands whose spouse is covered by compulsory insurance under that legislation shall be authorised to take out voluntary insurance under that legislation for periods during which the spouse is compulsorily insured.

This authorisation shall not cease where the spouse's compulsory insurance is terminated as a result of his death and where the survivor receives only a pension under the Algemene nabestaandenwet (General Surviving Relatives Act).

In any event, the authorisation in respect of voluntary insurance ceases on the date on which the person reaches the age of 65.

The contribution to be paid for voluntary insurance shall be set in accordance with the provisions relating to the determination of the contribution for voluntary insurance under the AOW. However, if the voluntary insurance follows on from a period of insurance as referred to in point 2(*b*), the contribution shall be set in accordance with the provisions relating to the determination of the contribution for compulsory insurance under the AOW, with the income to be taken into account being deemed to have been received in the Netherlands.

(*h*) The authorisation referred to in point 2(*g*) shall not be granted to anyone insured under another Member State's legislation on pensions or survivors' benefits.

(*i*) Anyone wishing to take out voluntary insurance under point 2(*g*) shall be required to apply for it to the Social Insurance Bank (Sociale Verzekeringsbank) not later than 1 year after the date on which the conditions for participation are fulfilled.

3. Application of the Algemene nabestaandenwet (ANW) (General Surviving Relatives Act)

(*a*) Where the surviving spouse is entitled to a survivor's pension under the Algemene Nabestaandenwet (ANW) (General Surviving Relatives Act) pursuant to Article 51(3) of this Regulation, that pension shall be calculated in accordance with Article 52(1)(*b*) of this Regulation. For the application of these provisions, periods of insurance prior to 1 October 1959 shall also be regarded as periods of insurance completed under Dutch legislation if during those periods the insured person, after the age of 15:

— resided in the Netherlands, or

— while resident in another Member State, worked in the Netherlands for an employer established in the Netherlands, or

— worked in another Member State during periods regarded as periods of insurance under the Dutch social security system.

(*b*) Account shall not be taken of the periods to be taken into consideration under point 3(a) which coincide with periods of compulsory insurance completed under the legislation of another Member State in respect of survivor's pensions.

(*c*) For the purposes of Article 52(1)(*b*) of this Regulation, only periods of insurance completed under Dutch legislation after the age of 15 shall be taken into account as periods of insurance.

(*d*) By way of derogation from Article 63a(1) of the ANW, a person resident in a Member State other than the Netherlands whose spouse is compulsorily insured under the ANW shall be authorised to take out voluntary insurance under the above legislation, provided that such insurance has already begun by the date of application of this Regulation, but only for periods during which the spouse is compulsorily insured.

This authorisation shall cease as from the date of termination of the spouse's compulsory insurance under the ANW, unless the spouse's compulsory insurance is terminated as a result of his death and where the survivor only receives a pension under the ANW.

In any event, the authorisation in respect of voluntary insurance ceases on the date on which the person reaches the age of 65.

NIC

The contribution to be paid for voluntary insurance shall be set in accordance with th provisions relating to the determination of contributions for voluntary insurance under the ANW However, if the voluntary insurance follows on from a period of insurance as referred to in poin 2(*b*), the contribution shall be set in accordance with the provisions relating to the determinatio of contributions for compulsory insurance under the ANW, with the income to be taken int account being deemed to have been received in the Netherlands.

4. Application of Dutch legislation relating to incapacity for work

(*a*) Where, pursuant to Article 51(3) of this Regulation, the person concerned is entitled to a Netherlands invalidity benefit, the amount referred to in Article 52(1)(*b*) of this Regulation for calculating that benefit shall be determined:

(*i*) where, prior to the occurrence of incapacity for work, the person last exercised an activity as an employed person within the meaning of Article 1(*a*) of this Regulation:

— in accordance with the provisions laid down in the Wet op arbeidsongeschiktheidsverzekering (WAO) (Disability Insurance Act) if the incapacity for work occurred before 1 January 2004, or

— in accordance with the provisions laid down in the Wet Werk en inkomen naar arbeidsvermogen (WIA) (Work and Income according to labour capacity Act) if the incapacity for work occurred on or after 1 January 2004;

(ii) where, prior to the occurrence of the incapacity for work, the person concerned last exercised an activity as a self-employed person within the meaning of Article 1 (b) of this Regulation, in accordance with the provisions laid down in the Wet arbeidsongeschiktheidsverzekering zelfstandigen (WAZ) (Self-employed Persons Disablement Benefits Act) if the incapacity for work occurred before 1 August 2004.

(*b*) In calculating benefits under either the WAO, WIA or the WAZ, the Netherlands institutions shall take account of:

— periods of paid employment, and periods treated as such, completed in the Netherlands before 1 July 1967,

— periods of insurance completed under the WAO,

— periods of insurance completed by the person concerned, after the age of 15, under the Algemene Arbeidsongeschiktheidswet (AAW) (General Act on Incapacity for Work), in so far as these do not coincide with the periods of insurance completed under the WAO,

— periods of insurance completed under the WAZ,

— periods of insurance completed under the WIA.

AUSTRIA

1. For the purpose of acquiring periods in the pension insurance, attendance at a school or comparable educational establishment in another Member State shall be regarded as equivalent to attendance at a school or educational establishment pursuant to Articles 227(1)(1) and 228(1)(3) of the Allgemeines Sozialversicherungsgesetz (ASVG) (General Social Security Act), Article 116(7) of the Gewerbliches Sozialversicherungsgesetz (GSVG) (Federal Act on Social Insurance for Persons engaged in Trade and Commerce) and Article 107(7) of the Bauern-Sozialversicherungsgesetz (BSVG) (Social Security Act for Farmers), when the person concerned was subject at some time to Austrian legislation on the grounds that he pursued an activity as an employed or self-employed person, and the special contributions provided for under Article 227(3) of the ASVG, Article 116(9) of the GSVG and Article 107(9) of the BSGV for the purchase of such periods of education, are paid.

2. For the calculation of the pro rata benefit referred to in Article 52(1)(b) of this Regulation, special increments for contributions for supplementary insurance and the miners' supplementary benefit under Austrian legislation shall be disregarded. In these cases the pro rata benefit calculated without those contributions shall, if appropriate, be increased by unreduced special increments for contributions for supplementary insurance and the miners' supplementary benefit.

3. Where pursuant to Article 6 of this Regulation substitute periods under an Austrian pension insurance scheme have been completed, but these cannot form a basis for calculation pursuant to Articles 238 and 239 of the Allgemeines Sozialversicherungsgesetz (ASVG) (General Social Security Act), Articles 122 and 123 of the Gewerbliches Sozialversicherungsgesetz (GSVG) (Federal Act on Social Insurance for Persons engaged in Trade and Commerce) and Articles 113 and 114 of the Bauern-Sozialversicherungsgesetz (BSVG) (Social Security Act for Farmers), the calculation basis for periods of childcare pursuant to Article 239 of the ASVG, Article 123 of the GSVG and Article 114 of the BSVG shall be used.

FINLAND

1. For the purposes of determining entitlement and of calculating the amount of the Finnish national pension under Articles 52 to 54 of this Regulation, pensions acquired under the legislation of another Member State are treated in the same way as pensions acquired under Finnish legislation.

2. When applying Article 52(1)(*b*)(i) of this Regulation for the purpose of calculating earnings for the credited period under Finnish legislation on earnings-related pensions, where an individual has pension insurance periods based on activity as an employed or self-employed person in another Member State for part of the reference period under Finnish legislation, the earnings for the credited period shall be equivalent to the sum of earnings obtained during the part of the reference period in Finland, divided by the number of months for which there were insurance periods in Finland during the reference period.

SWEDEN

1. When parental leave allowance is paid under Article 67 of this Regulation to a member of the family who is not employed, the parental leave allowance is paid at a level corresponding to the basic or lowest level.

2. For the purpose of calculating parental leave allowance in accordance with Chapter 4, paragraph 6 of the Lag (1962:381) om allmän försäkring (the National Insurance Act) for persons eligible for a work-based parental leave allowance, the following shall apply:

For a parent for whom sickness benefit generating income is calculated on the basis of income from gainful employment in Sweden, the requirement to have been insured for sickness benefit above the minimum level for at least 240 consecutive days preceding the child's birth shall be satisfied if, during the period mentioned, the parent had income from gainful employment in another Member State corresponding to insurance above the minimum level.

3. The provisions of this Regulation on the aggregation of insurance periods and periods of residence shall not apply to the transitional provisions in the Swedish legislation on entitlement to guarantee pension for persons born in or before 1937 who have been resident in Sweden for a specified period before applying for a pension (Act 2000:798).

4. For the purpose of calculating income for notional income-related sickness compensation and income-related activity compensation in accordance with Chapter 8 of the Lag (1962:381) om allmän försäkring (the National Insurance Act), the following shall apply:

(*a*) where the insured person, during the reference period, has also been subject to the legislation of one or more other Member States on account of activity as an employed or self-employed person, income in the Member State(s) concerned shall be deemed to be equivalent to the insured person's average gross income in Sweden during the part of the reference period in Sweden, calculated by dividing the earnings in Sweden by the number of years over which those earnings accrued;

(*b*) where the benefits are calculated pursuant to Article 46 of this Regulation and persons are not insured in Sweden, the reference period shall be determined in accordance with Chapter 8, paragraphs 2 and 8 of the abovementioned Act as if the person concerned were insured in Sweden. If the person concerned has no pension-generating income during this period under the Act on income-based old-age pension (1998:674), the reference period shall be permitted to run from the earlier point in time when the insured person had income from gainful activity in Sweden.

5.

(*a*) For the purpose of calculating notional pension assets for income-based survivor's pension (Act 2000:461), if the requirement in Swedish legislation for pension entitlement in respect of at least three out of the 5 calendar years immediately preceding the insured person's death (reference period) is not met, account shall also be taken of insurance periods completed in other Member States as if they had been completed in Sweden. Insurance periods in other Member States shall be regarded as based on the average Swedish pension base. If the person concerned has only 1 year in Sweden with a pension base, each insurance period in another Member State shall be regarded as constituting the same amount.

(*b*) For the purpose of calculating notional pension credits for widows' pensions relating to deaths on or after 1 January 2003, if the requirement in Swedish legislation for pension credits in respect of at least two out of the 4 years immediately preceding the insured person's death (reference period) is not met and insurance periods were completed in another Member State during the reference period, those years shall be regarded as being based on the same pension credits as the Swedish year.

UNITED KINGDOM

1. Where, in accordance with United Kingdom legislation, a person may be entitled to a retirement pension if:

(*a*) the contributions of a former spouse are taken into account as if they were that person's own contributions; or

(*b*) the relevant contribution conditions are satisfied by that person's spouse or former spouse, then provided, in each case, that the spouse or former spouse is or had been exercising an activity as an employed or self-employed person, and had been subject to the legislation of two or more Member States, the provisions of Chapter 5 of Title III of this Regulation shall apply in order to determine entitlement under United Kingdom legislation. In this case, references in the said Chapter 5 to 'periods of insurance' shall be construed as references to periods of insurance completed by:

(i) a spouse or former spouse where a claim is made by:
- a married woman, or
- a person whose marriage has terminated otherwise than by the death of the spouse; or

(ii) a former spouse, where a claim is made by:
- a widower who immediately before pensionable age is not entitled to widowed parent's allowance, or
- a widow who immediately before pensionable age is not entitled to widowed mother's allowance, widowed parent's allowance or widow's pension, or who is only entitled to an age-related widow's pension calculated pursuant to Article 52(1)(*b*) of this Regulation, and for this purpose 'age-related widow's pension' means a widow's pension payable at a reduced rate in accordance with section 39(4) of the Social Security Contributions and Benefits Act 1992.

2. For the purposes of applying Article 6 of this Regulation to the provisions governing entitlement to attendance allowance, carer's allowance and disability living allowance, a period of employment, self-employment or residence completed in the territory of a Member State other than the United Kingdom shall be taken into account in so far as is necessary to satisfy conditions as to required periods of presence in the United Kingdom, prior to the day on which entitlement to the benefit in question first arises.

3. For the purposes of Article 7 of this Regulation, in the case of invalidity, old age or survivors' cash benefits, pensions for accidents at work or occupational diseases and death grants, any beneficiary under United Kingdom legislation who is staying in the territory of another Member State shall, during that stay, be considered as if he resided in the territory of that other Member State.

4. Where Article 46 of this Regulation applies, if the person concerned suffers incapacity for work leading to invalidity while subject to the legislation of another Member State, the United Kingdom shall, for the purposes of Section 30A (5) of the Social Security Contributions and Benefits Act 1992, take account of any periods during which the person concerned has received, in respect of that incapacity for work:

(i) cash sickness benefits or wages or salary in lieu thereof; or

(ii) benefits within the meaning of Chapters 4 and 5 of Title III of this Regulation granted in respect of the invalidity which followed that incapacity for work, under the legislation of the other Member State, as though they were periods of short-term incapacity benefit paid in accordance with Sections 30A (1)-(4) of the Social Security Contributions and Benefits Act 1992.

In applying this provision, account shall only be taken of periods during which the person would have been incapable of work within the meaning of United Kingdom legislation.

5.

(1) For the purpose of calculating an earnings factor in order to determine entitlement to benefits under United Kingdom legislation, for each week of activity as an employed person under the legislation of another Member State, and which commenced during the relevant income tax year within the meaning of United Kingdom legislation, the person concerned shall be deemed to have paid contributions as an employed earner, or have earnings on which contributions have been paid, on the basis of earnings equivalent to two-thirds of that year's upper earnings limit.

(2) For the purposes of Article 52(1)(*b*)(ii) of this Regulation, where:

(*a*) in any income tax year starting on or after 6 April 1975, a person carrying out activity as an employed person has completed periods of insurance, employment or residence exclusively in a Member State other than the United Kingdom, and the application of point 5(1) above results in that year being counted as a qualifying year within the meaning of United Kingdom legislation for the purposes of Article 52(1)(*b*)(i) of this Regulation, he shall be deemed to have been insured for 52 weeks in that year in that other Member State;

(*b*) any income tax year starting on or after 6 April 1975 does not count as a qualifying year within the meaning of United Kingdom legislation for the purposes of Article 52(1)(b)(i) of this Regulation, any periods of insurance, employment or residence completed in that year shall be disregarded.

(3) For the purpose of converting an earnings factor into periods of insurance, the earnings factor achieved in the relevant income tax year within the meaning of United Kingdom legislation shall be divided by that year's lower earnings limit. The result shall be expressed as a whole

number, any remaining fraction being ignored. The figure so calculated shall be treated as representing the number of weeks of insurance completed under United Kingdom legislation during that year, provided that such figure shall not exceed the number of weeks during which in that year the person was subject to that legislation.

Amendments—[1] In entry for Netherlands, point *(fa)* inserted by Commission Regulation 1372/2013/EU art 1(2) with effect from 1 January 2014 (OJ L 346, 20.12.2013, p 27). Note that art 1(2) of Regulation 1372/2013/EU is repealed by Commission Regulation 1368/2014/EU art 2 with effect from 1 January 2015 (OJ L 366, 20.12.2014, p 15).

REGULATION (EC) NO 987/2009 OF THE EUROPEAN PARLIAMENT AND OF THE COUNCIL OF 16 SEPTEMBER 2009 LAYING DOWN THE PROCEDURE FOR IMPLEMENTING REGULATION (EC) NO 883/2004 ON THE COORDINATION OF SOCIAL SECURITY SYSTEMS

(987/2009/EC)

Note—The text of this Regulation includes amendments made by the following—

- Commission Regulation 1244/2010/EU with effect from 11 January 2011;
- Commission Regulation 465/2012/EU with effect from 28 June 2012;
- Commission Regulation 1224/2012/EU with effect from 8 January 2013; and
- Commission Regulation (EU) 2017/492 with effect from 11 April 2017.

This Regulation shall apply to nationals of third countries who are not already covered by these Regulations solely on the ground of their nationality, as well as to members of their families and to their survivors, provided that they are legally resident in the territory of a Member State and are in a situation which is not confined in all respects within a single Member State (Regulation 1231/2010/EU Art 1, OJ L 344, 29.12.2010, p 1).

(Text with relevance for the EEA and for Switzerland)

THE EUROPEAN PARLIAMENT AND THE COUNCIL OF THE EUROPEAN UNION,

Having regard to the Treaty establishing the European Community, and in particular Articles 42 and 308 thereof,

Having regard to Regulation (EC) No 883/2004 of the European Parliament and of the Council of 29 April 2004 on the coordination of social security systems [1], and in particular Article 89 thereof,

Having regard to the proposal from the Commission,

Having regard to the Opinion of the European Economic and Social Committee [2],

Acting in accordance with the procedure laid down in Article 251 of the Treaty [3],

Whereas:

(1) Regulation (EC) No 883/2004 modernises the rules on the coordination of Member States' social security systems, specifying the measures and procedures for implementing them and simplifying them for all the players involved. Implementing rules should be laid down.

(2) Closer and more effective cooperation between social security institutions is a key factor in allowing the persons covered by Regulation (EC) No 883/2004 to access their rights as quickly as possible and under optimum conditions.

(3) Electronic communication is a suitable means of rapid and reliable data exchange between Member States' institutions. Processing data electronically should help speed up the procedures for everyone involved. The persons concerned should also benefit from all the guarantees provided for in the Community provisions on the protection of natural persons with regard to the processing and free movement of personal data.

(4) Availability of the details (including electronic details) of those national bodies likely to be involved in implementing Regulation (EC) No 883/2004, in a form which allows them to be updated in real time, should facilitate exchanges between Member States' institutions. This approach, which focuses on the relevance of purely factual information and its immediate accessibility to citizens, is a valuable simplification which should be introduced by this Regulation.

(5) Achieving the smoothest possible operation and the efficient management of the complex procedures implementing the rules on the coordination of social security systems requires a system for the immediate updating of Annex 4. The preparation and application of provisions to that effect calls for close cooperation between the Member States and the Commission, and their implementation should be carried out rapidly, in view of the consequences of delays for citizens and administrative authorities alike. The Commission should therefore be empowered to establish and manage a database and ensure that it is operational at least from the date of entry into force of this Regulation. The Commission should, in particular, take the necessary steps to integrate into that database the information listed in Annex 4.

(6) Strengthening certain procedures should ensure greater legal certainty and transparenc for the users of Regulation (EC) No 883/2004. For example, setting common deadlines fo fulfilling certain obligations or completing certain administrative tasks should assist i clarifying and structuring relations between insured persons and institutions.

(7) The persons covered by this Regulation should receive from the competent institution timely response to their requests. The response should be provided at the latest within th time-limits prescribed by the social security legislation of the Member State in question, wher such time-limits exist. It would be desirable for Member States whose social security legislatio does not make provision for such time-limits to consider adopting them and making then available to the persons concerned as necessary.

(8) The Member States, their competent authorities and the social security institutions shoul have the option of agreeing among themselves on simplified procedures and administrativ arrangements which they consider to be more effective and better suited to the circumstance of their respective social security systems. However, such arrangements should not affect th rights of the persons covered by Regulation (EC) No 883/2004.

(9) The inherent complexity of the field of social security requires all institutions of the Member States to make a particular effort to support insured persons in order to avoic penalising those who have not submitted their claim or certain information to the institution responsible for processing this application in accordance with the rules and procedures set ou in Regulation (EC) No 883/2004 and in this Regulation.

(10) To determine the competent institution, namely the one whose legislation applies or which is liable for the payment of certain benefits, the circumstances of the insured person and those of the family members must be examined by the institutions of more than one Member State. To ensure that the person concerned is protected for the duration of the necessary communication between institutions, provision should be made for provisional membership of a social security system.

(11) Member States should cooperate in determining the place of residence of persons to whom this Regulation and Regulation (EC) No 883/2004 apply and, in the event of a dispute, should take into consideration all relevant criteria to resolve the matter. These may include criteria referred to in the appropriate Article of this Regulation.

(12) Many measures and procedures provided for in this Regulation are intended to ensure greater transparency concerning the criteria which the institutions of the Member States must apply under Regulation (EC) No 883/2004. Such measures and procedures are the result of the case-law of the Court of Justice of the European Communities, the decisions of the Administrative Commission and the experience of more than 30 years of application of the coordination of social security systems in the context of the fundamental freedoms enshrined in the Treaty.

(13) This Regulation provides for measures and procedures to promote the mobility of employees and unemployed persons. Frontier workers who have become wholly unemployed may make themselves available to the employment services in both their country of residence and the Member State where they were last employed. However, they should be entitled to benefits only from their Member State of residence.

(14) Certain specific rules and procedures are required in order to define the legislation applicable for taking account of periods during which an insured person has devoted time to bringing up children in the various Member States.

(15) Certain procedures should also reflect the need for a balanced sharing of costs between Member States. In particular in the area of sickness, such procedures should take account of the position of Member States which bear the costs of allowing insured persons access to their healthcare system and the position of Member States whose institutions bear the cost of benefits in kind received by their insured persons in a Member State other than that in which they are resident.

(16) In the specific context of Regulation (EC) No 883/2004, it is necessary to clarify the conditions for meeting the costs of sickness benefits in kind as part of scheduled treatments, namely treatments for which an insured person goes to a Member State other than that in which he is insured or resident. The obligations of the insured person with regard to the application for prior authorisation should be specified, as should the institution's obligations towards the patient with regard to the conditions of authorisation. The consequences for the chargeability of the costs of care received in another Member State on the basis of an authorisation should also be clarified.

(17) This Regulation, and especially the provisions concerning the stay outside the competent Member State and concerning scheduled treatment, should not prevent the application of more favourable national provisions, in particular with regard to the reimbursement of costs incurred in another Member State.

(18) More binding procedures to reduce the time needed for payment of these claims between Member States' institutions are essential in order to maintain confidence in the

exchanges and meet the need for sound management of Member States' social security systems. Procedures for the processing of claims relating to sickness and unemployment benefits should therefore be strengthened.

(19) Procedures between institutions for mutual assistance in recovery of social security claims should be strengthened in order to ensure more effective recovery and smooth functioning of the coordination rules. Effective recovery is also a means of preventing and tackling abuses and fraud and a way of ensuring the sustainability of social security schemes. This involves the adoption of new procedures, taking as a basis a number of existing provisions in Council Directive 2008/55/EC of 26 May 2008 on mutual assistance for the recovery of claims relating to certain levies, duties, taxes and other measures [4]. Such new recovery procedures should be reviewed in the light of the experience after five years of implementation and adjusted if necessary, in particular to ensure they are fully operable.

(20) For the purposes of provisions on mutual assistance regarding the recovery of benefits provided but not due, the recovery of provisional payments and contributions and the offsetting and assistance with recovery, the jurisdiction of the requested Member State is limited to actions regarding enforcement measures. Any other action falls under the jurisdiction of the applicant Member State.

(21) The enforcement measures taken in the requested Member State do not imply the recognition by that Member State of the substance or basis of the claim.

(22) Informing the persons concerned of their rights and obligations is a crucial component of a relationship of trust with the competent authorities and the Member States' institutions. Information should include guidance on administrative procedures. The persons concerned may include, depending on the situation, the insured persons, their family members and/or their survivors or other persons.

(23) Since the objective of this Regulation, namely the adoption of coordination measures in order to guarantee the effective exercise of the free movement of persons, cannot be sufficiently achieved by the Member States and can therefore, by reason of its scale and effects, be better achieved at Community level, the Community may adopt measures, in accordance with the principle of subsidiarity as set out in Article 5 of the Treaty. In accordance with the principle of proportionality, as set out in that Article, this Regulation does not go beyond what is necessary to achieve that objective.

(24) This Regulation should replace Council Regulation (EEC) No 574/72 of 21 March 1972 fixing the procedure for implementing Regulation (EEC) No 1408/71 on the application of social security schemes to employed persons and their families moving within the Community.[5]

1 OJ L 166, 30.4.2004, p. 1.
2 OJ C 324, 30.12.2006, p. 59.
3 Opinion of the European Parliament of 9 July 2008 (not yet published in the Official Journal), Council Common Position of 17 December 2008 (OJ C 38 E, 17.2.2009, p. 26) and Position of the European Parliament of 22 April 2009. Council Decision of 27 July 2009.
4 OJ L 150, 10.6.2008, p. 28.
5 OJ L 74, 27.3.1972, p. 1.

HAVE ADOPTED THIS REGULATION:

TITLE I
GENERAL PROVISIONS

CHAPTER I

DEFINITIONS

Article 1 Definitions

1. For the purposes of this Regulation:
   (*a*) "basic Regulation" means Regulation (EC) No 883/2004;
   (*b*) "implementing Regulation" means this Regulation; and
   (*c*) the definitions set out in the basic Regulation shall apply.
2. In addition to the definitions referred to in paragraph 1,
   (*a*) "access point" means an entity providing:
      (i) an electronic contact point;
      (ii) automatic routing based on the address; and
      (iii) intelligent routing based on software that enables automatic checking and routing (for example, an artificial intelligence application) and/or human intervention;
   (*b*) "liaison body" means any body designated by the competent authority of a Member State for one or more of the branches of social security referred to in Article 3 of the basic Regulation to respond to requests for information and assistance for the purposes of the application of the basic Regulation and the implementing Regulation and which has to fulfil the tasks assigned to it under Title IV of the implementing Regulation;

(*c*) "document" means a set of data, irrespective of the medium used, structured in such a way that it can be exchanged electronically and which must be communicated in order to enable the operation of the basic Regulation and the implementing Regulation;

(*d*) "Structured Electronic Document" means any structured document in a format designed for the electronic exchange of information between Member States;

(*e*) "transmission by electronic means" means the transmission of data using electronic equipment for the processing (including digital compression) of data and employing wires, radio transmission, optical technologies or any other electromagnetic means;

(*f*) "Audit Board" means the body referred to in Article 74 of the basic Regulation.

CHAPTER II

PROVISIONS CONCERNING COOPERATION AND EXCHANGES OF DATA

Article 2 Scope and rules for exchanges between institutions

1. For the purposes of the implementing Regulation, exchanges between Member States' authorities and institutions and persons covered by the basic Regulation shall be based on the principles of public service, efficiency, active assistance, rapid delivery and accessibility, including e-accessibility, in particular for the disabled and the elderly.

2. The institutions shall without delay provide or exchange all data necessary for establishing and determining the rights and obligations of persons to whom the basic Regulation applies. Such data shall be transferred between Member States directly by the institutions themselves or indirectly via the liaison bodies.

3. Where a person has mistakenly submitted information, documents or claims to an institution in the territory of a Member State other than that in which the institution designated in accordance with the implementing Regulation is situated, the information, documents or claims shall be re-submitted without delay by the former institution to the institution designated in accordance with the implementing Regulation, indicating the date on which they were initially submitted. That date shall be binding on the latter institution. Member State institutions shall not, however, be held liable, or be deemed to have taken a decision by virtue of their failure to act as a result of the late transmission of information, documents or claims by other Member States' institutions.

4. Where data are transferred indirectly via the liaison body of the Member State of destination, time limits for responding to claims shall start from the date when that liaison body received the claim, as if it had been received by the institution in that Member State.

Article 3 Scope and rules for exchanges between the persons concerned and institutions

1. Member States shall ensure that the necessary information is made available to the persons concerned in order to inform them of the changes introduced by the basic Regulation and by the implementing Regulation to enable them to assert their rights. They shall also provide for user friendly services.

2. Persons to whom the basic Regulation applies shall be required to forward to the relevant institution the information, documents or supporting evidence necessary to establish their situation or that of their families, to establish or maintain their rights and obligations and to determine the applicable legislation and their obligations under it.

3. When collecting, transmitting or processing personal data pursuant to their legislation for the purposes of implementing the basic Regulation, Member States shall ensure that the persons concerned are able to exercise fully their rights regarding personal data protection, in accordance with Community provisions on the protection of individuals with regard to the processing of personal data and the free movement of such data.

4. To the extent necessary for the application of the basic Regulation and the implementing Regulation, the relevant institutions shall forward the information and issue the documents to the persons concerned without delay and in all cases within any time limits specified under the legislation of the Member State in question.

The relevant institution shall notify the claimant residing or staying in another Member State of its decision directly or through the liaison body of the Member State of residence or stay. When refusing the benefits it shall also indicate the reasons for refusal, the remedies and periods allowed for appeals. A copy of this decision shall be sent to other involved institutions.

Article 4 Format and method of exchanging data

1. The Administrative Commission shall lay down the structure, content, format and detailed arrangements for exchange of documents and structured electronic documents.

2. The transmission of data between the institutions or the liaison bodies shall be carried out by electronic means either directly or indirectly through the access points under a common secure framework that can guarantee the confidentiality and protection of exchanges of data.

3. In their communications with the persons concerned, the relevant institutions shall use the arrangements appropriate to each case, and favour the use of electronic means as far as possible. The Administrative Commission shall lay down the practical arrangements for sending information, documents or decisions by electronic means to the person concerned.

Article 5 Legal value of documents and supporting evidence issued in another Member State

1. Documents issued by the institution of a Member State and showing the position of a person for the purposes of the application of the basic Regulation and of the implementing Regulation, and supporting evidence on the basis of which the documents have been issued, shall be accepted by the institutions of the other Member States for as long as they have not been withdrawn or declared to be invalid by the Member State in which they were issued.

2. Where there is doubt about the validity of a document or the accuracy of the facts on which the particulars contained therein are based, the institution of the Member State that receives the document shall ask the issuing institution for the necessary clarification and, where appropriate, the withdrawal of that document. The issuing institution shall reconsider the grounds for issuing the document and, if necessary, withdraw it.

3. Pursuant to paragraph 2, where there is doubt about the information provided by the persons concerned, the validity of a document or supporting evidence or the accuracy of the facts on which the particulars contained therein are based, the institution of the place of stay or residence shall, insofar as this is possible, at the request of the competent institution, proceed to the necessary verification of this information or document.

4. Where no agreement is reached between the institutions concerned, the matter may be brought before the Administrative Commission by the competent authorities no earlier than one month following the date on which the institution that received the document submitted its request. The Administrative Commission shall endeavour to reconcile the points of view within six months of the date on which the matter was brought before it.

Article 6 Provisional application of legislation and provisional granting of benefits

1. Unless otherwise provided for in the implementing Regulation, where there is a difference of views between the institutions or authorities of two or more Member States concerning the determination of the applicable legislation, the person concerned shall be made provisionally subject to the legislation of one of those Member States, the order of priority being determined as follows:

(*a*) the legislation of the Member State where the person actually pursues his employment or self-employment, if the employment or self-employment is pursued in only one Member State;

(*b*) the legislation of the Member State of residence if the person concerned pursues employment or self- employment in two or more Member States and performs part of his/her activity or activities in the Member State of residence, or if the person concerned is neither employed nor self-employed;

(*c*) in all other cases, the legislation of the Member State, the application of which was first requested if the person pursues an activity, or activities, in two or more Member States.

2. Where there is a difference of views between the institutions or authorities of two or more Member States about which institution should provide the benefits in cash or in kind, the person concerned who could claim benefits if there was no dispute shall be entitled, on a provisional basis, to the benefits provided for by the legislation applied by the institution of his place of residence or, if that person does not reside on the territory of one of the Member States concerned, to the benefits provided for by the legislation applied by the institution to which the request was first submitted.

3. Where no agreement is reached between the institutions or authorities concerned, the matter may be brought before the Administrative Commission by the competent authorities no earlier than one month after the date on which the difference of views, as referred to in paragraph 1 or 2 arose. The Administrative Commission shall seek to reconcile the points of view within six months of the date on which the matter was brought before it.

4. Where it is established either that the applicable legislation is not that of the Member State of provisional membership, or the institution which granted the benefits on a provisional basis was not the competent institution, the institution identified as being competent shall be deemed retroactively to have been so, as if that difference of views had not existed, at the latest from either the date of provisional membership or of the first provisional granting of the benefits concerned.

5. If necessary, the institution identified as being competent and the institution which provisionally paid the cash benefits or provisionally received contributions shall settle the financial situation of the person concerned as regards contributions and cash benefits paid provisionally, where appropriate, in accordance with Title IV, Chapter III, of the implementing Regulation.

Benefits in kind granted provisionally by an institution in accordance with paragraph 2 shall be reimbursed by the competent institution in accordance with Title IV of the implementing Regulation.

NIC

Article 7 Provisional calculation of benefits and contributions

1. Unless otherwise provided for in the implementing Regulation, where a person is eligible for a benefit, or is liable to pay a contribution in accordance with the basic Regulation, and the competent institution does not have all the information concerning the situation in another Member State which is necessary to calculate definitively the amount of that benefit or contribution, that institution shall, on request of the person concerned, award this benefit or calculate this contribution on a provisional basis, if such a calculation is possible on the basis of the information at the disposal of that institution.

2. The benefit or the contribution concerned shall be recalculated once all the necessary supporting evidence or documents are provided to the institution concerned.

CHAPTER III

OTHER GENERAL PROVISIONS FOR THE APPLICATION OF THE BASIC REGULATION

Article 8 Administrative arrangements between two or more Member States

1. The provisions of the implementing Regulation shall replace those laid down in the arrangements for the application of the conventions referred to in Article 8(1) of the basic Regulation, except the provisions concerning the arrangements concerning the conventions referred to in Annex II to the basic Regulation, provided that the provisions of those arrangements are included in Annex 1 to the implementing Regulation.

2. Member States may conclude between themselves, if necessary, arrangements pertaining to the application of the conventions referred to in Article 8(2) of the basic Regulation provided that these arrangements do not adversely affect the rights and obligations of the persons concerned and are included in Annex 1 to the implementing Regulation.

Article 9 Other procedures between authorities and institutions

1. Two or more Member States, or their competent authorities, may agree procedures other than those provided for by the implementing Regulation, provided that such procedures do not adversely affect the rights or obligations of the persons concerned.

2. Any agreements concluded to this end shall be notified to the Administrative Commission and listed in Annex 1 to the implementing Regulation.

3. Provisions contained in implementing agreements concluded between two or more Member States with the same purpose as, or which are similar to, those referred to in paragraph 2, which are in force on the day preceding the entry into force of the implementing Regulation and are included in Annex 5 to Regulation (EEC) No 574/72, shall continue to apply, for the purposes of relations between those Member States, provided they are also included in Annex 1 to the implementing Regulation.

Article 10 Prevention of overlapping of benefits

Notwithstanding other provisions in the basic Regulation, when benefits due under the legislation of two or more Member States are mutually reduced, suspended or withdrawn, any amounts that would not be paid in the event of strict application of the rules concerning reduction, suspension or withdrawal laid down by the legislation of the Member States concerned shall be divided by the number of benefits subjected to reduction, suspension or withdrawal.

Article 11 Elements for determining residence

1. Where there is a difference of views between the institutions of two or more Member States about the determination of the residence of a person to whom the basic Regulation applies, these institutions shall establish by common agreement the centre of interests of the person concerned, based on an overall assessment of all available information relating to relevant facts, which may include, as appropriate:

(*a*) the duration and continuity of presence on the territory of the Member States concerned;

(*b*) the person's situation, including:

- (i) the nature and the specific characteristics of any activity pursued, in particular the place where such activity is habitually pursued, the stability of the activity, and the duration of any work contract;
- (ii) his family status and family ties;
- (iii) the exercise of any non-remunerated activity;
- (iv) in the case of students, the source of their income;
- (*v*) his housing situation, in particular how permanent it is;
- (vi) the Member State in which the person is deemed to reside for taxation purposes.

2. Where the consideration of the various criteria based on relevant facts as set out in paragraph 1 does not lead to agreement between the institutions concerned, the person's intention, as it appears from such facts and circumstances, especially the reasons that led the person to move, shall be considered to be decisive for establishing that person's actual place of residence.

Article 12 Aggregation of periods

1. For the purposes of applying Article 6 of the basic Regulation, the competent institution shall contact the institutions of the Member States to whose legislation the person concerned has also been subject in order to determine all the periods completed under their legislation.

2. The respective periods of insurance, employment, self-employment or residence completed under the legislation of a Member State shall be added to those completed under the legislation of any other Member State, insofar as necessary for the purposes of applying Article 6 of the basic Regulation, provided that these periods do not overlap.

3. Where a period of insurance or residence which is completed in accordance with compulsory insurance under the legislation of a Member State coincides with a period of insurance completed on the basis of voluntary insurance or continued optional insurance under the legislation of another Member State, only the period completed on the basis of compulsory insurance shall be taken into account.

4. Where a period of insurance or residence other than an equivalent period completed under the legislation of a Member State coincides with an equivalent period on the basis of the legislation of another Member State, only the period other than an equivalent period shall be taken into account.

5. Any period regarded as equivalent under the legislation of two or more Member States shall be taken into account only by the institution of the Member State to whose legislation the person concerned was last compulsorily subject before that period. In the event that the person concerned was not compulsorily subject to the legislation of a Member State before that period, the latter shall be taken into account by the institution of the Member State to whose legislation the person concerned was compulsorily subject for the first time after that period.

6. In the event that the time in which certain periods of insurance or residence were completed under the legislation of a Member State cannot be determined precisely, it shall be presumed that these periods do not overlap with periods of insurance or residence completed under the legislation of another Member State, and account shall be taken thereof, where advantageous to the person concerned, insofar as they can reasonably be taken into consideration.

Article 13 Rules for conversion of periods

1. Where periods completed under the legislation of a Member State are expressed in units different from those provided for by the legislation of another Member State, the conversion needed for the purpose of aggregation under Article 6 of the basic Regulation shall be carried out under the following rules:

(*a*) the period to be used as the basis for the conversion shall be that communicated by the institution of the Member State under whose legislation the period was completed;

(*b*) in the case of schemes where the periods are expressed in days the conversion from days to other units, and vice versa, as well as between different schemes based on days shall be calculated according to the following table:

Scheme based on	1 day corresponds to	1 week corresponds to	1 month corresponds to	1 quarter corresponds to	Maximum of days in one calendar year
5 days	9 hours	5 days	22 days	66 days	264 days
6 days	8 hours	6 days	26 days	78 days	312 days
7 days	6 hours	7 days	30 days	90 days	360 days

(*c*) in the case of schemes where the periods are expressed in units other than days,

(i) three months or 13 weeks shall be equivalent to one quarter, and vice versa;

(ii) one year shall be equivalent to four quarters, 12 months or 52 weeks, and vice versa;

(iii) for the conversion of weeks into months, and vice versa, weeks and months shall be converted into days in accordance with the conversion rules for the schemes based on six days in the table in point (*b*);

(*d*) in the case of periods expressed in fractions, those figures shall be converted into the next smaller integer unit applying the rules laid down in points (*b*) and (*c*). Fractions of years shall be converted into months unless the scheme involved is based on quarters;

(*e*) if the conversion under this paragraph results in a fraction of a unit, the next higher integer unit shall be taken as the result of the conversion under this paragraph.

2. The application of paragraph 1 shall not have the effect of producing, for the total sum of the periods completed during one calendar year, a total exceeding the number of days indicated in the last column in the table in paragraph 1(*b*), 52 weeks, 12 months or four quarters.

If the periods to be converted correspond to the maximum annual amount of periods under the legislation of the Member State in which they have been completed, the application of paragraph 1 shall not result within one calendar year in periods that are shorter than the possible maximum annual amount of periods provided under the legislation concerned.

3. The conversion shall be carried out either in one single operation covering all those periods which were communicated as an aggregate, or for each year, if the periods were communicated on a year-by-year basis.
4. Where an institution communicates periods expressed in days, it shall at the same time indicate whether the scheme it administers is based on five days, six days or seven days.

TITLE II
DETERMINATION OF THE LEGISLATION APPLICABLE

Article 14 Details relating to Articles 12 and 13 of the basic Regulation

1. For the purposes of the application of Article 12(1) of the basic Regulation, a "person who pursues an activity as an employed person in a Member State on behalf of an employer which normally carries out its activities there and who is posted by that employer to another Member State" shall include a person who is recruited with a view to being posted to another Member State, provided that, immediately before the start of his employment, the person concerned is already subject to the legislation of the Member State in which his employer is established.
2. For the purposes of the application of Article 12(1) of the basic Regulation, the words "which normally carries out its activities there" shall refer to an employer that ordinarily performs substantial activities, other than purely internal management activities, in the territory of the Member State in which it is established, taking account of all criteria characterising the activities carried out by the undertaking in question. The relevant criteria must be suited to the specific characteristics of each employer and the real nature of the activities carried out.
3. For the purposes of the application of Article 12(2) of the basic Regulation, the words "who normally pursues an activity as a self-employed person" shall refer to a person who habitually carries out substantial activities in the territory of the Member State in which he is established. In particular, that person must have already pursued his activity for some time before the date when he wishes to take advantage of the provisions of that Article and, during any period of temporary activity in another Member State, must continue to fulfil, in the Member State where he is established, the requirements for the pursuit of his activity in order to be able to pursue it on his return.
4. For the purposes of the application of Article 12(2) of the basic Regulation, the criterion for determining whether the activity that a self-employed person goes to pursue in another Member State is "similar" to the self-employed activity normally pursued shall be that of the actual nature of the activity, rather than of the designation of employed or self-employed activity that may be given to this activity by the other Member State.
5. For the purposes of the application of Article 13(1) of the basic Regulation, a person who "normally pursues an activity as an employed person in two or more Member States" shall refer to a person who simultaneously, or in alternation, for the same undertaking or employer or for various undertakings or employers, exercises one or more separate activities in two or more Member States.
5a. For the purposes of the application of Title II of the basic Regulation, "registered office or place of business" shall refer to the registered office or place of business where the essential decisions of the undertaking are adopted and where the functions of its central administration are carried out.
For the purposes of Article 13(1) of the basic Regulation, an employed flight crew or cabin crew member normally pursuing air passenger or freight services in two or more Member States shall be subject to the legislation of the Member State where the home base, as defined in Annex III to Council Regulation (EEC) No 3922/91 of 16 December 1991 on the harmonization of technical requirements and administrative procedures in the field of civil aviation[1], is located.
5b. Marginal activities shall be disregarded for the purposes of determining the applicable legislation under Article 13 of the basic Regulation. Article 16 of the implementing Regulation shall apply to all cases under this Article.
6. For the purposes of the application of Article 13(2) of the basic Regulation, a person who "normally pursues an activity as a self-employed person in two or more Member States" shall refer, in particular, to a person who simultaneously or in alternation pursues one or more separate self-employed activities, irrespective of the nature of those activities, in two or more Member States.
7. For the purpose of distinguishing the activities under paragraphs 5 and 6 from the situations described in Article 12(1) and (2) of the basic Regulation, the duration of the activity in one or more other Member States (whether it is permanent or of an ad hoc or temporary nature) shall be decisive. For these purposes, an overall assessment shall be made of all the relevant facts including, in particular, in the case of an employed person, the place of work as defined in the employment contract.
8. For the purposes of the application of Article 13(1) and (2) of the basic Regulation, a "substantial part of employed or self-employed activity" pursued in a Member State shall mean a quantitatively substantial part of all the activities of the employed or self-employed person pursued there, without this necessarily being the major part of those activities.
To determine whether a substantial part of the activities is pursued in a Member State, the following indicative criteria shall be taken into account:
  (*a*) in the case of an employed activity, the working time and/or the remuneration; and

(*b*) in the case of a self-employed activity, the turnover, working time, number of services rendered and/or income.

In the framework of an overall assessment, a share of less than 25% in respect of the criteria mentioned above shall be an indicator that a substantial part of the activities is not being pursued in the relevant Member State.

9. For the purposes of the application of Article 13(2)(*b*) of the basic Regulation, the "centre of interest" of the activities of a self-employed person shall be determined by taking account of all the aspects of that person's occupational activities, notably the place where the person's fixed and permanent place of business is located, the habitual nature or the duration of the activities pursued, the number of services rendered, and the intention of the person concerned as revealed by all the circumstances.

10. For the determination of the applicable legislation under paragraphs 8 and 9, the institutions concerned shall take into account the situation projected for the following 12 calendar months.

11. If a person pursues his activity as an employed person in two or more Member States on behalf of an employer established outside the territory of the Union, and if this person resides in a Member State without pursuing substantial activity there, he shall be subject to the legislation of the Member State of residence.

[1] OJ L 373, 31.12.1991 p 4.

Article 15 Procedures for the application of Article 11(3)(*b*) and (*d*), Article 11(4) and Article 12 of the basic Regulation (on the provision of information to the institutions concerned)

1. Unless otherwise provided for by Article 16 of the implementing Regulation, where a person pursues his activity in a Member State other than the Member State competent under Title II of the basic Regulation, the employer or, in the case of a person who does not pursue an activity as an employed person, the person concerned shall inform the competent institution of the Member State whose legislation is applicable thereof, whenever possible in advance. That institution shall issue the attestation referred to in Article 19(2) of the implementing Regulation to the person concerned and shall without delay make information concerning the legislation applicable to that person, pursuant to Article 11(3)(b) or Article 12 of the basic Regulation, available to the institution designated by the competent authority of the Member State in which the activity is pursued.

2. Paragraph 1 shall apply *mutatis mutandis* to persons covered by Article 11(3)(*d*) of the basic Regulation.

3. An employer within the meaning of Article 11(4) of the basic Regulation who has an employee on board a vessel flying the flag of another Member State shall inform the competent institution of the Member State whose legislation is applicable thereof whenever possible in advance. That institution shall, without delay, make information concerning the legislation applicable to the person concerned, pursuant to Article 11(4) of the basic Regulation, available to the institution designated by the competent authority of the Member State whose flag, the vessel on which the employee is to perform the activity, is flying.

Article 16 Procedure for the application of Article 13 of the basic Regulation

1. A person who pursues activities in two or more Member States shall inform the institution designated by the competent authority of the Member State of residence thereof.

2. The designated institution of the place of residence shall without delay determine the legislation applicable to the person concerned, having regard to Article 13 of the basic Regulation and Article 14 of the implementing Regulation. That initial determination shall be provisional. The institution shall inform the designated institutions of each Member State in which an activity is pursued of its provisional determination.

3. The provisional determination of the applicable legislation, as provided for in paragraph 2, shall become definitive within two months of the institutions designated by the competent authorities of the Member States concerned being informed of it, in accordance with paragraph 2, unless the legislation has already been definitively determined on the basis of paragraph 4, or at least one of the institutions concerned informs the institution designated by the competent authority of the Member State of residence by the end of this two-month period that it cannot yet accept the determination or that it takes a different view on this.

4. Where uncertainty about the determination of the applicable legislation requires contacts between the institutions or authorities of two or more Member States, at the request of one or more of the institutions designated by the competent authorities of the Member States concerned or of the competent authorities themselves, the legislation applicable to the person concerned shall be determined by common agreement, having regard to Article 13 of the basic Regulation and the relevant provisions of Article 14 of the implementing Regulation.

Where there is a difference of views between the institutions or competent authorities concerned, those bodies shall seek agreement in accordance with the conditions set out above and Article 6 of the implementing Regulation shall apply.

5. The competent institution of the Member State whose legislation is determined to be applicable either provisionally or definitively shall without delay inform the person concerned.

6. If the person concerned fails to provide the information referred to in paragraph 1, this Article shall be applied at the initiative of the institution designated by the competent authority of the Member State of residence as soon as it is appraised of that person's situation, possibly via another institution concerned.

Article 17 Procedure for the application of Article 15 of the basic Regulation

Contract staff of the European Communities shall exercise the right of option provided for in Article 15 of the basic Regulation when the employment contract is concluded. The authority empowered to conclude the contract shall inform the designated institution of the Member State for whose legislation the contract staff member of the European Communities has opted.

Article 18 Procedure for the application of Article 16 of the basic Regulation

A request by the employer or the person concerned for exceptions to Articles 11 to 15 of the basic Regulation shall be submitted, whenever possible in advance, to the competent authority or the body designated by the authority of the Member State, whose legislation the employee or person concerned requests be applied.

Article 19 Provision of information to persons concerned and employers

1. The competent institution of the Member State whose legislation becomes applicable pursuant to Title II of the basic Regulation shall inform the person concerned and, where appropriate, his employer(s) of the obligations laid down in that legislation. It shall provide them with the necessary assistance to complete the formalities required by that legislation.

2. At the request of the person concerned or of the employer, the competent institution of the Member State whose legislation is applicable pursuant to Title II of the basic Regulation shall provide an attestation that such legislation is applicable and shall indicate, where appropriate, until what date and under what conditions.

Article 20 Cooperation between institutions

1. The relevant institutions shall communicate to the competent institution of the Member State whose legislation is applicable to a person pursuant to Title II of the basic Regulation the necessary information required to establish the date on which that legislation becomes applicable and the contributions which that person and his employer(s) are liable to pay under that legislation.

2. The competent institution of the Member State whose legislation becomes applicable to a person pursuant to Title II of the basic Regulation shall make the information indicating the date on which the application of that legislation takes effect available to the institution designated by the competent authority of the Member State to whose legislation that person was last subject.

Article 21 Obligations of the employer

1. An employer who has his registered office or place of business outside the competent Member State shall fulfil all the obligations laid down by the legislation applicable to his employees, notably the obligation to pay the contributions provided for by that legislation, as if he had his registered office or place of business in the competent Member State.

2. An employer who does not have a place of business in the Member State whose legislation is applicable and the employee may agree that the latter may fulfil the employer's obligations on its behalf as regards the payment of contributions without prejudice to the employer's underlying obligations. The employer shall send notice of such an arrangement to the competent institution of that Member State.

TITLE III

SPECIAL PROVISIONS CONCERNING THE VARIOUS CATEGORIES OF BENEFITS

CHAPTER I

SICKNESS, MATERNITY AND EQUIVALENT PATERNITY BENEFITS

Article 22 General implementing provisions

1. The competent authorities or institutions shall ensure that any necessary information is made available to insured persons regarding the procedures and conditions for the granting of benefits in kind where such benefits are received in the territory of a Member State other than that of the competent institution.

2. Notwithstanding Article 5(*a*) of the basic Regulation, a Member State may become responsible for the cost of benefits in accordance with Article 22 of the basic Regulation only if, either the insured person has made a claim for a pension under the legislation of that Member State, or in accordance with Articles 23 to 30 of the basic Regulation, he receives a pension under the legislation of that Member State.

Article 23 Regime applicable in the event of the existence of more than one regime in the Member State of residence or stay

If the legislation of the Member State of residence or stay comprises more than one scheme of sickness, maternity and paternity insurance for more than one category of insured persons, the provisions applicable under Articles 17, 19(1), 20, 22, 24 and 26 of the basic Regulation shall be those of the legislation on the general scheme for employed persons.

Article 24 Residence in a Member State other than the competent Member State

1. For the purposes of the application of Article 17 of the basic Regulation, the insured person and/or members of his family shall be obliged to register with the institution of the place of residence. Their right to benefits in kind in the Member State of residence shall be certified by a document issued by the competent institution upon request of the insured person or upon request of the institution of the place of residence.
2. The document referred to in paragraph 1 shall remain valid until the competent institution informs the institution of the place of residence of its cancellation.
The institution of the place of residence shall inform the competent institution of any registration under paragraph 1 and of any change or cancellation of that registration.
3. This Article shall apply *mutatis mutandis* to the persons referred to in Articles 22, 24, 25 and 26 of the basic Regulation.

Article 25 Stay in a Member State other than the competent Member State

A. *Procedure and scope of right*
1. For the purposes of the application of Article 19 of the basic Regulation, the insured person shall present to the health care provider in the Member State of stay a document issued by the competent institution indicating his entitlement to benefits in kind. If the insured person does not have such a document, the institution of the place of stay, upon request or if otherwise necessary, shall contact the competent institution in order to obtain one.
2. That document shall indicate that the insured person is entitled to benefits in kind under the conditions laid down in Article 19 of the basic Regulation on the same terms as those applicable to persons insured under the legislation of the Member State of stay.
3. The benefits in kind referred to in Article 19(1) of the basic Regulation shall refer to the benefits in kind which are provided in the Member State of stay, in accordance with its legislation, and which become necessary on medical grounds with a view to preventing an insured person from being forced to return, before the end of the planned duration of stay, to the competent Member State to obtain the necessary treatment.
B. *Procedure and arrangements for meeting the costs and providing reimbursement of benefits in kind*
4. If the insured person has actually borne the costs of all or part of the benefits in kind provided within the framework of Article 19 of the basic Regulation and if the legislation applied by the institution of the place of stay enables reimbursement of those costs to an insured person, he may send an application for reimbursement to the institution of the place of stay. In that case, that institution shall reimburse directly to that person the amount of the costs corresponding to those benefits within the limits of and under the conditions of the reimbursement rates laid down in its legislation.
5. If the reimbursement of such costs has not been requested directly from the institution of the place of stay, the costs incurred shall be reimbursed to the person concerned by the competent institution in accordance with the reimbursement rates administered by the institution of the place of stay or the amounts which would have been subject to reimbursement to the institution of the place of stay, if Article 62 of the implementing Regulation had applied in the case concerned.
The institution of the place of stay shall provide the competent institution, upon request, with all necessary information about these rates or amounts.
6. By way of derogation from paragraph 5, the competent institution may undertake the reimbursement of the costs incurred within the limits of and under the conditions of the reimbursement rates laid down in its legislation, provided that the insured person has agreed to this provision being applied to him/her.
7. If the legislation of the Member State of stay does not provide for reimbursement pursuant to paragraphs 4 and 5 in the case concerned, the competent institution may reimburse the costs within the limits of and under the conditions of the reimbursement rates laid down in its legislation, without the agreement of the insured person.
8. The reimbursement to the insured person shall not, in any event, exceed the amount of costs actually incurred by him/her.
9. In the case of substantial expenditure, the competent institution may pay the insured person an appropriate advance as soon as that person submits the application for reimbursement to it.
C. *Family Members*
10. Paragraphs 1 to 9 shall apply *mutatis mutandis* to the members of the family of the insured person.

Article 26 Scheduled treatment

A. *Authorisation procedure*

1. For the purposes of the application of Article 20(1) of the basic Regulation, the insured person shall present a document issued by the competent institution to the institution of the place of stay. For the purposes of this Article, the competent institution shall mean the institution which bears the cost of the scheduled treatment; in the cases referred to in Article 20(4) and 27(5) of the basic Regulation, in which the benefits in kind provided in the Member State of residence are reimbursed on the basis of fixed amounts, the competent institution shall mean the institution of the place of residence.

2. If an insured person does not reside in the competent Member State, he shall request authorisation from the institution of the place of residence, which shall forward it to the competent institution without delay.

In that event, the institution of the place of residence shall certify in a statement whether the conditions set out in the second sentence of Article 20(2) of the basic Regulation are met in the Member State of residence.

The competent institution may refuse to grant the requested authorisation only if, in accordance with the assessment of the institution of the place of residence, the conditions set out in the second sentence of Article 20(2) of the basic Regulation are not met in the Member State of residence of the insured person, or if the same treatment can be provided in the competent Member State itself, within a time-limit which is medically justifiable, taking into account the current state of health and the probable course of illness of the person concerned.

The competent institution shall inform the institution of the place of residence of its decision.

In the absence of a reply within the deadlines set by its national legislation, the authorisation shall be considered to have been granted by the competent institution.

3. If an insured person who does not reside in the competent Member State is in need of urgent vitally necessary treatment, and the authorisation cannot be refused in accordance with the second sentence of Article 20(2) of the basic Regulation, the authorisation shall be granted by the institution of the place of residence on behalf of the competent institution, which shall be immediately informed by the institution of the place of residence.

The competent institution shall accept the findings and the treatment options of the doctors approved by the institution of the place of residence that issues the authorisation, concerning the need for urgent vitally necessary treatment.

4. At any time during the procedure granting the authorisation, the competent institution shall retain the right to have the insured person examined by a doctor of its own choice in the Member State of stay or residence.

5. The institution of the place of stay shall, without prejudice to any decision regarding authorisation, inform the competent institution if it appears medically appropriate to supplement the treatment covered by the existing authorisation.

B. *Meeting the cost of benefits in kind incurred by the insured person*

6. Without prejudice to paragraph 7, Article 25(4) and (5) of the implementing Regulation shall apply *mutatis mutandis.*

7. If the insured person has actually borne all or part of the costs for the authorised medical treatment him or herself and the costs which the competent institution is obliged to reimburse to the institution of the place of stay or to the insured person according to paragraph 6 (actual cost) are lower than the costs which it would have had to assume for the same treatment in the competent Member State (notional cost), the competent institution shall reimburse, upon request, the cost of treatment incurred by the insured person up to the amount by which the notional cost exceeds the actual cost. The reimbursed sum may not, however, exceed the costs actually incurred by the insured person and may take account of the amount which the insured person would have had to pay if the treatment had been delivered in the competent Member State.

C. *Meeting the costs of travel and stay as part of scheduled treatment*

8. Where the national legislation of the competent institution provides for the reimbursement of the costs of travel and stay which are inseparable from the treatment of the insured person, such costs for the person concerned and, if necessary, for a person who must accompany him/her, shall be assumed by this institution when an authorisation is granted in the case of treatment in another Member State.

D. *Family members*

9. Paragraphs 1 to 8 shall apply *mutatis mutandis* to the members of the family of the insured persons.

Article 27 Cash benefits relating to incapacity for work in the event of stay or residence in a Member State other than the competent Member State

A. *Procedure to be followed by the insured person*

1. If the legislation of the competent Member State requires that the insured person presents a certificate in order to be entitled to cash benefits relating to incapacity for work pursuant to Article 21(1) of the basic Regulation, the insured person shall ask the doctor of the Member State of residence who established his state of health to certify his incapacity for work and its probable duration.

2. The insured person shall send the certificate to the competent institution within the time limit laid down by the legislation of the competent Member State.
3. Where the doctors providing treatment in the Member State of residence do not issue certificates of incapacity for work, and where such certificates are required under the legislation of the competent Member State, the person concerned shall apply directly to the institution of the place of residence. That institution shall immediately arrange for a medical assessment of the person's incapacity for work and for the certificate referred to in paragraph 1 to be drawn up. The certificate shall be forwarded to the competent institution forthwith.
4. The forwarding of the document referred to in paragraphs 1, 2 and 3 shall not exempt the insured person from fulfilling the obligations provided for by the applicable legislation, in particular with regard to his employer. Where appropriate, the employer and/or the competent institution may call upon the employee to participate in activities designed to promote and assist his return to employment.
B. *Procedure to be followed by the institution of the Member State of residence*
5. At the request of the competent institution, the institution of the place of residence shall carry out any necessary administrative checks or medical examinations of the person concerned in accordance with the legislation applied by this latter institution. The report of the examining doctor concerning, in particular, the probable duration of the incapacity for work, shall be forwarded without delay by the institution of the place of residence to the competent institution.
C. *Procedure to be followed by the competent institution*
6. The competent institution shall reserve the right to have the insured person examined by a doctor of its choice.
7. Without prejudice to the second sentence of Article 21(1) of the basic Regulation, the competent institution shall pay the cash benefits directly to the person concerned and shall, where necessary, inform the institution of the place of residence thereof.
8. For the purposes of the application of Article 21(1) of the basic Regulation, the particulars of the certificate of incapacity for work of an insured person drawn up in another Member State on the basis of the medical findings of the examining doctor or institution shall have the same legal value as a certificate drawn up in the competent Member State.
9. If the competent institution refuses the cash benefits, it shall notify its decision to the insured person and at the same time to the institution of the place of residence.
D. *Procedure in the event of a stay in a Member State other than the competent Member State*
10. Paragraphs 1 to 9 shall apply *mutatis mutandis* when the insured person stays in a Member State other than the competent Member State.

Article 28 Long-term care benefits in cash in the event of stay or residence in a Member State other than the competent Member State

A. *Procedure to be followed by the insured person*
1. In order to be entitled to long-term care benefits in cash pursuant to Article 21(1) of the basic Regulation, the insured person shall apply to the competent institution. The competent institution shall, where necessary, inform the institution of the place of residence thereof.
B. *Procedure to be followed by the institution of the place of residence*
2. At the request of the competent institution, the institution of the place of residence shall examine the condition of the insured person with respect to his need for long-term care. The competent institution shall give the institution of the place of residence all the information necessary for such an examination.
C. *Procedure to be followed by the competent institution*
3. In order to determine the degree of need for long-term care, the competent institution shall have the right to have the insured person examined by a doctor or any other expert of its choice.
4. Article 27(7) of the implementing Regulation shall apply *mutatis mutandis.*
D. *Procedure in the event of a stay in a Member State other than the competent Member State*
5. Paragraphs 1 to 4 shall apply *mutatis mutandis* when the insured person stays in a Member State other than the competent Member State.
E. *Family members*
6. Paragraphs 1 to 5 shall apply *mutatis mutandis* to the members of the family of the insured person.

Article 29 Application of Article 28 of the basic Regulation

If the Member State where the former frontier worker last pursued his activity is no longer the competent Member State, and the former frontier worker or a member of his family travels there with the purpose of receiving benefits in kind pursuant to Article 28 of the basic Regulation, he shall submit to the institution of the place of stay a document issued by the competent institution.

Article 30 Contributions by pensioners

If a person receives a pension from more than one Member State, the amount of contributions deducted from all the pensions paid shall under no circumstances be greater than the amount deducted in respect of a person who receives the same amount of pension from the competent Member State.

Article 31 Application of Article 34 of the basic Regulation

A. *Procedure to be followed by the competent institution*

1. The competent institution shall inform the person concerned of the provision contained in Article 34 of the basic Regulation regarding the prevention of overlapping of benefits. The application of such rules shall ensure that the person not residing in the competent Member State is entitled to benefits of at least the same total amount or value as those to which he would be entitled if he resided in that Member State.

2. The competent institution shall also inform the institution of the place of residence or stay about the payment of long-term care cash benefits where the legislation applied by the latter institution provides for the long-term care benefits in kind included in the list referred to in Article 34(2) of the basic Regulation.

B. *Procedure to be followed by the institution of the place of residence or stay*

3. Having received the information provided for in paragraph 2, the institution of the place of residence or stay shall without delay inform the competent institution of any long-term care benefit in kind intended for the same purpose granted under its legislation to the person concerned and of the rate of reimbursement applicable thereto.

4. The Administrative Commission shall lay down implementing measures for this Article where necessary.

Article 32 Special implementing measures

1. When a person or a group of persons are exempted upon request from compulsory sickness insurance and such persons are thus not covered by a sickness insurance scheme to which the basic Regulation applies, the institution of another Member State shall not, solely because of this exemption, become responsible for bearing the costs of benefits in kind or in cash provided to such persons or to a member of their family under Title III, Chapter I, of the basic Regulation.

2. For the Member States referred to in Annex 2, the provisions of Title III, Chapter I, of the basic Regulation relating to benefits in kind shall apply to persons entitled to benefits in kind solely on the basis of a special scheme for civil servants only to the extent specified therein.

The institution of another Member State shall not, on those grounds alone, become responsible for bearing the costs of benefits in kind or in cash provided to those persons or to members of their family.

3. When the persons referred to in paragraphs 1 and 2 and the members of their families reside in a Member State where the right to receive benefits in kind is not subject to conditions of insurance, or of activity as an employed or self-employed person, they shall be liable to pay the full costs of benefits in kind provided in their country of residence.

CHAPTER II

BENEFITS IN RESPECT OF ACCIDENTS AT WORK AND OCCUPATIONAL DISEASES

Article 33 Right to benefits in kind and in cash in the event of residence or stay in a Member State other than the competent Member State

1. For the purposes of the application of Article 36 of the basic Regulation, the procedures laid down in Articles 24 to 27 of the implementing Regulation shall apply *mutatis mutandis*.

2. When providing special benefits in kind in connection with accidents at work and occupational diseases under the national legislation of the Member State of stay or residence, the institution of that Member State shall without delay inform the competent institution.

Article 34 Procedure in the event of an accident at work or occupational disease which occurs in a Member State other than the competent Member State

1. If an accident at work occurs or an occupational disease is diagnosed for the first time in a Member State other than the competent Member State, the declaration or notification of the accident at work or the occupational disease, where the declaration or notification exists under national legislation, shall be carried out in accordance with the legislation of the competent Member State, without prejudice, where appropriate, to any other applicable legal provisions in force in the Member State in which the accident at work occurred or in which the first medical diagnosis of the occupational disease was made, which remain applicable in such cases. The declaration or notification shall be addressed to the competent institution.

2. The institution of the Member State in the territory of which the accident at work occurred or in which the occupational disease was first diagnosed, shall notify the competent institution of medical certificates drawn up in the territory of that Member State.

3. Where, as a result of an accident while travelling to or from work which occurs in the territory of a Member State other than the competent Member State, an inquiry is necessary in the territory of the first Member State in order to determine any entitlement to relevant benefits, a person may be appointed for that purpose by the competent institution, which shall inform the authorities of that Member State. The institutions shall cooperate with each other in order to assess all relevant information and to consult the reports and any other documents relating to the accident.

4. Following treatment, a detailed report accompanied by medical certificates relating to the permanent consequences of the accident or disease, in particular the injured person's present state and the recovery or stabilisation of injuries, shall be sent upon request of the competent institution. The relevant fees shall be paid by the institution of the place of residence or of stay, where appropriate, at the rate applied by that institution to the charge of the competent institution.
5. At the request of the institution of the place of residence or stay, where appropriate, the competent institution shall notify it of the decision setting the date for the recovery or stabilisation of injuries and, where appropriate, the decision concerning the granting of a pension.

Article 35 Disputes concerning the occupational nature of the accident or disease

1. Where the competent institution disputes the application of the legislation relating to accidents at work or occupational diseases under Article 36(2) of the basic Regulation, it shall without delay inform the institution of the place of residence or stay which provided the benefits in kind, which will then be considered as sickness insurance benefits.
2. When a final decision has been taken on that subject, the competent institution shall without delay inform the institution of the place of residence or stay which provided the benefits in kind.
Where an accident at work or occupational disease is not established, benefits in kind shall continue to be provided as sickness benefits if the person concerned is entitled to them.
Where an accident at work or occupational disease is established, sickness benefits in kind provided to the person concerned shall be considered as accident at work or occupational disease benefits from the date on which the accident at work occurred or the occupational disease was first medically diagnosed.
3. The second sub-paragraph of Article 6(5) of the implementing Regulation shall apply *mutatis mutandis*.

Article 36 Procedure in the event of exposure to the risk of an occupational disease in more than one Member State

1. In the case referred to in Article 38 of the basic Regulation, the declaration or notification of the occupational disease shall be sent to the competent institution for occupational diseases of the last Member State under the legislation of which the person concerned pursued an activity likely to cause that disease.
When the institution to which the declaration or notification was sent establishes that an activity likely to cause the occupational disease in question was last pursued under the legislation of another Member State, it shall send the declaration or notification and all accompanying certificates to the equivalent institution in that Member State.
2. Where the institution of the last Member State under the legislation of which the person concerned pursued an activity likely to cause the occupational disease in question establishes that the person concerned or his survivors do not meet the requirements of that legislation, inter alia, because the person concerned had never pursued in that Member State an activity which caused the occupational disease or because that Member State does not recognise the occupational nature of the disease, that institution shall forward without delay the declaration or notification and all accompanying certificates, including the findings and reports of medical examinations performed by the first institution to the institution of the previous Member State under the legislation of which the person concerned pursued an activity likely to cause the occupational disease in question.
3. Where appropriate, the institutions shall reiterate the procedure set out in paragraph 2 going back as far as the equivalent institution in the Member State under whose legislation the person concerned first pursued an activity likely to cause the occupational disease in question.

Article 37 Exchange of information between institutions and advance payments in the event of an appeal against rejection

1. In the event of an appeal against a decision to refuse benefits taken by the institution of one of the Member States under the legislation of which the person concerned pursued an activity likely to cause the occupational disease in question, that institution shall inform the institution to which the declaration or notification was sent, in accordance with the procedure provided for in Article 36(2) of the implementing Regulation, and shall subsequently inform it when a final decision is reached.
2. Where a person is entitled to benefits under the legislation applied by the institution to which the declaration or notification was sent, that institution shall make the advance payments, the amount of which shall be determined, where appropriate, after consulting the institution which made the decision against which the appeal was lodged, and in such a way that overpayments are avoided. The latter institution shall reimburse the advance payments made if, as a result of the appeal, it is obliged to provide those benefits. That amount will then be deducted from the benefits due to the person concerned, in accordance with the procedure provided for in Articles 72 and 73 of the implementing Regulation.
3. The second sub-paragraph of Article 6(5) of the implementing Regulation shall apply *mutatis mutandis*.

Article 38 Aggravation of an occupational disease

In the cases covered by Article 39 of the basic Regulation, the claimant must provide the institution in the Member State from which he is claiming entitlement to benefits with details concerning benefits previously granted for the occupational disease in question. That institution may contact any other previously competent institution in order to obtain the information it considers necessary.

Article 39 Assessment of the degree of incapacity in the event of occupational accidents or diseases which occurred previously or subsequently

Where a previous or subsequent incapacity for work was caused by an accident which occurred when the person concerned was subject to the legislation of a Member State which makes no distinction according to the origin of the incapacity to work, the competent institution or the body designated by the competent authority of the Member State in question shall:

(*a*) upon request by the competent institution of another Member State, provide information concerning the degree of the previous or subsequent incapacity for work, and where possible, information making it possible to determine whether the incapacity is the result of an accident at work within the meaning of the legislation applied by the institution in the other Member State;

(*b*) take into account the degree of incapacity caused by these previous or subsequent cases when determining the right to benefits and the amount, in accordance with the applicable legislation.

Article 40 Submission and investigation of claims for pensions or supplementary allowances

In order to receive a pension or supplementary allowance under the legislation of a Member State, the person concerned or his survivors residing in the territory of another Member State shall submit, where appropriate, a claim either to the competent institution or to the institution of the place of residence, which shall send it to the competent institution.

The claim shall contain the information required under the legislation applied by the competent institution.

Article 41 Special implementing measures

1. In relation to the Member States referred to in Annex 2, the provisions of Title III, Chapter 2 of the basic Regulation relating to benefits in kind shall apply to persons entitled to benefits in kind solely on the basis of a special scheme for civil servants, and only to the extent specified therein.

2. Article 32(2) second subparagraph and Article 32(3) of the implementing Regulation shall apply *mutatis mutandis*.

CHAPTER III

DEATH GRANTS

Article 42 Claim for death grants

For the purposes of applying Articles 42 and 43 of the basic Regulation, the claim for death grants shall be sent either to the competent institution or to the institution of the claimant's place of residence, which shall send it to the competent institution.

The claim shall contain the information required under the legislation applied by the competent institution.

CHAPTER IV

INVALIDITY BENEFITS AND OLD-AGE AND SURVIVORS' PENSIONS

Article 43 Additional provisions for the calculation of benefit

1. For the purposes of calculating the theoretical amount and the actual amount of the benefit in accordance with Article 52(1)(*b*) of the basic Regulation, the rules provided for in Article 12(3), (4), (5) and (6) of the implementing Regulation shall apply.

2. Where periods of voluntary or optional continued insurance have not been taken into account under Article 12(3) of the implementing Regulation, the institution of the Member State under whose legislation those periods were completed shall calculate the amount corresponding to those periods under the legislation it applies. The actual amount of the benefit, calculated in accordance with Article 52(1)(*b*) of the basic Regulation, shall be increased by the amount corresponding to periods of voluntary or optional continued insurance.

3. The institution of each Member State shall calculate, under the legislation it applies, the amount due corresponding to periods of voluntary or optional continued insurance which, under Article 53(3)(c) of the basic Regulation, shall not be subject to another Member State's rules relating to withdrawal, reduction or suspension.

Where the legislation applied by the competent institution does not allow it to determine this amount directly, on the grounds that that legislation allocates different values to insurance periods, a notional amount may be established. The Administrative Commission shall lay down the detailed arrangements for the determination of that notional amount.

Article 44 Taking into account of child raising-periods

1. For the purposes of this Article, "child-raising period" refers to any period which is credited under the pension legislation of a Member State or which provides a supplement to a pension explicitly for the reason that a person has raised a child, irrespective of the method used to calculate those periods and whether they accrue during the time of child-raising or are acknowledged retroactively.

2. Where, under the legislation of the Member State which is competent under Title II of the basic Regulation, no child-raising period is taken into account, the institution of the Member State whose legislation, according to Title II of the basic Regulation, was applicable to the person concerned on the grounds that he or she was pursuing an activity as an employed or self-employed person at the date when, under that legislation, the child-raising period started to be taken into account for the child concerned, shall remain responsible for taking into account that period as a child-raising period under its own legislation, as if such child-raising took place in its own territory.

3. Paragraph 2 shall not apply if the person concerned is, or becomes, subject to the legislation of another Member State due to the pursuit of an employed or self-employed activity.

Article 45 Claim for benefits

A. *Submission of the claim for benefits under type A legislation under Article 44(2) of the basic Regulation*

1. In order to receive benefits under type A legislation under Article 44(2) of the basic Regulation, the claimant shall submit a claim to the institution of the Member State, whose legislation was applicable at the time when the incapacity for work occurred followed by invalidity or the aggravation of such invalidity, or to the institution of the place of residence, which shall forward the claim to the first institution.

2. If sickness benefits in cash have been awarded, the expiry date of the period for awarding these benefits shall, where appropriate, be considered as the date of submission of the pension claim.

3. In the case referred to in Article 47(1) of the basic Regulation, the institution with which the person concerned was last insured shall inform the institution which initially paid the benefits of the amount and the date of commencement of the benefits under the applicable legislation. From that date benefits due before aggravation of the invalidity shall be withdrawn or reduced to the supplement referred to in Article 47(2) of the basic Regulation.

B. *Submission of other claims for benefits*

4. In situations other than those referred to in paragraph 1, the claimant shall submit a claim to the institution of his place of residence or to the institution of the last Member State whose legislation was applicable. If the person concerned was not, at any time, subject to the legislation applied by the institution of the place of residence, that institution shall forward the claim to the institution of the last Member State whose legislation was applicable.

5. The date of submission of the claim shall apply in all the institutions concerned.

6. By way of derogation from paragraph 5, if the claimant does not, despite having been asked to do so, notify the fact that he has been employed or has resided in other Member States, the date on which the claimant completes his initial claim or submits a new claim for his missing periods of employment or/and residence in a Member State shall be considered as the date of submission of the claim to the institution applying the legislation in question, subject to more favourable provisions of that legislation.

Article 46 Certificates and information to be submitted with the claim by the claimant

1. The claim shall be submitted by the claimant in accordance with the provisions of the legislation applied by the institution referred to in Article 45(1) or (4) of the implementing Regulation and be accompanied by the supporting documents required by that legislation. In particular, the claimant shall supply all available relevant information and supporting documents relating to periods of insurance (institutions, identification numbers), employment (employers) or self-employment (nature and place of activity) and residence (addresses) which may have been completed under other legislation, as well as the length of those periods.

2. Where, in accordance with Article 50(1) of the basic Regulation, the claimant requests deferment of the award of old-age benefits under the legislation of one or more Member States, he shall state that in his claim and specify under which legislation the deferment is requested. In order to enable the claimant to exercise that right, the institutions concerned shall, upon the request of the claimant, notify him of all the information available to them so that he can assess the consequences of concurrent or successive awards of benefits which he might claim.

3. Should the claimant withdraw a claim for benefits provided for under the legislation of a particular Member State, that withdrawal shall not be considered as a concurrent withdrawal of claims for benefits under the legislation of other Member States.

Article 47 Investigation of claims by the institutions concerned

A. *Contact institution*

1. The institution to which the claim for benefits is submitted or forwarded in accordance with Article 45(1) or (4) of the implementing Regulation shall be referred to hereinafter as the "contact institution". The institution of the place of residence shall not be referred to as the contact institution if the person concerned has not, at any time, been subject to the legislation which that institution applies.

In addition to investigating the claim for benefits under the legislation which it applies, this institution shall, in its capacity as contact institution, promote the exchange of data, the communication of decisions and the operations necessary for the investigation of the claim by the institutions concerned, and supply the claimant, upon request, with any information relevant to the Community aspects of the investigation and keep him/her informed of its progress.

B. *Investigation of claims for benefits under type A legislation under Article 44 of the basic Regulation*

2. In the case referred to in Article 44(3) of the basic Regulation, the contact institution shall send all the documents relating to the person concerned to the institution with which he was previously insured, which shall in turn examine the case.

3. Articles 48 to 52 of the implementing Regulation shall not be applicable to the investigation of claims referred to in Article 44 of the basic Regulation.

C. *Investigation of other claims for benefits*

4. In situations other than those referred to in paragraph 2, the contact institution shall, without delay, send claims for benefits and all the documents which it has available and, where appropriate, the relevant documents supplied by the claimant to all the institutions in question so that they can all start the investigation of the claim concurrently. The contact institution shall notify the other institutions of periods of insurance or residence subject to its legislation. It shall also indicate which documents shall be submitted at a later date and supplement the claim as soon as possible.

5. Each of the institutions in question shall notify the contact institution and the other institutions in question, as soon as possible, of the periods of insurance or residence subject to their legislation.

6. Each of the institutions in question shall calculate the amount of benefits in accordance with Article 52 of the basic Regulation and shall notify the contact institution and the other institutions concerned of its decision, of the amount of benefits due and of any information required for the purposes of Articles 53 to 55 of the basic Regulation.

7. Should an institution establish, on the basis of the information referred to in paragraphs 4 and 5 of this Article, that Article 46(2) or Article 57(2) or (3) of the basic Regulation is applicable, it shall inform the contact institution and the other institutions concerned.

Article 48 Notification of decisions to the claimant

1. Each institution shall notify the claimant of the decision it has taken in accordance with the applicable legislation. Each decision shall specify the remedies and periods allowed for appeals. Once the contact institution has been notified of all decisions taken by each institution, it shall send the claimant and the other institutions concerned a summary of those decisions. A model summary shall be drawn up by the Administrative Commission. The summary shall be sent to the claimant in the language of the institution or, at the request of the claimant, in any language of his choice recognised as an official language of the Community institutions in accordance with Article 290 of the Treaty.

2. Where it appears to the claimant following receipt of the summary that his rights may have been adversely affected by the interaction of decisions taken by two or more institutions, the claimant shall have the right to a review of the decisions by the institutions concerned within the time limits laid down in the respective national legislation. The time limits shall commence on the date of receipt of the summary. The claimant shall be notified of the result of the review in writing.

Article 49 Determination of the degree of invalidity

1. Where Article 46(3) of the basic Regulation is applicable, the only institution authorised to take a decision concerning the claimant's degree of invalidity shall be the contact institution, if the legislation applied by that institution is included in Annex VII to the basic Regulation, or failing that, the institution whose legislation is included in that Annex and to whose legislation the claimant was last subject. It shall take that decision as soon as it can determine whether the conditions for eligibility laid down in the applicable legislation are met, taking into account, where appropriate, Articles 6 and 51 of the basic Regulation. It shall without delay notify the other institutions concerned of that decision.

Where the eligibility criteria, other than those relating to the degree of invalidity, laid down in the applicable legislation are not met, taking into account Articles 6 and 51 of the basic Regulation, the contact institution shall without delay inform the competent institution of the last Member State to whose legislation the claimant was subject. The latter institution shall be authorised to take the decision concerning the degree of invalidity of the claimant if the conditions for eligibility laid down in the applicable legislation are met. It shall without delay notify the other institutions concerned of that decision.

When determining eligibility, the matter may, if necessary have to be referred back, under the same conditions, to the competent institution in respect of invalidity of the Member State to whose legislation the claimant was first subject.

2. Where Article 46(3) of the basic Regulation is not applicable, each institution shall, in accordance with its legislation, have the possibility of having the claimant examined by a medical doctor or other expert of its choice to determine the degree of invalidity. However, the institution of a Member State shall take into consideration documents, medical reports and administrative information collected by the institution of any other Member State as if they had been drawn up in its own Member State.

Article 50 Provisional instalments and advance payment of benefit

1. Notwithstanding Article 7 of the implementing Regulation, any institution which establishes, while investigating a claim for benefits, that the claimant is entitled to an independent benefit under the applicable legislation, in accordance with Article 52(1)(*a*) of the basic Regulation, shall pay that benefit without delay. That payment shall be considered provisional if the amount might be affected by the result of the claim investigation procedure.

2. Whenever it is evident from the information available that the claimant is entitled to a payment from an institution under Article 52(1)(*b*) of the basic Regulation, that institution shall make an advance payment, the amount of which shall be as close as possible to the amount which will probably be paid under Article 52(1)(*b*) of the basic Regulation.

3. Each institution which is obliged to pay the provisional benefits or advance payment under paragraphs 1 or 2 shall inform the claimant without delay, specifically drawing his attention to the provisional nature of the measure and any rights of appeal in accordance with its legislation.

Article 51 New calculation of benefits

1. Where there is a new calculation of benefits in accordance with Articles 48(3) and (4), 50(4) and 59(1) of the basic Regulation, Article 50 of the implementing Regulation shall be applicable *mutatis mutandis*.

2. Where there is a new calculation, withdrawal or suspension of the benefit, the institution which took the decision shall inform the person concerned without delay and shall inform each of the institutions in respect of which the person concerned has an entitlement.

Article 52 Measures intended to accelerate the pension calculation process

1. In order to facilitate and accelerate the investigation of claims and the payment of benefits, the institutions to whose legislation a person has been subject shall:

(*a*) exchange with or make available to institutions of other Member States the elements for identifying persons who change from one applicable national legislation to another, and together ensure that those identification elements are retained and correspond, or, failing that, provide those persons with the means to access their identification elements directly;

(*b*) sufficiently in advance of the minimum age for commencing pension rights or before an age to be determined by national legislation, exchange with or make available to the person concerned and to institutions of other Member States information (periods completed or other important elements) on the pension entitlements of persons who have changed from one applicable legislation to another or, failing that, inform those persons of, or provide them with, the means of familiarising themselves with their prospective benefit entitlement.

2. For the purposes of applying paragraph 1, the Administrative Commission shall determine the elements of information to be exchanged or made available and shall establish the appropriate procedures and mechanisms, taking account of the characteristics, administrative and technical organisation, and the technological means at the disposal of national pension schemes. The Administrative Commission shall ensure the implementation of those pension schemes by organising a follow-up to the measures taken and their application.

3. For the purposes of applying paragraph 1, the institution in the first Member State where a person is allocated a Personal Identification Number (PIN) for the purposes of social security administration should be provided with the information referred to in this Article.

Article 53 Coordination measures in Member States

1. Without prejudice to Article 51 of the basic Regulation, where national legislation includes rules for determining the institution responsible or the scheme applicable or for designating periods of insurance to a specific scheme, those rules shall be applied, taking into account only periods of insurance completed under the legislation of the Member State concerned.

2. Where national legislation includes rules for the coordination of special schemes for civil servants and the general scheme for employed persons, those rules shall not be affected by the provisions of the basic Regulation and of the implementing Regulation.

NIC

CHAPTER V
UNEMPLOYMENT BENEFITS

Article 54 Aggregation of periods and calculation of benefits

1. Article 12(1) of the implementing Regulation shall apply *mutatis mutandis* to Article 61 of the basic Regulation. Without prejudice to the underlying obligations of the institutions involved, the person concerned may submit to the competent institution a document issued by the institution of the Member State to whose legislation he was subject in respect of his last activity as an employed or self-employed person specifying the periods completed under that legislation.

2. For the purposes of applying Article 62(3) of the basic Regulation, the competent institution of the Member State to whose legislation the person concerned was subject in respect of his/her last activity as an employed or self- employed person shall, without delay, at the request of the institution of the place of residence, provide it with all the information necessary to calculate unemployment benefits which can be obtained in the Member State where it is situated, in particular the salary or professional income received.

3. For the purposes of applying Article 62 of the basic Regulation and notwithstanding Article 63 thereof, the competent institution of a Member State whose legislation provides that the calculation of benefits varies with the number of members of the family shall also take into account the members of the family of the person concerned residing in another Member State as if they resided in the competent Member State. This provision shall not apply where, in the Member State of residence of members of the family, another person is entitled to unemployment benefits calculated on the basis of the number of members of the family.

Article 55 Conditions and restrictions on the retention of the entitlement to benefits for unemployed persons going to another Member State

1. In order to be covered by Article 64 or Article 65a of the basic Regulation, the unemployed person going to another Member State shall inform the competent institution prior to his/her departure and request a document certifying that he/she retains his/her entitlement to benefits under the conditions laid down in Article 64(1)(*b*) of the basic Regulation.

That institution shall inform the person concerned of his obligations and shall provide the abovementioned document which shall include the following information:

(*a*) the date on which the unemployed person ceased to be available to the employment services of the competent State;

(*b*) the period granted in accordance with Article 64(1)(*b*) of the basic Regulation in order to register as a person seeking work in the Member State to which the unemployed person has gone;

(*c*) the maximum period during which the entitlement to benefits may be retained in accordance with Article 64(1)(*c*) of the basic Regulation;

(*d*) circumstances likely to affect the entitlement to benefits.

2. The unemployed person shall register as a person seeking work with the employment services of the Member State to which he goes in accordance with Article 64(1)(*b*) of the basic Regulation and shall provide the document referred to in paragraph 1 to the institution of that Member State. If he has informed the competent institution in accordance with paragraph 1 but fails to provide this document, the institution in the Member State to which the unemployed person has gone shall contact the competent institution in order to obtain the necessary information.

3. The employment services in the Member State to which the unemployed person has gone to seek employment shall inform the unemployed person of his obligations.

4. The institution in the Member State to which the unemployed person has gone shall immediately send a document to the competent institution containing the date on which the unemployed person registered with the employment services and his new address.

If, in the period during which the unemployed person retains entitlement to benefits, any circumstance likely to affect the entitlement to benefits arises, the institution in the Member State to which the unemployed person has gone shall send immediately to the competent institution and to the person concerned a document containing the relevant information.

At the request of the competent institution, the institution in the Member State to which the unemployed person has gone shall provide relevant information on a monthly basis concerning the follow-up of the unemployed person's situation, in particular whether the latter is still registered with the employment services and is complying with organised checking procedures.

5. The institution in the Member State to which the unemployed person has gone shall carry out or arrange for checks to be carried out, as if the person concerned were an unemployed person obtaining benefits under its own legislation. Where necessary, it shall immediately inform the competent institution if any circumstances referred to in paragraph 1(*d*) arise.

6. The competent authorities or competent institutions of two or more Member States may agree amongst themselves specific procedures and time-limits concerning the follow-up of the unemployed person's situation as well as other measures to facilitate the job-seeking activities of unemployed persons who go to one of those Member States under Article 64 of the basic Regulation.

7. Paragraphs 2 to 6 shall apply mutatis mutandis to the situation covered by Article 65a(3) of the basic Regulation.

Article 56 Unemployed persons who resided in a Member State other than the competent Member State

1. Where the unemployed person decides, in accordance with Article 65(2) or Article 65a(1) of the basic Regulation, to make himself/herself also available to the employment services in the Member State not providing the benefits, by registering there as a person seeking work, he/she shall inform the institution and the employment services of the Member State providing the benefits.

At the request of the employment services of the Member State not providing the benefits, the employment services in the Member State that is providing the benefits shall send the relevant information concerning the unemployed person's registration and his/her search for employment.

2. Where the legislation applicable in the Member States concerned requires the fulfilment of certain obligations and/or job-seeking activities by the unemployed person, the obligations and/or job-seeking activities by the unemployed person in the Member State providing the benefits shall have priority.

The non-fulfilment by the unemployed person of all the obligations and/or job-seeking activities in the Member State which does not provide the benefits shall not affect the benefits awarded in the other Member State.

3. For the purposes of applying Article 65(5)(*b*) of the basic Regulation, the institution of the Member State to whose legislation the worker was last subject shall inform the institution of the place of residence, when requested to do so by the latter, whether the worker is entitled to benefits under Article 64 of the basic Regulation.

Article 57 Provisions for the application of Articles 61, 62, 64 and 65 of the basic Regulation regarding persons covered by a special scheme for civil servants

1. Articles 54 and 55 of the implementing Regulation shall apply *mutatis mutandis* to persons covered by a special unemployment scheme for civil servants.

2. Article 56 of the implementing Regulation shall not apply to persons covered by a special unemployment scheme for civil servants. An unemployed person who is covered by a special unemployment scheme for civil servants, who is partially or wholly unemployed, and who, during his last employment, was residing in the territory of a Member State other than the competent State, shall receive the benefits under the special unemployment scheme for civil servants in accordance with the provisions of the legislation of the competent Member State as if he were residing in the territory of that Member State. Those benefits shall be provided by the competent institution, at its expense.

CHAPTER VI

FAMILY BENEFITS

Article 58 Priority rules in the event of overlapping

For the purposes of applying Article 68(1)(*b*)(i) and (ii) of the basic Regulation, where the order of priority cannot be established on the basis of the children's place of residence, each Member State concerned shall calculate the amount of benefits including the children not resident within its own territory. In the event of applying Article 68(1)(*b*)(i), the competent institution of the Member State whose legislation provides for the highest level of benefits shall pay the full amount of such benefits and be reimbursed half this sum by the competent institution of the other Member State up to the limit of the amount provided for in the legislation of the latter Member State.

Article 59 Rules applicable where the applicable legislation and/or the competence to grant family benefits changes

1. Where the applicable legislation and/or the competence to grant family benefits change between Member States during a calendar month, irrespective of the payment dates of family benefits under the legislation of those Member States, the institution which has paid the family benefits by virtue of the legislation under which the benefits have been granted at the beginning of that month shall continue to do so until the end of the month in progress.

2. It shall inform the institution of the other Member State or Member States concerned of the date on which it ceases to pay the family benefits in question. Payment of benefits from the other Member State or Member States concerned shall take effect from that date.

Article 60 Procedure for applying Articles 67 and 68 of the basic Regulation

1. The application for family benefits shall be addressed to the competent institution. For the purposes of applying Articles 67 and 68 of the basic Regulation, the situation of the whole family shall be taken into account as if all the persons involved were subject to the legislation of the Member State concerned and residing there, in particular as regards a person's entitlement to claim such benefits. Where a person entitled to claim the benefits does not exercise his right, an application for family benefits submitted by the other parent, a person treated as a parent, or a person or institution acting as guardian of the child or children, shall be taken into account by the competent institution of the Member State whose legislation is applicable.

NIC

2. The institution to which an application is made in accordance with paragraph 1 shall examine the application on the basis of the detailed information supplied by the applicant, taking into account the overall factual and legal situation of the applicant's family.
If that institution concludes that its legislation is applicable by priority right in accordance with Article 68(1) and (2) of the basic Regulation, it shall provide the family benefits according to the legislation it applies.
If it appears to that institution that there may be an entitlement to a differential supplement by virtue of the legislation of another Member State in accordance with Article 68(2) of the basic Regulation, that institution shall forward the application, without delay, to the competent institution of the other Member State and inform the person concerned; moreover, it shall inform the institution of the other Member State of its decision on the application and the amount of family benefits paid.
3. Where the institution to which the application is made concludes that its legislation is applicable, but not by priority right in accordance with Article 68(1) and (2) of the basic Regulation, it shall take a provisional decision, without delay, on the priority rules to be applied and shall forward the application, in accordance with Article 68(3) of the basic Regulation, to the institution of the other Member State, and shall also inform the applicant thereof. That institution shall take a position on the provisional decision within two months.
If the institution to which the application was forwarded does not take a position within two months of the receipt of the application, the provisional decision referred to above shall apply and the institution shall pay the benefits provided for under its legislation and inform the institution to which the application was made of the amount of benefits paid.
4. Where there is a difference of views between the institutions concerned about which legislation is applicable by priority right, Article 6(2) to (5) of the implementing Regulation shall apply. For this purpose the institution of the place of residence referred to in Article 6(2) of the implementing Regulation shall be the institution of the child's or childrens' place of residence.
5. If the institution which has supplied benefits on a provisional basis has paid more than the amount for which it is ultimately responsible, it may claim reimbursement of the excess from the institution with primary responsibility in accordance with the procedure laid down in Article 73 of the implementing Regulation.

Article 61 Procedure for applying Article 69 of the basic Regulation

For the purposes of applying Article 69 of the basic Regulation, the Administrative Commission shall draw up a list of the additional or special family benefits for orphans covered by that Article. If there is no provision for the institution competent to grant, by priority right, such additional or special family benefits for orphans under the legislation it applies, it shall without delay forward any application for family benefits, together with all relevant documents and information, to the institution of the Member State to whose legislation the person concerned has been subject, for the longest period of time and which provides such additional or special family benefits for orphans. In some cases, this may mean referring back, under the same conditions, to the institution of the Member State under whose legislation the person concerned has completed the shortest of his or her insurance or residence periods.

TITLE IV
FINANCIAL PROVISIONS

CHAPTER I

REIMBURSEMENT OF THE COST OF BENEFITS IN APPLICATION OF ARTICLE 35 AND ARTICLE 41 OF THE BASIC REGULATION

SECTION 1

REIMBURSEMENT ON THE BASIS OF ACTUAL EXPENDITURE

Article 62 Principles

1. For the purposes of applying Article 35 and Article 41 of the basic Regulation, the actual amount of the expenses for benefits in kind, as shown in the accounts of the institution that provided them, shall be reimbursed to that institution by the competent institution, except where Article 63 of the implementing Regulation is applicable.
2. If any or part of the actual amount of the expenses for benefits referred to in paragraph 1 is not shown in the accounts of the institution that provided them, the amount to be refunded shall be determined on the basis of a lump-sum payment calculated from all the appropriate references obtained from the data available. The Administrative Commission shall assess the bases to be used for calculation of the lump-sum payment and shall decide the amount thereof.
3. Higher rates than those applicable to the benefits in kind provided to insured persons subject to the legislation applied by the institution providing the benefits referred to in paragraph 1 may not be taken into account in the reimbursement.

SECTION 2

REIMBURSEMENT ON THE BASIS OF FIXED AMOUNTS

Article 63 Identification of the Member States concerned

1. The Member States referred to in Article 35(2) of the basic Regulation, whose legal or administrative structures are such that the use of reimbursement on the basis of actual expenditure is not appropriate, are listed in Annex 3 to the implementing Regulation.

2. In the case of the Member States listed in Annex 3 to the implementing Regulation, the amount of benefits in kind supplied to:

(*a*) family members who do not reside in the same Member State as the insured person, as provided for in Article 17 of the basic Regulation; and to

(*b*) pensioners and members of their family, as provided for in Article 24(1) and Articles 25 and 26 of the basic Regulation;

shall be reimbursed by the competent institutions to the institutions providing those benefits, on the basis of a fixed amount established for each calendar year. This fixed amount shall be as close as possible to actual expenditure.

Article 64 Calculation method of the monthly fixed amounts and the total fixed amount

1. For each creditor Member State, the monthly fixed amount per person (Fi) for a calendar year shall be determined by dividing the annual average cost per person (Yi), broken down by age group (i), by 12 and by applying a reduction (X) to the result in accordance with the following formula:

$$F_i = Y_i * 1/12 * (1-X)$$

Where:

— the index (i = 1, 2 and 3) represents the three age groups used for calculating the fixed amounts:

i = 1: persons aged under 20,
i = 2: persons aged from 20 to 64,
i = 3: persons aged 65 and over,

— Yi represents the annual average cost per person in age group i, as defined in paragraph 2,

— the coefficient X (0,20 or 0,15) represents the reduction as defined in paragraph 3,

2. The annual average cost per person (Yi) in age group i shall be obtained by dividing the annual expenditure on all benefits in kind provided by the institutions of the creditor Member State to all persons in the age group concerned subject to its legislation and residing within its territory by the average number of persons concerned in that age group in the calendar year in question. The calculation shall be based on the expenditure under the schemes referred to in Article 23 of the implementing Regulation.

3. The reduction to be applied to the monthly fixed amount shall, in principle, be equal to 20% (X = 0,20). It shall be equal to 15% (X = 0,15) for pensioners and members of their family where the competent Member State is not listed in Annex IV to the basic Regulation.

4. For each debtor Member State, the total fixed amount for a calendar year shall be the sum of the products obtained by multiplying, in each age group i, the determined monthly fixed amounts per person by the number of months completed by the persons concerned in the creditor Member State in that age group.

The number of months completed by the persons concerned in the creditor Member State shall be the sum of the calendar months in a calendar year during which the persons concerned were, because of their residence in the territory of the creditor Member State, eligible to receive benefits in kind in that territory at the expense of the debtor Member State. Those months shall be determined from an inventory kept for that purpose by the institution of the place of residence, based on documentary evidence of the entitlement of the beneficiaries supplied by the competent institution.

5. No later than 1 May 2015, the Administrative Commission shall present a specific report on the application of this Article and in particular on the reductions referred to in paragraph 3. On the basis of that report, the Administrative Commission may present a proposal containing any amendments which may prove necessary in order to ensure that the calculation of fixed amounts comes as close as possible to the actual expenditure incurred and the reductions referred to in paragraph 3 do not result in unbalanced payments or double payments for the Member States.

6. The Administrative Commission shall establish the methods for determining the elements for calculating the fixed amounts referred to in paragraphs 1 to 5.

7. Notwithstanding paragraphs 1 to 4, Member States may continue to apply Articles 94 and 95 of Regulation (EEC) No 574/72 for the calculation of the fixed amount until 1 May 2015, provided that the reduction set out in paragraph 3 is applied.

Article 65 Notification of annual average costs

1. The annual average cost per person in each age group for a specific year shall be notified to the Audit Board at the latest by the end of the second year following the year in question. If the notification is not made by this deadline, the annual average cost per person which the Administrative Commission has last determined for a previous year will be taken.

2. The annual average costs determined in accordance with paragraph 1 shall be published each year in the *Official Journal of the European Union*.

SECTION 3

COMMON PROVISIONS

Article 66 Procedure for reimbursement between institutions

1. The reimbursements between the Member States concerned shall be made as promptly as possible. Every institution concerned shall be obliged to reimburse claims before the deadlines mentioned in this Section, as soon as it is in a position to do so. A dispute concerning a particular claim shall not hinder the reimbursement of another claim or other claims.

2. The reimbursements between the institutions of the Member States, provided for in Articles 35 and 41 of the basic Regulation, shall be made via the liaison body. There may be a separate liaison body for reimbursements under Article 35 and Article 41 of the basic Regulation.

Article 67 Deadlines for the introduction and settlement of claims

1. Claims based on actual expenditure shall be introduced to the liaison body of the debtor Member State within 12 months of the end of the calendar half-year during which those claims were recorded in the accounts of the creditor institution.

2. Claims of fixed amounts for a calendar year shall be introduced to the liaison body of the debtor Member State within the 12-month period following the month during which the average costs for the year concerned were published in the *Official Journal of the European Union*. The inventories referred to Article 64(4) of the implementing Regulation shall be presented by the end of the year following the reference year.

3. In the case referred to in Article 6(5) second subparagraph of the implementing Regulation, the deadline set out in paragraphs 1 and 2 of this Article shall not start before the competent institution has been identified.

4. Claims introduced after the deadlines specified in paragraphs 1 and 2 shall not be considered.

5. The claims shall be paid to the liaison body of the creditor Member State referred to in Article 66 of the implementing Regulation by the debtor institution within 18 months of the end of the month during which they were introduced to the liaison body of the debtor Member State. This does not apply to the claims which the debtor institution has rejected for a relevant reason within that period.

6. Any disputes concerning a claim shall be settled, at the latest, within 36 months following the month in which the claim was introduced.

7. The Audit Board shall facilitate the final closing of accounts in cases where a settlement cannot be reached within the period set out in paragraph 6, and, upon a reasoned request by one of the parties, shall give its opinion on a dispute within six months following the month in which the matter was referred to it.

Article 68 Interest on late payments and down payments

1. From the end of the 18-month period set out in Article 67(5) of the implementing Regulation, interest can be charged by the creditor institution on outstanding claims, unless the debtor institution has made, within six months of the end of the month during which the claim was introduced, a down payment of at least 90% of the total claim introduced pursuant to Article 67(1) or (2) of the implementing Regulation. For those parts of the claim not covered by the down payment, interest may be charged only from the end of the 36-month period set out in Article 67(6) of the implementing Regulation.

2. The interest shall be calculated on the basis of the reference rate applied by the European Central Bank to its main refinancing operations. The reference rate applicable shall be that in force on the first day of the month on which the payment is due.

3. No liaison body shall be obliged to accept a down payment as provided for in paragraph 1. If however, a liaison body declines such an offer, the creditor institution shall no longer be entitled to charge interest on late payments related to the claims in question other than under the second sentence of paragraph 1.

Article 69 Statement of annual accounts

1. The Administrative Commission shall establish the claims situation for each calendar year in accordance with Article 72(*g*) of the basic Regulation, on the basis of the Audit Board's report. To this end, the liaison bodies shall notify the Audit Board, by the deadlines and according to the procedures laid down by the latter, of the amount of the claims introduced, settled or contested (creditor position) and the amount of claims received, settled or contested (debtor position).

2. The Administrative Commission may perform any appropriate checks on the statistical and accounting data used as the basis for drawing up the annual statement of claims provided for in paragraph 1 in order, in particular, to ensure that they comply with the rules laid down under this Title.

REIMBURSEMENT OF UNEMPLOYMENT BENEFITS PURSUANT TO ARTICLE 65 OF THE BASIC REGULATION

Article 70 Reimbursement of unemployment benefits

If there is no agreement in accordance with Article 65(8) of the basic Regulation, the institution of the place of residence shall request reimbursement of unemployment benefits pursuant to Article 65(6) and (7) of the basic Regulation from the institution of the Member State to whose legislation the beneficiary was last subject. The request shall be made within six months of the end of the calendar half-year during which the last payment of unemployment benefit, for which reimbursement is requested, was made. The request shall indicate the amount of benefit paid during the three or five month-period referred to in Article 65(6) and (7) of the basic Regulation, the period for which the benefits were paid and the identification data of the unemployed person. The claims shall be introduced and paid via the liaison bodies of the Member States concerned.

There is no requirement to consider requests introduced after the time-limit referred to in the first paragraph.

Articles 66(1) and 67(5) to (7) of the implementing Regulation shall apply *mutatis mutandis*.

From the end of the 18-month period referred to in Article 67(5) of the implementing Regulation, interest may be charged by the creditor institution on outstanding claims. The interest shall be calculated in accordance with Article 68(2) of the implementing Regulation.

The maximum amount of the reimbursement referred to in the third sentence of Article 65(6) of the basic Regulation is in each individual case the amount of the benefit to which a person concerned would be entitled according to the legislation of the Member State to which he was last subject if registered with the employment services of that Member State. However, in relations between the Member States listed in Annex 5 to the implementing Regulation, the competent institutions of one of those Member States to whose legislation the person concerned was last subject shall determine the maximum amount in each individual case on the basis of the average amount of unemployment benefits provided under the legislation of that Member State in the preceding calendar year.

CHAPTER III

RECOVERY OF BENEFITS PROVIDED BUT NOT DUE, RECOVERY OF PROVISIONAL PAYMENTS AND CONTRIBUTIONS, OFFSETTING AND ASSISTANCE WITH RECOVERY

SECTION 1

PRINCIPLES

Article 71 Common provisions

For the purposes of applying Article 84 of the basic Regulation and within the framework defined therein, the recovery of claims shall, wherever possible, be by way of offsetting either between the institutions of Member States concerned, or vis-à-vis the natural or legal person concerned in accordance with Articles 72 to 74 of the implementing Regulation. If it is not possible to recover all or any of the claim via this offsetting procedure, the remainder of the amount due shall be recovered in accordance with Articles 75 to 85 of the implementing Regulation.

SECTION 2

OFFSETTING

Article 72 Benefits received unduly

1. If the institution of a Member State has paid undue benefits to a person, that institution may, within the terms and limits laid down in the legislation it applies, request the institution of any other Member State responsible for paying benefits to the person concerned to deduct the undue amount from arrears or on-going payments owed to the person concerned regardless of the social security branch under which the benefit is paid. The institution of the latter Member State shall deduct the amount concerned subject to the conditions and limits applying to this kind of offsetting procedure in accordance with the legislation it applies in the same way as if it had made the overpayments itself, and shall transfer the amount deducted to the institution that has paid undue benefits.

2. By way of derogation from paragraph 1, if, when awarding or reviewing benefits in respect of invalidity benefits, old-age and survivors' pensions pursuant to Chapter 4 and 5 of Title III of the basic Regulation, the institution of a Member State has paid to a person benefits of undue sum, that institution may request the institution of any other Member State responsible for the payment of corresponding benefits to the person concerned to deduct the amount overpaid from the arrears

payable to the person concerned. After the latter institution has informed the institution that has paid an undue sum of these arrears, the institution which has paid the undue sum shall within two months communicate the amount of the undue sum. If the institution which is due to pay arrears receives that communication within the deadline it shall transfer the amount deducted to the institution which has paid undue sums. If the deadline expires, that institution shall without delay pay out the arrears to the person concerned.

3. If a person has received social welfare assistance in one Member State during a period in which he was entitled to benefits under the legislation of another Member State, the body which provided the assistance may, if it is legally entitled to reclaim the benefits due to the person concerned, request the institution of any other Member State responsible for paying benefits in favour of the person concerned to deduct the amount of assistance paid from the amounts which that Member State pays to the person concerned.

This provision shall apply *mutatis mutandis* to any family member of a person concerned who has received assistance in the territory of a Member State during a period in which the insured person was entitled to benefits under the legislation of another Member State in respect of that family member.

The institution of a Member State which has paid an undue amount of assistance shall send a statement of the amount due to the institution of the other Member State, which shall then deduct the amount, subject to the conditions and limits laid down for this kind of offsetting procedure in accordance with the legislation it applies, and transfer the amount without delay to the institution that has paid the undue amount.

Article 73 Provisionally paid benefits in cash or contributions

1. For the purposes of applying Article 6 of the implementing Regulation, at the latest three months after the applicable legislation has been determined or the institution responsible for paying the benefits has been identified, the institution which provisionally paid the cash benefits shall draw up a statement of the amount provisionally paid and shall send it to the institution identified as being competent.

The institution identified as being competent for paying the benefits shall deduct the amount due in respect of the provisional payment from the arrears of the corresponding benefits it owes to the person concerned and shall without delay transfer the amount deducted to the institution which provisionally paid the cash benefits.

If the amount of provisionally paid benefits exceeds the amount of arrears, or if arrears do not exist, the institution identified as being competent shall deduct this amount from ongoing payments subject to the conditions and limits applying to this kind of offsetting procedure under the legislation it applies, and without delay transfer the amount deducted to the institution which provisionally paid the cash benefits.

2. The institution which has provisionally received contributions from a legal and/or natural person shall not reimburse the amounts in question to the person who paid them until it has ascertained from the institution identified as being competent the sums due to it under Article 6(4) of the implementing Regulation.

Upon request of the institution identified as being competent, which shall be made at the latest three months after the applicable legislation has been determined, the institution that has provisionally received contributions shall transfer them to the institution identified as being competent for that period for the purpose of settling the situation concerning the contributions owed by the legal and/or natural person to it. The contributions transferred shall be retroactively deemed as having been paid to the institution identified as being competent.

If the amount of provisionally paid contributions exceeds the amount the legal and/or natural person owes to the institution identified as being competent, the institution which provisionally received contributions shall reimburse the amount in excess to the legal and/or natural person concerned.

Article 74 Costs related to offsetting

No costs are payable where the debt is recovered via the offsetting procedure provided for in Articles 72 and 73 of the implementing Regulation.

SECTION 3

RECOVERY

Article 75 Definitions and common provisions

1. For the purposes of this Section:

— "claim" means all claims relating to contributions or to benefits paid or provided unduly, including interest, fines, administrative penalties and all other charges and costs connected with the claim in accordance with the legislation of the Member State making the claim;

— "applicant party" means, in respect of each Member State, any institution which makes a request for information, notification or recovery concerning a claim as defined above,

— "requested party" means, in respect of each Member State, any institution to which a request for information, notification or recovery can be made,

2. Requests and any related communications between the Member States shall, in general, be addressed via designated institutions.
3. Practical implementation measures, including, among others, those related to Article 4 of the implementing Regulation and to setting a minimum threshold for the amounts for which a request for recovery can be made, shall be taken by the Administrative Commission.

Article 76 Requests for information

1. At the request of the applicant party, the requested party shall provide any information which would be useful to the applicant party in the recovery of its claim.
In order to obtain that information, the requested party shall make use of the powers provided for under the laws, regulations or administrative provisions applying to the recovery of similar claims arising in its own Member State.
2. The request for information shall indicate the name, last known address, and any other relevant information relating to the identification of the legal or natural person concerned to whom the information to be provided relates and the nature and amount of the claim in respect of which the request is made.
3. The requested party shall not be obliged to supply information:
(*a*) which it would not be able to obtain for the purpose of recovering similar claims arising in its own Member State;
(*b*) which would disclose any commercial, industrial or professional secrets; or
(*c*) the disclosure of which would be liable to prejudice the security of or be contrary to the public policy of the Member State.
4. The requested party shall inform the applicant party of the grounds for refusing a request for information.

Article 77 Notification

1. The requested party shall, at the request of the applicant party, and in accordance with the rules in force for the notification of similar instruments or decisions in its own Member State, notify the addressee of all instruments and decisions, including those of a judicial nature, which come from the Member State of the applicant party and which relate to a claim and/or to its recovery.
2. The request for notification shall indicate the name, address and any other relevant information relating to the identification of the addressee concerned to which the applicant party normally has access, the nature and the subject of the instrument or decision to be notified and, if necessary the name, address and any other relevant information relating to the identification of the debtor and the claim to which the instrument or decision relates, and any other useful information.
3. The requested party shall without delay inform the applicant party of the action taken on its request for notification and, particularly, of the date on which the decision or instrument was forwarded to the addressee.

Article 78 Request for recovery

1. The request for recovery of a claim, addressed by the applicant party to the requested party, shall be accompanied by an official or certified copy of the instrument permitting its enforcement, issued in the Member State of the applicant party and, if appropriate, by the original or a certified copy of other documents necessary for recovery.
2. The applicant party may only make a request for recovery if:
(*a*) the claim and/or the instrument permitting its enforcement are not contested in its own Member State, except in cases where the second subparagraph of Article 81(2) of the implementing Regulation is applied;
(*b*) it has, in its own Member State, applied appropriate recovery procedures available to it on the basis of the instrument referred to in paragraph 1, and the measures taken will not result in the payment in full of the claim;
(*c*) the period of limitation according to its own legislation has not expired.
3. The request for recovery shall indicate:
(*a*) the name, address and any other relevant information relating to the identification of the natural or legal person concerned and/or to the third party holding his or her assets;
(*b*) the name, address and any other relevant information relating to the identification of the applicant party;
(*c*) a reference to the instrument permitting its enforcement, issued in the Member State of the applicant party;
(*d*) the nature and amount of the claim, including the principal, the interest, fines, administrative penalties and all other charges and costs due indicated in the currencies of the Member States of the applicant and requested parties;
(*e*) the date of notification of the instrument to the addressee by the applicant party and/or by the requested party;
(*f*) the date from which and the period during which enforcement is possible under the laws in force in the Member State of the applicant party;
(*g*) any other relevant information.

4. The request for recovery shall also contain a declaration by the applicant party confirming that the conditions laid down in paragraph 2 have been fulfilled.
5. The applicant party shall forward to the requesting party any relevant information relating to the matter which gave rise to the request for recovery, as soon as this comes to its knowledge.

Article 79 Instrument permitting enforcement of the recovery

1. In accordance with Article 84(2) of the basic Regulation, the instrument permitting enforcement of the claim shall be directly recognised and treated automatically as an instrument permitting the enforcement of a claim of the Member State of the requested party.
2. Notwithstanding paragraph 1, the instrument permitting enforcement of the claim may, where appropriate and in accordance with the provisions in force in the Member State of the requested party, be accepted as, recognised as, supplemented with, or replaced by an instrument authorising enforcement in the territory of that Member State.
Within three months of the date of receipt of the request for recovery, Member States shall endeavour to complete the acceptance, recognition, supplementing or replacement, except in cases where the third sub-paragraph of this paragraph applies. Member States may not refuse to complete these actions where the instrument permitting enforcement is properly drawn up. The requested party shall inform the applicant party of the grounds for exceeding the three-month period.
If any of these actions should give rise to a dispute in connection with the claim and/or the instrument permitting enforcement issued by the applicant party, Article 81 of the implementing Regulation shall apply.

Article 80 Payment arrangements and deadlines

1. Claims shall be recovered in the currency of the Member State of the requested party. The entire amount of the claim that is recovered by the requested party shall be remitted by the requested party to the applicant party.
2. The requested party may, where the laws, regulations or administrative provisions in force in its own Member State so permit, and after consulting the applicant party, allow the debtor time to pay or authorise payment by instalment. Any interest charged by the requested party in respect of such extra time to pay shall also be remitted to the applicant party.
From the date on which the instrument permitting enforcement of the recovery of the claim has been directly recognised in accordance with Article 79(1) of the implementing Regulation, or accepted, recognised, supplemented or replaced in accordance with Article 79(2) of the implementing Regulation, interest shall be charged for late payment under the laws, regulations and administrative provisions in force in the Member State of the requested party and shall also be remitted to the applicant party.

Article 81 Contestation concerning the claim or the instrument permitting enforcement of its recovery and contestation concerning enforcement measures

1. If, in the course of the recovery procedure, the claim and/or the instrument permitting its enforcement issued in the Member State of the applicant party are contested by an interested party, the action shall be brought by this party before the appropriate authorities of the Member State of the applicant party, in accordance with the laws in force in that Member State. The applicant party shall without delay notify the requested party of this action. The interested party may also inform the requested party of the action.
2. As soon as the requested party has received the notification or information referred to in paragraph 1 either from the applicant party or from the interested party, it shall suspend the enforcement procedure pending the decision of the appropriate authority in the matter, unless the applicant party requests otherwise in accordance with the second sub-paragraph of this paragraph. Should the requested party deem it necessary, and without prejudice to Article 84 of the implementing Regulation, it may take precautionary measures to guarantee recovery insofar as the laws or regulations in force in its own Member State allow such action for similar claims.
Notwithstanding the first sub-paragraph, the applicant party may, in accordance with the laws, regulations and administrative practices in force in its own Member State, request the requested party to recover a contested claim, in so far as the relevant laws, regulations and administrative practices in force in the requested party's Member State allow such action. If the result of the contestation is subsequently favourable to the debtor, the applicant party shall be liable for the reimbursement of any sums recovered, together with any compensation due, in accordance with the legislation in force in the requested party's Member State.
3. Where the contestation concerns enforcement measures taken in the Member State of the requested party, the action shall be brought before the appropriate authority of that Member State in accordance with its laws and regulations.
4. Where the appropriate authority before which the action is brought in accordance with paragraph 1 is a judicial or administrative tribunal, the decision of that tribunal, insofar as it is favourable to the applicant party and permits recovery of the claim in the Member State of the

applicant party, shall constitute the "instrument permitting enforcement" within the meaning of Articles 78 and 79 of the implementing Regulation and the recovery of the claim shall proceed on the basis of that decision.

Article 82 Limits applying to assistance

1. The requested party shall not be obliged:
   (*a*) to grant the assistance provided for in Articles 78 to 81 of the implementing Regulation if recovery of the claim would, because of the situation of the debtor, create serious economic or social difficulties in the Member State of the requested party, insofar as the laws, regulations or administrative practices in force in the Member State of the requested party allow such action for similar national claims;
   (*b*) to grant the assistance provided for in Articles 76 to 81 of the implementing Regulation, if the initial request under Articles 76 to 78 of the implementing Regulation applies to claims more than five years old, dating from the moment the instrument permitting the recovery was established in accordance with the laws, regulations or administrative practices in force in the Member State of the applicant party at the date of the request. However, if the claim or instrument is contested, the time limit begins from the moment that the Member State of the applicant party establishes that the claim or the enforcement order permitting recovery may no longer be contested.
2. The requested party shall inform the applicant party of the grounds for refusing a request for assistance.

Article 83 Periods of limitation

1. Questions concerning periods of limitation shall be governed as follows:
   (*a*) by the laws in force in the Member State of the applicant party, insofar as they concern the claim and/or the instrument permitting its enforcement; and
   (*b*) by the laws in force in the Member State of the requested party, insofar as they concern enforcement measures in the requested Member State.

Periods of limitation according to the laws in force in the Member State of the requested party shall start from the date of direct recognition or from the date of acceptance, recognition, supplementing or replacement in accordance with Article 79 of the implementing Regulation.

2. Steps taken in the recovery of claims by the requested party in pursuance of a request for assistance, which, if they had been carried out by the applicant party, would have had the effect of suspending or interrupting the period of limitation according to the laws in force in the Member State of the applicant party, shall be deemed to have been taken in the latter State, in so far as that effect is concerned.

Article 84 Precautionary measures

Upon reasoned request by the applicant party, the requested party shall take precautionary measures to ensure recovery of a claim in so far as the laws and regulations in force in the Member State of the requested party so permit.

For the purposes of implementing the first paragraph, the provisions and procedures laid down in Articles 78, 79, 81 and 82 of the implementing Regulation shall apply *mutatis mutandis*.

Article 85 Costs related to recovery

1. The requested party shall recover from the natural or legal person concerned and retain any costs linked to recovery which it incurs, in accordance with the laws and regulations of the Member State of the requested party that apply to similar claims.
2. Mutual assistance afforded under this Section shall, as a rule, be free of charge. However, where recovery poses a specific problem or concerns a very large amount in costs, the applicant and the requested parties may agree on reimbursement arrangements specific to the cases in question.
3. The Member State of the applicant party shall remain liable to the Member State of the requested party for any costs and any losses incurred as a result of actions held to be unfounded, as far as either the substance of the claim or the validity of the instrument issued by the applicant party is concerned.

Article 86 Review clause

1. No later than the fourth full calendar year after the entry into force of the implementing Regulation, the Administrative Commission shall present a comparative report on the time limits set out in Article 67(2), (5) and (6) of the implementing Regulation.

On the basis of this report, the European Commission may, as appropriate, submit proposals to review these time limits with the aim of reducing them in a significant way.

2. No later than the date referred to in paragraph 1, the Administrative Commission shall also assess the rules for conversion of periods set out in Article 13 with a view to simplifying those rules, if possible.
3. No later than 1 May 2015, the Administrative Commission shall present a report specifically assessing the application of Chapters I and III of Title IV of the implementing Regulation, in particular with regard to the procedures and time limits referred to in Article 67(2), (5) and (6) of the implementing Regulation and to the recovery procedures referred to in Articles 75 to 85 of the implementing Regulation.

In the light of this report, the European Commission may, if necessary, submit appropriate proposals to make these procedures more efficient and balanced.

TITLE V

MISCELLANEOUS, TRANSITIONAL AND FINAL PROVISIONS

Article 87 Medical examination and administrative checks

1. Without prejudice to other provisions, where a recipient or a claimant of benefits, or a member of his family, is staying or residing within the territory of a Member State other than that in which the debtor institution is located, the medical examination shall be carried out, at the request of that institution, by the institution of the beneficiary's place of stay or residence in accordance with the procedures laid down by the legislation applied by that institution.

The debtor institution shall inform the institution of the place of stay or residence of any special requirements, if necessary, to be followed and points to be covered by the medical examination.

2. The institution of the place of stay or residence shall forward a report to the debtor institution that requested the medical examination. This institution shall be bound by the findings of the institution of the place of stay or residence.

The debtor institution shall reserve the right to have the beneficiary examined by a doctor of its choice. However, the beneficiary may be asked to return to the Member State of the debtor institution only if he or she is able to make the journey without prejudice to his health and the cost of travel and accommodation is paid for by the debtor institution.

3. Where a recipient or a claimant of benefits, or a member of his family, is staying or residing in the territory of a Member State other than that in which the debtor institution is located, the administrative check shall, at the request of the debtor institution, be performed by the institution of the beneficiary's place of stay or residence.

Paragraph 2 shall also apply in this case.

4. Paragraphs 2 and 3 shall also apply in determining or checking the state of dependence of a recipient or a claimant of the long-term care benefits mentioned in Article 34 of the basic Regulation.

5. The competent authorities or competent institutions of two or more Member States may agree specific provisions and procedures to improve fully or partly the labour-market readiness of claimants and recipients and their participation in any schemes or programmes available in the Member State of stay or residence for that purpose.

6. As an exception to the principle of free-of-charge mutual administrative cooperation in Article 76(2) of the basic Regulation, the effective amount of the expenses of the checks referred to in paragraphs 1 to 5 shall be refunded to the institution which was requested to carry them out by the debtor institution which requested them.

Article 88 Notifications

1. The Member States shall notify the European Commission of the details of the bodies defined in Article 1(m), (q) and (r) of the basic Regulation and Article 1(2)(*a*) and (*b*) of the implementing Regulation, and of the institutions designated in accordance with the implementing Regulation.

2. The bodies specified in paragraph 1 shall be provided with an electronic identity in the form of an identification code and electronic address.

3. The Administrative Commission shall establish the structure, content and detailed arrangements, including the common format and model, for notification of the details specified in paragraph 1.

4. Annex 4 to the implementing Regulation gives details of the public database containing the information specified in paragraph 1. The database shall be established and managed by the European Commission. The Member States shall, however, be responsible for the input of their own national contact information into this database. Moreover, the Member States shall ensure the accuracy of the input of the national contact information required under paragraph 1.

5. The Member States shall be responsible for keeping the information specified in paragraph 1 up to date.

Article 89 Information

1. The Administrative Commission shall prepare the information needed to ensure that the parties concerned are aware of their rights and the administrative formalities required in order to assert them. This information shall, where possible, be disseminated electronically via publication online on sites accessible to the public. The Administrative Commission shall ensure that the information is regularly updated and monitor the quality of services provided to customers.

2. The Advisory Committee referred to in Article 75 of the basic Regulation may issue opinions and recommendations on improving the information and its dissemination.

3. The competent authorities shall ensure that their institutions are aware of and apply all the Community provisions, legislative or otherwise, including the decisions of the Administrative Commission, in the areas covered by and within the terms of the basic Regulation and the implementing Regulation.

Article 90 Currency conversion

For the purposes of applying the basic Regulation and the implementing Regulation, the exchange rate between two currencies shall be the reference rate published by the European Central Bank. The date to be taken into account for determining the exchange rate shall be fixed by the Administrative Commission.

Article 91 Statistics

The competent authorities shall compile statistics on the application of the basic Regulation and the implementing Regulation and forward them to the secretariat of the Administrative Commission. Those data shall be collected and organised according to the plan and method defined by the Administrative Commission. The European Commission shall be responsible for disseminating the information.

Article 92 Amendment of the Annexes

Annexes 1, 2, 3, 4 and 5 to the implementing Regulation and Annexes VI, VII, VIII and IX to the basic Regulation may be amended by Commission Regulation at the request of the Administrative Commission.

Article 93 Transitional provisions

Article 87 of the basic Regulation shall apply to the situations covered by the implementing Regulation.

Article 94 Transitional provisions relating to pensions

1. Where the contingency arises before the date of entry into force of the implementing Regulation in the territory of the Member State concerned and the claim for pension has not been awarded before that date, such claim shall give rise to a double award, in as much as benefits must be granted, pursuant to such contingency, for a period prior to that date:

(*a*) for the period prior to the date of entry into force of the implementing Regulation in the territory of the Member State concerned, in accordance with Regulation (EEC) No 1408/71, or with agreements in force between the Member States concerned;

(*b*) for the period commencing on the date of entry into force of the implementing Regulation in the territory of the Member State concerned, in accordance with the basic Regulation.

However, if the amount calculated pursuant to the provisions referred to under point (*a*) is greater than that calculated pursuant to the provisions referred to under point (*b*), the person concerned shall continue to be entitled to the amount calculated pursuant to the provisions referred to under point (*a*).

2. A claim for invalidity, old age or survivors' benefits submitted to an institution of a Member State from the date of entry into force of the implementing Regulation in the territory of the Member State concerned shall automatically necessitate the reassessment of the benefits which have been awarded for the same contingency prior to that date by the institution or institutions of one or more Member States, in accordance with the basic Regulation; such reassessment may not give rise to any reduction in the amount of the benefit awarded.

Article 95 Transitional period for electronic data exchanges

1. Each Member State may benefit from a transitional period for exchanging data by electronic means as provided for by Article 4(2) of the implementing Regulation.

These transitional periods shall not exceed 24 months from the date of entry into force of the implementing Regulation.

However, if the delivery of the necessary Community infrastructure (Electronic Exchange of Social Security information — EESSI) is significantly delayed with regard to the entry into force of the implementing Regulation, the Administrative Commission may agree on any appropriate extension of these periods.

2. The practical arrangements for any necessary transitional periods referred to in paragraph 1 shall be laid down by the Administrative Commission with a view to ensuring the necessary data exchange for the application of the basic Regulation and the implementing Regulation.

Article 96 Repeal

1. Regulation (EEC) No 574/72 is repealed with effect from 1 May 2010.

However, Regulation (EEC) No 574/72 shall remain in force and continue to have legal effect for the purposes of:

(*a*) Council Regulation (EC) No 859/2003 of 14 May 2003 extending the provisions of Regulation (EEC) No 1408/71 and Regulation (EEC) No 574/72 to nationals of third countries who are not already covered by those provisions solely on the grounds of their nationality[1], until such time as that Regulation is repealed or amended;

(*b*) Council Regulation (EEC) No 1661/85 of 13 June 1985 laying down the technical adaptations to the Community rules on social security for migrant workers with regard to Greenland [2], until such time as that Regulation is repealed or amended;

(*c*) the Agreement on the European Economic Area [3], the Agreement between the European Community and its Member States, of the one part, and the Swiss Confederation, of the other, on the free movement of persons [4] and other agreements containing a reference to Regulation (EEC) No 574/72, until such time as those agreements are amended on the basis of the implementing Regulation.

2. In Council Directive 98/49/EC of 29 June 1998 on safeguarding the supplementary pension rights of employed and self-employed persons moving within the Community [5], and more generally in all other Community acts, the references to Regulation (EEC) No 574/72 shall be understood as referring to the implementing Regulation.

[1] OJ L 124, 20.5.2003, p. 1.
[2] OJ L 160, 20.6.1985, p. 7.
[3] OJ L 1, 3.1.1994, p. 1.
[4] OJ L 114, 30.4.2002, p. 6.
[5] OJ L 209, 25.7.1998, p. 46.

Article 97 Publication and entry into force

This Regulation shall be published in the *Official Journal of the European Union*. It shall enter into force on 1 May 2010.

This Regulation shall be binding in its entirety and directly applicable in all Member States.

Done at Strasbourg, ...16 September 2009.

ANNEX 1

IMPLEMENTING PROVISIONS FOR BILATERAL AGREEMENTS REMAINING IN FORCE AND NEW BILATERAL IMPLEMENTING AGREEMENTS

(referred to in Article 8(1) and Article 9(2) of the implementing Regulation)

BELGIUM — DENMARK

The Exchange of Letters of 8 May 2006 and 21 June 2006 on the Agreement of reimbursement with the actual amount of the benefit provided to members of the family of an employed or self-employed person insured in Belgium, where the family member resides in Denmark and to pensioners and/or members of their family insured in Belgium but residing in Denmark

BELGIUM — GERMANY

The Agreement of 29 January 1969 on the collection and recovery of social security contributions

BELGIUM — IRELAND

. . .

BELGIUM — SPAIN

The Agreement of 25 May 1999 on the reimbursement of benefits in kind according to the provisions of Regulations (EEC) No 1408/71 and No 574/72

BELGIUM — FRANCE

(*a*) The Agreement of 4 July 1984 relating to medical examinations of frontier workers resident in one country and working in another

(*b*) The Agreement of 14 May 1976 on the waiving of reimbursement of the costs of administrative checks and medical examinations, adopted pursuant to Article 105(2) of Regulation (EEC) No 574/72

(*c*) The Agreement of 3 October 1977 implementing Article 92 of Regulation (EEC) No 1408/71 (recovery of social security contributions)

(*d*) The Agreement of 29 June 1979 concerning the reciprocal waiving of reimbursement provided for in Article 70(3) of Regulation (EEC) No 1408/71 (costs of unemployment benefit)

(*e*) The Administrative Arrangement of 6 March 1979 on the procedures for the implementation of the Additional Convention of 12 October 1978 on social security between Belgium and France in respect of its provisions relating to self-employed persons

(*f*) The Exchange of Letters of 21 November 1994 and 8 February 1995 concerning the procedures for the settlement of reciprocal claims pursuant to Articles 93, 94, 95 and 96 of Regulation (EEC) No 574/72

BELGIUM — ITALY

(*a*) The Agreement of 12 January 1974 implementing Article 105(2) of Regulation (EEC) No 574/72

(*b*) The Agreement of 31 October 1979 implementing Article 18(9) of Regulation (EEC) No 574/72

(*c*) The Exchange of Letters of 10 December 1991 and 10 February 1992 concerning the reimbursement of reciprocal claims under Article 93 of Regulation (EEC) No 574/72

(*d*) The Agreement of 21.11.2003 on the terms for settling reciprocal claims under Articles 94 and 95 of Council Regulation (EEC) No 574/72

BELGIUM — LUXEMBOURG

(*a*) The Agreement of 28 January 1961 on the recovery of social security contributions

(*b*) The Agreement of 16 April 1976 on the waiving of reimbursement of the costs of administrative checks and medical examinations, as provided for in Article 105(2) of Regulation (EEC) No 574/72

BELGIUM — NETHERLANDS

(*a*) . . .

(*b*) The Agreement of 13 March 2006 on health care insurance

(*c*) The Agreement of 12 August 1982 on sickness, maternity and invalidity insurance

BELGIUM — UNITED KINGDOM

(*a*) The Exchange of Letters of 4 May and 14 June 1976 regarding Article 105(2) of Regulation (EEC) No 574/72 (waiving of reimbursement of the costs of administrative checks and medical examinations)

(*b*) The Exchange of Letters of 18 January and 14 March 1977 regarding Article 36(3) of Regulation (EEC) No 1408/71 (arrangement for reimbursement or waiving of reimbursement of the costs of benefits in kind provided under the terms of Chapter 1 of Title III of Regulation (EEC) No 1408/71) as amended by the Exchange of Letters of 4 May and 23 July 1982 (agreement for reimbursement of costs incurred under Article 22(1)(*a*) of Regulation (EEC) No 1408/71)

BULGARIA — CZECH REPUBLIC

Article 29(1) and (3) of the Agreement of 25 November 1998 and Article 5(4) of the Administrative Arrangement of 30 November 1999 on the waiving of reimbursement of the costs of administrative checks and medical examinations

BULGARIA — GERMANY

Articles 8 to 9 of the Administrative Agreement on implementing the Convention on social security of 17 December 1997 in the pension field

CZECH REPUBLIC — SLOVAKIA

Articles 15 and 16 of the Administrative Arrangement of 8 January 1993 concerning the specification of a seat of the employer and the place of residence for the purposes of application of Article 20 of the Convention of 29 October 1992 on social security

DENMARK — IRELAND

The Exchange of Letters of 22 December 1980 and 11 February 1981 on the reciprocal waiving of reimbursement of the costs of benefits in kind granted under insurance for sickness, maternity, accidents at work and occupational diseases, and of unemployment benefits and of the costs of administrative checks and medical examinations (Articles 36(3), 63(3) of Regulation (EEC) No 1408/71 and Article 105(2) of Regulation (EEC) No 574/72)

DENMARK — GREECE

DENMARK — SPAIN

Agreement of 11 December 2006 of advance payment, time-limits and reimbursement with the actual amount of the benefit provided to members of the family of an employed or self-employed person insured in Spain, where the family member resides in Denmark and to pensioners and/or members of their family insured in Spain but residing in Denmark

DENMARK — FRANCE

. . . [1]

DENMARK — ITALY

[2]

DENMARK — LUXEMBOURG

. . .

DENMARK — NETHERLANDS

. . . [1]

DENMARK — PORTUGAL

The Agreement of 17 April 1998 on the partial waiving of reimbursement of costs of benefits in kind under insurance for sickness, maternity, accidents at work and occupational diseases and administrative checks and medical examinations

DENMARK — FINLAND

Article 15 of the Nordic Convention on Social Security of 18 August 2003: Agreement on the reciprocal waiver of refund pursuant to Articles 36, 63 and 70 of Regulation (EEC) No 1408/71 (cost of benefits in kind in respect of sickness and maternity, accidents at work and occupational diseases, and unemployment benefits) and Article 105 of Regulation (EEC) No 574/72 (costs of administrative checks and medical examinations)

DENMARK — SWEDEN

Article 15 of the Nordic Convention on Social Security of 18 August 2003: Agreement on the reciprocal waiver of refund pursuant to Articles 36, 63 and 70 of Regulation (EEC) No 1408/71 (cost of benefits in kind in respect of sickness and maternity, accidents at work and occupational diseases, and unemployment benefits) and Article 105 of Regulation (EEC) No 574/72 (costs of administrative checks and medical examinations)

DENMARK — UNITED KINGDOM

The Exchange of Letters of 30 March and 19 April 1977 as modified by an Exchange of Letters of 8 November 1989 and of 10 January 1990 on agreement of waiving of reimbursement of the costs of benefits in kind and administrative checks and medical examinations

GERMANY — FRANCE

The Agreement of 26 May 1981 implementing Article 92 of Regulation (EEC) No 1408/71 (collection and recovery of social security contributions)

GERMANY — ITALY

The Agreement of 3 April 2000 on the collection and recovery of social security contributions

GERMANY — LUXEMBOURG

(*a*) The Agreement of 14 October 1975 on the waiving of reimbursement of the costs of administrative checks and medical examinations, adopted pursuant to Article 105(2) of Regulation (EEC) No 574/72

(*b*) The Agreement of 14 October 1975 on the collection and recovery of social security contributions

(*c*) The Agreement of 25 January 1990 relating to the application of Articles 20 and 22(1)(*b*) and (*c*) of Regulation (EEC) No 1408/71

GERMANY — NETHERLANDS

. . .

GERMANY — AUSTRIA

Section II, Number 1, and section III of the Agreement of 2 August 1979 on the implementation of the Convention on unemployment insurance of 19 July 1978 shall continue to apply to persons who have exercised an activity as a frontier worker on or before 1 January 2005 who become unemployed before 1 January 2011

GERMANY — POLAND

The Agreement of 11 January 1977 on the implementation of the Convention of 9 October 1975 on old-age pensions and benefits for accidents at work

ESTONIA — UNITED KINGDOM

The Arrangement finalised on 29 March 2006 between the Competent Authorities of the Republic of Estonia and of the United Kingdom under Articles 36(3) and 63(3) of Regulation (EEC) No 1408/71 establishing other methods of reimbursement of the costs of benefits in kind provided under this Regulation by both countries with effect from 1 May 2004

IRELAND — FRANCE

The Exchange of Letters of 30 July 1980 and 26 September 1980 concerning Articles 36(3) and 63(3) of Regulation (EEC) No 1408/71 (reciprocal waiving of reimbursement of the costs of benefits in kind) and Article 105(2) of Regulation (EEC) No 574/72 (reciprocal waiving of reimbursement of the costs of administrative checks and medical examinations)

IRELAND — LUXEMBOURG

The Exchange of Letters of 26 September 1975 and 5 August 1976 concerning Articles 36(3) and 63(3) of Regulation (EEC) No 1408/71and Article 105(2) of Regulation (EEC) No 574/72 (waiving of reimbursement of the costs of benefits in kind provided pursuant to Chapter 1 or 4 of Title III of Regulation (EEC) No 1408/71, and of the costs of administrative checks and medical examinations referred to in Article 105 of Regulation (EEC) No 574/72)

IRELAND — NETHERLANDS

The Exchange of Letters of 22 April and 27 July 1987 concerning Article 70(3) of Regulation (EEC) No 1408/71 (waiving of costs of reimbursement in respect of benefits awarded in application of Article 69 of Regulation (EEC) No 1408/71) and Article 105(2) of Regulation (EEC) No 574/72 (waiving of the reimbursement of the costs of administrative checks and medical examinations referred to in Article 105 of Regulation (EEC) No 574/72)

IRELAND — SWEDEN

The Agreement of 8 November 2000 on the waiving of reimbursement of the costs of benefits in kind of sickness, maternity, accidents at work and occupational diseases, and the costs of administrative and medical controls

IRELAND — UNITED KINGDOM

The Exchange of Letters of 9 July 1975 regarding Articles 36(3) and 63(3) of Regulation (EEC) No 1408/71 (arrangement for reimbursement or waiving of reimbursement of the costs of benefits in kind provided under the terms of Chapter 1 or 4 of Title III of Regulation (EEC) No 1408/71) and Article 105(2) of Regulation (EEC) No 574/72 (waiving of reimbursement of the costs of administrative checks and medical examinations)

GREECE — NETHERLANDS

. . .[1]

SPAIN — FRANCE

The Agreement of 17 May 2005 establishing the specific arrangements for the management and settlement of reciprocal claims in respect of health care benefits pursuant to Regulations (EEC) No 1408/71 and (EEC) No 574/72

SPAIN — ITALY

The Agreement on a new procedure for the improvement and simplification of reimbursements of costs for health care of 21 November 1997 concerning Article 36(3) of Regulation (EEC) No 1408/71 (reimbursement of sickness and maternity benefits in kind) and Articles 93, 94, 95, 100 and 102(5) of Regulation (EEC) No 574/72 (procedures for the refund and sickness and maternity insurance benefits and late claims)

SPAIN — NETHERLANDS

. . .[1]

SPAIN — PORTUGAL

(*a*) . . .

(*b*) The Agreement of 2 October 2002 laying down detailed arrangements for the management and settlement of reciprocal claims for health care with a view to facilitating and accelerating the settlement of these claims

SPAIN — SWEDEN

The Agreement of 1 December 2004 on the reimbursement of the costs of benefits in kind provided under Regulations (EEC) No 1408/71 and (EEC) No 574/72

SPAIN — UNITED KINGDOM

The Agreement of 18 June 1999 on the reimbursement of costs for benefits in kind granted pursuant to the provisions of Regulations (EEC) No 1408/71 and (EEC) No 574/72

FRANCE — ITALY

(*a*) The Exchange of Letters of 14 May and 2 August 1991 concerning the terms for settling reciprocal claims under Article 93 of Regulation (EEC) No 574/72

(*b*) The supplementary Exchange of Letters of 22 March and 15 April 1994 concerning the procedures for the settlement of reciprocal debts under the terms of Articles 93, 94, 95 and 96 of Regulation (EEC) No 574/72

(*c*) The Exchange of Letters of 2 April 1997 and 20 October 1998 modifying the Exchange of Letters mentioned under points (a) and (b) concerning the procedures for the settlement of reciprocal debts under the terms of Articles 93, 94, 95 and 96 of Regulation (EEC) No 574/72

(*d*) The Agreement of 28 June 2000 waiving reimbursement of the costs referred to in Article 105(1) of Regulation (EEC) No 574/72 for administrative checks and medical examinations requested under Article 51 of the abovementioned Regulation

[FRANCE — LUXEMBOURG

[(*a*) The Agreement of 2 July 1976 on the waiving of reimbursement of the costs of administrative checks and medical examinations provided for in Article 105(2) of Council Regulation (EEC) No 574/72 of 21 March 1972][1]

[(*b*) The Exchange of Letters of 17 July and 20 September 1995 concerning the terms for settling reciprocal claims under Articles 93, 95 and 96 of Regulation (EEC) No 574/72 and the Exchange of Letters dated 10 July and 30 August 2013][2]

FRANCE — NETHERLANDS

[(*a*) The Agreement of 28 April 1997 on the waiving of reimbursement of the costs of administrative checks and medical examinations pursuant to Article 105 of Regulation (EEC) No 574/72][1]

(*b*) . . .[2]

(*c*) . . .[2]

FRANCE — PORTUGAL

The Agreement of 28 April 1999 laying down special detailed rules governing the administration and settlement of reciprocal claims for medical treatment pursuant to Regulations (EEC) No 1408/71 and EEC No 574/72

FRANCE — UNITED KINGDOM

(*a*) The Exchange of Letters of 25 March and 28 April 1997 regarding Article 105(2) of Regulation (EEC) No 574/72 (waiving of reimbursement of the costs of administrative checks and medical examinations)

(*b*) The Agreement of 8 December 1998 on the specific methods of determining the amounts to be reimbursed for benefits in kind pursuant to Regulations (EEC) No 1408/71 and (EEC) No 574/72

ITALY — LUXEMBOURG

Article 4(5) and (6) of the Administrative Arrangement of 19 January 1955 on the implementing provisions of the General Convention on Social Security (sickness insurance for agricultural workers)

NIC

ITALY — NETHERLANDS

. . . [1]

ITALY — UNITED KINGDOM

The Arrangement signed on 15 December 2005 between the Competent Authorities of the Italian Republic and of the United Kingdom under Articles 36(3) and 63(3) of Regulation (EEC) No 1408/71 establishing other methods of reimbursement of the costs of benefits in kind provided under this Regulation by both countries with effect from 1 January 2005

LUXEMBOURG — NETHERLANDS

The Agreement of 1 November 1976 on the waiving of reimbursement of the costs of administrative checks and medical examinations adopted pursuant to Article 105(2) of Regulation (EEC) No 574/72

LUXEMBOURG — SWEDEN

The Arrangement of 27 November 1996 on the reimbursement of expenditure in the field of social security

LUXEMBOURG — UNITED KINGDOM

The Exchange of Letters of 18 December 1975 and 20 January 1976 regarding Article 105(2) of Regulation (EEC) No 574/72 (waiving of reimbursement of the costs entailed in administrative checks and medical examinations referred to in Article 105 of Regulation (EEC) No 574/72)

HUNGARY — UNITED KINGDOM

The Arrangement finalised on 1 November 2005 between the Competent Authorities of the Republic of Hungary and of the United Kingdom under Articles 35(3) and 41(2) of Regulation (EEC) No 883/2004 establishing other methods of reimbursement of the costs of benefits in kind provided under that Regulation by both countries with effect from 1 May 2004

MALTA — UNITED KINGDOM

The Arrangement finalised on 17 January 2007 between the Competent Authorities of Malta and of the United Kingdom under Articles 35(3) and 41(2) of Regulation (EEC) No 883/2004 establishing other methods of reimbursement of the costs of benefits in kind provided under that Regulation by both countries with effect from 1 May 2004

NETHERLANDS — PORTUGAL

. . .

NETHERLANDS — UNITED KINGDOM

[(*a*) The second sentence of Article 3 of the Administrative Arrangement of 12 June 1956 on the implementation of the Convention of 11 August 1954][1]

(*b*) . . . [1]

PORTUGAL — UNITED KINGDOM

The Arrangement of 8 June 2004 establishing other methods of reimbursement of the costs of benefits in kind provided by both countries with effect from 1 January 2003

FINLAND — SWEDEN

Article 15 of the Nordic Convention on Social Security of 18 August 2003: Agreement on the reciprocal waiver of refund pursuant to Articles 36, 63 and 70 of Regulation (EEC) No 1408/71 (cost of benefits in kind in respect of sickness and maternity, accidents at work and occupational diseases, and unemployment benefits) and Article 105 of Regulation (EEC) No 574/72 (costs of administrative checks and medical examinations)

FINLAND — UNITED KINGDOM

The Exchange of Letters 1 and 20 June 1995 concerning Articles 36(3) and 63(3) of Regulation (EEC) No 1408/71 (reimbursement or waiving of reimbursement of the cost of benefits in kind) and Article 105(2) of Regulation (EEC) 574/72 (waiving of reimbursement of the cost of administrative checks and medical examinations)

SWEDEN — UNITED KINGDOM

The Arrangement of 15 April 1997 concerning Article 36(3) and Article 63(3) of Regulation (EEC) No 1408/71 (reimbursement or waiving of reimbursement of the cost of benefits in kind) and Article 105(2) of Regulation (EEC) No 574/72 (waiving of refunds of the costs of administrative checks and medical examinations)

Amendments—[1] Sections "DENMARK — FRANCE", "DENMARK — NETHERLANDS", "GREECE — NETHERLANDS", "SPAIN — NETHERLANDS", "ITALY — NETHERLANDS" repealed, in section "FRANCE — LUXEMBOURG" point (a) substituted, in section "FRANCE — NETHERLANDS" point (a) inserted and points (b), (c) repealed, and in section "NETHERLANDS — UNITED KINGDOM" point (a) substituted and point (b) repealed, by Commission Regulation 1372/2013/EU art 2(1) with effect from 1 January 2014 (OJ L 346, 20.12.2013, p 27).

[2] Section "DENMARK — ITALY" repealed, and in section "FRANCE — LUXEMBOURG", point (b) substituted, by Commission Regulation 1368/2014/EU art 1 with effect from 1 January 2015 (OJ L 366, 20.12.2014, p 15).

ANNEX 2

SPECIAL SCHEMES FOR CIVIL SERVANTS

(referred to in Articles 31 and 41 of the implementing Regulation)

A. Special schemes for civil servants which are not covered by Title III, Chapter 1 of Regulation (EC) No 883/2004 concerning benefits in kind

Germany

Special sickness scheme for civil servants

B. Special schemes for civil servants which are not covered by Title III, Chapter 1 of Regulation (EC) No 883/2004, with the exception of Article 19, paragraph 1 of Article 27 and Article 35, concerning benefits in kind

Spain

Special scheme of social security for civil servants

Special scheme of social security for the armed forces

Special scheme of social security for the court officials and administrative staff

C. Special schemes for civil servants which are not covered by Title III, Chapter 2 of Regulation (EC) No 883/2004 concerning benefits in kind

Germany

Special accident scheme for civil servants

ANNEX 3

MEMBER STATES CLAIMING THE REIMBURSEMENT OF THE COST OF BENEFITS IN KIND ON THE BASIS OF FIXED AMOUNTS

(referred to in Article 63(1) of the implementing Regulation)

IRELAND

SPAIN

[CYPRUS]

. . .

PORTUGAL

. . .

SWEDEN

UNITED KINGDOM

Amendments—Entries for "The Netherlands" and "Finland" repealed by Commission Regulation 2017/492/EU Art 2(2) with effect from 1 January 2018 (OJ L 76, 22.3.2017, p 13).

ANNEX 4

DETAILS OF THE DATABASE REFERRED TO IN ARTICLE 88(4) OF THE IMPLEMENTING REGULATION

1. *Content of the database*

An electronic directory (URL) of the bodies concerned shall indicate:

(*a*) the names of the bodies in the official language(s) of the Member State as well as in English

(*b*) the identification code and the EESSI electronic addressing

(*c*) their function in respect of the definitions in Article 1(*m*), (*q*) and (*r*) of the basic Regulation and Article 1(*a*) and (*b*) of the implementing Regulation

(*d*) their competence as regards the different risks, types of benefits, schemes and geographical coverage

(*e*) which part of the basic Regulation the bodies are applying

(*f*) the following contact details: postal address, telephone, telefax, e-mail address and the relevant URL address

(*g*) any other information necessary for the application of the basic Regulation or the implementing Regulation.

2. *Administration of the database*

(*a*) The electronic directory is hosted in EESSI at the level of the European Commission.

(*b*) Member States are responsible for collecting and checking the necessary information of bodies and for the timely submission to the European Commission of any entry or change of the entries falling under their responsibility.

3. *Access*

Information used for operational and administrative purposes is not accessible to the public.

4. *Security*

All modifications to the database (insert, update, delete) shall be logged. Prior to accessing the Directory for the purposes of modifying entries, users shall be identified and authenticated. Prior to any attempt of a modification of an entry, the user's authorisation to perform this action will be checked. Any unauthorised action shall be rejected and logged.

5. *Language Regime*

The general language regime of the database is English. The name of bodies and their contact details should also be inserted in the official language(s) of the Member State.

ANNEX 5

MEMBER STATES DETERMINING, ON A RECIPROCAL BASIS, THE MAXIMUM AMOUNT OF REIMBURSEMENT REFERRED TO IN THE THIRD SENTENCE OF ARTICLE 65(6) OF THE BASIC REGULATION, ON THE BASIS OF THE AVERAGE AMOUNT OF UNEMPLOYMENT BENEFITS PROVIDED UNDER THEIR LEGISLATIONS IN THE PRECEDING CALENDAR YEAR

(referred to in Article 70 of the implementing Regulation)

BELGIUM
CZECH REPUBLIC
[DENMARK]
GERMANY
[NETHERLANDS][1]
AUSTRIA
SLOVAKIA
FINLAND

Amendments—[1] Section "NETHERLANDS" inserted by Commission Regulation 1372/2013/EU art 2(2) with effect from 1 January 2014 (OJ L 346, 20.12.2013, p 27).

Press Releases etc

NIC

Contents

List of press releases

Press Releases

INTEREST FOR NATIONAL INSURANCE CONTRIBUTIONS ALIGNED WITH RATES FOR TAX

31 January 1997

Interest rates for late payments and refunds of Class 1, Class 1A and Class 4 NICs are to change from the end of January 1997.

Inland Revenue regulations will change the way interest rates are calculated for income tax and capital gains tax from 31 January. The change will also apply to NICs.

From 31 January 1997, the rate of interest on late paid NICs will move closer to the average rate for borrowing and the rate paid on delayed refunds of NICs will move closer to the average rate for deposits.

The effect of the change will be that—

- the rate of interest charged on late payments of NICs will rise to 8.5% from 6.25%;
- the rate of interest paid in relation to overpaid NICs which are refunded will fall to 4.0% from 6.25%.

NOTES

1 The procedure and formulae for calculating interest rates for Revenue purposes are set out in FA 1989 s 178 and SI 1989/1297 entitled The Taxes (Interest Rate) Regulations 1989. Social Security Contributions and Benefits Act 1992 Sch 1 para 6(3) ties the rates of interest for the purposes of Class 1 and Class 1A NICs to the rate prescribed under FA 1989 s 178. This means that whatever rate is in force for income tax purposes applies also to Class 1 and Class 1A NICs.

2 Social Security Contributions and Benefits Act 1992 s 16 provides for all provisions of the Income Tax Acts to apply to Class 4 NICs and Sch 2 para 6(1) to the same Act specifically extends the Revenue's interest provisions to Class 4. Revenue interest rates are therefore relevant also for Class 4 NICs purposes.

3 The present method of calculating interest rates results in interest being charged at the same rate on—

- late paid NICs; and
- refunds of overpaid NICs.

The new method of calculation moves the rate of interest charged on late paid NICs nearer the average rate for borrowing, and the rate paid on delayed refunds of NICs nearer to the average rate of return on deposits. For the first time, therefore, the rates of interest applicable to late paid NICs and refunded NICs will be different.

4 On current bank base rates the rate chargeable on overdue sums will, with effect from 31 January 1997, rise to 8.5%. The rate payable in connection with refunds of overpaid NICs will fall to 4.0%.

THE CONTRIBUTIONS AGENCY—REVISED GUIDANCE TO EMPLOYERS ON PAYMENT INTO AND OUT OF FUNDED UNAPPROVED RETIREMENT BENEFIT SCHEMES (FURBS)

17 November 1997

In the light of legal advice, the Contributions Agency has revised its guidance on the NICs position of payments into Funded Unapproved Retirement Benefit Schemes (FURBS). The Agency now believes that most payments into FURBS being caught under legislation are earnings for national insurance purposes.

New guidance from the Contributions Agency accompanies this press release. In view of the Contributions Agency's existing guidance the Agency will only enforce arrears of NICs in respect of those FURBS clearly not providing a genuine pension.

The Government intends to make sure that FURBS cannot be used to avoid the employers' NICs and proposes to introduce further legislation to reinforce current regulations.

The Government has tabled an amendment to the Social Security Bill to enable it to introduce regulations which will provide for better apportionment of payments made to or for the benefit of two or more earners. A further package of regulations will follow, enabling the Contributions Agency to tackle remaining loopholes. The new legislation will come into force by April 1999. The Agency would expect all employers to comply by 6 April 1998 at the latest.

This package of revised practice and new legislation will ensure that only tax approved pension schemes fall outside NICs. The Government will not forgo NICs revenue to assist employers who wish to provide FURBS which are little more than deferred bonus schemes for well paid employees. Neither will it permit these schemes to be used to channel bonuses to employees in schemes to avoid paying NICs. Avoidance schemes are unfair on employers who pay full NICs on the remuneration of their employees. Action to bring FURBS into NICs will raise approximately £50 million each year.

FURTHER GUIDANCE

What are FURBS?

FURBS are funded unapproved retirement benefit schemes. They are outwith the scope of tax approved retirement benefit schemes. Typical FURBS consist of an employer securing future benefits through an insurance policy or the establishment of a separate trust. The former are common in the case of so-called "death benefit schemes" under which the insurance policies are written into trust for employees. In practice employers make contributions which the trustees apply towards the acquisition of an insurance policy providing a lump sum death benefit on the death of the specified person. The latter consists of the establishment of a trust fund specifically for participating employees/members.

Why some schemes attract NICs under current law

Separate trusts for each employee/member

Payments in

An employer's contributions to the separate trusts for each employee/member FURBS to be NIC-able earnings, being remuneration or profit derived from employment for the purposes of Social Security Contributions and Benefits Act 1992 s 3, and "paid to or for the benefit" of an employed earner for the purposes of s 6 of that Act. We take the same view where a third party makes a payment into FURBS in respect of an individual.

Payments out

Payments out of FURBS are earnings unless otherwise exempt in regulations. For instance, payments out in the form of a pension are exempt from the calculation of earnings for Class 1 NICs purposes by virtue of reg 19(1)(*g*) of the Social Security (Contributions) Regulations 1979. The Agency considers that payment by way of a pension for the purposes of reg 19(1)(*g*) can include pensions commuted to a lump sum.

Single trust fund—employee/members having a distinct and separate share

Payments in

An employer's contribution to the trust made for each employee/member is NIC-able earnings, being remuneration or profit derived from employment for the purposes of Social Security Contributions and Benefits Act 1992 s 3, and "paid to or for the benefit" of an employed earner for the purposes of s 6. We take the same view where a third party makes a payment into FURBS in respect of an individual.

Payments out

Payments out of FURBS are earnings unless otherwise exempt in regulations. For instance, payments out in the form of a pension are exempt from the calculation of earnings for Class 1

NICs purposes by virtue of reg 19(1)(*g*) of the Social Security (Contributions) Regulations 1979. The Agency considers that payment by way of a pension for the purposes of reg 19(1)(*g*) can include pensions commuted to a lump sum.

Single fund—discretionary benefit FURBS

The Contributions Agency closely scrutinise FURBS constructed under discretionary trust arrangements. If the Agency can establish a payment of earnings to or for an employee it will challenge the scheme and seek NICs.

In view of the terms of the Agency's previous guidance, the Agency will not be enforcing liability for unpaid NICs in respect of payments into FURBS where employers can show that they relied to their detriment on that guidance.

The Agency will seek to enforce liability for contributions in respect of payments made on or after 6 April 1998.

There are some FURBS schemes which the Agency considers are not and have never been intended as pension schemes. These schemes are only used in an attempt to pay bonuses avoiding NICs. Typically, in the schemes, the FURBS is short lived, payments out of that trust occur before the employee retires and a matter of weeks after the money is paid into the trust. The Agency considers that in this type of scheme it is highly unlikely that the employer could have been misled by guidance from the Agency. The Agency has always reserved its right to challenge FURBS which do not provide retirement benefits and it will continue to seek to enforce arrears. National insurance contributions avoidance schemes are unfair on those employers and employees who pay their share.

NIC

Tax approved pension schemes

There is no change in the Agency's treatment of tax approved pension schemes—

- payments into tax approved pension scheme—do not include in gross pay;
- payments from a tax approved scheme—do not include in gross pay.

TRAVEL AND SUBSISTENCE—EMPLOYERS URGED TO IMPLEMENT NATIONAL INSURANCE CHANGES FROM APRIL 1998

2 March 1998

In the Inland Revenue's Budget Press Release of 26 November 1996, the Department of Social Security (DSS) announced that it intended to change the national insurance rules regarding travel and subsistence. These changes would ensure that the national insurance rules mirror the tax changes being introduced from 6 April 1998.

The new T&S rules will cover changes relating to—

- site-based employees;
- temporary posting away from a permanent workplace; and
- "triangular" travel.

The new regulations are not likely to come into force until the Summer. Until they do, the Contributions Agency agrees that employers may apply the new rules from 6 April 1998. This will mean that, generally, the national insurance rules will mirror the tax rules from the start of the 1998–99 tax year.

NOTES: NEW TRAVEL AND SUBSISTENCE RULES IN DETAIL

Site-based employees

These are employees who have no permanent workplace; they work for a short period at one location before moving on to another. Currently, any amounts paid by the employer towards the costs of travel and/or subsistence are regarded as earnings as defined in Social Security Contributions and Benefits Act 1992 s 3(1). Under the new rules, any reasonable travel and subsistence costs paid by the employer can be excluded in calculating the amount of gross pay for national insurance purposes.

Temporary posting away from a permanent

Currently, a temporary posting is one where an employee spends 12 months or less away from their normal workplace. Under the new rules, this period is extended to 24 months.

"Triangular" travel

This occurs where an employee with a normal, permanent place of work travels directly from his/her home to another temporary place of work.

Under current rules, the amount which may be excluded from gross pay is normally the lesser of—

– the cost of travelling from the normal, permanent place of work to the temporary workplace; or
– the actual amounts of travelling costs incurred.

Under the new rules, reasonable travel and subsistence expenses paid by an employer can be excluded in calculating the amount of gross pay for national insurance purposes. A national insurance liability will only arise where an employer makes a travel and subsistence payment which exceeds that reasonable amount.

Further guidance, which includes various examples, can be found in booklet 490 "Employee travel—a tax and NICs guide for employers". Any employer who has not already received a copy can obtain one by telephoning the Employer's Annual Pack Orderline on 0345 646 646 (calls are charged at the local rate). The line is open until 25 July 1998, Monday–Friday 8am to 8pm and Saturday 10am to 1pm.

Employers who receive their booklet and would like further advice should call the Employers' Helpline on 0345 143 143. Calls are charged at the local rate.

1 For the sake of simplicity, the DSS intends that the wording of the new regulations will be based on and refer to the tax law changes which the Revenue proposes to include in the 1998 Finance Bill. As this is unlikely to become law until July/August, it will be the Summer before the national insurance regulations can come into force.

2 Therefore, between 6 April 1998 and the date on which the national insurance regulations come into force, employers may act as if those regulations were already in place.

3 The Contributions Agency is an Executive Agency of the Department of Social Security, and is responsible for the operational aspects of the NIC system.

Commentary—*Simon's Taxes* **E4.604**, **E4.710.**

NATIONAL INSURANCE CONTRIBUTIONS—TREATMENT OF MEDICAL EXPENSES ABROAD AND RELOCATION ALLOWANCES

16 March 1998

DSS Ministers today laid amendments to the Social Security (Contributions) Regulations 1979, which will take certain payments employers make to employees out of the scope of Class 1 NICs (SI 1998/680). The new regulations come into force from the start of the 1998–99 tax year, and are designed to make administration easier for employers. The amendments will cover two types of payment—

MEDICAL EXPENSES ABROAD

The regulations deal with the national insurance position of payments for medical costs and expenses an employee may incur when carrying out duties overseas, or insurance against such costs. Payments the employer makes towards these costs will be removed from liability for NICs.

RELOCATION ALLOWANCES

The regulations also deal with the various relocation allowances employees can receive when making a job-related move. Also published today is the Social Security Advisory Committee's report on the relocation allowance proposals.

John Denham, Minister with responsibility for national insurance said—

"Both these changes bring the tax and national insurance rules closer together.

The change to medical costs abroad is minor, affecting few employers and employees each year, but these changes will remove a source of potential uncertainty for employers.

I also announced on 30 July last year that we would be changing the rules on the treatment of relocation allowances from April 1998. National insurance contributions have not been collected on relocation allowances in the past but following legal advice we now believe that contributions are due under existing legislation. From 6 April 1998, the Contributions Agency will enforce the NIC liability on payments of relocation allowances in line with existing legislation. The regulations laid today exclude from liability for NICs those allowances that could qualify for tax relief as listed in tax legislation. These exclusions will make the system easier for employers to administer.

I am grateful to the Social Security Advisory Committee for their Report on the draft regulations. In response to the Report and to representations we have received from employers, we have decided to make two changes to our original proposals. The first is to exclude from contributions liability for a further year those relocation allowances that are taxed through Inland Revenue PAYE Settlement Agreements (PSAs). This change will minimise the administrative burdens on businesses that account for the tax on certain relocation allowances in this way. Subject to approval by Parliament, new legislation proposed in the current Social Security Bill will from 6 April 1999 align the national insurance treatment of items included in a PSA with the tax treatment, easing the administrative problems for those employers. The second change will ensure that, where there is no tax charge on relocation allowances for employees relocating abroad there will be no contributions liability."

The Department believes that payment of relocation allowances should generally have been subject to NICs in the past. Where these contributions have not been paid, the benefits position of some employees may have been affected. The DSS is ready to help those who think this may have happened to them. If any employee wishes to enquire about his or her own position then he or she should contact his or her local Contributions Agency office for advice. In Northern Ireland, contact the Contributions Unit Headquarters. To be affected, employees would need to have received relocation allowances on which contributions were not paid. Their normal earnings would also need to have been less than the upper earnings limit in the earnings period in which the relocation allowances were paid.

NIC

NOTES

1 The Contributions Agency is an Executive Agency of the Department of Social Security responsible for the operational aspects of the NICs scheme. The Contributions Unit is part of the Social Security Agency which is an Executive Agency of the Department of Health and Social Services responsible for the operational aspects of the national insurance scheme in Northern Ireland.

2 The NIC rules for relocation allowances will generally follow the tax rules, so that what is excluded from tax will also be excluded from NICs. Further, all qualifying allowances listed in tax legislation will be excluded from NICs, not just the first £8,000 as for tax.

3 Relocation allowances paid to employees who have already started work at the new location before 6 April 1998 will be excluded from NICs in line with published guidance to employers.

4 Employers who currently account for tax due on some relocation allowances through PAYE settlement agreements raised concerns about the original proposals, which they argued would require them to devise new payroll practices for one year only. Subject to Parliamentary approval, clause 52 of the Social Security Bill will allow employers to account for NICs in an annual lump sum settlement after the year end in respect of the same payments. Regulations bringing clause 52 into effect are planned to commence from 6 April 1999.

5 PAYE settlement agreements allow employers to account for any tax liability in respect of their employees on payments that are minor or irregular, or that are shared benefits on which it would be impractical to determine individual liability. Most taxable relocation allowances would fit one of these criteria. The exceptions would be regular and non-minor payments that employers make to employees who move to a more expensive housing cost area. These payments are commonly called additional housing cost allowances or mortgage subsidies.

6 If an employee has received relocation allowances in the past which should have attracted NICs liability, but contributions were not paid, the employee's benefit position may have been adversely affected. The Department believes that it is very unlikely that in any individual case

the contributions record has been affected significantly. Nevertheless, if an employee wh received relocation allowances wishes to check his or her own position the Contribution Agency is ready to help. Evidence of the amounts and dates of these payments would assist th Agency to make any corrections to a person's contributions record. Details of local Contribu tions Agency offices are in the phone book. In Northern Ireland, contact the Contributions Uni Headquarters, 24–42 Corporation Street, Belfast, BT1 3DP. Telephone number (01232 543301.

GOVERNMENT ANNOUNCES CHANGES TO NATIONAL INSURANCE RULES ON EARNINGS PAID IN SHARES AND SHARE OPTIONS

1 April 1998

John Denham, the Parliamentary Under Secretary of State for Social Security, yesterday announced proposals to change the national insurance rules relating to earnings paid in share and share options outside of Inland Revenue approved schemes. The changes will bring the national insurance rules into line with the tax changes announced by the Chancellor of the Exchequer in his Budget on 17 March.

In answer to a Parliamentary Question from Karen Buck (Regent's Park and Kensington North), John Denham said—

"We are proposing two changes to NIC rules which will bring them closer to the income tax rules in relation to shares and share options. This will make for greater clarity for employers and help reduce the administrative burden the system places on them.

First, we intend to bring forward at Report stage in the House of Lords a new clause for inclusion in the Social Security Bill. That clause will change the national insurance treatment of shares that are subject to the risk of forfeiture or that are convertible. The change will align the treatment of these shares under national insurance legislation with the tax legislation announced by my Rt Hon Friend, the Chancellor of the Exchequer in his Budget.

Alignment of national insurance with the income tax rules will bring forward some important changes to make the national insurance liability on shares and options easier for business to administer while guarding against their use in avoidance schemes.

The new clause will be tabled as soon as possible.

It will mirror the proposed income tax treatment of remuneration in shares subject to forfeiture or conversion. To keep to a minimum the period over which the tax and national insurance positions differ the clause will apply to shares awarded from the date on which it was tabled. We expect that to be before the end of the current Committee stage in the House of Lords.

The second change we propose is to match my Rt Hon Friend, the Chancellor's extension of the 'seven year rule' for share options when we align the national insurance treatment of share options with the income tax position. Under the current income tax arrangements the award of an option over shares is taxed at the time of grant rather than exercise only where the options can be exercised more than seven years later. My Rt Hon Friend, the Chancellor has announced his intention to extend that limit to ten years. We intend to mirror this in future national insurance legislation.

When the relevant regulations made under clause 50 of the Social Security Bill come into force they will replace the national insurance liability on grant of options with a liability on exercise, except in the case of options which can be exercised more than ten years later. This would take the great majority of options outside liability for national insurance on grant, thus reducing the administrative burden on business while continuing to protect the Exchequer.

Inland Revenue approved own-company share schemes remain excluded from liability for NICs."

DETAILS

Earnings in shares subject to forfeiture

Many companies offer their employees shares in the company they work for as part of their earnings. These shares often form part of a long-term incentive plan (LTIP), where the award of the shares depends on meeting certain performance criteria.

Usually such schemes involve an agreement that if the targets are met the employee will receive the shares. Sometimes, however, the employee is given the shares at the outset but subject to the condition that they will forfeit the shares if the targets are not met. If they are met, the risk of forfeiture is lifted, and the employee becomes the unconditional owner of the shares.

There will normally be no national insurance liability when shares carrying the risk of forfeiture are first awarded but there will be a national insurance liability on the market value of the shares when the risk of forfeiture is lifted or, if sooner, when the shares are sold.

There will also be a national insurance liability if the shares can still be subject to risk of forfeiture more than five years after they are first awarded. This is to stop national insurance liability being postponed indefinitely. As most LTIPs plans run for five years or less few employers and employees will, in fact, pay NICs when the shares are first awarded.

Earnings in convertible shares

Many companies issue shares of different classes which may, for example, have different voting or dividend rights. They may also allow their shares another class. Prior to the Budget changes employers devised schemes so that they could avoid or reduce the income tax charge on the shares. In such a scheme the employer would grant one class of shares which attracts little or no tax and then convert them to a more valuable class.

The Budget introduced an income tax charge when shares, awarded to an employee, convert from one class to another class, on the market value of the shares to which they convert, with an allowance for any income tax charged when the shares were first awarded. This will be matched by corresponding changes to national insurance liability. There will be national insurance liability when shares, awarded to an employee, convert from one class to another on the market value of the shares to which they convert, with an allowance for any national insurance paid when the shares were first awarded.

The new national insurance liability will—

- apply only to shares which are first awarded on or after the date on which the clause is tabled or 6 April 1998, whichever is the later;
- not apply if the majority of the shares of the class converting are not employees or directors.

The Contributions Agency will issue a further press release when the clause is tabled.

SHARE OPTIONS

The current income tax rules

Under normal tax rules when an employee is granted an option over shares, he or she pays no income tax at the time of grant, but instead pays income tax when the option is exercised and shares acquired. It is at this latter stage that the employee receives the benefit of the option.

However, when share options are granted which can be exercised more than seven years after the date of grant, there is a charge to income tax if the option price is less than the market value of the shares. This "seven year rule" is to prevent options with a high value being granted and left unexercised for very long periods.

Proposed changes to the tax rules

The Chancellor of the Exchequer announced on 17 March that he proposes to extend the "seven year rule" so that there will be a tax charge on the grant of an option only if the option is exercisable more than ten years later.

Current national insurance rules

The current national insurance rules differ from those for income tax. National insurance liability arises on the grant of an option and not on exercise.

Proposed changes to the national insurance rules

Under plans announced in July 1997, the Government intends to bring the national insurance treatment of options further into line with income tax. Clause 50 of the Social Security Bill will

NIC

enable the national insurance rules to be aligned with the income tax rules so that there will normally be a national insurance liability on exercise rather than grant. The Government planned to mirror the "seven year rule" for tax in national insurance. Instead it will mirror the new "ten year rule".

Inland Revenue approved schemes

These schemes will remain excluded from national insurance liability. Approved schemes are intended to encourage employee share ownership.

The contributions agency is an executive agency of the Department of Social Security, and is responsible for the operational aspects of the NIC system.

Details of the tax proposals were given in Revenue [Press] Release [dated] 17 March 1998.

Commentary—*Simon's Taxes* Division E4.5.

REMISSION OF INTEREST ON DISPUTED NATIONAL INSURANCE CONTRIBUTIONS LIABILITY

18 May 1999

The Inland Revenue today issued a temporary concession concerning interest on national insurance contributions (NICs) disputed by employers.

Where a decision on liability was requested under the pre-1 April 1999 procedures and interest on unpaid NICs did not accrue up to that date, it will continue to be remitted until 1 August 1999.

These cases will then be brought into the new decisions and appeals system when interest accrues during the appeals process. This completes the framework for a fairer and less cumbersome method of resolving disputes about NICs.

DETAILS

New scheme

1 Under the new NIC appeals procedure which came into effect from 1 April 1999 the amount of the disputed NICs liability and the interest on it need not be paid while an appeal to the tax appeal Commissioners is pending. If the liability is confirmed the whole becomes payable, with interest on the debt calculated from 14 days after the end of the tax year in which it became due.

Old scheme

2 Before 1 April 1999, interest was not charged on disputed amounts of NICs, pending a determination by the Secretary of State under the Social Security Administration Act 1992 s 17.

Pipeline cases

3 Where no determination had been made following an application for a Secretary of State's determination before 1 April, or following an agreement to be treated as if an application had been made, an appealable decision will be given by an officer of the Inland Revenue (under the new provisions). The temporary concession allows the interest remission to continue until 1 August 1999 or 14 days after the new decision—whichever is later.

4 Where a Secretary of State's determination had been made before 1 April 1999 confirming liability, but the contributor had not yet been provided with the Statement of Grounds on which to decide whether to pursue the matter to the High Court the concession also provides for remission of interest to 1 August 1999, or 14 days after the issue of the Statement of Grounds, whichever is the later.

5 The concession will apply to around 100 cases where a contributor had applied for a Secretary of State's determination before 1 April 1999, and to a further 2,300 cases where the same point arises and it had been agreed with the Contributions Agency, prior to the merger, that further action would be informed by the decision on a "lead" case. It also applies to around 40 contributors who had their liability confirmed by the Secretary of State and are considering taking the matter to the High Court.

6 Typically the cases to which the concession will apply are those where payments, mainly substantial bonuses, have been made in non-cash forms—such as rhodium or platinum sponge—in order to try and avoid NICs liability. Investigations of such schemes may be complex and lengthy, hence the reason for a number to be in the pipeline at the time the new appeals arrangements were introduced. Some £250–£300 million of NICs may be due from these cases.

Conclusion

7 The new decisions and appeals arrangements and associated interest provisions are much fairer than before. Under the old system no interest was payable at all on NICs eventually held to be payable for the period between an application for a determination and the determination being given. This gave an incentive for employers to request determinations in order to obtain a cash-flow advantage. It also gave an unfair advantage to those who disputed their liability over those who paid on time.

8 This concession on charging interest on outstanding liability provides those affected with notice of the date from which interest will accrue. It provides a fair balance between the expectation of contributors under the old system with our duty to collect the monies legally due. In total the concession will be worth around £5 million in interest foregone.

Notes

1 The Contributions Agency merged with the Inland Revenue on 1 April 1999. New arrangements for appeals about NICs were enacted in the Social Security Act 1998, but were replaced by provisions in the Social Security Contributions (Transfer of Functions, etc) Act 1999 Part II for such appeals to be made to the tax appeal Commissioners. Commencement Order SI 1999/527 paras 4(1) and (4) concern cases in the pipeline at 1 April 1999.

2 Before 1 April 1999 contributors could request a Secretary of State's determination on liability under Social Security Administration Act 1992 s 17. The Office for the Determination of Contribution Questions would make an examination of case, sometimes appointing an independent inquirer, and make a determination on behalf of the Secretary of State which could only be appealed to a court on a point of law.

3 The Social Security Contributions Regulations, SI 1979/591 Sch 1 reg 28D allows for the remission of interest—

- from the date on which a s 17 (above) has been made until 14 days after the Secretary of State has given his determination; and
- from the date on which the Secretary of State refers a matter to the High Court on a point of law under Social Security Administration Act s 18, until 14 days after the matter has been determined.

These rules will not apply to the new appeals arrangements and reg 28D will be amended shortly but the Regulations will continue to provide for the remission of interest in cases where there has been an official error.

ANNEX—TEMPORARY CONCESSION

Under the provisions of the Social Security Contributions (Transfer of Functions, etc) Act 1999 (the "Transfer Act") interest will no longer be remitted where there is a dispute over national insurance contributions (NICs) liability. However the Board of the Inland Revenue will, by concession, allow interest to be remitted in the following situations—

- Where, before 1 April 1999, a contributor had submitted an application for a Secretary of State's determination but had not received the determination by the time the new decisions and appeals procedures were introduced on 1 April, interest on the amount of NICs liability under dispute will continue to be remitted until 1 August 1999 or until the issue of the decision under the Transfer Act s 8—whichever is the later.
- Where, before 1 April 1999, a contributor had advised the Contributions Agency that they wished to challenge the assessment of liability, but an agreement had been reached with the Agency that they would not formally apply for a Secretary of State's determination pending the outcome of a lead case, interest will be remitted until 1 August 1999 or until a decision is given on the case formerly held pending the lead case under the Transfer Act s 8—whichever is the later.
- Where a Secretary of State's determination on NICs liability was made before 1 April 1999, but a Statement of Grounds requested from the Office for the Determination of Contribution Questions was only received by the contributor on or after that date, interest will be remitted until 1 August 1999 or 14 days after the Statement of Grounds has been issued—whichever is the later.

NATIONAL INSURANCE CONTRIBUTIONS—REMISSION OF INTEREST ON LATE PAYMENTS

5 July 1999

The Inland Revenue today announced that its practice in remitting interest on NICs has been brought into line with the equivalent tax practice.

The single practice will be applied where there is a late payment of tax or contributions as a result of a mistake or an unreasonable delay by officials. It represents a further step along the road of gradually aligning the tax and contributions rules with consequent benefits to employers.

Regulations laid today also repeal the provisions that provided remission of interest during disputes over NIC liability before the new framework for decisions and appeals was introduced on 1 April 1999.

DETAILS

1. The Inland Revenue's Code of Practice No 1 sets out the circumstances in which someone can apply to have interest remitted because of mistake or unreasonable delay. In essence, where there is no good reason for the delay by Inland Revenue officials and it has been more than six months in total, interest accruing during the period of the delay will be remitted.

2. The single Inland Revenue practice will be used in interpreting the statutory requirement to remit interest on NIC paid late as a result of a "mistake or omission" by an official. It replaces the set of practices previously applied by the Contributions Agency in applying this rule.

3. The wording of the statutory rule will not be materially changed as a result of the repeal of the provision remitting interest accruing during a period when NIC liability is under dispute.

4. An Inland Revenue press release dated 18 May announced the intention to repeal this provision and set out an extra-statutory concession in connection with NIC liability in dispute prior to 1 April 1999.

NOTES

1. The Regulations laid today are the Social Security (Contributions) (Amendment No 4) Regulations, SI 1999/1965 and the Social Security (Contributions) (Amendment No 4) (Northern Ireland) Regulations, SI 1999/1966. They will be available from the Stationery Office shortly, or may be found on the internet at www.inlandrevenue.gov.uk from Monday 13 July.

2. The Social Security Contributions Regulations, SI 1979/591 Sch 1 reg 28D allowed for the remission of interest—

– where the liability to pay interest on national insurance Class 1, Class 1A or Class 1B contributions arises because of an official error (a mistake or an omission). Interest is remitted from the date of the error to 14 days after it is rectified and the employer notified;
– from the date on which a Social Security Administration Act 1992 s 17 application has been made until 14 days after the Secretary of State has given his determination; and
– from the date on which the Secretary of State refers a matter to the High Court on a point of law under the Social Security Administration Act 1992 s 18, until 14 days after the matter has been determined.

3. The new Regulations repeal the last two circumstances for remission because of the new decisions and appeals arrangements introduced in the Social Security Contributions (Transfer of Functions, etc) Act 1999 Part II. The Social Security Administration Act 1992 ss 17, 18 no longer apply to national insurance. The first provision concerning official error remains broadly unchanged.

4. The Contributions Agency was transferred to the Inland Revenue on 1 April 1999.

NICS—AGGREGATION OF EARNINGS AND "NOT REASONABLY PRACTICABLE" TEST

August 2000. *IR Tax Bulletin issue 48*

Aggregation of earnings for National Insurance Contributions (NICs) purposes is an issue that is causing employers some problems, particularly in the Health and Local Government sectors. Our published advice in booklet CWG2 to employers about the issue is not comprehensive and it has been argued that the phrase "not reasonably practicable" is capable of more than one interpretation. The following article is a more detailed summary of our view on aggregation of earnings and the "not reasonably practicable" exception.

The starting point is that an employer has a duty to aggregate earnings when the employed earner has separate employments with the same employer SSCBA 1992 Sch 1 para 1(1)(*a*). Without the duty to aggregate, an incorrect liability might be paid and the individual's contributory benefit rights harmed because of separate earnings payments. The latter point is especially important if the person is low paid and the separate wages or salary are under the Lower Earnings Limit (LEL). However regulation 11 of the Social Security (Contributions) Regulations 1979 (SS(C) R 1979) (SI 1979/591) states that the earnings shall not be aggregated if such aggregation is not reasonably practicable. In order to satisfy the regulation, the earnings must be separately calculated and the impracticability arises because the earnings are separately calculated.

There is no definition of the phrase "not reasonably practicable" in NICs legislation. We are reliant on ordinary meaning and case law, the latter arising from Health & Safety legislation. The following views also take into account an unreported determination by the Secretary of State for Social Security on whether the earnings of 'Bank Nurses' should be aggregated.

If there is disagreement between the employer and the Inland Revenue it will be a question for the Commissioners to determine. The onus is on the employer to show that aggregation is not reasonably practicable because it is the employer making the judgement. It is not a once and for all decision because the duty to aggregate is an ongoing duty. Also, factors may change – such as the composition of the labour force—sufficiently to affect the judgement. The employer will need to take into account the costs, resources, and the effects on running the business. Cost is a material pointer but not decisive. The context is important so the employer will also need to be aware of the effect on the National Insurance Fund (NIF) and the benefit or pension entitlement of the employee.

The reported judgements have to be filtered on the basis of their specific legislation but *Mailier v Austin Rover Group* [1989] (2 All ER 1087) agreed on 3 principles—

- "reasonably practicable" is narrower than "physically possible"
- risk has to be measured against the cost of removing it, and
- account has to be taken of the likelihood of the risk arising.

Taking the principles in order—

- It is always possible to aggregate but that is not the test. And the "separately calculated" provision is not failed merely because it is the same employer or payroll system.
- Costs to the employer are not just financial. Time, effort and the effect on the business have to be considered because the weight of the cost of compliance should not be disproportionate to the loss of National Insurance Contributions and benefit entitlement.
- Mailier and other cases are generally considering whether there is a duty to guard against unknown and unexpected events. It is our view that employers have a very limited argument on the 3rd bullet point because aggregation is a known and recurring event. However that is not enough to negate any informed judgement by an employer that aggregation is not reasonably practicable.

The cases consider the balance between risk on one hand and the sacrifices necessary for averting the risk on the other hand. Basically, an employer needs to balance his employee's interests against his own costs. It is very important that the consequences for the primary contributor are considered, especially the low paid, because of the potential loss of benefits and pension rights.

The employer can only make an informed decision if all the facts are established because "reasonably practicable" is related to the individual circumstances. The evidence is that employers with computerised payrolls are the ones who find difficulty in complying with the need to aggregate. However the existence of such a payroll is not enough evidence that aggregation is not practicable. Manual or other fixes will have to be considered and costed especially when there will be similar risks in future years if aggregation is not done and the employer will have to revisit the issue.

Inland Revenue compliance staff will take account of the following points when comparing the costs of aggregation against the risks to contributors—

- Is it a fact, rather than an assumption, that payroll software cannot aggregate earnings?
- Is the payroll software an outside package, tailored package, provided by an internal IT section or able to be upgraded by internal resources?
- Has the payroll system been changed?
- If so, why was an aggregation requirement not part of the new specification?
- Does the provider of an outside or tailored package give an update service that includes aggregation?
- Is it possible to upgrade or would the employer have to buy a new system?
- What are the costs of upgrading the software?
- Is there a dedicated internal IT team that might be able to provide it cheaply subject to competing claims for their services?
- If the work has to be carried out manually what are the costs?
- Does the employer already have a manual support resource for payroll glitches, urgent payments and so on?
- Would new staff be required?
- What is entailed in staff years in manually calculating the NICs, which takes into account that experience will reduce the need for the initial, possibly untrained, resource?
- How many employees are potentially affected?
- What is the total number of employees on the payroll?
- Do employees have similar pay periods?
- Is aggregation a continuing requirement or a one-off consideration because of a particular project or task?
- What are the amounts of NICs at stake and the effect on NIF and primary contributors?
- How does this compare to the costs of compliance?
- Has there been a material change in the labour force since the decision not to aggregate was taken? Or a material change in the state benefits that aggregation could bring (State Second Pension may be relevant here).

The list is not exhaustive. We are not expecting employers to spend a lot of resources in detailed costings. Rather that we look for a reasoned consideration of the issue rather than, say, mere assertion that external change or constraints justify non-aggregation. We have seen the following issues raised in very general terms by employers—Equal Opportunities, Compulsory Competitive Tendering, Local Management of Schools, Internal Charging, De-Centralising payrolling and Security & Audit Requirements. It is difficult to judge their relevance when facts, legislation and detailed arguments are not known. But for example Equal Opportunities legislation might be a factor for aggregation especially if most workers with two jobs are female and their benefits are affected.

In summary, there is a duty to aggregate but the legislation recognises it might not be practicable in all circumstances. Employers, their advisers and Inland Revenue staff need to consider the costs and the risks based on all the facts of the individual cases. Future editions of CWG2 will be changed to reflect Inland Revenue views as expressed in this article.

Finally Inland Revenue compliance staff in the course of an employer review normally consider the issue of whether an employer aggregates. Assuming that it is agreed that aggregation is reasonably practicable, the question then arises on whether there should be retrospection. We normally expect that at least in-date years will be adjusted but that is subject of course to any relevant individual factors including any advice that employers might have relied upon from the Inland Revenue.

THE NATIONAL INSURANCE CONTRIBUTIONS AND STATUTORY PAYMENTS ACT

June 2004. *Tax Bulletin 71*

The National Insurance Contributions and Statutory Payments Bill was introduced in the House of Commons on 27 November 2003 and received Royal Assent on 13 May 2004. The Act has 5 measures. The first two measures will make the administration of National Insurance simpler when employers reward their employees with security based earnings. The three other measures help bring the National Insurance, Statutory Payments and equivalent tax regimes closer together. All these measures should make the administration of National Insurance less burdensome for both employers and individuals. This article gives a brief outline of the changes that are being made.

EXTENDING THE ABILITY OF THE EMPLOYER TO RECOVER PRIMARY NATIONAL INSURANCE CONTRIBUTIONS (NICS) FROM EMPLOYEES' SHARE BASED EARNINGS

The Social Security Act (1998) introduced legislation which allowed employers and employees to enter into written agreements allowing the employer, when making payment of the share based earnings, to retain or sell shares equal to the employee's NICs liability. Prior to the National Insurance and Statutory Payments Act this could only be done where:

- An employee had ceased employment and the payment of share based earnings was made after they left the employment but in the tax year of cessation; or
- An employee had received share based earnings and was ceasing employment in that tax year, and the employer was unable to recover the NICs from the employee's subsequent monetary earnings.

The Act has now extended this and the new legislation will now allow written agreements for the withholding of shares and other securities to be entered into for:

- All employees, including those in continuing employment, irrespective of whether the recovery could be made from the employees' subsequent monetary earnings;
- Employees who receive security based earnings in the year after they have ceased employment, as well as the year that they left.

All earnings that come under the definition of "securities" defined at Section 420 of the Income Tax (Earnings and Pensions) Act 2003 as amended by Schedule 22 to the Finance Act 2003 can be included. This definition of securities covers shares, company loan stock, Government gilts and a number of specialised financial instruments. It does not include such things as cash, cheques and leases. This will be set out in regulations following Royal Assent.

Regulations also govern how and when recovery can be made. To keep red tape to a minimum the regulations will only state that the employee has to have given prior written consent for the employer to withhold or sell an amount of securities equal to the employee's NICs liability. There is no set form that this has to be made on. The agreements can be entered into at any time up to the day that the earnings arise. It may therefore be possible for employers who, for instance, granted share options to an employee before this legislation came into force to make recovery by withholding shares. As long as the employee gives his/her written consent, and this consent was given after the legislation came into force but before the earnings were paid this method can be used.

The extension of the ability to recover from non monetary earnings does not impinge on the ability of the employer to recover the primary NICs that they have paid on the employee's behalf from their future monetary earnings. Statutory Instrument 2003 No. 1337 removed the limits on the amounts that could be recovered per pay period, and extended the time limit for recovery to the following tax year after share based earnings had been paid. This was subsequently amended by Statutory Instrument 2004 No. 770 which allowed this extension for all security based earnings. If employers prefer to recover by this method then they can continue to do so.

Detailed guidance on these changes to legislation will be made available shortly on the Employee Share Schemes pages of the Inland Revenue website.

EXTENSION OF JOINT AGREEMENTS AND ELECTIONS TO CONVERTIBLE AND RESTRICTED SHARES

Joint elections and agreements for National Insurance contributions were introduced in 2000 to allow the transfer of some or all of the employers' National Insurance liability (the "secondary liability") arising on share option gains to the employee, with the employee's agreement. Prior to the introduction of this facility, employers granting share options to their employees faced difficulties in accounting for the unquantifiable secondary NICs liability that arises when the option is exercised. These difficulties discouraged many employers from using share options to motivate and reward staff. When an employer and employee enter into a joint NICs election, the legal liability to pay the secondary NICs transfers from employer to employee. This removes the need for the employer to provide for the unquantifiable secondary liability in their accounts. Alternatively, employer and employee may enter into an agreement that the employee will reimburse the employer for the cost of the secondary NICs liability, but legal liability remains with the employer. This facility has proved popular, with over 1900 requests for approval of NICs elections submitted to the Inland Revenue to date.

NIC

More recently it was brought to our attention that employment-related awards of restricted and convertible shares can also expose the employer to an unquantifiable future NICs liability. This is because awards of such shares are subject to NICs liabilities when certain events arise after the time of award ("post-acquisition chargeable events"). Typically these events include the lifting of restrictions applying to the shares, thus increasing their value to the employee, or conversion of the shares into other more valuable shares.

The new legislation extends the existing joint election and agreement facility to restricted and convertible shares. As a result, employers awarding such shares to employees are able to ask those employees to bear the cost of secondary NICs liabilities arising after the employee acquires the shares.

Employees who agree to bear the secondary NIC liability arising on share option gains are entitled to an income tax relief on those gains, equivalent to the amount of employer's NICs they pay. The Finance Bill 2004 includes a measure proposing to extend this tax relief to employees who agree to bear secondary NICs liabilities arising on restricted and convertible shares.

In addition, statutory instruments will soon be laid before Parliament to:

- amend the National Insurance Regulations applying to joint NICs elections, so that they reflect the extended scope of this facility; and
- set the date from which this measure in the National Insurance Contributions and Statutory Payments Act will take legal effect.

Detailed guidance on these changes to legislation will be made available on the Employee Share Schemes pages of the Inland Revenue website following Royal Assent of Finance Bill 2004 (www.inlandrevenue.gov.uk/shareschemes/index.htm)

RECOVERY OF NATIONAL INSURANCE CONTRIBUTIONS

The measures relate to the approximately 3% of National Insurance contributions which are not collected through the PAYE and SA systems and to which the provisions governing the recovery of tax debt do not apply. Mostly these are the flat rate Class 2 contributions paid by the self employed, but they also include some Class 1A and Class 4 contributions which are not collected with tax. The current differences between the provisions governing the recovery of tax and those governing the recovery of contributions make it impracticable for the Inland Revenue to take a single recovery action where a person has both tax and contributions debts. The measures are designed to overcome this obstacle by:

- aligning the 30 day period of notice currently required under section 121A of the Social Security Administration Act 1992 for distraint action to recover contribution debt in England and Wales, with the 7 day period of notice which Inland Revenue guidance specifies for the recovery of tax under section 61 of the Taxes Management Act 1970;
- aligning the 30 day period of notice currently required under section 121B of the Social Security Administration Act 1992 for application for a summary warrant to recover contribution debt in Scotland, with the14 day period of notice required for the recovery of tax debt under section 63 of the Taxes Management Act 1970 and procedures for the recovery of debt generally under the Debt Arrangement and Attachment (Scotland) Act 2002; and
- replacing the current provisions of section 115A of the Social Security Administration (Northern Ireland) Act 1992 which provide for contributions debt in Northern Ireland to be recovered by the Enforcement of Judgements Office, with provisions which allow the Inland Revenue to levy distraint in Northern Ireland on the same basis as in England and Wales.

The changes will come into effect later this year.

Alignment of Officers' Information Powers

Inland Revenue powers to investigate National Insurance cases are contained in section 110ZA of the Social Security Administration Act 1992. These powers are considerably wider than those for tax and include a power to enter premises and examine (interview) persons on those premises as well as a power to compel the production of documents and information. We are now correcting this misalignment by removing the power of entry and examination and applying the section 20 TMA information powers to National Insurance.

This will allow the Inland Revenue to ask both primary and secondary contributors to provide documents and information about their liability for National Insurance. The Inland Revenue can also ask third parties to provide documents which are relevant to the contributions liability of another. But these requests must be made under a formal notice which needs the consent of a Tax Appeal Commissioner before it can be issued.

At the same time we are also introducing a regulation making power which will allow us to introduce powers to inspect SSP and SMP records on the same basis as we can currently inspect PAYE records.

Civil Penalties for Statutory Sick and Maternity Pay

Employers' failures to meet their obligations under Statutory Sick and Maternity Pay schemes are dealt with by a series of minor criminal offences. This is out of step with the compliance regimes that exist for tax, NICs, tax credits and the Statutory Paternity and Adoption Pay schemes. This Bill introduces a better and more proportionate response to employers who attempt to avoid their obligations by introducing a civil penalty system for the non-compliant which is identical to that introduced in the Employment Act 2002 for Statutory Paternity and Adoption Pay.

Commencement of the measures in the Act

The two measures enabling employers to choose how to meet their NICs liability when security based earnings have been paid will be commenced as soon as possible following Royal Assent of the Bill. Normal timing conventions indicate that this will be around two months after Assent.

The measures on distraint will also be introduced on the same timescale. We will ensure that proper notification is given for those affected, so that no one will be caught out unwillingly.

The measures which introduce the new officers' powers and the new compliance regime for statutory payments will commence in the tax year beginning 6 April 2005 to allow time for guidance for staff and employers to be issued on the new provisions.

Contact Details

Should you have any questions or queries on this article please phone Chris Davis on 020 7438 7823 or email him at Chris.Davis@ir.gsi.gov.uk.

NIC

TIPS, GRATUITIES, SERVICE CHARGES & TRONCS – THE NICS POSITION

April 2006. *Tax Bulletin 82*

INTRODUCTION

The Tax Bulletin issued in June 2005 provided guidance for employers regarding tips, gratuities and service charges. That bulletin included guidance on the National Insurance contributions (NICs) treatment of tips, gratuities and service charges.

Booklet E24 "Tips, Gratuities, Service Charges and Troncs: A guide to Income Tax, National Insurance contributions, National Minimum Wages issues and VAT" has been included on the Employer's pages in the HMRC website since February 2005.

Following further legal advice, the booklet was amended to exclude guidance about NICs. The changes were announced on HMRC's website. Leaflet E24 will be updated to reflect the changes. There are no changes to the Income Tax and VAT guidance contained within the leaflet. This article provides interim guidance about NICs liability.

In this guidance, where the word "tips" is used it is intended to refer to payments of tips, gratuities and voluntary service charges.

CHANGE OF VIEW ON NATIONAL INSURANCE CONTRIBUTIONS AND TIPS

If tips paid by customers are paid to employees through an independently-run tronc, they are not liable for Class 1 NICs even where they go to meet a—

– contractual obligation, or
– legal requirement such as the National Minimum Wage (NMW).

There are 2 reasons why such payments are not liable for Class 1 NICs—

(1) the amounts paid are in respect of tips ie gratuitous payments made by customers, and
(2) the employer has not allocated the tips directly or indirectly to his employees.

It is implicit in the phrase "independently-run" that the facts show that the employer has not allocated the tips directly or indirectly to his employees.

PAYMENTS OF TIPS, OR IN RESPECT OF TIPS

For a payment to be disregarded from earnings under paragraph 5 of Part 10 to Schedule 3 of the Social Security (Contributions) Regulations 2001 (SI 2001/1004), ("the tips disregard"), the payment made to the employee—

– must either be a tip or a payment in respect of a tip, and
– either condition 1 or 2 must be satisfied.

Where a payment is traceable to payments that were tips, for example, voluntary payments made by customers, the payment is "in respect of tips".

The conditions are that a payment is—

(1) not paid, directly or indirectly, to the employee by the employer and does not comprise or represent monies previously paid to the employer, or
(2) not allocated, directly or indirectly, to the employee by the employer.

Payments that are not—

– tips, or
– in respect of tips

cannot be excluded from earnings under the tips disregard. If not disregarded the payments must be added to any other earnings paid in the same earnings period for the purposes of calculating Class 1 NICs.

COMPULSORY SERVICE CHARGES

Customers are obliged to pay compulsory service charges so if such payments are the source of payments made to employees, they are not tips or in respect of tips. Such payments are earnings and liable for Class 1 NICs. This remains unchanged.

NICS AND NATIONAL MINIMUM WAGE (NMW) OBLIGATIONS

In the June 2005 edition of the Tax Bulletin you were told that HMRC did not consider that payments that count for NMW purposes could be disregarded from earnings under the tips disregard. Following further legal advice HMRC has changed its view. Where employees receive payments which are tips or payments in respect of tips and they are not—

– paid directly or indirectly to employees from sums previously paid to the employer; or
– allocated, directly or indirectly to employees, by the employer

the payments are not liable for Class 1 NICs.

The fact that payments are taken into account for NMW purposes does not determine whether the payments can be disregarded from earnings under the tips disregard for Class 1 NICs purposes. Payments can, in principle, count for NMW purposes but be disregarded from earnings and so not liable for Class 1 NICs.

Amounts paid by a customer as service charges, tips, gratuities and cover charges count towards NMW pay if they are paid by the employer to the employee via the employer's payroll and the amounts are shown on the pay slips issued by the employer.

Tips and gratuities given directly to the worker by a customer do not count towards NMW pay.

Tronc money paid directly from the tronc to an employee does not count towards NMW pay. However, if the tronc money is passed to the employer, and is both paid to the employee via the employer's payroll and reflected on payslips issued by the employer, then it will count towards

NMW pay. It will also count towards NMW pay where the troncmaster operates PAYE on tronc distributions and uses the employer to pass the net payments to each employee, provided the amounts are paid to the employee via the employer's payroll and are reflected on their payslips.

CONTRACTUAL PAYMENTS AND NICS

Our guidance currently advises that if an employee's contract of employment indicates that they can participate in a tronc, any payments made by a tronc are liable for Class 1 NICs because they are contractual payments and therefore not gratuitous.

Contractual terms may vary, but HMRC now accepts that where

- the terms of a contract do not entitle an employee to receive a specific amount from a tronc, and
- the employee is receiving payments from an independently-run tronc funded from tips paid by customers, and
- the employer is not allocating tips to the employee either directly or indirectly the tips disregard applies so no Class 1 NICs are due on payments from the tronc.

Payments do not cease to be tips or payments in respect of tips because an employee merely has a right to participate in a tronc.

In the event that an employer pays amounts to a tronc which exceed the total value of the tips paid by customers, the excess is not a payment of or in respect of a tip, so Class 1 NICs are due on the excess.

The tips disregard may also apply even where an earner's contract of service, whether written, verbal or implied, entitles an earner to a specific amount that originates from tips and the employer is obliged to pay the specified amount. In these types of cases, Class 1 NICs will only be due where the—

- payments are in respect of tips and the employer does not satisfy either of the conditions in the tips disregard, or
- the employer makes payments sourced from his own funds and not payments in respect of tips.

One of the conditions referred to above is that the employer must not allocate payments directly or indirectly to the earner. HMRC consider that where the employer promises or guarantees a certain amount from the tronc, that may indicate that the employer has sufficient de facto control over the operation of the tronc to constitute an indirect allocation by the employer. Further investigation may be required to establish the true nature of the arrangements.

ALLOCATING PAYMENTS DIRECTLY OR INDIRECTLY TO THE EARNER

Despite the fact that HMRC has changed its view about the types of payments that are payments of or in respect of tips, for payments to be excluded from Class 1 NICs liability, the employer must still satisfy one of the conditions in the tips disregard.

Liability for Class 1 NICs will depend on the specific arrangements regarding the distribution of the tips operated by individual employers. "Allocate" connotes deciding—

- who is to be the recipient of the payment and
- how much the recipient is to get.

The employer does not allocate a payment to a particular employee merely because it is a term or condition of the employment that the employee is entitled to share in a tronc run independently of the employer. Neither is it allocated just because the employer reserves the right to make certain deductions from the tips before they reach the tronc.

"Indirect allocation" refers to cases where the employer does not allocate payments in person or through an agent, which HMRC regard as "direct allocation". Rather, the employer establishes and controls a system that performs the allocation in such a way that the allocation can reasonably be said to reflect and give effect to the employer's wishes.

As noted above, if an employer promises or guarantees receipt of a certain amount from the tronc, that may suggest that the employer has sufficient de facto control over the operation of the tronc to constitute an indirect allocation of that amount to the employee.

NIC

If tips are paid by an independently run tronc and the employer is not involved in the allocation either directly or indirectly, there is no Class 1 NICs liability.

COMPLIANCE

HMRC compliance staff will, when looking at tips which an employer has not included in gross pay for Class 1 NICs, establish facts to help them determine whether the—

– payments are tips or in respect of tips, and
– the payments were made directly or indirectly by the employer from sums previously paid to him; and/or
– sthe employer allocated the payments either directly or indirectly.

As arrangements can vary it is not possible to be prescriptive about what conclusions can be drawn from certain facts.

NICS EXAMPLES

Booklet E24 will be amended to include examples which reflect HMRC's current views.

CLASS 1 NICS PAID IN ERROR

If employers consider that Class 1 NICs have been paid in error the action to take will depend upon whether the NICs were included in a contract settlement following a review of the employer's PAYE and NICs records.

CLASS 1 NICS PAID IN ERROR INCLUDED IN A CONTRACT SETTLEMENT

If some or all of the Class 1 NICs paid in error were included in a contract settlement, the employer can expect the local Revenue and Customs office that dealt with the settlement to write to the employer no later than 31 May 2006. The employer will be given the opportunity to apply for a refund.

Those Class 1 NICs paid in error included in a contract settlement will be returned to the employer together with the proportion of any penalty and interest that related to those Class 1 NICs included in the settlement. Where appropriate, repayment interest will be paid in accordance with paragraph 18 of Schedule 4 to the Social Security (Contributions) Regulations 2001 (SI 2001/1004).

If some Class 1 NICs paid in error were included in a contract settlement and some were paid and returned on forms P14 and P35

– those Class 1 NICs paid in error in a contract settlement will be refunded by HMRC's Accounts Office, and
– those returned on forms P14 and P35 will be refunded by the National Insurance Contributions Office Refunds Group.

If an employer does not receive a letter telling them about the changes and how to claim a refund before 1 June 2006, they should write to the local Revenue and Customs office that dealt with the contract settlement and request a refund.

CLASS 1 NICS PAID IN CURRENT TAX YEAR NOT INCLUDED IN A CONTRACT SETTLEMENT

Where Class 1 NICs have been paid in error in the current tax year the employer should take action as set out in paragraph 10 on page 17 of booklet CWG2(2006) "Employer's Further Guide to PAYE and NICs" to correct their records and refund overpaid employee's NICs to employees.

CLASS 1 NICS PAID AND RETURNED ON FORMS P14 AND P35

If all Class 1 NICs paid in error were not included in a contract settlement the person requesting the refund should write direct to H M Revenue and Customs, National Insurance Contributions Office, Refunds Group, Employers Team, Room BP1001, Benton Park View, Newcastle upon Tyne NE98 1ZZ. Refunds Group will tell the applicant what information is needed to process their request.

Employers should not write to Refunds Group if some Class 1 NICs paid in error were included in a contract settlement and some were returned on forms P14 and P35. The local Revenue and Customs office that dealt with the contract settlement will write to the employer no later than 31 May 2006 telling them what to do. See "Class 1 NICs paid in error included in a contract settlement" above.

RETURN OF CLASS 1 NICS PAID IN ERROR BY EMPLOYEES

We expect most refund requests to be initiated by employers but there is nothing preventing employees from requesting a refund of Class 1 NICs paid in error.

However, HMRC will ensure that when requests for refunds are made by employers that—

- where employees have paid primary Class 1 NICs in error, they will be returned to those employees subject to the provisions contained within regulations 51, 52 and 57 of the Social Security (Contributions) Regulations 2001 (SI 2001/1004). (Secondary Class 1 NICs and primary Class 1 NICs paid by the employer will be returned to the employer if the employer did not recover any of the NICs from the employees); and
- secondary Class 1 NICs paid by the employer will be returned to the employer.

LEGISLATION

For Class 1 NICs the legislation relating to "gratuities and offerings" is contained at paragraph 5, Part 10, Schedule 3 of the Social Security (Contributions) Regulations 2001 (SI 2001/1004).

The NMW legislation relating to service charges, tips, gratuities and cover charges that do not count for national minimum wage pay purposes is contained at regulation 31(1)(*e*) of the National Minimum Wage Regulations 1999 (SI 1999/584).

RETROSPECTIVE LIABILITY FOR PAYE AND NICS

16 May 2007. *HMRC Guidance*

Guidance for Employers where a retrospective liability to Income Tax (PAYE) and Class1 National Insurance Contributions (NICs) occurs.

GENERAL POINTS TO NOTE

A "closed tax year" is any year preceding 6 April of the tax year in which the legislation giving rise to both the tax and NICs liabilities has effect (the current year). For example, if the legislation giving rise to the tax and NICs liabilities has effect in 2008/09, the tax year ending 5 April 2008, and all preceding years, are closed tax years.

The dates that the legislation giving rise to the tax and NICs liabilities have effect will normally fall within different tax months (the tax by virtue of a Finance Act, and the NICs by subsequent Social Security regulations.) Where this occurs, payment of the PAYE and NICs will be due on different dates.

Since Social Security regulations will normally follow the enactment of retrospective tax legislation, employers are recommended to amend employees' closed year pay records simultaneously to reflect both the amended tax and NICs.

For **liabilities arising for 2006/07 and earlier years** by virtue of legislation given effect by a common operative date of 6 April 2007, **payments are due by 19 June 2007 and returns by 19 May 2008**. Similarly the 6 April 2007 determines the start of the 90 day period an employee has to make good to the employer the additional tax due and paid by the employer.

AMENDMENT OF PAY RECORDS

Closed tax years and current tax year

Where a pay record (form P11 or equivalent) already exists for an employee who received a payment retrospectively charged to tax and NICs, the employer must amend that pay record in accordance with the guidance below.

NIC

Where no pay record exists for an employee who received a payment retrospectively charged to tax and NICs, the employer must complete a P11 or equivalent in accordance with the guidance below.

Each year's pay record in which employees received payments subsequently charged to tax and NICs, must be amended.

The format of the amended pay record is for an employer to determine having regard to their existing payroll process. However, employers should be aware that for closed years, paper P14s and a paper P35(RL) are a mandatory requirement and this may influence their choice as to the format of the amended pay records.

CALCULATING THE LIABILITY

Points to note

PAYE should be calculated by reference to the code issued for the year in which the payment retrospectively charged to tax was actually paid. Where no code was issued, tax should be deducted at the Higher Rate of tax relating to the year in which the payment was actually paid.

National Insurance contributions (NICs) should be calculated by reference to the rates and thresholds of NICs applicable to the year in which the earnings subsequently charged to NICs were actually paid. Any such payment should be added to any other earnings paid to the earner in the earnings period in which the retrospective earnings were actually paid.

CLOSED TAX YEARS AND CURRENT TAX YEAR

PAYE

For tax purposes it is not necessary to calculate the PAYE separately where more than one payment retrospectively charged to tax was made to an employee in the same year. The total of such payments should be added to the gross pay at the final pay period of the year in question and the tax recalculated using the code issued/the Higher Rate for that year.

NICs

For the purposes of calculating the revised National Insurance contributions due, it is necessary to record on the revised pay record in the earnings period, or periods, in which the payment or payments of earnings retrospectively treated as earnings were actually paid. This is important in order to correctly calculate the NICs due. If more than one payment of earnings retrospectively treated as earnings was made to an employee in a year, it will be necessary to calculate the revised NICs on each payment separately and amend the total NICs figure for the year accordingly.

PAYING THE LIABILITY

Closed tax years

Payment to HM Revenue & Customs (HMRC) of both PAYE and NICs are due within 14 days of the end of the tax month, following the tax months in which the relevant tax and Social Security legislation giving rise to the liability has effect.

Example:

The Finance Act giving rise to a retrospective tax liability has effect on 20 July 2008. Payment of the PAYE will be due by 19 September 2008. The Social Security regulations have effect on 10 August 2008. Payment of the NICs will be due by 19 October 2008.

Irrespective of whether an employer pays their normal PAYE and NICs monthly or quarterly, payment of retrospective liabilities is due by reference to a month, as above.

Irrespective of whether an employer normally pays electronically or not, payment in respect of closed years can only be paid by cheque. A cheque should be sent, together with a letter clearly marked as relating to a retrospective PAYE/Class 1 NICs liability, giving the following information:

Name and address of employer
Accounts Office reference
The years to which the payment relates

For each year, a breakdown between the PAYE and the NICs.

Cheques should be made payable to "HM Revenue & Customs Only" followed immediately by the Accounts Office reference and sent to:

HM Revenue & Customs
Section 10 (RPL)
Accounts Office
Bradford
BD98 1YY

Interest will be due on any payment received after the relevant 19th of the month. Interest will be calculated once a return has been received by HMRC.

Current tax year

As with closed years, the payment dates are determined by the dates on which the relevant tax and Social Security legislation has effect.

Payments to HMRC of both PAYE and NICs are due within 14 days (or 17 if paid electronically) of the end of the tax month following the tax months in which the relevant tax and Social Security legislation giving rise to the liability has effect.

Employers should include the additional PAYE and NICs as part of their normal monthly payments to HMRC. If an employer normally pays quarterly, PAYE/NICs due in respect of retrospective liabilities cannot be paid quarterly but must be made out of turn by the statutory monthly due dates. If payment is normally made electronically, payment should be made electronically.

The normal interest provisions relating to PAYE and NICs apply to PAYE and NICs due in respect of retrospectively charged liabilities. That is interest will be due on any outstanding balance of PAYE or NICs unpaid by 19/22 April following the current tax year.

SUBMITTING RETURNS

Closed tax years

Employers must complete a separate form P35(RL) Employer Annual Return (PDF 98K) (including a certificate and declaration) for each closed year along with the "National Insurance" and "Tax" copies of form P14 for each employee affected by a retrospective payment in the tax year concerned. All forms P14 should be prominently marked "Revised".

Returns cannot be sent online, even where an employer normally submits their Return online. Instead you should use form P35(RL) (PDF 98K). If you are sending more than 8 forms P14 you will also need P35(RL)Continuation Sheets (PDF 42K).

Paper forms P14 can be obtained from our Employer Orderline:

Order online at Employer Orderline

Tel 0845 7 646 646
Fax 0870 2 406 406

Amended P14s should be completed from the amended forms P11 (or equivalent) to show for each affected employee: the employee's name, NI number, the tax year (that is the year in which the retrospectively charged earnings were actually paid), the revised gross earnings in the employment, the revised PAYE and NICs totals due, the tax code applied and, if applicable, the date of leaving.

The employer should then show on the P35(RL) the following details in respect of each affected employee:

their name

if the PAYE has not been fully recovered from the employee

the original total tax deducted

the revised total tax deducted

the original total NICs

the revised total NICs

The columns of the original and revised PAYE should then be totalled, with the original figure of PAYE subtracted from the revised figure of PAYE to arrive at the additional amount payable. The same process should then be undertaken to arrive at the additional NICs payable.

The form(s) P35(RL) must be signed and dated and sent, together with the P14s, to the following address by 19 May following the year in which the relevant tax and Social Security legislation giving rise to the liability has effect.

HM Revenue & Customs

NorthEast Metropolitan Area

Employers Section
Retrospective Liability Team

Fountain Court

119 Grange Road

Middlesborough
TS1 2AU

Penalties for the late or incorrect submission of a P35(RL) and associated P14s apply as they apply for the late or incorrect submission of a P35.

Current tax year

The amended P11 (or equivalent) figures for each affected employee should, in due course, be reflected on the P14 completed at the end of the year and summarised on the P35. There is therefore no need to make separate returns in respect of payments made in a current year

RECOVERY OF PAYE AND CLASS 1 NIC FROM AFFECTED EMPLOYEES

PAYE

Where an employer incurs an additional PAYE liability in respect of a named employee, that amount must be paid to HMRC by the statutory due date, irrespective of whether the employer:

– has recovered the sum from the employee
– believes the employee to have paid the tax directly to HMRC

Once a retrospective tax liability has been created (relating to any year) by the relevant Finance Act receiving Royal Assent, an employer may seek to recover the PAYE underpaid relating to a named employee, from the employee's net earnings paid in that tax month only. There is no restriction on the sum that can be recovered. (This also applies if the employee has actually left the employment but is still due a payment of earnings.)

Where an employer cannot recover the tax in full from the employee's net earnings, the employee must make good to the employer the tax due within 90 days otherwise the outstanding amount will become additional employment income and charged to tax on the employee. Where the employee does not make good the tax, the employer should report the additional employment income/earnings (the tax not recovered from the employee) on the current year's form P11D. The entry on the form P35(RL) relating to the appropriate employee should also be noted that the tax has not been recovered.

See "Class 1 National Insurance contributions" below regarding the National Insurance implications of an employee not making good the tax.

Example:

Royal Assent of a Finance Act is 20 July. This results in an additional PAYE liability of £100,000 in respect of employee A. Employee A's net monthly pay is £7,000 (salary being paid at the end of the calendar month.) The employer can recover from employee A a sum equivalent to the employee's net pay (£7,000 less the additional NICs due on the earnings giving rise to the £100,000 PAYE — see below) from the salary due on 31 July. Employee A has until 19 October to pay to the employer the remaining tax, failing which this becomes additional income to be declared by the employee on their Self Assessment tax return and an additional payment of earnings on which Class 1 NICs must be paid.

The unmet tax sum should be aggregated with any other earnings the employee receives in the earnings period which includes the 19th October. The total amount is then liable to Class 1 NICs.

Class 1 National Insurance contributions (NICs)

As with PAYE, where an employer incurs an additional NICs liability in respect of a named employee, that amount must be paid to HMRC by the statutory due date, irrespective of whether the employer recovers the primary contributions from the employee or not.

An employer has the remainder of the tax year in which the legislation giving rise to the retrospective NICs liability has effect, and all of the following year, to recover from the relevant employee's net earnings, that employee's primary contributions element of the additional NICs due. This is subject to the provision that the amount deducted cannot exceed the amount of NICs deducted from the employee's salary for the month.

These rules do not apply to any resulting increase in the employee's earnings arising from the employee's failure to make good to the employer any additional tax arising from payments retrospectively charged to tax. Under such circumstances the employer only has the earnings period in which the 90th day falls to recover any additional primary contributions.

Example:

Social Security legislation giving rise to retrospective earnings of £250,000 has effect on 10 August 2008. This results in an additional £34,500 NICs liability in respect of Employee A of which £2,500 represents primary contributions. Employee A's monthly salary, paid calendar monthly, is £3,000 on which £272.55 primary contributions are paid.

The employer can recover an additional £272.55 per month from August 2008 to March 2010 inclusive until the total £2,500 has been recovered. The employer will be able to recover the full amount of additional primary NICs in this example by May 2009.

The payment of tax by an employer on an employee's behalf is a payment of earnings for NICs purposes and should be aggregated with any other earnings an employee receives in an earnings period. This applies equally to cases where an employee fails to make good tax within 90 days. In these cases the sum of tax is treated as a payment of earnings on the 90th day and should be aggregated with any other earnings paid in the earnings period in which the 90th day falls.

Employers are able to recover the NICs due on these additional earnings as normal but there is no extended recovery period for these NICs if the total amount of primary NICs due cannot be recovered from the pay in the relevant earnings period.

INFORMATION TO BE PROVIDED TO EMPLOYEES

Closed tax years

Where an employer amends an employee's pay records for any closed tax year, for each year for which records are amended, the employer must provide the employee with details of the revised pay, tax and NICs as soon as possible after the amendments are made and no later than 31 December in the year in which the legislation giving rise to the retrospective liability has effect.

Where:

The employer previously issued the employee with a form P60, the employer must issue a revised P60. The form must be prominently marked that it supersedes the previous certificate relating to that year. On receipt of a revised P60, the employee must not use the original form

The employer has not previously issued the employee with a form P60, the employer must provide the employee with a copy of the revised P14 to be sent to HMRC as part of the statutory return due by 19 May.

Current tax year

Where an employer amends an employee's current year pay records, those amendments should be reflected in the revised figures on the form P60 provided at the end of the year, or P45 if the employee leaves during the year. As such there is no requirement to provide employees with separate certificates relating to retrospectively charged liabilities and the tax and NICs due on those liabilities.

LEAVERS

Recovery of tax from employee

Where an employee has left before the date on which legislation giving rise to a retrospective tax liability has effect, an employer should still attempt to seek repayment from the employee within 90 days by applying to the employee's last known address. If the ex-employee does not make good the tax, the same situation applies as if the employee were currently employed. That is the sum becomes additional income of the employee.

Recovery of NICs from employee

Where an employees has left before the date on which legislation giving rise to a retrospective NICs liability has effect, the employer cannot recover the primary contributions due on the retrospective earnings or on any amount of additional tax unpaid after the 90 days have expired unless he pays the employee any earnings after the date of leaving.

Code to be operated when calculating the additional PAYE due

Where a code was issued to an employer in respect of a named employee for the year in which the payment to that employee giving rise to the retrospective liability was actually paid, that code should be applied.

Where a code was not issued to an employer in respect of a named employee for the year in which the payment to that employee giving rise to the retrospective liability was actually paid, the Higher Rate tax should be applied to the payment.

Example:

> Employee A leaves the employment on 31 December 2006. On 6 April 2007 the employer makes a payment to employee A which on 20 July is retrospectively charged to tax. The employer has not been issued with a 2007/08 code in respect of the employee. The employer deducts tax at the Higher Rate applicable for 2007/08 on the payment made to employee A.

PROVIDING INFORMATION TO THE EMPLOYEE

The requirement to provide employees with details of revised earnings, tax and NICs, either by way of a revised P60 or copy P14, apply as equally to leavers as they do to current employees.

EMPLOYERS' TAX AND NIC FREE PAYMENTS TO HOMEWORKERS: INCREASE IN GUIDELINE RATE

9 April 2008. *HMRC Notice*

From 6 April 2008, HM Revenue & Customs (HMRC) has increased the tax and NIC free guideline rate employers can pay home working employees without keeping records from £2 to £3 per week.

Employers can reimburse their employees who work regularly from home for the additional household expenses they incur without incurring an extra tax or NICs charge. The additional expenses that the employer may reimburse are those connected with the day to day running of the employee's home. This might include additional costs of heating and lighting the work area, or additional insurance costs.

Because it might be difficult for employers to calculate the exact additional costs, HMRC has published a guideline rate that can be paid without the employer having to justify the amount paid or the employee having to keep any records to demonstrate the additional expenditure. The guideline rate is not a maximum amount and greater amounts can be paid where there is evidence to justify them.

Further guidance is available in the Employment Income Manual.

FRIDAY 13TH A GOOD DAY FOR THE UK'S BAR AND RESTAURANT WORKERS

13 June 2008. *HMRC press release*

Today the EAT ruled in HM Revenue & Customs' favour by supporting current National Minimum Wage legislation relating to tips, in the case of Annabel's restaurant and night club. The decision is good news for the UK's restaurant and bar workers.

This means that employers have to pay their staff at least the National Minimum Wage regardless of any tips, gratuities, service or cover charges, so long as the tips are not paid directly through the employer's pay-roll.

HMRC argued that payment via a "tronc" (an independent tips distribution scheme) does not count towards the National Minimum Wage.

The Judge determined that where restaurant or bar service charges are paid by the customer to the employer, but are then paid into a "troncmaster's" bank account for distribution in accordance with a "tronc" scheme agreed between the troncmaster and employees, the sums so distributed to employees are not "paid by the employer" for the purposes of being included in any National Minimum Wage calculation.

Denise Gaston of HM Revenue & Customs said:

"Our priority is to ensure that all workers are paid at least the National Minimum Wage. We are very pleased that the court has recognised HMRC's commitment to ensuring that tips are correctly and fairly distributed to the people who earn them. This is good news for bar and restaurant workers across the UK."

A spokesperson for the Department for Business said:

"It is essential that all UK workers receive the pay they are entitled to and that everyone earns at least the National Minimum Wage. Equally, it's important that tipping is fair and we are already examining what options are available to help ensure transparency."

HMRC vigorously enforces the minimum wage across all employment sectors including the catering and hospitality industry. Anyone who thinks they are not being paid National Minimum Wage rates should contact the confidential NMW Helpline on 0845 6000 678 and we will ensure the law is complied with.

NOTES

1. In October 2007 HM Revenue & Customs HMRC lost an Employment Tribunal appeal case against the restaurant/club Annabel's. The case involved the interaction between National Minimum Wage and Troncs. Troncs are a system of pooling and distributing tips to staff in the service industries. Under specific circum-stances payments made as tips may be included as part of the payroll by the employer and count toward NMW. However HMRC argued that tips paid via a tronc should not count towards national minimum wage. HMRC were given leave to take the case to the EAT.

2. The case was heard at the EAT today (13 June).

3. Annabel's have 14 days to seek permission to appeal the Judgment.

4. The National Minimum Wage Act 1998 has now been in force for nearly ten years. HM Revenue & Customs has operational responsibility for enforcing the minimum wage and has operated a helpline and network of compliance teams since 1 April 1999 to fulfil that role. The Department for Business, Enterprise and Regulatory Reform (BERR) is responsible for National Minimum Wage policy.

HMRC APPROVAL OF JOINT NATIONAL INSURANCE CONTRIBUTION ELECTIONS

10 November 2008. *HMRC Statement*

A facility to allow an employee to meet the employer's secondary Class 1 National Insurance contributions (NICs) liability arising on share option gains was introduced in the Child Support, Pensions and Social Security Act 2000 (CSPSSA) on 28 July 2000.[1] This can be achieved either by Agreement or Joint Election. However, unlike an agreement, a joint election

NIC

constitutes the legal transfer of liability for payment from the employer to the employee and the law requires that any joint election must be approved by an officer of HM Revenue & Customs (HMRC).

The Employee Shares and Securities Unit (ESSU) are responsible for the administration of the approval process and publish model forms of election (www.hmrc.gov.uk/manuals/ersmmanual/ERSM170750.htm) to facilitate it.[2] For various reasons the model elections may not always be suitable for a particular company's needs and practitioners may wish to customise them to suit a particular client. Whether or not the model election is used, HMRC still needs to approve whatever form of election is used by each company or group of companies. Before an election can be approved it must contain a number of elements to satisfy legislative requirements.

1. The parties to the election must be clearly identified. The Company (the "secondary contributor"), its registered office address and company registration number must be included in the draft election and provision made for the full name of the employee to be recorded along with their National Insurance number.

2. The purpose and scope of the joint election (see model document (www.hmrc.gov.uk/manuals/ersmmanual/ERSM170750.htm)) needs to be set out and this should clearly specify the option grant or award of securities which is subject to the election, the relevant legislation and the relevant employment income. An election will not be approved if it does not clearly identify the option grant or award to which it is to apply. For example, an election that is said to apply to all options whenever they may be granted will not be approved. This section also needs to include declarations (see model document (www.hmrc.gov.uk/manuals/ersmmanual/ERSM170750.htm)) concerning Chapter 3A of Part 7 and retrospection (section 4B(2) SSCBA 1992).

3. The election should also state what arrangements are in place as to how the employee will account for the secondary NICs liability and ensure that it is paid over to HMRC in good time. Where the relevant employment income will be received from a third party then the employee should authorise that party to withhold a sufficient amount of cash (or sell sufficient shares) to cover the liability, and this should be provided for in this section. A clear statement that the employee understands that they are personally liable for the secondary NICs covered by the election should also be included in this section.

4. A clear statement of the means for determining that the election is no longer in force (see model document (www.hmrc.gov.uk/manuals/ersmmanual/ERSM170750.htm)).

5. A clear statement that the election will continue in full force regardless of whether the employee ceases to be an employee of the company. Similarly a statement may be included concerning residency.

6. A declaration by both the company and the employee that they agree to be bound by the terms of the election which may be by deed if so required.

Recently a number of draft elections submitted for approval include other elements that are not within the scope of the legislation and they do not require HMRC approval. Including those elements within the election means that HMRC is being asked to recognise terms or clauses that are not a requirement of the legislation. Examples of terms or clauses which are being included are:

1. Transfer of employment within the group whereby the secondary contributor changes and the employee undertakes to enter into a new election with the new employer. This is not necessary as the joint election remains in force even if employment ceases (see section 5).

2. An indemnity in favour of the company against any expense incurred if the employee fails to satisfy their liability for secondary NIC. This expands the scope of the joint election and cannot be approved. If the company requires such an indemnity then it should be included within the option agreement or other similar document which does not require HMRC approval.

3. A power of attorney in order to enable enforcement of either of the above or any other aspect of the election. This again expands the scope of the election and cannot be approved. If required then it should be included in the option agreement or other similar document and could also be used to implement the joint election if required.

From the 1 December 2008 where draft elections are presented for approval that include additional elements not required by the legislation nor essential for the implementation of the election then approval will not be given. Further guidance on NIC Elections can be found in the

Employment Related Securities Manual (ERSM 170750 (www.hmrc.gov.uk/manuals/ersmmanual/ERSM170750.htm) and 170760 (www.hmrc.gov.uk/manuals/ersmmanual/ERSM170760.htm)).

Notes—[1] Subsequent changes to legislation increased the scope of NIC Joint Elections (& Agreements) so that they can include employment income arising from restricted securities (section 426 of ITEPA 2003) and convertible securities (section 438 of ITEPA 2003).

[2] Applications for approval should be sent to ESSU, HM Revenue and Customs, Room G52, 100 Parliament Street, London SW1A 2BQ. The application should include draft joint election, supporting documentation for grant or award and if the model documents are being used then a statement to that effect.

THE FIRST AID TRAINING SECTOR AND THE SOCIAL SECURITY (CATEGORISATION OF EARNERS) REGULATIONS 1978

1 April 2009. *HMRC Brief 25/09*

THE CURRENT POSITION

The Social Security (Categorisation of Earners) Regulations 1978 (the Regulations) need only be considered where there is a contract for services (self-employment).

HM Revenue & Customs' (HMRC) interpretation of the Regulations in terms of lecturers, teachers, instructors or others in a similar capacity who are engaged to provide instruction in an educational establishment is currently set out in guidance at ESM 4503 which will be shortly revised. The revised ESM 4503 is published below.

The comments below are by way of additional assistance. HMRC's view is that the Regulations apply where a lecturer, teacher or instructor etc provides instruction in:

– courses in a school, college or university
– courses of an academic/vocational nature at any place where the instruction is provided (for example, outdoors or at a client site)

A course is covered by the Regulations whether or not it leads to a certificate, diploma, degree or professional qualification. In practice, HMRC's view is that courses in the latter category fall within the Regulations where the completion of the course represents a substantive achievement. HMRC's view of what represents a 'substantive achievement' is the attainment of a recognised qualification, licence or skill which provides access to a particular job or the authority to conduct a particular activity in the workplace.

It is clear from discussions with the First Aid training sector, that the requirement that a course represents a substantive achievement is causing difficulty because of the diverse nature of courses provided by the sector (different courses being delivered by the same trainer in the same week), the nature of the courses, the circumstances under which they are provided, to whom they are provided and where they are provided. It is also clear that there are wide-ranging and firmly held views in the sector on the application of the Regulations.

HMRC need to have regard to the fact that the Regulations apply to training providers outside the First Aid sector. Accordingly HMRC propose to review whether the current Regulations should be amended in view of the nature of training delivery today.

THE WAY FORWARD

To inform the review and recommendations to Ministers, HMRC will undertake an informal consultation with the training sector, including the First Aid training sector, on the scope of the Regulations and their practical application.

HMRC will in due course publish an announcement about the consultation on its website. Simultaneously HMRC will write directly to identify interested stakeholders including those in the First Aid training sector with whom there has been discussion.

In the meantime, training providers in the First Aid sector should follow HMRC's revised ESM 4503, drawing on this bulletin as necessary, when deciding whether particular courses and instructors fall within the scope of the Regulations.

Where training providers cannot determine the status of their teachers, lecturers or trainers by applying the revised ESM 4503 and this bulletin, they should contact HMRC on Tel 08457 143

143 quoting this Revenue & Customs Brief 25/09 'The First Aid Training Sector and the Social Security (Categorisation of Earners) Regulations 1978'.

REVISED ESM 4503

ESM4503—Particular occupations: teachers, lecturers and instructors—NICs

SS (Categorisation of Earners) Regulations 1978 (SI 1978 No.1689) Regulation 1(2), Regulation 2, paragraph 4 in Part I of Schedule 1 and paragraph 6 in Schedule 3

Most teachers etc are engaged either part-time or full-time under a contract of service.

Where they are not, the above Regulations make provision for treating most teachers, who are not employed under a contract of service, as employees.

They provide for a teacher, lecturer or instructor who teaches in an 'educational establishment' to be treated as an employed earner if they teach in the presence of their students (unless they are working for the Open University); and are paid by the Education Authority or the person who provides the education.

Exceptions

Do not treat a teacher, lecturer or instructor as an employed earner if:

– the time the person spends teaching/lecturing is minimal in terms of the working time available or the instruction is given only occasionally. In practical terms this means that prior to giving the instruction, they have agreed to give it on not more than 3 days in 3 consecutive months; or
– the instruction is given as public lectures. A public lecture is regarded as one which any member of the public can attend without prior notice; that is, it is not part of a course or confined to a particular group or society.

What is an educational establishment?

An educational establishment is defined in Regulation 1(2) as including

– a place where instruction is given leading to a certificate, diploma, degree or professional qualification; or
– a place where instruction is given which follows substantially the same type of syllabus but which is not designed to lead to such a certificate, diploma, degree or professional qualification.

In practice, therefore, an educational establishment can be either a recognised educational establishment: for example a school, university or college or anywhere else (indoors or outdoors) where instruction is given. The case of St. John's School, Cambridge v Secretary of State for Social Security gives further guidance on this point – see ESM7230. What is important is the nature of the instruction.

The Regulations should be applied to all teachers, lecturers or instructors providing instruction in a school, college or university regardless of the nature of the instruction, whether it is given outside normal school hours or whether the particular course leads to a certificate, diploma, degree or professional qualification.

Where the instruction is given in a place which is not a recognised educational establishment such as a school, college or university, the Regulations should be applied only to those teachers, lecturers or instructors who are giving instruction on courses which result in the attainment of a recognised qualification, licence or skill which provides access to a particular job or authority to conduct a particular activity in the workplace. This is irrespective of whether such instruction results in the provision of a certificate, diploma or such similar document.

Who provides the education?

The teacher, lecturer or instructor delivering the instruction must be engaged by a person providing education. (Para 4, Part 1 of Schedule 1)

That person may be:

- A local authority, Board of Governors of a school or any other type of training organisation such as a company or partnership; or
- An individual (where they are engaged directly by the client to deliver the instruction)

Who pays the teacher, lecturer or instructor?

The earnings in respect of the employment must be paid by, or on behalf of, the person providing the education. (Para 4(c) Part 1 of Schedule 1)

Example 1—Recognised educational establishment

If a school engages a teacher, guarantees the payment of fees for that instruction and is responsible for ensuring that any fees due are paid by the parents, the school is paying the teacher.

If the teacher has contracted directly with the parents, receives his/her fees either via the school or direct from the parents and has to personally pursue non-payment of fees with the parents, the teacher is regarded as not being paid by the school. So the condition in paragraph 4(c) is not satisfied and the teacher continues to be a self-employed earner.

If it is stated that the previous paragraph applies, confirm the facts carefully and check for evidence before accepting that the provisions are not satisfied. Do not assume that the school is liable just because it includes the particular instruction in its syllabus or sets the fees but verify that it is also responsible for finding the teacher and any necessary replacements.

Example 2—Vocational or skills training in a non recognised educational establishment

Where a local authority or business contracts with a training organisation that provides a trainer to train its staff, that organisation receives payment direct from the local authority or business and pays the trainer for delivering the training, the Regulations will apply. In this situation the training organisation is treated as the secondary contributor.

Issuing opinions under the Regulations

Always use the draft letter at ESM0110 when giving an opinion under these Regulations.

HMRC WINS MINIMUM WAGE COURT BATTLE

7 May 2009. *HMRC press release*

The Court of Appeal has ruled that tips, gratuities and voluntary service charges paid to workers by a troncmaster via a tronc do not count towards the national minimum wage in the case of *Annabel's restaurant and night club and others*.

Bar and restaurant workers have today been given a helping hand by the Court of Appeal in their fight for fair pay. The court ruled in HM Revenue & Customs' favour by upholding current national minimum wage legislation relating to tips, gratuities and discretionary service charges in the case of *Annabel's restaurant and night club and others* [2009] All ER (D) 54 (May).

The judgment confirmed that employers must pay their staff at least the national minimum wage regardless of any tips, gratuities, service charges or cover charges, providing they are not paid by the employer to workers through the employer's payroll. This means that Annabel's and others must now pay over £125,000 in arrears to its workers.

HMRC had argued that payment via a "tronc" (an independent distribution scheme) does not count towards the national minimum wage.

The Court determined that where restaurant or bar service charges are paid by the customer to the employer, but are then paid into a "troncmaster's" bank account for distribution in accordance with a "tronc" scheme agreed between the troncmaster and workers, the sums distributed to workers are not "paid by the employer" and so cannot be included in national minimum wage pay.

Rt Hon Stephen Timms, Financial Secretary to the Treasury said—

"The Government's priority is to ensure that all workers are paid at least the national minimum wage. I am extremely pleased that the court has recognised HMRC's commitment to ensuring that tips are correctly and fairly distributed to the people who earn them. This is good news for bar and restaurant workers across the UK."

HMRC vigorously enforces the minimum wage across all employment sectors including the catering and hospitality industry. Anyone who thinks they are not being paid national minimum wage rates should contact the confidential NMW Helpline on 0845 6000 678.

NOTES

1. In June 2008 HM Revenue & Customs won an Employment Appeal Tribunal against the restaurant/club Annabel's and others. The case involved the calculation of national minimum wage pay where an independent tronc scheme was in operation. Troncs are a system of pooling and distributing service charges, tips and gratuities to staff in the service industries. Under specific circumstances, payments made as tips, gratuities, service charges and cover charges may count towards national minimum wage pay. However HMRC argued that tips, gratuities and voluntary service charges paid to workers by a troncmaster via a tronc did not count towards national minimum wage. Annabels and others were given leave to appeal against the ruling.

2. The case was heard at the Court of Appeal on 15 January 2009. The Court found in HMRC's favour and the judgment was handed down today (7 May 2009).

3. The judgment is legally binding and sets a precedent for other cases.

4. The National Minimum Wage Act 1998 has now been in force for ten years. HM Revenue & Customs has operational responsibility for enforcing the minimum wage and has operated a helpline and network of compliance teams since 1 April 1999 to fulfil that role. The Department for Business, Enterprise and Regulatory Reform (BERR) is responsible for national minimum wage policy.

5. The government announced yesterday that using tips to make up staff pay to minimum wage levels will be outlawed from October this year, giving thousands of workers fair wages, ensuring a fair and level playing field for employers and boosting consumer confidence in the use of tips. For more information on the government's plans, visit [the www.nds.coi.gov.uk website].

REFUNDS OF CLASS 1 NIC PAID IN ERROR BY LECTURERS, TEACHERS OR INSTRUCTORS

17 October 2012. *HMRC Brief 28/12*

ABSTRACT

The law requiring self-employed lecturers, teachers and instructors to be subject to Class 1 NICs was repealed with effect from 6 April 2012. However, HMRC recognises that certain individuals, likely to include First Aid and other training providers who were investigated by HMRC and ordered to pay Class 1 NICs under previous guidance, will now be entitled to a refund or set-off against Class 2/4 liabilities. Claims may be made in respect of the last two tax years and this brief sets out the arrangements for making such claims, including those by engagers in respect of secondary contributions.

FULL TEXT

The Social Security (Categorisation of Earners) Regulations 1978 in relation to lecturers, teachers, instructors or those in a similar capacity

Applications for refunds of National Insurance contributions paid in error or claims for financial redress

WHO SHOULD READ THIS?

Those who engage lecturers, teachers, instructors or trainers in a similar capacity, particularly, vocational and recreational training providers, including First Aid Training Providers.

Trainers particularly in the vocational and recreational fields who were engaged by their training provider under contracts for services (self-employment contracts) but who had Class 1 (employees') National Insurance contributions deducted.

NIC

BACKGROUND

1. The Social Security (Categorisation of Earners) Regulations 1978 (the Regulations) made provision for treating lecturers, teachers, instructors or those in a similar capacity in traditional educational establishments, such as schools, colleges or universities etc, who were not employed under a contract of service (an employment contract) as employees for NICs purposes.

2. With effect from 6 April 2012 the relevant provisions of the Regulations were repealed so that the Regulations no longer apply to lecturers, teachers, instructors or those in a similar capacity (SI 2012/816).

3. However, prior to repeal, it is possible that earlier published HMRC guidance may have led some training providers particularly in the vocational or recreational sector to incorrectly apply the Regulations to payments made to trainers engaged under self-employment contracts. If the Regulations were incorrectly applied, Class 1 NICs may have been accounted for and paid to HMRC in error. HMRC will now consider claims for the refund of any incorrectly paid contributions. Such claims are limited by statute so that refunds may only be made in respect of the last two tax years or, where a decision was requested/challenged and this remains undetermined, the tax year in which the challenge was made and the preceding tax year.

ARRANGEMENTS FOR CLAIMING REFUNDS OF CLASS 1 NATIONAL INSURANCE CONTRIBUTIONS PAID IN ERROR

WHO CAN CLAIM REFUNDS?

4. Refunds may be made by trainers or instructors, or those who engaged them, and where amounts of NICs were paid in error following HMRC's guidance. This is primarily going to affect those engaged in the provision of vocational or recreational training as set out in HMRC's guidance prior to repeal of the relevant provisions of the Regulations.

5. Refunds are not due where educational training providers applied the Regulations. This is because there is no dispute or doubt that the Regulations prior to 6 April 2012 applied to the providers of educational training. In this context educational training provider means a school, college, university or any such similar educational establishment.

6. Refunds are also not due where any trainer or instructor was engaged under an employment contract and Income Tax (PAYE) and Class 1 NICs were correctly accounted for.

7. Where a training provider owes HMRC any outstanding sums (including Income Tax, National Insurance contributions or VAT) any secondary Class 1 NICs refundable will, in the first instance, be set against those outstanding sums and only the balance repaid.

HOW DO I KNOW IF I AM ENTITLED TO APPLY FOR A REFUND?

VOCATIONAL AND RECREATIONAL TRAINING PROVIDERS

8. We believe there are likely to be three categories of training provider who may be eligible to apply for refunds:

– First Aid training providers who were subject to a compliance intervention by HMRC and Class 1 NICs were recovered under the Regulations where those amounts of NICs were paid in error following HMRC's guidance: HMRC is corresponding directly with these training providers. However, if you fall into this category and have not received a letter you should contact HMRC in writing at the address provided below.

– Other vocational and recreational training providers who were subject to a compliance intervention by HMRC, Class 1 NICs was recovered under the Regulations and where those amounts of NICs were paid in error following HMRC's guidance.

– Any other First Aid training or other vocational and recreational training providers not the subject of a compliance intervention but who wrote to HMRC requesting a decision as to the NICs category under which their trainers should be included.

APPLICATIONS FOR REFUNDS FROM TRAINERS AND ENGAGERS

9. Trainers who were engaged under self-employment contracts and who were subject to the Regulations by their training provider engager can choose not to have any primary contributions paid in error refunded to them but to let them count instead towards their contributory benefit entitlement as if they had been correctly paid. If a successful refund claim is received from a training provider which meets the statutory criteria, HMRC will write to the affected trainers asking them whether they wish the contributions refunded or not.

10. This does not prevent the engager from seeking a refund of the wrongly paid secondary contributions where one is due or the trainer notifying HMRC before they reach pension age that they now wish to apply for a refund. Any such claim in these circumstances would be subject to the statutory conditions for the claiming of refunds of erroneously paid contributions including those noted in paragraph 3 above.

11. Where trainers elect to have Class 1 contributions refunded, HMRC will offset the contributions refundable against the Class 2 and 4 National Insurance contributions correctly payable by virtue of the trainer's self-employed status. Additionally, where a trainer owes HMRC any outstanding sums (including Income Tax, NICs or VAT) any contributions refundable will be set against those outstanding sums and only the balance repaid.

HOW TO APPLY FOR A REFUND

12. Training providers who engaged trainers under self-employment contracts and accounted for Class 1 NICs under the Social Security (Categorisation of Earners) Regulations 1978 and who think that they fall into any of the categories identified above should contact HMRC in writing. When writing they should provide the information detailed below. This will help us to check that their particular circumstances meet the statutory qualifying rules governing the refunding of Class 1 NICs.

Please write to:

The Employment Status Team
HM Revenue & Customs
PT (Product & Process)
Area 1E 09
100 Parliament Street
London SW1A 2HQ

PLEASE PROVIDE THE FOLLOWING INFORMATION:

- training provider's name
- whether a company, partnership or sole trader
- address
- PAYE reference
- Accounts Office reference
- precise nature of business
- the years for which a refund is claimed
- the amount of refund being claimed
- the name, NI number and address of the actual training provider's trainers in respect of whom a refund is being sought
- full details of any written request made by the provider or the trainer to an officer of HMRC (including the date of the request) asking for a decision, or a variation of a previous decision, as to the category of earner under which any of the training providers workers should be included - this should be accompanied by a copy of any decision received from HMRC

FINANCIAL REDRESS

HMRC can make Financial Redress payments under its complaints policy. Our guiding principle when making such payments is to ensure that the customer is not out of pocket as a direct result of our mistake. In the majority of cases, this will mean reimbursing the additional costs incurred as a direct result of our mistake, to the extent that they are reasonable. Common examples include the cost of telephone calls, postage, and any additional professional fees incurred, again to the extent that they are reasonable and proportionate. We will also consider payments for demonstrable financial loss, but not for any loss which is hypothetical, speculative or insubstantial, or the value of any refundable Class1 NICs paid in error. Further information about our complaints processes can be found within the "Complaints" factsheet www.hmrc.gov.uk/factsheets/complaints-factsheet.pdf.

HMRC'S DATA-GATHERING POWERS AND DEPOSIT-TAKERS' RETURNS

7 January 2013. *HMRC Brief 39/12*

ABSTRACT

HMRC confirms that deposit-taking financial institutions will not be required to provide National Insurance numbers and other tax identification numbers in their "Type 17/18" annual returns of interest for accounts opened on or after 6 April 2013. The government had originally intended HMRC to collect this extra information under new powers in FA 2011, Sch 23, as specified in the draft Data-gathering Powers (Relevant Data) Regulations.

FULL TEXT

SCHEDULE 23 FINANCE ACT 2011 – COLLECTION OF NATIONAL INSURANCE NUMBERS AND OTHER TAX IDENTIFICATION NUMBERS BY FINANCIAL INSTITUTIONS

WHO SHOULD READ

Financial Institutions who make Type 17/18 annual returns of interest paid or collected.
Financial Institutions who make Type 17/18 annual returns of interest paid or collected.

Schedule 23 to the Finance Act 2011 (FA 2011) introduced a new framework of powers for HM Revenue & Customs (HMRC) to collect data to help in risk assessment.

One aim was to require UK Financial Institutions to collect and provide National Insurance numbers and other tax identification numbers for all interest bearing accounts opened on or after 6 April 2013.

Representations have been received from the financial sector and HMRC accept that Schedule 23 does not empower financial institutions to collect such information. HMRC will not now require this extra data to be provided.

Legislation will be required to empower the collection of such data. HMRC will discuss any such future legislation with the industry. There will be a suitable lead-in time to allow for the necessary system changes to be made.

This only applies to the new data collection requirements under Schedule 23 to FA 2011. All current reporting requirements involving National Insurance numbers and other tax identification numbers, on these and other returns, such as on ISA returns, continue to apply.

Further information on this subject can be obtained from the internet by following the link below.

Reports for sections 17 and 18 TMA and EUSD – www.hmrc.gov.uk/esd-guidance/s17-s18-si-reporting.htm

Or from Nick Wright on Tel 0161 475 8577.

NICS: HMRC'S POSITION FOLLOWING COURT OF APPEAL DECISION IN ITV SERVICES LTD

4 October 2013. *HMRC Brief 29/13*

ABSTRACT

This brief concerns HMRC's position on the employment status for NICs purposes of entertainers. HMRC confirms that guidance on retrospective application of the Court of Appeal decision in the ITV Services case remains as set out in R&C Brief 19/2012 and that no "concerted compliance activity" is planned for the media sector.

FULL TEXT

PURPOSE OF THE BRIEF

This Brief sets out HM Revenue & Customs' (HMRC) position following the decision by the Court of Appeal (CoA) in the case of ITV Services Ltd (ITV). The case concerned the employment status for National Insurance contributions purposes of actors engaged by ITV under specific contract types. The Court handed down its judgment on 23 July 2013 and found against ITV unanimously upholding the decisions of the First Tier Tribunal (FTT) and Upper Tribunal (UT) that the actors' contracts provided for remuneration by way of salary and there was liability for Class 1 National Insurance contributions on all the remuneration payable under the contract. See also Revenue & Customs Brief 19/12 issued 14 June 2012 (www.hmrc.gov.uk/briefs/national-insurance/brief1912.htm).

You can read the full text of the decision at [2013] EWCA Civ 867.

READERSHIP

All national broadcasters, film companies, theatre managers, independent production companies, their representative bodies and agents in the Film & TV Production Industries, Equity, individual entertainers and any other companies engaging entertainers to whom this judgement may also be relevant are encouraged to read this briefing.

BACKGROUND

By a decision released on 23 November 2010, the FTT dismissed the appeals by ITV against three determinations made by HMRC. ITV appealed the FTT decision to the UT. By a decision released on 7 February 2012, the UT upheld the decision of the FTT and dismissed ITV's appeal. On 25 May 2012 ITV was given permission to appeal the decision of the UT to the CoA. This appeal was heard on 12 and 13 December 2012 and 18 March 2013.

ITV's appeal to the CoA again focused primarily on whether actors engaged by ITV were to be treated as 'employed earners' for National Insurance purposes under the provisions of paragraph 5A of Part 1, Schedule 1 to the Social Security (Categorisation of Earners) Regulations 1978 (the Regulations) by virtue of the fact that the payments made to the actors by ITV were 'by way of salary' within the meaning of "salary" as defined in that paragraph of the Regulations.

THE COA DECISION

By a decision handed down on 23 July 2013, the Court unanimously dismissed ITV's appeal and upheld the principal position maintained by HMRC throughout that whether or not the provisions of the Regulations apply is to be determined at the outset of an actor's engagement by reference to the terms of their specific contract.

In particular, the Court decided that where contracts between the engager and the entertainer incorporated the payment provisions of collective agreements (that is, national standard agreements negotiated between producers' representatives and Equity) the effect of such provisions would be to include payments "by way of salary" as defined. Save for what was described as an "All Rights Contract" (which HMRC had previously agreed was not within the Regulations), the two "All Inclusive Fees Equity Agreements", the "Weekly Equity Agreement" and the "Option Equity Agreement", the Court found that the remuneration agreed to be paid under all other contracts presented to it included payments provided for in the collective agreements (for example production day and attendance day payments) and, therefore, included a payment by way of salary. Furthermore, except for the All Rights Contract, in all other contracts where the terms entitled the entertainer to receive payment on a contingent basis (for example on account of overage/overtime), that payment was a "payment by way of salary".

HMRC does not consider that Lord Justice Rimer's views expressed at paragraphs 35, 36 and 37 of the judgment (and the conclusions that he reached on the contracts based on those paragraphs) alter the decision reached by both Tribunals below that, under the terms of their contract, where an actor is required to make himself/herself available for work as and when required by the engager for the period of the engagement they are performing work (as defined in the Regulations). Both the other CoA judges (Sir Stanley Burnton and the President of the Family Division, Sir James Munby,) expressed reservations on Rimer LJ's comments on this issue but reserved their position, since it was not necessary to determine the point to determine the appeal.

FUTURE APPLICATION OF THE REGULATIONS FOLLOWING THE JUDGMENT

Although the specific contracts cited in the CoA judgment only concerned actors engaged by ITV, HMRC considers that the principles established in this and the previous decisions in the

Tribunals below cover all "entertainers" as statutorily defined in the Regulations – "a person employed as an actor, singer, or musician or in any similar performing capacity". HMRC now expects those in the industry engaging entertainers to comply with the Court's decision.

In particular all three judges agreed with the UT in its observation that hourly or daily payments such as overtime or overage payments, to which an entertainer is entitled under the contract, even though contingent and whether or not actually paid in practice, are computed by reference to the amount of time for which work is performed and are consequently payments by way of salary. This part of the judgment will have particular significance for those actors and musicians whose contracts are subject to the terms providing for payments under collective agreements with Equity and Musicians' Union respectively.

Given that HMRC now expects voluntary compliance with the Regulations, it does not intend to undertake concerted compliance activity in the media sector in respect of entertainers as a direct result of the *ITV* case. It will, however, continue to apply its normal risk-based approach to identifying individual cases which represent a high risk and reserves the right to investigate such cases. It will also continue to scrutinise those cases currently the subject of investigation.

Where HMRC is undertaking or undertakes an investigation into an entertainer or media company, it will apply the law in terms of the Regulations applying the decision and judgment of the UT and the CoA.

RETROSPECTIVE APPLICATION OF THE COURT OF APPEAL DECISION

HMRC's position regarding retrospective liability is that set out in Revenue & Customs Brief 19/12 on 14 June 2012, following the UT decision. As such the extent to which HMRC will seek to apply the CoA decision retrospectively will be determined by a number of different factors.

WRITTEN OPINION PREVIOUSLY GIVEN

Where HMRC has previously issued a written opinion to a party that Class 1 National Insurance contributions are not due in respect of payments made under a particular contract because HMRC did not consider those payments to be "by way of salary", it will not seek recovery retrospectively of the unpaid National Insurance contributions that were due and payable prior to 6 April 2011 (unless HMRC has expressly advised an engager that National Insurance contributions should be operated from an earlier date).

EXTENT OF WRITTEN OPINION

Where HMRC has previously provided a written opinion to an engager that Class 1 National Insurance contributions are not due in respect of a particular contract, and the engager used identical (other than for individual personal details) contract(s) to engage other entertainers, HMRC will not seek arrears of Class 1 National Insurance contributions due and payable prior to 6 April 2011 in respect of these other contracts.

NO WRITTEN OPINION PREVIOUSLY GIVEN

Where HMRC has not given such a written opinion, then it reserves the right to seek to recover any National Insurance contributions arrears under its normal compliance subject to the provisions of the Limitation Act 1980.

CONSULTATION ON NATIONAL INSURANCE AND SELF-EMPLOYED ENTERTAINERS

HMRC is mindful of the fact that it undertook a recent public consultation on options for amending the National Insurance treatment of entertainers at some point in the future and that its preferred option was to revoke those provisions of the Regulations that relate to entertainers with effect from 6 April 2014. If an amendment is made to the Regulations, such an amendment will only have prospective effect. The CoA judgment concerns the current and retrospective application of the relevant provisions in the Regulations and therefore will apply to any contracts entered into up until the point that any amendments to the current Regulations come into force. HMRC will be publishing a summary of the consultation responses and confirm the intended way forward later this year.

FURTHER INFORMATION

Under the terms of its Non-statutory clearance (www.hmrc.gov.uk/cap/nscg.htm) service to businesses, should an engager have material uncertainty on the National Insurance contributions consequences of a particular contractual engagement with an entertainer, if appropriate, HMRC can provide its view of how the law applies to that contract.

Any such requests should be made by formal 'Non-statutory clearance' application to Large Business Customer Relationship Managers, Film & Production or TV Broadcasting Units as appropriate enclosing details of the particular engagement and a copy of the relevant (signed) contract.

NICS IN RESPECT OF ENTERTAINERS FROM 6 APRIL 2014

18 November 2013. *HMRC Brief 35/13*

ABSTRACT

On 23 October, following consultation, HMRC confirmed it would treat entertainers, except those on an employment contract, as self-employed and subject to Class 2 and Class 4 NICs with effect from 6 April 2014. This brief sets out the position for entertainers, their engagers and advisers, including HMRC's intention to apply its 'normal risk-based approach' to investigating cases of non-compliance with the rules prior to 6 April 2014.

FULL TEXT

NATIONAL INSURANCE CONTRIBUTIONS (NICS): REPEAL OF THE SOCIAL SECURITY (CATEGORISATION OF EARNERS) REGULATIONS 1978 ("THE REGULATIONS") IN RESPECT OF ENTERTAINERS FROM 6 APRIL 2014

This Brief sets out HM Revenue & Customs (HMRC) position in relation to the liability of entertainers to pay National Insurance Contributions ("NICs") with effect from 6 April 2014 subject to the proposed changes in the Regulations being approved by Parliament.

READERSHIP

All national broadcasters, film companies, theatre managers, independent production companies, their representative bodies and agents in the Film & TV Production Industries, Equity, individual entertainers, companies engaging entertainers, and any other interested parties.

BACKGROUND

As a generality, entertainers (that is, those engaged as an actor, singer, or musician, or in any similar performing capacity) are engaged under self-employment terms and that their employment status, for both tax and NICs purposes, applying relevant case law criteria, is self-employment.

Since 1998 however, The Social Security (Categorisation of Earners) Regulations 1978 ("the Regulations") have deemed self-employed entertainers, in certain prescribed circumstances, to be employed earners for National Insurance purposes. The principal policy reason for this was to provide entertainers, through the payment of Class 1 NICs, with access to earnings-related contributory benefit entitlement when out of work.

In more recent years though, the manner in which entertainers have been and are being engaged and paid for their work has made it increasingly difficult for the Regulations to be applied and operated as intended, causing uncertainties and fundamental, problems for both entertainers and engagers in deciding whether Class 1 NICs should be deducted and accounted for on payments made to and by them.

PUBLIC CONSULTATION

Following 18 months of extensive engagement with representatives from all fields of the entertainment industry, HMRC published on 15 May 2013 a public consultation document: "National Insurance and Self-Employed Entertainers", which discussed the precise difficulties being caused by the current application of the Regulations. The consultation presented four possible options for simplifying the NICs treatment of entertainers going forwards.

The consultation ran for 12 weeks receiving 11,814 individual responses of which 99.1% supported the option of repealing the Social Security (Categorisation of Earners) Regulations in relation to the entertainers. On 23 October 2013 HMRC published a summary of the consultation responses which included the announcement of the Government's decision to repeal these Regulations insofar as they relate to entertainers from 6 April 2014 and a first draft of the legislation implementing this.

You can read the full consultation document and the summary of consultation responses on the central Government website.

HMRC consultation on NICs and entertainers (www.gov.uk/government/consultations/national-insurance-and-self-employed-entertainers)

THE CURRENT NICS POSITION FOR ENTERTAINERS UNTIL 5 APRIL 2014

The Regulations as articulated in the Upper Tribunal and Court of Appeal decision and judgement in the case of *ITV Services Ltd v HMRC* continue to apply up to and including 5 April 2014.

The Regulations are applied to entertainers on an engagement by engagement basis. This means each contract of engagement they enter into is looked at separately for the purposes of deciding whether the Regulations should apply to the payments to be made under its terms.

Where the Regulations currently apply to a particular contract of an entertainer, the earnings derived from that contract are presently subject to primary and secondary Class 1 NICs as defined in Section 6 of the Social Security Contributions and Benefits Act 1992 ("SSCBA 1992"). This includes any additional payments that derive from that engagement such as royalties or residuals payments that may continue to be paid to an entertainer for some time after their original performance/ engagement has ended.

Under the current Regulations the primary Class 1 NICs contributor is the entertainer, and the secondary contributor is the producer of the entertainment from which the entertainer's earnings are derived. The secondary contributor (that is, the producer of the entertainment) is liable to deduct and account for the primary Class 1 NICs from the entertainer at time of payment and to pay both these and the secondary Class 1 NICs due to HMRC.

Further details of when the Regulations currently apply to an entertainer's contract can be found in HMRC's published guidance for entertainers, available on its website.

- Entertainers - Guidelines on the Specials NIC Rules for Entertainers (www.hmrc.gov.uk/guidance/nicrules-ents.pdf)
- Revenue and Customs Brief 19/12 (www.hmrc.gov.uk/briefs/national-insurance/brief1912.htm)
- Revenue and Customs Brief 29/13 (www.hmrc.gov.uk/briefs/national-insurance/brief2913.htm)

HMRC expects engagers of entertainers to continue following this guidance and where the Regulations apply, operating primary and secondary Class 1 NICs on payments to entertainers up to and including 5 April 2014.

THE FUTURE NICS POSITION FOR ENTERTAINERS FROM 6 APRIL 2014

Subject to the proposed changes being approved by Parliament, from 6 April 2014, entertainers will no longer be included in the provisions of the Regulations. This in turn means that entertainers' earnings will no longer be brought within the ambit of Section 6 of SSCBA 1992 (which places a Class 1 NICs charge on them) from this date.

Where there is no Class 1 NICs charge under SSCBA 1992, the earnings will be self-employed earnings and subject to Class 2 NICs (subject to the existing Class 2 Small Earnings Exemption rules) and Class 4 NICs (subject to the existing the Class 4 Upper and Lower Earnings Limit rules).

As the point at which Class 1 NICs is charged is the time of payment (as opposed to the time of the engagement or the contract of engagement being entered into), the practical effect of repealing the Regulations for entertainers will be that from 6 April 2014 payments to entertainers paid under a contract for services (that, is self-employment) will be liable to Class 2 and Class 4 NICs under section 11 (Class 2) and sections 15 to 18 (Class 4) of SSCBA 1992 and subject to the existing Class 2 and Class 4 NICs rules.

The Regulations will not therefore apply to any payments made to entertainers after 6 April 2014.

These payments will not attract a Class 1 NICs liability from this date and will instead attract a Class 2 and (where applicable) Class 4 NICs liability as detailed above. This includes payments made to entertainers after 6 April 2014 but which derive from a contract for services entered into before this date.

WHAT HAPPENS NEXT?

IF YOU ARE AN ENTERTAINER

From 6 April 2014, producers engaging your performance services will not be required to deduct Class 1 NICs contributions from any payments they make to you. This includes additional use payments such as royalties. Your engager will make payments to you gross of tax and NICs and you must declare these earnings as part of your normal self-employed Self-Assessment return.

Please note that this guidance does not apply if you are on an employment contract, and receive a regular salary from your engager with tax and NICs deducted at source under the Pay As You Earn (PAYE) system.

IF YOU ENGAGE THE SERVICES OF ENTERTAINERS

From 6 April 2014, you will not be required to operate Class 1 NICs for the entertainers you engage. If you are currently deducting employees' Class 1 NICs from the payments you make to your entertainers (including additional use payments such as royalties), and paying the respective employers' Class 1 NICs on these payments, you should continue to do so up until 5 April 2014. From 6 April 2014 however you should cease to do this.

If you use an automated payroll system or an external payroll provider service you will need to ensure your systems or payroll arrangements are updated to ensure that Class 1 NICs continue to operate on payments you make to entertainers up to 5 April 2014, and cease to be operated from 6 April 2014.

IF YOU PROVIDE ADVICE TO THOSE IN THE ENTERTAINMENT INDUSTRY

You should refer any parties you advise to the contents of this Revenue and Customs brief and to HMRC's other published guidance on this issue as listed earlier in this brief.

RETROSPECTIVE RECOVERY OF CLASS 1 NICS

Revenue and Customs Brief 29/13 explains HMRC's position in respect of Class 1 NICs that are due for entertainers in respect of all periods up to 5 April 2014.

HMRC now expects voluntary compliance with the Regulations as detailed in Revenue and Customs brief 29/13 and therefore it does not intend to undertake concerted compliance activity in the media sector in respect of entertainers. It will, however, continue to apply its normal risk-based approach to identifying individual cases which represent a high risk and reserves the right to investigate such cases. HMRC will also continue to inspect those cases currently the subject of investigation.

Where HMRC is undertaking or undertakes an investigation into an entertainer or media company, it will apply the law in terms of the Regulations as they currently stand, applying the decision and judgement of the Upper Tribunal and the Court of Appeal in the case of *ITV Services Ltd v HMRC* for any relevant periods up to and including 5 April 2014.

HMRC will in due course publish separate guidance for entertainers with National Insurance records that may have been affected by this decision and judgement.

FURTHER INFORMATION

Under the terms of its Non-statutory clearance service to businesses, should an engager have material uncertainty on the NICs consequences of a particular contractual engagement with an entertainer, if appropriate, HMRC can provide its view of how the law applies to that contract.

Any such requests should be made by formal 'Non-statutory clearance' application to Large Business Customer Relationship Managers, Film & Production or TV Broadcasting Units as appropriate enclosing details of the particular engagement and a copy of the relevant (signed) contract.

INVITATION TO SPECIFIED ENTERTAINERS TO APPLY TO HAVE CLASS 1 NICS TREATED AS PAID

31 March 2014. *HMRC Brief 11/14*

ABSTRACT

This brief sets out the arrangements for entertainers, whom HMRC deemed not liable to pay Class 1 NICs for periods prior to April 2011 following the Court of Appeal decision in the *ITV Services* case, to apply to have Class 1 contributions treated as paid for the purposes of entitlement to contributory benefit. Individuals wishing to apply are invited to complete and submit form CA9184 to HMRC as soon as possible.

FULL TEXT

– The Social Security (Categorisation of Earners) Regulations in relation to entertainers.
– Regulation 60 of the Social Security (Contributions) Regulations 2001
– Invitation to specified entertainers to apply to have Class 1 employee's National Insurance contributions (NIC) treated as paid.

WHO SHOULD READ THIS?

Any individual engaged as an entertainer (i.e. actor, singer, musician or in any similar performing capacity) under standard Equity or Musicians' Union contract(s) for any period(s) between 6 April 2003 and 5 April 2011.

Agents or accountants acting for any entertainer described above who potentially may fall into one of the categories further described.

Equity, Musicians Union officials or other representative bodies able to identify any individual or groups of entertainers who potentially satisfy the qualifying conditions described below. In these circumstances it would be appreciated if this briefing was brought to the attention of the entertainers concerned.

BACKGROUND

The Social Security (Categorisation of Earners) Regulations 1978 made provision for treating entertainers who were not employed under a contract of service (an employee's contract) as employees for NIC purposes. The Regulations were revised in 2003 to their present format and it was announced in R&C Brief 35/13 that the regulations are to be revoked from 6 April 2014.

R&C Brief 19/12 issued on 14 June 2012 set out HMRC's position on the liability of entertainers following the decision of the Upper Tribunal (UT) to uphold the decision of the First Tier Tribunal (FTT) which dismissed an appeal in the case of *ITV Services Ltd v Commissioners for HMRC*. A further appeal by ITV Services Ltd to the Court of Appeal was also dismissed and the relevant details of this decision were reported in R&C Brief 29/13 on 2 October 2013. Both of these decisions effectively widened the scope of the legislation as it stood following the decision of the FTT on 23 November 2010 to the extent that some contracts previously considered not to fall within the legislation now did so. For that reason HMRC set out its position on the retrospective application of the UT and COA decisions in the above briefings as follows:

> 'Where HMRC had previously issued a written opinion to a party that Class 1 NICs were not due in respect of a particular contract (or identical contracts) because HMRC did not consider the relevant payments to be "by way of salary," it would not seek recovery retrospectively of the unpaid NICs that were due and payable prior to 6 April 2011.' This could potentially leave the individual entertainer with a shortfall in their NIC record through no fault of their own which HMRC is obliged to redress.

LEGISLATION

Where a liability to pay Class 1 NICs arises, those NICs should be paid and recorded to the individual's NI account. However, there are occasions, like those covered by this briefing, where despite their being a Class 1 liability, no NICs are recorded on an individual's account for that employment. Where this is the case it may be possible to record the missing NICs as "Treated as Paid".

Treating as paid is legislative and is provided for under the provisions of Regulation 60 of the Social Security (Contributions) Regulations 2001. This regulation allows for unpaid primary Class 1 NICs to be treated as paid, but only for the purpose of entitlement to contributory benefit.

Primary Class 1 NICs can be treated as paid provided the failure to pay was not:

– with the consent or connivance of the employee; or
– attributable to any negligence on the part of the employee

Treating NICs as paid under regulation 60 may only be considered when primary Class 1 NICs have *not* been paid to HMRC.

Regulation 60 therefore serves to protect the benefit entitlement of the individual where primary NICs have not been paid but the employee cannot be held responsible for that failure to pay.

Primary Class 1 NICs will therefore be treated as paid where we can establish that:

– there is a Class 1 NICs liability
– the primary Class 1 NICs have not been paid to HMRC
– the failure to pay was not due to the consent or connivance, or any negligence on the part of the employee

In the case of qualifying entertainers the above will apply and Primary NICs for those engagements can be treated as paid.

ARRANGEMENTS FOR APPLYING TO HAVE CLASS 1 EMPLOYEE'S NI CONTRIBUTIONS TREATED AS PAID

WHO CAN APPLY?

HMRC believes that the Regulation 60 provisions apply to a small number of entertainers who were engaged for periods between 6 April 2003 (when the current 'entertainers' regulations were introduced) and 5 April 2011 and, for the period(s) of the engagement(s), their engager did not pay employers and employees Class 1 NIC because HMRC had given a written opinion to their engager that there was no liability for Class1 NICs.

HOW DO I KNOW IF I AM ELIGIBLE TO HAVE CLASS 1 EMPLOYEE'S NI CONTRIBUTIONS TREATED AS PAID?

APPLICATIONS FOR TREATING CLASS 1 EMPLOYEE'S NI CONTRIBUTIONS AS PAID

HOW TO APPLY

Entertainers who were engaged to provide their services between 6 April 2003 and 5 April 2011 and were aware or have been made aware that a written opinion was given by HMRC between these dates that no Class 1 NICs were due for that engagement are invited to apply by downloading an application form CA9184 (www.hmrc.gov.uk/forms/ca9184.pdf).

When applying all sections of the form must be completed to enable us to check that your particular circumstances meet the criteria for entitlement to have employees' Class 1 NICs treated as paid. The form will ask you to provide:

– the name of the party that engaged you (if this was not the producer)
– the start and end dates that work was undertaken for the engagement, the title of the entertainment production and the engager's name (producer of the entertainment)
– information relating to the frequency of payment i.e. whether monies were received weekly/monthly etc...
– the amount of payment you received gross of any agent's or other fees for each tax year whilst employed by this engager
– details of any self employment undertaken during t he same period that you were engaged

A copy of the original written opinion from HMRC should also be included with the application where this is available.

Please address applications to:

Film & Production Unit, Floor 2
HM Revenue & Customs
Weardale House
Washington
Tyne & Wear NE37 1LW

The above location applies to ALL applications whether from entertainers in the TV industry, Film Industry or musicians. The special arrangements which HMRC is making in order to undertake action in these cases is expected to last no more than 2 years so it is important to apply as soon as possible.

If your application is accepted you will be notified once your NI record has been amended.

GUIDANCE ON ABOLITION OF EMPLOYER NICS FOR UNDER 21S

21 January 2015. *HMRC Notice*

ABSTRACT

Examples added on 21 January 2015. From 6 April 2015, employers will no longer have to pay secondary Class 1 NICs on earnings up to the Upper Secondary Threshold for employees under 21 years of age. This guide contains details of the 7 new NIC category letters employers will have to use when submitting payroll information for employees in the 16 to 20 age group.

1 KEY FACTS

From 6 April 2015 employers with employees under 21 years old will no longer have to pay Class 1 secondary National Insurance contributions on earnings up to the Upper Secondary Threshold (UST) for those employees.

The zero rate won't apply to Class 1A or Class 1B National Insurance contributions. Class 1 secondary National Insurance contributions will apply if the employee is earning above the UST.

2 NEW CATEGORY LETTERS

If you employ someone aged over 16 but under 21 you'll have to choose 1 of the 7 new National Insurance categories when assessing their secondary National Insurance contributions. It's the employer's responsibility to ensure the correct category letter has been applied based on the age and circumstances of the employee.

The 7 categories are—

- – M - not contracted-out standard rate contributions
- Z - not contracted-out deferred rate contributions
- Y - mariners not contracted-out standard rate contributions
- P - mariners not contracted-out deferred rate contributions
- V - mariners contracted-out salary related contributions
- I - contracted-out salary related standard rate contributions
- K - contracted-out salary related deferred rate contributions

Three of the new letters (V, I and K) will be removed in April 2016 in line with the ending of "contracted-out" status in relation to salary-related occupational pension schemes.

The structure of National Insurance will continue, but incorporate the changes introduced. There are no changes to the rules which set out how Class 1 National Insurance contributions are assessed. Bonus pay, holiday pay and other payments will continue to follow the same calculation principles as they do now.

3 DETAILS OF THE NEW RATES

Employees must be aged over 16 but under 21 years old for the new category letters to apply.

The current rate of secondary Class 1 National Insurance contributions for the tax year 2014 to 2015 is 13•8% on earnings above the Secondary Threshold (ST) of £153 per week - or its equivalent for pay periods that are longer than 1 week.

From 6 April 2015 that rate is reduced to 0% for those employees who are under the age of 21 with earnings between the ST and the UST. The value of the UST for the tax year 2015 to 2016 will be the same as the Upper Earnings Limit (UEL). There's no—

– statutory link to the UEL – this could change in subsequent years
– reduction in the rate of Class 1 secondary National Insurance contributions on earnings above this UST

Any decision on the level of the UST will be announced by the government. There's no reduction in the rate of Class 1 secondary National Insurance contributions on earnings above this UST.

The role of the secondary contributor isn't removed. They're still regarded as secondary contributors and will be legally required to carry out any other obligations (for example administering statutory payments) imposed by statute. This applies even though the amount of the contribution they will be required to pay is 0% on earnings up to the UST.

Introduction of the under 21 secondary rate coincides with the penultimate year of contracting-out before the new State Pension is implemented. Employers with employees under 21 years old and in contracted-out employment, will be entitled to a secondary contracted-out rebate on all earnings between the Lower Earnings Limit and the Upper Accrual Point. The rebate will cease on 5 April 2016 when all contracted-out category letters will be removed.

4 IF YOU NEED TO MAKE AN AMENDMENT

The process that's currently in place for any corrections will continue – the guidance can be found in helpbook CWG2.

5 WHAT YOU CAN TELL YOUR EMPLOYEES

Employees will continue to pay the standard rate of primary Class 1 National Insurance contributions through their salary. They won't see any reduction in their payments. It's employers who will benefit from this change. Employee's entitlement to contributory social security benefits, including State Pension won't be affected. Existing employees may notice a change to the National Insurance category letter recorded on their payslip.

6 EXAMPLES

Published 21 January 2014

A monthly paid employee is under the age of 21 at the time earnings of £1,600 are paid. The earnings fall above both the monthly, primary and secondary thresholds but beneath the monthly Upper Earnings Limit (UEL) and Upper Secondary Threshold (UST).

Primary	£1,600 - £672 = £928 x 12%	= £111.36
Secondary	£1,600 - £676 = £924 x 0%	= £0
Total NICs due		= £111.36

A monthly paid employee is under the age of 21 at the time earnings of £4,000 are paid. The earnings fall above the monthly UEL and UST.

Primary	£4,000 - £3,532 = £468 x 2%	=£9.36
	plus £3,532 - £672 = £2,860 x 12%	=£343.20
Secondary	£4,000 - £3,532 = £ 468 x 13.8%	=£64.58
	plus £3,532 - £676 = £2,856 x 0%	= £0
Total NICs due		= £417.14

A monthly paid employee is under the age of 21 at the time the earnings of £2,300 are paid and is a member of his employers contracted out salary related pension scheme. The earnings are above the primary and secondary threshold but below the UEL and UST.

Primary	£2,300 - £672 = £1,628 x 12%	= £195.36
	less £2,300 - £486 = £1,814 x 1.4%	= minus £25.40
Secondary	£2,300 - £676 = £1,624 x 0%	= £0
	less £2,300 - £486 = £1,814 x 3.4%	= minus £61.68
Total NICs due		= £108.28

The abolition of secondary NICs on earnings below the UST for those employees under the age of 21 does not alter any of the rules for assessing Class 1 NICs.

NIC rates and thresholds for tax year 2015 to 2016 will be available soon.

Further details will be in the 2015 to 2016 helpbook CWG2 which will be available early next year.

CLASS 1A NICS REFUNDS FOR CERTAIN OVERSEAS ACCOMMODATION PROVIDED THROUGH A COMPANY

27 April 2015 *HMRC Notice*

ABSTRACT

Between 6 April 2011 and 5 April 2015, company directors could submit refund claims for Class 1A NICs paid before the 2008/09 tax year in connection with overseas accommodation provided by their company in certain circumstances. This was intended to align the NICs position with that for income tax. HMRC has updated its contact details for claims.

www.gov.uk/government/publications/holiday-homes-purchased-abroad-through-a-ltd-company-potential-class-1a-refund

BACKGROUND

The Finance Act (FA) 2008 introduced new provisions to the Income Tax (Earnings and Pensions) Act 2003 (ITEPA): sections 100A and 100B. These provisions effectively provide an exemption from the living accommodation tax charge where living accommodation outside the UK is provided by a company for a director or other officer of the company (D) or a member of D's family or household where all of the following apply—

– the company is wholly owned by D or D and other individuals (and no interest in the company is partnership property),
– the company's main or only asset is a relevant interest in the property
– its only activities are ones that are incidental to its ownership of that interest

The new legislation was treated as having always had effect. In other words, the new legislation meant that since the coming into force of these provisions in the Finance Act 2008 a charge to Income Tax on the benefit provided through a qualifying overseas holiday home has never existed. As a consequence any liability to Class 1A National Insurance contributions, which was due on an amount equivalent to the general earnings charge in ITEPA, was also removed from 21 July 2008. At that time HM Revenue & Customs (HMRC) advised that refunds of tax could be claimed on the basis that the living accommodation tax charge was never intended to apply in these circumstances and the new legislation is treated as always having had effect. However the same wasn't the case for Class 1A National Insurance contributions (employer only). In the case of overseas holiday homes, it remained the case that for the years prior to the enactment of Finance Act 2008, Class 1A National Insurance contributions remained due on the benefit in kind chargeable to Income Tax. HMRC published Regulations on 17 March 2011 that align the National Insurance contributions position with that for Income Tax - The Social Security (Contributions) (Amendment No 3) Regulations 2011 (SI 2011/797). This means that it is now possible to claim a refund of Class 1A National Insurance contributions in the same way as it was possible for Income Tax. A refund of Class 1A National Insurance contributions can be claimed where contributions have been paid and an officer of HMRC is satisfied that the contribution was paid on the same amount treated as earnings that are now exempt under the relevant legislation in ITEPA.

REFUNDS

Any individual who can show that they have paid Class 1A National Insurance contributions for any year before 2008–09 on the benefit of living accommodation which qualifies for exemption in accordance with sections 100A and 100B of ITEPA should write giving the information listed below to—

National Insurance Contributions and Employers Office

HM Revenue and Customs

BX9 1BX

Information to be provided—

- name, address, National Insurance number and/or Unique Taxpayer's Reference
- if agent acting - agent's name and address
- details of the living accommodation outside the UK - address, type of property, uses made of the property
- details of the company through which living accommodation outside the UK is provided including name, address, nature of company/entity, place of incorporation, ownership and activities
- an explanation of why they consider that the exemption applies
- the years for which Class 1A National Insurance contributions have been paid on the benefit of this accommodation
- evidence that the benefit of the accommodation in question has been taxed - acceptable evidence would include for each year copies of one or more of the following documents which clearly show the benefit as taken into account as taxable income—
  - assessments/self-assessments
  - P11Ds and P11D(b)
  - correspondence with HMRC or the former Inland Revenue

Note that the above list is not intended to be exhaustive. HMRC will consider any other documentary evidence in the individual's possession that the individual believes can show that the benefit has been taxed as earnings and Class1A National Insurance contributions has been paid on the same amount treated as earnings.

TIME LIMIT FOR MAKING A REFUND CLAIM

Any application for a refund in these cases must be made in writing on or before 6 April 2015.

HMRC will take action to identify those customers who have previously claimed refunds of tax and Class 1A National Insurance contributions and arrange to refund the Class 1A National Insurance contributions already paid. However, if you wish to submit details of your original claim again please quote any reference number that you were given previously and send it to the above address.

Commentary—*Simon's Taxes* **E4.607**.

HMRC'S DIGITAL DISCLOSURE SERVICE

5 September 2016. *HMRC Notice*

ABSTRACT

HMRC has opened its digital disclosure service, which provides a single online access point for individuals and businesses to make voluntary disclosures relating to income tax, CGT, NICs and corporation tax, including the worldwide disclosure facility for offshore sources.

www.gov.uk/government/publications/hm-revenue-and-customs-disclosure-service

1 ABOUT THIS SERVICE

You can fill in the form yourself, as a nominated partner, as a trustee of a trust, or an officer of a company. Or you can notify or disclose on behalf of someone else.

2 NOTIFY OR DISCLOSE ON BEHALF OF SOMEONE ELSE

You can fill in this form on behalf of someone else if they've given you permission. For example, you're either—

- a tax adviser, accountant, agent or someone else
- an executor or the personal representative of a deceased person

3 WHEN TO USE THIS FORM

HMRC run a series of Campaigns to encourage people to tell us what they owe. Campaigns target particular business sectors or sources of income. The current campaigns are detailed below.

3.1 Let Property Campaign

The Let Property Campaign gives you an opportunity to bring your tax affairs up to date if you're an individual landlord letting out residential property in the UK or abroad and to get the best possible terms to pay the tax you owe.

3.2 Second Income Campaign

The Second Income Campaign gives you the chance to bring your tax affairs up to date if you're employed and have additional income that's not taxed.

3.3 Credit Card Sales Campaign

The Credit Card Sales Campaign is an opportunity to bring your tax affairs up to date if you accept credit or debit card payments.

3.4 Worldwide Disclosure Facility

If you want to disclose a UK tax liability that relates wholly or in part to an offshore issue, you can use the Worldwide Disclosure Facility. You can disclose unpaid or omitted tax on a foreign income or asset through to 30 September 2018.

An offshore issue includes unpaid or omitted tax relating to—

- income arising from a source in a territory outside the UK
- assets situated or held in a territory outside the UK
- activities carried on wholly or mainly in a territory outside the UK
- anything having effect as if it were income, assets or activities of a kind described above

An offshore issue also includes where you've transferred the funds connected to unpaid or omitted UK tax to a territory outside the UK.

3.5 Disclosures that aren't part of a current campaign

If you don't qualify for a current HMRC campaign, you can use the Voluntary Disclosure Opportunity and this form to tell us that you've not declared the right amount of one or more of the following—

- Income Tax
- Capital Gains Tax
- National Insurance contributions
- Corporation Tax

4 YOUR DISCLOSURE

Once you've told us why you're making a disclosure, for example, a particular campaign, we'll ask you what the reason for your outstanding liabilities was. The number of years you include in your disclosure depends upon why you didn't declare your liability at the right time.

5 CALCULATIONS OF LIABILITIES

The Digital Disclosure Service links to some calculators you may find useful in helping you complete your disclosure. Only use the calculators if your tax affairs are straightforward and you're only entitled to basic personal allowances.

We can't give individual advice on calculating how much you should pay so you may want to seek independent professional advice.

6 IMPACT ON TAX CREDITS OR OTHER MEANS TESTED BENEFITS

Any previously undisclosed income could impact any means tested benefits you get, such as housing or council tax benefit. You should contact your local authority directly to discuss this.

If you've made a joint claim for tax credits you may need to tell your partner that the award may be adjusted as a result of your disclosure.

7 INTEREST AND PENALTIES

HMRC charges interest when you pay any tax or National Insurance contributions later than due. We calculate interest daily and charge it from the original due date until the date you actually paid. The DDS form will link to a calculator to help you work out the amount of interest to pay.

There may be a penalty due on the outstanding liabilities. The penalty is a percentage of any additional amount due. The percentage is based on why you didn't tell HMRC about your tax liability, or why you sent in a return containing inaccuracies.

If we think the penalty you've applied isn't enough we may carry out a further check of your tax affairs. For example, we may not accept that someone who's been in business for many years earning significant undeclared amounts hasn't acted deliberately.

8 SUBMIT YOUR DISCLOSURE

Complete the declaration once you're sure that your disclosure is correct and complete and that you understand why you've been asked to include penalties in your disclosure.

If we decide that your disclosure is incorrect or incomplete, we'll work out what you owe and you'll have to pay the extra tax and interest. We may also charge you a higher penalty than the one you included in your disclosure. If you leave something significant out of your disclosure then HMRC may consider pursuing a criminal investigation. In such cases material in the disclosure could be used as evidence.

If you fail to submit a disclosure we may also take action.

9 PAY

When you pay, you'll need a Payment Reference Number. If you've already told HMRC that you intend to make a disclosure, HMRC will have included the Payment Reference Number on your acknowledgement letter.

If you're making a full disclosure now, we'll send you a Payment Reference Number once you've submitted your disclosure.

We won't accept your disclosure until you've paid your outstanding liabilities in full. HMRC expects you to pay what you owe when you make your disclosure.

If you can't pay the full amount, you'll need to let HMRC know as soon as possible and before you send in your disclosure. You should contact them on the relevant campaign helpline, which can be found in the guidance for each campaign.

When you phone, HMRC will want to talk to you about your current financial position so they can tell you what they think you should pay and when. To help HMRC decide, you'll need to tell them—

– your Disclosure Reference Number
– how and when you intend to pay HMRC what you owe
– what your current weekly/monthly income and outgoings are

- what you own, including your home, other property/land, vehicles, investments, money in the bank etc
- what you owe, including mortgages, loans, credit cards

If you can't pay the full amount don't submit your disclosure or payment until you've spoken to HMRC. Please use the Payment Reference Number we've sent you in order to make a full payment of your outstanding liabilities. We accept payment by a range of methods but recommend that you make your payment electronically as this is the most secure method.

Commentary—*Simon's Taxes* **A6.109**.

RESPONSES TO CONSULTATION ON ABOLISHING CLASS 2 AND REFORMING CLASS 4 NICS

5 December 2016. *Treasury Notice*

The government confirmed at Budget 2016 that it will abolish Class 2 NICs in April 2018. Self-employed individuals will be able to gain access to contributory benefits based on a profits test in Class 4 NICs. Draft clauses to implement these reforms in a National Insurance Contributions Bill were published on 5 December.

www.gov.uk/government/consultations/consultation-on-abolishing-class-2-national-insurance-and-introducing-a-contributory-benefit-test-to-class-4-national-insurance-for-the-self-employed

The government confirmed at Budget 2016 that it will abolish Class 2 NICs in April 2018. This followed recommendations from the Office for Tax Simplification, who noted that the abolition of Class 2 NICs would be a worthwhile simplification of the self-employed NICs system.

The government consulted between 9 December 2015 and 24 February 2016 on new contributory benefit tests that will be required to enable self-employed individuals to continue to gain access to the State Pension and other contributory benefits.

This government has confirmed that—

- from 2018/19, self-employed individuals will be able to gain access to contributory benefits based on a profits test in Class 4 NICs;
- a new zero-rate band will be introduced into Class 4 NICs on profits between the small profits limit (which replaces the Class 2 small profits threshold) and the lower profits limit;
- the standard rate of maternity allowance for the self-employed will be accessed using Class 3 voluntary NICs;
- those with profits below the small profits limit will continue to gain access to the new state pension through Class 1 NICs, NICs credits, or payment of Class 3 voluntary NICs;
- self-employed individuals with insufficient Class 4 NICs to qualify for contributory employment and support allowance will be able to do so using Class 3 voluntary NICs;
- foster carers' national insurance credit, which currently provides foster carers with access to the state pension, will be upgraded to a Class 1 credit, providing access to contributory jobseeker's allowance and employment and support allowance; and
- transitional arrangements until 1 January 2022 will enable individuals with low profits, share fishermen and volunteer development workers, to rely on their contribution record in the years prior to Class 2 abolition for longer than usual when claiming contribution-based jobseeker's allowance and contributory employment and support allowance.

Primary legislation to implement these reforms will be introduced in a National Insurance Contributions Bill. Draft clauses were published on 5 December.

The government will publish further information in due course on enabling the self-employed to access contributory employment and support allowance and maternity allowance by paying Class 3 NICs.

Note—See "National Insurance Contributions Bill delayed", Written Ministerial Statement, 2 November 2017 – confirming that abolition of Class 2 NICs will take effect from April 2019 (rather than April 2018 as originally intended).

SPORTING TESTIMONIALS—INCOME TAX AND NATIONAL INSURANCE PAYMENTS

6 April 2017. *HMRC Technical Note*

SPORTING TESTIMONIAL TAX CHANGES

From 6 April 2017, new rules apply to the treatment of sporting testimonial income.

Income tax is due on income from all sporting testimonial and benefit match events. Corporation Tax and VAT may also be due depending on the nature of the income or how payments are made.

The government has agreed to a "one-off" tax exempt amount of £100,000 for income from a non-contractual or non-customary sporting testimonial event (or year), if certain conditions are met.

The new rules cover income from events that take place on or after 6 April 2017, but only where the testimonial has been announced on or after 25 November 2015.

The new rules don't apply to National Insurance contributions (NICs), Matching changes for NICs will apply from 6 April 2018.

This means existing arrangements for the payment of NICs will apply until 5 April 2018.

WHO THE CHANGES AFFECT

These changes will apply to—

– sportspersons
– independent testimonial committees

CONDITIONS

CONTRACTUAL AND CUSTOMARY

In many cases, sportspersons have a contractual agreement with their employer for sporting testimonials. Often the agreement will be that if the sportsperson stays with the team or club for a specific number or years, they will be entitled to a testimonial, although it can also cover other matters.

If it's normal practice for a sportsperson to be awarded a testimonial in certain circumstances, this is what we refer to as "customary". It doesn't matter whether the testimonial is organised by the employer or by a third party.

For contractual and customary, all such income is treated as earnings from the employment, meaning—

– the employee should pay Income tax and Class 1 NICs
– the employer or testimonial committee has to pay employer NICs.

Read about employee and employer Income Tax rates and National Insurance contribution rates.

NON-CONTRACTUAL AND NON-CUSTOMARY

A non-contractual testimonial will be where there isn't a contractual arrangement between the employer and the sportsperson.

A non-customary testimonial will be where there isn't a contractual arrangement or a testimonial award which is considered to be normal practice.

These definitions remain the same as previously determined through case law and have not been altered by the new legislation.

HOW THE "ONE-OFF" EXEMPTION WORKS

A "one-off" exemption of £100,000 is available from 6 April 2017 to ensure that sportspersons on modest incomes (who are nearing end of career or have reached the end) are protected from the change.

A sportsperson will qualify for a "one-off" tax exemption of £100,000 on the income received if—

- they're an employed sportsperson
- they're a previously employed sportsperson and the testimonial relates to that employment
- the testimonial or benefit match is non-contractual or non-customary
- the events are held during a single testimonial or testimonial year
- the events are organised or controlled by an independent person (normally a testimonial committee)
- there has been no previous testimonial income to which the exemption applied

The exemption applies to income received from relevant events held in a maximum period of 12 calendar months only. This begins with the date the first event is held in a "testimonial year", even if that year covers more than one tax year.

Employed sportspersons who have a contractual entitlement or customary right to a **sporting testimonial** won't be affected by these changes. They'll be charged Income Tax on all their **sporting testimonial** income and the "one-off" exemption won't apply.

MORE THAN ONE EVENT

A second testimonial event and a second testimonial are not the same and are treated differently for tax purposes.

If a sportsperson has another benefit match within 12 calendar months of the first match, the event income can qualify for the £100,000 exemption. Any spare exemption from the first match can be used on income from the next if—

- it is part of a testimonial season being administered by the same controller (normally the independent testimonial committee)
- it is a second testimonial event rather than a separate sporting testimonial

For a different (separate) sporting testimonial the exemption cannot apply, no matter how close it is in timing to the first one.

RESPONSIBILITIES

Changes to the rules mean there can be more actions to take.

FOR A SPORTSPERSON

The independent testimonial committee should make the appropriate deductions from the sportsperson's testimonial income.

If the sportsperson isn't in employment elsewhere, they should give their P45 to the independent testimonial committee who will act like their employer in accounting for the income.

If the sportsperson doesn't have a current P45 to give to the independent testimonial committee, they should confirm their circumstances with the committee using a new starter declaration.

If the P45 hasn't been made available to the testimonial committee, the sportsperson may need to declare all of their income on a Self Assessment tax return. This is because the testimonial committee can only deduct basic rate tax in those circumstances and there may be more tax to pay.

INDEPENDENT TESTIMONIAL COMMITTEE

The independent testimonial committee should make the appropriate deductions from the sportsperson's testimonial income.

The independent testimonial committee should allow £100,000 of income tax free, then operate PAYE (see Second testimonial) if—

- the sporting testimonial is non-contractual or non-customary
- the testimonial was announced on or after 25 November 2015
- the income is from an event or events taking place on or after 6 April 2017

NIC

– the income relates to a testimonial event or a testimonial season lasting no more than 12 calendar months
– the sportsperson is employed or was formerly employed as such

If the amount of income within 12 calendar months has not used up all of the £100,000 exemption, it cannot be rolled forward to set against future testimonial income.

REPORTING

When the sporting testimonial falls within the new rules explained above, income in excess of £100,000 must be reported to HMRC.

You should report the sportsperson's income to HMRC online and in real time, either at the time you make the payment or beforehand. You will need a PAYE scheme to do this.

For the purposes of the testimonial or benefit match, the independent testimonial committee will be treated as an employer. The committee should operate PAYE on any income above £100,000 to collect the Income Tax due. You must have a PAYE scheme before you can make payments to the sportsperson.

You can register with HMRC for a PAYE scheme up to 2 months before you start making payments. Read about the Basic PAYE Tools that will enable you to meet your PAYE obligations.

The amount of income tax to deduct will depend on whether the sportsperson is still employed elsewhere. If they aren't employed elsewhere and they give you a current P45, you can use the tax code on it when you make a payment to them.

If you aren't given a current P45, you can work out your new employee's tax code and read the new starter checklist. You should pay over tax you have deducted to HMRC.

It's important to remember, the obligations you have as an employer are limited to accounting for the taxes due only. You don't have to—

– hold employers' liability insurance
– enrol the sportsperson into a workplace pension scheme
– provide a written statement (contract) of employment

Read about telling HMRC about a new employee.

FIND OUT IF THERE ARE VAT IMPLICATIONS

As a member of an independent testimonial committee, you'll need to consider whether any of the committee's activities result in transactions that may be subject to VAT.

Whether activities are subject to VAT will depend on the circumstances. For example, admission for spectators to sporting events is subject to VAT whereas donations are not.

EXAMPLES

EVENTS TAKING PLACE BEFORE AND AFTER 6 APRIL 2017

I'm involved in organising a testimonial season for a sportsperson. It was announced after 25 November 2015, but has events taking place both before and after 6 April 2017.

Only the income from events taking place on or after 6 April 2017 will be affected by the new rules. The income from events taking place before 6 April 2017 should be dealt with using previous rules.

RETIRED SPORTSPERSON'S TESTIMONIAL

I'm organising a testimonial for a sportsperson who has now retired. Will the new rules apply?

The new rules apply to income raised for sportspersons whether they're employees or former employees and as long as the main reason is to recognise their service as an employed professional sportsperson.

TESTIMONIAL FOR A DECEASED SPORTSPERSON

A sportsperson tragically died as a result of injuries received in a match. I'm arranging a sporting testimonial to raise funds for the family which will be paid directly to them. Will this fall into the new rules?

If payment is to be made direct to the family, it doesn't fall within the new rules and you won't have to account for Income Tax or NICs.

Any payment to the sportsperson's estate will fall into the new rules, meaning Income Tax will be due, but NICs will not. Corporation tax may apply in both cases because an independent testimonial committee is normally treated as an unincorporated company.

WORK OUT WHAT TO REPORT

Sportsperson A is awarded a testimonial match which raises £153,000 after costs. What should be reported to HMRC?

If the sportsperson qualifies for the £100,000 exemption, £53,000 should be reported to HMRC.

MAKE DEDUCTIONS BEFORE PAYMENT

The sporting testimonial has cleared the sum of £153,000. Can I pay the entire amount to Sportsperson A?

No, you should account for the relevant amount of Income Tax and employer NICs before the payment is made.

WHAT TO DO ABOUT NON-CASH BENEFITS

What if testimonial income comes in the form of cash and a non-cash benefit such as a car?

The value of any non-cash or cash benefit should be added to the amount of money raised to get to the total of the income received.

ALREADY HAD A TESTIMONIAL BEFORE 6 APRIL 2017

A sportsperson who'll have a testimonial after 6 April 2017 and who's previously had a testimonial prior to the new rules taking effect. Are they eligible for the £100,000 exemption and is the testimonial their first for tax purposes?

In this instance the testimonial would be their first for tax purposes, and the income raised would also be eligible for the £100,000 exemption as appropriate.

SECOND TESTIMONIAL

Sportsperson B was awarded a second testimonial. The first testimonial took place after 6 April 2017 and raised £70,000. As this income fell within the £100,000 exemption, it was paid tax-free and was not reported to HMRC. The second testimonial raised £83,000 after costs. Do I report £53,000 for tax purposes?

No. The unused exemption cannot be rolled forward to be used for a subsequent testimonial. The entire amount of £83,000 must be reported to HMRC.

Commentary—*Simon's Taxes* **B2.471A, E4.469**.

Note—See "National Insurance Contributions Bill delayed", Written Ministerial Statement, 2 November 2017, below.

SALARY SACRIFICE FOR EMPLOYERS

31 August 2017. *HMRC Guidance Note*

OVERVIEW

A salary sacrifice arrangement is an agreement to reduce an employee's entitlement to cash pay, usually in return for a non-cash benefit. As an employer, you can set up a salary sacrifice arrangement by changing the terms of your employee's employment contract. Your employee needs to agree to this change.

A salary sacrifice arrangement can't reduce an employee's cash earnings below the National Minimum Wage rates.

NIC

CHANGE THE TERMS OF A SALARY SACRIFICE ARRANGEMENT

If your employee wants to opt in or out of a salary sacrifice arrangement, you must alter their contract with each change. Your employee's contract must be clear on what their cash and non-cash entitlements are at any given time.

It may be necessary to change the terms of a salary sacrifice arrangement where a lifestyle change significantly alters an employee's financial circumstances. This may include marriage, divorce, or an employee's spouse or partner becoming redundant or pregnant. Salary sacrifice arrangements can allow opting in or out in the event of lifestyle changes like these.

As a general rule, if an employee can swap between cash earnings and a non-cash benefit whenever they like, any expected tax and National Insurance contributions (NICs) advantages under a salary sacrifice arrangement won't apply. There are some exceptions, please read Employment Income Manual 42755 for more information.

WORK OUT THE EFFECT ON TAX AND NICS

The impact on tax and NICs payable for any employee will depend on the pay and non-cash benefits that make up the salary sacrifice arrangement. You need to pay and deduct the right amount of tax and NICs for the cash and benefits you provide.

For the cash component, that means operating the PAYE system correctly through your payroll.

CALCULATE A NON-CASH BENEFIT

For any non-cash benefits, you need to calculate the value of the benefit.

From 6 April 2017, if you set up a new salary sacrifice arrangement, you'll need to work out the value of a non-cash benefit by using the higher of the—

- amount of the salary given up
- earnings charge under the normal benefit in kind rules

However, for cars with CO2 emissions of no more than 75g/km, you should always use the earnings charge under the normal benefit in kind rules.

TAX AND NICS EXEMPTIONS ON NON-CASH BENEFITS

Exemptions on benefits in kind don't apply to salary sacrifice schemes. The only benefits that you don't need to value for a salary sacrifice arrangement, as you don't have to report them to HMRC, are—

- payments into pension schemes
- employer provided pensions advice
- childcare vouchers, workplace nurseries and directly contracted employer provided childcare
- bicycles and cycling safety equipment (including cycle to work)

SALARY SACRIFICE ARRANGEMENTS SET UP BEFORE 6 APRIL 2017

If you set up a salary sacrifice arrangement with an employee before 6 April 2017, you can continue to calculate the value of the benefit as you did before. This only relates to specific arrangements with an employee, not to your overall salary sacrifice policy.

The arrangement will be subject to new rules if the arrangement is varied, renewed or modified unless the change is—

- connected to an employee's statutory sick pay
- connected to an employee's maternity, paternity, adoption or shared parental pay
- out of the control of the employee and employer (like a damaged contract)

Most existing arrangements set up before 6 April 2017 will automatically be subject to the new rules from 6 April 2018. However, arrangements will not be subject to the new rules until 6 April 2021 unless they are varied, renewed or modified if they are for—

- cars with CO2 emissions of more than 75g/km
- accommodation

– school fees (even if varied, renewed or modified as long as the arrangement relates to the same child and school)

REPORT A NON-CASH BENEFIT

Reporting requirements for many non-cash benefits are different to those for cash earnings. In general, benefits must be reported to HM Revenue and Customs (HMRC) at the end of the tax year using the end-of-year expenses and benefits online form.

ASK HMRC TO CONFIRM THE TAX AND NICS

Once a salary sacrifice arrangement is in place, employers can ask the HMRC Clearances Team to confirm the tax and NICs implications. HMRC won't comment on a proposed salary sacrifice arrangement before it has been put in place.

HMRC Clearances Team
Alexander House
21 Victoria Avenue
Southend-on-Sea
Essex SS99 1BD

Alternatively they can email the HMRC Clearances Team at hmrc.southendteam@hmrc.gsi.gov.uk

To be satisfied that the change has been effective at the right time and not applied retrospectively, HMRC would need to see—

– evidence of the variation of terms and conditions (if there is a written contract)
– payslips before and after the variation

EXAMPLES OF SALARY SACRIFICE

Salary	*Salary sacrificed*	*Non cash benefit received*	*Consequence*
£350 per week	£50 of that salary	Childcare voucher to the same value	Only £300 is subject to tax and NICs, childcare vouchers are exempt from both tax and Class 1 NICs up to a limit of £55 per week
£350 per week	£100 of that salary	Childcare vouchers to the same value	£295 is subject to tax and NICs - PAYE is operated on the £250 cash component, childcare vouchers are exempt from both tax and Class 1 NICs up to a limit of £55 per week, £45 is reported as a non-cash benefit at the end of the tax year using forms P11D or P9D

£5,000 bonus	£5,000	£5,000 employer contribution to registered pension scheme	No employment income tax or NICs charge to the employee - the full amount is invested in the pension fund

CHILDCARE VOUCHERS AND TAX CREDITS

Childcare vouchers from an employer may affect the amount of tax credits an employee gets. Employees can use a calculator to help them decide if they're better off taking the vouchers or not.

EFFECT OF SALARY SACRIFICE ON PAYMENTS AND BENEFITS

EARNINGS RELATED PAYMENTS

Employers usually decide how earnings related payments such as occupational pension contributions, overtime rates, pay rises, etc are calculated. Such payments can be based on the notional salary or the new reduced cash salary, but this must be made clear to the employee.

EARNINGS RELATED BENEFITS

Salary sacrifice can affect an employee's entitlement to earnings related benefits such as Maternity Allowance and Additional State Pension. The amount they receive may be less than the full standard rate or they may lose the entitlement altogether.

CONTRIBUTION BASED BENEFITS

Salary sacrifice may affect an employee's entitlement to contribution based benefits such as Incapacity Benefit and State Pension. Salary sacrifice may reduce the cash earnings on which NICs are charged. Employees may therefore pay – or be treated as paying – less or no NICs.

STATUTORY PAYMENTS

Salary sacrifice can affect the amount of statutory pay an employee receives. It can cause some employees to lose their entitlement altogether. If a salary sacrifice arrangement reduces an employee's average weekly earnings below the lower earnings limit, then the employer doesn't have to make any statutory payments to them.

WORKPLACE PENSION SCHEMES

The employer decides whether salary sacrifice affects contributions into a workplace pension scheme. Often, employers will use a notional level of pay to calculate employer and employee pension contributions, so that employees who participate in salary sacrifice arrangements are not put at a disadvantage.

However, employers should always check with their scheme provider to make sure any such arrangements are allowable. Other salary sacrifice arrangements are possible. For example, an employer might agree to pay more than the minimum amount required, to cover some or all of the employee's contribution. The employee may then become entitled to a lower cash salary.

AUTO-ENROLMENT

Where an employee has been automatically enrolled into a workplace pension scheme, it will be a registered pension scheme for tax purposes. No tax is charged on the contributions an employer pays to a registered pension scheme in respect of an employee.

Where an employee opts out of a workplace pension scheme, it is possible that they will have received reduced earnings under the salary sacrifice arrangement. If the employer "makes good" that shortfall to the employee then the payment should be made subject to tax and NICs.

TECHNICAL GUIDANCE

The following guides contain more detailed information:

Employment Income Manual - Salary sacrifice

Employment Income Manual - Particular benefits

Employment Income Manual - Salary sacrifice: contributions to a registered pension scheme: income tax effects

Tax Credits Technical Manual - Income: Employment Income Rules: Salary sacrifice

Commentary—*Simon's Taxes* **E4.602B**.

NATIONAL INSURANCE CONTRIBUTIONS BILL DELAYED

2 November 2017. *Written Ministerial Statement*

ABSTRACT

The government is to delay introduction of the NICs Bill announced in this year's Queen's speech until 2018, to allow more time to consult on the legislation abolishing Class 2 NICs, which will now take effect from April 2019. Other measures expected in the Bill include Class 1A exemption for sporting testimonials, pensions advice exemption and bringing NICs treatment of termination payments into line with tax.

hansard.parliament.uk/Commons/2017-11-02/debates/17110233000006/NationalInsurance-ContributionsBill

The Exchequer Secretary to the Treasury (Andrew Jones): The Government are announcing today that they will introduce the National Insurance Contributions (NICs) Bill in 2018. The measures it will implement will now take effect one year later, from April 2019. This includes the abolition of class 2 NICs, reforms to the NICs treatment of termination payments, and changes to the NICs treatment of sporting testimonials.

The Government have decided to implement a one-year delay to allow time to engage with interested parties and parliamentarians with concerns relating to the impact of the abolition of class 2 NICs on self-employed individuals with low profits. The Government have committed to abolishing class 2 NICs to simplify the system, so it is therefore right to take the time to ensure that there are no unintended consequences for the lowest paid.

Rates of National Insurance contributions for 2017–18

The table below shows the rates of National Insurance contributions for the year 2017–18.

Class 1 (Earnings related)		
Lower earnings limit (LEL)	£113 a week; £490 a month; £5,876 a year	
Primary threshold (PT)	£157 a week; £680 a month; £8,164 a year	
Secondary threshold (ST)	£157 a week; £680 a month; £8,164 a year	
Upper secondary threshold (UST)	£866 a week; £3,750 a month; £45,000 a year	
Upper earnings limit (UEL)	£866 a week; £3,750 a month; £45,000 a year	
RATES		
Employees' contributions[1]		
Weekly earnings:	£157.01–£866	12%
	Over £866	2%
Employers' contributions[1,3,4]		
Weekly earnings:	Over £157.00	13.8%
Women at reduced rate		
Employees' contributions		
Weekly earnings:	£157.01–£866	5.85%
	Over £866	2%
Employers' contributions	Normal employers' contributions apply as above	
Employment allowance[2]	**£3,000**	

Notes—[1] Employees' rates are nil for children under 16 and those over state pensionable age but employers' contributions are still payable. Employees' NICs are not payable on earnings up to the primary threshold, employers' NICs are not payable on earnings up to the secondary threshold.

[2] From 6 April 2014 an employment allowance applies for businesses, charities and CASCs to be offset against their employer Class 1 secondary NICs. The allowance is claimed as part of the normal payroll process through RTI. Only one company in a group may claim. There are some excluded employers such as certain employers of domestic staff, public authorities and those which carry out functions wholly or mainly of a public nature. From 6 April 2015 the allowance was extended to employers of care and support workers where the duties of employment relate to the employer's personal, family or household affairs. From 6 April 2016 the allowance is no longer available to companies whose only employee is the director.

[3] From 6 April 2015 employers with employees under the age of 21 are not required to pay Class 1 secondary NICs on earnings up to the upper secondary threshold for those employees.

[4] NICA 2015 s 1 provides for a zero rate of secondary contributions on earnings up to the upper secondary threshold for apprentices under the age of 25 from 6 April 2016.

Class 1A and Class 1B: 13.8%
Class 2 (self-employed): Flat rate £2.85 a week *Small profits threshold (2017–18 onwards)*: £6,025 a year *Volunteer development workers*: £5.65 a week *Share fishermen's special rate*: £3.50 a week
Class 3 (voluntary contributions): £14.25 a week
Class 4 (self-employed): 9% of profits between £8,164 and £45,000 a year, 2% above £45,000 per year Exempt if pensionable age reached by beginning of year of assessment
Maximum contributions *Class 1 or Class 1/Class 2:* £4,509.24 plus 2% of earnings over the upper earnings limit *Class 4 limiting amount:* £3,466.29 plus 2% of profits over the upper earnings limit

NIC Index

Defined words and phrases are listed separately at the end.

NIC

NIC

D

NIC

NIC

F

NIC

NIC

NIC

NIC

NIC

Words and phrases

Words in brackets indicate the context in which the word or phrase is used.

NIC

tax year—
contributions generally, SSCBA 1992 s 122(1), SSAA 1992 s 191
pension schemes, PSA 1993 s 181(1)
trade (public authority), SSCBA 1992 s 122(1)
trade union, SSCBA 1992 s 122(1)
training, SI 2001/1004 reg 1(2)
transfer provision, SSC(TF)A 1999 s 21(1)
transmission by electronic means, 987/2009/EC art 1

U

United Kingdom, SSA 1986 s 84(4), SSCBA 1992 s 172
upper earnings limit, SSCBA 1992 ss 5(1), 122(1)

V

volunteer development worker, SI 2001/1004 reg 149
voyage period, SI 2001/1004 reg 115

W

week—
contributions generally, SSCBA 1992 s 122(1), SI 2001/1004 reg 1(2)
statutory sick pay, SSCBA 1992 s 163(1)
unemployment benefit, SSCBA 1992 ss 25A(1)(*d*), 57(1)(*d*)

Y

year—
contributions, SI 2001/1004 reg 1(2), Sch 1 para 2(1)
credits, SI 1975/556 reg 2(1)
year of assessment, SI 2001/1004 reg 1(2)

Tax Credits

Contents

Statutes

Contents

TAX CREDITS ACT 2002

(2002 Chapter 21)

ARRANGEMENT OF SECTIONS

PART 1
TAX CREDITS

General

An Act to make provision for tax credits; to amend the law about child benefit and guardian's allowance; and for connected purposes.

[8 July 2002]

PART 1
TAX CREDITS

Modifications—Tax Credits (Polygamous Marriages) Regulations, SI 2003/742 regs 3–21 (modification of this Part in respect of members of polygamous units).

Prospective amendments—Part 1 to be repealed by the Welfare Reform Act 2012 s 147, Sch 14 Part 1 with effect from a date to be appointed.

General

1 Introductory

(1) This Act makes provision for—

(*a*) a tax credit to be known as child tax credit, and

(*b*) a tax credit to be known as working tax credit.

(2) In this Act references to a tax credit are to either of those tax credits and references to tax credits are to both of them.

(3) The following (which are superseded by tax credits) are abolished—

(*a*) children's tax credit under section 257AA of the Income and Corporation Taxes Act 1988 (c 1),

(*b*) working families' tax credit,

(*c*) disabled person's tax credit,

(*d*) the amounts which, in relation to income support and income-taxed jobseeker's allowance, are prescribed as part of the applicable amount in respect of a child or young person, the family premium, the enhanced disability premium in respect of a child or young person and the disabled child premium,

(*e*) increases in benefits in respect of children under sections 80 and 90 of the Social Security Contributions and Benefits Act 1992 (c 4) and sections 80 and 90 of the Social Security Contributions and Benefits (Northern Ireland) Act 1992 (c 7), and

(*f*) the employment credit under the schemes under section 2(2) of the Employment and Training Act 1973 (c 50) and section 1 of the Employment and Training Act (Northern Ireland) 1950 (c 29 NI)) known as "New Deal 50plus".

Order—See the Tax Credits Act 2002 (Commencement No 4, Transitional Provisions and Savings) Order, SI 2003/962 as amended by the Tax Credits Act 2002 (Further Commencement and Transitional Provisions) Order, SI 2011/2910 (TCA 2002 s 1(3)(*d*) comes into force on 31 December 2014).

Prospective amendments—Part 1 to be repealed by the Welfare Reform Act 2012 s 147, Sch 14 Part 1 with effect from a date to be appointed.

[2 Functions of Commissioners for Revenue and Customs

The Commissioners for Her Majesty's Revenue and Customs shall be responsible for the payment and management of tax credits.][1]

Commentary—*Simon's Taxes* **E2.250.**

Amendments—[1] This section substituted by CRCA 2005 s 50, Sch 4 para 88 with effect from 18 April 2005 (by virtue of SI 2005/1126).

Prospective amendments—Part 1 to be repealed by the Welfare Reform Act 2012 s 147, Sch 14 Part 1 with effect from a date to be appointed.

3 Claims

(1) Entitlement to a tax credit for the whole or part of a tax year is dependent on the making of a claim for it.

(2) Where the Board—

(*a*) decide under section 14 not to make an award of a tax credit on a claim, or

(*b*) decide under section 16 to terminate an award of a tax credit made on a claim,

(subject to any appeal) any entitlement, or subsequent entitlement, to the tax credit for any part of the same tax year is dependent on the making of a new claim.

(3) A claim for a tax credit may be made—

(*a*) jointly by the members of a [couple][1] both of whom are aged at least sixteen and are in the United Kingdom, or

(*b*) by a person who is aged at least sixteen and is in the United Kingdom but is not entitled to make a claim under paragraph (*a*) (jointly with another).

(4) Entitlement to a tax credit pursuant to a claim ceases—

(*a*) in the case of a joint claim, if the persons by whom it was made could no longer jointly make a joint claim, and

(*b*) in the case of a single claim, if the person by whom it was made could no longer make a single claim.

[(5A) In this Part "couple" means—

(*a*) a man and woman who are married to each other and are neither—

Tax Credits

(i) separated under a court order, nor
(ii) separated in circumstances in which the separation is likely to be permanent,

(*b*) a man and woman who are not married to each other but are living together as husband and wife,

(*c*) two people of the same sex who are civil partners of each other and are neither—
(i) separated under a court order, nor
(ii) separated in circumstances in which the separation is likely to be permanent, or

(*d*) two people of the same sex who are not civil partners of each other but are living together as if they were civil partners.][1]

(7) Circumstances may be prescribed in which a person is to be treated for the purposes of this Part as being, or as not being, in the United Kingdom.

(8) In this Part—
"joint claim" means a claim under paragraph (*a*) of subsection (3), and
"single claim" means a claim under paragraph (*b*) of that subsection.

Commentary—*Simon's Taxes* **E2.202, E2.251.**

HMRC Manuals—Tax Credit Technical Manual TCTM2002–2008 (entitlement: residence rules).
TCTM2003 (a person is ordinarily resident if they are normally residing in the United Kingdom (apart from temporary or occasional absences), and their residence here has been adopted voluntarily and for settled purposes as part of the regular order of their life for the time being. Lists factors in determining whether a claimant is ordinarily resident for tax credit purposes).
New Tax Credits Claimant Compliance Manual CCM6020–6200 (undeclared partners; Revenue's approach regarding status of claimants).

Regulations—Tax Credits (Residence) Regulations, SI 2003/654.
Tax Credits (Polygamous Marriages) Regulations, SI 2003/742.
Tax Credits (Miscellaneous Amendments) Regulations, SI 2012/848.
Child Benefit (General) and the Tax Credits (Residence) (Amendment) Regulations, SI 2014/1511.

Orders—Tax Credits Act 2002 (Transitional Provisions) Order, SI 2008/3151.

Modifications—Tax Credits (Polygamous Marriages) Regulations, SI 2003/742 reg 4 (modification of this section in respect of members of polygamous units).

Amendments—[1] Word in sub-s (3)(*a*) substituted, and sub-s (5A) substituted for sub-ss (5), (6) by the Civil Partnership Act 2004 s 254, Sch 24 para 144 with effect from 5 December 2005 (by virtue of SI 2005/3175).

Prospective amendments—Part 1 to be repealed by the Welfare Reform Act 2012 s 147, Sch 14 Part 1 with effect from a date to be appointed.

4 Claims: supplementary

(1) Regulations may—

(*a*) require a claim for a tax credit to be made in a prescribed manner and within a prescribed time,

(*b*) provide for a claim for a tax credit made in prescribed circumstances to be treated as having been made on a prescribed date earlier or later than that on which it is made,

(*c*) provide that, in prescribed circumstances, a claim for a tax credit may be made for a period wholly or partly after the date on which it is made,

(*d*) provide that, in prescribed circumstances, an award on a claim for a tax credit may be made subject to the condition that the requirements for entitlement are satisfied at a prescribed time,

(*e*) provide for a claim for a tax credit to be made or proceeded with in the name of a person who has died,

(*f*) provide that, in prescribed circumstances, one person may act for another in making a claim for a tax credit,

(*g*) provide that, in prescribed circumstances, a claim for a tax credit made by one member of a [couple][1] is to be treated as also made by the other member of [the couple][1], and

(*h*) provide that a claim for a tax credit is to be treated as made by a person or persons in such other circumstances as may be prescribed.

(2) The Board may supply to a person who has made a claim for a tax credit (whether or not jointly with another)—

(*a*) any information relating to the claim, to an award made on the claim or to any change of circumstances relevant to the claim or such an award,

(*b*) any communication made or received relating to such an award or any such change of circumstances, and

(*c*) any other information which is relevant to any entitlement to tax credits pursuant to the claim or any such change of circumstances or which appeared to be so relevant at the time the information was supplied.

Commentary—*Simon's Taxes* **E2.251.**

Regulations—Tax Credits (Claims and Notifications) Regulations, SI 2002/2014.
Tax Credits (Polygamous Marriages) Regulations, SI 2003/742.
Tax Credits (Miscellaneous Amendments) Regulations 2010, SI 2010/751.
Tax Credits (Miscellaneous Amendments) Regulations, SI 2012/848.
Tax Credits (Claims and Notifications) (Amendment) Regulations, SI 2015/669.
Tax Credits (Claims and Notifications) (Amendment) Regulations, SI 2017/597.

Modifications—Tax Credits (Polygamous Marriages) Regulations, SI 2003/742 reg 5 (modification of this section in respect of members of polygamous units).

Amendments—[1] Words in sub-s (1)(*g*) substituted by the Civil Partnership Act 2004 s 254, Sch 24 para 145 with effect from 5 December 2005 (by virtue of SI 2005/3175).

Prospective amendments—Part 1 to be repealed by the Welfare Reform Act 2012 s 147, Sch 14 Part 1 with effect from a date to be appointed.

5 Period of awards

(1) Where a tax credit is claimed for a tax year by making a claim before the tax year begins, any award of the tax credit on the claim is for the whole of the tax year.

(2) An award on any other claim for a tax credit is for the period beginning with the date on which the claim is made and ending at the end of the tax year in which that date falls.

(3) Subsections (1) and (2) are subject to any decision by the Board under section 16 to terminate an award.

Commentary—*Simon's Taxes* **E2.240.**

HMRC Manuals—Tax Credit Technical Manual TCTM7020, 7APPX4 (establishing the award period, with example where there is a change in tax credit eligibility).

Cross references—See the Tax Credits Act 2002 (Transitional Provisions) Order, SI 2005/773 (transitional provisions in connection with the commencement of the abolition of the child premia in respect of income support and Jobseekers Allowance).

Prospective amendments—Part 1 to be repealed by the Welfare Reform Act 2012 s 147, Sch 14 Part 1 with effect from a date to be appointed.

6 Notifications of changes of circumstances

(1) Regulations may provide that any change of circumstances of a prescribed description which may increase the maximum rate at which a person or persons may be entitled to a tax credit is to do so only if notification of it has been given.

(2) Regulations under subsection (1) may—

(*a*) provide for notification of a change of circumstances given in prescribed circumstances to be treated as having been given on a prescribed date earlier or later than that on which it is given,

(*b*) provide that, in prescribed circumstances, a notification of a change of circumstances may be given for a period wholly or partly after the date on which it is given, and

(*c*) provide that, in prescribed circumstances, an amendment of an award of a tax credit in consequence of a notification of a change of circumstances may be made subject to the condition that the requirements for entitlement to the amended amount of the tax credit are satisfied at a prescribed time.

(3) Regulations may require that, where a person has or persons have claimed a tax credit, notification is to be given if there is a change of circumstances of a prescribed description which may decrease the rate at which he is or they are entitled to the tax credit or mean that he ceases or they cease to be entitled to the tax credit.

(4) Regulations under this section may—

(*a*) require a notification to be given in a prescribed manner and within a prescribed time,

(*b*) specify the person or persons by whom a notification may be, or is to be, given, and

(*c*) provide that, in prescribed circumstances, one person may act for another in giving a notification.

Modifications—Tax Credits Notification of Changes of Circumstances (Civil Partnership) (Transitional Provisions) Order, SI 2005/828 (modification of this section for 2005–06 in respect of civil partnerships).

Regulations—Tax Credits (Claims and Notifications) Regulations, SI 2002/2014.
Tax Credits (Polygamous Marriages) Regulations, SI 2003/742.
Tax Credits (Miscellaneous Amendments) Regulations, SI 2012/848.

Prospective amendments—Part 1 to be repealed by the Welfare Reform Act 2012 s 147, Sch 14 Part 1 with effect from a date to be appointed.

7 Income test

(1) The entitlement of a person or persons of any description to a tax credit is dependent on the relevant income—

(*a*) not exceeding the amount determined in the manner prescribed for the purposes of this paragraph in relation to the tax credit and a person or persons of that description (referred to in this Part as the income threshold), or

(*b*) exceeding the income threshold by only so much that a determination in accordance with regulations under section 13(2) provides a rate of the tax credit in his or their case.

(2) Subsection (1) does not apply in relation to the entitlement of a person or persons to a tax credit for so long as the person, or either of the persons, is entitled to any social security benefit prescribed for the purposes of this subsection in relation to the tax credit.

(3) In this Part "the relevant income" means—

(*a*) if an amount is prescribed for the purposes of this paragraph and the current year income exceeds the previous year income by not more than that amount, the previous year income, (*b*) if an amount is prescribed for the purposes of this paragraph and the current year income exceeds the previous year income by more than that amount, the current year income reduced by that amount,

(*c*) if an amount is prescribed for the purposes of this paragraph and the previous year income exceeds the current year income by not more than that amount, the previous year income,

(*d*) if an amount is prescribed for the purposes of this paragraph and the previous year income exceeds the current year income by more than that amount, the current year income increased by that amount, and

(*e*) otherwise, the current year income.

(4) In this Part "the current year income" means—

(*a*) in relation to persons by whom a joint claim for a tax credit is made, the aggregate income of the persons for the tax year to which the claim relates, and

(*b*) in relation to a person by whom a single claim for a tax credit is made, the income of the person for that tax year.

(5) In this Part "the previous year income" means—

(*a*) in relation to persons by whom a joint claim for a tax credit is made, the aggregate income of the persons for the tax year preceding that to which the claim relates, and

(*b*) in relation to a person by whom a single claim for a tax credit is made, the income of the person for that preceding tax year.

(6) Regulations may provide that, for the purposes of this Part, income of a prescribed description is to be treated as being, or as not being, income for a particular tax year.

(7) In particular, regulations may provide that income of a prescribed description of a person for the tax year immediately before the preceding tax year referred to in subsection (5) is to be treated as being income of that preceding tax year (instead of any actual income of that description of the person for that preceding tax year).

(8) Regulations may for the purposes of this Part make provision—

(*a*) as to what is, or is not, income, and

(*b*) as to the calculation of income.

(9) Regulations may provide that, for the purposes of this Part, a person is to be treated—

(*a*) as having income which he does not in fact have, or

(*b*) as not having income which he does in fact have,

either generally or for a prescribed purposes.

(10) The Board may estimate the amount of the income of a person, or the aggregate income of persons, for any tax year for the purpose of making, amending or terminating an award of a tax credit; but such an estimate does not affect the rate at which he is, or they are, entitled to the tax credit for that or any other tax year.

Commentary—*Simon's Taxes* **E2.230.**

HMRC Manuals—Tax Credit Technical Manual TCTM7042 (explanation of how awards are assessed for all or part of the first tax year (2003–04) and later years, with worked example).

Regulations—Tax Credits (Definition and Calculation of Income) Regulations, SI 2002/2006.

Tax Credits (Polygamous Marriages) Regulations, SI 2003/742.

Tax Credits (Miscellaneous Amendments) Regulations, SI 2010/751.

Tax Credits (Miscellaneous Amendments) Regulations, SI 2011/721.

The Tax Credits Up-rating Regulations, SI 2011/1035

Tax Credits (Miscellaneous Amendments) Regulations, SI 2012/848.

Tax Credits Up-rating, etc. Regulations, SI 2013/750.

Tax Credits (Miscellaneous Amendments) Regulations, SI 2014/658.

Tax Credits Up-rating Regulations, SI 2014/845

Child Benefit (General) and Child Tax Credit (Amendment) Regulations, 2014/1231.

Child Benefit (General) and Tax Credits (Miscellaneous Amendments) Regulations, SI 2014/2924.

Social Security and Tax Credits (Miscellaneous Amendments) Regulations, SI 2015/175.

Tax Credits Up-rating Regulations, SI 2015/451.

Tax Credits and Child Benefit (Miscellaneous Amendments) Regulations, SI 2016/360.

Tax Credits (Income Thresholds and Determination of Rates) (Amendment) Regulations, SI 2016/393.

Tax Credits (Definition and Calculation of Income) (Amendment) Regulations, SI 2016/978.

Tax Credits (Definition and Calculation of Income) (Amendment) Regulations, SI 2017/396.

Modifications—Tax Credits (Polygamous Marriages) Regulations, SI 2003/742 reg 6 (modification of this section in respect of members of polygamous units).

Universal Credit (Transitional Provisions) Regulations, SI 2013/386 reg 17(2), Schedule, paras 1, 2 (modification of this section in respect of awards of universal credit and terminations of awards of tax credit in the same year).

Prospective amendments—Part 1 to be repealed by the Welfare Reform Act 2012 s 147, Sch 14 Part 1 with effect from a date to be appointed.

Child tax credit

8 Entitlement

(1) The entitlement of the person or persons by whom a claim for child tax credit has been made is dependent on him, or either or both of them, being responsible for one or more children or qualifying young persons.

(2) Regulations may make provision for the purposes of child tax credit as to the circumstances in which a person is or is not responsible for a child or qualifying young person.

(3) For the purposes of this Part a person is a child if he has not attained the age of sixteen; but regulations may make provision for a person who has attained that age to remain a child for the purposes of this Part after attaining that age for a prescribed period or until a prescribed date.

(4) In this Part "qualifying young person" means a person, other than a child, who—

(*a*) has not attained such age (greater than sixteen) as is prescribed, and

(*b*) satisfies prescribed conditions.

(5) Circumstances may be prescribed in which a person is to be entitled to child tax credit for a prescribed period in respect of a child or qualifying young person who has died.

Commentary—*Simon's Taxes* **E2.211.**

Regulations—Child Tax Credit Regulations, SI 2002/2007.

Tax Credits (Income Thresholds and Determination of Rates) Regulations, SI 2002/2008.

Tax Credits (Polygamous Marriages) Regulations, SI 2003/742.

Tax Credits (Miscellaneous Amendments) Regulations 2010, SI 2010/751.

Tax Credits (Miscellaneous Amendments) Regulations, SI 2012/848.

Child Benefit (General) and Tax Credits (Miscellaneous Amendments) Regulations, SI 2014/2924.

Tax Credits and Child Benefit (Miscellaneous Amendments) Regulations, SI 2016/360.

Modifications—Tax Credits (Polygamous Marriages) Regulations, SI 2003/742 reg 7 (modification of this section in respect of members of polygamous units).

Prospective amendments—Part 1 to be repealed by the Welfare Reform Act 2012 s 147, Sch 14 Part 1 with effect from a date to be appointed.

9 Maximum rate

(1) The maximum rate at which a person or persons may be entitled to child tax credit is to be determined in the prescribed manner.

(2) The prescribed manner of determination must involve the inclusion of—

(*a*) an element which is to be included in the case of all persons entitled to child tax credit, and

(*b*) an element in respect of each child or qualifying young person for whom the person is, or either or both of them is or are, responsible.

(3) The element specified in paragraph (*a*) of subsection (2) is to be known as the family element of child tax credit and that specified in paragraph (*b*) of that subsection is to be known as the individual element of child tax credit.

(4) The prescribed manner of determination may involve the inclusion of such other elements as may be prescribed.

(5) The prescribed manner of determination—

(*a*) may include provision for the amount of the family element of child tax credit to vary according to the age of any of the children or qualifying young persons or according to any such other factors as may be prescribed,

(*b*) may include provision for the amount of the individual element of child tax credit to vary according to the age of the child or qualifying young person or according to any such other factors as may be prescribed, and

(*c*) must include provision for the amount of the individual element of child tax credit to be increased in the case of a child or qualifying young person who is disabled and to be further increased in the case of a child or qualifying young person who is severely disabled.

(6) A child or qualifying young person is disabled, or severely disabled, for the purposes of this section only if—

(*a*) he satisfies prescribed conditions, or

(*b*) prescribed conditions exist in relation to him.

(7) If, in accordance with regulations under section 8(2), more than one claimant may be entitled to child tax credit in respect of the same child or qualifying young person, the prescribed manner of determination may include provision for the amount of any element of child tax credit included in the case of any one or more of them to be less than it would be if only one claimant were so entitled.

(8) "Claimant" means—

(*a*) in the case of a single claim, the person who makes the claim, and

(*b*) in the case of a joint claim, the persons who make the claim.

HMRC Manuals—Tax Credit Technical Manual TCTM2206 (guidance on elements of CTC).

Regulations—Child Tax Credit Regulations, SI 2002/2007.

Tax Credits Up-rating Regulations, SI 2005/681.

Tax Credits Up-rating Regulations, SI 2006/963.

Tax Credits Up-rating Regulations, SI 2007/828.

Tax Credits Up-rating Regulations, SI 2008/796.

Tax Credits Up-rating Regulations, SI 2009/800.

Tax Credits (Miscellaneous Amendments) Regulations 2010, SI 2010/751.

The Tax Credits Up-rating Regulations, SI 2011/1035

Tax Credits (Miscellaneous Amendments) Regulations, SI 2012/848.

Tax Credits Up-rating, etc. Regulations, SI 2013/750.

The Tax Credits Up-rating Regulations, SI 2014/845.

Child Benefit (General) and Tax Credits (Miscellaneous Amendments) Regulations, SI 2014/2924.
Tax Credits Up-rating Regulations, SI 2015/451.
Child Tax Credit (Amendment) Regulations, SI 2017/387.
Tax Credits and Guardian's Allowance Up-rating etc Regulations, SI 2017/406.
Modifications—Tax Credits (Polygamous Marriages) Regulations, SI 2003/742 reg 8 (modification of this section in respect of members of polygamous units).
Prospective amendments—The following amendments made by the Welfare Reform and Work Act 2016 s 13 with effect, for the purposes of making regulations, from 16 March 2016, and with effect for remaining purposes from 6 April 2017—

- in sub-s (2)(*a*), words "every person or persons entitled to child tax credit who is, or either or both of whom is or are, responsible for a child or qualifying young person who was born before 6 April 2017," to be substituted for words "all persons entitled to child tax credit, and";
- sub-s (2)(*c*) and preceding word to be inserted;
- sub-ss (3A), (3B) to be inserted; and
- sub-s (5)(*c*) to be substituted.

Sub-s (2)(*c*) as inserted to read as follows—

", and

(*c*) an element which is to be included in the case of a child or qualifying young person who is disabled or severely disabled.".

Sub-ss (3A), (3B) as inserted to read as follows—

"(3A) Subsection (3B) applies in the case of a person or persons entitled to child tax credit where the person is, or either or both of them is or are, responsible for a child or qualifying young person born on or after 6 April 2017.

(3B) The prescribed manner of determination in relation to the person or persons must not include an individual element of child tax credit in respect of the child or qualifying young person unless—

(*a*) he is (or they are) claiming the individual element of child tax credit for no more than one other child or qualifying young person, or

(*b*) prescribed exception applies.".

Sub-s (5)(*c*) as substituted to read as follows—

"(*c*) may include provision for the amount of the disability element of child tax credit to vary according to whether the child or qualifying young person is disabled or severely disabled.".

Part 1 to be repealed by the Welfare Reform Act 2012 s 147, Sch 14 Part 1 with effect from a date to be appointed.

Working tax credit

10 Entitlement

(1) The entitlement of the person or persons by whom a claim for working tax credit has been made is dependent on him, or either or both of them, being engaged in qualifying remunerative work.

(2) Regulations may for the purposes of this Part make provision—

(*a*) as to what is, or is not, qualifying remunerative work, and

(*b*) as to the circumstances in which a person is, or is not, engaged in it.

(3) The circumstances prescribed under subsection (2)(*b*) may differ by reference to—

(*a*) the age of the person or either of the persons,

(*b*) whether the person, or either of the persons, is disabled,

(*c*) whether the person, or either of the persons, is responsible for one or more children or qualifying young persons, or

(*d*) any other factors.

(4) Regulations may make provision for the purposes of working tax credit as to the circumstances in which a person is or is not responsible for a child or qualifying young person.

Commentary—*Simon's Taxes* **E2.220.**
HMRC Manuals—Tax Credit Technical Manual TCTM2301, 2401–2406 (guidance on qualifying remunerative work).
Regulations—Working Tax Credit (Entitlement and Maximum Rate) Regulations, SI 2002/2005.
Tax Credits (Miscellaneous Amendments) Regulations, SI 2012/848.
Working Tax Credit (Entitlement and Maximum Rate) (Amendment) Regulations, SI 2013/1736.
Working Tax Credit (Entitlement and Maximum Rate) (Amendment) Regulations, SI 2015/605.
Modifications—Tax Credits (Polygamous Marriages) Regulations, SI 2003/742 reg 9 (modification of this section in respect of members of polygamous units).
Prospective amendments—Part 1 to be repealed by the Welfare Reform Act 2012 s 147, Sch 14 Part 1 with effect from a date to be appointed.

11 Maximum rate

(1) The maximum rate at which a person or persons may be entitled to working tax credit is to be determined in the prescribed manner.

(2) The prescribed manner of determination must involve the inclusion of an element which is to be included in the case of all persons entitled to working tax credit.

(3) The prescribed manner of determination must also involve the inclusion of an element in respect of the person, or either or both of the persons, engaged in qualifying remunerative work—

(*a*) having a physical or mental disability which puts him at a disadvantage in getting a job, and

(*b*) satisfying such other conditions as may be prescribed.

(4) The element specified in subsection (2) is to be known as the basic element of working tax credit and the element specified in subsection (3) is to be known as the disability element of working tax credit.

(5) The prescribed manner of determination may involve the inclusion of such other elements as may be prescribed.

(6) The other elements may (in particular) include—

(*a*) an element in respect of the person, or either of the persons or the two of them taken together, being engaged in qualifying remunerative work to an extent prescribed for the purposes of this paragraph,

(*b*) an element in respect of the persons being the members of a [couple][1],

(*c*) an element in respect of the person not being a member of a married couple or an unmarried couple but being responsible for a child or qualifying young person,

(*d*) an element in respect of the person, or either or both of the persons, being severely disabled, and

(*e*) an element in respect of the person, or either or both of the persons, being over a prescribed age, satisfying prescribed conditions and having been engaged in qualifying remunerative work for not longer than a prescribed period.

(7) A person has a physical or mental disability which puts him at a disadvantage in getting a job, or is severely disabled, for the purposes of this section only if—

(*a*) he satisfies prescribed conditions, or

(*b*) prescribed conditions exist in relation to him.

Commentary—*Simon's Taxes* **E2.227.**

HMRC Manuals—Tax Credit Technical Manual TCTM2302 (guidance on elements of WTC).

Regulations—Working Tax Credit (Entitlement and Maximum Rate) Regulations, SI 2002/2005.
Tax Credits Up-rating Regulations, SI 2005/681.
Tax Credits Up-rating Regulations, SI 2006/963.
Tax Credits Up-rating Regulations, SI 2007/828.
Tax Credits Up-rating Regulations, SI 2008/796.
Tax Credits Up-rating Regulations, SI 2009/800.
Tax Credits (Miscellaneous Amendments) Regulations 2010, SI 2010/751.
The Tax Credits Up-rating Regulations, SI 2011/1035
Tax Credits (Miscellaneous Amendments) Regulations, SI 2012/848.
Tax Credits Up-rating, etc. Regulations, SI 2013/750.
Working Tax Credit (Entitlement and Maximum Rate) (Amendment) Regulations, SI 2013/1736.
Tax Credits (Miscellaneous Amendments) Regulations, SI 2014/658.
The Tax Credits Up-rating Regulations, SI 2014/845.
Child Benefit (General) and Tax Credits (Miscellaneous Amendments) Regulations, SI 2014/2924.
Tax Credits Up-rating Regulations, SI 2015/451.
Tax Credits and Guardian's Allowance Up-rating etc Regulations, SI 2017/406.

Modifications—Tax Credits (Polygamous Marriages) Regulations, SI 2003/742 reg 10 (modification of this section in respect of members of polygamous units).

Amendments—[1] Words in sub-s (6)(*b*) substituted by the Civil Partnership Act 2004 s 254, Sch 24 para 145 with effect from 5 December 2005 (by virtue of SI 2005/3175).

Prospective amendments—Part 1 to be repealed by the Welfare Reform Act 2012 s 147, Sch 14 Part 1 with effect from a date to be appointed.

12 Child care element

(1) The prescribed manner of determination of the maximum rate at which a person or persons may be entitled to working tax credit may involve the inclusion, in prescribed circumstances, of a child care element.

(2) A child care element is an element in respect of a prescribed proportion of so much of any relevant child care charges as does not exceed a prescribed amount.

(3) "Child care charges" are charges of a prescribed description incurred in respect of child care by the person, or either or both of the persons, by whom a claim for working tax credit is made.

(4) "Child care", in relation to a person or persons, means care provided—

(*a*) for a child of a prescribed description for whom the person is responsible, or for whom either or both of the persons is or are responsible, and

(*b*) by a person of a prescribed description.

(5) The descriptions of persons prescribed under subsection (4)(*b*) may include descriptions of persons approved in accordance with a scheme made by the appropriate national authority under this subsection.

(6) "The appropriate national authority" means—

(*a*) in relation to care provided in England, the Secretary of State,

(*b*) in relation to care provided in Scotland, the Scottish Ministers,

(*c*) in relation to care provided in Wales, the National Assembly for Wales, and

(*d*) in relation to care provided in Northern Ireland, the Department of Health, Social Services and Public Safety.

(7) The provision made by a scheme under subsection (5) must involve the giving of approvals, in accordance with criteria determined by or under the scheme, by such of the following as the scheme specifies—

(*a*) the appropriate national authority making the scheme,

(*b*) one or more specified persons or bodies or persons or bodies of a specified description, and

(*c*) persons or bodies accredited under the scheme in accordance with criteria determined by or under it.

(8) A scheme under subsection (5) may authorise—

(*a*) the making of grants or loans to, and

(*b*) the charging of reasonable fees by,

persons and bodies giving approvals.

Commentary—*Simon's Taxes* **E2.225.**

HMRC Manuals—New Tax Credits Claimant Compliance Manual CCM6210–6590 (Revenue's approach regarding child care issues).

Regulations—Working Tax Credit (Entitlement and Maximum Rate) Regulations, SI 2002/2005.
Tax Credits (Approval of Home Child Care Providers) Scheme, SI 2003/643.
Tax Credits (Approval of Child Care Providers) (Wales) Scheme, SI 2007/226.
Tax Credits (Child Care Providers) (Miscellaneous Revocation and Transitional Provisions) (England) Scheme, SI 2007/2481.
Tax Credits (Miscellaneous Amendments) Regulations 2010, SI 2010/751.
Tax Credits (Miscellaneous Amendments) Regulations, SI 2011/721.
Income Tax (Qualifying Child Care) Regulations 2011, SI 2011/775.
Tax Credits (Approval of Child Care Providers) (Wales) (Amendment) Scheme, SI 2011/993.
The Tax Credits Up-rating Regulations, SI 2011/1035
Tax Credits (Miscellaneous Amendments) Regulations, SI 2012/848.
Working Tax Credit (Entitlement and Maximum Rate) (Amendment) Regulations, SI 2013/1736.
Tax Credits (Approval of Child Care Providers) (Wales) (Amendment) Scheme, SI2013/2273.
Child Benefit (General) and Tax Credits (Miscellaneous Amendments) Regulations, SI 2014/2924.
Income Tax (Qualifying Child Care) Regulations, SI 2015/346.
Tax Credits and Child Benefit (Miscellaneous Amendments) Regulations, SI 2016/360.

Modifications—Tax Credits (Polygamous Marriages) Regulations, SI 2003/742 reg 11 (modification of this section in respect of members of polygamous units).

Prospective amendments—Part 1 to be repealed by the Welfare Reform Act 2012 s 147, Sch 14 Part 1 with effect from a date to be appointed.

Rate

13 Rate

(1) Where, in the case of a person or persons entitled to a tax credit, the relevant income does not exceed the income threshold (or his or their entitlement arises by virtue of section 7(2)), the rate at which he is or they are entitled to the tax credit is the maximum rate for his or their case.

(2) Regulations shall make provision as to the manner of determining the rate (if any) at which a person is, or persons are, entitled to a tax credit in any other case.

(3) The manner of determination prescribed under subsection (2)—

(*a*) may involve the making of adjustments so as to avoid fractional amounts, and

(*b*) may include provision for securing that, where the rate at which a person or persons would be entitled to a tax credit would be less than a prescribed rate, there is no rate in his or their case.

Commentary—*Simon's Taxes* **E2.256.**

Regulations—Tax Credits (Income Thresholds and Determination of Rates) Regulations, SI 2002/2008.
Tax Credits Up-rating Regulations, SI 2005/681.
Tax Credits Up-rating Regulations, SI 2006/963.
Tax Credits Up-rating Regulations, SI 2007/828.
Tax Credits Up-rating Regulations, SI 2008/796.
Tax Credits Up-rating Regulations, SI 2009/800.
Tax Credits (Miscellaneous Amendments) Regulations 2010, SI 2010/751.
The Tax Credits Up-rating Regulations, SI 2011/1035.
Tax Credits Up-rating, etc. Regulations, SI 2013/750.
The Tax Credits Up-rating Regulations, SI 2014/845

Prospective amendments—Part 1 to be repealed by the Welfare Reform Act 2012 s 147, Sch 14 Part 1 with effect from a date to be appointed.

Decisions

14 Initial decisions

(1) On a claim for a tax credit the Board must decide—

(*a*) whether to make an award of the tax credit, and

(*b*) if so, the rate at which to award it.

(2) Before making their decision the Board may by notice—

(*a*) require the person, or either or both of the persons, by whom the claim is made to provide any information or evidence which the Board consider they may need for making their decision, or (*b*) require any person of a prescribed description to provide any information or evidence of a prescribed description which the Board consider they may need for that purpose,

by the date specified in the notice.

(3) The Board's power to decide the rate at which to award a tax credit includes power to decide to award it at a nil rate.

Commentary—*Simon's Taxes* **E2.252.**

HMRC Manuals—New Tax Credits Claimant Compliance Manual CCM4000 (opening examinations).

CCM5000 (working examinations).

Regulations—Tax Credits (Claims and Notifications) Regulations, SI 2002/2014.

Modifications—Tax Credits (Immigration) Regulations, SI 2003/653 reg 4 (repeal of this section in relation to refugees whose asylum claims have been accepted).

Tax Credits (Polygamous Marriages) Regulations, SI 2003/742 reg 12 (modification of this section in respect of members of polygamous units).

Prospective amendments—Part 1 to be repealed by the Welfare Reform Act 2012 s 147, Sch 14 Part 1 with effect from a date to be appointed.

15 Revised provisional decisions after notifications

(1) Where notification of a change of circumstances increasing the maximum rate at which a person or persons may be entitled to a tax credit is given in accordance with regulations under section 6(1), the Board must decide whether (and, if so, how) to amend the award of the tax credit made to him or them.

(2) Before making their decision the Board may by notice—

(*a*) require the person by whom the notification is given to provide any information or evidence which the Board consider they may need for making their decision, or

(*b*) require any person of a prescribed description to provide any information or evidence of a prescribed description which the Board consider they may need for that purpose,

by the date specified in the notice.

Commentary—*Simon's Taxes* **E2.252.**

HMRC Manuals—New Tax Credits Claimant Compliance Manual CCM4000 (opening examinations).

CCM5000 (working examinations).

Regulations—Tax Credits (Claims and Notifications) Regulations, SI 2002/2014.

Modifications—Tax Credits (Immigration) Regulations, SI 2003/653 reg 4 (repeal of this section in relation to refugees whose asylum claims have been accepted).

Prospective amendments—Part 1 to be repealed by the Welfare Reform Act 2012 s 147, Sch 14 Part 1 with effect from a date to be appointed.

16 Other revised decisions

(1) Where, at any time during the period for which an award of a tax credit is made to a person or persons, the Board have reasonable grounds for believing—

(*a*) that the rate at which the tax credit has been awarded to him or them for the period differs from the rate at which he is, or they are, entitled to the tax credit for the period, or

(*b*) that he has, or they have, ceased to be, or never been, entitled to the tax credit for the period,

the Board may decide to amend or revoke the award.

(2) Where, at any time during the period for which an award of a tax credit is made to a person or persons, the Board believe—

(*a*) that the rate at which a tax credit has been awarded to him or them for the period may differ from the rate at which he is, or they are, entitled to it for the period, or

(*b*) that he or they may have ceased to be, or never been, entitled to the tax credit for the period,

the Board may give a notice under subsection (3).

(3) A notice under this subsection may—

(*a*) require the person, or either or both of the persons, to whom the tax credit was awarded to provide any information or evidence which the Board consider they may need for considering whether to amend or terminate the award under subsection (1), or

(*b*) require any person of a prescribed description to provide any information or evidence of a prescribed description which the Board consider they may need for that purpose,

by the date specified in the notice.

Commentary—*Simon's Taxes* **E2.252.**

HMRC Manuals—New Tax Credits Claimant Compliance Manual CCM4000 (opening examinations).

CCM5000 (working examinations).

Regulations—Tax Credits (Claims and Notifications) Regulations, SI 2002/2014.

Modifications—Tax Credits (Immigration) Regulations, SI 2003/653 reg 4 (repeal of this section in relation to refugees whose asylum claims have been accepted).

Tax Credits (Polygamous Marriages) Regulations, SI 2003/742 reg 13 (modification of this section in respect of members of polygamous units).

Prospective amendments—Part 1 to be repealed by the Welfare Reform Act 2012 s 147, Sch 14 Part 1 with effect from a date to be appointed.

17 Final notice

(1) Where a tax credit has been awarded for the whole or part of a tax year—

Tax Credits

(a) for awards made on single claims, the Board must give a notice relating to the tax year to the person to whom the tax credit was awarded, and

(b) for awards made on joint claims, the Board must give such a notice to the persons to whom the tax credit was awarded (with separate copies of the notice for each of them if the Board consider appropriate).

(2) The notice must either—

(a) require that the person or persons must, by the date specified for the purposes of this subsection, declare that the relevant circumstances were as specified or state any respects in which they were not, or

(b) inform the person or persons that he or they will be treated as having declared in response to the notice that the relevant circumstances were as specified unless, by that date, he states or they state any respects in which they were not.

(3) "Relevant circumstances" means circumstances (other than income) affecting—

(a) the entitlement of the person, or joint entitlement of the persons, to the tax credit, or

(b) the amount of the tax credit to which he was entitled, or they were jointly entitled,

for the tax year.

(4) The notice must either—

(a) require that the person or persons must, by the date specified for the purposes of this subsection, declare that the amount of the current year income or estimated current year income (depending on which is specified) was the amount, or fell within the range, specified or comply with subsection (5), or

(b) inform the person or persons that he or they will be treated as having declared in response to the notice that the amount of the current year income or estimated current year income (depending on which is specified) was the amount, or fell within the range, specified unless, by that date, he complies or they comply with subsection (5).

(5) To comply with this subsection the person or persons must either—

(a) state the current year income or his or their estimate of the current year income (making clear which), or

(b) declare that, throughout the period to which the award related, subsection (1) of section 7 did not apply to him or them by virtue of subsection (2) of that section.

(6) The notice may—

(a) require that the person or persons must, by the date specified for the purposes of subsection (4), declare that the amount of the previous year income was the amount, or fell within the range, specified or comply with subsection (7), or

(b) inform the person or persons that he or they will be treated as having declared in response to the notice that the amount of the previous year income was the amount, or fell within the range, specified unless, by that date, he complies or they comply with subsection (7).

(7) To comply with this subsection the person or persons must either—

(a) state the previous year income, or

(b) make the declaration specified in subsection (5)(b).

(8) The notice must inform the person or persons that if he or they—

(a) makes or make a declaration under paragraph (a) of subsection (4), or is or are treated as making a declaration under paragraph (b) of that subsection, in relation to estimated current year income (or the range within which estimated current year income fell), or

(b) states or state under subsection (5)(a) his or their estimate of the current year income,

he or they will be treated as having declared in response to the notice that the amount of the (actual) current year income was as estimated unless, by the date specified for the purposes of this subsection, he states or they state the current year income.

(9) "Specified", in relation to a notice, means specified in the notice.

(10) Regulations may—

(a) provide that, in prescribed circumstances, one person may act for another in response to a notice under this section, and

(b) provide that, in prescribed circumstances, anything done by one member of a [couple][1] in response to a notice given under this section is to be treated as also done by the other member of [the couple][1].

Commentary—*Simon's Taxes* **E2.256**.

HMRC Manuals—New Tax Credits Claimant Compliance Manual CCM11000 (Revenue end of year issues and s 17 notices).

Regulations—Tax Credits (Claims and Notifications) Regulations, SI 2002/2014.

Tax Credits (Miscellaneous Amendments) Regulations 2010, SI 2010/751.

Modifications—Tax Credits (Immigration) Regulations, SI 2003/653 reg 4 (repeal of this section in relation to refugees whose asylum claims have been accepted).

Tax Credits (Polygamous Marriages) Regulations, SI 2003/742 reg 14 (modification of this section in respect of members of polygamous units).

Universal Credit (Transitional Provisions) Regulations, SI 2013/386 reg 17(2), Schedule, paras 1, 3 (modification of this section in respect of awards of universal credit and terminations of awards of tax credit in the same year).

Amendments—[1] Word in sub-s (10)(*b*) substituted by the Civil Partnership Act 2004 s 254, Sch 24 para 145 with effect from 5 December 2005 (by virtue of SI 2005/3175).

Prospective amendments—Part 1 to be repealed by the Welfare Reform Act 2012 s 147, Sch 14 Part 1 with effect from a date to be appointed.

18 Decisions after final notice

(1) After giving a notice under section 17 the Board must decide—

(*a*) whether the person was entitled, or the persons were jointly entitled, to the tax credit, and

(*b*) if so, the amount of the tax credit to which he was entitled, or they were jointly entitled,

for the tax year.

(2) But, subject to subsection (3), that decision must not be made before a declaration or statement has been made in response to the relevant provisions of the notice.

(3) If a declaration or statement has not been made in response to the relevant provisions of the notice on or before the date specified for the purposes of section 17(4), that decision may be made after that date.

(4) In subsections (2) and (3) "the relevant provisions of the notice" means—

(*a*) the provision included in the notice by virtue of subsection (2) of section 17,

(*b*) the provision included in the notice by virtue of subsection (4) of that section, and

(*c*) any provision included in the notice by virtue of subsection (6) of that section.

(5) Where the Board make a decision under subsection (1) on or before the date referred to in subsection (3), they may revise it if a new declaration or statement is made on or before that date.

(6) If a person or persons to whom a notice under section 17 is given is or are within paragraph (*a*) or (*b*) of subsection (8) of that section, the Board must decide again—

(*a*) whether the person was entitled, or the persons were jointly entitled, to the tax credit, and

(*b*) if so, the amount of the tax credit to which he was entitled, or they were jointly entitled,

for the tax year.

(7) But, subject to subsection (8), that decision must not be made before a statement has been made in response to the provision included in the notice by virtue of subsection (8) of section 17.

(8) If a statement has not been made in response to the provision included in the notice by virtue of that subsection on or before the date specified for the purposes of that subsection, that decision may be made after that date.

(9) Where the Board make a decision under subsection (6) on or before the date referred to in subsection (8), they may revise it if a new statement is made on or before that date.

(10) Before exercising a function imposed or conferred on them by subsection (1), (5), (6) or (9), the Board may by notice require the person, or either or both of the persons, to whom the notice under section 17 was given to provide any further information or evidence which the Board consider they may need for exercising the function by the date specified in the notice.

(11) Subject to sections [19, 20, 21A and 21B][1] and regulations under section 21 (and to any revision under subsection (5) or (9) and any appeal)—

(*a*) in a case in which a decision is made under subsection (6) in relation to a person or persons and a tax credit for a tax year, that decision, and

(*b*) in any other case, the decision under subsection (1) in relation to a person or persons and a tax credit for a tax year,

is conclusive as to the entitlement of the person, or the joint entitlement of the persons, to the tax credit for the tax year and the amount of the tax credit to which he was entitled, or they were jointly entitled, for the tax year.

Commentary—*Simon's Taxes* **E2.252.**

HMRC Manuals—New Tax Credits Claimant Compliance Manual CCM11000 (end of year issues and making s 18 decisions).

Modifications—Tax Credits (Immigration) Regulations, SI 2003/653 reg 4 (modification of this section in relation to refugees whose asylum claims have been accepted).

Tax Credits (Polygamous Marriages) Regulations, SI 2003/742 reg 15 (modification of this section in respect of members of polygamous units).

Universal Credit (Transitional Provisions) Regulations, SI 2013/386 reg 17(2), Schedule paras 1, 4 (modification of this section in respect of awards of universal credit and terminations of awards of tax credit in the same year).

Amendments—[1] In sub-s (11), words substituted by the Tax Credits, Child Benefit and Guardian's Allowance Reviews and Appeals Order, SI 2014/886 art 2(1), (2) with effect from 6 April 2014.

Prospective amendments—Part 1 to be repealed by the Welfare Reform Act 2012 s 147, Sch 14 Part 1 with effect from a date to be appointed.

19 Power to enquire

(1) The Board may enquire into—

(*a*) the entitlement of a person, or the joint entitlement of persons, to a tax credit for a tax year, and

(*b*) the amount of the tax credit to which he was entitled, or they were jointly entitled, for the tax year,

if they give notice to the person, or each of the persons, during the period allowed for the initiation of an enquiry.

(2) As part of the enquiry the Board may by notice—

(*a*) require the person, or either or both of the persons, to provide any information or evidence which the Board consider they may need for the purposes of the enquiry, or

(*b*) require any person of a prescribed description to provide any information or evidence of a prescribed description which the Board consider they may need for those purposes,

by the date specified in the notice.

(3) On an enquiry the Board must decide—

(*a*) whether the person was entitled, or the persons were jointly entitled, to the tax credit, and

(*b*) if so, the amount of the tax credit to which he was entitled, or they were jointly entitled,

for the tax year.

(4) The period allowed for the initiation of an enquiry is the period beginning immediately after the relevant section 18 decision and ending—

(*a*) if the person, or either of the persons, to whom the enquiry relates is required by section 8 of the Taxes Management Act 1970 (c 9) to make a return, with the day on which the return becomes final (or, if both of the persons are so required and their returns become final on different days, with the later of those days), or

(*b*) in any other case, one year after the beginning of the relevant section 17 date.

(5) "The relevant section 18 decision" means—

(*a*) in a case in which a decision is to be made under subsection (6) of section 18 in relation to the person or persons and the tax year to which the enquiry relates, that decision, and

(*b*) in any other case, the decision under subsection (1) of that section in relation to the person or persons and that tax year.

(6) "The relevant section 17 date" means—

(*a*) in a case in which a statement may be made by the person or persons in response to provision included by virtue of subsection (8) of section 17 in the notice given to him or them under that section in relation to the award, the date specified in the notice for the purposes of that subsection, and

(*b*) in any other case, the date specified for the purposes of subsection (4) of that section in the notice given to him or them under that section in relation to the tax year.

(7) A return becomes final—

(*a*) if it is enquired into under section 9A of the Taxes Management Act 1970 (c 9), when the enquiries are completed (within the meaning of section 28A of that Act), or

(*b*) otherwise, at the end of the period specified in subsection (2) of that section in relation to the return.

(8) An enquiry is completed at the time when the Board give notice to the person or persons of their decision under subsection (3); but if the Board give notice to the persons at different times the enquiry is completed at the later of those times.

(9) The person, or either of the persons, to whom the enquiry relates may at any time before such notice is given apply for a direction that the Board must give such a notice.

[(10) Any such application is to be subject to the relevant provisions of Part 5 of the Taxes Management Act 1970 (see, in particular, section 48(2)(*b*) of that Act), and the tribunal must give the direction applied for unless satisfied that the Board have reasonable grounds for not making the decision or giving the notice.][1]

(11) Where the entitlement of a person, or the joint entitlement of persons, to a tax credit for a tax year has been enquired into under this section, it is not to be the subject of a further notice under subsection (1).

(12) Subject to [sections 20, 21A and 21B][2] and regulations under section 21 (and to any appeal), a decision under subsection (3) in relation to a person or persons and a tax credit for a tax year is conclusive as to the entitlement of the person, or the joint entitlement of the persons, to the tax credit for the tax year and the amount of the tax credit to which he was entitled, or they were jointly entitled, for the tax year.

Commentary—*Simon's Taxes* **E2.258.**

HMRC Manuals—New Tax Credits Claimant Compliance Manual CCM12000 (opening and working enquiries). CCM14000 (closing the enquiry).

Modifications—Tax Credits (Immigration) Regulations, SI 2003/653 reg 4 (modification of this section in relation to refugees whose asylum claims have been accepted).

Tax Credits (Polygamous Marriages) Regulations, SI 2003/742 reg 16 (modification of this section in respect of members of polygamous units).

Universal Credit (Transitional Provisions) Regulations, SI 2013/386 reg 17(2), Schedule paras 1, 5 (modification of this section in respect of awards of universal credit and terminations of awards of tax credit in the same year).

Amendments—[1] Sub-s (10) substituted by the Transfer of Tribunal Functions and Revenue and Customs Appeals Order, SI 2009/56 art 3, Sch 1 para 313 with effect from 1 April 2009.

[2] In sub-s (12), words substituted by the Tax Credits, Child Benefit and Guardian's Allowance Reviews and Appeals Order, SI 2014/886 art 2(1), (3) with effect from 6 April 2014.

Prospective amendments—Part 1 to be repealed by the Welfare Reform Act 2012 s 147, Sch 14 Part 1 with effect from a date to be appointed.

In sub-s (4)(*a*), words "to make a return under section 8 of the Taxes Management Act 1970" to be substituted for words "by section 8 of the Taxes Management Act 1970 (c. 9) to make a return" by F(No 2)A 2017 s 61(1), Sch 14 para 34 with effect from a day to be appointed.

20 Decisions on discovery

(1) Where in consequence of a person's income tax liability being revised the Board have reasonable grounds for believing that a conclusive decision relating to his entitlement to a tax credit for a tax year (whether or not jointly with another person) is not correct, the Board may decide to revise that decision.

(2) A person's income tax liability is revised—

(*a*) on the taking effect of an amendment of a return of his under section 9ZA(1) of the Taxes Management Act 1970,

(*b*) on the issue of a notice of correction under section 9ZB of that Act amending a return of his (provided that he does not give a notice of rejection before the end of the period of thirty days beginning with the date of issue of the notice of correction),

(*c*) on the amendment of an assessment of his by notice under section 9C of that Act,

(*d*) on the amendment of a return of his under section 12ABA(3)(*a*) of that Act,

(*e*) on the amendment of a return of his under subsection (6)(*a*) of section 12ABB of that Act after the correction of a partnership return under that section (provided that the amendment does not cease to have effect by reason of the rejection of the correction under subsection (4) of that section),

(*f*) on the issue of [a partial or final closure notice][2] under section 28A of that Act making amendments of a return of his,

(*g*) on the amendment of a return of his under section 28B(4)(*a*) of that Act,

(*h*) on the making of an assessment as regards him under section 29(1) of that Act,

(*i*) on the vacation of the whole or part of an assessment of his under section 32 of that Act,

(*j*) on giving him relief under section 33 of that Act, or

(*k*) on the determination (or settlement) of an appeal against the making, amendment or vacation of an assessment or return, or a decision on a claim for relief, under any of the provisions mentioned in paragraphs (*c*), (*f*) and (*h*) to (*j*).

(3) But no decision may be made under subsection (1)—

(*a*) unless it is too late to enquire into the person's entitlement under section 19, or

(*b*) after the period of one year beginning when the person's income tax liability is revised [as specified in subsection (1)][2].

(4) Where the Board have reasonable grounds for believing that—

(*a*) a conclusive decision relating to the entitlement of a person, or the joint entitlement of persons, to a tax credit for a tax year is not correct, and

(*b*) that is attributable to fraud or neglect on the part of the person, or of either of the persons, or on the part of any person acting for him, or either of them,

the Board may decide to revise that decision.

(5) But no decision may be made under subsection (4)—

(*a*) unless it is too late to enquire into the entitlement, or joint entitlement, under section 19, or

(*b*) after the period of five years beginning with the end of the tax year to which the conclusive decision relates.

(6) "Conclusive decision", in relation to the entitlement of a person, or joint entitlement of persons, to a tax credit for a tax year, means—

(*a*) a decision in relation to it under section 18(1), (5), (6) or (9) or 19(3) or a previous decision under this section, or

(*b*) a decision under regulations under section 21 relating to a decision within paragraph (*a*), [or][1]

[(*c*) a decision within paragraph (*a*) or (*b*) as varied under section 21A(5)(*b*), or

(*d*) a decision on an appeal against a decision within paragraph (*a*), (*b*) or (*c*).][1]

(7) Subject to any subsequent decision under this section and to regulations under section 21 [and to any review under section 21A][1] (and to any appeal), a decision under subsection (1) or (4) in relation to a person or persons and a tax credit for a tax year is conclusive as to the entitlement of the person, or the joint entitlement of the persons, to the tax credit for the tax year and the amount of the tax credit to which he was entitled, or they were jointly entitled, for the tax year.

Commentary—*Simon's Taxes* **E2.252.**

HMRC Manuals—New Tax Credits Claimant Compliance Manual CCM13000 (Revenue approach to discovery decisions).

Modifications—Tax Credits (Polygamous Marriages) Regulations, SI 2003/742 reg 17 (modification of this section in respect of members of polygamous units).

Universal Credit (Transitional Provisions) Regulations, SI 2013/386 reg 17(2), Schedule paras 1, 6 (modification of this section in respect of awards of universal credit and terminations of awards of tax credit in the same year).

Amendments—[1] In sub-s (6)(*b*), word inserted, sub-s (6)(*c*), (*d*),substituted for words following sub-s (6)(*b*), and in sub-s (7) words inserted, by the Tax Credits, Child Benefit and Guardian's Allowance Reviews and Appeals Order, SI 2014/886 art 2(1), (4), (5) with effect from 6 April 2014.

Tax Credits

[2] In sub-s (2)(*f*), words substituted for words "a closure notice", and in sub-s (3)(*b*), words inserted, by F(No 2)A 2017 s 63, Sch 15 para 35 with effect in relation to an enquiry under TMA 1970 ss 9A, 12ZM or 12AC or FA 1998 Sch 18 where notice of the enquiry is given on or after 16 November 2017 or the enquiry is in progress immediately before that day.

Prospective amendments—Part 1 to be repealed by the Welfare Reform Act 2012 s 147, Sch 14 Part 1 with effect from a date to be appointed.

21 Decisions subject to official error

Regulations may make provision for a decision under section 14(1), 15(1), 16(1), 18(1), (5), (6) or (9), 19(3) or 20(1) or (4) to be revised in favour of the person or persons to whom it relates if it is incorrect by reason of official error (as defined by the regulations).

Commentary—*Simon's Taxes* **E2.252.**

Regulations—Tax Credits (Official Error) Regulations, SI 2003/692.

Tax Credits (Miscellaneous Amendments) Regulations 2010, SI 2010/751.

Modifications—Universal Credit (Transitional Provisions) Regulations, SI 2013/386 reg 17(2), Schedule paras 1, 7 (modification of this section in respect of awards of universal credit and terminations of awards of tax credit in the same year).

Prospective amendments—Part 1 to be repealed by the Welfare Reform Act 2012 s 147, Sch 14 Part 1 with effect from a date to be appointed.

[21A Review of decisions

(1) The Commissioners for Her Majesty's Revenue and Customs must review any decision within section 38(1) if they receive a written application to do so that identifies the applicant and decision in question, and—

(*a*) that application is received within 30 days of the date of the notification of the original decision or of the date the original decision was made if not notified because of section 23(3), or

(*b*) it is received within such longer period as may be allowed under section 21B.

(2) The Commissioners must carry out the review as soon as is reasonably practicable.

(3) When the review has been carried out, the Commissioners must give the applicant notice of their conclusion containing sufficient information to enable the applicant to know—

(*a*) the conclusion on the review,

(*b*) if the conclusion is that the decision is varied, details of the variation, and

(*c*) the reasons for the conclusion.

(4) The conclusion on the review must be one of the following—

(*a*) that the decision is upheld;

(*b*) that the decision is varied;

(*c*) that the decision is cancelled.

(5) Where—

(*a*) the Commissioners notify the applicant of further information or evidence that they may need for carrying out the review, and

(*b*) the information or evidence is not provided to them by the date specified in the notice,

the review may proceed without that information or evidence.][1]

Amendments—[1] Sections 21A, 21B inserted by the Tax Credits, Child Benefit and Guardian's Allowance Reviews and Appeals Order, SI 2014/886 art 2(1), (6) with effect from 6 April 2014.

[21B Late application for a review

(1) The Commissioners for Her Majesty's Revenue and Customs may in a particular case extend the time limit specified in section 21A(1)(*a*) for making an application for a review if all of the following conditions are met.

(2) The first condition is that the person seeking a review has applied to the Commissioners for an extension of time.

(3) The second condition is that the application for the extension—

(*a*) explains why the extension is sought, and

(*b*) is made within 13 months of the notification of the original decision or of the date the original decision was made if not notified because of section 23(3).

(4) The third condition is that the Commissioners are satisfied that due to special circumstances it was not practicable for the application for a review to have been made within the time limit specified in section 21A(1)(*a*).

(5) The fourth condition is that the Commissioners are satisfied that it is reasonable in all the circumstances to grant the extension.

(6) In determining whether it is reasonable to grant an extension, the Commissioners must have regard to the principle that the greater the amount of time that has elapsed between the end of the time limit specified in section 21A(1)(*a*) and the date of the application, the more compelling should be the special circumstances on which the application is based.

(7) An application to extend the time limit specified in section 21A(1)(*a*) which has been refused may not be renewed.][1]

Amendments—[1] Sections 21A, 21B inserted by the Tax Credits, Child Benefit and Guardian's Allowance Reviews and Appeals Order, SI 2014/886 art 2(1), (6) with effect from 6 April 2014.

22 Information etc requirements: supplementary

(1) Regulations may make provision as to the manner and form in which—

(*a*) information or evidence is to be provided in compliance with a requirement imposed by a notice under section 14(2), 15(2), 16(3), 18(10) or 19(2), or

(*b*) a declaration or statement is to be made in response to a notice under section 17.

(2) Regulations may make provision as to the dates which may be specified in a notice under section 14(2), 15(2), 16(3), 17, 18(10) or 19(2).

Regulations—Tax Credits (Claims and Notifications) Regulations, SI 2002/2014.

Prospective amendments—Part 1 to be repealed by the Welfare Reform Act 2012 s 147, Sch 14 Part 1 with effect from a date to be appointed.

23 Notice of decisions

(1) When a decision is made under section 14(1), 15(1), 16(1), 18(1), (5), (6) or (9), 19(3) or 20(1) or (4) or regulations under section 21, the Board must give notice of the decision to the person, or each of the persons, to whom it relates.

(2) Notice of a decision must state the date on which it is given and include details of any right [to a review under section 21A and of any subsequent right][1] to appeal against the decision under section 38.

(3) Notice need not be given of a decision made under section 14(1) or 18(1) or (6) on the basis of declarations made or treated as made by the person or persons in response to the notice given to him or them under section 17 if—

(*a*) that notice, or

(*b*) in the case of a decision under subsection (6) of section 18, that notice or the notice of the decision under subsection (1) of that section,

stated what the decision would be and the date on which it would be made.

Commentary—*Simon's Taxes* **E2.252.**

Modifications—Universal Credit (Transitional Provisions) Regulations, SI 2013/386 reg 17(2), Schedule paras 1, 8 (modification of this section in respect of awards of universal credit and terminations of awards of tax credit in the same year).

Amendments—[1] Words inserted in sub-s (2) by the Tax Credits, Child Benefit and Guardian's Allowance Reviews and Appeals Order, SI 2014/886 art 2(1), (7) with effect from 6 April 2014.

Prospective amendments—Part 1 to be repealed by the Welfare Reform Act 2012 s 147, Sch 14 Part 1 with effect from a date to be appointed.

Payment

24 Payments

(1) Where the Board have made an award of a tax credit, the amount of the tax credit awarded must be paid to the person to whom the award is made, subject to subsections (2) and (3).

(2) Where an award of a tax credit is made to the members of a [couple][1], payments of the tax credit, or of any element of the tax credit, are to be made to whichever of them is prescribed.

(3) Where an award of a tax credit is made on a claim which was made by one person on behalf of another, payments of the tax credit, or of any element of the tax credit, are to be made to whichever of those persons is prescribed.

(4) Where an award of a tax credit has been made to a person or persons for the whole or part of a tax year, payments may, in prescribed circumstances, continue to be made for any period, after the tax year, within which he is or they are entitled to make a claim for the tax credit for the next tax year.

(5) Payments made under subsection (4) are to be treated for the purposes of this section and the following provisions of this Part as if they were payments of the tax credit for the next tax year.

(6) Subject to section 25, payments of a tax credit must be made by the Board.

(7) Regulations may make provision about the time when and the manner in which a tax credit, or any element of a tax credit, is to be paid by the Board.

(8) If the regulations make provision for payments of a tax credit, or any element of a tax credit, to be made by the Board by way of a credit to a bank account or other account notified to the Board, the regulations may provide that entitlement to the tax credit or element is dependent on an account having been notified to the Board in accordance with the regulations.

Commentary—*Simon's Taxes* **E2.255.**

Regulations—Working Tax Credit (Entitlement and Maximum Rate) Regulations, SI 2002/2005.

Tax Credits (Payments by the Board) Regulations, SI 2002/2173.

Tax Credits (Polygamous Marriages) Regulations, SI 2003/742.

Tax Credits (Miscellaneous Amendments) Regulations 2010, SI 2010/751.

Tax Credits (Miscellaneous Amendments) Regulations, SI 2012/848.

Modifications—Tax Credits (Polygamous Marriages) Regulations, SI 2003/742 reg 18 (modification of this section in respect of members of polygamous units).

Amendments—[1] Word in sub-s (2) substituted by the Civil Partnership Act 2004 s 254, Sch 24 para 145 with effect from 5 December 2005 (by virtue of SI 2005/3175).

Prospective amendments—Part 1 to be repealed by the Welfare Reform Act 2012 s 147, Sch 14 Part 1 with effect from a date to be appointed.

25 Payments of working tax credit by employers

(1) Regulations may require employers, when making [payments of, or on account of, PAYE income][1] and in any such other circumstances as may be prescribed, to pay working tax credit, or prescribed elements of working tax credit, to employees.

(2) The regulations may, in particular, include provision—

(*a*) requiring employers to make payments of working tax credit, or prescribed elements of working tax credit, in accordance with notices given to them by the Board,

(*b*) for the payment by the Board of working tax credit in cases where an employer does not make payments of working tax credit, or prescribed elements of working tax credit, in accordance with the regulations and with any notices given by the Board,

(*c*) prescribing circumstances in which employers are not required to make, or to continue making, payments of working tax credit, or prescribed elements of working tax credit,

(*d*) for the provision of information or evidence for the purpose of enabling the Board to be satisfied whether employers are complying with notices given by the Board and with the regulations,

(*e*) requiring employers to provide information to employees (in their itemised pay statements or otherwise),

(*f*) for the funding by the Board of working tax credit paid or to be paid by employers (whether by way of set off against income tax, national insurance contributions or student loan deductions for which they are accountable to the Board or otherwise),

(*g*) for the recovery by the Board from an employer of funding under paragraph (*f*) to the extent that it exceeds the amount of working tax credit paid by the employer,

(*h*) for the payment of interest at the prescribed rate on sums due from or to the Board, and for determining the date from which interest is to be calculated, and

(*i*) for appeals with respect to matters arising under the regulations which would otherwise not be the subject of an appeal.

(3), (4) . . .[2]

(5) In this Part—

"employee" means a person who receives any [payment of, or on account of, PAYE income][1], and "employer", in relation to an employee, means a person who makes any such payment to the employee.

(6) . . .[1]

(7) "Student loan deductions" means deductions in accordance with regulations under section 22(5) of the Teaching and Higher Education Act 1998 (c 30), section 73B(3) of the Education (Scotland) Act 1980 (c 44) or Article 3(5) of the Education (Student Support) (Northern Ireland) Order 1998 (SI 1998/1760 (NI 14)).

Commentary—*Simon's Taxes* **E2.255.**

Regulations—Working Tax Credit (Payment by Employers) Regulations, SI 2002/2172.

Amendments—[1] In sub-s (1), words substituted for the words "Schedule E payments"; in sub-s (5), words substituted for the words "Schedule E payment"; and sub-s (6) repealed; by ITEPA 2003 ss 722, 724, Sch 6 paras 264, 265, Sch 8 with effect, for income tax purposes, from 2003–04; and for corporation tax purposes, for accounting periods ending after 5 April 2003. For transitional provisions and savings see ITEPA 2003 s 723, Sch 7.

[2] Sub-ss (3), (4) repealed by FA 2008 s 113, Sch 36 para 90 with effect from 1 April 2009 (by virtue of SI 2009/404 art 2). In relation to a notice given on or before 31 March 2009, for the purposes of the application of TMA 1970 s 20 to this section, the amendments made by FA 2008 Sch 36 para 90 shall be disregarded (SI 2009/404 art 9).

Prospective amendments—Part 1 to be repealed by the Welfare Reform Act 2012 s 147, Sch 14 Part 1 with effect from a date to be appointed.

26 Liability of officers for sums paid to employers

(1) Regulations may provide that where—

(*a*) an employer which is a body corporate has failed to repay any funding to the Board in accordance with regulations made under section 24(2)(*g*), and

(*b*) the provision of the funding, or the failure by the employer to repay the funding, appears to the Board to be attributable to fraud or neglect on the part of one or more individuals who, at the time of the fraud or neglect, were officers of the body corporate ("culpable officers"),

the culpable officers are required to pay to the Board the amount of funding recoverable by the Board from the employer.

(2) Regulations under this section must include provision—

(*a*) for any amount paid to the Board by a culpable officer in accordance with the regulations to be deducted from the amount of funding liable to be repaid by the employer,

(*b*) for the amount which a culpable officer is liable to pay under the regulations to be reduced where the amount of funding recoverable from the employer is reduced by payments made to the Board by the employer, and

(*c*) for the Board to repay to a culpable officer the amount (if any) by which the amount that he has paid to the Board pursuant to the regulations exceeds the reduced amount that he is liable to pay by virtue of paragraph (*b*).

(3) Regulations under this section may include provision—

(*a*) requiring payments by culpable officers to be made in accordance with notices given to them by the Board,

(*b*) for determining, in cases of an employer in relation to which there is more than one culpable officer, the proportion of the amount of funding recoverable from the employer that is payable by each culpable officer,

(*c*) for the payment of interest at the prescribed rate on sums due to or from the Board, and for determining the date from which interest is to be calculated, and

(*d*) for appeals with respect to matters arising under the regulations.

(4) "Officer", in relation to a body corporate, means—

(*a*) any director, manager, secretary or other similar officer of the body corporate, or any person purporting to act as such, and

(*b*) in a case where the affairs of the body corporate are managed by its members, any member of the body corporate exercising functions of management with respect to it or purporting to do so.

Commentary—*Simon's Taxes* **E2.255.**

Prospective amendments—Part 1 to be repealed by the Welfare Reform Act 2012 s 147, Sch 14 Part 1 with effect from a date to be appointed.

27 Rights of employees

Schedule 1 (rights of employees not to suffer unfair dismissal or other detriment) has effect.

Prospective amendments—Part 1 to be repealed by the Welfare Reform Act 2012 s 147, Sch 14 Part 1 with effect from a date to be appointed.

28 Overpayments

(1) Where the amount of a tax credit paid for a tax year to a person or persons exceeds the amount of the tax credit to which he is entitled, or they are jointly entitled, for the tax year (as determined in accordance with the provision made by and by virtue of sections 18 to [21B][1]), the [Commissioners may][2] decide that the excess, or any part of it, is to be[—

(*a*) repaid to the Commissioners; or

(*b*) treated as if it were an amount recoverable by the Secretary of State under section 71ZB of the Administration Act or (as the case may be) by the relevant Northern Ireland Department under section 69ZB of the Administration (Northern Ireland) Act][2];

(2) In this Part such an excess is referred to as an overpayment.

(3) For overpayments made under awards on single claims, the person to whom the tax credit was awarded is liable to repay [to the Commissioners, the Secretary of State or (as the case may be) the relevant Northern Ireland Department, the amount which the Commissioners decide is to be repaid or treated as recoverable under subsection (1)(*b*)][2].

(4) For overpayments made under awards on joint claims, the persons to whom the tax credit was awarded are jointly and severally liable to repay [to the Commissioners, the Secretary of State or (as the case may be) the relevant Northern Ireland Department, the amount mentioned in subsection (3) unless the Commissioners decide that each is liable for][2] a specified part of that amount.

(5) Where it appears to the [Commissioners][2] that there is likely to be an overpayment of a tax credit for a tax year under an award made to a person or persons, the Board may, with a view to reducing or eliminating the overpayment, amend the award or any award of any tax credit made to the person or persons; but this subsection does not apply once a decision is taken in relation to the person or persons for the tax year under section 18(1).

(6) Where the [Commissioners][2] decide under section 16 to terminate an award of a tax credit made to a person or persons on the ground that at no time during the period to which the award related did the person or persons satisfy—

(*a*) section 8(1) (if the award related to child tax credit), or

(*b*) section 10(1) (if it related to working tax credit),

the Board may decide that the amount paid under the award, or any part of it, is to be treated for the purposes of this Part (apart from subsection (5)) as an overpayment.

[(7) In this section and in section 29—

"the Administration Act" means the Social Security Administration Act 1992;

"the Administration (Northern Ireland) Act" means the Social Security Administration (Northern Ireland) Act 1992;

"the relevant Northern Ireland Department" means the Department for Communities.

(8) In this section, "the Commissioners" means the Commissioners for Her Majesty's Revenue and Customs.][2]

Commentary—*Simon's Taxes* **E2.257.**

Modifications—Universal Credit (Transitional Provisions) Regulations, SI 2013/386 reg 17(2), Schedule paras 1, 9 (modification of this section in respect of awards of universal credit and terminations of awards of tax credit in the same year).

Universal Credit (Transitional Provisions) Regulations, SI 2014/1230 reg 12(2), (3) (modification of this section in repect of treatment of overpayment of tax credits).

Amendments—[1] In sub-s (1), reference substituted by the Tax Credits, Child Benefit and Guardian's Allowance Reviews and Appeals Order, SI 2014/886 art 2(1), (8) with effect from 6 April 2014.

Tax Credits

[2] The following amendments made by the Tax Credits (Exercise of Functions in relation to Northern Ireland and Notices for Recovery of Tax Credit Overpayments) Order, SI 2017/781 art 6(1), (2) with effect from 25 September 2017—
- in sub-s (1), words substituted for words "Board may" and words "repaid to the Board";
- in sub-s (3), words substituted for words "the amount which the Board decide is to be repaid";
- in sub-s (4), words substituted for words "the amount which the Board decide is to be repaid unless the Board decide that each is to repay";
- in sub-ss (5), (6), word substituted for word "Board"; and
- sub-ss (7), (8) inserted.

Prospective amendments—Part 1 to be repealed by the Welfare Reform Act 2012 s 147, Sch 14 Part 1 with effect from a date to be appointed.

29 Recovery of overpayments

(1) Where an amount is liable to be repaid [or paid][3] by a person or persons under section 28, the Board must give him, or each of them, a notice specifying the amount.

(2) The notice must state which of subsections (3) to (5) is to apply in relation to the amount or any specified part of the amount; and a notice may at any time be replaced by another notice containing a different statement.

(3) Where a notice states that this subsection applies in relation to an amount (or part of an amount), it is to be treated for the purposes of Part 6 of the Taxes Management Act 1970 (c 9) (collection and recovery) as if it were tax charged in an assessment and due and payable by the person or persons to whom the notice was given at the end of the period of thirty days beginning with the day on which the notice is given.

[(4) Where a notice states that this subsection applies in relation to an amount (or part of an amount), it may be recovered—

(*a*) subject to provision made by regulations, by deduction from payments of any tax credit under an award made for any period to the person, or either or both of the persons, to whom the notice was given;

(*b*) by the Secretary of State—

(i) by deductions under section 71ZC of the Administration Act (deduction from benefit);

(ii) by deductions under section 71ZD of that Act (deduction from earnings); or

(iii) as set out in section 71ZE of that Act (court action etc); or

(*c*) by the relevant Northern Ireland Department—

(i) by deductions under section 69ZC of the Administration (Northern Ireland) Act (deduction from benefit);

(ii) by deductions under section 69ZD of that Act (deduction from earnings); or

(iii) as set out in section 69ZE of that Act (court action etc).][3]

(5) Where a notice states that this subsection applies in relation to an amount (or part of an amount), [PAYE regulations][1] apply to it as if it were an underpayment of [income tax][2] for a previous year of assessment by the person or persons to whom the notice was given [that is not a relevant debt (within the meaning of section 684 of the Income Tax (Earnings and Pensions) Act 2003)][2].

Commentary—*Simon's Taxes* **E2.257.**

Regulations—Tax Credits and Child Benefit (Miscellaneous Amendments) Regulations, SI 2016/360.

Modifications—Tax Credits (Polygamous Marriages) Regulations, SI 2003/742 reg 19 (modification of this section in respect of members of polygamous units).

Universal Credit (Transitional Provisions) Regulations, SI 2013/386 reg 17(2), Schedule paras 1, 10 (modification of this section in respect of awards of universal credit and terminations of awards of tax credit in the same year).

Universal Credit (Transitional Provisions) Regulations, SI 2014/1230 reg 12(2), (3) (modification of this section in repect of treatment of overpayment of tax credits).

Amendments—[1] In sub-s (5), words substituted for the words "regulations under section 203(2)(*a*) of the Income and Corporation Taxes Act 1988 (c 1) (PAYE)" by ITEPA 2003 s 722, Sch 6 paras 264, 265 with effect, for income tax purposes, from 2003–04; and for corporation tax purposes, for accounting periods ending after 5 April 2003. For transitional provisions and savings see ITEPA 2003 s 723, Sch 7.

[2] In sub-s (5) words substituted for the word "tax" and words at the end inserted by FA 2009 s 110, Sch 58 para 8 with effect from 21 July 2009.

[3] In sub-s (1), words inserted, and sub-s (4) substituted, by the Tax Credits (Exercise of Functions in relation to Northern Ireland and Notices for Recovery of Tax Credit Overpayments) Order, SI 2017/781 art 6(1), (3) with effect from 25 September 2017. Sub-s (4) previously read as follows—

"(4) Where a notice states that this subsection applies in relation to an amount (or part of an amount), it may, subject to provision made by regulations, be recovered by deduction from payments of any tax credit under an award made for any period to the person, or either or both of the persons, to whom the notice was given.".

Prospective amendments—Part 1 to be repealed by the Welfare Reform Act 2012 s 147, Sch 14 Part 1 with effect from a date to be appointed.

30 Underpayments

(1) Where it has been determined in accordance with the provision made by and by virtue of sections 18 to [21B][1] that a person was entitled, or persons were jointly entitled, to a tax credit for a tax year and either—

(*a*) the amount of the tax credit paid to him or them for that tax year was less than the amount of the tax credit to which it was so determined that he is entitled or they are jointly entitled, or

(*b*) no payment of the tax credit was made to him or them for that tax year,

the amount of the difference, or of his entitlement or their joint entitlement, must be paid to him or to whichever of them is prescribed.

(2) Where the claim for the tax credit was made by one person on behalf of another, the payment is to be made to whichever of those persons is prescribed.

Commentary—*Simon's Taxes* **E2.257**.

Modifications—Universal Credit (Transitional Provisions) Regulations, SI 2013/386 reg 17(2), Schedule paras 1, 11 (modification of this section in respect of awards of universal credit and terminations of awards of tax credit in the same year).

Amendments—[1] In sub-s (1), reference substituted by the Tax Credits, Child Benefit and Guardian's Allowance Reviews and Appeals Order, SI 2014/886 art 2(1), (8) with effect from 6 April 2014.

Prospective amendments—Part 1 to be repealed by the Welfare Reform Act 2012 s 147, Sch 14 Part 1 with effect from a date to be appointed.

Penalties

31 Incorrect statements etc

(1) Where a person fraudulently or negligently—

(*a*) makes an incorrect statement or declaration in or in connection with a claim for a tax credit or a notification of a change of circumstances given in accordance with regulations under section 6 or in response to a notice under section 17, or

(*b*) gives incorrect information or evidence in response to a requirement imposed on him by virtue of section 14(2), 15(2), 16(3), 18(10) or 19(2) or regulations under section 25 [or in response to a notification under section 21A(5)][1],

a penalty not exceeding £3,000 may be imposed on him.

(2) Where a person liable to a penalty under subsection (1) is a person making, or who has made, a claim for a tax credit for a period jointly with another and the penalty is imposed—

(*a*) under paragraph (*a*) of that subsection in respect of the claim, a notification relating to the tax credit claimed or a notice relating to the tax credit awarded on the claim, or

(*b*) under paragraph (*b*) of that subsection in respect of a requirement imposed on him with respect to the tax credit for the period,

a penalty of an amount not exceeding £3,000 may be imposed on the other person unless subsection (3) applies.

(3) This subsection applies if the other person was not, and could not reasonably have been expected to have been, aware that the person liable to the penalty under subsection (1) had fraudulently or negligently made the incorrect statement or declaration or given the incorrect information or evidence.

(4) Where penalties are imposed under subsections (1) and (2) in respect of the same statement, declaration, information or evidence, their aggregate amount must not exceed £3,000.

(5) Where a person acts for another—

(*a*) in or in connection with a claim or notification referred to in subsection (1), or

(*b*) in response to a notice so referred to,

subsection (1) applies to him (as well as to any person to whom it applies apart from this subsection).

Commentary—*Simon's Taxes* **E2.259.**

HMRC Manuals—New Tax Credits Claimant Compliance Manual CCM10000 (Revenue approach to penalties and interest). CCM10040–10120 (Revenue approach to incorrect claims).

Cross references—See TCA 2002 Sch 2 para 6 (time limits for penalties under this section).

Modifications—Tax Credits (Polygamous Marriages) Regulations, SI 2003/742 reg 20 (modification of this section in respect of members of polygamous units).

Amendments—[1] Words inserted in sub-s (1)(*b*) by the Tax Credits, Child Benefit and Guardian's Allowance Reviews and Appeals Order, SI 2014/886 art 2(1), (9) with effect from 6 April 2014.

Prospective amendments—Part 1 to be repealed by the Welfare Reform Act 2012 s 147, Sch 14 Part 1 with effect from a date to be appointed.

32 Failure to comply with requirements

(1) Where a person fails—

(*a*) to provide any information or evidence which he is required to provide by virtue of section 14(2), 15(2), 16(3), 18(10) or 19(2) or regulations under section 25, or

(*b*) to comply with a requirement imposed on him by a notice under section 17 by virtue of subsection (2)(*a*), (4)(*a*) or (6)(*a*) of that section,

the penalties specifies in subsection (2) may be imposed on him.

(2) The penalties are—

(*a*) a penalty not exceeding £300, and

(*b*) if the failure continues after a penalty is imposed under paragraph (*a*), a further penalty or penalties not exceeding £60 for each day on which the failure continues after the day on which the penalty under that paragraph was imposed (but excluding any day for which a penalty under this paragraph has already been imposed).

Tax Credits

(3) Where a person fails to give a notification required by regulations under section 6(3), a penalty not exceeding £300 may be imposed on him.
(4) No penalty under subsection (2) may be imposed on a person in respect of a failure after the failure has been remedied.
(5) For the purposes of this section a person is to be taken not to have failed to provide information or evidence, comply with a requirement or give a notification which must be provided, complied with or given by a particular time—

(*a*) if he provided, complied with or gave it within such further time (if any) as the Board may have allowed,
(*b*) if he had a reasonable excuse for not providing, complying with or giving it by that time, or
(*c*) if, after having had such an excuse, he provided, complied with or gave it without unreasonable delay.

(6) Where the members of a [couple][1] both fail as mentioned in subsection (1)(*b*), the aggregate amount of any penalties under subsection (2) imposed on them in relation to their failures must not exceed the amounts specified in that subsection; and where the members of a married couple or an unmarried couple both fail as mentioned in subsection (3), the aggregate amount of any penalties imposed on them in relation to their failures must not exceed £300.

Commentary—*Simon's Taxes* **E2.259.**
HMRC Manuals—New Tax Credits Claimant Compliance Manual CCM10130–10200 (Revenue approach to failure to notify change of circumstances, with examples).
CCM10180 (examples of reasonable excuses within s 32(5)(*b*) above).
Cross references—See TCA 2002 Sch 2 para 3 (penalty proceedings).
TCA 2002 Sch 2 para 6 (time limits for penalties under this section).
Amendments—[1] Word in sub-s (6) substituted by the Civil Partnership Act 2004 s 254, Sch 24 para 145 with effect from 5 December 2005 (by virtue of SI 2005/3175).
Prospective amendments—Part 1 to be repealed by the Welfare Reform Act 2012 s 147, Sch 14 Part 1 with effect from a date to be appointed.

33 Failure by employers to make correct payments

(1) Where an employer refuses or repeatedly fails to make to an employee payments of tax credits which he is required to make to him by regulations under section 25 and, as a result, the Board make payments to the employee in accordance with regulations under subsection (2)(*b*) of that section, a penalty not exceeding £3,000 may be imposed on the employer.
(2) Where an employer has, by reason of his fraud or neglect, not paid to an employee for a tax year the correct amount of any tax credit which he is required by regulations under section 25 to pay to him for that tax year, a penalty not exceeding £3,000 may be imposed on the employer.
(3) But no penalty may be imposed on an employer under subsection (2) in respect of payments which are incorrect only because of a refusal or failure in respect of which a penalty is imposed on him under subsection (1).

Commentary—*Simon's Taxes* **E2.259.**
Cross references—See TCA 2002 Sch 2 para 6 (time limits for penalties under this section).
Prospective amendments—Part 1 to be repealed by the Welfare Reform Act 2012 s 147, Sch 14 Part 1 with effect from a date to be appointed.

34 Supplementary

Schedule 2 (penalties: supplementary) has effect.

Fraud

35 Offence of fraud

(1) A person commits an offence if he is knowingly concerned in any fraudulent activity undertaken with a view to obtaining payments of a tax credit by him or any other person.
(2) A person who commits an offence under subsection (1) is liable—

(*a*) on summary conviction, to imprisonment for a term not exceeding six months, or a fine not exceeding the statutory maximum, or both, or
(*b*) on conviction on indictment, to imprisonment for a term not exceeding seven years, or a fine, or both.

Commentary—*Simon's Taxes* **E2.259.**
Prospective amendments—New sub-ss (2)–(12) to be substituted for existing sub-s (2) by the Welfare Reform Act 2012 s 124 with effect from a date to be appointed. New sub-ss (2)–(12) to read as follows—

"(2) Where a person is alleged to have committed an offence under this section in relation to payments of a tax credit not exceeding £20,000, the offence is triable summarily only.

(3) A person who commits an offence under this section is liable on summary conviction pursuant to subsection (2) to imprisonment for a term not exceeding the applicable term, or a fine not exceeding level 5 on the standard scale, or both.

(4) In subsection (3) the applicable term is—

(a) for conviction in England and Wales, 51 weeks;
(b) for conviction in Scotland or Northern Ireland, 6 months.

(5) Where a person is alleged to have committed an offence under this section in any other case, the offence is triable either on indictment or summarily.

(6) A person who commits an offence under this section is liable—

(a) on summary conviction pursuant to subsection (5), to imprisonment for a term not exceeding the applicable term, or a fine not exceeding the statutory maximum, or both;

(b) on conviction on indictment pursuant to subsection (5) to imprisonment for a term not exceeding 7 years, or a fine, or both.

(7) In subsection (6)(a) the applicable term is—

(a) for conviction in England and Wales or Scotland, 12 months;

(b) for conviction in Northern Ireland, 6 months.

(8) In relation to an offence under this section committed in England and Wales before the commencement of section 281(5) of the Criminal Justice Act 2003, the reference in subsection (4)(a) to 51 weeks is to be read as a reference to 6 months.

(9) In relation to an offence under this section committed in England and Wales before the commencement of section 154(1) of the Criminal Justice Act 2003, the reference in subsection (7)(a) to 12 months is to be read as a reference to 6 months.

(10) In England and Wales—

(a) subsection (1) of section 116 of the Social Security Administration Act 1992 (legal proceedings) applies in relation to proceedings for an offence under this section;

(b) subsections (2)(a) and (3)(a) of that section apply in relation to proceedings for an offence under this section which is triable summarily only pursuant to subsection (2) above.

(11) In Scotland, subsection (7)(a) and (b) of section 116 of the Social Security Administration Act 1992 (legal proceedings) apply in relation to proceedings for an offence under this section which is triable summarily only pursuant to subsection (2) above.

(12) In Northern Ireland—

(a) subsection (1) of section 110 of the Social Security Administration (Northern Ireland) Act 1992 (legal proceedings) applies in relation to proceedings for an offence under this section;

(b) subsections (2)(a) and (3)(a) of that section apply in relation to proceedings for an offence under this section which is triable summarily only pursuant to subsection (2) above.".

Part 1 to be repealed by the Welfare Reform Act 2012 s 147, Sch 14 Part 1 with effect from a date to be appointed.

36 Powers in relation to documents

(1) Section 20BA of the Taxes Management Act 1970 (c 9) (orders for delivery of documents) applies (with Schedule 1AA and section 20BB) in relation to offences involving fraud in connection with, or in relation to, tax credits as in relation to offences involving serious fraud in connection with, or in relation to, tax.

(2), (3) . . . [1]

(4) Any regulations under Schedule 1AA to the Taxes Management Act 1970 which are in force immediately before the commencement of subsection (1) apply, subject to any necessary modifications, for the purposes of that Schedule as they apply by virtue of that subsection (until amended or revoked).

Commentary—*Simon's Taxes* **E2.258.**

Amendments—[1] Sub-ss (2), (3) repealed by FA 2007 ss 84, 114, Sch 22 paras 3, 14, Sch 27 Pt 5(1) with effect from 1 December 2007 (by virtue of SI 2007/3166 art 3(a)).

Prospective amendments—Part 1 to be repealed by the Welfare Reform Act 2012 s 147, Sch 14 Part 1 with effect from a date to be appointed.

[Loss of tax credit provisions

36A Loss of working tax credit in case of conviction etc for benefit offence

(1) Subsection (4) applies where a person ("the offender")—

(*a*) is convicted of one or more benefit offences in any proceedings, or

(*b*) after being given a notice under subsection (2) of the appropriate penalty provision by an appropriate authority, agrees in the manner specified by the appropriate authority to pay a penalty under the appropriate penalty provision to the appropriate authority, in a case where the offence to which the notice relates is a benefit offence, or

(*c*) is cautioned in respect of one or more benefit offences.

(2) In subsection (1)(*b*)—

(*a*) "the appropriate penalty provision" means section 115A of the Social Security Administration Act 1992 (penalty as alternative to prosecution) or section 109A of the Social Security Administration (Northern Ireland) Act 1992 (the corresponding provision for Northern Ireland);

(*b*) "appropriate authority" means—

(i) in relation to section 115A of the Social Security Administration Act 1992, the Secretary of State or an authority which administers housing benefit or council tax benefit, and

Tax Credits

(ii) in relation to section 109A of the Social Security Administration (Northern Ireland) Act 1992, the Department (within the meaning of that Act) or the Northern Ireland Housing Executive.

(3) Subsection (4) does not apply by virtue of subsection (1)(*a*) if, because the proceedings in which the offender was convicted constitute the current set of proceedings for the purposes of section 36C, the restriction in subsection (3) of that section applies in the offender's case.

(4) If this subsection applies and the offender is a person who would, apart from this section, be entitled (whether pursuant to a single or joint claim) to working tax credit at any time within the disqualification period, then, despite that entitlement, working tax credit shall not be payable for any period comprised in the disqualification period—

(*a*) in the case of a single claim, to the offender, or

(*b*) in the case of a joint claim, to the offender or the other member of the couple.

(5) Regulations may provide in relation to cases to which subsection (4)(*b*) would otherwise apply that working tax credit shall be payable, for any period comprised in the disqualification period, as if the amount payable were reduced in such manner as may be prescribed.

(6) For the purposes of this section, the disqualification period, in relation to any disqualifying event, means the relevant period beginning with such date, falling after the date of the disqualifying event, as may be determined by or in accordance with regulations.

(7) For the purposes of subsection (6) the relevant period is—

(*a*) in a case falling within subsection (1)(*a*) where the benefit offence, or one of them, is a relevant offence, the period of three years,

(*b*) in a case falling within subsection (1)(*a*) (but not within paragraph (a) above)), the period of 13 weeks, or

(*c*) in a case falling within subsection (1)(*b*) or (*c*), the period of 4 weeks.

(8) The Treasury may by order amend subsection (7)(*a*), (*b*) or (*c*) to substitute a different period for that for the time being specified there.

(9) This section has effect subject to section 36B.

(10) In this section and section 36B—

"benefit offence" means any of the following offences committed on or after the day specified by order made by the Treasury—

(*a*) an offence in connection with a claim for a disqualifying benefit;

(*b*) an offence in connection with the receipt or payment of any amount by way of such a benefit;

(*c*) an offence committed for the purpose of facilitating the commission (whether or not by the same person) of a benefit offence;

(*d*) an offence consisting in an attempt or conspiracy to commit a benefit offence;

"disqualifying benefit" has the meaning given in section 6A(1) of the Social Security Fraud Act 2001;

"disqualifying event" means—

(*a*) the conviction falling within subsection (1)(*a*);

(*b*) the agreement falling within subsection (1)(*b*);

(*c*) the caution falling within subsection (1)(*c*);

"relevant offence" has the meaning given in section 6B of the Social Security Fraud Act 2001.][1]

Orders—Loss of Tax Credits (Specified Day) Order, SI 2013/524 (the day specified under ss 36A(10) and 36C(7), for the purposes of ss 36A–36D, is 6 April 2013). Where an offence is of a type mentioned in s 36A(10) or 36C(7), and is committed on or after 6 April 2013, it is a "benefit offence" for the purposes of ss 36A to 36D (see Explanatory Note to SI 2013/524).

Regulations—Loss of Tax Credits Regulations, SI 2013/715.

Amendments—[1] Sections 36A–36D inserted by the Welfare Reform Act 2012 s 120 with effect from 6 April 2013 (see SI 2013/178). Note that the insertion of ss 36A–36D has effect from 1 February 2013 only for the purpose of making regulations and orders.

Prospective amendments—Sub-s (1)(*c*) is to be repealed by the Welfare Reform Act 2012 s 121(2) with effect from a date to be appointed.

Part 1 to be repealed by the Welfare Reform Act 2012 s 147, Sch 14 Part 1 with effect from a date to be appointed.

In sub-s (7)(*a*), words "or (*c*)" to be repealed, and in sub-s (1), in definition of "disqualifying event", para (*c*) to be repealed, by the Welfare Reform Act 2012 s 147, Sch 14 Part 12 with effect from a date to be appointed.

[36B Section 36A: supplementary

(1) Where—

(*a*) the conviction of any person of any offence is taken in account for the purposes of the application of section 36A in relation to that person, and

(*b*) that conviction is subsequently quashed,

all such payments and other adjustments shall be made as would be necessary if no restriction had been imposed by or under section 36A that could not have been imposed if the conviction had not taken place.

(2) Where, after the agreement of any person ("P") to pay a penalty under the appropriate penalty provision is taken into account for the purposes of the application of section 36A in relation to that person—

(*a*) P's agreement to pay the penalty is withdrawn under subsection (5) of the appropriate penalty provision, or

(*b*) it is decided on an appeal or in accordance with regulations under the Social Security Act 1992 or the Social Security (Northern Ireland) Order 1998 (SI 1998/1506 (N.I. 10)) that the overpayment to which the agreement relates is not recoverable or due,

all such payments and other adjustments shall be made as would be necessary if no restriction had been imposed by or under section 36A that could not have been imposed if P had not agreed to pay the penalty.

(3) Where, after the agreement ("the old agreement") of any person ("P") to pay a penalty under the appropriate penalty provision is taken into account for the purposes of the application of section 36A in relation to P, the amount of any overpayment made to which the penalty relates is revised on an appeal or in accordance with regulations under the Social Security Act 1998 or the Social Security (Northern Ireland) Order 1998—

(*a*) section 36A shall cease to apply by virtue of the old agreement, and

(*b*) subsection (4) shall apply.

(4) Where this subsection applies—

(*a*) if there is a new disqualifying event consisting of—

(i) P's agreement to pay a penalty under the appropriate penalty regime in relation to the revised overpayment, or

(ii) P being cautioned in relation to the offence to which the old agreement relates,

the disqualification period relating to the new disqualifying event shall be reduced by the number of days in so much of the disqualification period relating to the old agreement as had expired when subsection 36A ceased to apply by virtue of the old agreement, and

(*b*) in any other case, all such payments and other adjustments shall be made as would be necessary if no restriction had been imposed by or under section 36A that could not have been imposed if P had not agreed to pay the penalty.

(5) For the purposes of section 36A—

(*a*) the date of a person's conviction in any proceedings of a benefit offence shall be taken to be the date on which the person was found guilty of that offence in those proceedings (whenever the person was sentenced) or in the case mentioned in paragraph (*b*)(ii) the date of the order for absolute discharge, and

(*b*) references to a conviction include references to—

(i) a conviction in relation to which the court makes an order for absolute or conditional discharge,

(ii) an order for absolute discharge made by a court of summary jurisdiction in Scotland under section 246(3) of the Criminal Procedure (Scotland) Act 1995 without proceeding to a conviction, and

(iii) a conviction in Northern Ireland.

(6) In this section "the appropriate penalty provision" has the meaning given by section 36A(2)(*a*).][1]

Orders—Loss of Tax Credits (Specified Day) Order, SI 2013/524 (the day specified under ss 36A(10) and 36C(7), for the purposes of ss 36A–36D, is 6 April 2013). Where an offence is of a type mentioned in s 36A(10) or 36C(7), and is committed on or after 6 April 2013, it is a "benefit offence" for the purposes of ss 36A to 36D (see Explanatory Note to SI 2013/524).

Amendments—[1] Sections 36A–36D inserted by the Welfare Reform Act 2012 s 120 with effect from 6 April 2013 (see SI 2013/178). Note that the insertion of ss 36A–36D has effect from 1 February 2013 only for the purpose of making regulations and orders.

Prospective amendments—Part 1 to be repealed by the Welfare Reform Act 2012 s 147, Sch 14 Part 1 with effect from a date to be appointed.

Sub-s (4)(*a*)(ii) and preceding word "or", to be repealed by the Welfare Reform Act 2012 s 147, Sch 14 Part 12 with effect from a date to be appointed.

[36C Loss of working tax credit for repeated benefit fraud

(1) If—

(*a*) a person ("the offender") is convicted of one or more benefit offences in a set of proceedings ("the current set of proceedings"),

(*b*) within the period of five years ending on the date on which the benefit offence was, or any of them were, committed, one or more disqualifying events occurred in relation to the offender (the event, or the most recent of them, being referred to in this section as "the earlier disqualifying event"),

(*c*) the current set of proceedings has not been taken into account for the purposes of any previous application of this section in relation to the offender,

(*d*) the earlier disqualifying event has not been taken into account as an earlier disqualifying event for the purposes of any previous application of this section in relation to the offender, and (*e*) the offender is a person who would, apart from this section, be entitled (whether pursuant to a single or joint claim) to working tax credit at any time within the disqualification period,

then, despite that entitlement, the restriction in subsection (3) shall apply in relation to the payment of that benefit in the offender's case.

(2) The restriction in subsection (3) does not apply if the benefit offence referred to in subsection (1)(*a*), or any of them, is a relevant offence.

(3) Working tax credit shall not be payable for any period comprised in the disqualification period—

(*a*) in the case of a single claim, to the offender, or

(*b*) in the case of a joint claim, to the offender or the other member of the couple.

(4) Regulations may provide in relation to cases to which subsection (3)(*b*) would otherwise apply that working tax credit shall be payable, for any period comprised in the disqualification period, as if the amount payable were reduced in such manner as may be prescribed.

(5) For the purposes of this section the disqualification period, in an offender's case, means the relevant period beginning with a prescribed date falling after the date of the conviction in the current set of proceedings.

(6) For the purposes of subsection (5) the relevant period is—

(*a*) in a case where, within the period of five years ending on the date on which the earlier disqualifying event occurred, a previous disqualifying event occurred in relation to the offender, the period of three years;

(*b*) in any other case, 26 weeks.

(7) In this section and section 36D—

"appropriate penalty provision" has the meaning given in section 36A(2)(*a*);

"benefit offence" means any of the following offences committed on or after the day specified by order made by the Treasury—

(*a*) an offence in connection with a claim for a disqualifying benefit;

(*b*) an offence in connection with the receipt or payment of any amount by way of such a benefit;

(*c*) an offence committed for the purpose of facilitating the commission (whether or not by the same person) of a benefit offence;

(*d*) an offence consisting in an attempt or conspiracy to commit a benefit offence;

"disqualifying benefit" has the meaning given in section 6A(1) of the Social Security Fraud Act 2001;

"disqualifying event" has the meaning given in section 36A(10);

"relevant offence" has the meaning given in section 6B of the Social Security Fraud Act 2001.

(8) Where a person is convicted of more than one benefit offence in the same set of proceedings, there is to be only one disqualifying event in respect of that set of proceedings for the purposes of this section and—

(*a*) subsection (1)(*b*) is satisfied if any of the convictions take place in the five year period there;

(*b*) the event is taken into account for the purposes of subsection (1)(*d*) if any of the convictions have been taken into account as mentioned there;

(*c*) in the case of the earlier disqualifying event mentioned in subsection (6)(*a*), the reference there to the date on which the earlier disqualifying event occurred is a reference to the date on which any of the convictions take place;

(*d*) in the case of the previous disqualifying event mentioned in subsection (6)(*a*), that provision is satisfied if any of the convictions take place in the five year period mentioned there.

(9) The Treasury may by order amend subsection (6) to substitute different periods for those for the time being specified there.

(10) An order under subsection (9) may provide for different periods to apply according to the type of earlier disqualifying event or events occurring in any case.

(11) This section has effect subject to section 36D.][1]

Orders—Loss of Tax Credits (Specified Day) Order, SI 2013/524 (the day specified under ss 36A(10) and 36C(7), for the purposes of ss 36A–36D, is 6 April 2013). Where an offence is of a type mentioned in s 36A(10) or 36C(7), and is committed on or after 6 April 2013, it is a "benefit offence" for the purposes of ss 36A to 36D (see Explanatory Note to SI 2013/524).

Regulations—Loss of Tax Credits Regulations, SI 2013/715.

Amendments—[1] Sections 36A–36D inserted by the Welfare Reform Act 2012 s 120 with effect from 6 April 2013 (see SI 2013/178). Note that the insertion of ss 36A–36D has effect from 1 February 2013 only for the purpose of making regulations and orders.

Prospective amendments—Part 1 to be repealed by the Welfare Reform Act 2012 s 147, Sch 14 Part 1 with effect from a date to be appointed.

[36D Section 36C: supplementary

(1) Where—

(*a*) the conviction of any person of any offence is taken into account for the purposes of the application of section 36C in relation to that person, and

(*b*) that conviction is subsequently quashed,

all such payments and other adjustments shall be made as would be necessary if no restriction had been imposed by or under section 36C that could not have been imposed if the conviction had not taken place.

(2) Subsection (3) applies where, after the agreement of any person ("P") to pay a penalty under the appropriate penalty provision is taken into account for the purposes of the application of section 36C in relation to that person—

(*a*) P's agreement to pay the penalty is withdrawn under subsection (5) of the appropriate penalty provision,

(*b*) it is decided on an appeal or in accordance with regulations under the Social Security Act 1998 or the Social Security (Northern Ireland) Order 1998 (SI 1998/1506 (N.I. 10)) that any overpayment made to which the agreement relates is not recoverable or due, or

(*c*) the amount of any over payment to which the penalty relates is revised on an appeal or in accordance with regulations under the Social Security Act 1998 or the Social Security (Northern Ireland) Order 1998 and there is no new agreement by P to pay a penalty under the appropriate penalty provision in relation to the revised overpayment.

(3) In those circumstances, all such payments and other adjustments shall be made as would be necessary if no restriction had been imposed by or under section 36C that could not have been imposed if P had not agreed to pay the penalty.

(4) For the purposes of section 36C—

(*a*) the date of a person's conviction in any proceedings of a benefit offence shall be taken to be the date on which the person was found guilty of that offence in those proceedings (whenever the person was sentenced) or in the case mentioned in paragraph (b)(ii) the date of the order for absolute discharge, and

(*b*) references to a conviction include references to—

(i) a conviction in relation to which the court makes an order for absolute or conditional discharge,

(ii) an order for absolute discharge made by a court of summary jurisdiction in Scotland under section 246(3) of the Criminal Procedure (Scotland) Act 1995 without proceeding to a conviction, and

(iii) a conviction in Northern Ireland.

(5) In section 36C references to any previous application of that section—

(*a*) include references to any previous application of a provision having an effect in Northern Ireland corresponding to provision made by that section, but

(*b*) do not include references to any previous application of that section the effect of which was to impose a restriction for a period comprised in the same disqualification period.][1]

Orders—Loss of Tax Credits (Specified Day) Order, SI 2013/524 (the day specified under ss 36A(10) and 36C(7), for the purposes of ss 36A–36D, is 6 April 2013). Where an offence is of a type mentioned in s 36A(10) or 36C(7), and is committed on or after 6 April 2013, it is a "benefit offence" for the purposes of ss 36A to 36D (see Explanatory Note to SI 2013/524).

Amendments—[1] Sections 36A–36D inserted by the Welfare Reform Act 2012 s 120 with effect from 6 April 2013 (see SI 2013/178). Note that the insertion of ss 36A–36D has effect from 1 February 2013 only for the purpose of making regulations and orders.

Prospective amendments—Part 1 to be repealed by the Welfare Reform Act 2012 s 147, Sch 14 Part 1 with effect from a date to be appointed.

Interest

37 Interest

(1) If an overpayment of a tax credit for a period is attributable to fraud or neglect on the part of the person, or either or both of the persons, to whom the award of the tax credit was made (or a person acting for him, or for either or both of them, in making the claim for the tax credit), the Board may decide that the whole or any part of the overpayment is to carry interest.

(2) Where the Board so decide the overpayment (or part of the overpayment) carries interest at a prescribed rate from a date thirty days after the appropriate date.

(3) "The appropriate date" is—

(*a*) in the case of an amount treated as an overpayment by virtue of section 28(6), the date of the decision under section 16 to terminate the award, and

(*b*) in any other case, the date specified for the purposes of subsection (4) of section 17 in the notice given to the person or persons under that section in relation to the tax credit.

(4) The Board must give notice of a decision under subsection (1) to the person, or each of the persons, to whom it relates; and the notice must state the date on which it is given and include details of the right to appeal against the decision under section 38.

(5) A penalty under any of sections 31 to 33 carries interest at the prescribed rate from the date on which it becomes due and payable; but the Board may in their discretion mitigate any interest or entirely remit any interest which would otherwise be carried by a penalty.

(6) Any interest carried under this section by an overpayment or penalty is to be regarded for the purposes of section 29(3) to (5) or paragraph 7 of Schedule 2 as if it were part of the overpayment or penalty.

Commentary—*Simon's Taxes* **E2.257**.
HMRC Manuals—New Tax Credits Claimant Compliance Manual CCM10390, 10400 (Revenue approach to interest).
Regulations—Tax Credits (Interest Rate) Regulations, SI 2003/123.
Modifications—Tax Credits (Polygamous Marriages) Regulations, SI 2003/742 reg 21 (modification of this section in respect of members of polygamous units).
Prospective amendments—Part 1 to be repealed by the Welfare Reform Act 2012 s 147, Sch 14 Part 1 with effect from a date to be appointed.

Appeals

38 Appeals

(1) An appeal may[, subject to subsection (1A),][2] be brought against—

(*a*) a decision under section 14(1), 15(1), 16(1), 19(3) or 20(1) or (4) or regulations under section 21,

(*b*) the relevant section 18 decision in relation to a person or persons and a tax credit for a tax year and any revision of that decision under that section,

(*c*) a determination of a penalty under paragraph 1 of Schedule 2, . . . [1]

[(*ca*) a decision under section 36A or 36C that working tax credit is not payable (or is not payable for a particular period), and][1]

(*d*) a decision under section 37(1).

[(1A) An appeal may not be brought by virtue of subsection (1) against a decision unless a review of the decision has been carried out under section 21A and notice of the conclusion on the review has been given under section 21A(3).

(1B) If in any case the conclusion of a review under section 21A is to uphold the decision reviewed, an appeal by virtue of subsection (1) in that case may be brought only against the original decision.

(1C) If in any case the conclusion of a review under section 21A is to vary the decision reviewed, an appeal by virtue of subsection (1) in that case may be brought only against the decision as varied.][2]

(2) "The relevant section 18 decision" means—

(*a*) in a case in which a decision must be made under subsection (6) of section 18 in relation to the person or persons and the tax credit for the tax year, that decision, and

(*b*) in any other case, the decision under subsection (1) of that section in relation to the person or persons and the tax credit for the tax year.

Commentary—*Simon's Taxes* **E2.254.**
Modifications—Universal Credit (Transitional Provisions) Regulations, SI 2013/386 reg 17(2), Schedule paras 1, 12 (modification of this section in respect of awards of universal credit and terminations of awards of tax credit in the same year).
Amendments—[1] In sub-s (1), word "and" at end of para (*c*) repealed, and para (*ca*) inserted, by the Welfare Reform Act 2012 s 120(1), (3) with effect from 6 April 2013 (by virtue of SI 2013/178 art 2).
[2] Words inserted in sub-s (1) inserted, and sub-ss (1A)–(1C) inserted, by the Tax Credits, Child Benefit and Guardian's Allowance Reviews and Appeals Order, SI 2014/886 art 2(1), (10), (11) with effect from 6 April 2014.
Prospective amendments—Part 1 to be repealed by the Welfare Reform Act 2012 s 147, Sch 14 Part 1 with effect from a date to be appointed.

39 Exercise of right of appeal

(1) . . . [2]

(2) . . . [2]

(3)–(5) . . . [1]

(6) Part 5 of the Taxes Management Act 1970 [(appeals and other proceedings)][1] applies in relation to appeals under section 38 (as in relation to appeals under the Taxes Acts, within the meaning of that Act), but subject to such modifications as are prescribed.

(7) . . . [1]

Commentary—*Simon's Taxes* **E2.254.**
Regulations—Tax Credits (Notice of Appeal) Regulations, SI 2002/3119.
Tax Credits (Employer Penalty Appeals) Regulations, SI 2003/1382.
Amendments—[1] Sub-ss (3), (4), (5), (7) repealed; in sub-s (6) words substituted for the words "(appeals to Commissioners)" by the Transfer of Tribunal Functions and Revenue and Customs Appeals Order, SI 2009/56 art 3, Sch 1 para 314 with effect from 1 April 2009.
[2] Sub-ss (1), (2) repealed by the Tax Credits, Child Benefit and Guardian's Allowance Reviews and Appeals Order, SI 2014/886 art 2(1), (10), (12) for England and Wales and Scotland with effect from 6 April 2014. Note that sub-ss (1), (2) continue to apply in relation to Northern Ireland as follows (with amendments by SI 2014/886 art 2(13) with effect from 3 November 2014 in square brackets)—

> "(1) Notice of an appeal under section 38 against a decision must be given to the Board in the prescribed manner within the period of thirty days after the date on which notice of the decision was given (or, in the case of a decision to which section 23(3) applies, the date of the decision) [notice under section 21A(3) was given of the conclusion on the review of the decision].
>
> (2) Notice of such an appeal must specify the grounds of appeal.".

Prospective amendments—Part 1 to be repealed by the Welfare Reform Act 2012 s 147, Sch 14 Part 1 with effect from a date to be appointed.

[39A Late appeals

(1) The Commissioners for Her Majesty's Revenue and Customs may treat a late appeal under section 38 as made in time where the conditions specified in subsections (2) to (6) are satisfied, except that the Commissioners may not do so in the case of an appeal made more than one year after the expiration of the time (original or extended) for appealing.

(2) An appeal may be treated as made in time if the Commissioners are satisfied that it is in the interests of justice to do so.

(3) For the purposes of subsection (2) it is not in the interests of justice to treat an appeal as made in time unless—

(*a*) the special circumstances specified in subsection (4) are relevant; or

(*b*) some other special circumstances exist which are wholly exceptional and relevant,

and as a result of those special circumstances it was not practicable for the appeal to be made in time.

(4) The special circumstances mentioned in subsection (3)(*a*) are—

(*a*) the appellant or a partner or dependant of the appellant has died or suffered serious illness;

(*b*) the appellant is not resident in the United Kingdom; or

(*c*) normal postal services were disrupted.

(5) In determining whether it is in the interests of justice to treat an appeal as made in time, regard shall be had to the principle that the greater the amount of time that has elapsed between the expiration of the time for appealing and the submission of the notice of appeal, the more compelling should be the special circumstances.

(6) In determining whether it is in the interests of justice to treat an appeal as made in time, no account shall be taken of the following—

(*a*) that the appellant or any other person acting for the appellant was unaware of or misunderstood the law applicable to the appellant's case (including ignorance or misunderstanding of any time limit); or

(*b*) that the Upper Tribunal or a court has taken a different view of the law from that previously understood and applied.

(7) If in accordance with the preceding provisions of this section the Commissioners for Her Majesty's Revenue and Customs treat a late appeal under section 38 as made in time, it is to be treated as having been brought within any applicable time limit.][1]

Amendments—[1] Section 39A inserted by the Tax Credits (Late Appeals) Order, SI 2014/885 art 2 with effect from 2 April 2014.

40 Annual reports

(1) The Board must make to the Treasury an annual report about—

(*a*) . . . [1]

(*b*) the number of awards of child tax credit and of working tax credit,

(*c*) the number of enquiries conducted under section 19,

(*d*) the number of penalties imposed under this Part, and

(*e*) the number of prosecutions and convictions for offences connected with tax credits.

(2) The Treasury must publish each annual report made to it under subsection (1) and lay a copy before each House of Parliament.

Commentary—*Simon's Taxes* **E2.250.**

Amendments—[1] Sub-s (1)(*a*) repealed by CRCA 2005 s 50, Sch 4 para 89, s 52 Sch 5 with effect from 18 April 2005 (by virtue of SI 2005/1126).

Prospective amendments—Part 1 to be repealed by the Welfare Reform Act 2012 s 147, Sch 14 Part 1 with effect from a date to be appointed.

41 Annual review

(1) The Treasury must, in each tax year, review the amounts specified in subsection (2) in order to determine whether they have retained their value in relation to the general level of prices in the United Kingdom as estimated by the Treasury in such manner as it considers appropriate.

(2) The amounts are monetary amounts prescribed—

(*a*) under subsection (1)(*a*) of section 7,

(*b*) for the purposes of any of paragraphs (*a*) to (*d*) of subsection (3) of that section,

(*c*) under section 9,

(*d*) under section 11, otherwise than by virtue of section 12, or

(*e*) under subsection (2) of section 13, otherwise than by virtue of subsection (3) of that section.

(3) The Treasury must prepare a report of each review.

(4) The report must include a statement of what each amount would be if it had fully retained its value.

(5) The Treasury must publish the report and lay a copy of it before each House of Parliament.

Commentary—*Simon's Taxes* **E2.250.**

Cross references—See the Welfare Reform and Work Act 2016 s 12 (a review under this section in the tax years 2015–16 to 2018–2019 need not cover relevant amounts of Working Tax Credit or Child Tax Credit: see the Welfare Reform and Work Act 2016 Sch 1 para 2).

Tax Credits

Prospective amendments—Part 1 to be repealed by the Welfare Reform Act 2012 s 147, Sch 14 Part 1 with effect from a date to be appointed.

42 Persons subject to immigration control

(1) Regulations may make provision in relation to persons subject to immigration control or in relation to prescribed descriptions of such persons—

(*a*) for excluding entitlement to, or to a prescribed element of, child tax credit or working tax credit (or both), or

(*b*) for this Part to apply subject to other prescribed modifications.

(2) "Person subject to immigration control" has the same meaning as in section 115 of the Immigration and Asylum Act 1999 (c 33).

Regulations—Tax Credits (Immigration) Regulations, SI 2003/653.
Tax Credits (Polygamous Marriages) Regulations, SI 2003/742.
Tax Credits (Miscellaneous Amendments) Regulations, SI 2012/848.
Tax Credits (Miscellaneous Amendments) Regulations, SI 2014/658.

Prospective amendments—Part 1 to be repealed by the Welfare Reform Act 2012 s 147, Sch 14 Part 1 with effect from a date to be appointed.

43 Polygamous marriages

(1) Regulations may make provision for this Part to apply in relation to persons who are parties to polygamous marriages subject to prescribed modifications.

(2) A person is a party to a polygamous marriage if—

(*a*) he is a party to a marriage entered into under a law which permits polygamy, and

(*b*) either party to the marriage has a spouse additional to the other party.

Regulations—Tax Credits (Polygamous Marriages) Regulations, SI 2003/742.
Child Tax Credit (Amendment) Regulations, SI 2017/387.

Prospective amendments—Part 1 to be repealed by the Welfare Reform Act 2012 s 147, Sch 14 Part 1 with effect from a date to be appointed.

44 Crown employment

This Part applies in relation to persons employed by or under the Crown (as in relation to other employees).

Prospective amendments—Part 1 to be repealed by the Welfare Reform Act 2012 s 147, Sch 14 Part 1 with effect from a date to be appointed.

45 Inalienability

(1) Every assignment of or charge on a tax credit, and every agreement to assign or charge a tax credit, is void; and, on the bankruptcy of a person entitled to a tax credit, the entitlement to the tax credit does not pass to any trustee or other person acting on behalf of his creditors.

(2) In the application of subsection (1) to Scotland—

(*a*) the reference to assignment is to assignation ("assign" being construed accordingly), and

(*b*) the reference to the bankruptcy of a person is to the sequestration of his estate or the appointment on his estate of a judicial factor under section 41 of the Solicitors (Scotland) Act 1980 (c 46).

Prospective amendments—Part 1 to be repealed by the Welfare Reform Act 2012 s 147, Sch 14 Part 1 with effect from a date to be appointed.

46 Giving of notices by Board

The Board may give any notice which they are required or permitted to give under this Part in any manner and form which the Board consider appropriate in the circumstances.

Prospective amendments—Part 1 to be repealed by the Welfare Reform Act 2012 s 147, Sch 14 Part 1 with effect from a date to be appointed.

47 Consequential amendments

Schedule 3 (consequential amendments) has effect.

Prospective amendments—Part 1 to be repealed by the Welfare Reform Act 2012 s 147, Sch 14 Part 1 with effect from a date to be appointed.

48 Interpretation

[(1)] [1] In this Part—

"child" has the meaning given by section 8(3),

["couple" has the meaning given by section 3(5A),][1]

"the current year income" has the meaning given by section 7(4),

"employee" and "employer" have the meaning given by section 25(5),

. . . [2]

"the income threshold" has the meaning given by section 7(1)(*a*),

"joint claim" has the meaning given by section 3(8),

. . . [1]

"overpayment" has the meaning given by section 28(2) and (6),

"the previous year income" has the meaning given by section 7(5), "qualifying remunerative work", and being engaged in it, have the meaning given by regulations under section 10(2),

"qualifying young person" has the meaning given by section 8(4),

"the relevant income" has the meaning given by section 7(3),

"responsible", in relation to a child or qualifying young person, has the meaning given by regulations under section 8(2) (for the purposes of child tax credit) or by regulations under section 10(4) (for the purposes of working tax credit),

"single claim" has the meaning given by section 3(8),

. . . [2]

"tax year" means a period beginning with 6th April in one year and ending with 5th April in the next, and

. . . [1]

[(2) For the purposes of this Part, two people of the same sex are to be regarded as living together as if they were civil partners if, but only if, they would be regarded as living together as husband and wife were they instead two people of the opposite sex.][1]

Modifications—Universal Credit (Transitional Provisions) Regulations, SI 2013/386 reg 17(2), Schedule paras 1, 13 (modification of this section in respect of awards of universal credit and terminations of awards of tax credit in the same year).

Universal Credit (Transitional Provisions) Regulations, SI 2014/1230 reg 12(2), (3) (modification of this section in repect of treatment of overpayment of tax credits).

Amendments—[1] Sub-s (1) numbered as such, definition of "couple" inserted, definitions of "married couple" and "unmarried couple" repealed, and sub-s (2) inserted, by the Civil Partnership Act 2004 s 254, 261(4), Sch 24 para 147, Sch 30 with effect from 5 December 2005 (by virtue of SI 2005/3175).

[2] In sub-s (1) definitions of "the General Commissioners" and "the Special Commissioners" repealed by the Transfer of Tribunal Functions and Revenue and Customs Appeals Order, SI 2009/56 art 3, Sch 1 para 315 with effect from 1 April 2009.

Prospective amendments—Part 1 to be repealed by the Welfare Reform Act 2012 s 147, Sch 14 Part 1 with effect from a date to be appointed.

PART 2
CHILD BENEFIT AND GUARDIAN'S ALLOWANCE

Transfer of functions etc

49 Functions transferred to Treasury

(1) The functions of the Secretary of State under—

(*a*) section 77 of the Social Security Contributions and Benefits Act 1992 (c 4) (guardian's allowance: Great Britain),

(*b*) Part 9 of that Act (child benefit: Great Britain), except . . . [1] paragraphs 5 and 6(1) of Schedule 10,

(*c*) section 80 of the Social Security Administration Act 1992 (c 5) (overlap with benefits under legislation of other member States: Great Britain), and

(*d*) section 72 of the Social Security Act 1998 (c 14) (power to reduce child benefit for lone parents: Great Britain),

are transferred to the Treasury.

(2) The functions of the Northern Ireland Department under—

(*a*) section 77 of the Social Security Contributions and Benefits (Northern Ireland) Act 1992 (c 7) (guardian's allowance: Northern Ireland),

(*b*) Part 9 of that Act (child benefit: Northern Ireland), . . . [1] paragraphs 5 and 6(1) of Schedule 10,

(*c*) section 76 of the Social Security Administration (Northern Ireland) Act 1992 (c 8) (overlap with benefits under legislation of other member States: Northern Ireland), and

(*d*) Article 68 of the Social Security (Northern Ireland) Order 1998 (1998/1506 (NI 10)) (power to reduce child benefit for lone parents: Northern Ireland),

are transferred to the Treasury.

(3) The functions of the Secretary of State under Part 10 of the Social Security Administration Act 1992 (c 5) (review and alteration of benefits: Great Britain) so far as relating to child benefit and guardian's allowance are transferred to the Treasury.

(4) The functions of the Northern Ireland Department under sections 132 to 134 of the Social Security Administration (Northern Ireland) Act 1992 (c 8) (review and alteration of benefits: Northern Ireland) so far as relating to child benefit and guardian's allowance are transferred to the Treasury.

Amendments—[1] Words in sub-ss (1)(*b*), (2)(*b*) repealed by the Child Benefit Act 2005 s 3, Sch 2 with effect from 10 April 2006: see the Child Benefit Act 2005 s 6.

50 Functions transferred to Board

(1) The functions of the Secretary of State and the Northern Ireland Department under the provisions specified in subsection (2), so far as relating to child benefit and guardian's allowance, are transferred to the Board.

(2) The provisions referred to in subsection (1) are—

(*a*) the Social Security Contributions and Benefits Act 1992 (c 4), (*b*) the Social Security Administration Act 1992, except Part 13 (advisory bodies and consultation: Great Britain),

(*c*) the Social Security Contributions and Benefits (Northern Ireland) Act 1992 (c 7),

(*d*) the Social Security Administration (Northern Ireland) Act 1992, except Part 12 (advisory bodies and consultation: Northern Ireland),

(*e*) Chapter 2 of Part 1 of the Social Security Act 1998 (c 14) (social security decisions and appeals: Great Britain),

(*f*) Chapter 2 of Part 2 of the Social Security (Northern Ireland) Order 1998 (1998/1506 (NI 10)) (social security decisions and appeals: Northern Ireland), and

(*g*) any subordinate legislation made under any of the provisions specified in section 49 or any of the preceding provisions of this subsection.

(3) This section has effect subject to section 49.

51 Consequential amendments

Schedule 4 (amendments consequential on transfer of functions made by sections 49 and 50) has effect.

52 Transfer of property, rights and liabilities

(1) This subsection transfers to and vests in the Treasury the property, rights and liabilities to which the Secretary of State or the Northern Ireland Department is entitled or subject in connection with functions transferred to the Treasury by section 49 immediately before they are transferred.

(2) This subsection transfers to and vests in the Board the property, rights and liabilities to which the Secretary of State or the Northern Ireland Department is entitled or subject in connection with functions transferred to the Board by section 50 immediately before they are transferred.

(3) A certificate given by the Treasury that any property has been transferred by subsection (1) is conclusive evidence of the transfer; and a certificate given by the Board that any property has been transferred by subsection (2) is conclusive evidence of the transfer.

(4) Subsections (1) and (2) have effect in relation to property, rights and liabilities in spite of any provision (of whatever nature) which would prevent or restrict transfer otherwise than by this section.

(5) Subsections (1) and (2) do not apply to contracts within subsection (6); but any term of such a contract about the provision of goods or services to the Secretary of State (or a government department) or the Northern Ireland Department is to be taken to refer also to the Board in connection with any function transferred by section 49 or 50.

(6) The contracts within this subsection are contracts for the supply of goods or services to the Secretary of State or the Northern Ireland Department—

(*a*) which relate partly to functions transferred by section 49 or 50 and partly to other functions, or

(*b*) the terms of which are wholly or partly determined by a contract within paragraph (*a*).

(7) Her Majesty may by Order in Council make such provision for the transfer to [the statutory home civil service][1] of persons employed in the Northern Ireland Civil Service as appears to Her Majesty to be appropriate in consequence of the transfer of functions made by sections 49 and 50.

[(8) In subsection (7) "the statutory home civil service" means the civil service (excluding Her Majesty's diplomatic service) within the meaning of Chapter 1 of Part 1 of the Constitutional Reform and Governance Act 2010 (see section 1(4) of that Act).][1]

Amendments—[1] In sub-s (7) words substituted for words "Her Majesty's Home Civil Service", and sub-s (8) inserted, by the Constitutional Reform and Governance Act 2010 s 19, Sch 2 para 13 with effect from 11 November 2010 (by virtue of SI 2010/2703, art 2(*a*)).

[53 General functions of Commissioners for Revenue and Customs

The Commissioners for Her Majesty's Revenue and Customs shall be responsible for the payment and management of child benefit and guardian's allowance.][1]

Amendments—[1] This section substituted by CRCA 2005 s 50, Sch 4 para 90 with effect from 18 April 2005 (by virtue of SI 2005/1126).

54 Transitional provisions

(1) Any function covered by section 49 which is a function of making subordinate legislation may be exercised by the Treasury at any time after the passing of this Act if the subordinate legislation made in the exercise of the function comes into force after the commencement of that section.

(2) Any function covered by section 50 which is a function of making subordinate legislation may be exercised by the Board at any time after the passing of this Act if the subordinate legislation made in the exercise of the function comes into force after the commencement of that section.

(3) Nothing in section 49 or 50 affects the validity of anything done by or in relation to the Secretary of State or the Northern Ireland Department before its commencement.

(4) Anything (including legal proceedings) relating to any functions transferred by section 49, or any property, rights or liabilities transferred by section 52(1), which is in the course of being done or carried on by or in relation to the Secretary of State or the Northern Ireland Department immediately before the transfer may be continued by or in relation to the Treasury.

(5) Anything (including legal proceedings) relating to any functions transferred by section 50, or any property, rights or liabilities transferred by section 52(2), which is in the course of being done or carried on by or in relation to the Secretary of State or the Northern Ireland Department immediately before the transfer may be continued by or in relation to the Board.
(6) Anything done by the Secretary of State or the Northern Ireland Department for the purposes of or in connection with any functions transferred by section 49, or any property, rights or liabilities transferred by section 52(1), which is in effect immediately before the transfer has effect afterwards as if done by the Treasury.
(7) Anything done by the Secretary of State or the Northern Ireland Department for the purposes of or in connection with any functions transferred by section 50, or any property, rights or liabilities transferred by section 52(2), which is in effect immediately before the transfer has effect afterwards as if done by the Board.
(8) The Treasury is substituted for the Secretary of State or the Northern Ireland Department in any subordinate legislation, any contracts or other documents and any legal proceedings relating to any functions transferred by section 49, or any property, rights or liabilities transferred by section 52(1), made or commenced before the transfer.
(9) The Board are substituted for the Secretary of State or the Northern Ireland Department in any subordinate legislation, any contracts or other documents and any legal proceedings relating to any functions transferred by section 50, or any property, rights or liabilities transferred by section 52(2), made or commenced before the transfer.
(10) Any order made under section 8 of the Electronic Communications Act 2000 (c 7) which—

(*a*) modifies provisions relating to child benefit or guardian's allowance, and
(*b*) is in force immediately before the commencement of this subsection,

is to continue to have effect for the purposes of child benefit and guardian's allowance, despite subsection (7) of that section, until regulations made by the Board under section 132 of the Finance Act 1999 (c 16) which are expressed to supersede that order come into force.

Minor amendments

55 Continuing entitlement after death of child

(1) Insert the section set out in subsection (2)—

(*a*) in the Social Security Contributions and Benefits Act 1992 (c 4) after section 145 (as section 145A), and
(*b*) in the Social Security Contributions and Benefits (Northern Ireland) Act 1992 (c 7) after section 141 (as section 141A).

(2) The section is—

"Entitlement after death of child

(1) If a child dies and a person is entitled to child benefit in respect of him for the week in which his death occurs, that person shall be entitled to child benefit in respect of the child for a prescribed period following that week.

(2) If the person entitled to child benefit under subsection(1) dies before the end of that prescribed period and, at the time of his death, was—

(*a*) a member of a married couple and living with the person to whom he was married, or
(*b*) a member of an unmarried couple,

that other member of the married couple or unmarried couple shall be entitled to child benefit for the period for which the dead person would have been entitled to child benefit under subsection (1) above but for his death.

(3) If a child dies before the end of the week in which he is born, subsections (1) and (2) apply in his case as if references to the person entitled to child benefit in respect of a child for the week in which his death occurs were to the person who would have been so entitled if the child had been alive at the beginning of that week (and if any conditions which were satisfied, and any facts which existed, at the time of his death were satisfied or existed then).

(4) Where a person is entitled to child benefit in respect of a child under this section, section 77 applies with the omission of subsections (4) to (6).

(5) In this section—

"married couple" means a man and a woman who are married to each other and are neither—

(*a*) separated under a court order, nor
(*b*) separated in circumstances in which the separation is likely to be permanent, and

"unmarried couple" means a man and a woman who are not a married couple but are living together as husband and wife."

56 Presence in United Kingdom

(1) For section 146 of the Social Security Contributions and Benefits Act 1992 (c 4) (persons outside Great Britain) substitute—

"146 Presence in Great Britain

(1) No child benefit shall be payable in respect of a child for a week unless he is in Great Britain in that week.

(2) No person shall be entitled to child benefit for a week unless he is in Great Britain in that week.

(3) Circumstances may be prescribed in which a child or other person is to be treated for the purposes of this section as being, or as not being, in Great Britain."

(2) For section 142 of the Social Security Contributions and Benefits (Northern Ireland) Act 1992 (c 7)(persons outside Northern Ireland) substitute—

"142 Presence in Northern Ireland

(1) No child benefit shall be payable in respect of a child for a week unless he is in Northern Ireland in that week.

(2) No person shall be entitled to child benefit for a week unless he is in Northern Ireland in that week.

(3) Circumstances may be prescribed in which a child or other person is to be treated for the purposes of this section as being, or as not being, in Northern Ireland."

57 Abolition of exclusion of tax exempt persons

In Schedule 9 to—

(*a*) the Social Security Contributions and Benefits Act 1992, and

(*b*) the Social Security Contributions and Benefits (Northern Ireland) Act 1992,

omit paragraph 4 (person not entitled to child benefit if he or other prescribed person is exempt from tax under prescribed provisions).

PART 3
SUPPLEMENTARY

Information etc

58 Administrative arrangements

(1) This section applies where regulations under—

(*a*) section 4 or 6 of this Act,

(*b*) section 5 of the Social Security Administration Act 1992 (c 5), or

(*c*) section 5 of the Social Security Administration (Northern Ireland) Act 1992 (c 8),

permit or require a claim or notification relating to a tax credit, child benefit or guardian's allowance to be made or given to a relevant authority.

(2) Where this section applies, regulations may make provision—

(*a*) for information or evidence relating to tax credits, child benefit or guardian's allowance to be provided to the relevant authority (whether by persons by whom such claims and notifications are or have been made or given, by the Board or by other persons),

(*b*) for the giving of information or advice by a relevant authority to persons by whom such claims or notifications are or have been made or given, and

(*c*) for the recording, verification and holding, and the forwarding to the Board or a person providing services to the Board, of claims and notifications received by virtue of the regulations referred to in subsection (1) and information or evidence received by virtue of paragraph (*a*),

(3) "Relevant authority" means—

(*a*) the Secretary of State,

(*b*) the Northern Ireland Department, or

(*c*) a person providing services to the Secretary of State or the Northern Ireland Department.

Regulations—Tax Credits (Administrative Arrangements) Regulations, SI 2002/3036.

59 Use and disclosure of information

Schedule 5 (use and disclosure of information) has effect.

Other supplementary provisions

60 Repeals

Schedule 6 (repeals) has effect.

61 Commencement

Apart from section 54(1) and (2), the preceding provisions of this Act come into force in accordance with orders made by the Treasury.

Orders—See the Tax Credits Act 2002 (Commencement No 1) Order, SI 2002/1727.
Tax Credits Act 2002 (Commencement No 2) Order, SI 2003/938.

Tax Credits Act 2002 (Commencement No 3 and Transitional Provisions and Savings) Order, SI 2003/392.
Tax Credits Act 2002 (Commencement No 4, Transitional Provisions and Savings) Order, SI 2003/962.
Tax Credits Act 2002 (Further Commencement and Transitional Provisions) Order, SI 2011/2910.
Tax Credits Act 2002 (Commencement and Transitional Provisions)(Partial Revocation) Order, SI 2014/1848.

62 Transitional provisions and savings

(1) The Secretary of State may by order make as respects England and Wales and Scotland, and the Northern Ireland Department may by order make as respects Northern Ireland, any transitional provisions or savings which appear appropriate in connection with the commencement of the abolition of the increases referred to in section 1(3)(*e*).

(2) Subject to any provision made by virtue of subsection (1), the Treasury may by order make any transitional provisions or savings which appear appropriate in connection with the commencement of any provision of this Act.

Orders—See the Tax Credits Act 2002 (Commencement No 1) Order, SI 2002/1727.
Tax Credits Act 2002 (Commencement No 4, Transitional Provisions and Savings) Order, SI 2003/962.
Tax Credits Act 2002 (Child Tax Credit) (Transitional Provisions) Order, SI 2003/2170.
Tax Credits Act 2002 (Further Commencement and Transitional Provisions) Order, SI 2011/2910.
Tax Credits Act 2002 (Commencement and Transitional Provisions)(Partial Revocation) Order, SI 2014/1848.

63 Tax credits appeals etc: temporary modifications

(1) Until such day as the Treasury may by order appoint, Part 1 of this Act has effect subject to the modifications specified in this section; and an order under this subsection may include any transitional provisions or savings which appear appropriate.

[(2) Except in the case of an appeal against an employer penalty, an appeal under section 38 is to—

(*a*) in Great Britain, the First-tier Tribunal; or

(*b*) in Northern Ireland, the appeal tribunal;

and in either case section 39(6) shall not apply.][2]

[(3) The function of giving a direction under section 19(10) is a function of—

(*a*) in Great Britain, the First-tier Tribunal; or

(*b*) in Northern Ireland, the appeal tribunal;

and in either case the relevant provisions of Part 5 of the Taxes Management Act 1970 shall not apply.][2]

[(4) In Northern Ireland, except in the case of an employer information penalty, proceedings under paragraph 3 of Schedule 2 are by way of information in writing, made to the appeal tribunal (rather than to the tribunal), and upon summons issued by them to the defendant to appear before them at a time and place stated in the summons; and they must hear and decide each case in a summary way.][2]

(5) So far as is appropriate in consequence of subsections (2) to (4)—

(*a*) the references to [tribunal in section 19(10)][2] and paragraphs 2 and 3(2) of Schedule 2 are to [the First-tier Tribunal or][3] the [appeal tribunal][1, 2], . . . [2]

(*b*) . . . [2]

[(6) In Northern Ireland, an appeal under paragraph 2(2) or 4(1) of Schedule 2 from a decision of, or against the determination of a penalty by, the [First-tier Tribunal or}[3] appeal tribunal lies to the Northern Ireland Social Security Commissioner (rather than to the Upper Tribunal).][2]

(7) So far as is appropriate in consequence of subsection (6), the references in paragraphs 2(2) and 4 of Schedule 2 [to the Upper Tribunal are to the Northern Ireland Social Security Commissioner][2]][1].

(8) Regulations may apply any provision contained in—

(*a*) Chapter 2 of Part 1 of the Social Security Act 1998 (c 14) (social security appeals: Great Britain),

(*b*) Chapter 2 of Part 2 of the Social Security (Northern Ireland) Order 1998 (SI 1998/1506 (NI 10)) (social security appeals: Northern Ireland), or

(*c*) section 54 of the Taxes Management Act 1970 (c 9) (settling of appeals by agreement),

in relation to appeals which, by virtue of this section, are to [the First-tier Tribunal or][3] [the [appeal tribunal or lie to][2] a Northern Ireland Social Security Commissioner][1], but subject to such modifications as are prescribed.

(9) . . . [2]

[(10) "Appeal tribunal" means an appeal tribunal constituted under Chapter 1 of Part 2 of the Social Security (Northern Ireland) Order 1998.][2]

(11) "Employer penalty" means—

(*a*) a penalty under section 31 or 32 relating to a requirement imposed by virtue of regulations under section 25, or

(*b*) a penalty under section 33.

(12) "Employer information penalty" means a penalty under section 32(2)(*a*) relating to a requirement imposed by virtue of regulations under section 25.

(13) ["Northern Ireland Social Security Commissioner" means][1] the Chief Social Security Commissioner or any other Social Security Commissioner appointed under the Social Security Administration (Northern Ireland) Act 1992 (c 8) or a tribunal of two or more Commissioners constituted under Article 16(7) of the Social Security (Northern Ireland) Order 1998 (SI 1998/1506 (NI 10)).

[(14) "tribunal" (other than in the expression "appeal tribunal") shall have the meaning in section 47C of the Taxes Management Act 1970.][2]

Regulations—Tax Credits (Payments by the Board) Regulations, SI 2002/2173.

Tax Credits (Appeals) Regulations, SI 2002/2926.

Tax Credits (Settlement of Appeals) Regulations, SI 2014/1933.

Amendments—[1] In sub-ss (2), (3), (4), (6), (8) words substituted for words "an appeal tribunal", in sub-s (5)(*a*) words substituted for words "appeal tribunal", in sub-ss (6), (8) words substituted for words "a Social Security Commissioner", in sub-s (7) words substituted for words "the Social Security Commissioner", sub-s (10) substituted, in sub-s (13) words substituted for the words from the beginning to "in Northern Ireland,", by the Transfer of Tribunal Functions Order, SI 2008/2833 art 6, Sch 3 paras 143, 191 with effect from 3 November 2008.

[2] The following amendments made by the Transfer of Tribunal Functions and Revenue and Customs Appeals Order, SI 2009/56 art 3, Sch 1 para 316 with effect from 1 April 2009—

- sub-ss (2)–(4), (6), (10) substituted;
- in sub-s (5)(*a*)(i) words in the first place substituted for the words "the General Commissioners or Special Commissioners in sections 19(10) and 39(5)", words in the second place substituted for the words "appropriate tribunal";
- sub-s (5)(*b*) and the word "and" immediately preceding it repealed;
- words in sub-s (7) substituted for the words "to the High Court and the Court of Session are to [the Upper Tribunal or the Northern Ireland Social Security Commissioner";
- words in sub-s (8) substituted for the words "appropriate tribunal] or lie to [the Upper Tribunal ";
- sub-s (9) repealed; sub-s (14) inserted.

[3] In sub-ss (5), (8), words inserted by the Revenue and Customs Appeals Order, SI 2012/533 art 2 with effect from 1 March 2012.

64 Northern Ireland

(1) The Northern Ireland Act 1998 (c 47) has effect subject to the amendments in subsections (2) and (3).

(2) In Schedule 2 (excepted matters), after paragraph 10 insert—

"10A.

Tax credits under Part 1 of the Tax Credits Act 2002.

10B.

Child benefit and guardian's allowance."

(3) In section 87 (consultation and co-ordination on social security matters), after subsection (6) insert—

"(6A) But this section does not apply to the legislation referred to in subsection (6) to the extent that it relates to child benefit or guardian's allowance."

(4) For the purposes of that Act, a provision of—

(*a*) an Act of the Northern Ireland Assembly, or

(*b*) a Bill for such an Act,

which amends or repeals any of the provisions of the Employment Rights (Northern Ireland) Order 1996 (SI 1996/1919 (NI 16)) dealt with in Schedule 1 shall not be treated as dealing with tax credits if the Act or Bill deals with employment rights conferred otherwise than by that Schedule in the same way.

65 Regulations, orders and schemes

(1) Any power to make regulations under sections 3, 7 to 13, 42 and 43, and any power to make regulations under this Act prescribing a rate of interest, is exercisable by the Treasury.

(2) Any other power to make regulations under this Act is exercisable by the Board.

(3) Subject to subsection (4), any power to make regulations, orders or schemes under this Act is exercisable by statutory instrument.

(4) The power—

(*a*) of the Department of Health, Social Services and Public Safety to make schemes under section 12(5), and

(*b*) of the Northern Ireland Department to make orders under section 62(1),

is exercisable by statutory rule for the purposes of the Statutory Rules (Northern Ireland) Order 1979 (SI 1979/1573 (NI 12)).

(5) Regulations may not be made under section 25 or 26 in relation to appeals in Scotland without the consent of the Scottish Ministers.

(6) Regulations may not be made under section 39(6) or 63(8) without the consent of the Lord Chancellor[, the Department of Justice in Northern Ireland][1] and the Scottish Ministers.

(7) Any power to make regulations under this Act may be exercised—

(*a*) in relation to all cases to which it extends, to all those cases with prescribed exceptions or to prescribed cases or classes of case,

(*b*) so as to make as respects the cases in relation to which it is exercised the full provision to which it extends to any less provision (whether by way of exception or otherwise),

(*c*) so as to make the same provision for all cases in relation to which it is exercised or different provision for different cases or classes of case or different provision as respects the same case or class of case for different purposes,

(*d*) so as to make provision unconditionally or subject to any prescribed condition,

(*e*) so as to provide for a person to exercise a discretion in dealing with any matter.

8) Any regulations made under a power under this Act to prescribe a rate of interest may—

(*a*) either themselves specify a rate of interest or make provision for any such rate to be determined by reference to such rate or the average of such rates as may be referred to in the regulations,

(*b*) provide for rates to be reduced below, or increased above, what they otherwise would be by specified amounts or by reference to specified formulae,

(*c*) provide for rates arrived at by reference to averages to be rounded up or down,

(*d*) provide for circumstances in which alteration of a rate of interest is or is not to take place, and

(*e*) provide that alterations of rates are to have effect for periods beginning on or after a day determined in accordance with the regulations in relation to interest running from before that day as well as from or from after that day.

9) Any power to make regulations or a scheme under this Act includes power to make any ncidental, supplementary, consequential or transitional provision which appears appropriate for the ›urposes of, or in connection with, the regulations or scheme.

Regulations—Working Tax Credit (Entitlement and Maximum Rate) Regulations, SI 2002/2005.
'ax Credits (Definition and Calculation of Income) Regulations, SI 2002/2006.
'hild Tax Credit Regulations, SI 2002/2007.
'ax Credits (Income Thresholds and Determination of Rates) Regulations, SI 2002/2008.
'ax Credits (Claims and Notifications) Regulations, SI 2002/2014.
Vorking Tax Credit (Payment by Employers) Regulations, SI 2002/2172.
'ax Credits (Payments by the Board) Regulations, SI 2002/2173.
'ax Credits (Appeals) Regulations, SI 2002/2926.
'ax Credits (Administrative Arrangements) Regulations, SI 2002/3036.
'ax Credits (Notice of Appeal) Regulations, SI 2002/3119.
'ax Credits (Interest Rate) Regulations, SI 2003/123.
'ax Credits (Approval of Home Child Care Providers) Scheme, SI 2003/643.
'ax Credits (Immigration) Regulations, SI 2003/653.
'ax Credits (Residence) Regulations, SI 2003/654.
'ax Credits (Official Error) Regulations, SI 2003/692.
'ax Credits (Provision of Information) (Functions Relating to Health) Regulations, SI 2003/731.
'ax Credits (Polygamous Marriages) Regulations, SI 2003/742.
'ax Credits (Employer Penalty Appeals) Regulations, SI 2003/1382.
'ax Credits (Provision of Information) (Functions Relating to Health) (No 2) Regulations, SI 2003/1650.
'ax Credits (Provision of Information) (Function Relating to Employment and Training) Regulations, SI 2003/2041.
'ax Credits (Provision of Information) (Evaluation and Statistical Studies) Regulations, SI 2003/3308.
'ax Credits (Provision of Information) (Function Relating to Employment and Training) Regulations, SI 2005/66.
'ax Credits (Miscellaneous Amendments) Regulations 2010, SI 2010/751.
'ax Credits (Miscellaneous Amendments) Regulations, SI 2011/721.
'he Tax Credits Up-rating Regulations, SI 2011/1035
'ax Credits (Miscellaneous Amendments) Regulations, SI 2012/848.
.oss of Tax Credits Regulations, SI 2013/715.
'ax Credits Up-rating, etc. Regulations, SI 2013/750.
Vorking Tax Credit (Entitlement and Maximum Rate) (Amendment) Regulations, SI 2013/1736.
'ax Credits (Miscellaneous Amendments) Regulations, SI 2014/658.
'ax Credits Up-rating Regulations, SI 2014/845
'hild Benefit (General) and Child Tax Credit (Amendment) Regulations, 2014/1231.
'hild Benefit (General) and the Tax Credits (Residence) (Amendment) Regulations, SI 2014/1511.
'ax Credits (Settlement of Appeals) Regulations, SI 2014/1933.
'hild Benefit (General) and Tax Credits (Miscellaneous Amendments) Regulations, SI 2014/2924.
'ax Credits Up-rating Regulations, SI 2015/451.
Vorking Tax Credit (Entitlement and Maximum Rate) (Amendment) Regulations, SI 2015/605.
'ax Credits (Claims and Notifications) (Amendment) Regulations, SI 2015/669.
'ax Credits and Child Benefit (Miscellaneous Amendments) Regulations, SI 2016/360.
'ax Credits (Income Thresholds and Determination of Rates) (Amendment) Regulations, SI 2016/393.
'ax Credits (Definition and Calculation of Income) (Amendment) Regulations, SI 2016/978.
'hild Tax Credit (Amendment) Regulations, SI 2017/387.
'ax Credits (Definition and Calculation of Income) (Amendment) Regulations, SI 2017/396.
'ax Credits and Guardian's Allowance Up-rating etc Regulations, SI 2017/406.
'ax Credits (Claims and Notifications) (Amendment) Regulations, SI 2017/597.

.mendments—[1] In sub-s (6), words inserted by the Northern Ireland Act 1998 (Devolution of Policing and Justice Functions) Order, SI 2010/976 art 15(5), Sch 18 paras 59, 60 with effect from 12 April 2010.

66 Parliamentary etc control of instruments

(1) No [order or][1] regulations to which this subsection applies may be made unless a draft of th instrument containing [the order or regulations][1] (whether or not together with other provisions) ha been laid before, and approved by a resolution of, each House of Parliament.

(2) Subsection (1) applies to—

[(*za*) an order made by the Treasury under section 36A(8) or 36C(9),

(*zb*) regulations made under section 36A(5) or 36C(4),][1]

(*a*) regulations prescribing monetary amounts that are required to be reviewed under section 41

(*b*) regulations made by virtue of subsection (2) of section 12 prescribing the amount in excess o which charges are not taken into account for the purposes of that subsection, and

(*c*) the first regulations made under sections 7(8) and (9), 9, 11, 12 and 13(2).

(3) A statutory instrument containing—

(*a*) [an order or][1] regulations under this Act,

(*b*) a scheme made by the Secretary of State under section 12(5), or

(*c*) an Order in Council under section 52(7),

is (unless a draft of the instrument has been laid before, and approved by a resolution of, each Hous of Parliament) subject to annulment in pursuance of a resolution of either House of Parliament.

(4) A statutory instrument containing a scheme made by the Scottish Ministers under section 12(5) is subject to annulment in pursuance of a resolution of the Scottish Parliament.

(5) A statutory rule containing a scheme made by the Department of Health, Social Services an Public Safety under section 12(5) is subject to negative resolution within the meaning o section 41(6) of the Interpretation Act (Northern Ireland) 1954 (c 33 (NI)).

Amendments—[1] In sub-s (1), words inserted after word "no", and words substituted for word "them", in sub-s (2), new paras (*za*), (*zb*) inserted, and in sub-s (3)(*a*) words inserted, by the Welfare Reform Act 2012 s 120(1), (4) with effect from 1 February 2013 (by virtue of SI 2013/178 art 2(1), (3)).

67 Interpretation

In this Act—

"the Board" means the Commissioners of Inland Revenue,

["cautioned", in relation to any person and any offence, means cautioned after the persor concerned has admitted the offence; and "caution" is to be interpreted accordingly;][1]

"modifications" includes alterations, additions and omissions, and "modifies" is to be construec accordingly,

"the Northern Ireland Department" means the Department for Social Development in Northerr Ireland,

"prescribed" means prescribed by regulations, and

"tax credit" and "tax credits" have the meanings given by section 1(2).

Regulations—Working Tax Credit (Entitlement and Maximum Rate) Regulations, SI 2002/2005.
Tax Credits (Definition and Calculation of Income) Regulations, SI 2002/2006.
Child Tax Credit Regulations, SI 2002/2007.
Tax Credits (Income Thresholds and Determination of Rates) Regulations, SI 2002/2008.
Tax Credits (Claims and Notifications) Regulations, SI 2002/2014.
Working Tax Credit (Payment by Employers) Regulations, SI 2002/2172.
Tax Credits (Notice of Appeal) Regulations, SI 2002/3119.
Tax Credits (Interest Rate) Regulations, SI 2003/123.
Working Tax Credit (Payment by Employers) (Amendment) Regulations, SI 2003/715.
Tax Credits (Provision of Information) (Functions Relating to Health) Regulations, SI 2003/731.
Tax Credits (Employer Penalty Appeals) Regulations, SI 2003/1382.
Tax Credits (Provision of Information) (Functions Relating to Health) (No 2) Regulations, SI 2003/1650.
Tax Credits (Provision of Information) (Function Relating to Employment and Training) Regulations, SI 2003/2041.
Tax Credits (Provision of Information) (Evaluation and Statistical Studies) Regulations, SI 2003/3308.
Tax Credits (Provision of Information) (Function Relating to Employment and Training) Regulations, SI 2005/66.
Tax Credits (Miscellaneous Amendments) Regulations 2010, SI 2010/751.
Tax Credits (Miscellaneous Amendments) Regulations, SI 2011/721.
Tax Credits Up-rating Regulations, SI 2011/1035.
Tax Credits Up-rating Regulations, SI 2012/849.
Tax Credits (Miscellaneous Amendments) Regulations, SI 2012/848.
Loss of Tax Credits Regulations, SI 2013/715.
Tax Credits Up-rating, etc. Regulations, SI 2013/750.
Tax Credits (Miscellaneous Amendments) Regulations, SI 2014/658.
Tax Credits Up-rating Regulations, SI 2014/845
Child Benefit (General) and Child Tax Credit (Amendment) Regulations, 2014/1231.
Child Benefit (General) and Tax Credits (Miscellaneous Amendments) Regulations, SI 2014/2924.
Tax Credits Up-rating Regulations, SI 2015/451.
Working Tax Credit (Entitlement and Maximum Rate) (Amendment) Regulations, SI 2015/605.
Tax Credits (Claims and Notifications) (Amendment) Regulations, SI 2015/669.
Tax Credits and Child Benefit (Miscellaneous Amendments) Regulations, SI 2016/360.
Tax Credits (Income Thresholds and Determination of Rates) (Amendment) Regulations, SI 2016/393.
Child Tax Credit (Amendment) Regulations, SI 2017/387.

Tax Credits (Definition and Calculation of Income) (Amendment) Regulations, SI 2017/396.
Tax Credits and Guardian's Allowance Up-rating etc Regulations, SI 2017/406.
Tax Credits (Claims and Notifications) (Amendment) Regulations, SI 2017/597.

Amendments—[1] Definition of "cautioned" inserted by the Welfare Reform Act 2012 s 120(1), (5) with effect from 6 April 2012 (by virtue of SI 2013/178 art 2(1)).

Prospective amendments—Definition of "cautioned" to be repealed by the Welfare Reform Act 2012 s 147, Sch 14 Part 12 with effect from a date to be appointed.

68 Financial provision

(1) There is to be paid out of money provided by Parliament—

(*a*) any expenditure of a Minister of the Crown or government department under this Act, and

(*b*) any increase attributable to this Act in sums payable out of money provided by Parliament under any other Act.

(2) There is to be paid into the Consolidated Fund any sums received by a government department by virtue of this Act (apart from any required by any other enactment to be paid into the National Insurance Fund).

69 Extent

(1) The amendments, repeals and revocations made by this Act have the same extent as the enactments or instruments to which they relate.

(2) Subject to that, this Act extends to Northern Ireland (as well as to England and Wales and Scotland).

70 Short title

This Act may be cited as the Tax Credits Act 2002.

SCHEDULES

SCHEDULE 1

RIGHTS OF EMPLOYEES

Section 27

The amendments made by this Schedule, so far as relevant to this publication, have been noted in the relevant legislation. Amendments beyond the scope of this publication have been omitted.

SCHEDULE 2

PENALTIES: SUPPLEMENTARY

Section 34

Determination of penalties by Board

1—(1) The Board may make a determination—

(*a*) imposing a penalty under section 31, 32(2)(*b*) or (3) or 33, and

(*b*) setting it at such amount as, in their opinion, is appropriate.

(2) The Board must give notice of a determination of a penalty under this paragraph to the person on whom the penalty is imposed.

(3) The notice must state the date on which it is given and give details of the right to appeal against the determination under section 38.

(4) After the notice of a determination under this paragraph has been given the determination must not be altered except on appeal.

(5) A penalty determined under this paragraph becomes payable at the end of the period of thirty days beginning with the date on which the notice of determination is given.

2—(1) On an appeal [. . .][1] under section 38 against the determination of a penalty under [paragraph 1 that is notified to the First-tier tribunal, the tribunal][1] may—

(*a*) if it appears that no penalty has been incurred, set the determination aside,

(*b*) if the amount determined appears to be appropriate, confirm the determination,

(*c*) if the amount determined appears to be excessive, reduce it to such other amount (including nil) as [the First-tier Tribunal considers][1] appropriate, or

(*d*) if the amount determined appears to be insufficient, increase it to such amount not exceeding the permitted maximum as [the First-tier Tribunal considers][1] appropriate.

[(2) In addition to any right of appeal on a point of law under section 11(2) of the Tribunals, Courts and Enforcement Act 2007, the person liable to the penalty may appeal to the Upper Tribunal against the amount of the penalty which has been determined under sub-paragraph (1), but not against any decision which falls under section 11(5)(*d*) or (*e*) of that Act and was made in connection with the determination of the amount of the penalty.

(2A) Section 11(3) and (4) of the Tribunals, Courts and Enforcement Act 2007 applies to the right of appeal under sub-paragraph (2) as it applies to the right of appeal under section 11(2) of that Act.

Tax Credits

(2B) On an appeal under this paragraph the Upper Tribunal has the same powers as are conferred on the First-tier Tribunal by virtue of this paragraph.][1]

Amendments—[1] In sub-para (1) words "to them" repealed and words substituted for the words "paragraph 1, the General Commissioners or Special Commissioners"; in sub-para (1)(*c*), (*d*) words substituted for the words "they consider"; sub-paras (2)–(2B) substituted for former sub-para (2) by the Transfer of Tribunal Functions and Revenue and Customs Appeals Order, SI 2009/56 art 3, Sch 1 para 317 with effect from 1 April 2009.

Penalty proceedings before [tribunal]

3—(1) The Board may commence proceedings for a penalty under section 32(2)(*a*) [before the tribunal][1].
[(2) The person liable to the penalty shall be a party to the proceedings.][1]
[(3) "tribunal" is to be read in accordance with section 47C of the Taxes Management Act 1970.][1]

Amendments—[1] In heading, word substituted for the word "Commissioners"; sub-para (1) words inserted; sub-para (2) substituted; sub-para (3) inserted by the Transfer of Tribunal Functions and Revenue and Customs Appeals Order, SI 2009/56 art 3, Sch 1 para 319 with effect from 1 April 2009.

4—[(1) In addition to any right of appeal on a point of law under section 11(2) of the Tribunals, Courts and Enforcement Act 2007, the person liable to the penalty may appeal to the Upper Tribunal against the determination of a penalty in proceedings under paragraph 2(1), but not against any decision which falls under section 11(5)(*d*) or (*e*) of that Act and was made in connection with the determination of the amount of the penalty.
(1A) Section 11(3) and (4) of the Tribunals, Courts and Enforcement Act 2007 applies to the right of appeal under sub-paragraph (1) as it applies to the right of appeal under section 11(2) of that Act.][1]
(2) On any such appeal the [Upper Tribunal][1] may—
(*a*) if it appears that no penalty has been incurred, set the determination aside,
(*b*) if the amount determined appears to be appropriate, confirm the determination,
(*c*) if the amount determined appears to be excessive, reduce it to such other amount (including nil) as the [Upper Tribunal][1] considers appropriate, or
(*d*) if the amount determined appears to be insufficient, increase it to such amount not exceeding the permitted maximum as the [Upper Tribunal][1] considers appropriate.

Amendments—[1] Sub-paras (1), (1A) substituted for former sub-para (1) words inserted; in sub-para (2) words substituted in each place for word "court" by the Transfer of Tribunal Functions and Revenue and Customs Appeals Order, SI 2009/56 art 3, Sch 1 para 320 with effect from 1 April 2009.

Mitigation of penalties

5 The Board may in their discretion mitigate any penalty under this Part or stay or compound any proceedings for any such penalty and may also, after judgment, further mitigate or entirely remit any such penalty.

Time limits for penalties

6—(1) In the case of a penalty under section 31 relating to a tax credit for a person or persons for the whole or part of a tax year (other than a penalty to which sub-paragraph (3) applies), the Board may determine the penalty at any time before the latest of—
(*a*) the end of the period of one year beginning with the expiry of the period for initiating an enquiry under section 19 into the entitlement of the person, or the joint entitlement of the persons, for the tax year,
(*b*) if such an enquiry is made, the end of the period of one year beginning with the day on which the enquiry is completed, and
(*c*) if a decision relating to the entitlement of the person, or the joint entitlement of the persons, for the tax year is made under section 20(1) or (4), the end of the period of one year beginning with the day on which the decision is made.
(2) In the case of a penalty under section 32 relating to a tax credit for a person or persons for the whole or part of a tax year (other than a penalty to which sub-paragraph (3) applies), the Board may determine the penalty, or commence proceedings for it, at any time before—
(*a*) if an enquiry into the entitlement of the person, or the joint entitlement of the persons, for the tax year is made under section 19, the end of the period of one year beginning with the day on which the enquiry is completed, and
(*b*) otherwise, the end of the period of one year beginning with the expiry of the period for initiating such an enquiry.
(3) In the case of—
(*a*) a penalty under section 31 or 32 relating to a requirement imposed by virtue of regulations under section 25, or
(*b*) a penalty under section 33,

the Board may determine the penalty, or commence proceedings for it, at any time before the end of the period of six years after the date on which the penalty was incurred or began to be incurred.

Modifications—Universal Credit (Transitional Provisions) Regulations, SI 2013/386 reg 17(2), Schedule paras 1, 14 (modification of this section in respect of awards of universal credit and terminations of awards of tax credit in the same year).
Universal Credit (Transitional Provisions) Regulations, SI 2014/1230 reg 12(2), (3) (modification of this section in repect of treatment of overpayment of tax credits).

Recovery of penalties

7—(1) A penalty payable under this Part is to be treated for the purposes of Part 6 of the Taxes Management Act 1970 (c 9) (collection and recovery) as if it were tax charged in an assessment and due and payable.

(2) Regulations under section 203(2)(*a*) of the Income and Corporation Taxes Act 1988 (c 1) (PAYE) apply to a penalty payable under this Part as if it were an underpayment of tax for a previous year of assessment.

SCHEDULE 3
TAX CREDITS: CONSEQUENTIAL AMENDMENTS

Section 47

The amendments made by this Schedule, so far as relevant to this publication, have been noted in the relevant legislation. Amendments beyond the scope of this publication have been omitted.

SCHEDULE 4
TRANSFER OF FUNCTIONS: CONSEQUENTIAL AMENDMENTS

Section 51

The amendments made by this Schedule, so far as relevant to this publication, have been noted in the relevant legislation. Amendments beyond the scope of this publication have been omitted.
Paras 2 and 8 of this Schedule are repealed by the Welfare Reform Act 2012 s 107(3) with effect from 8 May 2012.

SCHEDULE 5
USE AND DISCLOSURE OF INFORMATION

Section 59

Powers to use information

1 Information which is held for the purposes of any functions relating to tax credits, child benefit or guardian's allowance—

(*a*) by the Board, or

(*b*) by a person providing services to the Board, in connection with the provision of those services,

may be used, or supplied to any person providing services to the Board, for the purposes of, or for any purposes connected with, the exercise of any such functions.

2 . . .

Amendment—This paragraph repealed by CRCA 2005 s 50, Sch 4 paras 88, 91, s 52 Sch 5 with effect from 18 April 2005 (by virtue of SI 2005/1126).

3—(1) Information which is held for the purposes of any functions relating to social security (including child benefit and guardian's allowance) or tax credits—

(*a*) by the Secretary of State or the Northern Ireland Department, or

(*b*) by a person providing services to the Secretary of State or the Northern Ireland Department, in connection with the provision of those services,

may be used, or supplied to any person providing services to the Secretary of State or the Northern Ireland Department, for the purposes of, or for any purposes connected with, the exercise of any functions under relevant regulations.

(2) In this paragraph "relevant regulations" are regulations made under—

(*a*) section 4, 6 or 58 of this Act,

(*b*) section 5 of the Social Security Administration Act 1992 (c 5), or

(*c*) section 5 of the Social Security Administration (Northern Ireland) Act 1992 (c 8).

Exchange of information between Board and Secretary of State or Northern Ireland Departments

4—(1) This paragraph applies to information which is held for the purposes of functions relating to tax credits, child benefit or guardian's allowance—

Tax Credits

(*a*) by the Board, or

(*b*) by a person providing services to the Board, in connection with the provision of those services.

[(2) Information to which this paragraph applies may be supplied—

(*a*) to the Secretary of State, or

(*b*) to a person providing services to the Secretary of State,

for use for the purposes of functions relating to . . . [2] war pensions or for such purposes relating to evaluation or statistical studies as may be prescribed.

(3) An authorised officer may require information to which this paragraph applies to be supplied—

(*a*) to the Secretary of State, or

(*b*) to a person providing services to the Secretary of State,

for use for the purposes of functions relating to social security.[2]

(3A) Information to which this paragraph applies may be supplied—

(*a*) to the Northern Ireland Department, or

(*b*) to a person providing services to the Northern Ireland Department,

for use for the purposes of functions relating to . . . [2] child support or war pensions or for such purposes relating to evaluation or statistical studies as may be prescribed.

(3B) An authorised officer may require information to which this paragraph applies to be supplied—

(*a*) to the Northern Ireland Department, or

(*b*) to a person providing services to the Northern Ireland Department,

for use for the purposes of functions relating to . . . [2] child support.][1]

(4) In [sub-paragraphs . . . [2] (3B)][1] "authorised officer" means an officer of the Secretary of State or the Northern Ireland Department authorised for the purposes of this paragraph by the Secretary of State or the Northern Ireland Department.

(5) In this paragraph "war pension" has the meaning given by section 25(4) of the Social Security Act 1989 (c 24).

Regulations—Tax Credits (Provision of Information) (Evaluation and Statistical Studies) Regulations, SI 2003/3308.

Amendments—[1] Sub-paras (2)–(3B) substituted for previous sub-paras (2), (3), and in sub-para (4) words substituted for words "sub-paragraph (3)", by the Child Maintenance and Other Payments Act 2008 s 57, Sch 7 para 4(1)–(3) with effect from 1 June 2009 (by virtue of SI 2009/1314, art 2(2)(*b*)(i)).

[2] In sub-para (2) words "social security or", whole of sub-para (3), in sub-para (3A) words "social security,", in sub-para (3B) words "social security or", and in sub-para (4) words "(3) and", repealed, by the Welfare Reform Act 2012 s 247, Sch 14 Part 13 with effect from 8 May 2012.

5—(1) This paragraph applies to information which is held for the purposes of functions relating to tax credits, child benefit or guardian's allowance—

(*a*) by the Board, or

(*b*) by a person providing services to the Board, in connection with the provision of those services.

(2) Information to which this paragraph applies may be supplied—

(*a*) to the Secretary of State or the Department for Employment and Learning in Northern Ireland, or

(*b*) to a person providing services to the Secretary of State or that Department,

for use for the purposes of such functions relating to employment or training as may be prescribed.

Regulations—Tax Credits (Provision of Information) (Function Relating to Employment and Training) Regulations, SI 2003/2041.

Tax Credits (Provision of Information) (Function Relating to Employment and Training) Regulations, SI 2005/66.

6—[(1) This paragraph applies to information which is held for the purposes of functions relating to . . . [2] war pensions or employment or training—

(*a*) by the Secretary of State, or

(*b*) by a person providing services to the Secretary of State, in connection with the provision of those services.

(1A) This paragraph also applies to information which is held for the purposes of functions relating to . . . [2] child support, war pensions or employment or training—

(*a*) by the Northern Ireland Department or the Department for Employment and Learning in Northern Ireland, or

(*b*) by a person providing services to either of those Departments, in connection with the provision of those services.][1]

(2) Information to which this paragraph applies may be supplied—

(*a*) to the Board, or

(*b*) to a person providing services to the Board,

for use for the purposes of functions relating to tax credits, child benefit or guardian's allowance.

(3) The Board may require information to which this paragraph applies to be so supplied if the information is held for the purposes of functions relating to . . . [2] child support.

(4) In this paragraph "war pension" has the meaning given by section 25(4) of the Social Security Act 1989.

Amendments—[1] Sub-paras (1), (1A) substituted for previous sub-para (1) by the Child Maintenance and Other Payments Act 2008 s 57, Sch 7 para 4(1), (4) with effect from 1 June 2009 (by virtue of SI 2009/1314, art 2(2)(*b*)(i)).

[2] In sub-paras (1), (1A) words "social security", and in sub-para (3) words "social security or", repealed, by the Welfare Reform Act 2012 s 247, Sch 14 Part 13 with effect from 8 May 2012.

Exchange of information between Board and authorities administering certain benefits

7—(1) This paragraph applies to information which is held for the purposes of functions relating to tax credits, child benefit or guardian's allowance—

(*a*) by the Board, or

(*b*) by a person providing services to the Board, in connection with the provision of those services.

(2) Information to which this paragraph applies may be supplied by or under the authority of the Board—

(*a*) to an authority administering housing benefit or council tax benefit, or

(*b*) to a person authorised to exercise any function of such an authority relating to such a benefit,

for use in the administration of such a benefit.

(3) Information supplied under this paragraph is not to be supplied by the recipient to any other person or body unless it is supplied—

(*a*) to a person to whom the information could be supplied directly by or under the authority of the Board,

(*b*) for the purposes of any civil or criminal proceedings relating to the Social Security Contributions and Benefits Act 1992 (c 4), the Social Security Administration Act 1992 (c 5) or the Jobseekers Act 1995 (c 18) or to any provision of Northern Ireland legislation corresponding to any of them, or

(*c*) under paragraph 8 below.

8—(1) The Board may require—

(*a*) an authority administering housing benefit or council tax benefit, or

(*b*) a person authorised to exercise any function of such an authority relating to such a benefit,

to supply benefit administration information held by the authority or other person to, or to a person providing services to, the Board for use for any purpose relating to tax credits, child benefit or guardian's allowance.

(2) In sub-paragraph (1) "benefit administration information", in relation to an authority or other person, means any information which is relevant to the exercise of any function relating to housing benefit or council tax benefit by the authority or other person.

Provision of information by Board for health purposes

9—(1) This paragraph applies to information which is held for the purposes of functions relating to tax credits, child benefit or guardian's allowance—

(*a*) by the Board, or

(*b*) by a person providing services to the Board, in connection with the provision of those services.

(2) Information to which this paragraph applies may be supplied—

(*a*) to the Secretary of State, the National Assembly for Wales, the Scottish Ministers or the Department of Health, Social Services and Public Safety in Northern Ireland, or

(*b*) to persons providing services to, or exercising functions on behalf of, the Secretary of State, the National Assembly for Wales, the Scottish Ministers or that Department,

for use for the purposes of such functions relating to health as may be prescribed.

(3) Information supplied under this paragraph is not to be supplied by the recipient to any other person or body unless it is supplied—

(*a*) to a person to whom the information could be supplied directly by or under the authority of the Board, or

(*b*) for the purpose of civil or criminal proceedings,

and is not to be so supplied in those circumstances without the authority of the Board.

(4) A person commits an offence if he discloses information supplied to him under this paragraph unless the disclosure is made—

(*a*) in accordance with sub-paragraph (3),

(*b*) in accordance with an enactment or an order of a court,

(*c*) with consent given by or on behalf of the person to whom the information relates, or (*d*) in such a way as to prevent the identification of the person to whom it relates.

(5) It is a defence for a person charged with an offence under sub-paragraph (4) to prove that he reasonably believed that his disclosure was lawful.

(6) A person guilty of an offence under sub-paragraph (4) is liable—

(*a*) on conviction on indictment, to imprisonment for a term not exceeding two years, to a fine or to both, or

(*b*) on summary conviction, to imprisonment for a term not exceeding six months, to a fine not exceeding the statutory maximum or to both.

Regulations—Tax Credits (Provision of Information) (Functions Relating to Health) Regulations, SI 2003/731.
Tax Credits (Provision of Information) (Functions Relating to Health) (No 2) Regulations, SI 2003/1650.
Tax Credits (Miscellaneous Amendments) Regulations, SI 2011/721.

Provision of information by Board for education purposes

10—

Amendments—Para 10 repealed by the Education and Skills Act 2008 s 169, Sch 1 para 78, Sch 2 with effect from 26 January 2009.

[Provision of information by Board for purposes relating to welfare of children

10A—*(1) This paragraph applies to information, other than information relating to a person's income, which is held for the purposes of functions relating to tax credits, child benefit or guardian's allowance–*

(a) by the Board, or

(b) by a person providing services to the Board, in connection with the provision of those services.

(2) Information to which this paragraph applies may be supplied to—

(a) a local authority in England and Wales for use for the purpose of any enquiry or investigation under Part 5 of the Children Act 1989 relating to the welfare of a child;

(b) a local authority in Scotland for use for the purpose of any enquiry or investigation under Chapter 3 of Part 2 of the Children (Scotland) Act 1995[, or Part 5, 6, 13 or 14 of the Children's Hearings (Scotland) Act 2011][2] *relating to the welfare of a child;*

(c) an authority in Northern Ireland for use for the purpose of any enquiry or investigation under Part 6 of the Children (Northern Ireland) Order 1995 (SI 1995/755 (NI 2)) relating to the welfare of a child.

(3) Information supplied under this paragraph is not to be supplied by the recipient to any other person or body unless it is supplied—

(a) for the purpose of any enquiry or investigation referred to in sub-paragraph (2) above,

(b) for the purpose of civil or criminal proceedings, or

*(c) where paragraph (*a*) or (*b*)* does not apply, to a person to whom the information could be supplied directly by or under the authority of the Board.

*(4) Information may not be supplied under sub-paragraph (3)(*b*)* or (*c*) without the authority of the Board.

(5) A person commits an offence if he discloses information supplied to him under this paragraph unless the disclosure is made—

(a) in accordance with sub-paragraph (3),

(b) in accordance with an enactment or an order of a court,

(c) with consent given by or on behalf of the person to whom the information relates, or

(d) in such a way as to prevent the identification of the person to whom it relates.

(6) It is a defence for a person charged with an offence under sub-paragraph (5) to prove that he reasonably believed that his disclosure was lawful.

(7) A person guilty of an offence under sub-paragraph (5) is liable—

(a) on conviction on indictment, to imprisonment for a term not exceeding two years, to a fine or to both;

(b) on summary conviction in England and Wales, to imprisonment for a term not exceeding twelve months, to a fine not exceeding the statutory maximum or to both;

(c) on summary conviction in Scotland or Northern Ireland, to imprisonment for a term not exceeding six months, to a fine not exceeding the statutory maximum or to both.

(8) In sub-paragraph (2) "child" means a person under the age of eighteen and—

(a) in paragraph (a), "local authority" has the meaning given by section 105(1) of the Children Act 1989;

(b) in paragraph (b), "local authority" has the meaning given by section 93(1) of the Children (Scotland) Act 1995; and

(c) in paragraph (c), "authority" has the meaning given by Article 2 of the Children (Northern Ireland) Order 1995 (SI 1995/755 (NI 2)).

(7) The reference to an enactment in sub-paragraph (5)(b) includes a reference to an enactment comprised in, or in an instrument made under, an Act of the Scottish Parliament.][1]

Amendments—[1] Para 10A inserted by the Children Act 2004, s 63(1) with effect from 15 November 2004.
[2] In sub-s (2)(*b*), words inserted by the Children's Hearings (Scotland) Act 2011 (Consequential and Transitional Provisions and Savings) Order, SI 2013/1465 art 17, Sch 1 para 8 with effect from 24 June 2013 (the day on which the Children's Hearings (Scotland) Act 2011 s 7 came into force: see SSI 2013/195 art 2 and art 1(2)).

Unauthorised disclosure of information

11 (*amends* FA 1989 s 182)

Consequential amendments

12 (*amends* SSAA 1992 s 122(1) and SSA(NI)A 1992 s 116(1)(*a*); sub-para (*a*) repealed by the Welfare Reform Act 2012 s 247, Sch 14 Part 13)

13 (*amends* FA 1997 s 110(5A))

Prospective amendment—This paragraph to be repealed by the Welfare Reform (Northern Ireland) Order, SI 2015/2006 art 140, Sch 12 Pt 12 with effect from a date to be appointed.

SCHEDULE 6

REPEALS AND REVOCATIONS

Section 60

The repeals in this Schedule, so far as relevant to this publication, have been noted in the relevant legislation. Amendments beyond the scope of this publication have been omitted.

CIVIL PARTNERSHIP ACT 2004

(2004 Chapter 33)

An Act to make provision for and in connection with civil partnership.

[18 November 2004]

PART 7
MISCELLANEOUS

254 Social security, child support and tax credits

(1) Schedule 24 contains amendments relating to social security, child support and tax credits.

(2) Subsection (3) applies in relation to any provision of any Act, Northern Ireland legislation or subordinate legislation which—

(*a*) relates to social security, child support or tax credits, and

(*b*) contains references (however expressed) to persons who are living or have lived together as husband and wife.

(3) The power under section 259 to make orders amending enactments, Northern Ireland legislation and subordinate legislation is to be treated as including power to amend the provision to refer to persons who are living or have lived together as if they were civil partners.

(4) Subject to subsection (5), section 175(3), (5) and (6) of the Social Security Contributions and Benefits Act 1992 (c 4) applies to the exercise of the power under section 259 in relation to social security, child support or tax credits as it applies to any power under that Act to make an order (there being disregarded for the purposes of this subsection the exceptions in section 175(3) and (5) of that Act).

(5) Section 171(3), (5) and (6) of the Social Security Contributions and Benefits (Northern Ireland) Act 1992 (c 7) applies to the exercise by a Northern Ireland department of the power under section 259 in relation to social security and child support as it applies to any power under that Act to make an order (there being disregarded for the purposes of this subsection the exceptions in section 171(3) and (5) of that Act).

(6) The reference in subsection (2) to an Act or Northern Ireland legislation relating to social security is to be read as including a reference to—

(*a*) the Pneumoconiosis etc (Workers' Compensation) Act 1979 (c 41), and

(*b*) the Pneumoconiosis, etc, (Workers' Compensation) (Northern Ireland) Order 1979 (SI 1979/925 (NI 9));

and the references in subsections (4) and (5) to social security are to be construed accordingly.

PART 8
SUPPLEMENTARY

262 Extent

(1) Part 2 (civil partnership: England and Wales), excluding section 35 but including Schedules 1 to 9, extends to England and Wales only.

(2) Part 3 (civil partnership: Scotland), including Schedules 10 and 11, extends to Scotland only.

(3) Part 4 (civil partnership: Northern Ireland), including Schedules 12 to 19, extends to Northern Ireland only.

(4) In Part 5 (civil partnerships formed or dissolved abroad etc)—

(*a*) sections 220 to 224 extend to England and Wales only;

(*b*) sections 225 to 227 extend to Scotland only;

(*c*) sections 228 to 232 extend to Northern Ireland only.

(5) In Part 6—

(*a*) any amendment made by virtue of section 247(1)(*a*) and Schedule 21 has the same extent as the provision subject to the amendment;

(*b*) section 248 and Schedule 22 extend to Northern Ireland only.

(6) Section 251 extends to England and Wales and Scotland only.

(7) Section 252 extends to Northern Ireland only.

(8) Schedule 28 extends to Scotland only.

(9) Schedule 29 extends to Northern Ireland only.

(10) Any amendment, repeal or revocation made by Schedules 24 to 27 and 30 has the same extent as the provision subject to the amendment, repeal or revocation.

263 Commencement

(1) Part 1 comes into force in accordance with provision made by order by the Secretary of State, after consulting the Scottish Ministers and the Department of Finance and Personnel.

(2) Part 2, including Schedules 1 to 9, comes into force in accordance with provision made by order by the Secretary of State.

(3) Part 3, including Schedules 10 and 11, comes into force in accordance with provision made by order by the Scottish Ministers, after consulting the Secretary of State.

(4) Part 4, including Schedules 12 to 19, comes into force in accordance with provision made by order by the Department of Finance and Personnel, after consulting the Secretary of State.

(5) Part 5, excluding section 213(2) to (6) but including Schedule 20, comes into force in accordance with provision made by order by the Secretary of State, after consulting the Scottish Ministers and the Department of Finance and Personnel.

(6) Section 213(2) to (6) comes into force on the day on which this Act is passed.

(7) In Part 6—

(*a*) sections 246 and 247(1) and Schedule 21 come into force in accordance with provision made by order by the Secretary of State, after consulting the Scottish Ministers and the Department of Finance and Personnel,

(*b*) section 248(1) and Schedule 22 come into force in accordance with provision made by order by the Department of Finance and Personnel, after consulting the Secretary of State, and

(*c*) sections 247(2) to (7) and 248(2) to (5) come into force on the day on which this Act is passed.

(8) In Part 7—

(*a*) sections 249, 251, 253, 256 and 257 and Schedules 23, 25 and 26 come into force in accordance with provision made by order by the Secretary of State,

(*b*) section 250 comes into force in accordance with provision made by order by the Secretary of State, after consulting the Scottish Ministers and the Department of Finance and Personnel,

(*c*) section 252 comes into force in accordance with provision made by the Department of Finance and Personnel, after consulting the Secretary of State,

(*d*) subject to paragraph (*e*), section 254(1) and Schedule 24 come into force in accordance with provision made by order by the Secretary of State,

(*e*) the provisions of Schedule 24 listed in subsection (9), and section 254(1) so far as relating to those provisions, come into force in accordance with provision made by the Department of Finance and Personnel, after consulting the Secretary of State, and

(*f*) sections 254(2) to (6) and 255 come into force on the day on which this Act is passed.

(9) The provisions are—

(*a*) Part 2;

(*b*) in Part 5, paragraphs 67 to 85, 87, 89 to 99 and 102 to 105;

(*c*) Part 6;

(*d*) Parts 9 and 10;

(*e*) Part 15.

(10) In this Part—

(*a*) sections 258, 259, 260 and 262, this section and section 264 come into force on the day on which this Act is passed,

(*b*) section 261(1) and Schedule 27 and, except so far as relating to any Acts of the Scottish Parliament or any provision which extends to Northern Ireland only, section 261(4) and Schedule 30 come into force in accordance with provision made by order by the Secretary of State, (*c*) section 261(2) and Schedule 28 and, so far as relating to any Acts of the Scottish Parliament, section 261(4) and Schedule 30 come into force in accordance with provision made by order by the Scottish Ministers, after consulting the Secretary of State,

(*d*) section 261(3) and Schedule 29 and, so far as relating to any provision which extends to Northern Ireland only, section 261(4) and Schedule 30 come into force in accordance with provision made by order by the Department of Finance and Personnel, after consulting the Secretary of State.

(11) The power to make an order under this section is exercisable by statutory instrument.

264 Short title

This Act may be cited as the Civil Partnership Act 2004.

SCHEDULES

SCHEDULE 24

SOCIAL SECURITY, CHILD SUPPORT AND TAX CREDITS

Section 254

PART 14

AMENDMENTS OF THE TAX CREDITS ACT 2002 (C 21)

Prospective amendments—Paras 144–147 to be repealed by the Welfare Reform Act 2012 s 147, Sch 14 Part 1 with effect from a date to be appointed.

144—(1) Amend section 3 (claims) as follows.
(2) (*amends* TCA 2002 s 3(3)(*a*)).
(3) (*substitutes* TCA 2002 s 3(5A)).

Prospective amendments—Paras 144–147 to be repealed by the Welfare Reform Act 2012 s 147, Sch 14 Part 1 with effect from a date to be appointed.

145 (*amends* TCA 2002 ss 4(1)(*g*), 11(6)(*b*), (*c*), 17(10)(*b*), 24(2), 32(6)).

Prospective amendments—Paras 144–147 to be repealed by the Welfare Reform Act 2012 s 147, Sch 14 Part 1 with effect from a date to be appointed.

146 (*amends* TCA 2002 ss 4(1)(*g*), 17(10)(*b*)).

Prospective amendments—Paras 144–147 to be repealed by the Welfare Reform Act 2012 s 147, Sch 14 Part 1 with effect from a date to be appointed.

147—(1) (*amends* TCA 2002 s 48(1)).
(2) (*amends* TCA 2002 s 48(1)).
(3) (*inserts* TCA 2002 s 48(2)).

Prospective amendments—Paras 144–147 to be repealed by the Welfare Reform Act 2012 s 147, Sch 14 Part 1 with effect from a date to be appointed.

WELFARE REFORM ACT 2012

(2012 Chapter 5)

An Act to make provision for universal credit and personal independence payment; to make other provision about social security and tax credits; to make provision about the functions of the registration service, child support maintenance and the use of jobcentres; to establish the Social Mobility and Child Poverty Commission and otherwise amend the Child Poverty Act 2010; and for connected purposes.

[8th March 2012]

BE IT ENACTED by the Queen's most Excellent Majesty, by and with the advice and consent of the Lords Spiritual and Temporal, and Commons, in this present Parliament assembled, and by the authority of the same, as follows:—

PART 3

OTHER BENEFIT CHANGES

Working tax credit

Tax Credits

PART 3

OTHER BENEFIT CHANGES

Working tax credit

76 Calculation of working tax credit

(1) Step 5 in regulation 7(3) of the 2002 Regulations has effect in relation to awards of working tax credit for the whole or part of the relevant year as if from the beginning of the day on 6 April 2011 the percentage to be applied under step 5 in finding the amount of the reduction were 41% (instead of 39%).

(2) Anything done by the Commissioners before the coming into force of this section in relation to awards of working tax credit for the whole or part of the relevant year is to be treated as having been duly done, if it would have been duly done but for being done on the basis that from the beginning of the day on 6 April 2011 the percentage to be applied under step 5 was 41%.

(3) In this section—

"the 2002 Regulations" means the Tax Credits (Income Thresholds and Determination of Rates) Regulations 2002 (SI 2002/2008);

"the Commissioners" means the Commissioners for Her Majesty's Revenue and Customs;

"the relevant year" means the year beginning with 6 April 2011.

PART 5

SOCIAL SECURITY: GENERAL

Recovery of benefits

107 Recovery of child benefit and guardian's allowance

(1) In section 71(8) of the Social Security Administration Act 1992 (recovery of benefits by deduction from prescribed benefits), the words ", other than an amount paid in respect of child benefit or guardian's allowance," are repealed.

(2) In section 69(8) of the Social Security Administration (Northern Ireland) Act 1992 (recovery of benefits by deduction from prescribed benefits), the words ", other than an amount paid in respect of child benefit or guardian's allowance," are repealed.

(3) In the Tax Credits Act 2002, in Schedule 4, paragraphs 2 and 8 are repealed.

Loss of benefit

120 Loss of tax credits

(1) The Tax Credits Act 2002 is amended as follows.

(2) After section 36 there is inserted—

"Loss of tax credit provisions

36A Loss of working tax credit in case of conviction etc for benefit offence

(1) Subsection (4) applies where a person ("the offender")—

(*a*) is convicted of one or more benefit offences in any proceedings, or

(*b*) after being given a notice under subsection (2) of the appropriate penalty provision by an appropriate authority, agrees in the manner specified by the appropriate authority to pay a penalty under the appropriate penalty provision to the appropriate authority, in a case where the offence to which the notice relates is a benefit offence, or

(*c*) is cautioned in respect of one or more benefit offences.

(2) In subsection (1)(*b*)—

(*a*) "the appropriate penalty provision" means section 115A of the Social Security Administration Act 1992 (penalty as alternative to prosecution) or section 109A of the Social Security Administration (Northern Ireland) Act 1992 (the corresponding provision for Northern Ireland);

(*b*) "appropriate authority" means—

(i) in relation to section 115A of the Social Security Administration Act 1992, the Secretary of State or an authority which administers housing benefit or council tax benefit, and

(ii) in relation to section 109A of the Social Security Administration (Northern Ireland) Act 1992, the Department (within the meaning of that Act) or the Northern Ireland Housing Executive.

(3) Subsection (4) does not apply by virtue of subsection (1)(*a*) if, because the proceedings in which the offender was convicted constitute the current set of proceedings for the purposes of section 36C, the restriction in subsection (3) of that section applies in the offender's case.

(4) If this subsection applies and the offender is a person who would, apart from this section, be entitled (whether pursuant to a single or joint claim) to working tax credit at any time within the disqualification period, then, despite that entitlement, working tax credit shall not be payable for any period comprised in the disqualification period—

(*a*) in the case of a single claim, to the offender, or

(*b*) in the case of a joint claim, to the offender or the other member of the couple.

(5) Regulations may provide in relation to cases to which subsection (4)(*b*) would otherwise apply that working tax credit shall be payable, for any period comprised in the disqualification period, as if the amount payable were reduced in such manner as may be prescribed.

(6) For the purposes of this section, the disqualification period, in relation to any disqualifying event, means the relevant period beginning with such date, falling after the date of the disqualifying event, as may be determined by or in accordance with regulations.

(7) For the purposes of subsection (6) the relevant period is—

(*a*) in a case falling within subsection (1)(*a*) where the benefit offence, or one of them, is a relevant offence, the period of three years,

(*b*) in a case falling within subsection (1)(*a*) (but not within paragraph (*a*) above)), the period of 13 weeks, or

(*c*) in a case falling within subsection (1)(*b*) or (*c*), the period of 4 weeks.

(8) The Treasury may by order amend subsection (7)(*a*), (*b*) or (*c*) to substitute a different period for that for the time being specified there.

(9) This section has effect subject to section 36B.

(10) In this section and section 36B—

"benefit offence" means any of the following offences committed on or after the day specified by order made by the Treasury—

(*a*) an offence in connection with a claim for a disqualifying benefit;

(*b*) an offence in connection with the receipt or payment of any amount by way of such a benefit;

(*c*) an offence committed for the purpose of facilitating the commission (whether or not by the same person) of a benefit offence;

(*d*) an offence consisting in an attempt or conspiracy to commit a benefit offence;

"disqualifying benefit" has the meaning given in section 6A(1) of the Social Security Fraud Act 2001;

"disqualifying event" means—

(*a*) the conviction falling within subsection (1)(*a*);

Tax Credits

(*b*) the agreement falling within subsection (1)(*b*);

(*c*) the caution falling within subsection (1)(*c*);

"relevant offence" has the meaning given in section 6B of the Social Security Fraud Act 2001.

36B Section 36A: supplementary

(1) Where—

(*a*) the conviction of any person of any offence is taken in account for the purposes of the application of section 36A in relation to that person, and

(*b*) that conviction is subsequently quashed,

all such payments and other adjustments shall be made as would be necessary if no restriction had been imposed by or under section 36A that could not have been imposed if the conviction had not taken place.

(2) Where, after the agreement of any person ("P") to pay a penalty under the appropriate penalty provision is taken into account for the purposes of the application of section 36A in relation to that person—

(*a*) P's agreement to pay the penalty is withdrawn under subsection (5) of the appropriate penalty provision, or

(*b*) it is decided on an appeal or in accordance with regulations under the Social Security Act 1992 or the Social Security (Northern Ireland) Order 1998 (SI 1998/1506 (N.I. 10)) that the overpayment to which the agreement relates is not recoverable or due,

all such payments and other adjustments shall be made as would be necessary if no restriction had been imposed by or under section 36A that could not have been imposed if P had not agreed to pay the penalty.

(3) Where, after the agreement ("the old agreement") of any person ("P") to pay a penalty under the appropriate penalty provision is taken into account for the purposes of the application of section 36A in relation to P, the amount of any overpayment made to which the penalty relates is revised on an appeal or in accordance with regulations under the Social Security Act 1998 or the Social Security (Northern Ireland) Order 1998—

(*a*) section 36A shall cease to apply by virtue of the old agreement, and

(*b*) subsection (4) shall apply.

(4) Where this subsection applies—

(*a*) if there is a new disqualifying event consisting of—

(i) P's agreement to pay a penalty under the appropriate penalty regime in relation to the revised overpayment, or

(ii) P being cautioned in relation to the offence to which the old agreement relates,

the disqualification period relating to the new disqualifying event shall be reduced by the number of days in so much of the disqualification period relating to the old agreement as had expired when subsection 36A ceased to apply by virtue of the old agreement, and

(*b*) in any other case, all such payments and other adjustments shall be made as would be necessary if no restriction had been imposed by or under section 36A that could not have been imposed if P had not agreed to pay the penalty.

(5) For the purposes of section 36A—

(*a*) the date of a person's conviction in any proceedings of a benefit offence shall be taken to be the date on which the person was found guilty of that offence in those proceedings (whenever the person was sentenced) or in the case mentioned in paragraph (*b*)(ii) the date of the order for absolute discharge, and

(*b*) references to a conviction include references to—

(i) a conviction in relation to which the court makes an order for absolute or conditional discharge,

(ii) an order for absolute discharge made by a court of summary jurisdiction in Scotland under section 246(3) of the Criminal Procedure (Scotland) Act 1995 without proceeding to a conviction, and

(iii) a conviction in Northern Ireland.

(6) In this section "the appropriate penalty provision" has the meaning given by section 36A(2)(*a*).

36C Loss of working tax credit for repeated benefit fraud

(1) If—

(*a*) a person ("the offender") is convicted of one or more benefit offences in a set of proceedings ("the current set of proceedings"),

(*b*) within the period of five years ending on the date on which the benefit offence was, or any of them were, committed, one or more disqualifying events occurred in relation to the offender (the event, or the most recent of them, being referred to in this section as "the earlier disqualifying event"),

(*c*) the current set of proceedings has not been taken into account for the purposes of any previous application of this section in relation to the offender,

(*d*) the earlier disqualifying event has not been taken into account as an earlier disqualifying event for the purposes of any previous application of this section in relation to the offender, and

(*e*) the offender is a person who would, apart from this section, be entitled (whether pursuant to a single or joint claim) to working tax credit at any time within the disqualification period,

then, despite that entitlement, the restriction in subsection (3) shall apply in relation to the payment of that benefit in the offender's case.

(2) The restriction in subsection (3) does not apply if the benefit offence referred to in subsection (1)(*a*), or any of them, is a relevant offence.

(3) Working tax credit shall not be payable for any period comprised in the disqualification period—

(*a*) in the case of a single claim, to the offender, or

(*b*) in the case of a joint claim, to the offender or the other member of the couple.

(4) Regulations may provide in relation to cases to which subsection (3)(*b*) would otherwise apply that working tax credit shall be payable, for any period comprised in the disqualification period, as if the amount payable were reduced in such manner as may be prescribed.

(5) For the purposes of this section the disqualification period, in an offender's case, means the relevant period beginning with a prescribed date falling after the date of the conviction in the current set of proceedings.

(6) For the purposes of subsection (5) the relevant period is—

(*a*) in a case where, within the period of five years ending on the date on which the earlier disqualifying event occurred, a previous disqualifying event occurred in relation to the offender, the period of three years;

(*b*) in any other case, 26 weeks.

(7) In this section and section 36D—

"appropriate penalty provision" has the meaning given in section 36A(2)(*a*);

"benefit offence" means any of the following offences committed on or after the day specified by order made by the Treasury—

(*a*) an offence in connection with a claim for a disqualifying benefit;

(*b*) an offence in connection with the receipt or payment of any amount by way of such a benefit;

(*c*) an offence committed for the purpose of facilitating the commission (whether or not by the same person) of a benefit offence;

(*d*) an offence consisting in an attempt or conspiracy to commit a benefit offence;

"disqualifying benefit" has the meaning given in section 6A(1) of the Social Security Fraud Act 2001;

"disqualifying event" has the meaning given in section 36A(10);

"relevant offence" has the meaning given in section 6B of the Social Security Fraud Act 2001.

(8) Where a person is convicted of more than one benefit offence in the same set of proceedings, there is to be only one disqualifying event in respect of that set of proceedings for the purposes of this section and—

(*a*) subsection (1)(*b*) is satisfied if any of the convictions take place in the five year period there;

(*b*) the event is taken into account for the purposes of subsection (1)(*d*) if any of the convictions have been taken into account as mentioned there;

(*c*) in the case of the earlier disqualifying event mentioned in subsection (6)(*a*), the reference there to the date on which the earlier disqualifying event occurred is a reference to the date on which any of the convictions take place;

(*d*) in the case of the previous disqualifying event mentioned in subsection (6)(*a*), that provision is satisfied if any of the convictions take place in the five year period mentioned there.

(9) The Treasury may by order amend subsection (6) to substitute different periods for those for the time being specified there.

(10) An order under subsection (9) may provide for different periods to apply according to the type of earlier disqualifying event or events occurring in any case.

(11) This section has effect subject to section 36D.

36D Section 36C: supplementary

(1) Where—

(*a*) the conviction of any person of any offence is taken into account for the purposes of the application of section 36C in relation to that person, and

(*b*) that conviction is subsequently quashed,

all such payments and other adjustments shall be made as would be necessary if no restriction had been imposed by or under section 36C that could not have been imposed if the conviction had not taken place.

(2) Subsection (3) applies where, after the agreement of any person ("P") to pay a penalty under the appropriate penalty provision is taken into account for the purposes of the application of section 36C in relation to that person—

(*a*) P's agreement to pay the penalty is withdrawn under subsection (5) of the appropriate penalty provision,

(*b*) it is decided on an appeal or in accordance with regulations under the Social Security Act 1998 or the Social Security (Northern Ireland) Order 1998 (SI 1998/1506 (N.I. 10)) that any overpayment made to which the agreement relates is not recoverable or due, or

(*c*) the amount of any over payment to which the penalty relates is revised on an appeal or in accordance with regulations under the Social Security Act 1998 or the Social Security (Northern Ireland) Order 1998 and there is no new agreement by P to pay a penalty under the appropriate penalty provision in relation to the revised overpayment.

(3) In those circumstances, all such payments and other adjustments shall be made as would be necessary if no restriction had been imposed by or under section 36C that could not have been imposed if P had not agreed to pay the penalty.

(4) For the purposes of section 36C—

(*a*) the date of a person's conviction in any proceedings of a benefit offence shall be taken to be the date on which the person was found guilty of that offence in those proceedings (whenever the person was sentenced) or in the case mentioned in paragraph (*b*)(ii) the date of the order for absolute discharge, and

(*b*) references to a conviction include references to—

(i) a conviction in relation to which the court makes an order for absolute or conditional discharge,

(ii) an order for absolute discharge made by a court of summary jurisdiction in Scotland under section 246(3) of the Criminal Procedure (Scotland) Act 1995 without proceeding to a conviction, and

(iii) a conviction in Northern Ireland.

(5) In section 36C references to any previous application of that section—

(*a*) include references to any previous application of a provision having an effect in Northern Ireland corresponding to provision made by that section, but

(*b*) do not include references to any previous application of that section the effect of which was to impose a restriction for a period comprised in the same disqualification period."

(3) In section 38 (appeals), in subsection (1)—

(*a*) the "and" immediately following paragraph (*c*) is repealed;

(*b*) after that paragraph there is inserted—

"(*ca*) a decision under section 36A or 36C that working tax credit is not payable (or is not payable for a particular period), and".

(4) In section 66 (parliamentary etc control of instruments)—

(*a*) in subsection (1)—

(i) after "no" there is inserted "order or";

(ii) for "them" there is substituted "the order or regulations";

(*b*) in subsection (2) before paragraph (*a*) there is inserted—

"(*za*) an order made by the Treasury under section 36A(8) or 36C(9),

(*zb*) regulations made under section 36A(5) or 36C(4),";

(*c*) in subsection (3)(*a*) at the beginning there is inserted "an order or".

(5) In section 67 (interpretation), at the appropriate place there is inserted—

""cautioned", in relation to any person and any offence, means cautioned after the person concerned has admitted the offence; and "caution" is to be interpreted accordingly;".

Commencement—Welfare Reform Act 2012 (Commencement No 7) Order, SI 2013/178 (section 120 comes into force on 6 April 2013, subject to the following: sub-s (2), and sub-s (1) in so far as it relates to sub-s (2), come into force on 1 February 2013 only for the purpose of making regulations and orders; sub-s (4), and sub-s (1) in so far as it relates to sub-s (4), come into force on 1 February 2013).

Prospective amendments—Sub-s (5) to be repealed by s 147, Sch 14 Pt 12 of this Act, with effect from a date to be appointed.

121 Cautions

(1) In section 6B of the Social Security Fraud Act 2001 (loss of benefit in case of conviction, penalty or caution for benefit offence)—

(*a*) in the heading, for "penalty or caution" there is substituted "or penalty";

(*b*) in subsection (1), after paragraph (*a*) there is inserted "or";

(*c*) subsection (1)(*c*) (cautions) is repealed;

(*d*) in subsection (13), in the definition of "disqualifying event", after "(1)(*a*)" there is inserted "or".

(2) In section 36A of the Tax Credits Act 2002 (loss of tax working tax credit in case of conviction, penalty or caution for benefit offence) subsection (1)(c) (cautions) is repealed.

Administration of tax credits

122 Tax credit fraud: investigation

In section 109A of the Social Security Administration Act 1992 (authorisations for investigators), at the end there is inserted—

"(9) This section and sections 109B to 109C below apply as if—

(*a*) the Tax Credits Act 2002 were relevant social security legislation, and

(*b*) accordingly, child tax credit and working tax credit were relevant social security benefits for the purposes of the definition of "benefit offence"."

Commencement—Welfare Reform Act 2012 (Commencement No 2) Order, SI 2012/1246 (6 June 2012 is the day appointed for the coming into force of ss 122, 123 and 125).

123 Information-sharing for prevention etc of tax credit fraud

(1) Section 122B of the Social Security Administration Act 1992 (supply of government information for fraud prevention etc) is amended as follows.

(2) In subsection (2)(*a*), after "social security" there is inserted "or tax credits".

(3) In subsection (3)—

(*a*) in paragraph (*b*), after "1995" there is inserted ", the Tax Credits Act 2002",

(*b*) in that paragraph, the final "or" is repealed, and

(*c*) after paragraph (*c*) there is inserted

"or

(*d*) it is supplied under section 127 of the Welfare Reform Act 2012."

Commencement—Welfare Reform Act 2012 (Commencement No 2) Order, SI 2012/1246 (6 June 2012 is the day appointed for the coming into force of ss 122, 123 and 125).

124 Tax credit fraud: prosecution and penalties

In section 35 of the Tax Credits Act 2002 (offence of fraud), for subsection (2) there is substituted—

"(2) Where a person is alleged to have committed an offence under this section in relation to payments of a tax credit not exceeding £20,000, the offence is triable summarily only.

(3) A person who commits an offence under this section is liable on summary conviction pursuant to subsection (2) to imprisonment for a term not exceeding the applicable term, or a fine not exceeding level 5 on the standard scale, or both.

(4) In subsection (3) the applicable term is—

(*a*) for conviction in England and Wales, 51 weeks;

(*b*) for conviction in Scotland or Northern Ireland, 6 months.

(5) Where a person is alleged to have committed an offence under this section in any other case, the offence is triable either on indictment or summarily.

(6) A person who commits an offence under this section is liable—

(*a*) on summary conviction pursuant to subsection (5), to imprisonment for a term not exceeding the applicable term, or a fine not exceeding the statutory maximum, or both;

(*b*) on conviction on indictment pursuant to subsection (5) to imprisonment for a term not exceeding 7 years, or a fine, or both.

(7) In subsection (6)(*a*) the applicable term is—

(*a*) for conviction in England and Wales or Scotland, 12 months;

Tax Credits

(*b*) for conviction in Northern Ireland, 6 months.

(8) In relation to an offence under this section committed in England and Wales before the commencement of section 281(5) of the Criminal Justice Act 2003, the reference in subsection (4)(*a*) to 51 weeks is to be read as a reference to 6 months.

(9) In relation to an offence under this section committed in England and Wales before the commencement of section 154(1) of the Criminal Justice Act 2003, the reference in subsection (7)(*a*) to 12 months is to be read as a reference to 6 months.

(10) In England and Wales—

(*a*) subsection (1) of section 116 of the Social Security Administration Act 1992 (legal proceedings) applies in relation to proceedings for an offence under this section;

(*b*) subsections (2)(*a*) and (3)(*a*) of that section apply in relation to proceedings for an offence under this section which is triable summarily only pursuant to subsection (2) above.

(11) In Scotland, subsection (7)(*a*) and (*b*) of section 116 of the Social Security Administration Act 1992 (legal proceedings) apply in relation to proceedings for an offence under this section which is triable summarily only pursuant to subsection (2) above.

(12) In Northern Ireland—

(a) subsection (1) of section 110 of the Social Security Administration (Northern Ireland) Act 1992 (legal proceedings) applies in relation to proceedings for an offence under this section;

(b) subsections (2)(*a*) and (3)(*a*) of that section apply in relation to proceedings for an offence under this section which is triable summarily only pursuant to subsection (2) above."

125 Unauthorised disclosure of information relating to tax credit offences

In Schedule 4 to the Social Security Administration Act 1992 (persons employed in social security administration or adjudication), in paragraph 1 of Part 2, after "security," there is inserted "to the investigation or prosecution of offences relating to tax credits,".

Commencement—Welfare Reform Act 2012 (Commencement No 2) Order, SI 2012/1246 (6 June 2012 is the day appointed for the coming into force of ss 122, 123 and 125).

126 Tax credits: transfer of functions etc

(1) Her Majesty may by Order in Council—

(*a*) transfer to the Secretary of State any tax credit function of the Treasury or the Commissioners;

(*b*) direct that any tax credit function of the Treasury or the Commissioners is to be exercisable concurrently with the Secretary of State or is to cease to be so exercisable.

(2) Provision within subsection (1) may be limited so as to apply only in relation to cases within a specified description.

(3) Her Majesty may by Order in Council, as Her Majesty considers appropriate—

(*a*) make provision in connection with a transfer or direction under subsection (1);

(*b*) make other provision within one or more of the following sub-paragraphs—

(i) provision applying (with or without modifications) in relation to tax credits any provision of primary or secondary legislation relating to social security;

(ii) provision combining or linking any aspect of the payment and management of tax credits with any aspect of the administration of social security;

(iii) provision about the use or supply of information held for purposes connected with tax credits, including (in particular) provision authorising or requiring its use or supply for other purposes;

(iv) in relation to information held for purposes not connected with tax credits, provision authorising or requiring its use or supply for purposes connected with tax credits.

(4) An Order may make provision under subsection (3)(*b*) only if—

(*a*) the Order also makes provision under subsection (1), or

(*b*) a previous Order has made provision under subsection (1).

(5) Provision within subsection (3)—

(*a*) may confer functions on, or remove functions from, the Secretary of State, the Treasury, the Commissioners, a Northern Ireland department or any other person;

(*b*) may (in particular) authorise the Secretary of State and the Commissioners to enter into arrangements from time to time under which the Commissioners are to provide services to the Secretary of State in connection with tax credits.

(6) Provision within subsection (3)—

(*a*) may expand the scope of the conduct which constitutes an offence under any primary or secondary legislation, but may not increase the scope of any punishment for which a person may be liable on conviction for the offence;

(*b*) may expand the scope of the conduct in respect of which a civil penalty may be imposed under any primary or secondary legislation, but may not increase the maximum amount of the penalty.

(7) An Order under this section may include such consequential, supplementary, incidental or transitional provision as Her Majesty considers appropriate including (for example)—

(*a*) provision for transferring or apportioning property, rights or liabilities (whether or not they would otherwise be capable of being transferred or apportioned);

(*b*) provision for substituting any person for any other person in any instrument or other document or in any legal proceedings;

(*c*) provision with respect to the application in relation to the Crown of provision made by the Order.

(8) A certificate issued by the Secretary of State that any property, rights or liabilities set out in the certificate have been transferred or apportioned by an Order under this section as set out in the certificate is conclusive evidence of the matters so set out.

(9) An Order under this section may amend, repeal or revoke any primary or secondary legislation.

(10) A statutory instrument containing an Order under this section is subject to annulment in pursuance of a resolution of either House of Parliament.

(11) In this section references to tax credits are to child tax credit or working tax credit or both.

(12) In this section references to primary or secondary legislation are to such legislation whenever passed or made.

(13) In this section—

"the Commissioners" means the Commissioners for Her Majesty's Revenue and Customs;

"primary legislation" means an Act (including this Act) or Northern Ireland legislation;

"secondary legislation" means an instrument made under primary legislation (including an Order under this section);

"tax credit functions" means functions so far as relating to tax credits conferred by or under any primary or secondary legislation.

(14) In section 5A(3) of the Ministers of the Crown Act 1975, for "section 5(1)" there is substituted "section 5(1)(*a*) or (*b*)".

Orders—Tax Credits (Exercise of Functions) Order 2014, SI 2014/3280.

Tax Credits (Exercise of Functions in relation to Northern Ireland and Notices for Recovery of Tax Credit Overpayments) Order, SI 2017/781.

Information-sharing: Secretary of State and HMRC

127 Information-sharing between Secretary of State and HMRC

(1) This subsection applies to information which is held for the purposes of any HMRC functions—

(a) by the Commissioners for Her Majesty's Revenue and Customs, or

(b) by a person providing services to them.

(2) Information to which subsection (1) applies may be supplied—

(a) to the Secretary of State, or to a person providing services to the Secretary of State, or

(b) to a Northern Ireland Department, or to a person providing services to a Northern Ireland Department,

for use for the purposes of departmental functions.

(3) This subsection applies to information which is held for the purposes of any departmental functions—

(a) by the Secretary of State, or by a person providing services to the Secretary of State, or

(b) by a Northern Ireland Department, or by a person providing services to a Northern Ireland Department.

(4) Information to which subsection (3) applies may be supplied—

(a) to the Commissioners for Her Majesty's Revenue and Customs, or

(b) to a person providing services to them,

for use for the purposes of HMRC functions.

(5) Information supplied under this section must not be supplied by the recipient of the information to any other person or body without—

(a) the authority of the Commissioners for Her Majesty's Revenue and Customs, in the case of information supplied under subsection (2);

(b) the authority of the Secretary of State, in the case of information held as mentioned in subsection (3)(a) and supplied under subsection (4);

(c) the authority of the relevant Northern Ireland Department, in the case of information held as mentioned in subsection (3)(b) and supplied under subsection (4).

(6) Where information supplied under this section has been used for the purposes for which it was supplied, it is lawful for it to be used for any purposes for which information held for those purposes could be used.

(7) In this section—

"departmental functions" means functions relating to—

(*a*) social security,

(*b*) employment or training, . . .[1]
(*c*) the investigation or prosecution of offences relating to tax credits; [or
(*d*) child support;][1]

"HMRC function" means any function—
(a) for which the Commissioners for Her Majesty's Revenue and Customs are responsible by virtue of section 5 of the Commissioners for Revenue and Customs Act 2005, . . .[3]
(b) which relates to a matter listed in Schedule 1 to that Act, . . .[4]
[(c) which is conferred by or under the Childcare Payments Act 2014][3] [, or
(d) which is conferred by or under section 2 of, or Schedule 2 to, the Savings (Government Contributions) Act 2017 (bonuses in respect of savings in Help-to-Save accounts);][4]

"Northern Ireland Department" means any of the following—
(a) the Department for Social Development;
(b) the Department of Finance and Personnel;
(c) the Department for Employment and Learning.

(8) For the purposes of this section any reference to functions relating to social security includes a reference to functions relating to—
(a) statutory payments as defined in section 4C(11) of the Social Security Contributions and Benefits Act 1992;
(b) maternity allowance under section 35 of that Act;
(c) statutory payments as defined in section 4C(11) of the Social Security Contributions and Benefits (Northern Ireland) Act 1992;
(d) maternity allowance under section 35 [or 35B][2] of that Act.

(9) This section does not limit the circumstances in which information may be supplied apart from this section.

(10) (*inserts* SSA 1998 s 3(1A)(*d*))

Commencement—This section came into effect on 8 May 2012 (two months after the Act was passed by virtue of s 150(2)(*f*).

Amendments—[1] In sub-s (7), in definition "departmental functions", word "or" in para (*b*) repealed, and para (*d*) and preceding word "or" inserted, by the Public Bodies (Child Maintenance and Enforcement Commission: Abolition and Transfer of Functions) Order, SI 2012/2007 art 3(2), Schedule paras 101, 102 with effect from 1 August 2012.

[2] Words inserted in sub-s (8)(d) by the Social Security (Maternity Allowance) (Participating Wife or Civil Partner of Self-employed Earner) Regulations, SI 2014/606 reg 4 with effect in relation to the payment of maternity allowance in cases where a woman's expected week of confinement (within the meaning of SSCBA 1992 s 35) begins on or after 27 July 2014.

[3] In sub-s (7), in definition of "HMRC function", word ", or" at the end of para (a) repealed, and para (c) and preceding word "or" inserted, by the Childcare Payments Act 2014 s 27(6)(a) with effect for the powers to make regulations only, from 17 December 2014, and for remaining purposes, from a date to be appointed (the Childcare Payments Act 2014 s 75(1)(c), (2)).

[4] In sub-s (7), in definition of "HMRC function", words ", or" at the end of para (b) repealed, and para (d) and preceding word "or" inserted, by the Savings (Government Contributions) Act 2017 s 2, Sch 2 para 17(8) with effect from 17 January 2017.

PART 7
FINAL

147 Repeals

Schedule 14 contains consequential repeals.

148 Financial provision

There shall be paid out of money provided by Parliament—
(*a*) sums paid by the Secretary of State by way of universal credit or personal independence payment;
(*b*) any other expenditure incurred in consequence of this Act by a Minister of the Crown or the Commissioners for Her Majesty's Revenue and Customs;
(*c*) any increase attributable to this Act in the sums payable under any other Act out of money so provided.

149 Extent

(1) This Act extends to England and Wales and Scotland only, subject as follows.
(2) The following provisions extend to England and Wales, Scotland and Northern Ireland—
(*a*) section 32 (power to make consequential and supplementary provision: universal credit);
(*b*) section 33 (abolition of benefits);
(*c*) section 76 (calculation of working tax credit);
(*d*) section 92 (power to make consequential and supplementary provision: personal independence payment);
(*e*) section 126(1) to (13) (tax credits: transfer of functions etc);
(*f*) section 127(1) to (9) (information-sharing between Secretary of State and HMRC);
(*g*) this Part, excluding Schedule 14 (repeals).
(3) Sections 128 and 129 extend to England and Wales only.

(4) Any amendment or repeal made by this Act has the same extent as the enactment to which it relates.

150 Commencement

(1) The following provisions of this Act come into force on the day on which it is passed—

(*a*) section 76 (calculation of working tax credit);
(*b*) section 103 and Schedule 12 (supersession of decisions of former appellate bodies) (but see section 103(2));
(*c*) section 108 (application of Limitation Act 1980) (but see section 108(4));
(*d*) section 109 (recovery of fines etc by deductions from employment and support allowance) (but see section 109(3));
(*e*) section 126 (tax credits: transfer of functions etc);
(*f*) this Part, excluding Schedule 14 (repeals).

(2) The following provisions of this Act come into force at the end of the period of two months beginning with the day on which it is passed—

(*a*) section 50 (dual entitlement to employment and support allowance and jobseeker's allowance);
(*b*) section 60 and Part 6 of Schedule 14 (claimants dependent on drugs etc);
(*c*) sections 71 and 72 (social fund: purposes of discretionary payments and determination of amount or value of budgeting loan);
(*d*) section 107 (recovery of child benefit and guardian's allowance);
(*e*) section 111 (time limit for legal proceedings);
(*f*) section 127 and Part 13 of Schedule 14 (information-sharing between Secretary of State and HMRC);
(*g*) section 134 (information-sharing for social security or employment purposes etc);
(*h*) section 135 (functions of registration service);
(*i*) section 142 (exclusion of child support maintenance from individual voluntary arrangements);
(*j*) section 145 and Schedule 13 (Social Mobility and Child Poverty Commission);
(*k*) Part 2 of Schedule 14 (entitlement to jobseeker's allowance without seeking employment).

(3) The remaining provisions of this Act come into force on such day as the Secretary of State may by order made by statutory instrument appoint.

(4) An order under subsection (3) may—

(*a*) appoint different days for different purposes;
(*b*) appoint different days for different areas in relation to—
   (i) any provision of Part 1 (universal credit) or of Part 1 of Schedule 14;
   (ii) section 61 or 62 (entitlement to work: jobseeker's allowance and employment and support allowance);
   (iii) any provision of Part 4 (personal independence payment) or of Part 9 of Schedule 14;
   (iv) section 102 (consideration of revision before appeal);
(*c*) make such transitory or transitional provision, or savings, as the Secretary of State considers necessary or expedient.

Orders—Welfare Reform Act 2012 (Commencement No 1) Order, SI 2012/863.
Welfare Reform Act 2012 (Commencement No 2) Order, SI 2012/1246.
Welfare Reform Act 2012 (Commencement No 2) (Amendment) Order, SI 2012/1440.
Welfare Reform Act 2012 (Commencement No 3, Savings Provision) Order, SI 2012/1651.
Welfare Reform Act 2012 (Commencement No 4) Order, SI 2012/2530.
Welfare Reform Act 2012 (Commencement No 5) Order, SI 2012/2946.
Welfare Reform Act 2012 (Commencement No 6 and Savings Provisions) Order, SI 2012/3090.
Welfare Reform Act 2012 (Commencement No 7) Order, SI 2013/178.
Welfare Reform Act 2012 (Commencement No 8 and Savings and Transitional Provisions) Order, SI 2013/358.
Welfare Reform Act 2012 (Commencement No 9 and Transitional and Transitory Provisions and Commencement No 8 and Savings and Transitional Provisions (Amendment)) Order 2013, SI 2013/983.
Welfare Reform Act 2012 (Commencement No 10) Order 2013, SI 2013/1250.
Welfare Reform Act 2012 (Commencement No 11 and Transitional and Transitory Provisions and Commencement No 9 and Transitional and Transitory Provisions (Amendment)) Order 2013, SI 2013/1511.
Welfare Reform Act 2012 (Commencement No 12) Order 2013, SI 2013/2534.
Welfare Reform Act 2012 (Commencement No 13 and Transitional and Transitory Provisions) Order, SI 2013/2657.
Welfare Reform Act 2012 (Commencement No 14 and Transitional and Transitory Provisions) Order 2013, SI 2013/2846.
Child Maintenance and Other Payments Act 2008 (Commencement No 12 and Savings Provisions) and the Welfare Reform Act 2012 (Commencement No 15) Order 2013, SI 2013/2947.
Welfare Reform Act 2012 (Commencement No 16 and Transitional and Transitory Provisions) Order 2014, SI 2014/209.
Welfare Reform Act 2012 (Commencement No 9, 11, 13, 14 and 16 and Transitional and Transitory Provisions (Amendment)) Order 2014, SI 2014/1452
Welfare Reform Act 2012 (Commencement No 17 and Transitional and Transitory Provisions) Order 2014, SI 2014/1583
Child Maintenance and Other Payments Act 2008 (Commencement No 14 and Transitional Provisions) and the Welfare Reform Act 2012 (Commencement No 18 and Transitional and Savings Provisions) Order, SI 2014/1635.

Welfare Reform Act 2012 (Commencement No 9, 11, 13 14, 16 and 17 and Transitional and Transitory Provisions (Amendment)) Order 2014, SI 2014/1661.

Welfare Reform Act 2012 (Commencement No 9, 11, 13, 14, 16 and 17 and Transitional and Transitory Provisions (Amendment) (No 2)) Order 2014, SI 2014/1923.

Welfare Reform Act 2012 (Commencement No 19 and Transitional and Transitory Provisions and Commencement No 9 and Transitional and Transitory Provisions (Amendment)) Order 2014, SI 2014/2321.

Welfare Reform Act 2012 (Commencement No 9, 11, 13 14, 16, 17 and 19 and Transitional and Transitory Provisions (Amendment)) Order 2014, SI 2014/3067.

Welfare Reform Act 2012 (Commencement No 9, 11, 13, 14, 16, 17 and 19 and Transitional and Transitory Provisions (Amendment)) Order 2015, SI 2015/32.

Welfare Reform Act 2012 (Commencement No 21 and Transitional and Transitory Provisions) Order 2015, SI 2015/33.

Welfare Reform Act 2012 (Commencement No 22 and Transitional and Transitory Provisions) Order 2015, SI 2015/101.

Welfare Reform Act 2012 (Commencement No 23 and Transitional and Transitory Provisions) Order 2015, SI 2015/634.

Welfare Reform Act 2012 (Commencement No 23 and Transitional and Transitory Provisions) (Amendment) Order 2015, SI 2015/740.

Welfare Reform Act 2012 (Commencement No 24 and Transitional and Transitory Provisions and Commencement No 9 and Transitional and Transitory Provisions (Amendment)) Order 2015, SI 2015/1537.

Welfare Reform Act 2012 (Commencement No 25 and Transitional and Transitory Provisions) Order, SI 2015/1930.

Welfare Reform Act 2012 (Commencement No 26 and Transitional and Transitory Provisions and Commencement No 22, 23 and 24 and Transitional and Transitory Provisions (Modification)) Order, SI 2016/33.

Welfare Reform Act 2012 (Commencement No 27 and Transitional and Transitory Provisions and Commencement No 22, 23 and 24 and Transitional and Transitory Provisions (Modification)) Order, SI 2016/407.

Welfare Reform Act 2012 (Commencement No 28) Order, SI 2016/511.

Welfare Reform Act 2012 (Commencement No 13, 14, 16, 19, 22, 23 and 24 and Transitional and Transitory Provisions (Modification)) Order, SI 2016/596.

151 Short title

This Act may be cited as the Welfare Reform Act 2012.

SCHEDULE 14

REPEALS

Section 147

PART 1

ABOLITION OF BENEFITS SUPERSEDED BY UNIVERSAL CREDIT

Short title and chapter	*Extent of repeal*
Tax Credits Act 2002 (c 21)	Part 1 (but not Schedule 1 or 3).
Civil Partnership Act 2004 (c 33)	In Schedule 24, paragraphs 42 to 46, 55, 118 to 122 and 144 to 147.

PART 13

INFORMATION-SHARING BETWEEN SECRETARY OF STATE AND HMRC

Short title and chapter	*Extent of repeal*
Tax Credits Act 2002 (c 21).	In Schedule 5— (*a*) in paragraph 4(2) "social security or"; (*b*) paragraph 4(3) (*c*) in paragraph 4(3A) "social security,"; (*d*) in paragraph 4(3B), "social security or"; (*e*) in paragraph 4(4), "(3) and"; (*f*) in paragraph 6(1), "social security,"; (*g*) in paragraph 6(1A), "social security," (*h*) in paragraph 6(3) "social security or"; (*i*) paragraph 12(*a*).

CHILDCARE PAYMENTS ACT 2014

2014 Chapter 28

An Act to make provision for and in connection with the making of payments to persons towards the costs of childcare; and to restrict the availability of an exemption from income tax in respect of the provision for an employee of childcare, or vouchers for obtaining childcare, under a scheme operated by or on behalf of the employer.

[17th December 2014]

Special rules affecting tax credit and universal credit claimants

30 Termination of tax credit awards

(1) In this section "the relevant day", in relation to a person who has made a declaration of eligibility for an entitlement period, means—

(*a*) the first day of the entitlement period, or

(*b*) if later, the day on which the declaration of eligibility for the entitlement period was made.

(2) This subsection applies where—

(*a*) a person ("P") has made a valid declaration of eligibility for an entitlement period,

(*b*) an award of a tax credit is or has been made—

(i) to P or to a person who is P's partner on the relevant day (whether on a single claim or a joint claim), or

(ii) to both of them on a joint claim, and

(*c*) the award is for a period that includes the relevant day.

(3) Where subsection (2) applies, the award of the tax credit terminates immediately before the relevant day, regardless of whether the decision on the claim was made before or after the relevant day.

This is subject to subsections (4) to (7).

(4) Where a person has made a valid declaration of eligibility for more than one entitlement period beginning during the determination period (see subsection (5)), the award of the tax credit is terminated immediately before the day which is the relevant day in relation to the first of those entitlement periods.

(5) In subsection (4) the "determination period", in relation to an award of a tax credit, means the period—

(*a*) beginning with the day on which the claim for the tax credit was made, and

(*b*) ending with the day on which the decision on the claim was made.

(6) Where—

(*a*) a person has applied for a review under section 21A of the Tax Credits Act 2002 of a decision not to make an award of a tax credit or to terminate such an award, and

(*b*) the conclusion on the review is that the decision is varied or cancelled,

subsection (3) does not apply in respect of the award in relation to any entitlement period beginning before the day on which the person is notified of the conclusion on the review.

(7) Where—

(*a*) a person has brought an appeal under section 38 of the Tax Credits Act 2002 against a decision not to make an award of a tax credit or to terminate such an award, and

(*b*) the appeal is upheld,

subsection (3) does not apply in respect of the award in relation to any entitlement period beginning before the day on which the person is notified of the decision on the appeal.

(8) Where an award of a tax credit made to a person is terminated by virtue of this section—

(*a*) HMRC must notify the person of that fact,

(*b*) the tax credits legislation applies in relation to the person with such modifications as may be made in regulations, and

(*c*) the amount of any tax credit to which the person is entitled is to be calculated in accordance with the tax credits legislation, subject to any such modifications of that legislation.

(9) Regulations may make further provision for the purpose of securing that, where a person makes a valid declaration of eligibility, any entitlement of the person, or a person who is the person's partner, to payments under the tax credits legislation ceases immediately before the relevant day.

(10) Regulations under subsection (9) may, in particular—

(*a*) provide that the tax credits legislation applies in relation to the person whose entitlement to such payments has ceased with such modifications as may be specified in the regulations, and

(*b*) apply any provision of this section with such modifications as may be so specified.

(11) If—

(*a*) a person makes a declaration of eligibility for an entitlement period, and

(*b*) at any time after the relevant day HMRC determine that the declaration was not valid,

that does not affect anything done by virtue of this section as a result of the making of the declaration.

Tax Credits

(12) In this section—

"joint claim" and "single claim" have the same meaning as in the Tax Credits Act 2002;

"the tax credits legislation" means the Tax Credits Act 2002 and any provision made under that Act.

(13) This section ceases to have effect when the repeal of Part 1 of the Tax Credits Act 2002 made by Schedule 14 to the Welfare Reform Act 2012 has fully come into force.

Commencement—Childcare Payments Act 2014 (Commencement No 2) Regulations, SI 2016/1083 reg 2(*d*) (the day appointed for the coming into force of this section is 14 November 2016, with effect only for the purposes of the trial of the childcare payment scheme taking place between 14 November 2016 and 15 May 2017).

Childcare Payments Act 2014 (Commencement No 3 and Transitional Provisions) Regulations, SI 2017/578 reg 3(*d*) (the day appointed for the coming into force of this section, in so far as it is not already in force, is 21 April 2017).

32 Power to disqualify tax credit claimants from obtaining top-up payments

(1) This section applies in relation to a person ("P") if—

(*a*) P, or a person who is P's partner, makes a claim (whether a single or a joint claim) that results in an award of a tax credit being made for a relevant period (see subsection (2)),

(*b*) the claim is made during an entitlement period for which P or P's partner has made a valid declaration of eligibility,

(*c*) there has not been a change of circumstances in relation to P or P's partner since the beginning of the entitlement period, and

(*d*) P, or a person who is P's partner, makes a declaration of eligibility within the period of 12 months beginning with the day on which the claim was made.

(2) In subsection (1)(*a*) "relevant period", in relation to an entitlement period, means a period that includes the whole or any part of the entitlement period.

(3) If this section applies in relation to a person, HMRC may give the person a warning notice.

(4) A warning notice is a notice stating that, if this section or section 33 (power to disqualify universal credit claimants from obtaining top-up payments) applies in relation to the person at any time during the period of 4 years beginning with the day on which the notice is given, HMRC may give the person a disqualification notice (see section 34).

(5) Regulations may make provision—

(*a*) about what is, or is not, to be regarded as a change of circumstances in relation to a person for the purposes of this section;

(*b*) specifying cases in which something which would otherwise be a change of circumstances is not to be treated as such for the purposes of this section.

(6) Regulations may amend subsection (1)(*d*) so as to substitute a different period for the period for the time being specified there.

(7) In this section "joint claim" and "single claim" have the same meaning as in the Tax Credits Act 2002.

Commencement—Childcare Payments Act 2014 (Commencement No 2) Regulations, SI 2016/1083 reg 2(*e*) (the day appointed for the coming into force of this section is 14 November 2016, with effect only for the purposes of the trial of the childcare payment scheme taking place between 14 November 2016 and 15 May 2017).

Childcare Payments Act 2014 (Commencement No 3 and Transitional Provisions) Regulations, SI 2017/578 reg 3(*d*) (the day appointed for the coming into force of this section, in so far as it is not already in force, is 21 April 2017).

Regulations—Childcare Payments (Eligibility) Regulations, SI 2015/448.

Cross references—Childcare Payments (Eligibility) Regulations, SI 2015/448 reg 18 (change of circumstances for the purposes of this section).

34 Disqualification notices

(1) If—

(*a*) a person has been given a warning notice under section 32(3) or 33(3), and

(*b*) section 32 or 33 applies in relation to the person at any time during the period of 4 years beginning with the day on which the notice is given,

HMRC may give the person a disqualification notice under this section.

(2) Where a person has been given a disqualification notice—

(*a*) the person may not open a childcare account,

(*b*) no qualifying payments may be made into any childcare account held by the person, and

(*c*) any declaration of eligibility made by the person for an entitlement period for which the notice has effect is not valid.

(3) A disqualification notice has effect for the period specified in the notice.

(4) But a disqualification notice may not have effect for a period longer than 3 years.

(5) The period specified in a disqualification notice—

(*a*) may begin before the day on which the notice is given, but

(*b*) may not begin before the start of the entitlement period for which the declaration of eligibility that resulted in the giving of the notice was made.

(6) If HMRC give a person a disqualification notice, HMRC must give a copy of the notice to any person or body which provides childcare accounts.

(7) HMRC may revoke a disqualification notice.

Commencement—Childcare Payments Act 2014 (Commencement No 2) Regulations, SI 2016/1083 reg 2(*e*) (the day appointed for the coming into force of this section is 14 November 2016, with effect only for the purposes of the trial of the childcare payment scheme taking place between 14 November 2016 and 15 May 2017).

Childcare Payments Act 2014 (Commencement No 3 and Transitional Provisions) Regulations, SI 2017/578 reg 3(*d*) (the day appointed for the coming into force of this section, in so far as it is not already in force, is 21 April 2017).

Recovery of top-up payments

35 Recovery of top-up payments where tax credits award made on a review

(1) This section applies where—

(*a*) a person ("P"), or (in the case of a joint claim) P or P's partner at the time of the claim, applies for a review under section 21A of the Tax Credits Act 2002 of a decision not to make an award of a tax credit or to terminate such an award, and

(*b*) the conclusion on the review is that the decision is varied or cancelled.

(2) P is liable to pay HMRC an amount equal to the sum of—

(*a*) any top-up payments made to P for an entitlement period falling wholly within the relevant period, and

(*b*) the relevant proportion of the sum of any top-up payments made to P for an entitlement period falling partly within the relevant period.

(3) The "relevant period" means the period in relation to which the following conditions are met—

(*a*) it falls within the review period (see subsection (4)),

(*b*) it is a period for which an award of a tax credit is made, or continues, as a result of the variation or cancellation of the decision, and

(*c*) where the award has been made to P and P's partner on a joint claim, the person who was P's partner at the time of the claim has been P's partner throughout the period.

(4) The "review period" means the period which—

(*a*) begins with the day on which the decision was made, and

(*b*) ends with—

(i) the day on which the person who applied for the review is notified of its conclusions, or

(ii) if that day falls within an entitlement period for which P has made a valid declaration of eligibility, the last day of the entitlement period.

(5) In subsection (2)(*b*) the "relevant proportion", in relation to top-up payments made for an entitlement period, means a proportion equal to the proportion of the entitlement period which falls within the relevant period.

(6) In this section "joint claim" has the same meaning as in the Tax Credits Act 2002.

(7) For provision about terminating an award of a tax credit when a declaration of eligibility is made for a subsequent entitlement period, see section 30.

Commencement—Childcare Payments Act 2014 (Commencement No 2) Regulations, SI 2016/1083 reg 2(*e*) (the day appointed for the coming into force of this section is 14 November 2016, with effect only for the purposes of the trial of the childcare payment scheme taking place between 14 November 2016 and 15 May 2017).

Childcare Payments Act 2014 (Commencement No 3 and Transitional Provisions) Regulations, SI 2017/578 reg 3(*d*) (the day appointed for the coming into force of this section, in so far as it is not already in force, is 21 April 2017).

36 Recovery of top-up payments where tax credits award made on appeal

(1) This section applies where—

(*a*) a person ("P"), or (in the case of a joint claim) P or P's partner at the time of the claim, has brought an appeal under section 38 of the Tax Credits Act 2002 against a decision not to make an award of a tax credit or to terminate such an award, and

(*b*) the appeal is upheld.

(2) P is liable to pay HMRC an amount equal to the sum of—

(*a*) any top-up payments made to P for an entitlement period falling wholly within the relevant period, and

(*b*) the relevant proportion of the sum of any top-up payments made to P for an entitlement period falling partly within the relevant period.

(3) The "relevant period" means the period in relation to which the following conditions are met—

(*a*) it falls within the appeal period (see subsection (4)),

(*b*) it is a period for which an award of a tax credit is made, or continues, as a result of the appeal being upheld, and

(*c*) where the award has been made to P and P's partner on a joint claim, the person who was P's partner at the time of the claim has been P's partner throughout the period.

(4) The "appeal period" means the period which—

(*a*) begins with the day on which the decision was made, and

(*b*) ends with—

(i) the day on which the person who brought the appeal is notified of the decision on the appeal, or

(ii) if that day falls within an entitlement period for which P has made a valid declaration of eligibility, the last day of the entitlement period.

(5) In subsection (2)(*b*) the "relevant proportion", in relation to top-up payments made for an entitlement period, means a proportion equal to the proportion of the entitlement period which falls within the relevant period.

(6) In this section "joint claim" has the same meaning as in the Tax Credits Act 2002.

(7) For provision about terminating an award of a tax credit when a declaration of eligibility is made for a subsequent entitlement period, see section 30.

Commencement—Childcare Payments Act 2014 (Commencement No 2) Regulations, SI 2016/1083 reg 2(*e*) (the day appointed for the coming into force of this section is 14 November 2016, with effect only for the purposes of the trial of the childcare payment scheme taking place between 14 November 2016 and 15 May 2017).

Childcare Payments Act 2014 (Commencement No 3 and Transitional Provisions) Regulations, SI 2017/578 reg 3(*d*) (the day appointed for the coming into force of this section, in so far as it is not already in force, is 21 April 2017).

41 Assessment and enforcement of recoverable amounts

(1) Where a person is liable under any of sections 35 to 40 ("the relevant section") to pay an amount to HMRC—

(*a*) HMRC may assess the amount, and

(*b*) if they do so, they must notify the person.

(2) No assessment may be made under this section after—

(*a*) the end of the period specified in subsection (3), or

(*b*) if earlier, the end of the period of 12 months beginning with the day on which HMRC first believed, or had reasonable grounds for believing, that the person was liable under the relevant section to pay an amount to HMRC.

(3) The period referred to in subsection (2)(*a*) is—

(*a*) the period of 4 years beginning with the day on which the person became liable under the relevant section to pay an amount to HMRC, or

(*b*) in a case where the person became liable under the relevant section to pay an amount to HMRC as a result of the person's dishonesty, the period of 20 years beginning with that day.

(4) Where two or more persons—

(*a*) are liable under section 40(3) or (4) to pay an amount to HMRC, and

(*b*) have each been notified of an assessment under this section in respect of the amount,

each of those persons is jointly and severally liable to pay the amount assessed under this section.

(5) Where a person is notified of an assessment under this section, the amount payable as a result of the assessment must be paid—

(*a*) in a case where the person does not apply for a review of the assessment within the period specified in section 57(2)(*a*), before the end of that period,

(*b*) in a case where the person applies for a review of the assessment but does not give notice of an appeal against the assessment, before the end of the period in which notice of such an appeal could have been given, or

(*c*) in a case where notice of such an appeal has been given, on the day on which the appeal is determined or withdrawn.

(6) A requirement to pay an amount to HMRC under any of sections 35 to 40 may be enforced as if the amount were income tax charged in an assessment and due and payable.

See also sections 52 to 54 (which contain further powers to recover amounts owed to HMRC).

Commencement—Childcare Payments Act 2014 (Commencement No 2) Regulations, SI 2016/1083 reg 2(*f*) (the day appointed for the coming into force of this section is 14 November 2016, with effect only for the purposes of the trial of the childcare payment scheme taking place between 14 November 2016 and 15 May 2017).

Childcare Payments Act 2014 (Commencement No 3 and Transitional Provisions) Regulations, SI 2017/578 reg 3(*d*) (the day appointed for the coming into force of this section, in so far as it is not already in force, is 21 April 2017).

Other enforcement powers

52 Deduction of recoverable amounts from tax credit awards

(1) This section applies where, as a result of a review of, or an appeal against, a tax credits decision—

(*a*) a person is required to pay an amount ("the relevant debt") to HMRC under section 35 or 36, and

(*b*) an amount of tax credit ("the award") is payable to the person or to the person and the person's partner jointly.

(2) The relevant debt may be deducted from the award before it is paid.

(3) The requirement to pay the relevant debt is discharged to the extent that it is deducted from the award under this section.

(4) In this section "tax credits decision" means a decision not to make an award of a tax credit or to terminate such an award.

(5) This section ceases to have effect when the repeal of Part 1 of the Tax Credits Act 2002 made by Schedule 14 to the Welfare Reform Act 2012 has fully come into force.

Commencement—Childcare Payments Act 2014 (Commencement No 2) Regulations, SI 2016/1083 reg 2(*g*) (the day appointed for the coming into force of this section is 14 November 2016, with effect only for the purposes of the trial of the childcare payment scheme taking place between 14 November 2016 and 15 May 2017).

Childcare Payments Act 2014 (Commencement No 3 and Transitional Provisions) Regulations, SI 2017/578 reg 3(*e*) (the day appointed for the coming into force of this section, in so far as it is not already in force, is 21 April 2017).

54 Set-off

(1) This section applies where—

(*a*) an amount ("the relevant debt") is due and payable to HMRC under this Act by a person who holds a childcare account in respect of a child,

(*b*) the childcare account is not active (see section 17(3)), and

(*c*) the relevant debt consists of an amount which the person is liable to pay HMRC under any of sections 35 to 39 or section 40(1) (recovery of top-up payments) as a result of something done, or omitted to be done, in connection with that account or any other childcare account which the person has held in respect of the child.

(2) If the account-holder makes a withdrawal from the childcare account, the amount payable to HMRC under section 22 (the "corresponding top-up amount" of the withdrawal) is to be set off against the relevant debt.

(3) In a case where the whole or part of the corresponding top-up amount of a withdrawal ("the set-off amount") is set off against the relevant debt, so much of the withdrawal as generated the set-off amount is to be ignored for the purposes of section 19(8).

Commencement—Childcare Payments Act 2014 (Commencement No 2) Regulations, SI 2016/1083 reg 2(*g*) (the day appointed for the coming into force of this section is 14 November 2016, with effect only for the purposes of the trial of the childcare payment scheme taking place between 14 November 2016 and 15 May 2017).

Childcare Payments Act 2014 (Commencement No 3 and Transitional Provisions) Regulations, SI 2017/578 reg 3(*e*) (the day appointed for the coming into force of this section, in so far as it is not already in force, is 21 April 2017).

55 Order in which payments are taken to discharge debts

(1) This section applies where an amount (a "relevant debt") is due and payable to HMRC under this Act by a person.

(2) For the purposes of this section—

(*a*) a relevant debt is within this paragraph if it consists of a penalty or other amount not falling with paragraph (*b*) or (*c*),

(*b*) a relevant debt is within this paragraph if it consists of an amount of recoverable top-up payments, and

(*c*) a relevant debt is within this paragraph if it consists of an amount of interest payable under section 51.

(3) In determining whether a relevant debt is an amount of recoverable top-up payments for the purposes of section 53 or 54, any amount paid to HMRC by the person in the discharge of a relevant debt is to be taken to have discharged a relevant debt within paragraph (*b*) of subsection (2) only if any relevant debt within paragraph (*a*) of that subsection has been discharged.

(4) Any amount paid to HMRC by the person in the discharge of a relevant debt is to be taken to have discharged any relevant debt within paragraph (*c*) of subsection (2) only if any relevant debt within paragraph (*a*) or (*b*) of that subsection has been discharged.

(5) Any amount paid to HMRC in accordance with a direction under section 53 made in respect of a relevant debt within paragraph (*b*) or (*c*) of subsection (2) is to be taken to have discharged any relevant debt within paragraph (*c*) only if any relevant debt within paragraph (*b*) has been discharged.

(6) In this section an "amount of recoverable top-up payments" means an amount which a person is liable to pay HMRC under any of sections 35 to 39 or section 40(1) (recovery of top-up payments).

Commencement—Childcare Payments Act 2014 (Commencement No 2) Regulations, SI 2016/1083 reg 2(*g*) (the day appointed for the coming into force of this section is 14 November 2016, with effect only for the purposes of the trial of the childcare payment scheme taking place between 14 November 2016 and 15 May 2017).

Childcare Payments Act 2014 (Commencement No 3 and Transitional Provisions) Regulations, SI 2017/578 reg 3(*e*) (the day appointed for the coming into force of this section, in so far as it is not already in force, is 21 April 2017).

Reviews and appeals

56 Appealable decisions

(1) A person who is affected by an appealable decision (see subsection (3)) may appeal against the decision.

(2) But a person may not appeal against any decision unless—

(*a*) the person has applied under section 57 for a review of the decision, and

(*b*) either—

(i) the person has been notified of the conclusion on the review, or

(ii) the person has not been notified of the conclusion on the review and the period for notifying the person of that conclusion has ended.

(3) The following decisions are "appealable decisions"—

(*a*) a decision not to open a childcare account;

(*b*) a decision that a declaration of eligibility is not valid;

(*c*) a decision as to whether or not to make or revoke an account restriction order under section 24;

(*d*) a decision to give a person a notice under section 26;

Tax Credits

(*e*) a decision to give a person a disqualification notice under section 34;
(*f*) a decision to make an assessment, or to make an assessment of a particular amount, under section 41;
(*g*) a decision to assess a penalty, or to assess a penalty of a particular amount, under section 47;
(*h*) a decision to make a disqualification order under section 49;
(*i*) a decision to make a direction under section 50;
(*j*) a decision to give a person a notice under section 51;
(*k*) a decision to give a direction under section 53.

(4) Where a person is notified of an appealable decision under this Act, the notification must include details of the person's right to apply for a review of the decision and to appeal against the decision.

(5) The effect of an appealable decision falling within paragraph (*d*), (*f*), (*g*), (*j*) or (*k*) of subsection (3) is suspended by—
(*a*) the making of an application for a review of the decision, or
(*b*) the making of an appeal against the decision.

(6) The effect of any other appealable decision is not suspended by the making of such an application or appeal.

Commencement—Childcare Payments Act 2014 (Commencement No 2) Regulations, SI 2016/1083 reg 2(*g*) (the day appointed for the coming into force of this section is 14 November 2016, with effect only for the purposes of the trial of the childcare payment scheme taking place between 14 November 2016 and 15 May 2017).
Childcare Payments Act 2014 (Commencement No 3 and Transitional Provisions) Regulations, SI 2017/578 reg 3(*e*) (the day appointed for the coming into force of this section, in so far as it is not already in force, is 21 April 2017).

57 Review of decisions

(1) A person who is affected by an appealable decision ("the applicant") may apply to the Commissioners for Her Majesty's Revenue and Customs for a review of the decision.

(2) The application must be made—
(*a*) within the period of 30 days beginning with the day on which the applicant was notified of the decision, or
(*b*) if the period for making the application has been extended under section 58, within the extended period.

(3) The application must—
(*a*) be made in writing,
(*b*) contain sufficient information to identify the applicant and the decision, and
(*c*) set out the reasons for seeking a review of the decision.

[(3A) Regulations may make provision specifying, or enabling HMRC to specify, the form and manner in which the application may be made (subject to subsection (3)(a)).][1]

(4) If an application for a review of a decision is made to the Commissioners in accordance with this section [(and any provision made under subsection (3A))][1], the Commissioners must review the decision.

(5) On a review under this section, the Commissioners may—
(*a*) uphold the decision,
(*b*) vary the decision, or
(*c*) cancel the decision.

(6) If the applicant makes any representations to the Commissioners at a stage which gives the Commissioners a reasonable opportunity to consider them, the Commissioners must take account of them when carrying out the review.

(7) Where—
(*a*) the Commissioners notify the applicant of further information or evidence which they may need for carrying out the review, and
(*b*) the information or evidence is not provided to them within the period of 15 days beginning with the day on which the notice is given,

the review may proceed without that information or evidence.

(8) The Commissioners must notify the applicant of the matters set out in subsection (9) within—
(*a*) the period of 30 days beginning with the day on which the Commissioners received the application for the review,
(*b*) if the applicant has been given a notice under subsection (7), the period of 45 days beginning with that day, or
(*c*) such other period as the applicant and the Commissioners may agree.

(9) The matters referred to in subsection (8) are—
(*a*) the conclusion on the review,
(*b*) if the conclusion is that the decision is varied, details of the variation, and
(*c*) the reasons for the conclusion.

(10) If the Commissioners do not comply with subsection (8), the review is to be treated as having concluded that the decision is upheld.

In such a case, the Commissioners must notify the applicant of that conclusion.

Commencement—Childcare Payments Act 2014 (Commencement No 2) Regulations, SI 2016/1083 reg 2(*g*) (the day appointed for the coming into force of this section is 14 November 2016, with effect only for the purposes of the trial of the childcare payment scheme taking place between 14 November 2016 and 15 May 2017).

Childcare Payments Act 2014 (Commencement No 3 and Transitional Provisions) Regulations, SI 2017/578 reg 3(*e*) (the day appointed for the coming into force of this section, in so far as it is not already in force, is 21 April 2017).

Amendments—[1] Sub-s (3A) inserted, and in sub-s (4), words inserted, by the Small Charitable Donations and Childcare Payments Act 2017 s 5(1), (3) with effect for the tax year 2017–18 and subsequent tax years.

58 Extension of time limit for applications for review

(1) A person who wishes to make an application for a review under section 57 may apply to the Commissioners for an extension of the period for making the application.

(2) An application under this section—

(*a*) must be made before the end of the period of 6 months beginning with the day after the last day of the period mentioned in section 57(2)(a) ("the standard period"), and

(*b*) must set out the reasons for seeking the extension.

[(2A) Regulations may make provision specifying, or enabling HMRC to specify, the form and manner in which an application under this section may be made.][1]

(3) The Commissioners may grant an extension under this section if they are satisfied that—

(*a*) due to special circumstances, it was not practicable for the person to make the application under section 57 within the standard period, and

(*b*) it is reasonable in all the circumstances to grant the extension.

(4) If an application under this section is refused, it may not be renewed.

Commencement—Childcare Payments Act 2014 (Commencement No 2) Regulations, SI 2016/1083 reg 2(*g*) (the day appointed for the coming into force of this section is 14 November 2016, with effect only for the purposes of the trial of the childcare payment scheme taking place between 14 November 2016 and 15 May 2017).

Childcare Payments Act 2014 (Commencement No 3 and Transitional Provisions) Regulations, SI 2017/578 reg 3(*e*) (the day appointed for the coming into force of this section, in so far as it is not already in force, is 21 April 2017).

Amendments—[1] Sub-s (2A) inserted by the Small Charitable Donations and Childcare Payments Act 2017 s 5(1), (4) with effect for the tax year 2017–18 and subsequent tax years.

59 Exercise of right of appeal

(1) An appeal under section 56 is to the appropriate tribunal.

(2) "The appropriate tribunal" means—

(*a*) the First-tier Tribunal, or

(*b*) in Northern Ireland, the appeal tribunal.

(3) "Appeal tribunal" means an appeal tribunal constituted under Chapter 1 of Part 2 of the Social Security (Northern Ireland) Order 1998 (SI 1998/1506 (N.I. 10)).

(4) Regulations may provide for any provision contained in or made under the following legislation to apply in relation to appeals under section 56, with such modifications as may be specified in regulations—

(*a*) Chapter 2 of Part 1 of the Social Security Act 1998 (social security appeals: Great Britain);

(*b*) Chapter 2 of Part 2 of the Social Security (Northern Ireland) Order 1998 (social security appeals: Northern Ireland);

(*c*) section 54 of the Taxes Management Act 1970 (settling of appeals by agreement).

Commencement—Childcare Payments Act 2014 (Commencement No 2) Regulations, SI 2016/1083 reg 2(*g*) (the day appointed for the coming into force of this section is 14 November 2016, with effect only for the purposes of the trial of the childcare payment scheme taking place between 14 November 2016 and 15 May 2017).

Childcare Payments Act 2014 (Commencement No 3 and Transitional Provisions) Regulations, SI 2017/578 reg 3(*e*) (the day appointed for the coming into force of this section, in so far as it is not already in force, is 21 April 2017).

60 Powers of tribunal

(1) This section applies where a person is appealing to the Tribunal under section 56 against an appealable decision.

(2) In a case where the appealable decision is a decision under section 47 to assess a penalty, or to assess a penalty of a particular amount, the Tribunal may do any of the following—

(*a*) uphold the penalty;

(*b*) set aside the penalty;

(*c*) substitute for the penalty a penalty of an amount decided by the Tribunal.

(3) In any other case, the Tribunal must either—

(*a*) dismiss the appeal, or

(*b*) quash the whole or part of the decision to which the appeal relates.

(4) The Tribunal may act as mentioned in subsection (3)(*b*) only to the extent that it is satisfied that the decision was wrong on one or more of the following grounds—

(*a*) that the decision was based, wholly or partly, on an error of fact;

(*b*) that the decision was wrong in law.

(5) If the Tribunal quashes the whole or part of a decision, it may either—

(*a*) refer the matter back to HMRC with a direction to reconsider and make a new decision in accordance with its ruling, or

(*b*) substitute its own decision for that of HMRC.

This is subject to section 61(8).

(6) The Tribunal may not direct HMRC to take any action which they would not otherwise have the power to take in relation to the decision.

(7) A decision of the Tribunal made by virtue of this section has the same effect as, and may be enforced in the same manner as, a decision of HMRC.

(8) In this section "the Tribunal" means—

(*a*) the First-tier Tribunal, or

(*b*) in Northern Ireland, the appeal tribunal (within the meaning of section 59(3)).

Commencement—Childcare Payments Act 2014 (Commencement No 2) Regulations, SI 2016/1083 reg 2(*g*) (the day appointed for the coming into force of this section is 14 November 2016, with effect only for the purposes of the trial of the childcare payment scheme taking place between 14 November 2016 and 15 May 2017).

Childcare Payments Act 2014 (Commencement No 3 and Transitional Provisions) Regulations, SI 2017/578 reg 3(*e*) (the day appointed for the coming into force of this section, in so far as it is not already in force, is 21 April 2017).

61 Cases where there is more than one eligible person

(1) This section applies in the following cases.

(2) The first case is where—

(*a*) two or more persons ("the applicants") have applied to open a childcare account in respect of the same child, and

(*b*) any of the applicants is appealing against a decision not to allow the applicant to open a childcare account in respect of the child.

(3) The second case is where—

(*a*) one or more persons ("the applicants") have applied to open a childcare account in respect of a child,

(*b*) another person ("the existing account-holder") holds a childcare account in respect of the child, and

(*c*) any of the applicants is appealing against a decision not to allow the applicant to open a childcare account in respect of the child.

(4) The third case is where—

(*a*) a person is appealing against a decision not to make an account restriction order in relation to another person, or

(*b*) a person is appealing against a decision to make an account restriction order in relation to the person so as to enable another person to open a childcare account or make a declaration of eligibility in relation to such an account.

(5) In this section "the affected parties" means—

(*a*) in the case described in subsection (2), the applicants;

(*b*) in the case described in subsection (3), the applicants and the existing account-holder;

(*c*) in the case described in subsection (4), each of the persons mentioned in paragraph (*a*) or (*b*) of that subsection (as the case may be).

(6) Notice of the appeal must be given to each of the affected parties (other than the person bringing the appeal).

(7) Each of the affected parties is to be treated as a party to the appeal.

(8) If the Tribunal quashes the whole or part of the decision, it must substitute its own decision for that of HMRC.

(9) A decision of the Tribunal made by virtue of this section has the same effect as, and may be enforced in the same manner as, a decision of HMRC.

(10) In this section "the Tribunal" has the same meaning as in section 60.

Commencement—Childcare Payments Act 2014 (Commencement No 2) Regulations, SI 2016/1083 reg 2(*g*) (the day appointed for the coming into force of this section is 14 November 2016, with effect only for the purposes of the trial of the childcare payment scheme taking place between 14 November 2016 and 15 May 2017).

Childcare Payments Act 2014 (Commencement No 3 and Transitional Provisions) Regulations, SI 2017/578 reg 3(*e*) (the day appointed for the coming into force of this section, in so far as it is not already in force, is 21 April 2017).

Final provisions

69 Regulations: general

(1) Any power to make regulations under this Act is exercisable by statutory instrument.

(2) Any power to make regulations under the following provisions of this Act is exercisable by the Treasury—

(*a*) section 1(5) (power to amend rate of top-up payment);

(*b*) section 2(3)(*b*) to (*d*) (qualifying childcare);

(*c*) sections 3, 7 to 11 and 13 (eligibility);

(*d*) section 5(2) (power to alter length of entitlement period);

(*e*) section 14 (qualifying child);

(*f*) section 19(7) (power to amend the relevant maximum);

(*g*) section 30 (termination of tax credit awards);

(*h*) section 31 (power to provide for automatic termination of universal credit);

(*i*) sections 32 and 33 (disqualification of tax credit or universal credit claimants from obtaining top-up payments);
(*j*) sections 43(5), 44(6) and 46(5) (powers to vary certain penalties);
(*k*) section 50(4) (power to alter period for which directions under section 50 have effect);
(*l*) section 62(6) (power to amend rate of compensatory payments);
(*m*) section 72 (power to make consequential amendments);
(*n*) section 75 (commencement).

(3) Any power to make regulations under a provision of this Act that is not mentioned in subsection (2) is exercisable by the Commissioners for Her Majesty's Revenue and Customs.

(4) Regulations under this Act may—
(*a*) make different provision for different purposes or in relation to different areas,
(*b*) contain incidental, supplemental, consequential or transitional provision or savings, and
(*c*) provide for a person to exercise a discretion in dealing with any matter.

(5) Subsection (4) does not apply to regulations under section 75 (see instead subsection (3) of that section).

Regulations—Childcare Payments (Eligibility) Regulations, SI 2015/448.
Childcare Payments Act 2014 (Amendment) Regulations, SI 2015/537.
Childcare Payments Act 2014 (Commencement No 1) Regulations, SI 2016/763.
Childcare Payments Act 2014 (Commencement No 2) Regulations, SI 2016/1083.
Childcare Payments Act 2014 (Commencement No 3 and Transitional Provisions) Regulations, SI 2017/578.
Childcare Payments Act 2014 (Commencement No 4) Regulations, SI 2017/750.

70 Regulations: Parliamentary control

(1) A statutory instrument containing regulations under this Act is subject to annulment in pursuance of a resolution of either House of Parliament, unless the instrument—
(*a*) is required by subsection (3) or any other enactment to be laid in draft before, and approved by a resolution of, each House, or
(*b*) contains only regulations under section 75.

(2) Subsection (3) applies to a statutory instrument that contains (with or without other provisions)—
(*a*) regulations under section 1(5);
(*b*) regulations under section 2(3)(*b*), (*c*) or (*d*);
(*c*) the first regulations under each of sections 3 and 7 to 10;
(*d*) regulations under section 5(2);
(*e*) the first regulations under section 14;
(*f*) regulations under section 19(7) which substitute a lower amount for any amount for the time being specified in section 19(5);
(*g*) regulations under section 31;
(*h*) the first regulations under each of sections 32(5) and 33(5);
(*i*) regulations under section 32(6) or 33(6);
(*j*) regulations under section 43(5), 44(6) or 46(5);
(*k*) regulations under section 50(4);
(*l*) regulations under section 62(6);
(*m*) regulations under section 72.

(3) A statutory instrument to which this subsection applies may not be made unless a draft of the instrument has been laid before, and approved by a resolution of, each House of Parliament.

Tax Credits

74 Extent

(1) Except as provided by subsection (2), this Act extends to England and Wales, Scotland and Northern Ireland.

(2) Any amendment or repeal made by this Act has the same extent as the provision amended or repealed.

75 Commencement and short title

(1) The following provisions of this Act come into force on the day on which this Act is passed—
(*a*) sections 65 and 68;
(*b*) sections 69 to 72, 73(1), 74 and this section;
(*c*) any power to make regulations under this Act.

(2) The remaining provisions of this Act come into force in accordance with provision contained in regulations.

(3) Regulations under subsection (2) may—
(*a*) make different provision for different purposes or in relation to different areas;
(*b*) make such transitory or transitional provision, or savings, as the Treasury consider necessary or expedient, including (in particular) such adaptations of provisions of this Act brought into force as appear to be necessary or expedient in consequence of other provisions of this Act not yet having come into force.

(4) This Act may be cited as the Childcare Payments Act 2014.

Regulations—Childcare Payments Act 2014 (Amendment) Regulations, SI 2015/537.
Childcare Payments Act 2014 (Commencement No 1) Regulations, SI 2016/763.

Childcare Payments Act 2014 (Commencement No 2) Regulations, SI 2016/1083.
Childcare Payments Act 2014 (Commencement No 3 and Transitional Provisions) Regulations, SI 2017/578.
Childcare Payments Act 2014 (Commencement No 4) Regulations, SI 2017/750.

Statutory Instruments

Tax Credits

Contents

Tax Credits

SI 2008/2169 *Tax Credits (Miscellaneous Amendments) (No 2) Regulations 2008*
SI 2008/2684 First-tier Tribunal and Upper Tribunal (Chambers) Order 2008 (revoked)
SI 2008/2707 Appeals (Excluded Decisions) Order 2008
SI 2008/3151 *Tax Credits Act 2002 (Transitional Provisions) Order 2008*
SI 2009/697 Tax Credits (Miscellaneous Amendments) Regulations 2009
SI 2009/800 *Tax Credits Up-rating Regulations 2009*
SI 2009/1829 *Working Tax Credit (Entitlement and Maximum Rate) (Amendment) Regulations 2009*
SI 2009/697 *Tax Credits (Miscellaneous Amendments) Regulations 2009*
SI 2009/2887 *Tax Credits (Miscellaneous Amendments) (No 2) Regulations 2009*
SI 2010/42 First-tier Tribunal (Gambling) Fees Order 2010
SI 2010/644 Tax Credits Act 2002 (Transitional Provisions) Order 2010
SI 2010/751 *Tax Credits (Miscellaneous Amendments) Regulations 2010*
SI 2010/918 *Working Tax Credit (Entitlement and Maximum Rate) (Amendment) Regulations 2010*
SI 2010/981 *Tax Credits Up-rating Regulations 2010*
SI 2010/2494 *Tax Credits (Miscellaneous Amendments) (No 2) Regulations 2010*
SI 2011/721*Tax Credits (Miscellaneous Amendments) Regulations 2011*
SI 2011/1502 Taxation of Equitable Life (Payments) Order 2011
SI 2011/2910 Tax Credits Act 2002 (Further Commencement and Transitional Provisions) Order 2011
SI 2012/533 Revenue and Customs Appeals Order 2012
SI 2012/848 Tax Credits (Miscellaneous Amendments) Regulations 2012
SI 2012/849 Tax Credits Up-rating Regulations 2012
SI 2013/386 Universal Credit (Transitional Provisions) Regulations 2013 (extracts)
SI 2013/524 Loss of Tax Credits (Specified Day) Order 2013
SI 2013/591 Armed Forces and Reserve Forces Compensation Scheme (Consequential Provisions: Subordinate Legislation) Order 2013
SI 2013/715 Loss of Tax Credits Regulations 2013
SI 2013/750 Tax Credits Up-rating, etc. Regulations 2013
SI 2013/1736 Working Tax Credit (Entitlement and Maximum Rate) (Amendment) Regulations 2013
SI 2014/384 Child Benefit and Tax Credits Up-rating Order 2014
SI 2014/658 Tax Credits (Miscellaneous Amendments) Regulations 2014
SI 2014/845 Tax Credits Up-rating Regulations 2014
SI 2014/885 Tax Credits (Late Appeals) Order 2014
SI 2014/886 Tax Credits, Child Benefit and Guardian's Allowance Reviews and Appeals Order 2014
SI 2014/1230 Universal Credit (Transitional Provisions) Regulations 2014
SI 2014/1231 Child Benefit (General) and Child Tax Credit (Amendment) Regulations 2014
SI 2014/1511 Child Benefit (General) and the Tax Credits (Residence) (Amendment) Regulations 2014
SI 2014/1848 Tax Credits Act 2002 (Commencement and Transitional Provisions) (Partial Revocation) Order 2014
SI 2014/1933 Tax Credits (Settlement of Appeals) Regulations 2014
SI 2014/2881 Tax Credits, Child Benefit and Guardian's Allowance Appeals (Appointed Day) (Northern Ireland) Order 2014
SI 2014/2924 Child Benefit (General) and Tax Credits (Miscellaneous Amendments) Regulations 2014
SI 2014/3280 Tax Credits (Exercise of Functions) Order 2014
SI 2015/175 Social Security and Tax Credits (Miscellaneous Amendments) Regulations 2015
SI 2015/451 Tax Credits Up-rating Regulations 2015
SI 2015/567 Child Benefit and Tax Credits Up-rating Order 2015
SI 2015/669 Tax Credits (Claims and Notifications) (Amendment) Regulations 2015
SI 2015/1985 Pensions Act 2014 (Consequential, Supplementary and Incidental Amendments) Order 2015
SI 2016/232 Universal Credit (Transitional Provisions) (Amendment) Regulations 2016 (revoked)
SI 2016/360 Tax Credits and Child Benefit (Miscellaneous Amendments) Regulations 2016
SI 2016/393 Tax Credits (Income Thresholds and Determination of Rates) (Amendment) Regulations

Statutory Instruments

1999/3219

TAX CREDITS (PAYMENT BY EMPLOYERS) REGULATIONS 1999

Made by the Commissioners of Inland Revenue under the Tax Credits Act 1999, s 6

Made ....*2 December 1999*
Laid before Parliament ....*3 December 1999*
Coming into force ....*6 April 2000*

Commentary—*Simon's Taxes* **E4.902.**

1 Citation and commencement

These Regulations may be cited as the Tax Credits (Payment by Employers) Regulations 1999 and shall come into force on 6th April 2000 immediately after the coming into force of section 6 of the Tax Credits Act 1999.

2 Interpretation

[(1)] [1] In these Regulations unless the context otherwise requires—

"award period" means—

(*a*) where the award is of working families' tax credit, the period for which amounts are payable to a person by virtue of section 128(3) of the Social Security Contributions and Benefits Act 1992 or section 127(3) of the Social Security Contributions and Benefits (Northern Ireland) Act 1992, or

(*b*) where the award is of disabled person's tax credit, the period for which amounts are payable to a person by virtue of section 129(6) of the Social Security Contributions and Benefits Act 1992 or section 128(6) of the Social Security Contributions and Benefits (Northern Ireland) Act 1992;

"the Board" means the Commissioners of Inland Revenue;

"certificate of payments" shall be construed in accordance with regulation 4(3);

"Contributions Regulations" means the Social Security (Contributions) Regulations 1979 or, in Northern Ireland, the Social Security (Contributions) Regulations (Northern Ireland) 1979;

"deductions working sheet" shall be construed in accordance with regulation 2 of the Employments Regulations;

"emoluments" means any income assessable to income tax under Schedule E;

"employer" and "employee" shall be construed in accordance with section 6(1) of the Tax Credits Act 1999;

"Employments Regulations" means the Income Tax (Employments) Regulations 1993;

"income tax month" means the period beginning on the 6th day of any calendar month and ending on the 5th day of the following calendar month;

"income tax period" has the same meaning as in regulation 2 of the Employments Regulations;

"income tax quarter" means the period beginning on the 6th day of April and ending on the 5th day of July, or beginning on the 6th day of July and ending on the 5th day of October, or beginning on the 6th day of October and ending on the 5th day of January, or beginning on the 6th day of January and ending on the 5th day of April;

"Management Act" means the Taxes Management Act 1970;

"notice" means notice in writing;

"partner" has the same meaning as in regulation 2 of the Family Credit (General) Regulations 1987 or, in Northern Ireland, the Family Credit (General) Regulations (Northern Ireland) 1987, and in regulation 2 of the Disability Working Allowance (General) Regulations 1991 or, in Northern Ireland, the Disability Working Allowance (General) Regulations (Northern Ireland) 1992;

"pay period" means the period by reference to which an employee's emoluments are paid, whether weekly, monthly or otherwise;

"relevant employer" and "relevant subsequent employer" have the meanings given by regulation 3;

"start notification" shall be construed in accordance with regulation 4(2);

"stop notice" shall be construed in accordance with regulation 9(2);

"tax credit" means working families' tax credit or disabled person's tax credit;

"tax year" means a year beginning with 6th April in any year and ending with 5th April in the following year.

Tax Credits

[(2) References in these Regulations to entitlement to tax credit or to an award of tax credit do not include either of the following cases.][1]

[(3) The first case is where—

(*a*) the entitlement arises from, or the award is made in consequence of, a claim made following and by reason of the birth of a child to the claimant or the adoption by the claimant of a child or young person or the granting of a parental order for a surrogate child, and

(*b*) the previous award of tax credit was terminated by virtue of—

(i) regulation 54A of the Disability Working Allowance (General) Regulations 1991 or regulation 54A of the Disability Working Allowance (General) Regulations (Northern Ireland) 1992, or

(ii) regulation 49ZA of the Family Credit (General) Regulations 1987 or regulation 49ZA of the Family Credit (General) Regulations (Northern Ireland) 1987.][1]

[(4) The second case is where the claimant is entitled at the date of the claim to statutory maternity pay within the meaning of Part XII of the Social Security Contributions and Benefits Act 1992 or maternity allowance within the meaning of section 35 of that Act.][1]

[(5) In paragraph (3)(*a*) "surrogate child" means a child in respect of whom an order has been made under section 30 of the Human Fertilisation and Embryology Act 1990.][1]

Amendments—[1] Regulation renumbered as para (1), paras (2)–(5) added by the Tax Credits (Miscellaneous Amendments No 3) Regulations, SI 2001/892 reg 19 with effect for claims made after 3 April 2001.

3 Definition of "relevant employer" and "relevant subsequent employer"

(1) Subject to paragraph (2) "relevant employer" means an employer who, at the time an award of tax credit is made, or renewed for a further award period, is required, on making any payment of or on account of any income assessable to income tax under Schedule E to any person, to deduct tax in accordance with the Employments Regulations or to deduct contributions in accordance with the Contributions Regulations and, in the case of an employee with more than one such employer, means in addition—

(*a*) where the award is of working families' tax credit, the employer by whom, at the date of application, the larger (or largest) amount of net earnings as construed in accordance with the Family Credit (General) Regulations 1987 or, in Northern Ireland, the Family Credit (General) Regulations (Northern Ireland) 1987 is payable, or

(*b*) where the award is of disabled person's tax credit, the employer by whom, at the date of application, the larger (or largest) amount of net earnings as construed in accordance with the Disability Working Allowance (General) Regulations 1991 or, in Northern Ireland, the Disability Working Allowance (General) Regulations (Northern Ireland) 1992 is payable.

(2) "Relevant employer" does not include an employer who is authorised to make deductions in accordance with regulation 20 of the Employments Regulations.

(3) Subject to paragraph (4) "relevant subsequent employer" means an employer who, at the time that the employee notifies the Board in accordance with regulation 10(4) that he has commenced work for that employer (being a time falling after the date on which the employee ceased to be employed by the relevant employer but falling within the same award period), is required, on making any payment of or on account of any income assessable to income tax under Schedule E to any person, to deduct tax in accordance with the Employments Regulations or to deduct contributions in accordance with the Contributions Regulations.

(4) "Relevant subsequent employer" does not include an employer who is authorised to make deductions in accordance with regulation 20 of the Employments Regulations.

4 Notification to relevant employer or relevant subsequent employer of employee's entitlement to payment of tax credit

(1) Where—

(*a*) an employee of a relevant employer becomes entitled to tax credit, or has an award of tax credit renewed for a further award period, or

(*b*) a person who—

(i) is entitled to tax credit, and

(ii) was an employee of a relevant employer at the date on which he became entitled to that tax credit,

commences employment with a relevant subsequent employer,

the Board shall notify the relevant employer or, as the case may be, the relevant subsequent employer of that employee's entitlement to payment of tax credit in accordance with paragraphs (2) to (4).

(2) A notification of entitlement furnished to the relevant employer or the relevant subsequent employer under paragraph (1) ("start notification") shall be in a form provided by the Board and shall contain the following particulars—

(*a*) the date of issue of the start notification;

(*b*) the name of the employee concerned;

(*c*) the employee's national insurance number and (if known) his payroll number;

(*d*) the commencement date and the termination date of the period during which the employer is to be responsible for payment of tax credit to the employee;
(*e*) the daily rate of tax credit applicable to each calendar day falling within that period and a table showing the multiples from 1 to 31 of that daily rate;
(*f*) the total amount of tax credit to be paid to the employee by the employer.

(3) A start notification shall be accompanied by a certificate of payments in a form provided by the Board to be completed by the relevant employer or the relevant subsequent employer in accordance with regulation 9 (termination of relevant employer's or relevant subsequent employer's obligation to pay tax credit prior to the termination date contained in the start notification), and such certificate shall contain the following particulars—
(*a*) the name of the employee concerned;
(*b*) the employee's national insurance number and (if known) his payroll number;
(*c*) the date of issue of the certificate of payments.

(4) The commencement date contained in the start notification—
(*a*) where the employee's pay period is one week or of shorter duration, shall not be earlier than 14 days from the date of issue of the start notification, and
(*b*) in all other cases, shall not be earlier than 42 days from the date of issue of the start notification.

5 Notification to employee of relevant employer or relevant subsequent employer of employee's entitlement to tax credit

(1) Where an employee of a relevant employer becomes entitled to tax credit, or has an award of tax credit renewed for a further award period, the Board shall notify the employee of his entitlement to payment of tax credit in accordance with paragraph (2).

(2) A notification under paragraph (1) shall be in a form provided by the Board and shall contain the following particulars—
(*a*) the weekly amount of tax credit to which the employee is entitled;
(*b*) the dates (if any) between which the Board will be responsible for payment of tax credit to the employee;
(*c*) the dates (if any) between which a named employer of the employee will be responsible for payment of tax credit to the employee;
(*d*) the daily rate of tax credit applicable to each calendar day during the period of the award of tax credit to the employee and a table showing the multiples from 1 to 31 of that daily rate;
(*e*) the total amount of tax credit to be paid to the employee by a named employer.

(3) Where a person who—
(*a*) is entitled to tax credit, and
(*b*) was an employee of a relevant employer at the date on which he became entitled to that tax credit,

commences employment with a relevant subsequent employer, the Board shall notify the employee of his entitlement to payment of tax credit in accordance with paragraph (4).

(4) A notification under paragraph (3) shall be in a form provided by the Board and shall contain the following particulars—
(*a*) the dates (if any) between which the Board will be responsible for payment of tax credit to the employee;
(*b*) the dates (if any) between which a named employer of the employee will be responsible for payment of tax credit to the employee;
(*c*) the total amount of tax credit to be paid to the employee by a named employer.

6 Relevant employer's or relevant subsequent employer's obligation to pay tax credits

(1) On receipt of a start notification in respect of an employee the relevant employer or the relevant subsequent employer shall, if he reasonably expects that employee to remain in his employment and receive payment for three or more consecutive pay periods commencing with the pay period in which the commencement date contained in that start notification falls, calculate the tax credit to which that employee is entitled to be paid in each pay period during which the employer will be responsible for paying tax credit to that employee in accordance with the start notification.

(2) Subject to paragraph (3), where the employer—
(*a*) has received a start notification in respect of an employee, and
(*b*) makes a payment of emoluments to that employee on or after the commencement date contained in that start notification,

he shall pay to that employee the tax credit to which the employee is entitled during the pay period to which the payment of emoluments relates.

(3) Where the employer—

(*a*) has received a start notification in respect of an employee but does not reasonably expect that employee to remain in his employment and receive payment for three or more consecutive pay periods as mentioned in paragraph (1); or

(*b*) becomes aware before the first date on which a payment of emoluments is due following the commencement date contained in that start notification that an employee in respect of whom a start notification has been received has left, or will leave, his employment before the end of the third consecutive pay period,

he shall return the start notification and the uncompleted form of certificate of payments to the Board, indicating on the start notification his reasons for doing so.

(4) The employer shall record on the employee's payslip for the relevant pay period, as a credit described as a "tax credit", any payment made under paragraph (2).

(5) Any amount paid under paragraph (2) shall be recorded on the deductions working sheet for the employee which the employer is required to prepare under regulation 38 of the Employments Regulations.

(6) The employer shall record on the certificate referred to in regulation 39 of the Employments Regulations the total tax credit paid to each employee for the tax year to which the certificate relates.

(7) The employer shall record on the certificate referred to in regulation 43 of the Employments Regulations the total tax credit paid for the tax year to which the certificate relates.

(8) Where the employer makes a payment to an employee of an amount of tax credit which exceeds the amount of tax credit which that employee is entitled to be paid in accordance with the start notification, the employer may recover from that employee an amount not exceeding the excess.

(9) No payment of tax credit under paragraph (2) shall be capable of attachment under any enactment, or shall be used by way of set-off or otherwise reduced, extinguished or terminated except in accordance with these Regulations.

Cross references—See Income Tax (Electronic Communications) (Incentive Payments) Regulations, SI 2001/56 reg 5 (incentive payments to be made to individuals and employers who submit returns to the Inland Revenue using electronic communications).

7 Funding of payment by relevant employer or relevant subsequent employer of tax credit

(1) Subject to paragraphs (2), (3) and (4), the relevant employer or the relevant subsequent employer shall fund payments of tax credit under regulation 6(2) for a pay period from the total amounts of tax which the employer is required to pay to the collector of taxes in respect of the deductions from the emoluments of his employees in accordance with the Employments Regulations for the same pay period, and the amount which the employer is required to pay to the collector of taxes in respect of that pay period in accordance with those Regulations shall be reduced by the amount of tax credit which the employer has paid in respect of that same pay period.

(2) If the total amount of tax credit which the employer is required to pay to an employee or employees for a pay period exceeds the total amount of tax which the employer is required to pay to the collector of taxes in respect of the deductions from the emoluments of his employees in accordance with the Employments Regulations for the same pay period, the employer shall fund the payment of the tax credit (or so much of it as remains outstanding) from any deductions made by the employer from the emoluments of his employees for the same pay period in accordance with regulations under section 22(5) of the Teaching and Higher Education Act 1998 or section 73B of the Education (Scotland) Act 1980 (student loan repayments), or in accordance with Article 3(5) of the Education (Student Support) (Northern Ireland) Order 1998, and the aggregate amount which the employer is required to pay to the collector of taxes in respect of that pay period in accordance with those enactments shall be reduced by the amount which the employer has deducted from them and paid in tax credit in respect of the same pay period.

(3) If the total amount of tax credit which the employer is required to pay to an employee or employees for a pay period exceeds the aggregate of—

(*a*) the total amount of tax which the employer is required to pay to the collector of taxes in respect of the deductions from the emoluments of his employees in accordance with the Employments Regulations for the same pay period, and

(*b*) the total amount of the deductions made by the employer from the emoluments of his employees for the same pay period in accordance with regulations under section 22(5) of the Teaching and Higher Education Act 1998 or section 73B of the Education (Scotland) Act 1980 or in accordance with Article 3(5) of the Education (Student Support) (Northern Ireland) Order 1998,

the employer shall fund the payment of the tax credit (or so much of it as remains outstanding) from the total amounts of earnings-related contributions which the employer is required to pay to the collector of taxes in respect of the emoluments of his employees (whether by means of deduction or otherwise) for the same pay period in accordance with the Contributions Regulations, and the aggregate amount which the employer is required to pay to the collector of taxes in respect of that pay period in accordance with those enactments shall be reduced by the amount which the employer has deducted from them and paid in tax credit in respect of the same pay period.

(4) If the total amount of tax credit which the employer is required to pay to an employee or employees for a pay period exceeds the aggregate of—

(*a*) the total amount of tax which the employer is required to pay to the collector of taxes in respect of the deductions from the emoluments of his employees in accordance with the Employments Regulations for the same pay period,

(*b*) the total amount of the deductions made by the employer from the emoluments of his employees for the same pay period in accordance with regulations under section 22(5) of the Teaching and Higher Education Act 1998 or section 73B of the Education (Scotland) Act 1980 or in accordance with Article 3(5) of the Education (Student Support) (Northern Ireland) Order 1998, and

(*c*) the total amounts of earnings-related contributions which the employer is required to pay to the collector of taxes in respect of the emoluments of his employees (whether by means of deduction or otherwise) in accordance with the Contributions Regulations for the same pay period,

the employer may apply to the Board in accordance with regulation 8 for funds to pay the tax credit (or so much of it as remains outstanding) to the employee or employees.

8 Application for funding from the Board

(1) Where—

(*a*) the condition in regulation 7(4) is satisfied, or

(*b*) the relevant employer or the relevant subsequent employer considers that the condition in regulation 7(4) will be satisfied on the date of any subsequent payment of emoluments to one or more employees who are entitled to payment of tax credit,

the employer may apply to the Board for funding on a form provided, or approved, for that purpose by the Board.

(2) An application by an employer under paragraph (1) shall be for any amount up to, but not exceeding, the total sum required by the employer to pay tax credit under regulation 6(2) to his employee or employees entitled to payment of tax credit for—

(*a*) the period of 6 months immediately following the date of the employer's application, or

(*b*) a period of 6 months commencing not earlier than 6 months before the date of the employer's application but not later than that date.

(3) If an application by an employer under paragraph (1) is accepted the Board shall pay to the employer the amount applied for or such other amount as the Board may determine in the circumstances to be reasonable having regard to all relevant matters including—

(*a*) the past obligations and the likely future obligations of the employer under the enactments specified in regulation 7, and

(*b*) the obligations of the employer under any start notification issued to him in the period of 6 months ending with the date of the application under paragraph (1).

(4) An officer of the Board may vary a determination under paragraph (3) if he has reason to believe that it was incorrect at the time that it was made.

(5) An officer of the Board may make a determination superseding an earlier determination, whether as originally made or as varied in accordance with paragraph (4), which has become inappropriate for any reason.

(6) The Board shall notify the employer of any decision or variation of a determination they make in respect of—

(*a*) an application under paragraph (1), or

(*b*) the amount determined by the Board under paragraph (3).

(7) An employer may appeal to the General Commissioners against—

(*a*) the Board's refusal of an application under paragraph (1),

(*b*) an amount determined by the Board under paragraph (3), or

(*c*) an amount determined by the Board under paragraph (3) as varied under paragraph (4);

by giving notice to the Board within thirty days of the receipt by him of notice of the Board's decision.

(8) An appeal under paragraph (7) shall be heard by the General Commissioners for the division in which the place of employment is situated.

(9) The provisions of Part V of the Management Act and of the General Commissioners (Jurisdiction and Procedure) Regulations 1994 shall apply with any necessary modifications to the appeal as they apply to appeals against assessments.

(10) On appeal, the General Commissioners, having regard to the matters set out in paragraph (3) may—

(*a*) confirm the Board's refusal of an application under paragraph (1), or allow the appeal against that refusal;

(*b*) confirm, increase or reduce the amount determined under paragraph 3 or that amount as varied under paragraph (4).

(11) Subject to paragraph (9), the determination of the General Commissioners shall be final.

(12) Where—

(*a*) an employer appeals to the General Commissioners under paragraph (7); and

(*b*) the General Commissioners determine the appropriate amount of funding in a sum which exceeds the amount determined by the Board under paragraph (3),

the Board shall pay to that employer a sum equal to the excess.

(13) An amount which is paid to an employer by the Board under paragraph (12) shall carry interest at the rate applicable under section 178 of the Finance Act 1989 for the purposes of section 824 or, as the case may be, section 826 of the Income and Corporation Taxes Act 1988 from the date on which the condition in regulation 7(4) is satisfied until payment.

(14) Funds provided to an employer by the Board in accordance with this regulation shall be for the purpose only of payment by that employer of tax credit under regulation 6(2) to one or more employees.

9 Termination of relevant employer's or relevant subsequent employer's obligation to pay tax credit prior to the termination date contained in the start notification

(1) In any of the circumstances specified in paragraph (2) and subject to paragraphs (9) and (10), the relevant employer or relevant subsequent employer shall cease to make payments of tax credit to an employee in accordance with regulation 6(2) prior to the termination date contained in the start notification.

(2) The circumstances specified in this paragraph are—

(*a*) where the employer has received notification from the Board to cease payment of tax credit ("stop notice") in respect of that employee;

(*b*) the death of the employee;

(*c*) the employee ceasing to be employed by the employer otherwise than by reason of the employee's death.

(3) In the circumstances specified in paragraph (2)(*a*) and subject to paragraph (9), the employer shall not pay tax credit to the employee at any time following the latest payable date specified in the stop notice.

(4) In the circumstances specified in paragraph (2)(*b*) the employer shall not pay tax credit to the employee at any time following the date on which the employer became aware of the death.

(5) In the circumstances specified in paragraph (2)(*c*) and subject to paragraph (10), the employer shall not pay tax credit to the employee either—

(*a*) at any time following the last day on which that employee was in his employment, or

(*b*) at any time following the last day of the pay period in which the employee ceased to be employed,

whichever the employer chooses.

(6) Subject to paragraphs (9) and (10), where two or more of the circumstances specified in paragraph (2) occur in respect of the same employee the relevant employer or relevant subsequent employer shall not pay tax credit to that employee at any time following the earliest of the dates specified in paragraphs (3), (4) and (5)(*b*).

(7) A stop notice shall be in a form provided by the Board and shall contain the following particulars—

(*a*) the date of issue of the stop notice;

(*b*) the name of the employee concerned;

(*c*) the employee's national insurance number and (if known) his payroll number;

(*d*) the latest date for which tax credit is payable to that employee ("the latest payable date").

(8) Except where an earlier date has been agreed between the Board and the employer, the latest payable date—

(*a*) where the employee's pay period is one week or of shorter duration, shall not be earlier than 14 days from the date of issue of the stop notice, and

(*b*) in all other cases, shall not be earlier than 42 days from the date of issue of the stop notice.

(9) In the circumstances specified in paragraph (2)(*a*) the employer may, after the latest payable date, make a payment to the employee of tax credit that is outstanding at that date in respect of any period which falls within the award period in which the circumstances specified in paragraph 2(*a*) arise.

(10) In the circumstances specified in paragraph (2)(*c*) the employer may, after the date chosen by the employer in accordance with paragraph (5), make a payment to the employee of tax credit that is outstanding at that date in respect of any period which falls within the award period in which the circumstances specified in paragraph (2)(*c*) arise.

(11) A stop notice shall be effective in respect of an employee unless and until a new start notification is received from the Board in respect of that employee.

(12) Where no payment of emoluments is due from the relevant employer or relevant subsequent employer to an employee for a complete pay period the employer shall either—

(*a*) cease to make payments of tax credit to that employee in accordance with regulation 6(2) prior to the termination date contained in the start notification, or

(*b*) continue to pay tax credit in accordance with regulation 6(2) as if payment of emoluments had been made in that pay period,

whichever the employer chooses.

10 Obligations of relevant employer or relevant subsequent employer and employee on termination of employer's obligation to pay tax credit prior to the termination date contained in the start notification

(1) On the death of an employee the employer shall, not later than 7 days following the date on which the employer became aware of the death—

(*a*) enter the following details on either the certificate of payments referred to in regulation 4(3) or on a certificate which has been approved for this purpose by the Board—

(i) the total tax credit paid to the employee in accordance with the start notification in force at the time; and

(ii) the date of the final payment of tax credit and the pay period to which that final payment of tax credit related; and

(*b*) sign, date and send the completed certificate to the Board after retaining a copy.

(2) In the circumstances referred to in regulation 9(2)(*c*) the employer shall, not later than 7 days following the date on which payments of tax credit ceased in accordance with regulation 9(5)—

(*a*) enter the details set out in paragraph (1)(*a*) on either the certificate of payments referred to in regulation 4(3) or on a certificate which has been approved for this purpose by the Board, and

(*b*) sign, date and send the completed certificate to the employee after retaining a copy.

(3) Where the employer ceases payment in accordance with regulation 9(12) the employer shall, not later than 7 days following the last day of the pay period following the pay period in which the last payment of tax credit was made—

(*a*) enter the details set out in paragraph (1)(*a*) on either the certificate of payments referred to in regulation 4(3) or on a certificate which has been approved for this purpose by the Board, and

(*b*) sign, date and send the completed certificate to the employee after retaining a copy.

(4) Where the employee ceases to be employed by the employer as mentioned in regulation 9(2)(*c*) and commences work for another employer during the same award period, the employee shall notify the Board that he has commenced work for that other employer.

(5) A notification by the employee under paragraph (4) shall contain the following particulars—

(*a*) the new employer's name and address;

(*b*) (if known) the new employer's PAYE reference number;

(*c*) (if known) the employee's new payroll number;

(*d*) the date on which the new employment has commenced or will commence;

(*e*) (if known) the new employer's pay period.

11 Board's obligations following termination of employer's obligation to pay tax credit prior to the termination date contained in the start notification

(1) Subject to paragraph (2), where a relevant employer or relevant subsequent employer has ceased to make payment of tax credit in accordance with regulation 9 the Board shall pay to the employee the tax credit to which he is entitled until the termination of the award period or the commencement date referred to in a new start notification, whichever first occurs.

(2) Where—

(*a*) a relevant employer or relevant subsequent employer has ceased to make payment of tax credit by reason of the death of the employee, and

(*b*) that employee is survived by a partner,

the Board shall make payment to that partner of the amount of tax credit to which that employee would have been entitled but for his death.

12 Formal determination of tax credit funding

(1) This regulation applies where funds have been provided to the employer under regulation 8 in respect of one or more employees and it appears to the inspector or other officer of the Board that the employer may have retained some or all of those funds.

(2) Where this regulation applies the inspector or other officer of the Board shall determine the amount of funds provided under regulation 8 and retained by the employer to the best of his judgment and shall serve notice of his determination on the employer.

(3) A determination under this regulation may cover the funds provided under regulation 8—

(*a*) for any one or more pay periods in a tax year, and

(*b*) in respect of a class or classes of employees specified in the notice of determination (without naming the individual employees) or of one or more named employees so specified.

(4) An appeal against a determination under this regulation that is to be brought before the General Commissioners shall be brought before the General Commissioners for the division in which the place given by the provisions of this regulation ("the relevant place") is situated.

(5) Parts IV, V, except section 55, and VI of the Management Act shall apply with any necessary modifications to a determination under this regulation as if it were an assessment and as if the amount of funds determined were income tax charged on the employer.

(6) The relevant place is whichever of the places specified in paragraph (7) is identified by an election made by the employer.

(7) Those places are—

(*a*) the place (if any) in the United Kingdom which, at the time when the election is made, is the employer's place of business;

(*b*) the place (if any) which at that time is the employer's place of residence in the United Kingdom.

(8) Where the employer fails to make an election for the purposes of paragraph (4) before the time limit given in paragraph (9)(*b*) an officer of the Board may elect which of the places specified in paragraph (7) is to be the relevant place.

(9) An election by an employer for the purposes of this regulation—

(*a*) shall be made by notice to an officer of the Board;

(*b*) shall be made at the time when notice of appeal is given or before such later date as the Board allow; and

(*c*) shall be irrevocable.

(10) Where there is no place falling within paragraph (7) an officer of the Board may give directions for determining the relevant place.

(11) A direction given under paragraph (10) shall not have effect in relation to an appeal unless the officer of the Board has served on the employer a notice stating the effect of the direction in relation to the appeal.

(12) In paragraph (7)(*a*) "place of business" means—

(*a*) the place where the trade, profession, vocation or business of the employer is carried on, or

(*b*) if the trade, profession, vocation or business is carried on at more than one place, the head office or place where it is mainly carried on.

13 Recovery of tax credit funding

(1) Subject to paragraph (3), the provisions of any enactments relating to the recovery of income tax charged under Schedule E shall apply to the recovery of the amount of funds provided under regulation 8 specified in paragraph (2) as if the amount of funds provided under regulation 8 were tax charged under Schedule E by way of an assessment on the employer.

(2) The amount of funds provided under regulation 8 specified in this paragraph is any amount of funds which an employer is deemed liable under regulation 12 to pay to the collector for any income tax period.

(3) Summary proceedings for the recovery of funds determined under regulation 12 may be brought in England, Wales or Northern Ireland at any time before the expiry of twelve months after the date on which the amount of funds provided under regulation 8 was determined.

(4) Proceedings may be brought for the recovery of funds determined under regulation 12 without distinguishing the amounts which the employer is liable to repay in respect of each employee and without specifying the employees in question, and the amount of funds provided under regulation 8 shall be one cause of action or one matter of complaint for the purpose of proceedings under section 65, 66 or 67 of the Management Act.

(5) Nothing in paragraph (4) shall prevent the bringing of separate proceedings for the recovery of each amount of the several amounts of funds determined under regulation 12 which the employer is liable to pay for any income tax period in respect of his several employees.

(6) A certificate of the collector that the amount of funds determined under regulation 12 has not been paid to him, or to the best of his knowledge and belief, to any other collector or to any person acting on his behalf or on behalf of another collector, shall be sufficient evidence that the sum mentioned in the certificate is unpaid and due to the Crown.

(7) Any document purporting to be a certificate under paragraph (6) shall be deemed to be such a certificate until the contrary is proved.

14 Inspection of employer's records

(1) Every relevant employer or relevant subsequent employer, whenever called upon to do so by any authorised officer of the Board, shall produce the records specified in paragraph (2) to that officer for inspection, at such time as that officer may reasonably require, at the prescribed place.

(2) The records specified in this paragraph are—

(*a*) all wages sheets, deductions working sheets and other documents and records whatsoever relating to the calculation or payment of the tax credits of his employees in respect of the tax years or income tax months specified by the authorised officer; or

(*b*) such of those wages sheets, deductions working sheets or other documents and records as may be specified by the authorised officer.

(3) "The prescribed place" mentioned in paragraph (1) means—

(*a*) such place in the United Kingdom as the employer and the authorised officer may agree upon; or

(*b*) in default of such agreement, the place in the United Kingdom at which the documents and records referred to in paragraph (2)(*a*) are normally kept; or

(*c*) in default of such agreement and if there is no such place as is referred to in sub-paragraph (*b*), the employer's principal place of business in the United Kingdom.

(4) The authorised officer may—

(*a*) take copies of, or make extracts from, any document produced to him for inspection in accordance with paragraphs (1) and (2); and

(*b*) remove any document so produced if it appears to him to be necessary to do so, at a reasonable time and for a reasonable period.

(5) Where any document is removed in accordance with paragraph (4)(*b*), the authorised officer shall provide a receipt for that document.

(6) Where any document is removed in accordance with paragraph (4)(*b*) which is reasonably required for the proper conduct of a business, the authorised officer shall, not later than seven days following the date on which the document was so removed, provide a copy of the document, free of charge, to the person by whom it was produced or caused to be produced.

(7) Where a lien is claimed on a document produced in accordance with paragraphs (1) and (2), the removal of the document in accordance with paragraph (4)(*b*) shall not be regarded as breaking the lien.

(8) Where records are maintained by computer, the person required to make them available for inspection shall provide the authorised officer with all facilities necessary for obtaining information from them.

(9) For the purposes of paragraphs (1) and (2), the wage sheets, deductions working sheets and other documents and records mentioned in those paragraphs shall be retained by the employer for not less than three years after the end of the tax year to which they relate.

2001/253

FINANCE ACT 1989, SECTION 178(1), (APPOINTED DAY) ORDER 2001

Made by the Treasury under FA 1989 s 178(7)

Made . . . . *1 February 2001*

1 This Order may be cited as the Finance Act 1989, section 178(1), (Appointed Day) Order 2001.

2—(1) The day appointed for the enactments specified in paragraph (2) for periods beginning on or after which section 178(1) of the Finance Act 1989 shall have effect is 7th March 2001.

(2) The enactments specified are—

(*a*) section 71(8A) of the Social Security Administration Act 1992;

(*b*) section 69(8A) of the Social Security Administration (Northern Ireland) Act 1992;

(*c*) paragraph 8 of Schedule 4 to the Tax Credits Act 1999.

2002/1727

TAX CREDITS ACT 2002 (COMMENCEMENT NO 1) ORDER 2002

Made by the Treasury under TCA 2002 ss 61, 62

Made . . . . *8 July 2002*

1 Citation and interpretation

(1) This Order may be cited as the Tax Credits Act 2002 (Commencement No. 1) Order 2002.

(2) In this Order—

"the Act" means the Tax Credits Act 2002;

"award" means an award of a tax credit for a period commencing on or after 6th April 2003.

2 Commencement of certain provisions of the Act

The following provisions of the Act come into force on the dates and for the purposes mentioned in relation to each provision:

Provision	*Date*	*Purposes*
Section 1(1) and (2) (introductory)	9th July 2002	All purposes of Part 1 of the Act and, as respects tax credits, Part 3 of the Act
Section 2 (functions of Board)	9th July 2002	All purposes of Part 1 of the Act and, as respects tax credits, Part 3 of the Act
Section 3(1) and (3) (claims)	9th July 2002	Making regulations about claims
Section 3(1) and (3)	1st August 2002	Making claims
Section 3(1) and (3)	1st January 2003	Making decisions on claims

Tax Credits

Provision	*Date*	*Purposes*
Section 3(1) and (3)	6th April 2003	All other purposes of Part 1 of the Act and, as respects tax credits, Part 3 of the Act
Section 3(2)(*a*)	1st January 2003	All purposes of Part 1 of Act and, as respects tax credits, Part 3 of the Act
Section 3(2)(*b*)	1st January 2003	All purposes of Part 1 of the Act and, as respects tax credits, Part 3 of the Act
Section 3(4)	1st August 2002	Entitlement to make a claim
Section 3(5) to (8)	9th July 2002	All purposes of Part 1 of the Act and, as respects tax credit, Part 3 of the Act
Section 4(1) (claims—supplementary)	9th July 2002	Making regulations
Section 4(2)	1st August 2002	All purposes mentioned in section 4(2) of the Act
Section 5(1) and (3) (Period of awards)	1st January 2003	Making decisions on claims made before beginning of tax year
Section 5(2) and (3)	6th April 2003	Making decisions on other claims
Section 6 (notifications of changes of circumstances)	9th July 2002	Making regulations
Section 7(1) to (5) (income test)	9th July 2002	Making regulations
Section 7(1) to (5)	1st August 2002	Making claims
Section 7(1) to (5)	1st January 2003	Making decisions on claims
Section 7(1) to (5)	6th April 2003	Entitlement to payment award
Section 7(6) to (9)	9th July 2002	Making regulations
Section 7(10)	1st August 2002	Estimating income for the purposes of making, amending or terminating awards
Section 8 (entitlement to child tax credit)	9th July 2002	Making regulations
Section 8	1st August 2002	Making claims
Section 8	1st January 2003	Making decisions on claims
Section 8	6th April 2003	Entitlement to payment award
Section 9 (maximum rate child tax credit)	9th July 2002	Making regulations
Section 9	1st August 2002	Making claims
Section 9	1st January 2003	Making decisions on claims
Section 9	6th April 2003	Entitlement to payment of award
Section 10 (entitlement to working tax credit)	9th July 2002	Making regulations
Section 10	1st August 2002	Making claims
Section 10	1st January 2003	Making decisions on claims
Section 10	6th April 2003	Entitlement to payment of award
Section 11 (maximum rate working tax credit)	9th July 2002	Making regulations
Section 11	1st August 2002	Making claims
Section 11	1st January 2003	Making decisions on claims
Section 11	6th April 2003	Entitlement to payment of award
Section 12(1) to (5) (child care element working tax credit)	9th July 2002	Making regulations
Section 12(1) to (5)	1st August 2002	Making claims
Section 12 (1) to (5)	1st January 2003	Making decisions on claims
Section 12(1) to (5)	6th April 2003	Entitlement to payment of award
Section 12(5) to (8)	9th July 2002	Making schemes
Section 13 (rate of tax credit)	9th July 2002	Making regulations
Section 13	1st August 2002	Making claims

Provision	*Date*	*Purposes*
Section 13	1st January 2003	Making decisions on claims
Section 13	6th April 2003	Entitlement to payment of award
Section 14(1) and (3) (initial decisions on claims)	1st January 2003	Making decisions on claims
Section 14(2)	9th July 2002	Making regulations
Section 14(2)	1st August 2002	Dealing with claims
Section 15(1) (revised decisions after notifications)	1st January 2003	Making decisions on whether to amend awards
Section 15(2)	9th July 2002	Making regulations
Section 15(2)	1st August 2002	Dealing with notifications of change of circumstances
Section 16(1) (other revised decisions)	1st January 2003	Making decisions on whether to amend or terminate awards
Section 16(2) and (3)	1st January 2003	Giving of notice under section 16(2) and (3) of the Act
Section 16(3)	9th July 2002	Making regulations
Section 17(1) to (9) (final notice)	6th April 2003	Giving final notice on award
Section 17(10)	9th July 2002	Making regulations
Section 18 (decisions after final notice)	6th April 2003	Making decisions after final notice
Section 19 (power to enquire into awards)	6th April 2003	Enquiring into awards
Section 19(2)	9th July 2002	Making regulations
Section 20 (decisions on discovery)	6th April 2003	Making decisions under section 20(1) and (4) of the Act
Section 21 (decisions subject to official error)	9th July 2002	Making regulations for the purposes of revising decisions under sections 14(1), 15(1), 16(1), 18(1), (5), (6) and (9), 19(3) and 20(1) and (4) of the Act
Section 22 (information etc. requirements— supplementary)	9th July 2002	Making regulations
Section 23 (notice of decisions)	1st January 2003	Giving notices of decisions under sections 14(1), 15(1) and 16(1) of the Act, and of revised decisions under those sections by virtue of regulations under section 21 of the Act
Section 23	6th April 2003	Giving notices of decisions under sections 18(1), (5), (6) and (9), 19(3) and 20(1) and (4) of the Act, and of revised decisions under those sections by virtue of regulations under section 21 of the Act
Section 24 (payments of a tax credit)	9th July 2002	Making regulations
Section 24	1st August 2002	Making claims
Section 24	1st January 2003	Making decisions on claims
Section 24	6th April 2003	Entitlement to payment of award
Section 25(1), (2) and (5) to (7) (payments of working tax credit by employers)	9th July 2002	Making regulations
Section 25(3), (4), and (5)	6th April 2003	Power to call for documents etc. in relation to employer's compliance with regulations under section 25
Section 26 (liability of officers for sums paid to employers)	1st January 2003	Making regulations
Section 27 and Schedule 1 (rights of employees)	1st September 2002	Rights conferred on employees by virtue of regulations under section 25 of the Act

Provision	*Date*	*Purposes*
Sections 28 to 30 (overpayments, recovery of overpayments and underpayments of a tax credit)	6th April 2003	Liability to repay overpayments or to be paid full entitlement where underpayment
Section 30 (underpayments)	1st January 2003	Making regulations under section 30 of the Act
Section 31 (incorrect statements etc)	1st August 2002	Imposition of penalties for incorrect statement or declaration in or in connection with a claim for a tax credit or a notification given in accordance with regulations under section 6 of the Act, or for incorrect information or evidence in response to a requirement imposed by virtue of regulations under section 25 of the Act
Section 31	1st January 2003	Imposition of penalties for incorrect information or evidence in response to a requirement imposed by virtue of section 14(2), 15(2) or 16(3) of the Act
Section 31	6th April 2003	Imposition of penalties for incorrect information or evidence in response to a requirement imposed by virtue of section 18(10) or 19(2) of the Act, or for incorrect statement or declaration in response to a notice under section 17 of the Act
Section 32 (failure to comply with requirements)	1st August 2002	Imposition of penalty for failure to provide information or evidence required by regulations under section 25 of the Act, or for failure to give notification required by regulations under section 6(3) of the Act
Section 32	1st January 2003	Imposition of penalty for failure to provide information or evidence under section 14(2), 15(2) or 16(3) of the Act
Section 32	6th April 2003	Imposition of penalty for failure to provide information or evidence under section 18(10) or 19(2) of the Act, or to comply with requirement imposed by notice under section 17 of the Act by virtue of subsection (2)(a), (4)(a) or (6)(a) of that section
Section 33 (failure by employers to make correct payments)	6th April 2003	Imposition of penalty for failure by employer to make correct payment to employee
Section 34 and Schedule 2 (penalties—supplementary)	1st August 2002	Imposition of penalties under section 31 of the Act for incorrect statement or declaration in or in connection with a claim for a tax credit or a notification given in accordance with regulations under section 6 of the Act, or for incorrect information or evidence in response to a requirement imposed by regulations under section 25 of the Act; mitigation of such penalties, appeals against such penalties and recovery of such penalties
Section 34 and Schedule 2	1st January 2003	Imposition of penalties under section 31 of the Act for incorrect information or evidence in response to a requirement imposed by virtue of section 14(2), 15(2) or 16(3) of the Act; mitigation of such penalties, appeals against such penalties and recovery of such penalties

Provision	*Date*	*Purposes*
Section 34 and Schedule 2	6th April 2003	Imposition of penalties under section 31 of the Act for incorrect information or evidence in response to a requirement imposed by virtue of section 18(10) or 19(2) of the Act, or for incorrect statement or declaration in response to a notice under section 17 of the Act; mitigation of such penalties, appeals against such penalties and recovery of such penalties
Section 34 and Schedule 2	1st August 2002	Imposition of penalties under section 32(2)(*b*) or (3) of the Act for failure to provide information or evidence required by regulations under section 25 of the Act, or for failure to give notification required by regulations under section 6(3) of the Act; bringing of proceedings for penalties under section 32(2)(*a*) before Commissioners for failure to provide information or evidence required by regulations under section 25 of the Act; mitigation of such penalties, appeals against such penalties and recovery of such penalties
Section 34 and Schedule 2	1st January 2003	Imposition of penalties under section 32(2)(*b*) of the Act for failure to provide information or evidence under section 14(2), 15(2) or 16(3) of the Act; bringing of proceedings for such penalties under section 32(2)(*a*) before Commissioners; mitigation of such penalties, appeals against such penalties and recovery of such penalties
Section 34 and Schedule 2	6th April 2003	Imposition of penalties under section 32(2)(*b*) of the Act for failure to provide information or evidence under section 18(10) or 19(2) of the Act, or for failure to comply with requirement imposed by notice under section 17 of the Act by virtue of subsection (2)(*a*), (4)(*a*) or (6)(*a*) of that section; bringing of proceedings for such penalties under section 32(2)(*a*) before Commissioners; mitigation of such penalties, appeals against such penalties and recovery of such penalties
Section 34 and Schedule 2	6th April 2003	Imposition of penalties under section 33 of the Act for failure by employer to make correct payment to employee; mitigation of such penalties, appeals against such penalties and recovery of such penalties
Section 35 (offence of fraud)	1st August 2002	Instituting criminal proceedings for fraud in connection with obtaining payments of a tax credit
Section 36 (powers in relation to documents)	1st August 2002	Obtaining of documents in relation to offences involving fraud or serious fraud in connection with, or in relation to, tax credits
Section 37(1) to (4) and (6) (interest)	6th April 2003	Interest on overpayment of a tax credit
Section 37(2) and (5)	9th July 2002	Making regulations to prescribe rates of interest

Provision	*Date*	*Purposes*
Section 37(5) and (6)	1st August 2002	Interest on penalties under section 31 of the Act for incorrect statement or declaration in or in connection with a claim for a tax credit or a notification given in accordance with regulations under section 6 of the Act, or for incorrect information or evidence in response to a requirement imposed by virtue of regulations under section 25 of the Act
Section 37(5) and (6)	1st January 2003	Interest on penalties under section 31 of the Act for incorrect information or evidence in response to a requirement imposed by virtue of section 14(2), 15(2) or 16(3) of the Act
Section 37(5) and (6)	6th April 2003	Interest on penalties under section 31 of the Act for incorrect information or evidence in response to a requirement imposed by virtue of section 18(10) or 19(2) of the Act, or for incorrect statement or declaration in response to a notice under section 17 of the Act
Section 37(5) and (6)	1st August 2002	Interest on penalties under section 32 of the Act for failure to provide information or evidence required by regulations under section 25 of the Act, or for failure to give notification required by regulations under section 6(3) of the Act
Section 37(5) and (6)	1st January 2003	Interest on penalties under section 32 of the Act for failure to provide information or evidence under section 14(2), 15(2) or 16(3) of the Act
Section 37 (5) and (6)	6th April 2003	Interest on penalties under section 32 of the Act for failure to provide information or evidence under section 18(10) or 19(2) of the Act, or to comply with requirement imposed by notice under section 17 of the Act by virtue of subsection (2)(*a*), (4)(a) or (6)(*a*) of that section
Section 37(5) and (6)	6th April 2003	Interest on penalties under section 33 of the Act for failure by employer to make correct payment to employee
Sections 38 and 39 (appeals and exercise of right of appeal)	1st September 2002	Appeal against determination of penalty under paragraph 1 of Schedule 2 to the Act where the penalty is imposed under section 31 of the Act for incorrect statement or declaration in or in connection with a claim for a tax credit or a notification given in accordance with regulations under section 6 of the Act, or for incorrect information or evidence in response to a requirement imposed by virtue of regulations under section 25 of the Act
Sections 38 and 39	1st January 2003	Appeal against determination of penalty under paragraph 1 of Schedule 2 to the Act where the penalty is imposed under section 31 of the Act for incorrect information or evidence in response to a requirement imposed by virtue of section 14(2), 15(2) or 16(3) of the Act

Provision	*Date*	*Purposes*
Sections 38 and 39	6th April 2003	Appeal against determination of penalty under paragraph 1 of Schedule 2 to the Act where the penalty is imposed under section 31 of the Act for incorrect information or evidence in response to a requirement imposed by virtue of section 18(10) or 19(2) of the Act, or for incorrect statement or declaration in response to a notice under section 17 of the Act
Sections 38 and 39	1st September 2002	Appeal against determination of penalty under paragraph 1 of Schedule 2 to the Act where the penalty is imposed under section 32(2)(*b*) or (3) of the Act for failure to provide information or evidence required by regulations under section 25 of the Act, or for failure to give notification required by regulations under section 6(3) of the Act
Sections 38 and 39	1st January 2003	Appeal against determination of penalty under paragraph 1 of Schedule 2 to the Act where the penalty is imposed under section 32(2)(*b*) of the Act for failure to provide information or evidence under section 14(2), 15(2) or 16(3) of the Act
Sections 38 and 39	6th April 2003	Appeal against determination of penalty under paragraph 1 of Schedule 2 to the Act where the penalty is imposed under section 32(2)(*b*) of the Act for failure to provide information or evidence under section 18(10) or 19(2) of the Act, or to comply with requirement imposed by notice under section 17 of the Act by virtue of subsection (2)(*a*), (4)(*a*) or (6)(*a*) of that section
Sections 38 and 39	6th April 2003	Appeal against a determination of a penalty under paragraph 1 of Schedule 2 to the Act where the penalty is imposed under section 33 of the Act for failure by employer to make correct payment to employee
Sections 38 and 39	1st January 2003	Appeal against a decision under section 14(1), 15(1) or 16(1) of the Act, or under regulations under section 21 of the Act
Sections 38 and 39	6th April 2003	Appeal against a decision under section 18 (falling within section 38(1)(*b*)), 19(3), 20(1) to (4) or 37(1) of the Act
Section 40 (annual reports)	6th April 2004	Making of annual report by the Board to the Treasury
Section 41 (annual review)	6th April 2003	Review of prescribed monetary amounts
Sections 42 and 43 (persons subject to immigration control and polygamous marriages)	9th July 2002	Making regulations
Section 44 (Crown employment)	9th July 2002	Application of Part 1 of the Act to persons employed by or under the Crown
Section 45 (inalienability)	1st January 2003	All purposes of Part 1 of the Act and, as respects tax credits, Part 3 of the Act
Section 46 (giving of notices by Board)	1st August 2002	All purposes of Part 1 of the Act and, as respects tax credits, Part 3 of the Act
Section 48 (interpretation)	9th July 2002	All purposes of Part 1 of the Act
Section 58 (administrative arrangements)	9th July 2002	For the purposes of making regulations in relation to tax credits only
Section 59 and Schedule 5 (use and disclosure of information)	1st August 2002	All purposes of Part 1 of the Act and, as respects tax credits, Part 3 of the Act

Tax Credits

Provision	*Date*	*Purposes*
Section 60 and Schedule 6 (repeals) so far as concerns section 6 of the Tax Credits Act 1999 (c.10) (payment of tax credit by employers etc.) and regulations made under that section	27th August 2002	For the purposes of awards of working families' tax credit and disabled person's tax credit commencing on or after 27th August 2002
Section 60 and Schedule 6 so far as concerns section 6 of the Tax Credits Act 1999 and regulations made under that section	The day immediately following the expiry of the period of 26 weeks from the date of commencement of the award	For the purposes of awards of working families' tax credit and disabled person's tax credit that commence on or after 4th June 2002 but before 27th August 2002 and are existing on 27th August 2002

3 [Claims for a tax credit relating to the tax year 2003–04—transitional provision

(1) For the purposes of the definition of "the previous year income" in section 7(5) of the Act—

(*a*) any claim under the Act for a tax credit relating to the tax year 2003–04 shall be treated as if it were a claim for the tax year 2002–03, and

(*b*) accordingly the previous year income in relation to such a claim shall be income for the tax year 2001–02.

(2) In paragraph (1)—

"the tax year 2001–02" means the tax year beginning on 6th April 2001 and ending on 5th April 2002,

"the tax year 2002–03" means the tax year beginning on 6th April 2002 and ending on 5th April 2003, and

"the tax year 2003–04" means the tax year beginning on 6th April 2003 and ending on 5th April 2004.][1]

Amendments—[1] Substituted by the Tax Credits (Claims) (Transitional Provision) (Amendment) Order, SI 2002/2158 with effect from 20 August 2002 in the absence of any specific commencement provision.

2002/2005

WORKING TAX CREDIT (ENTITLEMENT AND MAXIMUM RATE) REGULATIONS 2002

Made by the Treasury under TCA 2002 ss 10, 11, 12, 65(1), (7), 67

Made . . . . *30 July 2002*

Coming into force in accordance with . . . . *regulation 1*

Commentary—*Simon's Taxes* **E2.220, E2.221**.

PART 1
GENERAL

1 Citation, commencement and effect

These Regulations may be cited as the Working Tax Credit (Entitlement and Maximum Rate) Regulations 2002 and shall come into force—

(*a*) for the purpose of enabling claims to be made, on 1st August 2002;

(*b*) for the purpose of enabling decisions on claims to be made, on 1st January 2003; and

(*c*) for all other purposes, on 6th April 2003;

and shall have effect for the tax year beginning on 6th April 2003 and subsequent tax years.

2 Interpretation

(1) In these Regulations, except where the context otherwise requires—

"the Act" means the Tax Credits Act 2002, and a reference without more to a numbered section is a reference to the section of the Act bearing that number;

["armed forces independence payment" means armed forces independence payment under the Armed Forces and Reserve Forces (Compensation Scheme) Order 2011;][10]

"the Board" means the Commissioners of Inland Revenue;

"the Contributions and Benefits Act" means the Social Security Contributions and Benefits Act 1992;

"child" has the same meaning as it has in the Child Tax Credit Regulations 2002;

"claim" means a claim for working tax credit and "joint claim" and "single claim" have the meanings respectively assigned in [section 3(8)][1];

"claimant" means the person making a claim and, in the case of a joint claim, means either of the claimants;

["contributory employment and support allowance" means a contributory allowance under Part 1 of the Welfare Reform Act [("the 2007 Act") as amended by the provisions of Schedule 3, and Part 1 of Schedule 14, to the Welfare Reform Act 2012 that remove references to an income-related allowance, and a contributory allowance under Part 1 of the 2007 Act as that Part has effect apart from those provisions][11];][6]

["couple" has the meaning given by section 3(5A) of the Act][3]

"the determination of the maximum rate" means the determination of the maximum rate of working tax credit;

["employed", except in the expression "self-employed", means employed under a contract of service or apprenticeship where the earnings under the contract are chargeable to income tax as employment income under Parts 2 to 7 of the Income Tax (Earnings and Pensions) Act 2003;][1] [otherwise than by reason of Chapter 8 of Part 2 of that Act (deemed employment in respect of arrangements made by intermediaries).][2]

["employment zone" means an area within Great Britain—

(*a*) subject to a designation for the purposes of the Employment Zones Regulations 2003 by the Secretary of State, or

[(*b*) listed in the Schedule to the Employment Zones (Allocation to Contractors) Pilot Regulations 2006][5]

pursuant to section 60 of the Welfare Reform and Pensions Act 1999;][4]

"employment zone programme" means a programme which is—

(*a*) established for one or more employment zones, and

(*b*) designed to assist claimants for a jobseeker's allowance to obtain sustainable employment;

["initial claim" shall be construed in accordance with regulation 9A;][1]

["limited capability for work credit" refers to a credit under regulation 8B(1) of the Social Security (Credits) Regulations 1975 where paragraph (2)(*a*)(iv) or (2)(*a*)(v) of that regulation applies, and which follows the cessation of the entitlement period of contributory employment and support allowance;][8]

"local authority" means—

(*a*) in relation to England, the council of a county or district, a metropolitan district, a London Borough, the Common Council of the City of London or the Council of the Isles of Scilly;

(*b*) in relation to Wales, the council of a county or county borough; or,

(*c*) in relation to Scotland, a council constituted under section 2 of the Local Government, etc (Scotland) Act 1994;

["partner" means a member of a . . . [3] couple making a joint claim;][1]

"patient" means a person (other than a person who is serving a sentence, imposed by a court, in a prison or youth custody institution or, in Scotland, a young offenders' institution) who is regarded as receiving free in-patient treatment within the meaning of the Social Security (Hospital In-Patients) Regulations [2005][8];

"period of award" shall be construed in accordance with [section 5][1];

["personal independence payment" means personal independence payment under Part 4 of the Welfare Reform Act 2012;][9]

"qualifying young person" means a person who satisfies regulation 5 of the Child Tax Credit Regulations 2002;

"relevant child care charges" has the meaning given by regulation 14;

. . . [1]

["self-employed" means engaged in carrying on a trade, profession or vocation on a commercial basis and with a view to the realisation of profits, either on one's own account or as a member of a business partnership and the trade, profession or vocation is organised and regular;][12]

"sports award" means an award made by one of the Sports Councils named in section 23(2) of the National Lottery etc Act 1993 out of sums allocated to it for distribution under that section;

"surrogate child" means a child in respect of whom an order has been made under section 30 of the Human Fertilisation and Embryology Act 1990 [(parental orders) or section 54 of the Human Fertilisation and Embryology Act 2008 (parental orders)][7];

. . . [1]

"training allowance" means an allowance (whether by way of periodical grants or otherwise) payable—

Tax Credits

(*a*) out of public funds by a Government department or by or on behalf of the Secretary of State, Scottish Enterprise or Highlands and Islands Enterprise or the Department for Employment and Learning ("the relevant paying authority");

(*b*) to a person in respect of his maintenance or in respect of a member of his family; and

(*c*) for the period, or part of the period, during which he is following a course of training or instruction—

(i) provided by, or in pursuance of arrangements made with, the relevant paying authority, or

(ii) approved by the relevant paying authority in relation to him,

but does not include an allowance, paid by a Government department, Northern Ireland department or the Scottish Executive to or in respect of a person by reason of the fact that he is training as a teacher, or is following a course of full-time education, other than under arrangements made under section 2 of the Employment and Training Act 1973, section 2 or 3 of the Disabled Persons (Employment) Act (Northern Ireland) 1945, or section 1(1) of the Employment and Training Act (Northern Ireland) 1950;

["training for work" shall be construed in accordance with regulation 9B;][1]

"week" means a period of seven days beginning with midnight between Saturday and Sunday;

["the Welfare Reform Act" means the Welfare Reform Act 2007.][6]

(2) For the purposes of these Regulations a person is responsible for a child or qualifying young person if he is treated as being responsible for that child or qualifying young person in accordance with the rules contained in regulation 3 of the Child Tax Credit Regulations 2002.

(3) A reference in these Regulations to an enactment applying to Great Britain but not to Northern Ireland shall, unless the context otherwise requires, include a reference to the corresponding enactment applying in Northern Ireland.

[(4) In these Regulations as they apply to an office a reference to being employed includes a reference to being the holder of an office.][1]

[(5) For the purpose of these Regulations—

(*a*) two or more periods of entitlement to employment and support allowance are linked together if they satisfy the conditions in regulation 145 of the Employment and Support Allowance Regulations 2008 [or regulation 86 of the Employment and Support Allowance Regulations 2013][11]; and

(*b*) a period of entitlement to employment and support allowance is linked together with a period of entitlement to statutory sick pay if it follows that period within 12 weeks.][6]

Modifications—Tax Credits (Polygamous Marriages) Regulations, SI 2003/742 regs 26, 27 (modification of this regulation for the purposes of polygamous marriages).

Amendments—[1] In para (1), words in definitions of "claim" and "period of award" substituted, definitions of "employed" and "initial claim" substituted, definitions of "partner" and "training for work" inserted, definitions of "Schedule E" and "the Taxes Act" revoked; and para (4) inserted; by the WTC (Entitlement and Maximum Rate) (Amendment) Regulations, SI 2003/701 regs 2, 3 with effect from 6 April 2003.

[2] Words in definition of "employed" inserted by the Tax Credits (Miscellaneous Amendments No 2) Regulations, SI 2003/2815 regs 12, 13 with effect from 26 November 2003.

[3] In para (1), definition of "couple" substituted, and words in definition of "partner" revoked, by the Civil Partnership Act 2004 (Tax Credits, etc) (Consequential Amendments) Order, SI 2005/2919 art 2(1), (2) with effect from 5 December 2005.

[4] Definition of "employment zone" substituted by the Tax Credits (Miscellaneous Amendments) Regulations, SI 2006/766 reg 20(1), (2) with effect from 6 April 2006.

[5] Words in definition of "employment zone" substituted by the Tax Credits (Miscellaneous Amendments) Regulations, SI 2007/824 regs 2, 3 with effect from 6 April 2007.

[6] In para (1), definitions of "contributory employment and support allowance" and "the Welfare Reform Act", and whole of para (5), inserted, by the Employment and Support Allowance (Consequential Provisions) (No 3) Regulations, SI 2008/1879, reg 20(1), (2)(*a*), (*b*) with effect from 27 October 2008.

[7] In para (1), in definition of "surrogate child" words inserted by the Human Fertilisation and Embryology (Parental Orders) (Consequential, Transitional and Saving Provisions) Order, SI 2010/986 art 2, Schedule para 7 with effect from 6 April 2010.

[8] In para (1), the entry for "limited capability for work credit" inserted with effect from 1 May 2012, and in the entry for "patient" words substituted with effect from 6 April 2012, by the Tax Credits (Miscellaneous Amendments) Regulations, SI 2012/848 regs 1(2), (4), 2(1), (2).

[9] In para (1), definition of "personal independence payment" inserted by the Personal Independence Payment (Supplementary Provisions and Consequential Amendments) Regulations, SI 2013/388 reg 28(1), (2) with effect from 8 April 2013.

[10] In para (1), definition of "armed forces independence payment" inserted by the Armed Forces and Reserve Forces Compensation Scheme (Consequential Provisions: Subordinate Legislation) Order, SI 2013/591 art 7, Schedule para 24(1), (2) with effect from 8 April 2013.

[11] In paras (1), (5)(*a*), words inserted by the Universal Credit (Consequential, Supplementary, Incidental and Miscellaneous Provisions) Regulations, SI 2013/630 reg 77(1), (2) with effect from 29 April 2013.

[12] In para (1), definition of "self-employed" substituted by the Working Tax Credit (Entitlement and Maximum Rate) (Amendment) Regulations, SI 2015/605 regs 2, 3 with effect from 6 April 2015.

3 Other elements of working tax credit

(1) For the purposes of determining the maximum rate of working tax credit, in addition to the basic element and the disability element, the following elements are prescribed—

(*a*) a 30 hour element;
(*b*) a second adult element;
(*c*) a lone parent element;
(*d*) a child care element; [and][1]
(*e*) a severe disability element; . . . [1]
(*f*) . . . [1]

(2) It is a condition of entitlement to the other elements of working tax credit that the person making the claim for working tax credit is entitled to the basic element.

(3) If the claim for working tax credit is a joint claim, and both members of the couple satisfy the conditions of entitlement for—

(*a*) the disability element, [or][1]
(*b*) the severe disability element, . . . [1]
(*c*) . . . [1]

the award must include two such elements.

Commentary—*Simon's Taxes* **E2.221, E2.228.**

Modifications—Tax Credits (Polygamous Marriages) Regulations, SI 2003/742 regs 26, 28 (modification of para (3) above for the purposes of polygamous marriages).

Amendments –[1] In para (1), in sub-para (*d*) word inserted and sub-para (*f*) and preceding word revoked, and in para (3) in sub-para (*a*) word inserted and sub-para (*c*) and preceding word revoked, by the Tax Credits (Miscellaneous Amendments) Regulations, SI 2012/848 reg 1(2). 2(1), (3) with effect from 6 April 2012.

PART 2
CONDITIONS OF ENTITLEMENT

BASIC ELEMENT

4 Entitlement to basic element of Working Tax Credit: qualifying remunerative work

(1) Subject to the qualification in paragraph (2), a person shall be treated as engaged in qualifying remunerative work if, and only if, he satisfies all of the following conditions [(and in the case of the Second condition, one of the variations in that condition)][7].

First condition

The person [is employed or self-employed and][9]

(*a*) is working at the date of the claim; or
(*b*) has an offer of work which he has accepted at the date of the claim and the work is expected to commence within 7 days of the making of the claim.

In relation to a case falling within sub-paragraph (b) of this condition, references in the second third and fourth conditions below to work which the person undertakes are to be construed as references to the work which the person will undertake when it commences.

In such a case the person is only to be treated as being in qualifying remunerative work when he begins the work referred to in that sub-paragraph.

Second condition

[First variation: In the case of a single claim, the person—][7]

[(*a*) is aged at least 16 and—
(i) undertakes work for not less than 16 hours per week,
(ii) . . . [7] is responsible for a child or qualifying young person, or he has a physical or mental disability which puts him at a disadvantage in getting a job and satisfies regulation 9(1)(*c*),][1]

(*b*) . . . [7]
(*c*) is aged at least 25 and undertakes not less than 30 hours work per week . . . [6][, or
(*d*) is aged at least 60 and undertakes not less than 16 hours work per week][6].

[Second variation: In the case of a joint claim where neither person is responsible for a child or qualifying young person, the person— :

(*a*) is aged at least 16 and undertakes work for not less than 16 hours per week and has a physical or mental disability which puts that person at a disadvantage in getting a job and satisfies regulation 9(1)(*c*);
(*b*) is aged at least 25 and undertakes work for not less than 30 hours per week; or
(*c*) is aged at least 60 and undertakes work for not less than 16 hours per week.

Third variation: In the case of a joint claim where a person or that person's partner is responsible for a child or qualifying young person, the person—

(*a*) is aged at least 16 and is a member of a couple where at least one partner undertakes work for not less than 16 hours per week and the aggregate number of hours for which the couple undertake work is not less than 24 hours per week;
(*b*) is aged at least 16 and undertakes work for not less than 16 hours per week and has a physical or mental disability which puts that person at a disadvantage in getting a job and satisfies regulation 9(1)(*c*);

Tax Credits

(*c*) is aged at least 16 and undertakes work for not less than 16 hours per week and that person's partner is—
(i) incapacitated and satisfies any of the circumstances in [regulation 13(4) to (12)][8]; or
(ii) an in-patient in hospital; or
(iii) in prison (whether serving a custodial sentence or remanded in custody awaiting trial or sentence); or
(iv) entitled to carer's allowance under section 70 of the Social Security Contributions and Benefits Act 1992;

(*d*) is aged at least 60 and undertakes work for not less than 16 hours per week.][7]

Third condition

The work which the person undertakes is expected to continue for at least 4 weeks after the making of the claim or, in a case falling within sub-paragraph (*b*) of the first condition, after the work starts.

Fourth condition

The work is done for payment or in expectation of payment.

. . .[7]

[A social security benefit is not payment for the purposes of satisfying this condition.][5]

[(1A) For the purposes of interpretation of paragraph (1)—

(*a*) paragraphs (3) and (4) provide the method of determining the number of hours of qualifying remunerative work that a person undertakes;
(*b*) regulations 5, 5A, 6 and 7A and 7B apply in relation to periods of absence from work connected with childbirth or adoption, sickness, strike periods or suspension from work;
(*c*) regulations 7 and 7C apply to term time and seasonal workers and where pay is received in lieu of notice;
(*d*) regulation 7D applies where a person or, in the case of a joint claim, one or both persons cease to work or reduce their hours to the extent that they no longer satisfy the Second condition in paragraph (1);
(*e*) regulation 8 applies where there is a gap between jobs;
(*f*) regulation 9 prescribes the conditions which must be satisfied by, or exist in relation to, a person so that he is to be treated as having a physical or mental disability which puts him at a disadvantage in getting a job.][7]

(2) A person who would otherwise satisfy the conditions in paragraph (1) shall not be regarded as engaged in qualifying remunerative work to the extent that he is—

(*a*) engaged by a charitable or voluntary organisation, or is a volunteer, if the only payment received by him or due to be paid to him is a payment by way of expenses which falls to be disregarded under item 1 in Table 7 in regulation 19 of the Tax Credits (Definition and Calculation of Income) Regulations 2002;
(*b*) engaged in caring for a person who is not a member of his household but is temporarily residing with him if the only payment made to him for providing that care is disregarded income by virtue of item 3 or 4 in Table 8 in regulation 19 of the Tax Credits (Definition and Calculation of Income) Regulations 2002;
(*c*) engaged on a scheme for which a training allowance is being paid;
(*d*) participating in the Intensive Activity Period specified in regulation 75(1)(*a*)(iv) of the Jobseeker's Allowance Regulations 1996 or the Preparation for Employment Programme specified in regulation 75(1)(*a*)(v) of the Jobseeker's Allowance Regulations (Northern Ireland) 1996;
(*e*) engaged in an activity in respect of which—
(i) a sports award has been made, or is to be made, to him, and
(ii) no other payment is made, or is expected to be made, to him; or
(*f*) participating in an employment zone programme, that is to say a programme established for one or more areas designated pursuant to section 60 of the Welfare Reform and Pensions Act 1999, and subject to [the Employment Zones Regulations 2003 and the Employment Zones (Allocation to Contractors) Pilot Regulations 2005][3] if he receives no payments under that programme other than—
(i) discretionary payments disregarded in the calculation of a claimant's income under item 6(*b*) in [Table 6][1] in regulation 19 of the Tax Credits (Definition and Calculation of Income) Regulations 2002; or
(ii) training premiums.
[(*g*) a person who—
(i) is serving a custodial sentence or has been remanded in custody awaiting trial or sentence, and
(ii) is engaged in work (whether inside or outside a prison) while he is serving the sentence or remanded in custody.][4]

[This is subject to the following qualification.][2]

[(2A) Neither sub-paragraph (*c*) nor sub-paragraph (*d*) of paragraph (2) applies if—

(*a*) in a case falling within sub-paragraph (*c*), the training allowance, or
(*b*) in a case falling within sub-paragraph (d), any payment made by the Secretary of State, or, in Northern Ireland, by the Department for Social Development, in connection with the Intensive Activity Period,

is chargeable to income tax as the profits of a trade, profession or vocation.][2]

(3) The number of hours for which a person undertakes qualifying remunerative work is—
(*a*) in the case of an apprentice, employee or office-holder the number of hours of such work which he normally performs—
(i) under the contract of service or of apprenticeship under which he is employed; or
(ii) in the office in which he is employed;
(*b*) in the case of an agency worker, the number of hours in respect of which remuneration is normally paid to him by an employment agency with whom he has a contract of employment; or
(*c*) in the case of a person who is self-employed, the number of hours he normally performs for payment or in expectation of payment.

This is subject to the following qualification.

(4) In reckoning the number of hours of qualifying remunerative work which a person normally undertakes—
(*a*) any period of customary or paid holiday, and
(*b*) any time allowed for meals or refreshment, unless the person is, or expects to be paid earnings in respect of that time,

shall be disregarded.

[(5) In reckoning the number of hours of qualifying remunerative work which a person normally undertakes, any time allowed for visits to a hospital, clinic or other establishment for the purpose only of treating or monitoring the person's disability shall be included; but only if the person is, or expects to be, paid in respect of that time.][1]

[(6) In this regulation "work" shall be construed as a reference to any work that the person undertakes whether as a person who is employed or self-employed or both.][9]

Commentary—*Simon's Taxes* **E2.222.**

HMRC Manuals—Tax Credit Technical Manual TCTM2401 (normal conditions for treatment as being in qualifying remunerative work, with example).

TCTM2403 (guidance on students, student nurses, carers, trainees, intensive activity periods, sports awards and employment zone programmes).

TCTM2404 (guidance on working at home, foster parents, employment schemes and deciding whether a scheme provides employment).

TCTM2405 (guidance on calculating the hours worked, with examples).

New Tax Credits Claimant Compliance Manual CCM 6600–6820 (Revenue's approach to questions surrounding remunerative work and hours).

Modifications—See SI 2002/2005 reg 10(3) (modification of para (1) above for the purposes of determining whether the condition in SI 2002/2005 reg 10(2)(*c*) is met).

Tax Credits (Polygamous Marriages) Regulations, SI 2003/742 regs 26, 29 (modification of para (1) Second Condition for the purposes of polygamous marriages).

Amendments—[1] Words in paras (1), (2)(*f*)(i) substituted, and para (5) inserted, by the WTC (Entitlement and Maximum Rate) (Amendment) Regulations, SI 2003/701 regs 2, 4 with effect from 6 April 2003.

[2] Words in para (2) inserted, and para (2A) inserted, by the Tax Credits (Miscellaneous Amendments) Regulations, SI 2004/762 regs 4, 5 with effect from 6 April 2004.

[3] Words in para (2)(*f*) substituted by the Tax Credits (Miscellaneous Amendments) Regulations, SI 2006/766 reg 20(1), (3) with effect from 6 April 2006.

[4] Para (2)(*g*) inserted by the Tax Credits (Miscellaneous Amendments) Regulations, SI 2007/824 regs 2, 4 with effect from 6 April 2007.

[5] In para (1), fourth condition, words inserted by the Tax Credits (Miscellaneous Amendments) Regulations, SI 2009/697 regs 2, 3 with effect from 6 April 2009.

[6] In para (1), in second condition, at end of sub-para (*b*) word revoked, in sub-para (*c*) words revoked, and sub-para (*d*) and preceding word inserted, by the Tax Credits (Miscellaneous Amendments) (No 3) Regulations, SI 2010/2914 regs 10, 11 with effect from 6 April 2011.

[7] In para (1), words inserted, in the "Second condition", words substituted, words in para (*a*)(ii) and whole of para (*b*) revoked, "Second variation" and "Third variation" inserted, words in Fourth Condition revoked, and para (1A) inserted, by the Tax Credits (Miscellaneous Amendments) Regulations, SI 2012/848 regs 1(2), 2(1), (4), (5) with effect from 6 April 2012.

[8] In para (1), in Second condition, Third variation, sub-para (*c*)(i), words substitutedby the Working Tax Credit (Entitlement and Maximum Rate) (Amendment) Regulations, SI 2013/1736 reg 2 with effect from 5 August 2013.

[9] Words inserted in para (1), First Condition, and para (6) inserted by the Working Tax Credit (Entitlement and Maximum Rate) (Amendment) Regulations, SI 2015/605 regs 2, 4, 5 with effect from 6 April 2015.

5 [Time off in connection with [childbirth]

Amendments—Words in Heading substituted by the Tax Credits (Miscellaneous Amendments) Regulations, SI 2004/762 regs 4, 6 with effect from 6 April 2004.

(1) This regulation applies for any period during which a person—
(*a*) is paid maternity allowance,
(*b*) is paid statutory maternity pay,

(*c*) is absent from work during an ordinary maternity leave period under section 71 of the Employment Rights Act 1996 or Article 103 of the Employment Rights (Northern Ireland) Order 1996,

[(*ca*) is absent from work during the first 13 weeks of an additional maternity leave period under section 73 of the Employment Rights Act 1996 or article 105 of the Employment Rights (Northern Ireland) Order 1996,][2]

(*d*) is paid [. . . [6] statutory paternity pay][4],

(*da*) . . . [6]

[(*e*) is absent from work during [a][6] paternity leave period under . . . [6] Articles 112A or 112B of the Employment Rights (Northern Ireland) Order 1996,][4]

[(*ea*) is absent from work during an additional paternity leave period under sections 80AA or 80BB of the Employment Rights Act 1996 or Articles 112AA or 112BB of the Employment Rights (Northern Ireland) Order 1996,][4]

(*f*) is paid statutory adoption pay, . . . [2]

(*g*) is absent from work during an ordinary adoption leave period under section 75A of the Employment Rights Act 1996 or Article 107A of the Employment Rights (Northern Ireland) Order 1996[, or]

[(*ga*) is absent from work during the first 13 weeks of an additional adoption leave period under section 75B of the Employment Rights Act 1996 or article 107B of the Employment Rights (Northern Ireland) Order 1996,][2]

[(*h*) is paid statutory shared parental pay,][6]

[(*I*) is absent from work during a period of shared parental leave under section 75E or 75G of the Employment Rights Act 1996][6].

(2) For the purposes of the [conditions of entitlement in this Part][3], the person is treated as being engaged in qualifying remunerative work during the period. This is subject to [paragraphs (3), (3A) and regulation 7D][5].

(3) The person must have been engaged in qualifying remunerative work immediately before the beginning of the period.

[(3A) A person shall only be treated as being engaged in qualifying remunerative work by virtue of paragraph (1)(*ea*) for such period as that person would have been paid additional statutory paternity pay had the conditions of entitlement in . . . [6] Parts 2 or 3 of the Additional Statutory Paternity Pay (General) Regulations (Northern Ireland) 2010 been satisfied.][4]

[(3B) A person shall only be treated as being engaged in qualifying remunerative work by virtue of paragraph (1)(*i*) for such period as that person would have been paid statutory shared parental pay had the conditions of entitlement in Parts 2 or 3 of the Statutory Shared Parental Pay (General) Regulations 2014 been satisfied.][6]

(4) A person who is self-employed is treated as engaged in qualifying remunerative work for the requisite number of hours during any period for which paragraph (1) would have applied in his case but for the fact that the work he performed in the week immediately before the period began, although done for payment or in the expectation of payment, was not performed under a contract of service or apprenticeship.][1]

Commentary—*Simon's Taxes* **E2.222.**

HMRC Manuals—Tax Credit Technical Manual TCTM2402 (lists time off in connection with childbirth).

Amendments—[1] This regulation substituted by the WTC (Entitlement and Maximum Rate) (Amendment) Regulations, SI 2003/701 regs 2, 5 with effect from 6 April 2003.

[2] Paras (1)(*ca*), (*ga*) and preceding word "or" inserted, and in para (1)(*f*) word "or" revoked, by the Tax Credits (Miscellaneous Amendments) Regulations, SI 2007/824 regs 2, 5 with effect from 6 April 2007.

[3] In para (2), words substituted by the Working Tax Credit (Entitlement and Maximum Rate) (Amendment) Regulations, SI 2009/1829 regs 2, 3 with effect from 31 July 2009.

[4] In para (1)(*d*), words substituted , para (1)(*e*) substituted, paras (1)(*da*), (*ea*), (3A) inserted, and former words in para (2) substituted by the Tax Credits (Miscellaneous Amendments) (No 2) Regulations, SI 2010/2494, regs 2, 3, with effect from 14 November 2010.

[5] In para (2) words substituted by the Tax Credits (Miscellaneous Amendments) Regulations, SI 2012/848 regs 1(2), 2(1), (6) with effect from 6 April 2012.

[6] The following amendments made by the Working Tax Credit (Entitlement and Maximum Rate) (Amendment) Regulations, SI 2014/3255 reg 11 with effect from 5 April 2015—

- in sub-para (1)(*d*), word revoked;
- sub-para (1)(*da*), revoked;
- in sub-para (1)(*e*), word substituted;
- in sub-paras (1)(*ea*), (3A) words revoked; and
- sub-paras (1)(*h*), (*I*), (3B) inserted.

5A [Time off in connection with childbirth and placement for adoption: further provisions

(1) This regulation applies to a person for any period—

(*a*) which falls within a period to which regulation 5 applies; and

(*b*) which follows the birth or the placement for adoption of the child in connection with whose birth or placement entitlement to the allowance, pay or leave mentioned in regulation 5(1) arises.

(2) [A person who would have been treated as being engaged in qualifying remunerative work if they or, in the case of a joint claim, they or their partner had been responsible for a child or qualifying young person][3], immediately before the beginning of a period to which regulation 5 applies, shall be treated as [being engaged in qualifying remunerative work for the purposes of the conditions of entitlement in this Part][2] during the period mentioned in paragraph (1) above.
(3) Paragraph (4) of regulation 5 applies for the purpose of this regulation as it applies for the purpose of that regulation.][1]
[(4) This regulation is subject to regulation 7D.][3]

HMRC Manuals—Tax Credit Technical Manual TCTM2402 (lists time off in connection with childbirth).

Amendments—[1] This regulation inserted by the Tax Credits (Miscellaneous Amendments) Regulations, SI 2004/762 regs 4, 7 with effect from 6 April 2004.

[2] In para (2), words substituted by the Working Tax Credit (Entitlement and Maximum Rate) (Amendment) Regulations, SI 2009/1829 regs 2, 4 with effect from 31 July 2009.

[3] In para (2), words substituted, and para (4) inserted, by the Tax Credits (Miscellaneous Amendments) Regulations, SI 2012/848 regs 1(2), 2(1), (7) with effect from 6 April 2012.

6 [Periods of illness[, incapacity for work or limited capability for work]

(1) This regulation applies for any period during which a person—
(*a*) is paid statutory sick pay,
(*b*) is paid short-term incapacity benefit at the lower rate under sections 30A to 30E of the Contributions and Benefits Act,
(*c*) is paid income support on the grounds of incapacity for work under paragraphs 7 and 14 of Schedule 1B to the Income Support (General) Regulations 1987,
[(*cc*) is paid an employment and support allowance under Part 1 of the Welfare Reform Act, or][2]
(*d*) receives national insurance credits on the grounds of incapacity for work [or limited capability for work][2] under regulation 8B of the Social Security (Credits) Regulations 1975.
(2) For the purposes of the [conditions of entitlement in this Part][2], the person is treated as being engaged in qualifying remunerative work during the period. This is subject to [paragraphs (3), (4) and regulation 7D][3].
(3) The person must have been engaged in qualifying remunerative work immediately before the beginning of the period.
(4) If the person is paid income support as specified in paragraph (1)(*c*) [or employment and support allowance as specified in paragraph (1)(*cc*)][2] or receives national insurance credits as specified in paragraph (1)(*d*) he is treated as being engaged in qualifying remunerative work for a period of 28 weeks only, beginning with the day on which he is first paid income support [or employment and support allowance][2] or receives national insurance credits (as the case may be).
(5) A person who is self-employed is treated as engaged in qualifying remunerative work for the requisite number of hours during any period for which paragraph (1) would have applied in his case but for the fact that the work he performed in the week immediately before the period began, although done for payment or in the expectation of payment, was not performed under a contract of service or apprenticeship.][1]

Commentary—*Simon's Taxes* **E2.222.**

Amendments—[1] This regulation substituted by the WTC (Entitlement and Maximum Rate) (Amendment) Regulations, SI 2003/701 regs 2, 6 with effect from 6 April 2003.

[2] Words in heading substituted, para (1)(*cc*) substituted, in para (1)(*d*), words inserted, and in para (4), words inserted, by the Employment and Support Allowance (Consequential Provisions) (No 3) Regulations, SI 2008/1879 reg 20(1), (3) with effect from 27 October 2008.

[3] In para (2) words substituted by the Tax Credits (Miscellaneous Amendments) Regulations, SI 2012/848 regs 1(2), 2(1), (8) with effect from 6 April 2012.

7 Term time and other seasonal workers

(1) For the purposes of the [conditions of entitlement in this Part][1], paragraph (2) applies if a person—
(*a*) works at a school, other educational establishment or other place of employment,
(*b*) there is a recognisable cycle to his employment there; and
(*c*) the length of that recognisable cycle is one year and includes periods of school holidays or similar vacations during which he does not work.
(2) If this paragraph applies, the periods mentioned in paragraph (1)(*c*) are disregarded in determining whether the [conditions of entitlement in this Part][1] are satisfied.

Commentary—*Simon's Taxes* **E2.222.**

HMRC Manuals—Tax Credit Technical Manual TCTM2405 (examples of term time workers).

Amendments—[1] In paras (1), (2), words substituted by the Working Tax Credit (Entitlement and Maximum Rate) (Amendment) Regulations, SI 2009/1829 regs 2, 6 with effect from 31 July 2009.

7A [Strike periods

(1) This regulation applies for any period during which a person is on strike.
(2) For the purposes of the [conditions of entitlement in this Part][2], the person is treated as being engaged in qualifying remunerative work during the period.
This is subject to [paragraph (3) and regulation 7D][3].

(3) The person—

(*a*) must have been engaged in qualifying remunerative work immediately before the beginning of the period, and

(*b*) must not be on strike for longer than a period of ten consecutive days on which he should have been working.][1]

Commentary—*Simon's Taxes* **E2.222.**

Amendments—[1] Regulations 7A, 7B, 7C inserted by the WTC (Entitlement and Maximum Rate) (Amendment) Regulations, SI 2003/701 regs 2, 7 with effect from 6 April 2003.

[2] In para (2), words substituted by the Working Tax Credit (Entitlement and Maximum Rate) (Amendment) Regulations, SI 2009/1829 regs 2, 7 with effect from 31 July 2009.

[3] In para (2), words substituted by the Tax Credits (Miscellaneous Amendments) Regulations, SI 2012/848 regs 1(2), 2(1), (9) with effect from 6 April 2012.

7B [Persons suspended from work

(1) This regulation applies for any period during which a person is suspended from work while complaints or allegations against him are investigated.

(2) For the purposes of the [conditions of entitlement in this Part][2], the person is treated as being engaged in qualifying remunerative work during the period.

This is subject to [paragraph (3) and regulation 7D][3]

(3) The person must have been engaged in qualifying remunerative work immediately before the beginning of the period.][1]

Commentary—*Simon's Taxes* **E2.222.**

Amendments—[1] Regulations 7A, 7B, 7C inserted by the WTC (Entitlement and Maximum Rate) (Amendment) Regulations, SI 2003/701 regs 2, 7 with effect from 6 April 2003.

[2] In para (2), words substituted by the Working Tax Credit (Entitlement and Maximum Rate) (Amendment) Regulations, SI 2009/1829 regs 2, 7 with effect from 31 July 2009.

[3] In para (2), words substituted by the Tax Credits (Miscellaneous Amendments) Regulations, SI 2012/848 regs 1(2), 2(1), (9) with effect from 6 April 2012.

7C [Pay in lieu of notice

(1) This regulation applies if a person stops work and receives pay in lieu of notice.

(2) For the purposes of the [conditions of entitlement in this Part][3], the person shall not be treated as being engaged in qualifying remunerative work during the period for which he receives the pay.][1]

[(3) This regulation is subject to regulation 7D.][2]

Commentary—*Simon's Taxes* **E2.222.**

Amendments—[1] Regulations 7A, 7B, 7C inserted by the WTC (Entitlement and Maximum Rate) (Amendment) Regulations, SI 2003/701 regs 2, 7 with effect from 6 April 2003.

[2] Para (3) inserted by the WTC (Entitlement and Maximum Rate) (Amendment) Regulations, SI 2007/968 reg 2(1), (2) with effect from 6 April 2007.

[3] In para (2), words substituted by the Working Tax Credit (Entitlement and Maximum Rate) (Amendment) Regulations, SI 2009/1829 regs 2, 7 with effect from 31 July 2009.

7D [Ceasing to undertake work or working for less than 16[, 24][2] or 30 hours per week

(1) This regulation applies for the four-week period immediately after—

(*a*) a person, not being a member of a couple, who is engaged in qualifying remunerative work for not less than 16 hours per week, ceases to work or starts to work less than 16 hours per week,

(*b*) a person, being a member of a couple only one of whom is engaged in qualifying remunerative work for not less than 16 hours per week, ceases to work or starts to work less than 16 hours per week,

(*c*) both members of a couple, each of whom is engaged in qualifying remunerative work for not less than 16 hours per week, cease to work or start to work less than 16 hours per week,

(*d*) a person, being a member of a couple who is entitled to the childcare element of working tax credit each of whom is engaged in qualifying remunerative work for not less than 16 hours per week, ceases to work or start to work less than 16 hours per week, or

(*e*) a person who satisfies paragraph (*c*) [of the first variation or paragraph (*b*) of the second variation][2] of the second condition in regulation 4(1) and who is engaged in qualifying remunerative work for not less than 30 hours per week, ceases to work or starts to work less than 30 hours per week.

[(*f*) one or both members of a couple who satisfy paragraph (*a*) of the third variation of the Second condition in regulation 4(1) and are engaged in qualifying remunerative work cease to work or reduce their hours to the extent that they cease to meet the condition that one member of the couple works not less than 16 hours per week and the aggregate number of hours for which the couple are engaged in qualifying remunerative work is not less than 24 hours per week.][2]

(2) For the purposes of the conditions of entitlement in this Part, the person is treated as being engaged in qualifying remunerative work during that period.][1]

Amendments—[1] This reg substituted by the Working Tax Credit (Entitlement and Maximum Rate) (Amendment) Regulations, SI 2009/1829 regs 2, 8 with effect from 31 July 2009.

[2] In heading, words inserted; in para (1)(*e*), words inserted; and para (1)(*f*) inserted; by the Tax Credits (Miscellaneous Amendments) Regulations, SI 2012/848 regs 1(2), 2(1), (10) with effect from 6 April 2012.

8 Gaps between jobs

For the purposes of the [conditions of entitlement in this Part][1] a person shall be treated as being engaged in qualifying remunerative work for the requisite number of hours if he has been so engaged within the past 7 days.

Commentary—*Simon's Taxes* **E2.222.**

Amendments—[1] Words substituted by the Working Tax Credit (Entitlement and Maximum Rate) (Amendment) Regulations, SI 2009/1829 regs 2, 9 with effect from 31 July 2009.

9 [Disability element and workers who are to be treated as at a disadvantage in getting a job

(1) The determination of the maximum rate must include the disability element if the claimant, or, in the case of a joint claim, one of the claimants—

(*a*) undertakes qualifying remunerative work for at least 16 hours per week;

(*b*) has any of the disabilities listed in Part 1 of Schedule 1, or in the case of an initial claim, satisfies the conditions in Part 2 of Schedule 1; and

(*c*) is a person who satisfies any of Cases A to G on a day for which the maximum rate is determined in accordance with these Regulations.

[(2) Case A is where the person has, for at least one day in the preceding 182 days ("the qualifying day"), been in receipt of—

(*a*) higher rate short-term incapacity benefit;

(*b*) long-term incapacity benefit;

(*c*) severe disablement allowance; or

(*d*) employment and support allowance [or a limited capability for work credit,][5] where entitlement to employment and support allowance [or that credit][5] or statutory sick pay [or a benefit or allowance mentioned in sub-paragraphs (*a*) to (*c*) or the income support payable under paragraph (3)(*a*),][5] has existed for a period of 28 weeks immediately preceding the qualifying day comprising one continuous period or two or more periods which are linked together.][4]

(3) Case B is where, for at least one day in the preceding 182 days, the person has been a person [for whom at least one of the following benefits has been payable and for whom the applicable amount][2] included a higher pensioner or disability premium [in respect of him][2] determined—

(*a*) in the case of income support, in accordance with [paragraphs 10(1)(*b*) or (2)(*b*) or 11, and where applicable, 12,][2] of Part III of Schedule 2 to the Income Support (General) Regulations 1987;

(*b*) in the case of income-based jobseeker's allowance, in accordance with [paragraphs 12(1)(*a*), or (*b*)(ii), or (*c*), or 13, and where applicable 14 of Part 3 of][2] Schedule 1 to the Jobseeker's Allowance Regulations 1996;

(*c*) in the case of housing benefit, in accordance with [paragraphs 11(1)(*b*) or 11(2)(*b*) or 12, and where applicable, 13 of Part 3 Schedule 3 of the Housing Benefit Regulations 2006][3];

(*d*) . . . [9]

(4) Case C is where the person is a person to whom at least one of the following is payable—

(*a*) a disability living allowance;

(*b*) an attendance allowance;

(*c*) a mobility supplement or a constant attendance allowance which is paid, in either case, in conjunction with a war pension or industrial injuries disablement benefit.

[(*d*) personal independence payment.][6]

[(*e*) armed forces independence payment.][7]

(5) Case D is where the person has an invalid carriage or other vehicle provided under—

(*a*) section 5(2)(*a*) of, and Schedule 2 to, the National Health Service Act 1977,

(*b*) section 46 of the National Health Service (Scotland) Act 1978, or

(*c*) Article 30(1) of the Health and Personal Social Services (Northern Ireland) Order 1972.

(6) Case E is where the person—

[(*a*) has received—

(i) on account of his incapacity for work, statutory sick pay, occupational sick pay, short-term incapacity benefit payable at the lower rate or income support, for a period of 140 qualifying days, or has been credited with Class 1 or Class 2 contributions under the Contributions and Benefits Act for a period of 20 weeks on account of incapacity for work, and where the last of those days or weeks (as the case may be) fell within the preceding 56 days; or

(ii) on account of his [incapacity for work or][5]having limited capability for work, an employment and support allowance [, or the pay or benefit mentioned in paragraph (i),][5] or a period of 140 qualifying days, or has been credited with Class 1 or Class 2 contributions under the Contributions and Benefits Act for a period of 20 weeks on account of [incapacity for work or][5] having limited capability for work, and where the last of those days or weeks (as the case may be) fell within the preceding 56 days;][4]

Tax Credits

(*b*) has a disability which is likely to last for at least six months, or for the rest of his life if his death is expected within that time; and

(*c*) has gross earnings which are less than they were before the disability began by at least the greater of 20 per cent. and £15 per week. For the purpose of this Case "qualifying days" are days which form part of a single period of incapacity for work within the meaning of Part 11 of the Contributions and Benefits Act [or a period of limited capability for work within the meaning of regulation 2(1) of the Employment and Support Allowance Regulations 2008][4].

(7) Case F is where the person—

(*a*) has undertaken training for work for at least one day in the preceding 56 days; and

[(*b*) has, within 56 days before the first day of that period of training for work, received—

(i) higher rate short-term incapacity benefit;

(ii) long-term incapacity benefit;

(iii) severe disablement allowance; or

(iv) contributory employment and support allowance [or a limited capability for work credit,][5] where entitlement to that allowance [or credit][5] or statutory sick pay [or a benefit or allowance mentioned in paragraphs (i) to (iii),][5] has existed for a period of 28 weeks comprising one continuous period or two or more periods which are linked together provided that, if the person received statutory sick pay, the person satisfied the first and second contribution conditions set out in paragraphs 1 and 2 of Schedule 1 to the Welfare Reform Act.][4]

[(7A) In paragraph (7)(*b*)(iv), the reference to contributory employment and support allowance is a reference to an allowance under Part 1 of the Welfare Reform Act 2007 ("the 2007 Act") as amended by the provisions of Schedule 3, and Part 1 of Schedule 14, to the Welfare Reform Act 2012 that remove references to an income-based allowance, and a contributory allowance under Part 1 of the 2007 Act as that Part has effect apart from those provisions.][8]

(8) Case G is where the person was entitled, [for at least one day in the preceding 56 days][2], to the disability element of working tax credit or to disabled person's tax credit by virtue of his having satisfied the requirements of Case A, B, E or F at some earlier time. For the purposes of this Case a person is treated as having an entitlement to the disability element of working tax credit if that element is taken into account in determining the rate at which the person is entitled to a tax credit.

(9) For the purposes of the Act, a person who satisfies paragraph (1)(*b*) is to be treated as having a physical or mental disability which puts him at a disadvantage in getting a job.][1]

Commentary—*Simon's Taxes* **E2.227.**

HMRC Manuals—Tax Credit Technical Manual TCTM2501 (summary of entitlement to disability element of WTC). TCTM2502 (reg 9(2)–(8): explanation of "qualifying benefits" test and fast-track).

Amendments—[1] Regulations 9, 9A, 9B substituted for regulation 9 as originally enacted, by the WTC (Entitlement and Maximum Rate) (Amendment) Regulations, SI 2003/701 regs 2, 8 with effect from 6 April 2003.

[2] Words in para (3) substituted and inserted, and words in para (8) substituted, by the Tax Credits (Miscellaneous Amendments No 2) Regulations, SI 2003/2815 regs 12, 14 with effect from 26 November 2003.

[3] Words in para (3)(*c*), (*d*) substituted by the Housing Benefit and Council Tax Benefit (Consequential Provisions) Regulations 2006, SI 2006/217 reg 5 Sch 2 para 22(2) with effect from 6 March 2006.

[4] Paras (2), (6)(*a*), (7)(*b*) substituted, and words in para (6) inserted, by the Employment and Support Allowance (Consequential Provisions) (No 3) Regulations, SI 2008/1879 reg 20(1), (4) with effect from 27 October 2008.

[5] In para (2)(*d*) and para (7)(*b*)(iv), words "or a limited capability for work credit,", "or that credit" and "or credit" inserted with effect from 1 May 2012, and other words in those paras and words in para (6)(*a*)(ii) inserted with effect from 6 April 2012, by the Tax Credits (Miscellaneous Amendments) Regulations, SI 2012/848 regs 1(2), 2(1), (11), (12), (13).

[6] Para (4)(*d*) inserted by the Personal Independence Payment (Supplementary Provisions and Consequential Amendments) Regulations, SI 2013/388 reg 28(1), (3) with effect from 8 April 2013.

[7] Para (4)(*e*) inserted by the Armed Forces and Reserve Forces Compensation Scheme (Consequential Provisions: Subordinate Legislation) Order, SI 2013/591 art 7, Schedule para 24(1), (3) with effect from 8 April 2013.

[8] Para (7A) inserted by the Universal Credit (Consequential, Supplementary, Incidental and Miscellaneous Provisions) Regulations, SI 2013/630 reg 77(1), (3) with effect from 29 April 2013.

[9] Para (3)(*d*) revoked by the Tax Credits (Miscellaneous Amendments) Regulations, SI 2014/658 reg 2 with effect from 6 April 2014.

9A [Initial claims

(1) In regulation 9(1)(*b*) an "initial claim" means a claim which—

(*a*) is made for the disability element of working tax credit, and

(*b*) relates to a person who has not had an entitlement to that element or to disabled person's tax credit during the two years immediately preceding the making of the claim.

(2) In paragraph (1) any reference to the making of a claim includes the giving of notification, in accordance with regulation 20 of the Tax Credits (Claims and Notifications) Regulations 2002, of a change of circumstances falling within that regulation.

(3) For the purposes of paragraph (1)(*b*) a person is treated as having an entitlement to the disability element of working tax credit if, by virtue of the person being a person who satisfies regulation 9, that element is taken into account in determining the rate at which the person is entitled to a tax credit.][1]

Amendments—[1] Regulations 9, 9A, 9B substituted for regulation 9 as originally enacted, by the WTC (Entitlement and Maximum Rate) (Amendment) Regulations, SI 2003/701 regs 2, 8 with effect from 6 April 2003.

9B [Training for work etc

(1) In [regulation 9][2] "training for work" means training for work received—

(*a*) in pursuance of arrangements made under—

(i) section 2(1) of the Employment and Training Act 1973,

(ii) section 2(3) of the Enterprise and New Towns (Scotland) Act 1990, or

(iii) section 1(1) of the Employment and Training Act 1950, or

(*b*) on a course whose primary purpose is the teaching of occupational or vocational skills, and which the person attends for 16 hours or more a week.

(2) For the purposes of regulation 9(7) a period of training for work means a series of consecutive days of training for work, there being disregarded any day specified in paragraph (3).

(3) Those days are any day on which the claimant was—

(*a*) on holiday;

(*b*) attending court as a justice of the peace, a party to any proceedings, a witness or a juror;

(*c*) suffering from some disease or bodily or mental disablement as a result of which he was unable to attend training for work, or his attendance would have put at risk the health of other persons;

(*d*) unable to participate in training for work because—

(i) he was looking after a child because the person who usually looked after that child was unable to do so;

(ii) he was looking after a member of his family who was ill;

(iii) he was required to deal with some domestic emergency; or

(iv) he was arranging or attending the funeral of his partner or a relative; or

(*e*) authorised by the training provider to be absent from training for work.

(4) For the purposes of paragraph (3)(*d*)(iv) "relative" means close relative, grandparent, grandchild, uncle, aunt, nephew or niece; and in this paragraph "close relative" means parent, parent-in-law, son, son-in-law, daughter, daughter-in-law, step-parent, step-son, step-daughter, brother, sister, or the spouse of any of the preceding persons or, if that person is one of an unmarried couple, the other member of that couple.][1]

Commentary—*Simon's Taxes* **E2.227.**

Amendments—[1] Regulations 9, 9A, 9B substituted for regulation 9 as originally enacted, by the WTC (Entitlement and Maximum Rate) (Amendment) Regulations, SI 2003/701 regs 2, 8 with effect from 6 April 2003.

[2] Words substituted by the Tax Credits (Miscellaneous Amendments) Regulations, SI 2004/762 regs 4, 8 with effect from 6 April 2004.

10 30 hour element

(1) The determination of the maximum rate must include a 30 hour element if the claimant, or in the case of a joint claim, at least one of the claimants, is engaged in qualifying remunerative work for at least 30 hours per week.

(2) The determination of the maximum rate must also include the 30 hour element if—

(*a*) the claim is a joint claim,

(*b*) at least one of the claimants is responsible for one or more children or qualifying young people,

(*c*) the aggregate number of hours for which the couple engage in qualifying remunerative work is at least 30 hours per week, and

(*d*) at least one member of the couple engages in qualifying remunerative work for at least 16 hours per week.

(3) . . . [1]

HMRC Manuals—Tax Credit Technical Manual TCTM2405 (examples illustrating the 30 hour element).

Modifications—Tax Credits (Polygamous Marriages) Regulations, SI 2003/742 regs 26, 30 (modification of para (2) above for the purposes of polygamous marriages).

Amendments—[1] Para (3) revoked by the Tax Credits (Miscellaneous Amendments) Regulations, SI 2012/848 regs 1(2), 2(1), (14) with effect from 6 April 2012.

11 [Second adult element

(1) The determination of the maximum rate must include the second adult element if the claim is a joint claim. This is subject to the following provisions of this regulation.

(2) . . . [5]

(3) . . . [5]

[(4) The determination of the maximum rate shall . . .[5] not include the second adult element if neither claimant has responsibility for a child or qualifying young person, and

(*a*) one claimant is serving a custodial sentence of more than twelve months, or

(*b*) one claimant is subject to immigration control within the meaning of [section 115(9)][3] of the Immigration and Asylum Act 1999.][2]

[(5) Paragraph (4)(b) does not apply where the claimant subject to immigration control is a person to whom Case 4 of regulation 3(1) of the Tax Credits (Immigration) Regulations 2003 applies.][3]][1]

Tax Credits

Commentary—*Simon's Taxes* **E2.224.**

Modifications—Tax Credits (Polygamous Marriages) Regulations, SI 2003/742 regs 26, 31 (modification of paras (1), (2) and (4) above for the purposes of polygamous marriages).

Amendments—[1] This regulation substituted by the WTC (Entitlement and Maximum Rate) (Amendment) Regulations, SI 2003/701 regs 2, 10 with effect from 6 April 2003.

[2] Para (4) substituted by the Tax Credits (Miscellaneous Amendments) Regulations, SI 2009/697 regs 2, 4 with effect from 6 April 2009.

[3] In para (4)(*b*), words substituted for words "section 115(9)(*a*)", and para (5) inserted, by the Tax Credits (Miscellaneous Amendments) (No 2) Regulations, SI 2009/2887 regs 2, 3 with effect from 6 April 2010.

[4] In former para (3), word "or" at end of sub-para (*a*) revoked, and sub-para (*c*) and preceding word ", or" inserted, by the Tax Credits (Miscellaneous Amendments) (No 3) Regulations, SI 2010/2914 regs 10, 12 with effect from 31 December 2010.

[5] Para (2), (3) and word in para (4) revoked by the Tax Credits (Miscellaneous Amendments) Regulations, SI 2012/848 regs 1(2), 2(1), (15) with effect from 6 April 2012.

12 Lone parent element

The determination of the maximum rate must include the lone parent element if—

(*a*) the claim is a single claim; and

(*b*) the claimant is responsible for [a child or qualifying young person][1].

Commentary—*Simon's Taxes* **E2.224.**

Amendments—[1] Words substituted by the WTC (Entitlement and Maximum Rate) (Amendment) Regulations, SI 2003/701 regs 2, 11 with effect from 6 April 2003.

CHILD CARE ELEMENT

13 Entitlement to child care element of working tax credit

(1) The determination of the maximum rate must include a child care element where that person, or in the case of a joint claim at least one of those persons, is incurring relevant child care charges and—

(*a*) is a person, not being a member of a . . . [3] couple, engaged in [qualifying remunerative work][1];

[(*b*) is a member or are members of a . . . [3] couple where both are engaged in qualifying remunerative work [for not less than 16 hours per week][6]; or][1]

[(*c*) is a member or are members of a . . . [3] couple where one is engaged in qualifying remunerative work [for not less than 16 hours per week][6] and the other—

(i) is incapacitated;

(ii) is an in-patient in hospital; or

(iii) is in prison (whether serving a custodial sentence or remanded in custody awaiting trial or sentence)][1][; or

[(iv) is entitled to carer's allowance under section 70 of the Social Security Contributions and Benefits Act 1992.][6]

(2) For the purposes of paragraph (1) a person is not treated as incurring relevant child care charges where the average weekly charge calculated in accordance with regulation 15 is nil or where an agreement within regulation 15(4) has not yet commenced.

(3) . . . [2]

[(4) For the purposes of paragraph (1)(*c*)(i) the other member of a couple is incapacitated in any of the circumstances specified in [paragraphs (5) to (12)][7].][1]

[(5) The circumstances specified in this paragraph are where housing benefit is payable under Part 7 of the Contributions and Benefits Act to the other member or the other member's partner and the applicable amount of the person entitled to the benefit includes a disability premium on account of the other member's incapacity or regulation 28(1)(*c*) of the Housing Benefit Regulations 2006 (treatment of child care charges) applies in that person's case.][7]

(6) The circumstances specified in this paragraph are where there is payable [or – in the case of a credit – an entitlement][6] in respect of him one or more of the following[6] . . . —

(*a*) short-term incapacity benefit [payable at the higher rate][1] under section 30A of the Contributions and Benefits Act;

(*b*) long term incapacity benefit under section 40 or 41 of the Contributions and Benefits Act;

(*c*) attendance allowance under section 64 of that Act;

(*d*) severe disablement allowance under section 68 of that Act;

(*e*) disability living allowance under section 71 of that Act;

(*f*) increase of disablement pension under section 104 of that Act;

(*g*) a pension increase under a war pension scheme or an industrial injuries scheme which is analogous to an allowance or increase of disablement pension under sub-paragraph (b), (d) or (e) above;

[(*h*) contributory employment and support allowance [or a limited capability for work credit,][6] where entitlement to that allowance [or credit][6] or statutory sick pay [or a benefit or allowance mentioned in sub-paragraph (*a*) or (*b*) or (*d*),][6] has existed for a period of 28 weeks comprising one continuous period or two or more periods which are linked together provided that, if the person received statutory sick pay, the person satisfied the first and second contribution conditions set out in paragraphs 1 and 2 of Schedule 1 to the Welfare Reform Act][5].

[(*i*) personal independence payment.][8]

[(*j*) armed forces independence payment.][9]

[(6A) In paragraph (6)(h), the reference to contributory employment and support allowance is a reference to an allowance under Part 1 of the Welfare Reform Act 2007 ("the 2007 Act") as amended by the provisions of Schedule 3, and Part 1 of Schedule 14, to the Welfare Reform Act 2012 that remove references to an income-related allowance, and a contributory allowance under Part 1 of the 2007 Act as that Part has effect apart from those provisions.][10]

(7) The circumstances specified in this paragraph are where a pension or allowance to which sub-paragraph [(*c*)][1], (*d*), (*e*) or (*f*) of paragraph (6) refers, was payable on account of his incapacity but has ceased to be payable only in consequence of his becoming a patient.

(8) The circumstances specified in this paragraph are where he has an invalid carriage or other vehicle provided to him under section 5(2)(*a*) of and Schedule 2 to the National Health Service Act 1977, section 46 of the National Health Service (Scotland) Act 1978; or Article 30(1) of the Health and Personal Social Services (Northern Ireland) Order 1972.

[(9) The circumstances specified in this paragraph are where, on 31st March 2013, council tax benefit was payable under Part 7 of the Contributions and Benefits Act (as then in force) to the other member or the other member's partner and the applicable amount of the person entitled to the benefit included a disability premium on account of the other member's incapacity.

(10) Paragraph (9) is subject to paragraphs (11) and (12).

(11) Paragraph (9) does not apply unless the other member of the couple was incapacitated (for the purposes of paragraph (1)(c)(i) and regulation 4(1) Second condition, Third variation (c)(i)) solely by virtue of that person or their partner having been in receipt, on 31st March 2013, of council tax benefit which included a disability premium on account of the other member's incapacity, and none of the other circumstances specified in paragraphs (5) to (8) applied on that date.

(12) If—

(*a*) the other member of the couple is incapacitated in the circumstances specified in paragraph (9), and

(*b*) the couple ceases to be entitled to working tax credit (for any reason) on or after 1st April 2013,

that member of the couple shall not be treated as incapacitated in the circumstances specified in paragraph (9) in relation to any subsequent claim.][7]

Commentary—*Simon's Taxes* **E2.225.**

HMRC Manuals—Tax Credit Technical Manual TCTM2610 (summary of above).
TCTM2620 (meaning of incapacitated).

Modifications—Tax Credits (Polygamous Marriages) Regulations, SI 2003/742 regs 26, 32 (modification of paras (1), (4), and (5) above for the purposes of polygamous marriages).

Amendments—[1] Words in para (1)(*a*), and reference in para (7) substituted, para (1)(*b*), (*c*), and paras (3), (4) substituted, and words in para (6)(*a*) inserted, by the WTC (Entitlement and Maximum Rate) (Amendment) Regulations, SI 2003/701 regs 2, 12 with effect from 6 April 2003.

[2] Para (3) revoked by the Tax Credits (Miscellaneous Amendments) Regulations, SI 2004/762 regs 4, 9 with effect from 6 April 2004.

[3] Words in para (1) revoked by the Civil Partnership Act 2004 (Tax Credits, etc) (Consequential Amendments) Order, SI 2005/2919 art 2(1), (3) with effect from 5 December 2005.

[4] Words in para (5) substituted by the Housing Benefit and Council Tax Benefit (Consequential Provisions) Regulations 2006, SI 2006/217 reg 5 Sch 2 para 22(3) with effect from 6 March 2006.

[5] Para (6)(*h*) inserted by the Employment and Support Allowance (Consequential Provisions) (No 3) Regulations, SI 2008/1879 reg 20(1), (5) with effect from 27 October 2008.

[6] In para (1) words inserted, and sub-para (iv) inserted, with effect from 6 April 2012; in para (6) words "or a benefit or allowance mentioned in sub-paragraph (*a*) or (*b*) or (*d*)," inserted with effect from 6 April 2012, and other words inserted and revoked with effect from 1 May 2012, by the Tax Credits (Miscellaneous Amendments) Regulations, SI 2012/848 regs 1(2), (4), 2(1), (16), (17).

[7] In para (4), words substituted, para (5) substituted, and paras (9)–(12) inserted by the Working Tax Credit (Entitlement and Maximum Rate) (Amendment) Regulations, SI 2013/1736 reg 3 with effect from 5 August 2013.

[8] Para (6)(*l*) inserted by the Personal Independence Payment (Supplementary Provisions and Consequential Amendments) Regulations, SI 2013/388 reg 28(1), (4) with effect from 8 April 2013.

[9] Para (6)(*j*) inserted by the Armed Forces and Reserve Forces Compensation Scheme (Consequential Provisions: Subordinate Legislation) Order, SI 2013/591 art 7, Schedule para 24(1), (4) with effect from 8 April 2013.

[10] Para (6A) inserted by the Universal Credit (Consequential, Supplementary, Incidental and Miscellaneous Provisions) Regulations, SI 2013/630 reg 77(1), (4) with effect from 29 April 2013.

14—(1) [Subject to paragraph (1A),][1] for the purposes of section 12 of the Act charges incurred for child care are charges paid by the person, or in the case of a joint claim, by either or both of the persons, for child care provided for any child for whom the person, or at least one of the persons, is responsible [within the meaning of regulation 3 of the Child Tax Credit Regulations 2002][2].

Tax Credits

In these Regulations, such charges are called "relevant child care charges".

[(1A) Child care charges do not include charges in respect of care provided by [—

(*a*) a relative of the child, wholly or mainly in the child's home, or

(*b*) . . . [11]][4]][1]

[(*c*) a provider mentioned in regulation 14(2)(*c*)(v), in circumstances where the care is excluded from being qualifying child care by Article 4(2)(*c*) of the Tax Credits (Approval of Home Child Care Providers) Scheme (Northern Ireland) 2006.][6]

[(*d*) a provider mentioned in [regulation 14(2)(*f*)(vii)][12], in circumstances where the care is excluded from being qualifying child care by Article 5(3)(*d*) of the Tax Credits (Approval of Child Care Providers) (Wales) Scheme 2007.][7]

[(*e*) a foster parent[, a foster carer or a kinship carer][12] in respect of a child whom [that person is fostering or is looking after as the child's kinship carer][12].][11]

[(1B) For the purposes of this regulation—

(*a*) "relative" means parent, grandparent, aunt, uncle, brother or sister whether by blood, half blood, marriage[, civil partnership][5] or affinity;

(*b*) "the child's home" means the home of the person, or in the case of a joint claim of either or both of the persons, responsible for the child.][1]

[(*c*) "foster parent" in relation to a child—

(i) in relation to England, means a person with whom the child is placed under the Fostering Services Regulations 2002;

(ii) in relation to Wales, means a person with whom the child is placed under the Fostering Services (Wales) Regulations 2003;

(iii) in relation to Northern Ireland, means a person with whom the child is placed under the Foster Placement (Children) Regulations (Northern Ireland) 1996; and

(*d*) "foster carer" and "kinship carer" have the meanings given in regulation 2 of the Looked After Children (Scotland) Regulations 2009.][12]

(2) "Child care" means care provided for a child—

(*a*) in England[9] . . . —

(i) . . . [11]

(ii) . . . [10]

[(ii*a*) by a person registered under Part 3 of the Childcare Act 2006;][10]

[(iii) in respect of any period on or before the last day the child is treated as a child for the purpose of this regulation by or under the direction of the proprietor of a school on the school premises [(subject to paragraph (2B))][11];][10]

(iv) . . . [11] . . . [9]

(v) . . . [11]

(vi) . . . [11]

(vii) by a domiciliary care worker under the Domiciliary Care Agencies Regulations 2002; . . . [10]

(viii) . . . [10]][9]

(*b*) in Scotland—

(i) by a person in circumstances where the care service provided by him consists of child minding or of day care of children within the meaning of [schedule 12 to the Public Services Reform (Scotland) Act 2010 and is registered under Part 5 of that Act;][15] . . . [3]

[(ia) by a child care agency where the service consists of or includes supplying, or introducing to persons who use the service, child carers within the meaning of [paragraph 5 of schedule 12 to the Public Services Reform (Scotland) Act 2010; or][15]][6]

(ii) by a local authority in circumstances where the care service provided by the local authority consists of child minding or of day care of children within the meaning of [schedule 12 to the Public Services Reform (Scotland) Act 2010 and is registered under Part 5 of that Act; or][15] . . . [14]

(iii) . . . [14]

(*c*) in Northern Ireland—

(i) by persons registered under Part XI of the Children (Northern Ireland) Order 1995; . . . [3]

(ii) by institutions and establishments exempt from registration under that Part by virtue of Article 121 of that Order;

[(iii) in respect of any period ending on or before the day on which he ceases to be a child for the purposes of this regulation, where the care is provided out of school hours by a school on school premises or by an Education and Library Board or a Health and Social Services Trust; or][3]

(iv) . . . [14]

[(v) by a child care provider approved in accordance with the Tax Credits (Approval of Home Child Care Providers) Scheme (Northern Ireland) 2006][6][; or

(vi) by a foster parent in relation to a child (other than one whom the foster parent is fostering) in circumstances where, but for the fact that the child is too old, the care would fall within one of the descriptions in paragraph (2C);][14]

(*d*) [anywhere outside the United Kingdom[1]]—

(i) by a child care provider approved by an accredited organisation within the meaning given by regulation 4 of the Tax Credit (New Category of Child Care Provider) Regulations 2002; or

(ii) . . . [1]

[(*e*) . . . [9]

[(*f*) in Wales—

(i) by persons registered under [Part 2 of the Children and Families (Wales) Measure 2010][14];

[(ii) by a person in circumstances where, but for article 11, 12 or 14 of the Child Minding and Day Care Exceptions (Wales) Order 2010, the care would be day care for the purposes of Part 2 of the Children and Families (Wales) Measure 2010;][14]

(iii) in respect of any period on or before the last day he is treated as a child for the purposes of this regulation, where the care is provided out of school hours, by a school on school premises or by a local authority;

(iv) by a child care provider approved by an accredited organisation within the meaning given by regulation 4 of the Tax Credit (New Category of Child Care Provider) Regulations 1999;

(v) . . . [14]

(vi) by a domiciliary care worker under the Domiciliary Care Agencies (Wales) Regulations 2004; . . . [14]

(vii) by a child care provider approved under the Tax Credits (Approval of Child Care Providers) (Wales) Scheme 2007][9][; or

(viii) by a foster parent in relation to a child (other than one whom the foster parent is fostering) in circumstances where, but for the fact that the child is too old, the care would fall within one of the descriptions in paragraph (2D).][14]

[(2A) In paragraph (2)(*a*)(iii)—

"proprietor", in relation to a school, means—

(*a*) the governing body incorporated under section 19 of the Education Act 2002, or

(*b*) if there is no such body, the person or body of persons responsible for the management of the school;

"school" means a school that Her Majesty's Chief Inspector of Education, Children's Services and Skills (the "Chief Inspector") is or may be required to inspect;

"school premises" means premises that may be inspected as part of an inspection of the school by the Chief Inspector.

(2B) Care provided for a child in England is not [child care][11] under paragraph (2)(*a*)(iii) if—

(*a*) it is provided during school hours for a child who has reached compulsory school age, or

(*b*) it is provided in breach of a requirement to register under Part 3 of the Childcare Act 2006.][10]

[(2C) The descriptions referred to in paragraph (2)(*c*)(vi) are—

(*a*) child minding or day care for the purposes of Part 11 of the Children (Northern Ireland) Order 1995; and

(*b*) qualifying child care for the purposes of the Tax Credits (Approval of Home Child Care Providers) Scheme (Northern Ireland) 2006.

(2D) The descriptions referred to in paragraph (2)(*f*)(viii) are—

(*a*) child minding, or day care, for the purposes of Part 2 of the Children and Families (Wales) Measure 2010; and

(*b*) qualifying child care for the purposes of the Tax Credits (Approval of Child Care Providers) (Wales) Scheme 2007.][14]

(3) For the purposes of this regulation a person is a child until the last day of the week in which falls the 1st September following that child's fifteenth birthday (or sixteenth birthday if the child is disabled).

(4) For the purposes of paragraph (3) a child is disabled where—

(*a*) a disability living allowance is payable in respect of that child, or has ceased to be payable solely because he is a patient;

[(*b*) the child is certified as severely sight impaired or blind by a consultant ophthalmologist;][18]

(*c*) the child ceased to be [certified as severely sight impaired or blind by a consultant ophthalmologist][18] within the 28 weeks immediately preceding the date of claim[; . . . [17]

Tax Credits

(*d*) personal independence payment is payable in respect of that child, or would be payable but for regulations under section 86(1) (hospital in-patients) of the Welfare Reform Act 2012;][16] [or

(*e*) armed forces independence payment is payable in respect of that child.][17]

(5) Charges paid in respect of the child's compulsory education or charges paid by a person to a partner or by a partner to the person in respect of any child for whom either or any of them is responsible are not relevant child care charges.

(6) Where regulation 15(4) (agreement for the provision of future child care) applies—

(*a*) the words "charges paid" in paragraph (1) include charges which will be incurred, and

(*b*) the words "child care provided" in paragraph (1) include care which will be provided.

(7) . . . [2]

(8) Relevant child care charges are calculated on a weekly basis in accordance with regulation 15.

Commentary—*Simon's Taxes* **E2.225.**

HMRC Manuals—Tax Credit Technical Manual TCTM2630 (meaning of child care).

Modifications—Tax Credits (Polygamous Marriages) Regulations, SI 2003/742 regs 26, 33 (modification of paras (1), (1B) and (5) above for the purposes of polygamous marriages).

Amendments—[1] Words in para (1) inserted, paras (1A), (1B) inserted; words in para (2)(*d*) substituted, sub-para (2)(*d*)(ii) revoked; by the WTC (Entitlement and Maximum Rate) (Amendment) Regulations, SI 2003/701 regs 2, 13 with effect from 6 April 2003.

[2] Words in para (1) inserted, and para (7) revoked, by the Tax Credits (Miscellaneous Amendments) Regulations, SI 2004/762 regs 4, 10 with effect from 6 April 2004.

[3] In para (2), words substituted, revoked and inserted by the Working Tax Credit (Entitlement and Maximum Rate) (Amendment) Regulations, SI 2004/1276 with effect from 1 June 2004.

[4] Words in para (1A) substituted, by the WTC (Entitlement and Maximum Rate) (Amendment) Regulations, SI 2005/769 regs 3, 4(*b*) with effect from 6 April 2005.

[5] In para (1B)(*a*), words inserted in the definition of "relative" by the Civil Partnership Act 2004 (Tax Credits, etc) (Consequential Amendments) Order, SI 2005/2919 art 2(1), (4) with effect from 5 December 2005.

[6] Paras (1A)(*c*), (2)(*b*)(ia), (*c*)(v) inserted by the Tax Credits (Miscellaneous Amendments) Regulations, SI 2006/766 reg 20(1), (4)–(6) with effect from 6 April 2006.

[7] Para (1A)(*d*) inserted, by the Tax Credits (Miscellaneous Amendments) Regulations, SI 2007/824 regs 2, 6 with effect from 6 April 2007.

[9] In para (2), in sub-para (*a*), words before para (i), word "or" in para (iv), and paras (vii), (viii) inserted; sub-para (*e*) revoked; and sub-para (*f*) substituted; by the Tax Credits (Miscellaneous Amendments) Regulations, SI 2008/604 reg 3 with effect from 6 April 2008.

[10] In para (2)(*a*), para (ii) revoked, para (ii*a*) inserted, para (iii) substituted, and para (viii) and preceding word "or" revoked, and paras (2A), (2B) inserted, by the Tax Credits (Miscellaneous Amendments) (No 2) Regulations, SI 2008/2169 reg 2 with effect from 1 September 2008.

[11] In para (1A), sub-para (*b*) revoked, sub-para (*e*) inserted, in para (2)(*a*), sub-paras (i), (v), (vi) revoked and words in sub-para (iii) substituted, and in para (2B), words substituted, by the Tax Credits (Miscellaneous Amendments) Regulations, SI 2009/697 regs 2, 5 with effect from 6 April 2009.

[12] In para (1A)(*d*), words substituted, in para (1A)(*e*), words inserted and words substituted; para (1B)(*c*), (*d*) inserted; by the Tax Credits (Miscellaneous Amendments) (No 2) Regulations, SI 2009/2887 regs 2, 4 with effect from 21 November 2009.

[14] In para (2), sub-para (*b*)(iii) and preceding word "or" revoked, in sub-para (*c*) para (iv) revoked, para (vi) and preceding word "or" inserted, in sub-para (*f*) in para (i) words substituted, para (ii) substituted, para (v) revoked, word "or" at end of para (vi) revoked, para (viii) and preceding word "or" inserted; and paras (2C), (2D) inserted; by the Tax Credits (Miscellaneous Amendments) Regulations, SI 2011/721 reg 3 with effect from 6 April 2011.

[15] In para (2)(b), words substituted by the Public Services Reform (Scotland) Act 2010 (Consequential Modifications of Enactments) Order, SI 2011/2581 art 2, Sch 2 para 36 with effect from 28 October 2011.

[16] In para (4), sub-para (*d*) and preceding word "or" inserted by the Personal Independence Payment (Supplementary Provisions and Consequential Amendments) Regulations, SI 2013/388 reg 28(1), (5) with effect from 8 April 2013.

[17] In para (4), word "or" at end of sub-para (*c*) revoked, and sub-para (*e*) and preceding word "or" inserted, by the Armed Forces and Reserve Forces Compensation Scheme (Consequential Provisions: Subordinate Legislation) Order, SI 2013/591 art 7, Schedule para 24(1), (5) with effect from 8 April 2013.

[18] In para (4), sub-para (*b*) substituted, and in sub-para (*c*) words substituted by the Child Benefit (General) and Tax Credits (Miscellaneous Amendments) Regulations, SI 2014/2924 reg 4(1), (2) with effect from 28 November 2014.

15 Calculation of relevant child care charges

(1) Relevant child care charges are calculated by aggregating the average weekly charge paid for child care for each child in respect of whom charges are incurred [and rounding up the total to the nearest whole pound][1].

This is subject to [paragraphs (1A) and (2)][1].

[(1A) In any case in which the charges in respect of child care are paid weekly, the average weekly charge for the purposes of paragraph (1) is established—

(*a*) where the charges are for a fixed weekly amount, by aggregating the average weekly charge paid for child care for each child in respect of whom charges are incurred in the most recent four complete weeks; or

(*b*) where the charges are for variable weekly amounts, by aggregating the charges for the previous 52 weeks and dividing the total by 52.][1]

(2) In any case in which the charges in respect of child care are paid monthly, the average weekly charge for the purposes of paragraph (1) is established—

(*a*) where the charges are for a fixed monthly amount, by multiplying that amount by 12 and dividing the product by 52; or

(*b*) where the charges are for variable monthly amounts, by aggregating the charges for the previous 12 months and dividing the total by 52.

(3) In a case where there is insufficient information for establishing the average weekly charge paid for child care in accordance with paragraphs (1) and (2), an officer of the Board shall estimate the charge—

(*a*) in accordance with information provided by the person or persons incurring the charges; and

(*b*) by any method which in the officer's opinion is reasonable.

(4) If a person—

(*a*) has entered into an agreement for the provision of child care; and

(*b*) will incur under that agreement relevant child care charges in respect of child care during the period of the award,

the average weekly charge for child care is based upon a written estimate of the future weekly charges provided by that person.

Commentary—*Simon's Taxes* **E2.225.**

HMRC Manuals—Tax Credit Technical Manual TCTM2640 (where there is no or insufficient information to calculate relevant child care charges, the Revenue officer will estimate the relevant child care charges in accordance with relevant information provided by the person or persons incurring the charges and by any method which in the officer's opinion is reasonable).

Amendments—[1] Words in para (1) substituted, and para (1A) inserted, by the WTC (Entitlement and Maximum Rate) (Amendment) Regulations, SI 2003/701 regs 2, 14 with effect from 6 April 2003.

16 Change of circumstances

(1) There is a relevant change in circumstances if—

(*a*) . . . [1]

(*b*) [during the period of an award, the weekly relevant child care charges, rounded up to the nearest whole pound[1]]—

(i) exceed the average weekly charge calculated in accordance with regulation 15 by £10 a week or more;

(ii) are less than the average weekly charge calculated in accordance with regulation 15 by £10 a week or more; or

(iii) are nil.

If there is a relevant change in circumstances, the amount of the child care element of working tax credit shall be recalculated with effect from the specified date.

[(2) For the purposes of paragraph (1), the weekly relevant child care charge—

(*a*) where the child care charges are for a fixed weekly amount, is the aggregate of the weekly charge paid for child care for each child in respect of whom charges are incurred in each of the four consecutive weeks in which the change occurred; or

(*b*) where the child care charges are for variable weekly amounts, is established by aggregating the anticipated weekly charge paid for child care for each child in respect of whom charges will be incurred for the following 52 weeks and dividing the total by 52.][1]

(3) If in any case the charges in respect of child care are paid monthly, the weekly relevant child care charge for the purposes of paragraph (1) is established—

(*a*) where the charges are for a fixed monthly amount, by multiplying that amount by 12 and dividing the product by 52; or

(*b*) where the charges are for variable monthly amounts, by aggregating the [anticipated][1] charges for the [next][1] 12 months and dividing the total by 52.

(4) In a case where there is insufficient information for establishing the weekly relevant child care charge paid for child care in accordance with paragraphs (2) and (3), an officer of the Board shall estimate the charge—

(*a*) in accordance with information provided by the person or persons incurring the charges; and

(*b*) by any method which in the officer's opinion is reasonable.

(5) For the purpose of paragraph (1) the specified date is—

(*a*) where the child care charges are increased, the later of—

(i) the first day of the week in which the change occurred, and

(ii) the first day of the week in which falls the day which is [one month][3] prior to the date notification of the change is given;

[(*b*) where the child care charges are decreased—

(i) in a case where an award of child care charges is a fixed period, the length of which is known when the award is first made, the first day of the week following the end of that fixed period, and

(ii) in all other cases, the first day of the week following the four consecutive weeks in which the change occurred.][2]

Commentary—*Simon's Taxes* **E2.225.**

HMRC Manuals—Tax Credit Technical Manual TCTM5200 (examples of changes in circumstances that should be notified).

Amendments—[1] Para (1)(*a*) revoked, words in para (1)(*b*) substituted, para (2) substituted, and words in para (3)(*b*) inserted and substituted, by the WTC (Entitlement and Maximum Rate) (Amendment) Regulations, SI 2003/701 regs 2, 15 with effect from 6 April 2003.

[2] Para (5)(*b*) substituted by the Working Tax Credit (Entitlement and Maximum Rate) (Amendment) Regulations, SI 2010/918, regs 2, 3, with effect from 15 April 2010.

[3] Words in para (5)(*a*)(ii) substituted by the Tax Credits (Miscellaneous Amendments) Regulations, SI 2012/848 regs 1(2), 2(1), (18) with effect from 6 April 2012.

17 Severe disability element

(1) The determination of the maximum rate must include the severe disability element if the claimant, or, in the case of a joint claim, one of the claimants satisfies paragraph (2) [or (3)][1] [or (4)][2].

(2) A person satisfies this paragraph if a disability living allowance, attributable to the care component payable at the highest rate prescribed under section 72(3) of the Contributions and Benefits Act or an attendance allowance at the higher rate prescribed under section 65(3) of that Act—

(*a*) is payable in respect of him; or

(*b*) would be so payable but for a suspension of benefit by virtue of regulations under section 113(2) of the Contributions and Benefits Act (suspension during hospitalisation), or an abatement as a consequence of hospitalisation.

[(3) A person satisfies this paragraph if the enhanced rate of the daily living component of personal independence payment under section 78(2) of the Welfare Reform Act 2012—

(*a*) is payable in respect of that person; or

(*b*) would be so payable but for regulations made under section 86(1) (hospital inpatients) of that Act.][1]

[(4) A person satisfies this paragraph if an armed forces independence payment is payable in respect of him.][2]

Amendments—[1] In para (1) words inserted, and para (3) inserted, by the Personal Independence Payment (Supplementary Provisions and Consequential Amendments) Regulations, SI 2013/388 reg 28(1), (6) with effect from 8 April 2013.

[2] Words in para (1), and whole of para (4), inserted, by the Armed Forces and Reserve Forces Compensation Scheme (Consequential Provisions: Subordinate Legislation) Order, SI 2013/591 art 7, Schedule para 24(1), (6) with effect from 8 April 2013.

18 50 plus element

. . .[1]

Commentary—*Simon's Taxes* **E2.228.**

HMRC Manuals—Tax Credit Technical Manual TCTM2700–2704 (summary of WTC entitlement to 50 plus element).

Amendments—[1] This regulation revoked by the Tax Credits (Miscellaneous Amendments) Regulations, SI 2012/848 regs 1(2), 2(1), (19) with effect from 6 April 2012.

DEATH OF A CHILD OR QUALIFYING YOUNG PERSON FOR WHOM THE CLAIMANT IS RESPONSIBLE

19 Entitlement after death of a child or qualifying young person for whom the claimant is responsible

(1) Paragraph (2) applies if—

(*a*) the death occurs of a child or qualifying young person,

(*b*) working tax credit is payable to a person who was, or to a couple at least one of whom was, immediately before the death responsible for that child or qualifying young person;

(*c*) the prescribed conditions for an element of working tax credit were satisfied because the claimant, or at least one of the claimants, was responsible for that child or qualifying person, but would not have been satisfied but for that responsibility; and

(*d*) the prescribed conditions would have continued to be satisfied but for the death.

(2) If this paragraph applies, working tax credit shall continue to be payable, as if the child or qualifying young person had not died, for the period for which child tax credit continues to be payable in accordance with regulation 6 of the Child Tax Credit Regulations 2002.

PART 3
MAXIMUM RATE

20 Maximum rates of elements of working tax credit

(1) The maximum annual rate of working tax credit (excluding the child care element) payable to a single claimant or to a couple making a joint claim is the sum of whichever of the following elements are applicable—

(*a*) the basic element specified in column (2) of the table in Schedule 2 at paragraph 1;

(*b*) in respect of a claimant who satisfies regulation 9(1), the disability element specified in column (2) of the table in Schedule 2 at paragraph 2;

(*c*) the 30 hour element specified in column (2) of the table in Schedule 2 at paragraph 3 in respect of—

(i) a single claimant who works for not less than 30 hours per week,

(ii) a couple either or both of whom work for not less than 30 hours per week; or

(iii) a couple, at least one of whom is responsible for a child or a qualifying young person and at least one of whom works for 16 hours per week if their hours of work when aggregated amount to at least 30 hours per week;

(*d*) the second adult element specified in column (2) of the table in Schedule 2 at paragraph 4 where regulation 11 so provides;

(*e*) the lone parent element specified in column (2) of the table in Schedule 2 at paragraph 5 where regulation 12 applies; [and][4]

(*f*) the severe disability element specified in column (2) of the table in Schedule 2 at paragraph 6—

(i) in respect of a single claimant who satisfies regulation 17; or

(ii) in respect of a member of a couple making a joint claim who satisfies regulation 17.

. . . [4]

(*g*) . . . [4]

(2) The maximum rate of the child care element of a working tax credit is [70 per cent][3] of the maxima specified in paragraph (3).

(3) The maxima are—

(*a*) [£175][2].00 per week, where the [claimant or, in the case of a joint claim, at least one of the claimants, is responsible for][1] only one child in respect of whom relevant child care charges are paid; and

(*b*) [£300][2].00 per week where the [claimant or, in the case of a joint claim, at least one of the claimants, is responsible for][1] more than one child in respect of whom relevant child care charges are paid.

Commentary—*Simon's Taxes* **E2.221, E2.225.**

HMRC Manuals—Tax Credit Technical Manual TCTM2601, 3101 (summary of above).

Modifications—Tax Credits (Polygamous Marriages) Regulations, SI 2003/742 regs 26, 34 (modification of para (1) above for the purposes of polygamous marriages).

Amendments—[1] Words in para (3) substituted by the WTC (Entitlement and Maximum Rate) (Amendment) Regulations, SI 2003/701 regs 2, 16 with effect from 6 April 2003.

[2] Figures in para (3) substituted by the Tax Credits Up-rating Regulations, SI 2005/681 reg 3(1). The amendments have effect in relation to awards of tax credits for the tax year beginning on 6 April 2005 and subsequent tax years: SI 2005/681 reg 1(3).

[3] Figure in para (2) substituted by the Tax Credits Up-rating Regulations, SI 2011/1035 reg 3 with effect in relation to awards of tax credits for the year beginning on 6 April 2011. This amendment continues to have effect in relation to awards of tax credits for the tax year beginning on 6 April 2012 and subsequent tax years (SI 2012/849 reg 5(*b*)).

[4] In para (1), in sub-para (*e*) word inserted and sub-para (*g*) and preceding word "and" revoked, by the Tax Credits (Miscellaneous Amendments) Regulations, SI 2012/848 regs 1(2), 2(1), (20) with effect from 6 April 2012.

SCHEDULES

SCHEDULE 1

DISABILITY WHICH PUTS A PERSON AT A DISADVANTAGE IN GETTING A JOB

Regulation 9(1)

PART 1

1 When standing he cannot keep his balance unless he continually holds onto something.

2 Using any crutches, walking frame, walking stick, prosthesis or similar walking aid which he habitually uses, he cannot walk a continuous distance of 100 metres along level ground without stopping or without suffering severe pain.

3 He can use neither of his hands behind his back as in the process of putting on a jacket or of tucking a shirt into trousers.

4 He can extend neither of his arms in front of him so as to shake hands with another person without difficulty.

5 He can put neither of his hands up to his head without difficulty so as to put on a hat.

6 Due to lack of manual dexterity he cannot, with one hand, pick up a coin which is not more than 2½ centimetres in diameter.

7 He is not able to use his hands or arms to pick up a full jug of 1 litre capacity and pour from it into a cup, without difficulty.

8 He can turn neither of his hands sideways through 180 degrees.

[9 He is certified as severely sight impaired or blind by a consultant ophthalmologist.][1]

Amendments—[1] Para 9 substituted by the Child Benefit (General) and Tax Credits (Miscellaneous Amendments) Regulations, SI 2014/2924 reg 4(1), (3) with effect from 28 November 2014.

10 He cannot see to read 16 point print at a distance greater than 20 centimetres, if appropriate, wearing the glasses he normally uses.

11 He cannot hear a telephone ring when he is in the same room as the telephone, if appropriate, using a hearing aid he normally uses.

12 In a quiet room he has difficulty in hearing what someone talking in a loud voice at a distance of 2 metres says, if appropriate, using a hearing aid he normally uses.

13 People who know him well have difficulty in understanding what he says.

14 When a person he knows well speaks to him, he has difficulty in understanding what that person says.

15 At least once a year during waking hours he is in a coma or has a fit in which he loses consciousness.

16 He has a mental illness for which he receives regular treatment under the supervision of a medically qualified person.

17 Due to mental disability he is often confused or forgetful.

18 He cannot do the simplest addition and subtraction.

19 Due to mental disability he strikes people or damages property or is unable to form normal social relationships.

20 He cannot normally sustain an 8 hour working day or a 5 day working week due to a medical condition or intermittent or continuous severe pain.

PART 2

21 As a result of an illness or accident he is undergoing a period of habilitation or rehabilitation.

Commentary—*Simon's Taxes* **E2.227.**

HMRC Manuals—Tax Credit Technical Manual TCTM2504, 2505 (explanation, with examples, of tests used in determining whether the above disabilities exist).

SCHEDULE 2

MAXIMUM RATES OF THE ELEMENTS OF A WORKING TAX CREDIT

Commentary—*Simon's Taxes* **E2.221.**

HMRC Manuals—Tax Credit Technical Manual TCTM7APPX2 (maximum rates, with daily rates and income thresholds).

Regulation 20(1)

[Relevant element of working tax credit	*Maximum annual rate*
1. Basic element	[£1,960][2]
2. Disability element	[£3,000][3]
3. 30 hour element	[£810][2]
4. Second adult element	[£2,010][2]
5. Lone parent element	[£2,010][2]
6. Severe disability element	[£1,290][3]][1]

Amendments—[1] Table substituted by the Tax Credits Up-rating, etc. Regulations, SI 2013/750 reg 3 with effect in relation to awards of tax credits for the tax year beginning on 6 April 2013 and subsequent tax years.

[2] Figure in items 1, 3, 4, 5 substituted by the Child Benefit and Tax Credits Up-rating Order, SI 2015/567 art 4 with effect from 6 April 2015.

[3] Figures in items 2, 6 substituted by the Tax Credits and Guardian's Allowance Up-rating etc Regulations, SI 2017/406 reg 2 with effect in relation to awards of tax credits for the tax year beginning on 6 April 2017 and subsequent tax years. Figures were previously £2,970 and £1,275 respectively.

2002/2006

TAX CREDITS (DEFINITION AND CALCULATION OF INCOME) REGULATIONS 2002

Made by the Treasury under TCA 2002 ss 7(8) and (9), 65(1), (7) and (9) and 67

Made . . . . *30 July 2002*

Coming into force in accordance with . . . . *regulation 1*

PART 1

GENERAL PROVISIONS

1 Citation, commencement and effect

These Regulations may be cited as the Tax Credits (Definition and Calculation of Income) Regulations 2002 and shall come into force—

(*a*) for the purpose of enabling claims to be made, on 1st August 2002;

(*b*) for the purpose of enabling awards to be made, on 1st January 2003; and

(*c*) for all other purposes, on 6th April 2003;

and shall have effect for the tax year beginning on 6th April 2003 and subsequent tax years.

2 Interpretation

(1) In these Regulations, unless the context otherwise requires—

"the Act" means the Tax Credits Act 2002;

"the Contributions and Benefits Act" means the Social Security Contributions and Benefits Act 1992; . . .[3]

"the Employment Act" means the Employment and Training Act 1973[; and

"the Northern Ireland Contributions and Benefits Act" means the Social Security Contributions and Benefits (Northern Ireland) Act 1992.][3]

(2) In these Regulations except where the context otherwise requires—

"the 1992 Fund" means moneys made available from time to time by the Secretary of State for Social Security for the benefit of persons eligible for payment in accordance with the provisions of a scheme established by him on 24th April 1992 as respects England and Wales and Northern Ireland and on 10th April 1992 as respects Scotland;

["the Board" means the Commissioners for Her Majesty's Revenue and Customs;][5]

"child" has the meaning given in the Child Tax Credit Regulations 2002;

"claim" means a claim for child tax credit or working tax credit and "joint claim" and "single claim" shall be construed in accordance with [section 3(8)][2] of the Act and "claimant" shall be construed accordingly;

["couple" has the meaning given by section 3(5A) of the Act;][4]

["earnings" shall be construed in accordance with section 62 of the ITEPA;][1]

"the Eileen Trust" means the charitable trust of that name established on 29th March 1993 out of funds provided by the Secretary of State for Social Security for the benefit of persons eligible in accordance with its provisions;

. . .[1]

["employment zone" means an area within Great Britain—

(i) subject to a designation for the purposes of the Employment Zones Regulations 2003 by the Secretary of State, or

[(ii) listed in the Schedule to the Employment Zones (Allocation to Contractors) Pilot Regulations 2006,][7]

pursuant to section 60 of the Welfare Reform and Pensions Act 1999;][5]

"employment zone programme" means a programme which is—

(*a*) established for one or more employment zones, and

(*b*) designed to assist claimants for a jobseeker's allowance to obtain sustainable employment;

"family" means—

(*c*) in the case of a joint claim, the . . .[4] couple by whom the claim is made and any child or qualifying young person for whom at least one of them is responsible, in accordance with regulation 3 of the Child Tax Credit Regulations 2002; and

(*d*) in the case of a single claim, the claimant and any child or qualifying young person for whom he is responsible in accordance with regulation 3 of the Child Tax Credit Regulations 2002;

"the Independent Living Fund" means the charitable trust of that name established out of funds provided by the Secretary of State for Social Services for the purpose of providing financial assistance to those persons incapacitated by or otherwise suffering from very severe disablement who are in need of such assistance to enable them to live independently;

Tax Credits

["ITA" means the Income Tax Act 2007;][8]

["the Independent Living Fund (2006)" means the Trust of that name established by a deed dated 10th April 2006 and made between the Secretary of State for Work and Pensions of the one part and Margaret Rosemary Cooper, Michael Beresford Boyall and Marie Theresa Martin of the other part;][9]

"the Independent Living Funds" means the Independent Living Fund, [the Independent Living (Extension) Fund, the Independent Living (1993) Fund and the Independent Living Fund (2006)][9];

"the Independent Living (Extension) Fund" means the trust of that name established on 25th February 1993 by the Secretary of State for Social Security and Robin Glover Wendt and John Fletcher Shepherd;

"the Independent Living (1993) Fund" means the trust of that name established on 25th February 1993 by the Secretary of State for Social Security and Robin Glover Wendt and John Fletcher Shepherd;

["ITEPA" means the Income Tax (Earnings and Pensions) Act 2003;][1]

["ITTOIA" means the Income Tax (Trading and Other Income) Act 2005;][5]

"the Macfarlane (Special Payments) Trust" means the trust of that name established on 29th January 1990 partly out of funds provided by the Secretary of State for Health for the benefit of certain persons suffering from haemophilia;

"the Macfarlane (Special Payments) (No 2) Trust" means the trust of that name established on 3rd May 1991 partly out of funds provided by the Secretary of State for Health for the benefit of certain persons suffering from haemophilia and other beneficiaries;

"the Macfarlane Trust" means the charitable trust established partly out of funds provided by the Secretary of State for Health to the Haemophilia Society for the relief of poverty or distress among those suffering from haemophilia;

"the Macfarlane Trusts" means the Macfarlane Trust, the Macfarlane (Special Payments) Trust and the Macfarlane (Special Payments) (No 2) Trust;

"pensionable age" has the meaning given by the rules in paragraph 1 of Schedule 4 to the Pensions Act 1995;

"pension fund holder", in relation to a [registered pension scheme][6], means the trustees, managers or scheme administrators of the scheme . . .[6];

. . .[6]

["qualifying care receipts" has the meaning given to that expression by section 805 of the Income Tax (Trading and Other Income) Act 2005;][12]

"qualifying young person" has the meaning given in the Child Tax Credit Regulations 2002;

["registered pension scheme" has the meaning given by section 150(2) of the Finance Act 2004;][6]

. . .[6]

. . .[6]

. . .[5]

. . .[1]

["Saving Gateway account" has the meaning given by section 1 of the Saving Gateway Accounts Act 2009;][10]

. . .[11]

"tax year" means a period beginning with the 6th April in one year and ending with 5th April in the next;

"the Taxes Act" means the Income and Corporation Taxes Act 1988;

"voluntary organisation" means a body, other than a public or local authority, the activities of which are carried on otherwise than for profit;

"war pension" has the meaning given in section 25(4) of the Social Security Act 1989.

(3) For the purposes of these Regulations, whether a person is responsible for a child or a qualifying young person is determined in accordance with regulation 3 of the Child Tax Credit Regulations 2002.

(4) In these Regulations—

(*a*) a reference to a claimant's partner is a reference to a claimant's spouse [or civil partner][4] or a person with whom the claimant lives as a spouse [or civil partner][4]; and

(*b*) a reference to a claimant's former partner is a reference to a claimant's former spouse [or civil partner][4] or a person with whom the claimant has lived as a spouse [or civil partner][4]; and

(*c*) a reference in these Regulations to an Extra Statutory Concession is a reference to that Concession as published by the Inland Revenue on 1st July 2002.

Modifications—Tax Credits (Polygamous Marriages) Regulations, SI 2003/742 regs 35, 36 (in para (2), definition of "family" amended, definitions of "joint claim" and "polygamous unit" inserted, and words in para (4)(*a*), (*b*) substituted for the purposes of polygamous marriages).

Universal Credit (Transitional Provisions) (Amendment) Regulations, SI 2014/1626

Universal Credit (Transitional Provisions) Regulations, SI 2013/386 reg 17(1), (2), Schedule paras 15, 16 (modification of this regulation in respect of awards of universal credit and terminations of awards of tax credit in the same year).
Universal Credit (Transitional Provisions) Regulations, SI 2014/1626 reg 4 (modification of this regulation in respect of awards of universal credit and terminations of awards of tax credit in the same year).

Amendments—[1] Definitions of "earnings" and "ITEPA" inserted, and definitions of "emoluments" and "Schedule E" revoked by the Tax Credits (Definition and Calculation of Income) (Amendment) Regulations, SI 2003/732, regs 1, 3 and 4, with effect from 6 April 2003.

[2] In para (2), reference in the definition of "claim" substituted by the Tax Credits (Miscellaneous Amendments No 2) Regulations, SI 2003/2815 regs 2, 3 with effect from 26 November 2003.

[3] In para (1), word revoked, and definition of "the Northern Ireland Contributions and Benefits Act" inserted, by the Tax Credits (Miscellaneous Amendments) Regulations, SI 2004/762 regs 12, 13 with effect from 6 April 2004.

[4] In para (2), definition of "couple" inserted, and words in the definition of "family" revoked, and words inserted in para (4), by the Civil Partnership Act 2004 (Tax Credits, etc) (Consequential Amendments) Order, SI 2005/2919 art 3 with effect from 5 December 2005.

[5] In para (2), definition of "the Board" and "employment zone" substituted; definition of "ITTOIA" inserted; and definition of "Schedule D" revoked; by the Tax Credits (Miscellaneous Amendments) Regulations, SI 2006/766 regs 6, 7 with effect from 6 April 2006.

[6] In para (2), words substituted and revoked in definition of "pension fund holder", definition of "personal pension scheme", "retirement annuity contract" and "retirement benefits scheme" revoked, and definition of "registered pension scheme" inserted, by the Taxation of Pension Schemes (Consequential Amendments) Order, SI 2006/745 art 26(1), (2) with effect from 6 April 2006.

[7] Words in definition of "employment zone" substituted by the Tax Credits (Miscellaneous Amendments) Regulations, SI 2007/824 regs 7, 8 with effect from 6 April 2007.

[8] In para (2), definition of "ITA" inserted by the Tax Credits (Definition and Calculation of Income) (Amendment) Regulations, SI 2007/1305 regs 2, 3 with effect from 16 May 2007.

[9] In para (2), definition of "the Independent Living Fund (2006)" inserted, and words in the definition of "the Independent Living Funds" substituted, by the Independent Living Fund (2006) Order, SI 2007/2538 art 7 with effect from 1 October 2007.

[10] Definition inserted by the Tax Credits (Miscellaneous Amendments) Regulations, SI 2010/751 regs 2, 3 with effect from 6 April 2010.

[11] In para (2), definition of "the Service Pensions Order" revoked by the Tax Credits (Miscellaneous Amendments) (No 3) Regulations, SI 2010/2914 regs 2, 3 with effect from 31 December 2010.

[12] In para (2), definition of "qualifying care receipts" inserted by the Tax Credits (Miscellaneous Amendments) Regulations, SI 2011/721 reg 2(1), (2) with effect from 6 April 2011.

PART 2
INCOME FOR THE PURPOSES OF TAX CREDITS

CHAPTER 1

GENERAL

3 Calculation of income of claimant

(1) The manner in which income of a claimant or, in the case of a joint claim, the aggregate income of the claimants, is to be calculated for a tax year for the purposes of Part 1 of the Act is as follows.

Step One

Calculate and then add together—

(*a*) the pension income (as defined in regulation 5(1)),
(*b*) the investment income (as defined in regulation 10),
(*c*) the property income (as defined in regulation 11),
(*d*) the foreign income (as defined in regulation 12) and
(*e*) the notional income (as defined in regulation 13)

of the claimant, or, in the case of a joint claim, of the claimants.

If the result of this step is £300 or less, it is treated as nil.

If the result of this step is more than £300, only the excess is taken into account in the following steps.

Step Two

Calculate and then add together—

(*a*) the employment income (as defined in regulation 4),
(*b*) the social security income (as defined in regulation 7),
(*c*) the student income (as defined in regulation 8) and
(*d*) the miscellaneous income (as defined in regulation 18)

of the claimant, or in the case of a joint claim, of the claimants.

Step Three

Add together the results of Steps One and Two.

Step Four

Calculate the trading income (as defined in regulation 6) of the claimant, or in the case of a joint claim, of the claimants.

Add the result of this step to that produced by Step Three . . . [1]

If there has been a trading loss in the year, [subtract][2] the amount of that loss from the result of Step Three.

[A loss shall not be available for tax credits purposes, unless the trade was being carried on upon a commercial basis and with a view to the realisation of profits in the trade or, where the carrying on of the trade formed part of a larger undertaking, in the undertaking as a whole.][8]

[Any trading loss in the year not set off as a result of the calculations in Steps One to Four above due to an insufficiency of income may be carried forward and set off against trading income (if any) of the same trade, profession or vocation in subsequent years (taking earlier years first) for the purposes of calculation of income under this regulation.][7]

(2) Subject to the qualifications in the following paragraphs of this regulation, and the provisions of Part 3, the result of Step Four in paragraph (1) is the income of the claimant, or, in the case of a joint claim, of the claimants, for the purposes of the Act.

(3) Income which—

(*a*) arises in a territory outside the United Kingdom and

(*b*) is, for the time being, unremittable for the purposes of [Chapter 4 of Part 8 of ITTOIA,][8]

is disregarded in calculating the income of the claimant or, in the case of a joint claim, of the claimants.

(4) Paragraph (5) applies in the case of a claimant who is[, for income tax purposes[3]]—

(*a*) resident [and domiciled . . . [12]][3] in the United Kingdom, . . . [7]

(*b*) resident . . . [12] but not domiciled in the United Kingdom . . . [12]

(*c*) . . . [12]

(5) In the case of a person to whom this paragraph applies—

[(*a*) any income arising outside the United Kingdom is to be taken into account, subject to any specific provision of these Regulations, regardless of the domicile or residence of the claimant; and][4]

(*b*) references to a sum being [taken into account][4] are to be construed as including a sum which would be taxable if he were resident . . . [12] and domiciled in the United Kingdom.

[(5A) Any income is to be taken into account, subject to any specific provision of these Regulations, notwithstanding the provision of any Order in Council under section 788 of the Taxes Act (double taxation agreements).][5]

(6) In the case of a claimant who would be chargeable to income tax but for some special exemption or immunity from income tax, income shall be calculated on the basis of the amounts which would be so chargeable but for that exemption or immunity.

[(6A) Income paid to a claimant in a currency other than sterling shall be converted into sterling at the average of the exchange rates applicable for the conversion of that currency into sterling in the period of 12 months [ending on 31st March][10] in the tax year in which the income arises.][5]

(7) In calculating income under this Part there shall be deducted[6] . . . —

(*a*) [the amount of][6] any banking charge or commission payable in converting to sterling a payment of income which is made in a currency other than sterling;

(*b*) [the grossed-up amount of][6] any qualifying donation (within the meaning of [Chapter 2 of Part 8 of ITA (gift aid)][11]), made by the claimant or, in the case of a joint claim, by either or both of the claimants; . . . [7] [and][9]

[(*c*) the amount of any contribution made by the claimant, or in the case of a joint claim, by either or both of the claimants to a registered pension scheme together with the amount of any tax relief due on those contributions.][9]

(*d*) . . . [9].

[(8) If—

(*a*) a claimant has sustained a loss in relation to a [UK property business][8] or an overseas property business; and

(*b*) the relief to which he is entitled in accordance with [section 120 of ITA (deduction of property losses from general income)][11] exceeds the amount of his property income or foreign income for tax credits purposes, for the year in question;

the amount of his total income for tax credit purposes, computed in accordance with the preceding provisions of this regulation, shall be reduced by the amount of the excess.

[In this paragraph "UK property business" and "overseas property business" have the same meanings as they have in Chapter 2 of Part 3 of ITTOIA.][8]][7]

Commentary—*Simon's Taxes* **E2.232.**

HMRC Manuals—Tax Credit Technical Manual TCTM4001, 4002 (summary of above; any trading loss in the year which is not set off as a result of the calculation in Steps 1 to 4 above due to an insufficiency of income may be carried forward and set off against trading income of the same trade, profession or vocation in subsequent years, taking earlier years first).

Modifications—Tax Credits (Polygamous Marriages) Regulations, SI 2003/742 regs 35, 37 (modification of para (7) for the purposes of polygamous marriages).

Universal Credit (Transitional Provisions) Regulations, SI 2013/386 reg 17(1), (2), Schedule paras 15, 17 (modification of this regulation in respect of awards of universal credit and terminations of awards of tax credit in the same year).

Universal Credit (Transitional Provisions) Regulations, SI 2014/1626 reg 4 (modification of this regulation in respect of awards of universal credit and terminations of awards of tax credit in the same year).

Amendments—[1] Words in sub-para (1), Step Four revoked by virtue of the Tax Credits (Definition and Calculation of Income) (Amendment) Regulations, SI 2003/732, regs 3, 5(1), (2)(*a*) with effect from 6 April 2003.

2 Word in sub-para (1), Step Four substituted by SI 2003/732, regs 3, 5(1), (2)(*b*) with effect from 6 April 2003.

3 Words in sub-para (4) inserted and words in sub-para (4)(*a*) substituted by SI 2003/732, regs 3, 5(1), (3) with effect from 6 April 2003.

4 Sub-para (5)(*a*) and words in (5)(*b*) substituted by SI 2003/732, regs 3, 5(1), (4) with effect from 6 April 2003.

5 Sub-paras (5A), (6A) inserted by SI 2003/732, regs 3, 5(1), (5), (6) with effect from 6 April 2003.

6 Words in sub-para (7) revoked, words in sub-para (7)(*a*), (*b*), (*c*) inserted, and words in sub-para (7)(*c*)(iii) substituted, by SI 2003/732, regs 3, 5(1), (7) with effect from 6 April 2003.

7 Words in para (1) inserted, in para (4); word in sub-para (*a*) revoked, word in sub-para (*b*) inserted, and sub-para (*c*) inserted; in para (7), word in sub-para (*b*) revoked, word in sub-para (*c*)(iii) inserted, and sub-para (*d*) inserted; and para (8) inserted; by the Tax Credits (Miscellaneous Amendments No 2) Regulations, SI 2003/2815 regs 2, 4 with effect from 26 November 2003.

8 In para (1), words in Step Four inserted; and words in paras (3), (8) substituted; by the Tax Credits (Miscellaneous Amendments) Regulations, SI 2006/766 regs 6, 8 with effect from 6 April 2006.

9 In para (7), word in sub-para (*b*) inserted, sub-para (*c*) substituted, and sub-para (*d*) revoked, by the Taxation of Pension Schemes (Consequential Amendments) Order, SI 2006/745 art 26(1), (3) with effect from 6 April 2006.

10 Words in para (6A) substituted by the Tax Credits (Miscellaneous Amendments) Regulations, SI 2007/824 regs 7, 9 with effect from 6 April 2007.

11 Words in paras (7)(*b*), (8)(*b*) substituted by the Tax Credits (Definition and Calculation of Income) (Amendment) Regulations, SI 2007/1305 regs 2, 4 with effect from 16 May 2007.

12 In paras (4)(*a*), (*b*), (5)(*b*) words revoked, and para (4)(*c*) and preceding word "or" revoked, by the Tax Credits (Miscellaneous Amendments) Regulations, SI 2014/658 reg 4(1)–(4) with effect from 6 April 2014.

CHAPTER 2

EMPLOYMENT INCOME

4 Employment income

(1) In these regulations "employment income" means—

(*a*) any [earnings][1] from an office or employment received in the tax year;

(*b*) so much of any payment made to a claimant in that year in respect of expenses as is chargeable to income tax [by virtue of section 62 or section 72 of ITEPA][1];

(*c*) [the cash equivalent of][1] any non-cash voucher received by the claimant in that year and chargeable to income tax under [section 87 of ITEPA][1] [or, where there is an optional remuneration arrangement, the relevant amount,][18];

(*d*) [the cash equivalent of][1] any credit-token received by the claimant in that year and chargeable to income tax under [section 94 of ITEPA][1] [or, where such a credit-token is provided pursuant to an optional remuneration arrangement, the relevant amount][18];

(*e*) [the cash equivalent of][1] any cash voucher received by the claimant in that year and chargeable to income tax under [section 81 of ITEPA][1] [or, where there is an optional remuneration arrangement, the relevant amount,][18];

[(*f*) any amount chargeable to tax under Chapter 3 of Part 6 of ITEPA;][1]

(*g*) so much of a payment of statutory sick pay, received by the claimant during the year, as is subject to income tax [by virtue of section 660 of ITEPA][1];

[(*h*) the amount (if any) by which a payment of statutory maternity pay, statutory paternity pay, statutory shared parental pay or statutory adoption pay exceeds £100 per week;][17]

(*i*) any amount charged to income tax for that year [under section 120 or section 149 of ITEPA][1];

[(*ia*) the relevant amount in cases where a car is made available to the claimant or a member of the claimant's family pursuant to an optional remuneration arrangement where the car's CO_2 emissions figure exceeds 75 grams per kilometre;][18]

[(*j*) any sum to which section 225 of ITEPA applies;][1]

(*k*) any amount paid in that year by way of strike pay to the claimant as a member of a trade union.

[(*l*) any amount charged to income tax for that year under Part 7 of ITEPA.][4]

[(*m*) any amount paid to a person serving a custodial sentence or remanded in custody awaiting trial or sentence, for work done while serving the sentence or remanded in custody.][8]

For the purposes of this paragraph, references to the receipt of a payment of any description are references to its receipt by or on behalf of the claimant, or in the case of a joint claim of either of the claimants, in any part of the world.

This paragraph is subject to the following qualifications.

(2) Employment income does not include pension income.

(2A), (2B) . . . [7]

[(3) This paragraph applies if (apart from section 64 of ITEPA) the same benefit would give rise to two amounts ("A" and "B")—

Tax Credits

(*a*) "A" being an amount of earnings from a claimant's employment as defined in section 62 of ITEPA, and

(*b*) "B" being an amount to be treated as earnings under any provision of Chapter 10 of Part 3 of ITEPA.

In such a case, the amount to be taken into account in computing the claimant's employment income is the greater of A and B, and the lesser amount shall be disregarded.][4]

(4) In calculating employment income, the payments and benefits listed in Table 1 shall be disregarded [except where the payment or benefit is provided pursuant to optional remuneration arrangements and is neither a special case benefit nor an excluded benefit][18].

TABLE 1
PAYMENTS [AND BENEFITS][2] DISREGARDED IN THE CALCULATION OF EMPLOYMENT INCOME

1	Any payment in respect of qualifying removal expenses, or the provision of any qualifying removal benefit, within the meaning of [Chapter 7 of Part 4 of ITEPA][2].
[2A	The payment or reimbursement of expenses incurred in the provision of transport to a disabled employee (as defined in section 246(4) of ITEPA) by his employer, if no liability to income tax arises in respect of that payment or reimbursement (as the case may be) by virtue of section 246 of ITEPA.
2B	The provision to a disabled employee (as defined in section 246(4) of ITEPA) by his employer of a car, the provision of fuel for the car, or the reimbursement of expenses incurred in connection with the car, if no liability to income tax arises in respect of that provision or reimbursement (as the case may be) by virtue of section 247 of ITEPA.
2C	The payment or reimbursement of expenses incurred on transport, if no liability to income tax arises in respect of that payment or reimbursement (as the case may be) by virtue of section 248 of ITEPA.][2]
3	Travel facilities provided for the claimant as a member of the naval, military or air forces of the Crown for the purpose of going on, or returning from, leave.
[3A	The payment [under a Royal Warrant made under section 333 of the Armed Forces Act 2006][14] of an operational allowance to a member of Her Majesty's forces in respect of service in an operational area specified by the Secretary of State for Defence.][8]
[3B	A payment designated [under a Royal Warrant made under section 333 of the Armed Forces Act 2006][14] as Council Tax Relief and made by the Secretary of State for Defence to a member of Her Majesty's forces.][9]
[3C	The payment under a Royal Warrant made under section 333 of the Armed Forces Act 2006, of the Continuity of Education Allowance to or in respect of members of the armed forces of the Crown during their employment under the Crown or after their deaths.][13]
4	Payment or reimbursement of expenses in connection with the provision for, or use by, the claimant as a person holding an office or employment of a car parking space at or near his place of work.
5	Any benefit or non-cash voucher provided to the claimant, or to any member of his family or household, [in respect of which no liability to income tax arises by virtue of Chapter 5 of Part 4 of ITEPA][2].
6	Any payment of incidental overnight expenses [in respect of which no liability to income tax arises by virtue of section 240 of ITEPA][2].
[7	Food, drink and mess allowances for the armed forces and training allowances payable to members of the reserve forces in respect of which no liability to income tax arises by virtue of section 297 or 298 of ITEPA.][2]
8	The value of meal vouchers issued to the claimant as an employee, [if section 89 of ITEPA applies to the vouchers][2].
9	Any cash payment received by the claimant as a miner in lieu of free coal, or the provision of the coal itself, [in respect of which no liability to income tax arises by virtue of section 306 of ITEPA][2].
10	An award made to the claimant as a director or employee by way of a testimonial to mark long service, [if, or to the extent that, no liability to income tax arises in respect of it by virtue of section 323 of ITEPA][2].
11	Payment of a daily subsistence allowance [in respect of which no liability to income tax arises by virtue of section 304 of ITEPA][2].

[11A The payment or reimbursement of reasonable expenses incurred by an employee who has a permanent workplace at an offshore installation, on transfer transport, related accommodation and subsistence or local transport, if no liability to income tax arises in respect of that payment or reimbursement (as the case may be) by virtue of section 305 of ITEPA.

For the purposes of this item, expressions which are defined in section 305 of ITEPA have the same meaning here as they do there.

11B Payment of an allowance to a person in employment under the Crown in respect of which no liability to income tax arises by virtue of section 299 of ITEPA.

11C The payment or reimbursement to an employee of any sum in connection with work-related training, or individual learning account training (as respectively defined in sections 251 and 256 of ITEPA) if no liability to income tax arises in respect of that payment or reimbursement (as the case may be) by virtue of any provision of Chapter 4 of Part 4 of ITEPA.

11D The provision for an employee of a non-cash voucher or a credit-token, to the extent that liability to income tax does not arise in respect of that voucher or credit-token (as the case may be), under Chapter 4 of [Part 3 of ITEPA, by virtue of any provision of Chapter 6 of Part 4 of ITEPA][4]

11E The provision for an employee of free or subsidised meal vouchers or tokens (within the meaning of section 317(5) of ITEPA), if no liability to income tax arises in respect of that provision by virtue of section 317 of ITEPA.][2]

[11F The provision of one mobile telephone for an employee in respect of which no liability to income tax arises by virtue of section 319 of ITEPA.][8]

12 An award made to the claimant under a Staff Suggestion Scheme, if the conditions specified in [sections 321 and 322 of ITEPA][2] [are satisfied][5].

13 Travelling and subsistence allowances paid to or on behalf of the claimant by his employer [in respect of which no liability to income tax arises by virtue of section 245 of ITEPA][2].

14 Any gift consisting of goods, or a voucher or token to obtain goods, [in respect of which no liability to income tax arises by virtue of section 270 or 324 of ITEPA][2].

[14A Any payment or reimbursement of expenses incurred in connection with an employment-related asset transfer (as defined in section 326(2) of ITEPA), if no liability to income tax arises in respect of that payment or reimbursement (as the case may be) by virtue of section 326 of ITEPA.

14B Any payment of expenses incurred by an employee in connection with a taxable car if no liability to income tax arises in respect of the payment by virtue of section 239(2) of ITEPA.][2]

[14C The discharge of any liability of an employee in connection with a taxable car if no liability to income tax arises by virtue of section 239(1) of ITEPA.

[14D A benefit connected with a taxable car if no liability to income tax arises by virtue of section 239(4) of ITEPA.][4]

15 A cash voucher, non-cash voucher or credit-token to the extent that it is used by the recipient for the provision of child care, the costs of which if borne by the recipient would be relevant child care charges within the meaning of regulation 14 of the Working Tax Credit (Entitlement and Maximum Rate) Regulations 2002.

[16 A payment made by the Department for Work and Pensions under section 2 of the Employment Act—

(*a*) by way of In-Work Credit[, Better Off In-Work Credit][10], Job Grant or Return to Work Credit, . . . [10]

(*b*) under the Employment Retention and Advancement Scheme or the Working Neighbourhoods Pilot.][5]

[(*c*) under the City Strategy Pathfinder Pilots,

(*d*) by way of an In-Work Emergency Discretion Fund payment pursuant to arrangements made by the Secretary of State, . . . [11]

(*e*) by way of an Up-front Childcare Fund payment pursuant to arrangements made by the Secretary of State][10][, or

(*f*) under the Future Capital pilot scheme.][11]

Tax Credits

[16A A payment made by the Department for Employment and Learning in Northern Ireland under section 1 of the Employment and Training Act (Northern Ireland) 1950 by way of Return to Work Credit.][7]

[16B Any In-Work Emergency Fund payment made to a person pursuant to arrangements made by the Department of Economic Development under section 1 of the Employment and Training Act (Northern Ireland) 1950.][10]

[17 The payment or reimbursement of reasonable additional household expenses incurred by an employee who works from home, within the meaning of section 316A of ITEPA.][4]

[18 The payment or reimbursement of retraining course expenses within the meaning of section 311 of ITEPA.][4]

[19 Provision of computer equipment in respect of which no liability to income tax arises by virtue of section 320 of ITEPA.][6]

[20 Pay As You Earn (PAYE) settlement agreements made under Part 6 of the Income Tax (PAYE) Regulations ("the PAYE Regulations") 2003. For the purposes of this item the special arrangements under regulation 141 of the PAYE Regulations also apply.][10]

[21 The payment or reimbursement of a fee within section 326A(1) of ITEPA (fees relating to vulnerable persons' monitoring schemes).][13]

[22 The payment of a qualifying bonus within section 312A of ITEPA (limited exemption for qualifying bonus payments).][15]

(5) From the amount of employment income, calculated in accordance with the preceding provisions of this regulation, there shall be deducted the amount of any deduction permitted in [calculating earnings by virtue of any provision of sections [231 to 232,][4] 336 to 344, or section 346, 347, 351, 352, 362, 363, 367, 368, 370, 371, 373, 374, 376, 377 or 713 of ITEPA][3].

[(6) For the purposes of this regulation, a benefit is provided pursuant to optional remuneration arrangements if it is provided under either—

(*a*) arrangements under which, in return for the benefit, the claimant gives up the right (or a future right) to receive an amount of earnings within Chapter 1 of Part 3 of ITEPA ("Type A arrangements"), or

(*b*) arrangements (other than Type A arrangements) under which the claimant agrees to be provided with the benefit rather than an amount of earnings within Chapter 1 of Part 3 of ITEPA.

(7) The relevant amount, in relation to a benefit provided pursuant to an optional remuneration arrangement, means the amount treated for income tax purposes as earnings from employment for the tax year by reason of the benefit being provided pursuant to optional remuneration arrangements.

(8) A benefit is a special case benefit if it is exempted from a charge to income tax by any of the following provisions in ITEPA—

(*a*) section 289A (exemption for paid or reimbursed expenses),

(*b*) section 289D (exemption for other benefits),

(*c*) section 308B (independent advice in respect of conversions and transfers of pension scheme benefits),

(*d*) section 312A (limited exemption for qualifying bonus payments),

(*e*) section 317 (subsidised meals),

(*f*) section 320C (recommended medical treatment), and

(*g*) section 323A (trivial benefits provided by employers).

(9) A benefit is an excluded benefit if—

(*a*) it is exempted from a charge to income tax by any of the following provisions in ITEPA—

(i) section 239 (payments and benefits connected with taxable cars and vans and exempt heavy goods vehicles),

(ii) section 244 (cycles and cyclist's safety equipment),

(iii) section 266(2)(*c*) (non-cash voucher regarding entitlement to exemption under section 244),

(iv) section 270A (limited exemption for qualifying childcare vouchers),

(v) section 308 (exemption of contribution to registered pension scheme),

(vi) section 308A (exemption of contribution to overseas pension scheme),

(vii) section 309 (limited exemptions for statutory redundancy payments),

(viii) section 310 (counselling and other outplacement services),

(ix) section 311 (retraining courses),

(x) section 318 (childcare: exemption for employer-provided care), or

(xi) section 318A (childcare: limited exemption for other care), or (*b*) it is a payment, or reimbursement of costs incurred by the claimant, in respect of pension advice and that payment or reimbursement is exempt from a charge to income tax under Chapter 9 of Part 4 of ITEPA.

(10) A car's CO_2 emissions figure is to be determined in accordance with sections 133 to 138 of ITEPA (cars: the appropriate percentage).][18]

Commentary—*Simon's Taxes* **E2.233.**

HMRC Manuals—Tax Credit Technical Manual TCTM4101–4140 (employment income rules, including benefits in kind, earnings under the "money's worth" principle, earnings within the "pecuniary liability" principle and allowable deductions).

TCTM4106 (specific payments and benefits in kind included as income for tax credits purposes).

TCTM4110–4135 (specific payments and benefits in kind excluded as income for tax credits purposes).

TCTM4140 (summary of deductions allowable under reg 4(5) above).

TCTM4141 (allowable deductions under reg 4(5) above for ministers of religion).

Modifications—Tax Credits (Polygamous Marriages) Regulations, SI 2003/742 regs 35, 38 (modification of para (1) for the purposes of polygamous marriages).

Universal Credit (Transitional Provisions) Regulations, SI 2013/386 reg 17(1), (2), Schedule paras 15, 18 (modification of this regulation in respect of awards of universal credit and terminations of awards of tax credit in the same year).

Universal Credit (Transitional Provisions) Regulations, SI 2014/1626 reg 4 (modification of this regulation in respect of awards of universal credit and terminations of awards of tax credit in the same year).

Amendments—[1] Words in sub-para (1) inserted/substituted by the Tax Credits (Definition and Calculation of Income) (Amendment) Regulations, SI 2003/732, regs 3, 6(1), (2) with effect from 6 April 2003.

[2] Words in Table 1 substituted and inserted and items 2A–2C, 11A–11E, 14A, 14B and 16 inserted by SI 2003/732, regs 3, 6(1), (4) with effect from 6 April 2003.

[3] Words in sub-para (5) substituted by SI 2003/732, regs 3, 6(1), (5) with effect from 6 April 2003.

[4] Sub-para (1)(*l*) inserted; para (3) substituted; in Table 1, words in item 11D substituted, and items 14C, 14D, 17 and 18 inserted; and references in para (5) inserted; by the Tax Credits (Miscellaneous Amendments No 2) Regulations, SI 2003/2815 regs 2, 5 with effect from 26 November 2003.

[5] In Table 1, words in item 12 inserted, and item 16 substituted, by the Tax Credits (Miscellaneous Amendments) Regulations, SI 2004/762 regs 12, 14 with effect from 6 April 2004.

[6] In Table 1, item 19 inserted by the Tax Credits (Miscellaneous Amendments No 3) Regulations, SI 2004/2663 reg 2 with effect from 3 November 2004.

[7] Paras (2A), (2B) revoked, and item 16A in Table 1 inserted, by the Tax Credits (Miscellaneous Amendments) Regulations, SI 2006/766 regs 6, 9 with effect from 6 April 2006.

[8] Para (1)(*m*), and items 3A, 11F in Table 1, inserted by the Tax Credits (Miscellaneous Amendments) Regulations, SI 2007/824 regs 7, 10 with effect from 6 April 2007.

[9] In Table 1, item 3B inserted by the Tax Credits (Miscellaneous Amendments) Regulations, SI 2008/604 reg 2(1), (2) with effect from 1 April 2008.

[10] In Table 1, in item 16 words in para (*a*) and whole of paras (*c*)–(*e*) inserted, and items 16B and 20 inserted, by the Tax Credits (Miscellaneous Amendments) (No 2) Regulations, SI 2008/2169 regs 3, 4 with effect from 1 September 2008.

[11] In Table 1, in item 16 word "or" at end of para (*d*) revoked, and para (*f*) and preceding word "or" inserted, by the Tax Credits (Miscellaneous Amendments) (No 2) Regulations, SI 2009/2887 regs 5, 6 with effect from 21 November 2009.

[12] In para (1)(*h*) words substituted by the Tax Credits (Miscellaneous Amendments) (No 2) Regulations, SI 2010/2494, regs 4, 5, with effect from 14 November 2010.

[13] In para (4) in Table 1, items 3C and 21 inserted by the Tax Credits (Miscellaneous Amendments) Regulations, SI 2012/848 regs 1(2), 3(1), (2) with effect from 6 April 2012.

[14] In para (4) in Table 1, words in items 3A, 3B substituted by the Tax Credits (Miscellaneous Amendments) Regulations, SI 2014/658 reg 4(1), (5) with effect from 6 April 2014.

[15] In para (4) in Table 1, item 22 inserted by the Child Benefit (General) and Tax Credits (Miscellaneous Amendments) Regulations, SI 2014/2924 reg 5 with effect from 28 November 2014.

[16] In para 1(*h*), words revoked and substituted by the Shared Parental Leave and Statutory Shared Parental Pay (Consequential Amendments to Subordinate Legislation) Order, SI 2014/3255 art 12(1), (2) with effect from 5 April 2015.

[17] Para 1(*h*) substituted by the Social Security and Tax Credits (Miscellaneous Amendments) Regulations, SI 2015/175 reg 7 with effect from 5 April 2015. These amendments do not have effect where they relate to ordinary statutory paternity pay or additional statutory paternity pay, or ordinary statutory paternity pay or additional statutory paternity pay paid on or after 5 April 2015: SI 2015/175 reg 9.

[18] In paras (1), (4), words inserted, and paras (6)–(10) inserted, by the Tax Credits (Definition and Calculation of Income) (Amendment) Regulations, SI 2017/396 regs 2, 3 with effect in relation to awards of tax credit for the tax year 2017–18 and subsequent tax years.

CHAPTER 3

PENSION INCOME

5 Pension Income

[(1) In these Regulations, except where the context otherwise require, "pension income" means—

(*a*) any pension to which section 577 or 629 of ITEPA applies;

(*b*) any pension to which section 569 of ITEPA applies;

(*c*) any voluntary annual payment to which section 633 of ITEPA applies;

[(*d*) any pension, annuity or income withdrawal to which section 579A of ITEPA applies;][5]

[(*e*) any unauthorised member payments to which section 208(2)(*a*) or (*b*) of the Finance Act 2004 applies;][5]

(*f*) any periodical payment to which section 619 of ITEPA applies;

(*g*)–(*j*) . . .[5]

Tax Credits

[(*k*) any annuity paid under a retirement annuity contract to which Chapter 9 of Part 9 of ITEPA applies;][5]

(*l*) any annuity to which section 609, 610 or 611 of ITEPA applies; . . .

(*m*) . . . [6]][1]

[(*n*) any social security pension lump sum to which section 7 of the Finance (No 2) Act 2005 applies; and][4]

[(*o*) any lump sum payment to which section 636B or 636C of ITEPA applies.][4]

(2) In calculating the amount of a person's pension income there shall be disregarded any [payment or benefit mentioned][1] in Column 1 of Table 2 to the extent specified in the corresponding entry in Column 2.

TABLE 2
[PENSIONS, OTHER PAYMENTS AND BENEFITS][2] DISREGARDED IN THE CALCULATION OF PENSION INCOME

1 Payment	*2 Extent of disregard*
1 A wounds pension or disability pension to which [section 641 of ITEPA][2] applies.	So much of the payment as is disregarded by virtue of [section 641 of ITEPA][2].
2 An annuity or additional pension payable to a holder of the Victoria Cross, George Cross or any other decoration mentioned in [section 638 of ITEPA][2].	The whole of the annuity or additional pension and, if both are payable, the whole of both such annuity and additional pension.
3 A pension or allowance to which [section 639 of ITEPA][2] applies.	[The amount of the pension or allowance.][2]
4 A pension or allowance by reason of payment of which a pension or allowance specified in [section 639 of ITEPA][2] is withheld or abated.	[The amount treated as falling within section 639 of ITEPA by virtue of section 640(2) of that Act.][2]
. . . [7]	. . . [7]
6 A mobility supplement, or a payment in respect of attendance, paid in conjunction with a war pension.	The amount of the supplement or payment.
. . . [7]	. . . [7]
8 A pension awarded at the supplementary rate under article 27(3) of the Personal Injuries (Civilians) Scheme 1983.	The amount for the time being specified in paragraph 1(c) of Schedule 4 to the Scheme.
9 A pension awarded on retirement through disability caused by injury on duty or by a work-related illness.	[The exempt amount of the pension calculated in accordance with section 644(3) of ITEPA.][2]
[10 A lump sum on which no liability to income tax arises by virtue of [section 636A of ITEPA][5].	The amount of the lump sum.][2]
[11 Coal or smokeless fuel provided as mentioned in section 646(1) of ITEPA, or an allowance in lieu of such provision.	The amount on which no liability to income tax arises by virtue of that section.][2]

[(3) From the amount of pension income, calculated in accordance with the preceding provisions of this regulation, there shall be deducted any amount deductible for income tax purposes in computing pension income (as defined in ITEPA) under section 713 of that Act.][3]

Commentary—*Simon's Taxes* **E2.232.**

HMRC Manuals—Tax Credit Technical Manual TCTM4201–4203 (summary of pension income rules).

Modifications—Universal Credit (Transitional Provisions) Regulations, SI 2013/386 reg 17(1), (2), Schedule paras 15, 19 (modification of this regulation in respect of awards of universal credit and terminations of awards of tax credit in the same year).

Universal Credit (Transitional Provisions) Regulations, SI 2014/1626 reg 4 (modification of this regulation in respect of awards of universal credit and terminations of awards of tax credit in the same year).

Amendments—[1] Sub-para (1) and words in sub-para (2) substituted by the Tax Credits (Definition and Calculation of Income) (Amendment) Regulations, SI 2003/732, regs 3, 7 with effect from 6 April 2003.

[2] Words in heading and Table 2 substituted, and entries 10 and 11 inserted, by SI 2003/732, regs 3, 7(1), (4) with effect from 6 April 2003.

[3] Sub-para (3) inserted by SI 2003/732, regs 3, 7(1), (5) with effect from 6 April 2003.

[4] Para (1)(*n*), (*o*) inserted by the Tax Credits (Miscellaneous Amendments) Regulations, SI 2006/766 regs 6, 10 with effect from 6 April 2006.

[5] Para (1)(*d*), (*e*), (*k*) substituted, para (1)(*g*), (*h*), (*i*), (*j*) revoked, and words in Table 2, item 10 substituted, by the Taxation of Pension Schemes (Consequential Amendments) Order, SI 2006/745 art 26(1), (4) with effect from 6 April 2006.

6 Para (1)(*m*) and preceding word "and" revoked by the Tax Credits (Miscellaneous Amendments) Regulations, SI 2008/604 reg 2(1), (3) with effect from 6 April 2008.

7 In Table 2, items 5, 7 revoked by the Tax Credits (Miscellaneous Amendments) (No 3) Regulations, SI 2010/2914 regs 2, 4 with effect from 31 December 2010.

CHAPTER 4

TRADING INCOME

6 Trading income

The claimant's trading income is—

(*a*) the amount of his taxable profits for the tax year from—

(i) any trade carried on in the United Kingdom or elsewhere;

(ii) any profession or vocation the income from which does not fall under any other provisions of these Regulations; or

(*b*) if the claimant is a partner in the trade, profession or vocation, his taxable profit for the year arising from his share of the partnership's trading or professional income.

[Here "taxable profits" has the same meaning as it has in Part 2 of ITTOIA but disregarding Chapter 16 of that Part (averaging profits of farmers and creative artists).][1]

Commentary—*Simon's Taxes* **E2.334.**

HMRC Manuals—Tax Credit Technical Manual TCTM4300 (summary of trading income rules. Where there is a trading loss, any portion of that loss which remains unrelieved after the sideways set-off described in Step 4 of reg 3 above can be set-off against future income of the same trade, profession or vocation).

Modifications—Universal Credit (Transitional Provisions) Regulations, SI 2013/386 reg 17(1), (2), Schedule paras 15, 20, 21 (modification of this regulation in respect of awards of universal credit and terminations of awards of tax credit in the same year).

Universal Credit (Transitional Provisions) Regulations, SI 2014/1626 reg 4 (modification of this regulation in respect of awards of universal credit and terminations of awards of tax credit in the same year).

Amendments—[1] Words substituted by the Tax Credits (Miscellaneous Amendments) Regulations, SI 2006/766 regs 6, 11 with effect from 6 April 2006.

CHAPTER 5

SOCIAL SECURITY INCOME

7 Social security income

(1) The claimant's social security income is the total amount payable—

(*a*) under any provision of the Social Security Act 1988, the Contributions and Benefits Act[, the Jobseekers Act 1995 or Part 1 of the Welfare Reform Act 2007][5] or under section 69 of the Child Support, Pensions and Social Security Act 2000;

[(*aa*) under Part 3 of the Welfare Supplementary Payments Regulations (Northern Ireland) 2016 or Part 2 of the Welfare Supplementary Payment (Loss of Carer Payments) Regulations (Northern Ireland) 2016;][13]

(*b*) [1] . . .

(*c*) by the Secretary of State in respect of the non-payment of a payment which ought to have been made under a provision mentioned in sub-paragraph (*a*); and

(*d*) by way of an ex gratia payment made by the Secretary of State, or in Northern Ireland by the [Department for Communities][13], in connection with a benefit, pension or allowance under the Contributions and Benefits Act.

This is subject to the following provisions of this regulation.

(2) Pensions under the Contributions and Benefits Act which are pension income by virtue of regulation 5(1)(*a*) are not social security income.

(3) In calculating the claimant's social security income the payments in Table 3 shall be disregarded.

TABLE 3

PAYMENTS UNDER, OR IN CONNECTION WITH, THE ACT, THE SOCIAL SECURITY ACT 1988, THE CONTRIBUTIONS AND BENEFITS ACT[, THE JOBSEEKERS ACT 1995 OR PART 1 OF THE WELFARE REFORM ACT 2007][5] DISREGARDED IN CALCULATION OF SOCIAL SECURITY INCOME

1	An attendance allowance under section 64 of the Contributions and Benefits Act.
2	A back to work bonus under section 26 of the Jobseekers Act 1995.
[3	A bereavement support payment under section 30 of the Pensions Act 2014.][14]
4	Child benefit under Part 2 of the Act.
5	A Christmas bonus under section 148 of the Contributions and Benefits Act.
6	Council tax benefit under section 131 of the Contributions and Benefits Act.
7	A disability living allowance under section 71 of the Contributions and Benefits Act.

8	Disabled person's tax credit under section 129 of the Contributions and Benefits Act.
9	Any discretionary housing payment pursuant to regulation 2(1) of the Discretionary Financial Assistance Regulations 2001.
10	An ex-gratia payment by the Secretary of State or, in Northern Ireland, the [Department for Communities][13], to a person over pensionable age by way of supplement to incapacity benefit.
11	A guardian's allowance under section 77 of the Contributions and Benefits Act.
12	Housing benefit under section 130 of the Contributions and Benefits Act.
13	Income support under section 124 of the Contributions and Benefits Act, unless it is chargeable to tax under [section 665 of ITEPA][2].
14	Incapacity benefit which is— (*a*) short term incapacity benefit payable at the lower rate; or (*b*) payable to a person who had received invalidity benefit before 13th April 1995 if the period of incapacity for work is treated, by virtue of regulation 2 of the Social Security (Incapacity Benefit) (Transitional) Regulations 1995 (days to be treated as days of incapacity for work) as having begun before that date.
15	Industrial injuries benefit [(except industrial death benefit)][2] under section 94 of the Contributions and Benefits Act.
16	A contribution-based jobseeker's allowance under the Jobseekers Act 1995 [as amended by the provisions of Part 1 of Schedule 14 to the Welfare Reform Act 2012 that remove references to an income-based allowance, and a contribution-based allowance under the Jobseekers Act 1995 as that Act has effect apart from those provisions][9], to the extent that it exceeds the maximum contained in [section 674 of ITEPA][2].
17	An income-based jobseeker's allowance under the Jobseekers Act 1995.
18	A maternity allowance under section 35 of the Contributions and Benefits Act.
19	A severe disablement allowance under section 68 or 69 of the Contributions and Benefits Act.
20	A social fund payment under Part 8 of the Contributions and Benefits Act.
[20A	Statutory adoption pay under Part 12ZB of the Contributions and Benefits Act.][2]
21	Statutory maternity pay under Part 12 of the Contributions and Benefits Act.
[21A	[. . . [11] statutory paternity pay . . . [11] . . . [12]][7] under Part 12ZA of the Contributions and Benefits Act.][2]
[21B	Statutory shared parental pay under Part 12ZC of the Contributions and Benefits Act.][11]
22	Statutory sick pay under Part 11 of the Contributions and Benefits Act.
23	Working families' tax credit under section 128 of the Contributions and Benefits Act.
24	A payment by way of compensation for the non-payment of, or in respect of loss of entitlement (whether wholly or partly) of, income support, jobseeker's allowance, [or housing benefit][4].
25	A payment in lieu of milk tokens or the supply of vitamins under the Welfare Foods Regulations 1996.
[26	An income-related employment and support allowance payable under Part 1 of the Welfare Reform Act 2007.][5]
[27	A payment by way of health in pregnancy grant made pursuant to Part 8A of the Contributions and Benefits Act.][6]
[28.	Personal independence payment under Part 4 of the Welfare Reform Act 2012.][8]

(4) If an increase in respect of a child dependant is payable with an allowance, benefit, pension or other payment ("the main payment") listed in Table 3, the increase shall also be wholly disregarded in calculating the income of the recipient of the main payment.

(5) . . . [3]

[(5A) From the amount of social security income, calculated in accordance with the preceding provisions of this regulation, there shall be deducted any amount deductible for income tax purposes in computing social security income (as defined in ITEPA) under section 713 of ITEPA.][3]

(6) A reference in this regulation to an enactment applying only in Great Britain includes a reference to a corresponding enactment applying in Northern Ireland.

Commentary—*Simon's Taxes* **E2.233.**

HMRC Manuals—Tax Credit Technical Manual TCTM4400–4403 (summary of social security income rules. Pensions paid under the Contributions and Benefits Act, which are pension income under reg 5(1)(*a*) above, are not social security income. Statutory maternity pay, statutory sick pay, statutory paternity pay and statutory adoption pay are excluded from social security income for tax credit purposes but are instead dealt with as employment income).

Modifications—Universal Credit (Transitional Provisions) Regulations, SI 2013/386 reg 17(1), (2), Schedule paras 15, 22 (modification of this regulation in respect of awards of universal credit and terminations of awards of tax credit in the same year).

Universal Credit (Transitional Provisions) Regulations, SI 2014/1626 reg 4 (modification of this regulation in respect of awards of universal credit and terminations of awards of tax credit in the same year).

Amendments—[1] Sub-para (1)(*b*) revoked by the Tax Credits (Definition and Calculation of Income) (Amendment) Regulations, SI 2003/732, regs 3, 8(1), (2) with effect from 6 April 2003.

[2] Words in Table 3 substituted, and items 20A, 21A inserted by SI 2003/732, regs 8(1), (3).

[3] Sub-para (5) revoked, and sub-para (5A) inserted, by SI 2003/732, regs 3, 8(1), (4), (5) with effect from 6 April 2003.

[4] Words in Table 3, item 24 substituted by the Tax Credits (Miscellaneous Amendments No 2) Regulations, SI 2003/2815 regs 2, 6 with effect from 26 November 2003.

[5] In para (1)(*a*), words substituted, in para (3), in table 3, in heading words substituted, and entry number 26 inserted, by the Employment and Support Allowance (Consequential Provisions) (No 3) Regulations, SI 2008/1879 reg 21(1), (2) with effect from 27 October 2008.

[6] In Table 3, item 27 inserted by the Tax Credits (Miscellaneous Amendments) Regulations, SI 2009/697 regs 6, 7 with effect from 6 April 2009.

[7] In Table 3, Item 21A, words substituted by the Tax Credits (Miscellaneous Amendments) (No 2) Regulations, SI 2010/2494, regs 4, 6, with effect from 14 November 2010.

[8] In Table 3, Item 28 inserted by the Personal Independence Payment (Supplementary Provisions and Consequential Amendments) Regulations, SI 2013/388 reg 29 with effect from 8 April 2013.

[9] In Table 3, words in Item 16 inserted by the Universal Credit (Consequential, Supplementary, Incidental and Miscellaneous Provisions) Regulations, SI 2013/630 reg 78(1), (2) with effect from 29 April 2013.

[10] In Table 3, words in Item 18 inserted by the Tax Credits (Miscellaneous Amendments) Regulations, SI 2014/658 reg 4(1), (5) with effect from 6 April 2014.

[11] In Table 3, Item 21A, words revoked, and Item 21B inserted by the Shared Parental Leave and Statutory Shared Parental Pay (Consequential Amendments to Subordinate Legislation) Order, SI 2014/3255 art 12(1), (3) with effect from 5 April 2015.

[12] In Table 3, Item 21A, word revoked by the Tax Credits and Child Benefit (Miscellaneous Amendments) Regulations, SI 2016/360 reg 3(1), (2) with effect from 6 April 2016.

[13] Para (1)(*aa*) inserted, and in para (1)(*d*), Table 3, Item 10, words substituted for words "Department for Social Development", by the Tax Credits (Definition and Calculation of Income) (Amendment) Regulations, SI 2016/978 reg 2(1), (2) with effect from 31 Octoner 2016.

[14] In Table 3, Item 3 substituted by the Pensions Act 2014 (Consequential, Supplementary and Incidental Amendments) Order, SI 2017/422 art 22 with effect from 6 April 2017 (the day on which Pensions Act 2014 s 30 comes into effect for all purposes).

CHAPTER 6

STUDENT INCOME

8 [Student income

"Student income" means, in relation to a student—

[(*a*) in England, any adult dependant's grant payable [pursuant to regulations under section 22 of the Teaching and Higher Education Act 1998;][4]][3]

(*b*) in Scotland, any dependant's grant payable under regulation 4(1)(*c*) of the Students' Allowances (Scotland) Regulations [2007];[4] . . . [2]

(*c*) in Northern Ireland, any grant which corresponds to income treated as student income in England . . . [4] by virtue of paragraph (*a*); [and

[(*d*) in Wales, any adult dependant's grant payable [pursuant to regulations under section 22 of the Teaching and Higher Education Act 1998][4]][3]

Commentary—*Simon's Taxes* **E2.233.**

HMRC Manuals—Tax Credit Technical Manual TCTM4500 (summary of student income rules).

Modifications—Universal Credit (Transitional Provisions) Regulations, SI 2013/386 reg 17(1), (2), Schedule paras 15, 23 (modification of this regulation in respect of awards of universal credit and terminations of awards of tax credit in the same year).

Universal Credit (Transitional Provisions) Regulations, SI 2014/1626 reg 4 (modification of this regulation in respect of awards of universal credit and terminations of awards of tax credit in the same year).

Amendments—[1] Substituted by the Tax Credits (Miscellaneous Amendments No 2) Regulations, SI 2003/2815 regs 2, 7 with effect from 26 November 2003.

[2] Word in para (*b*) revoked, and word in para (*c*) inserted, by the Tax Credits (Miscellaneous Amendments) Regulations, SI 2006/766 regs 6, 12 with effect from 6 April 2006.

[3] Paras (*a*), (*d*) substituted by the Tax Credits (Miscellaneous Amendments) (No 2) Regulations, SI 2008/2169 reg 5 with effect from 1 September 2008.

[4] In paras (*a*), (*d*) words substituted, in para (*b*), year substituted, and in para (*c*) words revoked, by the Tax Credits (Miscellaneous Amendments) Regulations, SI 2012/848 regs 1(2), 3(3) with effect from 6 April 2012.

9 [Payments of income in connection with students to be disregarded for the purposes of regulation 3

Income which is exempt from income tax by virtue of section 753 or 776 of ITTOIA (which deal respectively with interest on the repayment of student loans and scholarship income) is disregarded in calculating a claimant's income under regulation 3.][1]

Commentary—*Simon's Taxes* **E2.233.**

HMRC Manuals—Tax Credit Technical Manual TCTM4500 (list of student income disregarded).
Amendments—[1] Regulation 9 substituted by the Tax Credits (Miscellaneous Amendments) Regulations, SI 2006/766 regs 6, 13 with effect from 6 April 2006.

CHAPTER 7

INVESTMENT INCOME

10 Investment income

(1) In these Regulations "investment income" means the gross amount of—

(*a*) any interest of money, whether yearly or otherwise, or any annuity or other annual payment, whether such payment is payable within or out of the United Kingdom, either as a charge on any property of the person paying it by virtue of any deed or will or otherwise, or as a reservation out of it, or as a personal debt or obligation by virtue of any contract, or whether the payment is received and payable half-yearly or at any shorter or longer periods, but not including property income;

(*b*) any discounts on securities;

(*c*) any income from securities payable out of the public revenues of the United Kingdom or Northern Ireland;

(*d*) dividends and other distributions of a company resident in the United Kingdom and any tax credit associated with that payment; and

(*e*) any amount treated as forming part of the individual's income for the year for income tax purposes by virtue of [Chapter 9 of Part 4 of ITTOIA disregarding section 535 (top slicing relief)][3].

This is subject to the following qualification.

(2) In calculating investment income, there shall be disregarded—

(*a*) any amount listed in column 1 of Table 4 to the extent shown in the corresponding entry in column 2;

(*b*) any amount listed in column 1 of Table 5 during the period shown in the corresponding entry in column 2;

(*c*) any income arising from savings certificates, and interest on tax reserve certificates, exempted from tax by [section 692, 693 or 750 of ITTOIA][3] (savings certificates and tax reserve certificates);

(*d*) the first £70 in any tax year of interest on deposits with National Savings and Investments, exempted from income tax by [section 691 of ITTOIA (National Savings Bank ordinary account interest).][3].

(*e*) any payment to a claimant which does not form part of his income for the purposes of income tax by virtue of [section 727 of ITTOIA (certain annual payments by individuals).][3]

TABLE 4
PAYMENTS DISREGARDED IN THE CALCULATION OF INVESTMENT INCOME

1 Description of income to be disregarded	*2 Extent of disregard*
1 Any interest, dividends, distributions, profits or gains in respect of investments under— (*a*) a Personal Equity Plan, or (*b*) an Individual Savings Account, in respect of which the claimant is entitled to relief from income tax under [Chapter 3 of Part 6 of ITTOIA][3], or which is taxed only in accordance with regulation 23 of the Individual Savings Account Regulations 1998.	The whole amount, unless it is interest under a personal equity plan to which regulation 17A(2) of the Personal Equity Plan Regulations 1989 applies. Interest to which that paragraph applies is disregarded only to the extent that it does not exceed the annual limit of £180 mentioned in that regulation.
2 . . . [3]	. . . [3]
[3 Any interest payable under a certified SAYE savings arrangement for the purposes of Chapter 4 of Part 6 of ITTOIA.][3]	The whole amount.
4 Any winnings from betting, including pool betting, or lotteries or games with prizes.	The whole amount.
5 Any interest on a payment of £10,000 made by the Secretary of State to a person who was held prisoner by the Japanese during the Second World War or to the spouse of such a person, if the payment is held in a distinct account and no payment (other than interest) has been added to the account.	The whole amount of the interest.

6 Any interest on a payment made to the claimant by, or on behalf of a government of a country outside the United Kingdom, either from its own resources or with contributions from any other organisation, by way of compensation for a victim of National Socialism if the payment is held in a distinct account and no payment (other than interest) has been added to the account. Here a reference to a victim of National Socialism is a reference to a person who was required to work as a slave or a forced labourer for National Socialists or their sympathisers during the Second World War, or suffered property loss, or suffered injury or is the parent of a child who died, at the hands of National Socialists or their sympathisers during the Second World War.	The whole amount of the interest.
7 Any monies paid to the claimant by a bank or building society as compensation in respect of an unclaimed account held by a Holocaust victim and which vested in the Custodian of Enemy Property under section 7 of the Trading with the Enemy Act 1939 and treated as exempt from income tax by [section 756A of ITTOIA][4].	The amount [of interest exempted from income tax under section 756A of ITTOIA][4].
8 Any interest, or payment . . .[3], which is disregarded for income tax purposes by virtue of— [(*a*) section 751 of ITTOIA (interest on damages for personal injury), or][3] (*b*) [section 731 of ITTOIA (periodical payments of personal injury damages)][3] (personal injury damages in the form of periodical payments).	The amount so disregarded.
[9][1] Annuity payments under an award of compensation made under the Criminal Injuries Compensation Scheme (within the meaning of [section 732(3) of ITTOIA][3]).	The amount of any payment which is treated as not being income of the claimant or his partner by virtue of [section 731 of ITTOIA][3].
[10][1] A payment under a life annuity.	The amount of interest eligible for relief under section 353 of the Taxes Act by virtue of section 365 of that Act.
[11][1] Any interest, or payment in respect of interest, which is compensation to a person who is under the age of 18 years for the death of one or both of his parents.	The whole of the interest or payment.
[12 A purchased life annuity to which [Chapter 7 of Part 4 of ITTOIA][3] applies.	[The amount exempted under section 717 of ITTOIA as calculated under section 719 of that Act.][3]][2]
[13 Any payments which are exempt from income tax by virtue of— (*a*) section 725 of ITTOIA (annual payments under immediate needs annuities), or (*b*) section 735 of ITTOIA (health and employment insurance payments).	The whole amount.][3]
[14 Any income arising from or payment made in respect of a Saving Gateway account.	The whole amount.][5]
[15. Any payment of, or in respect of, a government bonus under section 1 of the Savings (Government Contributions) Act 2017.	The whole amount.][6]

TABLE 5
PAYMENTS IN CONNECTION WITH VERY SEVERE DISABLEMENT, CREUTZFELDT-JAKOB DISEASE AND HAEMOPHILIA

1 Description of income to be disregarded	*2 Applicable period*
1 A trust payment made to— (*a*) a diagnosed person; (*b*) the diagnosed person's partner; or (*c*) the person who was his partner at the date of his death.	The period beginning on the date on which the trust payment is made and ending with the death of the person to whom the payment is made.
2 A trust payment made to a parent of a deceased diagnosed person, or a person acting in the place of his parent.	The period beginning on the date on which the trust payment is made and ending two years after that date.
3 The amount of any payment out of the estate of a person to whom a trust payment has been made, which is made to the person who was the diagnosed person's partner at the date of his death.	The period beginning on the date on which the payment is made and ending on the date on which that person dies.
4 The amount of any payment out of the estate of a person to whom a trust payment has been made, which is made to a parent of a deceased diagnosed person, or a person acting in the place of his parent.	The period beginning on the date on which the payment is made and ending two years after that date.

(3) The amounts disregarded under items 3 and 4 in Table 5 shall not exceed the total amount of any trust payments made to the person to whom the trust payment had been made.

(4) In this regulation "diagnosed person" means—

(*a*) a person who has been diagnosed as suffering from, or who after his death has been diagnosed has having suffered from, variant Creutzfeldt-Jakob disease;

(*b*) a person who is suffering or has suffered from haemophilia; or

(*c*) a person in respect of whom a payment has been made from the 1992 Fund, the Eileen Trust or the Independent Living Funds; and

a reference to a person being a member of the diagnosed person's household at the date of the diagnosed person's death includes a person who would have been a member of his household but for the diagnosed person being in residential accommodation, a residential care home or a nursing home on that date.

(5) In this regulation—

"relevant trust" means—

(*a*) a trust established out of funds provided by the Secretary of State in respect of persons who suffered, or who are suffering, from variant Creutzfeldt-Jakob disease for the benefit of persons eligible for payments in accordance with its provisions;

(*b*) the Macfarlane Trusts, or

(*c*) the 1992 Fund, the Eileen Trust or the Independent Living Funds.

"residential accommodation", "residential care home" and "nursing home" have the meanings given by regulation 2(1) of the Income Support (General) Regulations 1987; and

"trust payment" means a payment under a relevant trust.

Commentary—*Simon's Taxes* **E2.232.**

HMRC Manuals—Tax Credit Technical Manual TCTM4600–4652 (summary of investment income rules, including matters covered in tables 4 and 5 above).

TCTM4653 (treatment of vaccine damage payments).

Modifications—Universal Credit (Transitional Provisions) Regulations, SI 2013/386 reg 17(1), (2), Schedule paras 15, 24 (modification of this regulation in respect of awards of universal credit and terminations of awards of tax credit in the same year).

Universal Credit (Transitional Provisions) Regulations, SI 2014/1626 reg 4 (modification of this regulation in respect of awards of universal credit and terminations of awards of tax credit in the same year).

Amendment—[1] In Table 4 items 9, 10, 11 renumbered correctly by the Tax Credits (Definition and Calculation of Income) (Amendment) Regulations, SI 2003/732, reg 9 with effect from 6 April 2003.

[2] In Table 4, item 12 inserted by the Tax Credits (Miscellaneous Amendments No 2) Regulations, SI 2003/2815 regs 2, 8 with effect from 26 November 2003.

[3] Words in paras (1)(*e*), (2)(*c*), (*d*), (*e*) substituted; in Table 4, items 1, 8, 9, 12 amended, item 2 revoked, item 3 substituted, and item 13 inserted; by the Tax Credits (Miscellaneous Amendments) Regulations, SI 2006/766 regs 6, 14 with effect from 6 April 2006.

[4] Words in item 7 of Table 4 substituted by the Tax Credits (Miscellaneous Amendments) Regulations, SI 2007/824 regs 7, 12 with effect from 6 April 2007.

[5] In Table 4, item 14 inserted by the Tax Credits (Miscellaneous Amendments) Regulations, SI 2010/751 regs 2, 4 with effect from 6 April 2010.

6 In Table 4, item 15 inserted by the Tax Credits (Definition and Calculation of Income) (Amendment) Regulations, SI 2017/396 regs 2, 4 with effect in relation to awards of tax credit for the tax year 2017–18 and subsequent tax years.

CHAPTER 8

PROPERTY INCOME

11 Property income

(1) In these Regulations "property income" means the annual taxable profits arising from a business carried on for the exploitation, as a source of rents or other receipts, of any estate, interest or rights in or over land in the United Kingdom.

Expressions which are used in this paragraph which are defined in [Part 3 of ITTOIA][2] for the purposes of [that Part][2] bear the same meaning here as they bear in [that Part][2].

This paragraph is subject to the following [qualifications][1].

[(2) In calculating property income there shall be disregarded any profits—

(*a*) treated as nil by section 791 to 794 of ITTOIA (full rent-a-room relief); or

(*b*) excluded from profits by section 795 to 798 of ITTOIA (alternative calculation of profits if amount exceeds limit).][2]

[(2A) In calculating property income, the restrictions in section 272A of ITTOIA (restricting deductions for finance costs related to residential property) and section 399A of ITA (property partnerships: restriction of relief for investment loan interest) shall be disregarded.][4]

[(3) [Where a property business (as defined in Part 3 of ITTOIA)][2] makes a loss to which the relief provisions [contained in sections 118 (carry forward against subsequent property business profits) and 119 (how relief works) of ITA][3] apply, then such relief as may arise under [those sections][3] shall be applied in calculating property income for the purposes of this regulation.][1]

Commentary—*Simon's Taxes* **E2.232.**

HMRC Manuals—Tax Credit Technical Manual TCTM4700 (calculating property income and deductions in computing profits from property income).

Modifications—Universal Credit (Transitional Provisions) Regulations, SI 2013/386 reg 17(1), (2), Schedule paras 15, 25 (modification of this regulation in respect of awards of universal credit and terminations of awards of tax credit in the same year).

Universal Credit (Transitional Provisions) Regulations, SI 2014/1626 reg 4 (modification of this regulation in respect of awards of universal credit and terminations of awards of tax credit in the same year).

Amendments—1 Word in para (1) substituted, and para (3) inserted, by the Tax Credits (Miscellaneous Amendments No 2) Regulations, SI 2003/2815 regs 2, 9 with effect from 26 November 2003.

2 Words in para (1), (3) substituted; and para (2) substituted; by the Tax Credits (Miscellaneous Amendments) Regulations, SI 2006/766 regs 6, 15 with effect from 6 April 2006.

3 Words in para (3) substituted by the Tax Credits (Definition and Calculation of Income) (Amendment) Regulations, SI 2007/1305 regs 2, 6 with effect from 16 May 2007.

4 Para (2A) inserted by the Tax Credits (Definition and Calculation of Income) (Amendment) Regulations, SI 2017/396 regs 2, 5 with effect in relation to awards of tax credit for the tax year 2017–18 and subsequent tax years.

CHAPTER 9

FOREIGN INCOME

12 Foreign income

(1) In these Regulations "foreign income" means income arising, in the year in question, from [a source outside the United Kingdom or from foreign holdings][3] which is not—

(*a*) employment income;

(*b*) trading income; or

(*c*) investment income falling within regulation 10(1)(*e*).

This is subject to the following provisions of this regulation.

[(2) The reference in paragraph (1) to "foreign holdings" shall be construed in accordance with section 571 of ITTOIA.][3]

(3) In calculating the claimant's foreign income there shall be disregarded—

(*a*) any payment by way of an annuity or pension payable under any special provision for victims of National Socialist persecution which is made by the law of the Federal Republic of Germany, or any part of it, or of Austria;

[(*aa*) any monies paid by a bank or building society which are exempted from income tax under section 756A of ITTOIA (interest on certain deposits of victims of National-Socialist persecution).][4]

[(*bb*) any pension, annuity, allowance or other payment provided in accordance with the provisions of the scheme established under the law of the Netherlands and known as *Wet uitkeringen vervolgingsslachtoffers 1940–1945* (Netherlands Benefit Act for Victims of Persecution 1940–1945).][6]

[(*b*) the amount authorised to be deducted by the relevant provision if the claimant's foreign income comprises or includes a pension to which the following provisions of ITEPA apply—

(i) section 567(5) and 617 (deduction allowed from taxable pension income);

(ii) section 575(2) (taxable pension income: foreign pensions);

(iii) section 613(3) (taxable pension income: foreign annuities); and

(iv) section 635(3) (taxable pension income: foreign voluntary annual payments); and][3]

(*c*) any amount which would be disregarded for the purposes of income tax by virtue of—

(i) Extra Statutory Concession A10 (lump sums paid by overseas pension schemes);

[(ii) section 681 of ITEPA;][1]

(iii) [section 751(1)(*c*) of ITTOIA][3] (interest on damages for personal injuries awarded by a foreign court); . . .[3]

(iv) Extra Statutory Concession A44 (education allowances payable to public officials of overseas territories) [or

(v) section 730 of ITTOIA (foreign maintenance payments).][3]

[(4) Where an overseas property business [(within the meaning of Part 3 of ITTOIA)][3] makes a loss to which the relief provisions [contained in sections 118 (carry forward against subsequent property business profits) and 119 (how relief works) of ITA apply][5], then such relief as may arise under [those sections][5] shall be applied in calculating foreign income for the purposes of this regulation.][2]

Commentary—*Simon's Taxes* **E2.232.**

HMRC Manuals—Tax Credit Technical Manual TCTM4800 (calculating foreign income).

Modifications—Universal Credit (Transitional Provisions) Regulations, SI 2013/386 reg 17(1), (2), Schedule paras 15, 26 (modification of this regulation in respect of awards of universal credit and terminations of awards of tax credit in the same year).

Universal Credit (Transitional Provisions) Regulations, SI 2014/1626 reg 4 (modification of this regulation in respect of awards of universal credit and terminations of awards of tax credit in the same year).

Note—See Part 2 of this publication for the text of the above Concessions.

Amendments—[1] Words in sub-para (3)(*b*) revoked, and words inserted, and sub-para 3(*c*)(ii) substituted, by the Tax Credits (Definition and Calculation of Income) (Amendment) Regulations, SI 2003/732, regs 3, 10 with effect from 6 April 2003.

[2] Para (4) inserted by the Tax Credits (Miscellaneous Amendments No 2) Regulations, SI 2003/2815 regs 2, 10 with effect from 26 November 2003.

[3] Words in paras (1), (3)(*c*), (4) substituted; para (2) substituted; and words in para (3)(*c*) inserted; by the Tax Credits (Miscellaneous Amendments) Regulations, SI 2006/766 regs 6, 16 with effect from 6 April 2006.

[4] Para (3)(*aa*) inserted by the Tax Credits (Miscellaneous Amendments) Regulations, SI 2007/824 regs 7, 13 with effect from 6 April 2007.

[5] Words in para (4) substituted by the Tax Credits (Definition and Calculation of Income) (Amendment) Regulations, SI 2007/1305 regs 2, 7 with effect from 16 May 2007.

[6] Para (3)(*bb*) inserted by the Tax Credits and Child Benefit (Miscellaneous Amendments) Regulations, SI 2016/360 reg 3(1), (3) with effect from 6 April 2016.

CHAPTER 10

NOTIONAL INCOME

13 Introduction

In these Regulations "notional income" means income which, by virtue of regulations 14 to 17 a claimant is treated as having, but which he does not in fact have.

Commentary—*Simon's Taxes* **E2.232.**

HMRC Manuals—Tax Credit Technical Manual TCTM4900–4905 (summary of notional income rules).

Modifications—Universal Credit (Transitional Provisions) Regulations, SI 2013/386 reg 17(1), (2), Schedule paras 15, 27 (modification of this regulation in respect of awards of universal credit and terminations of awards of tax credit in the same year).

Universal Credit (Transitional Provisions) Regulations, SI 2014/1626 reg 4 (modification of this regulation in respect of awards of universal credit and terminations of awards of tax credit in the same year).

14 Claimants treated for any purpose as having income by virtue of the Income Tax Acts

(1) If an amount is treated for any purpose as the claimant's income under any provision mentioned in paragraph (2), he is to be treated as having that amount of income.

(2) The provisions mentioned in paragraph (1) are—

(*a*) the following provisions of the Taxes Act—

(i)–(viii) . . .[1]

(ix) section 714 (transfers of securities: treatment of deemed sums and reliefs) or 716 (transfer of unrealised interest);

(x) section 730 (transfer of income arising from securities);

(xi)–(xiii) . . .[2]

(xiv) section 761 (charge to income tax of offshore income gain); and

(xv) . . .[2]

[(*b*) the following provisions of ITTOIA—

(i) sections 277 to 283 (amounts treated as receipts: leases);

(ii) Chapter 5 of Part 4 (stock dividends from UK resident companies);

(iii) Chapter 6 of Part 4 (release of loan to participator in close company);

(iv) section 427 (charge to tax on profits from deeply discounted securities);

(v) Chapter 11 of Part 4 (transactions in deposits);
(vi) sections 624 to 628 (income treated as income of settlor: retained interests);
(vii) sections 629 to 632 (income treated as income of settlor: unmarried children);
(viii) section 633 (capital sums paid to settlor by trustees of settlement);
(ix) section 641 (capital sums paid to settlor by body connected with settlement);
(x) section 652 (estate income: absolute interests in residue); and
(xi) sections 654 to 655 (estate income: interests in residue); and][1]

[(*ba*) the following provisions of ITA—
(i) Chapter 5 of Part 11 (price differences under repos);
(ii) Chapter 2 of Part 13 (transfer of assets abroad); and
(iii) Chapter 3 of Part 13 (transactions in land).][2]

[(*c*) section 84 and Schedule 15 to the Finance Act 2004 (charge to income tax by reference to enjoyment of property previously owned).][1]

Commentary—*Simon's Taxes* **E2.232.**

Amendments—[1] Para (2)(*a*)(i)–(viii) revoked; and para (2)(*b*), (*c*) substituted for para (2)(*b*); by the Tax Credits (Miscellaneous Amendments) Regulations, SI 2006/766 regs 6, 17 with effect from 6 April 2006.

[2] Para (2)(*a*)(xi)–(xiii), (xv) revoked, and para (2)(*ba*) inserted, by the Tax Credits (Definition and Calculation of Income) (Amendment) Regulations, SI 2007/1305 regs 2, 7 with effect from 16 May 2007.

15 Claimants depriving themselves of income in order to secure entitlement

If a claimant has deprived himself of income for the purpose of securing entitlement to, or increasing the amount of, a tax credit, he is treated as having that income.

Commentary—*Simon's Taxes* **E2.232.**

HMRC Manuals—Tax Credit Technical Manual TCTM4903 (if the claimant has various reasons for disposing of the income, one of which is to obtain tax credit or more tax credit, then reg 15 applies if securing or increasing entitlement to tax credit is a **significant** reason for the disposal).

16 Claimants to whom income becomes available upon the making of a claim

(1) If income would become available to a claimant upon the making of an application for that income he is treated as having that income.

This is subject to the following qualification.

(2) Paragraph (1) does not apply in relation to income—
(*a*) under a trust derived from a payment made in consequence of a personal injury;
(*b*) under a personal pension scheme or retirement annuity contract;
(*c*) consisting in a sum to which item 8 of Table 4 in regulation 10 refers (compensation for personal injuries which is administered by the Court); or
(*d*) consisting in a rehabilitation allowance made under section 2 of the Employment Act.

[(3) Paragraph (1) also does not apply to income by way of—
(*a*) a Category A or Category B retirement pension,
[(*aa*) a state pension under Part 1 of the Pensions Act 2014 or Part 1 of the Pensions Act (Northern Ireland) 2015,][2]
(*b*) a graduated retirement benefit, or
(*c*) a shared additional pension, payment of which has been deferred. Here—

"Category A retirement pension" means a pension to which a person is entitled by virtue of section 44 of the Contributions and Benefits Act or the Northern Ireland Contributions and Benefits Act;

"Category B retirement pension" means a pension to which a person is entitled by virtue of any of sections 48A to 48C of the Contributions and Benefits Act or sections 48A to 48C of the Northern Ireland Contributions and Benefits Act;

"graduated retirement benefit" means a pension payable under—
(*a*) sections 36 and 37 of the National Insurance Act 1965; or
(*b*) sections 35 and 36 of the National Insurance Act (Northern Ireland) 1966; and

"shared additional pension" means a pension to which a person is entitled by virtue of section 55A [or 55AA][2] of the Contributions and Benefits Act or section 55A [or 55AA][2] of the Northern Ireland Contributions and Benefits Act.][1]

Commentary—*Simon's Taxes* **E2.232.**

Amendments—[1] Para (3) inserted by the Tax Credits (Miscellaneous Amendments) Regulations, SI 2004/762 regs 12, 15 with effect from 6 April 2004.

[2] Para (3)(*aa*) inserted, and in para (3)(*c*), in definition of "shared additional pension", words inserted in both places, by the Pensions Act 2014 (Consequential, Supplementary and Incidental Amendments) Order, SI 2015/1985 art 25 with effect from 6 April 2016.

17 Claimants providing services to other persons for less than full earnings

(1) If a claimant provides a service for another person and—
(*a*) the other person makes no payment of earnings or pays less than those paid for a comparable employment (including self-employment) in the area; and

(*b*) the Board are satisfied that the means of the other person are sufficient for him to pay for, or to pay more for, the service,

the claimant is to be treated as having such an amount of employment income, or in the case of a service provided in the course of a trade or business, such an amount of trading income as is reasonable for the employment of the claimant to provide the service.

This is subject to the following qualification.

(2) Paragraph (1) does not apply where—

(*a*) the claimant is a volunteer or is engaged to provide the service by a charitable or voluntary organisation and the Board are satisfied that it is reasonable for the claimant to provide the service free of charge; or

(*b*) the service is provided in connection with the claimant's participation in an employment or training programme—

[(i) in Great Britain, which is approved by the Secretary of State;][1]

(ii) in Northern Ireland in accordance with regulation 19(1)(p) of the Jobseeker's Allowance Regulations (Northern Ireland) 1996 other than where it is provided in connection with the claimant's participation in the Preparation for Employment Programme specified in regulation 75(1)(*a*)(v) of those Regulations.

Commentary—*Simon's Taxes* **E2.232.**

Amendments—[1] Para (2)(*b*)(i) substituted by the Universal Credit (Consequential, Supplementary, Incidental and Miscellaneous Provisions) Regulations, SI 2013/630 reg 78(1), (3) with effect from 29 April 2013.

CHAPTER 11

MISCELLANEOUS INCOME

18 Miscellaneous income

In these Regulations "miscellaneous income" means income which does not fall within any other provision of these Regulations and which is subject to income tax under [Part 5 of ITTOIA][1].

Commentary—*Simon's Taxes* **E2.233.**

HMRC Manuals—Tax Credit Technical Manual TCTM4800A (miscellaneous income includes copyright royalties received by individuals whose activities do not amount to a profession).

Modifications—Universal Credit (Transitional Provisions) Regulations, SI 2013/386 reg 17(1), (2), Schedule paras 15, 28 (modification of this regulation in respect of awards of universal credit and terminations of awards of tax credit in the same year).

Universal Credit (Transitional Provisions) Regulations, SI 2014/1626 reg 4 (modification of this regulation in respect of awards of universal credit and terminations of awards of tax credit in the same year).

Amendments—[1] Words substituted by the Tax Credits (Miscellaneous Amendments) Regulations, SI 2006/766 regs 6, 18 with effect from 6 April 2006.

PART 3

SUMS DISREGARDED IN THE CALCULATION OF INCOME

19 General disregards in the calculation of income

(1) For the purposes of regulation 3—

(*a*) the sums specified in Table 6 are disregarded in the calculation of income;

(*b*) the sums specified in column 1 of Table 7 are disregarded in the calculation of income if the condition in the corresponding entry in column 2 of that Table is satisfied; and

(*c*) the sums specified in column 1 of Table 8 are disregarded in the calculation of income to the extent specified in the corresponding entry in column 2 of that Table.

(2) In this regulation—

"the JSA Regulations" means the Jobseeker's Allowance Regulations 1996; and

"the JSA (NI) Regulations" means the Jobseeker's Allowance (Northern Ireland) Regulations 1996.

TABLE 6

SUMS DISREGARDED IN THE CALCULATION OF INCOME

1 Any payment of an employment credit under a scheme under section 2(2) of the Employment Act known as "New Deal 50 plus" or the corresponding scheme under section 1 of the Employment and Training Act (Northern Ireland) 1950.
2 Any payment made— (*a*) under section 15 of the Disabled Persons (Employment Act) 1944 or section 15 of the Disabled Persons (Employment) Act (Northern Ireland) 1945; or (*b*) in accordance with arrangements made under section 2 of the Employment Act or section 1 of the Employment and Training Act (Northern Ireland) 1950 to assist disabled persons to obtain or retain employment despite their disability.
3 Any mandatory top-up payment made pursuant to—

(*a*) section 2 of the Employment Act [or section 1 of the Employment and Training Act (Northern Ireland) 1950][4] in respect of the claimant's participation in—

(i) an employment programme specified in regulation 75(1)(*a*)(ii)(*bb*) of the JSA Regulations or regulation 75(1)(*a*)(ii) of the JSA (NI) Regulations (Voluntary Sector Option of the New Deal);

(ii) an employment programme specified in regulation 75(1)(*a*)(ii)(*cc*) of the JSA Regulations (Environmental Task Force Option of the New Deal) or regulation 75(1)(*a*)(iii) of the JSA (NI) Regulations; . . .[9]

[(iia) an employment programme specified in regulation 75(1)(*a*)(ii)(*dd*) of the JSA Regulations (Community Task Force);][9]

(iii) the Intensive Activity Period of the New Deal Pilots for 25 plus specified in regulation 75(1)(*a*)(iv) of the JSA Regulations or, in Northern Ireland, the Preparation for Employment Programme specified in regulation 75(1)(*a*)(v) of the JSA (NI) Regulations; . . .[8] [or

(iv) the Backing Young Britain programme pursuant to arrangements made under section 2 of the Employment Act;][9]

(*b*) a written arrangement entered into between—

(i) the Secretary of State and the person who has arranged for the claimant's participation in the Intensive Activity Period of the New Deal for 25 plus and which is made in respect of his participation in that Period; or

(ii) the Department for Employment and Learning and the person who has arranged for the claimant's participation in the Preparation for Employment Programme and which is made in respect of the claimant's participation in the Programme[; or

(*c*) the Steps to Work Programme specified in regulation 75(1)(*a*)(vi) of the Jobseeker's Allowance Regulations (Northern Ireland) 1996.][8]

[This item applies only to the extent that the payment is not taxable as a profit of a trade, profession or vocation.][4]

4 Any discretionary payment pursuant to section 2 of the Employment Act, or, in Northern Ireland, section 1(1) of the Employment and Training Act (Northern Ireland) 1950 to meet, or help to meet, special needs in respect of the claimant's participation in the Full-Time Education and Training Option of the New Deal as specified in regulation 75(1)(*b*)(ii) of the JSA Regulations or of the JSA (NI) Regulations.

5 Any—

(*a*) education maintenance allowance in accordance with regulations made under section 518 of the Education Act 1996 (payment of school expenses; grant of scholarships etc); or

(*b*) payment (not within sub-paragraph (*a*)) in respect of a course of study attended by a child or qualifying young person payable—

(i) in accordance with regulations made under section 518 of the Education (Scotland) Act 1980 (power to assist persons to take advantage of educational facilities) or section 12(2)(*c*) of the Further and Higher Education (Scotland) Act 1992 (provision of financial assistance to students); or

(ii) by virtue of regulations made Article 50, 51 or 55(1) of the Education and Libraries (Northern Ireland) Order 1986 (provisions to assist persons to take advantage of educational facilities).

6 Any payment made by an employment zone contractor payable in respect of the claimant's participation in the employment zone programme by way of—

(*a*) a training premium;

(*b*) a discretionary payment, being a fee, grant, loan or otherwise; or

(*c*) any arrears of subsistence allowance paid as a lump sum.

7 . . .[4]

8 An amount of income equal to any qualifying maintenance payment within section 347B of the Taxes Act.

[9 Any payment by way of qualifying care receipts to the extent that those receipts qualify for relief under Chapter 2 of Part 7 of the Income Tax (Trading and Other Income) Act 2005.][11]

10 Any payment of maintenance, whether under a court order or not, which is made or due to be made by—

(*a*) the claimant's former partner, or the claimant's partner's former partner; or

(*b*) the parent of a child or qualifying young person where that child or qualifying young person is a member of the claimant's household except where that parent is the claimant or the claimant's partner.

11 Any payment in respect of a child or qualifying young person who is a member of the claimant's household made—

[(*a*) to adopters which is exempt from income tax by virtue of [sections 744 to 746 of ITTOIA;][6]][3]

(*b*) by a local authority in pursuance of paragraph 15(1) of Schedule 1 to the Children Act 1989 (local authority contribution to child's maintenance);

[(*bb*) by a local authority by way of special guardianship support services pursuant to regulations under section 14F(1)(*b*) of the Children Act 1989; or][4]

(*c*) by an authority, as defined in Article 2 of the Children (Northern Ireland) Order 1995, in pursuance of Article 15 of, and paragraph 17 of Schedule 1 to, that Order (contribution by an authority to child's maintenance).

[12 Any payment in respect of travelling expenses—

(*a*) in relation to England under regulation 5, 6 or 12 of the National Health Service (Travel Expenses and Remission of Charges) Regulations 2003;

(*b*) in relation to Wales under regulation 5, 6 or 11 of the National Health Service (Travelling Expenses and Remission of Charges) (Wales) Regulations 2007;

(*c*) in relation to Scotland, under regulation 3, 5, or 11 of the National Health Service (Travelling Expenses and Remission of Charges) (Scotland) (No 2) Regulations 2003;

(*d*) in relation to Northern Ireland, under regulation 5, 6 or 11 of the Travelling Expenses and Remission of Charges Regulations (Northern Ireland) 2004; or

(*e*) made by the Secretary of State for Health, the Scottish Ministers, the Welsh Ministers or the Department of Health, Social Services and Public Safety and which is analogous to a payment specified in paragraph (a), (b), (c) or (d).][10]

13 Any payment made by the Secretary of State or the Scottish Ministers under a scheme established to assist relatives and other persons to visit persons in custody.

[14 Any payment under the Community Care (Direct Payments) Act 1996, section 57 of the Health and Social Care Act 2001, . . . [12] Article 15A of the Health and Personal Social Services (Direct Payments) (Northern Ireland) Order 1996 [or regulations made under section 57 of the Health and Social Care Act 2001 (direct payments)][5][, sections 50 to 53 of the Social Services and Well-being (Wales) Act 2014][13] or section 8 of the Carers and Direct Payments Act (Northern Ireland) 2002 [or as a direct payment as defined in section 4(2) of the Social Care (Self-directed Support) (Scotland) Act 2013][12].][3].

[14A Any payment made under the "Supporting People" programme—

(*a*) in England and Wales, under section 93 of the Local Government Act 2000;

(*b*) in Scotland, under section 91 of the Housing (Scotland) Act 2001; or

(*c*) in Northern Ireland, under Article 4 of the Housing Support Services (Northern Ireland) Order 2002.][1]

15 [Any payment or a voucher][1] provided under section 95 or 98 of the Immigration and Asylum Act 1999 for any former asylum-seeker or his dependants.

16 Any payment of a provident benefit by a trade union.

Here—

"provident benefit" has the meaning given in section 467(2) of the Taxes Act; and

"trade union" has the meaning given in section 467(4) of the Taxes Act.

[17. Armed forces independence payment under the Armed Forces and Reserve Forces (Compensation Scheme) Order 2011.][14]

[18. Any payment made under the Welfare Supplementary Payment (Loss of Disability Living Allowance) Regulations (Northern Ireland) 2016, the Welfare Supplementary Payment (Loss of Disability-Related Premiums) Regulations (Northern Ireland) 2016, Part 2 of the Welfare Supplementary Payments Regulations (Northern Ireland) 2016, or Parts 3 to 5 of the Welfare Supplementary Payment (Loss of Carer Payments) Regulations (Northern Ireland) 2016][17]

TABLE 7
SUMS DISREGARDED IN CALCULATING INCOME IF CONDITIONS ARE SATISFIED

1 Description of payment	*2 [Conditions][4] that must be satisfied*
1 Any payment in respect of any expenses incurred by a claimant who is engaged by a charitable or voluntary organisation or is a volunteer.	The claimant does not receive remuneration or profit from the engagement and is not treated as possessing any employment income under regulation 17 in respect of that engagement.

2 A payment by way of— (*a*) travelling expenses reimbursed to the claimant; (*b*) a living away from home allowance under section 2(2)(*d*) of the Employment Act, section 2(4)(*c*) of the Enterprise and New Towns (Scotland) Act 1990 or section 1 of the Employment and Training Act (Northern Ireland) 1950; (*c*) training grant; . . . [8] (*d*) child care expenses reimbursed to the claimant in respect of his participation in—	The claimant (*a*) participates in arrangements for training made under— (i) section 2 of the Employment Act; (ii) section 2 of the Enterprise and New Towns (Scotland) Act 1990; or (iii) section 1 of the Employment and Training Act (Northern Ireland) 1950; or (*b*) attends a course at an employment rehabilitation centre established under section 2 of the Employment Act.
(i) a New Deal option, (ii) the Intensive Activity Period of the New Deal Pilots for 25 plus, . . . [7] (iii) the Preparation for Employment Programme[; . . . [9] (iv) the Flexible New Deal specified in regulation 75(1)(a)(v) of the [JSA Regulations][9]][7][; or [(v) the Community Task Force specified in regulation 75(1)(*a*)(ii)(dd) of the JSA Regulations; or][9] (*e*)child care expenses under the Steps to Work Programme specified in regulation 75(1)(a)(vi) of the [JSA (NI) Regulations][9]][8]	[The payment is not taxable as a profit of a trade, profession or vocation.][4]

TABLE 8
SUMS PARTLY DISREGARDED IN THE CALCULATION OF INCOME

Type of payment to be disregarded	*Limit on, or exception to, the extent of disregard*
1 Any discretionary payment made pursuant to section 2 of the Employment Act, or, in Northern Ireland section 1(1) of the Employment and Training Act (Northern Ireland) 1950 to meet, or help meet, the claimant's special needs in undertaking a qualifying course within the meaning of regulation 17A(7) of the JSA Regulations or regulation 17A(7) of the JSA (NI) Regulations.	A payment is not within this item to the extent that it relates to travel expenses incurred as a result of the claimant's attendance on the course if an amount in respect of those expenses has already been disregarded pursuant to regulation 8.
2 Any payment made in respect of a career development loan paid pursuant to section 2 of the Employment Act.	A payment is not within this item to the extent that the loan has been applied for or paid in respect of living expenses for the period of education and training supported by the loan.
3 Any payment made to the claimant or his partner in respect of a person who is not normally a member of the claimant's household but is temporarily in his care, by— (*a*) a health authority; (*b*) a local authority; (*c*) a voluntary organisation; (*d*) that person pursuant to section 26(3A) of the National Assistance Act 1948;	A payment is only to be disregarded by virtue of this item if [(*a*)][2] any profits . . . [6] arising from the payment mentioned in column 1 are treated as nil by [section 791 to 794 of ITTOIA (full rent-a-room relief)][6] [; or (*b*) excluded from profits [by section 795 to 798 of ITTOIA (alternative calculation of profits if amount exceeds limit)][6]][2].

[(*dza*) that person where the payment is for the provision of accommodation in respect of the meeting of that person's needs under section 18 or 19 of the Care Act 2014 (duty and power to meet needs for care and support) [or section 35 or 36 of the Social Services and Well-being (Wales) Act 2014 (duty and power to meet care and support needs of an adult)][16];][15]	
[(*da*) a clinical commissioning group established under section 14D of the National Health Service Act 2006;	
(*db*) the National Health Service Commissioning Board;][13]	
(*e*) a primary care trust established under section 16A of the National Health Service Act 1977.	
4 Any payment made in Northern Ireland to the claimant or his partner in respect of a person who is not normally a member of the claimant's household but is temporarily in his care— (*a*) pursuant to Article 36(7) of the Health and Personal Social Services (Northern Ireland) Order 1972 by an authority; a voluntary organisation; or the person concerned, or (*b*) by a training school within the meaning of section 137 of the Children and Young Persons Act (Northern Ireland) 1968. In this item "an authority" has the meaning given by Article 2 of the Children (Northern Ireland) Order 1995.	A payment is only to be disregarded by virtue of this item if [(*a*)] any profits . . . [6] arising from the payment mentioned in column 1 are treated as nil by [section 791 to 794 of ITTOIA (full rent-a-room relief)][6][; or (*b*) excluded from profits [by section 795 to 798 of ITTOIA (alternative calculation of profits if amount exceeds limit)][6]][2].
5 Any payment under an insurance policy taken out to insure against the risk of being unable to maintain the repayments— (*a*) on a loan which is secured on the dwelling house which the claimant occupies as his home; or (*b*) under a regulated agreement or under a hire-purchase agreement or a conditional sale agreement. For the purposes of paragraph (*b*)— "regulated agreement" has the meaning given in the Consumer Credit Act 1974; and "hire-purchase agreement" and "conditional sale agreement" have the meanings given in Part 3 of the Hire-Purchase Act 1964.	A payment is only to be disregarded by virtue of this item to the extent that it is used to— (*a*) maintain the repayments referred to in column (1); and (*b*) meet any amount due by way of premiums on— (i) that policy; or (ii) in a case to which paragraph (*a*) of this item applies, an insurance policy taken out to insure against loss or damage to any building or part of a building which is occupied by the claimant as his home and which is required as a condition of the loan referred to in column (1).
[6][2] Any payment in respect of the claimant's attendance at court as a juror or witness.	This item applies only to the extent that the payment is not compensation for loss of earnings or for the loss of payment of social security income.
[7][2] Any payment of a sports award except to the extent that it has been made in respect of living expenses.	For the purposes of this item "living expenses" does not include— (*a*) the cost of vitamins, minerals or other special dietary supplements intended to enhance the performance of the claimant in the sport in respect of which the award was made; or

	(*b*) accommodation costs incurred as a consequence of living away from home whilst training for, or competing in, the sport in respect of which the award was made.

Commentary—*Simon's Taxes* **E2.335.**

HMRC Manuals—Tax Credit Technical Manual TCTM4910A–4957A (guidance on items listed in tables 6, 7 and 8).

Amendments—[1] In Table 6, item 14A inserted and words in item 15 substituted by the Tax Credits (Definition and Calculation of Income) (Amendment) Regulations, SI 2003/732, regs 3, 11(1), (2) with effect from 6 April 2003.

[2] Words in Table 8 inserted, and items 6, 7 renumbered, by SI 2003/732, regs 3, 11(1), (3)(*a*), (*b*) with effect from 6 April 2003.

[3] In Table 6, items 11(*a*) and 14 substituted by the Tax Credits (Miscellaneous Amendments No 2) Regulations, SI 2003/2815 regs 2, 11 with effect from 26 November 2003.

[4] In Table 6, words inserted in items 3 and 11, and item 7 revoked; and in Table 7, word substituted, and words inserted, by the Tax Credits (Miscellaneous Amendments) Regulations, SI 2004/762 regs 12, 16 with effect from 6 April 2004.

[5] In Table 6, words inserted in item 14 by the Community Care, Services for Carers and Children's Services (Direct Payments) (Wales) Regulations, SI 2004/1748 reg 3 with effect from 1 November 2004.

[6] In Table 6, item, 11(*a*) amended, and in Table 8, items 3 and 4 amended, by the Tax Credits (Miscellaneous Amendments) Regulations, SI 2006/766 regs 6, 19 with effect from 6 April 2006.

[7] In Table 7, in item 2(*d*), in para (ii) word "or" revoked, and para (iv) and preceding word "or" inserted, by the Tax Credits (Miscellaneous Amendments) Regulations, SI 2009/697 regs 6, 8 with effect from 5 October 2009.

[8] In Table 6, in item 3 word "or" at end of para (*a*) revoked and para (*c*) and preceding word "or" inserted; in Table 7, in item 2 of column 1 word "or" at end of para (*c*) revoked, and para (*e*) and preceding word "or" inserted, by the Tax Credits (Miscellaneous Amendments) (No 2) Regulations, SI 2009/2887 regs 5, 7 with effect from 21 November 2009.

[9] In Table 6 in item 3, paras (*a*)(iia), (iv) inserted, in Table 7 in item 2 para (*d*)(v) inserted, and in paras (*d*)(iv), (*e*) words substituted for "Jobseeker's Allowance Regulations 1996", and "Jobseeker's Allowance Regulations (Northern Ireland) 1996", by the Tax Credits (Miscellaneous Amendments) Regulations, SI 2010/751 regs 2, 5 with effect from 6 April 2010.

[10] In Table 6, item 12 substituted by the Tax Credits (Miscellaneous Amendments) (No 3) Regulations, SI 2010/2914 regs 2, 5 with effect from 31 December 2010.

[11] In Table 6, item 9 substituted by the Tax Credits (Miscellaneous Amendments) Regulations, SI 2011/721 reg 2(1), (2) with effect from 6 April 2011.

[12] In Table 6, item 14, words revoked and words inserted by the Social Care (Self-directed Support) (Scotland) Act 2013 (Consequential Modifications and Savings) Order, SI 2014/513 art 2, Sch para 8 with effect from 1 April 2014.

[13] In Table 8, item 3(*da*), (*db*) inserted by the National Treatment Agency (Abolition) and the Health and Social Care Act 2012 (Consequential, Transitional and Saving Provisions) Order, SI 2013/235 art 11, Sch 2 Pt 1 para 55(*a*) with effect from 1 April 2013

[14] In Table 6, item 17 inserted by the Armed Forces and Reserve Forces Compensation Scheme (Consequential Provisions: Subordinate Legislation) Order, SI 2013/591 art 7, Schedule para 25 with effect from 8 April 2013.

[15] In Table 8, item 3(*dza*) inserted by the Care Act 2014 (Consequential Amendments) (Secondary Legislation) Order, SI 2015/643 art 2, Schedule para 20 with effect from 1 April 2015.

[16] In Table 8, item 3(*dza*), words inserted by the Tax Credits and Child Benefit (Miscellaneous Amendments) Regulations, SI 2016/360 reg 3(1), (4) with effect from 6 April 2016.

[17] In Table 6, item 18 inserted by the Tax Credits (Definition and Calculation of Income) (Amendment) Regulations, SI 2016/978 reg 2(1), (3) with effect from 31 October 2016.

2002/2007

CHILD TAX CREDIT REGULATIONS 2002

Made by the Treasury under TCA 2002 ss 8, 9, 65, 67

Made . . . . *30 July 2002*

Coming into force in accordance with . . . . *regulation 1*

1 Citation, commencement and effect

These Regulations may be cited as the Child Tax Credit Regulations 2002 and shall come into force—

(*a*) for the purpose of enabling claims to be made, on 1st August 2002;

(*b*) for the purpose of enabling awards to be made, on 1st January 2003; and

(*c*) for all other purposes on 6th April 2003;

and shall have effect for the tax year beginning on 6th April 2003 and subsequent tax years.

HMRC Manuals—Tax Credit Technical Manual TCTM2200–2207 (CTC entitlement).

2 Interpretation

(1) In these Regulations, unless the context otherwise requires—

["A", as a noun, has the meaning given by regulation 7(2A);][14]

"the Act" means the Tax Credits Act 2002;

"advanced education" means[12] . . . —

(*a*) a course in preparation for a degree, a diploma of higher education, a higher national diploma, a higher national diploma or higher national certificate of Edexcel or the Scottish Qualifications Authority, or a teaching qualification; or

Tax Credits

(*b*) any other course which is of a standard above ordinary national diploma, a national diploma or national certificate of Edexcel . . . [2], a general certificate of education (advanced level), [or Scottish national qualifications at higher or advanced higher level][2];

["approved training" has the meaning given by regulation 1(3) of the Child Benefit (General) Regulations 2006;][4]

["armed forces independence payment" means armed forces independence payment under the Armed Forces and Reserve Forces (Compensation Scheme) Order 2011;][10]

["the Board" means the Commissioners [for Her Majesty's Revenue and Customs][4];][1]

"the Careers Service" means—

(*a*) in England and Wales, a person with whom the Secretary of State or the National Assembly of Wales has made arrangements under section 10(1) of the Employment Act, and a [local authority][7] to whom the Secretary of State or the National Assembly of Wales has given a direction under section 10(2) of that Act,

(*b*) in Scotland, a person with whom the Scottish Ministers have made arrangements under section 10(1) of the Employment Act and any education authority to which a direction has been given by the Scottish Ministers under section 10(2) of that Act, and

(*c*) . . . [1]

"child" means a person who has not attained the age of sixteen . . . [5];

"claimant" has the meaning in section 9(8) of the Act, [except in regulations 7 and 9 to 14 (for which see regulations 7(1) and 13(13) to (15))][14];

"the Connexions Service" means a person of any description with whom the Secretary of State has made an arrangement under section 114(2)(*a*) of the Learning and Skills Act 2000 and section 10(1) of the Employment Act, and any person to whom he has given a direction under section 114(2)(*b*) of the former Act and section 10(2) of the latter Act;

"the Contributions and Benefits Act" means the Social Security Contributions and Benefits Act 1992;

["couple" has the meaning given by section 3(5A) of the Act;][3]

"custodial sentence"—

(*a*) in England and Wales, has the meaning in section 76 of the Powers of Criminal Courts (Sentencing) Act 2000,

(*b*) in Scotland, means detention under a sentence imposed by a court under sections 44, 205, 207 or 208 of the Criminal Procedure (Scotland) Act 1995, and

(*c*) in Northern Ireland, means a custodial sentence under the Criminal Justice (Children) (Northern Ireland) Order 1998;

"disability living allowance" means a disability living allowance under section 71 of the Contributions and Benefits Act;

"the Employment Act" means the Employment and Training Act 1973;

"the family element of child tax credit" and "the individual element of child tax credit" shall be construed in accordance with section 9(3) of the Act;

. . . [12]

["income support" means income support under section 124 of the Contributions and Benefits Act;][14]

"joint claim" and "single claim" shall be construed in accordance with section 3(8) of the Act;

"looked after by a local authority" has the meaning in section 22 of the Children Act 1989, [section 74 of the Social Services and Well-being (Wales) Act 2014,][13] section 17(6) of the Children (Scotland) Act 1995 or (in Northern Ireland) Article 25 of the Children (Northern Ireland) Order 1995 (with the modification that for the reference to a local authority there is substituted a reference to an authority within the meaning in Article 2 of that Order)[, and (in Scotland) includes a child in respect of which a child assessment order within the meaning of section 35 of the Children's Hearings (Scotland) Act 2011 has been made or a child protection order within the meaning of section 37 of that Act has been made][12];

the "main responsibility test" has the meaning given in Rule 2.2. of regulation 3;

the "normally living with test" has the meaning given in Rule 1.1. of regulation 3;

["old style JSA" means a jobseeker's allowance under the Jobseekers Act 1995(c) as that Act has effect apart from the amendments made by Part 1 of Schedule 14 to the Welfare Reform Act 2012(d) that remove references to an income-based allowance;][14]

"Part 1" means Part 1 of the Act;

"patient" means a person (other than a person who is serving a custodial sentence) who is regarded as receiving free in-patient treatment within the meaning of the Social Security (Hospital In-patients) Regulations 1975, or the Social Security (Hospital In-patients) Regulations (Northern Ireland) 1975;

[personal independence payment" means personal independence payment under Part 4 of the Welfare Reform Act 2012;][9]

["placing for adoption" means placing for adoption in accordance with—

(*a*) the Adoption Agencies Regulations 2005,

(*b*) the Adoption Agencies (Wales) Regulations 2005

(*c*) the Adoption Agencies (Scotland) Regulations 2009, or

(*d*) the Adoption Agencies Regulations (Northern Ireland) 1989,][8]

["qualifying body" means—

(*a*) the Careers Service or Connexions Service;

(*b*) the Ministry of Defence;

(*c*) in Northern Ireland, the Department for Employment and Learning or an Education and Library Board established under Article 3 of the Education and Libraries (Northern Ireland) Order 1986; or

(*d*) for the purposes of applying Council Regulation (EEC) No 1408/71 [and Regulation (EC) No 883/2004 of the European Parliament and of the Council][6], any corresponding body in another member state;][5]

"qualifying young person" means a person, other than a child, who—

(*a*) has not attained the age of [twenty][4], and

(*b*) satisfies the conditions in regulation 5(3) and (4);

. . . [5]

. . . [4]

"remunerative work" means work which is—

(*a*) done for payment or in expectation of payment,

(*b*) undertaken for not less than 24 hours a week, calculated in accordance with regulation 4(3) of the Working Tax Credit (Entitlement and Maximum Rate) Regulations 2002, and

(*c*) not excluded from the meaning of engagement in remunerative work by regulation 4(2) of those Regulations;

["step-parent", in relation to A, means a person who is not A's parent but—

(*a*) is a member of a couple, the other member of which is a parent of A, where both are responsible for A; or

(*b*) was previously a member of—

(i) a couple, the other member of which was a parent of A, or

(ii) a polygamous unit (within the meaning of the Tax Credits (Polygamous Marriages) Regulations 2003), another member of which was a parent of A,

if immediately prior to ceasing to be a member of that couple or that polygamous unit the person was, and has since remained, responsible for A;][14]

and other expressions have the same meanings as defined in the Act.

(2) In the application of these Regulations to Northern Ireland, a reference to a provision of an enactment which applies only to Great Britain or England and Wales, shall be construed, so far as necessary, as including a reference to the corresponding enactment applying to Northern Ireland.

HMRC Manuals—Tax Credit Technical Manual TCTM2204 (lists types of recognised educational establishments, non-advanced education etc).

Modifications—Tax Credits (Polygamous Marriages) Regulations, SI 2003/742 regs 22, 23 (definition of "joint claim" substituted and definition of "polygamous unit" inserted; for the purposes of polygamous marriages).

Amendments—[1] Definition of "the Board" inserted, para (*c*) in definition of "Careers Service" repealed, and in definition of "relevant training programme", para (*aa*) inserted, by CTC (Amendment) Regulations, SI 2003/738 regs 2, 3 with effect from 6 April 2003.

[2] In the definition of "advanced education", words revoked and substituted by the Tax Credits (Miscellaneous Amendments No 2) Regulations, SI 2003/2815 reg 17 with effect from 26 November 2003.

[3] In para (1), definition of "couple" inserted by the Civil Partnership Act 2004 (Tax Credits, etc) (Consequential Amendments) Order, SI 2005/2919 art 4(1), (2) with effect from 5 December 2005.

[4] Definition of "approved training" inserted; words substituted in the definitions of "the Board" and "qualifying young person"; and definition of "relevant training programme" revoked; by CTC (Amendment) Regulations, SI 2006/222 regs 2, 3 with effect from 6 April 2006.

However, a person aged 19 or over on 6 April 2006 is not a qualifying young person, regardless of these amendments: SI 2006/222 reg 1.

[5] In para (1), words in definition of "child" revoked, definitions of "full-time education" and "qualifying body" inserted, and definition of "recognised educational establishment" revoked, by the Tax Credits (Miscellaneous Amendments) (No 2) Regulations, SI 2008/2169 regs 6, 7 with effect from 1 September 2008.

[6] In para (1), in definition of "qualifying body", in para (*d*), words inserted, by the Tax Credits (Miscellaneous Amendments) (No 3) Regulations, SI 2010/2914 regs 8, 9 with effect from 31 December 2010.

[7] In para (1), in definition of "the careers service", in para (*a*), words substituted by the Local Education Authorities and Children's Services Authorities (Integration of Functions) (Local and Subordinate Legislation) Order, SI 2010/1172 art 5, Sch 3 para 46 with effect from 5 May 2010.

[8] In para (1), definition of "placing for adoption" substituted by the Tax Credits (Miscellaneous Amendments) Regulations, SI 2012/848 regs 1(2), 4(1), (2) with effect from 6 April 2012.

[9] In para (1), definition of "personal independence payment" inserted by the Personal Independence Payment (Supplementary Provisions and Consequential Amendments) Regulations, SI 2013/388 reg 30(1), (2) with effect from 8 April 2013.

[10] In para (1), definition of "armed forces independence payment" inserted by the Armed Forces and Reserve Forces Compensation Scheme (Consequential Provisions: Subordinate Legislation) Order, SI 2013/591 art 7, Schedule para 26(1), (2) with effect from 8 April 2013.

[11] In sub-para (1), in definition of "looked after by a local authority", words inserted by the Children's Hearings (Scotland) Act 2011 (Consequential and Transitional Provisions and Savings) Order, SI 2013/1465 art 17, Sch 1 para 19(1), (2) with effect from 24 June 2013 (the day the Children's Hearings (Scotland) Act 2011 s 7 came into force: SSI 2013/195 art 2).

[12] In para (1), in definition of "advanced education", words revoked, and definition of "full-time education revoked by the Child Benefit (General) and Child Tax Credit (Amendment) Regulations, 2014/1231, reg 3(1), (2) with effect from 4 June 2014.

[13] In para (1), in definition of "looked after by a local authority", words inserted by the Tax Credits and Child Benefit (Miscellaneous Amendments) Regulations, SI 2016/360 reg 4(1), (2) with effect from 6 April 2016.

[14] In para (1), definitions of "A", "income support", "old style JSA" and "step-parent" inserted, and in definition of "claimant" words substituted, by the Child Tax Credit (Amendment) Regulations, SI 2017/387 regs 2, 3 with effect from 6 April 2017.

3 Circumstances in which a person is or is not responsible for a child or qualifying young person

(1) For the purposes of child tax credit the circumstances in which a person is or is not responsible for a child or qualifying young person shall be determined in accordance with the following Rules.

Rule 1

1.1 A person shall be treated as responsible for a child or qualifying young person who is normally living with him (the "normally living with test").

1.2 This Rule is subject to Rules 2 to 4.

Rule 2 (Competing claims)

2.1 This Rule applies where—

(*a*) a child or qualifying young person normally lives with two or more persons in—

(i) different households, or

(ii) the same household, where those persons are not limited to the members of a . . . [2] couple, or

(iii) a combination of (i) and (ii), and

(*b*) two or more of those persons make separate claims (that is, not a single joint claim made by a . . . [2] couple) for child tax credit in respect of the child or qualifying young person.

2.2 The child or qualifying young person shall be treated as the responsibility of—

(*a*) only one of those persons making such claims, and

(*b*) whichever of them has (comparing between them) the main responsibility for him (the "main responsibility test"),

subject to Rules 3 and 4.

Rule 3

3.1 The persons mentioned in Rule 2.2. (other than the child or qualifying young person) may jointly elect as to which of them satisfies the main responsibility test for the child or qualifying young person, and in default of agreement the Board may determine that question on the information available to them at the time of their determination.

Rule 4

4.1 A child or qualifying young person shall be treated as not being the responsibility of any person during any period in which any of the following Cases applies.

Case A	The child or qualifying young person is provided with, or placed in, accommodation under Part III of the Children Act 1989, [Parts 4 or 6 of the Social Services and Well-being (Wales) Act 2014,][11] Part II of the Children (Scotland) Act 1995 [by virtue of a requirement in a child assessment order within the meaning of section 35 of the Children's Hearings (Scotland) Act 2011, a child protection order within the meaning of section 37 of that Act, a compulsory supervision order within the meaning of section 83 of that Act or an interim compulsory supervision order within the meaning of section 86 of that Act,][10] or Part IV of the Children (Northern Ireland) Order 1995, and the cost of that child's or qualifying young person's accommodation or maintenance is borne wholly or partly— (i) out of local authority funds under [section 22C(10) . . . [11] of the Children Act 1989 [or section 81(13) of the Social Services and Wellbeing (Wales) Act 2014][11] or [regulation 33 of the Looked After Children (Scotland) Regulations 2009][8] , (ii) in Northern Ireland, by an authority, within the meaning in Article 2, and under Article 27, of that Order, or (iii) out of other public funds. . . . [4]
Case B	The child or qualifying young person— (i) is being looked after by a local authority, and (ii) has been placed for adoption by that authority in the home of a person proposing to adopt him,

and a local authority is making a payment in respect of the child's or qualifying young person's accommodation or maintenance, or both, under [section 22C(10) . . . [11] of the Children Act 1989, [section 81(13) of the Social Services and Well-being (Wales) Act 2014,][11] [regulation 33 of the Looked After Children (Scotland) Regulations 2009][8] or Article 27 of the Children (Northern Ireland) Order 1995.

This Case applies in Northern Ireland with the modification that for references to a local authority there are substituted references to an authority (within the meaning in Article 2 of that Order).

Case C — A custodial sentence—

(*a*) for life,

(*b*) without limit of time,

(*c*) of detention during Her Majesty's pleasure,

(*d*) in Northern Ireland, of detention during the pleasure of the Secretary of State, or

(*e*) for a term or period of more than four months,

has been passed on the child or qualifying young person.

Case D — The . . . [5] qualifying young person claims and is awarded child tax credit in his or her own right, in respect of a child for whom he or she is responsible, for that period.

[Case E — . . . [5] the qualifying young person, claims incapacity benefit [or contributory employment and support allowance payable under Part 1 of the Welfare Reform Act 2007][6] in his or her own right and that benefit is paid to or in respect of him or her for that period.

This Case does not apply at any time ("the later time") during a period of incapacity for work which began before 6th April 2004 in the case of a person in respect of whom, at a time—

(*a*) during that period of incapacity, and

(*b*) before that date,

both incapacity benefit and child tax credit were payable, if child tax credit has been payable in respect of him or her continuously since 5th April 2004 until that later time.

For the purposes of this Case "period of incapacity" shall be construed in accordance with section 30C of the 1992 Act (incapacity benefit: days and periods of incapacity for work) but disregarding subsections (5) and (5A) of that section.][1]

[Case F — . . . [5] the qualifying young person claims and receives working tax credit in his or her own right (whether alone or on a joint claim). . . . [5]][3]

[Case G — The qualifying young person has a spouse, civil partner or partner with whom they are living and the spouse, civil partner or partner is not in full-time education or approved training as provided for under regulation 5(3).

Case H — The responsible person is the spouse, civil partner or partner of a qualifying young person with whom they are living.

[Cases G and H do][7] not apply to persons in receipt of child tax credit for a qualifying young person who is living with a partner on the day before 1st September 2008.][5]

[4.2 Where a child or qualifying young person is in residential accommodation referred to in regulation 9 of the Child Benefit (General) Regulations 2006 and in the circumstances prescribed in paragraphs (*a*) or (*b*) of that regulation, he shall be treated as being the responsibility of any person who was treated as being responsible for him immediately before he entered that accommodation.][4]

(2) Where—

(*a*) a claimant is treated as responsible for a child or qualifying young person by virtue of the preceding Rules, and

(*b*) the child or qualifying young person has a child of his or her own, normally living with him or her,

the claimant shall also be treated as responsible for, and as having made a claim for child tax credit in respect of, the child of the child or qualifying young person (but without prejudice to the facts as to which of them is mainly responsible for that child).

Commentary—*Simon's Taxes* **E2.212.**

HMRC Manuals—Tax Credit Technical Manual TCTM2201 (reg 3(1): the terms "normally lives with you" and "main responsibility" should be given their ordinary every day meaning; factors listed which Revenue consider in deciding who has main responsibility, eg who the child normally lives with and where they keep the majority of their belongings such as clothes, toys).

TCTM2202 (guidance on rule 4; a child or young person treated as normally living with a family if he or she is a patient in long term care unless, during that time, the family ceases to have main responsibility for the child or young person)

Modifications—Tax Credits (Polygamous Marriages) Regulations, SI 2003/742 regs 22, 24 (in para (1) Rule 2.1 above, "polygamous unit" to be substituted for "married couple or unmarried couple" wherever occurring, for the purposes of polygamous marriages).

1 In para (1), Rule 4, Case E inserted by the Tax Credits (Miscellaneous Amendments) Regulations, SI 2004/762 reg 2 with effect from 6 April 2004.

2 In para (1), words in Rule 2 revoked by the Civil Partnership Act 2004 (Tax Credits, etc) (Consequential Amendments) Order, SI 2005/2919 art 4(1), (3) with effect from 5 December 2005.

3 Words in para (1) inserted by the Child Tax Credit (Amendment No 2) Regulations, SI 2006/1163 with effect from 24 May 2006.

4 Words in para (1), Rule 4, Case A revoked, and Rule 4.1 inserted, by the Child Tax Credit (Amendment) Regulations, SI 2007/2151 regs 2, 3 with effect from 16 August 2007.

5 In para (1), Rule 4.1, words in Cases D, E, F revoked, and Cases G, H inserted, by the Tax Credits (Miscellaneous Amendments) (No 2) Regulations, SI 2008/2169 regs 6, 8 with effect from 1 September 2008.

6 Words in para (1) inserted by the Employment and Support Allowance (Consequential Provisions) (No 3) Regulations, SI 2008/1879 reg 22(1), (2) with effect from 27 October 2008.

7 In para (1), Rule 4.1, Case H, words substituted by the Tax Credits (Miscellaneous Amendments) Regulations, SI 2009/697 regs 9, 10 with effect from 6 April 2009.

8 In para (1), in Rule 4, in Case A para (i) and Case B para (ii), words substituted for words "section 26 of the Children (Scotland) Act 1995", by the Adoption and Children (Scotland) Act 2007 (Consequential Modifications) Order, SI 2011/1740 art 2 Sch 1 para 29(1), (3) with effect from 15 July 2011.

9 In Rule 4.1, in Case A in sub-para (i), and in Case B, words inserted, by the Tax Credits (Miscellaneous Amendments) Regulations, SI 2012/848 regs 1(2), 4(1), (3) with effect from 6 April 2012.

10 In para (1), Rule 4.1, Case A, inserted by the Children's Hearings (Scotland) Act 2011 (Consequential and Transitional Provisions and Savings) Order, SI 2013/1465 art 17, Sch 1 para 19(1), (3) with effect from 24 June 2013 (the day the Children's Hearings (Scotland) Act 2011 s 7 came into force: SSI 2013/195 art 2).

11 In para (1), Rule 4.1, Case A, Case B, words inserted and revoked by the Tax Credits and Child Benefit (Miscellaneous Amendments) Regulations, SI 2016/360 reg 4(1), (3) with effect from 6 April 2016.

4 [Period for which a person who attains the age of sixteen is a qualifying young person

(1) [Subject to paragraph (1A), a][2] person who attains the age of sixteen is a qualifying young person from the date on which that person attained that age until 31st August which next follows that date.

[(1A) A person who attains the age of sixteen on 31st August is a qualifying young person from the date on which that person attained that age.][2]

(2) Paragraph (1) is subject to regulation 5 but as if there were no requirement to satisfy the first condition specified in paragraph (3) of that regulation.][1]

[(2A) Paragraph (1A) is subject to regulation 5.][2]

Amendments—[1] Reg 4 substituted by the Tax Credits (Miscellaneous Amendments) (No 2) Regulations, SI 2008/2169 regs 6, 9 with effect from 1 September 2008.

2 In para (1), words substituted, and paras (1A), (2A) inserted, by the Tax Credits (Miscellaneous Amendments) Regulations, SI 2012/848 regs 1(2), 4(1), (4) with effect from 6 April 2012.

5 Maximum age and prescribed conditions for a qualifying young person

(1) For the purposes of Part 1 a person ceases to be a qualifying young person (unless disqualified earlier under the following paragraphs) on the date on which he attains the age of [twenty][2].

(2) A person who is not a child, but has not attained the age of [twenty][2] years, is a qualifying young person for any period during which the following conditions are satisfied with regard to him [(and once a person falls within the terms of paragraph (3)(*b*), he shall be treated as having satisfied the first condition from the [relevant leaving date][3] mentioned in that paragraph)][1].

(3) The first condition is that he is[2] . . . —

(*a*) receiving full-time education, not being—

(i) advanced education, or

(ii) education received by that person by virtue of his employment or of any office held by him; . . . [2]

[(*ab*) undertaking approved training[, is enrolled or has been accepted to undertake such training,][4] which is not provided [by means of a contract of employment][5]; or][2]

(*b*) under the age of eighteen years and—

[(i) he ceased to receive full-time education or to undertake approved training (the date of that event being referred to as "the relevant leaving date");][2]

[(ii) within 3 months of the [relevant leaving date][2], he has notified the Board (in the manner prescribed by regulation 22 of the Tax Credits (Claims and Notifications) Regulations 2002) that he is registered for work or training with [a qualifying body][5], and][1]

[(iii) not more than 20 weeks has elapsed since the [relevant leaving date][2].][1]

[(3A) A person who has attained the age of nineteen years satisfies paragraph (3)(*a*) or (*ab*) only where the course of education or training began before he attained that age[, or he enrolled or was accepted to undertake that course before he attained that age][4].][2]

(4) The second condition is that the period in question is not (and does not include)—

(*a*) a week in which he (having ceased to receive full-time education [or approved training][2]) becomes engaged in remunerative work [or][2];

(*b*) . . . [2]

(*c*) a period in respect of which that person receives income support[, income-related employment and support allowance payable under Part 1 of the Welfare Reform Act 2007][6][,][7] income-based jobseeker's allowance within the meaning of section 1(4) of the Jobseekers Act 1995 [or universal credit under Part 1 of the Welfare Reform Act 2012][7].

[(5) For the purposes of paragraphs (3) and (4) a person shall be treated as being in full-time education if full-time education is received by that person by undertaking a course—

(*a*) at a school or college, or

(*b*) where that person has been receiving that education prior to attaining the age of sixteen, elsewhere, if approved by the Board,][5]

where in pursuit of that course, the time spent receiving instruction or tuition, undertaking supervised study, examination or practical work or taking part in any exercise, experiment or project for which provision is made in the curriculum of the course, exceeds or exceeds on average 12 hours a week in normal term-time [and shall include gaps between the ending of one course and the commencement of another, where the person enrols on and commences the latter course][9] . . . [4].

[(5A) If paragraph (5) does not apply, then for the purposes of paragraphs (3) and (4) a person shall be treated as being in full-time education if that person is being provided with "appropriate full-time education" in England within section 4 (appropriate full-time education or training) of the Education and Skills Act 2008.][8]

(6) In calculating the time spent in pursuit of the course, no account shall be taken of time occupied by meal breaks or spent on unsupervised study.

[(7) In determining whether a person is undertaking a course of full-time education or approved training, there shall be disregarded any interruption—

(*a*) for a period of up to 6 months, whether beginning before or after the person concerned attains age 16, to the extent that it is reasonable in the opinion of the Board to do so; and

(*b*) for any period due to illness or disability of the mind or body of the person concerned provided that it is reasonable in the opinion of the Board to do so.][2]

Commentary—*Simon's Taxes* **E2.211.**

HMRC Manuals—Tax Credit Technical Manual TCTM2203 (reg 5(1)–(4): definition of a young person). TCTM2204 ("normal term time" in reg 5(5) takes its natural meaning; in calculating the time spent in pursuit of the course in reg 5(6), do not take account of meal breaks or unsupervised study or homework which is undertaken outside normal hours).

Amendments—[1] Words in paras (2) and (5)(*b*) inserted, and sub-paras (3)(*b*)(i)–(iii) substituted by CTC (Amendment) Regulations, SI 2003/738 regs 2, 4–6 with effect from 6 April 2003.

[2] Words in paras (1)–(3) substituted; words in paras (3), (4) revoked and inserted; paras (3A), (7) inserted; by CTC (Amendment) Regulations, SI 2006/222 regs 2, 4 with effect from 6 April 2006.
However, a person aged 19 or over on 6 April 2006 is not a qualifying young person, regardless of these amendments: SI 2006/222 reg 1.

[3] Words in para (2) substituted by the Tax Credits (Miscellaneous Amendments) Regulations, SI 2006/766 reg 3 with effect from 6 April 2006.

[4] Words in paras (3)(*ab*), (3A) inserted, and words in para (5) revoked, by the Child Tax Credit (Amendment) Regulations, SI 2007/2151 regs 2, 4 with effect from 16 August 2007.

[5] Words in paras (3)(*ab*), (*b*)(ii), (5) substituted by the Tax Credits (Miscellaneous Amendments) (No 2) Regulations, SI 2008/2169 regs 6, 10 with effect from 1 September 2008.

[6] Words in para (4)(*c*) inserted by the Employment and Support Allowance (Consequential Provisions) (No 3) Regulations, SI 2008/1879 reg 22(1), (3) with effect from 27 October 2008.

[7] In para (4)(*c*), comma substituted for word "or", and words inserted after words "Jobseekers Act 1995" by the Universal Credit (Consequential, Supplementary, Incidental and Miscellaneous Provisions) Regulations, SI 2013/630 reg 79 with effect from 29 April 2013.

[8] Para (5A) inserted by the Child Benefit (General) and Child Tax Credit (Amendment) Regulations, 2014/1231, reg 3(1), (3) with effect from 4 June 2014.

[9] Words in para (5) inserted by the Child Benefit (General) and Tax Credits (Miscellaneous Amendments) Regulations, SI 2014/2924 reg 3(1), (2) with effect from 28 November 2014.

6 Entitlement to child tax credit after death of child or qualifying young person

If—

(*a*) a child or qualifying young person dies, and

(*b*) a person is (or would, if a claim had been made, have been) entitled to child tax credit in respect of the child or qualifying young person immediately before the death,

that person shall be entitled to child tax credit in respect of the child or qualifying young person for the period of eight weeks immediately following the death or, in the case of a qualifying young person, until the date on which he or she would have attained the age of [twenty][1], if earlier.

Amendments—[1] Word substituted by CTC (Amendment) Regulations, SI 2006/222 regs 2, 5 with effect from 6 April 2006. However, a person aged 19 or over on 6 April 2006 is not a qualifying young person, regardless of these amendments: SI 2006/222 reg 1.

7 Determination of the maximum rate at which a person or persons may be entitled to child tax credit

(1) In the following paragraphs [and in regulations 9 to 12 and 14][4]—

(*a*) in the case of a single claim (but not a joint claim), the person making the claim is referred to as the "claimant"; and

(*b*) in the case of a joint claim, the members of the . . . [1] couple making the claim are referred to as the "joint claimants".

(2) The maximum rate at which a claimant or joint claimants may be entitled to child tax credit shall be the aggregate of—

(*a*) the family element of child tax credit [if the claimant is, or either or both the joint claimants are, responsible for a child or qualifying young person who was born before 6th April 2017][4], and

(*b*) an individual element of child tax credit, in respect of each child or qualifying young person for whom—

(i) the claimant, or

(ii) either or both of the joint claimants,

as the case may be, is or are [responsible, but subject to paragraph (2A);][4]

[(*c*) a disability element of child tax credit in the case of each child or qualifying young person who is disabled or severely disabled.][4]

[(2A) Where the claimant, or either or both of the joint claimants, is or are responsible for a child or qualifying young person born on or after 6th April 2017 ("A"), the maximum rate referred to in paragraph (2) shall not include an individual element of child tax credit in respect of A unless—

(*a*) the claimant is, or the joint claimants are, claiming the individual element of child tax credit for no more than one other child or qualifying young person; or

(*b*) an exception applies in relation to A in accordance with regulation 9.][4]

[(3) The family element of child tax credit is £545.][2]

(4) The individual element of child tax credit for any child or qualifying young person referred to in paragraph (2)(*b*) above—

(*a*) . . . [4]

(*b*) . . . [4]

(*c*) in the case of [a][4] child, is [£2,780][3];

(*d*) . . . [4]

(*e*) . . . [4] and

(*f*) in the case of [a][4] qualifying young person, is [£2,780][3].

[(5) The disability element of child tax credit—

(*a*) where the child or qualifying young person is disabled, is £3,175;

(*b*) where the child or qualifying young person is severely disabled, is £4,465.][5]

Commentary—*Simon's Taxes* **E2.213, E2.214, E2.215.**

HMRC Manuals—Tax Credit Technical Manual TCTM3001 (summary of maximum rates of CTC).

Modifications—Tax Credits (Polygamous Marriages) Regulations, SI 2003/742 regs 22, 25 (words in paras (1)(*b*), (2)(*b*) substituted for the purposes of polygamous marriages).

Amendments—[1] In para (1)(*b*), words revoked by the Civil Partnership Act 2004 (Tax Credits, etc) (Consequential Amendments) Order, SI 2005/2919 art 4(1), (4) with effect from 5 December 2005.

[2] Sub-para (3) substituted by the Tax Credits Up-rating Regulations, SI 2011/1035 reg 2 with effect in relation to awards of tax credits for the year beginning on 6 April 2011. This amendment continues to have effect in relation to awards of tax credits for the tax year beginning on 6 April 2012 and subsequent tax years (SI 2012/849 reg 5(*a*)).

[3] In para (4)(*c*), (*f*), figure substituted by the Child Benefit and Tax Credits Up-rating Order, SI 2015/567 art 3 with effect from 6 April 2015. Figure was previously £2,750.

[4] In paras (1), (2), words inserted; whole of para (2A) inserted; in paras (2)(*b*), (4)(*c*), (*f*), words substituted; and paras (4)(*a*), (*b*), (*d*), (*e*) revoked; by the Child Tax Credit (Amendment) Regulations, SI 2017/387 regs 2, 4 with effect from 6 April 2017.

[5] Para (5) inserted by the Tax Credits and Guardian's Allowance Up-rating etc Regulations, SI 2017/406 reg 3 with effect in relation to awards of tax credits for the tax year beginning on 6 April 2017 and subsequent tax years.

8 Prescribed conditions for a disabled or severely disabled child or qualifying young person

(1) For the purposes of section 9 of the Act a child or qualifying young person—

(*a*) is disabled if he satisfies the requirements of paragraph (2); and

(*b*) is severely disabled if he satisfies the requirements of paragraph (3) [or (4)][1] [or (5)][2].

(2) A person satisfies the requirements of this paragraph if—

(*a*) disability living allowance is payable in respect of him, or has ceased to be so payable solely because he is a patient; or

[(*b*) he is certified as severely sight impaired or blind by a consultant ophthalmologist;][3]

(*c*) he ceased to be so . . . [3] certified as [severely sight impaired or][3] blind within the 28 weeks immediately preceding the date of claim[; or

(*d*) personal independence payment is payable in respect of that person, or would be so payable but for regulations made under section 86(1) (hospital in-patients) of the Welfare Reform Act 2012][1].

(3) A person satisfies the requirements of this paragraph if the care component of disability living allowance—

(*a*) is payable in respect of him, or

(*b*) would be so payable but for either a suspension of benefit in accordance with regulations under section 113(2) of the Contributions and Benefits Act or an abatement as a consequence of hospitalisation,

at the highest rate prescribed under section 72(3) of that Act.

[(4) A person satisfies the requirements of this paragraph if the daily living component of personal independence payment—

(*a*) is payable in respect of that person, or

(*b*) would be so payable but for regulations made under section 86(1) (hospital inpatients) of the Welfare Reform Act 2012,

at the enhanced rate under section 78(2) of that Act.][1]

[(5) A person satisfies the requirements of this paragraph if an armed forces independence payment is payable in respect of him.][2]

Commentary—*Simon's Taxes* **E2.216.**

HMRC Manuals—Tax Credit Technical Manual TCTM2203 (reg 8(2)–(3): definitions of a disabled and severely disable young person or child).

Amendments—[1] In para (1)(*b*) words inserted, para (2)(*d*) and preceding word "or" inserted, and para (4) inserted, by the Personal Independence Payment (Supplementary Provisions and Consequential Amendments) Regulations, SI 2013/388 reg 30(1), (3) with effect from 8 April 2013.

[2] Words in para (1)(*b*), and whole of para (5), inserted, by the Armed Forces and Reserve Forces Compensation Scheme (Consequential Provisions: Subordinate Legislation) Order, SI 2013/591 art 7, Schedule para 26(1), (3) with effect from 8 April 2013.

[3] Para (2)(*b*) substituted, and in para (2)(*c*) words revoked and words inserted, by the Child Benefit (General) and Tax Credits (Miscellaneous Amendments) Regulations, SI 2014/2924 reg 3(1), (3) with effect from 28 November 2014.

[Individual element: exceptions to the restriction on numbers

9 Exceptions for the purposes of regulation 7(2A)(*b*)

(1) For the purposes of regulation 7(2A)(*b*), an exception applies in relation to A if—

(*a*) A is (in accordance with paragraphs (5) and (6)) the third or subsequent child or qualifying young person for whom the claimant, or either or both of the joint claimants, is or are responsible and any of regulations 10 to 14 applies in relation to A; or

(*b*) A is (in accordance with paragraphs (5) and (6)) the first or second child or qualifying young person for whom the claimant, or either or both of the joint claimants, is or are responsible and the condition in paragraph (2) is met.

(2) The condition in this paragraph is met—

(*a*) where A is the second child or qualifying young person, if—

(i) there is another child or qualifying young person for whom the claimant, or either or both of the joint claimants, is or are responsible;

(ii) that other child or qualifying young person was born before 6th April 2017;

(iii) the claimant, or either or both of the joint claimants, was or were already responsible for A before the date on which the claimant, or either or both of the joint claimants, became responsible for that other child or qualifying young person; and

(iv) regulation 11 or 12 would have applied in relation to that other child or qualifying young person if references in those regulations to A were references to that other child or qualifying young person;

(*b*) where A is the first child or qualifying young person, if there is more than one child or qualifying young person who fulfils the description set out in paragraphs (i) to (iv) of sub-paragraph (*a*).

(3) Where an exception applies in relation to A by virtue of paragraph (1), an exception applies also in relation to any other child or qualifying young person who was born on or after 6th April 2017 and for whom the claimant, or either or both of the joint claimants, is or are responsible, if—

(*a*) regulation 7(2A) would (apart from this paragraph) prevent the inclusion of an individual element of child tax credit in respect of that other child or qualifying young person, but would not do so if A were disregarded; and

(*b*) the claimant, or either or both of the joint claimants, was or were already responsible for that other child or qualifying young person before the date on which the claimant, or either or both of the joint claimants, became responsible for A.

(4) Where any of regulations 10 to 14 applies in relation to more than one child or qualifying young person, or different ones apply in relation to different children or qualifying young persons—

(*a*) the reference to A in paragraph (3)(*a*) is a reference to all the children or qualifying young persons in respect of whom at least one of those regulations applies; and

(*b*) the date referred to in paragraph (3)(*b*) is the date on which the claimant, or either or both of the joint claimants, became responsible for the first such child or qualifying young person for whom the claimant, or either or both of the joint claimants, became responsible.

Tax Credits

(5) For the purposes of paragraphs (1) and (2), whether A is the first, second, third or subsequent child or qualifying young person is determined by treating children and qualifying persons as forming a single class and, subject to paragraph (6), the order of the members within that class is determined by the following date in relation to each member, taking the earliest date first:—

(*a*) where the claimant, or at least one of the joint claimants, is the member's parent or step-parent (in either case, other than by adoption), the member's date of birth; or

(*b*) in any other case, the date on which the claimant, or either or both of the joint claimants, became responsible for the member.

(6) In a case where—

(*a*) the date determined under paragraph (5) is the same in respect of two or more members, or

(*b*) the claimant, or either of the joint claimants, gave birth to a member less than 10 months after becoming responsible for a member in relation to whom regulation 12 applies,

their order (as between themselves only) is to be such as the Board determines to be appropriate to ensure that the individual element of child tax credit is included in respect of the greatest number of members.

(7) Where joint claimants became responsible for a child or qualifying young person on different dates, any reference in this regulation to the date on which either or both of the joint claimants became responsible for that child or qualifying young person is a reference to the earliest of those dates.

(8) In paragraph (2)(*a*)(iv), the reference to regulation 11 includes a reference to regulation 14, but only where regulation 14 would have applied because—

(*a*) the reference to regulation 11 in regulation 14(2)(*b*) is the reason why the criterion in regulation 14(2)(*b*) or (5)(b) would have been satisfied; or

(*b*) the reference to regulation 11 in regulation 14(4)(*b*) is the reason why the criterion in that sub-paragraph would have been satisfied.][1]

Amendments—[1] Regulations 9–14 inserted by the Child Tax Credit (Amendment) Regulations, SI 2017/387 with effect from 6 April 2017.

[10 Multiple births

This regulation applies in relation to A if—

(*a*) the claimant, or at least one of the joint claimants, is a parent (other than an adoptive parent) of A;

(*b*) A was one of two or more children born as a result of the same pregnancy;

(*c*) the claimant, or either or both of the joint claimants, is or are responsible for at least two of the children or qualifying young persons born as a result of that pregnancy; and

(*d*) A is not the first in the order of those children or qualifying young persons as determined in accordance with regulation 9.][1]

Amendments—[1] Regulations 9–14 inserted by the Child Tax Credit (Amendment) Regulations, SI 2017/387 with effect from 6 April 2017.

[11 Adoption

(1) This regulation applies in relation to A if A has been—

(*a*) placed for adoption with the claimant or either or both of the joint claimants; or

(*b*) adopted by the claimant, or either or both of the joint claimants, in accordance with—

(i) the Adoption and Children Act 2002 ("the 2002 Act");

(ii) the Adoption and Children (Scotland) Act 2007 ("the 2007 Act"); or

(iii) the Adoption (Northern Ireland) Order 1987 ("the 1987 Order").

(2) But this regulation does not apply in relation to A if—

(*a*) the claimant or at least one of the joint claimants—

(i) was a step-parent of A immediately prior to the adoption; or

(ii) has been a parent of A (other than by adoption) at any time;

(*b*) the adoption order was made as a Convention adoption order within the meaning of—

(i) section 144 of the 2002 Act;

(ii) section 119(1) of the 2007 Act; or

(iii) article 2(2) of the 1987 Order; or

(*c*) prior to the adoption, A was adopted by the claimant, or either or both of the joint claimants, under the law of any country or territory outside the British Islands.][1]

Amendments—[1] Regulations 9–14 inserted by the Child Tax Credit (Amendment) Regulations, SI 2017/387 with effect from 6 April 2017.

[12 Non-parental caring arrangements

(1) This regulation applies in relation to A if the claimant or at least one of the joint claimants—

(*a*) is a friend or family carer in relation to A; or

(*b*) is responsible for a child or qualifying young person who is a parent of A.

(2) But this regulation does not apply in relation to A if the claimant, or at least one of the joint claimants, is—

(*a*) a parent of A; or

(*b*) a step-parent of A.

(3) In this regulation, "friend or family carer" means a person who is responsible for A and—

(*a*) is named, in—

(i) a child arrangements order under section 8 of the Children Act 1989, or

(ii) a residence order under article 8 of the Children (Northern Ireland) Order 1995,

as a person with whom A is to live;

(*b*) is a guardian of A appointed under—

(i) section 5 of the Children Act 1989;

(ii) section 7 of the Children (Scotland) Act 1995; or

(iii) article 159 or 160 of the Children (Northern Ireland) Order 1995;

(*c*) is a special guardian of A appointed under section 14A of the Children Act 1989;

(*d*) is entitled to a guardian's allowance under section 77 of the Contributions and Benefits Act or section 77 of the Contributions and Benefits (Northern Ireland) Act 1992 in respect of A;

(*e*) is a person in whose favour a kinship care order, as defined in section 72(1) of the Children and Young People (Scotland) Act 2014, subsists in relation to A;

(*f*) is a person in whom one or more of the parental responsibilities or parental rights described in section 1 or 2 of that Act are vested by a permanence order made in respect of A under section 80 of the Adoption and Children (Scotland) Act 2007;

(*g*) fell within any of paragraphs (*a*) to (*f*) immediately prior to A's 16th birthday and has since continued to be responsible for A; or

(*h*) has undertaken the care of A in circumstances in which it is likely that A would otherwise be looked after by a local authority.][1]

Amendments—[1] Regulations 9–14 inserted by the Child Tax Credit (Amendment) Regulations, SI 2017/387 with effect from 6 April 2017.

[13 Non-consensual conception

(1) This regulation applies in relation to A if—

(*a*) the claimant is A's parent; and

(*b*) the Board determines that—

(i) A is likely to have been conceived as a result of sexual intercourse to which the claimant did not agree by choice, or did not have the freedom and capacity to agree by choice; and

(ii) the claimant is not living at the same address as the other party to that intercourse ("B").

Control or coercion

(2) For the purposes of paragraph (1)(*b*)(i), the circumstances in which the claimant is to be treated as not having the freedom or capacity to agree by choice are to include (but are not limited to) circumstances in which, at or around the time A was conceived—

(*a*) B was—

(i) personally connected to the claimant; and

(ii) repeatedly and continuously engaging in behaviour towards the claimant that was controlling or coercive; and

(*b*) that behaviour had a serious effect on the claimant.

(3) For the purposes of paragraph (2)(*a*)(i), B is personally connected to the claimant if—

(*a*) B is in an intimate personal relationship with the claimant; or

(*b*) B and the claimant live together and—

(i) are members of the same family; or

(ii) have previously been in an intimate personal relationship with each other.

(4) For the purposes of paragraph (2)(*b*), behaviour has a serious effect on the claimant if—

(*a*) it causes the claimant to fear, on at least two occasions, that violence will be used against the claimant; or

(*b*) it causes the claimant serious alarm or distress which has a substantial adverse effect on the complainant's day-to-day activities.

(5) For the purposes of paragraph (3)(*b*)(i), B and the claimant are members of the same family if—

(*a*) they are, or have been, married to each other;

(*b*) they are, or have been, civil partners of each other;

(*c*) they are relatives (within the meaning of section 63(1) of the Family Law Act 1996);

(*d*) they have agreed to marry each other (whether or not the agreement has been terminated);

(*e*) they have entered into a civil partnership agreement (within the meaning of section 73 or 197 of the Civil Partnership Act 2004), whether or not the agreement has been terminated;

(*f*) they are both parents of the same child;

(*g*) they have, or have had, parental responsibility (within the meaning of section 3 of the Children Act 1989 or article 6 of the Children (Northern Ireland) Order 1995) for the same child; or (*h*) they have, or have had, in respect of the same child, one or more of the parental responsibilities or parental rights described in section 1 or 2 of the Children (Scotland) Act 2007.

Determinations

(6) The Board may make a determination under paragraph (1)(*b*)(i) if, and only if—

(*a*) the claimant provides evidence from an approved person which demonstrates that—

(i) the claimant has had contact with that person or another approved person; and

(ii) the claimant's circumstances are consistent with those of a person to whom paragraph (1)(*a*) and (*b*)(i) apply; or

(*b*) there has been—

(i) a conviction for—

(*aa*) an offence of rape under section 1 of the Sexual Offences Act 2003, section 1 of the Sexual Offences (Scotland) Act 2009 or article 5 of the Sexual Offences (Northern Ireland) Order 2008,

(*bb*) an offence of controlling or coercive behaviour in an intimate or family relationship under section 76 of the Serious Crime Act 2015, or

(*cc*) any offence under the law of any jurisdiction outside the United Kingdom that the Board considers to be analogous to an offence mentioned in paragraph (*aa*) or (*bb*), or

(ii) an award under the Criminal Injuries Compensation Scheme in respect of a relevant criminal injury sustained by the claimant,

and it appears to the Board to be likely (disregarding the matters mentioned in paragraph (7)) that the offence was committed, or the relevant criminal injury was caused, by B and either resulted in the conception of A or diminished the claimant's freedom or capacity to agree by choice to the sexual intercourse which resulted in that conception.

(7) In considering, for the purposes of paragraph (6)(b), the likelihood that the offence or injury resulted in the conception of A the matters to be disregarded are any possibilities that the conception of A may have resulted from another such offence or injury, regardless of whether any conviction or award has occurred in respect of that other offence or injury.

(8) In paragraph (6)(*a*), "approved person" means a person of a description specified on a list approved by the Board for the purposes of this regulation and acting in the capacity referred to in the description.

(9) In paragraph (6)(*b*)(ii), "relevant criminal injury" means—

(*a*) a sexual offence (including a pregnancy sustained as a direct result of being the victim of a sexual offence),

(*b*) physical abuse of an adult, including domestic abuse, or

(*c*) mental injury,

as described in the tariff of injuries in the Criminal Injuries Compensation Scheme.

(10) In paragraphs (6)(*b*)(ii) and (9), "Criminal Injuries Compensation Scheme" means the Criminal Injuries Compensation Scheme or the Northern Ireland Criminal Injuries Compensation Scheme as established from time to time under the Criminal Injuries Compensation Act 1995 or the Criminal Injuries Compensation (Northern Ireland) Order 2002 respectively.

(11) The Board may treat the condition in paragraph (6)(*a*) as met if the Board are satisfied that the claimant has provided the evidence to the Secretary of State for corresponding purposes in relation to universal credit, income support or old style JSA.

(12) The Board may make a determination under paragraph (1)(*b*)(ii) if the claimant confirms that the criterion in paragraph (1)(*b*)(ii) is met.

Application to single and joint claims

(13) In this regulation, "claimant", in relation to a single claim, means the person who makes the claim.

(14) In relation to a joint claim—

(*a*) paragraph (1)(*b*)(i) applies if it applies to either of the joint claimants; and

(*b*) references in the other provisions of this regulation to "the claimant" mean the joint claimant to whom paragraph (1)(*b*)(i) applies (and, in paragraphs (6) and (11) include a joint claimant who purports to meet that criterion).

(15) In paragraph (14), "joint claimant" means a member of the couple making the claim.][1]

Amendments—[1] Regulations 9–14 inserted by the Child Tax Credit (Amendment) Regulations, SI 2017/387 with effect from 6 April 2017.

[14 Continuation of certain exceptions

(1) This regulation applies in relation to A if—

(*a*) no other exception applies in relation to A under these Regulations;

(*b*) the claimant, or at least one of the joint claimants, is A's step-parent (and, in this Regulation, "C" means the claimant or a joint claimant who is A's step-parent); and

(c) paragraph (2), (4) or (5) applies.

(2) This paragraph applies if—

(a) C has previously been entitled to child tax credit jointly with a parent of A;

(b) immediately before that joint entitlement ceased, an exception applied under regulation 9(1) by virtue of regulation 10, 11 or 13 applying in relation to A;

(c) since that joint entitlement ceased, C has continuously been entitled to child tax credit (whether or not jointly with another person); and

(d) where the criterion in sub-paragraph (b) is met by virtue of its reference to regulation 10, the condition in paragraph (3) is met.

(3) The condition in this paragraph is that—

(a) the claimant, or either or both of the joint claimants, is or are responsible for one or more other children or qualifying young persons born as a result of the same pregnancy as A; and

(b) A is not the first in the order of those children as determined in accordance with regulation 9.

Where a corresponding exception previously applied for the purposes of another benefit

(4) This paragraph applies if—

(a) within the 6 months immediately preceding the day on which a relevant CTC entitlement began—

(i) C was entitled to an award of universal credit as a member of a couple jointly with a parent of A; or

(ii) C and a parent of A were a couple and either of them was entitled to an award of income support or old style JSA;

(b) immediately before the entitlement mentioned in sub-paragraph (a)(i) or (ii) ceased, the amount of that entitlement included an amount in respect of A by virtue of any exception corresponding, for the purposes of that entitlement, to an exception under regulation 9(1) by virtue of regulation 10, 11 or 13 applying in relation to A;

(c) C has continuously been entitled to child tax credit (whether or not jointly with another person) since the relevant CTC entitlement mentioned in sub-paragraph (a); and

(d) where the criterion in sub-paragraph (b) is met by virtue of its reference to regulation 10, the condition in paragraph (3) is met.

(5) This paragraph applies if—

(a) within the 6 months immediately preceding the day on which a relevant CTC entitlement began—

(i) C was entitled to an award of universal credit (whether or not as a member of a couple jointly with another person); or

(ii) C was entitled to an award of income support or old style JSA (whether or not C was in a couple with another person);

(b) immediately before the entitlement mentioned in sub-paragraph (a)(i) or (ii) ceased, the amount of that entitlement included an amount in respect of A by virtue of any exception corresponding, for the purposes of that entitlement, to the exception that, under regulation 9(1), applies where this regulation applies;

(c) C has continuously been entitled to child tax credit (whether or not jointly with another person) since the relevant CTC entitlement mentioned in sub-paragraph (a); and

(d) where the criterion in sub-paragraph (b) is met by virtue of the reference to regulation 10 in paragraph (2), the condition in paragraph (3) is met.

Interpretation

(6) In this regulation—

"couple" has the same meaning as in Part 1 of the Welfare Reform Act 2012; and

"relevant CTC entitlement" means an entitlement of C (whether or not jointly with another person) to child tax credit.

(7) For the purposes of this regulation, an entitlement of C to child tax credit is to be regarded as continuous despite any interruption of less than 6 months in such an entitlement.][1]

Amendments—[1] Regulations 9–14 inserted by the Child Tax Credit (Amendment) Regulations, SI 2017/387 with effect from 6 April 2017.

2002/2008

TAX CREDITS (INCOME THRESHOLDS AND DETERMINATION OF RATES) REGULATIONS 2002

Made by the Treasury under TCA 2002 ss 8(1)–(3), 13(2) and (3), 65(1) and (7) and 67

Made . . . . *30 July 2002*

Coming into force in accordance with . . . . *regulation 1*

Commentary—*Simon's Taxes* **E2.241–E2.244.**

HMRC Manuals—Tax Credit Technical Manual TCTM7000–7050, 7APPX3 (calculation of awards, including income thresholds).

1 Citation, commencement and effect

(1) These Regulations may be cited as the Tax Credits (Income Thresholds and Determination of Rates) Regulations 2002 and shall come into force—

(*a*) for the purpose of enabling claims to be made, on 1st August 2002;

(*b*) for the purpose of enabling decisions on claims to be made, on 1st January 2003; and

(*c*) for all other purposes, on 6th April 2003.

(2) These Regulations shall have effect for the tax year beginning with 6th April 2003 and subsequent tax years.

2 Interpretation

In these Regulations—

"the Act" means the Tax Credits Act 2002;

"the income threshold" has the meaning given by section 7(1)(*a*) of the Act;

"period of award" shall be construed in accordance with section 5 of the Act;

"the relevant income" has the meaning given by section 7(3) of the Act;

"tax year" means a period beginning with 6th April in one year and ending with 5th April in the next.

Modifications—Universal Credit (Transitional Provisions) Regulations, SI 2013/386 reg 17(1), (2), Schedule paras 29, 30 (modification of this regulation in respect of awards of universal credit and terminations of awards of tax credit in the same year).

Universal Credit (Transitional Provisions) Regulations, SI 2014/1626 reg 4 (modification of this regulation in respect of awards of universal credit and terminations of awards of tax credit in the same year).

3 Manner in which amounts to be determined for the purposes of section 7(1)(a) of the Act

(1) This regulation prescribes the manner in which amounts are to be determined for the purposes of section 7(1)(*a*) of the Act.

(2) In the case of a person or persons entitled to working tax credit, the amount in relation to that tax credit is [£6,420][1].

(3) In the case of a person or persons entitled to child tax credit, the amount in relation to that tax credit is [£16,105][2].

Note—Note that the proposed reductions to the income thresholds in paras (2) and (3), announced by the Chancellor in the 8 July 2015 Budget and set out in the Draft Tax Credits (Income Thresholds and Determination of Rates) (Amendment) Regulations 2015, were subsequently abandoned.

Amendments—[1] Figure in para (2) substituted by the Tax Credits Up-rating Regulations, SI 2008/796 reg 4(1)–(3) with effect from 6 April 2008. These Regulations have effect in relation to awards of tax credits for the tax year beginning on 6 April 2008 and subsequent tax years.

[2] Figure in para (3) substituted by the Tax Credits Up-rating Regulations, SI 2015/541 reg 4(1), (2) with effect in relation to awards of tax credits for the tax year beginning on 6 April 2015 and subsequent tax years. Previous figure was £16,010.

4 Social security benefits prescribed for the purposes of section 7(2) of the Act

[(1)] [3] [Subject to paragraph (2),][3] the following are social security benefits prescribed for the purposes of section 7(2) of the Act in relation to child tax credit and working tax credit—

(*a*) income support under Part 7 of the Social Security Contributions and Benefit Act 1992 other than income support to which a person is entitled only by virtue of regulation 6(2) and (3) of the Income Support (General) Regulations 1987;

(*b*) income support under Part 7 of the Social Security Contributions and Benefit (Northern Ireland) Act 1992 other than income support to which a person is entitled only by virtue of regulation 6(2) and (3) of the Income Support (General) Regulations (Northern Ireland) 1987;

(*c*) an income-based jobseeker's allowance within the meaning of the Jobseekers Act 1995 or the Jobseekers (Northern Ireland) Order 1995.

[(*d*) state pension credit within the meaning of the State Pension Credit Act 2002 or the State Pension Credit Act (Northern Ireland) 2002.][1]

[(*e*) an income-related employment and support allowance payable under Part 1 of the Welfare Reform Act 2007.][2]

[(2) Paragraph (1) shall not apply in relation to working tax credit during the four-week period described in regulation 7D of the Working Tax Credit (Entitlement and Maximum Rate) Regulations 2002 (ceasing to undertake work or working for less than 16 or 30 hours per week).][3]

Amendments—[1] Sub-para (*d*) inserted by the Tax Credits (Miscellaneous Amendments No 2) Regulations, SI 2003/2815 reg 18 with effect from 26 November 2003.

[2] Para (*e*) inserted by the Employment and Support Allowance (Consequential Provisions) (No 3) Regulations, SI 2008/1879 reg 23 with effect from 27 October 2008.

[3] Para (1) designated as such, and in para (1) words inserted at beginning, and para (2) inserted, by the Tax Credits (Miscellaneous Amendments) Regulations, SI 2010/751, regs 16, 17(1), (2) with effect from 6 April 2010.

[5 [Amounts prescribed for the purposes of section 7(3) of the Act]

The amount prescribed—

(*a*) for the purposes of section 7(3)(*a*) and (*b*) of the Act is [£2,500][2]; and

(*b*) for the purposes of section 7(3)(*c*) and (*d*) of the Act is £2,500.][1]

Amendments—[1] Reg 5 and preceding heading substituted by the Tax Credits Up-rating Regulations, SI 2012/849 reg 4(1)–(3) with effect in relation to awards of tax credits for the tax year beginning on 6 April 2012 and subsequent tax years.
[2] Figure in para (*a*) substituted by the Tax Credits (Income Thresholds and Determination of Rates) (Amendment) Regulations, SI 2016/393 reg 2 with effect in relation to awards of tax credits for the tax year beginning on 6 April 2016 and subsequent tax years. Figure was previously "£5,000".

6 Manner of determining the rate at which a person is, or persons are, entitled to a tax credit

Regulations 7, 8 and 9 make provision as to the manner of determining the rate (if any) at which a person is, or persons are, entitled to a tax credit in any case where—

(*a*) the relevant income exceeds the income threshold; and
(*b*) his or their entitlement does not arise by virtue of section 7(2) of the Act.

7 Determination of rate of working tax credit

(1) In relation to a person or persons entitled to working tax credit, the rate shall be determined by finding the rate for each relevant period and, where necessary, adding together those rates.

(2) "Relevant period" means any part of the period of award throughout which—

(*a*) the elements of working tax credit (other than the child care element) to which the person or persons may be entitled, remain the same; and
(*b*) there is no relevant change of circumstances for the purposes of the child care element of working tax credit, within the meaning of regulation 16(1) of the Working Tax Credit (Entitlement and Maximum Rate) Regulations 2002 (change of circumstances for the purposes of child care element).

(3) The rate for each relevant period shall be found in accordance with the following steps—

Step 1—finding the daily maximum rate for each element other than the child care element

For each element of the tax credit (other than the child care element) to be included in the case of the person or persons entitled to the tax credit, find the daily maximum rate using the following formula—

$$\frac{MR}{N1}$$

where—

"MR" is the maximum rate in relation to that element for the tax year to which the claim for the tax credit relates;
"N1" is the number of days in that tax year.

Step 2—finding the maximum rate for the relevant period for each element other than the child care element

For each element of the tax credit to be so included, find the amount produced by multiplying the daily maximum rate (found under Step 1 and rounded up to the nearest penny) by the number of days in the relevant period.

Step 3—finding the income for the relevant period

Find the income for the relevant period by using the following formula—

$$\frac{I}{N1} \times N2$$

where—

"I" is the relevant income for the tax year to which the claim for the tax credit relates;
"N1" is the number of days in that tax year;
"N2" is the number of days in the relevant period.

Step 4—finding the threshold for the relevant period

Find the threshold for the relevant period using the following formula—

$$\frac{[£6,420]^1}{N1} \times N2$$

where—

"N1" is the number of days in that tax year;
"N2" is the number of days in the relevant period.

Step 5—finding the amount of the reduction

Find the amount which is [41%][2] of the amount by which the income for the relevant period (found under Step 3 and rounded down to the nearest penny) exceeds the threshold for the relevant period (found under Step 4 and rounded up to the nearest penny).

Step 6—reducing the elements of the tax credit (other than any child care element)

Tax Credits

If the amount found under Step 5 (rounded down to the nearest penny) is less than or equal to the total of the amounts found under Step 2 for the elements of the tax credit, deduct the amount found under Step 5 (rounded down to the nearest penny) from the total of those amounts found under Step 2.

Step 7—finding the actual weekly child care costs for the relevant period

Find the relevant child care charges for the relevant period in accordance with regulation 15 of the Working Tax Credit (Entitlement and Maximum Rate) Regulations 2002.

Step 8—finding the actual child care costs for the relevant period

Multiply the result of Step 7 by 52/N1 × N2.

Here N1 and N2 have the same meanings as in Step 3.

The result of this step is the amount of actual child care costs for the relevant period.

Step 9—finding the prescribed maximum child care costs for the relevant period

Divide whichever of the maxima in regulation 20(3) of the Working Tax Credit (Entitlement and Maximum Rate) Regulations 2002 is applicable by 7, round the result up to the nearest penny and multiply the resulting figure by the number of days in the relevant period.

The result of this is the prescribed maximum child care costs for the relevant period.

Step 10—finding the child care element for the period

Take the lesser of the results of Steps 8 and 9.

Multiply that figure by [70%][1] and round the result up to the nearest penny.

The result of this step is the maximum rate of the child care element for the relevant period.

Step 11—reducing the elements of the tax credit (including any child care element)

If the amount found under Step 5 (rounded down to the nearest penny) exceeds the total of the amounts found under Step 2 for the elements of the tax credit—

(*a*) deduct the excess from the amount found under Step 10 for any child care element; and

(*b*) reduce the total of the amounts found under Step 2 for the other elements of the tax credit to nil.

Step 12—finding the rate for the relevant period

Add together—

(*a*) the total of the amounts found under Step 2 for the elements of the tax credit (other than any child care element) after reduction in accordance with Step 6 or Step 11; and

(*b*) the amount found under Step 10 for any child care element after any reduction in accordance with Step 11.

This is the rate for the relevant period.

(4) "Child care element" has the meaning given by section 12(2) of the Act.

Commentary—*Simon's Taxes* **E2.242.**

Note—In para (3), note that the proposed reduction to the income threshold in Step 4 and the proposed increase in the withdrawal rate in Step 5, announced by the Chancellor in the 8 July 2015 Budget and set out in the Draft Tax Credits (Income Thresholds and Determination of Rates) (Amendment) Regulations 2015, were subsequently abandoned.

HMRC Manuals—Tax Credit Technical Manual TCTM7010–7050, 7APPX4 (steps in calculation of award, with worked example).

Modifications—Universal Credit (Transitional Provisions) Regulations, SI 2013/386 reg 17(1), (2), Schedule paras 29, 31 (modification of this regulation in respect of awards of universal credit and terminations of awards of tax credit in the same year).

Universal Credit (Transitional Provisions) Regulations, SI 2014/1626 reg 4 (modification of this regulation in respect of awards of universal credit and terminations of awards of tax credit in the same year).

Amendments—[1] Figure in Step 10 substituted by the Tax Credits Up-rating Regulations, SI 2011/1035 reg 4(1), (4) with effect in relation to awards of tax credits for the year beginning on 6 April 2011. This amendment continues to have effect in relation to awards of tax credits for the tax year beginning on 6 April 2012 and subsequent tax years (SI 2012/849 reg 5(*c*)).

[2] In para (3), figure in Step 5 substituted by the Tax Credits Up-rating Regulations, SI 2012/849 reg 4(1), (4) with effect in relation to awards of tax credits for the tax year beginning on 6 April 2012 and subsequent tax years.

8 Determination of rate of child tax credit

(1) In relation to a person or persons entitled to child tax credit, the rate shall be determined by finding the rate for each relevant period and, where necessary, adding together those rates.

(2) "Relevant period" means—

(*a*) in the case of a person or persons entitled to child tax credit only, any part of the period of award throughout which the maximum rate at which he or they may be entitled to the tax credit remains the same;

(*b*) in the case of a person or persons entitled to both child tax credit and working tax credit, any part of the period of award throughout which the maximum rate of child tax credit to which he or they may be entitled remains the same and both sub-paragraphs (*a*) and (*b*) of regulation 7(2) are met.

(3) The rate for each relevant period shall be found in accordance with the following steps—

Step 1—finding the daily maximum rate for each element

For each element of the tax credit to be included in the case of the person or persons entitled to the tax credit, find the daily maximum rate using the following formula—

$$\frac{MR}{N1}$$

where—

"MR" is the maximum rate in relation to that element for the tax year to which the claim for the tax credit relates;

"N1" is the number of days in that tax year.

Step 2—finding the maximum rate for the relevant period for each element

For each element of the tax credit to be so included, find the amount produced by multiplying the maximum rate (found under Step 1 and rounded up to the nearest penny) by the number of days in the relevant period.

Step 3—finding income for the relevant period

Find the income for the relevant period by using the following formula—

$$\frac{I}{N1} \times N2$$

where—

"I" is the relevant income for the tax year to which the claim for the tax credit relates;

"N1" is the number of days in that tax year;

"N2" is the number of days in the relevant period.

Step 4—finding the threshold for the relevant period

Find the amount produced by the following formula—[3]

$$\frac{[£16,105]}{N1} \times N2$$

where—

"N1" is the number of days in that tax year;

"N2" is the number of days in the relevant period.

The threshold for the relevant period is—

(*a*) in the case of a person or persons entitled to child tax credit only, that amount;

(*b*) in the case of a person or persons entitled to both child tax credit and working tax credit—

(i) that amount; or

(ii) if greater, the lowest amount of income for the relevant period (found under Step 3) which, disregarding regulation 9, would result in a determination in accordance with regulation 7 providing for no rate of working tax credit in his or their case for that period.

Step 5—finding the amount of the reduction of the elements of the tax credit . . .[2]

Find the amount (if any) which is [41%][1] of the amount by which the income for the relevant period (found under Step 3 and rounded down to the nearest penny) exceeds the threshold for the relevant period (found under Step 4 and rounded up to the nearest penny).

Step 6—reducing the elements of the tax credit . . .[2]

If the amount found under Step 5 (rounded down to the nearest penny) is less than the total of the amounts found under Step 2 for the elements of the tax credit . . .[2], deduct the amount found under Step 5 (rounded down to the nearest penny) from the total of those amounts.

Step 7—reducing the elements of the tax credit . . .[2] *to nil*

If the amount found under Step 5 (rounded down to the nearest penny) is equal to or exceeds the total of the amounts found under Step 2 for the elements of the tax credit . . .[2], reduce the total of those amounts to nil.

...[2]

[Step 8]—[2]finding the rate for the relevant period

[The rate for the relevant period is the total of the amounts found under Step 2 for the elements of the tax credit after any reduction in accordance with Step 6 or Step 7.][2]

(4) "The family element" means the family element of child tax credit within the meaning given by section 9(3) of the Act.

Commentary—*Simon's Taxes* **E2.243.**

Note—In para (3), note that the proposed reduction to the income threshold in Step 4 and the proposed increase in the withdrawal rate in Step 5, announced by the Chancellor in the 8 July 2015 Budget and set out in the Draft Tax Credits (Income Thresholds and Determination of Rates) (Amendment) Regulations 2015, were subsequently abandoned.

Tax Credits

HMRC Manuals—Tax Credit Technical Manual TCTM7010–7050, 7APPX4 (steps in calculation of award, with worked example).

Modifications—Universal Credit (Transitional Provisions) Regulations, SI 2013/386 reg 17(1), (2), Schedule paras 29, 32 (modification of this regulation in respect of awards of universal credit and terminations of awards of tax credit in the same year).

Universal Credit (Transitional Provisions) Regulations, SI 2014/1626 reg 4 (modification of this regulation in respect of awards of universal credit and terminations of awards of tax credit in the same year).

Amendments—[1] In para (3), in Step 5, figure substituted by the Tax Credits Up-rating Regulations, SI 2011/1035 reg 4(1), (5) with effect in relation to awards of tax credits for the year beginning on 6 April 2011. This amendment continues to have effect in relation to awards of tax credits for the tax year beginning on 6 April 2012 and subsequent tax years (SI 2012/849 reg 5(*c*)).

[2] In para (3), in the headings before Steps 5, 6, 7, and in Steps 6, 7, words revoked, Steps 8, 9, 10 revoked, Step 8 (previously Step 11) renumbered as such, and in renumbered Step 8 words substituted, by the Tax Credits Up-rating Regulations, SI 2012/849 reg 4(1), (5) with effect in relation to awards of tax credits for the tax year beginning on 6 April 2012 and subsequent tax years.

[3] In para (3), figure in Step 4 substituted by the Tax Credits Up-rating Regulations, SI 2015/541 reg 4(1), (3) with effect in relation to awards of tax credits for the tax year beginning on 6 April 2015 and subsequent tax years. Previous figure was £16,010.

9 Cases in which there is no rate of tax credit

(1) In the case of a person or persons entitled to working tax credit only or child tax credit only, where the rate at which the person or persons would be entitled to the tax credit (as determined in accordance with regulation 7 or 8) would be less than £26.00, there is no rate in his or their case.

(2) In the case of a person or persons entitled to both working tax credit and child tax credit, where the total of the rates at which the person or persons would be entitled to the tax credits (as determined in accordance with regulations 7 and 8) would be less than £26.00, there are no rates in his or their case.

Commentary—*Simon's Taxes* **E2.244.**

2002/2014

TAX CREDITS (CLAIMS AND NOTIFICATIONS) REGULATIONS 2002

Made by the Commissioners of Inland Revenue under TCA 2002 ss 4(1), 6, 14(2), 15(2), 16(3), 17(10), 19(2), 22(1)(*b*) and (2), 65(1), (2) and (7) and 67

Made .... *31 July 2002*
Laid before Parliament .... *31 July 2002*
Coming into force .... *12 August 2002*

Commentary—*Simon's Taxes* **E2.251, E2.253.**

HMRC Manuals—Tax Credit Technical Manual TCTM5000–5500 (changes of circumstances).
TCTM6000–6110 (claims and notifications).

PART 1
GENERAL

1 Citation, commencement and effect

(1) These Regulations may be cited as the Tax Credits (Claims and Notifications) Regulations 2002 and shall come into force on 12th August 2002.

(2) These Regulations have effect in relation to claims for a tax credit for periods of award beginning on or after 6th April 2003.

2 Interpretation

In these Regulations—

"the Act" means the Tax Credits Act 2002;

["appropriate office" means Comben House, Farriers Way, Netherton, Merseyside or any other office specified in writing by the Board.][3]

["armed forces independence payment" means armed forces independence payment under the Armed Forces and Reserve Forces (Compensation Scheme) Order 2011;][5]

"the Board" means the Commissioners of Inland Revenue;

["couple" has the meaning given by section 3(5A) of the Act;][2]

"disability element" shall be construed in accordance with section 11(4) of the Act;

"joint claim" has the meaning given by section 3(8) of the Act;

. . . [2]

["personal independence payment" means personal independence payment under Part 4 of the Welfare Reform Act 2012;][4]

["relevant authority" means—

(*a*) the Board;

(*b*) the Secretary of State or the Department for Social Development in Northern Ireland; or

(*c*) a person providing services to the Board, the Secretary of State or that Department in connection with tax credits;][1]

"severe disability element" has the meaning in regulation 17 of the Working Tax Credit Regulations;

"single claim" has the meaning given by section 3(8) of the Act;

"tax year" means a period beginning on 6th April in one year and ending with 5th April in the next;

. . . [2]

"the Working Tax Credit Regulations" means the Working Tax Credit (Entitlement and Maximum Rate) Regulations 2002.

Modifications—Tax Credits (Polygamous Marriages) Regulations, SI 2003/742 regs 39, 40 (definition of "joint claim" substituted, and definition of "polygamous unit" inserted, for the purposes of polygamous marriages).

Amendments—[1] Definition of "relevant authority" inserted by the Tax Credits (Claims and Notifications and Payments by the Board) (Amendment) Regulations, SI 2003/723 regs 2, 3(1) with effect from 6 April 2003.

[2] Definition of "couple" inserted, and definitions of "married couple" and "unmarried couple" revoked, by the Civil Partnership Act 2004 (Tax Credits, etc) (Consequential Amendments) Order, SI 2005/2919 art 5(1), (2) with effect from 5 December 2005.

[3] Definition of "appropriate office" substituted by the Tax Credits (Miscellaneous Amendments) Regulations, SI 2009/697 regs 11, 12 with effect from 6 April 2009.

[4] Definition of "personal independence payment" inserted by the Personal Independence Payment (Supplementary Provisions and Consequential Amendments) Regulations, SI 2013/388 reg 31(1), (2) with effect from 8 April 2013.

[5] Definition of "armed forces independence payment" inserted by the Armed Forces and Reserve Forces Compensation Scheme (Consequential Provisions: Subordinate Legislation) Order, SI 2013/591 art 7, Schedule para 27(1), (2) with effect from 8 April 2013.

3 Use of electronic communications to make claims or to give notices or notifications

(1) In these Regulations "writing" includes writing produced by electronic communications that are approved by directions issued by or on behalf of the Board.

(2) If a claim which is required by these Regulations to be made to [a relevant authority at an appropriate office][1] is made in writing produced by electronic communications, it shall be treated for the purposes of these Regulations as having been made to, and received by, [a relevant authority at an appropriate office][1] on the date on which it is recorded on an official computer system.

(3) If a notice or notification which is required by these Regulations to be given to [a relevant authority at an appropriate office][1] is given in writing produced by electronic communications, it shall be treated for the purposes of these Regulations as having been given to, and received by, [a relevant authority at an appropriate office][1] on the date on which it is recorded on an official computer system.

(4) In this regulation—

(*a*) "electronic communications" has the meaning given by section 132(10) of the Finance Act 1999;

(*b*) "official computer system" means a computer system maintained by or on behalf of the Board to—

(i) send or receive information, or

(ii) process or store information.

Amendments—[1] Words substituted by the Tax Credits (Claims and Notifications and Payments by the Board) (Amendment) Regulations, SI 2003/723 regs 2, 3(2)(*a*) with effect from 6 April 2003.

PART 2

CLAIMS

4 Interpretation of this Part

In this Part (and Part 3) "the relevant date", in relation to a claim for a tax credit, means—

(*a*) in cases where regulation 6 applies, the date on which the claim would be treated as being made by that regulation disregarding [regulations 7, 7A and 8][3];

(*b*) in cases where sub-paragraph [(*d*)][2] of regulation 11(3) applies, the date on which the claim would be treated as being made by that sub-paragraph disregarding [regulations 7, 7A and 8][3];

(*c*) in any other case, the date on which the claim is received by [a relevant authority at an appropriate office[1]].

Modifications—Universal Credit (Transitional Provisions) Regulations, SI 2013/386 reg 17(1), (2), Schedule paras 33, 34 (modification of this regulation in respect of awards of universal credit and terminations of awards of tax credit in the same year).

Universal Credit (Transitional Provisions) Regulations, SI 2014/1626 reg 4 (modification of this regulation in respect of awards of universal credit and terminations of awards of tax credit in the same year).

Amendments—[1] Words substituted by the Tax Credits (Claims and Notifications and Payments by the Board) (Amendment) Regulations, SI 2003/723 regs 2, 3(2)(*b*) with effect from 6 April 2003.

[2] In para (*b*), reference substituted by the Tax Credits (Miscellaneous Amendments) Regulations, SI 2009/697 regs 11, 13 with effect from 6 April 2009.

[3] In paras (*a*), (*b*), words substituted by the Tax Credits (Claims and Notifications) (Amendment) Regulations, SI 2015/669 reg 3 with effect from 6 April 2015.

5 Manner in which claims to be made

(1) This regulation prescribes the manner in which a claim for a tax credit is to be made.

(2) A claim must be made to [a relevant authority at an appropriate office[1]]—

(*a*) in writing on a form approved or authorised by the Board for the purpose of the claim, or

[(*b*) in such other manner as the Board may decide having regard to all the circumstances.][2]

(3) A claim must contain the information requested on the form (or such of that information as the Board may accept as sufficient in the circumstances of the particular case).

(4) In particular, a claim must include in respect of every person by whom the claim is made—

(*a*) a statement of the person's national insurance number and information or evidence establishing that that number has been allocated to the person; or

(*b*) information or evidence enabling the national insurance number that has been allocated to the person to be ascertained; or

(*c*) an application for a national insurance number to be allocated to the person which is accompanied by information or evidence enabling such a number to be so allocated.

This paragraph is subject to [paragraphs (6) and (8)][3].

(5) "National insurance number" means the national insurance number allocated within the meaning of regulation 9 of the Social Security (Crediting and Treatment of Contributions, and National Insurance Numbers) Regulations 2001.

(6) Paragraph (4) does not apply if the Board are satisfied that the person or persons by whom the claim was made had a reasonable excuse for making a claim which did not comply with the requirements of that paragraph.

(7) At any time after a claim has been made but before the Board have given notice of their decision under section 14(1) of the Act in relation to the claim, the person or persons by whom the claim was made may amend the claim by giving notice orally or in writing to [a relevant authority at an appropriate office][1].

[(8) Paragraph (4) does not apply to any person who is subject to immigration control within the meaning set out in section 115(9)(*a*) of the Immigration and Asylum Act 1999 and to whom a national insurance number has not been allocated.][3]

HMRC Manuals—Tax Credit Technical Manual TCTM6100 (summary of making a claim).

TCTM6102 (if a claim contains insufficient information, it is rejected and a new claim must be made, but there is discretion to accept a claim that contains sufficient information to proceed. If a claim is accepted, and further information is sought in order to reach an initial decision, the original claim is a valid claim.)

TCTM6107 (amendments to claims permitted under reg 5(7) above are unlikely to be very common in view of the short time between receiving a claim and the initial award notice being sent out; they may mostly occur where a claim has been delayed due to pre-payment checking).

TCTM6110 (provision and verification of national insurance number which is required when making a claim).

Amendments—[1] Words substituted by the Tax Credits (Claims and Notifications and Payments by the Board) (Amendment) Regulations, SI 2003/723 regs 2, 3(2)(*c*) with effect from 6 April 2003.

[2] Para (2)(*b*) substituted by the Tax Credits (Miscellaneous Amendments) (No 2) Regulations, SI 2008/2169 regs 11, 12 with effect from 1 September 2008.

[3] In para (4), words substituted, and para (8) inserted, by the Tax Credits (Miscellaneous Amendments) Regulations, SI 2009/697 regs 11, 14 with effect from 6 April 2009.

6 Amended claims

(1) In the circumstances prescribed by paragraph (2) a claim for a tax credit which has been amended shall be treated as having been made as amended and, subject to [regulations 7, 7A and 8][2], as having been made on the date prescribed by paragraph (3).

(2) The circumstances prescribed by this paragraph are where a person has amended or persons have amended the claim in accordance with regulation 5(7).

(3) The date prescribed by this paragraph is the date on which the claim being amended was received by [a relevant authority at an appropriate office][1].

Amendments—[1] Words substituted by the Tax Credits (Claims and Notifications and Payments by the Board) (Amendment) Regulations, SI 2003/723 regs 2, 3(2)(*d*) with effect from 6 April 2003.

[2] In para (1), words substituted by the Tax Credits (Claims and Notifications) (Amendment) Regulations, SI 2015/669 reg 3 with effect from 6 April 2015.

7 Time limit for claims (if otherwise entitled to tax credit up to [[31] days] earlier)

(1) In the circumstances prescribed by paragraph (2) a claim for a tax credit received by [a relevant authority at an appropriate office][1] shall be treated as having been made on the date prescribed by paragraph (3).

(2) The circumstances prescribed by this paragraph are those where the person or persons by whom the claim is made would (if a claim had been made) have been entitled to the tax credit either—

(*a*) on the date falling [[31][3] days][2] before the relevant date (or on 6 April 2003, if later); or

(*b*) at any later time in the period beginning on the date in sub-paragraph (a) and ending on the relevant date.

(3) The date prescribed by this paragraph is the earliest date falling within the terms of paragraph (2)(*a*) or (*b*) when the person or the persons by whom the claim is made would (if a claim had been made) have become entitled to the tax credit.

HMRC Manuals—Tax Credit Technical Manual TCTM6103, 6104 (circumstances when claim is backdated).

Cross references—Tax Credits Act 2002 (Transitional Provisions) Order, SI 2005/773 (transitional provisions in connection with the commencement of the abolition of the child premia in respect of income support and Jobseekers Allowance).

Tax Credits Act 2002 (Transitional Provisions) (No.2) Order, SI 2005/776 (transitional provisions in connection with the commencement of the abolition of the child premia in respect of income support and Jobseekers Allowance).

Tax Credits Act 2002 (Transitional Provisions) Order, SI 2008/3151 (transitional provisions in respect of eligibility for tax credits).

Amendments—[1] Words substituted by the Tax Credits (Claims and Notifications and Payments by the Board) (Amendment) Regulations, SI 2003/723 regs 2, 3(2)(*e*) with effect from 6 April 2003.

[2] In heading and para (2)(*a*), words substituted by the Tax Credits (Miscellaneous Amendments) (No 2) Regulations, SI 2009/2887 reg 8(1), (2)(*a*), (*b*) with effect from 21 November 2009.

[3] In heading, and in para (2)(*a*), number substituted by the Tax Credits (Miscellaneous Amendments) Regulations, SI 2012/848 regs 1(3), 5(1), (2)(*a*), (*b*) with effect from 6 April 2012.

[7A Time limit for claims – the Childcare Payments Act 2014

(1) Subject to [paragraphs (2A) to (4)][2], regulation 7 does not apply where the claim for a tax credit made by a person or persons is received by a relevant authority at an appropriate office during an entitlement period where the person making the claim, or in the case of joint claimants either person, has for that entitlement period made a valid declaration of eligibility under section 4(2) of the Childcare Payments Act 2014 (declarations of eligibility).

(2) Subject to [paragraphs (2A) to (4)][2], where a claim for tax credits is received by a relevant authority at an appropriate office during the period of 31 days beginning with the last day of the entitlement period for which the person making the claim or, in the case of joint claimants either person, has made a valid declaration of eligibility under section 4(2) of the Childcare Payments Act 2014, regulation 7 shall apply but the date prescribed by paragraph (3) of regulation 7 may be no earlier than the day following the last day of that entitlement period

[(2A) Where–

(*a*) a claim for a tax credit is received by a relevant authority at an appropriate office and the person making the claim, or in the case of joint claimants either person, has made a valid declaration of eligibility under section 4(2) of the Childcare Payments Act 2014,

(*b*) no payments under section 20(1)(*a*) of the Childcare Payments Act 2014 have been made out of any childcare account held by the person making the claim, or in the case of joint claimants either person, and

(*c*) all the childcare accounts held by the person making the claim for tax credits, or in the case of joint claimants both persons, have been closed,

regulation 7 shall apply .][2]

(3) For the purposes of this regulation, the "appropriate date" is the date on which—

(*a*) Her Majesty's Revenue and Customs makes an account restriction order in accordance with section 24 of the Childcare Payments Act 2014 (imposing restrictions on childcare accounts) for the purposes of giving effect to a determination made under section 18(2) of that Act (cases where there is more than one eligible person) and regulations made thereunder,

(*b*) a childcare account is closed in accordance with regulations made under section 25 of the Childcare Payments Act 2014 (closure of childcare accounts), or

(*c*) a child ceases to be a "qualifying child" for the purposes of the Childcare Payments Act 2014 as defined in regulation 5 of the Childcare Payments (Eligibility) Regulations 2015 except in the case where they cease to be a "disabled child" as defined in regulation 5(5) of those Regulations.

(4) Where a claim for tax credits is received by a relevant authority at an appropriate office—

(*a*) during an entitlement period relating to a childcare account where the person making the claim, or in the case of joint claimants either person, has for that entitlement period made a valid declaration of eligibility under section 4(2) of the Childcare Payments Act 2014, or

(*b*) during the period of 31 days beginning with the day following the last day of that entitlement period,

regulation 7 shall apply but the date prescribed in paragraph (3) of regulation 7 may be no earlier than the appropriate date.

(5) For the purposes of this regulation, the terms "childcare account" and "entitlement period" have the same meanings as they have for the purposes of the Childcare Payments Act 2014 and regulations made thereunder.][1]

Amendments—[1] Regulation 7A inserted by the Tax Credits (Claims and Notifications) (Amendment) Regulations, SI 2015/669 reg 2 with effect from 6 April 2015.

[2] In paras (1), (2), words substituted for words "paragraphs (3) and (4)", and para (2A) inserted, by the Tax Credits (Claims and Notifications) (Amendment) Regulations, SI 2017/597 reg 2 with effect from 17 May 2017.

8 [Date of claims—disability element of working tax credit

(1) In the circumstances prescribed by paragraph (2), the claim referred to in paragraph (2)(*a*) shall be treated as having been made on the date prescribed by paragraph (3).

(2) The circumstances prescribed by this paragraph are where—

(*a*) a claim for working tax credit including the disability element ("the tax credits claim") is made by a person or persons ("the claimants") which results in the Board making an award of working tax credit including the disability element;

(*b*) the claim is made within [[31][3] days][2] of the date that a claim for any of the benefits referred to in regulation 9(2) to (8) of the Working Tax Credit Regulations ("the benefits claim") is determined in favour of the claimants (or one of them); and

(*c*) the claimants would (subject to making a claim) have been entitled to working tax credit if (and only if) they had satisfied the requirements of regulation 9(1)(*c*) of the Working Tax Credit Regulations, on any day in the period—

(i) beginning on the date of the benefits claim, and

(ii) ending on the date of the tax credits claim.

(3) The date prescribed by this paragraph is—

(*a*) the first date in respect of which the benefit claimed is payable; or

(*b*) if later, the date falling [[31][3] days][2] before the claim for the benefit is made; or

(*c*) if later, the first day identified under paragraph (2)(*c*).][1]

Amendments—[1] Reg 8 substituted by the Tax Credits (Miscellaneous Amendments) Regulations, SI 2009/697 regs 11, 15 with effect from 6 April 2009.

[2] In paras (2)(*b*), (3)(*b*), words substituted by the Tax Credits (Miscellaneous Amendments) (No 2) Regulations, SI 2009/2887 reg 8(1), (2)(*c*) with effect from 21 November 2009.

[3] In paras (2)(*b*), (3)(*b*), number substituted by the Tax Credits (Miscellaneous Amendments) Regulations, SI 2012/848 regs 1(3), 5(1), (2)(*c*), (*d*) with effect from 6 April 2012.

9 Advance claims before the year begins

(1) In the circumstances prescribed by paragraph (2) a claim for a tax credit may be made for a period after the relevant date.

(2) The circumstances prescribed by this paragraph are where a tax credit is claimed for a tax year by making a claim before the tax year begins.

(3) This regulation shall cease to have effect in relation to the tax year beginning on 6 April 2004 and subsequent tax years

10 Advance claims—working tax credit

(1) In the circumstances prescribed by paragraph (2) a claim for a tax credit may be made for a period after the relevant date.

(2) The circumstances prescribed by this paragraph are where—

(*a*) the tax credit in question is working tax credit; and

(*b*) the case falls within sub-paragraph (*b*) of the First Condition in regulation 4(1) of the Working Tax Credit Regulations (person who has accepted an offer of work which is expected to commence within 7 days).

(3) In the circumstances prescribed by paragraph (2)—

(*a*) an award on a claim for tax credit may be made subject to the condition that the requirements for entitlement are satisfied no later than the date prescribed by paragraph (4); and

(*b*) if those requirements are satisfied no later than that date, the claim shall be treated as being made on the date on which they are satisfied.

Modifications—Universal Credit (Transitional Provisions) Regulations, SI 2013/386 reg 17(1), (2), Schedule paras 33, 35 (modification of this regulation in respect of awards of universal credit and terminations of awards of tax credit in the same year).

(4) The date prescribed by this paragraph is the date falling seven days after the relevant date.

11 Circumstances in which claims to be treated as made—notices containing provision under section 17(2)(*a*), (4)(*a*) or (6)(*a*) of the Act

(1) In the circumstances prescribed by paragraph (2) a claim for a tax credit is to be treated as made.

(2) The circumstances prescribed by this paragraph are where (in the case where there has been a previous single claim) a person has or (in the case where there has been a previous joint claim) [either person or][4] both persons have made a declaration in response to provision included in a notice under section 17 of the Act by virtue of—

(*a*) subsection (2)(*a*) of that section;

(*b*) subsection (4)(*a*) of that section;

(*c*) subsection (6)(*a*) of that section; or

(*d*) any combination of those subsections.

The declaration made shall (subject to regulation 5(3)) be treated as a claim for tax credit by that person or persons for the tax year following that to which the notice relates.

[(3) The claim shall be treated as made—

(*a*) in a case where the declaration is made by [the date specified on the section 17 notice][4] on 6th April [following the period to which the section 17 notice relates][4];

(*aa*) . . . [4]

(*b*) in a case where the declaration, not having been made by [the date specified on the section 17 notice][4], is made within 30 days following the date on the notice to the claimant that payments of tax credit under section 24(4) of the Act have ceased due to the claimant's failure to make the declaration, [on 6th April . . .[4] following [the period to which the section 17 notice relates][4]][3];

(*c*) in a case where the declaration, not having been made by [the date specified on the section 17 notice][4] or within the 30 days specified in sub-paragraph (*b*), is made before [31st January in the tax year following the period to which the section 17 notice relates][4], and, in the opinion of the Board, the claimant had good cause for not making the declaration as mentioned in sub-paragraphs (*a*) or (*b*), [on 6th April following the period to which the section 17 notice relates][4]; or

(*d*) in any other case, on the latest date on which the declaration is received by a relevant authority at an appropriate office (subject to the application of [regulations 7 and 7A][5]).][2]

[(4) Paragraph (3) does not apply—

(*a*) in the case where there has been a previous single claim (to which the notice referred to in paragraph (2) relates) if the person by whom it was made could no longer make a single claim; . . .[4]

(*b*) in the case where there has been a previous joint claim (to which the notice referred to in paragraph (2) relates) if the persons by whom it was made could no longer make a joint claim.][1] [or

(*c*) in the case where the response to the notice referred to in paragraph (2) specifies that such response is not to be treated as a new claim for the tax year beginning 6th April following the period to which the section 17 notice relates.][4]

Modifications—Tax Credits (Polygamous Marriages) Regulations, SI 2003/742 regs 39, 41 (modification of para (2) above for the purposes of polygamous marriages).

Universal Credit (Transitional Provisions) Regulations, SI 2013/386 reg 17(1), (2), Schedule paras 33, 36 (modification of this regulation in respect of awards of universal credit and terminations of awards of tax credit in the same year).

Universal Credit (Transitional Provisions) Regulations, SI 2014/1626 reg 4 (modification of this regulation in respect of awards of universal credit and terminations of awards of tax credit in the same year).

Amendments—[1] Para (4) inserted by the Tax Credits (Miscellaneous Amendments) Regulations, SI 2004/762 reg 3(1), (2) with effect from 6 April 2004.

[2] Para (3) substituted by the Tax Credits (Miscellaneous Amendments) Regulations, SI 2008/604 reg 4 with effect from 6 April 2008.

[3] In para (3), sub-para (*aa*) inserted and words in sub-para (*b*) substituted, by the Tax Credits (Miscellaneous Amendments) Regulations, SI 2009/697 regs 11, 16 with effect from 6 April 2009.

[4] Words inserted in para (2); words in para (3)(*a*), (*b*), (*c*) substituted ; para (4)(*c*) inserted, and para (3)(*aa*) repealed, by the Tax Credits (Miscellaneous Amendments) Regulations, SI 2010/751 regs 6, 7 with effect from 6 April 2010.

[5] In para (3)(*d*), words substituted by the Tax Credits (Claims and Notifications) (Amendment) Regulations, SI 2015/669 reg 4 with effect from 6 April 2015.

12 Circumstances in which claims to be treated as made—notices containing provision under section 17(2)(*b*), (4)(*b*) and (6)(*b*) of the Act

(1) In either of the circumstances prescribed by paragraphs (2) and (4) a claim for a tax credit is to be treated as made.

(2) The circumstances prescribed by this paragraph are where a person is or persons are treated as having made a declaration in response to provision included in a notice under section 17 of the Act by virtue of—

(*a*) subsection (2)(*b*) of that section, and

(*b*) subsection (4)(*b*) of that section,

or a combination of those subsections and subsection (6)(b) of that section.

(3) The declaration referred to in paragraph (2) shall (subject to regulation 5(3)) be treated as a claim by that person or persons for tax credit for the tax year following that to which the notice relates.

(4) The circumstances prescribed by this paragraph are where a person or any of the persons has—

(*a*) made a statement under paragraph (*b*) of subsection (2) of section 17 of the Act in response to such a notice by the date specified for the purposes of that subsection, or

(*b*) made a statement under paragraph (*b*) of subsection (4) of that section in response to such a notice by the date specified for the purposes of that subsection,

or a combination of any of those subsections and subsection (6)(*b*) of that section.

(5) The notice referred to in paragraph (4), together with (and as corrected by) the statement or statements there referred to, shall (subject to regulation 5(3)) be treated as a claim for tax credit by that person or persons for the tax year following that to which the notice relates.

(6) The claim shall be treated as made on the 6 April preceding the dates specified in the notice for the purposes of subsections (2) or (4) of section 17 of the Act.

(7) [Paragraphs (3) and (5) shall not apply][2]

(*a*) in the case where there has been a previous single claim (to which the notice relates), the person by whom it was made could no longer make a single claim; . . .[1]

Tax Credits

(*b*) in the case where there has been a previous joint claim (to which the notice relates), the persons by whom it was made could no longer jointly make a joint claim; . . . [2]

[(*c*) in the case where, before the specified date, the person or persons to whom a notice under section 17 of the Act is given advise the Board that the person or persons do not wish to be treated as making a claim for tax credit for the tax year following that to which the notice relates; or][2]

[(*d*) in the case where there has been a previous single claim to which a notice under section 17 of the Act relates—

(i) a relevant notification is given to the person by whom the claim was made; and

(ii) the person fails to make a relevant request; and

(*e*) in the case where there has been a previous joint claim to which a notice under section 17 of the Act relates—

(i) a relevant notification is given to the persons by whom the claim was made; and

(ii) they fail to make a relevant request.][2]

[(8) In this regulation—

(*a*) "relevant notification" means a written notification to a person or persons by whom a claim for tax credit was made which—

(i) is given by the Board at least 35 days before the Board gives notice under section 17 of the Act to the person or persons;

(ii) states the date on which it is given;

(iii) advises that the Board intends to give such a notice to the person or persons; and

(iv) advises that this regulation will not have effect to treat the person or persons as making a claim for tax credit for the tax year following that to which the notice relates unless a relevant request is made;

(*b*) "relevant request" means a request made to the Board by a person or persons to whom a relevant notification is given that—

(i) is made in response to the relevant notification within 30 days of the date on which it is given; and

(ii) requests that the person or persons will be treated by virtue of this regulation as making a claim for tax credit for the tax year following that to which the notice relates;

(*c*) "specified date" means the date specified for the purposes of section 17(2) and (4) of the Act or, where different dates are specified, the later of them.][2]

Modifications—Universal Credit (Transitional Provisions) Regulations, SI 2013/386 reg 17(1), (2), Schedule paras 33, 37 (modification of this regulation in respect of awards of universal credit and terminations of awards of tax credit in the same year).

Universal Credit (Transitional Provisions) Regulations, SI 2014/1626 reg 4 (modification of this regulation in respect of awards of universal credit and terminations of awards of tax credit in the same year).

Amendments—[1] Word "or" at the end of para (7)(*a*) repealed, by the Tax Credits (Miscellaneous Amendments) Regulations, SI 2010/751 regs 6, 8 with effect from 6 April 2010.

[2] In para (7), words substituted, word "or" at end of sub-para (*b*) revoked, sub-para (*c*) substituted and sub-paras (*d*), (*e*) inserted, and para (8) inserted, by the Tax Credits (Miscellaneous Amendments) (No 3) Regulations, SI 2010/2914 regs 13–15 with effect from 31 December 2010.

13 Circumstances in which claims made by one member of a couple to be treated as also made by the other member of the couple

(1) In the circumstances prescribed by paragraph (2) [or (3)][2] a claim for a tax credit made by one member of a . . . [1] couple is to be treated as also made by the other member of the . . . [1] couple.

(2) The circumstances prescribed by this paragraph are those where one member of a . . . [1] couple is treated by [regulation 11 or][3] regulation 12 as having made a claim for a tax credit in response to a notice under section 17 of the Act given to both members of the couple.

[(3) A claim for a tax credit made by one member of a couple is to be treated as also made by the other member of the couple in such manner and in such circumstances as the Board may decide.][2]

Modifications—Tax Credits (Polygamous Marriages) Regulations, SI 2003/742 regs 39, 42 (modification of this regulation for the purposes of polygamous marriages).

Universal Credit (Transitional Provisions) Regulations, SI 2013/386 reg 17(1), (2), Schedule paras 33, 38 (modification of this regulation in respect of awards of universal credit and terminations of awards of tax credit in the same year).

Universal Credit (Transitional Provisions) Regulations, SI 2014/1626 reg 4 (modification of this regulation in respect of awards of universal credit and terminations of awards of tax credit in the same year).

Amendments—[1] Words revoked by the Civil Partnership Act 2004 (Tax Credits, etc) (Consequential Amendments) Order, SI 2005/2919 art 5(1), (3) with effect from 5 December 2005.

[2] Words in para (1), and whole of para (3), inserted, by the Tax Credits (Miscellaneous Amendments) (No 2) Regulations, SI 2008/2169 regs 11, 13 with effect from 1 September 2008.

[3] Words in para (2) inserted by the Tax Credits (Miscellaneous Amendments) Regulations, SI 2010/751 regs 6, 9 with effect from 6 April 2010.

14 Circumstances in which awards to be conditional and claims treated as made—decisions under section 14(1) of the Act made before 6 April 2003

(1) In the circumstances prescribed by paragraph (2) an award on a claim for a tax credit may be made subject to the condition that the requirements for entitlement are satisfied on 6 April 2003.

(2) The circumstances prescribed by this paragraph are those where—

(*a*) an advance claim (under regulation 9) for a tax credit has been made for the tax year beginning on 6 April 2003; and

(*b*) the Board give notice of their decision under section 14(1) of the Act before that date.

(3) Where, in a case falling within the terms of paragraph (2),—

(*a*) notification is given before 6 April 2003 of a change of circumstances (other than one increasing the maximum rate at which a person or persons may be entitled to a tax credit) which is expected to continue at that date, or

(*b*) the Board have reasonable grounds before that date for believing that the requirements for entitlement are otherwise expected to differ on that date from those in the claim,

the person or persons making the claim shall be treated as making a new claim (on the basis of the altered requirements for entitlement, together with so much of those requirements stated in the original claim as remain unchanged) in the place of the original claim.

15 Persons who die after making a claim

(1) This regulation applies where any person who has made a claim for a tax credit dies—

(*a*) before the Board have made a decision in relation to that claim under section 14(1) of the Act;

(*b*) having given a notification of a change of circumstances increasing the maximum rate at which a person or persons may be entitled to the tax credit, before the Board have made a decision whether (and, if so, how) to amend the award of tax credit made to him or them; or

(*c*) where the tax credit has been awarded for the whole or part of a tax year, after the end of that tax year but before the Board have made a decision in relation to the award under section 18(1), (5), (6) or (9) of the Act.

(2) In the case of a single claim, the personal representatives of the person who has died may proceed with the claim in the name of that person.

(3) In the case of a joint claim where only one of the persons by whom the claim was made has died, the other person with whom the claim was made may proceed with the claim in the name of the person who has died as well as in his own name.

(4) In the case of a joint claim where both the persons by whom the claim was made have died, the personal representatives of the last of them to die may proceed with the claim in the name of both persons who have died.

(5) For the purposes of paragraph (4), where persons have died in circumstances rendering it uncertain which of them survived the other—

(*a*) their deaths shall be presumed to have occurred in order of seniority; and

(*b*) the younger shall be treated as having survived the elder.

Modifications—Tax Credits (Polygamous Marriages) Regulations, SI 2003/742 regs 39, 43 (modification of paras (3), (4) for the purposes of polygamous marriages).

Universal Credit (Transitional Provisions) Regulations, SI 2013/386 reg 17(1), (2), Schedule paras 33, 39 (modification of this regulation in respect of awards of universal credit and terminations of awards of tax credit in the same year).

Universal Credit (Transitional Provisions) Regulations, SI 2014/1626 reg 4 (modification of this regulation in respect of awards of universal credit and terminations of awards of tax credit in the same year).

16 Persons who die before making joint claims

(1) This regulation applies where one member of a . . . [1] couple dies and the other member of the . . . [1] couple wishes to make a joint claim for a tax credit

(2) The member who wishes to make the claim may make and proceed with the claim in the name of the member who has died as well as in his own name.

(3) Any claim made in accordance with this regulation shall be for a tax credit for a period ending with—

(*a*) the date of the death of the member of the . . . [1] couple who has died; or

(*b*) if earlier, 5 April in the tax year to which the claim relates.

HMRC Manuals—Tax Credit Technical Manual TCTM6108 (if it is a joint claim and both partners die, the personal representative of the last person to die can proceed with the claim; it is a joint claim and both partners have died and it is uncertain which of them were the last to die then the personal representative of the younger of the couple can proceed with the claim).

Modifications—Tax Credits (Polygamous Marriages) Regulations, SI 2003/742 regs 39, 44 (words in paras (1), (3)(*a*) substituted, para (2) substituted, and words in para (3)(a) inserted for the purposes of polygamous marriages).

Amendments—[1] Words in paras (1), (3)(*a*) revoked by the Civil Partnership Act 2004 (Tax Credits, etc) (Consequential Amendments) Order, SI 2005/2919 art 5(1), (4) with effect from 5 December 2005.

17 Circumstances where one person may act for another in making a claim—receivers etc

(1) In the circumstances prescribed by paragraph (2) any receiver or other person mentioned in sub-paragraph (*b*) of that paragraph may act for the person mentioned in sub-paragraph (*a*) of that paragraph in making a claim for a tax credit.

(2) The circumstances prescribed by this paragraph are where—

(*a*) a person is, or is alleged to be, entitled to a tax credit but is unable for the time being to make a claim for a tax credit; and

(*b*) there are any of the following—

(i) a receiver appointed by the Court of Protection with power to make a claim for a tax credit on behalf of the person;

(ii) in Scotland, a tutor, curator or other guardian acting or appointed in terms of law who is administering the estate of the person; and

(iii) in Northern Ireland, a controller appointed by the High Court, with power to make a claim for a tax credit on behalf of the person.

18 Circumstances where one person may act for another in making a claim—other appointed persons

(1) In the circumstances prescribed by paragraph (2) any person mentioned in sub-paragraph (*b*) of that paragraph may act for the person mentioned in sub-paragraph (*a*) of that paragraph in making a claim for a tax credit.

(2) The circumstances prescribed by this paragraph are where—

(*a*) a person is, or is alleged to be, entitled to a tax credit but is unable for the time being to make a claim for a tax credit; and

(*b*) in relation to that person, there is a person appointed under—

(i) regulation 33(1) of the Social Security (Claims and Payments) Regulations 1987;

(ii) regulation 33(1) of the Social Security (Claims and Payments) Regulations (Northern Ireland) 1987; or

(iii) paragraph (3).

(3) Where there is no person mentioned in regulation 17(2)(*b*) in relation to the person who is unable to act, the Board may appoint under this paragraph a person who—

(*a*) has applied in writing to the Board to be appointed to act on behalf of the person who is unable to act; and

(*b*) if a natural person, is aged 18 years or more.

(4) An appointment under paragraph (3) shall end if—

(*a*) the Board terminate it;

(*b*) the person appointed has resigned from the appointment having given one month's notice in writing to the Board of his resignation; or

(*c*) the Board are notified that a receiver or other person mentioned in regulation 17(2)(*b*) has been appointed in relation to the person who is unable to make a claim.

PART 3

NOTIFICATIONS OF CHANGES OF CIRCUMSTANCES

19 Interpretation of this Part

In this Part "the notification date", in relation to a notification, means—

(*a*) the date on which the notification is given to [a relevant authority at an appropriate office][1]; or

(*b*) in cases where regulation 24 applies, the date on which the notification would be treated by that regulation as being given disregarding regulations 25 and 26.

Amendments—[1] Words substituted by the Tax Credits (Claims and Notifications and Payments by the Board) (Amendment) Regulations, SI 2003/723 regs 2, 3(2)(*g*) with effect from 6 April 2003.

20 Increases of maximum rate of entitlement to a tax credit as a result of changes of circumstances to be dependent on notification

(1) Any change of circumstances of a description prescribed by paragraph (2) which may increase the maximum rate at which a person or persons may be entitled to tax credit is to do so only if notification of it has been given in accordance with this Part.

(2) The description of changes of circumstances prescribed by this paragraph are changes of circumstances other than those in consequence of which the Board have given notice of a decision under section 16(1) of the Act in accordance with section 23 of the Act.

21 Requirement to notify changes of circumstances which may decrease the rate at which a person or persons is or are entitled to tax credit or mean that entitlement ceases

(1) [Subject to paragraph (1A),][1] where a person has or persons have claimed a tax credit, notification is to be given within the time prescribed by paragraph (3) if there is a change of circumstances of the description prescribed by paragraph (2) which may decrease the rate at which he is or they are entitled to the tax credit or mean that he ceases or they cease to be entitled to the tax credit.

[(1A) Paragraph (1) does not apply where advance notification has been given under regulation [27(2), (2A) or (3)][2].][1]

[(2) The changes of circumstances described by this paragraph are those where—

(*a*) entitlement to the tax credit ceases by virtue of section 3(4), or regulations made under section 3(7), of the Act;

(*b*) there is a change in the relevant child care charges which falls within regulation 16(1)(*b*) (omitting paragraph (i)) of the Working Tax Credit Regulations;

(*c*) a person ceases to undertake work for at least 16 hours per week for the purposes of—

(i) the Second Condition in regulation 4(1) (read with regulations 4(3) to (5) and 5 to 8) [except where that person falls within paragraph (*a*) of the third variation of the Second Condition][4] or

(ii) regulation 13(1),

of the Working Tax Credit Regulations;

[(*d*) person ceases to undertake work for at least 30 hours per week for the purposes of the first or second variation of the Second Condition in regulation 4(1) of the Working Tax Credit Regulations (read with regulations 4(3) to (5) and 5 to 8), except in a case where that person still falls within the terms of paragraph (*a*) or (*d*) of the first variation or paragraph (*a*) or (*c*) of the second variation of that Condition;][4]

(*e*) a person ceases to undertake, or engage in, qualifying remunerative work for at least 16 hours per week for the purposes of—

(i) regulation 9(1)(*a*) (disability element), [or][4]

(ii) regulation 10(2)(*d*) (30 hour element), . . . [4]

(iii) . . . [4]

(*f*) a person ceases to engage in qualifying remunerative work for at least 30 hours per week, for the purposes of—

(i) regulation 10(1) (30 hour element), or

(ii) regulation 11(2)(*c*) (second adult element), in a case where the other claimant mentioned in that provision is not so engaged for at least 30 hours per week,

of the Working Tax Credit Regulations;

(*g*) a couple cease to engage in qualifying remunerative work for at least 30 hours per week, for the purposes of regulation 10(2)(*c*) (30 hour element) of the Working Tax Credit Regulations;

(*h*) a person ceases to be treated as responsible for a child or qualifying young person, for the purposes of child tax credit or of the Working Tax Credit Regulations;

(*i*) in a case where a person has given advance notification under regulation 27(2B) that a child is expected to become a qualifying young person, the child does not become a qualifying young person for the purposes of Part 1 of the Act;

(*j*) a person ceases to be a qualifying young person for the purposes of Part 1 of the Act, other than by attaining the age of twenty; or

(*k*) a child or qualifying young person dies.][3]

[(*l*) one or both members of a couple who satisfy paragraph (*a*) of the third variation of the Second Condition in regulation 4(1) of the Working Tax Credit Regulations (read with regulations 4(3) to (5) and 5 to 8) and are engaged in qualifying remunerative work cease to meet the condition that one member of the couple works not less than 16 hours per week and the aggregate number of hours for which the couple are engaged in qualifying remunerative work is not less than 24 hours per week, except in a case where the person or their partner still falls within the terms of paragraph (*b*), (*c*) or (*d*) of the third variation of that Condition.][4]

(3) The time prescribed by this paragraph is the period of [one][3] months beginning on the date on which the change of circumstances occurs or [except in the case of paragraph (2)(*j*))][2], if later, the period of [one][3] months beginning on [the date on which the person first becomes aware of the change in circumstances][2].

Modifications—Universal Credit (Transitional Provisions) Regulations, SI 2013/386 reg 17(1), (2), Schedule paras 33, 40 (modification of this regulation in respect of awards of universal credit and terminations of awards of tax credit in the same year).

Amendments—[1] Words in para (1) inserted, and para (1A) inserted, by the Tax Credits (Claims and Notifications and Payments by the Board) (Amendment) Regulations, SI 2003/723 regs 2, 4 with effect from 6 April 2003.

2 Words in paras (1A), (3) substituted, and para (2) substituted, by the Tax Credits (Claims and Notifications) (Amendment) Regulations, SI 2006/2689 regs 2–5 with effect from 1 November 2006.

3 In para (3), word substituted in both places by the Tax Credits (Claims and Notifications) (Amendment) Regulations, SI 2006/2689 regs 2, 6 with effect from 6 April 2007.

4 In para (2), in sub-para (*c*)(i) words inserted, sub-para (*d*) substituted, word at end of sub-para (*e*)(i) inserted, sub-para (*e*)(iii) and preceding word "or" revoked, and sub-para (*l*) inserted, by the Tax Credits (Miscellaneous Amendments) Regulations, SI 2012/848 regs 1(3), 5(1), (3) with effect from 6 April 2012.

22 Manner in which notifications to be given

(1) This regulation prescribes the manner in which a notification is to be given.

(2) A notification must be given to [a relevant authority at an appropriate office][1].

(3) A notification may be given orally or in writing.

(4) At any time after a notification has been given but before the Board have made a decision under section 15(1) or 16(1) of the Act in consequence of the notification, the person or persons by whom the notification was given may amend the notification by giving notice orally or in writing to [a relevant authority at an appropriate office][1].

Definition—"Appropriate office", reg 2.

HMRC Manuals—Tax Credit Technical Manual TCTM5400 (a notification can be by telephone or in person. It can also include notifications made by fax, E-mail or via the internet).

Amendments—[1] Words substituted by the Tax Credits (Claims and Notifications and Payments by the Board) (Amendment) Regulations, SI 2003/723 regs 2, 3(2)(*h*) with effect from 6 April 2003.

23 Person by whom notification may be, or is to be, given

(1) In the case of a single claim, notification is to be given by the person by whom the claim for a tax credit was made.

(2) In the case of a joint claim, notification may be given by either member of the . . .[1] couple by whom the claim for a tax credit was made.

HMRC Manuals—Tax Credit Technical Manual TCTM5500 (in practice, the change can also be notified by any person appointed by the Board of Inland Revenue, or the Secretary of State for Social Security to act as appointees for claimant(s) who are unable to act for themselves).

Modifications—Tax Credits (Polygamous Marriages) Regulations, SI 2003/742 regs 39, 45 (modification of para (2) for the purposes of polygamous marriages).

Amendments—[1] Words in para (2) revoked by the Civil Partnership Act 2004 (Tax Credits, etc) (Consequential Amendments) Order, SI 2005/2919 art 5(1), (5) with effect from 5 December 2005.

24 Amended notifications

(1) In the circumstances prescribed by paragraph (2) a notification which has been amended shall be treated as having been given as amended and, subject to regulations [25, 26 and 26A][2], as having been given on the date prescribed by paragraph (3).

(2) The circumstances prescribed by this paragraph are where the person or persons by whom the notification is given amends or amend the notification in accordance with regulation 22(4).

(3) The date prescribed by this paragraph is the date on which the notification being amended was given to [a relevant authority at an appropriate office][1].

Amendments—[1] Words substituted by the Tax Credits (Claims and Notifications and Payments by the Board) (Amendment) Regulations, SI 2003/723 regs 2, 3(2)(*i*) with effect from 6 April 2003.

2 References substituted by the Tax Credits (Miscellaneous Amendments) Regulations, SI 2004/762 reg 3(1), (3) with effect from 6 April 2004.

25 Date of notification—cases where change of circumstances which may increase the maximum rate

(1) Where a notification of a change of circumstances which may increase the maximum rate at which a person or persons may be entitled to tax credit is given in the circumstances prescribed by paragraph (2), that notification is to be treated as having been given on the date specified by paragraph (3).

(2) The circumstances prescribed by this paragraph are where notification is given to [a relevant authority at an appropriate office][1] of a change of circumstances which has occurred other than in the circumstances prescribed by [regulations][2] 26(2) [and 26A(2)][2].

(3) The date specified by this paragraph is—

(*a*) the date falling [one month][3] before the notification date; or

(*b*) if later, the date of the change of circumstances.

HMRC Manuals—Tax Credit Technical Manual TCTM5300 (effective dates of changes in circumstances; the two cases where an increase in an award can be backdated for more than 3 months before the date of notifying the change).

Amendments—[1] Words substituted by the Tax Credits (Claims and Notifications and Payments by the Board) (Amendment) Regulations, SI 2003/723 regs 2, 3(2)(*j*) with effect from 6 April 2003.

2 In para (2), word substituted and words inserted, by the Tax Credits (Miscellaneous Amendments) Regulations, SI 2009/697 regs 11, 17 with effect from 6 April 2009.

3 In para (3)(*a*), words substituted by the Tax Credits (Miscellaneous Amendments) Regulations, SI 2012/848 regs 1(3), 5(1), (4)(*a*) with effect from 6 April 2012.

26 [Date of notification—disability element and severe disability element of working tax credit

[(1) In the circumstances prescribed by paragraph (2), the notification of a change in circumstances is to be treated as having been given on the date prescribed by paragraph (3).

(2) The circumstances prescribed by this paragraph are where—

(*a*) a notification is given of a change of circumstances in respect of a claim to working tax credit, which results in the Board making an award of the disability element or the severe disability element of working tax credit (or both of them) in favour of a person or persons; and

(*b*) the notification date is within [one month][2] of the date that a claim for any of the benefits referred to in regulation 9(2) to (8) or 17(2) of the Working Tax Credit Regulations is determined in favour of those persons (or one of them).

(3) The date prescribed by this paragraph is the latest of the following:

(*a*) the first date in respect of which the benefit claimed was payable;

(*b*) the date falling [one month][2] before the claim for the benefit was made;

(*c*) the date the claim for working tax credit was made (or treated as made under [regulations 7 and 7A][3]);

(*d*) (for the purposes of the disability element only), the first date that the person or persons satisfied the conditions of entitlement for the disability element.][1]

Amendments—[1] Reg 26 substituted by the Tax Credits (Miscellaneous Amendments) Regulations, SI 2009/697 regs 11, 18 with effect from 6 April 2009.

[2] In paras (2)(*b*), (3)(*b*) words substituted by the Tax Credits (Miscellaneous Amendments) Regulations, SI 2012/848 regs 1(3), 5(1), (4)(b), (c) with effect from 6 April 2012.

[3] In para (3)(*c*), words substituted by the Tax Credits (Claims and Notifications) (Amendment) Regulations, SI 2015/669 reg 4 with effect from 6 April 2015.

26A [Date of notification—disability element and severe disability element of child tax credit

[(1) In the circumstances prescribed by paragraph (2), the notification of a change in circumstances is to be treated as having been given on the date prescribed by paragraph (3).

(2) The circumstances prescribed by this paragraph are where—

(*a*) a notification is given of a change of circumstances in respect of a claim to child tax credit which results in the Board making an award of the disability element or the severe disability element of child tax credit (or both of those elements) in favour of a person or persons, in respect of a child; and

(*b*) the notification date is within [one month][2] of the date that a claim for a disability living allowance [or personal independence payment][3] [or armed forces independence payment][5] in respect of the child is determined in favour of those persons (or one of them).

(3) The date prescribed by this paragraph is the latest of the following:

(*a*) the first date in respect of which the disability living allowance [or personal independence payment][3] [or armed forces independence payment][5] was payable;

(*b*) the date falling [one month][2] before the claim for the disability living allowance [or personal independence payment][3] [or armed forces independence payment][5] was made;

(*c*) the date the claim for child tax credit was made (or treated as made under [regulations 7 and 7A][4]).][1]

Amendments—[1] Reg 26A substituted by the Tax Credits (Miscellaneous Amendments) Regulations, SI 2009/697 regs 11, 19 with effect from 6 April 2009.

[2] In paras (2)(*b*), (3)(*b*) words substituted by the Tax Credit (Miscellaneous Amendments) Regulations, SI 2012/848 regs 1(3), 5(1), (4)(*d*), (*e*) with effect from 6 April 2012.

[3] Words inserted by the Personal Independence Payment (Supplementary Provisions and Consequential Amendments) Regulations, SI 2013/388 reg 31(1), (3) with effect from 8 April 2013.

[4] In para (3)(*c*), words substituted by the Tax Credits (Claims and Notifications) (Amendment) Regulations, SI 2015/669 reg 4 with effect from 6 April 2015.

[5] Words inserted in each place by the Armed Forces and Reserve Forces Compensation Scheme (Consequential Provisions: Subordinate Legislation) Order, SI 2013/591 art 7, Schedule para 27(1), (3) with effect from 8 April 2013.

27 Advance notification

(1) In [any][1] of the circumstances prescribed by paragraphs (2)[to][2] (3) a notification of a change of circumstances may be given for a period after the date on which it is given.

(2) The circumstances prescribed by this paragraph are those prescribed by regulation 10(2) (working tax credit: person who has accepted an offer of work expected to commence within seven days), the reference to "the claim" being read as a reference to the notification.

[(2A) The circumstances prescribed by this paragraph are where either regulation 15(4) (agreement for the provision of future child care) or regulation 16(1) (relevant change in circumstances) of the Working Tax Credit Regulations applies.][1]

[(2B) The circumstances prescribed by this paragraph are those where a child is expected to become a qualifying young person for the purposes of Part 1 of the Act.][2]

(3) The circumstances prescribed by this paragraph are where a tax credit has been claimed for the tax year beginning on 6 April 2003 by making a claim before that tax year begins, and the notification relates to that tax year and is given before that date.

(4) In the circumstances prescribed by paragraph (2), an amendment of an award of a tax credit in consequence of a notification of a change of circumstances may be made subject to the condition that the requirements for entitlement to the amended amount of the tax credit are satisfied at the time prescribed by paragraph (5).

(5) The time prescribed by this paragraph is the latest date which—

(*a*) is not more than 7 days after the date on which the notification is given; and

(*b*) falls within the period of award in which the notification is given.

[(5A) In the circumstances prescribed by paragraph (2A), an amendment of an award of tax credit in consequence of a notification of a change of circumstances may be made subject to the condition that the requirements for entitlement to the amended amount of the tax credit are satisfied at the time prescribed by paragraph (5B).][1]

[(5B) The time prescribed by this paragraph is the first day of the week—

(*a*) in which the agreement within regulation 15(4) of the Working Tax Credit Regulations commences or the relevant change of circumstances occurs; and

(*b*) which is not more than 7 days after the date on which notification is given and falls within the period of award in which the notification is given.][1]

[(5C) For the purposes of paragraph (5B), "week" means a period of 7 days beginning with midnight between Saturday and Sunday.][1]

(6) "Period of award" shall be construed in accordance with section 5 of the Act.

Modifications—Universal Credit (Transitional Provisions) Regulations, SI 2013/386 reg 17(1), (2), Schedule paras 33, 41 (modification of this regulation in respect of awards of universal credit and terminations of awards of tax credit in the same year).

Amendments—[1] Word in para (1) substituted, and paras (2A), (5A)–(5C) inserted, by the Tax Credits (Claims and Notifications and Payments by the Board) (Amendment) Regulations, SI 2003/723 regs 2, 5 with effect from 6 April 2003.

[2] Word in para (1) substituted, and para (2B) inserted, by the Tax Credits (Claims and Notifications) (Amendment) Regulations, SI 2006/2689 regs 2, 7 with effect from 1 November 2006.

28 Circumstances where one person may act for another in giving a notification—receivers etc

(1) In the circumstances prescribed by paragraph (2) any receiver or other person mentioned in sub-paragraph (*b*) of that paragraph may act for the person mentioned in sub-paragraph (*a*) of that paragraph in giving a notification.

(2) The circumstances prescribed by this paragraph are where—

(*a*) a person is unable for the time being to give a notification; and

(*b*) there are any of the following—

(i) a receiver appointed by the Court of Protection with power to proceed with a claim for a tax credit on behalf of the person;

(ii) in Scotland, a tutor, curator or other guardian acting or appointed in terms of law who is administering the estate of the person; and

(iii) in Northern Ireland, a controller appointed by the High Court, with power to proceed with a claim for a tax credit on behalf of the person.

29 Circumstances where one person may act for another in giving a notification—other appointed persons

(1) In the circumstances prescribed by paragraph (2) any person mentioned in sub-paragraph (*b*) of that paragraph may act for the person mentioned in sub-paragraph (*a*) of that paragraph in giving a notification.

(2) The circumstances prescribed by this paragraph are where—

(*a*) a person is unable for the time being to give a notification; and

(*b*) in relation to that person, there is a person appointed under—

(i) regulation 33(1) of the Social Security (Claims and Payments) Regulations 1987;

(ii) regulation 33(1) of the Social Security (Claims and Payments) Regulations (Northern Ireland) 1987; or

(iii) regulation 18(3);

and the provisions of regulation 18(3) shall apply to notifications and (under regulation 36) responses to notices under section 17 of the Act, as they apply to claims.

PART 4
NOTICES TO PROVIDE INFORMATION OR EVIDENCE

29A [Form in which evidence of birth or adoption to be provided

If the Board require the person, or either or both of the persons, by whom a claim is made to provide a certificate of a child's birth or adoption, the certificate so produced must be either an original certificate or a copy authenticated in such manner as would render it admissible in proceedings in any court in the jurisdiction in which the copy was made.][1]

Amendments—[1] This regulation inserted by the Tax Credits (Miscellaneous Amendments No 2) Regulations, SI 2004/1241 regs 2, 4 with effect from 1 May 2004.

30 Employers

(1) For the purposes of sections 14(2)(*b*), 15(2)(*b*), 16(3)(*b*) and 19(2)(*b*) of the Act the persons specified in paragraph (2) are prescribed, and, in relation to those persons, the information or evidence specified in paragraph (4) is prescribed.

(2) The persons specified in this paragraph are—

(*a*) any person named by a person or either of the persons by whom a claim for a tax credit is made as his employer or the employer of either of them; and

(*b*) any person whom the Board have reasonable grounds for believing to be an employer of a person or either of the persons by whom such a claim is made.

(3) "Employer" has the meaning given by section 25(5) of the Act.

(4) The information or evidence specified in this paragraph is information or evidence, including any documents or certificates, which relates to—

(*a*) the claim for the tax credit in question;

(*b*) the award of the tax credit in question; or

(*c*) any question arising out of, or under, that claim or award.

Modifications—Tax Credits (Polygamous Marriages) Regulations, SI 2003/742 regs 39, 46 (modification of para (2) for the purposes of polygamous marriages).

31 Persons by whom child care is provided

(1) For the purposes of sections 14(2)(*b*), 15(2)(*b*), 16(3)(*b*) and 19(2)(*b*) of the Act the persons specified in paragraph (2) are prescribed, and, in relation to those persons, the information or evidence specified in paragraph (3) is prescribed.

(2) The persons specified in this paragraph are—

(*a*) any person named by a person or persons by whom a claim for the child care element of working tax credit is made as being, in relation to him or either of them, a person by whom child care is provided; and

(*b*) any person whom the Board have reasonable grounds for believing to be, in relation to a person or persons by whom such a claim is made, a person by whom child care is provided.

(3) The information or evidence specified in this paragraph is information or evidence, including any documents or certificates, which relates to—

(*a*) the claim for the tax credit in question;

(*b*) the award of the tax credit in question; or

(*c*) any question arising out of, or under, that claim or award.

(4) "Child care" has the meaning given by regulation 14(2) of the Working Tax Credit Regulations.

Modifications—Tax Credits (Polygamous Marriages) Regulations, SI 2003/742 regs 39, 47 (modification of para (2)(*a*) for the purposes of polygamous marriages).

32 Dates to be specified in notices under section 14(2), 15(2), 16(3), 18(10) or 19(2) of the Act

In a notice under section 14(2), 15(2), 16(3), 18(10) or 19(2) of the Act, the date which may be specified shall not be less than 30 days after the date of the notice.

PART 5
FINAL DECISIONS

33 [Dates to be specified in notices under section 17 of the Act

In a notice under section 17 of the Act—

(*a*) the date which may be specified for the purposes of subsection (2) or subsection (4) shall be not later than [31st July][2] following the end of the tax year to which the notice relates, or 30 days after the date on which the notice is given, if later; and

(*b*) the date which may be specified for the purposes of subsection (8) shall be not later than 31st January following the end of the tax year to which the notice relates, or 30 days after the date on which the notice is given, if later.][1]

Modifications—Universal Credit (Transitional Provisions) Regulations, SI 2013/386 reg 17(1), (2), Schedule paras 33, 42 (modification of this regulation in respect of awards of universal credit and terminations of awards of tax credit in the same year).

Universal Credit (Transitional Provisions) Regulations, SI 2014/1626 reg 4 (modification of this regulation in respect of awards of universal credit and terminations of awards of tax credit in the same year).

Tax Credits

Amendments—[1] Regulations 33, 34 substituted by the Tax Credits (Miscellaneous Amendments) Regulations, SI 2004/762 reg 3(1), (5) with effect from 6 April 2004.

[2] Words in para (*a*) substituted by the Tax Credits (Miscellaneous Amendments) Regulations, SI 2007/824 reg 14(1), (3) with effect from 6 April 2007.

34 [Manner in which declaration or statement in response to a notice under section 17 of the Act to be made

(1) This regulation prescribes the manner in which a declaration or statement in response to a notice under section 17 of the Act must be made.

(2) A declaration or statement must be made—

(*a*) in writing in a form approved by the Board for that purpose;

(*b*) orally to an officer of the Board; or

(*c*) in such other manner as the Board may accept as sufficient in the circumstances of any particular case.

(3) In a case falling within paragraph (2)(*b*) one of two joint claimants may act for both of them in response to a notice under section 17 if, at the time the declaration or statement is made, a joint claim could be made by both of them.][1]

Amendments—[1] Regulations 33, 34 substituted by the Tax Credits (Miscellaneous Amendments) Regulations, SI 2004/762 reg 3(1), (5) with effect from 6 April 2004.

35 Circumstances where one person may act for another in response to a notice under section 17 of the Act—receivers etc

(1) In the circumstances prescribed by paragraph (2) any receiver or other person mentioned in sub-paragraph (*b*) of that paragraph may act for the person mentioned in sub-paragraph (*a*) of that paragraph in response to a notice under section 17 of the Act.

(2) The circumstances prescribed by this paragraph are where—

(*a*) a person is unable for the time being to act in response to a notice under section 17 of the Act; and

(*b*) there are any of the following—

(i) a receiver appointed by the Court of Protection with power to proceed with a claim for a tax credit on behalf of the person;

(ii) in Scotland, a tutor, curator or other guardian acting or appointed in terms of law who is administering the estate of the person; and

(iii) in Northern Ireland, a controller appointed by the High Court, with power to proceed with a claim for a tax credit and proceed with the claim on behalf of the person.

36 Circumstances where one person may act for another in response to a notice under section 17 of the Act

(1) In the circumstances prescribed by paragraph (2) any person mentioned in sub-paragraph (*b*) of that paragraph may act for the person mentioned in sub-paragraph (*a*) of that paragraph in response to a notice under section 17 of the Act.

(2) The circumstances prescribed by this paragraph are where—

(*a*) a person is unable for the time being to act in response to a notice under section 17 of the Act; and

(*b*) in relation to that person, there is a person appointed under—

(i) regulation 33(1) of the Social Security (Claims and Payments) Regulations 1987;

(ii) regulation 33(1) of the Social Security (Claims and Payments) Regulations (Northern Ireland) 1987; or

(iii) regulation 18(3).

2002/2172

WORKING TAX CREDIT (PAYMENT BY EMPLOYERS) REGULATIONS 2002

Made by the Commissioners of Inland Revenue under TCA 2002 ss 25(1), (2), 65, 67

Made . . . .*20 August 2002*

Laid before Parliament . . . .*21 August 2002*

Coming into force . . . .*1 March 2003*

Amendment—These regulations, so far as not already revoked, are revoked by the Tax Credit (Payment by Employers, etc) (Amendment) Regulations, SI 2005/2200 reg 9(2)(*a*) with effect from 6 April 2006.

2002/2173

TAX CREDITS (PAYMENTS BY [THE COMMISSIONERS]) REGULATIONS 2002

Made by the Commissioners of Inland Revenue under TCA 2002 ss 24(2), (3), (4), (7) and (8), 65(1), (2) and (7) and 67

Made . . . .*20 August 2002*
Laid before Parliament . . . .*21 August 2002*
Coming into force . . . .*6 April 2003*

Note—The title of these regulations has been changed by the Tax Credit (Payment by Employers, etc) (Amendment) Regulations, SI 2005/2200 reg 7(1), (2). Also, by virtue of SI 2005/2200 reg 7(1), (4), in regs 3–14 below, the words "the Commissioners" have been substituted throughout for the words "the Board". These amendments have effect from 29 August 2005.

Commentary—*Simon's Taxes* **E2.255.**

HMRC Manuals—Tax Credit Technical Manual TCTM8001–8105 (direct payments of tax credits).

1 Citation, commencement and effect

(1) These Regulations may be cited as the Tax Credits (Payments by [the Commissioners][2]) Regulations 2002 and shall come into force on 6th April 2003.

(2) These Regulations have effect in relation to payments of a tax credit, or any element of a tax credit, which must be made . . . [1] in relation to the tax year beginning with 6th April 2003 and subsequent tax years.

[(3) Regulations 8 to 14 have effect only in relation to such payments as must be made by the Board.][1]

Amendments—[1] Word in para (2) revoked, and para (3) inserted, by the Tax Credits (Claims and Notifications and Payments by the Board) (Amendment) Regulations, SI 2003/723 regs 6, 7 with effect from 6 April 2003.

[2] Words substituted by the Tax Credit (Payment by Employers, etc) (Amendment) Regulations, SI 2005/2200 reg 7(1), (2) with effect from 29 August 2005.

2 Interpretation

In these Regulations—

"the Act" means the Tax Credits Act 2002;

. . . [1]

["the Commissioners" means Commissioners for Her Majesty's Revenue and Customs (see section 1 of the Commissioners for Revenue and Customs Act 2005);][1]

["couple" has the meaning given by section 3(5A) of the Act;][2]

"employee" and "employer" have the meaning given by section 25(5) of the Act;

. . . [2]

"period of award" shall be construed in accordance with section 5 of the Act;

"the relevant tax year" means the whole or part of the tax year for which an award of a tax credit has been made to a person or persons (referred to in section 24(4) of the Act);

"tax year" means a period beginning with 6th April in one year and ending with 5th April in the next;

. . . [2]

Modifications—Tax Credits (Polygamous Marriages) Regulations, SI 2003/742 regs 48, 49 (definitions of "married couple" and "unmarried couple" revoked, and definition of "polygamous unit" inserted, for the purposes of polygamous marriages).

Amendments—[1] Definition of "the Board" revoked, and definition of "the Commissioners" inserted, by the Tax Credit (Payment by Employers, etc) (Amendment) Regulations, SI 2005/2200 reg 7(1), (3) with effect from 29 August 2005.

[2] Definition of "couple" inserted, and definitions of "married couple" and "unmarried couple" revoked, by the Civil Partnership Act 2004 (Tax Credits, etc) (Consequential Amendments) Order, SI 2005/2919 art 6(1), (2) with effect from 5 December 2005.

3 Child tax credit and child care element—member of a couple prescribed for the purposes of section 24(2) of the Act

(1) This regulation has effect in relation to payments of—

(*a*) child tax credit; and

(*b*) any child care element of working tax credit.

(2) Subject to regulation 5, the member of a [couple][3] prescribed by paragraph (3) is prescribed for the purposes of section 24(2) of the Act.

(3) The member of a [couple][3] [prescribed by this paragraph is—

(*a*) where the [couple][3] are for the time being resident at the same address—

(i) the member who is identified by both members of the [couple][3] as the main carer;

(ii) in default of a member being so identified, the member who appears to [the Commissioners] to be the main carer; and

(*b*) where—

(i) the members of the [couple][3] are for the time being resident at different addresses, or

Tax Credits

(ii) one member of the [couple][3] is temporarily absent from the address at which they live together,

the member who appears to [the Commissioners] to be the main carer.

Here "main carer" means the member of the [couple][3] who is the main carer for the children and qualifying young persons for whom either or both of the members is or are responsible.][2]

(4) "Children" means persons who have not attained the age of sixteen or who fall within the terms of regulation 4 of the Child Tax Credit Regulations 2002.

(5) "Qualifying young persons" means persons, other than children, who—

(*a*) have not attained the age of nineteen, and

(*b*) satisfy the conditions in regulation 5(3) and (4) of the Child Tax Credit Regulations 2002.

(6) Where payments are being made to the member of a [couple][3] prescribed by virtue of paragraph (3) and the members of the [couple][3] jointly give notice to [the Commissioners] that, as a result of a change of circumstances, the payments should be made to the other member as the main carer, the other member shall[, except where the notice appears to [the Commissioners] to be unreasonable,][2] be treated as prescribed by virtue of paragraph (3).

[(7) For the purposes of this regulation, a person is responsible for a child or qualifying young person if he is treated as being responsible for that child or qualifying young person in accordance with the rules contained in regulation 3 of the Child Tax Credit Regulations 2002.][1]

HMRC Manuals—Tax Credit Technical Manual TCTM2207 (CTC can only be paid to one person; where the claim is made by a couple then it can only be paid to the person in that couple who is the main carer for all the children of that couple. The "main carer" is someone who is normally answerable for, or called to account for, the child or young person).

Modifications—Tax Credits (Polygamous Marriages) Regulations, SI 2003/742 regs 48, 50 (word in heading substituted, and paras (2)–(6) substituted, for the purposes of polygamous marriages).

Amendments—[1] Para (7) inserted by the Tax Credits (Claims and Notifications and Payments by the Board) (Amendment) Regulations, SI 2003/723 regs 6, 8 with effect from 6 April 2003.

[2] Words in para (3) substituted, and words in para (6) inserted, by the Tax Credits (Miscellaneous Amendments No 2) Regulations, SI 2004/1241 reg 5 with effect from 1 May 2004.

[3] Word in paras (2), (3), (6) substituted by the Civil Partnership Act 2004 (Tax Credits, etc) (Consequential Amendments) Order, SI 2005/2919 art 6(1), (3)(*a*) with effect from 5 December 2005.

4 Working tax credit (excluding any child care element)—member of a couple prescribed for the purposes of section 24(2) of the Act

(1) This regulation has effect in relation to payments of working tax credit other than payments of any child care element.

(2) Subject to regulation 5, the member of a [couple][1] prescribed by paragraph (3) is prescribed for the purposes of section 24(2) of the Act.

(3) The member of a [couple][1] prescribed by this paragraph is—

(*a*) if only one member of the [couple][1] is engaged in remunerative work, that member;

(*b*) if both members of the [couple][1] are engaged in remunerative work—

(i) the member elected jointly by them; or

(ii) in default of any election, such of them as appears to [the Commissioners] to be appropriate.

(4) Where payments are being made to the member of a [couple][1] prescribed by virtue of paragraph (3)(*b*) and the members of the [couple][1] jointly give notice to [the Commissioners] that, as a result of a change of circumstances, they wish payments to be made to the other member, the other member shall be treated as prescribed by virtue of paragraph (3)(*b*).

(5) For the purposes of paragraph (3), a member of a [couple][1] is engaged in remunerative work if—

(*a*) he is engaged in qualifying remunerative work; or

(*b*) he works not less than 16 hours per week and the other member of the married or unmarried couple is engaged in qualifying remunerative work.

(6) "Qualifying remunerative work", and being engaged in it, have the meaning given by regulation 4 of the Working Tax Credit (Entitlement and Maximum Rate) Regulations 2002.

Amendments—[1] Word in paras (2), (3), (4) and (5) substituted by the Civil Partnership Act 2004 (Tax Credits, etc) (Consequential Amendments) Order, SI 2005/2919 art 6(1), (3)(*b*) with effect from 5 December 2005.

5 Member of a couple prescribed for the purposes of section 24(2) of the Act where one of the members of the couple has died

(1) This regulation applies where one of the members of a [couple][1] has died.

(2) The member of the [couple][1] prescribed by paragraph (3) is prescribed for the purposes of section 24(2) of the Act.

(3) The member of the [couple][1] prescribed by this paragraph is the member who survives.

(4) For the purposes of this regulation, where persons have died in circumstances rendering it uncertain which of them survived the other—

(*a*) their deaths shall be presumed to have occurred in order of seniority; and

(*b*) the younger shall be treated as having survived the elder.

Amendments—[1] Word in paras (1), (2) and (3) substituted by the Civil Partnership Act 2004 (Tax Credits, etc) (Consequential Amendments) Order, SI 2005/2919 art 6(1), (3)(*c*) with effect from 5 December 2005.

6 Person prescribed for the purposes of section 24(3) of the Act where an award of a tax credit is made on a claim which is made by one person on behalf of another

For the purposes of section 24(3) of the Act, the person prescribed is—

(*a*) the person by whom the claim on behalf of another was made; or

(*b*) if at any time [the Commissioners] do not consider it appropriate for payments of the tax credit to be made to that person, the person on behalf of whom the claim was made.

7 Prescribed circumstances for the purposes of section 24(4) of the Act

(1) Either of the circumstances prescribed by paragraphs (2) and (3) are prescribed circumstances for the purposes of section 24(4) of the Act.

(2) The circumstances prescribed by this paragraph are where—

(*a*) a claim for a tax credit for the next tax year has been made or treated as made by the person or persons by the date specified for the purposes of subsection (4) of section 17 of the Act in the notice given to him or them under that section in relation to the relevant tax year; and

(*b*) [the Commissioners] have not made a decision under section 14(1) of the Act in relation to that claim.

(3) The circumstances prescribed by this paragraph are where—

(*a*) a claim for a tax credit for the next tax year has not been made or treated as made by the person or persons; and

(*b*) [the Commissioners] have not made a decision under section 18(1) of the Act in relation to the person and persons for the relevant tax year.

Modifications—Universal Credit (Transitional Provisions) Regulations, SI 2013/386 reg 17(1), (2), Schedule paras 43, 44 (modification of this regulation in respect of awards of universal credit and terminations of awards of tax credit in the same year).

Universal Credit (Transitional Provisions) Regulations, SI 2014/1626 reg 4 (modification of this regulation in respect of awards of universal credit and terminations of awards of tax credit in the same year).

8 Time of payment by way of a credit to a bank account or other account

(1) . . . [2] this regulation applies where the tax credit or element is to be paid by way of a credit to a bank account or other account notified to [the Commissioners].

(2) [Subject to paragraphs (2A) and (2B)][3] the tax credit or element shall be paid—

(*a*) each week; or

(*b*) every four weeks,

in accordance with any election given by the person to whom payment is to be made.

[(2A) If a person makes elections under paragraph (2) for child tax credit and any child care element of working tax credit to be paid at differing intervals, the elections shall have no effect and [the Commissioners] may pay the child tax credit and any child care element together either each week or every four weeks as appears to them to be appropriate.][1]

[(2B) Notwithstanding the terms of any election under paragraph (2), the Commissioners may pay the tax credit or element either each week or every four weeks as appears to them to be appropriate.][3]

(3) . . . [2]

(4) This regulation is subject to regulations 10 and 11.

Amendments—[1] Words in para (2) inserted, and para (2A) inserted, by the Tax Credits (Claims and Notifications and Payments by the Board) (Amendment) Regulations, SI 2003/723 regs 6, 9 with effect from 6 April 2003.

[2] Para (3) and words in para (1) revoked by the Tax Credit (Payment by Employers, etc) (Amendment) Regulations, SI 2005/2200 reg 9(2)(*b*), (*c*) with effect from 6 April 2006.

[3] In para (2), words substituted , and para (2B) inserted, by the Tax Credits (Miscellaneous Amendments) (No 3) Regulations, SI 2010/2914 regs 6, 7 with effect from 31 December 2010.

9 Time of payment other than by way of a credit to a bank account or other account etc

(1) This regulation applies where—

(*a*) the tax credit or element is to be paid other than by way of a credit to a bank account or other account notified to [the Commissioners]; or

(*b*) . . . [1]

(2) The tax credit or element shall be paid at such times as appear to [the Commissioners] to be appropriate.

Amendments—[1] Para (1)(*b*) revoked by the Tax Credit (Payment by Employers, etc) (Amendment) Regulations, SI 2005/2200 reg 9(2)(*b*) with effect from 6 April 2006.

10 [Single payment of small sums of tax credit

The tax credit or element may be paid by way of a single payment, and at such time, and in such manner, as appear to [the Commissioners] to be appropriate, in any of the following cases—

(*a*) where [the Commissioners] are paying only child tax credit to a person and the weekly rate at which it is payable is less than £2.00;

(*b*) where [the Commissioners] are paying both any child care element (but no other element) of working tax credit and child tax credit to a person and the total weekly rate at which they are payable is less than £2.00;

(*c*) where [the Commissioners] are paying only working tax credit (apart from any child care element) to a person and the weekly rate at which it is payable (excluding any such child care element) is less than £2.00;

(*d*) where [the Commissioners] are paying both working tax credit (including elements other than, or in addition to, any child care element) and child tax credit to a person who has elected under regulation 8(2) to have them paid at the same intervals and the total weekly rate at which they are payable is less than £2.00;

(*e*) where [the Commissioners] are paying both working tax credit (apart from any child care element) and child tax credit to a person who has elected under regulation 8(2) to have them paid at differing intervals and—

(i) the total weekly rate at which any such child care element and the child tax credit are payable is less than £2.00; or

(ii) the weekly rate at which the working tax credit is payable (excluding any such child care element) is less than £2.00.][1]

Amendments—[1] This regulation substituted by the Tax Credits (Claims and Notifications and Payments by the Board) (Amendment) Regulations, SI 2003/723 regs 6, 10 with effect from 6 April 2003.

11 Postponement of payment

(1) [The Commissioners] may postpone payment of the tax credit or element in any of the circumstances specified in [paragraphs (2), (2A), (3) and (3A)][3].

(2) The circumstances specified in this paragraph are where there is a pending determination of an appeal against a decision of [[the First-tier Tribunal, the appeal tribunal, the][2] Upper Tribunal, the Northern Ireland][1] Social Security Commissioner or a court relating to—

(*a*) the case in question; or

(*b*) another case where it appears to [the Commissioners] that, if the appeal were to be determined in a particular way, an issue would arise as to whether the award in the case in question should be amended or terminated under section 16(1) of the Act.

[(2A) The circumstances specified in this paragraph are where—

(*a*) a notice in writing has been given by the Commissioners to a person to notify a bank account or other account to which the Commissioners may make payment of a tax credit or element to which the person is entitled;

(*b*) a period of [four] weeks has elapsed since the day on which the Commissioners gave their notice; and

(*c*) no bank account or other account has been[4] notified to the Commissioners pursuant to their notice.][3]

(3) The circumstances specified in this paragraph are where confirmation is pending of—

(*a*) the details of a bank account or other account by way of a credit to which payment is to be made; or

(*b*) the address of the person to whom payment is to be made,

where it appears to [the Commissioners] that such details or address as were previously notified to them are incorrect.

[(3A) The circumstances specified in this paragraph are where—

(*a*) a notice under section 16(3) of the Tax Credits Act 2002 has been issued to the person, or either or both of the persons, to whom the tax credit or element was awarded, and

(*b*) such person or persons have not provided the information or evidence requested in that notice by the date specified in such notice.][3]

(4) For the purposes of paragraph (2), the circumstances where a determination of an appeal is pending include circumstances where a decision of [[the First-tier Tribunal, the appeal tribunal, the][2] Upper Tribunal, the Northern Ireland][1] Social Security Commissioner or a court has been made and [the Commissioners]—

(*a*) are awaiting receipt of the decision;

(*b*) in the case of a decision by [the [First-tier Tribunal or the appeal tribunal][2]][1], are considering whether to apply for a statement of reasons or have applied for, and are awaiting receipt of, a statement of reasons; or

(*c*) have received the decision or statement of reasons and are considering—

(i) whether to apply for permission to appeal; or

(ii) where permission is not needed or has been given, whether to appeal.

(5) "[Appeal tribunal[2]]" has the meaning given by section 63(10) of the Act.

(6) "[Northern Ireland Social][1] Security Commissioner" has the meaning given by section 63(13) of the Act.

[(7) The postponement of payment pursuant to the circumstances specified in paragraph (2A) shall cease at the earlier of the time when—

(*a*) a bank account or other account is notified to the Commissioners; or (*b*) the entitlement to the tax credit or element ceases in accordance with regulation 14.][3]

Amendments—[1] In paras (2), (4), (6), words substituted by the Tribunals, Courts and Enforcement Act 2007 (Transitional and Consequential Provisions) Order, SI 2008/2683 art 6(1), Sch 1 para 190 with effect from 3 November 2008.

[2] In paras (2), (4), (5), words substituted by the Transfer of Tribunal Functions and Revenue and Customs Appeals Order, SI 2009/56 art 3, Sch 2 para 78 with effect from 1 April 2009.

[3] Words in para (1) substituted and paras (2A), (3A) and (7) inserted, by the Tax Credits (Miscellaneous Amendments) Regulations, SI 2010/751 reg 10(1)–(5) with effect from 6 April 2010.

[4] In para (2A)(*b*), word substituted by the Tax Credits (Miscellaneous Amendments) Regulations, SI 2012/848 regs 1(3), 6 with effect in relation to a notice given on or after 6 April 2012 within para (2A)(*a*).

12 Amounts of payments

(1) The tax credit or element shall be paid in accordance with the most recent decision by [the Commissioners] under section 14(1), 15(1) or 16(1) of the Act.

(2) Where the tax credit or element is to be paid other than by way of a single payment, it shall be paid so far as possible in such amounts as will result in the person to whom payment is to be made receiving regular payments of similar amounts over the entire period of award.

(3) Where an award of tax credit is amended, the total amount paid prior to the award being amended [may][1] be taken into account by [the Commissioners] in determining the amount of any further payments for the remainder of the period of award.

[(4) Where payments under section 24(4) of the Act are to be made the Commissioners may take any or both of the following factors into account in determining the amount of those payments—

(*a*) the rate at which the person or persons were entitled to the tax credit for the relevant tax year;

(*b*) the estimated amount of income the person or persons referred to above may receive in the current tax year.][2]

Amendment—[1] Word in para (3) substituted by the Tax Credits (Miscellaneous Amendments) Regulations, SI 2007/824 reg 15 with effect from 6 April 2007.

[2] Para (4) substituted by the Tax Credits (Miscellaneous Amendments) Regulations, SI 2008/604 reg 5 with effect from 6 April 2008.

12A [Recovery of overpayments of tax credit from other payments of tax credit

(1) This regulation applies where notice is given to a person or persons under subsection (4) of section 29 of the Act (deduction of overpayments from payments of tax credit).

(2) The maximum rate at which an overpayment may be recovered from payments of tax credit is—

(*a*) where the only amount of tax credit to which the person is, or, in the case of a joint claim, the persons are, entitled, is the family element of child tax credit, 100% of that tax credit;

(*b*) where the total amount of tax credit to which the person is, or, in the case of a joint claim, the persons are, entitled is not subject to reduction—

(i) by virtue of section 7(2) of the Act; or

(ii) because their income for the relevant year does not exceed the relevant income threshold prescribed in his or their case in regulation 3 of the Tax Credits (Income Thresholds and Determination of Rates) Regulations 2002;

10% of that tax credit; and

(*c*) in any other case, [the income-related percentage][2] of the tax credit to which the person is, or in the case of a joint claim, the persons are, entitled.

[(2A) In paragraph (2)(*c*), "the income-related percentage" means—

(*a*) 50% if annual income exceeds £20,000; and

(*b*) 25% in any other case.

(2B) For the purposes of paragraph (2A)(*a*), "annual income"—

(*a*) means the annual income of the person or, in the case of a joint claim, the aggregate annual income of the persons, mentioned in paragraph (2)(*c*); and

(*b*) is to be taken to be the amount that the Commissioners are for the time being treating that income to be for the purposes of Part 1 of the Act, regardless of whether that amount is also "the relevant income" (as defined by section 7(3) of the Act) on which the entitlement to the tax credit mentioned in paragraph (2)(*c*) is dependent.][2]

(3) In paragraph (2) a reference to the amount to which a person is, or persons are, entitled is a reference to the amount to which they would be entitled but for the operation of that paragraph.][1]

Amendments—[1] This regulation inserted by the Tax Credits (Miscellaneous Amendments) Regulations, SI 2004/762 reg 18 with effect from 6 April 2004.

[2] In para (2)(*c*), words substituted, and paras (2A), (2B) inserted by the Tax Credits and Child Benefit (Miscellaneous Amendments) Regulations, SI 2016/360 reg 5 with effect from 6 April 2016.

13 Manner of payment

(1) Subject to paragraph (2), the tax credit or element shall be paid by way of a credit to a bank account or other account notified to [the Commissioners] by the person to whom payment is to be made.

(2) Where [it does not appear to [the Commissioners] to be appropriate][1] for the tax credit or element to be paid by way of a credit to a bank account or other account notified to [the Commissioners] by the person to whom payment is to be made, the tax credit or element may be paid in such manner as appears to [the Commissioners] to be appropriate.

(3) Subject to regulation 14, if no bank account or other account has been notified to [the Commissioners], the tax credit or element shall be paid in such manner as appears to [the Commissioners] to be appropriate.

Amendments—[1] Words in para (2) substituted by the Tax Credits (Claims and Notifications and Payments by the Board) (Amendment) Regulations, SI 2003/723 regs 6, 11 with effect from 6 April 2003.

14 Entitlement to tax credit or element dependent on a bank account or other account having been notified to [the Commissioners]

[(1) Subject to paragraph (3), where—

(*a*) payment of a tax credit or element is postponed pursuant to the circumstances specified in regulation 11(2A), and

(*b*) before the relevant time determined in accordance with this regulation, no bank account or other account is notified to the Commissioners by the person to whom a tax credit or element would have been paid if payment of it had not been postponed,

that person shall cease to be entitled to the tax credit or element for the remainder of the period of the award beginning on the day from which the Commissioners decide to postpone payment.][1]

(2) . . . [1]

(3) Where there are exceptional circumstances which are expected to result in a person not being able to obtain a bank account or other account throughout the period of award, paragraph (1) shall not have effect in relation to that person's entitlement to a tax credit or element for the period of award.

(4) . . . [1]

[(4A) Subject to paragraphs (4C) and (4E), the relevant time is the earlier of—

(*a*) three months after the time when the Commissioners decide to postpone payment of a tax credit or element; or

(*b*) immediately after the end of the relevant tax year.

(4B) This paragraph applies where, before the time determined in accordance with paragraph (4A), the person entitled to payment of the tax credit or element—

(*a*) requests from the Commissioners authority to open an account for which such authority is required; and

(*b*) provides sufficient information from which the Commissioners can give that authority.

(4C) Subject to paragraph (4E), where paragraph (4B) applies, the relevant time is the later of—

(*a*) the time determined in accordance with paragraph (4A); and

(*b*) the expiry of the period of 3 weeks from the day on which the Commissioners give their authority following a request described in paragraph (4B)(*a*).

(4D) This paragraph applies where a person to whom a notice described in regulation 11(2A)(*a*) has been given has a reasonable excuse—

(*a*) for not being able to take all necessary steps to obtain a bank account or other account before a time determined in accordance with paragraphs (4A) or (4C), or

(*b*) for not being able to notify to the Commissioners the bank account or other account before a time determined in accordance with paragraphs (4A) or (4C).

(4E) Where paragraph (4D) applies, the relevant time is the later of—

(*a*) the time determined in accordance with paragraph (4A);

(*b*) where paragraph (4B) applies, the time determined in accordance with paragraph (4C); and

(*c*) the date by which the account can reasonably be expected to be notified to the Commissioners.][1]

(5) "Writing" includes writing produced by electronic communications that are approved by [the Commissioners].

Amendments—[1] Para (1) substituted, paras (4A)–(4E) inserted, and paras (2), (4) repealed, by the Tax Credits (Miscellaneous Amendments) Regulations, SI 2010/751 reg 10(1), (6)–(8) with effect from 6 April 2010.

2002/2926

TAX CREDITS (APPEALS) REGULATIONS 2002

Made by the Commissioners of Inland Revenue under TCA 2002 ss 63(8), 65(2), (6)

Made . . . . *26 November 2002*

Laid before Parliament . . . . *26 November 2002*

Coming into force . . . . *17 December 2002*

1 Citation, commencement and duration

(1) These Regulations may be cited as the Tax Credits (Appeals) Regulations 2002 and shall come into force on 17th December 2002.

(2) These Regulations shall cease to have effect on such day as is appointed by order made under section 63(1) of the Tax Credits Act 2002 (tax credits appeals etc. temporary modifications).

2 Interpretation

In these Regulations—

"appeal tribunal" means an appeal tribunal constituted—

(*a*) . . . [1]

(*b*) [1] in Northern Ireland, under Chapter 1 of Part 2 of the Social Security (Northern Ireland) Order 1998 (social security appeals: Northern Ireland);

"tax credit appeal" means an appeal which, by virtue of section 63 of the Tax Credits Act 2002 or of provisions applied by these Regulations, is to an appeal tribunal or lies to a Social Security Commissioner;

"Social Security Commissioner" means—

(*a*) in Great Britain, the Chief Social Security Commissioner or any other Social Security Commissioner appointed under the Social Security Act 1998 or a tribunal of three or more Commissioners constituted under section 16(7) of that Act, and

(*b*) in Northern Ireland, the Chief Social Security Commissioner or any other Social Security Commissioner appointed under the Social Security Administration (Northern Ireland) Act 1992 or a tribunal of two or more Commissioners constituted under Article 16(7) of the Social Security (Northern Ireland) Order 1998;

"the 1998 Act" means the Social Security Act 1998;

"the 1998 Order" means the Social Security (Northern Ireland) Order 1998.

Amendments—[1] In definitions of "appeal tribunal" and "Social Security Commissioner", sub-para (*a*) revoked, and in sub-para (*b*) letter "(*b*)" revoked, by the Tribunals, Courts and Enforcement Act 2007 (Transitional and Consequential Provisions) Order, SI 2008/2683 art 6(1), Sch 1 paras 191, 192 with effect from 3 November 2008.

3 Application of section 54 of the Taxes Management Act 1970

(1) Section 54 of the Taxes Management Act 1970 (settling of appeals by agreement) shall apply to a tax credit appeal to an appeal tribunal [or the First-tier Tribunal][1] with the modifications prescribed by paragraphs (2) to (8).

(2) In subsection (1) for "[tribunal[2]]", in both places where that word occurs, substitute the words "appeal tribunal [or the First-tier Tribunal[1]]".

(3) In subsections (1) and (4) omit the words "assessment or", in each place where they occur.

(4) In subsections (1), (2) and (4)(*a*) for "inspector or other proper officer of the Crown" substitute the words "officer of the Board".

(5) For subsection (3) substitute the following subsection—

"(3) Where an agreement is not in writing—

(*a*) the preceding provisions of this section shall not apply unless the Board give notice, in such form and manner as they consider appropriate, to the appellant of the terms agreed between the officer of the Board and the appellant; and

(*b*) the references in those preceding provisions to the time when the agreement was come to shall be construed as references to the date of that notice.".

(6) In subsection (4)(*b*) for "inspector or other proper officer giving" substitute the words "officer of the Board giving".

(7) In subsection (4) for "inspector or other proper officer had come" substitute the words "officer of the Board had come".

(8) After subsection (5) add the following subsection—

"(6) In subsection (1) "appeal tribunal" means an appeal tribunal constituted—

(a) . . . [1]

(*b*) [1]in Northern Ireland, under Chapter 1 of Part 2 of the Social Security (Northern Ireland) Order 1998 (social security appeals: Northern Ireland).".

Amendments—[1] In paras (1), (2), words inserted, and in para (8), in inserted sub-s (6), sub-para (*a*) revoked, and in sub-para (*b*) letter "(*b*)" revoked, by the Tribunals, Courts and Enforcement Act 2007 (Transitional and Consequential Provisions) Order, SI 2008/2683 art 6(1), Sch 1 paras 191, 193 with effect from 3 November 2008.

[2] In para (2), word substituted by the Transfer of Tribunal Functions and Revenue and Customs Appeals Order, SI 2009/56 art 3, Sch 2 paras 80, 81 with effect from 1 April 2009.

4 Application of section 12 of the 1998 Act and Article 13 of the 1998 Order

(1) Section 12 of the 1998 Act and Article 13 of the 1998 Order (appeals to an appeal tribunal [or the First-tier Tribunal][1]) shall apply to a tax credit appeal to an appeal tribunal [or the First-tier Tribunal][1] with the modifications prescribed by paragraphs (2) to (8).

(2) For subsections (1) and (2) of that section substitute the following subsections—

Tax Credits

"(1) An appeal which is to [the First-tier Tribunal][1] by virtue of section 63 of the Tax Credits Act 2002, including an application for a direction under section 19(9) of that Act, (a "tax credit appeal") may be brought by—

(*a*) a claimant whose claim for a tax credit is the subject of the appeal;
(*b*) the person on whom the penalty to which the appeal relates was imposed;
(*c*) the person applying for the direction under section 19(9) of that Act; or
(*d*) such other person as may be prescribed.".

(3) For paragraphs (1) and (2) of that Article substitute the following paragraph—

"(1) An appeal which is to an appeal tribunal by virtue of section 63 of the Tax Credits Act 2002, including an application for a direction under section 19(9) of that Act, (a "tax credit appeal") may be brought by—

(*a*) a claimant whose claim for a tax credit is the subject of the appeal;
(*b*) the person on whom the penalty to which the appeal relates was imposed;
(*c*) the person applying for a direction under section 19(9) of that Act; or
(*d*) such other person as may be prescribed.".

(4) Omit subsections (3) to (6) of that section and paragraphs (3) to (6) of that Article.

(5) In subsection (7) of that section and paragraph (7) of that Article add at the end ", and may in particular extend the time limit for giving notice of appeal specified in section 39(1) of the Tax Credits Act 2002".

(6) In subsection (8) of that section for "an appeal under this section" substitute "a tax credit appeal".

(7) In paragraph (8) of that Article for "an appeal under this Article" substitute "a tax credit appeal".

(8) Omit subsections (8)(*a*) and (9) of that section and paragraphs (8)(*a*) and (9) of that Article.

Amendments—[1] In para (1), words inserted, and in para (2), words substituted for words "an appeal tribunal", by the Tribunals, Courts and Enforcement Act 2007 (Transitional and Consequential Provisions) Order, SI 2008/2683 art 6(1), Sch 1 paras 191, 194 with effect from 3 November 2008.

5 Application of section 13 of the 1998 Act and Article 14 of the 1998 Order

(1) Section 13 of the 1998 Act and Article 14 of the 1998 Order (redetermination etc. of appeals by tribunal) shall apply to a decision of an appeal tribunal [or the First-tier Tribunal][1] on a tax credit appeal (other than a decision on a tax credit appeal under Schedule 2 to the Tax Credits Act 2002) with the modifications prescribed by paragraphs (2) to (4).

(2) Omit subsection (3) of that section and paragraph (3) of that Article.

(3) In subsection (4) of that section—

(*a*) omit the words "this section and";
(*b*) omit paragraph (*b*) and the word "and" immediately preceding it.

(4) In paragraph (4) of that Article—

(*a*) omit the words "this Article and";
(*b*) omit sub-paragraph (*a*);
(*c*) for sub-paragraph (*b*) substitute the following sub-paragraph—

"(*b*) the Board and the persons mentioned in paragraph (3)(*b*) of that Article.".

Amendments—[1] In para (1), words inserted by the Tribunals, Courts and Enforcement Act 2007 (Transitional and Consequential Provisions) Order, SI 2008/2683 art 6(1), Sch 1 paras 191, 195 with effect from 3 November 2008.

6 Application of section 14 of the 1998 Act and Article 15 of the 1998 Order

(1) Section [14(2) to (6)][1] of the 1998 Act and Article 15(1) to (10) of the 1998 Order (appeal from tribunal to Commissioner) shall apply to a decision of an appeal tribunal [or the First-tier Tribunal][1] on a tax credit appeal (other than a decision on a tax credit appeal under Schedule 2 to the Tax Credits Act 2002) with the modifications prescribed by paragraphs (2) and (3).

(2) In that section—

(*a*) . . . [1]
(*b*) in subsection (3)(*a*) for "Secretary of State" substitute "Board";
(*c*) omit subsections (3)(*d*), (4) and (5)(*c*).

(3) In that Article—

(*a*) in paragraph (1) omit the words "under Article 13 or 14";
(*b*) in paragraph (3)(*a*) for "Department" substitute "Board";
(*c*) omit paragraphs (3)(*d*), (4) and (5)(*c*).

Amendments—[1] In para (1), words substituted and inserted, and para (2)(*a*) revoked, by the Tribunals, Courts and Enforcement Act 2007 (Transitional and Consequential Provisions) Order, SI 2008/2683 art 6(1), Sch 1 paras 191, 196 with effect from 3 November 2008.

7—(1) . . . [2] Article 15(11) to (13) of the 1998 Order (appeals and procedure before Commissioner) shall apply to a decision of an appeal tribunal on a tax credit appeal (including a decision on a tax credit appeal under Schedule 2 to the Tax Credits Act 2002) with the modifications prescribed by paragraphs (2) and (3).

(2) So far as concerns decisions on tax credit appeals under Schedule 2 to the Tax Credits Act 2002, . . . [2] paragraph (11) of that Article omit the words "and applications made for leave to appeal".

(3) . . . [1]

Amendments—[1] Para (3) revoked by the Tax Credits (Appeals) (Amendment) Regulations, SI 2004/372 with effect from 16 March 2004.

[2] In pars (1), (2), words revoked by the Tribunals, Courts and Enforcement Act 2007 (Transitional and Consequential Provisions) Order, SI 2008/2683 art 6(1), Sch 1 paras 191, 197 with effect from 3 November 2008.

8 Application of section 15 of the Social Security Act 1998

Section 15 of the 1998 Act ([applications for permission to appeal against a decision of the Upper Tribunal][1]) shall apply to a decision of [the Upper Tribunal][1] on a tax credit appeal.

Amendments—[1] Words substituted by the Tribunals, Courts and Enforcement Act 2007 (Transitional and Consequential Provisions) Order, SI 2008/2683 art 6(1), Sch 1 paras 191, 198 with effect from 3 November 2008.

9 Application of section 16 of the 1998 Act and Article 16 of the 1998 Order

(1) Section 16 of, and Schedule 5 to, the 1998 Act and Article 16 of, and Schedule 4 to, the 1998 Order (procedure) shall apply for the purposes of a tax credit appeal with the modifications prescribed by paragraphs (2) to (6).

[(2) Omit subsection (3) of section 16.][1]

(3) Omit paragraph (3)(*b*) of that Article and the word "and" immediately preceding it.

(4) Omit subsections (4) and (5) of that section and paragraphs (4) and (5) of that Article.

(5) In Schedule 5 to the 1998 Act—

(*a*) in paragraph 1, omit the words "the Secretary of State,", in both places where they occur;

(*b*) in paragraph 4(*b*), add at the end ", including provision extending the time limit for giving of notice of appeal specified in section 39(1) of the Tax Credits Act 2002".

(6) In Schedule 4 to the 1998 Order—

(*a*) in paragraph 1, omit the words "the Department", in both places where they occur;

(*b*) in paragraph 4(*b*), add at the end ", including provision for extending the time limit for giving notice of appeal specified in section 39(1) of the Tax Credits Act 2002".

Amendments—[1] Para (2) substituted by the Tribunals, Courts and Enforcement Act 2007 (Transitional and Consequential Provisions) Order, SI 2008/2683 art 6(1), Sch 1 paras 191, 199 with effect from 3 November 2008.

10 Application of section 17 of the 1998 Act and Article 17 of the 1998 Order

(1) Section 17 of the 1998 Act and Article 17 of the 1998 Order (finality of decisions) shall apply to a decision of an appeal tribunal [the First-tier Tribunal, the Upper Tribunal][1] or a Social Security Commissioner on a tax credit appeal with the modifications prescribed by paragraphs (2) to (4).

(2) For subsection (1) of that section substitute the following subsection—

"(1) Subject to the provisions of—

(*a*) sections 12 to 16 of this Act, and

(*b*) the Tax Credits Act 2002,

[(*c*) any provision made by or under Chapter 2 of Part 1 of the Tribunals, Courts and Enforcement Act 2007,][1]

any decision made in accordance with those provisions in respect of an appeal which, by virtue of section 63 of the Tax Credits Act 2002 (or of provisions of this Act applied by regulations made under that section), is to [the First-tier Tribunal or lies to the Upper Tribunal][1], shall be final.".

(3) For paragraph (1) of that Article substitute the following paragraph—

"(1) Subject to the provisions of—

(*a*) Articles 13 to 16 of this Order, and

(*b*) the Tax Credits Act 2002,

any decision made in accordance with those provisions in respect of an appeal which, by virtue of section 63 of the Tax Credits Act 2002 (or of provisions of this Order applied by regulations made under that section), is to an appeal tribunal or lies to a Commissioner, shall be final.".

(4) Omit subsection (2)(*b*) and (*c*) of that section and paragraph (2)(*b*) and (*c*) of that Article.

Amendments—[1] In para (1), words inserted, in para (2), words inserted and words substituted, by the Tribunals, Courts and Enforcement Act 2007 (Transitional and Consequential Provisions) Order, SI 2008/2683 art 6(1), Sch 1 paras 191, 200 with effect from 3 November 2008.

11 Application of . . . and Article 28 of the 1998 Order

(1) . . . [1] Article 28 of the 1998 Order (correction of errors and setting aside of decisions) shall apply to a decision by an appeal tribunal or a Social Security Commissioner on a tax credit appeal with the modifications prescribed by paragraphs (2) to (4).

(2) . . . [1]

(3) For paragraph (3) of that Article substitute the following paragraph—

"(3) In this Article "relevant statutory provision" means—

(*a*) any of Articles 13 to 17 above, and

(*b*) any statutory provision contained or referred to in section 19(10), 38 or 39 of, or Schedule 2 to, the Tax Credits Act 2002.".

(4) Omit . . . [1] paragraph (1A) of that Article.

Tax Credits

Amendments—[1] In heading and paras (1), (4), words revoked, and para (2) revoked, by the Tribunals, Courts and Enforcement Act 2007 (Transitional and Consequential Provisions) Order, SI 2008/2683 art 6(1), Sch 1 paras 191, 201 with effect from 3 November 2008.

12 Application of section 39 of the 1998 Act and Article 39 of the 1998 Order

(1) Section 39 of the 1998 Act and Article 39 of the 1998 Order (interpretation etc. of Chapter 2) shall apply for the purposes of a tax credit appeal with the modifications prescribed by paragraphs (2) to (4).

(2) In subsection (1) of that section—

(*a*) [in the appropriate place][1] insert—

" "the Board" means the Commissioners of Inland Revenue;";

(*b*) for the definition of "claimant" substitute—

" "claimant" means a person who makes (whether or not jointly with another) a claim for a tax credit in accordance with sections 3 and 4 of the Tax Credits Act 2002, and includes a person entitled to make such a claim on behalf of another person by virtue of regulation 17 or 18 of the Tax Credits (Claims and Notifications) Regulations 2002;";

[(*c*) omit the definition of "relevant benefit"][2]

(3) In paragraph (1) of that Article—

(*a*) for the definition of "Inland Revenue" substitute—

" "the Board" means the Commissioners of Inland Revenue;

"claimant" means a person who makes (whether or not jointly with another) a claim for a tax credit in accordance with sections 3 and 4 of the Tax Credits Act 2002, and includes a person entitled to make such a claim on behalf of another person by virtue of regulation 17 or 18 of the Tax Credits (Claims and Notifications) Regulations 2002;";

[(*b*) omit the definition of "relevant benefit"][2]

(4) Omit subsections (2) and (3) of that section and paragraphs (2) and (3) of that Article.

Amendments—[1] In para (2)(*a*), words substituted by the Tribunals, Courts and Enforcement Act 2007 (Transitional and Consequential Provisions) Order, SI 2008/2683 art 6(1), Sch 1 paras 191, 202 with effect from 3 November 2008.

[2] Paras (2)(*c*), (3)(*b*) substituted by the Transfer of Tribunal Functions and Revenue and Customs Appeals Order, SI 2009/56 art 3, Sch 2 paras 80, 82 with effect from 1 April 2009.

2002/3036

TAX CREDITS (ADMINISTRATIVE ARRANGEMENTS) REGULATIONS 2002

Made by the Commissioners of the Inland Revenue under TCA 2002 ss 58 and 65(1), (2), (7) and (9)

Made . . . . *9 December 2002*

Laid before Parliament . . . . *10 December 2002*

Coming into force . . . . *1 January 2003*

1 Citation and commencement

These Regulations may be cited as the Tax Credits (Administrative Arrangements) Regulations 2002 and shall come into force on 1st January 2003.

2 Interpretation

In these Regulations—

"the Board" means the Commissioners of Inland Revenue;

"the principal Regulations" means the Tax Credits (Claims and Notifications) Regulations 2002;

"relevant authority" means—

(*a*) the Secretary of State;

(*b*) the Department for Social Development in Northern Ireland; or

(*c*) a person providing services to the Secretary of State or that Department.

3 Provision of information or evidence to relevant authorities

(1) Information or evidence relating to tax credits which is held—

(*a*) by the Board; or

(*b*) by a person providing services to the Board, in connection with the provision of those services,

may be provided to a relevant authority for the purposes of, or for any purposes connected with, the exercise of that relevant authority's functions under the principal Regulations.

(2) Information or evidence relating to tax credits may be provided to a relevant authority by persons other than the Board (whether or not persons by whom claims or notifications relating to tax credits are or have been made or given).

4 Giving of information or advice by relevant authorities

A relevant authority to which a claim or notification is or has been made or given by a person in accordance with the principal Regulations may give information or advice relating to tax credits to that person.

5 Recording, verification and holding, and forwarding, of claims etc received by relevant authorities

(1) A relevant authority may record and hold claims and notifications received by virtue of the principal Regulations and information or evidence received by virtue of regulation 3(2).

(2) Subject to paragraphs (3) and (4), a relevant authority must forward to the Board or a person providing services to the Board such a claim or notification, or such information or evidence, as soon as reasonably practicable after being satisfied that it is complete.

(3) Before forwarding a claim in accordance with paragraph (2), a relevant authority must verify—

(*a*) that any national insurance number provided in respect of the person by whom the claim is made exists and has been allocated to that person;

(*b*) that the matters verified in accordance with sub-paragraph (*a*) accord with—

(i) its own records; or

(ii) in the case of a person providing services to the Secretary of State or the Department for Social Development in Northern Ireland, records held by the Secretary of State or that Department; and

(*c*) whether the details of any relevant claim for benefit that have been provided are consistent with those held by it.

(4) If a relevant authority cannot locate any national insurance number in respect of a person by whom such a claim is made, it must forward to the Board or a person providing services to the Board the claim (notwithstanding that it is not complete).

(5) "National insurance number" means the national insurance number allocated within the meaning of—

(*a*) regulation 9 of the Social Security (Crediting and Treatment of Contributions, and National Insurance Numbers) Regulations 2001; or

(*b*) regulation 9 of the Social Security (Crediting and Treatment of Contributions, and National Insurance Numbers) Regulations (Northern Ireland) 2001.

(6) "Claim for benefit" means a claim for—

(*a*) a benefit in relation to which—

(i) the Secretary of State has functions under the Social Security Contributions and Benefits Act 1992; or

(ii) the Department for Social Development in Northern Ireland has functions under the Social Security Contributions and Benefits (Northern Ireland) Act 1992; . . . [1]

(*b*) a jobseeker's allowance under—

(i) the Jobseekers Act 1995; or

(ii) the Jobseekers (Northern Ireland) Order 1995[; or

(*c*) universal credit under Part 1 of the Welfare Reform Act 2012][1].

Amendments—[1] In para (6), word "or" revoked, and by the Universal Credit (Consequential, Supplementary, Incidental and Miscellaneous Provisions) Regulations, SI 2013/630 reg 79 with effect from 29 April 2013.

2002/3119

TAX CREDITS (NOTICE OF APPEAL) REGULATIONS 2002

Amendments—These regulations revoked by the Tax Credits, Child Benefit and Guardian's Allowance Reviews and Appeals Order, SI 2014/886, art 3 with effect in relation to England, Wales and Scotland from 6 April 2014.

2002/3196

TAX CREDITS (APPEALS) (NO 2) REGULATIONS 2002

Made by the Secretary of State for Work and Pensions under SSA 1998 ss 7(6), 12(2) and (7), 14(10) and (11), 16(1), 28(1), 39(1), 79(1) and (3) to (7) and 84, and Sch 1 paras 11, 12 and Sch 5, and after consultation with the Council on Tribunals in accordance with section 8 of the Tribunals and Inquiries Act 1992

Made . . . . *18 December 2002*

Coming into force . . . . *1 January 2003*

Tax Credits

PART 1
GENERAL

1 Citation, commencement, duration and interpretation

(1) These Regulations may be cited as the Tax Credits (Appeals) (No 2) Regulations 2002 and shall come into force on 1st January 2003.

(2) These Regulations shall cease to have effect on such day as is appointed by order made under section 63(1) of the Tax Credits Act 2002 (tax credits appeals etc: temporary modifications).

(3) In these Regulations, unless the context otherwise requires—

"the Act" means the Social Security Act 1998;

"the 2002 Act" means the Tax Credits Act 2002;

"the Appeals Regulations" means the Tax Credits (Appeals) Regulations 2002;

"the Decisions and Appeals Regulations" means the Social Security and Child Support (Decisions and Appeals) Regulations 1999;

"the Working Tax Credit Regulations" means the Working Tax Credit (Entitlement and Maximum Rate) Regulations 2002;

"appeal" means an appeal under section 38 of the 2002 Act;

"an application for a direction" means an application for a direction to close down an enquiry made under section 19(9) of the 2002 Act;

. . . [2]

. . . [2]

["couple" means—

(*a*) a man and woman who are married to each other and are members of the same household;

(*b*) a man and woman who are not married to each other but are living together as husband and wife;

(*c*) two people of the same sex who are civil partners of each other and are members of the same household; or

(*d*) two people of the same sex who are not civil partners of each other but are living together as if they were civil partners,

and for the purposes of paragraph (*d*), two people of the same sex are to be regarded as living together as if they were civil partners if, but only if, they would be regarded as living together as husband and wife were they instead two people of the opposite sex;][1]

"court" means the High Court, the Court of Appeal, the Court of Session, the High Court or Court of Appeal in Northern Ireland, the House of Lords or the Court of Justice of the European Community;

. . . [2]

. . . [2]

. . . [2]

"joint claim" means a claim made under section 3(3)(*a*) of the 2002 Act and any reference in these Regulations to "joint claimant" shall be construed accordingly;

. . . [2]

. . . [2]

. . . [2]

. . . [2]

. . . [2]

"partner" means . . . [1] the other member of [a couple][1];

"party to the proceedings" means the Board and any other person—

(*a*) who is an appellant in an appeal brought against a decision or determination set out in section 38 of the 2002 Act;

(*b*) who is an applicant for a direction to close down an enquiry under section 19(9) of the 2002 Act;

(*c*) who is a defendant (or defender) in penalty proceedings brought under paragraph 3 of Schedule 2 to the 2002 Act;

(*d*) who is a person with a right of appeal or a right to make an application for a direction under regulation 3;

. . . [2]

. . . [2]

. . . [2]

"single claim" means a claim made under section 3(3)(*b*) of the 2002 Act;

"tax credit" means child tax credit or working tax credit, construing those terms in accordance with section 1(1) and (2) of the 2002 Act, and any reference in these Regulations to "child tax credit" or "working tax credit" shall be construed accordingly.

Amendments—[1] Definition of "couple" inserted, words in definition of "partner" revoked and substituted by the Civil Partnership (Pensions, Social Security and Child Support) (Consequential, etc Provisions) Order 2005, SI 2005/2877 reg 2(2), Sch 3 para 36(2) with effect from 5 December 2005.

[2] Definitions of "a case", "clerk to the appeal tribunal", "the date of notification", "decision", "financially qualified panel member", "legally qualified panel member", "medically qualified panel member", "panel", "panel member", "panel member with a disability qualification", "penalty determination", "penalty proceedings" and "President" revoked, by the Tribunals, Courts and Enforcement Act 2007 (Transitional and Consequential Provisions) Order, SI 2008/2683 art 6(1), Sch 1 paras 204, 205 with effect from 3 November 2008.

2 Service of notices or documents

Where, by any provision of these Regulations—

(*a*) any notice or other document is required to be given or sent . . . [1] to the Board, that notice or document shall be treated as having been so given or sent on the day that it is received . . . [1] by the Board, and

(*b*) any notice or other document is required to be given or sent to any person other than . . . [1] the Board, that notice or document shall, if sent to that person's last known address, be treated as having been given or sent on the day that it was posted.

Amendments—[1] In sub-para (*a*), (*b*), words revoked by the Tribunals, Courts and Enforcement Act 2007 (Transitional and Consequential Provisions) Order, SI 2008/2683 art 6(1), Sch 1 paras 204, 206 with effect from 3 November 2008.

PART 2

GENERAL APPEAL MATTERS

3 Other persons with a right of appeal or a right to make an application for a direction

For the purposes of section 12(2) of the Act (as applied and modified by the Appeals Regulations), where—

(*a*) a person has made a claim for a tax credit but is unable for the time being to make an appeal against a decision in respect of that tax credit; or

(*b*) a person is the person in respect of whom an enquiry has been initiated under section 19(1) of the 2002 Act, but is unable for the time being to make an application for a direction,

the following other persons have a right of appeal to [the First-tier Tribunal][2] or a right to make an application for a direction—

(i) a receiver appointed by the Court of Protection with power to make a claim for a tax credit on behalf of the person;

(ii) in Scotland, a [judicial factor, or guardian acting or appointed under the Adults with Incapacity (Scotland) Act 2000 who has power to claim, or as the case may be, receive a tax credit on his behalf][1] who is administering the estate of the person;

(iii) a person appointed under regulation 33(1) of the Social Security (Claims and Payments) Regulations 1987 (persons unable to act);

(iv) where there is no person mentioned in sub-paragraph (iii) in relation to the person who is unable to act, a person who has applied in writing to the Board to be appointed to act on behalf of the person who is unable to act and, if a natural person, is aged 18 years or more and who has been so appointed by the Board for the purposes of this sub-paragraph.

Amendments—[1] Words substituted by the Social Security, Child Support and Tax Credits (Miscellaneous Amendments) Regulations, SI 2005/337 reg 4(1), (2) with effect from 18 March 2005.

[2] Words substituted by the Tribunals, Courts and Enforcement Act 2007 (Transitional and Consequential Provisions) Order, SI 2008/2683 art 6(1), Sch 1 paras 204, 207 with effect from 3 November 2008.

4 Time within which an appeal is to be brought

(1) Where a dispute arises as to whether an appeal was brought within the time limit specified in section 39(1) of the 2002 Act, the dispute shall be referred to, and be determined by, [the First-tier Tribunal][1].

(2) The time limit specified in section 39(1) of the 2002 Act may be extended in accordance with regulation 5.

Amendments—[1] Words substituted by the Tribunals, Courts and Enforcement Act 2007 (Transitional and Consequential Provisions) Order, SI 2008/2683 art 6(1), Sch 1 paras 204, 208 with effect from 3 November 2008.

5 Late appeals

(1) [The Board may treat a late appeal as made in time][1] where the conditions specified in paragraphs [(4)][1] to (8) are satisfied, but no appeal shall in any event be brought more than one year after the expiration of the last day for appealing under section 39(1) of the 2002 Act.

(2), (3) . . . [1]

[(4) An appeal may be treated as made in time if the Board is satisfied that it is in the interests of justice.][1]

(5) For the purposes of paragraph (4) it is not in the interests of justice to [treat the appeal as made in time unless the Board are][1] satisfied that—

(*a*) the special circumstances specified in paragraph (6) are relevant . . . [1]; or

(*b*) some other special circumstances exist which are wholly exceptional and relevant . . . [1],

Tax Credits

and as a result of those special circumstances, it was not practicable for the appeal to be made within the time limit specified in section 39(1) of the 2002 Act.

(6) For the purposes of paragraph (5)(*a*), the special circumstances are that—

(*a*) the applicant or a partner or dependant of the applicant has died or suffered serious illness;

(*b*) the [appellant][1] is not resident in the United Kingdom; or

(*c*) normal postal services were disrupted.

(7) In determining whether it is in the interests of justice to [treat the appeal as made in time][1], regard shall be had to the principle that the greater the amount of time that has elapsed between the expiration of the time within which the appeal is to be brought under section 39(1) of the 2002 Act and the [submission of the notice of appeal, the more compelling should be the special circumstances.][1]

(8) In determining whether it is in the interests of justice to [treat the appeal as made in time][1], no account shall be taken of the following—

(*a*) that the applicant or any person acting for him was unaware of or misunderstood the law applicable to his case (including ignorance or misunderstanding of the time limit imposed by section 39(1) of the 2002 Act); or

(*b*) that [the Upper Tribunal][1] or a court has taken a different view of the law from that previously understood and applied.

(9)–(11) [1]

Amendments—[1] In para (1), words substituted , reference substituted, paras (2), (3), (9)–(11) revoked, para (4) substituted, in para (5), words substituted and words revoked in both places, in paras (6) (7),(8) words substituted, by the Tribunals, Courts and Enforcement Act 2007 (Transitional and Consequential Provisions) Order, SI 2008/2683 art 6(1), Sch 1 paras 204, 209 with effect from 3 November 2008.

6 Making of an application for an extension of time

Amendments—Paras 6, 7, 9–27 revoked by the Tribunals, Courts and Enforcement Act 2007 (Transitional and Consequential Provisions) Order, SI 2008/2683 art 6(1), Sch 1 paras 204, 210 with effect from 3 November 2008.

7 Making an application for a direction

Amendments—Paras 6, 7, 9–27 revoked by the Tribunals, Courts and Enforcement Act 2007 (Transitional and Consequential Provisions) Order, SI 2008/2683 art 6(1), Sch 1 paras 204, 210 with effect from 3 November 2008.

8 Death of a party to an appeal or an application for a direction

(1) In any proceedings relating to an appeal or an application for a direction, on the death of a party to those proceedings (other than the Board) the following persons may proceed with the appeal or application for a direction in the place of such deceased party—

(*a*) where the proceedings are in relation to a single claim, the personal representatives of the person who has died;

(*b*) where the proceedings are in relation to a joint claim, where only one of the persons by whom the claim was made has died, the other person with whom the claim was made;

(*c*) where the proceedings are in relation to a joint claim where both the persons by whom the claim was made have died, the personal representatives of the last of them to die;

(*d*) for the purposes of paragraph (*c*), where persons have died in circumstances rendering it uncertain which of them survived the other—

(i) their deaths shall be presumed to have occurred in order of seniority; and

(ii) the younger shall be treated as having survived the elder.

(2) Where there is no person mentioned in paragraphs (1)(*a*) to (1)(*c*) to proceed with the appeal or application for a direction, the Board may appoint such person as they think fit to proceed with that appeal or that application in the place of such deceased party referred to in paragraph (1).

(3) A grant of probate, confirmation or letters of administration to the estate of the deceased party, whenever taken out, shall have no effect on an appointment made under paragraph (2).

(4) Where a person appointed under paragraph (2) has, prior to the date of such appointment, taken any action in relation to the appeal or application for a direction on behalf of the deceased party, the effective date of appointment by the Board shall be the day immediately prior to the first day on which such action was taken.

PART 3
APPEAL TRIBUNALS FOR TAX CREDITS

CHAPTER 1

APPEAL TRIBUNALS

9 Composition of appeal tribunals

Amendments—Paras 6, 7, 9–27 revoked by the Tribunals, Courts and Enforcement Act 2007 (Transitional and Consequential Provisions) Order, SI 2008/2683 art 6(1), Sch 1 paras 204, 210 with effect from 3 November 2008.

0 *Assignment of clerks to appeal tribunals: function of clerks*

mendments—Paras 6, 7, 9–27 revoked by the Tribunals, Courts and Enforcement Act 2007 (Transitional and Consequential Provisions) Order, SI 2008/2683 art 6(1), Sch 1 paras 204, 210 with effect from 3 November 2008.

CHAPTER 2

PROCEDURE IN CONNECTION WITH DETERMINATION OF APPEALS, APPLICATIONS FOR DIRECTIONS AND PENALTY PROCEEDINGS

1 *Consideration and determination of appeals, applications for a direction and enalty proceedings*

mendments—Paras 6, 7, 9–27 revoked by the Tribunals, Courts and Enforcement Act 2007 (Transitional and Consequential Provisions) Order, SI 2008/2683 art 6(1), Sch 1 paras 204, 210 with effect from 3 November 2008.

2 *Choice of hearing*

mendments—Paras 6, 7, 9–27 revoked by the Tribunals, Courts and Enforcement Act 2007 (Transitional and Consequential Provisions) Order, SI 2008/2683 art 6(1), Sch 1 paras 204, 210 with effect from 3 November 2008.

3 *Withdrawal of application for a direction or penalty proceedings*

mendments—Paras 6, 7, 9–27 revoked by the Tribunals, Courts and Enforcement Act 2007 (Transitional and Consequential Provisions) Order, SI 2008/2683 art 6(1), Sch 1 paras 204, 210 with effect from 3 November 2008.

4 *Non-disclosure of medical advice or evidence*

mendments—Paras 6, 7, 9–27 revoked by the Tribunals, Courts and Enforcement Act 2007 (Transitional and Consequential Provisions) Order, SI 2008/2683 art 6(1), Sch 1 paras 204, 210 with effect from 3 November 2008.

5 *Summoning of witnesses and administration of oaths*

mendments—Paras 6, 7, 9–27 revoked by the Tribunals, Courts and Enforcement Act 2007 (Transitional and Consequential Provisions) Order, SI 2008/2683 art 6(1), Sch 1 paras 204, 210 with effect from 3 November 2008.

CHAPTER 3

STRIKING OUT APPEALS AND APPLICATIONS FOR A DIRECTION

6 *Cases which may be struck out*

mendments—Paras 6, 7, 9–27 revoked by the Tribunals, Courts and Enforcement Act 2007 (Transitional and Consequential Provisions) Order, SI 2008/2683 art 6(1), Sch 1 paras 204, 210 with effect from 3 November 2008.

7 *Reinstatement of struck out cases*

mendments—Paras 6, 7, 9–27 revoked by the Tribunals, Courts and Enforcement Act 2007 (Transitional and Consequential Provisions) Order, SI 2008/2683 art 6(1), Sch 1 paras 204, 210 with effect from 3 November 2008.

CHAPTER 4

ORAL HEARINGS

18 *Procedure at oral hearings*

mendments—Paras 6, 7, 9–27 revoked by the Tribunals, Courts and Enforcement Act 2007 (Transitional and Consequential Provisions) Order, SI 2008/2683 art 6(1), Sch 1 paras 204, 210 with effect from 3 November 2008.

19 *Manner of providing expert assistance*

mendments—Paras 6, 7, 9–27 revoked by the Tribunals, Courts and Enforcement Act 2007 (Transitional and Consequential Provisions) Order, SI 2008/2683 art 6(1), Sch 1 paras 204, 210 with effect from 3 November 2008.

20 *Postponement and adjournment*

mendments—Paras 6, 7, 9–27 revoked by the Tribunals, Courts and Enforcement Act 2007 (Transitional and Consequential Provisions) Order, SI 2008/2683 art 6(1), Sch 1 paras 204, 210 with effect from 3 November 2008.

CHAPTER 5

DECISIONS OF APPEAL TRIBUNALS AND RELATED MATTERS

21 *Decisions of appeal tribunals*

Amendments—Paras 6, 7, 9–27 revoked by the Tribunals, Courts and Enforcement Act 2007 (Transitional and Consequential Provisions) Order, SI 2008/2683 art 6(1), Sch 1 paras 204, 210 with effect from 3 November 2008.

22 *Late applications for a statement of reasons of tribunal decision*

Amendments—Paras 6, 7, 9–27 revoked by the Tribunals, Courts and Enforcement Act 2007 (Transitional and Consequential Provisions) Order, SI 2008/2683 art 6(1), Sch 1 paras 204, 210 with effect from 3 November 2008.

23 *Record of tribunal proceedings*

Amendments—Paras 6, 7, 9–27 revoked by the Tribunals, Courts and Enforcement Act 2007 (Transitional and Consequential Provisions) Order, SI 2008/2683 art 6(1), Sch 1 paras 204, 210 with effect from 3 November 2008.

24 *Correction of accidental errors*

Amendments—Paras 6, 7, 9–27 revoked by the Tribunals, Courts and Enforcement Act 2007 (Transitional and Consequenti Provisions) Order, SI 2008/2683 art 6(1), Sch 1 paras 204, 210 with effect from 3 November 2008.

25 *Setting aside decisions on certain grounds*

Amendments—Paras 6, 7, 9–27 revoked by the Tribunals, Courts and Enforcement Act 2007 (Transitional and Consequenti Provisions) Order, SI 2008/2683 art 6(1), Sch 1 paras 204, 210 with effect from 3 November 2008.

26 *Provisions common to regulations 24 and 25*

Amendments—Paras 6, 7, 9–27 revoked by the Tribunals, Courts and Enforcement Act 2007 (Transitional and Consequenti Provisions) Order, SI 2008/2683 art 6(1), Sch 1 paras 204, 210 with effect from 3 November 2008.

26A *[Service of decision notice by electronic mail*

Amendments—Paras 6, 7, 9–27 revoked by the Tribunals, Courts and Enforcement Act 2007 (Transitional and Consequenti Provisions) Order, SI 2008/2683 art 6(1), Sch 1 paras 204, 210 with effect from 3 November 2008.

27 *Application for leave to appeal to a Commissioner from a decision of an appeal tribunal*

Amendments—Paras 6, 7, 9–27 revoked by the Tribunals, Courts and Enforcement Act 2007 (Transitional and Consequenti Provisions) Order, SI 2008/2683 art 6(1), Sch 1 paras 204, 210 with effect from 3 November 2008.

2002/3237

SOCIAL SECURITY COMMISSIONERS (PROCEDURE) (TAX CREDITS APPEALS) REGULATIONS 2002

Made by the Lord Chancellor under SSA 1998 ss 14, 15, 16, 28 39, 79(2) and 84, and Schs 4 and 5 and after consultation with the Council on Tribunals in accordance with section 8 of the Tribunals and Inquiries Act 1992

Made . . . . *18 December 2002*
Laid before Parliament . . . . *28 November 2002*
Coming into force . . . . *1 January 2003*

PART 1
GENERAL PROVISIONS

1 Citation, commencement and duration

(1) These Regulations may be cited as the Social Security Commissioners (Procedure) (Tax Credits Appeals) Regulations 2002 and shall come into force on 1st January 2003.

(2) These Regulations shall cease to have effect on such day as is appointed by order made under section 63(1) of the Tax Credits Act 2002 (tax credit appeals etc: temporary modifications).

2 Interpretation

In these Regulations, unless the context otherwise requires—

"the 1998 Act" means the Social Security Act 1998, as applied and modified by the Tax Credits (Appeals) Regulations 2002;

"the 2002 Act" means the Tax Credits Act 2002;

"appeal" means an appeal which by virtue of section 63 of the 2002 Act is from an appeal tribunal to a Social Security Commissioner;

"appeal tribunal" means an appeal tribunal constituted under Chapter 1 of Part 1 of the 1998 Act;

"authorised officer" means an officer authorised by the Lord Chancellor, or in Scotland by the Secretary of State, in accordance with paragraph 6 of Schedule 4 to the 1998 Act;

"chairman" means—

(i) the person who was the chairman or the sole member of the appeal tribunal which gave the decision against which leave to appeal is being sought; or

(ii) any other person authorised to deal with applications for leave to appeal to a Commissioner against that decision under section 14 of the 1998 Act;

["funding notice" means the notice or letter from the Legal Services Commission confirming that legal services are to be funded;][1]

"joint claimant" means a person making a claim under section 3(3)(*a*) of the 2002 Act;

["legal aid certificate" means the certificate issued by the Scottish Legal Aid Board confirming that legal services are to be funded;][1]

"legally qualified" means being a solicitor or barrister, or in Scotland, a solicitor or advocate;

["Legal Services Commission" means the Legal Services Commission established under section 1 of the Access to Justice Act 1999;][1]

["live television link" means a television link or other audio and video facilities which allow a person who is not physically present at an oral hearing to see and hear proceedings and be seen and heard by all others who are present (whether physically present or otherwise);][1]

"month" means a calendar month;
"office" means an Office of the Social Security Commissioners;
"party" means a party to the proceedings;
"penalty proceedings" means proceedings taken under Schedule 2 of the 2002 Act;
"proceedings" means any proceedings before a Commissioner, whether by way of an application for leave to appeal to, or from, a Commissioner, or by way of an appeal, or otherwise;
"respondent" means—

(i) any person or organisation other than the applicant or appellant who is one of the principal parties as defined in section 13 of the 1998 Act;

(ii) any other person taking part in the proceedings in accordance with section 14 of the 1998 Act or at the direction or with the leave of the Commissioner;

["Scottish Legal Aid Board" means the Scottish Legal Aid Board established under section 1 of the Legal Aid (Scotland) Act 1986;][1]
"summons", in relation to Scotland, corresponds to "citation" and regulation 20 shall be construed accordingly;
"tax credit" means a child tax credit or a working tax credit, construing those terms in accordance with section 1(1) and (2) of the 2002 Act.

Amendments—[1] Definitions inserted by the Social Security and Child Support Commissioners (Procedure) (Amendment) Regulations, SI 2005/207 reg 4(1), (3) with effect from 28 February 2005. However, this amendment ceases to have effect on such day as is appointed by order made under TCA 2002 s 63(1): SI 2005/207 reg 1.

3 General powers of a Commissioner

(1) Subject to the provisions of these Regulations, a Commissioner may adopt any procedure in relation to proceedings before him.

(2) A Commissioner may—

(*a*) extend or abridge any time limit under these Regulations (including, subject to regulations 7(3) and 11(2), granting an extension where the time limit has expired);

(*b*) expedite, postpone or adjourn any proceedings.

(3) Subject to paragraph (4), a Commissioner may, on or without the application of a party, strike out any proceedings for want of prosecution or abuse of process.

(4) Before making an order under paragraph (3), the Commissioner shall send notice to the party against whom it is proposed that it should be made giving him an opportunity to make representations why it should not be made.

(5) A Commissioner may, on application by the party concerned, give leave to reinstate any proceedings which have been struck out in accordance with paragraph (3) and, on giving leave, he may give directions as to the conduct of the proceedings.

(6) Nothing in these Regulations shall affect any power which is exercisable apart from these Regulations.

4 Transfer of proceedings between Commissioners

If it becomes impractical or inexpedient for a Commissioner to continue to deal with proceedings which are or have been before him, any other Commissioner may rehear or deal with those proceedings and any related matters.

5 Delegation of functions to authorised officers

(1) The following functions of the Commissioners may be exercised by legally qualified authorised officers, to be known as legal officers to the Commissioners—

(*a*) giving directions under regulations 6 and 16;

(*b*) determining requests for or directing hearings under regulation 18;

(*c*) summoning witnesses, and setting aside a summons made by a legal officer, under regulation 20;

(*d*) postponing a hearing under regulation 3;

(*e*) giving leave to withdraw or reinstate applications or appeals under regulation 21;

(*f*) waiving irregularities under regulation 22 in connection with any matter being dealt with by a legal officer;

(*g*) extending or abridging time, directing expedition, giving notices, striking out and reinstating proceedings under regulation 3.

(2) Any party may, within 14 days of being sent notice of the direction or order of a legal officer, make a written request to a Commissioner asking him to reconsider the matter and confirm or replace the direction or order with his own, but, unless ordered by a Commissioner, a request shall not stop proceedings under the direction or order.

6 Manner of and time for service of notices, etc

(1) A notice to or document for any party shall be deemed duly served if it is—

(*a*) delivered to him personally; or

(*b*) properly addressed and sent to him by prepaid post at the address last notified by him for this purpose, or to his ordinary address; or

[(*ba*) subject to paragraph (1A), sent by email; or][1]

Tax Credits

(*c*) served in any other manner a Commissioner may direct.

[(1A) A document may be served by email on any party if the recipient has informed the person sending the email in writing—

(*a*) that he is willing to accept service by email;

(*b*) of the email address to which the documents should be sent; and

(*c*) if the recipient wishes to so specify, the electronic format in which documents must be sent.][1]

(2) A notice to or other document for a Commissioner shall be[—

(*a*) delivered to the office in person;

(*b*) sent to the office by prepaid post;

(*c*) sent to the office by fax; or

(*d*) where the office has given written permission in advance, sent to the office by email][1].

(3) For the purposes of any time limit, a properly addressed notice or other document sent by prepaid post, fax or email is effective from the date it is sent.

Amendments—[1] Paras (1)(*ba*) and (1A) inserted, and words in para (2) substituted, by the Social Security and Child Support Commissioners (Procedure) (Amendment) Regulations, SI 2005/207 reg 4(1), (4) with effect from 28 February 2005. However, this amendment ceases to have effect on such day as is appointed by order made under TCA 2002 s 63(1): SI 2005/207 reg 1(2): SI 2005/207 reg 1.

6A [Funding of legal services

If a party is granted funding of legal services at any time, he shall—

(*a*) where funding is granted by the Legal Services Commission, send a copy of the funding notice to the office;

(*b*) where funding is granted by the Scottish Legal Aid Board, send a copy of the legal aid certificate to the office; and

(*c*) notify every other party that funding has been granted.][1]

Amendments—[1] This regulation inserted by the Social Security and Child Support Commissioners (Procedure) (Amendment) Regulations, SI 2005/207 reg 4(1), (5) with effect from 28 February 2005. However, this amendment ceases to have effect on such day as is appointed by order made under TCA 2002 s 63(1): SI 2005/207 reg 1(2).

PART 2

APPLICATIONS FOR LEAVE TO APPEAL AND APPEALS

6B [Application of this Part

In this Part

(*a*) regulations 7, 8 and 9 apply to appeals other than an appeal against a determination in penalty proceedings;

(*b*) regulations 10, 11 and 12 apply to all appeals.][1]

Amendments—[1] This regulation inserted by the Social Security and Child Support Commissioners (Procedure) (Amendment) Regulations, SI 2005/207 reg 4(1), (6) with effect from 28 February 2005. However, this amendment ceases to have effect on such day as is appointed by order made under TCA 2002 s 63(1): SI 2005/207 reg 1(2).

7 Application to a Commissioner for leave to appeal

(1) An application to a Commissioner for leave to appeal against the decision of an appeal tribunal may be made only where the applicant has sought to obtain leave from the chairman and leave has been refused or the application has been rejected.

(2) Subject to paragraph (3) an application to a Commissioner shall be made within one month of notice of the refusal or rejection being sent to the applicant by the appeal tribunal.

(3) A Commissioner may for special reasons accept a late application or an application where the applicant failed to seek leave from the chairman within the specified time, but did so on or before the final date.

(4) In paragraph (3) the final date means the end of a period of 13 months from the date on which the decision of the appeal tribunal or, if later, any separate statement of the reasons for it, was sent to the applicant by the appeal tribunal.

8 Notice of application to a Commissioner for leave to appeal

(1) An application to a Commissioner for leave to appeal shall be made by notice in writing, and shall contain—

(*a*) the name and address of the applicant;

(*b*) the grounds on which the applicant intends to rely;

(*c*) if the application is made late, the grounds for seeking late acceptance; and

(*d*) an address for sending notices and other documents to the applicant.

(2) The notice in paragraph (1) shall have with it copies of—

(*a*) the decision against which leave to appeal is sought;

(*b*) if separate, the written statement of the appeal tribunal's reasons for it; and

(*c*) the notice of refusal or rejection sent to the applicant by the appeal tribunal.

(3) Where an application for leave to appeal is made by the Board, they shall send each respondent a copy of the notice of application and any documents sent with it when they are sent to the Commissioner.

9 Determination of application

(1) The office shall send written notice to the applicant and each respondent of the determination of an application for leave to appeal to a Commissioner.

(2) Subject to a direction by a Commissioner, where a Commissioner grants leave to appeal under regulation 7—

(*a*) notice of appeal shall be deemed to have been sent on the date when notice of the determination is sent to the applicant; and

(*b*) the notice of application shall be deemed to be a notice of appeal sent under regulation 10.

(3) If a Commissioner grants an application for leave to appeal he may, with the consent of the applicant and each respondent, treat and determine the application as an appeal.

10 Notice of appeal

(1) Subject to regulation 9(2), an appeal shall be made by notice in writing and shall contain—

(*a*) the name and address of the appellant;

(*b*) [where applicable,][1] the date on which the appellant was notified that leave to appeal had been granted;

(*c*) the grounds on which the appellant intends to rely;

(*d*) if the appeal is made late, the grounds for seeking late acceptance; and

(*e*) an address for sending notices and other documents to the appellant.

(2) The notice in paragraph (1) shall have with it copies of—

(*a*) the notice informing the appellant that leave to appeal has been granted;

(*b*) the decision against which leave to appeal has been granted; and

(*c*) if separate, the written statement of the appeal tribunal's reasons for it.

Amendments—[1] Words in para (1)(*b*) inserted by the Social Security and Child Support Commissioners (Procedure) (Amendment) Regulations, SI 2005/207 reg 4(1), (7) with effect from 28 February 2005. However, this amendment ceases to have effect on such day as is appointed by order made under TCA 2002 s 63(1): SI 2005/207 reg 1(2).

[11 Time limit for appealing . . .

(1) In the case of an appeal against a determination in penalty proceedings, the notice of appeal shall not be valid unless it is sent to a Commissioner within one month of the decision of the appeal tribunal being sent to the applicant.

(2) For all other appeals, a notice of appeal shall not be valid unless it is sent to a Commissioner within one month of the date on which the appellant was sent written notice that leave to appeal had been granted.

(3) A Commissioner may for special reasons accept late notice of appeal.][1]

Amendments—[1] Words in cross-heading revoked, and regulation substituted, by the Social Security and Child Support Commissioners (Procedure) (Amendment) Regulations, SI 2005/207 reg 4(1), (8), (9) with effect from 28 February 2005. However, this amendment ceases to have effect on such day as is appointed by order made under TCA 2002 s 63(1): SI 2005/207 reg 1(2).

12 Acknowledgement of a notice of appeal and notification to each respondent

The office shall send—

(*a*) to the appellant, an acknowledgement of the receipt of the notice of appeal;

(*b*) to each respondent, a copy of the notice of appeal.

PART 3
PROCEDURE

13 Representation

A party may conduct his case himself (with assistance from any person if he wishes) or be represented by any person whom he may appoint for the purpose.

14 Respondent's written observations

(1) A respondent may submit to a Commissioner written observations on an appeal within one month of being sent written notice of it.

(2) Written observations shall include—

(*a*) the respondent's name and address and address for sending documents;

(*b*) a statement as to whether or not he opposes the appeal; and

(*c*) the grounds upon which the respondent proposes to rely.

(3) The office shall send a copy of any written observations from a respondent to every other party.

(4) Where there is more than one respondent, the order of and time for written observations shall be as directed by a Commissioner under regulation 16.

15 Written observations in reply

(1) Any party may submit to a Commissioner written observations in reply within one month of being sent written observations under regulation 14.

(2) The office shall send a copy of any written observations in reply to every other party.

(3) Where—

(*a*) written observations have been received under regulation 14; and (*b*) each of the principal parties expresses the view that the decision appealed against was erroneous in point of law;

a Commissioner may make an order under section 14(7) of the 1998 Act setting aside the decision and may dispense with the procedure in paragraphs (1) and (2).

16 Directions

(1) Subject to paragraph (2), where a Commissioner considers that an application or appeal made to him gives insufficient particulars to enable the question at issue to be determined, he may direct the party making the application or appeal, or any respondent, to furnish any further particulars which may be reasonably required.

(2) No person shall be compelled to give any evidence or produce any document or other material that he could not be compelled to give or produce on a trial of an action in a court of law in that part of Great Britain where the hearing takes place.

(3) A Commissioner may, before determining the application or appeal, direct the appeal tribunal to submit a statement of such facts or other matters as he considers necessary for the proper determination of that application or appeal.

(4) At any stage of the proceedings, a Commissioner may, on or without an application, give any directions as he may consider necessary or desirable for the efficient despatch of the proceedings.

(5) Without prejudice to regulations 14 and 15, or to paragraph (4), and subject to paragraph (2), a Commissioner may direct any party before him, to make any written observations as may seem to him necessary to enable the question at issue to be determined.

(6) An application under paragraph (4) shall be made in writing to a Commissioner and shall set out the direction which the applicant seeks.

(7) Unless a Commissioner shall otherwise determine, the office shall send a copy of an application under paragraph (4) to every other party.

17 Non-disclosure of medical evidence

(1) Where, in any proceedings, there is before a Commissioner medical evidence relating to a person which has not been disclosed to that person and in the opinion of the Commissioner the disclosure to that person of that evidence would be harmful to his health, such evidence shall not be disclosed to that person.

(2) Evidence such as is mentioned in paragraph (1)—

(*a*) shall not be disclosed to any person acting for or representing the person to whom it relates;

(*b*) shall not be disclosed to a joint claimant of the person to whom it relates or any person acting for or representing that joint claimant;

(*c*) in a case where a claim for a tax credit is made by reference to the disability of a person other than the claimant or joint claimant and the evidence relates to that other person, shall not be disclosed to the claimant, joint claimant or any person acting for or representing the claimant or joint claimant;

unless the Commissioner considers that it is in the interests of the person to whom the evidence relates to disclose it.

(3) Non-disclosure under paragraphs (1) or (2) does not preclude the Commissioner from taking the evidence concerned into account for the purpose of the proceedings.

18 Requests for hearings

(1) Subject to paragraphs (2), (3), (4) and (5), a Commissioner may determine any proceedings without a hearing.

(2) In appeals against a determination in penalty proceedings, where a request for a hearing is made by the party on whom the penalty has been imposed, a Commissioner shall grant the request.

(3) Where a request for a hearing is made by any party other than as provided by paragraph (2), a Commissioner shall grant the request unless he is satisfied that the proceedings can properly be determined without a hearing.

(4) Where a Commissioner refuses a request for a hearing, he shall send written notice to the person making the request, either before or at the same time as making his determination or decision.

(5) A Commissioner may, without an application and at any stage, direct a hearing.

19 Hearings

(1) This regulation applies to any hearing of an application or appeal to which these Regulations apply.

(2) Subject to paragraph (3), the office shall give reasonable notice of the time and place of any hearing before a Commissioner.

(3) Unless all the parties concerned agree to a hearing at shorter notice, the period of notice specified under paragraph (2) shall be at least 14 days before the date of the hearing.

(4) If any party to whom notice of a hearing has been sent fails to appear at the hearing, the Commissioner may proceed with the case in that party's absence, or may give directions with a view to the determination of the case.

(5) Any hearing before a Commissioner shall be in public, unless the Commissioner for special reasons directs otherwise.

(6) Where a Commissioner holds a hearing the following persons or organisations shall be entitled to be present and be heard—

(*a*) the person or organisation making the application or appeal;
(*b*) the claimant;
(*c*) the Board;
(*d*) a trade union, employers' association or other association which would have had a right of appeal under the 1998 Act;
(*e*) a person acting for another in making a claim for a tax credit, or acting for another in making an application for a direction under section 19(9) of the 2002 Act;
(*f*) a person acting for another in giving notification of a change of circumstances;
(*g*) a person acting for another in response to a notice given under section 17 of the 2002 Act; and
(*h*) with the leave of the Commissioner, any other person.

[(6A) Subject to the direction of a Commissioner—

(*a*) any person or organisation entitled to be present and be heard at a hearing; and
(*b*) any representatives of such a person or organisation,

may be present by means of a live television link.][1]

[(6B) Any provision in these Regulations which refers to a party or representative being present is satisfied if the party or representative is present by means of a live television link.][1]

(7) Any person entitled to be heard at a hearing may address the Commissioner and—

(*a*) in the case of an appeal against a determination in penalty proceedings, the party on whom the penalty has been imposed may give evidence, call witnesses and put questions directly to any other person called as a witness;
(*b*) in all other cases, a person entitled to be heard may with the leave of the Commissioner, give evidence, call witnesses and put questions directly to any other person called as a witness.

(8) Nothing in these Regulations shall prevent a member of the Council on Tribunals or of the Scottish Committee of the Council in his capacity as such from being present at a hearing before a Commissioner which is not held in public.

Amendments—[1] Paras (6A), (6B) substituted by the Social Security and Child Support Commissioners (Procedure) (Amendment) Regulations, SI 2005/207 reg 4(1), (10) with effect from 28 February 2005. However, this amendment ceases to have effect on such day as is appointed by order made under TCA 2002 s 63(1): SI 2005/207 reg 1(2).

20 Summoning of witnesses

(1) Subject to paragraph (2), a Commissioner may summon any person to attend a hearing as a witness, at such time and place as may be specified in the summons, to answer any questions or produce any documents in his custody or under his control which relate to any matter in question in the proceedings.

(2) A person shall not be required to attend in obedience to a summons under paragraph (1) unless he has been given at least 14 days' notice before the date of the hearing or, if less than 14 days, has informed the Commissioner that he accepts such notice as he has been given.

(3) Upon the application of a person summoned under this regulation, a Commissioner may set the summons aside.

(4) A Commissioner may require any witness to give evidence on oath and for this purpose an oath may be administered in due form.

21 Withdrawal of applications for leave to appeal and appeals

(1) At any time before it is determined, an applicant may withdraw an application to a Commissioner for leave to appeal against a decision of an appeal tribunal by giving written notice to a Commissioner.

(2) At any time before the decision is made, the appellant may withdraw his appeal with the leave of a Commissioner.

(3) A Commissioner may, on application by the party concerned, give leave to reinstate any application or appeal which has been withdrawn in accordance with paragraphs (1) and (2) and, on giving leave, he may make directions as to the conduct of the proceedings.

22 Irregularities

Any irregularity resulting from failure to comply with the requirements of these Regulations shall not by itself invalidate any proceedings, and the Commissioner, before reaching his decision, may waive the irregularity or take steps to remedy it.

PART 4
DECISIONS

23 Determinations and decisions of a Commissioner

(1) The determination of a Commissioner on an application for leave to appeal shall be in writing and signed by him.

Tax Credits

(2) The decision of a Commissioner on an appeal shall be in writing and signed by him and, unless it was a decision made with the consent of the parties or an order setting aside a tribunal's decision under section 14(7) of the 1998 Act, he shall include the reasons.

(3) The office shall send a copy of the determination or decision and any reasons to each party.

(4) Without prejudice to paragraphs (2) and (3), a Commissioner may announce his determination or decision at the end of a hearing.

24 Correction of accidental errors in decisions

(1) Subject to regulations 4 and 26, the Commissioner who gave the decision may at any time correct accidental errors in any decision or record of a decision.

(2) A correction made to, or to the record of, a decision shall become part of the decision or record and the office shall send a written notice of the correction to any party to whom notice of the decision has been sent.

25 Setting aside decisions on certain grounds

(1) Subject to regulations 4 and 26, on an application made by any party, the Commissioner who gave the decision in proceedings may set it aside where it appears just to do so on the ground that—

(*a*) a document relating to the proceedings was not sent to, or was not received at an appropriate time by, a party or his representative or was not received at an appropriate time by the Commissioner; or

(*b*) a party or his representative was not present at a hearing before the Commissioner.

(2) An application under this regulation shall be made in writing to a Commissioner within one month from the date on which the office gave written notice of the decision to the party making the application.

(3) Unless the Commissioner considers that it is unnecessary for the proper determination of an application made under paragraph (1), the office shall send a copy of it to each respondent, who shall be given a reasonable opportunity to make representations on it.

(4) The office shall send each party written notice of a determination of an application to set aside a decision and the reasons for it.

26 Provisions common to regulations 24 and 25

(1) In regulations 24 and 25, the word "decision" shall include determinations of applications for leave to appeal, orders setting aside tribunal decisions under section 14(7) of the 1998 Act and decisions on appeals.

(2) There shall be no appeal against a correction or a refusal to correct under regulation 24 or a determination given under regulation 25.

PART 5

APPLICATIONS FOR LEAVE TO APPEAL TO THE APPELLATE COURT

27 Application to a Commissioner for leave to appeal to the Appellate Court

(1) Subject to paragraph (2), an application to a Commissioner under section 15 of the 1998 Act for leave to appeal against a decision of a Commissioner shall be made in writing, stating the grounds of the application, within three months from the date on which the applicant was sent written notice of the decision.

[(2) Where—

(*a*) any decision or record of a decision is corrected under regulation 24; or

(*b*) an application for a decision to be set aside under regulation 25 is refused for reasons other than that the application was made outside the period specified in regulation 25(2),

the period specified in paragraph (1) shall run from the date on which written notice of the correction or refusal of the application to set aside is sent to the applicant.][1]

(3) A person who under regulation 18 of the Tax Credits (Claims and Notifications) Regulations 2002 may act for another in making a claim for a tax credit is authorised for the purposes of section 15 of the 1998 Act to apply for leave to appeal against the decision of a Commissioner.

(4) Regulations 21(1) and 21(3) shall apply to an application to a Commissioner for leave to appeal from a Commissioner's decision as they apply to the proceedings in that regulation.

Amendments—[1] Para (2) substituted by the Social Security and Child Support Commissioners (Procedure) (Amendment) Regulations, SI 2005/207 reg 4(1), (11) with effect from 28 February 2005. However, this amendment ceases to have effect on such day as is appointed by order made under TCA 2002 s 63(1): SI 2005/207 reg 1(2).

2003/123

TAX CREDITS (INTEREST RATE) REGULATIONS 2003

Made by the Treasury under TCA 2002 ss 37(2), (5), 65(1), (8) and 67

Made . . . . *28 January 2003*
Laid before Parliament . . . . *28 January 2003*
Coming into force . . . . *18 February 2003*

1 Citation and commencement
These Regulations may be cited as the Tax Credits (Interest Rate) Regulations 2003 and shall come into force on 18th February 2003.

2 Interpretation
(1) In these Regulations—

"the Board" means the Commissioners of Inland Revenue;

"established rate" means—

(*a*) on the coming into force of these Regulations, 6.5 per cent. per annum;

(*b*) in relation to any date after the first reference date after the coming into force of these Regulations, the reference rate found on the immediately preceding reference date;

"operative date" means the sixth day of each month;

"reference date" means the day of each month which is the twelfth working day before the sixth day of the following month;

"tax credit" means child tax credit or, as the case may be, working tax credit, provision for which is made by the Tax Credits Act 2002;

"working day" means any day other than a non-business day within the meaning of section 92 of the Bills of Exchange Act 1882.

(2) For the purposes of regulation 4(2) the reference rate found on a reference date is the percentage per annum found by averaging the base lending rates at close of business on that date of—

(*a*) Bank of Scotland;
(*b*) Barclays Bank plc;
(*c*) Lloyds Bank plc;
(*d*) HSBC Bank plc;
(*e*) National Westminster Bank plc;
(*f*) The Royal Bank of Scotland plc,

and, if the result is not a whole number, rounding the result to the nearest such number, with any result midway between two whole numbers rounded down.

3 Interest on overpayments of tax credit and penalties
(1) Where the Board decide in accordance with section 37(1) of the Tax Credits Act 2002 that the whole or part of an overpayment of a tax credit which is attributable to fraud or neglect is to carry interest, the rate of interest for the purposes of section 37(2) of that Act is that prescribed by regulation 4.
(2) The rate of interest for the purposes of section 37(5) of the Tax Credits Act 2002 (interest on a penalty under any of sections 31 to 33 of that Act) is that prescribed by regulation 4.

4 Prescribed rate of interest
(1) The rate of interest which is prescribed is, subject to paragraph (2), 6.5 per cent per annum.
(2) Where, on a reference date after the coming into force of these Regulations, the reference rate found on that date ("RR") differs from the established rate, the rate of interest which is prescribed shall, on and after the next operative date, be the percentage per annum found by applying the formula—

$$RR + 2.5$$

2003/463

TAX CREDITS (APPROVAL OF HOME CHILD CARE PROVIDERS) SCHEME 2003

Made by the Secretary of State for Education and Skills under TCA 2002 ss 12(5)–(8) and 65(9), and after consultation with the Council of Tribunals in accordance with section 8(1) of the Tribunals and Inquiries Act 1992

Made . . . . .25 February 2003
Laid before Parliament . . . . .4 March 2003
Coming into force:
All articles (except for articles 17 to 20) . . . . .25 March 2003
Articles 17 to 20 . . . . .1 April 2003

Revocation—This Scheme revoked by the Tax Credits (Approval of Child Care Providers) Scheme, SI 2005/93 reg 13 with effect from 6 April 2005. However, any approval granted to any child care provider under this Scheme and which is in force on that date shall continue to have effect in respect of that provider under this Scheme until whichever is the earliest of—

(a) the date on which the approval is withdrawn or suspended in accordance with this Scheme;

(b) the date on which the child care provider concerned is given an approval by the approval body pursuant to the Tax Credits (Approval of Child Care Providers) Scheme, SI 2005/93 art 6; or

(c) 31 December 2005: SI 2005/93 reg 13(2), (3).

SCHEDULE 1

MATTERS TO BE ADDRESSED BY APPROVAL CRITERIA

Article 8

(1) The suitability of the child care provider to look after children.
(2) Working in partnership with parents.
(3) Acting with integrity and maintaining confidentiality.
(4) Organisational skills.
(5) Awareness of care, learning and play.
(6) Health, safety and welfare of children.
(7) Equal opportunities.
(8) Special needs.
(9) Managing behaviour.
(10) Child protection.
(11) Keeping of records.

2003/653

TAX CREDITS (IMMIGRATION) REGULATIONS 2003

Made by the Treasury under TCA 2002 ss 42, 65(1), (3), (7) and (9)

Made . . . . *11 March 2003*
Laid before Parliament . . . . *11 March 2003*
Coming into force . . . . *6 April 2003*

1 Citation and commencement

These Regulations may be cited as the Tax Credits (Immigration) Regulations 2003 and shall come into force on 6th April 2003.

Commentary—*Simon's Taxes* **E2.203.**
HMRC Manuals—Tax Credit Technical Manual TCTM2101–2106 (entitlement: immigration rules).

2 Interpretation

In these Regulations–

"the Act" means the Tax Credits Act 2002;

"the Child Tax Credit Regulations" means the Child Tax Credit Regulations 2002;

["couple" has the meaning given by section 3(5A) of the Act;][1]

"immigration rules" has the meaning given by section 33 of the Immigration Act 1971;

"joint claim" has the meaning given by section 3(8) of the Act;

"limited leave" has the meaning given by section 33 of the Immigration Act 1971;

. . .[1]

"person subject to immigration control" has the meaning in section 115(9) of the Immigration and Asylum Act 1999;

"refugee" means a person who has been recorded by the Secretary of State as a refugee within the definition in Article 1 of the Convention relating to the Status of Refugees done at Geneva on 28th July 1951 as extended by Article 1(2) of the Protocol relating to the Status of Refugees done at New York on 31st January 1967;

"tax credit" refers to either child tax credit or working tax credit and references to tax credits are to both of them;

"the Working Tax Credit Regulations" means the Working Tax Credit (Entitlement and Maximum Rate) Regulations 2002.

Modifications—Tax Credits (Polygamous Marriages) Regulations, SI 2003/742 regs 53, 54 (definition of "joint claim" substituted, and definition of "polygamous unit" inserted, for the purposes of polygamous marriages).

Amendments—[1] Definition of "couple" inserted, and definitions of "married couple" and "unmarried couple" revoked, by the Civil Partnership Act 2004 (Tax Credits, etc) (Consequential Amendments) Order, SI 2005/2919 art 7(1), (2) with effect from 5 December 2005.

3 Exclusion of persons subject to immigration control from entitlement to tax credits

(1) No person is entitled to child tax credit or working tax credit while he is a person subject to immigration control, except in the following Cases, and subject to paragraphs (2) to (9).

Case 1

He is a person who–

(*a*) has been given leave to enter, or remain in, the United Kingdom by the Secretary of State upon the undertaking of another person or persons, pursuant to the immigration rules, to be responsible for his maintenance and accommodation, and

(*b*) has been resident in the United Kingdom for a period of at least 5 years commencing on or after the date of his entry into the United Kingdom, or the date on which the undertaking was given in respect of him, whichever is the later.

Case 2

He is a person who—

(*a*) falls within the terms of paragraph (a) of Case 1, and

(*b*) has been resident in the United Kingdom for less than the 5 years mentioned in paragraph (b) of Case 1, but the person giving the undertaking has died or, where the undertaking was given by more than one person, they have all died.

. . . [3]

Case 4

Where the claim is for working tax credit, he is—

(*a*) a national of a state which has ratified the European Convention on Social and Medical Assistance (done in Paris on 11th December 1953) or of a state which has ratified the Council of Europe Social Charter (signed in Turin on 18th October 1961), and

(*b*) lawfully present in the United Kingdom.

The Case so described also applies where—

(*a*) the claim is for child tax credit,

(*b*) the award of child tax credit would be made on or after 6th April 2004, and

(*c*) immediately before the award is made (and as part of the transition of claimants entitled to elements of income support and income-based jobseeker's allowance, to child tax credit) the person is, or will on the making of a claim be, entitled to any of the amounts in relation to income support or income-based jobseeker's allowance which are described in section 1(3)(*d*) of the Act.

Case 5

Where the claim is for child tax credit, he is—

(*a*) a person who is lawfully working in the United Kingdom, and

(*b*) a national of a State with which the Community has concluded an Agreement under Article 310 of the Treaty of Amsterdam amending the Treaty on European Union, the Treaties establishing the European Communities and certain related Acts providing, in the field of social security, for the equal treatment of workers who are nationals of the signatory State and their families.

(2) Where one member of a . . . [1] couple is a person subject to immigration control, and the other member is not or is within any of Cases 1 to 5 or regulation 5—

(*a*) the calculation of the amount of tax credit under the Act, the Child Tax Credit Regulations and the Working Tax Credit Regulations (including any second adult element or other element in respect of, or determined by reference to, that person),

(*b*) the method of making (or proceeding with) a joint claim by the couple, and

(*c*) the method of payment of the tax credit, shall, subject to paragraph (3), be determined in the same way as if that person were not subject to such control.

(3) Where the other member is within Case 4 or 5 or regulation 5, paragraph (2) shall only apply to the tax credit to which he (in accordance with those provisions) is entitled.

(4) Where a person has submitted a claim for asylum as a refugee and in consequence is a person subject to immigration control, in the first instance he is not entitled to tax credits, subject to paragraphs (5) to (9).

(5) If that person—

(*a*) is notified that he has been recorded by the Secretary of State as a refugee, and

(*b*) claims tax credit within [one month][2] of receiving that notification, paragraphs (6) to (9) and regulation 4 shall apply to him.

(6) He shall be treated as having claimed tax credits—

(*a*) on the date when he submitted his claim for asylum, and

(*b*) on every 6th April (if any) intervening between the date in sub-paragraph (a) and the date of the claim referred to in paragraph (5)(*b*), rather than on the date on which he makes the claim referred to in paragraph (5)(*b*).

(7) [Regulations 7, 7A and 8][4] of the Tax Credits (Claims and Notifications) Regulations 2002 shall not apply to claims treated as made by virtue of paragraph (6).

(8) He shall have his claims for tax credits determined as if he had been recorded as a refugee on the date when he submitted his claim for asylum.

(9) The amount of support provided under—

(*a*) section 95 or 98 of the Immigration and Asylum Act 1999,

(*b*) regulations made under Schedule 9 to that Act, by the Secretary of State in respect of essential living needs of the claimant and his dependants (if any), or (*c*) regulations made under paragraph 3 of Schedule 8 to that Act, (after allowing for any deduction for that amount under regulation 21ZB(3) of the Income Support (General) Regulations 1987) shall be deducted from any award of tax credits due to the claimant by virtue of paragraphs (6) and (8).

HMRC Manuals—Tax Credit Technical Manual TCTM2103 (reg 3 excludes from entitlement to tax credits, subject to certain exceptions, persons whose right to remain in the UK is subject to a limitation or restrictions. This includes persons "subject to immigration control" within the meaning of the Immigration and Asylum Act 1999 s 115).

TCTM2104 (exceptions to the general exclusion).

TCTM2105 (reg 3(4)–(8): treatment of refugees).

TCTM2106 (reg 3(2), (3): treatment of family members).

Modifications—Tax Credits (Polygamous Marriages) Regulations, SI 2003/742 regs 53, 55 (modification of reg (2) above for the purposes of polygamous marriages).

Amendments—[1] Words in para (2) revoked by the Civil Partnership Act 2004 (Tax Credits, etc) (Consequential Amendments) Order, SI 2005/2919 art 7(1), (3) with effect from 5 December 2005.

[2] In para (5)(*b*), words substituted by the Tax Credit (Miscellaneous Amendments) Regulations, SI 2012/848 regs 1(2), 7 with effect from 6 April 2012.

[3] In para (1), entry for "Case 3" revoked by the Tax Credits (Miscellaneous Amendments) Regulations, SI 2014/658 reg 3 with effect from 6 April 2014.

[4] In para (7), words substituted by the Tax Credits (Claims and Notifications) (Amendment) Regulations, SI 2015/669 reg 5 with effect from 6 April 2015.

4 Modifications of Part 1 of the Act for refugees whose asylum claims have been accepted

(1) For the purposes of claims falling within paragraph (2), Part 1 of the Act shall apply subject to the modifications set out in paragraphs (3) to (5).

(2) A claim falls within this paragraph if it is a claim for tax credits which a person is treated as having made by virtue of regulation 3(6), other than a claim which he is treated as having made in the tax year in which he made his claim under regulation 3(5).

(3) Omit sections 14 to 17 (initial decisions, revised decisions and final notices).

(4) In section 18 (decisions after final notices)—

(*a*) in subsection (1) for "After giving a notice under section 17" substitute "In relation to each claim for a tax credit made by a person or persons for the whole or part of a tax year";

(*b*) omit subsections (2) to (9);

(*c*) for subsection (10) substitute—

"(10) Before making their decision the Board may by notice—

(*a*) require the person, or either or both of the persons, by whom the claim is made to provide any information or evidence which the Board consider they may need for making their decision, or

(*b*) require any person of a prescribed description to provide any information or evidence of a prescribed description which the Board consider they may need for that purpose,

by the date specified in the notice.";

(*d*) in subsection (11) omit—

(i) "any revision under subsection (5) or (9) and";

(ii) paragraph (*a*);

(iii) in paragraph (*b*), "in any other case,".

(5) In section 19 (enquiries)—

(*a*) in subsection (4), for paragraphs (*a*) and (*b*) substitute

"one year after that decision or, if—

(*a*) the person, or either of the persons, to whom the enquiry relates is required by section 8 of the Taxes Management Act 1970 to make a return, and

(*b*) the return becomes final on a day more than one year after that decision,

with that day (or, if both of the persons are so required and their returns become final on different days, with the later of those days).";

(*b*) in subsection (5) omit paragraph (*a*) and, in paragraph (*b*) "in any other case,";

(*c*) omit subsection (6).

HMRC Manuals—Tax Credit Technical Manual TCTM2105 (if a person is granted refugee status, there are limited cases where tax credits may be claimed for the period beginning with the date he first submitted his claim for asylum).

Modifications—Tax Credits (Polygamous Marriages) Regulations, SI 2003/742 regs 53, 56 (modification of reg (1) above for the purposes of polygamous marriages).

5 Transitional relief – claimants moving from income support and income-based jobseeker's allowance to child tax credit

In relation to child tax credit, a person is not treated for the purposes of these Regulations as subject to immigration control where—

(*a*) the award of child tax credit would be made on or after 6th April 2004;

(*b*) immediately before the award of child tax credit is made, he is, or will on the making of a claim be, entitled to any of the amounts in relation to income support or income-based jobseeker's allowance which are described in section 1(3)(*d*) of the Act; and

(*c*) he is a person who, immediately before the award of child tax credit is made —

(i) was receiving or entitled to income support by virtue of regulation 12(1) of the Social Security (Persons From Abroad) Miscellaneous Amendments Regulations 1996, and his claim for asylum has not been recorded by the Secretary of State as having been decided (other than on appeal) or abandoned; or

(ii) was receiving or entitled to income support or income-based jobseeker's allowance by virtue of regulation 12(3) of the Social Security (Immigration and Asylum) Consequential Amendments Regulations 2000, and his claim for asylum has not been so recorded as having been decided (other than on appeal) or abandoned.

HMRC Manuals—Tax Credit Technical Manual TCTM2104 (transitional rules).

2003/654

TAX CREDITS (RESIDENCE) REGULATIONS 2003

Made by the Treasury under TCA 2002 ss 3(7), 65(1), (7) and (9)

Made . . . .*11 March 2003*
Laid before Parliament . . . .*11 March 2003*
Coming into force . . . .*6 April 2003*

1 Citation and commencement

These Regulations may be cited as the Tax Credits (Residence) Regulations 2003 and shall come into force on 6th April 2003.

Commentary—*Simon's Taxes* **E2.203.**
HMRC Manuals—Tax Credit Technical Manual TCTM2002–2008 (entitlement: residence rules).

2 Interpretation

(1) In these Regulations—

"the Act" means the Tax Credits Act 2002;
"child" has the same meaning as it has in the Child Tax Credit Regulations 2002;
["couple" has the meaning given by section 3(5A) of the Act;][1]
"Crown servant posted overseas" has the meaning given in regulation 5(2);
"partner" means where a person is a member of a . . . [1] couple, the other member of that couple;
"qualifying young person" has the meaning given in regulation 2, read with regulation 5, of the Child Tax Credit Regulations 2002;
"relative" means brother, sister, ancestor or lineal descendant.

(2) In these Regulations a person is responsible for a child or qualifying young person if he is treated as being responsible for that child or qualifying young person in accordance with the rules contained in regulation 3 of the Child Tax Credit Regulations 2002.

Commentary—*Simon's Taxes* **E2.203.**
Modifications—Tax Credits (Polygamous Marriages) Regulations, SI 2003/742 regs 51, 52 (words in definition of "partner" substituted, and definition of "polygamous unit" inserted, for the purposes of polygamous marriages).
Amendments—[1] Definition of "couple" inserted, and words in the definition of "partner" revoked, by the Civil Partnership Act 2004 (Tax Credits, etc) (Consequential Amendments) Order, SI 2005/2919 art 8 with effect from 5 December 2005.

3 Circumstances in which a person is treated as not being in the United Kingdom

(1) A person shall be treated as not being in the United Kingdom for the purposes of Part 1 of the Act if he is not ordinarily resident in the United Kingdom.
(2) [Paragraphs (1) and (6) do][5] not apply to a Crown servant posted overseas or his partner.
(3) A person who is in the United Kingdom as a result of his deportation, expulsion or other removal by compulsion of law from another country to the United Kingdom shall be treated as being ordinarily resident in the United Kingdom [and paragraph (6) shall not apply][5].
(4) For the purposes of working tax credit, a person shall be treated as being ordinarily resident if he is exercising in the United Kingdom his rights as a worker pursuant to [Parliament and Council Regulation (EU) No 492/2011][3] or he is a person with a right to reside in the United Kingdom pursuant to [Council Directive No 2004/38/EC][2].
[(5) A person shall be treated as not being in the United Kingdom for the purposes of Part 1 of the Act where he—

(*a*) makes a claim for child tax credit (other than being treated as making a claim under regulation 11 or 12 of the Tax Credits (Claims and Notifications) Regulations 2002 or otherwise), on or after 1st May 2004; and

(*b*)

(i) does not have a right to reside in the United Kingdom; or

Tax Credits

(ii) has a right to reside in the United Kingdom under—

regulation 15A(1) of the Immigration (European Economic Area) Regulations 2006, but only in a case where the right exists under that regulation because the person satisfies the criteria in regulation 15A(4A) of those Regulations; or

Article 20 of the Treaty on the Functioning of the European Union (in a case where the right to reside arises because a British citizen would otherwise be deprived of the genuine enjoyment of the substance of their rights as a European Union citizen)][4].][1]

[(6) Subject to paragraph (7), a person is to be treated as being in the United Kingdom for the purposes of Part 1 of the Act where he makes a claim for child tax credit only if that person has been living in the United Kingdom for 3 months before that claim plus any time taken into account by regulation 7 of the Tax Credits (Claims and Notifications) Regulations 2002 for determining for the purpose of that regulation when the claim is treated as having been made.

(7) Paragraph (6) shall not apply where the person—

(*a*) most recently entered the United Kingdom before 1st July 2014;

(*b*) is a worker or a self-employed person in the United Kingdom for the purposes of Council Directive 2004/38/EC (rights of citizens of the European Union and their family members to move and reside freely within the territory of the Member States);

(*c*) retains the status of a worker or self-employed person in the United Kingdom pursuant to Article 7(3) of Council Directive 2004/38/EC;

(*d*) is treated as a worker in the United Kingdom pursuant to regulation 5 of the Accession of Croatia (Immigration and Worker Authorisation) Regulations 2013 (right of residence of a Croatian who is an "accession State national subject to worker authorisation");

(*e*) is a family member of a person referred to in sub-paragraphs (*b*), (*c*), (*d*) or (*i*);

(*f*) is a person to whom regulation 4 applies (persons temporarily absent from the United Kingdom) and who returns to the United Kingdom within 52 weeks starting from the first day of the temporary absence;

(*g*) returns to the United Kingdom after a period abroad of less than 52 weeks where immediately before departing from the United Kingdom that person had been ordinarily resident in the United Kingdom for a continuous period of 3 months;

(*h*) returns to the United Kingdom otherwise as a worker or self-employed person after a period abroad and where, otherwise than for a period of up to 3 months ending on the day of returning, that person has paid either Class 1 or Class 2 contributions pursuant to regulation 114, 118, 146 or 147 of the Social Security (Contributions) Regulations 2001 or pursuant to an Order in Council having effect under section 179 of the Social Security Administration Act 1992;

(*i*) is not a national of an EEA State and would be a worker or self-employed person in the United Kingdom for the purposes of Council Directive 2004/38/EC if that person were a national of an EEA State;

(*j*) is a refugee as defined in Article 1 of the Convention relating to the Status of Refugees done at Geneva on 28th July 1951, as extended by Article 1(2) of the Protocol relating to the Status of Refugees done at New York on 31st January 1967;

(*k*) has been granted leave, or is deemed to have been granted leave, outside the rules made under section 3(2) of the Immigration Act 1971 where that leave is—

(i) granted by the Secretary of State with recourse to public funds, or

(i) deemed to have been granted by virtue of regulation 3 of the Displaced Persons (Temporary Protection) Regulations 2005;

(*l*) has been granted leave to remain in the United Kingdom by the Secretary of State pending an application for indefinite leave to remain as a victim of domestic violence;

(*m*) has been granted humanitarian protection by the Secretary of State under Rule 339C of Part 11 of the rules made under section 3(2) of the Immigration Act 1971.

(8) In this regulation, a "family member" means a person who is defined as a family member of another person in Article 2 of Council Directive 2004/38/EC.

(9) In this regulation, "EEA State", in relation to any time, means a state which at that time is a member State, or any other state which at that time is a party to the agreement on the European Economic Area signed at Oporto on 2nd May, together with the Protocol adjusting that Agreement signed at Brussels on 17th March 1993, as modified or supplemented from time to time.][5]

Commentary—*Simon's Taxes* **E2.203.**

HMRC Manuals—Tax Credit Technical Manual TCTM2007 (reg 3(4) above: entitlement in respect of people with rights under Community law).

Modifications—Universal Credit (Transitional Provisions) Regulations, SI 2013/386 reg 17(1), (2), Schedule paras 45, 46 (modification of this regulation in respect of awards of universal credit and terminations of awards of tax credit in the same year).

Amendments—[1] Para (5) inserted by the Tax Credits (Residence) (Amendment) Regulations, SI 2004/1243 with effect from 1 May 2004. SI 2004/1243 was expressed to cease to have effect on 1 May 2006, unless revoked with effect from an earlier date: SI 2004/1243 reg 1. SI 2004/1423 reg 1(2) has been revoked by the Tax Credits (Miscellaneous Amendments) Regulations, SI 2006/766 reg 5 with effect from 6 April 2006. The effect is that para (5) as inserted does not lapse on 1 May 2006.

2 Words in para (4) substituted by the Tax Credits (Miscellaneous Amendments) Regulations, SI 2006/766 reg 4 with effect from 6 April 2006.

3 Words in para (4) substituted by the Tax Credits (Miscellaneous Amendments) Regulations, SI 2012/848 regs 1(2), 8 with effect from 6 April 2012.

4 Para (5)(*b*) substituted by the Child Benefit and Child Tax Credit (Miscellaneous Amendments) Regulations, SI 2012/2612 regs 5, 6 with effect from 8 November 2012.

5 In para (2), words substituted, in para (3), words inserted, and paras (6)–(9) inserted by the Child Benefit (General) and the Tax Credits (Residence) (Amendment) Regulations, SI 2014/1511 regs 5, 6 with effect from 1 July 2014.

4 Persons temporarily absent from the United Kingdom

(1) A person who is ordinarily resident in the United Kingdom and is temporarily absent from the United Kingdom shall be treated as being in the United Kingdom during the first—

(*a*) 8 weeks of any period of absence; or

(*b*) 12 weeks of any period of absence where that period of absence, or any extension to that period of absence, is in connection with—

(i) the treatment of his illness or physical or mental disability;

(ii) the treatment of his partner's illness or physical or mental disability;

(iii) the death of a person who, immediately prior to the date of death, was his partner;

(iv) the death, or the treatment of the illness or physical or mental disability, of a child or qualifying young person for whom either he or his partner is, or both of them are, responsible; or

(v) the death, or the treatment of the illness or physical or mental disability, of his or his partner's relative.

(2) A person is temporarily absent from the United Kingdom if at the beginning of the period of absence his absence is unlikely to exceed 52 weeks.

Commentary—*Simon's Taxes* **E2.203.**

HMRC Manuals—Tax Credit Technical Manual TCTM2004 (for the extension to 12 weeks in reg 4(*b*) to apply, the absence, or its extension, must be **in connection** with the death or with the treatment of an illness or disability. It is not enough for the two things simply to coincide. Where the extended absence coincides with the death of someone's child, partner or relative, the Revenue normally accept that the two are connected).

Modification—See SI 2003/654 reg 6 (modification of this regulation in relation to partners of Crown servants posted overseas).

5 Crown servants posted overseas

(1) A Crown servant posted overseas shall be treated as being in the United Kingdom.

(2) A Crown servant posted overseas is a person performing overseas the duties of any office or employment under the Crown in right of the United Kingdom —

(*a*) who is, or was, immediately prior to his posting or his first of consecutive postings, ordinarily resident in the United Kingdom; or

(*b*) who, immediately prior to his posting or his first of consecutive postings, was in the United Kingdom in connection with that posting.

Commentary—*Simon's Taxes* **E2.203.**

HMRC Manuals—Tax Credit Technical Manual TCTM2005 (Crown servants posted overseas).

6 Partners of Crown servants posted overseas

(1) The partner of a Crown servant posted overseas who is accompanying the Crown servant posted overseas shall be treated as being in the United Kingdom when he is either—

(*a*) in the country where the Crown servant is posted, or

(*b*) absent from that country in accordance with regulation 4 as modified by paragraphs (3) and (4).

(2) Regulation 4 applies to the partner of a Crown servant posted overseas with the modifications set out in paragraphs (3) and (4).

(3) Omit the words "ordinarily resident in the United Kingdom and is".

(4) In relation to a partner who is accompanying the Crown servant posted overseas the references to "United Kingdom" in the phrase "temporarily absent from the United Kingdom", in both places where it occurs, shall be construed as references to the country where the Crown servant is posted.

Commentary—*Simon's Taxes* **E2.203.**

HMRC Manuals—Tax Credit Technical Manual TCTM2005 (whether the partner of the Crown servant is present in the UK or accompanying their partner overseas, reg 6(1)(*b*), (2)–(4) ensure that the usual flexibility for temporary absences apply to them).

7 Transitional Provision – income support and income-based jobseeker's allowance

A person is exempt from the requirement to be ordinarily resident in the United Kingdom (which is set out in regulation 3(1)) in respect of child tax credit on and for three years after the date on which the award of child tax credit is made where—

(*a*) the award of child tax credit would be made on or after 6th April 2004;

Tax Credits

(*b*) immediately before the award of child tax credit is made, he is, or will be on the making of a claim, entitled to any of the amounts in relation to income support and income-based jobseeker's allowance which are described in section 1(3)(d) of the Act; and

(*c*) he is a person to which one or more of the following provisions applies—

(i) paragraph (*b*) or (*c*) in the definition of "person from abroad" in regulation 21(3) of the Income Support (General) Regulations 1987;

(ii) paragraph (*b*) or (*c*) in the definition of "person from abroad" in regulation 85(4) of the Jobseeker's Allowance Regulations 1996;

(iii) paragraph (*b*) or (*c*) in the definition of "person from abroad" in regulation 21(3) of the Income Support (General) (Northern Ireland) Regulations 1987;

(iv) paragraph (*b*) or (*c*) in the definition of "person from abroad" in regulation 85(4) of the Jobseeker's Allowance Regulations (Northern Ireland)1996.

Commentary—*Simon's Taxes* **E2.203.**

HMRC Manuals—Tax Credit Technical Manual TCTM2006 (transitional protection).

2003/692

TAX CREDITS (OFFICIAL ERROR) REGULATIONS 2003

Made by the Commissioners of Inland Revenue under TCA 2002 ss 21 and 65(2), (3), (7) and (9)

Made . . . . *13 March 2003*

Laid before Parliament . . . . *13 March 2003*

Coming into force . . . . *6 April 2003*

1 Citation and commencement

These Regulations may be cited as the Tax Credits (Official Error) Regulations 2003 and shall come into force on 6th April 2003.

2 Interpretation

(1) In these Regulations—

"the Board" means the Commissioners of Inland Revenue;

"official error" means an error relating to a tax credit made by—

(*a*) an officer of the Board,

(*b*) an officer of the Department for Work and Pensions,

(*c*) an officer of the Department for Social Development in Northern Ireland, or

(*d*) a person providing services to the Board or to an authority mentioned in paragraph (*b*) or (*c*) of this definition, in connection with a tax credit or credits,

to which the claimant, or any of the claimants, or any person acting for him, or any of them, did not materially contribute, excluding any error of law which is shown to have been an error by virtue of a subsequent decision by a Social Security Commissioner or by a court;"

"Social Security Commissioner" has the meaning given by section 63(13);

"tax year" means a period beginning with 6th April in one year and ending with 5th April in the next.[1]

(2) In these Regulations references to a section are to that section of the Tax Credits Act 2002.

Amendments—[1] Definition repealed by the Tax Credits (Miscellaneous Amendments) Regulations, SI 2010/751 regs 11, 12 with effect from 6 April 2010.

3—(1) A decision under section 14(1), 15(1), 16(1), 18(1), (5), (6) or (9), 19(3) or 20(1) or (4) may be revised in favour of the person or persons to whom it relates if it is incorrect by reason of official error, subject to the following paragraphs.

(2) In revising a decision, the officer or person in question need not consider any issue that is not raised by the application for revision by the claimant or claimants or, as the case may be, did not cause him to act on his own initiative.

(3) A decision mentioned in paragraph (1) may be revised at any time not later than five years after [the date of the decision][1].

Amendments—[1] Words in para (3) substituted by the Tax Credits (Miscellaneous Amendments) Regulations, SI 2010/751 regs 11, 12 with effect from 6 April 2010.

2003/731

TAX CREDITS (PROVISION OF INFORMATION) (FUNCTIONS RELATING TO HEALTH) REGULATIONS 2003

Made by the Commissioners of Inland Revenue under TCA 2002 ss 65(2) and 67 and Sch 5 para 9(2)

Made . . . . *14 March 2003*
Laid before Parliament . . . . *14 March 2003*
Coming into force . . . . *6 April 2003*

1 Citation and commencement

These Regulations may be cited as the Tax Credits (Provision of Information) (Functions Relating to Health) Regulations 2003 and shall come into force on 6th April 2003.

2 Interpretation

In these Regulations—

"child tax credit" shall be construed in accordance with section 8 of the Tax Credits Act 2002;

"disability element" means the disability element of working tax credit as specified in section 11(3) of the Tax Credits Act 2002;

["couple" has the meaning given by section 3(5A) of the Tax Credits Act 2002;][1]

"family" means—

(*a*) in the case of a joint claim for a tax credit under the Tax Credits Act 2002, the . . . [1] couple by whom the claim is made and any child or qualifying young person for whom at least one of them is responsible, in accordance with regulation 3 of the Child Tax Credit Regulations 2002;

(*b*) in the case of a single claim for a tax credit under the Tax Credits Act 2002, the claimant and any child or qualifying young person for whom he is responsible in accordance with regulation 3 of the Child Tax Credit Regulations 2002;

"qualifying family" means a family—

[(*a*) that has a relevant income of £16,190 or less, and

(*b*) one member of which is a person who—

(i) is receiving child tax credit, and

(ii) is not eligible for working tax credit;][2]

"qualifying young person" has the meaning given by regulation 2(1), read with regulation 5(3) and (4), of the Child Tax Credit Regulations 2002;

"relevant income" has the same meaning as in section 7(3) of the Tax Credits Act 2002;

"working tax credit" shall be construed in accordance with section 10 of the Tax Credits Act 2002.

Amendments—[1] Definition of "couple" inserted, and words in the definition of "family" revoked, by the Civil Partnership Act 2004 (Tax Credits, etc) (Consequential Amendments) Order, SI 2005/2919 art 9 with effect from 5 December 2005.

[2] In definition of "qualifying family", sub-paras (*a*), (*b*) substituted by the Tax Credits (Miscellaneous Amendments) Regulations, SI 2011/721 reg 4(1), (2) with effect from 6 April 2011.

3 Prescribed functions relating to health

The following functions are prescribed for the purposes of paragraph 9 of Schedule 5 to the Tax Credits Act 2002 (provision of information by the Board of Inland Revenue for health purposes)—

(*a*) the issue by or on behalf of the Secretary of State, the National Assembly for Wales, the Scottish Ministers or the Department of Health, Social Services, and Public Safety in Northern Ireland of a certificate confirming that the family is a qualifying family;

(*b*) verification by or on behalf of the Secretary of State, the National Assembly for Wales, the Scottish Ministers or that Department at any time that a family is a qualifying family at that time;

[(*ba*) the provision of benefits by or on behalf of the Secretary of State or the Department of Health, Social Services and Public Safety under a scheme established pursuant to section 13 of the Social Security Act 1988 or article 13 of the Social Security (Northern Ireland) Order 1988 in so far as such a scheme relates to the health of pregnant women, mothers or children.][1]

(*c*)–(*e*) . . . [1]

Amendments—[1] Paras (*c*)–(*e*) revoked, and para (*ba*) inserted, by the Tax Credits (Miscellaneous Amendments) Regulations, SI 2011/721 reg 4(1), (3) with effect from 6 April 2011.

2003/742

TAX CREDITS (POLYGAMOUS MARRIAGES) REGULATIONS 2003

Made by the Treasury under TCA 2002 ss 3(7), 7(8) and (9), 8, 10 to 12, 42, 43 and 65(1), (3), (7) and (9), and the Commissioners of Inland Revenue under TCA 2002 ss 4(1), 6, 24 and 65(2), (3), (7) and (9)

Made . . . . *14 March 2003*
Laid before Parliament . . . . *14 March 2003*

Tax Credits

Coming into force . . . . .6 *April 2003*

1 Citation, commencement and effect

(1) These Regulations may be cited as the Tax Credits (Polygamous Marriages) Regulations 2003 and shall come into force on 6th April 2003, immediately after the coming into force of the Child Tax Credit (Amendment) Regulations 2003.

(2) Regulations 22 to 56 only have effect in relation to members of polygamous units (and in the case of regulations 35 to 38, former members of such units).

2 Interpretation

In these Regulations—

"the Act" means the Tax Credits Act 2002;

"polygamous couple" means a man and a woman who are married under a law which permits polygamy where—

(*a*) they are not separated under a court order or in circumstances in which the separation is likely to be permanent, and

(*b*) either of them has an additional spouse;

"polygamous unit" means—

(*a*) a polygamous couple, and

(*b*) any person who is married to either member of the polygamous couple and who is not separated from that member under a court order or in circumstances in which the separation is likely to be permanent.

3 Modifications to Part 1 of the Act for members of polygamous units

Regulations 4 to 21 prescribe modifications to Part 1 of the Act so far as it applies to members of polygamous units.

4 In section 3—

(*a*) in subsection (3)(*a*) after "United Kingdom" insert "(and neither of whom are members of a polygamous unit)";

(*b*) after subsection (3)(*a*) insert—

"(*aa*) jointly by the members of a polygamous unit all of whom are aged at least sixteen and are in the United Kingdom, or";

(*c*) in subsection (3)(*b*) after "paragraph (*a*)" insert "or (*aa*)";

(*d*) after subsection (4)(*a*) insert—

"(*aa*) in the case of a joint claim under subsection (3)(*a*), if a member of the married or unmarried couple becomes a member of a polygamous unit, and

(*ab*) in the case of a joint claim under subsection (3)(*aa*), if there is any change in the persons who comprise the polygamous unit, and";

(*e*) after subsection (6) insert—

"(6A) In this Part "polygamous unit" has the meaning given by regulation 2 of the Tax Credits (Polygamous Marriages) Regulations 2003.";

(*f*) in subsection (8), in the definition of "joint claim", after "paragraph (*a*)" insert "or paragraph (*aa*)".

5 In section 4(1)(*g*)—

(*a*) for "member of a married couple or an unmarried couple" substitute "or more members of a polygamous unit";

(*b*) for "of the married couple or unmarried couple" substitute "or members".

6 In section 7(2) for "either" substitute "any".

7 In section 8(1) for "either or both" substitute "any or all".

8 In [both section 9(2)(*b*) and (3A)][1] for "either or both" substitute "any or all".

Amendments—[1] Words substituted by the Child Tax Credit (Amendment) Regulations, SI 2017/387 regs 6, 7 with effect from 6 April 2017.

9 In section 10—

(*a*) in subsection (1) for "either or both" substitute "any or all".

(*b*) in subsection (3) for "either" wherever it appears substitute "any".

10 In section 11—

(*a*) in subsection (3) for "either or both" substitute "any or all";

(*b*) in subsection (6)(*a*) for "either of the persons or the two" substitute "any of the persons or all";

(*c*) in subsection (6)(*b*) for "married couple or unmarried couple" substitute "polygamous unit";
(*d*) omit subsection (6)(*c*);
(*e*) in both subsection (6)(*d*) and (*e*) for "either or both" substitute "any or all".

11 In both section 12(3) and (4)(*a*) for "either or both" substitute "any or all".

12 In section 14(2)(*a*) for "either or both" substitute "any or all".

13 In section 16(3)(*a*) for "either or both" substitute "any or all".

14 In section 17(10)(*b*)—
(*a*) for "member of a married couple or an unmarried couple" substitute "or more members of a polygamous unit";
(*b*) for " married couple or unmarried couple" substitute "or members".

15 In section 18(10) for "either or both" substitute "any or all".

16 In section 19—
(*a*) in subsection (2)(*a*) for "either or both" substitute "any or all";
(*b*) in subsection (4)(*a*) for "either" substitute "any" and for "both" substitute "more than one";
(*c*) in subsection (9) for "either" substitute "any".

17 In section 20(4)(*b*) for "either" (wherever it appears) substitute "any".

18 In section 24(2)—
(*a*) for "married couple or an unmarried couple" substitute "polygamous unit";
(*b*) for "whichever of them" substitute "one or more of those persons as".

19 In section 29(4) for "either or both" substitute "any or all".

20 In section 31(2)—
(*a*) after "another" insert "or others";
(*b*) for "unless subsection (3) applies" substitute "or each of them unless subsection (3) applies to the person in question".

21 In section 37(1) for "either or both" (in each place they appear) substitute "any or all".

22 Amendments to the Child Tax Credit Regulations 2002

Amend the Child Tax Credit Regulations 2002 (for members of polygamous units only) as follows.

23 In regulation 2(1)—
(*a*) for the definition of "joint claim" substitute the following definition—
" "joint claim" means a claim under section 3(3)(*aa*) of the Act, as inserted by regulation 4(*b*) of the Tax Credits (Polygamous Marriages) Regulations 2003;";
(*b*) insert at the appropriate place the following definition—
" "polygamous unit" has the meaning in the Tax Credits (Polygamous Marriages) Regulations 2003;".
[(*c*) in the definition of "step-parent", in paragraph (*a*) only, for "couple, the other" substitute "polygamous unit, another".][1]

Amendments—[1] Para (*c*) inserted by the Child Tax Credit (Amendment) Regulations, SI 2017/387 regs 6, 8 with effect from 6 April 2017.

24 In regulation 3(1), in Rule 2.1., for "married couple or unmarried couple" in each place it appears substitute "polygamous unit".

25 In regulation 7—
(*a*) in paragraph (1)(*b*) for "married couple or unmarried couple" substitute "polygamous unit";
(*b*) in [both paragraph (2)(*a*) and (*b*)(ii)][1] for "either or both" substitute "any or all";
[(*c*) in paragraph (2A) for "either or both" substitute "any or all".][1]

Amendments—[1] Words in para (*b*) substituted, and para (*c*) inserted, by the Child Tax Credit (Amendment) Regulations, SI 2017/387 regs 6, 9 with effect from 6 April 2017.

[25A In regulation 9—
(*a*) in paragraphs (1) to (5) for "either or both" (in each place they appear) substitute "any or all";
(*b*) in paragraph (6)(b) for "either" substitute "any";
(*c*) in paragraph (7) for "either or both" substitute "any or all".][1]

Tax Credits

Amendments—[1] Regulations 25A–25E inserted by the Child Tax Credit (Amendment) Regulations, SI 2017/387 regs 6, 10 with effect from 6 April 2017.

[25B In regulation 10(*c*) for "either or both" substitute "any or all".][1]

Amendments—[1] Regulations 25A–25E inserted by the Child Tax Credit (Amendment) Regulations, SI 2017/387 regs 6, 10 with effect from 6 April 2017.

[25C In regulation 11 for "either or both" (in each place they appear) substitute "any or all".][1]

Amendments—[1] Regulations 25A–25E inserted by the Child Tax Credit (Amendment) Regulations, SI 2017/387 regs 6, 10 with effect from 6 April 2017.

[25D In regulation 13—

(*a*) in paragraph (14)(*a*) for "either" substitute "any";

(*b*) in paragraph (15) for "couple" substitute "polygamous unit".][1]

Amendments—[1] Regulations 25A–25E inserted by the Child Tax Credit (Amendment) Regulations, SI 2017/387 regs 6, 10 with effect from 6 April 2017.

[25E In regulation 14(3)(*a*) for "either or both" substitute "any or all".][1]

Amendments—[1] Regulations 25A–25E inserted by the Child Tax Credit (Amendment) Regulations, SI 2017/387 regs 6, 10 with effect from 6 April 2017.

26 Amendments to the Working Tax Credit (Entitlement and Maximum Rate) Regulations 2002

Amend the Working Tax Credit (Entitlement and Maximum Rate) Regulations 2002 (for members of polygamous units only) as follows.

27 In regulation 2(1)—

(*a*) for the definition of "joint claim" substitute the following definition—

" "joint claim" means a claim under section 3(3)(*aa*) of the Act (as inserted by regulation 4(*b*) of the Tax Credits (Polygamous Marriages) Regulations 2003);";

(*b*) insert at the appropriate place the following definition—

" "polygamous unit" has the meaning in the Tax Credits (Polygamous Marriages) Regulations 2003;".

28 In regulation 3(3)—

(*a*) for "both members of the couple satisfy" substitute "more than one member of the polygamous unit satisfies"; and

(*b*) for "two such elements" substitute "one such element for each of them that satisfies those conditions".

[29 In regulation 4(1) in the third variation of the Second Condition—

(*a*) in the introduction, for "that person's partner" substitute: "any other member of the polygamous unit"; and

(*b*) in paragraph (*a*)—

(i) for "couple" (in both places) substitute: "polygamous unit"; and

(ii) for "partner" substitute: "member of the unit".][1]

Amendments—[1] Reg 29 substituted by the Tax Credits (Miscellaneous Amendments) Regulations, SI 2012/848 regs 1(2), 9 with effect from 6 April 2012.

30 In regulation 10(2)—

(*a*) in sub-paragraph (*c*) for "couple" substitute "members of the polygamous unit";

(*b*) in sub-paragraph (*d*) for "couple" substitute "unit".

31 In regulation 11—

(*a*) in paragraph (1) after "element" insert "(and an additional such element for each member of the polygamous unit exceeding two in number)";

(*b*) in paragraph (2)(*c*) for "neither of the claimants" substitute "no claimant";

(*c*) in paragraph (4) in the words preceding sub-paragraph (*a*) after "adult element" insert "for any claimant";

(*d*) in paragraph (4)(*a*) for "neither claimant" substitute "none of the claimants"; and

(*e*) in paragraph (4)(*b*) for "one claimant" substitute "the claimant in question".

32 In regulation 13—

(*a*) omit paragraph (1)(*a*);

(*b*) in paragraph (1)(*b*) for "married or unmarried couple where both" substitute "polygamous unit where at least two of them";

(*c*) in paragraph (1)(*c*) for the words preceding paragraph (i) substitute "is a member or are members of a polygamous unit where at least one member is engaged in qualifying remunerative work and at least one other".
(*d*) in paragraph (4) for "the other member of a couple" substitute "another member of the polygamous unit";
(*e*) in paragraph (5) for "the other member or his partner" substitute "him or another member of the polygamous unit".

33 In regulation 14—
(*a*) in paragraph (1) for "either or both" substitute "any or all";
(*b*) in paragraph (1B) for "either or both" substitute "any or all";
(*c*) in paragraph (5) for "a partner or by a partner" substitute "another member of the same polygamous unit or".

34 In regulation 20—
(*a*) in paragraph (1) for "single claimant or to a couple" substitute "polygamous unit";
(*b*) omit paragraph (1)(*c*)(i);
(*c*) in paragraph (1)(*c*)(ii) for "a couple either or both" substitute "the members of a polygamous unit, any or all of whom";
(*d*) in paragraph (1)(*c*)(iii) for "a couple" substitute "the members of a polygamous unit";
(*e*) omit paragraph (1)(*e*);
(*f*) omit paragraph (1)(*f*)(i);
(*g*) in paragraph (1)(*f*)(ii) for "couple" substitute "polygamous unit".

35 Amendments to the Tax Credits (Definition and Calculation of Income) Regulations 2002
Amend the Tax Credits (Definition and Calculation of Income) Regulations 2002 (for members or former members of polygamous units only) as follows.

36 In regulation 2 (interpretation)—
(*a*) in paragraph (2) in the definition of "family" for "married or unmarried couple" substitute "members of the polygamous unit";
(*b*) in paragraph (2) insert at the appropriate places the following definitions—
" "joint claim" means a claim under section 3(3)(*aa*) of the Act, as inserted by regulation 4(*b*) of the Tax Credits (Polygamous Marriages) Regulations 2003;
"polygamous unit" has the meaning in the Tax Credits (Polygamous Marriages) Regulations 2003;";
(*c*) in paragraph (4)(*a*) for the words from "a claimant's spouse" to the end substitute "another member of the same polygamous unit";
(*d*) in paragraph (4)(*b*) for the words from "claimant's former spouse" to the end substitute "person who was formerly a member with the claimant of the same polygamous unit".

37 In regulation 3(7) (calculation of income of claimant)—
(*a*) in sub-paragraph (*b*) for "either or both" substitute "any or all";
(*b*) in sub-paragraph (*c*) for "either or both" substitute "any or all".

38 In regulation 4(1) (employment income), in the words succeeding sub-paragraph (k) for "either" substitute "any".

39 Amendments to the Tax Credits (Claims and Notifications) Regulations 2002
Amend the Tax Credits (Claims and Notifications) Regulations 2002 (for members of polygamous units only) as follows.

40 In regulation 2 (interpretation)—
(*a*) for the definition of "joint claim" substitute the following definition—
" "joint claim" means a claim under section 3(3)(*aa*) of the Act, as inserted by regulation 4(*b*) of the Tax Credits (Polygamous Marriages) Regulations 2003;";
(*b*) insert at the appropriate place the following definition—
" "polygamous unit" has the meaning in the Tax Credits (Polygamous Marriages) Regulations 2003;".

41 In regulation 11(2) for "both" substitute "all of the".
42 In regulation 13—

Tax Credits

(*a*) in paragraph (1) for the words from "one member" to the end substitute "one or more members of a polygamous unit is to be treated as also made by the other member or members of that unit";

(*b*) in paragraph (2)—

(i) for "member of a married couple or an unmarried couple" substitute "or more members of a polygamous unit";

(ii) for "both members of the couple" substitute "all the members of the unit".

43 In regulation 15—

(*a*) in paragraph (3) for the words from "only one" to the end substitute "one or more members of a polygamous unit die, the other member or members of the unit may proceed with the claim in the name or names of the person or persons who have died, as well as in their own name or names";

(*b*) in paragraph (4) for "both" (in each place it appears) substitute "all of".

44 In regulation 16—

(*a*) in paragraph (1) for the words from "member of a" to the end substitute "or more members of a polygamous unit die and the other member or members of the unit wish to make a joint claim for a tax credit";

(*b*) for paragraph (2) substitute—

"(2) The survivor or survivors may make and proceed with the claim in the name of the member or members who have died as well as in his or their own names.;"

(*c*) in paragraph (3)(*a*)—

(i) for "married couple or unmarried couple" substitute "polygamous unit";

(ii) add at the end "(or the earliest such date if more than one)".

45 In regulation 23(2) for "either member of the married couple or unmarried couple" substitute "any member of the polygamous unit".

46 In regulation 30(2) for "either" (in each place it appears) substitute "any".

47 In regulation 31(2)(*a*) for "either" substitute "any".

[47A In regulation 34(3)—

(*a*) for "one of two joint claimants" substitute "any member of a polygamous unit"; and

(*b*) for "both" (in each place where it occurs) substitute "all".][1]

Amendments—[1] This regulation inserted by the Tax Credits (Miscellaneous Amendments) Regulations, SI 2004/762 reg 19 with effect from 6 April 2004.

48 Amendments to the Tax Credits (Payment by the Board) Regulations 2002

Amend the Tax Credits (Payments by the Board) Regulations 2002 (for members of polygamous units only) as follows.

49 In regulation 2 (interpretation)—

(*a*) omit the definitions of "married couple" and "unmarried couple";

(*b*) insert at the appropriate place the following definition—

" "polygamous unit" has the meaning in the Tax Credits (Polygamous Marriages) Regulations 2003;".

50 In regulation 3—

(*a*) in the heading, for "couple" substitute "polygamous unit";

(*b*) for paragraphs (2) to (6) substitute—

"(2) There shall be established, for each particular child or qualifying young person for whom any or all of the members of the polygamous unit is or are responsible—

(*a*) the member of that unit who is (for the time being) identified by all the members of the unit as the main carer for that child or qualifying young person; or

(*b*) in default of such a member, the member of that unit who appears to the Board to be the main carer for that child or qualifying young person.

(3) The individual element[, and any disability element,][1] of child tax credit for any child or qualifying young person shall be paid to the main carer of that child or qualifying young person.

(4) The family element of child tax credit for any polygamous unit shall be divided (pro rata) by the number of children and qualifying young persons for whom any or all of the members of that unit is or are responsible, and the proportion so attributable to each such child or qualifying young person shall be paid to the main carer of that child or qualifying young person.

(5) Any child care element of working tax credit shall be divided (pro rata) by the number of children referred to in paragraph (2) in respect of whom relevant child care charges are paid, and the proportion so attributable to each such child shall be paid to the main carer of that child.

(6) In this regulation—

"child" has the meaning given by the Child Tax Credit Regulations 2002;

"qualifying young person" has the meaning given by those Regulations; and

"relevant child care charges" has the meaning given by regulation 14(1) of the Working Tax Credit (Entitlement and Maximum Rate) Regulations 2002."

Amendments—[1] Words in para (3) inserted by the Child Tax Credit (Amendment) Regulations, SI 2017/387 regs 6, 11 with effect from 6 April 2017.

51 Amendments to the Tax Credits (Residence) Regulations 2003

Amend the Tax Credits (Residence) Regulations 2003 (for members of polygamous units only) as follows.

52 In regulation 2 (Interpretation)—

(*a*) in the definition of "partner" for the words from "married" to the end substitute "polygamous unit, any other member of that unit";

(*b*) insert at the appropriate place the following definition—

" "polygamous unit" has the meaning in the Tax Credits (Polygamous Marriages) Regulations 2003;".

53 Amendments to the Tax Credits (Immigration) Regulations 2003

Amend the Tax Credits (Immigration) Regulations 2003 (for members of polygamous units only) as follows.

54 In regulation 2 (Interpretation)—

(*a*) for the definition of "joint claim" substitute the following definition—

" "joint claim" means a claim under section 3(3)(*aa*) of the Act, as inserted by regulation 4(*b*) of the Tax Credits (Polygamous Marriages) Regulations 2003;";

(*b*) insert at the appropriate place the following definition—

" "polygamous unit" has the meaning in the Tax Credits (Polygamous Marriages) Regulations 2003;".

55 In regulation 3(2)—

(*a*) for the words from "married couple" to "and the other" substitute "polygamous unit is a person subject to immigration control and any other";

(*b*) in sub-paragraph (*b*) for "couple" substitute "unit".

56 In regulation 4(1) (modifications to the Tax Credits Act 2002) add at the end "(which, in the case of a claim by the members of a polygamous unit, are subject to the modifications made by regulations 4 to 21 of the Tax Credits (Polygamous Marriages) Regulations 2003)".

2003/962

TAX CREDITS ACT 2002 (COMMENCEMENT NO 4, TRANSITIONAL PROVISIONS AND SAVINGS) ORDER 2003

Made by the Treasury under TCA 2002 ss 61, 62(2)

Made .... *31 March 2003*

1 Citation and interpretation

(1) This Order may be cited as the Tax Credits Act 2002 (Commencement No 4, Transitional Provisions and Savings) Order 2003.

(2) In this Order—

"the Act" means the Tax Credits Act 2002;

"the 1999 Act" means the Tax Credits Act 1999; and

"the superseded tax credits" means working families' tax credit and disabled person's tax credit.

2 Commencement of provisions of the Act

(1) Subject to the provisions of articles 3 and 4 (savings and transitional provisions), the provisions of the Act specified in this article shall come into force in accordance with the following paragraphs of this article.

(2) Section 47 (consequential amendments), so far as it relates to paragraphs 4 to 7 of Schedule 3, shall come into force on 1st April 2003.

Tax Credits

(3) The following provisions of the Act shall come into force on 6th April 2003—

(*a*) section 1(3)(*a*) and (*f*) (abolition of children's tax credit under section 257AA of the Income and Corporation Taxes Act 1988 and employment credit);

(*b*) section 47, so far as it relates to the provisions of Schedule 3 specified in sub-paragraph (*d*);

(*c*) section 60 (repeals), so far as it relates to the provisions of Schedule 6 specified in sub-paragraph (*e*);

(*d*) in Schedule 3 (consequential amendments)—

(i) paragraphs 1 to 3,

(ii) paragraphs 8 and 9, and

(iii) paragraphs 13 to 59; and

(*e*) in Schedule 6, the entries relating to the enactments specified in column 1 of Schedule 1 to this Order to the extent shown in column 2 of that Schedule.

(4) The following provisions of the Act shall come into force on 8th April 2003—

(*a*) section 1(3)(*b*) and (*c*) (abolition of working families' tax credit and disabled person's tax credit);

(*b*) section 47 so far as concerns the provisions of Schedule 3 mentioned in this paragraph;

(*c*) section 60 so far as concerns the entries in Schedule 6 referred to in sub-paragraph (*e*);

(*d*) paragraphs 10 to 12 of Schedule 3 to the Act; and

(*e*) in Schedule 6 to the Act, the entries relating to the enactments specified in column 1 of Schedule 2 to this Order to the extent shown in column 2 of that Schedule.

(5) . . . [1]

Amendments—[1] Para 5 revoked by the Tax Credits Act 2002 (Commencement and Transitional Provisions)(Partial Revocation) Order, SI 2014/1848 art 2 with effect from 14 July 2014.

3 Savings

(1) This article applies to any claim for either of the superseded tax credits made—

(*a*) on or before 6th July 2003; and

(*b*) in respect of a period ending on or before 7th April 2003.

Such a claim is referred to in the following provisions of this article as "a relevant claim".

(2) Notwithstanding the commencement of the repeals specified in paragraph (6)—

(*a*) a relevant claim may be made, inquired into by an officer of the Board, or decided by an officer of the Board; and

(*b*) a decision of an officer of the Board on a relevant claim may be—

(i) revised,

(ii) superseded, or

(iii) the subject of an appeal,

in accordance with the provisions specified in paragraph (3) as if the repeals specified in paragraph (6) had not taken place.

(3) The provisions specified are—

(a) Chapter 2 of Part 1 of the Social Security Act 1998;[1]

(*b*) in Northern Ireland, Chapter II of Part II of the Social Security (Northern Ireland) Order 1998; and

(*c*) regulations under the provisions mentioned in sub-paragraphs (*a*) and (*b*), as applied for the purposes of the superseded tax credits by section 21 or 23 of the 1999 Act (as the case may be).

(4) Notwithstanding the commencement of the repeals specified in paragraph (6), payment of a superseded tax credit may be made on or after 8th April 2003 in pursuance of a decision of an officer of the Board on a relevant claim (including such a decision as revised, superseded or varied on appeal).

(5) Notwithstanding the commencement of the repeals specified in paragraph (6)—

(*a*) an officer of the Board may make any decision in respect of an overpayment of a superseded tax credit, the recovery of such an overpayment, or the imposition of any penalty in respect of a superseded tax credit which he might have made but for the repeal in question, and

(*b*) the like consequences shall flow from the decision mentioned in sub-paragraph (*a*), including any right of appeal, as would have flowed but for the repeal in question.

(6) The repeals specified in this paragraph are those contained in Schedule 6 to the Act relating to—

(*a*) the 1999 Act, other than section 6;

(*b*) sections 122(1), 123(1), 128, 129 and 135(5) of the Social Security Contributions and Benefits Act 1992;

(*c*) sections 5(2), 11, 71(11), 121DA(1), 124(2), 154(2), 163(2), 179(5), and 191 of the Social Security Administration Act;

(*d*) sections 121(1), 122(1), 127, 128 and 131(5) of the Social Security Contributions and Benefits (Northern Ireland) Act 1992; and

(*e*) sections 5(2), 9, 69(11), 115CA(1), 134(2), 155(5) and 167(1) of the Social Security Administration (Northern Ireland) Act 1992.

Amendments—[1] Para 3(*a*) revoked by the Tax Credits Act 2002 (Commencement and Transitional Provisions)(Partial Revocation) Order, SI 2014/1848 art 2 with effect from 14 July 2014.

4 Notwithstanding the repeal in Schedule 6 of words in section 84 of the Finance Act 2000, section 84 of that Act shall apply to a payment of an employment credit made on or after 6th April 2003 as if the repeal had not occurred.

5 Transitional provisions

(1) If a claim has been made for a tax credit under the Act by two (or more) persons, at least one of whom was in receipt of either or both of the superseded tax credits immediately before the repeal of the 1999 Act, the Board may make any payment of a tax credit, due to them under the Act on or before 5th October 2003, to either or any of them, notwithstanding any provision of the Tax Credits (Payment by Employers) Regulations 2002 or the Working Tax Credit (Payment by the Board) Regulations 2002.

(2) In respect of a person who claims the higher rate of short-term incapacity benefit, or long term incapacity benefit on or before 6th April 2005 section 30C of the Social Security Contributions and Benefits Act 1992 and section 30C of the Social Security Contributions and Benefits (Northern Ireland) Act 1992 shall have effect as if, after subsection (5A) there were inserted—

"(5B) A person also satisfies the relevant tax credit conditions on any day before 7th April 2003 if that day falls within a week for which he is entitled to a disabled person's tax credit.".

(3) In respect of a person who claims incapacity benefit on or before 6th April 2005 under section 40 or 41 of either the Social Security Contributions and Benefits Act 1992 or the Social Security Contributions and Benefits (Northern Ireland) Act 1992, section 42 of the respective Act shall have effect as if, after subsection (1A), there were inserted—

"(1B) A person also satisfies the relevant tax credit conditions on any day before 7th April 2003 if that day falls within a week for which he is entitled to a disabled person's tax credit.".

(4) . . . [2]

Amendments—[1] Para (4)(*a*) substituted by the Tax Credits Act 2002 (Transitional Provisions) Order, SI 2008/3151 art 3(1), (3).

[2] Para (4) repealed by the Tax Credits Act 2002 (Transitional Provisions) Order, SI 2010/644 art 5, with effect from 1 April 2010.

SCHEDULE 1

PROVISIONS OF SCHEDULE 6 TO THE ACT COMING INTO FORCE ON 6TH APRIL 2003

Article 2(3)(*e*)

Enactment	*Extent of repeal or revocation commenced*
Taxes Management Act 1970	The whole entry in Schedule 6.
Income and Corporation Taxes Act 1988	The whole entry in Schedule 6.
Children Act 1989	The whole entry in Schedule 6.
Education Reform (Northern Ireland) Order 1989	The whole entry in Schedule 6.
Disability Living Allowance and Disability Working Allowance Act 1991	The whole entry in Schedule 6.
Child Support Act 1991	The whole entry in Schedule 6.
Disability Living Allowance and Disability Working Allowance (Northern Ireland) Order 1991	The whole entry in Schedule 6.
Child Support (Northern Ireland) Order 1991	The whole entry in Schedule 6.
Social Security Contributions and Benefits Act 1992	So much of the entry in Schedule 6 as concerns sections 21(5A)(*b*) and 45A.
Social Security Administration Act 1992	So much of the entry in Schedule 6 as concerns sections 3(3) and 189(1).
Social Security Contributions and Benefits (Northern Ireland) Act 1992	So much of the entry in Schedule 6 as concerns sections 20(1), 21(5A)(*b*), 30B(3), 45A, 56(1), 60(6), 61(1) and (2), 63(*c*) and (*f*)(i), 77(1), 78(4)(*d*), 80, 81, 89(1), 90, 91(1)(*b*) and Schedules 4 and 5.
Social Security Administration (Northern Ireland) Act 1992	So much of the entry in Schedule 6 as concerns section 3(3).
Local Government Finance Act 1992	The whole entry in Schedule 6.
Finance Act 1994	The whole entry in Schedule 6.

Enactment	*Extent of repeal or revocation commenced*
Social Security (Incapacity for Work) Act 1994	The whole entry in Schedule 6
Social Security (Incapacity for Work) (Northern Ireland) Order 1994	The whole entry in Schedule 6.
Pensions Act 1995	The whole entry in Schedule 6.
Pensions (Northern Ireland) Order 1995	The whole entry in Schedule 6.
Employment Tribunals Act 1996	The whole entry in Schedule 6.
Employment Rights (Northern Ireland) Order 1996	The whole entry in Schedule 6.
Finance Act 1999	The whole entry in Schedule 6.
Access to Justice Act 1999	The whole entry in Schedule 6.
Welfare Reform and Pensions Act 1999	The whole entry in Schedule 6.
Welfare Reform and Pensions (Northern Ireland) Order 1999	The whole entry in Schedule 6.
Finance Act 2000	The whole entry in Schedule 6.
Finance Act 2001	The whole entry in Schedule 6.

SCHEDULE 2

PROVISIONS OF SCHEDULE 6 TO THE ACT COMING INTO FORCE ON 8TH APRIL 2003

Article 2(4)(*e*)

Enactment	*Extent of repeal or revocation commenced*
Social Security Contributions and Benefits Act 1992	So much of the entry in Schedule 6 as relates to sections 122(1), 123(1), 128, 129 and 135(5).
Social Security Administration Act 1992	So much of the entry in Schedule 6 as relates to sections 5(2), 11, 71(11), 121DA(1), 124(2), 163(2), 179(5) and 191.
Social Security Contributions and Benefits (Northern Ireland) Act 1992	So much of the entry in Schedule 6 as relates to sections 121(1), 122(1), 127, 128 and 131(5).
Social Security Administration (Northern Ireland) Act 1992	So much of the entry in Schedule 6 as relates to sections 5(2), 9, 69(11), 115CA(1), 134(2), 155(5) and 167(1).
Jobseekers Act 1995	The whole entry in Schedule 6.
Jobseekers (Northern Ireland) Order 1995	The whole entry in Schedule 6.
Finance Act 1997	The whole entry in Schedule 6.
Social Security Act 1998	The whole entry in Schedule 6.
Tax Credits (Initial Expenditure) Act 1998	The whole entry in Schedule 6.
Social Security (Northern Ireland) Order 1998	The whole entry in Schedule 6.
Tax Credits Act 1999	The whole entry in Schedule 6, insofar as it has not already been commenced.
Employment Relations Act 1999	The whole entry in Schedule 6.
Immigration and Asylum Act 1999	The whole entry in Schedule 6.
Employment Relations (Northern Ireland) Order 1999	The whole entry in Schedule 6.
Government Resources and Accounts Act 2000	The whole entry in Schedule 6.
Social Security Fraud Act 2001	The whole entry in Schedule 6.
Social Security Fraud Act (Northern Ireland) 2001	The whole entry in Schedule 6.
Employment Act 2002	The whole entry in Schedule 6.
Criminal Injuries Compensation (Northern Ireland) Order 2002	The whole entry in Schedule 6.

2003/1382

TAX CREDITS (EMPLOYER PENALTY APPEALS) REGULATIONS 2003

Made by the Commissioners of Inland Revenue under TCA 2002 ss 39(6), 65(2) and (6) and 67 of the Tax Credits Act 2002, with the consent of the Lord Chancellor and the Scottish Ministers

Made . . . . *23 May 2003*
Laid before Parliament . . . . *28 May 2003*
Coming into force . . . . *18 June 2003*

1 Citation and Commencement

These Regulations may be cited as the Tax Credits (Employer Penalty Appeals) Regulations 2003 and shall come into force on 18th June 2003.

2 Interpretation

In these Regulations—

"the Act" means the Taxes Management Act 1970; and

"employer penalty" has the meaning given in section 63(11) of the Tax Credits Act 2002.

3 Part 5 of the Taxes Management Act

Part 5 of the Act [(appeals)][1] applies to an appeal under section 38 of the Tax Credits Act 2002 against an employer penalty subject to the modifications set out in these Regulations.

Amendments—[1] Words substituted by the Transfer of Tribunal Functions and Revenue and Customs Appeals Order, SI 2009/56 art 3, Sch 2 paras 84, 85 with effect from 1 April 2009.

4–6

Amendments—Regulations 4–6 revoked by the Transfer of Tribunal Functions and Revenue and Customs Appeals Order, SI 2009/56 art 3, Sch 2 paras 84, 86 with effect from 1 April 2009.

7 In section 48 of the Act—

(*a*) in subsection (1) for the definition of appeal substitute—

" "appeal" means an appeal against an employer penalty (as defined in section 63(11) of the Tax Credits Act 2002) to the [tribunal][1];"; and

(*b*) omit subsection (2).

Amendments—[1] Word substituted by the Transfer of Tribunal Functions and Revenue and Customs Appeals Order, SI 2009/56 art 3, Sch 2 paras 84, 87 with effect from 1 April 2009.

8

Amendments—Regulation 8 revoked by the Transfer of Tribunal Functions and Revenue and Customs Appeals Order, SI 2009/56 art 3, Sch 2 paras 84, 88 with effect from 1 April 2009.

9 In section 54 of the Act—

(*a*) in subsection (1) for the words "discharged or cancelled" substitute "set aside" and for the words "had discharged or cancelled it" substitute "had set it aside";

(*b*) for the words "the inspector or other proper officer of the Crown" and the words "the inspector or other proper officer", in each place where they occur, substitute "the officer of the Board"; and

(*c*) omit the words "assessment or" in each place where they occur.

10 [Omit section 56 of the Act][1]

Amendments—[1] Reg 10 substituted by the Transfer of Tribunal Functions and Revenue and Customs Appeals Order, SI 2009/56 art 3, Sch 2 paras 84, 89 with effect from 1 April 2009.

2003/1650

TAX CREDITS (PROVISION OF INFORMATION) (FUNCTIONS RELATING TO HEALTH) (NO 2) REGULATIONS 2003

Made by the Commissioners of Inland Revenue under TCA 2002 ss 65(2) and 67 and Sch 5 para 9

Made . . . . *25 June 2003*
Laid before Parliament . . . . *26 June 2003*
Coming into force . . . . *17 July 2003*

1 Citation, commencement and extent

(1) These Regulations may be cited as the Tax Credits (Provision of Information) (Functions Relating to Health) (No 2) Regulations 2003 and shall come into force on 17th July 2003.

(2) These Regulations do not extend to Northern Ireland.

2 Prescribed functions relating to health

(1) The function specified in paragraph (2) is prescribed for the purposes of paragraph 9 of Schedule 6 to the Tax Credits Act 2002 (provision of information by the Board of Inland Revenue for health purposes).

(2) The function specified in this paragraph is the conduct, by a person providing services to the Secretary of State and the Scottish Ministers, of a survey of the mental health of persons in Great Britain who are under the age of 17 on 1st September 2003.

(3) Nothing in these Regulations limits the operation of the Tax Credits (Provision of Information Relating to Health) Regulations 2003.

2003/2041

TAX CREDITS (PROVISION OF INFORMATION) (FUNCTION RELATING TO EMPLOYMENT AND TRAINING) REGULATIONS 2003

Made by the Commissioners of Inland Revenue under TCA 2002 ss 65(2), 67, Sch 5 para 5(2)

Made .... *6 August 2003*
Laid before Parliament .... *8 August 2003*
Coming into force .... *29 August 2003*

1 Citation, commencement and extent

(1) These Regulations may be cited as the Tax Credits (Provision of Information) (Function Relating to Employment and Training) Regulations 2003 and shall come into force on 29th August 2003.

(2) These Regulations do not extend to Northern Ireland.

2 Prescribed function relating to employment and training

(1) The function specified in paragraph (2) is prescribed for the purposes of paragraph 5 of Schedule 5 to the Tax Credits Act 2002 (provision of information by the Board of Inland Revenue for employment and training purposes).

(2) The function specified in this paragraph is the operation of the Employment Retention and Advancement Scheme, that is to say the scheme for assisting persons to improve their job retention or career advancement, established by the Secretary of State under section 2 of the Employment and Training Act 1973.

2003/2077

CHILDREN ACT 1989, SECTION 17(12) REGULATIONS 2003

Made by the Treasury under the Children Act 1989 ss 17(12) and 104

Made .... *11 August 2003*
Laid before Parliament .... *11 August 2003*
Coming into force .... *1 September 2003*

1 Citation and commencement

These Regulations may be cited as the Children Act 1989, Section 17(12) Regulations 2003 and shall come into force on 1st September 2003.

2 Interpretation

In these Regulations—

"child care" has the meaning in the Working Tax Credit (Entitlement and Maximum Rate) Regulations 2002;

"relevant child care charges" has the meaning given in regulation 14(1) of those Regulations.

3 Treating a person as in receipt of working tax credit or of any element of child tax credit other than the family element

A person shall be treated, for the purposes of Part 3 of the Children Act 1989, as in receipt of working tax credit, or of any element of child tax credit other than the family element, where—

(*a*) the person is in receipt of assistance under section 17 of that Act, or of a direct payment or voucher under section 17A or 17B of that Act; and

(*b*) that assistance consists in the provision (or a direct payment or voucher to secure the provision) of child care, the cost of which (if paid for by the person out of his own resources) would—

(i) be relevant child care charges in relation to that person, and

(ii) cause that person (in circumstances where, but for that cost, he would otherwise not be) to be entitled to working tax credit, or to any element of child tax credit other than the family element.

2003/2170

TAX CREDITS ACT 2002 (CHILD TAX CREDIT) (TRANSITIONAL PROVISIONS) ORDER 2003

Made by the Treasury under TCA 2002 s 62(2)

Made . . . .*21 August 2003*
Coming into force . . . .*22 August 2003*

1 Citation and commencement

This Order may be cited as the Tax Credits Act 2002 (Child Tax Credit) (Transitional Provisions) Order 2003 and shall come into force on 22nd August 2003.

2 Transitional provision

(1) This article applies in the case of a person who throughout the period beginning on 22nd August 2003 and ending on 28th September 2003 is—

(*a*) in receipt of income support;
(*b*) aged not less than 60; and
(*c*) responsible for a child (within the meaning of regulation 3 of the Child Tax Credit Regulations 2002).

(2) Where this article applies to a person, he shall be treated as having made a claim for child tax credit in respect of the child for whom he is responsible as mentioned in paragraph (1)(*c*) of this article—

(*a*) on 22nd August 2003 for the purposes of enabling the Board to make an initial decision on the claim; and
(*b*) on the first day of the first benefit week in relation to income support beginning on or after 29th September 2003 for all other purposes.

(3) In paragraph (2) "benefit week" has the same meaning—

(*a*) in relation to a person in Great Britain, as it bears in regulation 2(1) of the Income Support (General) Regulations 1987; and
(*b*) in relation to a person in Northern Ireland, as it bears in regulation 2(1) of the Income Support (General) Regulations (Northern Ireland) 1987.

2003/3308

TAX CREDITS (PROVISION OF INFORMATION) (EVALUATION AND STATISTICAL STUDIES) REGULATIONS 2003

Made by the Commissioners of Inland Revenue under TCA 2002 ss 65(2) and 67, and Sch 5, para 4(2)

Made . . . .*18 December 2003*
Laid before Parliament . . . .*19 December 2003*
Coming into force . . . .*9 January 2004*

1 Citation, commencement and extent

(1) These Regulations may be cited as the Tax Credits (Provision of Information) (Evaluation and Statistical Studies) Regulations 2003 and shall come into force on 9th January 2004.

(2) These Regulations do not extend to Northern Ireland.

2 Purposes for which information may be provided

The purposes of conducting evaluation and statistical studies in relation to—

(*a*) the education of children and young people under the age of 17; and
(*b*) the provision and use of child care, are prescribed under paragraph 4 of Schedule 5 to the Tax Credits Act 2002 (provision of information by the Board of Inland Revenue for evaluation and statistical studies).

Here "child care" means any care provided for a child whether or not of a description prescribed for any purpose under the Act.

Tax Credits

2004/575

TAXATION OF BENEFITS UNDER GOVERNMENT PILOT SCHEMES (WORKING NEIGHBOURHOODS PILOT AND IN WORK CREDIT) ORDER 2004

Made by the Treasury under FA 1996 s 151(1)(a) and (7)(a)

Made . . . .*4 March 2004*
Laid before the House of Commons . . . .*5 March 2004*
Coming into force . . . .*6 April 2004*

1 Citation and commencement

(1) This Order may be cited as the Taxation of Benefits under Government Pilot Schemes (Working Neighbourhoods Pilot and In Work Credit) Order 2004.

(2) This Order shall come into force on 6th April 2004.

2 Interpretation

In this Order—

"benefit" has the meaning given by subsection (6) of section 151 of the Finance Act 1996;

"Government pilot scheme" has the meaning given by subsections (3) and (4) of section 151 of the Finance Act 1996;

"In-Work Credit" and "Working Neighbourhoods Pilot" mean benefits under the Government pilot schemes known by those names.

3 Exemptions from income tax

The Income Tax Acts shall have effect in relation to any amount of payment by way of In-Work Credit or by way of the Working Neighbourhoods Pilot, as if that amount were wholly exempt from income tax and accordingly to be disregarded in computing the amount of any receipts brought into account for income tax purposes.

2005/66

TAX CREDITS (PROVISION OF INFORMATION) (FUNCTION RELATING TO EMPLOYMENT AND TRAINING) REGULATIONS 2005

Made by the Commissioners of Inland Revenue under TCA 2002 ss 65(2), 67, Sch 5 para 5(2)

Made . . . .*17 January 2005*
Laid before House of Commons . . . .*18 January 2005*
Coming into force . . . .*8 February 2005*

1 Citation and commencement

These Regulations may be cited as the Tax Credits (Provision of Information) (Function Relating to Employment and Training) Regulations 2005 and shall come into force on 8th February 2005.

2 Prescribed function relating to employment and training

(1) The function specified in paragraph (2) is prescribed for the purposes of paragraph 5 of Schedule 5 to the Tax Credits Act 2002 (provision of information by the Board of Inland Revenue for employment and training purposes).

(2) The function specified in this paragraph is evaluation of, and research in relation to, the employment and training programmes administered—

(*a*) in Great Britain, by the Department for Work and Pensions; or

(*b*) in Northern Ireland, the Department for Employment and Learning.

2005/93

TAX CREDITS (APPROVAL OF CHILD CARE PROVIDERS) SCHEME 2005

Made . . . .*24 January 2005*
Laid before Parliament . . . .*1 February 2005*
Coming into force . . . .*6 April 2005*

Made by the Secretary of State for Education and Skills under Tax Credits Act 2002 ss 12(5), (7) and (8) and 65(9), in accordance with Tribunals and Inquiries Act 1992 s 8(1)

Revocation—Revoked, in relation to England, by the Tax Credits (Child Care Providers) (Miscellaneous Revocation and Transitional Provisions) (England) Scheme, SI 2007/2481 art 4(1) with effect from 1 October 2007: SI 2007/2481 reg 1(2). The Scheme continues to have effect, however, in relation to any approval granted to a childcare provider under the Scheme which is valid immediately before 1 October 2007, and any application for approval under the Scheme which has not been granted before that date.

1 *Citation, commencement and application*

(1) This Scheme shall be known as the Tax Credits (Approval of Child Care Providers) Scheme 2005 and shall come into force on 6th April 2005.

(2) This Scheme applies in relation to England.

Revocation—Revoked, in relation to England, by the Tax Credits (Child Care Providers) (Miscellaneous Revocation and Transitional Provisions) (England) Scheme, SI 2007/2481 art 4(1) with effect from 1 October 2007: SI 2007/2481 reg 1(2).

The Scheme continues to have effect, however, in relation to any approval granted to a childcare provider under the Scheme which is valid immediately before 1 October 2007, and any application for approval under the Scheme which has not been granted before that date.

2 *Definitions*

In this Scheme—

"the 1989 Act" means the Children Act 1989;

"approval body" means the body referred to in article 3;

"approval criteria" has the meaning given to it in article 7;

"child" has the meaning attributed to it by the Child Tax Credit Regulations 2002;

"domestic premises" means any premises which are wholly or mainly used as a private dwelling and "premises" includes any area and any vehicle;

"parent" includes a person who—

- *(a) has parental responsibility for a child;*
- *(b) is a local authority foster parent in relation to a child;*
- *(c) is a foster parent with whom a child has been placed by voluntary organisation; or*
- *(d) fosters a child privately;*

"parental responsibility" and "fosters a child privately" have the meanings attributed to those respective expressions by sections 3 and 66 of the 1989 Act;

"qualifying child care" has the meaning ascribed to it in article 5;

"relative" in relation to a child means a grand-parent, brother, sister, uncle or aunt (whether of the full blood or half blood or by affinity) or a step-parent;

"relevant first-aid certificate" means a certificate in respect of a course of first-aid training—

- *(a) which is suitable to the care of babies and children;*
- *(b) which includes training in the following areas: dealing with emergencies; resuscitation; shock; choking; anaphylactic shock; and*
- *(c) which has been undertaken by the applicant not more than three years before the date upon which the application for approval is made;*

"the Tribunal" means the Tribunal established by section 9 of the Protection of Children Act 1999;

"the Tribunal Regulations" means the Protection of Children and Vulnerable Adults and Care Standards Tribunal Regulations 2002.

Revocation—Revoked, in relation to England, by the Tax Credits (Child Care Providers) (Miscellaneous Revocation and Transitional Provisions) (England) Scheme, SI 2007/2481 art 4(1) with effect from 1 October 2007: SI 2007/2481 reg 1(2).

The Scheme continues to have effect, however, in relation to any approval granted to a childcare provider under the Scheme which is valid immediately before 1 October 2007, and any application for approval under the Scheme which has not been granted before that date.

3 *Specified body*

The body specified for the purpose of giving approvals under this Scheme is Nestor Primecare Services Limited.

Revocation—Revoked, in relation to England, by the Tax Credits (Child Care Providers) (Miscellaneous Revocation and Transitional Provisions) (England) Scheme, SI 2007/2481 art 4(1) with effect from 1 October 2007: SI 2007/2481 reg 1(2).

The Scheme continues to have effect, however, in relation to any approval granted to a childcare provider under the Scheme which is valid immediately before 1 October 2007, and any application for approval under the Scheme which has not been granted before that date.

4 *Requirements of the Scheme*

For the purposes of regulations made under section 12 of the Tax Credits Act 2002, a person shall be a child care provider approved in accordance with this Scheme only—

- *(a) if he is for the time being approved by the approval body; and*
- *(b) in respect of the provision by him of qualifying child care.*

Tax Credits

Revocation—Revoked, in relation to England, by the Tax Credits (Child Care Providers) (Miscellaneous Revocation and Transitional Provisions) (England) Scheme, SI 2007/2481 art 4(1) with effect from 1 October 2007: SI 2007/2481 reg 1(2).

The Scheme continues to have effect, however, in relation to any approval granted to a childcare provider under the Scheme which is valid immediately before 1 October 2007, and any application for approval under the Scheme which has not been granted before that date.

5 *Qualifying Child Care*

(1) Qualifying child care means care for a child provided by an individual on domestic premises for reward but does not include care referred to in paragraph (2).

(2) Qualifying child care does not include—

- *(a) childminding which is subject to registration pursuant to Part 10A of the 1989 Act;*
- *(b) child care provided wholly or mainly in the child's own home in respect of a child to whom the provider is a parent or relative; or*
- *(c) child care provided wholly or mainly in the home of a relative of the child where such care is usually provided solely in respect of one or more child to whom the provider is a parent or relative.*

Revocation—Revoked, in relation to England, by the Tax Credits (Child Care Providers) (Miscellaneous Revocation and Transitional Provisions) (England) Scheme, SI 2007/2481 art 4(1) with effect from 1 October 2007: SI 2007/2481 reg 1(2).

The Scheme continues to have effect, however, in relation to any approval granted to a childcare provider under the Scheme which is valid immediately before 1 October 2007, and any application for approval under the Scheme which has not been granted before that date.

6 *Approved person*

(1) A person shall be given approval as a child care provider under this Scheme if the approval body is satisfied that the approval criteria are met in relation to that person.

(2) A person who has been given approval under paragraph (1) shall cease to be so approved if that approval is withdrawn by the approval body.

(3) The approval body may withdraw an approval if satisfied that the approval criteria are no longer met in relation to that person.

Revocation—Revoked, in relation to England, by the Tax Credits (Child Care Providers) (Miscellaneous Revocation and Transitional Provisions) (England) Scheme, SI 2007/2481 art 4(1) with effect from 1 October 2007: SI 2007/2481 reg 1(2).

The Scheme continues to have effect, however, in relation to any approval granted to a childcare provider under the Scheme which is valid immediately before 1 October 2007, and any application for approval under the Scheme which has not been granted before that date.

7 *Approval criteria*

In relation to an application for approval as a child care provider the approval criteria are—

- *(a) that the applicant is 18 years of age or over;*
- *(b) that the applicant—*
  - *(i) has obtained one of the qualifications from time to time specified in a list maintained by the Department for Education and Skills for the purpose of this article; or*
  - *(ii) has attended a basic course of training in the care of children being one specified in a list maintained by the Department for Education and Skills for the purpose of this article;*
- *(c) that the applicant has obtained a relevant first-aid certificate; and*
- *(d) that the applicant is not considered unsuitable to work with or have unsupervised access to children.*

Revocation—Revoked, in relation to England, by the Tax Credits (Child Care Providers) (Miscellaneous Revocation and Transitional Provisions) (England) Scheme, SI 2007/2481 art 4(1) with effect from 1 October 2007: SI 2007/2481 reg 1(2).

The Scheme continues to have effect, however, in relation to any approval granted to a childcare provider under the Scheme which is valid immediately before 1 October 2007, and any application for approval under the Scheme which has not been granted before that date.

8 *Approval system*

(1) The approval body shall operate a system for the determination of applications for approval made to it under this Scheme and shall make adequate arrangements to publicise the details of that system.

(2) Without prejudice to the generality of paragraph (1), the approval system referred to in that paragraph shall in particular—

- *(a) provide for a procedure by which an applicant may apply for approval;*
- *(b) set out requirements relating to the provision by an applicant of documentary or other evidence necessary to demonstrate that the approval criteria are met;*
- *(c) provide for a procedure whereby approvals may be withdrawn;*
- *(d) provide for the applicant to be given notice in writing in respect of a determination to grant, refuse or withdraw an approval;*
- *(e) provide for a procedure whereby it may be ascertained whether an individual is for the time being approved under the Scheme; and*

(f) provide for the keeping of appropriate records relating to applications for approvals and to the grant, refusal or withdrawal of such approvals.

(3) The approval body shall maintain a record of those persons to whom an approval is granted for the time being under this Scheme.

(4) The records referred to in paragraphs (2) and (3) may be kept by means of a computer.

Revocation—Revoked, in relation to England, by the Tax Credits (Child Care Providers) (Miscellaneous Revocation and Transitional Provisions) (England) Scheme, SI 2007/2481 art 4(1) with effect from 1 October 2007: SI 2007/2481 reg 1(2).

The Scheme continues to have effect, however, in relation to any approval granted to a childcare provider under the Scheme which is valid immediately before 1 October 2007, and any application for approval under the Scheme which has not been granted before that date.

9 Provision of information by approval body

The approval body shall supply to the Commissioners of Inland Revenue such information as they may require for the discharge of any of their functions relating to working tax credit and which is information relating to the approval, or the refusal or withdrawal of approval, of persons under this Scheme.

Revocation—Revoked, in relation to England, by the Tax Credits (Child Care Providers) (Miscellaneous Revocation and Transitional Provisions) (England) Scheme, SI 2007/2481 art 4(1) with effect from 1 October 2007: SI 2007/2481 reg 1(2).

The Scheme continues to have effect, however, in relation to any approval granted to a childcare provider under the Scheme which is valid immediately before 1 October 2007, and any application for approval under the Scheme which has not been granted before that date.

10 Period of approval

(1) An approval given under this Scheme shall state the period of its validity which shall not exceed a period of 12 months.

(2) Nothing in this article shall prejudice the application of article 6(2).

Revocation—Revoked, in relation to England, by the Tax Credits (Child Care Providers) (Miscellaneous Revocation and Transitional Provisions) (England) Scheme, SI 2007/2481 art 4(1) with effect from 1 October 2007: SI 2007/2481 reg 1(2).

The Scheme continues to have effect, however, in relation to any approval granted to a childcare provider under the Scheme which is valid immediately before 1 October 2007, and any application for approval under the Scheme which has not been granted before that date.

11 Appeals

(1) Where the approval body refuses an application for the grant of an approval or withdraws an approval previously granted, an appeal shall lie to the Tribunal against that decision.

(2) The provisions of the Tribunal Regulations shall apply to an appeal under paragraph (1) as they apply to an appeal under section 79M of the 1989 Act and as if those provisions were set out in this Scheme, but with the modifications referred to in paragraph (3).

(3) Schedule 2 to the Tribunal Regulations shall apply as if—

(a) any reference to an appeal under the 1989 Act were a reference to an appeal under article 11(1) of this Scheme;

(b) any reference to any registration were a reference to an approval given under this Scheme;

(c) any reference to the cancellation of registration were a reference to the withdrawal of an approval under this Scheme;

(d) any reference to the registration body or the respondent were a reference to the approval body; and

(e) paragraph 3(3)(c) of that Schedule were modified as specified in paragraph (4) of this article and any reference to the said paragraph 3 were a reference to that paragraph as so modified.

(4) The said paragraph 3(3)(c) shall apply as if—

(a) the decision referred to in sub-paragraph (ii) of that paragraph were to the decision to refuse to grant or to withdraw an approval under this Scheme; and

(b) sub-paragraph (iii) of that paragraph did not apply.

(5) On an appeal, the Tribunal may—

(a) confirm the refusal to grant the approval or the withdrawal of the approval;

(b) direct that the said refusal or withdrawal shall not have, or shall cease to have, effect; or

(c) direct the approval body to reconsider any decision which is the subject of the appeal.

Revocation—Revoked, in relation to England, by the Tax Credits (Child Care Providers) (Miscellaneous Revocation and Transitional Provisions) (England) Scheme, SI 2007/2481 art 4(1) with effect from 1 October 2007: SI 2007/2481 reg 1(2).

The Scheme continues to have effect, however, in relation to any approval granted to a childcare provider under the Scheme which is valid immediately before 1 October 2007, and any application for approval under the Scheme which has not been granted before that date.

12 Fees

The approval body may charge any person seeking approval under this Scheme such reasonable fee as it shall, subject to the approval of the Secretary of State, determine.

Revocation—Revoked, in relation to England, by the Tax Credits (Child Care Providers) (Miscellaneous Revocation and Transitional Provisions) (England) Scheme, SI 2007/2481 art 4(1) with effect from 1 October 2007: SI 2007/2481 reg 1(2).

The Scheme continues to have effect, however, in relation to any approval granted to a childcare provider under the Scheme which is valid immediately before 1 October 2007, and any application for approval under the Scheme which has not been granted before that date.

13 Revocation and saving

(1) Subject to paragraph (2), the Tax Credit (Approval of Home Child Care Providers) Scheme 2003 (hereinafter referred to as "the 2003 Scheme") is hereby revoked.

(2) The provisions of the 2003 Scheme shall continue to have effect to the extent necessary to give full effect to paragraph (3).

(3) Any approval granted to any child care provider under the 2003 Scheme and which is in force on 6th April 2005 shall continue to have effect in respect of that provider under that Scheme until whichever is the earliest of—

- *(a) the date on which the approval is withdrawn or suspended in accordance with the 2003 Scheme;*
- *(b) the date on which the child care provider concerned is given an approval by the approval body pursuant to article 6 of this Scheme; or*
- *(c) 31st December 2005.*

Revocation—Revoked, in relation to England, by the Tax Credits (Child Care Providers) (Miscellaneous Revocation and Transitional Provisions) (England) Scheme, SI 2007/2481 art 4(1) with effect from 1 October 2007: SI 2007/2481 reg 1(2).

The Scheme continues to have effect, however, in relation to any approval granted to a childcare provider under the Scheme which is valid immediately before 1 October 2007, and any application for approval under the Scheme which has not been granted before that date.

2005/773

TAX CREDITS ACT 2002 (TRANSITIONAL PROVISIONS) ORDER 2005

Made by the Treasury under Tax Credits Act 2002 s 62(2)

Made .... *17 March 2005*

Revocation—These regulations revoked by the Tax Credits Act 2002 (Transitional Provisions) Order, SI 2010/644 art 5 with effect from 1 April 2010.

2005/776

TAX CREDITS ACT 2002 (TRANSITIONAL PROVISIONS) (NO 2) ORDER 2005

Revocation—This Order revoked by the Tax Credits Act 2002 (Commencement and Transitional Provisions) Order, SI 2006/3369 art 5.

2005/828

TAX CREDITS NOTIFICATION OF CHANGES OF CIRCUMSTANCES (CIVIL PARTNERSHIP) (TRANSITIONAL PROVISIONS) ORDER 2005

Made by the Treasury, under Civil Partnership Act 2004 s 259(1), (11)

Made .... *17 March 2005*

Laid before Parliament .... *18 March 2005*

Coming into force .... *8 April 2005*

1 Citation and commencement

This Order may be cited as the Tax Credits Notification of Changes of Circumstances (Civil Partnership) (Transitional Provisions) Order 2005 and shall come into force on 8th April 2005.

2 Modification of section 6 of the Tax Credits Act 2002

(1) For the tax year 2005/06, section 6 of the Tax Credits Act 2002 (notification of changes of circumstances) shall be modified as follows.

(2) After subsection (3) insert—

"(3A) For the purposes of this section, a change of circumstances shall be treated as having occurred where by virtue of the coming into force of Part 14 of Schedule 24 to the Civil Partnership Act 2004 (amendments of the Tax Credits Act 2002) two people of the same sex are treated as a couple.

(3B) In subsection (3A), "couple" has the meaning given in paragraph 144(3) of Part 14 of Schedule 24 to the Civil Partnership Act 2004.".

2007/2481

TAX CREDITS (CHILD CARE PROVIDERS) (MISCELLANEOUS REVOCATION AND TRANSITIONAL PROVISIONS) (ENGLAND) SCHEME 2007

The Secretary of State for Children, Schools and Families, being the appropriate national authority under section 12(6) of the Tax Credits Act 2002, and in exercise of the powers conferred by sections 12(5), (7) and (8) and 65(9) of that Act, makes the following Scheme:

Made . . . . *28 August 2007*
Laid before Parliament . . . . *3 September 2007*
Coming into force in accordance with . . . . *article 1(2)*

1 Citation, commencement and application

(1) This Scheme may be cited as the Tax Credits (Child Care Providers) (Miscellaneous Revocation and Transitional Provisions) (England) Scheme 2007.

(2) This Scheme comes into force—

(*a*) to the extent that it revokes the 2005 Scheme and the provisions of the 1999 Regulations other than regulations 11(*a*) and (*b*) and 12, on 1st October 2007; and

(*b*) to the extent that it revokes regulations 11(*a*) and (*b*) and 12 of the 1999 Regulations, on 1st October 2009.

(3) This Scheme applies in relation to England only.

2 Interpretation

In this Scheme—

"the 1999 Regulations" means the Tax Credit (New Category of Child Care Provider) Regulations 1999;

"the 2005 Scheme" means the Tax Credits (Approval of Child Care Providers) Scheme 2005;

"the inspection provisions" means regulations 11(a) and (b) and 12 of the 1999 Regulations (access to information and records by officers of the Secretary of State and Her Majesty's Revenue and Customs); and

"the transitional period" means the period beginning on 1st October 2007 and ending on 1st October 2009.

3 Partial revocation of the 1999 Regulations and transitional provision

(1) The 1999 Regulations are revoked to the extent that they make a Scheme for determining the description of persons by whom child care is provided, and whose charges fall to be taken into account in computing the child care element of working tax credit, subject to paragraph (3) of this article.

(2) Any accreditation of an organisation by the Secretary of State pursuant to the Scheme provided for by the 1999 Regulations, and any approval granted by such an organisation, shall lapse on 1st October 2007, except for the purposes of the inspection provisions.

(3) During the transitional period the inspection provisions shall have effect as if—

(*a*) the reference in regulation 11 to the period for which an organisation is accredited were a reference to the transitional period; and

(*b*) the reference in regulation 12 to the period during which a child care provider is approved by an accredited organisation were a reference to the transitional period.

4 Revocation of the 2005 Scheme and transitional provision

(1) The 2005 Scheme is revoked, subject to paragraph (2).

(2) The provisions of the 2005 Scheme continue to have effect[, with the modifications in paragraph (3),][1] in relation to—

(*a*) any approval granted to a child care provider under that Scheme which is valid immediately before 1st October 2007; and

(*b*) any application for approval under that Scheme which has not been granted before 1st October 2007.

[(3) For the purposes of paragraph (2) the 2005 Scheme is amended as follows—

(*a*) in article 2 omit the definitions of "the Tribunal" and "the Tribunal Regulations";

(*b*) in article 11—

(i) in paragraphs (1) and (5) for "Tribunal" substitute "First-tier Tribunal";

(ii) for paragraph (2) substitute—

"(2) Tribunal Procedure Rules shall apply to an appeal under paragraph (1) as they apply to an appeal under section 79M of the 1989 Act."; and

(*c*) omit paragraphs (3) and (4).][1]

Amendments—[1] In para (2), words inserted, and para (3) inserted, by the Tribunals, Courts and Enforcement Act 2007 (Transitional and Consequential Provisions) Order, SI 2008/2683 art 6(1), Sch 1 para 329 with effect from 3 November 2008.

2008/2684

FIRST-TIER TRIBUNAL AND UPPER TRIBUNAL (CHAMBERS) ORDER 2008

Made . . . .*13 October 2008*
Laid before Parliament . . . .*15 October 2008*
Coming into force . . . .*3 November 2008*

Revocation—This Order revoked by the First-tier Tribunal and Upper Tribunal (Chambers) Order, SI 2010/2655 art 1(2), Schedule with effect from 29 November 2010.

2008/2707

APPEALS (EXCLUDED DECISIONS) ORDER 2008

Made by the Lord Chancellor under the Tribunals, Courts and Enforcement Act 2007 s 11(5)(*f*)

Made . . . .*13 October 2008*
Laid before Parliament . . . .*15 October 2008*
Coming into force . . . .*3 November 2008*

1 This Order may be cited as the Appeals (Excluded Decisions) Order 2008 and shall come into force on 3rd November 2008.

2 For the purposes of section 11(1) of the Tribunals, Courts and Enforcement Act 2007, the following decisions of the First-tier Tribunal are excluded decisions—

(*a*) any decision on an appeal under section 102 of the Immigration and Asylum Act 1999;
(*b*) any decision on an appeal under section 63(6) of the Tax Credits Act 2002;
(*c*) any decision on an appeal under section 24(2) of the Child Trust Funds Act 2004.

2010/42

FIRST-TIER TRIBUNAL (GAMBLING) FEES ORDER 2010

Made . . . .*10 January 2010*
Laid before Parliament . . . .*12 January 2010*
Coming into force . . . .*18 January 2010*

The Lord Chancellor makes the following Order in exercise of the power conferred by section 42 of the Tribunals, Courts and Enforcement Act 2007.

In accordance with section 42(5) of that Act the Lord Chancellor has consulted the Senior President of Tribunals and the Administrative Justice and Tribunals Council.

1 Citation and commencement

This Order may be cited as the First-tier Tribunal (Gambling) Fees Order 2010 and comes into force on 18 January 2010.

2 Fee for bringing an appeal under the Gambling Act 2005

(1) Subject to paragraph (2) and articles 3 and 4, the fees set out in column 2 of the table in [Schedule 1][1] are payable in relation to an appeal to the First-tier Tribunal under the Gambling Act 2005 listed in column 1 of that table.

(2) Where an appeal relates to a combination of any of the licences listed in fees 1.1 to 1.12 of column 1 of the table in [Schedule 1][1] , only one fee is payable, and if those fees are different, only the highest fee is payable.

Amendments—[1] Words substituted by the Courts and Tribunals Fee Remissions Order, SI 2013/2302 art 9(1), (2) with effect from 7 October 2013.

[3 Remissions and part remissions

Schedule 2 applies for the purpose of ascertaining whether a party is entitled to a remission or part remission of a fee prescribed by this Order.][1]

Amendments—[1] Article 3 substituted by the Courts and Tribunals Fee Remissions Order, SI 2013/2302 art 9(1), (3) with effect from 7 October 2013.

4, 5 . . . [1]

Amendments—[1] Articles 4, 5 revoked by the Courts and Tribunals Fee Remissions Order, SI 2013/2302 art 9(1), (4) with effect from 7 October 2013.

[[SCHEDULE 1]

FEES TO BE TAKEN

Article 2

Appeal	*Column A*	*Column B*
	New fee	*Old fee*
1 On filing an appeal under section 141 of the Gambling Act 2005 in relation to—		
1.1 a casino operating licence referred to in section 65(2)(*a*) of that Act	£14,000	£13,070
1.2 a bingo operating licence referred to in section 65(2)(*b*) of that Act	£3,100	£2,905
1.3 a general betting operating licence referred to in section 65(2)(*c*) of that Act	£10,000	£9,335
1.4 a pool betting operating licence referred to in section 65(2)(*d*) of that Act	£10,000	£9,335
1.5 a betting intermediary operating licence referred to in section 65(2)(*e*) of that Act	£10,000	£9,335
1.6 a gaming machine general operating licence for an adult gaming centre referred to in section 65(2)(*f*) of that Act	£1,600	£1,450
1.7 a gaming machine general operating licence for a family entertainment centre referred to in section 65(2)(*g*) of that Act	£1,600	£1,450
1.8 a gaming machine technical operating licence referred to in section 65(2)(*h*) of that Act	£1,600	£1,450
1.9 a gambling software operating licence referred to in with section 65(2)(i) of that Act	£1,600	£1,450
1.10 a lottery operating licence referred to in section 65(2)(j) of that Act	£9,400	£8,710
1.11 a personal management office licence referred to in section 127 of that Act	£1,600	£1,450
1.12 a personal operational function licence referred to in section 127 of that Act	£800	£755
2 On filing an appeal under section 337(1) of the Gambling Act 2005 against the Gambling Commission's order to void a bet under section 336(1) of that Act	£9,400	£8,710]

Amendments—Schedule substituted by the First-tier Tribunal (Gambling) Fees (Amendment) Order, SI 2010/633 art 2, Schedule with effect from 6 April 2010.

Schedule 1 numbered as such by the Courts and Tribunals Fee Remissions Order, SI 2013/2302 art 9(1), (5) with effect from 7 October 2013.

[SCHEDULE 2

REMISSIONS AND PART REMISSIONS

Amendments—Schedule 2 inserted by the Courts and Tribunals Fee Remissions Order, SI 2013/2302 art 9(1), (6), Schedule with effect from 7 October 2013.

[1 Interpretation

(1) In this Schedule—

"child" means a person—

(*a*) whose main residence is with a party and who is aged—

(i) under 16 years; or

(ii) 16 to 19 years; and is—

(*aa*) not married or in a civil partnership; and

(*bb*) enrolled or accepted in full-time education that is not advanced education, or approved training; or

(*b*) in respect of whom a party or their partner pays child support maintenance or periodic payments in accordance with a maintenance agreement,

and "full-time education", "advanced education" and "approved training" have the meaning given by the Child Benefit (General) Regulations 2006;

"child support maintenance" has the meaning given in section 3(6) of the Child Support Act 1991;

"couple" has the meaning given in section 3(5A) of the Tax Credits Act 2002;

"disposable capital" has the meaning given in paragraph 5;

["excluded benefits" means any of the following—

(*a*) any of the following benefits payable under the Social Security Contributions and Benefits Act 1992 or the corresponding provisions of the Social Security Contributions and Benefits (Northern Ireland) Act 1992—

(i) attendance allowance under section 64;

(ii) severe disablement allowance;

(iii) carer's allowance;

(iv) disability living allowance;

(v) constant attendance allowance under section 104 as an increase to a disablement pension;

(vi) any payment made out of the social fund;

(vii) housing benefit;

(viii) widowed parents allowance;

(*b*) any of the following benefit payable under the Tax Credits Act 2002—

(i) any disabled child element or severely disabled child element of the child tax credit;

(ii) any childcare element of the working tax credit;

(*c*) any direct payment made under the Community Care, Services for Carers and Children's Services (Direct Payments) (England) Regulations 2009, the Community Care, Services for Carers and Children's Services (Direct Payments) (Wales) Regulations 2011, the Carers and Direct Payments Act (Northern Ireland) 2002, or section 12B(1) of the [the Social Care (Self–directed Support) (Scotland) Act 2013][3];

(*d*) a back to work bonus payable under section 26 of the Jobseekers Act 1995, or article 28 of the Jobseekers (Northern Ireland) Order 1995;

(*e*) any exceptionally severe disablement allowance paid under the Personal Injuries (Civilians) Scheme 1983;

(*f*) any payments from the Industrial Injuries Disablement Benefit;

(*g*) any pension paid under the Naval, Military and Air Forces etc (Disablement and Death) Service Pension Order 2006;

(*h*) any payment made from the Independent Living Funds;

(*i*) any payment made from the Bereavement Allowance;

(*j*) any financial support paid under an agreement for the care of a foster child;

(*k*) any housing credit element of pension credit;

(*l*) any armed forces independence payment;

(*m*) any personal independence payment payable under the Welfare Reform Act 2012;

(*n*) any payment on account of benefit as defined in the Social Security (Payments on Account of Benefit) Regulations 2013;

(*o*) any of the following amounts, as defined by the Universal Credit Regulations 2013, that make up an award of universal credit—

(i) an additional amount to the child element in respect of a disabled child;

(ii) a housing costs element;

(iii) a childcare costs element;

(iv) a carer element;

(v) a limited capability for work or limited capacity for work and work-related activity element.][2]

"family help (higher)" has the meaning given in paragraph 15(3) of the Civil Legal Aid (Merits Criteria) Regulations 2013;

"family help (lower)" has the meaning given in paragraph 15(2) of the Civil Legal Aid (Merits Criteria) Regulations 2013;

"gross monthly income" has the meaning given in paragraph 13;

"Independent Living Funds" means the funds listed at regulation 20(2)(*b*) of the Criminal Legal Aid (Financial Resources) Regulations 2013;

"legal representation" has the meaning given in paragraph 18(2) of the Civil Legal Aid (Merits Criteria) Regulations 2013;

"maintenance agreement" has the meaning given in subsection 9(1) of the Child Support Act 1991;

"partner" means a person with whom the party lives as a couple and includes a person with whom the party is not currently living but from whom the party is not living separate and apart;

"party" means the individual who would, but for this Schedule, be liable to pay a fee under this Order;

"restraint order" means—

(*a*) an order under section 42(1A) of the Senior Courts Act 1981;

(*b*) an order under section 33 of the Employment Tribunals Act 1996;

(*c*) a civil restraint order made under rule 3.11 of the Civil Procedure Rules 1998, or a practice direction made under that rule; or

(*d*) a civil restraint order under rule 4.8 of the Family Procedure Rules 2010, or the practice direction referred to in that rule.

(2) References to remission of a fee are to be read as including references to a part remission of a fee as appropriate and remit and remitted shall be construed accordingly.][1]

Amendments—[1] Schedule 2 inserted by the Courts and Tribunals Fee Remissions Order, SI 2013/2302 art 9(1), (6), Schedule with effect from 7 October 2013.

[2] Definition of "excluded benefits" substituted by the Courts and Tribunals Fees (Miscellaneous Amendments) Order, SI 2014/590 art 6 with effect from 6 April 2014.

[3] In definition of "excluded benefits", para (*e*), words substituted by the Social Care (Self-directed Support) (Scotland) Act 2013 (Consequential Modifications and Savings) Order, SI 2014/513 art 2, Schedule para 20 with effect from 1 April 2014. Publisher's note: notwithstanding the substitution of the definiton of "excluded benefirts" with effect from 6 April 2014 (see amendment note 1 above), the Social Work (Scotland) Act 1968 s 12B was repealed by the Social Care (Self–directed Support) (Scotland) Act 2013 s 25 with effect from 1 April 2014 (by virtue of SSI 2014/32)).

[2 Fee remission

If a party satisfies the disposable capital test, the amount of any fee remission is calculated by applying the gross monthly income test.][1]

Amendments—[1] Schedule 2 inserted by the Courts and Tribunals Fee Remissions Order, SI 2013/2302 art 9(1), (6), Schedule with effect from 7 October 2013.

[Disposable capital test

3 Disposable capital test

(1) Subject to paragraph 4, a party satisfies the disposable capital test if—

(*a*) the fee payable by the party and for which an application for remission is made, falls within a fee band set out in column 1 of Table 1; and

(*b*) the party's disposable capital is less than the amount in the corresponding row of column 2.

Table 1

Column 1 (fee band)	*Column 2 (disposable capital)*
Up to and including £1,000	£3,000
£1,001 to £1,335	£4,000
£1,336 to £1,665	£5,000
£1,666 to £2,000	£6,000
£2,001 to £2,330	£7,000
£2,331 to £4,000	£8,000
£4,001 to £5,000	£10,000
£5,001 to £6,000	£12,000
£6,001 to £7,000	£14,000
£7,001 or more	£16,000][1]

Amendments—[1] Schedule 2 inserted by the Courts and Tribunals Fee Remissions Order, SI 2013/2302 art 9(1), (6), Schedule with effect from 7 October 2013.

[4

Subject to paragraph 14, if a party or their partner is aged 61 or over, that party satisfies the disposable capital test if that party's disposable capital is less than £16,000.][1]

Tax Credits

Amendments—[1] Schedule 2 inserted by the Courts and Tribunals Fee Remissions Order, SI 2013/2302 art 9(1), (6), Schedule with effect from 7 October 2013.

5 [Disposable capital

Subject to paragraph 14, disposable capital is the value of every resource of a capital nature belonging to the party on the date on which the application for remission is made, unless it is treated as income by this Order, or it is disregarded as excluded disposable capital.][1]

Amendments—[1] Schedule 2 inserted by the Courts and Tribunals Fee Remissions Order, SI 2013/2302 art 9(1), (6), Schedule with effect from 7 October 2013.

[6 Disposable capital—non-money resources

The value of a resource of a capital nature that does not consist of money is calculated as the amount which that resource would realise if sold, less—

(*a*) 10% of the sale value; and

(*b*) the amount of any borrowing secured against that resource that would be repayable on sale.][1]

Amendments—[1] Schedule 2 inserted by the Courts and Tribunals Fee Remissions Order, SI 2013/2302 art 9(1), (6), Schedule with effect from 7 October 2013.

[7 Disposable capital—resources held outside the United Kingdom

(1) Capital resources in a country outside the United Kingdom count towards disposable capital.

(2) If there is no prohibition in that country against the transfer of a resource into the United Kingdom, the value of that resource is the amount which that resource would realise if sold in that country, in accordance with paragraph 6.

(3) If there is a prohibition in that country against the transfer of a resource into the United Kingdom, the value of that resource is the amount that resource would realise if sold to a buyer in the United Kingdom.][1]

Amendments—[1] Schedule 2 inserted by the Courts and Tribunals Fee Remissions Order, SI 2013/2302 art 9(1), (6), Schedule with effect from 7 October 2013.

[8 Disposable capital—foreign currency resources

Where disposable capital is held in currency other than sterling, the cost of any banking charge or commission that would be payable if that amount were converted into sterling, is deducted from its value.][1]

Amendments—[1] Schedule 2 inserted by the Courts and Tribunals Fee Remissions Order, SI 2013/2302 art 9(1), (6), Schedule with effect from 7 October 2013.

[9 Disposable capital—jointly owned resources

Where any resource of a capital nature is owned jointly or in common, there is a presumption that the resource is owned in equal shares, unless evidence to the contrary is produced.][1]

Amendments—[1] Schedule 2 inserted by the Courts and Tribunals Fee Remissions Order, SI 2013/2302 art 9(1), (6), Schedule with effect from 7 October 2013.

[10 Excluded disposable capital

The following things are excluded disposable capital—

(*a*) a property which is the main or only dwelling occupied by the party;

(*b*) the household furniture and effects of the main or only dwelling occupied by the party;

(*c*) articles of personal clothing;

(*d*) any vehicle, the sale of which would leave the party, or their partner, without motor transport;

(*e*) tools and implements of trade, including vehicles used for business purposes;

(*f*) the capital value of the party's or their partner's business, where the party or their partner is self-employed;

(*g*) the capital value of any funds or other assets held in trust, where the party or their partner is a beneficiary without entitlement to advances of any trust capital;

(*h*) a jobseeker's back to work bonus;

(*i*) a payment made as a result of a determination of unfair dismissal by a court or tribunal, or by way of settlement of a claim for unfair dismissal;

(*j*) any compensation paid as a result of a determination of medical negligence or in respect of any personal injury by a court, or by way of settlement of a claim for medical negligence or personal injury;

(*k*) the capital held in any personal or occupational pension scheme;

(*l*) any cash value payable on surrender of a contract of insurance;

(*m*) any capital payment made out of the Independent Living Funds;

(*n*) any bereavement payment;

(*o*) any capital insurance or endowment lump sum payments that have been paid as a result of illness, disability or death;

(*p*) any student loan or student grant;

(*q*) any payments under the criminal injuries compensation scheme.][1]

Amendments—[1] Schedule 2 inserted by the Courts and Tribunals Fee Remissions Order, SI 2013/2302 art 9(1), (6), Schedule with effect from 7 October 2013.

[Gross monthly income test

11 Remission of fees—gross monthly income

(1) If a party satisfies the disposable capital test, no fee is payable under this Order if, at the time when the fee would otherwise be payable, the party or their partner has the number of children specified in column 1 of Table 2 and—

(*a*) if the party is single, their gross monthly income does not exceed the amount set out in the appropriate row of column 2; or

(*b*) if the party is one of a couple, the gross monthly income of that couple does not exceed the amount set out in the appropriate row of column 3.

Table 2

Column 1 *Number of children of party*	*Column 2* *Single*	*Column 3* *Couple*
no children	£1,085	£1,245
1 child	£1,330	£1,490
2 children	£1,575	£1,735

(2) If a party or their partner has more than 2 children, the relevant amount of gross monthly income is the appropriate amount specified in Table 2 for 2 children, plus the sum of £245 for each additional child.

(3) For every £10 of gross monthly income received above the appropriate amount in Table 2, including any additional amount added under sub-paragraph (2), the party must pay £5 towards the fee payable, up to the maximum amount of the fee payable.

(4) This paragraph is subject to paragraph 12.][1]

Amendments—[1] Schedule 2 inserted by the Courts and Tribunals Fee Remissions Order, SI 2013/2302 art 9(1), (6), Schedule with effect from 7 October 2013.

[12 Gross monthly income cap

(1) No remission is available if a party or their partner has the number of children specified in column 1 of Table 3 and—

(*a*) if the party is single, their gross monthly income exceeds the amount set out in the appropriate row of column 2 of Table 3; or

(*b*) if the party is one of a couple, the gross monthly income of that couple exceeds the amount set out in the appropriate row of column 3 of Table 3.

Table 3

Column 1 *Number of children of party*	*Column 2* *Single*	*Column 3* *Couple*
no children	£5,085	£5,245
1 child	£5,330	£5,490
2 children	£5,575	£5,735

(2) If a party or their partner has more than 2 children, the relevant amount of gross monthly income is the appropriate amount specified in Table 3 for 2 children, plus the sum of £245 for each additional child.][1]

Amendments—[1] Schedule 2 inserted by the Courts and Tribunals Fee Remissions Order, SI 2013/2302 art 9(1), (6), Schedule with effect from 7 October 2013.

13 [Gross monthly income

(1) Subject to paragraph 14, gross monthly income means the total monthly income, for the month preceding that in which the application for remission is made, from all sources, other than receipt of any of the excluded benefits.

(2) Income from a trade, business or gainful occupation other than an occupation at a wage or salary is calculated as—

(*a*) the profits which have accrued or will accrue to the party; and

(*b*) the drawings of the party;

in the month preceding that in which the application for remission is made.

(3) In calculating profits under sub-paragraph (2)(*a*), all sums necessarily expended to earn those profits are deducted.][1]

Amendments—[1] Schedule 2 inserted by the Courts and Tribunals Fee Remissions Order, SI 2013/2302 art 9(1), (6), Schedule with effect from 7 October 2013.

[General

14 Resources and income treated as the party's resources and income

(1) Subject to sub-paragraph (2), the disposable capital and gross monthly income of a partner of a party is to be treated as disposable capital and gross monthly income of the party.

(2) Where the partner of a party has a contrary interest to the party in the matter to which the fee relates, the disposable capital and gross monthly income of that partner, if any, is not treated as the disposable capital and gross monthly income of the party.][1]

Amendments—[1] Schedule 2 inserted by the Courts and Tribunals Fee Remissions Order, SI 2013/2302 art 9(1), (6), Schedule with effect from 7 October 2013.

15 [Application for remission of a fee

(1) An application for remission of a fee must be made at the time when the fee would otherwise be payable.

(2) Where an application for remission of a fee is made, the party must—

(*a*) indicate the fee to which the application relates;

(*b*) declare the amount of their disposable capital; and

(*c*) provide documentary evidence of their gross monthly income and the number of children relevant for the purposes of paragraphs 11 and 12.

(3) Where an application for remission of a fee is made on or before the date on which a fee is payable, the date for payment of the fee is disapplied.

(4) Where an application for remission is refused, or if part remission of a fee is granted, the amount of the fee which remains unremitted must be paid within the period notified in writing to the party.][1]

Amendments—[1] Schedule 2 inserted by the Courts and Tribunals Fee Remissions Order, SI 2013/2302 art 9(1), (6), Schedule with effect from 7 October 2013.

[16 Remission in exceptional circumstances

A fee specified in this Order may be remitted where the Lord Chancellor is satisfied that there are exceptional circumstances which justify doing so.][1]

Amendments—[1] Schedule 2 inserted by the Courts and Tribunals Fee Remissions Order, SI 2013/2302 art 9(1), (6), Schedule with effect from 7 October 2013.

[17 Refunds

(1) Subject to sub-paragraph (3), where a party pays a fee at a time when that party would have been entitled to a remission if they had provided the documentary evidence required by paragraph 15, the fee, or the amount by which the fee would have been reduced as the case may be, must be refunded if documentary evidence relating to the time when the fee became payable is provided at a later date.

(2) Subject to sub-paragraph (3), where a fee has been paid at a time when the Lord Chancellor, if all the circumstances had been known, would have remitted the fee under paragraph 15, the fee or the amount by which the fee would have been reduced, as the case may be, must be refunded to the party.

(3) No refund shall be made under this paragraph unless the party who paid the fee applies within 3 months of the date on which the fee was paid.

(4) The Lord Chancellor may extend the period of 3 months mentioned in sub-paragraph (3) if the Lord Chancellor considers that there is a good reason for a refund being made after the end of the period of 3 months.][1]

Amendments—[1] Schedule 2 inserted by the Courts and Tribunals Fee Remissions Order, SI 2013/2302 art 9(1), (6), Schedule with effect from 7 October 2013.

[18 Legal Aid

A party is not entitled to a fee remission if, under Part 1 of the Legal Aid, Sentencing and Punishment of Offenders Act 2012, they are in receipt of the following civil legal services—

(*a*) Legal representation; or

(*b*) Family help (higher); or

(*c*) Family help (lower) in respect of applying for a consent order.][1]

Amendments—[1] Schedule 2 inserted by the Courts and Tribunals Fee Remissions Order, SI 2013/2302 art 9(1), (6), Schedule with effect from 7 October 2013.

[19 Vexatious litigants

(1) This paragraph applies where—

(*a*) a restraint order is in force against a party; and

(*b*) that party makes an application for permission to—
   (i) issue proceedings or take a step in proceedings as required by the restraint order;
   (ii) apply for amendment or discharge of the order; or
   (iii) appeal the order.

(2) The fee prescribed by this Order for the application is payable in full.

(3) If the party is granted permission, they are to be refunded the difference between—
   (*a*) the fee paid; and
   (*b*) the fee that would have been payable if this Schedule had been applied without reference to this paragraph.][1]

Amendments—[1] Schedule 2 inserted by the Courts and Tribunals Fee Remissions Order, SI 2013/2302 art 9(1), (6), Schedule with effect from 7 October 2013.

[20 Exceptions

No remissions or refunds are available in respect of the fee payable for—
   (a) copy or duplicate documents;
   (b) searches.][1]

Amendments—[1] Schedule 2 inserted by the Courts and Tribunals Fee Remissions Order, SI 2013/2302 art 9(1), (6), Schedule with effect from 7 October 2013.

2010/644

TAX CREDITS ACT 2002 (TRANSITIONAL PROVISIONS) ORDER 2010

Made . . . . *8 March 2010*
Coming into force . . . . *1 April 2010*

The Treasury make the following Order in exercise of the powers conferred by section 62(2) of the Tax Credits Act 2002.

1 Citation and commencement

This Order may be cited as the Tax Credits Act 2002 (Transitional Provisions) Order 2010 and shall come into force on 1st April 2010.

2 Interpretation

(1) In this Order—

"benefit week" has the meaning given in—
   (*a*) regulation 2(1) of the Income Support Regulations 1987 in relation to income support, and
   (*b*) regulation 1(3) of the Jobseeker's Allowance Regulations 1996 in relation to income-based jobseeker's allowance;

"child premia" means the amounts in respect of income support or income-based jobseeker's allowance referred to in section 1(3)(*d*) of the Tax Credits Act 2002;

"polygamous unit" has the meaning given in regulation 2 of the Tax Credits (Polygamous Marriages) Regulations 2003;

"specified date" has the meaning given by paragraph (2);

"specified person" has the meaning given by paragraph (3).

(2) For the purposes of this Order the "specified date" is the day following the date notified to an officer of Revenue and Customs as the final day of the last benefit week for which the child premia is to be paid to the specified person—
   (*a*) by the Department for Work and Pensions, if the specified person is claiming in Great Britain, or
   (*b*) by the Department for Social Development, if the specified person is claiming in Northern Ireland.

(3) For the purposes of this Order a "specified person" is a person who—
   (*a*) until the specified date was receiving the child premia, and
   (*b*) has not made a claim for child tax credit.

3 Transitional provisions

(1) Notwithstanding section 5(2) of the Tax Credits Act 2002, an award on a claim for child tax credit made by a person who until the specified date was receiving the child premia is for the period specified in paragraph (2)

(2) The period is a period beginning with the specified date and ending at the end of the tax year in which that date falls.

(3) Notwithstanding regulation 7 of the Tax Credits (Claims and Notifications) Regulations 2002, a person shall not be entitled to child tax credit in respect of any day prior to the day on which that person makes a claim for it ("the earlier day") if—
   [(*a*) the earlier day falls before 31st December 2014, and][1]

(*b*) the claimant is entitled, or in the case of a joint claim, either of the claimants is entitled, to the child premia on the earlier day.

Amendments—[1] Para (3)(*a*) substituted by the Tax Credits Act 2002 (Further Commencement and Transitional Provisions) Order, SI 2011/2910, art 3.

4 Deemed claims for tax credits

(1) A claim shall be deemed to be made under section 3(1) of the Tax Credits Act 2002 if Her Majesty's Revenue and Customs receive a claim for child tax credit from the Department of Work and Pensions or the Department for Social Development and the claim—

(*a*) is in respect of a specified person,

(*b*) complies with regulation 5(2) of the Tax Credits (Claims and Notifications) Regulations 2002, and

(*c*) contains the information required in paragraphs (3) to (5) of regulation 3 of those Regulations.

(2) The claim shall be deemed to be made by the person in respect of whom it is made.

(3) If the specified person is a member of a married couple or an unmarried couple or a polygamous unit, the specified person and the other member of the couple or member or members of the polygamous unit are treated as making a joint claim.

(4) The specified person is treated as being responsible for the child or children or qualifying young person or persons to whom that person's entitlement to the child premia relates.

(5) The claim shall be deemed to be made on the specified date.

(6) This article is subject to article 3.

5 Revocation of previous commencement and transitional provisions orders

The instruments listed in the Table below are revoked to the extent specified in the third column of that Table.

(1)	(2)	(3)
Instruments revoked	References	Extent of revocation
The Tax Credits Act 2002 (Commencement No 4, Transitional Provisions and Savings) Order 2003	SI 2003/962	Article 5(4)
The Tax Credits Act 2002 (Transitional Provisions) Order 2005	SI 2005/773	The whole Order
The Tax Credits Act 2002 (Commencement and Transitional Provisions) Order 2006	SI 2006/3369	The whole Order
The Tax Credits Act 2002 (Transitional Provisions) Order 2008	SI 2008/3151	Articles 2 and 3(3)

2011/1502

TAXATION OF EQUITABLE LIFE (PAYMENTS) ORDER 2011

Made . . . . 15 June 2011

Coming into force in accordance with article 1(1)

The Treasury make the following Order in exercise of the powers conferred by section 1(3) and (4) of the Equitable Life (Payments) Act 2010

In accordance with section 1(5) of that Act, a draft of this Order was laid before Parliament and approved by a resolution of each House of Parliament.

1 Citation, commencement, effect and interpretation

(1) This Order may be cited as the Taxation of Equitable Life (Payments) Order 2011 and shall come into force on the day after the day on which it is made.

(2) This Order has effect in relation to authorised payments made after the day on which this Order is made.

(3) In this Order "authorised payment" means a payment to which section 1 of the Equitable Life (Payments) Act 2010 applies.

2 Capital gains tax

An authorised payment shall be disregarded for the purposes of capital gains tax.

3 Corporation tax

An authorised payment shall be disregarded for the purposes of the Corporation Tax Acts.

4 Income tax

An authorised payment shall be disregarded for the purposes of the Income Tax Acts.

5 Inheritance tax

(1) For the purposes of the Inheritance Tax Act 1984—

(*a*) in determining the value of a person's estate immediately before that person's death, no account shall be taken of any value attributable to a right to, or interest in, an authorised payment made after that person's death; and

(*b*) in determining the value of relevant property immediately before a ten-year anniversary for the purposes of the charge under section 64 of the Inheritance Tax Act 1984, no account shall be taken of any value attributable to a right to, or interest in, an authorised payment made on or after that ten-year anniversary.

(2) In this article—

"estate" has the meaning given by section 272 of the Inheritance Tax Act 1984;

"relevant property" has the meaning given by section 58 of that Act; and

"ten-year anniversary" has the meaning given by section 61 of that Act.

6 Tax Credits

In calculating investment income in accordance with regulation 10 of the Tax Credits (Definition and Calculation of Income) Regulations 2002, an authorised payment shall be disregarded.

2013/715

LOSS OF TAX CREDITS REGULATIONS 2013

Made . . . . *26 March 2013*

Coming into force. . . . . *6 April 2013*

The Commissioners for Her Majesty's Revenue and Customs make these Regulations in the exercise of the powers conferred by sections 36A(5) and (6), 36C(4) and (5), 65(2) and 67 of the Tax Credits Act 2002.

A draft of this instrument was laid before and approved by a resolution of each House of Parliament in accordance with section 66(1) and (2)(*zb*) of the Tax Credits Act 2002.

1 Citation, commencement and interpretation

(1) These Regulations may be cited as the Loss of Tax Credits Regulations 2013 and come into force on 6th April 2013.

(2) In these Regulations, references to sections of the Act are to sections of the Tax Credits Act 2002.

2 Loss of working tax credit for benefit offence and repeated benefit fraud: beginning of disqualification periods

(1) For the purposes of section 36A(6) of the Act, the date on which the relevant period begins is the thirtieth day after the day on which the Commissioners for Her Majesty's Revenue and Customs ("the Commissioners") are notified of the disqualifying event mentioned in section 36A(1)—

(*a*) in relation to England and Wales and Scotland, by the Secretary of State or by an authority which administers housing benefit or council tax benefit,

(*b*) in relation to Northern Ireland, by the Department for Social Development, the Department of Finance and Personnel or the Northern Ireland Housing Executive.

(2) For the purposes of section 36C(5) of the Act, the prescribed date is the thirtieth day after the day on which the Commissioners are notified of the offender's conviction mentioned in that section, by the prosecuting authority responsible for bringing the current set of proceedings in which the offender was convicted.

3 Loss of working tax credit for benefit offence and repeated benefit fraud

For the duration of any period—

(a) comprised in the offender's disqualification period for the purposes of section 36A(4)(*b*) or 36C(3)(*b*) of the Act, and

(b) not comprising any such disqualification period of the other member of the couple mentioned in either section,

the working tax credit in question shall be payable, but as if the amount payable were reduced by 50%.

2014/1230

UNIVERSAL CREDIT (TRANSITIONAL PROVISIONS) REGULATIONS 2014

Made . . . . *12 May 2014*

Laid before Parliament . . . . *14 May 2014*

Coming into force . . . . .16 *June 2014*

The Secretary of State for Work and Pensions makes the following Regulations in exercise of the powers conferred by section 42(2) and (3) of and paragraphs 1(1) and (2)(*b*), 3(1)(*a*) to (*c*), 4(1)(*a*), 5(1), (2)(*c*) and (*d*) and (3)(*a*) and 6 of Schedule 6 to the Welfare Reform Act 2012.

In accordance with section 172(1) of the Social Security Administration Act 1992 ("the 1992 Act"), the Secretary of State has referred proposals in respect of these Regulations to the Social Security Advisory Committee.

In accordance with section 176(1) of the 1992 Act and, in so far as these Regulations relate to housing benefit, the Secretary of State has consulted with organisations appearing to him to be representative of the authorities concerned in respect of proposals for these Regulations.

PART 1
INTRODUCTORY

1 Citation and commencement

(1) These Regulations may be cited as the Universal Credit (Transitional Provisions) Regulations 2014.

(2) These Regulations come into force on 16th June 2014.

PART 2
TRANSITION TO UNIVERSAL CREDIT

CHAPTER 2

ENTITLEMENT TO OTHER BENEFITS

11 Ongoing awards of tax credits

(1) For the purposes of regulations 7(7) and 8(4)—

(*a*) a person is to be treated as being entitled to working tax credit with effect from the start of the current tax year even though a decision has not been made under section 14 of the 2002 Act in respect of a claim for that tax credit for that tax year, if the person was entitled to working tax credit for the previous tax year and any of the cases specified in paragraph (2) applies; and

(*b*) a person is to be treated as being entitled to child tax credit with effect from the start of the current tax year even though a decision has not been made under section 14 of the 2002 Act in respect of a claim for that tax credit for that tax year, if the person was entitled to child tax credit for the previous tax year and any of the cases specified in paragraph (2) applies.

(2) The cases are—

(*a*) a final notice has not been given to the person under section 17 of the 2002 Act in respect of the previous tax year;

(*b*) a final notice has been given, which includes provision by virtue of subsection (2) or (4) of section 17, or a combination of those subsections and subsection (6) and—

(i) the date specified in the notice for the purposes of section 17(2) and (4) or, where different dates are specified, the later of them, has not yet passed and no claim for a tax credit for the current tax year has been made, or treated as made; or

(ii) a claim for a tax credit has been made, or treated as made, on or before the date mentioned in paragraph (i), but no decision has been made in relation to that claim under section 14(1) of the 2002 Act;

(*c*) a final notice has been given, no claim for a tax credit for the current year has been made, or treated as made, and no decision has been made under section 18(1) of the 2002 Act in respect of entitlement to a tax credit for the previous tax year; or

(*d*) a final notice has been given and—

(i) the person did not make a declaration in response to provision included in that notice by virtue of section 17(2)(*a*), (4)(*a*) or (6)(*a*), or any combination of those provisions, by the date specified in the notice;

(ii) the person was given due notice that payments of tax credit under section 24(4) of the 2002 Act had ceased due to his or her failure to make the declaration; and

(iii) the person's claim for universal credit is made during the period of 30 days starting with the date on the notice referred to in paragraph (ii) or, where the person is a new claimant partner, notification of formation of a couple with a person entitled to universal credit is given to the Secretary of State during that period.

12 Modification of tax credits legislation: overpayments and penalties

(1) This regulation applies where—

(*a*) a claim for universal credit is made, or is treated as having been made;

(*b*) the claimant is, or was at any time during the tax year in which the claim is made or treated as made, entitled to a tax credit; and

(*c*) the Secretary of State is satisfied that the claimant meets the basic conditions specified in section 4(1)(*a*) to (*d*) of the Act (other than any of those conditions which the claimant is not required to meet by virtue of regulations under section 4(2) of the Act).

(2) Where this regulation applies, the 2002 Act applies in relation to the claimant with the following modifications.

(3) In section 28—

(*a*) in subsection (1)—

(i) after "tax year" in both places where it occurs, insert "or part tax year";

[(ii) in paragraph (*b*), for the words from "as if it were" to the end substitute "as an overpayment of universal credit";][2]

(b) in subsections (3) and (4), after "repaid" insert "to the Board or, as the case may be, to the Secretary of State";[2]

(*c*) omit subsection (5);

(*d*) in subsection (6) omit "(apart from subsection (5))".

[(4) For section 29(4) substitute—

"(4) Where a notice states that this subsection applies in relation to an amount (or part of an amount), it may be recovered—

(*a*) subject to provision made by regulations, by deduction from payments of any tax credit under an award made for any period to the person, or either or both of the persons, to whom the notice was given; or

(*b*) subject to regulations made by the Secretary of State under the Social Security Administration Act 1992—

(i) by deductions under section 71ZC of that Act (Deduction from benefit—including universal credit);

(ii) by deductions under section 71ZD of that Act (Deduction from earnings); or

(iii) as set out in section 71ZE of that Act (Court action etc).".[2]

(5) In section 48 after the definition of "overpayment" insert—

""part tax year" means a period of less than a year beginning with 6th April and ending with the date on which the award of a tax credit terminated,".

(6) In Schedule 2, in paragraph 6(1)(*a*) and (*c*) and (2)(*a*), after "for the tax year" insert "or part tax year".

Amendments—[1] Para 4 substituted by the Universal Credit (Transitional Provisions) (Amendment) Regulations, SI 2016/232 reg 2 with effect from 1 April 2016.

[2] Para (3)(*a*)(ii) substituted, and paras (3)(*b*), (4) revoked by the Tax Credits (Exercise of Functions in relation to Northern Ireland and Notices for Recovery of Tax Credit Overpayments) Order, SI 2017/781 art 7 with effect from 25 September 2017. Para (3)(*a*)(ii) previously read as follows—

"(ii) at the end insert "or treated as an overpayment of universal credit";".

[12A Modification of tax credits legislation: finalisation of tax credits

(1) This regulation applies where—

(*a*) a claim for universal credit is made, or is treated as having been made;

(*b*) the claimant is, or was at any time during the tax year in which the claim is made or treated as made, entitled to a tax credit; and

(*c*) the Secretary of State is satisfied that the claimant meets the basic conditions specified in section 4(1)(*a*) to (*d*) of the Act (other than any of those conditions which the claimant is not required to meet by virtue of regulations under section 4(2) of the Act).

(2) Subject to paragraph (3), where this regulation applies, the amount of the tax credit to which the person is entitled is to be calculated in accordance with the 2002 Act and regulations made under that Act, as modified by the Schedule to these Regulations ("the modified legislation").

(3) Where, in the opinion of the Commissioners for Her Majesty's Revenue and Customs, it is not reasonably practicable to apply the modified legislation in relation to any case or category of cases, the 2002 Act and regulations made under that Act are to apply without modification in that case or category of cases.][1]

Amendments—[1] Reg 12A inserted by the Universal Credit (Transitional Provisions) (Amendment) Regulations, SI 2014/1626 reg 4 with effect from 13 October 2014.

13 Appeals etc relating to certain existing benefits

(1) This regulation applies where, after an award of universal credit has been made to a claimant—

(*a*) an appeal against a decision relating to the entitlement of the claimant to income support, housing benefit or a tax credit (a "relevant benefit") is finally determined;

(*b*) a decision relating to the claimant's entitlement to income support is revised under section 9 of the Social Security Act 1998 ("the 1998 Act") or superseded under section 10 of that Act;

(*c*) a decision relating to the claimant's entitlement to housing benefit is revised or superseded under Schedule 7 to the Child Support, Pensions and Social Security Act 2000; or (*d*) a decision relating to the claimant's entitlement to a tax credit is revised under section 19 or 20 of the 2002 Act, or regulations made under section 21 of that Act, or is varied or cancelled under section 21A of that Act.

(2) Where the claimant is a new claimant partner and, as a result of determination of the appeal or, as the case may be, revision or supersession of the decision the claimant would (were it not for the effect of these Regulations) be entitled to income support or housing benefit during the relevant period mentioned in regulation 7(3), awards of those benefits are to terminate in accordance with regulation 7.

(3) Where the claimant is not a new claimant partner and, as a result of determination of the appeal or, as the case may be, revision, supersession, variation or cancellation of the decision, the claimant would (were it not for the effect of these Regulations) be entitled to a relevant benefit on the date on which the claim for universal credit was made, awards of relevant benefits are to terminate in accordance with regulation 8.

(4) The Secretary of State is to consider whether it is appropriate to revise under section 9 of the 1998 Act the decision in relation to entitlement to universal credit or, if that decision has been superseded under section 10 of that Act, the decision as so superseded (in either case, "the UC decision").

(5) Where it appears to the Secretary of State to be appropriate to revise the UC decision, it is to be revised in such manner as appears to the Secretary of State to be necessary to take account of—

(a) the decision of the First-tier Tribunal, Upper Tribunal or court, or, as the case may be, the decision relating to entitlement to a relevant benefit, as revised, superseded, varied or cancelled; and

(b) any finding of fact by the First-tier Tribunal, Upper Tribunal or court.

[SCHEDULE

MODIFICATION OF TAX CREDITS LEGISLATION (FINALISATION OF TAX CREDITS)

Regulation 12A

Amendments—[1] Schedule inserted by the Universal Credit (Transitional Provisions) (Amendment) Regulations, SI 2014/1626 reg 4 with effect from 13 October 2014.

Modifications to the Tax Credits Act 2002

1 Paragraphs 2 to 10 prescribe modifications to the application of the 2002 Act where regulation 12A of these Regulations applies.

2 In section 7 (income test)—

(*a*) in subsection (3), before "current year income" in each place where it occurs, insert "notional";

(*b*) in subsection (4)—

(i) for "current year" substitute "current part year";

(ii) in paragraphs (*a*) and (*b*), before "tax year" insert "part";

(*c*) after subsection (4), insert—

"(4A) In this section "the notional current year income" means—

(*a*) in relation to persons by whom a joint claim for a tax credit is made, the aggregate income of the persons for the part tax year to which the claim relates, divided by the number of days in that part tax year, multiplied by the number of days in the tax year in which the part tax year is included and rounded down to the next whole number of pence; and

(*b*) in relation to a person by whom a single claim for a tax credit is made, the income of the person for that part tax year, divided by the number of days in that part tax year, multiplied by the number of days in the tax year in which the part tax year is included and rounded down to the next whole number of pence.".

3 In section 17 (final notice)—

(*a*) in subsection (1)—

(i) omit "the whole or"; and

(ii) in sub-paragraph (*a*), before "tax year" insert "part";

(*b*) in subsection (3), before "tax year" insert "part";

(*c*) in subsections (4)(*a*) and (4)(*b*), for "current year" in both places where it occurs, substitute "current part year";

(*d*) in subsection (5)(*a*) for "current year" in both places where it occurs, substitute "current part year";

(*e*) omit subsection (8).

4 In section 18 (decisions after final notice)—

(*a*) in subsection (1), before "tax year" insert "part";
(*b*) omit subsections (6) to (9);
(*c*) in subsection (10), for "subsection (1), (5), (6) or (9)" substitute "subsection (1) or (5)";
(*d*) in subsection (11)—
(i) after "subsection (5)" omit "or (9)";
(ii) omit paragraph (*a*);
(iii) in paragraph (*b*) omit "in any other case,";
(iv) before "tax year" in each place where it occurs, insert "part".

In section 19 (power to enquire)—
(*a*) in subsection (1)(*a*) and (*b*), before "tax year" insert "part";
(*b*) in subsection (3), before "tax year" insert "part";
(*c*) for subsection (5) substitute—
"(5) "The relevant section 18 decision" means the decision under subsection (1) of section 18 in relation to the person or persons and the part tax year.";
(*d*) for subsection (6) substitute—
"(6) "The relevant section 17 date" means the date specified for the purposes of subsection (4) of section 17 in the notice given to a person or persons under that section in relation to the part tax year.";
(*e*) in subsection (11), before "tax year" insert "part";
(*f*) in subsection (12), before "tax year" in each place where it occurs, insert "part".

In section 20 (decisions on discovery)—
(*a*) in subsection (1), before "tax year" insert "part";
(*b*) in subsection (4)(*a*), before "tax year" insert "part";
(*c*) in subsection (5)(*b*), before "tax year" insert "part";
(*d*) in subsection (6)—
(i) before "tax year" insert "part";
(ii) in paragraph (a), for "section 18(1), (5), (6) or (9)" substitute "section 18(1) or (5)";
(*e*) in subsection (7), before "tax year" in each place where it occurs, insert "part".

In section 21 (decisions subject to official error), for "18(1), (5), (6) or (9)" substitute "18(1) or 5)".

In section 23 (notice of decisions)—
(*a*) in subsection (1), for "18(1), (5), (6) or (9)" substitute "18(1) or (5)";
(*b*) in subsection (3)—
(i) after "18(1)" omit "or (6)";
(ii) for paragraph (b) substitute—
"(**b**) the notice of the decision under subsection (1) of section 18,".

In section 30(1) (underpayments), before "tax year" in each place where it occurs, insert "part".

0 In section 38 (appeals)—
(*a*) in subsection (1)(*b*), before "tax year" insert "part";
(*b*) for subsection (2), substitute—
"(2) "The relevant section 18 decision" means the decision under subsection (1) of section 18 in relation to the person or persons and the tax credit for the part tax year.".

lodifications to the Tax Credits (Definition and Calculation of Income) Regulations 2002

1 Paragraphs 12 to 23 prescribe modifications to the application of the Tax Credits (Definition and alculation of Income) Regulations 2002 where regulation 12A of these Regulations applies.

2 In regulation 2(2) (interpretation), after the definition of "the Macfarlane Trusts" insert—
""part tax year" means a period of less than a year beginning with 6th April and ending with the date on which the award of a tax credit terminated;".

3 In regulation 3 (calculation of income of claimant)—
(*a*) in paragraph (1)—
(i) before "tax year" insert "part";
(ii) in Steps 1 and 2, after "of the claimant, or, in the case of a joint claim, of the claimants" insert "received in or relating to the part tax year";
(iii) in the second and third sentences of Step 4, before "year" insert "part";
(*b*) in paragraph (6A), for the words from "ending on 31st March" to the end, substitute "ending on the last day of the month in which the claimant's award of a tax credit terminated";

(*c*) in paragraph (8)(*b*), before "year" insert "part".

14 In regulation 4 (employment income)—

(*a*) in paragraph (1)(*a*), before "tax year" insert "part";

(*b*) in paragraph (1)(*b*), (*c*), (*d*), (*e*), (*g*) and (*k*), before "year" insert "part";

(*c*) in paragraph (1)(*f*), after "ITEPA" insert "which is treated as received in the part tax year an in respect of which the charge arises in the part tax year";

(*d*) in paragraph (1)(*h*), after "week" insert "in the part tax year";

(*e*) in paragraph (1)(*i*), for "that year" substitute "the tax year" and after "ITEPA" insert "whic is treated as received in the part tax year";

(*f*) in paragraph (1)(*j*), after "applies" insert "which is received in the part tax year";

(*g*) in paragraph (1)(*l*), for "that year" substitute "the tax year" and after "ITEPA" insert "i respect of which the charge arises in the part tax year";

(*h*) in paragraph (1)(*m*), after "paid" insert "in the part tax year";

(*i*) in paragraph (4), in the first sentence and in the title of Table 1, after "employment income insert "received in the part tax year";

(*j*) in paragraph (5), after "calculating earnings" insert "received in the part tax year".

15 In regulation 5 (pension income)—

(*a*) in paragraph (1), after ""pension income" means" insert "any of the following received in c relating to the part tax year";

(*b*) in paragraph (2), in the first sentence and in the title of Table 2, after "pension income" inse "received in or relating to the part tax year";

(*c*) in paragraph (3), after "income tax purposes", insert "in relation to the part tax year".

16 In regulation 6 (trading income)—

(*a*) re-number the existing regulation as paragraph (1);

(*b*) in paragraph (1) (as so re-numbered)—

(i) in sub-paragraph (*a*), for "taxable profits for the tax year" substitute "actual or estimate taxable profits attributable to the part tax year";

(ii) in sub-paragraph (*b*), for "taxable profit for the" substitute "actual or estimated taxab profit attributable to the part tax";

(*c*) after paragraph (1) insert—

"(2) Actual or estimated taxable profits attributable to the part tax year ("the relevant tradin income") is to be calculated by reference to the basis period (determined by reference to th rules in Chapter 15 of Part 2 of ITTOIA) ending during the tax year in which the claimant mad or was treated as making, a claim for universal credit.

(3) The relevant trading income is to be calculated by—

(*a*) taking the figure for the actual or estimated taxable income earned in the bas period;

(*b*) dividing that figure by the number of days in the basis period to give the dai figure; and

(*c*) multiplying the daily figure by the number of days in the part tax year on which th trade, profession or vocation was carried on.".

17 In regulation 7 (social security income)—

(*a*) in paragraph (1), after "social security income" insert "received in the part tax year";

(*b*) in paragraph (3), in the opening words and in the title of Table 3, after "social securit income" insert "received in the part tax year".

18 In regulation 8 (student income), after "in relation to a student" insert ", any of the followir which is received in the part tax year".

19 In regulation 10 (investment income)—

(*a*) in paragraph (1), after "gross amount" insert "received in the part tax year";

(*b*) in paragraph (1)(*e*), before "year" insert "part tax";

(*c*) in paragraph (2), in the opening words and in the title of Table 4, after "investment incom insert "received in the part tax year".

20 In regulation 11(1) (property income)—

(*a*) omit "annual";

(*b*) after "taxable profits" insert "for the part tax year".

21 In regulation 12(1) (foreign income), before "year" insert "part tax".

22 In regulation 13 (notional income), after "means income" insert "received in the part tax year

23 In regulation 18 (miscellaneous income), after "means income" insert "received in the part tax year".

Modifications to the Tax Credits (Income Thresholds and Determination of Rates) Regulations 2002

24 Paragraphs 25 to 27 prescribe modifications to the application of the Tax Credits (Income Thresholds and Determination of Rates) Regulations 2002 where regulation 12A of these Regulations applies.

25 In regulation 2 (interpretation)—

(*a*) after the definition of "the income threshold" insert—

""part tax year" means a period of less than a year beginning with 6th April and ending with the date on which the award of a tax credit terminated;";

(*b*) in the definition of "the relevant income" insert "as modified by the Universal Credit (Transitional Provisions) Regulations 2014" at the end.

26 In regulation 7(3) (determination of rate of working tax credit)—

(*a*) in Step 1, in the definition of "MR", after "maximum rate" insert "(determined in the manner prescribed at the date on which the award of the tax credit terminated)";

(*b*) in Step 3—

(i) in the definition of "I", before "tax year" insert "part";

(ii) in the definition of "N1", before "tax year" insert "part".

27 In regulation 8(3) (determination of rate of child tax credit)—

(*a*) in Step 1, in the definition of "MR", after "maximum rate" insert "(determined in the manner prescribed at the date on which the award of the tax credit terminated)";

(*b*) in Step 3—

(i) in the definition of "I", before "tax year" insert "part";

(ii) in the definition of "N1", before "tax year" insert "part".

Modifications to the Tax Credits (Claims and Notifications) Regulations 2002

28 Paragraphs 29 to 34 prescribe modifications to the application of the Tax Credits (Claims and Notifications) Regulations 2002 where regulation 12A of these Regulations applies.

29 In regulation 4 (interpretation), omit paragraph (*b*).

30 Omit regulation 11 (circumstances in which claims to be treated as made).

31 Omit regulation 12 (further circumstances in which claims to be treated as made).

32 In regulation 13 (circumstances in which claims made by one member of a couple to be treated as also made by the other)—

(*a*) in paragraph (1), after "prescribed by paragraph" omit "(2) or";

(*b*) omit paragraph (2).

33 In regulation 15(1)(*c*) (persons who die after making a claim)—

(*a*) omit "the whole or" and "after the end of that tax year but"; and

(*b*) for "section 18(1), (5), (6) or (9)" substitute "section 18(1) or (5)".

34 In regulation 33 (dates to be specified in notices)—

(*a*) in paragraph (*a*), for the words from "not later than 31st July" to "if later", substitute "not less than 30 days after the date on which the notice is given";

(*b*) omit paragraph (*b*) and the "and" which precedes it.

Modification to the Tax Credits (Payment by the Commissioners) Regulations 2002

35 Paragraph 36 prescribes a modification to the application of the Tax Credits (Payment by the Commissioners) Regulations 2002 where regulation 12A of these Regulations applies.

36 Omit regulation 7 (prescribed circumstances for certain purposes).

Modification to the Tax Credits (Residence) Regulations 2003

37 Paragraph 38 prescribes a modification to the application of the Tax Credits (Residence) Regulations 2003 where regulation 12A of these Regulations applies.

38 In regulation 3(5)(a) (circumstances in which a person is treated as not being in the United Kingdom), omit "under regulation 11 or 12 of the Tax Credits (Claims and Notifications) Regulations 2002 or otherwise".][1]

Amendments—[1] Schedule inserted by the Universal Credit (Transitional Provisions) (Amendment) Regulations, SI 2014/1626 reg 4 with effect from 13 October 2014.

2014/1933

TAX CREDITS (SETTLEMENT OF APPEALS) REGULATIONS 2014

Made . . . . *21 July 2014*
Laid before Parliament . . . . *22 July 2014*
Coming into force . . . . *12 August 2014*

The Commissioners for Her Majesty's Revenue and Customs in exercise of the powers conferred by sections 63(8) and 65(2) and (6) of the Tax Credits Act 2002 and with the consent of the Lord Chancellor, the Department of Justice in Northern Ireland and the Scottish Ministers, make the following Regulations.

1 Citation, commencement and extent

(1) These Regulations may be cited as the Tax Credits (Settlement of Appeals) Regulations 2014 and come into force on 12th August 2014

(2) These Regulations extend to England and Wales and Scotland only.

2 Interpretation

In these Regulations—

"tax credits appeal" means an appeal which, by virtue of section 63 of the Tax Credits Act 2002 (tax credits appeals etc: temporary modifications), is to the First-tier Tribunal.

3 Application of section 54 of the Taxes Management Act 1970

(1) Section 54 of the Taxes Management Act 1970 (settling of appeals by agreement) shall apply to a tax credits appeal, with the modifications prescribed by paragraphs (2) to (7).

(2) In subsection (1) for "tribunal" (in both places) substitute "First-tier Tribunal".

(3) In subsections (1) and (4) for "assessment" (in each place) substitute "determination".

(4) In subsections (1), (2) and (4)(*a*) for "the inspector or other proper officer of the Crown" substitute "an officer of Revenue and Customs".

(5) For subsection (3) substitute—

"(3) Where an agreement is not in writing—

(*a*) the preceding provisions of this section shall not apply unless the Board give notice, in such form and manner as they consider appropriate, to the appellant of the terms agreed between the officer of Revenue and Customs and the appellant; and

(*b*) the references in those preceding provisions to the time when the agreement was come to shall be construed as references to the date of that notice.".

(6) In subsection (4)(*b*) for "the inspector or other proper officer" substitute "an officer of Revenue and Customs".

(7) In subsection (4), in the words after paragraph (b), for "the inspector or other proper officer" substitute "an officer of Revenue and Customs".

2014/3280

TAX CREDITS (EXERCISE OF FUNCTIONS) ORDER 2014

Made . . . . *10 December 2014*
Laid before Parliament . . . . *17 December 2014*
Coming into force . . . . *1 April 2015*

At the Court at Buckingham Palace, the 10th day of December 2014

Present,

The Queen's Most Excellent Majesty in Council

This Order in Council is made in exercise of the powers conferred by section 126(1), (2), (3)(a) and (b)(i) and (9) of the Welfare Reform Act 2012.

Accordingly, Her Majesty is pleased, by and with the advice of Her Privy Council to order as follows:

1 Citation and commencement

This Order may be cited as the Tax Credits (Exercise of Functions) Order 2014 and comes into force on 1st April 2015.

2 Interpretation

(1) In this Order—

"the 2002 Act" means the Tax Credits Act 2002;

"the Administration Act" means the Social Security Administration Act 1992;

"the 2013 Regulations" means the Social Security (Overpayments and Recovery) Regulations 2013;

"notice" means a notice given under section 29 of the 2002 Act (recovery of overpayments of tax credits);

"penalty" means a penalty imposed under section 31 (incorrect statements etc) or 32 (failure to comply with requirements) of the 2002 Act.

(2) Any interest carried under section 37 of the 2002 Act on an amount specified in a notice or on a penalty is to be regarded for the purpose of this Order as if it were specified in the notice or formed part of the penalty respectively.

3 Functions exercisable by the Secretary of State

(1) The functions of the Commissioners under section 2 of the 2002 Act specified in paragraph (2) are to be exercisable concurrently with the Secretary of State.

(2) The functions are those that relate to—

(*a*) the recovery from a person to whom a notice has been given of the amount specified in a notice;

(*b*) the recovery from a person on whom a penalty has been imposed of the amount of the penalty.

4 Application of the Administration Act

(1) Subject to paragraph (2), the amount specified in a notice or, as the case may be, the amount of a penalty is, for the purposes of the Administration Act, to be treated as if it were an amount recoverable under section 71ZB of that Act.

(2) Section 71ZB of the Administration Act has effect in relation to the amount specified in a notice or, as the case may be, the amount of a penalty, as if subsection (3) were omitted.

5 Application of the 2013 Regulations

(1) The amount specified in a notice is, for the purposes of the 2013 Regulations, to be treated as if it were an overpayment as defined in regulation 2 of those Regulations.

(2) The amount of a penalty is, for the purposes of the 2013 Regulations, to be treated as if it were an amount recoverable under a provision of the Administration Act specified in regulation 3(2) of those Regulations.

6 Amendment of the 2013 Regulations

In the definition of "overpayment" in regulation 2 of the 2013 Regulations (interpretation) omit paragraph (*b*).

Miscellaneous Non-Statutory Material

Contents

Tax Credits: Miscellaneous Material

THE EQUITABLE LIFE PAYMENT SCHEME: TAX AND TAX CREDIT IMPLICATIONS

27 July 2011. *HMRC Brief 26/11*

ABSTRACT

This HMRC brief explains the impact for taxes and tax credits of payments under the Equitable Life Payment Scheme, covering: the background to the scheme; how ELPS will work; and tax and the effect of tax credit, including reporting requirements.

FULL TEXT

WHAT THIS BRIEF COVERS

This brief explains the impact for taxes and tax credits of payments under the Equitable Life Payment Scheme (ELPS). It covers:

- background to the scheme
- how ELPS will work
- tax and tax credit effects, including reporting requirements

BACKGROUND

The Coalition's Programme for Government issued in May 2010 promised to implement the Parliamentary Ombudsman's recommendation to make fair and transparent payments to Equitable Life policy holders, through an independent payment scheme, for their relative loss as a consequence of regulatory failure. On 20 October 2010 the Financial Secretary, Mark Hoban, announced in a written ministerial statement that £1.5 billion will be available for payment under ELPS. He also announced that the payments will be free of tax.

On 16 December 2010 the Equitable Life (Payments) Act 2010 came into force. The Act authorises the Treasury to incur expenditure when making ELPS payments and enables those payments to be made by National Savings and Investments (on the Treasury's behalf). The Act also allows the Treasury to make an order to provide for ELPS payments to be free of tax and to disregard them for tax credit purposes.

A Statutory Instrument, the Taxation of Equitable Life (Payments) Order 2011, SI 2011 No 1502 (the SI), makes the necessary provision to exempt authorised payments under ELPS. The SI was made on 15 June 2011 and came into force the following day. The SI can be found by following the link below.

HOW ELPS WILL WORK

The Treasury published full scheme design documentation on 16 May. A link to the full document ca be found by following the link below.

Equitable Life Payment Scheme - important next steps: www.hm-treasury.gov.uk/fin_equitable-_life.htm

In outline, the ELPS will work as follows:

- Payments will be made to individuals who have suffered relative loss as a result of Government maladministration in the regulation of Equitable Life.
- Relative loss is the difference between the actual returns received, or expected to be received, from Equitable Life and the assumed returns that the policyholder would have received, if they had invested the same amount in a similar product in a comparable company. Policyholders with With Profits Annuities (WPAs) will receive payments covering 100 per cent of their loss. Those with Accumulation With Profits (AWP),

Conventional With Profits (CWP), or group scheme policies, will receive lump sum payments of 22.4 per cent of their loss, subject to a £10 de minimis on payments.
- First payments will be made by the end of June 2011. Payments to traceable AWP, CWP group scheme policyholders should be made over the first three years of the scheme. WPAs will receive their payments on an ongoing annual basis.

TAX AND TAX CREDIT EFFECTS

SI 2011/1502 provides that authorised payments under ELPS are disregarded for the purposes of:

- Income Tax
- calculating investment income for tax credits
- Capital Gains Tax
- Corporation

The SI also ensures that Inheritance Tax is not chargeable on the value of any right to receive an ELPS payment.

All direct payments from the scheme to payees as identified in the scheme documentation are authorised payments.

Payments from trusts to beneficiaries of trust will retain their tax free status where the beneficiary is entitled as of right to receive the payment under the terms of the trust.

Payments made by trustees in exercise of a power or discretion given to them by the trust deed are not authorised payments as they do not flow directly from the receipt of the payment. They will therefore be subject to the usual tax treatment for such payments.

The main practical effects of the exemptions under the SI are as follows.

INCOME TAX AND CORPORATION TAX ON INCOME

Payments under ELPS to individuals and companies are free of Income Tax and should be excluded from Self Assessment tax returns or claims for repayment of tax on form R40.

The position for trustees of pension schemes is set out below. In other cases, if the trust is a bare trust or interest in possession trust it is the beneficiary of the trust who is potentially liable to tax on the trust income. The position is therefore as in the previous paragraph: payments are free of Income Tax and should be excluded from tax returns or claims for repayment of tax. Trustees of accumulation or discretionary trusts are also exempt from Income Tax on payments made to them under ELPS and should exclude the payments from the Trust and Estate tax return.

PAYMENTS INVOLVING REGISTERED PENSION SCHEMES

"Authorised payment" and "trustee" in this context mean a payment as authorised by the ELPS and the recipient of that payment under the Equitable Life (Payments) Act 2010. An authorised payment under this Act is not the same as an authorised payment under the Registered Pension Schemes tax legislation in Finance Act 2004.

DIRECT PAYMENTS TO INDIVIDUALS

In a registered pension scheme case the authorised payment will generally be made to the member to whom the policy relates. All payments to individual payees will be free of tax. However, in certain circumstances, the payee will not be the individual member of the scheme. In these cases the principles for identifying the payee are shown below.

PAYMENTS IN GROUP PENSION SCHEMES

Payments will be made to group pension schemes in three ways:

- Payments will be made to group pension schemes in three ways:
- In some cases payments will be made to the trustee and they will be asked to distribute payments amongst their members. (For example, this will happen when the pension scheme has a single policy, which represents the investment of a number of members, for whom Equitable Life will not have contact details.) The trustee will receive the payment

from the ELPS as their paying agent and will then pass the payment on to members. These payments will not be held as part of the pension scheme and will not be treated as payments from the pension scheme.

– Where the policy has been held by a defined benefits scheme (for example, a final salary scheme), payments will be made directly to the trustee as it is the scheme that has suffered the loss.

In all these cases, payments will remain free of tax to the final recipient, whether that is an individual scheme member, or the pension scheme trustee.

RETURNS AND REPORTING

In all pension cases the payments should be excluded from tax returns. The payments should not be included in any returns or reports made by a registered pension scheme administrator, for example event report, Pension Scheme Return.

NON-PENSION LIFE INSURANCE POLICIES/ANNUITY CONTRACTS

Payments under ELPS are disregarded for the purpose of Income Tax when calculating gains under the chargeable event gain regime. The payments will not be included in chargeable event certificates issued to policyholders by Equitable Life when gains arise. They do not have to be included in the parts of tax returns dealing with life insurance gains for persons liable to Income Tax on the gains, whether individuals, trustees or personal representatives.

Payments under ELPS are also disregarded for the purpose of Corporation Tax in the application of the loan relationships rules to investment life assurance contracts to which a company is a party.

TAX CREDITS

Authorised payments are disregarded as investment income for the purposes of the child and working tax credits and will not affect eligibility for such support. Consequently, authorised payments will not have to be reported by tax credit claimants as part of their annual income.

CAPITAL GAINS TAX AND CORPORATION TAX ON CHARGEABLE GAINS

Payments under ELPS to Equitable Life policy holders are disregarded for the purposes of Capital Gains Tax and Corporation Tax on chargeable gains. This treatment applies whether the payment is received by an individual, trustee, personal representative or company. The payments do not have to be shown on the capital gains pages of the recipient's tax return or otherwise reported to HMRC. They do not represent a disposal or part disposal of the policy for tax purposes, so any allowable cost of the policy is unaffected going forward.

INHERITANCE TAX

Where a payment is made to the estate of someone who has already died, the right to receive the payment is disregarded in establishing the value of the estate for Inheritance Tax purposes. There is no need to tell HMRC Trusts and Estates that the executors have received such a payment. A payment that is made to someone whilst they are alive, however, forms part of their estate and will be subject to Inheritance Tax in the normal way.

A similar treatment applies where the trustees of a "relevant property" trust receive a payment. "Relevant property" has the meaning given by section 58 of the Inheritance Tax Act 1984. The right to receive the payment should be disregarded in determining the value of relevant property that is subject to a 10 year charge. Again, there is no need to tell HMRC Trusts and Estates that the trustees have received such a payment after a 10 year charge has fallen due. Once the trustees have received the payment, however, it forms part of the assets of the trust and will be subject to Inheritance Tax in the normal way.

UNIVERSAL CREDIT—WRITTEN MINISTERIAL STATEMENT

2 November 2011. *Written Ministerial Statement*

The Secretary of State for Work and Pensions has announced the government's plans to introduce the Universal Credit in three phases, between October 2013 and the end of 2017.

The Secretary of State for Work and Pensions (Mr Iain Duncan Smith): Today the Department for Work and Pensions announces its strategy for moving 12 million working-age benefit and credit recipients on to universal credit by 2017.

Universal credit is intended to provide a streamlined welfare system which makes the financial advantages of taking work or increasing hours clear to claimants. We recognise that the move from one welfare system to another needs to be carefully managed to ensure social outcomes are maximised and no one is left without support.

The transition from the old benefit system to universal credit will therefore take place in three phases over four years, ending in 2017 with around 7.7 million households receiving more support to find more work and be more self-sufficient.

Between October 2013 and April 2014, 500,000 new claimants will receive universal credit in place of jobseekers allowance, employment support allowance, housing benefit, working tax credit and child tax credit. At the same time a further 500,000 existing claimants (and their partners and dependants) will also move on to universal credit as and when their circumstances change significantly, such as when they find work or when a child is born.

From April 2014 the second phase will give priority to households who will benefit most from the transition, such as those working tax credit claimants who currently work a small number of hours a week but could work more hours with the support that universal credit brings. Overall 3.5 million existing claimants (and their partners and dependents) will be transferred on to universal credit during this second phase.

The last and final phase, which begins at the end of 2015 and runs through to the end of 2017, will see around 3 million households being transferred to universal credit by local authority boundary. This phase will have the flexibility to respond to the circumstances of particular local authorities as they change and will focus on safeguarding financial support, such as housing benefit payments, to claimants as the old benefit system winds down.

The Department for Work and Pensions will continue to work with HMRC and local authorities to settle on a precise timing schedule of the move to universal credit. Once agreed, the schedule will be kept under regular review

HMRC ISSUE BRIEFING: TAX CREDITS OVERPAYMENTS

10 February 2014. *HMRC Issue Briefing*

We pay tax credits to support nearly five million households with eight million children. The amount of tax credits an eligible household receives depends upon its individual circumstances. To avoid overpayments, penalties and debt, tax credits claimants need to tell us about changes to their circumstances. This briefing explains how overpayments occur, how they can be avoided and what to do if a claimant has been paid money they are not entitled to.

Claimants can call the Tax Credit Helpline on 0345 300 3900 or write to us at Tax Credit Office, Preston, PR1 4AT. Those who want to apply for more time to pay should contact our Payments Helpline on 0845 302 1429. More information is also available at www.hmrc.gov.uk.

1. HOW OVERPAYMENTS HAPPEN

There are two types of tax credits: Child Tax Credit helps people bringing up children, while Working Tax Credit helps those working on low pay, regardless of whether they have children.

Overpayments can happen if:

– claimant don't tell us about a change to their personal circumstances that would affect their payments
– the claimant gave us the wrong information
– claimants have not renewed their tax credits on time
– we made a mistake and recorded the wrong information about a claimant or did not act on the information given to us

2. AVOIDING OVERPAYMENTS

Claimants should take steps to avoid an overpayment, such as:

- reporting any changes to their circumstances. Claimants have a legal responsibility to report certain changes of circumstances within one month of the date when the change happened
- carefully checking any award notice we send them. Claimants should tell us within a month if something is missing, wrong or incomplete, or if there is anything they don't understand
- telling us about any payments they receive that do not match the amount on their award notice
- renewing their tax credits each year by 31 July, if required to do so. We send out renewal packs between April and June. The pack tells claimants what they need to do to renew their claim

3. CHECKING CLAIMS

We may check the information that claimants have already given us to make sure we are paying them the correct amount. We can do this by asking them to supply evidence to confirm their details and we will ask them to respond to us within 30 days. If they have any questions or concerns about this, they can contact us by post or by phone. Our contact details are provided on the letter we send to them.

4. WHEN SOMEONE HAS BEEN OVERPAID

Claimants must pay back any money that has been overpaid. We do this by reducing their ongoing payments or by requiring them to make a direct payment, depending upon whether they are still claiming tax credits. There are limits on the amount by which we can reduce ongoing payments.

5. LIMITS FOR REDUCING ONGOING PAYMENTS

Claimants who get the maximum tax credits with no reduction due to income	All other tax credits claimants
up to 10% (maximum)	up to 25%

Any customer experiencing hardship as a result of this type of recovery can contact the Tax Credit Office to discuss their circumstances.

Where someone is no longer receiving tax credits, we will send them a Notice to Pay requiring them to repay the full amount within 30 days. If they are unable to meet this requirement, they should contact the Tax Credit Office.

6. DISPUTES

If a claimant feels that they have met their responsibilities and that we have made a mistake or given them incorrect advice, they can ask us to look at our decision on their overpayment again. This is called a 'dispute' and it must be made within three months of receiving a final decision notice.

To make a dispute the claimant can fill out and return form TC846, which they can request from us or download from our website. We will continue to recover repayment from the claimant while the overpayment is being disputed and reviewed.

Claimants who have received a decision on their dispute and still disagree with the outcome can ask for it to be reviewed. They can only ask for one review and they will have 30 days to provide further evidence to support their case.

RECOVERING TAX CREDITS OVERPAYMENTS FROM PREVIOUS AWARDS

7 November 2014. *HMRC Brief 40/14*

ABSTRACT

This brief sets out how HMRC recover some tax credit overpayments through a reduction in current payments, ranging from 10% up to a maximum of 25%.

Tax Credits

FULL TEXT

PURPOSE OF THIS BRIEF

To provide an update on changes to how HM Revenue and Customs (HMRC) will recover some tax credit overpayments.

READERSHIP

Advisers and intermediaries who may deal with tax credit customers.

THE CHANGES

HMRC is changing the way it recovers tax credits overpayments.

Claimants who have been overpaid tax credits may have their tax credits award reduced to repay outstanding debts from previous claims.

Depending on a person's circumstances, outstanding overpayment(s) may be from one or more previous awards.

HMRC will continue this recovery until the overpayment(s) is repaid or the claimant is no longer entitled to tax credits.

HMRC wrote to claimants about these overpayment(s) at the time it identified them. If claimants have an arrangement in place to repay debts they will not be affected by this change.

HMRC will apply a different rate of recovery depending on a household's circumstances and income. Those on lowest incomes will have their debt repayments spread over a longer timeframe.

The maximum recovery rate is 25% of current payments; however households with a limited income who are receiving a maximum tax credits award may only experience a 10% reduction in payments.

FURTHER INFORMATION

Claimants suffering severe hardship can contact the Tax Credit Helpline on Telephone: 0345 300 3900 (Textphone: 0345 300 3909) to discuss their individual circumstances and any help that may be available.

For more information read Tax credits overpayments: www.gov.uk/tax-credits-overpayments.

NEW RULES FOR SELF-EMPLOYED CLAIMING WORKING TAX CREDIT

25 March 2015. *HMRC Brief 7/15*

ABSTRACT

New regulations having effect from 6 April 2015 tighten up the eligibility conditions for those claiming working tax credit on the basis of self-employment. New claimants will have to show that they are trading on a commercial basis and their business is done with a view to achieving profits. This may require submission of a business plan in support of a claim.

www.gov.uk/government/publications/revenue-and-customs-brief-7-2015-new-rules-for-the-self-employed-claiming-working-tax-credit

1. INTRODUCTION

From April to get Working Tax Credit (WTC) self-employed people will need to meet new criteria (see SI 2015/605). This brief provides further details on these changes.

2. WHO NEEDS TO READ THIS?

Self-employed WTC claimants or advisers who support claimants.

3. THE CHANGES

From 6 April 2015, all new claimants who are using self-employed work to meet the qualifying remunerative work test for WTC, must show that they are trading on a commercial basis and their business is done with a view to achieving profits. The self-employment should also be structured, regular and ongoing.

For example, if their business activity is a hobby it is not likely to be considered commercial or have an expectation of realising a profit.

These checks are about ensuring HM Revenue and Customs (HMRC) only pay tax credits to those who are entitled. WTC will continue to support those who are carrying on a genuine business activity. These changes will not affect the rules for claiming Child Tax Credit.

4. HOW THE CHANGES WILL APPLY

Self-employed WTC claimants with earnings below a threshold (this will be based on working hours and the National Minimum Wage) will be asked by HMRC to provide evidence that they are in a regular and organised trade, profession or vocation on a commercial basis and with a view to achieving a profit.

The information we ask for should be available as part of normal business activity, for example receipts and expenses, records of sales and purchases. We may also ask for supporting documents such as a business plan, planned work, cash flow and profit projections.

During the early stages of self-employment it may prove difficult to make a profit. If someone in this situation claims WTC they may be asked to show that they have a commercial approach and how their business would become profitable. This could be demonstrated in a business plan.

HMRC will use the information provided to reach a decision about the claimants' current WTC award.

Claimants may lose their WTC if they cannot provide the evidence we ask for and may have to repay any tax credits they are not entitled to.

Claimants who disagree with our decision can ask for us to look at the decision again.

5. FURTHER INFORMATION

All claimants affected will receive information from HMRC about the new rules and the action they need to take before any awards are changed.

COP26 WHAT HAPPENS IF WE'VE PAID YOU TOO MUCH TAX CREDIT?

April 2017. *HMRC Code of Practice*

This leaflet explains why overpayments happen and how to pay them back. It also tells you when you don't have to pay them back and how to dispute an overpayment.

INTRODUCTION

MANDATORY RECONSIDERATION

An overpayment means we've paid you more money than you're entitled to.

If you think the amount of tax credits is wrong, you can ask us to look at the decision again. This is called mandatory reconsideration and you must normally contact us within 30 days of the date shown on your decision notice. You can also ask us to look at any penalty we've imposed in connection with your tax credits claim or if we decided to charge interest on your overpayment.

When we've looked at the decision again we'll send you a Mandatory Reconsideration Notice explaining what we've done. This will include all the information you need to appeal to HM Courts and Tribunals Service in England, Scotland and Wales or The Appeals Service in Northern Ireland, if you're still unhappy with our decision.

Appeals to the Tribunals or Appeals Service must be made in writing and within 30 days of the date of the Mandatory Reconsideration Notice.

We'll put any recovery action on hold while we carry out the reconsideration or while your appeal is being considered.

For more information see our leaflet WTC/AP, 'What to do if you think your Child Tax Credit or Working Tax Credit is wrong'.

- go to https://www.gov.uk/ and search for WTC/AP
- or phone the Tax Credit Helpline on 0345 300 3900 for a copy.

WHEN YOU SHOULD DISPUTE AN OVERPAYMENT

If you think our decision is right, but you don't agree that you should repay the overpayment, read pages 8 to 12 of this leaflet for more information about whether you should dispute our decision to recover the overpayment.

Please contact us (see below) if you don't:

- agree that you have been overpaid
- know if you should ask us to look at the decision that generated the overpayment again under mandatory reconsideration or **dispute** the decision to recover an overpayment

HOW WE WORK OUT THE AMOUNT OF YOUR TAX CREDITS

Tax credits depend on your income and your family circumstances. When your income or family circumstances change then your entitlement or the amount we pay you may change.

We pay you tax credits for a tax year – from 6 April one year to 5 April the next. When we first work out what to pay you, we look at your family's circumstances now and your income for the last tax year. If you think your income for the current tax year is going to be different than in the last year you can give us an estimate of what it will be. If we use this estimated figure it's important you tell us as straightaway if you think your income is going to be lower or higher than the estimate you provided. If you don't, we may not be paying you enough tax credits or you may be overpaid.

After 5 April each year, we send you a renewal pack asking you to:

- check the information we hold about you is up to date
- tell us how much income you had in the last tax year

If your tax credits award is renewed automatically and you're in PAYE employment, we may have used income figures given to us by your employer. It's important that you check these figures are correct for tax credits. Your renewal notes will help you do this. Contact us if you think they're not and tell us why.

You should fill in and return your renewal form straightaway. We'll then work out the actual amount due to you for the year that has just ended and also the amount for the year that started on 6 April.

If you claim Universal Credit, we may end your tax credits during the year rather than wait until the end of the year. We'll write to you to tell you what you need to do.

HOW AN OVERPAYMENT HAPPENS

An overpayment can happen if:

- you don't give us the right information either when you claim or when you renew your claim at the end of the year
- you're late telling us about a change in your circumstances
- your income in 2017 to 2018 is more than £2,500 higher than it was in 2016 to 2017
- you gave us an estimated current year income which turns out to be too low
- you give us wrong information when you tell us about a change in your circumstances or income
- we make a mistake when we record the information you give us
- we don't act on information you give us

CHANGES IN YOUR CIRCUMSTANCES OR INCOME

You should keep us up to date with any changes in your income and your family circumstances. The law says that you must tell us about certain changes **within one month** of them happening.

Sometimes it might not be clear exactly when there has been a change so you must tell us **within one month** of the date when you realised a change has happened.

You should use the checklist TC602(SN) 'Check your tax credits award notice now' that we sent with your award notice to check what changes you need to tell us about. If you need to tell s about a change, you may find it helpful to keep a note of the date you contacted us, the name f the person you spoke to and details of the change.

.fter you tell us about a change we'll work out the new amount of tax credits payments you're ue and send you a new award notice.

Vhere a change of circumstances means you have already received more than we estimate for our full year entitlement, tax credits payments will normally stop. Normal hardship rules will till apply and be assessed on a case by case basis (read below: 'Financial hardship').

IF YOU START LIVING WITH A PARTNER, YOU SEPARATE FROM YOUR PARTNER OR YOUR PARTNER DIES

'ou must let us know **within one month** if:

- you marry or enter into a civil partnership or start living with someone as though you are married or in a civil partnership
- you are married, or in a civil partnership, and you separate legally or in circumstances likely to be permanent
- you stop living with someone as though you are married or in a civil partnership
- your partner dies

'our claim will legally end in these circumstances. If you can still claim tax credits, you'll need o make a new claim. If you do make a new claim, it may be backdated up to one month.

The longer you delay telling us about this type of change, the bigger any overpayment may be. f you've started a new claim we may consider reducing the amount that you have to pay back. Ve'll work out how much you would have been paid in your new claim if you'd told us about he change on time and take that amount off your overpayment.

OUR RESPONSIBILITIES AND YOURS

To help get your award right and to help avoid building up an overpayment, it's important that we meet our responsibilities and you meet yours.

OUR RESPONSIBILITIES

When you contact us we should:

- give you correct advice based on the information you give us when you contact us for information
- accurately record and use the information you give us when you make or renew your claim, to work out your tax credits and pay you the correct amount
- include information you've given us about your family and your income when we send you an award notice – if you tell us that there's a mistake or something missing on your award notice, we should put it right and send you a corrected award notice
- accurately record what you've told us and send you a new award notice **within 30 days** when you tell us about a change of circumstance – the 30 days doesn't start until we get all of the information we need from you to make the change so it's important you give us all of the information about a change

YOUR RESPONSIBILITIES

You should:

- give us accurate, complete and up-to-date information
- tell us about any changes of circumstance throughout the year so we've accurate and up-to-date information, the law says you must tell us about certain changes **within one month** of them happening (you should use the checklist TC602(SN) we sent with your award notice to check what these changes are) – to reduce the chance of building up an overpayment, we recommend that you tell us about any changes in income as soon as possible
- use the checklist TC602(SN) we send with each award notice to check all the items listed and tell us straightaway if anything is wrong, missing or incomplete

You must tell us about some changes within one month of them happening – these are listed on the back of the checklist.

Tax Credits

- if it's a joint award (for you and your partner) or a single award (based on your individual circumstances)
- the hours you work
- if you get Income Support, income-based Jobseeker's Allowance, income-related Employment and Support Allowance or Pension Credit
- that a disability element is shown if you, or anyone in the household, is entitled to it
- the number and age of any children in your household
- any childcare costs
- your total household income for the period shown on the award notice

We'll send you a corrected award notice if you tell us anything is wrong, missing or incomplete. **If you don't get an award notice within 30 days of telling us about a change in circumstance let us know as soon as possible.**

You should check that the payments you get match what we said they should be on your award notice. Tell us if you get any payments that don't match what is shown on your award notice.

If anything is wrong, missing or incomplete you must tell us straight away. Make a note of when you got your award notice and when you told us about the mistake. We may ask you for this information to show that you acted **within 30 days.**

If you had difficult personal circumstances that meant you couldn't check your award notice or bank payments, for example, a member of your family has been seriously ill, let us know as soon as possible.

If you don't understand your award notice, phone our helpline (read below).

IF WE FAIL TO MEET OUR RESPONSIBILITIES

If we fail to meet our responsibilities, but you meet **all** of yours, we won't ask you to pay back all of an overpayment caused by our failure.

However – you must tell us about any mistakes on your award notice within 30 days of the date on your award notice. If you do, then you won't be responsible for an overpayment caused by our mistake. If you tell us about a mistake **more than 30** days after the date on your award notice we may ask you to pay back an overpayment up to the date you contacted us.

EXAMPLE 1

On 1 September you tell us about a change in your circumstances but we don't change your award until 16 October. We won't collect back any overpayment that arises after 30 September.

EXAMPLE 2

On 12 August you tell us about a change in your income. We send you a new award notice which you get on 19 August, but we haven't correctly recorded the information you gave us. If you spot this and tell us about the mistake by 18 September (30 days from 19 August) we won't collect any overpayment caused by our mistake.

EXAMPLE 3

On 12 August you tell us about a change in your income. We send you a new award notice which you get on 19 August, but we haven't correctly recorded the information you gave us. If you spot this and don't tell us about the mistake until 27 September (39 days from 19 August) you may be responsible for the overpayment up to the date you contacted us.

Whenever you tell us about a mistake we won't collect an overpayment that may build up if we don't correct our mistake from this time.

IF YOU FAIL TO MEET YOUR RESPONSIBILITIES

If you fail to meet your responsibilities, but we meet **all** of ours, we'll normally ask you to pay back all of an overpayment. For example, if you tell us about a mistake on your award notice **more than 30 days** after the date on your award notice, then you may have to pay back an overpayment which has built up until the time you contacted us. But also read 'Exceptional circumstances' below.

IF WE BOTH FAIL TO MEET OUR RESPONSIBILITIES

If we both fail to meet one or more of our responsibilities, we'll look at the circumstances of your case and may write off parts of an overpayment.

IF WE BOTH MEET OUR RESPONSIBILITIES

If we both meet our responsibilities, we'll still ask you to pay back the overpayment

EXAMPLE 4

On 12 August you told us your income increased from 15 July. We updated your tax credit record on 11 September. We'll still ask you to pay back any overpayments made during the period 15 July to 11 September.

IF IT TAKES YOU SOME TIME TO TELL US WE DIDN'T MEET OUR RESPONSIBILITIES

We ask you to tell us about any mistakes we've made **within 30 days** of the date on your award notice. If you don't tell us **within 30 days**, we'll ask you to pay back an overpayment up to the date you told us. **We won't ask you to pay back an overpayment, which is caused by our mistake, after the date you told us.**

EXCEPTIONAL CIRCUMSTANCES

We understand that exceptional circumstances may prevent you from meeting your responsibilities on time. For example, you or a close family member may have been seriously ill so you couldn't report a change, check your award notice or tell us about our mistake **within 30 days** of the date on your award notice. Let us know, as soon as it becomes possible, if you think this applies to you, or if you're not sure whether we've made a mistake.

If you don't understand why there's an overpayment, contact us. We can give you an explanation over the phone or in writing. Our leaflet WTC8, 'Why overpayments happen' gives more information about things that can cause overpayments. You can get a copy:

- online, go to GOV.UK and search for WTC8
- by phoning our helpline (read below) if you don't have access to the internet

We know that some customers may not be able to manage their own affairs, handle money or understand or complete forms. In such circumstances another person may act on their behalf. These people are called appointees.

APPOINTEES

Appointees can sometimes be appointed by:

- a court or government department, for example the Department for Work and Pensions
- an individual who decides that they need help in dealing with their affairs
- a carer, a voluntary sector organisation or a mental health or social care professional who would be able to act in all dealings with us

For more information, go to www.gov.uk/getting-help-with-yourtax-credits-claim/appointees

CHALLENGING THE RECOVERY OF AN OVERPAYMENT

HOW TO DISPUTE AN OVERPAYMENT

If you don't agree that we should ask you to pay back an overpayment you can ask us to look at this again. We call this **disputing** an overpayment. To do this, complete and return form TC846, 'Tax credits overpayment'. You can get a copy:

- online, go to GOV.UK and search for TC846
- by phoning our helpline (read page 17) if you don't have access to the internet

You can write to us instead, but you must make sure you give us full details including

- in what tax year the overpayment being disputed happened
- if and when you contacted us
- why you think the overpayment happened
- why you think you shouldn't have to pay back the overpayment

Usually you have to dispute recovery of an overpayment within 3 months from the date of:

- your final decision notice

Tax Credits

- the decision on your Annual Review notice (if your award is renewed automatically)
- your Statement of Account
- the decision on your Award Review notice (if your award is ended automatically due to a claim for Universal Credit)
- the letter which gives you our decision on your mandatory reconsideration
- the letter from the Tribunals or Appeals Service which gives you their decision on your appeal

You can only dispute recovery of an overpayment that happened in the tax year the notice or letter relates to. You won't normally be able to dispute overpayments from earlier tax years. We'll only accept a late dispute in exceptional circumstances, for example, if you were in hospital for that 3-month period. If you do send us a dispute, we'll continue to seek recovery of the overpayment while we're considering your dispute.

If we later change our decision and you receive another decision notice for the same year, you have 3 months from the date of that notice to dispute recovery of an overpayment.

EXAMPLE 5

Mary and Alan have overpayments from 2012 to 2013 and 2013 to 2014 tax years. They're paying the overpayments back from their tax credits award in 2016 to 2017. They were late reporting a change of circumstances in 2016 to 2017 and there's a new overpayment shown on their final 2016 to 2017 award notice. Their final award notice also shows the overpayments from the earlier tax years.

Mary and Alan have 3 months from the date of their 2016 to 2017 decision notice to dispute the new overpayment only. But they'll not be able to dispute the overpayments from 2012 to 2013 and 2013 to 2014 tax years.

HISTORIC DEBT

If you no longer get tax credits, you'll have been informed on past notices that, if you want to dispute an overpayment, you should do so as quickly as possible. If you didn't do this, you can't dispute overpayments from previous awards where it's been more than 3 months since you received your final decision notice. However, if you can show there are exceptional circumstances why you didn't previously dispute the overpayment, such as being in hospital, we'll consider the dispute.

If you no longer get tax credits, but have received a final decision notice from us in the last 3 months you'll only be able to dispute the overpayment occurring in the tax year the notice relates to.

If you reclaim tax credits and receive payments, we'll tell you if we are recovering historic debts from your ongoing award. You'll only be able to dispute the overpayment in the 3 months after you received the final decision notice relating to your previous award. Read page 13 'Paying back an overpayment'.

EXAMPLE 6

You receive your tax credits renewal pack on 21 May 2017 which requires you to confirm family circumstances and income for the previous 12 months ending 5 April 2017. You check your household details and decide you've no changes to report. We then send out a final decision notice on 15 August 2017. This shows you have been overpaid tax credits because your eldest child left school in September 2016 though your award was only changed in January 2017.

You don't notice the information about the overpayment until December 2017 when you realise your monthly tax credits payments are being reduced to pay it back. You agree there's been an overpayment but believe you shouldn't have to pay it back because you told HMRC about your daughter leaving school in September 2016 and we didn't change your award until January 2017. You had 3 months to dispute the overpayment from 15 August 2017, when we sent the final decision notice. This means that you needed to dispute the overpayment by 15 November 2017. As you're now out of time you can't dispute the overpayment unless you can show there are exceptional circumstances for missing the deadline, such as being in hospital.

WHERE WE GOT A DECISION WRONG

In some cases we may revise the decision which caused the overpayment. We can only do this where the decision is incorrect as a result of an error by us and we find that you didn't materially contribute to the error. We call this type of error an 'official error'. However, we won't revise a decision which is incorrect due to official error if more than 5 years have passed from the date of the decision, or if the revised decision wouldn't be in your favour.

Where a dispute is found in your favour, we'll refund the amount already recovered.

EXAMPLE 7

You have received Working Tax Credit since 2012. You became entitled to Disability Living Allowance in 2013 and asked us whether you were entitled to the disability element of Working Tax Credit.

We incorrectly advised you and said you were not entitled to the disability element. In 2015 you visited Citizens Advice with a query about your tax credits award. The adviser noticed that you qualified for the disability element but it wasn't included on your award. You contacted us and asked about our original advice. Since our decision was wrong, solely because of our error, your awards would be revised all the way back to 2013.

HOW WE DECIDE IF YOU SHOULD PAY BACK SOME OR ALL OF AN OVERPAYMENT

When we're deciding if you should pay back an overpayment we'll check:

- that we accurately recorded and acted on any information you gave us **within 30 days** of you telling us about a change of circumstance
- that we accurately worked out and paid you your correct entitlement
- that the information we included on your award notice was accurate at the date of the notice
- what you told us if you contacted us, and whether the advice we gave you based on that information was correct
- whether you contacted us to discuss any queries on your award notice, and whether we answered them correctly
- that you gave us accurate and up-to-date information when you claimed tax credits
- that you told us about any changes of circumstance at the right time
- that you checked your award notice **within 30 days** of the date on your award notice and if and when you told us about any mistakes
- that you checked that the payments you got matched the amounts on your award notice and if not, that you told us **within 30 days** of the date on your award notice
- if you told us of any exceptional circumstances that meant you couldn't tell us about a change of circumstance or about our mistake **within 30 days**

Once we've checked whether we've met our responsibilities and you've met yours, we'll decide if:

- an overpayment should be paid back
- you must pay back all or only part of an overpayment

We'll normally give you our decision, along with our reasons, in writing. However, we won't stop collecting an overpayment while we do this.

We may not ask you to pay back an overpayment if you contacted us to tell us that your exceptional personal circumstances meant you couldn't check your award notice or bank payments. For example, a member of your family may have been seriously ill. If this is the case let us know as soon as possible.

IF YOU STILL THINK YOU SHOULDN'T PAY BACK AN OVERPAYMENT

If you're still unhappy that we've decided to continue collecting an overpayment you can ask us to look at the decision again if you give us new and relevant information. You can only ask us to review the decision once and you'll have to do this within 30 days of receiving your dispute decision letter. Your overpayment will continue to be collected while we do this. We'll only accept a late request for a review in exceptional circumstances, for example, if you were in hospital for that 30 day period.

If you don't have any new information to give us, but you're still unhappy with our decision, you can contact a professional adviser or organisation, for example, Citizens Advice. You can consider what options are open to you, including any through the courts.

If you're not happy with our service, read 'Customer service' below.

PAYING BACK AN OVERPAYMENT

We may collect back an overpayment from you in a number of ways including:

- reducing your payments from an ongoing tax credits award

- asking you to make direct payments to us
- adjusting your tax code

If you claim Universal Credit we may ask the Department for Work and Pensions or the Department for Communities (in Northern Ireland) to recover your tax credits overpayment.

In exceptional circumstances we may recover the overpayment directly from your bank account.

In some exceptional cases we may ask you to do more than one of the above.

From an ongoing tax credits award

If you're still getting tax credits payments we'll automatically reduce these payments to recover an overpayment from your ongoing tax credits. Overpayments we'll recover may be from awards you:

- or your partner have had as single people
- and your partner have had together either now or previously

We won't recover from your ongoing tax credits, any overpayments from awards you or your partner have had with other partners.

Recovery from an on-going tax credits award only takes place where an overpayment is established at the end of the year and that overpayment falls for cross year recovery.

If an overpayment still exists at the end of the year we'll recover from the award starting at 6 April of the following year.

How much we reduce your payments by will depend on how much you're getting. We reduce awards at different levels, read the table below to see the different rates used to recover overpayment.

If you want help understanding which recovery rate applies to you, contact us (see below).

Type of award	*The most we'll take back from your award*
For those entitled to the maximum tax credits with no reduction due to income	10%
If you're getting Child Tax Credit or Working Tax Credit below the maximum and your total household income is £20,000 or less	25%
If your total household income exceeds £20,000	50%
If you're only getting the family element of Child Tax Credit	100%

By direct payment

If you're no longer entitled to tax credits, we'll ask you to make a direct payment to us. We'll also ask you to make a direct payment to us if your tax credits award has ended (this might happen if there's a change in your household, for example, you were in a couple and now you're single).

From an ongoing tax credits award and by direct payment

This may happen if you have an overpayment from an old award which ended and you also have an overpayment from a current award. For example, you and your partner separated and you then made another claim as a single person or in a new couple. We could ask you to pay back an overpayment from your current award as well as a direct payment from your previous award. If this happens to you, you can ask for the direct payment to be put on hold until you have paid back the overpayment from your ongoing tax credits payments.

If you do have an outstanding overpayment from an old claim, in some circumstances we may recover this from your ongoing award, instead of asking you to pay this overpayment back directly

Asking for more time to pay back a direct payment

If we've asked you to pay back an overpayment from a previous award directly, but you need more time to pay it back, phone our Payment Helpline on 0345 302 1429 as soon as possible. We can arrange for you to pay it back in equal instalments. If you'd like more details on different direct payment options, tell us when you phone.

By an adjustment to your tax code

If you're in PAYE employment or getting pension income and have a tax credits overpayment we may be able to adjust your tax code to collect your overpayment. We'll write to you and let you know if we can collect your overpayment this way. If we do write to you and you would prefer not to have your tax code adjusted, you can contact us to pay in full or agree an instalment arrangement. The amount that is recovered depends on your income.

If you claim Universal Credit

If you claim Universal Credit we may transfer your tax credits debt(s) to the Department for Work and Pensions or the Department for Communities (in Northern Ireland) for them to recover. This includes where we've previously agreed a payment plan with you. If this is going to happen we'll write to you with more details. For more information go to www.gov.uk/tax-credits-overpayments

Financial hardship

If you need to discuss financial hardship with us, phone us to explain this.

When you phone we may ask you about any family circumstances that may lead to extra living costs. For example, if you're looking after someone who is chronically ill or disabled. In some exceptional circumstances, we may cancel an overpayment altogether.

If you can't pay for your essential living expenses

If you can't pay for your essential living expenses such as your rent, gas or electricity and:

- you're paying back an overpayment directly
- we've asked you to pay back an overpayment

phone the Payment Helpline on **0345 302 1429**. We'll ask you about your circumstances in more detail.

If we've reduced your ongoing payments so you can pay back an overpayment you can find more information at www.gov.uk/taxcredits-overpayments or you can phone us on 0345 300 3900. You may be asked for more information regarding your income and living costs.

Whether you're repaying your overpayment through a reduction in your tax credits payments or through a direct payment, we may offer you an option for extending the period of time over which you pay back the overpayment. We can do this by reducing the amount being recovered each month. If we do reduce the monthly amount of your repayment, it'll take you longer to pay off the overpayment.

If you can't pay for your essential living expenses and you're getting Universal Credit, you should contact the Department for Work and Pensions or the Department for Communities (in Northern Ireland).

If you and your partner separate

If you and your partner separate and your joint claim ends, we'll work out if you've been overpaid. If you have, we'll write to you both, usually at the end of the tax year to:

- tell you how much we've overpaid you by
- ask you to contact us to arrange to pay back the money

You and your ex-partner are both responsible for paying back an overpayment from your joint claim. The letter sent to each of you will show the total overpayment that you both owe.

You should try to agree with your ex-partner how much each of you should pay. The options are that:

- each of you pays half
- each of you pays a different amount
- one of you pays the full amount

When you have reached an agreement with your ex-partner, you should phone the Payment Helpline on **0345 302 1429** to arrange repaying the overpayment. You'll then get a letter confirming what you have to pay back.

You might not be able to talk it over with your ex-partner, either because you don't want to contact them or you don't know where they are. Even if you do speak to them, you might not be able to agree on what each of you should pay back. If this happens, you should speak to the Payment Helpline as quickly as possible. You'll then be asked to pay back half of the overpayment, with your partner being asked to pay back the rest. You won't be asked to pay back more than half of the overpayment.

If you and your partner separate, you may decide to make a new claim as a single person or with a new partner.

We can't reduce your payments from your new claim to collect back an overpayment that you had with your previous partner. You must pay this overpayment back directly by ringing the Payment Helpline.

However, if you get back together with your ex-partner and claim again, we can reduce your payments to recover the overpayment.

CONTACT US

When you contact us tell us:

- your full name
- your National Insurance number
- a daytime phone number

By phone

Tax Credits Helpline 0345 300 3900

Payment Helpline 0345 302 1429

Textphone 0345 300 3909

If you prefer to speak in Welsh, phone 0300 200 1900

If you're abroad and can't get through on the helpline, phone +44 2890 538 192

In writing

You can write to the address shown on your award notice, or to the address below.

Tax Credits Office

HM Revenue and Customs

BX9 1ER

CUSTOMER SERVICE

Your rights and obligations

For information about our complaints procedure,

go to www.gov.uk/complain-to-hm-revenue-and-customs

'Your Charter' explains what you can expect from us and what we expect from you. For more information,

go to www.gov.uk/hmrc/your-charter

Tax Credits Index

Defined words and phrases are listed separately at the end.

A

APPEALS
consideration, SI 2002/3196 reg 11
death of party, SI 2002/3196 reg 8
decisions, against, TCA 2002 s 38
determination, SI 2002/3196 reg 11
directions applications—
death of party, SI 2002/3196 reg 8
general, SI 2002/3196 regs 7, 11
withdrawal, SI 2002/3196 reg 13
employer penalty, against, SI 2003/1382
excluded decisions, SI 2008/2707
exercise of right, TCA 2002 s 39
extension of time—
applications, SI 2002/3196 reg 6
generally, SI 2014/886
late appeals, SI 2002/3196 reg 5
meaning, SI 2002/2926 reg 2, SI 2002/3196 reg 1(3)
medical advice or evidence—
non-disclosure, SI 2002/3196 reg 14
notices, SI 2002/3119
oral hearings—
adjournment, SI 2002/3196 reg 20
directions, SI 2002/3196 reg 12
expert assistance provision, SI 2002/3196 reg 19
postponement, SI 2002/3196 reg 20
procedure, SI 2002/3196 reg 18
penalty proceedings—
consideration, SI 2002/3196 reg 11
withdrawal of application, SI 2002/3196 reg 13
persons with right, SI 2002/3196 reg 3
regulations, SI 2002/2926, SI 2002/3196
service of notices or documents, SI 2002/3196 reg 2
settlement, SI 2014/1933
striking out—
cases subject to, SI 2002/3196 reg 16
reinstatement, SI 2002/3196 reg 17
temporary modifications, TCA 2002 s 63
timing, SI 2002/3196 reg 4
tribunal—
application for leave to appeal, SI 2002/3196 reg 27
clerks, SI 2002/3196 reg 10
composition, SI 2002/3196 reg 9
correction of accidental errors, SI 2002/3196 regs 24, 26
decisions, SI 2002/3196 reg 21

APPEALS – *cont.*
tribunal— – *cont.*
late applications for statement of reasons, SI 2002/3196 reg 22
meaning, SI 2002/2926 reg 2
record of proceedings, SI 2002/3196 reg 23
setting aside, SI 2002/3196 regs 25, 26
statement of reasons, SI 2002/3196 reg 22
witnesses, SI 2002/3196 reg 15

APPEALS (SOCIAL SECURITY COMMISSIONERS)
application to for leave to appeal—
Appellate Court, to, SI 2002/3237 reg 27
determination, SI 2002/3237 reg 9
generally, SI 2002/3237 reg 7
notice of, SI 2002/3237 reg 8
time limit for appeal, SI 2002/3237 reg 11
withdrawal, SI 2002/3237 reg 21
authorised officers, delegation of functions between, SI 2002/3237 reg 5
determinations and decisions—
correction of accidental errors, SI 2002/3237 regs 24, 26
generally, SI 2002/3237 reg 23
setting aside, SI 2002/3237 regs 25, 26
directions, SI 2002/3237 reg 16
general powers, SI 2002/3237 reg 3
hearings—
generally, SI 2002/3237 reg 19
request, SI 2002/3237 reg 18
witnesses, SI 2002/3237 reg 20
irregularities, SI 2002/3237 reg 22
non-disclosure of medical evidence, SI 2002/3237 reg 17
notice of appeal, SI 2002/3237 regs 10, 12
representation, SI 2002/3237 reg 13
service of notices, SI 2002/3237 reg 6
transfer of proceedings, SI 2002/3237 reg 4
written observations, SI 2002/3237 reg 15

APPOINTEES
management of affairs, HMRC COP26

C

CHILD BENEFIT
administrative arrangements, TCA 2002 s 58
Board, functions transferred to, TCA 2002 ss 50, 53, Sch 4
death of child, TCA 2002 s 55

Tax Credits

Words and phrases

Words in brackets indicate the context in which the word or phrase is used.

Petroleum Revenue Tax

PRT

Contents

Statutes

Contents

TAXES MANAGEMENT ACT 1970

(1970 Chapter 9)

Note—Reference should be made to the following in connection with PRT—

TMA 1970 s 43D (Claims for double taxation relief in relation to petroleum revenue tax)

TMA 1970 Pt 7A (ss 77B–77K) (Holders of licences under the Petroleum Act 1998).

The full text of TMA 1970 is reproduced in Part 1a of this publication.

FINANCE ACT 1973

(1973 Chapter 51)

An Act to grant certain duties, to alter other duties, and to amend the law relating to the National Debt and the Public Revenue, and to make further provision in connection with Finance.

[25th July 1973]

PART III

INCOME TAX, CORPORATION TAX AND CAPITAL GAINS TAX

38 Territorial extension of charge to income tax, capital gains tax and corporation tax

. . .

Rewrite destinations—This section rewritten to TMA 1970 Pt 7A (ss 77B–77K).

Amendments—This section repealed by TIOPA 2010 ss 371, 378, Sch 7 paras 6, 7, Sch 10 Pt 12. TIOPA 2010 has effect for corporation tax purposes for accounting periods ending on or after 1 April 2010, for income and capital gains tax purposes for the tax year 2010–11 and subsequent tax years, and for petroleum revenue tax purposes for chargeable periods beginning on or after 1 July 2010.

SCHEDULES

SCHEDULE 15

TERRITORIAL EXTENSION OF CHARGE TO TAX—SUPPLEMENTARY PROVISIONS

Section 38

Rewrite destinations—This Schedule rewritten to TMA 1970 Pt 7A (ss 77B–77K).

Amendments—This Schedule repealed by TIOPA 2010 ss 371, 378, Sch 7 paras 6, 8, Sch 10 Pt 12. TIOPA 2010 has effect for corporation tax purposes for accounting periods ending on or after 1 April 2010, for income and capital gains tax purposes for the tax year 2010–11 and subsequent tax years, and for petroleum revenue tax purposes for chargeable periods beginning on or after 1 July 2010.

OIL TAXATION ACT 1975

(1975 Chapter 22)

An Act to impose a new tax in respect of profits from substances won or capable of being won under the authority of licences granted under the Petroleum (Production) Act 1934 or the Petroleum (Production) Act (Northern Ireland) 1964; to make in the law relating to income tax and corporation tax amendments connected with such substances or with petroleum companies; and for connected purposes

[8th May 1975]

PART I

PETROLEUM REVENUE TAX

Cross references—See FA 2011 Sch 23 para 23(*b*) (relevant data-holders: the responsible person in relation to an oil field within the meaning of this Part is a relevant data-holder for the purposes of FA 2011 Sch 23 (data-gathering powers).

1 Petroleum revenue tax

(1) A tax, to be known as petroleum revenue tax, shall be charged in accordance with this Part of this Act in respect of profits from oil won under the authority of a licence granted under either [Part I of the Petroleum Act 1998][5] or the Petroleum (Production) Act (Northern Ireland) 1964; and in this Part of this Act "oil" means any substance so won or capable of being so won other than methane gas won in the course of operations for making and keeping mines safe.

(2) For each oil field [which is a taxable field][3] the tax shall, in the case of each participator, be charged at the rate of [[0]][4] per cent][2] on the assessable profit accruing to him in any chargeable period from that field, as reduced under section 7 of this Act by any allowable losses and under section 8 of this Act by reference to his share, if any, of the oil allowance for that period, subject however to the limit imposed in his case by section 9 of this Act.

(3) In relation to any oil field—

PRT

(*a*) the first chargeable period is the period ending at the end of the critical half year (including an unlimited time prior to the beginning of that half year); and

(*b*) each subsequent half year is a chargeable period.

(4) In this section—

"the critical half year", in relation to an oil field means the first half year ending after 12 November 1974 at the end of which the total amount of oil ever won and saved from the field exceeds 1,000 [metric tonnes][1] (counting [1,100 cubic metres][1] of gas at a temperature of 15 degrees centigrade and pressure of one atmosphere as equivalent to one [metric tonne][1]);

"half year" means a period of six months ending at the end of June or December.

(5) Schedule 1 to this Act shall have effect with respect to the determination of oil fields, and Schedule 2 to this Act shall have effect with respect to the management and collection of the tax; and this Part of this Act shall have effect subject to the further provisions in Schedule 3 to this Act and, in connection with certain gas sold to the British Gas Corporation, to section 10 of this Act.

HMRC Manuals—Oil Taxation Manual OT03100 (Definitions).
OT04005 (first chargeable period, critical half year).
OT05075 (currency translation).
OT05501 (royalty).
OT17200 (oil allowance: "oil won and saved").
OT17250 (treatment of gas for oil allowance purposes).

Amendments—[1] Words substituted by F(No 2)A 1979 s 21(2), (4).
[2] In sub-s (2) words substituted by FA 1982 s 132.
[3] In sub-s (2) words inserted by FA 1993 s 185(4)(a).
[4] In sub-s (2),figure substituted by FA 2016 s 140(1) with effect in relation to chargeable periods ending after 31 December 2015.
[5] In sub-s (4) words substituted by the Petroleum Act 1998 Sch 4 para 7 with effect from 15 February 1999 (by virtue of SI 1999/161 art 2).

2 Assessable profits and allowable losses

(1) For the purposes of the tax the assessable profit or allowable loss accruing to a participator in any chargeable period from an oil field shall be computed in accordance with the following provisions of this section.

(2) The assessable profit or allowable loss so accruing in the period is the difference (if any) between the sum of the positive amounts for the period and the sum of the negative amounts for the period; and that difference (if any) is an assessable profit if the sum of the positive amounts is greater than the sum of the negative amounts, and is otherwise an allowable loss.

(3) For the period—

(*a*) the positive amounts for the purposes of this section are the following (as defined in this section), namely the gross profit (if any) accruing to the participator in the period, his licence credit (if any) for the period, and any amount to be credited to him for the period in respect of expenditure; and

(*b*) the negative amounts for those purposes are the following (as so defined) namely the gross loss (if any) so accruing, his licence debit (if any) for the period, and any amount to be debited to him for the period in respect of expenditure.

(4) [For the purposes of the tax (including advance petroleum revenue tax)][2] the gross profit or loss (if any) accruing to the participator in the period is the difference (if any) between—

(*a*) the aggregate of the amounts mentioned in subsection (5) below; and

(*b*) one-half of the market value, [on the last business day][11] of the preceding chargeable period, of so much of his share of oil won from the field as he had [at the end of that period][6] either—

(i) not disposed of and not relevantly appropriated; or

(ii) disposed of but not delivered,

and the difference (if any) is a gross profit if the said aggregate is greater than one-half of the said market value, and is otherwise a gross loss.

(5) [Subject to [subsections (5A) and (5B)][12] below][2] the amounts referred to in subsection (4)(*a*) above are—

(*a*) the price received or receivable for so much of any oil won from the field and disposed of by him crude in sales at arm's length as was delivered by him in the period (excluding oil delivered before 13 November 1974);

(*b*) the aggregate market value, ascertained in accordance with Schedule 3 to this Act, of so much of any oil [(not being light gases)][9] so won and disposed of by him crude otherwise than in sales at arm's length as was delivered by him in the period (excluding oil delivered before 13 November 1974);

(*c*) the aggregate market value, ascertained in accordance with Schedule 3 to this Act, of so much of any oil [(not being light gases)][9] so won as was relevantly appropriated by him in the period without being disposed of (excluding oil so appropriated before 13 November 1974); and [(*ca*) the market value, ascertained in accordance with paragraph 3A of Schedule 3 to this Act, of so much of any light gases so won and disposed of by him otherwise than in sales at arm's length as was delivered by him in the period; and

(*cb*) the market value, ascertained in accordance with paragraph 3A of Schedule 3 to this Act, of so much of any light gases so won as was relevantly appropriated by him in the period without being, disposed of; and][9]

(*d*) one-half of the market value, [on the last business day][11] of the period, of so much of his share of oil so won as he had [at the end of that period][6] either—

(i) not disposed of and not relevantly appropriated; or

(ii) disposed of but not delivered [and

(*e*) the excess of the nominated proceeds for that period, as defined in section 61 of the Finance Act 1987][5].

[(5A) In any case where [oil][10] is disposed of in a sale at arm's length and the terms of the contract are such that the seller is required to transport the [oil][10] from a place on land in the United Kingdom [or another country[, or from its place of extraction (where that is in the territorial sea of the United Kingdom or a designated area),][11] for delivery at another place in or][10] outside the United Kingdom or to meet some or all of the costs of or incidental to its transportation from and to such places then, for the purposes of this Part of this Act—

(*a*) the price received or receivable for the [oil][10] shall be deemed to be that for which it would have been sold, and

(*b*) the [oil][10] shall be deemed to be delivered at the time it would have been delivered,

if the terms of the contract [did not require the seller to meet any such costs as are mentioned above but did require the [oil][10] to be delivered—

(i) in the case of [oil][10] extracted in the United Kingdom, at the place of extraction; or

(ii) in the case of [oil][10] extracted from strata in the sea bed and subsoil of the territorial sea of the United Kingdom or of a designated area, at the place in the United Kingdom [or, in the case of oil first landed in another country, at the place in that or any other country][10] at which the seller could reasonably be expected to deliver it or, if there is more than one such place, the one nearest to the place of extraction][7].][3]

[(5B) The Board may by regulations make provision for the purposes of subsection (5)(*a*) to (*c*) for determining to which fields and in what proportions blended oil to which subsection (5C) applies is attributable.

(5C) This subsection applies to blended oil within the meaning of section 63(1A) of the Finance Act 1987 (other than light gases) which—

(*a*) is not gaseous at a temperature of 15 degrees Centigrade and a pressure of one atmosphere, and

(*b*) is not normally disposed of crude by deliveries in quantities of 25,000 metric tonnes or less.

(5D) Regulations under subsection (5B)—

(*a*) may apply generally or only to specified cases or circumstances,

(*b*) may make different provision for different cases or circumstances,

(*c*) may make incidental, consequential, or transitional provision,

(*d*) shall be made by statutory instrument, and

(*e*) may not be made unless a draft has been laid before and approved by resolution of the House of Commons.][12]

(6) The participator's licence debit or credit (if any) for the period is the difference (if any) between—

(*a*) the sum of the amounts mentioned in subsection (7) below; and

(*b*) the sum of—

(i) the amount taken into account under paragraph (*a*) of that subsection in computing his licence debit or credit for the preceding chargeable period; and

(ii) the amount of any royalty repaid to the participator [in or before the period][1] in respect of the field;

and that difference (if any) is a licence debit if the sum mentioned in paragraph (a) above is greater than the sum mentioned in paragraph (b) above, and is otherwise a licence credit.

(7) The amounts referred to in subsection (6)(*a*) above are—

(*a*) the amount shown in the return for the period made under paragraph 2 of Schedule 2 to this Act as the amount of royalty payable for the period in respect of the participator's share of oil won from the field;

(*b*) the amount of royalty paid [in or before the period][1] in respect of that share; and

(*c*) any amount paid in the period in respect of any periodic payment payable to the [OGA][14] under any relevant licence otherwise than by way of royalty.

[(8) The amount (if any) to be debited or credited to the participator for the period in respect of expenditure is the sum of the amounts mentioned in subsection (9) below.][13]

PRT

(9) [Subject to section 192 of the Finance Act 1993][8] the amounts referred to in subsection (8)(*a*) above are—

(*a*) . . . [13]

(*b*) the participator's share, as determined on a claim under Schedule 5 to this Act, of the aggregate of—

(i) any expenditure allowable under section 3 or 4 of this Act for the field which has been allowed on such a claim before the Board have made an assessment to tax or a determination on or in relation to him for the period in respect of the field; and

(ii) an amount equal to [35 per cent][1] of so much of that expenditure as has been so allowed on such a claim as qualifying for supplement under this sub-paragraph by virtue of subsection (5) of the said section 3,

so far as that share has not been taken into account in any previous assessment to tax or determination;

(*c*) the aggregate of—

(i) any expenditure allowable in the case of the participator under section 3 or 4 of this Act which has, on a claim made by him under Schedule 6 to this Act, been allowed before the Board have made an assessment to tax or a determination on or in relation to him for the period in respect of the field; and

(ii) an amount equal to [35 per cent][1] of so much of that expenditure as has been so allowed on such a claim as qualifying for supplement under this sub-paragraph by virtue of subsection (5) of the said section 3,

so far as that expenditure and amount have not been taken into account in any previous assessment to tax or determination;

(*d*) any abortive exploration expenditure allowable in the case of the participator under section 5 of this Act which on a claim made by him under Schedule 7 to this Act has been allowed under that Schedule before the Board have made an assessment to tax or a determination on or in relation to him for the period in respect of the field, so far as that expenditure has not been taken into account in any previous assessment to tax or determination; and

(*e*) any unrelievable field losses allowable in the case of the participator under section 6 of this Act which on a claim made by him under Schedule 8 to this Act have been allowed under that Schedule before the Board have made an assessment to tax or a determination on or in relation to him for the period in respect of the field, so far as those losses have not been taken into account in any previous assessment to tax or determination [; and

(*f*) any exploration and appraisal expenditure allowable in the case of the participator under section 5A of this Act which, on a claim made by him under Schedule 7 to this Act, has been allowed under that Schedule before the Board have made an assessment to tax or a determination on or in relation to him for the period in respect of the field, so far as that expenditure has not been taken into account in any previous assessment to tax or determination][4] [; and

(*g*) any research expenditure allowable in the case of the participator under section 5B of this Act which, on a claim made by him under Schedule 7 to this Act, has been allowed under that Schedule before the Board have made an assessment to tax or a determination on or in relation to him for the period in respect of the field, so far as that expenditure has not been taken into account in any previous assessment to tax or determination][5].

(10), (11) . . . [13]

HMRC Manuals—Oil Taxation Manual OT03150 (computation of PRT charge).
OT05199 (nomination scheme).
OT05600 (commingling).

Cross references—See FA 1980, Sch 17 para 6, 11, 12, 20 (Transfers of interests in oil fields).
FA 1981 s 111 (Restriction of expenditure supplement).
FA 1981 s 118 (Licence payments other than royalties).
FA 1984 s 114 (Sales of gas: treatment of certain payments).
FA 1987 s 61, Sch 10 (Nomination of disposals and appropriations).
FA 1987 s 63, Sch 12 (Blends of oil from two or more fields).

Simon's Tax Cases—s 2(9), *Amoco (UK) Exploration Co v IRC* [1983] STC 634.

Modification—Modified, in relation to transfers of interests in oil fields after 1 August 1980, by FA 1980 s 106, Sch 17 Pt II para 6 Pt III paras 11, 12, 20.

Amendments—[1] In sub-ss (6), (7), (9)(*b*), (*c*) words substituted by F(No 2)A 1979 ss 19(1)–(3), 22(1)(*a*), (2).
[2] Words in sub-ss (4), (5) inserted by FA 1982 ss 133(1), (3) 139(6) Sch 19 Pt III para 18.
[3] Sub-s (5A) inserted by FA 1982 s 133(1), (3), with respect to chargeable periods ending after 31 December 1981.
[4] Sub-s (9)(*f*), and word "and" preceding it, inserted by FA 1983 s 37, Sch 8 Pt II para 1.
[5] Sub-ss (5)(*e*), (9)(*g*), and word "and" preceding them, inserted by FA 1987 ss 61(5), 64, Sch 13 Pt II para 1.
[6] Words in sub-s (5)(*d*) substituted, by FA 1987 s 62(1), (2), (9), 72, Sch 16 Part X, with respect to chargeable periods ending after 31 December 1986.
[7] In sub-s (5A), words substituted by F(No 2)A 1992 s 74, Sch 15 para 1 with effect in accordance with s 74(5) thereof.
[8] Words in sub-s (9) inserted by FA 1993 s 192(3).

9 Words in sub-s (5)(*b*), (*c*), (9)(*a*) and sub-s (5)(*ca*), (*cb*) inserted, by FA 1994 ss 236, 258, Sch 23 para 1(1), (2), Sch 26 Pt VI.

10 In sub-s (5A) words substituted or inserted, in relation to chargeable periods ending after 31 December 1993, by FA 1994 s 235(1).

11 In sub-ss (4)(*b*), (5)(*d*) words substituted; in sub-s (5A) words inserted; by FA 2006 s 146, Sch 18 para 2 with effect—

(a) in relation to oil delivered or appropriated on or after 1 July 2006 (disregarding section 12A of this Act); and

(b) for the purpose of determining for any chargeable period ending on or after 31 December 2006—

(i) the value to be brought into account under section 2(4)(*b*) of OTA 1975 by reference to a previous chargeable period ending on or after 30 June 2006, and

(ii) the value to be brought into account under section 2(5)(*d*) of that Act,

subject to transitional provisions in FA 2006 s 147(4)–(8).

12 Words in sub-s (5) substituted for words "subsection (5A)" and sub-ss (5B)–(5D) inserted by FA 2006 s 148 with effect from 19 July 2006. The regulations under section 2(5B) may have effect for the purpose of calculating profits in relation to a chargeable period ending at any time on or after 1 July 2006 (FA 2006 s 148(3)).

13 Sub-s (8) substituted, and sub-ss (9)(*a*), (10), (11) repealed, by FA 2009 s 89, Sch 43 para 3 with effect in relation to a chargeable period beginning after 30 June 2009, subject to transitional provisions in FA 2009 Sch 43 para 4. Sub-s (8) previously read as follows—

"(8) The amount (if any) to be debited or credited to the participator for the period in respect of expenditure is the difference (if any) between—

(*a*) the sum of the amounts mentioned in subsection (9) below; and

(*b*) subject to subsection (10) below, any amount taken into account under paragraph (*a*) of the said subsection (9) in computing the assessable profit or allowable loss accruing to the participator in the last but one preceding chargeable period;

and that difference (if any) is an amount to be debited as aforesaid if the sum mentioned in paragraph (a) above is greater than the amount mentioned in paragraph (b) above, and is otherwise an amount to be credited as aforesaid.".

Sub-s (9)(*a*) previously read as follows—

"(*a*) subject to subsection (11) below, an amount equal to 5 per cent. of the aggregate of—

(i) the sum of the amounts which, in the participator's return under paragraph 2 of Schedule 2 to this Act for the period, are, in the case of deliveries falling within sub-paragraph (2)(*a*) of that paragraph, stated to be the price received for the oil, its market value as determined in accordance with Schedule 3 to this Act for each of the deliveries or (in the case of light gases) its market value as determined in accordance with paragraph 3A of that Schedule to this Act, as the case may require; and

(ii) the sum of the amounts which, in that return, are, in the case of appropriations falling within sub-paragraph (2)(*b*) of that paragraph, stated to be the market value of the oil as determined in accordance with Schedule 3 to this Act for each of the appropriations or (in the case of light gases) the market value as determined in accordance with paragraph 3A of that Schedule;".

Sub-ss (10), (11) previously read as follows—

"(10) If, for the period, the expenditure falling within paragraph (*b*)(i) or (*c*)(i) of subsection (9) above includes an amount of expenditure ("the relevant amount") incurred in the preceding chargeable period, then—

(*a*) the amount which would otherwise be taken into account under subsection (8)(*b*) above for the first-mentioned period shall be increased by the smaller of the following amounts, namely the relevant amount and the amount (if any) taken into account under paragraph (*a*) of subsection (9) above in computing the assessable profit or allowable loss accruing to the participator in the preceding chargeable period; and

(*b*) the amount which would otherwise be taken into account under subsection (8)(*b*) above for the chargeable period following the first-mentioned chargeable period shall be reduced by an amount equal to that increase.

(11) If, for the period, the expenditure falling within paragraph (*b*)(i) or (*c*)(i) of subsection (9) above includes an amount of expenditure incurred in the period, the amount mentioned in paragraph (*a*) of that subsection shall be reduced by that amount.".

14 In sub-s (7)(*c*), word substituted for words "Secretary of State" by the Petroleum (Transfer of Functions) Regulations, SI 2016/898 reg 4(1), (2) with effect from 1 October 2016.

3 Allowance of expenditure (other than expenditure on long-term assets and abortive exploration expenditure)

(1) Subject to the provisions of this section and Schedules 4, 5 and 6 to this Act, the expenditure allowable under this section for any oil field is any expenditure (whether or not of a capital nature) which, not being expenditure to which section 4 of this Act applies, is incurred by a person at or before the time when he is a participator in the field to the extent [subject to subsection (7) below][3] that it is incurred for one or more of the following purposes, namely—

(*a*) searching for oil anywhere within the area of the field as subsequently determined under Schedule 1 to this Act or not more than 5,000 metres beyond the boundary of that area;

(*b*) making to the [OGA][7] any payment under or for the purpose of obtaining a relevant licence, not being a payment by way of royalty or other periodic payment;

(*c*) ascertaining (whether before or after the determination of the field under Schedule 1 to this Act) the extent or characteristics of any oil-bearing area wholly or partly included in the field, or what the reserves of oil of any such oil-bearing area are;

(*d*) winning oil from the field;

(*e*) measuring the quantity of oil won or to be won from the field;

(*f*) in the case of oil won from the field that was so won from strata in the sea bed and subsoil of either the territorial sea of the United Kingdom or a designated area, transporting it [(i)] [10] to the place where it is first landed in the United Kingdom [[or

(ii) to the place in the United Kingdom or, in the case of oil first landed in another country, to the place in that or any other country (other than the United Kingdom)][10] at which the seller in a sale at arm's length could reasonably be expected to deliver it or, if there is more than one place at which he could reasonably be expected to deliver it, the one nearest to the place of extraction][1];

(*g*) the initial treatment or initial storage of oil won from the field;

(*h*) disposing of any oil won from the field which is disposed of crude in sales at arm's length;

[(*hh*) obtaining an abandonment guarantee, as defined in section 104 of the Finance Act 1991;][8]

[(*i*) closing down, decommissioning, abandoning or wholly or partially dismantling or removing any qualifying asset;

(*j*) carrying out qualifying restoration work consequential upon the closing down of the field or any part of it][9].

[(1A) In this section "qualifying asset" has the same meaning as in the Oil Taxation Act 1983; and, in the case of a qualifying asset which was leased or hired, the reference in subsection (1)(i) above to decommissioning includes a reference to carrying out any restoration or similar work which is required to be carried out to comply with the terms of the contract of lease or hire.

(1B) In subsection (1)(*j*) above "qualifying restoration work", in relation to a participator in an oil field, means—

(*a*) restoring (including landscaping) land on which a qualifying asset is or was situated; or

(*b*) restoring the seabed (including the subsoil thereof) on which a qualifying asset is or was situated.

[(1C) In any case where—

(*a*) any expenditure incurred by a participator in a taxable field would, apart from this subsection, be allowable for the field under subsection (1)(*i*) or (*j*) above, and

(*b*) the qualifying asset that is relevant to the incurring of that expenditure has at some time been used otherwise than [for a qualifying purpose][14],

only the relevant portion of the expenditure is allowable for the field under subsection (1)(i) or (j) above.][11]

[(1D) In subsection (1C) above "the relevant portion" of the expenditure is the portion of the expenditure that it is just and reasonable to apportion to use of the asset that is use [for a qualifying purpose.][14]][11]

[(1DA) In subsections (1C) and (1D) a reference to use for a qualifying purpose is a reference to—

(*a*) use in connection with the taxable field mentioned in subsection (1C), and

(*b*) other use in—

(i) the United Kingdom,

(ii) the territorial sea of the United Kingdom, or

(iii) a designated area,

except use wholly or partly for an ineligible oil purpose.

(1DB) In subsection (1DA)(*b*) the reference to use for an ineligible oil purpose is a reference to—

(*a*) use in connection with an oil field other than the taxable field mentioned in subsection (1C), and

(*b*) use for any other purpose (apart from a purpose falling within section 3(1)(*b*)) of a separate trade consisting of activities falling within [the definition of "oil-related activities" in section 274 of CTA 2010][15].

(1DC) In subsections (1DA) and (1DB) a reference to use in connection with a taxable field or other oil field includes use giving rise to receipts which, for the purposes of the Oil Taxation Act 1983, are tariff receipts.][14]

[(1E) Subsections (1C) and (1D) above have effect subject to the transitional provisions in section 100(5) to (11) of the Finance Act 2001.][11]

(2) Subject to the following provisions of this section and Schedules 4, 5 and 6 to this Act, where any amount is . . . [13] [or under section 77 of the Income Tax (Trading and Other Income) Act 2005 ("ITTOIA 2005") [or section 77 of the Corporation Tax Act 2009][13]][12] (statutory redundancy payments) allowable as a deduction in computing for any accounting period the profits or losses of the relevant trade carried on by a person who was in that period a participator in an oil field, or would be so allowable under . . . [13] [that section][12] if it were not otherwise so allowable, then that amount . . . [12] shall be expenditure allowable under this section for that field.

In this subsection "the relevant trade", in relation to a participator in an oil field, means the separate trade which by virtue of [section 16 of ITTOIA 2005 or section 279 of CTA 2010 consists of activities carried on by the participator that fall within the definition of "oil-related activities" in section 16(2) of ITTOIA 2005 or section 274 of CTA 2010 or which would have so consisted if those sections][15] had additionally had effect as regards all past chargeable periods [(as defined by section 1119 of CTA 2010)][15].

(3) Expenditure is not allowable under this section for any oil field if, or to the extent that, it has been allowed under Schedule 5 or 6 to this Act for any other oil field or has been allowed under Schedule 7 to this Act in connection with any oil field [but where expenditure allowable under section 5A [or section 5B][6] of this Act has been allowed on a claim under Schedule 7 to this Act, nothing in this subsection shall prevent a claim being made for an allowance under this section in respect of the same expenditure unless the person making the claim is the participator who made the claim under that Schedule][4].

(4) The expenditure allowable under this section for any oil field does not include—

(*a*) expenditure in respect of interest or any other pecuniary obligation incurred in obtaining a loan or any other form of credit; or

(*b*) the cost of acquiring any land or interest in land, other than the cost of making to the [OGA][7] any payment falling within subsection (1)(*b*) above; or

(*c*) the cost of acquiring or erecting any building or structure on land, except—

(i) a structure to be subsequently placed on the sea bed . . . [10]; or

(ii) a building or structure used or to be used wholly in the process of winning oil from strata in or under land or of measuring the quantity of oil won or to be won from such strata; or

(iii) a building or structure used or to be used for initial treatment or initial storage of oil; or

[(iv) a building or structure used or to be used for transporting such oil as is mentioned in subsection (1)(*f*) above from the place where it is first landed [to the place in the United Kingdom or in the case of oil first landed in another country, to the place in that or any other country (other than the United Kingdom)][10] at which the seller in a sale at arm's length could reasonably be expected to deliver it or, if there is more than one place at which he could reasonably be expected to deliver it, the one nearest to the place of extraction; or][2]

(*d*) any expenditure wholly or partly depending on or determined by reference to the quantity, value or proceeds of, or the profits from, oil won from the field; . . . [5]

(*e*) any payment made for the purpose of obtaining a direct or indirect interest in oil won or to be won from the field, other than a payment made to the [OGA][7]; [or

(*f*) any payment made in pursuance of a notice under section 77C of the Taxes Management Act 1970 (notice requiring licence-holder to pay unpaid tax assessed on non-UK resident);][16]

but nothing in paragraph (e) above shall be taken to apply to a payment made by a participator in pursuance of a contract whereby expenditure incurred for any of the purposes mentioned in subsection (1) above is to be shared between that participator and any of the other participators in the field.

(5) [Subject to subsection (5A) below][3] expenditure allowable under this section for an oil field qualifies for supplement under section 2(9)(*b*)(ii) or (*c*)(ii) of this Act if and to the extent that it is incurred for one or more of the following purposes, namely—

(*a*) bringing about the commencement of the winning of oil from the field or the commencement of the transporting of oil won from it to the United Kingdom [or another country][10];

(*b*) ascertaining (whether before or after the determination of the field under Schedule 1 to this Act) any of the matters mentioned in subsection (1)(*c*) above;

(*c*) carrying out works for, or acquiring an asset or an interest in an asset to be used for the purpose of, substantially improving the rate at which oil can be won or transported to the United Kingdom [or another country][10] from the field, or preventing or substantially reducing a decline in that rate; or

(*d*) providing any installation for the initial treatment or initial storage of oil won from the field;

but expenditure incurred in hiring an asset shall not so qualify unless the asset is used in carrying out works for a purpose mentioned in paragraph (a), (b) or (c) above or works for the provision of any such installation as is mentioned in paragraph (d) above.

[(5A) Where expenditure incurred in relation to an asset is incurred—

(*a*) in part for one of the purposes specified in subsection (5) above (or for what would be one of those purposes if section 10(2) below were disregarded), and

(*b*) in part for the purpose of enabling the asset to be used in a way giving rise to tariff receipts within the meaning of the Oil Taxation Act 1983,

then, to the extent that the expenditure is incurred for the purpose mentioned in paragraph (b) above, it shall be treated for the purposes of this Part of this Act as incurred for one of the purposes specified in subsection (5) above].[3]

[(5B) Expenditure incurred by a participator in an oil field shall be taken to be incurred for the purpose mentioned in paragraph (*hh*) of subsection (1) above if, and only if,—

PRT

(*a*) it consists of fees, commission or incidental costs incurred wholly and exclusively for the purposes of obtaining an abandonment guarantee; and

(*b*) the abandonment guarantee is obtained in order to comply with a term of a relevant agreement relating to that field under which the participator is required to provide security (whether or not specifically in the form of an abandonment guarantee) in respect of his liabilities to contribute to field abandonment costs;

and expressions used in this subsection shall be construed in accordance with section 104 of the Finance Act 1991][8].

(6) [Without prejudice to any apportionment under [subsections (1C) and (1D)][11] above][9] for the purposes of subsections (1) and (5) above [other than paragraph (*hh*) of subsection (1)][8] expenditure incurred partly for one or more of the purposes there mentioned and partly not shall [subject to subsection (7) below][3] be apportioned in such manner as is just and reasonable [and where, in the case of oil won as mentioned in paragraph (*f*) of subsection (1) above, expenditure is incurred in transporting—

(*a*) oil first landed in the United Kingdom to a place in the United Kingdom which is not the nearest place referred to in sub-paragraph (ii) of that paragraph, or

(*b*) oil first landed in another country to a place in that or any other country (other than the United Kingdom) which is not the nearest place so referred to,

so much of that expenditure as does not exceed what would have been the expenditure incurred in transporting it to that nearest place shall be regarded as falling within the said paragraph (f)][10].

[(7) In any case where—

(*a*) expenditure which is incurred by any person as mentioned in subsection (6) above is so incurred in connection with a long-term asset, and

(*b*) the long-term asset gives rise to receipts which, for the purposes of the Oil Taxation Act 1983, are tariff receipts of that person attributable to the field for which any of that expenditure is so allowable,

then, so far as relates to that field, in making in accordance with subsection (6) above any apportionment for the purposes of either or both of subsections (1) and (5) above, the whole of the relevant expenditure shall be apportioned to one or more of the purposes mentioned in that subsection or, as the case may be, those subsections.

(8) In subsection (7) above—

(*a*) "long-term asset" means an asset whose useful life continues after the end of the claim period for which a claim is first made for an allowance in respect of expenditure incurred in connection with the asset; and

(*b*) "relevant expenditure" means that portion of the expenditure in connection with the asset which is reasonably attributable to the use of the asset which gives rise to the receipts referred to in subsection (7)(*b*) above][3].

Simon's Tax Cases—s 3(1), *BP Exploration Operating Co Ltd v IRC* [2000] STC (SCD) 466.
s 3(1)(*a*) *Amerada Hess Ltd v IRC* [2001] STC 420.

HMRC Manuals—Oil Taxation Manual OT09000 (allowable expenditure).
OT09300 (relief for redundancy payments).
OT12000 (supplement).

Cross references—See FA 1987 s 65, Sch 14 (cross-field allowance of certain expenditure incurred on new fields).
FA 1991 ss 62, 103, 104 (expenditure on and under abandonment guarantees).
FA 1991 s 108(4) (reimbursement by defaulter in respect of certain abandonment expenditure).
F(No 2)A 1992 s 74 (oil exported direct from UK offshore fields).
FA 1994 Sch 22, para 11(2) (supplementary provisions as to elections by reference to pipeline usage).
FA 1999, s 95 (restriction on allowable expenditure: sale and leasebacks).
FA 2001 s 102(5)–(11) (transitional provisions ensuring that sub-s (1C) above does not apply if certain conditions are met).
FA 2001 Sch 32, para 6(2) (general rule for determining unrelievable portion of a loss).

Modification—This section is modified by the Oil Taxation Act 1983 s 12, Sch 4 para 11(3).

Amendments—[1] Words in sub-s (1)(*f*) inserted by F(No 2)A 1979 s 20(1), (3).

[2] Sub-s (4)(*c*)(iv) inserted by FA 1981 s 119.

[3] Words in sub-ss (1), (5), (6) and sub-ss (5A), (7), (8) inserted by the Oil Taxation Act 1983 s 5(1), (2), (3), (5), in relation to expenditure incurred after 30 June 1982.

[4] Words in sub-s (3) inserted by FA 1983 s 37, Sch 8 Pt II para 2.

[5] In sub-s (4)(*d*) word repealed by FA 1984 ss 124, 128(6), Sch 23 Pt XIV.

[6] Words in sub-s (3) inserted by FA 1987 s 64, Sch 13 Pt II para 2.

[7] Word substituted for words "Secretary of State" in each place by the Petroleum (Transfer of Functions) Regulations, SI 2016/898 reg 4(1), (3) with effect from 1 October 2016.

[8] Sub-ss (1)(*hh*), (5B) and words in sub-s (6) inserted, with respect to expenditure incurred after 18 March 1991, by FA 1991 s 103(2), (5), (6), (8).

[9] Sub-s (1)(*i*), (*j*) substituted for para (i) as originally enacted, and word in sub-s (6) inserted, with respect to expenditure incurred after 30 June 1991, by FA 1991 s 103(3), (4), (8).

[10] In sub-s (1)(*f*), sub-para (i) numbered as such, and words therein substituted, in sub-s (4)(*c*)(i) words repealed, words in sub-s (4)(*c*)(iv) substituted, and words in sub-ss (5), (6) inserted, by F(No 2)A 1992 ss 74, 82, Sch 15 para 2(1)–(4), Sch 18 with effect in accordance with s 74(5) thereof.

11 Sub-ss (1C)–(1E) substituted for sub-ss (1C), (1D), and words in sub-s (6) substituted, by FA 2001 s 102(1), (2) and (4) with effect for expenditure incurred after 6 March 2001.

12 In sub-s (2), words inserted and words repealed by ITTOIA 2005 ss 882(1), 884, Sch 1 paras 391, 392, Sch 3 with effect from 6 April 2005. ITTOIA 2005 has effect—

(a) for income tax purposes, for 2005–06 and subsequent tax years, and

(b) for corporation tax purposes, for accounting periods ending after 5 April 2005: ITTOIA 2005 s 883(1).

13 In sub-s (2), words "under subsection (2) of section [579] of the Taxes Act" and "that subsection or" repealed, and words inserted by CTA 2009 ss 1322, 1326, Sch 1 paras 313, 314, Sch 3 Part 1. CTA 2009 applies for accounting periods ending on or after 1 April 2009 (for corporation tax purposes) and for tax years 2009–10 onwards (for income and capital gains tax purposes).

14 Sub-ss (1DA)–(1DC) inserted, and in sub-ss (1C)(*b*), (1D) words substituted for words "in connection with the field", by FA 2009 s 87, Sch 41 para 1 with effect in relation to chargeable periods beginning after 30 June 2009.

15 In sub-s (1DB)(*b*) words substituted for words "section 492(1) of the Income and Corporation Taxes Act 1988", in sub-s (2) words substituted for words "subsection (1) of section 492 of the Taxes Act or by virtue of section 16 of ITTOIA 2005 consists of activities carried on by him that fall within paragraph (*a*) or (*b*) of that subsection or within the definition of "oil-related activities" in section 16(2) of ITTOIA 2005 or which would have so consisted if that subsection or section" and "(within the meaning of the Taxes Acts)" by CTA 2010 s 1177, Sch 1 paras 160, 161. CTA 2010 has effect for corporation tax purposes for accounting periods ending on or after 1 April 2010, and for income and capital gains tax purposes for the tax year 2010–11 and subsequent tax years.

16 Sub-s (4)(*f*) and the word "or" preceding it substituted by TIOPA 2010 s 371, Sch 7 paras 8, 10. TIOPA 2010 has effect for corporation tax purposes for accounting periods ending on or after 1 April 2010, for income and capital gains tax purposes for the tax year 2010–11 and subsequent tax years, and for petroleum revenue tax purposes for chargeable periods beginning on or after 1 July 2010.

4 Allowance of expenditure on long-term assets

(1) Subject to subsection (13) below, this section applies to expenditure (whether or not of a capital nature) which is incurred by a person at or before the time when he is a participator in an oil field, being expenditure incurred in acquiring, bringing into existence, or enhancing the value of an asset which is to be or is subsequently used in connection with the field and whose useful life continues after the end of the claim period in which it is first so used:

Provided that this section shall not apply to expenditure incurred as aforesaid in any case where the Board consider that its application to that expenditure would have only a negligible effect on the total expenditure allowable under this Part of this Act for the field and so notify the responsible person.

(2) The following provisions of this section are subject to Schedules 4, 5 and 6 to this Act.

(3), (4) . . .

(5) Subject to the following provisions of this section, a proportion of the expenditure shall be allowable under this section on a claim for the first relevant claim period, and that proportion is—

(*a*) if, at the end of that period, a reasonable estimate can be made of the proportion which the time during which the asset will eventually have been used in connection with the field in the period between the incurring of the expenditure or the asset's first use in that connection (whichever is later) and the date on which its useful life is reasonably likely to end bears to the time between the incurring of the expenditure and that date, the same proportion as that estimated proportion;

(*b*) in any other case, the proportion which the time during which the asset has been used in that connection in the period between the incurring of the expenditure or the asset's first use in that connection (whichever is later) and the end of the first relevant claim period bears to the time between the incurring of the expenditure and the date when the asset's useful life is reasonably likely to end:

Provided that, where the asset was not used for any purpose in the period between the incurring of the expenditure and the asset's first use in connection with the field, the expenditure shall for the purposes of this subsection be treated as having been incurred on the date when the asset was first used in connection with the field.

(6) . . .

(7) Whether or not the whole of the expenditure is by virtue of subsection (3) above allowable under this section on a claim for the first relevant claim period, for each subsequent claim period up to and including that in which use of the asset in connection with the field permanently ceases, the proportion of the expenditure allowable under this section for the relevant period shall be computed by applying the provisions of subsections (5) and (6) above with the omission of the words "on a claim" (wherever occurring) and the substitution of references to the relevant period for references to the first relevant claim period.

For the purposes of this subsection "the relevant period", in relation to a claim period, means the period consisting of that claim period and each earlier claim period back to and including that in which the expenditure was incurred.

(8) If, as computed under subsection (7) above for any claim period, the proportion of the expenditure allowable for the relevant period exceeds the amount thereof which (taking into account any previous adjustments made under the following subsection) has been allowed on claims made for earlier claim periods falling within the relevant period, the excess shall be allowable under this section on a claim for that claim period.

(9) If, as computed under subsection (7) above for any claim period, the proportion of the expenditure allowable for the relevant period is exceeded by the amount thereof which (taking into account any previous adjustments made under this subsection) has been allowed on claims made for earlier claim periods falling within the relevant period, the total amount of expenditure allowable under this and the preceding section on a claim for the first-mentioned claim period shall be reduced by an amount equal to the excess.

(10) Subsections (3) to (5) of section 3 of this Act shall apply for the purposes of this section as they apply for the purposes of that section; and where in accordance with subsection (9) above the total amount of the expenditure allowable under this and the preceding section on a claim for any claim period is reduced, the amount falling to be taken into account under section 2(9)(b)(ii) or (c)(ii) of this Act by reference to that expenditure shall be reduced by a proportion equal to the proportion by which the total amount of that expenditure is so reduced.

(11) For the purposes of subsections (5) and (6) above (including those subsections as they apply under subsection (7) above) an asset which is throughout any period of time simultaneously used partly in connection with the field and partly otherwise shall be treated as being used in connection with the field for a proportion of that period equal to the proportion which the extent of its use in the period in that connection bears to the extent of its use in the period in that connection and otherwise.

(12) For the purposes of this section—

(*a*) the asset is a brought-in asset if, between the time when it was acquired or brought into existence and its first use in connection with the field, the asset was used otherwise than in connection with the field; and

(*b*) "the first relevant claim period"—

(i) in the case of expenditure incurred in acquiring or bringing into existence a brought-in asset, means the claim period in which the asset was first used in connection with the field; and

(ii) in the case of any other expenditure, means the claim period in which the expenditure was incurred.

(13) The preceding provisions of this section, and any other provisions in this Part of this Act as to which it is provided that this subsection applies, shall, with any necessary modifications, apply in relation to expenditure incurred by a person in acquiring an interest in an asset, or in bringing into existence an asset in which he is to have an interest, or in enhancing the value of an asset in which he has an interest, as the provisions in question apply in relation to expenditure incurred by a person in acquiring, bringing into existence, or enhancing the value of an asset, as the case may be.

HMRC Manuals—Oil Taxation Manual OT11000 (long term assets).

Cross references—See FA 1987 s 65, Sch 14 (cross-field allowance of certain expenditure incurred on new fields).

FA 1999, s 95 (restriction on allowable expenditure: sale and leasebacks).

Modification—This section is modified by the Oil Taxation Act 1983 s 12, Sch 4 para 11(3).

5 Allowance of abortive exploration expenditure

(1) Subject to the following provisions of this section and Schedule 7 to this Act, the abortive exploration expenditure allowable in the case of a person who is a participator in an oil field is any expenditure (whether or not of a capital nature) incurred on or after 1 January 1960 [and before 16 March 1983][2] which—

(*a*) was incurred by that person or, if that person is a company, by that company or a company associated with it in respect of the expenditure; and

(*b*) was incurred wholly and exclusively for the purpose of searching for oil in the United Kingdom, the territorial sea thereof or a designated area; and

(*c*) is not, and is unlikely to become, allowable under section 3 or 4 of this Act for any oil field,

but so that any expenditure to which subsection (2) below applies shall not be allowable under this section except to the extent that it falls by virtue of that subsection to be treated as incurred wholly and exclusively for the purpose mentioned in paragraph (b) above.

(2) Where any person has incurred expenditure in acquiring, bringing into existence, or enhancing the value of an asset which is subsequently used by him for the purpose mentioned in paragraph (*b*) of subsection (1) above, then—

(*a*) subject to paragraph (*b*) below, if the useful life of the asset continues after the end of the twelve months beginning with the day on which he acquired the asset or brought it into existence, he shall be treated for the purposes of that subsection as having incurred wholly and exclusively for that purpose a fraction of that expenditure on each day after the expenditure was incurred on which the asset is used by him wholly and exclusively for that purpose, and that fraction is the fraction of which the numerator is 1 and the denominator is the number of days in the period beginning with the day on which he incurred that expenditure and ending with the day on which the asset's useful life is reasonably likely to end;

(*b*) if a subsequent disposal of the asset by that person otherwise than to a person connected with him gives rise to the receipt of a sum that falls to be taken into account under subsection (6) below, being a sum not less than the price which the asset might reasonably have been expected to fetch if sold in the open market at the time of the disposal, paragraph (*a*) above shall apply with the substitution, for the reference to the day on which the asset's useful life is reasonably likely to end, of a reference to the day on which the disposal was made.

Section 4(13) of this Act applies to the preceding provisions of this subsection.

[(2A) For the purpose only of determining under paragraph (*c*) of subsection (1) above whether expenditure is or is likely to become allowable for any oil field, it shall be assumed that any oil field which, apart from this subsection, would be a non-taxable field is or, as the case may be, will be a taxable field and, accordingly, that section 185(4)(*e*) of the Finance Act 1993 (no expenditure allowable for non-taxable fields) does not apply].[3]

(3) Expenditure is not allowable under this section in connection with an oil field if, or to the extent that, it has been allowed under Schedule 7 to this Act in connection with any oil field.

(4) Subsection (4) of section 3 of this Act shall apply for the purposes of this section with the following modifications, that is to say—

(*a*) in paragraph (*c*) the words from "except" to the end of sub-paragraph (iii) shall be omitted;

(*b*) paragraph (*d*) shall be omitted;

(*c*) in paragraph (*e*), the reference to oil won or to be won from the field shall be read as a reference to oil won or to be won from any area whatsoever.

(5) Paragraph 2 of Schedule 4 to this Act shall . . . [1] apply in relation to this section as it applies in relation to sections 3 and 4 of this Act.

(6) Where any expenditure which would otherwise be allowable under this section gives rise to the receipt of any sum (whether or not of a capital nature) by the person who incurred the expenditure or any person connected with him, that expenditure shall for the purposes of this section be reduced by an amount equal to that sum.

(7) For the purposes of this section—

(*a*) "company" means any body corporate;

(*b*) [section 1122 of CTA 2010][4] (connected persons) shall apply; and

(*c*) a company which is a participator in an oil field is associated with another company in respect of expenditure incurred by the other company if—

(i) throughout that part of the relevant period in which both were in existence, one was a 51 per cent. subsidiary of the other and the other was not a 51 per cent. subsidiary of any company; or

(ii) each of them was, throughout that part of the relevant period in which it was in existence, a 51 per cent. subsidiary of a third company which was not itself a 51 per cent. subsidiary of any company.

(8) For the purposes of subsection (7)(*c*) above—

(*a*) "the relevant period" is the period beginning immediately before the expenditure was incurred and ending with the end of whichever of the following periods ends later, that is to say—

(i) the earliest chargeable period in which the company which is a participator in the oil field in question was a participator in that field; and

(ii) the chargeable period (for that field) in which the expenditure was incurred,

(or, if they are the same period, with the end of that period); and

(*b*) [Chapter 3 of Part 24 of CTA 2010][4] (subsidiaries) shall apply.

HMRC Manuals—Oil Taxation Manual OT13950 (abortive expenditure: basic conditions).

Cross references—See FA 1980 Sch 17, para 16 (transfers of interests in oil fields).

FA 1983 s 37, Sch 8 (receipts to be set against allowable expenditure).

FA 1984 s 113 (restriction on PRT relief: expenditure incurred before qualifying date).

Modification—This section is modified, in relation to transfers of interests in oil fields after 1 August 1980, by FA 1980 s 106, Sch 17 Pt III para 16.

Amendments—[1] In sub-s (5) words repealed by FA 1980 s 122, Sch 20, Part XIII.

[2] Words in sub-s (1) inserted by FA 1983 s 37, Sch 8 Pt II para 3.

[3] Sub-s (2A) inserted by FA 1994 s 237(1) and deemed to have had effect from 27 July 1993.

[4] In sub-s (7)(*b*) words substituted for words "section 839 of the Taxes Act", in sub-s (8)(*b*) words substituted for words "section 838 of the Taxes Act" by CTA 2010 s 1177, Sch 1 paras 160,162. CTA 2010 has effect for corporation tax purposes for accounting periods ending on or after 1 April 2010, and for income and capital gains tax purposes for the tax year 2010–11 and subsequent tax years.

[5A Allowance of exploration and appraisal expenditure

(1) The exploration and appraisal expenditure which, subject to the provisions of this section and Schedule 7 to this Act, is allowable in the case of a person who is a participator in an oil field is any expenditure (whether or not of a capital nature) which—

(*a*) is incurred after 15 March 1983 by that person or, if that person is a company, by that company or a company associated with it in respect of the expenditure; and

[(*aa*) either is incurred before 16 March 1993 or is incurred within the period of two years beginning on that date and is expenditure to which that person or, if that person is a company, that company or a company associated with it in respect of the expenditure, is committed immediately before that date; and][5] (*b*) is so incurred wholly and exclusively for one or more of the purposes specified in subsection (2) below; and

(*c*) at the time it is so incurred, does not relate to a field for which a development decision has previously been made.

[(1A) For the purposes of subsection (1)(aa) above, in respect of expenditure incurred on or after 16 March 1993, a person is to be regarded as committed to that expenditure immediately before that date if—

(*a*) he has an obligation under an exploration and appraisal contract entered into before that date to incur the expenditure; or

(*b*) the expenditure is incurred wholly and exclusively for the same purpose as that for which the contract referred to in paragraph (*a*) above was entered into and is so incurred pursuant to an obligation under an exploration and appraisal contract entered into on or after 16 March 1993 and before 16 June 1993.

(1B) In considering whether a person has at any time such a contractual obligation as is referred to in paragraph (*a*) or paragraph (*b*) of subsection (1A) above in respect of any expenditure,

(*a*) if the contract contains a power (however exercisable) by virtue of which the person concerned, or a company associated with him in respect of the expenditure, is able to bring any contractual obligations to an end, he shall not be regarded as committed to any expenditure which, if the power were to be exercised, would not be incurred; and

(*b*) if the person concerned (or a company associated with him in respect of the expenditure) has an option (however described) which was not exercised before 16 March 1993 but the exercise of which would increase his expenditure under the contract, he shall not be regarded as committed to any expenditure which would be incurred only as a result of the exercise of the option.

(1C) For the purposes of subsection (1A) above a contract is an exploration and appraisal contract if it is a contract for the provision of any services or other business facilities or assets for any of the purposes specified in subsection (2) below][5].

(2) The purposes referred to in [subsections (1) to (1C)][5] above are—

(*a*) the purpose of searching for oil in [the territorial sea of the United Kingdom][3] or a designated area;

(*b*) the purpose of ascertaining the extent or characteristics of any oil-bearing area in [the territorial sea of the United Kingdom][3] or a designated area;

(*c*) the purpose of ascertaining what are the reserves of oil of any such oil-bearing area; and

(*d*) subject to subsection (3) below, the purpose of making to the [OGA][7] any payment under or for the purpose of obtaining a licence (not being a payment by way of royalty or other periodic payment).

[(2A) Any reference in subsection (2) above to a designated area does not include a sector which, by virtue of subsection (3)(*b*) of section 107 of the Finance Act 1980 (transmedian fields), is deemed to be a designated area].[2]

(3) Expenditure incurred for the purpose mentioned in subsection (2)(*d*) above is not allowable under this section unless, at the time the allowance is claimed,—

(*a*) the licence to which the expenditure related has expired or has been determined or revoked; or

(*b*) part of the licensed area has been surrendered;

and where paragraph (b) above applies only that proportion of the expenditure which corresponds to the proportion of the licensed area which has been surrendered is expenditure falling within subsection (1) above.

(4) Subject to subsection (5) below, subsections (2) and (4) to (8) of section 5 of this Act apply for the purposes of this section as they apply for the purposes of that section.

(5) In the application for the purposes of this section of the provisions of section 5 of this Act referred to in subsection (4) above,—

(*a*) any reference in subsection (2) of section 5 to the purpose mentioned in subsection (1)(*b*) of that section shall be construed as a reference to any of the purposes specified in subsection (2) of this section;

(*b*) the reference in subsection (2)(*a*) of section 5 to subsection (1) of that section shall be construed as a reference to subsection (1) of this section; and

(*c*) the reference in subsection (6) of section 5 to a sum received—

[(i) includes a reference to a sum received, or treated by virtue of subsection (5A) below as received, from the disposal of oil won in the course of operations carried out for any of the purposes in paragraphs (*a*) to (*c*) of subsection (2) of this section; but

(ii) does not include a reference to a sum received for the assignment of any of the rights conferred by a licence or of any interest in a licensed area][2].

[(5A) Subsection (5B) below applies in any case where—

(*a*) oil which is won as mentioned in paragraph (*c*)(i) of subsection (5) above is either disposed of otherwise than in sales at arm's length or appropriated to refining or to any use except for production purposes of an oil field, and

(*b*) if that oil had been disposed of in a sale at arm's length, then, by virtue of section 5(6) of this Act as applied by subsection (5) above, certain expenditure would have been reduced by reference to the receipt of a sum from that disposal.

(5B) Where this subsection applies, the oil concerned shall be treated for the purposes of subsection (5)(*c*)(i) above and section 5(6) of this Act as having been disposed of for a sum equal to its market value . . . [4] [determined in accordance with Schedule 3 to this Act for the disposal or appropriation mentioned][6] in subsection (5A)(*a*) above and, accordingly, for those purposes—

(*a*) a sum equal to that market value shall be treated as having been received from that disposal; and

(*b*) no account shall be taken of any sum actually received from the disposal of any of that oil.

(5C) In the application of Schedule 3 to this Act for the purpose of ascertaining the market value of oil as mentioned in subsection (5B) above,—

(*a*) . . . [6]

(*b*) [sub-paragraph (4)][6] of paragraph 2 shall be omitted; . . . [6]

(*c*) any reference in paragraphs 2 and 2A to oil being relevantly appropriated shall be construed as a reference to its being appropriated as mentioned in subsection (5A)(*a*) above[; and

(*d*) any reference in paragraph 2 to the notional delivery day for the actual oil shall be construed as a reference to the day on which the oil is disposed of or appropriated as mentioned in subsection (5A)(*a*) above.][6]][2]

(6) Expenditure is not allowable under this section in connection with an oil field if, or to the extent that, it has been allowed under Schedule 5, Schedule 6 or Schedule 7 to this Act in connection with any oil field.

(7) For the purposes of subsection (1)(*c*) above, a development decision is made when—

(*a*) consent for development is granted to a licensee by the [OGA][7] in respect of the whole or part of an oil field; or

(*b*) a programme of development is served on a licensee or approved by the [OGA][7] for the whole or part of an oil field;

and subsections (4) and (5) of section 36 of the Finance Act 1983 (meaning of development etc) apply in relation to this subsection as they apply in relation to subsections (2) and (3) of that section.

(8) If, at the time when it is incurred, expenditure relates to an area—

(*a*) which is not then an oil field, but

(*b*) in respect of which notice of a proposed determination has previously been given under paragraph 2(*a*) of Schedule 1 to this Act,

that area shall be treated for the purposes of this section as having become an oil field at the time the notice was given unless, when the actual determination is made, the area is not included in an oil field][1].

HMRC Manuals—Oil Taxation Manual OT13975 (exploration and appraisal expenditure: basic conditions).

Cross references—See FA 1980 Sch 17, para 16A (transfers of interests in oil fields).

FA 1983 s 37, Sch 8 (receipts to be set against allowable expenditure).

FA 1987 s 64 (relief for research expenditure).

FA 1987 s 65 (cross field allowance may not include exploration and appraisal expenditure).

FA 1984 s 113 (restriction on PRT relief: expenditure incurred before qualifying date).

FA 1993 s 189 (transitional relief for certain exploration and appraisal expenditure).

Modification—This section is modified, in relation to transfers of interests in oil fields after 1 August 1980, by FA 1980 s 106, Sch 17 Pt III para 16.

Amendments—[1] This section inserted by FA 1983 s 37, Sch 8 Pt I.

[2] Sub-ss (2A), (5A)–(5C) inserted, and words in sub-s (5) substituted, by FA 1985 s 90, with respect to expenditure incurred on or after 19 March 1985.

[3] Words in sub-s (2) substituted by FA 1985 s 90(2), in relation to expenditure on or after 1 April 1986.

[4] In sub-s (5B) words repealed, in relation to chargeable periods ending after 31 December 1986, by FA 1987 s 62, Sch 11 Pt II para 4, Sch 16 Pt X.

[5] Words in sub-ss (1), (2) and whole of sub-ss (1A)–(1C) inserted by FA 1993 s 188(1)–(3).

[6] In sub-s (5B) words substituted for the words "in the calendar month in which it was disposed of or appropriated as mentioned"; in sub-s (5C) para (*a*) and the word "and" at the end of para (*b*) repealed, words in para (*b*) substituted for words "sub-paragraphs (3) and (4)" and para (*d*) inserted by FA 2006 s 146, Sch 18 para 3, s 178, Sch 26 Pt 5(1) with effect—

(a) in relation to oil delivered or appropriated on or after 1 July 2006 (disregarding section 12A of this Act); and

(b) for the purpose of determining for any chargeable period ending on or after 31 December 2006—

(i) the value to be brought into account under section 2(4)(*b*) of OTA 1975 by reference to a previous chargeable period ending on or after 30 June 2006, and

(ii) the value to be brought into account under section 2(5)(*d*) of that Act,

subject to transitional provisions in FA 2006 s 147(4)–(8).

Sub-s (5)(*a*) previously read as follows–

"(a) in paragraph 2, in paragraph [(f)] of sub-paragraph (2) for the words from the beginning to "paragraph in question" there shall be substituted "the contract is for the sale of the whole quantity of oil whose market value

PRT

falls to be ascertained for the purposes of section 5A(5B) of this Act";".

7 Word substituted for words "Secretary of State" in each place by the Petroleum (Transfer of Functions) Regulations, SI 2016/898 reg 4(1), (4) with effect from 1 October 2016.

[5B Allowance of research expenditure

(1) Subject to the following provisions of this section and Schedule 7 to this Act, the research expenditure which is allowable in the case of a person who is a participator in an oil field is any expenditure (whether or not of a capital nature) which—

(*a*) is incurred by him on or after 17 March 1987; and

(*b*) at the expiry of the period of three years from the time at which it was incurred, has not become allowable under section 3 or section 4 of this Act or section 3 of the Oil Taxation Act 1983; and

(*c*) was not incurred for purposes relating to a particular oil field; and

(*d*) was not incurred wholly and exclusively for one or more of the purposes which, subject to subsection (2) below, are specified in section 5A(2) of this Act; and

(*e*) was incurred for the purpose of research of such a description that, if it had been incurred by the participator in relation to a particular field, it would have been allowable for that field under section 3 or section 4 of this Act or section 3 of the Oil Taxation Act 1983; and

(*f*) was incurred wholly or partly for United Kingdom purposes.

(2) For the purposes only of subsection (1)(*d*) above, any reference in section 5A(2) of this Act to the territorial sea of the United Kingdom shall be taken to include a reference to the United Kingdom itself.

(3) Where expenditure falling within paragraphs (*a*) to (*e*) of subsection (1) above is incurred partly for United Kingdom purposes and partly for other purposes, only such part of the expenditure as it is just and reasonable to apportion to United Kingdom purposes shall be allowable by virtue of this section.

(4) In subsections (1)(*f*) and (3) above, "United Kingdom purposes" means purposes relating to the United Kingdom, the territorial sea thereof or designated areas, excluding any sector which, by virtue of subsection (3)(*b*) of section 107 of the Finance Act 1980 (transmedian fields), is deemed to be a designated area.

(5) Expenditure is not allowable under this section if, or to the extent that, it has been allowed under Schedule 5, Schedule 6 or Schedule 7 to this Act for or in connection with an oil field.

(6) To the extent that it is reasonable to assume that expenditure which, apart from this subsection, would be allowable under this section has been incurred for purposes relating to excluded oil, within the meaning of section 10(1) of this Act [or for purposes relating to non-taxable fields][2], that expenditure is not allowable under this section.

(7) Subject to subsection (3) above, subsections (2) and (6) of section 5 of this Act apply for the purposes of this section as they apply for the purposes of that section except that—

(*a*) any reference in subsection (2) of section 5 to the purpose mentioned in subsection (1)(*b*) of that section shall be construed as a reference to the purpose referred to in subsection (1)(*e*) of this section;

(*b*) the reference in paragraph (*a*) of subsection (2) to subsection (1) of that section shall be construed as a reference to subsection (1) of this section; and

(*c*) where any expenditure falls to be apportioned under subsection (3) of this section, any receipt to which it gives rise shall be similarly apportioned in the application of subsection (6) of section 5.

(8) Paragraph 2 of Schedule 4 to this Act applies in relation to this section as it applies in relation to sections 3 and 4 of this Act].[1]

HMRC Manuals—Oil Taxation Manual OT14100 (research expenditure: outline).
Cross references—See FA 1980 Sch 17, para 16A (transfers of interests in oil fields).
FA 1984 s 113 (restriction on PRT relief: expenditure incurred before qualifying date).
Modification—This section is modified, in relation to transfers of interests in oil fields after 1 August 1980, by FA 1980 s 106, Sch 17 Pt III para 16.
Amendments—1 This section inserted by FA 1987 s 64, Sch 13 Pt I.
2 Words in sub-s (6) inserted by FA 1993 s 185(4)(c).

6 Allowance of unrelievable loss from abandoned field

[(1) In the case of a participator in an oil field, an allowable unrelievable field loss is the unrelievable portion of an allowable loss falling within subsection (1B) below.][3]

[(1A) Subsection (1) above is subject to subsections (5) to (9) below and Schedule 8 to this Act.][3] [and [paragraph 6][7] of [Schedule 20B][6] to the Finance Act 1993].[5]

[(1B) An allowable loss falls within this subsection if—

(*a*) the loss accrued in any chargeable period from another field ("the abandoned field"),

(*b*) the person to whom the loss accrued is—

(i) the participator, or

(ii) if the participator is a company, a company associated with the participator in respect of the loss (see subsection (3) below), (*c*) the loss accrued to that person as a participator in the abandoned field, and

(*d*) the winning of oil from the abandoned field has permanently ceased.][3]

[(1C) The "unrelievable portion" of an allowable loss falling within subsection (1B) above is so much of that loss as cannot under the provisions of section 7 of this Act be relieved against assessable profits accruing from the abandoned field to the person to whom the loss accrued.][3]

[(1D) Subsection (1C) above is subject to Schedule 31 to the Finance Act 2001 (determination of unrelievable portion where Parts II and III of Schedule 17 to the Finance Act 1980 did not apply to transfer of interest in abandoned field).][3]

(2) In determining for the purposes of this section whether an allowable loss as accrued as mentioned in [subsection (1B) above][3] from an oil field from which the winning of oil permanently ceased before the total amount of oil ever won and saved from it reached the amount by reference to which the critical half year is defined in section 1(4) of this Act, the first chargeable period for that field shall be taken to have been the period ending at the end of the half year in which the winning of oil from the field so ceased (including an unlimited time prior to the beginning of that half year).

In this subsection "half year" has the same meaning as in section 1 of this Act.

(3) For the purposes of this section—

(*a*) "company" means any body corporate; and

(*b*) a company which is a participator in an oil field is associated with another company in respect of an allowable loss which accrued to that other company in a chargeable period from another oil field if—

(i) throughout that part of the relevant period in which both were in existence one was a 51 per cent subsidiary of the other and the other was not a 51 per cent. subsidiary of any company; or

(ii) each of them was, throughout that part of the relevant period in which it was in existence, a 51 per cent. subsidiary of a third company which was not itself a 51 per cent subsidiary of any company;

and in this section and Schedule 8 to this Act any reference to the winning of oil from an oil field permanently ceasing includes a reference to the permanent cessation of operations for the winning of oil from the field.

(4) For the purposes of subsection (3)(*b*) above—

(*a*) the relevant period is the period beginning with the chargeable period in which the allowable loss accrued to the other company referred to in that paragraph and ending with the end of whichever of the following period ends later, that is to say—

(i) the earliest chargeable period in which the company which is a participator in the oil field in question was a participator in that field; and

(ii) the chargeable period in which the allowable loss accrued,

(or, if they are the same period, with the end of that period); and

(*b*) [Chapter 3 of Part 24 of CTA 2010][1] (subsidiaries) shall apply.

[(4A) For the purposes of this section and Schedule 8 to this Act, the winning of oil from an oil field shall not be regarded as having permanently ceased until all the oil wells in the field have been permanently abandoned.][4]

[(5) Subsections (6) to (9) below apply if—

(*a*) a claim is made for the allowance of an unrelievable field loss; and

(*b*) the person to whom the loss accrued made a claim or election for the allowance of any expenditure unrelated to that field; and

(*c*) that claim or election was received by the Board on or after 29 November 1994; and

(*d*) the whole or a part of the expenditure to which the claim or election relates is allowed and, accordingly, falls to be taken into account under section 2(8)(*a*) of this Act for a chargeable period (whether beginning before or after 29 November 1994).

(6) Subject to subsection (7) below, where this subsection applies, from the amount which, apart from this subsection. would be the amount of the unrelievable field loss referred to in paragraph (*a*) of subsection (5) above there shall be deducted an amount equal to so much of any expenditure unrelated to the field as is allowed on a claim or election as mentioned in paragraph (*d*) of that subsection.

(7) If—

(*a*) claims are made for the allowance of more than one unrelievable field loss derived from the same abandoned field, and

(*b*) the person to whom the loss accrued is the same in respect of each of the unrelievable field losses,

subsection (6) above shall have effect as if the deduction referred to in that subsection fell to be made from the aggregate amount of those losses.

(8) Where subsection (7) above applies, the deduction shall be set against the unrelievable field losses in the order in which the claims for the allowance of each of those losses were received by the Board.

PRT

(9) In subsections (5) and (6) above, "expenditure unrelated to the field" means—

(*a*) expenditure allowable under any of sections 5, 5A and 5B of this Act;

(*b*) expenditure allowable under this section (derived from a different abandoned field); or

(*c*) expenditure falling within section 65 of the Finance Act 1987 which is accepted by the Board as allowable in accordance with Schedule 14 to that Act;

and in relation to expenditure falling within section 65 of the Finance Act 1987, "election" means an election under Part I of Schedule 14 to that Act][2].

HMRC Manuals—Oil Taxation Manual OT16250 (unrelievable field loss).

Cross references—FA 1984 s 113 (restriction on PRT relief: expenditure incurred before qualifying date).

FA 1987 s 65 and Sch 14 (cross field allowance).

FA 2001 Sch 32 (unrelievable field losses).

Amendments—[1] In sub-s (4)(*b*) words substituted for words "section 838 of the Taxes Act" by CTA 2010 s 1177, Sch 1 para 163. CTA 2010 has effect for corporation tax purposes for accounting periods ending on or after 1 April 2010, and for income and capital gains tax purposes for the tax year 2010–11 and subsequent tax years.

[2] Words in sub-ss (5)–(9) inserted by FA 1995 s 146(1)–(3).

[3] Sub-ss (1)–(1D) substituted for sub-ss (1), (1A), and words in sub-s (2) substituted by FA 2001 s 101(1), (2), and (5) with effect from 7 March 2001.

[4] Sub-s (4A) inserted by FA 2007 s 104, and deemed to come into force on 1 July 2007.

[5] Words in sub-s (1A) inserted by FA 2008 s 107, Sch 33 para 2 with effect from 21 July 2008.

[6] In sub-s (1A) words substituted for words "Schedule 20A" by FA 2009 s 91, Sch 45 para 3(2)(*a*) with effect from 21 July 2009.

[7] In sub-s (1A), words substituted by F(No 2)A 2017 s 44(2) with effect from 23 November 2016.

7 Relief for allowable losses

(1) Where the Board have determined under Schedule 2 to this Act that an allowable loss has accrued to a participator in a chargeable period from an oil field, then, subject to the following provisions of this section, the assessable profit accruing to him from the field in any succeeding chargeable period shall be treated as reduced by the amount of that allowable loss, or by so much of that amount as cannot, under this subsection or on a claim (if made) under subsection (2) below, be relieved against the assessable profit accruing to him from the field in any earlier chargeable period.

(2) Where the Board have determined under Schedule 2 to this Act that an allowable loss has accrued to a participator in a chargeable period from an oil field, the participator may make a claim requiring that the loss be in the first instance set against any assessable profit which accrued to him from the field in any preceding chargeable period; and the assessable profit which so accrued to him in any such period shall then be treated as reduced by the amount of the loss, or by so much of that amount as cannot be relieved under this subsection against any assessable profit accruing to him from the field in a later chargeable period.

(3) Where—

(*a*) the Board have determined under Schedule 2 to this Act that an allowable loss has accrued to a participator in a chargeable period from an oil field; and

(*b*) the winning of oil from that field has permanently ceased,

then so much of that allowable loss as cannot under subsection (1) or (2) above be relieved against assessable profits accruing to the participator from the field shall be relieved under this subsection by treating the assessable profit accruing to him from the field in any chargeable period as reduced by the amount of the loss, or by so much of that amount as cannot be relieved under this section against the assessable profit so accruing to him in a later chargeable period.

HMRC Manuals—Oil Taxation Manual OT16000 (allowable losses).

Cross references—See FA 1980 Sch 17 paras 7, 14, 15 (transfers of interests in oil fields).

8 Oil allowance

(1) Subject to the provisions of this section and paragraphs 10 and 11 of Schedule 3 to this Act, where a participator in an oil field would, apart from this section and section 9 of this Act, be chargeable to tax for any chargeable period on an amount ("the said amount") consisting of the assessable profit accruing to him in the period from the field or that profit as reduced under section 7 of this Act by any allowable losses, then for the purpose of determining his liability, if any, to tax for that period, the said amount shall be treated as reduced or further reduced as follows, that is to say—

(*a*) if the said amount exceeds the cash equivalent of his share of the oil allowance for the field for that period, to an amount equal to the excess; or

(*b*) if the said amount does not exceed the cash equivalent of his share of that allowance, to nil.

(2) The oil allowance for an oil field is, for each chargeable period, [250,000 metric tonnes][1], and shall be divided between the participators in shares proportionate to their shares of the oil won and saved from the field during the period.

(3) For the purposes of this section the cash equivalent of a participator's share of the oil allowance for an oil field for a chargeable period is (subject to subsection (4) below) the amount given by the formula—

$$A \times \frac{B}{C}$$

where—

A is the gross profit accruing to him in the period or, if a gross loss (or neither a gross profit nor a gross loss) accrues to him in the period, nil (in which case the cash equivalent itself will be nil);

B is his share of the allowance, in [metric tonnes][1]; and

C is his share, exclusive of excluded oil within the meaning of section 10 of this Act, of the oil won and saved from the field during the period, in [metric tonnes][1].

(4) If a participator in an oil field so elects by notice in writing given to the Board at the time when he makes his return under paragraph 2 of Schedule 2 to this Act for a chargeable period, then the cash equivalent of his share of the oil allowance for the field for that period shall be determined under subsection (3) above—

[(*a*) to the extent that his share of that oil allowance does not exceed his share of the oil (other than gas) won and saved from the field in the period, as if—

(i) in computing the gross profit or gross loss accruing to him in the period all amounts relating to gas fell to be disregarded, and

(ii) in the definition of C, for "the oil won and saved" there were substituted "the oil (other than gas) won and saved"; and

(*b*) to the extent, if any, that his share of that oil allowance exceeds his share of the oil (other than gas) so won and saved, as if—

(i) in computing the gross profit or gross loss so accruing all amounts relating to oil other than gas fell to be disregarded, and

(ii) in the definition of C, for "the oil won and saved" there were substituted "the gas won and saved".][2]

(5) For the purposes of this section the amount of the oil allowance for an oil field utilised by a participator in any chargeable period is—

(*a*) if in his case a reduction is made for that period under subsection (1)(*a*) above, an amount in [metric tonnes][1] equal to his share of the oil allowance for the field for that period;

(*b*) if in his case a reduction is made for that period under subsection (1)(*b*) above, the amount in [metric tonnes][1] arrived at by multiplying his share of the oil allowance for the field for that period (in [metric tonnes][1]) by the fraction of which the numerator is the amount of that reduction and the denominator is the cash equivalent of his share of the said oil allowance;

(*c*) in any other case, nil.

(6) The total oil allowance for an oil field shall not exceed [5 million metric tonnes][1], and accordingly—

(*a*) for each chargeable period there shall be determined the aggregate of the amounts of the oil allowance for the field utilised by the participators in that period; and

(*b*) as regards the earliest chargeable period such that the sum of the aggregate determined under paragraph (*a*) above for that period and the aggregates so determined for each earlier chargeable period would, apart from this subsection, exceed [5 million metric tonnes][1], the necessary restriction shall be apportioned between the participators in such manner as may be notified to the Board by the responsible person or, in default of such notification, as may be determined by the Board.

In this subsection "the necessary restriction" means the restriction necessary to secure that the aggregate determined under paragraph (*a*) above for the chargeable period to which paragraph (*b*) above applies will, when added to the sum of the aggregates so determined for each earlier chargeable period, produce a total of [5 million metric tonnes][1].

(7) For the purpose of this section [1,100 cubic metres][1] of oil consisting of gas at the temperature and pressure mentioned in section 1(4) of this Act shall be counted as equivalent to one [metric tonne][1] of oil other than gas.

(8) Any reduction to be made under subsection (1) above shall be made before applying the provisions of section 9 of this Act.

Concession—ESC I1 (where a participator elects for oil allowance to be set against oil in priority to gas, gas also excluded from the total of oil won and saved).

HMRC Manuals—Oil Taxation Manual OT17000 (oil allowance).

Cross references—See OTA 1975 s 9A(3) (operating expenditure incurred while safeguard relief applies: for the purposes of sub-s (6), certain amounts of oil allowance that would not have been utilised are disregarded).

FA 1980 Sch 17 para 17 (transfers of interests in oil fields).

FA 1987, s 66 (oil allowance: adjustment for final periods).

FA 1988 s138 (reduced oil allowance for certain Southern Basin and onshore fields).

FA 2013 s 85 (no additional relief under this section as a result of the operation of FA 2013 s 83).

Modification—This section is modified by FA 1983 s 36, and by FA 1988 s 138.

Amendments—[1] Words in sub-ss (2), (3), (5)–(7) substituted by F(No 2)A 1979 s 21.

PRT

2 Sub-s (4)(*a*), (*b*) substituted by the Enactment of Extra-Statutory Concessions Order, SI 2009/730 art 15 with effect in relation to chargeable periods ending on or after 6 April 2009.

[9 Restriction of limit on amount of tax payable

(1) The tax payable by a participator in an oil field for any chargeable period to which this subsection applies shall not exceed 80 per cent. of the amount (if any) by which his adjusted profit for that period (as defined in this section) exceeds 15 per cent. of his accumulated capital expenditure at the end of that period (as so defined).

(1A) Subsection (1) above applies to—

(*a*) any chargeable period from the first chargeable period up to and including the period which is the participator's net profit period for the field for the purposes of section 111 of the Finance Act 1981 or where section 113 of that Act applies, up to and including the earlier of the periods mentioned in subsection (2) of that section; and

(*b*) any subsequent chargeable period up to such number of periods as is equal to half the number of chargeable periods [which are included in paragraph (*a*) above and in which the amount of oil won and saved from the field exceeds 1,000 metric tonnes][3] (counting any resulting fraction of a period as a whole period)

[and for the purposes of paragraph (*b*) above 1,100 cubic metres of gas at a temperature of 15 degrees centigrade and pressure of one atmosphere shall be counted as equivalent to one metric tonne][3].

(2) The adjusted profit of a participator in an oil field for any chargeable period shall be determined as follows—

(*a*) there shall be ascertained—

(i) the assessable profit (without any reduction under section 7 or 8 of this Act) or allowable loss accruing to him in that period; and

(ii) the total amount taken into account under section 2(9)(*b*), (*c*), (*d*)[, (*e*) [(*f*) and (*g*)][4]][2] of this Act in computing that profit or loss, excluding expenditure so taken into account under section 2(9)(*b*)(i) or (*c*)(i) which was not allowed as qualifying for supplement under section 2(9)(*b*)(ii) or (*c*)(ii)(*e*);

(*b*) if there is a profit under paragraph (*a*)(i) above, the sum of that profit and the total ascertained under paragraph (*a*)(ii) above is his adjusted profit for the period;

(*c*) if there is a loss under paragraph (*a*)(i) above smaller than the total ascertained under paragraph (*a*)(ii) above, the difference is his adjusted profit for the period.

(3) The accumulated capital expenditure of a participator in an oil field at the end of any chargeable period is the total amount of expenditure taken into account under section 2(9)(*b*)(i) and (*c*)(i) of this Act in computing the assessable profit or allowable loss accruing to him in that period and all earlier chargeable periods excluding all expenditure so taken into account which was not allowed as qualifying for supplement under section 2(9)(*b*)(ii) or (*c*)(ii).

(4) . . . [5]][1]

HMRC Manuals—Oil Taxation Manual OT17500 (safeguard).

Cross references—See FA 1980 Sch 17, paras 8, 18 (transfers of interests in oil fields).

FA 1999 ss 95(4), 97(2)(*e*) (sale and leaseback).

Amendments—[1] This section substituted by FA 1981 s 114.

2 Words in sub-s (2)(*a*) substituted by FA 1983 s 37, Sch 8 Pt II para 4.

3 Words in sub-s (1A) substituted or inserted, with respect to any oil field where the first chargeable period ends after 30 June 1985, by FA 1985 s 91(1), (2).

4 Words in sub-s (2)(*a*) substituted by FA 1987 s 64, Sch 13 Pt II para 3.

5 Sub-s (4) repealed by FA 2009 s 91, Sch 45 para 1(1), (3) with effect in relation to chargeable periods beginning after 30 June 2009.

[9A Operating expenditure incurred while section 9 applies

(1) Subsections (2) and (3) below apply where—

(*a*) operating expenditure is incurred by a participator in an oil field during a chargeable period to which section 9(1) of this Act applies ("the relevant chargeable period");

(*b*) a claim for the allowance of the expenditure is made under Schedule 5 or 6 for the claim period which coincides with the relevant chargeable period ("the relevant claim period"); and

(*c*) the claim is made more than four months after the end of the relevant claim period.

(2) The Board shall not allow the expenditure except to such extent (if any) as they consider necessary to secure that the participator's overall liability to tax is no greater than it would have been if the claim had been allowed before the Board had made an assessment to tax or a determination on or in relation to the participator in respect of the field for the relevant chargeable period.

(3) Any amounts of oil allowance which, if the claim had been allowed before the Board had made an assessment to tax or a determination on or in relation to the participator in respect of the field for the relevant chargeable period, would not have been utilised by him in that period, or any subsequent chargeable period, shall be disregarded for the purposes of section 8(6) of this Act.

(4) Where—

(*a*) the participator transfers the whole or part of his interest in the oil field to another person; and

(*b*) Parts II and III of Schedule 17 to the Finance Act 1980 apply to the transfer, subsections (2) and (3) above shall have effect as if references to the participator included references to that other person.

(5) In this section—

"acquisition", in relation to an asset, includes acquisition of an interest in the asset;

"capital expenditure" means expenditure on the acquisition or construction of an asset which is to be used for any of the following purposes—

(*a*) for ascertaining the extent or characteristics of any oil-bearing area wholly or partly included in the field, or what the reserves of oil of any such oil-bearing area are;

(*b*) for winning oil from the field;

(*c*) for transporting oil won from the field, whether to a place in the United Kingdom or to a place in another country; or

(*d*) for the initial treatment or initial storage of oil won from the field;

"operating expenditure" means any expenditure other than capital expenditure.

(6) Where a claim period is a period of twelve months, this section shall have effect as if—

(*a*) that period were two separate claim periods of six months each;

(*b*) any claim for that period under Schedule 5 or 6 were two separate claims, one for each of those separate periods; and

(*c*) the operating expenditure to which that claim relates were apportioned between those separate periods and those separate claims in such manner as may be just and reasonable.][1]

HMRC Manuals—Oil Taxation Manual OT17750 (deferred expenditure claims).

Amendments—[1] This section inserted by FA 2000 s 139(1) with effect for expenditure incurred after 20 March 2000.

10 Modifications of Part I in connection with certain gas sold to British Gas Corporation

(1) In computing under section 2 of this Act the gross profit or loss (if any) accruing to a participator in any chargeable period from an oil field—

(*a*) any oil consisting of gas sold to the British Gas Corporation under a contract made before the end of June 1975 shall be disregarded; and

(*b*) if at the end of that chargeable period the participator's share exclusive of oil falling within paragraph (*a*) above or used for production purposes, of the total amount of oil ever won and saved from the field does not exceed 5 per cent. of his share of the total amount of oil so falling which was ever so won and saved, his share of the oil won and saved from the field but not so falling shall also be disregarded;

and in the following provisions of this section any oil which falls to be disregarded under this subsection is referred to as "excluded oil".

(2) Excluded oil shall be deemed not to be oil for the purposes of the following provisions of this Act, namely section 2(7) and (9), section 3 (except paragraphs (*a*) to (*c*) [(*hh*), (i) and (*j*) of subsection (1) and [subsections (1C) and (1D)][3]][2] and section 4 (including, in the case of any expression used in any of those provisions which is defined elsewhere, its definition so far as it has effect for the purpose of that provision); and in computing under section 2 of this Act the licence debit or credit (if any) of a participator in an oil field for any chargeable period, any royalty repaid to him in the period in respect of excluded oil shall be disregarded.

[(3) Subsections (3A) to (3H) below apply where, in the case of any taxable field, the oil—

(*a*) won and saved from the field, or

(*b*) expected to be won and saved from the field,

includes oil falling within subsection (1)(a) above.][4]

[(3A) Any expenditure allowable under section 3 of this Act for the field by virtue of any of paragraphs (*a*) to (*c*) of section 3(1) of this Act shall be a proportion of what it would otherwise have been.][4]

[(3B) The proportion mentioned in subsection (3A) above is that which, according to estimates submitted to the [OGA][5] after the end of June 1975 and approved by [it][5] as reasonable, the field's original reserves of oil exclusive of oil falling within subsection (1)(*a*) above bear to the field's original reserves of oil inclusive of oil so falling.][4]

[(3C) Until estimates have been submitted and approved for the purpose of subsection (3B) above, the expenditure allowable for the field under section 3 of this Act by virtue of section 3(1)(*a*), (*b*) or (*c*) of this Act shall be deemed to be nil.][4]

[(3D) Any expenditure allowable under section 3 of this Act for the field by virtue of section 3(1)(*hh*) of this Act shall be a portion of what it would otherwise have been.][4]

[(3E) That portion is determined in accordance with the following rules—

1. Identify the abandonment guarantee (within the meaning given by section 104 of the Finance Act 1991) on the obtaining of which the expenditure was incurred.
2. Identify the liabilities covered by the guarantee.
3. Identify which of those liabilities relate to qualifying assets.
4. Identify the portion of the expenditure that it is just and reasonable to apportion to the liabilities identified under rule 3.
5. Identify the qualifying assets to which the liabilities identified under rule 3 relate.

PRT

6. Identify the use of those qualifying assets that has been (or is expected to be) non-excluded use.
7. Assume that expenditure is incurred on the provision of those qualifying assets and identify the proportion of the hypothetical expenditure that it would be just and reasonable to apportion to the use of those assets identified under rule 6.
8. The portion mentioned in subsection (3D) above is then determined by multiplying—
(i) the portion identified under rule 4, by
(ii) the proportion (expressed as a fraction) identified under rule 7.][4]

[(3F) Any expenditure allowable under section 3 of this Act for the field by virtue of section 3(1)(*i*) or (*j*) of this Act shall be a portion of what it would otherwise have been.][4]

[(3G) That portion is determined in accordance with the following rules—
1. Identify the qualifying asset that is relevant to the incurring of the expenditure.
2. Identify the use of that qualifying asset that has been non-excluded use.
3. Assume that expenditure is incurred on the provision of that qualifying asset and identify the proportion of the hypothetical expenditure that it would be just and reasonable to apportion to the use of that asset identified under rule 2.
4. The portion mentioned in subsection (3F) above is then determined by multiplying—
(i) the expenditure, by
(ii) the proportion (expressed as a fraction) identified under rule 3.][4]

[(3H) In subsections (3E) and (3G) above—
"non-excluded use" means—
(*a*) use in connection with the winning and saving of oil, other than excluded oil, from the field, or
(*b*) use giving rise to receipts that, for the purposes of the Oil Taxation Act 1983, are tariff receipts attributable to a participator in the field;
"qualifying asset" has the same meaning as it has for the purposes of the Oil Taxation Act 1983 (see section 8 of that Act).][4]

(4) A return made under paragraph 2 of Schedule 2 to this Act by a participator in an oil field need not, in the case of oil falling within subsection (1)(*a*) above, state the price received or receivable for the oil.

(5) For the purposes of this section [1,100 cubic metres][1] of oil consisting of gas at the temperature and pressure mentioned in section 1(4) of this Act shall be counted as equivalent to one [metric tonne][1] of oil other than gas.

HMRC Manuals—Oil Taxation Manual OT13200 (exempt gas).
Cross references—See FA 1980 Sch 17, para 9 (transfers of interests in oil fields).
FA 1981 s 118(2)(*d*) (licence payments other than royalties).
FA 1999 s 94(2) (for the purposes of sub-s (1)(*a*) a replacement contract shall be treated as the same contract as the old contract unless the rights and liabilities are so different that the replacement contract cannot be regarded as the same contract).
Amendments—[1] Words in sub-s (5) substituted by F(No 2)A 1979 s 21.
[2] Words in sub-ss (2), (3) substituted, so far as they relate to s 3(1)(*hh*), with respect to expenditure incurred on or after 19 March 1991, and for remaining purposes with respect to expenditure incurred after 30 June 1991, by FA 1991 s 103(7), (8).
[3] Words in sub-s (2) substituted by FA 2001 s 102(3) with effect for expenditure incurred after 6 March 2001.
[4] Sub-ss (3)–(3H) substituted for original sub-s (3) by FA 2001 s 103 with effect for expenditure incurred after 6 March 2001.
[5] In sub-s (3B), word substituted for words "Secretary of State" and word "him" by the Petroleum (Transfer of Functions) Regulations, SI 2016/898 reg 4(1), (5) with effect from 1 October 2016.

11 Application of Provisional Collection of Taxes Act 1968

Section 1 of the Provisional Collection of Taxes Act 1968 shall apply to petroleum revenue tax; and accordingly, in subsection (1) of that section after the words "income tax" there shall be inserted the words "petroleum revenue tax".

12 Interpretation of Part I

(1) In this Part of this Act—
["business day" has the same meaning as in the Bills of Exchange Act 1882;][10]
["calendar month" (where those words are used) means a month of the calendar year;][10]
["Category 1 oil" and "Category 2 oil" have the meaning given by paragraph 2(1B) of Schedule 3 to this Act;][10]
"chargeable period", in relation to an oil field, has the meaning given by section 1(3) of this Act;
"claim period", in relation to an oil field, has the meaning given by paragraph 1 of Schedule 5 to this Act;
"crude", where the reference is to oil being disposed of or appropriated crude, refers to its being so dealt with without having been refined (whether or not it has previously undergone initial treatment);
"determination", in a context relating to an assessment or determination on or in relation to a participator, means a determination under Schedule 2 to this Act that a loss is allowable to him or that neither an assessable profit nor an allowable loss has accrued to him;

"initial storage", in relation to oil won from an oil field, means the storage . . . [6] of a quantity of oil won from the field not exceeding, in the case of storage in the United Kingdom [or another country][6], a quantity equal to ten times the maximum daily production rate of oil for the field as planned or achieved (whichever is the greater), but does not include—

(*a*) the storing of oil as part of or in conjunction with the operation of an oil refinery; or

(*b*) deballasting; or

(*c*) conveying oil in a pipe-line;

"initial treatment", in relation to oil from an oil field, means the doing, at any place . . . [6] of any of the following things, that is to say—

(*a*) subjecting oil won from the field to any process of which the sole purpose is to enable the oil to be safely stored, safely loaded into a tanker or safely accepted by an oil refinery; or

[(*b*) separating oil so won and consisting of gas from other oil so won; or

(*c*) separating oil so won and consisting of gas of a kind that is transported and sold in normal commercial practice from other oil so won and consisting of gas; or

(*d*) liquifying oil so won and consisting of gas of such a kind as aforesaid for the purpose of transporting it; or

(*e*) subjecting oil so won to any process of which the purpose is to secure that oil disposed of crude has the quality that is normal for oil so disposed of from the field,][2]

but does not include—

(i) the storing of oil even where this involves the doing to the oil of things within [any of paragraphs (*a*) to (*e*) of this definition][2] or

[(ii) any activity carried on as part of, or in association with, the refining of oil not consisting of gas or any activity the sole or main purpose of which is to achieve a chemical reaction in respect of oil consisting of gas; or][2]

(iii) deballasting;

"land" includes land in the United Kingdom [or another country][6] covered with water;

"licence" means a licence under [Part I of the Petroleum Act 1998][9] or the Petroleum (Production) Act (Northern Ireland) 1964 authorising the winning of oil, and "licensed area" shall be construed accordingly;

"licensee" means—

(*a*) the person entitled to the benefit of a licence or, where two or more persons are entitled to the benefit of a licence, each of those persons; and

(*b*) a person who has rights under an agreement which is approved by the Board and is certified by the [OGA][14] to confer on that person rights which are the same as, or similar to, those conferred by a licence;

["light gases", except in relation to an election under section 134 of the Finance Act 1982 or section 109 of the Finance Act 1986, means oil consisting of gas of which the largest component by volume over any chargeable period, measured at a temperature of 15 degrees centigrade and a pressure of one atmosphere, is methane or ethane or a combination of those gases].[8]

["the OGA" means the Oil and Gas Authority;][14]

"oil" has the meaning given by section 1(1) of this Act;

"oil field" shall be construed in accordance with Schedule 1 to this Act [(which also includes provision about areas that are to be treated as continuing to be oil fields)][13]; [and "taxable field" and "non-taxable field" have the same meaning as in Part III of the Finance Act 1993][7];

"participator" (except in paragraph 4 of Schedule 2 to this Act) means, in relation to an oil field and [a][12] chargeable period [("the relevant chargeable period")[11]]—

(*a*) a person who is or was at any time in [the relevant chargeable period][11] a licensee in respect of any licensed area then wholly or partly included in the field; and

[(*aa*) a person who is no longer a licensee in respect of any licensed area wholly or partly included in the field, but who—

(i) was such a licensee at any time in any chargeable period preceding the relevant chargeable period, and

(ii) ceased to be such a licensee because of a cessation event; and][12]

(*b*) a person who is no longer a licensee in respect of any licensed area wholly or partly included in the field [(and who does not fall within paragraph (*aa*) of this definition)][12], but who was such a licensee at any time in either of the two chargeable periods preceding [the relevant chargeable period][11]; and

(*c*) a person who is no longer a licensee in respect of any licensed area wholly or partly included in the field (and who does not fall within paragraph [(*aa*) or][12] (*b*) of this definition), but who has or had at any time in [the relevant chargeable period][11] a share

PRT

of oil won (whether or not in that period) from the field, being a share with respect to any part of which either of the following conditions is or was satisfied at that time, that is to say—

(i) he has or had neither disposed of that part nor relevantly appropriated it; or

(ii) he has or had disposed of, but not delivered, that part;[and

(*d*) a former participator to whom an amount is attributed under paragraph 2A(2) of Schedule 5 in respect of a default payment made in relation to the field in the relevant chargeable period; and

(*e*) a former participator to whom an amount was attributed under paragraph 2A(2) of Schedule 5 in respect of a default payment made in relation to the field in either of the two chargeable periods preceding the relevant chargeable period; and

(*f*) a person who—

(i) made a default payment in relation to the field (whether the person was then a current participator or former participator),

(ii) is not a participator during the relevant chargeable period under any of paragraphs (*a*) to (*e*) of this definition, and

(iii) receives, in the relevant chargeable period, reimbursement expenditure (within the meaning of section 108(1)(*c*) of the Finance Act 1991) in respect of the default payment; and

(*g*) a person who—

(i) made a default payment in relation to the field (whether the person was then a current participator or former participator),

(ii) is not a participator during the relevant chargeable period under any of paragraphs (*a*) to (*f*) of this definition, and

(iii) received, in either of the two chargeable periods preceding the relevant chargeable period, reimbursement expenditure (within the meaning of section 108(1)(*c*) of the Finance Act 1991) in respect of the default payment;

. . . [12]

"pipe-line" means a pipe-line as defined in section 65 of the Pipelines Act 1962;

"production purposes", in relation to an oil field, means any of the following purposes, that is to say—

(*a*) carrying on drilling or production operations within the field; or

(*b*) in the case of oil won from the field that was so won from strata in the sea bed and subsoil of either the territorial sea of the United Kingdom or a designated area, pumping it to the place where it is first landed in the United Kingdom [or to the place in the United Kingdom [or another country][5] at which the seller in a sale at arm's length could reasonably be expected to deliver it or, if there is more than one place at which he could reasonably be expected to deliver it, the one nearest to the place of extraction][1]; or

(*c*) the initial treatment of oil won from the field;

["refining", in relation to oil, does not include subjecting it to initial treatment and "refined" and "refinery" shall be construed accordingly;][2]

"relevant licence", in relation to a participator in an oil field, means any licence held or previously held by him in respect of a licensed area wholly or partly included in the field;

"relevantly appropriated", in relation to oil won from an oil field, means appropriated to refining or to any use except use for production purposes [in relation to that or any other oil field][4], and "relevant appropriation" shall be construed accordingly;

"the responsible person", in relation to an oil field, has the meaning given by paragraph 4 of Schedule 2 to this Act;

"royalty", in relation to a participator in an oil field, means royalty payable (but not, it is hereby declared, oil delivered) to the Secretary of State under any relevant licence;

"tax" or "the tax" means petroleum revenue tax.

[(1A) In the definition of "participator" in subsection (1)—

(*a*) "cessation event", in relation to an oil field to which a licence relates, means any of the following—

(i) determination of the licence by the licensee,

(ii) revocation of the licence by the [OGA][14] or a Northern Ireland Department,

(iii) expiry of the licence at the end of its term,

(iv) the licensed area ceasing to include any relevant area whatsoever, by reason of the licensee surrendering the licence so far as it relates to the whole of the relevant area, and

(v) the licence ceasing to apply to the oil field by reason of the operation of the licence;

and for the purposes of sub-paragraph (iv) "relevant area" means an area which is, or combination of areas each of which is, included in the oil field (whether or not such an area falls partly outside the oil field);

(*b*) "current participator", "former participator" and "default payment" have the same meanings as in paragraph 2A of Schedule 5.][12]

(2) In this Part of this Act any reference to the use of an asset in connection with an oil field is a reference to its use in connection with that field for one or more of the purposes mentioned in section 3(1) of this Act (excluding section 3(1)(*b*)).

(3) In this Part of this Act any reference (however worded) to the doing of anything in a chargeable period in connection with an oil field or with oil won from an oil field shall . . .[3] be construed as including the doing of that thing in connection with the area of the field as subsequently determined under Schedule 1 to this Act or, as the case may be, with oil won from that area.

(4) In so far as a person is a participator in an oil field by virtue of a licence under the Petroleum (Production) Act (Northern Ireland) 1964, references in this Part of this Act to the Secretary of State [or the OGA][14] (except references in Schedule 1) shall be construed in his case as references to the Department of Commerce for Northern Ireland.

Simon's Tax Cases—s 12(1), (2) *BP Exploration Operating Co Ltd v IRC* [2000] STC (SCD) 466.

Amendments—[1] In sub-s (1) words in definition of "production purposes" inserted by F(No 2)A 1979 s 20(1), (3).

[2] In sub-s (1) in definition of "initial treatment" paras (*b*)–(*e*), words in para (i), and whole of para (ii) substituted, and definition of "refining" inserted, by FA 1980 s 109(2)–(5).

[3] Words in sub-s (3) repealed by FA 1982 ss 135(4), (5), 157, Sch 22 Pt IX.

[4] In sub-s (1) in definition of "relevantly appropriated" words inserted by FA 1983 s 39.

[5] In sub-s (1) in definition of "production purposes" words inserted by F(No 2)A 1992 s 74, Sch 15 para 3(d) with effect in accordance with s 74(5) thereof.

[6] In definitions of "initial storage" and "initial treatment" words repealed and in definitions of "initial storage" and "land" words inserted by F(No 2)A 1992 ss 55(3), 74, Sch 15 para 3, with effect in accordance with ss 55(3), 74(5) thereof.

[7] In sub-s (1) in definition of "oil field" words inserted by FA 1993 s 185(5).

[8] In sub-s (1) definition of "light gases" inserted by FA 1994 s 236(2), (4).

[9] In definition of "licence" words substituted by the Petroleum Act 1998 s 50, Sch 4 para 7(3) with effect from 15 February 1999 (by virtue of SI 1999/161, art 2).

[10] In sub-s (1) definitions of "business day" and "Category 1 oil and Category 2 oil" inserted and definition of "calendar month" substituted by FA 2006 s 146, Sch 18 para 4 with effect—

(a) in relation to oil delivered or appropriated on or after 1 July 2006 (disregarding section 12A of this Act); and

(b) for the purpose of determining for any chargeable period ending on or after 31 December 2006—

(i) the value to be brought into account under section 2(4)(*b*) of OTA 1975 by reference to a previous chargeable period ending on or after 30 June 2006, and

(ii) the value to be brought into account under section 2(5)(*d*) of that Act,

subject to transitional provisions in FA 2006 s 147(4)–(8).

Definition of "calendar month" previously read as follows—

" "calendar month" (where those words are used) [has] the meaning given by paragraph 3(2) of Schedule 3 to this Act;".

[11] In sub-s (1), in definition of "participator", words and paras (*d*)–(*g*) inserted, and words substituted for words "that chargeable period", by FA 2008 s 102(1)–(4) with effect in relation to expenditure incurred after 30 June 2008.

[12] In sub-s (1) in the definition of "participator" word substituted for word "any", sub-para (*aa*) inserted, words in sub-paras (*b*), (c) inserted, in sub-para (*g*) words repealed, and sub-s (1A) inserted, by FA 2009 s 88 Sch 42 paras 1, 2 with effect in relation to persons who cease to be licensees because of cessation events occurring in chargeable periods that begin after 30 June 2009.

[13] In sub-s (1), in the definition of "oil field", words inserted by FA 2009 s 88 Sch 42 paras 5, 6 with effect in relation to areas that cease to be oil fields, or parts of oil fields, in chargeable periods that begin after 30 June 2009.

[14] In sub-ss (1), in definition of "licensee", and (1A)(*a*)(ii), word substituted for words "Secretary of State", in sub-s (1), definition of "the OGA" inserted, and in sub-s (4), words inserted, by the Petroleum (Transfer of Functions) Regulations, SI 2016/898 reg 4(1), (6) with effect from 1 October 2016.

Prospective amendments—In sub-s (1A)(*a*)(ii), words ", the Scottish Ministers" to be inserted after words "Secretary of State" by the Scotland Act 2016 s 48(18), (19) with effect from a date to be appointed.

In sub-s (1), in definition of "licensee" para (*b*), words substituted for words "the OGA", and in sub-s (1A)(a)(ii), words ", the Welsh Ministers" to be inserted after words "Scottish Ministers", by the Wales Act 2017 s 69, Sch 6 para 19 with effect from a day to be appointed. Words as substituted to read as follows—

"—

(i) the Welsh Ministers, where the rights relate to oil in the Welsh onshore area (as defined in section 8A of the Petroleum Act 1998), or

(ii) the OGA, where the rights relate to oil elsewhere,".

[12A Date of delivery or appropriation: shipped oil not sold at arm's length

(1) This section has effect for the purpose of determining the date on which any oil to which it applies is to be regarded for the purposes of this Part as delivered or relevantly appropriated.

(2) This section applies to—

(*a*) oil (not being light gases) won from a field and disposed of crude by a participator otherwise than in sales at arm's length, and

(*b*) oil (not being light gases) so won and relevantly appropriated by a participator,

if the condition in subsection (3)(a) or (b) below is met.

(3) The condition is that the oil is or has been, or is to be,—

PRT

(*a*) transported by ship from the place of extraction to a place in the United Kingdom or elsewhere, or

(*b*) transported by pipeline to a place in the United Kingdom and loaded on to a ship there.

(4) The date on which the oil is to be taken to be delivered, or (as the case may be) relevantly appropriated, by the participator is—

(*a*) the date of completion of load, in a case where the condition in subsection (3)(*a*) above is met,

(*b*) the date of the bill of lading, in a case where the condition in subsection (3)(*b*) above is met.][1]

Amendments—[1] This section inserted by FA 2006 s 146, Sch 18 para 5 with effect in relation to oil which would (apart from this paragraph) fall to be regarded for the purposes of Part 1 of OTA 1975 as delivered or appropriated on a date after 30 June 2006.

PART II
PROVISIONS RELATING TO THE EXTRACTION OF PETROLEUM IN THE UNITED KINGDOM OR A DESIGNATED AREA

Amendments—This Part repealed by TA 1988 s 844, Sch 31.

PART III
MISCELLANEOUS AND GENERAL

21 Citation, interpretation and construction

(1) This Act may be cited as the Oil Taxation Act 1975.

(2) In this Act—

["the Board" means the Commissioners for Her Majesty's Revenue and Customs;][2]

["CTA 2010" means the Corporation Tax Act 2010;][3]

"designated area" means an area designated by Order in Council under section 1(7) of the Continental Shelf Act 1964;

"the Taxes Act" means the Income and Corporation Taxes Act [1988].[3]

(3) Parts II and III of this Act, so far as they relate to income tax, shall be construed as one with the Income Tax Acts and, so far as they relate to corporation tax, shall be construed as one with the Corporation Tax Acts.

(4) Except so far as the context otherwise requires, any reference in this Act to any enactment shall be construed as a reference to that enactment as applied, by or under any other enactment, including this Act.

(5) . . . [1]

Amendments—[1] Sub-s (5) repealed by the Petroleum Act 1998 ss 50, 51, Sch 4 para 7(4), Sch 5 Pt I with effect from 15 February 1999 (by virtue of SI 1999/161, art 2).

[2] In sub-s (2) definition of "the Board" substituted by FA 2006 s 146, Sch 18 para 6 with effect from 19 July 2006.

[3] In sub-s (2) definition inserted and definition of "the Taxes Act" repealed by CTA 2010 ss 1177, 1181, Sch 1 para 164, Sch 3 Pt 1. CTA 2010 has effect for corporation tax purposes for accounting periods ending on or after 1 April 2010, and for income and capital gains tax purposes for the tax year 2010–11 and subsequent tax years.

SCHEDULES

SCHEDULE 1
DETERMINATION OF OIL FIELDS

Section 1

[Areas that are oil fields]

Amendments—Heading inserted by FA 2009 s 88, Sch 42 paras 5, 7 with effect in relation to areas that cease to be oil fields, or parts of oil fields, in chargeable periods that begin after 30 June 2009.

1—(1) For the purposes of this Part of this Act an oil field is any area which the appropriate authority may determine to be an oil field, being an area of which every part is, or is part of, a licensed area.

(2) For the purposes of this Schedule the appropriate authority, in relation to any area—

(*a*) is the [OGA][2] if the area is such that licences can be granted for all of it under [Part I of the Petroleum Act 1998][1];

(*b*) is the Department of Commerce for Northern Ireland if the area is such that licences can be granted for all of it under the Petroleum (Production) Act (Northern Ireland) 1964; and

(*c*) is the [OGA][2] and that Department acting jointly if the area is such that licences can be granted for part of it under one and for part of it under the other of those Acts;

and any reference in this Schedule to the making of representations to the appropriate authority is, in a case falling within (*c*) above, a reference to the making of them to either the [OGA][2] or the said Department.

HMRC Manuals—Oil Taxation Manual OT01007 (field determination process).

Amendments—[1] Words in sub-para (2)(*a*) substituted by the Petroleum Act 1998 s 50, Sch 4 para 7(5) with effect from 15 February 1999 (by virtue of SI 1999/161, art 2).

[2] In sub-para (2), word substituted for words "Secretary of State" in each place by the Petroleum (Transfer of Functions) Regulations, SI 2016/898 reg 4(1), (7) with effect from 1 October 2016.

Prospective amendments—In sub-para (2)(*a*), words "by the Secretary of State" to be inserted after word "granted", and sub-para (2)(*aa*), (*ab*) to be inserted by the Scotland Act 2016 s 48(1), (2) with effect from a date to be appointed. Sub-s (2)(*aa*), (*ab*) as inserted to read as follows—

"(*aa*) is the Scottish Ministers if the area is such that licences can be granted by the Scottish Ministers for all of it under Part 1 of the Petroleum Act 1998;

(*ab*) is the Secretary of State and the Scottish Ministers acting jointly if the area is such that licences can be granted for part of it by the Secretary of State and for part of it by the Scottish Ministers;".

Sub-para (2)(*ac*), (*ad*) to be inserted by the Wales Act 2017 s 69, Sch 6 para 20 with effect from a day to be appointed. Sub-para (2)(*ac*), (*ad*) as inserted to read as follows—

"(*ac*) is the Welsh Ministers if the area is such that licences can be granted by the Welsh Ministers for all of it under Part 1 of the Petroleum Act 1998;

(*ad*) is the OGA and the Welsh Ministers acting jointly if the area is such that licences can be granted for part of it by the OGA and for part of it by the Welsh Ministers;".

2 Before determining an area to be an oil field the appropriate authority—

(*a*) shall give notice in writing of the proposed determination to every person who is a licensee in respect of a licensed area wholly or partly included in that area and to any other licensee whose interests appear to the authority to be affected; and

(*b*) shall consider any representations in writing which a person to whom a notice under this paragraph has been given may make to the authority within sixty days of receiving the notice,

and the determination may be made either as proposed or with such modifications as appear to the authority to be appropriate after considering any representations made to the authority in accordance with this paragraph.

3 A determination under this Schedule shall be in such form as the appropriate authority thinks fit and shall for purposes of identification assign to the field to which it relates a distinguishing number or other designation.

4 The appropriate authority shall give notice of any determination made by the authority under this Schedule to each of the persons to whom notice of the proposed determination was given.

HMRC Manuals—Oil Taxation Manual OT04030 (appointment of responsible person).

5 A determination under this Schedule may from time to time be varied by a new determination thereunder made by the appropriate authority, and paragraphs 2 to 4 above shall apply to any such new determination.

[Areas treated as continuing to be oil fields

6—(1) This paragraph applies if an area has ceased to be—

(*a*) an oil field within the meaning of paragraph 1(1), or

(*b*) part of such an oil field.

(2) The area is to be treated as continuing to be—

(*a*) the oil field, or

(*b*) the part of the oil field, that it actually was.

(3) Accordingly, whilst the area is treated in accordance with sub- paragraph (2), any reference to an oil field is to include a reference to the area.

(4) Sub-paragraph (2) ceases to apply to the area—

(*a*) in accordance with sub-paragraph (5), and

(*b*) if or to the extent that it has not ceased to apply in accordance with sub-paragraph (5), in accordance with sub-paragraph (6).

(5) Sub-paragraph (2) ceases to apply to the area if, or to the extent that, it again becomes—

(*a*) an oil field within the meaning of paragraph 1(1), or

(*b*) part of such an oil field.

(6) Sub-paragraph (2) ceases to apply to the area at the end of the second chargeable period that falls after the chargeable period in which the area is decommissioned.][1]

Amendments—[1] Paragraphs 6 and 7 inserted by FA 2009 s 88, Sch 42 paras 5, 7 with effect in relation to areas that cease to be oil fields, or parts of oil fields, in chargeable periods that begin after 30 June 2009.

[**7**—(1) A relevant area is decommissioned for the purposes of paragraph 6 if all qualifying assets of the relevant area are decommissioned.

(2) If, and to the extent that, a UK offshore decommissioning regime applies to qualifying assets of the relevant area, those assets are decommissioned if—

PRT

(*a*) the Secretary of State has approved one or more abandonment programmes under the regime in relation to those assets, and

(*b*) those programmes have been carried out to the satisfaction of the Secretary of State.

(3) If, and to the extent that, a UK offshore decommissioning regime does not apply to qualifying assets of the relevant area, those assets are decommissioned if the Board are satisfied that they have been decommissioned.

(4) For the purposes of sub-paragraph (3), the Board must have regard to any obligations to decommission the qualifying assets which arise under the law applicable to [those qualifying assets][2] (whether the law of any part of the United Kingdom or of any other state or territory), including any obligations imposed by an authority having functions under that law in respect of such decommissioning.

(5) If sub-paragraph (3) applies (to any extent) to any qualifying assets, the Board must give the responsible person notice of any decision the Board make under that sub-paragraph.

(6) The responsible person may appeal against such a decision by notice in writing given to the Board within three months of the responsible person receiving the notice under sub-paragraph (5).

(7) An appeal under sub-paragraph (6) may, before it is notified to the tribunal, be abandoned by notice in writing given to the Board by the responsible person.

(8) The provisions of paragraphs 14A to 14I of Schedule 2 apply to appeals under sub-paragraph (6) subject to any necessary modifications.

(9) In this paragraph—

"qualifying assets" means assets that are qualifying assets within the meaning of OTA 1983;

"relevant area" means an area that is treated as being an oil field, or part of an oil field, under paragraph 6;

"UK offshore decommissioning regime" means—

(*a*) Part 4 of the Petroleum Act 1998, and

(*b*) Part 1 of the Petroleum Act 1987.][1]

Amendments—[1] Paragraphs 6 and 7 inserted by FA 2009 s 88, Sch 42 paras 5, 7 with effect in relation to areas that cease to be oil fields, or parts of oil fields, in chargeable periods that begin after 30 June 2009.

[2] In sub-para (4) words substituted for words "the relevant area" by FA 2011 s 61 with effect in relation to chargeable periods beginning after 30 June 2009.

SCHEDULE 2

MANAGEMENT AND COLLECTION OF PETROLEUM REVENUE TAX

Section 1

Management of tax

1—(1) The tax shall be under the care and management of the Board; and the provisions of the Taxes Management Act 1970 specified in the first column of the following Table shall apply in relation to the tax as they apply in relation to a tax within the meaning of that Act, subject to any modifications specified in the second column of that Table and with the substitution, for references to Part IX of that Act or to the Taxes Acts, of references to this Part of this Act and, for references to chargeable periods within the meaning of that Act, of references to chargeable periods within the meaning of this Part of this Act.

Table

Provisions applied	*Modifications*
Section	
1(3)	—
[...	...][8]
[...	...][7]
. . .[6]	. . .[6]
[47C	—][6]
48	—
49 . . .[6]	—
. . .[4]	. . .[4]
. . .[6]	. . .[6]
. . .[4]	. . .[4]
[[56][6]	—][3]
. . .[6]	. . .[6]
60	In subsection (1), omit the words following "charged therewith".

Provisions applied	*Modifications*
61	In subsection (1), omit the words from "distrain upon" to "is charged or".
62(1)	Omit "or which are payable for the year in which the seizure is made" and for "one year" and "one whole year" substitute "two chargeable periods".
(2)	For "one whole year" substitute "two chargeable periods".
63	—
64(1)	For "one year" and "one whole year" substitute "two chargeable periods".
(2)	For "one whole year" substitute "two chargeable periods".
66	—
67	—
68	—
69	In paragraph (*a*), substitute a reference to section 68 as applied by this paragraph for the reference to the sections there specified.
70(1)[5]	—
(2)[5]	*For the reference to section 86 or 87 substitute a reference to paragraph 15 of this Schedule.*[5]
. . . [1]	. . . [1]
90	—
. . . [4]	. . . [4]
. . . [9]	. . . [9]
[100C][6]	[In subsection (1) omit the words after "penalty"][6]
101	For the reference to income or chargeable gains substitute a reference to assessable profits.
102	—
103(1)	For the words from the beginning to "court" substitute "Where the amount of a penalty is to be ascertained by reference to tax payable by a person for any period, proceedings for the penalty may be commenced before the [tribunal][6]".
(4)	For the words from the beginning to "court," substitute "Proceedings for a penalty to which subsection (1) above does not apply may be commenced before the [tribunal][6]".[2]
104	—
105	—
107(1)–(3)	—
108	In subsection (2), for the words from the beginning to "Acts" substitute "The tax chargeable".
112	In subsection (1), after "assessment to tax" and "the assessment" insert "or determination" and after "duplicate of assessment to tax" and "duplicate of assessment" insert "or of determination".
113(1A)	—
(3)	After "assessment" insert "determination" and after "notice of assessment" insert "notice of determination".
114	After "assessment" wherever occurring insert "or determination".
115(1)–(3)	—
118(1)	—
(2)	—

(2) Any expression to which a meaning is given in this Part of this Act which is used in a provision of the Taxes Management Act 1970 applied by this paragraph shall, in that provision as so applied, have the same meaning as in this Part of this Act.

Amendments—[1] Words repealed, in relation to periods beginning on or after 18 August 1989, by FA 1989 s 187, Sch 17, Part X.

[2] Entry relating to s 103 substituted by FA 1991 s 109.

[3] Entries relating to ss 46A, 56A inserted by F(No 2)A 1992 s 76, Sch 16 para 6.

[4] Entries relating to ss 50(1), 51, 52, 56, 98 repealed, by the General and Special Commissioners (Amendment of Enactments) Regulations, SI 1994/1813, reg 2, Sch 1 para 18(a), Sch 2 Pt I.

PRT

5 Entries relating to s 70(1), (2) repealed by FA 2008 s 138, Sch 44 para 2 with effect from 21 July 2008. Note: FA 2008 Sch 44 para 2 instructs the repeal of entries relating to s 70(1), (2) in "the table in paragraph 2(1) of Schedule 2". As there is no table in para 2(1), the publisher has taken the view that this amendment was intended to be carried through in the table in para 1(1).

6 Entries relating to sections 46A, 53, 56B, 56C, 56D, 58(2B), 58(2C) and 58(3) repealed, entry relating to section 47C inserted, in entry for section 49(1), figure "(1)" repealed, figure "56" substituted for figure "56A", entry relating to section 100C amended, entries relating to section 100C(2)–(5) repealed, and in the entries relating to section 103(1), (4) word substituted for words "Special Commissioners", by the Transfer of Tribunal Functions and Revenue and Customs Appeals Order, SI 2009/56 art 3, Sch 1 paras 68–70 with effect from 1 April 2009.

7 In the former entry relating to TMA 1970 s 33, in the second column, entry for sub-s (1) substituted, and former entries relating to TMA 1970 ss 34, 36 repealed, by FA 2009 s 99, Sch 51 paras 17, 18 with effect from 1 April 2011 (SI 2010/867).

8 Former entry relating to TMA 1970 s 33 repealed by F(No 3)A 2010 s 28, Sch 12 Pt 2 paras 6, 7 with effect in relation to claims made on or after 1 April 2011.

9 Entry relating to TMA 1970 s 99 repealed by FA 2012 s 223, Sch 38 para 51 with effect from 1 April 2013 (by virtue of SI 2013/279 art 2).

Note—The provisions of TMA 1970 that apply for the purposes of PRT in the table are not affected by amendments to TMA 1970 made by FA 2009 s 100, Sch 52 para 11 (note that FA 2009 Sch 52 para 11 is repealed by F(No 3)A 2010 s 28, Sch 12 Pt 2 para 13 (*b*) with effect in relation to claims made on or after 1 April 2011).

Returns by participators

2—(1) Every participator in [a taxable field][4] shall, for each chargeable period, prepare and, within two months after the end of the period [or within such longer period as the Board may allow][7], deliver to the Board a return complying with the following provisions of this paragraph; but nothing in this sub-paragraph shall require a participator to deliver a return under this paragraph before 31 August 1975.

(2) A return under this paragraph for a chargeable period shall give the following information in relation to oil which is or was included in the participator's share of any oil won from [the taxable field][4] (whether or not in that period), that is to say—

(*a*) in the case of each delivery (other than one made before 13 November 1974) in the period of oil disposed of by him crude (other than oil delivered as mentioned in (*c*) of this sub-paragraph), the return shall—

(i) state the quantity of oil delivered;

(ii) state the person to whom the oil was disposed of;

(iii) in the case of oil disposed of in a sale at arm's length, state the price received or receivable for the oil or, in the case of oil disposed of otherwise than in a sale at arm's length, state the market value of the oil . . .[2] [as determined in accordance with Schedule 3 to this Act in the case of the delivery][8] [or (in the case of light gases) the market value as determined in accordance with paragraph 3A of Schedule 3 to this Act][5]; and

(iv) contain such other particulars of or relating to the disposal as the Board may prescribe;

(*b*) in the case of each relevant appropriation of crude oil (other than one made before 13 November 1974) in the period (not being oil disposed of by him), the return shall—

(i) state the quantity of oil appropriated;

(ii) state the market value of the oil . . .[2] [as determined in accordance with Schedule 3 to this Act in the case of the appropriation][8] [or (in the case of light gases) the market value as determined in accordance with paragraph 3A of Schedule 3 to this Act][5]; and

(iii) contain such other particulars of or relating to the appropriation as the Board may prescribe;

(*c*) in the case of crude oil delivered to the [OGA][9] in the period under the terms of a licence granted under [Part I of the Petroleum Act 1998][6], the return shall state the total quantity of the oil;

(*d*) in the case of crude oil which, at the end of the period, has either not been disposed of and not relevantly appropriated or has been disposed of but not delivered, the return shall—

(i) state the quantity of the oil;

(ii) state the market value of the oil [on the last business day][8] of the period; and

(iii) contain such other particulars relating to the oil as the Board may prescribe.

[(2A) Every participator in [a taxable field][4] shall, in the first return under this paragraph which he makes for that field, state whether any and, if any, how much [expenditure to which section 5A or section 5B][3] of this Act applies and which relates to, or to a licence for, any part of the field has been claimed under Schedule 7 to this Act—

(*a*) by him, or

(*b*) by a company associated with him in respect of that expenditure, or

(*c*) if he or such a company is the new participator, within the meaning of Schedule 17 to the Finance Act 1980, by the old participator, within the meaning of that Schedule, or by a company associated with him in respect of that expenditure, and subsection (7) of section 5 of this Act applies for the purposes of this sub-paragraph as it applies for the purposes of that section][1].

(3) A return under this paragraph for a chargeable period shall state—

(*a*) the amount of royalty payable by the participator for that period in respect of his share of oil won from the field as shown in the return or returns made by him to the Secretary of State under the relevant licence or licences;

(*b*) the amount of royalty paid by the participator in that period in respect of that share;

(*c*) the amount of any royalty paid under any relevant licence in respect of the field which was repaid to the participator in that period; and

(*d*) the amount of any periodic payment made by the participator to the [OGA][9] in that period under each relevant licence otherwise than by way of royalty.

[(3A) A return under this paragraph for a chargeable period shall—

(*a*) state the amount (if any) which, in the case of the participator, is to be brought into account for that period in accordance with section 2(5)(*e*) of this Act;

(*b*) contain such particulars as the Board may prescribe (whether before or after the passing of the Finance Act 1987) with respect to any nominated transaction under Schedule 10 to that Act—

(i) the effective volume of which forms part of the participator's aggregate effective volume (construing those terms in accordance with that Schedule) for any calendar month comprised in that chargeable period; and

(ii) which has not led to deliveries of oil or relevant appropriations of which particulars are included in the return by virtue of sub-paragraph (2) above; and

(*c*) contain such other particulars as the Board may prescribe (as mentioned above) in connection with the application of section 61 of and Schedule 10 to the Finance Act 1987.][3]

(4) A return under this paragraph shall be in such form as the Board may prescribe and shall include a declaration that the return is correct and complete.

[(5) The power of the Board to allow an extension of time under sub-paragraph (1) above shall include power—

(*a*) to allow an extension for an indefinite period; and

(*b*) to provide for the period of any extension to end at such time as may be stipulated in a notice given by the Board.][7]

HMRC Manuals—Oil Taxation Manual OT04090 (returns by participators).

Cross references—FA 2009 Sch 55 (penalty for failure to make returns etc).

Amendments—[1] Sub-para (2A) inserted by FA 1983 s 37, Sch 8 Pt II para 5.

[2] Words in sub-para (2)(*a*)(iii), (*b*)(ii) repealed, with respect to chargeable periods ending after 31 December 1986, by FA 1987 ss 62, 72, Sch 16 Pt X.

[3] Words in sub-para (2A) substituted and sub-para (3A) inserted by FA 1987 ss 61, 64, Sch 10 para 13, Sch 13 Pt II para 4.

[4] In sub-paras (1), (2), (2A) words substituted by FA 1993 s 187(1)(*a*), (*b*).

[5] Words in sub-para (2)(*a*)(iii), (*b*)(ii) inserted by FA 1994 s 236, Sch 23 para 2.

[6] Words in sub-para (2)(*c*) substituted by the Petroleum Act 1998 s 50, Sch 4 para 7(6) with effect from 15 February 1999 (by virtue of SI 1999/161 art 2).

[7] Words in sub para (1), and whole of sub-para (5), inserted by FA 1999 s 102(1) with effect in relation to chargeable periods ending on or after 30 June 1999.

[8] Words in sub-para (2)(*a*)(iii) substituted for words "in the calendar month in which the delivery was made"; words in sub-para (2)(*b*)(ii) substituted for words "in the calendar month in which the appropriation was made"; words in sub-para (2)(*d*)(ii) substituted for words "in the last calendar month" by FA 2006 s 146, Sch 18 para 7 with effect—

(a) in relation to oil delivered or appropriated on or after 1 July 2006 (disregarding section 12A of this Act); and

(b) for the purpose of determining for any chargeable period ending on or after 31 December 2006—

(i) the value to be brought into account under section 2(4)(*b*) of OTA 1975 by reference to a previous chargeable period ending on or after 30 June 2006, and

(ii) the value to be brought into account under section 2(5)(*d*) of that Act,

subject to transitional provisions in FA 2006 s 147(4)–(8).

Note—FA 2006 Sch 18 para 7(3), which substitutes para (2)(*b*)(ii), makes reference to substitution of the word "delivery". The publisher considers that this is an error and should refer to substitution of the word "appropriation".

[9] In sub-paras (2)(*c*), (3)(*d*), word substituted for words "Secretary of State" by the Petroleum (Transfer of Functions) Regulations, SI 2016/898 reg 4(1), (8) with effect from 1 October 2016.

3—(1) If a participator fails to deliver a return within the time allowed for doing so under paragraph 2(1) above he shall be liable, subject to sub-paragraph (3) below—

(*a*) to a penalty not exceeding, except in the case mentioned in sub-paragraph (2) below, £500; and

(*b*) if the failure continues after it has been declared by the court or the [tribunal before which][1] proceedings for the penalty have been commenced, to a further penalty not exceeding £100 for each day on which the failure so continues.

(2) If the failure continues after the end of six months from the time by which the return ought to have been delivered, the penalty under sub-paragraph (1)(*a*) above shall be an amount not exceeding the aggregate of £500 and the total amount of the tax with which the participator is charged for the chargeable period in question.

(3) Except in the case mentioned in sub-paragraph (2) above, the participator shall not be liable to any penalty incurred under this paragraph for failure to deliver a return if the failure is remedied before proceedings for the recovery of the penalty are commenced.

HMRC Manuals—Oil Taxation Manual OT18810 (incorrect statement of payment on account).

Amendments—[1] In sub-para (1), words substituted for words "Commissioners before whom", by the Transfer of Tribunal Functions and Revenue and Customs Appeals Order, SI 2009/56 art 3, Sch 1 paras 68, 69, 71 with effect from 1 April 2009.

Appointment of responsible person for each oil field

4—(1) For each oil field a body corporate or partnership shall be appointed in accordance with this paragraph as the responsible person for that field to perform, in relation to the field, any functions conferred on it as such by this Part of this Act; and the body or partnership which for the time being holds that appointment is in this Part of this Act referred to as "the responsible person".

(2) No body corporate shall be eligible for appointment as the responsible person for [a taxable field][1] unless it is resident in the United Kingdom, and no partnership shall be so eligible unless all its members are resident there.

(3) The participators in [a taxable field][1] shall, by notice in writing to the Board within the initial period, nominate a body corporate or a partnership for appointment as the responsible person for that oil field and, if the Board approve the nomination, the Board shall appoint that body or partnership as the responsible person and give it notice that it has been so appointed.

(4) If—

(*a*) the participators have made no nomination within the initial period; or

(*b*) the Board do not appoint the body or partnership nominated under sub-paragraph (3) above,

the Board shall appoint one of the participators in [the taxable field][1] as the responsible person for the field and shall give notice to that participator that he has been so appointed.

(5) For the purposes of the preceding provisions of this paragraph, the initial period is the period of thirty days beginning with the latest date on which notice of determination of [the taxable field][1] is given to any of the participators under paragraph 4 of Schedule 1 to this Act.

(6) The Board may at any time, on the application of all the participators in [a taxable field][1], appoint a body corporate or partnership nominated by the participators as the responsible person for that field in place of the body corporate or partnership which is the responsible person at that time, and shall give the body or partnership so appointed notice that it has been so appointed.

(7) The Board may, by notice in writing to the body corporate or partnership which is for the time being the responsible person for [a taxable field][1], revoke the appointment of that body or partnership as the responsible person for that field; and where they do so the Board shall appoint one of the participators in [the taxable field][1] as the responsible person for that field and shall give notice to the participator that he has been so appointed.

(8) In this paragraph "participator", in relation to [a taxable field][1], means a person who is a licensee in respect of any licensed area wholly or partly included in the field.

HMRC Manuals—Oil Taxation Manual OT04030 (appointment of responsible person).

Cross-reference—FA 1993 Sch 20A para 8(7) (as inserted by FA 2008 Sch 33 para 1) (definition of "initial period" for the purposes of this para).

Amendments—[1] Words substituted by, or by virtue of, FA 1993 s 187(1).

Returns by the responsible person

5—(1) The responsible person for [a taxable field][3] shall, for each chargeable period, prepare and, within one month after the end of the period [or within such longer period as the Board may allow][4], deliver to the Board a return for that period complying with sub-paragraphs (2) and (3) below; but nothing in this sub-paragraph shall require the responsible person to deliver a return under this paragraph before 31 July 1975.

(2) A return under this paragraph for a chargeable period shall—

(*a*) state the quantity of oil won and saved from [the taxable field][3] during the period;

(*b*) state the respective interests of the participators in the field in that oil;

(*c*) state what, in accordance with those interests, is each participator's share of that oil; and

(*d*) contain such other particulars of or relating to the field as the Board may require.

[(2A) The reference in sub-paragraph (2)(*d*) above to particulars of or relating to the field includes a reference to particulars required for determining the amount by which any qualifying tariff receipts, within the meaning of section 9 of the Oil Taxation Act 1983, are to be treated as reduced by virtue of that section].[1]

[(2B) If in any chargeable period oil won from [the taxable field][3] is mixed as mentioned in section 63 of the Finance Act 1987 so as to give rise to blended oil, within the meaning of that section, then, as respects that chargeable period, for paragraph (*a*) of sub-paragraph (2) above there shall be substituted the following paragraph—

"(*a*) state the total of the shares of the participators in [the taxable field][3] of the oil won from the field during the period less so much of the oil won from the field as is not saved"].[2]

(3) A return under this paragraph shall be in such form as the Board may prescribe and shall include a declaration that the return is correct and complete.

[(4) The power of the Board to allow an extension of time under sub-paragraph (1) above shall include power—

(*a*) to allow an extension for an indefinite period; and

(*b*) to provide for the period of any extension to end at such time as may be stipulated in a notice given by the Board.][1]

HMRC Manuals—Oil Taxation Manual OT04060 (returns by responsible person).

Amendments—[1] Sub-para (2A) inserted by the Oil Taxation Act 1983 s 10(4), with respect to chargeable periods ending after 1 December 1983.

[2] Sub-para (2B) inserted by F(No 2)A 1987 s 101(4), with respect to chargeable periods ending after 1 January 1987.

[3] Words in sub-paras (1), (2)(*a*), (2B) substituted by FA 1993 s 187(1).

[4] Words in sub-para (1) and sub-para (4) inserted by FA 1999 s 102(2) with effect in relation to chargeable periods ending on or after 30 June 1999.

6—(1) If the responsible person fails to deliver a return within the time allowed for doing so under paragraph 5(1) above he shall be liable—

(*a*) to a penalty not exceeding £500, and

(*b*) if the failure continues after it has been declared by the court or [the tribunal before which][1] proceedings for the penalty have been commenced, to a further penalty not exceeding £100 for each day on which the failure so continues.

(2) The responsible person shall not be liable to any penalty incurred under sub-paragraph (1) above for failure to deliver a return if the failure is remedied before proceedings for the recovery of the penalty are commenced.

Amendments—[1] In sub-para (1), words substituted for words "Commissioners before whom", by the Transfer of Tribunal Functions and Revenue and Customs Appeals Order, SI 2009/56 art 3, Sch 1 paras 68, 69, 72 with effect from 1 April 2009.

Production of accounts, books and other information

7 (*repealed* by FA 1993 s 187(1)).

Incorrect returns, accounts, etc

8— . . .

HMRC Manuals—Oil Taxation Manual OT18770 (incorrect returns).

Amendments—This para repealed by FA 2008 s 122, Sch 40 para 21(*a*) with effect from 1 April 2009 (by virtue of SI 2009/571 art 2).

9— . . .

HMRC Manuals—Oil Taxation Manual OT18780 (meaning of fraudulently or negligently).

Amendments—This para repealed by FA 2008 s 122, Sch 40 para 21(*a*) with effect from 1 April 2009 (by virtue of SI 2009/571 art 2).

Assessments to tax and determinations of loss, etc

10—(1) Where it appears to the Board that, in accordance with the provisions of this Part of this Act, an assessable profit has accrued to a participator in a chargeable period from [a taxable field][1], they shall make an assessment to tax on the participator and shall give him notice of the assessment.

[1A) An assessment under sub-paragraph (1) may be made at any time not more than 4 years after the end of the chargeable period to which it relates (subject to paragraphs 12A[, 12B and 13E][3]).][2]

(2) Where it appears to the Board that, in accordance with those provisions, an allowable loss has accrued to a participator in a chargeable period from [a taxable field][1], they shall make a determination that the loss is allowable to the participator and shall give him notice of the determination.

(3) Where it appears to the Board that, in accordance with those provisions, neither an assessable profit nor an allowable loss has accrued to a participator in a chargeable period, they shall make a determination to that effect and shall give him notice of the determination.

(4) A notice of assessment for a chargeable period shall state the amount of any allowable losses which, in accordance with those provisions, have been set against the assessable profit for that period.

(5) A notice of assessment or determination shall state that the participator may appeal against the assessment or determination in accordance with paragraph 14 below.

PRT

(6) After the service of the notice of assessment or the notice of determination the assessment or determination, as the case may be, shall not be altered except in accordance with the express provisions of this Part of this Act (including the provisions applied by paragraph 1 above).

Simon's Tax Cases—*Amoco (UK) Exploration Co v IRC* [1983] STC 634.

Amendments—[1] Words substituted by, or by virtue of, FA 1993 s 187(1).

[2] Sub-para (1A) inserted by FA 2009 s 99, Sch 51 paras 17, 19 with effect from 1 April 2011 (SI 2010/867).

[3] In sub-para (1A) (as inserted by FA 2009) words substituted by F(No 3)A 2010 s 28, Sch 12 Pt 2 paras 6, 8 with effect in relation to claims made on or after 1 April 2011.

11—(1) Where a participator has under paragraph 2 above delivered to the Board a return for a chargeable period and the Board are satisfied that the information given in the return is correct in so far as it is material for the purpose of computing his assessable profit or allowable loss (if any) for that period, the Board shall (in so far as the computation falls to be made by reference to the matters dealt with in the return) make the assessment or determination under paragraph 10 above in accordance with the return.

(2) Where the Board are not so satisfied in relation to a participator's return or a participator fails to deliver to the Board a return for a chargeable period as required by paragraph 2 above, the Board shall, in so far as the computation of his assessable profit or allowable loss (if any) for that period falls to be made by reference to the matters which were dealt with in the return or, as the case may be, ought to have been dealt with in a return, make the assessment or determination under paragraph 10 above to the best of their judgment.

(3) Nothing in sub-paragraph (2) above or in paragraph 5 above shall be taken, in a case where the participator has delivered a return as to which the Board are not satisfied as mentioned in sub-paragraph (1) above, to prevent the Board from basing their assessment or determination on the participator's having had an interest in oil won and saved from the field different from that on which he based his return.

Cross references—FA 2009 Sch 56 (penalty for failure to make payments on time).

12—(1) Where it appears to the Board—

(*a*) that the assessable profit charged to tax by or stated in an assessment ought to be or to have been larger or smaller; or

(*b*) that the allowable loss stated in an assessment or a determination of loss ought to be or to have been larger or smaller; or

(*c*) that, where they made a determination that neither an assessable profit nor an allowable loss accrued in a chargeable period, they ought to have made an assessment to tax or a determination of loss for that period, [or

(*d*) that for any chargeable period they ought to have made an assessment to tax instead of a determination of loss or a determination of loss instead of an assessment to tax][1];

the Board may make such assessments or determinations or such amendments of assessments or determinations as may be necessary; and where the Board exercise any of their powers under this paragraph in relation to a chargeable period, they may make such [assessments or determinations or amendments of assessments or determinations][1] for other chargeable periods as may be necessary in consequence of the exercise of those powers.

[(1A) An assessment (or an amendment of an assessment) under sub- paragraph (1) may be made at any time not more than 4 years after the end of the chargeable period to which the assessment relates (subject to sub-paragraph (1B) and paragraphs 12A and 12B).

(1B) The time limits in sub-paragraph (1A) and paragraphs 12A and 12B do not apply to an amendment of an assessment where the amendment is made in consequence (directly or indirectly) of—

(*a*) the granting of relief under section 7(2) or (3) to any participator for allowable losses accruing in any chargeable period, [...][3]

[(*aa*) a claim under paragraph 13A (see paragraph 13E), or][3].

(*b*) a notice of variation served under paragraph 9 of Schedule 5 on any responsible person in respect of a claim for any claim period.][2]

(2) Where under sub-paragraph (1) above it appears to the Board that the assessable profit for a chargeable period ought to have been larger and that the deficiency resulted from an excessive allowable loss accruing in a subsequent period having been set against the profit for that period, the Board may [...][2] make a further assessment by virtue of sub-paragraph (1) above at any time not later than [four years][2]after the end of the chargeable period in which the allowable loss accrued [(subject to paragraphs 12A and 12B)][2].

[(3) Where under this paragraph the Board make an assessment or determination or amend an assessment or determination they shall give notice thereof to the participator concerned; and sub-paragraphs (4), (5) and (6) of paragraph 10 above shall apply in relation to any such assessment, determination or amendment as they apply in relation to an assessment or determination under that paragraph].[1]

HMRC Manuals—Oil Taxation Manual OT04330 (amended assessments).
Amendments—[1] Words inserted or substituted by FA 1976 s 130.
[2] Sub-paras (1A), (1B) inserted, in sub-para (2) words repealed, words "substituted and words inserted by FA 2009 s 99, Sch 51 paras 17, 20 with effect from 1 April 2011 (SI 2010/867).
[3] In sub-para (1B) (as inserted by FA 2009), in para (*a*) word at the end repealed, and para (*aa*) inserted, by F(No 3)A 2010 s 28, Sch 12 Pt 2 paras 6, 9 with effect in relation to claims made on or after 1 April 2011.

[12A—(1) Where—

(*a*) the Board has extended the period for the delivery of any return that is required under paragraph 2 of this Schedule to be delivered for any chargeable period, and

(*b*) the relevant time falls more than one year after the end of the chargeable period,

the period within which the Board may make an assessment under this Schedule for that chargeable period shall not expire before the end of the period of [four][2] years beginning with the relevant time.

(2) In this paragraph "the relevant time" means the earlier of—

(*a*) the time which, as a result of the extension, is the latest time for the delivery of the return; and

(*b*) the time when the return is delivered.][1]

Modification—FA 1993 Sch 20A para 8 (as inserted by FA 2008 Sch 33 para 1) (If the Commissioners specify the period within which a PRT return must be delivered, this para applies to the specified period as if it were a period for the delivery of a PRT return that has been extended under OTA 1975 Sch 2 para 2).
Amendments—[1] Para 12A inserted by FA 1999 s 102(3) with effect in relation to chargeable periods ending on or after 30 June 1999.
[2] In sub-para (1) words substituted by FA 2009 s 99, Sch 51 paras 17, 21 with effect from 1 April 2011 (SI 2010/867).

[12B—(1) In a case involving a relevant situation brought about carelessly by a participator (or a person acting on behalf of a participator), an assessment (or an amendment of an assessment) under this Schedule on the participator may be made at any time not more than 6 years after the end of the relevant chargeable period (subject to sub-paragraph (2) [and (2A)][2]).

(2) In a case involving a relevant situation brought about deliberately by a participator (or a person acting on behalf of a participator), an assessment (or an amendment of an assessment) on the participator may be made at any time not more than 20 years after the end of the relevant chargeable period.

[(2A) In a case involving a relevant situation brought about by arrangements which were expected to give rise to a tax advantage in respect of which a participator (or a person acting on behalf of a participator) was under an obligation to notify the Board under section 253 of the Finance Act 2014 (duty to notify Commissioners of promoter reference number) but failed to do so, an assessment (or an amendment of an assessment) on the participator may be made at any time not more than 20 years after the end of the relevant chargeable period.][2]

(3) "Relevant situation" means a situation in which—

(*a*) there is a loss of tax,

(*b*) the assessable profit charged to tax by or stated in an assessment for a chargeable period ought to be or to have been larger,

(*c*) the allowable loss stated in an assessment or a determination of loss for a chargeable period ought to be or to have been smaller, or

(*d*) an assessment to tax should have been made for a chargeable period but was not made.

(4) "Relevant chargeable period" means—

(*a*) in the case of a further assessment under paragraph 12(2), the chargeable period in which the excessive allowable loss accrued, and

(*b*) in any other case, the chargeable period to which the assessment relates.

(5) Where the participator carried on a trade or business with one or more other persons at any time in the chargeable period for which the assessment under sub-paragraph (1)[, (2) or (2A)][2] is made, an assessment to tax in respect of the profits of that trade or business may also be made on any of the participator's partners.

(6) In determining the amount of the tax to be charged on a person for a chargeable period in an assessment in a case mentioned in sub- paragraph (1)[, (2) or (2A)][2] (including an assessment under sub- paragraph (5)), effect must be given to any relief or allowance to which that person would have been entitled for that period if a valid claim or application had been made.

(7) Sub-paragraph (6) only applies if the person on whom the assessment is made so requires.

(8) Subsections (5) to (7) of section 118 of the Taxes Management Act 1970 (losses and situations brought about carelessly or deliberately) apply for the purposes of this paragraph as they apply for the purposes of that Act.

(9) In subsection (6)(*b*) of that section (as it applies for the purposes of this paragraph), the reference to the person who provides the information has effect as if it included any person who becomes the responsible person for the oil field after the information is provided.][1]

Amendments—[1] Para (12B) inserted by FA 2009 s 99, Sch 51 paras 17, 22 with effect from 1 April 2011 (SI 2010/867).

[2] Words inserted in sub-para (1), sub-para (2A) inserted, and words in sub-paras (5), (6) substituted for words "or (2)", by FA 2014 s 277(2) with effect from 17 July 2014.

Payment of tax

13 Subject to paragraph 14 below, the tax charged in an assessment made on a participator for any chargeable period [and payable shall be due within six months][1] after the end of that chargeable period or, if later, thirty days after the date of issue of the notice of assessment; but no tax shall be payable by virtue of this paragraph before 30 April 1976.

HMRC Manuals—Oil Taxation Manual OT04150 (payments on account).
Cross references—FA 2009 Sch 56 (penalty for failure to make payments on time).
Amendments—[1] Words substituted by FA 1982 s 139(6) Sch 19 Pt III para 19, with respect to chargeable periods ending on or after 30 June 1983.

[Claim for relief for overpaid tax etc

13A—(1) This paragraph applies where—

(*a*) a participator has paid an amount by way of tax but believes that the tax was not due, or

(*b*) a participator has been assessed as liable to pay an amount by way of tax but believes that the tax is not due.

(2) The participator may make a claim to the Commissioners for Her Majesty's Revenue and Customs ("HMRC") for repayment or discharge of the amount.

(3) Paragraph 13B makes provision about cases in which HMRC are not liable to give effect to a claim under this paragraph.

(4) Paragraphs 13C to 14I make further provision about making and giving effect to claims under this paragraph.

(5) Paragraph 13F makes provision about the application of this paragraph and paragraphs 13B to 13E to amounts paid under contract settlements.

(6) HMRC are not liable to give relief in respect of a case described in sub-paragraph (1)(*a*) or (*b*) except as provided—

(*a*) by this Schedule (following a claim under this paragraph), or

(*b*) by or under another provision of the Oil Taxation Acts.

(7) For the purposes of this paragraph and paragraphs 13B to 13F, an amount paid by one person on behalf of another is treated as paid by the other person.

(8) In this paragraph and paragraphs 13B to 13F, "the Oil Taxation Acts" means—

(*a*) Parts 1 and 3 of this Act,

(*b*) the Oil Taxation Act 1983, and

(*c*) any other enactment relating to petroleum revenue tax.][1]

Amendments—[1] Paras 13 and preceding cross-heads inserted by F(No 3)A 2010 s 28, Sch 12 Pt 2 paras 6, 10 with effect in relation to claims made on or after 1 April 2011.

[Cases in which HMRC not liable to give effect to a claim

13B—(1) HMRC are not liable to give effect to a claim under paragraph 13A if or to the extent that the claim falls within a case described in this paragraph.

(2) Case A is where the amount paid, or liable to be paid, is excessive by reason of—

(*a*) a mistake in a claim, election or notice or a nomination under Schedule 10 to FA 1987, or

(*b*) a mistake consisting of making or giving, or failing to make or give, a claim, election or notice or a nomination under Schedule 10 to FA 1987.

(3) Case B is where the participator—

(*a*) has or could have sought relief by making a claim for expenditure to be allowed under section 3 or 4 (allowance of expenditure), or

(*b*) is or will be able to seek relief by taking other steps under the Oil Taxation Acts.

(4) Case C is where the participator—

(*a*) could have sought relief by taking such steps within a period that has now expired, and

(*b*) knew, or ought reasonably to have known, before the end of that period that such relief was available.

(5) Case D is where the claim is made on grounds that—

(*a*) have been put to a court or tribunal in the course of an appeal by the participator relating to the amount paid or liable to be paid, or

(*b*) have been put to HMRC in the course of an appeal by the participator relating to that amount that is treated as having been determined by a tribunal (by virtue of paragraph 14(9) (settling of appeals by agreement)).

(6) Case E is where the participator knew, or ought reasonably to have known, of the grounds for the claim before the latest of the following—

(*a*) the date on which an appeal by the participator relating to the amount paid, or liable to be paid, in the course of which the ground could have been put forward (a "relevant appeal") was determined by a court or tribunal (or is treated as having been so determined),

(*b*) the date on which the participator withdrew a relevant appeal to a court or tribunal, and

(*c*) the end of the period in which the participator was entitled to make a relevant appeal to a court or tribunal.

(7) Case F is where the amount in question was paid or is liable to be paid—

(*a*) in consequence of proceedings enforcing the payment of that amount brought against the participator by HMRC, or

(*b*) in accordance with an agreement between the participator and HMRC settling such proceedings.

(8) Case G is where—

(*a*) the amount paid, or liable to be paid, is excessive by reason of a mistake in calculating the participator's liability to tax, and

(*b*) liability was calculated in accordance with the practice generally prevailing at the time.][1]

[(9) Case G does not apply where the amount paid, or liable to be paid, is tax which has been charged contrary to EU law.

(10) For the purposes of sub-paragraph (9), an amount of tax is charged contrary to EU law if, in the circumstances in question, the charge to tax is contrary to—

(*a*) the provisions relating to the free movement of goods, persons, services and capital in Titles II and IV of Part 3 of the Treaty on the Functioning of the European Union, or

(*b*) the provisions of any subsequent treaty replacing the provisions mentioned in paragraph (*a*).][2]

Amendments—[1] Paras 13B inserted by F(No 3)A 2010 s 28, Sch 12 Pt 2 paras 6, 10 with effect in relation to claims made on or after 1 April 2011.

[2] Sub-ss (9), (10) inserted by FA 2013 s 231(2) with effect in relation to any claim (in respect of overpaid tax, excessive assessment etc) made after the end of the six month period beginning with 17 July 2013.

[Making a claim

13C—(1) A claim under paragraph 13A may not be made more than 4 years after the end of the relevant chargeable period.

(2) In relation to a claim made in reliance on paragraph 13A(1)(*a*), the relevant chargeable period is—

(*a*) where the amount paid, or liable to be paid, is excessive by reason of a mistake in a return or returns under paragraph 2 or 5, the chargeable period to which the return (or, if more than one, the first return) relates, and

(*b*) otherwise, the chargeable period in respect of which the amount was paid.

(3) In relation to a claim made in reliance on paragraph 13A(1)(*b*), the relevant chargeable period is[—

(*a*) where the amount liable to be paid is excessive by reason of a mistake in a return or returns under paragraph 2 or 5, the chargeable period to which the return (or, if more than one, the first return) relates, and

(*b*) otherwise,][2] the chargeable period to which the assessment relates.

(4) A claim under paragraph 13A must be in such form as the HMRC may prescribe.][1]

Amendments—[1] Paras 13C inserted by F(No 3)A 2010 s 28, Sch 12 Pt 2 paras 6, 10 with effect in relation to claims made on or after 1 April 2011.

[2] Words in sub-para (3) inserted by FA 2013 s 232(2) with effect in relation to any claim (in respect of overpaid tax, excessive assessment etc) made after the end of the six month period beginning with 17 July 2013.

[Decision on claim

13D HMRC must—

(*a*) make a decision on the claim, and

(*b*) by notice inform the participator of their decision.][1]

Amendments—[1] Paras 13D inserted by F(No 3)A 2010 s 28, Sch 12 Pt 2 paras 6, 10 with effect in relation to claims made on or after 1 April 2011.

[Assessment of claimant in connection with claim

13E—(1) This paragraph applies where—

(*a*) a claim is made under paragraph 13A,

(*b*) the grounds for giving effect to the claim also provide grounds for making an assessment or determination under paragraph 10 or 12, or an amendment of such an assessment or determination, on the participator in respect of any accounting period, and

PRT

(*c*) such an assessment, determination or amendment could be made but for the expiry of a time limit in paragraph 10(1A), 12(1A), 12A or 12B.

(2) Where this paragraph applies—

(*a*) the time limit does not apply, and

(*b*) the assessment, determination or amendment is not out of time if it is made before the final determination of the claim.

(3) A claim is not finally determined until it, or the amount to which it relates, can no longer be varied (whether on appeal or otherwise).][1]

Amendments—[1] Paras 13E inserted by F(No 3)A 2010 s 28, Sch 12 Pt 2 paras 6, 10 with effect in relation to claims made on or after 1 April 2011.

[Contract settlements

13F—(1) In paragraph 13A(1)(*a*) the reference to an amount paid by a participator by way of tax includes an amount paid by a person under a contract settlement in connection with tax believed to be due.

(2) Sub-paragraphs (3) to (6) apply if the person who paid the amount under the contract settlement ("the payer") and the person from whom the tax was due ("the taxpayer") are not the same person.

(3) In relation to a claim under paragraph 13A in respect of that amount—

(*a*) the references to the participator in paragraph 13B(5) to (7) (Cases D, E and F) have effect as if they included the taxpayer,

(*b*) the reference to the participator in paragraph 13B(8) (Case G) has effect as if it were a reference to the taxpayer, and

(*c*) the reference to the participator in paragraph 13E(1)(*b*) has effect as if it were a reference to the taxpayer.

(4) Sub-paragraph (5) applies where the grounds for giving effect to a claim by the payer in respect of the amount also provide grounds for making an assessment or determination under paragraph 10 or 12, or an amendment of such an assessment or determination, on the taxpayer in respect of any chargeable period.

(5) HMRC may set any amount repayable to the payer by virtue of the claim against any amount payable by the taxpayer by virtue of the assessment, determination or amendment.

(6) The obligations of HMRC and the taxpayer are discharged to the extent of any set-off under sub-paragraph (5).

(7) "Contract settlement" means an agreement made in connection with any person's liability to make a payment to HMRC under or by virtue of an enactment.]

Amendments—Paras 13F inserted by F(No 3)A 2010 s 28, Sch 12 Pt 2 paras 6, 10 with effect in relation to claims made on or after 1 April 2011.

Appeals

14—(1) A participator may appeal . . .[2] against an assessment or determination [or an amendment of an assessment or determination][1] made on or in relation to him by notice of appeal in writing given to [HMRC][2] within thirty days after the date of issue of the notice of assessment or determination [or of the notice of the amendment][1].

[(1A) A participator who has made a claim under paragraph 13A may appeal from the decision on the claim by notice in writing given to HMRC within 30 days after the date of issue of the notice of the decision.][4]

[(2) The notice of appeal must specify the grounds of appeal.][2]

(3) A participator who has given notice of appeal under sub-paragraph (1) above against an assessment charging him with any tax for a chargeable period may, if he delivered a return for that period as required by paragraph 2 above, withhold, until the determination or abandonment of the appeal, so much of the tax charged in the assessment as is the smaller of—

(*a*) the amount of the tax so charged; and

(*b*) tax on the difference between—

(i) the aggregate of the consideration received or receivable for oil as stated in the participator's return in pursuance of sub-paragraph (2) of that paragraph and, subject to sub-paragraph (4) below, the market value of oil as so stated; and

(ii) the aggregate of the corresponding consideration and value as included in the assessment.

(4) Subject to sub-paragraph (5) below, where the market value of all the oil for which a market value is stated in the participator's return is, as stated in that return, less than the value which is produced for that oil by applying to it the average price mentioned in sub-paragraph (6) below, sub-paragraph (3) above shall have effect as if, for the reference to the market value of oil as so stated, there were substituted a reference to the value which is so produced for that oil.

(5) The comparison of values and the substitution required by sub-paragraph (4) above shall, in the case of an appeal by a participator whose return relates both to gas and to other oil, be made separately for the gas and for the other oil.
(6) The average price referred to in sub-paragraph (4) above is the average price at which all oil included in the relevant returns as oil delivered in the period covered by the returns and disposed of in sales at arm's length was so disposed of.
(7) The relevant returns for the purposes of sub-paragraph (6) above are all the returns of all the participators in all oil fields which—

(*a*) were made for the chargeable period preceding that to which the appeal relates; and
(*b*) were delivered before the end of the chargeable period to which the appeal relates.

(8) The participator may at any time, if [HMRC][2] do not object to his doing so, abandon an appeal instituted by him; and for this purpose he shall notify his desire to do so to [HMRC][2] who may, within thirty days after being so notified, object by notice in writing to the participator.
(9) Where, at any time between—

(*a*) the giving of a notice of appeal against the assessment [determination or amendment][1] or from a decision of [HMRC][2] on a claim under [paragraph 13A][4] , and
(*b*) the determination of the appeal by the [tribunal][2],

[HMRC][2] and the participator agree [on how the assessment, determination, amendment or decision should be varied or on what assessment or determination should be substituted in relation to the chargeable period in question, the same consequences shall ensue as if the [tribunal][2] had determined the appeal to that effect][1].
[(10) If [[an appeal under sub-paragraph (1)][4] is notified to the tribunal and][2] it appears to [the tribunal][2] that the assessment, determination or amendment is wrong—

(*a*) because no, or a smaller, assessable profit or a, or a larger, allowable loss has accrued for the chargeable period in question; or
(*b*) because a, or a larger, assessable profit or no, or a smaller, allowable loss has accrued for that period,

the [tribunal[2] shall vary the assessment, determination or amendment in such manner, or substitute such assessment or determination, as may be required; and it shall be for the participator to satisfy the [tribunal[2] as to any matter within paragraph (a) above].[1]
[(10A) If an appeal under sub-paragraph (1A) is notified to the tribunal and it appears to the tribunal that the decision is wrong, the tribunal shall substitute such decision as may be required.][4]
[(11) When an appeal is notified to the tribunal, the decision of the tribunal on the appeal is final and conclusive.
(12) But sub-paragraph (11) is subject to—

(*a*) sections 9 to 14 of the Tribunals, Courts and Enforcement Act 2007,
(*b*) Tribunal Procedure Rules, and
(*c*) any provision of this Schedule.][3]

HMRC Manuals—Oil Taxation Manual OT04360 (appeals against assessments).
Simon's Tax Cases—Sub-paras (8), (9), *R v Special Comrs, ex p Fina Exploration Ltd* [1992] STC 1.
Amendments—[1] Words inserted or substituted by FA 1976 s 130.
[2] In sub-para (1), words "to the Special Commissioners" repealed, and word substituted for words "the Board", sub-para (2) substituted, in sub-para (8), word substituted for words "the Board" (in both places), in sub-para (9), words substituted for words "the Board" (in both places), "Special Commissioners" and "Commissioners" respectively, and in sub-para (10), words substituted for words ", on the appeal,", "a majority of the Commissioners present at the hearing" and "Commissioners" (in both places) respectively, by the Transfer of Tribunal Functions and Revenue and Customs Appeals Order, SI 2009/56 art 3, Sch 1 paras 68, 69, 74 with effect from 1 April 2009.
[3] Sub-paras (11), (12) substituted for previous sub-para (11), by the Revenue and Customs Appeals Order, SI 2009/777 art 2 with effect from 1 April 2009.
[4] Sub-paras (1A), (10A) inserted, in sub-para (9) and (10) words substituted by F(No 3)A 2010 s 28, Sch 12 Pt 2 paras 6, 11 with effect in relation to claims made on or after 1 April 2011.

[Appeal: HMRC review or determination by tribunal

14A—(1) This paragraph applies if notice of appeal has been given to HMRC.
(2) In such a case—

(*a*) the participator may notify HMRC that the participator requires HMRC to review the matter in question (see paragraph 14B),
(*b*) HMRC may notify the participator of an offer to review the matter in question (see paragraph 14C), or
(*c*) the participator may notify the appeal to the tribunal (see paragraph 14D).

(3) See paragraphs 14G and 14H for provision about notifying appeals to the tribunal after a review has been required by the participator or offered by HMRC.
(4) This paragraph does not prevent the matter in question from being dealt with in accordance with paragraph 14(9).][1]

Amendments—[1] Paras 14A–14I inserted by the Transfer of Tribunal Functions and Revenue and Customs Appeals Order, SI 2009/56 art 3, Sch 1 paras 68, 69, 75 with effect from 1 April 2009.

[Participator requires review by HMRC

14B—(1) Sub-paragraphs (2) and (3) apply if the participator notifies HMRC that the participator requires HMRC to review the matter in question.

(2) HMRC must, within the relevant period, notify the participator of HMRC's view of the matter in question.

(3) HMRC must review the matter in question in accordance with paragraph 14E.

(4) The participator may not notify HMRC that the participator requires HMRC to review the matter in question and HMRC shall not be required to conduct a review if—

(*a*) the participator has already given a notification under this paragraph in relation to the matter in question,

(*b*) HMRC have given a notification under paragraph 14C in relation to the matter in question, or

(*c*) the participator has notified the appeal to the tribunal under paragraph 14D.

(5) In this paragraph "relevant period" means—

(*a*) the period of 30 days beginning with the day on which HMRC receive the notification from the participator, or

(*b*) such longer period as is reasonable.][1]

Amendments—[1] Paras 14A–14I inserted by the Transfer of Tribunal Functions and Revenue and Customs Appeals Order, SI 2009/56 art 3, Sch 1 paras 68, 69, 75 with effect from 1 April 2009.

[HMRC offer review

14C—(1) Sub-paragraphs (2) to (5) apply if HMRC notify the participator of an offer to review the matter in question.

(2) When HMRC notify the participator of the offer, HMRC must also notify the participator of HMRC's view of the matter in question.

(3) If, within the acceptance period, the participator notifies HMRC of acceptance of the offer, HMRC must review the matter in question in accordance with paragraph 14E.

(4) If the participator does not give HMRC such a notification within the acceptance period, HMRC's view of the matter in question is to be treated as if it were contained in an agreement in writing under paragraph 14(9) for the settlement of that matter.

(5) Sub-paragraph (4) does not apply to the matter in question if, or to the extent that, the participator notifies the appeal to the tribunal under paragraph 14H.

(6) HMRC may not notify the participator of an offer to review the matter in question (and, accordingly, HMRC shall not be required to conduct a review) if—

(*a*) HMRC have already given a notification under this paragraph in relation to the matter in question,

(*b*) the participator has given a notification under paragraph 14B in relation to the matter in question, or

(*c*) the participator has notified the appeal to the tribunal under paragraph 14D.

(7) In this paragraph "acceptance period" means the period of 30 days beginning with the date of the document by which HMRC notify the participator of the offer to review the matter in question.][1]

Amendments—[1] Paras 14A–14I inserted by the Transfer of Tribunal Functions and Revenue and Customs Appeals Order, SI 2009/56 art 3, Sch 1 paras 68, 69, 75 with effect from 1 April 2009.

[Notifying appeal to the tribunal

14D—(1) This paragraph applies if notice of appeal has been given to HMRC.

(2) The participator may notify the appeal to the tribunal.

(3) If the participator notifies the appeal to the tribunal, the tribunal is to decide the matter in question.

(4) Sub-paragraphs (2) and (3) do not apply in a case where—

(*a*) HMRC have given a notification of their view of the matter in question under paragraph 14B, or

(*b*) HMRC have given a notification under paragraph 14C in relation to the matter in question.

(5) In a case falling within sub-paragraph (4)(a) or (b), the participator may notify the appeal to the tribunal, but only if permitted to do so by paragraph 14G or 14H.][1]

Amendments—[1] Paras 14A–14I inserted by the Transfer of Tribunal Functions and Revenue and Customs Appeals Order, SI 2009/56 art 3, Sch 1 paras 68, 69, 75 with effect from 1 April 2009.

[Nature of review etc

14E—(1) This paragraph applies if HMRC are required by paragraph 14B or 14C to review the matter in question.

(2) The nature and extent of the review are to be such as appear appropriate to HMRC in the circumstances.
(3) For the purpose of sub-paragraph (2), HMRC must, in particular, have regard to steps taken before the beginning of the review—
(*a*) by HMRC in deciding the matter in question, and
(*b*) by any person in seeking to resolve disagreement about the matter in question.
(4) The review must take account of any representations made by the participator at a stage which gives HMRC a reasonable opportunity to consider them.
(5) The review may conclude that HMRC's view of the matter in question is to be—
(*a*) upheld,
(*b*) varied, or
(*c*) cancelled.
(6) HMRC must notify the participator of the conclusions of the review and their reasoning within—
(*a*) the period of 45 days beginning with the relevant day, or
(*b*) such other period as may be agreed.
(7) In sub-paragraph (6) "relevant day" means—
(*a*) in a case where the participator required the review, the day when HMRC notified the participator of HMRC's view of the matter in question,
(*b*) in a case where HMRC offered the review, the day when HMRC received notification of the participator's acceptance of the offer.
(8) Where HMRC are required to undertake a review but do not give notice of the conclusions within the time period specified in sub-paragraph (6), the review is to be treated as having concluded that HMRC's view of the matter in question (see paragraphs 14B(2) and 14C(2)) is upheld.
(9) If sub-paragraph (8) applies, HMRC must notify the participator of the conclusion which the review is treated as having reached.][1]

Amendments—[1] Paras 14A–14I inserted by the Transfer of Tribunal Functions and Revenue and Customs Appeals Order, SI 2009/56 art 3, Sch 1 paras 68, 69, 75 with effect from 1 April 2009.

[Effect of conclusions of review

14F—(1) This paragraph applies if HMRC give notice of the conclusions of a review (see paragraph 14E(6) and (9)).
(2) The conclusions are to be treated as if they were an agreement in writing under paragraph 14(9) for the settlement of the matter in question.
(3) Sub-paragraph (2) does not apply to the matter in question if, or to the extent that, the participator notifies the appeal to the tribunal under paragraph 14G.][1]

Amendments—[1] Paras 14A–14I inserted by the Transfer of Tribunal Functions and Revenue and Customs Appeals Order, SI 2009/56 art 3, Sch 1 paras 68, 69, 75 with effect from 1 April 2009.

[Notifying appeal to tribunal after review concluded

14G—(1) This paragraph applies if—
(*a*) HMRC have given notice of the conclusions of a review in accordance with paragraph 14E, or
(*b*) the period specified in paragraph 14E(6) has ended and HMRC have not given notice of the conclusions of the review.
(2) The participator may notify the appeal to the tribunal within the post-review period.
(3) If the post-review period has ended, the participator may notify the appeal to the tribunal only if the tribunal gives permission.
(4) If the participator notifies the appeal to the tribunal, the tribunal is to determine the matter in question.
(5) In this paragraph "post-review period" means—
(*a*) in a case falling within sub-paragraph (1)(*a*), the period of 30 days beginning with the date of the document in which HMRC give notice of the conclusions of the review in accordance with paragraph 14E(6), or
(*b*) in a case falling within sub-paragraph (1)(*b*), the period that—
(i) begins with the day following the last day of the period specified in paragraph 14E(6), and
(ii) ends 30 days after the date of the document in which HMRC give notice of the conclusion of the review in accordance with paragraph 14E(9).][1]

Amendments—[1] Paras 14A–14I inserted by the Transfer of Tribunal Functions and Revenue and Customs Appeals Order, SI 2009/56 art 3, Sch 1 paras 68, 69, 75 with effect from 1 April 2009.

[Notifying appeal to tribunal after review offered but not accepted

14H—(1) This paragraph applies if—

PRT

(*a*) HMRC have offered to review the matter in question (see paragraph 14C), and

(*b*) the participator has not accepted the offer.

(2) The participator may notify the appeal to the tribunal within the acceptance period.

(3) But if the acceptance period has ended, the participator may notify the appeal to the tribunal only if the tribunal gives permission.

(4) If the participator notifies the appeal to the tribunal, the tribunal is to determine the matter in question.

(5) In this paragraph "acceptance period" has the same meaning as in paragraph 14C.][1]

Amendments—[1] Paras 14A–14I inserted by the Transfer of Tribunal Functions and Revenue and Customs Appeals Order, SI 2009/56 art 3, Sch 1 paras 68, 69, 75 with effect from 1 April 2009.

[Interpretation of paragraphs 14A to 14H

14I—(1) In paragraphs 14A to 14H—

(*a*) "matter in question" means the matter to which an appeal relates;

(*b*) a reference to a notification is a reference to a notification in writing.

(2) In paragraphs 14A to 14H, a reference to the participator includes a person acting on behalf of the participator except in relation to—

(*a*) notification of HMRC's view under paragraph 14B(2);

(*b*) notification by HMRC of an offer of review (and of their view of the matter) under paragraph 14C;

(*c*) notification of the conclusions of a review under paragraph 14E(6); and

(*d*) notification of the conclusions of a review under paragraph 14E(9).

(3) But if a notification falling within sub-paragraph (2) is given to the participator, a copy of the notification may also be given to a person acting on behalf of the participator.][1]

Amendments—[1] Paras 14A–14I inserted by the Transfer of Tribunal Functions and Revenue and Customs Appeals Order, SI 2009/56 art 3, Sch 1 paras 68, 69, 75 with effect from 1 April 2009.

Interest on tax

15—(1) Subject to sub-paragraph (2) below, tax charged in an assessment for a chargeable period shall carry interest at the [rate applicable under section 178 of the Finance Act 1989][2] from [two months][1] after the end of the period until payment.

(2) Nothing in sub-paragraph (1) shall authorise or require interest to be charged from any time before 30 April 1976.

(3) Where, under paragraph 14(3) above, tax may be withheld until the determination or abandonment of an appeal, the interest on that tax may also be withheld until the determination or abandonment of the appeal.

HMRC Manuals—Oil Taxation Manual OT04270 (interest on tax).

Amendments—[1] Words substituted by the Petroleum Revenue Tax Act 1980 s 2(1).

[2] Words substituted, in relation to periods beginning on or after 18 August 1989, by FA 1989 s 179.

16 [Subject to paragraph 17 below][5] where any amount of tax charged by an assessment to tax [or paid on account of tax so charged][1] becomes repayable under any provision of this Part of this Act that amount shall carry interest at the [rate applicable under section 178 of the Finance Act 1989][3] [from—

(*a*) two months after the end of the chargeable period for which the assessment was made; or

(*b*) the date on which it was paid,

whichever is the later, until [the order for repayment is issued][4]][2].

HMRC Manuals—Oil Taxation Manual OT04270 (interest on tax).

Amendments—[1] Words inserted by the Petroleum Revenue Tax Act 1980 s 2(2).

[2] Words substituted by the Petroleum Revenue Tax Act 1980 s 2(2).

[3] Words substituted, in relation to periods beginning on or after 18 August 1989, by FA 1989 s 179.

[4] Words substituted, with retrospective effect, by FA 1989 s 180(2), (3).

[5] Words inserted by FA 1990 s 121(2).

[**17**—(1) This paragraph applies where—

(*a*) an assessment made on a participator for a chargeable period or an amendment of such an assessment (in this paragraph referred to as "the relevant assessment or amendment") gives effect to relief under subsection (2) or subsection (3) of section 7 of this Act for one or more allowable losses accruing in a later chargeable period (in this paragraph referred to, in relation to the relevant assessment or amendment, as "the relief for losses carried back"); and

(*b*) the later chargeable period referred to in paragraph (*a*) above ends after 30 June 1991; and

(*c*) an amount of tax becomes repayable to the participator by virtue of the relevant assessment or amendment (whether wholly or partly by reason of giving effect to the relief for losses carried back).

(2) In the following provisions of this paragraph, so much of the repayment of tax referred to in sub-paragraph (1)(*c*) above as is attributable to giving effect to the relief for losses carried back is referred to as "the appropriate repayment" [and, in relation to the appropriate repayment, the chargeable period for which the relevant assessment or amendment is made is referred to as "the repayment period"][2].

(3) For the purpose of determining the amount of the appropriate repayment in a case where the relevant assessment or amendment not only gives effect to the relief for losses carried back but also takes account of any other matter (whether a relief or not) which goes to reduce the assessable profit of the period in question or otherwise to reduce the tax payable for that period, the amount of the repayment which is attributable to the relief for losses carried back is the difference between—

(*a*) the total amount of tax repayable by virtue of the relevant assessment or amendment; and

(*b*) the amount of tax (if any) which would have been so repayable if no account had been taken of the relief for losses carried back.

(4) [Subject to sub-paragraph (6) below][2] where this paragraph applies, the amount of interest which, by virtue of paragraph 16 above, is carried by the appropriate repayment shall not exceed the difference between—

(*a*) [the relevant percentage of the amount][3] of the allowable loss or losses referred to in sub-paragraph (1)(*a*) above [which is treated as reducing the assessable profit of the repayment period][2]; and

(*b*) the amount of the appropriate repayment.

[(5) For the purposes of sub-paragraph (4)(*a*) above—

(*a*) where the repayment period ends on or before 30 June 1993, the relevant percentage, in relation to the amount of the loss or losses which is treated as reducing the assessable profit accruing to the participator for that period is 85 per cent; and

(*b*) in relation to the amount of the loss or losses which is treated as reducing the assessable profit accruing to the participator for any later repayment period, the relevant percentage is 60 per cent . . .[4].

(6) If, in order to give effect to the relief for losses carried back, a repayment of APRT falls, or will on the making of a claim fall, to be made with respect to a chargeable period which is the repayment period in relation to the appropriate repayment, the reference in sub-paragraph (4)(*b*) above to the appropriate repayment shall be construed as a reference to the aggregate of that repayment and the repayment of APRT.

(7) In sub-paragraph (6) above "APRT" means advance petroleum revenue tax paid under Chapter II of Part VI of the Finance Act 1982].[1]

HMRC Manuals—Oil Taxation Manual OT04270 (interest on tax, interest cap).

Simon's Tax Cases—Sub-paras (1), (4)–(7), *Texaco Britain Ltd v IRC* [1994] STC 785.

Modification—This paragraph is modified in relation to transmedian fields by FA 1980 s 107, and in relation to foreign fields by the Oil Taxation Act 1983 s 12, Sch 4 paras 13, 14.

Amendments—[1] Para 17 inserted by FA 1990 s 121(3).

[2] Words in sub-paras (2), (4), and whole of sub-paras (5)–(7), inserted by FA 1993 s 186(3), (4).

[3] Words in sub-para (4) substituted by FA 1993 s 186(3), (4).

[4] In sub-para (5), words "if that later repayment period ends on or before 31 December 2015, and 45 per cent if it ends after 31 December 2015" repealed by FA 2016 s 140(2) with effect from 15 September 2016.

SCHEDULE 3

PETROLEUM REVENUE TAX: MISCELLANEOUS PROVISIONS

Section 1

Definition of sale of oil at arm's length

1—(1) For the purposes of this Part of this Act a sale of any oil is a sale at arm's length if, but only if, the following conditions are satisfied with respect to the contract of sale, that is to say—

(*a*) the contract price is the sole consideration for the sale;

(*b*) the terms of the sale are not affected by any commercial relationship (other than that created by the contract itself) between the seller or any person connected with the seller and the buyer or any person connected with the buyer; and

(*c*) neither the seller nor any person connected with him has, directly or indirectly, any interest in the subsequent resale or disposal of the oil or any product derived therefrom.

(2) [Section 1122 of CTA 2010][1] (connected persons) shall apply for the purposes of the preceding sub-paragraph.

HMRC Manuals—Oil Taxation Manual OT05025 (disposals in sales at arm's length).

Amendments—[1] In sub-para (2) words substituted for words "Section [839] of the Taxes Act" by CTA 2010 s 1177, Sch 1 para 165(2). CTA 2010 has effect for corporation tax purposes for accounting periods ending on or after 1 April 2010, and for income and capital gains tax purposes for the tax year 2010–11 and subsequent tax years.

PRT

[Determination of market value: the notional delivery day for a quantity of oil

1A—(1) This paragraph has effect for determining, for the purposes of this Schedule, the day which is the "notional delivery day" in the case of any particular quantity of oil of any particular kind whose market value falls to be determined in accordance with the provisions of this Schedule in the case of any chargeable period.

(2) The notional delivery day need not be a day in the chargeable period.

(3) In the case of a quantity of oil which, at the end of the chargeable period,—

(*a*) has neither been disposed of nor relevantly appropriated in the period, or

(*b*) has been disposed of but not delivered in the period,

the notional delivery day is the last business day of the chargeable period.

(4) In the case of—

(*a*) a quantity of oil won and disposed of which is delivered on a day in the chargeable period, or

(*b*) a quantity of oil—

(i) relevantly appropriated on a day in the chargeable period, but

(ii) not disposed of in the chargeable period,

the notional delivery day is to be determined in accordance with sub-paragraphs (5) to (7) below.

(5) If that oil is—

(*a*) oil transported by ship from the place of extraction to a place in the United Kingdom or elsewhere, or

(*b*) oil transported by pipeline to a place in the United Kingdom and loaded on to a ship there,

and there is a loading slot for it (see sub-paragraph (8)), the notional delivery day is the middle day of the loading slot.

(6) If sub-paragraph (5) above does not apply to that oil, then—

(*a*) if it is oil delivered on a day in the chargeable period, the notional delivery day is the date of the delivery, or

(*b*) if it is oil relevantly appropriated on a day in the chargeable period, the notional delivery day is the date of the appropriation.

(7) The Treasury may by regulations make provision for or in connection with substituting as the notional delivery day in such circumstances as may be prescribed—

(*a*) in the case of oil transported by ship from the place of extraction to a place in the United Kingdom or elsewhere, the date of completion of load, or

(*b*) in the case of oil transported by pipeline to a place in the United Kingdom and loaded on to a ship there, the date of the bill of lading.

(8) The "loading slot" for any oil is the period of three days within which the loading of the oil on to the ship is or was to take place—

(*a*) as duly published by the operator of the facility at which that loading is or was to take place (unless paragraph (*b*) below applies), or

(*b*) as subsequently finally duly varied to give effect to any modifications duly notified to that operator by the participator concerned.

(9) In sub-paragraph (8) above, "duly" means in accordance with the arrangements for the time being governing the time and manner of—

(*a*) publication, or variation, of the final loading schedule for the calendar month in which loading is or was to take place, or

(*b*) notification of modifications to that schedule,

and, in any case, before the end of the calendar month immediately preceding that in which loading is to take place.

(10) If the Treasury consider that, for the purpose of defining "loading slot", any period of days for the time being specified by or under this Act as the period of days within which loading of oil on to a ship is to take place is, or is to be, no longer appropriate, they may by regulations make provision for, or in connection with,—

(*a*) varying the number of days in the period,

(*b*) determining the day that is to be the notional delivery day if the number, as varied, is an even number.

The power conferred by this sub-paragraph includes power to make amendments to, or modifications of, this Schedule.][1]

Amendments—[1] This paragraph inserted by FA 2006 s 146(1) with effect—

(a) in relation to oil delivered or appropriated on or after 1 July 2006 (disregarding section 12A of this Act); and

(b) for the purpose of determining for any chargeable period ending on or after 31 December 2006—

(i) the value to be brought into account under section 2(4)(*b*) of OTA 1975 by reference to a previous chargeable period ending on or after 30 June 2006, and

(ii) the value to be brought into account under section 2(5)(*d*) of that Act,

subject to transitional provisions in FA 2006 s 147(4)–(8).

Definition of market value of oil

2—[(1) [Except in the case of light gases][3] the market value of [any particular quantity of oil of any kind on any day][4] shall be determined for the purposes of this Part of this Act in accordance with this paragraph [and, accordingly, references in the following provisions of this paragraph to oil do not apply to light gases][3]][2].

[(1A) This paragraph makes different provision according to whether the oil is—

(*a*) Category 1 oil of any kind, or

(*b*) Category 2 oil of any kind.

(1B) For the purposes of this Act—

(*a*) Category 1 oil is oil of any of one or more kinds specified as such in regulations made for the purpose by the Board;

(*b*) Category 2 oil is oil of any other kind.

(1C) The Board may specify oil of any particular kind as Category 1 oil only if they are satisfied that reports of prices for sales of oil of that kind are published and widely available (whether or not on payment of a fee).][4]

[(2) The market value of any particular quantity of Category 1 oil of any kind is the price for which that quantity of oil of that kind might reasonably have been expected to be sold under a contract of sale that meets the following conditions—

(*a*) the contract is for the sale of the oil at arm's length to a willing buyer;

(*b*) the contract is for delivery of a single standard cargo of the oil;

(*c*) the contract specifies a period of three days within which loading of the oil is to take place and that period includes the notional delivery day for the actual oil;

(*d*) the contract requires the oil to have been subjected to appropriate initial treatment before delivery;

(*e*) the contract requires the oil to be delivered—

(i) in the case of oil extracted in the United Kingdom, at the place of extraction; or

(ii) in the case of oil extracted from strata in the sea bed and subsoil of the territorial sea of the United Kingdom or of a designated area, at the place in the United Kingdom or another country at which the seller could reasonably be expected to deliver it or, if there is more than one such place, the one nearest to the place of extraction.

The terms as to payment which are to be implied in the contract are those which are customarily contained in contracts for the sale at arm's length of oil of the kind in question.

(2AA) The market value of any particular quantity of Category 2 oil of any kind is the price for which that quantity of oil of that kind might reasonably have been expected to be sold under a contract of sale that meets the following conditions—

(*a*) the contract is for the sale of the oil at arm's length to a willing buyer;

(*b*) the contract provides for delivery of the oil on the notional delivery day for the actual oil or within such period that includes that day as is normal under a contract at arm's length for the sale of oil of that kind (or, if there is more than one such period, the shortest of them);

(*c*) the contract is made on a date such that the period between that date and the notional delivery day for the actual oil is the normal period between contract and delivery in the case of a contract at arm's length for the sale of oil of that kind (or, if there is more than one such period, the shortest of them);

(*d*) the contract requires the oil to have been subjected to appropriate initial treatment before delivery;

(*e*) the contract requires the oil to be delivered—

(i) in the case of oil extracted in the United Kingdom, at the place of extraction; or

(ii) in the case of oil extracted from strata in the sea bed and subsoil of the territorial sea of the United Kingdom or of a designated area, at the place in the United Kingdom or another country at which the seller could reasonably be expected to deliver it or, if there is more than one such place, the one nearest to the place of extraction.

The terms as to payment which are to be implied in the contract are those which are customarily contained in contracts for the sale at arm's length of oil of the kind in question.][4]

[(2E) For the purposes of sub-paragraph (2) or (2AA) above, the price of any quantity of Category 1 or Category 2 oil of any kind shall be determined in such manner, on the basis of such information, and by reference to such factors, as may be prescribed for oil of that Category and kind in regulations made by the Board.

(2F) The provision that may be made by regulations under subsection (2E) above includes provision for or in connection with any or all of the following—

PRT

(*a*) determining the price by reference to prices, or an average of prices, for sales of oil (whether or not oil of the Category or kind in question, and whether the prices are prices under actual contracts, prices that are published and widely available (whether on payment of a fee or otherwise) or prices ascertained or determined in some other way);
(*b*) the prices to be taken into account;
(*c*) the descriptions of contracts to be taken into account;
(*d*) the method to be used for determining an average of prices;
(*e*) the day or days, or period or periods, by reference to which prices, or any average of prices, is to be determined;
(*f*) the application of a prescribed price differential, in cases where the price of oil of one kind falls to be determined in whole or in part by reference to prices for oil of some other kind.

(2G) Sub-paragraph (2I) below has effect if, or in so far as, the Board are satisfied that it is impracticable or inappropriate to determine for the purposes of sub-paragraph (2) or (2AA) above the price of any oil in accordance with the provisions of regulations for the time being in force under sub-paragraph (2E) above.

(2H) For that purpose it is immaterial whether the impracticability or inappropriateness is by virtue of—
(*a*) an insufficiency of contracts or published prices that satisfy the conditions,
(*b*) an insufficiency of information relating to such contracts or published prices, or
(*c*) the nature of the market for oil of the kind in question, or for any other reason.

(2I) Where this sub-paragraph has effect, the price is to be determined—
(*a*) so far as it is practicable and appropriate to do so by reference to other contracts or published prices (whether or not relating to oil of the same kind) and in accordance with the principles set out in the regulations for determining an average of prices; and
(*b*) so far as it is not practicable or appropriate to determine it as mentioned in paragraph (*a*) above, in such other manner as appears to the Board to be appropriate in the circumstances.][4]

(3) . . . [7]

[(3A) Where all or any of the oil whose market value falls to be ascertained in accordance with [sub-paragraph (1) and sub-paragraph (2) or (2AA) above][4] has been subjected to initial treatment before being disposed of or relevantly appropriated, the appropriate initial treatment referred to in [sub-paragraph (2)(*d*) or (2AA)(*d*) above][4] shall, as respects that oil, include the whole of that treatment][1].

(4) The provisions of [sub-paragraphs (2) and (2AA)][4] above shall apply for the ascertainment of the market value of oil in any case mentioned in paragraph 2(2) of Schedule 2 to this Act as they apply in relation to the corresponding case mentioned in those provisions.

[(5) In this paragraph "prescribed" means specified in, or determined in accordance with, regulations.][4]

Statement of Practice—SP 14/93 (Valuation of oil disposed of otherwise than at arm's length).
HMRC Manuals—Oil Taxation Manual OT05300 (valuation of non arm's length disposals).
Cross references—See FA 1982 s 134, Sch 18 (alternative valuation of ethane used for petrochemical purposes).
FA 1986 s 109 and Schedule 21 (alternative valuation of light gases)
FA 1987 s 62 (market value of oil to be determined on a monthly basis)
See Inland Revenue Notice 23/1/04 (updated statutory market values for disposal of oil and gas from Brent and Forties fields through December 2002).

Amendments—[1] Sub-para (3A) inserted by FA 1980 s 109, in relation to any chargeable period ending after 31 December 1979.
[2] Sub-para (1) substituted, with respect to chargeable periods ending after 31 December 1986, by FA 1987 s 62, Sch 11 Pt I para 1, Sch 16 Pt X.
[3] In sub-para (1) words inserted by FA 1994 s 236, Sch 23 para 3(1).
[4] Words in sub-para (1) substituted for the words "any oil in any calendar month"; sub-paras (1A)–(1C) inserted; sub-paras (2)–(2AA) substituted for former sub-para (2); sub-paras (2E)–(2I) substituted for former sub-paras (2A)–(2D); sub-para (3) repealed; words in sub-para 3A substituted for the words "sub-paragraphs (1) and (2) above" and "sub-paragraph (2)(*a*) above"; words in sub-para (4) substituted for the words "sub-paragraphs (2)and (3)"; and sub-para (5) inserted by FA 2006 s 146(2)–(10), s 178, Sch 26 Pt 5(1) with effect—
(a) in relation to oil delivered or appropriated on or after 1 July 2006 (disregarding section 12A of that Act); and
(b) for the purpose of determining for any chargeable period ending on or after 31 December 2006—
(i) the value to be brought into account under section 2(4)(*b*) of OTA 1975 by reference to a previous chargeable period ending on or after 30 June 2006, and
(ii) the value to be brought into account under section 2(5)(*d*) of that Act,
subject to transitional provisions in FA 2006 s 147(4)–(8). Former sub-paras (2)–(2D), (3) previously read—

"[(2) Subject to the following provisions of this paragraph, the market value of any oil in a calendar month (in this paragraph referred to as "the relevant month") is the price at which oil of that kind might reasonably have been expected to be sold under a contract of sale satisfying the following conditions—
(*a*) the contract is for the sale of the oil at arm's length to a willing buyer;
(*b*) the contract is for the delivery of the oil at a time in the relevant month;
(*c*) the contract is entered into within the period beginning at the beginning of the month preceding the relevant month and ending on the middle day of the relevant month or, if the Treasury by order so direct, within such other period as may be specified in the order;

(*d*) the contract requires the oil to have been subjected to appropriate initial treatment before delivery;

(*e*) the contract requires the oil to be delivered]—

(i) in the case of oil extracted in the United Kingdom, at the place of extraction; or

(ii) in the case of oil extracted from strata in the sea bed and subsoil of the territorial sea of the United Kingdom or of a designated area, at the place in the United Kingdom [or another country] at which the seller could reasonably be expected to deliver it or, if there is more than one such place, the one nearest to the place of extraction;

[(*f*)] in the case of oil whose market value falls to be ascertained [as in a particular month] for the purposes of paragraph (*b*) of section 2(4) or paragraph (*d*) of section 2(5) of this Act or, subject to sub-paragraph (3) below, under paragraph 3 below for the purposes of paragraph (*b*) or (*c*) of the said section 2(5), the contract is for the sale of the whole quantity of oil whose market value falls to be ascertained [as in that month][3] for the purposes of the paragraph in question, and of no other oil;

[and, for the avoidance of doubt, it is hereby declared that the terms as to payment which are to be implied in the contract shall be those which are customarily contained in contracts for the sale at arm's length of oil of the kind in question] [and, for the purposes of paragraph (c) above, the middle day of a month containing an even number of days shall be taken to be the last day of the first half of the month, and the power to make an order under that paragraph shall be exercisable by statutory instrument which shall be subject to annulment in pursuance of a resolution of the Commons House of Parliament].

[(2A) For the purpose of sub-paragraph (2) above, the price of any oil in a calendar month shall be determined, subject to sub-paragraphs (2B) and (2C) below, by taking the average of the prices under actual contracts for the sale of oil of that kind—

(*a*) which are contracts for the sale of oil by a participator in an oil field or by a company which, for the purposes of section 115(2) of the Finance Act 1984, is associated with such a participator; and

(*b*) which, subject to sub-paragraph (2B) below, satisfy the conditions in paragraphs (*a*) to (*e*) of sub-paragraph (2) above; and

(*c*) which do not contain terms as to payment which differ from those customarily contained in contracts for the sale at arm's length of oil of the kind in question.

(2B) For the purposes of sub-paragraph (2A)(*b*) above, a contract shall be treated as fulfilling the condition in paragraph (*c*) of sub-paragraph (2) above if it contains provisions under which the price for oil to be delivered in the relevant month either is determined or subject to review in the period relevant for the purposes of that paragraph or is determined by reference to other prices which are themselves determined in that period, being prices for oil to be delivered in the relevant month.

(2C) The average referred to in sub-paragraph (2A) above shall be determined—

(*a*) by establishing an average price for oil of the kind in question for each business day within the period relevant for the purposes of sub-paragraph (2)(*c*) above; and

(*b*) by taking the arithmetic mean of the average prices so established;

and in this sub-paragraph "business day" has the same meaning as in the Bills of Exchange Act 1882.

(2D) If or in so far as the Board are satisfied that it is impracticable or inappropriate to determine for the purposes of sub-paragraph (2) above the price of any oil in a calendar month as mentioned in sub-paragraph (2A) above (whether by virtue of an insufficiency of contracts satisfying the conditions or of information relating to such contracts or by virtue of the nature of the market for oil of the kind in question or for any other reason), that price shall be determined,—

(*a*) so far as it is practicable and appropriate to do so by reference to such other contracts (whether or not relating to oil of the same kind) and in accordance with the principles in sub-paragraph (2C) above; and

(*b*) so far as it is not practicable or appropriate to determine it as mentioned in paragraph (*a*) above, in such other manner as appears to the Board to be appropriate in the circumstances].

(3) If oil whose market value falls to be ascertained [as in a particular month] under paragraph 3 below for the purposes of paragraph (*b*) of the said section 2(5) was not all disposed of to the same person, then the market value at that time of so much of that oil as was disposed of [in that month] to any one person shall be ascertained in accordance with sub-paragraphs (1) [to (2D)] above as if that were the only oil whose market value fell to be ascertained [as in that month][3] for those purposes (with sub-paragraph [(2)(*f*)] above applying accordingly)."

[2A—(1) Paragraph 2 above shall have effect in accordance with this paragraph where the oil whose market value falls to be ascertained at any time in accordance with sub-paragraphs [(1) to [(2I)][5]][2] of that paragraph . . . [5] consists of or includes gas.

[(1A) Sub-paragraphs (2) and (3) below also apply where the market value of any light gases falls to be ascertained under paragraph 3A below].[4]

(2) [Sub-paragraph (2)(*d*) or (as the case may be) (2AA)(*d*) of paragraph 2 above][5] [or, as the case may require, sub-paragraph (2)(*b*) of paragraph 3A below][4] shall not apply to so much of the oil as consists of gas unless—

(*a*) it has been subjected to initial treatment before being disposed of or relevantly appropriated; or

(*b*) it has, after being disposed of or relevantly appropriated, been subjected to initial treatment by or on behalf of the participator in question or by or on behalf of a person who is connected with him within the meaning of [section 1122 of CTA 2010][6];

and where oil consisting of gas has, whether before or after being disposed of or relevantly appropriated, been subjected to initial treatment by or on behalf of the participator in question or by

PRT

or on behalf of a person who is connected with him as aforesaid the appropriate initial treatment referred to in sub-paragraph [(2)][2] [or (2AA)][5] of paragraph 2 above [or, as the case may require, sub-paragraph (2)(b) of paragraph 3A below][4] shall include the treatment to which it has been so subjected.

(3) Where the initial treatment mentioned in sub-paragraph (2) [or (2AA)][5] above includes treatment in order to separate gas of one or more kinds which are transported and sold in normal commercial practice, the market value of the gas of each such kind which is separated shall be ascertained in accordance with sub-paragraphs [(1) to [(2I)][5]][2] of paragraph 2 [or, as the case may require, in accordance with paragraph 3A below][4] as if that were the only oil whose market value fell to be ascertained at the time in question . . . [5].

(4) . . . [4]][1]

HMRC Manuals—Oil Taxation Manual OT05310 (valuation of gas other than light gas).

Cross references—See FA 1982 s 134, Sch 18 (alternative valuation of ethane used for petrochemical purposes).

FA 1986 s 109 and Schedule 21 (alternative valuation of light gases).

FA 1987 s 62 (market value of oil to be determined on a monthly basis).

Amendments—[1] Para 2A inserted by FA 1980 s 109, in relation to any chargeable period ending after 31 December 1979.

[2] Words in sub-paras (1), (2) (3) substituted, with respect to chargeable periods ending after 31 December 1986, by FA 1987 s 62, Sch 11 Pt I para 2.

[4] Sub-para (1A) and words in sub-paras (2), (3) inserted, and sub-para (4) repealed, by FA 1994 ss 236, 258, Sch 23 para 3(2)–(5), Sch 26 Pt VI.

[5] In sub-para (1) number substituted for "(2D)" and words ", or in accordance with those sub-paragraphs as modified by sub-paragraph (3) of that paragraph," repealed; in sub-para (2) words substituted for words "Sub-paragraph (2)(*d*)(*e*) of paragraph 2 above" and words inserted; in sub-para (3) words inserted, number substituted for "(2D)" and words "(with sub-paragraphs (2)(*f*) of paragraph 2 applying accordingly)" repealed by FA 2006 s 146, Sch 18 para 8, s 178, Sch 26 Pt 5(1) with effect—

(a) in relation to oil delivered or appropriated on or after 1 July 2006 (disregarding section 12A of this Act); and

(b) for the purpose of determining for any chargeable period ending on or after 31 December 2006—

(i) the value to be brought into account under section 2(4)(*b*) of OTA 1975 by reference to a previous chargeable period ending on or after 30 June 2006, and

(ii) the value to be brought into account under section 2(5)(*d*) of that Act,

subject to transitional provisions in FA 2006 s 147(4)–(8).

[6] In sub-para (2)(b) words substituted for words "section839 of the Taxes Act" by CTA 2010 s 1177, Sch 1 para 165(3). CTA 2010 has effect for corporation tax purposes for accounting periods ending on or after 1 April 2010, and for income and capital gains tax purposes for the tax year 2010–11 and subsequent tax years.

Aggregate market value of oil for purposes of section 2(5)

[3—(1) For the purposes of subsection (5) of section 2 of this Act, the aggregate market value of any oil falling within paragraph (*b*) or (*c*) of that subsection is arrived at as follows.

(2) In the case of oil falling within paragraph (*b*) of that subsection and delivered as there mentioned in the chargeable period in question—

(*a*) for each delivery, find (in accordance with paragraph 2 above (read, where applicable, with paragraph 2A above)) the market value of the quantity of oil delivered, and

(*b*) aggregate the market values so found.

(3) In the case of oil falling within paragraph (*c*) of that subsection and appropriated as there mentioned in the chargeable period in question—

(*a*) for each appropriation, find (in accordance with paragraph 2 above (read, where applicable, with paragraph 2A above)) the market value of the quantity of oil appropriated, and

(*b*) aggregate the market values so found.][1]

HMRC Manuals—Oil Taxation Manual OT05305 (light gas).

Cross references—See FA 1982 s 134, Sch 18 (alternative valuation of ethane used for petrochemical purposes).

FA 1986 s 109 and Schedule 21 (alternative valuation of light gases).

FA 1987 s 62 (market value of oil to be determined on a monthly basis).

Amendments—[1] This paragraph substituted by FA 2006 s 146, Sch 18 para 9 with effect—

(a) in relation to oil delivered or appropriated on or after 1 July 2006 (disregarding section 12A of this Act); and

(b) for the purpose of determining for any chargeable period ending on or after 31 December 2006—

(i) the value to be brought into account under section 2(4)(*b*) of OTA 1975 by reference to a previous chargeable period ending on or after 30 June 2006, and

(ii) the value to be brought into account under section 2(5)(*d*) of that Act,

subject to transitional provisions in FA 2006 s 147(4)–(8).

Paragraph (3) formerly read as follows—

"3—(1)For the purposes of subsection (5) of section 2 of this Act the aggregate market value of any oil falling within paragraph (*b*) or (*c*) of that subsection shall be arrived at by ascertaining, for each calendar month in the chargeable period in question, the market value at the material time of so much, if any, of that oil as was—

(a) in the case of oil falling within the said paragraph (b), delivered as there mentioned in that month;

(b) in the case of oil falling within the said paragraph (c), appropriated as there mentioned in that month,

and, in either case, aggregating the market values so ascertained.

(2) In this paragraph and elsewhere in this Part of this Act "calendar month" (where those words are used) means a month of the calendar year . . . ."

Definition of market value of light gases

[3A—(1) The market value of any light gases for the purposes of this Part of this Act is the price at which, having regard to all the circumstances relevant to the disposal or appropriation in question, light gases of that kind might reasonably have been expected to be sold under a contract of sale satisfying the conditions specified in sub-paragraph (2) below.

(2) The conditions referred to in sub-paragraph (1) above are that—

(*a*) the contract is for the sale of the gases at arm's length to a willing buyer;

(*b*) the contract requires the gases to have been subjected to appropriate initial treatment before delivery; and

(*c*) the contract requires the gases to be delivered—

(i) in the case of gases extracted in the United Kingdom, at the place of extraction; or

(ii) in the case of gases extracted from strata in the sea bed and subsoil of the territorial sea of the United Kingdom or of a designated area, at the place in the United Kingdom or another country at which the seller could reasonably be expected to deliver the gases or, if there is more than one such place, the one nearest to the place of extraction.

(3) If the circumstances referred to in sub-paragraph (1) above are such that the price referred to in that sub-paragraph might reasonably be expected to include—

(*a*) any such payments as are referred to in subsection (2) of section 114 of the Finance Act 1984 (treatment of certain payments relating to gas sales), or

(*b*) any capacity payments, as defined in subsection (5) of that section,

section 114 of the Finance Act 1984 shall apply accordingly in relation to the notional contract specified in sub-paragraph (1) above as it applies in relation to an actual contract.

[(3A) The circumstances referred to in sub-paragraph (1) above include—

(*a*) the timing of the making, and of any subsequent variations, of the actual contract or other arrangements under which the disposal or appropriation was made;

(*b*) the terms of that contract or, as the case may be, of those arrangements, and the terms of any such variations; and

(*c*) the extent to which the circumstances to which regard is to be had by virtue of paragraphs (*a*) and (*b*) above are circumstances that might reasonably have been expected to exist in the case of a contract satisfying the conditions specified in sub-paragraph (2) above.][2]

(4) This paragraph has effect subject to sub-paragraphs (2) and (3) of paragraph 2A above].[1]

Amendments—[1] Para 3A inserted by FA 1994 s 236, Sch 23 para 4.3A.

[2] Sub-para (3A) inserted by FA 1998 s 152(1) and deemed always to have had effect.

Oil delivered in place of royalties to be disregarded for certain purposes

4 Oil delivered to the [OGA][2] under the terms of a licence granted under [Part I of the Petroleum Act 1998][1] shall be disregarded for the purposes of section 2(5) of this Act and for the purposes of the references in section 8(3) and (4) of this Act to a participator's share of the oil won and saved from an oil field in a chargeable period.

Amendments—[1] Words substituted by the Petroleum Act 1998 s 50, Sch 4 para 7(7) with effect from 15 February 1999 (by virtue of SI 1999/161 art 2).

[2] Word substituted for words "Secretary of State" by the Petroleum (Transfer of Functions) Regulations, SI 2016/898 reg 4(1), (9) with effect from 1 October 2016.

Effect of transfer to an associated company of participator's rights etc in connection with an oil field or relevant licence

5—(1) This paragraph applies to any agreement or other arrangement between a participator in an oil field and a company associated with the participator whereby—

(*a*) ownership of all or any of the participator's share of the oil won and saved from the field is transferred to the company; and

(*b*) the company obtains or assumes all or any of the participator's other rights, interests and obligations in connection with the field or any relevant licence.

(2) As regards any chargeable period in which a participator in an oil field is a party to an arrangement to which this paragraph applies, the other party to the arrangement shall be treated for all purposes of this Part of this Act (except this paragraph) and for the purposes of [sections 299 to 301 of CTA 2010][1] as having been a participator in the field at all times when the actual participator was such a participator (including times before the arrangement was made), and shall be assessable and chargeable to tax and entitled to make any claim under this Part of this Act, and any deduction or claim under [sections 299 to 301 of CTA 2010][1], accordingly.

(3) Where a participator in an oil field is or has been a party to an arrangement to which this paragraph applies then for all purposes of this Part of this Act—

(*a*) anything done by or in relation to the participator in connection with the field or any relevant licence shall be treated as being or having been done by or, as the case may be, in relation to the other party to the arrangement; and

(*b*) all rights, interests or obligations of the participator in connection with the field or any relevant licence shall be treated as being or having been rights, interests or obligations of the other party.

(4) Where a participator in an oil field is or has been a party to an arrangement to which this paragraph applies, then, if any tax or interest payable under this Part of this Act by the other party to the arrangement is not paid within thirty days after the date on which it becomes payable, the Board may by notice in writing require the participator to pay that tax or interest; and where such a notice is served on the participator, the tax or interest in question shall be payable by him forthwith, but without prejudice to the Board's right to recover it from the other party.

(5) For the purposes of this paragraph "company" means any body corporate, and a participator in an oil field and another company are associated with one another if—

(*a*) the participator has control over or is under the control of the other company; or

(*b*) the participator and the other company are both under the control of the same person or persons;

and in this sub-paragraph "control" has the meaning given by [section 1124 of CTA 2010][1].

HMRC Manuals—Oil Taxation Manual OT18000 (transfers of licences interests).

Amendments—[1] In sub-para (2) words substituted in each place for words "section 500 of the Taxes Act", in sub-para (5) words substituted for words "section 840 of the Taxes Act" by CTA 2010 s 1177, Sch 1 para 165(4), (5). CTA 2010 has effect for corporation tax purposes for accounting periods ending on or after 1 April 2010, and for income and capital gains tax purposes for the tax year 2010–11 and subsequent tax years.

Oil owned by a person other than a participator in the oil field from which it was won

6—(1) Where a proportion of a participator's share in the oil won and saved from an oil field (as distinct from a specific quantity of oil comprised in that share) is owned by [a person (in this paragraph referred to as "the owner") who is not a participator and][1] who acquired it (whether directly or indirectly) under an agreement to which paragraph 5 above does not apply, the following provisions of this paragraph shall have effect.

(2) For the purposes of this Part of this Act the oil acquired by the owner under the agreement shall be treated in every case as having been disposed of to him by the participator otherwise than in a sale at arm's length.

(3) Where any oil which the owner owns in right of the agreement is in pursuance of the agreement—

(*a*) delivered to the owner by the participator; or

(*b*) delivered to a third person by the participator acting on behalf of the owner,

the delivery shall for the purposes of this Part of this Act be regarded as a delivery by the participator although he does not own the oil.

(4) This sub-paragraph applies to all such oil (if any) as, being owned by the owner in right of the agreement, is in any chargeable period delivered by the participator as mentioned in the preceding sub-paragraph and would accordingly, apart from the following sub-paragraph, fall to be brought into account under section 2(5)(*b*) of this Act in computing the assessable profit or allowable loss accruing to the participator in that period (in the following sub-paragraph referred to as "the relevant period").

(5) If on a claim made by the participator within two months after the end of the relevant period—

(*a*) it is shown that some or all of the oil to which sub-paragraph (4) above applies has been disposed of by or on behalf of the owner crude in sales at arm's length; and

(*b*) the Board are satisfied that the oil with respect to which it is so shown includes the whole of so much of the oil to which that sub-paragraph applies as has been so disposed of,

then, in computing the assessable profit or allowable loss accruing to the participator in the relevant period, the oil with respect to which it is so shown shall be brought into account by reference to the price received or receivable for it by the owner instead of by reference to its market value.

HMRC Manuals—Oil Taxation Manual OT18370 (unitisations and redeterminations).

Amendments—[1] Words in sub-para (1) substituted by FA 1977 s 54(2).

[Effect of certain transactions between participators

6A Where the whole or part of the share of a participator ("the transferor") of oil won from an oil field became the share, or part of the share, of another participator ("the transferee") in pursuance of an agreement between them under which the transferor undertook to remain responsible for carrying out the transferee's obligations in connection with the field so far as they relate to the transferred share or part, then, for the purposes of this Part of this Act—

(*a*) the shares of the transferor and the transferee of oil won from the field shall be taken to be the same as they would have been if the transfer had not occurred, and (*b*) any oil comprised in the transferred share or part and taken up by or on the authority of the transferee in pursuance of the agreement shall be regarded as being disposed of and delivered to him by the transferor at the time when it is taken up].[1]

HMRC Manuals—Oil Taxation Manual OT18200 (participation rights).

Amendments—[1] Para 6A inserted by FA 1977 s 54(1).

Exclusion from section 2(4)(b) and (5)(d) of offshore oil in transit to place of first landing . . .[1]

7 In computing the assessable profit or allowable loss accruing to a participator in a chargeable period from an oil field, the market value of any oil won as mentioned in section 3(1)(*f*) of this Act—

(*a*) shall not be taken into account under section 2(4)(*b*) of this Act if and to the extent that at the end of the preceding chargeable period the oil was in the course of being transported to the place where it was first landed in the United Kingdom [or to the place referred to in section 3(1)(*f*)(ii) of this Act][1]; and

(*b*) shall not be taken into account under section 2(5)(*d*) of this Act if and to the extent that at the end of the first-mentioned chargeable period the oil was in the course of being so transported.

HMRC Manuals—Oil Taxation Manual OT17200 (oil allowance).

Amendments—[1] Words in heading repealed and words inserted by F(No 2)A 1992 ss 74, 82, Sch 15 para 4(2), Sch 18 Pt VIII, with effect in accordance with s 74(5) thereof.

Certain subsidised expenditure to be disregarded

8—(1) Expenditure shall not be regarded for any of the purposes of this Part of this Act as having been incurred by any person in so far as it has been or is to be met directly or indirectly by the Crown or by any government or public or local authority, whether in the United Kingdom or elsewhere, or by any person other than the first-mentioned person . . .[1]

[(1A) But sub-paragraph (1) above does not apply to any expenditure for which the relevant participator is liable that has been or is to be met directly or indirectly out of a payment made by the guarantor under an abandonment guarantee.

(1B) In sub-paragraph (1A) above—

"abandonment guarantee" has the same meaning as it has for the purposes of section 3 of this Act (see section 104 of the Finance Act 1991), and

"the guarantor" and "the relevant participator" have the same meaning as in section 104 of that Act.][2]

(2) In considering, for the purposes of this paragraph, how far any expenditure has been or is to be met directly or indirectly by the Crown or by any authority or person other than the person incurring the expenditure, there shall be left out of account any insurance or compensation payable in respect of the loss or destruction of any asset.

HMRC Manuals—Oil Taxation Manual OT09350 (insurance recoveries: partial damage).

Amendments—[1] Words in sub-para (1) repealed by FA 1982 ss 137, 157, Sch 22 Pt IX.

[2] Sub-paras (1A), (1B) inserted by FA 2013 s 89(1), Sch 31 para 3 with effect in relation to expenditure incurred on or after 17 July 2013.

Election to have amounts mentioned in section 2(9)(b) and (c) spread

9, 10

Amendments—Paras 9, 10 repealed by FA 2009 s 91, Sch 45 para 1(1), (2) with effect in relation to chargeable periods beginning after 30 June 2009.

Restriction of amount of reduction under section 8(1)

11 Where—

(*a*) a claim under Schedule 5 or 6 to this Act is made after the relevant time; and

(*b*) the reduction which would, apart from this paragraph, fall to be made under subsection (1) of section 8 of this Act for any chargeable period is greater than it would have been if the expenditure and other amounts allowed on the claim had been claimed before and allowed at the relevant time,

then, if the Board so direct, the reduction made under that sub-section for that chargeable period shall be only what it would have been if the expenditure and other amounts allowed on the claim had been claimed before and allowed at the relevant time.

In this paragraph "the relevant time" means the end of twelve months from the end of the claim period to which the claim mentioned in sub-paragraph (*a*) above relates.

HMRC Manuals—Oil Taxation Manual OT17350 (late expenditure claims).

[Power to make regulations under this Schedule

12—(1) Any power to make regulations under this Schedule is exercisable by statutory instrument.

(2) A statutory instrument containing regulations under this Schedule may not be made unless a draft of the instrument has been laid before, and approved by a resolution of, the House of Commons.

(3) Any power to make regulations under this Schedule includes power—

(*a*) to make different provision for different Categories or kinds of oil or for different cases, or

(*b*) to make incidental, consequential, supplemental, or transitional provision or savings.][1]

Amendments—[1] Para 12 inserted by FA 2006 s 146, Sch 18 para 10 with effect—

(a) in relation to oil delivered or appropriated on or after 1 July 2006 (disregarding section 12A of this Act); and

(b) for the purpose of determining for any chargeable period ending on or after 31 December 2006—

(i) the value to be brought into account under section 2(4)(*b*) of OTA 1975 by reference to a previous chargeable period ending on or after 30 June 2006, and

(ii) the value to be brought into account under section 2(5)(*d*) of that Act,

subject to transitional provisions in FA 2006 s 147(4)–(8).

SCHEDULE 4

PROVISIONS SUPPLEMENTARY TO SECTIONS 3 AND 4

Sections 3, 4

Restrictions on expenditure allowable under section 3 or 4

1—(1) Expenditure incurred by any person in the acquisition of an asset is not allowable under section 3 or 4 of this Act for an oil field if expenditure previously incurred by another person in acquiring, bringing into existence, or enhancing the value of that asset is allowable under that section for that field.

Section 4(13) of this Act applies to the preceding provisions of this sub-paragraph.

(2) Sub-paragraph (1) above shall, with any necessary modifications, have effect in relation to expenditure incurred by a person—

(*a*) in renting or hiring an asset or any interest in an asset; or

(*b*) for the provision of services or other business facilities of whatever kind; or

(*c*) for the grant or transfer to him of any right, licence or interest (other than an interest in an asset),

as it has effect in relation to expenditure incurred in the acquisition of, or of an interest in, an asset.

2—[(1) Where, in a transaction to which this paragraph applies, a person has incurred expenditure in acquiring, bringing into existence or enhancing the value of an asset, he shall at any time be treated for the purposes of—

(*a*) sections 3 and 4 of this Act, and

(*b*) sections 3 and 4 of and Schedule 1 to the Oil Taxation Act 1983,

[as having incurred that expenditure only to the extent that it does not exceed the lowest of the amounts described in sub-paragraph (1ZA) below which is applicable in the particular case.][3]

[(1ZA) Those amounts are—

(*a*) the amount of expenditure (other than loan expenditure) incurred up to the time mentioned in sub-paragraph (1) above in a transaction to which this paragraph does not apply (or, if there has been more than one such transaction, the later or latest of them) in acquiring, bringing into existence, or enhancing the value of, the asset;

(*b*) the amount of the open market consideration for the acquisition, bringing into existence, or enhancement of the value, of the asset;

(*c*) in a case where the other party to the transaction is a participator in a taxable field and in the case of that participator either—

(i) an amount is brought into account under section 2 of this Act in accordance with section 7(1) of the Oil Taxation Act 1983 as disposal receipts in respect of the transaction, or

(ii) no amount is so brought into account by reason of reductions falling to be made in the amount that would have been so brought into account apart from those reductions,

the amount so brought into account or, as the case may be, nil;

(*d*) in a case where the other party to the transaction is not a participator in a taxable field but—

(i) the transaction is the latest in a series of transactions in respect of the asset (or in respect of an asset or assets in which the asset was comprised),

(ii) those transactions are transactions to which this paragraph applies,

(iii) in the case of at least one of those transactions, there is a party who is a participator in an oil field, and

(iv) in the case of any such party, an amount either is brought into account as mentioned in paragraph (*c*)(i) above in respect of the transaction or would have been so brought into account but for such reductions as are mentioned in paragraph (*c*)(ii) above, so much of the amount so brought into account in respect of that transaction (or, where there are two or more such transactions, the later or latest of them) as is justly and reasonably referable to the asset mentioned in sub-paragraph (1) above (taking that amount as being nil in the case of any transaction where no amount is so brought into account by reason of any such reductions).][3]

(1A) Subsections (1) to (3) of section 191 of the Finance Act 1993 apply to determine for the purposes of this paragraph what expenditure has at any time been incurred under a transaction to which this paragraph does not apply, as they apply in relation to expenditure for the allowance of which a claim is received by the Board after 16 March 1993.

(1B) In sub-paragraph [(1ZA)(*a*)][3] above "loan expenditure" means expenditure in respect of interest or any other pecuniary obligation incurred in obtaining a loan or any other form of credit].[2]

[(1C) The reference in sub-paragraph (1ZA)(*b*) above to the open market consideration for the acquisition, bringing into existence, or enhancement of the value, of an asset is a reference to the consideration which might reasonably have been given for the acquisition, bringing into existence, or enhancement of the value, of the asset (whatever the nature of the acquisition, bringing into existence or enhancement of the value) had it been made in a transaction to which this paragraph does not apply.][3]

(2) This paragraph applies to any transaction between connected persons and to any transaction made otherwise than at arm's length; and for the purposes of this paragraph a person is connected with another person if [they are connected within the meaning of [section 1122 of CTA 2010][4]][1].

[(3) The preceding provisions of this section shall, with any necessary modification, apply in relation to expenditure incurred by any person in acquiring an interest in an asset or in bringing into existence an asset in which he is to have an interest, or in enhancing the value of an asset in which he has an interest, as those provisions apply in relation to expenditure incurred by a person in acquiring, bringing into existence, or enhancing the value of an asset, as the case may be.

(4) The provisions of sub-paragraphs (1) to (2) above shall, with any necessary modification, apply in relation to expenditure incurred by any person in respect of—

(*a*) the use of an asset (including expenditure on renting or hiring), or

(*b*) the provision of services or other business facilities of whatever kind in connection with the use, otherwise than by that person, of an asset,

as they have effect in relation to expenditure incurred in the acquisition of, or of an interest in, an asset].[2]

HMRC Manuals—Oil Taxation Manual OT14740 (associated party transactions: insurance).

Amendments—[1] In sub-para (2) words substituted by F(No 2)A 1979 s 20.

2 Sub-paras (1)–(1B) substituted, for sub-para (1) as originally enacted and sub-paras (3), (4) substituted, for sub-para (3) as originally enacted, where transactions to which this para applies take place on or after 16 March 1993, by FA 1993 s 191(4).

3 Words in sub-para (1)(*b*) substituted, reference in sub-para (1B) substituted, and sub-paras (1ZA), (1C) inserted, by FA 2004 s 287 with effect for expenditure incurred after 16 March 2004.

4 In sub-para (2) words substituted for words "section 839 of the Taxes Act" by CTA 2010 s 1177, Sch 1 para 166(2). CTA 2010 has effect for corporation tax purposes for accounting periods ending on or after 1 April 2010, and for income and capital gains tax purposes for the tax year 2010–11 and subsequent tax years.

3— . . .

Amendments—This para repealed by FA 2009 s 91, Sch 45 para 1(1), (4) with effect in relation to chargeable periods beginning after 30 June 2009.

Disposal of long-term asset formerly used in connection with an oil field

4—(1) Where an asset is used in connection with an oil field in circumstances such that section 4 of this Act applies to any expenditure incurred in acquiring, bringing into existence, or enhancing the value of that asset, then if—

(*a*) the asset is disposed of for valuable consideration while in use in that connection or not more than two years after its use in that connection permanently ceases;

(*b*) the person making the disposal is either a participator in the field or a person connected with a participator;

(*c*) the person to whom the disposal is made is not a person connected with a participator; and

(*d*) the amount or value of the consideration received or receivable for the disposal is not less than the price which the asset might reasonably have been expected to fetch if sold in the open market at the time of the disposal,

sub-paragraphs (2) to (4) below shall have effect.

(2) If the disposal occurs without the asset permanently ceasing to be used in connection with the field, its use in that connection shall for the purposes of section 4 of this Act and the following provisions of this paragraph be deemed to have permanently ceased at the time of the disposal.

(3) If the disposal takes place not later than the end of the claim period in which the use of the asset in connection with the field permanently ceases, the proportion of the expenditure allowable under section 4 of this Act for the relevant period (that is to say the period which, in relation to that claim

PRT

period, is the relevant period for the purposes of subsection (7) of that section) or, if the claim period in question is the first relevant claim period (as defined in that section), the proportion of the expenditure so allowable for that claim period shall be computed under that section subject to the provisions of sub-paragraph (5) below.

(4) If the disposal takes place after the end of the claim period in which the use of the asset in connection with the field permanently ceases, then, as regards the claim period in which the disposal takes place—

(*a*) subsection (7) of section 4 of this Act shall have effect in relation to the asset as if its use in that connection had permanently ceased in that claim period (but so that for the purposes of subsections (5) and (6) of that section as applied by the said subsection (7) the asset shall not be treated as having been used in that connection at any time when it was not so used); and

(*b*) the proportion of the expenditure allowable under that section for the relevant period (that is to say the period which, in relation to that claim period is the relevant period for the purposes of the said subsection (7)) shall be computed under that section subject to the provisions of sub-paragraph (5) below.

(5) For the purposes of the computation mentioned in sub-paragraph (3) or (4) above, as the case may be—

(*a*) the amount of the expenditure incurred in acquiring, bringing into existence, or enhancing the value of the asset which would otherwise fall to be taken into account shall be treated as reduced by the amount or value of the consideration received or receivable for the disposal (or, if equal to or smaller than the amount or value of that consideration, as reduced to nil); and

(*b*) the asset's useful life shall be treated as having ended at the time of the disposal or, if the asset permanently ceased to be used in connection with the field before that time and was neither used nor available for use by anyone in the interval between its permanently ceasing to be so used and the time of the disposal, at the time when it permanently ceased to be so used.

(6) In any case where, for different parts of the expenditure incurred in the case of an asset as mentioned in sub-paragraph (1) above, different proportions thereof would be allowable under section 4 of this Act apart from sub-paragraph (5)(*a*) above (including a case where, for some but not all of that expenditure, the proportion thereof so allowable would be 100 per cent.), the amount of value of the consideration received or receivable for the disposition shall for the purposes of this paragraph be treated as referable to those different parts in such proportions as may be just and reasonable.

(7) Section 4(13) of this Act applies to the preceding provisions of this paragraph; and those provisions shall, with any necessary modifications, apply in relation to a disposal of an interest in an asset as they apply in relation to a disposal of an asset.

(8) [Section 1122 of CTA 2010][1] (connected persons) shall apply for the purposes of this paragraph.

Amendments—[1] In sub-para (8) words substituted for words "Section 839 of the Taxes Act" by CTA 2010 s 1177, Sch 1 para 166(3). CTA 2010 has effect for corporation tax purposes for accounting periods ending on or after 1 April 2010, and for income and capital gains tax purposes for the tax year 2010–11 and subsequent tax years.

Long-term assets used in connection with more than one oil field

5 (*repealed* by OTA 1983 s 15(6), Sch 6).

Provisions supplementary to section 4(9) of this Act and paragraph 5(2) above

6—(1) Where in the case of an oil field, the total amount of the expenditure allowable under sections 3 and 4 of this Act on a claim for a claim period—

(*a*) is, under one or more of the relevant provisions, reduced to nil; and

(*b*) would, under one or more of those provisions, have fallen to be reduced by a further amount if the total amount of that expenditure had been sufficient to enable the maximum reduction thereunder to be made,

that further amount shall be apportioned between the participators in proportions corresponding to what for that claim period would be their respective shares of any expenditure falling within section 2(9)(b)(i) of this Act; and in computing the assessable profit or allowable loss accruing to any participator in the earliest chargeable period which ends after the end of that claim period, the aggregate mentioned in section 2(4)(a) of this Act shall be increased by an amount equal to the amount apportioned to him under this paragraph.

(2) In this paragraph "the relevant provisions" means section 4(9) of this Act and paragraph 5(2) above.

Insurance or compensation in respect of loss or destruction of long-term asset formerly used in connection with oil field

7—(1) Where, in consequence of the loss or destruction at any time within the period mentioned in sub-paragraph (1) of paragraph 4 above of such an asset as is mentioned in that sub-paragraph, any insurance or compensation in respect of the loss or destruction is receivable by a participator in the field or a person connected with a participator, paragraphs 4 and 6 above shall apply as if at that time the person by whom the insurance or compensation is receivable had disposed of the asset or his interest in it for an amount equal to the insurance or compensation.

(2) [Section 1122 of CTA 2010][1] (connected persons) shall apply for the purposes of this paragraph.

Amendments—[1] In sub-para (2) words substituted for words "Section 839 of the Taxes Act" by CTA 2010 s 1177, Sch 1 para 166(4). CTA 2010 has effect for corporation tax purposes for accounting periods ending on or after 1 April 2010, and for income and capital gains tax purposes for the tax year 2010–11 and subsequent tax years.

Assets acquired jointly by participators in different oil fields

8 Where an asset was acquired jointly by persons who are participators in two or more different oil fields (whether or not any one of those persons is a participator in more than one of those fields), then in determining for the purposes of section 4 of this Act, in the case of any one of those fields, the use which has been, or which it is reasonable to assume will be, made of the asset otherwise than in connection with that field, no regard shall be had to its use or possible use in connection with any other of those fields.

SCHEDULE 5

ALLOWANCE OF EXPENDITURE (OTHER THAN ABORTIVE EXPLORATION EXPENDITURE)

Sections 3 and 4

Claim periods and claims

1—(1) In relation to any oil field—

(*a*) the first claim period is whichever of the following periods the responsible person elects, namely the period ending at the end of June following the determination of the field or the period ending at the end of December following that determination (including, in either case, an unlimited time prior to that determination);

(*b*) each subsequent claim period is whichever of the following periods the responsible person elects, namely the period of six months or the period of twelve months from the end of the preceding claim period:

Provided that unless and until the responsible person elects the period of six months from the end of any particular claim period, the claim period next after that claim period shall be taken to be the period of twelve months from the end of it.

(2) An election under this paragraph must be made by notice in writing to the Board.

HMRC Manuals—Oil Taxation Manual OT04420 (claims by responsible person, first claim period).

2—(1) A claim under this Schedule for the allowance of any expenditure allowable under section 3 or 4 of this Act for an oil field must be made by the responsible person to the Board and, subject to the provisions of this Part of this Act, must be made in a claim or claims for the claim period in which the expenditure is incurred, but may not be made before the determination of the field or more than [4 years][3] after the end of the claim period in which the expenditure is incurred.

(2) A claim under this Schedule for the allowance of any expenditure allowable under section 3 or 4 of this Act for an oil field which was incurred by a person before he became a participator in the field must be made in a claim for the claim period in which he became a participator.

(3) A claim under this Schedule shall not include any expenditure allowable under section 3 or 4 of this Act which has been included in a claim under Schedule 6 to this Act.

(4) A claim must state—

(*a*) what part (if any) of the expenditure is claimed as qualifying for supplement under section 2(9)(*b*)(ii) of this Act; and

(*b*) [Subject for paragraph 2A below][1] the shares in which, in accordance with their respective interests in the oil field, the participators propose to divide between them, for the purposes of paragraph (*b*) of section 2(9) of this Act, the expenditure allowed on the claim and the amount which will arise under sub-paragraph (ii) of that paragraph if some or all of that expenditure is allowed on the claim as so qualifying.

(5) Where a claim for the allowance of any expenditure under section 4 of this Act for an oil field was made in relation to any asset for the claim period which, in the case of that asset, is the first relevant claim period (as defined in that section), then any claim with respect to that field made under

this Schedule for any subsequent claim period must give all such information as is relevant for the purpose of enabling the Board to carry into effect the provisions of that section in relation to that asset.

(6) A claim must be in such form as the Board may prescribe and must include a declaration that all statements contained in it are correct to the best of the knowledge and belief of the person making the claim.

[(7) Where—

(*a*) the claim period in which any expenditure allowable under section 3 or 4 of this Act for an oil field is incurred coincides with or includes a chargeable period, and

(*b*) the Board has extended the period for the delivery of the return that is required under paragraph 5 of Schedule 2 to this Act to be delivered for that chargeable period by the responsible person, and

(*c*) the relevant time falls more than [2 years][3] after the end of the claim period,

sub-paragraph (1) above shall have effect as if the reference to [4 years][3] after the end of the claim period in which the expenditure is incurred were a reference to two years after the relevant time.

(8) In sub-paragraph (7) above "the relevant time" means the earlier of—

(*a*) the time which, as a result of the extension mentioned in that sub-paragraph, is the latest time for the delivery of the return there mentioned; and

(*b*) the time when that return is delivered.][2]

HMRC Manuals—Oil Taxation Manual OT04420 (claims by responsible person).
OT04390 (claims outline).

Press releases etc—IR 16-12-87 (Petroleum Revenue Tax: Safeguard and Deferred Expenditure Claims).
IR Tax Bulletin April 1996 (withdrawal of PRT expenditure claims).

Modification—FA 1993 Sch 20A para 8 (as inserted by FA 2008 Sch 33 para 1) (If the Commissioners specify the period within which a PRT return must be delivered, sub-paras (7), (8) (including these provisions as applied to Sch 6 by Sch 6 para 2) apply to the specified period as if it were a period for the delivery of a PRT return that has been extended under OTA 1975 Sch 2 para 2).

Amendments—[1] Words in sub-para (4) inserted by FA 1991 s 107(1).
[2] Sub-paras (7), (8) inserted by FA 1999 s 102(4) with effect in relation to chargeable periods ending on or after 30 June 1999.
[3] In sub-para (1) and words after sub-para (7)(*c*), words substituted by FA 2009 s 99, Sch 51 paras 17, 23 with effect from 1 April 2011 (SI 2010/867).

[2A—(1) This paragraph applies if—

(*a*) a current participator ("the defaulter") has defaulted on a liability under—

(i) a relevant agreement, or

(ii) an abandonment programme,

to make a payment towards abandonment expenditure, and

(*b*) a current or former participator ("the contributing participator") pays an amount in or towards meeting the whole or part of the default ("a default payment").

(2) If a claim is made under this Schedule for the allowance of the abandonment expenditure, the amount of the default payment is to be attributed to the contributing participator for the purposes of paragraphs 2(4)(*b*) and 3(1)(*c*).

(3) But the amount attributed under sub-paragraph (2) may not exceed—

(*a*) so much of the sum in default as the contributing participator is required to meet in accordance with—

(i) the relevant agreement, or

(ii) the abandonment programme, or

(*b*) such other amount as the participator may be required to meet in accordance with a direction given under Part 4 of the Petroleum Act 1998.

(4) Sub-paragraph (2) is subject to paragraph 2B.

(5) In determining the amount which is to be attributed to the contributing participator under sub-paragraph (2), account shall be taken of the whole of the defaulter's interest in the relevant oil field.

(6) But in determining the share of the abandonment expenditure to be attributed to the defaulter under paragraph 2(4)(*b*), the amount which would be attributed by reference to the defaulter's interest in the relevant oil field is to be reduced or (as the case may be) extinguished by the deduction of the aggregate of—

(*a*) the amount attributed to the contributing participator under sub-paragraph (2), and

(*b*) any other amounts attributed under sub-paragraph (2) to other current or former participators who make default payments in respect of the defaulter's default.][1]

Amendments—[1] Paras 2A–2C substituted for para 2A by FA 2008 s 103 with effect in relation to expenditure incurred after 30 June 2008.

[2B—(1) No amount is to be attributed to a contributing participator under paragraph 2A(2) unless the following conditions are all met.

(2) The first condition is that the contributing participator is not connected with the defaulter, applying [section 1122 of CTA 2010][2] (connected persons) for the purposes of this sub-paragraph.

(3) The second condition is that, at the end of the claim period for which the claim is made, the defaulter still has an interest in the relevant oil field which, under paragraph 2(4)(*b*), falls to be taken into account in determining the shares in the abandonment expenditure.

(4) The third condition is that the relevant participators have taken all reasonable steps by way of legal remedy—

(*a*) to secure that the defaulter meets the whole of the liability referred to in paragraph 2A(1)(*a*), and

(*b*) to enforce any guarantee or other security provided in respect of that liability.

(5) In sub-paragraph (4) "relevant participators" means—

(*a*) each current participator (other than the defaulter), and

(*b*) each former participator who makes a default payment in respect of the defaulter's default.][1]

Amendments—[1] Paras 2A–2C substituted for para 2A by FA 2008 s 103 with effect in relation to expenditure incurred after 30 June 2008.

[2] In sub-para (2) words substituted for words "section 839 of the Taxes Act" by CTA 2010 s 1177, Sch 1 para 167. CTA 2010 has effect for corporation tax purposes for accounting periods ending on or after 1 April 2010, and for income and capital gains tax purposes for the tax year 2010–11 and subsequent tax years.

[2C—(1) An amount attributed under paragraph 2A(2) is—

(*a*) in the case of a current participator, to be an addition to the share of the abandonment expenditure referable to the current participator's interest in the oil field, or

(*b*) in the case of a former participator, to be the share of the abandonment expenditure referable to the former participator's interest in the oil field.

(2) In paragraphs 2A and 2B and this paragraph—

"abandonment expenditure" means expenditure which is allowable for an oil field by virtue of section 3(1)(*i*) or (*j*);

"abandonment programme" means an abandonment programme approved under Part 4 of the Petroleum Act 1998 (including any such programme as revised);

"current participator" means a person who is, by virtue of paragraph (*a*), [(*aa*),][2] (*b*) or (*c*) of the definition in section 12, a participator in the relevant oil field in the chargeable period in which the abandonment expenditure is incurred;

"former participator" means a person who—

(*a*) is not a current participator, but

(*b*) was, by virtue of paragraph (*a*), [(*aa*),][2] (*b*) or (*c*) of the definition in section 12, a participator in the relevant oil field in any chargeable period before the chargeable period in which the abandonment expenditure is incurred;

"relevant agreement" has the meaning given by section 104(5)(*a*) of the Finance Act 1991;

"relevant oil field" means the oil field to which the abandonment expenditure relates;

"sum in default" means the amount of the payment which the defaulter is liable to make as mentioned in paragraph 2A(1)(*a*), [less so much of that payment as has been made by the defaulter][3]

(3) For the purposes of paragraph 2A, a current participator is to be regarded as defaulting on a liability to make a payment towards abandonment expenditure if the following conditions are met.

(4) The first condition is that the current participator has failed to make the payment in full on the due day.

(5) The second condition is that—

(*a*) any of the payment remains unpaid on the sixtieth day after the due day, or

(*b*) before that sixtieth day, the current participator's interest in a relevant licence becomes liable under the relevant agreement to be sold or forfeited, in whole or in part, by reason of the failure to meet the liability.

(6) In sub-paragraphs (4) and (5) "due day" means the day on which the payment towards abandonment expenditure becomes due under the relevant agreement or the abandonment programme.][1]

Amendments—[1] Paras 2A–2C substituted for para 2A by FA 2008 s 103 with effect in relation to expenditure incurred after 30 June 2008.

[2] In sub-para (2) words inserted by FA 2009 s 88, Sch 42 paras 1, 3 with effect in relation to persons who cease to be licensees because of cessation events occurring in chargeable periods that begin after 30 June 2009.

[3] In sub-para (2), in definition of "sum in default", words substituted by FA 2013 s 89(1), Sch 31 para 4 with effect in relation to expenditure incurred on or after 17 July 2013.

3—(1) The Board shall by notice in writing to the responsible person inform him of their decision on the claim, stating in the notice—

(*a*) the amount of the expenditure allowed by them on the claim;

PRT

(*b*) the amount, if any, of that expenditure allowed by them on the claim as qualifying for supplement under section 2(9)(*b*)(ii) of this Act; and

(*c*) the shares determined by the Board to be the shares in which, in the opinion of the Board, the amount stated under (*a*) above or, as the case may be, the aggregate of that amount and an amount equal to the relevant percentage of the amount stated under (*b*) above, is divisible between the participators for the purposes of section 2(9)(*b*) of this Act;

and where the decision relates to part only of the expenditure claimed, or claimed as so qualifying, the Board shall give a further notice or notices in relation to the remainder.

(2) In this paragraph "the relevant percentage" means the percentage mentioned in the said section 2(9)(*b*)(ii);

HMRC Manuals—Oil Taxation Manual OT04630 (decisions).

4 If, in a case where sub-paragraph (5) of paragraph 2 above requires a claim made for a particular claim period to give all such information as is relevant for the purpose there mentioned in relation to an asset, a claim satisfying the requirements of that sub-paragraph is not made within twelve months after the end of that period, then, in carrying into effect the provisions of section 4 of this Act in relation to that asset for that claim period, the Board may proceed accordingly to the best of their judgment, and may make any adjustments under any of the provisions mentioned in paragraph 6(2) of Schedule 4 to this Act accordingly.

HMRC Manuals—Oil Taxation Manual OT04630 (decisions).

Appeals

5—(1) If—

(*a*) the amount or total of the amounts stated under sub-paragraph (1)(*a*) of paragraph 3 above in the notice or notices given by the Board under that paragraph on a claim, or the amount or total of the amounts so stated under sub-paragraph (1)(*b*) of that paragraph, is less than the amount claimed; or

(*b*) the shares so stated under sub-paragraph (1)(*c*) of that paragraph in the notice or latest of the notices so given differ from the shares stated under paragraph 2(4)(*b*) above in the claim,

the responsible person may [appeal][1] by notice in writing given to the Board not more than three years after the making of the claim . . . [1]; but the bringing of an appeal under this paragraph shall not affect the operation of any notice so given by the Board.

(2) On an appeal [that is notified to the tribunal][1] against a decision on a claim brought on the ground mentioned in sub-paragraph (1)(*b*) above, and in any proceedings arising out of such an appeal, any participator in the oil field to which the claim relates shall be entitled to [be a party][1].

(3) An appeal against a decision on a claim may at any time [before it is notified to the tribunal][1] be abandoned by a notice in writing given to the Board by the responsible person.

(4) On an appeal [that is notified to the tribunal][1] against a decision on a claim, the [tribunal][1] may vary the decision appealed against whether or not the variation is to the advantage of all or any of the participators in the oil field to which the claim relates.

[(5) The provisions of paragraphs 14A to 14I of Schedule 2 shall apply to appeals under this paragraph subject to any necessary modifications.][1]

HMRC Manuals—Oil Taxation Manual OT04690 (appeals against claim decisions).

Amendments—[1] In sub-para (1), words inserted and words substituted for words "appeal to the Special Commissioners", in sub-para (2), words inserted and words substituted for words "appear and be heard", in sub-para (3), words inserted, in sub-para (4), words inserted and words substituted for words "Special Commissioners", and sub-para (5) inserted, by the Transfer of Tribunal Functions and Revenue and Customs Appeals Order, SI 2009/56 art 3, Sch 1 paras 68, 76, 77 with effect from 1 April 2009.

6—(1) Where the responsible person gives notice of appeal against a decision on a claim on one or both of the grounds mentioned in paragraph 5(1)(*a*) above and, before the appeal is determined by the [tribunal][1], the Board and the responsible person agree on—

(*a*) the amount of the expenditure that ought to be allowed on the claim; or

(*b*) the amount, if any, of the expenditure claimed which ought to be so allowed as qualifying for supplement under section 2(9)(*b*)(ii) of this Act;

the appropriate amount (if any) of the expenditure claimed or, as the case may be, claimed as so qualifying shall be treated for the purposes of this Part of this Act as having been allowed by the Board on the claim, and as having been so allowed on the date on which the notice of appeal was given.

For the purposes of this sub-paragraph the appropriate amount (if any) of the expenditure claimed or, as the case may be, claimed as so qualifying, is an amount thereof equal to the excess, if any, of the amount so agreed on over the corresponding amount or the total of the corresponding amounts allowed by the notice or notices previously given by the Board under paragraph 3 above.

(2) Where the responsible person gives notice of appeal against a decision on a claim on the ground mentioned in paragraph 5(1)(*b*) above and, before the appeal is determined by the [tribunal[1], the Board and the responsible person agree on the shares in which the amount of any expenditure allowed on the claim, or so allowed as qualifying for supplement under section 2(9)(*b*)(ii) of this Act, ought to be divided between the participators for the purposes of section 2(9)(*b*) of this Act, the shares so agreed on shall be deemed to be the shares stated in any notice previously given by the Board under paragraph 3 above on the claim, and shall apply in the case of any part of the expenditure claimed, or claimed as so qualifying, which is by virtue of this or the following paragraph treated as having been allowed on the claim;

(3) Where the Board and the responsible person agree on the matter mentioned in sub-paragraph (1)(*a*), sub-paragraph (1)(*b*) or sub-paragraph (2) above in the circumstances there mentioned, the corresponding ground of appeal shall be treated as having been abandoned; and where by virtue of this sub-paragraph all the grounds of the appeal fall to be so treated, the appeal itself shall be treated as having been abandoned.

HMRC Manuals—Oil Taxation Manual OT04690 (appeals against claim decisions).

Amendments—[1] In sub-paras (1), (2), word substituted for words "Special Commissioners", by the Transfer of Tribunal Functions and Revenue and Customs Appeals Order, SI 2009/56 art 3, Sch 1 paras 68, 76, 78 with effect from 1 April 2009.

7—(1) Where[,][1] on an appeal under paragraph 5 above [that is notified to the tribunal, the tribunal determines][1] that any amount or part of an amount in dispute is allowable under section 3 or 4 of this Act or qualifies for supplement under section 2(9)(*b*)(ii) of this Act, the following provisions of this paragraph shall apply;

(2) Subject to paragraph 8(2) below, the said amount or part shall be treated for the purposes of this Part of this Act as having been allowed on the claim to which the appeal relates, and as having been so allowed on the date on which the notice of appeal was given.

(3) There shall be made in any computation made under section 2 of this Act, and in any assessment to tax or determination, all such adjustments as are necessary in consequence of the determination of the [tribunal][1].

HMRC Manuals—Oil Taxation Manual OT04690 (appeals against claim decisions).

Amendments—[1] In sub-para (1), comma inserted, and words substituted for words "the Special Commissioners determine", and in sub-para (3), word substituted for words "Special Commissioners", by the Transfer of Tribunal Functions and Revenue and Customs Appeals Order, SI 2009/56 art 3, Sch 1 paras 68, 76, 79 with effect from 1 April 2009.

8—(1) Where—

[(*a*) an appeal is made against a determination by the tribunal on an appeal under paragraph 5 above; and][4]

(*b*) in the proceedings on the [appeal so made][3], or in any proceedings arising out of those proceedings, any matter which was determined by the [tribunal][4] on that appeal is finally determined otherwise than in accordance with their determination on [the appeal under paragraph 5 above][3],

the following provisions of this paragraph shall apply.

(2) Any expenditure allowable under section 3 or 4 of this Act, which, if the decision of the Board on the claim to which the appeal under paragraph 5 above related had been in accordance with the final determination of that matter, would have been allowed by that decision, or allowed by it as qualifying for supplement under section 2(9)(*b*)(ii) of this Act, shall be treated for the purposes of this Part of this Act as having been allowed by the Board on the claim to the extent that it has not been previously allowed on the claim, and as having been so allowed to that extent on the date on which the original notice of appeal was given under paragraph 5 above.

(3) There shall be made in any computation made under section 2 of this Act and in any assessment to tax or determination all such adjustments or further adjustments as are necessary in consequence of the final determination.

(4) Any tax which becomes payable in consequence of any adjustment made under sub-paragraph (3) above in an assessment for a chargeable period shall carry interest at the [rate applicable under section 178 of the Finance Act 1989][2] from [two months][1] after the end of that period to the date of payment.

(5) For the purposes of this paragraph a matter shall not be deemed to be finally determined in any such proceedings as are mentioned in sub-paragraph (1)(*b*) above until a determination thereof made in any such proceedings can no longer be varied or overruled by the order of any court [or the tribunal][4].

HMRC Manuals—Oil Taxation Manual OT04690 (appeals against claim decisions).

Amendments—[1] Words in sub-para (4) substituted by the Petroleum Revenue Tax Act 1980 s 2(1).

[2] Words in sub-para (4) substituted, in relation to periods beginning on or after 18 August 1989, by FA 1989 s 179.

[3] Words in sub-para (1) substituted by SI 1994/1813, reg 2(1), Sch 1 para 19.

[4] Sub-para (1)(*a*) substituted, in sub-para (1)(*b*) word substituted for words "Special Commissioners", and in sub-para (5), words inserted, by the Transfer of Tribunal Functions and Revenue and Customs Appeals Order, SI 2009/56 art 3, Sch 1 paras 68, 76, 80 with effect from 1 April 2009.

[9—(1) If ...[4] it appears to the Board that the relevant amount was incorrectly stated [in a notice of a decision under paragraph 3 above given to the responsible person for an oil field][4] the Board may before the expiry of [the permitted period][4] serve on the responsible person a notice stating what appears to the Board to be the correct amount (referred to below as "the notice of variation").

...[2]

(2) In this paragraph "the relevant amount", in relation to a notice of a decision on a claim under paragraph 3 above, means any one or more of the following—

(*a*) the amount of expenditure allowed on the claim;

(*b*) the amount of that expenditure allowed as qualifying for supplement under section 2(9)(*b*)(ii) of this Act;

(*c*) where different percentages were stated in that notice to apply to different parts of that expenditure for the purpose of calculating the supplement, each of those parts of that expenditure.

...[2]

[(2B) In this paragraph "permitted period" means the period of 4 years beginning with the date on which the notice of the decision under paragraph 3 was given (but see sub-paragraph (2C)).

(2C) Where the relevant amount was overstated in the notice of decision as a result of an inaccuracy in a statement or declaration made by the responsible person (or a person acting on behalf of the responsible person) in connection with the claim—

(*a*) if the inaccuracy was careless, the permitted period is extended to 6 years, and

(*b*) if the inaccuracy was deliberate, the permitted period is extended to 20 years.][4]

(3) The responsible person may, by notice in writing given to the Board not more than thirty days after the notice of variation was served on him, appeal . . .[3] against the notice of variation.

(4) A notice of appeal under sub-paragraph (3) shall state the grounds on which the appeal is brought.

(5) An appeal under this paragraph may at any time [before it is notified to the tribunal][3] be abandoned by notice in writing given to the Board by the responsible person.

(6) A notice of variation may be withdrawn at any time before it becomes effective.

(7) In any case where—

(*a*) the responsible person gives notice of appeal against a notice of variation, and

(*b*) before the appeal is determined by the [tribunal][3], the Board and the responsible person agree as to what the relevant amount ought to be,

the notice of variation shall have effect subject to such modifications as may be necessary to give effect to that agreement; and thereupon the appeal shall be treated as having been abandoned.

(8) On an appeal [that is notified to the tribunal][3] against a notice of variation the [tribunal][3] may vary the notice, quash the notice or dismiss the appeal; and the notice may be varied whether or not the variation is to the advantage of all or any of the participators in the oil field in question.

(9) Where a notice of variation relating to a decision on a claim becomes effective, the relevant amount shall be taken for the purposes of this Part of this Act as having been reduced or increased, as the case may require, on the date on which notice of the decision was given, by such amount as may be necessary to give effect to that notice, and the Board may make such computations under section 2 of this Act and such assessments or determinations or such amendments of assessments or determinations as may be necessary in consequence of that reduction or increase.

(10) A notice of variation becomes effective for the purposes of this paragraph either—

(*a*) on the expiry of the period during which notice of appeal against the notice of variation may be given . . .[3] under sub-paragraph (3) above without such notice of appeal being given; or

(*b*) where such notice of appeal is given, when the notice of variation can no longer be varied or quashed by the [tribunal][3] or by the order of any court.

...[2].][1]

[(12) For the purposes of this section, an inaccuracy in a statement or declaration made by the responsible person (or a person acting on behalf of the responsible person) is careless if it is due to a failure by the person to take reasonable care.

(13) An inaccuracy in a statement or declaration made by the responsible person (or a person acting on behalf of the responsible person) is to be treated as careless if—

(*a*) the responsible person, the person who acted on behalf of the responsible person or any person who becomes the responsible person for the oil field after the statement or declaration is made discovers the inaccuracy some time after it is made, and

(*b*) that person fails to take reasonable steps to inform Her Majesty's Revenue and Customs.][4]

HMRC Manuals—Oil Taxation Manual OT04750 (notices of variations).

Amendments—[1] Para 9 inserted by FA 1983 s 40(1).

[2] Sub-paras (1A)–(1C), (2A), (11) omitted by FA 2009 s 99 and Sch 51 para 24(3) with effect from 1 April 2011 (SI 2010/867). Paras previously inserted, and sub-para (11) substituted, by FA 1990 s 122(1)–(4).

3 In sub-paras (3), (10)(*a*) words "to the Special Commissioners" repealed, in sub-para (5) words inserted, in sub-paras (7), (10)(*b*), word substituted for words "Special Commissioners", in sub-para (8), words inserted, and word substituted for words "Special Commissioners", by the Transfer of Tribunal Functions and Revenue and Customs Appeals Order, SI 2009/56 art 3, Sch 1 paras 68, 76, 81 with effect from 1 April 2009.

4 In sub-para (1), words omitted and words substituted and sub-paras (2B), (2B), (12) and (13) inserted by FA 2009 s 99, Sch 51 paras 17, 24 with effect from 1 April 2011 (SI 2010/867).

[10 In this Schedule "tribunal" means the First-tier Tribunal or, where determined by or under Tribunal Procedure Rules, the Upper Tribunal.][1]

Amendments—[1] This para inserted by the Transfer of Tribunal Functions and Revenue and Customs Appeals Order, SI 2009/56 art 3, Sch 1 paras 68, 76, 82 with effect from 1 April 2009.

SCHEDULE 6

ALLOWANCE OF EXPENDITURE (OTHER THAN ABORTIVE EXPLORATION EXPENDITURE) ON CLAIM BY PARTICIPATOR

Sections 3 and 4

1—(1) A claim for the allowance of any expenditure allowable under section 3 or 4 of this Act for an oil field may be made to the Board under this Schedule by the participator who incurred it (instead of under Schedule 5 to this Act by the responsible person for that field) if the participator satisfies the Board that, for reasons of trade secrecy, it would be unreasonable for him to have to provide the responsible person with the information necessary for the making of a claim under that Schedule.

(2) A claim by a participator under this Schedule for the allowance of any such expenditure incurred by him must, subject to the provisions of this Part of this Act, be made in a claim or claims for the claim period in which the expenditure is incurred, but may not be made before the determination of the field or more than [4 years][1] after the end of the claim period in which the expenditure is incurred.

(3) A claim by a participator under this Schedule for the allowance of any such expenditure incurred by him before he became a participator in the field must be made in a claim for the claim period in which he became a participator.

HMRC Manuals—Oil Taxation Manual OT04480 (claims by participators).

Modification—Sub-para (1) modified by FA 1991 s 108(6), in relation to claims by a defaulter for the allowance of reimbursement expenditure.

Amendments—[1] In sub-para (2) words substituted by FA 2009 s 99, Sch 51 paras 17, 25(1), (2) with effect from 1 April 2011 (SI 2010/867).

2 The provisions of Schedule 5 to this Act specified in the first column of the following Table shall apply in relation to a claim under this Schedule as they apply in relation to a claim under that Schedule subject to any modifications specified in the second column of that Table and with the substitution, for references to the responsible person, of references to the participator by whom the claim under this Schedule is made and, for references to section 2(9)(*b*)(ii) of this Act, of references to section 2(9)(*c*)(ii) of this Act.

TABLE

Provisions applied	**Modifications**
Paragraph	
2(3)	For the reference to this Schedule substitute a reference to Schedule 5 to this Act.
(4)	Omit paragraph.
(5)	—
(6)	—
[(7)	For the reference to paragraph 5 of Schedule 2 to this Act substitute a reference to paragraph 2 of that Schedule; for the reference to paragraph 2(1) of Schedule 5 to this Act substitute a reference to paragraph 1(2) of this Schedule.][3]
[8	—][3]
3(1)	Omit paragraph (*c*).
4	—
5(1)	Omit paragraph.
(3)	—
(4)	For the reference to all or any of the participators substitute a reference to the participator by whom the claim is made.
[5(5)	—][4]

Provisions applied	Modifications
Paragraph	
6(1)	—
(3)	Omit the reference to paragraph 6(2).
7	—
8	—
[9][1]	...[5].][2]

HMRC Manuals—Oil Taxation Manual OT04600 (PRT administration).

Amendments—[1] In column 1 of the Table, entry for "9" inserted by FA 1983 s 40(2).

[2] In column 2 of the Table, words in the entry for "9" inserted by FA 1990 s 122(5).

[3] Entries in Table relating to paras 2(7) and (8) inserted by FA 1999 s 102(5) with effect in relation to chargeable periods ending on or after 30 June 1999.

[4] Entry inserted by the Transfer of Tribunal Functions and Revenue and Customs Appeals Order, SI 2009/56 art 3, Sch 1 paras 68, 83 with effect from 1 April 2009.

[5] In Table in entry in second column relating to para 9 repealed by FA 2009 s 99, Sch 51 paras 17, 25(1), (3) with effect from 1 April 2011 (SI 2010/867).

SCHEDULE 7

ALLOWANCE OF ABORTIVE EXPLORATION EXPENDITURE

Section 5

Allowance of abortive exploration expenditure

1— (1) A claim for the allowance, in connection with an oil field,

[(*a*) of any abortive exploration expenditure allowable under section 5 of this Act, or

(*b*) of any exploration and appraisal expenditure allowable under section 5A of this Act][1], [or

(*c*) of any research expenditure allowable under section 5B of this Act][2]

in the case of a participator in that field must be made by the participator to the Board, . . . [1].

(2) Where a claim under this Schedule has been made and the participator by whom it was made subsequently discovers that an error or mistake has been made in the claim, he may make a supplementary claim . . . [1].

(3) The provisions of Schedule 5 to this Act specified in the first column of the following Table shall apply in relation to a claim under this Schedule as they apply in relation to a claim under that Schedule, subject to any modifications specified in the second column of that Table and with the substitution, for references to the responsible person, of references to the participator by whom the claim under this Schedule is made and, for references to section 3 or 4 of this Act, of references to section 5 [or, as the case may be, section 5A [or section 5B][2]][1] of this Act.

Table

Provisions applied	Modifications
Paragraph	
2(6)	—
3(1)	Omit paragraphs (*b*) and (*c*).
5(1)	Omit the words from "or the amount" to "(1)(*b*) of that paragraph" and paragraph.
(3)	—
(4)	For the reference to all or any of the participators substitute a reference to the participator by whom the claim is made.
[5(5)	—][4]
6(1)	For "one or both of the grounds" substitute "the ground", and omit paragraph (*b*) and the words "or, as the case may be, claimed as so qualifying" (wherever occurring).
(3)	Omit "sub-paragraph (1)(*b*) or sub-paragraph (2)", and for the words from "the corresponding" to "itself" substitute "the appeal".
7	In sub-paragraph (1), omit the words from "or qualifies" to "2(9)(*b*)(ii) of this Act".
8	In sub-paragraph (2) omit the words from "or allowed by it" to "section 2(9)(*b*)(ii) of this Act".

Provisions applied	**Modifications**
Paragraph	
[9	...[2] in sub-paragraph (2) omit paragraphs (*b*) and (*c*), ...[3] in sub-paragraph (8) for the reference to all or any of the participators substitute a reference to the participator by whom the claim is made[5] ..."][2].

HMRC Manuals—Oil Taxation Manual OT04510 (claims by participators).

Amendments—[1] Sub-para (1)(*a*), (*b*) substituted, words in sub-paras (1), (2) repealed, and words in sub-para (3) inserted by FA 1983 ss 37, 48, Sch 8 Pt II para 6, Sch 10 Pt III.

[2] Sub-para (1)(*c*), words in sub-para (2), and entry in Table relating to para 9 inserted by FA 1987 ss 64, 67, Sch 13 Pt II para 5. Words in entry in column 2 of Table relating to para 9 subsequently omitted by FA 2009 s 99, Sch 51 para 26(a) with effect from 1 April 2011 (SI 2010/867).

[3] Words in entry in column 2 of Table relating to para 9 omitted by FA 2009 s 99, Sch 51 para 26(a) with effect from 1 April 2011 (SI 2010/867). Words previously inserted by FA 1990 s 122(6).

[4] Entry inserted by the Transfer of Tribunal Functions and Revenue and Customs Appeals Order, SI 2009/56 art 3, Sch 1 paras 68, 84 with effect from 1 April 2009.

[5] Words in entry relating to para 9 omitted by FA 2009 s 99, Sch 51 para 26(b) with effect from 1 April 2011 (SI 2010/867).

SCHEDULE 8

ALLOWANCE OF UNRELIEVABLE FIELD LOSS

Section 6

Reference and determination of question of abandonment of oil field

1 Where it appears to the responsible person for an oil field that the winning of oil from the field has permanently ceased he may by notice in writing given to the Board refer to them for their decision the question whether the winning of oil from that field has permanently ceased.

HMRC Manuals—Oil Taxation Manual OT16350 (permanent cessation of winning oil).

2— (1) The Board shall, by notice in writing given to the responsible person, inform him of their decision on the question and, if their decision is that the winning of oil has so ceased, shall state the date which they are satisfied is that on which the winning of oil from the field in question ceased.

(2) The responsible person shall, within one month of his receiving a notice under sub-paragraph (1) above informing him of the Board's decision, furnish a copy of that notice to every person who was at any time a participator in the field in question.

HMRC Manuals—Oil Taxation Manual OT16350 (permanent cessation of winning oil).

3—(1) The responsible person may appeal . . . [1] against the Board's decision by notice in writing given to the Board within three months of his receiving the notice under paragraph 2(1) above informing him thereof.

(2) An appeal under sub-paragraph (1) above may at any time [before it is notified to the tribunal][1] be abandoned by notice in writing given to the Board by the responsible person.

[(3) The provisions of paragraphs 14A to 14I of Schedule 2 shall apply to appeals under this paragraph subject to any necessary modifications.][1]

HMRC Manuals—Oil Taxation Manual OT16350 (permanent cessation of winning oil).

Amendments—[1] In sub-para (1), words "to the Special Commissioners" repealed, in sub-para (2), words inserted, and sub-para (3) inserted, by the Transfer of Tribunal Functions and Revenue and Customs Appeals Order, SI 2009/56 art 3, Sch 1 paras 68, 84 with effect from 1 April 2009.

Claims by participators for allowance of unrelievable field losses

4—(1) A claim for the allowance, in connection with an oil field, of any unrelievable field loss allowable under section 6 of this Act in the case of a participator in that field must be made by the participator to the Board [at any time after][1] the date of the decision (whether of the Board or on appeal from the Board) that the winning of oil from the oil field in the case of which the loss accrued has permanently ceased, . . . [1]

(2) Where a claim under this Schedule has been made and the participator by whom it was made subsequently discovers that an error or mistake has been made in the claim, he may make a supplementary claim . . . [1]

(3) The provisions of Schedule 5 to this Act specified in the first column of the Table set out in paragraph 1(3) of Schedule 7 to this Act shall apply in relation to a claim under this Schedule as they apply in relation to a claim under the said Schedule 5, subject to any modifications specified in the second column of that Table and with the substitution, for references to the responsible person, of references to the participator by whom the claim under this Schedule is made, for references to the claiming or allowance of expenditure, of references to the claiming or allowance of an unrelievable field loss and, for references to section 3 or 4 of this Act, of references to section 6 of this Act.

HMRC Manuals—Oil Taxation Manual OT16400 (permanent cessation of production but further assessable income).

PRT

Amendments—[1] In sub-paras (1), (2) words omitted repealed and words substituted, in relation to claims made on or after 1 May 1995, by FA 1995 ss 147, 162, Sch 29 Pt IX.

FINANCE (NO 2) ACT 1979

(1979 Chapter 47)

PART III

PETROLEUM REVENUE TAX

19 Reduction of uplift for allowable expenditure

(1) (*amends* OTA 1975 s 2(9)(*b*)(ii) and (*c*)(ii)).

(2) Subject to subsection (3) below, subsection (1) above has effect in relation to expenditure incurred in pursuance of a contract entered into on or after 1 January 1979.

(3) Where expenditure is incurred in pursuance of a contract entered into before the said 1st January but is attributable to a request for an alteration or addition made, or other instruction given, on or after that date by or on behalf of the person incurring the expenditure to another party to the contract, subsection (1) above shall have effect in relation to that expenditure as if the percentage to be substituted for 75 per cent. were 66 2/3 per cent.

(4) Where under paragraph 2(4)(*a*) of Schedule 5 to the said Act of 1975 or that paragraph as applied by Schedule 6 to that Act (claims for allowable expenditure) a claim states that any expenditure is claimed as qualifying for supplement under section 2(9)(*b*)(ii) or (*c*)(ii) of that Act, then, if by virtue of this section those provisions have effect in relation to different parts of that expenditure with different percentages—

(*a*) the claim shall distinguish between those parts;

(*b*) in paragraphs 3(1)(*b*), 6(1)(*b*), 6(2), 7(1) and 8(2) of that Schedule, and in those paragraphs as applied by the said Schedule 6, references to expenditure allowed or which ought to be allowed as qualifying for supplement or to expenditure which does so qualify shall be construed as referring separately to each of those parts; and

(*c*) in paragraph 5(1)(*a*) of that Schedule, and in that paragraph as so applied, the reference to the amount or total of the amounts stated under the said paragraph 3(1)(*b*) shall be construed as a reference to any amount so stated by virtue of paragraph (*b*) above.

(5) Where by virtue of subsection (4) above different amounts are stated under paragraph 3(1)(*b*) of the said Schedule 5 the reference in paragraph 3(1)(*c*) of that Schedule to an amount equal to the relevant percentage of the amount stated under paragraph 3(1)(*b*) shall be construed as a reference to an amount arrived at by applying the appropriate percentage to each of those amounts and aggregating the result.

20 Extension of allowable expenditure

(1), (2) (*amend* OTA 1975 s 3(1)(*f*) and 12(1), Sch 4, para 2).

(3) This section shall have effect in relation to any expenditure in respect of which a claim is made after 31 December 1978.

21 Reduction of oil allowance and metrication of measurements

(1) (*amends* OTA 1975 s 8).

(2) (*amends* OTA 1975 s 1(4)).

(3) (*amends* OTA 1975 s 10(5)).

(4) Subsections (1) and (2) above shall have effect respectively in relation to chargeable periods ending after 31 December 1978 and half years ending after that date and subsection (3) above shall be deemed to have come into force on 1 January 1979.

PART IV

MISCELLANEOUS AND SUPPLEMENTARY

Short title, interpretation, construction and repeals

25—

(1) This Act may be cited as the Finance (No 2) Act 1979.

(2), (3) [not reproduced]

(4) Part III of this Act shall be construed as one with Part I of the Oil Taxation Act 1975.

PETROLEUM REVENUE TAX ACT 1980

(1980 Chapter 1)

An Act to make new provision in respect of petroleum revenue tax so as to require payments on account of tax to be made in advance of the making of an assessment, to bring forward the date from which interest is payable on unpaid and overpaid tax and to provide for altering the rate at which such interest is payable

[31st January 1980]

1 Payments on account of tax

(1) Every participator in an oil field shall, at the time when he delivers to the Board the return for a chargeable period required by paragraph 2 of Schedule 2 to the Oil Taxation Act 1975—

(*a*) deliver to the Board a statement showing whether any, and if so what, amount of tax is payable by him in accordance with the Schedule to this Act for that period in respect of the field; and

(*b*) pay to the Board a sum equal to the amount of tax if any, shown in the statement [less an amount equal to his APRT credit for that chargeable period in respect of that oil field][1].

(2) The statement under subsection (1)(*a*) above shall be in such form as the Board may prescribe.

(3) The sum paid under subsection (1)(*b*) above shall constitute a payment on account of the tax charged in any assessment made on the participator in respect of the assessable profit accruing to him for the chargeable period from the oil field; and if the payment on account exceeds the tax so charged [less the amount of the APRT credit deducted in accordance with subsection (1)(*b*) above from the tax shown in the statement][1]; the excess shall be repaid to the participator.

[(3A) In subsections (1) and (3) above "APRT credit" has the meaning given by section 139(4) of the Finance Act 1982.

(3B) Paragraphs 3 . . . [2] of Schedule 2 of the principal Act (penalties for failure to make returns under paragraph 2 of that Schedule) shall apply in relation to statements required to be made under subsection (1)(*a*) above as they apply in relation to returns required to be made under paragraph 2 of that Schedule][1].

(4) (*amends* the Oil Taxation Act 1975, Sch 2, para 13).

(5) Where a participator gives notice of appeal under paragraph 14 of the said Schedule 2 against an assessment charging tax in respect of which he has made a payment on account, the amount, if any, to be repaid under subsection (3) above shall be calculated as if the tax charged in the assessment were limited to the tax which he would not be entitled to withhold under sub-paragraph (3) of that paragraph.

(6) Certificates of tax deposit issued by the Treasury under section 12 of the National Loans Act 1968 on terms published on or before 14 May 1979 may be used for making payments on account under this section; and for that purpose those terms shall have effect with the necessary modifications and as if the tax in or towards the payment of which a certificate is used were due two months after the end of the chargeable period to which it relates.

HMRC Manuals—Oil Taxation Manual OT04150 (payments on account).

Cross references—FA 2009 Sch 55 (penalty for failure to make returns etc).

Amendments—[1] Words in sub-ss (1), (3), and whole of sub-ss (3A), (3B), inserted by FA 1982 s 139(6), Sch 19 Pt III para 21, with effect in accordance with s 139 thereof.

[2] In sub-s (3B), words ", 8 and 9" repealed by FA 2008 s 122, Sch 40 para 21(*b*) with effect from 1 April 2009 (by virtue of SI 2009/571 art 2).

2 Interest on tax and on repayments

(1), (2) (*amends* OTA 1975 Sch 2 para 15(1), 16, Sch 5 para 8(4)).

(3) Any alteration made under section 89(2) of the Taxes Management Act 1970 in the rate of interest mentioned in the said paragraph 15(1) shall apply also to the rate of interest mentioned in the said paragraphs 8(4) and 16.

3 Short title construction and commencement

(1) This Act may be cited as the Petroleum Revenue Tax Act 1980.

(2) This Act shall be construed as one with Part I of the Oil Taxation Act 1975.

(3) Section 1 above has effect in relation to chargeable periods ending on or after 31 December 1979, section 2(1) and (2) above have effect in relation to tax charged for any such period and section 2(3) above has effect from 1 January 1980.

SCHEDULE

Computation of payment on account

Modification—This Schedule is modified by FA 1980 s 106, Sch 17 para 13(1), by FA 1981 s 111(6) and by the Oil Taxation Act 1983 s 12, Sch 4 para 15.

PRT

1 For the purposes of section 1(1)(*a*) of this Act the tax payable by a participator for any chargeable period in respect of an oil field shall be determined as provided in the following provisions of this Schedule; and references in those provisions to any section or Schedule is a reference to that section or Schedule in the Oil Taxation Act 1975.

2—(1) There shall first be determined whether a computation made in accordance with section 2 as modified by the following provisions of this paragraph would result in an assessable profit, an allowable loss or neither an assessable profit or allowable loss and, if it would result in an assessable profit or allowable loss, the amount of that profit or loss.

(2) The market value, price and amounts referred to in section 2(5), (6)(*b*)(ii) and (7)(*b*) and (*c*) shall be taken from the particulars included in the return in pursuance of paragraph 2(2) and (3) of Schedule 2.

[(2A) The amount of any tariff or disposal receipts, within the meaning of the Oil Taxation Act 1983, shall be taken from the particulars included in the return referred to in sub-paragraph (2) above, and any amount by which any of those tariff receipts are to be treated as reduced under section 9 of that Act shall be determined accordingly].[1]

(3) The amount referred to in section 2(8)(*b*) shall be treated as nil and section 2(9)(*a*), (10) and (11) shall be omitted.

(4) Any expenditure in respect of which a claim has been made under Schedule 5, 6 or 7 and in respect of which the Board have not notified their decision under that Schedule may be treated for the purposes of section 2(9)(*b*), (*c*)[, (*d*), [(*f*) or (*g*)][3]][2]—

(*a*) as having been allowed; and

(*b*) in the case of expenditure claimed as qualifying for supplement under section 2(9)(*b*)(ii) or (*c*)(ii), as having been allowed as so qualifying.

(5) The participator's share of any expenditure which by virtue of sub-paragraph (4) above is treated as having been allowed on a claim under Schedule 5 shall be the share proposed in the claim in pursuance of paragraph 2(4)(*b*) of that Schedule.

(6) Any loss in respect of which a claim has been made under Schedule 8 and in respect of which the Board have not notified their decision under that Schedule may be treated for the purposes of section 2(9)(*e*) as having been allowed.

(7) No expenditure or loss shall be taken into account under sub-paragraph (4), (5) or (6) above in relation to more than one chargeable period or more than one oil field.

Amendments—[1] Sub-para (2A) inserted by the Oil Taxation Act 1983 s 10(6).

[2] In sub-para (4) reference to "(*d*)" substituted by FA 1983 s 37, Sch 8 Pt II para 7.

[3] Reference to "(*f*) or (*g*)" substituted by FA 1987 s 64, Sch 13 para 6.

3 The amount of any assessable profit resulting from the computation under paragraph 2 above may be reduced by any allowable loss in accordance with section 7(1) and shall be reduced in accordance with section 8 by reference to the participator's share, if any, of the oil allowance for the chargeable period.

4—(1) The tax payable shall be arrived at by—

(*a*) calculating the tax on the amount of assessable profit resulting from the computation under paragraph 2 above as reduced under paragraph 3 above; and

(*b*) applying the limit imposed by section 9.

(2) In applying section 9 under this paragraph[1] . . .—

(*a*) the assessable profit or allowable loss referred to in subsection (2)(*a*)(i) of that section shall be computed as provided in paragraph 2 above; and

(*b*) the expenditure to be excluded under subsection (2)(*a*)(ii) and (3) of that section from the expenditure taken into account in computing the assessable profit or allowable loss for that period shall not include any expenditure treated under paragraph 2(4)(*b*) above as having been allowed as qualifying for supplement.

Amendments—[1] Words repealed by FA 1981 s 139, Sch 19 Pt X.

FINANCE ACT 1980

(1980 Chapter 48)

PART VI

OIL TAXATION

106 Transfers of interests in oil fields

Schedule 17 to this Act shall have effect for supplementing and modifying Part I of the Oil Taxation Act 1975 where after the passing of this Act a participator in an oil field transfers the whole or part of his interest in the field.

107 Transmedian fields

(1) The Oil Taxation Acts shall have effect in accordance with this section where provision is made by an agreement between the government of the United Kingdom and the government of another country for—

(*a*) the exploitation as a single unit of oil in strata in the sea bed and subsoil of an area consisting of—

(i) an oil field within the meaning of Part I of the Oil Taxation Act 1975; and

(ii) a sector under the jurisdiction of the other country; and

(*b*) the apportionment of the oil between—

(i) the participators in that field; and

(ii) the persons who are, or have rights, interests or obligations of, licensees in respect of that sector under the law of the other country.

(2) The share of a participator in the oil won from the oil field shall be determined as if the oil won from the field consisted of so much of the oil won from the area as a whole as is apportioned to the participators in accordance with the agreement; and in section 10(3)(*b*) of the said Act of 1975 (restriction of allowable expenditure) and paragraphs 5(2)(*a*) and 7 of Schedule 2 to that Act (returns and information as to oil won from the field) references to oil won from the field shall be construed as references to so much of the oil won from the area as a whole as is so apportioned.

(3) Subject to subsection (2) above—

(*a*) the oil field shall be deemed to include the sector mentioned in subsection (1)(*a*)(ii) above;

(*b*) that sector shall be deemed to be a designated area; and

(*c*) references to oil shall include references to any substance that would be oil within the meaning of the said Act of 1975 if the enactments mentioned in section 1(1) extended to that sector;

but paragraph (a) above does not affect section 10(3)(a) of that Act or paragraph 4 of Schedule 2 to that Act (appointment of responsible person), and paragraph (b) above does not affect section 5(1)(b) of that Act (abortive exploration expenditure) or operate so as to apply section 38(4) of the Finance Act 1973 (taxation of non-residents engaged in activities in designated areas) to the persons referred to in subsection (1)(b)(ii) above.

(4) Where under the agreement there is a re-determination of the apportionment mentioned in subsection (1)(*b*) above and in consequence thereof the participators in the field receive a repayment in respect of expenditure which has been allowed for the field under section 3 of the said Act of 1975, the total amount of expenditure allowable under that section and section 4 of that Act for the field in the claim period in which the repayment is received shall be reduced by the amount of the repayment; and paragraph 6 of Schedule 4 to that Act (recovery of deductions from allowable expenditure) shall have effect as if the foregoing provisions of this subsection were relevant provisions within the meaning of that paragraph.

(5) . . . [1]

(6) In subsections (4) . . . [1] above references to a repayment include references to a credit or set-off.

(7) In this section "the Oil Taxation Acts" means the Oil Taxation Act 1975, any other enactment relating to petroleum revenue tax and the provisions of the Income Tax Acts and Corporation Tax Acts in their application to oil extraction activities and oil rights within the meaning of [Part 8 of the Corporation Tax Act 2010 or][2] [Chapter 16A of Part 2 of the Income Tax (Trading and Other Income) Act 2005][3].

(8) This section has effect whether the agreement mentioned in subsection (1) above is made before or after the passing of this Act and applies in relation to a chargeable period ending before the coming into force of this Act as well as to a chargeable period ending later.

HMRC Manuals—Oil Taxation Manual 13450 (transmedian fields).

Amendments—[1] Words repealed in sub-ss (5), (6) by the Oil Taxation Act 1983 s 15(6) Sch 6.

[2] In sub-s (7) words inserted by CTA 2010 s 1177, Sch 1 para 171. CTA 2010 has effect for corporation tax purposes for accounting periods ending on or after 1 April 2010, and for income and capital gains tax purposes for the tax year 2010–11 and subsequent tax years.

[3] In sub-s (7) words substituted by TIOPA 2010 s 374, Sch 8 paras 175, 176. TIOPA 2010 has effect for corporation tax purposes for accounting periods ending on or after 1 April 2010, for income and capital gains tax purposes for the tax year 2010–11 and subsequent tax years, and for petroleum revenue tax purposes for chargeable periods beginning on or after 1 July 2010.

108 Gas banking schemes

(1) Subject to the provisions of this section, the Board may by regulations made by statutory instrument modify the operation of the Oil Taxation Acts in their application to cases where—

(*a*) a gas banking scheme is in force between the participators in two or more oil fields; and

(*b*) the participators in those fields elect that the modifications prescribed by the regulations shall apply.

PRT

(2) Subject to subsection (3)(*a*) below, a gas banking scheme for the purposes of this section is any scheme which provides for the transfer of oil consisting of gas won from one of the oil fields to which the scheme applies to or to the order of the participators in another of those fields in consideration wholly or mainly of the subsequent transfer of oil consisting of gas won from the other field to or to the order of the participators in the first-mentioned field.

(3) Regulations under this section may—

(*a*) prescribe additional conditions required to be satisfied for a scheme to constitute a gas banking scheme, including conditions requiring the gas to be of a description specified in the regulations;

(*b*) prescribe conditions subject to which, and the manner in which, an election may be made under this section and the time for which any such election is to continue in force; and

(*c*) contain such incidental, supplementary or transitional provisions as appear to the Board to be necessary or expedient.

(4) The foregoing provisions of this section shall apply to an international gas banking scheme as they apply to a gas banking scheme within the meaning of those provisions except that only the participators in the oil field or oil fields to which the scheme applies need make the election referred to in subsection (1)(*b*) above; and for the purposes of this section an international gas banking scheme is any scheme which—

(*a*) applies to areas that include both one or more oil fields and one or more areas under the jurisdiction of a country other than the United Kingdom; and

(*b*) would be a gas banking scheme within the meaning of the foregoing provisions if all the areas were oil fields and all the persons who are, or have rights, interests or obligations of, licensees in respect of those areas were participators.

(5) Regulations under this section may be made so as to apply only to gas banking schemes other than international gas banking schemes or so as to apply only to the latter; and regulations applying to a scheme of either description may differ from those applying to the other.

(6) No regulations shall be made under this section unless a draft of the regulations has been laid before, and approved by a resolution of, the House of Commons.

(7) In this section "the Board", "oil", "oil field" and "participator" have the same meaning as in Part I of the Oil Taxation Act 1975 and "the Oil Taxation Acts" has the same meaning as in section 107 above.

HMRC Manuals—Oil Taxation Manual 05445 (gas banking)

Cross references—See SI 1982/92, SI 1982/1858 (Gas Banking Schemes regulations).

109 Fractionation

(1)–(7) (*amend* the Oil Taxation Act 1975 s 12, Sch 3, para 2).

(8) Subject to the following provisions of this section, this section has effect—

(*a*) as respects Part I of the Oil Taxation Act 1975, in relation to chargeable periods (within the meaning of that Part) ending after 31 December 1979; and

(*b*) as respects [Chapter V of Part XII of the Taxes Act 1988][1], in relation to chargeable periods (within the meaning of that Part) ending after that date.

(9) Expenditure shall not by virtue of this section be allowable under section 3 of the said Act of 1975 unless it was incurred after the said 31st December or would have been allowable under section 4 of that Act but for the proviso to subsection (1) of that section.

(10) For the purposes of section 4 of the said Act of 1975 expenditure incurred in acquiring, bringing into existence or enhancing the value of an asset which before the passing of this Act was used for the purpose of any process which, if this Act had been in force, would by virtue of this section have constituted initial treatment of oil won from an oil field shall be treated as having been incurred on the date when the asset was first so used; and for the purposes of that section (but not of the foregoing provisions of this subsection) the use of the asset in connection with the field shall be treated as having begun—

(*a*) on 1 January 1980; or

(*b*) the date on which the asset was first used for that purpose,

whichever is the later.

Subsection (13) of the said section 4 shall apply for the purposes of this subsection.

(11) (*repealed* by TA 1988 s 844 Sch 31).

Amendments—[1] Words in sub-s (8)(*b*) substituted by FA 1988 s 146, Sch 13 Pt II para 20.

SCHEDULES

SCHEDULE 17

TRANSFERS OF INTERESTS IN OIL FIELDS

Section 106

PART I
PRELIMINARY

Interpretation

1—(1) For the purposes of this Schedule a participator in an oil field transfers the whole or part of his interest in the field whenever as a result of a transaction or event other than—

(*a*) the making of an agreement or arrangement of the kind mentioned in paragraph 5 of Schedule 3 to the Oil Taxation Act 1975; or

(*b*) a re-determination under a unitisation agreement,

the whole or part of his share in the oil to be won and saved from the field becomes the share or part of the share of another person who is or becomes a participator in the field.

(2) In sub-paragraph (1) above a "unitisation agreement" means an agreement for the exploitation of—

(*a*) an oil field falling within two or more licensed areas; or

(*b*) any such area as is mentioned in subsection (1)(*a*) of section 107 of this Act,

and a "re-determination" means, in a case within paragraph (a) above, a re-determination of the apportionment of oil from the field as between the different licensed areas and, in a case within paragraph (b) above, a re-determination of the apportionment mentioned in subsection (1)(b) of that section.

(3) In this Schedule "the old participator" means the participator whose interest is wholly or partly transferred, "the new participator" means the person to whom it is transferred and ["the transfer period" means the chargeable period in which the transfer takes place][1].

HMRC Manuals—Oil Taxation Manual 18020 (PRT consequences of change of field ownership).

Amendments—[1] Words in sub-para (3) substituted by FA 1981 s 114.

2 This Schedule shall be construed as one with Part I of the said Act of 1975, and any reference in this Schedule to a section or Schedule not otherwise identified is a reference to that section or Schedule of that Act.

Notice of transfer

3—(1) The old and new participators shall within two months after the end of the transfer period deliver to the Board a notice in such form and containing such particulars with respect to the transfer as the Board may prescribe.

(2) Where as a result of the same transaction or event—

(*a*) the whole or part of the interest of two or more persons in an oil field becomes the interest or part of the interest of another person; or

(*b*) parts of a participator's interest in an oil field are transferred to two or more other persons,

a single notice relating to all the transfers shall be given under this paragraph by all the old participators and new participators, and in relation to any such notice references in paragraphs 4 and 5 below to the old and new participators shall be construed accordingly.

HMRC Manuals—Oil Taxation Manual 18030 (procedures).

Exclusion of transfer rules

4—(1) Parts II and III of this Schedule shall not apply in relation to a transfer if the old and new participators make an application in that behalf in the notice under paragraph 3 above and the Board consider that those provisions would not materially affect the total tax chargeable in respect of the field.

(2) The Board shall give notice of their decision under this paragraph to the old and new participators.

Partial transfers

5—(1) Where the transfer is of part of the old participator's interest in the field the notice under paragraph 3 above shall state what the old and new participators propose should be the corresponding part of the amounts to be transferred to the new participator under paragraphs 6, 7 and 8 below and of the old participator's share of oil to be treated as that of the new participator under paragraph 9 below; and subject to the following provisions of this paragraph, the corresponding part shall for the purposes of those provisions be taken to be such part as is determined by the Board and specified in a notice given to the old and new participators.

(2) If the corresponding part determined by the Board differs from that proposed by the old and new participators they or any of them [may appeal by notice][1] in writing given to the Board not more than three months after the notice given by the Board under sub-paragraph (1) above . . . [1]; but the bringing of an appeal shall not affect the operation of the notice given by the Board.

(3) The old participator or the new participator shall, whether or not himself the appellant, be entitled to [be a party to][1] the appeal and in any proceedings arising out of it.

(4) An appeal may be abandoned [before it is notified to the tribunal][1] by notice in writing to the Board; and if before an appeal is determined the old and new participators agree with the Board on what should be the corresponding part referred to above the Board's notice under subsection (1) above shall have effect as if that were the part specified in it.

(5) Where the corresponding part referred to above as specified in the Board's notice under sub-paragraph (1) is varied on appeal, the Board's notice shall have effect as if the varied part had been specified in it; and all such assessments or determinations or adjustments shall be made as are necessary in consequence of the variation.

[(6) The provisions of paragraphs 14A to 14I of Schedule 2 to the Oil Taxation Act 1975 shall apply to appeals under this paragraph subject to any necessary modifications.][1]

Amendments—[1] In sub-para (2), words substituted for words "may by notice" and words "appeal to the Special Commissioners" repealed, in sub-para (3), words substituted for words "appear and be heard on", words in sub-para (4) inserted, and sub-para (5) inserted, by the Transfer of Tribunal Functions and Revenue and Customs Appeals Order, SI 2009/56 art 3, Sch 1 paras 94, 95 with effect from 1 April 2009.

PART II
TRANSFER OF OLD PARTICIPATOR'S EXPENDITURE RELIEF, LOSSES AND EXEMPTIONS

Unused expenditure relief

6—(1) There shall be transferred to the new participator the whole or, if the transfer is of part of the old participator's interest in the field, a corresponding part of any amount which—

(*a*) would, apart from this paragraph, fall to be taken into account under section 2(9)(*b*) in computing the assessable profit or allowable loss accruing to the old participator from the field in the transfer period or a later chargeable period; and

(*b*) is attributable to expenditure allowed to the old participator under Schedule 5 in accordance with his interest in the field before the transfer.

(2) If the whole of the old participator's interest in the field is transferred in the transfer period (whether to one new participator or partly to one and partly to another or others) there shall be transferred to the new participator the whole or, as the case may be, to each of them a corresponding part, of any amount which—

(*a*) would, apart from this paragraph, fall to be taken into account under section 2(9)(*c*) in computing the assessable profit or allowable loss accruing to the old participator from the field in the transfer period or a later chargeable period; and

(*b*) is attributable to expenditure incurred by the old participator before the transfer and allowed to him under Schedule 6.

(3) Any amount transferred to the new participator under this paragraph shall, instead of being taken into account as mentioned in sub-paragraph (1)(*a*) or (2)(*a*) above, be taken into account in computing the assessable profit or allowable loss accruing to the new participator from the field.

HMRC Manuals—Oil Taxation Manual 18040 (unused expenditure relief).

Unused losses

7—(1) There shall be transferred to the new participator the whole or, if the transfer is of part of the old participator's interest in the field, a corresponding part of any loss which the Board have determined under Schedule 2 has accrued to the old participator from the field [in the transfer period or any earlier chargeable period][2] to the extent that it has not been relieved against assessable profits accruing to him in the transfer period or an earlier chargeable period.

(2) [Subject to the following provisions of this paragraph][3] any amount of a loss transferred to the new participator under this paragraph may be relieved under section 7 against assessable profits accruing to the new participator in the transfer period or a later chargeable period and shall not be set off against assessable profits of the old participator [and, for the purposes of effecting such relief, subsection (1) of section 7 shall have effect as if the word "succeeding" were omitted][1].

[(3) If, in the case of a transfer of the whole or part of an interest on or after 29 November 1994,—

(*a*) the old participator made a claim or election for the allowance of any expenditure unrelated to the field, and (*b*) the claim or election was received by the Board on or after that date, and

(*c*) the expenditure allowed on the claim or election fell to be taken into account in computing the assessable profit or allowable loss of the old participator for the transfer period or any earlier chargeable period,

then, from the sum which, apart from this sub-paragraph, would be the aggregate of all the losses transferred to the new participator under this paragraph there shall be deducted (subject to sub-paragraphs (5) and (6) below) so much of the expenditure referred to in paragraph (a) above as is allowed on the claim or election (and, accordingly, the amount so deducted shall not fall to be transferred to the new participator under this paragraph).

(4) In this paragraph "expenditure unrelated to the field" means expenditure allowable under any of the following provisions—

(*a*) section 5 (abortive exploration expenditure);

(*b*) section 5A (exploration and appraisal expenditure);

(*c*) section 5B (research expenditure);

(*d*) section 6 (unrelievable loss from abandoned field); and

(*e*) section 65 of the Finance Act 1987 (cross-field allowance of certain expenditure incurred on new fields);

and in relation to any such expenditure, "claim" means a claim under Schedule 7 or Schedule 8 and "election" means an election under Part I of Schedule 14 to the Finance Act 1987 and, in relation to such an election, expenditure shall be regarded as allowed if it is accepted by the Board as allowable in accordance with that Schedule.

(5) Where, in accordance with sub-paragraph (1) above, only a part of a loss (corresponding to the part of the interest transferred) falls to be transferred under this paragraph, only a corresponding part of the expenditure referred to in sub-paragraph (3) above shall be deducted under that sub-paragraph.

(6) Where the amount of the deduction under sub-paragraph (3) above equals or exceeds the sum from which it is to be deducted, no part of any loss shall be transferred to the new participator under this paragraph].[3]

HMRC Manuals—Oil Taxation Manual 18050 (unused losses).

Amendments—[1] Words inserted by FA 1983 s 41.

[2] Words in sub-para (1) substituted by FA 1993 s 41.

[3] Words in sub-para (2), and whole of sub-paras (3)–(6), inserted by FA 1995 s 148(2), (3).

Accumulated capital expenditure

8—(1) There shall be transferred to the new participator the whole or, if the transfer is of part of the old participator's interest in the field, a corresponding part of the amount which under section 9(3) is the old participator's accumulated capital expenditure at the end of [the last chargeable period before the transfer period][1].

(2) Subject to paragraph 18 below, any amount transferred under this paragraph shall be treated for the purposes of section 9(3) as, or as part of, the new participator's accumulated capital expenditure at the end of the transfer [period][1] and later [chargeable periods][1] and not as, or as part of, the old participator's accumulated capital expenditure at the end of any such [period][1].

HMRC Manuals—Oil Taxation Manual 18060 (accumulated capital expenditure).

Amendments—[1] Words substituted by FA 1981 s 114.

Excluded oil

9 For the purpose of determining under section 10(1)(*b*) what oil is to be disregarded in computing a participator's gross profit or loss attributable to oil won from the field after the transfer there shall be treated as if it were the new participator's, and not the old participator's, the whole or, if the transfer is of part of the old participator's interest in the field, a corresponding part of the old participator's share of oil won and saved from the field before the transfer.

HMRC Manuals—Oil Taxation Manual 18070 (exempt gas).

Successive transfers

10—(1) Where the old participator transfers the whole or part of his interest in a field in which he has himself acquired an interest by a previous transfer, the amounts to be taken into account in determining what is to be transferred to the new participator under paragraphs 6, 7 and 8 above and what is to be the share of oil treated as the new participator's under paragraph 9 above shall include—

(*a*) any amount which falls to be transferred to the old participator under paragraph 6 or 7 above by reference to the previous transfer and has not been taken into account or relieved in relation to him under paragraph 6(3) or 7(2) above; and

(*b*) any amount or share which falls to be transferred to the old participator or treated as his under paragraph 8 or 9 above by reference to the previous transfer.

(2) Where the old participator makes successive transfers of parts of his interest, the amounts to be transferred to the new participator under paragraphs 6, 7 and 8 above and the share of oil to be treated as the new participator's under paragraph 9 above by reference to each transfer shall be that amount or share after deducting any of it which falls to be so transferred or treated by reference to a previous transfer.

HMRC Manuals—Oil Taxation Manual 18080 (successive transfers).

PART III
OTHER RULES

Provisional relief for expenditure

11 Where at the end of the transfer period the old participator has no interest in the field—

(a) the assessable profit or allowable loss accruing to him from the field in the transfer period shall be computed as if—

(i) the amount referred to in section 2(8)(b) were increased by any amount taken into account under section 2(9)(a) in computing the assessable profit or allowable loss accruing to him from the field in the preceding chargeable period; and

(ii) the amount referred to in section 2(9)(a) were nil; and

(b) the assessable profit or allowable loss accruing to him from the field in any later chargeable period in which he has no such interest shall be computed as if the amount referred to in section 2(8)(b) and (9)(a) were nil.[1]

HMRC Manuals—Oil Taxation Manual 18090 (provisional expenditure allowance).

Amendments—[1] This paragraph (and the heading before it) repealed by FA 2009 s 89, Sch 43 para 3(4) with effect in relation to a chargeable period beginning after 30 June 2009, subject to transitional provisions in FA 2009 Sch 43 para 4.

Royalty payments

12—(1) Where at the end of the transfer period the old participator has no interest in the field—

(*a*) any licence debit or credit which, apart from this paragraph, would fall to be taken into account under subsection (6) of section 2 in computing the assessable profit or allowable loss accruing to him from the field in any later chargeable period in which he has no such interest shall not be so taken into account; but

(*b*) that subsection shall have effect in relation to the transfer period as if the amount of—

(i) any such licence debit or credit as is mentioned in paragraph (*a*) above; and

(ii) any licence debit or credit that would have fallen to be taken into account as there mentioned for a later chargeable period if the old participator were still a participator,

were an amount to be included in the sum referred to in paragraph (a) or, as the case may be, paragraph (b) of that subsection.

(2) Sub-paragraph (1) above does not affect the amount of any loss transferred under paragraph 7 above.

(3) Notwithstanding anything in section 34 of the Taxes Management Act 1970 (ordinary time limit for assessments) any further assessment or determination or amendment of an assessment or determination required in consequence of sub-paragraph (1) above may be made at any time not later than six years after the end of the later chargeable period referred to in sub-paragraph (1)(*a*) or (*b*)(ii) above.

HMRC Manuals—Oil Taxation Manual 18100 (royalty payments).

Payments on account and advance payments

13—(1) For the purpose of computing under the Schedule to the Petroleum Revenue Tax Act 1980 (computation of payment on account) whether any, and if so what, amount of tax is payable under that Act by the old participator and the new participator for the transfer period or any later chargeable period—

(*a*) it shall be assumed that any application or proposal made in relation to the transfer under paragraph 4 or 5(1) above and in respect of which the Board have not notified their decision will be accepted by the Board; and

(*b*) the computation under that Schedule shall be made as if paragraph 6 above applied in relation to expenditure which under paragraph 2(4) of that Schedule is treated as having been allowed under Schedule 5 or 6 as well as to expenditure which has been so allowed.

(2) Where at the end of the transfer period the old participator has no interest in the field he shall not be liable under section 105 of this Act to pay any amount as an advance payment of tax in respect of the field for any subsequent chargeable period in which he has no such interest.

(3) The old participator shall not be entitled to interest under subsection (7) of that section by reason of any such excess as is there mentioned for the transfer period or either of the next two chargeable periods if he and the new participator are connected within the meaning of [section 1122 of the Corporation Tax Act 2010][1].

HMRC Manuals—Oil Taxation Manual 18110 (payments on account).

Amendments—[1] In sub-para (3) words substituted for words "section 839 of the Taxes Act 1988" by CTA 2010 s 1177, Sch 1 para 172(2). CTA 2010 has effect for corporation tax purposes for accounting periods ending on or after 1 April 2010, and for income and capital gains tax purposes for the tax year 2010–11 and subsequent tax years.

Losses of new participator

14—(1) Where the Board have determined under Schedule 2 that an allowable loss has accrued to the new participator from the field in the transfer period or a later chargeable period, then, if—

(*a*) the loss has been computed by reference to an amount taken into account by virtue of paragraph 6 above; and

(*b*) the old participator has no interest in the field at the end of the transfer period,

the old and new participators may jointly elect that the loss shall be surrendered to the old participator to the extent that it does not exceed whichever is the lesser of the amount referred to in paragraph (a) above and the total assessable profits as reduced under section 7 that accrued to the old participator from the field in chargeable periods up to and including the chargeable period after the transfer period.

(2) Where any amount of a loss is surrendered under this paragraph it shall be treated—

(*a*) in relation to the old participator, as an allowable loss accruing to him in the chargeable period next but one after the transfer period; and

(*b*) in relation to the new participator, as if it has been relieved against assessable profits accruing to him from the field in chargeable periods before that in which it accrued.

HMRC Manuals—Oil Taxation Manual 18120 (surrender of new participator's loss).

[Terminal losses

15—(1) This paragraph applies in any case where—

(*a*) such an allowable loss as falls to be relieved under section 7(3) accrues to the new participator from the field in a chargeable period ending after 17th March 2004, but

(*b*) some or all of the loss cannot be relieved under section 7(3) against assessable profits accruing to him from the field.

(2) So much of the loss as cannot be so relieved ("the remaining loss") shall be regarded as an allowable unrelievable field loss in relation to the new participator ("the loss-maker") only to the extent that—

(*a*) so much of it as cannot be relieved in accordance with sub- paragraphs (3) to (6) below, exceeds

(*b*) the aggregate of any relevant previous participators' expenditure unrelated to the field (see sub-paragraphs (10) and (11) below).

(3) The remaining loss shall be treated as an allowable loss which falls to be relieved under section 7(3) against so much of any assessable profits accruing to the old participator from the field as is attributable to his represented interest (see sub-paragraphs (9) and (12) below).

(4) Where a person is the new participator in relation to two or more old participators—

(*a*) the remaining loss shall be apportioned between those old participators in such manner as is just and reasonable having regard to the interests respectively transferred by them to the new participator,

(*b*) sub-paragraph (3) above shall have effect separately in relation to each of them (and the part of the remaining loss apportioned to him).

(5) Any relief by virtue of sub-paragraph (3) above shall be given against the assessable profits accruing to the old participator in an earlier chargeable period only to the extent to which it cannot be given against the assessable profits accruing to him in a later chargeable period.

(6) If—

(*a*) the old participator acquired some or all of his interest in the field by a previous transfer in relation to which he was the new participator,

(*b*) Parts 2 and 3 of this Schedule applied in relation to that previous transfer, and

(*c*) some or all of the part of the remaining loss treated as an allowable loss of his cannot be relieved in accordance with sub-paragraph (3) above,

sub-paragraphs (3) to (5) above shall apply in relation to so much of that part of the remaining loss as cannot be so relieved as they apply in relation to the remaining loss, but construing the references in those sub-paragraphs to the new participator and the old participator by reference to that previous transfer and the parties to it, and then applying this sub-paragraph accordingly (and so on).

(7) But where—

(*a*) the person who is the old participator in relation to a transfer made before 17th March 2004 ("the later transfer") is also the new participator in relation to a previous transfer, and

(*b*) Parts 2 and 3 of this Schedule applied in relation to both of those transfers,

sub-paragraph (3) above shall not apply by virtue of sub-paragraph (6) above in relation to so much of the assessable profits of the person who is the old participator in relation to that previous transfer as is attributable to so much of his interest as constitutes the whole or part of his represented interest by virtue of the later transfer.

(8) Where losses accruing to each of two or more participators fall to be relieved by virtue of sub-paragraph (3) above against the same assessable profits, a loss accruing to the person who last had an interest representing the whole or part of the transferred interest at an earlier time shall be so relieved before one accruing to a person who last had such an interest at a later time.

In this sub-paragraph "the transferred interest" means the interest transferred by the person against whose assessable profits the losses fall to be relieved.

(9) In determining for the purposes of this paragraph the assessable profits of a participator that are attributable to his represented interest, the assessable profits shall be apportioned between—

(*a*) the represented interest, and

(*b*) the remainder of the participator's interest,

using such method as is just and reasonable, having regard to the respective sizes of those interests.

[(9A) This paragraph is subject to [paragraph 6][4] of [Schedule 20B][3] to the Finance Act 1993.][2]

(10) For the purposes of this paragraph "relevant previous participators' expenditure unrelated to the field" means so much of each relevant previous participator's allowed expenditure unrelated to the field as is referable to his represented interest, other than excepted old expenditure.

(11) For the purposes of sub-paragraph (10) above—

"allowed expenditure unrelated to the field", in relation to a participator, is expenditure unrelated to the field which is allowed on a claim or election made by the participator;

"excepted old expenditure" is expenditure which has been allowed in pursuance of a claim or election for its allowance received by the Board before 17th March 2004;

"relevant previous participator" means a participator against any of whose assessable profits relief is given in accordance with sub-paragraphs (3) to (6) above;

and sub-paragraph (9) above shall apply in relation to allowed expenditure unrelated to the field as it applies in relation to assessable profits.

(12) In this paragraph—

"expenditure unrelated to the field" has the meaning given by section 6(9);

"the loss-maker" shall be construed in accordance with sub- paragraph (2) above;

"previous owner" means a person from whom the loss-maker directly or indirectly derives his title to the whole or any part of his interest;

"represented interest", in the case of a previous owner, means so much of the interest which that previous owner transferred, by a transfer to which Parts 2 and 3 of this Schedule apply, as is represented in the loss-maker's interest by virtue only of—

(*a*) that transfer, or

(*b*) that transfer and one or more subsequent transfers to which those Parts apply,

making, for the purposes of paragraph (b) above, such apportionments as are just and reasonable, having regard to the interests transferred by each of the transferors.][1]

Cross-references—See FA 2013 s 84(2) (terminal losses accruing by virtue of another company's default: this para does not apply in relation to any allowable loss accruing to the other company from the oil field).

Amendments—[1] Paragraph 15 substituted by FA 2004 s 288(2) with effect for losses accruing in chargeable periods ending after 17 March 2004.

[2] Sub-para (9A) inserted by FA 2008 s 107, Sch 33 para 3 with effect from 21 July 2008.

[3] In sub-s (9A) words substituted for words "Schedule 20A" by FA 2009 s 91, Sch 45 para 3(2)(*b*) with effect from 21 July 2009.

[4] In sub-para (9A), words substituted by F(No 2)A 2017 s 44(3) with effect from 23 November 2016.

Abortive exploration expenditure

16—(1) Subject to sub-paragraph (2) below, there shall be allowed under section 5 in the case of the new participator, in connection with any field in which an interest is transferred to him by the old participator, any expenditure incurred—

(*a*) by the old participator; or

(*b*) if the old participator is a company, by a company which is within the meaning of that section associated with the old participator in respect of the expenditure,

if no claim in respect of it has been made under Schedule 7 by the old participator or any such company and the expenditure would be allowable under that section in the case of the new participator if he had himself incurred it.

(2) Sub-paragraph (1) above—

(*a*) does not apply so long as the old participator or, if the old participator is a company, any company associated with the old participator has an interest in a licence; and

(*b*) applies to the new participator only if the transfer to him was the last transfer made by the old participator.

(3) For the purposes of sub-paragraph (2) above a company is associated with the old participator if—

(*a*) one is a 51 per cent. subsidiary of the other and the other is not a 51 per cent subsidiary of any company; or

(*b*) each of them is a 51 per cent. subsidiary of a third company which is not itself a 51 per cent subsidiary of any company;

and [Chapter 3 of Part 24 of the Corporation Tax Act 2010][1] (subsidiaries) shall apply for the purposes of this sub-paragraph.

(4) This paragraph is without prejudice to the application of section 5 in cases where the old participator is a company and the new participator is within the meaning of that section a company associated with the old participator in respect of the expenditure in question.

Amendments—[1] In sub-para (3) words substituted for words "section 838 of the Taxes Act 1988" by CTA 2010 s 1177, Sch 1 para 172(3). CTA 2010 has effect for corporation tax purposes for accounting periods ending on or after 1 April 2010, and for income and capital gains tax purposes for the tax year 2010–11 and subsequent tax years.

[Exploration and appraisal expenditure

16A In relation to exploration and appraisal expenditure to which section 5A applies, paragraph 16 above has effect as if any reference therein to section 5 were a reference to section 5A].[1]

HMRC Manuals—Oil Taxation Manual 18140 (non-field expenditure).

Amendments—[1] Para 16A inserted by FA 1983 s 37, Sch 8 Pt II para 8.

[Research expenditure

16B In relation to research expenditure to which section 5B applies, paragraph 16 above has effect as if any reference therein to section 5 were a reference to section 5B].[1]

HMRC Manuals—Oil Taxation Manual 18140 (non-field expenditure).

Amendments—[1] Para 16B inserted by FA 1987 s 64, Sch 13 Pt II para 7.

Oil allowance

17 If the transfer period is one of the first three chargeable periods of the field section 8 shall not apply to the old participator for that period or any earlier period.

HMRC Manuals—Oil Taxation Manual 18150 (oil allowance).

Limit on tax payable in transfer year

18—(1) For the purposes of section 9 in its application to the transfer [period][1], the accumulated capital expenditure at the end of that [period][1] of the old participator and the new participator respectively shall be treated as equal to the aggregate of—

(*a*) the pre-transfer fraction of what (apart from this paragraph) would be the amount of his accumulated capital expenditure for the purposes of that section at the end of that [period][1] if any transfer from or to him under paragraph 6 or 8 above were disregarded; and

(*b*) the post-transfer fraction of what (apart from this paragraph) would be that amount having regard to any transfer from or to him in that [period][1] under those paragraphs.

(2) For the purposes of this paragraph the pre-transfer and post-transfer fractions are respectively the fractions of the [period][1] (reckoned in days) which elapse before and begin with the date of the transfer; and if there are two or more transfers in the [period][1] those fractions shall be determined—

(*a*) for a participator who is the old participator as respects any of the transfers, by reference to the first transfer as respects which he is the old participator;

(*b*) for a participator who is the new participator as respects any of the transfers, by reference to the last transfer as respects which he is the new participator;

(*c*) for a participator who is the old participator as respects one or more of the transfers and the new participator as respects another or others, by reference to whichever results in the smallest amount of accumulated capital expenditure under this paragraph.

Amendments—[1] Words substituted by FA 1981 s 114.

Disposal of long-term assets

19—(1) [Neither][1] paragraph 4 of Schedule 4 [nor section 7 of the Oil Taxation Act 1983 shall][1] apply to the disposal of an asset used in connection with an oil field if the disposal is by the old participator (or a person connected with him) to the new participator (or a person connected with him) and the disposal is in pursuance of the transfer by the old participator to the new participator of an interest in the field.

(2) Section [839 of the Taxes Act 1988][2] (connected persons) shall apply for the purposes of this paragraph.

HMRC Manuals—Oil Taxation Manual 18160 (long-term asset disposal).

Amendments—[1] First words in sub-para (1) inserted and second words substituted by the Oil Taxation Act 1983 ss 6, 7, Sch 2 para 6;

[2] Words in sub-para (2) substituted by TA 1988 s 844, Sch 29 para 32.

Transfers of oil

20 Where in pursuance of the transfer of the whole or part of his interest in the field the old participator transfers his right to any oil already won from the field to the new participator, that oil—

(*a*) shall not be taken into account under section 2(5) in computing the old participator's assessable profit or allowable loss in the transfer period; but

(*b*) shall be taken into account under section 2(5) in computing the new participator's assessable profit or allowable loss as if it were included in his share of the oil won from the field.

HMRC Manuals—Oil Taxation Manual 18170 (transfers of oil).

Retention of share of oil

21 Where the old participator retains a share of the oil won from the field in pursuance of an agreement between him and the new participator under which the latter undertakes to be responsible for carrying out the old participator's obligations in connection with the field so far as they relate to that share—

(*a*) that share shall be taken to belong to the new participator; and

(*b*) any oil comprised in that share shall be treated as oil acquired by the old participator under an agreement to which paragraph 6 of Schedule 3 applies.

FINANCE ACT 1981

(1981 Chapter 35)

An Act to grant certain duties, to alter other duties, and to amend the law relating to the National Debt and the Public Revenue, and to make further provision in connection with Finance.

[27 July 1981].

PART VII
PETROLEUM REVENUE TAX

111 Restriction of expenditure supplement

(1) Expenditure taken into account under section 2(9)(*b*)(i) or (*c*)(i) of the Oil Taxation Act 1975 ("the principal Act") in computing the assessable profit or allowable loss accruing to a participator in a chargeable period from an oil field shall not qualify for supplement under section 2(9)(*b*)(ii) or (*c*)(ii) of that Act if it is incurred after the end of the chargeable period ("the net profit period") [which is the earliest chargeable period ending after a development decision has been made for the field in which—

(*a*) the amount of oil won and saved from the field exceeds 1,000 metric tonnes (counting 1,100 cubic metres of gas at a temperature of 15 degrees centigrade and pressure of one atmosphere as equivalent to one metric tonne); and

(*b*) a net profit from the field accrues to the participator;

and subsection (7) of section 5A of the principal Act (time when development decision is made) shall apply for the purposes of this subsection as it applies for the purposes of subsection (1)(c) of that section][3].

(2) Subject to subsections (3) and (4) below, a net profit shall be treated as having accrued to a participator from an oil field in a chargeable period when the total assessable profits (without any reduction under section 7 or 8 of the principal Act) that have accrued to him from the field in chargeable periods up to and including that period [exceed the aggregate of the total allowable losses that have so accrued to him and the total amount of advance petroleum revenue tax paid by him in respect of that field for chargeable periods up to and including that period][1].

[(2A) For the purposes of subsection (2) above the total amount of advance petroleum revenue tax paid by the participator does not include any amount of that tax repaid to him before the end of the chargeable period first referred to in that subsection or any amount of that tax subsequently repaid to him under section 142(1) of the Finance Act 1982 or under paragraph 9 of Schedule 19 to that Act][1].

(3) In determining for the purposes of subsection (2) above whether any, and if so what, assessable profit or allowable loss has accrued to a participator from an oil field in a chargeable period—

(*a*) there shall be excluded from its computation any expenditure allowed under Schedule 7 and any loss allowed under Schedule 8 to the principal Act . . .[4];

(*b*) any election under paragraph 9(1) of Schedule 3 to that Act (spreading of allowable expenditure) shall be disregarded; and

(*c*) in the case of the last chargeable period taken into account in deciding what is the net profit period there shall be included in that computation any amount which, by reason of an adjustment under section 4(9) of that Act (long-term assets) for a claim period ending not later than that period, will fall to be taken into account under paragraph 6 of Schedule 4 to that Act for the next chargeable period [and

(*d*) if any qualifying tariff receipts, within the meaning of section 9 of the Oil Taxation Act 1983, are received or receivable by the participator for that period, any amount by which those receipts are treated as reduced by virtue of that section shall be brought into account in that computation as an addition to the positive amounts referred to in section 2(3)(*a*) of the principal Act][2].

(4) A net profit shall not by virtue of subsection (2) above be treated as having accrued to a participator from an oil field in a chargeable period if—

(*a*) after an assessment or determination has been made in respect of that period under paragraph 10 of Schedule 2 to the principal Act any expenditure incurred before the end of that period is allowed on a claim under Schedule 5 or Schedule 6 to that Act; and

(*b*) a net profit would not have accrued to the participator from the field in that period if that expenditure (or, as respects expenditure allowed under Schedule 5, his share of it) had been taken into account in the assessment or determination together with any amount falling to be taken into account under section 2(9)(*b*)(ii) or (*c*)(ii) of the principal Act by reference to (or, as the case may be, to his share of) that expenditure.

(5) The expenditure referred to in subsection (4) above does not include expenditure allowed for any claim period beginning after the chargeable period in respect of which the assessment or determination was made.

(6) In the following provisions, that is to say—

(*a*) paragraphs 2(4)(*a*) and 3(1)(*b*) of Schedule 5 to the principal Act (claims for and determination of expenditure qualifying for supplement), including those paragraphs as applied by Schedule 6 to that Act; and

(*b*) paragraph 2(4)(*b*) of the Schedule to the Petroleum Revenue Tax Act 1980 (computation of payment on account),

references to expenditure qualifying for supplement shall include references to expenditure that would so qualify apart from this section; but the responsible person need not make a claim under paragraph 2(4)(a) of the said Schedule 5 if it appears to him that none of the expenditure is likely to qualify because of this section.

(7) This section applies whether the net profit period ends before or after the passing of this Act but subsection (1) above shall not disqualify any expenditure which was incurred before 1 January 1981 or which is incurred before 1 January 1983 in pursuance of a contract entered into before 1 January 1981.

Amendments—[1] Words in sub-s (2) and sub-s (2A) substituted by FA 1982 s 139(6), Sch 19 Pt II para 16(2), with effect in accordance with s 139 thereof.

[2] Words in sub-s (3) inserted by the Oil Taxation Act 1983 s 9(8).

[3] Words in sub-s (1) substituted by FA 1985 s 91(3), (4).

[4] Words in sub-s (3) repealed by FA 1987 ss 64, 72, Sch 13 para 8, Sch 16, Part X.

112 Restriction of expenditure supplement: transfers of interests

(1) Section 111 above shall have effect in accordance with this section where a participator in an oil field has acquired the whole or part of his interest in the field as a result of one or more transfers to him within the meaning of Schedule 17 to the Finance Act 1980, and in this section "the new participator" and "the old participator" mean respectively the first-mentioned participator and any participator from whom he has acquired the whole or part of his interest.

(2) The new participator's net profit period shall be whichever is the earlier of—

(*a*) his own net profit period as determined in accordance with section 111 above and subsections (3) and (4) below; or

(*b*) subject to subsection (5) below, the chargeable period which is the net profit period of the old participator or, if there are two or more old participators, of whichever of them has the earliest net profit period.

(3) Where the old participator has transferred the whole of his interest in the field to the new participator, the net profit period of the new participator shall be determined by treating as if they were his the total assessable profits and allowable losses of the old participator as determined for the purposes of section 111 above.

(4) Where the old participator has transferred part of his interest in the field to the new participator, the net profit period of the old and new participators shall be determined by treating as if they were the new participator's and not the old participator's such part of the total assessable profits and allowable losses of the old participator (as determined for the purposes of section 111 above) as may be just and reasonable.[(4A) Subsections (2) and (2A) of section 111 shall have effect as if references to the amount of advance petroleum revenue tax paid by the new participator or repaid to him included references to the amount of that tax paid by or repaid to the old participator or, where the old participator has transferred part of his interest, such part of that amount as is just and reasonable].

[(4A) Subsections (2) and (2A) of section 111 shall have effect as if references to the amount of advance petroleum revenue tax paid by the new participator or repaid to him included references to the amount of that tax paid by or repaid to the old participator or, where the old participator has transferred part of his interest, such part of that amount as is just and reasonable.]

(5) The net profit period of an old participator shall not be taken into account under subsection (2)(*b*) above if the new participator's own net profit period, as determined without reference under subsection (3) or (4) above to the old participator's assessable profits or allowable losses, fell before the chargeable period in which the new participator acquired the whole or part of the old participator's interest.

Amendments—[1] Sub-s (4A) inserted by FA 1982 s 139(6) Sch 19 Pt II para 16(3), with effect in accordance with s 139 thereof.

113 Restriction of expenditure supplement: loss following net profit period

[(1) This section has effect where the aggregate of—

(*a*) the total allowable losses that have accrued to a participator from an oil field in chargeable periods up to and including a chargeable period ending not more than three years after his net profit period, and

(*b*) the amount of advance petroleum revenue tax paid by him in respect of that field for those periods less any such tax repaid to him before the end of those periods or repaid subsequently under section 142(1) of the Finance Act 1982 or paragraph 9 of Schedule 19 to that Act,

exceeds the total assessable profits (without any reduction under section 7 or 8 of the principal Act) that have so accrued to him].(2) Section 111(1) above shall not disqualify for supplement under section 2(9)(b)(ii) or (c)(ii) of the principal Act expenditure which is incurred up to the end of—

(*a*) the last chargeable period in the three years mentioned in subsection (1) above; or

(*b*) the chargeable period in which a net profit next accrues to the participator from the field after the chargeable period mentioned in that subsection,

whichever is the earlier.

(3) Subsection (3) of section 111 above shall apply for the purposes of subsection (1) above as it applies for the purposes of subsection (2) of that section and subsections (3), (4) and (5) of that section shall apply for the purposes of subsection (2)(*b*) above as they apply for the purposes of subsection (2) of that section.

114 Restriction of limit on amount of tax payable

(1) (*amends* OTA 1975 s 9).

(2) (*amends* FA 1980 Sch 17).

(3) This section applies whether the net profit period ends before or after the passing of this Act.

115 Contracts with deferred payment

(1) Expenditure incurred in pursuance of a contract to which this section applies shall not qualify for supplement under section 2(9)(*b*)(ii) or (*c*)(ii) of the principal Act.

(2) This section applies to any contract which is entered into after 1 July 1980 unless—

(*a*) the amount required to be paid under it by the person incurring the expenditure is less than £10 million; or

(*b*) it is reasonable to expect, at the time when the contract is entered into—

(i) that not less than 90 per cent. of that amount will be paid within nine months of the date on which the other party begins to perform the contract; or

(ii) that a payment or payments in respect of that amount will be made which comply with subsection (3) below;

and for the purposes of paragraph (a) above there may be disregarded any provision of the contract allowing for variations in the amount payable to take account of changes in costs or design.

(3) The payment or payments referred to in subsection (2)(*b*)(ii) above must be such that the amount to be paid up to any time after the date on which the other party to the contract begins to perform it is equal to not less than 75 per cent. of the amount that would have become payable up to that time if—

(*a*) the payments required to be made under the contract were such that the first of them was payable within six months after that date and each subsequent one within six months after the previous one; and

(*b*) the first of the payments were required to be of an amount proportionate to the extent to which the contract has been performed by that party since that date and each subsequent one to be of an amount proportionate to the extent to which the contract has been so performed since the previous payment was required to be made.

(4) Where a contract requires a payment in respect of any period or in respect of the completion of any stage in the performance of the contract to be made within three months after the end of that period or within three months after the completion of that stage the amount to be paid up to any time shall be determined for the purposes of subsection (3) above as if the payment were required to be made at the end of that period or on completion of that stage.

(5) Where a contract provides for payments in respect of the completion of stages in the performance of separate parts of the work specified in the contract, the payments under the contract shall be treated as complying with subsection (3) above if the payments attributable to each part of the contract would have complied with that subsection if that part had been the subject of a separate contract.

116 Spreading of capital expenditure

(1), (2) (*amend* OTA 1975 Sch 3 paras 9, 10).

(3) This section has effect in relation to any chargeable period ending after 31 December 1979.

117 Spreading of capital expenditure: transitional provisions

(1) Where allowable losses have accrued to a participator from an oil field in chargeable periods ending before 1 January 1980 he may by notice in writing given to the Board elect that so much of those losses as would, apart from this section, be available for set-off under section 7 of the principal Act against assessable profits accruing to him from the field in chargeable periods beginning on or after that date shall instead be treated as an amount of relief for supplemented expenditure which, subject to any election under paragraph 9 of Schedule 3 to that Act, falls to be taken into account in computing the assessable profit or allowable loss accruing to him from the field in the chargeable period ending on 30 June 1980.

(2) The amount to which an election under this section applies shall not exceed the total amount of relief for supplemented expenditure taken into account in computing the assessable profits or allowable losses accruing to the participator in chargeable periods ending before 1 January 1980.

(3) Any notice under this section shall be in such form as the Board may prescribe and shall be given before 1 April 1982; and—

(*a*) any notice under paragraph 9 of Schedule 3 to the principal Act in respect of a chargeable period ending before that date shall not be out of time if given before that date;

(*b*) any tax charged or repayable in respect of any such chargeable period in consequence of an election under that paragraph shall not carry interest under paragraph 15 or 16 of Schedule 2 to that Act in respect of any period before the date of the election.

(4) In section 111(3)(*b*) above and in section 9(4) of, and paragraph 10 of Schedule 3 to, the principal Act references to an election under paragraph 9(1) of that Schedule shall include references to an election under this section.

(5) This section shall be construed as one with Part I of the principal Act and paragraph 9(7) of Schedule 3 to that Act shall apply for the interpretation of subsections (1) and (2) above.

118 Licence payments other than royalties

(1) For the purpose of computing under section 2 of the principal Act the assessable profit or allowable loss accruing to a participator in any chargeable period from an oil field—

(*a*) there shall be included as a positive amount any allowable sum paid to the participator in the period by the Secretary of State [or the OGA][2].

(*b*) there shall be included as a negative amount any allowable sum paid by the participator in the period to the [OGA][2].

(2) In this section "chargeable sum" and "allowable sum" mean any sum which after 31 December 1980 is paid to a participator by the Secretary of State [or the OGA][2] or, as the case may be, by the participator to the [OGA][2] by reference to a relevant licence except—

(*a*) any sum falling to be taken into account under section 2(6) of the principal Act (licence debit or credit) or section 3(1)(*b*) of that Act (payment under or for the purpose of obtaining a relevant licence);

(*b*) any sum consisting of interest on a sum payable to or by the [OGA][2];

(*c*) any repayment by the Secretary of State under [section 6(1) of the Petroleum Act 1998][1] (repayment of royalty for facilitating or maintaining the development of United Kingdom petroleum resources); and

(*d*) any payment or repayment of royalty in respect of excluded oil (as defined in section 10 of the principal Act) and any other payment attributable to such oil.

(3) Where the relevant licence by reference to which a chargeable sum or allowable sum is paid relates to a licensed area comprising the whole or part of two or more oil fields, that sum shall for the purposes of this section be apportioned between all or any of those fields, or attributed wholly to one of them, as may be just and reasonable.
(4) A return under paragraph 2 of Schedule 2 to the principal Act shall include a statement of the chargeable sums and allowable sums, if any, paid to or by the participator in the chargeable period to which the return relates.
(5) In considering for the purposes of paragraph 8(1) of Schedule 3 to the principal Act (subsidised expenditure) how far any expenditure has been or is to be met directly or indirectly by the Crown or by any authority or person other than the person incurring the expenditure, any chargeable sum shall be left out of account.
(6) This section shall be construed as one with Part I of the principal Act.

Amendments—[1] Words in sub-s (1) substituted by the Petroleum Act 1998 s 50, Sch 4 para 16 with effect from 15 February 1999 (by virtue of SI 1999/161, art 2).
[2] In sub-ss (1)(*a*), (2), words inserted, and in sub-ss (1)(*b*), (2), word substituted for words "Secretary of State" by the Petroleum (Transfer of Functions) Regulations, SI 2016/898 reg 5 with effect from 1 October 2016.

119 Transportation costs for off-shore oil

(1) (*amends* OTA 1975 s 3(4)).
(2) This section shall have effect in relation to any expenditure in respect of which a claim is made after 31 December 1978.

. . .

121 Gas banking schemes

Regulations under section 108 of the Finance Act 1980 (gas banking schemes) may provide for the modifications made by them to have effect from a date before the regulations are made and for any election made under that section to have effect from a date before the election is made.

PART X

MISCELLANEOUS AND SUPPLEMENTARY

139 Short title, interpretation, construction and repeals

(1) This Act may be cited as the Finance Act 1981.
(2) In this Act "the Taxes Act" means the Income and Corporation Taxes Act [1988].
(3) Part IV of this Act, so far as it relates to income tax, shall be construed as one with the Income Tax Acts, so far as it relates to corporation tax, shall be construed as one with the Corporation Tax Acts and, so far as it relates to capital gains tax, shall be construed as one with the Capital Gains Tax Act 1979.
(4) Part V of this Act shall be construed as one with Part III of the Finance Act 1975.
(5) In Parts VII and VIII of this Act "the principal Act" means the Oil Taxation Act 1975.
(6) [not reproduced].

FINANCE ACT 1982

(1982 Chapter 39)

PART VI

OIL TAXATION

CHAPTER I

GENERAL

132 Increase of petroleum revenue tax and ending of supplementary petroleum duty

(1) (*amends* OTA 1975 s 1(2)).
(2) (*amends* FA 1981 s 122(5)).

133 Export sales of gas

(1) (*amends* OTA 1975 s 2(5A)).
(2) (*amends* FA 1981 s 122(3)).
(3) This section has effect with respect to chargeable periods ending after 31 December 1981.

134 Alternative valuation of ethane used for petrochemical purposes

(1) Where an election is made under this section and accepted by the Board, the market value for taxation purposes of any ethane to which the election applies shall be determined, not in accordance with paragraphs 2, 2A and 3 of Schedule 3 to the principal Act (value under a notional contract), but in accordance with a price formula specified in the election; and, in relation to any such ethane, any reference to market value in any other provision of the principal Act[, in Part 8 of the Corporation Tax Act 2010][3] [or [Chapter 16A of Part 2 of the Income Tax (Trading and Other Income) Act 2005][4]][1] shall be construed accordingly.

(2) Subject to subsection (3) below, an election under this section [must be made before 1 January 1994 and][2] applies only to ethane—

(*a*) which, during the period covered by the election, is either disposed of otherwise than in sales at arm's length or relevantly appropriated; and

(*b*) which is used or to be used for petrochemical purposes by or on behalf of the person to whom it is so disposed of or, as the case may be, by or on behalf of the participator by whom it is appropriated; and

(*c*) which is not subjected to fractionation between the time at which it is disposed of or appropriated as mentioned in paragraph (*a*) above and the time at which it is used as mentioned in paragraph (*b*) above.

(3) In any case where—

(*a*) at a time during the period covered by an election, a market value falls to be determined for ethane to which subsection (4)(*b*) or subsection (5)(*d*) of section 2 of the principal Act applies (oil stocks at the end of chargeable periods), and

(*b*) after the expiry of the chargeable period in question, the ethane is disposed of or appropriated and used as mentioned in subsection (2) above,

the market value of that ethane at the time referred to in paragraph (a) above shall be determined as if it were then ethane to which the election applies.

(4) Where any ethane is used principally for the petrochemical purposes specified in the election but some of it used for fuel, as an incident of the principal use, the whole of it shall be regarded as ethane to which the election applies; but, subject thereto, the market value of ethane used otherwise than for those purposes shall be determined as if no election had been made.

(5) The provisions of Schedule 18 to this Act shall have effect for supplementing this section.

(6) In the preceding provisions of this section—

(*a*) "ethane" means oil consisting of gas of which the largest component by volume over any chargeable period is ethane and which—

(i) before being disposed of or appropriated as mentioned in subsection (2)(*a*) above either is not subjected to initial treatment or is subjected to initial treatment which does not include fractionation, or

(ii) results from the fractionation of gas before it is disposed of or relevantly appropriated;

(*b*) "taxation purposes" means the purposes of Part I of the principal Act and of Part VIII of the Finance Act 1981 (supplementary petroleum duty).

(7) In this section "fractionation" means the treatment of gas in order to separate gas of one or more kinds as mentioned in paragraph 2A(3) of Schedule 3 to the principal Act; and for the purposes of subsection (6)(*a*) above,—

(*a*) the proportion of ethane in any gas shall be determined at a temperature of 15 degrees centigrade and at a pressure of one atmosphere; and

(*b*) "component" means ethane, methane or liquified petroleum gas.

Amendments—[1] Words in sub-s (1) inserted by TA 1988 s 844, Sch 29 para 29.

[2] Words in sub-s (2) inserted by FA 1994 s 236(3) with effect from 31 December 1993.

[3] In sub-s (1) words inserted by CTA 2010 s 1177, Sch 1 para 177. CTA 2010 has effect for corporation tax purposes for accounting periods ending on or after 1 April 2010, and for income and capital gains tax purposes for the tax year 2010–11 and subsequent tax years.

[4] In sub-s (1) words substituted by TIOPA 2010 s 374, Sch 8 paras 177, 178. TIOPA 2010 has effect for corporation tax purposes for accounting periods ending on or after 1 April 2010, for income and capital gains tax purposes for the tax year 2010–11 and subsequent tax years, and for petroleum revenue tax purposes for chargeable periods beginning on or after 1 July 2010.

135 Determination of oil fields

(1) In any case where a determination of an oil field is made under Schedule 1 to the principal Act and before the date of the determination oil has been won from the oil field so determined,—

(*a*) Part I of the principal Act, except Schedule 7, and Part VIII of the Finance Act 1981 (supplementary petroleum duty) shall apply as if the determination had been made immediately before oil was first won from the field;

(*b*) where the actual date of the determination is later than the date which by virtue of paragraph (*a*) above is the end of a chargeable period for the oil field, then as respects that chargeable period sections 33(1) and 34 of the Taxes Management Act 1970 (in their application by virtue of paragraph 1 of Schedule 2 to the principal Act), paragraphs 2(1), 5(1) and 13 of Schedule 2 to the principal Act and paragraph 9 of Schedule 16 to the Finance Act 1981 shall have effect as if any reference to the end of a chargeable period were a reference to the actual date of the determination;

(*c*) where the actual date of the determination is later than the date which by virtue of paragraph (*a*) above is the end of a claim period in relation to the oil field, then as respects that claim period paragraph 2(1) of Schedule 5 to the principal Act and paragraph 1(2) of Schedule 6 to that Act shall have effect as if any reference to the end of the claim period in which the expenditure is incurred were a reference to that actual date; and (*d*) where the actual date of the determination is later than the date which by virtue of paragraph (*a*) above is the end of the transfer period, within the meaning of Schedule 17 to the Finance Act 1980, in relation to the oil field, then as respects that transfer period paragraph 3(1) of that Schedule shall have effect as if the reference to the end of the transfer period were a reference to that actual date.

(2) In any case where—

(*a*) a determination is made under paragraph 5 of Schedule 1 to the principal Act (variation of fields) varying an earlier determination; and

(*b*) in consequence of that variation an existing oil field is altered to any extent;

then Part I of the principal Act and Part VIII of the Finance Act 1981 shall apply in relation to the oil field subject only to the modifications provided by subsection (3) below.

(3) Where subsection (2) above applies—

(*a*) the time allowed—

(i) by paragraph 2 or paragraph 5 of Schedule 2 to the principal Act for making returns, or

(ii) by paragraph 3 of Schedule 17 to the Finance Act 1980 for delivering notices—

shall as respects returns or notices containing such particulars as may be required in consequence of the later determination be extended to a period ending, in the case of a return under paragraph 2 or a notice under paragraph 3, two months and, in the case of a return under paragraph 5, one month after the actual date of that determination;

(*b*) any claim falling to be made in accordance with Schedule 5 or 6 to the principal Act in respect of any expenditure incurred before the actual date of the later determination which could not have been made before that determination may be made at any time before the expiry of the period of six years beginning with that date;

(*c*) section 1 of the Petroleum Revenue Tax Act 1980 (payments of tax on account), section 105 of the Finance Act 1980 (advance payments of tax) and paragraph 10 of Schedule 16 to the Finance Act 1981 (payments on account of supplementary petroleum duty) shall not apply in relation to any return made under paragraph 2 of Schedule 2 to the principal Act in so far as it is made by virtue of paragraph (*a*) above; and

(*d*) section 139 below (advance petroleum revenue tax) shall not apply in relation to so much of the gross profit as accrues to any person in a chargeable period ending before the actual date of the later determination by virtue only of that later determination.

(4) (*amends* the Oil Taxation Act 1975 s 12(3)).

(5) This section has effect in relation to determinations made after 31 December 1981.

CHAPTER II

ADVANCE PETROLEUM REVENUE TAX

139 Liability for APRT and credit against liability for petroleum revenue tax

(1) For each of the following chargeable periods, namely—

(*a*) the first chargeable period ending after 31 December 1982 [and before 1 January 1987][1] in which, subject to sections 140 and 141 below, a gross profit accrues to a participator from an oil field, and

(*b*) every one out of the [immediately succeeding chargeable periods (if any) which ends before 1 January 1987 and][1] in which, subject to those sections, a gross profit accrues to him from that field,

the participator shall be liable to pay an amount of petroleum revenue tax (to be known as "advance petroleum revenue tax" and in this Chapter referred to as "APRT") in accordance with this section.

(2) Subject to sections 140 and 141 below, APRT shall be payable on the gross profit accruing to the participator in the chargeable period in question and shall be payable

[(*a*) for the chargeable period ending on 30 June 1983, at the rate of 20 per cent;

(*b*) for subsequent chargeable periods ending on or before 31 December 1984, at the rate of 15 per cent;

(*c*) for chargeable periods ending in 1985, at the rate of 10 per cent; and

(*d*) for chargeable periods ending in 1986, at the rate of 5 per cent][1].

(3) The aggregate of—

(*a*) [any APRT which is payable and paid][1] by a participator in respect of any chargeable period and not repaid, and

(*b*) any APRT which is carried forward from the previous chargeable period by virtue of subsection (4) below,

shall be set against the participator's liability for petroleum revenue tax charged in any assessment made on him in respect of the assessable profit accruing to him in the period referred to in paragraph (a) above from the oil field in question (which liability is in this Chapter referred to as his liability for petroleum revenue tax for a chargeable period) and shall, accordingly, discharge a corresponding amount of that liability.

(4) If, for any chargeable period, the aggregate of—

(*a*) [any APRT which is payable and paid][1] by a participator for that period and not repaid, and

(*b*) any APRT carried forward from the previous chargeable period by virtue of this subsection,

exceeds the participator's liability for petroleum revenue tax for that period, the excess shall be carried forward as an accretion to [any APRT paid][1] (and not repaid) for the next chargeable period; and any reference in this Chapter to a participator's APRT credit for a chargeable period is a reference to the aggregate of [any APRT paid][1] for that period and not repaid and any APRT carried forward from the previous chargeable period by virtue of this subsection.

(5) The references in section 1 of the Provisional Collection of Taxes Act 1968 to petroleum revenue tax include a reference to APRT.

(6) The provisions of Schedule 19 to this Act shall have effect for supplementing this section and, accordingly, section 105 of the Finance Act 1980 (advance payments of petroleum revenue tax) shall cease to have effect with respect to chargeable periods ending after 30 June 1983.

(7) This Chapter shall be included in the Oil Taxation Acts for the purposes of sections 107 and 108 of the Finance Act 1980 (transmedian fields and gas banking schemes).

Amendments—[1] Words in sub-ss (1)–(4) inserted or substituted by FA 1983 s 35.

140 Increase of gross profit by reference to royalties in kind

(1) This section applies where part of a participator's share of the oil won and saved from an oil field is delivered by him in a chargeable period to the [OGA][1] pursuant to a requirement imposed under the terms of a licence granted under the Petroleum (Production) Act 1934.

(2) In determining for the purposes of APRT the gross profit accruing to the participator from the field in the chargeable period the aggregate of the amounts mentioned in paragraphs (*a*), (*b*) and (*c*) of subsection (5) of section 2 of the principal Act shall be increased by multiplying it by a fraction of which—

(*a*) the numerator is the total of the quantity of oil won from the field which is delivered or relevantly appropriated by him in the period including the oil delivered to the [OGA][1]; and

(*b*) the denominator is that total excluding the oil delivered to the [OGA][1].

(3) Where oil is delivered pursuant to a requirement which relates to oil of one or more kinds but not to others, subsection (2) above shall apply only in relation to oil of the kind or kinds to which the requirement relates; and where oil is delivered pursuant to a requirement which specifies different proportions in relation to different kinds of oil, that subsection shall apply separately in relation to each of those kinds.

(4) For the purposes of subsection (5) of section 2 of the principal Act as it applies in determining for the purposes of APRT the gross profit accruing to a participator, the exclusion by paragraph 4 of Schedule 3 to that Act of oil delivered to the [OGA][1] under the terms of a licence granted under the said Act of 1934 shall be deemed to extend to oil which is inadvertently delivered to him in excess of the amount required; and oil so delivered shall be treated for the purposes of this section as delivered pursuant to a requirement imposed under the terms of such a licence.

(5) Any reference in this section or in section 141 below to the purposes of APRT includes a reference to the purpose of determining whether APRT is payable for a chargeable period by virtue of section 139(1) above.

Amendments—[1] Word substituted for words "Secretary of State" in each place by the Petroleum (Transfer of Functions) Regulations, SI 2016/898 reg 6(1), (2) with effect from 1 October 2016.

141 Reduction of gross profit by reference to exempt allowance

(1) For the purposes of APRT there shall be for each oil field in each chargeable period an exempt allowance of 500,000 metric tonnes of oil divided between the participators in shares proportionate to their shares of the oil won and saved from the field during the period.

(2) If the gross profit accruing to a participator in a chargeable period from a field exceeds the cash equivalent of his share of the exempt allowance, the gross profit shall be reduced to an amount equal to the excess.

(3) If the gross profit accruing to a participator in a chargeable period from a field does not exceed the cash equivalent of his share of the exempt allowance, the gross profit shall be reduced to nil.

(4) Subject to subsection (5) below, the cash equivalent of a participator's share of the exempt allowance for an oil field for a chargeable period shall be equal to such proportion of the gross profit accruing to him from the field in that period (before any reduction under this section) as his share of the exempt allowance bears to his share, exclusive of excluded oil within the meaning of section 10 of the principal Act, of the oil won and saved from the field during the period.

(5) If a participator in an oil field so elects by notice in writing given to the Board at the time when he makes his return under paragraph 2 of Schedule 2 to the principal Act for a chargeable period, the cash equivalent of his share of the exempt allowance for the field for that period shall be determined under subsection (4) above—

(*a*) to the extent that his share of that exempt allowance does not exceed his share of the oil (other than gas) won and saved from the field in the period, as if in computing the gross profit accruing to him in the period all amounts relating to gas fell to be disregarded; and (*b*) to the extent, if any, that his share of that allowance exceeds his share of the oil (other than gas) so won and saved, as if in computing the gross profit so accruing all amounts relating to oil other than gas fell to be disregarded.

(6) In this section references to a participator's share of the oil won and saved from a field are to his share as expressed in metric tonnes and for that purpose 1,100 cubic metres of oil consisting of gas at a temperature of 15 degrees centigrade and pressure of one atmosphere shall be counted as equivalent to one metric tonne of oil other than gas.

142 Consequences of crediting APRT against liability for petroleum revenue tax

(1) If it appears to the Board—

(*a*) that any amount of APRT credit which has been set off against a participator's assessed liability to petroleum revenue tax for any chargeable period ought not to have been so set off, or that the amount so set off has become excessive, or

(*b*) that, disregarding any liability to or credit for APRT, a participator is entitled to a repayment of petroleum revenue tax for any chargeable period,

then, for the purpose of securing that the liabilities of the participator to petroleum revenue tax and APRT (including interest on unpaid tax) for the chargeable period in question are what they ought to have been, the Board may make such assessments to, and shall make such repayments of, petroleum revenue tax and APRT as in their judgment are necessary in the circumstances.

(2) In a case falling within paragraph (*a*) of subsection (1) above, any necessary assessment to petroleum revenue tax may, where the revised amount of set off is ascertained as a result of an appeal, be made at any time before the expiry of the period of six years beginning at the end of the chargeable period in which the appeal is finally determined; and in a case falling within paragraph (*b*) of that subsection any necessary assessment to APRT may be made at any time before the expiry of the period of six years beginning at the end of the chargeable period in which the participator became entitled as mentioned in that paragraph.

(3), (4) (*amends* OTA 1975 s 17).

(5) Paragraphs 13, 14 and 15 of Schedule 2 to the principal Act (payment of tax, appeals and interest on tax) apply in relation to an assessment to petroleum revenue tax under subsection (1) above as they apply to an assessment under that Schedule.

PART VII
MISCELLANEOUS AND SUPPLEMENTARY

157 Short title, interpretation, construction and repeals

(1) This Act may be cited as the Finance Act 1982.

(2)–(4) [not reproduced].

(5) Part VI of this Act shall be construed as one with Part I of the Oil Taxation Act 1975 . . . [1] and references in Part VI to the principal Act are references to that Act.

(6) The enactments and Orders mentioned in Schedule 22 to this Act (which include spent enactments) are hereby repealed to the extent specified in the third column of that Schedule, but subject to any provision at the end of any part of that Schedule.

Amendments—[1] In sub-s (5) words repealed by TA 1988 s 844, Sch 31.

SCHEDULES

SCHEDULE 18

ALTERNATIVE VALUATION OF ETHANE USED FOR PETROCHEMICAL PURPOSES

Section 134

The election

1—(1) An election shall be made—

(*a*) in so far as it is to apply to ethane which is relevantly appropriated, by the participator alone; and

(*b*) in so far as it is to apply to ethane which is disposed of, by the participator and the person to whom it is disposed of.

(2) An election shall be made in such form as may be prescribed by the Board and shall—

(*a*) identify, by reference to volume, chemical composition and initial treatment, the ethane to which the election is to apply;

(*b*) specify the period, beginning on or after the date of the election and not exceeding fifteen years, which is covered by the election;

(*c*) specify the price formula which is to apply for determining the market values of ethane during that period;

(*d*) specify the petrochemical purposes for which ethane to which the election applies will be used; and (*e*) specify the place to or at which any such ethane is to be delivered or appropriated.

(3) The reference in sub-paragraph (2)(*a*) above to initial treatment is a reference to such initial treatment (if any) as the ethane will have been subjected to before it is disposed of or relevantly appropriated.

Conditions for acceptance of an election

2—(1) Subject to sub-paragraphs (2) and (3) below, the Board shall accept an election if they are satisfied that, under a relevant contract (as defined in paragraph 3 below) for the sale at arm's length of the ethane to which the election applies, the contract prices would not differ materially from the market values determined in accordance with the price formula specified in the election; and if the Board are not so satisfied they shall reject the election.

(2) The Board shall reject an election if they are not satisfied that the price formula specified in the election is such that the market value of ethane disposed of or relevantly appropriated at any time during the period covered by the election will be readily ascertainable either by reference to the price formula alone or by reference to that formula and to information—

(*a*) which is, or is expected to be at that time, publicly available; and

(*b*) which is not related or dependent, in whole or to any substantial degree, to or on the activities of the person or persons making the election or any person connected or associated with him or them.

(3) The Board shall reject an election if, after receiving notice in writing from the Board, the person or, as the case may be, either of the persons by whom the election was made—

(*a*) fails to furnish to the Board, before the appropriate date, any information which the Board may reasonably require for the purpose of determining whether the election should be accepted; or

(*b*) fails to make available for inspection, before the appropriate date, by an officer authorised by the Board any books, accounts or documents in his possession or power which contain any information relevant for that purpose.

(4) In sub-paragraph (3) above "the appropriate date" means such date as may be specified in the notice concerned, being a date not earlier than one month after the date on which the notice was given.

(5) Any notice under sub-paragraph (3) above shall be given within the period of three months beginning on the date of the election in question.

3—(1) In paragraph 2 above "relevant contract" means a contract which is entered into,—

(*a*) if the price formula specified in the election is derived from an actual contract which is identified in the election and was entered into not more than two years before the date of the election, at the time at which that contract was entered into, and

(*b*) in any other case, at the time of the election in question,

and which incorporates the terms specified in sub-paragraph (2) below, but is not necessarily a contract for the sale of ethane for petrochemical purposes.

(2) The terms referred to in sub-paragraph (1) above are—

(*a*) that the ethane is required to be delivered at the place in the United Kingdom [or another country][1] at which the seller could reasonably be expected to deliver it or, if there is more than one such place, the one nearest to the place of extraction; and

(*b*) that the price formula may be varied only in the event of a substantial and lasting change in the economic circumstances surrounding or underlying the contract and that any such variation may not take place before the expiry of the period of five years beginning on the date of the first delivery of ethane during the period covered by the election.

Amendments—[1] Words in sub-para (2) inserted by F(No 2)A 1992 s 74, Sch 15 para 5.

Notice of acceptance or rejection

4—(1) Notice of the acceptance or rejection of an election shall be given to the party or, as the case may be, each of the parties to the election before the expiry of the period of three months beginning on—

(*a*) the date of the election, or

(*b*) if a notice has been given under paragraph 2(3) above relating to the election, the date or, as the case may be, the last date which is the appropriate date, as defined in paragraph 2(4) above, in relation to such a notice.

(2) If no such notice of acceptance or rejection is so given, the Board shall be deemed to have accepted the election and to have given notice of their acceptance on the last day of the period referred to in sub-paragraph (1) above.

(3) After notice of the acceptance of an election has been given under this paragraph, a change in the identity of the participator or, where appropriate, of the person to whom the ethane in question is disposed of shall not, of itself, affect the continuing operation of the election.

Market value ceasing to be readily ascertainable

5—(1) In any case where—

(*a*) it appears to the Board that, at some time during the period covered by an election, the market value of ethane to which the election applies has ceased or is ceasing to be readily ascertainable as mentioned in paragraph 2(2) above, and

(*b*) the Board give notice of that fact to the party or, as the case may be, each of the parties to the election and in that notice specify a date for the purposes of this paragraph (which may be a date earlier than that on which the notice is given),

then, subject to sub-paragraph (2) below, on the date so specified the election shall cease to have effect.

(2) If—

(*a*) within the period of three months beginning on the date of a notice under sub-paragraph (1)(*b*) above, the party or parties to the election by notice in writing given to the Board specify a new price formula, and

(*b*) the new price formula is accepted by the Board in accordance with paragraph 7 below,

the election shall continue to have effect and, subject to paragraph 9 below, for the purpose of determining the market value, on and after the date specified in the notice under sub-paragraph (1)(b) above, of ethane to which the election applies, section 134 of this Act shall have effect as if the new price formula were the formula specified in the election.

Price formula ceasing to give realistic market values

6—(1) If, at any time after the expiry of the period of five years beginning on the date of the first delivery or relevant appropriation of ethane during the period covered by an election,—

(*a*) it appears to the party or parties to the election or, as the case may be, to the Board that, by reason of any substantial and lasting change in any economic circumstances which were relevant at the time referred to in paragraph 3(1) above, the market values determined in accordance with the price formula specified in the election are no longer realistic; and

(*b*) the party or parties to the election give notice of that fact to the Board, or the Board give notice of that fact to the party or, as the case may be, each of the parties to the election,

then, subject to the following provisions of this paragraph, sub-paragraph (2) below shall apply.

(2) Where this sub-paragraph applies, the election shall not have effect with respect to any chargeable period beginning after the date of the notice under sub-paragraph (1)(*b*) above.

(3) Before the expiry of the period of three months beginning on the date on which a notice under sub-paragraph (1)(*b*) above given by the party or parties to the election is received by the Board, the Board shall give notice of acceptance or rejection of that notice to the party or parties concerned; and

(*a*) if the Board give notice of rejection, sub-paragraph (2) above shall not apply; and

(*b*) if no notice of acceptance or rejection is in fact given as required by this sub-paragraph, the Board shall be deemed to have given notice of acceptance on the last day of the period of three months referred to above.

(4) If a notice under sub-paragraph (1)(*b*) above which has been given by the party or parties to the election contains a new price formula, the Board shall first consider the notice without regard to that formula and if, following upon that consideration, the Board give a notice of acceptance under sub-paragraph (3) above, they shall then proceed to consider the new price formula.

(5) In any case where—

(*a*) sub-paragraph (4) above applies and the new price formula contained in the notice under sub-paragraph (1)(*b*) above is accepted by the Board in accordance with paragraph 7 below, or

(*b*) within the period of three months beginning on the date of a notice given by the Board under sub-paragraph (1)(*b*) above, the party or parties to the election by notice in writing given to the Board specify a new price formula which is accepted by the Board in accordance with paragraph 7 below,

sub-paragraph (2) above shall not apply and for the purpose of determining, for any chargeable period beginning after the date of the notice under sub-paragraph (1)(b) above, the market value of ethane to which the election applies, section 134 of this Act shall have effect as if the new price formula were the formula specified in the election.

(6) If, by virtue of sub-paragraph (5) above or an appeal under paragraph 8 below, a new price formula has effect for determining the market value of ethane to which an election applies, sub-paragraph (1) above shall thereafter have effect in relation to the market value of any such ethane as if—

(*a*) the reference therein to the date of the first delivery or relevant appropriation of ethane during the period covered by the election, and

(*b*) the reference therein to the time referred to in paragraph 3(1) above, were each a reference to the beginning of the first chargeable period for which the new price formula has effect.

Acceptance or rejection of new price formula

7—(1) Subject to sub-paragraph (3) below, the Board shall accept a new price formula specified in a notice under paragraph 5(2) above if they are satisfied that the new formula provides for readily ascertainable market values which correspond, so far as practicable, with those which were intended to be provided for under the original price formula; and if the Board are not so satisfied they shall reject such a new price formula.

(2) Subject to sub-paragraph (3) below, sub-paragraphs (1) and (2) of paragraph 2 above and paragraph 3 above shall apply to determine whether the Board shall accept—

(*a*) a new price formula contained in a notice under paragraph 6(1)(*b*) above which has been accepted by the Board under paragraph 6(3) above, or

(*b*) if the Board have given notice under paragraph 6(1)(*b*) above, a new price formula specified in a notice under paragraph 6(5)(*b*) above,

as if the new price formula were specified in an election made at the time the notice under paragraph 6(1)(b) above was given.

(3) The Board shall reject such a new price formula as is referred to in sub-paragraph (1) or sub-paragraph (2) above if, after receiving notice in writing from the Board, the party or, as the case may be, either of the parties to the election—

(*a*) fails to furnish to the Board, before the appropriate date, any information which the Board may reasonably require for the purpose of determining whether the new formula should be accepted in accordance with sub-paragraph (1) or, as the case may be, sub-paragraph (2) above, or

(*b*) fails to make available for inspection, before the appropriate date, by an officer authorised by the Board any books, accounts or documents in his possession or power which contain information relevant for that purpose.

(4) Sub-paragraph (4) of paragraph 2 above applies in relation to sub-paragraph (3) above as it applies in relation to sub-paragraph (3) of that paragraph.

(5) Notice of the acceptance or rejection of a new price formula—

(*a*) specified in a notice under paragraph 5(2) or paragraph 6(5)(*b*) above, or

(*b*) contained in a notice under paragraph 6(1)(*b*) above which has been accepted by the Board by a notice under paragraph 6(3) above,

shall be given to the party or, as the case may be, each of the parties to the election concerned before the expiry of the period of three months beginning on the relevant date (as defined in sub-paragraph (6) below), and if no notice of acceptance or rejection is in fact given as required by this sub-paragraph, the Board shall be deemed to have accepted the formula and to have given notice of their acceptance on the last day of that period.

(6) In sub-paragraph (5) above "the relevant date" means—

(*a*) if a notice has been given under sub-paragraph (3) above relating to the price formula in question, the date or, as the case may be, the last date which is the appropriate date, within the meaning of that sub-paragraph, in relation to such a notice; and

(*b*) if no such notice has been given, then—

(i) in relation to a new price formula, falling within paragraph (*a*) of sub-paragraph (5) above, the date on which the notice referred to in that paragraph was received by the Board; and

(ii) in relation to a new price formula falling within paragraph (*b*) of that sub-paragraph, the date of the notice from the Board under paragraph 6(3) above.

8—(1) Where the Board give notice to any person or persons—

(*a*) under paragraph 4 above, rejecting an election; or

(*b*) under paragraph 5 above, that the value of any ethane has ceased or is ceasing to be readily ascertainable; or

(*c*) under paragraph 6(1)(*b*) above, that a price formula is no longer realistic; or

(*d*) under paragraph 6(3) above, rejecting a notice given under paragraph 6(1)(*b*) above; or

(*e*) under paragraph 7(5) above, rejecting a new price formula;

that person or, as the case may be, those persons acting jointly may appeal . . . [1] against the notice.

(2) An appeal under sub-paragraph (1) above shall be made by notice in writing given to the Board within thirty days after the date of the notice in respect of which the appeal is brought.

(3) Where at any time after the giving of notice of appeal under this paragraph and before the determination of the appeal by the [tribunal][1], the Board and the appellant agree that the notice in respect of which the appeal is brought should be accepted or withdrawn or varied, the same consequences shall ensue as if the [tribunal][1] had determined the appeal to that effect.

(4) [If an appeal under this paragraph is notified to the tribunal and the tribunal determines][1] that the appeal should be allowed [it][1] shall allow the appeal and—

(*a*) where the appeal is against a notice of rejection of an election or proposed new price formula, [the tribunal shall][1] substitute a notice of acceptance of the election or price formula without modification or with such modifications as [the tribunal thinks][1] fit;

(*b*) where the appeal is against a notice under paragraph 5 or paragraph 6(1)(*b*) above, [the tribunal may direct][1] that the price formula in question shall continue to have effect as if the notice had not been given; and

(*c*) where the appeal is against a notice under paragraph 6(3) above rejecting a notice under paragraph 6(1)(*b*) above, the [tribunal][1] shall substitute a notice of acceptance.

(5) Sub-paragraphs (2), (8) and (11) of paragraph 14 of Schedule 2 to the principal Act[, and paragraphs 14A to 14I of that Schedule][1] shall apply in relation to an appeal against any such notice as is referred to in sub-paragraph (1) above as they apply in relation to an appeal against an assessment or determination made under the principal Act, but with the substitution, for any reference to the participator, of a reference to the person or persons who gave notice of appeal under sub-paragraph (2) above [and, in the case of paragraphs 14A to 14I of Schedule 2, with such other modifications as may be necessary][1].

(6) Where notice of appeal is duly given against a notice given by the Board under paragraph 5 or paragraph 6(1)(*b*) above, the period of three months referred to in paragraph 5(2)(*a*) or, as the case may be, paragraph 6(5)(*b*) above shall not begin to run until the appeal is withdrawn or finally determined.

(7) Any reference in section 134 of this Act or the preceding provisions of this Schedule to an election accepted by the Board shall be construed as including a reference to an election accepted in pursuance of an appeal under this paragraph.

Amendments—[1] In sub-para (1) words "to the Special Commissioners" repealed, in sub-para (3), word substituted for word "Commissioners", in both places, in sub-para (4), in words before para (*a*), words substituted for words "If, on a hearing of an appeal under this paragraph it appears to the majority of the Commissioners present at the hearing", and word substituted for word "they", in sub-para (4)(*a*) words substituted for words "they shall" and "they think" respectively, in sub-para (4)(*b*), words substituted for words "they may direct", in sub-para (4)(*c*), word substituted for word "Commissioners", and in sub-para (5), words inserted, by the Transfer of Tribunal Functions and Revenue and Customs Appeals Order, SI 2009/56 art 3, Sch 1 paras 100, 101 with effect from 1 April 2009.

Returns

9 In any case where a notice under paragraph 5(1)(*b*) above or paragraph 6(1)(*b*) above relating to an election has been given to a party to the election or to the Board then, unless the notice has been withdrawn (whether in pursuance of an appeal or otherwise) or a price formula different from that to which the notice referred has effect as if specified in the election, any party to the election, in making a return under paragraph 2 of Schedule 2 to the principal Act with respect to ethane to which that election applies or which by virtue of that election falls within section 134(3) of this Act—

(*a*) where the notice was given under paragraph 5 above, may include the market value on and after the date specified in the notice of any such ethane determined on such basis as appears to him to be the best practical alternative to that provided by the price formula to which the notice referred; and

(*b*) where the notice was given under paragraph 6 above, shall include the market value of any such ethane determined in accordance with the price formula to which the notice referred.

Penalties for incorrect information etc

10—(1) [Schedule 24 to the Finance Act 2007 (which penalises inaccurate documents and is in this paragraph referred to as "the penalty provisions")][1] shall apply, in accordance with sub-paragraph (2) or sub-paragraph (3) below, in relation to inaccurate information—

(*a*) contained in an election; or

(*b*) furnished pursuant to a notice under paragraph 2(3) or paragraph 7(3) above; or

(*c*) contained in any books, accounts or documents made available as mentioned in paragraph 2(3)(*b*) or paragraph 7(3)(*b*) above.

(2) Where the inaccurate information is provided by a participator, the penalty provisions shall apply—

(*a*) as they apply in relation to an incorrect return under paragraph 2 of Schedule 2 to the principal Act; and

(*b*) *as if the reference in paragraph 8(2)(a)(i) of that Schedule to the chargeable period to which the return relates were a reference to each chargeable period which falls within the period covered by the election and which is affected by any decision of the Board in connection with which the provision of the information was material.*[1]

(3) Where the incorrect information is provided by a person other than a participator, the penalty provisions shall apply—

(*a*) as they apply to an incorrect return under paragraph 5 of Schedule 2 to the principal Act; and (*b*) as if that person were the responsible person for an oil field.

Amendments—[1] In sub-s (1), words substituted for words "Paragraphs 8 and 9 of Schedule 2 to the principal Act (which penalise inaccurate returns etc and are in this paragraph referred to as "the penalty provisions")", and sub-para (2)(*b*) repealed, by the Finance Act 2008, Schedule 40 (Appointed Day, Transitional Provisions and Consequential Amendments) Order, SI 2009/571 art 8, Sch 1 paras 17, 18 with effect from 1 April 2009.

Interpretation

11—(1) Subsection (6) of section 134 of this Act has effect in relation to this Schedule as it has effect in relation to the preceding provisions of that section.

(2) In this Schedule, any reference to an election is a reference to an election under section 134 of this Act; and any reference to the date of an election is a reference to the date on which the election (made as mentioned in paragraph 1 above) is received by the Board.

(3) Any reference in the preceding provisions of this Schedule to the party to an election is relevant only to an election applying to ethane which is relevantly appropriated and is a reference to the participator by whom the ethane is for the time being so appropriated.

(4) Any reference in the preceding provisions of this Schedule to the parties to an election is relevant only to an election applying to ethane which is disposed of as mentioned in section 134(2)(*a*) of this Act and is a reference to the participator by whom and the person to whom the ethane is for the time being so disposed of.

SCHEDULE 19

SUPPLEMENTARY PROVISIONS RELATING TO APRT

Section 139(6)

PART I
COLLECTION OF TAX

Payment of tax

1—(1) APRT which a participator is liable to pay in respect of any chargeable period for an oil field shall be due on the date on which the return for that period and that field is made by the participator in accordance with paragraph 2 of Schedule 2 to the principal Act or, if a return is not so made, on the last day of the second month following that period; and APRT which is due shall be payable without the making of an assessment.

(2) Subject to sub-paragraph (3) below, every participator in an oil field shall, at the time when he delivers to the Board the return for a chargeable period required by paragraph 2 of Schedule 2 to the principal Act—

(*a*) deliver to the Board a statement showing whether any, and if so what, amount of APRT is payable by him for that chargeable period in respect of the field; and

(*b*) subject to the following provisions of this Schedule, pay to the Board the amount of APRT, if any, shown in the statement.

(3) In relation to any oil field, sub-paragraph (2) above does not apply with respect to any chargeable period after the last of the . . . [1] chargeable periods referred to in section 139(1)(*b*) of this Act.

(4) The statement under sub-paragraph (2)(*a*) above shall be in such form as the Board may prescribe.

(5) Paragraphs 3, 8 and 9 of Schedule 2 to the principal Act shall apply in relation to statements required to be made under this paragraph as they apply in relation to returns required to be made under paragraph 2 of that Schedule.

Amendments—[1] Words in sub-para (3) repealed by FA 1983 ss 35, 48, Sch 7 para 1, Sch 10 Pt III.

2—(1) Subject to sub-paragraph (2) below, if for any chargeable period for an oil field ending on or after 30 June 1983—

(*a*) an amount of APRT is shown to be payable by the participator in the statement delivered by him in accordance with paragraph 1 above in respect of that period and that field; or

(*b*) an amount is payable by the participator on account of petroleum revenue tax in accordance with section 1 of the Petroleum Revenue Tax Act 1980 in respect of that period and that field; or

(*c*) both such amounts are so payable by the participator,

then the participator shall pay to the Board six monthly instalments commencing in the second month of the next chargeable period each equal to one-eighth of the amount referred to in paragraph (a) or paragraph (b) above or, where paragraph (c) applies, of the aggregate of those amounts.

(2) With respect to [any chargeable period ending on or after 31 December 1984][1] sub-paragraph (1) above shall have effect as if—

PRT

(*a*) for paragraphs (*a*) to (*c*) there were substituted the words "an amount of tax is shown to be payable in the statement delivered in respect of that period in accordance with section 1(1)(*a*) of the Petroleum Revenue Tax Act 1980"; and

(*b*) for the words from "the amount referred to in paragraph (*a*)" onwards there shall be substituted the words "that amount".

(3) Instalments paid in accordance with sub-paragraph (1) above shall be regarded as being paid in respect of the next chargeable period referred to in that sub-paragraph.

(4) The aggregate amount paid by a participator in accordance with sub-paragraph (1) above in respect of a chargeable period for an oil field—

(*a*) to the extent that it is equal to or less than his liability, if any, to pay an amount of APRT under paragraph 1 above in respect of that oil field for that chargeable period shall be deemed to be an amount of APRT paid by him in respect of that field for that period; and

(*b*) to the extent that it exceeds any such liability of his to pay an amount of APRT and is equal to or less than his liability, if any, to pay an amount in respect of that field for that period in accordance with paragraph (*b*) of subsection (1) of section 1 of the Petroleum Revenue Tax Act 1980 (payments on account of petroleum revenue tax), shall be deemed to be an amount paid by him under that paragraph.

[(4A) In sub-paragraph (1) the reference to any chargeable period for an oil field ending on or after 30th June 1983 does not include a chargeable period ending on 31st December 2015.][2]

Amendments—[1] Words in sub-para (2) substituted by FA 1983 s 35, Sch 7 para 2.

[2] Sub-para (4A) inserted by FA 2016 s 140(3) with effect from 15 September 2016.

3—(1) [Subject to sub-paragraph (1A) below][1] if in any month [(the relevant month)[1] a participator in an oil field—

(*a*) has not delivered (otherwise than to the [OGA][2]) any of the oil which has been won from the field and disposed of by him at any time in or before that month; and

(*b*) has not relevantly appropriated any of the oil which has been so won by him at any such time,

he shall be entitled to withhold the instalment due, under paragraph 2 above, for that field in the following month.

[(1A) Sub-paragraph (1) above does not apply if the relevant month is a month in which any consideration (whether in the nature of income or capital) is received or receivable by the participator in respect of any such matter as is mentioned in paragraph (*a*) or (*b*) in section 6(2) of the Oil Taxation Act 1983 (chargeable tariff receipts).][1]

(2) An instalment shall not be withheld by virtue of the conditions in sub-paragraph (1) above being fulfilled in any month unless a notice to that effect, in such form as the Board may prescribe, is given to the Board before the end of the following month and—

(*a*) where the Board are not satisfied with any such notice, the powers conferred by paragraph 7 of Schedule 2 to the principal Act (production of accounts etc) shall be exercisable as if the notice were a return under paragraph 2 of that Schedule; and

(*b*) paragraph 8 of that Schedule (penalties) shall apply to an incorrect notice as it applies to an incorrect return under paragraph 2.

Concessions I5—Petroleum revenue tax instalments.

Amendments—[1] Words in sub-para (1) and whole of sub-para (1A) inserted by FA 1999 s 99 with effect in respect of chargeable periods ending after 30 December 1999.

[2] In sub-para (1)(*a*), word substituted for words "Secretary of State" in each place by the Petroleum (Transfer of Functions) Regulations, SI 2016/898 reg 6(1), (3) with effect from 1 October 2016.

4 Certificates of tax deposit issued by the Treasury under section 12 of the National Loans Act 1968 on terms published on or before 14 May 1979 may be used for making payments of APRT and of instalments under paragraph 2 above; and for that purpose those terms shall have effect with the necessary modifications and as if the tax in or towards the payment of which a certificate is used were due—

(*a*) in the case of APRT payable under paragraph 1 above, two months after the end of the chargeable period to which it relates;

(*b*) in the case of an instalment payable under paragraph 2 above, at the end of the month in which the instalment is required to be paid.

Assessments and appeals

5—(1) Where it appears to the Board that any APRT payable in accordance with paragraph 1 above has not been paid on the due date they may make an assessment to tax on the participator and shall give him notice of any such assessment.

(2) APRT due under an assessment under this paragraph shall be due within thirty days of the issue of the notice of assessment.

(3) A notice of assessment shall state that the participator may appeal against the assessment in accordance with paragraph 7 below.

(4) After the service of a notice of assessment the assessment shall not be altered except in accordance with the express provisions of this Part of this Schedule or any of the provisions of the Taxes Management Act 1970 which apply by virtue of paragraph 1 of Schedule 2 to the principal Act in relation to the assessment.

6—(1) Where it appears to the Board that any gross profit charged to tax on a participator for any chargeable period in respect of an oil field by an assessment under paragraph 5 above ought to have been larger or smaller or that no gross profit accrued to the participator from that oil field during that chargeable period, they may make such amendments to the assessment or withdraw the assessment, as the case may require.
(2) Where the Board amend an assessment under sub-paragraph (1) above they shall give notice to the participator of the amendment; and sub-paragraphs (2) to (4) of paragraph 5 above shall apply in relation to any such notice as they apply in relation to a notice of assessment under paragraph 5.

7—(1) A participator may appeal . . . [1] against an assessment or amendment of an assessment under paragraph 5 or paragraph 6 above by notice of appeal in writing to the Board given within thirty days of the date of issue of the notice of the assessment or amendment of assessment.
(2) Sub-paragraphs (2) to (11) of paragraph 14 of [and paragraphs 14A to 14I of][1] Schedule 2 to the principal Act shall apply in relation to an appeal under this paragraph as they apply in relation to an appeal under sub-paragraph (1) of that paragraph except that—

(*a*) for each reference in [paragraph 14(3)][1] to tax there shall be substituted a reference to APRT;
(*b*) where in determining the gross profit accruing to a participator from a field in a chargeable period the aggregate of the amounts mentioned in paragraphs (*a*) to (*c*) of subsection (5) of section 2 of the principal Act falls to be increased under section 140 of this Act (whether as respects all oil or as respects a particular kind or kinds of oil), the difference mentioned in [paragraph 14(3)(b)][1] (or as the case may be, the difference so far as relating to oil of the particular kind or kinds in question) shall be increased by multiplying it by the fraction mentioned in subsection (2) of section 140;
(*c*) for each reference in [paragraph 14(10)][1] to an assessable profit there shall be substituted a reference to a gross profit; . . . [1]
(*d*) any reference in [paragraph 14(10)][1] to an allowable loss shall be omitted[; and
(*e*) in the case of paragraphs 14A to 14I of Schedule 2, with such modifications as may be necessary][1].

Amendments—[1] In sub-para (1), words "to the Special Commissioners" repealed, in sub-para (2), in words before para (*a*) words inserted, in para (*a*), words substituted for words "sub-paragraph (3)", in para (*b*), words substituted for words "sub-paragraph (3)(*b*)", in para (*c*), word "and" repealed, in paras (*c*), (*d*), words substituted for words "sub-paragraph 10" in both places, and para (*e*) and preceding word "and" inserted, by the Transfer of Tribunal Functions and Revenue and Customs Appeals Order, SI 2009/56 art 3, Sch 1 paras 100, 102 with effect from 1 April 2009.

8 Paragraphs 5(2) to (4) and 7 above shall apply in relation to an assessment to APRT under section 142(1) of this Act as if it were an assessment under paragraph 5.

Overpayment of tax

9—(1) Where in respect of any oil field a participator has paid an amount of APRT for a chargeable period which exceeds the amount of APRT payable therefor the amount of that excess shall be repaid to him.
(2) Where in respect of any oil field the amount paid for any chargeable period by a participator by way of instalments under paragraph 2 above exceeds the aggregate of his liabilities mentioned in sub-paragraph (4) of that paragraph, the amount of that excess shall be repaid to him.

Interest

10—(1) APRT payable for a chargeable period but not paid before the end of the second month after the end of that period shall carry interest from the end of that month until payment.
(2) Any amount payable by a participator as an instalment in respect of a chargeable period for a field and not paid by him in the month in which it ought to be paid shall carry interest from the end of that month until—

(*a*) payment of the amount, or
(*b*) two months after the end of that period, whichever is the earlier.

(3) Where, in accordance with paragraph 14 of Schedule 2 to the principal Act as applied by paragraph 7 above, APRT may be withheld until the determination or abandonment of an appeal, the interest on that APRT may also be withheld until the determination or abandonment of that appeal.
(4) Where an amount of APRT or an amount paid by way of instalment becomes repayable, that amount shall carry interest from—

(*a*) two months after the end of the chargeable period in respect of which the APRT or the instalment was paid, or

PRT

(*b*) the date on which the amount was paid, whichever is the later, until [the order for repayment is issued][1].

(5) For the purposes of sub-paragraph (2) above a payment on account of an overdue instalment shall, so far as possible, be attributed to the earliest month for which an instalment is overdue; and for the purposes of sub-paragraph (4) above any instalment or part of an instalment that becomes repayable shall, so far as possible, be regarded as consisting of the instalment most recently paid.

(6) In its application (by virtue of paragraph 1 of Schedule 2 to the principal Act) to interest payable under sub-paragraph (1) or sub-paragraph (2) above, section 69 of the Taxes Management Act 1970 shall have effect with the omission of the words "charged and due and payable under the assessment to which it relates".

(7) . . . [2]

(8) Any reference in this paragraph to interest is a reference to interest at the rate applying under paragraph 15 of Schedule 2 to the principal Act.

Rewrite destination—Sub-para (7) rewritten to CTA 2010 s 302(2), (3).

Amendments—[1] Words in sub-para (4) substituted, with retrospective effect, by FA 1989 s 180(2), (7).

[2] Sub-para (7) repealed by CTA 2010 ss 1177, 1181, Sch 1 para 178, Sch 3 Pt 2 with effect for corporation tax purposes only, for accounting periods ending on or after 1 April 2010.

Transitional provisions

11—(1) In any case where, by virtue of section 105 of the Finance Act 1980, a sum is paid by a participator as an advance payment of tax in respect of an oil field for the chargeable period ending on 30 June 1983 then,—

(*a*) to the extent that the sum so paid does not exceed his liability to APRT for that period, it shall be deemed to be a payment of APRT for that period; and

(*b*) subsection (5) of that section (treatment of advance payments) shall apply to any such sum only to the extent that it exceeds that liability to APRT.

(2) In subsection (7) of that section the reference to tax assessed on a participator in respect of a field for a chargeable period shall include, for the chargeable period ending on 30 June 1983, a reference to the amount (if any) of APRT payable by him in respect of that field for that period.

12—(1) Every participator in an oil field shall in March 1983 and in each of the four succeeding months pay to the Board an amount equal to one-fifth of the amount, if any, shown in the statement delivered by the participator under paragraph 10(1)(*a*) of Schedule 16 to the Finance Act 1981 as supplementary petroleum duty payable by him in respect of the field for the chargeable period ending on 31 December 1982.

(2) Paragraphs 2(4) and 9 above shall apply in relation to any payment made by the participator under sub-paragraph (1) above as if it were an instalment under paragraph 2 above paid in respect of the chargeable period ending on 30 June 1983; but for the purposes of this sub-paragraph the amount of the participator's liability to pay any APRT as mentioned in paragraph 2(4) above shall be reduced by the amount of any APRT deemed to have been paid by him in accordance with paragraph 11 above.

(3) Paragraphs 3, 4 and 10 above shall apply in relation to a payment under sub-paragraph (1) above as if it were an instalment under paragraph 2 above.

13—(1) If, in respect of the chargeable period ending on 30 June 1983, any sum is payable by a participator in accordance with section 1 of the Petroleum Revenue Tax Act 1980, then, so far as the net amount of that sum is concerned, only one-fifth shall become payable at the time specified in that section and the remaining four-fifths shall be paid in four equal monthly instalments in the months of September to December 1983, inclusive.

(2) The reference in sub-paragraph (1) above to the net amount of any sum payable in accordance with section 1 of the Petroleum Revenue Tax Act 1980 is a reference to the sum specified in paragraph (*b*) of subsection (1) of that section less any amount which is treated as (or deemed to be) paid as part of that sum—

(*a*) by virtue of section 105(5) of the Finance Act 1980, as applied by paragraph 11(1)(*b*) above; or

(*b*) by virtue of paragraph 2(4)(*b*) above, as applied by paragraph 12(2) above.

(3) Any amount payable by a participator as an instalment by virtue of sub-paragraph (1) above and not paid by him in the month in which it ought to be paid shall carry interest from the end of that month until payment.

(4) Paragraph 15 of Schedule 2 to the principal Act (interest on assessed tax) shall not apply in relation to so much of the tax charged in an assessment on the participator for the chargeable period referred to in sub-paragraph (1) above (excluding any APRT so charged) as is equal to or less than the net amount referred to in that sub-paragraph and payable by him, and in relation to so much if any of that tax as exceeds that net amount paragraph 15 shall apply with the substitution for the words "two months after the end of the period" of the words "the end of October 1983".

(5) If, in respect of the chargeable period referred to in sub-paragraph (1) above, any amount of tax charged by an assessment to tax or paid on account of tax so charged becomes repayable under any provision of Part I of the principal Act, paragraph 16 of Schedule 2 to the principal Act (interest on such repayments) shall have effect in relation to that amount with the substitution for the words following "per annum" of the words "from the end of October 1983 until repayment".

(6) Sub-paragraphs (5) to (8) of paragraph 10 above shall apply for the purposes of sub-paragraphs (3) and (5) above as they apply for the purposes of sub-paragraphs (2) and (4) of paragraph 10.

PART II
MISCELLANEOUS

Repayment of APRT

14—(1) If a participator in an oil field has an excess of APRT credit [for the ninth chargeable period following the first chargeable period referred to in section 139(1)(*a*)][1] of this Act, then, on the making of a claim the amount of that excess shall be repaid to him.

(2) For the purposes of this paragraph there is an excess of APRT credit for [the ninth chargeable period referred to in sub-paragraph (1) above][1] if any of that credit would, apart from this paragraph, fall to be carried forward to the next chargeable period in accordance with [section 139(4) of this Act][1]; and the amount of the excess is the amount of the credit which would fall to be so carried forward.

(3) A claim under sub-paragraph (1) above shall be made not earlier than two months after the expiry of [the ninth chargeable period][1] referred to in that sub-paragraph.

(4) In any case where—

(*a*) a claim is made under sub-paragraph (1) above before an assessment is made for [the ninth chargeable period][1] referred to in that sub-paragraph, and

(*b*) the APRT credit for that period exceeds the amount of tax which, in the statement delivered under section 1(1)(*a*) of the Petroleum Revenue Tax Act 1980, is shown to be payable by the participator concerned in accordance with the Schedule to that Act for that period in respect of the oil field in question,

the amount of the excess shall be repaid to the participator and that repayment shall be regarded as a payment on account of any amount which may fall to be repaid to him by virtue of sub-paragraph (1) above.

(5) Paragraph 10(4) above shall not apply to any amount of APRT which is repayable only on the making of a claim under sub-paragraph (1) above.

(6) Amounts repaid to a participator by virtue of this paragraph shall be disregarded in computing his income for the purposes of income tax or corporation tax.

Amendments—[1] Words in sub-paras (2), (3), (4)(*a*) substituted by FA 1983 s 35, Sch 7 paras 3, 4.

Transfer of interest in fields

15—(1) This paragraph has effect in a case where Part I of Schedule 17 to the Finance Act 1980 applies (transfer of interests in oil fields) and expressions used in the following provisions in this paragraph have the same meaning as in that Schedule.

(2) For the purpose of determining whether the new participator is liable to pay an amount of APRT, but for no other purpose, subsection (1) of section 139 of this Act shall apply as if any gross profit which at any time before the transfer had accrued to the old participator from the field had accrued at that time to the new participator or, if the transfer is of part of the old participator's interest in the field, as if a corresponding part of that gross profit had at that time accrued to the new participator.

(3) There shall be treated as the APRT credit of the new participator the whole or, if the transfer is of part of the old participator's interest in the field, a corresponding part of so much, if any, of the old participator's APRT credit in respect of that field for the transfer period as exceeds his liability for petroleum revenue tax for that period.

(4) For the purposes of computing whether any, and if so what, amount of APRT is payable by the old participator and the new participator for the transfer period or any later chargeable period it shall be assumed that any application or proposal made in relation to the transfer under paragraph 4 or paragraph 5(1) of Schedule 17 to the Finance Act 1980 and in respect of which the Board have not notified their decision will be accepted by the Board.

Net profit periods

16—(1) For the purposes of sections 111, 112 and 113 of the Finance Act 1981 (determination of net profit periods etc) the total assessable profits which have accrued to a participator from an oil field at the end of a chargeable period may in addition to being set against allowable losses be set against the APRT paid by the participator in respect of that oil field for chargeable periods up to and including that period and accordingly those sections shall have effect subject to the following modifications.

PRT

(2)–(4) (*amend* FA 1981 ss 111(2A), 112(4A), 113(1)).

Abandoned fields

17—(1) The provisions of this paragraph apply where—

(*a*) the responsible person for an oil field has given notice under paragraph 1 of Schedule 8 to the principal Act that the winning of oil from the field has permanently ceased;

(*b*) he has been notified of a decision (whether of the Board or on appeal from the Board) that the winning of oil has so ceased; and

(*c*) the date stated in that decision as the date on which the winning of oil from the field ceased is earlier than the expiry of the [ninth chargeable period following the first chargeable period referred to in section 139(1)(*a*)][1] of this Act.

(2) Where a participator in the field in question has an amount of APRT credit—

(*a*) which cannot be set against a liability for petroleum revenue tax under section 139(3) of this Act, and

(*b*) which is not repayable by virtue of any other provision of this Schedule,

then, on the making of a claim, that amount shall be repaid to him.

(3) Paragraph 10(4) above shall not apply to any amount of APRT which is repayable only on the making of a claim under sub-paragraph (2) above.

(4) Any claim under sub-paragraph (2) above shall be made before any claim for any unrelievable field loss allowance under section 6 of the principal Act; and any amount of APRT which is repayable by virtue of such a claim shall be left out of account in determining the amount of any such loss.

(5) Amounts repaid to a participator under this paragraph shall be disregarded in computing his income for the purposes of income tax and corporation tax.

Amendments—[1] Words in sub-para (1)(*c*) substituted by FA 1983 s 35, Sch 7 paras 3, 4.

PART III
AMENDMENTS

18 (*amends* OTA 1975 s 2).

19—(1) In paragraph 13 of Schedule 2 to the principal Act for the words from "so far as" to "four months" there shall be substituted the words "and payable shall be due within six months".

(2) This paragraph has effect with respect to chargeable periods ending on or after 30 June 1983.

20 In sub-paragraph (2) and (4) of paragraph 5 of Schedule 3 to the principal Act (liability for petroleum revenue tax and interest in the case of transfers to associated companies) the references to tax and to interest payable under Part I of that Act shall include references to APRT and to interest payable under paragraph 10 or paragraph 13 above.

21 In section 1 of the Petroleum Revenue Tax Act 1980 (payments on account of petroleum revenue tax)—

(*a*)–(*c*) (*amend* PRTA 1980 s 1(1), (3), (3A), (3B)).

FINANCE ACT 1983

(1983 Chapter 28)

An Act to grant certain duties, to alter other duties, and to amend the law relating to the National Debt and the Public Revenue, and to make further provision in connection with Finance.

[13 May 1983]

PART III
OIL TAXATION

35 Phasing out of APRT

(1)–(3) (*amends* FA 1982 s 139(1)–(4), Sch 19).

36 Increased oil allowance for certain new fields

(1) For all relevant new fields, as defined in subsection (2) below, section 8 of the principal Act (the oil allowance) shall have effect subject to the following modifications:—

(*a*) in subsection (2) (the amount of the allowance for each chargeable period) for "250,000 metric tonnes" there shall be substituted "500,000 metric tonnes"; and

(*b*) in subsection (6) (the total allowance for a field) for "5 million metric tonnes" there shall be substituted "10 million metric tonnes".

(2) Subject to subsection (3) below, in this section "relevant new field" means an oil field—

(*a*) no part of which lies in a landward area, within the meaning of the Petroleum (Production) Regulations 1982 or in an area to the East of the United Kingdom and between latitudes 52 degrees and 55 degrees North; and

(*b*) for no part of which consent for development has been granted to the licensee by the Secretary of State before 1 April 1982; and

(*c*) for no part of which a programme of development had been served on the licensee or approved by the Secretary of State before that date.

(3) In determining, in accordance with subsection (2) above, whether an oil field (in this subsection referred to as "the new field") is a relevant new field, no account shall be taken of a consent for development granted before 1 April 1982 or a programme of development served on the licensee or approved by the Secretary of State before that date if—

(*a*) in whole or in part that consent or programme related to another oil field for which a determination under Schedule 1 to the principal Act was made before the determination under that Schedule for the new field; and

(*b*) on or after 1 April 1982, a consent for development is or was granted or a programme of development is or was served on the licensee or approved by the [OGA][1] and that consent or programme relates, in whole or in part, to the new field.

(4) In subsections (2) and (3) above "development" means—

(*a*) the erection or carrying out of permanent works for the purpose of getting oil from the field or for the purpose of conveying oil won from the field to a place on land; or

(*b*) winning oil from the field otherwise than in the course of searching for oil or drilling wells;

and consent for development does not include consent which is limited to the purpose of testing the characteristics of an oil-bearing area and does not relate to the erection or carrying out of permanent works.

(5) In subsection (4) above "permanent works" means any structures or other works whatsoever which are intended by the licensee to be permanent and are neither designed to be moved from place to place without major dismantling nor intended by the licensee to be used only for searching for oil.

Amendments—[1] In sub-s (3)(*b*), word substituted for words "Secretary of State" by the Petroleum (Transfer of Functions) Regulations, SI 2016/898 reg 7 with effect from 1 October 2016.

37 Reliefs for exploration and appraisal expenditure etc

(1) The section set out in Part I of Schedule 8 to this Act shall be inserted in the principal Act after section 5 for the purpose of setting up a new allowance by virtue of which a participator in an oil field may obtain relief for certain expenditure which is incurred otherwise than in connection with that field.

(2) For the purpose of giving effect to, and in consequence of, the new allowance, the enactments specified in Part II of Schedule 8 to this Act shall have effect subject to the amendments there specified.

(3) Part III of Schedule 8 to this Act shall have effect with respect to sums received after 15 March 1983 and falling to be set off against expenditure which would otherwise be allowable under section 5 of the principal Act or under the new section set out in Part I of that Schedule.

(4) (*amends* OTA 1975 Sch 7 para 1).

38 Terms of payment to be implied in determining market value

(*amended* OTA 1975 Sch 3 para 2(2) and *is repealed* by FA 2006 s 178, Sch 26 Pt 5(1)).

39 Exclusion of oil appropriated for production purposes in other fields

(1) (*amends* OTA 1975 s 12(1)).

(2) This section has effect, and shall be deemed to have had effect, for chargeable periods ending after 31 December 1977.

40 Variation of decisions on claims for allowable expenditure

(*amends* OTA 1975 Sch 5 para 9, Sch 6 para 2, Table).

41 Transfers of interests in oil fields

(1), (2) (*amend* FA 1980 Sch 17 para 7(1), (2)).

(3) This section has effect in relation to transfer periods (within the meaning of paragraph 1 of Schedule 17 to the Finance Act 1980) ending after 31 December 1982.

PART IV
MISCELLANEOUS AND SUPPLEMENTARY

48 Short title, interpretation, construction and repeals

(1) This Act may be cited as the Finance Act 1983.

(2), (3) [not reproduced].

(4) Part III of this Act shall be construed as one with Part I of the Oil Taxation Act 1975 and references in Part III to the principal Act are references to that Act.

(5) The enactments specified in Schedule 10 to this Act are hereby repealed to the extent specified in the third column of that Schedule, but subject to any provision at the end of any Part of that Schedule.

SCHEDULES

SCHEDULE 7

APRT: MODIFICATIONS OF FA 1982, SCHEDULE 19

Section 35

1–4 (*amend* FA 1982 Sch 19 paras 1(3), 2(2), 14(1)–(3), 17(1)(*c*)).

SCHEDULE 8

RELIEFS FOR EXPLORATION AND APPRAISAL EXPENDITURE, ETC

Section 37

PART I

SECTION TO BE INSERTED AFTER SECTION 5 OF THE PRINCIPAL ACT

[*inserts* OTA 1975 s 5A].

PART II

AMENDMENTS RELATING TO THE NEW ALLOWANCE

The principal Act

1–6 (*amend* OTA 1975 s 2(9), 3(3), 5(1), 9(2)(*a*)(ii), Sch 2 para 2(2A), Sch 7 para 1(1), (3)).

The Petroleum Revenue Tax Act 1980

7 (*amends* PRTA 1980 Sch para 2(4)).

The Finance Act 1980

8 (*amends* FA 1980 Sch 17 para 16A).

The Finance Act 1981

9 (*amends* FA 1981 s 111(3)(*a*)).

PART III

RECEIPTS TO BE SET AGAINST ALLOWABLE EXPENDITURE

10 In this Part of this Schedule—

"allowable expenditure" means expenditure which, in accordance with section 5 or section 5A of the principal Act, is allowable on a claim made by a participator under Schedule 7 to that Act; and

"qualifying receipt" means a sum the amount of which falls, by virtue of subsection (6) of section 5 of the principal Act, to be applied by way of reduction in the amount of expenditure which would otherwise be allowable expenditure.

11—(1) A return made by a participator for a chargeable period under paragraph 2 of Schedule 2 to the principal Act shall give details of any qualifying receipt (whether received by him or by a person connected with him) of which details have not been given in a return made by him for an earlier chargeable period.

(2) [Section 1122 of the Corporation Tax Act 2010][1] (connected persons) applies for the purposes of this paragraph.

Amendments—[1] In sub-para (2) words substituted for words "Section 839 of the Income and Corporation Taxes Act 1988" by CTA 2010 s 1177, Sch 1 para 179. CTA 2010 has effect for corporation tax purposes for accounting periods ending on or after 1 April 2010, and for income and capital gains tax purposes for the tax year 2010–11 and subsequent tax years.

12—(1) This paragraph applies where—

(*a*) a claim for allowable expenditure has been made by a participator under Schedule 7 to the principal Act; and

(*b*) as a result of the receipt (whether before or after the making of the claim) of a qualifying receipt, the amount allowed by way of allowable expenditure on the claim exceeds what it should have been.

(2) In determining, in a case where this paragraph applies, the assessable profit or allowable loss accruing to the participator in the chargeable period in which the qualifying receipt is received, the amount of the excess referred to in sub-paragraph (1)(*b*) above shall be taken into account under section 2 of the principal Act as an amount which is to be included among the positive amounts referred to in subsection (3)(*a*) of that section.

(3) In the application of section 9 of the principal Act (limit on amount of tax payable) to a chargeable period in respect of which sub-paragraph (2) above applies, the amount of the excess referred to in sub-paragraph (1)(*b*) above shall be deducted from the amount which would otherwise be the total ascertained under subsection (2)(*a*)(ii) of that section and, if the amount of that excess is greater than the amount which would otherwise be that total, that total shall be a negative amount equal to the difference.

OIL TAXATION ACT 1983

(1983 Chapter 56)

An Act to vary the reliefs available for certain expenditure incurred in connection with assets used or to be used in connection with oil fields; to bring into charge to petroleum revenue tax certain sums received or receivable in respect of such assets and of certain other assets situated in the United Kingdom, the territorial sea thereof or a designated area, within the meaning of the Continental Shelf Act 1964; to amend Part II of the Oil Taxation Act 1975 in relation to sums so received or receivable; and for connected purposes.

[1 December 1983]

RELIEFS FOR EXPENDITURE

1 Expenditure incurred on non-dedicated mobile assets

(1) Subject to subsection (3) below, with respect to expenditure which is or was incurred after 30 June 1982 in acquiring, bringing into existence or enhancing the value of an asset, section 4 of the principal Act (allowance of expenditure on long-term assets) shall apply only where—

(*a*) the asset is a mobile asset which is not dedicated to the oil field referred to in subsection (1) of that section; or

(*b*) the expenditure is incurred as mentioned in section 13(1)(*b*) below.

(2) Where section 4 of the principal Act applies as mentioned in subsection (1)(*a*) above, it shall so apply with the following modifications:—

(*a*) in subsection (1), after the words "subsection (13) below" there shall be inserted the words "and section 1 of the Oil Taxation Act 1983" and for the words from "whose useful life" to "used" there shall be substituted the words "which, at the end of the first relevant claim period, is or is expected to be a long-term asset as defined in section 3(8) of the Oil Taxation Act 1983";

(*b*) subsections (3) and (4) shall be omitted;

(*c*) in subsection (5), paragraph (*a*) and the words "in any other case" in paragraph (*b*) shall be omitted and, in paragraph (*b*), for the words "that connection" there shall be substituted the words "connection with the field";

(*d*) subsection (6) shall be omitted;

(*e*) in subsection (7), for the words from the beginning to "each subsequent claim period" there shall be substituted the words "For each claim period subsequent to the first relevant claim period and" and for the words "subsections (5) and (6)" there shall be substituted the words "subsection (5)"; and

(*f*) in subsection (11) for the words from "subsections (5)" to "they apply" there shall be substituted the words "subsection (5) above (including that subsection as it applies".

(3) If the asset referred to in subsection (1)(*a*) above becomes dedicated to the oil field referred to in subsection (1) of section 4 of the principal Act or is or becomes dedicated to another oil field,—

(*a*) expenditure incurred as mentioned in subsection (1) above shall not be allowable under section 4 of the principal Act for a claim period for which it is allowable under section 3 below nor, subject to paragraph (*b*) below, for a claim period which falls wholly or partly within a claim period of another field to which the asset is or becomes dedicated, being a claim period for which the expenditure is allowable; and

(*b*) where expenditure incurred in relation to the asset becomes allowable under section 3 below, no part of that expenditure shall be allowable under section 4 of the principal Act for any claim period ending less than six months before the end of a claim period for which the expenditure is allowable under section 3 below.

(4) Paragraph 4 of Schedule 4 to the principal Act (reduction of allowable expenditure on disposal of long-term asset formerly used in connection with an oil field) does not apply to any disposal of an asset after 30 June 1982 unless the asset is a mobile asset which is not dedicated to the oil field referred to in section 4(1) of the principal Act.

HMRC Manuals—Oil Taxation Manual OT11100 (non-dedicated mobile assets).

Cross references—FA 1993 s 190 (allowance of expenditure on certain assets limited by reference to taxable field use).

2 Dedicated mobile assets

(1) For the purposes of this Act and Part I of the principal Act a mobile asset becomes dedicated to a particular oil field in a claim period if—

(*a*) the asset is used in connection with that field during the whole or part of that claim period; and

(*b*) the asset was not, at the beginning of that period, already dedicated to that field; and

(*c*) at the end of that period it is reasonable to make the assumptions in subsection (2) below.

(2) The assumptions referred to in paragraph (*c*) of subsection (1) above are—

(*a*) that during the whole or substantially the whole of the relevant period, the asset will be used in connection with the field referred to in that subsection (whether or not that use will be exclusive to that field); and

(*b*) that the main use of the asset during the whole of the relevant period will be in connection with that field or with two or more oil fields of which that field is one.

(3) In any case where—

(*a*) at or before the time when he is a participator in an oil field, a person incurs expenditure in bringing into existence a mobile asset, and

(*b*) that expenditure is so incurred in a claim period for that field which is earlier than that in which the asset is first used by that person in connection with that field, and

(*c*) at the end of that claim period, it is reasonable to make the assumptions in subsection (2) above, and

(*d*) the circumstances are such that the asset is not a brought-in asset, as defined in section 4(12)(*a*) of the principal Act, then, as respects any claim for the allowance of the expenditure referred to in paragraph (*a*) above which is made before the asset is first used as mentioned in paragraph (*b*) above, the asset shall be regarded for the purposes of this Act and Part I of the principal Act as becoming dedicated to the oil field in question in the claim period referred to in paragraphs (*b*) and (*c*) above.

(4) In subsection (2) above "the relevant period" means the period beginning at the end of the claim period referred to in subsection (1) above or, where subsection (3) above applies, at the end of the claim period in which it can reasonably be expected that the asset will be first used, and ending—

(*a*) at the end of the useful life of the asset, or

(*b*) when the winning of oil from the field in question permanently ceases,

whichever first occurs.

(5) If, in the case of a mobile asset which would not be dedicated to a particular oil field but for the provisions of subsection (3) above, it becomes apparent at any time that it is no longer reasonable to make the assumptions in subsection (2) above, then the asset concerned shall be regarded for the purposes of this Act and Part I of the principal Act as never having been dedicated to that field; and the provisions of paragraph 9 of Schedule 5 to the principal Act (variations of decisions on claims for allowable expenditure) shall have effect accordingly.

HMRC Manuals—Oil Taxation Manual OT11150 (dedicated mobile assets).

Cross references—FA 1993 s 190 (allowance of expenditure on certain assets limited by reference to taxable field use).

3 Expenditure incurred on long-term assets other than non-dedicated mobile assets

(1) Subject to section 13 below, this section applies to expenditure (whether or not of a capital nature) which is or was incurred by a person after 30 June 1982 and at or before the time when he is or was a participator in an oil field, being expenditure incurred, subject to subsection (2) below, in acquiring, bringing into existence, or enhancing the value of an asset—

(*a*) which, at the end of the relevant claim period, is being or is expected to be used in connection with the field; and

(*b*) which, at the end of the relevant claim period, is or is expected to be a long-term asset; and

(*c*) which either is not a mobile asset or is a mobile asset which became dedicated to that field in the relevant claim period or in any earlier claim period.

(2) This section does not apply to expenditure incurred as mentioned in subsection (1) above in any case where the Board consider that its application to that expenditure would have only a negligible effect on the total expenditure allowable under Part I of the principal Act for the field and so notify the responsible person.

(3) Part I of Schedule 1 to this Act shall have effect for the purpose of allowing relief for certain expenditure which would not otherwise fall within this section or, as the case may be, section 3 of the principal Act.

(4) Except as provided by subsections (6) and (7) and [sections 3A and 4][1] below and Part II of Schedule 1 to this Act, the whole of any expenditure to which this section applies shall be allowable on a claim under Schedule 5 or Schedule 6 to the principal Act for the relevant claim period.

(5) The relevant claim period referred to in subsections (1) and (4) above is—

(*a*) the claim period which is appropriate under paragraph 2 of Schedule 5 or, as the case may be, paragraph 1 of Schedule 6 to the principal Act; or

(*b*) if the asset is a brought-in asset, as defined in section 4(12)(*a*) of the principal Act, and the expenditure has not already been allowable for an earlier claim period by virtue of paragraph (*a*) above, the claim period in which the asset is first used in connection with the field in question, discounting, in the case of a mobile asset, any claim period in which it was not dedicated to that field; or (*c*) if the asset is a mobile asset and paragraph (*b*) above does not apply and the expenditure has not already been allowable for an earlier claim period by virtue of paragraph (*a*) above, the claim period in which the asset became dedicated to the field in question.

(6) Subsections (3) to (5A) of section 3 of the principal Act apply for the purposes of this section and Schedule 1 to this Act as they apply for the purposes of that section; and, except in so far as section 5 below provides to the contrary, any reference to section 4 of the principal Act (but not a reference to any specific provision of that section) in—

(*a*) Part I of that Act,

(*b*) any enactment, other than this Act, which is to be construed as one with that Part, or

(*c*) section 107 of the Finance Act 1980 (transmedian fields),

shall be construed as including a reference to this section, section 4 below and Schedule 1 to this Act.

(7) Section 4(13) of the principal Act (interests in assets) applies to the preceding provisions of this section and the provisions of Schedule 1 to this Act; and those provisions are subject to paragraph 2 of Schedule 4 and to Schedules 5 and 6 to the principal Act.

(8) In this section "long-term asset" means an asset the useful life of which continues after the end of the claim period in which it is first used in connection with the oil field in question.

Simon's Tax Cases—s 3(1), *BP Exploration Operating Co Ltd v IRC* [2000] STC (SCD) 466.

HMRC Manuals—Oil Taxation Manual OT11250 (associated assets).

Cross references—See FA 1987 s 65, Sch 14 (cross-field allowance of certain expenditure incurred on new fields). FA 1999 s 95(2) (limit on allowable expenditure associated with certain sale and lease-back transactions occurring on or after 9 March 1999).

Amendments—[1] Words in sub-s (4) substituted by FA 2004 s 285, Sch 37 para 2 with effect for expenditure incurred after 31 December 2003.

[3A Exclusion from section 3(4) of expenditure on assets giving rise to tax-exempt tariffing receipts

(1) This section applies where—

(*a*) expenditure incurred on or after 1st January 2004 falls within section 3(1) above, but

(*b*) some of the use (or expected use) of the asset in relation to which the expenditure was incurred is use in a way that gives rise to tax-exempt tariffing receipts (see section 6A(2) below).

(2) In any such case, such part of the expenditure as it is just and reasonable to apportion to the use mentioned in subsection (1)(*b*) above shall be excluded from the expenditure which is allowable as mentioned in section 3(4) above.][1]

Amendments—[1] Section 3A inserted by FA 2004 s 285, Sch 37 para 3 with effect for expenditure incurred after 31 December 2003.

4 Expenditure related to exempt gas and deballasting

(1) In any case where expenditure falls within section 3(1) above, but by reason of section 10(2) of the principal Act (exempt gas) some of the use (or expected use) of the asset is not use in connection with an oil field, such part of that expenditure as it is just and reasonable to apportion to that use (or expected use) shall be excluded from the expenditure which is allowable as mentioned in section 3(4) above.

(2) In any case where expenditure—

(*a*) falls within section 3(1) above, or

(*b*) by virtue of any provision of Part I of Schedule 1 to this Act, falls within section 3 of the principal Act,

but some of the use (or expected use) of the asset is use for deballasting, such part of that expenditure as it is just and reasonable to apportion to that use (or expected use) shall be excluded from the expenditure which is allowable as mentioned in section 3(4) above or, as the case may be, from the expenditure which is allowable under section 3 of the principal Act.

(3) In any case where—

(*a*) expenditure does not fall within section 3(1) above or section 3 of the principal Act by reason only of section 10(2) of that Act (exempt gas), but

(*b*) the asset in relation to which the expenditure was incurred is or is expected to be used in a way which gives rise to tariff receipts,

then, so far as relates to so much of that expenditure as it is just and reasonable to apportion to the use referred to in paragraph (b) above, that use of the asset shall be treated for the purposes of section 3 above, Schedule 1 to this Act and section 3 of the principal Act as use in connection with the field from which the excluded oil, within the meaning of section 10 of that Act, is won.

(4) References in subsection (3) above to the use of an asset (other than the final reference to use in connection with a field) include references to the provision, in connection with the use of the asset, of services or other business facilities of any kind.

(5) In any case where—

(*a*) expenditure is incurred in enhancing the value of an asset with a view to the subsequent disposal of it or of an interest in it, and

PRT

(*b*) by reason only of section 10(2) of the principal Act (exempt gas), the expenditure does not fall within section 3(1) above or section 3 of that Act, and

(*c*) the subsequent disposal of, or of an interest in, the asset gives or is expected to give rise to disposal receipts, then, such part of the use of the asset as it is just and reasonable to apportion to the expenditure referred to in paragraph (*a*) above shall be treated for the purposes of section 3 above, Schedule 1 to this Act and section 3 of the principal Act as use in connection with the field from which the excluded oil, within the meaning of section 10 of that Act, is won.

[(6) But where—

(*a*) expenditure would (apart from this subsection) fall within paragraph (*a*) of subsection (5) above, and

(*b*) the asset has, at any time in the period of 6 years ending with the date on which the expenditure was incurred, been used in a way that gives rise to tax-exempt tariffing receipts,

the expenditure shall not be regarded for the purposes of that subsection as expenditure incurred in enhancing the value of the asset with a view to the subsequent disposal of the asset, or of an interest in it, to the extent that the amount of the expenditure falls to be reduced in accordance with subsection (7) below.][1]

[(7) The reduction is to be made by applying section 7A below in relation to the expenditure as it applies in relation to disposal receipts in respect of a disposal, but with the substitution—

(*a*) for references to the disponor, of references to the person incurring the expenditure ("the relevant participator"),

(*b*) for references to the amount or value (apart from that section) of any disposal receipts of the disponor in respect of the disposal, of references to the amount which would, apart from subsection (6) above, be the amount of the expenditure incurred by the relevant participator with a view to the subsequent disposal of the asset or of an interest in it,

(*c*) for references to the interest disposed of, of references to the asset or interest whose subsequent disposal gives or is expected to give rise to disposal receipts,

(*d*) for references to the date of the disposal, of references to the date on which the expenditure was incurred,

and taking the reference in subsection (6)(*b*) of that section to a reduction made by virtue of that section as a reference to a reduction made by virtue of that section for the purposes of section 7(9) of this Act.][1]

HMRC Manuals—Oil Taxation Manual OT11200 (exempt gas and deballasting).

Amendments—[1] Sub-ss (6), (7) inserted by FA 2004 s 285, Sch 37 para 4 with effect for expenditure incurred after 31 December 2003.

5 Miscellaneous amendments relating to reliefs

(1)–(3) (*amend* OTA 1975 s 3).

(4) Paragraph 1 of Schedule 4 to the principal Act (expenditure not allowable under section 3 or section 4 of that Act if relief already allowable for another person) does not apply to any expenditure which—

(*a*) consists of a payment made to a participator or a person connected with him; and

(*b*) constitutes a tariff receipt or disposal receipt of the participator.

(5) Subsections (1) to (4) above apply with respect to expenditure which is or was incurred after 30 June 1982.

(6) (*amend* OTA 1975 Sch 4).

(7) Notwithstanding anything in section 3(6) above, any reference to section 4 of the principal Act in—

(*a*) paragraph 4 of Schedule 4 to that Act (disposal of certain long-term assets), or

(*b*) paragraph 2(5) or paragraph 4 of Schedule 5 to that Act (claims and appeals relating to allowance of expenditure),

does not include a reference to sections 3 and 4 above or Schedule 1 to this Act.

(8) Paragraph 5 of Schedule 4 to the principal Act (treatment of payments for hire of assets) shall not apply in any case where the payments are or were received after 30 June 1982 (whenever the expenditure was incurred).

CHARGE OF RECEIPTS

6 Chargeable tariff receipts

(1) In computing under section 2 of the principal Act the assessable profit or allowable loss accruing to a participator from an oil field in any chargeable period ending after 30 June 1982, the positive amounts for the purposes of that section (as specified in subsection (3)(*a*) thereof) shall be taken to include any tariff receipts of the participator attributable to that field for that period.

(2) Subject to the provisions of this section [and section 6A below][1], for the purposes of this Act the tariff receipts of a participator in an oil field which are attributable to that field for any chargeable period are the aggregate of the amount or value of any consideration (whether in the nature of income or capital) received or receivable by him in that period (and after 30 June 1982) in respect of—

(*a*) the use of a qualifying asset; or

(*b*) the provision of services or other business facilities of whatever kind in connection with the use, otherwise than by the participator himself, of a qualifying asset.

(3) Any reference in this Act to the asset to which any tariff receipts are referable is a reference to the qualifying asset referred to in paragraph (*a*) or, as the case may be, paragraph (*b*) of subsection (2) above.

(4) Notwithstanding anything in subsection (2) above, any amount which—

(*a*) is, in relation to the person giving it, expenditure in respect of interest or any other pecuniary obligation incurred in obtaining a loan or any other form of credit, or

(*b*) is referable to the use of an asset for, or the provision of services or facilities in connection with, deballasting [or][2],

[(*c*) is referable to other use of an asset, except use wholly or partly for an oil purpose,][2]

does not constitute a tariff receipt for the purposes of this Act; and, accordingly, any consideration which includes such an amount shall be apportioned in such manner as is just and reasonable.

[(4A) In this section the reference to use of an asset for an oil purpose is a reference to—

(*a*) use in connection with an oil field, and

(*b*) use for any other purpose (apart from a purpose falling within section 3(1)(*b*) of the principal Act) of a separate trade consisting of activities falling within [the definition of "oil-related activities" in section 274 of the Corporation Tax Act 2010][3].

(4B) In subsection (4A) the reference to use in connection with an oil field includes use giving rise to receipts which, for the purposes of this Act, are tariff receipts.][2]

(5) Schedule 2 to this Act shall have effect for supplementing the provisions of this section and of sections 7 and 8 below.

HMRC Manuals—Oil Taxation Manual OT15025 (tariff receipts: definition).

Cross references—See FA 1993 s 193 (tariff receipts in non-taxable fields; connected parties).

FA 1994 s 231, Sch 22 (election by reference to pipe-line with excess capacity).

FA 1999 s 98 (qualifying assets).

Amendments—[1] Words inserted by FA 2004 s 285 (2) with effect from 22 July 2004.

[2] Sub-ss (4)(*c*) and preceding word "or", and sub-ss (4A), (4B) inserted, by FA 2009 s 87, Sch 41 para 2 with effect in relation to chargeable periods beginning after 30 June 2009.

[3] In sub-s (4A)(*b*) words substituted for words "section 492(1) of the Income and Corporation Taxes Act 1988" by CTA 2010 s 1177, Sch 1 para 181. CTA 2010 has effect for corporation tax purposes for accounting periods ending on or after 1 April 2010, and for income and capital gains tax purposes for the tax year 2010–11 and subsequent tax years.

[6A Tax-exempt tariffing receipts

(1) An amount which is a tax-exempt tariffing receipt (see subsection (2) below) does not constitute a tariff receipt for the purposes of the Oil Taxation Acts.

(2) An amount is a "tax-exempt tariffing receipt" for the purposes of the Oil Taxation Acts if—

(*a*) it would, apart from this section, be a tariff receipt of a participator in an oil field,

(*b*) it is received or receivable by the participator in a chargeable period ending on or after 30th June 2004 under a contract entered into on or after 9th April 2003, and

(*c*) it is in respect of tax-exempt business (see subsection (3) below).

(3) For the purposes of this section an amount is in respect of tax-exempt business if it is an amount received or receivable by a participator in an oil field in respect of—

(*a*) the use of a qualifying asset, or

(*b*) the provision of services or other business facilities of whatever kind in connection with the use, otherwise than by the participator himself, of a qualifying asset,

and that use of the qualifying asset falls within subsection (4) below.

(4) Use of a qualifying asset falls within this subsection if it is—

(*a*) use in relation to a new field (see subsection (5) below) or oil won from such a field, or

(*b*) use in relation to a qualifying existing field (see subsection (5) below) or oil won from such a field [or

(*c*) use in relation to a UK recommissioned field (see subsection (5) below) or oil won from such a field.][2]

(5) In this section—

"existing field" means any oil field or foreign field which is not a new field;

"foreign field" means, subject to subsection (6) below (treatment of transmedian fields), any hydrocarbon accumulation which is not under the jurisdiction of the government of the United Kingdom;

"licensee", in relation to a foreign field, means a person who has rights, interests or obligations in respect of the foreign field under a licence or other authority granted by the government of a country other than the United Kingdom;

"new field" means—

(*a*) an oil field for no part of which had—

(i) consent for development been granted to a licensee by the Secretary of State before 9th April 2003; or

PRT

(ii) a programme of development been served on a licensee or approved by the Secretary of State before that date; or

(*b*) a foreign field for no part of which had—

(i) any consent for development been granted to a licensee by the government of a country other than the United Kingdom before 9th April 2003; or

(ii) a programme of development been served on a licensee or approved by such a government before that date;

and subsections (4) and (5) of section 36 of the Finance Act 1983 (which define "development" for the purposes of subsections (2) and (3) of that section) shall apply also for the purposes of this definition;

"the Oil Taxation Acts" means—

(*a*) Parts 1 and 3 of the principal Act;

(*b*) this Act; and

(*c*) any other enactment relating to petroleum revenue tax;

"qualifying existing field" means an existing field as respects which the condition in section 6B(1) below is satisfied.

["UK recommissioned field" means any oil field which is not a new field or qualifying existing field but as respects which the conditions in section 185(1A) of the Finance Act 1993 are satisfied (fields recommissioned after earlier decommissioning).][2]

(6) For the purposes of this section, in the case of an oil field which, by virtue of section 107 of the Finance Act 1980 (transmedian fields), is deemed to include the sector mentioned in subsection (1)(*a*)(ii) of that section—

(*a*) that sector shall be treated as a foreign field, and

(*b*) the remainder of that field shall be treated as a separate oil field.

(7) In the application of provisions of the Oil Taxation Acts relating to tax- exempt tariffing receipts, references to oil, in relation to a foreign field, are references to any substance that would be oil within the meaning of the principal Act if the enactments mentioned in section 1(1) of that Act extended to the foreign field.

(8) This section is subject to the transitional provisions in Part 2 of Schedule 35 to the Finance Act 2004 (expenditure incurred between 9th April and 31st December 2003: treatment of initial portion of tax-exempt tariffing receipts as tariff receipts).][1]

Amendments—[1] This section inserted by FA 2004 s 285 (3) with effect from 22 July 2004.
[2] Sub-s (4)(*c*) and preceding word "or", and in sub-s (5) definition of "UK recommissioned field", inserted, by FA 2007 s 103 and deemed to have come into force on 1 July 2007.

[6B The condition for being a qualifying existing field

(1) The condition for an existing field to be a qualifying existing field for the purposes of section 6A above is that at no time in the period of 6 years ending with 8th April 2003 ("the 6 year period") was there—

(*a*) any use of a disqualifying asset (see subsection (2) below) in a UK area (see subsection (11) below) in relation to the field or oil won from it, or

(*b*) any provision of any services or other business facilities of whatever kind in connection with the use of a disqualifying asset in a UK area in relation to the field or oil won from it.

(2) For the purposes of subsection (1) above "disqualifying asset", in relation to an existing field and any time in the 6 year period, means an asset which at that time—

(*a*) was a qualifying asset in relation to a participator in an oil field; and

(*b*) was not an excepted asset (see subsection (3) below).

(3) For the purposes of subsection (2) above "excepted asset", in relation to an existing field and any time in the 6 year period, means any of the following—

(*a*) any asset (other than a tanker) which at that time was wholly situated in the existing field;

(*b*) any tanker which at that time was a non-dedicated tanker (see subsection (10) below) being used for transporting from the existing field oil which had been won from that field;

(*c*) any asset which at that time was being used in relation to oil which had been won from the existing field and transported from that field by a non-dedicated tanker;

(*d*) if the existing field is an oil field and is expected not to be a tanker loading field (see subsection (7) below)—

(i) any tanker which at that time was a dedicated tanker (see subsection (9) below) being used for transporting from the existing field oil which had been won from that field;

(ii) any asset which at that time was being used in relation to oil which had been won from the existing field and transported from that field by a dedicated tanker;

(iii) any asset which at that time was being used to transport from the existing field oil consisting of gas won from that field to another oil field for the purpose of enabling that oil to be used for assisting the extraction of oil from that other field;

(*e*) if at that time the existing field was not a taxable field, any asset by reference to which an election under section 231 of the Finance Act 1994 (election by reference to asset with excess capacity) was at that time in operation with respect to an oil field.

(4) Where any use of an asset is, by virtue of subsection (3) above, use of an excepted asset, the provision of any services or other business facilities of whatever kind in connection with that use of that asset accordingly falls to be disregarded for the purposes of subsection (1)(*b*) above.

(5) Where an asset in a UK area—

(*a*) is a qualifying asset in relation to a participator in such an oil field as is mentioned in section 107 of the Finance Act 1980 (a "participator in the UK sector"), and

(*b*) is also, by virtue of paragraph 3 of Schedule 4 to this Act, a chargeable asset in relation to a participator in a foreign field (a "participator in the foreign sector"),

subsection (6) below applies in relation to use of the asset in relation to the existing field or oil won from it.

(6) Where this subsection applies, then, in determining for the purposes of subsection (1) above whether there has been any use of a disqualifying asset in relation to the existing field or oil won from it, any use of the asset in relation to that field or oil won from it shall be treated—

(*a*) as use of a qualifying asset in relation to a participator in an oil field, if or to the extent that the use is attributable, on a just and reasonable basis, to a participator in the UK sector, or

(*b*) as use of an asset which was not a qualifying asset in relation to a participator in an oil field, if or to the extent that the use is attributable, on a just and reasonable basis, to a participator in the foreign sector.

(7) For the purposes of subsection (3) above, the existing field is expected not to be a tanker loading field if, at the time when the relevant contract is entered into, it is expected that all (or virtually all) of the oil (other than oil consisting of gas) to be won from that field and transported from it after the beginning of the operational period will be so transported otherwise than by tanker.

(8) For the purposes of subsection (7) above—

(*a*) "the relevant contract" means the contract mentioned in section 6A(2)(*b*) above; and

(*b*) "the beginning of the operational period" means the time at which the qualifying asset to which that contract relates begins to be used under that contract in relation to the existing field or oil won from that field.

(9) For the purposes of subsection (3) above a tanker is a dedicated tanker at any time if—

(*a*) the existing field mentioned in that subsection is an oil field, and

(*b*) at that time the tanker is a mobile asset dedicated to that oil field (see section 2 above).

(10) For the purposes of subsection (3) above a tanker is a non-dedicated tanker—

(*a*) at any time, if the existing field mentioned in that subsection is not an oil field, or

(*b*) where that field is an oil field, at any time when the tanker is not a mobile asset dedicated to that oil field.

(11) In this section "UK area" means each of the following—

(*a*) the United Kingdom;

(*b*) the territorial sea of the United Kingdom;

(*c*) a designated area, to the extent that it does not fall to be treated by virtue of section 6A(6) above as a foreign field.

(12) This section shall be construed as one with section 6A above.][1]

Amendments—[1] This section inserted by FA 2004 s 285 (3) with effect from 22 July 2004.

7 Chargeable receipts from disposals

(1) In computing under section 2 of the principal Act the assessable profit or allowable loss accruing to a participator from an oil field in any chargeable period ending after 30 June 1982, the positive amounts for the purposes of that section (as specified in subsection (3)(*a*) thereof) shall be taken to include any disposal receipts of the participator attributable to that field for that period.

(2) Subject to the provisions of this section, for the purposes of this Act the disposal receipts of a participator in an oil field which are attributable to that field for any chargeable period are the aggregate of the amount or value of any consideration received or receivable by him in respect of the disposal in that period of a qualifying asset or of an interest in such an asset.

(3) Where there is such a redetermination as is mentioned in subsection (4) of section 107 of the Finance Act 1980 (transmedian fields) and in consequence thereof the participators in the field receive a repayment, credit or set-off in respect of expenditure which was incurred in acquiring, bringing into existence or enhancing the value of a qualifying asset or an interest in it, the repayment shall be regarded as consideration received as mentioned in subsection (2) above in respect of the disposal of an interest in the asset.

(4) No account shall be taken under subsection (2) above of any disposal of, or of an interest in, a qualifying asset which takes place more than two years after the time at which the asset—

(*a*) ceases to be used in connection with any oil field whatsoever, or

(*b*) ceases to give rise to tariff receipts of the participator referred to in that subsection, [or

(*c*) ceases to give rise to tax-exempt tariffing receipts of that participator,][1]

whichever is the [latest][1].

PRT

(5) Notwithstanding anything in subsection (2) or subsection (3) above, any amount which, in relation to the person paying it,—

(*a*) is expenditure in respect of interest or any other pecuniary obligation incurred in obtaining a loan or any other form of credit, or(*b*) is a payment made for the purpose of obtaining a direct or indirect interest in oil won or to be won from an oil field,

does not constitute a disposal receipt for the purposes of this Act; and accordingly, any consideration which includes such an amount shall be apportioned in such manner as is just and reasonable.

(6) If in any claim period a qualifying asset gives rise to disposal receipts of a participator and any expenditure incurred by the participator is expenditure which in that period qualifies for supplement under paragraph (*b*)(ii) or paragraph (*c*)(ii) of subsection (9) of section 2 of the principal Act, then, except in so far as it is expenditure falling within section 111(7) of the Finance Act 1981 (certain expenditure incurred before 1 January 1983),—

(*a*) the amount which, apart from this subsection, would in his case be taken into account under either or both of those paragraphs shall be reduced by deducting therefrom a fraction thereof determined under subsection (7) below or, if that fraction exceeds unity, shall be taken to be nil; and

(*b*) references in subsections (2) and (3) of section 9 of the principal Act (limit on amount of tax payable) to expenditure which was not allowed as qualifying for supplement under section 2(9)(*b*)(ii) or (*c*)(ii) shall be construed accordingly.

(7) For the claim period referred to in subsection (6) above, the fraction referred to in paragraph (*a*) of that subsection is that of which—

(*a*) the numerator, subject to subsection (8) below, is the disposal receipts of the participator in question for that period in respect of the qualifying asset referred to in subsection (6) above or, if it is less, the expenditure allowed or allowable to the participator in respect of that asset under section 3 above or section 4 of the principal Act; and

(*b*) the denominator is so much of the total amount of expenditure allowable for the field on a claim for the claim period referred to in subsection (6) above as, in the case of the participator in question, falls to be taken into account under paragraphs (*b*)(i) and (*c*)(i) of subsection (9) of section 2 of the principal Act;

and in paragraph (b) above "allowable" means allowable under section 3 or section 4 of the principal Act or under section 3 above.

(8) If the disposal receipts in question relate to a disposal of an interest in the asset, rather than the asset itself, then the reference in subsection (7)(*a*) above to certain expenditure shall be construed as a reference to such proportion only of that expenditure as it is just and reasonable to apportion to the interest disposed of.

[(9) In determining the amount or value of the disposal receipts of the participator in question in a case where the qualifying asset has been used in a way that gives rise to tax-exempt tariffing receipts, the amount or value (apart from this subsection) of any disposal receipts of his in respect of the disposal shall be reduced in accordance with section 7A below.][1]

HMRC Manuals—Oil Taxation Manual OT15060 (disposal receipts).

Cross references—See FA 1999 s 98 (qualifying assets).

Amendments—[1] Sub-s (4)(*c*) inserted, in sub-s (4), word substituted for the word "later", and sub-s (9) inserted, by FA 2004 s 285, Sch 37 para 5(1)–(3) with effect for disposals in chargeable periods ending after 29 June 2004.

[7A Reduction of disposal receipts: use giving rise to tax-exempt tariffing receipts

(1) Where this section applies, the amount or value (apart from this section) of any disposal receipts of the participator ("the disponor") in respect of the disposal shall be reduced in accordance with the following provisions of this section.

(2) The reduction is to be made by multiplying that amount or value by the fraction that is equal to—

$$1 - \frac{T}{A}$$

(3) In that formula—

T is the aggregate of the tax-exempt tariffing use of the asset in the reference period by—

(*a*) the disponor, so far as referable to the interest disposed of, and

(*b*) each of the previous owners, so far as referable to that previous owner's represented interest, and

A is the aggregate of all use of the asset in the reference period by—

(*a*) the disponor, so far as referable to the interest disposed of, and

(*b*) each of the previous owners, so far as referable to that previous owner's represented interest,

but only taking into account for this purpose use of the asset by a person at a time when he is or was a participator in a taxable field.

(4) For the purposes of this section—

"the interest disposed of" means the asset, or the interest in an asset, the disposal of which gives rise to the disposal receipts mentioned in sub-paragraph (1) above;

"previous owner" means any person from whom the disponor directly or indirectly derives his title to the whole or any part of the interest disposed of;

"the reference period" means the shortest of the following periods ending with the date of the disposal—

(*a*) the period of 6 years; or

(*b*) the period beginning with the bringing into existence of the asset;

"represented interest", in the case of a previous owner, means so much of the interest which that previous owner had in the asset as is represented in the interest disposed of;

"tax-exempt tariffing use", in relation to an asset, means use of the asset in a way that gives rise to tax-exempt tariffing receipts.

(5) Any apportionment that falls to be made for the purpose of determining a previous owner's represented interest shall be made using a method which is just and reasonable, having regard to—

(*a*) the proportion of any person's interest that was acquired from any particular person, and

(*b*) the proportion of any person's interest that was transferred to any particular person.

(6) Where—

(*a*) the disponor or any previous owner acquired the asset or an interest in the asset from another person, and

(*b*) on that other person's corresponding disposal of the asset or interest a reduction was made by virtue of this section,

use of the asset shall not be brought into account in determining T or A in the formula in subsection (2) above to the extent that it was so brought into account in relation to that corresponding disposal.

(7) Where paragraph 9 of Schedule 2 to this Act (reduction of disposal receipts in respect of brought-in assets) applies in relation to an asset, no account shall be taken for the purposes of this section of any use of the asset during the initial period.

In this subsection "the initial period", in relation to an asset, has the same meaning as it has in relation to that asset in paragraph 7 of Schedule 1 to this Act (restriction on allowable expenditure on brought-in asset).

(8) For the purposes of this section, the amount of use of an asset—

(*a*) where the use is in relation to oil, is to be determined by reference to the volume of oil in relation to which the asset is used, and

(*b*) where the use is otherwise than in relation to oil, is to be determined on a just and reasonable basis.

(9) For the purposes of this section, the extent to which use of an asset is referable to—

(*a*) the interest disposed of, or

(*b*) the represented interest of a previous owner,

shall be determined on a just and reasonable basis, having regard to the size of the interest in question and the size from time to time of the whole interest in the asset of the disponor or, as the case may be, that previous owner.][1]

Amendments—[1] This section inserted by FA 2004 s 285, Sch 37 para (4) with effect for disposals in chargeable periods ending after 29 June 2004.

8 Qualifying assets

(1) Subject to paragraph 4 of Schedule 2 to this Act, for the purposes of this Act a "qualifying asset", in relation to a participator in an oil field, means [subject to subsection (1A) below][1] an asset—

(*a*) which either is not a mobile asset or is a mobile asset dedicated to that oil field; and

(*b*) in respect of which expenditure incurred by the participator is allowable, or has been allowed, for that field under section 3 above, section 4 of the principal Act or, subject to subsection (2) below, section 3 of that Act.

[(1A) Notwithstanding anything in subsection (1) above, the following assets are not qualifying assets for the purposes of this Act, namely—

(*a*) land or an interest in land; and

(*b*) a building or structure which is situated on land and which does not fall within any of sub-paragraphs (i) to (iv) of paragraph (*c*) of subsection (4) of section 3 of the principal Act].[1]

(2) If, in respect of any asset, the only expenditure which falls within subsection (1)(*b*) above is expenditure allowable or allowed under section 3 of the principal Act, the asset shall not be a qualifying asset unless, at the time the expenditure was incurred, it was expected that the useful life of the asset would continue after the end of the claim period in which the asset was to be first used in a way which would constitute use in connection with an oil field for the purposes of that section.

(3) Subject to subsection (4) below, the oil field to which are attributable tariff receipts or disposal receipts referable to a qualifying asset is that field for which the expenditure referred to in subsection (1)(*b*) above is allowable; and, if there is more than one such field, then,—

(*a*) in the case of a mobile asset, no account shall be taken of a field to which it is not dedicated; and

PRT

(*b*) no account shall be taken of a field in relation to which the asset is a qualifying asset by virtue only of paragraph 1 of Schedule 1 to this Act; and

(*c*) subject to paragraphs (*a*) and (*b*) above [and subsection (3A) below][2], it is that one of those fields in relation to which a development decision was first made;

and subsection (7) of section 5A of the principal Act (time when development decision is made) shall have effect for the purposes of paragraph (c) above [and subsection (3A) below][2] as it has effect for the purposes of subsection (1)(c) of that section.

[(3A) If development decisions were first made in relation to two or more oil fields on the same day then, for the purposes of subsection (3)(*c*) above, it shall be conclusively presumed that the first of those decisions was made in relation to that one of those fields in connection with which it appeared—

(*a*) at the time of the decision, or

(*b*) if it is later, at the time the asset was acquired or brought into existence by the participator in question for use in connection with an oil field,

that the participator in question would make the most use of the asset.][2]

(4) In the case of an asset which, in relation to the participator in question, is a qualifying asset by virtue only of paragraph 1 of Schedule 1 to this Act, the oil field to which are attributable tariff receipts or disposal receipts referable to the asset is that to which (in accordance with subsection (3) above) those receipts would be attributable if they were referable to the other asset referred to in sub-paragraph (1)(*d*) of that paragraph (that is to say, the asset in association with which the first asset is, or is expected to be, used).

(5) In relation to a qualifying asset or the tariff receipts or disposal receipts referable to it, in this Act "chargeable field" means the field referred to in subsection (3) or, as the case may be, subsection (4) above.

HMRC Manuals—Oil Taxation Manual OT15100 (definition of qualifying assets).

Amendments—[1] Words in sub-s (1) and whole of sub-s (1A) inserted by FA 1985 s 92(1), (2), (5), as respects consideration received or receivable after 19 March 1985.

[2] Words in sub-s (3) and whole of sub-s (3A) inserted with retrospective effect by FA 1986 s 110.

9 Tariff receipts allowance

(1) Subject to the provisions of this section and Schedule 3 to this Act if, in computing the assessable profit or allowable loss accruing to a participator from an oil field (in this section referred to as "the principal field") in any chargeable period, account would be taken, apart from this section, of an amount of qualifying tariff receipts received or receivable by him for that period from a user field, then, for the purpose of determining his liability (if any) to tax for that period, the amount of those qualifying tariff receipts shall be treated as reduced as follows, that is to say,—

(*a*) if that amount exceeds the cash equivalent of his share of the tariff receipts allowance in respect of that user field for that period, to an amount equal to the excess; or

(*b*) if that amount equals the cash equivalent of his share of that allowance, to nil.

(2) Subject to [subsection (4)][3] below, for the participators in the principal field there shall be, for each chargeable period, a separate tariff receipts allowance of 250,000 metric tonnes in respect of each user field.

(3) . . . [3]

(4) Schedule 3 to this Act shall have effect—

(*a*) for determining for the purposes of this section the cash equivalent of a participator's share of the tariff receipts allowance in respect of a user field for a chargeable period; and

(*b*) generally for supplementing [subsections (1) and (2) above][3].

(5) Any reference in this section or in Schedule 3 to this Act to a user field is a reference—

(*a*) to an oil field [other than—

(i) the principal field, or

(ii) an oil field that is a non-taxable field by virtue of section 185(1) or (1A) of the Finance Act 1993.][2]

(*b*) to an area which is not under the jurisdiction of the government of the United Kingdom but which, by an order made by statutory instrument by the Secretary of State for the purposes of this Act, is specified as a foreign field.

[(5A) No order may be made under subsection (5)(*b*) above on or after 1 July 1993.][1]

(6) In this section—

(*a*) "qualifying tariff receipts" means tariff receipts in relation to which the principal field is the chargeable field and which are attributable to, or to the provision of services or other business facilities in connection with, the use of any asset for extracting transporting, initially treating or initially storing oil won otherwise than from the principal field; and

(*b*) any reference to qualifying tariff receipts received from a user field is a reference to any of those receipts which are received from a participator in the user field in respect of the use of an asset for extracting, transporting, initially treating or initially storing oil won from that field or the provision of services or other business facilities in connection with that use;

and, for the purposes of this section and Schedule 3 to this Act, an oil field which, by virtue of section 107 of the Finance Act 1980 (transmedian fields), is deemed to include the sector mentioned in subsection (1)(a)(ii) of that section, shall be treated as two separate oil fields, one being that sector and the other being the rest of the field.

(7) In relation to any user field which is not an oil field within the meaning of the principal Act,—

(*a*) references to oil are references to any substance that would be oil within the meaning of that Act if the enactments mentioned in section 1(1) thereof extended to the user field; and

(*b*) references to a participator are references to a person who is, or has rights, interests or obligations of, a licensee in respect of the user field under the law of a country outside the United Kingdom.

(8) (*amends* FA 1981 s 111(3)).

(9) For the purposes of this section and Schedule 3 to this Act 1,100 cubic metres of oil consisting of gas at the temperature and pressure mentioned in section 1(4) of the principal Act shall be counted as equivalent to one metric tonne of oil other than gas.

(10) In any case where there is in force a scheme which, for the purposes of section 108 of the Finance Act 1980 (gas banking schemes) is either a gas banking scheme or an international gas banking scheme, then, whether or not an election is made under that section, in determining for the purposes of this section and Schedule 3 to this Act what oil is won from a particular user field oil consisting of gas which is transferred to a user field pursuant to the scheme shall be treated as won from that field.

Concession I4—Tariff receipts in respect of foreign user fields.

HMRC Manuals—Oil Taxation Manual OT15600 (tariff receipts allowance).

Regulations—See SI 1986/1644, SI 1986/1645, SI 1987/545, SI 1989/2384, SI 1991/1982, SI 1991/1983, SI 1991/1984, SI 1993/1408, SI 1993/1566 (Foreign Fields).

Simon's Tax Cases—*BP Oil Development Ltd v IRC* [1992] STC 28; *Chevron UK Ltd v IRC* [1995] STC 712.

Amendments—[1] Sub-s (5A) inserted by FA 1993 s 193(1).

[2] Sub-s (5)(*a*)(i), (ii) and preceding words "other than—" substituted by FA 2008 s 107, Sch 33 para 4 with effect from 21 July 2008.

[3] Sub-s (3) repealed, in sub-s (2) words substituted for words "subsections (3) and (4)", and in sub-s (4)(*b*) words substituted for words "subsections (1) to (3)", by FA 2009 s 91, Sch 45 para 2(1)–(3) with effect from 21 July 2009.

10 Returns relating to tariff and disposal receipts

(1) A return made by a participator in an oil field under paragraph 2 of Schedule 2 to the principal Act shall contain the following particulars—

(*a*) a statement of the amount or value and the source of any tariff receipts or disposal receipts of the participator which are attributable to that field for the chargeable period to which the return relates; and

(*b*) a statement of the assets to which any such tariff receipts or disposal receipts are referable; and

(*c*) such other particulars as the Board may prescribe with respect to any such tariff receipts or disposal receipts.

(2) In any case where—

(*a*) before the commencement of this Act, a participator in an oil field has made a return under paragraph 2 of Schedule 2 to the principal Act in respect of a chargeable period, and

(*b*) if subsection (1) above had been in force at the time that the return was made, the return would have been required to contain the particulars referred to in paragraphs (*a*) to (*c*) of that subsection,

the participator shall prepare and before 30 June 1984 deliver to the Board a supplementary return for that chargeable period identifying it and containing those particulars.

(3) Paragraphs 2(4) and 3 of Schedule 2 to the principal Act shall apply in relation to a supplementary return under subsection (2) above with the substitution of a reference to that subsection for the reference in paragraph 3(1) to paragraph 2(1) of that Schedule.

(4) (*amends* OTA 1975, 2 Sch 5(2A)).

(5) In the return under paragraph 5 of Schedule 2 to the principal Act for the chargeable period ending on 30 June 1984, the Board may require the responsible person to include particulars required for determining the amount by which any qualifying tariff receipts, within the meaning of section 9 above, are to be treated as reduced by virtue of that section for earlier chargeable periods.

(6) (*amends* PRTA 1980, Sch 2(2A)).

11

(*repealed* by TA 1988 s 844, Sch 31).

12 Charge of receipts attributable to UK use of foreign field assets

(1) The provisions of Schedule 4 to this Act have effect for the purpose of bringing into charge to tax the amount or value of certain consideration (whether in the nature of income or capital) which is received or receivable after 30 June 1982 by a participator in a foreign field—

(*a*) in respect of the United Kingdom use of a field asset; or

PRT

(*b*) in respect of the provision, in connection with the United Kingdom use of a field asset, of services or other business facilities of whatever kind, or

(*c*) in respect of the disposal of a field asset or an interest in such an asset where either the asset has already been in United Kingdom use or it is reasonable to expect that, after the disposal, the asset will be in United Kingdom use.

(2) In this section and Schedule 4 to this Act—

(*a*) "foreign field" means, subject to subsection (3) below, an area which is not under the jurisdiction of the government of the United Kingdom but which, by an order made by statutory instrument by the Secretary of State for the purposes of this Act, is specified as a foreign field; and

(*b*) in relation to a foreign field, "participator" means a person who is, or has rights, interests or obligations of, a licensee in respect of the foreign field under the law of a country outside the United Kingdom.

(3) For the purposes of this section and Schedule 4 to this Act, in the case of an oil field [which is a taxable field and][1] which, by virtue of section 107 of the Finance Act 1980 (transmedian fields) is deemed to include the sector mentioned in subsection (1)(*a*)(ii) of that section—

(*a*) that sector shall be treated as a foreign field; and

(*b*) the remainder of that field shall be treated as a separate oil field.

[(3A) No order may be made under subsection (2)(*a*) above on or after 1 July 1993.][1]

(4) In this section and Schedule 4 to this Act—

(*a*) "field asset", in relation to a foreign field, means an asset which—

(i) is not a mobile asset, and

(ii) is situated in the United Kingdom, the territorial sea thereof or a designated area, and

(iii) subject to subsection (6) below, is, has been or is expected to be used in a way which, on the assumptions in subsection (5) below, would be use in connection with the foreign field; and

(*b*) "United Kingdom use", in relation to a field asset, means the use of the asset in connection with the exploration or exploitation of so much of the seabed and subsoil and their natural resources as is situated in the territorial sea of the United Kingdom or a designated area.

(5) The assumptions referred to in subsection (4)(*a*) above are—

(*a*) that every foreign field is situated in a designated area and is an oil field within the meaning of Part I of the principal Act; and

(*b*) that references in Part I of the principal Act to oil are references to any substance that would be oil if the enactments mentioned in section 1(1) thereof extended to the foreign field.

(6) For the purposes of this section and Schedule 4 to this Act an asset which falls within sub-paragraphs (i) and (ii) of paragraph (*a*) of subsection (4) above but does not fall within sub-paragraph (iii) of that paragraph is nevertheless a field asset if—

(*a*) its use gives rise or is expected to give rise to consideration which, assuming the asset to be a field asset, would fall within subsection (1) above; and

(*b*) its useful life continues, or is expected to continue, for more than six months after the time at which the consideration referred to in paragraph (*a*) above is first received or receivable; and

(*c*) it is, or is expected to be, used in association with another asset which is a field asset.

(7) For the purposes of subsection (6)(*c*) above, an asset shall not be regarded as used in association with a field asset unless it is so used in a way which constitutes use in connection with an oil field or would constitute such use but for section 10(2) of the principal Act (exempt gas).

Regulations—SI 1986/1644, SI 1986/1645, SI 1987/545, SI 1989/2384, SI 1991/1982, SI 1991/1983, SI 1991/1984, SI 1993/1408, SI 1993/1566 (Foreign Fields).

HMRC Manuals—Oil Taxation Manual OT15025 (tariff receipts; foreign field assets).

Cross references—FA 1993 s 194 (double taxation relief in relation to PRT in respect of amounts chargeable under s 12).

Amendments—[1] Words in sub-s (3) and whole of sub-s (3A) inserted by FA 1993 s 193(4), (5).

Supplementary

13 Transitional provisions

Amendments—Sections 13, 14 repealed by FA 2009 s 91, Sch 45 para 2(1), (4) with effect from 21 July 2009.

14 Re-opening of decisions for periods before the passing of this Act

Amendments—Sections 13, 14 repealed by FA 2009 s 91, Sch 45 para 2(1), (4) with effect from 21 July 2009.

15 Short title, interpretation, construction and repeals

(1) This Act may be cited as the Oil Taxation Act 1983.

(2) In this Act "the principal Act" means the Oil Taxation Act 1975.

(3) In this Act—

"chargeable field" shall be construed in accordance with section 8(5) above;

"disposal receipts" shall be construed in accordance with section 7(2) above;

"qualifying asset" shall be construed in accordance with [section 8][1] above; and

"tariff receipts" shall be construed, subject to Schedule 5 to this Act, in accordance with section 6(2) above.

(4) [Section 1122 of the Corporation Tax Act 2010][2] (connected persons) applies for the purposes of this Act.

(5) This Act shall be construed as one with Part I of the principal Act.

(6) The enactments specified in Schedule 6 to this Act are hereby repealed to the extent specified in the third column of that Schedule.

HMRC Manuals—Oil Taxation Manual OT15010 (tariff receipts: outline).

Amendments—[1] Words in sub-s (3) substituted by FA 1985 s 92(3), (5).

[2] In sub-s (4) words substituted for words "Section 839 of the Taxes Act" by CTA 2010 s 1177, Sch 1 para 182. CTA 2010 has effect for corporation tax purposes for accounting periods ending on or after 1 April 2010, and for income and capital gains tax purposes for the tax year 2010–11 and subsequent tax years.

SCHEDULES

SCHEDULE 1
ALLOWABLE EXPENDITURE

Section 3

PART I
EXTENSIONS OF ALLOWABLE EXPENDITURE FOR ASSETS GENERATING RECEIPTS

Associated assets

1—(1) This paragraph applies where, after 30 June 1982, a participator in an oil field (in this paragraph referred to as "the principal field") incurs or incurred expenditure in acquiring, bringing into existence or enhancing the value of an asset—

(*a*) which is not a mobile asset and which, apart from this paragraph, does not fall within subsection (1)(*a*) of section 3 of this Act; and

(*b*) the use of which gives rise, or is expected to give rise, to receipts which, assuming the asset to be a qualifying asset, would be tariff receipts; and

(*c*) the useful life of which continues, or is expected to continue, after the end of the first chargeable period in which the receipts referred to in paragraph (*b*) above arise; and

(*d*) which is, or is expected to be, used in association with another asset which itself is, has been, or is expected to be, used in connection with the principal field;

and, where this paragraph applies, the asset on which the expenditure is or was incurred is in the following provisions of this paragraph referred to as "the associated asset".

(2) Subject to section 4(2) of this Act, for the purposes of section 3 of this Act, Part II below and section 3 of the principal Act, the use of the associated asset to give rise to the receipts referred to in sub-paragraph (1)(*b*) above shall be assumed to be use in connection with the principal field.

(3) For the purposes of this paragraph, an asset shall not be regarded as used in association with another asset which is, has been or is expected to be used in connection with the principal field unless it is used in a way—

(*a*) which constitutes use in connection with another oil field; or

(*b*) which would constitute such use but for section 10(2) of the principal Act (exempt gas); or

(*c*) which, on the assumptions in sub-paragraph (4) below, would constitute use in connection with an external field;

and for the purposes of paragraph (c) above, an external field is an area which is not under the jurisdiction of the government of the United Kingdom.

(4) The assumptions referred to in sub-paragraph (3)(*c*) above are—

(*a*) that every external field is situated in a designated area and is an oil field within the meaning of Part I of the principal Act; and

(*b*) that references in Part I of the principal Act to oil are references to any substance that would be oil if the enactments mentioned in section 1(1) thereof extended to the external field; . . . [1]

(*c*) . . . [1]

HMRC Manuals—Oil Taxation Manual OT11250 (associated assets).

Amendments—[1] Words in sub-para (4) repealed by F(No 2)A 1992 ss 74, 82, Sch 15 para 6, Sch 18 Pt VIII with effect in accordance with s 74(5) thereof.

Restriction of relief for remote associated assets

2—(1) The provisions of this paragraph apply where some part of the associated asset is situated more than 100 metres from the nearest part of another asset—

(*a*) in association with which the associated asset is or is expected to be used; and

(*b*) which is, has been or is expected to be used in a way which otherwise than by virtue of paragraph 1 above, constitutes use in connection with the principal field;

PRT

and sub-paragraphs (3) and (4) of paragraph 1 above have effect for the purposes of this sub-paragraph as they have effect for the purposes of that paragraph.

(2) In sub-paragraph (1) above,—

(*a*) "the associated asset" has the meaning assigned to it by sub-paragraph (1) of paragraph 1 above;

(*b*) "the principal field" has the same meaning as in that paragraph;

and where the associated asset falls within sub-paragraph (1) above it is in the following provisions of this paragraph referred to as "the remote asset".

(3) For the purpose of determining, in accordance with subsection (8) of section 2 of the principal Act, the amount to be debited or credited to a participator for a chargeable period in respect of expenditure, where any expenditure which is or was incurred by the participator in respect of the remote asset—

(*a*) is expenditure to which section 3 of this Act or section 3 of the principal Act applies by virtue only of paragraph 1 above, and

(*b*) has been allowed on a claim under Schedule 5 or Schedule 6 to the principal Act before the Board have made an assessment to tax or a determination on or in relation to the participator for a chargeable period earlier than that referred to in sub-paragraph (5) below,

the expenditure shall be treated for the purposes of paragraph (b) or paragraph (c) of subsection (9) of the said section 2 as having been allowed immediately before the Board made an assessment to tax or a determination on or in relation to the participator for the period specified in sub-paragraph (5) below and not at any earlier time.

(4) In determining under subsection (4) of section 111 of the Finance Act 1981 (restriction of expenditure supplement) whether, if account were to be taken of certain expenditure, a net profit would not have accrued to a participator in a chargeable period, expenditure which—

(*a*) is or was incurred by the participator in respect of the remote asset, and

(*b*) is expenditure to which section 3 of this Act or section 3 of the principal Act applies by virtue only of paragraph 1 above,

shall be disregarded unless the chargeable period in question is, or is later than, the period specified in sub-paragraph (5) below.

(5) The chargeable period referred to in sub-paragraphs (3) and (4) above is the first in which either—

(*a*) by virtue of section 6(1) of this Act, the positive amounts for the purposes of section 2 of the principal Act include (after taking account of any reduction under section 9 of this Act) an amount of tariff receipts derived, in whole or in part, from the remote asset; or

(*b*) by virtue of section 7(1) of this Act, the positive amounts for the purposes of section 2 of the principal Act include an amount of disposal receipts in respect of the disposal of, or of an interest in, that asset.

(6) For any chargeable period in which expenditure incurred by a participator in respect of the remote asset falls to be brought into account under paragraph (*b*) or paragraph (*c*) of subsection (9) of section 2 of the principal Act the amount of that expenditure which is to be so brought into account shall not exceed the aggregate of—

(*a*) the amount of the tariff receipts (if any) which are derived, in whole or in part, from the remote asset, and

(*b*) the amount of the disposal receipts (if any) in respect of the disposal of, or of an interest in, the remote asset,

which (after taking account of any reduction under section 9 of this Act) are included in the positive amounts for that chargeable period for the purposes of that section.

(7) In any case where—

(*a*) for any chargeable period the positive amounts for the purposes of section 2 of this Act include an amount (in this sub-paragraph referred to as "the reduced amount") which represents an amount of qualifying tariff receipts which were received from one user field and which have been reduced by virtue of section 9 of this Act, and

(*b*) those qualifying tariff receipts include tariff receipts which are derived, in whole or in part, from the remote asset as well as other tariff receipts,

the portion of the reduced amount which is to be regarded for the purpose of the preceding provisions of this paragraph as tariff receipts derived, in whole or in part, from the remote asset shall bear to the whole of the reduced amount the same proportion as, before the reduction, the tariff receipts so derived bore to the whole of the qualifying tariff receipts in question.

(8) For the purpose of the preceding provisions of this paragraph a tariff receipt is derived, in whole or in part, from the remote asset if it consists of or includes consideration in respect of—

(*a*) the use of the remote asset; or

(*b*) the provision of services or other business facilities of whatever kind in connection with the use of that asset;

and subsection (6) of section 9 of this Act shall have effect for the purposes of sub-paragraph (7) above as it has effect for the purposes of that section.

HMRC Manuals—Oil Taxation Manual OT11300 (remote associated assets).

Assets no longer in use for the principal field

3—(1) This paragraph applies where—

(*a*) a participator in an oil field (in this paragraph referred to as "the principal field") incurs expenditure in enhancing the value of [or otherwise in connection with][1] an asset which is not a mobile asset; and

(*b*) before the expenditure was incurred the asset had already been used or was expected to be used in connection with the principal field (and, accordingly, is a qualifying asset); and

(*c*) at the end of the claim period in which the expenditure is incurred, the asset is no longer being, and is not expected to be, used in connection with the principal field; and

(*d*) [either the use of the asset][1] gives rise or is expected to give rise to tariff receipts or [the expenditure][1] is incurred with a view to the subsequent disposal of the asset or of an interest in it.

(2) For the purposes of section 3 of this Act, Part II below and section 3 of the principal Act,—

(*a*) the use of the asset referred to in sub-paragraph (1) above to give rise to tariff receipts shall be assumed to be use in connection with the principal field; and

(*b*) if the subsequent disposal of, or of an interest in, the asset gives or is expected to give rise to disposal receipts, the asset shall be assumed to be being used in connection with the principal field throughout the claim period in which the expenditure is incurred.

[(2A) But where—

(*a*) the expenditure would (apart from this sub-paragraph) be regarded as incurred with a view to the subsequent disposal of the asset or of an interest in it, and

(*b*) the asset has, at any time in the period of 6 years ending with the date on which the expenditure was incurred, been used in a way that gives rise to tax-exempt tariffing receipts,

the expenditure shall not be regarded for the purposes of this paragraph as expenditure incurred with a view to the subsequent disposal of the asset or of an interest in it, to the extent that the amount of the expenditure falls to be reduced in accordance with sub-paragraph (2B) below.][2]

[(2B) The reduction is to be made by applying section 7A of this Act in relation to the expenditure as it applies in relation to disposal receipts in respect of a disposal, but with the substitution—

(*a*) for references to the disponor, of references to the participator incurring the expenditure ("the relevant participator"),

(*b*) for references to the amount or value (apart from that section) of any disposal receipts of the disponor in respect of the disposal, of references to the amount which would, apart from sub-paragraph (2A) above, be the amount of the expenditure incurred by the relevant participator with a view to the subsequent disposal of the asset or of an interest in it,

(*c*) for references to the interest disposed of, of references to the asset or interest whose subsequent disposal gives or is expected to give rise to disposal receipts,

(*d*) for references to the date of the disposal, of references to the date on which the expenditure was incurred,

and taking the reference in subsection (6)(*b*) of that section to a reduction made by virtue of that section as a reference to a reduction made by virtue of that section for the purposes of section 7(9) of this Act.][2]

(3) References in sub-paragraphs (1) and (2) above to use in connection with the principal field include references to use which would constitute use in connection with that field but for section 10(2) of the principal Act (exempt gas).

HMRC Manuals—Oil Taxation Manual OT11350 (assets no longer in use for the principal field).

Amendments—[1] Words in sub-para (1)(*a*) inserted and sub-para (1)(*d*) substituted, in relation to expenditure incurred on or after 15 March 1988, by FA 1988 s 139.

[2] Sub-paras (2A), (2B) inserted by FA 2004 s 285, Sch 37 para 6 with effect for expenditure incurred after 31 December 2003.

PART II

SPECIAL RULES AS TO EXPENDITURE ALLOWABLE IN RESPECT OF FIXED ASSETS AND DEDICATED MOBILE ASSETS

Interpretation

4 In this Part of this Schedule—

"allowable expenditure" means expenditure which, subject to the provisions of this Part, is allowable as mentioned in subsection (4) of the principal section;

"the new asset" means the asset referred to in subsection (1) of the principal section which was acquired or brought into existence, or the value of which was enhanced, as a result of the incurring of the allowable expenditure;

"the principal section" means section 3 of this Act;

"the purchaser" means the person referred to in subsection (1) of the principal section as the person incurring the allowable expenditure; and

"the relevant claim period", in relation to any allowable expenditure, has the same meaning as, by virtue of subsection (5) of the principal section, it has for the purposes of subsection (1) of that section.

Assets acquired etc for two or more fields

5—(1) Subject to sub-paragraphs (2) and (3) below, where the purchaser is a participator in two or more oil fields (in this paragraph referred to as "the purchaser's fields") and, at the end of the relevant claim period, it appears that the new asset is or is expected to be used in connection with two or more of those fields then, unless it seems just and reasonable to attribute all of the allowable expenditure relevant to the new asset to only one of those fields, that expenditure shall be apportioned, in such manner as may be just and reasonable, between those of the purchaser's fields in connection with which the new asset is or is expected to be used.

(2) If, in a case falling within sub-paragraph (1) above, the use of the new asset in connection with one of the purchaser's fields (in this paragraph referred to as "the paying field") gives, or is at the end of the relevant claim period expected to give, rise to receipts which, by virtue of section 8 of this Act, are to be attributed to another of those fields, as being the chargeable field, so much (if any) of the allowable expenditure as, apart from this sub-paragraph, would be apportioned to the paying field and as is reasonably attributable to the use of the new asset which gives rise to the receipts shall be apportioned to the chargeable field.

(3) If, in a case falling within sub-paragraph (1) above, it appears, at the end of the relevant claim period, that the new asset also is or is expected to be used otherwise than in connection with a field in which the purchaser is a participator, then—

(*a*) in the apportionment made by virtue of sub-paragraph (1) above, such a percentage of the allowable expenditure as is just and reasonable shall be apportioned to that use; and

(*b*) for the purpose of any claim for an allowance in respect of any of the allowable expenditure, the percentage of that expenditure which under paragraph (*a*) above was apportioned to that use shall be added to the percentage of that expenditure which, under sub-paragraph (1) above, was apportioned to that one of the purchaser's fields which, in relation to the new asset, is the chargeable field.

(4) If, in relation to the allowable expenditure, the relevant claim periods of the purchaser's fields are not the same, references in the preceding provisions of this paragraph to the end of the relevant claim period are references to the end of that relevant claim period which ends earlier or earliest.

HMRC Manuals—Oil Taxation Manual OT11400 (assets acquired for more than one field).

6—(1) In any case where—

(*a*) the new asset is or is expected to be used in connection with two or more oil fields, and

(*b*) no apportionment of the allowable expenditure falls to be made by virtue of paragraph 5 above,

the allowable expenditure shall be treated as wholly attributable to the use of the asset in connection with that field in which the purchaser is a participator or, if there is more than one such field, that one of them in relation to which a development decision is or was first made.

(2) Subsection (7) of section 5A of the principal Act (time when development decision is made) shall have effect for the purposes of sub-paragraph (1) above as it has effect for the purposes of subsection (1)(*c*) of that section.

[(3) Subsection (3A) of section 8 of this Act applies for the purposes of sub-paragraph (1) above as it applies for the purposes of subsection (3)(*c*) of that section.][1]

HMRC Manuals—Oil Taxation Manual OTO11400 (assets acquired for more than one field; supplement).

Amendments—[1] Sub-para (3) inserted with retrospective effect by FA 1986 s 110(4).

Brought-in assets

7—(1) The provisions of this paragraph apply where—

(*a*) the allowable expenditure is (in whole or in part) referable to the use of the new asset in connection with an oil field which is not an exempt field; and

(*b*) the allowable expenditure was incurred at a time before the new asset was first used in connection with that oil field, discounting, in the case of a mobile asset, any use in a claim period when it was not dedicated to that oil field; and (*c*) during the period (in this paragraph referred to as "the initial period") between the time when the new asset was acquired or brought into existence and that first use, the new asset was used—

[(i)] [2] otherwise than in connection with [a taxable field][1], [or][2]

[(ii) in connection with a taxable field in a way that gives rise to tax-exempt tariffing receipts,][2]

by the purchaser or a person connected with him.

(2) In any case where—

(*a*) at some time during the initial period the new asset was used in a way which, disregarding section 10(2) of the principal Act (exempt gas), would be use in connection with an exempt field, and

(*b*) at the beginning of the initial period it was not reasonable to expect that the asset would be used in connection with an oil field,

the amount which, apart from this sub-paragraph, would be the amount of the allowable expenditure in respect of the expected use referred to in sub-paragraph (1)(a) above, shall be reduced to nil.

(3) In determining whether the condition in sub-paragraph (2)(*b*) above is fulfilled, no account shall be taken of use which, by virtue only of subsection (3) or subsection (5) of section 4 of this Act, is treated as use in connection with an exempt field.

(4) In a case where sub-paragraph (2) above does not apply, the amount which, apart from this sub-paragraph, would be the amount of the allowable expenditure shall be reduced by multiplying it by the fraction of which—

(*a*) the numerator is a reasonable estimate of so much of the useful life of the asset as remains after the date on which it was first used as mentioned in sub-paragraph (1)(*b*) above; and

(*b*) the denominator is the aggregate of that reasonable estimate and the initial period.

(5) In this paragraph an "exempt field" means an oil field from which all the oil won is excluded oil, as defined in section 10(1) of the principal Act.

HMRC Manuals—Oil Taxation Manual OTO11500 (brought in assets).

Amendments—[1] Words in sub-para (1) substituted by FA 1993 s 190(3).

[2] In sub-para (1)(*c*), sub-para (i) renumbered as such, word "or" and sub-para (ii) inserted by FA 2004 s 285, Sch 37 para 7 with effect for expenditure incurred after 31 December 2003.

Subsequent use of new asset otherwise than in connection with [a taxable field]

8—(1) Subject to sub-paragraph (3) below,—

(*a*) if at any time the new asset ceases to be used by the purchaser in a way which either constitutes use [for a qualifying purpose][3] or would constitute such use but for section 10(2) of the principal Act (exempt gas), and

(*b*) thereafter, the new asset is or is expected to be used otherwise than [for a qualifying purpose][3] and is not disposed of in circumstances giving rise to disposal receipts,

the amount which, apart from this paragraph, would be the amount of the allowable expenditure shall be taken to be reduced by multiplying it by the fraction specified in sub-paragraph (2) below.

(2) The fraction referred to in sub-paragraph (1) above is that of which—

(*a*) the numerator is a reasonable estimate of the period beginning when the purchaser first used the asset in connection with [a taxable field][1] or, if it was earlier, when the asset first gave rise to tariff receipts of the purchaser and ending when the asset is or is expected to be first used as mentioned in paragraph (*b*) of sub-paragraph (1) above after the cessation referred to in paragraph (*a*) of that sub-paragraph; and

(*b*) the denominator is a reasonable estimate of the useful life of the asset or, where sub-paragraph (4) of paragraph 7 above applies, of so much of that useful life as falls after the date on which the asset was first used as mentioned in sub-paragraph (1)(*a*) of that paragraph.

[(2A) In sub-paragraph (1) a reference to use for a qualifying purpose is a reference to—

(*a*) use in connection with a taxable field, and

(*b*) other use in—

(i) the United Kingdom,

(ii) the territorial sea of the United Kingdom, or

(iii) a designated area,

except use wholly or partly for an ineligible oil purpose.

(2B) In this Act a reference to use of an asset for an ineligible oil purpose is a reference to—

(*a*) use in connection with an oil field that is not a taxable field, and

(*b*) use for any other purpose (apart from a purpose falling within section 3(1)(*b*) of the principal Act) of a separate trade consisting of activities falling within [the definition of "oil-related activities" in section 274 of the Corporation Tax Act 2010][4].

(2C) In sub-paragraphs (2A) and (2B) a reference to use in connection with a taxable field or other oil field includes use giving rise to receipts which, for the purposes of this Act, are tariff receipts.][3]

(3) If and so long as an asset gives rise to—

[(*a*)] [2] tariff receipts of the purchaser attributable to [a taxable field][1], [or][2]

[(*b*) tax-exempt tariffing receipts which, if they were tariff receipts (and expenditure were or had been allowable accordingly), would be tariff receipts of the purchaser attributable to a taxable field,][2]

the asset shall be treated, for the purposes of sub-paragraph (1) above, as if it were used by him in connection with [a taxable field].

(4) If, in any case where the amount of any expenditure falls to be reduced under sub-paragraph (1) above, so much of the expenditure as has been previously allowed on a claim for any claim period exceeds the reduced allowable expenditure, an amount equal to the excess shall be treated (otherwise than for the purposes of paragraph (*b*) of that sub-paragraph) as disposal receipts of the purchaser arising from the asset in the chargeable period in which the asset ceased to be used as mentioned in paragraph (*a*) of that sub-paragraph.

(5) In the case of an asset which has been used in connection with two or more oil fields for which any of the purchaser's allowable expenditure is or has been allowed or allowable, the chargeable period referred to in sub-paragraph (4) above shall be determined in relation to that one of those fields—

(*a*) in connection with which the asset was last used by the purchaser; or

(*b*) if it is later, in respect of which the asset last gave rise to tariff receipts of the purchaser; [or

(*c*) if it is later than paragraph (*a*) and (where otherwise applicable) paragraph (*b*) above, in respect of which the asset would have last given rise to tariff receipts of the purchaser had tax-exempt tariffing receipts of the purchaser been tariff receipts of his (and if expenditure were or had been allowable accordingly);][2]

and the reference in that sub-paragraph to disposal receipts shall accordingly be construed as a reference to disposal receipts attributable to that field.

(6) In any case where—

(a) at a time before the new asset is brought into use by the purchaser in such a way as is mentioned in sub-paragraph (1)(*a*) above, it ceases to be expected to be used in such a way, and

(*b*) thereafter the new asset is or is expected to be used otherwise than in connection with [a taxable field][1] and is not disposed of in circumstances giving rise to disposal receipts,

the amount which, apart from this paragraph, would be the amount of the allowable expenditure shall be taken to be reduced to nil.

(7) In any case where the amount of any expenditure falls to be reduced to nil under sub-paragraph (6) above, an amount equal to so much of the expenditure as has been previously allowed on a claim for any claim period shall be treated (otherwise than for the purposes of paragraph (*b*) of that sub-paragraph) as disposal receipts of the purchaser arising from the asset in the chargeable period in which the asset ceased to be expected to be used in such a way as is mentioned in sub-paragraph(1)(*a*) above.

HMRC Manuals—Oil Taxation Manual OT11600 (subsequent use of new asset outside Taxable Field).

Amendments—[1] Words in heading and sub-paras (2), (3), (6) substituted by FA 1993 s 190(4).

[2] In sub-para (3), sub-para (a) renumbered as such, word "or" and sub-para (b) inserted, sub-para (5)(*c*) and the word "or" immediately preceding it inserted, by FA 2004 s 285, Sch 37 para 8 with effect for expenditure incurred after 31 December 2003.

[3] In sub-para (1)(*a*), (*b*) words substituted for words "in connection with a taxable field", and sub-paras (2A)–(2C) inserted, by FA 2009 s 87, Sch 41 para 3 with effect in relation to chargeable periods beginning after 30 June 2009.

[4] In sub-para (2B)(*b*) words substituted for words "section 492(1) of the Income and Corporation Taxes Act 1988" by CTA 2010 s 1177, Sch 1 para 183. CTA 2010 has effect for corporation tax purposes for accounting periods ending on or after 1 April 2010, and for income and capital gains tax purposes for the tax year 2010–11 and subsequent tax years.

Mobile assets becoming dedicated assets

9—(1) Subject to sub-paragraph (2) below, where any expenditure in connection with a mobile asset has been allowed or is allowable under section 4 of the principal Act and the asset becomes dedicated to an oil field, the expenditure which would otherwise be allowable under the principal section shall be reduced by so much of that expenditure as has been allowed or is allowable under the said section 4.

(2) Sub-paragraph (1) above does not apply in any case where—

(*a*) paragraph 7 above applies; and

(*b*) sub-paragraph (4) of that paragraph applies to reduce the amount of expenditure which is allowable expenditure.

SCHEDULE 2

SUPPLEMENTAL PROVISIONS AS TO RECEIPTS FROM QUALIFYING ASSETS

Sections 6–8

Interpretation

1—(1) Any reference in this Schedule to the use of an asset includes a reference to the provision, in connection with that use, of services or other business facilities of whatever kind.

(2) Any reference in this Schedule to the disposal of an asset includes a reference to the disposal of an interest in it.

Consideration received by connected persons under avoidance schemes

2—(1) This paragraph applies if consideration in respect of the use or disposal of an asset which, in relation to a participator or two or more participators in an oil field, is a qualifying asset is received or receivable—

(*a*) by a person in relation to whom the asset is not a qualifying asset but who is connected with the participator or, as the case may be, with each of them; and

(*b*) under or in consequence of a scheme or arrangements the main purpose or one of the main purposes of which is the avoidance of petroleum revenue tax or corporation tax.

(2) In relation to the participator or, as the case may be, each of the participators referred to in sub-paragraph (1) above, any reference in section 6 or section 7 of this Act or in the following provisions of this Schedule to consideration received or receivable by him in respect of the use or disposal of the asset referred to in that sub-paragraph includes, subject to sub-paragraph (3) below, a reference to the consideration referred to in sub-paragraph (1) above or, if there is more than one participator, such portion of that consideration as it is just and reasonable to apportion to the participator in question.

(3) In any case where—

(*a*) the tariff receipts or disposal receipts of a participator in respect of the use or disposal of a qualifying asset include consideration which is received or receivable from a person who is connected with the participator, and

(*b*) consideration is received or receivable from a person who is not connected with the participator by a person who is so connected (whether the person referred to in paragraph (*a*) above or not), and

(*c*) apart from this sub-paragraph, the consideration referred to in paragraph (*b*) above or (where there is more than one connected participator) a portion of that consideration would, by virtue of sub-paragraph (2) above, be included in the tariff receipts or disposal receipts of the participator which are referable to the use or disposal of the qualifying asset concerned,

only so much of the consideration or, as the case may be, of the portion of it referred to in paragraph (b) above as exceeds the consideration referred to in paragraph (a) above shall be included (by virtue of sub-paragraph (2) above) in the tariff receipts or, as the case may be, the disposal receipts of the participator.

HMRC Manuals—Oil Taxation Manual OT15400 (anti-avoidance: tariff or disposal receipts received by connected person).

Apportionment of consideration in respect of use or disposal

3 In any case where—

(*a*) consideration received or receivable by a participator in an oil field in respect of the use or disposal of a qualifying asset includes an element that is unquantified but which does not constitute a tariff receipt or disposal receipt of his, and

(*b*) the consideration does not fall to be apportioned by virtue of section 6(4) or section 7(5) of this Act,

the portion of the consideration which constitutes a tariff receipt or disposal receipt of the participator shall be determined in such manner as is just and reasonable.

Cases where all the oil is disregarded under section 10 of the principal Act

4—(1) This paragraph applies in any case where, in computing under section 2 of the principal Act the gross profit or loss accruing to a participator in any chargeable period from the chargeable field, all the oil which, apart from section 10 of that Act (exempt gas), would be taken into account falls to be disregarded under subsection (1) of that section.

(2) In any case where this paragraph applies, subsection (1) of section 8 of this Act shall have effect in relation to the participator as if—

(*a*) in paragraph (*a*) the word "either" and the words "or is a mobile asset dedicated to that oil field" were omitted; and

(*b*) in paragraph (*b*) for the words "is allowable, or has" there were substituted the words "would, apart from section 10(2) of the principal Act, be allowed or have";

PRT

and, in relation to the participator, tariff receipts and disposal receipts shall be construed accordingly.

[(2A) In any case where this paragraph applies, paragraph (*b*) of subsection (1A) of section 8 of this Act shall have effect in relation to the participator as if—

(*a*) for the words "does not" there were substituted "would not"; and

(*b*) at the end there were added the words "even if section 10(2) of the principal Act were disregarded.][1]

(3) Subsections (6) to (8) of section 7 of this Act shall not apply where the asset is a qualifying asset by reason only of sub-paragraph (2) above.

HMRC Manuals—Oil Taxation Manual OT13250 (exempt gas fields).

Amendments—[1] Sub-para (2A) inserted by FA 1985 s 92(4), (5).

Acquisition otherwise than at arm's length: limit on tariff and disposal receipts

5—(1) In any case where—

(*a*) in a transaction to which paragraph 2 of Schedule 4 to the principal Act applies (restriction on allowable expenditure where asset acquired in a transaction not at arm's length) a participator in [a taxable field][1] makes a disposal of a qualifying asset, and

(*b*) the disposal gives rise to what would, apart from this paragraph be tariff receipts or disposal receipts of the participator for a chargeable period, and

(*c*) those receipts are received from a person who is also a participator in [a taxable field][1] (whether the same field or not), [and

(*d*) the use of the asset will be wholly by that person in connection with a taxable field in which he is a participator (and accordingly, and in particular, there will be no use giving rise to tariff receipts);][2]

[the receipts referred to in paragraphs (b) and (c) above][2] shall not be regarded as tariff receipts or disposal receipts if and to the extent that their aggregate in the period beginning with the transaction and ending with the end of that chargeable period exceeds relevant expenditure.

(2) In this paragraph "relevant expenditure" means expenditure (other than expenditure in respect of interest or any other pecuniary obligation incurred in obtaining a loan or any other form of credit) incurred by the participator referred to in sub-paragraph (1)(*a*) above or by another person in acquiring, bringing into existence, or enhancing the value of the asset in a transaction to which paragraph 2 of Schedule 4 to the principal Act does not apply (or, if there has been more than one such transaction, the later or latest of them).

(3) In any case where—

(*a*) in a transaction to which paragraph 2 of Schedule 4 to the principal Act applies, a participator in [a taxable field][1] makes a disposal of a qualifying asset, and

[(*b*) the disposal does not fall within sub-paragraph (1) above, and][2]

(*c*) the disposal either gives rise to tariff receipts or disposal receipts of the participator for a chargeable period or is made for no consideration,

the disposal shall be treated as giving rise to disposal receipts or tariff receipts (according to the nature of the disposal) equal to the open market consideration for the disposal and any actual receipts falling within paragraph (c) above shall be disregarded.

(4) Without prejudice to paragraph 1(2) above, in this paragraph "disposal", in relation to a qualifying asset, includes the hiring of it or any similar transaction by which the use of the asset gives rise, or might reasonably be expected to give rise, to receipts (whether in the nature of income or capital).

(5) The reference in sub-paragraph (3) above to the open market consideration for a disposal is a reference to the consideration which might reasonably have been obtained for the disposal in question (whatever its nature) had it been made in a transaction to which paragraph 2 of Schedule 4 to the principal Act does not apply.

HMRC Manuals—Oil Taxation Manual OT15450 (tariff and disposal receipts not at arm's length).

Amendments—[1] Words in sub-paras (1), (3) substituted by FA 1993 s 190(5).

[2] Sub-para (1)(*d*) inserted and words in sub-para (1) and sub-para (3)(*b*) substituted, with respect to disposals made after 30 November 1993, by or by virtue of FA 1994 ss 238, 258, Sch 26, Part VI.

Transfers of interests in fields

6 (*amends* FA 1980 Sch 17 para 19).

Insurance and compensation payments

7 Any payment by way of insurance or compensation in respect of the loss or destruction of an asset which, in relation to a participator in an oil field, is a qualifying asset, shall be brought into account for the purposes of section 7 of this Act and this Schedule as consideration in respect of a disposal of the asset taking place at the time the payment is received or receivable.

HMRC Manuals—Oil Taxation Manual OT15350 (insurance receipts).

Dedicated mobile assets ceasing to be used in connection with participator's oil field

8—(1) This paragraph applies in any case where—

(*a*) a mobile asset which, in relation to a participator in an oil field, is a qualifying asset gives rise to receipts which, apart from the provisions of this paragraph, would be tariff receipts of the participator; and

(*b*) the asset has ceased to be used in connection with any oil field whatsoever in which the participator or a person connected with him is a participator.

(2) In any case where this paragraph applies, so much of what would, apart from this paragraph, be tariff receipts of the participator arising from the asset and which are neither—

(a) received or receivable before the end of the chargeable period in which falls the second anniversary of the date on which the asset ceased to be used as mentioned in sub-paragraph (1)(*b*) above, nor

(*b*) received or receivable after the end of that chargeable period in respect of the use of the asset before the end of that period,

shall not form part of the tariff receipts of the participator for any chargeable period in which the asset is not used as mentioned in sub-paragraph (1)(b) above.

Disposal receipts in respect of brought-in assets

9 If paragraph 7(4) of Schedule 1 to this Act applies to reduce the allowable expenditure, within the meaning of Part II of that Schedule, in respect of an asset and any disposal receipt is received or receivable in respect of the asset, the amount which, apart from this paragraph, would be the amount of that receipt shall be taken to be reduced by multiplying it by the same fraction as, by virtue of the said paragraph 7(4), was applied to that allowable expenditure.

HMRC Manuals—Oil Taxation Manual OT15060 (disposal receipts).

Disposal receipts: assets used for deballasting

10 In any case where—

(*a*) section 4(2) of this Act applies to reduce the expenditure allowable as mentioned in section 3(4) of this Act in respect of an asset, and

(*b*) any disposal receipt is received or receivable in respect of the asset,

the amount which, apart from this paragraph, would be the amount of that receipt shall be taken to be reduced in the proportion in which the expenditure so allowable was reduced by virtue of section 4(2) of this Act.

HMRC Manuals—Oil Taxation Manual OT15060 (disposal receipts).

Use by connected or associated person: avoidance devices

11—(1) This paragraph applies in any case where—

(*a*) any consideration in respect of the use of an asset is received or receivable by a person (in this paragraph referred to as "the recipient") in relation to whom the asset is not a qualifying asset; and

(*b*) the asset is at any time used in connection with an oil field by a person (in this paragraph referred to as "the user") who is connected or associated with the recipient and who is a participator in that or any other oil field; and(*c*) the consideration is so received or receivable under or in consequence of a scheme or arrangements the main purpose or one of the main purposes of which is the avoidance of petroleum revenue tax or corporation tax.

(2) Subject to sub-paragraphs (5) and (6) below, the user shall be treated for the purposes of this Act and Part I [of the principal Act and [sections 299 to 301 of the Corporation Tax Act 2010][2]][1] as if—

(*a*) any consideration arising from the use of the asset and received or receivable at any time by the recipient or a person connected or associated with him, other than consideration received or receivable from the user himself, had been received or receivable at that time by the user; and

(*b*) such proportion of any expenditure incurred by the recipient at any time in connection with the asset as it is just and reasonable to apportion to the use which gives rise to the consideration had been incurred at that time by the user for the purpose for which it was in fact incurred by the recipient.

(3) For the purposes of this paragraph, a participator in an oil field is associated with another person if the participator, by acting together with a person who is, or two or more persons each of whom is, a participator in that oil field or in any other relevant field, would be able to secure or exercise control of that other person, and for this purpose—

(*a*) "control" shall be construed in accordance with [sections 450 and 451 of the Corporation Tax Act 2010][2]; and

PRT

(*b*) "relevant field" means an oil field in connection with which the asset referred to in sub-paragraph (1)(*a*) above has been, is, or is expected to be, used.

(4) For the purposes of sub-paragraph (3) above—

(*a*) a foreign field, within the meaning of section 12 of this Act, shall be treated as an oil field, and

(*b*) an asset is used in connection with a relevant field which is a foreign field if it is used in a way which, on the assumptions set out in subsection (5) of that section, would be use in connection with the foreign field,

and, in relation to a relevant field which is a foreign field, the reference in sub-paragraph (3) above to a participator shall be construed in accordance with section 12(2)(b) of this Act.

(5) If, in relation to the recipient, there is more than one person who is the user, any consideration or expenditure falling within paragraph (*a*) or paragraph (*b*) of sub-paragraph (2) above shall be apportioned between those persons in such manner as is just and reasonable.

(6) Sub-paragraph (2)(*b*) above does not apply if the asset is a mobile asset which is not dedicated to an oil field.

HMRC Manuals—Oil Taxation Manual OT15500 (use by connected or associated persons).

Amendments—[1] Words substituted by TA 1988 s 844, Sch 29 para 32.

[2] In sub-para (2) words substituted for words "section 500 of the Taxes Act", in sub-para (3)(*a*) words substituted for words "section 416 of the Taxes Act" by CTA 2010 s 1177, Sch 1 para 184(2), (3). CTA 2010 has effect for corporation tax purposes for accounting periods ending on or after 1 April 2010, and for income and capital gains tax purposes for the tax year 2010–11 and subsequent tax years.

Purchase at place of extraction

12—(1) [Subject to sub-paragraphs (4) to (6)][4] below, in any case where—

(*a*) a participator in an oil field or any person connected with him purchases any oil, otherwise than in pursuance of such an agreement as is mentioned in paragraph 6A of Schedule 3 to the principal Act (transactions between participators), and takes delivery of that oil at the place of extraction, and

(*b*) any of that oil is transported, initially treated or initially stored (or subjected to any two or more of those operations) by means of any asset which is a qualifying asset in relation to that field, and

(*c*) when the oil is disposed of or relevantly appropriated by the participator or the person connected with him, the selling price of the oil exceeds the price paid for it on the purchase referred to in paragraph (*a*) above,

the participator shall be treated for the purposes of this Act and Part I [of the principal Act and [sections 299 to 301 of the Corporation Tax Act 2010][5]][1] as having received an amount equal to that excess as tariff receipts which arise in the chargeable period in which the selling price falls to be determined and are attributable to the use of the asset for carrying out the operation or operations referred to in paragraph (b) above.

(2) In this paragraph "selling price", in relation to any oil, means the aggregate of the amounts determined in relation to that oil in accordance with [paragraphs (*a*) to (*cb*)][3] of subsection (5) of section 2 of the principal Act; and for the purpose of the application of those paragraphs and of determining whether any oil falling within sub-paragraph (1) above is relevantly appropriated,—

(*a*) a person who is connected with the participator and who purchases oil as mentioned in sub-paragraph (1)(*a*) above shall be deemed to be a participator; and

(*b*) oil falling within sub-paragraph (1) above shall be treated, for the purposes of section 2(5) of the principal Act and the definition of "relevantly appropriated" in section 12 of that Act as if it were oil won from the field referred to in paragraph (*a*) of that sub-paragraph.

(3) A person who takes delivery of oil [before it has been transported—

(*a*) to the place at which it is first landed in the United Kingdom; or

(*b*) to the place referred to in section 3(1)(*f*)(ii) of the principal Act][2],

shall be treated for the purposes of sub-paragraph (1)(a) above as having taken delivery of the oil at the place of extraction.

(4) Sub-paragraph (1) above does not apply to oil if, at a time before the participator's selling price for that oil falls to be determined as mentioned in sub-paragraph (2) above, the oil is either—

(*a*) stored in the field referred to in paragraphs (*a*) and (*b*) of sub-paragraph (1) above; or

(*b*) used for the purpose of assisting the extraction of oil from that field.

(5) Sub-paragraph (1) above does not apply to oil if, by virtue of [2(5)(*b*) or (ca) of the principal Act (oil disposed of otherwise than in sales at arm's length),][3] the market value of the oil is taken into account in calculating the gross profit and loss (if any) accruing to a participator from an oil field in any chargeable period.

[(6) In any chargeable period ending on or after 30th June 2004, sub-paragraph (1) above does not apply to oil in a case where—

(*a*) had the operation or operations to which the oil was subjected as mentioned in paragraph (*b*) of that sub-paragraph been carried out under a contract entered into on or after 9th April 2003, and

(*b*) had an amount been received or receivable under the contract in that chargeable period by the participator,

that amount would have been a tax-exempt tariffing receipt.][4]

HMRC Manuals—Oil Taxation Manual OT15540 (purchase at place of extraction).

Amendments—[1] Words in sub-para (1) substituted by TA 1988 s 844, Sch 29 para 32.

[2] Words in sub-para (3) substituted by F(No 2)A 1992 s 74, Sch 15 para 7 with effect in accordance with s 74(5) thereof.

[3] Words in sub-paras (2), (5) substituted by FA 1998 s 152(2)(*a*) and is deemed always to have had effect in relation to light gases disposed of or appropriated at any time after 2 May 1994: see FA 1998 s 152(2).

[4] In sub-para (1), words substituted for the words "Subject to sub-paragraphs (4) and (5)", and sub-para (6) inserted, by FA 2004 s 285 (4) with effect from 22 July 2004.

[5] In sub-para (1) words substituted for words "section 500 of the Taxes Act" by CTA 2010 s 1177, Sch 1 para 184(4). CTA 2010 has effect for corporation tax purposes for accounting periods ending on or after 1 April 2010, and for income and capital gains tax purposes for the tax year 2010–11 and subsequent tax years.

SCHEDULE 3

TARIFF RECEIPTS ALLOWANCE

Section 9

The participator's share

1—(1) In this Schedule—

"the principal section" means section 9 of this Act;

"receipts from existing contracts" means qualifying tariff receipts under a contract or contracts made as mentioned in subsection (3) of the principal section;

and other expressions have the same meaning as in the principal section.

(2) In relation to a user field, any reference in the following provisions of this Schedule to the oil to which any qualifying tariff receipts which are received or receivable in a chargeable period relate is a reference to the oil won from that user field which, in that chargeable period, is extracted, transported, initially treated or initially stored (or subjected to two or more of those operations) by means of the asset to which the qualifying tariff receipts are referable.

HMRC Manuals—Oil Taxation Manual OT15600 (tariff receipts allowance).

Simon's Tax Cases—Sub-para (2), *BP Oil Development Ltd v IRC* [1992] STC 28; *Chevron UK Ltd v IRC* [1995] STC 712.

2—(1) Subject to paragraphs 3 and 6 below, where an amount of qualifying tariff receipts received or receivable by a participator in a chargeable period from a user field falls to be treated, for the purpose mentioned in subsection (1) of the principal section, as reduced in accordance with paragraph (*a*) or paragraph (*b*) of that subsection, the cash equivalent of his share of the tariff receipts allowance in respect of that user field for that period is the amount given, subject to sub-paragraph (2) below, by the formula—

$$A \times \frac{B}{C}$$

where—

"A" is the amount of those qualifying tariff receipts;

"B" is the tariff receipts allowance in respect of that user field, expressed in metric tonnes; and

"C" is the amount, in metric tonnes, of the oil to which those qualifying tariff receipts relate.

(2) If, apart from this sub-paragraph, the fraction B/C in the formula in sub-paragraph (1) above would exceed unity, it shall be treated as unity for the purposes of this Schedule.

HMRC Manuals—Oil Taxation Manual OT15675 (calculation of participator's share of TRA).

Simon's Tax Cases—Sub-para (2), *BP Oil Development Ltd v IRC* [1992] STC 28; *Chevron UK Ltd v IRC* [1995] STC 712.

3 . . .

Amendments—This para repealed by FA 2009 s 91, Sch 45 para 2(1) with effect from 21 July 2009.

Qualifying tariff receipts referable to different periods

4—(1) This paragraph applies if any qualifying tariff receipts which are received or receivable by a participator for a chargeable period from a user field are referable to the use of a qualifying asset for a period (in this paragraph and paragraph 5 below referred to as "the period of use") which is not wholly comprised in that chargeable period.

(2) If, apart from this sub-paragraph, the period of use would exceed ten years, it shall be treated for the purposes of the following provisions of this paragraph as ending immediately before the tenth anniversary of the first day of the period.

PRT

(3) In a case where this paragraph applies, the qualifying tariff receipts referred to in sub-paragraph (1) above shall be treated for the purpose mentioned in subsection (1) of the principal section as reduced in accordance with paragraph 5 below and not in accordance with paragraph (*a*) or paragraph (*b*) of that subsection.

(4) For the purpose of determining the amount of the reduction under paragraph 5 below,—

(*a*) the qualifying tariff receipts shall be regarded as wholly received in the period of use; and

(*b*) if the period of use is not wholly comprised in a chargeable period, a portion of those receipts shall be regarded as received in each chargeable period which, in whole or in part, is comprised in the period of use;

and any chargeable period which, in whole or in part, is comprised in the period of use is in the following provisions of this paragraph and paragraph 5 below referred to as a "relevant chargeable period".

(5) For the relevant chargeable period or, as the case may be, for each of them, there shall be determined the amount of oil won from the user field in question which is expected to be qualifying oil for that period; and in this paragraph and paragraph 5 below "qualifying oil", in relation to a chargeable period, means oil which in that period is extracted, transported, initially treated or initially stored by means of any asset or assets giving rise to the qualifying tariff receipts referred to in sub-paragraph (1) above.

(6) In a case falling within paragraph (*b*) of sub-paragraph (4) above, the portion of the qualifying tariff receipts which is to be regarded as received in each of the relevant chargeable periods shall bear to each of those receipts the same proportion as the amount of the qualifying oil for that period bears to the total of the qualifying oil for all the relevant chargeable periods.

(7) In any case where, apart from this sub-paragraph, it is not practicable to determine for the purpose of sub-paragraph (5) above how much of the oil won from a user field is for any period expected to be qualifying oil, such a determination shall be made on the assumption that any asset which gives rise to qualifying tariff receipts falling within that sub-paragraph will at all times be used to the full extent which, by reference to the receipts, is available for the extraction, transport, initial treatment or initial storage of oil won from the user field in question.

HMRC Manuals—Oil Taxation Manual OT15750 (qualifying tariff receipts referable to different periods).

5—(1) For the purpose of calculating the reduction referred to in paragraph 4(3) above, there shall be determined, in accordance with paragraphs 2 and 3 above and sub-paragraphs (2) and (3) below, the amount which would be the cash equivalent of the participator's share of the tariff receipts allowance in respect of the user field in question for the relevant chargeable period or, if there is more than one such period, for each of them.

(2) For a relevant chargeable period, the determination referred to in sub-paragraph (1) above shall be made on the basis—

(*a*) that "A" in the formula in paragraph 2 above is the amount of the qualifying tariff receipts determined for the period under sub-paragraph (6) of paragraph 4 above or, if that sub-paragraph does not apply, the whole of the qualifying tariff receipts referred to in sub-paragraph (1) of that paragraph; and

(*b*) that "C" in the formula in paragraph 2 above is the amount of the qualifying oil for that period.

(3) If, on the determination under sub-paragraph (1) above, the cash equivalent of the participator's share of the tariff receipts allowance in respect of the user field in question would, apart from this sub-paragraph, exceed the qualifying tariff receipts for that period (as calculated under sub-paragraph (2) above) then, for the purposes of this paragraph, the amount of that cash equivalent shall be taken to be reduced to an amount equal to those qualifying tariff receipts.

(4) The amount of the reduction referred to in paragraph 4(3) above shall be an amount equal to the cash equivalent of the participator's share of the tariff receipts allowance in respect of the user field in question for the relevant chargeable period, as determined under this paragraph, or, if there is more than one relevant chargeable period, the aggregate of the cash equivalents as so determined for each of the relevant chargeable periods.

HMRC Manuals—Oil Taxation Manual OT15750 (qualifying tariff receipts referable to different periods).

6—(1) In any case where—

(*a*) there are normal qualifying tariff receipts from a user field for a chargeable period which, for the purpose of determining the amount of a reduction under paragraph 5 above in an amount of straddling qualifying tariff receipts from that field, was a relevant chargeable period as defined in paragraph 4(4) above, and

(*b*) those normal qualifying tariff receipts relate to oil to which the straddling qualifying tariff receipts do not relate,

the amount which, apart from this paragraph, would be the cash equivalent of the participator's share of the tariff receipts allowance in respect of that user field for that chargeable period shall be varied in accordance with the following provisions of this paragraph.

(2) In the first instance, the cash equivalent of the participator's share of the tariff receipts allowance for the chargeable period in question shall be determined, in accordance with paragraphs 2 and 3 above, on the basis that—

(*a*) there is to be added to the normal qualifying tariff receipts for that period that portion of the straddling qualifying tariff receipts which, in accordance with sub-paragraph (6) of paragraph 4 above, is to be regarded as received in that period or, if that sub-paragraph does not apply, the whole of those receipts; and

(*b*) there is to be added to the oil referred to in sub-paragraph (1)(*b*) above the oil which, by reference to the straddling qualifying tariff receipts, is qualifying oil for that chargeable period for the purposes of paragraphs 4 and 5 above.

(3) The cash equivalent of the participator's share referred to in sub-paragraph (1) above shall be the amount produced by deducting from the cash equivalent of that share, as determined under sub-paragraph (2) above, the amount of the cash equivalent of his share for the period in question as determined under paragraph 5 above.

(4) For the purposes of this paragraph, qualifying tariff receipts are "normal" if they fall to be treated as reduced in accordance with paragraph (*a*) or paragraph (*b*) of subsection (1) of the principal section and "straddling" if they fall to be treated as reduced in accordance with paragraph 5 above.

HMRC Manuals—Oil Taxation Manual OT15750 (straddling tariff receipts).

SCHEDULE 4

RECEIPTS ATTRIBUTABLE TO UNITED KINGDOM USE OF FOREIGN FIELD ASSETS

Section 12

Interpretation

1 In this Schedule—

(*a*) "the principal section" means section 12 of this Act;

(*b*) "the relevant assumptions" means—

(i) those specified in subsection (5) of the principal section; and

(ii) the assumption that a participator in a foreign field is a participator within the meaning of Part I of the principal Act;

(*c*) "United Kingdom field" means an oil field within the meaning of Part I of the principal Act.

Chargeable receipts

2 A participator in a foreign field is chargeable to tax in accordance with this Schedule in respect of consideration falling within subsection (1) of the principal section if, and only if—

(*a*) the field asset which gives rise to that consideration is, in accordance with paragraph 3 below, a chargeable asset in relation to him; and

(*b*) the consideration constitutes, in accordance with paragraph 4 below, a receipt for which he is accountable;

and, where the conditions in paragraphs (a) and (b) above are fulfilled, the consideration is in this Schedule referred to as a chargeable receipt of the participator.

3—(1) Subject to sub-paragraph (2) below, a field asset is a chargeable asset in relation to a participator in a foreign field if, on the relevant assumptions, expenditure incurred by the participator in respect of the asset would be or would have been allowable for that foreign field—

(*a*) under section 3 of this Act or section 4 of the principal Act, or

(*b*) in the case of an asset the useful life of which was, at the time the expenditure was incurred, expected to exceed six months, under section 3 of the principal Act.

(2) An asset which is a field asset by virtue of subsection (6) of the principal section is a chargeable asset in relation to that participator in that foreign field in relation to whom and to which the asset referred to in paragraph (*c*) of that subsection is a chargeable asset.

4—(1) Consideration falling within subsection (1) of the principal section constitutes a receipt for which a participator in a foreign field is accountable if, and only if,—

(*a*) on the relevant assumptions, and

(*b*) on the further assumption that the field asset which gives rise to the consideration is a qualifying asset,

the consideration would constitute, for the purposes of this Act, a tariff receipt or disposal receipt of the participator attributable to the foreign field.

(2) In applying section 7 of this Act to determine whether any consideration falling within subsection (1)(*c*) of the principal section would, on the assumptions in sub-paragraph (1) above, constitute a disposal receipt the reference in section 7(4)(*b*) of this Act to tariff receipts of the participator shall

PRT

be construed as a reference to consideration falling within paragraph (*a*) or paragraph (*b*) of subsection (1) of the principal section which, on those assumptions, would constitute a tariff receipt of his.

5—(1) Schedule 2 to this Act, except paragraphs 4 and 6 to 8, applies in relation to chargeable receipts on the relevant assumptions and also on the further assumptions—

(*a*) that any reference in that Schedule to tariff receipts or disposal receipts includes a reference to chargeable receipts;

(*b*) that, except in paragraphs 5 and 11(3), any reference in that Schedule to an oil field or a participator applies only to a foreign field or, as the case may be, a participator in a foreign field; and

(*c*) that any reference in that Schedule to a qualifying asset is a reference to a field asset which, in accordance with paragraph 3 above, is a chargeable asset.

(2) In Schedule 2 to this Act, as applied by sub-paragraph (1) above, any reference to any of the provisions specified in sub-paragraph (2) of paragraph 8 below shall be construed as a reference to that provision as it has effect by virtue of that sub-paragraph.

(3) In its application by virtue of sub-paragraph (1) above, paragraph 2 of Schedule 2 to this Act shall have effect as if the reference in sub-paragraph (2) of that paragraph to section 6 or section 7 of this Act included a reference to the principal section.

(4) Notwithstanding anything in paragraph (*a*) of sub-paragraph (1) above, paragraph 9 of Schedule 2 to this Act, in its application by virtue of that sub-paragraph, shall have effect as if the reference in that paragraph to any disposal receipt were a reference to any chargeable receipt falling within paragraph (*c*) of subsection (1) of the principal section.

(5) In its application by virtue of sub-paragraph (1) above, paragraph 10 of Schedule 2 to this Act shall have effect as if,—

(*a*) notwithstanding anything in paragraph (*a*) of that sub-paragraph, the reference in that paragraph to any disposal receipt were a reference to any chargeable receipt falling within paragraph (*c*) of subsection (1) of the principal section; and

(*b*) in the application of paragraph 4 above for the purposes of paragraph 10 below, section 6(4)(*b*) of this Act were disregarded.

(6) In its application by virtue of sub-paragraph (1) above, paragraph 11 of Schedule 2 to this Act shall have effect as if sub-paragraph (4) of that paragraph were omitted.

6—(1) Subject to sub-paragraph (2) below, the chargeable receipts of a participator in a foreign field are attributable to that field for which expenditure incurred by him in respect of the field asset concerned would be or would have been allowable as mentioned in paragraph 3(1) above; and if there is more than one such foreign field, then the receipts are attributable to that one of those fields in connection with which, on the relevant assumptions, the field asset would have been first used.

(2) The foreign field to which are attributable chargeable receipts referable to an asset which is a field asset by virtue of subsection (6) of the principal section is that field to which are attributable chargeable receipts referable to the field asset referred to in paragraph (*c*) of that subsection.

The charge to tax

7—(1) In relation to a foreign field, every half year beginning on or after 1 July 1982 shall be taken to be a chargeable period.

(2) In this paragraph "half year" has the same meaning as in section 1 of the principal Act.

(3) Any reference in this Schedule to the chargeable period to which any chargeable receipts of a participator in a foreign field are attributable is,—

(*a*) in the case of chargeable receipts falling within paragraph (*c*) of subsection (1) of the principal section a reference to the chargeable period in which the disposal referred to in that paragraph occurs; and

(*b*) in any other case, a reference to the chargeable period in which the receipts are received or receivable by him.

HMRC Manuals—Oil Taxation Manual OT13525 (PRT: foreign fields).

8—(1) For each chargeable period of a foreign field beginning with that in which a participator in that field has chargeable receipts, there shall be determined, subject to the following provisions of this Schedule but otherwise in accordance with section 2 of the principal Act, what is the assessable profit or allowable loss accruing to the participator from the foreign field on the basis that—

(*a*) the positive amounts for the purposes of section 2 of the principal Act consist of any chargeable receipts of his attributable to that field for that period; and

(*b*) the negative amounts for those purposes are any amounts referred to in paragraphs (*b*), (*c*) and (*f*) of subsection (9) of that section.

(2) For the purpose of the determination referred to in sub-paragraph (1) above, the provisions of Part I of the principal Act and sections 3 and 4 of and Part II of Schedule 1 to this Act shall have effect—

(*a*) on the relevant assumptions; and

(*b*) on the further assumption that any reference in those provisions to an oil field or a participator applies only to a foreign field or, as the case may be, a participator in a foreign field.

(3) Without prejudice to sub-paragraph (2) above, in computing the assessable profit or allowable loss accruing to a participator in a foreign field, section 9 of and Schedule 3 to this Act shall apply—

(*a*) on the relevant assumptions; and

(*b*) on the further assumption that any chargeable receipts of his, other than those falling within subsection (1)(*c*) of the principal section, are tariff receipts.

(4) In any case where, apart from this sub-paragraph, the whole or any part of any consideration which constitutes a chargeable receipt of a participator in a foreign field would also fall to be treated, by virtue of paragraph 2 or paragraph 11 of Schedule 2 to this Act, as a tariff or disposal receipt of a participator in a United Kingdom field, it shall not be so treated.

(5) In any case where, apart from this sub-paragraph, the whole or any part of any consideration which constitutes a tariff or disposal receipt of a participator in a United Kingdom field would also fall to be treated, by virtue of paragraph 2 or paragraph 11 of Schedule 2 to this Act, as applied by paragraph 5(1) above, as a chargeable receipt of a participator in a foreign field, it shall not be so treated.

HMRC Manuals—Oil Taxation Manual OT13525 (PRT: foreign fields).

9—(1) Subject to sub-paragraph (2) below,—

(*a*) the principal Act, and

(*b*) the provisions of the Taxes Management Act 1970 which are applied by paragraph 1 of Schedule 2 to the principal Act,

shall have effect in relation to any assessable profit or allowable loss of a participator in a foreign field determined for a chargeable period under paragraph 8(1) above as if it were such an assessable profit or allowable loss as is referred to in section 1(2) of the principal Act.

(2) No reduction shall be made by virtue of section 8 of the principal Act (oil allowance) in the assessable profit accruing to a participator in a foreign field for any chargeable period.

HMRC Manuals—Oil Taxation Manual OT13560 (foreign fields: oil allowance).

Expenditure relief

10—(1) For the purpose of the determination referred to in sub-paragraph (1) of paragraph 8 above, no expenditure shall be allowable by virtue of paragraph (*b*) of that sub-paragraph, under section 3 of the principal Act or section 3 of this Act unless—

(*a*) the expenditure relates to a field asset which is a chargeable asset which gives rise, or is expected to give rise, to chargeable receipts; and

(*b*) the expenditure is incurred either for the purpose of enabling the asset to be used in a way which gives rise, or is expected to give rise, to chargeable receipts falling within paragraph (*a*) or paragraph (*b*) of subsection (1) of the principal section, or for the purpose of enhancing the value of the asset with a view to the subsequent disposal of it or of an interest in it.

(2) Where expenditure falling within paragraph (*a*) of sub-paragraph (1) above is incurred partly for one or both of the purposes referred to in paragraph (*b*) of that sub-paragraph and partly for other purposes, only so much of that expenditure as it is just and reasonable to apportion to a purpose referred to in that paragraph shall be regarded as falling within those paragraphs.

(3) References in the preceding provisions of this paragraph to the use of an asset in a way which gives rise, or is expected to give rise, to chargeable receipts include references to the provision, in connection with the use of that asset, of services or other business facilities of any kind which give rise, or are expected to give rise, to chargeable receipts.

(4) To the extent only that expenditure falls within paragraphs (*a*) and (*b*) of sub-paragraph (1) above, the field asset to which the expenditure relates shall be regarded for the purposes of section 3 of the principal Act and section 3 of this Act as used in connection with the foreign field.

11—(1) In the following provisions of this Schedule expenditure which falls within paragraphs (*a*) and (*b*) of sub-paragraph (1) of paragraph 10 above is referred to as "qualifying expenditure".

(2) In relation to qualifying expenditure, references in section 3 of the principal Act to tariff receipts shall be construed as references to chargeable receipts falling within paragraph (*a*) or paragraph (*b*) of subsection (1) of the principal section.

(3) If, on the relevant assumptions . . . [1] expenditure which was incurred in relation to a field asset but which is not qualifying expenditure would have qualified for supplement as mentioned in subsection (5) of section 3 of the principal Act, then, in relation to qualifying expenditure which relates to that field asset, subsection (5A) of that section shall have effect with the omission of paragraph (*a*).

(4) . . . [1]

PRT

(5) In relation to qualifying expenditure which is allowable expenditure within the meaning of Part I of Schedule 1 to this Act, in paragraph 8 of that Schedule—

(*a*) any reference to disposal receipts shall be construed as a reference to chargeable receipts falling within subsection (1)(*c*) of the principal section; and

(*b*) any reference to tariff receipts shall be construed as a reference to other descriptions of chargeable receipts.

Amendment—[1] Words repealed by F(No 2)A 1992 ss 74, 82, Sch 15 para 8, Sch 18, Part VIII, with effect in accordance with s 74(5) thereof.

Claims for expenditure relief

12 In relation to a claim for the allowance of any qualifying expenditure, and in relation to the foreign field in connection with which, by virtue of paragraph 10(4) above, the field asset concerned is to be regarded as used, the first claim period shall be the period ending on 30 June 1982 and each subsequent claim period shall be the period of six months from the end of the preceding claim period.

The responsible person

13 In relation to a foreign field, paragraph 4 of Schedule 2 to the principal Act shall have effect as if—

(*a*) for sub-paragraphs (1) to (5) there were substituted the following sub-paragraph—

"(1) For each oil field the Board may, by notice in writing given to him, appoint one of the participators in the field as the responsible person for that field, to perform in relation to the field, any functions conferred on the responsible person as such by this Part of this Act; and the participator who for the time being holds that appointment is in this Part of this Act referred to as 'the responsible person'";

(*b*) in sub-paragraphs (6) and (7) for any reference to a body corporate or partnership there were substituted a reference to a participator; and

(*c*) sub-paragraph (8) (which varies the definition of "participator" in relation to a United Kingdom field) were omitted.

Management and collection

14—(1) In its application to tax chargeable only by virtue of the provisions of the principal section and this Schedule, Schedule 2 to the principal Act (in this paragraph referred to as "Schedule 2") shall have effect as if—

(*a*) any reference in that Schedule to an oil field or a participator were a reference only to a foreign field or, as the case may be, a participator in a foreign field, and

(*b*) any reference in that Schedule to a chargeable period (within the meaning of Part I of the principal Act) were a reference only to a chargeable period within the meaning of this Schedule to which there are attributable any chargeable receipts of a participator in a foreign field,

and subject to the modifications made in the following provisions of this paragraph.

(2) Notwithstanding anything in sub-paragraph (2) of paragraph 1 of Schedule 2, sub-paragraph (1) above shall have effect in relation to those provisions of the Taxes Management Act 1970 which are applied by that paragraph as it has effect in relation to Schedule 2 itself.

(3) Paragraph 2 of Schedule 2 shall have effect as if for sub-paragraphs (2) and (3) there were substituted the following sub-paragraph—

"(2) A return under this paragraph for a chargeable period shall contain the following particulars—

(*a*) a statement of the amount or value and the source of any receipts which are, within the meaning of Schedule 4 to the Oil Taxation Act 1983, chargeable receipts of the participator attributable to the chargeable period to which the return relates; and

(*b*) a statement of the assets giving rise to any such receipts; and

(*c*) such other particulars as the Board may prescribe with respect to any such receipts";

and accordingly subsections (1) to (3) of section 10 of this Act shall not apply in relation to a return made under that paragraph by virtue of this Schedule.

(4) Paragraph 5 of Schedule 2 shall have effect as if for sub-paragraphs (2) and (2A) there were substituted the following sub-paragraph—

"(2) A return under this paragraph shall contain such particulars of or relating to the oil field as the Board may require for the purpose of determining the amount by which any chargeable receipts, within the meaning of Schedule 4 to the Oil Taxation Act 1983 are to be treated as reduced by virtue of section 9 of that Act, as applied by paragraph 8(3) of that Schedule."

(5) Paragraph 7(1) of Schedule 2 shall have effect with the omission of the words "or to oil won therefrom", in both places where they occur.

(6) Paragraph 14 of Schedule 2 shall have effect as if for sub-paragraphs (i) and (ii) of paragraph (*b*) of sub-paragraph (3) there were substituted the following sub-paragraphs—

"(i) the aggregate of the receipts as stated in the participator's return in pursuance of sub-paragraph (2)(*a*) of that paragraph; and

(ii) the aggregate of the corresponding receipts as included in the assessment";

and with the omission of sub-paragraphs (4) to (7).

Payment on account

15 In its application to tax chargeable only as mentioned in paragraph 14(1) above, paragraph 2 of the Schedule to the Petroleum Revenue Tax Act 1980 shall have effect as if, in place of the sub-paragraph (2A) set out in section 10(6) of this Act, there were substituted the following sub-paragraph—

"(2A) The amount of any chargeable receipts, within the meaning of Schedule 4 to the Oil Taxation Act 1983, shall be taken from the particulars included in the return referred to in sub-paragraph (2) above, and any amount by which any of those receipts are to be treated as reduced under section 9 of that Act, as applied by paragraph 8(3) of that Schedule, shall be determined accordingly."

Income and corporation taxes

16—(1) Section 11 of this Act shall have effect as if—

(*a*) any reference therein to an oil field included a reference to a foreign field; and

(*b*) any reference therein to a participator were to be construed, in relation to a foreign field, in accordance with subsection (2)(*b*) of the principal section; and

(*c*) any reference therein to a tariff receipt included a reference to a chargeable receipt consisting of consideration received or receivable as mentioned in paragraph (*a*) or paragraph (*b*) of subsection (1) of the principal section.

(2) Paragraphs (*a*) and (*b*) of sub-paragraph (1) above apply in relation to paragraph 11(3) of Schedule 2 to this Act in so far as that paragraph has effect for the purposes of section 11 of this Act by virtue of subsection (4) thereof.

SCHEDULE 5

TRANSITIONAL PROVISIONS

Section 13

Amendments—This Schedule repealed by FA 2009 s 91, Sch 45 para 2(1), (4) with effect from 21 July 2009.

FINANCE ACT 1984

(1984 Chapter 43)

An Act to grant certain duties, to alter other duties, and to amend the law relating to the National Debt and the Public Revenue, and to make further provision in connection with Finance.

[26th July 1984]

PART V
OIL TAXATION

113 Restriction on PRT reliefs

(1) Subject to subsection (3) below, in determining whether any . . .[1] expenditure is allowable in the case of a participator in an oil field under section 5 or section 5A [or section 5B][1] of the principal Act, no account shall be taken of any expenditure incurred before his qualifying date.

(2) Subject to subsection (3) below, in determining whether any unrelievable field losses are allowable in the case of a participator in an oil field under section 6 of that Act, no account shall be taken of any allowable loss [falling within subsection (1B)][3] of that section unless the date on which the winning of oil [from the abandoned field][3] permanently ceased fell on or after his qualifying date.

(3) Subsections (1) and (2) above do not apply in the case of a participator in an oil field if his qualifying date falls before 14 September 1983 or before the end of the first chargeable period in relation to the field.

(4) In this section "qualifying date", in relation to a participator in an oil field, means [(subject to subsection (6) below)][2] whichever of the following dates is applicable in his case or (if there is more than one) the earliest of them—

(*a*) the date on which the participator first qualified in respect of any licensed area, being an area which is wholly or partly included in the field;

(*b*) if the participator is a company, the date on which another company first satisfied both of the following conditions, that is to say—

(i) it qualified in respect of any licensed area, being an area which is wholly or partly included in the field; and

(ii) it was connected with the participator; and

(*c*) if he is a participator in the field by reason of an arrangement between him and another company, being an arrangement to which paragraph 5 of Schedule 3 to the principal Act applies (transfer of rights etc to associated company), the date on which the arrangement was made or, if later, the date on which that other company first qualified in respect of any licensed area, being an area which is wholly or partly included in the field.

(5) For the purposes of subsection (4) above, a person qualifies in respect of a licensed area when, in respect of that area—

(*a*) he is, or is one of those, entitled to the benefit of a licence, or

(*b*) he enjoys rights under an agreement, being an agreement which has been approved by the Board and certified by the [OGA][5] to confer on him rights which are the same as, or similar to, those conferred by a licence.

(6) Where (apart from this section) expenditure would be allowable under section 5 or section 5A [or section 5B][1] of the principal Act in the case of a participator in an oil field (in this subsection referred to as "the new participator") by virtue only of [paragraphs 16 to 16B][1] of Schedule 17 to the Finance Act 1980 (transfers of interests in oil fields) then, for the purpose of determining whether the expenditure is allowable in his case in accordance with this section, the date which was the qualifying date in relation to the old participator (within the meaning of that Schedule)[, rather than the date given by subsection (4) above, shall be taken to be the qualifying date in relation to the new participator.][2]

(7) For the purposes of subsection (2) above the date on which the winning of oil from an oil field has permanently ceased is the date stated in a decision (whether of the Board or on appeal from the Board) under Schedule 8 to the principal Act to be that date.

(8) For the purposes of this section, one company is connected with another if—

(*a*) one is a 51 per cent subsidiary of the other and the other is not a 51 per cent subsidiary of any company; or

(*b*) each of them is a 51 per cent subsidiary of a third company which is not itself a 51 per cent subsidiary of any company;

and [Chapter 3 of Part 24 of the Corporation Tax Act 2010][4] (subsidiaries) applies for the purposes of this subsection.

(9) In this section—

(*a*) "company" means any body corporate; and

(*b*) any reference to the winning of oil from an oil field permanently ceasing includes a reference to the permanent cessation of operations for the winning of oil from the field.

(10) This section shall have effect in relation to any expenditure or losses in respect of which a claim is made after 13 September 1983.

Amendments—[1] Words repealed in sub-s (1), and words in sub-ss (1), (6) inserted and substituted, by FA 1987 ss 64, 72, Sch 13 para 9, Sch 16 Pt X.

[2] Words in sub-s (4) inserted, and words in sub-s (6) substituted, by FA 1997 s 107(2), (4), in relation to any expenditure in respect of which a claim is made after 22 July 1996.

[3] Words in sub-s (2) substituted by FA 2001 s 101(3), (5) with effect from 7 March 2001.

[4] In sub-s (8) words substituted for words "section 838 of the Taxes Act 1988" by CTA 2010 s 1177, Sch 1 para 186. CTA 2010 has effect for corporation tax purposes for accounting periods ending on or after 1 April 2010, and for income and capital gains tax purposes for the tax year 2010–11 and subsequent tax years.

[5] In sub-s (5)(*b*), word substituted for words "Secretary of State" by the Petroleum (Transfer of Functions) Regulations, SI 2016/898 reg 8 with effect from 1 October 2016.

114 Sales of gas: treatment of certain payments

(1) This section applies only in relation to oil consisting of gas and references in the following provisions of this section to oil shall be construed accordingly.

(2) In any case where, under a contract for the sale of oil won from an oil field, the consideration includes any sum—

(*a*) which is payable by the buyer in respect of a quantity of oil to be delivered at a specified time or in a specified period, and

(*b*) which is payable whether or not the buyer takes delivery of the whole of the oil at that time or in that period, and

(*c*) which, in the event that the buyer does not take delivery of the whole of the oil, entitles the buyer to delivery of oil free of charge at a later time or in a later period,

then, to the extent that the sum is payable in respect of oil which is not delivered at the time or in the period in question, the sum shall be treated for the purposes of the principal Act as an advance payment for the oil to be delivered free of charge and, accordingly, that oil shall be treated for those purposes as sold for a price which (subject to any additional element arising under the following provisions of this section) is equal to that advance payment.

(3) Where, in a case falling within subsection (2) above, an amount of oil is delivered free of charge in pursuance of the entitlement referred to in paragraph (*c*) of that subsection, the proportion of the advance payment referred to in that subsection which is to be attributed to that amount of oil shall be that which that amount of oil bears to the total quantity of oil of which the buyer is entitled to delivery free of charge by virtue of the payment of the sum in question.

(4) In any case where—

(*a*) by virtue of subsection (2) above a sum falls to any extent to be treated as an advance payment for oil to be delivered free of charge, but

(*b*) at the latest date at which oil could be delivered free of charge in pursuance of the entitlement referred to in paragraph (*c*) of that subsection, the whole or any part of the oil to which that entitlement relates has not been so delivered,

then at that latest date, one tonne of oil shall be deemed to be delivered as mentioned in paragraph (b) above and so much of the advance payment as has not, under subsection (3) above, been attributed to oil actually delivered shall be attributed to that one tonne.

(5) Where, under a contract for the sale of oil won from an oil field, the consideration includes any sums (in this section referred to as "capacity payments")—

(*a*) which are payable by the buyer at specified times or in respect of specified periods, and

(*b*) which, though they may vary in amount by reference to deliveries of oil or other factors, are payable whether or not oil is delivered under the contract at particular times or in particular periods, and

(*c*) which do not, under the terms of the contract or by virtue of subsection (2) above, fall to be treated, in whole or in part, as advance payments for oil to be delivered at some time after the times or periods at or in respect of which the sums are payable,

then, in so far as they would not do so apart from this subsection, the capacity payments shall be treated for the purposes of the principal Act as an additional element of the price received or receivable for the oil sold under the contract.

(6) For the purpose of determining, in a case where there are capacity payments under a contract for the sale of oil won from an oil field, the assessable profit or allowable loss accruing in a particular chargeable period to the participator by whom oil is sold under the contract, each capacity payment shall be treated as an additional element of the price received or receivable for the oil delivered by him under the contract in the chargeable period in which the capacity payment is paid or payable; and if no oil is in fact so delivered in a chargeable period in which a capacity payment is paid or payable, one tonne of oil shall be deemed to be so delivered in that period and, accordingly, the capacity payment shall be treated for the purposes of the principal Act as the price for which that tonne is sold.

(7) If, by virtue of subsection (4) or subsection (6) above, one tonne of oil is deemed to be delivered in any chargeable period of the oil field referred to in subsection (2) or, as the case may be, subsection (5) above, a return for that period by the participator concerned under paragraph 2 of Schedule 2 to the principal Act shall give the like information in relation to that tonne as in relation to any other oil falling within sub-paragraph (2)(*a*) of that paragraph.

115 Information relating to sales at arm's length and market value of oil

(1) The Board may, by notice in writing given to a company which is or has been a participator in an oil field, require that company to give to the Board, within such time (not being less than thirty days) as may be specified in the notice, such particulars (which may include details of relevant documents) as may be so specified of any related transaction which appears to the Board to be relevant for the purpose of—

(*a*) determining whether a disposal of any oil is a sale at arm's length, or

(*b*) ascertaining the market value of any oil.

(2) For the purposes of a notice under subsection (1) above a transaction is a related transaction if, but only if, it is one to which the company to whom the notice is given or a company associated with that company was a party; and for the purposes of this subsection two companies are associated with one another if—

(*a*) one is under the control of the other; or

(*b*) both are under the control of the same person or persons;

and in this subsection "control" has the meaning given by [section 1124 of the Corporation Tax Act 2010][2].

(3) In any case where a company (in this subsection and subsection (4) below referred to as "the participator company") is or has been a participator in an oil field and—

(*a*) the participator company is a 51 per cent. subsidiary of another company, or

(*b*) another company is a 51 per cent. subsidiary of the participator company, or

(*c*) the participator company and another company are both 51 per cent. subsidiaries of a third company,

the Board may, by notice in writing given to any company referred to in paragraphs (a) to (c) above which is resident in the United Kingdom, require it to make available for inspection any relevant books, accounts or other documents or records whatsoever of the company itself or, subject to

PRT

subsection (5) below, of any other company which is its 51 per cent. subsidiary.

(4) In subsection (3) above "relevant" means relating to any transaction which is relevant for the purpose of—

(*a*) determining whether a disposal of any oil by the participator company is a sale at arm's length; or

(*b*) ascertaining the market value of oil won by the participator company.

(5) In any case where—

(*a*) under subsection (3) above a company is by notice required to make available for inspection any books, accounts, documents or records of one of its 51 per cent. subsidiaries which is resident outside the United Kingdom, and

(*b*) it appears to the Board, on the application of the company, that the circumstances are such that the requirement ought not to have effect,

the Board shall direct that the company need not comply with the requirement.

(6) If, on an application under subsection (5) above, the Board refuse to give a direction under that subsection, the company concerned [may appeal, by notice][1] in writing given to the Board within thirty days after the refusal, [and, where such an appeal is notified to the tribunal, the tribunal][1], if satisfied that the requirement in question ought in the circumstances not to have effect, may determine accordingly.

[(6A) The provisions of paragraphs 14A to 14I of Schedule 2 to the principal Act shall apply to appeals under this paragraph subject to any necessary modifications.][1]

(7) In this section—

"company" means any body corporate; and

"51 per cent. subsidiary" shall be construed in accordance with [Chapter 3 of Part 24 of the Corporation Tax Act 2010][2] (subsidiaries).

HMRC Manuals—Oil Taxation Manual 04790 (information powers).

Amendments—[1] In sub-s (6), words substituted for words "may, by notice" and "appeal to the Special Commissioners who" respectively, and sub-s (6A) inserted, by the Transfer of Tribunal Functions and Revenue and Customs Appeals Order, SI 2009/56 art 3, Sch 1 paras 103, 104 with effect from 1 April 2009.

[2] In sub-s (2) words substituted for words "section 840 of the Taxes Act 1988", in sub-s (7) words substituted for words "section 838 of the Taxes Act 1988" by CTA 2010 s 1177, Sch 1 para 187. CTA 2010 has effect for corporation tax purposes for accounting periods ending on or after 1 April 2010, and for income and capital gains tax purposes for the tax year 2010–11 and subsequent tax years.

116 Offences relating to section 115

(1) Where a company has been required by notice under subsection (1) or subsection (3) of section 115 above to give any particulars or, as the case may be, to make available for inspection any books, accounts, documents or records and fails to comply with the notice, the company shall be liable, subject to subsection (3) below—

(*a*) to a penalty not exceeding £500; and

(*b*) if the failure continues after it has been declared by the court or the [tribunal][1] before whom proceedings for the penalty have been commenced, to a further penalty not exceeding £100 for each day on which the failure so continues.

(2) Where a company fraudulently or negligently furnishes, gives, produces or makes any incorrect information, document or record of a kind mentioned in subsection (1) or subsection (3) of section 115 above, the company shall be liable to a penalty not exceeding £2,500 or, in the case of fraud on its part, £5,000.

(3) A company shall not be liable to any penalty incurred under subsection (1) above for failure to comply with a notice if the failure is remedied before proceedings for the recovery of the penalty are commenced.

(4) In this section "company" has the same meaning as in section 115 above.

Amendments—[1] In sub-s (1)(*b*), word substituted for word "Commissioners" by the Transfer of Tribunal Functions and Revenue and Customs Appeals Order, SI 2009/56 art 3, Sch 1 paras 103, 105 with effect from 1 April 2009.

PART VI

MISCELLANEOUS AND SUPPLEMENTARY

Miscellaneous

124 Recovery of certain tax assessed on non-residents

. . .

Amendments—This section repealed by TIOPA 2010 s 378, Sch 10 Pt 12. TIOPA 2010 has effect for corporation tax purposes for accounting periods ending on or after 1 April 2010, for income and capital gains tax purposes for the tax year 2010–11 and subsequent tax years, and for petroleum revenue tax purposes for chargeable periods beginning on or after 1 July 2010.

128 Short title, interpretation, construction and repeals

(1) This Act may be cited as the Finance Act 1984.

(2)–(4) [not reproduced].

(5) Part V of this Act shall be construed as one with Part I of the Oil Taxation Act 1975 and references in Part V of this Act to the principal Act are references to that Act.

(6) The enactments specified in Schedule 23 to this Act are hereby repealed to the extent specified in the third column of that Schedule, but subject to any provision at the end of any Part of that Schedule.

FINANCE ACT 1985

(1985 Chapter 54)

PART IV

OIL TAXATION

90 Limitations on relief for exploration and appraisal expenditure

(1) With respect to expenditure incurred on or after 19 March 1985, section 5A of the Oil Taxation Act 1975 (allowance of exploration and appraisal expenditure) shall be amended in accordance with subsections (3) to (5) below.

(2) With respect to expenditure incurred on or after 1 April 1986, in subsection (2) of the said section 5A (the purposes for which expenditure is to be incurred to qualify for relief), for the words "the United Kingdom, the territorial sea thereof", in each place where they occur, there shall be substituted "the territorial sea of the United Kingdom".

(3)–(5) (*amend* OTA 1975 s 5A).

91 Chargeable periods relevant to limit on tax payable and expenditure supplement

(1) (*amends* OTA 1975 s 9(1A));

(2) The amendment made by subsection (1) above has effect with respect to any oil field in respect of which the first chargeable period ends after 30 June 1985.

(3) (*amends* FA 1981 s 111(1)).

(4) The amendment made by subsection (3) above has effect with respect to chargeable periods ending after 30 June 1985.

92 Qualifying assets: exclusion of land and certain buildings

(1)–(4) (*amend* OTA 1983 ss 8, 15, Sch 2 para 4(2A)).

(5) This section has effect for determining whether any consideration which is received or receivable after 19 March 1985 constitutes tariff receipts or disposal receipts within the meaning of the Oil Taxation Act 1983.

PART V

MISCELLANEOUS AND SUPPLEMENTARY

98 Short title, interpretation, construction and repeals

(1) This Act may be cited as the Finance Act 1985.

(2)–(4) [not reproduced].

(5) Part IV of this Act shall be construed as one with Part I of the Oil Taxation Act 1975.

FINANCE ACT 1986

(1986 Chapter 41)

PART VI

OIL TAXATION

108 The on-shore/off-shore boundary

(1) For the purposes of the enactments relating to oil taxation, land lying between the landward boundary of the territorial sea and the shoreline of the United Kingdom (as defined below) shall be treated as part of the bed of the territorial sea of the United Kingdom and any reference in those enactments to the territorial sea or the subsoil beneath it shall be construed accordingly.

(2) Any reference to the United Kingdom in the enactments relating to oil taxation, where that reference is a reference to a geographical area, shall be treated as a reference to the United Kingdom exclusive of the land referred to in subsection (1) above and of any waters for the time being covering that land.

(3) In this section—

(*a*) "the landward boundary of the territorial sea" means the line for the time being ordered by Her Majesty in Council to be the baseline from which the breadth of the territorial sea is measured; and

(*b*) "the shoreline of the United Kingdom" means, subject to subsection (4) below, the high-water line along the coast, including the coast of all islands comprised in the United Kingdom.

(4) In the case of waters adjacent to a bay, as defined in the Territorial Waters Order in Council 1964, the shoreline means—

PRT

(*a*) if the bay has only one mouth and the distance between the high-water lines of the natural entrance points of the bay does not exceed 5,000 metres, a straight line joining those high-water lines;

(*b*) if, because of the presence of islands, the bay has more than one mouth and the distances between the high-water lines of the natural entrance points of each mouth added together do not exceed 5,000 metres, a series of straight lines across each of the mouths drawn so as to join those high-water lines; and

(*c*) if neither paragraph (*a*) nor paragraph (*b*) above applies, a straight line 5,000 metres in length drawn from high-water line to high-water line within the bay in such a manner as to enclose the maximum area of water that is possible with a line of that length.

(5) If, by virtue of this section, it becomes necessary at any time to establish the high-water line at any place, it shall be taken to be the line which, on the current Admiralty chart showing that place, is depicted as "the coastline"; and for this purpose,—

(*a*) an Admiralty chart means a chart published under the superintendence of the Hydrographer of the Navy;

(*b*) if there are two or more Admiralty charts of different scales showing the place in question and depicting the coastline, account shall be taken only of the largest scale chart; and

(*c*) subject to paragraph (*b*) above, the current Admiralty chart at any time is that most recently published before that time.

(6) In this section "the enactments relating to oil taxation" means Part I of the Oil Taxation Act 1975 and any enactment which is to be construed as one with that Part.

(7) This section shall be deemed to have come into force on 1 April 1986.

109 Alternative valuation of light gases

(1) Where an election is made under this section [before 1 January 1994][1] and accepted by the Board, the market value for the purposes of the Oil Taxation Acts of any light gases to which the election applies shall be determined, not in accordance with paragraphs 2, 2A and 3 of Schedule 3 to the principal Act (value under a notional contract), but by reference to a price formula specified in the election; and, in relation to any such light gases, any reference to market value in any other provision of the Oil Taxation Acts shall be construed accordingly.

(2) No election may be made under this section in respect of light gases which are "ethane" as defined in subsection (6)(*a*) of section 134 of the Finance Act 1982 (alternative valuation of ethane used for petrochemical purposes) if the principal purpose for which the gases are being or are to be used is that specified in subsection (2)(*b*) of the said section 134 (use for petrochemical purposes).

(3) Subject to subsection (4) below, an election under this section applies only to light gases—

(*a*) which, during the period covered by the election, are either disposed of otherwise than in sales at arm's length or relevantly appropriated; and

(*b*) which are not subject to fractionation between the time at which they are so disposed of or appropriated and the time at which they are applied or used for the purposes specified in the election.

(4) In any case where,—

(*a*) at a time during the period covered by an election, a market value falls to be determined for light gases to which subsection (4)(*b*) or (5)(*d*) of section 2 of the principal Act applies (oil stocks at the end of chargeable periods), and

(*b*) after the expiry of the chargeable period in question, the light gases are disposed of or appropriated as mentioned in subsection (3) above,

the market value of those light gases at the time referred to in paragraph (a) above shall be determined as if they were gases to which the election applies.

(5) Schedule 18 to the Finance Act 1982 (which applies to elections under section 134 of that Act relating to ethane used or to be used for petrochemical purposes) shall have effect for supplementing this section but subject to the modifications in Schedule 21 to this Act (in which "the 1982 Schedule" means the said Schedule 18).

(6) This section shall be construed as one with Part I of the principal Act and in this section—

(*a*) "light gases" means oil consisting of gas of which the largest component by volume over any chargeable period is methane or ethane or a combination of those gases and which—

(i) results from the fractionation of gas before it is disposed of or appropriated as mentioned in subsection (3)(*a*) above, or

(ii) before being so disposed of or appropriated, is not subjected to initial treatment or is subjected to initial treatment which does not include fractionation;

(*b*) "the principal Act" means the Oil Taxation Act 1975; and

(*c*) "the Oil Taxation Acts" means Part I of the principal Act and any enactment which is to be construed as one with that Part.

(7) In this section "fractionation" means the treatment of gas in order to separate gas of one or more kinds as mentioned in paragraph 2A(3) of Schedule 3 to the principal Act; and for the purposes of subsection (6)(*a*) above,—

(*a*) the proportion of methane, ethane or a combination of the two in any gas shall be determined at a temperature of 15 degrees C and at a pressure of one atmosphere; and

(*b*) any component other than methane, ethane or liquified petroleum gas shall be disregarded.

Amendments—[1] Inserted by FA 1994 s 236(3) with effect from 31 December 1993.

110 Attribution of certain receipts and expenditure between oil fields

(1) Section 8 of the Oil Taxation Act 1983 (qualifying assets) shall have effect, and be deemed always to have had effect, subject to the amendments in subsections (2) and (3) below.

(2)–(4) (*amend* OTA 1983 s 8, Sch 1).

SCHEDULES

SCHEDULE 21

MODIFICATIONS OF FINANCE ACT 1982, SCHEDULE 18 IN RELATION TO ELECTIONS UNDER SECTION 109 OF THIS ACT

General modifications

1—(1) For any reference in the 1982 Schedule to ethane there shall be substituted a reference to light gases, as defined in section 109 of this Act.

(2) Except as provided below, any reference in the 1982 Schedule to section 134 of the Finance Act 1982 shall be construed as a reference to section 109 of this Act.

Specific modifications

2—(1) In paragraph 1 (provisions as to the election), in sub-paragraph (2)(*b*) for the words "and not exceeding fifteen years" there shall be substituted "or in the case of an election made before 31 December 1986 beginning on 1 July 1986" and for sub-paragraph (2)(*d*) there shall be substituted—

"(*d*) specify the purposes for which the light gases to which the election applies will be applied or used,".

(2) At the end of that paragraph there shall be inserted the following sub-paragraph—

"(4) If an election relates to light gases, then, in addition to the matters referred to in sub-paragraph (2) above, the election shall contain—

(*a*) a description of the characteristics of the supply by which the disposal or appropriation is intended to be effected; and

(*b*) if that supply is of such a description that, if it were under a contract at arm's length, it is reasonable to expect that the price of the gas would vary with the level of the supply, a description of the pattern of supply which the party or parties to the election consider most probable."

3—(1) In paragraph 2 (conditions for acceptance of an election) in sub-paragraph (1) after the words "and (3)" there shall be inserted "and paragraph 2A".

(2) In sub-paragraph (2) of that paragraph, after the words "such that" there shall be inserted "subject to paragraphs 2A and 3A below".

4 After paragraph 2 there shall be inserted the following paragraph—

"2A—

(1) The provisions of this paragraph apply if, having regard to the pattern of supply described in an election as mentioned in paragraph 1(4)(*b*) above, it is reasonable to assume that, under a contract for the sale at arm's length of the light gases to which the election applies, the consideration would include—

(*a*) any such payments as are referred to in subsection (2) of section 114 of the Finance Act 1984 ("take or pay" payments), or

(*b*) any capacity payments, as defined in subsection (5) of that section.

(2) The relevant contract—

(*a*) shall be assumed to be for the delivery of gas according to the pattern of supply described in the election; and

(*b*) shall be assumed to contain provision for such of the payments referred to in sub-paragraph (1) above as are appropriate to that pattern of supply.

(3) Sub-paragraph (1) of paragraph 2 above shall have effect as if for the words following "sale at arm's length" there were substituted "of the light gases to which the election applies, the total sums payable under the contract in respect of deliveries of gas in any chargeable period would not

PRT

differ materially from the sums determined in accordance with the price formula specified in the election for gases disposed of or appropriated in that period; and if the Board are not so satisfied they shall reject the election".

(4) The price formula specified in the election shall contain provisions for determining sums corresponding to such of the payments referred to in sub-paragraph (1) above as, by virtue of sub-paragraph (2) above, are assumed to be provided for by the relevant contract."

5—(1) In paragraph 3 (definition of "the relevant contract") [in sub-paragraph (1)][1] in paragraph (*a*) after the word "and", in the first place where it occurs, there shall be inserted the words "which, subject to sub-paragraph (3) below" and in the words following paragraph (*b*) for the words from "is not" onwards, there shall be substituted "which, subject to paragraph 2A(2) above, is not necessarily a contract for the sale of light gases for the purposes specified in the election".

(2) At the end of that paragraph there shall be added the following sub-paragraphs—

"(3) In the case of an election which relates to light gases which are "excluded oil", as defined in section 10(1) of the principal Act, sub-paragraph (1)(*a*) above shall have effect with the omission of the words from "and which" to "date of the election".

(4) Sub-paragraph (4) of paragraph 2A of Schedule 3 to the principal Act (assumptions as to consents in determining price under an arm's length contract) shall apply for the purposes of paragraphs 2 and 2A above as it applies for the purposes of paragraph 2 of that Schedule, substituting a reference to a relevant contract (as defined above) for any reference to the contract mentioned in paragraph 2(2) of that Schedule."

Amendments—[1] Words inserted by F(No 2)A 1992 s 74, Sch 15 para 9, in relation, as regards expenditure, to claim periods ending after 27 November 1991, and in relation to any other matter, to chargeable periods ending after 30 June 1992.

6 After paragraph 3 there shall be inserted the following paragraph—

"3A Market value where paragraph 2A applies

(1) Where an election is accepted by the Board and the price formula contains provision for the determination of sums as mentioned in paragraph 2A(4) above, then, for the purpose of determining the market value of gas to which the election applies, section 114 of the Finance Act 1984 (which deals with the treatment of such payments as are referred to in paragraph 2A(1) above) shall have effect in relation to those sums and that gas as if—

(*a*) those sums were part of the consideration under a contract for the sale of gas to which the election applies, and

(*b*) that contract provided for delivery of the gas according to the pattern of supply described in the election,

and where the said section 114 has effect by virtue of this sub-paragraph, subsections (4), (6) and (7) of that section (which provide for and relate to the deemed delivery of one tonne of oil in certain periods) shall be treated for the purposes of the principal Act as providing for and relating to the deemed disposal or appropriation of one tonne of gas to which the election applies.

(2) Where sub-paragraph (1) above applies, the market value of the gas to which the election applies which is disposed of or appropriated in any chargeable period shall consist of—

(*a*) such amount (if any) as is determined in accordance with the price formula by reference to the quantity of gas disposed of or appropriated in that chargeable period; and

(*b*) any sums which, by virtue of sub-paragraph (1) above, either are treated as payments for gas supplied free of charge in that period or are treated as an additional element of the price received or receivable for gas disposed of or appropriated in that period.

(3) Where the market value of gas is determined as mentioned in sub-paragraph (2) above, any reference in the following provisions of this Schedule (however expressed) to the market value determined in accordance with the price formula is a reference to that value determined as mentioned in that sub-paragraph (that is to say, in accordance with the formula and section 114 of the Finance Act 1984 as applied by sub-paragraph (1) above).

(4) Where the market value of light gases to which an election applies is determined for a chargeable period as mentioned in sub-paragraph (2) above then, as respects a return for that period under paragraph 2 of Schedule 2 to the principal Act which is made by the participator who is the party or one of the parties to the election,—

(*a*) sub-paragraphs (2)(*a*)(iii) and (2)(*b*)(ii) of that paragraph (which require information with respect to each delivery or relevant appropriation of oil in the period) shall not apply in relation to the light gases to which the election applies; and (*b*) there shall be included in his return a statement of the market value (determined as mentioned in sub-paragraph (2) above) of the light gases relevantly appropriated or disposed of by him in that period.

(5) Notwithstanding that, under sub-paragraph (2) above, a market value is determined for all the gas disposed of or appropriated in a particular chargeable period, for the purposes of determining—

(*a*) the market value referred to in section 2(5)(*d*) of the principal Act (stocks at the end of a period), and

(*b*) the market value referred to in subsection (1) or, as the case may be, subsection (2) of section 14 of that Act (valuation for corporation tax purposes of oil disposed of or appropriated),

then, except in a case where the only gas disposed of or appropriated in a particular chargeable period is a single tonne which, by virtue of sub-paragraph (1) above, is treated as being disposed of or appropriated, the market value determined as mentioned in sub-paragraph (2) above shall be apportioned rateably to each quantity of gas disposed of or appropriated in that period."

7 After paragraph 6 there shall be inserted the following paragraph—

"6A Price formula no longer appropriate for pattern of supply, etc

(1) In any case where it appears to the Board—

(*a*) that light gases to which an election applies are being disposed of or appropriated in a manner, to an extent or by a pattern of supply which is different from that which was taken into consideration in the acceptance of the election, and

(*b*) that if, at the time the Board were considering whether the election should be accepted, they had taken into account as a probability the manner, extent or pattern of supply by which the gases are in fact being disposed of, they would have rejected the election,

then, subject to sub-paragraph (4) below, the election shall not have effect with respect to any chargeable period beginning after the date on which the Board give notice under this paragraph to each of the parties to the election.

(2) Without prejudice to the generality of sub-paragraph (1) above, if at any time in a chargeable period the extent to which gases to which an election applies are disposed of or relevantly appropriated (including the case where none is so disposed of or appropriated) is such that, if the gas were being delivered under a contract at arm's length,—

(*a*) the seller would be likely to incur financial penalties by reason of a failure to meet requirements arising from the pattern of supply described in the election, and

(*b*) those penalties would not be insubstantial,

that shall be a ground for the Board to give notice under this paragraph.

(3) A notice under this paragraph shall state that, by reason of the matters referred to in sub-paragraph (1) above, the Board are no longer satisfied that the price formula specified in the election is appropriate to the disposals or appropriations actually being made of gases to which the election applies.

(4) If, within the period of three months beginning on the date of a notice under this paragraph, the party or parties to the election give notice in writing to the Board—

(*a*) specifying a new price formula taking account of the manner, extent or pattern of supply by which the gases to which the election applies are being disposed of or appropriated, and

(*b*) containing, if appropriate, a description of the changed pattern of supply which, at the time of the notice, the party or parties to the election consider most probable,

then, if that new price formula is accepted by the Board in accordance with paragraph 7 below, so much of sub-paragraph (1) above as provides that the election shall not have effect with respect to certain periods shall not apply.

(5) If notice has been given under sub-paragraph (4) above and a new price formula has been accepted as mentioned in that sub-paragraph, then, for the purpose of determining, for any chargeable period beginning after the date on which the Board gave notice as mentioned in sub-paragraph (1) above, the market value of light gases to which the election applies, section 109 of the Finance Act 1986 shall have effect as if the new price formula were the formula specified in the election."

8—(1) In paragraph 7 (acceptance or rejection of new price formula) in sub-paragraph (2) after the words "paragraph 3" there shall be inserted "and, where appropriate, paragraphs 2A and 3A"; and at the end of paragraph (*b*) of that sub-paragraph there shall be inserted

PRT

"or

(*c*) a new price formula specified in a notice under paragraph 6A(4) above";

and for the words from "were specified" onwards there shall be substituted "had been specified in, and at the time of, the election and as if the circumstances giving rise to the new price formula had been in contemplation at that time".

(2) In sub-paragraph (5) of that paragraph, after "6(5)(*b*)" there shall be inserted "or paragraph 6A(4)".

9—(1) In paragraph 8 (appeals) in sub-paragraph (1) after paragraph (*d*) there shall be inserted the following paragraph—

"(*dd*) under paragraph 6A above, that a price formula is no longer appropriate".

(2) In sub-paragraph (4)(*b*) of that paragraph after "6(1)(*b*)" there shall be inserted "or paragraph 6A".

10 In paragraph 9 (returns)—

(*a*) after "6(1)(*b*)" there shall be inserted "or paragraph 6A"; and

(*b*) for the words "section 134(3) of this Act" there shall be substituted "section 109(4) of the Finance Act 1986"; and

(*c*) in paragraph (*b*) after "6" there shall be inserted "or paragraph 6A".

11—(1) In paragraph 11 (interpretation) sub-paragraph (1) shall be omitted.

(2) In sub-paragraph (2) of that paragraph the words from "to an election" to "and any reference" shall be omitted.

(3) In sub-paragraph (4) of that paragraph for the words "section 134(2)(*a*) of this Act" there shall be substituted "section 109(3)(*a*) of the Finance Act 1986".

FINANCE ACT 1987

(1987 Chapter 16)

PART V
OIL TAXATION

61 Nomination of disposals and appropriations

(1) The provisions of Schedule 10 to this Act shall have effect, being provisions for and in connection with the establishment of a scheme of nominations by participators in oil fields of certain proposed sales . . . [1] of oil.

(2) Nothing in this section or Schedule 10 to this Act applies—

(*a*) to oil which is gaseous at a temperature of 15 degrees centigrade and pressure of one atmosphere; or

(*b*) to oil of a kind which is normally disposed of crude by deliveries in quantities of 25,000 metric tonnes or less; or

(*c*) to oil which is excluded from this section by regulations under subsection (8) below;

and references to oil in this section and Schedule 10 to this Act shall be construed accordingly.

[(3) If the market value of a relevant delivery ascertained in accordance with Schedule 3 to the principal Act exceeds a participator's delivery proceeds of a relevant delivery (within the meaning given by Schedule 10), the excess shall be brought into account by him in accordance with section 2(5)(*e*) of the principal Act.

(4) If a relevant delivery is a delivery of blended oil within the meaning of section 63, regulations under section 2(5B) of the principal Act shall apply for the purposes of determining the proportion of the excess attributable to a field.

(4A) For each month in which a participator makes a relevant delivery, his monthly excess is the sum of his excesses (if any) calculated in accordance with subsection (3).

(4B) For each chargeable period of an oil field "the excess of nominated proceeds for the period" means, in relation to a participator in the oil field, that proportion of the sum of his monthly excesses for the chargeable period (if any) which is attributable to the field.][1]

(5) (*amends* OTA 1975 s 2(5)(*e*)).

(6) . . . [1]

(7) . . . [1]

(8) The Board may by regulations made by statutory instrument make provision, including provision having effect with respect to things done on or after [1st July 2006][1],—

(*a*) as to oil which is excluded from this section, as mentioned in subsection (2) above; and

(*b*) for any purpose for which regulations, other than those described as "Treasury regulations", may be made under Schedule 10 to this Act;

and regulations made by virtue of paragraph (a) above may amend paragraphs (a) and (b) of subsection (2) above.

(9) A statutory instrument made in the exercise of the power conferred by . . . [1] subsection (8) above shall [(unless otherwise expressly provided)][1] be subject to annulment in pursuance of a resolution of the Commons House of Parliament.

Cross references—See SI 1987/1338 (Nomination Scheme regulations).
SI 2000/1072 (amendment to Nomination Scheme regulations).

Amendments—[1] Words ", supplies and appropriations" in sub-s (1) repealed; sub-ss (3)–(4B) substituted for former sub-ss (3), (4); sub-ss (6), (7) repealed; words in sub-s (8) substituted for words "9th February 1987"; in sub-s (9) words "subsection (7) or" repealed and words inserted by FA 2006 s 149, s 178, Sch 26 Pt 5(2) with effect in relation to chargeable periods ending on or after 1 July 2006.

62 Market value of oil to be determined on a monthly basis

(1), (2) (*amend* the Oil Taxation Act 1975, ss 2, 5A, 14, Sch 2, para 2 and *repealed* in part by FA 2006 s 178, Sch 26 Pt 5(1)).

(3) In Schedule 3 to the principal Act (miscellaneous provisions relating to petroleum revenue tax) paragraphs 2, 2A and 3 (market value of oil) shall be amended in accordance with Part I of Schedule 11 to this Act; and the consequential amendments of the principal Act in Part II of that Schedule shall have effect.

[(3A) Subsection (4) applies to a participator in an oil field in any case where—

(*a*) paragraph 2 of Schedule 2 to the principal Act requires the participator to make a return for any chargeable period (including cases where the latest time for the delivery of that return is deferred), and

(*b*) there are any relevant sales of Category 2 oil (as defined in subsection (6) below).][4]

[(4) [In such a case, that participator shall also be required, not later than the end of the second month after the end of that chargeable period, to deliver to the Board a return of all relevant sales of Category 2 oil stating—][4]

(*a*) the date of the contract of sale;

(*b*) the name of the seller;

(*c*) the name of the buyer;

(*d*) the quantity of [Category 2 oil][4] actually sold and, if it is different, the quantity of oil contracted to be sold;

(*e*) the price receivable for that [Category 2 oil][4];

(*f*) the date which, under the contract, was the date or, as the case may be, the latest date for delivery of the [Category 2 oil][4] and the date on which the [Category 2 oil][4] was actually delivered; and

(*g*) such other particulars as the Board may prescribe.

(5) Where two or more companies which are participators in the same oil field are members of the same group of companies, within the meaning of section [413][2] of the Taxes Act, a return made for the purposes of subsection (4) above by one of them and expressed also to be made on behalf of the other or others shall be treated for the purposes of this section as a return made by each of them.

(6) For the purposes of the return required by subsection (4) above from a participator in an oil field, a relevant sale of [Category 2 oil][4] is a contract for the sale of [Category 2 oil][4] [at arm's length][1] to which the participator or any company which is resident in the United Kingdom and associated with the participator for the purposes of section 115(2) of the Finance Act 1984 is a party (as seller, buyer or otherwise), being a sale of [Category 2 oil][4] —

(*a*) for delivery at any time during the chargeable period referred to in [subsection (3A)][4] above; and

[(*b*) details of which are not included in a return for the period under paragraph 2 of Schedule 2 to the principal Act which is delivered to the Board at the same time as the return required by subsection (4) above or which was delivered to them previously; and][3]

(*c*) which is for the delivery of at least 500 metric tonnes of [Category 2 oil][4]; . . .

(7) A return under subsection (4) above shall be in such form as the Board may prescribe and shall include a declaration that the return is correct and complete; and if a participator fails to deliver a return under that subsection he shall be liable—

(*a*) to a penalty not exceeding £500; and

(*b*) if the failure continues after it has been declared by the court or the [tribunal before which][5] proceedings for the penalty have been commenced, to a further penalty not exceeding £100 for each day on which the failure so continues;

except that a participator shall not be liable to a penalty under this subsection if the failure is remedied before proceedings for the recovery of the penalty are commenced.

(8) Where a participator fraudulently or negligently delivers an incorrect return under subsection (4) above, he shall be liable to a penalty not exceeding £2,500 or, in the case of fraud, £5,000.

[(8A) For provision about the meaning of "Category 2 oil", see paragraph 2 of Schedule 3 to the principal Act (which applies by virtue of section 72(6) below).][4]

(9) This section has effect with respect to chargeable periods ending after 31 December 1986.

Amendments—[1] Words in sub-s (6) inserted, with respect to chargeable periods ending after 1 January 1987, by the F(No 2)A 1987 s 101.

PRT

[2] Number in sub-s (5) substituted by TA 1988 s 844, Sch 29 para 32.
[3] Words in sub-s (6)(*b*) substituted by FA 1999 s 102(6), (7) with effect for chargeable periods ending on or after 30 June 1999.
[4] The following amendments are made by FA 2008 s 106 in relation to expenditure incurred after 30 June 2008—
(a) Sub-ss (3A), (8A) inserted.
(b) Opening words in sub-s (4) substituted.
(c) In sub-ss (4)(*d*)–(*f*), (6), words "Category 2 oil" substituted for word "oil".
(d) In sub-s (6)(*a*), words "subsection (3A)" substituted for words "subsection (4)".
(e) Sub-s (6)(*d*) and preceding word "and" repealed.
[5] In sub-s (7)(*b*), words substituted for words "Commissioners before whom" by the Transfer of Tribunal Functions and Revenue and Customs Appeals Order, SI 2009/56 art 3, Sch 1 paras 126, 127 with effect from 1 April 2009.

[63 Blends of oil from two or more fields

(1) This section applies if, at any time before its disposal or relevant appropriation, oil won from an oil field ("the relevant field") in a chargeable period ("the relevant period") is mixed with oil won from one or more other oil fields.

(2) A relevant participator's share of oil won from the relevant field in the relevant period is to be taken to be the amount of the blended oil that it is just and reasonable (for the purposes of the oil taxation legislation) to allocate to the participator in respect of the relevant period.

(3) In making the allocation regard must be had (in particular) to the quantity and quality of the oil derived from each of the originating fields.

(4) If the participators in the originating fields select a method for making the allocation, that method is to be used to determine that allocation.

(5) But that is subject to Schedule 12.

(6) If the participators in the originating fields fail to select a method for making the allocation, HMRC may select a method.

(7) In a case where only some oil won from the relevant field in the relevant period is, before its disposal or relevant appropriation, mixed with oil won from one or more other fields, subsection (2) has effect for the purpose of determining the amount of the blended oil that is to be taken to be included in a relevant participator's share of oil won from the relevant field.

(8) Schedule 12 contains provision supplementing this section.

(9) In this section and Schedule 12—

"blended oil" means oil that consists of oil from two or more oil fields that has been mixed;

"foreign field" means an area which is a foreign field for the purposes of section 12 of the Oil Taxation Act 1983;

"oil" includes any substance which would be oil if the enactments mentioned in section 1(1) of the principal Act extended to a foreign field;

"oil field" includes a foreign field;

"oil taxation legislation" means Part 1 of the principal Act and any enactment construed as one with that Part;

"originating fields", in relation to any blended oil, means the oil fields from which oil which has been mixed as mentioned in subsection (1);

"relevant participator" means a person who is a participator in the relevant field at any time in the relevant period.][1]

Amendments—[1] Section 63 substituted by FA 2009 s 85, Sch 39 paras 1, 2 with effect in relation to chargeable periods beginning after 30 June 2009.

64 Relief for research expenditure

(1) The section set out in Part I of Schedule 13 to this Act shall be inserted in the principal Act after section 5A for the purpose of setting up a new allowance by virtue of which a participator in an oil field may obtain relief for certain research expenditure which is incurred otherwise than in connection with that field.

(2) For the purpose of giving effect to, and in consequence of, the new allowance, the enactments specified in Part II of Schedule 13 to this Act shall have effect subject to the amendments there specified.

(3) Part III of Schedule 13 to this Act shall have effect with respect to sums falling to be set off against expenditure which would otherwise be allowable under the new section set out in Part I of that Schedule.

65 Cross-field allowance of certain expenditure incurred on new fields

(1) Where an election is made by a participator in an oil field (in this section referred to as "the receiving field"), up to 10 per cent. of certain expenditure incurred on or after 17 March 1987 in connection with another field, being a field which is for the purposes of this section a relevant new field, shall be allowable in accordance with this section in respect of the receiving field; and in the following provisions of this section the relevant new field in connection with which the expenditure was incurred is referred to as "the field of origin".

(2) An election under this section may be made only in respect of expenditure which—

(*a*) was incurred by the participator making the election or, if that participator is a body corporate, by an associated company; and (*b*) as regards the field of origin, is allowable under section 3 or section 4 of the principal Act or section 3 of the Oil Taxation Act 1983; and

(*c*) as regards the field of origin, has been allowed as qualifying for supplement under section 2(9)(*b*)(ii) or (*c*)(ii) of the principal Act (in the following provisions of this section referred to as "supplement"); and

(*d*) is not expenditure falling within subsection (1) of section 5A of the principal Act (allowance of exploration and appraisal expenditure);

and Part I of Schedule 14 to this Act shall have effect with respect to elections under this section.

(3) A participator may not make an election under this section in respect of expenditure which was incurred before the date which is his qualifying date, within the meaning of section 113 of the Finance Act 1984 (restriction of PRT reliefs), in relation to the receiving field unless that date falls before the end of the first chargeable period in relation to that field.

(4) Where, by virtue of an election by a participator under this section, an amount of expenditure is allowable in respect of the receiving field, it shall be allowable as follows—

(*a*) it shall be taken into account in that assessment to tax or determination relating to a chargeable period of the receiving field which is specified in Part II of Schedule 14 to this Act; and

(*b*) it shall be so taken into account under subsection (8) of section 2 of the principal Act (allowable expenditure etc) as if, for the chargeable period in question, it were an addition to the sum mentioned in paragraph (*a*) of that subsection; and

(*c*) it shall be excluded in determining for the purposes of section 111(2) of the Finance Act 1981 (restriction of expenditure supplement) whether any, and if so what, assessable profit or allowable loss accrues to the participator in any chargeable period of the receiving field.

(5) Where, by virtue of an election by a participator under this section, an amount of expenditure is allowable in respect of the receiving field, that amount shall be disregarded in determining, as regards the field of origin, the amounts referred to (in relation to the participator or the associated company, as the case may be) in paragraph (*b*) or paragraph (*c*) of subsection (9) of section 2 of the principal Act (allowable expenditure and supplement thereon).

(6) In Schedule 14 to this Act—

(*a*) Part III has effect to determine for the purposes of this section what is a relevant new field and who is an associated company of a participator making an election;

(*b*) Part IV contains provisions supplemental to and consequential upon the allowance of expenditure by virtue of an election under this section, including provisions applicable where a notice of variation is served in respect of expenditure which is already the subject of such an election;

(*c*) "the receiving field" and "the field of origin" have the meaning assigned by subsection (1) above;

(*d*) "the principal section" means this section;

(*e*) "election" means an election under this section; and

(*f*) "supplement" has the meaning assigned by subsection (2)(*c*) above.

HMRC Manuals—Oil Taxation Manual OT13040 (cross field allowances).

66 Oil allowance: adjustment for final periods

(1) For the purposes of this section—

(*a*) "the final allocation period", in relation to an oil field, means the chargeable period of that field in which section 8(6)(*b*) of the principal Act applies (the earliest chargeable period in which oil allowance is subject to "the necessary restriction" in order to confine it within the overall maximum); and

(*b*) "the penultimate period", in relation to an oil field, means the chargeable period of that field which immediately precedes the final allocation period;

and any reference in this section to the two final periods is a reference to the final allocation period and the penultimate period.

(2) The following provisions of this section apply if the responsible person gives notice to the Board (in this section referred to as an "apportionment notice") specifying the manner in which the oil allowance for the field is to be apportioned between the participators in each of the two final periods, being a manner designed—

(*a*) to produce, so far as practicable, the result specified in subsection (4) below, being a result which, in the circumstances of the case, could not be achieved under section 8(6)(*b*) of the principal Act; and

(*b*) to secure that adjustments in a participator's share of the oil allowance are made in the final allocation period in preference to the penultimate period.

(3) An apportionment notice shall be of no effect unless—

(*a*) it is given not later than six months after the expiry of the final allocation period; and

PRT

(*b*) not later than the date of the notice the responsible person notifies the Board in accordance with paragraph (*b*) of subsection (6) of section 8 of the principal Act of the manner in which the necessary restriction, as defined in that subsection, is to be apportioned between the participators; and

(*c*) it specifies a period for each of paragraphs (*a*) and (*b*) of subsection (4) below; and

(*d*) it contains such information as the Board may prescribe for the purpose of showing how, or to what extent, the apportionment of the oil allowance achieves the result specified in subsection (4) below.

(4) The result referred to in subsection (2) above is that the respective shares of the oil allowance utilised by each of two or more participators specified in the apportionment notice bear to each other the same proportion as their respective shares in oil won and saved from the field and, for this purpose—

(*a*) a participator's share of the oil allowance means the total amount of the allowance utilised by him over the period specified for the purpose of this paragraph in the apportionment notice; and

(*b*) a participator's share in oil won and saved from the field means the total of the oil included in his share of oil won and saved from the field (as specified in returns under Schedule 2 to the principal Act) over the period specified for the purposes of this paragraph in the apportionment notice, being a period which includes that specified for the purposes of paragraph (*a*) above.

(5) If the Board are satisfied that an apportionment notice complies with subsections (2) to (4) above, they shall give notice to the responsible person accepting the apportionment notice and, on the giving of that notice—

(*a*) the apportionment specified in the apportionment notice shall, as respects the two final periods, have effect as if it were the apportionment resulting from section 8(2) of the principal Act; and

(*b*) all such amendments of assessments to tax and determinations shall be made as may be necessary in consequence of paragraph (*a*) above.

(6) If the Board are not satisfied that an apportionment notice complies with subsections (2) to (4) above, they shall give notice to the responsible person rejecting the apportionment notice and, where the Board give such a notice, the responsible person may, by notice in writing given to the Board within thirty days after the date of the notice of rejection, appeal . . . [1] against the notice.

(7) Where notice of appeal is given under subsection (6) above—

(*a*) if, at any time after the giving of the notice and before the determination of the appeal by the [tribunal][1], the Board and the appellant agree that the apportionment notice should be accepted or withdrawn or varied, the same consequences shall ensue as if the [tribunal][1] had determined the appeal to that effect;

(*b*) if [the appeal is notified to the tribunal and][1] it appears to [tribunal][1] that the apportionment notice should be accepted, with or without modifications, [the tribunal shall][1] allow the appeal and, where appropriate, make such modifications of the apportionment specified in the notice as [the tribunal thinks][1] fit; and

(*c*) where the appeal is allowed, subsection (5) above shall apply as if the apportionment notice (subject to any modifications made by the [tribunal][1]) had been accepted by the Board.

[(8) Paragraphs 14(2), (8) and (11) and 14A to 14I of Schedule 2 to the principal Act shall apply in relation to an appeal under subsection (6) as they apply in relation to an appeal against an assessment or determination made under that Act subject to the following modifications—

(*a*) any reference in those paragraphs to a participator is to be construed as a reference to the responsible person by whom notice of appeal is given;

(*b*) any reference to an agreement under paragraph 14(9) shall be construed as a reference to an agreement under subsection (7)(*a*) above;

(*c*) any other modifications that are necessary.][1]

(9) This section applies where the final allocation period ends on or after 30 June 1987.

Amendments—[1] In sub-s (6), words "to the Special Commissioners" repealed, in sub-s (7), in para (*a*) word substituted for word "Commissioners" in each place, in para (*b*) words substituted for words ", on the hearing of the appeal,", "the majority of Commissioners present at the hearing", "they shall" and "they think" respectively, and in para (*c*) word substituted for word "Commissioners", and sub-s (8) substituted, by the Transfer of Tribunal Functions and Revenue and Customs Appeals Order, SI 2009/56 art 3, Sch 1 paras 126, 129 with effect from 1 April 2009.

67 Variation of decisions on claims for allowable expenditure

(*amends* OTA 1975 Sch 7 para 1(3) Table).

PART VI

MISCELLANEOUS AND SUPPLEMENTARY

72 Short title, interpretation, construction and repeals

(1) This Act may be cited as the Finance Act 1987.

(2)–(5) [not reproduced].

(6) Part V of this Act shall be construed as one with Part I of the Oil Taxation Act 1975 and in that Part "the principal Act" means that Act.

(7) The enactments specified in Schedule 16 to this Act (which include enactments which are spent or otherwise unnecessary) are hereby repealed to the extent specified in the third column of that Schedule, but subject to any provision at the end of any Part of that Schedule.

SCHEDULES

SCHEDULE 10

NOMINATION SCHEME FOR DISPOSALS AND APPROPRIATIONS

Section 61

Cross references—See SI 1987/1338 (Nomination Scheme regulations).

SI 2000/1072 (amendment to Nomination Scheme regulations).

Modifications—This Schedule is modified in relation to a nomination of a proposed transaction in blended oil by the Petroleum Revenue Tax (Nomination Scheme for Disposals and Appropriations) Regulations 1987, SI 1987/1338, reg 20.

Interpretation

1—(1) In this Schedule—

"month" means calendar month;

"nominal volume" shall be construed in accordance with paragraph 7 below;

"nominated price" shall be construed in accordance with paragraph 6 below;

"nomination" means a nomination made in such manner as may be prescribed by regulations made by the Board;

"proposed sale" . . . [2] shall be construed in accordance with [paragraph (*a*)][2] of sub-paragraph (1) of paragraph 2 below;

"proposed delivery month" shall be construed in accordance with [paragraph 12A below][2];

"proposed transaction" means one falling within paragraph 2(1) below;

"regulations made by the Board" means regulations under section 61(8) of this Act; and

"Treasury regulations" means regulations under section 61(7) of this Act.

(2) . . . [2]

[(3) Where an amount of oil is required to be delivered to the Secretary of State pursuant to a notice served by him, any oil which is inadvertently delivered to him in excess of the amount required shall be treated for the purposes of sub-paragraph (2) above as delivered pursuant to the notice].[1]

Amendments—[1] Sub-para (3) inserted, with respect to calendar months in chargeable periods beginning with March 1987, by F(No 2)A 1987 s 101, Sch 8 para 1.

[2] In sub-para (1) words "proposed supply" and "proposed appropriation" repealed and words substituted for words "paragraph 3 below" and "paragraphs (*a*) to (*c*)"; sub-para (2) repealed by FA 2006 s 150(2), s 178, Sch 26 Pt 5(2) with effect in relation to a transaction whenever proposed, but not with effect in relation to a proposed transaction with a transaction base date (within the meaning given by regulations under Sch 10 para 4 of this Act) on or before 30 June 2006. Sub-para (2) previously read—

"For the purposes of this Schedule, a participator's equity production from an oil field in any month is his share of the oil won from the field which, in that month, is either delivered or relevantly appropriated, other than oil which is delivered to the Secretary of State pursuant to a notice served by him."

[3] In sub-para (3), word substituted for words "Secretary of State" and word "him" by the Petroleum (Transfer of Functions) Regulations, SI 2016/898 reg 9(1), (2) with effect from 1 October 2016.

Transactions which may be nominated

2—(1) The proposed transactions which may be nominated by a participator in an oil field for the purposes of this Schedule are—

(*a*) proposed sales at arm's length by the participator of specified quantities of oil for delivery from that oil field; and

(*b*)–(*d*) . . . [1]

. . . [1]

(2) Where a proposed sale is nominated before a contract of sale comes into being, any reference in this Schedule to the contract of sale is a reference to the subsequent contract for the sale of oil in accordance with the terms of the nomination; and, accordingly, if no such contract of sale comes into being, the nomination of the proposed sale shall be of no effect.

(3) A participator may not nominate a proposed sale if—

(*a*) under the terms of the contract of sale as originally entered into, the party undertaking to sell the oil is someone other than the participator; or

(*b*) it is of a description prescribed for the purposes of this sub-paragraph by regulations made by the Board.

HMRC Manuals—Oil Taxation Manual 05205 (transactions which may be nominated).

Amendments—[1] Sub-para (1)(*b*)–(*d*) and words following sub-para (2)(*d*) repealed by FA 2006 s 150(3), s 178, Sch 26 Pt 5(2) with effect in relation to a transaction whenever proposed, but not with effect in relation to a proposed transaction with a transaction base date (within the meaning given by regulations under Sch 10 para 4 of this Act) on or before 30 June 2006. Sub-para (1)(*b*)–(*d*) and following words previously read—

"(*b*) proposed supplies by the participator (being a company) to another company which is associated with the participator of specified quantities of oil for delivery from that oil field for use for refining either by that other company or by a third company associated with the participator; and

(*c*) proposed relevant appropriations by the participator of specified quantities of oil won from that field; and

(*d*) any other proposed transactions specified for the purposes of this sub-paragraph by Treasury regulations;

and two companies are associated with each other for the purposes of paragraph (*b*) above if they would be so associated for the purposes of section 115(2) of the Finance Act 1984."

Period for which nomination has effect

3 . . . [1]

Amendments—[1] This paragraph repealed by FA 2006 s 150(4), s 178, Sch 26 Pt 5(2) with effect in relation to a transaction whenever proposed, but not with effect in relation to a proposed transaction with a transaction base date (within the meaning given by regulations under Sch 10 para 4 of this Act) on or before 30 June 2006. Para 3 previously read—

"3—

(1) Subject to sub-paragraph (3) below, a nomination shall have effect with respect to proposed deliveries and appropriations of oil in one month only and, accordingly, where a nomination is of a proposed sale and the contract of sale provides for the supply of oil in more than one month, the nomination shall be effective only in relation to oil proposed to be delivered in the month for which the nomination has effect.

(2) Subject to sub-paragraph (3) below, in relation to a nomination, "the proposed delivery month" means the month for which the nomination has effect in accordance with sub-paragraph (1) above.

(3) In relation to a contract of sale of a description specified in the regulations, regulations made by the Board may permit a nomination to have effect as a nomination of a proposed sale for each of a number of months and, in relation to such a nomination, this Schedule shall have effect subject to such modifications as may be prescribed in the regulations."

Timing of nominations

4—[(1) If a nomination is made during business hours it shall be effective only if—

(*a*) it is made within the period of two hours beginning with the transaction base time, and

(*b*) it satisfies the requirements of paragraph 5.

(1A) If a nomination is made outside business hours it shall be effective only if—

(*a*) it is made within the period of two hours beginning with the transaction base time, and

(*b*) it satisfies the requirements of paragraph 5 or 5A.

(1B) For the purposes of this paragraph—

(*a*) the transaction base time of a proposed transaction is such time on such date as the Board shall prescribe by regulations, and

(*b*) "business hours" means the period beginning with 09.00 and ending with 17.00 (UK time) on a business day (within the meaning of the Bills of Exchange Act 1882 (c 61)).][1]

(2) . . . [1]

[(2A) . . . [1]

(3) The [transaction base time][1] prescribed for a proposed sale may be a [time][1] earlier than the [time][1] on which a legally binding agreement for the sale of the oil in question comes into being but may not be later than the [time][1] on which there is an agreed price at which any oil which is to be delivered pursuant to the contract of sale will be sold.

(4) . . . [1]

HMRC Manuals—Oil Taxation Manual 05220 (when a nomination should be made).

Amendments—[1] Sub-paras (1)–(1B) substituted for former sub-para (1); sub-paras (2), (2A), (4) repealed and words in sub-para (3) substituted for words "transaction base date" and "date" by FA 2006 s 150(5), s 178, Sch 26 Pt 5(2) with effect in relation to a transaction whenever proposed, but not with effect in relation to a proposed transaction with a transaction base date (within the meaning given by regulations under this para) on or before 30 June 2006. Regulations under para 4(1B) may have retrospective effect (FA 2006 s 150(15)).

Sub-paras (1), (2), (2A), (4) previously read—

"(1) Subject to [sub-paragraphs (2) and (2)(A)] below, a nomination shall be effective only if it is made not later than five o'clock in the afternoon of the second business day following the date which, in relation to a proposed transaction of that description, is prescribed as the transaction base date.

(2) Sub-paragraph (1) above does not apply to a nomination made on or before 16 February 1987 which specified a proposed transaction having a transaction base date earlier than 12 February 1987.

[(2A) Where the proposed transaction has a transaction base date later than 31 December 1993, sub-paragraph (1) above has effect with the substitution for the reference to the second business day of a reference to the first business day].

In this paragraph—

(*a*) "business day" has the same meaning as in the Bills of Exchange Act 1882;

(*b*) "prescribed" means prescribed by regulations made by the Board."

Content of nomination

5—(1) [The requirements of this paragraph for a nomination in respect of a proposed transaction are][2],—

(*a*) the name of the participator;

(*b*) [. . . [2]][1] the name of the person to whom the oil is to be [sold][1];

(*c*) the field from which the oil is to be delivered . . . [2];

(*d*) the nominated price of the oil to be [delivered][2] . . . [2];

(*e*) the nominal volume of that oil;

(*f*) the proposed delivery month;

[(*g*) the transaction base time; and][2]

(*h*) such other information as may be prescribed by the Board.

(2) A nomination [made under this paragraph][2] shall include a declaration that it is correct and complete and, in the case of a nomination of a proposed sale which is made before the contract of sale comes into being, shall also include a declaration that, to the best of the knowledge and belief of the participator making the nomination, a contract of sale will come into being in accordance with the terms of the nomination.

(3) Where a participator fraudulently or negligently furnishes any incorrect information or makes any incorrect declaration in or in connection with a nomination [made under this paragraph][2] he shall be liable to a penalty not exceeding £50,000 or, in the case of fraud, £100,000 [and the nomination shall not be effective][1].

HMRC Manuals—Oil Taxation Manual 05215 (how a nomination should be made).

Amendments—[1] Words in sub-para (1) substituted and words in sub-para (3) inserted by F(No 2)A 1987 s 101, Sch 8 para 2 with respect to calendar months in chargeable periods beginning with March 1987.

[2] Words at the beginning of sub-para (1) substituted for words "A nomination of a proposed transaction shall not be effective unless it specifies, with respect to that transaction"; words "in the case of a proposed sale" in sub-para (1)(*b*) and words "or relevantly appropriated" in sub-para (1)(*c*), (*d*) repealed, word in sub-para (1)(*d*) substituted for the word "supplied" and the whole of sub-para (1)(*g*) substituted; words in sub-paras (2), (3) inserted by FA 2006 s 150(6), s 178, Sch 26 Pt 5(2) with effect in relation to a transaction whenever proposed, but not with effect in relation to a proposed transaction with a transaction base date (within the meaning given by regulations under para 4) on or before 30 June 2006. Sub-para (1)(*g*) previously read—

"(*g*) the transaction base date; and".

[5A—(1) The requirements of this paragraph for a nomination in respect of a proposed transaction are—

(*a*) the name of the participator or of the group of which the participator is a member;

(*b*) the name of the person to whom the oil is to be sold, or the name of the group of which that person is a member;

(*c*) the blend or grade of oil to be delivered;

(*d*) the nominated price of the oil to be delivered;

(*e*) the nominal volume of the oil;

(*f*) the proposed delivery month;

(*g*) the transaction base time; and

(*h*) such other information as may be prescribed by the Board.

(2) In sub-paragraph (1) "group" has the meaning given by section 53 of the Companies Act 1989.][1]

Amendments—[1] This paragraph inserted by FA 2006 s 150(7) with effect in relation to a transaction whenever proposed, but not with effect in relation to a proposed transaction with a transaction base date (within the meaning given by regulations under para 4) on or before 30 June 2006.

[5B—(1) A nomination of a transaction shall not be effective unless oil is delivered pursuant to a contract at arm's length the terms of which incorporate the information specified in the nomination in accordance with paragraph 5(1) or 5A(1).

(2) But—

(*a*) a contract need not refer to the transaction base time, and

(*b*) the nomination shall be effective whether or not delivery takes place in the proposed delivery month specified in the nomination and the contract.][1]

Amendments—[1] This paragraph inserted by FA 2006 s 150(7) with effect in relation to a transaction whenever proposed, but not with effect in relation to a proposed transaction with a transaction base date (within the meaning given by regulations under para 4) on or before 30 June 2006.

Nominated price

6—(1) . . . [1] in the case of a proposed sale, the "nominated price", in relation to the oil which is to be delivered pursuant to the sale, is the price specified in the contract of sale (expressed as a unit price) or, as the case may be, the formula under which, in accordance with the contract, the price of that oil (as so expressed) is to be determined.
(2), (3) . . . [1]

Amendments—[1] Words "Subject to sub-paragraph (3) below," in sub-para (1) and the whole of sub-paras (2), (3), repealed by FA 2006 s 150(8), s 178, Sch 26 Pt 5(2) with effect in relation to a transaction whenever proposed, but not with effect in relation to a proposed transaction with a transaction base date (within the meaning given by regulations under para 4) on or before 30 June 2006. Sub-paras (2), (3) previously read—

"(2) Subject to sub-paragraph (3) below, in the case of a proposed supply or proposed appropriation, the "nominated price" of the oil concerned means the market value of that oil, ascertained in accordance with Schedule 3 to the principal Act and expressed as a unit price; and for the purposes of paragraph 5(1)(*d*) above a statement that the nominated price of oil is its "market value" shall be sufficient.

(3) Treasury regulations may—

(*a*) vary the meaning of "nominated price" in relation to a proposed sale, supply or appropriation and, for that purpose, amend sub-paragraph (1) or sub-paragraph (2) above; and

(*b*) make provision as to the meaning of "nominated price" in relation to a proposed transaction falling within paragraph 2(1)(*d*) above."

Nominal volume

7—(1) Subject to sub-paragraph (3) below, in the case of a proposed sale, the nominal volume means the quantity of oil which it is proposed should be delivered under the contract of sale in the proposed delivery month.
(2) . . . [1]
(3) In the case of any proposed transaction, the nominal volume means the quantity of oil expressed in such manner as may be prescribed by regulations made by the Board.
(4) In any case where—

(*a*) apart from this sub-paragraph, the nominal volume in any proposed transaction would be expressed as a specific volume of oil, plus or minus a particular tolerance, and

(*b*) that tolerance exceeds the limits prescribed for the purposes of this Schedule by regulations made by the Board,

the nominal volume shall for those purposes be taken to be the specific volume referred to in paragraph (a) above, plus or minus the maximum tolerance permitted by the regulations.
(5) . . . [1]
[(6) The Board may by regulations prescribe that in specified circumstances the nominal volume in relation to a delivery shall be treated as greater or less than the nominal volume ascertained in accordance with the preceding provisions of this paragraph.
(7) Regulations under sub-paragraph (6)—

(*a*) shall be made by statutory instrument, and

(*b*) may not be made unless a draft has been laid before and approved by resolution of the House of Commons.][1]

Amendments—[1] Sub paras (2), (5), repealed and sub-paras (6), (7) inserted by FA 2006 s 150(9), (10) with effect in relation to a transaction whenever proposed, but not with effect in relation to a proposed transaction with a transaction base date (within the meaning given by regulations under para 4) on or before 30 June 2006. Sub-paras (2), (5) previously read—

"(2) Subject to sub-paragraph (3) below, in the case of a proposed supply or proposed appropriation, the nominal volume means the quantity of oil which the participator making the nomination proposes to supply or relevantly appropriate (as the case may be) in the proposed delivery month.

(5) Where a nominal volume is expressed as a specific volume of oil, plus or minus a tolerance, any reference in paragraph 9 below to the maximum nominal volume or the minimum nominal volume is a reference to that specific volume of oil, plus or minus the tolerance respectively."

Revision of nominations

8—*(1) Except as provided by this paragraph, a nomination may not be amended or withdrawn.*
(2) If a participator who has made a nomination of a proposed sale does not, in whole or in part, fulfil his obligations under the contract of sale by the delivery of oil forming part of his equity production for the proposed delivery month, then, in accordance with regulations made by the Board, he may amend or withdraw the nomination if in his opinion—

(*a*) *there were good commercial reasons for the failure to fulfil those obligations; or*

(*b*) *the failure was occasioned by circumstances over which neither he nor any person connected or associated with him had control.*

[(2A) If a participator who has made a nomination of a proposed supply, proposed appropriation or a proposed transaction falling within paragraph 2(1)(d) above fails, in whole or in part, to supply, to appropriate or otherwise to complete the proposed transaction by the delivery or appropriation of oil forming part of his equity production for the proposed delivery month, then, in accordance with regulations made by the Board, he may amend or withdraw the nomination as mentioned in sub-paragraph (2B) below.

(2B) The circumstances in which, in a case falling within sub-paragraph (2A) above, a participator may amend or withdraw a nomination are,—

(a) in the case of a nomination of a proposed supply or proposed appropriation, if the participator is of the opinion that the failure referred to in that sub-paragraph was caused by circumstances over which neither he nor any person connected or associated with him had control; or

(b) in the case of a nomination of a proposed transaction falling within paragraph 2(1)(d) above, in such circumstances as may be prescribed by regulations made by the Board; or

(c) in any case where the nomination is of a proposed supply or proposed appropriation and the participator is either the field operator or the operator of a relevant system, if the participator is of the opinion that the failure referred to in sub-paragraph (2A) above was caused by action necessarily taken by him in the interests of safety or the prevention of pollution or in accordance with good oil field practice.

(2C) In relation to such a nomination as is referred to in sub-paragraph (2B)(c) above,—

(a) a participator is the field operator, if, in relation to the field specified in the nomination, he is the person having the function of organising or supervising operations for searching or boring for or getting oil in pursuance of a licence; and

(b) the expression "relevant system" is applicable only where the oil to which the nomination relates is blended oil and is a reference to any system by which blended oil (in relation to which the field specified in the nomination is one of the originating fields) is transported, treated or stored prior to its disposal or relevant appropriation; and

(c) a participator in an oil field is an operator of a relevant system, as defined above, if he is the person charged, or principally charged, with the operation of the system;

and expressions used in paragraph (b) above have the same meaning as in section 63 of this Act].[2]

(3) An amendment or withdrawal of a nomination by a participator in accordance with [the preceding provisions of this paragraph][2] *above shall not be effective unless the Board give notice to the participator that the amendment or withdrawal is accepted, and the Board shall not give such a notice unless they are satisfied—*

(a) as to the matters mentioned in either paragraph (a) or paragraph (b) of sub-paragraph (2) above [or, where sub-paragraph (2B) above applies, that the failure was caused as mentioned in paragraph (a) or paragraph (c) of that sub-paragraph or that the circumstances prescribed for the purposes of paragraph (b) of that sub-paragraph exist][2]*; and*

(b) [except where sub-paragraph (2)(b) or sub-paragraph (2B)(a)][2] *above applies, that the failure was not part of a scheme or arrangement the main purpose of which was the avoidance of tax.*

(4) For the purposes of sub-paragraph (2)(b) [and sub-paragraph (2B)][2] *above,—*

(a) section [839][1] *of the Taxes Act (connected persons) applies; and*

(b) two companies of which one is a participator in an oil field are associated with each other if one has control over the other or both are under the control of the same person or persons;

and in paragraph (b) above "control" shall be construed in accordance with section [416][1] *of the Taxes Act.*

(5) Where a nomination is amended in accordance with this paragraph, the [provisions of this Schedule (other than this paragraph)][1] *shall apply in relation to it subject to such modifications as may be specified in regulations made by the Board.*[3]

Amendments—[1] Words in sub-para (4) substituted by TA 1988 s 844, Sch 29 para 32

[2] Sub-paras (2A)–(2C) and words in sub-paras (3)(*a*), (4) inserted and other words in sub-paras (3), (5) substituted by F(No 2)A 1987 s 101, Sch 8 para 3 with respect to calendar months in chargeable periods beginning with March 1987.

[3] Paragraphs 8–11 repealed by FA 2006 s 150(11), s 178, Sch 26 Pt 5(2) with effect in relation to a transaction whenever proposed, but not with effect in relation to a proposed transaction with a transaction base date (within the meaning given by regulations under para 4) on or before 30 June 2006.

Effective volume for nominated transactions

9—*(1) The provisions of this paragraph have effect to determine, in relation to each nominated transaction, what is the effective volume of oil.*

(2) In relation to a proposed sale where the nominal volume is expressed as mentioned in paragraph 7(5) above and oil is in fact delivered under the contract of sale, the effective volume is whichever is the greater of—

(a) the minimum nominal volume; and

PRT

(b) so much of the total volume of oil actually delivered under the contract as does not exceed the maximum nominal volume.

(3) In relation to any proposed sale which does not fall within sub-paragraph (2) above, the effective volume shall be taken to be the nominal volume.

[(4) In relation to a proposed supply or proposed appropriation where the nominal volume is expressed as mentioned in paragraph 7(5) above and oil is in fact supplied or, as the case may be, relevantly appropriated as proposed in the nomination, the effective volume is whichever is the greater of—

(a) the minimum nominal volume; and

(b) so much of the total volume of oil supplied or relevantly appropriated as does not exceed the maximum nominal volume.

(5) In relation to a proposed supply or proposed appropriation which does not fall within sub-paragraph (4) above, the effective volume is the nominal volume].[1,2]

Amendments—[1] Sub-paras (4), (5) substituted for original sub-para (4) by F(No 2)A 1987 s 101, Sch 8 para 4 with respect to calendar months in chargeable periods beginning with March 1987.

[2] Paragraphs 8–11 repealed by FA 2006 s 150(11), s 178, Sch 26 Pt 5(2) with effect in relation to a transaction whenever proposed, but not with effect in relation to a proposed transaction with a transaction base date (within the meaning given by regulations under para 4) on or before 30 June 2006.

Aggregate effective volume for a month

10—*(1) Subject to the provisions of this paragraph, for each month the aggregate effective volume of a participator's nominated transactions is the sum of the effective volumes of all of the proposed transactions nominated by him for that month.*

(2) If a participator's aggregate effective volume for any month, as determined under sub-paragraph (1) above, would exceed his equity production for that month—

(a) his nominated transactions for that month shall be taken to be reduced by cancelling later nominations in priority to earlier ones until the cancellation of the next nominated transaction would produce an aggregate effective volume less than the participator's equity production; and

(b) the effective volume of the latest remaining nominated transaction shall be taken to be reduced so far as necessary to secure that the aggregate effective volume is equal to the participator's equity production.[1]

Amendments—[1] Paragraphs 8–11 repealed by FA 2006 s 150(11), s 178, Sch 26 Pt 5(2) with effect in relation to a transaction whenever proposed, but not with effect in relation to a proposed transaction with a transaction base date (within the meaning given by regulations under para 4) on or before 30 June 2006.

Aggregate nominated proceeds for a month

11—*(1) For each month, a participator's aggregate nominated proceeds for the purposes of section 61 of this Act is the sum of—*

(a) the proceeds of each nominated transaction falling within sub-paragraph (2) below; and

(b) the market value of any excess falling within sub-paragraph (3) below.

(2) For each nominated transaction, the effective volume of which forms part of the participator's aggregate effective volume for the month, as defined in paragraph 10 above, the proceeds of the transaction means the effective volume multiplied by the nominated price.

(3) If the participator's equity production for a month exceeds his aggregate effective volume for that month, as defined in paragraph 10 above, the market value of the excess shall be determined in accordance with Schedule 3 to the principal Act.

(4) The reference in sub-paragraph (2) above to the nominated price is a reference to that price expressed in sterling; and regulations made by the Board shall make provision with respect to the conversion into sterling of any nominated price which is expressed in a currency other than sterling.[1]

Amendments—[1] Paragraphs 8–11 repealed by FA 2006 s 150(11), s 178, Sch 26 Pt 5(2) with effect in relation to a transaction whenever proposed, but not with effect in relation to a proposed transaction with a transaction base date (within the meaning given by regulations under para 4) on or before 30 June 2006.

Blended oil

12—[(1) If a person is a participator in two or more oil fields which, in relation to any blended oil, are or are included among the originating fields then, in accordance with regulations made by the Board, he may make a nomination, having effect with respect to all the originating fields in which he is a participator, of a proposed sale . . .[2] of the blended oil][1]; and the preceding provisions of this Schedule shall have effect in relation to such a nomination subject to such modifications as may be prescribed by regulations made by the Board.

[(2) In sub-paragraph (1) above "blended oil" and "the originating fields" have the same meaning as in section 63 of this Act.][1]

HMRC Manuals—Oil Taxation Manual 05260 (blended oil).

Amendments—[1] Words in sub-para (1) substituted and sub-para (2) inserted by F(No 2)A 1987 s 101, Sch 8 para 6 with respect to calendar months in chargeable periods beginning with March 1987.

[2] Words ", supply or appropriation" in sub-para (1) repealed by FA 2006 s 150(12), s 178, Sch 26 Pt 5(2) with effect in relation to a transaction whenever proposed, but not with effect in relation to a proposed transaction with a transaction base date (within the meaning given by regulations under para 4) on or before 30 June 2006.

[Interpretation

12A For the purposes of section 61 and this Schedule—

(*a*) a reference to the proposed delivery month in relation to a proposed transaction is a reference to the month in which delivery is to take place,

(*b*) "relevant delivery" means a delivery of oil under a contract made at arm's length in respect of which there has been no effective nomination, and

(*c*) "delivery proceeds" means the price received for a relevant delivery.][1]

Amendments—[1] This paragraph inserted by FA 2006 s 150(13) with effect in relation to a transaction whenever proposed, but not with effect in relation to a proposed transaction with a transaction base date (within the meaning given by regulations under para 4) on or before 30 June 2006.

Returns

13 (*amends* OTA 1975 Sch 2 para 2(3A)).

SCHEDULE 11

MARKET VALUE OF OIL

Section 62

PART I

AMENDMENT OF PARAGRAPHS 2, 2A AND 3 OF SCHEDULE 3 TO THE PRINCIPAL ACT

(*amends* the Oil Taxation Act 1975 Sch 3; *repealed* in part by TA 1988, s 844, Sch 31 and by FA 2006 s 178, Sch 26 Pt 5(1)).

PART II

CONSEQUENTIAL AMENDMENTS OF PRINCIPAL ACT

(*amends* the Oil Taxation Act 1975 ss 5A, 12, 14, Sch 9, para 6).

SCHEDULE 12

SUPPLEMENTARY PROVISIONS AS TO BLENDED OIL

Section 63

[Interpretation

1—(1) In this Schedule—

"HMRC" means Her Majesty's Revenue and Customs; "method of allocation" means a method for making an allocation of blended oil for the purposes of section 63 that has been selected by the participators in the originating fields (including such a method that has been amended in accordance with this Schedule).

(2) In this Schedule a reference to a suitable method of allocation is a reference to a method which secures that allocation of blended oil is just and reasonable (for the purposes of the oil taxation legislation).][1]

Amendments—[1] Paragraphs 1 and 2 substituted by FA 2009 s 85, Sch 39 paras 1, 3 with effect in relation to chargeable periods beginning after 30 June 2009.

[Method of allocation not suitable

2—(1) This paragraph applies if it appears to HMRC that—

(*a*) a method of allocation that has been used in respect of a chargeable period was not suitable, or

(*b*) a method of allocation that is proposed to be used in respect of a chargeable period would not be suitable.

(2) HMRC may give notice to each of the participators in the originating fields—

(*a*) informing the participators of what appears to HMRC to be the case, and

(*b*) proposing amendments to the method of allocation.

(3) If HMRC give notice, the allocation of the blended oil for the purposes of section 63 in respect of the chargeable period is to be re determined, or determined, using the method of allocation as amended in accordance with the notice.

(4) Sub-paragraph (3) is subject to—

(*a*) the following provisions of this Schedule,

(*b*) any subsequent notice given under this paragraph, and

(*c*) any amendment to the method of allocation made by the participators in the originating fields.][1]

Amendments—[1] Paragraphs 1 and 2 substituted by FA 2009 s 85, Sch 39 paras 1, 3 with effect in relation to chargeable periods beginning after 30 June 2009.

Appeals

3—(1) Where [HMRC][2] give notice to the participators in the originating fields under [paragraph 2(2)][2] above, any of those participators may appeal . . . [1] against the notice by giving notice in writing to [HMRC][2] within thirty days after the date of the notice given by [HMRC][2].

(2) Where notice of appeal is given under sub-paragraph (1) above—

(*a*) [HMRC][2] shall give notice in writing to all those participators in the originating fields who have not given notice of appeal and they shall, by virtue of that notice, become parties to the appeal . . . [1];

(*b*) if, before the determination of the appeal by the [tribunal][1], [HMRC][2] and the participators in the originating fields agree that the method of allocation concerned should not be amended or should have effect with particular amendments the same consequences shall ensue as if the [tribunal][1] had determined the appeal to that effect;

(*c*) [if, on an appeal notified to the tribunal, it appears to the tribunal][1] that the method of allocation concerned is satisfactory, with or without modifications, for the purposes of the oil taxation legislation [the tribunal][1] shall allow the appeal and, where appropriate, shall amend the method of allocation accordingly for those purposes; and

[(*d*) paragraphs 14(2), (8) and (11) and 14A to 14I of Schedule 2 to the principal Act shall apply in relation to the appeal as they apply in relation to an appeal against an assessment or determination made under that Act subject to the following modifications—

(i) any reference to an agreement under paragraph 14(9) shall be construed as a reference to an agreement under sub-paragraph (2)(*b*) above;

(ii) any other modifications that are necessary.][1]

[(3) If the method of allocation is amended in accordance with this paragraph, the allocation of the blended oil for the purposes of section 63 in respect of the chargeable period is to be re determined, or determined, using the method of allocation as so amended.

(4) Sub-paragraph (3) is subject to—

(*a*) any subsequent notice given under this paragraph, and

(*b*) any amendment to the method of allocation made by the participators in the originating fields.][2]

Amendments—[1] In sub-para (1), words "to the Special Commissioners" repealed; in sub-para (2), in para (*a*) words "and be entitled to appear accordingly" repealed; in para (*b*) word substituted for words "Special Commissioners" and "Commissioners" respectively; in sub-para (2)(*c*), words substituted for words "if, on the hearing of the appeal, it appears to the majority of the Commissioners present" and "they" respectively; and sub-para (2)(*d*) substituted, by the Transfer of Tribunal Functions and Revenue and Customs Appeals Order, SI 2009/56 art 3, Sch 1 paras 126, 130 with effect from 1 April 2009.

[2] Word substituted for words "the Board" in each place; in sub-s (1) words substituted for words "paragraph 2(*a*)"; and sub-paras (3), (4) inserted, by FA 2009 s 85, Sch 39 paras 1, 3 with effect in relation to chargeable periods beginning after 30 June 2009.

4 *Any method or amended method of allocation having effect by virtue of paragraph 3(2) above shall have effect with respect to any such chargeable period as is referred to in paragraph 2(b) above.*[1]

Amendments—[1] Paragraph 4 repealed by FA 2009 s 85, Sch 39 paras 1, 4 with effect in relation to chargeable periods beginning after 30 June 2009.

SCHEDULE 13

RELIEF FOR RESEARCH EXPENDITURE

Section 64

PART I

SECTION TO BE INSERTED AFTER SECTION 5A OF THE PRINCIPAL ACT

(*inserts* OTA 1975 s 5B).

PART II

AMENDMENTS RELATING TO THE NEW ALLOWANCE

The principal Act

1–5 (*amends* OTA 1975 ss 2, 3, 9, Schs 2, 7).

The Petroleum Revenue Tax Act 1980

6 (*amends* PRTA 1980 Sch para 2(4)).

The Finance Act 1980

7 (*amends* FA 1980 Sch 17 para 16B).

The Finance Act 1981

8 (*amends* FA 1981 s 111(3)(*a*)).

The Finance Act 1984

9 (*amends* FA 1984 s 113).

PART III

RECEIPTS TO BE SET AGAINST ALLOWABLE EXPENDITURE

10 In this Part of this Schedule—

"allowable expenditure" means expenditure which, in accordance with section 5B of the principal Act, is allowable on a claim made by a participator under Schedule 7 to that Act; and

"qualifying receipt" means a sum the amount of which falls, by virtue of subsection (6) of section 5 of the principal Act, to be applied by way of reduction in the amount of expenditure which would otherwise be allowable expenditure.

11—(1) A return made by a participator for a chargeable period under paragraph 2 of Schedule 2 to the principal Act shall give details of any qualifying receipt (whether received by him or by a person connected with him) of which details have not been given in a return made by him for an earlier chargeable period.

(2) [Section 1122 of the Corporation Tax Act 2010][1] (connected persons) applies for the purposes of this paragraph.

Amendments—[1] In sub-para (2) words substituted for words "Section 839 of the Taxes Act 1988" by CTA 2010 s 1177, Sch 1 para 204. CTA 2010 has effect for corporation tax purposes for accounting periods ending on or after 1 April 2010, and for income and capital gains tax purposes for the tax year 2010–11 and subsequent tax years.

12—(1) This paragraph applies where—

(*a*) a claim for allowable expenditure has been made by a participator under Schedule 7 to the principal Act; and

(*b*) as a result of the receipt (whether before or after the making of the claim) of a qualifying receipt, the amount allowed by way of allowable expenditure on the claim exceeds what it should have been.

(2) In determining, in a case where this paragraph applies, the assessable profit or allowable loss accruing to the participator in the chargeable period in which the qualifying receipt is received, the amount of the excess referred to in sub-paragraph (1)(*b*) above shall be taken into account under section 2 of the principal Act as an amount which is to be included among the positive amounts referred to in subsection (3)(*a*) of that section.

(3) In the application of section 9 of the principal Act (limit on amount of tax payable) to a chargeable period in respect of which sub-paragraph (2) above applies, the amount of the excess referred to in sub-paragraph (1)(*b*) above shall be deducted from the amount which would otherwise be the total ascertained under subsection (2)(*a*)(ii) of that section and, if the amount of that excess is greater than the amount which would otherwise be that total, that total shall be a negative amount equal to the difference.

SCHEDULE 14

CROSS-FIELD ALLOWANCE

Section 65

PART I

ELECTIONS

General

1—(1) An election shall be made in such form as may be prescribed by the Board.

(2) Without prejudice to sub-paragraph (1) above, an election shall specify—

(*a*) the expenditure in respect of which it is made and the amount of that expenditure (in this Part of this Schedule referred to as "the elected amount"), which shall not exceed 10 per cent., which is to be allowable under the principal section;

(*b*) the field of origin and the receiving field;

(*c*) the notice, agreement or determination which, under paragraph 2 below, determines the earliest date on which the election could be made;

(*d*) in a case where the elected amount is to be allowable in respect of more than one receiving field, the proportions in which that amount is to be apportioned between those fields; and

(*e*) in the case of expenditure incurred by a company which is an associated company of the participator for the purposes of the principal section, the name of that company.

(3) An election shall be irrevocable.

HMRC Manuals—Oil Taxation Manual 13060 (procedures).

Earliest date for an election

2—(1) No election may be made in respect of an amount of expenditure until a final decision as to supplement has been made on a claim in respect of that amount under Schedule 5 or Schedule 6 to the principal Act.

(2) For the purposes of this paragraph, a final decision as to supplement is made in relation to an amount of expenditure when—

(*a*) the Board give to the responsible person or, as the case may be, the participator notice under paragraph 3 of Schedule 5 to the principal Act stating that amount of expenditure as an amount qualifying for supplement; or

(*b*) after notice of appeal has been given against a decision on a claim, an agreement is made as mentioned in sub-paragraph (1) of paragraph 6 of Schedule 5 to the principal Act and that amount of expenditure is, for the purposes of that sub-paragraph, the appropriate amount of the expenditure claimed as qualifying for supplement; or

(*c*) on an appeal against a decision on a claim, there is a determination by the [tribunal][1] or the court by virtue of which that amount of expenditure falls (under paragraph 7(2) or paragraph 8(2) of Schedule 5 to the principal Act) to be treated for the purposes of Part I of that Act as qualifying for supplement.

(3) Nothing in Schedule 5 to the principal Act relating to the date on which an amount of expenditure is to be treated as having been allowed as qualifying for supplement applies for the purposes of sub-paragraph (2) above.

Amendments—[1] In sub-para (2)(*c*), word substituted for words "Special Commissioners", by the Transfer of Tribunal Functions and Revenue and Customs Appeals Order, SI 2009/56 art 3, Sch 1 paras 126, 131 with effect from 1 April 2009.

Latest date for election

3—(1) Subject to sub-paragraph (2) below, an election by a participator in respect of a particular amount of expenditure may be made at any time before—

(*a*) the Board make, for a chargeable period of the field of origin, an assessment or determination which takes account of that amount of expenditure as qualifying for supplement; and

(*b*) notice of that assessment or determination is given to the participator or, as the case may be, the associated company, under paragraph 10 of Schedule 2 to the principal Act.

(2) Where the earliest date for the making of an election in respect of a particular amount of expenditure is a date determined under paragraph 2(2)(*b*) or paragraph 2(2)(*c*) above, such an election may be made at any time before notice is given as mentioned in sub-paragraph (1)(*b*) above or, if it is later, before the expiry of the period of thirty days beginning on the day following that earliest date.

Two or more elections relating to same expenditure

4 Where more than one election is made in respect of the same amount of expenditure—

(*a*) the maximum of 10 per cent specified in paragraph 1(2)(*a*) above shall be cumulative; and

(*b*) if the elected amount specified in a second or subsequent election is such that, when aggregated with the elected amount or amounts specified in the earlier election or elections, it would exceed 10 per cent, that second or subsequent election shall have effect as if it specified such an elected amount as would, when so aggregated, be equal to 10 per cent of the expenditure concerned; and

(*c*) an election shall be of no effect if it is made after one or more earlier elections have specified (or been treated by paragraph (*b*) above as having specified) an elected amount or an aggregate of elected amounts equal to 10 per cent.

PART II
ELECTION RECEIVING FIELD

5—(1) In relation to an election, the assessment to tax or determination referred to in subsection (4)(*a*) of the principal section is that which is first made after the relevant date on or in relation to the participator by whom the election is made.

(2) Subject to paragraphs 6 and 7 below, the relevant date for the purposes of sub-paragraph (1) above is the date of the election.

6 In any case where—

(*a*) an election is made in the period of thirty days beginning on the day following that on which the Board give notice under paragraph 3 of Schedule 5 to the principal Act stating the expenditure in respect of which the election is made as expenditure qualifying for supplement, and

(*b*) after the date of that notice but on or before the date of the election, an assessment to tax or determination for the receiving field is made on or in relation to the participator making the election,

the relevant date for the purposes of paragraph 5(1) above is the date of the notice referred to in paragraph (a) above; and the assessment or determination referred to in paragraph (b) above shall be amended accordingly.

7 In any case where, following the giving of a notice of appeal, an election is made in respect of expenditure which (under paragraph 6(1), paragraph 7(2) or paragraph 8(2) of Schedule 5 to the principal Act) is treated for the purposes of Part I of that Act as having been allowed as qualifying for supplement on the date on which the notice of appeal was given, the relevant date for the purposes of paragraph 5(1) above is the date on which that notice was given; and in any assessment to tax or determination (relating to the field of origin or the receiving field) all such adjustments or further adjustments shall be made as are necessary in consequence of the election.

PART III
RELEVANT NEW FIELDS AND ASSOCIATED COMPANIES

Relevant new fields

8—(1) For the purposes of the principal section "relevant new field" means, subject to sub-paragraph (2) below, an oil field—

(*a*) no part of which lies in a landward area, within the meaning of the Petroleum (Production) Regulations 1982 or in an area to the East of the United Kingdom and between latitudes 52 degrees and 55 degrees North; and

(*b*) for no part of which consent for development has been granted to the licensee by the Secretary of State before 17 March 1987; and

(*c*) for no part of which a programme of development had been served on the licensee or approved by the Secretary of State before that date.

(2) In determining, in accordance with sub-paragraph (1) above, whether an oil field (in this sub-paragraph referred to as "the new field") is a relevant new field, no account shall be taken of a consent for development granted before 17 March 1987 or a programme of development served on the licensee or approved by the Secretary of State before that date if—

(*a*) in whole or in part that consent or programme related to another oil field for which a determination under Schedule 1 to the principal Act was made before the determination under that Schedule for the new field; and

(*b*) on or after 17 March 1987 a consent for development is or was granted or a programme of development is or was served on the licensee or approved by the [OGA][1] and that consent or programme relates, in whole or in part, to the new field.

Amendments—[1] In sub-para (2)(*b*), word substituted for words "Secretary of State" and word "him" by the Petroleum (Transfer of Functions) Regulations, SI 2016/898 reg 9(1), (3) with effect from 1 October 2016.

9—(1) In paragraph 8 above "development" means—

(*a*) the erection or carrying out of permanent works for the purpose of getting oil from the field or for the purpose of conveying oil won from the field to a place on land; or

(*b*) winning oil from the field otherwise than in the course of searching for oil or drilling wells;

and consent for development does not include consent which is limited to the purpose of testing the characteristics of an oil-bearing area and does not relate to the erection or carrying out of permanent works.

(2) In sub-paragraph (1) above "permanent works" means any structures or other works whatsoever which are intended by the licensee to be permanent and are neither designed to be moved from place to place without major dismantling nor intended by the licensee to be used only for searching for oil.

Associated companies

10—(1) For the purposes of the principal section, a company is an associated company of a participator (being itself a company) making an election under that section if—

PRT

(*a*) throughout that part of the relevant period in which both were in existence one was a 51 per cent subsidiary of the other and the other was not a 51 per cent subsidiary of any company; or

(*b*) each of them was, throughout that part of the relevant period in which it was in existence, a 51 per cent subsidiary of a third company which was not itself a 51 per cent subsidiary of any company.

(2) In this paragraph "company" means any body corporate and [Chapter 3 of Part 24 of the Corporation Tax Act 2010][1] (subsidiaries) applies for the purposes of this paragraph.

(3) For the purposes of this paragraph the relevant period ends on the date on which the election in question is made and begins—

(*a*) in the case of an election relating to expenditure incurred in the first claim period of the field of origin, on the date on which any part of that field was first determined under Schedule 1 to the principal Act; and

(*b*) in the case of an election relating to expenditure incurred in any other claim period of the field of origin, at the beginning of that claim period.

Amendments—[1] In sub-para (2) words substituted for words "section 838 of the Taxes Act 1988" by CTA 2010 s 1177, Sch 1 para 205. CTA 2010 has effect for corporation tax purposes for accounting periods ending on or after 1 April 2010, and for income and capital gains tax purposes for the tax year 2010–11 and subsequent tax years.

PART IV
SUPPLEMENTAL AND CONSEQUENTIAL PROVISIONS

Notice of variation reducing expenditure qualifying for supplement

11—(1) This paragraph applies in any case where—

(*a*) an amount of expenditure is allowed as qualifying for supplement as regards the field of origin; and

(*b*) one or more elections is made in respect of that expenditure; and(*c*) a notice of variation is served under paragraph 9 of Schedule 5 to the principal Act; and

(*d*) on that notice of variation becoming effective for the purposes of the said paragraph 9, the amount of the expenditure referred to in paragraph (*a*) above is taken for the purposes of Part I of the principal Act as having been reduced.

(2) In sub-paragraph (3) below—

(*a*) "the original expenditure" means the amount of expenditure referred to in sub-paragraph (1)(*a*) above, disregarding the effect of the notice of variation;(*b*) "the reduced expenditure" means the amount of that expenditure after the notice of variation became effective for the purposes of paragraph 9 of Schedule 5 to the principal Act; and

(*c*) "the expenditure originally allowable" means the amount of the original expenditure which, having regard to the election or elections in respect of that expenditure but disregarding the effect of the notice of variation, was allowable in accordance with the principal section.

(3) If the expenditure originally allowable exceeds 10 per cent. of the reduced expenditure, the principal section shall have effect as if the election or elections had specified an amount of that expenditure equal (or equal in the aggregate) to 10 per cent. of the reduced expenditure and, where there was more than one election, paragraph 4 above shall be taken to have applied accordingly.

(4) Such amendments of assessments to tax or determinations (relating to the field of origin or the receiving field) shall be made as may be necessary in consequence of the preceding provisions of this paragraph.

Elections following variation increasing expenditure qualifying for supplement

12—(1) In any case where—

(*a*) an amount of expenditure is allowed as qualifying for supplement as regards the field of origin, and

(*b*) one or more elections is made in respect of that expenditure, and

(*c*) a notice of variation is served under paragraph 9 of Schedule 5 to the principal Act, and

(*d*) on that notice of variation becoming effective for the purposes of the said paragraph 9, the amount of the expenditure referred to in paragraph (*a*) above is taken for the purposes of Part I of the principal Act as having been increased,

an election may be made in respect of the amount of the increase as if it were a separate amount of expenditure.

(2) In the circumstances referred to in sub-paragraph (1) above an election may be made by the participator in question at any time before—

(*a*) notice is given to the participator or, as the case may be, the associated company of the making of that assessment or determination or that amendment of an assessment or determination which takes account of the increase resulting from the notice of variation; or (*b*) if it is later, the expiry of the period of thirty days beginning on the date on which the notice of variation becomes effective for the purposes of paragraph 9 of Schedule 5 to the principal Act.

(3) Where an election is made by a participator in the circumstances referred to in sub-paragraph (1) above—

(*a*) paragraph 1(2)(*c*) above shall have effect as if it referred to the notice of variation;

(*b*) subsection (4)(*a*) of the principal section shall not apply; and

(*c*) the expenditure allowable as a result of the election shall be taken into account in the first assessment to tax or determination relating to a chargeable period of the receiving field which is made on or in relation to the participator after the date of the decision to which the notice of variation relates.

(4) Such amendments of assessments to tax or determinations (relating to the field of origin or the receiving field) shall be made as may be necessary in consequence of the preceding provisions of this paragraph.

Limit on amount of tax payable in respect of receiving field

13—(1) Where an election has been made by a participator, this paragraph has effect with respect to the determination under section 9 of the principal Act (limit on amount of tax payable) of the adjusted profit of the participator in respect of the receiving field.

(2) For the chargeable period in which the amount of expenditure allowable by virtue of the election is taken into account as mentioned in subsection (4) of the principal section, that amount shall also be taken into account as if it were an addition to the total amount mentioned in section 9(2)(*a*)(ii) of the principal Act.

FINANCE (NO 2) ACT 1987

(1987 Chapter 51)

PART I

INCOME TAX, CORPORATION TAX AND CAPITAL GAINS TAX

CHAPTER V

TAXES MANAGEMENT PROVISIONS

Interest etc

86 Supplementary provisions as to interest on overdue tax

(1) (*amended* TMA 1970 s 69, *repealed by* FA 2001 s 110, Sch 33 Pt 2(14).)

(7) This section has effect with respect to accounting periods ending after the appointed day.

Miscellaneous

94 Failure to do things within a limited time

(*amends* TMA 1970 s 118(2)).

95 Interpretation of Chapter V and consequential and supplementary provisions

(1) In this Chapter "the Management Act" means the Taxes Management Act 1970.

(2) Subject to subsection (3) below, any reference in this Chapter to the appointed day is a reference to such day as the Treasury may by order made by statutory instrument appoint, and different days may be so appointed for different provisions of this Chapter.

(3) No day may be appointed by virtue of subsection (2) above which falls earlier than 31 March 1992.

PART III

MISCELLANEOUS AND SUPPLEMENTARY

101 Oil taxation

(1) Schedule 10 to the Finance Act 1987 (nomination scheme for disposals and appropriations of oil) shall have effect subject to the amendments in Schedule 8 to this Act.

(2) In section 62 of the Finance Act 1987 (market value of oil to be determined on a monthly basis) subsection (6) (meaning of relevant sale of oil in relation to the additional return required by subsection (4) of that section) shall have effect subject to the following modifications—

(*a*) (*amends* FA 1987 s 62(6)).

(*b*) . . . [1]

(3) (*amends* FA 1987 s 63(1A)).

(4) (*amends* OTA 1975 Sch 2 para 5(2B)).

(5) Subsections (2) to (4) above have effect with respect to chargeable periods ending after 1 January 1987 and . . . [2] Schedule 8 to this Act has effect with respect to calendar months in chargeable periods beginning with March 1987.

PRT

(6) . . .[2]

Amendments—[1] Sub-s (2)(*b*) repealed by FA 1999 s 139, Sch 20 Pt IV(1) with effect in relation to any chargeable period ending after 29 June 1999.

[2] Words ", subject to subsection (6) below" in sub-s (5) and the whole of sub-s (6) repealed by FA 2006 s 178, Sch 26 Pt 5(1) with effect—

(a) in relation to oil delivered or appropriated on or after 1 July 2006 (disregarding section 12A of this Act); and

(b) for the purpose of determining for any chargeable period ending on or after 31 December 2006—

(i) the value to be brought into account under section 2(4)(*b*) of OTA 1975 by reference to a previous chargeable period ending on or after 30 June 2006, and

(ii) the value to be brought into account under section 2(5)(*d*) of that Act,

subject to transitional provisions in FA 2006 s 147(4)–(8).

Sub-s (6) previously read as follows—

"Paragraph 5 of Schedule 8 to this Act has effect with respect to chargeable periods ending after such date as the Treasury may by order made by statutory instrument appoint; but no order shall be made under this subsection unless a draft of it has been laid before and approved by a resolution of the House of Commons."

104 Short title, interpretation, construction and repeals

(1) This Act may be cited as the Finance (No 2) Act 1987.

(2), (3) [not reproduced].

(4) The enactments specified in Schedule 9 to this Act (which include enactments which are spent or otherwise unnecessary) are hereby repealed to the extent specified in the third column of that Schedule but subject to any provision at the end of any Part of that Schedule.

SCHEDULE 8

Section 101

Amendments of Schedule 10 to Finance Act 1987

1–6 (*amended* FA 1987 Sch 10 and *repealed* in part by FA 2006 s 146, Sch 18 para 11, s 178, Sch 26 Pt 5(1)).

INCOME AND CORPORATION TAXES ACT 1988

(1988 Chapter 1)

Note—Reference should be made to the following in connection with PRT—

TA 1988 Schedule 19B (Petroleum Extraction Activities: Exploration Expenditure Supplement).

The full text of TA 1998, as amended, is reproduced in Part 1a of this publication.

FINANCE ACT 1988

(1988 Chapter 39)

PART IV

MISCELLANEOUS AND GENERAL

Petroleum revenue tax

138 Reduced oil allowance for certain Southern Basin and onshore fields

(1) For every relevant Southern Basin or onshore field, as defined in subsection (2) below, section 8 of the Oil Taxation Act 1975 (the oil allowance) shall have effect subject to the following modifications—

(*a*) in subsection (2) (the amount of the allowance for each chargeable period) for "250,000 metric tonnes" there shall be substituted "125,000 metric tonnes"; and

(*b*) in subsection (6) (the total allowance for a field) for "5 million metric tonnes" there shall be substituted "2.5 million metric tonnes".

(2) Subject to subsection (3) below, for the purposes of this section a "relevant Southern Basin or onshore field" is any oil field other than one—

(*a*) which is a relevant new field for the purposes of section 36 of the Finance Act 1983 (increased oil allowance for certain new fields); or

(*b*) for any part of which consent for development was granted to the licensee by the Secretary of State before 1 April 1982; or

(*c*) for any part of which a programme of development was served on the licensee or approved by the Secretary of State before that date.

(3) In determining, in accordance with subsection (2) above, whether an oil field (in this subsection referred to as "the field in question") is a relevant Southern Basin or onshore field, no account shall be taken of a consent for development granted before 1 April 1982 or a programme of development served on the licensee or approved by the Secretary of State before that date if—

(*a*) in whole or in part that consent or programme related to another oil field for which a determination under Schedule 1 to the Oil Taxation Act 1975 was made before the determination under that Schedule for the field in question; and

(*b*) on or after 1 April 1982, a consent for development is or was granted or a programme of development is or was served on the licensee or approved by the [OGA][1] and that consent or programme relates, in whole or in part, to the field in question.

(4) Subsections (4) and (5) of section 36 of the Finance Act 1983 (which define "development" for the purposes of subsections (2) and (3) of that section) shall apply also for the purposes of subsections (2) and (3) of this section.

(5) This section shall have effect in relation to chargeable periods ending after 30 June 1988.

(6) This section shall be construed as one with Part I of the Oil Taxation Act 1975.

Amendments—[1] In sub-s (3)(*b*), word substituted for words "Secretary of State" by the Petroleum (Transfer of Functions) Regulations, SI 2016/898 reg 10 with effect from 1 October 2016.

139 Assets generating tariff receipts: extension of allowable expenditure

(*amends* OTA 1983 Sch 1 para 3(1)(*a*)).

SCHEDULES

SCHEDULE 13

POST-CONSOLIDATION AMENDMENTS

Section 146

PART II

AMENDMENTS OF OTHER ENACTMENTS

The Finance Act 1980

20 (*amends* FA 1980 s 109(8)(*b*)).

The Finance Act 1984

22 (*amends* FA 1984 s 80).

Commencement

25 The amendments made by paragraphs 16 to 23 of this Schedule shall be treated for the purposes of their commencement as if they had been made by the Taxes Act 1988.

FINANCE ACT 1989

(1989 Chapter 26)

PART III

MISCELLANEOUS AND GENERAL

Interest etc

178 Setting of rates of interest

(1) The rate of interest applicable for the purposes of an enactment to which this section applies shall be the rate which for the purposes of that enactment is provided for by regulations made by the Treasury under this section.

(2) This section applies to—

[(*aa*) section 15A of the Stamp Act 1891;][12]

(*a*) section 8(9) of the Finance Act 1894,

(*b*) section 18 of the Finance Act 1896,

(*c*) section 61(5) of the Finance (1909–10) Act 1910,

(*d*) section 17(3) of the Law of Property Act 1925,

(*e*) . . . [20]

(*f*) [sections . . . [23] 86, 86A, 87, 87A, . . . [9] and [103A][10]][8] of the Taxes Management Act 1970,

(*g*) paragraph 3 of Schedule 16A to the Finance Act 1973,

[(*ga*) section 48(1) of the Finance Act 1975,][21]

[(*gg*) [paragraph 6 of Schedule 1 to the Social Security Contributions and Benefits Act 1992][4],][1]

[(*gh*) section 71(8A) of the Social Security Administration Act 1992, and section 69(8A) of the Social Security Administration (Northern Ireland) Act 1992, as they have effect in any case where the overpayment was made in respect of working families' tax credit or disabled person's tax credit;][15]

(*h*) paragraphs 15 and 16 of Schedule 2, and paragraph 8 of Schedule 5, to the Oil Taxation Act 1975,

[(*i*) section 283 of the Taxation of Chargeable Gains Act 1992;][5]

(*j*) paragraph 59 of Schedule 8 to the Development Land Tax Act 1976,

(*k*) sections 233[, 235(1)][21] and 236(3) and (4) of the Inheritance Tax Act 1984,

(*l*) section 92 of the Finance Act 1986, and

(*m*) sections . . . [16] *160*[17], 824, 825 [826 and 826A(1)(*b*)][11] of . . .,[7] and paragraph 3 of Schedule 19A to, the Taxes Act 1988 [and][2].

[(*n*) . . .][6] [and][3]

[(*o*) section 14(4) of the Ports Act 1991][3]

[(*p*) paragraph 8 of Schedule 4 to the Tax Credits Act 1999][13] [, *and*[17]

[(*q*)] [17] section 110 of the Finance Act][14][, and

[(*q*) paragraph 8 of Schedule 1 to the Employment Act 2002][18]

(*r*) Chapter 7 of Part 3 of the Income Tax (Earnings and Pensions) Act 2003][17]

[(*r*) sections 87, 88 and 89 of the Finance Act 2003][19] . . . [25]

(*u*) paragraph 11 of Schedule 35 to the Finance Act 2014][24][, and

[(*v*) section 79 of FA 2015.][25]

(3) Regulations under this section may—

(*a*) make different provision for different enactments or for different purposes of the same enactment,

(*b*) either themselves specify a rate of interest for the purposes of an enactment or make provision for any such rate to be determined by reference to such rate or the average of such rates as may be referred to in the regulations,

(*c*) provide for rates to be reduced below, or increased above, what they otherwise would be by specified amounts or by reference to specified formulae,

(*d*) provide for rates arrived at by reference to averages to be rounded up or down,

(*e*) provide for circumstances in which alteration of a rate of interest is or is not to take place, and

(*f*) provide that alterations of rates are to have effect for periods beginning on or after a day determined in accordance with the regulations in relation to interest running from before that day as well as from or from after that day.

(4) The power to make regulations under this section shall be exercisable by statutory instrument which shall be subject to annulment in pursuance of a resolution of the House of Commons.

(5) Where—

(a) *the rate provided for by regulations under this section as the rate applicable for the purposes of any enactment is changed, and*

(*b*) *the new rate is not specified in the regulations,*

the Board shall by order specify the new rate and the day from which it has effect.[21]

(6) (amends TA 1988 s 828(2)).[22]

(7) Subsection (1) shall have effect for periods beginning on or after such day as the Treasury may by order made by statutory instrument appoint and shall have effect in relation to interest running from before that day as well as from or from after that day; and different days may be appointed for different enactments.

Commentary—*Simon's Taxes* **A4.621**.

Regulations—Taxes (Interest Rate) Regulations, SI 1989/1297.

Finance Act 1989, section 178(1), (Appointed Day No 1) Order, SI 1989/1298.

Finance Act 1989, section 178(1), (Appointed Day) Order, SI 1992/2073.

Finance Act 1989, section 178(1), (Appointed Day) Order, SI 1993/754.

Taxes (Interest Rate) (Amendment No 3) Regulations, SI 1993/2212.

Taxes (Interest Rate) (Amendment) Regulations, SI 1994/1307.

Taxes (Interest Rate) (Amendment No 4) Regulations, SI 1996/3187.

Taxes (Interest Rate) (Amendment No 2) Regulations, SI 1997/2707.

Finance Act 1989, section 178(1), (Appointed Day) Order, SI 1997/2708.

Taxes (Interest Rate) (Amendment) Regulations, SI 1998/310.

Finance Act 1989, section 178(1), (Appointed Day) Order, SI 1998/311.

Taxes (Interest Rate) (Amendment No 2) Regulations, SI 1998/3176.

Taxes (Interest Rate) (Amendment) Regulations, SI 1999/419.

Taxes (Interest Rate) (Amendment No 2) Regulations, SI 1999/1928.

Taxes (Interest Rate) (Amendment No 4) Regulations, SI 1999/2637.

Taxes (Interest Rate) (Amendment) Regulations, SI 2000/893.

Taxes (Interest Rate) (Amendment No 1) Regulations, SI 2001/204.

Finance Act 1989, Section 178(1), (Appointed Day) Order, SI 2001/253.

Taxes (Interest Rate) (Amendment) Regulations, SI 2005/2462.

Taxes (Interest Rate) (Amendment) Regulations, SI 2008/778.

Taxes and Duties (Interest Rate) (Amendment) Regulations, SI 2008/3234.

Taxes (Interest Rate) (Amendment) Regulations, SI 2009/199.

Taxes and Duties (Interest Rate) (Amendment) Regulations, SI 2009/2032.

Taxes (Interest Rate) (Amendment) Regulations, SI 2010/415.

Taxes (Interest Rate) (Amendment) Regulations, SI 2014/496.

Taxes (Interest Rate) (Amendment) Regulations, SI 2015/441.
Taxes (Interest Rate) (Amendment) Regulations, SI 2017/305.

Note—The appointed day for the purposes of all the enactments mentioned in sub-s (2) above (with such exceptions as mentioned in the **Amendments** note below) and appointed under sub-s (7) above is 18 August 1989; FA 1989 s 178(1) (Appointed Day No 1) Order, SI 1989/1298.

Amendments—[1] Sub-s (2)(*gg*) inserted by the Social Security Act 1990 s 17(10) with effect from 6 April 1992.

[2] Word "and" added by FA 1990 s 118(8) with effect from 26 July 1990.

[3] Sub-s (2)(*o*) and preceding word "and" added by the Ports Act 1991 s 14(5) with effect from 15 July 1991.

[4] Words in sub-s (2)(*gg*) substituted by the Social Security (Consequential Provisions) Act 1992 s 4, Sch 2 para 107 with effect from 1 July 1992.

[5] Sub-s (2)(*i*) substituted by TCGA 1992 Sch 10 para 19(4) with effect from the year 1992–93.

[6] Sub-s (2)(*n*) (inserted by FA 1990 s 118(8)) repealed by FA 1995 Sch 29 Pt XII.

[7] Words in sub-s (2)(*m*) repealed by FA 1996 Sch 7 para 30 and Sch 41 Pt V(2) with effect for income tax for the year 1996–97 and for corporation tax for accounting periods ending after 31 March 1996.

[8] Words in sub-s (2)(*f*) substituted by FA 1994 ss 196, 199 and Sch 19 para 44 with effect from the year 1996–97 in relation to income tax and capital gains tax and, in relation to corporation tax, for accounting periods ending after 30 June 1999 (by virtue of Finance Act 1994, Section 199, (Appointed Day) Order, SI 1998/3173 art 2).

[9] Word "88" in sub-s (2)(*f*) repealed by FA 1996 Sch 18 para 13 and Sch 41 Pt V(8) with effect for the year 1996–97, and in relation to any income tax or capital gains tax which is charged by an assessment made after 5 April 1998 which is for the year 1995–96 or any earlier year of assessment, and so far as relating to partnerships whose trades, professions or businesses were set up and commenced before 6 April 1994 from the year 1997–98 in relation to any income tax which is charged by an assessment made after 5 April 1998 which is for the year 1995–96 or any earlier year of assessment.

[10] The appointed day for the purposes of TMA 1970 ss 59C and 103A and appointed under sub-s (7) above is 9 March 1998; Finance Act 1989, section 178(1), (Appointed Day) Order 1998, SI 1998/311.

[11] Words substituted by FA 1998 Sch 4 para 1(3) with effect for accounting periods ending on or after 1 July 1999 (the date appointed under FA 1994 s 199, by virtue of SI 1998/3173, for the purposes of corporation tax self-assessment).

[12] Sub-s (2)(*aa*) inserted by FA 1999 s 109(2), (4) with effect for instruments executed after 30 September 1999.

[13] Sub-s (2)(*p*) inserted by Tax Credits Act 1999 Sch 4 para 8(1) with effect from 7 March 2001 (by virtue of SI 2001/253).

[14] Sub-s (2)(*p*) and preceding word ", and" inserted by FA 1999 s 110(8), (9) with effect for instruments executed after 30 September 1999. It would appear that this paragraph has been incorrectly numbered.

[15] Sub-s (2)(*gh*) inserted in relation to the transfer of functions concerning the working families' tax credit and the disabled person's tax credit by Tax Credits Act 1999 s 2(3), Sch 2 para 10(2) with effect from 5 October 1999.

[16] Words in sub-s (2)(*m*) repealed by FA 2000 s 156, Sch 40 Pt II(17) with effect for relevant payments or receipts in relation to which the chargeable date for the purposes of TA 1988 Pt IV, Ch VIIA is after 31 March 2001.

[17] In sub-s (2), in para (*m*), reference "160" repealed, in para (*p*), word in italics repealed, para (*q*) numbered as such, and para (*r*) and word preceding it inserted by ITEPA 2003 ss 722, 724, Sch 6 paras 156, 162, Sch 8 with effect, for income tax purposes, from 2003–04; and for corporation tax purposes, for accounting periods ending after 5 April 2003. For transitional provisions and savings see ITEPA 2003 s 723, Sch 7.

[18] Sub-s (2)(*q*), which appears to have been numbered incorrectly, inserted by EA 2002 ss 11, 12, Sch 1 para 8(1) with effect from 8 December 2002 (by virtue of SI 2002/2866).

[19] Sub-s (2)(*r*) inserted by FA 2003 s 123(1), Sch 18 para 4 with effect in accordance with FA 2003 s 124, Sch 19. It would appear that this provision has been incorrectly numbered.

[20] Sub-s (2)(*e*) repealed by the Land Registration Act 2002 ss 135, 136(2), Sch 13 with effect from 13 October 2003 (by virtue of SI 2003/1725).

[21] Sub-s (2)(*ga*) and words in sub-s (2)(*k*) inserted, and sub-s (5) repealed, by FA 2009 s 105(5), (6)(a) with effect from 21 July 2009.

[22] Sub-s (6) repealed by CTA 2010 s 1181, Sch 3 Pt 1. CTA 2010 has effect for corporation tax purposes for accounting periods ending on or after 1 April 2010, and for income and capital gains tax purposes for the tax year 2010–11 and subsequent tax years.

[23] In sub-s (2)(*f*), reference "59C," repealed by the Finance Act 2009, Schedules 55 and 56 (Income Tax Self Assessment and Pension Schemes) (Appointed Days and Consequential and Savings Provisions) Order, SI 2011/702 art 12 with effect from 1 April 2011. This amendment has no effect in relation to a return or other document which is required to be made or delivered to HMRC or an amount of tax which is payable in relation to the tax year 2009–10 or any previous tax year (SI 2011/702 art 20).

[24] Sub-s (2)(*u*) and preceding word "and" inserted by FA 2014 s 274, Sch 35 para 11 with effect from 17 July 2014.

[25] In sub-s (2), word "and" previously preceding para (*u*) repealed, and para (*v*) and preceding word inserted, by FA 2015 s 115(4) with effect in relation to accounting periods beginning on or after 1 April 2015. For accounting periods that straddle that date, see FA 2015 s 116(2), (3).

179 Provisions consequential on section 178

(1)–(3) [not reproduced]

(4) Any amendment made by subsection (1), (2) or (3) above shall have effect in relation to any period for which section 178(1) above has effect for the purposes of the enactment concerned.

(5) [not reproduced]

180 Repayment interest: period of accrual

(1) [not reproduced].

(2)

(*a*) (*amends* OTA 1975 Sch 2 para 16).

(*b*) (*amends* FA 1980 s 105(7)).

(*c*) (*amends* FA 1981 Sch 16 para 13(4), (5)).

(*d*) (*amends* FA 1982 Sch 19 para 10(4)).

(7) The amendments made by this section shall be deemed always to have had effect.

General

186 Interpretation etc

(1) In this Act "the Taxes Act 1970" means the Income and Corporation Taxes Act 1970 and "the Taxes Act 1988" means the Income and Corporation Taxes Act 1988.

(3) Part II of this Act, so far as it relates to capital gains tax, shall be construed as one with the Capital Gains Tax Act 1979.

188 Short title

This Act may be cited as the Finance Act 1989.

FINANCE ACT 1990

(1990 Chapter 29)

PART II

INCOME TAX, CORPORATION TAX AND CAPITAL GAINS TAX

CHAPTER I

GENERAL

Oil industry

62 CT treatment of PRT repayment

(*amends* TA 1988 ss 500, 502).

Miscellaneous

89 Correction of errors in Taxes Act 1988

Schedule 14 to this Act shall have effect.

CHAPTER II

MANAGEMENT

Claims by companies

99 Loss relief

(1) The Taxes Act 1988 shall be amended as follows.

(2) (*amends* TA 1988 s 393(1), (11)).

(4) This section applies in relation to accounting periods ending after the day appointed for the purposes of section 10 of the Taxes Act 1988 (pay and file).

PART IV

MISCELLANEOUS AND GENERAL

Petroleum revenue tax

121 Limit on PRT repayment interest where loss carried back

(1) Schedule 2 to the Oil Taxation Act 1975 (management and collection of PRT) shall be amended as follows.

(2) (*amends* OTA 1975 Sch 2 para 16).

(3) (*amends* OTA 1975 Sch 2 para 17).

122 Variation, on account of fraudulent or negligent conduct, of decision on expenditure claim etc

. . .

Amendments—This section repealed by FA 2009 s 99, Sch 51 para 43(*a*) with effect from 1 April 2010 (SI 2010/867, art 2(1)).

General

131 Interpretation etc

(1) In this Act "the Taxes Act 1970" means the Income and Corporation Taxes Act 1970 and "the Taxes Act 1988" means the Income and Corporation Taxes Act 1988.

(2) [not reproduced].

(3) Part II of this Act, so far as it relates to capital gains tax, shall be construed as one with the Capital Gains Tax Act 1979.

133 Short title

This Act may be cited as the Finance Act 1990.

SCHEDULES

SCHEDULE 14

AMENDMENTS CORRECTING ERRORS IN THE TAXES ACT 1988

Section 89

PART I

AMENDMENTS OF THE TAXES ACT 1988

1 The Taxes Act 1988 shall have effect, and shall be deemed always to have had effect, subject to the amendments made by this Part of this Schedule.

PART II

AMENDMENTS OF OTHER ENACTMENTS

16 The Oil Taxation Act 1975
(*amends* OTA 1975 Sch 3 para 5(2)).

19 Commencement
(1) Subject to the following provisions of this paragraph, the amendments made by this Part of this Schedule shall be treated for the purposes of their commencement as if they had been made by the Taxes Act 1988.

FINANCE ACT 1991

(1991 Chapter 31)

PART II

INCOME TAX, CORPORATION TAX AND CAPITAL GAINS TAX

CHAPTER I

GENERAL

Oil industry

62–65

. . .

Amendments—Sections repealed for corporation tax purposes by CTA 2010 ss 1177, 1181, Sch 1 paras 221, 222, Sch 3 Pt 2. CTA 2010 has effect for corporation tax purposes for accounting periods ending on or after 1 April 2010, and for income and capital gains tax purposes for the tax year 2010–11 and subsequent tax years.

Sections repealed by TIOPA 2010 ss 374, 378, Sch 8 paras 185, 186, Sch 10 Pt 6; . TIOPA 2010 has effect for corporation tax purposes for accounting periods ending on or after 1 April 2010, for income and capital gains tax purposes for the tax year 2010–11 and subsequent tax years, and for petroleum revenue tax purposes for chargeable periods beginning on or after 1 July 2010.

66 Restrictions on setting ACT against liability to corporation tax on profits from oil extraction activities etc
(*amends* TA 1988 s 497).

Miscellaneous

73 Relief for company trading losses

(1), (2) (*insert* TA 1988 s 393A, *repeal* ss 393(2)–(6), 394).

(3) Schedule 15 to this Act shall have effect.

(4) This section shall have effect only in relation to losses incurred in accounting periods ending on or after 1 April 1991.

(5) Any enactment amended by this section or that Schedule shall, in its application in relation to losses so incurred, be deemed to have had effect at all times with that amendment; and where any such enactment is the re-enactment of a repealed enactment, the repealed enactment shall, in its application in relation to losses so incurred, be deemed to have had effect at all times with a corresponding amendment.

Amendments—Sub-s (1) repealed by CTA 2010 s 1181, Sch 3 Pt 1. CTA 2010 has effect for corporation tax purposes for accounting periods ending on or after 1 April 2010, and for income and capital gains tax purposes for the tax year 2010–11 and subsequent tax years.

PART III
OIL TAXATION

Abandonment etc

103 Allowance of certain expenditure relating to abandonment, decommissioning assets, etc

(1)–(7) (*amends* OTA 1975 ss 3, 10, *part repealed* by FA 2001 s 110, Sch 33 Pt III(2) with effect for expenditure incurred after 6 March 2001).

(8) So far as they relate to the paragraph (*hh*) inserted by subsection (2) above, the amendments in subsections (5) to (7) above have effect with respect to expenditure incurred on or after 19 March 1991 and, subject to that, the amendments in subsections (4) to (7) above have effect with respect to expenditure incurred after 30 June 1991.

104 Abandonment guarantees

(1) Subject to subsection (2) below, for the purposes of section 3 of the principal Act . . . [2], an abandonment guarantee is a contract under which a person ("the guarantor") undertakes to make good any default by a participator in an oil field ("the relevant participator") in meeting the whole or any part of those liabilities of his which—

(*a*) arise under a relevant agreement relating to that field; and

(*b*) are liabilities to contribute to field abandonment costs;

and such a contract is an abandonment guarantee regardless of the form of the undertaking of the guarantor and, in particular, whether or not it is expressed as a guarantee or arises under a letter of credit, a performance bond or any other instrument.

(2) For the purposes of section 3 of the principal Act . . . [2] a contract is not an abandonment guarantee—

(*a*) unless it is entered into in good faith and on terms reasonably appropriate to the nature and extent of the guarantee; or

(*b*) if the guarantor undertakes any liability beyond that of making good any such default as is referred to in subsection (1) above; or

(*c*) if it can be revoked by the guarantor otherwise than on account of some fraud, misrepresentation or other fault on the part of the relevant participator occurring prior to the making of the contract; or

(*d*) if, subject to subsection (3) below, the guarantor is, or is a person connected with, a participator in one or more oil fields.

(3) Paragraph (*d*) of subsection (2) above does not apply if—

(*a*) the main business carried on by the guarantor is such that it is in the ordinary course of that business to provide guarantees; and

(*b*) the relevant participator is not connected with the guarantor;

and [section 1122 of the Corporation Tax Act 2010][1] (connected persons) applies for the purposes of this subsection and subsection (2) above.

(4) Without prejudice to the generality of paragraph (*a*) of subsection (2) above, a contract shall not be regarded as entered into in good faith if, as a result of any arrangement, the liability to make good any such default as is referred to in subsection (1) above will be met, directly or indirectly, by such a person that, if he were the guarantor under the contract, the contract could not be an abandonment guarantee by virtue of paragraph (*d*) of subsection (2) above.

(5) In this section and in section 3(5B) of the principal Act—

(*a*) in relation to an oil field, a "relevant agreement" means a joint operating agreement, a unitisation agreement (within the meaning of paragraph 1(1) of Schedule 17 to the Finance Act 1980) or an agreement entered into by some or all of the parties to a joint operating agreement or such a unitisation agreement; and

(*b*) in relation to an oil field, "field abandonment costs" means costs incurred in closing down the field or any part of it, together with any costs incurred in discharging any continuing liabilities resulting directly from that closure.

Amendments—[1] In sub-s (3) words substituted for words "section 839 of the Taxes Act 1988" by CTA 2010 s 1177, Sch 1 para 223. CTA 2010 has effect for corporation tax purposes for accounting periods ending on or after 1 April 2010, and for income and capital gains tax purposes for the tax year 2010–11 and subsequent tax years.

[2] In sub-s (1), words "and sections 105 and 106 below" repealed, and in sub-s (2), words "and section 106 (but not section 105) below" repealed, by FA 2013 s 89(1), Sch 31 para 11 with effect in relation to expenditure incurred on or after 17 July 2013.

105 Restriction of expenditure relief by reference to payments under abandonment guarantees

Amendments—Section 105 repealed by FA 2013 s 89(1), Sch 31 para 5(1), (2) with effect in relation to expenditure incurred on or after 17 July 2013.

106 Relief for reimbursement expenditure under abandonment guarantees

Amendments—Section 106 repealed by FA 2013 s 89(1), Sch 31 para 5(1), (3) with effect in relation to expenditure incurred on or after 17 July 2013.

[1] Section 106 repealed by FA 2013 s 89(1), Sch 31 para 5(1), (3) with effect in relation to expenditure incurred on or after 17 July 2013.

107 Allowance of expenditure of participator meeting defaulter's field abandonment expenditure

(1) (*amends* OTA 1975 Sch 5 para 2(4)(*b*)).

(2) (*inserts* OTA 1975 Sch 5 para 2A)).

108 Reimbursement by defaulter in respect of certain abandonment expenditure

Amendments—Section 108 repealed by FA 2013 s 89(1), Sch 31 para 8 with effect in relation to expenditure incurred on or after 17 July 2013.

Penalties

109 PRT: proceedings for penalties

(1) In Schedule 2 to the principal Act (management and collection of petroleum revenue tax) the Table in paragraph 1(1) shall be amended as follows.

(2), (3) (*amends* OTA 1975 Sch 2 para 1(1)).

PART V

MISCELLANEOUS AND GENERAL

General

122 Interpretation etc

(1) In this Act "the Taxes Act 1988" means the Income and Corporation Taxes Act 1988.

(2) Part II of this Act, so far as it relates to capital gains tax, shall be construed as one with the Capital Gains Tax Act 1979.

(3) Part III of this Act shall be construed as one with Part I of the Oil Taxation Act 1975 and in that Part of this Act "the principal Act" means that Act.

124 Short title

This Act may be cited as the Finance Act 1991.

SCHEDULES

SCHEDULE 15

RELIEF FOR COMPANY TRADING LOSSES

Section 73

The Income and Corporation Taxes Act 1988

8 (*amends* TA 1988 s 393).

17 (*amends* TA 1988 s 492).

24 (*amends* TA 1988 s 843).

TAXATION OF CHARGEABLE GAINS ACT 1992

(1992 Chapter 12)

Note—For the purposes of oil and gas taxation, the following provisions should be referred to—

TCGA 1992 s 194 (Disposals of oil licences relating to undeveloped areas);
TCGA 1992 s 195 (Allowance of certain drilling expenditure etc);
TCGA 1992 s 195A (Oil licence swaps);
TCGA 1992 s 195B (Licence-consideration swap);
TCGA 1992 s 195C (Company that receives mixed consideration: N exceeds C);
TCGA 1992 s 195D (Company that receives mixed consideration: N does not exceed C);
TCGA 1992 s 195E (Company that gives mixed consideration);
TCGA 1992 s 195F (Reimbursed expenditure);
TCGA 1992 s 196 (Interpretation of TCGA 1992 ss 194 and 195);
TCGA 1992 s 197 (Disposals of interests in oil fields etc: ring fence provisions);
TCGA 1992 s 198 (Replacement of business assets used in connection with oil fields);
TCGA 1992 s 198A (Ring fence reinvestment: whole consideration reinvested);
TCGA 1992 s 198B (Ring fence reinvestment: part of consideration reinvested);
TCGA 1992 s 198C (Provisional application of sections 198A and 198B);
TCGA 1992 s 198D (No double claims);
TCGA 1992 s 198E (Ring fence reinvestments and disposal consideration);
TCGA 1992 s 198F (Qualification for roll-over relief);
TCGA 1992 s 198G (Qualification for section 153 relief);
TCGA 1992 s 198H (Acquisition by member of same group);
TCGA 1992 s 198I (Exploration, appraisal and development expenditure);
TCGA 1992 s 198J (Oil and gas: reinvestment after pre-trading disposal);
TCGA 1992 s 198K (Provisional application of section 198J);

TCGA 1992 s 198L (Expenditure by member of same group);
TCGA 1992 s 199 (Exploration or exploitation assets: deemed disposals);
TCGA 1992 s 201 (Mineral leases: royalties)
TCGA 1992 s 202 (capital losses);
TCGA 1992 s 203 (Provisions supplementary to TCGA 1992 ss 201 and 202);
TCGA 1992 s 276 (The territorial sea and the continental shelf).
The full text of TCGA 1992 is reproduced in Part 1a of this publication.

FINANCE (NO 2) ACT 1992

(1992 Chapter 48)

PART II
INCOME TAX, CORPORATION TAX AND CAPITAL GAINS TAX

CHAPTER I
Miscellaneous

55 Oil extraction activities: extended transportation

. . .

Amendments—This section repealed by CTA 2010 s 1181, Sch 3 Pt 2. CTA 2010 has effect for corporation tax purposes for accounting periods ending on or after 1 April 2010, and for income and capital gains tax purposes for the tax year 2010–11 and subsequent tax years.

PART III
MISCELLANEOUS AND GENERAL

Petroleum revenue tax

74 Oil exported direct from United Kingdom off-shore fields

(1) The enactments specified in Schedule 15 to this Act (being enactments relating to oil taxation) shall have effect subject to the amendments in that Schedule, being amendments—

(*a*) which take account, for the purpose of determining assessable profits and allowable losses, of certain cases where oil which is won from an off-shore oil field is, or could reasonably be expected to be, first landed in a country other than the United Kingdom; or

(*b*) which are consequential upon, or incidental to, the amendments referred to in paragraph (*a*) above.

(2) For the purposes of subsection (1)(*a*) above an oil field is an off-shore oil field if the whole of it is situated outside the geographical area of the United Kingdom (as determined under section 108 of the Finance Act 1986—the on-shore/off-shore boundary).

(3) In the amendments in Schedule 15 to this Act, any reference to a country other than the United Kingdom shall be treated as a reference to the geographical area of that country exclusive of any land (or waters) to the seaward side of the high-water line along the coast of that country, including the coast of all islands comprised in that country.

(4) For the purpose of subsection (3) above, section 108(5) of the Finance Act 1986 (which provides a means of determining the high-water line at any place in the United Kingdom) shall, with any necessary modifications, apply to determine the high-water line at any place in a country other than the United Kingdom.

(5) Except in so far as they have effect in relation to corporation tax or income tax, the amendments in Schedule 15 to this Act take effect as follows—

(*a*) in so far as they relate to expenditure incurred, they take effect for claim periods ending after 27 November 1991; and

(*b*) in so far as they relate to any other matter, they take effect for chargeable periods ending after 30 June 1992.

(6) This section shall be construed as one with Part I of the Oil Taxation Act 1975.

SCHEDULES

SCHEDULE 15

AMENDMENTS RELATING TO OIL EXPORTED DIRECTLY FROM OFF-SHORE FIELDS

Section 74

The Oil Taxation Act 1975

1 (*amends* OTA 1975 s 2(5A)).

2 (amends OTA 1975 s 3).

3 (amends OTA 1975 s 12(1)).

4 (amended OTA 1975 Sch 3 and is *repealed* in part by FA 2006 s 178, Sch 26 Pt 5(1)).

The Finance Act 1982

5 (*amends* FA 1982 Sch 18 para 3(2)).

The Oil Taxation Act 1983

6–8 (*amends* OTA 1983 Sch 1 para 1(4), Sch 2 para 12(3)(*a*), (*b*), Sch 4 para 11).

The Finance Act 1986

9 (*amends* FA 1986 Sch 21 para 5(1)).

SCHEDULE 16

GENERAL AND SPECIAL COMMISSIONERS

Section 76

Amendments—This Schedule repealed by the Transfer of Tribunal Functions and Revenue and Customs Appeals Order, SI 2009/56 art 3, Sch 1 para 186(*c*) with effect from 1 April 2009.

FINANCE ACT 1993

(1993 Chapter 34)

PART III

OIL TAXATION

185 Abolition of PRT for oil fields with development consents on or after 16 March 1993

[(A1) In this Part of this Act—

"non-taxable oil field" means an oil field which meets the conditions in subsection (1), (1ZA) or (1A), and

"taxable oil field" means an oil field which is not a non-taxable field.][2]

[(1) An oil field meets the conditions in this subsection if it is an oil field—][2]

(*a*) for no part of which consent for development was granted to a licensee by the Secretary of State before 16 March 1993; and

(*b*) for no part of which a programme of development was served on a licensee or approved by the Secretary of State before that date;

. . . [2]

[(1ZA) An oil field meets the conditions in this subsection if—

(*a*) the field does not meet the conditions in subsection (1), and

(*b*) an election under [Schedule 20B][3] that the field is to be non-taxable is in effect.][2]

[(1A) An oil field meets the conditions in this subsection if—

[(*za*) the field does not meet the conditions in subsection (1),][2]

(*a*) the Secretary of State has at any time approved one or more abandonment programmes under Part 4 of the Petroleum Act 1998 (or Part 1 of the Petroleum Act 1987) in relation to all assets of the field which are relevant assets;

(*b*) those programmes have been carried out to the satisfaction of the Secretary of State;

(*c*) a development decision is made in relation to the field; and

(*d*) that decision is made on or after 16th March 1993 and after those programmes have been so carried out.

(1B) For the purposes of subsection (1A)(*a*) above, an asset is a relevant asset of an oil field if—

(*a*) it has at any time been a qualifying asset (within the meaning of the 1983 Act) in relation to any participator in the field; and

(*b*) it has at any time been used for the purpose of winning oil from the field.

(1C) For the purposes of subsection (1A)(*c*) and (*d*) above, a development decision is made in relation to an oil field when—

(*a*) consent for development is granted to a licensee by the [OGA][4] in respect of the whole or part of the field; or

(*b*) a programme of development is served on a licensee or approved by the [OGA][4] for the whole or part of the field.][1]

(2) For the purposes of subsection (1) above, no account shall be taken, in relation to an oil field, of a consent for development granted before 16 March 1993 or a programme of development served on a licensee or approved by the Secretary of State before that date if—

(*a*) in whole or in part that consent or programme related to another oil field for which a determination under Schedule 1 to the principal Act was made before the determination under that Schedule for the field in question; and

PRT

(*b*) on or after 16 March 1993, a consent for development is or was granted or a programme of development is or was served on a licensee or approved by the [OGA][4] and that consent or programme relates, in whole or in part, to the field in question.

(3) Petroleum revenue tax shall not be charged in accordance with the Oil Taxation Acts in respect of—

(*a*) profits from oil won from a non-taxable field under the authority of such a licence as is referred to in section 1(1) of the principal Act; or

(*b*) any receipts accruing to a participator in a non-taxable field which, in the case of a taxable field, would be tariff receipts or disposal receipts attributable to the field for any period.

(4) Without prejudice to the generality of subsection (3) above—

(*a*)–(*c*) (*amends* OTA 1975 ss 1(2), 3(1D), 5B(6).

(*d*) no computation shall be made under the Oil Taxation Acts of the assessable profit or allowable loss accruing to a participator in any period from a non-taxable field; and

(*e*) no expenditure shall be regarded as allowable (or allowed) for a non-taxable field under the Oil Taxation Acts.

(5) (*amends* OTA 1975 s 12(1)).

(6) Subject to paragraphs (*b*) and (*c*) of subsection (4) above, where, apart from this section, expenditure incurred on or after 16 March 1993 would fall to be apportioned (as being allowable expenditure) between two or more oil fields, at least one of which is a non-taxable field, the apportionment shall be made as if all the fields were taxable fields, but subsection (4)(*e*) above shall then apply to any amount of expenditure apportioned to a non-taxable field.

(7) In [this section][1] above "development", in relation to an oil field, means—

(*a*) the erection or carrying out of permanent works for the purpose of getting oil from the field or for the purpose of conveying oil won from the field to a place on land; or

(*b*) winning oil from the field otherwise than in the course of searching for oil or drilling wells; and consent for development does not include consent which is limited to the purpose of testing the characteristics of an oil-bearing area and does not relate to the erection or carrying out of permanent works.

(8) In subsection (7) above "permanent works" means any structures or other works whatsoever which are intended by the licensee to be permanent and are neither designed to be moved from place to place without major dismantling nor intended by the licensee to be used only for searching for oil.

Amendments—[1] Sub-ss (1A)–(1C) inserted, and words in sub-s (7) substituted by FA 2007 s 102 with effect for an oil field which meets the conditions in sub-s (1A) that becomes a non-taxable field for the purposes of any enactment relating to petroleum revenue tax—

(a) in any case where the development decision is made before 1 July 2007, on that date, and

(b) in any other case, on the date on which the development decision is made.

[2] Sub-ss (A1), (1ZA), (1A)(*za*) inserted, and words in sub-s (1) substituted and repealed, by FA 2008 s 107 with effect from 21 July 2008.

[3] In sub-s (1ZA) words substituted for words "Schedule 20A" by FA 2009 s 91, Sch 45 para 3(2)(*c*) with effect from 21 July 2009.

[4] In sub-ss (1C)(*a*), (*b*), (2)(*b*), word substituted for words "Secretary of State" by the Petroleum (Transfer of Functions) Regulations, SI 2016/898 reg 12 with effect from 1 October 2016.

Prospective amendments–In sub-ss (1C)(*a*), (*b*), (2)(*b*), words "appropriate authority" to be substituted for word "OGA", and sub-s (2A) to be inserted, by the Wales Act 2017 s 69, Sch 6 para 22 with effect from a day to be appointed. Sub-s (2A) as inserted to read as follows—

"(2A) In subsections (1C) and (2), "the appropriate authority" means—

(*a*) in relation to a field that is wholly within the Welsh onshore area (as defined in section 8A of the Petroleum Act 1998), the Welsh Ministers;

(*b*) otherwise, the OGA."

186 Reduction of rates of PRT and interest repayments for taxable oil fields

(*amends* the Oil Taxation Act 1975, s 1(2), Sch 2, para 17(2), (4), and adds Sch 2, para 17(5)–(7)).

HMRC Manuals—Oil Taxation Manual 03515 (abolition of PRT: taxable and non-taxable fields).

187 Returns and information

(1) (*amends* OTA 1975 Sch 2 para 1; *repeals* OTA 1975 Sch 2 para 7).

(2) The Board may by notice in writing require a person—

(a) to deliver to a named officer of the Board such documents as are in the person's possession or power and as (in the Board's reasonable opinion) contain, or may contain, information relevant to—

(i) any tax liability to which that person is or may be subject, or

(ii) the amount of any such liability; or

(b) to furnish to a named officer of the Board such particulars as the Board may reasonably require as being relevant to, or to the amount of, any such liability.

(3) The Board may, for the purpose of enquiring into the tax liability of any person ("the taxpayer"), by notice in writing require any other person to deliver to or, if the person to whom the notice is given so elects, to make available for inspection by, a named officer of the Board, such documents—

(a) as are in his possession or power; and

(b) as (in the Board's reasonable opinion) contain, or may contain, information relevant to—

(i) any tax liability to which the taxpayer is or may be or may have been subject; or

(ii) the amount of any such liability.

(4) Subject to subsection (5) below, a notice under subsection (3) above shall name the taxpayer with whose liability the Board is concerned; and (for the avoidance of doubt) a company which has ceased to exist may be so named.

(5) If, on an application made by the Board, [the tribunal consents][1], the Board may give such a notice as is mentioned in subsection (3) above but without naming the taxpayer to whom the notice relates; but such a consent shall not be given unless the [tribunal][1] is satisfied—

(a) that the notice relates to a taxpayer whose identity is not known to the Board or to a class of taxpayers whose individual identities are not so known;

(b) that there are reasonable grounds for believing that the taxpayer or any of the class of taxpayers to whom the notice relates may have failed or may fail to comply with any provision of the Oil Taxation Acts;

(c) that any such failure is likely to have led or to lead to serious prejudice to the proper assessment or collection of tax; and

(d) that the information which is likely to be contained in any documents to which the notice relates is not readily available from another source.

(6) A person to whom a notice is given under subsection (5) above may, by notice in writing given to the Board within thirty days after the date of the notice under that subsection, object to that notice on the ground that it would be onerous for him to comply with it; and, if the matter is not resolved by agreement, it shall be referred to the [tribunal which][1] Special Commissioners who may confirm vary or cancel that notice.

(7) Subsections (2) to (6) above (which, in relation to petroleum revenue tax, contain provisions similar to those of section 20 of the Taxes Management Act 1970) shall have effect subject to Part I of Schedule 21 to this Act (which contains provisions similar to those of section 20B of that Act); and the provisions of Part II of that Schedule relating to the meaning of "documents" (which are derived from provisions of sections 20 and 20D of that Act) shall have effect.

(8) Section 98 of the Taxes Management Act 1970 (penalties, etc in relation to special returns) shall have effect as if, in the first column of the Table in that section, there were included a reference to subsections (2) to (6) above.[2]

Amendments—[1] In sub-s (5) words substituted in the first instance for the words "a Special Commissioner gives his consent" and in the second instance for "Special Commissioner"; in sub-s (6) words substituted for the words "Special Commissioner" by the Transfer of Tribunal Functions and Revenue and Customs Appeals Order, SI 2009/56 art 3, Sch 1 para 193 with effect from 1 April 2009.

[2] Sub-ss (2)–(8) repealed by the Finance Act 2009, Section 96 and Schedule 48 (Appointed Day, Savings and Consequential Amendments) Order, SI 2009/3054 art 3, Schedule para 5(a) with effect from 1 April 2010. Note that, in relation to a notice given under this section before 1 April 2010, sub-ss (6), (8) continue to have effect on and after 1 April 2010 despite their repeal by the Schedule to SI 2009/3054 (SI 2009/3054 art 5).

188 Exploration and appraisal expenditure

(*amends* the Oil Taxation Act 1975 s 5A(1), (2), adds s 5A(1A)–(1C)).

189 Transitional relief for certain exploration and appraisal expenditure

(1) This section applies in any case where—

(*a*) a participator in an oil field or an associate incurs expenditure on or after 16 March 1993 and before 1 January 1995; and

(*b*) apart from this section, that expenditure would not be allowable under section 5A of the principal Act (as amended by section 188 above); and

(*c*) if section 188 above had not been enacted, the expenditure would be allowable in the case of the participator under section 5A of the principal Act; and

(*d*) on 16 March 1993 the participator or the associate was a licensee in respect of the area to which the expenditure related.

(2) In the following provisions of this section—

(*a*) expenditure falling within subsection (1) above is referred to as "transitional E and A expenditure"; and

(*b*) the participator in whose case that expenditure would be allowable as mentioned in paragraph (*c*) of that subsection is referred to as "the claimant".

(3) Subject to the following provisions of this section, so much of the transitional E and A expenditure incurred by the claimant or an associate as does not in the aggregate exceed £10 million shall be allowable in the case of the claimant under section 5A of the principal Act (as exploration and appraisal expenditure).

(4) In subsections (1) to (3) above any reference to an associate of a participator applies only where the participator is a company and is a reference to another company—

(*a*) which on 16 March 1993 was a member of the same group of companies as the participator; and

PRT

(*b*) with which the participator is associated in respect of expenditure incurred by the other company;

and subsections (7) and (8) of section 5 of the principal Act (companies and associates etc) apply for the purposes of this section as they apply for the purposes of that section.

(5) Where—

(*a*) the claimant is a company, and

(*b*) on 16 March 1993 the claimant was a member of a group of companies, and

(*c*) at least one other company which was a member of the group on that date was then a participator in an oil field, and

(*d*) that other company is also the claimant in relation to an amount of transitional E and A expenditure,

subsection (3) above shall have effect as if references therein to the claimant were references to the aggregate of all those companies which on that date were members of the group and are the claimants in relation to any transitional E and A expenditure.

(6) In this section, a group of companies means a company which is not a 51 per cent subsidiary of any other company, together with each company which is its 51 per cent subsidiary; and section 838 of the Taxes Act 1988 (subsidiaries) applies for the purposes of this section as it applies for the purposes of the Tax Acts (within the meaning of that Act).

HMRC Manuals—Oil Taxation Manual 14040 (exploration and appraisal expenditure: transitional provisions).

190 Allowance of expenditure on certain assets limited by reference to taxable field use

(1) Where, in the case of expenditure incurred as mentioned in section 1(1) of the 1983 Act (expenditure incurred on non-dedicated mobile assets),—

(*a*) the expenditure would, apart from this subsection, be allowable under section 4 of the principal Act for a claim period of a taxable field, and

(*b*) during that claim period, the asset becomes dedicated to a non-taxable field,

that proportion of the expenditure which is equal to the proportion of the claim period during which the asset is dedicated to a non-taxable field shall not be allowable as mentioned in paragraph (a) above.

(2) For the purpose of determining whether an asset becomes at any time dedicated to a non-taxable field, it shall be assumed that, in relation to a non-taxable field, any reference in section 2 of the 1983 Act (dedicated mobile assets) to a claim period is a reference to—

(*a*) the period ending at the end of December following the determination of the field; or

(*b*) the period of twelve months ending at the end of December in any later year.

(3)–(5) (*amend* OTA 1983 Sch 1 paras 7(1)(*c*), 8, Sch 2 para 5).

191 Time when expenditure is incurred

(1) Subject to the following provisions of this section, where a claim is made under the principal Act for the allowance of any expenditure and the claim is received by the Board after 16 March 1993, an amount of expenditure is to be taken to be incurred for the purposes of the Oil Taxation Acts on the date on which the obligation to pay that amount becomes unconditional (whether or not there is a later date on or before which the whole or any part of that amount is required to be paid).

(2) Subject to subsection (3) below, where the amount of any expenditure incurred by any person at any time after 16 March 1993 under a contract—

(*a*) for the acquisition from any other person of, or of an interest in, an asset, or

(*b*) for the provision by any other person of services or other business facilities of whatever kind (whether in connection with the use of an asset or not), or

(*c*) for the grant or transfer to that person by any other person of any right, licence or interest (other than an interest in an asset)

is disproportionate to the extent to which that other person has, at or before that time, performed his obligations under the contract then, for the purposes of the Oil Taxation Acts, only so much of the expenditure shall be taken to have been incurred at that time as is proportionate to those obligations which have been so performed.

(3) If, in the case of a contract entered into after 16 March 1993 and falling within paragraph (*a*) or paragraph (*b*) of subsection (2) above—

(*a*) the expenditure referred to in that subsection is incurred before 1 July 1993, and

(*b*) the other person referred to in paragraph (*a*) or paragraph (*b*) ("the contractor") has performed his obligations by entering into one or more further contracts,

the contractor shall be treated for the purposes of subsection (2) above as having at any time performed his obligations under the contract only to the extent that, at that time, the asset or interest in question has been acquired by, or, as the case may be, the services or other business facilities have been provided to, the person incurring the expenditure.

(4), (5) (*amend* OTA 1975 Sch 4 para 2).

(6) The amendments made by subsections (4) and (5) above have effect where the transaction to which paragraph 2 of Schedule 4 to the principal Act applies takes place on or after 16 March 1993.

192 Chargeable periods in which expenditure may be brought into account

(1) Where a claim which—

(*a*) is made under Schedule 5 or Schedule 6 to the principal Act for the allowance of any expenditure, and

(*b*) is received by the Board after 16 March 1993,

has been allowed, the expenditure shall not be brought into account in determining the assessable profit or allowable loss of any chargeable period which ends earlier than the last day of the claim period in which the expenditure was incurred.

(2) Where a claim has been made under Schedule 7 to the principal Act for the allowance of any expenditure incurred after 31 March 1993 and that claim has been allowed, the expenditure shall not be brought into account in determining the assessable profit or allowable loss of any chargeable period which ends before the date on which the expenditure was incurred.

(3) The preceding provisions of this section have effect notwithstanding anything in subsection (9) of section 2 of the principal Act (under which expenditure which had been allowed might in certain cases be taken into account in earlier chargeable periods) and, accordingly, at the beginning of that subsection there shall be inserted "Subject to section 192 of the Finance Act 1993".

193 Tariff receipts etc

(1) (*amends* OTA 1983 s 9(5), *inserts* s 9(5A)).

(2) Where a participator in a taxable field incurs any expenditure and,—

(*a*) apart from this subsection, the expenditure would be taken into account in determining the assessable profit or allowable loss accruing to that participator from the taxable field in any chargeable period, and

(*b*) in the hands of the recipient, the expenditure would, on the relevant assumptions, constitute tariff receipts or disposal receipts of a participator in a non-taxable field attributable to that field for any period, and

(*c*) at the time the expenditure is incurred, the participator referred to in paragraph (*a*) above is or is connected with a participator in the non-taxable field referred to in paragraph (*b*) above,

the expenditure shall be disregarded in determining the assessable profit or allowable loss referred to in paragraph (a) above.

(3) For the purposes of subsection (2) above, the relevant assumptions are—

(*a*) that the non-taxable field is a taxable field; and(*b*) that the asset which gives rise to the expenditure (by virtue of its use, the provision of services or other business facilities in connection with its use or its disposal) is a qualifying asset in relation to the participator in question.

(4) (*amends* OTA 1983 s 12(3)).

(5) (*inserts* OTA 1983 s 12(3A)).

(6) In this section "disposal receipts", "qualifying asset" and "tariff receipts" have the same meaning as in the 1983 Act; and [section 1122 of the Corporation Tax Act 2010][1] (connected persons) applies for the purposes of subsection (2)(*c*) above.

Amendments—[1] In sub-s (6) words substituted for words "section 839 of the Taxes Act 1988" by CTA 2010 s 1177, Sch 1 para 278. CTA 2010 has effect for corporation tax purposes for accounting periods ending on or after 1 April 2010, and for income and capital gains tax purposes for the tax year 2010–11 and subsequent tax years.

194 Double taxation relief in relation to petroleum revenue tax

. . .

Rewrite destinations—Sub-s (1) rewritten to TIOPA 2010 ss 2(1)–(3), 3(1)–(3), 6(4), 124(1), 125(1).
Sub-s (3) rewritten to TIOPA 2010 s 6(4).
Sub-s (4) rewritten to TIOPA 2010 s Sch 8 para 7.
Sub-s (5) rewritten to TIOPA 2010 s 129(1)–(4).

Amendments—This section repealed by TIOPA 2010 ss 374, 378, Sch 8 paras 48, 49, Sch 10 Pt 1. TIOPA 2010 has effect for corporation tax purposes for accounting periods ending on or after 1 April 2010, for income and capital gains tax purposes for the tax year 2010–11 and subsequent tax years, and for petroleum revenue tax purposes for chargeable periods beginning on or after 1 July 2010.

195 Interpretation of Part III and consequential amendments of assessments etc

(1) In this Part—

(*a*) "the principal Act" means the Oil Taxation Act 1975;(*b*) "the 1983 Act" means the Oil Taxation Act 1983;

(*c*) "the Oil Taxation Acts" means Parts I and III of the principal Act, the 1983 Act and any other enactment relating to petroleum revenue tax; and

(*d*) "taxable field" and "non-taxable field" shall be construed in accordance with section 185 above.

(2) The Board may make all such amendments of assessments or determinations or of decisions on claims as may be necessary in consequence of the provisions of this Part.

(3) This Part . . . [1] shall be construed as one with Part I of the principal Act.

Amendments—[1] In sub-s (3), words ", other than section 194," repealed by TIOPA 2010 ss 374, 378, Sch 8 paras 48, 50, Sch 10 Pt 1. TIOPA 2010 has effect for corporation tax purposes for accounting periods ending on or after 1 April 2010, for income and capital gains tax purposes for the tax year 2010–11 and subsequent tax years, and for petroleum revenue tax purposes for chargeable periods beginning on or after 1 July 2010.

PART VI
MISCELLANEOUS AND GENERAL

Statutory effect of resolutions etc

205 The 1968 Act

(1) The Provisional Collection of Taxes Act 1968 shall be amended as follows.
(2)–(5) (*amends* PCTA 1968 s 1).
(6) (*amends* PCTA 1968 s 5).
(7) This section shall apply in relation to resolutions passed after the day on which this Act is passed.

Miscellaneous

209 Gas levy

Amendments—This section repealed with effect in relation to gas levy for the year 1998–99 and subsequent years of assessment subject to savings in relation to sub-s (3) which read as follows—

"(3) Where a person ceases to be liable to pay gas levy in respect of any gas won by him by virtue of the fact that winning the gas, in accordance with a contract or document, has ceased to be commercially viable, then, with respect to any chargeable period which ends—
(*a*) after that cessation of liability to pay gas levy, and
(*b*) after 30 June 1993,
any oil (whether or not consisting of gas) won and saved from the field from which the gas is won shall cease to be disregarded under section 10(1)(*b*) of the Oil Taxation Act 1975 (PRT disregard of up to 5 per cent of oil production incidental to the production of gas sold to the British Gas Corporation).".

SCHEDULES
[SCHEDULE 20[B][2]
PRT: ELECTIONS FOR OIL FIELDS TO BECOME NON-TAXABLE][1]

Amendments—[1] Schedule 20A inserted by FA 2008 s 107, Sch 33 para 1 with effect from 21 July 2008.
[2] Sch 20A renumbered as Sch 20B by FA 2009 s 91, Sch 45 para 3(1) with effect from 21 July 2009.

[Election by responsible person

1—(1) The responsible person for a taxable field may make an election that the field is to be non-taxable.
(2) An election is irrevocable.
(3) The responsible person may not make an election unless each person who is a participator at the time the election is made agrees to the election being made.
(4) If the responsible person makes an election, the Commissioners may assume that each participator agrees to the election being made (unless it appears to the Commissioners that a participator does not agree).][1]

Amendments—[1] Schedule 20A inserted by FA 2008 s 107, Sch 33 para 1 with effect from 21 July 2008.

[Method of election

2 An election must be made in writing.][1]

Amendments—[1] Sub-paras (2)–(7) substituted for sub-paras (2)–(12) by F(No 2)A 2017 s 44(1) with effect from 23 November 2016.

[3 An election must be notified to the Commissioners.][1]

Amendments—[1] Sub-paras (2)–(7) substituted for sub-paras (2)–(12) by F(No 2)A 2017 s 44(1) with effect from 23 November 2016.

[4 An election is deemed to have been made on the date on which notification of the election was sent to the Commissioners.][1]

Amendments—[1] Sub-paras (2)–(7) substituted for sub-paras (2)–(12) by F(No 2)A 2017 s 44(1) with effect from 23 November 2016.

[Effect of election

5 If an election is made, the field ceases to be taxable with effect from the start of the first chargeable period to begin after the election is made.][1]

Amendments—[1] Sub-paras (2)–(7) substituted for sub-paras (2)–(12) by F(No 2)A 2017 s 44(1) with effect from 23 November 2016.

[No unrelievable field losses from field

6 From the start of the first chargeable period to begin after an election is made, no allowable loss that accrues from the oil field is an allowable unrelievable field loss for the purposes of petroleum revenue tax.][1]

Amendments—[1] Sub-paras (2)–(7) substituted for sub-paras (2)–(12) by F(No 2)A 2017 s 44(1) with effect from 23 November 2016.

[Interpretation

7 (1) In this Schedule—

"Commissioners" means the Commissioners for Her Majesty's Revenue and Customs;

"participator", in relation to a particular time, means a person who is a participator in the chargeable period which includes that time.

(2) Expressions used in this Schedule and in Part 1 of the Oil Taxation Act 1975 have the same meaning in this Schedule as in Part 1 of that Act.][1]

Amendments—[1] Sub-paras (2)–(7) substituted for sub-paras (2)–(12) by F(No 2)A 2017 s 44(1) with effect from 23 November 2016.

SCHEDULE 21

OIL TAXATION: SUPPLEMENTARY PROVISIONS ABOUT INFORMATION

Section 187

Amendments—This Schedule repealed by the Finance Act 2009, Section 96 and Schedule 48 (Appointed Day, Savings and Consequential Amendments) Order, SI 2009/3054 art 3, Schedule para 5(b) with effect from 1 April 2010.

FINANCE ACT 1994

(1994 Chapter 9)

PART V
OIL TAXATION

CHAPTER I

ELECTION BY REFERENCE TO PIPE-LINE USAGE

231 Election by reference to pipe-line with excess capacity

(1) The provisions of this Chapter apply where, on or before 1 January 1996, a participator in a taxable field makes, in accordance with Part I of Schedule 22 to this Act, an election with respect to that field by reference to a pipe-line—

(*a*) which is a qualifying asset;

(*b*) which is used or intended to be used for transporting oil in circumstances which give rise or are expected to give rise to tariff receipts;

(*c*) which, at the date of the election, is at least 25 kilometres in length; and

(*d*) for which the initial usage fraction does not exceed one-half.

(2) A participator may not make an election—

(*a*) unless the field to which the election applies is (or, as the case may be, is intended to be) the chargeable field in relation to the tariff receipts referred to in subsection (1)(*b*) above; or

(*b*) if the first chargeable period of that field ended on or before 30 June 1982; or

(*c*) if the participator's net profit period with respect to that field ended on or before 30 June 1993;

and for the purposes of paragraph (c) above no account shall be taken of the operation of section 113 of the Finance Act 1981 (loss following net profit period).

(3) If there is more than one pipe-line by reference to which the electing participator could, apart from this subsection, make an election (with respect to the same field) he may make an election only by reference to that pipe-line which is the longer or longest.

(4) In this Chapter, in relation to a pipe-line or an election made by reference to a pipe-line, "the initial usage fraction" means the fraction of which—

(*a*) the numerator is the daily contracted and production throughput of oil in relation to the pipe-line on 16 March 1993; and

(*b*) the denominator is the design capacity of the pipe-line, expressed on a daily basis.

(5) Subject to subsection (6) below, where an election is in operation it shall apply to all those assets which, by reference to the field to which the election applies, are at the date of the election or subsequently become—

(*a*) qualifying assets in relation to the electing participator; and (*b*) assets to which are or are expected to be referable any tariff receipts of the electing participator attributable to that field.

(6) If the electing participator specifies in his election that the election is to be limited to oil which is, or is expected to be, transported by the pipe-line by reference to which the election is made, the election shall apply only to such of the assets referred to in subsection (5) above as, in whole or in part, are or subsequently become used in connection with that oil.

(7) For the purposes of this Chapter, unless it is just and reasonable to determine some other quantity of oil, the daily contracted and production throughput of oil in relation to a pipe-line on 16 March 1993 is the aggregate of—

(*a*) the maximum daily capacity specified in contracts then in force for the use of the pipe-line (whether at that date or in the future) for transporting oil won from any taxable field (including the field to which the election applies); and

(*b*) the maximum expected daily throughput, otherwise than pursuant to such contracts, of oil transported by the pipe-line and won from the field to which the election applies or any other taxable field, being the throughput ascertained by reference to what was at that date the most recent development plan applicable to the field to which the election applies or, as the case may be, the other taxable field.

(8) For the purposes of this Chapter, unless it is just and reasonable to determine some other capacity, the design capacity of a pipe-line is that which is specified for the pipe-line as a whole in what was, on 16 March 1993, the most recent development plan applicable to the field to which the election applies or, as the case may be, the pipe-line itself.

232 Restriction on electing participator's allowable expenditure on elected assets

(1) This section has effect in relation to expenditure which is incurred on an asset to which an election applies; and in this section "allowable or allowed", in relation to any expenditure, means allowable or allowed under any of the expenditure relief provisions.

(2) Subject to the following provisions of this section, in the case of expenditure incurred before the date of the election, the amount which, apart from this section, would be allowable or allowed in the case of the electing participator shall be reduced by multiplying it by the initial usage fraction.

(3) Subject to subsection (5) below, in the case of expenditure incurred on or after the date of the election, the amount which, apart from this section, would be allowable or allowed in the case of the electing participator shall be reduced to nil.

(4) Where, after 30 November 1993 and before the date of the election, expenditure was incurred on an asset to which the election applies and—

(*a*) apart from this section, that expenditure would have qualified for supplement by virtue of paragraph (*c*) or paragraph (*d*) of subsection (5) of section 3 of the principal Act, and

(*b*) the effect of the expenditure is to increase the maximum capacity of the pipe-line by reference to which the election was made above its design capacity or to increase the capacity of any asset used or to be used for the initial treatment or initial storage of oil transported by the pipe-line above its development plan capacity,

that expenditure shall be treated for the purposes of the application of subsections (2) and (3) above as if it had been incurred after the date of the election.

(5) Where, at the date of the election, an asset to which the election applies is for the time being leased or hired under a contract which was entered into before 16 March 1993, any expenditure—

(*a*) which is incurred on or after the date of the election on the leasing or hiring of the asset under the contract, and

(*b*) which is not of a description falling within paragraphs (*a*) and (*b*) of subsection (4) above,

shall be treated for the purposes of the application of subsections (2) and (3) above as if it had been incurred before the date of the election.

(6) For the purposes of subsection (4)(*b*) above, the development plan capacity of any asset used or to be used for the initial treatment or initial storage of oil transported by a pipe-line is—

(*a*) the maximum capacity of that asset as specified in what, on 16 March 1993, was the most recent development plan applicable to the field to which the election applies or, as the case may be, to the asset itself; or

(*b*) if no such maximum capacity was so specified in relation to an asset, its actual maximum capacity on that date or, if there was no such capacity on that date, nil.

(7) Where a claim under Schedule 5 or Schedule 6 to the principal Act relates to the allowance of any expenditure to which subsection (2) above applies, the amount claimed shall take account of the operation of that subsection; and where subsection (3) above applies to any expenditure, no such claim shall be made with respect to it.

(8) Where a claim has been made under Schedule 5 or Schedule 6 to the principal Act with respect to any expenditure and, subsequently, an election is made which has the effect of altering the amount of expenditure which is allowable or allowed,—

(*a*) a notice of variation such as is mentioned in paragraph 9 of Schedule 5 to the principal Act may be served after the end of the period referred to in sub-paragraph (1) of that paragraph if it is served before the expiry of the period of three years beginning on the date of the election; and

(*b*) if the effect of such a notice is that the net profit period with respect to the field to which the election applies is changed, the change shall not (by virtue of section 231(2) above) affect the validity of the election.

(9) Nothing in this section affects the determination of the question whether an asset is a qualifying asset for the purposes of the 1983 Act and, accordingly, for that purpose, the preceding provisions of this section shall be disregarded in determining whether any expenditure is allowable or allowed.

233 Tax relief for certain receipts of an electing participator

(1) If any sum—

(*a*) is received or receivable by the electing participator on or after the date of an election, and

(*b*) is so received or receivable from [any person][1] in respect of the use, [otherwise than in connection with a taxable field][1], of an asset to which the election applies or the provision of services or other business facilities of whatever kind in connection with that use, and

(*c*) would, apart from this section, constitute a tariff receipt attributable to the field to which the election applies,

that sum shall not be regarded as a tariff receipt for the purposes of the Oil Taxation Acts.

(2) If any sum—

(a) is received or receivable by the electing participator on or after the date of an election, and

(*b*) is so received or receivable in respect of the disposal of an asset to which the election applies or of an interest in such an asset, and

(*c*) constitutes a disposal receipt of the electing participator attributable to the field to which to the election applies,

that sum shall, for the purposes of the Oil Taxation Acts, be taken to be reduced in accordance with subsection (4) below.

(3) Any reference in subsection (1) or subsection (2) above to a sum received or receivable includes a reference to an amount which (apart from this section) would be treated as a tariff receipt or disposal receipt by virtue of paragraph 5 of Schedule 2 to the 1983 Act (acquisition and disposal of qualifying assets otherwise than at arm's length).

(4) Unless it is just and reasonable to make a different reduction, the reduction referred to in subsection (2) above shall be determined by reference to that applicable under subsection (2) or subsection (3) of section 232 above to the expenditure incurred on the asset concerned so that if, for the purposes of determining under those subsections the amount of that expenditure which was allowed or allowable,—

(*a*) the whole or any part of that expenditure was reduced by multiplying it by the initial usage fraction, or

(*b*) the whole or any part of that expenditure was reduced to nil,

a similar reduction shall apply to the whole or, as the case may require, to each correspondingly proportionate part of any sum falling within subsection (2) above.

(5) In this section "the Oil Taxation Acts" means Parts I and III of the principal Act, the 1983 Act and any other enactment relating to petroleum revenue tax.

Amendments—[1] Words in sub-s (1)(*b*) substituted by FA 1999 s 101 with effect in relation to sums received or receivable in any chargeable period ending on or after 31 December 1999.

234 Interpretation of Chapter and supplementary provisions

(1) In this Chapter "the 1983 Act" means the Oil Taxation Act 1983 and expressions used in this Chapter have the same meaning as in that Act.

(2) In this Chapter—

(*a*) "election" means an election under section 231 above and "electing participator" means a participator who makes or has made an election;

(*b*) "the expenditure relief provisions" means sections 3 and 4 of the principal Act and section 3 of the 1983 Act; and

(*c*) "the initial usage fraction" shall be construed in accordance with section 231(4) above.

(3) In this Chapter—

(*a*) any reference to the assets to which an election applies is a reference to the pipe-line by reference to which the election is made together with the assets determined in accordance with subsections (5) and (6) of section 231 above;

(*b*) any reference to the net profit period is a reference to the chargeable period which is the net profit period for the purposes of section 111 of the Finance Act 1981 (restriction of expenditure supplement); and

(*c*) any reference to a development plan is a reference to a consent for, or programme of, development granted, served or approved by the Secretary of State.

(4) Any reference in this Chapter to expenditure incurred on an asset is a reference to expenditure (whether or not of a capital nature) which—

(*a*) is incurred in acquiring, bringing into existence or enhancing the value of the asset, or

(*b*) is incurred (for any of the purposes mentioned in section 3(1) of the principal Act) by reference to the use of the asset in connection with a taxable field,

other than expenditure which, in the hands of the recipient, constitutes a tariff receipt.

(5) For the purposes of this Chapter—

(*a*) an election is "in operation" if it has been accepted by the Board; and

(*b*) the date of an election which is in operation is the date on which the election was received by the Board.

(6) The provisions of Part II of Schedule 22 to this Act shall have effect for supplementing the preceding provisions of this Chapter.

(7) The Board may make all such amendments of assessments or determinations or of decisions on claims as may be necessary in consequence of the provisions of this Chapter.

CHAPTER II

MISCELLANEOUS

235 Valuation of oil

(1) (*amends* OTA 1975 s 2(5A) and is *repealed* in part by FA 2006 s 178, Sch 26 Pt 5(1)).

(2)–(5) (*amend* OTA Sch 3 paras 2, 2A, Sch 10 paras 4, 11 and is *repealed* in part by FA 2006 s 178, Sch 26 Pt 5(1)).

236 Valuation of certain light gases

(1) Subject to subsection (2) below, the principal Act shall have effect subject to the amendments in Schedule 23 to this Act, being—

(*a*) amendments altering the rules for determining the market value of certain light gases for the purposes of petroleum revenue tax; and

(*b*) amendments consequential upon, or incidental to, those amendments.

(2) The amendments in Schedule 23 to this Act do not have effect in relation to any light gases if, before 1 January 1994, an election was made under section 134 of the Finance Act 1982 (alternative valuation of certain ethane) or section 109 of the Finance Act 1986 (alternative valuation of certain light gases) and the election applies to those gases.

(3) No election may be made after 31 December 1993 under section 134 of the Finance Act 1982 or section 109 of the Finance Act 1986; and, accordingly—

(*a*), (*b*) (*amend* FA 1982 s 134(2) and FA 1986 s 109(1)).

(4) (*amends* OTA 1975 s 12(1)).

237 Abortive exploration expenditure

(1) (*adds* OTA 1975 s 5(2A)).

(2) Subsection (1) above shall be deemed to have come into force at the same time as Part III of the Finance Act 1993 (27 July 1993).

(3) The Board may make all such amendments of assessments or determinations or of decisions on claims as may be necessary in consequence of the preceding provisions of this section.

238 Disposals of assets producing tariff receipts

(1) With respect to disposals made after 30 November 1993, paragraph 5 of Schedule 2 to the Oil Taxation Act 1983 (acquisition and disposal of qualifying assets otherwise than at arm's length: limit on tariff and disposal receipts) shall be amended in accordance with subsections (2) and (3) below; and in this subsection "disposal" has the same meaning as in that paragraph.

(2), (3) (*amend* OTA 1983 Sch 2 para 5).

(4) The Board may make all such amendments of assessments or determinations or of decisions on claims as may be necessary in consequence of the preceding provisions of this section.

SCHEDULES

SCHEDULE 22

SUPPLEMENTARY PROVISIONS AS TO ELECTIONS BY REFERENCE TO PIPE-LINE USAGE

Sections 231, 234

PART I

PROCEDURE FOR AND IN CONNECTION WITH AN ELECTION

The election

1—(1) An election shall be made by serving it on the Board, shall be in such form as may be prescribed by the Board and shall contain such information as the Board may reasonably require with respect to—

(*a*) the oil field to which the election is to apply, the pipe-line by reference to which the election is being made and whether the election is to be with subsection (6) of section 231 of this Act;

(*b*) all other assets which, if the election were to be accepted, would at the date of the election be assets to which the election applies;

(*c*) the electing participator's interest in those assets;

(*d*) the sums to which, if the election is accepted, it is reasonable to expect that section 233 of this Act will apply and the sources, quantities and descriptions of oil which will give rise to those sums;

(*e*) any other oil field (whether taxable or non-taxable) in connection with which any of the assets referred to in paragraph (*b*) above is or is expected to be used or in respect of which services or other business facilities in connection with that use are or are expected to be provided; and

(*f*) the initial usage fraction and the amounts which make up the numerator and the denominator of that fraction.

(2) The reference in sub-paragraph (1)(*e*) above to an oil field includes a reference to any area which the electing participator expects might be determined as an oil field under Schedule 1 to the principal Act.

(3) An election shall include a declaration that it is correct and complete to the best of the knowledge and belief of the electing participator.

(4) An election shall be irrevocable.

2—(1) The Board shall reject an election if they are not satisfied—

(*a*) that the conditions relating to the pipe-line in paragraphs (*a*) to (*d*) of subsection (1) or in subsection (3) of section 231 of this Act are fulfilled; or

(*b*) that the conditions relating to the oil field or the participator in subsection (2) of that section are fulfilled; or

(*c*) that, if the election were to be accepted, the assets to which the election would apply (having regard to any limitation under subsection (6) of that section) have the capacity and characteristics, and are otherwise suitable, to handle the quantities and descriptions of oil specified in accordance with paragraph 1(1)(*d*) above.

(2) Subject to sub-paragraph (3) below, the Board shall also reject an election if it appears to them—

(*a*) that any of the information required to be contained in the election by virtue of paragraph 1(1) above is incorrect; or

(*b*) that, after receiving notice in writing from the Board, the electing participator has failed to furnish to the Board on or before the specified date any information which the Board have reasonably required either with respect to the matters specified in paragraph 1(1) above or for the purpose of satisfying themselves as to the matters referred to in sub-paragraph (1) above.

(3) Before rejecting an election under sub-paragraph (2)(*a*) above the Board may, if they think fit, by notice in writing give the electing participator an opportunity to correct any error in the information and, if he does so, the information shall then be treated as having been provided in the correct form.

(4) In sub-paragraph (2)(*b*) above "the specified date" means such date as may be specified in the notice concerned, being a date not earlier than one month after the date on which the notice was given.

(5) A notice under sub-paragraph (2)(*b*) above shall be given within the period of three months beginning on the date on which the election was received by the Board.

3—(1) Notice of the acceptance or rejection of an election shall be served on the electing participator before the expiry of the period of three months beginning on whichever of the following dates is the later or latest—

(*a*) the date on which the election was received by the Board;

PRT

(*b*) if a notice was given under paragraph 2(2)(*b*) above relating to the election, the date or, as the case may be, the last date which is the specified date, as defined in paragraph 2(4) above, in relation to such a notice;

(*c*) if a notice was given under paragraph 2(3) above relating to the election, the date on which that notice was given.

(2) If no such notice of acceptance or rejection is so served, the Board shall be deemed to have accepted the election and to have served notice of their acceptance on the last day of the period referred to in sub-paragraph (1) above.

4—(1) Where the Board serve notice on an electing participator under paragraph 3 above rejecting an election, he may appeal . . . [1] against the notice.

(2) An appeal under sub-paragraph (1) above shall be made by notice of appeal served on the Board within thirty days beginning on the date of the notice in respect of which the appeal is brought.

(3) Where, at any time after the service of notice of appeal under this paragraph and before the determination of the appeal by the [tribunal][1], the Board and the appellant agree that the notice in respect of which the appeal is brought should stand or that the election to which it related should be accepted with or without modification, the same consequences shall ensue as if the [tribunal][1] had determined the appeal to that effect.

(4) On the hearing of an appeal under this paragraph, the [tribunal][1] shall either dismiss the appeal or allow it; and if the [tribunal allows][1] the appeal, [the tribunal shall][1] direct either—

(*a*) that the election shall be accepted; or

(*b*) that the election shall have effect subject to such modifications as may be specified in the direction and shall be accepted in its modified form.

[(5) In an appeal under sub-paragraph (1)—

(*a*) paragraphs 14(2), (8) and (11) and 14A to 14I of Schedule 2 to the principal Act shall apply as they apply in relation to an appeal against an assessment or determination made under that Act subject to any necessary modifications including the following;

(*b*) any reference in those paragraphs to an agreement under paragraph 14(9) shall be construed as a reference to an agreement under sub-paragraph (3) above.][1]

(6) Any reference in this Chapter to an election accepted by the Board shall be construed as including a reference to an election accepted in pursuance of an appeal under this paragraph.

Amendments—[1] In sub-para (1), words "to the Special Commissioners" repealed, in sub-paras (3), (4), word substituted for word "Commissioners", in sub-para (4) words substituted for words "Commissioners allow" and "they shall", and sub-para (5) substituted, by the Transfer of Tribunal Functions and Revenue and Customs Appeals Order, SI 2009/56 art 3, Sch 1 paras 196, 211 with effect from 1 April 2009.

5—(1) Within thirty days of the relevant date, the electing participator shall furnish to the responsible person for the field to which the election applies (or would apply if the election were accepted) a copy of—

(*a*) any election made by him; and

(*b*) any notice under paragraph 3 above accepting or rejecting the election.

(2) For the purposes of sub-paragraph (1) above, the relevant date is—

(*a*) in the case of an election made by the electing participator, the date on which it was served on the Board; and

(*b*) in the case of a notice under paragraph 3 above, the date on which the electing participator received it.

(3) In a case where paragraph 9 below applies (or would apply if an election were accepted) sub-paragraphs (1) and (2) above shall require the electing participator additionally to furnish copies of the same documents to the responsible person for any non-chargeable field mentioned in sub-paragraph (3) of that paragraph.

(4) In a case where paragraph 11 below applies (or would apply if an election were accepted) sub-paragraphs (1) and (2) above shall require the electing participator additionally to furnish copies of the same documents to the old participator referred to in that paragraph.

6 Where a participator fraudulently or negligently furnishes any incorrect information or makes any incorrect declaration in or in connection with an election he shall be liable to a penalty not exceeding—

(*a*) in the case of negligence, £50,000, and

(*b*) in the case of fraud, £100,000.

Re-opening election decisions on grounds of incorrect information

7—(1) Without prejudice to paragraph 6 above, this paragraph applies if, at any time after notice of the acceptance of an election has been served by the Board, it appears to the Board that, as a result of an error in the information furnished to the Board, the election should not have been accepted.

(2) If, in a case where this paragraph applies, either—

(*a*) the error was attributable, in whole or in part, to the fraudulent or negligent conduct of the electing participator or a person acting on his behalf, or

(*b*) on the error coming to the notice of the electing participator, or a person acting on his behalf, the error was not remedied without unreasonable delay,

the Board may serve on the electing participator and on the responsible person for the field to which the election applies a notice rescinding the acceptance and stating what appears to the Board to be the correct position,

(3) When a notice under sub-paragraph (2) above becomes effective, the election shall be treated as having been rejected in accordance with paragraph 3 above.

(4) If, in a case where this paragraph applies,—

(*a*) neither of the conditions in sub-paragraph (2) above is fulfilled, and

(*b*) the Board are of the opinion that, if the correct information had been furnished, the election could have been accepted, the election shall be treated as having been made and accepted subject to such modifications (being modifications to correct the effect of the error) as the Board may direct, by notice served on the electing participator and on the responsible person for the field to which the election applies.

(5) A notice served under sub-paragraph (2) or sub-paragraph (4) above shall become effective either—

(*a*) on the expiry of the period during which notice of appeal against the notice may be served on the Board under paragraph 8 below without such notice of appeal being served; or

(*b*) where such notice of appeal is served, when the notice can no longer be varied or quashed by the [tribunal][1] or by the order of any court.

Amendments—[1] In sub-para (5)(*b*), words substituted for words "Special Commissioners", by the Transfer of Tribunal Functions and Revenue and Customs Appeals Order, SI 2009/56 art 3, Sch 1 paras 196, 212 with effect from 1 April 2009.

Appeals against re-opening notices

8—(1) This paragraph applies where the Board serve notice under sub-paragraph (2) or sub-paragraph (4) of paragraph 7 above; and in the following provisions of this paragraph such a notice is referred to as a "re-opening notice".

(2) The electing participator may, by notice of appeal served on the Board within thirty days beginning on the date of the re-opening notice, appeal to the Special Commissioners against the re-opening notice.

(3) A notice of appeal under sub-paragraph (2) above shall state the grounds on which the appeal is brought.

(4) An appeal under this paragraph may at any time [before it is notified to the tribunal][1] be abandoned by notice served on the Board by the electing participator.

(5) A re-opening notice may be withdrawn at any time before it becomes effective.

(6) In any case where—

(*a*) the electing participator serves notice of appeal against a re-opening notice served under sub-paragraph (4) of paragraph 7 above, and

(*b*) before the appeal is determined by the [tribunal][1], the Board and the electing participator agree as to the modifications necessary to correct the effect of the error concerned,

the re-opening notice shall take effect subject to such modifications as may be necessary to give effect to that agreement; and thereupon the appeal shall be treated as having been abandoned.

(7) Subject to sub-paragraph (8) below, on an appeal against a re-opening notice the [tribunal][1] may vary the notice, quash the notice or dismiss the appeal; and the notice may be varied whether or not the variation is to the advantage of the electing participator.

(8) The provisions relating to the variation of a re-opening notice referred to in sub-paragraph (7) above shall not apply in respect of any such notice served under sub-paragraph (2) of paragraph 7 above.

[(9) In an appeal under sub-paragraph (2)—

(*a*) paragraphs 14A to 14I of Schedule 2 to the principal Act shall apply as they apply in relation to an appeal against an assessment or determination made under that Act subject to any necessary modifications including the following;

(*b*) any reference in those paragraphs to an agreement under paragraph 14(9) shall be construed as a reference to an agreement under sub-paragraph (6) above.][1]

Amendments—[1] In sub-para (2), words "to the Special Commissioners" repealed, in sub-para (4), words inserted, in sub-paras (6)(*b*), (7), word substituted for words "Special Commissioners", and sub-para (9) inserted, by the Transfer of Tribunal Functions and Revenue and Customs Appeals Order, SI 2009/56 art 3, Sch 1 paras 196, 213 with effect from 1 April 2009.

PART II
SUPPLEMENTARY PROVISIONS

Assets used in connection with more than one taxable field

9—(1) The provisions of this paragraph apply where—

(*a*) an election is in operation; and

(*b*) any of the assets to which the election applies is used or expected to be used in connection with two or more taxable fields.

(2) Any reference in this paragraph to allowable expenditure has the same meaning as in Part II of Schedule 1 to the 1983 Act and is a reference to expenditure incurred on an asset to which the election applies.

(3) Sub-paragraph (4) below applies if, by virtue of paragraph 5 of Schedule 1 to the 1983 Act (which, in a case falling within this paragraph, provides for the apportionment of allowable expenditure between two or more fields), any part of the allowable expenditure is apportioned to a taxable field (a "non-chargeable field") other than the field to which the election applies.

(4) Where this sub-paragraph applies, then, so far as concerns the electing participator (as a participator in a non-chargeable field), section 232 of this Act shall apply in relation to that part of the allowable expenditure which is apportioned to the non-chargeable field as it applies in relation to the part apportioned to the field to which the election applies.

Transfer of interests

10—(1) If, while an election is in operation, the electing participator (or a person who is treated as an electing participator by virtue of this paragraph) transfers the whole or part of his interest in the field to which the election applies, then, so far as concerns that interest or part, the new participator shall thereafter be treated as the electing participator for the purposes of this Chapter, other than paragraph 11 below, and, in particular,—

(*a*) any restriction on the amount of expenditure allowed or allowable by virtue of section 232 of this Act shall continue to apply to any expenditure relief transferred to the new participator under paragraph 6 of Schedule 17 to the Finance Act 1980; and

(*b*) any relief from tax under section 233 of this Act shall apply in relation to the new participator as it applied in relation to the old participator.

(2) If, in a case where paragraph 9 above applies, the electing participator, as a participator in the non-chargeable field (within the meaning of that paragraph) transfers the whole or part of his interest in that field, sub-paragraph (1) above (except paragraph (*b*)) shall apply in relation to that transfer as if—

(*a*) any reference to the field to which the election applies were a reference to the non-chargeable field; and

(*b*) any reference to the electing participator were a reference to him in his capacity as a participator in the non-chargeable field.

(3) In sub-paragraph (1) above the expressions "the old participator" and "the new participator" have the same meaning as in Schedule 17 to the Finance Act 1980.

11—(1) This paragraph applies in any case where—

(*a*) the electing participator acquired the whole or any part of his interest in the field to which the election applies as a result of a transfer to which Part I of Schedule 17 to the Finance Act 1980 applies (so that the electing participator is the new participator); and

(*b*) some or all of the relief in respect of any expenditure incurred (before the transfer) on any asset to which the election applies did not fall to be transferred to the electing participator (whether by virtue of paragraph 6 or paragraph 7 of that Schedule).

(2) With regard to so much of the expenditure referred to in sub-paragraph (1)(*b*) above as falls to be taken into account under paragraph (*b*)(i) or paragraph (*c*)(i) of subsection (9) of section 2 of the principal Act in computing, for any chargeable period ending before the transfer period, the assessable profit or allowable loss accruing to the old participator or any predecessor of his, section 232 of this Act, shall apply in the case of the old participator or, as the case may be, his predecessor as it is expressed to apply in the case of the electing participator.

(3) If, as a result of the operation of sub-paragraph (2) above, there is a reduction in the amount which would otherwise be the accumulated capital expenditure of the old participator at the end of the last chargeable period before the transfer period, paragraph 8 of Schedule 17 to the Finance Act 1980 shall be taken to have transferred a correspondingly reduced amount to the electing participator.

(4) In this paragraph—

(*a*) the expressions "the old participator", "the new participator" and "the transfer period" have the same meaning as in Schedule 17 to the Finance Act 1980; and (*b*) any reference to a predecessor of the old participator is a reference to a person who (before the transfer referred to in sub-paragraph (1)(*a*) above) transferred the whole or part of his interest in the field to which the election applies either to the old participator or to another person who is a predecessor in title of the old participator in respect of that interest or part.

Transfer of elected assets

12—(1) This paragraph applies if there is a disposal of an asset which, immediately before the disposal or at an earlier time, was an asset to which an election applies; and in this paragraph—

(*a*) "the asset transferred" means the asset so disposed of;

(*b*) "the vendor" means the electing participator or other person by whom the asset is disposed of.

(2) Where a person has incurred expenditure on the acquisition of a transferred asset, he shall be treated for the purposes of the expenditure relief provisions as having incurred that expenditure only to the extent that it does not exceed the amount which, having regard to section 232 of this Act or the previous operation of this paragraph, was (in the case of the vendor) allowable under those provisions immediately before the disposal in respect of his expenditure on the asset.

(3) Any expenditure incurred on the asset after the disposal shall be left out of account for the purposes of the expenditure relief provisions.

Restriction of relief for expenditure incurred after 30 November 1993 and before the date of an election

13—(1) This paragraph applies if, after 30 November 1993 and before the date of an election, expenditure was incurred by the electing participator under a contract—

(*a*) for the acquisition from any other person of, or of an interest in, an asset to which the election applies; or

(*b*) for the provision by any other person of services or other business facilities of whatever kind in connection with the use of an asset to which the election applies.

(2) If, in a case where this paragraph applies, the other person referred to in paragraph (*a*) or paragraph (*b*) of sub-paragraph (1) above ("the contractor") has performed his obligations by entering into one or more further contracts, the contractor shall be treated for the purposes of subsection (2) of section 191 of the Finance Act 1993 (time when expenditure is incurred) as having performed his obligations under the contract only to the extent that, at that time, the asset or interest in question has been acquired by or, as the case may be, the services or other business facilities have been provided to, the electing participator.

SCHEDULE 23

AMENDMENTS OF THE PRINCIPAL ACT RELATING TO VALUATION OF LIGHT GASES

Section 23

(*amends* OTA 1975 s 2(5), (9), Sch 2 para 2, Sch 3 paras 2, 2A, 3 and adds Sch 3 para 3A.)

FINANCE ACT 1995

(1995 Chapter 4)

PART IV

PETROLEUM REVENUE TAX

146 Restriction of unrelievable field losses

(*amends* OTA 1975 s 6; *part repealed* by FA 2001 s 110, Sch 33 Pt III(2) with effect from 7 March 2001).

147 Removal of time limits for claims for unrelievable field losses

(1) (*amends* OTA 1975 Sch 8 para 4).

(2) This section applies to claims made on or after the day on which this Act is passed.

148 Transfer of interests in fields: restriction of transferred losses

(*amends* FA 1980 Sch 17 para 7).

FINANCE ACT 1996

(1996 Chapter 8)

180 Scientific research expenditure: oil licences

Amendment—This section repealed by CAA 2001 ss 579, 580, Sch 4 with effect for corporation tax, as respects allowances and charges falling to be made for chargeable periods ending after 31 March 2001, and for income tax, as respects allowances and charges falling to be made for chargeable periods ending after 5 April 2001.

181 Overseas petroleum

(1) (*amends* TCGA 1992 s 196(1)).

(2) (*inserts* TCGA 1992 s 196(1A) and *amends* s 196(2)).

(3) (*amends* TCGA 1992 s 196(5), (5A)).

(4) Subsections (1) to (3) above shall have effect in relation to any disposal on or after 13 September 1995 and subsection (3) shall also have effect, and be deemed always to have had effect, for the construction of section 195 of the Taxation of Chargeable Gains Act 1992 in its application to disposals before that date.

(5) Where enactments re-enacted in the Taxation of Chargeable Gains Act 1992 apply, instead of that Act, in the case of any disposal before 13 September 1995, this section shall have effect as if it required amendments equivalent to those made by subsection (3) above to have effect, and be deemed always to have had effect, for the construction of any enactment corresponding to section 195 of that Act.

FINANCE ACT 1997

(1997 Chapter 16)

PART VIII

MISCELLANEOUS AND SUPPLEMENTAL

Petroleum revenue tax

107 Non-field expenditure allowable after transfer

(1)–(3) (*amend* FA 1984 s 113).

(4) This section has effect in relation to any expenditure in respect of which a claim is made on or after 23rd July 1996.

FINANCE ACT 1998

(1998 Chapter 36)

An Act to grant certain duties, to alter other duties, and to amend the law relating to the National Debt and the Public Revenue, and to make further provision in connection with Finance.

[31 July 1998]

Petroleum revenue tax etc

152 Gas valuation

(1) (*inserts* OTA 1975 Sch 3 para 3A).

(2) (*amends* OTA 1983 Sch 2 para 12).

(3) (*inserts* TA 1988 s 493(6)).

Amendments—Sub-s (3) repealed by CTA 2010 s 1181, Sch 3 Pt 2 with effect for corporation tax purposes only for accounting periods ending on or after 1 April 2010.

FINANCE ACT 1999

(1999 Chapter 16)

An Act to grant certain duties, to alter other duties, and to amend the law relating to the National Debt and the Public Revenue, and to make further provision in connection with Finance.

[27 July 1999]

PART IV

OIL TAXATION

94 Excluded oil

(1) This section applies where—

(*a*) a contract ("the old contract") provides for the sale by a person ("A") of oil consisting of gas to the British Gas Corporation or one of its successors ("the purchaser");

(*b*) the old contract is a contract made, or treated (by virtue of this section) as made, before the end of June 1975;

(*c*) the old contract is replaced by a contract ("the new contract") for the sale of oil consisting of gas to the purchaser made after the end of June 1975; and

(*d*) any of the rights and liabilities which, under the old contract, were rights and liabilities of A are, under the new contract, rights and liabilities of another person ("B").

(2) The new contract shall be treated for the purposes of section 10(1)(*a*) of the Oil Taxation Act 1975 as the same contract as the old contract unless the rights and liabilities of B under the new contract are so different from those of A under the old contract that a contract conferring those rights and imposing those liabilities on A could not have been regarded as the same contract as the old contract.

(3) For the purposes of subsection (1) above the successors of the British Gas Corporation are—

(*a*) British Gas plc; and

(*b*) British Gas Trading Limited.

(4) This section shall be deemed always to have had effect.

95 Sale and lease-back

(1) This section applies to a lease ("the lease in question") of an asset ("the relevant asset") where—

(*a*) a person ("the seller") who is a participator in an oil field ("the seller's oil field") has made a disposal in a chargeable period of the relevant asset or an interest in it;

(*b*) the relevant asset was a qualifying asset in relation to the seller and the seller's oil field is the chargeable field in relation to it;

(*c*) the relevant asset is used in connection with an oil field ("the lessee's oil field") by a participator in that field ("the lessee") under the lease in question;

(*d*) the seller, or a person connected with him at any time in the relevant period, is the lessee; and

(*e*) the lessee uses the relevant asset before the end of the period of two years beginning with the disposal.

(2) Subject to subsection (8) below, to the extent that the expenditure falling within subsection (3) below exceeds the amount of the cap, that expenditure shall not be allowable under section 3 or 4 of the principal Act or section 3 of the Oil Taxation Act 1983 for the lessee's oil field.

(3) That expenditure is the aggregate of the following—

(*a*) the total expenditure, excluding operating expenditure, incurred by the lessee under the lease in question; and

(*b*) if at any time after the disposal he acquires the relevant asset or an interest in it, the total expenditure (not falling within paragraph (*a*) above) incurred by him in acquiring the asset or interest.

(4) Subject to subsections (5) to (7) below—

(*a*) if the period in which the disposal was made is one in which the seller has benefited from safeguard relief, the amount of the cap is the smaller of—

(i) the amount given by dividing the marginal tax on the disposal receipts by the applicable rate of tax; and

(ii) the amount of the disposal receipts; and

(*b*) in any other case the amount of the cap is the amount of the disposal receipts.

(5) Subject to subsection (7) below, where at the relevant time there are, in relation to the relevant asset, two or more leases to which this section applies, the amount of the cap for the lease in question shall be the appropriate proportion of the cap found by applying subsection (4) above.

(6) For the purposes of subsection (5) above the appropriate proportion is the proportion given by the formula—

$$\frac{A}{B}$$

where—

A is the proportion of the total use of the relevant asset during the term of the lease in question that is expected to be use under the lease; and

B is—

(*a*) in a case where the seller disposed of the whole of the relevant asset, one; and

(*b*) in any other case, the proportion that the value of the interest disposed of by him bore to the total value of the relevant asset.

(7) Where at the relevant time the relevant asset is used, or is expected to be used, by the lessee under the lease in question in connection with two or more oil fields, the amount of the cap for each of the fields shall be so much of the cap found by applying subsections (4) to (6) above as accords with the proportion of the use of the asset under the lease that is expected, at that time, to be—

(*a*) use in connection with that field; or

(*b*) use giving rise to tariff receipts of the lessee attributable to that field.

(8) Where—

(*a*) expenditure falling within subsection (3) above has been allowed for the lessee's oil field, on a claim under Schedule 5 or 6 to the principal Act, on the basis that the cap was of a particular amount;

(*b*) information later becomes available to the Board which establishes that the cap is not of that amount; and

PRT

(*c*) the amount that was allowed exceeds the amount (if any) of the expenditure falling within that subsection that would have been allowed on the claim if the information had been available when the expenditure was allowed,

the excess shall continue to be allowable.

(9) Subject to subsection (10) below, this section and sections 96 and 97 below apply to assets, or interests in assets, disposed of on or after 9th March 1999.

(10) This section and those sections do not apply to assets, or interests in assets, disposed of pursuant to an agreement made before that date if—

(*a*) the agreement is not conditional; or

(*b*) the agreement is conditional and the condition is satisfied before that date.

96 Transfer of field interest

(1) This section applies where—

(*a*) section 95 above has applied to a lease;

(*b*) the lessee has transferred the whole or part of his interest in the lessee's oil field; and

(*c*) pursuant to the transfer, the relevant asset is used in connection with that oil field under a lease ("the new participator's lease") by the person who is the new participator in relation to the transfer.

(2) Subject to subsection (4) below, section 95 above shall have effect as if the new participator were the lessee and the new participator's lease were the lease in question.

(3) The reference in subsection (1)(*b*) above to the lessee includes a reference to a successor of his; and subject to subsection (4) below, the expenditure that the new participator is treated by virtue of subsection (2) above as having incurred includes—

(*a*) any expenditure, excluding operating expenditure, incurred by the lessee or a successor of his under the lease in question or a lease of the relevant asset; and

(*b*) any expenditure (not falling within paragraph (*a*) above) incurred by the lessee or a successor of his after the disposal mentioned in section 95(1)(*a*) above in acquiring the relevant asset or an interest in it.

(4) Where the transfer mentioned in subsection (1)(*b*) above, or any antecedent transfer, was a transfer of part of the transferor's interest in the lessee's oil field—

(*a*) the amount of the cap which is applicable by virtue of subsection (2) above shall be so much of the cap that would be applicable apart from this subsection as accords with the proportion of the lessee's interest in the field that is represented by the new participator's interest in the field; and

(*b*) the expenditure incurred (as mentioned in subsection (3) above) by the lessee or any successor of his that is treated, by virtue of subsection (2) above, as expenditure incurred by the new participator shall be so much of the expenditure incurred (as so mentioned) by the person concerned as accords with the proportion of that person's interest in the field that is represented by the new participator's interest in the field.

(5) A person is a successor of the lessee for the purposes of this section if and only if—

(*a*) this section has applied to an earlier transfer by the lessee or a successor of his of the whole or part of his interest in the lessee's oil field; and

(*b*) that person was the new participator in relation to the earlier transfer and used the relevant asset under the lease in connection with that oil field.

(6) In this section "antecedent transfer" means a transfer (other than the transfer mentioned in subsection (1)(*b*) above) by the lessee or a successor of his of the whole or part of his interest in the lessee's oil field, pursuant to which the relevant asset was used as mentioned in subsection (1)(*c*) above.

97 Provisions supplementary to ss 95 and 96

(1) For the purposes of section 95 above the marginal tax on the disposal receipts is the difference between—

(*a*) the amount of tax to which the seller is chargeable on the assessable profit accruing to him from the seller's oil field in the period in which the asset or interest was disposed of; and

(*b*) the amount of tax to which the seller would have been so chargeable if the amount or value of the consideration received or receivable by him in respect of the disposal in that period of the asset or interest had been nil.

(2) For the purposes of that section—

(*a*) any question whether a person is connected with the seller shall be determined in accordance the provisions of [section 1122 of the Corporation Tax Act 2010][1];

(*b*) the relevant period is the period beginning with the time of the disposal of the asset or interest and ending with the time when the first claim is made for the allowance, for the lessee's oil field, of expenditure incurred by the lessee or a successor of his under the lease in question or a lease of the relevant asset (and in this paragraph the reference to the lessee includes a reference to a person who is treated as the lessee by virtue of section 96 above);

(*c*) the applicable rate of tax is the rate at which tax is charged under section 1(2) of the principal Act at the time of the disposal of the asset or interest;

(*d*) the amount of the disposal receipts is the aggregate of the amount or value of any consideration received or receivable by the seller in respect of the disposal of the asset or interest;

(*e*) a chargeable period is a period in which the seller benefits from safeguard relief if and only if the tax payable by the seller for that period is less than it would have been if section 9 of the principal Act (safeguard relief) had not been enacted;

(*f*) the relevant time is the end of the earliest claim period for which a claim such as is mentioned in paragraph (*b*) above is made; and

(*g*) tariff receipts of the lessee shall be taken to be attributable to an oil field if and only if they are attributable to the field for any chargeable period for the purposes of the Oil Taxation Act 1983.

(3) In section 96 above references—

(*a*) to the transfer by a person of the whole or part of his interest in the lessee's oil field; or

(*b*) in relation to a transfer, to the new participator,

shall be construed in accordance with Schedule 17 to the Finance Act 1980.

(4) The expenditure which for the purposes of sections 95 and 96 above shall be taken to be operating expenditure shall be so much of the expenditure incurred by the lessee or, as the case may be, a successor of his under the lease concerned as appears, on a just and reasonable estimate, to be operating expenditure.

(5) References in this section to a successor of the lessee shall be construed in accordance with section 96(5) above.

(6) In this section and sections 95 and 96 above—

"the chargeable field" has the same meaning as in the Oil Taxation Act 1983;

"lease", in relation to an asset, has the same meaning as in sections 781 to 784 of the Taxes Act 1988 [Chapter 3 of Part 19 of CTA 2010 (see section 868)][2];

"the lease in question", "the lessee", "the lessee's oil field", "the relevant asset", "the seller" and "the seller's oil field" shall be construed in accordance with section 95(1) above;

"operating expenditure" means expenditure (for example, in respect of the provision of staff or crew or the maintenance or operation of the relevant asset) of such a nature that the lessee or, as the case may be, his successor would or might have incurred it, otherwise than under any arrangements to finance his ownership, if he had been the owner of the asset;

"the new participator's lease" shall be construed in accordance with section 96(1) above;

"the principal Act" means the Oil Taxation Act 1975;

"qualifying asset" has the same meaning as in the Oil Taxation Act 1983; and

"tariff receipts" has the same meaning as in that Act.

(7) This section and sections 95 and 96 above shall be construed as one with Part I of the principal Act.

Amendments—[1] In sub-s (2)(*a*) words substituted for words "section 839 of the Taxes Act 1988" by CTA 2010 s 1177, Sch 1 para 301. CTA 2010 has effect for corporation tax purposes for accounting periods ending on or after 1 April 2010, and for income and capital gains tax purposes for the tax year 2010–11 and subsequent tax years.

[2] In sub-s (6), words substituted by TIOPA 2010 s 374, Sch 8 paras 247, 248;. TIOPA 2010 has effect for corporation tax purposes for accounting periods ending on or after 1 April 2010, for income and capital gains tax purposes for the tax year 2010–11 and subsequent tax years, and for petroleum revenue tax purposes for chargeable periods beginning on or after 1 July 2010.

98 Qualifying assets

(1) Subsection (2) below applies where—

(*a*) an asset which is not a mobile asset is a qualifying asset for the purposes of the Oil Taxation Act 1983 in relation to a person ("the taxpayer") who is a participator in an oil field ("the field");

(*b*) tariff receipts[, tax-exempt tariffing receipts][1] or disposal receipts of the taxpayer which are referable to the asset are attributable to the field for a chargeable period ("the earlier period");

(*c*) receipts of the taxpayer which are referable to the asset for a subsequent chargeable period ("the later period") would not, apart from this section, be tariff receipts[, tax-exempt tariffing receipts][1] or disposal receipts attributable to the field for that period as a result of—

(i) the taxpayer's ceasing to be a participator in the field; or

(ii) his becoming a participator in another oil field; and

(*d*) not more than two chargeable periods intervene between the earlier period and the later period.

(2) The Oil Taxation Acts shall have effect, in relation to the later period and any subsequent chargeable period, as if—

(*a*) receipts of the taxpayer which are referable to the asset for the period concerned were tariff receipts[, tax-exempt tariffing receipts][1] or disposal receipts attributable to the field for that period; and

PRT

(*b*) in a case falling within subsection (1)(*c*)(i) above, the taxpayer continued to be a participator in the field.

(3) Subsection (4) below applies where—

(*a*) an asset which is not a mobile asset is a qualifying asset for the purposes of the Oil Taxation Act 1983 in relation to a person ("the taxpayer") who is a participator in an oil field ("the field");

(*b*) tariff receipts[, tax-exempt tariffing receipts][1] or disposal receipts of the taxpayer which are referable to the asset are attributable to the field for a chargeable period ("the earlier period");

(*c*) in a subsequent chargeable period ("the later period") the taxpayer disposes of—

(i) the asset; or

(ii) an interest in the asset,

to another person ("the transferee") in circumstances such that section 7 of the Oil Taxation Act 1983 does not apply to the disposal; and

(*d*) not more than two chargeable periods intervene between the earlier period and the later period.

(4) The Oil Taxation Acts shall have effect, in relation to the later period and any subsequent chargeable period, as if—

(*a*) receipts of the transferee which are referable to the asset for the period concerned were tariff receipts[, tax-exempt tariffing receipts][1] or disposal receipts attributable to the field for that period; and

(*b*) the transferee were a participator in the field.

(5) Subject to subsection (6) below, any reference in this section to receipts of any person which are referable to the asset for a period is a reference to any sums which—

(*a*) are received or receivable by that person in that period in respect of the use of the asset, or the provision of services or other business facilities of whatever kind in connection with its use; or

(*b*) are received or receivable by that person in respect of the disposal in that period of the asset, or an interest in the asset.

(6) In a case falling within subsection (3)(*c*)(ii) above—

(*a*) any sums which are received or receivable by the transferee otherwise than by virtue of his acquisition of the interest shall not be regarded for the purposes of subsection (4) above as receipts of his which are referable to the asset for any period; and

(*b*) for the purposes of paragraph (*a*) above, such apportionments shall be made as may be just and reasonable.

[(6A) In relation to tax-exempt tariffing receipts, any reference in this section—

(*a*) to being attributable to a field for a period, or

(*b*) to being referable to an asset,

shall be construed as if tax-exempt tariffing receipts were tariff receipts (and expenditure were or had been allowable accordingly).][1]

(7) This section shall be construed as one with Part I of the Oil Taxation Act 1975; and in this section "the Oil Taxation Acts" means—

(*a*) the enactments relating to petroleum revenue tax (including this section);

[(*aa*) Part 8 of the Corporation Tax Act 2010 (oil activities); and][2].

[(*ba*) Chapter 16A of Part 2 of the Income Tax (Trading and Other Income) Act 2005 (oil activities)][3].

(8) Nothing in this section shall be taken to affect the meaning of "participator" in paragraph 4 of Schedule 2 to the principal Act.

(9) Subject to subsection (11) below, subsection (1) above applies where—

(*a*) the disposal by virtue of which the taxpayer ceased to be a participator in the field; or

(*b*) the acquisition by virtue of which he became a participator in the other oil field,

was made on or after 1st July 1999.

(10) Subject to subsection (11) below, subsection (3) above applies where the asset, or the interest in the asset, was disposed of on or after that date.

(11) Neither subsection (1) nor subsection (3) above applies where the disposal or acquisition concerned was made pursuant to an agreement which was made before 1st July 1999 and either—

(*a*) the agreement was not conditional; or

(*b*) the agreement was conditional and the condition was satisfied before that date.

Amendments—[1] In sub-ss 1(b), (c), 2(a), 3(b), 4(a), words inserted, and sub-s (6A) inserted, by FA 2004 s 285, Sch 37 para 12 with effect for chargeable periods, within the meaning of FA 1999 s 98, ending after 29 June 2004.

[2] Sub-s (7)(*aa*) inserted by CTA 2010 s 1177, Sch 1 para 302. CTA 2010 has effect for corporation tax purposes for accounting periods ending on or after 1 April 2010, and for income and capital gains tax purposes for the tax year 2010–11 and subsequent tax years.

[3] Sub-s (7)(*ba*), substituted for previous sub-s (7)(*b*), (*c*) by TIOPA 2010 s 374, Sch 8 paras 187, 188. TIOPA 2010 has effect for corporation tax purposes for accounting periods ending on or after 1 April 2010, for income and capital gains tax purposes

for the tax year 2010–11 and subsequent tax years, and for petroleum revenue tax purposes for chargeable periods beginning on or after 1 July 2010.

99 PRT instalments

(1) (*amend* FA 1982 Sch 19 para 3).

(2) Subsection (1) above applies for the purpose of determining whether instalments are payable in respect of chargeable periods ending on or after 31st December 1999.

100 Sale and lease-back: ring fence profits

. . .

Amendments—This section repealed by CTA 2010 s 1181, Sch 3 Pt 1. CTA 2010 has effect for corporation tax purposes for accounting periods ending on or after 1 April 2010, and for income and capital gains tax purposes for the tax year 2010–11 and subsequent tax years.

101 Pipe-line elections

(1) (*amend* FA 1994 s 233).

(2) Subsection (1) above applies to sums received or receivable in any chargeable period ending on or after 31st December 1999.

102 PRT returns

(1)–(5) (*amend* OTA 1975 Sch 2 paras 2, 5, Sch 6 para 2 Table, and insert Sch 2 para 12A, Sch 5 para 2(7), (8)).

(6), (7) (*amend* FA 1987 s 62).

(8) The preceding provisions of this section apply in relation to chargeable periods ending on or after 30th June 1999.

103 Business assets: roll-over relief

(1) (*repeal* TCGA 1992 s 193).

(2) This section has effect in relation to—

(*a*) a disposal of a licence or an interest in a licence which occurs on or after 1st July 1999;

(*b*) an acquisition of a licence or an interest in a licence which occurs on or after 1st July 1999.

FINANCE ACT 2001

(2001 Chapter 9)

An Act to grant certain duties, to alter other duties, and to amend the law relating to the National Debt and the Public Revenue, and to make further provision in connection with Finance.

[11 May 2001]

PART IV
OTHER TAXES

Petroleum revenue tax

101 PRT: unrelievable field losses

(1), (2) (*substitute* OTA 1975 s 6(1)–(1D) for sub-ss (1), (1A) and *amend* sub-s (2))

(3) (*amends* FA 1984 s 113(2))

(4) Schedule 32 to this Act has effect.

(5) The provisions of this section shall be deemed to have come into force on 7th March 2001.

102 PRT: allowable decommissioning expenditure

(1)–(3) (*substitute* OTA 1975 s 3(1C)–(1E) for sub-ss (1C), (1D) and *amend* sub-s (6) and s 10).

(4) The amendments made by subsections (1) to (3) apply to expenditure incurred on or after 7th March 2001.

(5) Subsections (6) to (8) apply where—

(*a*) on or after 7th March 2001 a participator in a taxable field ("the transitional participator") incurs expenditure that falls to be apportioned under the new provision,

(*b*) the transitional participator was a participator in the field both immediately before, and at the beginning of, 7th March 2001,

(*c*) the qualifying asset that is relevant to the incurring of the expenditure was, at both of the times mentioned in paragraph (*b*), a qualifying asset in relation to the transitional participator and the field, and

(*d*) at a time before 7th March 2001—

(i) a person was a participator in two or more oil fields, and

(ii) the asset was a qualifying asset in relation to that person and each of at least two of those fields.

(6) If there would be no apportionment of the expenditure under the old provision, for the purpose of applying the new provision to the expenditure "the relevant portion" of the expenditure is the taxable field portion.

(7) If the expenditure would be apportioned between two or more oil fields under the old provision, for the purpose of applying the new provision to the expenditure "the relevant portion" of the expenditure is the portion of the taxable field portion which it is just and reasonable to apportion to use of the asset in connection with the field.

(8) In carrying out that apportionment of the taxable field portion, ignore use of the asset in connection with an oil field that is not one of the oil fields between which the expenditure would be apportioned under the old provision.

(9) In subsections (6) to (8) "the taxable field portion" means the portion of the expenditure that it is just and reasonable to apportion to use of the asset in connection with a taxable field.

(10) In subsections (5) to (8)—

"the new provision" means section 3(1C) of the Oil Taxation Act 1975 as substituted by subsection (1);

"the old provision" means section 3(1C) of that Act as it would have effect apart from the amendments made by subsections (1) to (3);

"qualifying asset" has the same meaning as it has for the purposes of the Oil Taxation Act 1983 (see section 8 of that Act).

(11) Subsections (5) to (10) shall be construed as one with Part I of the Oil Taxation Act 1975.

103 PRT: expenditure in certain gas-producing fields

(1) (*substitutes* OTA 1975 s 10(3)–(3H) for sub-s (3))

(2) The amendments made by this section apply to expenditure incurred on or after 7th March 2001.

PART V

MISCELLANEOUS AND SUPPLEMENTARY PROVISIONS

Supplementary

110 Repeals and revocations

(1) The enactments mentioned in Schedule 33 to this Act (which include provisions that are spent or of no practical utility) are repealed or revoked to the extent specified.

(2) The repeals and revocations specified in that Schedule have effect subject to the commencement provisions and savings contained or referred to in the notes set out in that Schedule.

SCHEDULES

SCHEDULE 32

PETROLEUM REVENUE TAX: UNRELIEVABLE FIELD LOSSES

Section 101

Schedule applies where there has been a transfer to which Parts II and III of Schedule 17 to the Finance Act 1980 do not apply

1—(1) This Schedule applies where—

(*a*) there has been a transfer of the whole or part of the interest in an oil field of a participator in the field (see paragraph 4),

(*b*) the transfer is an excluded transfer (see paragraph 2), and

(*c*) an allowable loss has accrued from the field to—

(i) the old participator,

(ii) the new participator, or

(iii) a subsequent new owner (see paragraph 3).

(2) In this Schedule—

"the loss-maker" means the person to whom the allowable loss accrues;

"the old participator" means the person whose interest is wholly or partly transferred by the transfer and "the new participator" means the person to whom the interest or part is transferred by the transfer;

"the transferred interest" means—

(*a*) where the transfer is of the whole of the old participator's interest in the field, that interest, and

(*b*) where the transfer is of part of the old participator's interest in the field, that part.

Meaning of "excluded transfer"

2 For the purposes of this Schedule, a transfer of the whole or part of the interest in an oil field of a participator in the field is an "excluded transfer" if—

(*a*) Parts II and III of Schedule 17 to the Finance Act 1980 do not apply to the transfer, and

(*b*) either—

(i) the transfer is made pursuant to an agreement made on or after 7th March 2001, or

(ii) the transfer is made pursuant to a conditional agreement made before 7th March 2001 and the condition is satisfied on or after 7th March 2001.

Meaning of "subsequent new owner"

3 For the purposes of this Schedule, a "subsequent new owner" is any participator in the field who has the transferred interest, or any part of the transferred interest, as a result of—

(*a*) a transfer by the new participator of the whole or part of the transferred interest, or

(*b*) the combination of such a transfer as is mentioned in paragraph (*a*) and—

(i) a transfer by a subsequent new owner of the whole or part of the transferred interest, or

(ii) two or more such transfers as are mentioned in sub-paragraph (i).

Transfers of interests in oil fields: interpretation

4—(1) For the purposes of this Schedule, a participator in an oil field transfers the whole or part of his interest in the field whenever as a result of a transaction or event other than—

(*a*) the making of an agreement or arrangement of the kind mentioned in paragraph 5 of Schedule 3 to the Oil Taxation Act 1975 (agreement or arrangement for transfer of participator's rights to associated company), or

(*b*) a re-determination under a unitisation agreement,

the whole or part of his share in the oil to be won and saved from the field becomes the share or part of the share of another person who is or becomes a participator in the field.

(2) Paragraph 1(2) of Schedule 17 to the Finance Act 1980 (meaning of "unitisation agreement" and "re-determination") applies for the purposes of sub-paragraph (1) above as for those of paragraph 1(1) of that Schedule.

Schedule applies in place of section 6(1C) of the Oil Taxation Act 1975

5 Where this Schedule makes provision for determining the unrelievable portion of an allowable loss, that portion is determined in accordance with the provisions of this Schedule instead of in accordance with the provisions of section 6(1C) of the Oil Taxation Act 1975.

General rule for determinations under this Schedule of "unrelievable portion" of loss

6—(1) The unrelievable portion of the allowable loss is so much of the intermediate unrelieved loss as cannot be relieved under paragraph 7 against relevant profits.

(2) In this Schedule—

"the intermediate unrelieved loss" is so much of the allowable loss as cannot be relieved under section 7 of the Oil Taxation Act 1975 against assessable profits accruing from the field to the loss-maker;

"relevant profits" means assessable profits—

(*a*) accruing from the field to any participator in the field other than the loss-maker,

(*b*) computed as if the amounts mentioned in section 2(8)(*a*) of that Act did not include expenditure unrelated to the field except where it has been allowed in pursuance of a claim or election for its allowance received by the Board before 29th November 1994, and

(*c*) reduced (after being so computed) under section 7 of that Act.

(3) In sub-paragraph (2) "expenditure unrelated to the field" has the meaning given by section 6(9) of that Act.

Loss to be relieved against other participators' profits

7—(1) The intermediate unrelieved loss shall (but only for the purposes of determinations under this Schedule) be relieved against relevant profits accruing to a different owner.

(2) The provisions of paragraphs 8 to 10 apply for the purposes of relieving the intermediate unrelieved loss under this paragraph.

(3) In this paragraph and paragraph 8, a "different owner" means any participator in the field who—

(*a*) has the loss-maker's interest at any time (whether before or after the transfer) when the loss-maker does not have that interest, or

(*b*) has a part of the loss-maker's interest at any time (whether before or after the transfer) when the loss-maker does not have that part.

(4) In sub-paragraph (3) "the loss-maker's interest" means—

(*a*) if the loss-maker is the old participator or the new participator, the transferred interest;

(*b*) if the loss-maker is a subsequent new owner and at any time (whether before or after the transfer) has the whole of the transferred interest, that interest; and

PRT

(*c*) if the loss-maker is a subsequent new owner and paragraph (*b*) does not apply, the aggregate of each part of the transferred interest that at any time (whether before or after the transfer) is a part that the loss-maker has.

Extent to which losses to be relieved

8—(1) Where the interest in the field of a different owner is the transferred interest, the intermediate unrelieved loss is to be relieved against the whole of any relevant profits accruing to the different owner.

(2) Where the interest in the field of a different owner is part of the transferred interest, the corresponding part (but only that part) of the intermediate unrelieved loss is to be relieved against the whole of any relevant profits accruing to the different owner.

(3) Where—

(*a*) a different owner's interest in the field includes the transferred interest, but

(*b*) the transferred interest is only part of the different owner's interest in the field,

the intermediate unrelieved loss is to be relieved against the corresponding part (but no other part) of any relevant profits accruing to the different owner.

(4) Sub-paragraph (5) applies where—

(*a*) a different owner's interest in the field includes part only of the transferred interest ("the owned part of the transferred interest"), and

(*b*) the owned part of the transferred interest is only part of the different owner's interest in the field.

(5) Only the part of the intermediate unrelieved loss corresponding to the owned part of the transferred interest is to be relieved, and it is to be relieved against (but only against) the part of any relevant profits accruing to the different owner that corresponds to the part which the owned part of the transferred interest forms of the different owner's interest in the field.

Profits not to be utilised more than once

9 The intermediate unrelieved loss may not be relieved against relevant profits to the extent that those profits have already been utilised for the purposes of paragraph 7.

Relieving different losses against the same profits

10—(1) Where intermediate unrelieved losses accruing to each of two or more persons fall to be relieved under paragraph 7 against the same relevant profits, such a loss accruing to a person who last had the transferred interest (or part of it) at an earlier time shall be so relieved before one accruing to a person who last had the interest (or part) at a later time.

(2) Where—

(*a*) two or more persons each last had a part of the transferred interest at the same time, and

(*b*) intermediate unrelieved losses accruing to each of them fall to be relieved under paragraph 7 against the same relevant profits,

those losses shall be so relieved in such a manner as ensures that the same proportion of each is so relieved.

(3) In this paragraph, references to an intermediate unrelieved loss accruing to a person are to the intermediate unrelieved loss in respect of an allowable loss accruing to the person.

Construction as one with Part I of the Oil Taxation Act 1975

11 This Schedule shall be construed as one with Part I of the Oil Taxation Act 1975.

SCHEDULE 33

REPEALS

Section 110

PART III

OTHER TAXES

(2)

PETROLEUM REVENUE TAX

Note—All repeals relevant to petroleum revenue tax are already in effect and have therefore been omitted.

FINANCE ACT 2002

(2002 Chapter 23)

Note—For the purposes of UK oil and gas taxation, reference should be made to the following provisions of FA

2002—
FA 2002 s 92 (Assessment, recovery and postponement of supplementary charge);
FA 2002 s 93 (Supplementary charge: transitional provisions).
FA 2002 is reproduced in Part 1a of this publication.

FINANCE ACT 2004

(2004 Chapter 12)

An Act to Grant certain duties, to alter other duties, and to amend the law relating to the National Debt and the Public Revenue, and to make further provision in connection with finance.

[22 July 2004]

PART 5
OIL

285 Certain receipts not to be tariff receipts

(1) The Oil Taxation Act 1983 is amended as follows.
(2) (*amends* s 6(2)).
(3) (*inserts* ss 6A, 6B).
(4) (*amends* Sch 2 para 12).
(5) Schedule 37 to this Act has effect; and in that Schedule—
Part 1 makes amendments to the Oil Taxation Act 1983 (c. 56) relating to allowable expenditure and disposal receipts;
Part 2 makes transitional provision;
Part 3 makes amendments to the Taxes Act 1988;
Part 4 makes amendments to other enactments.
(6) In Part 1 of Schedule 37 to this Act—
(*a*) the amendments made by paragraph 5 (which relate to disposal receipts) have effect in relation to disposals in chargeable periods ending on or after 30th June 2004, and
(*b*) the other amendments made by that Part have effect in relation to expenditure incurred on or after 1st January 2004.
(7) The amendments made by Part 3 of that Schedule have effect in relation to chargeable periods, within the meaning of the Taxes Act 1988, ending on or after 1st January 2004.[1], [2]
(8) The amendments made by Part 4 of that Schedule have effect in relation to chargeable periods (within the meaning of section 98 of the Finance Act 1999 (c 16)) ending on or after 30th June 2004.

Amendments—[1] Sub-s (7) repealed for corporation tax purposes by CTA 2010 s 1181, Sch 3 Pt 2. CTA 2010 has effect for corporation tax purposes for accounting periods ending on or after 1 April 2010, and for income and capital gains tax purposes for the tax year 2010–11 and subsequent tax years.
[2] Sub-s (7) repealed by TIOPA 2010 s 378, Sch 10 Pt 6. TIOPA 2010 has effect for corporation tax purposes for accounting periods ending on or after 1 April 2010, for income and capital gains tax purposes for the tax year 2010–11 and subsequent tax years, and for petroleum revenue tax purposes for chargeable periods beginning on or after 1 July 2010.

286 Petroleum extraction activities: exploration expenditure supplement

(1) Chapter 5 of Part 12 of the Taxes Act 1988 (petroleum extraction activities) is amended as follows.
(2) (*inserts* s 496A)
(3) (*inserts* Sch 19B)

287 Restrictions on expenditure allowable

(1) In Schedule 4 to the Oil Taxation Act 1975 (c. 22), paragraph 2 (restrictions on expenditure allowable where acquisition etc from connected person or otherwise not at arm's length) is amended as follows.
(2)–(5 (*amend* sub-paras (1), (1B), *insert* sub-para (1ZA), (1C)).
(6) The amendments made by this section have effect in relation to expenditure incurred on or after 17th March 2004.

288 Terminal losses

(1) Schedule 17 to the Finance Act 1980 (c. 48) (transfers of interests in oil fields) is amended as follows.
(2) (*substitutes* para 15).
(3) The amendment made by this section has effect in relation to losses accruing in chargeable periods ending after 17th March 2004.

PART 9
SUPPLEMENTARY PROVISIONS

326 Repeals

(1) The enactments mentioned in Schedule 42 to this Act (which include provisions that are spent or of no practical utility) are repealed to the extent specified.

(2) The repeals specified in that Schedule have effect subject to the commencement provisions and savings contained or referred to in the notes set out in that Schedule.

327 Interpretation

In this Act "the Taxes Act 1988" means the Income and Corporation Taxes Act 1988 (c 1).

SCHEDULES

SCHEDULE 37

OIL TAXATION: TAX-EXEMPT TARIFFING RECEIPTS AND ASSETS PRODUCING THEM

Section 285

PART 1

AMENDMENTS OF THE OIL TAXATION ACT 1983 RELATING TO ALLOWABLE EXPENDITURE AND DISPOSAL RECEIPTS

Introductory

1 The Oil Taxation Act 1983 (c. 56) is amended in accordance with the following provisions of this Part.

Expenditure incurred on long-term assets other than non-dedicated mobile assets

2—(1) Section 3 (expenditure incurred on long-term assets other than non- dedicated mobile assets) is amended as follows.

(2) (*amends* sub-s (4)).

Exclusion from s 3(4) of expenditure on assets giving rise to tax-exempt tariffing receipts

3 (*inserts* s 3A).

Expenditure related to exempt gas: asset use giving rise to tax-exempt tariffing receipts

4—(1) Section 4 (expenditure related to exempt gas and deballasting) is amended as follows.

(2) (*inserts* sub-ss (6), (7)).

Disposal receipts from assets used in a way that gives rise to tax-exempt tariffing receipts

5—(1) Section 7 (chargeable receipts from disposals) is amended as follows.

(2), (3) (*amend* sub-s (4), *insert* sub-s (9)).

(4) (*inserts* s 7A).

Assets no longer in use for the principal field

6—(1) In Schedule 1 (allowable expenditure) in Part 1 (extensions of allowable expenditure for assets generating receipts) paragraph 3 is amended as follows.

(2) (*inserts* sub-paras (2A), (2B)).

Brought-in assets

7—(1) In Part 2 of Schedule 1, paragraph 7 is amended as follows.

(2) (*amends* sub-para (1)(*c*)).

Subsequent use of new asset otherwise than in connection with a taxable field

8—(1) In Part 2 of Schedule 1, paragraph 8 is amended as follows.

(2), (3) (*amend* sub-paras (3), (5)).

PART 2

TRANSITIONAL PROVISION

Expenditure incurred in transitional period: restriction of tax-exempt tariffing receipts

9—(1) In this paragraph—

"claim period" has the same meaning as in Part 1 of the Oil Taxation Act 1975 (c 22);

"relevant receipts" means each of the following—

(*a*) tax-exempt tariffing receipts;

(*b*) amounts that would be tax-exempt tariffing receipts apart from sub-paragraph (4);

"the transitional period" means the period—

(*a*) beginning with 9th April 2003, and

(*b*) ending with 31st December 2003.

(2) This paragraph applies where—

(*a*) expenditure was incurred in the transitional period by a participator in an oil field in acquiring, bringing into existence or enhancing the value of an asset,

(*b*) the asset is one whose useful life continues, or is expected to continue, after the end of the claim period in which the expenditure was incurred,

(*c*) the expenditure is allowable for a claim period ending after 9th April 2003,

(*d*) at the time the expenditure was incurred, the asset was being, or was expected to be, used to any extent in relation to—

(i) an oil field or foreign field (a "user field"), or

(ii) oil won from such a field, and

(*e*) that use (or expected use) is use in such a way as, in a chargeable period ending on or after 30th June 2004, gives rise, or would have given rise, to relevant receipts of the participator or, where sub- paragraph (3) applies, of a successor.

(3) This sub-paragraph applies where—

(*a*) after the incurring of the expenditure, there is or has been a transfer of an interest of the participator's in the asset, and

(*b*) as a result of that transfer (or of any subsequent transfer of the whole or any part of that interest), relevant receipts ("consequential relevant receipts") arise, or are expected to arise, to a person (a "successor") who is a participator in an oil field.

(4) In the case of each user field, the initial portion of the aggregate of the relevant receipts of the participator, and the consequential relevant receipts of each successor, that are referable to—

(*a*) use of the asset in relation to that field or oil won from it, or

(*b*) the provision of services or other business facilities of whatever kind in connection with any such use of the asset (otherwise than by the participator or the successor himself),

shall not be tax-exempt tariffing receipts (and shall accordingly continue to be tariff receipts).

(5) In this paragraph—

"the initial portion", in relation to the aggregate of any relevant receipts, means so much of that aggregate as does not exceed the qualifying threshold for the user field in question;

and for this purpose amounts received or receivable at an earlier date are to be attributed to the initial portion before amounts received or receivable at a later date;

"the qualifying threshold", in relation to a user field, means an amount equal to such part of the aggregate of the expenditure—

(*a*) incurred by the participator in relation to the asset in question, and

(*b*) falling within sub-paragraph (2),

as it is just and reasonable to apportion to the use (or expected use) of the asset, in relation to that user field or oil won from it, in a way that gives rise to relevant receipts of the participator or consequential relevant receipts of any successor.

(6) Expressions used in this paragraph and in section 6A of the Oil Taxation Act 1983 (c. 56) have the same meaning in this paragraph as they have in that section.

PART 3

AMENDMENTS OF THE TAXES ACT 1988

Introductory

10 The Taxes Act 1988 is amended in accordance with the following provisions of this Part.[1], [2]

Amendments—[1] Part 3 repealed for corporation tax purposes by CTA 2010 s 1181, Sch 3 Pt 2. CTA 2010 has effect for corporation tax purposes for accounting periods ending on or after 1 April 2010, and for income and capital gains tax purposes for the tax year 2010–11 and subsequent tax years.

[2] Part 3 repealed by TIOPA 2010 s 378, Sch 10 Pt 6. TIOPA 2010 has effect for corporation tax purposes for accounting periods ending on or after 1 April 2010, for income and capital gains tax purposes for the tax year 2010–11 and subsequent tax years, and for petroleum revenue tax purposes for chargeable periods beginning on or after 1 July 2010.

Section 496: treatment of tax-exempt tariffing receipts for income and corporation tax

11—(1) Section 496 (tariff receipts) is amended as follows.

(2)–(5) (*amend* sub-ss (1)(*a*), (2), (3), Heading).[1], [2]

Amendments—[1] Part 3 repealed for corporation tax purposes by CTA 2010 s 1181, Sch 3 Pt 2. CTA 2010 has effect for corporation tax purposes for accounting periods ending on or after 1 April 2010, and for income and capital gains tax purposes for the tax year 2010–11 and subsequent tax years.

[2] Part 3 repealed by TIOPA 2010 s 378, Sch 10 Pt 6. TIOPA 2010 has effect for corporation tax purposes for accounting periods ending on or after 1 April 2010, for income and capital gains tax purposes for the tax year 2010–11 and subsequent tax years, and for petroleum revenue tax purposes for chargeable periods beginning on or after 1 July 2010.

PART 4

AMENDMENTS OF OTHER ENACTMENTS

FINANCE ACT 1999

Qualifying assets

12—(1) Section 98 of the Finance Act 1999 is amended as follows.
(2), (3) (*substitute* words throughout section and *insert* sub-s (6A)).

SCHEDULE 38

Note—This Schedule contained the text of TA 1988 Sch 19B as inserted by FA 2004 s 286(1), (3).

COMMISSIONERS FOR REVENUE AND CUSTOMS ACT 2005

(2005 Chapter 11)

An Act to make provision for the appointment of Commissioners to exercise functions presently vested in the Commissioners of Inland Revenue and the Commissioners of Customs and Excise; for the establishment of a Revenue and Customs Prosecutions Office; and for connected purposes.

[7 April 2005]

Note—Please see Part 1 of this publication for the text of this Act.

INCOME TAX (TRADING AND OTHER INCOME) ACT 2005

(2005 Chapter 5)

Note—Reference should be made to the following in connection with PRT—
ITTOIA 2005 Part 2 Chapter 16A (ss 225A–225V) (Oil Activities).
ITTOIA 2005 s 342 (Extended meaning of "mineral royalties" etc in Northern Ireland).
The full text of ITTOIA 2005 is reproduced in Part 1b of this publication.

FINANCE ACT 2006

(2006 Chapter 25)

An Act to Grant certain duties, to alter other duties, and to amend the law relating to the National Debt and the Public Revenue, and to make further provision in connection with finance.

[19 July 2006]

PART 5

OIL

New basis for determining market value

146 New basis for determining the market value of oil

(1) (*inserts* OTA 1975 Sch 3 para 1A)
(2) Paragraph 2 of that Schedule (definition of market value of oil) is amended as follows.
(3) (*amends* OTA 1975 Sch 3 para 2)
(4) (*inserts* OTA 1975 Sch 3 para 2(1A), (1B))
(5) (*substitutes* OTA 1975 Sch 3 para 2(2), (2AA))
(6) (*substitutes* OTA 1975 Sch 3 para 2(2E)–(2I))
(7) (*repeals* OTA 1975 Sch 3 para 2(3))
(8) (*amends* OTA 1975 Sch 3 para 2(3A))
(9) (*amends* OTA 1975 Sch 3 para 2(4))
(10) (*inserts* OTA 1975 Sch 3 para 2(5))
(11) Schedule 18 (which makes minor and consequential amendments) has effect.

147 Section 146: commencement and transitional provisions

(1) The amendments made by section 146 and Schedule 18 have effect in relation to oil delivered or appropriated on or after 1st July 2006 (disregarding section 12A of that Act).
(2) Those amendments also have effect for the purpose of determining for any chargeable period ending on or after 31st December 2006—

(*a*) the value to be brought into account under section 2(4)(*b*) of OTA 1975 by reference to a previous chargeable period ending on or after 30th June 2006, and

(*b*) the value to be brought into account under section 2(5)(*d*) of that Act.

(3) Subsections (1) and (2) are subject to any express provision in Schedule 18 as to the commencement or application of any provision of that Schedule.

(4) In the following provisions of this section—
(*a*) "the last old period" means the chargeable period that ends on 30th June 2006, and
(*b*) "the first new period" means the chargeable period that ends on 31st December 2006.
(5) Subsection (6) applies in relation to oil which was won from an oil field before 1st July 2006 and which—
(*a*) was loaded on to a ship before 1st July 2006 and transported from the place of extraction to a place in the United Kingdom or elsewhere, or
(*b*) was transported by pipeline from the place of extraction to a place in the United Kingdom and there loaded on to a ship before that date.
(6) If the oil is or was disposed of crude by a participator in sales otherwise than at arm's length, but the market value of the oil—
(*a*) does not fall to be brought into account for the purposes of section 2(5)(*b*) of OTA 1975 for the last old period by reason only that the oil was not delivered in that period, and
(*b*) would not (apart from this subsection) fall to be brought into account for the purposes of that provision in the first new period by reason only that the date on which the oil is to be regarded by virtue of section 12A of that Act as delivered falls in the last old period,
the date on which the oil is to be taken for the purposes of section 2(5)(b) of that Act to have been delivered is instead to be the first business day of the first new period.
(7) Any power to make regulations that is conferred under or by virtue of any of the amendments made by section 146 or Schedule 18 includes power to make regulations having effect for, or in relation to,—
(*a*) the first new period, or
(*b*) for the purpose mentioned in subsection (2), the last old period,
notwithstanding that the period in question has begun or ended before the making of the regulations.
(8) Any regulations made by virtue of subsection (7) must be made before 31st December 2006.

Regulations—Oil Taxation (Market Value of Oil) Regulations 2006, SI 2006/3313.

Attribution of blended crude oil

148 Crude oil: power to make regulations

(1) (*amends* OTA 1975 s 2(5))
(2) (*inserts* OTA 1975 s 2(5B)–(5D))
(3) Regulations under section 2(5B) of OTA 1975 (inserted by subsection (2) above) may have effect for the purpose of calculating profits in relation to a chargeable period ending at any time on or after 1st July 2006.

Regulations—Petroleum Revenue Tax (Attribution of Blended Crude Oil) Regulations 2006, SI 2006/3312.

Nomination scheme

149 Nomination scheme

(1) Section 61 of FA 1987 (oil taxation: nominations) shall be amended as follows.
(2) (*amends* FA 1987 s 61(1))
(3) (*substitutes* FA 1987 s 61(3)–(4B))
(4) (*repeals* FA 1987 s 61(6), (7))
(5) (*amends* FA 1987 s 61(8))
(6) (*amends* FA 1987 s 61(9))
(7) This section shall have effect in relation to chargeable periods ending on or after 1st July 2006.

150 Amendment of Schedule 10 to FA 1987

(1) Schedule 10 to FA 1987 (oil taxation: nominations) shall be amended as follows.
(2) In paragraph 1—
(*a*) (*amends* FA 1987 Sch 10 para 1(1))
(*b*) (*repeals* FA 1987 Sch 10 para 1(2))
(3) In paragraph 2 omit—
(*a*) (*repeals* FA 1987 Sch 10 para 2(1)(*b*), (*c*) and (*d*))
(*b*) (*amends* FA 1987 Sch 10 para 2(1))
(4) (*repeals* FA 1987 Sch 10 para 3)
(5) In paragraph 4—
(*a*) (*substitutes* FA 1987 Sch 10 para 4(1)–(1B))
(*b*) (*repeals* FA 1987 Sch 10 para 4(2), (2A))
(*c*) (*amends* FA 1987 Sch 10 para 4(3))
(*d*) (*repeals* FA 1987 Sch 10 para 4(4))
(6) In paragraph 5—
(*a*) (*amends* FA 1987 Sch 10 para 5(1))
(*b*) (*amends* FA 1987 Sch 10 para 5(1)(*b*))
(*c*) (*amends* FA 1987 Sch 10 para 5(*c*), (*d*))
(*d*) (*amends* FA 1987 Sch 10 para 5(1)(*d*))
(*e*) (*substitutes* FA 1987 Sch 10 para 5(1)(*g*))

(*f*) (*amends* FA 1987 Sch 10 para 5(2))
(*g*) (*amends* FA 1987 Sch 10 para 5(3))
(7) (*inserts* FA 1987 Sch 10 paras 5A, 5B)
(8) In paragraph 6—
(*a*) (*amends* FA 1987 Sch 10 para 6(1))
(*b*) (*repeals* FA 1987 Sch 10 para 6(2), (3))
(9) (*repeals* FA 1987 Sch 10 para 7(2), (5))
(10) (*inserts* FA 1987 Sch 10 para 7(6), (7))
(11) (*repeals* FA 1987 Sch 10 paras 8 to 11)
(12) (*amends* FA 1987 Sch 10 para 12(1))
(13) (*inserts* FA 1987 Sch 10 para 12A)
(14) This section shall have effect in relation to a transaction whenever proposed, but shall not have effect in relation to a proposed transaction with a transaction base date (within the meaning given by regulations under paragraph 4 of Schedule 10 to FA 1987) on or before 30th June 2006.
(15) Regulations under paragraph 4(1B) of Schedule 10 to FA 1987 (inserted by subsection (5) above) may have retrospective effect.

151 Nomination excesses and corporation tax

. . .

Amendments—This section repealed for corporation tax purposes by CTA 2010 s 1181, Sch 3 Pt 2. CTA 2010 has effect for corporation tax purposes for accounting periods ending on or after 1 April 2010, and for income and capital gains tax purposes for the tax year 2010–11 and subsequent tax years.
This section repealed by TIOPA 2010 s 378, Sch 10 Pt 6. TIOPA 2010 has effect for corporation tax purposes for accounting periods ending on or after 1 April 2010, for income and capital gains tax purposes for the tax year 2010–11 and subsequent tax years, and for petroleum revenue tax purposes for chargeable periods beginning on or after 1 July 2010.

Ring fence trades

152 Increase in rate of supplementary charge

(1) (*amends* TA 1988 s 501A(1))
(2) The amendment made by subsection (1) has effect in relation to any accounting period beginning on or after 1st January 2006 (but see also subsection (3)).
(3) For the purpose of calculating the amount of the supplementary charge on a company for an accounting period (a "straddling period") beginning before 1st January 2006 and ending on or after that date—
(*a*) so much of the straddling period as falls before 1st January 2006, and so much of the straddling period as falls on or after that date, are treated as separate accounting periods, and
(*b*) the company's adjusted ring fence profits for the straddling period are apportioned to the two separate accounting periods in proportion to the number of days in those periods.
(4) The amount of the supplementary charge on the company for the straddling period is the sum of the amounts of supplementary charge that would, in accordance with subsection (3), be chargeable on the company for those separate accounting periods.
(5) In the case of a company's straddling period—
(*a*) the Instalment Payments Regulations apply as if the amendment made by subsection (1) had not been made, but
(*b*) those Regulations also apply separately, in accordance with the following subsection, in relation to the increase in the amount of any supplementary charge on the company for that period that arises as a result of that amendment.
(6) In that separate application of those Regulations as mentioned in subsection (5)(*b*), those Regulations have effect as if, for the purposes of those Regulations,—
(*a*) the straddling period were an accounting period beginning on 1st January 2006,
(*b*) supplementary charge were chargeable on the company for that period, and
(*c*) the amount of that charge were equal to the increase in the amount of the supplementary charge for the straddling period that arises as a result of the amendment made by subsection (1).
(7) Any reference in the Instalment Payments Regulations to the total liability of a company is, accordingly, to be read—
(*a*) in their application as a result of subsection (5)(*a*), as a reference to the amount that would be the company's total liability for the straddling period if the amendment made by subsection (1) had not been made, and
(*b*) in their application as a result of subsection (5)(*b*), as a reference to the amount of the supplementary charge on the company for the deemed accounting period under subsection (6)(*a*).
(8) For the purposes of the Instalment Payments Regulations—
(*a*) a company is to be regarded as a large company as respects the deemed accounting period under subsection (6)(*a*) if (and only if) it is a large company for those purposes as respects the straddling period, and

(*b*) any question whether a company is a large company as respects the straddling period is to be determined as it would have been determined if the amendment made by subsection (1) had not been made.

(9) If the Instalment Payments Regulations—

(*a*) apply in relation to a company's liability to supplementary charge for the deemed accounting period under subsection (6)(*a*), and

(*b*) would (but for this subsection) treat any instalment payment in respect of that liability as being due and payable on a date falling on or before 22nd March 2006,

those Regulations have effect as if the payment were due and payable instead at the end of the period of 14 days beginning with that date.

(10) In this section—

"adjusted ring fence profits" has the meaning given by section 501A of ICTA,

"the Instalment Payments Regulations" means the Corporation Tax (Instalment Payments) Regulations 1998 (SI 1998/ 3175),

"supplementary charge" means any sum chargeable under section 501A(1) of ICTA as if it were an amount of corporation tax.

153 Election to defer capital allowances

(1) This section applies if—

(*a*) a company carries on a ring fence trade in an accounting period beginning on or after 1st January 2006,

(*b*) relevant expenditure is incurred for the purposes of or in relation to the ring fence trade (see subsections (4) to (7)), and

(*c*) the relevant expenditure would (but for this section) be treated as incurred for the purposes of CAA 2001 in the period of 12 months ending with 31st December 2005.

(2) The company may elect for the relevant expenditure to be treated instead as if it were incurred on the first day of the company's first accounting period beginning on or after 1st January 2006.

(3) The election—

(*a*) has effect for the purposes of CAA 2001 other than those of section 45G (expenditure not first-year qualifying expenditure under section 45F if plant or machinery used for less than 5 years in a ring fence trade), and

(*b*) must be made by notice given to an officer of Revenue and Customs on or before 31st December 2007.

(4) Expenditure is relevant expenditure if it falls within any of Cases A to C.

(5) Expenditure falls within Case A if—

(*a*) it is first-year qualifying expenditure on the provision of plant or machinery under section 45F of CAA 2001 (expenditure on plant and machinery for use wholly in a ring fence trade), and

(*b*) no disposal event (see subsection (8)) in relation to the plant or machinery occurs in the relevant period.

(6) Expenditure falls within Case B—

(*a*) if it is first-year qualifying expenditure under section 416B of CAA 2001 (mineral extraction allowances: expenditure incurred by a company for purposes of a ring fence trade),

(*b*) if no disposal event in relation to any asset representing the expenditure occurs in the relevant period,

(*c*) if (or so far as) it is expenditure to which no part of any capital sum received by the company in the relevant period is reasonably attributable under section 425(2) of CAA 2001, and

(*d*) if no entitlement to a balancing allowance for a chargeable period in respect of the expenditure arises under any of sections 426 to 431 of CAA 2001 as a result of an event that occurs in the relevant period (as well as in that chargeable period).

The reference in paragraph (*b*) to any asset representing the expenditure is to be read in accordance with section 416B(4) of CAA 2001.

(7) Expenditure falls within Case C if—

(*a*) it is qualifying expenditure on research and development under Part 6 of CAA 2001 where the ring fence trade is the trade by reference to which the expenditure is qualifying expenditure, and

(*b*) no disposal event in relation to any asset representing the expenditure occurs in the relevant period.

(8) In this section—

"disposal event"—

(*a*) in relation to first-year qualifying expenditure under section 45F of CAA 2001, means an event of a kind that requires a disposal value to be brought into account under Part 2 of that Act (whether under section 61(1) or otherwise),

PRT

(*b*) in relation to first-year qualifying expenditure under section 416B of CAA 2001, means an event of a kind that requires a disposal value to be brought into account under section 421 or 422 of that Act,

(*c*) in relation to qualifying expenditure on research and development under Part 6 of CAA 2001, means an event of a kind that requires a disposal value to be brought into account under section 443(1) of that Act,

"the relevant period", in relation to any expenditure for the purposes of or in relation to a company's ring fence trade, means the period—

(*a*) beginning with the day on which the expenditure would (but for this section) be treated as incurred for the purposes of CAA 2001, and

(*b*) ending with the first day of the company's first accounting period beginning on or after 1st January 2006,

"ring fence trade" means a ring fence trade in respect of which tax is chargeable under section 501A of ICTA (supplementary charge in respect of ring fence trades).

154 Ring fence expenditure supplement

(1) Chapter 5 of Part 12 of ICTA (petroleum extraction activities) is amended as follows.
(2) (*inserts* TA 1988 s 496B)
(3) Schedule 19B (petroleum extraction activities: exploration expenditure supplement) is amended as follows.
(4) In paragraph 1 (about the Schedule)—
(*a*) (*amends* TA 1988 Sch 19B para 1(1))
(*b*) (*amends* TA 1988 Sch 19B para 1(2))
(5) In paragraph 3 (accounting periods)—
(*a*), (*b*) (*amend* TA 1988 Sch 19B para 3(1))
(*c*) (*inserts* TA 1988 Sch 19B para 3(3), (4))
(6) (*amends* TA 1988 Sch 19B para 6(2))
(7) (*amends* TA 1988 Sch 19B para 15(2))
(8) (*inserts* TA 1988 Sch 19B para 16(2A))
(9) (*inserts* TA 1988 Sch 19B para 18A)
(10) (*inserts* TA 1988 Sch 19B para 22(4)–(7))
(11) After Schedule 19B insert the Schedule 19C set out in Schedule 19 to this Act.

PART 10
SUPPLEMENTARY PROVISIONS

178 Repeals

(1) The enactments mentioned in Schedule 26 (which include provisions that are spent or of no practical utility) are repealed to the extent specified.
(2) The repeals specified in that Schedule have effect subject to the commencement provisions and savings contained or referred to in the notes set out in that Schedule.

SCHEDULES

SCHEDULE 18
OIL TAXATION: MARKET VALUE OF OIL

Section 146

PART 1
AMENDMENTS OF THE OIL TAXATION ACT 1975

Introductory

1 OTA 1975 is amended as follows.

Assessable profits and allowable losses

2—(1) Section 2 is amended as follows.
(2) (*amends* OTA 1975 s 2(4)(*b*))
(3) (*amends* OTA 1975 s 2(5)(*d*))
(4) (*amends* OTA 1975 s 2(5A))
(5) (*amends* OTA 1975 s 2(9)(*a*)(i))
(6) (*amends* OTA 1975 s 2(9)(*a*)(ii))

Allowance of exploration and appraisal expenditure

3—(1) Section 5A is amended as follows.
(2) (*amends* OTA 1975 s 5A(5B))

(3) Amend subsection (5C) (application of Schedule 3 with modifications for ascertaining market value for the purposes of subsection (5B)) as follows.
(4) (*repeals* OTA 1975 s 5A(5C)(*a*))
(5) (*amends* OTA 1975 s 5A(5C)(*b*))
(6) (*inserts* OTA 1975 s 5A(5C)(*d*))

Interpretation

4—(1) In section 12 (interpretation of Part 1 of the Act) subsection (1) (general definitions) is amended as follows.
(2) (*amends* OTA 1975 s 12)
(3) (*amends* OTA 1975 s 12)

Date of delivery or appropriation for shipped oil not disposed of in sales at arm's length

5—(1) (*inserts* OTA 1975 s 12A)
(2) The amendment made by this paragraph has effect in relation to oil which would (apart from this paragraph) fall to be regarded for the purposes of Part 1 of OTA 1975 as delivered or appropriated on a date after 30th June 2006.

"The Board"

6—(1) In section 21 (citation, interpretation and construction of the Act) subsection (2) is amended as follows.
(2) (*amends* OTA 1975 s 21(2))
(3) The amendment made by this paragraph comes into force on the day on which this Act is passed.

Returns by participators

7—(1) In Schedule 2 (management and collection) paragraph 2 is amended as follows.
(2) (*amends* OTA 1975 Sch 2 para 2(2)(*a*)(iii))
(3) (*amends* OTA 1975 Sch 2 para 2(2)(*b*)(ii))
(4) (*amends* OTA 1975 Sch 2 para 2(2)(*d*)(ii))

Gas fractionation

8—(1) In Schedule 3 (petroleum revenue tax: miscellaneous provisions) paragraph 2A (market value of oil that consists of or includes gas) is amended as follows.
(2) (*amends* OTA 1975 Sch 3 para 2A(1))
(3) (*amends* OTA 1975 Sch 3 para 2A(2))
(4) (*amends* OTA 1975 Sch 3 para 2A(3))

Aggregate market value of oil for purposes of section 2(5)

9 (*substitutes* OTA 1975 Sch 3 para 3)

Power to make regulations

10 (*inserts* OTA 1975 Sch 3 para 12)

PART 2

AMENDMENTS OF OTHER ENACTMENTS

FINANCE (NO 2) ACT 1987

The designated fraction for the month

11—(1) Schedule 8 to F(No 2)A 1987 (amendments of Schedule 10 to FA 1987) is amended as follows.
(2) (*repeals* F(No 2)A 1987 para 5)
(3) The amendment made by this paragraph has effect for chargeable periods beginning on or after 1st July 2006.

INCOME AND CORPORATION TAXES ACT 1988

Valuation of oil disposed of or appropriated in certain circumstances.

12—(1) Section 493 of ICTA (valuation of oil disposed of or appropriated in certain circumstances) is amended as follows.
(2) (inserts TA 1988 s 493(A1)–(A3))
(3) (*amends* TA 1988 s 493(1))

(4) (*amends* TA 1988 s 493(2))
(5) (*amends* TA 1988 s 493(3))
(6) (*amends* TA 1988 s 493(4))
(7) (substitutes TA 1988 s 493(5))

Amendments—Sub-para (2) repealed by CTA 2010 s 1181, Sch 3 Pt 1. CTA 2010 has effect for corporation tax purposes for accounting periods ending on or after 1 April 2010, and for income and capital gains tax purposes for the tax year 2010–11 and subsequent tax years.

Sub-paras (3)(*b*), (7) repealed for corporation tax purposes by CTA 2010 s 1181, Sch 3 Pt 2. CTA 2010 has effect for corporation tax purposes for accounting periods ending on or after 1 April 2010, and for income and capital gains tax purposes for the tax year 2010–11 and subsequent tax years.

Sub-paras (3)(*b*), (7) repealed by TIOPA 2010 s 378, Sch 10 Pt 6. TIOPA 2010 has effect for corporation tax purposes for accounting periods ending on or after 1 April 2010, for income and capital gains tax purposes for the tax year 2010–11 and subsequent tax years, and for petroleum revenue tax purposes for chargeable periods beginning on or after 1 July 2010.

SCHEDULE 19

SCHEDULE TO BE INSERTED AS SCHEDULE 19C TO ICTA

Section 154

(inserts TA 1988 Sch 19C)

Repeal—This Schedule repealed by CTA 2010 s 1181, Sch 3 Pt 1. CTA 2010 has effect for corporation tax purposes for accounting periods ending on or after 1 April 2010, and for income and capital gains tax purposes for the tax year 2010–11 and subsequent tax years.

SCHEDULE 26

REPEALS

Section 178

PART 5
OIL

Note—The repeals made by this Schedule are already in force and have therefore been omitted.

FINANCE ACT 2007

(2007 Chapter 11)

An Act to Grant certain duties, to alter other duties, and to amend the law relating to the National Debt and the Public Revenue, and to make further provision in connection with finance.

[19 July 2007]

PART 7
MISCELLANEOUS

Petroleum revenue tax

102 Abolition of PRT for fields recommissioned after earlier decommissioning

(1) Section 185 of FA 1993 (abolition of PRT for oil fields with development consents on or after 16th March 1993) is amended as follows.
(2) (*amends* FA 1993 s 185(1))
(3) (*inserts* FA 1993 s 185(1A)–(1C))
(4) (*amends* FA 1993 s 185(7))
(5) An oil field which meets the conditions in subsection (1A) of section 185 of FA 1993 (as inserted by subsection (3) above) becomes a non-taxable field for the purposes of any enactment relating to petroleum revenue tax—

(*a*) in any case where the development decision is made before 1st July 2007, on that date, and
(*b*) in any other case, on the date on which the development decision is made.

103 Tax-exempt tariffing receipts

(1) Section 6A of the Oil Taxation Act 1983 (c 56) (tax-exempt tariffing receipts) is amended as follows.
(2) (*inserts* OTA 1983 s 6A(4)(*c*))
(3) (*amends* OTA 1983 s 6A(5))
(4) The amendments made by this section are deemed to have come into force on 1st July 2007.

104 Allowance of unrelievable loss from abandoned field

(1) (*inserts* OTA 1975 s 6(4A))
(2) The amendment made by subsection (1) is deemed to have come into force on 1st July 2007.

FINANCE ACT 2008

(2008 Chapter 9)

An Act to Grant certain duties, to alter other duties, and to amend the law relating to the National Debt and the Public Revenue, and to make further provision in connection with finance.

[21 July 2008]

PART 6
OIL

Petroleum revenue tax

102 Meaning of "participator"

(1) In section 12 of OTA 1975 (interpretation of Part 1), the definition of "participator" is amended as follows.

(2)–(4) (*amend* OTA 1975 s 12(1) definition of "participator")

(5) The amendments made by this section have effect in relation to expenditure incurred after 30 June 2008.

103 Abandonment expenditure: default by participator met by former participator

(1) (*substitutes* OTA 1975 Sch 5 paras 2A–2C)

(2) The amendment made by subsection (1) has effect in relation to expenditure incurred after 30 June 2008.

104 Abandonment expenditure: deductions from ring fence income

. . .

Amendments—This section repealed for corporation tax purposes by CTA 2010 s 1181, Sch 3 Pt 2. CTA 2010 has effect for corporation tax purposes for accounting periods ending on or after 1 April 2010, and for income and capital gains tax purposes for the tax year 2010–11 and subsequent tax years.

This section repealed by TIOPA 2010 s 378, Sch 10 Pt 6. TIOPA 2010 has effect for corporation tax purposes for accounting periods ending on or after 1 April 2010, for income and capital gains tax purposes for the tax year 2010–11 and subsequent tax years, and for petroleum revenue tax purposes for chargeable periods beginning on or after 1 July 2010.

105 Abandonment expenditure: former participator reimbursed by defaulter

(1) Section 108 of FA 1991 (reimbursement by defaulter in respect of certain abandonment expenditure) is amended as follows.

(2) (amends FA 1991 s 108(1)(*a*))

(3) (substitutes FA 1991 s 108(1)(*b*))

(4) (amends FA 1991 s 108(1)(*c*))

(5) (amends FA 1991 s 108(4))

(6) (amends FA 1991 s 108(5))

(7) (amends FA 1991 s 108(7))

(8) The amendments made by this section have effect in relation to expenditure incurred after 30 June 2008.[1]

Amendments—[1] Section 105 repealed by FA 2013 s 89(1), Sch 31 para 12 with effect in relation to expenditure incurred on or after 17 July 2013.

106 Returns of relevant sales of oil

(1) Section 62 of FA 1987 (returns of relevant sales of oil) is amended as follows.

(2) (*inserts* FA 1987 s 62(3A))

(3), (4) (*amend* FA 1987 s 62(4))

(5) (*amends* FA 1987 s 62(6))

(6) (*inserts* FA 1987 s 62(8A))

(7) The amendments made by this section have effect in relation to chargeable periods ending on or after 30 June 2008.

107 Elections for oil fields to become non-taxable

(1) Section 185 of FA 1993 is amended as follows.

(2) (*inserts* FA 1993 s 185(A1))

(3) (*amends* FA 1993 s 185(1))

(4) (*inserts* FA 1993 s 185(1ZA))

(5) (*inserts* FA 1993 s 185(1A(*za*))

(6) (*inserts* FA 1993 Sch 20A)

(7) Part 2 of Schedule 33 contains other amendments relating to the amendments made by this section.

Corporation tax

108 Capital allowances: plant and machinery for use in ring fence trade

(1) (*amends* CAA 2001 s 52(3))

(2) The amendment made by subsection (1) has effect in relation to expenditure incurred on or after 12 March 2008.

109 Capital allowances: decommissioning expenditure

(1) Section 163 of CAA 2001 (meaning of "abandonment expenditure") is amended as follows.
(2) (*amends* CAA 2001 s 163 heading)
(3) (*substitutes* CAA 2001 s 163(1)–(3))
(4) (*inserts* CAA 2001 s 163(4ZA)–(4ZC))
(5) (*amends* CAA 2001 s 163 (5)(*b*))
(6) Schedule 34 contains amendments consequential on this section.
(7) The amendments made by this section and that Schedule have effect in relation to expenditure incurred on or after 12 March 2008.

110 Capital allowances: abandonment expenditure after ceasing ring fence trade

(1) Section 165 of CAA 2001 (abandonment expenditure within 3 years of ceasing ring fence trade) is amended as follows.
(2) (*amends* CAA 2001 s 165 heading)
(3) (*substitutes* CAA 2001 s 165(2)–(2C))
(4) (*inserts* CAA 2001 s 165(4A))
(5) (*inserts* CAA 2001 s 165(6), (7))
(6) Section 393A of ICTA (losses: set off against profits of the same, or an earlier, accounting period) is amended as follows.
(7) (*amends* TA 1988 s 393A(11))
(8) (*inserts* TA 1988 s 393A(11A))
(9) The amendments made by this section have effect in relation to ring fence trades that cease to be carried on or after 12 March 2008.

111 Losses: set off against profits of earlier accounting periods

. . .

Amendments—This section repealed by CTA 2010 s 1181, Sch 3 Pt 1. CTA 2010 has effect for corporation tax purposes for accounting periods ending on or after 1 April 2010, and for income and capital gains tax purposes for the tax year 2010–11 and subsequent tax years.

112 Ring fence trade: no deduction for expenses of investment management

. . .

Amendments—This section repealed by CTA 2010 s 1181, Sch 3 Pt 1. CTA 2010 has effect for corporation tax purposes for accounting periods ending on or after 1 April 2010, and for income and capital gains tax purposes for the tax year 2010–11 and subsequent tax years.

SCHEDULES

SCHEDULE 33

PRT: ELECTIONS FOR OIL FIELDS TO BECOME NON-TAXABLE

Section 107

PART 1
NEW SCHEDULE 20A TO FA 1993

1 (*inserts* FA 1993 Sch 20A)

PART 2
OTHER AMENDMENTS

OTA 1975

2 (*amends* OTA 1975 s 6(1A))

FA 1980

3 (*inserts* FA 1980 Sch 17 para 15(9))

Oil Taxation Act 1983

4 (*amends* OTA 1983 s 9(5)(*a*))

SCHEDULE 34

OIL DECOMMISSIONING EXPENDITURE: CONSEQUENTIAL AMENDMENTS

Section 109

ICTA

1 (*amends* TA 1988 s 393A)

CAA 2001

2 CAA 2001 is amended as follows.

3 (*amends* CAA 2001 s 26(5))

4 (*amends* CAA 2001 s 57)

5 (*amends* CAA 2001 s 164)

6 (*amends* CAA 2001 s 165)

SCHEDULE 35

SET OFF AGAINST OIL PROFITS: MINOR AND CONSEQUENTIAL AMENDMENTS

Section 111

TMA 1970

1 (amends TMA 1970 s 87A(6)(*a*))

Amendments—This para repealed by CTA 2010 s 1181, Sch 3 Pt 1. CTA 2010 has effect for corporation tax purposes for accounting periods ending on or after 1 April 2010, and for income and capital gains tax purposes for the tax year 2010–11 and subsequent tax years.

ICTA

2 ICTA is amended as follows.

3 (amends TA 1988 s 343(3))

Amendments—This para repealed by CTA 2010 s 1181, Sch 3 Pt 1. CTA 2010 has effect for corporation tax purposes for accounting periods ending on or after 1 April 2010, and for income and capital gains tax purposes for the tax year 2010–11 and subsequent tax years.

4 (amends TA 1988 s 393(1))

Amendments—This para repealed by CTA 2010 s 1181, Sch 3 Pt 1. CTA 2010 has effect for corporation tax purposes for accounting periods ending on or after 1 April 2010, and for income and capital gains tax purposes for the tax year 2010–11 and subsequent tax years.

5 (inserts TA 1988 s 393A(2D))

Amendments—This para repealed by CTA 2010 s 1181, Sch 3 Pt 1. CTA 2010 has effect for corporation tax purposes for accounting periods ending on or after 1 April 2010, and for income and capital gains tax purposes for the tax year 2010–11 and subsequent tax years.

6 (amends TA 1988 s 768A(1))

Amendments—This para repealed by CTA 2010 s 1181, Sch 3 Pt 1. CTA 2010 has effect for corporation tax purposes for accounting periods ending on or after 1 April 2010, and for income and capital gains tax purposes for the tax year 2010–11 and subsequent tax years.

7 (*amends* TA 1988 s 826(7A)(*b*))

8—(1) Schedule 19B (petroleum extraction activities: exploration expenditure supplement) is amended as follows.
(2) (*amends* TA 1988 Sch 19B para 1(7)(*b*))
(3) (*inserts* TA 1988 Sch 19B para 17(2)(*b*))

9—(1) Schedule 19C (petroleum extraction activities: ring fence expenditure supplement) is amended as follows.
(2) (amends TA 1988 Sch 19C para 1)
(3) (amends TA 1988 Sch 19C para 17)

Amendments—This para repealed by CTA 2010 s 1181, Sch 3 Pt 1. CTA 2010 has effect for corporation tax purposes for accounting periods ending on or after 1 April 2010, and for income and capital gains tax purposes for the tax year 2010–11 and subsequent tax years.

FA 2000

10—(1) Schedule 20 to FA 2000 (tax relief for expenditure on research and development) is amended as follows.
(2), (3) (amend FA 2000 Sch 20 paras 15(4)(b), (5)(b), 23(2))[1]

Amendments—[1] Para 10 repealed by CTA 2009 s 1326, Sch 3 Pt 1. CTA 2009 applies for accounting periods ending on or after 1 April 2009 (for corporation tax purposes) and for tax years 2009–10 onwards (for income and capital gains tax purposes).

SCHEDULE 36

INFORMATION AND INSPECTION POWERS

Section 113

Note—Schedule 36, as amended, is reproduced in full in Part 1 of this work.

FINANCE ACT 2009

(2009 Chapter 10)

PART 6

OIL

PART 7

ADMINISTRATION

Assessments, claims etc

An Act to Grant certain duties, to alter other duties, and to amend the law relating to the National Debt and the Public Revenue, and to make further provision in connection with finance.

[21 July 2009]

PART 6

OIL

84 Capital allowances for oil decommissioning expenditure

Schedule 38 contains provision about capital allowances for oil decommissioning expenditure.

85 Blended oil

Schedule 39 contains provision about the treatment of blended oil for the purposes of petroleum revenue tax.

86 Chargeable gains

Schedule 40 contains provision about chargeable gains in oil trades.

87 Oil assets put to other uses

Schedule 41 contains provision about oil production assets put to certain other uses.

88 Former licensees and former oil fields

Schedule 42 contains provision about the treatment of certain former licensees and former oil fields for the purposes of petroleum revenue tax.

89 Abolition of provisional expenditure allowance

Schedule 43 contains provision abolishing provisional expenditure allowance.

90 Supplementary charge: reduction for certain new oil fields

. . .

Amendments—This section repealed by CTA 2010 ss 1177,1181, Sch 1 paras 706, 711, Sch 3 Pt 1. CTA 2010 has effect for corporation tax purposes for accounting periods ending on or after 1 April 2010, and for income and capital gains tax purposes for the tax year 2010–11 and subsequent tax years.

91 Miscellaneous amendments

Schedule 45 contains miscellaneous amendments relating to oil taxation.

PART 7

ADMINISTRATION

Assessments, claims etc

99 Time limits for assessments, claims etc

(1) Schedule 51 contains provision about time limits for assessments, claims etc

(2) The amendments made by that Schedule come into force on such day as the Treasury may by order made by statutory instrument appoint.

(3) An order under subsection (2)—

(*a*) may make different provision for different purposes, and

(*b*) may include transitional provision and savings.

Commencement—Finance Act 2009, Schedule 51 (Time Limits for Assessments, Claims, etc) (Appointed Days and Transitional Provisions) Order 2010, SI 2010/867 (appointed days for the purposes of amendments made by Sch 51 are—

(a) 1 April 2010 for amendments made by paras 1 to 4 and 27 to 43 (insurance premium tax, aggregates levy, climate change levy, landfill tax and minor and consequential provision); and

(b) 1 April 2011 for amendments made by paragraphs 5 to 26 (inheritance tax, stamp duty land tax and petroleum revenue tax.))

SCHEDULES

SCHEDULE 39

PRT: BLENDED OIL

Section 85

1 Part 5 of FA 1987 (oil taxation) is amended as follows.

2 (*substitutes* FA 1987 s 63)

3—(1) Schedule 12 (supplementary provisions as to blended oil) is amended as follows.

(2) (*substitutes* FA 1987 Sch 12 paras 1, 2)

(3) In paragraph 3(1)—

(*a*) for "the Board" (in each place) substitute "HMRC", and

(*b*) for "paragraph 2(*a*)" substitute "paragraph 2(2)".

(4) In paragraph 3(2), for "the Board" (in each place) substitute "HMRC".

(5) (*inserts* FA 1987 Sch 12 para 3(3), (4))

(6) Omit paragraph 4.

4 The amendments made by this Schedule have effect in relation to chargeable periods beginning after 30 June 2009.

SCHEDULE 40

OIL: CHARGEABLE GAINS

Section 86

PART 1

LICENCE SWAPS

1–7 (*amend* TCGA 1992: see *Part 1a* of this publication)

8 The amendments made by this Part have effect in relation to disposals made on or after 22 April 2009.

PART 2

REINVESTMENT OF RING FENCE ASSETS

Amendment of TCGA 1992

9–12 (*amend* TCGA 1992: see *Part 1a* of this publication)

Alternative to roll-over relief

13 The amendments made by this Part have effect in relation to disposals made on or after 22 April 2009 (whether the acquisition in which the consideration is reinvested takes place before, on or after that date).

SCHEDULE 41

OIL ASSETS PUT TO OTHER USES

Section 87

PART 1
PETROLEUM REVENUE TAX

Allowance of decommissioning and restoration expenditure

1—(1) Section 3 of OTA 1975 (allowance of expenditure) is amended as follows.
(2) In subsection (1C)(*b*), for "in connection with the field" substitute "for a qualifying purpose".
(3) In subsection (1D), for "in connection with the field" substitute "for a qualifying purpose".
(4) (*inserts* OTA 1975 s 3(1DA)–(1DC))

Amounts which are not chargeable tariff receipts

2—(1) Section 6 of OTA 1983 (amounts which are not chargeable tariff receipts) is amended as follows.
(2) In subsection (4)—

(*a*) in paragraph (*b*), insert at the end "or", and

(*b*) after that paragraph insert—

"(*c*) is referable to other use of an asset, except use wholly or partly for an oil purpose,".

(3) (*inserts* OTA 1983 s 6(4A), (4B))

No reduction of allowable expenditure

3—(1) Paragraph 8 of Schedule 1 to OTA 1983 (allowable expenditure: use of new asset otherwise than in connection with taxable field) is amended as follows.
(2) In sub-paragraph (1)(*a*) and (*b*), for "in connection with a taxable field" substitute "for a qualifying purpose".
(3) (*inserts* OTA 1983 Sch 1 para 8(2A)–(2C))

Commencement

4 The amendments made by this Part have effect in relation to chargeable periods beginning after 30 June 2009.

SCHEDULE 42

PRT: FORMER LICENSEES AND FORMER OIL FIELDS

Section 88

PART 1
PERSONS WHO CEASE TO BE LICENSEES BECAUSE OF CESSATION EVENTS

1 OTA 1975 is amended as follows.

2—(1) Section 12 (interpretation of Part 1) is amended as follows.
(2) In subsection (1), in the definition of "participator"—

(*a*) for "any", in the first place, substitute "a",

(*b*) (*inserts* OTA 1975 s 12 "participator" (*aa*))

(*c*) in paragraph (*b*), after "field" insert "(and who does not fall within paragraph (*aa*) of this definition)",

(*d*) in paragraph (*c*), after "paragraph" insert "(*aa*) or", and

(*e*) omit the words after paragraph (*g*).

(3) (*inserts* OTA 1975 s 12(1A))

3 In Schedule 5 (allowance of expenditure other than abortive exploration expenditure), in paragraph 2C(2)—

(*a*) in the definition of "current participator", after "paragraph (*a*)," insert "(*aa*),", and

(*b*) in paragraph (*b*) of the definition of "former participator", after "paragraph (*a*)," insert "(*aa*),".

4 The amendments made by this Part have effect in relation to persons who cease to be licensees because of cessation events occurring in chargeable periods that begin after 30 June 2009.

PART 2

AREAS TREATED AS CONTINUING TO BE OIL FIELDS

5 OTA 1975 is amended as follows.

6 In section 12(1) (interpretation of Part 1), in the definition of "oil field", after "this Act" insert "(which also includes provision about areas that are to be treated as continuing to be oil fields)".

7—(1) Schedule 1 (determination of oil fields) is amended as follows.
(2) Before paragraph 1 insert—

"Areas that are oil fields"

(3) (*inserts* OTA 1975 Sch 1 paras 6, 7))

8 The amendments made by this Part have effect in relation to areas that cease to be oil fields, or parts of oil fields, in chargeable periods that begin after 30 June 2009.

SCHEDULE 43

PRT: ABOLITION OF PROVISIONAL EXPENDITURE ALLOWANCE

Section 89

Interpretation

1 In this Schedule—

"future chargeable period" means a chargeable period beginning after 30 June 2009;

"provisional expenditure allowance" means an amount calculated under section 2(9)(*a*) of OTA 1975.

Abolition of allowance

2 No provisional expenditure allowance is to be calculated in respect of a future chargeable period.

Amendments consequential on abolition

3 (1) Section 2 of OTA 1975 (assessable profits and allowable losses) is amended as follows.
(2) For subsection (8) substitute—

"(8) The amount (if any) to be debited or credited to the participator for the period in respect of expenditure is the sum of the amounts mentioned in subsection (9) below."

(3) Omit subsections (9)(*a*), (10) and (11).
(4) In Schedule 17 to FA 1980 (transfers of interests in oil fields), omit paragraph 11 (and the heading before it).
(5) This paragraph has effect in relation to future chargeable periods.
(6) But this paragraph is subject to paragraph 4.

Savings

4 (1) This paragraph applies if provisional expenditure allowance has been calculated in respect of a pre-abolition chargeable period ("the relevant allowance").
(2) The saved provisions continue to have effect in future chargeable periods in relation to the relevant allowance and the relevant participator as if those provisions had not been amended by paragraph 3.
(3) In this paragraph—

"pre-abolition chargeable period" means a chargeable period that begins before 30 June 2009;

"relevant participator" means the participator in respect of which the relevant allowance has been calculated;

"the saved provisions" means—

(*a*) section 2(8) and (10) of OTA 1975, and

(*b*) paragraph 11 of Schedule 17 to FA 1980.

SCHEDULE 44

SUPPLEMENTARY CHARGE: REDUCTION FOR CERTAIN NEW OIL FIELDS

Section 90

Amendments—This Schedule repealed by CTA 2010 ss 1177, 1181, Sch 1 paras 706, 720, Sch 3 Part 1. CTA 2010 has effect for corporation tax purposes for accounting periods ending on or after 1 April 2010, and for income and capital gains tax purposes for the tax year 2010–11 and subsequent tax years.

SCHEDULE 45

OIL: MISCELLANEOUS AMENDMENTS

Section 91

OTA 1975

1—(1) OTA 1975 is amended as follows.

(2) Omit paragraphs 9 and 10 of Schedule 3 (election to have amounts mentioned in section 2(9)(*b*) and (*c*) spread).

(3) In consequence of the omission of paragraph 9 of Schedule 3, omit section 9(4).

(4) Omit paragraph 3 of Schedule 4 (allowable expenditure incurred before 13 November 1974).

(5) The repeals made by this paragraph have effect in relation to chargeable periods beginning after 30 June 2009.

OTA 1983

2—(1) OTA 1983 is amended as follows.

(2) Omit section 9(3) and paragraph 3 of Schedule 3 (receipts from contracts made before 8 May 1982).

(3) In consequence of the omission of subsection (3) of section 9—

(*a*) in subsection (2) of that section, for "subsections (3) and (4)" substitute "subsection (4)", and

(*b*) in subsection (4)(*b*) of that section, for "subsections (1) to (3)" substitute "subsections (1) and (2)".

(4) Omit sections 13 and 14 and Schedule 5 (transitional provision for expenditure incurred on or before 31 December 1983).

FA 1993

3—(1) Schedule 20A to FA 1993 (as inserted by Part 1 of Schedule 33 to FA 2008) is renumbered as Schedule 20B to that Act.

(2) In the following provisions, for "Schedule 20A" substitute "Schedule 20B"—

(*a*) section 6(1A) of OTA 1975,

(*b*) paragraph 15(9A) of Schedule 17 to FA 1980, and

(*c*) section 185(1ZA)(*b*) of FA 1993.

ICTA

4— . . .

Amendments—This para repealed by CTA 2010 s 1181, Sch 3 Pt 1. CTA 2010 has effect for corporation tax purposes for accounting periods ending on or after 1 April 2010, and for income and capital gains tax purposes for the tax year 2010–11 and subsequent tax years.

SCHEDULE 51

TIME LIMITS FOR ASSESSMENTS, CLAIMS ETC

Section 99

Order—Finance Act 2009, Schedule 51 (Time Limits for Assessments, Claims, etc) (Appointed Days and Transitional Provisions) Order, SI 2010/867 (appointed day for amendments made by FA 2009 Sch 51 paras 5–26 is 1 April 2011).

Petroleum revenue tax

17 OTA 1975 is amended as follows.

18—(1) The Table in paragraph 1(1) of Schedule 2 (applying provisions of TMA 1970 in relation to management and collection of petroleum revenue tax) is amended as follows.

(2) [...][1]

(3) Omit the entries relating to sections 34 and 36 of TMA 1970.

Amendments—[1] Sub-para (2) repealed by F(No 3)A 2010 s 28, Sch 12 Pt 2 para 13(*a*) with effect in relation to claims made on or after 1 April 2011.

19 In paragraph 10 of Schedule 2 (assessments to tax and determinations of loss etc), after sub-paragraph (1) insert—

"(1A) An assessment under sub-paragraph (1) may be made at any time not more than 4 years after the end of the chargeable period to which it relates (subject to paragraphs 12A and 12B)."

20—(1) Paragraph 12 of Schedule 2 (further assessments and determinations) is amended as follows.

(2) After sub-paragraph (1) insert—

"(1A) An assessment (or an amendment of an assessment) under sub-paragraph (1) may be made at any time not more than 4 years after the end of the chargeable period to which the assessment relates (subject to sub-paragraph (1B) and paragraphs 12A and 12B).

(1B) The time limits in sub-paragraph (1A) and paragraphs 12A and 12B do not apply to an amendment of an assessment where the amendment is made in consequence (directly or indirectly) of—

(*a*) the granting of relief under section 7(2) or (3) to any participator for allowable losses accruing in any chargeable period, or

(*b*) a notice of variation served under paragraph 9 of Schedule 5 on any responsible person in respect of a claim for any claim period."

(3) In sub-paragraph (2)—

(*a*) omit "(notwithstanding anything in section 34 of the Taxes Management Act 1970 (ordinary time limit for assessment))",

(*b*) for "six years" substitute "4 years", and

(*c*) insert at the end "(subject to paragraphs 12A and 12B)".

21 In paragraph 12A(1) of Schedule 2 (time limit for assessment following extension of time for delivery of return), for "five years" substitute "4 years".

22 In that Schedule, after paragraph 12A insert—

"12B—

(1) In a case involving a relevant situation brought about carelessly by a participator (or a person acting on behalf of a participator), an assessment (or an amendment of an assessment) under this Schedule on the participator may be made at any time not more than 6 years after the end of the relevant chargeable period (subject to sub-paragraph (2)).

(2) In a case involving a relevant situation brought about deliberately by a participator (or a person acting on behalf of a participator), an assessment (or an amendment of an assessment) on the participator may be made at any time not more than 20 years after the end of the relevant chargeable period.

(3) "Relevant situation" means a situation in which—

(*a*) there is a loss of tax,

(*b*) the assessable profit charged to tax by or stated in an assessment for a chargeable period ought to be or to have been larger,

(*c*) the allowable loss stated in an assessment or a determination of loss for a chargeable period ought to be or to have been smaller, or

(*d*) an assessment to tax should have been made for a chargeable period but was not made.

(4) "Relevant chargeable period" means—

(*a*) in the case of a further assessment under paragraph 12(2), the chargeable period in which the excessive allowable loss accrued, and

(*b*) in any other case, the chargeable period to which the assessment relates.

(5) Where the participator carried on a trade or business with one or more other persons at any time in the chargeable period for which the assessment under sub-paragraph (1) or (2) is made, an assessment to tax in respect of the profits of that trade or business may also be made on any of the participator's partners.

(6) In determining the amount of the tax to be charged on a person for a chargeable period in an assessment in a case mentioned in sub-paragraph (1) or (2) (including an assessment under sub-paragraph (5)), effect must be given to any relief or allowance to which that person would have been entitled for that period if a valid claim or application had been made.

(7) Sub-paragraph (6) only applies if the person on whom the assessment is made so requires.

(8) Subsections (5) to (7) of section 118 of the Taxes Management Act 1970 (losses and situations brought about carelessly or deliberately) apply for the purposes of this paragraph as they apply for the purposes of that Act.

PRT

(9) In subsection (6)(*b*) of that section (as it applies for the purposes of this paragraph), the reference to the person who provides the information has effect as if it included any person who becomes the responsible person for the oil field after the information is provided."

23—(1) Paragraph 2 of Schedule 5 (allowance of expenditure other than abortive exploration expenditure: claim period) is amended as follows.

(2) In sub-paragraph (1), for "six years" substitute "4 years".

(3) In sub-paragraph (7)—

(*a*) in paragraph (*c*), for "four years" substitute "2 years", and

(*b*) in the words after that paragraph, for "six years" substitute "4 years".

24—(1) Paragraph 9 of Schedule 5 (allowance of expenditure other than abortive exploration expenditure: notice of variation) is amended as follows.

(2) In sub-paragraph (1)—

(*a*) omit the words from ", within" to "field,",

(*b*) for "in the notice" substitute "in a notice of a decision under paragraph 3 above given to the responsible person for an oil field", and

(*c*) for "that period" substitute "the permitted period".

(3) Omit sub-paragraphs (1A) to (1C) and (2A).

(4) After sub-paragraph (2A) insert—

"(2B) In this paragraph "permitted period" means the period of 4 years beginning with the date on which the notice of the decision under paragraph 3 was given (but see sub-paragraph (2C)).

(2C) Where the relevant amount was overstated in the notice of decision as a result of an inaccuracy in a statement or declaration made by the responsible person (or a person acting on behalf of the responsible person) in connection with the claim—

(*a*) if the inaccuracy was careless, the permitted period is extended to 6 years, and

(*b*) if the inaccuracy was deliberate, the permitted period is extended to 20 years."

(5) Omit sub-paragraph (11).

(6) Insert at the end—

"(12) For the purposes of this section, an inaccuracy in a statement or declaration made by the responsible person (or a person acting on behalf of the responsible person) is careless if it is due to a failure by the person to take reasonable care.

(13) An inaccuracy in a statement or declaration made by the responsible person (or a person acting on behalf of the responsible person) is to be treated as careless if—

(*a*) the responsible person, the person who acted on behalf of the responsible person or any person who becomes the responsible person for the oil field after the statement or declaration is made discovers the inaccuracy some time after it is made, and

(*b*) that person fails to take reasonable steps to inform Her Majesty's Revenue and Customs."

25—(1) Schedule 6 (allowance of expenditure (other than abortive exploration expenditure) on claim by participator) is amended as follows.

(2) In paragraph 1(2) (claim period), for "six years" substitute "4 years".

(3) In paragraph 2 (applying provisions of Schedule 5), in the Table, in the entry relating to paragraph 9 of Schedule 5, omit the words in the second column.

26 In paragraph 1(3) of Schedule 7 (re), in the Table, in the entry relating to paragraph 9 of Schedule 5, in the second column omit—

(*a*) the words "In sub-paragraph (1C) omit paragraph (*c*)" and "omit sub-paragraph (2A)", and

(*b*) the words from "and in sub-paragraph (11)" to the end.

SCHEDULE 53

LATE PAYMENT INTEREST

Section 101

PART 2

SPECIAL PROVISION: LATE PAYMENT INTEREST START DATE

[Instalments of petroleum revenue tax

11A The late payment interest start date in respect of an instalment of petroleum revenue tax payable under paragraph 2 of Schedule 19 to FA 1982 (payment for tax) is the last day of the month in which that instalment is payable.]

Prospective amendment—Paras 11A, 11B and preceding cross-heads to be inserted by F(No 3)A 2010 s 25, Sch 9 Pt 2 paras 13, 16, 17 with effect from a day to be appointed by Treasury order (F(No 3)A 2010 s 25).

[Other amounts of petroleum revenue tax

11B The late payment interest start date in respect of any other amount of petroleum revenue tax is the date falling two months after the end of the chargeable period in respect of which the amount is due.]

Prospective amendment—Paras 11A, 11B and preceding cross-heads to be inserted by F(No 3)A 2010 s 25, Sch 9 Pt 2 paras 13, 16, 17 with effect from a day to be appointed by Treasury order (F(No 3)A 2010 s 25).

PART 3

SPECIAL PROVISION: DATE TO WHICH LATE PAYMENT INTEREST RUNS

[Instalments of petroleum revenue tax

14A—(1) An instalment of petroleum revenue tax payable under paragraph 2 of Schedule 19 to FA 1982 (payment for tax) carries late payment interest until the earlier of—

(*a*) the date on which the instalment is paid, and

(*b*) the date falling two months after the end of the chargeable period in respect of which the instalment is due.

(2) An instalment which remains unpaid after the date mentioned in sub-paragraph (1)(*b*) carries interest as an amount payable on account under section 1 of PRTA 1980.

(3) For the purposes of determining the date on which an overdue instalment is paid, a payment on account of one or more such instalments is to be attributed, so far as possible, to the earliest month for which an instalment is overdue.]

Prospective amendment—Para 14A and preceding cross-head to be inserted by F(No 3)A 2010 s 25, Sch 9 Pt 2 paras 13, 16, 18 with effect from a day to be appointed by Treasury order (F(No 3)A 2010 s 25).

SCHEDULE 54

REPAYMENT INTEREST

Section 102

PART 2

SPECIAL PROVISION AS TO REPAYMENT INTEREST START DATE

[Petroleum revenue tax

12A—(1) The repayment interest start date in respect of any amount of petroleum revenue tax is the later of—

(*a*) the date falling two months after the end of the chargeable period in respect of which the amount was paid, and

(*b*) the date on which the amount was paid.

(2) Sub-paragraph (1) is subject to paragraph 12B (limit on amount of repayment interest carried by certain repayments generated by carry back reliefs).

(3) For the purposes of this paragraph any instalment or part of an instalment that becomes repayable is to be regarded, so far as possible, as consisting of the instalment most recently paid.]

Prospective amendment—Paras 12A, 12B and preceding cross-head to be inserted by F(No 3)A 2010 s 25, Sch 9 Pt 2 paras 13, 19 with effect from a day to be appointed by Treasury order (F(No 3)A 2010 s 25).

[12B—(1) This paragraph applies where—

(*a*) an assessment for a chargeable period ("the earlier period") gives effect to relief under section 7(2) or (3) of OTA 1975 for one or more allowable losses accruing in a later chargeable period, and

(*b*) by virtue of that assessment, an amount of tax becomes repayable to the participator in question (whether wholly or partly by reason of giving effect to that relief).

(2) The amount of repayment interest carried by the appropriate repayment is not to exceed the difference between—

(*a*) 60% of the amount of the allowable loss or losses which is treated as reducing the assessable profit of the earlier period, and

(*b*) the amount of the appropriate repayment.

(3) In this paragraph "the appropriate repayment" means so much of the repayment as is attributable to giving effect to the relief (but this is subject to sub-paragraphs (4) and (5)).

(4) Sub-paragraph (5) applies where the assessment (as well as giving effect to the relief mentioned in sub-paragraph (1)) takes account of any other matter, whether a relief or not, which goes—

(*a*) to reduce the assessable profit of the earlier period, or

(*b*) otherwise to reduce the tax payable for that period.

(5) The appropriate repayment is to be taken to be the difference between—

(*a*) the total amount of tax repayable by virtue of the assessment, and

PRT

(*b*) the amount of tax (if any) which would have been repayable if no account had been taken of that relief.

(6) If the earlier period ends on or before 30 June 1993, sub-paragraph (2) has effect as if the percentage specified in paragraph (*a*) were 85%.

(7) In this paragraph references to an assessment include an amendment of an assessment.]

Prospective amendment—Paras 12A, 12B and preceding cross-head to be inserted by F(No 3)A 2010 s 25, Sch 9 Pt 2 paras 13, 19 with effect from a day to be appointed by Treasury order (F(No 3)A 2010 s 25).

SCHEDULE 55

PENALTY FOR FAILURE TO MAKE RETURNS ETC

Section 106

Note—For Schedule 55 see Part 1 of this work.

SCHEDULE 56

PENALTY FOR FAILURE TO MAKE PAYMENTS ON TIME

Section 107

Note—For Schedule 56 see Part 1 of this work.

CORPORATION TAX ACT 2010

(2010 Chapter 4)

Note—Reference should be made to the following in connection with PRT—

CTA 2010 Parts 8 and 8ZA (ss 270–356NG).

The full text of CTA 2010 is reproduced in Part 1c of this publication.

TAXATION (INTERNATIONAL AND OTHER PROVISIONS) ACT 2010

(2010 Chapter 8)

Note—Reference should be made to the following in connection with PRT—

TIOPA 2010 Part 4 Chapter 7 (ss 205–206A) (Oil-related Ring-fence Trades).

TIOPA 2010 s 318 (Companies engaged in oil extraction activities).

TIOPA 2010 s 333 (Group members with income from oil extraction subject to particular tax treatment in UK).

TIOPA 2010 s 364 (Oil activities).

The full text of TIOPA 2010 is reproduced in Part 1c of this publication.

FINANCE (NO 3) ACT 2010

(2010 Chapter 33)

An ACT TO Grant certain duties, to alter other duties, and to amend the law relating to the National Debt and the Public Revenue, and to make further provision in connection with finance.

[16 December 2010]

PART 3

ADMINISTRATION

25 Interest: corporation tax and petroleum revenue tax

(1) Schedule 9 contains amendments of FA 2009 relating to late payment interest and repayment interest on amounts of corporation tax and petroleum revenue tax.

(2) That Schedule comes into force on such day as the Treasury may by order appoint.

(3) An order under subsection (2)—

(*a*) may commence a provision generally or only for specified purposes, and

(*b*) may appoint different days for different provisions or for different purposes.

(4) The Treasury may by order make any incidental, supplemental, consequential, transitional, transitory or saving provision which appears appropriate in consequence of, or otherwise in connection with, that Schedule.

(5) An order under subsection (4) may—

(*a*) make different provision for different purposes, and

(*b*) make provision amending, repealing or revoking any Act or subordinate legislation whenever passed or made (including this Act and any Act amended by it).

(6) An order under this section is to be made by statutory instrument.

(7) A statutory instrument containing an order under subsection (4) which includes provision amending or repealing any provision of an Act is subject to annulment in pursuance of a resolution of the House of Commons.

28 Recovery of overpaid stamp duty land tax and petroleum revenue tax etc

(1) Schedule 12 contains—

(*a*) provision amending Part 4 of FA 2003 (stamp duty land tax) in respect of the recovery of overpaid tax etc, and

(*b*) provision amending Schedule 2 to OTA 1975 (management and collection of petroleum revenue tax) in respect of the recovery of overpaid tax etc.

(2) The amendments made by Schedule 12 have effect in relation to claims made on or after 1 April 2011.

(3) The Treasury may by order make any incidental, supplemental, consequential, transitional, transitory or saving provision which appears appropriate in consequence of, or otherwise in connection with, that Schedule.

(4) An order under this section may—

(*a*) make different provision for different purposes, and

(*b*) make provision amending, repealing or revoking any Act or subordinate legislation whenever passed or made (including this Act and any Act amended by it).

(5) An order under this section is to be made by statutory instrument.

(6) A statutory instrument containing an order under this section which includes provision amending or repealing any provision of an Act is subject to annulment in pursuance of a resolution of the House of Commons.

SCHEDULE 9

INTEREST

Section 25

PART 2

PETROLEUM REVENUE TAX

13 FA 2009 is amended as follows.

14 In section 101 (late payment interest on sums due to HMRC), omit subsection (2)(*b*).

15 In section 102 (repayment interest on sums to be paid by HMRC), omit subsection (2)(*b*).

16 Schedule 53 (late payment interest) is amended as follows.

17 After paragraph 11 insert—

"Instalments of petroleum revenue tax

11A

The late payment interest start date in respect of an instalment of petroleum revenue tax payable under paragraph 2 of Schedule 19 to FA 1982 (payment for tax) is the last day of the month in which that instalment is payable.

Other amounts of petroleum revenue tax

11B

The late payment interest start date in respect of any other amount of petroleum revenue tax is the date falling two months after the end of the chargeable period in respect of which the amount is due."

18 After paragraph 14 insert—

"Instalments of petroleum revenue tax

14A

(1) An instalment of petroleum revenue tax payable under paragraph 2 of Schedule 19 to FA 1982 (payment for tax) carries late payment interest until the earlier of—

(*a*) the date on which the instalment is paid, and

TIOPA 2010

(*b*) the date falling two months after the end of the chargeable period in respect of which the instalment is due.

(2) An instalment which remains unpaid after the date mentioned in sub-paragraph (1)(*b*) carries interest as an amount payable on account under section 1 of PRTA 1980.

(3) For the purposes of determining the date on which an overdue instalment is paid, a payment on account of one or more such instalments is to be attributed, so far as possible, to the earliest month for which an instalment is overdue."

19 In Schedule 54 (repayment interest), after paragraph 12 insert—

"Petroleum revenue tax

12A

(1) The repayment interest start date in respect of any amount of petroleum revenue tax is the later of—

(*a*) the date falling two months after the end of the chargeable period in respect of which the amount was paid, and

(*b*) the date on which the amount was paid.

(2) Sub-paragraph (1) is subject to paragraph 12B (limit on amount of repayment interest carried by certain repayments generated by carry back reliefs).

(3) For the purposes of this paragraph any instalment or part of an instalment that becomes repayable is to be regarded, so far as possible, as consisting of the instalment most recently paid.

12B

(1) This paragraph applies where—

(*a*) an assessment for a chargeable period ("the earlier period") gives effect to relief under section 7(2) or (3) of OTA 1975 for one or more allowable losses accruing in a later chargeable period, and

(*b*) by virtue of that assessment, an amount of tax becomes repayable to the participator in question (whether wholly or partly by reason of giving effect to that relief).

(2) The amount of repayment interest carried by the appropriate repayment is not to exceed the difference between—

(*a*) 60% of the amount of the allowable loss or losses which is treated as reducing the assessable profit of the earlier period, and

(*b*) the amount of the appropriate repayment.

(3) In this paragraph "the appropriate repayment" means so much of the repayment as is attributable to giving effect to the relief (but this is subject to sub-paragraphs (4) and (5)).

(4) Sub-paragraph (5) applies where the assessment (as well as giving effect to the relief mentioned in sub-paragraph (1)) takes account of any other matter, whether a relief or not, which goes—

(*a*) to reduce the assessable profit of the earlier period, or

(*b*) otherwise to reduce the tax payable for that period.

(5) The appropriate repayment is to be taken to be the difference between—

(*a*) the total amount of tax repayable by virtue of the assessment, and

(*b*) the amount of tax (if any) which would have been repayable if no account had been taken of that relief.

(6) If the earlier period ends on or before 30 June 1993, sub-paragraph (2) has effect as if the percentage specified in paragraph (*a*) were 85%.

(7) In this paragraph references to an assessment include an amendment of an assessment."

SCHEDULE 12

RECOVERY OF UNPAID TAX

Section 28

PART 2

PETROLEUM REVENUE TAX

Claims for recovery of overpaid tax etc

6 Schedule 2 to OTA 1975 (management and collection of petroleum revenue tax) is amended as follows.

7 In the Table in paragraph 1(1) (applying provisions of TMA 1970 in relation to management and collection of petroleum revenue tax), omit the entry relating to section 33 of TMA 1970.

8 In paragraph 10(1A) (time limit for assessments and determinations) for "and 12B" substitute ", 12B and 13E".

9 In paragraph 12(1B) (disapplication of time limits for further assessments and determinations)—

(*a*) omit the "or" at the end of paragraph (*a*), and

(*b*) after that paragraph insert—

"(*aa*) a claim under paragraph 13A (see paragraph 13E), or".

10 After paragraph 13 insert—

"Claim for relief for overpaid tax etc

13A

(1) This paragraph applies where—

(*a*) a participator has paid an amount by way of tax but believes that the tax was not due, or

(*b*) a participator has been assessed as liable to pay an amount by way of tax but believes that the tax is not due.

(2) The participator may make a claim to the Commissioners for Her Majesty's Revenue and Customs ("HMRC") for repayment or discharge of the amount.

(3) Paragraph 13B makes provision about cases in which HMRC are not liable to give effect to a claim under this paragraph.

(4) Paragraphs 13C to 14I make further provision about making and giving effect to claims under this paragraph.

(5) Paragraph 13F makes provision about the application of this paragraph and paragraphs 13B to 13E to amounts paid under contract settlements.

(6) HMRC are not liable to give relief in respect of a case described in sub-paragraph (1)(*a*) or (*b*) except as provided—

(*a*) by this Schedule (following a claim under this paragraph), or

(*b*) by or under another provision of the Oil Taxation Acts.

(7) For the purposes of this paragraph and paragraphs 13B to 13F, an amount paid by one person on behalf of another is treated as paid by the other person.

(8) In this paragraph and paragraphs 13B to 13F, "the Oil Taxation Acts" means—

(*a*) Parts 1 and 3 of this Act,

(*b*) the Oil Taxation Act 1983, and

(*c*) any other enactment relating to petroleum revenue tax.

Cases in which HMRC not liable to give effect to a claim

13B

(1) HMRC are not liable to give effect to a claim under paragraph 13A if or to the extent that the claim falls within a case described in this paragraph.

(2) Case A is where the amount paid, or liable to be paid, is excessive by reason of—

(*a*) a mistake in a claim, election or notice or a nomination under Schedule 10 to FA 1987, or

(*b*) a mistake consisting of making or giving, or failing to make or give, a claim, election or notice or a nomination under Schedule 10 to FA 1987.

(3) Case B is where the participator—

(*a*) has or could have sought relief by making a claim for expenditure to be allowed under section 3 or 4 (allowance of expenditure), or

(*b*) is or will be able to seek relief by taking other steps under the Oil Taxation Acts.

(4) Case C is where the participator—

(*a*) could have sought relief by taking such steps within a period that has now expired, and

(*b*) knew, or ought reasonably to have known, before the end of that period that such relief was available.

(5) Case D is where the claim is made on grounds that—

(*a*) have been put to a court or tribunal in the course of an appeal by the participator relating to the amount paid or liable to be paid, or (*b*) have been put to HMRC in the course of an appeal by the participator relating to that amount that is treated as having been determined by a tribunal (by virtue of paragraph 14(9) (settling of appeals by agreement)).

(6) Case E is where the participator knew, or ought reasonably to have known, of the grounds for the claim before the latest of the following—

(*a*) the date on which an appeal by the participator relating to the amount paid, or liable to be paid, in the course of which the ground could have been put forward (a "relevant appeal") was determined by a court or tribunal (or is treated as having been so determined),

(*b*) the date on which the participator withdrew a relevant appeal to a court or tribunal, and

(*c*) the end of the period in which the participator was entitled to make a relevant appeal to a court or tribunal.

(7) Case F is where the amount in question was paid or is liable to be paid—

(*a*) in consequence of proceedings enforcing the payment of that amount brought against the participator by HMRC, or

(*b*) in accordance with an agreement between the participator and HMRC settling such proceedings.

(8) Case G is where—

(*a*) the amount paid, or liable to be paid, is excessive by reason of a mistake in calculating the participator's liability to tax, and

(*b*) liability was calculated in accordance with the practice generally prevailing at the time.

Making a claim

13C

(1) A claim under paragraph 13A may not be made more than 4 years after the end of the relevant chargeable period.

(2) In relation to a claim made in reliance on paragraph 13A(1)(*a*), the relevant chargeable period is—

(*a*) where the amount paid, or liable to be paid, is excessive by reason of a mistake in a return or returns under paragraph 2 or 5, the chargeable period to which the return (or, if more than one, the first return) relates, and

(*b*) otherwise, the chargeable period in respect of which the amount was paid.

(3) In relation to a claim made in reliance on paragraph 13A(1)(*b*), the relevant chargeable period is the chargeable period to which the assessment relates.

(4) A claim under paragraph 13A must be in such form as the HMRC may prescribe.

Decision on claim

13D

HMRC must—

(*a*) make a decision on the claim, and

(*b*) by notice inform the participator of their decision.

Assessment of claimant in connection with claim

13E

(1) This paragraph applies where—

(*a*) a claim is made under paragraph 13A,

(*b*) the grounds for giving effect to the claim also provide grounds for making an assessment or determination under paragraph 10 or 12, or an amendment of such an assessment or determination, on the participator in respect of any accounting period, and

(*c*) such an assessment, determination or amendment could be made but for the expiry of a time limit in paragraph 10(1A), 12(1A), 12A or 12B.

(2) Where this paragraph applies—

(*a*) the time limit does not apply, and

(*b*) the assessment, determination or amendment is not out of time if it is made before the final determination of the claim.

(3) A claim is not finally determined until it, or the amount to which it relates, can no longer be varied (whether on appeal or otherwise).

Contract settlements

13F

(1) In paragraph 13A(1)(*a*) the reference to an amount paid by a participator by way of tax includes an amount paid by a person under a contract settlement in connection with tax believed to be due.

(2) Sub-paragraphs (3) to (6) apply if the person who paid the amount under the contract settlement ("the payer") and the person from whom the tax was due ("the taxpayer") are not the same person.

(3) In relation to a claim under paragraph 13A in respect of that amount—

(*a*) the references to the participator in paragraph 13B(5) to (7) (Cases D, E and F) have effect as if they included the taxpayer,

(*b*) the reference to the participator in paragraph 13B(8) (Case G) has effect as if it were a reference to the taxpayer, and

(*c*) the reference to the participator in paragraph 13E(1)(*b*) has effect as if it were a reference to the taxpayer.

(4) Sub-paragraph (5) applies where the grounds for giving effect to a claim by the payer in respect of the amount also provide grounds for making an assessment or determination under paragraph 10 or 12, or an amendment of such an assessment or determination, on the taxpayer in respect of any chargeable period.

(5) HMRC may set any amount repayable to the payer by virtue of the claim against any amount payable by the taxpayer by virtue of the assessment, determination or amendment.

(6) The obligations of HMRC and the taxpayer are discharged to the extent of any set-off under sub-paragraph (5).

(7) "Contract settlement" means an agreement made in connection with any person's liability to make a payment to HMRC under or by virtue of an enactment."

11 (1) Paragraph 14 (appeals) is amended as follows.

(2) After sub-paragraph (1) insert—

"(1A) A participator who has made a claim under paragraph 13A may appeal from the decision on the claim by notice in writing given to HMRC within 30 days after the date of issue of the notice of the decision."

(3) In sub-paragraph (9) for "section 33 of the Taxes Management Act 1970 as applied by paragraph 1 above" substitute "paragraph 13A".

(4) In sub-paragraph (10) for "the appeal that" substitute "an appeal under subparagraph (1)".

(5) After sub-paragraph (10) insert—

"(10A) If an appeal under sub-paragraph (1A) is notified to the tribunal and it appears to the tribunal that the decision is wrong, the tribunal shall substitute such decision as may be required."

Consequential amendments

12 (1) Schedule 24 to FA 2007 (penalties for errors) is amended as follows.

(2) In the Table in paragraph 1, after the first entry relating to petroleum revenue tax insert—

"Petroleum revenue tax	Statement or declaration in connection with a claim under paragraph 13A of Schedule 2 to the Oil Taxation Act 1975."

(3) In paragraph 1(5), after "Oil Taxation Act 1975" insert "or a statement or declaration under paragraph 13A of that Schedule".

13 In FA 2009—

(*a*) in Schedule 51 (time limits for assessments, claims etc), omit paragraph 18(2), and

(*b*) in Schedule 52 (recovery of overpaid tax etc), omit paragraph 11.

FINANCE ACT 2011

(2011 Chapter 11)

[19 July 2011]

PART 3

OIL

61 PRT: areas treated as continuing to be oil fields

(1) (*amends* OTA 1975 Sch 1 para 7(4))

(2) The amendment made by this section has effect in relation to chargeable periods that begin after 30 June 2009.

63 Reduction of supplementary charge for certain new oil fields

(1) (*amends* CTA 2010 s 337(1))

(2) (*substitutes* CTA 2010 s 350)

(3) . . . [1]

(4) The amendments made by this section have effect in relation to accounting periods ending on or after 1 April 2010.

(5) Corresponding amendments, having effect in relation to accounting periods ending on or after 22 April 2009, are to be treated as having been made in Schedule 44 to FA 2009.

Commentary—*Simon's Taxes* **D7.923**.

Amendment—[1] Sub-s (3) repealed by FA 2012 s 184, Sch 22 para 20 with effect from 1 April 2013 (by virtue of SI 2013/744 art 2).

PART 7

ADMINISTRATION ETC

86 Data-gathering powers

(*see* IHT section)

SCHEDULE 23

DATA-GATHERING POWERS

Section 86(1)

(*see* IHT section)

FINANCE ACT 2012

(2012 Chapter 14)

CONTENTS

An Act to grant certain duties, to alter other duties, and to amend the law relating to the National Debt and the Public Revenue, and to make further provision in connection with finance.

[17 July 2012]

PART 5

OIL

181 Transfers within a group by companies carrying on ring fence trade

(1) Section 171A of TCGA 1992 (election to reallocate gain or loss to another member of group) is amended as follows.

(2) (*amends* TCGA 1992 s 171A(4))

(3) (*inserts* TCGA 1992 s 171A(4A), (4B))

(4) The amendments made by this section have effect in relation to chargeable gains accruing, or treated by virtue of section 197(4) of TCGA 1992 as accruing, in chargeable periods ending on or after 6 December 2011 (but see also subsection (5)).

(5) In relation to a chargeable period of a company beginning before 6 December 2011 and ending on or after that date ("the straddling period"), the amendments made by this section have effect as if, for the purposes of section 197 of TCGA 1992, so much of the straddling period as falls before 6 December 2011, and so much of that period as falls on or after that date, were separate chargeable periods.

Commentary—*Simon's Taxes* **D2.329**.

182 Supplementary charge

(1) (*amends* CTA 2010 s 330(2))

(2) This section is treated as having come into force on 6 December 2011.

Commentary—*Simon's Taxes* **D7.903**.

183 Relief in respect of decommissioning expenditure

Schedule 21 contains provision about the relief available in respect of decommissioning expenditure.

184 Reduction of supplementary charge for certain oil fields

Schedule 22 contains provision extending the availability of field allowances for oil fields.

PART 9

MISCELLANEOUS MATTERS

Administration

223 Tax agents: dishonest conduct

Commentary—*Simon's Taxes* **A6.321**.

Note—*Please see the IHT section for the full text of this section.*

SCHEDULE 21

RELIEF IN RESPECT OF DECOMMISSIONING EXPENDITURE

Section 183

Restriction of relief available in respect of decommissioning expenditure

1 Part 8 of CTA 2010 (oil activities) is amended as follows.

2 (*amends* CTA 2010 s 330(2))

3 (*inserts* CTA 2010 ss 330A–330C)

Commentary—*Simon's Taxes* **D7.903**.

4 (*amends* FA 2011 s 7(6))

Extension of loss relief available in respect of decommissioning expenditure

5 (1) In Chapter 2 of Part 4 of CTA 2010 (relief for trade losses), section 40 (ring fence trades: extension of periods for which relief may be given) is amended as follows.

(2) (*amends* CTA 2010 s 40(1)(b))

(3) (*amends* CTA 2010 s 40(3))

(4) (*inserts* CTA 2010 s 40(3A))

Application

6 (1) The amendments made by this Schedule have effect in relation to expenditure incurred in connection with decommissioning carried out on or after 21 March 2012.

(2) In sub-paragraph (1) "decommissioning" means anything falling within any of paragraphs (a) to (e) of section 330C(1) of CTA 2010 (as inserted by this Schedule).

SCHEDULE 22

REDUCTION OF SUPPLEMENTARY CHARGE FOR CERTAIN OIL FIELDS

Section 184

Amendments of Chapter 7 of Part 8 of CTA 2010

Commentary—*Simon's Taxes* **D7.923**.

1 In Part 8 of CTA 2010 (oil activities), Chapter 7 (reduction of supplementary charge for certain new oil fields) is amended as follows.

2 (*amends* CTA 2010 s 334)

3 (*amends* CTA 2010 s 337)

4 (*amends* CTA 2010 s 338)

5 (*amends* CTA 2010 s 339)

6 (*amends* CTA 2010 s 340)

7 (*amends* CTA 2010 s 341)

8 (*amends* CTA 2010 s 342)

9 (*amends* CTA 2010 s 343)

10 (*amends* CTA 2010 s 344)

11 (*amends* CTA 2010 s 345)

12 (*amends* CTA 2010 s 346)

13 (*amends* CTA 2010 s 347)

14 (*amends* CTA 2010 s 349)

15 (*inserts* CTA 2010 s 349A

16 (*amends* CTA 2010 s 357)

17 The heading of the Chapter becomes "REDUCTION OF SUPPLEMENTARY CHARGE FOR ELIGIBLE OIL FIELDS".

Consequential amendments

18 (1) Part 8 of CTA 2010 (oil activities) is amended as follows.
(2) (*amends* CTA 2010 s 270)
(3) (*amends* CTA 2010 s 330)

19 (*amends* CTA 2010 Sch 4)

20 (*amends* FA 2011 s 63)

Commencement

21 (1) The amendments made by paragraphs 14, 15 and 16(3) come into force on the day on which this Act is passed.
(2) The other amendments made by this Schedule come into force in accordance with provision contained in an order made by the Treasury.
(3) An order made under sub-paragraph (2) may—
  (a) make different provision for different purposes;
  (b) provide for such amendments to have effect in relation to times before the order is made.

Commencement—Finance Act 2012, Schedule 22 (Reduction of Supplementary Charge for Certain Oil Fields) (Appointed Day) Order, SI 2013/744 (appointed day under sub-para (2) for the purposes amendments of CTA 2012 Pt 8 Ch 7 made by FA 2012 Sch 22 (other than those made by paras 14, 15, 16(3)) is 1 April 2013).

Commentary—*Simon's Taxes* **D7.923**.

22 (1) The Commissioners for Her Majesty's Revenue and Customs may by order make any incidental, supplemental, consequential, transitional or saving provision in consequence of the amendments made by this Schedule.
(2) An order under this paragraph may—
  (a) amend, repeal or revoke any provision made by or under CTA 2010;
  (b) include provision having effect in relation to times before it is made, provided that it does not increase any person's liability to tax.

SCHEDULE 38

TAX AGENTS: DISHONEST CONDUCT

Section 223

Commentary—*Simon's Taxes* **A6.321**.

Note—*Please see the IHT section for the full text of this Schedule.*

PART 7

CONSEQUENTIAL PROVISIONS

OTA 1975

51 (*amends* OTA 1975 Sch 2)

FINANCE ACT 2013

(2013 Chapter 29)

AN ACT TO Grant certain duties, to alter other duties, and to amend the law relating to the National Debt and the Public Revenue, and to make further provision in connection with finance.

[17 July 2013]

CONTENTS

PART 2

OIL

Decommissioning relief agreements

80 Decommissioning relief agreements

(1) There are to be paid out of money provided by Parliament any sums which a Minister of the Crown is liable to pay under a decommissioning relief agreement.

(2) A "decommissioning relief agreement" is an agreement which—

(*a*) is made between a Minister of the Crown and a qualifying company, and

(*b*) provides that, in such circumstances as are specified in the agreement, if the amount of tax relief in respect of any decommissioning expenditure incurred by that or another qualifying company is less than an amount determined in accordance with the agreement ("the reference amount"), the difference is payable to the company that incurred the expenditure.

(3) "Qualifying company" means—

(*a*) any company that has at any time carried on a ring fence trade,

(*b*) any company that is associated with a company carrying on a ring fence trade,

(*c*) any company that has at any time been associated with a company that was carrying on a ring fence trade at that time, and

(*d*) in the case of decommissioning expenditure incurred in connection with any plant or machinery, or any land, situated in the UK sector of a cross-boundary field, any company that is a party to a joint operating agreement or unitisation agreement in relation to that field.

(4) For the purposes of subsection (2)(*b*) the amount of tax relief in respect of any decommissioning expenditure is to be determined in accordance with the agreement; and in making such a determination tax relief in respect of expenditure incurred by the qualifying company that is not decommissioning expenditure may, in such circumstances as are specified in the agreement, be treated as if it were tax relief in respect of decommissioning expenditure.

(5) A payment made to a company under a decommissioning relief agreement is not to be regarded as income or a gain of the company for any purpose of the Tax Acts.

(6) Section 18(1) of CRCA 2005 (restriction on disclosure by Revenue and Customs officials) does not prevent—

(*a*) disclosure to a Minister of the Crown for the purpose of enabling the Minister of the Crown to determine the extent of any liability under a decommissioning relief agreement, or

(*b*) disclosure to a company that has rights under a decommissioning relief agreement for the purpose of enabling the company to determine the reference amount.

(7) In this section—

"company" has the meaning given by section 1121 of CTA 2010,

"cross-boundary field" has the meaning given by section 10(9) of the Petroleum Act 1998,

"decommissioning expenditure" has the meaning given by section 81,

"Minister of the Crown" includes the Treasury,

"ring fence trade" has the same meaning as in Part 8 of CTA 2010 (see section 277 of that Act),

"the UK sector of a cross-boundary field" means that part of a cross-boundary field lying within the UK marine area (as defined by section 42 of the Marine and Coastal Access Act 2009), and

"unitisation agreement" has the meaning given by paragraph 1(2) of Schedule 17 to FA 1980.

(8) Subsections (8) to (9) of section 30 of the Petroleum Act 1998 (which specifies when one body corporate is associated with another) apply for the purposes of this section as they apply for the purposes of that section.

Definitions—Decommissioning expenditure: see FA 2013 s 81 below.

81 Meaning of "decommissioning expenditure"

(1) In section 80 "decommissioning expenditure" means expenditure incurred in connection with—

(*a*) demolishing any plant or machinery,

(*b*) preserving any plant or machinery pending its reuse or demolition,

(*c*) preparing any plant or machinery for reuse,

(*d*) arranging for the reuse of any plant or machinery, or

(*e*) the restoration of any land.

(2) It is immaterial for the purposes of subsection (1)(*b*) whether the plant or machinery is reused, is demolished or is partly reused and partly demolished.

(3) It is immaterial for the purposes of subsection (1)(*c*) and (*d*) whether the plant or machinery is in fact reused.

(4) In subsection (1)(*e*) "restoration" includes landscaping.

(5) The Treasury may by order amend this section.

(6) An order under subsection (5) may include transitional provision and savings.

(7) The power to make an order under subsection (5) is exercisable by statutory instrument.

(8) A statutory instrument containing an order under subsection (5) is subject to annulment in pursuance of a resolution of the House of Commons.

82 Annual report

(1) For each financial year the Treasury must prepare a report containing the information in subsection (2).

(2) The information is—

(*a*) the number of decommissioning relief agreements entered into in that year,

(*b*) the total number of decommissioning relief agreements in force at the end of that year,

(*c*) the number of payments made under any decommissioning relief agreements during that year, and the amount of each payment,

(*d*) the total number of payments that have been made under any decommissioning relief agreements as at the end of that year, and the total amount of those payments, and

(*e*) an estimate of the maximum amount liable to be paid under any decommissioning relief agreements.

(3) The report for a financial year must be laid before the House of Commons as soon as is reasonably practicable after the end of that year.

(4) In this section "decommissioning relief agreement" has the same meaning as in section 80.

(5) This section has effect in relation to financial years ending on or after 31 March 2014.

83 Effect of claim on PRT

(1) This section applies where a sum is payable to a company ("the claimant") under a decommissioning relief agreement.

(2) Subsection (3) applies where the reference amount is calculated by reference to what the claimant's assessable profit in any chargeable period would be if any expenditure incurred by it were used to reduce its profit in a particular way (rather than in any way that it has in fact been used).

(3) For the purposes of petroleum revenue tax—

(*a*) the expenditure is treated as having been used to reduce the claimant's profit in that way (rather than in any way that it has in fact been used), and

(*b*) the claimant is treated as if it had received the tax relief it would receive if its profit were reduced in that way (so no repayment of tax is to be made by virtue of this subsection).

(4) Subsection (5) applies where the reference amount is calculated by reference to what any other company's assessable profit in any chargeable period would be if any expenditure incurred by the claimant—

(*a*) had been incurred by the other company, and

(*b*) were used to reduce the other company's profit in a particular way.

(5) For the purposes of petroleum revenue tax—

(*a*) the expenditure is treated as incurred by the other company (and not the claimant),

(*b*) the expenditure is treated as having been used by the other company to reduce its profit in that way, and

(*c*) the other company is treated as if it had received the tax relief it would receive if its profit were reduced in that way (so no repayment of tax is to be made by virtue of this subsection).

(6) In this section—

"assessable profit" and "chargeable period" have the same meaning as in Part 1 of OTA 1975,

"company" has the meaning given by section 1121 of CTA 2010,

"decommissioning relief agreement" has the same meaning as in section 80, and

"the reference amount" means the reference amount (within the meaning of that section) that relates to the sum mentioned in subsection (1).

84 Terminal losses accruing by virtue of another's default

(1) This section applies where—

(*a*) a company defaults on a liability under—

(i) a relevant agreement, or

(ii) an abandonment programme,

to make a payment towards decommissioning expenditure in respect of an oil field,

(*b*) in consequence of the default, another company ("the other company") that has rights under a decommissioning relief agreement at the time of the default incurs decommissioning expenditure in respect of that oil field, and (*c*) but for paragraph 15 of Schedule 17 to FA 1980 (terminal losses), a sum (or a sum of a greater amount) would be payable to the other company under the decommissioning relief agreement.

(2) Paragraph 15 of Schedule 17 to FA 1980 does not apply in relation to any allowable loss accruing to the other company from that oil field.

(3) Any allowable unrelievable field loss (within the meaning of section 6 of OTA 1975) that—

(*a*) consists of the unrelieved portion of an allowable loss within subsection (2), and

(*b*) would (in the absence of this subsection) arise as a result of subsection (2),

is not to be regarded as arising.

(4) Nothing in this section affects the operation of section 83(3) or (5).

(5) In this section—

"abandonment programme" means an abandonment programme approved under Part 4 of the Petroleum Act 1998 (including such a programme as revised),

"company" has the meaning given by section 1121 of CTA 2010,

"decommissioning expenditure" has the same meaning as in section 80,

"decommissioning relief agreement" has the same meaning as in that section,

"oil field" has the same meaning as in OTA 1975,

"relevant agreement" has the meaning given by section 104(5)(*a*) of FA 1991, and

"unrelieved portion", in relation to an allowable loss, is to be read in accordance with section 6 of OTA 1975.

85 Claims under agreement not to affect oil allowance

(1) This section applies where—

(*a*) a company defaults on a liability under—

(i) a relevant agreement, or

(ii) an abandonment programme,

to make a payment towards decommissioning expenditure in respect of an oil field,

(*b*) in consequence of the default, another company that has rights under a decommissioning relief agreement at the time of the default incurs decommissioning expenditure in respect of that oil field, and

(*c*) by virtue of section 83, any expenditure incurred by that company (whether or not that decommissioning expenditure) is treated as having been used by that company or any other company ("the affected company") to reduce its assessable profit in a chargeable period in a particular way.

(2) If, in the absence of section 83, the assessable profit accruing to the affected company from an oil field in that chargeable period would be reduced under section 8(1) of OTA 1975, the amount of the oil allowance for the oil field utilised by the affected company in that chargeable period for the purposes of section 8 of that Act is to be determined as if section 83 did not apply.

(3) In this section—

"abandonment programme" means an abandonment programme approved under Part 4 of the Petroleum Act 1998 (including such a programme as revised),

"company" has the meaning given by section 1121 of CTA 2010,

"decommissioning expenditure" has the same meaning as in section 80,

"decommissioning relief agreement" has the same meaning as in that section,

"oil field" has the same meaning as in OTA 1975, and

"relevant agreement" has the meaning given by section 104(5)(*a*) of FA 1991.

Decommissioning security settlements

86 Removal of IHT charges in respect of decommissioning security settlements

(1) In Chapter 3 of Part 3 of IHTA 1984 (settled property: settlements without interests in possession etc), section 58 (relevant property) is amended as follows.

(2) (*inserts* IHTA 1984 s 58(1)(*eb*))

(3) (*inserts* IHTA 1984 s 58(6), (7))

(4) This section is treated as having come into force on 20 March 1993.

(5) For the purposes of section 58 of IHTA 1984—

(*a*) any reference in that section to Part 4 of the Petroleum Act 1998 has effect, in relation to any period before the coming into force of that Part, as a reference to Part 1 of the Petroleum Act 1987, and

(*b*) section 38A of the Petroleum Act 1998 is to be treated as having come into force at the same time as this section.

(6) There is to be no charge to tax under section 65 of IHTA 1984 if the only reason for such a charge would be that property ceases to be relevant property by virtue of the coming into force of this section.

87 Loan relationships arising from decommissioning security settlements

(1) (*inserts* CTA 2010 s 287A)

(2) (*amends* CTA 2009 s 464(3)(*e*))

(3) The amendments made by this section have effect in relation to accounting periods beginning on or after the day on which this Act is passed.

Decommissioning expenditure etc

88 Decommissioning expenditure taken into account for PRT purposes

(1) Section 330B of CTA 2010 (decommissioning expenditure taken into account for PRT purposes) is amended as follows.

(2) (*inserts* CTA 2010 s 330B(1)(*c*))

(3) (*substitutes* CTA 2010 s 330B(2))

(4) (*amends* CTA 2010 s 330B(3))

(5) (*amends* CTA 2010 s 330B(4))

(6) (*amends* CTA 2010 s 330B(7))

(7) The amendments made by this section have effect in relation to expenditure incurred in connection with decommissioning carried out on or after the day on which this Act is passed.

89 Miscellaneous amendments relating to decommissioning

(1) Part 1 of Schedule 31 contains provision about expenditure on and under abandonment guarantees and abandonment expenditure.

(2) Part 2 of Schedule 31 contains provision about calculating the profits of a ring fence trade carried on by a person who incurs expenditure on meeting another person's decommissioning liabilities.

Capital allowances

90 Expenditure on decommissioning onshore installations

(1) Section 163 of CAA 2001 (meaning of "general decommissioning expenditure") is amended as follows.

(2) In subsection (1)—

(*a*) the words after "if" become paragraph (*a*) of that subsection,

(*b*) in that paragraph, for "subsections (3) to (4)" substitute "subsections (3), (3A) and (4)", and

(*c*) at the end of that paragraph insert ", or

(*b*) the conditions in subsections (3B) and (4) are met."

(3) After subsection (3A) insert—

"(3B) The expenditure must have been incurred on decommissioning plant or machinery—

(*a*) which has been brought into use wholly or partly for the purposes of a ring fence trade, and

(*b*) which—

(i) is, or forms part of, a relevant onshore installation, or

(ii) when last in use for the purposes of a ring fence trade, was, or formed part of, such an installation.

(3C) In subsection (3B) "relevant onshore installation" means any building or structure which—

(*a*) falls within any of sub-paragraphs (ii) to (iv) of section 3(4)(*c*) of OTA 1975,

(*b*) is not an offshore installation, and

(*c*) is or has been used for purposes connected with the winning of oil from an oil field any part of which lies within—

(i) the boundaries of the territorial sea of the United Kingdom, or

(ii) an area designated under section 1(7) of the Continental Shelf Act 1964."

(4) In subsection (5)(*a*), for ""oil field" has" substitute ""oil" and "oil field" have".

(5) The amendments made by this section have effect in relation to expenditure incurred on decommissioning carried out on or after the day on which this Act is passed.

Commentary—*Simon's Taxes* **B3.354**.

91 Expenditure on decommissioning certain redundant plant or machinery

(Please see Part 1 of this work.)

Commentary—*Simon's Taxes* **B3.354**.

92 Expenditure on site restoration

(Please see Part 1 of this work.)

Commentary—*Simon's Taxes* **B3.406**.

93 Restrictions on allowances for certain oil-related expenditure

Schedule 32 contains provision in connection with restrictions on allowances for certain oil-related expenditure.

PART 5
GENERAL ANTI-ABUSE RULE

Note—*(Please see IHT section for the full text of this Part.)*

PART 6
OTHER PROVISIONS

Powers

228 Data-gathering from merchant acquirers etc

Note—*(Please see IHT section for the full text of this section.)*

Payment

231 Overpayment relief: generally prevailing practice exclusion and EU law

(1) (*inserts* TMA 1970 Sch 1AB para 2(9A), (9B))
(2) (*inserts* OTA 1975 Sch 2 para 13B(9), (10))
(3) (*inserts* FA 1998 Sch 18 para 51A(9), (10))
(4) (*inserts* FA 2003 Sch 10 para 34A(9), (10))
(5) The amendments made by this section have effect in relation to any claim (in respect of overpaid tax, excessive assessment etc) made after the end of the six month period beginning with the day on which this Act is passed.

Commentary—*Simon's Taxes* **A4.218**.

232 Overpayment relief: time limit for claims

(1) (*amends* TMA 1970 Sch 1AB para 3)
(2) (*amends* OTA 1975 Sch 2 para 13C)
(3) (*amends* FA 1998 Sch 18 para 51B)
(4) The amendments made by this section have effect in relation to any claim (in respect of overpaid tax, excessive assessment etc) made after the end of the six month period beginning with the day on which this Act is passed.

Commentary—*Simon's Taxes* **A4.218**.

Interim remedies

234 Restrictions on interim payments in proceedings relating to taxation matters

(1) This section applies to an application for an interim remedy (however described), made in any court proceedings relating to a taxation matter, if the application is founded (wholly or in part) on a point of law which has yet to be finally determined in the proceedings.
(2) Any power of a court to grant an interim remedy (however described) requiring the Commissioners for Her Majesty's Revenue and Customs, or an officer of Revenue and Customs, to pay any sum to any claimant (however described) in the proceedings is restricted as follows.
(3) The court may grant the interim remedy only if it is shown to the satisfaction of the court—
- (*a*) that, taking account of all sources of funding (including borrowing) reasonably likely to be available to fund the proceedings, the payment of the sum is necessary to enable the proceedings to continue, or
- (*b*) that the circumstances of the claimant are exceptional and such that the granting of the remedy is necessary in the interests of justice.

(4) The powers restricted by this section include (for example)—
- (*a*) powers under rule 25 of the Civil Procedure Rules 1998 (S.I. 1998/3132);
- (*b*) powers under Part II of Rule 29 of the Rules of the Court of Judicature (Northern Ireland) (Revision) 1980 (S.R. 1980 No.346).

(5) This section applies in relation to proceedings whenever commenced, but only in relation to applications made in those proceedings on or after 26 June 2013.
(6) This section applies on and after 26 June 2013.
(7) Subsection (8) applies where, on or after 26 June 2013 but before the passing of this Act, an interim remedy was granted by a court using a power which, because of subsection (6), is to be taken to have been restricted by this section.
(8) Unless it is shown to the satisfaction of the court that paragraph (*a*) or (*b*) of subsection (3) applied at the time the interim remedy was granted, the court must, on an application made to it under this subsection—
- (*a*) revoke or modify the interim remedy so as to secure compliance with this section, and
- (*b*) if the Commissioners have, or an officer of Revenue and Customs has, paid any sum as originally required by the interim remedy, order the repayment of the sum or any part of the sum as appropriate (with interest from the date of payment).

(9) For the purposes of this section, proceedings on appeal are to be treated as part of the original proceedings from which the appeal lies.

(10) In this section "taxation matter" means anything, other than national insurance contributions, the collection and management of which is the responsibility of the Commissioners for Her Majesty's Revenue and Customs (or was the responsibility of the Commissioners of Inland Revenue or Commissioners of Customs and Excise).

SCHEDULE 31

MISCELLANEOUS AMENDMENTS RELATING TO DECOMMISSIONING

Section 89

PART 1

ABANDONMENT GUARANTEES AND ABANDONMENT EXPENDITURE

Expenditure on abandonment guarantees

1 (1) In Part 2 of ITTOIA 2005 (trading income), Chapter 16A (oil activities) is amended as follows.
(2) (*amends* ITTOIA 2005 s 225N)
(3) (*amends* ITTOIA 2005 s 225R)

2 (1) In Part 8 of CTA 2010 (oil activities), Chapter 4 (calculation of profits) is amended as follows.
(2) (*amends* CTA 2010 s 292)
(3) (*amends* CTA 2010 s 296)

Expenditure under abandonment guarantees

3 (*inserts* OTA 1975 Sch 3 para 8(1A), (1B))

4 (*amends* OTA 1975 Sch 5 para 2C(2))

5 (1) Part 3 of FA 1991 (oil taxation) is amended as follows.
(2) (*repeals* FA 1991 s 105)
(3) (*repeals* FA 1991 s 106)

6 (1) In Part 2 of ITTOIA 2005 (trading income), Chapter 16A (oil activities) is amended as follows.
(2) (*repeals* ITTOIA 2005 s 225N(3), (4))
(3) (*repeals* ITTOIA 2005 s 225O)

7 (1) In Part 8 of CTA 2010 (oil activities), Chapter 4 (calculation of profits) is amended as follows.
(2) (*repeals* CTA 2010 s 292(3), (4))
(3) (*repeals* CTA 2010 s 293)

Reimbursement by defaulter in respect of abandonment expenditure

8 (*repeals* FA 1991 s 108)

9 (*repeals* ITTOIA 2005 s 225T)

10 (*repeals* CTA 2010 s 298)

Consequential amendments

11 (1)–(3) (*amend* FA 1991 s 104)

12 (*repeals* FA 2008 s 105)

13 In Part 2 of ITTOIA 2005, Chapter 16A is amended as follows.

14 (1)–(4) (*amends* ITTOIA 2005 s 225N)

15 (*repeals* ITTOIA 2005 ss 225P, 225Q)

16 (*amends* ITTOIA 2005 s 225R)

17 In Part 8 of CTA 2010, Chapter 4 is amended as follows.

18 (1)–(4) (*amend* CTA 2010 s 292)

19 (*repeals* CTA 2010 ss 294, 295)

20 (*amends* CTA 2010 s 296)

PART 2

RECEIPTS ARISING FROM DECOMMISSIONING

Calculation of profits chargeable to corporation tax and supplementary charge

21 (*inserts* CTA 2010 s 298A)

Calculation of profits chargeable to income tax

22 (*inserts* ITTOIA 2005 s 225V)

PART 3

COMMENCEMENT

23 The amendments made by this Schedule have effect in relation to expenditure incurred on or after the day on which this Act is passed.

SCHEDULE 32

RESTRICTIONS ON ALLOWANCES FOR CERTAIN OIL-RELATED EXPENDITURE

Section 93

PART 1

DECOMMISSIONING EXPENDITURE

(Please see Part 1 of this work.)

PART 2

EXPENDITURE ON SITE RESTORATION

(Please see Part 1 of this work.)

PART 3

AMENDMENTS OF TIOPA 2010

12 Part 4 of TIOPA 2010 (transfer pricing) is amended as follows.

13 (*amends* TIOPA 2010 s 147(6))

14 (*inserts* TIOPA 2010 s 206A)

15 (*inserts* TIOPA 2010 s 213(3))

16 The amendments made by this Part have effect for accounting periods ending on or after the day on which this Act is passed.

SCHEDULE 43

GENERAL ANTI-ABUSE RULE: PROCEDURAL REQUIREMENTS

Section 209

Note—*(Please see IHT section for the full text of this Schedule.)*

FINANCE ACT 2014

(2014 Chapter 26)

AN ACT TO Grant certain duties, to alter other duties, and to amend the law relating to the National Debt and the Public Revenue, and to make further provision in connection with finance.

[17 July 2014]

CONTENTS

CHAPTER 4

OTHER PROVISIONS

Oil and gas

PART 7

FINAL PROVISIONS

PART 1

INCOME TAX, CORPORATION TAX AND CAPITAL GAINS TAX

CHAPTER 2

INCOME TAX: GENERAL

Other provisions

21 Oil and gas workers on the continental shelf: operation of PAYE

(1) ITEPA 2003 is amended as follows.

(2) In section 222 (payments by employer on account of tax where deduction not possible)—

(a) in subsection (1)(a), after "689" insert ", 689A", and

(b) in subsection (3), after "employer)" insert "or section 689A(3) (deemed payments of PAYE income of continental shelf workers by person other than employer)".

(3) In section 421L (persons to whom certain duties to provide information and returns apply)—

(a) in subsection (3), after paragraph (b) insert—

"(ba) if the employee in question is a continental shelf worker and PAYE regulations do not apply to the employer in question, any person who is a relevant person in relation to the employee in question,", and

(b) after subsection (5) insert—

"(5A) In subsection (3)(ba) "continental shelf worker" and "relevant person" have the meaning given by section 689A(11) (PAYE: oil and gas workers on the continental shelf)."

(4) In section 689 (provision about PAYE for employees of non-UK employers), after subsection (1) insert—

"(1ZA) But this section does not apply if section 689A applies or would apply but for a certificate issued under regulations made under subsection (7) of that section."

(5) After that section insert—

"689A Oil and gas workers on the continental shelf

(1) This section applies if—

(a) any payment of, or on account of, PAYE income of a continental shelf worker in respect of a period is made by a person who is the employer or an intermediary of the employer or of the relevant person,

(b) PAYE regulations do not apply to the person making the payment or, if that person makes the payment as an intermediary of the employer or of the relevant person, to the employer, and

(c) income tax and any relevant debts are not deducted, or not accounted for, in accordance with PAYE regulations by the person making the payment or, if that person makes the payment as an intermediary of the employer or of the relevant person, by the employer.

(2) Subject to subsection (5), subsection (1)(a) does not apply in relation to a payment so far as the sum paid is employment income under Chapter 2 of Part 7A.

TIOPA 2010

(3) The relevant person is to be treated, for the purposes of PAYE regulations, as making a payment of PAYE income of the continental shelf worker of an amount equal to the amount given by subsection (4).

(4) The amount referred to is—

(a) if the amount of the payment actually made is an amount to which the recipient is entitled after deduction of income tax and any relevant debts under PAYE regulations, the aggregate of the amount of the payment and the amount of any income tax due and any relevant debts deductible, and

(b) in any other case, the amount of the payment.

(5) If, by virtue of any of sections 687A and 693 to 700, an employer would be treated for the purposes of PAYE regulations (if they applied to the employer) as making a payment of any amount to a continental shelf worker, this section has effect as if—

(a) the employer were also to be treated for the purposes of this section as making an actual payment of that amount, and

(b) paragraph (a) of subsection (4) were omitted.

(6) For the purposes of this section a payment of, or on account of, PAYE income of a continental shelf worker is made by an intermediary of the employer or of the relevant person if it is made—

(a) by a person acting on behalf of the employer or the relevant person and at the expense of the employer or the relevant person or a person connected with the employer or the relevant person, or

(b) by trustees holding property for any persons who include, or a class of persons which includes, the continental shelf worker.

(7) PAYE regulations may make provision for, or in connection with, the issue by Her Majesty's Revenue and Customs of a certificate to a relevant person in respect of one or more continental shelf workers—

(a) confirming that, in respect of payments of, or on account of, PAYE income of the continental shelf workers specified or described in the certificate, income tax and any relevant debts are being deducted, or accounted for, as mentioned in subsection (1)(c), and

(b) disapplying this section in relation to payments of, or on account of, PAYE income of those workers while the certificate is in force.

(8) Regulations under subsection (7) may, in particular, make provision about—

(a) applying for a certificate;

(b) the circumstances in which a certificate may, or must, be issued or cancelled;

(c) the form and content of a certificate;

(d) the effect of a certificate (including provision modifying the effect mentioned in subsection (7)(b) or specifying further effects);

(e) the effect of cancelling a certificate.

(9) Subsection (10) applies if—

(a) there is more than one relevant person in relation to a continental shelf worker, and

(b) in consequence of the same payment within subsection (1)(a), each of them is treated under subsection (3) as making a payment of PAYE income of the worker.

(10) If one of the relevant persons complies with section 710 (notional payments: accounting for tax) in respect of the payment that person is treated as making, the other relevant persons do not have to comply with that section in respect of the payments they are treated as making.

(11) In this section—

"continental shelf worker" means a person in an employment some or all of the duties of which are performed—

(a) in the UK sector of the continental shelf (as defined in section 41), and

(b) in connection with exploration or exploitation activities (as so defined);

"employer" means the employer of the continental shelf worker;

"relevant person", in relation to a continental shelf worker, means—

(a) if the employer has an associated company (as defined in section 449 of CTA 2010) with a place of business or registered office in the United Kingdom, the associated company, or

(b) in any other case, the person who holds the licence under Part 1 of the Petroleum Act 1998 in respect of the area of the UK sector of the continental shelf where some or all of the duties of the continental shelf worker's employment are performed."

(6) In section 690 (employee non-resident etc), in subsection (10)—

(a) after "689", in the first place it appears, insert "or 689A", and
(b) after "689", in the second place it appears, insert "or (as the case may be) 689A".

(7) In section 710 (notional payments: accounting for tax), in subsection (2)—
(a) in paragraph (a)—
(i) after "689" insert ", 689A", and
(ii) for "or 689(3)(a)" substitute ", 689(3)(a) or 689A(4)(a)", and
(b) in paragraph (b), after "689(2)" insert "or 689A(3)".

(8) In section 689A (inserted by subsection (5)), at the end insert—

"(12) The Treasury may by regulations modify the definitions of "continental shelf worker" and "relevant person", as the Treasury thinks appropriate.

(13) Regulations under subsection (12) may—
(a) make different provision for different cases or different purposes,
(b) make incidental, consequential, supplementary or transitional provision or savings, and
(c) amend this section."

(9) The amendment made by subsection (5) is treated as having come into force—
(a) on 26 March 2014 for the purposes of making regulations under section 689A(7) of ITEPA 2003, and
(b) on 6 April 2014 for remaining purposes.

(10) The amendments made by subsections (2), (4), (6) and (7) are treated as having come into force on 6 April 2014.

Commentary—*Simon's Taxes* **E4.1128**.

CHAPTER 4

OTHER PROVISIONS

Oil and gas

69 Extended ring fence expenditure supplement for onshore activities

Schedule 14 contains provision about an extended ring fence expenditure supplement in connection with onshore oil-related activities.

70 Supplementary charge: onshore allowance

Schedule 15 contains provision about the reduction of adjusted ring fence profits by means of an onshore allowance.

71 Oil and gas: reinvestment after pre-trading disposal

(1) In Chapter 2 of Part 6 of TCGA 1992 (oil and mineral industries), after section 198I insert—

"198J Oil and gas: reinvestment after pre-trading disposal

(1) This section applies if a company which is an E&A company makes a disposal of, or of the company's interest in, relevant E&A assets and that disposal is—
(a) a disposal of, or of an interest in, a UK licence which relates to an undeveloped area, or
(b) a disposal of an asset used in an area covered by a licence under Part 1 of the Petroleum Act 1998 or the Petroleum (Production) Act (Northern Ireland) 1964 which authorises the company to undertake E&A activities.

(2) If—
(a) the consideration which the company obtains for the disposal is applied by the company, within the permitted reinvestment period—
(i) on E&A expenditure at a time when the company is an E&A company, or
(ii) on oil assets taken into use, and used only, for the purposes of a ring fence trade carried on by it, and
(b) the company makes a claim under this subsection in relation to the disposal,

any gain accruing to the company on the disposal is not a chargeable gain.

(3) If part only of the amount or value of the consideration for the disposal is applied as described in subsection (2)(a)—
(a) subsection (2) does not apply, but
(b) subsection (4) applies if all of the amount or value of the consideration is so applied except for a part which is less than the amount of the gain (whether all chargeable gain or not) accruing on the disposal.

(4) If the company makes a claim under this subsection in relation to the disposal, the company is to be treated for the purposes of this Act as if the amount of the gain accruing on the disposal were reduced to the amount of the part mentioned in subsection (3)(b) (and, if not all chargeable gain, with a proportionate reduction in the amount of the chargeable gain).

(5) The incurring of expenditure is within "the permitted reinvestment period" if the expenditure is incurred in the period beginning 12 months before and ending 3 years after the disposal, or at such earlier or later time as the Commissioners for Her Majesty's Revenue and Customs may by notice allow.

(6) Subsections (6), (7), (10) and (11) of section 152 apply for the purposes of this section as they apply for the purposes of section 152, except that—

- (a) in subsection (6) the reference to a trade is to be read as a reference to E&A activities or a ring fence trade,
- (b) in subsection (7), the reference to the old assets is to be read as a reference to the assets disposed of as mentioned in subsection (1) of this section, and
- (c) in subsection (7), the references to the trade are to be read as references to the E&A activities.

(7) In this section—

"E&A activities" means oil and gas exploration and appraisal in the United Kingdom or an area designated by Order in Council under section 1(7) of the Continental Shelf Act 1964;

"E&A company" means a company which carries on E&A activities and does not carry on a ring fence trade;

"E&A expenditure" means expenditure on E&A activities which is treated as such under generally accepted accounting practice;

"oil asset" has the same meaning as in section 198E, and section 198I applies for the purposes of this section as it applies for the purposes of section 198E;

"relevant E&A assets" means assets which—

- (a) are used, and used only, for the purposes of E&A activities carried on by the company throughout the period of ownership, and
- (b) are within the classes of assets listed in section 155 (with references to "the trade" in that section being read as references to the E&A activities);

"ring fence trade" has the meaning given by section 277 of CTA 2010;

"UK licence" means a licence within the meaning of Part 1 of the Oil Taxation Act 1975;

and a reference to a UK licence which relates to an undeveloped area has the same meaning as in section 194 (see section 196).

198K Provisional application of section 198J

(1) This section applies where a company for a consideration disposes of, or of an interest in, any assets at a time when it is an E&A company and declares, in the company's return for the chargeable period in which the disposal takes place—

- (a) that the whole or any specified part of the consideration will be applied, within the permitted reinvestment period—
  - (i) on E&A expenditure at a time when the company is an E&A company, or
  - (ii) on expenditure on oil assets which are taken into use, and used only, for the purposes of the company's ring fence trade, and
- (b) that the company intends to make a claim under section 198J(2) or (4) in relation to the disposal.

(2) Until the declaration ceases to have effect, section 198J applies as if the expenditure had been incurred and the person had made such a claim.

(3) The declaration ceases to have effect as follows—

- (a) if and to the extent that it is withdrawn before the relevant day, or is superseded before that day by a valid claim under section 198J, on the day on which it is so withdrawn or superseded, and
- (b) if and to the extent that it is not so withdrawn or superseded, on the relevant day.

(4) On the declaration ceasing to have effect in whole or in part, all necessary adjustments—

- (a) are to be made by making or amending assessments or by repayment or discharge of tax, and
- (b) are to be so made despite any limitation on the time within which assessments or amendments may be made.

(5) In this section "the relevant day" means the fourth anniversary of the last day of the accounting period in which the disposal took place.

(6) For the purposes of this section—

- (a) sections (6), (10) and (11) of section 152 apply as they apply for the purposes of that section, except that in subsection (6) the reference to a trade is to be read as a reference to E&A activities or a ring fence trade, and

(b) terms used in this section which are defined in section 198J have the meaning given by that section.

198L Expenditure by member of same group

(1) Section 198J applies where—

(a) the disposal is by a company which, at the time of the disposal, is a member of a group of companies (within the meaning of section 170),

(b) the E&A expenditure or expenditure on oil assets is by another company which, at the time the expenditure is incurred, is a member of the same group, and

(c) the claim under section 198J is made by both companies,

as if both companies were the same person.

(2) "E&A company", "E&A expenditure" and "oil assets" have the meaning given by section 198J."

(2) The amendment made by this section has effect in relation to disposals made on or after 1 April 2014.

Commentary—*Simon's Taxes* **D7.928**.

72 Substantial shareholder exemption: oil and gas

(1) In Schedule 7AC to TCGA 1992 (exemption for disposals by companies with substantial shareholding), in paragraph 15A (effect of transfer of trading assets within a group), after sub-paragraph (2) insert—

"(2A) For the purposes of sub-paragraph (2)(b) and (d), "trade" includes oil and gas exploration and appraisal."

(2) The amendment made by this section has effect in relation to disposals made on or after 1 April 2014.

Commentary—*Simon's Taxes* **D1.1014A**.

73 Oil contractor activities: ring-fence trade etc

Schedule 16 contains provision about the corporation tax treatment of oil contractor activities.

PART 7

FINAL PROVISIONS

301 Power to update indexes of defined terms

(1) The Treasury may by order amend any index of defined expressions contained in an Act relating to taxation, so as to make amendments consequential on any enactment.

(2) In this section—

"enactment" means any provision made by or under an Act (whether before or after the passing of this Act);

"index of defined expressions" means a provision contained in an Act relating to taxation which lists where expressions used in the Act, or in a particular part of the Act, are defined or otherwise explained.

(3) The power to make an order under this section is exercisable by statutory instrument.

Commentary—*Simon's Taxes* **A1.150**.

(4) An order under this section is subject to annulment in pursuance of a resolution of the House of Commons.

302 Interpretation

(1) In this Act—

"ALDA 1979" means the Alcoholic Liquor Duties Act 1979,

"BGDA 1981" means the Betting and Gaming Duties Act 1981,

"CAA 2001" means the Capital Allowances Act 2001,

"CEMA 1979" means the Customs and Excise Management Act 1979,

"CRCA 2005" means the Commissioners for Revenue and Customs Act 2005,

"CTA 2009" means the Corporation Tax Act 2009,

"CTA 2010" means the Corporation Tax Act 2010,

"F(No 3)A 2010" means the Finance (No 3) Act 2010,

"IHTA 1984" means the Inheritance Tax Act 1984,

"ITA 2007" means the Income Tax Act 2007,

"ITEPA 2003" means the Income Tax (Earnings and Pensions) Act 2003,

"ITTOIA 2005" means the Income Tax (Trading and Other Income) Act 2005,

"OTA 1975" means the Oil Taxation Act 1975,

"TCGA 1992" means the Taxation of Chargeable Gains Act 1992,

"TIOPA 2010" means the Taxation (International and Other Provisions) Act 2010,

"TMA 1970" means the Taxes Management Act 1970,

"TPDA 1979" means the Tobacco Products Duty Act 1979,

"VATA 1994" means the Value Added Tax Act 1994, and

"VERA 1994" means the Vehicle Excise and Registration Act 1994.

(2) In this Act—

"FA", followed by a year, means the Finance Act of that year, and

"F(No 2)A", followed by a year, means the Finance (No 2) Act of that year.

303 Short title

This Act may be cited as the Finance Act 2014.

SCHEDULE 14

EXTENDED RING FENCE EXPENDITURE SUPPLEMENT FOR ONSHORE ACTIVITIES

Section 69

1 In Part 8 of CTA 2010 (oil activities), after Chapter 5 insert—

"CHAPTER 5A

EXTENDED RING FENCE EXPENDITURE SUPPLEMENT FOR ONSHORE ACTIVITIES

Introduction

329A Overview of Chapter

(1) This Chapter entitles a company carrying on a ring fence trade, on making a claim in respect of an accounting period, to an additional supplement in respect of—

(a) qualifying pre-commencement onshore expenditure incurred before the date the trade is set up and commenced,

(b) losses incurred in the trade which relate to onshore oil-related activities,

(c) some or all of the supplement allowed in respect of earlier periods under Chapter 5, and

(d) the additional supplement allowed in respect of earlier periods under this Chapter.

(2) Sections 329B to 329H make provision about the application and interpretation of this Chapter.

(3) Sections 329I to 329M make provision about additional supplement in relation to expenditure incurred by the company—

(a) with a view to carrying on a ring fence trade, but

(b) in an accounting period before the company sets up and commences that trade.

(4) Sections 329N to 329T make provision about additional supplement in relation to losses incurred in carrying on the ring fence trade.

(5) There is a limit (of 4) on the number of accounting periods in respect of which a company may claim additional supplement.

(6) In determining the amount of additional supplement allowable, reductions fall to be made in respect of—

(a) disposal receipts in respect of any asset representing qualifying pre-commencement onshore expenditure,

(b) onshore ring fence losses that could be deducted under section 37 (relief for trade losses against total profits) or section 42 (ring fence trades: further extension of period for relief) from ring fence profits of earlier periods,

(c) onshore ring fence losses incurred in earlier periods that fall to be used under section 45 (carry forward of trade loss against subsequent trade profits) to reduce profits of succeeding periods, and

(d) unrelieved group ring fence profits.

Application and interpretation

329B Qualifying companies

(1) This Chapter applies in relation to any company which—

(a) carries on a ring fence trade, or

(b) is engaged in any activities with a view to carrying on a ring fence trade.

(2) In this Chapter such a company is referred to as a "qualifying company".

329C Onshore and offshore oil-related activities

(1) This section applies for the purposes of this Chapter.

(2) "Onshore oil-related activities" has the same meaning as in Chapter 8 (supplementary charge: onshore allowance) (see section 356BA).

(3) "Offshore oil-related activities" means oil-related activities that are not onshore oil-related activities.

329D Accounting periods and straddling periods

(1) In this Chapter, in the case of a qualifying company—

"the commencement period" means the accounting period in which the company sets up and commences its ring fence trade,

"post-commencement period" means an accounting period ending on or after 5 December 2013—

(a) which is the commencement period, or

(b) which ends after the commencement period, and

"pre-commencement period" means an accounting period ending—

(a) on or after 5 December 2013, and

(b) before the commencement period.

(2) For the purposes of this Chapter, a company not within the charge to corporation tax which incurs any expenditure is to be treated as having such accounting periods as it would have if—

(a) it carried on a trade consisting of the activities in respect of which the expenditure is incurred, and

(b) it had started to carry on that trade when it started to carry on the activities in the course of which the expenditure is incurred.

(3) In this Chapter, "straddling period" means an accounting period beginning before and ending on or after 5 December 2013.

329E The relevant percentage

(1) For the purposes of this Chapter, the relevant percentage for an accounting period is 10%.

(2) The Treasury may by order vary the percentage for the time being specified in subsection (1) for such accounting periods as may be specified in the order.

329F Restrictions on accounting periods for which additional supplement may be claimed

(1) A company may claim additional supplement under this Chapter in respect of no more than 4 accounting periods.

(2) The accounting periods in respect of which claims are made need not be consecutive.

(3) The additional supplement under this Chapter—

(a) is additional to any supplement allowed under Chapter 5, but

(b) may only be claimed for accounting periods which fall after 6 accounting periods for which supplement is allowed as a result of claims by the company under Chapter 5.

329G Qualifying pre-commencement onshore expenditure

(1) For the purposes of this Chapter, expenditure is "qualifying pre-commencement onshore expenditure" if it meets Conditions A to D.

(2) Condition A is that the expenditure is incurred on or after 5 December 2013.

(3) Condition B is that the expenditure is incurred in the course of oil extraction activities which are onshore oil-related activities.

(4) Condition C is that the expenditure is incurred by a company with a view to carrying on a ring fence trade, but before the company sets up and commences that ring fence trade.

(5) Condition D is that the expenditure—

(a) is subsequently allowable as a deduction in calculating the profits of the ring fence trade for the commencement period (whether or not any part of it is so allowable for any post-commencement period), or

(b) is relevant R&D expenditure incurred by an SME.

(6) For the purposes of this section, expenditure incurred by a company is "relevant R&D expenditure incurred by an SME" if—

(a) the company makes an election under section 1045 of CTA 2009 (alternative treatment for pre-trading expenditure: deemed trading loss) in respect of that expenditure, but

(b) the company does not make a claim for an R&D tax credit under section 1054 of that Act in respect of that expenditure.

(7) In the case of any qualifying pre-commencement onshore expenditure which is relevant R&D expenditure incurred by an SME, the amount of that expenditure is treated for the purposes of this Chapter as being equal to 150% of its actual amount.

(8) In the case of any qualifying pre-commencement onshore expenditure which is relevant R&D expenditure incurred by a large company, the amount of that expenditure is treated for the purposes of this Chapter as being equal to 125% of its actual amount.

(9) In subsection (8) "relevant R&D expenditure incurred by a large company" means qualifying Chapter 5 expenditure, as defined in section 1076 of CTA 2009.

329H Unrelieved group ring fence profits

In this Chapter "unrelieved group ring fence profits" has the same meaning as in Chapter 5 (see sections 313 and 314).

Pre-commencement additional supplement

329I Additional supplement in respect of a pre-commencement accounting period

(1) If—

(a) a qualifying company incurs qualifying pre-commencement onshore expenditure in respect of a ring fence trade, and

(b) the expenditure is incurred before the commencement period,

the company may claim additional supplement under this section ("pre-commencement additional supplement") in respect of one or more pre-commencement periods.

This is subject to section 329F(3)(b).

(2) Any pre-commencement additional supplement allowed on a claim in respect of a pre-commencement period is to be treated as expenditure—

(a) which is incurred by the company in the commencement period, and

(b) which is allowable as a deduction in calculating the profits of the ring fence trade for that period.

(3) The amount of the additional supplement for any pre-commencement period in respect of which a claim under this section is made is the relevant percentage for that period of the reference amount for that period.

(4) Sections 329J to 329M have effect for the purpose of determining the reference amount for a pre-commencement period.

(5) If a pre-commencement period is a period of less than 12 months, the amount of the additional supplement for the period (apart from this subsection) is to be reduced proportionally.

(6) Any claim for pre-commencement additional supplement in respect of a pre-commencement period must be made as a claim for the commencement period.

(7) Paragraph 74 of Schedule 18 to FA 1998 (company tax returns etc: time limit for claims for group relief) applies in relation to a claim for pre-commencement additional supplement as it applies in relation to a claim for group relief.

329J The mixed pool of qualifying pre-commencement onshore expenditure and supplement previously allowed

(1) For the purpose of determining the amount of any pre-commencement additional supplement, a qualifying company is to be taken to have had, at all times in the pre-commencement periods of the company, a continuing mixed pool of—

(a) qualifying pre-commencement onshore expenditure,

(b) pre-commencement supplement under Chapter 5, and

(c) pre-commencement additional supplement under this Chapter.

(2) The pool is to be taken to have consisted of—

(a) the company's qualifying pre-commencement onshore expenditure, allocated to the pool for each pre-commencement period in accordance with subsection (3),

(b) the company's pre-commencement supplement allowed under Chapter 5, allocated to the pool in accordance with subsections (4) to (7), and

(c) the company's pre-commencement additional supplement allowed under this Chapter, allocated to the pool in accordance with subsection (8).

(3) To allocate qualifying pre-commencement onshore expenditure to the pool for any pre-commencement period, take the following steps—

Step 1

Count as eligible expenditure for that period so much of the qualifying pre-commencement onshore expenditure mentioned in section 329I(1) as was incurred in that period.

Step 2

Find the total of all the eligible expenditure for that period (amount E).

Step 3

If section 329K (reduction in respect of disposal receipts under CAA 2001) applies, reduce amount E in accordance with that section.

Step 4

If section 329L (reduction in respect of unrelieved group ring fence profits) applies, reduce (or, as the case may be, further reduce) amount E in accordance with that section.

And so much of amount E as remains after making those reductions is to be taken to have been added to the pool in that period.

(4) If any pre-commencement supplement is allowed on a claim under Chapter 5 in respect of a pre-commencement period, the appropriate proportion of that supplement is to be taken to have been added to the pool in that period.

(5) "The appropriate proportion" means—

(a) if, before the end of the pre-commencement period, the company has incurred qualifying pre-commencement expenditure (within the meaning of section 312) on offshore oil-related activities, such proportion of the pre-commencement supplement under Chapter 5 as it is just and reasonable to attribute (directly or indirectly) to the company's qualifying pre-commencement onshore expenditure, and

(b) in any other case, 100%.

(6) In the case of a straddling period—

(a) the appropriate proportion of the pre-commencement supplement allowed on a claim under Chapter 5 in respect of the period is apportioned between so much of that period as falls before 5 December 2013 and so much of it as falls on or after that date, on the basis of the number of days in each part, and

(b) only so much of the appropriate proportion of the supplement as is apportioned to the later period is taken to have been added to the pool under subsection (4).

(7) But if the basis of the apportionment in subsection (6)(a) would work unjustly or unreasonably in the company's case, the company may elect for the apportionment to be made on another basis that is just and reasonable and specified in the election.

(8) If any pre-commencement additional supplement is allowed on a claim under this Chapter in respect of a pre-commencement period, the amount of that supplement is to be taken to have been added to the pool in that period.

329K Reduction in respect of disposal receipts under CAA 2001

(1) This section applies in the case of the qualifying company if—

(a) it incurs qualifying pre-commencement onshore expenditure in respect of a ring fence trade in any pre-commencement period,

(b) it would, on the relevant assumption, be entitled to an allowance under any provision of CAA 2001 in respect of that expenditure,

(c) an event occurs in relation to any asset representing the expenditure in any pre-commencement period, and

(d) the event would, on the relevant assumption, require a disposal value to be brought into account under any provision of CAA 2001 for any pre-commencement period.

(2) The relevant assumption is that the company was carrying on the ring fence trade—

(a) when the expenditure was incurred, and

(b) when the event giving rise to the disposal value occurred.

(3) For the purpose of allocating qualifying pre-commencement onshore expenditure to the pool for each pre-commencement period—

(a) find the total amount of the disposal values in the case of all such events (amount D), and

(b) taking later periods before earlier periods, reduce (but not below nil) amount E for any pre-commencement period by setting against it so much of amount D as does not fall to be set against amount E for a later pre-commencement period.

(4) Where the asset represented by the qualifying pre-commencement onshore expenditure is a mixed-activities asset, subsection (3) applies as if the disposal value required to be brought into account as mentioned in subsection (1)(d) were such proportion of the actual disposal value as is just and reasonable having regard to that expenditure.

(5) The asset is a "mixed-activities asset" if it also represents expenditure on offshore oil-related activities which is incurred by the company in a pre-commencement period and in respect of which the company would, on the relevant assumption, be entitled to an allowance under any provision of CAA 2001.

329L Reduction in respect of unrelieved group ring fence profits

(1) This section applies if there is an amount of unrelieved group ring fence profits for a pre-commencement period.

(2) For the purpose of allocating qualifying pre-commencement onshore expenditure to the pool for that period—

(a) find so much (if any) of amount E for that period as remains after any reduction falling to be made under section 329K ("the amount of the net onshore expenditure"), and

(b) reduce the amount of the net onshore expenditure (but not below nil) by setting against it a sum equal to the aggregate of the amounts of unrelieved group ring fence profits for the period.

(3) If the pre-commencement period is a straddling period, the unrelieved group ring fence profits for that period are to be determined as if the period began on 5 December 2013 and ended at the same time as the straddling period.

(4) Subsection (5) applies where in the pre-commencement period the company carries on both onshore oil-related activities and offshore oil related activities.

(5) The sum to be set against the net onshore expenditure under subsection (2)(b) is first to be reduced (but not below nil) by the amount of the company's net offshore expenditure for the period.

(6) "The net offshore expenditure" of the company for the period is determined as follows—

Step 1

Determine the amount of the company's total pre-commencement offshore expenditure incurred in the period.

Step 2

Make any reduction in that amount required by subsection (9).

So much as remains is the net offshore expenditure of the company for the period.

(7) "Pre-commencement offshore expenditure" means expenditure which—

(a) is incurred in the course of oil extraction activities which are offshore oil-related activities, and

(b) meets Conditions A, C and D in section 329G.

(8) Subsection (9) applies if—

(a) the qualifying company incurs pre-commencement offshore expenditure in respect of a ring fence trade in any pre-commencement period,

(b) it would, on the relevant assumption in section 329K, be entitled to an allowance under any provision of CAA 2001 in respect of that expenditure,

(c) an event occurs in relation to any asset representing the expenditure in any pre-commencement period, and

(d) the event would, on that assumption, require a disposal value to be brought into account under any provision of CAA 2001 for any pre-commencement period.

(9) For the purposes of Step 2 in subsection (6)—

(a) find the total amount of the disposal values in the case of all such events (amount D), and

(b) taking later periods before earlier periods, reduce (but not below nil) the amount of pre-commencement offshore expenditure for any pre-commencement period by setting against it so much of amount D as does not fall to be set against that total for a later pre-commencement period.

(10) Where the asset represented by the pre-commencement offshore expenditure is a mixed-activities asset, subsection (9) applies as if the disposal value required to be brought into account as mentioned in subsection (8)(d) were such proportion of the actual disposal value as is just and reasonable having regard to that expenditure.

(11) The asset is a "mixed-activities asset" if it also represents expenditure on onshore oil-related activities which is incurred by the company in a pre-commencement period and in respect of which the company would, on the relevant assumption in section 329K, be entitled to an allowance under any provision of CAA 2001.

329M The reference amount for a pre-commencement period

For the purposes of section 329I, the reference amount for a pre-commencement period is the amount in the pool at the end of the period—

(a) after the addition to the pool of any qualifying pre-commencement onshore expenditure allocated to the pool for that period in accordance with section 329J(3), but

(b) before determining, and adding to the pool, the amount of any pre-commencement additional supplement claimed in respect of the period under this Chapter.

Post-commencement additional supplement

329N Supplement in respect of post-commencement period

(1) A qualifying company which incurs an onshore ring fence loss (see section 329P) in any post-commencement period may claim supplement under this section ("post-commencement additional supplement") in respect of—

(a) that period, or

(b) any subsequent accounting period in which it carries on its ring fence trade.

(2) Any post-commencement additional supplement allowed on a claim in respect of a post-commencement period is to be treated for the purposes of the Corporation Tax Acts (other than the post-commencement additional supplement provisions) as if it were a loss—

(a) which is incurred in carrying on the ring fence trade in that period, and

(b) which falls in whole to be used under section 45 (carry forward of trade loss against subsequent trade profits) to reduce trading income from the ring fence trade in succeeding accounting periods.

(3) Paragraph 74 of Schedule 18 to FA 1998 (company tax returns etc: time limit for claims for group relief) applies in relation to a claim for post-commencement additional supplement as it applies in relation to a claim for group relief.

(4) In this Chapter "the post-commencement additional supplement provisions" means this section and sections 329O to 329T.

329O Amount of post-commencement additional supplement for a post-commencement period

(1) The amount of the post-commencement additional supplement for any post-commencement period in respect of which a claim under section 329N is made is the relevant percentage for that period of the reference amount for that period.

(2) Sections 329P to 329T have effect for the purpose of determining the reference amount for a post-commencement period.

(3) If the post-commencement period is a period of less than 12 months, the amount of the post-commencement additional supplement for the period (apart from this subsection) is to be reduced proportionally.

329P Onshore ring fence losses

(1) If—

(a) in a post-commencement period ("the period of the loss") a qualifying company carrying on a ring fence trade consisting solely of onshore oil-related activities incurs a loss in the trade, and

(b) some or all of the loss falls to be used under section 45 (carry forward of trade loss against subsequent profits) to reduce trading income from the trade in succeeding accounting periods,

so much of the loss as falls to be so used is an "onshore ring fence loss" of the company.

This is subject to subsection (4).

(2) If—

(a) in a post-commencement period ("the period of the loss") a qualifying company carrying on a ring fence trade consisting of both onshore oil-related activities and offshore oil-related activities incurs a loss in the trade, and

(b) some or all of the loss falls to be used under section 45 (carry forward of trade loss against subsequent profits) to reduce trading income from the trade in succeeding accounting periods,

the appropriate proportion of so much of the loss as falls to be so used is an "onshore ring fence loss" of the company.

This is subject to subsection (4).

(3) "The appropriate proportion" means such proportion as it is just and reasonable to attribute to the company's onshore oil-related activities carried out in the course of its ring fence trade.

(4) In the case of a straddling period—

(a) the amount of the onshore ring fence loss determined under subsection (1) or (2) in respect of the period is apportioned between so much of that period as falls before 5 December 2013 and so much of it as falls on or after that date, on the basis of the number of days in each part, and

(b) only so much of the loss as is apportioned to the later part of the period is an onshore ring fence loss of the company for the straddling period.

(5) But if the basis of the apportionment in subsection (4)(a) would work unjustly or unreasonably in the company's case, the company may elect for the apportionment to be made on another basis that is just and reasonable and specified in the election.

(6) In determining for the purposes of the post-commencement additional supplement provisions how much of a loss incurred in a ring fence trade falls to be used as mentioned in subsection (1)(b) or (2)(b), the following assumptions are to be made.

(7) The first assumption is that every claim is made that could be made by the company under section 37 (relief for trade losses against total profits) to deduct losses incurred in the ring fence trade from ring fence profits of post-commencement periods which are earlier than the period of the loss.

(8) The second assumption is that (where appropriate) section 42 (ring fence trades: further extension of period for relief) applies in relation to every such claim under section 37.

(9) This section has effect for the purposes of the post-commencement additional supplement provisions.

329Q The onshore ring fence pool

(1) For the purpose of determining the amount of any post-commencement additional supplement, a qualifying company is to be taken at all times in its post-commencement periods to have a continuing mixed pool (the "onshore ring fence pool") of—

(a) the company's onshore ring fence losses,

(b) post-commencement supplement under Chapter 5,

(c) post-commencement additional supplement under this Chapter.

(2) The onshore ring fence pool continues even if the amount in it is nil.

(3) The onshore ring fence pool consists of—

(a) the company's onshore ring fence losses, allocated to the pool in accordance with subsection (4)(a),

(b) the company's post-commencement supplement allowed under Chapter 5, allocated to the pool in accordance with subsections (4)(b) and (5) to (7), and

(c) the company's post-commencement additional supplement allowed under this Chapter, allocated to the pool in accordance with subsection (4)(c).

(4) The allocation to the pool is made as follows—

(a) the amount of an onshore ring fence loss is added to the pool in the period of the loss,

(b) if any post-commencement supplement is allowed on a claim under Chapter 5 in respect of a post-commencement period, the appropriate proportion of the amount of that supplement is added to the pool in that period, and

(c) if any post-commencement additional supplement is allowed on a claim under this Chapter in respect of a post-commencement period, the amount of that supplement is added to the pool in that period.

(5) "The appropriate proportion" is—

(a) if the ring fence trade carried on by the company includes, or has at any time included, offshore oil-related activities, such proportion of the supplement as it is just and reasonable to attribute (directly or indirectly) to the company's onshore oil-related activities carried on in the period for which the supplement is allowed or an earlier post-commencement period, and

(b) in any other case, 100%.

(6) In the case of a straddling period—

(a) the appropriate proportion of the post-commencement supplement allowed on a claim under Chapter 5 in respect of the period is apportioned between so much of that period as falls before 5 December 2013 and so much of it as falls on or after that date, on the basis of the number of days in each part, and

(b) only so much of the appropriate proportion of the supplement as is apportioned to the later period is added to the pool under subsection (4)(b).

(7) But if the basis of the apportionment in subsection (6)(a) would work unjustly or unreasonably in the company's case, the company may elect for the apportionment to be made on another basis that is just and reasonable and specified in the election

(8) The amount in the onshore ring fence pool is subject to reductions in accordance with the following provisions of this Chapter.

(9) If a reduction in the amount in the onshore ring fence pool falls to be made in any accounting period, the reduction is made—

(a) after the addition to the pool of—

(i) the amount of any onshore ring fence losses allocated to the pool in that period in accordance with subsection (4)(a), and

(ii) any amount of post-commencement supplement under Chapter 5 claimed in respect of the period and allocated to the pool in accordance with subsection (4)(b), but

(b) before determining and adding to the pool under subsection (4)(c) the amount of any post-commencement additional supplement under this Chapter claimed in respect of the period,

and references to the amount in the pool are to be read accordingly.

329R Reductions in respect of utilised onshore ring fence losses

(1) If one or more losses incurred by a qualifying company in its ring fence trade in a post-commencement period are used under section 45 (carry forward of trade loss against subsequent trade profits) to reduce any profits of a post-commencement period, a reduction is to be made in that period in accordance with this section.

(2) To the extent that the losses used as mentioned in subsection (1) are onshore ring fence losses, the amount in the onshore ring fence pool is to be reduced (but not below nil) by setting against it a sum equal to such amount of those onshore ring fence losses as is so used.

(3) For the purposes of determining the extent to which losses used as mentioned in subsection (1) are onshore ring fence losses, relevant offshore losses are to be treated as so used in priority to onshore ring fence losses.

(4) For this purpose "relevant offshore loss" means so much (if any) of a loss used as mentioned in subsection (1) as is given by—

$$X - Y$$

where—

X is the amount of the loss so used, and

Y is so much of that loss as (ignoring section 329P(4)) is an onshore ring fence loss.

(5) In the case of a loss incurred in a straddling period—

(a) the amount of the relevant offshore loss is apportioned between so much of that period as falls before 5 December 2013 and so much of it as falls on or after that date, on the basis of the number of days in each part, and

(b) only so much of the loss as is apportioned to the later part of the period is a relevant offshore loss of the company for the straddling period.

(6) But if the basis of the apportionment in subsection (5)(a) would work unjustly or unreasonably in the company's case, the company may elect for the apportionment to be made on another basis that is just and reasonable and specified in the election.

329S Reductions in respect of unrelieved group ring fence profits

(1) If there is an amount of unrelieved group ring fence profits for a post-commencement period, reductions are to be made in that period in accordance with this section.

(2) After making any reductions that fall to be made in accordance with section 329R, the remaining amount in the onshore ring fence pool is to be reduced (but not below nil) by setting against it a sum equal to the aggregate of the amounts of unrelieved group ring fence profits for the period.

This is subject to subsection (4).

(3) If the post-commencement period is a straddling period, the unrelieved group ring fence profits for that period are to be determined as if the period began on 5 December 2013 and ended at the same time as the straddling period.

(4) If the ring fence trade carried on by the company includes, or has at any time included, offshore oil-related activities, the sum to be set against the onshore ring fence pool under subsection (2) is first to be reduced by the notional offshore loss pool.

(5) "The notional offshore loss pool" means—

(a) the sum of the relevant offshore losses (see section 329R(4)) for the post-commencement period mentioned in subsection (1) and earlier post-commencement periods, less

(b) the sum of—

(i) so much of those losses as is to be treated (see section 329R(3)) as used as mentioned in section 329R, and

TIOPA 2010

(ii) any reductions previously made under subsection (2) of this section.

329T The reference amount for a post-commencement period

For the purposes of section 329O the reference amount for a post-commencement period is so much of the amount in the onshore ring fence pool as remains after making any reductions required by sections 329R and 329S."

2 In section 270 of CTA 2010 (overview of Part 8), after subsection (5) insert—

"(5A) Chapter 5A makes provision about onshore additional ring fence expenditure supplement."

3 In Schedule 4 to CTA 2010 (index of defined expressions), at the appropriate place insert—

[FTB

"the commencement period (in Chapter 5A of Part 8)	section 329D(1)";
"offshore oil-related activities (in Chapter 5A of Part 8)	section 329C(3)";
"onshore oil-related activities (in Chapter 5A of Part 8)	section 329C(2)";
"onshore ring fence loss (in Chapter 5A of Part 8)	section 329P";
"the onshore ring fence pool (in Chapter 5A of Part 8)	section 329Q";
"the period of the loss (in Chapter 5A of Part 8)	section 329P";
"post-commencement additional supplement (in Chapter 5A of Part 8)	section 329N(1)";
"the post-commencement additional supplement provisions (in Chapter 5A of Part 8)	section 329N(4)";
"post-commencement period (in Chapter 5A of Part 8)	section 329D(1)";
"pre-commencement additional supplement (in Chapter 5A of Part 8)	section 329I(1)";
"pre-commencement period (in Chapter 5A of Part 8)	section 329D(1)";
"qualifying company (in Chapter 5A of Part 8)	section 329B";
"qualifying pre-commencement onshore expenditure (in Chapter 5A of Part 8)	section 329G";
"the relevant percentage (in Chapter 5A of Part 8)	section 329E";
"straddling period (in Chapter 5A of Part 8)	section 329D(3)";
"unrelieved group ring fence profits (in Chapter 5A of Part 8)	section 329H".

4 The amendments made by this Schedule have effect in relation to accounting periods ending on or after 5 December 2013.

SCHEDULE 15

SUPPLEMENTARY CHARGE: ONSHORE ALLOWANCE

Section 70

PART 1

AMENDMENTS OF PART 8 OF CTA 2010

1 Part 8 of CTA 2010 (oil activities) is amended as follows.

Onshore allowance

2 Section 357 (other definitions) is renumbered as section 356AA.

3 After Chapter 7 insert—

"CHAPTER 8
SUPPLEMENTARY CHARGE: ONSHORE ALLOWANCE
Introduction

356B Overview

This Chapter sets out how relief for certain capital expenditure incurred for the purposes of onshore oil-related activities is given by way of reduction of a company's adjusted ring fence profits, and includes provision about—

(a) the need for allowance held for a site to be activated by relevant income from the same site in order for the allowance to be available for reducing adjusted ring fence profits,

(b) elections by a company to transfer allowance between different sites in which it is a licensee (see section 356F), and

(c) mandatory transfers of allowance where shares in the equity in a licensed area are disposed of (see sections 356H to 356HB and the related provisions in sections 356G to 356GD).

356BA "Onshore oil-related activities"

(1) In this Chapter "onshore oil-related activities" means activities of a company which are carried on onshore and—

(a) fall within any of subsections (1) to (4) of section 356BB, or

(b) consist of the acquisition, enjoyment or exploitation of oil rights.

(2) Activities of a company are carried on "onshore" if they are authorised—

(a) under a landward licence under Part 1 of the Petroleum Act 1998 or the Petroleum (Production) Act 1934, or

(b) under a licence under the Petroleum (Production) Act (Northern Ireland) 1964.

(3) In subsection (2)(a), "landward licence" means a licence in respect of an area which falls within the definition of "landward area" in the regulations pursuant to which the licence was applied for.

356BB The activities

(1) Activities of a company in searching for oil or causing such searching to be carried out for the company.

(2) Activities of a company in extracting oil, or causing oil to be extracted for it, under rights which—

(a) authorise the extraction, and

(b) are held by it or by a company associated with it.

(3) Activities of a company in transporting, or causing to be transported for it, oil extracted under rights which—

(a) authorise the extraction, and

(b) are held as mentioned in subsection (2)(b),

but only if the transportation meets the condition in subsection (5).

(4) Activities of the company in effecting, or causing to be effected for it, the initial treatment or initial storage of oil won from any site under rights which—

(a) authorise its extraction, and

(b) are held as mentioned in subsection (2)(b).

(5) The condition mentioned in subsection (3) is that the transportation is to a place at which the seller in a sale at arm's length could reasonably be expected to deliver it (or, if there is more than one such place, the one nearest to the place of extraction).

(6) In this section "initial storage"—

(a) means, in relation to oil won from a site, the storage of a quantity of oil won from the site not exceeding 10 times the relevant share of the maximum daily production rate of oil for the site as planned or achieved (whichever is greater), but

(b) does not include the matters excluded by paragraphs (a) to (c) of the definition of "initial storage" in section 12(1) of OTA 1975;

and in this subsection "the relevant share" means a share proportionate to the company's share of oil won from the site concerned.

(7) In this section "initial treatment" has the meaning given by section 12(1) of OTA 1975; but for this purpose that definition is to be read as if the references in it to an oil field were to a site.

356BC "Site"

In this Chapter "site" (except in the expression "drilling and extraction site") means—

(a) a drilling and extraction site that is not used in connection with any oil field, or

(b) an oil field (whether or not one or more drilling and extraction sites are used in connection with it).

Onshore allowance

356C Generation of onshore allowance

(1) Subsection (2) applies where a company incurs any relievable capital expenditure in relation to a qualifying site.

(2) The company is to hold an amount of allowance equal to 75% of the amount of the expenditure.

(3) "Qualifying site" means a site whose development (in whole or in part) is authorised for the first time on or after 5 December 2013.

(4) Capital expenditure incurred by a company is "relievable" only if, and so far as—

(a) it is incurred for the purposes of onshore oil-related activities (see section 356BA), and

(b) neither of the disqualifying conditions is met at the beginning of the day on which the expenditure is incurred (see section 356CA).

(5) Allowance held under this Chapter is called "onshore allowance".

(6) Onshore allowance is said in this Chapter to be "generated" at the time when the capital expenditure is incurred (see section 356JA).

(7) Onshore allowance is referred to in this Chapter as being generated—

(a) "by" the company concerned,

(b) "at" the site concerned.

(8) Where capital expenditure is incurred only partly for the purposes of onshore oil-related activities, or the onshore oil-related activities for the purposes of which capital expenditure is incurred are carried on only partly in relation to a particular site, the expenditure is to be attributed to the site concerned on a just and reasonable basis.

(9) In this section, references to authorisation of development of a site—

(a) in the case of a site which is an oil field, are to be read in accordance with section 351;

(b) in the case of a drilling and extraction site, are to be read in accordance with section 356J.

356CA Disqualifying conditions for section 356C(4)(b)

(1) The first disqualifying condition is that production from the site is expected to exceed 7,000,000 tonnes.

(2) The second disqualifying condition is that production from the site has exceeded 7,000,000 tonnes.

(3) For the purposes of this section 1,100 cubic metres of gas at a temperature of 15 degrees celsius and pressure of one atmosphere is to be counted as equivalent to one tonne.

356CB Expenditure not related to an established site

(1) A company may make an election under this section in relation to capital expenditure incurred by it for the purposes of onshore oil-related activities if the appropriate condition is met.

(2) The appropriate condition is that at the time of the election no site can be identified as a site in relation to which the expenditure has been incurred.

(3) An election may not be made before the beginning of the third accounting period of the company after that in which the expenditure is incurred.

(4) An election must specify—

(a) the expenditure in question,

(b) a site ("the specified site") every part of which is, or is part of, an area in which the company is a licensee, and

(c) an accounting period of the company ("the specified accounting period").

(5) The specified accounting period must not be earlier than the accounting period in which the election is made.

(6) Where a company makes an election under this section in relation to an amount of expenditure, that amount is treated for the purposes of this Chapter as incurred by the company—

(a) in relation to the specified site, and

(b) at the beginning of the specified accounting period.

Reduction of adjusted ring fence profits

356D Reduction of adjusted ring fence profits

(1) A company's adjusted ring fence profits for an accounting period are to be reduced by the cumulative total amount of activated allowance for the accounting period (but are not to be reduced below zero).

(2) In relation to a company and an accounting period, the "cumulative total amount of activated allowance" is—

A + C

where—

A is the total of any amounts of activated allowance the company has, for any sites, for the accounting period (see section 356E(2)) or for reference periods within the accounting period (see section 356GB(1)), and

C is any amount carried forward to the period under section 356DA.

356DA Carrying forward of activated allowance

(1) This section applies where, in the case of a company and an accounting period—

(a) the cumulative total amount of activated allowance (see section 356D(2)), is greater than

(b) the adjusted ring fence profits.

(2) The difference is carried forward to the next accounting period.

356DB Companies with both field allowances and onshore allowance

(1) This section applies where a company's adjusted ring fence profits for an accounting period are reducible both—

(a) under section 333(1) (by the amount of the company's pool of field allowances for the period), and

(b) under section 356D(1) (by the cumulative total amount of activated allowance for the period).

(2) The company may choose the order in which the different allowances are to be used.

(3) If the company chooses to apply section 333(1) first, then—

(a) Chapter 7 and this Chapter are to be ignored in calculating the "adjusted ring fence profits" in accordance with section 356AA, and

(b) if section 356D(1) is also applied: this Chapter, but not Chapter 7, is to be ignored in calculating the adjusted ring fence profits in accordance with section 356JB.

(4) If the company chooses to apply section 356D(1) first, then—

(a) this Chapter and Chapter 7 are to be ignored in calculating the adjusted ring fence profits in accordance with section 356JB, and

(b) if section 333(1) is also applied: Chapter 7, but not this Chapter, is to be ignored in calculating the "adjusted ring fence profits" in accordance with section 356AA.

Activated and unactivated allowance: basic calculation rules

356E Activation of allowance: no change of equity share

(1) This section applies where—

(a) a company is a licensee in a licensed area for the whole or part ("the licensed part") of an accounting period,

(b) the company's share of the equity in the site is the same throughout the accounting period or, as the case requires, throughout the licensed part of the accounting period,

(c) the licensed area is or contains a site,

(d) the company holds, for the accounting period and the site, a closing balance of unactivated allowance (see section 356EA) that is greater than zero, and

(e) the company has relevant income from the site for the accounting period.

(2) The amount of activated allowance the company has for that accounting period and that site is the smaller of—

(a) the closing balance of unactivated allowance held for the accounting period and the site;

(b) the company's relevant income for that accounting period from that site.

(3) In this Chapter "relevant income", in relation to a site and an accounting period of a company, means production income of the company from any oil extraction activities carried on at the site that is taken into account in calculating the company's adjusted ring fence profits for the accounting period.

356EA The closing balance of unactivated allowance for an accounting period

The closing balance of unactivated allowance held by a company for an accounting period and a site is—

P + Q – R

where—

P is the amount of onshore allowance generated by the company in the accounting period at the site (including any amount treated under section 356F(7) or 356HB(1) as generated by the company in that accounting period at that site);

Q is any amount carried forward from an immediately preceding accounting period under section 356EB(2) or from an immediately preceding reference period under section 356GC;

R is any amount deducted in accordance with section 356GD(1) (reduction of allowance if equity disposed of).

356EB Carrying forward of unactivated allowance

(1) This section applies where X is greater than Y in the case of an accounting period of a company and a site, where—

X is the closing balance of unactivated allowance for the accounting period and the site;

Y is the company's relevant income for the accounting period from that site.

(2) An amount equal to the difference between X and Y is treated as onshore allowance held by the company for that site for the next accounting period (and is treated as held with effect from the beginning of that period).

Transfer of allowances between sites

356F Transfer of allowances between sites

(1) This section applies if a company has, with respect to a site, an amount ("N") of onshore allowance available to carry forward to an accounting period—

(a) under section 356EB(2), or

(b) by virtue of section 356GC(3).

(2) The company may elect to transfer the whole or part of that amount to another site ("site B"), if the appropriate conditions are met.

(3) The appropriate conditions are that—

(a) every part of site B is, or is part of, an area in which the company is a licensee, and

(b) the election is made no earlier than the beginning of the third accounting period of the company after that in which the allowance was generated.

(4) For the purposes of subsection (3)(b), a company may regard an amount of onshore allowance held by it for a site as generated in a particular accounting period if the amount does not exceed—

A – T

where—

A is the amount of onshore allowance generated in that accounting period for that site;

T is the total amount of onshore allowance generated in that period for that site that has already been transferred under this section.

(5) An election must specify—

(a) the amount of onshore allowance to be transferred;

(b) the site at which it was generated;

(c) the site to which it is transferred;

(d) the accounting period in which it was generated.

(6) Where a company makes an election under subsection (2), then—

(a) if the company elects to transfer the whole of N, no amount is available to be carried forward under section 356EB(2) or (as the case may be) by virtue of section 356GC(3);

(b) if the company elects to transfer only part of N, the amount available to be carried forward as mentioned in subsection (1) is reduced by the amount transferred.

(7) Where an amount of onshore allowance is transferred to a site as a result of an election, this Chapter has effect as if the allowance is generated at that site at the beginning of the accounting period in which the election is made.

Changes in equity share: activation of allowance

356G Introduction to sections 356GA to 356GD

(1) Sections 356GA to 356GD apply to a company in respect of an accounting period and a licensed area that is or contains a site, if the following conditions are met—

(a) the company is a licensee in the licensed area for the whole, or for part, of the accounting period;

(b) the company has different shares (greater than zero) of the equity in the licensed area at different times during the accounting period.

(2) In a case where a company has three or more different shares of the equity in a licensed area during a particular day, sections 356GA to 356GD (in particular, provisions relating to the beginning or end of a day) have effect subject to the necessary modifications.

356GA Reference periods

(1) For the purposes of sections 356GB to 356GD, the accounting period, or (if the company is not a licensee for the whole of the accounting period) the part or parts of the accounting period for which the company is a licensee, are to be divided into reference periods (each of which "belongs to" the site concerned).

(2) A reference period is a period of consecutive days that meets the following conditions—

(a) at the beginning of each day in the period, the company is a licensee in the licensed area;

(b) at the beginning of each day in the period, the company's share of the equity in the licensed area is the same;

(c) each day in the period falls within the accounting period.

356GB Activation of allowance: reference periods

(1) The amount (if any) of activated allowance that a company has with respect to a site for a reference period is the smaller of the following—

(a) the company's relevant income from the site in the reference period;

(b) the total amount of unactivated allowance that is attributable to the reference period and the site (see section 356GD).

(2) The company's relevant income from the site in the reference period is—

I x (R / L)

where—

I is the company's relevant income from the site in the whole of the accounting period;

R is the number of days in the reference period;

L is the number of days in the accounting period for which the company is a licensee in the licensed area concerned.

356GC Carry-forward of unactivated allowance from a reference period

(1) If, in the case of a reference period ("RP1") of a company, the amount mentioned in subsection (1)(b) of section 356GB exceeds the amount mentioned in subsection (1)(a) of that section, an amount equal to the difference between those amounts is treated as onshore allowance held by the company for the site concerned for the next period.

(2) If RP1 is immediately followed by another reference period of the company (belonging to the same site), "the next period" means that reference period.

(3) If subsection (2) does not apply, "the next period" means the next accounting period of the company.

356GD Unactivated amounts attributable to a reference period

(1) For the purposes of section 356GB(1)(b), the total amount of unactivated allowance attributable to a reference period and a site is—

P + Q – R

where—

P is the amount of allowance generated by the company in the reference period at the site (including any amount treated under section 356F(7) or 356HB(1) as generated by the company in that accounting period at that site);

Q is the amount given by subsection (2) or (3);

R is any amount to be deducted under section 356HA(1) in respect of a disposal of the whole or part of the company's share of the equity in a licensed area that is or contains the site.

(2) Where the reference period is not immediately preceded by another reference period but is preceded by an accounting period of the company, Q is equal to the amount (if any) that is to be carried forward from that preceding accounting period under section 356EB(2).

(3) Where the reference period is immediately preceded by another reference period, Q is equal to the amount carried forward by virtue of section 356GC(2).

Transfers of allowance on disposal of equity share

356H Introduction to sections 356HA and 356HB

(1) Sections 356HA and 356HB apply where a company ("the transferor")—

(a) disposes of the whole or part of its share of the equity in a licensed area that is or contains a site;

(b) immediately before the disposal holds (unactivated) onshore allowance for the site concerned.

(2) Each company to which a share of the equity is disposed of is referred to in section 356HB as "a transferee".

356HA Reduction of allowance if equity disposed of

(1) The following amount is to be deducted, in accordance with section 356GD(1), in calculating the total amount of unactivated allowance attributable to a reference period and a site—

F × ((E1 – E2) / E1)

where—

F is the pre-transfer total of unactivated allowance for the reference period that ends with the day on which the disposal is made;

E1 is the transferor's share of the equity in the licensed area immediately before the disposal;

E2 is the transferor's share of the equity in the licensed area immediately after the disposal.

(2) The "pre-transfer total of unactivated allowance" for a reference period is—

P + Q

where P and Q are the same as in section 356GD.

356HB Acquisition of allowance if equity acquired

(1) A transferee is treated as generating at the site concerned, at the beginning of the reference period or accounting period of the transferee that begins with, or because of, the disposal, onshore allowance of the amount given by subsection (2).

(2) The amount is—

R × (E3 / (E1 – E2))

where—

R is the amount determined for the purposes of the deduction under section 356HA(1);

E3 is the share of equity in the licensed area that the transferee has acquired from the transferor;

E1 and E2 are the same as in section 356HA.

Miscellaneous

356I Adjustments

(1) This section applies if there is any alteration in a company's adjusted ring fence profits for an accounting period after this Chapter has effect in relation to the profits.

(2) Any necessary adjustments to the operation of this Chapter (whether in relation to the profits or otherwise) are to be made (including any necessary adjustments to the effect of section 356D on the profits or to the calculation of the amount to be carried forward under section 356DA).

356IA Orders

(1) The Treasury may by order substitute a different percentage for the percentage that is at any time specified in section 356C(2) (calculation of allowance as a percentage of capital expenditure).

(2) The Treasury may by order amend the number that is at any time specified in section 356CA(1) or (2) (cap on production, or estimated production, at a site for the purposes of onshore allowance).

(3) An order under subsection (1) or (2) may include transitional provision.

Interpretation

356J "Authorisation of development": drilling and extraction sites

(1) References in this Chapter to authorisation of development of a site are to be interpreted as follows in relation to a drilling and extraction site that is situated in, or used in connection with, a licensed area.

(2) The references are to be read as references to a national authority—

(a) granting a licensee consent for development of the licensed area,

(b) serving on a licensee a programme of development for the licensed area, or

(c) approving a programme of development for the licensed area.

(3) References in subsection (2) to a "licensee" are to a licensee in the licensed area mentioned in subsection (1).

(4) In this section—

"consent for development", in relation to a licensed area, does not include consent which is limited to the purpose of testing the characteristics of an oil-bearing area;

"development", in relation to a licensed area, means winning oil from the licensed area otherwise than in the course of searching for oil or drilling wells;

"national authority" means—

(a) the Secretary of State, or

(b) a Northern Ireland Department.

356JA When capital expenditure is incurred

Section 5 of CAA 2001 (when capital expenditure is incurred) applies for the purposes of this Chapter as for the purposes of that Act.

356JB Other definitions

In this Chapter (except where otherwise specified)—

"adjusted ring fence profits", in relation to a company and an accounting period, means the adjusted ring fence profits that would (if this Chapter were ignored) be taken into account in calculating the supplementary charge on the company under section 330(1) for the accounting period (but see also section 356DB);

"cumulative total amount of activated allowance" has the meaning given by section 356D(2);

"licence" has the same meaning as in Part 1 of OTA 1975 (see section 12(1) of that Act);

"licensed area" has the same meaning as in Part 1 of OTA 1975;

"licensee" has the same meaning as in Part 1 of OTA 1975;

"onshore allowance" has the meaning given by section 356C(5);

"relevant income", in relation to an onshore site and an accounting period, has the meaning given by section 356E(3);

"site" has the meaning given by section 356BC."

Restriction of field allowance to offshore fields

4 (1) Section 352 (meaning of "qualifying oil field") is amended as follows.

(2) Renumber section 352 as subsection (1) of section 352.

(3) In section 352(1) (as renumbered), after "an oil field" insert ", other than an onshore field,".

(4) After subsection (1) insert—

"(2) An oil field is an "onshore field" for the purposes of subsection (1) if—

(a) the authorisation day is on or after 5 December 2013, and

(b) on the authorisation day every part of the oil field is, or is part of, an onshore licensed area;

but see the transitional provisions in paragraph 7 of Schedule 15 to FA 2014.

(3) A licensed area is an "onshore licensed area" if it falls within the definition of "landward area" in the regulations pursuant to which the application for the licence was made."

PART 2

MINOR AND CONSEQUENTIAL AMENDMENTS

5 (1) CTA 2010 is amended as follows.

(2) In section 270 (overview of Part)—

(a) after subsection (7) insert—

"(7A) Chapter 8 makes provision about the reduction of supplementary charge by an allowance for capital expenditure incurred for the purposes of onshore oil-related activities.";

(b) in subsection (8)(c), for "357" substitute "356AA".

(3) In section 333 (reduction of adjusted ring fence profits)—

(a) in subsection (1), after "reduced" insert "(but not below zero)";

(b) omit subsection (2).

(4) In section 356AA (as renumbered by paragraph 2)(definitions for Chapter 7), in the definition of "adjusted ring fence profits", at the end insert "; but see also section 356DB (companies with allowances under Chapter 8 as well as this Chapter)".

(5) In Schedule 4 (index of defined expressions)—

(a) at the appropriate places insert—

[FTB

"adjusted ring fence profits (in Chapter 8 of Part 8)	section 356JB";
"cumulative total amount of activated allowance (in Chapter 8 of Part 8)	section 356JB";
"onshore allowance (in Chapter 8 of Part 8)	section 356JB";
"onshore oil-related activities (in Chapter 8 of Part 8)	section 356BA";
"relevant income (in Chapter 8 of Part 8)	section 356E(3)";
"site (in Chapter 8 of Part 8)	section 356BC";

(b) in the entries for "adjusted ring fence profits", "authorisation day", "eligible oil field", "licensee" and "relevant income" (in each case, as those expressions are defined for Chapter 7 of Part 8 of CTA 2010), for "357" substitute "356AA".

PART 3

COMMENCEMENT AND TRANSITIONAL PROVISION

Commencement of onshore allowance

6 (1) The amendments made by paragraphs 3 and 5(1), (2)(a), (3) and (4) have effect in relation to capital expenditure incurred on or after 5 December 2013.

(2) The amendments made by paragraph 4 have effect in relation to any accounting period of a company in which a post-commencement authorisation day falls.

(3) In sub-paragraph (2) "post-commencement authorisation day" means an authorisation day (as defined for Chapter 7 of Part 8 of CTA 2010) that is 5 December 2013 or a later day.

(4) Section 5 of CAA 2001 (when capital expenditure is incurred) applies for the purposes of this paragraph as for the purposes of that Act.

Option to defer commencement

7 (1) This paragraph applies in relation to any oil field whose development (in whole or in part) is authorised for the first time on or after 5 December 2013 but before 1 January 2015.

(2) At any time before 1 January 2015, the companies that are licensees in the oil field may jointly elect that the law is to have effect in relation to each of those companies as if the date specified in—

(a) section 352(2)(a) of CTA 2010 (as inserted by paragraph 4(4) of this Schedule),

(b) section 356C(3) of CTA 2010 (as inserted by paragraph 3 of this Schedule), and

(c) paragraph 6(3),

were 1 January 2015.

(3) Expressions used in this paragraph and in Chapter 7 of Part 8 of CTA 2010 have the same meaning in this paragraph as in that Chapter.

Straddling accounting periods

8 (1) Paragraphs 9 and 10 apply where a company has an accounting period (the "straddling accounting period") that begins before and ends on or after commencement day.

(2) In paragraphs 9 and 10 "commencement day" means—

(a) 5 December 2013 (except where paragraph (b) applies);

(b) 1 January 2015, in relation to a company that makes an election under paragraph 7.

(3) Expressions used in paragraph 9 or 10 and in Chapter 8 of Part 8 of CTA 2010 (as inserted by paragraph 3) have the same meaning in the paragraph concerned as in that Chapter.

9 (1) The amount (if any) by which the company's adjusted ring fence profits for the straddling accounting period are reduced under section 356D of CTA 2010 (as inserted by paragraph 3) cannot exceed the appropriate proportion of those profits.

(2) Section 356DA of CTA 2010 (carrying forward of activated allowance) applies in relation to the company and the accounting period as if the reference in subsection (1)(b) of that section to the adjusted ring fence profits were to the appropriate proportion of those profits.

(3) The "appropriate proportion" of the company's adjusted ring fence profits for the straddling accounting period is—

$(D / Y) \times N$

where—

D is the number of days in the straddling accounting period that fall on or after commencement day;

Y is the number of days in the straddling accounting period;

N is the amount of the company's adjusted ring fence profits for the accounting period.

(4) If the basis of apportionment in sub-paragraph (3) would work unjustly or unreasonably in the company's case, the company may elect for its adjusted ring fence profits to be apportioned on another basis that is just and reasonable and specified in the election.

10 (1) For the purpose of determining the amount of activated allowance the company has with respect to any site—

(a) for the straddling accounting period (see section 356E of CTA 2010, as inserted by paragraph 3), or

(b) for a reference period that is part of the straddling accounting period (see section 356GB of CTA 2010, as so inserted),

the company's relevant income from the site in the straddling accounting period is taken to be the appropriate proportion of the actual amount of that relevant income.

(2) Accordingly, in relation to the company, the straddling accounting period and the site in question, section 356EB of CTA 2010 (carrying forward of unactivated allowance) has effect as if Y in subsection (1) of that section were defined as the appropriate proportion of the company's relevant income for the straddling accounting period from that site.

(3) The "appropriate proportion" of the company's relevant income from a site in the straddling accounting period is—

$(D / Y) \times I$

where—

D is the number of days in the straddling accounting period that fall on or after commencement day;

Y is the number of days in the straddling accounting period;

I is the amount of the company's relevant income from the site in the straddling accounting period.

(4) If the basis of apportionment in sub-paragraph (3) would work unjustly or unreasonably in the company's case, the company may elect for its adjusted ring fence profits to be apportioned on another basis that is just and reasonable and specified in the election.

SCHEDULE 16

OIL CONTRACTORS: RING-FENCE TRADE ETC

Section 73

Press releases etc—UK oil and gas—offshore bareboat chartering—draft legislation and TIIN: HMRC Technical Note 3 April 2014 (see *SWTI 2014, Issue 14*)

CTA 2010

1 CTA 2010 is amended as follows.

2 In section 1 (overview of Act), in subsection (3), after paragraph (a) insert—

"(aa) oil contractor activities (see Part 8ZA),

(ab) profits arising from the exploitation of patents etc (see Part 8A),".

3 In Chapter 4 of Part 8 (oil activities: calculation of profits), after section 285 insert—

"Hire of relevant assets

285A Restriction on hire etc of relevant assets to be brought into account

(1) This section applies if—

(a) oil contractor activities are, or are to be, carried out, and

(b) a company that carries on a ring fence trade makes, or is to make, one or more payments under a lease of a relevant asset, or part of a relevant asset, which is, or is to be, provided, operated or used in the relevant offshore service in question.

(2) The total amount that may be brought into account in respect of the payments for the purposes of calculating the company's ring fence profits in an accounting period is limited to the hire cap.

(3) The "hire cap" is an amount equal to the relevant percentage of TC for the accounting period, subject to subsection (4).

(4) If payments in relation to which subsection (2) or section 356N(2) (restriction on hire for oil contractors under Part 8ZA) applies are also made, or to be made, by one or more other companies in respect of the relevant asset or part, the "hire cap" is to be such proportion of the amount mentioned in subsection (3) as is just and reasonable, having regard (in particular) to the amounts of the payments made, or to be made, by each company.

(5) The "relevant percentage" and TC are to be determined in accordance with section 356N(5) to (16).

(6) To the extent that, by virtue of this section, payments within subsection (1)(b) cannot be brought into account for the purposes of calculating the company's ring fence profits in an accounting period, the payments may be—

(a) allowed as a deduction from the company's total profits for the accounting period, or

(b) treated as a surrenderable amount of the company for the accounting period for the purposes of Part 5 (group relief) (see section 99(7)) as if they were a trading loss,

but this is subject to subsection (7).

(7) No deduction may be made by virtue of subsection (6) from total profits so far as they are ring fence profits or contractor's ring fence profits.

(8) If the company or an associated person enters into arrangements the main purpose or one of the main purposes of which is to secure that subsection (2) does not apply in relation to one or more payments to any extent, that subsection applies in relation to the payments to the extent that it would not otherwise do so.

(9) In subsection (8) "arrangements" includes any agreement, understanding, scheme, transaction or series of transactions (whether or not legally enforceable).

(10) In this section—

"associated person" has the meaning given by section 356LB;

"contractor's ring fence profits" has the meaning given by section 356LD;

"oil contractor activities" and "relevant offshore service" have the meaning given by section 356L;

"relevant asset" has the meaning given by section 356LA;

"lease" has the meaning given by section 868."

4 After Part 8 (oil activities) insert—

"PART 8ZA
OIL CONTRACTORS

CHAPTER 1
INTRODUCTION

356K Overview of Part

(1) This Part is about the corporation tax treatment of oil contractor activities.
(2) Chapter 2 contains basic definitions used in this Part.
(3) Chapter 3 treats oil contractor activities as a separate trade.
(4) Chapter 4 makes provision about the calculation of profits from oil contractor activities.
(5) For the meaning of oil contractor activities, see section 356L.

CHAPTER 2
BASIC DEFINITIONS

356L "Oil contractor activities" etc

(1) The definitions in this section have effect for the purposes of this Part.
(2) "Oil contractor activities" means activities carried on by a company ("the contractor"), which are not oil-related activities (within the meaning of section 274), but are—

(a) exploration or exploitation activities in, or in connection with, which the contractor provides, operates or uses a relevant asset (see section 356LA) in a relevant offshore service, or
(b) otherwise carried on in, or in connection with, the provision by the contractor of a relevant offshore service.

(3) The contractor provides a "relevant offshore service" if the contractor provides, operates or uses a relevant asset in, or in connection with, the carrying on of exploration or exploitation activities in a relevant offshore area by the contractor or any other associated person.
(4) "Exploration or exploitation activities" means activities carried on in connection with the exploration or exploitation of the seabed and subsoil and their natural resources.
(5) "Relevant offshore area" means—

(a) the territorial sea of the United Kingdom;
(b) the areas designated by Order in Council under section 1(7) of the Continental Shelf Act 1964.

356LA "Relevant asset"

(1) In this Part "relevant asset" means an asset within subsection (2) in respect of which conditions A and B are met.
(2) An asset is within this subsection if it is a structure that—

(a) can be moved from place to place (whether or not under its own power) without major dismantling or modification, and
(b) can be used to—
 (i) drill for the purposes of searching for, or extracting, oil, or
 (ii) provide accommodation for individuals who work on or from another structure used in a relevant offshore area for, or in connection with, exploration or exploitation activities ("offshore workers").

(3) But an asset is not within subsection (2)(b)(ii) if it is reasonable to suppose that its use to provide accommodation for offshore workers is unlikely to be more than incidental to another use, or other uses, to which the asset is likely to be put.
(4) In subsection (2)—

"oil" means any substance capable of being won under the authority of a licence granted under Part 1 of the Petroleum Act 1998 or the Petroleum (Production) Act (Northern Ireland) 1964;
"structure" includes a ship or other vessel.

(5) Condition A is that the asset, or any part of the asset, is leased (whether by the contractor or not) from an associated person other than the contractor.
(6) Condition B is that the asset is of the requisite value.
(7) The asset is of the "requisite value" if its market value is £2,000,000 or more.
(8) The Treasury may by regulations modify the meaning of "requisite value".
(9) Regulations under subsection (8) may—

(a) amend this section,
(b) make different provision for different cases or different purposes, and

(c) make incidental, consequential, supplementary or transitional provision or savings.

356LB "Associated person"

(1) For the purposes of this Part each of the following is an "associated person"—

(a) the contractor,

(b) any person who is, or has been, connected with the contractor,

(c) any person who has acted, acts or is to act, together with the contractor to provide a service, and

(d) any person who is connected with a person falling within paragraph (b) or (c).

(2) A person does not act together with the contractor to provide a service by reason only of leasing an asset, to any person, which is provided, operated or used in the service.

356LC "Lease"

In this Part "lease" has the meaning given by section 868 and "leased" and "leasing" are to be construed accordingly.

356LD "Contractor's ring fence profits"

In this Part the "contractor's ring fence profits", in relation to an accounting period, means the contractor's income arising from oil contractor activities for that period.

CHAPTER 3

DEEMED SEPARATE TRADE

356M Oil contractor activities treated as separate trade

If the contractor carries on oil contractor activities as part of a trade, those activities are treated for the purposes of the charge to corporation tax on income as a separate trade, distinct from all other activities carried on by the contractor as part of the trade.

CHAPTER 4

CALCULATION OF PROFITS

Hire of relevant assets

356N Restriction on hire etc of relevant assets to be brought into account

(1) This section applies if the contractor makes, or is to make, one or more payments under a lease of—

(a) a relevant asset, or

(b) part of a relevant asset.

(2) The total amount that may be brought into account in respect of the payments for the purposes of calculating the contractor's ring fence profits in an accounting period is limited to the hire cap.

(3) The "hire cap" is an amount equal to the relevant percentage of TC for the accounting period, subject to subsection (4).

(4) If payments in relation to which subsection (2) or section 285A(2) (restriction on hire for company carrying on a ring fence trade under Part 8) applies are also made, or to be made, by one or more other companies in respect of the relevant asset or part, the "hire cap" is to be such proportion of the amount mentioned in subsection (3) as is just and reasonable, having regard (in particular) to the amounts of the payments made, or to be made, by the contractor and each other company.

(5) Subject to subsection (7), the "relevant percentage" is—

$$\frac{UROS}{TU} \times 7.5\%$$

where—

UROS is the number of days in the accounting period that the relevant asset is provided, operated or used in a relevant offshore service, and

TU is the number of days in the accounting period that the relevant asset is provided, operated or used (whether or not in a relevant offshore service).

(6) Accordingly, the relevant percentage is zero if the relevant asset is not provided, operated or used in the accounting period.

(7) If the accounting period is less than 12 months, the relevant percentage is to be proportionally reduced.

(8) TC is—

OC + CE

(9) Unless subsection (11) applies, OC is the sum of—

(a) any consideration given for the acquisition of the relevant asset or part when it was first acquired by an associated person, and

(b) any expenses incurred by an associated person in connection with that acquisition (other than the costs of financing the acquisition).

This is subject to subsections (12) and (13).

(10) Subsection (11) applies if the relevant asset or part—

(a) is leased by an associated person from a person who is not an associated person, and

(b) has never been owned by an associated person.

(11) OC is the sum of—

(a) the consideration that it is reasonable to suppose would have been given for the acquisition of the relevant asset or part, if it had been acquired by an associated person by way of a bargain at arm's length at the time it was first leased as mentioned in subsection (10)(a), and

(b) the expenses (other than the costs of financing the acquisition) that it is reasonable to suppose would have been incurred by an associated person in connection with such an acquisition.

This is subject to subsections (12) and (13).

(12) If the relevant asset or part was first acquired by an associated person, or (as the case may be) first leased as mentioned in subsection (10)(a), before the beginning of the accounting period, OC does not include any part of the consideration mentioned in subsection (9)(a) or (as the case may be) (11)(a) that it is reasonable to attribute to anything that no longer forms part of the relevant asset or part at the beginning of the accounting period.

(13) If the relevant asset or part was first acquired by an associated person, or (as the case may be) first leased as mentioned in subsection (10)(a), in the accounting period, OC for the accounting period is—

$$OC \times \frac{D - DBA}{D}$$

where—

D is the total number of days in the accounting period,

DBA is the number of days in the accounting period before the day on which the relevant asset or part was first acquired or first leased, and

OC is the amount given by subsection (9) or (as the case may be) (11).

(14) CE is capital expenditure on the relevant asset or part (other than capital expenditure in respect of its acquisition or the acquisition of a lease of it) incurred by an associated person—

(a) after it was first acquired by an associated person or (as the case may be) was first leased as mentioned in subsection (10)(a), and

(b) before the end of the accounting period.

This is subject to subsections (15) and (16).

(15) CE does not include any capital expenditure mentioned in subsection (14) that is—

(a) incurred before the beginning of the accounting period, and

(b) not reflected in the state or nature of the relevant asset or part at the beginning of the accounting period.

(16) If any capital expenditure mentioned in subsection (14) is incurred on a day in the accounting period, the amount of CE for the accounting period in respect of that capital expenditure is—

$$CEA \times \frac{D - DBI}{D}$$

where—

D is the total number of days in the accounting period,

DBI is the number of days in the accounting period before the day on which that capital expenditure is incurred, and

CEA is the amount of that capital expenditure.

356NA Restriction on hire: further provision

(1) The Treasury may by regulations modify the "relevant percentage" for the purposes of section 356N or 285A.

(2) Regulations under subsection (1) may—

(a) amend section 356N or section 285A,

(b) make different provision for different cases or different purposes, and

(c) make incidental, consequential, supplementary or transitional provision or savings.

(3) To the extent that, by virtue of section 356N, payments within subsection (1) of that section cannot be brought into account for the purposes of calculating the contractor's ring fence profits in an accounting period, the payments may be—

(a) allowed as a deduction from the contractor's total profits for the accounting period, or

(b) treated as a surrenderable amount of the contractor for the accounting period for the purposes of Part 5 (group relief) (see section 99(7)) as if they were a trading loss,

subject to subsection (4).

(4) No deduction may be made by virtue of subsection (3) from total profits so far as they are contractor's ring fence profits or ring fence profits for the purposes of Part 8.

(5) If an associated person enters into arrangements the main purpose or one of the main purposes of which is to secure that section 356N(2) does not apply in relation to one or more payments to any extent, that provision applies in relation to the payments to the extent it would not otherwise do so.

(6) In subsection (5) "arrangements" includes any agreement, understanding, scheme, transaction or series of transactions (whether or not legally enforceable).

Loan relationships

356NB Restriction on debits to be brought into account

(1) Debits may not be brought into account for the purposes of Part 5 of CTA 2009 (loan relationships) in respect of the contractor's loan relationships in any way that results in a reduction of what would otherwise be the contractor's ring fence profits, but this is subject to subsections (2) to (4).

(2) Subsection (1) does not apply so far as a loan relationship is in respect of money borrowed by the contractor which has been—

(a) used to meet expenditure incurred by the contractor in carrying on oil contractor activities, or

(b) appropriated to meeting expenditure to be so incurred by the contractor.

(3) Subsection (1) does not apply, in the case of debits falling to be brought into account as a result of section 329 of CTA 2009 (pre-loan relationship and abortive expenses) in respect of a loan relationship that has not been entered into, so far as the relationship would have been one entered into for the purpose of borrowing money to be used or appropriated as mentioned in subsection (2).

(4) Subsection (1) does not apply, in the case of debits in respect of a loan relationship to which Chapter 2 of Part 6 of CTA 2009 (relevant non-lending relationships) applies, so far as—

(a) the payment of interest under the relationship is expenditure incurred as mentioned in subsection (2)(a), or

(b) the exchange loss arising from the relationship is in respect of a money debt on which the interest payable (if any) is, or would be, such expenditure.

(5) If a debit—

(a) falls to be brought into account for the purposes of Part 5 of CTA 2009 in respect of a loan relationship of the contractor, but

(b) as a result of this section cannot be brought into account in a way that results in any reduction of what would otherwise be the contractor's ring fence profits,

the debit is to be brought into account for those purposes as a non-trading debit despite anything in section 297 of that Act.

(6) References in this section to a loan relationship, in relation to the borrowing of money, do not include a relationship to which Chapter 2 of Part 6 of CTA 2009 (relevant non-lending relationships) applies.

356NC Restriction on credits to be brought into account

(1) Credits in respect of exchange gains from the contractor's loan relationships may not be brought into account for the purposes of Part 5 of CTA 2009 (loan relationships) in any way that results in an increase of what would otherwise be the contractor's ring fence profits, but this is subject to subsections (2) to (4).

(2) Subsection (1) does not apply so far as a loan relationship is in respect of money borrowed by the contractor which has been—

(a) used to meet expenditure incurred by the contractor in carrying on oil contractor activities, or

(b) appropriated to meeting expenditure to be so incurred by the contractor.

(3) Subsection (1) does not apply, in the case of credits falling to be brought into account as a result of section 329 of CTA 2009 (pre-loan relationship and abortive expenses) in respect of a loan relationship that has not been entered into, so far as the relationship would have been one entered into for the purpose of borrowing money to be used or appropriated as mentioned in subsection (2).

(4) Subsection (1) does not apply, in the case of credits in respect of a loan relationship to which Chapter 2 of Part 6 of CTA 2009 (relevant non-lending relationships) applies, so far as—

(a) the payment of interest under the relationship is expenditure incurred as mentioned in subsection (2)(a), or

(b) the exchange gain arising from the relationship is in respect of a money debt on which the interest payable (if any) is, or would be, such expenditure.

(5) If a credit—

(a) falls to be brought into account for the purposes of Part 5 of CTA 2009 in respect of a loan relationship of the contractor, but

(b) as a result of this section cannot be brought into account in a way that results in any increase of what would otherwise be the contractor's ring fence profits,

the credit is to be brought into account for those purposes as a non-trading credit despite anything in section 297 of that Act.

(6) Section 356NB(6) applies for the purposes of this section.

Relief

356ND Management expenses

No deduction under section 1219 of CTA 2009 (expenses of management of a company's investment business) is to be allowed from the contractor's ring fence profits.

356NE Losses

Relief in respect of a loss incurred by the contractor may not be given under section 37 (relief for trade losses against total profits) against the contractor's ring fence profits except so far as the loss arises from oil contractor activities.

356NF Group relief

(1) On a claim for group relief made by a claimant company in relation to a surrendering company, group relief may not be allowed against the claimant company's contractor's ring fence profits except so far as the claim relates to losses incurred by the surrendering company that arose from oil contractor activities.

(2) In section 105 (restriction on surrender of losses etc within section 99(1)(d) to (g)) the references to the surrendering company's gross profits of the surrender period do not include the company's relevant contractor's ring fence profits for that period.

(3) The company's "relevant contractor's ring fence profits" for that period are—

(a) if for that period there are no qualifying charitable donations made by the company that are allowable under Part 6 (charitable donations relief), the company's contractor's ring fence profits for that period, or

(b) otherwise, so much of the contractor's ring fence profits of the company for that period as exceeds the amount of the qualifying charitable donations made by the company that are allowable under section 189 for that period.

(4) In this section "claimant company" and "surrendering company" are to be read in accordance with Part 5 (group relief) (see section 188).

356NG Capital allowances

A capital allowance may not to any extent be given effect under section 259 or 260 of CAA 2001 (special leasing) by deduction from the contractor's ring fence profits."

5 In Schedule 4 (index of defined expressions), insert the following entries at the appropriate places—

"associated person (in Part 8ZA)	section 356LB"
"contractor (in Part 8ZA)	section 356L(2)"
"contractor's ring fence profits (in Part 8ZA)	section 356LD"
"exploration or exploitation activities (in Part 8ZA)	section 356L(4)"
"lease (in Part 8ZA)	section 356LC"
"oil contractor activities (in Part 8ZA)	section 356L(2)"
"relevant asset (in Part 8ZA)	section 356LA"
"relevant offshore area (in Part 8ZA)	section 356L(5)"
"relevant offshore service (in Part 8ZA)	section 356L(3)"

Commencement etc

6 This Schedule is to be treated as having come into force on 1 April 2014 ("the commencement date").

7 Section 356L of CTA 2010 has effect in relation to activities carried out on or after the commencement date.

8—(1) If, on the commencement date, a company was carrying on a trade that consisted of, or included, carrying out oil contractor activities, an accounting period ends (if it would not otherwise do so) with 31 March 2014.

(2) Sub-paragraph (3) applies if—

(a) but for sub-paragraph (1), a company would have had an accounting period that began before the commencement date and ended on or after that date ("the split accounting period"), and

(b) the company's accounting period beginning with 1 April 2014 ends when the split accounting period would have ended but for that sub-paragraph.

(3) For the purposes of Chapter 4 of Part 22 of CTA 2010 (surrender of tax refund within group)—

(a) the company is to be treated as having the split accounting period,

(b) any tax refund due to the company for—

(i) the accounting period ending with 31 March 2014, or

(ii) the accounting period beginning with 1 April 2014,

is to be treated as if it were a tax refund due to the company for the split accounting period, and

(c) if the company surrenders a tax refund that is so treated (or part of such a refund), the references in section 964(6) of CTA 2010 to the date on which corporation tax became due and payable are to be treated as references to the date on which corporation tax would have become due and payable had the company had the split accounting period.

9—(1) A company may be given relief under section 45 of CTA 2010 (carry forward of trade loss against subsequent trade profits) for a loss made in an accounting period ending before the commencement date against profits of a ring fence trade so far as (and only so far as) the loss would have been a loss of the ring fence trade had section 356L of that Act had effect in relation to activities carried out before the commencement date and Part 8ZA therefore applied.

(2) In sub-paragraph (1) "ring fence trade" means oil contractor activities that constitute a separate trade (whether by virtue of section 356M of that Act or otherwise).

FINANCE ACT 2015

2015 Chapter 11

An Act to grant certain duties, to alter other duties, and to amend the law relating to the National Debt and the Public Revenue, and to make further provision in connection with finance.

26 March 2015

CONTENTS

WE, Your Majesty's most dutiful and loyal subjects, the Commons of the United Kingdom in Parliament assembled, towards raising the necessary supplies to defray Your Majesty's public expenses, and making an addition to the public revenue, have freely and voluntarily resolved to give and to grant unto Your Majesty the several duties hereinafter mentioned; and do therefore most humbly beseech Your Majesty that it may be enacted, and be it enacted by the Queen's most Excellent Majesty, by and with the advice and consent of the Lords Spiritual and Temporal, and Commons, in this present Parliament assembled, and by the authority of the same, as follows:—

PART 2

EXCISE DUTIES AND OTHER TAXES

Petroleum Revenue Tax

52 Reduction in rate of petroleum revenue tax

(1) OTA 1975 is amended as follows.

(2) In section 1(2) (rate of petroleum revenue tax) for "50" substitute "35".

(3) In paragraph 17(5)(*b*) of Schedule 2 (relevant percentage in relation to the amount of loss which is treated as reducing assessable profit) after "60 per cent" insert "if that later repayment period ends on or before 31 December 2015, and 45 per cent if it ends after 31 December 2015".

(4) The amendment made by subsection (2) has effect with respect to chargeable periods ending after 31 December 2015.

FINANCE ACT 2016

2016 Chapter 24

An Act to grant certain duties, to alter other duties, and to amend the law relating to the National Debt and the Public Revenue, and to make further provision in connection with finance.

15 September 2016

CONTENTS

PART 2

CORPORATION TAX

Oil and gas

58 Reduction in rate of supplementary charge

(1) In section 330 of CTA 2010 (supplementary charge in respect of ring fence trades), in subsection (1), for "20%" substitute "10%".

(2) The amendment made by subsection (1) has effect in relation to accounting periods beginning on or after 1 January 2016 (but see also subsection (3)).

(3) Subsections (4) and (5) apply where a company has an accounting period beginning before 1 January 2016 and ending on or after that date ("the straddling period").

(4) For the purpose of calculating the amount of the supplementary charge on the company for the straddling period—

(*a*) so much of that period as falls before 1 January 2016, and so much of that period as falls on or after that date, are treated as separate accounting periods, and

(*b*) the company's adjusted ring fence profits for the straddling period are apportioned to the two separate accounting periods in proportion to the number of days in those periods.

(5) The amount of the supplementary charge on the company for the straddling period is the sum of the amounts of supplementary charge that would, in accordance with subsection (4), be chargeable on the company for those separate accounting periods.

(6) In this section—

"adjusted ring fence profits" has the same meaning as in section 330 of CTA 2010;

"supplementary charge" means any sum chargeable under section 330(1) of CTA 2010 as if it were an amount of corporation tax.

59 Investment allowance: disqualifying conditions

(1) Section 332D of CTA 2010 (expenditure on acquisition of asset: disqualifying conditions) is amended as follows.

(2) In subsection (1) after "an asset" insert "("the acquisition concerned")".

(3) In subsection (2)—

(*a*) for "acquisition," substitute "acquisition concerned," and

(*b*) after "acquiring," insert "leasing,".

(4) In subsection (3)(*b*)—

(*a*) for "acquisition," substitute "acquisition concerned,", and

(*b*) after "acquiring," insert "leasing,".

(5) After subsection (4) insert—

"(5) In subsection (3)(*c*) "this Chapter" means the provisions of this Chapter, and of any regulations made under this Chapter, as those provisions have effect at the time when the investment expenditure mentioned in subsection (1) is incurred.

(6) Subsections (7) and (8) apply where investment expenditure mentioned in subsection (1) would, in the absence of this section, be relievable under section 332C by reason of section 332CA (treatment of expenditure incurred before field is determined).

(7) Where this subsection applies—

(*a*) subsection (2) is to be read as if after "was" there were inserted ", or has become,", and

(*b*) in determining for the purposes of subsection (2) or (3)(*b*) whether particular expenditure was incurred "before" the acquisition concerned—

(i) paragraph (*b*) of section 332CA(3) is to be ignored, and

(ii) accordingly, that expenditure is to be taken (for the purposes of determining whether it was incurred before the acquisition concerned) to have been incurred when it was actually incurred.

(8) Where this subsection applies, in determining whether the second disqualifying condition applies to the asset—

(*a*) the reference in subsection (3)(*a*)(i) to a qualifying oil field is to be read as including an area which, at the time of the acquisition concerned, had not been determined to be an oil field but which has subsequently become a qualifying oil field,

(*b*) the reference in subsection (3)(*a*)(ii) to a qualifying oil field is to be read as including an area which, at the time of the transfer, had not been determined to be an oil field but which has subsequently become a qualifying oil field,

(*c*) the reference in subsection (3)(*c*)(i) to "the qualifying oil field" is to be read accordingly, and

(*d*) the following sub-paragraph is to be treated as substituted for subsection (3)(*c*)(ii)—

"(ii) would have been relievable under section 332C if this Chapter had been fully in force and had applied to expenditure incurred at the time when that expenditure was actually incurred and the area in question had been a qualifying oil field at that time."

(9) In subsection (8)(*a*) and (*b*) "determined" means determined under Schedule 1 to OTA 1975.

(10) In this section any reference to expenditure which was incurred by a company in "leasing" an asset is to expenditure incurred by the company under an agreement under which the asset was leased to the company."

(6) The amendments made by this section have effect for the purposes of determining whether any expenditure—

(*a*) incurred by a company on or after 16 March 2016 on the acquisition of an asset, or

(*b*) treated under section 332CA of CTA 2010 as so incurred,

is relievable expenditure for the purposes of section 332C of CTA 2010.

60 Investment allowance: power to expand meaning of "relevant income"

(1) Section 332F of CTA 2010 (activation of investment allowance) is amended as follows.

(2) In subsection (2)(*b*) before "the company's relevant income" insert "the total amount of".

(3) For subsection (3) substitute—

"(3) For the purposes of this Chapter, income is relevant income of a company from a qualifying oil field for an accounting period if it is—

(*a*) production income of the company from any oil extraction activities carried on in that oil field that is taken into account in calculating the company's adjusted ring fence profits for the accounting period, or

(*b*) income that—

(i) is income of such description (whether or not relating to the oil field) as may be prescribed by the Treasury by regulations, and

(ii) is taken into account as mentioned in paragraph (*a*).

(4) The Treasury may by regulations make such amendments of this Chapter as the Treasury consider appropriate in consequence of, or in connection with, any provision contained in regulations under subsection (3)(*b*).

(5) Regulations under subsection (3)(*b*) or (4) may provide for any of the provisions of the regulations to have effect in relation to accounting periods ending before (or current when) the regulations are made.

(6) But subsection (5) does not apply to—

(*a*) any provision of amending or revoking regulations under subsection (3)(*b*) which has the effect that income of any description is to cease to be treated as relevant income of a company from a qualifying oil field for an accounting period, or (*b*) provision made under subsection (4) in consequence of or in connection with provision within paragraph (*a*).

(7) Regulations under this section may make transitional provision or savings.

(8) Regulations under this section may not be made unless a draft of the instrument containing them has been laid before, and approved by a resolution of, the House of Commons."

61 Onshore allowance: disqualifying conditions

(1) CTA 2010 is amended as follows.

(2) In section 356C after subsection (4) insert—

"(4A) Subsections (1) to (4) are subject to section 356CAA (which prevents expenditure on the acquisition of an asset from being relievable in certain circumstances)."

(3) After section 356CA insert—

"356CAA Expenditure on acquisition of asset: further disqualifying conditions

(1) Capital expenditure incurred by a company ("the acquiring company") on the acquisition of an asset ("the acquisition concerned") is not relievable capital expenditure for the purposes of section 356C if subsection (2), (3) or (8) applies to the asset.

(2) This subsection applies to the asset if capital expenditure incurred before the acquisition concerned, by the acquiring company or another company, in acquiring, bringing into existence or enhancing the value of the asset was relievable under section 356C.

(3) This subsection applies to the asset if—

(*a*) the asset—

(i) is the whole or part of the equity in a qualifying site, or

(ii) is acquired in connection with a transfer to the acquiring company of the whole or part of the equity in a qualifying site,

(*b*) capital expenditure was incurred before the acquisition concerned, by the acquiring company or another company, in acquiring, bringing into existence or enhancing the value of the asset, and

(*c*) any of that expenditure—

(i) related to the qualifying site, and

(ii) would have been relievable under section 356C if this Chapter had been fully in force and had applied to expenditure incurred at that time.

(4) For the purposes of subsection (3)(*a*)(ii) it does not matter whether the asset is acquired at the time of the transfer.

(5) In subsection (3)(*c*) "this Chapter" means the provisions of this Chapter as those provisions have effect at the time when the capital expenditure mentioned in subsection (1) is incurred.

(6) The reference in subsection (3)(*c*)(i) to the qualifying site includes an area that, although not a qualifying site when the expenditure mentioned in subsection (3)(*b*) was incurred, subsequently became the qualifying site.

(7) Where expenditure mentioned in subsection (3)(*b*) related to an area which subsequently became the qualifying site, the following subparagraph is to be treated as substituted for subsection (3)(*c*)(ii)—

"(ii) would have been relievable under section 356C if the area in question had been a qualifying site when the expenditure was incurred, or if the area in question had been such a site at that time and this Chapter had been fully in force and had applied to expenditure incurred at that time."

(8) This subsection applies to the asset if—

(*a*) capital expenditure mentioned in subsection (1) would, in the absence of this section, be relievable under section 356C by reason of an election under section 356CB (treatment of expenditure not related to an established site), and

(*b*) capital expenditure which was incurred before the acquisition concerned, by the acquiring company or another company, in acquiring, bringing into existence or enhancing the value of the asset, either—

(i) has become relievable under section 356C by reason of an election under section 356CB, or

(ii) would be so relievable if such an election were made in respect of that expenditure.

(9) In determining for the purposes of subsection (8)(*b*) whether particular expenditure was incurred "before" the acquisition concerned—

(*a*) paragraph (*b*) of section 356CB(6) is to be ignored, and

(b) accordingly, that expenditure is to be taken (for the purposes of determining whether it was incurred before the acquisition concerned) to have been incurred when it was actually incurred.

(10) For the purposes of subsection (8)(b)(ii) it does not matter if an election is not in fact capable of being made."

(4) The amendments made by this section have effect for the purposes of determining whether any expenditure—

(a) incurred by a company on or after 16 March 2016 on the acquisition of an asset, or

(b) treated by reason of an election under section 356CB as so incurred,

is relievable expenditure for the purposes of section 356C of CTA 2010.

62 Cluster area allowance: disqualifying conditions

(1) Section 356JFA of CTA 2010 (expenditure on acquisition of asset: disqualifying conditions) is amended as follows.

(2) In subsection (2) after "acquiring," insert "leasing,".

(3) In subsection (3)(b) after "acquiring," insert "leasing,".

(4) After subsection (4) insert—

"(5) In this section any reference to expenditure which was incurred by a company in "leasing" an asset is to expenditure incurred by the company under an agreement under which the asset was leased to the company."

(5) The amendments made by this section have effect for the purposes of determining whether any expenditure incurred by a company on or after 16 March 2016 on the acquisition of an asset is relievable expenditure for the purposes of section 356JF of CTA 2010.

63 Cluster area allowance: power to expand meaning of "relevant income"

(1) Section 356JH of CTA 2010 (activation of cluster area allowance) is amended as follows.

(2) In subsection (2)(b) before "the company's relevant income" insert "the total amount of".

(3) For subsection (3) substitute—

"(3) For the purposes of this Chapter, income is relevant income of a company from a cluster area for an accounting period if it is—

(a) production income of the company from any oil extraction activities carried on in that area that is taken into account in calculating the company's adjusted ring fence profits for the accounting period, or

(b) income that—

(i) is income of such description (whether or not relating to the cluster area) as may be prescribed by the Treasury by regulations, and

(ii) is taken into account as mentioned in paragraph (a).

(4) The Treasury may by regulations make such amendments of this Chapter as the Treasury consider appropriate in consequence of, or in connection with, any provision contained in regulations under subsection (3)(b).

(5) Regulations under subsection (3)(b) or (4) may provide for any of the provisions of the regulations to have effect in relation to accounting periods ending before (or current when) the regulations are made.

(6) But subsection (5) does not apply to—

(a) any provision of amending or revoking regulations under subsection (3)(b) which has the effect that income of any description is to cease to be treated as relevant income of a company from a cluster area for an accounting period, or

(b) provision made under subsection (4) in consequence of or in connection with provision within paragraph (a).

(7) Regulations under this section may make transitional provision or savings.

(8) Regulations under this section may not be made unless a draft of the instrument containing them has been laid before, and approved by a resolution of, the House of Commons."

PART 9
OTHER TAXES AND DUTIES

Petroleum revenue tax

140 Petroleum revenue tax: rate

(1) In section 1(2) of OTA 1975 (rate of petroleum revenue tax) for "35" substitute "0".

(2) In paragraph 17 of Schedule 2 to that Act (cap on interest on repayments of tax), in sub-paragraph (5)(b) omit the words from "if that" to the end.

(3) In paragraph 2 of Schedule 19 to FA 1982 (duty to pay instalments based on amount of tax payable in previous chargeable period), after sub-paragraph (4) insert—

"(4A) In sub-paragraph (1) the reference to any chargeable period for an oil field ending on or after 30th June 1983 does not include a chargeable period ending on 31st December 2015."

(4) The amendment made by subsection (1) has effect with respect to chargeable periods ending after 31 December 2015.

FINANCE (NO 2) ACT 2017

An Act To Grant certain duties, to alter other duties, and to amend the law relating to the national debt and the public revenue, and to make further provision in connection with finance.

PART 2

INDIRECT TAXES

44 Petroleum revenue tax: elections for oil fields to become non-taxable

(1) In Schedule 20B to FA 1993, for paragraphs 2 to 12 substitute—

"Method of election

2

An election must be made in writing.

3

An election must be notified to the Commissioners.

4

An election is deemed to have been made on the date on which notification of the election was sent to the Commissioners.

Effect of election

5

If an election is made, the field ceases to be taxable with effect from the start of the first chargeable period to begin after the election is made.

No unrelievable field losses from field

6

From the start of the first chargeable period to begin after an election is made, no allowable loss that accrues from the oil field is an allowable unrelievable field loss for the purposes of petroleum revenue tax.

Interpretation

7

(1) In this Schedule—

"Commissioners" means the Commissioners for Her Majesty's Revenue and Customs;

"participator", in relation to a particular time, means a person who is a participator in the chargeable period which includes that time.

(2) Expressions used in this Schedule and in Part 1 of the Oil Taxation Act 1975 have the same meaning in this Schedule as in Part 1 of that Act."

(2) In OTA 1975, in section 6(1A), for "paragraph 5" substitute "paragraph 6".

(3) In FA 1980, in paragraph 15(9A) of Schedule 17, for "paragraph 5" substitute "paragraph 6".

(4) The amendment made by this section is to be treated as having come into force on 23 November 2016.

PART 4

ADMINISTRATION, AVOIDANCE AND ENFORCEMENT

Avoidance etc

65 Penalties for enablers of defeated tax avoidance

(Please see IHT section for the full text of this section.)

SCHEDULE 16
PENALTIES FOR ENABLERS OF DEFEATED TAX AVOIDANCE
Section 65

(Please see IHT section for the full text of this Schedule.)

Statutory Instruments

PRT

Contents

Chronological list of printed statutory instruments

Chronological list of statutory instruments

Statutory Instruments

1982/92

OIL TAXATION (GAS BANKING SCHEMES) REGULATIONS 1982

Made by the Commissioners of Inland Revenue under FA 1980 s 108

Made . . . .*29 January 1982*
Laid before the House of Commons . . . .*in draft*
Coming into Operation . . . .*1 February 1982*

1 Citation and commencement

These Regulations may be cited as the Oil Taxation (Gas Banking Schemes) Regulations 1982 and shall come into operation on 1 February 1982.

2 Interpretation

In these Regulations, unless the context otherwise requires—

"associated gas" means gas found in an oil field in association with oil other than gas, which has been won from the field at a rate dependent on that at which the oil other than gas is so won;

"election" means an election under the principal section;

"gas" means oil consisting of gas;

"gas banking scheme" means such a scheme as is defined in subsection (2) of the principal section as a gas banking scheme for the purposes of the section;

"the modifications" means the modifications to the operation of the Oil Taxation Acts prescribed by Regulation 3 below;

"the Oil Taxation Acts" has the same meaning as in the principal section;

"the principal section" means section 108 of the Finance Act 1980;

"relevant field" means, in relation to a gas banking scheme, an oil field to which the scheme applies;

"responsible persons" means the bodies corporate or partnerships appointed in accordance with paragraph 4 of Schedule 2 to the Oil Taxation Act 1975 as the responsible persons for the oil fields to which a gas banking scheme applies;

"transferor field" and "transferee field" mean, in relation to a transfer of gas won from a relevant field by the participators in that field to the participators in another relevant field under a gas banking scheme, the first-mentioned field and the last-mentioned field respectively;

other expressions have the same meaning as in the Oil Taxation Act 1975.

3 Modifications to the operation of the Oil Taxation Acts

(1) This Regulation shall apply for the purposes of modifying the operation of the Oil Taxation Acts in their application to cases where—

(*a*) a gas banking scheme which satisfies the additional conditions contained in Regulation 4 below is in force between the participators in two or more relevant fields;

(*b*) the participators in those fields have elected under the principal section in the manner prescribed by Regulation 6 below that the modifications prescribed by this Regulation shall apply; and

(*c*) gas won from a relevant field is transferred by the participators in that field to the participators in another relevant field under the scheme.

(2) Gas which is transferred in the circumstances described in paragraph (1)(*c*) above (in this Regulation referred to as "transferred gas") shall be disregarded in determining—

(*a*) the gross profit or gross loss for the purposes of petroleum revenue tax . . . [1] accruing to a participator from the transferor field in a chargeable period;

[(*b*) the cash equivalent of the share of a participator in a transferor field of the oil allowance referred to in section 8 of the Oil Taxation Act 1975 and the exempt allowance referred to in section 141 of the Finance Act 1982 for that field for a chargeable period; and][1]

(*c*) the total amount of oil ever won and saved from the transferor field referred to in section 10(1)(*b*) of the Oil Taxation Act 1975.

(3) For all the purposes of petroleum revenue tax . . . [1], transferred gas shall be treated as having been won and saved from the transferee field by the participators in the field in the chargeable period in which it is transferred to them, in shares proportionate to their shares of oil actually won and saved from the field during the period.

(4) For the purposes of income tax and of the charge of corporation tax on income, transferred gas shall be treated—

(*a*) as not having been extracted from the transferor field by the participators in the field in the course of oil extraction activities carried on by them nor as having been acquired by those participators by virtue of oil rights held by them; and

(*b*) as having been extracted from the transferee field by the participators in the field in the course of oil extraction activities carried on by them.

Amendments—[1] Words in paras (2)(*a*), (3) revoked and para (2)(*b*) substituted by the Oil Taxation (Gas Banking Schemes) (No 2) Regulations, SI 1982/1858, reg 4.

4 Additional conditions for gas banking schemes

(1) The additional conditions to be satisfied for a scheme to constitute a gas banking scheme are—

(*a*) that the scheme provides that the transfer of gas won from a relevant field to or to the order of the participators in another relevant field, in consideration for which gas won from the other field is subsequently transferred to or to the order of the participators in the first-mentioned field, is to be transfer of associated gas;

(*b*) that the scheme provides that gas won from a relevant field and transferred to or to the order of the participators in another relevant field under the scheme is to be of a kind which, after it has been subjected to initial treatment, would be suitable for use by the British Gas Corporation in the National Gas Transmission System; and

(*c*) that the scheme is a separate scheme constituted by one or more agreements under which it enters into force between the participators in each relevant field as from the same date.

(2) For the purposes of this Regulation there will be a separate scheme whenever the participators in a relevant field who have entered into an agreement constituting a scheme enter into a further agreement with the participator in an oil field to which the first agreement did not apply; but a further agreement which is entered into solely for the purpose of replacing a participator as a party to a scheme by another person or of adding another person as a party to a scheme, on his becoming a participator in a relevant field by virtue of the transfer to him of the first participator's interest in the field, or part of that interest as the case may be, shall not constitute a separate scheme.

5 Conditions for elections

(1) The consent of the Board shall be obtained before an election is made by the participators in the relevant fields that the modifications shall apply in the case of a gas banking scheme.

(2) An application for the consent of the Board to the making of an election—

(*a*) shall be made, in such form as the Board may prescribe, jointly by the responsible persons within three months after the end of the chargeable period in which gas is first transferred under the scheme . . .[1]; and

(*b*) shall be accompanied by the agreement or agreements constituting the scheme, the undertakings referred to in paragraph (5) below and such other documents and information as the Board may require.

(3) A separate application under paragraph (2) above shall be made on behalf of all the participators in the relevant fields in respect of each scheme that is in force between them.

(4) If the Board are of the opinion that the documents or information accompanying an application under paragraph (2) above are not sufficient to enable them to decide whether to consent to the making of an election, they shall within three months of the receipt thereof notify in writing to the responsible persons what further documents or information they require for that purpose.

(5) In connection with an application under paragraph (2) above the participators in each relevant field shall undertake to the Board, in consideration of the Board's consent to the making of an election in respect of the scheme to which the application relates—

(*a*) that they will, within three months after the making of an election, accept a variation of the provisions of any licence granted under the Petroleum (Production) Act 1934 or the Petroleum (Production) Act (Northern Ireland) 1964 in respect of the licensed area of which the relevant field in which they are participators forms part, in terms proposed by the [appropriate authority][2], to the effect that gas transferred under the scheme shall, so long as the election is in force, be—

(i) disregarded in determining the value of petroleum relating to any chargeable period for the purpose of the payment of royalty, and the quantity of petroleum won and saved in any half-year for the purpose of delivery of petroleum to the [appropriate authority][2], under a licence in respect of a licensed area of which a transferor field forms part, and

(ii) taken into account in determining the value of petroleum relating to the chargeable period, and the quantity of petroleum won and saved in the half-year, in which it is so transferred for the purpose of the payment of royalty and delivery of petroleum to the [appropriate authority][2] under a licence in respect of a licensed area of which a transferee field forms part; and

(*b*) that they will each use gas which is transferred to them under the scheme for one or more of the following purposes, and for no purpose other than these, namely—

(i) sale to the British Gas Corporation,

(ii) production purposes in relation to the transferee field on the footing that such gas has been won from the field, or

(iii) in an emergency, flaring or venting at any place outside the transferor field.

[(5A) In paragraph (5)(*a*), "the appropriate authority" means—

(*a*) in the case of a licence granted under the Petroleum (Production) Act 1934, the Oil and Gas Authority;

(*b*) in the case of a licence granted under the Petroleum (Production) Act (Northern Ireland) 1964, the Department for the Economy.][2]

(6) The Board shall not consent to the making of an election in respect of a gas banking scheme unless the participators in each relevant field show to the satisfaction of the Board that they entered into the scheme for bona fide commercial reasons.

(7) The Board shall within three months from the receipt of an application under paragraph (2) above give notice of their decision in writing to the responsible persons consenting to or refusing consent to the making of an election and, subject to paragraph (8) below, if no such notice has been given within the said period of three months, the Board will be deemed to have so consented.

(8) In any case where the Board have notified to the responsible persons that they require further documents or information in accordance with paragraph (4) above the period of three months referred to in the preceding paragraph shall not commence until the Board have received the further documents or information so required.

(9) If a participator in a relevant field is in breach of an undertaking given by him to the Board under paragraph (5)(*a*) above or ceases to be a party to the scheme other than on the transfer of his interest in the field to another person who becomes a party to it or the scheme ceases to be a gas banking scheme, the Board may at any time thereafter by notice in writing to the responsible persons revoke their consent to the making of an election in respect of the scheme and any election which has been made shall thereupon cease to be in force and be treated as if it never was in force and the Board may make such assessments or determinations or such amendments of assessments or determinations in relation to petroleum revenue tax and supplementary petroleum duty and the inspector may make such assessments or adjustments to assessments to income tax or corporation tax (notwithstanding that the assessments concerned may have become final or that the time for making assessments may have expired) as may be necessary in the circumstances.

Amendments—[1] Words in para (2) revoked by the Oil Taxation (Gas Banking Schemes) (No 2) Regulations, SI 1982/1858, reg 4.

[2] In para (5)(*a*), words substituted, in para (5)(*a*)(i), (ii), word substituted, and para (5A) inserted, by the Energy (Transfer of Functions, Consequential Amendments and Revocation) Regulations, SI 2016/912 reg 4 with effect from 1 October 2016.

6 Election under the principal section

(1) On being notified of the decision of the Board consenting to the making of an election, or on the expiration of the period of three months referred to in paragraph (7) of Regulation 5 above, the responsible persons shall forthwith inform the participators in the relevant fields that the Board have, or are to be deemed to have, so consented and the participators in each relevant field may within one month of such notification make an election in the manner prescribed by this Regulation.

(2) An election shall be made by all the participators in the relevant fields in the form of a notice to the Board signed by each of them stating that they have elected that the modifications shall apply in the case of the scheme.

(3) Following the making of an election the modifications shall, subject to paragraph (4) below, apply—

(*a*) for the purposes of petroleum revenue tax . . . [1], for chargeable periods beginning with that in which gas is first transferred under the scheme, and

(*b*) for the purposes of income tax and the charge of corporation tax on income, in relation to any gas transferred under the scheme.

(4) Where gas has been transferred under a gas banking scheme before these Regulations come into operation and an election is subsequently made in accordance with this Regulation the modifications shall apply—

(*a*) for the purposes of petroleum revenue tax . . . [1], for chargeable periods before these Regulations came into operation beginning with that in which gas was first transferred under the scheme, and

(*b*) for the purposes of income tax and the charge of corporation tax on income, in relation to any gas transferred under the scheme whether before or after these Regulations came into operation,

and the Board shall make such assessments and determinations or such amendments of assessments and determinations in relation to petroleum revenue tax . . . [1] and the inspector shall make such assessments or adjustments to assessments to income tax or corporation tax (notwithstanding that the assessments in question may have become final) as may be necessary in the circumstances.

(5) An election shall continue in force so long as gas is transferred under the gas banking scheme in respect of which the election was made and the Board have not revoked their consent to the making of the election; and any person to whom a participator in a relevant field transfers his interest, or part

of his interest, in the field and who is or becomes a participator in that field shall be treated by virtue of the transfer as having joined in the election and as having given the same undertakings to the Board under paragraph (5)(*b*) of Regulation 5 above as were given by the participators in connection with the application for the Board's consent to the making of the election.

(6) No election may be made otherwise than in accordance with this Regulation.

Amendments—[1] Words in paras (3), (4) revoked by the Oil Taxation (Gas Banking Schemes) (No 2) Regulations, SI 1982/1858, reg 4.

7 Appeals

(1) The responsible persons may [appeal][1] by notice in writing given to the Board not more than two months after receipt of notice of a decision of the Board refusing or revoking consent to the making of an election in respect of a gas banking scheme . . . [1]; but the bringing of an appeal under this paragraph shall not affect the operation of any revocation of consent under paragraph (9) of Regulation 5 above.

(2) A participator in a relevant field, whether or not himself an appellant, shall be entitled to appear and be heard on the appeal and any proceedings arising out of it.

(3) An appeal against a decision of the Board refusing or revoking consent to the making of an election may at any time be abandoned by a notice in writing given to the Board by the appellants.

(4) On an appeal against a decision of the Board refusing or revoking consent to the making of an election the [tribunal][1] may vary the decision appealed against, whether or not the variation is to the advantage of all or any of the participators in the relevant fields, and the provisions of the Taxes Management Act 1970 shall apply in relation to such an appeal as they apply in relation to an appeal under Part I of the Oil Taxation Act 1975.

[(5) The provisions of paragraphs 14A to 14I of Schedule 2 to the Oil Taxation Act 1975 shall apply in relation to appeals under this regulation, subject to any necessary modifications.][1]

Amendments—[1] In para (1), word inserted, and words revoked, in para (4), words substituted, and para (5) inserted, by the Transfer of Tribunal Functions and Revenue and Customs Appeals Order, SI 2009/56 art 3, Sch 2 para 8 with effect from 1 April 2009.

8 [Payment on account

In computing for the purposes of the statements to be delivered to the Board under section 1(1)(*a*) of the Petroleum Revenue Tax Act 1980 and paragraph 1(2)(*a*) of Schedule 19 to the Finance Act 1982 the tax payable for any chargeable period in respect of an oil field, it shall be assumed that the consent of the Board to the making of an election in respect of a gas banking scheme, for which application has been made under paragraph (2) of Regulation 5 above at the time when any such statement is to be delivered, will be forthcoming and that such an election will be made by the participators in the relevant fields in the manner prescribed by Regulation 6.][1]

Amendments—[1] This regulation substituted by the Oil Taxation (Gas Banking Schemes) (No 2) Regulations, SI 1982/1858, reg 4.

9 International gas banking schemes

These Regulations do not apply to international gas banking schemes as defined for the purposes of the principal section by subsection (4) of the section.

1982/1858

OIL TAXATION (GAS BANKING SCHEMES) (NO 2) REGULATIONS 1982

Made by the Commissioners of Inland Revenue under FA 1980 s 108(6)

Made . . . . *23 December 1982*

Coming into operation . . . . *1 January 1983*

1 Citation and commencement

These Regulations may be cited as the Oil Taxation (Gas Banking Schemes) (No 2) Regulations 1982 and shall come into operation on 1 January 1983.

2 Interpretation

In these Regulations, unless the context otherwise requires—

"APRT" has the same meaning as in Chapter II of Part VI of the Finance Act 1982;

"the Principal Regulations" means The Oil Taxation (Gas Banking Schemes) Regulations 1982;

other expressions have the same meaning as in the Principal Regulations.

3 Amendments to the Principal Regulations

The references in the Principal Regulations to petroleum revenue tax shall, in relation to each of the chargeable periods referred to in section 139(1) of the Finance Act 1982, include a reference to APRT.

4 (*amends* SI 1982/92, regs 3, 5, 6, 8).

5 Supplementary and transitional provisions
Where an application for the consent of the Board to the making of an election is made before 1 April 1983 in respect of a gas banking scheme under which gas was first transferred in the chargeable period ending 31 December 1982 and an election is subsequently made (or it is to be assumed for the purposes of Regulation 8 of the Principal Regulations that an election will be made) by the participators in the relevant fields in the manner prescribed by Regulation 6 of the Principal Regulations that the modifications should apply in the case of the scheme, Regulation 3 of those Regulations shall apply in the case of the scheme as it was before amendment by these Regulations for the chargeable period ending 31 December 1982 only.

6 Participators in two or more oil fields who, before these Regulations came into operation, made an election in the manner prescribed by Regulation 6 of the Principal Regulations that the modifications should apply in the case of a gas banking scheme in force between them shall be treated for chargeable periods ending after 31 December 1982 as having made a further election on the coming into operation of these Regulations that the modifications as amended by these Regulations should apply in the case of the scheme and Regulation 3 of the Principal Regulations shall apply accordingly for such chargeable periods.

1986/1644

FOREIGN FIELDS (SPECIFICATION) (NO 1) ORDER 1986

Made by the Secretary of State under the Oil Taxation Act 1983 ss 9(5), 12(2)

Made . . . . *9 September 1986*

1 This Order may be cited as the Foreign Fields (Specification) (No 1) Order 1986.

2 In this Order the "Heimdal Field" means the hydrocarbon accumulation above a depth of 7,200 feet beneath mean sea level within the boundary defined by a set of lines of latitude and longitude joining the surface co-ordinates set out in the Schedule hereto together with any additional hydrocarbon accumulations outside the boundary which are subsequently discovered above the said depth of 7,200 feet and which are not separated from the main accumulation by an aquifer.

3 The Heimdal Field, being an area which is not under the jurisdiction of the government of the United Kingdom, is for the purposes of the Act hereby specified as a foreign field.

SCHEDULE

Article 2

Heimdal field co-ordinates

Latitude North	Longitude East	Latitude North	Longitude East
59°38'00"	02°10'00"	59°32'00"	02°16'00"
59°38'00"	02°17'00"	59°32'00"	02°08'00"
59°37'00"	02°17'00"	59°35'00"	02°08'00"
59°37'00"	02°20'00"	59°35'00"	02°09'00"
59°35'00"	02°20'00"	59°37'00"	02°09'00"
59°35'00"	02°17'00"	59°37'00"	02°10'00"
59°34'00"	02°17'00"	59°38'00"	02°10'00"
59°34'00"	02°16'00"		

1986/1645

FOREIGN FIELDS (SPECIFICATION) (NO 2) ORDER 1986

Made by the Secretary of State under the Oil Taxation Act 1983 ss 9(5), 12(2)

Made . . . . *9 September 1986*

1 This Order may be cited as the Foreign Fields (Specification) (No 2) Order 1986.

2 In this Order the "North East Frigg Field" means the hydrocarbon accumulation within the boundary defined by a set of lines of latitude and longitude joining the surface co-ordinates set out in the Schedule hereto.

PRT

3 The North East Frigg Field, being an area which is not under the jurisdiction of the government of the United Kingdom, is for the purposes of the Act hereby specified as a foreign field.

SCHEDULE

Article 2

North east frigg field co-ordinates

Latitude North	Longitude East	Latitude North	Longitude East
60°03'00"	02°17'15"	59°58'00"	02°12'00"
60°02'45"	02°17'15"	59°58'00"	02°12'15"
60°02'45"	02°17'00"	59°57'45"	02°12'15"
60°02'30"	02°17'00"	59°57'45"	02°13'30"
60°02'30"	02°16'15"	59°58'00"	02°13'30"
60°02'15"	02°16'15"	59°58'00"	02°14'30"
60°02'15"	02°16'00"	59°58'15"	02°14'30"
60°02'00"	02°16'00"	59°58'15"	02°15'15"
60°02'00"	02°16'15"	59°58'30"	02°15'15"
60°01'30"	02°16'15"	59°58'30"	02°15'30"
60°01'30"	02°16'00"	59°58'45"	02°15'30"
60°01'15"	02°16'00"	59°58'45"	02°16'15"
60°01'15"	02°15'45"	59°59'00"	02°16'15"
60°00'45"	02°15'45"	59°59'00"	02°16'45"
60°00'45"	02°15'30"	59°59'15"	02°16'45"
60°00'30"	02°15'30"	59°59'15"	02°17'30"
60°00'30"	02°15'00"	59°59'45"	02°17'30"
60°00'15"	02°15'00"	59°59'45"	02°17'45"
60°00'15"	02°14'45"	60°00'00"	02°17'45"
60°00'00"	02°14'45"	60°00'00"	02°18'45"
60°00'00"	02°14'30"	60°00'15"	02°18'45"
59°59'30"	02°14'30"	60°00'15"	02°19'00"
59°59'30"	02°13'45"	60°00'45"	02°19'00"
59°59'15"	02°13'45"	60°00'45"	02°18'45"
59°59'15"	02°13'30"	60°01'15"	02°18'45"
59°59'00"	02°13'30"	60°01'15"	02°19'15"
59°59'00"	02°13'15"	60°01'45"	02°19'15"
59°58'45"	02°13'15"	60°01'45"	02°19'45"
59°58'45"	02°13'00"	60°03'00"	02°19'45"
59°58'30"	02°13'00"	60°03'00"	02°17'15"
59°58'30"	02°12'00"		

1987/545

FOREIGN FIELDS (SPECIFICATION) (NO 1) ORDER 1987

Made by the Secretary of State under the Oil Taxation Act 1983 ss 9(5), 12(2)

Made . . . . *18 March 1987*

1 This Order may be cited as the Foreign Fields (Specification) (No 1) Order 1987.

2 In this Order the "Ekofisk Area Fields" means the hydrocarbon accumulations, known as the Albuskjell, Cod, Edda, Ekofisk, Eldfisk, Tor and West Ekofisk Fields respectively, the boundaries of which are defined by the sets of lines of latitude and longitude joining the surface co-ordinates set out in the Schedule hereto.

3 Each of the Ekofisk Area Fields being an area which is not under the jurisdiction of the government of the United Kingdom, is for the purposes of the Act hereby specified as a foreign field.

SCHEDULE

Article 2

Ekofisk Area fields co-ordinates:

Albuskjell field

Latitude North	Longitude East	Latitude North	Longitude East
56°36’18.9”	03°06’01.0”	56°38’14.9”	02°53’40.9”
56°36’49.6”	03°05’44.0”	56°37’52.6”	02°54’21.0”
56°37’12.8”	03°04’55.9”	56°37’33.7”	02°55’18.4”
56°37’35.8”	03°03’59.1”	56°37’17.8”	02°56’27.0”
56°37’53.2”	03°02’59.1”	56°37’19.7”	02°57’33.4”
56°38’12.6”	03°01’47.1”	56°37’19.6”	02°58’30.0”
56°38’24.0”	03°00’56.2”	56°37’14.0”	02°59’23.8”
56°38’38.7”	02°59’52.4”	56°37’02.4”	03°00’19.1”
56°38’49.7”	02°58’43.6”	56°36’50.1”	03°01’19.7”
56°38’59.9”	02°57’39.7”	56°36’38.2”	03°02’22.8”
56°39’07.8”	02°56’42.8”	56°36’23.9”	03°03’28.5”
56°39’16.5”	02°55’46.0”	56°36’09.0”	03°04’33.9”
56°39’24.5”	02°54’27.6”	56°36’06.4”	03°05’34.3”
56°39’25.2”	02°53’27.5”	56°36’18.9”	03°05’58.5”
56°39’12.2”	02°52’44.4”	56°36’18.9”	03°06’01.0”
56°38’43.0”	02°52’59.8”		

COD Field

Latitude North	Longitude East	Latitude North	Longitude East
57°02’08.8”	02°28’20.7”	57°05’40.4”	02°23’53.4”
57°02’11.3”	02°29’20.3”	57°05’03.0”	02°23’19.7”
57°02’35.6”	02°30’09.5”	57°04’36.1”	02°23’01.3”
57°02’57.2”	02°29’45.6”	57°03’59.3”	02°22’47.1”
57°02’52.9”	02°28’55.8”	57°03’20.1”	02°23’01.1”
57°03’04.4”	02°28’26.9”	57°02’54.4”	02°23’39.8”
57°03’39.1”	02°28’35.0”	57°02’35.4”	02°24’26.7”
57°04’04.6”	02°28’42.0”	57°02’18.4”	02°25’25.8”
57°04’42.1”	02°28’32.4”	57°02’11.2”	02°26’17.6”
57°05’12.8”	02°28’07.1”	57°02’16.0”	02°27’01.2”
57°05’33.4”	02°27’06.4”	57°02’15.3”	02°27’42.8”
57°05’43.2”	02°26’13.2”	57°02’09.5”	02°28’18.9”
57°05’53.7”	02°24’59.3”	57°02’08.8”	02°28’20.7”

EDDA field

Latitude North	Longitude East	Latitude North	Longitude East
56°27’33.4”	03°05’12.9”	56°29’13.6”	03°07’03.1”
56°27’12.2”	03°06’03.9”	56°29’12.4”	03°06’17.9”
56°27’09.8”	03°06’56.0”	56°29’02.5”	03°05’34.2”
56°27’15.9”	03°08’02.7”	56°28’47.5”	03°04’54.2”
56°27’37.4”	03°08’53.3”	56°28’23.6”	03°04’29.4”
56°27’53.2”	03°09’27.9”	56°28’03.8”	03°04’33.7”
56°28’11.1”	03°10’04.9”	56°27’51.4”	03°04’50.5”
56°28’36.2”	03°10’20.9”	56°27’44.6”	03°04’58.6”
56°28’59.7”	03°10’11.4”	56°27’38.7”	03°05’05.7”
56°29’11.5”	03°09’28.8”	56°27’33.4”	03°05’12.9”

Latitude North	Longitude East	Latitude North	Longitude East
56°29'12.4"	03°08'16.7"		

Ekofisk Field

Latitude North	Longitude East	Latitude North	Longitude East
56°29'30.8"	03°13'28.4"	56°34'22.1"	03°10'44.9"
56°29'32.1"	03°14'05.7"	56°33'50.9"	03°10'24.1"
56°29'59.1"	03°14'17.5"	56°33'19.3"	03°10'25.5"
56°30'29.1"	03°14'20.7"	56°32'50.2"	03°10'21.9"
56°31'03.5"	03°14'41.0"	56°32'17.0"	03°10'34.6"
56°31'32.6"	03°14'58.5"	56°31'57.5"	03°10'58.9"
56°31'52.1"	03°15'13.4"	56°31'39.1"	03°11'22.8"
56°32'24.5"	03°15'28.1"	56°31'20.3"	03°11'48.7"
56°32'57.6"	03°15'39.0"	56°30'57.5"	03°12'16.1"
56°33'31.3"	03°15'40.5"	56°30'41.2"	03°12'35.6"
56°34'05.4"	03°15'25.5"	56°30'20.1"	03°12'56.4"
56°34'27.8"	03°14'59.6"	56°29'58.5"	03°13'09.4"
56°34'44.1"	03°14'14.8"	56°29'40.6"	03°13'17.5"
56°34'53.2"	03°13'17.2"	56°29'31.5"	03°13'27.7"
56°34'57.4"	03°12'16.5"	56°29'30.8"	03°13'28.4"
56°34'46.6"	03°11'24.9"		

Eldfisk field

Latitude North	Longitude East	Latitude North	Longitude East
56°21'09.8"	03°16'44.2"	56°25'22.2"	03°11'50.1"
56°21'23.7"	03°17'14.6"	56°24'56.8"	03°12'05.4"
56°21'51.3"	03°17'28.8"	56°24'34.0"	03°12'25.8"
56°22'19.8"	03°17'11.3"	56°24'07.6"	03°12'54.4"
56°22'42.6"	03°16'45.7"	56°23'36.2"	03°13'08.1"
56°23'09.8"	03°16'15.6"	56°23'13.1"	03°13'06.2"
56°23'33.7"	03°15'48.3"	56°22'49.1"	03°13'22.3"
56°24'03.2"	03°15'34.9"	56°22'23.9"	03°13'44.9"
56°24'37.2"	03°15'37.2"	56°22'00.1"	03°14'13.6"
56°25'07.6"	03°15'19.8"	56°21'38.9"	03°14'41.3"
56°25'31.5"	03°14'42.6"	56°21'19.0"	03°15'21.0"
56°25'43.2"	03°13'56.4"	56°21'10.9"	03°15'58.7"
56°25'59.8"	03°13'06.0"	56°21'07.3"	03°16'26.4"
56°26'10.4"	03°12'17.4"	56°21'09.4"	03°16'42.1"
56°26'07.7"	03°11'39.9"	56°21'09.8"	03°16'44.2"
56°25'43.9"	03°11'33.8"		

Tor field

Latitude North	Longitude East	Latitude North	Longitude East
56°37'32.3"	03°18'32.9"	56°39'21.0"	03°20'28.4"
56°37'41.3"	03°19'22.2"	56°39'26.6"	03°19'40.4"
56°37'47.1"	03°20'01.1"	56°39'18.9"	03°18'38.3"
56°37'58.6"	03°20'26.0"	56°39'00.1"	03°17'48.8"
56°38'14.5"	03°21'03.0"	56°38'48.6"	03°17'13.7"
56°38'07.4"	03°21'56.5"	56°38'16.9"	03°16'57.6"
56°38'23.1"	03°22'25.3"	56°37'49.3"	03°17'19.8"

Latitude North	Longitude East	Latitude North	Longitude East
56°38'32.6"	03°22'56.8"	56°37'47.9"	03°18'00.6"
56°38'48.8"	03°22'53.6"	56°37'32.2"	03°18'30.5"
56°38'52.3"	03°21'52.8"	56°37'32.3"	03°18'32.9"
56°38'51.9"	03°21'05.3"		

West ekofisk field

Latitude North	Longitude East	Latitude North	Longitude East
56°32'42.3"	03°04'37.6"	56°34'26.1"	03°04'06.6"
56°32'46.3"	03°05'18.0"	56°34'12.2"	03°03'31.2"
56°32'56.8"	03°05'47.7"	56°33'50.0"	03°03'11.2"
56°33'07.3"	03°06'11.3"	56°33'27.0"	03°03'04.6"
56°33'18.3"	03°06'37.7"	56°33'03.8"	03°03'22.8"
56°33'28.2"	03°06'58.2"	56°32'52.2"	03°03'48.6"
56°33'34.6"	03°06'57.2"	56°32'45.2"	03°04'07.6"
56°33'48.0"	03°06'33.4"	56°32'42.7"	03°04'22.2"
56°34'01.9"	03°06'16.4"	56°32'41.7"	03°04'36.1"
56°34'20.9"	03°05'44.1"	56°32'42.3"	03°04'37.6"
56°34'30.6"	03°04'53.7"		

1987/1338

[OIL TAXATION] (NOMINATION SCHEME FOR DISPOSALS . . .) REGULATIONS 1987

Made by the Commissioners of Inland Revenue under FA 1987 s 61(8) and Sch 10

Made . . . .*28 July 1987*
Laid before the House of Commons . . . .*30 July 1987*
Coming into force . . . .*22 August 1987*

Commentary—*Simon's Taxes* **D7.906**.

Amendments—Words in title substituted and revoked by the PRT (Nomination Scheme for Disposals and Appropriations) (Amendment) Regulations, SI 2006/3089 regs 2, 3 with effect from 1 July 2006 in relation to proposed sales whose transaction base time is a time on or after that date, and not in relation to proposed transactions with a transaction base date before that date.

1 Citation and commencement

These Regulations may be cited as the [Oil Taxation][1] (Nomination Scheme for Disposals . . . [1]) Regulations 1987 and shall come into force on 22 August 1987 but shall have effect with respect to things done on or after 9 February 1987.

Amendments—[1] Words substituted and revoked by the PRT (Nomination Scheme for Disposals and Appropriations) (Amendment) Regulations, SI 2006/3089 regs 2, 3 with effect from 1 July 2006 in relation to proposed sales whose transaction base time is a time on or after that date, and not in relation to proposed transactions with a transaction base date before that date.

2 Interpretation

In these Regulations unless the context otherwise requires—

"blended oil" has the meaning given to it by [section 63(1A)(*c*)][1] of the Finance Act 1987;

["the Commissioners" means the Commissioners for Her Majesty's Revenue and Customs;][2]

. . . [2]

"the originating fields" has the meaning given to it by [section 63(1A)(*d*)][1] of the Finance Act 1987; and

"Schedule 10" means Schedule 10 to the Finance Act 1987.

Amendments—[1] Words in definitions of "blended oil" and "the originating fields" substituted by the Petroleum Revenue Tax (Nomination Scheme for Disposals and Appropriations) (Amendment) Regulations, SI 1990/2469, reg 3.

[2] Definition "the Commissioners" substituted for definition "the Board", and definition "composite nomination" revoked, by the PRT (Nomination Scheme for Disposals and Appropriations) (Amendment) Regulations, SI 2006/3089 regs 2, 4 with effect from 1 July 2006 in relation to proposed sales whose transaction base time is a time on or after that date, and not in relation to proposed transactions with a transaction base date before that date.

2A [Excluded oil

(1) Oil which forms part of a participator's equity production from an oil field (within the meaning in paragraph 1(2) of Schedule 10, immediately before the coming into force of section 150 of the Finance Act 2006, but omitting references to a month) shall be excluded from section 61 of the Finance Act 1987 if it is sold otherwise than under a Brent-Forties-Oseberg forward contract [or a Brent- Forties-Oseberg-Ekofisk forward contract][2].

(2) In paragraph (1) "a Brent-Forties Oseberg forward contract" means a contract which provides for settlement, at least 21 days after the date on which it is made, by the delivery of a volume of oil comprising, at the seller's election, Brent blend, Forties blend or oil of Oseberg grade, or a cash payment.][1]

[(3) In paragraph (1) "a Brent-Forties-Oseberg-Ekofisk forward contract" means a contract which provides for settlement, at least 21 days after the date on which it is made, by the delivery of a volume of oil comprising, at the seller's election, Brent blend, Forties blend or oil of Oseberg grade or oil of Ekofisk blend, or a cash payment.][2]

Amendments—[1] This Regulation substituted by the PRT (Nomination Scheme for Disposals and Appropriations) (Amendment) Regulations, SI 2006/3089 regs 2, 5 with effect from 1 July 2006 in relation to proposed sales whose transaction base time is a time on or after that date, and not in relation to proposed transactions with a transaction base date before that date.

[2] Words in para (1), and whole of para (3) inserted, by the Oil Taxation (Nomination Scheme for Disposals) (Amendment) Regulations, SI 2007/1454 regs 2, 3 with effect from 8 June 2007.

3 Manner of making nominations

(1) This regulation prescribes the manner in which a nomination of a proposed transaction by a participator may be made for the purposes of the scheme established by Schedule 10.

[(2) A nomination shall—

(*a*) be made in writing—

(i) in the case of a nomination made during business hours, by or on behalf of the participator who is proposing to carry out the sale in respect of which the nomination is made; and

(ii) in the case of a nomination made outside business hours, by or on behalf of the participator, where the participator (or group of which the participator is a member) is proposing to carry out the sale in respect of which the nomination is made; and

(*b*) be transmitted to the Commissioners—

(i) at the e-mail address published by the Commissioners for the receipt of such nominations, from time to time, by e-mail electronic communications; or

(ii) in the case of disruption of e-mail communications, by telephonic facsimile transmission to the number published by the Commissioners for the receipt of such nominations, from time to time.

(3) For the purpose of determining whether the nomination is made within the period of two hours mentioned in paragraph 4(1)(*a*) or (1A)(*a*) of Schedule 10, the time of sending the transmission is to be used.

(3A) But transmission shall not be regarded as having been effected for the purposes of paragraph (2) until the nomination is received by the Commissioners at that address or number.][3]

[(4) In paragraph (2) . . . [3] ["electronic communications" includes any communications conveyed by means of an electronic communications network][2].][1]

Amendments—[1] Para (4) inserted by the PRT (Nomination Scheme for Disposals and Appropriations) (Amendment) Regulations, SI 2000/1072 reg 4 with effect in relation to nominations made for the purposes of the scheme established by FA 1987 Sch 10 in respect of transactions for which the transaction base date prescribed by reg 7 below falls in a chargeable period beginning

[2] Words in para (4) substituted by the Communications Act 2003 (Consequential Amendments) Order, SI 2003/2155 art 3(1), Sch 1 para 23(1)(*a*), (2) with effect from 17 September 2003.

[3] Paras (2)–(3A) substituted for previous paras (2), (3), and words in para (4) revoked, by the PRT (Nomination Scheme for Disposals and Appropriations) (Amendment) Regulations, SI 2006/3089 regs 2, 6, 7 with effect from 1 July 2006 in relation to proposed sales whose transaction base time is a time on or after that date, and not in relation to proposed transactions with a transaction base date before that date.

4–6 . . .

Amendments—Regulations 4–6 revoked by the PRT (Nomination Scheme for Disposals and Appropriations) (Amendment) Regulations, SI 2006/3089 regs 2, 8 with effect from 1 July 2006 in relation to proposed sales whose transaction base time is a time on or after that date, and not in relation to proposed transactions with a transaction base date before that date.

7 [Transaction base time

(1) This regulation prescribes the transaction base time for a proposed sale for the purposes of paragraph 4 of Schedule 10.

(2) The transaction base time is the time (and date) at which there is an agreed price (in the form of a unit price or formula for determination of the price) at which oil is to be delivered pursuant to the contract of sale (irrespective of whether or not a legally binding agreement has come into being).][1]

Amendments—[1] Regulation 7 substituted for previous regs 7, 8, by the Petroleum Revenue Tax (Nomination Scheme for Disposals and Appropriations) (Amendment) Regulations, SI 2006/3089 regs 2, 9 with effect from 1 July 2006 in relation to proposed sales whose transaction base time is a time on or after that date, and not in relation to proposed transactions with a transaction base date before that date.

8 . . . [1]

Amendments—[1] Regulation 7 substituted for previous regs 7, 8, by the PRT (Nomination Scheme for Disposals and Appropriations) (Amendment) Regulations, SI 2006/3089 regs 2, 9 with effect from 1 July 2006 in relation to proposed sales whose transaction base time is a time on or after that date, and not in relation to proposed transactions with a transaction base date before that date.

9 Nominal volume

(1) This regulation prescribes the manner in which the quantity of oil which it is proposed to deliver under the contract of sale . . . [1] is to be expressed for the purpose of specifying the nominal volume with respect to a proposed transaction.

(2) The quantity of oil may be expressed for that purpose—

(*a*) as a specific volume plus or minus a tolerance expressed as a percentage of that specific volume; . . . [1]

. . . [1]

. . . [1]

Amendments—[1] Words in para (1), para (2)(*b*)–(*d*) and preceding word "or", and para (3), revoked by the PRT (Nomination Scheme for Disposals and Appropriations) (Amendment) Regulations, SI 2006/3089 regs 2, 10 with effect from 1 July 2006 in relation to proposed sales whose transaction base time is a time on or after that date, and not in relation to proposed transactions with a transaction base date before that date.

10 The maximum tolerance prescribed for the purposes of Schedule 10 is [1][1] per cent of a volume of oil.

Amendments—[1] Figure substituted by the PRT (Nomination Scheme for Disposals and Appropriations) (Amendment) Regulations, SI 2006/3089 regs 2, 11 with effect from 1 July 2006 in relation to proposed sales whose transaction base time is a time on or after that date, and not in relation to proposed transactions with a transaction base date before that date.

11–18

Amendments—Regulations 11–18 revoked by the PRT (Nomination Scheme for Disposals and Appropriations) (Amendment) Regulations, SI 2006/3089 regs 2, 12 with effect from 1 July 2006 in relation to proposed sales whose transaction base time is a time on or after that date, and not in relation to proposed transactions with a transaction base date before that date.

19 Nominations of proposed transactions in blended oil having effect with respect to more than one field

(1) [A][1] person who is a participator in two or more fields which, in relation to any blended oil, are or are included among the originating fields may make a nomination, having effect with respect to all the originating fields in which he is a participator, of a proposed sale . . . [1] of the blended oil in the manner prescribed by regulation 3 . . . [1]

(2) . . . [1]

Amendments—[1] In para (1) words substituted and revoked, and para (2) revoked, by the PRT (Nomination Scheme for Disposals and Appropriations) (Amendment) Regulations, SI 2006/3089 regs 2, 13 with effect from 1 July 2006 in relation to proposed sales whose transaction base time is a time on or after that date, and not in relation to proposed transactions with a transaction base date before that date.

20 . . .

Amendments—This regulation revoked by the PRT (Nomination Scheme for Disposals and Appropriations) (Amendment) Regulations, SI 2006/3089 regs 2, 14 with effect from 1 July 2006 in relation to proposed sales whose transaction base time is a time on or after that date, and not in relation to proposed transactions with a transaction base date before that date.

1989/1297

TAXES (INTEREST RATE) REGULATIONS 1989

Made by the Treasury under FA 1989 s 178

Made . . . .*27 July 1989*

Laid before the House of Commons . . . .*28 July 1989*

Coming into Force . . . .*18 August 1989*

Commentary—*Simon's Taxes* **A4.523; E4.632; I11.405, I11.532.**

1 Citation and commencement

These Regulations may be cited as the Taxes (Interest Rate) Regulations 1989 and shall come into force on 18th August 1989.

PRT

2 Interpretation

(1) In these Regulations unless the context otherwise requires—

["the 1998 Regulations" means the Corporation Tax (Instalment Payments Regulations 1998;][1]

"established rate" means—

(*a*) on the coming into force of these Regulations, 14 per cent per annum; and

(*b*) in relation to any date after the first reference date after the coming into force of these Regulations, the reference rate found on the immediately preceding reference date;

["operative date" means—

(*a*) the [twelfth][3] working day after the reference date, or

(*b*) where regulation 3ZA or 3BA applies—

(i) where the reference date is the first Tuesday, the day which is the Monday next following the first Tuesday, or

(ii) where the reference date is the second Tuesday, the day which is the Monday next following the second Tuesday;][2]

["reference date" means—

(*a*) the . . . [3] working day following the day on which the most recent meeting of the Monetary Policy Committee of the Bank of England took place, or

(*b*) where regulation 3ZA or 3BA applies—

(i) the day which is the Tuesday next following the day on which that meeting took place ("the first Tuesday"), and

(ii) the day which is the Tuesday ("the second Tuesday") occurring two weeks after the first Tuesday;][2]

"section 178" means section 178 of the Finance Act 1989;

"working day" means any day other than a non-business day within the meaning of section 92 of the Bills of Exchange Act 1882.

[(2) In these Regulations the reference rate found on a reference date is the official bank rate determined by the most recent meeting of the Monetary Policy Committee of the Bank of England.][3]

Amendments—[1] Words in para (1) inserted by the Taxes (Interest Rate) (Amendment No 2) Regulations, SI 1998/3176 reg 3 with effect for accounting periods ending on or after 1 July 1999 by virtue of the Finance Act 1994, Section 199 (Appointed Day) Order, SI 1998/3173 art 2.

[2] In para (1), definitions of "operative date" and "reference date" substituted by the Taxes and Duties (Interest Rate) (Amendment) Regulations, SI 2008/3234 reg 2 with effect from 7 January 2009.

[3] In definition of "operative date" word substituted, in definition of "reference date" word revoked, and para (2) substituted, by the Taxes and Duties (Interest Rate) (Amendment) Regulations, SI 2009/2032 regs 2, 3 with effect from 12 August 2009.

2A [Applicable rate of interest equal to zero

In determining the rate of interest applicable under section 178 for any purposes mentioned in these Regulations, if the result is less than zero the rate shall be treated as zero for those purposes.][1, 2]

Amendments—[1] This para inserted by the Taxes and Duties (Interest Rate) (Amendment) Regulations, SI 2008/3234 reg 2 with effect from 7 January 2009.

[2] This reg revoked by the Taxes and Duties (Interest Rate) (Amendment) Regulations, SI 2009/2032 regs 2, 4 with effect from 12 August 2009.

[3 [Applicable rates of interest on unpaid tax, tax repaid and repayment supplement]1

(1) For the purposes of—

(*a*) [section 86 (except where regulation 3AA(1)(*aa*) applies) and section 88][5] of the Taxes Management Act 1970,

[*(aa) section 59C of the Taxes Management Act 1970, as it applies to any income tax or capital gains tax which has become payable in accordance with—*

(i) section 55 of that Act, so far as it relates to an amendment or an assessment referred to in paragraphs (*a*) and (*b*) of subsection (1) of that section, or

(ii) section 59B of that Act,[8]

...[9]][3]

(*b*) [section 118F of, and paragraph 6B of Schedule 3 to][2] the Income and Corporation Taxes Act 1988, . . . [4]

[(*ba*) section 71(8A) of the Social Security Administration Act 1992 and section 69(8A) of the Social Security Administration (Northern Ireland) Act 1992, as they have effect in any case where the amount recoverable referred to in each of those sections is in respect of working families' tax credit or disabled person's tax credit, and paragraph 8 of Schedule 4 to the Tax Credits Act 1999;][6]

(*c*) paragraph 6(2)(*a*) of Schedule 1 to the Social Security Contributions and Benefits Act 1992, [. . . [7]

(*d*) section 15A of the Stamp Act 1891,] [4][; and][7]

[(*e*) sections 87 and 88 of the Finance Act 2003.][7]

the rate applicable under section 178 shall, subject to paragraph (2), be 8.5 per cent per annum.

(2) Where, on a reference date after 1st January 1997, the reference rate found on that date differs from the established rate, the rate applicable under section 178 for the purposes of the enactments referred to in paragraph (1) shall, on and after the next operative date, be the percentage per annum found by applying the formula specified in paragraph (3).

(3) The formula specified in this paragraph is—

$$RR + 2.5$$

where RR is the reference rate referred to in paragraph (2).][1]

Note—The rate of interest under this Regulation changes periodically in accordance with the specified formula. Changes are announced by HMRC press release. The rate applicable at any given time can be obtained from *Simon's Taxes*, Binder 1 and from *Simon's Weekly Tax Intelligence*.

Amendments—[1] This regulation substituted by the Taxes (Interest Rate) (Amendment No 4) Regulations, SI 1996/3187, with effect from 31 January 1997.

[2] Words in sub-para (1)(*b*) inserted by the Taxes (Interest Rate) (Amendment No 2) Regulations, SI 1997/2707 with effect from 9 December 1997.

[3] Sub-paragraphs 3(1)(*aa*) and (*ab*) inserted by the Taxes (Interest Rate) (Amendment) Regulations, SI 1998/310, with effect from 9 March 1998.

[4] In para (1), word "and" in sub-para (*b*) revoked, word "and" in sub-para (*c*), and the whole of sub-para (*d*) inserted by the Taxes (Interest Rate) (Amendment No 3) Regulations, SI 1999/2538 reg 3 with effect from 1 October 1999.

[5] Words in para (1)(*a*) substituted by the Taxes (Interest Rate) (Amendment No 1) Regulations, SI 2001/204 reg 3, with effect from 6 March 2001. Words previously read "sections 86 and 88".

[6] Para (1)(*ba*) inserted by the Taxes (Interest Rate) (Amendment No 2) Regulations, SI 2001/254 reg 3, with effect from 7 March 2001.

[7] In para (1), words in sub-para (*c*) revoked, word in sub-para (*d*) inserted, and sub-para (*e*) inserted, by the Taxes (Interest Rate) (Amendment) Regulations, SI 2005/2462 regs 2, 3 with effect from 26 September 2005.

[8] Para (1)(*aa*) repealed by the Finance Act 2009, Schedules 55 and 56 (Income Tax Self Assessment and Pension Schemes) (Appointed Days and Consequential and Savings Provisions) Order, SI 2011/702 art 16 with effect from 1 April 2011. This amendment has no effect in relation to a return or other document which is required to be made or delivered to HMRC or an amount of tax which is payable in relation to the tax year 2009–10 or any previous tax year (SI 2011/702 art 20).

[9] Para (1)(*ab*) revoked by the Finance Act 2009, Sections 101 to 103 (Income Tax Self Assessment) (Appointed Days and Transitional and Consequential Provisions) Order, SI 2011/701 art 10 with effect from 31 October 2011.

[3AA—(1) For the purposes of—

(*a*) sections 86A and 87 of the Taxes Management Act 1970,

[(*aa*) section 86 of the Taxes Management Act 1970 as it has effect in relation to accounting periods of companies ending before 1st October 1993 (interest on unpaid assessed corporation tax),][4]

(*b*) paragraph 3 of Schedule 16A to the Finance Act 1973,

(*c*) paragraphs 15 . . . [5] of Schedule 2, and paragraph 8 of Schedule 5, to the Oil Taxation Act 1975,

(*d*) *paragraph 59 of Schedule 8 to the Development Land Tax Act 1976,*[5]

(*e*) . . . [2]

(*f*) *section 825 of, and paragraph 3 of Schedule 19A to, the Income and Corporation Taxes Act 1988,*[5]

rate applicable under section 178 shall, [except where regulation 3AC applies and][3] subject to paragraph (2), [be—

(i) where paragraph (*aa*) above applies, 6.5 per cent per annum;

(ii) in all other cases, 6.25 per cent per annum.][4]

(2) Where, on a reference date after 1st January 1997, the reference rate found on that date differs from the established rate, the rate applicable under section 178 for the purposes of the enactments referred to in paragraph (1) shall, on and after the next operative date, be the percentage per annum found by applying the formula specified in paragraph (3) . . . [5]

[(3) The formula specified in this paragraph is—

$$RR + 2.5,$$

where RR is the reference rate referred to in paragraph (2).][5]][1]

Note—The rate of interest under this Regulation changes periodically in accordance with the specified formula. Changes are announced by HMRC press release. The rate applicable at any given time can be obtained from *Simon's Taxes*, Binder 1 and from *Simon's Weekly Tax Intelligence*.

Amendments—[1] This regulation inserted by Taxes (Interest Rate) (Amendment No 4) Regulations, SI 1996/3187, with effect from 31 January 1997.

[2] Sub-para (1)(*e*) revoked by the Taxes (Interest Rate) (Amendment No 3) Regulations, SI 1999/2538 reg 4 with effect from 1 October 1999.

[3] Words inserted by Taxes (Interest Rate) (Amendment No 4) Regulations, SI 1999/2637 reg 4 with effect from 14 October 1999.

[4] Para (1)(*aa*) inserted and words at end of para (1) substituted by the Taxes (Interest Rate) (Amendment No 1) Regulations, SI 2001/204 reg 4, with effect from 6 March 2001. Words previously read "be 6.25% per annum".

[5] In para (1)(*c*), words revoked, para (1)(*d*), (*f*) revoked, in para (2), words revoked, and para (3) substituted, by the Taxes and Duties (Interest Rate) (Amendment) Regulations, SI 2009/2032 regs 2, 5 with effect from 12 August 2009.

[3AB—(1) For the purposes of—

(*a*) section 824 of the Income and Corporation Taxes Act 1988,

(*b*) paragraph 6(2)(*b*) of Schedule 1 to the Social Security Contributions and Benefits Act 1992, . . . [2]

(*c*) section 283 of the Taxation of Chargeable Gains Act 1992.

[(*d*) section 92 of the Finance Act 1986, . . . [3]

(*e*) section 110 of the Finance Act 1999,][2] [; and][3]

[(*f*) section 89 of the Finance Act 2003.][3]

the rate applicable under section 178 shall, subject to paragraph (2), be 4 per cent per annum.

(2) Where, on a reference date after 1st January 1997, the reference rate found on that date differs from the established rate, the rate applicable under section 178 for the purposes of the enactments referred to in paragraph (1) shall, on and after the next operative date, be the [higher of—

(*a*) 0.5% per annum, and

(*b*) the percentage per annum found by applying the formula specified in paragraph (3).][4]

[(3) The formula specified in this paragraph is—

$$RR - 1,$$

where RR is the reference rate referred to in paragraph (2).][4]][1]

Note—The rate of interest under this Regulation changes periodically in accordance with the specified formula. Changes are announced by HMRC press release. The rate applicable at any given time can be obtained from *Simon's Taxes*, Binder 1 and from *Simon's Weekly Tax Intelligence*.

Amendments—[1] This regulation inserted by the Taxes (Interest Rate) (Amendment No 4) Regulations, SI 1996/3187, with effect from 31 January 1997.

[2] Word "and" in sub-para (1)(*b*) revoked, and sub-paras (1)(*d*), (*e*) inserted, by the Taxes (Interest Rate) (Amendment No 3) Regulations, SI 1999/2538 reg 5 with effect from 1 October 1999.

[3] In para (1), word in sub-para (*d*) revoked, word in sub-para (*e*) inserted, and sub-para (*f*) inserted, by the Taxes (Interest Rate) (Amendment) Regulations, SI 2005/2462 regs 2, 4 with effect from 26 September 2005.

[4] In para (2), words substituted, and para (3) substituted, by the Taxes and Duties (Interest Rate) (Amendment) Regulations, SI 2009/2032 regs 2, 7 with effect from 12 August 2009.

[3AC—(1) For the purposes of section 87 of the Taxes Management Act 1970 in so far as it relates to tax that becomes due and payable on or after 14th October 1999, the rate applicable under section 178 shall, subject to paragraph (2), be 7.5 per cent per annum.

(2) Where on a reference date after 14th October 1999 the reference rate found on that date differs from the established rate, the rate applicable under section 178 for the purposes mentioned in paragraph (1) shall, on and after the next operative date, be the percentage per annum found by applying the formula specified in paragraph (3).

(3) The formula specified in this paragraph is—

$$RR + 2.5,$$

where RR is the reference rate referred to in paragraph (2).][1]

Amendments—[1] This regulation inserted by Taxes (Interest Rate) (Amendment No 4) Regulations, SI 1999/2637 reg 4 with effect from 14 October 1999.

[3A [Applicable rate of interest on overdue corporation tax

(1) For the purposes of section 87A of the Taxes Management Act 1970 the rate applicable under section 178 shall, [except where regulation 3ZA or 3ZB applies and][2] subject to paragraph(2), be 6.25 per cent per annum.

(2) Where, on a reference date after 1st October 1993, the reference rate found on that date differs from the established rate, the rate applicable under section 178 for the purposes of the enactment referred to in paragraph (1) shall, on and after the next operative date, be the percentage per annum found by applying the formula specified in paragraph (3) . . . [3]

[(3) The formula specified in this paragraph is—

$$RR + 2.5,$$

where RR is the reference rate referred to in paragraph (2).][3]][1]

Note—The rate of interest under this Regulation changes periodically in accordance with the specified formula. Changes are announced by HMRC press release. The rate applicable at any given time can be obtained from *Simon's Taxes*, Binder 1 and from *Simon's Weekly Tax Intelligence*.

Amendments—[1] This regulation inserted by the Taxes (Interest Rate) (Amendment No 3) Regulations, SI 1993/2212 with effect from 1 October 1993.

[2] Words in para (1) inserted by the Taxes (Interest Rate) (Amendment No 2) Regulations, SI 1998/3176 reg 5 with effect for accounting periods ending on or after 1 July 1999 by virtue of FA 1994 s 199 (Appointed Day) Order, SI 1998/3173 art 2.

3 In para (2), words revoked, and para (3) substituted, by the Taxes and Duties (Interest Rate) (Amendment) Regulations, SI 2009/2032 regs 2, 8 with effect from 12 August 2009.

[3AAA—(1) For the purposes of—

(*a*) paragraph 16 of Schedule 2 to the Oil Taxation Act 1975,

(*b*) paragraph 59 of Schedule 8 to the Development Land Tax Act 1976, and

(*c*) section 825 of, and paragraph 3 of Schedule 19A to, the Income and Corporation Taxes Act 1988,

the rate applicable under section 178 shall, subject to paragraph (3), be the percentage per annum found by applying the formula specified in paragraph (2), but if the result is not a multiple of one-quarter the result shall be rounded down to the nearest amount which is such a multiple.

(2) The formula specified for the purposes of paragraph (1) is—

$$((RR + 2.5) \times 80) / 100,$$

where RR is the official bank rate determined at the meeting of the Monetary Policy Committee of the Bank of England which immediately preceded the coming into force of these Regulations.

(3) Where on a reference date after the coming into force of these Regulations, the reference rate found on that date differs from the established rate, the rate applicable under section 178 for the purposes of the enactments referred to in paragraph (1) shall, on and after the next operative date, be the higher of—

(*a*) 0.5% per annum, and

(*b*) the percentage per annum found by applying the formula specified in paragraph (4).

(4) The formula specified in this paragraph is—

$$RR - 1,$$

where RR is the reference rate referred to in paragraph (3).][1]

Amendments—[1] Regulation inserted, by the Taxes and Duties (Interest Rate) (Amendment) Regulations, SI 2009/2032 regs 2, 6 with effect from 12 August 2009.

[3ZA—(1) For the purposes of section 87A of the Taxes Management Act 1970 in so far as it relates, by virtue of subsection (1A) of that section, to an amount or amounts treated as becoming due and payable in respect of the total liability of a large company for an accounting period ending on or after 1st July 1999 in accordance with regulation 5 of the 1998 Regulations, the rate applicable under section 178 shall, subject to paragraph (2), be 8.25 per cent per annum.

(2) Where on a reference date after 7th January 1999 the reference rate found on that date differs from the established rate, the rate applicable under section 178 for the purposes mentioned in paragraph (1) shall, on and after the next operative date and as respects the period specified in paragraph (3), be the percentage per annum found by applying the formula specified in paragraph (4).

(3) The period specified in this paragraph is any period falling between—

(*a*) the date on which the first instalment payment is treated as becoming due and payable for the accounting period concerned under regulation 5 of the 1998 Regulations, and

(*b*) the day following the expiry of nine months from the end of that accounting period,

during which any amount treated as becoming due and payable in accordance with regulation 5 of those Regulations for that accounting period remains unpaid.

(4) The formula[2] specified in this paragraph is—

$$[RR + 1],$$

where RR is the reference rate referred to in paragraph (2).][1]

Amendments—[1] This regulation inserted by the Taxes (Interest Rate) (Amendment No 2) Regulations, SI 1998/3176 reg 6 with effect for accounting periods ending on or after 1 July 1999 by virtue of FA 1994 s 199 (Appointed Day) Order, SI 1998/3173 art 2.

2 Formula substituted by the Taxes (Interest Rate) (Amendment) Regulations, SI 2000/893 reg 2(1), with effect as from 20 April 2000 in relation to interest running from before that day as well as to interest running from, or from after, that day.

[3ZB—(1) For the purposes of section 87A of the Taxes Management Act 1970 in so far as it relates to an unpaid amount in respect of the total liability of a company for an accounting period ending on or after 1st July 1999, other than an amount to which regulation 3ZA applies, the rate applicable under section 178 shall, subject to paragraph (2), be 8.5 per cent per annum.

(2) Where on a reference date after 7th January 1999 the reference rate found on that date differs from the established rate, the rate applicable under section 178 for the purposes mentioned in paragraph (1) shall, on and after the next operative date, be the percentage per annum found by applying the formula specified in paragraph (3).

(3) The formula specified in this paragraph is—

PRT

$$RR + 2.5,$$

where RR is the reference rate referred to in paragraph (2).] [1]

Amendments—[1] This regulation inserted by the Taxes (Interest Rate) (Amendment No 2) Regulations, SI 1998/3176 reg 6 with effect for accounting periods ending on or after 1 July 1999 by virtue of FA 1994 s 199 (Appointed Day) Order, SI 1998/3173 art 2.

3B [Applicable rate of interest on tax overpaid

(1) For the purposes of section 826 of the Income and Corporation Taxes Act 1988 the rate applicable under section 178 shall, [except where regulation 3BA or 3BB applies and][2] subject to paragraph(2), be 3·25 per cent per annum.

(2) Where, on a reference date after 1st October 1993, the reference rate found on that date differs from the established rate, the rate applicable under section 178 for the purposes of the enactment referred to in paragraph (1) shall, on and after the next operative date, be the [higher of—

(*a*) 0.5% per annum, and

(*b*) the percentage per annum found by applying the formula specified in paragraph (3).][3]

[(3) The formula specified in this paragraph is—

$$RR - 1,$$

where RR is the reference rate referred to in paragraph (2).][3]][1]

Note—The rate of interest under this Regulation changes periodically in accordance with the specified formula. Changes are announced by HMRC press release. The rate applicable at any given time can be obtained from *Simon's Taxes*, Binder 1 and from *Simon's Weekly Tax Intelligence*.

Amendments—[1] This regulation inserted by the Taxes (Interest Rate) (Amendment No 3) Regulations, SI 1993/2212 with effect from 1 October 1993.

[2] Words in para (1) inserted by the Taxes (Interest Rate) (Amendment No 2) Regulations, SI 1998/3176 reg 5 with effect for accounting periods ending on or after 1 July 1999 by virtue of FA 1994 s 199 (Appointed Day) Order, SI 1998/3173 art 2.

[3] In para (2), words substituted, and para (3) substituted, by the Taxes and Duties (Interest Rate) (Amendment) Regulations, SI 2009/2032 regs 2, 9 with effect from 12 August 2009.

3BA, 3BB, 4

Note—These regulations are not relevant to this work.

5 [Applicable rate of official rate of interest

[(1) Subject to paragraph (2), the rate applicable under section 178 for the purposes of Chapter 7 of Part 3 of the Income Tax (Earnings and Pensions) Act 2003 ("Chapter 7") shall, [on and after 6th April 2017, be 2.50 per cent per annum][4].][3]

(2) In relation to a loan outstanding for the whole or part of a year of assessment where—

(*a*) the loan was made in the currency of a country or territory specified in the Table below,

(*b*) the benefit of the loan is obtained by reason of the employment of a person who normally lives in that country or territory, and

(*c*) that person has lived in that country or territory at some time in the period of six years ending with that year,

the rate applicable under section 178 for the purposes of [Chapter 7][3] and the date on and after which that rate has effect shall be ascertained from the entries in the Table below relating to the country or territory concerned.

TABLE

Country or territory	*Date on and after which applicable rate has effect*	*Applicable rate*
Japan	6th June 1994	3·9 per cent per annum
Switzerland	[6th July 1994][2]	[5·5 per cent per annum][2]][1]

Notes—The rate of interest under this Regulation is subject to occasional changes made by statutory instruments. The rate applicable at any given time may be obtained from *Simon's Taxes*, Binder 1 and from *Simon's Weekly Tax Intelligence*.

TA 1988 s 160 has been replaced by ITEPA 2003 s 181.

Amendments—[1] This regulation substituted by the Taxes (Interest Rate) (Amendment) Regulations, SI 1994/1307.

[2] Words and percentage in Table substituted by SI 1994/1567.

[3] Para (1) substituted, and in para (2), words substituted, by the Taxes (Interest Rate) (Amendment) Regulations, SI 2009/199 reg 2 with effect from 1 March 2009.

[4] Words in para (1) substituted by the Taxes (Interest Rate) (Amendment) Regulations, SI 2017/305 reg 2 with effect from 6 April 2017.

6 Effect of change in applicable rate

Where the rate applicable under section 178 for the purpose of any of the enactments referred to in [these Regulations][1] changes on an operative date by virtue of these Regulations, that change shall have effect for periods beginning on or after the operative date in relation to interest running from before that date as well as from or from after that date.

Amendments—[1] Words substituted by the Taxes and Duties (Interest Rate) (Amendment) Regulations, SI 2009/2032 regs 2, 14 with effect from 12 August 2009.

1989/2384

FOREIGN FIELDS (SPECIFICATION) ORDER 1989

Made . . . . 16 December 1989

The Secretary of State, in exercise of the powers conferred on him by sections 9(5) and 12(2) of the Oil Taxation Act 1983 (hereinafter referred to as "the Act"), and all other powers enabling him in that behalf, hereby makes the following Order:

1 This Order may be cited as the Foreign Fields (Specification) Order 1989.

2 In this Order, the "Gullfaks Field" means the hydrocarbon accumulation within the boundary defined by lines of latitude and longitude joining the surface co-ordinates set out in the Schedule hereto.

3 The Gullfaks Field, being an area which is not under the jurisdiction of the government of the United Kingdom, is hereby specified as a foreign field for the purposes of the Act.

SCHEDULE

Article 2

Gullfaks field co-ordinates

Latitude North	Longitude East	Latitude North	Longitude East
61°13'12"	2°9'54"	61°11'18"	2°18'12"
61°13'12"	2°10'18"	61°11'18"	2°18'0"
61°13'6"	2°10'18"	61°11'12"	2°18'0"
61°13'6"	2°10'36"	61°11'12"	2°17'48"
61°13'0"	2°10'36"	61°11'6"	2°17'48"
61°13'0"	2°11'6"	61°11'6"	2°17'36"
61°13'18"	2°11'6"	61°11'0"	2°17'36"
61°13'18"	2°11'12"	61°11'0"	2°17'30"
61°13'24"	2°11'12"	61°10'54"	2°17'30"
61°13'24"	2°11'18"	61°10'54"	2°17'18"
61°13'42"	2°11'18"	61°10'48"	2°17'18"
61°13'42"	2°11'24"	61°10'48"	2°17'6"
61°13'54"	2°11'24"	61°10'42"	2°17'6"
61°13'54"	2°11'30"	61°10'42"	2°16'54"
61°14'0"	2°11'30"	61°10'6"	2°16'54"
61°14'0"	2°11'42"	61°10'6"	2°15'48"
61°14'6"	2°11'42"	61°10'12"	2°15'48"
61°14'6"	2°12'18"	61°10'12"	2°15'36"
61°14'12"	2°12'18"	61°10'18"	2°15'36"
61°14'12"	2°12'24"	61°10'18"	2°15'30"
61°14'24"	2°12'24"	61°10'48"	2°15'30"
61°14'24"	2°12'30"	61°10'48"	2°15'6"
61°14'36"	2°12'30"	61°10'36"	2°15'6"
61°14'36"	2°13'6"	61°10'36"	2°15'0"
61°14'24"	2°13'6"	61°10'30"	2°15'0"
61°14'24"	2°13'36"	61°10'30"	2°14'54"
61°14'30"	2°13'36"	61°10'24"	2°14'54"
61°14'30"	2°14'18"	61°10'24"	2°14'42"

PRT

Latitude North	Longitude East	Latitude North	Longitude East
61°14'36"	2°14'18"	61°10'18"	2°14'42"
61°14'36"	2°16'12"	61°10'18"	2°14'36"
61°14'30"	2°16'12"	61°10'12"	2°14'36"
61°14'30"	2°16'18"	61°10'12"	2°14'30"
61°14'24"	2°16'18"	61°10'6"	2°14'30"
61°14'24"	2°16'24"	61°10'6"	2°14'0"
61°14'18"	2°16'24"	61°10'0"	2°14'0"
61°14'18"	2°16'36"	61°10'0"	2°13'48"
61°14'6"	2°16'36"	61°9'54"	2°13'48"
61°14'6"	2°17'0"	61°9'54"	2°13'30"
61°14'0"	2°17'0"	61°9'48"	2°13'30"
61°14'0"	2°17'18"	61°9'48"	2°13'18"
61°13'54"	2°17'18"	61°9'36"	2°13'18"
61°13'54"	2°17'30"	61°9'36"	2°12'54"
61°13'48"	2°17'30"	61°9'30"	2°12'54"
61°13'48"	2°18'30"	61°9'30"	2°10'36"
61°13'42"	2°18'30"	61°9'54"	2°10'36"
61°13'42"	2°18'54"	61°9'54"	2°10'24"
61°13'36"	2°18'54"	61°9'48"	2°10'24"
61°13'36"	2°19'6"	61°9'48"	2°10'6"
61°13'30"	2°19'6"	61°9'42"	2°10'6"
61°13'30"	2°19'18"	61°9'42"	2°9'42"
61°13'0"	2°19'18"	61°9'36"	2°9'42"
61°13'0"	2°19'6"	61°9'36"	2°9'30"
61°12'54"	2°19'6"	61°9'30"	2°9'30"
61°12'54"	2°18'54"	61°9'30"	2°8'54"
61°12'48"	2°18'54"	61°9'36"	2°8'54"
61°12'48"	2°18'42"	61°9'36"	2°8'48"
61°12'0"	2°18'42"	61°9'42"	2°8'48"
61°12'0"	2°18'54"	61°9'42"	2°8'30"
61°11'30"	2°18'54"	61°9'48"	2°8'30"
61°11'30"	2°18'42"	61°9'48"	2°8'6"
61°11'24"	2°18'42"	61°10'36"	2°8'6"
61°11'24"	2°18'12"	61°10'36"	2°8'18"
61°11'6"	2°8'18"	61°11'42"	2°9'42"
61°11'6"	2°8'24"	61°11'54"	2°9'42"
61°11'12"	2°8'24"	61°11'54"	2°9'54"
61°11'12"	2°8'30"	61°12'0"	2°9'54"
61°11'18"	2°8'30"	61°12'0"	2°10'0"
61°11'18"	2°8'36"	61°12'6"	2°10'0"
61°11'24"	2°8'36"	61°12'6"	2°10'6"
61°11'24"	2°8'42"	61°12'42"	2°10'6"
61°11'30"	2°8'42"	61°12'42"	2°10'0"
61°11'30"	2°9'30"	61°12'48"	2°10'0"
61°11'42"	2°9'30"	61°12'48"	2°9'54"
		61°13'12"	2°9'54"

1991/1982

FOREIGN FIELDS (SPECIFICATION) ORDER 1991

Made by the Secretary of State under the Oil Taxation Act 1983 ss 9(5), 12(2)
Made . . . . *22 August 1991*

1 This Order may be cited as the Foreign Fields (Specification) Order 1991.

2 In this Order, "the Odin Field" means the hydrocarbon accumulation within the boundary defined by lines of latitude and longitude joining the surface co-ordinates set out in the Schedule hereto.

3 The Odin Field, being an area which is not under the jurisdiction of the government of the United Kingdom, is hereby specified as a foreign field for the purpose of the Act.

[SCHEDULE

Article 3

Odin field co-ordinates

Latitude North	Longitude East	Latitude North	Longitude East
60°05'50"	02°07'15"	60°01'30"	02°10'50"
60°05'50"	02°08'10"	60°01'30"	02°10'30"
60°06'00"	02°08'10"	60°00'25"	02°10'30"
60°06'00"	02°08'45"	60°00'25"	02°10'10"
60°06'10"	02°08'45"	60°00'10"	02°10'10"
60°06'10"	02°09'15"	60°00'10"	02°09'45"
60°06'20"	02°09'15"	59°59'55"	02°09'45"
60°06'20"	02°09'35"	59°59'55"	02°09'25"
60°06'30"	02°09'35"	59°59'45"	02°09'25"
60°06'30"	02°09'45"	59°59'45"	02°09'05"
60°06'40"	02°09'45"	59°59'05"	02°09'05"
60°06'40"	02°09'55"	59°59'05"	02°07'55"
60°06'50"	02°09'55"	60°00'30"	02°07'55"
60°06'50"	02°11'15"	60°00'30"	02°08'30"
60°06'40"	02°11'15"	60°00'40"	02°08'30"
60°06'40"	02°11'45"	60°00'40"	02°08'50"
60°06'30"	02°11'45"	60°01'55"	02°08'50"
60°06'30"	02°12'15"	60°01'55"	02°08'10"
06°05'55"	02°12'15"	60°02'40"	02°08'10"
60°05'55"	02°12'00"	60°02'40"	02°09'05"
60°05'40"	02°12'00"	60°02'25"	02°09'05"
60°05'40"	02°12'10"	60°02'25"	02°09'30"
60°05'30"	02°12'10"	60°02'40"	02°09'30"
60°05'30"	02°12'20"	60°02'40"	02°09'45"
60°05'20"	02°12'20"	60°03'00"	02°09'45"
60°05'20"	02°12'30"	60°03'00"	02°09'10"
60°05'10"	02°12'30"	60°03'10"	02°09'10"
60°05'10"	02°12'45"	60°03'10"	02°08'50"
60°05'00"	02°12'45"	60°03'20"	02°08'50"
60°05'00"	02°12'55"	60°03'20"	02°08'35"
60°04'15"	02°12'55"	60°03'30"	02°08'35"
60°04'15"	02°12'45"	60°03'30"	02°08'05"
60°03'55"	02°12'45"	60°03'40"	02°08'05"
60°03'55"	02°12'55"	60°03'40"	02°07'50"
60°03'25"	02°12'55"	60°03'50"	02°07'50"
60°03'25"	02°12'40"	60°03'50"	02°07'40"
60°03'00"	02°12'40"	60°04'00"	02°07'40"

PRT

Latitude North	Longitude East	Latitude North	Longitude East
60°03'00"	02°11'35"	60°04'00"	02°07'25"
60°02'05"	02°11'35"	60°04'10"	02°07'25"
60°02'05"	02°11'15"	60°04'10"	02°07'15"
60°01'50"	02°11'15"	60°05'50"	02°07'15"
60°01'50"	02°10'50"][1]		

Amendments—[1] This Schedule substituted by the Foreign Fields (Specification) (Amendment) Order, SI 1993/1565 art 3 Schedule with effect from 18 June 1993.

1991/1983

FOREIGN FIELDS (SPECIFICATION) (NO 2) ORDER 1991

Made by the Secretary of State under the Oil Taxation Act 1983 ss 9(5), 12(2)

Made . . . . *22nd August 1991*

1 This Order may be cited as the Foreign Fields (Specification) (No 2) Order 1991.

2 In this Order—

"the East Frigg Alpha Field" means the hydrocarbon accumulation within the boundary defined by lines of latitude and longitude joining the surface co-ordinates set out in Part I of the Schedule hereto; and "the East Frigg Beta Field" means the hydrocarbon accumulation within the boundary defined by the lines of latitude and longitude joining the surface co-ordinates set out in Part II of the Schedule hereto.

3 The East Frigg Alpha Field and the East Frigg Beta Field, both being areas which are not under the jurisdiction of the government of the United Kingdom, are hereby specified as foreign fields for the purposes of the Act.

SCHEDULE

Article 2

PART I

East frigg alpha field co-ordinates

Latitude North	Longitude East	Latitude North	Longitude East
59° 54' 55" N	2° 18' 10" E	59° 55' 35" N	2° 24' 55" E
59° 54' 55" N	2° 18' 35" E	59° 55' 0" N	2° 24' 55" E
59° 55' 0" N	2° 18' 35" E	59° 55' 0" N	2° 23' 55" E
59° 55' 0" N	2° 18' 45" E	59° 55' 5" N	2° 23' 55" E
59° 55' 25" N	2° 18' 45" E	59° 55' 5" N	2° 23' 35" E
59° 55' 25" N	2° 18' 50" E	59° 54' 50" N	2° 23' 35" E
59° 55' 35" N	2° 18' 50" E	59° 54' 50" N	2° 23' 5" E
59° 55' 35" N	2° 19' 10" E	59° 54' 35" N	2° 23' 5" E
59° 55' 40" N	2° 19' 10" E	59° 54' 35" N	2° 23' 15" E
59 ° 55' 40" N	2° 20' 40" E	59° 54' 10" N	2° 23' 15" E
59° 55' 45" N	2° 20' 40" E	59° 54' 10" N	2° 23' 0" E
59° 55' 45" N	2° 21' 30" E	59° 53' 55" N	2° 23' 0" E
59° 55' 55" N	2° 21' 30" E	59° 53' 55" N	2° 21' 55" E
59° 55' 55" N	2° 22' 5" E	59° 54' 5" N	2° 21' 55" E
59° 56' 15" N	2° 22' 5" E	59° 54' 5" N	2° 21' 35" E
59° 56' 15" N	2° 22' 35" E	59° 54' 15" N	2° 21' 35" E
59° 56' 20" N	2° 22' 35" E	59° 54' 15" N	2° 21' 10" E
59° 56' 20" N	2° 23' 5" E	59° 54' 25" N	2° 21' 10" E
59° 56' 15" N	2° 23' 5" E	59° 54' 25" N	2° 20' 40" E
59° 56' 15" N	2° 24' 30" E	59° 54' 10" N	2° 20' 40" E
59° 56' 5" N	2° 24' 30" E	59° 54' 10" N	2° 20' 5" E

Latitude North	Longitude East	Latitude North	Longitude East
59° 56' 5" N	2° 24' 50" E	59° 54' 0" N	2° 20' 5' E
59° 55' 50" N	2° 24' 50" E	59° 54' 0" N	2° 18' 10" E
59° 55' 50" N	2° 24' 40" E	59° 54' 55" N	2° 18' 10" E
59° 55' 35" N	2° 24' 40" E		

PART II

East frigg beta field co-ordinates

Latitude North	Longitude East	Latitude North	Longitude East
59° 53' 25" N	2° 18' 50" E	59° 53' 5" N	2° 25' 5" E
59° 53' 25" N	2° 19' 15" E	59° 53' 5" N	2° 24' 30" E
59° 53' 35" N	2° 19' 15" E	59° 52' 55" N	2° 24' 30" E
59° 53' 35" N	2° 19' 25" E	59° 52' 55" N	2° 24' 5" E
59° 53' 45" N	2° 19' 25" E	59° 52' 45" N	2° 24' 5" E
59° 53' 45" N	2° 22' 5" E	59° 52' 45" N	2° 21' 35" E
59° 53' 50" N	2° 22' 5" E	59° 52' 50" N	2° 21' 35" E
59° 53' 50" N	2° 23' 20" E	59° 52' 50" N	2° 19' 10" E
59° 53' 45" N	2° 23' 20" E	59° 53' 0" N	2° 19' 10" E
59° 53' 45" N	2° 24' 25" E	59° 53' 0" N	2° 18' 50" E
59° 53' 40" N	2° 24' 25" E	59° 53' 25" N	2° 18' 50" E
59° 53' 40" N	2° 25' 5" E		

1991/1984

FOREIGN FIELDS (SPECIFICATION) (NO 3) ORDER 1991

Made by the Secretary of State under the Oil Taxation Act 1983 ss 9(5), 12(2)

Made . . . . *22nd August 1991*

1 This Order may be cited as the Foreign Fields (Specification) (No 3) Order 1991.

2 In this Order, "the Snorre Field" means the hydrocarbon accumulation within the boundary defined by lines of latitude and longitude joining the surface co-ordinates set out in the Schedule hereto.

3 The Snorre Field, being an area which is not under the jurisdiction of the government of the United Kingdom, is hereby specified as a foreign field for the purposes of the Act.

SCHEDULE

Article 2

Snorre field co-ordinates

Latitude North	Longitude East	Latitude North	Longitude East
61° 24' 30" N	02° 06' 00" E	61° 32' 00" N	02° 18' 00" E
61° 25' 00" N	02° 06' 00" E	61° 32' 00" N	02° 17' 00" E
61° 25' 00" N	02° 04' 00" E	61° 29' 00" N	02° 17' 00" E
61° 27' 00" N	02° 04' 00" E	61° 29' 00" N	02° 16' 00" E
61° 27' 00" N	02° 05' 00" E	61° 28' 00" N	02° 16' 00" E
61° 28' 00" N	02° 05' 00" E	61° 28' 00" N	02° 15' 00" E
61° 28' 00" N	02° 06' 00" E	61° 27' 00" N	02° 15' 00" E
61° 29' 00" N	02° 06' 00" E	61° 27' 00" N	02° 13' 00" E
61° 29' 00" N	02° 07' 00" E	61° 26' 00" N	02° 13' 00" E
61° 32' 00" N	02° 07' 00" E	61° 26' 00" N	02° 12' 00" E
61° 32' 00" N	02° 10' 00" E	61° 25' 00" N	02° 12' 00" E
61° 34' 00" N	02° 10' 00" E	61° 25' 00" N	02° 11' 00" E

Latitude North	Longitude East	Latitude North	Longitude East
61° 34' 00" N	02° 12' 00" E	61° 24' 30" N	02° 11' 00" E
61° 35' 00" N	02° 12' 00" E	61° 24' 30" N	02° 06' 00" E
61° 35' 00" N	02° 18' 00" E		

1993/1408

FOREIGN FIELDS (SPECIFICATION) ORDER 1993

Made by the Secretary of State under the Oil Taxation Act 1983 ss 9(5), 12(2)

Made . . . . *7 June 1993*

1 This Order may be cited as the Foreign Fields (Specification) Order 1993.

2 In this Order the "Lille Frigg Field" means the hydrocarbon accumulation between the depths of 3,570 metres and 3,700 metres beneath mean sea level within the boundary defined by a set of lines of latitude and longitude joining the surface co-ordinates set out in the Schedule hereto.

3 The Lille Frigg Field, being an area which is not under the jurisdiction of the government of the United Kingdom, is for the purposes of the Act hereby specified as a foreign field.

SCHEDULE

Article 2

Latitude North	Longitude East	Latitude North	Longitude East
59°59°40"	02°23'20"	59°56'10"	02°22'15"
59°59'40"	02°23'40"	59°56'40"	02°22'15"
59°59'05"	02°23'40"	59°56'40"	02°22'25"
59°59'05"	02°23'35"	59°57'00"	02°22'25"
59°58'50"	02°23'35"	59°57'00"	02°22'20"
59°58'50"	02°23'30"	59°57'20"	02°22'20"
59°58'30"	02°23'30"	59°57'20"	02°22'15"
59°58'30"	02°23'35"	59°57'40"	02°22'15"
59°58'25"	02°23'35"	59°57'40"	02°22'25"
59°58'25"	02°23'40"	59°57'55"	02°22'25"
59°57'55"	02°23'40"	59°57'55"	02°22'20"
59°57'55"	02°23'45"	59°58'10"	02°22'20"
59°57'45"	02°23'45"	59°58'10"	02°22'25"
59°57'45"	02°23'50"	59°58'25"	02°22'25"
59°57'40"	02°23'50"	59°58'25"	02°22'35"
59°57'40"	02°23'55"	59°58'30"	02°22'35"
59°57'35"	02°23'55"	59°58'30"	02°22'30"
59°57'35"	02°24'00"	59°58'35"	02°22'30"
59°57'30"	02°24'00"	59°58'35"	02°22'25"
59°57'30"	02°24'05"	59°58'45"	02°22'25"
59°57'25"	02°24'05"	59°58'45"	02°22'30"
59°57'25"	02°24'10"	59°58'55"	02°22'30"
59°56'50"	02°24'10"	59°58'55"	02°22'40"
59°56'50"	02°24'05"	59°59'05"	02°22'40"
59°56'45"	02°24'05"	59°59'05"	02°22'50"
59°56'45"	02°24'00"	59°59'10"	02°22'50"
59°56'35"	02°24'00"	59°59'10"	02°22'55"
59°56'35"	02°23'55"	59°59'15"	02°22'55"
59°56'30"	02°23'55"	59°59'15"	02°23'00"
59°56'30"	02°23'20"	59°59'20"	02°23'00"
59°56'25"	02°23'20"	59°59'20"	02°23'05"

Latitude North	Longitude East	Latitude North	Longitude East
59°56’25”	02°23’00”	59°59’25”	02°23’05”
59°56’20”	02°23’00”	59°59’25”	02°23’10”
59°56’20”	02°22’50”	59°59’30”	02°23’10”
59°56’10”	02°22’50”	59°59’30”	02°23’15”
59°56’10”	02°22’45”	59°59’35”	02°23’15”
59°56’05”	02°22’45”	59°59’35”	02°23’20”
59°56’05”	02°22’20”	59°59’40”	02°23’20”
59°56’10”	02°22’20”		

1993/1566

FOREIGN FIELDS (SPECIFICATION) (NO 2) ORDER 1993

Made by the Secretary of State under the Oil Taxation Act 1983 ss 9(5), 12(2)

Made . . . . .18 June 1993

1 This Order may be cited as the Foreign Fields (Specification) Order 1993.

2 In this Order the “Froy Field” means the hydrocarbon accumulation between the depths of 2,920 metres and 3,200 metres beneath mean sea level within the boundary defined by a set of lines of latitude and longitude joining the surface co-ordinates set out in the Schedule hereto.

3 The Froy Field, being an area which is not under the jurisdiction of the government of the United Kingdom, is for the purposes of the Act hereby specified as a foreign field.

SCHEDULE

Article 2

Froy field co-ordinates

Latitude North	Longitude East	Latitude North	Longitude East
59°46’15”	02°33’40’	59°42’50”	02°34’05”
59°46’15”	02°33’55”	59°42’50”	02°34’00”
59°46’05”	02°33’55”	59°42’40”	02°34’00”
59°46’05”	02°34’05”	59°42’40”	02°33’55”
59°46’00”	02°34’05”	59°42’35”	02°33’55”
59°46’00”	02°34’15”	59°42’35”	02°33’50”
59°45’55”	02°34’15”	59°42’30”	02°33’50”
59°45’55”	02°34’30”	59°42’30”	02°33’45”
59°45’50”	02°34’30”	59°42’25”	02°33’45”
59°45’50”	02°34’35”	59°42’25”	02°33’40”
59°45’40”	02°34’35”	59°42’20”	02°33’40”
59°45’40”	02°34’40”	59°42’20”	02°33’35”
59°45’30”	02°34’40”	59°42’15”	02°33’35”
59°45’30”	02°34’45”	59°42’15”	02°33’30”
59°45’15”	02°34’45”	59°42’10”	02°33’30”
59°45’15”	02°34’50”	59°42’°10”	02°33’15”
59°45’05”	02°34’50”	59°42’05”	02°33’15”
59°45’05”	02°34’55”	59°42’05”	02°33’05”
59°44’55”	02°34’55”	59°42’00”	02°33’05”
59°44’55”	02°35’00”	59°42’00”	02°32’35”
59°44’35”	02°35’00”	59°41’55”	02°32’35”
59°44’35”	02°35’05”	59°41’55”	02°32’25”
59°44’20”	02°35’05”	59°41’50”	02°32’25”
59°44’20”	02°34’55”	59°41’50”	02°32’20”
59°44’15”	02°34’55”	59°41’45”	02°32’20”

Latitude North	Longitude East	Latitude North	Longitude East
59°44’15”	02°34’50”	59°41’45”	02°32’15”
59°44’10”	02°34’50”	59°41’25”	02°32’15”
59°44’10”	02°34’45”	59°41’25”	02°32’10”
59°44’05”	02°34’45”	59°41’20”	02°32’10”
59°44’05”	02°34’40”	59°41’20”	02°31’05”
59°44’00”	02°34’40”	59°41’25”	02°31’05”
59°44’00”	02°34’30”	59°41’25”	02°31’00”
59°43’55”	02°34’30”	59°41’40”	02°31’00”
59°43’55”	02°34’25”	59°41’40”	02°30’55”
59°43’40”	02°34’25”	59°42’05”	02°30’55”
59°43’40”	02°34’30”	59°42’05”	02°31’10”
59°43’20”	02°34’30”	59°42’10”	02°31’10”
59°43’20”	02°34’25”	59°42’10”	02°31’20”
59°43’15”	02°34’25”	59°42’15”	02°31’20”
59°43’15”	02°34’20”	59°42’15”	02°31’30”
59°43’10”	02°34’20”	59°42’25”	02°31’30”
59°43’10”	02°34’15”	59°42’25”	02°31’25”
59°43’05”	02°34’15”	59°42’40”	02°31’25”
59°43’05”	02°34’10”	59°42’40”	02°32’00”
59°43’00”	02°34’10”	59°42’50”	02°32’00”
59°43’00”	02°34’05”	59°42’50”	02°31’55”
59°43’05”	02°31’55”	59°45’10”	02°32’45”
59°43’05”	02°32’00”	59°45’10”	02°32’50”
59°43’10”	02°32’00”	59°45’15”	02°32’50”
59°43’10”	02°32’05”	59°45’15”	02°32’55”
59°43’15”	02°32’05”	59°45’20”	02°32’55”
59°43’15”	02°32’10”	59°45’20”	02°33’00”
59°43’30”	02°32’10”	59°45’25”	02°33’00”
59°43’30”	02°32’15”	59°45’25”	02°33’05”
59°43’35”	02°32’15”	59°45’30”	02°33’05”
59°43’35”	02°32’20”	59°45’30”	02°33’10”
59°43’45”	02°32’20”	59°45’35”	02°33’10”
59°43’45”	02°32’15”	59°45’35”	02°33’15”
59°44’10”	02°32’15”	59°45’45”	02°33’15”
59°44’10”	02°32’20”	59°45’45”	02°33’20”
59°44’15”	02°32’20”	59°45’50”	02°33’20”
59°44’15”	02°32’25”	59°45’50”	02°33’25”
59°44’30”	02°32’25”	59°46’00”	02°33’25”
59°44’30”	02°32’30”	59°46’00”	02°33’30”
59°44’50”	02°32’30”	59°46’05”	02°33’30”
59°44’50”	02°32’35”	59°46’05”	02°33’35”
59°44’55”	02°32’35”	59°46’10”	02°33’35”
59°44’55”	02°32’40”	59°46’10”	02°33’40”
59°45’00”	02°32’40”	59°46’15”	02°33’40”
59°45’00”	02°32’45”		

2003/2718

PETROLEUM REVENUE TAX (ELECTRONIC COMMUNICATIONS) REGULATIONS 2003

Made by the Inland Revenue under FA 1999 s 132

Made . . . .*23 October 2003*
Laid before the House of Commons . . . .*23 October 2003*
Coming into force . . . .*13 November 2003*

PART 1
INTRODUCTION

1 Citation, commencement and interpretation

(1) These Regulations may be cited as the Petroleum Revenue Tax (Electronic Communications) Regulations 2003 and shall come into force on 13th November 2003.

(2) In these Regulations—

"the Act" means the Oil Taxation Act 1975 and references, without more, to a numbered section or Schedule are to the section of, or Schedule to, the Act bearing that number;

"approved" means approved, for the purposes of these Regulations and for the time being, by means of a general or specific direction of the Board;

"the Management Act" means the Taxes Management Act 1970;

"the Board" means the Commissioners of Inland Revenue;

"field" means an oil field as defined in Schedule 1;

"official computer system" means a computer system maintained by or on behalf of the Board—

(*a*) to send or receive information, or

(*b*) to process or store information; "participator" has the meaning given in section 12; and

"responsible person" has the meaning given in paragraph 4 of Schedule 2.

(3) References in these Regulations to information and to the delivery of information shall be construed in accordance with section 132(8) of the Finance Act 1999.

2 Scope

These Regulations apply for the purposes of delivering information in, or in connection with, the claims, elections, notices and returns specified in the Schedule to these Regulations.

PART 2
ELECTRONIC COMMUNICATIONS—GENERAL PROVISIONS

3 Restriction on the use of electronic communications

(1) The Board may only use electronic communications in connection with the matters referred to in regulation 2 if—

(*a*) the recipient has indicated that he consents to the Board using electronic communications in connection with those matters; and

(*b*) the Board have not been informed that that consent has been withdrawn.

(2) A person other than the Board may only use electronic communications in connection with the matters referred to in regulation 2 if the conditions specified in paragraphs (3) to (6) are satisfied.

(3) The first condition is that the person is for the time being permitted to use electronic communications for the purpose in question by a general or specific direction of the Board.

(4) The second condition is that the person uses—

(*a*) an approved method for authenticating the identity of the sender of the communication;

(*b*) an approved method of electronic communications; and

(*c*) an approved method for authenticating any information delivered by means of electronic communications.

(5) The third condition is that any information sent by means of electronic communications is in a form approved.

Here "form" includes the manner in which the information is presented.

(6) The fourth condition is that the person maintains such records in written or electronic form as may be specified in a general or specific direction of the Board.

4 Use of intermediaries

The Board may use intermediaries in connection with—

(*a*) the delivery of information by means of electronic communications in connection with the matters referred to in regulation 2, and

(*b*) the authentication or security of anything transmitted by such means,

and may require other persons to use intermediaries in connection with those matters.

PART 3

ELECTRONIC COMMUNICATIONS—EVIDENTIAL PROVISIONS

5 Effect of delivering information by means of electronic communications

(1) Information to which these Regulations apply, and which is delivered by means of electronic communications, shall be treated as having been delivered, in the manner or form required by any provision of the Act or the Management Act which applies of the purpose of petroleum revenue tax if, but only if, all the conditions imposed by—

(*a*) these Regulations,

(*b*) any other applicable enactment (except to the extent that the condition thereby imposed is incompatible with these Regulations), and

(*c*) any specific or general direction given by the Board, are satisfied.

(2) Information delivered by means of electronic communications shall be treated as having been delivered on the day on which the last of the conditions imposed as mentioned in paragraph (1) is satisfied.

This is subject to paragraphs (3) and (4).

(3) The Board may by a general or specific direction provide for information to be treated as delivered upon a different date (whether earlier or later) than that given by paragraph (2).

(4) Information shall not be taken to have been delivered to an official computer system by means of electronic communications unless it is accepted by the system to which it is delivered.

6 Proof of content

(1) A document certified by an officer of the Board to be a printed-out version of any information delivered by means of electronic communications under these Regulations on any occasion shall be evidence, unless the contrary is proved, that that information—

(*a*) was delivered by means of electronic communications on that occasion; and

(*b*) constitutes the entirety of what was delivered on that occasion.

(2) A document purporting to be a certificate given in accordance with paragraph (1) shall be presumed to be such a certificate unless the contrary is proved.

7 Proof of sender or recipient

The identity of—

(*a*) the sender of any information delivered to an official computer system by means of electronic communications under these Regulations, or

(*b*) the recipient of any information delivered by means of electronic communications from an official computer system,

shall be presumed, unless the contrary is proved, to be the person recorded as such on an official computer system.

8 Information delivered electronically on another's behalf

Any information delivered by an approved method of electronic communications on behalf of any person shall be deemed to have been delivered by him unless he proves that it was delivered without his knowledge or connivance.

9 Proof of delivery of information

(1) The use of an authorised method of electronic communications shall be presumed, unless the contrary is proved, to have resulted in the delivery of information—

(*a*) in the case of information falling to be delivered to the Board, if the delivery of the information has been recorded on an official computer system; and

(*b*) in the case of information falling to be delivered by the Board, if the despatch of that information has been recorded on an official computer system.

(2) The use of an authorised method of electronic communications shall be presumed, unless the contrary is proved, not to have resulted in the delivery of information—

(*a*) in the case of information falling to be delivered to the Board, if the delivery of the information has not been recorded on an official computer system; and

(*b*) in the case of information falling to be delivered by the Board, if the despatch of that information has not been recorded on an official computer system.

(3) The time of receipt of any information sent by an authorised means of electronic communications shall be presumed, unless the contrary is proved, to be that recorded on an official computer system.

10 Use of unauthorised means of electronic communications

(1) Paragraph (2) applies to information which is required to be delivered to the Board in connection with the matters mentioned in regulation 2.

(2) The use of a means of electronic communications, for the purpose of delivering any information to which this paragraph applies, shall be conclusively presumed not to have resulted in the delivery of that information, unless—

(*a*) that means of electronic communications is for the time being approved for delivery of information of that kind; and (*b*) the sender is approved for the use of that means of electronic communications in relation to information of that kind.

SCHEDULE

Regulation 2

Information permitted to be delivered to the Board by means of electronic communications

1 A return by a participator under paragraph 2 of Schedule 2.

2 A return by a responsible person under paragraph 5 of Schedule 2.

3 An election by a responsible person under paragraph 1 of Schedule 5.

4 A claim made by a responsible person for expenditure under paragraph 2 of Schedule 5.

5 A claim made by a participator for expenditure under paragraph 1 of Schedule 6.

6 A claim by a participator for under paragraph 1 of Schedule 7 for the allowance of expenditure of any of the classes mentioned in that paragraph.

7 A notice by a responsible person under paragraph 1 of Schedule 8.

8 A claim by a participator under paragraph 4 of Schedule 8 for the allowance under section 6 of an unrelievable field loss.

9 A statement of tax payable on account under section 1 of the Petroleum Revenue Tax Act 1980.

10 A notice to the Board of the transfer of an interest in a field under paragraph 3 of Schedule 17 to the Finance Act 1980.

11 A return by a participator under section 62(4) of the Finance Act 1987.

12 An election by a participator under section 65 of the Finance Act 1987 for the allowance of expenditure as mentioned in subsection (1) of that section.

13 A participator's undertaking under regulation 5(5) of the Oil Taxation (Gas Banking Schemes) Regulations 1982 in connection with an application under regulation 5(2) of those Regulations.

14 An election under regulation 6 of the Oil Taxation (Gas Banking Schemes) Regulations 1982. For the purpose of this paragraph, regulation 6(2) of the 1982 Regulations shall have effect, in relation to an election which is made electronically, as if for "signed" there were substituted "authenticated in such manner as the Board may approve".

2006/3312

PETROLEUM REVENUE TAX (ATTRIBUTION OF BLENDED CRUDE OIL) REGULATIONS 2006

Made . . . . *13 December 2006*

Coming into force . . . . *14 December 2006*

A draft of these Regulations was laid before the House of Commons in accordance with section 2(5B) and (5D) of the Oil Taxation Act 1975.

The draft was approved by a resolution of that House.

Accordingly the Commissioners for Her Majesty's Revenue and Customs make the following Regulations in exercise of the powers conferred upon them by section 2(5B) to (5D) of the Oil Taxation Act 1975 and section 148(3) of the Finance Act 2006.

1 Citation and commencement

These Regulations may be cited as the Petroleum Revenue Tax (Attribution of Blended Crude Oil) Regulations 2006, shall come into force on the day following that on which they are made and shall have effect in respect of chargeable periods ending on or after 1st July 2006.

2 Interpretation

(1) In these Regulations—

"the Act" means the Finance Act 1987;

"balancing parcel" is the difference between—

(*a*) the volume of blended oil which a purchaser has notified to the participator as being required under the contract; and

(*b*) the volume of blended oil actually lifted under that contract;

"blended oil" has the meaning given by section 63(1A) of the Act;

PRT

"lifting" is—

(*a*) the loading of a volume of blended oil onto a tanker from an offshore loading point or an onshore oil terminal, or

(*b*) the transfer of a volume of blended oil by means of a pipeline to an onshore oil terminal,

and cognate expressions shall be construed accordingly;

"loading schedule" is the schedule produced each month by the terminal operator based upon the projected monthly production entitlement for each participator for the blended oil in question;

"month" is a calendar month and "monthly" shall be construed accordingly;

"nomination excess" is the amount by which the market value of a relevant delivery exceeds the participator's delivery proceeds of that relevant delivery (within the meaning of section 61(3) of the Act);

"opening stock"—

(*a*) in relation to the first month to which these Regulations apply in relation to a participator's interest in a particular originating field, is so much of the amount found by the latest computation of a participator's production entitlement in that field, used in constructing a loading schedule, as has not been lifted at the start of that month (and which may accordingly be a positive or negative value); and

(*b*) in relation to any later month to which these Regulations apply in relation to such an interest is—

(i) the participator's production entitlement in respect of that interest at the start of the preceding month; less

(ii) the total volume of oil lifted during the previous month and allocated, in accordance with these Regulations to that field;

"originating field" has the meaning given by section 63(1A) of the Act;

"period of entitlement contract" is a contract under which a participator sells its projected oil entitlement over a fixed period to a purchaser in return for regular payment, and under which the purchaser has discretion as to when to lift that oil;

"production entitlement" in relation to an originating field means the sum of—

(*a*) the participator's opening stock of oil from that field; and

(*b*) his qualifying production from that field;

"qualifying production" means—

(*a*) in the case of oil in a blend where oil is normally allocated to an originating field in advance of lifting, the projected production referred to in the loading schedule for the period in question; and

(*b*) in any other case, the amount of oil actually won by the participator from that field;

"relevant delivery" has the meaning given by paragraph 12A of Schedule 10 to the Act;

"term contract" is a contract for the sale of a volume of oil within a specified period which is subject to more than one delivery.

(2) Section 839 of the Income and Corporation Taxes Act 1988 (connected persons) applies to determine whether persons are connected with each other for the purposes of these Regulations.

3 Volume of oil

(1) For the purposes of the following provisions of these Regulations references to the volume of oil lifted shall be construed—

(*a*) if the conditions in paragraph (2) are satisfied, as a reference to the nominated volume; and

(*b*) in any other case, as a reference to the volume actually lifted.

(2) The conditions are that—

(*a*) the contract under which the oil is to be lifted entitles the purchaser to notify the participator of the volume of oil to be lifted under it ("the nominated volume");

(*b*) the agreement between the participator and the operator of the terminal from which the oil is actually to be lifted entitles the participator to allocate the nominated volume between the participator's field interests and provides for different treatment of the balancing parcel; and

(*c*) the nominated volume is allocated as mentioned in sub-paragraph (*b*).

(3) Regulation 6 (treatment of balancing parcels) applies where the conditions in paragraph (2) are satisfied.

(4) Any references in these Regulations to a volume of oil is to a volume calculated in barrels. For this purpose a barrel is a volume of 0.158987 cubic metres of oil.

4 Allocation of blended oil lifted

(1) For each lifting of blended oil by a participator in an originating field, the amount to be allocated to each originating field in respect of that lifting is—

$$A \times \frac{B}{C}$$

Here—

A is the volume of blended oil of a particular blend lifted by the participator in that lifting;

B is the total volume of the participator's production entitlement for that blend from the originating field for that month; and

C is the sum of—

(*a*) the participator's production entitlements from all originating fields for that blend, and

(*b*) so much of the seller's production entitlement in respect of oil of that blend for that period as the participator is entitled to lift under period of entitlement contracts,

but where an entitlement in respect of an originating field is a negative amount that entitlement shall be treated as zero in computing C.

These definitions are subject to the following qualifications.

(2) Where oil is lifted under a period of entitlement contract or a term contract regulation 5 applies.

(3) The final volume produced by application of the formula in paragraph (1) may be adjusted (up or down) by the participator by up to a maximum of 1000 barrels.

But the sum of the adjusted volumes in respect of each allocation must equal the total volume of blended oil lifted.

5 Period of Entitlement Contracts and Term Contracts

(1) Where a participator in an originating field sells blended oil under a period of entitlement contract or a term contract, and the contract relates to oil from more than one field, the following formula applies to determine how much of the volume of oil lifted and sold under the contract must be allocated to each originating field in the blend—

$$A \times \frac{B}{C}$$

Here—

A is the volume of blended oil lifted in the lifting in question;

B is the total volume of the participator's production entitlement for that blend from the originating field for that month under the terms of the contract; and

C is the sum of the participator's production entitlements from that blend from all originating fields for that month under the contract, but where an entitlement in respect of an originating field is a negative amount, that entitlement shall be treated as zero in computing C.

(2) The final volume produced by application of the formula in paragraph (1) may be adjusted (up or down) by the participator to a maximum of 1000 barrels.

But the sum of the adjusted volumes in respect of each allocation must be equal to the total volume of oil of the particular blend lifted.

6 Balancing parcels

(1) Where this regulation applies—

(*a*) the participator must notify Her Majesty's Revenue and Customs of an originating field ("the receiving field") to which balancing parcels of the particular blend of oil are to be attributed, and

(*b*) every balancing parcel in respect of that blend must be allocated to the receiving field, but subject to the following provisions of this regulation.

(2) When a receiving field ceases oil production, the participator must allocate balancing parcels to another originating field ("the substituted field"), and thereafter this regulation applies to the substituted field as it applied to the receiving field.

(3) Where the allocation, or continuing allocation, of a balancing parcel to a receiving field becomes impossible having regard to the terms of the agreement between the participator and the terminal operator for that field, the participator must notify Her Majesty's Revenue and Customs that another originating field is to be treated as the receiving field while those conditions persist.

(4) A notice under paragraph (3) must be given before the first allocation of a balancing parcel to the other originating field which is to be treated as the receiving field.

7 Sale of field interests

(1) If a participator ("the seller") agrees to sell a field interest to an unconnected party ("the buyer") the seller must notify Her Majesty's Revenue and Customs in writing of—

(*a*) the names of the buyer and seller;

(*b*) the field interest in question;

(*c*) the proposed completion date of the sale; and

(*d*) the cessation date.

(2) In this regulation "the cessation date" means the date after which, in accordance with the contract for the sale of the field interest, the seller will make no further lifting of oil won from that field interest, except as required by the terminal operator, prior to completion of the sale.
(3) The information must be provided to Her Majesty's Revenue and Customs no later than the first day of the month preceding the month in which the cessation date falls.
(4) From the later of the cessation date, or the end of the month in which falls the date on which the information specified in paragraph (1) is received by Her Majesty's Revenue and Customs—

- (*a*) any amounts lifted from that field interest ("the separated interest")shall be separated from the seller's other field interests for the purposes of calculating the allocation entitlements for that field; and
- (*b*) the entitlements in respect of the separated interest shall be calculated on the basis of the formula set out in paragraph (5).

(5) For each lifting of blended oil from the separated interest in a month, the following formula applies to determine the quantity of oil lifted from each of the fields from which the oil is derived—

$$A \times \frac{B}{C}$$

Here—

A is the volume of oil lifted;
B is the total amount of the seller's production entitlement for the separated interest for that month; and
C is the sum of the seller's production entitlement from all his separated interests for that month.

8 Sale of field interest—further provisions

(1) This regulation applies when, during a chargeable period—

- (*a*) a field interest, from which oil is used to produce blended crude oil, is sold to a buyer with whom the seller is not connected; and
- (*b*) the seller retains another field interest forming part of the same blend.

(2) Where this regulation applies, the adjustment to the closing stock is calculated as follows.
Step 1
Find the operational closing stock, that is to say the amount found by the formula E – L.
Here—
E is the sum of—

- (*a*) the participator's operational stock of oil won from that field interest at the start of the month in which the field interest is sold; and
- (*b*) the amount of oil actually won by the participator from that field interest during that month; and

L is the amount of oil actually lifted in that month and won from that field interest.
In paragraph (*a*) of the definition of E "operational stock" is so much of the amount found by the latest computation of a participator's production entitlement in that field, used in constructing a loading schedule, as has not been lifted at the start of that month (and which may accordingly be a positive or negative value).
Step 2
Find the tax closing stock, that is to say the amount found by the formula O + W – A
Here—

O is the opening stock at the start of the month in which the field interest is sold;
W is the amount of oil actually won by the participator from that field interest during that month; and
A is the amount of oil allocated to that field under regulations 4 to 6.

Step 3
Subtract the result of Step 2 from that of Step 1.
(3) The amount found under Step 3 (whether positive or negative) must be allocated to the other field interests in the blend of which the field interest to be sold is a part, in accordance with regulation 4 but, for the purposes of calculating C in regulation 4(1), the participator's production entitlement for the field interest being sold shall be zero.

9 Sale of field interest not proceeding

(1) In the event that it appears to the proposed seller that the sale of a field interest or interests will not proceed, the seller shall notify Her Majesty's Revenue and Customs, no later than the due date for his petroleum revenue tax return for the period in which the seller is first aware of this, that it will not proceed.
(2) Where a sale does not proceed—

(*a*) from the beginning of the month following that in which the seller is first aware that the sale will not proceed the separation of the field interest or interests which were the subject matter of the sale will cease; and

(*b*) thereafter the formula set out in regulation 4 will again apply for the purposes of allocating any lifting from that field or those fields.

10 Allocation of Nomination Excesses

Where a participator makes a relevant delivery of blended oil the following provisions apply to determine how much of his nomination excess to attribute to each originating field.

Step 1

Calculate the respective volumes of blended lifted oil to be allocated to individual originating fields applying the formula in regulation 4(1).

Step 2

Establish the total volume of the relevant delivery of blended oil.

Step 3

Divide each of the volumes calculated in Step 1 by the amount found under Step 2.

Step 4

Multiply each result of Step 3 by the nomination excess.

The result is the nomination excess to be allocated to the individual originating field in question.

2006/3313

OIL TAXATION (MARKET VALUE OF OIL) REGULATIONS 2006

Made . . . . 13 December 2006

Coming into force in accordance with . . . . regulation 1(1)

A draft of these Regulations was laid before the House of Commons in accordance with paragraph 10 of Schedule 3 to the Oil Taxation Act 1975.

The draft was approved by a resolution of that House.

Accordingly, the Commissioners for Her Majesty's Revenue and Customs make the following Regulations in exercise of the powers conferred by section 21(2) of, and paragraph 2(1B), (1C), (2E) and (2F) of Schedule 3 to that Act, and section 147(4) and (7) of the Finance Act 2006.

Introduction

1 Citation, commencement and effect

(1) These Regulations may be cited as the Oil Taxation (Market Value of Oil) Regulations 2006, and shall come into force on the day after that on which they are made.

(2) These Regulations have effect in relation to the first new period, within the meaning of section 147(4)(*b*) of FA 2006 (commencement and transitional provisions for amendments to Schedule 3 to OTA by section 146 of, and Schedule 18 to, FA 2006) and subsequent periods.

2 Interpretation

(1) This paragraph gives the meaning of the abbreviated references used in these Regulations—

"FA 2006" means the Finance Act 2006;

"ICTA" means the Income and Corporation Taxes Act 1988; and

"OTA" means the Oil Taxation Act 1975.

(2) This paragraph gives the meaning of other terms used in these Regulations—

"bank holiday" means a day which is a bank holiday in England and Wales under the Banking and Financial Dealings Act 1971;

"Category 1 oil" is oil of any of the kinds specified in regulation 3;

"relevantly appropriated" has the meaning given by section 12(1) of OTA.

(3) A sale of oil is at arm's length if (but only if) it satisfies paragraph 1 of Schedule 3 to OTA.

3 Category 1 oil

(1) Category 1 oil is oil of any of the following kinds—

(*a*) Brent blend;

(*b*) Ekofisk blend;

(*c*) Flotta blend;

(*d*) Forties blend;

(*e*) Statfjord oil.

(2) In these Regulations—

"Brent blend" means the blend of crude oils landed at Sullom Voe in Shetland via either the Brent or Ninian pipeline systems;

"Ekofisk blend" means the blend of crude oils landed at the Teesside Oil Terminal at Seal Sands via the Norpipe pipeline;

"Flotta blend" means the blend of crude oils landed at the Flotta Oil Terminal in Orkney and originating from the Flotta catchment area;

"Forties blend" means the blend of crude oils landed at Cruden Bay, Aberdeenshire via the Forties pipeline system;

"Statfjord oil" means oil to which article 23 of the Agreement between Her Majesty's Government of the United Kingdom and Northern Ireland and the Government of the Kingdom of Norway relating to the exploitation of the Statfjord Field Reservoirs signed at Oslo on 16th October 1979 applies.

4 Interpretation—reports and factors used in calculations

(1) In these Regulations the terms defined in the following paragraphs, which relate to the way in which the market value of a Category 1 oil is determined, have the meanings given there.

(2) "The relevant reports" means—

(*a*) Argus Crude published by Argus Media Limited, whose registered office is Argus House, St John Street London EC1V 4LW;

(*b*) ICIS (the Independent Chemical Information Services' World Crude Report), published by Reed Elsevier Group plc whose registered office is Quadrant House, The Quadrant, Sutton, Surrey, SM2 5AS; and

(*c*) Platts Oilgram published by Platts, a division of the McGraw-Hill Companies, whose registered office is Two Penn Plaza, 25th Floor, New York, NY 10121–2298.

(3) "The reference value" is the value quoted—

(*a*) in the case of Argus Crude as "Dated BFO" in the section of the report entitled "Atlantic Basin Crudes, London 16.30 hours, North Sea";

(*b*) in the case of ICIS, as "Dated BFO" in the North Sea 3rd Update; and

(*c*) in the case of Platts Oilgram, as "Brent (DTD)" in the International section of the report.

(4) "Adjustment factor" means the differential, upon the day in question, from the reference value—

(*a*) found, in the case of Brent blend, in accordance with regulation 14;

(*b*) for any other Category 1 oil, shown—

(i) in the case of Argus Crude, in the report under "Atlantic Basin Crudes, London 16.30 hours North Sea";

(ii) in the case of ICIS, in North Sea 3rd Update; and

(iii) in the case of Platts Oilgram, as the assessment of the spread against forward dated Brent blend (described in the report as "spread vs fwd DTD Brent").

Scope

5 General scope of these Regulations

These Regulations apply for the purpose of determining the market value of oil won from a field to which section 2(5)(*b*) or (*c*) of OTA applies and which is—

(*a*) delivered, or relevantly appropriated, on or after 1st July 2006; or

(*b*) held by a participator and not delivered at the end of a chargeable period.

Valuing Category 1 Oil

6 General

The method of determining the market value of Category 1 oil to which these Regulations apply is as follows—

(*a*) find the notional delivery day (see regulations 7 and 8);

(*b*) find the average reference value for that day (see regulations 9 to 12);

(*c*) add the adjustment factor (see regulations 13 to 15); and

(*d*) find the total market value of the oil (see regulation 16).

7 The notional delivery day: the general rule

(1) The general rule is that the notional delivery day is found in accordance with paragraph 1A of Schedule 3 to OTA (determination of market value: notional delivery day for a quantity of oil).

(2) The general rule is subject to regulation 8.

8 The notional delivery day: additional rule

(1) Paragraph (2) applies to a delivery of Category 1 oil by way of a sale otherwise than at arm's length if—

(*a*) during any period of 24 months, beginning on or after 1st July 2006, the total quantity of equity oil of that type disposed of by a participator and persons connected with him is not less than 4,000,000 barrels;

(*b*) a lower price would fall to be taken into account in determining the participator's gross profit under section 2(1) of OTA for the delivery from that which would have applied if it had been by way of a sale at arm's length;

(c) the reason for that lower price is because the notional delivery day is a day other than that on which the actual delivery takes place;

(d) the whole or main benefit which might reasonably be expected to be obtained from a sale otherwise than at arm's length, when compared with a sale at arm's length, is a tax advantage within the meaning of section 709 of ICTA.

2) The notional delivery day is the day specified in paragraph (a) or (b) (as the case requires) of paragraph 1A(7) of Schedule 3 to OTA.

3) In this regulation—

"barrel" means a volume of 0.158987 cubic metres of oil; and

"equity oil" means oil forming part of the trading stock of a participator or a person connected with him which has been won by that participator or a person connected with him from a field in the United Kingdom sector of the North Sea.

(4) Section 839 of ICTA (connected persons) applies for determining whether persons are connected for the purposes of this regulation.

9 The average reference value: notional delivery day one for which reference values available

(1) If the notional delivery day is a day for which reference values are available find the daily average of the reference values from each of the three relevant reports for—

(a) each of the two dates immediately preceding the notional delivery day;

(b) the notional delivery day; and

(c) each of the two dates immediately following notional delivery day.

(2) If any of the relevant reports contains more than one reference value for any of these dates, the result for that report for that date is the arithmetical mean of those values.

(3) Find the average of the daily averages found for each of the five days referred to in paragraph (1).

(4) The result is the average reference value for the notional delivery day.

10 The average reference value: notional delivery day a Saturday, or a Bank Holiday which is not a Monday, and for which reference values not available

(1) If the notional delivery day is not a day for which reference values are available but is a Saturday, or a bank holiday which is not a Monday, find the daily average of the reference values from each of the three relevant reports for—

(a) each of the three business days immediately preceding the notional delivery day; and

(b) each of the two business days immediately following the notional delivery day.

(2) If any of the relevant reports contains more than one reference value for any of these dates, the result for that report for that date is the arithmetical mean of those values.

(3) Find the average of the daily averages found for each of the five days referred to in paragraph (1).

(4) The result is the average reference value for the notional delivery day.

11 The average reference value: notional delivery day a Sunday, or a Bank Holiday which is a Monday

(1) If the notional delivery day is not a day for which reference values are available but is a Sunday, or a bank holiday which is a Monday, find the daily average of the reference values from each of the three relevant reports for—

(a) each of the two business days immediately preceding the notional delivery day; and

(b) each of the three business days immediately following the notional delivery day.

(2) If any of the relevant reports contains more than one reference value for any of these dates, the result for that report for that date is the arithmetical mean of those values.

(3) Find the average of the daily averages found for each of the five days referred to in paragraph (1).

(4) The result is the average reference value for the notional delivery day.

12 The average reference value: additional provisions

(1) If in respect of any of the days specified in a provision of regulation 9, 10 or 11 one or two of the relevant reports is not published, that provision has effect as if references to the relevant reports were to such of the relevant reports as are actually published in respect of that day.

(2) If in respect of any of the days specified in a provision of regulation 9, 10 or 11 other than the notional delivery day, none of the relevant reports is published ("a non-publication day"), that provision has effect as if—

(a) references to a day which is a non-publication day falling before the notional delivery day were to the day falling next before that day on which at least one of the relevant reports is published; and

(b) references to a day which is a non-publication day falling after the notional delivery day were to the day falling next after that day on which at least one of the relevant reports is published.

(3) If the application of the rule in paragraph (2) would lead to the reports for a day being taken into account more than once, a reference to the day falling next before, or after, the non-publication day shall be read as a reference to the first day falling next before or after (as the case may be) the non-publication day which would not otherwise be taken into account for the purposes of this regulation.

(4) In cases where the date of completion of load or the date of the bill of lading is substituted for the notional delivery day under regulation 8, references in this regulation to the notional delivery day are to be read as references to the day substituted under that regulation.

13 The adjustment factors—general

(1) The adjustment factor applicable to the Category 1 oil in question must be added to the average reference value.

(2) The adjustment factor is found—

(*a*) in accordance with regulation 14 in the case of Brent blend; and

(*b*) in accordance with regulation 15 in the case of other Category 1 oil.

14 Adjustment factor—Brent blend

(1) The adjustment factor for Brent blend is found as follows.

(2) Find the daily average of the differentials from the reference value quoted in the relevant reports for each of the days—

(*a*) during the period which begins 21 days, and ends 14 days before the notional delivery day and

(*b*) in respect of which at least one such report is produced,

as follows.

(3) Find the Argus Crude differential for a particular day by taking the value shown as the "Brent" assessment and subtracting from it the value shown as "Dated BFO" in that report.

(4) Find the ICIS differential for a particular day by taking the value shown as the "Brent" assessment and subtracting from it the value shown as "Dated BFO" in that report.

(5) Find the Platts differential for a particular day by taking the value for "Brent Assessment 10–21 days out" in Platts Crude Oil Marketwire and subtracting from it the value for "North Sea Dated Strip" in that report.

(6) In this regulation "Platts Crude Oil Marketwire" means the report of that name published by Platts, a division of the McGraw-Hill Companies, whose registered office is Two Penn Plaza, 25th Floor, New York, NY 10121–2298.

(7) If any of the reports referred to in this regulation contains more than one value for the relevant quote for any of these days, the result for that report for that day is the arithmetical mean of those values.

(8) Find the average of the daily averages found in accordance with this regulation for each of the days specified in paragraph (2).

(9) The result is the adjustment factor for Brent blend.

15 Adjustment factor—other Category 1 oil

(1) The adjustment factor for a Category 1 oil other than Brent blend is found as follows.

(2) Find the daily average of the differentials, from reference value, for the Category 1 oil in question quoted in the three relevant reports for each of the days—

(*a*) during the period which begins 21 days, and ends 14 days before the notional delivery day, and

(*b*) in respect of which at least one such report is produced.

(3) If any of the relevant reports contains more than one value for the Category 1 oil in question for any of these days, the result for that report for that day is the arithmetical mean of those values.

(4) Find the average of the daily averages found by paragraphs (2) and (3) for each of the days specified in paragraph (2).

(5) The result is the adjustment factor for the relevant Category 1 oil.

16 The total market value of the oil

(1) The total market value of a volume of Category 1 oil to which these Regulations apply is found as follows—

(*a*) take the average reference value for the notional delivery day (see regulations 9 to 12);

(*b*) add the adjustment factor applicable to the Category 1 oil in question (see regulations 13 to 15); and

(*c*) multiply the sum found by sub-paragraph (*b*) by the volume of Category 1 oil in question.

(2) The result is the total market value of the oil.

Valuing Category 2 Oils

17 Market value: Category 2 oils

The market value of a quantity of Category 2 oil to which these Regulations apply is found by whichever of the methods in regulation 18 (method 1) or regulations 19 to 23 (method 2) would produce a sum which more closely reflects the price which would normally apply in a sale at arm's length for a similar quantity of that oil on the notional delivery day (found in accordance with paragraph 1A of Schedule 3 to OTA), but subject to the special rules in regulation 24.

18 Method 1

The first method is to find the average unit price for actual sales at arm's length of the relevant Category 2 oil under contracts meeting the conditions set out in paragraphs (*a*) to (*e*) of paragraph 2(2AA) of Schedule 3 to OTA.

19 Method 2: general

The second method is as follows—

(*a*) find the relevant reference oils ("the marker crudes") for the relevant Category 2 oil (see regulation 20);

(*b*) find the average marker crude price quoted in respect of the relevant Category 2 oil (see regulation 21);

(*c*) adjust the average marker crude price (see regulation 22);

(*d*) find the total market value of the oil (see regulation 23).

20 Finding the relevant reference oils for the Category 2 oil in question

Ascertain which crude oils are normally used as marker crudes for the purposes of determining the market value of the relevant Category 2 oil under contracts at arm's length.

21 Finding the average marker crude price

(1) Find the average of the prices quoted by the relevant reports for the sale of the marker crudes in respect of trades during the reference period in contracts for the sale at arm's length of the relevant Category 2 oil.

(2) In paragraph (1) "the reference period" means the period ordinarily used to find the market value of oils, by reference to which the price of the oil in question is determined, in a contract for the sale of that oil at arm's length.

22 Adjusting the average marker crude price

Add to the result of regulation 21 differential or combination of differentials normally applied in a contract for the sale at arm's length of the relevant Category 2 oil.

23 Total value of the Category 2 oil sold or relevantly appropriated

(1) Multiply the result of regulation 22 by the volume of Category 2 oil to which these Regulations apply in the particular case.

(2) The product so found is the market value of the Category 2 oil in question.

(3) This is subject to regulation 24.

24 Special rules

(1) If a participator's contracts for the sale of Category 2 oil in sales at arm's length normally provide for the price to be determined—

(*a*) in the case of oil transported by ship from the place of extraction to a place in the United Kingdom or elsewhere, by reference to the actual date of the completion of the load, or completion of the discharge, of the cargo; or

(*b*) in the case of oil transported by pipeline to a place in the United Kingdom and loaded on to a ship there, by reference to the date of the bill of lading;

references to the notional delivery day in regulation 17 are to be construed, in relation to that participator as references to the day mentioned in sub-paragraph (a) or (b) (as the case requires).

(2) The modification in paragraph (1) also applies where Category 2 oil is loaded onto a ship at least 7 days later than the date provided for by the contract for sale by reason of circumstances wholly beyond the control of the parties.

2010/610

FIELD ALLOWANCE FOR NEW OIL FIELDS ORDER 2010

Made . . . . *4 March 2010*

Coming into force in accordance with . . . . *article 1(1)*

Revocation—This Order revoked by the Qualifying Oil Fields Order, SI 2012/3153 art 7 with effect from 21 December 2012.

2013/2910

ADDITIONALLY-DEVELOPED OIL FIELDS ORDER 2013

Made . . . . *15 November 2013*

Coming into force in accordance with article 1

The Commissioners for Her Majesty's Revenue and Customs make the following Order, in exercise of the powers conferred by sections 349 and 349A of the Corporation Tax Act 2010 and paragraph 22 of Schedule 22 to the Finance Act 2012.

PRT

In accordance with sections 349 and 349A of the Corporation Tax Act 2010, a draft of this Order was laid before the House of Commons and approved by a resolution of that House.

1 Citation, commencement and interpretation

(1) This Order may be cited as the Additionally-developed Oil Fields Order 2013 and is treated as having come into force on 1st April 2013.

(2) In this Order "CTA 2010" means the Corporation Tax Act 2010.

2 Additionally-developed oil field

(1) The conditions which a project that is described in a consent for development of an oil field must meet for the purposes of section 349A(1)(*b*) of CTA 2010 are as follows.

(2) Condition A is that the project was authorised as mentioned in section 349A(1)(*a*) of CTA 2010 on or after 7th September 2012.

(3) Condition B is that the cost per tonne of the project is more than £60.

(4) Condition C is that the additional reserves of oil which the field has as a result of the project have not been taken into account in calculating the cost per tonne of any qualifying project that has previously been authorised in relation to the field.

(5) A project authorised in relation to an oil field is a "qualifying project" for the purposes of paragraph (4) if a field allowance has at any time been held for the field as a result of the project.

(6) Condition D is that, as at the authorisation day, the whole of the oil field lies on the seaward side of the baselines from which the territorial sea is measured.

(7) Condition E is that the project does not involve enhanced oil recovery using carbon dioxide.

(8) For the purposes of this article the "cost per tonne" of a project authorised in relation to an oil field means the amount given by—

E/*R*

where—

E is the expected capital expenditure of the project (see paragraph (9)), and

R is the sum of the amounts of additional reserves of oil (in tonnes) which the field and any other oil fields have as a result of the project.

(9) The expected capital expenditure of a project is to be determined as follows—

Step 1

Calculate the amount of capital expenditure which it is reasonably expected, as at the authorisation day, will be incurred in carrying out the project.

In calculating that amount, ignore any expenditure incurred before the authorisation day which, if the project had not been authorised, would have been wasted expenditure.

Step 2

Calculate the amount of any capital expenditure which it is reasonably expected, as at the authorisation day, would have been incurred on or after that day if the project had not been authorised.

In calculating that amount, ignore any expenditure which—

(*a*) would have been incurred under an agreement entered into before the authorisation day, and

(*b*) would not have been wasted expenditure.

Step 3

Deduct the amount given by step 2 from the amount given by step 1.

But if the amount given by step 2 is greater than the amount given by step 1, the expected capital expenditure of the project is nil.

(10) In determining the expected capital expenditure of a project—

(*a*) where an amount attributed to an item of expenditure includes an amount for contingencies, the amount so included may not exceed 20% of the amount that would be attributed to that item of expenditure in the absence of any amount for contingencies,

(*b*) expenditure is not to be treated as wasted expenditure to the extent that it is recoverable, and

(*c*) the following are to be disregarded—

(i) any decommissioning expenditure (within the meaning of section 330C of CTA 2010), and

(ii) any payments of interest.

(11) For the purposes of this article—

(*a*) the amount of additional reserves of oil which a field has is to be determined on the authorisation day,

(*b*) 1,100 cubic metres of gas at a temperature of 15 degrees celsius and pressure of one atmosphere is to be counted as equivalent to one tonne,

(*c*) "authorisation day", in relation to a project, means the day when the project is authorised as mentioned in section 349A(1)(*a*) of CTA 2010, and

(*d*) "territorial sea" means the territorial sea of the United Kingdom.

3–12 Amendments of CTA 2010

(the amendments to CTA 2010 are already in force and are therefore not reproduced here — see Yellow Tax Handbook Part 1)

Extra-Statutory Concessions

PRT

Contents

PRT

Extra-statutory Concessions

I5 PETROLEUM REVENUE TAX INSTALMENTS

Finance Act 1982 Sch 19 para 3(1), entitles a participator, on giving notice to the Board, to withhold the instalment due for a month under paragraph 2 of the Schedule if, in the previous month, he did not deliver or relevantly appropriate any of the oil won from the field. By concession, a participator is also entitled, again on giving notice to the Board, to withhold the instalment for a month if in the previous or an earlier month, oil actually ceased to be won from the field as a result of some sudden catastrophic loss of or damage to production, transportation or initial treatment facilities relating to the field, and has not recommenced.

Statements of Practice

Note—This statement has no binding force and does not affect a taxpayer's right of appeal on points concerning liability to tax.

PRT

Contents

Statements of Practice

SP 6/84 NON-RESIDENT LESSORS—TA 1988 S 830

Where mobile drilling rigs, vessels or equipment leased by a non-resident lessor are used in connection with exploration or exploitation activities carried on in the UK or in a designated area, the question of whether the profits or gains arising from the lease constitute income from such activities depends on the facts and circumstances of each particular case. However, the practice of HMRC is not to seek to charge such profits or gains to tax under TA 1988 s 830 if all of the following conditions are satisfied—

1 the contract is concluded outside the UK and the designated areas;

2 the lessor's obligations are limited to the provision of the asset, eg, a rig on "bare-boat" terms, that is to say, if the lessor has not undertaken to provide any facilities, service or personnel;

3 the lessee takes delivery of the asset outside the designated areas, and is responsible for moving it to the place where it is used, and is not restricted to using it solely in the UK or a designated area;

4 the lessee and lessor are not connected persons, and no facilities, services or personnel related to the operation of the asset are provided by any person connected with the lessor.

Commentary—*Simon's Taxes* **D4.401.**

Press Releases etc

PRT

Contents

Press Releases etc

SAFEGUARD AND DEFERRED EXPENDITURE CLAIMS

16 December 1987

In reply to a Parliamentary Question today, asked whether he intended to introduce legislation to amend the rules for the claiming and allowance of PRT relief for field expenditure incurred by oil companies before the end of a chargeable period where the special safeguard relief provision reduces or cancels PRT payable, the Economic Secretary Mr Peter Lilley gave the following written answer—

"No. I asked the Revenue to carry out a review of the interaction between the timing of claims for PRT expenditure relief and the special safeguard relief which can reduce or cancel a company's PRT liability during a number of chargeable periods once a field reaches payback (the net profit period as defined in FA 1981 s 11). In respect of these periods it can be advantageous for a company not to claim relief for field expenditure in time for it to be allowed in the assessment for the chargeable period in which it was incurred. The expenditure is then available to be claimed against PRT liability for a later chargeable period. The safeguard relief was introduced as a special overriding relief designed to ensure that PRT—calculated after taking account of all other available reliefs and allowances—does not reduce a participator's return on capital in any chargeable period (up to a prescribed time limit) to 15% or less. It was not originally intended that further benefit should be available by deferring field expenditure claims so that expenditure incurred before the end of a chargeable period where PRT is reduced or cancelled by safeguard is claimed and allowed against profits of a later chargeable period.

Nevertheless, the Government has decided, in the light of representations received during the review and in the current situation in the oil market, not to bring forward legislation in next year's Finance Bill to prevent extra relief from being obtained by means of deferring expenditure claims. The Revenue have a choice over the timing of assessments which could also be exercised to counteract the benefit of deferring expenditure claims, but they will not use this power in these special circumstances to defer assessments for periods from payback where safeguard relief reduces or cancels liability. This decision in relation to safeguard does not have any application to the timing of assessments in other circumstances."

NOTE

Safeguard, introduced as the Oil Taxation Act 1975 s 9, is one of the special reliefs in PRT designed to protect less profitable fields. It cancels or limits PRT liability until a few years after a field reaches payback if profits fall below a given level in relation to the capital investment in the field. It operates for chargeable periods up to payback and for half as many chargeable periods again. In any of these periods, if the PRT charge would otherwise reduce the return on a field before corporation tax to less than 15% of cumulative upliftable expenditure, the charge is to be cancelled. A tapering provision ensures that the PRT charge will not be more than 80% of the amount (if any) by which the profit exceeds 15% of the cumulative upliftable expenditure.

Safeguard is only applied where it is to a company's advantage. To decide that, the PRT (if any) due under the safeguard rules is compared with the PRT due under the normal rules. Under the latter, PRT is charged after taking account of expenditure (including uplift) which is both claimed and allowed. Where safeguard reduces or cancels PRT liability for a chargeable period it can be beneficial for companies not to claim relief for field expenditure incurred before the end of that period in time for it to be allowed in the assessment on the profits earned in that period. Instead the company can save it for a claim against PRT liability in a later period. This is not the way in which it was originally intended that the safeguard relief rules should operate.

Nevertheless, in the light of the current situation in the oil market, Ministers have decided not to legislate in next year's Finance Bill to prevent companies from obtaining extra relief by means of deferring expenditure claims. Nor will the Revenue, who have a choice over the timing of assessments, use that power to defer assessments for chargeable periods from payback where safeguard reduces or cancels liability, in order to counteract the deferring of expenditure claims. This decision does not have any application to the timing of assessments in other circumstances.

Ministers' decision not to legislate in the 1988 Finance Bill will mean that some companies in less profitable fields which have been adversely affected by the fall in oil prices will not only be able to have their PRT liability reduced or eliminated by safeguard in the early years but will also be able to get more expenditure relief later on.

OIL TAXATION

27 November 1991

The Economic Secretary to the Treasury, John Maples, announced today that the Government intend to introduce legislation in the 1992 Finance Bill to amend the Petroleum Revenue Tax (PRT) and North Sea 'ring fence' corporation tax (CT) rules. In a written reply to a Parliamentary Question the Economic Secretary said:

> "Some future North Sea projects may involve the landing of gas outside the United Kingdom, or its initial treatment or storage outside the UK or the UK continental shelf. At present, the Petroleum Revenue Tax (PRT) and 'ring fence' corporation tax (CT) rules do not cater for these situations. To ensure that these tax rules do not distort the economics of such investments, we propose bringing forward legislation in the next Finance Bill to take account of new developments of this kind. In particular PRT relief, and CT relief within the "ring fence", will be given for the cost of transporting oil or gas to the nearest reasonable place of delivery outside the United Kingdom; and relief for initial treatment and storage costs will similarly be extended to costs incurred outside the United Kingdom or the United Kingdom continental shelf. Relevant expenditure already incurred will qualify for this new relief.
>
> A double charge to both PRT and gas levy could arise if gas were sold, under a new contract, from a reservoir which was previously exploited under a contract which pre-dated PRT and so was subject to gas levy instead. Although production under the new contract would be within the scope of PRT, gas levy would under the present law still be payable. To remove this unintended double charge, the proposed legislation will cancel gas levy when a PRT exempt gas contract which already contains a single fixed termination date comes to an end at that date, and gas from the reservoir begins to be sold under a new contract which is not exempt from PRT.
>
> These changes should encourage companies to proceed with worthwhile and substantial North Sea investments."

DETAILS

1. For both PRT and ring fence CT, the costs of transporting oil and gas to shore, and, if further, to the first "reasonable place of delivery" are allowable, as well as initial treatment and initial storage costs. But this only applies where the landfall is in the UK, and any initial treatment and storage are in the UK or on the UK continental shelf. Some future North Sea developments are likely to involve the direct landing in other countries of UK oil or gas produced offshore, and also initial treatment either on another country's continental shelf or abroad. Where oil or gas are landed overseas, the taxable price or value will reflect the cost of getting it to shore. The changes the Government propose will ensure that the corresponding costs – transport and treatment – are allowable for tax and that the place at which oil or gas is valued, where necessary, for tax purposes corresponds with the place to which transport costs are allowed. Further minor related changes will also be proposed to ensure essentially equivalent treatment whatever arrangements are made for the sale and transport to shore of oil or gas.

2. Double taxation issues could arise in the future in connection with any tariffs from third party use of UK field assets on a foreign continental shelf for which PRT expenditure relief has been given under this proposal. Such issues, if they arise, would need to be discussed with the foreign country concerned in the context of the relevant bilateral Double Taxation Convention. Depending on the outcome of any such discussions it might be necessary at some future date for the Government to introduce measures to ensure that excessive PRT relief was not given on assets giving rise to tariff receipts in this way.

3. Oil and gas projects are major investments with long planning and development time scales. Work is already under way on some projects which, if they went ahead, would benefit from the changes outlined above. That is why the Government have announced these changes now, and why expenditure incurred before today will qualify for the new reliefs.

IR NOTES

When PRT was introduced in 1975, it contained an exemption for gas sold to British Gas under contracts entered into before July 1975. In 1981, gas levy (administered by the Department of Energy) became payable by the purchaser of gas from reservoirs where there was a PRT-exempt contract. If gas from the reservoir were sold other than under the PRT-exempt contract (for example where the contract reached its intended termination date but the field was not yet exhausted) gas levy would continue, but would then be payable by the producer. Since the new contract would not be exempt from PRT, the double charge could impose effective taxation of over 100% on gas produced after the PRT-exempt contract came to an end. Abolition of the unintended double charge in these circumstances will remove a hindrance to long-term substantial incremental investment in levy-paying fields.

EXPENDITURE CLAIMS—CHANGE OF PRACTICE

April 1996. *Tax Bulletin*

Qualifying expenditure is relieved for Petroleum Revenue Tax (PRT) under rules set out in the Oil Taxation Act 1975. The previous practice of the department was to allow an expenditure claim to be withdrawn only in limited circumstances. But, in the light of recent legal advice, the Board now accepts that a claimant may withdraw any claim or part of any claim to the extent that a decision has not been taken on it in respect of the withdrawn expenditure in question.

Oil industry representative bodies were recently advised of this change of view in the following terms—

> "Withdrawal of Expenditure Claims
>
> You will be aware that we have recently received advice on this topic. I am writing now to confirm our change of practice following that advice. We are advised that any claim can be withdrawn to the extent that a decision has not been taken on it in respect of the withdrawn expenditure. But where a decision has been taken to allow some, or all, of the claimed expenditure, that claim, or part of the claim as appropriate, cannot be withdrawn. The withdrawn expenditure may be included in a fresh claim, provided that the conditions for making such a claim are still satisfied (for example that the time limit for claiming the expenditure relief has not expired).
>
> There is no change in the Board's view of a claim for supplement, which, if it is claimed, must be included in a claim for the associated expenditure. It follows that if a claim for expenditure qualifying for supplement is withdrawn, then so also is any associated supplement claim. To the extent that a decision has not been taken on the claim in respect of expenditure identified as qualifying for supplement, the claimant can withdraw the claim which must include the associated supplement. The claimant may make a fresh claim for the expenditure (subject to the conditions for submitting the claim still being satisfied) without the expenditure necessarily being identified as qualifying for supplement."

TAX CREDIT RELIEF

10 April 2007. *HMRC Brief 35/07*

SHARJAH – PETROLEUM REVENUE TAX

HMRC has changed its view on the admissibility of the Petroleum Revenue Tax charged in Sharjah on profits arising out of production sharing contracts or petroleum concession agreements entered into between companies and the Emirate of Sharjah.

We now consider this tax to be paid under the law of a territory outside the United Kingdom and computed by reference to income arising in Sharjah. It will therefore qualify for unilateral relief under Section 790 Income and Corporation Taxes Act 1988.

The amount of relief due in a particular case (including any further claims arising from this change of view) should be agreed in the usual way with:

PRT

CT & VAT
Underlying Tax Group
Fitz Roy House
PO Box 46
Nottingham NG2 1BD

(DT16751) will be amended shortly to reflect this change of The Double Taxation Relief guidance manual view.

If you have any queries arising from this change please contact:

Kevin Madley
HMRC
Frontiers & International Tax Treaty Team
100 Parliament Street
London SW1A 2BQ
Tel: 020 7147 2661

NEW FIELD ALLOWANCE FOR GAS IN THE NORTH SEA

25 July 2012. *HMRC Notice*

The Chancellor of the Exchequer has today announced a new tax relief to support gas investment in the UK Continental Shelf.

A £500m field allowance for large shallow-water gas fields will be established with the aim of securing future investment in North Sea gas, creating jobs and bolstering the UK's energy security.

The Government has pledged to publish a gas strategy later in the year with the aim of giving certainty to investors on the UK's long-term commitment to gas as a vital part of the transition towards low-carbon energy generation.

The Chancellor said:

"Gas is the single biggest source of energy in the UK. Today the government is signalling its long-term commitment to the role it can play in delivering a stable, secure and lower-carbon energy mix. At the Budget, we announced an ambitious package of support to stimulate billions of investment in oil and gas production in the North Sea. Today's news is a further sign of the Government's determination to get the most out of a huge national asset."

The Energy Secretary has today also announced the level of the Renewables Obligation Certification (ROC) banding for onshore wind electricity generation until March 2014 and confirmed the ongoing importance of gas as part of the UK's energy mix.

Taken together, these announcements are intended to give investors the long-term certainty needed to make decisions on investment in both gas and renewable power.

NOTES

1. At Budget 2011, the Chancellor said that he would consider the case for introducing a new category of field allowance for marginal gas fields. Today's allowance will apply to new large shallow-water gas fields, defined as fields:

- Whose development is authorised for the first time on or after 25 July 2012;
- With a share of gas reserves greater than 95% based on the central estimates of oil and gas reserves at the time of development authorisation;
- With water depth less than 30 metres.

The maximum allowance will be available to fields with a central estimate of gas reserves between 10 billion cubic metres (bcm) and 20 bcm, tapering to no allowance at 25 bcm.

Two or more fields qualifying on the same day will be considered together for the purpose of meeting the gas reserves criterion, with the total allowance to be allocated between them in proportion to their respective central estimates of gas reserves.

2. The allowance will protect £500m of income from qualifying fields from the 32 per cent Supplementary Charge (SC) tax rate. These fields will still pay 30 per cent Ring Fence Corporation Tax (RFCT) on all income from the field, in addition to SC on all income not protected by the field allowance.

3. This measure is expected to cost approximately £20 million per annum. The final costing will be subject to scrutiny by the Office for Budget Responsibility, and will be set out at Autumn Statement 2012.

4. As the Chancellor announced at Budget 2012, the Government will continue to work with the oil and gas industry to consider how a potential brown field allowance could be structured to unlock investment, while protecting Exchequer revenues. It is also consulting on a contractual approach to provide greater certainty on decommissioning tax relief.

REVIEW OF UK OFFSHORE OIL AND GAS RECOVERY

10 June 2013. *Written Ministerial Statement*

Rt Hon Edward Davey MP: Secretary of State for Energy and Climate Change - The UK's oil and gas industry is of national importance. It plays a vital part in our economic life and makes a substantial contribution to our energy security. For decades the oil and gas sector has been one of the UK's major industrial success stories, a key contributor to growth, jobs and tax revenue. The industry supports 440,000 jobs directly or indirectly and paid £11.2 billion in direct taxes in 2011 – 2012, almost a quarter of all corporation taxes received by the Exchequer. Investment in the UK Continental Shelf has risen substantially in recent years, and investment in 2013, up to £14 billion, will reach an all-time high.

Some 41 billion barrels of oil and gas have already been produced from the UK Continental Shelf, and 20 billion or more could still to be produced. Although peak production is now behind us, we must maintain our momentum and make the most of the huge opportunity that the UK Continental Shelf still represents. In addition to the economic importance, maximising recovery of the UK's indigenous supplies of oil and gas will also help maintain security of supply as we continue on our journey to a low-carbon future.

While investment levels are rising and the near-term prospects for the UK Continental Shelf are strong, it is one of the most mature offshore basins in the world, and therefore faces unprecedented challenges that require new thinking. For example declining exploration and production rates, ageing infrastructure and declining production efficiency, and the risk of premature decommissioning of key infrastructure all need to be addressed if we are to extract the maximum economic benefit for the UK.

Government already has an excellent working relationship with the oil and gas industry through our PILOT partnership, which has made significant contributions to addressing some of these challenges over the last decade. However, I have come to the view that the challenges we now face are of sufficient importance that they merit a focused, in-depth review. Such a review has not been conducted since the early 1990s when the challenges faced were very different to those we face now.

I have therefore invited Sir Ian Wood, recently-retired chair of Wood Group, a leading UK oil services company, to lead such a review. Sir Ian will bring huge experience to the task following a career spanning four decades of leadership in the UK Continental Shelf. He will work with leaders across industry, Government and elsewhere to produce robust analysis, conclusions and recommendations for improving future economic recovery of UK Continental Shelf oil and gas.

Since 2011 there has been a range of changes to the tax regime which industry has welcomed and which has led to significant new investment. It is too soon to review the effectiveness of these changes and so this review will focus on other factors such as the licensing regime, optimising use of and extending life of infrastructure, production efficiency, better collaboration across the industry, increasing the exploration effort and maximising the use of enhanced oil recovery techniques. It will also look at the current structure, scale and effectiveness of the Government stewardship regime in line with the increased technical and commercial complexity of the mature market. While the Review will not make recommendations on taxation, its conclusions may nevertheless be drawn upon in future tax policy considerations by HM Treasury.

I expect emerging conclusions from the review to be published in the autumn and the final report and recommendations to be published in early 2014.

This is an exciting time for the UK's offshore oil and gas industry and its extensive supply chain, and I look forward to seeing the recommendations of Sir Ian's important work.

OIL AND GAS: DECOMMISSIONING RELIEF DEED AND GUIDANCE ON APPLICATIONS

7 November 2013. *HM Treasury Notice*

Introduced by Finance Act 2013, the Decommissioning Relief Deed (DRD) is a contract between the government and qualifying companies operating in the UK and UK Continental Shelf, to provide certainty on the tax relief they will receive when decommissioning assets.

The DRD provides that, in such circumstances as are specified in the agreement, if the amount of tax relief in respect of any decommissioning expenditure incurred by the qualifying company is less than an amount determined in accordance with the agreement, the difference is payable to the company.

The government has now published a final version of the model DRD and guidance for applications.

— Decommissioning Relief Deed: www.gov.uk/government/uploads/system/uploads/attachment_data/file/255650/Decommissioning_Relief_Deed.DOC

— Guidance on applying for a Decommissioning Relief Deed: www.gov.uk/government/uploads/system/uploads/attachment_data/file/255651/131029_-_HMG_guidance_on_applying_for_a_Decommissioning_Relief_Deed.doc

WRITTEN MINISTERIAL STATEMENT: DECOMMISSIONING RELIEF DEEDS

21 July 2014. *Written Ministerial Statement.*

The Exchequer Secretary to the Treasury (Priti Patel): At Budget 2013, the government announced it would begin signing decommissioning relief deeds. These deeds represent a new contractual approach to provide oil and gas companies with certainty on the level of tax relief they will receive on future decommissioning costs.

Since October last year, the government has entered into 61 decommissioning relief deeds (50 were signed in financial year 2013-14). Oil & Gas UK estimates that these deeds have so far unlocked at least £2.2bn of capital, which can now be invested elsewhere.

The government committed to report to Parliament every year on progress with the deeds. The report for financial year 2013-14 is provided below.

(a) The number of decommissioning relief agreements entered into: the government entered into fifty decommissioning relief agreements in 2013-14.

(b) The total number of decommissioning relief agreements in force at the end of that year: fifty decommissioning relief agreements were in force at the end of the year.

(c) The number of payments made under any decommissioning relief agreements during that year, and the amount of each payment: no payments were made under any decommissioning relief agreements in 2013-14.

(d) The total number of payments that have been made under any decommissioning relief agreements as at the end of that year, and the total amount of those payments: no payments had been made under any decommissioning relief agreement as at the end of the 2013-14 financial year.

(e) An estimate of the maximum amount liable to be paid under any decommissioning relief agreements: the government has not made any changes to the tax regime that would generate a liability to be paid under any decommissioning relief agreements.

OIL AND GAS TAXATION—REDUCTION IN PETROLEUM REVENUE TAX AND SUPPLEMENTARY CHARGE

16 March 2016. *Tax Information and Impact Note.*

Who is likely to be affected

Oil and gas companies that operate in the UK or on the UK Continental Shelf (UKCS).

General description of the measure

This package of measures will permanently zero rate Petroleum Revenue Tax (PRT) payable in respect of profits from oil and gas production in the UK and UKCS - a reduction from 35%, and further reduces the rate of supplementary charge payable in respect of adjusted ring fence profits from 20% to 10%.

Additionally, it will give HM Revenue and Customs (HMRC) a power to extend the definition of "relevant income" for the cluster area and investment allowances by secondary legislation, to enable tariff income to be included to activate the allowances.

Policy objective

Building on the £1•3 billion package of fiscal reforms delivered at March Budget 2015, these measures deliver the next stage of reform and ensure the UK is in a strong and competitive position, protecting jobs and investment and safeguarding the future of the North Sea industry. These measures support the government's objective of providing the right conditions to maximise the economic recovery of the UK's oil and gas resources at a time when the industry is facing considerable challenges.

The cuts to headline tax rates will simplify the tax regime for investors, and level the playing field between investment opportunities in older fields and infrastructure and new developments. They will increase the attractiveness of projects in the UKCS relative to investment opportunities elsewhere, encouraging investment in the UK and UKCS, and could lead to increased production of oil and gas, helping to increase the UK's energy security, balance of payments and supporting jobs and supply chain opportunities.

The extension to relevant income will encourage investment in infrastructure maintained for third parties. Enabling allowances to be activated by tariff income (payments by a third party for access) will improve the incentive for owners to maintain investment in infrastructure which is critical to the protection of existing production and development of new projects.

The taking of a power to introduce this extension by secondary legislation will provide the opportunity for government to take representations from industry on how best to address issues of allocation and transparency, whilst not being bound to a Finance Bill timetable.

Background to the measure

At Autumn Statement 2014, the government published the conclusions of the HM Treasury review of the oil and gas fiscal regime in "Driving investment: a plan to reform the oil and gas fiscal regime." The Review concluded that the government should keep the rate of PRT under review and consider reducing the rate when fiscal conditions allow, to level the playing-field between investment opportunities in fields which are subject to PRT and opportunities in other fields and ensure key assets attract the right level of investment. A reduction in the rate of PRT from 50% to 35% was announced at Budget 2015.

"Driving Investment" also recognised that the government would need to reduce the overall tax burden on the industry over time to maximise economic recovery. The government announced a reduction in the rate of supplementary charge to 30% at Autumn Statement 2014, and set out its aim to reduce the rate further in an affordable way. Delivering on that aim, Budget 2015 announced a further reduction to 20%.

Budget 2015 also announced the introduction of the cluster area and investment allowance. The legislation did not cover tariff income, owing to the complexities of identifying and apportioning capital expenditure between infrastructure owners and users, and insufficient transparency around the commercial arrangements in place. The response to the consultation on the investment allowance, published on 22 January 2015, confirmed that further work would be carried out to permit tariff income to activate generated allowance in addition to production income.

Detailed proposal

Operative date

The reduction in the rate of PRT will have effect for all chargeable periods ending after 31 December 2015.

PRT

The reduction in the rate of supplementary charge will have effect for accounting periods commencing on and after 1 January 2016. There are transitional rules for accounting periods beginning before the operative date.

The power to extend the scope of relevant income will have effect from Royal Assent and will allow a retrospective effective date of the extension.

Current law

Section 1 of Oil Taxation Act 1975 imposes a PRT charge on a participator's assessable profits in respect of a taxable field at the rate of 35%.

Corporation Tax Act (CTA) 2010 Part 8 Chapter 6 section 330 imposes a supplementary charge on a company's adjusted ring fence profits at the rate of 20%.

CTA 2010 sections 332F(3) and 356JH(3) define "relevant income" for the purposes of the investment and cluster area allowances.

Proposed revisions

Legislation will be introduced in Finance Bill 2016 to amend section 1 of the Oil Taxation Act 1975 to reduce the rate of PRT to 0%, to amend section 330 of CTA 2010 to reduce the rate of the supplementary charge to 10%, and to enable HMRC to amend the cluster area and investment allowance by secondary legislation to extend the definition of "relevant income" and to make any amendments in consequence of, or in connection with, this extension.

Monitoring and evaluation

The measure will be kept under review through regular communication with affected taxpayer groups and the monitoring of tax receipts from activity in the North Sea oil and gas sector.

Further advice

If you have any questions about this change, please contact Nicola Garrod on Telephone: 03000 589251 or email: nicola.garrod@hmrc.gsi.gov.uk.

Commentary—*Simon's Taxes* **D7.903**.

OIL AND GAS COMPANIES' DECOMMISSIONING EXPENDITURE—TECHNICAL NOTE ON TAX RELIEF

16 March 2016. *HMRC Technical Note*

This note clarifies HMRC's views on relief for decommissioning expenditure incurred following the transfer of a licence in an oil field. It is not necessary to retain a licence interest in the field in order to claim relief for the decommissioning expenditure incurred; nor is it necessary to have been either served with, or to hold, a "section 29 notice", provided that the costs were incurred directly and the claimant can demonstrate compliance with all the conditions for "general decommissioning expenditure" in CAA 2001, s 163.

www.gov.uk/government/publications/oil-and-gas-companies-tax-relief-for-decommissioning-expenditure

1 The purpose of this technical note is to clarify certain aspects of HM Revenue and Customs (HMRC's) view of the legislation that provides tax relief for decommissioning expenditure incurred by oil and gas companies.

2 This should provide companies with greater certainty over the tax treatment of expenditure incurred following the transfer of a licence in an oil field.

3 The relevant legislation can be found in Chapter 13 of Part 2 of the Capital Allowances Act (CAA) 2001, in particular, sections 162 to 165. All statutory references are to CAA 2001 unless stated otherwise.

4 Broadly, tax relief is available under section 164 where—

– a person who is carrying on a ring fence trade
– incurs "general decommissioning expenditure" and

- the plant and machinery concerned has been brought into use for the purpose of that ring fence trade

5 Section 165 provides relief for decommissioning expenditure after a person has ceased to carry on a ring fence trade.

6 "General decommissioning expenditure" is defined in section 163 as—

- expenditure incurred on decommissioning plant and machinery which
- has been brought into use wholly or partly for the purpose of a ring fence trade
- forms (or did form when last in use) part of an offshore installation or a submarine pipeline and
- has not been replaced, and
- expenditure which has been incurred wholly or substantially in complying with—
  - an approved abandonment programme
  - a condition to which the approval of an abandonment programme is subject, or
  - a condition imposed by the Secretary of State, or an agreement made with the Secretary of State
    - (I) before the approval of an abandonment programme, and
    - (II) in relation to the decommissioning of the plant or machinery

7 There may be circumstances where a person disposes of the licence interest in a particular field or area, but under the terms of a commercial agreement, agrees to retain some or all of the decommissioning liability for any plant and machinery transferred.

8 Relief will be due where the above conditions are met and the claimant directly incurs the decommissioning costs. It is not sufficient for the claimant to have contributed to costs incurred by others; the claimant must directly incur the decommissioning costs. HMRC will normally accept that the expenditure has been incurred where the claimant is directly liable for the costs charged by those carrying out the decommissioning work, such that legal action could be taken against the claimant in the event that those costs are not met. Further guidance on contributions can be found at in the Capital Allowances Manual CA 14100.

9 HMRC's view is that it is not necessary for the claimant to retain a licence interest in the field on which assets are later decommissioned in order to claim relief for the decommissioning expenditure incurred under sections 164 (where a ring fence trade is carried on) or 165 (where the ring fence trade has ceased).

10 HMRC's view is that it is not necessary for the claimant to have been either served with, or to remain a holder of, a notice under section 29 of the Petroleum Act 1998 ("section 29 notice"), for relief for decommissioning expenditure to be allowed, although it will usually be the case that the claimant will be a section 29 notice holder in these circumstances. In order for relief to be allowed, the claimant must demonstrate that the expenditure has been incurred in complying with an approved abandonment programme (whether or not named on the programme) and the other conditions imposed by section 163 (see paragraph 6 above.)

11 If you have any questions on this note, please contact Nicola Garrod on email nicola.garrod@hmrc.gsi.gov.uk.

Commentary—*Simon's Taxes* **D7.925**.

PRT

Petroleum Revenue Tax Index

Defined words and phrases are listed separately at the end.

PRT

OIL TAXATION – *cont.*
petroleum revenue tax—
deduction for corporation tax, TA 1988 s 500
interest on repayment, TA 1988 s 501
receipts from qualifying assets—
purchase at place of extraction, OTA 1983 Sch 2 para 12
taxpayer becoming participator in another field, FA 1999 s 98
taxpayer ceasing to be participator in field, FA 1999 s 98
use by connected or associated person, OTA 1983 Sch 2 para 11
regional development grants, FA 1982 s 137; TA 1988 s 495
roll-over relief—
exclusion of oil licence, FA 1999 s 103
ring fence trade, TCGA 1992 s 198
sale and leaseback, FA 1999 s 95
tariff receipts, TA 1988 s 496
valuation of oil disposed of otherwise than at arm's length, SP 14/93
ONSHORE ACTIVITIES
ring fence expenditure supplement, FA 2014 s 69, Sch 14
ONSHORE ALLOWANCE
supplementary charge, FA 2014 s 70, Sch 15

P

PAYMENT OF TAX
instalments, withholding of, FA 1982 Sch 19 para 3(1); ESC I5
late payment interest, FA 2009 Sch 53
repayment interest, FA 2009 Sch 54
PETROLEUM REVENUE TAX
appeals, OTA 1975 Sch 2 paras 14–14I
assessment to tax, OTA 1975 Sch 2 para 10
capital expenditure on field development—
election for spread of relief over a period, OTA 1975 Sch 3 para 9; ESC I3
contract settlements, OTA 1975 Sch 2 para 13F
deduction for—
generally, TA 1988 s 500
supplementary duty, FA 1989 s 127
transport of oil from tanker-loading field, deduction for, OTA 1975 s 3(1)(*f*)
expenditure claims, Tax Bulletin Apr 1996
interest, OTA 1975 Sch 2 paras 15–17, F(No 3)A 2010 s 25, Sch 9
overpayment relief, OTA 1975 Sch 2 paras 13A–13E, F(No3)A 2010 s 28
management, OTA 1975 Sch 2 para 1
payment, OTA 1975 Sch 2 para 13
repayment—
interest exempt from corporation tax, TA 1988 s 501
reviews, OTA 1975 Sch 2 paras 14A–14I
supplementary duty, FA 1989 s 127
PETROLEUM REVENUE TAX – *cont.*
transport of oil from tanker-loading field, OTA 1975 s 3(1)(*f*)
withdrawal of expenditure claims, Tax Bulletin Apr 1996

R

RATE
payable, OTA 1975 s 1(2); FA 2016 Pt 9 s 140
REINVESTMENT AFTER PRE-TRADING DISPOSAL
amendment of provisions, FA 2014 s 71
RESPONSIBLE PERSON
appointment, OTA 1975 Sch 2 para 4
RETURNS
incorrect, OTA 1975 Sch 2 paras 8, 9
participators, OTA 1975 Sch 2 paras 2, 3
responsible person, OTA 1975 Sch 2 paras 5, 6
RING FENCE CORPORATION TAX
relief for, IR PR 27/11/91
sale and leaseback, TA 1988 s 494AA
RING FENCE EXPENDITURE SUPPLEMENT
accounting periods—
generally, TA 1988 Sch 19C para 3
limit on number for which claimed, TA 1988 Sch 19C para 5
pre-commencement, supplement in respect of, TA 1988 Sch 19C para 9
taxable ring fence profits, TA 1988 Sch 19C para 8
unrelieved group ring fence profits, TA 1988 Sch 19C para 7
onshore activities, FA 2014 s 69, Sch 14
post-commencement, TA 1988 Sch 19C paras 15–23
pre-commencement, TA 1988 Sch 19C paras 9–14
qualifying companies, TA 1988 Sch 19C para 2
qualifying pre-commencement expenditure, TA 1988 Sch 19C para 6
relevant percentage, TA 1988 Sch 19C para 4

S

SAFEGUARD RELIEF
deferred expenditure claims, IR PR 16/12/87
limit on amount payable, restrictions, OTA 1975 s 9
operating expenditure incurred while applying, OTA 1975 s 9A
SHARJAH
tax credit relief, PR 10/4/07
SUBSTANTIAL SHAREHOLDER EXEMPTION
onshore allowance, FA 2014 s 72
SUPPLEMENTARY CHARGE
onshore allowance, FA 2014 s 70, Sch 15

T

TARIFF RECEIPTS
Allowance—
foreign 'user' fields, OTA 1983 s 9(5); ESC I4
tax-exempt, OTA 1983 s 6A
assets giving rise to, OTA 1983 s 3A
disposal receipts, reduction of, OTA 1983 s 7A
qualifying existing fields, OTA 1983 s 6B
transitional period, expenditure in, FA 2004 Sch 37 Pt 2

V

VALUATION
gas, market value of light gases, OTA 1975 Sch 3 para 3A; FA 1998 s 152

VALUATION – *cont.*
oil disposed of at non-arm's length, OTA 1975 Sch 3 para 2; SP 14/93
oil, market value of—
Category 1 oil, SI 2006/3313, regs 3, 8–16
Category 2 oil, SI 2006/3313, reg 17–24
definitions, SI 2006/3313, reg 2
reports and accounts used in calculations, SI 2006/3313, reg 4
scope of regulations, SI 2006/3313, reg 5

Words and phrases